Different:
rules

D1518849

Different:
defies

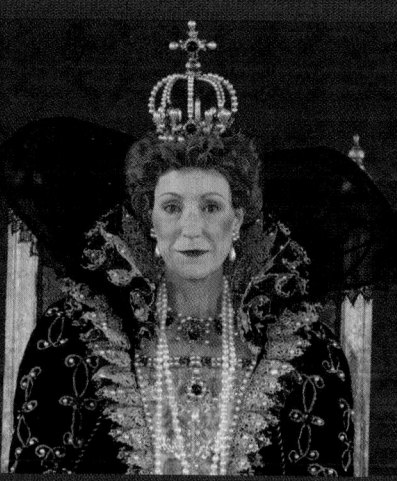

Discover 2011
One Tank Trips

A road trip through this area is a voyage through history, with stops at some of the most important sites in our nation's past. Explore America's origins by traveling the same roads taken by our nation's forefathers, treat yourself to some of New England's world-famous seafood and savor the tranquility to be found at the seaside communities that date back to Colonial days. New England is where the past and the present combine to create that special blend of old world and new, where past and present combine to create a vacationer's delight.

There's something for everyone in the Mid-Atlantic area, whether it's matters of state in Washington, D.C. or fly-fishing in the waters of Virginia's crystal-clear lakes. In Philadelphia, visit the Liberty Bell then enjoy a cheese steak sandwich for which this area is widely renowned. Head over to New Jersey and bask in the sunshine along miles of white sandy beaches, then take in a show at a casino resort in Atlantic City, or camp out in the mountains and just enjoy nature. Fans of outdoor as well as indoor recreation will find something to amuse themselves here in this nexus of relaxing entertainment.

Old times may not be forgotten in the South, but don't think this area stays mired in the past. Today's South is a hotbed of current events, from being the home of some of the biggest names in major league baseball to hosting exciting NASCAR races. There's definitely an appreciation for its heritage, with fabulous antebellum homes, blooming magnolias and historical sites aplenty. From cheering the ponies to victory at the Kentucky Derby to hearing the blues on Memphis' Beale Street, the South will easily provide something to suit every taste and style, from the fast paced to the leisurely.

All five senses will go on overload when they come in contact with the sweet-scented wildflowers of Iowa, the deep blue skies over Ohio and the smooth, creamy cheeses of Wisconsin. This area presents a wealth of opportunities to fish for trout and catfish, or go sailing across the glassy smooth waters of the Great Lakes. It's a land of warm and friendly people, where you can relax and enjoy the peace that only being out in nature's embrace can bring.

Saddle up! You're heading through the territory made famous by such rugged characters as Wyatt Earp, Bat Masterson and all the outlaws of Deadwood. This area drew them all to it, some of whom are permanent residents of Boot Hill. You'll walk the streets where gunfights erupted, where gamblers won and lost fortunes with a single turn of a card and can venture along part of the trail blazed by Lewis and Clark. There are enough mountain ranges running through here than you can enjoy in one trip, so whether it's the Rockies, the Ozarks or Yellowstone, you'll experience the same rugged frontier spirit that shaped our nation.

This region is easily one of the most diverse when it comes to the range of activities, from glacier-hiking in Alaska or sipping a margarita by the beaches of Old Mexico. Leave your heart in the City by the Bay then take Lady Luck for a night on the town and cry "Viva Las Vegas!" The rich, thick forests of the Pacific Northwest are just waiting to show off their wonders and Arizona's thriving spa culture will reveal just how relaxing a soak in hot mud can be. In the Far West, boredom is not an option.

There's no need to hop on a plane in order to enjoy exotic foreign travel when a land of wild, undiscovered adventure lies just across America's northern border. This unspoiled territory remains much as it was in the days of the Klondike Trail, when prospectors and fur trappers plied their trade hoping for that One Big Score. History lives on with live re-creations of bygone days, and the environment is so clean and clear that it's as if modern man never set foot within this area's boundaries. Canada remains one of our final frontiers, just waiting to be explored for the first time.

Published by Woodall's Publications Corp.
2575 Vista Del Mar, Ventura, CA 93001
Phone: 805-667-4100 or 800-323-9076
Website: www.woodalls.com

Also Publishers of
Annual Woodall's Camping Life,
Woodall's Campground Management: (219) 457-3370;
Woodall's RV Buyer's Guide: (800) 323-9076, ext. 284.

President of Affinity Clubs,
Sr.Vice President for Affinity Media Joe Daquino

MULTI-MEDIA DIVISION
Vice President & Publisher Ann Emerson

Sr. Director of Production and Editorial Christine Bucher
Sr. Database Manager Clarinda Pham
Systems and Editorial Staff Susan Shapiro

Director of Production Yvette L. Schulz
Electronic Prepress Systems Specialist Milt Phelps
Graphic Designers Gary Guthrie, Jessa Riley
Traffic Supervisor Tanya Paz

Production/Editorial Assistants Sabrina Leal, Jennifer Marquez, Princesa Rodriguez

Cover Design Quad Graphics
Feature Writers Angie Norris, Timothy Morrison
Feature Designs Jessa Riley

EMD Web Specialist Jonathan Blackburn
Director of Marketing Genevieve Branco

Marketing Manager Donna Brown
Marketing Fulfillment Coordinator Brittny Jensen

Director of Sales Dawn Watanabe
Business Manager Christine Distl
Account Coordinators Nelly Beraun, Corey Grant, Veronica Heikes, Raz Cumbe

Marketing Consultants Jim & Sally Bryan

NATIONAL ADVERTISING
Scott Oakes - Eastern Sales
(206) 283-9545
1818 Westlake Ave. N., Ste. 420
Seattle, WA 98109
John Marciano - Western Sales
(206) 235-7555
1818 Westlake Ave. N., Ste. 420
Seattle, WA 98109

WOODALL REPRESENTATIVES
- Larry & Glenna Baird
- Greg & Maureen Baron
- Randy & Debbie Block
- John & Shirley Bujnovsky
- Dave & Jaynie Carlson
- Joe & Rita Comer
- Jim & Betty Croson
- Chip & Pat Dennis
- Dave & Femke Durham
- John & Jean Everett
- Duane & Bev Finger
- Lee & Mary Franck
- A.J. & Kathleen Goodale
- Clyde & Carolyn Greene
- Chuck & Nancy Hanson
- Johnny & Nancy Johnson
- Frank & Linda Mintken
- Fred & Joanne Playle
- John & Michele Pynenburg
- Dave & Kate Reikofski
- John & Carla Skolburg
- Kim & Debi Smith
- Marcia Waggoner
- Kevin & Susan Weber
- Gary & Sherry Wilcox

PRINTED IN THE U.S.A.
Book Trade Distribution by The Globe-Pequot Press
246 Goose Lane
P.O. Box 480
Guilford, CT 06437 (203) 458-4500
ISBN-13: 978-0-7627-6136-4

Printed on Recyclable Paper.

2011 Eastern Edition Directory Listings

WOODALL'S

2011 Discover One Tank Trips

Dear Readers~

A lot can happen in 75 years. Forgive me as I wax nostalgic, but let's go backward a bit in time. In 1936 America was still reeling from the Great Depression, Franklin Delano Roosevelt was elected to his second term as President in a landslide, the Hoover Dam was finally completed, Jesse Owens put an exclamation point in the Berlin Olympics by winning 4 gold medals, and the first stock car race was held in Dayton Beach. Around this time, the fledging RV industry was beginning to come into its own. In 1936 Wally Byam built an RV for his wife that would become an iconic symbol of the RV lifestyle—the Airstream Clipper, one of the best selling RVs of all time. Accompanying the increased production and buying of Travel Trailers, RV Parks and Campgrounds began popping up around the country. Land owner and businessman Ollie Trout opened one of the first premier luxury RV resorts in Miami, FL during these early days. For $5 a day, Ollie guaranteed RVers would have "a palm tree at every camping spot" while employees raced from the clubhouse to bring guests cold drinks and sandwiches. However, for pioneering RVers, finding these new RV parks or campgrounds was like looking for the proverbial needle in a haystack. Enter Karl Hale Dixon, who founded Woodall's Publications and published its first campground directory in 1936, connecting wandering RVers with welcoming RV parks.

While fads and trends have come and gone in the last 75 years, North America's love of RV travel has never dimmed, and it shows in the growing and vibrant RV Industry that we have today. And while the way people camp and travel has evolved some over the years, the classics still remain. Airstream RVs are still considered fun and stylish, RV resorts are still attracting travelers from all over the world, and RV enthusiasts still trust Woodall's Directories as their guide to places to go and things to see.

In that spirit, we are pleased to publish this 2011 edition of the Woodall's Directory, celebrating 75 years of connecting RVers to parks and business throughout North America. Within these pages you will find all the features that have set Woodall's apart—our industry standard 5W ratings, helpful information about specific states and provinces, and thousands of private and public campgrounds detailing the amenities they offer and how to find them. This special edition of the Directory demonstrates how Woodall's has not only grown up with the RV Industry, but has led the way in Campground Publications. Bold, eye-catching full color ads can be seen throughout the entire Directory. And to assist "green" campers, we have highlighted those RV parks that practice ecology-friendly habits.

Our faithful RV followers will also find even MORE exciting items on woodalls.com, including Visual Tours of campgrounds, social media links, helpful camping articles, beautiful photos, and all the resources to plan a perfect RV trip. From woodalls.com, readers can now access our Family Camping blog, which is jam-packed with delicious recipes, camping tips, great travel destinations, and also provides RVers and Campers the chance to interact with the entire RV community.

It is remarkable to see how the RV industry has changed. From the Great Depression to the Great Recession, RVers have continued enjoy the lifestyle. I think camping taps into that pioneering spirit which drove explorers across North America in covered wagons, and now drives RVers to new places across the country. Woodall's is grateful to have been part of this tradition and is eagerly anticipating what the next decades will bring to this way of life we love.

Thank you, loyal readers, for bringing Woodall's with you on your road adventures, and allowing us to be your guide for the journey for all these years. Enjoy this 2011 edition of the Woodall's Directory. We think Mr. Dixon would be proud of this one.

Sincerely,

Ann Emerson
Vice President & Publisher

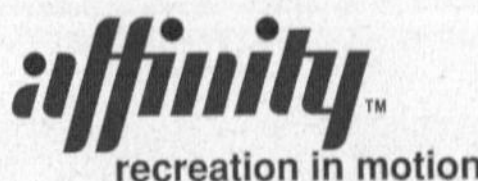

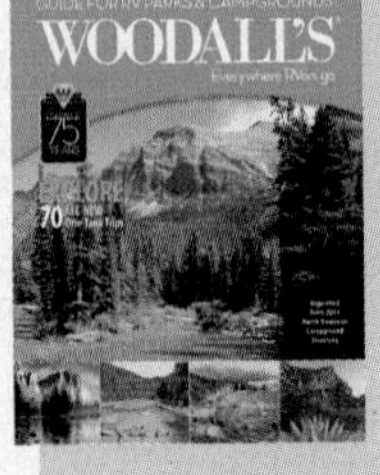

Please see page two for the Table of Contents for *Discover 2011—One Tank Trips*

WOODALL'S IS THE OFFICIAL CAMPGROUND DIRECTORY RECOGNIZED by the FAMILY MOTOR COACH ASSOCIATION and FAMILY CAMPERS AND RVERS

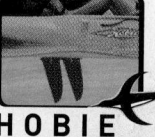

Cheaper to Keep'er
I was ready to trade my Rig for lack of power. A friend installed Banks on his Rig and bragged so much, I had to try it on mine. Banks PowerPack works great and improved the power to my satisfaction. Believe me, I'm not ready to trade anymore.
Harold Case; Londonderry, NH
PowerPack Owner

Shown: Big Hoss Bundle for '01-04 Chevy/GMC 6.6L Duramax LB7
banks
TECHNI-COOLER
banks RAM-AIR

WOODALL'S
ONE TANK TRIPS
Discover New York/New England!

CONNECTICUT

Don't shy away from Connecticut because of its size. As the third smallest state, it might be a little more than a dot on a map, but within its borders lies a wealth of rural landscapes, colonial villages, and beautiful coastal villages. With such an inspiring landscape, it's not surprising that Mark Twain wrote his greatest work here, "The Adventures of Huckleberry Finn". Who knows what inspiration a visit to this incredible state will give you?

Our trip starts off in Clinton, a charming New England town overlooking the Long Island Sound. Like many coastal New England towns, life here centers around shipbuilding, farming and fishing, which can still be enjoyed as a leisurely pursuit in the Sound. Visitors can also enjoy hiking on the many trails in Peters Memorial Woods, where you can test yourself and your endurance on one of the more physically demanding trails, or leisurely stroll and enjoy the beauty of the New England countryside.

From Clinton, we move onto Old Lyme via US-1 N with a merge onto I-95 N. Exit onto CT-156 E, and in no time, you'll be right in the heart of our next stop! Filled with beautiful old buildings, Old Lyme is a great place to spend a few days, particularly if you're fond of the arts and ITS history. During the late 1800s and early 1900s, Old Lyme was a favorite to many painters, and if you stop by the art museum (which is also the former home of Miss Florence Griswold), you'll be treated to some of the finest American Impressionist works to be found anywhere.

For our next stop, take I-95 N out of Old Lyme. After several miles, exit left for CT-184/CT-12 and after several miles, merge onto CT-184 E and make a left at CT-117 N to arrive at Ledyard Center. For visitors to this sleepy New England town, you'll find surprisingly diverse choices for recreation including wineries, a casino, and Sawmill Park, which spans 11 acres and gives visitors a chance to see a working blacksmith, a gristmill, shingle mill and a mill museum located in a beautifully restored building. The park is open year-round, and to witness the mill in action, plan your trip in April or October. Late fall would be the perfect time to experience the spectacular fall foliage. The brilliant hues are something you won't want to miss!

As one of the original 13 colonies, Connecticut just seems to keep getting better with age. With an amazing coastline, several wonderful historical sites, and various renowned museums, it's easy to see why Connecticut is one of the most visited states in the nation.

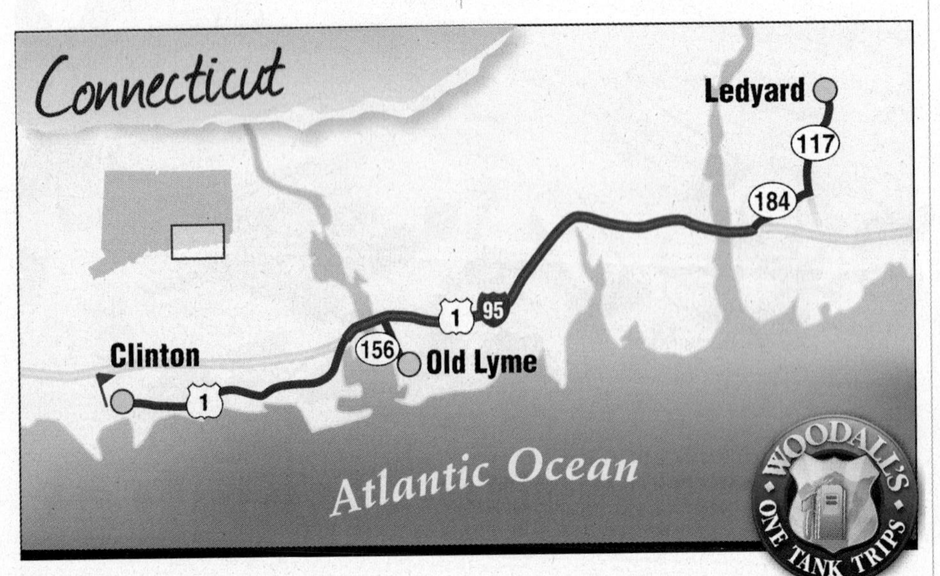

OTHER AREA LOCATIONS

BOZRAH

Odetah Camping Resort

PRESTON

Hidden Acres Family Campground

MAINE

Maine is a state that epitomizes the look and feel of New England. Some of the most beautiful landscapes in the country can be found here; from the picturesque harbor towns, to rugged coastlines, to the heavily forested interior of the state, travelers will be won over at every corner. Maine is an experience like no other, and you just haven't lived until you dive head first into the freshest seafood to be found anywhere in the US!

We begin our trip today in the city of Millinocket. From humble beginnings as a mill town, Millinocket embodies the natural beauty of Maine. It was this town that famous New Hampshire writer and naturalist, Henry David Thoreau, visited on his excursion into the Maine wilderness, and Millinocket would find it's way into the novel "The Maine Woods". What did Thoreau find here? Beautiful rolling hills and scenic vistas that seem to be endless. It's easy to fall in love with this area, and many travelers find themselves coming back to this tranquil haven again and again. Anglers will find this area both challenging and rewarding with the lakes teeming with bass, salmon, lake and brook trout, and many others. Nearby Baxter State Park provides the outdoor enthusiast with ample opportunities for hiking, boating, cross-country skiing and ice fishing. The northern terminus of the Appalachian Trail is located on top of breathtaking Mt.Katahdin's peak, and the mountain provides a scenic backdrop for your getaway.

Moving on to our next stop, Houlton, take ME-157 E to I-95 N. In approximately an hour and a half, you will have arrived. In the early 1900s, this charming town was one of the richest communities in the US. Victorian mansions constructed during Houlton's heyday can be found throughout the city, and the beautifully maintained Market Square District contains an impressive collection of historic buildings worth exploring during your visit. For the outdoor enthusiast,

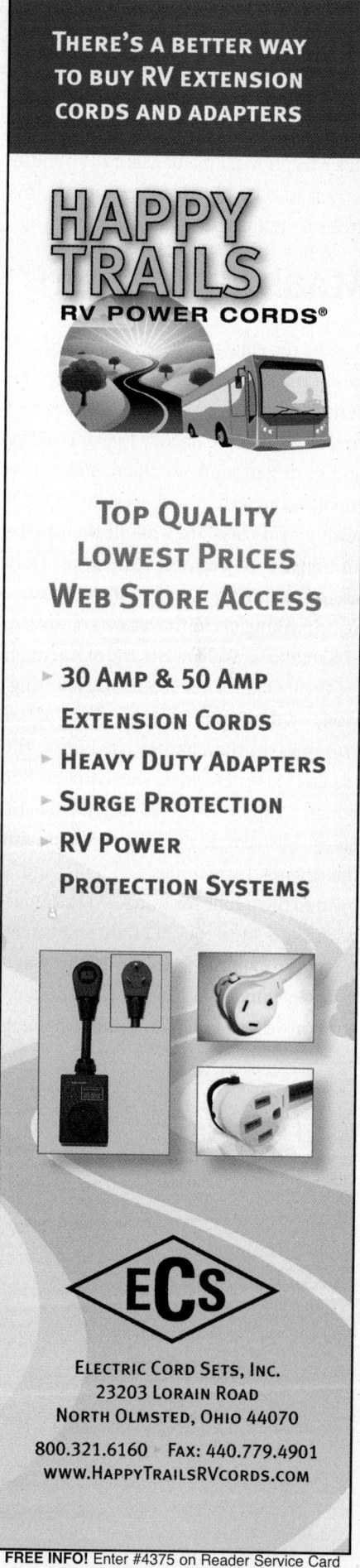

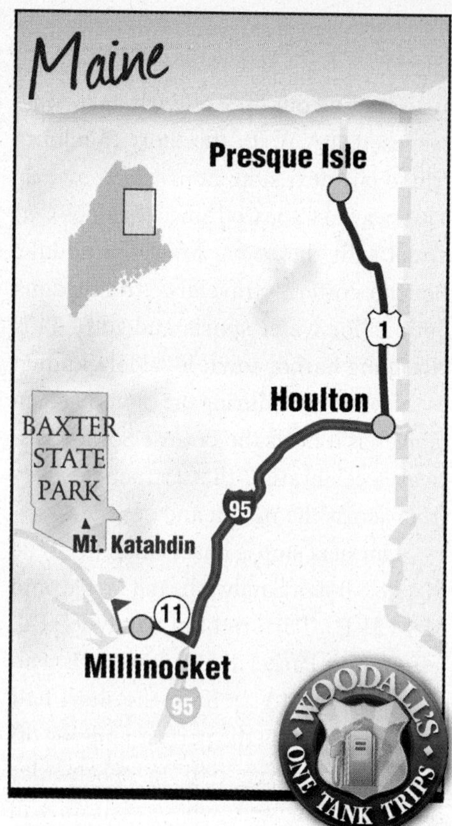

Houlton will impress with some of the best snowmobiling and ATV trail riding in the Northeast, as well as canoeing and hiking. Don't forget your fishing pole! You'll want to cast a line and try your angling skills!

The last stop on our journey is the city of Presque Isle. Taking US-1 N out of Houlton, continue on US-1 N for approximately 42 miles. Because Northern Maine is the closest landmass to Europe, Presque Isle was chosen as a take-off for planes and equipment headed overseas during WWII, and in 1978, Presque Isle was once again chosen as a take-off point for Double Eagle II, the first hot air balloon to cross the Atlantic Ocean. Is it any wonder that Presque Isle should be a favorite spot to celebrate taking to the air at the Crown of Maine Balloon Fest? Visitors come from across the state and beyond, for a weekend of food, music, fun, and of course, balloons! Usually held in late August, it's an event you won't want to miss. For more outdoor fun than you can handle, head over to the Nordic Heritage Center. This four-season recreation facility will challenge and delight all visitors with over 20 miles of mountain bike trails, cross country ski and biathalon opportunities, and much more.

You don't need to be an expert in wilderness survival to get the most out of this exceptional area of Maine. From the largest lake, to the tallest mountain, this area will tempt the outdoor lover in you!

MASSACHUSETTS

As the epicenter of several major and important chapters in history, Massachusetts is something special. Visitors will find an abundance of New England charm and beauty to captivate them, major metropolitan areas that will overwhelm them with world-class art, and all the hustle-and-bustle they crave, while beautifully intermingling the past and the present.

Speaking of charm, let's start our trip in Sandwich. Welcome to the oldest town on Cape Cod! This beautiful New England town is home to some of the oldest buildings in the country, including the Hoxie House, the oldest surviving saltbox house. Built in the 1600s, the Hoxie House has been beautifully restored with the original furnishings and tools, and is open to the public for tours. At the Sandwich Glass Museum, not only will you be treated to exhibits from the 1800s, you'll also see wonderful glassblowing demonstrations. Both fascinating and enlightening, it's a museum you won't want to miss!

Heading out of Sandwich, take Massachusetts 6A W for the short 15 minute trip to our next stop; Bourne. Known as a gateway to Cape Cod since the Cape Cod Canal split the town down the middle, Bourne offers travelers tremendous options for water sports and golf. This charming harbor town is widely known as the place to be during the month of September as it hosts the Bourne Scallop Festival, a celebration that attracts visitors from across the nation and beyond.

Our next stop is East Falmouth. Take MA-28 S out of Sandwich, and merge onto MA-151 E. Turn right at Sandwich Rd, left at John Parker Rd and left at E. Falmouth Hwy/MA-28 S for the short half hour trip. This is the perfect jumping off point for a ferry trip to spectacular Martha's Vineyard, where visitors will find themselves surrounded by peaceful beauty, miles of beaches, and all the charm and allure Martha's Vineyard is known for.

Barnstable is our next stop, and to get there, hop onto MA-28 S for the short, scenic drive through the beautiful New England countryside. In no time at all you will have arrived, and what an incredible stop! Barnstable lies just a few miles southwest of beautiful Wequaquet Lake, where all sorts of water activities lie at your fingertips; from swimming and fishing, to boating and lounging by the water, soaking up some sun.

For our next destination, Hyannisport, return to MA-28 S, take a right at Pitchers Way and continue onto Scudder Avenue. Take a left at Marston Avenue, turn right to stay on Marston Avenue and take the 2nd left onto Edge Hill Rd. This trip should take you less than 20 minutes. Hyannis is the largest village of Barnstable, and probably best known as the Kennedy's favorite getaway location, and for good reason. In Hyannisport there is no shortage of ferries to be taken, fishing and sailing charters to hitch a ride on, and charming shops and restaurants to explore. Visitors can also find the JFK memorial here, and in no time at all, you'll understand why the Kennedy's were drawn back to the beauty and peace of this area.

Leaving Hyannisport, take Ocean Avenue out of town, which turns into Sea Street. Continue on Sea Street, turning right at South Street, then a left at Lewis Bay Rd. Take the 3rd right onto Main Street, which should turn into MA-28 S. After several miles, take a right onto Sea Street, and in around a half hour, we will arrive at our next location, Dennis Port. The Cape is a well-known haven for artists, and in Dennis Port travelers will find many galleries and stores that display local wares. From its location on the coast, Dennis Port is the perfect place to enjoy the mild New England weather, charter a fishing boat, dig your toes in the sand, or watch the surf. There are few things as peaceful and serene as grazing out into the ocean, and whatever daily stress you've brought with you is sure to melt away in this incredible town.

Moving on, we're going to back-track a little on Sea Street and head back to MA-28 S/Main Street and head to our next location, Chatham. Located at the ragged elbow of the Cape, Chatham embodies the quintessential New England town with pristine beaches, sandbars, tidal shoals and saltwater inlets. Decidedly old fash-

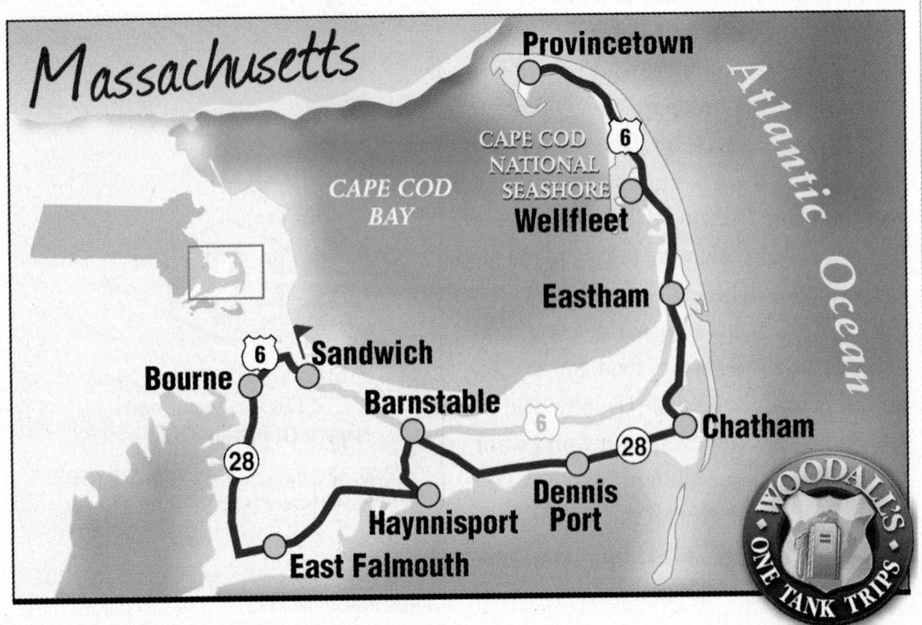

ioned, Chatham has gotten the reputation as a shopper's paradise in recent years. For the curious, head down to the fishing pier for a first hand look at the backbone of this wonderful village.

Leaving Chatham, take Old Harbor Road out of town, taking a left onto MA-28 S/Orleans Rd. At the traffic circle, take the 1st exit onto Mid-Cape Hwy/US-6 E. The entire trip should take you around a half-hour, and before you know it, you'll have arrived in Eastham. Eastham may catch first time visitors a little off guard. With no discernable town center, and no formal Main Street, you can see that Eastham is made for those looking to get far from the craziness of everyday life. As one of the four original settlements on the Cape, Eastham still remains relatively undiscovered, and that's just the way locals prefer it. One of the wonders that draw travelers to this region (aside from the miles of beaches, cool New England breezes, and laidback vibe) is the National Seashore where visitors are free to explore and birdwatch. Also here is the Cape's oldest remaining windmill, the beautiful Swift-Daley House. For history buffs, take a trip to First Encounter Beach where Myles Standish and his Pilgrim scouts first came in contact with the Nauset Indians in 1620.

From Eastham we continue to Wellfleet taking Mid-Cape Hwy/US-6 E out of town. Once a whaling port, Wellfleet still manages to uphold its reputation as a fishing village, while supporting a healthy art community. After exploring the several historical residences within the city, head over to the Wellfleet Oyster and dig into some of that famous New England cuisine. For the nature lover, Wellfleet has something for you, too, and you'll find it in the Wellfleet Bay Sanctuary. With 1,000 acres and several hiking trails, it's where you'll want to head to either work off all the calories you've just consumed or work up an appetite for more!

Our last stop takes us back to US-6 E. Turn left toward Massachusetts 6A W/Shore Rd, and right at Massachusetts 6A W. This trip should take less than 30 minutes, and what better place to end our journey than Provincetown. If you're looking to truly get away from it all, this is about as far as you can get. As the last stop on the continent, Provincetown has drawn a number of different types; from Pilgrims and fishermen, to artists and beach lovers, all of them finding something beautiful and peaceful here. Well known as the spot where the Pilgrims first landed, travelers will find the tallest granite structure in the nation commemorating their landing. What better way to end our trip than in the place where it all began.

NEW HAMPSHIRE

Long and lean, New Hampshire supplies enough year-round appeal to rival some of the larger states. From beautiful, majestic beaches to mountainous regions and metropolitan areas, all surrounded by that famous New England countryside. New Hampshire can fulfill all of your getaway expectations and more.

Let's start our journey in Wolfeboro. Located on the eastern shores of Lake Winnipesaukee, Wolfeboro is touted as the "Four Seasons Getaway" and is the oldest summer resort in America. Visitors here will enjoy the peace and quiet of beautiful Lake Winnipesaukee, a huge array of water sports including swimming, fishing, and boating. Also available are antique boat rides on the lake - what better way to enjoy all of the amazing, pristine beauty?

Let's move on to our next location, Tamworth. Take NH-28 N out of Wolfeboro, and merge left onto NH-16 S. After several miles, merge left again onto NH-25 W, taking a right at NH-113 E. Tamworth enjoys a steady stream of visitors due to its location at the base of the White Mountains. There are hundreds of miles of trails for biking, and thousands of miles for hiking, ranging from simple walks in the woods to challenging moun-

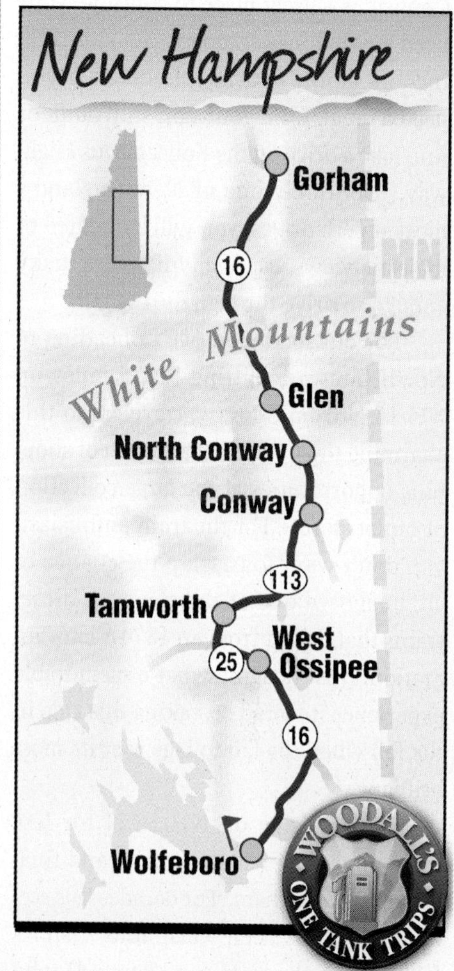

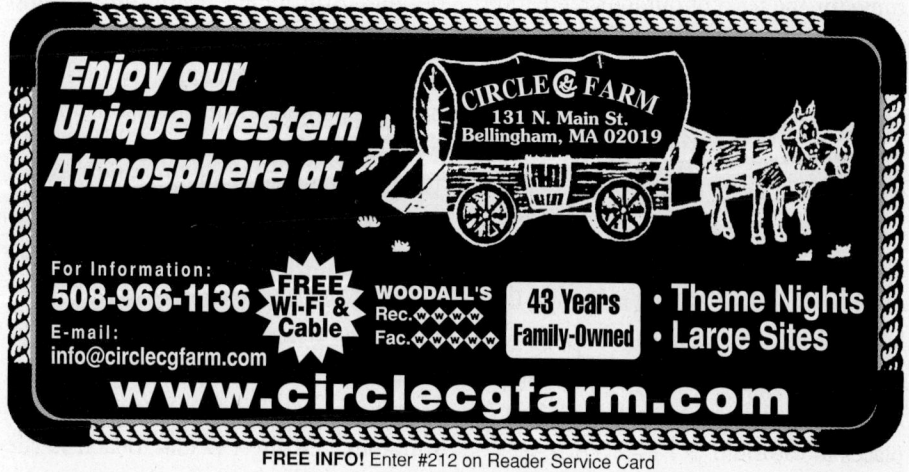

taineering opportunities, all the while surrounded by indescribable beauty. The winter months bring even more outdoor recreation including snowshoeing, alpine and cross country skiing. Now matter what time of year you visit, you'll find more than enough to challenge and delight!

Our next location takes us back to US-113 N to the town of Conway. Keeping up the pace we started in Tamworth, Conway is a great place to continue your need for all things outdoors. Yet more hiking and skiing is available here. If you need a break from your non-stop outdoor fun, take a drive on the Kancamagus Highway. Definitely one of New England's most superb drives, you will be treated to majestic views, especially if you're lucky enough to drive through during fall.

For our next stop, we're heading to North Conway. Sitting just 6 miles up NH-16 N from Conway, travelers to this charming town will find a wealth of shopping opportunities at the large collection of outlet stores. For the train enthusiast, you don't want to pass up the chance to climb aboard one of the steam or diesel trains that depart from an 1874 Victorian Station. Just imagine what a memorable experience it would be, taking this ride in the fall when the fall foliage is at its most brilliant.

We continue on NH-16 N for less than an hour to reach our next and final destination, Gorham. For decades this scenic beauty has been welcoming visitors from across the state (and beyond) who come for the feast of outdoor recreation, such as rock climbing, hiking, kayaking, canoeing, fishing and hunting. Whether you're looking to relax and take it easy, or to exhaust yourself with activities, Gorham will never disappoint.

Within it's slender borders, New Hampshire is a vacation wonderland full of rugged outdoor beauty and New England charm. New Hampshire has so much beauty and recreation to offer, that it easily becomes one of the East Coast's Top 10 places to vacation.

NEW YORK

Situated in the northeast corner of the US, New York is home to spectacular and diverse landscapes, as well as diverse cultures and cities. New York City is a natural tourist draw for travelers across the globe, and for good reason. But if you extend yourself past the hustle-and-bustle of this major metropolitan city, you'll find the beauty of the Adirondack Mountains, charming cities and towns, and a wealth of outdoor activities.

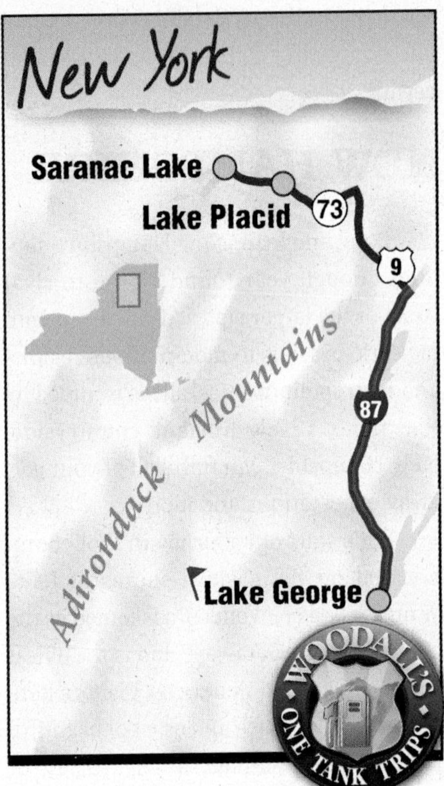

Beginning in one of the most breathtaking areas of the state, the village of Lake George is ideally located at the edge of the Adirondack Mountains, and perched at the mouth of the lake from which the town was named, Lake George provides outdoor enthusiasts and anglers with endless recreation possibilities. With approximately 32 miles of beautiful water, it's no wonder canoers, kayakers, fishermen, and sailors flock to this area. Scuba divers love to explore the depths of the lake where historic shipwrecks abound. If you're looking to soak up some rays, make sure you bring plenty of sunblock! Million Dollar Beach is the place you'll want to lay out your towel and work on your tan. Inside the city, the power shopper will find the several factory outlet stores are just the place to keep them busy finding the next great bargain.

Our next stop is equally as beautiful and serene as our first, and a short trip on I-87 N, taking the exit for US-9, and a slight left at NY-73 W will get you there before you can say, "Two time host of the Winter Olympics". Lake Placid is a city proud of its heritage, and proud to have been the host of two Winter Olympic games. It's at this very location in 1932 that Sonja Henie won her second gold medal, and inspired many little girls to become figure skaters themselves. Who could forget the "Miracle on Ice" when the 1980 US hockey team pulled off one of the biggest upsets in history by defeating the Soviet Union. A visit to the Olympic Sports Complex just might be the thing to awaken the athlete in you. Test your skills at downhill and cross country skiing, take a heart stopping bobsled ride, or get a few lessons to see if you have what it takes to be a biathlete. After a day of adventure, stop in at any number of the restaurants, spas and shops that will tempt you with their relaxing services, delicious food, or interesting wares.

Heading to our last stop - Saranac Lake - take NY-86 W, and in less than a half hour you will have arrived. For the outdoor enthusiast, Saranac Lake is like paradise, loaded with hiking trails, canoe routes and plenty of outfitters to help you along your adventure. Other notable attractions (depending on the season) are golf, downhill and cross-country skiing, and cycling. If you're looking for something a little quieter and maybe a little more relaxed, Saranac Lake has an array of unique shops and restaurants that tempt the shopper and the palate. Literary types shouldn't leave this area without perusing the Robert Louis Stevenson cottage, and for the train enthusiast, a trip along the Adirondack Scenic Railroad is sure to bowl you over with spectacular views of the mountains that surround this area.

The Adirondacks have been luring visitors for centuries, long before there was the wealth of activities to be found there now. The delicate beauty, pristine lakes, and its promise to help any traveler shed the worries of the daily grind make it an easy draw for those looking to relax, wind down and recharge.

OTHER AREA LOCATIONS

LAKE GEORGE
Ledgeview RV Park
NEWBURGH
KOA-Newburgh/
New York City North

RHODE ISLAND

Like so much of New England, Rhode Island offers an array of natural beauty, cultural offerings and wonderful history. The very name of the Ocean State conjures images of long, sandy beaches, tucked away vineyards, and seafood so fresh, nothing else will ever come close to it!

Our trip begins in Westerly. Straddling the state line of Connecticut, Westerly is a city with a proud granite mining heritage, and a haven for historians, foodies, and antique hunters alike. For the summer months, visitors flock to Watch Hill for its beautiful beaches, historic homes, and the Watch Hill Lighthouse. If you're in need of a quiet place to stroll, collect your thoughts, or just enjoy the warm New England sun, head over to Wilcox Park where you can lose yourself amongst the dwarf conifer collection and fragrant flower beds. There are several annual events held within the park, including Summer Pops and Shakespeare in the Park.

Let's head to our next stop, Narragansett. Head out of Westerly on Post Rd/US-1 N. Take the exit toward Narragansett/Point Judith. Take a right at Woodruff Ave, and a left at Old Point Judith Rd. At the traffic circle, take the 1st exit onto Kingstown Rd/Rhode Island 1A N. Turn left at Beach St. This part of our trip is less than an hour drive. Narragansett was once a thriving resort destination in the 1800s and still enjoys its share of travelers who come for the wide variety of fun to be found here. Some of the finest recreation, including sport fishing, as well as spectacular beaches, are right around the corner. And for the shopper, the Narragansett Pier provides more than a few places where you can find a wonderful souvenir, or great bargain, to remind you of your trip.

The next portion of our trip takes us back to Rhode Island 1A N/Boston Neck Rd. Turn left to merge onto RI-138 E. Take a slight right at Tashtassuck Rd to arrive in beautiful Jamestown. Located on Conanicut Island in the Narragansett Bay, this sleepy island city hosts summer travelers who flock to enjoy the quiet rural feel and wonderful New England charm. You'll discover many old neighborhoods, farms, and several historic buildings worth exploring via bike or foot. Jamestown has a wonderful laid-back feel to it that just might be the thing to jump start your summer in the right direction.

The last stop on our trip takes us back to RI-138R, and across the Newport Bridge. Be prepared for tolls and partial tolls as we travel to Newport. Take the Rhode Island 238 Scenic S ramp to Newport, take a right at RI-138 Scenic/RI-238 S to arrive. Newport is considered to be a gem of the Rhode Island coast. Here travelers will find some spectacular coastal scenery, exceptional architecture, scenic vineyards, and enough photo opportunities to keep you snapping pictures all day! One of the biggest draws to this fine city by the sea is the beautiful Gilded Age Mansions. No matter what else you do here, you don't want to pass up the chance to take a tour (or several) of these former

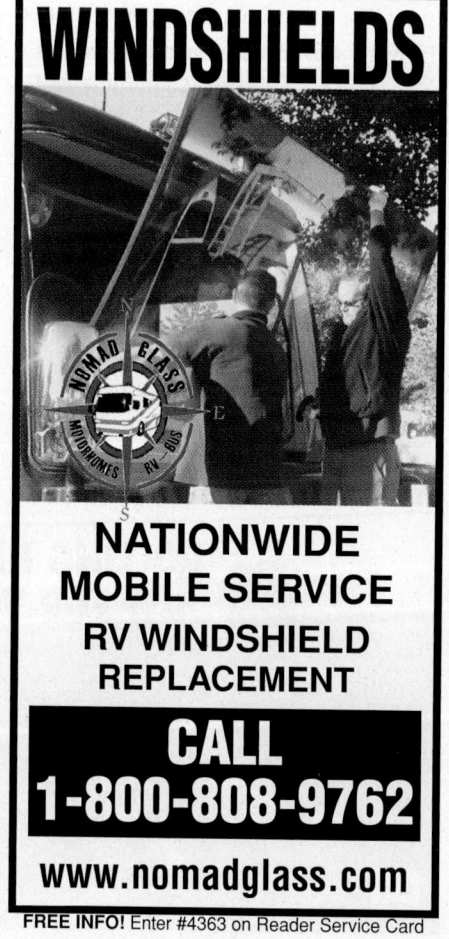

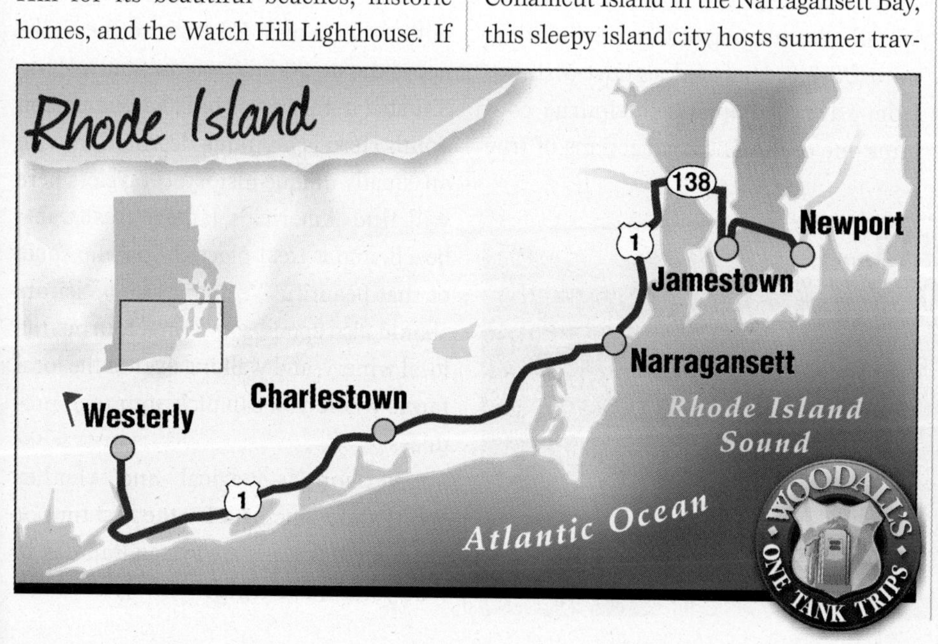

homes to wealthy industrialists. Walking through the cobblestone streets of this city is sure to make any traveler feel as if they'd stepped back in time. It provides the perfect atmosphere for a nice romantic stroll.

No matter if you're looking for a quick getaway, a romantic journey, or to surround yourself with the beauty and serenity of the New England countryside, Rhode Island should get top billing for your next traveling adventure!

VERMONT

Are you looking to sweeten up your adventures? Vermont is the place for you! Famous for country inns, covered bridges, and some of the most incredibly scenic areas in the country, Vermont offers visitors more beauty and recreation than should be legal! Oh, and did I mention the syrup? Mmmmm...

Today we start in Waterbury, a tiny village located on the shores of the Winooski River within the Green Mountains. The views here are spectacular, and although the town is small, it lies in a prime spot for a wealth of activities. Who doesn't like ice cream? Ben & Jerry's Ice Cream factory is located here, and no one should pass up the opportunity for a little tour and a little taste of the stuff that made Waterbury famous. Just as sweet and delicious is the Cold Hollow Cider Mill, where you can watch crates of apples being pressed. And don't forget to pick up some of that famous Vermont maple syrup! There are plenty of activities to help you work off all that good stuff you just munched on, right in, and around, town. At the Waterbury Reservoir, fishing, canoeing, boating, and swimming are just a few of the things you can immerse yourself in. Since the majority of Waterbury is beautifully forested, it makes for the perfect place to do some hiking, cycling and birdwatching as well.

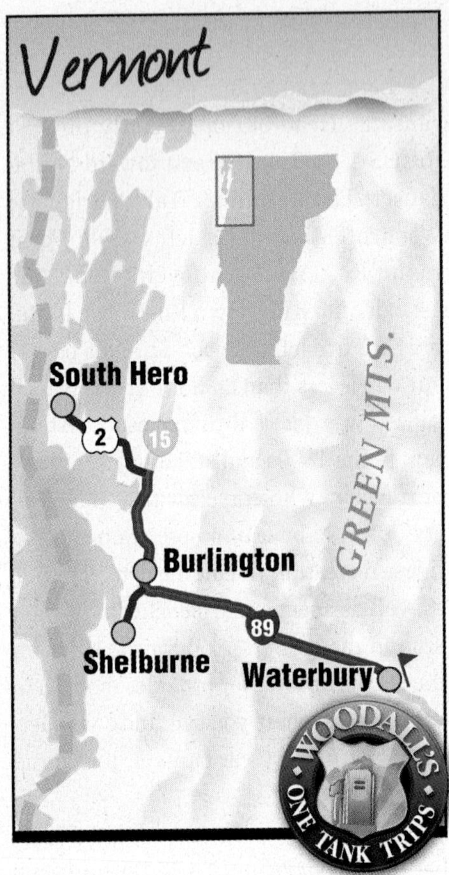

Dry yourself off as we move on to our next stop, Shelburne. Take I-89 N out of Waterbury, merging onto I-189 and then onto US-7 S. Located a short distance from Lake Champlain, Shelburne contains one of the finest collections of true Americana items and displays at the Shelburne Museum, and is more than worthy of a visit. With lush valley and mountain views, Shelburne is a true jewel of the valley. Visitors here will also find The Vermont Teddy Bear Company, a great place to pick up a traveling buddy or gift for some lucky person. And for a very unique experience, pay a visit to Shelburne Farms, a 1,400-acre working farm, a National Historic Landmark, and one of the most spectacular places within the state. Created as a model agricultural estate in 1886, the farm urges visitors of all ages to come and explore the trails, the farmyard, inn, and restaurant at their leisure.

Return to US-7 N for the short trip to our next stop, Burlington. The largest city in Vermont, but small according to big city standards, Burlington is a popular destination due to its location to Lake Champlain, as well as the Green and Adirondack Mountains. These areas offer a host of recreational activities year-round. Visitors are welcome to indulge in any number of water sports from boating to swimming, while the surrounding mountains are a great spot for hiking, mountain biking, camping and climbing. Winter months bring some incredible skiing opportunities, and no matter what activity suits you, the beauty of Burlington provides a breathtaking backdrop.

Our last stop takes us back to I-89 N with a merge onto US-2 W for the short, approximate 20-mile trip to South Hero. Situated in the center of Lake Champlain, South Hero is a unique destination with an equally unique history. Travelers here will find America's largest freshwater beach, and a great place to soak up some of that beautiful Vermont sun. Visitors should also spend some time touring the local winery, and walking over to the local farms where you can pick your own produce.

Vermont is magical, and whether you're experiencing it for the first time or the hundredth, it's always guaranteed to take your breath away.

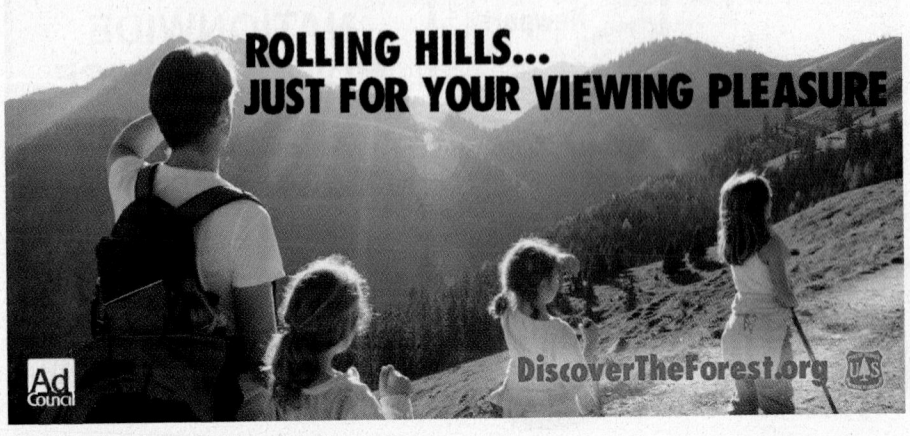

what in the world is a QR CODE?

Welcome to the Future

From the Desk of Yvette L. Schulz

Have you noticed these weird spotty square images showing up on business doors, flashing across the TV and even on soda cans? You are going to start seeing a lot more of them. Technology continues to develop and people continue to be mesmerized with the hi-tech, hands-on experience. The best thing about QR Codes is that they bridge the physical world directly to the virtual world with the click of a button. They will bring the curious smartphone user to webpages, videos and so much more.

How QR Codes Work

In layman's terms, a Quick Response Code is a barcode containing encoded information that can be scanned by a "QR Reader" and decoded by a smartphone (like the Android, the i-Phone, Nokia, etc). Some smartphones already have the software installed and some require a simple application download of a QR Reader.

Other FREE apps include I-nigma, Bee Tag and MobileTag. Listed below are the suggested FREE apps for the different types of phones:

- Androids~Barcode Scanner
- iPhones~ Neo reader
- Windows Phone~Microsoft Tag

QR Codes are not a new technology. It was actually created by Japanese corporation DENSO-Wave in 1994 and was originally intended for use in tracking the complex task of automobile parts manufacturing and sourcing throughout the automobile assembly process. They quickly became popular when people realized they could be used to create a hardlink, a link from the physical world to the internet. They spread through Japan and Europe and are now sweeping across the United States.

With smartphones becoming the more prominent choice of the consumer, and with society's love of technology, it won't be long before we see these QR Codes everywhere!

Apple Computer®

Nike®

There are 4X as many mobile phones
as there are PCs, and 1.8 billion people already
have access to the mobile Web. Make no mistake,
"mobile" is the wave of the future...
- GoDaddy

How are they being used?

There are many ways QR codes are being used to connect easily to mobile content. We have listed a few:

URLs: Scan a QR code on an ad, on a poster, in an article or even on the side of a building and you could go straight to a website for more information or even a youtube video.
Business Cards: Scan and upload contact information off a business card into your phone.
Downloads: Download a coupon for the grocery store or a movie trailer at the theatre.
Instant TXT: Scan and instantly send a pre-populated TXT to enter a promotion.
Display TXT: Scan the QR code on a concert poster and some promoters are sending out the tour dates.

Find Woodall's QR codes throughout the book and gain access to our many online resources via your smartphone.

HBO's "True Blood®"

With the widespread use of iPhones, Androids and other smartphones, are US brands and businesses finally ready to embrace QR codes in a big way? Some restaurants have started using them on their packaging to identify nutritional information. The Multi-Media Industry has started to use them as well with the movie "Iron Man 2®," "9®," and HBO Series "True Blood®" and "Boardwalk Empire®." Calvin Klein®, Ralph Lauren®, Louis Vuitton®, Adidas®, General Mills®, Pepsi® and even the Detroit Red Wings® have used the QR Codes in some way!

Now that you know what these weird spotty square images are, if you have a smartphone, you might find yourself searching for a QR Code to scan when you're out in the real world, eager to have that virtual experience again. They certainly are engaging! If you're a smartphone user, rest assured, we've scattered some throughout our publication for you find! The idea of digitally connecting readers of our paper-based content to the internet is a powerful concept. Welcome to the Future!

DELAWARE

There's nothing wrong with being first, and the first state, Delaware, proves that again and again with first-class hospitality, scenic beauty, and some of the most important historical sites in the country. Wherever your travels take you, Delaware should be at the top of your list.

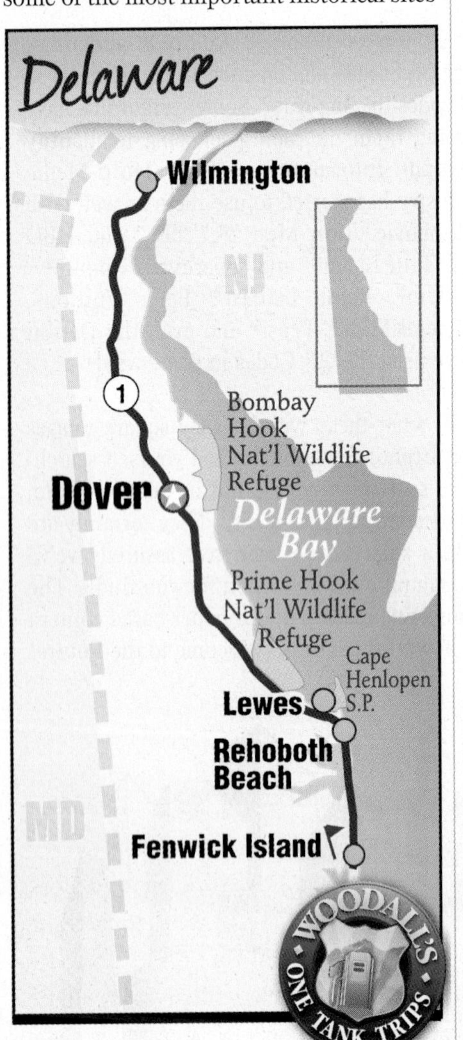

Fenwick Island is one of the most relaxing and serene places you're likely to find anywhere. Do yourself a big favor and make camp where you have an unobstructed view of the incredible sunset. Such eye-popping wonder should be savored. After the sun goes down, head into town and enjoy a fine dinner at any of the local restaurants, all of which offer fish that were caught – frequently on that very day – by fishermen from town.

After a great night's sleep and a hearty breakfast, point the rig north on Highway 1 and drive for a little less than 20 miles into the town of Rehoboth Beach. This is a thriving beachside community, and fun-in-the-sun is the name of the game. Local outlets will gladly rent you a kayak or a bike so you can go out on the water or enjoy the bike trails running along the beach. This town is all about relaxation, so soak in a mud bath at any of the local spas, or whack a few balls around the green at your pick of several golf courses in the area.

Eight miles further north on Highway 1 awaits the seaside village of Lewes. This historic town was established in the early 1600s and still retains a great deal of that period's charm and elegance, while still being rooted firmly in the 21st century. Continuing the tradition of the nearby cities of Rehoboth Beach and Fenwick Island, here you can find wide expanses of sand for you to spread out a blanket and enjoy the sunshine. The local wildlife refuge is a prime spot to go bird watching, or perhaps you'd like to hike or bike around town on one of the trails. You can rent a fishing boat, or take part in a crabbing expedition and take dinner home with you (just watch your fingers).

Leaving Lewes via the northbound Highway 1, drive for about 34 miles until you come to the city limits of Dover, Delaware's state capital. In addition to touring the state capitol building, you'll find the Dover Air Force Base and Air Mobility Command Museum to be a fascinating visit. The museum is an impressive facility, showcasing three-dozen aircraft, ranging from WWII-era fighters to the high-tech, present day combat aircraft. The Dover Downs Casino is also a popular destination, featuring Vegas-style opulence, with all manner of gambling, including a vast array of slot machines and horse racing. There's no better way to watch the ponies race around the track than in person, under the shade, with a cool beverage in your hand.

With a few winnings in your pocket, it's time to continue north on Highway 1 and take it for about 50 miles to your final stop, Wilmington. History buffs will enjoy the Wilmington and Western Railroad Museum, which displays the railroad that was completed in the mid 1800s, and offers visitors the chance to ride in vintage locomotives. There are also several botanical and herb gardens in town that feature a variety of flora in various stages of bloom throughout the year.

Without a doubt, Delaware lives up to its "First State" status, making it a fun, peaceful and scenic destination with ample opportunities for recreation and relaxation!

OTHER AREA LOCATIONS

LEWES

Tall Pines Campground Resort

MARYLAND

If you're looking for a unique and purely authentic American experience, you've come to the right place! The Maryland/Washington, D.C. area is the most popular destination for its unsurpassed beauty, warm sandy beaches, some of the most significant US historic landmarks in the country, and the place where history is made everyday.

While not technically part of Maryland, Washington, D.C. is most famous for such monuments like the Lincoln and Jefferson Memorials, the Washington Monument, the Smithsonian, the Capitol Building, and of course, the White House. These are impressive places to visit, and are sources of inspiration and wonder to all who experience them, so be sure to allow more than just a day to see them all. Another popular destination is the College Park Aviation Museum, which features original aircraft, as well as reproductions of every type of aircraft from aviation history. Interestingly enough, this is also America's oldest, still-functioning airport, conducting takeoffs and landings since 1909. In fact, you can watch current arrivals and departures from the museum windows.

Annapolis is just a short hop east on the US-50, a little over 20 miles. The state capitol building is an excellent place to start checking out the local sights, and you'll definitely want to stop by the Annapolis Maritime Museum. This facility contains fascinating exhibits showcasing the region's seafaring history, from the colonial days to its present contributions to the fishing industry. Annapolis is also the home of the prestigious U.S. Naval Academy, which has been producing the finest naval officers in the world since its founding in the mid-1800s. Tours are available, but it's best to call ahead for times and date availability.

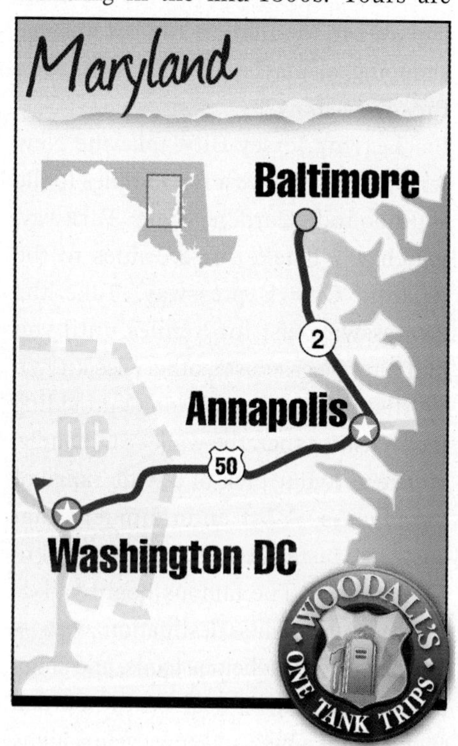

Head north on the MD-2 for about 20 miles and you'll pull into your next stop, Baltimore. This is another city that's rich with history and culture, and you'll most likely want to spend a day or two enjoying such interesting places as the B & O Railroad Museum, which has been devoted to showcasing the American railroad system since the late 1800s. The collection of artifacts and memorabilia is easily the largest and most comprehensive in the world, covering everything from the tiniest tools to a full collection of 19th century locomotives. This is a must-see for every type of train enthusiast. Fort McHenry is another popular visitors' destination; now a national monument, it was pivotal during the War of 1812's Battle of Baltimore, when it successfully repelled an assault by British naval forces. This battle gave Francis Scott Key the inspiration to write "The Star Spangled Banner," an anthem that is sung with pride around the country. Standing on Fort McHenry's grounds will definitely give you goosebumps.

While in Baltimore, be sure to look in on the 1,500 creatures, from over 200 species, that make up the animal population of the Maryland Zoo. They've got everything from A for aardvark to Z for zebra, and a whole lot in between. The animals roam about in created environments that replicate their own natural habitats, ranging from Arctic climes to the African plains. The National Aquarium is another fascinating way to spend a day; you'll see specimens of undersea animal and plant life that you'd normally need a snorkel or scuba gear to enjoy.

While the area's square mileage may be relatively small, you'll be hard pressed to visit all the museums and historic sites in both of these regions in just one trip, but what say we give it our best college try? History awaits...

OTHER AREA LOCATIONS

COLLEGE PARK

Cherry Hill Park

OCEAN CITY

Castaways RV Resort & Campground

Frontier Town Campground

WHALEYVILLE

Fort Whaley Campground

WOODBINE

Ramblin' Pines Family Campground & RV Park

NEW JERSEY

It's true New Jersey is widely known as a gateway to New York, but those lucky enough to spend some time exploring the Garden State will find quite a few surprises. As the most densely populated state in the nation, New Jersey is a state

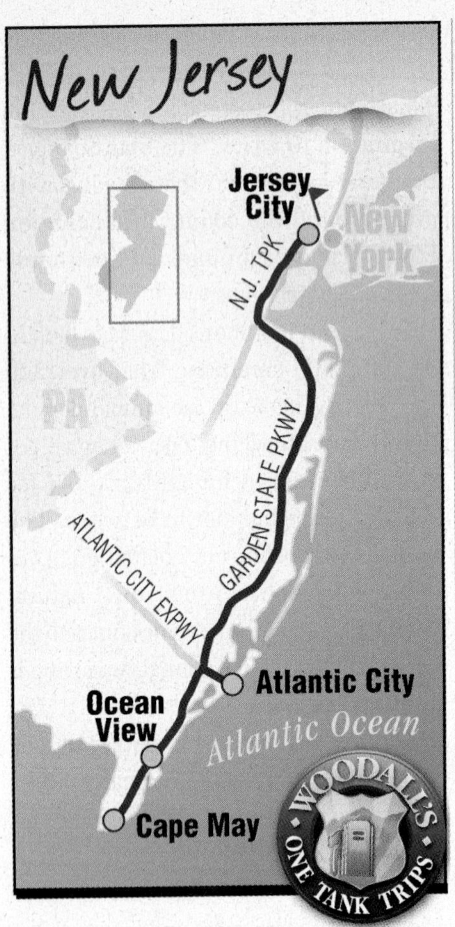

filled with important history, beautiful beaches, and a 72-mile leg of the Appalachian Trail. And there's nothing quite like seeing Lady Liberty from afar for the first time; it gives one a sense of what ship-bound immigrants must have felt upon arrival in America.

Jersey City makes for a great beginning for this southbound trip through New Jersey, via the Garden State Parkway. From Jersey City, you can take a harbor cruise across New York Harbor and get some of those previously mentioned spectacular views of Manhattan and Liberty Island. Or, take a short ferry ride to Ellis Island, which greeted more than 12 million immigrants who would one day become American citizens. Today, Ellis Island serves as a monument and museum to those brave individuals who sought a fresh start in the Land of Opportunity. While seeing the Statue of Liberty from afar is truly amazing, seeing New Jersey and New York from the top of the statue is equally impressive. It's a view you'll never forget. While you're in the neighborhood, how about a day trip over to Manhattan and get in some shopping, or maybe pick up tickets for a Broadway show?

Leaving Jersey City, take the New Jersey Turnpike west for 15 miles to the southbound Garden State Parkway, which you'll take for 25 miles to the Atlantic City Expressway. Take the Expressway east for 8 miles until you pull into "Vegas East", otherwise known as Atlantic City. In addition to providing more casinos than the wallet can handle, you've got your pick of a wide range of world-class, A-list entertainment that suits any taste, from Wayne Newton to Mötley Crüe. The famous Boardwalk is a definite don't-miss destination, with its classic arcades, delicious foods, and shopping galore. Take a walk on the Garden Pier, or rent a bike and go bicycling along the Boardwalk. The beaches all along the Jersey Coast are some of the most beautiful in the nation, so why not set up camp and enjoy some fun-in-the-sun for the day, then take in a show at night?

When you've had enough of flashy neon signs for a while, head west on the Atlantic City Expressway, then take the Garden State Parkway south for 20 miles to the town of Ocean View. This is a good spot to pull over and set up camp, and spend a bit more time at the beach. Take a sightseeing cruise across the clear, blue ocean, or try a little deep sea fishing or crabbing. Bring a camera along if you go out on the water, as whales and dolphins are frequently spotted in these waters.

Continuing south on the Garden State Parkway, it's another 20 miles before you come to your final destination on this route, Cape May. This town is widely renowned for its Victorian architecture, and one of the best – and most enjoyable – ways to see as much of it as possible is by taking an old-fashioned trolley tour of the historic Old Town district. The lighthouse at Cape May is also well worth a visit, and the view from its pinnacle has been described as spectacular. Originally built in the late 1800s, and recently restored to its original condition, this historic lighthouse beckons you to climb its 200 steps to the top, where you can see the Delaware Bay and the Atlantic Ocean stretching for miles and miles into the distance. Afterward, head over to any of the local wineries and relax with a wine tasting, featuring several samples of excellent local vintages.

As you can see, while New Jersey may be thought to be the gateway to Manhattan, the Garden State's equal to the Big City in entertainment and recreation.

CAPE MAY
Seashore Campsites

CLARKSBORO
Timberlane Campground

JERSEY CITY
Liberty Harbor RV Park

MAYS LANDING
Winding River Campground

NEW GRETNA
Timberline Lake Camping Resort

OCEAN VIEW
Ocean View Resort Campground

PENNSYLVANIA

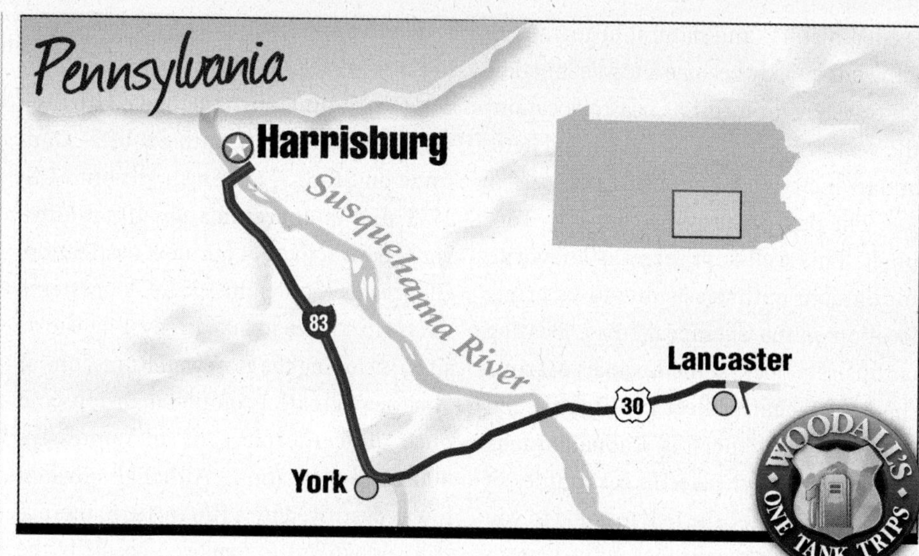

From its confluence of three rivers, Pennsylvania lures travelers with a wealth of historic attractions, craggy mountain ranges like the Allegheny and Appalachians, and the beauty of Dutch Country, represented by a large Amish and Mennonite communities. Not to be outdone, Mother Nature makes a brilliant display here in every corner of the state with dramatic colors (especially in the fall), and enough outdoor recreation to keep Pennsylvania at the top of your list.

There is no place better to start our adventure than in Lancaster, right in the heart of Pennsylvania's Dutch Country. Visitors here will find a beautiful blend of old world charm and modern day attractions, most notably the wonders of the Amish Farm and House, the Mennonite Information Center, and the Lancaster Quilt and Textile Museum. At each location, visitors can familiarize themselves with the Amish people who call this area home and the simplicity with which they live their lives. Well known for its covered bridges, this area has an abundance of these beauties to drive through, explore, and photograph. For the kiddies - or just the young at heart - stop by Dutch Wonderland, a kingdom for the little ones to enjoy over 30 kid-friendly rides, plenty of live entertainment, and a bunch of memories to be made.

The next stop on our Pennsylvania journey is the city of York, less than an hours drive on US-30 W. If you've ever had an interest in colonial or Revolutionary War history, you've come to the right place. Surrounded by the beauty of rolling hills and several Amish communities, this city was once America's first capital, a history you can trace through the amazing architecture downtown, which spans two and a half centuries. It's here you'll find the Colonial Courthouse, the place where the Continental Congress signed the Articles of Confederation in 1777. Another not to miss attraction is the Central Market, where locals and visitors have been shopping for more than a century. For the outdoor enthusiasts, golf, cycling and kayaking are just a few of the offerings to be found here.

Leaving York on I-83 N, continue on through the scenic Dutch countryside, and in less than an hour you will have arrived at the final destination of our journey, Harrisburg. Located on the beautiful Susquehanna River, Harrisburg has been the capital of Pennsylvania since 1812. Exquisite examples of Victorian, Antebellum, Tudor and Georgian styles can be found throughout the diverse neighborhoods within the city. The crowning jewel is the city's capitol building whose dome dominates the skyline, and was inspired by St. Peter's Basilica in Rome. Visitors are offered the opportunity to board an old-fashioned paddlewheeler and take a lazy cruise down the Susquehanna River, and Harrisburg's streets are lined with small shops, quaint cafes, and beautiful old buildings; the perfect place to leisurely stroll, grab some lunch, or look for a great bargain or perfect souvenir to remind you of your trip to this incredible city.

If you've never been to the Keystone State, you don't know what you've been missing! Full of history and beauty, Pennsylvania is hard to resist, whether it's your first time or your hundredth. Give Pennsylvania the chance to charm you once, and guaranteed it will charm you again and again.

VIRGINIA

They say "Virginia is for lovers", and never was there a truer statement. It's a state for lovers of vast mountain ranges, southern hospitality, grassy plains, deep-

seeded history, and natural beauty. Virginia has quickly become a top destination for travelers for its prime coastal location, the wealth of recreation to be found here, and its incredible beauty.

The perfect start for our trip is Topping. This well-kept secret is a favorite for outdoor enthusiasts due to its prime location on the Chesapeake Bay. Boating enthusiasts flock to the Locklies Marina, the largest charter fleet in Virginia, and for the angler there is Rappahannock River, the perfect place to cast a line, sit back, and wait for the fish to come to you while you dangle your feet in the water.

Head out of Topping via VA-3 E, merge onto VA-33 W, and after several miles, turn right onto VA-227 N to arrive at our next stop, Urbanna. Picturesque Urbanna is located on the Rappahannock River, and was established as a port for the shipment of tobacco to England. Travelers can find remnants of the past at the tobacco warehouse, built in 1766, which now serves as a visitor center. Another architectural beauty is the Urbanna courthouse. Built in 1784, the building is on the National Register of Historic Places, and is one of only 11 colonial era courthouses still standing in Virginia. For those lucky enough to visit in November, you won't want to miss the Urbanna Oyster Festival. Attracting thousands every year, you will be treated to several oyster specialties and other exquisite Chesapeake Bay seafood, as well as a parade, art exhibit, and several fine crafts from local artisans. This is a huge event, and one worth spending some time exploring.

Continuing our trip, leave Urbanna via SR-602, and left onto SR-615. Continue on SR-615, making a left onto US-17 S, and in approximately 40 minutes, you'll have arrived at our next destination, Gloucester. Settled in 1651, Gloucester is the perfect place to take in several historic sites, including the Rosewell Ruins, one of America's greatest colonial mansions and once the centerpiece of an impressive 3000-acre plantation. Although much of it was destroyed by a fire in 1916, there is still enough left to explore, especially the intricate 18th century brickwork. For the angler, there is no place better than the 625-acre Beaverdam Park. This is the only public freshwater fishing on the Middle Peninsula, and a great place to cast your line or do some hiking on the scenic nature trail.

Our next stop is Yorktown. A short drive on US-17 S will get you there in around a half an hour. If you're looking for total immersion in 300 years of history, you've come to the right place! Yorktown is filled with plenty of 18th Century homes and Revolutionary War battlefields for you to explore. A great place to start your walk through history is in the Yorktown Victory Center, which chronicles the history of the last battle that secured our great nation from British rule and covers the rest of the Revolutionary War as well. All that history is sure to spark your appetite, and the town's picturesque streets are filled with charming restaurants, many of which have a wonderful view of the York River. After you've sated yourself, stroll along the scenic riverwalk, or browse through the many antique and specialty shops where you're sure to find something you just can't live without.

Heading onward, take Colonial National Historic Parkway out of Yorktown. Turn left onto VA-132 S to arrive at our next destination, Williamsburg. For those that want to get a glimpse of where America, democracy, and revolution began, take a tour of Jamestown, the first permanent English settlement in the New World. Colonial Williamsburg is the nation's largest living history museum, encompassing 301 acres rife with stores, homes, taverns and buildings painstakingly restored to their beautiful 18th-century appearance. Along the way, travelers will experience historical interpreters and character actors, as well as 90 acres of gardens and greens. Williamsburg is an experience for all ages, and one that is sure to hold everyone's attention (even those who don't love history). Watch out, you just might learn something after a visit here!

Leaving Williamsburg, take US60 E out of town and directly to our next location, Newport News. An exceptional Peninsula city with much to offer on land and sea, it is a history lover's paradise with several key Civil War battle locations, including the site of General McClellan's only major attempt to break through the Confederate defenses. For history and military buffs alike, visit the Virginia War Museum, which traces American military history from the Revolutionary War to the present. An impressive collection of over 65,000 artifacts is contained within the museum.

Heading out on I-664 S with a slight left at I-264 E to Virginia Beach. Way before the Spring Break crowd discovered Virginia Beach as the go-to place for fun, Europeans settled in this gorgeous area in 1607, and they've been flocking here ever since! Maybe it's the beautiful beaches, the incredible history or wealth of outdoor recreation? It's probably all of these, and then some. On the boardwalk, visitors get spectacular views of the ocean on one side, and an endless array of attractions on the other—from amusement parks to shops! Visitors can take guided tours and come face-to-face with dolphins and whales, or kayak, golf, fish or swim. Sightseers will enjoy taking in some of the oldest homes in the country, or the first government lighthouse. The possibilities are endless in Virginia Beach!

Our last stop takes us to US-60 out of Virginia Beach, and after a partial toll, turning right on US-13 N. Continue across the Chesapeake Bay Bridge, and when you get to VA-184, go west towards Cape Charles. With one of the largest concentrations of late Victorian and turn of the century buildings on the east coast, the entire town of Cape Charles has been designated as a Historic District on the Virginia Landmarks Register and the beauty of this area will stun you. For the birder, head over to Kiptopeke State Park for viewing opportunities, especially during the fall migratory season.

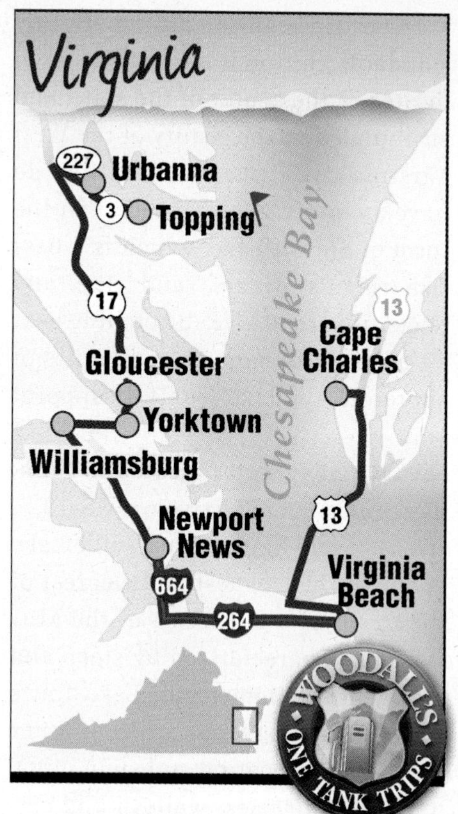

Once you've had a little time in Virginia, it will soon be clear what all the fuss is about, and Virginia will make a lover out of you, too!

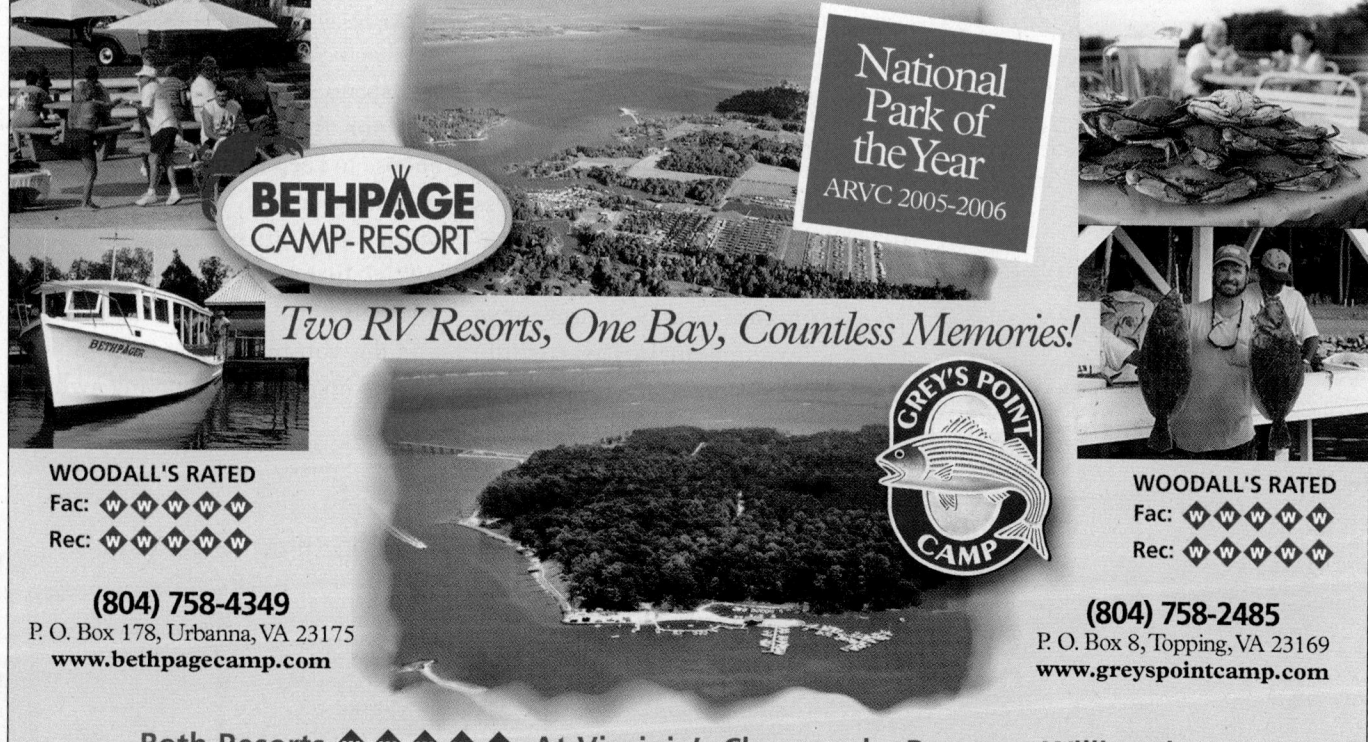

OTHER AREA LOCATIONS

BROADWAY

Harrisonburg / Shenandoah Valley KOA

CENTREVILLE

Bull Run Regional Park

CHERITON

Cherrystone Family Camping Resort

FAIRFAX

Burke Lake Park (Fairfax County Park Authority)

Lake Fairfax Park (Fairfax County Park)

GREY'S POINT

Grey's Point Camp RV Adventures

LORTON

Pohick Bay Regional Park

STAFFORD

Aquia Pines Camp Resort

URBANNA

Bethpage Mini-Golf & Ice Creamery

RV Adventures

VIRGINIA BEACH

Holiday Trav-L-Park of Virginia Beach

WILLIAMSBURG

KOA-Colonial Central

KOA-Williamsburg

WEST VIRGINIA

Any savvy traveler will tell you, West Virginia has it all. With the heart of the graceful Appalachian Mountains providing a breathtaking backdrop, West Virginia is one of the best kept secrets within the eastern US. Here you'll find the beauty of rural locales, scenic and serene vistas, a host of outdoor activity, and four distinct seasons to do it in.

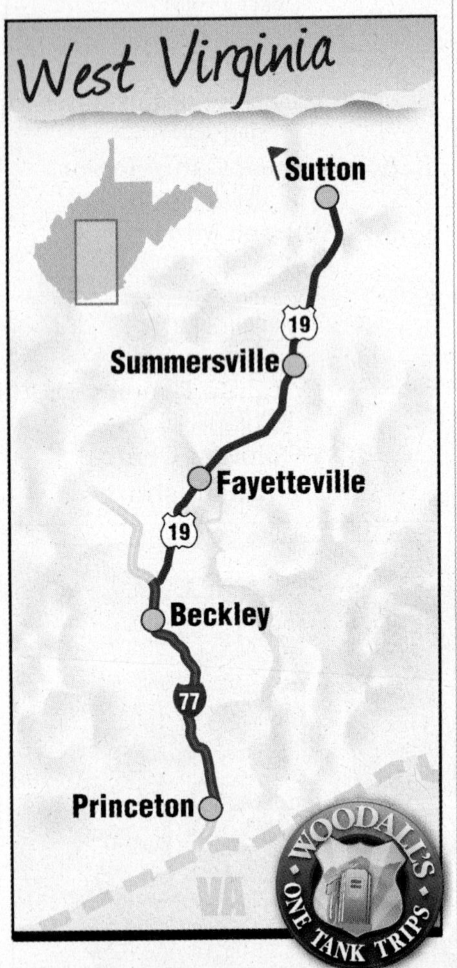

Our trip begins in Sutton. By any standards, Sutton is a tiny little town located in the center of the state, and surrounded by the beauty of the West Virginia countryside. But they do have a closely guarded secret in the form of Sutton Lake, which is a bass fisherman's dream, and one any angler is sure to love. Stretching over 14 miles, with more than 40 miles of shoreline, the lake won't disappoint you!

Our next stop takes us to Summersville, a short drive on US-19 S. It's been said that Summersville Lake is one of the cleanest and clearest of the freshwater lakes east of the Mississippi. Characterized by steep and rocky cliffs, Summersville Lake draws travelers looking for a variety of water sports - from boating and swimming, to fishing for bass, walleye and catfish. Due to the clarity of the lake, divers and snorkelers are drawn to this area as well. For the history buffs, you'll find the Carnifex Ferry Battlefield war site nearby, and the area provides a wealth of opportunities for hiking with many interpretive signs throughout the trails provide some insight into the historic battle fought here.

Return to US-19 S for the less than an hour drive to our next location, Fayetteville. You will exhaust yourself before you ever run out of fun and excitement in Fayetteville! Due to its location in the heart of one of the most sought after locales in the state, Fayetteville is at the very center of exciting outdoor recreation opportunities including mountain biking, rock climbing, bird watching, hiking, hunting, fishing, and for the true adventurer, white water rafting. And if you're looking for something a little tamer as far as adventure goes, don't worry; Fayetteville has a wonderfully historic downtown area waiting to be explored, several exceptional and eclectic restaurants to entice you, and some first class shopping opportunities to be had as well.

Moving further down US-19 S takes us to our last stop, Beckley. It's hard not to feel the relaxed, quaint vibe of this city from the moment you set foot within its borders. If you want to get a feel for what coal mining is all about, you can tour around in a coal car at the Exhibition Coal Mine, which takes you on an underground tour. Or if you're making your trip in the summertime, pack up a picnic and head over to the blueberry farm, where you can pick blueberries to your heart's content. There is also no shortage of excitement or outdoor fun in Beckley. You can choose to keep it mild with some birdwatching or golf, or go full out with whitewater rafting, rock climbing or ATVs. Just pick your poison, and it's all right here! With so much to see and do, you just might find yourself setting up camp and staying awhile.

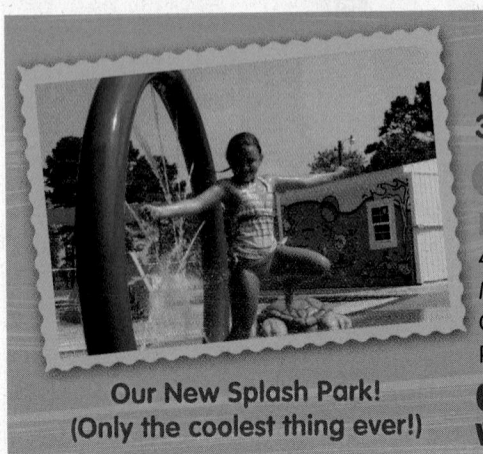

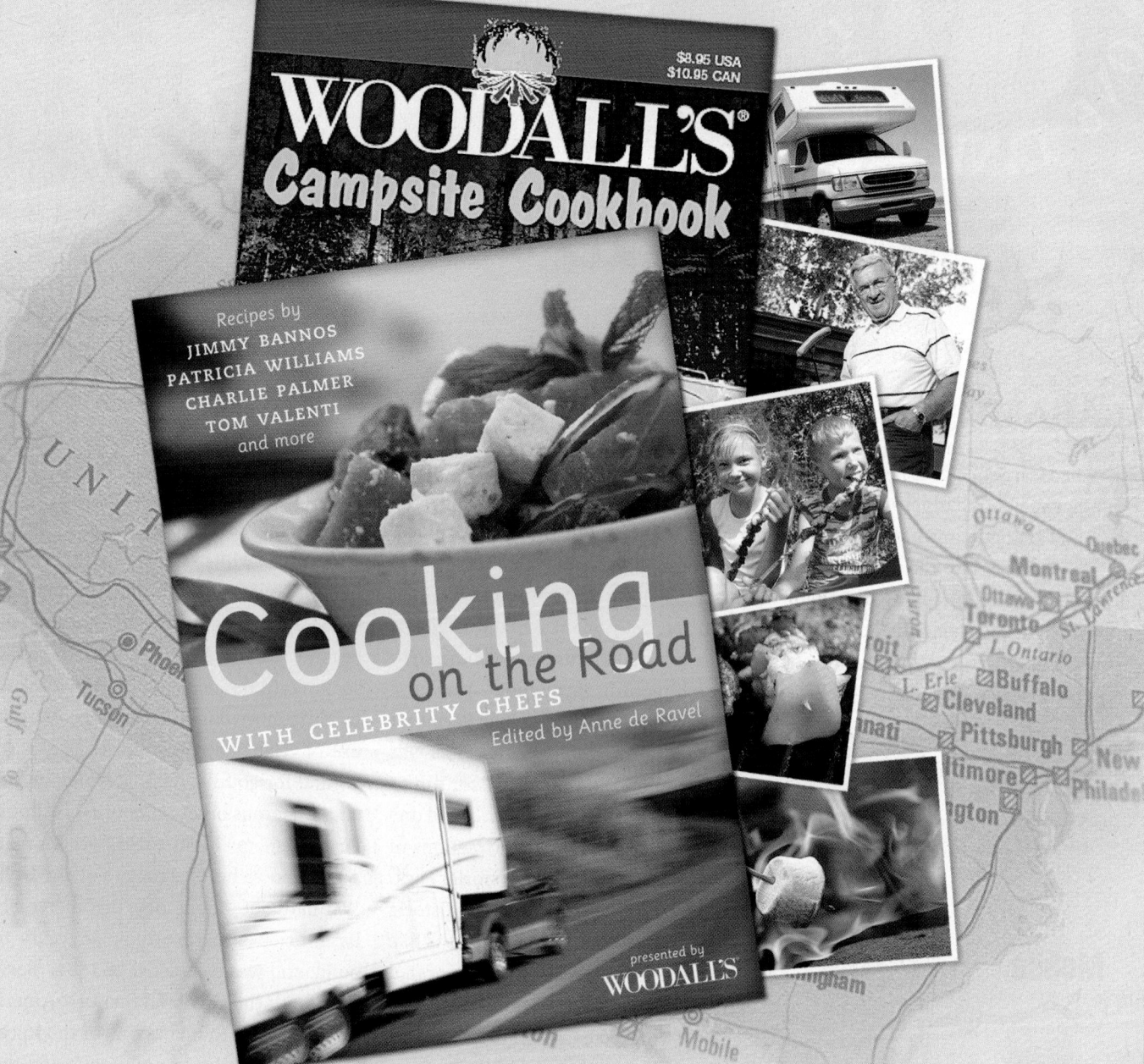

ALABAMA

The Heart of Dixie is nestled firmly between Mississippi and Georgia, and shares a long and interesting past. The birthplace of the Confederacy, and the state which first brought to light the Civil Rights Movement, Alabama is known for its diverse geography and its wonderful Southern Hospitality. Visitors here are encouraged to slow down, relax, and ask, "what's the rush?"

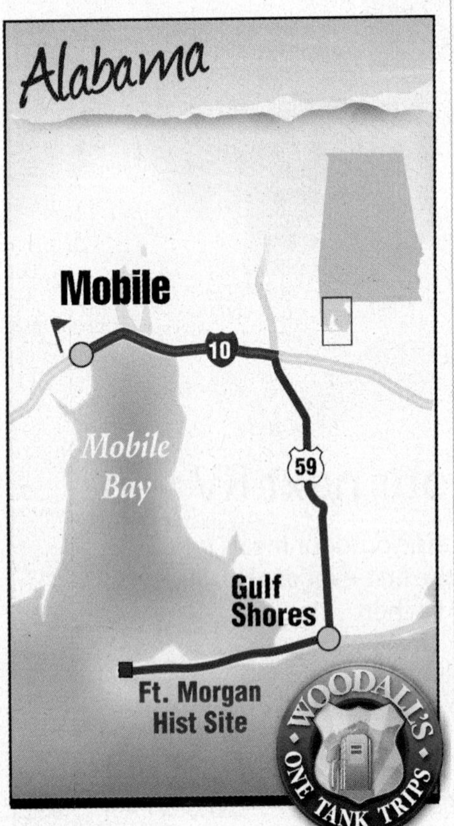

Our trip begins in Mobile, once the first capital of colonial French Louisiana in 1702, it is also one of the 14th oldest cities in the United States. For its first 100 years, Mobile was a colony of France, then Britain and lastly Spain, and the influence of these early landlords can still be seen in the architecture throughout the city. Located on the Mobile Bay, the very first organized celebration of Mardi Gras was celebrated here, and the party continues to this day. It's here visitors will find one of the most unique military attractions in the world, the Battleship Memorial Park. You can walk the flight decks of historic vessels, and get a taste of what it was like aboard one of America's most decorated battleships. Don't miss the Bellingrath Gardens! A 65 acre Garden Estate started in 1932, the gardens are always in bloom with beautiful and delicate flowers. A self-guided tour is available for the gardens, as well as at the Bellingrath Home, and it just might be the thing to inspire the gardener in you. For the mad scientist (or just the science enthusiast), The Gulf Coast Exploreum Science Center is the place to entertain you. With more than 150 interactive exhibits, IMAX films, and hands on educational programming, the Science Center is perfect for the whole family to learn about science and the world around us.

Leaving Mobile, take I-10 E to Hwy-59 S, and in a little over an hour, you'll arrive at our next stop, Gulf Shores. Some of the finest white sand beaches are found here in Gulf Shores. Wait, Alabama has beaches? Oh yes, it does, and nothing can be more relaxing than sitting on the beach, soaking up the rays, and letting all your troubles move out with the tide. A treasure of Alabama, Gulf Shores is a playground for golfing, fishing, water sports, and numerous other outdoor recreations. Pay a visit to the historic Fort Morgan while you're here. The site of the Civil War battle of Mobile Bay, this incredibly large brick structure took 15 years to build, and was completed in 1834. Servicing both the Civil and Spanish-American Wars, it is touted as one of the finest examples of military architecture in the world. The craftsmanship alone is a marvel for it's time, and shouldn't be missed on any trip to this area. There are many cruise companies that offer dolphin excursions, and any visit to Gulf Shores wouldn't be complete without joining one. Get up close and personal with the beautiful porpoises that call the Gulf home, and depending on the company, you just might get the chance to go snorkeling or the opportunity for a midnight rendezvous with these delightful creatures. Many visitors will also enjoy Waterville, USA. The largest water park in the area, and the perfect place for a cool down, the park is 20 acres of nonstop wet fun. The wave machine produces gigantic waves, and the lazy river is just the place to sit back and relax in the sun. A great place for the whole family, and well worth a visit.

No matter the reason you pay a visit to Alabama, whether for some much needed rest, or the thrill of a lifetime, Alabama has the thing you're looking for, and much, much more.

FLORIDA - CENTRAL

The Sunshine State is a destination high on the list for many travelers. Endless blue skies, months of warm weather, and miles of beaches make this beautiful state irresistible for even the most jaded traveler. Oh, and did I mention it's also home to Disney World, the largest amusement park on the planet? Grab your sandals, and don't forget the sunscreen, we're off to explore Central Florida!

Located on the beautiful coast of the Atlantic, Titusville is a popular destination for travelers seeking many of the year-round recreation activities available, including fishing, swimming, canoeing, surfing, and hiking on many of the nature and historical trails offered at the Canaveral National Seashore. Stretching approximately 24 miles, it is the longest stretch of undeveloped public beach on the east coast, drawing thousands for it's scenic beauty and ecological and historic value. If you find yourself staring up at the stars at night, wondering exactly what is out there in all that wide-open space, you might find some answers by paying a visit to the Cape Canaveral Space Center. Here you can explore the early beginnings of space exploration, and the most recent leaps in technology. Walk through a full-scale replica of a shuttle obiter, see real moon rocks, and be blown away by movies seen on the giant IMAX screen. Cape Canaveral shares space with the Merritt Island National Wildlife Refuge, which consists of 140,000 acres of coastal dunes, saltwater estuaries, pine flatwoods and hardwood hammocks that provide a home to more than 1,500 species of plants and animals. There are many recreation opportunities provided at the Refuge, including bird and wildlife observation, a manatee observation deck, as well as hunting and fishing.

Our next destination is Orlando; a short but scenic drive on US-50 W will get you there in no time. Travelers here will find the world famous Walt Disney World Resort, which includes four major theme parks-Magic Kingdom, Epcot Center, Disney MGM Studios and Disney Animal Kingdom. More than just attractions, this giant amusement park is an adventure, welcoming visitors from across the globe and from all age groups for a unique and exhilarating experience. What's a visit to Florida without some up close and personal time with gators? Pay a visit to Gatorland, a protected habitat, a 110-acre theme park, and a nature conservatory, complete with breeding marsh, boardwalk and observation tower - it is the best and safest way to learn about these incredible creatures, and one of the few places you can observe some good ol' fashioned gator wrestlin'! Sea World, home of Shamu the killer whale, offers visitors some amazing fun with aquarium exhibits, thrill rides, and water shows. Don't forget to jump aboard the Wild Arctic helicopter while you're there for an amazing view of the North Pole exhibit, where polar bears run and play in their very own recreated environment.

A less than 2-hour drive on US-50 W will bring you to our next destination, Brooksville. Nestled among rolling hills and wide open spaces, and with Withlacoochee State Forest as it's back yard, this quaint town is just the thing we need to slow it down a bit after the nonstop fun in Orlando. Nearby Homosassa Spring State Wildlife Park is what draws most visitors, and a place where you can discover the real Florida with sightseeing tours, fishing and snorkeling, and many other outdoor activities.

Now that we've rested a bit, let's move on to US-19 S, and merge onto I-275 E to Tampa. One of the most beautiful and exotic locations in Florida, Tampa Bay

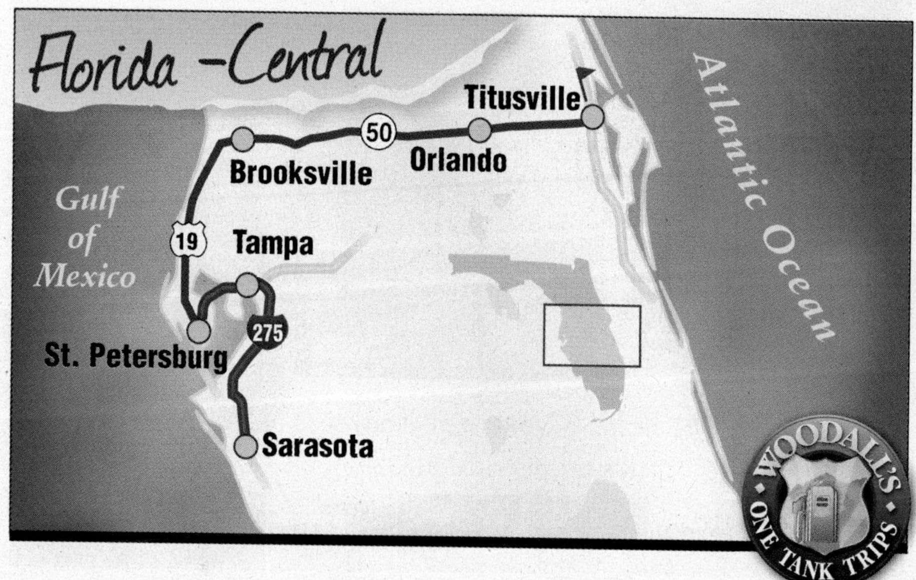

is filled with breathtaking views, and has a little of everything you're looking for. Tampa is home to the beautiful Busch Garden & Theme Park, where visitors can have up-close and personal encounters with some amazing creatures, or set off on a safari on the Serengeti Plains, or feel your heart jump out of your chest on one of the many coasters here. For a purely exotic experience, visitors should head over to Tampa's Latin Quarter, Ybor City. Once a cigar manufacturing center, the city is one of only two National Historic Landmark Districts in the Sunshine State, and a great place to discover the delightful Latin culture that has left it's mark throughout this area. Watch experienced artisans roll their handmade cigars, and have a cup of that famous Cuban coffee while you relax in the sun.

Moving along down I-275 S, our next stop is Tampa's sister city, St. Petersburg. A city with as much grace, style and sophistication as her sister across the bay, this amazing city is well known for its beautiful emerald waters, never ending outdoor recreation, and its ability to weave a tropical spell on anyone who happens to be traveling through. The Salvador Dali Museum is a must see for culture seekers, and houses the world's largest collected works of the great Surrealist artist. At the St. Petersburg Museum of History, you can retrace the history of this city and surrounding areas. Another must see for culture buffs is the Sunken Gardens. The oldest living museum, this lovely 100-year-old garden is home to some of the oldest tropical plants within the region. A wonderful place for a stroll among the more than 50,000 plants, this peaceful and serene garden also has cascading waterfalls, and offers tours.

Back on I-275 S, we are headed to our last destination, Sarasota. Sarasota, although not as big as the other cities on our trip, has a wonderful concentration of culture and outdoor fun that you can enjoy for a few sweet days or for years. The Ringling Museum, one of the most remarkable museums in the world, calls Sarasota home, and should be placed high on your list of things to see here. Built by John Ringling, of the Ringling Bros. fame, the collection houses many incredible pieces of art, and as a bonus, on the 66 acre grounds there is also a theater and two circus museums.

The possibilities for fun and excitement in this exquisite state are endless. The sand, sun and warm tropical breezes have a way of turning the most serious traveler into a run away hedonist!

OTHER AREA LOCATIONS

LAKE BUENA VISTA

Disney's Fort Wilderness Resort & Campground

LAKE PLACID

Camp Florida Resort

MARATHON

Grassy Key RV Park & Resort

Jolly Roger Travel Park

NAPLES

Neapolitan Cove RV Resort

SARASOTA

Turtle Beach Campground at Turtle Beach Park

TAMPA

Bay Bayou RV Resort

Lazydays RV Campground

TITUSVILLE

The Great Outdoors RV-Nature & Golf Resort

VENICE

Myakka RV Resort - KOA

WESLEY CHAPEL

Quail Run RV Resort

FLORIDA - NORTH

North Florida contains some of the oldest settlements in the state, as well as in all of the US. The number one tourist destination in the world welcomes millions every year to soak up the sun, tee up, bird watch and fish, and with year-round mild temperatures in most of the state, millions more seek it out as part of their permanent vacation.

Today we start in St. Augustine, the nation's oldest city, and one filled with a deep rooted history and unparalleled beauty. Throughout the city, St. Augustine continues to pay homage to its past with several attractions. If you're looking for a hands-on approach to history, stop by the Old Florida Museum where visitors get the chance to write with a quill pen or work on an Indian dug out canoe. Don't miss a visit to The Castillo de San Marcos. Built to protect the Spaniards' claim to the New World, it is an architectural wonder, and the oldest masonry and only extant

17th century fort in North America. The Fort Matanzas National Monument is another fascinating place worth exploring, and was also built under Spanish rule. The city of St. Augustine is filled with amazing sights to study, and a very colorful and enduring history to fall in love with.

Moving on, take US-1 S along the breathtaking coast to our next stop, Palm Coast. A unique city lush in native trees and an old Florida feel, this city is full of charm, with beautiful canals that move both salt and freshwater through this area. Palm Coast has several championship golf courses to test your skills, as well as several tennis courts. And of course, there is plenty of fishing and boating to go around! A charter is the best way to try your fishing skills, and offers the chance to catch blue marlin, king mackerel, wahoo, and many others. Many travelers come here for the quiet and serene nature of this area, and to get away from the stress of everyday life.

A little further down US-1 S, we arrive at our next stop, Flagler Beach. Another beautiful and peaceful place, Flagler Beach is reminiscent of old Florida. Travelers can immerse themselves in kayaking, canoeing, hiking, biking, horseback riding, birdwatching and fishing. Flagler Beach is one of those rare, virtually untouched places where the peace that surrounds it moves through you, instantly relaxing and calming you.

Continuing on scenic US-1 S, the next destination on our trip is Ormond Beach. Once home to the likes of John D. Rockefeller, as well as many early auto pioneers who tested their inventions here, Ormond Beach celebrates its racing heritage annually with reenactments of the early days of racing on the beach. Visitors should tour the former winter home of Rockefeller, and then sprint outdoors for some fun in the sun.

Can you feel the ground shake? Earthquake? Nope, but close! A little further down US-1 S leads us to every racing fans dream; Daytona Beach. If you have the need for speed, make sure you make a stop to the raceway for some heart pounding, earth shaking racing: it's an experience you won't soon forget! Every racing fan should pay a visit to the Halifax Historical Museum, a fascinating place where you can trace the history of auto racing. Ponce Inlet is well known as a surfer's haven, drawing crowds who can't wait to paddle out and ride some waves. Travelers should visit Florida's tallest lighthouse, which is located here, and if you can handle the 203 steps to the top, you will be aptly rewarded with an amazing 360-degree view of the Atlantic. Don't worry, the trip down is much easier!

Heading to our last stop, we continue down the coast on US-1 S to New Smyrna Beach. Quaint New Smyrna has a wonderful historic hometown feel, and its harbors are a reminder of the Sugar Mill Ruins. Apollo Beach is part of the extensive and beautiful Canaveral National Seashore, which is all-natural and remains minimally developed. Visitors will enjoy

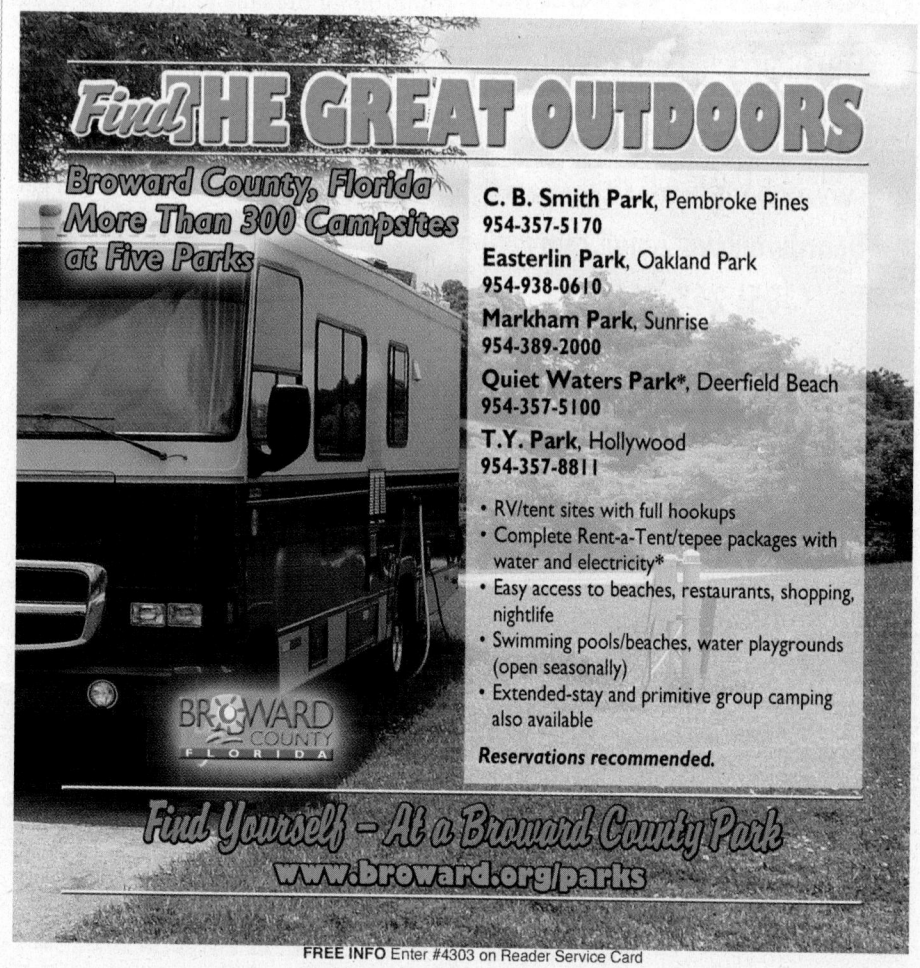

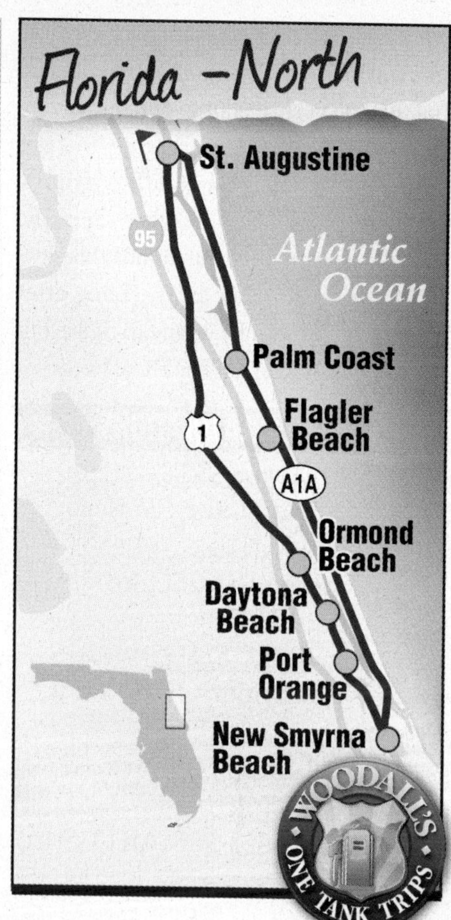

walking the many trails, and participating in many of the water sports offered, making this the perfect spot to end our adventure.

Florida has much to offer visitors: endless sun, sandy beaches and the incredible beauty that surrounds this state make it hard to stay away. Long after you've gone, you'll be trying to figure out how soon you can get back!

FLORIDA - SOUTH

Southern Florida is magical. In less than an hour into your visit here, you'll want to trade in the rat race for a pair of Bermuda shorts, a Hawaiian shirt, and just a fishing pole to keep you company. Don't fret, it happens to just about everyone who comes here. The fresh air, warm, humid breezes and perfectly sunny days are intoxicating.

Today we begin in the city of Okeechobee. Located on the northern tip of Lake Okeechobee, the name is derived from the Seminole language, and literally means, 'Big Water'. In English, that can only mean one thing: good fishing! The second largest freshwater lake in the US, Okeechobee is an angler's paradise, offering great fishing opportunities. For the adventurous, take one of the airboat rides offered, and tour this incredible lake. You just might see a gator or two, as well as some endangered species. In the mood for a hike? The Florida Trail is the perfect way to see this beautiful body of water in its entirety. There are many points along the lake to access the trail, and plenty of covered benches along the route if you want to stop and marvel at the beauty or have a picnic.

Our next destination is the city of Clewiston. Taking Hwy-78 S, you'll get an incredible view of Lake Okeechobee. Merge onto Hwy-27 E, and in no time, we'll have arrived. Clewiston is located on the southern shore of Lake Okeechobee, and if you didn't catch anything up on the north side of the lake, feel free to cast your line on this side and give it a go. A must visit when in this area is the Big Cypress Seminole Reservation. Home to the Billie Swamp Safari, a 2,200 acre eco-heritage wildlife park located in the Everglades, visitors can take a tour on an airboat or swamp buggy, watch some swamp critter shows, hike the nature trail, and marvel over the reptile and animal exhibits. The Swamp Safari is located on some of the reservation's wildest land, an area that hasn't changed much over the last 150 years. If you close your eyes, you can just imagine what it was like when cowboys herded their cattle through the scrub, and warriors ruled the swamps. The Reservation is also host to a casino, and the Ah-Tah-Thi-Ki Museum, a wonderful place to learn about the life and customs of the great Seminole tribe.

Take Hwy-27 S out of Clewiston, and merge onto Hwy-997 S, and in about an hour you'll arrive at our next destination, Homestead. This amazing city sits on the edge of the Everglades, and it's here that travelers can kayak through the mangrove tunnels, and spot some of the 200 species of birds that migrate through the area. Also known as a great site for fishing, visitors enjoy the half-mile hike on the Anhinga Trail. Be on the look for alligators, birds, and turtles as you hike. If you're a racing fan, then you have to take a trip to the Homestead-Miami Speedway for some heart-pounding fun. Considered one of the most beautiful tracks in the country, the speedway hosts several major races, and is a racing fan's dream.

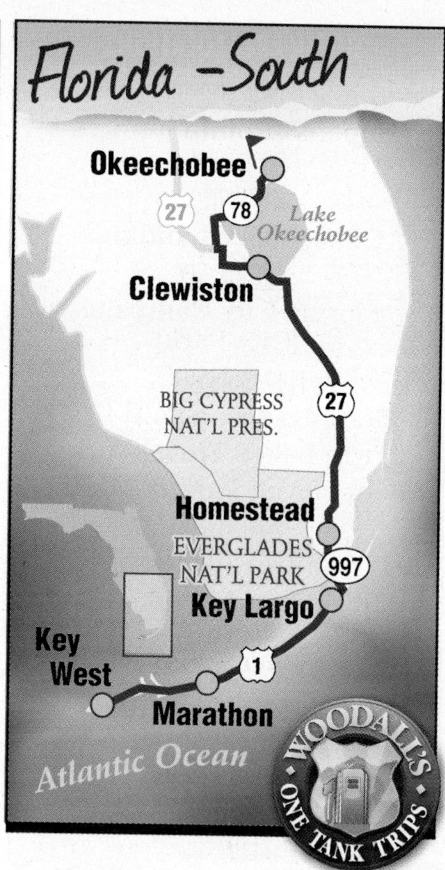

Moving on, take US-1 S through the beautiful Everglades to arrive at our next stop, Key Largo. Upon arriving, you'll notice right away why so many people include a trip to the Keys as part of their vacation. Home to the only living coral barrier reef in North America, Key Largo offers some of the finest diving and snorkeling opportunities in the Keys, and there are many guided trips available. Key Largo is nearly as famous as a sport-fishing destination as it is for diving. Offshore, anglers can test their fishing skills on any number of charters available in the area, and with the some of the best charter fishing guides and captains at the ready, it should make for a wonderful experience.

Returning to US-1 S, get your camera ready, as this is one of the most incredibly scenic and breathtaking stretches of highway anywhere in the world. If you weren't in love with this area before, you will be! In a little over an hour, you should arrive at our next destination, Marathon. Scenic Marathon is home to the Dolphin Research Center, and a place you won't want to miss. Better than any regular sightseeing tour, visitors here can experience one-on-one time with these amazing mammals, and even swim with them! Also home to several sea lions, it is a great place to learn more about their fragile habitat, as well as these endearing creatures themselves.

The last stop on our tour takes us to Key West, just a little further on US-1 S. If this is your first visit to the city, you are in for a real treat. Aside from more great fishing and even more great diving and snorkeling, Key West is a perfect place to sample some spectacular seafood. At the Theater of the Sea, you'll get another great opportunity to swim with the dolphins, stingrays, and sea lions. The Key West Aquarium is another must see, and one of the most unique aquariums in the world. This fascinating place has been delighting visitors since 1934. And if after all this, South Florida isn't your favorite runaway destination, stay for the sunset...it's awe-inspiring!

OTHER AREA LOCATIONS

BONITA SPRINGS
Imperial Bonita Estates RV Resort

CLEWISTON
Okeechobee Landings

FLORIDA CITY
Florida City Campsite (City Park)

FORT LAUDERDALE
Paradise Island
Twin Lakes Travel Park
Yacht Haven Park & Marina

FORT MYERS
Raintree RV Resort
Riverbend Motorcoach Resort
Seminole Campground
Woodsmoke Camping Resort

FORT MYERS BEACH
San Carlos Island Resort

KEY LARGO
Calusa Campground Condominium Association

KEY WEST
Bluewater Key RV Resort
Boyd's Key West Campground

LA BELLE
The Glades RV, Golf & Marina Resort

OKEECHOBEE
Okeechobee County Tourism Development Council
Silver Palms RV Village
Zachary Taylor RV Resort

WEST PALM BEACH
Vacation Inn Resort

GEORGIA

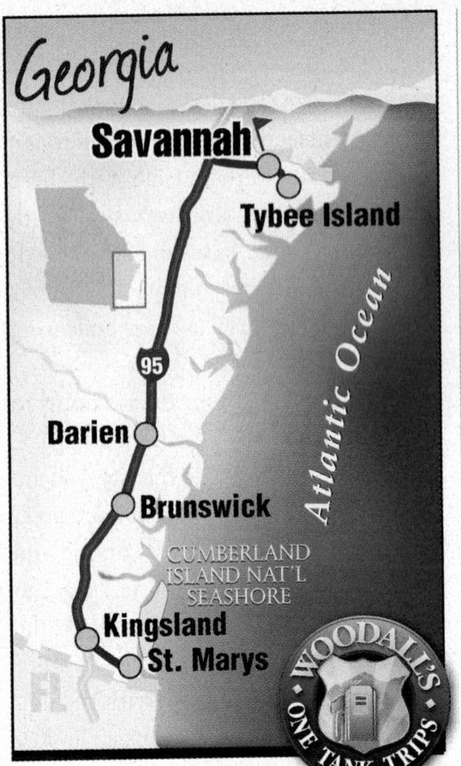

If you have Georgia on your mind, there's good reason. Warm Southern nights, Spanish Moss gently swinging from the trees, antebellum mansions, friendly people, and mint juleps sipped on the porch. Sounds good, doesn't it? So let's get moving!

There is no better starting place for our trip than Savannah. Draped in Southern charm, with a long and interesting history, Savannah is an experience to be treasured. With numerous parks, attractions, and several landmarks, it's one of the few places that can be best discovered by a walking, boat or trolley tour. The historic district alone encompasses a huge area that has been well preserved and is one of the most expansive historic districts in the nation. River Street comes highly recommended during your visit. Stroll along the water, or visit any of the 100 shops, galleries or restaurants that line the cobblestone streets. Savannah is home to 22 public squares, and any one of them is a perfect place to kick off your shoes and enjoy a picnic. Another great attraction is the Gray's Reef National Marine Sanctuary. One of largest near shore live-bottom reefs in the southeastern US, it is also one of 14 marine protected areas, and the only natural area protected off the Georgia coast.

Moving on to our next stop, take US-80 E to Tybee Island. From kayaking to sunbathing, Tybee Island can accommodate many desires. A great area for dolphin viewing and for fishing, many chartered tours are offered, and an array of boats await to take travelers on an unforgettable ride around this beautiful area. Aside from all the sun, fun and water sports that can be had here, there are several historic sites to visit as well. The Marine Science Center offers aquariums, interactive and interpretive programs, and nearby restaurants offer a feast for seafood lovers. Another must see is the Tybee Island Lighthouse, one of only a few 18th century lighthouses still in operation

Backtracking on US-80 W, merge onto I-95 S to reach our next location, Darien. Located on the Altamaha Scenic Byway, Darien offers a striking view of one (if not the most important) tidal estuarine environments in the world. Nearby Wolf Island National Wildlife Refuge provides protection for migratory birds and such endangered species as the loggerhead turtle and the piping plover. Darien is a nature lovers dream! Boat tours, deep sea fishing, dock fishing, birdwatching or biking are just some of what this great place has to offer. Another interesting site is the amazing Fort King George, the oldest remaining English fort on Georgia's coast. A great place to explore, and you just might catch a reenactment while you're there.

Heading back to I-95 S, we continue our trip onto our next destination, Brunswick. Like many of the cities along the Georgia coastline, Brunswick is another jewel. There are miles of sun-kissed beaches, hundreds of holes of golf to be played, cruises of the local waters aboard working shrimp boats, and a lot of relaxing and fun to be had. Nearby St. Simons Island is a wonderful place to explore some interesting historical sites and attractions, including St. Simons Lighthouse. And nearby

Jekyll Island, the southernmost of the Golden Isles, is a must see. Once an exclusive winter retreat for some of America's wealthiest families, it's now a popular destination for travelers from all over.

Our last stop takes us back on the I-95 S to Kingsland. This city will make you feel like you're in another moment in time. Downtown is listed on the National Register of Historic Places, and has a look and feel of the 1930s, which makes for a very charming, and unique experience. Taking a sort ferry ride to Cumberland Island, visitors will come up close and personal with the wild horses that roam free here. With abundant rivers and streams, Kingsland offers visitors a wealth of kayaking, boating and fishing. Don't miss a visit to the Okefenokee Swamp, which encompasses over 400,000 acres of canals, cypress tress and lily pad prairies. Guided tours are offered, or if you're feeling adventurous, you can paddle your own canoe.

St. Marys, a short distance away, is home to the Submarine Museum, and a great opportunity for history buffs to immerse themselves in the 3,500 items housed in the museum including photographs, and artifacts.

Georgia is filled with beauty, beaches, and some incredible history you can find tucked away throughout the state. If the peaches don't get you, the hospitality and warmth of this state will!

KENTUCKY

Home to Bluegrass music, the Kentucky Derby, some of the finest Bourbon in the world, and the birthplace of Abe Lincoln, this serene state prides itself on the natural environment and beauty found throughout. Boasting one of the most geologically diverse landscapes in the US, Kentucky also contains some of the longest and most beautiful stretches of rivers and streams in the country, making it the most water filled state in the Continental US, and a outdoor lovers paradise.

Today, we begin in the city of Florence. Situated in the far northern part of the state, Florence's close proximity to Cincinnati, Ohio offers the metropolitan amenities of city life, while maintaining its peacefully rural feel. What's a visit to Kentucky without getting a glimpse of some of the graceful and beautiful horses this state is known for? Turfway Park is a thoroughbred horse racing track where you can watch some of Kentucky's finest race around the track at incredible speeds. If you're feeling lucky, place a bet or two. Florence is also home to several golf courses and the nation's first arboretum, Boone County Arboretum. Peaceful and serene, the Arboretum has more than 2 miles of walking trails through various plant and shrub collections contained within an amazing 121 acre park.

Moving on down I-75 S will take you to our next location, Lexington. This friendly city is home to the Kentucky Horse Park, an actual working museum where visitors can see over 50 different breeds of horses and discover how much work goes into the care and training of these beautiful animals. With two out-

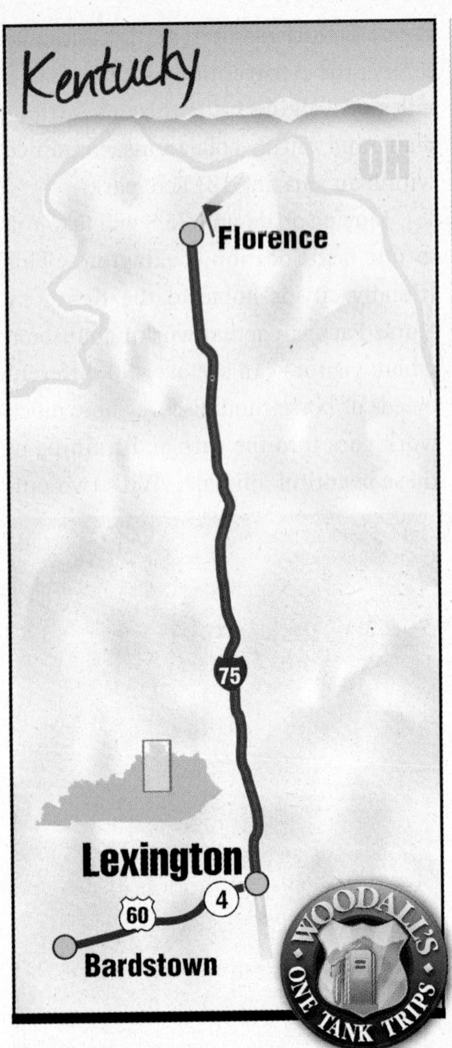

standing museums, twin theaters, and an array of horse shows, it's a fascinating place for any horse admirer. Another must see on your trip is the Headley-Whitney Museum, located on the lush grounds of what was once the Headley farm. This wonderful museum houses an amazing collection of dollhouses, and several pieces of jewelry created by George Headley. This also gives you a chance to wander around the grounds, marvel at the beauty of the Kentucky countryside, and enjoy a piece of Lexington history. For the nature lover, the perfect place for you is the Raven Run Nature Center, a 734-acre nature sanctuary dedicated to preserving all the natural beauty of the Kentucky River Palisades and early history. Visitors here are free to commune with nature, hike, bird watch, and explore some of the early remnants of 19th century settlers.

Continuing our trip, take KY-4 W and merge onto US-60 W to our last stop, Bardstown. Tranquil and scenic, historic Bardstown offers a wealth of cultural activities for travelers to this area. Starting at the Bardstown's Civil War Museum, visitors will discover the rich Civil War narrative through displays of historical documents, artifacts and exhibits. It is the fourth largest Civil War Museum in the US, so you won't want to miss it. Another must see is the Women of the Civil War Museum, which is dedicated specifically to the role women played during the war as spies, nurses and soldiers: A fascinating place to learn the little known story of these brave women. Even teetotalers can appreciate a tour at one of the many Bourbon distilleries in Bardstown. At the Heaven Hill Distilleries Bourbon Heritage Center, visitors can get a behind the scenes tour of a Bourbon aging brick house, a guide of the cistern room where barrels are filled, and a little taste of the stuff that made Kentucky famous. If you're a lover of trains, you've come to the perfect place! In Bardstown, visitors can still ride the rails aboard vintage train cars pulled by beautifully restored L & N steam locomotives, or relax and enjoy a meal aboard one of the luxurious 1940s dining car as it winds its way through the beautiful Kentucky countryside. Is there a more perfect way to end our trip?

With all the beauty and splendor of this state laid out before you, it's easy to see why so many travelers to Kentucky get caught up in her spell.

LOUISIANA

There is no other place in the world like Louisiana. Known the world over as a place to kick up your heels at Mardis Gras, it also offers attractions to travelers of all types, from history buffs to jazz fans. The iconic swamps of Louisiana are where you'll find excellent fishing, and some of the most unique and spicy cuisine anywhere in the south. C'mon, y'all! Let's laissez les bons temps rouler!

Ah, New Orleans! New Orleans is a city that requires little introduction, and there are few other places in the world that so gracefully blend their history and culture together. New Orleans is the stuff legends are made of, and nowhere is that more evident than on historic Bourbon Street. Running the length of the French Quarter, it is the most well known street in New Orleans. Bourbon Street is generally quiet during the day, which gives you time to have a look around at the unique and beautiful architecture, and to sample some world class cuisine. It's interesting to note that many of the buildings along Bourbon Street are authentic, dating back to the 1700s. You'll notice a very heavy Spanish influence due to a very brief period in time when this area was under Spanish rule. There are many city tours offered, and they are highly recommended. At night, the streets quickly fill up with people on their way to shows, dinner, or to catch some of that famous New Orleans jazz that can be heard in many of the bars and restaurants in this area.

Leaving New Orleans on I-10 W will take us to the next incredible city, Baton Rouge. Baton Rouge, whose name literally means, 'red stick', became the capital of Louisiana in 1849. As culturally diverse as the rest of the state, Baton Rouge is a popular tourist attraction, with most travelers coming to see the breathtaking plantations that are scattered throughout the area. Two of the most popular are Magnolia Mound Plantation, a Creole style house with a museum where visitors can get a glimpse into the grandeur and history of the 18th century. The other is Mount Hope Plantation, which was used as the set for the film, "Gone With the Wind," and is a spectacular example of the classic antebellum house. Another great place to stop is the St. Joseph's Cathedral, a historic church founded some 250 years ago, and contains a wealth of historic furnishings.

From Baton Rouge, we head to Lafayette by way of I-10 W, which will take us straight into the Heart of Cajun Country. The largest city in Acadiana, Lafayette contains a beautiful mix of Cajun and Creole cultures. Visitors should start by touring the recreation of an 1800s Cajun village called "Vermillionville". An active living history museum set on 23 acres, Vermillionville comes complete with storytellers, chefs, interpreters and one amazing history about the very early beginnings of this state and it's people. You can't go to Lafayette without experiencing a swamp tour! The perfect trip for birdwatchers, photographers and nature lovers to get up close to the Louisiana flora and fauna. Lafayette is a thriving metropolis, but there are several more activities available for the outdoor lover - from golf and cycling, to birding and canoeing.

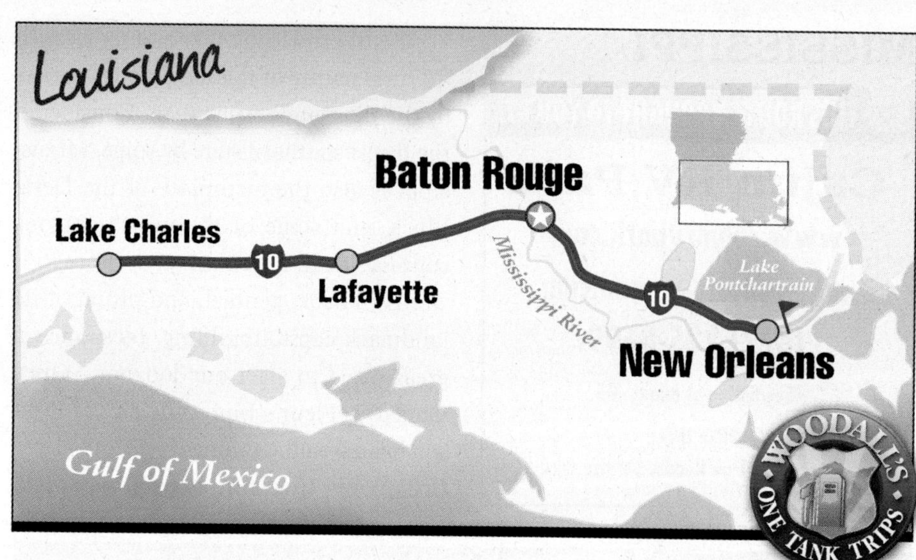

Leaving beautiful Lafayette, our final stop is Lake Charles, just a little further down I-10 W. In the heart of the Festival Capital, Lake Charles is full of the same culinary delights and wonderful music that make this region so much fun. The city overlooks a large freshwater lake that bears the titular name and offers numerous watersport and recreation activities. Home to the only white sand beach on the Gulf Coast, Lake Charles is a favorite spot for locals and travelers. Around the area, there are many more outdoor recreation opportunities such as hunting and fishing, and golfers will love the popular courses they have to choose from. The beautiful and historic Charpentier District of the city contains nearly 20 blocks of some of the most beautiful Victorian-era homes to be found anywhere in the state, with architecture that is unique to this area, and is a definite must see!

Louisiana is infectious. Long after you've come and gone, you'll soon be thinking of a way to get back for the cuisine, the beauty, and those wonderful, fun loving Cajuns who provide a warmth and color to their great state.

MISSISSIPPI

Southern Hospitality and the beautiful rural nature of this state draw tourists by the thousands every year. Considered the truest southern state by some, Mississippi is also the birthplace of the Delta Blues, and some of the most gorgeous countryside in the country.

Laid back, genteel, and proud of its landmark capitol building, Jackson is a great place to start our journey. Once named 'LeFleur's Bluff', the city of Jackson has a wealth of things to do and places to explore. If culture is what you seek, Jackson has what you need! The city has several museums, namely the Mississippi Museum of Art, which houses an impressive collection from Warhol to O'Keefe, and if you get lucky, you just might catch a live jazz performance that are occasionally held there. Eudora Welty, one of Mississippi's most famous writers, called Jackson home, and it's here that you can tour her historic Belhaven home and gardens she built with her mother. Also notable is the Russel C. Davis Planetarium. One of the most impressive and largest in the world, a distinct feature of the planetarium is the huge wrap-around screen that presents regular Sky Shows on astronomy, astronauts, and space exploration. Downtown, you'll find the Governor's Mansion, the second oldest, continuously occupied governor's residence in the US. Many historians consider this mansion to be one of the best surviving examples of Greek revival architecture.

The next stop on our trip is the city of Gulfport, just a short scenic drive on SH-49 S. Not only does the city have some incredible beaches, there are several championship golf courses, museums, historical buildings, cultural displays and exhibits, and casinos. The Stennis Space Center is a top attraction in this city, and the perfect place to discover interesting facts regarding oceanographic, environmental, and space studies. The Crosby Arboretum is another spectacular attraction, featuring 64 acres of nature trails, 300 species of plants, and a picturesque pavilion designed by famous architect, Frank Lloyd Wright. The Ship Island Ferry will take you from the Gulfport Small Craft Harbor to an incredible expanse of white sand beach on Sand Island. There is no place better to do some fishing, or just lounge on the beach and gaze out at the beautiful emerald green water.

Heading off to our next stop, take I-10 E along the beautiful Gulf Coast to Biloxi. The chief destination on the Gulf, Biloxi is the state's oldest city, founded by the

French in 1699. If you're looking for a peek at true Southern culture, you've come to the right place. Biloxi boasts several gorgeous homes, many of which were built in the mid 1800s, and are open to the public for tours. Beach lovers will relish the nearly 30 miles of stunning beach, and the endless array of water sports to be had here. The barrier islands that sit off the coast of Biloxi are the perfect place to do some hiking, fishing, beach combing, and bird watching. Biloxi also features a 44,000 gallon Gulf of Mexico exhibit, a Mardi Gras museum, and is the location of Beauvoir, the home and library of Confederate President, Jefferson Davis.

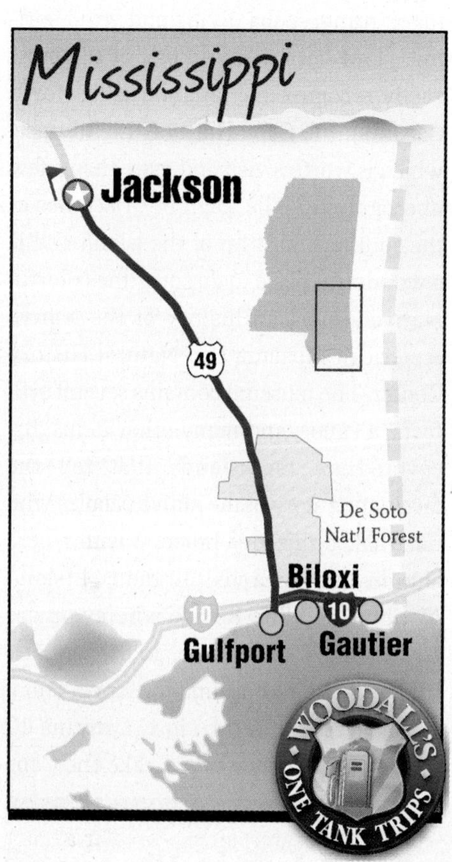

A hop, skip, and a jump on I-10 E from Biloxi brings us to our last stop, Gautier. If you want to look at the beautiful local wildlife in their natural settings, take a trip to the Sandhill Crane National wildlife Refuge. Here, you can walk trails that lead you through several different habitats in this expansive 19,000-acre facility. Also available are eco-tours along the Pascagoula River, the longest unimpeded river in the lower 48, which flows 80 miles from its confluence to the Gulf of Mexico. Interpretive tours will introduce you to the natural habitats of the Cyprus swamps and salt marshes of the river. Visitors will see an abundance of migratory birds - pelicans, herons, osprey, egrets, and bald eagles, and maybe just a few alligators as well!

Mississippi offers every traveler a very unique experience, whether you're looking for some amazing outdoor experience, culture, or just plain fun. Mississippi does it all with the grace and generosity the South is known for.

OTHER AREA LOCATIONS

BILOXI

Mazalea Travel Park

Parker's Landing RV Park

GAUTIER

Indian Point RV Resort

GULFPORT

Baywood RV Park and Campground, Inc.

SOUTHAVEN

EZ Daze RV Park

NORTH CAROLINA

Are you looking for diversity? Searching for a charming destination filled with coastal getaways, incredible mountainous regions, and a never-ending supply of recreation opportunities? Look no further; North Carolina has exactly what you crave and so much more!

By far, one of the most spectacular areas in North Carolina is the captivating Outer Banks, and the perfect starting point for our journey is Roanoke Island, and the historic city of Manteo. Beautiful and serene, Manteo is a town steeped in mystery, history, and recreation galore. It's here visitors can rediscover the "Lost Colony", the site of the mysterious disappearance of early colonists. The area is frequented by archaeologists, historians and scientists alike, all trying to discover the reasons for one of the greatest disappearing acts in history. Visitors to Manteo should take in the longest running outdoor theater production in America, 'The Lost Colony', which tells the baffling story. Aviation enthusiasts can't leave this area without a stop at Kill Devil Hills, the site of the Wright Brothers National Memorial, which commemorates the four powered airplane flights that began our fascination with flying. Other notables on this small, but charming, island are the North Carolina Aquarium and the beautiful Roanoke Marshes Lighthouse. Both are a definite must see, as well as a tour through the restored homes and inns along the historic district.

Leaving Manteo, take N Carolina 12 S along the spectacular chain of islands to our next destination, Rodanthe. Sitting on tip of the Southern Outer Banks, Rodanthe is a place of unspoiled beaches, lush flora and fauna, and the perfect place to swing in a hammock and watch the water. Visitors are attracted to this tranquil town for its wonderful location, relaxed atmosphere, and a plethora of water sports, including fishing, wind surfing, kite boarding, boating, and much more. The nearby Cape Hatteras National Seashore, travelers will find sea turtles that nest on the sandy beaches, and other creatures both large and small, as well as a myriad of plant life. Here, you can look for shells, do some fishing, and enjoy the peaceful serenity of this area. Don't pass up the chance to visit the Chicamacomico Lifesaving Station Historic Site located here. The original 1847 life station has many rescue stories to share and offers a unique glimpse into life on this tiny island.

Moving on, our next destination is Cape Hatteras, and a short drive along N Carolina 12 S will get you there in a snap! Cape Hatteras is a delicate blend of natural beauty and simple, quiet attitudes. Don't let the size of the island fool you; there is plenty to do here, including, fishing, birding, scuba diving and wind surfing. Travelers will find one of the most easily recognizable landmarks in North Carolina, the Cape Hatteras Lighthouse, which is worth a visit and more than a few photographs. The town of Frisco lies at the southernmost tip of the island and is a wonderful place to discover the colorful Native American history at the Native American Museum and Natural History Center. The museum contains several artifacts, a canoe, and many other items discovered on the islands that tell the fascinating story of the native peoples who once called this area home. Visitors here should also pay a visit to the Pea Island National Wildlife Refuge where you are free to take a canoe tour, go on a guided bird walk, or hike around the North Pond.

Moving on, return to N Carolina 12 S, and in just a few miles, take the Cape

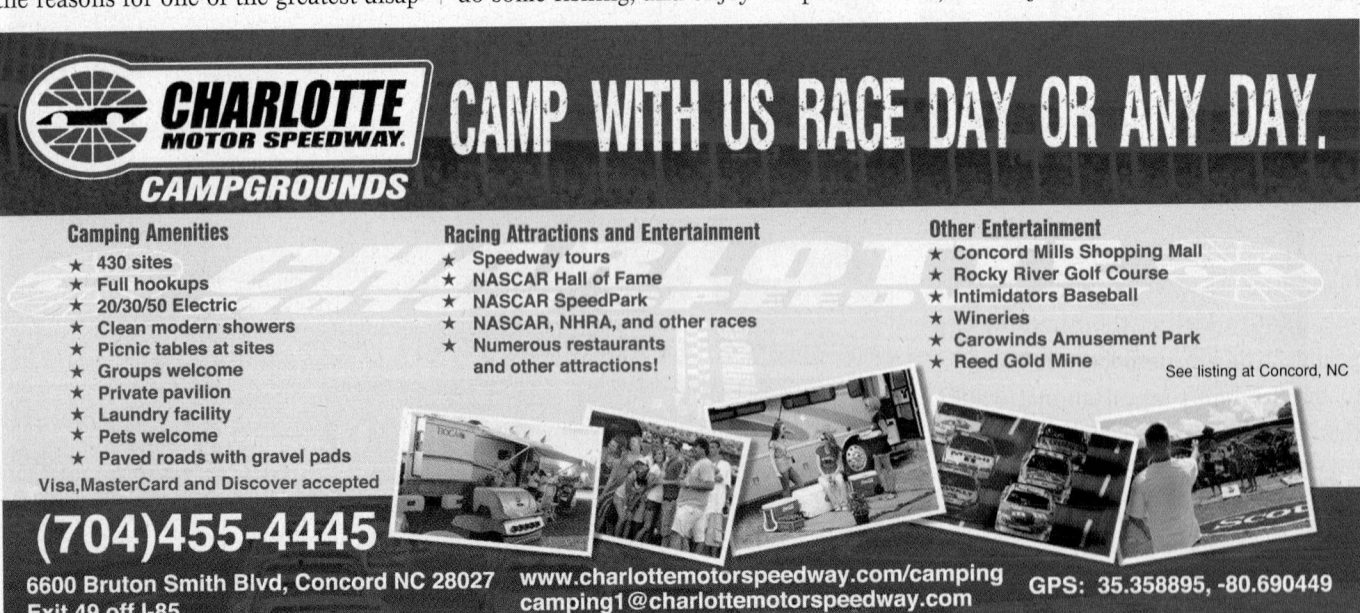

Hatteras-Ocracoke ferry to our next stop, Ocracoke. What a beautiful place to linger! Ocracoke has a character all its own. Visitors here will find the Ocracoke Preservation Society Museum, located in a former Coast Guard captain's home. The museum features exhibits about the local history and culture, and is well worth a visit. Also of note is the Ocracoke Lighthouse, the oldest sea sentry still in use in the state, dating back to 1823.

Take the Cedar Island-Ocracoke ferry from Ocracoke to Cedar Island, and return to N Carolina 12 S, which turns into US-70 W, and in a little over 2 hours you will arrive at our next destination, Morehead City. Located on the breathtaking Crystal Coast, Morehead City is home to The History Place, which features a wide and varied collection reflecting the cultural history of North Carolina's coast; from the indigenous peoples who roamed the lands, all the way through World War II. No traveler should miss this, as the museum also contains an extensive library filled with local history and genealogy records.

Leaving Morehead City, take N Carolina 24 W along the beautiful Emerald Isle coast to arrive at Jacksonville, just around an hour drive away. Located on the Atlantic, this incredible city is a favorite location for travelers seeking an ocean playground setting. Visitors to this area will find Hammocks Beach State Park, which boasts one of the most scenic and breathtaking stretches of unspoiled beaches on the Atlantic Coast. Just a short ferry ride away, travelers can enjoy fishing on the endless rows of breakers, stroll the beach, or discover tiny specimens of marine life hidden in tidal pools and mudflats. If you're looking for a secluded and tranquil place to slow your pace, this is the perfect place!

Continuing our trip, take US-17 S to our next stop, Surf City. Quiet and uncrowded, this sleepy coastal town boasts more than 30 public beach accesses, and is a great destination for those looking to head off of the beaten path, and find there own little hideaway. Here, you can laze the days away on the beach, do some fishing, enjoy some tasty culinary delights at any of the many restaurants, or enjoy shopping at any of the unique boutiques in town.

The last stop on our trip is Wilmington, less than an hour away on US-17 S. A fascinating history, coupled with majestic scenery, makes this dynamic city a perfect destination. Wedged between Cape Fear and the Atlantic Ocean, Wilmington has a host of surprises in store for travelers. From battleships and riverboats, Civil War history to ghost walks, Wilmington is a jewel on the coast. Visitors to historic downtown will be charmed by cobblestone streets, several well preserved buildings, romantic carriage rides, and several restaurants, boutiques and shops. A must see in this captivating city is the Bellamy Man-

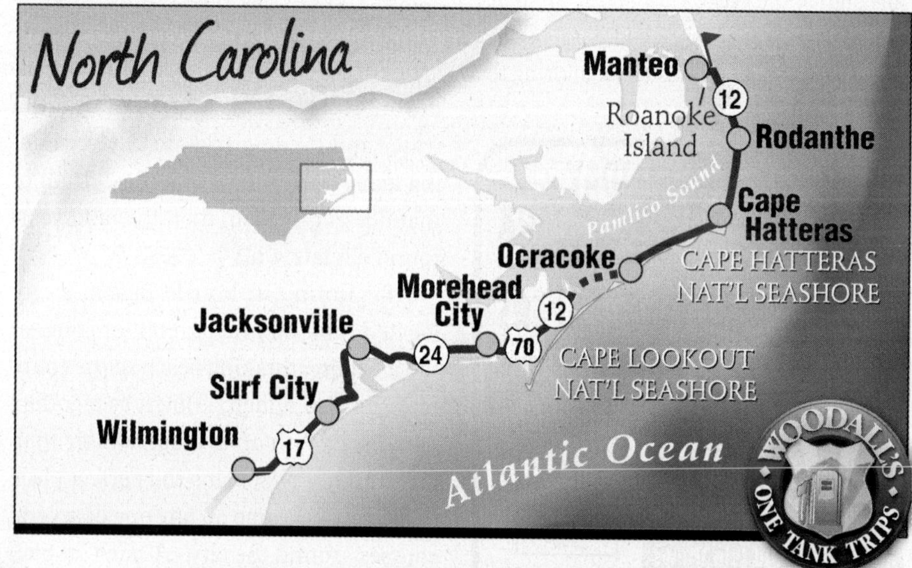

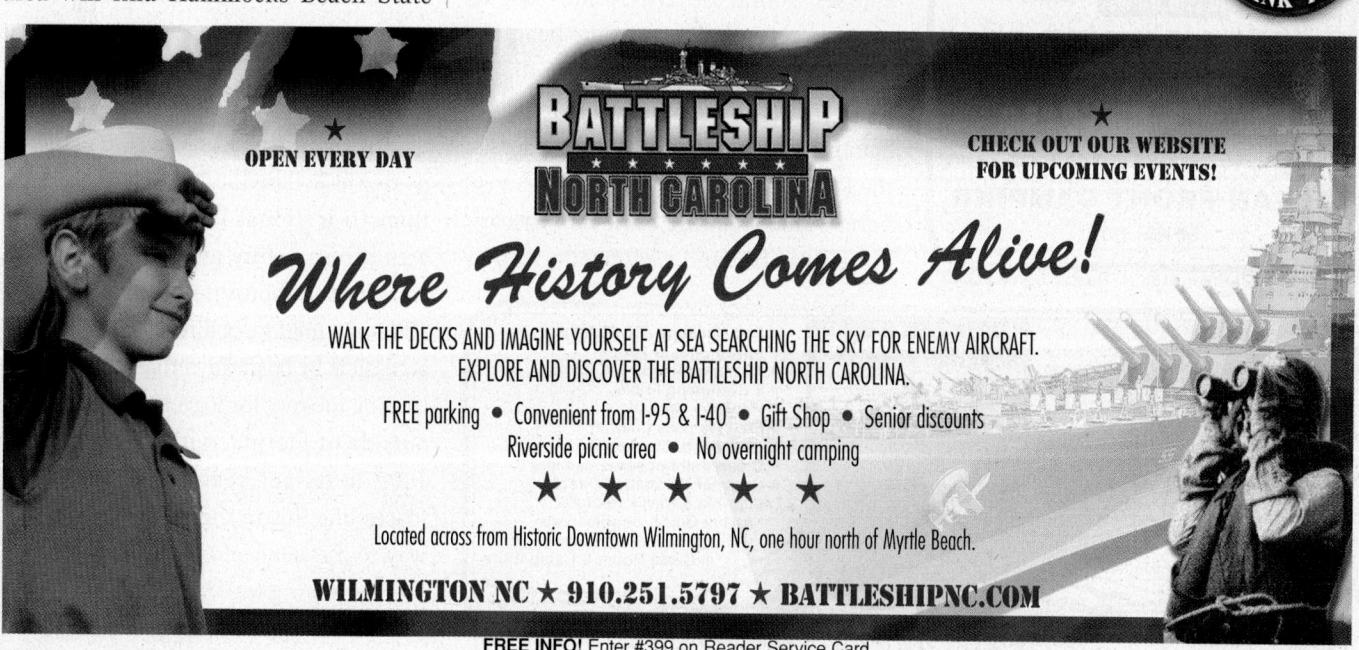

sion, one of the most spectacular examples of antebellum architecture in the state. Now a museum, visitors can retrace the history of the building through several exhibitions. Another notable destination, and one history and nautical buffs alike are sure to enjoy, is the Battleship North Carolina. Visitors can walk the decks, and encounter many of the stories of the young men who served their country during WWII aboard this massive ship. And no visit would be complete without a tour of the incredible Airlie Gardens. The Gardens amaze all that come for a visit with the beautiful mix of formal gardens, historic structures, walking trails, 10 acres of freshwater lakes, and the grandeur of the 462-year-old Arlie Oak. After a whirlwind of fun, sun, and incredible sights, the Arlie Oak is just the place to kick back, rest in the shade, and bask in the glow of one fabulous trip exploring the Outer Banks.

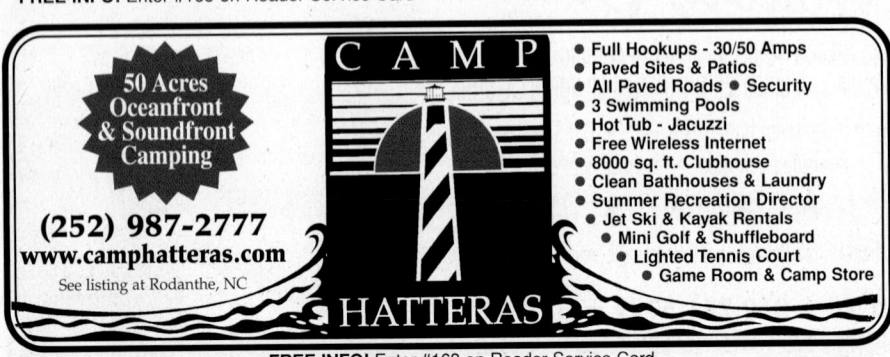

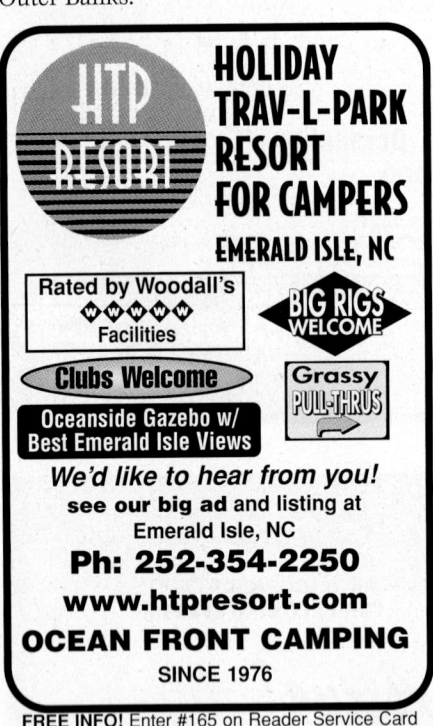

SOUTH CAROLINA

It's hard not to fall in love with South Carolina. A rich, and exotic blend of world renowned southern hospitality, centuries old history, and idyllic ocean settings makes this state one of the most sought after locations for an amazing array of activities. Entertainment venues are found throughout the state, from water and theme parks, to a never-ending array of outdoor activities. If all of that doesn't get you, then the mild year-round climate will!

Beginning in Myrtle Beach, a city located on a 60 mile stretch of some of the most breathtaking beach in the country, it is also widely known as a golfers paradise. With an average winter temperature in the 50s, it's the perfect place to refine your game on any one of several courses around the city. A must stop on a visit to Myrtle Beach is the beautiful Hopsewee Plantation. Built in 1740, this regal plantation was the birthplace of Thomas Lynch, Jr., one of the signers of the Declaration of Independence. A visit here is like stepping back into history. For a little fun and excitement, stop by the Freestyle Amusement Park. A 55-acre park, with music themed attractions, like "The Time Machine", a 150-foot tall, 65-mph steel coaster, with built-in speakers that blast a variety of songs from the 70s, 80s, and 90s. A great way to combine a love of music, with the hair-raising experience of an amusement park ride!

Once your stomach has settled, let's hit the road to our next stop, Murrells Inlet. A short drive on US-17 S along the beautiful coast will get you there in no time, and it is the perfect place to slow it down a bit after all that excitement in Myrtle Beach. Murrells Inlet is a historic fishing village where you can indulge on some of the finest, and freshest fish you have ever had. Local fishing markets offer the catch of the day for those looking for something to throw on the grill later, or bring your pole and try to wrestle in your own catch of the day from the peaceful waters of the inlet. Travelers here will also enjoy the amazing Brookgreen Gardens. Originally four rice plantations, and boasting some 10,000 acres, Brookgreen is home to several themed gardens, sculptures, the Lowcountry Zoo, and trails that run through several ecosystems on the property. The perfect place to relax, take a stroll and unwind! Murrells Inlet is a stop widely known to birdwatchers as one of the best places to get a glimpse of some rare and beautiful creatures.

Back onto US-17 S, and a little further down the breathtaking coast, brings us to McClellanville. Home to the Cape Romain National Wildlife Refuge, this area brings nature and birding enthusiasts, by the thousands. Established in 1932 as a migratory bird refuge, and only accessible by boat, the refuge is the largest nesting rookery for loggerhead sea turtles outside of Florida, with approximately 1000 nests per year. There are few places like this in the world, and a great way to see some endangered wildlife.

Returning to US-17 S, we continue our trip along the coast to the incompa-

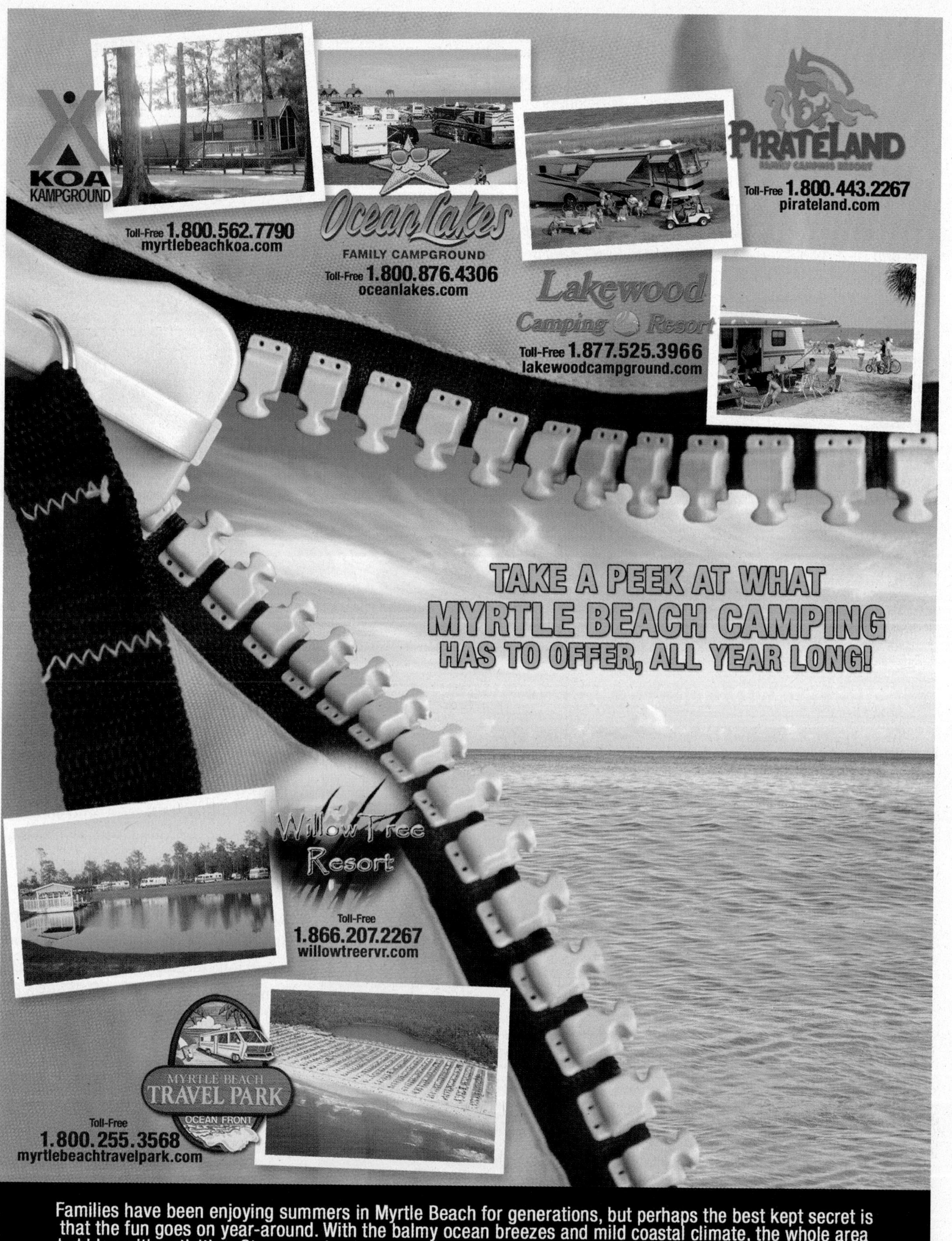
KOA
KAMPGROUND
Toll-Free 1.800.562.7790
myrtlebeachkoa.com
Ocean Lakes
FAMILY CAMPGROUND
Toll-Free 1.800.876.4306
oceanlakes.com
PIRATELAND
Toll-Free 1.800.443.2267
pirateland.com
Lakewood
Camping Resort
Toll-Free 1.877.525.3966
lakewoodcampground.com
TAKE A PEEK AT WHAT
MYRTLE BEACH CAMPING
HAS TO OFFER, ALL YEAR LONG!
Willow Tree
Resort
Toll-Free
1.866.207.2267
willowtreervr.com
MYRTLE BEACH
TRAVEL PARK
OCEAN FRONT
Toll-Free
1.800.255.3568
myrtlebeachtravelpark.com
Families have been enjoying summers in Myrtle Beach for generations, but perhaps the best kept secret is that the fun goes on year-around. With the balmy ocean breezes and mild coastal climate, the whole area bubbles with activities. Stay a week, stay a month or stay all winter and fill every day with a special treat!
Choose from the area's six best campgrounds. 1-888-621-0102 • campmyrtlebeach.com

FREE INFO! Enter #322 on Reader Service Card

rable Charleston. Upon arrival, it's difficult not to notice the 300-year-old history reflected in this coastal city. In the historic district of Charleston, there are some 2000 historic buildings, and all of them are surrounded by several beautiful plantation homes, many of which are still in use today. Highly recommended is a walking tour of old Charleston, and travelers will find the haunting legends and folk tales tour particularly fascinating. Filled with Gullah superstitions, stories of resident ghosts, and haunted inns, it just might make the hair on the back of your neck stand up a little!

For our last stop, it's back to US-17 S to Hilton Head. One of the most family friendly destinations in the world, Hilton Head offers an assortment of outdoor fun, and was named one of the top ten family beaches in the country. Only 12 miles wide, it's amazing what is packed into such a narrow strip of land! Besides the incredible beaches, golfers will be in heaven on any one of the 24 courses to be found here. World class shopping, some exquisite dining, sandy beaches, and much, much more await. Hilton Head is a little piece of paradise, and one that will cater to just about any interest or lifestyle.

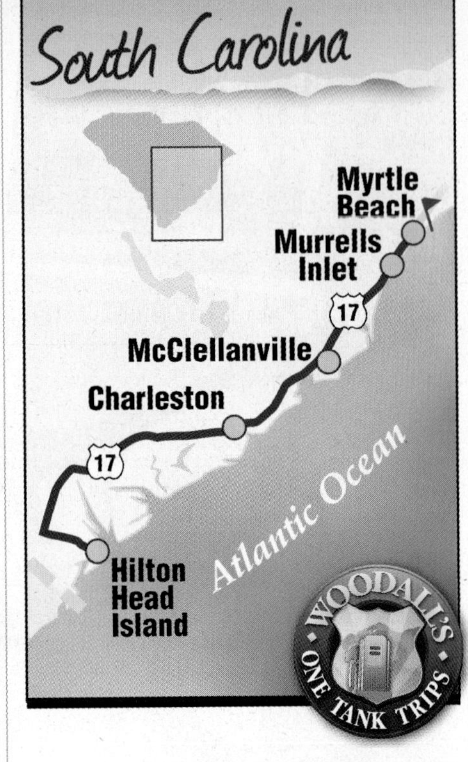

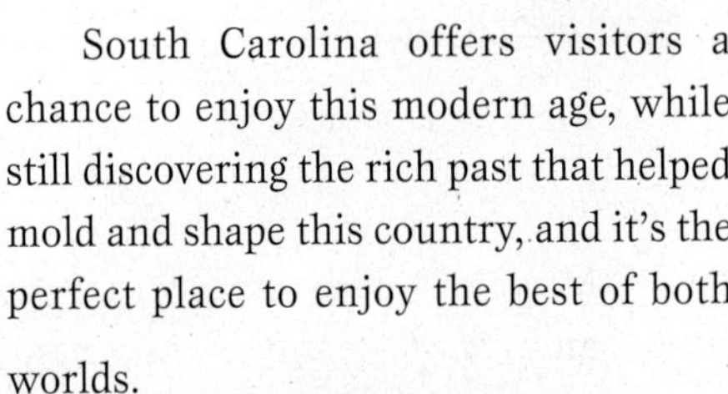

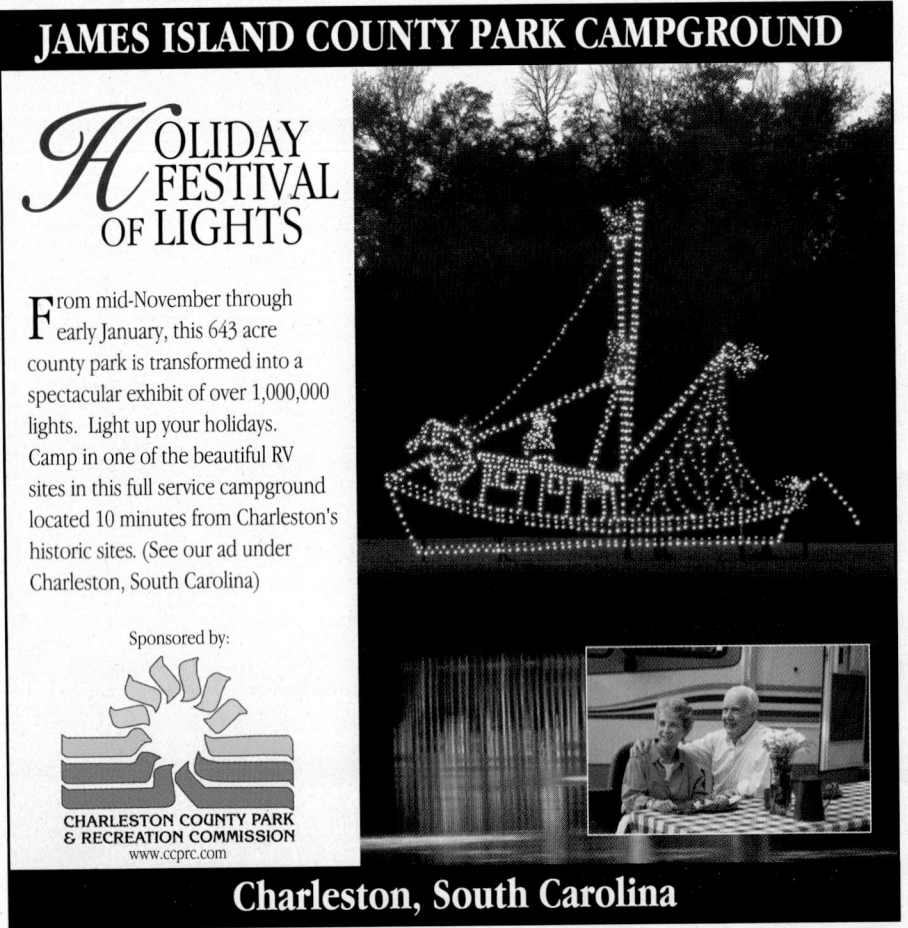

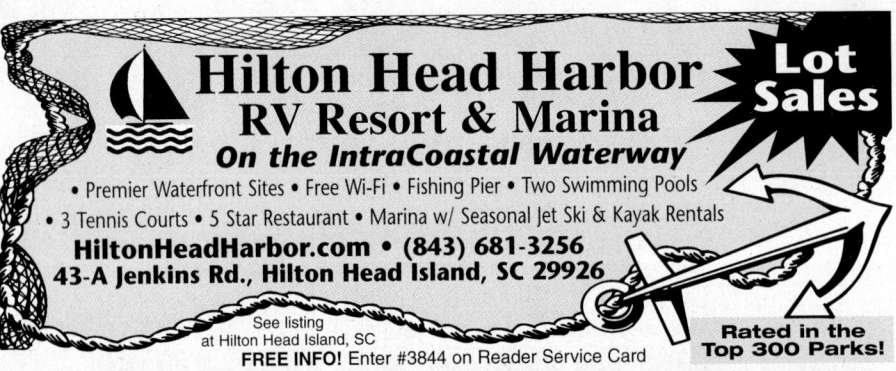

South Carolina offers visitors a chance to enjoy this modern age, while still discovering the rich past that helped mold and shape this country, and it's the perfect place to enjoy the best of both worlds.

TENNESSEE

Tennessee has long been the focal point for blues, bluegrass, and country-western music, but the state is also home to some of the most beautiful scenery in the US. Depending on your interest, Tennessee offers a wide variety of opportunities - from great food, music, outdoor recreation, to many cultural offerings. From the Great Smoky Mountains to the lush interior, this is one Southern state that has to be experienced to be truly appreciated.

Today we begin in the city of Chattanooga. Its location on the banks of the Tennessee River makes it the ideal place for boating, fishing, and a list of other water activities. Are you looking for a jaw-dropping thrill? You'll find it inside Lookout Mountain at Ruby Falls, the nations largest and deepest waterfall, located over 1120 feet beneath the surface. Dropping from a height of 145 ft., this underground waterfall is surrounded by ancient geological formations, and one you won't want to miss. Located atop Lookout Mountain, visitors will also discover Rock City; a marvel of nature featuring ancient rock structures, gardens, and over 400 species of plants. Visitors can also see a breathtaking panoramic view from its location, which is sure to be awe-inspiring.

Heading out of Chattanooga on US-64 E, merge onto TN-153 S, and then onto I-75 N, and in less than an hour and a half, you should arrive at our next stop, Sweetwater. A visit to this area wouldn't be complete without visiting the Lost Sea. The Lost Sea is a network of fascinating caverns, which are part of a historic cave system called the Craighead Caverns.

Moving on, take I-75 N, continuing on I-40 E, exit on Winfield Dunn Pkwy to arrive at our next destination, Sevierville. Nestled at the base of the Smoky Mountains, Sevierville attracts more than it's fair share of visitors who come to visit the hometown of Country music legend Dolly Parton, but they are also drawn to the wealth of outdoor activities offered here. If you're looking to do some hiking, nearby Smoky Mountain National Park has over 800 miles of trails for you to wander around on. Other offerings include golf, kayaking, canoeing, fishing and swimming.

Our next destination is Pigeon Forge, just a short drive away. Taking the Dolly Parton Pkwy out of town, take a right at Veterans Rd, and you'll be there in minutes. This stunning city is home to Dollywood, a massive park that spans 125 acres. You'll soon realize there are more than enough shows, rides, and some of the best live entertainment in the world to keep you busy for hours! Travelers here might also be interested in the Old Mill. A national historic site more than 150 years old, it is one of the country's most photographed mills, and by far the most gorgeous. Tours are available so you can see how corn meal is made, and there is an on-site village, plenty of restaurants, and many shops filled with the works of local artisans.

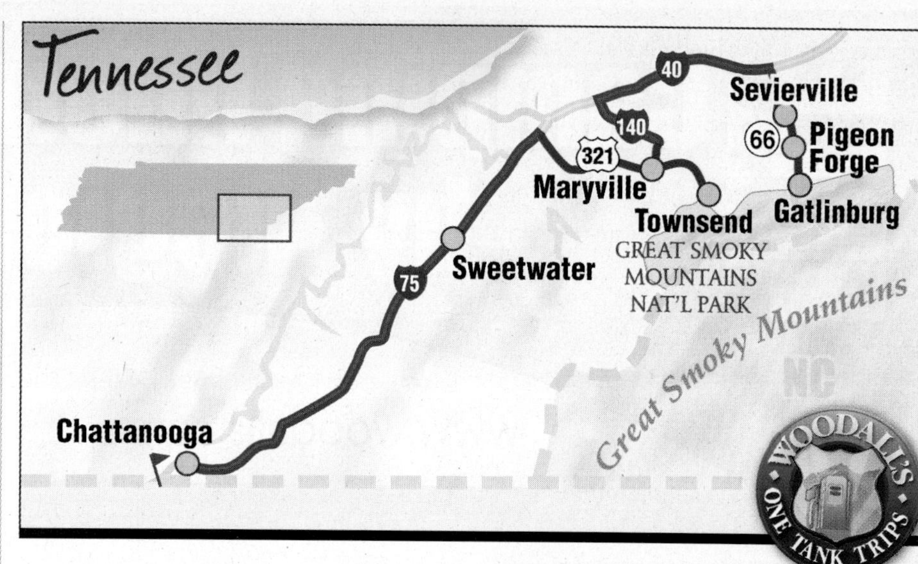

For our last stop, take TN-71 S, and in just a few short minutes you'll be in the very scenic city of Gatlinburg. Known as one of the gateway cities due to its close proximity to the Smoky Mountain National Park, Gatlinburg is a breathtaking city that offers much in the way of recreation.

Tennessee is surprisingly beautiful, and has all of the grace and hospitality you'd expect from a great Southern state, and a wealth of culture and outdoor fun that any visitor is sure to appreciate.

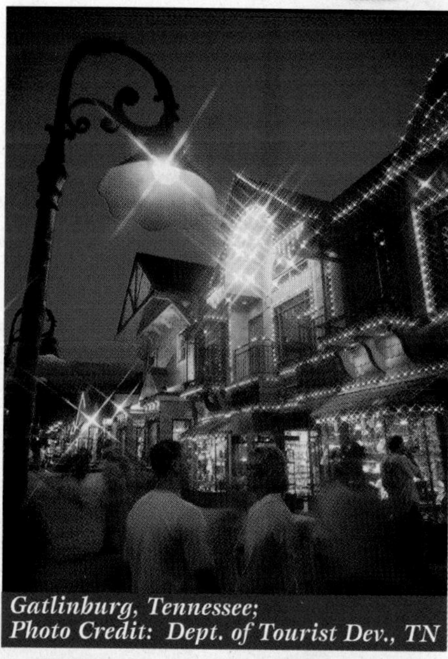

Gatlinburg, Tennessee; Photo Credit: Dept. of Tourist Dev., TN

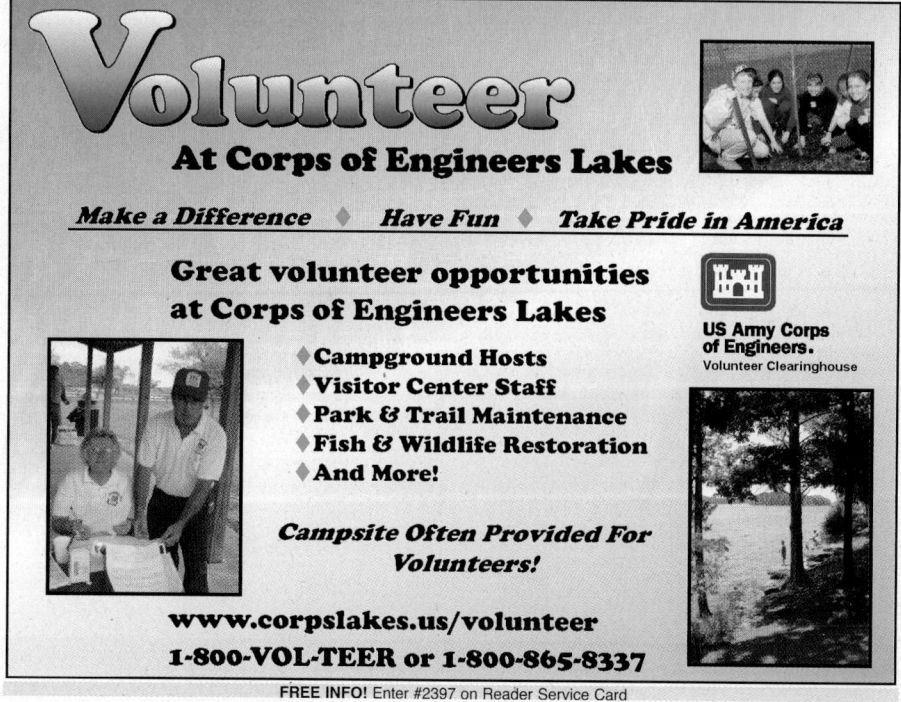

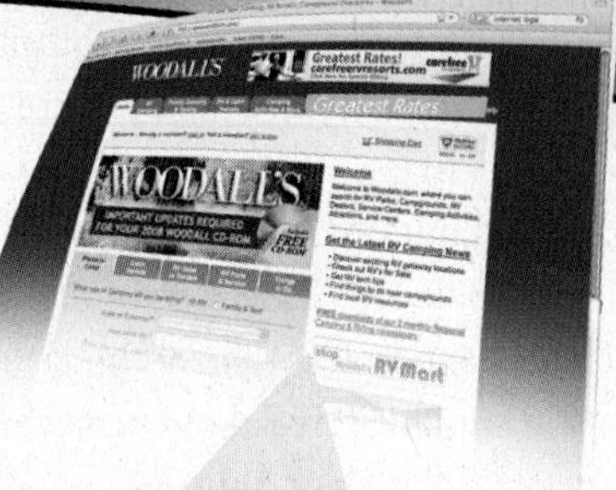

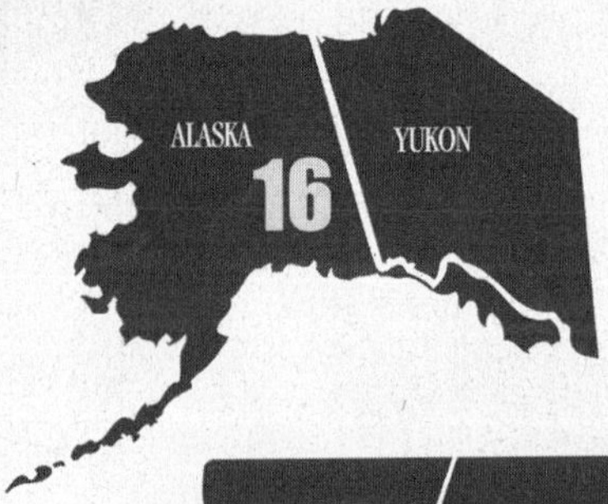

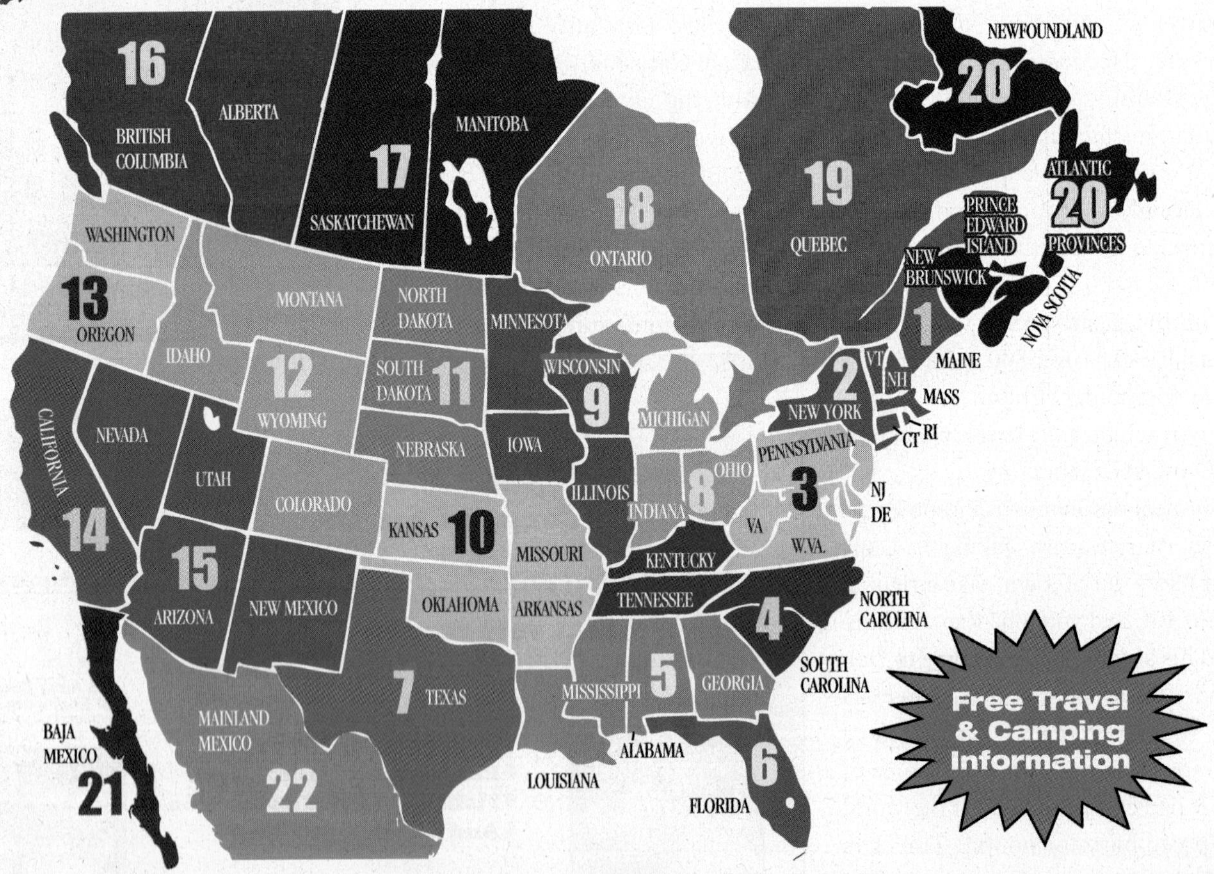

GET FREE INFORMATION ABOUT PRODUCTS & SERVICES FOUND IN THIS DIRECTORY

WOODALL'S READER QUESTIONNAIRE

Please enter your response or circle the appropriate number on the reader service card indicating your answer to our questions below. This will help us determine how to serve you better. Thank you!

1. Age________
2. What is your approximate annual gross family income?________
3. What is your approximate family net worth?________
4. Approximately how many years have you been camping / RVing? ________
5. What was your camping pattern over the last 12 months? (best estimate)
   a. Number of camping trips_____
   b. Total number of nights camped____
   c. Total number of miles traveled_____
   d. Number of different parks at which you stayed_____
   e. Number of Amusement/Tourist Attractions visited while on camping trips_____
   f. Total money spent on Amusement/ Tourist Attractions_______
6. How close to your home did you buy your present RV?
   a. Within 50 miles b. 50 to 99 miles
   c. 100 or more miles away
7. Are you considering buying a new RV in the next 12 months?
   a. yes b. no

If yes, please indicate the type which interests you most: (select only one)

a. Travel Trailer
b. Park Model (Trailer)
c. Class A motor home – gas
d. Class A motor home – diesel
e. Fold-Down Trailer (Tent Trailer)
f. Truck Camper
g. Fifth Wheel
h. Class C motor home
i. Van Conversion
j. Class B motor home
l. Other-Please specify_________

(continued on back)

To receive valuable information from our advertisers, simply write in the numbers on the attached card that correspond to the advertisers which interest you. Then, fill out your name and address and drop it in the mail.

Receive FREE Product Information Online at

WWW.WOODALLS.COM

The #1 Site For RVers On The Internet

(Tell all your friends to "Bookmark" this site!)

READER SERVICE
EXPIRES: DEC. 31, 2012

NAME ____________
ADDRESS ____________
CITY & STATE/PROV. ____________ ZIP/P.C. ____________
PHONE (____) ____________
E-MAIL ____________

PRINT READER SERVICE NUMBERS OF THE ADVERTISERS FROM WHOM YOU WANT MORE INFORMATION.

ENTER REGION FROM PAGE NUMBER 48 TO RECEIVE INFO. FROM ALL ADVERTISERS IN THE REGION (Max. of 8):

READER QUESTIONNAIRE: Please circle the appropriate response number for each question.

1. ________. **2.** ____________. **3.** ____________. **4.**________.
5. a_____,b_____,c________,d_____,e_____,f_________. **6.** a,b,c. **7.** a,b.
8. a,b,c,d,e,f,g,h,i,j,l________. **9.** a,b,c,d. **10.** a,b,c,d,e. **11.** a,b. **12.** a,b.
13. a,b,c,d,e,f. **14.** __________ **15.** __________ **16.** a,b. **17.** a,b,c,d,e,f,g.
18. a,b. **19.** a,b. **20.** a,b.

CD-11

Use this card for additional information or fill it out for a friend.

READER SERVICE
EXPIRES: DEC. 31, 2012

NAME ____________
ADDRESS ____________
CITY & STATE/PROV. ____________ ZIP/P.C. ____________
PHONE (____) ____________
E-MAIL ____________

PRINT READER SERVICE NUMBERS OF THE ADVERTISERS FROM WHOM YOU WANT MORE INFORMATION.

ENTER REGION FROM PAGE NUMBER 48 TO RECEIVE INFO. FROM ALL ADVERTISERS IN THE REGION (Max. of 8):

READER QUESTIONNAIRE: Please circle the appropriate response number for each question.

1. ________. **2.** ____________. **3.** ____________. **4.**________.
5. a_____,b_____,c________,d_____,e_____,f_________. **6.** a,b,c. **7.** a,b.
8. a,b,c,d,e,f,g,h,i,j,l________. **9.** a,b,c,d. **10.** a,b,c,d,e. **11.** a,b. **12.** a,b.
13. a,b,c,d,e,f. **14.** __________ **15.** __________ **16.** a,b. **17.** a,b,c,d,e,f,g.
18. a,b. **19.** a,b. **20.** a,b.

CD-11

Receive FREE Product Information Online at

WWW.WOODALLS.COM

The #1 Site For RVers On The Internet

(Tell all your friends to "Bookmark" this site!)

NO POSTAGE NECESSARY IF MAILED IN THE UNITED STATES

BUSINESS REPLY MAIL
FIRST-CLASS MAIL PERMIT NO 398 NAPLES FL
POSTAGE WILL BE PAID BY ADDRESSEE

WOODALLS CAMPGROUND DIRECTORY
PO BOX 413050
NAPLES FL 34101-6804

NO POSTAGE NECESSARY IF MAILED IN THE UNITED STATES

BUSINESS REPLY MAIL
FIRST-CLASS MAIL PERMIT NO 398 NAPLES FL
POSTAGE WILL BE PAID BY ADDRESSEE

WOODALLS CAMPGROUND DIRECTORY
PO BOX 413050
NAPLES FL 34101-6804

9. How far from your home would you consider driving in order to buy the right RV for your needs?
a. Within 50 miles
b. 50 to 99 miles
c. 100 or more miles away
d. Mileage would not be a factor in locating the right RV

10. What portion of your campground stops do you pre-plan before leaving home?
a. None b. 1/4 c. 1/2
d. 3/4 e. All

11. When pre-planning your camping trips at home, do you also plan what to do and see on your trip?
a. yes b. no

12. Are you inclined to select locations that advertise their unique features over those who don't?
a. yes b. no

13. How often do you/will you buy a new WOODALL'S Campground Directory?
a. Every year b. Every 2 years
c. Every 3 years d. Every 4 years
e. Every 5 years f. More than 5 yrs

14. How many times did you use your WOODALL'S Campground Directory in the past 12 months?_____

15. How many times have others used your WOODALL'S Campground Directory in the past 12 months? (Including how many times you have loaned out your WOODALL'S Campground Directory)_____

16. Do you belong to any RV camping clubs?
a. yes b. no

17. If yes, please select which one (check all that apply)
a. FCRV
b. FMCA
c. Good Sam
d. KOA Value Kard
e. Camp Club USA
f. Escapees
g. Other(s)_______________

18. Do you access the internet while on RV camping trips?
a. yes b. no

19. Have you ever searched for RV camping info on woodalls.com?
a. yes b. no

20. Do you access websites found in advertisements to learn more about that business?
a. yes b. no

USE READER SERVICE TO GET FREE INFORMATION ABOUT THE ADVERTISERS IN THIS DIRECTORY!

Here is a quick and easy way to receive free travel and camping information. Enter the Reader Service Number (listed below) on the Reader Service Card, which is located opposite page 48. Your request will be forwarded to the businesses you've indicated. You'll receive information, sent directly to your home. It's the no-hassle way to plan your next trip!

Enter RS Number		Page Number
FAR WEST		
3243	Pueblo El Mirage Resort & Country Club	91
2881	Rio Bend RV & Golf Resort	99
3771	River Rock Casino	95
3385	Superstition Sunrise	88
1023	Westwind RV & Golf Resort	92
FRONT WEST/GREAT PLAINS & MTN		
3628	Isleta Lakes & Recreation Area	73
326	Port Isabel Park Center	76
4192	Texas State Parks & Wildlife Department	77
GREAT LAKES		
4273	Bigfoot Construction	55
MID ATLANTIC		
220	Bethpage Camp Resort	27
216	Cherrystone Family Camping Resort	28
401	Lake In Wood Resort	25
2119	Liberty Harbor RV Park	24
3773	PRVCA	26
NATIONAL		
4361	Advanced Elements	81
721	Born Free Motorcoach	89
2584	Cal Am Properties	Insert
3490	Camp Club USA	118
3490	Camp Club USA	119
3817	Camping Life	65
109	Camping World	116
109	Camping World	117
4059	Camping World Roadcare	120
4032	Carefree RV Resorts	C3
4307	Carefree RV Resorts	Insert
4374	CEA Solar	85
4362	Coleman Company	59
4060	Dahon USA	58
3496	Escapees Club	9
167	Essex Credit	64
129	Family Campers & RVers	39
4218	Fleetwood	10
123	FMCA (Family Motor Coach Association)	96
4349	Gale Banks Engineering	11
4025	Geico	3
3808	Hobie Cat	5
3648	Honda Generators	C2
4061	Hopkins Mfg	19
111	Kampgrounds of America	C4
207	Leisure Systems	7
4369	Levelease	40
4213	Microsoft Corporation	6
4363	Nomad Glass	17
4370	Relief Mart	57
3823	Roadmaster	101
3609	RVSearch.com	56
4211	Sea Eagle	61
4360	SteadyFast	60
4367	Titan International	8
3814	Transfer Flow	97
NEW YORK & NEW ENGLAND		
212	Circle CG Farm Adult RV Park	15
SOUTH		
399	Battleship North Carolina	43
282	Big Pine Key & Florida's Lower Keys	35
4303	Broward County Parks	33
163	Camp Hatteras	44
302	Campground at James Island County Park	46
4357	Charlotte Motor Speedway Campground	42
412	Harrah's Casino RV Resort	41
3844	Hilton Head Harbor RV Resort	46
165	Holiday Trav L Park Resort for Campers	44
4366	Lazydays RV Campground	32
348	Lee County Visitors & Convention Bureau	34
322	Myrtle Beach Campground Association	45
3399	Outer Banks Visitors Bureau	1
365	Paragon Casino RV Resort	37
2397	US Army Corps of Engineers/Volunteers	47
CANADA		
258	Campark Resorts	112
2842	Nova Scotia Department of Tourism	109
218	Yogi Bear's Jellystone Park Camp-Resort	114

FREE Camping Information
TRAVEL SECTION

SAVE HOURS OF RESEARCH—USE READER SERVICE!

Here is a quick and easy way to receive free travel and camping information. Enter the Reader Service Number (listed below) on the Reader Service Card, which is located opposite page 48. Your request will be forwarded to the businesses you've indicated. You'll receive information, sent directly to your home. It's the no-hassle way to plan your next trip!

Enter Number	
ALASKA	
3713	Adventure Bound Alaska
3424	Alaska Campground Owners Association
684	Alaska Marine Highway System
3512	Alaska's Inter-Island Ferry Authority
780	Fairbanks Convention & Visitors Bureau
4023	Haines Convention & Visitors Bureau
3434	Orca Enterprises
3111	Stan Stephens Glacier & Wildlife Cruises
ALABAMA	
4223	Auburn-Opelika Convention & Visitors
4221	Bella Terra of Gulf Shores
4304	Lake Osprey
472	Noccalula Falls Park & Campground
4234	Point Mallard Campground (City Park)
ARKANSAS	
3449	Fort Smith Visitors Center
ARIZONA	
2163	Arizona ARVC
3570	Desert Oasis MH & RV Park
4272	Rusty's RV Ranch
CALIFORNIA	
607	California Travel Park Assoc
4290	Jelly Belly Candy Co.
3040	San Bernardino County Parks
4013	Silent Valley Club
COLORADO	
2969	Colorado Campground & Lodging Owners Assoc
3208	Colorado State Parks
4041	Loveland RV Resort
CONNECTICUT	
457	Connecticut Campground Owners Assoc
4333	Lake Compounce Family Theme Park
3984	Scranton Motors, Inc.
DISTRICT OF COLUMBIA	
683	Aquia Pines Camp Resort
781	Bethpage Camp Resort
3323	Capitol KOA Washington DC NE
462	Cherry Hill Park
460	Duncan's Family Campground
565	Fredericksburg / Washington DC KOA
562	Greenville Farm Family Campground
564	Travel Trailer Village
FLORIDA	
4219	Aztec RV Resort
3477	Big Cypress RV Resort
3784	Broward County Parks
4300	Broward County Parks
4263	Camping on the Gulf
3671	Como Truck & RV Sales & Service
4176	Disney's Fort Wilderness Resort & Campground
671	Dunedin RV Resort
4322	Emerald Coast RV Beach Resort
3583	Flagler County Chamber of Commerce
2173	Florida Association of RV Parks and Campgrounds
4265	Goethe Trailhead Ranch & RV Park
4130	Hammondell Campsites & RV Sales
672	Lake Marian Paradise
4355	Lazy Days RV Campground
4245	Outdoor Resorts at Orlando
4255	Pelican's Landing
3666	Quail Run RV Resort
4270	Rainbow Resort
3872	Revels Nationwide RV Sales
3806	Sarasota Sunny South
4253	Seasons in the Sun RV & Motorcoach Resort
3374	Sonrise Palms Christian RV Park
4341	The Floridian RV Resort
3670	Wilderness RV Park Estates
440	Zachary Taylor Resort
GEORGIA	
4251	Brickyard Plantation RV Park
3696	Cedar Creek RV Park & Outdoor Center
3221	Flynn's Inn Camping Village
473	Georgia Mountain Fairgrounds Campground
849	Georgia Power Company Parks
IOWA	
4000	Amana Colonies Visitors Center
3276	Iowa ARVC
3458	Truck Country
IDAHO	
3633	Idaho RV Campground Association
4285	Village of Trees RV Resort
KANSAS	
2724	Hays Convention & Visitors Bureau
458	Kansas Association RV Parks & Campgrounds
3326	Kansas RV Parks & Travel Inc
3431	Prairie Band Casino & Resort RV Park
3430	Rolling Hills Zoo & Wildlife Museum
LOUISIANA	
4256	Bayou LaFourche Area CVB
2687	Cajun Coast Visitors & Convention Bureau
4065	Coushatta Luxury RV Resort at Red Shoes Park
396	Houma Area Convention & Visitors Bureau
2843	Lafayette Convention & Visitors Commission
3013	Lake Charles/Southwest Louisiana Convention & Visitors Bureau
3255	Louisiana Campground Owners Assoc
3767	Louisiana Travel Promotion Association
4314	Mississippi State Parks
2589	Paragon Casino RV Resort
153	St. Tammany Parish Tourist & Convention Commission
MASSACHUSETTS	
2222	Massachusetts Association of Campground Owners
MARYLAND	
461	Cherry Hill Park
4106	Cherrystone Family Camping Resort
3482	Yogi Bear's Jellystone Camp Resort Williamsport
MAINE	
2613	Libby's Oceanside Camp
709	Maine Campground Owner Assoc.
716	Point Sebago Golf & Beach RV Resort
MICHIGAN	
4332	Bay Mills Resort & Casino
469	Cran-Hill Ranch Family Campground
4282	Haas Lake Park
3804	Hidden Ridge RV Resort
4179	Lake Chemung Outdoor Resort
3022	Little River Casino
4057	Oak Beach County Park
MINNESOTA	
4174	Fortune Bay Resort Casino & RV Park
3298	Grand Casino Hinckley RV Resort
647	Lebanon Hills Campground
3420	Minnesota Resort Campground Association
3560	Prairie View RV Park & Campground
4315	Treasure Island Resort & Casino
MISSOURI	
4271	Boomland RV Park & Campground

FREE Camping Information
TRAVEL SECTION

Enter Number	
3766	Branson Lakes Area Chamber of Commerce & CVB
3028	Division of State Parks Missouri
3465	Lady Luck RV Park & Nature Trail
3147	Missouri Association of RV Parks
3338	Missouri Division of Tourism

MISSISSIPPI

754	Mississippi State Parks

MONTANA

495	Campground Owners of Montana

NORTH CAROLINA

3591	Carolina RV Parks & Campground Association
3527	Daly RV
3617	Franklin RV Park & Campground
3398	Outer Banks Visitors Bureau
3707	The Refuge

NORTH DAKOTA

804	Medora Campground
3145	Norsk Hostfest

NEBRASKA

2999	Cabela's RV Park

NEW HAMPSHIRE

4309	Great Bay Camping/Shell
4331	Tamworth Camping Area
730	White Mountain Attractions

NEW JERSEY

574	New Jersey Campground Association
958	Ocean View Resort Campground
4021	Seashore Campsites

NEW MEXICO

3769	Lordsburg Hildago Chamber of Commerce

NEVADA

4266	Elko CVA
4352	Nevada Magazine
3665	Nevada Treasure RV Resort & Spa

NEW YORK

4364	Ausable Chasm
4029	Black Bear Campground
456	Campground Owners of New York (CONY)
689	Sullivan County Tourism
3574	The Villages at Turning Stone RV Park
659	Yogi Bear's Jellystone Park Camp Resort at Mexico

OHIO

2807	Cedar Point Camper Village/Lighthouse Point
411	Ohio Campground Owners Association
4277	Ohio Department of Natural Resources
3779	RV Wholesalers

OKLAHOMA

4320	Chisholm Trail RV Park
4164	WinStar RV Park

OREGON

3827	Schroeder Josephine & County Park
3717	Seven Feathers RV Resort
3741	The Mill Casino RV Park

PENNSYLVANIA

3568	Bear Run Campground
3739	Boyer RV Center
3743	Dale Smith's Camper Sales
3704	Mellott Brothers RV
515	Pennsylvania Campground Owners' Association
3584	The Foote Rest Campground

SOUTH CAROLINA

3592	Carolina Campground Association
3667	Magnolia RV Park & Campground
4278	Myrtle Beach Campground Association

SOUTH DAKOTA

4267	American RV Park & Motel
3709	Hart Ranch RV Resort
2665	Lake Mitchell Campground (City Park)
2467	Rafter J Bar Ranch Camping Resort
2805	South Dakota Department of Game, Fish & Parks
3688	The Journey Museum
2754	Wylie Park Campground

TENNESSEE

4340	Tennessee ARVC
3342	Tennessee State Parks Department

TEXAS

4233	Casa Del Sol
4227	Guadalupe River RV Resort
4224	Kerrville Convention & Visitors Bureau
4225	Midessa Oil Patch RV Park
4301	Northlake Village RV Park
2840	Port Aransas Chamber of Commerce
4268	Southern Oaks
4226	Spring Creek Marina & RV Park
3328	Texas Association of Campground Owners
3813	Texas State Parks & Wildlife Dept
4356	WinStar RV Park

UTAH

2685	Cedar City Brian Head Tourism Bureau
4187	St. George Area Visitors Bureau
3631	Uintah County Tourism

VIRGINIA

568	Bethpage Camp Resort
538	Cherrystone Family Camping Resort
4319	KOA Williamsburg
3757	Virginia Campground Association

VERMONT

4302	Greenwood Lodge & Campsites
4342	Lone Pine Campsites
2293	Quechee Pine Valley KOA
3148	Vermont Campground Owners Assoc

WASHINGTON

3689	Lakeshore RV Park & Marina
3744	Ocean Park Area Chamber of Commerce
4160	Silver Cove RV Resort
3720	Washington State Parks and Recreation
3471	Yakama Nation RV Resort

WISCONSIN

4291	Jelly Belly Candy Co.
3456	Truck Country
3256	Wisconsin Association of Campgrounds

WYOMING

690	Buffalo Bill's Cody
3652	Cheyenne Area Convention & Visitors Bureau

CANADA

ALBERTA

4030	Radium Valley Vacation Resort
3422	Southern Alberta Historic Sites

BRITISH COLUMBIA

4173	BC Lodging & Campground Association
4323	Camperland RV Resort
3453	District of Chetwynd
4259	Riverside RV Resort & Campground
4313	Wells Gray Golf Resort and RV Park

MANITOBA

741	Communications Services Manitoba

NORTHWEST TERRITORIES

4334	Northwest Territories Tourism

ONTARIO

466	Ontario Private Campground Association
4325	Sherkston Shores

PRINCE EDWARD ISLAND

4294	PEI Provincial Parks

QUEBEC

627	Conseil De Development du Camping au Quebec
4231	Okeechobee Landings

SASKATCHEWAN

798	Saskatchewan South East Tourism
2532	Saskatchewan West Central Tourism

FREE Camping Information
EXTENDED STAY SECTION

SAVE HOURS OF RESEARCH!

The campgrounds/RV parks, RV service centers and attractions listed below want your business! Here is a quick and easy way to receive free information about seasonal camping, fun things to do, and where to service your RV or buy a new one. Simply enter their **Reader Service Number** (listed below) on the **Reader Service Card**, which is located opposite page 48 in the front of the **Discover Section**. Your request will be forwarded to the names you've indicated. Then, you'll receive brochures and/or pricing information, sent directly to your home. It's the no-hassle way to shop for the campground, attraction or RV dealership you are interested in!

Enter Number	
ARIZONA	
3835	Desert Gold RV Resort
3834	Holiday Palms RV Park
CALIFORNIA	
4260	KOA San Francisco North/Petaluma
4305	Lake Elsinore West Marina & RV Resort
3590	Sunland RV Resorts
FLORIDA	
4365	Arrowhead Campsites
4246	Forest Lake Estates & RV Park
4232	Imperial Bonita Estates RV Resort
4033	Lakeland RV Resort
3554	Mill Creek RV Resort
4230	Okeechobee Landings
3884	Paradise Island
4244	Quail Run RV Resort
906	Road Runner Travel Resort
3889	Sun 'N' Shade Campground
3753	The Boardwalk
919	Upriver RV Resort
4237	Woodsmoke Camping Resort
439	Zachary Taylor Resort
GEORGIA	
4275	Cecil Bay RV Park
3058	River's End Campground & RV Park
MAINE	
1050	Beach Acres Campground
MICHIGAN	
926	Creek Valley
1076	Greenwood Acres Family Campground
4287	Houghton Lake Travel Park
3441	Lake Chemung Outdoor Resort
4212	Shady Shores Resort
MISSISSIPPI	
3792	Indian Point RV Resort
4359	Nanabe Creek Campground
4288	River Town Campground
4358	Santa Maria RV Park
NEW HAMPSHIRE	
4368	The Bluffs Adult RV Resort
NEW MEXICO	
4284	Kiva RV Park and Horse Motel
TEXAS	
3669	Parkview Riverside
4239	Sea Breeze RV Park

Reserve Online at Woodalls.com

ALASKA
CANTWELL
Cantwell RV Park LLC (800)940-2210
HAINES
Oceanside RV Park (907)766-2437
KENAI
Diamond M Ranch Resort (907)283-9424
TOK
Tok RV Village (907)883-5877
VALDEZ
Eagle's Rest RV Park & Cabins (800)553-7275
WASILLA
Alaskan Trails RV & Camper Park (907)376-5504

ALABAMA
FOLEY
Magnolia Springs RV Hideaway (251)965-6777
ROBERTSDALE
Wilderness RV Park (251)960-1195
WOODVILLE
Parnell Creek RV Park (256)776-2348

ARKANSAS
HARRISON
Parkers RV Park (870)743-2267

ARIZONA
GILA BEND
Augie's Quail Trail RV Park (928)683-2850
MARANA
Valley of The Sun RV Resort (520)682-3434
MARICOPA
John Wayne RV Ranch (520)424-3813
MESA
Val Vista Village RV Resort (888)940-8989
NACO
Turquoise Valley Golf & RV Resort (520)432-3091
PICACHO
Picacho Peak RV Resort (520)466-7841
QUARTZSITE
Desert Sunset RV Park (928)927-6443
La Paz Valley RV Park (928) 927-6661
Split Rail RV Park (928)927-5296
WILLCOX
Lifestyle RV Resort (520)384-3303

CALIFORNIA
BAKERSFIELD
Bakersfield River Run RV Park (888)748-7786
Bakersfield RV Travel Park (877)361-3550
Orange Grove RV Park (661)366-4662
BLYTHE
Hidden Beaches River Resort (877)922-7276
BORREGO SPRINGS
Blu In Park RV Resort and Restaurant (760)561-1370
The Springs at Borrego RV Resort & Golf Course (866)330-0003
BOULEVARD
Sacred Rocks RV Park (619)766-4480
COLEVILLE
Meadowcliff Lodge & RV Resort (530)495-2255
EL CAJON
Rancho Los Coches RV Park (800)630-0448
GRAND TERRACE
Terrace Village RV Park (909)783-4580
ISLETON
Delta Shores Resort & Marina (916)777-5577
KLAMATH
Kamp Klamath (866)KLAMATH
LIKELY
Likely Place RV & Golf Resort (888)350-3848
MENDOCINO
Caspar Beach RV Park and Campground (707)964-3306
NOVATO
Novato RV Park (415)897-1271
OLEMA
Olema RV Resort & Campground (415)663-8106
QUINCY
Pioneer RV Park (888)216-3266
RED BLUFF
Durango RV Resort (866)770-7001
REDDING
Mountain Gate RV Park (800)404-6040
SAN DIEGO
Santa Fe RV Resort (800)959-3787
SANTA NELLA
Santa Nella RV Park (888)826-3105
VACAVILLE
Vineyard RV Park (866)447-8797

COLORADO
COLORADO SPRINGS
Goldfield RV Park (888)471-0495
MONTROSE
Country Village RV Park (970)249-6382
SEIBERT
Shady Grove Wi-Fi Campground (970)664-2218

FLORIDA
ARCADIA
Cross Creek Country Club & RV Resort (863)494-7300
CLERMONT
Bee's RV Resort (352)429-2116
FOUNTAIN
Pine Lake RV Park (850)722-1401
JASPER
Florida Gateway Resort (877)253-0114
OCKLAWAHA
Lake Bryant MH & RV Park (352)625-2376

GEORGIA
PERRY
Fair Harbor RV Park & Campground (877)988-8844

IOWA
NEWTON
Newton KOA (877)792-2428

Reserve Online at Woodalls.com

IDAHO
EDEN
Anderson Camp RV Park (888)480-9400
GRANGEVILLE
Bear Den RV Resort (800)530-3658

ILLINOIS
CARBONDALE
Little Grassy Lake Campground & Marina (618)457-6655
JOSLIN
Sunset Lakes Resort (800)747-5253

INDIANA
HOWE
Twin Mills Camping Resort (866)562-3212
NEW CARLISLE
Lakeside RV Resort (574)654-3260

KANSAS
KINSLEY
Four Aces RV Park (620)659-2321

KENTUCKY
BENTON
Big Bear Resort (800)922-BEAR

LOUISIANA
FENTON
Quiet Oaks RV Park (888)755-2230
MONROE
Shiloh Campground & RV Resort (318)343-6098
WEST MONROE
Pavilion RV Park (888)322-4216

MASSACHUSETTS
SOUTH DENNIS
Old Chatham Road RV Resort (508)385-3616

MAINE
BAR HARBOR
Mt. Desert Narrows Camping Resort (866)917-4300
Narrows Too Camping Resort (866)917-4300
ELLSWORTH
Patten Pond Camping Resort (866)917-4300
GEORGETOWN
Sagadahoc Bay Campground (207)371-2014
OLD ORCHARD BEACH
Pinehirst RV Resort (207)934-5526

MICHIGAN
CADILLAC
Camp Cadillac (231)775-9724
HOWELL
Taylor's Beach Campground (517)546-2679
MANISTEE
Insta-Launch Campground & Marina (866)452-8642
MUNITH
The Oaks Resort (517)596-2747

MINNEOSTA
ST. CLOUD
St. Cloud Campground & RV Park (320)251-4463

MISSOURI
BRANSON
Pea Patch RV Park (417)335-3958
LEBANON
Happy Trails RV Park (417)532-3422
OSAGE BEACH
Osage Beach RV Park (573)348-3445
VAN BUREN
Big Spring RV Camp (800)354-6295

MISSISSIPPI
BILOXI
Cajun RV Park (877)225-8699
PICAYUNE
Sun Roamers RV Resort (601)798-5818

MONTANA
BOZEMAN
Bear Canyon Campground (800)438-1575
TROUT CREEK
Trout Creek Motel & RV Park (406)827-3268

NORTH CAROLINA
ABERDEEN
Long Leaf Pine Oasis (910)266-8372
CAPE CARTERET
Goose Creek Resort Family Campground (252)393-2628
CHEROKEE
Fort Wilderness Campground and RV Resort(828)497-9331
WASHINGTON
Twin Lakes Camping Resort and Yacht Basin (252)946-5700

NEBRASKA
HENDERSON
Prairie Oasis Campground (402)723-5227

NEW HAMPSHIRE
CONTOOCOOK
Sandy Beach RV Resort (603)746-3591
EPSOM
Circle 9 Ranch (603)736-9656
EXETER
Exeter Elms Family Campground (603)778-7631
SOUTH HAMPTON
Tuxbury Pond Resort (800)585-7660

NEW JERSEY
CAPE MAY COURT HOUSE
Big Timber Lake Camping Resort (609)465-4456

NEVADA
RENO
Bonanza Terrace RV Park (775)329-9624
WINNEMUCCA
Hi Desert RV Park (775)623-4513

NEW YORK
CORINTH
Alpine Lake RV Resort, LLC (518)654-6260
JAVA CENTER
Beaver Meadow Family Campground (585)457-3101
LAKE GEORGE
Lake George Escape Resort (800)327-3188
ONEONTA
Susquehanna Trail Campground (607)432-1122
PULASKI
Brennan Beach RV Resort (888)891-5979

OHIO
BLUFFTON
Twin Lakes Park (888)436-3610
PORT CLINTON
Shade Acres Campground & Cottages (419)797-4681
SANDUSKY
Sandusky Bayshore KOA (800)562-2486

OKLAHOMA
HUGO
Hugo Lake State Park (580)326-0303

OREGON
ASHLAND
Glenyan RV Park of Ashland (541)488-1785
BANDON
Robbin's Nest RV Park (541)347-2175
MYRTLE CREEK
Tri City RV Park (541)860-5000
OAKLAND
Rice Hill RV Park (541)849-2335
SUTHERLIN
Hi-Way Haven RV Park (541)459-4557
SWEET HOME
Edgewater RV Resort & Marina (541)818-0431
TILLAMOOK
Tillamook Bay City RV Park (503)377-2124
WINCHESTER BAY
Surfwood RV Campground (541)271-4020

PENNSYLVANIA
COVINGTON
Tanglewood Camping (570)549-8299
KINZERS
Roamers' Retreat Campground (800)525-5605
NEW HOLLAND
Spring Gulch Resort Campground (717)354-3100
SHEFFIELD
Whispering Winds Campground (814)968-4377

SOUTH CAROLINA
JOANNA
Magnolia RV Park & Campground (864)697-1214

SOUTH DAKOTA
HILL CITY
Crooked Creek Resort (800)252-8486

TENNESSEE
BRISTOL
Lakeview RV Park (866)800-0777
GATLINBURG
Smoky Bear Campground (800)850-8372

TEXAS
ARLINGTON
Arlington Forest Acres RV & MH (817)478-5805
COLUMBUS
Columbus KOA (979)732-9494
CONCAN
Parkview Riverside RV Park (877)374-6748
FORT DAVIS
RV Resort MacMillen in the Highlands (432)426-2056
FORT STOCKTON
Parkview RV Park (432)336-7733
GLADEWATER
Antique Capital RV Park (903)845-7378
GONZALES
Hill Shade RV Park (830)437-2428
GUNBARREL CITY
Lakeridge RV Park (877)451-4304
KERRVILLE
Johnson Creek RV Resort & Park (800)933-6578
MANSFIELD
Texan RV Ranch (817)473-1666
MISSION
Mission Bell Tradewinds RV Resort (956)585-4833
NEWTON
Artesian Springs Resort (409)379-8826
ROCKPORT
A Raintree RV Park (361)729-7005
TEXARKANA
Shady Pines RV Park (903)832-1268

UTAH
TORREY
Wonderland RV Park (877)854-0184

VIRGINIA
GORDONSVILLE
Shenandoah Crossing Resort & Country Club (540)832-9506
LOUISA
Small Country Campground (540)967-2431

VERMONT
ASCUTNEY
Running Bear Camping Area (802)674-6417

WISCONSIN
BARABOO
Fox Hill RV Park (888)236-9445
FREMONT
Yogi Bear Jellystone Park Camp-Resort (800)258-3315
STURGEON BAY
Tranquil Timbers Camping Retreat (800)986-2267
WISCONSIN DELLS
Arrowhead Resort Campground (608)254-7344
Yogi Bear's Jellystone Park Camp-Resort (800)462-9644
Yukon Trails Camping (608)666-3261

WEST VIRGINIA
MOOREFIELD
Riverside Cabins & RV Park (304)538-6467

MEXICO BAJA
LORETO (B.C.S.)
Loreto Shores Villas & RV Park 011-52-613-135-1513

BRITISH COLUMBIA
ALDERGROVE
Eagle Wind RV Park (604)856-6674
BARRIERE
Dee Jay RV Park & Campground (866)872-5685

NEWFOUNDLAND & LABRADOR
DEER LAKE
Gateway to the North RV Park (888)818-8898

NOVA SCOTIA
AYLESFORD
Klahanie Kamping (902)847-9316

ILLINOIS

Bounded by five states, Illinois is often called the "Crossroads State", where east meets west. Rich in beauty, history and architectural wonders, Illinois is a state where progress, diversity, and small town sensibility work hand-in-hand to create a true cross section of American living.

The first stop on our journey is the charming town of Geneseo. Located near the historic Hennepin Canal State Park, travelers can enjoy a wealth of outdoor activities including fishing, boating, swimming, kayaking and hiking. For the culture seeker, Geneseo has a wonderful historical museum worth exploring. The Geneseo Historical Museum features 27 rooms, and 9,000 square feet in which to display their entire collection, ranging from local artifacts to general store and dentist office replicas.

The next stop on our journey is a short 50-mile drive away. Leave Geneseo via IL-82 N, turn left at IL-92 W, making a right turn to merge onto I-88 E. Take a left off of I-88 E onto IL-40 N. Rock Falls sits on the banks of the Rock River, and offers more great opportunities for canoeing, kayaking, fishing, biking and hiking. For those travelers looking to try their hand at homesteading, stop by the Muller Lane Farm where you'll get your chance to learn exactly what it takes to be a farmer through tours and demonstrations, including soap making, buttermilk churning, and much more. Not far from Rock Falls, in the town of Dixon, you'll find Ronald Reagan's boyhood home, which is worth a visit, and the John Deere Historic Site, which is filled with fascinating tidbits of information on some of the innovative tools John Deere built.

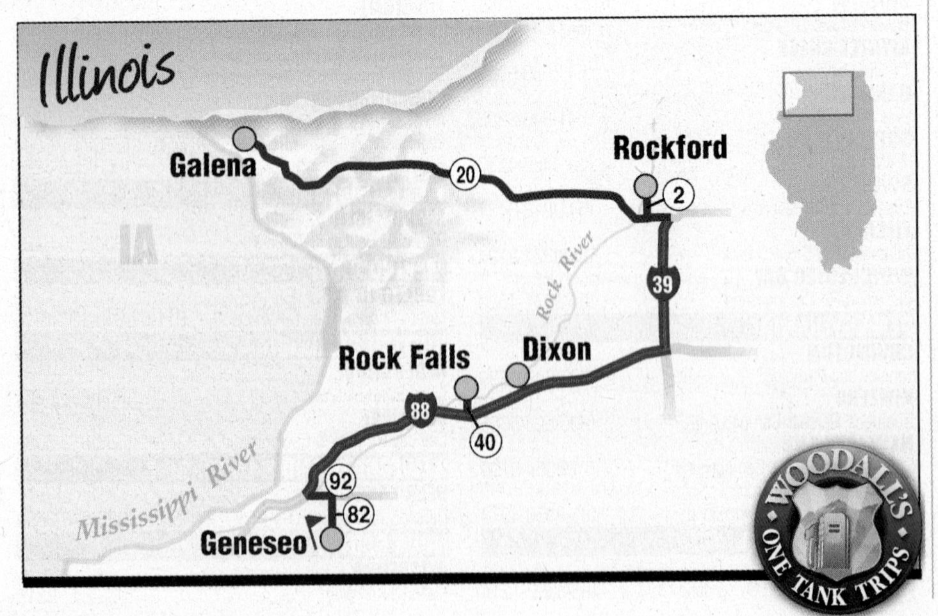

Let's move on to our next stop, Rockford. Backtrack a little on US-40 heading south, and turn left onto US-30 E to return to I-88 E. Exit onto I-39 N, and then onto US-20 W toward Freeport/Rockford, then exit again onto IL-2 N for the 70-mile trip into Rockford. This incredible town is literally overflowing with great stuff! Here you'll find fascinating museums, like the Burpee Museum of Natural History and the Discovery Center Museum. The town also has beautiful gardens, like the Anderson Japanese Garden, the ravishing Klehm Arboretum, or the Sinnissippi; all which have earned Rockford a reputation as a garden city. To get an up close and personal glimpse of the stately homes gracing the waterfront, climb aboard a riverboat and take a tour where you'll learn about Rockford's humble beginnings. For the outdoor enthusiast, there is no shortage of great opportunities for you. There are several outfitters in the area just waiting to aid you in your exploration of the Kishwaukee River. Or head over to the Winnebago County Forest Preserve where you have miles and miles of hiking trails to explore.

Our last stop is Galena, about an hour and a half drive away on US-20 W. Galena is a spectacular destination filled with rich history and exceptional architecture surrounded by the beautiful Illinois countryside. This is wine country, so feel free to take tours, do some sampling, and enjoy the hills and valleys of this area. At the Galena Historical Society and Museum visitors can take special ghost tours, which offer a wonderful opportunity to learn more about this historic city. Well known as the home to a variety of artists, Galena has numerous galleries and craft stores worth exploring, and the main street offers many fun and unique shopping experiences. No matter where you look in Galena, you'll find a wealth of beauty and history worth immersing yourself into. This town is a perfect exclamation point to a great trip through Illinois.

INDIANA

There may be a few long running arguments on how the Hoosier State got it's name, but there is no disputing the vast Midwestern beauty that this state contains, or the wealth of recreational fun around every bend!

We're going to start it off in Elkhart, a vibrant riverside city rich with turn-of-the-century architecture mixed with modern day touches. Downtown you'll find an abundance of tasty eats and a burgeoning arts district waiting to be explored. At the Midwest Museum of American Art, travelers will find everything, from pop art, to an extensive collection of Norman Rockwell paintings. At the National New York Central Railroad Museum travelers can ride the rails of history. For those looking to enjoy the outdoors, Elkhart is home to several parks, many of them in close proximity to the Elkhart and St. Joseph rivers that merge downtown. Here you can jog, ride your bike, or spread out a blanket and enjoy a picnic. Elkhart easily caters to a variety of travelers, with a pace much slower, and far less crowded, than most other larger metropolitan areas.

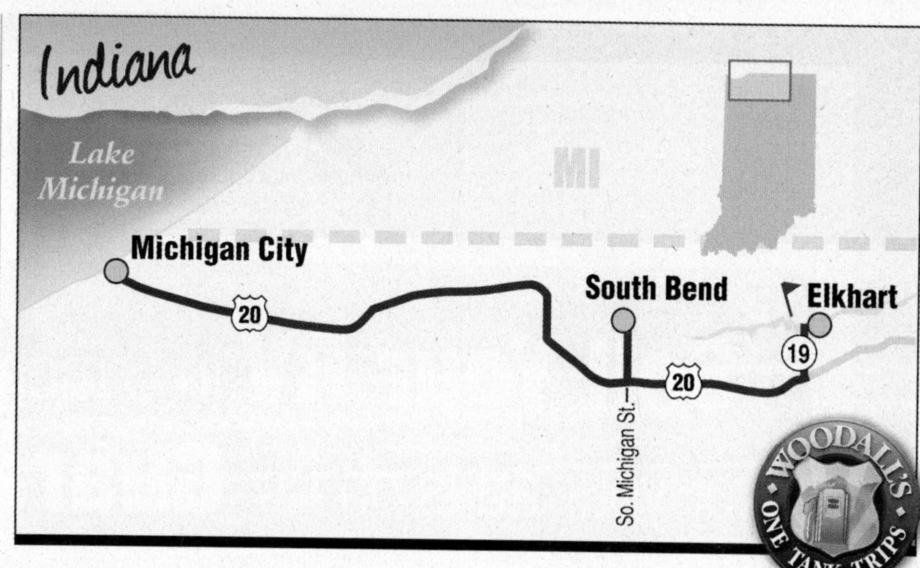

Let's move on to our next stop; South Bend. Head out of Elkhart on IN-19 S, and merge onto US-20 W. Exit onto S. Michigan Street. This leg of our trip clocks in at about 20 miles. Named for the large southern curve in the St. Joseph River, which borders South Bend, the river has always been an important part of the city's growth, from the sawmills of long ago, to providing travelers and locals a spectacular place to gather for outdoor recreation. Throughout the city of South Bend you'll find a number of public parks suitable for walking, mountain biking and jogging. Home to the University of Notre Dame, football fans will delight in some pigskin history at the College Football Hall of Fame, while nature lovers can enjoy the rushing rapids of the East Race Waterway, the first artificial whitewater rafting course. But the sweetest destination in South Bend has to be the Chocolate Museum, specializing in all things cocoa: from posters and tins, to a behind the scenes look at making that smooth, creamy good stuff!

Moving onto our next stop, return to US-20 W for the approximate 36-mile trip into Michigan City. Bordering the southernmost tip of Lake Michigan, Michigan City is a spectacular destination for any traveler. Michigan City is home to several parks where outdoor recreation abounds, from hiking, biking, horseback riding, fishing, to yes, even golf! In the summer months, head over to Mt. Baldy where you can wiggle your toes in the sand, work on your tan, or immerse yourself in the many water sports offered here. It's said that on a clear day, you can see the Chicago skyline from atop the giant dune located here, and the sunsets in this location are some of the most beautiful in the area. You won't want to leave without a visit to Indiana's only working lighthouse located in a 99 acre park, where there are still more incredible recreation opportunities! This is one area with so much to do, you just might have to plan a return trip. See you next year!

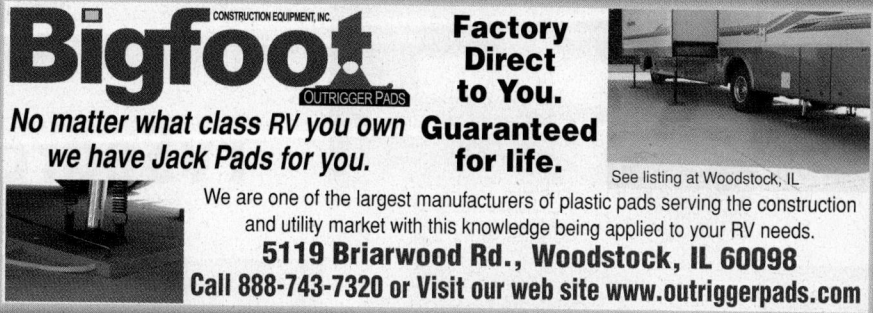

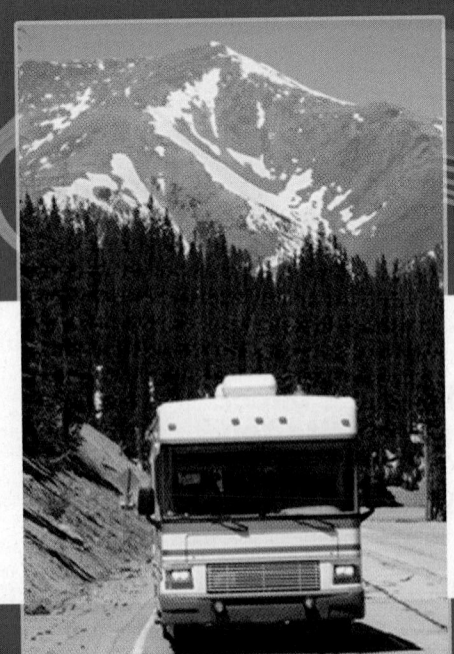

IOWA

Often referred to as "America's Heartland", Iowa has an incredible beauty all its own. Filled with friendly, hardworking Midwesterners, Iowa has a way of making each visitor feel like their coming home again with warmth and hospitality that will make you want to live here!

Let's start our trip in West Branch, where you'll find Midwestern living at its best! Made famous as the hometown of Herbert Hoover, visitors can visit the President's humble beginnings at the tiny two-room cottage he was born in, and explore the several other historical buildings surrounding it. At the Herbert Hoover Presidential Library and Museum, visitors can further explore the life of this great man, and his incredible career through the many exhibits here.

Our next stop takes us west on I-80, with a merge onto I-380 N/IA-27 N to Cedar Rapids, with this leg of our trip taking less than an hour. This city holds a rich history and diverse culture waiting to be explored! Travelers will find many wonderful museums worth a visit, including the National Czech and Slovak Museum and Library, The Iowa Masonic Library and Museum, and the Cedar Rapids Museum of Art. Make sure to put Brucemore at the top of your list of must see places! Built in 1886, this beautiful Queen Anne building sits on 26 incredible acres. Visitors can tour the mansion, stroll through the gardens, attend one of the many outdoor theater events, or bring a picnic and spread out under the warm Iowa sun. Not a bad way to spend the day, is it? Cedar Rapids has something for you nature lovers, too. Head over to the Indian Creek Nature Center where you will find 210 acres of restored savannas, prairies and woodlands, and four miles of trails where you can explore to your heart's content.

The last stop on our Iowa journey takes us to the Amana Colonies, by way of US-151. Amana Colonies began in 1855 by a group of Pietists who sought

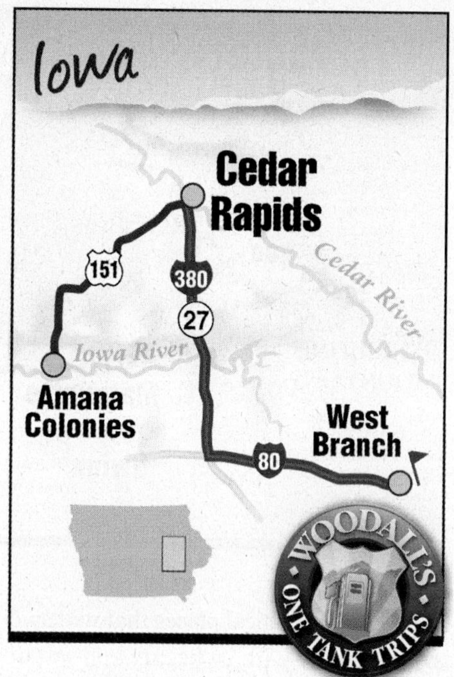

refuge from religious persecution in their native Germany and settled in the beautiful Iowan countryside and would eventually become one of America's oldest and largest religious communal societies. Visitors are free to tour the surrounding buildings, which include a communal kitchen, general store, and church; each one beautifully maintained as it was when the Amanas lived and worked here. It's a fascinating place filled with an amazing history, one that is sure to keep you enthralled for the duration of your trip.

From just the little time we've spent in this wonderful state, it's easy to see there's far more to Iowa than just corn!

MICHIGAN

As travelers, there are times when we choose the hustle-and-bustle of heavy tourist areas and there are other times when what we seek is something more serene, more peaceful, and more soul-centering. The Upper Peninsula of Michigan is definitely the latter. Some of the most breathtaking and awe-inspiring natural beauty can be found here. The kind of thing that lifts your spirits, and shakes the tensions of daily life away.

We're going to begin in Sault Sainte Marie, a place that has been touted as one

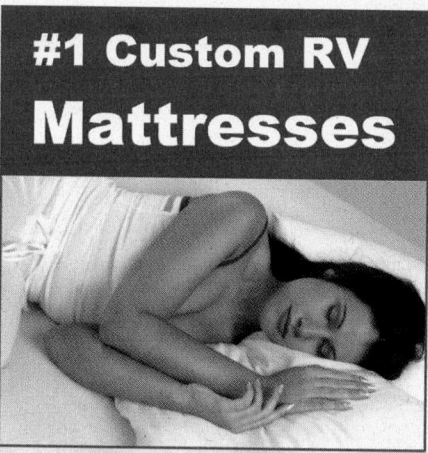

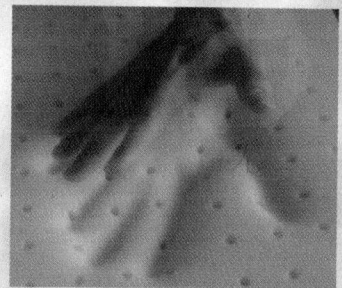

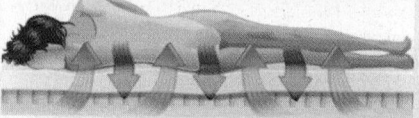

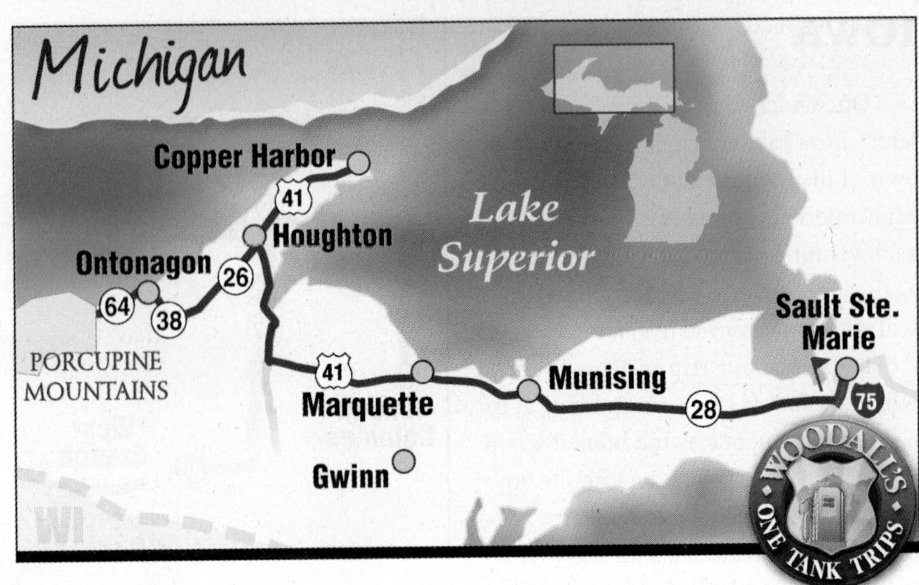

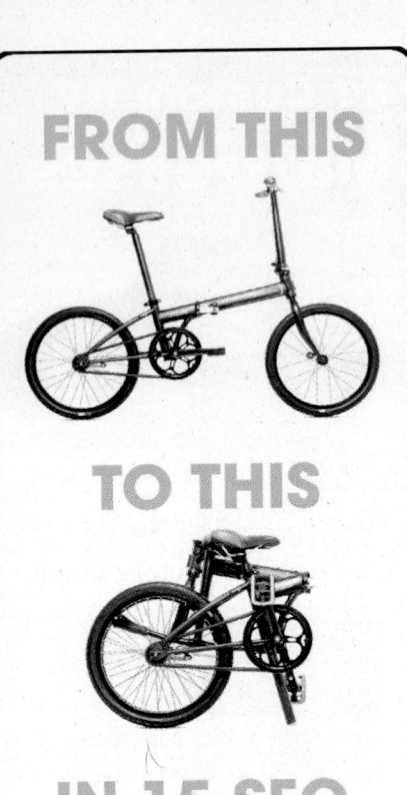

of those rare magical places that will awe every traveler with its beauty and serenity. You'll find rushing waterfalls, majestic forests, miles of rocky coastline, and some of the most picturesque scenery here. One of the greatest attractions in the region is the Soo Locks, often referred to as one of the greatest wonders in the world, and still the largest waterway traffic system on earth. Consisting of two canals and four locks, visitors will be amazed as they watch huge vessels sail through this passageway. Sault Sainte Marie is the oldest city in Michigan, and with that comes a rich maritime heritage, part of which can be explored at the Point Iroquois Lighthouse, which was first illuminated in 1857. Now part of the Hiawatha National Forest (also known as the Great Lakes National Forest), visitors are free to roam the grounds and explore this exceptional lighthouse, as well as the other five lighthouses that can be found within the area. Also available is hiking, hunting, fishing, birdwatching, and access to some of the most incredible, undeveloped shores in the world.

From Sault Sainte Marie, we move on to Munising, taking I-75 S toward St. Ignace, exit for MI-28 toward Newberry/Munising, and turn right at MI-28 W. This part of our journey is about a 3-and-a-half hour trip, weather permitting. Munising is a small, quiet little city, where time and troubles seem to take pause and allow you to relax and enjoy all this area has to offer. There are no long lines, thrill rides, or traffic in Munising; just the rich beauty of the Upper Peninsula to help you recenter yourself during your much needed time off. In Munising, travelers are urged to explore the beauty of this area on the numerous hiking trails, and don't be surprised if you're out on a hike and discover a waterfall - or several. This area seems to be filled with them! Also available are opportunities for swimming, fishing, boating, and the winter months bring incredible snowfall, and skiing and snowmobile riding on the many trails. Nearby Grand Island National Recreation Area and Pictured Rocks National Lakeshore are two favorite spots amongst travelers.

From Munising we move on to Marquette by heading northwest on MI-28 W. Turn right at MI-28 W/US-41 N and you should enjoy this spectacular drive! This route hugs the shores of Lake Superior, and offers incredible opportunities to take a few snap shots! Marquette is located on the southern shores of Lake Superior, where remnants of it's past can be found throughout its historic downtown, and at the Marquette Maritime Museum. Here, the rich heritage of the city comes to life with exhibits, which include birch bark canoes, antique outboard and inboard motors, shipwreck charts, and an amazing array of other items. You don't want to miss this one! Like the rest of the Upper Peninsula, fishing and charters are readily available, as well as hiking and biking, and winter months bring opportunities for ice fishing and skiing.

Return to MI-28 W/US-41 N, taking a left at MI-38 W/Michigan Ave, and another left at MI-26 S/MI038 W to arrive at beautiful Ontonagon. This city, with a most unusual name, has a rich mining history and is surrounded by the splendor of the Porcupine Mountains. For the winter travelers, Ontonagon offers incredible winter sports. The Porcupine Mountains treat skiers to some of the highest vertical slopes within the Midwest, and for the Nordic skier, there is plenty of adventure waiting for you on the cross-country trails throughout the area. Summer and spring offer hiking, swimming, fishing and boating opportunities. Lake of the Clouds is one of the most scenic spots in Michigan, and from Summit Peak Observation Tower, visitors can see miles and miles of pristine, virgin forest, and views of far off Apostle Islands. For those interested in history, there are self-guided hiking trails to old mining sites on the Union Mine Scenic Trail that are definitely worth exploring.

The next leg of our trip has us backtracking a bit on MI-38 heading east. Continue on to MI-26 N to arrive at our next stop, Houghton. From its location within the Keweenaw Peninsula, Houghton is an outdoor and scenic wonderland. Surrounded by water, it provides an ample amount of water sports, and for the winter traveler, Houghton receives about 180 inches of snowfall on average, making it the focal point for amazing winter activities. Accessible only by boat, ferries are offered to Isle Royale, a beautifully primitive and isolated island, where many hiking trails worth exploring and first-class fishing are available.

Our last stop takes us to the very tip of the Upper Peninsula; Copper Harbor. Return to MI-26 N/US-41 N for the quick hour or so trip. Visitors have called this particular area of the Upper Peninsula "The Best of the Lake", and for good reason. The views of the Keweenaw Peninsula are spectacular. Here travelers are overwhelmed with opportunities to hike, fish, canoe, kayak, bike, or even go agate hunting! Don't be surprised if you catch a glimpse of the local wildlife during your stay. For the truly adventurous, explore a real mine at the Delaware Mine and learn about the history of copper mining, or venture over to the Copper Harbor Lighthouse Museum. And for those taking a trip in the winter months, Copper Harbor gets a whopping 250 inches of dry powder on average, making it a winter wonderland, filled with cross-country skiing, snow-shoeing, snowmobile and snow-boarding opportunities. There is no shortage of fun here, no matter what time of year you visit. This area of Michigan is so spectacular, no one would blame you if you backtrack and start this trip over from the beginning!

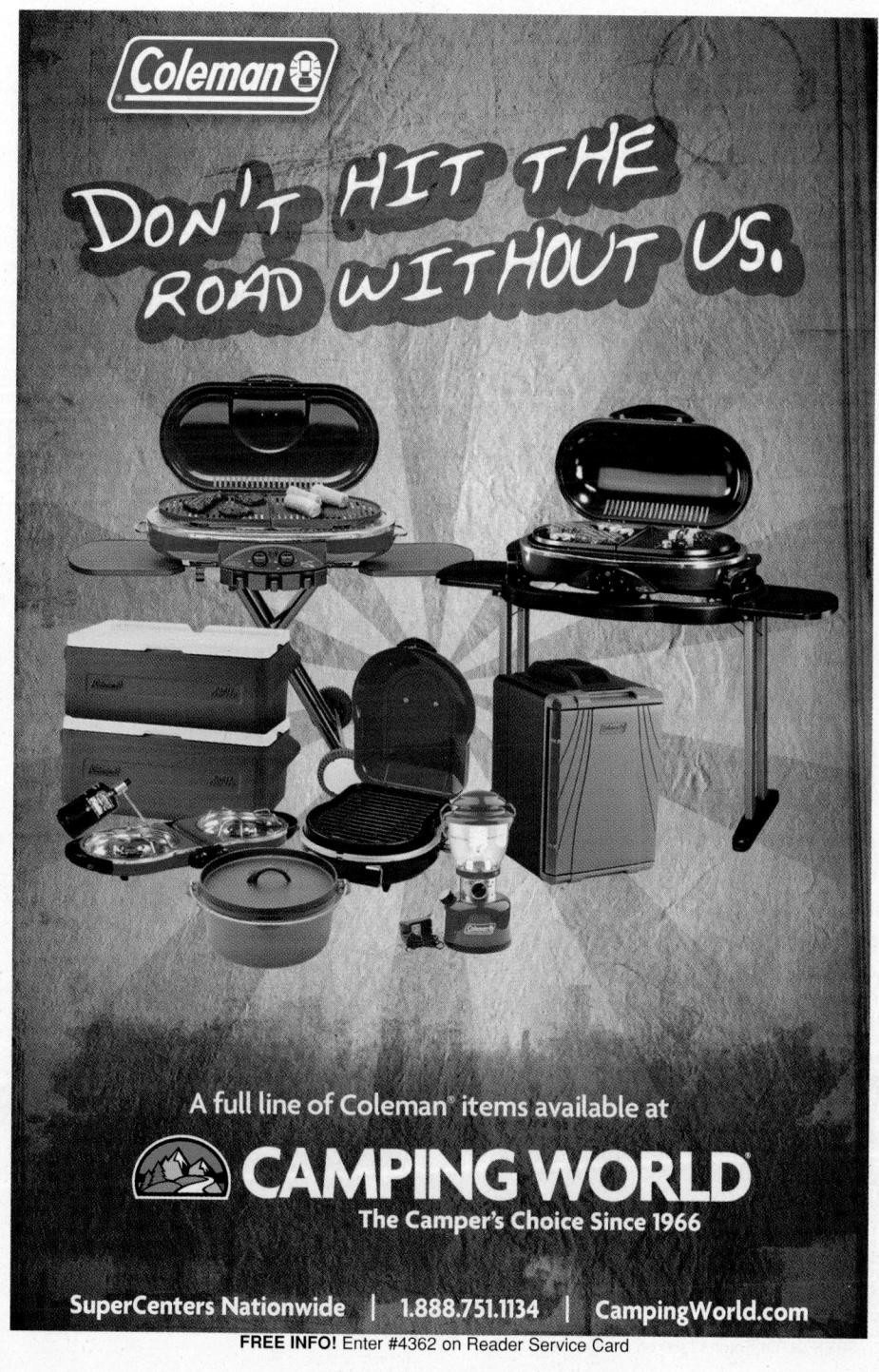

OTHER AREA LOCATIONS

BRIMLEY
Bay Mills Resort & Casinos
CHAMPION
Michigamme Shores Campground Resort
GWINN
Horseshoe Lake Campground & RV Park
KINROSS
Kinross RV Park East
NEW HUDSON
Haas Lake Park
SAULT STE. MARIE
Aune-Osborn RV Park

MINNESOTA

Known as the "Land of Ten Thousand Lakes", Minnesota is a virtual outdoor paradise, attracting thrill seekers, wilderness lovers and anglers alike. With warm, friendly locals, and spectacular beauty, a visit to this great state just might have you hook, line and sinker!

The perfect start for our journey today is the charming town of Chisholm. Located in the northeast part of the state, Chisholm provides travelers with ample recreation, including hiking, mountain biking, boating and fishing - this is the Land of Ten Thousand Lakes, remember! Also notable is the Minnesota Museum of Mining and the Minnesota Discover Center, where visitors can learn the fascinating mining past of Chisholm and the surrounding area.

The next stop on our trip takes us to Duluth, via US-169 N. Turn right to merge onto US-53 S. Take the ramp to I-35 N, keeping left. Duluth clocks in at approximately an hour and 45 minutes away from Chisholm. Located on the western-most tip of massive Lake Superior, it is no wonder travelers are drawn to this area in droves, not only for the water recreation found here, but also for the incredible beauty. One very unique attraction in Duluth is Canal Park, which showcases an aerial life bridge that rises

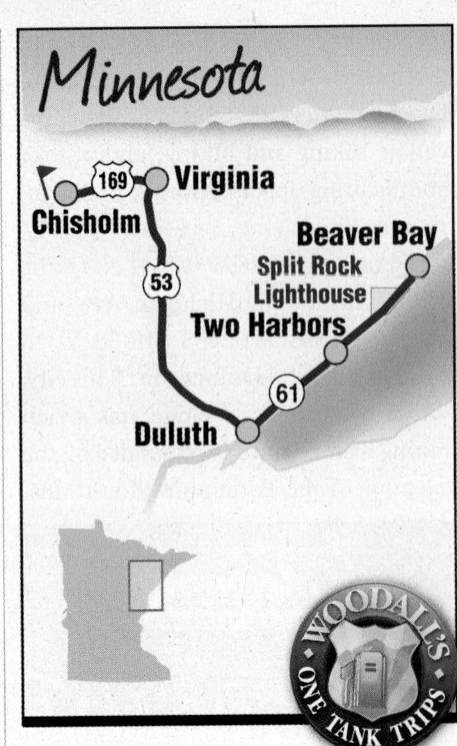

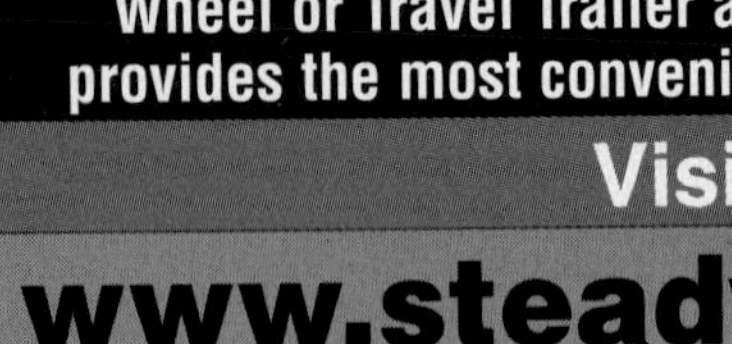

to allow massive vessels to enter the harbor. Tours are available that highlight these huge vessels, and is something you won't want to pass up during your visit. You'll also want to make time to stop by the Great Lakes Aquarium. It's the only fresh water aquarium in the US, and a place the whole family will enjoy!

Our next location is Two Harbors, less than an hour drive on MN-61 N. Considered by many to be the Gateway to the North Shore, Two Harbors is an awesome location for those looking to do some exceptional hiking, or indulge in some great fishing. A trip to Gooseberry Falls, located along the North Shore, will bring you face-to-face with a spectacular view of the Gooseberry River that drops approximately 90 feet as it cascades over the upper and lower falls. It is the featured attraction at the park, and one you should definitely experience for yourself. At Split Rock State Park, there are many more hiking opportunities, and visitors will also find Split Rock Lighthouse here. It is one of Minnesota's best-known landmarks, and fully restored to the beauty of its original 1920s appearance.

Return to MN-61 N for the short trip along the breathtaking coast to our final destination, Beaver Bay. Once the most active harbor along the North Shore, Beaver Bay was the first established community on the Minnesota shore of Lake Superior. The pace has slowed somewhat in Beaver Bay, but don't let that fool you; it's still a fantastic location for a variety of outdoor activity including biking, hiking, fishing, kayaking, and the winter months always bring their own chilly fun along the North Shore with snowmobiling, snowshoeing, and dog sledding!

The Land of Ten Thousand Lakes is one of those special states, that no matter how many times you've visited, you'll always find something wonderful, unique, and special to bring you back.

OHIO

For those of you who have passed on visiting the Buckeye State before, you don't know what you've been missing! Surprisingly diverse, Ohio shares the Allegheny and Appalachian Mountain ranges with its eastern neighbors, and is bordered by Lake Erie to the north, and the Ohio River to the south giving this Midwestern state a charm and graceful beauty all its own.

We're going to start it off in New Philadelphia, and from the moment you step foot in this pretty Ohio town, you're surrounded by history. Starting with Schoenbrunn Village, visitors will come face-to-face with the past. Began by the Moravian church in 1772 as a mission to the Delaware Indians, Schoenbrunn gives you a glimpse into rural life before the Revolutionary War. Completely reconstructed, travelers will find the original mission cemetery, several log buildings to explore, and a museum. Within this area you will also find the beauty and simplicity of the Amish people. In fact, Ohio supports the largest Amish community in the US, and you'll find many opportunities for purchasing delicate Amish crafts here, as well as delicious bologna and cheese.

Let's head out to our next destination, Canton. To get there, take OH-39 W out of New Philadelphia and turn right onto I-77 N/US-250 W exiting onto OH-172 E. Any football fan knows, Canton is the birthplace of a great American sport, and the city is proud of its pigskin heritage. A stop by the Pro Football Hall of Fame will get you in touch with your inner athlete by perusing the world's largest collection of pro-football memorabilia. There's plenty more sites worth exploring in Canton, most notably the Wm. McKinley Presidential Library and Museum, and the Canton Classic Car Museum, where thousands of piece of nostalgia are just waiting to be enjoyed!

Our next stop has us return to I-77 N to arrive at Akron. Today, Akron is known as the "City of Invention", but in the past it's also been known as the "Rubber Capital of the World", and the original home of Quaker Oats. Here you can take a walk through history at the Mustill Store and House, an exceptional canal-era building built around 1850, containing many fascinating exhibits on the history of Akron's beginnings. Also notable is the home of John Brown, the famous aboli-

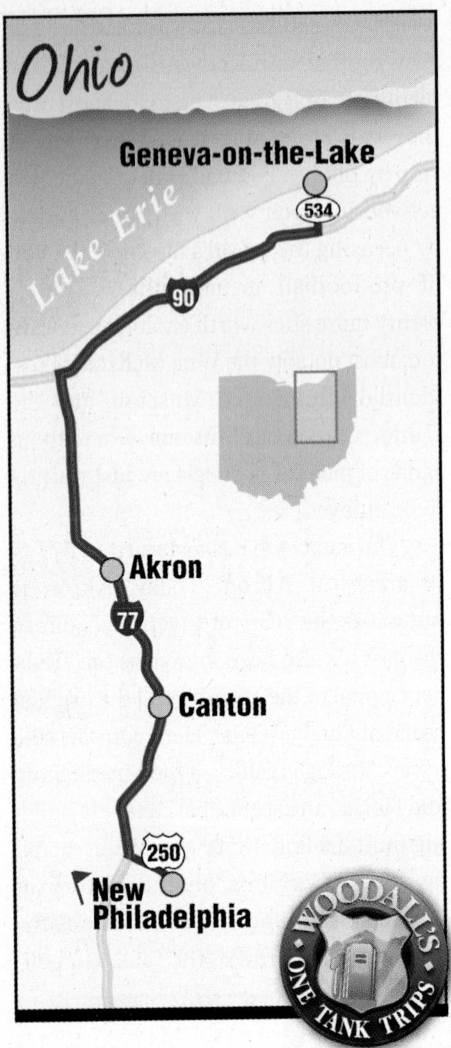

tionist, where visitors can catch a glimpse of one man's fight against slavery. Another must see is the Hower House, an incredible Second Empire Italianate-style mansion, and once home to the famous Akron industrialist, John Hower. Tours are available, and it's one both architecture and history buffs will both enjoy.

For our last stop, take OH-59 E/OH-8 N out of Akron. Merge onto I-271 N and then onto I-90 E. Exit for OH-534 toward Geneva. This leg of the trip is our longest, but well worth it when you finally arrive at this jewel on the shores of Lake Erie: Geneva-on-the-Lake. A veritable paradise for outdoor recreation, Geneva is a great destination for a weekend away, or a far lengthier stay. Travelers here will have all the canoeing, fishing, boating, hiking, birdwatching and kayaking they can handle on the beautiful waters of Lake Erie. Ohio may not be the first name you think of when you hear "wine", but Geneva lies in the heart of wine country, containing over 20 wineries to tempt your palate. You'll soon discover why Ohio Wine Country produces some of the best wines in the country. And with the Amish cheese and bologna we picked up in New Philadelphia, and a fine local wine, we've got everything we need for a relaxing day on the shores of Lake Erie.

OTHER AREA LOCATIONS

COLUMBUS

Cross Creek Camping Resort

WISCONSIN

It's true: Wisconsin is proud of its cheese, boasting the largest variety of award winning cheeses in the country. But there is more to America's Dairyland than the fine cheese produced here. Sometimes referred to as the Midwest's Cape Cod, Wisconsin's beautiful countryside and rolling hills resemble Europe more than the Midwest, and visitors here are often surprised to find a wealth of unique culture and beauty unlike any other place.

We're going to start our journey in Sturgeon Bay. Depending on who you ask, Sturgeon Bay was either named for its resemblance to a sturgeon, or because of the abundance of fish found in both Green Bay and Lake Michigan. Whatever the reason, Sturgeon Bay remains one of the most popular destinations within the state, drawing thousands who come to enjoy the endless water sports and fishing opportunities to be found here. Being surrounded by so much inspirational beauty, it should be no surprise that Sturgeon Bay also has a very healthy art community, with several local artisans displaying their works in the galleries found throughout the area. No trip to Sturgeon Bay would be complete without exploring the rich maritime heritage that still flourishes today, including a trip to the Door County Maritime Museum where the history of this area comes to life. Within the museum, you'll have the opportunity to explore each of the four diverse galleries within the 20,000 sq. ft. building, ranging from shipbuilding to the Great Storm of 1913. While parked on the waterfront, you'll find a beautifully restored 1919 big red tug, which is now open for tours.

Heading on to our next destination, take WI-42 N out of Sturgeon Bay, taking a left at Co Rd G. You'll have to take another left to stay on Co Rd G, and in less than an hour you should have arrived at beautiful Egg Harbor. What a charmer! A stroll through this village, and you'll soon discover why it's a popular destination for travelers. A wide variety of shops and galleries (all of which maintain that wonderful old Wisconsin charm), an exquisite variety of restaurants where you can sample the local fair, and all set against the dramatic beauty of the coast make Egg Harbor a spectacular destination for a wide variety of travelers. In case you're wondering, Egg Harbor was named for a good-natured "war" that broke out among a landing party in 1825 that ended in a huge egg fight that left everyone - from traders to spectators - covered in eggs, and the shoreline littered with eggshells.

Our next stop takes us back to Co Rd G toward E Shore Rd. Turn right at Co Rd E, and left WI-57 N to arrive at Baileys Harbor. Located on what locals refer to as "the quiet side of the harbor", Baileys Harbor is an awesome destination for relaxing or getting your fill of the many activities to be found here, including kayaking, canoeing, hiking, and fishing. One of the most popular attractions in this area is the Cana Island Lighthouse, where visitors can explore the original keeper's house. Nearby, you'll find Ridges Sanctuary, a 1200-acre nature preserve boasting some 5 miles of hiking trails and a variety of native flowers which add to the beauty of the walk.

Let's move onto Sister Bay, a short drive along WI-42 N. By far one of the most popular villages in the county, Sister Bay's beautiful natural environment beckons travelers of varied interests. The waters bordering Green Bay and Lake Michigan offer many opportunities for fishing and kayaking, and if you've never had the pleasure of a Door County Fish Boil, you don't know what you've been missing. Don't leave this area without indulging yourself in at least one!

Our last stop takes us to beautiful Ellison Bay, a short drive away on WI-42 N. Visitors to this incredible location will find a wealth of unique shopping opportunities, many of which come from local artisans and potters. For the shopper, this is nirvana! Nearby Newport State Park is a semi-wilderness area that contains some great hiking along secluded trails, and 11 miles of Lake Michigan shoreline, which offers some peace and quiet from the commotion. There is plenty to explore here, including headlands, coves, and lots and lots of beaches.

Words just don't seem to do this scenic and exciting section of Wisconsin justice. This area is by far one of the most spectacular destinations within the state, and the options for recreation and good old-fashioned fun are as numerous as the fish in Lake Michigan!

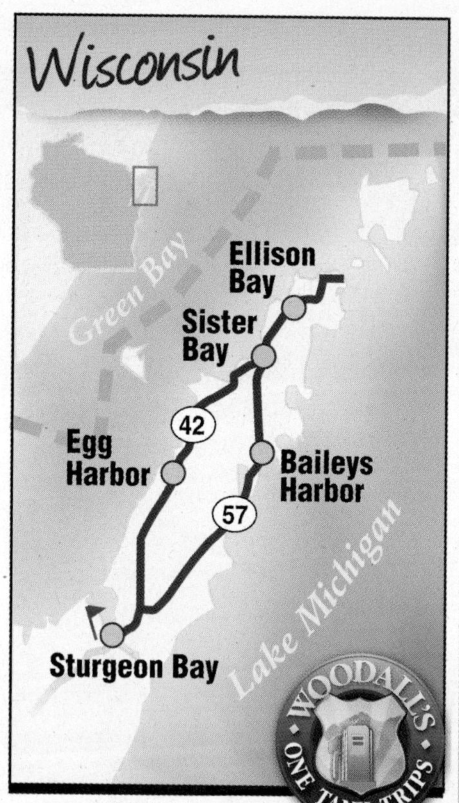

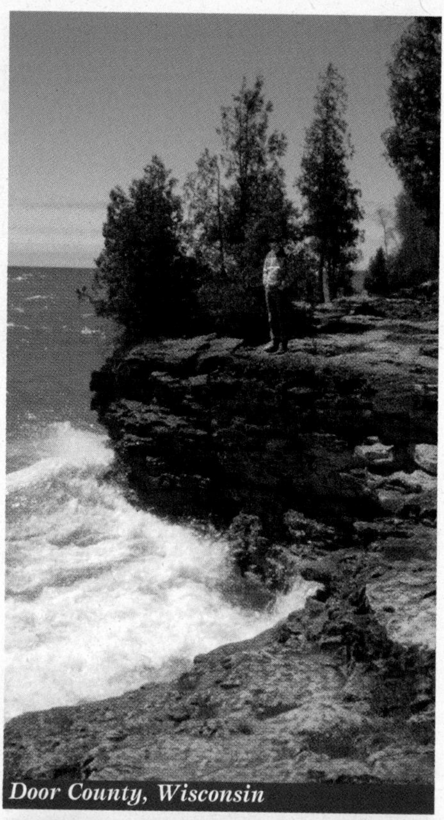
Door County, Wisconsin

OTHER AREA LOCATIONS

DOOR COUNTY

Door County Visitor Bureau

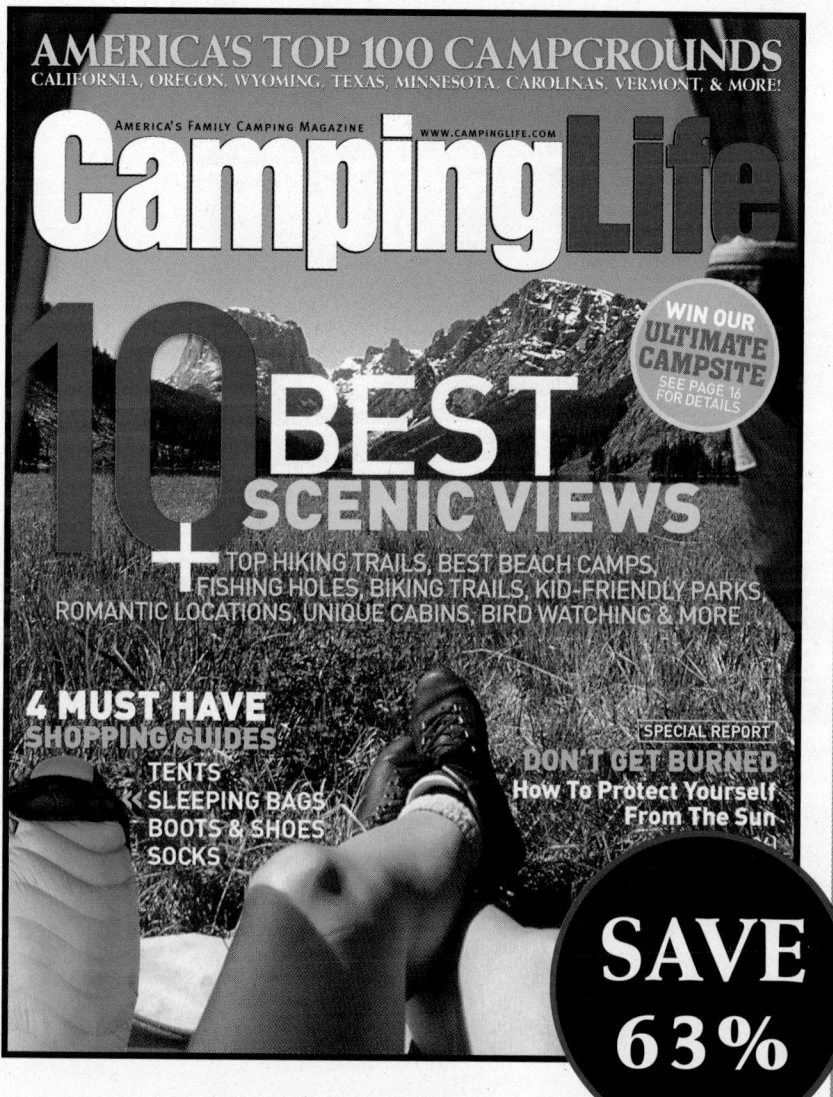

ARKANSAS

Hiding between the Midwest and the Deep South is one of America's best kept secrets. From the worn slopes of the Ozarks and Ouachita Mountains to sweeping vistas, dense forests and rolling pastures, "The Natural State" is bursting with beauty. The abundance of rivers, lakes, and miles of forest draw outdoor enthusiasts every year, but one of the most unique treasures in the state includes the world's only public diamond mine where over 75,000 diamonds have been discovered by lucky treasure seekers.

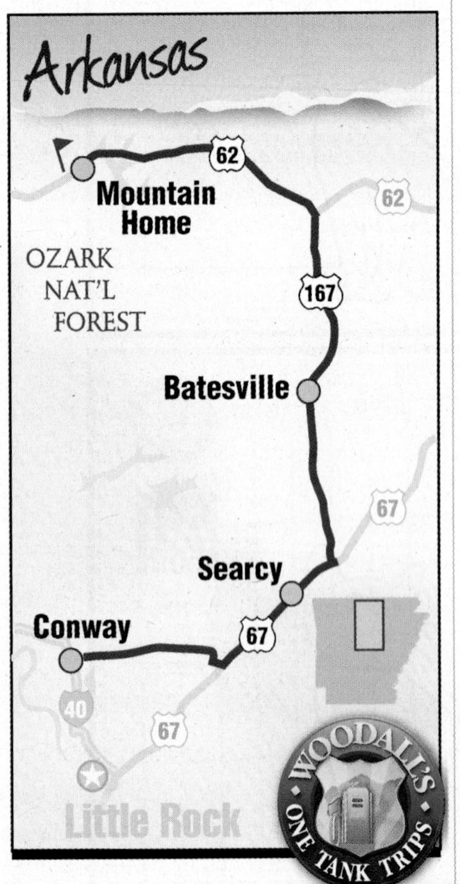

Tucked within the Ozark Mountains, and surrounded by Norfolk and Bull Shoals Lakes lies beautiful Mountain Home, and the perfect place to start our journey. The area surrounding Mountain Home is a nature lover's paradise. Voted one of the top fishing towns, thousands of anglers flock to this area for it's endless fishing possibilities, and for the never ending supply of record trout pulled from the lakes every year. For all of Mountain Home's small town feel, charm, and the natural beauty that lures visitors in, it also has several historic attractions, golf, world-class dining and shopping that even the most discriminating travelers will appreciate.

Take US-412 E/ US-62 E out of Mountain Home, and after several miles, turn onto N/US-167, which brings us to our next stop, Batesville. The oldest existing city in Arkansas, it is also known as the "Gateway to the Ozarks". There is always something interesting going on in Batesville, from the Ozark Scottish Festival held every spring, to the Batesville Air Festival held each autumn, featuring thirty hot-air balloons, along with unique and rare aircraft. Visitors should stop at the Independence Regional Museum, a 12,500 square-foot building made of stone and built in 1931, which is a genealogist's dream. Representing a twelve county area, the collection contains an archival vault which houses some rare and fragile documents, as well as a large gallery house for major exhibits. If you're lucky enough to be in Batesville at the end of March, you cannot miss the Ozark Hawg BBQ Championship featuring the best BBQ champs from Arkansas as well as the Mid-South. Don't let the small town feel fool you; underneath the warm inviting exterior lies the Batesville Motor Speedway. If you have the need for speed, and love the sound of street stock motors burning through your ears, consider Batesville heaven! From March to October there are races with top dollar prizes, and something you won't want to miss.

Our next stop is a little further down US-167 S, with a merge onto US-67 S, which takes us to Searcy. Searcy is just northeast of Little Rock, and the perfect place for those seeking quieter surroundings. Nestled between the Ozark Mountains, Searcy offers more than enough outdoor activities to keep you occupied, and is the perfect place for a quiet weekend getaway, or an extended family vacation with all the peace and quiet to help you relax and unwind.

From Searcy, get back on US-167 S and after several miles, merge onto US-64 W to find your way to our last stop, Conway. Conway is home to not one, but three colleges, which means there is always something going on in this town worth seeing and experiencing, from the Conway Symphony Orchestra to theatrical productions. But the one thing Conway is most known for (and any traveler to this area can't miss) is the Toad Suck Daze Festival held every May. The largest and most popular in the state, it derives it's name from the captains and crew of steamboats who would dock their boats where the Toad Suck Lock and Dam now spans the river and wait for the water to rise. Meanwhile, the crew would carouse the local tavern to the great displeasure of the locals who would complain, "They suck on the bottle 'til they swell up like toads." The tavern is long gone, but the legend remains.

It's true what they say: Arkansas is for lovers, but it's fair to say that the beauty and allure brings a whole host of travelers seeking a taste of history, some outdoor adventures, and a dose of culture which is just a small portion of what the Natural State has to offer.

COLORADO

Want to know what's so great about Colorado? Everything! Sharing its borders with seven states, Colorado is a beautiful mix of urban delights, scenic natural beauty, natural attractions, and is a premier destination for an amazing array of outdoor sports. With more than 40,000 acres of skiable real estate, it's no wonder travelers far and wide make this breathtaking state their first stop for a whirlwind of winter activities. I hope you brought your skis!

If there is one city that is truly synonymous with skiing, it has to be Vail. Established less than 50 years ago, Vail has quickly surpassed all other locations as the place to be for skiing, snowboarding, huge annual events, scenic mountain views, or just rubbing elbows with celebrities. From its location in the heart of Vail Valley, it's literally a town that has been created for skiing, and travelers here will find a wealth of outdoor fun, first class resorts and lodges, and enough beauty and luxury to win over the most reluctant of travelers.

It's going to be hard to leave Vail, but we have so much more to see and do, so take I-170 W to Glenwood Springs, then SE on Hwy-82 to arrive at Aspen. This exceptional town, along with its sister town of Snowmass Village, services four major ski areas, the highest concentration anywhere in Colorado. A free shuttle service will take you between areas, making it easy for you to enjoy the mountain of your choice - or all of them! The surrounding peaks of the area are some of this state's most picturesque, so don't be surprised if you catch yourself staring in awe more than once during your visit. And to wow you even more, take a ride on the Silver Queen Gondola, and you'll be treated to spectacular panoramic views of Aspen and the beautiful Elk Mountain Range. Aside from world-class skiing opportunities, visitors in the summer months can hike, bike, fish, or do some rafting on the nearby Colorado River. A must see is the John Denver Sanctuary. This beautiful commemorative park was built to remember one of Aspen's most famous residents, and is filled with rolling grassy mounds, containing huge granite rocks. Take a closer look at the rocks and you'll notice the lyrics to John Denver's songs carved into them. Peaceful and serene, it's a wonderful place to sit and reflect. If you're lucky enough to visit in October, you'll be treated to a celebration of John Denver's life and music, which brings fans from all over the world.

From Aspen, we head to our last stop, Leadville. Returning to CO-82 E, after several miles merge onto US-24 W, and in less than two hours, you'll be right in the heart of Leadville. If ever there was a well-kept secret in Colorado, it's this city. Located along the top of the

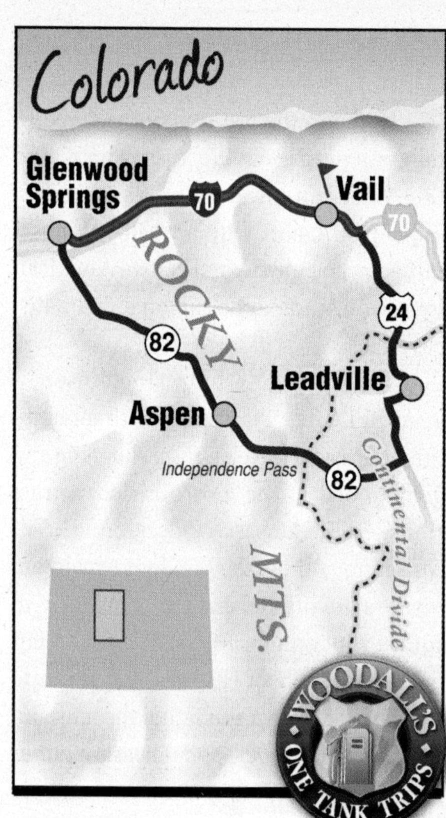

Rockies Scenic and Historic Byway, Leadville (as it's name suggests) is a legendary frontier mining town, and easily accommodates a variety of travelers. Located within the city are 70 square blocks of incredible Victorian architecture, and an adjacent 20 square miles of mining district, which overflows with rich history, from Doc Holliday to Soapy Smith. Rumor has it that some may have even struck it rich here, so cross your fingers and keep your eyes open. For the adventurous, take a tour of one of the mines in the area, and get a real sense of what it must've been like for miners over 100 years ago, who had to travel some 1,000 feet into a mountain to work. This is one trip not cut out for the claustrophobic, but what an awesome glimpse into history!

Colorado has been wooing travelers for centuries with its scenic beauty, wide array of outdoor activities and Old West history. No matter what you're looking for, you'll find it here, and with some of the most majestic and breathtaking mountain ranges in the country. Colorado is a state that's hard to resist, and it's hard to imagine why anyone one would want to!

KANSAS

Home to the last remaining stand of tallgrass prairies in North America, and the American bison, Kansas is a picturesque plains state with a wealth of museums, cowboy towns, and Native American legacies waiting to be explored and rediscovered.

We begin our trip in Hutchinson, a beautiful Great Plains city with much to offer the savvy traveler, from shopping and golf, to one of the most unusual attractions, the Kansas Underground Salt Museum. Taking the 650-foot trip down, visitors are offered a rare opportunity to tour a functional salt mill, and one that helped the town of Hutchinson grow into the city it is today. You'll find the museum underground as well, and it boasts a rather nice collection of Hollywood memorabilia that visitors are encouraged to peruse while there. Also housed at the museum are several masters for classics like The Wizard of Oz, Gone With The Wind, Star Wars, and many others. It's a fascinating and fun place, and one no traveler should miss. Another great attraction for visitors to this area is the Kansas Cosmosphere & Space Center. If you want an unbiased account of the space race, then you've come to the right place. Housed at this fascinating museum is the largest collection of Russian Space artifacts outside of Moscow, and the second largest collection of US space artifacts. It is one of only three museums in the world to display flown spacecraft from all three early manned American space programs. And keep in mind as you wander through this incredible place, you are looking at less than 10% of this very large and impressive collection, the rest of which is stored in the museum's vault.

Once you come back down to Earth and get out of your spacesuit, take KS-61 N out of Hutchinson, and merge onto I-135 N to arrive at our next destination, Salina, which is nearly the geographical center of the US. Historic Salina has a host of offerings for travelers, including some

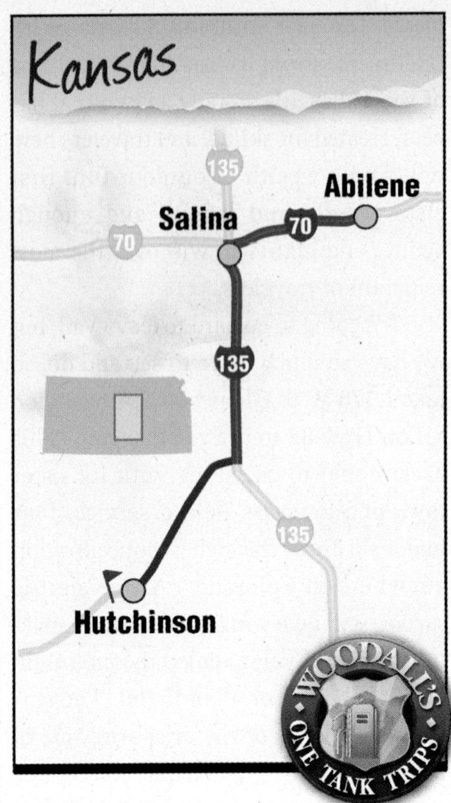

excellent shopping, dining and cultural attractions. One of the most impressive is the Rolling Hills Wildlife Adventures, a 65-acre zoological park nestled right here in the Kansas prairie. With more than 300 animals on exhibit, and a new, world-class wildlife museum, it's something you won't want to miss. Only a handful of people get to experience the majestic beauty of the American bison, but here in Salina, you can do just that at the Smoky Hill Bison Visitor's Center. An honest-to-goodness working bison ranch, visitors can watch bison roam the grounds from the porch of the visitor's center, shop in the gift shop for their favorite buffalo related trinket, and purchase some of the best buffalo steaks or jerky this side of the Mississippi! The chance to see these impressive creatures up close and personal is a once-in-a-lifetime opportunity, and should be taken advantage of when visiting this area.

Moving on to our last stop, take I-135 N out of Salina, and merge onto I-70 E, and in a little over a half hour, you'll arrive at Abilene. Steeped in history, Abilene was once a rough-and-tumble place where Wild Bill Hickock and Tom Smith made their famous attempts to maintain some semblance of order on these mean streets, and over 3 million heads of Texas Longhorn cattle moved through this town to be shipped by rail. Today, things are much calmer in Abilene. The outlaws and cattle are long gone, but the city has preserved its very colorful and long history in many of its museums and historic homes. One such beautifully preserved place visitors should tour is the Eisenhower Presidential Library & Eisenhower Museum, which houses the beautifully preserved Eisenhower family home. The museum contains a war gallery, and covers Ike's election and presidential years. In the library, visitors will find an enormous collection of motion picture films, audiotapes, books and oral history transcripts. At the nearby Place of Meditation located on the grounds, visitors will find the tombs of Abilene's favorite son, and his wife Mamie, as well as a chapel.

This beautiful state is full of surprises and a wild beauty that beckoned to the first pioneers and settlers who first discovered it. From the rolling hills to the vast, expansive plains that seem to roll on into infinity, Kansas offers travelers much to see, do, and discover, and there's always something special waiting just around the corner.

MISSOURI

Missouri may be something of a surprise for most visitors. The Show Me State has plenty to offer those that travel here, including world-class barbecue, smooth, sultry jazz, lazy days floating on rivers, and some of the best fishing spots in the world.

Our trip begins in the incomparable Kansas City. Straddling the border of Kansas and Missouri, this double city lies at the junction of the Kansas and Missouri Rivers. Once, this city was lined with stockyards, but all of that has given way to a graceful skyline, and a modern city with much to offer visitors. Now, there is barbecue, and then there is Kansas City barbecue, and once you've had it here, you'll soon understand what all the fuss is about, so grab as much as you can while you are here. Visitors will also enjoy the wealth of cultural activities this city has to offer, and for some wet and wild fun, pay a visit to Worlds of Fun. It is packed with more than 175 acres of twisting inner tube slides, a gigantic super pool, and much, much more. What a great place to cool off in those hot Missouri summer days! If it's world-class shopping and dining you're looking for, visit The Country Club Plaza, Kansas City's premier shopping, dining and entertainment district. Spanning 15 blocks, the Plaza is filled with big name stores, charming boutiques, special events, and it's a great place to get one of those famous Kansas City steaks you've probably heard so much about, and will need after all that splashing at Worlds of Fun!

Heading off to our next destination, take I-70 E out of Kansas City. After several miles, merge onto MO-7 S and follow this road to our next merge onto MO-13 S. In a few hours, you will have arrived at Springfield. The city of Springfield has a compelling past, which can be discovered in a wealth of places throughout the city. Outdoor enthusiasts will get a thrill out of the Wonders of Wildlife, a museum dedicated to hunting and fishing. With an aquarium, several displays, and hundreds of live animals in natural habitats, it's a place worth exploring. The Wilson's Creek National Civil War Battlefield commemorates the first major Civil War engagement west of the Mississippi involving thousands of troops, and visitors can

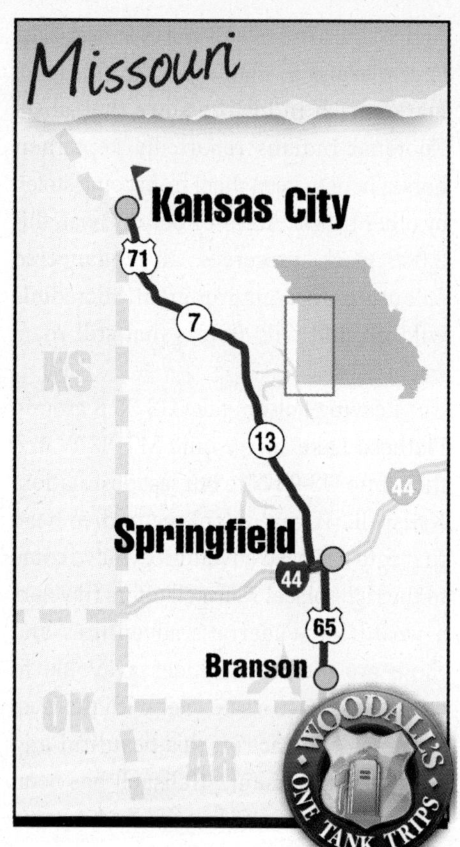

tour the grounds of the battleground site, and explore the museum located here. The site is a fascinating look into this city's interesting past, and a definite must see.

Moving on to our last stop, take US-65 S to US-65 N, and in a little over an hour you'll have arrived in Branson. From it's location nestled along the Ozarks, Branson has been widely known as an area outdoor enthusiasts flock to all year for the wealth of camping, fishing, canoeing, kayaking and other wonderful outdoor opportunities. Lake Taneycomo is one such jewel where anglers will find some of the finest trout fishing in the world. It's from these waters that numerous state records have been earned, and all methods of trout fishing can be used here year-round. It's a fantastic opportunity for any fish chaser, and one you should take advantage of during your visit. In recent years, Branson has become a city with a reputation as a family oriented entertainment mecca right here in the Midwest. There are an enormous amount of theatrical performances ranging through every genre of music imaginable. One of the most popular destinations in Branson is Silver Dollar City. This incredible place transports visitors back to the simple times of the 1880s with a craft village filled with numerous rides, attractions, and festivals. One thing is for sure, this place will keep you moving with so much to do and see!

If you make Missouri a destination spot, one thing is for sure; you'll be surprised by the natural beauty, friendly people, and incredible wealth of outdoor recreation to be found here.

OTHER AREA LOCATIONS

BRANSON

America's Best Campground
Compton Ridge Campground
Cooper Creek Campground

MONTANA

Dubbed the "last best place", Montana is filled with inspiring landscapes, short grass prairies, and some of the most breathtaking mountain ranges in the nation. Montana is Big Sky country where antelope and buffalo still roam freely, and the spirit and allure of the Old West is alive and well.

Our first stop, Missoula, sits along the Clark Fork River and upon an ancient glacial lake bed surrounded by millions of acres of forest, and just 30 miles of Montana's most intact ghost town, Garnet. As the largest city in western Montana, visitors are attracted to extraordinary opportunities for recreation and the inspiring scenery. You can't visit Missoula without having a look at the first fully hand-carved carousel to be built in the US since the Great Depression. Created by hundreds of volunteers, over 100,000 hours were spent laboring over this amazing piece of art, which will definitely make you feel like a kid again. When you need a break from all the fishing, hiking, skiing, kayaking, and other activities, stop by the Fort Missoula National Historic Site. Nestled on 32 acres at the core of historic Fort Missoula, visitors can explore several historic

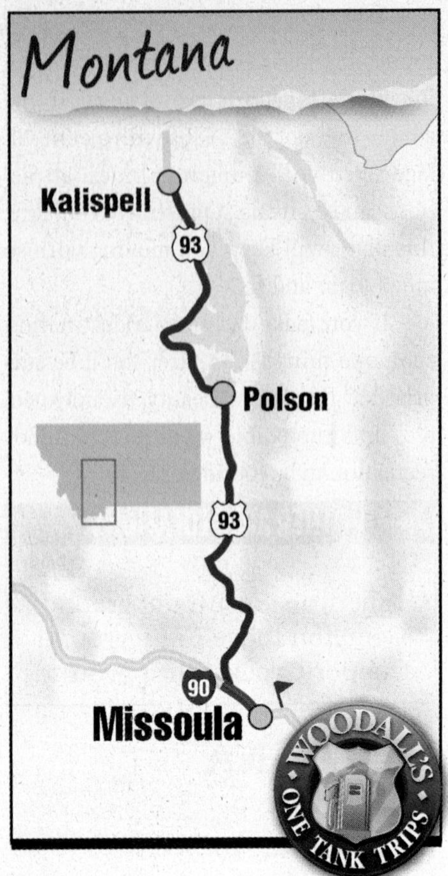

structures on the site as well as a collection of artifacts in the museum that tell the fascinating history of this wonderful city and surrounding area. For bird enthusiasts, or those looking for a great place for a leisurely stroll or bike ride, the Eureka Riverwalk is the place you want to be. The Riverwalk spans 2 acres, includes a bridge over Sinclair Creek, and is a great place to see the natural beauty of this area at its best.

Leaving Missoula, take Old US 93 E to I-90 W, and merge onto US-93 N to arrive at our next breathtaking stop, Polson. Nestled on the banks of Flathead Lake - the largest body of freshwater found west of the Continental Divide - this charming city is surrounded by cherry orchards, and hosts the annual Cherry Festival. Flathead Lake is a great place to do some boating, trout fishing, as well as many other water sports, and for the bird enthusiast, Pablo Wildlife Refuge is the place you'll want to visit for some excellent bird spotting. For a taste of Polson's past, The Miracle of America and Polson-Flathead Historical Museum offers many displays and memorabilia. Visitors may also find Wild Horse Island worth a visit. The largest island in Flathead Lake, this landmark is rich in history since the Salish-Kootenai Indians reportedly kept their horses here to keep them from being stolen by other tribes. Accessed only by boat, this 2,000 park preserves an endangered palouse prairie environment, incredible wildlife, and wild horses that still roam freely here.

Leaving Polson, take US-35 S around Flathead Lake, merge onto MT-82 W and then onto US-93 N to our last destination, Kalispell. If you're looking to dive head first into a rugged adventure, you've come to the right place! Kalispell offers travelers a wealth of wilderness adventures and there are plenty of guides available to ensure you have a safe visit with the least amount of impact on this beautiful and fragile environment. Kalispell has been growing in leaps and bounds, and is home to a flourishing art community, boasting several art galleries and studios. Visitors will also find the Conrad Mansion here, a beautifully preserved pre-1900 mansion, offering a glimpse into a bygone era of elegance. On display throughout the home are several period pieces of furniture, as well as clothing, giving visitors a peek into several generations of the family who once lived there. A short drive from Kalispell is Glacier National Park, one of the most exquisite and pristine pieces of wilderness left in the nation. Boasting 1.4 million acres of rugged landscape shaped by slow moving glaciers millions of years ago (50 of which are still active), travelers here are sure to be blown away by the sweeping landscape and grand vistas.

If you like your recreation a little wilder, a little more rugged and a bit more breathtaking, you've come to the right place! Montana can challenge even the most experienced outdoorsman, and immediately leaves you with an overwhelming desire to do it all again.

OTHER AREA LOCATIONS

ANACONDA

Fairmont RV Park

NEBRASKA

The Cornhusker State is filled with vast plains extending from the prairies of the east to the scenic Rocky Mountains in the west, and in between lie charming small towns, and incredible metropolis areas waiting to be explored.

Kicking things off in Omaha, this wonderful city is the state's largest riverfront community. Sitting on the west bank of the Missouri River, Omaha was once a prairie outpost, but it's hard to imagine this beautiful city having such humble beginnings. Travelers to this incredible city have to take a walk on the longest pedestrian bridge that links two states, the Bob Kerrey Pedestrian Bridge. This is no ordinary sidewalk; with over 150 miles of trails on both sides, this amazing cable stay bridge connects Iowa and Nebraska, and is the perfect place to jog, bike ride, walk, or just take a stroll. History buffs will love the General Crook House. Authentically restored and complete with garden, museum and exhibits, it's one you shouldn't miss. For the shopper, Omaha has something special for you! The Old Market district was once historic warehouses, and has been completely refurbished into the premiere shopping destination for this area. The uneven brick streets are lined with unique shops, boutiques, restaurants, and pubs, and are a fabulous place to shop 'til you drop.

Heading out of Omaha, take I-80 W, after several miles, merge onto I-180 E, and then onto US-34 E to arrive at our next stop, Lincoln. This wonderful capital city has much to offer travelers, from shopping, exquisite dining, several wineries to tour, many historical sites, and a wealth of museums. Most notable is the Nebraska History Museum, where visitors can explore ancient Native American artifacts, and peruse the past of this enchanting state. For an offbeat adventure, head over to the National Museum of Roller Skating, with the largest collection of roller skates and memorabilia in the world. Shoppers will love historic Haymarket. Once the site of the original market square, visitors can stroll past lines of shops, have a look at the historic Burlington railroad depot, maybe grab a tasty bite to eat, and slow down the pace a little before heading off to our next stop, Hastings.

Backtracking a little, take US-34 W out of town, and merge onto I-80 W, and after several miles, merge onto US-34 S. In about two hours, you'll have arrived at Hastings. This charming Midwestern town is the agricultural heartland of the area. Many birders come from around the world to take in the spectacular migration of cranes and waterfowl as they stop over along the Platte River annually, and it's an incredible sight to behold. A premiere attraction here is the Hastings Museum of Natural and Cultural History, where visitors will find the largest whooping crane display in the US, Native American and pioneer memorabilia, a planetarium, and the five stories tall Lied Super Screen Theatre, which offers many documentary style features several times a day.

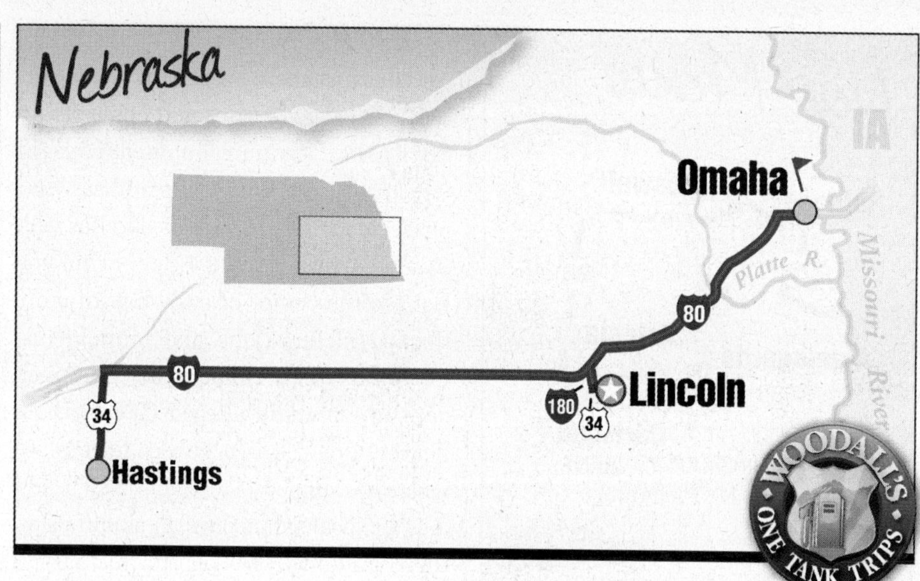

Nebraska is literally bursting at the seams with unsurpassed beauty and a wealth of recreational, cultural and historical activities, and the written word just can't do them all justice. One thing is for sure; spend a little time in Nebraska, and you'll come back again and again!

NEW MEXICO

The Land of Enchantment is aptly named. From the white sand dunes to the high mountains in the north, New Mexico is the canvas on which nature uses her most brilliant colors. Wherever you look, history is tucked in every nook and cranny, just waiting to be rediscovered.

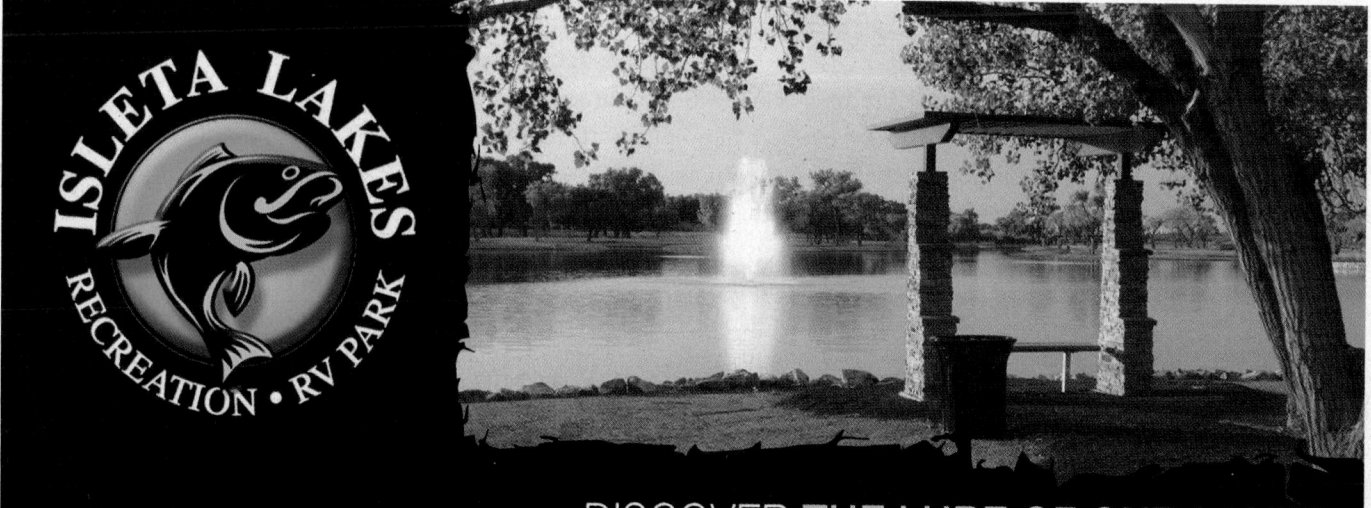

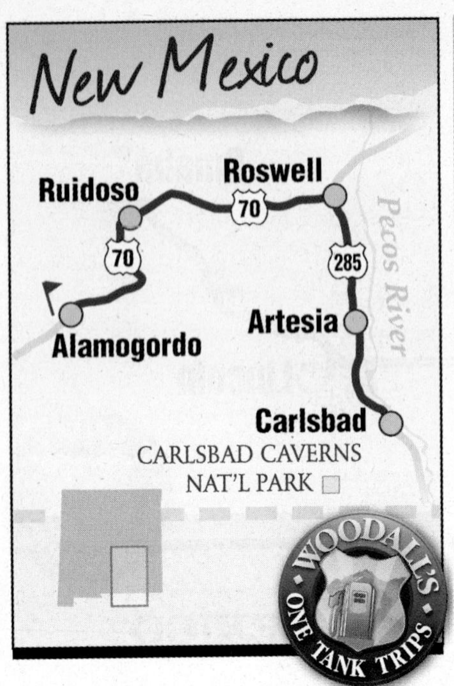

Our trip begins in Alamogordo, a city surrounded by the majestic Organ, San Andres, and Sacramento mountain ranges. Voted one of the healthiest places to live in the US, and with an average temperature of 75, Alamogordo sees more than its share of travelers from the north trying to shed the winter blues. It's here in this gorgeous city that you'll find the New Mexico Space Museum. Literally several museums within one building, space enthusiasts can find a wealth of information on space history, exploration, and the men and women who have made it their life's work. There are amazing archives and a library within the Hubbard Space and Science Research Building, with a huge collection of photos, collections and NASA publications.

We're heading out of Alamogordo, and off to our next destination, Ruidoso. A short drive on US-70 E will get us there in no time. The mild climate here makes it perfect for a plethora of year round outdoor activities, including golf, tennis, fishing, horseback riding, mountain biking and skiing. If you need a little break from the never-ending list of fun, head over to the Hubbard Museum of the American West. If you've ever had an interest in the history of this area, or of the Wild, Wild West in general, then you won't want to miss this! The collection at the museum contains just about everything from spurs and saddles, to wagons and horse drawn carriages, all spanning hundreds of years.

Load up the spaceship and set your phasers to stun, we're headed to Roswell! A short trip on US-70 E will bring you right to the center of a town with more than a little mystique, and a unique history all its own. Home to the 1947 incident in which an alleged UFO crashed nearby, Roswell is a quirky little place where the lampposts resemble alien heads, and the local stores have alien murals on their windows. No trip to this part of New Mexico would be complete without a stop by the International UFO Museum & Research Center. It's here that you can discover all sorts of other-worldly information about crop circles, UFO sightings and abductions, the famed Area 51, and the town of Roswell itself. Don't forget to pose for a picture with an alien ship waiting to beam you aboard their craft! Roswell is a town that doesn't take itself too seriously, and that makes for a very light and entertaining stop.

Our next destination is the town of Artesia. Taking US-285 out of Roswell, you'll be there in no time, and quicker if you're going by UFO. Artesia is nothing, if not charming. Quiet and laid back, it's a good stop for anyone looking to move at a slower, more relaxed pace. Artesia was named for the artesian wells discovered nearby, and they give the town the feel of being a natural oasis in the middle of the desert.

Taking US-285 S will lead us to our final destination, Carlsbad. Sitting on the banks of the Pecos River, the biggest tourist draw to the area is the nearby Carlsbad Caverns. This is not any ordinary cave, and on the surface, it might look deceptively normal, until you step inside the elevator and plunge 75 stories underground. Thankfully, you don't have to enter the caverns via an old guano mining bucket like they did when it was first discovered. There are 113 caves beneath the surface, and accessible by guided tours, or if you're a seasoned spelunker, you can take a self-guided tour. The park itself is a beautiful setting for some back country hiking, with many visitors hanging around during the summer dusk to watch the bats migrate. If you've never seen such a spectacle, you don't know what you're missing!

New Mexico is the kind of place you could get lost in. Its mild temperatures, deep-rooted history, colorful Mexican and Native American influences and expansive beauty are enough to hold any traveler under its spell.

NORTH DAKOTA

Bordering on Canada, North Dakota is a beautiful, expansive state that hasn't changed much since the days of Lewis and Clark. In fact, Lewis and Clark spent more time here than any other place on their journeys, and today, we're going to find out just what they saw here that had them so intrigued.

Beginning in Bismarck, the capital of North Dakota, the city is rich with historic sites, educational attractions and cultural events. The North Dakota Heritage Center is a fascinating place with many static and traveling exhibits, and archives of manuscripts and books that tell the exciting history of this state. Many visitors will also find Camp Hancock of interest. Once a military post, it offered protection for working gangs building the Northern Pacific Railroad. Another must see is the Double Ditch Indian Village, an incredible site, which contains the ruins of a large Mandan Indian earthlodge village, believed to have been inhabited for nearly 300 years. For the birding enthusiast, Bismarck will be of particular interest; it's here you can follow the paths of renowned early explorers by searching the Bismarck-Mandan Birding Drive for the wealth of birds that can be found here.

Moving on, we're heading to Washburn, about an hour and a half away on Hwy-83 N. Peaceful and serene, Washburn is located on the banks of the Missouri River and offers travelers a wide variety of sights and experiences. Fishing is abundant throughout much of the state, but the most popular place to set a line is here at Lake Sakakawea. The largest lake built by the Corp of Engineers, it has more than 1,600 miles of shoreline and extends westward almost 200 miles, and is one of the 3 largest man-made reservoirs in the nation. All of this makes Lake Sakakawea an angler's paradise, and a great place for a number of other water activities. Of great interest in this area is the Knife River Indian Village. A historic site, this fascinating place holds important, and historic, archaeological remnants of the Northern Plains Indians who once used this area as a major trading and agricultural center. The National Lewis & Clark Interpretive Center is a must see on this trip. The Center provides an overview of the Lewis & Clark expedition, and contains many Native American artifacts of significant interest, all telling the story of the discovery and the settling of this wonderful city.

The last stop on our journey takes us to the wonderful city of Minot, just a short drive on Hwy-83 N. Travelers here should visit the Scandinavian Heritage Center and Park. Built to honor North Dakota's very large Scandinavian ancestry, this incredible park features remembrances and replicas from each of the Scandinavian countries. Every September Minot welcomes thousands of people to celebrate their Scandinavian culture at the Norsk Hostfest, the largest of its kind in North America. Featuring many exhibits, cuisine, art and jewelry, it's a wonderful experience, and shouldn't be missed! For birders, this is another exceptional place to do some great viewing. Located in the middle of five National Wildlife Refuges, Minot is a birding utopia.

No matter what time of year you visit, North Dakota has a wealth of activities waiting for you including birding, camping, fishing, and plenty of winter fun!

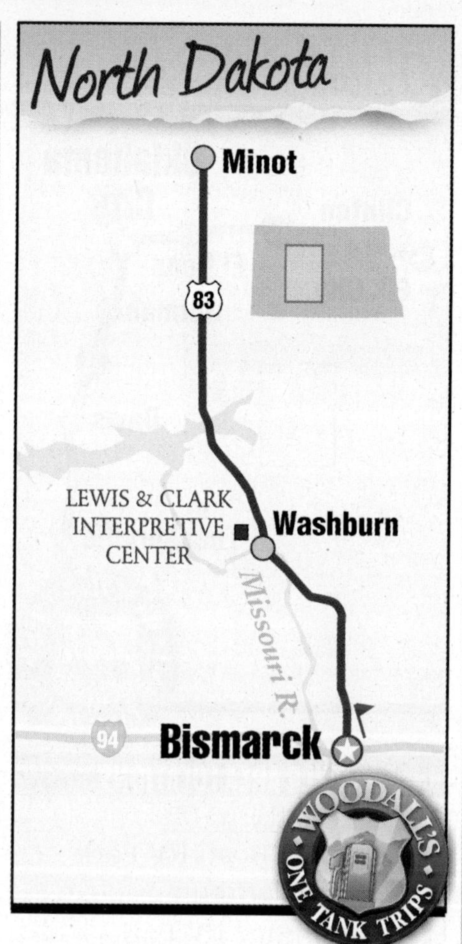

OKLAHOMA

Oklahoma! The very name conjures up images of settlers, the Wild West, and pioneers. Travelers here will find one of the most geologically diverse terrains in the nation, and the perfect place for the ultimate outdoor adventure. Whether you're looking for a step back in time, an urban thrill, or to experience rich Native American heritage, your adventure starts here!

Located on historic Route 66, Elk City has a well-deserved reputation for hospitality, and is very proud of its history. There are several museums in town that spotlight Elk City's colorful past, including the Old Town Museum, which is dedicated to telling the tale of Western pioneers who settled the area in the late 1800s, and the National Route 66 Museum, which highlights the highway that cuts through eight states, running from Chicago to California.

Heading on I-40 E, your next stop of Clinton is waiting for you a little over 20 miles away. In addition to great shopping and golfing, Clinton is home to Foss Lake, which boasts a large population of striped bass and catfish. Rent a boat and try your luck, or maybe fasten on a pair of water skis and skim across the water on a sunny afternoon. Grab a tasty lunch at the floating restaurant, a popular attraction here at the lake. If you've had no luck with fishing, you just might be able to turn it around at the casino located on Indian land, or enjoy the great buffet there.

Driving fifty miles further east on the I-40 takes you to the city limits of El Reno, a fun little city located between Route 66 and the Chisholm Trail. The historic Old Town district has a wide selection of shops where you'll find souvenirs and antiques from the Victorian era and the days of the Old West. You can tour this area either by foot or with the trolley system that takes you from downtown to Heritage Park. We recommend taking the trolley, as it's the best way to see this city. While you're here, head over to Lake El Reno and see the herd of buffalo that calls this area home, or enjoy the 300-acre lake by jet skiing, boating, or taking a swim. Once you take a look around town, you'll see why this town is growing in popularity as a tourist destination.

Time to hit the big city. The state capital of Oklahoma City is 25 miles east of El Reno via the I-40, and is packed with so many adventures to occupy your time that there's no way to cover it adequately. For the history buff, there are museums and monuments aplenty, ranging from the Oklahoma Railway Museum to the Governor's Mansion. Arcadia Lake and the Chesapeake Boathouse are two of the many places geared towards pleasing the fan of water-borne activities, and for those looking to peruse around town and see the sights, make sure not to miss the Adventure District. This spot features an eclectic selection of botanical gardens, a zoo, and a 20-screen theater multiplex, packed into a mere two miles. When you factor in the golf courses, ice skating arenas, art galleries, shopping districts, and even a roller coaster heavy theme park, you can see that several return trips are in order to enjoy everything that Oklahoma City has to offer.

Heading south on the I-35 takes you 13 miles from Oklahoma City into the community of Norman. This town is stocked with casinos, one being the largest in all of Oklahoma – and that's saying something! This area is also the heart of Oklahoma's wine country, so treat your palate to a tasting of some of the region's finest wines, then head over to Lake Thunderbird and watch the sky change colors as the sun sinks past the water's glassy surface.

Seeing everything Oklahoma has to offer is next to impossible on one vacation trip, but one thing you can count on is that the warm and friendly people will welcome you back again "Sooner" rather than later!

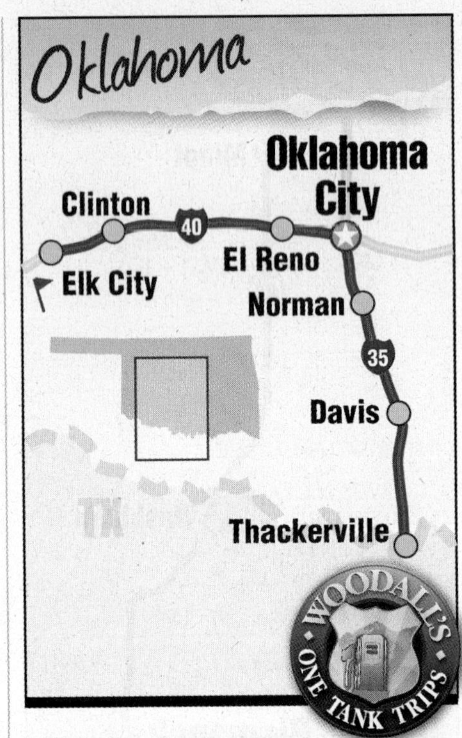

OTHER AREA LOCATIONS

OKLAHOMA CITY
Council Road RV Park

THACKERVILLE
WinStar RV Park

Route 66 Museum, Elk City, OK • Photo Credit: Oklahoma Travel & Tourism

SOUTH DAKOTA

One of the most breathtaking states in North America, South Dakota offers a complimentary blend of outdoor adventure, scenic beauty, and cultural heritage that delights visitors again and again.

Our trip begins in Rapid City, a city whose central location to the Black Hills Mountains makes it a popular vacation and tourist destination. For the outdoors enthusiast, Rapid City offers a long list of activities including, camping, mountain biking, water sports, hiking, fishing, rock climbing, and the list just goes on! No visit to this area would be complete without visiting Bear Country, USA. Home to 20 species of North American mammals, including black bear, cougars, elk, and buffalo, every effort has been made to imitate a wild environment for these amazing creatures, who have been captive born and hand raised. Larger species roam freely throughout 250 acres of drive-thru park, and offer visitors a rare glimpse into the behaviors of not just bears, but many other animals as well. The park can be explored on foot, and for your daily dose of cuteness, make sure you pay a visit to the Babyland area inside the park where you will see black bear cubs and wolf pups romping around. Another must see is the Reptile Gardens. Hope you're not squeamish about snakes! There is something for everyone here, and the Reptile Gardens boasts the finest collection of tropical plants and reptiles in the world. In fact, they have more species and subspecies of these venomous reptiles than any other zoo or park anywhere! For those that favor more of the cultural excitement (and less of the slithering kind), head over to the Journey Museum, an incredible place that will take you on a trek through time where you will witness the saga of the Western Frontier, and the upheaval that formed the Black Hills billions of years ago.

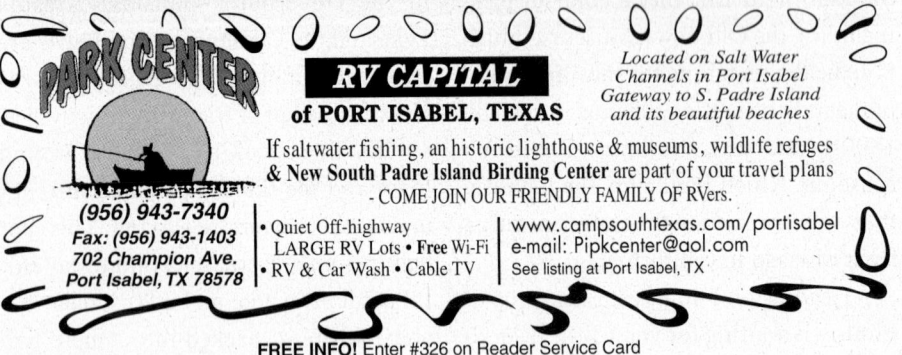

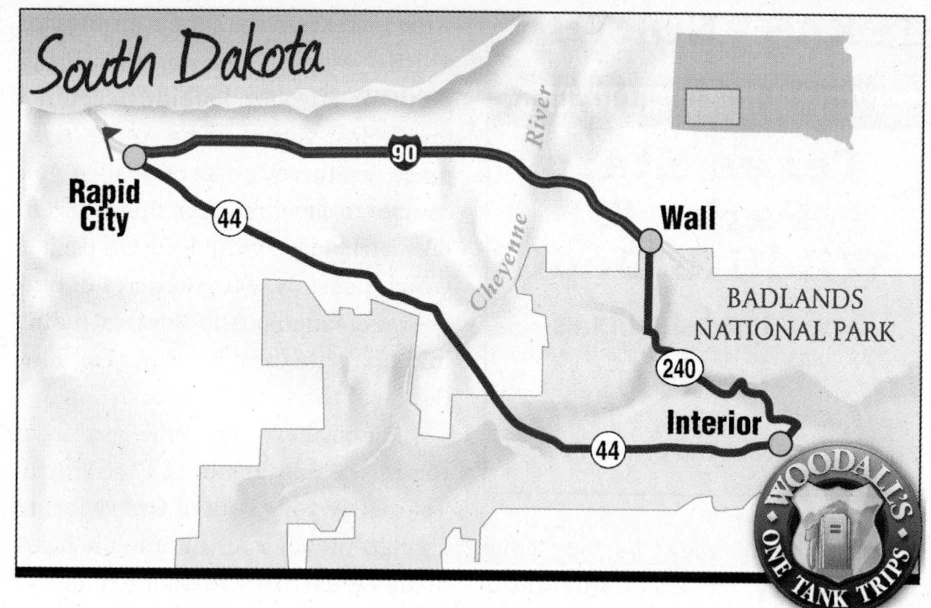

Heading out of Rapid City, take I-90 E to our next destination, Wall. One of the most interesting and unique sights in Wall is the Wall Drug store. What began in 1931 as a tiny drug store that drew passing travelers with a "free water" sign, has morphed into a 76,000 square foot slice of Americana, complete with an animated T-Rex, a chance to pan and mine for fossils and gem stones, an art gallery restaurant, and so much more. There is still a pharmacy inside, and it's the only one for 50 miles, and yes, you can still load up on free water and 5-cent coffee, but it's a place you have to experience to appreciate. Oh, and don't forget to get your picture taken in front of the 80 ft. dinosaur before you go. For the history buff, pay a visit to the Wounded Knee Massacre Museum, a wonderful narrative museum that seeks to educate all visitors about the history of the Native American relocation.

Continuing on I-90 E, we come to our last destination, Interior. Perched at the edge of the ruggedly beautiful Badlands National Park, this small town welcomes visitors from the four corners who are looking to experience this striking, moon-like landscape. Covering 244,000 acres, the park is one of the largest protected mixed-grass prairies in the US, and is home to several species of wildlife. The evolutionary stories of several mammals can be found here among the buttes and formations. For more than 11,000 years, Native Americans have used this site as their hunting grounds, and today the area is of great paleontological importance. Visitors are free to roam the park by car, foot, or on horseback, but be prepared, this prairie is very rugged and you'll need a good pair of hiking boots for exploring, and for the inexperienced hiker, it's best to stay close; it's named "The Badlands" for a reason! Don't leave without stopping by the Visitors Center/Museum located at the east entrance of the park; it's a great place to learn about the ever-changing visual wonder that is this fascinating region.

South Dakota has many different sights and experiences to discover. The Wild West is still very much alive in this region, and as you peer out over the vast prairie, you can almost imagine wagon trains, renegade cowboys, and the early tribes of the great Sioux Nation who roamed this land.

OTHER AREA LOCATIONS

HILL CITY
Crooked Creek Resort
KOA-Mount Rushmore
Rafter J Bar Ranch Camping Resort

PIERRE
South Dakota Dept of Game, Fish & Parks

RAPID CITY
KOA-Rapid City

SPEARFISH
Chris' Camp

TEXAS - NORTH

J.R. Ewing might be long gone from this area, but Northern Texas is alive and well. This is prairie land, filled with oil wells and cattle that help fuel the economy, but don't let that scare you off! There's a wealth of things to do in Texas, so let's get started!

The first stop on our trip is historic Grapevine, and there is no better place to start our journey. Grapevine is a quaint, charming Texas town, nestled between Dallas and Fort Worth, a convenient escape from the daily grind without having to go very far to do it. Downtown Grapevine is filled with lovely shops, an incredible array of restaurants, and quite a few tasting rooms that showcase some of Texas' finest wines. That's right, they make wine in Texas, so be sure to arrange for a little sample. You won't be disappointed! If you're looking to get in a few holes, you've come to the right place, as there are several nice golf courses to choose from in this area. Or, take a trip to beautiful Lake Grapevine, which boasts 8,000-plus acres of outdoor recreation possibilities, including hiking, fishing and boating. For a little town, there sure is a lot to do!

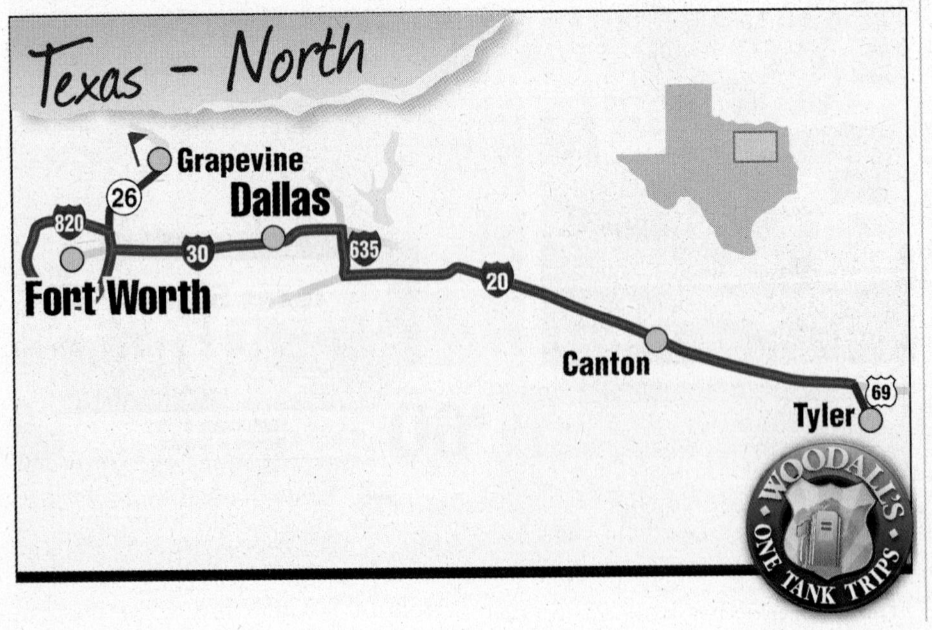

For our next stop, we're heading to the hustle and bustle of Fort Worth. Taking Hwy 26 S out of Grapevine, to US-820 W will lead you into the heart of this great city. With a wonderful mix of cowboys and culture, Fort Worth is a city you won't soon forget. Fort Worth has an impressive amount of restaurants, shopping opportunities, and museums, like the Cattle Raisers Museum. If you've ever wanted to know what it was like in the early days of six-shooters and cow punching, look no further. Artifacts, photos, and film tell the amazing history of Fort Worth, and the people who settled here. Want to live the cowboy way? How about the world's only daily cattle drive, where the Old West comes alive along Exchange Avenue? You don't want to miss this one!

Heading out of Forth Worth via US-30 east it's a straight shot to the equally grand city of Dallas. Welcome to the number one traveler destination in Texas, and what a destination! A major center for oil and gas, Dallas is also known for it's incredible cultural and entertainment district. Old City Park is a wonderful historical village sitting on 13 acres just south of downtown, and a perfect place to view many Victorian Era homes, and other restored structures. You've never seen any zoo like the Dallas Zoo! With 95 acres to explore, it's one exciting experience after another. Founded in 1888, it's also the first zoological park in the Southwest, and worth every minute you spend exploring.

Leaving Dallas, take US-20 E to our next stop, Canton. Canton is a town that moves much slower than Dallas or Fort Worth, but is popular for the First Monday Trade days. Open the first weekend of every month, thousands of bargain shoppers flock looking for some great deals, and to wander around and have a look at some of the most interesting and rare collectibles found anywhere. Started over 150 years ago as a flea market, the Trade Days has slowly morphed into something much bigger and grander than ever imagined. First time visitors are usually left speechless, but always return again and again!

For our last stop, continue on US-20 E out of Canton, and right to the heart of Tyler. The city of Tyler is most famous as the Rose Capital of America, with one out of every five roses sold in North America coming from in and around this lovely town. A botanical lovers dream, Tyler is host to the Texas Rose Festival, as well as the Azalea Trails event, which is a walking tour of local residents gardens. This area is also well known for its prime location to numerous lakes and parks that offer plenty of recreational opportunities.

Texas is a state widely known for doing things big, and that seems to be the case with just about everything that goes on here, especially in the hospitality and friendliness towards travelers from far and wide. The great expanse of this state is sure to draw you in, and the kindness of those lucky enough to call Texas home is sure to blow you away!

TEXAS - SOUTH

Southern Texas is made up of more level terrain, broken up by mesquite and brush. Compared to Northern Texas, this region has a much flatter landscape, but there is nothing "plain" about this region! It is rich in history and culture, with enough sights and experiences that will entice and intrigue you throughout your visit.

We begin our trip in stunning Corpus Christi. Located on the Gulf of Mexico, visitors here will be swept away by the incredible ocean views, and the never-ending number of water sports offered in the area. Swimming, fishing, sailing, windsurfing, and just some plain old relaxing on the beach are just a few of the exciting activities this fabulous city has to offer. It's here where visitors will also find the USS Lexington. Once you step foot on this historic vessel, you're in for an amazing experience and an adventure around every corner. If you think you have what it takes to handle the USS Lexington, the virtual battle stations will test your wits and your reflexes! When you're done shooting down enemy planes, pay a visit to Padre Island National Seashore, the largest remaining natural barrier island in the world. One of Corpus Christi's most striking attractions, the Seashore covers 130,000 acres and is home to sea turtles, and is a paradise for avid birdwatchers. There is no place better to experience the beauty and charm of the Texas Gulf Coast.

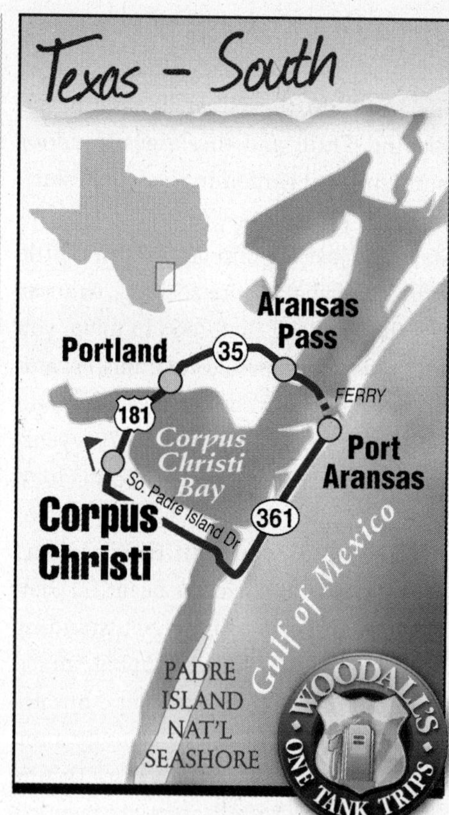

Our next stop is Portland. Traveling on US-181 N you'll notice the stunning waters of the Nueces Bay on your left, and the equally beautiful Corpus Christi Bay to your right. What a view! Due to its location on two bays, Portland is a playground for water sport enthusiasts. Fishing, boating, sailing, swimming and skiing are just of the few things this town has to offer. A beautiful 333-acre public park, called Sunset Lake, provides an ecologically rich wetland combined with a saltwater lake; the perfect place to have some fun! The lake, and its marshlands provide nesting grounds for several migratory birds. On the out-skirts of Portland, travelers will find the Fred Jones Sanctuary, a hidden treasure and a rich protected area. This sanctuary is one of many hot spots in the area for the birding enthusiast.

Heading out on TX-35 E, will bring us to Aransas Pass. A stunning and laid-back town, Aransas Pass is named for the pass between Mustang and St. Joseph islands. There is some great fishing to be had in this area, so bring the poles! Of the more than 700 different species of birds in North America, the coast of

Texas is visited by 500, making it a perfect place for birders. With three viewing spots on the Great Texas Coastal Birding Trail, and the largest outdoor hummingbird garden in the whole state, this area is a must see for birding enthusiasts, or just the bird curious. If a little culture is what you're seeking, Aransas Pass has some of that, too. In town, you can find some superb restaurants, theater productions, and art displays. With an average temperature in the 70s year-round, there is no bad time to come for a visit.

The last stop on our trip is a short drive on TX-361 S across beautiful Redfish Bay to Port Aransas. Outstanding dining, nightlife, great shopping, mixed with opportunities for anglers, birders and beachcombers, makes this city a top destination for visitors. Deep-sea fishing is big here, and the waters are teeming with red snapper, king, pompano, and several others worth playing tug of war with. Due to its location in the heart of the spring and fall migrations, nearby Mustang Island has one of the highest bird counts on the Gulf. With four sites on the Great Texas Coastal Birding Trail, it's a must see for all birders. It's here that you can also experience some coastal cuisine at its finest. You won't leave hungry, that's for sure!

Texas is full of all sorts of surprises, and this area is definitely one of them. The beautiful waters of the Gulf combined with mild temperatures, gentle breezes and a wealth of beauty as far as the eye can see make it easy to see why the travelers who have discovered it want to keep it a secret. But, sshhh...you didn't hear that from me!

UTAH

This incredible state is known the world over for its diverse range of landscapes, and visitors from all over are enticed by the beauty and year round recreation. Whether you're looking for world class skiing at any of the many ski resorts, or simply want to marvel at the beauty of the natural stone arches and canyons, Utah is definitely the place you want to be.

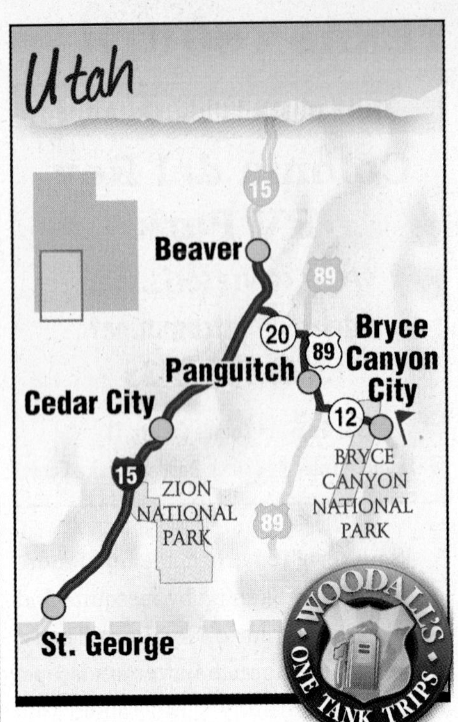

Ruby's Inn in Bryce Canyon is a great starting point for our trip. This wonderful RV park offers travelers easy access to all points of interest in this area, and is a favorite among RVers and campers alike. Visitors here can enjoy horseback riding, mountain biking, guided ATV tours and helicopter tours. The views are spectacular in this region, and it's the perfect place to get you warmed up for the rest of our adventure.

Leaving Ruby's Inn, take UT-12 W and merge onto US-89 N, and in around an hour you will have arrived in Panguitch. This quiet and unassuming town (with a most unusual name) is centered in the highest concentration of scenic natural wonders in the US, giving Panguitch the fitting title - "Center of Scenic Utah". Visitors here can enjoy a plethora of outdoor fun! From snowshoe hikes along the rim to guided tours, which will take you through some of the most beautifully diverse flora and fauna found anywhere. There is an incredible fishing adventure waiting for you at Panguitch Lake, a natural 1,250-acre lake surrounded by forests and lava flows. The lake, just like the city, derives its name from the Paiute Indian word meaning, "Big Fish", which gives you a hint to what's waiting for you in the waters, so make sure you bring the poles!

Leaving Panguitch, take US-89 N to UT-20 W, and merge onto I-15 N. In a little over an hour, you should arrive at our next destination; Beaver. Sitting on the northern edge of Utah's spectacular Color Country, Beaver sometimes goes unnoticed to many travelers who often whiz by towards larger locations, but this area is packed with many outdoor wonders worth exploring. There is no place better for those seeking a quieter locale, and Beaver is the perfect year-round destination retreat for hiking, backpacking, fishing, hunting, and a laundry list of other great adventures. Visitors will find the famous 230-mile Paiute Trail here, and a great opportunity for the ultimate ATV excursion. In the winter months, many come to Beaver to escape the crowded ski areas and enjoy snowmobiling and some spectacular Alpine and Nordic skiing in peace and near solitude. Surrounded by so much scenic and awe-inspiring beauty, Beaver is a well-kept secret in this area.

Back-tracking a little on I-15 S, a little over an hour's drive will bring you to our next scenic stop; Cedar City. This large and gorgeous city sits on the edge of flat rangeland next to the heavily forested highland of the Markagunt Plateau, and is a convenient base for exploring the countryside. In warmer months, this area is the perfect place for hiking, biking, fishing, ATV and horseback riding, and the winter months bring a wealth of powdery snow and some of the best skiing in the world. For those lucky enough to visit in late summer, Cedar City comes alive with the extremely popular Utah Shakespearean Festival which brings visitors from the four corners and then some!

The last stop on our whirlwind adventure is St. George, a city known affectionately as "Utah's Dixie". Continue on I-15 S, and it will get you there in no time. St. George is an incredible city boasting a beautifully temperate climate, making it the perfect location for year-round golf, camping, hiking, boating, fishing and much, much more. St. George is filled with many historic buildings waiting to be explored, plenty of shopping opportunities, and wonderful restaurants to tempt your taste buds. Downtown visitors will find the St. George Tabernacle and the summer home of Brigham Young, both of which should be high on the list of places to visit. Also notable is the sprawling Rosenbruch Wildlife Museum that will delight you with their many detailed dioramas of over 300 species.

There is a saying about Utah: "If you can't do it here, it's probably not worth doing." For the outdoor enthusiast, Utah is a mecca of recreational activities, surrounded by the beauty of alpine wilderness, majestic plateaus, natural stone arches, canyons with deep, rich red colors, and views so spectacular, it's impossible not to be awe-struck. Now, all that's worth an extra 10 hours in the day, isn't it?

OTHER AREA LOCATIONS

BRYCE CANYON
Ruby's Inn RV Park & Campground

WYOMING

If there was just one word to describe Wyoming, it would have to be stunning...beautiful...picturesque. Alright, it's impossible to pick just one word to describe the beauty of this area, and there is no end to the activities that go on, either! Whatever you're looking for, whether it's snowboarding, skiing, mountain biking, kayaking, or just looking to sit breathless as you stare at some of the most gorgeously rugged landscape to be found anywhere, Wyoming has got the cure for what ails you!

Today, we start in Cody, a city rich in frontier past and named after its founder, Buffalo Bill Cody. As a gateway city, Cody is in a prime location for many travelers seeking a little winter recreation, some outdoor adventure, and maybe even some relaxation, if they have the time! For those who seek culture, Cody has something for you, too. There are museums, and then there is the Buffalo Bill Historical Center, featuring five acclaimed museums under one roof. Consisting of the Whitney Gallery of Western Art, the Buffalo Bill Museum, the Plains Indian Museum, the Cody Firearms Museum, and the Draper Museum of Natural History, this is the finest western center anywhere in the world, and there is so much packed in these five incredible museums, your admission is good for two days. A great place to wind down your day, or to take a break from all that winter fun.

Grand Teton National Park, Wyoming • Photo Credit: Egret Communications

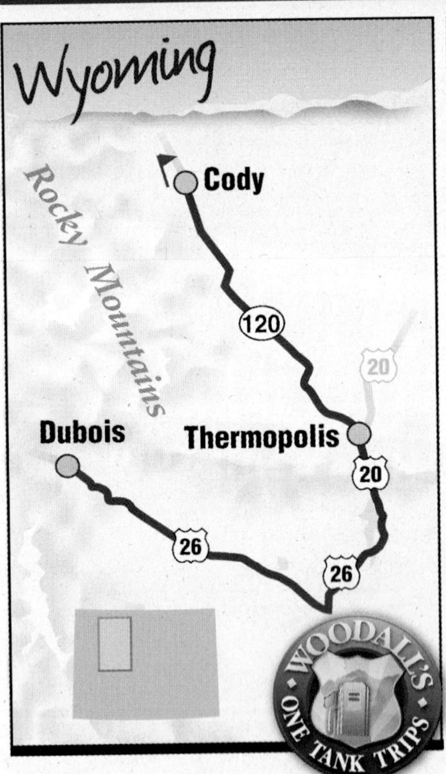

Heading out of Cody on WY-120 E, travelers are in for a spectacular drive on our way to our next destination, Thermopolis. If this is your first time to this amazing city, you're in for a real treat! Home to the world's largest mineral hot springs, Thermopolis draws millions who want to combine the wonders of the springs with the many other indoor, outdoor, and cultural activities that are offered here. For a wonderful thrill, stop in at the Wyoming Dinosaur Center. This fascinating museum has over 30 mounted skeletons, hundreds of displays and dioramas, and a dig site where visitors get to see actual dinosaurs buried in the ground. Where else could you get up close and personal with a T-Rex? The Wind River Scenic Byway offers travelers 34 miles of unspoiled views of this great state, and offers the outdoor enthusiast a place to get lost in canyon fishing, float trips, camping, and many other activities. Native Americans, explorers and pioneers once used this scenic canyon as a travel corridor between the central and northwest areas of Wyoming. What better stretch of highway to lead us to our next destination!

To our last stop, take the Wind River Scenic Byway, better known as US-20 E and merge onto US-26 W, and in a few hours you'll have arrived at stunning Dubois. Nestled along the Wind River, Dubois is surrounded by the Wind River and Absaroka mountains, a place once well known as the headquarters for old time cow outfits and railroad tie crews. Today, Dubois is the social center for Wind River dude ranches, and many travelers venture this way for the incredible scenery, fishing, horseback riding, dogsledding, hiking and to participate in the best big game hunting in the western US. The Big Horn Sheep Interpretive Center is the main attraction in town and tours are offered to show off the Whiskey Mountain herd of bighorn sheep, the largest wintering herd in the world. Don't pass up the opportunity to catch a glimpse of these fascinating creatures. Don't let Dubois' rustic look fool you - this charming town offers accommodations to fit every taste, including dining and shopping.

Wyoming is rugged and beautiful; there is no doubt about it. It's a veritable playground for those who enjoy an exciting array of outdoor activities. With all of its beauty and rich old west history, Wyoming manages to hold onto its mystique and charm that bring visitors back again and again.

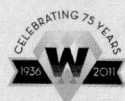

ALASKA

Alaska is one of the few places left on the planet where the veil between man and nature is decidedly thin, and where Mother Nature shows the power of her might with awe inspiring mountain ranges, pristine lakes and waters, and massive, majestic glaciers. This is where men come to test their will and endurance from iditarods to hunting, proving that the Land of the Midnight Sun can provide you with all you're looking for and more. Purchased from Russia in 1867 for roughly two cents an acre, Americans back then thought such a purchase was a complete waste of money. Ask any die-hard outdoor enthusiast today, and they'd tell you it was the best purchase we ever made. There are few places with as much grace, grandeur and beauty as Alaska, and whether you're looking for the challenge of a life time, or the opportunity to get lost in the sights and adventures that seem to be at every turn, Alaska will leave you breathless, and wanting more.

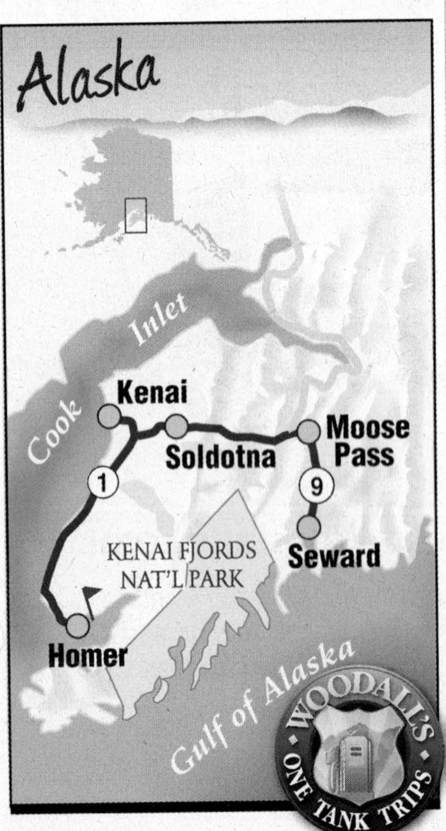

Just four miles into the breathtaking Kachemak Bay lies the city of Homer, where our trip begins. With dramatic snowcapped mountains and glaciers as a backdrop, this city was once a prospecting camp in the 1800s, and was later used as a coal mining headquarters. Today, the town of Homer is an eclectic community of commercial fishing facilities and a thriving group of local artists. In Homer you'll find big fish and bigger bears, and some of the best scenery to be found anywhere. Homer is a hot spot for a long list of outdoor activities, including kayaking, golf, whitewater rafting, and horseback riding. When you're ready to rest your paddles, stop by the only natural history museum in the Kenai Peninsula - the Pratt Museum - which focuses on native cultures, homesteading, fishing and marine ecology, and welcomes roughly 40,000 visitors each year for it's unique and amazing collection.

A scenic 80 miles along the coast of the Cook Inlet on AK- 1 north brings us to our next stop known affectionately as "Alaska's Playground." A city of rugged beauty, Kenai provides stunning views of mountain ranges, and active volcanoes from its point on the inlet. Hailed as the King Salmon capital of the world, anglers come from the four corners of the earth to fish these waters. They say you're not really an angler until you've wrestled a King Salmon, most of which can reach an average of 50 pounds. The largest King Salmon ever caught here was a whopping 97 pounds, so there's nowhere better to try your skills than here in Kenai. This is one fish story you'll never have to embellish! Kenai is also home to the beautifully preserved Holy Assumption Russian Orthodox Church. Built in 1894 in a common rural Russian design, the church has been virtually unchanged since 1905, and shouldn't be missed.

Heading out of Kenai on Highway 9 east for roughly 76 miles brings us to our next destination, Moose Pass. Nestled on the shores of Trail Lake, and beginning as a small log cabin and roadhouse in the 1900s, the original iditarod trail was built through this area in 1910. With only 200 year-round residents, Moose Pass is quiet and breathtaking, and surrounded by towering mountains; a perfect place for the amateur or professional photographer to catch more than a few amazing shots of the alpine vistas, or pristine lakes in the area. Here, there is no end to the combinations of outdoor activities, like hiking, fishing, hunting, birdwatching and camping. Most popular is a 'flight-seeing' tour. Not for the faint of heart, this tour will take your breath away as you fly over mountain ranges and see more incredible jaw dropping sites from the air.

Once you've gotten your land legs back, jump back on Highway 9 and head south to our final destination of Seward. Make sure you have your camera ready, the drive from Moose Pass to Seward has some incredible views of mountain ranges on both sides as you drive. You'll want to make frequent stops along this route for some amazing shots. Sandwiched between the Kenai Mountains on Resurrection Bay is where you'll find Seward. This is one of Alaska's oldest and most scenic communities. Behind this quiet seaside village, Mt. Marathon rises steeply, and is the stage for America's second oldest foot race held every July. Not to be outdone by Kenai for fishing, casting your line here just might land you a mammoth Halibut weighing several hundred pounds. The fish here are so numerous, it's been said they jump into your boat! Seward is also home to the Alaska SeaLife Center, where you can go nose-to-glass with many creatures you'd otherwise only see from a distance, including puffins, sea lions, harbor seals, and much more. The SeaLife Center is a one-of-a-kind research, rehab and education facility where you can actually observe research as it's being conducted. From Lowell Point, you can slice through glassy waters on kayak, gliding past sea otters and harbor seals; a perfect way to marvel at the grace and beauty of Alaska.

ARIZONA

Traveling through Arizona, it's hard not to try and imagine what it would have been like when Native Americans roamed this land, and the likes of Doc Holliday and Wyatt Earp etched out their place in history. Luckily for visitors to this beautiful state, Arizona manages to hold on to it's 'Wild West' history while adding a modern flair that allows the past and the present to stand side-by-side, each one unique and intriguing. Whether you're hot on the trail of a gunslinger named Billy the Kid, looking to stand breathlessly on the edge of the Grand Canyon, or search for modern creature comforts like world-class golf, Arizona has something for you.

To start our trip, we begin in Quartzsite, a sleepy little desert town where not much happens for most of the year, but every January thru February this tiny town swells with over a million visitors. Why? Since the 60s, Quartzsite has been known to many RVers as a rock hound's paradise. Eight major gem and mineral shows, as well as vendors of raw and handcrafted merchandise, peddle their wares to collectors and enthusiasts who flock from all over the country. If rocks just aren't your thing, Quartzsite has plenty of other great events to keep you busy, including an RV show, crafts fairs and a pow wow that are all within the same time frame.

Heading north on AZ-95 will bring you to our next destination, beautiful Lake Havasu City. This city has a reputation as a popular destination for college kids on Spring Break, but it's also a thriving tourist town with more than 400 miles of coastline and enough water sports, hiking, off-roading and fishing to keep you busy for more than a little while. But, the one thing any traveler should see while visiting this beautiful city is the London Bridge. That's right, the actual London Bridge. Built in 1831, it was purchased by an enterprising man who had the entire bridge dismantled, numbered, then moved 7,000 miles from London and rebuilt in its present location in Lake Havasu City in 1972. Today, the bridge is a huge tourist draw, and under the bridge is English Village, with plenty of shops and restaurants to keep you busy for hours.

Taking AZ-95 N out of Lake Havasu City, merge onto I-40 W, and after several miles we'll arrive at our next destination, Bull Head City. Covering 46 miles along the Arizona/Nevada border, Bull Head City's desert climate makes it one of the hottest cities in the US, with summer temperatures sometimes exceeding 125 degrees. Steer clear of the heat by paying a visit to the Colorado River Museum, and explore the incredible history of the steamboats that traveled the Colorado River, the gold and silver mines, ranching, and local Native American history. Despite the heat, more than 5 million travelers make their way through Bull Head City annually for it's year-round sun, and the vast water recreation opportunities.

Making our way out of Bull Head City, via AZ-68 E, we make our way to the last destination of our trip, Kingman. Beautiful Kingman is the heart of Historic Route 66, and one of the true treasures of Arizona. There is so much to see and do, where do we start? How about exploring the Historic Route 66 Museum, located on the longest remaining stretch of The Mother Road? The museum offers the evolution of Route 66 with photos, murals and dioramas. Make sure to visit the Mohave Museum of History and Arts. Founded in 1961, the museum is dedicated to preserving the heritage of the area through its collection of documents, maps, photos and manuscripts. Before you leave the Museum of History and Arts, make sure you grab a map for a walking tour of the 60 buildings Kingman has on the historic register. And of course, no trip to this town would be complete without visiting good old Engine No. 3759 at the Locomotive Park. Built in 1928, the engine is a coal burning steam locomotive that ran passengers between Los Angeles and Kansas City. It was retired after 20 years, but had run over 2.5 million miles in the course of its service. A popular relaxation spot for both tourists and locals who can sit back and relax in the shade of

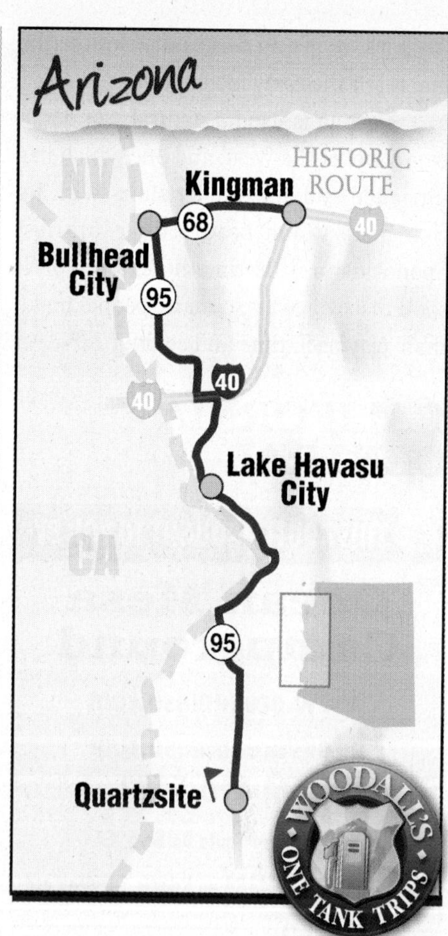

the park, or get up close and examine the marvel of the early locomotive.

Arizona is itself a natural wonder, a true jewel of the West, and one which has intrigued and delighted visitors with its rich history and beauty for centuries. Spend just a little time here, and you'll soon discover why so many people make their way back time and again.

CALIFORNIA - CENTRAL

There are some that say Central California is paradise. Rolling hills, mild temperatures, incredible beaches make this area a draw for surfers, shoppers, golfers and wine enthusiasts alike. The breathtaking beauty of this region, and relaxed pace makes it the perfect place to relax and unwind.

Today, we start our journey in Santa Barbara. This part of the California Coast is sometimes referred to as the "American Rivera", and with the low ridge of hills with spectacular views of the harbor nearly surrounding the city, it's easy to see why. Sightseers will love exploring the Old Spanish Presidio and Mission Santa Barbara in the older area of the city. And being in the heart of wine country, there is a long list of local wineries worth a visit to taste some of the best wines in the world.

Heading out on Hwy-1 N, which has some spectacular views of the Pacific and is one of the most scenic drives in the country, will lead us to our next stop, Pismo Beach. A scenic, sleepy seaside town, with unspoiled beaches and rolling sand dunes makes Pismo a top destination for sun worshipers and outdoor enthusiasts. One of the most heavily fished of the central coast piers - with clamming opportunities below - the Pismo Beach Pier also offers an incredible 360-degree view of the Pacific Ocean. California's largest

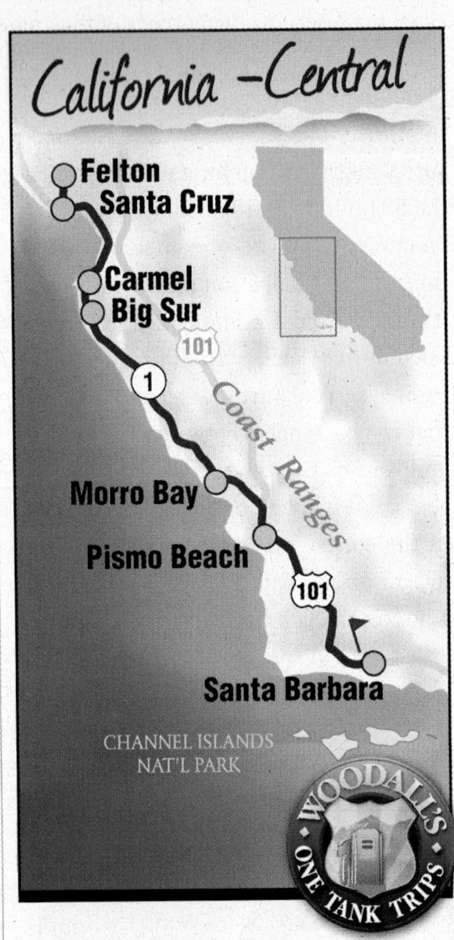

Monarch Butterfly Grove is also located in the city, and if you visit between November and February you will get the chance to tour local eucalyptus trees inhabited by thousands of beautiful Monarchs.

Heading a little further north on Hwy-1 will bring you to Morro Bay. In the heart of the region known as California's Natural Escape, Morro Bay has unlimited outdoor recreation opportunities, including surfing, kayaking, windsurfing, bicycling, and golf. The sentinel of this historic fishing village is Morro Rock. A volcanic peak, which stands 576 feet high, and is over 21 million years old, the peak also acts as a preserve for the peregrine falcons that nest on top. The town is also home to the Morro Bay National Estuary, a bird sanctuary that is home to more than 250 species. Some of the best and freshest seafood can be had here at many local area markets and restaurants due to Morro Bay having one of the largest, and most productive commercial fishing fleets. Eat up! It doesn't get better than this!

Back on the road and continuing our scenic drive on Hwy-1 N, our next location is Big Sur. There are few places left in the world left like Big Sur, and visitors here are in for a spectacular and rare treat. Big Sur boasts a population in the neighborhood of about 1,000 people year-round, which is surprising given the beauty of this area. Big Sur is also devoid of the usual urban areas, due mostly to the land along the coast being privately owned. The environmentally conscious residents have worked hard to keep Big Sur unspoiled, which allows it to retain its isolated and frontier mystique.

Back to our scenic drive along Hwy-1 N, and just a short, but beautiful trip away lies Carmel. Carmel-by-the-Sea is an area steeped in Bohemian History. Long known as a haven for artists, residential districts have no streetlights or sidewalks, and many homes lack street addresses. Carmel is home to numerous art galleries that showcase original works by established artists. We highly recommend the walking tour through Carmel's eclectic gardens, courtyards and area artist's residences. Like much of the rest of California, Carmel enjoys a moderate year round temperature, which makes it perfect for several outdoor activities, including golf and scuba diving.

Continuing on Hwy-1 N, less than 30 minutes away is the city of Marina. Home to an environmentally sensitive habitat, this oceanfront city is well known for it's fabulous dunes where hang gliders lift off on their aerial journey above the Pacific Ocean. There are several outdoor activities to keep you entertained, including surfing, fishing, bird and whale watching. Once home to the Army training base, Fort Ord, today the 8,000 acres of the former base are considered public land, and intricate trails running through the area can be enjoyed on foot, bike, or horse.

Back to beautiful Hwy-1 N, we continue on to Santa Cruz. This serene city boasts one of only two oceanfront amusement parks in California, and draws adults and children to the many attractions of the seaside park. Within the park is an old fashioned wooden roller coaster, The Big Dipper, which is one of the most famous coasters in the country. And, if you can manage to keep your eyes open and keep your heart in your chest, you'll see a breathtaking 20-second view of the hills above Santa Cruz, as well as the Pacific Ocean from atop the Big Dipper. A popular destination for surfers, thousands have been known to converge on Santa Cruz for the annual surf competition. It is a heart pounding, nail biting competition for those that are lucky enough to watch the incredible towers of waves, and those brave enough to ride them.

For our last stop, we continue on Hwy-1 N to beautiful Felton. Surrounded by beautiful redwood groves and forests, most of them over 1500 years old, Felton welcomes visitors from across the globe who come to marvel at the beauty of the area. Many visitors come to take advantage of several outdoor opportunities including biking, fishing, shopping, and yes, even train rides. Here, visitors have the chance to ride one of the oldest and most historic rail lines in California, which transports you back in time. Opened in 1875, the route was designed to carry picnickers and tourists to the Big Trees and Santa Cruz. The Steam Train narrow-gauge excursions to Bear Mountain are equally popular, and most of these engines date back to the 1890s.

From the coast to the redwood forests, Central California is full of delicate and incredible beauty. Many come for the peace and quiet and for the laid back, slower pace, but whatever the reason, you're sure to discover something to bring you back again and again.

CALIFORNIA - NORTH

Northern California's geography is as eclectic as the people who call this area home. Here, there are spectacular sandy beaches on the Pacific coast. To the east, lie the ruggedly beautiful Sierra Nevada mountains, and in the center, one of the most vital agricultural areas in the country. It's this kind of diversity that brings millions of travelers to this area every year.

Starting off in San Francisco, it's easy to see why so many people left their hearts here after a visit to this incredible city. If you can imagine, San Francisco started off as a small town of only 1,000 people, and has steadily grown to be one of the most diverse cities in the nation. Well known for it's steep streets, beautiful architecture, and chilly summer fog, it is also the most densely populated city in the US. One of the most popular destinations in the city is historic Fisherman's Wharf. If the views of the Bay don't draw you in, then the great seafood will! Now stripped of the traditional waterfront life that once existed here, today the Wharf is an open shopping mall. The atmosphere here is mesmerizing, attracting visitors from all over California (and beyond) for the world class dining, shopping, street performers and vendors. What would a trip to San Francisco be without a trip to Chinatown? A residential area that includes authentic markets, restaurants and more, it's the quickest trip you'll ever take to Hong Kong's past and present. And of course, there is one of the most easily recognized bridges in the world, the Golden Gate Bridge. Built in 1937, this suspension bridge connects the northern tip of the San Francisco Peninsula to Marin County, and is one of the most beautiful examples of modern engineering. Who can pass up a tour to one of the most famous former prisons in the world - Alcatraz – where the mere mention causes thoughts of one of the most famous unsolved prison breaks in history? Alcatraz and the people who lived, worked and were incarcerated here, have an enduring and fascinating history worth exploring.

Leaving San Francisco, we're heading south to Point Reyes via CA-1N, turning left at Sir Francis Drake Blvd. This leg of our trip is a little less than 2 hours, but will definitely be high on your list as one of the most scenic. Point Reyes National Seashore encompasses over 71,000 acres of breathtaking shoreline filled with estuaries, windswept beaches, grasslands and salt marshes, and is home to a rich biological diversity you'd be hard pressed to experience anywhere else. Over 45% of North American bird species have been sighted here, making it a natural stop for any bird enthusiast. Containing a haven of 80 miles of the most pristine and unspoiled coastline makes Point Reyes a wonderful spot to glimpse any number of native wildlife including white deer, fox, river otter and maybe even a coyote. The city is also home to the Point Reyes Lighthouse, built in 1780, where travelers are free to tour this beautiful historic treasure and are encouraged to explore the grounds.

Heading out to our next destination, double back on Sir Francis Drake Blvd and take a left onto CA-1N for the scenic trip to Bodega Bay. From its location on the stunning coast, travelers to the town are treated to some of the most spectacular views of the Pacific Ocean and Sonoma Coast, complete with the sight of migrating whales. It's here travelers can indulge themselves in the best Northern California has to offer. Whether you're looking to ride horseback on the beach, dust your board off and hit the waves, kayak the local waters or indulge yourself in regional coastal cuisine, Bodega Bay has a little taste of all the greatest things that make this area so special.

From Bodega Bay, we're heading out on CA-1 S and merging on to CA-12 E. Merge onto US-101 N via the ramp to Eureka and in no time, you'll be right in the heart of our next destination, Santa Rosa.

Santa Rosa is a place of convergence, where wine and farm country mingle with the beauty of redwood forests and ocean views. Newcomers will find deliciously scenic vistas and a plate full of activities right in the heart of Sonoma Wine Country, which is sure to delight even the pickiest of travelers. There is no shortage of great adventures here! Start at the Charles M. Schulz Museum and Research Center, where the most loved comic strip characters of all times are preserved and displayed. Next, get a taste of history at the Sonoma County Museum where you'll find art exhibits from fine local artists. If museums don't do it for you, how about shopping at the Historic Railroad Square? You'll feel like you stepped back in time as you shop for antiques, dine in local restaurants and wander this beautiful square. Oh, and if you're a railroad buff, you should definitely pay a visit to the Northwestern Pacific Rail Room Gallery located in the historic Train Depot. If you're looking for something a little more rugged, the Armstrong Redwoods State Reserve is an 805-acre park which contains some of the

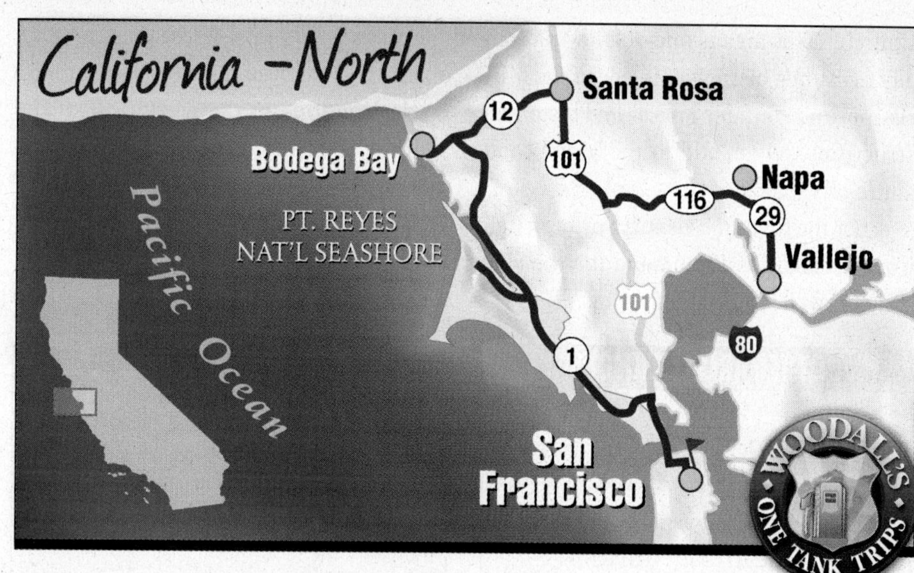

oldest and tallest redwoods in the state, and you won't want to pass up the opportunity to see these majestic beauties up close and personal. Of course, being in the heart of wine country gives travelers to this area ample opportunity to tour local wineries, taste some samples and buy a few bottles to take home with them! Some of the finest wines in the country are made right here in this region, and after spending just a few hours exploring, you'll soon discover what makes this area so special. Of course, the only thing that would make a trip to Santa Rosa even more unforgettable would be for you to take a balloon ride for spectacular views of wineries and the surrounding areas.

Once you've gotten your land legs back, we're back on the road to our next stop, Napa. Head out on US-101 S, taking the exit for Ca-116 E toward Sonoma/Napa. Turn left at CA-121 N/Fremont Dr, and left again at CA-121 N/CA-29 N. Finally, take the first exit toward Downtown Napa. Napa is one of the premiere destinations in the world and no matter what time of year you visit, you'll be surrounded by breathtaking beauty and plenty of opportunities to indulge yourself in some of the finer things (including wines), this area has to offer. By far, the most popular way to explore Napa is by bicycle. Napa just can't be fully appreciated by car, and you'll be glad you took the opportunity for a leisurely bike ride on country lanes through some of the most well known wineries in the country. Once you're finished with your mobile tour, those tight muscles could probably use some spa time, and Napa has you covered! Or how about some leisure time at the Historic Napa Mill? This downtown riverfront delight is filled with music, wine, and award-winning restaurants, the perfect way to round out our trip with a little jazz and a bite to eat.

Heading out of Napa on CA-29 S, the last stop on our adventure is the city of Vallejo, an approximate half-hour drive away. As the most famous naval shipbuilding and repair facility on the west coast, and the first permanent home of California's state government, Vallejo has a rich and varied history. Vallejo is a city filled with the beauty of historic buildings, cultural diversity, and some non-stop adventures! Art galleries, casinos, golf, museums, amusement parks; no matter what your adventure tastes, Vallejo has an impressive sampling of opportunities for any traveler. You won't want to pass up a tour to historic Mare Island. Visitors will find incredibly beautiful and historic buildings including St. Peter's Chapel, renowned for its Tiffany designed stained glass windows. Mare Island has a fascinating maritime history, and one worth exploring on your visit. Make your way to St. Vincent's Hill Historic District, a 33-square block area surrounding the St. Vincent's Catholic

Church. This area is one of a few nationally registered districts this side of the Mississippi and contains houses and historical structures, which add to the beauty and allure of Vallejo.

For the first time visitor, Northern California feels like Eden...and for the seasoned traveler? They know it is.

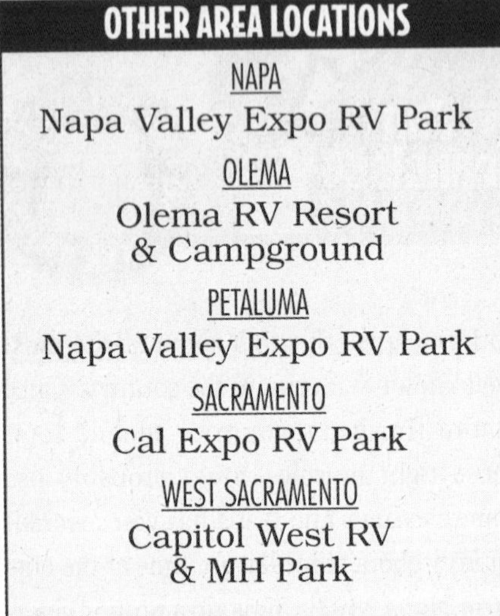

CALIFORNIA - SOUTH

California is a land of geographical extremes, from the Sierra Mountain ranges, to the beaches along the coast, and the desert area nestled between. And with such extremes comes a wealth of adventures, incredible sights, and awe-inspiring beauty. Whatever it is you're looking to experience while visiting, you're guaranteed to find in the Golden State.

We begin our trip in Anaheim, a city made famous as the home of Disneyland. Ask most kids, and they'd be able to find Anaheim on a map blindfolded, and one-handed. Disneyland is The Happiest Place on Earth, and one of the most popular family destinations in the world. With the addition of Disney's California Adventure, which occupies 55 of the original 100 acre Disneyland parking lot, and located immediately south of Magic Kingdom, it's just one more reason to pack up and head to

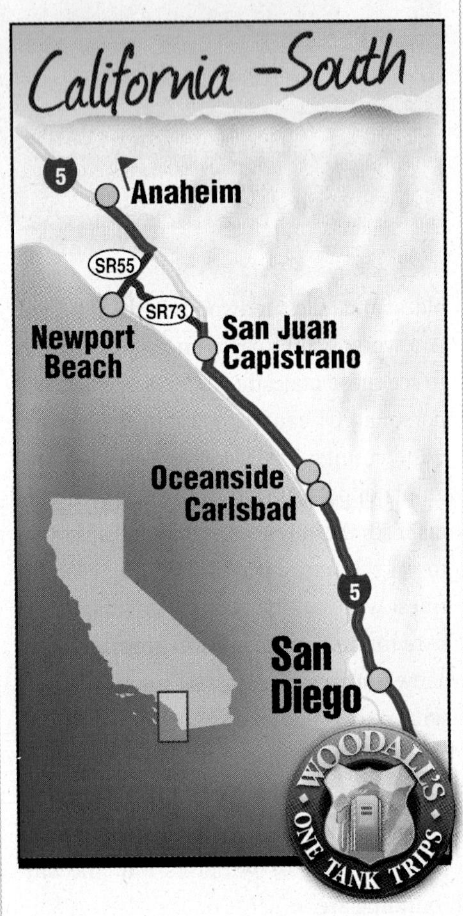

Disney! For most, Disneyland is a once in a lifetime opportunity, and no matter how old you are, it shouldn't be missed!

Say goodbye to the Disney gang - we're off to our next stop, beautiful Newport Beach. A short, but scenic trip on I-5 S, with a merge onto CA-55 S gets you there in no time. Did you bring your surfboard? Newport Beach is an incredible location to ride some waves, sometimes reaching up to 30 feet! But if surfing isn't your thing, there are plenty of other activities to experience. Feeling a little romantic? Then a gondola ride around the bay and canals of Newport is the perfect activity for you. Witness spectacular views beneath the picturesque skyline, and for a fraction of the time and money it would take you to experience the real thing in Italy. Newport Beach is a wonderful city with a boatload of things to do and see, from endless water sports, to some great upscale shopping. It's a perfect place to soak up some world famous California sun.

For the next leg of our trip, backtrack on CA-55 heading south, and merge onto CA-73 S. After a partial toll, merge onto I-5 S. In no time, you'll have arrived in stunning San Juan Capistrano. Visitors here can't miss a visit to the beautiful Mission San Juan Capistrano. Built around a series of 18th century arcades, with each arcade enclosing gorgeous fountains and lush gardens. The charming Serra Chapel, a white-washed building with vivid and beautiful frescoes inside is considered the oldest building in the state of California, and is set against the endless blue skies. It's treasure worth admiring.

The I-5 S will take us along the beautiful coast and to our next stop, Oceanside. Known as the gateway to San Diego, Oceanside is a classic California beach community. Warm sandy beaches, historic pier, and a Cape Cod style harbor village, which comes complete with unlimited water sports and recreation opportunities - the perfect place to escape the hustle and bustle, and experience the casualness that made this beach culture legendary. A little further down I-5 S is Oceanside's sister city, Carlsbad. Known affectionately as the "Village by the Sea," Carlsbad offers visitors all the charm and allure of a European town, but with the amenities of a large city. Filled with antique stores, boutiques and sidewalk cafes, Carlsbad's wonderfully mild climate offers a variety of unique events and activities, from street fairs to art walks. With miles of coastline, perfect for sunbathing and surfing, as well as beautiful lagoons just waiting for you to drop in a fishing line, Carlsbad is the perfect place to sit back, relax, and shake off your worries!

Now that you're nice and relaxed, let's get on the road to our final destination, San Diego. Getting back on I-5 S, with a merge onto I-805 S, and another merge onto CA-

163 S leads us straight to this appealing southern California city. What's a trip to San Diego without a visit to Sea World, the Home of Shamu, the killer whale. Where else can you interact with animals in such an exciting and unique way? There are plenty of shows, displays and exhibits to make for a very exciting and educational day. Another must see in San Diego is the incredible Balboa Park. This is the largest urban cultural park in the nation, and home to 15 major museums, many performing arts venues, gardens, and the San Diego Zoo. There's always something happening here, and is well worth a visit. The city is a fabulously sunny and beautiful place to end our journey!

OTHER AREA LOCATIONS

ANAHEIM
Newport Dunes Waterfront Resort

CHULA VISTA
Chula Vista RV Resort & Marina

NEWPORT BEACH
Newport Dunes Waterfront Resort

POMONA
Fairplex KOA/Los Angeles

SAN DIEGO
Campland on the Bay
Mission Bay RV Resort

SANTEE
Santee Lakes Recreation Preserve

IDAHO

If you've never had the pleasure of taking a trip to Idaho, you're probably wondering what's so great about it. That's where they grow potatoes right? But there is more to the state than just growing delicious vegetables! Encompassing the western side of the continental divide of the Rocky Mountains, Idaho is filled with emerald hillsides, timbered mountains, pristine lakes, and jagged peaks in the central area of the state. Idaho is an outdoorsman's dream, and one of the best kept secrets in the nation.

Beginning in Idaho Falls, a city situated at the base of the graceful Blackfoot Mountains, it's hard not to be overwhelmed by the beauty of this area. Literally at the doorstep of some of the most beautiful landmarks in North America, Idaho Falls is an outdoor enthusiast's wish come true. You'll run out of steam long before you ever run out of things to do! Biking, fishing, skiing, snowmobiling, rafting, and horseback riding are just a few things to keep you busy. Idaho Falls has more than a few opportunities for shopping and dining, with many other cultural offerings as well, including the Museum of Idaho. Here, visitors will learn all about this beautiful state; from the times of pioneers Lewis & Clark, to the present day, with many exhibits on display, including giant insects and the Columbian mammoth. If you're looking to get your pole wet, cast your line in the nearby Green River, one of the best places in the country to land a trout or two, or ride your bike, run, or just stroll leisurely around this lovely park which spans 14 miles along the river.

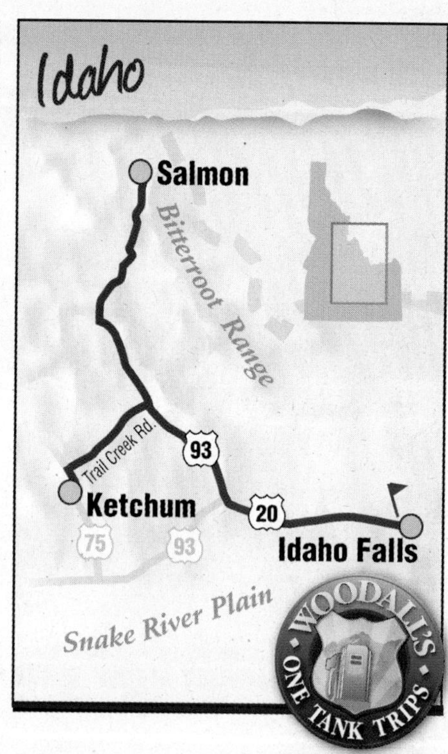

The next stop on our trip is the equally serene city of Ketchum, less than a four hour drive on US-93 N out of Idaho Falls. Ketchum is a year-round recreation area, and is a gateway to the internationally renowned Sun Valley. Visitors here can not

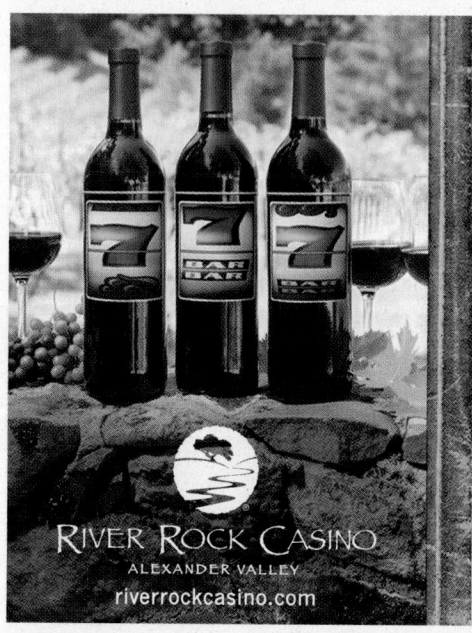

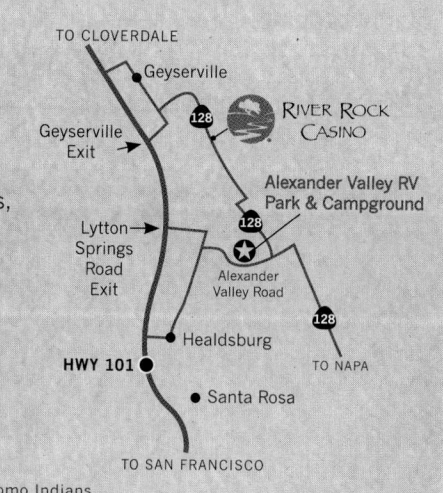

only enjoy some first class skiing, but also hiking, ice skating, trail riding, tennis, cycling, or mush a pack of huskies. Author Ernest Hemingway reportedly wrote his greatest novel here, and is it any wonder? The view is inspirational! Hemingway loved the town of Ketchum so much, he eventually relocated here, and fans can find his grave in the nearby Ketchum Cemetery. The city of Ketchum is filled with art galleries, featuring the works of local and national artists, world class shopping, and many fine restaurants. The town has a little bit for everyone who travels here, no matter the interest. For a view of the valley that will just blow you away, head up to Galena Summit Overlook. Completed in 1881, this route was once a toll road known as Sawtooth Grade. The view from the summit is spectacular!

Take scenic Trail Creek Rd out of Ketchum, merge onto US-93 N to arrive at our last stop, Salmon. Can you guess what the city of Salmon is known for? That's right, this incredible little town is known as the "Whitewater Capital of the World," and lies in a prime wild river fishing region at the base of the breathtaking Bitterroot Mountains. The nearby Salmon River is one of the few rivers that escaped being dammed in North America, and is a prime spot for anglers. Spawning season sees tremendous numbers of salmon in the gravel beds, but this river is also filled with rainbow trout, as well as steelhead. Not to be outdone by our other stops, Salmon is also a gateway to the mountains, lakes, streams and rivers that surround this area. There are many guides and outfitters available if you're looking to hunt, fish, raft, or horsepack, and they are more than willing to give you the thrill of a lifetime by escorting you into the back country.

Idaho is much, much more than the farmland that stretches across most of the state. The natural beauty and wealth of activities draw visitors by the thousands looking to have some fun, and no matter what the season, Idaho has some incredible things in store for everyone. From the majestic mountains to the salmon filled streams, Idaho should be on every traveler's list of getaways.

NEVADA

Nevada is truly for the ambitious. It's one of the few places you can ski in the morning, play golf in the afternoon, hike some trails, jump on an ATV, and kayak down river...all in one day. From the rugged and untamed Cowboy Country in the north, to the gambler's paradise in the south, one visit here, and you just might never want to leave!

Our first stop has been widely known as a playground for the rich, and those looking to get rich with the perfect hand, the perfect roll of the dice, or the perfect pull of a lever. Las Vegas is a nonstop, day and night, year-round destination full of five star dining, top notch shopping, and some of the best live entertainment you will ever see. If you're seeking to mix a little education with your vacation, make a stop to the Nevada State Museum. Here, you can discover the whole story behind the glitz and neon of Vegas, and the long list of unique characters who helped mold and shape it into the mecca it is today. The Liberace Museum is also here in Vegas, and whether you loved him or hated him, you'll want to see the collection of memorabilia from one of the most flamboyant entertainers who ever lived. Make sure you stop by the Chinatown Plaza. If you enjoy Asian culture, this is a must see! The plaza is filled with unique shops, a bakery, a jade store, and a wide variety of Asian food. You cannot leave Las Vegas without checking out the Fremont Street Experience. If you want a little taste of what Vegas used to be when the Rat Pack roamed these streets, this is the place for you! It is vintage Vegas as its best. This is where the tiny town of Vegas all began, at the corner of Fremont and Main. In fact, Fremont was the first paved street in the city. There is some

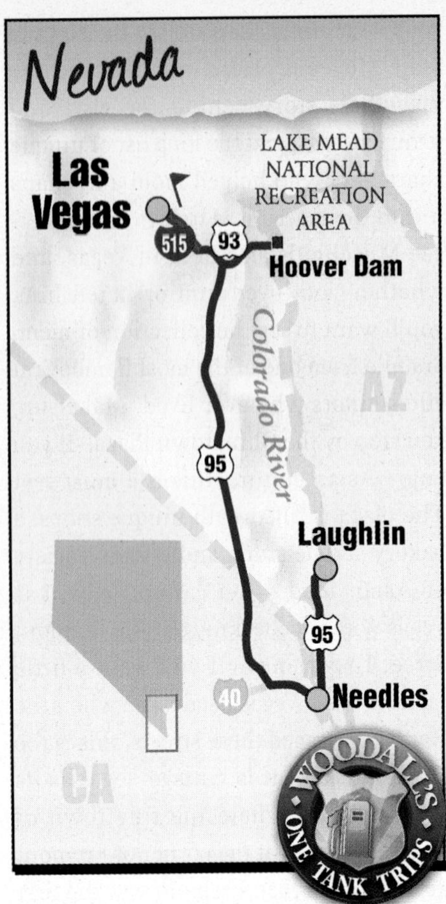

quality fun to be had in downtown, and a very unique experience. As Elvis once sang, "Viva Las Vegas!"

Like another song says, "we're leaving Las Vegas!" For the next leg of our trip, take I-515 S/ US-93 S to our next stop, the Hoover Dam. Straddling the Colorado and Black Canyon Rivers, this modern marvel is one of the largest dams in the world. Originally called the Boulder Dam, it is 726 feet high and 1244 feet long. If you don't fear heights, US-93 crosses over the top of the dam, winding its way back up and out on the Arizona side of the Colorado River. As you can imagine, the view from the top is spectacular! If you just can't get yourself to drive over it, (or maybe you did), make sure to stop by the Visitor's Center. Here you can learn what a pivotal role the construction of the dam played in making that little town called Las Vegas possible. Started in 1928, and completed in 1936, this amazing structure was not only built a full two years ahead of schedule, but also $15 million under budget, which might qualify it as a "Wonder of the Fiscal World". Lake Mead is a reservoir lake that resulted from the building of the dam. Converging with Lake Mead is Lake Mohave to the south, which was formed by the destruction of the Davis Dam, and together the two lakes comprise 291 square miles, drawing about 9 million visitors a year on average. Lake Mead alone extends about 110 miles upstream, and it's the perfect place for a wide variety of water sports.

Once you dry off from your dip in Lake Mead, it's back on the road! Take US-93 N to US-95 S toward Searchlight/Needles, then turn left onto US-95 N. After several miles, turn left on NV-163 E and follow that road until we reach our final destination, Laughlin. This city started off as little more than a motel and a bar that catered to the local miners and the many construction workers who toiled away on the Davis Dam. The motel soon fell into disrepair until a wealthy club owner bought the property, and in two years turned it into the Riverside Resort where you could get an all-you-can-eat chicken dinner for 98 cents. From those humble beginnings, Laughlin grew into a quite a tourist draw, attracting in the neighborhood of 3 million visitors every year who come to gamble, and enjoy several water sport activities on the Colorado River. If you're looking for a little more relaxed, laid back approach to gambling and shopping, Laughlin might be just the speed for you. It may not have all that Las Vegas has to offer, but it will be enough to make you want to plan on dropping by again real soon!

This area of Nevada is one of the most popular destinations in the whole state. Not all come for the gambling, although most do. The rest come for the lights, the people, the awesome food and the experience that will leave you reeling for days. The list of things to see and do in this area gets longer every year, and you may not be able to see it all, but you'll have a blast trying!

OTHER AREA LOCATIONS

RENO

Bordertown Casino & RV Resort

Silver Sage RV Park

SPARKS

Rivers Edge RV Park

OREGON

Left largely unspoiled, Oregon prides itself on its wild and serene reputation. Visitors here will never go without some incredible sight to see, a powdery slope to master, a challenging river to kayak, or another hill to hike. One thing is for sure, a visit to Oregon will make you wish you had at least 10 more hours in a day to experience all that this beautiful and rugged state has to offer.

Our trip through Oregon starts along the coast in Lincoln City. For those that have never been to this particular area of Oregon, you don't know what you've been missing! The coast of Oregon is nothing, if not striking. Miles and miles of sandy beaches, evergreen trees, and fresh clean air - the perfect place to relax and unwind. The beautiful mix of sea, beach, marshlands, coastal forest, rocky cliffs and hills also create the perfect habitat for bird viewing along the coast. Most notable are the peregrine falcon and the delicate murre. But there is a host of other beautiful species to be seen along the coast, and the mild temperate climate here makes it perfect for year-round viewing. Lincoln City also boasts several biking trails, and more than a few of the most scenic and breathtaking hiking trails in the country, so make sure you bring your hiking shoes!

Heading out on US-101 N, in less than an hour you will arrive at our next stop, Pacific City. This incredible area is perfect for more than a few activities, including fishing, beachcombing, and if you're feeling really brave, hang gliding. The view on the ground is amazing, but from the air it has to be jaw-dropping! A visit to the Nestucca Bay National Wildlife Refuge should be a high on the list for the nature observer. This beautiful area supports one-tenth of the world's Dusky Canada Goose population and contains at least seven types of habitat. The Cape Meares Lighthouse and Wildlife Refuge is a wonderful place to view whales, watch offshore rocks for native birds, and hike through many of the trails located here. Make sure you check out the lighthouse during your visit; there's a rumor that it just might be haunted!

Continuing our trip on US-101 N, another short drive up the coast will bring you to Netarts, our next destination. Netarts is a tiny seaside town, but there is a wealth of fun to be had here! Located on the Three Capes Scenic Loop, the area is a popular destination for scuba diving, fishing, crabbing, clamming, boating, and another great spot to do some bird watching.

Moving on, head back to US-101 N for a short drive continuing up the stunning coast to our next place of interest, Cannon Beach. This charming city is nestled between the Coast Mountain range, and the Pacific Ocean, offering some spectacular views and some amazing outdoor recreation opportunities. The most distinguishing landmark of the area is the Haystack Rock, a marvel of nature towering 235 ft above sea level, and just off the shoreline. Surfing, biking, golfing, horseback riding, swimming and hiking are just a few of the things you will enjoy during your visit. In town, visitors will enjoy wonderful restaurants, and an abundance of local art galleries featuring glass, photography and sculptures.

Returning to US-101 N, our last destination is less than an hour away at Warrenton. Beautifully situated at both the mouth of the Columbia River and the Pacific Coast, Warrenton is the perfect place to relax, bask in the scenery or enjoy a wealth of outdoor recreation. For the history buff, you'll find the winter headquarters of Lewis and Clark: Fort Stevens. Built in 1863 during the Civil War, Fort Stevens remained in service

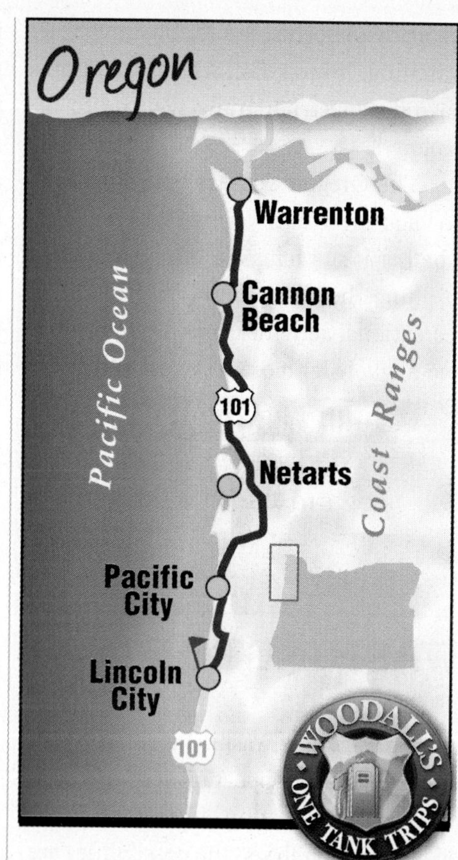

until World War II, and is definitely worth exploring. Warrenton also offers travelers many opportunities for boating, birdwatching, hiking, fishing, and contains several equestrian trails waiting to be explored.

The Oregon Coast is stunning, and no matter what you're looking for, whether it's to relax and slow your pace, or plunge headlong into a whirlwind of recreational activities, you'll find it here, and a whole lot more.

OTHER AREA LOCATIONS

LINCOLN CITY
Logan Road RV Park
SALEM
Happy Valley RV Park

WASHINGTON

Breathtaking Washington offers wonderfully diverse opportunities for travelers. From relaxation, to recreation, to adventure, you'll find the possibilities are as endless as the graceful beauty of this scenic state.

Our first stop is a beautiful area known as the Tri-Cities region, which includes the cities of Richland, Pasco and Kennewick. Within this small area there are more than 160 wineries within a 50-mile radius, which makes it the perfect place to do a little winery touring and tasting, or take some time to admire the expansive beauty of the vineyards. With the confluence of the Yakima, Columbia and Snake rivers, visitors will also find a wealth of recreation year-round including skiing, hunting, fishing and kayaking. The possibilities here will delight any traveler!

Taking US-395 N out of the Tri-Cities, merge onto WA-17 N, then merge onto WA-26 W and in less than 2 hours you will arrive at our next destination, Othello. Abundant in wildlife and outdoor recreation, Othello is also home to the Columbia National Wildlife Refuge where bird enthusiasts will delight in the large numbers of migrating and wintering fowl to be found here. With over 23,000 acres to play and explore, travelers will find the rugged beauty of this area the perfect place for hiking, biking, and fishing as well.

From Othello, return to WA-17 N, and in about an hour, you'll have arrived in beautiful Moses Lake. Reenact your favorites scenes from "Lawrence of Arabia" here at one of the largest sand dune

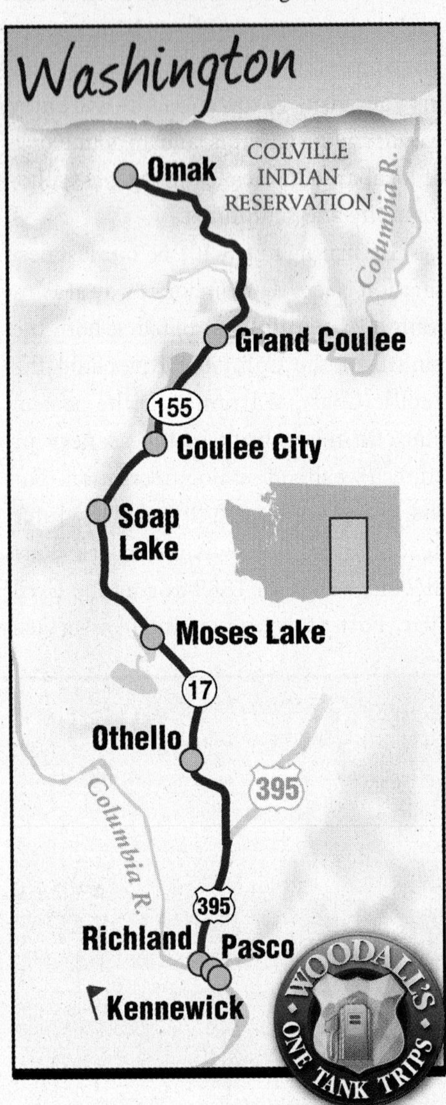

areas in the region, or better yet, put on your eye gear and do some off-road driving and exploring of the dunes. If off-roading isn't your thing, you'll find a wealth of other incredible activities including golf, fishing and water skiing.

Leaving Lake Moses, take WA-17 N to Soap Lake. Welcome to the most unique stop on our trip! At the turn of the century, this unusual lake (that takes its name from the minerals within the lake giving it a soapy texture) was widely known as mineral spa, and people with all sorts of ills came from miles around to soak in the water, and play in the creamy mud. Today, visitors can still come to this peaceful area to get a massage, sit on the beach and relax their cares away; just the thing for those tired muscles after all the excitement in Lake Moses.

Now that you've soaked your troubles and sore muscles, it's back to WA-17 N with a merge onto US-2 E to scenic Coulee City. Nestled on the shores of Banks Lake, Coulee City is the oldest city in the county, and one that provides visitors with some incredible outdoor fun. Birdwatching, fishing, hiking, and guided hunting are most popular in this area. Visitors will also find the famous Dry Falls in this region, and although no water flows now, it was once the sight of the largest waterfall known to have existed on earth. Viewing the 3.5 miles of sheer cliffs that drop 400 feet, it's easy to imagine the roar of water pouring over the side.

Our next stop is a short drive on Washington-155 N to Grand Coulee. Sitting two miles above the incredible 550-foot-high walls of the largest concrete dam in America, the city of Grand Coulee welcomes visitors from the four corners for some serious outdoor fun. Lake Roosevelt, the backwater of the dam, has 630 miles of shoreline and is 150 miles long, providing anglers and water sports enthusiasts with more than enough to keep them busy for hours. Guided tours are offered of the impressive dam and if you get lucky enough to hang around after the sun goes down, there is an incredible light show on the dam you won't want to miss!

A little over an hour away on Washington 155 N you'll find our last stop, Omak. Ruggedly beautiful and serene, Omak offers visitors many water activities including fishing, skiing and hunting. This lovely area of the Okanogan Valley offers plenty of wineries and breweries to visit, and a wonderful Native American history that is celebrated through Pow Wows and other events. The beauty and charm of this small town can win over the pickiest traveler, as there truly is something for everyone!

Miles and miles of untouched forests and the tranquil natural beauty make the Evergreen State irresistible to nature lovers and outdoorsmen alike. No matter where you travel in this state, you'll look forward to every turn in the road.

OTHER AREA LOCATIONS

BOTHELL
Lake Pleasant RV Park

CLARKSTON
Granite Lake Premier RV Resort

GIG HARBOR
Gig Harbor RV Resort

KENT
Rivers Edge RV Park

MEXICO - BAJA

At the southernmost tip of California lies a gateway to another world. A land rich with culture, fine food, music, and endless opportunities for fun-in-the-sun. This exotic and inviting land is just a step over the border in Baja, Mexico.

Today we begin in Tecate, the oldest border city in Baja. The pace here in Tecate moves slower than much of the rest of the world, and travelers here are encouraged to relax, take their time, soak in some of the endless sun, and savor each step. Many visitors come to experience the Guadalupe Hot Springs, an area which is also popular with the locals. Rustic rock rimmed hot tubs filled with sparkling clear geothermal mineral water is the perfect way to soak away your troubles. This area of Baja is widely known for several ancient Indian caves, cascading waterfalls, and endless opportunities for hiking. Tecate is also a gateway city into the beautiful expanse of land where some of the finest wines in Mexico are made, and the land is covered in row after stunning row of vineyards.

Leaving Tecate, take Mexico-3 S to arrive at our next stop, Francisco Zarco. As quiet and sleepy as our previous stop, Francisco Zarco lies in the heart of Mexican wine country. Many travelers venture this way for the idyllic beauty, and to visit any one of the several vineyards in the area. Connoisseurs come here from around the world to sample wines, or to laze their days away amongst the vineyards, and who could blame them? This area invites you to tap into your inner hedonist and take in a tour or two, and bask in the sun while sipping some of Mexico's finest wines.

Heading back to Mexico-3 S brings us to our last stop, Ensenada. The third largest city in Baja, Ensenada is a scenic coastal town with incredible beaches,

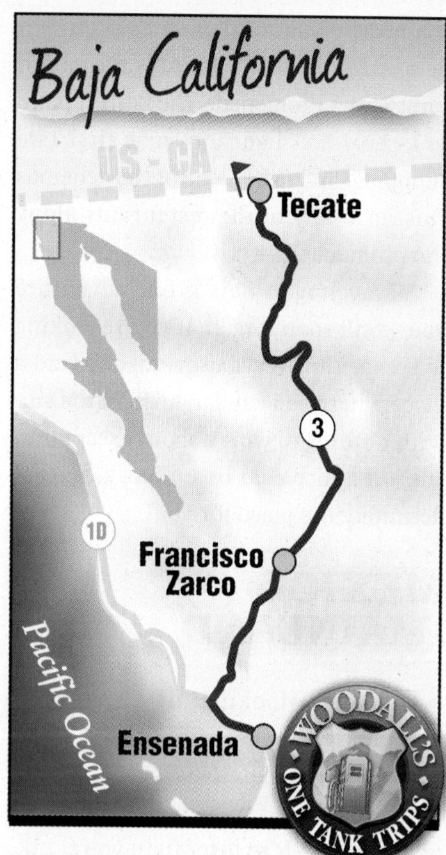

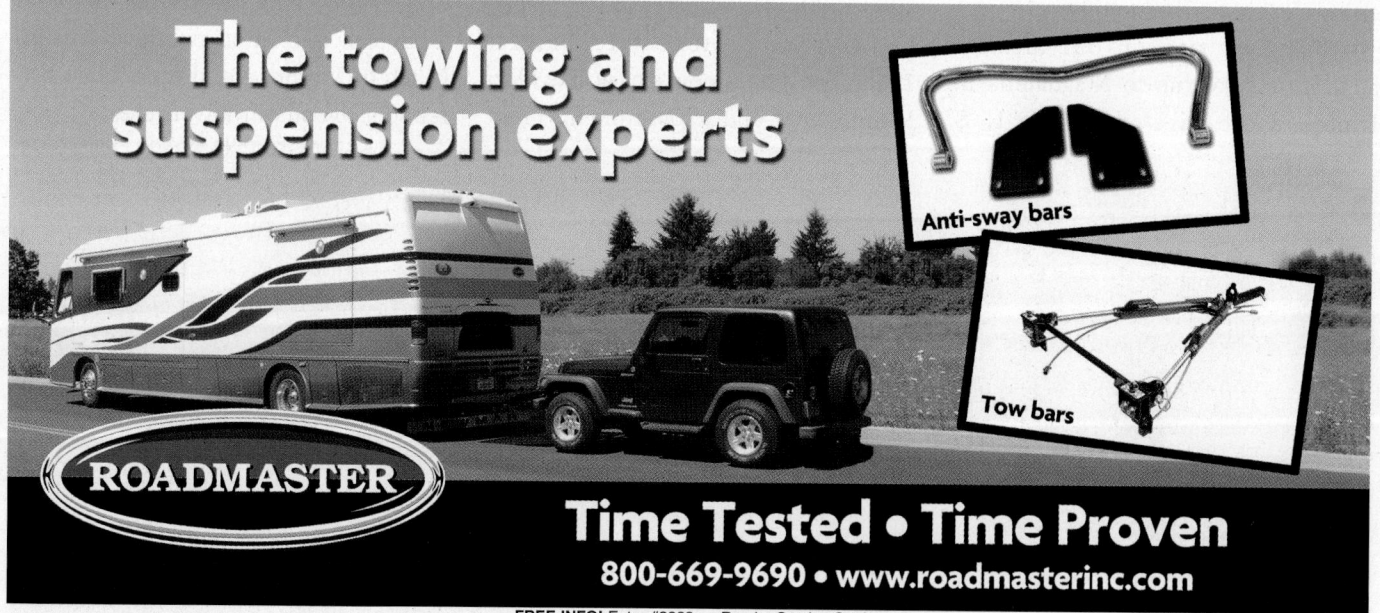

numerous boutiques, and some excellent fishing, making it a premier destination in Baja. Like our other two stops before, Ensenada is also well known for its many vineyards and tasting tours, but many visitors also come for the opportunity to whale watch, and to explore La Bufadora, a natural blowhole formed by marine erosion that throws a gush of water up to 24 feet in the air. There are observation decks for safe viewing and the nearby botanical gardens shouldn't be missed. Also of interest is the quaint First Street Promenade, the perfect place to laze in the shade, do some first rate shopping, and taste some of the delicious cuisine at any of the restaurants along the promenade.

Traveling to Baja is one adventure you won't soon forget. If you're looking to escape the everyday grind, and find a place where you can languish in the sun with nothing to worry about except putting on a nice coat of sunblock, Baja is definitely the place for you!

MEXICO -MAINLAND

If you're looking for a change of venue, why not head south of the border where warm breezes, swaying palm trees and some fantastic cuisine await your arrival. It's closer than you think, and you can be there quicker than you can say, Viva Mexico!

Kicking off our trip in charming Nogales, visitors here will be treated to an amazing array of sights, sounds, colors and experiences. Sitting just across the border from Arizona, Nogales enjoys its fair share of travelers looking for exquisite food and several bargains. With so many beautiful sights and shops, plan on taking several hours to enjoy all this city has to offer.

The next stop on our Mexican adventure takes us to Magdalena de Kino, a short drive on Mexico 15 S. Although many tourists rush by, Magdalena is a town worth a stop. This is the resting place of the Italian missionary and explorer, Padre Eusebio Kino, who founded numerous missions

within the area, and in Arizona, in the 1600-1700s. His remains are on display in a crypt where they were found in 1966. The area is now a park-like Plaza Monumental, and across from the plaza, visitors will find the graceful Temple of Santa Maria de Magdalena. Numerous small shops surround the plaza, and each year this oasis is host to thousands of pilgrims who gather during the religious festival dedicated to San Francisco Javier.

Moving on, return to Mexico 15 S and in less than two hours, you will have arrived at our next stop, Hermosillo. This beautiful capital city is one of the largest in Mexico, and a placed well loved for travelers. A point of interest here is the Catedral de la Asuncion, built in 1912 - a beautiful example of religious architecture, and the pride of the city. Another is the Sonora Museum, which was once a military penitentiary, but now travelers can observe all the history and culture of the area in freedom.

Moving on, our next stop is Bahia de Kino, a short drive on HWY-16. Bahia de Kino is a beautiful area with no shortage of excitement. Travelers can do plenty of fishing, diving, skiing, sailing and swimming, and what a beautiful backdrop for this adventure!

Our last stop takes us a short distance down HWY-24 to Guaymas. There are many cultural draws in this city, including Plaza de San Fernando, where many good shopping bargains are just waiting to be discovered, and plenty of golf and water activities abound. Guaymas is located on the beautiful beach of Miramar, and there is no better spot to end our adventure.

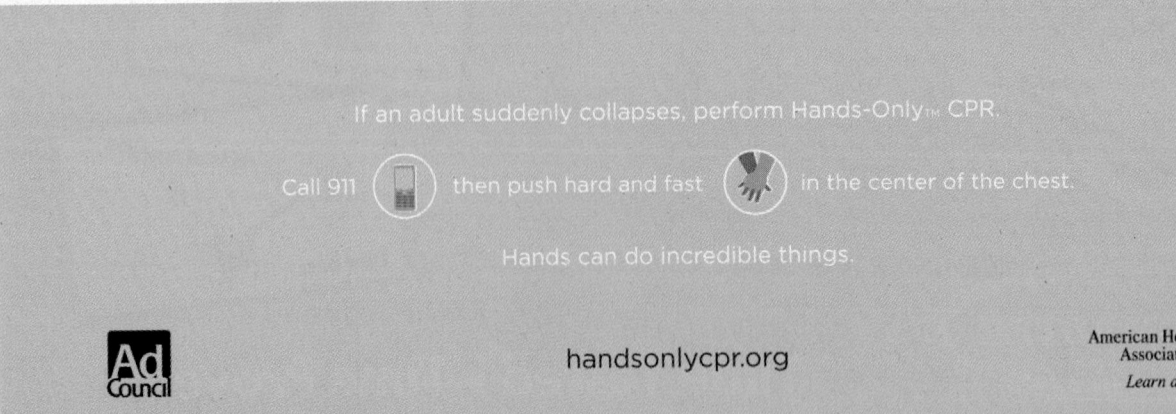

ALBERTA

Alberta's grandeur and beauty are obvious from the moment you arrive. Awe-inspiring mountain ranges, rolling foothills, lush farmland, and even a desert topography dot this area. Alberta has long been known as the perfect place to play during the winter months, offering a wide variety of sports, from skiing to dog sledding. And if that doesn't win you over, the hospitality will. Alberta is among the friendliest places you'll ever visit. What are you waiting for? Let's head to Alberta!

Lloydminster is unusual in that it lies in both the Alberta and Saskatchewan Provinces, but it's a great place for us to begin our trip. The line separating both Provinces runs directly down the center of the city, giving it the unique distinction of being Canada's only "border city", and one of the few places you can claim to have been in two separate towns, and two separate provinces, at the same time! Being the only border city, Lloydminster is also home to the world's largest (100 ft.) survey markers, which can be found in Lloydminster's City Hall. Once a Barr Colony, the city takes pride in its pioneer heritage, and nowhere is this more evident than at the Barr Colony Heritage Cultural Centre, found on the Saskatchewan side of town. This impressive collection houses over 250 religious and historical artworks, and is a good way to glimpse into the past of this unique place.

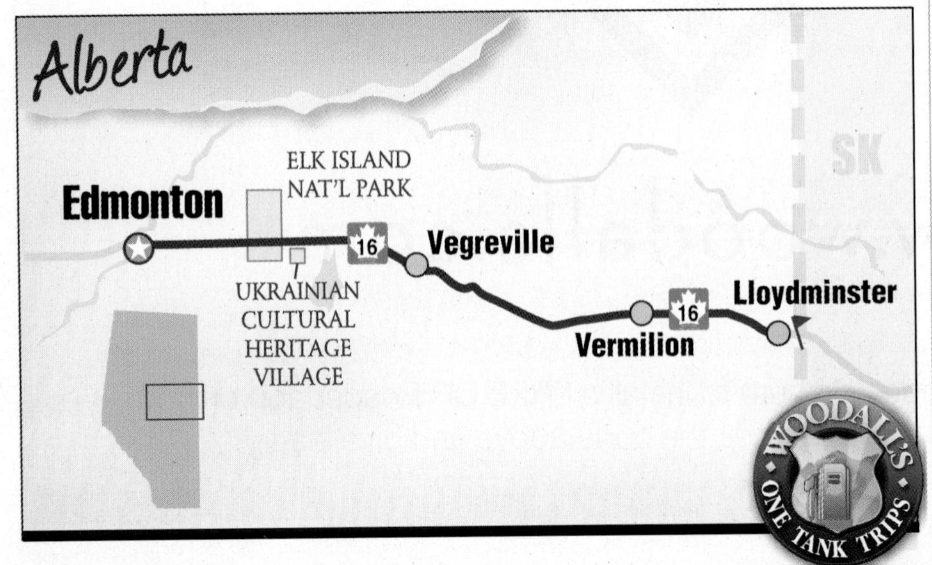

Saying goodbye to Lloydminster, take BC-Yellowhead Hwy/Hwy-16 W to our next location, Vegreville. Named after Father Valentin Vegreville, a missionary in Western Canada, the first settlers arrived here in 1894. One of the most unusual aspects of this small town is the cultural diversity and the harmony with which the locals live and work together. By the 1950s, there were more than thirty different ethnic groups living in the area, the four largest being English, French, German and Ukrainian. The other amazing notable fact about Vegreville is that it's home to the world's largest pysanka, or Ukrainian Easter egg. Measuring some 25.7 feet long, 18.3 feet wide, and 31.6 feet high with the massive internal structure weighing 3,000 pounds. It is the premiere attraction of Vegreville, and one that thousands of visitors come to marvel at every year for its beauty, size and engineering. Now, try and picture the 300-foot chicken that would have laid it...........

Continuing on Hwy 16 W, we come to our next stop, the Ukrainian Cultural Heritage Village. This little village is not like any other you'll encounter; in fact, you might want to check your calendar, just to make sure what year it is. An open-air museum, the Ukrainian Cultural Heritage Village was built to resemble the pioneer settlements in East Central Alberta. Buildings from surrounding communities have been moved to the village and painstakingly restored to various years within the first part of the twentieth century. Guides at the village are in full historic costume, and remain in character at all times, answering questions as if it is the year their building portrays, usually from the year 1930 or earlier. Many of the structures are homes of three important settler families, as well as farmsteads, and town buildings. Activities at the Village change from day-to-day and week-to-week according to the season so that no two visits to the site are ever quite the same.

Making your way back to present time, it's time to get back on Hwy 16 W to the final destination of our trip, Edmonton. The capital of Alberta, Edmonton is known for its scenic river valley, and a thriving art and music community. But the most incredible sight is the mammoth West Edmonton Mall. Much more than any shopping center you've probably ever seen, this complex has a giant water park, a man-made lake, a skating rink, two mini-golf courses, 21 theaters, a casino, and an amusement park with 25 rides and attractions. With all of this, is it any wonder that it's also North America's largest shopping and entertainment complex? This is one place that will provide you with more than just your run-of-the-mill shopping adventure. Make sure you bring your walking shoes!

Beautiful Alberta, with its charming, warm people, beautiful landscapes and deep-rooted history, offers broad possibilities for any travelers. Whether you're looking to escape the grind of every day life in the wilderness, or to dive head first into metropolitan creature comforts, Alberta's door is always open.

BRITISH COLUMBIA - NORTH

For outdoor enthusiasts, it's almost impossible to pick a location that offers more heart-pounding, endless recreation and serene beauty than Northern British Columbia. The wilderness alone covers more than half of the province, it is larger than the state of California, and is filled with raging rivers, pristine lakes, and jagged mountain peaks. If ever there was a heaven for the outdoorsman, this region is definitely it.

Let's start our trip in Prince Rupert, a small marine city with a lot to offer those in need of some one-on-one time with Mother Nature. Well known as a popular stop on various cruises, Prince Rupert is one of the few places where you will see tame deer roaming the streets, and wild grizzly bears seen safely via boats. Surrounded by lush, old-growth rainforest, there are little treasures to be found throughout the town, from petroglyphs to beautiful architecture. For the angler, Prince Rupert is a paradise of saltwater fishing opportunities and enough Halibut, Chinook and Coho to keep you busy for hours. Many anglers opt for charters that will take them out on a fishing experience they won't soon forget. For the culture seeker, you won't want to miss the Museum of Northern British Columbia, which will take you on an incredible journey of exploration through the Northwest Coast dating back to the last ice age. The museum is packed with archaeological discoveries, works of art, and unique artifacts that will keep you spellbound. The Northern Pacific Cannery is a historic site, which protects the oldest surviving salmon cannery village along the coast. If you've ever wondered what it must have been like to spend long summer seasons working in a cannery, now is your chance! The plant closed in the 1960s, but you can still take a self-guided tour through the 30 buildings still standing, which include primitive living quarters, bunkhouses, and the main cannery building.

For our next stop, we're heading down HWY-16 E through some spectacular mountain ranges to Terrace. Depending on the weather, and the number of stops you take for photos, this trip will take you about 2 hours. No matter what time of year you visit Terrace, it has something incredible to offer. From its location along the Skeena River, anglers won't be able to resist casting a line for salmon. The summer months also bring hiking, rock climbing, kayaking, and canoeing. Winter has deep powder downhill skiing in store for you, as well as cross-country skiing, snowboarding, and snowshoeing. And if you're lucky, you'll catch a glimpse of the Kermode bear, a rare black bear born with a pure white coat. This rare beauty is also known as the Spirit Bear and holds a special place in the hearts of the locals.

Our next stop takes us to Kitimat. Take HWY-37 out of Terrace, and turn right at Haisla Blvd, then take the first left to stay on Haisla Blvd. This leg of our trip is about 2 hours, weather permitting. What Kitimat lacks in population, it

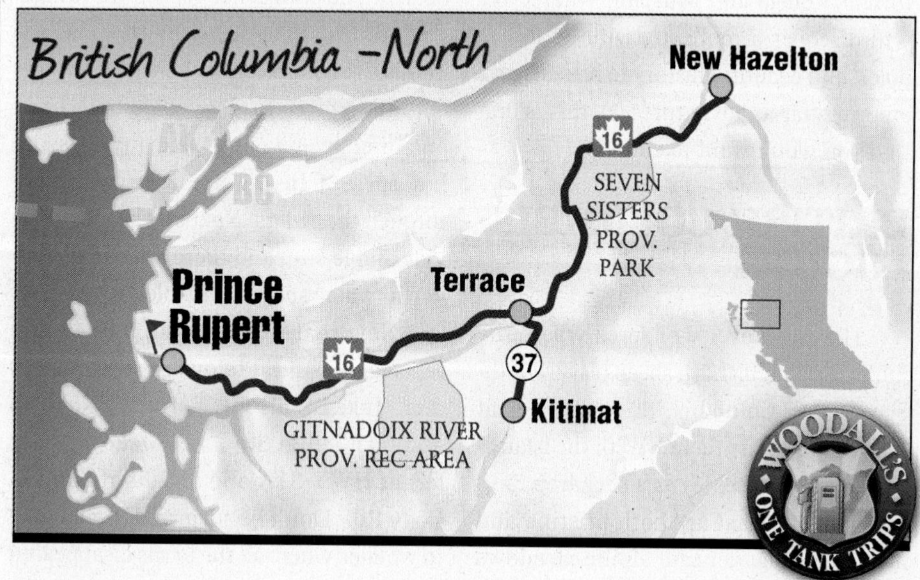

makes up for in some of the most scenic and peaceful views found anywhere on earth. The nearby Kitimat River and ocean channels are perfect for a variety of water sports, including fresh and saltwater fishing, kayaking, canoeing, boating, and even a visit to the hot springs. The surrounding area is beautifully untouched, and hikers and rock climbers will find themselves drawn to the many trails and climbing opportunities. And it's on one of these hikes that you just might run into the jewel of the Kitimat Valley, a Giant Sitka Spruce, which is over 500 years old. Now, that's worth an hours hike, isn't it?

Our last destination has us backtracking on HWY-37, and returning to HWY-16 where you need to take a right. After several miles, turn left at Churchill and continue onto HWY 62/New Hazelton Hi-Level Rd. This is the longest leg of our trip and should take you in excess of 3 hours. Hazelton is one of a group of towns that comprise an area known simply as The Hazeltons, and is a true hidden gem just waiting to be discovered by those curious enough to venture off of HWY-16. It's here that travelers will discover the beauty of the First Nations culture surrounded by serene natural beauty. There is a wealth of activities available to the outdoorsman including boating, hiking, and fishing for both steelhead and salmon. For those looking to dive head first into local aboriginal culture, pay a visit to 'Ksan Historical Village and Museum where you will discover a replicated village, totem poles, and beautiful history to be rediscovered. As far as adventures go, this is one that you won't want to end.

BRITISH COLUMBIA - SOUTH

Have you ever wondered where the mule deer and bighorn sheep play? Southern British Columbia, of course! And who could blame them? With the beautiful Kootenay Rockies as a backdrop, providing views that are both pristine and awe-inspiring, delicate alpine meadows and waterfalls found throughout the region, it is a place like no other.

We're going to begin in Revelstoke. If you're looking to go extreme, Revelstoke has what you need! Surrounded by some of the most spectacular mountain ranges in Canada, Revelstoke will easily appeal to a wide variety of outdoorsman. Winter months will delight you with heli, Nordic, cat, backcountry and downhill skiing, as well as snowmobiling, so no excuses for staying indoors here, especially after you find out Revelstoke is home to the longest vertical ski run in North America. The summer months will lure you into the mountains for some first class hiking and mountain biking. Don't worry about your aching muscles - Revelstoke is widely known for having incredible local mineral hot springs for you to sooth your aches and pains. If you're looking for a cultural injection in your trip, try the Revelstoke Railway Museum where you'll see the history of railroading through the Rockies unfold through artifacts and galleries.

Let's move on to our next stop, Nakusp. Head out of Revelstoke on HWY-1 W, and turn left at HWY-23. Take the Shelter Bay-Galena Bay ferry and continue straight onto HWY-23. This leg of our trip clocks in at over two hours, depending on the weather. Nakusp is a small village located on the shores of the Arrow Lake and surrounded by the Selkirk and Monashee mountain ranges. Once caught up in the mining boom of the 1800s, travelers now venture to this charming place to rejuvenate both body and mind by enjoying the many spas and hot springs in the area, or by hiking through the cedars. Nakusp's beaches provide ample sun, and there are some wonderful water sports available as well.

Now that we're rested, tanned and relaxed, let's head to our next stop, Sandon. Take BC-6E/HWY 6 out of Nakusp, and turn left at 8th Ave. Make another left at HWY 31A and a right at Sandon Cody Rd. Don't be surprised if you start to wonder where all the locals disappeared to once you arrive! Sandon is a bona fide ghost town, and one of several in the area that were once part of a mining boom but have slowly lost their residents over the years. Like most ghost towns, feel free to look around and wonder what life must have been like for those that braved the elements and came to these remote areas with little more than a dream in their pocket. It's a fascinating part of history and well worth the stop.

Moving on, we're going to backtrack on Sandon Cody Rd toward HWY 31A. Once at HWY 31A, take a right for the remainder of this leg of our trip to Kaslo, which should take about an hour. Kaslo is a tiny lakeside village with some incredible opportunities for outdoor adventure, including boating, kayaking, sailboating and canoeing, and the surrounding mountains provide breathtaking views and challenging hikes. This sleepy village is also home to several important cultural sites, including the SS Moyie, the world's oldest intact passenger sternwheeler. This is a rare opportunity to climb aboard and enjoy an international treasure.

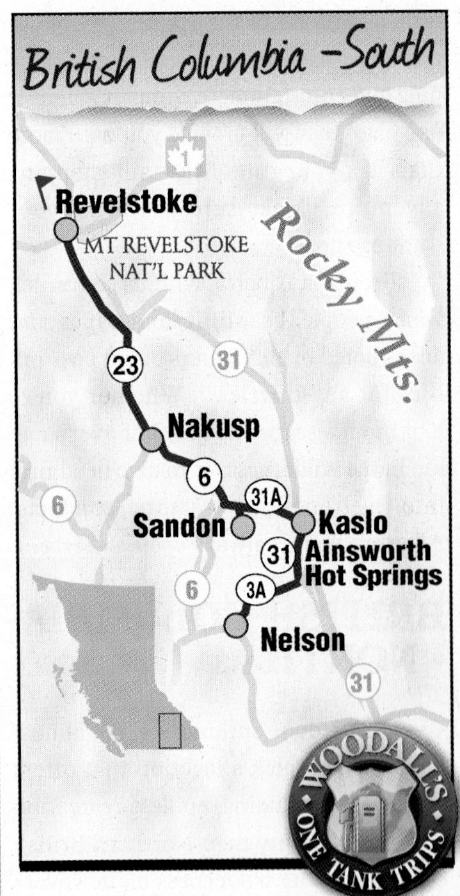

Heading out, take HWY 31 southeast out of Kaslo and right to the heart of Ainsworth Hot Springs. This part of our journey should take about 35 minutes. From its location along the Kootenay Lake, it's easy to see why so many travelers make their way to this inspiring location to recharge their worn down batteries. No matter what time of year you visit, it's sure to be an amazing experience.

Our last stop takes us back to HWY 31 heading southeast again and continuing onto HWY 3A/HWY 3B into Nelson. Nelson, by far, is one of the most eclectic places within British Columbia, offering an incredible arts community, as well as an impressive array of outdoor fun to get caught up in. With a downtown that is small, walkable, and filled with all sorts of goodies, there can be no better end to this trip than a little shopping, a little art, and a bite to eat at one of the excellent restaurants located here.

OTHER AREA LOCATIONS

BURNABY

Burnaby Cariboo RV Park

SURREY

Hazelmere RV Park & Campground

MANITOBA

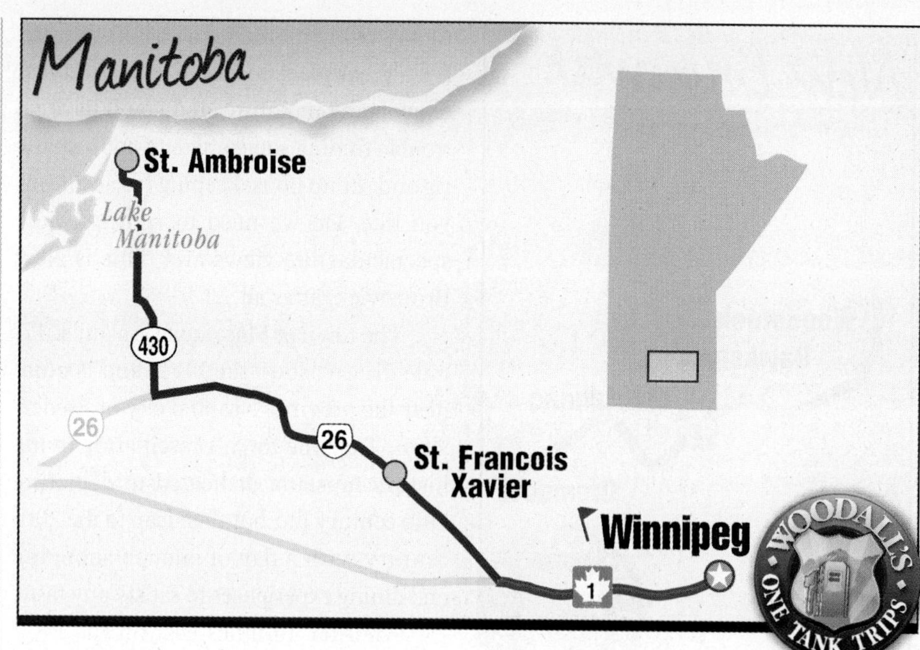

As the geographical heart of Canada, Manitoba is renowned for its dramatic, scenic landscapes, warm friendly people, and beautiful cultural heritage. Surprisingly, Manitoba is home to some of North America's most stunning beaches and lures travelers the world over wanting to catch a glimpse of the majestic polar bear, one of the most elusive and endangered creatures. With four distinct seasons, and a plethora to see and do, it's no wonder Manitoba is a top destination for many travelers. Whether you're looking for a total break from civilization, or want to divide your time between the old world and the modern, Manitoba can more than accommodate you.

Winnipeg is a good choice for a starting point. The province's capital city is filled with exciting things to occupy you, including a self-guided tour of Winnipeg's thriving arts and culture district, which is filled with museums and galleries showcasing every imaginable type of artwork. Fort Gibraltar is a fascinating place to visit, as costumed interpreters give you a glimpse into the days of the Canadian frontier and the fur trade. In June, the annual Cool Jazz Winnipeg festival draws thousands of attendees who enjoy listening to some of the world's finest jazz and blues artists in various clubs and theaters in, and around, town.

Travel 20 miles west on Highway 1 and you'll soon arrive at St. Francois Xavier, known by locals as "White Horse Plain." Once it was home to the Cree and Sioux tribes, but then was founded as a town in the late 1800s. Today, it remains relatively unchanged from the days of old. It's close enough to the big city's conveniences, but is rural enough for a relaxing getaway. The town is a terrific place to set up camp by the Assiniboine River, where you can fish, kayak, or go boating to your heart's content.

From St. Francois Xavier, drive northwest on the PR-430 for about 25 miles into St. Ambroise. This beachside community will provide you with ample opportunities to enjoy time in the sunshine. You can either stay on land and stroll down the boardwalk past the marshlands, where you'll be treated to glimpses of local wildlife including geese, pelicans and American finches, or take a canoe out to any of the local islets off shore. This is a west-facing beach, so prepare yourself for some truly awesome sunsets.

It's this mix of rural and metropolitan that keeps travelers coming back to Manitoba year after year, seeking that perfect blend of the wild and the civilized, the rural and the metropolitan; all within a short drive from each other. When you choose Manitoba, you'll witness this duality at work, and be amazed at how far removed you seem to be, while not really being so distant at all.

NEW BRUNSWICK

Located on the far eastern shore of Canada, New Brunswick is an enchanting cluster of provinces that are widely known for their rugged coastline and charming maritime culture. Filled with diverse landscapes and cultures, visitors will be swept away by the idyllic fishing villages, the bustling metropolitan areas, and the amazing natural beauty.

Starting off in Woodstock (which has the distinction of being New Brunswick's

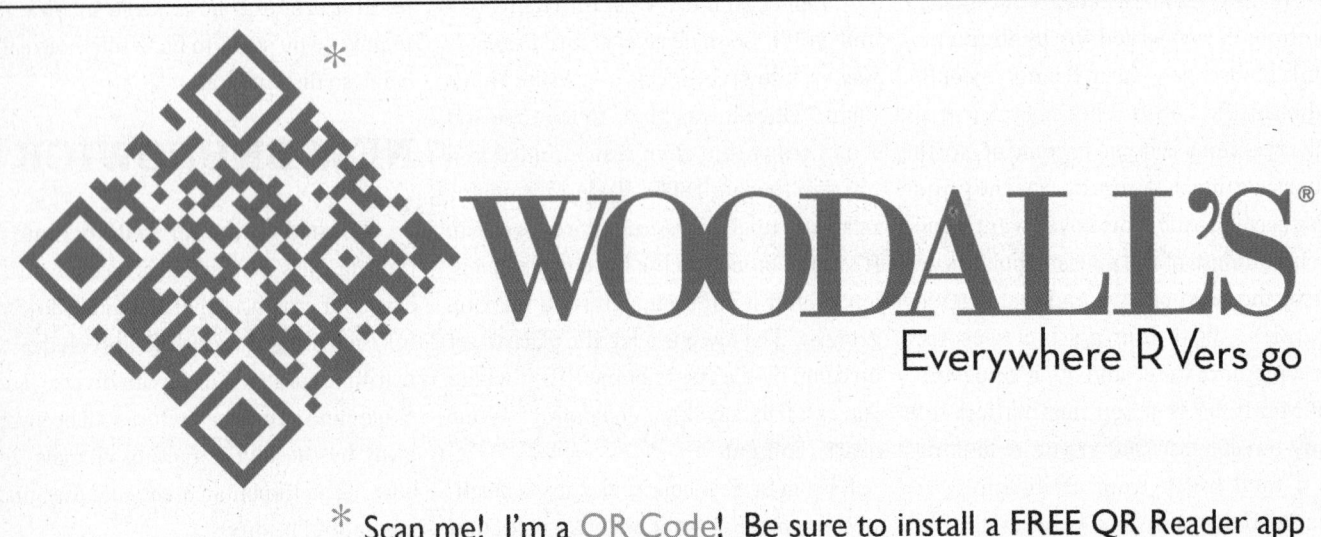

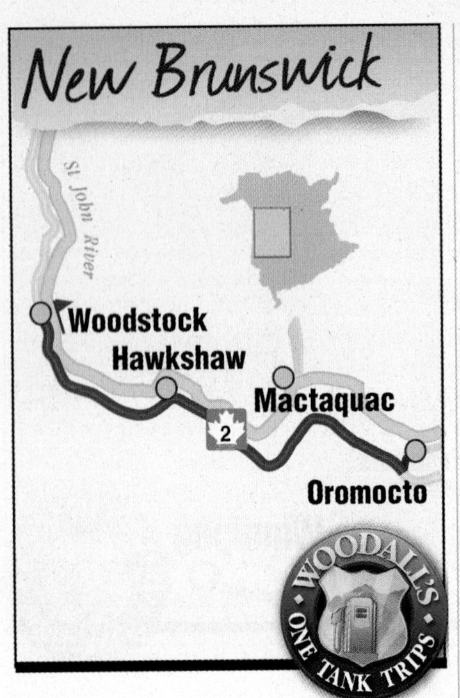

first town), you'll find a community rich in character and proud of its history. There are several Victorian homes available for touring, and both the Meduxnekeag and St. John's Rivers join near downtown Woodstock. Rent a paddleboat or kayak and take a cruise along the water's edge, or enjoy the view from any of the waterside eateries that serve some of the finest French food in Canada.

Getting out on the road, drive southeast on Provincial Route 2 for a little more than 20 miles, which will bring you into Hawkshaw. This area brings the quietness of a remote getaway, while remaining close to any conveniences you might require. It's a great place to set up camp and just enjoy being in nature, and you'll have no trouble finding somewhere to hook up the rig and set up housekeeping for as long as you like. Do we need to mention how spectacular the views are? This is New Brunswick, after all…

The town of Mactaquac is a quick 17-mile drive east on the PR-2, and is quite near the province's capital city of Fredericton. Tour the town's fascinating living history museum dedicated to depicting 19th century life, but then leap to the 20th century with a day of enough shopping and dining experiences to satisfy any taste.

Another 10 miles east on the PR-2 takes you to Oromocto, a small and beautiful community with a population of around 9,000. This town features a wide range of outdoor activities, from hiking and mountain biking trails, to fishing and camping. It's one of Canada's undiscovered jewels, so treat yourself and pay it a visit before everyone gets in on the act!

NEWFOUNDLAND

There are few places on this planet that can boast about remaining relatively untouched for thousands of years. And there are those of us that relish the opportunity to explore such places, while respecting the grace and beauty of the area. Newfoundland is one of those rare places. Rich in history, sprawling with natural beauty, and embraced by all of those lucky enough to happen upon this province, Newfoundland has a piece of heaven around every bend just waiting to be discovered by some fortunate traveler willing to take the leap.

This route runs east along Canada's Highway 1, and kicks off in the town of Grand Falls-Windsor. This community is renowned for being one of Newfoundland's chief tourist attractions and the home of Thunder Brook, a fantastic place to go fishing and swimming, and Beothuk Park, where you can experience the feeling of camping out in the wild while remaining close to modern conveniences.

In Bishop's Falls - which lies 11 miles to the east via Highway 1 - you can enjoy camping beside the Exploits River, with a fantastic view of the waterfalls for which the town is named. The Bishop's Falls Heritage Centre offers a variety of exhibits and artifacts showcasing the waterways, logging industry, and contributions to the sports industry that have stemmed from the town.

The town of Gander awaits you after a 40-mile eastbound drive through some truly eye-popping scenic countryside along Highway 1. Here you'll find the fishing waters to be rich and plentiful. No doubt you'll find the sunset views to be breathtaking, each one more beautiful than the previous one. Prepare to be enthralled by the peacefulness of the region, and allow at least a couple of days to savor the serenity.

Glovertown is your next stop, at the end of a 35-mile drive further east on Highway 1. This is a sailing community, situated right next to Bloody Bay Reach. Launch your boat along the waters, pack your rod and reel, and see how many tasty Atlantic salmon you can haul in for the day.

Angling south, but remaining on Highway 1 for 15 miles, brings you to your final stop, Terra Nova. Take a nature hike, visit the bogs and marshlands for some wildlife watching, or drop a kayak in the Atlantic waters and get a staggering view from offshore – just you, the sea, and the sunset. There are miles upon miles of hiking trails just waiting to be explored, and in the wintertime you can even go dogsledding!

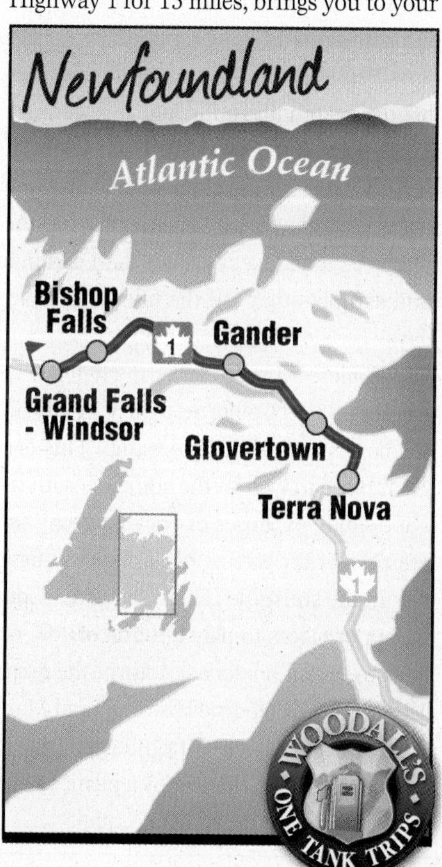

When you come to Newfoundland, prepare to be amazed. It's like a candy store for all five senses – minus the cavities and sticky fingers.

NOVA SCOTIA

Nova Scotia is widely known as a land of fun and adventure, but also of quietude and restoration. Renowned for its breathtaking beauty, Nova Scotia is a land filled with seaside inns, vineyards that dot the countryside, and an incredible amount of annual festivals. There is no bad time for a trip to this remarkable place, so let's get going; adventure awaits!

In Louisbourg, a particular highlight is the Fortress of Louisbourg, which served as a base of operations for the British and helped them achieve victory over the French in the 18th century. Now, it is a well-visited tourist attraction, and features large-scale reenactments of some of the battles the fortress has seen. If you plan your visit in early August, you can take part in the annual Crab Fest, a delicious festival celebrating all things crab-related, featuring the crustaceans cooked in all manner of mouth-watering ways.

Drive north on Highway 22 for 10 miles into Albert Bridge, a fantastic place

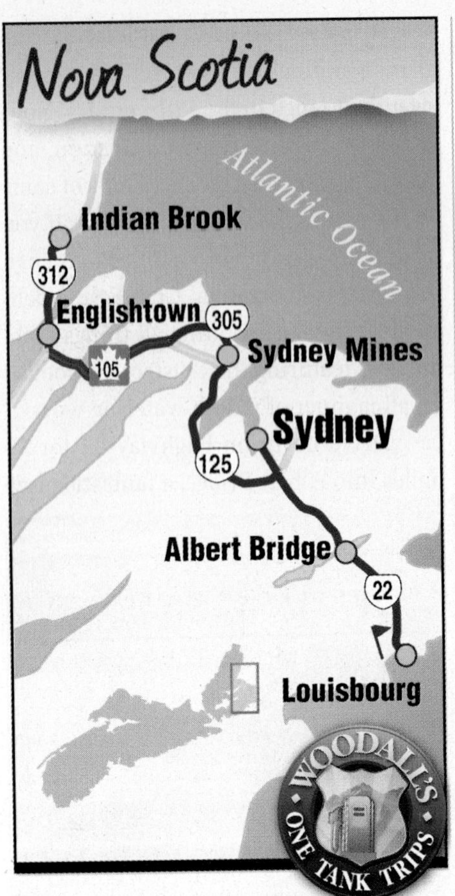

to set up camp and enjoy the outdoors. Located near Mira River, you'll have your pick of all kinds of water-based recreation. Nearby parks feature a multitude of hiking trails and bike paths for you to get some exercise and – if you brought your furry little four-legged friends along – go for a run!

A short 12-mile drive further north on Highway 22 takes you to Sydney, which has a wealth of activities to enjoy, ranging from orchestra performances to the Alexander Graham Bell Museum in nearby Baddeck. The Bras d'Or Lake is close by, if you fancy a day on, or near, the water with either a fishing pole in hand or a kayak carrying you across the surface. This area mixes the metropolitan with the rural in a very deft, and unique, fashion.

Head west on Highway 125 for 12 miles, then take the westbound 305 for another 3 miles into Sydney Mines. This quaint resort community features a selection of bed and breakfast inns, a thriving art culture, and some incredible Georgian architecture. Stroll through some of the most colorful and well-maintained English gardens to be found on this side of the Atlantic, then smack a few balls around at any of the local world-class golf courses.

Next stop, Englishtown. Bear west on Provincial Route 105 for 20 miles, then drive north on Highway 312 for the remaining 3 miles into town. This is the home of the Englishtown Mussel Fest, where you can stuff yourself silly with mussels, prepared every way imaginable (and a few ways that aren't!) The nearby Cabot Trail region will keep you occupied exploring its back country, so take a picnic lunch and enjoy the feeling of the sun on your face and the wind at your back.

Proceeding north on highway 312, a 5-mile drive takes you straight to the aforementioned Cabot Trail, which runs for 2 miles to your final stop, Indian Brook. Everywhere you look there are telltale signs of the local Indian tribes that once called this area home. Explore the nearby caves and take a walk along Bird Island, or kick back by the ocean and watch the ebb and flow of the Atlantic as it crashes onto the shoreline.

Nova Scotia is a land of rugged adventure, but brings with it a rarely seen element of style and sophistication guaranteed to appeal to travelers of all tastes.

ONTARIO - NIAGARA

Without a doubt, this amazing section of Ontario is one of the richest historical areas in all of Canada, preserved and readily available to those lucky enough to cross these borders. From wine routes and breathtaking gardens, to sandy beaches and quaint villages that offer exquisite culinary delights and wonderful artisan treasures; you'll find it here, all nestled within one of the most popular tourist destinations in Canada.

From Niagara Falls, head south on Highway 190 for 14 miles, then take the westbound Highway 3 for 6 more miles until you come to Ridgeway. This charming town gets quite a few tourists during the summer, who come to enjoy the quiet atmosphere and visit the local wineries. Fort Erie is a popular place to visit here, having been built in the late 18th century by British Imperial Loyalists, where it served them well in their war against the French. Today, it continues to serve the public as a history museum with exhibits and artifacts that tell the tale of its glory days.

A mere 13 miles west on Highway 3, you'll find Port Colborne, a thriving city on the banks of the Welland Canal. This is a great place to visit in the summer, with its wide sandy expanses of Nickel Beach that are perfect for getting out and enjoying a day in the sunshine. There's a water slide, plenty of places to play a round of golf, or sites to take a horseback tour of the area. Visit the Port Colborne Historical and Maritime Museum for an intriguing glimpse at the area's history, then enjoy a picnic lunch by the banks of the Welland Canal.

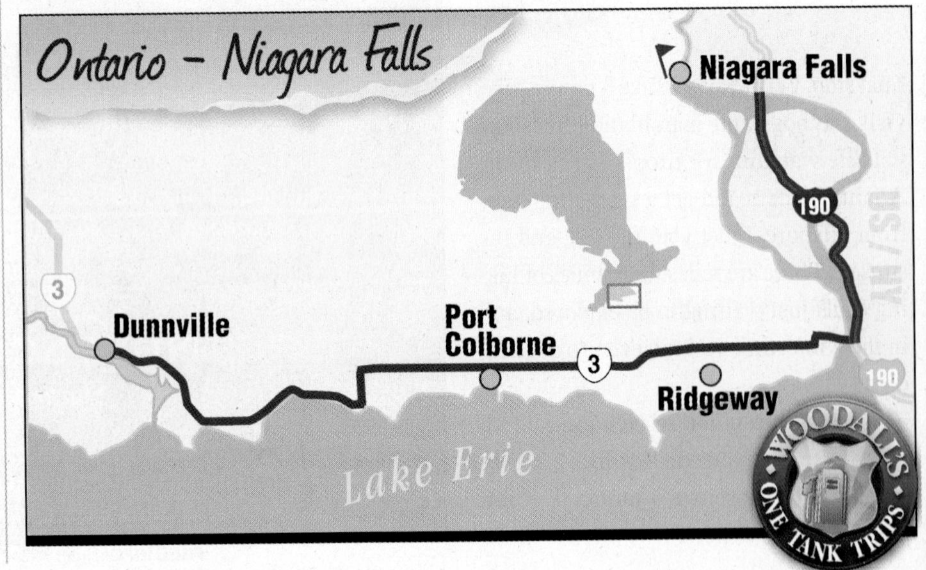

Dunnville awaits your arrival, located at the end of a westbound 20-mile drive across Highway 3. It's easily accessed from the U.S., being just an hour's drive north of the border. Lake Erie's just a short drive away as well, so this is a beautiful spot to put the rig in park and make camp. Dunnville is a quaint throwback to Victorian times, with streets lit by coachlight lanterns. There are several festivals and events going on throughout the year, such as June's yearly Mudcat Festival. This gala features parades, carnival attractions, and a nightly fireworks extravaganza. The Port Maitland Pier is a good place to take a leisurely stroll and look out over the waters, or take a wildlife hike through the Byng Island Conservation Area.

Once you've experienced Niagara Falls and its surrounding communities, you can't help but fall in love with the area. If this isn't your first time visiting, prepare to fall in love with the place all over again.

OTHER AREA LOCATIONS

CHERRY VALLEY
Quinte's Isle Campark
NIAGARA FALLS
Yogi Bear's Jellystone Park Camp-Resort
PORT COLBORNE
Sherkston Shores

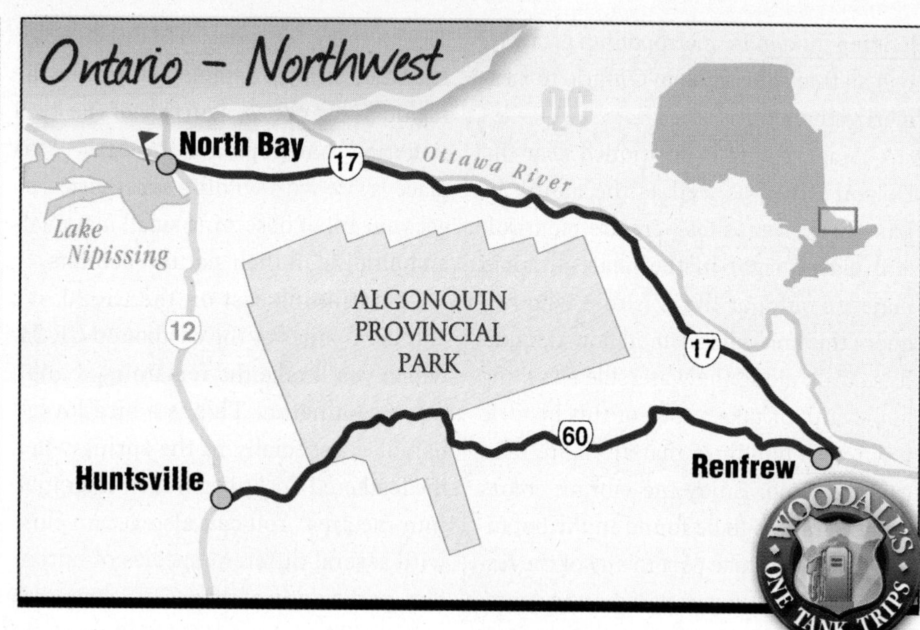

ONTARIO - NW LOOP

For the angler, this area of Ontario has long been known as the place to be for some of the most incredible fishing experiences imaginable, but it's quickly becoming a getaway for many other outdoor enthusiasts looking to immerse themselves in endless outdoor fun, set against landscapes fantastic enough to inspire both poets and painters alike. It's a destination like no other!

North Bay has been attracting tourists "in the know" for quite some time. Situated near Lake Nipissing, water sport enthusiasts venture here to go boating, water skiing, and kayaking in the summer, while in the winter the Laurentian Ski Hill is a big draw to snowboarders and skiers. No matter what time of year, there's plenty of opportunity to stretch your legs along the miles upon miles of trails near the waterfront.

Getting out on the road, the next leg of your journey takes you through 160 miles of mountains, grassy plains, and past beautiful rivers and streams. Highway 17 takes you east from North Bay to your next stop, Renfrew. Sitting beside the banks of the Bonnechere River, this quaint and friendly town is a frequent stopover point for visitors on their way to Ottawa. Whitewater rafting, golfing, and fishing are prevalent in the more temperate months, but in the winter you'll have a great time skiing, snowboarding, or just rolling around in the snow. Renfrew stages a variety of festivals throughout the year, including Valleyfest, a multiple-day event that celebrates over a century of Renfrew's contributions to the logging industry, and September's Renfrew Fair, which provides rides, attractions, and vendors with all types of food and live music.

Get your camera ready, because the next leg of your trip takes you along 150 miles of Ontario's back country, where all kinds of wildlife can be seen grazing by the roadside. At the end of this westbound cruise down Highway 60, your final stop on the route awaits: Huntsville. Somebody really knew what they were doing when they decided to build this town next to the Muskoka River, because not only are the water views gorgeous, but you can also rent a kayak or small boat from any of the local rental shops and spend some time testing your skill against the river, or just kick back along its banks in a lawn chair and a good book. If you didn't come prepared for an activity you'd like to try, there's no shortage of outfitters to fill in the blanks. The surrounding wilderness area is a big hit with hikers and campers, and the town itself has an eclectic array of shops and dining opportunities for when you're ready for a little city life.

This part of Ontario is all about enjoying life's little pleasures, which are the best and most precious of all.

ONTARIO - SOUTHEAST

As one of Canada's most heavily populated provinces, Ontario is also a prime destination for travelers because of its abundance of cultural and recreational activities and breathtaking beauty. Outdoor enthusiasts, sightseers, and those looking for a more metropolitan getaway, will all find something in Ontario to mesmerize them!

Amherstburg is positioned near the Detroit River, as well as the mouth of Lake Erie. Campsites here are plentiful, and placed right in the heart of some majestic outdoor life. Visitors who frequent this area comment on how tranquil it is. Walk along the waterside shopping boulevard, or take a tour of this historic town with buildings that are more than a century old. Enjoy the vibrant colors and fragrances to be found in the botanical garden, or take part in any of the festivals that are always going on in town. It's easy to see why this area is growing in popularity as a tourist destination.

Leaving Amherstburg via the eastbound CR-20, cruise along 24 miles until you come to Kingsville, which is within walking distance of Lake Erie. This charming town is filled to its borders with Victorian architecture, so feel free to walk through the streets and admire. Take a ferry for a day trip out to Pelee Island or enjoy a sample of some of the region's best wines, courtesy of the local wineries that populate the area. This place is rife with wildlife sanctuaries, so get your fill of observing small mammals and bird life in their natural habitats.

Continuing east on the CR-20, it's another 5 miles to the eastbound CR-34, which you'll take the remaining 3 miles into Leamington. This is a bird lover's paradise, especially in the spring when the feathered flocks begin their migration into the area. You can also get up close with several different species of butterflies, particularly of the majestic monarch variety. The Marina Park Promenade offers shops and dining, or you can drop a fishing line in the water from off the pier, or rent a boat and take a relaxing cruise across the water.

An eight-mile eastbound drive on the CR-34 brings you into Wheatley, your final stop on this route through southeast Ontario. In addition to being close to Lake Erie, Wheatley has several parks, with over 20 miles of trails that take you on a winding boardwalk path through forests and hills. This town is considered by bird watching enthusiasts to be the

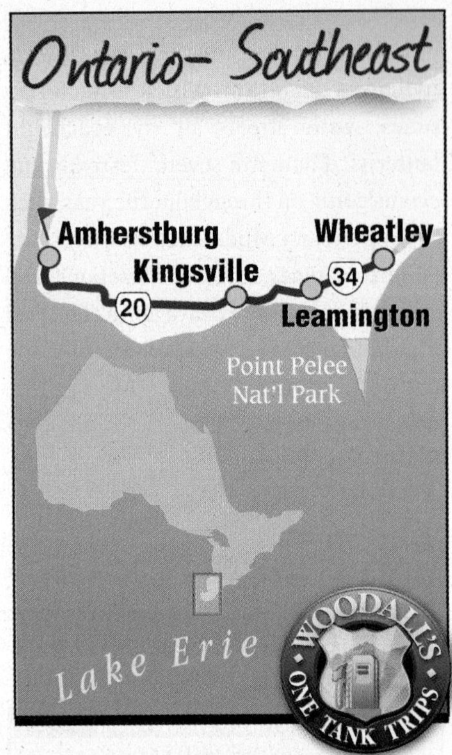

best spot in Ontario for spotting birds, and apparently the fish are biting pretty well here, too.

PRINCE EDWARD ISLAND

Prince Edward Island may be the smallest province in Canada, but it's by no means small in beauty, charm, or character. Travelers here will find some of the most awe-inspiring scenery in all of Canada, culinary delights that will tempt your taste buds and leave your mouth watering, and a relaxed pace and atmosphere that is sure to make anyone want to drop anchor and stay a while.

The trip starts in Wood Islands, which is easily accessed via Canada Highway 1. This is a small farming and fishing town, just a short ferry ride away from Caribou, Nova Scotia. Wood Islands is a great place to get away from it all, and enjoy the clean air and the ebb and flow of the tides. The Wood Islands Lighthouse and Museum features a fully functional lighthouse with eleven rooms, each with a different theme. One room is a meticulously recreated 1950s kitchen, another is filled entirely with "Sea Glass," which are oddities formed by the motion of the sea. Another room is devoted to the legend of the Phantom Burning Ship, which has allegedly been sighted in the Northumberland Strait.

From Wood Islands, head east for 12 miles on Provincial Route 4 until you pull into the town of Murray River. This is another place devoted to peace and quiet, located on the banks of the Murray River itself. Take a river cruise, or hike around the town and visit the surrounding wetlands for some excellent bird watching. The sunset views are truly spectacular, so sit back and prepare to feast your eyes on nature's magic.

Drive east for 4 miles on Highway 18 until you come to the next stop,

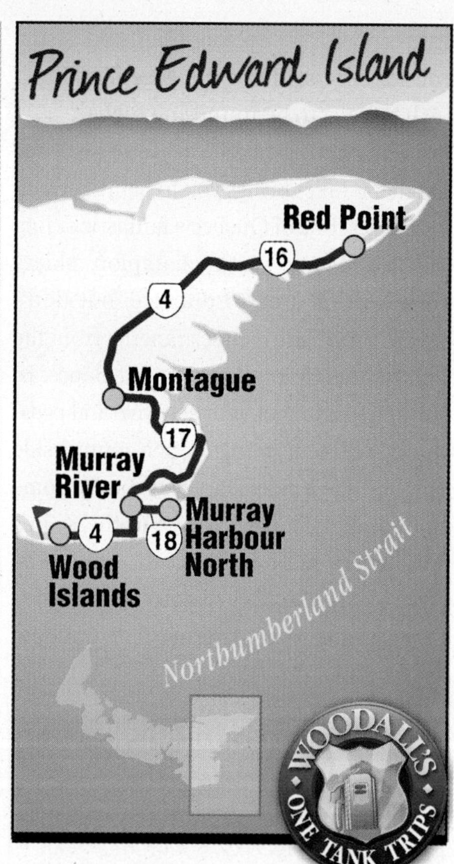

Murray Harbour North. Like many towns in the area, this is a fishing village, and there are many wharves and fisheries along the waterfront. From here, take Highway 17 north for 15 miles to Montague, a charming town bisected by the Montague River. Get a splendid view of the water from the bridge that connects the town's two halves, and if you plan your visit during Montague Days you'll see the town converted into a large carnival, with parades, traveling musicians, and fireworks.

From Montague, head north on Highway 4 for 3 miles, then merge with the northbound Highway 313 for 14 miles until you come to the eastbound Highway 16, which takes you the remaining 15 miles to the last stop on the route, Red Point. This area boasts some of the most magnificent white sand beaches on the island, and incredible ocean views. Set up camp and enjoy the serenity and calm that washes over you as you look out on the ocean, and let the tide take all your cares away.

Prince Edward Island is proud to be known as "The Gentle Island", and once you experience it, you'll understand why that moniker fits so perfectly.

OTHER AREA LOCATIONS
DARNLEY
Twin Shores Camping Area

QUEBEC

World renowned for its exceptional beauty, Quebec is a province steeped in tradition and history – a place where the past and the present are beautifully entwined, creating a destination filled with a European flair all its own.

Starting things off in Quebec City, you've got your choice of world-class museums, filled with art and sculpture ranging from classic to modern. This is one of the most romantic cities in the world, with a definite European flavor that is reminiscent of Paris or Prague. Take a river cruise down the St. Lawrence Seaway, or sample some exquisite cuisine at any of the five-star restaurants here in Quebec City.

Heading north on Route 138, you'll drive along 13 miles of Quebec's scenic route until you come to your next stop, L'Ange-Gardien. This predominantly French-speaking community is a winter wonderland during the latter part of the year, resembling many towns in the French Alps. The rest of the time, it's home to some of the most picture-postcard scenery you'll find anywhere. The Du Lievre River runs through the city, providing opportunities for fishing and kayaking, and local wineries provide excellent vintages to please even the most discriminating palates.

From here, it's onward to Ste-Anne-De-Beaupre, which awaits you 10 miles further north on Route 138. The sanctuary here is the site of the oldest pilgrimage in all of North America, and is a magnificent place to tour, regardless of religious affiliation. The Gothic architec-

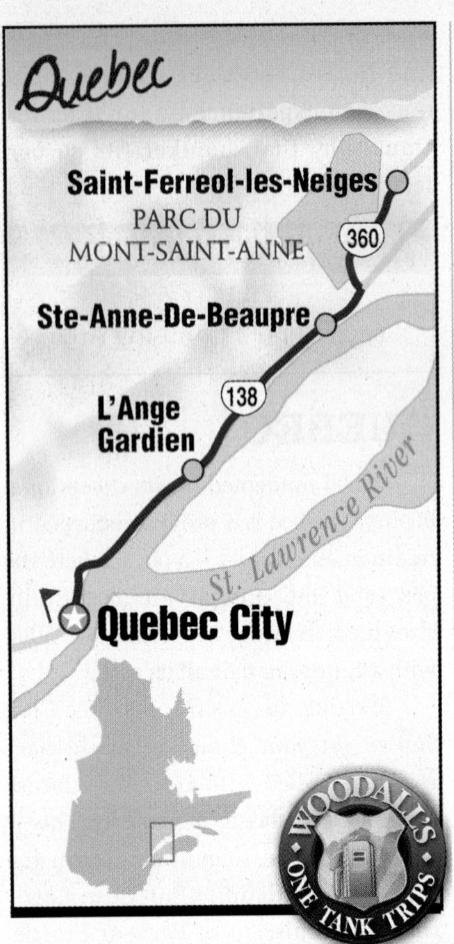

ture is positively eye-popping, and is surrounded by some of the greenest, most lush terrain to be found in Quebec.

Continuing north on Route 138 for another 3 miles brings you to Saint-Ferreol-les-Neiges, one of Quebec's fantastic skiing villages. Many world-champion skiers come to this area to practice, but don't worry – there are courses ranging from the bunny runs to serious downhill slopes. In spring and summer, rent a bicycle and pedal through this charming French countryside village. Take a picnic lunch and savor some fine, locally produced wine and cheese in a soft green meadow, or just enjoy the embrace of Mother Nature from your campsite and revel in the absolute tranquility this town provides.

OTHER AREA LOCATIONS

BROMONT

Camping du Village Bromont RV Resort

SAINT-MATHIEU-DE-BELOEIL

Camping Alouette Inc

SASKATCHEWAN

Nestled between Alberta and Manitoba, Saskatchewan lies in the heart of the Canadian Prairies. Beautifully rural and forested, Saskatchewan is infectious. With so much wide, open sky, this amazing province leaves every visitor with a sense of calm that will invariably draw them back to explore all of the beauty and cultural diversity that makes this area so unique.

Today, our trip starts in Weyburn, a definite charmer of a city, and host to some incredible possibilities for some outdoor fun. Travelers will find no shortage of hiking, camping, and golfing in the area. For the culture seeker, Weyburn is host to some interesting sights, like the King George Hotel, which was once riddled with bullets by Billy the Kid. And of course, you won't want to leave Weyburn without a stop to the Soo Line Historical Museum, which houses a wide display of theme items, from old general store products, to agricultural and mental hospital displays. Both fascinating and educational!

Let's head out to our next stop - Estevan - by heading south on Govern-

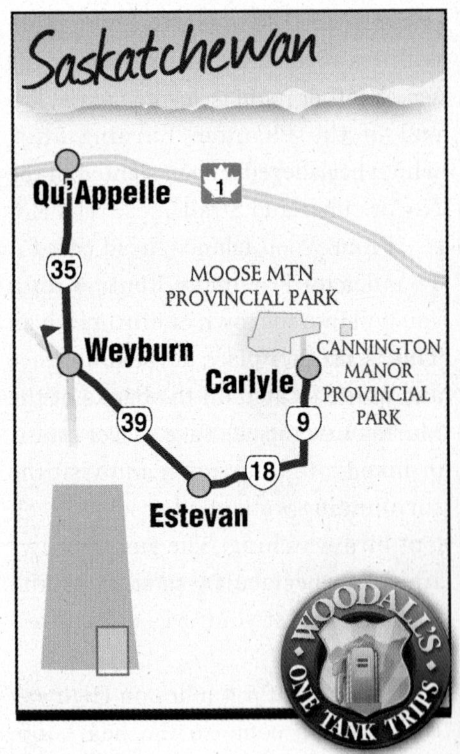

ment Rd, and taking a left at HWY 39. In a little over an hour, you should be smack in the middle of Estevan, the eighth largest city in the province. For anglers and boating enthusiasts, head over to the Boundry or Rafferty Dam. Both are favorites of the locals, and ideal fishing spots. To immerse yourself in local history, head over to the Souris Valley Museum where you'll encounter an array of historical artifacts. To discover why Estevan is also known as "Energy City", tours can be taken of local power stations and greenhouse. It's an entertaining tour, and one that just might surprise you.

Moving on to our last stop, take HWY 47 out of Estevan, and take a right onto HWY 13. Small and peaceful, Carlyle is located just south of Moose Mountain Provincial Park, one of Saskatchewan's five original provincial parks. The town has had a status as a vacation spot well before its establishment in 1931. Visitors are surrounded by the beauty of aspen, white birch and ash trees, and within the park there are multiple opportunities for hiking, fishing, cooling off in the big waterslide complex, horseback riding, and even golf and tennis. The local casino draws quite a crowd and there are quite a few first-class restaurants to dine in, and wonderful shops to peruse. If you want to extend your trip just a little further past Carlyle, stop by the Cannington Manor Provincial Park. Once the dream of British settlers to build a society on Victorian social values complete with poetry clubs and fox hunts, Cannington manor enjoyed a brief, but successful life prior to the 1900s. Today, you can wander through period buildings and original artifacts, and costumed staff are onsite to bring the whole experience to life through demonstrations and interpretive programs.

The beauty of the Saskatchewan prairie has a way of instilling a gentle calm from the very moment you visit. Here, within this province, time seems to slow down, making for a relaxing, one-of-a-kind experience.

YUKON TERRITORIES

If you're looking for an adventure that will test you, try you and inspire you, the Yukon Territories are the place you'll want to plan your next trip. Make no mistake; this area is the northern gem of Canada, but also one of the most rugged areas in the world, reserved especially for those of us looking to come nose-to-nose with Mother Nature and all she has to offer.

Today we begin in Yukon's capital, Whitehorse, whose long history is owed mostly to the boom of the Klondike Gold Rush of the late 19th Century. As remote as it is beautiful, Whitehorse welcomes thousands of visitors who come to marvel at the 24-hour sunlight and pay a visit to the Yukon Beringia Interpretive Centre. A fascinating place, the Interpretive Centre tells the tale of the first arctic people of North America, giant mammals and ice that covered the land, and interpretive information and dioramas. Another highlight you should be sure to take in is the MacBride museum, which spans a whopping four city blocks and features some incredible moments in history of the Yukon region.

Moving on, take Alaska Hwy/HWY 1 out of Whitehorse and make a right onto HWY 2/S Klondike Hwy. This leg of the trip should take you approximately an hour-and-a-half, weather permitting. Located on the north end of Bennett Lake and at the mouth of the Natasaheenie River, Carcross is a year-round destination for travelers seeking the peaceful beauty of the mountainous area that surrounds it. Your outdoor recreation possibilities are endless in Carcross, with the summer months bringing boating, canoeing, fishing, hiking, biking, and a whole list of other

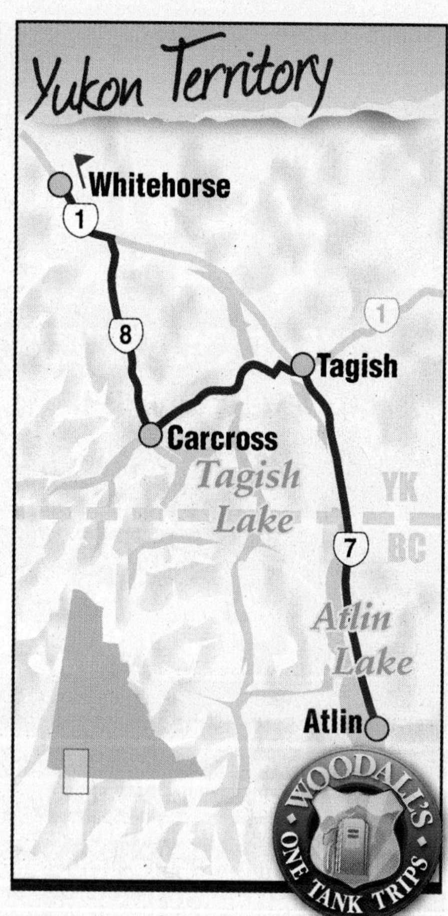

goodies. Let's head out to our last stop, Tagish. Taking Carcross Hwy/HWY 8 out of Carcross, this leg of the trip should take you around 40 minutes. Tagish, in Athabascan means "fish trap", and with a local lake bearing the same name, you can bet there is some good fishing to be had in these waters! Measuring some 60 miles long, Tagish Lake is one of the most popular trout fishing areas within the Territories, and if fishing doesn't do much for you, there is a list of other activities to do in scenic Tagish, including hiking, boating, biking, skiing, and kayaking, just to name a few. If you're feeling more than a little adventurous, there are several dogsledding outfitters that will take you out from one hour, to several days (if you really want a once-in-a-lifetime experience).

For first timers, the Yukon is alarmingly beautiful, inspiring, and has all the wild adventure you can handle. If you really have the urge to get away from it all, you've come to the right place.

RV VIEW
ODYSSEY

CAMPING WORLD
$5 OFF
any purchase of $50 or more
Cannot be combined with any other offer. Regular President's Club 10% discount applies. Offer redeemable at Camping World SuperCenters and through call center only. Not redeemable for cash. Good one time only. Offer is not retroactive. Mention this coupon at time of purchase. Limit one per customer.
Offer expires 12/31/11.
Discount Code: 1412

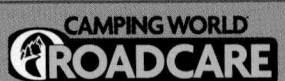

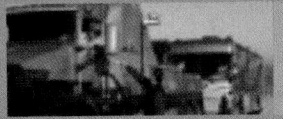

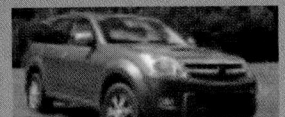

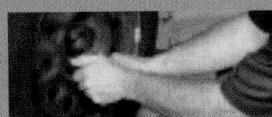

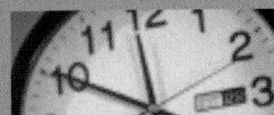

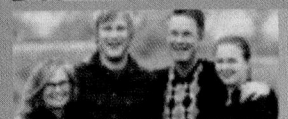

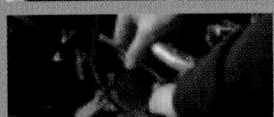

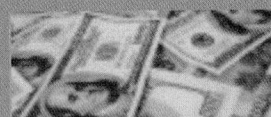

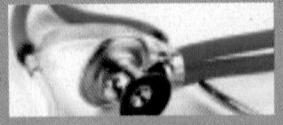

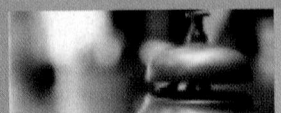

CAL-AM RESORTS
Arizona RV Resorts™

If You Run Out Of Things To Do, We Have Some More...

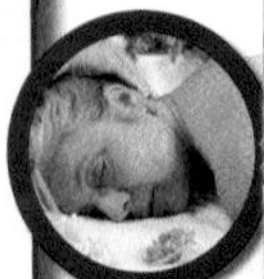

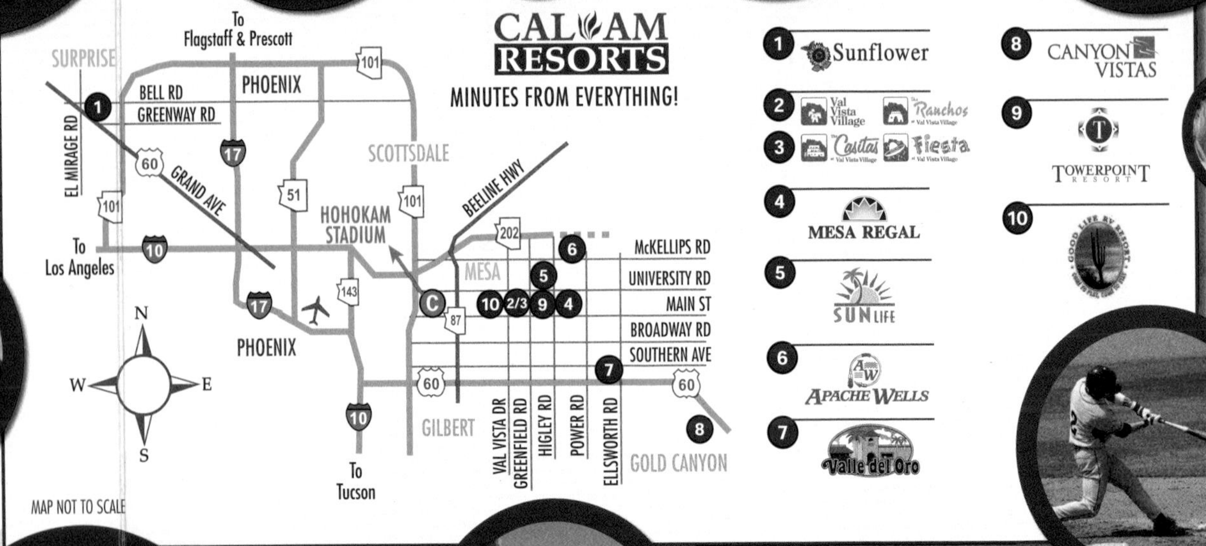

CAL AM RESORTS
MINUTES FROM EVERYTHING!

To Flagstaff & Prescott
SURPRISE
BELL RD
GREENWAY RD
PHOENIX
EL MIRAGE RD
GRAND AVE
SCOTTSDALE
BEELINE HWY
HOHOKAM STADIUM
To Los Angeles
MESA
McKELLIPS RD
UNIVERSITY RD
MAIN ST
BROADWAY RD
SOUTHERN AVE
PHOENIX
GILBERT
To Tucson
VAL VISTA DR
GREENFIELD RD
HIGLEY RD
POWER RD
ELLSWORTH RD
GOLD CANYON
MAP NOT TO SCALE

1 Sunflower
2 Val Vista Village; Los Ranchos at Val Vista Village
3 Casitas at Val Vista Village; Fiesta at Val Vista Village
4 MESA REGAL
5 SUN LIFE
6 APACHE WELLS
7 Valle del Oro
8 CANYON VISTAS
9 TOWERPOINT RESORT
10 GOOD LIFE RV RESORT

Cal-Am's Arizona RV Resorts Have it ALL!

If any place on earth could be described as a vacation wonderland, it's Arizona. From the breathtaking vistas of the Grand Canyon and Sedona, to the old west history of Prescott, Tombstone and Bisbee you could spend a lifetime here and never see it all. Arizona has long been a destination and haven for visitors from around the world. Cal-Am's Arizona RV Resorts are centrally located near Phoenix in the lush Valley of the Sun allowing you to explore the local entertainment, shopping, sporting and recreational events or venture out on day trips to dozens of exciting destinations. When you stay at a Cal-Am Resort you're literally surrounded by enjoyment!

Call 888.940.8989 or visit www.cal-am.com/resorts

Look for Cal-Am Resort specific information in the Arizona section.

How to Use This Directory

Find it Quickly!

WOODALL'S Campground Directory
is organized alphabetically:
First by U.S. state
Then by Canadian province
Followed by Mexico.

Under these categories, the information is alphabetized by town. Each town name is followed by a letter and number (i.e., A-1) which refers to a grid coordinate on the maps found at the beginning of each state or province.

The campgrounds, RV sales/service centers and attractions/tourism locations are alphabetized under those towns.

Travel Sections are found at the beginning of each state/province

Each state/province begins with travel information and a map, both of which are updated annually. The sole purpose of the state/provincial maps is to show towns where campgrounds (indicated by diamonds ◆), attractions/tourism locations (indicated by flags ⚑), RV sales/service centers (indicated by gears ✿) and CampClub USA parks (indicated by the CampClub USA logo) are located.

We recommend that you always travel with an official state or provincial highway map or a current road atlas. The WOODALL maps are meant to help you identify towns where parks, attractions and/or RV sales/service centers are located. Use them in conjunction with the listings to plan your travel itinerary.

The North American Split

The North American edition is split into Eastern and Western sections, each organized alphabetically starting with Alabama in the East and Alaska in the West. At the end of each section, you'll find an alphabetical index of all facilities listed in that section. The "WOODALL Alphabetical Quick Reference" provides the name of each listed campground/RV park, RV sales/service center or attraction/tourism location — in name order. It's useful when you know the name of the location you want to visit, but don't remember the town under which it's listed. Symbols in front of each name indicate the availablilty of ® RV /park trailer rentals; ∅ tent rentals; □ cabin rentals; ★ RV sales/service centers; ● attractions/tourism locations. You'll also find the map coordinate after each town name for ease in using our maps. Find it quickly at the end of the Eastern and the end of the Western sections.

WOODALL Representatives make Personal Inspections

All privately-owned RV parks/campgrounds are personally inspected each year by one of our 25 Rep Teams. **Their detailed inspection reports provide the listing information and recommend the WOODALL ratings. These WOODALL Rep Teams have had years of RVing experience before joining WOODALL'S. They are professionally trained and are brought together each year for additional training. The privately-operated RV park/campground listings in this Directory are based upon Rep Teams' personal inspections made in the spring and summer of 2010. In addition to compiling information on a detailed listing form for each park, the Rep Teams also complete an evaluation form (sample shown on pages IV and V) to recommend the ratings.**

Our Rep Teams also personally visit and gather information on RV sales/service centers and attractions/toursim locations. Those listed in this Directory are the facilities particularly interested in your business.

The listings for government campgrounds (federal, state, provincial, municipal and military) are based upon information collected from public resources.

WOODALL'S Dual Rating System

What do all those ◆s mean?

Ratings help you choose the park you are looking for.

WOODALL'S assigns two ratings to each privately-owned campground/RV park. One rating is assigned to the facilities at the park (sites, roads, service buildings, restrooms, hookups, etc.). A separate recreation rating is also assigned. Both facilities and recreation ratings range from 1◆ to 5◆. (This ◆ is WOODALL'S copyrighted rating symbol.) Keep in mind the final ratings are a composite of several different areas of interest.

The WOODALL Rating System is detailed on pages IV and V with an example of how our representatives complete an evaluation form.

What do the Woodall Ratings indicate?

Ratings depend on the quality and quantity of our criteria elements. The more ◆s a park has generally reflects the presence of more development at the park, and usually more facilities. HOWEVER, THE MAINTENANCE OF THE CAMPGROUND WEIGHS HEAVILY IN ALL RATINGS ASSIGNMENTS. Cleanliness is a major factor in determining if you and your family will have an enjoyable vacation. The maintenance level at a park must meet or exceed the recommended ratings or the rating cannot be assigned at that level.

Do more ◆s mean a better park?

Emphatically, NO! The WOODALL rating system does NOT indicate good, better, best. Each RV/camping family needs to decide how much development is going to make their trip enjoyable. WOODALL lists a wide range of parks from rustic, natural settings to resort-like RV parks. Different factors may make a park attractive: convenience to the Interstate; width of sites; located near a popular attraction; a swimming pool, lake or other on-site recreation. Please take the time to understand the WOODALL Rating System and consider the ratings, along with other factors, when choosing the parks in which you want to stay. Be sure to read the listings carefully to make sure they have the facilities and amenities you want, and be sure to let the park owner know you found them in WOODALL'S.

How to Use This Directory

WOODALL'S features 7 Different Types of Listings

The top line of every listing identifies the type of listing.

Privately-owned campgrounds are rated.

(SW) BUTTONWOOD BAY—(Highlands) *From jct Hwy 17 & US 27 & 98: Go 5 mi S on US 27. Enter on R.*

◆◆◆◆◆ FACILITIES: 534 Sites, typical site width 40 ft, 534 full hkups, (30/50 amps), cable TV ($), Wi-Fi instant internet at site, phone/cable on-site, internet (needs activ), phone internet central location, dump station, laundry, ice, picnic tables, patios.

◆◆◆◆◆ RECREATION: rec hall, rec room/area, pavilion, 2 swim pools, boating, ramp, dock, lake fishing, mini-golf, golf nearby, bskball, 14 shuffleboard courts, activities, tennis, horseshoes, sports field, hiking trails, v-ball, local tours.

Pets welcome, breed restrict, quantity restrict. Partial handicap access. No tents. Age restrictions may apply. Open all yr. Big rigs welcome. Escort to site. Clubs welcome. Green friendly. Rate in 2010 $36-56 for 2 persons. MC/VISA/DISC. CCUSA discount.

Phone: (866) 655-5565
Address: 10001 US 27 S.,
Sebring, FL 33876
Lat/Lon: 27.40710/-81.41693
Email: sunresv@aol.com
Web: www.buttonwoodbay.com

SEE AD TRAVEL SECTION PAGE 73

✔ ADVERTISER LISTING:

Name is in dark, all capital letters. Shown with a Welcome diamond at the beginning of the listing.

Advertisers Want Your Business

The listings in this Directory are provided at no charge to the campground owner. Any campground which meets our minimum criteria requirements receives a listing. Many campground owners want to tell you more about their campground than the listing includes. These campgrounds have purchased advertising for that purpose. These ads can be a great help to you in choosing where to stay – they describe the special features and uniqueness of that campground. They can also tell you about nearby attractions, shopping and restaurants. Remember to say you "saw them in WOODALL'S."

(SW) Sunnyvale RV Resort—(Pinal) *From jct I-10 (exit 194) & Hwy 287: Go 7 mi E on Hwy 287, then 1 1/4 mi S on Eleven Mill Corner Rd, then 1/2 mi E on Sunscape Way. Enter on L.* ◆◆◆ FACILITIES: 215 sites, typical site width 28 ft, 159 full hkups, 56 E (30 & 50 amps), dump station, laundry. ◆◆◆ RECREATION: swim pool, boating, canoeing, ramp, dock, play equipment. Partial handicap access. No tents. Open mid Sep thru early May. Big rigs welcome. No pets. Green friendly. Age restrict may apply. Rate in 2010 $20 per vehicle. Phone: (555)429-0490.

✔ PRIVATE CAMPGROUND (NON-ADVERTISER):

Name is in dark type, capital and lower case letters.

COPAKE FALLS AREA (Taconic SP)—*From business center: Go 13 mi NE on Hwy 22 & Hwy 344.* FACILITIES: 112 sites, 22 ft. max RV length, 112 no hkups, tenting, dump station, tables. RECREATION: river swimming, boating, canoeing, river fishing, playground. No pets. Green friendly. Open mid May thru mid Dec. Phone: (555)329-3993.

✔ PUBLICLY-OWNED CAMPGROUND:

Operated by a federal, state or local government agency. Name appears in light capital letters.

MILITARY PARK (Lake Martinez Recreation Area-Yuma MCAS)—*Off base. Located on Colorado River, off US 95.* FACILITIES: 20 sites, 17 W & E, 3 no hkups, tenting. RECREATION: lake swimming, boating, fishing. Open all yr. Reservations required. For Military Use Only- w/ Military ID Card. Phone: (555)341-2278.

✔ MILITARY CAMPGROUND:

Career-military personnel and U.S. Dept. of Defense personnel (active or retired) may camp at these parks. Proper ID is required for admittance. Call ahead to ensure eligibility.
Note: use the Alphabetical Quick Reference to locate these parks — look under "M" for MILITARY PARK.

⚑(E) JUSTIN'S WATER WORLD—*From jct I-10 & I-19: Go 1 1/2 mi S on I-19, then 9 mi W on Hwy 86 (Ajo Way), then 2 1/2 mi NW on San Joaquin Rd. Enter on R.* Eight swimming pools and seven giant slides in the rural Sonoran Desert. Located adjacent to Saguaro National Park. Open late May thru late Aug.

Phone: (866) 883-8340
Address: 3451 S. San Joaquin Rd.,
Tucson, AZ 85735
Lat/Lon: 32.18106/-111.15085
Email: info@justinswater.com
Website: www.justinswaterworld.com

SEE AD PAGE 42

✔ ATTRACTIONS AND TOURISM LOCATIONS (ADVERTISER FORMAT):

Identified by a flag symbol. Also shown with a Welcome diamond at the beginning of the listing.

✱(W) 1 STOP AUTOMOTIVE & RV REPAIR—*From jct I-40 (exit 48) & Historic Route 66/Business I-40 (W Beale St.): Go 100 feet S on Historic Route 66. Enter on L.* SERVICES: full-time mech, engine/chassis repair, RV appliance repair, body work/collision repair, LP gas by meter. Open all yr. MC/VISA/DISC/AMEX.

Phone: (928) 718-1400
Address: 290 Metacalfe Rd.,
Kingman, AZ 86401
Lat/Lon: 32.19122/-114.06528
Email: info@1stoprv.com
Website: www.1stoprv.com

SEE AD THIS PAGE

✔ RV SALES/SERVICE CENTER (ADVERTISER FORMAT):

Identified by a gear symbol. Also shown with a Welcome diamond at the beginning of the listing.

✱(S) Giant RV World—*From jct I-495 (exit 6) & US-44: Go 3 mi W on US 44. Enter on R.* SALES: travel trailers, 5th wheels, toy haulers, Class A motor homes, Class C motor homes, Class B motor homes, fold-down camping trailers, pre-owned unit sales. SERVICES: full-time mech, engine/chassis repair, RV appliance repair, body work/collision repair, LP gas by weight/by meter, RV storage, sells parts/accessories. Open all yr. MC/VISA/DISC/AMEX. Phone: (508)555-3338. FMCA discount.

✔ RV SALES/SERVICE CENTER (NON-ADVERTISER FORMAT):

Identified by a gear symbol.

Abbreviation Key

You'll see a few selected abbreviations incorporated into some of our listings. Our editors have made every attempt to keep them simple and easy to read and understand.

mech	mechanic
emerg rd svc	emergency road service
L	left
R	right
W	water
E	electric
v-ball	volleyball
bsktball	basketball
hkups	hookups
need activ	needs activation
yr	year
wkends	weekends
Auth	Authority
BLM	Bureau of Land Management
COE	Corps of Engineers
Cons	Conservation
NF	National Forest
NP	National Park
NRA	National Recreation Area
PF	Provincial Forest
PP	Provincial Park
Reg	Regional
SF	State Forest
SNA	State Natural Area
SP	State Park
SRA	State Recreation Area

A word about camping fees...

Neither WOODALL'S nor the campground operator intends the published rate as a guaranteed rate. These rates were gathered by WOODALL Representatives during their inspections in 2010. The rates will almost always be higher by the time you get there because operators' costs have increased just like those of any other business. Rates are provided to give you a comparative overview of the camping fees within a general area. The fee will most often be shown as a range of rates for either a specific number of persons, a family (2 adults, 2 children) or per vehicle. The range represents the low to high ranges and may or may not include hookups.

How to Use This Directory

How to read the listings

1. WELCOME:
The Welcome symbol before a listing identifies those parks that have purchased an advertisement because they want to tell you more about their business.

2. FACILITIES:
The ratings range from 1 to 5 ◈s. All of the facilities listed are available on site.

3. PARTIAL HANDICAP ACCESS:
Indicates the park has been adapted in one or more ways to accommodate RVers/campers with disabilities. May include showers with benches and handrails, sinks and toilets that allow wheelchair access, wide doorways with no curbs or steps, wheelchair ramps, signs on buildings and/or hiking trails printed in Braille, TDD equipment, etc. If you or a family member has special needs, please call ahead to determine the type of services/facilities available.

4. TENT/RV/PARK TRAILERS/ CABIN RENTALS:
You may rent a tent, RV/park trailer or cabin at this park.

5. RECREATION:
The ratings range from 1 to 5 ◈s. All recreation listed is available right at the campground.

6. RATE INFORMATION:
Most often this will show as a range of rates from low to high which the privately-owned campground charged in 2009 (the year in which these inspections were made). THESE ARE NOT GUARANTEED RATES.

7. NATIONAL AND STATE/ PROVINCIAL CAMPGROUND AFFILIATION:
This directory identifies the campgrounds which belong to the National Association of RV Parks & Campgrounds (ARVC) and also those which are members of U.S. state or Canadian province campground associations.

8. ADVERTISER REFERENCE:
This line will refer you to the specific page for this listing's advertisement.

9. CONTACT THE PARK:
Easy, at-a-glance information. This highly visible section gives you everything you need to contact and research the park.

10. DISCOUNTS:
KOA-10% Value Card Discount, CCUSA, FCRV & FMCA Discounts are shown.

11. ADDITIONAL INFO:
Information such as age restrictions, operating season and pet policy. If the listing reads "no pets" then the park has a strict policy that prevents RVers from bringing pets of any kind on the premise. If the listing reads "pets welcome" this indicates the park does accept some pets. ($) indicates charges for pets. If you are traveling with a large or unusual pet, or with several pets, we recommend you call ahead to be sure your pet is welcome. If your 6-foot iguana is your best pal, call ahead to make sure he'll be welcome.

12. BIG RIGS WELCOME:
Factors evaluated by WOODALL Requirements are: minimum 50 amps, road width, overhead access clearance, site clearance to accommodate the tallest and widest rigs built. Often, not every site at the park can accommodate a big rig, so we recommend you call ahead for availability.

13. CLUBS WELCOME:
If the park's management welcomes camping clubs, we'll indicate that in the listing.

14. TENTING:
This campground welcomes tenters. NOTE: Tenters are welcome at most campgrounds. If a campground does not have facilities for tenters, its listing will indicate "no tents" in the special info section or "accepts full hookup units only" in the facilities section.

15. DIRECTIONS/ENTRANCE:
Detailed, easy-to-read locator directions to guide you right to the park entrance. Directly following these directions, we tell you whether the park's entrance is on the left, right, or at the end of the street.

16. MAP COORDINATES:
Matching grids on each state/provincial map help you to locate the listing town.

17. TYPICAL SITE WIDTH/ MAX RV LENGTH:
Most parks have sites of varying sizes. The listing shows the most commonly occurring site width at a park. The maximum length of RV (excluding the tow vehicle) that the campground can accommodate is shown (if under 40 ft.). Factors are turns, access and site sizes, based on the skills of an average RVer.

18. INTERNET ACCESS:
More and more RVers are staying in touch via email and utilizing the Internet. This has prompted many parks to provide Internet access at their sites and/or at a central location in the park, usually in the office or rec hall area. ($) indicates a fee may apply. Some site hookups may need activation by a service provider or the local phone/cable company before you can use them. Others noted "Instant Internet access" are immediately available.

19. COUNTY:
This appears in parentheses after the park name. May be useful when severe weather occurs as you travel, since most broadcast weather warnings are given by county.

24 **PEACEFUL VALLEY – A-2** 16

(NW) **CAREFREE CAMPING RV PARK**—(DuPage) 19

1 WELCOME *From jct I-94 (exit 24) & Hwy 120: Go 1/2 mi N on Hwy 120 (Golden Eagle Road), then 4 mi W on Hwy 80, then 1 mi N on Carefree Rd. Enter on R.* 15

JUST LIKE NEW!
We've completely renovated our park for this season! Come relax in our new swimming pool or take advantage of our deluxe new bathhouses. Don't miss our annual festivities such as Christmas in July & end-of-season pig roast. 23

2 ◈◈◈◈◈ FACILITIES: 320 sites, typical site width 40 ft, 175 full hkups, 100 W & E, 25 E, (20/30/50 amp), 50 amps ($), 20 no hkups, some extd stay sites, 50 pull-thrus, heater not allowed, cable TV, Wi-Fi Instant Internet at site ($), phone/cable on-site Internet (needs activ), cable Internet access central location, family camping, tenting, RV/park model rentals, cabins, dump, non-guest dump ($), laundry, groceries, LP gas by weight/meter, LP bottle exch, ice, picnic tables, wood. 17 18 4 25 14 21

5 CAMPCLUB USA 26 ◈◈◈◈◈ RECREATION: rec hall, equipped pavilion, coin games, 2 swim pools, wading pool, lake swim, hot tub, boating, 10 motorboat rentals, lake fishing, fishing supplies, mini-golf ($), 25 bike rentals, playground, activities, tennis, hiking trails, local tours. 3

11 Pets welcome, breed restrict, size restrict, quantity restrict ($). Partial handicap access. Escort to site. Open all year. Big rigs welcome. Clubs welcome. Green friendly. Rate in 2010 $18.50-23.50 per family. MC/VISA/DISC/AMEX. ATM. Member of ARVC. FCRV discount. FMCA discount. 12 6 20 22 13 27 10 7

Phone: (999)555-6200.
Address: 27 Carefree Rd., Zephyr Hills, FL 34875 9
LAT/LON: 28.27213/-82.17965
Email: cmpn@carefree.com
Website: www.carefreecamping.com
8 **SEE AD THIS PAGE**

20. CREDIT CARDS/ATMs:
MC=MasterCard;
VISA;
DISC=Discover;
AMEX=American Express;
ATM=Automated Teller Machine;
Debit=Debit Card.

21. NON-GUEST DUMPING:
If the park management allows travelers to come in off the road (non-guests) and empty their holding tanks, this is indicated in the listing. If the park charges for this service, you'll see a "$" after the phrase, i.e., non-guest dumping ($).

22. ESCORT TO SITE:
If management escorts your RV right to your site, we let you know.

23. SPECIAL INFORMATION:
Unique information provided by park owners who want you to know about special features and offers at their park. These individualized messages are highlighted in yellow and give you that little extra nugget of information not found in our standardized listing information.

24. DIRECTION LOCATOR:
The abbreviation before the facility's name indicates the direction from town. For example, "(NW)" means the facility is northwest of their listed town; "(C)" means center of town.

25. FAMILY CAMPING:
Family campers are adults that camp with their children 18 years or younger, traveling to outdoor destinations with their families and engaging in active outdoor activities.

26. CAMP CLUB USA:
The Camp Club USA logo identifies parks that are part of the CCUSA network and offer 50% off nightly rates to members.

27.GREEN FRIENDLY:
As more and more outdoor enthusiasts engage in "green practices," parks also have taken steps to become more environmentally responsible. Parks with "Green Friendly" noted in their listing meet at least 50% of the "Green Friendly" criteria.

Special Notes

Toilets? Showers?

• Unless otherwise noted, all campgrounds have flush toilets and hot showers. If the showers in the restroom are coin operated, the listing will indicate "shower$."

Seasonal Sites?

• Many parks can accommodate seasonal or extended stay RVers. If less than 10% of a park's sites are occupied by extended stay RVers, the listing won't mention seasonals. If 10% to 49% are usually occupied by extended stay RVers, the listing will indicate "some extended stay sites." Between 50% and 74%, the listing will indicate "many extended stay sites," and between 75% to 99%, the listing will indicate "mostly extended stay sites."

Age Restrictions?

• WOODALL'S lists "Age Restrictions May Apply" based upon information believed to be correct at the time of WOODALL'S inspections. Some sunbelt area parks cater to senior adults only. Since these classifications may change because of developing legislation, we suggest that you confirm this status by telephone, if it's important to you.

STATE/PROV.:

TOWN:

CG NAME:

AREAS OF INTEREST	NOT QUALIFIED	Level 1	Level 2	Level 3
ENTRANCE Includes an assessment of the following: Sign, Entrance, Access into CG, Entry Roads.	If any of these exist: No Sign, Access or Entry Roads too Difficult or Dangerous – **Not Qualified for Listing**	Requires the following: 1 ___ Sign ___ Reasonable Access	Requires 2 of the following (in addition to Level 1): 2 ___ Commercial Quality Sign Lighted ___ Developed Entrance ___ Wide Easy Access ___ All Weather Entry Roads	Requires 3 of the following: 3 ___ Commercial Quality Sign Lighted ___ Developed Entrance ___ Wide Easy Access ___ All Weather Entry Roads
SERVICES Includes an assessment of Registration & Laundry.	If No registration system – **Not Qualified for Listing**	Requires the following: 1 ___ Some system of registration (self-service accepted)	Requires the following: 2 ___ Part-time Management (no regular office hours)	Requires 1 of the following: 3 ✓ Management with reg. office hours ✓ Laundry (under a roof but not enclosed by walls is acceptable)
RESTROOMS AFHO/ASCO listings do not require restrooms. If restrooms are provided, numbers can be waived, but construction requirements apply for rating level suggested. If none, assign same level as hookups.	If No restroom (unless AFHO/ASCO) – **Not Qualified for Listing**	May be crude construction. Non-flush permitted. May not have showers. 3	May be non-professional finish. Standard Flush, marine or recirculating toilets. Showers & basins required. 6	Over 50% professional finish. Standard flush toilets, showers & basins required. 9
DUMP/FACILITY/METHOD If park has all Full Hookup Sites or Accepts Self-Contained units only, or if all non-full hookup sites are for tents only, No Requirement. If provided, assign the higher of either the dump station or hookups. If none, assign same level as Hookups.		Some method available such as: 1 ___ Sewer site, if vacant OR ___ Portable dump If NONE, Assign 0 point value: 0	Some method available on daily basis such as 2 ___ Permanent facility OR ___ Portable dump	Good quality facility with concrete pad sloped to flush inlet, closure and flushing water. 3 Posted, scheduled, daily management provided pump out service acceptable substitute.
SITES Includes an assessment of Picnic Tables and/or Patios. Also Shade and/or Plantings and/or Landscaping. If sites for *tents only* exist, disregard those sites for the purpose of determining the SITES rating.		10% of the sites must 2 ___ be level ___ have reasonable access ___ have picnic table (patio substitute) ___ have shade and/or plantings and/or landscaping If Less than Level 1 Assign 0 point value 0	25% of the sites must: 4 ___ be level ___ have good access ___ have picnic table (patio substitute) ___ have shade and/or plantings and/or landscaping	50% of the sites must: 6 ___ be level ___ have good access ___ have picnic table (patio substitute) ___ have shade and/or plantings and/or landscaping ___ have surface preparation
HOOKUPS If sites for *tents only* exist, disregard those sites for the purpose of determining the SITES rating for assigning Bonus Points.	If No water available – **Not Qualified for Listing**	Adequate water taps 2	25% electric hookups plus adequate water taps. 4	25% electric and water hookups, plus 25% electric hookups. 6

BONUS POINTS: 1 PT – If at least 20% of Total (RV) Sites have a separate 50 amp receptacle per site. 1 PT – If at least 50% of Total (RV) Sites offer (instant)

AREAS OF INTEREST	NOT QUALIFIED	Level 1	Level 2	Level 3
INTERIOR ROADS An assessment of the roads within the park utilized by RVs or the towing of RVs.		Roads are not All-Weather (may be a track through grass) 1 If less than Level 1 Assign 0 point value 0	Some are All-Weather or paved 2	High-use roads are All-Weather or paved 3
GROUNDS & LIGHTING This refers to non-camping, non-recreational areas. These are the public & common areas. Include in this element an assessment of the lighting that exists overall in the campground.	If No Lighting – **Not Qualified for Listing**	A lighted area 1	Requires both: 2 ___ grounds development ___ lighting outside at central building	Requires All of the following: 3 ___ grounds development Lighting at: ___ registration ___ restrooms
RECREATION		1 Major recreation or 3 minors	2 Major recreations	Indoor Recreation OR Swimming TOTAL REQUIREMENT 4 Major recreations

REC HALL	(M)	MN	NC	ITC	BOATING	M	MN	NC	ITC	PUTTING GREEN	M	MN	NC	ITC
REC ROOM/AREA	M	MN	NC	ITC	FLOAT TRIPS	M	MN	NC	ITC	PLAYGROUND	M	MN	NC	ITC
PAVILION	M	MN	NC	ITC	CANOEING	M	MN	NC	ITC	PLAY EQUIPMENT	M	MN	NC	ITC
EQUIPPED PAVILION	M	MN	NC	ITC	KAYAKING	M	MN	NC	ITC	MINI GOLF	M	MN	NC	ITC
COIN GAMES	M	MN	NC	ITC	BOAT RENTALS	M	MN	NC	ITC	SHUFFLEBOARD CT.	M	MN	NC	ITC
SWIM	(M)	MN	NC	ITC	FISHING	(M)	MN	NC	ITC	BIKE RENTALS	M	MN	NC	ITC
WADING POOL	M	MN	NC	ITC	FISHING GUIDES	M	MN	NC	ITC	PLANNED GROUP ACTIVITIES	M	MN	NC	ITC
WHIRLPOOL	M	MN	NC	ITC	FISHING SUPPLIES	M	MN	NC	ITC					

- The circles shown above indicate the level of each AREA OF INTEREST that exists at this Campground/RV Park.
- The underlined words indicate what is lacking in each AREA OF INTEREST that does not allow it to be circled at the next level.
- Point values are given to the park based on each AREA OF INTEREST circled.
- A 4◈ Facility Rating would be assigned to the above park.

Remember: A park may have particular AREAS OF INTEREST that are at different levels than the rating assigned. The overall rating is a composite of all AREAS OF INTEREST.

Level 4	Level 5	TOTAL	MAINTENANCE: unacceptable / minimal / fair / good / very good / superior	2010 CD
Requires All of the following: (4) ✓ Commercial Quality Sign Lighted ✓ Landscaped Entrance ✓ Wide Easy Access ✓ Wide, All Weather Entry Roads	Requires All of the following: (5) ✓ Superior Commercial Quality Sign Lighted ✓ Superior Landscaped Entrance ✓ Superior Paved Wide Easy Access ___ Superior Paved Wide Entry Roads	4	0 1 2 3 4 (5)	
Requires Both of the following (4) ✓ Management with Posted Daily office hrs. ___ Laundry (Enclosed)	Requires Both of the following: (5) ___ Management w/ Posted daily office hours and separate registration building or area ___ Superior Laundry (Commercial Quality Laundromat)	3	0 1 2 (3) 4 5	
Only a trace of non-professional finish acceptable. (12) RATIO OF 1:10 NON SEWER SITES PLUS 1:50 SEWER SITES	Full professional finish inside & out. Ceramic tile floors, showers & 4 feet up the walls. Ceramic tile, Formica or Corian counters. Factory built partitions. (Certain quality equivalent materials acceptable as substitute for ceramic tile.) (15) RATIO SAME AS LEVEL 4	12	0 2 4 6 (8) 10 (F) W (C) (Cn) S P (circle Prof. Items)	
4' x 6' Concrete pad sloped to flush inlet; self-closing cap, flushing water; if drinking water available, it must be at least 30' from dump. (4) Note: Pump-out service is not an acceptable substitute at this level.	Same as Level 4, except must have easy access & be clearly signed. (5) NOTE: Pump-out service is not an acceptable substitute at this level.	5	0 1 2 3 (4) 5	
50% of the sites must: (8) ✓ be level ✓ have easy access ✓ have picnic table (patio substitute) ✓ have shade and/or plantings and/or landscaping 75% of the sites must: ✓ have surface preparation	75% of the sites must: (10) ✓ be level ✓ have easy access ✓ have picnic table (patio substitute) ✓ have shade and/or plantings and/or landscaping 100% of the sites must: ✓ have surface preparation	8	0 1 2 3 4 (5)	
25% full hookups plus 25% electric & water hookups plus 25% electric plus adequate water taps. Logical hookup relationship. Will accept 2 RVs per full hookup cluster. Will accept 4 RVs per non-full hookup cluster. (8) ✓ Minimum 20 amp receptacles at all sites with electrical hookups.	50% individual full hookups plus 50% electric & water hookups with a water tap and electric stanchion for each 4 non-full hookup spaces. Logical hookup relationship. (10) ___ Minimum 30 amp receptacle at all full hookups AND ✓ Minimum 20 amp receptacle at all electrical hookups	8	0 1 2 3 (4) 5	
Access upon arrival via wireless, phone or cable hookup.				
High-use roads are wide and All-Weather or paved. (4)	All roads are wide and All-Weather or paved. (5)	4	0 1 2 (3) 4 5	
Requires All of the following: (4) ___ grounds development Lighting at: ___ registration ___ restrooms ___ camping areas	Requires All of the following: (5) ✓ Extensive grounds development Lighting at: ✓ registration ✓ restrooms ✓ camping areas ✓ some activity areas	5	0 1 2 3 (4) 5	
Indoor Recreation (with 4 items) AND Swimming TOTAL REQUIREMENT 6 Major Recreations	Indoor Recreation (with 6 items), Planned Group Activities AND Swimming TOTAL REQUIREMENT 10 Major Recreations	51	**FACILITIES TOTALS** 36	

Recreation				
HORSESHOES	M	MN	NC	ITC
TENNIS	M	(MN)	NC	ITC
BASKETBALL	M	(MN)	NC	ITC
VOLLEYBALL	M	(MN)	NC	ITC
SPRAYGROUND	M	MN	NC	ITC
SPORT FIELD	M	MN	NC	ITC
HIKING TRAILS	M	MN	NC	ITC
LOCAL TOURS	M	MN	NC	ITC
___	M	MN	NC	ITC
___	M	MN	NC	ITC
___	M	MN	NC	ITC
___	M	MN	NC	ITC
___	M	MN	NC	ITC
___	M	MN	NC	ITC
___	M	MN	NC	ITC
___	M	MN	NC	ITC

AREAS OF INTEREST	MAINTENANCE Delete 0-8
1W 12-21	1W 9-15
2W 22-33	2W 16-24
3W 34-45	3W 25-33
(4W 46-56)	(4W 34-42)
5W 57-62	5W 43-45
REC. LEVEL 4	REC. MAINT. 3

COMMENTS:

F-3-9

- The lower portion of the form is used to tally the recreation.
- Recreation items are assigned Major (M), Minor (MN) or No Count (NC) value based on the investment and/or quantity and/or usage of that recreation item at the park.
- The recreation items shown for the above park would result in a 3W Recreation Rating due to maintenance.
- The maintenance level at a Campground/RV Park must meet or exceed the recommended rating or the ratings cannot be assigned at that level.
- Remember: Ratings are recommended by WOODALL'S Rep Teams, and are approved (or declined) by the WOODALL Rating Committee.

Free Camping Information

✔ **FREE INFORMATION**

Use our Reader Service Card opposite page 48 /Discover Section as an easy way to write for FREE travel and camping information and more information about advertisers' products and services. This card also gives you the opportunity to be a part of WOODALL by sharing with us how far you travel, for how long, and in what type of unit so that we can better meet your needs.

✔ **EXTENDED STAY GUIDE**

When looking for a park in which to spend a month or an entire season, also refer to WOODALL'S Extended Stay Guide to RV Parks/Campgrounds (the yellow pages in the middle of this directory).

Detailed listings include locator directions, facilities and recreation available on-site, and more, all verified through personal visits by WOODALL'S representatives.

Many facilities have purchased advertising in this section to tell you about its unique features, special rates, and nearby attractions. All ads are reader serviced, so you can obtain even more information, FREE!, direct from the parks.

✔ **PERSONAL INSPECTIONS**

And most important, WOODALL'S 25 Representative Teams spent over 5,000 days, traveling half a million miles to update our information by personal inspection. And as a result, our dependable WOODALL ratings for both facilities and recreation have been assigned to privately-operated campgrounds.

✔ **TRAVEL SECTIONS**

When planning your next trip be sure to refer to the travel sections located at the beginning of each state and province. You'll find helpful information on climate, topography, time zone, travel information sources, recreational information, places to see and things to do, and events.

✔ **100% MONEY BACK GUARANTEE**

WOODALL has been publishing RV/camping guides, directories and magazines for over 70 years! We take pride in our efforts to provide you with the most complete, accurate and up-to-date Campground Directory available on the market. However, if for any reason you're not satisfied with this Directory, please return it to us by December 31, 2011, along with your sales receipt, and we will reimburse you for the amount you paid for the Directory. Also please share with us the reason for your dissatisfaction.

TYPES OF NON-RATED LISTINGS:

1. RV SPACES: Spaces reserved for overnight travelers as an adjunct to the main business operation. To be listed, there must be a minimum of 20 spaces for RV's; reasonable access for all units; water available; level, lighted area and evidence of maintenance.

2. TOO NEW TO RATE: These parks have been inspected by WOODALL and are fully operational, but before a rating is assigned, we want each park to have the opportunity to fully complete its development and maintenance regime.

3. UNDER CONSTRUCTION, PLANNED, REBUILDING, NOT VISITED: Please write or phone ahead when considering a stay at these parks to confirm their ability to accommodate you.

4. CAMP RESORT: Usually fewer than 20 spaces are available to non-members. Phone ahead for site availability and for more information about purchasing a site.

5. NUDIST RESORTS: WOODALL lists a few nudist and clothing-optional RV parks/campgrounds.

Do all parks qualify for a listing in WOODALL'S Campground Directory?

No, not all parks are listed. A campground must meet our standards for maintenance, access into the park, and have a minimum of 20 designated sites available for overnight camping. Parks that are deleted are re-visited after three years.

Why is a new WOODALL'S Campground Directory needed each year?

During each inspection season, our representative teams delete several hundred listings because they do not meet our minimum requirements and we think they wouldn't meet yours. Hundreds of new parks are added each year, too. And, each year over 300,000 changes are made to the listings from the previous edition involving changes in phone numbers, ratings, open and close dates, facilities and recreation available, park policy, and more—important reasons to ALWAYS use a current WOODALL'S Campground Directory.

We'd like to hear from you!

We are always glad to hear from you for any reason and we respond to all correspondence and phone calls, whether you have a suggestion, a compliment or a complaint. Your comments continue to help us improve our directory each year. There are several ways to get in touch with us, so pick the method most convenient to you:

- **Visit our Web Site at: www.woodalls.com**
- Phone us at: 877/680-6155
- Fax us at: 805/667-4468
- Write us at: WOODALL Publications Corporation
  Woodall Correspondent
  64 Inverness Dr. E.
  Englewood, CO 80112

Every attempt is made to ensure that all phone numbers are correct. However, due to numerous changes in area codes throughout North America, your call might not go through. Please call Directory Assistance for more information.

Comment Utiliser ce Guide

L'organisation du guide WOODALL

Toutes les informations dans le **WOODALL'S CAMPGROUND DIRECTORY** sont classées par ordre alphabétique. Vous y trouverez en premier lieu les états américains, suivent les provinces canadiennes et, finalement, le Mexique. L'ordre alphabétique se maintient au niveau des états et provinces ainsi que des villes et, sous celles-ci, des inscriptions des établissements tels que terrains de camping, centres de service de véhicules récréatifs et attractions touristiques. Chaque nom de ville est suivi d'une lettre et d'un chiffre (ex: A-1) vous permettant de situer la ville que vous recherchez sur la carte géographique au début de chaque état et province.

L'édition Nord-Américaine est divisée en deux sections: Est et Ouest. Chacune de ces sections est aussi classée par ordre alphabétique en débutant par l'Alabama à l'Est et par l'Alaska à l'Ouest. L'index "WOODALL'S ALPHABETICAL QUICK REFERENCE" que vous retrouverez à la fin de chaque section fournit le nom des terrains de camping, des services et locations d'équipements ainsi que des attractions touristiques. Cet index facilite les recherches si vous connaissez le nom de l'établissement mais non la ville où il est situé. Dans cet index, le symbole ® signifie location de véhicules récréatifs; ∅ location de tentes; □ location de chalets; ★ centre de services; • attractions touristiques. Vous y trouverez aussi la référence vous permettant de repérer la ville sur la carte.

Chaque état et province, ainsi que le Mexique, débute par une carte géographique et des informations pertinentes à la région. Sur la carte, les villes où sont localisés les terrains de camping sont identifiées par le losange ◈; les attractions touristiques par le drapeau ⚑ et les centres de services pour véhicules récréatifs par un ✲ . Ces cartes doivent être utilisées en complément des cartes routières officielles. Nous vous invitons à consulter les listes d'attractions touristiques et de points d'intérêt lorsque vous planifiez votre voyage.

Les représentants WOODALL effectuent des inspections annuelles

Tous les terrains de camping privés répertoriés dans ce guide sont inspectés chaque année par une équipe WOODALL.

Ces équipes comptent déjà de nombreuses années d'expérience en camping et véhicules récréatifs avant de joindre WOODALL. En plus d'être familiers avec le territoire qui leur est assigné, ils reçoivent une formation initiale intensive à laquelle vient s'ajouter une formation annuelle. Le rapport détaillé recueilli à chaque inspection complète les informations nécessaires au classement recommandé par WOODALL. Le répertoire des terrains de camping privés de ce présent guide est établi à la suite des inspections faites au printemps et à l'été 2010. En complément aux informations recueillies pour chaque terrain de camping, les représentants complètent une formule d'évaluation (exemple en pages IV et V) permettant d'attribuer la cote d'évaluation de WOODALL.

Les représentants WOODALL visitent aussi les centres de service de véhicules récréatifs et les attractions touristiques d'importance dont la liste s'ajoute à celle des terrains de camping.

Le répertoire des terrains de camping publics (fédéraux, provinciaux, municipaux et militaires) d'informations de public.

Le système d'évaluation jumelée de WOODALL

Les cotes d'évaluation vous aident à choisir le terrain de camping que vous recherchez.

WOODALL fixe deux cotes d'évaluation à chacue terrain de camping privé. Le système d'évaluation exclusif à WOODALL est expliqué en pages **IV** et **V** à l'aide de la formule dont se servent les représentants sur le terrain. La première cote tient compte des caractéristiques de chaque terrain de camping (ex: sites, routes, toilettes, eau, égouts, électricité, etc.). La seconde cote évalue les services récréatifs. Les deux cotes vont de 1◈ à 5◈. Le ◈ est un symbole exclusif à WOODALL. La cote finale tient compte du degré d'entretien que présente le terrain de camping.

Que signifient les cotes d'évaluation WOODALL?

Les cotes dépendent non seulement des caractéristiques d'un terrain de camping donné, mais aussi du degré d'entretien qui lui est consacré. Mieux un terrain de camping est coté, non seulement plus nombreuses sont ses caractéristiques mais aussi en meilleur état d'entretien. En vue de vous assurer une satisfaction complète, à vous et à votre famille, WOODALL porte une attention particulière à la propreté et en tient compte dans sa cote d'évaluation. Le niveau d'entretien et de propreté doit être supérieur, du moins égal à la cote des caractéristiques sinon la cote générale devient celle de l'entretien.

Plusieurs ◈ indiquent-ils un meilleur terrain de camping?

Définitivement NON! Tous les terrains de camping répertoriés dans le Guide WOODALL rencontrent les normes minimales de WOODALL; cependant la cote d'évaluation ne permet pas de déterminer si un terrain de camping est bien, très bien ou excellent. Chaque campeur doit fixer son choix selon les caractéristiques énumérées dans le Guide. Plusieurs facteurs entrent alors en ligne de compte: la description des sites, la proximité d'une autoroute, d'attractions touristique, une piscine, un lac, etc. Assurez-vous de bien saisir le système de cotation exclusif à WOODALL'S; il facilitera votre choix et assurera votre satisfaction. Et ne manquez surtout pas de mentionner lors de votre inscription que vous avez fait votre choix à l'aide des informations contenues dans le Guide WOODALL.

Encouragez Nos Annoneurs

WELCOME

L'inscription dans le Guide WOODALL est offerte sans frais aux propriétaires de terrains de camping qui rencontrent les normes minimales de WOODALL. Les propriétaires qui désirent faire mieux connaître leur terrain le font à l'aide d'annonces publiées dans nos pages. Cette publicité additionnelle est destinée à vous seconder dans votre choix en mettant l'accent sur des particularités dont ils sont fiers. Si c'est le cas, n'oubliez pas d'aviser les propriétaires que vous avez fait votre choix à l'aide de leur publicité.

Comment Utiliser Ce Guide

Nous sommes à l'écoute de nos lecteurs. Basée sur les commentaires et les suggestions que vous nous avez soumis, voici une description des éléments contenus dans une inscription. Ces éléments sont ceux que vous jugez importants.

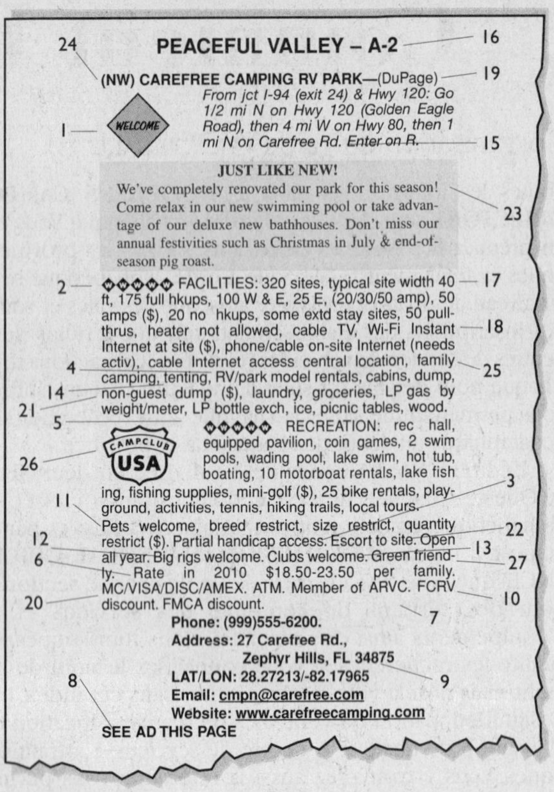

1. LE LOSANGE WELCOME:
Le losange WELCOME devant une inscription indique que le propriétaire de ce terrain de camping dispose d'une annonce publicitaire pour vous offrir des renseignements supplémentaires à propos de son terrain.

2. CARACTÉRISTIQUES:
Évaluées et cotées de 1à 5 ◈.Toutes les caractéristiques énumérées dans l'inscription sont offertes sur ce terrain de camping.

3. ACCES PARTIEL AUX HANDICAPÉS:
Indique que le terrain présente certains éléments pouvant accommoder les personnes avec des incapacités physiques. Soit des douches avec bancs et rampes murales, des lavabos et toilettes donnant accès aux chaises roulantes, des portes admettant des chaises roulantes, des trottoirs avec rampes, signalisation en Braille. Pour en connaître davantage, informez-vous avant votre départ.

4. LOCATION DE TENTE, DE VÉHICULE RÉCRÉATIF ET DE CHALET:
Vous pouvez louer une tente, un véhicule récréatif ou un chalet à ce terrain de camping.

5. ACTIVITÉS RÉCRÉATIVES:
Évaluées et cotées de 1à 5◈,Toutes ces activités récréatives sont offertes sur ce terrain de camping.

6. CONCERNANT LES TARIFS:
Les tarifs indiquent les prix minimum et maximum au cours de la saison précédente, en vigueur lors de l'inspection par les représentants WOODALL. Ces tarifs sont sujets à changement.

7. AFFILIATIONS:
Identifie les associations que patronise ce terrain de camping.

8. PUBLICITÉ ADDITIONNELLE:
Vous réfère à la page où paraît l'annonce publicitaire.

9. CONTACTER LE PARC:
Facile, en un clin d'il INFORMATIONS. Cette trés visible section vous donne tout ce dont vous avez besoin de contact et de recherche du parc.

10. RABAIS:
Rabais offerts aux membres d'organismes particuliers.

11. INFORMATIONS SPÉCIFIQUES:
Restrictions telles qu'animaux interdits, motocyclistes interdits, âge minimum, dates d'ouverture, etc. Si la mention NO PETS n'apparaît pas, les animaux sont acceptés. Cependant, si vous possédez un animal domestique peu commun il vous serait préférable de vous informer au préalable.

12. GRANDS VÉHICULES ACCEPTÉS:
Si le terrain de camping est en mesure d'accueillir les grands véhicules récréatifs l'inscription l'indique. Les principaux facteurs pris en considération sont: la largeur et la longueur des sites, le dégagement vertical, l'ampérage, les routes d'accès et l'accès aux sites.

13. BIENVENUE AUX CLUBS:
Cette mention indique que le terrain accueille des clubs et des caravanes.

14. BIENVENUE AUX TENTES:
Cette mention indique que le terrain accepte les tentes. Ces campeurs sont acceptés dans la plupart des terrains, cependant si un terrain ne les accepte pas la mention NO TENTS ou ACCEPTS FULL HOOKUP UNITS ONLY paraîtra dans les informations spécifiques.

15. DIRECTIONS POUR S'Y RENDRE:
Des informations faciles et détaillées vous conduiront au terrain.

16. POINT DE RÉFÉRENCE:
Vous permet de situer la ville sur la carte géographique de l'état ou de la province.

17. LONGUEUR ET LARGEUR DES SITES:
La dimension des sites varie d'un parc à l'autre. Vous trouverez ici les dimensions les plus communes de ce terrain. Si la longueur du site est inférieure à 40 pieds elle sera précisée. L'on a tenucompte de l'habileté d'un conducteur moyen.

18. L'INTERNET::
De plus en plus de VR'S veulent utiliser leur courriel ainsi que internet. Maintenant plusieurs Parcs offrent ce service directement a votre emplacement / ou a un endroit central, qui est normalement situe a l'Office ou dans la Salle Communautaire nous designons ce Parc comme "*Instant Internet access.*" Aussi un autre service, directement a votre emplacement, peut etre offert dans ce Parc mais vous devrez activer la ligne telephonique en vous abonnant au service local de la Compagnie de telephone; ceci est surtout pour ceux qui veulent y resider a long terme.

19. COMTÉS:
Le nom du comté dans lequel le parc estsitué apparaît entre parenthèses. Aux États-Unis, le nom des comtés est utilisé lors d'alertes.

20. CARTES DE CRÉDIT:
MC=MasterCard;
VISA;
DISC=Discover;
DC=Diner's Club;
AMEX=American Express;
ATM=Automated Teller Machine.
Debit=Debit Card

21. VIDANGE DES RÉSERVOIRS D'ÉGOUT:
Si le terrain accepte les voyageurs non clients ou non et s'il y a des frais ($) pour ce service

---

24 **PEACEFUL VALLEY – A-2** 16

(NW) CAREFREE CAMPING RV PARK—(DuPage) 19
1 WELCOME *From jct I-94 (exit 24) & Hwy 120: Go 1/2 mi N on Hwy 120 (Golden Eagle Road), then 4 mi W on Hwy 80, then 1 mi N on Carefree Rd. Enter on R.* 15

JUST LIKE NEW!
We've completely renovated our park for this season! Come relax in our new swimming pool or take advantage of our deluxe new bathhouses. Don't miss our annual festivities such as Christmas in July & end-of-season pig roast. 23

2 ◈◈◈◈◈ FACILITIES: 320 sites, typical site width 40 ft, 175 full hkups, 100 W & E, 25 E, (20/30/50 amp), 50 amps ($), 20 no hkups, some extd stay sites, 50 pull-thrus, heater not allowed, cable TV, Wi-Fi Instant Internet at site ($), phone/cable on-site Internet (needs activ), cable Internet access central location, family camping, tenting, RV/park model rentals, cabins, dump, non-guest dump ($), laundry, groceries, LP gas by weight/meter, LP bottle exch, ice, picnic tables, wood. 17 18 25 4 14 21

5 ◈◈◈◈◈ RECREATION: rec hall, equipped pavilion, coin games, 2 swim pools, wading pool, lake swim, hot tub, boating, 10 motorboat rentals, lake fish ing, fishing supplies, mini-golf ($), 25 bike rentals, playground, activities, tennis, hiking trails, local tours. 26 CAMPCLUB USA 3

11 Pets welcome, breed restrict, size restrict, quantity restrict ($). Partial handicap access. Escort to site. Open all year. Big rigs welcome. Clubs welcome. Green friendly. Rate in 2010 $18.50-23.50 per family. MC/VISA/DISC/AMEX. ATM. Member of ARVC. FCRV discount. FMCA discount. 22 13 27 10 7 12 6 20

Phone: (999)555-6200.
Address: 27 Carefree Rd., Zephyr Hills, FL 34875
LAT/LON: 28.27213/-82.17965 9
Email: cmpn@carefree.com
Website: www.carefreecamping.com
8 **SEE AD THIS PAGE**

---

22. ESCORTER AU SITE:
Ceci vous indique que la Direction vous reconduit a votre emplacement designe pour votre VR.

23. L'INFORMATION SPECIALE:
Nouveau dans notre édition 2006 est l'information fournie par les propriétaires de Parc qui veulent vous informer des caractéristiques et des offres spéciales à leur Parc. Ces messages individualisés sont surlignés en 'jaune' et vous donnent des détails supplémentaires qui ne se retrouvent pas dans les informations régulières.

24. LOCALISATEUR DE LA DIRECTION:
L'abréviation avant la facilite indique la position de cette facilite versus la direction de la Ville. Par exemple, "(NW)" veut dire que cette facilite est situee au Nord-ouest de la ville ou est son inscription;"(C)" signifie le centre de la ville.

25. CAMPER DE FAMILLE:
Les campeurs de famille sont des adultes qui campent avec leurs enfants 18 ans ou plus jeunes, voyager aux destinations extérieures avec leurs familles et s'engageant dans des activités en plein air actives.

26. CAMP CLUB USA:
Le Camp Club USA logo identifie les parcs qui font partie du réseau CCUSA et offrent 50% de réduction des tarifs de nuit pour les membres.

27. VERT AMICALE:
Comme de plus en plus amateurs de plein air se librer a des "pratiques vertes," les parcs ont également pres des mesures pour devenir plus respectueux de l'environment. Parcs avec "Vert bienvenus," a souligné dans leur annonce se réunir au moins 50% de "Vert Amicale" criteres

Special Notes

Toilettes? Douches?

• À moins d'indication contraire, tous les terrains de camping énumérés sont munis de toilettes à l'eau courante et de douches à l'eau chaude. Si les douches sont payantes, l'inscription "shower$" le précise.

Sites saisonniers

Plusieurs Parcs peuvent offrir des emplacements pour saisonniers ou ceux qui desirent prolonger leur sejour. Si le Parc a moins de 10% de son occupation en saisonnier cela ne sera pas mentionner dans la description de nos Guides. S'il y a entre 10% et 49% la mention se lira comme suit "some extended stay sites." S'il y a entre 50% et 74% la mention se lira comme suit "many extended stay sites." S'il y a entre 75% et 99% la mention se lira comme suit "mostly extended stay sites."

Restriction d'âge

• La mention "Age Restrictions May Apply" paraîtra si le terrain en question n'offre pas des services qu'aux personnes d'un certain âge. Ces restrictions étant sujettes à certaines législations, nous vous recommandons donc de vérifier auprès des responsables.

LES CARACTÉRISTIQUES SPÉCIALES

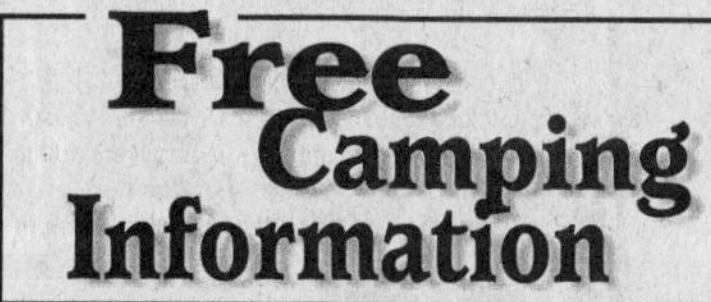

✔ INFORMATION GRATUITE

Pour obtenir de l'information supplémentaire sur les produits et services offerts dans ce guide, il vous suffit d'utiliser notre carte "READER SERVICE CARD" de la page 48. De plus, cette carte vous offre l'opportunité de partager, avec WOODALL'S, vos informations voyage telle que la durée de votre voyage, la distance parcourue, le genre de véhicule récréatif que vous utilisez. Tous ces renseignements nous permettent de mieux répondre à vos besoins.

✔ LES SECTIONS VOYAGE

Lors de la planification de votre prochain voyage, consultez la section voyage située au début de tous les états et provinces. Vous y trouverez des informations, concernant la région que vous désirez visiter, sur le climat, la topographie, les fuseaux horaires, les bureaux d'informations touristiques,

LES RAISONS POUR LESQUELLES CERTAINS TERRAINS DE CAMPING NE SONT PAS ÉVALUÉS ET INSCRITS.

1. ESPACES POUR VÉHICULES RÉCRÉATIFS: Les terrains de camping doivent offrir un minimum de 20 sites disponibles pour les voyageurs d'un soir, tel qu'indiqué plus haut, pour être inscrits. De plus, ils doivent offrir une facilité d'accès pour tous types de véhicules récréatifs, une disponibilité d'eau, des sites bien éclairés mais surtout propres et bien entretenus.

2. SITES TROP RÉCENTS POUR ÊTRE ÉVALUÉS: Ces terrains ont été inspectés par nos représentants et sont entièrement opérationnels mais, avant de leur attribuer une cote, nous désirons leur laisser l'opportunité de compléter leur développement.

3. TERRAINS EN CONSTRUCTION, EN RÉNOVATION OU NON-VISITÉS: S'il-vous-plaît, veuillez communiquer avec ces terrain pour vous assurer qu'ils sont en mesure de vous accueillir.

4. RESORT: Habituellement, ces terrains de camping comptent moins de 20 sites disponibles pour les non-membres. Veuillez communiquer avec les responsables du terrain pour vous assurer qu'ils sont en mesure de vous accueillir.

5. PARC NATURISTE: WOODALL'S inscrit quelques-uns de ces terrains de camping dans le guide.

Priére de Noter

Nous tentons de nous assurer que les numéros de téléphone inscrits sont exacts. Cependant, dû aux changements de codes régionaux en Amérique du Nord, votre appel peut ne pas être acheminé. Si cela se produit, demandez l'aide des téléphonistes.

WOODALL'S EXTENDED STAY
WEEKLY MONTHLY SEASONAL WEEKLY MONTHLY SEASONAL WEEKLY MONTHLY SEASONAL
SPRING SUMMER AUTUMN WINTER SPRING SUMMER AUTUMN WINTER SPRING
GUIDE TO RV PARKS/CAMPGROUNDS 2011

les attractions et points d'intérêt, etc.

Quand vous regardez pour un Parc ou vous voudriez sejourner un mois ou une saison entiere, vous pourrez vous referer dans la section du Guide de WOODALL'S Extended Stay (les pages jaune qui se trouve a la fin de nos Guides).

Les details qui vous y retrouverez comprendront: la direction, les facilites, les recreations et un peu plus; que nos Representants auront verifies personnellement lors de leur inspection.

Certains Parcs ont voulu se demarquer en placant une publicite qui leur permet de vous donner encore plus de details comme: leur offre speciale, leur tarif, les attractions dans les environs et plus encore. Ils benificient aussi du service du "reader's service" qui vous est offert "GRATUITEMENT" en vous permettant d'obtenir plus amples informations.

✔ INSPECTIONS PERSONNALISÉES

Et, le plus important, 25 représentants dévoués de WOODALL'S parcourent plus d'un demi million de milles pendant près de 5,000 jours dans le but de mettre à jour les informations contenues dans ce guide. Suite à leurs inspections personnalisées, les cotes sont émises pour chacun des terrains de camping privés, autant pour les facilités que les activités offertes.

✔ SATISFACTION GARANTIE OU ARGENT REMIS

¡WOODALL'S publie ce guide plus de 70 ans! Nous sommes fiers de vous procurer un guide des plus complets et mis à jour annuellement. Toutefois, si, pour quelques raisons que ce soit, vous n'êtes pas satisfait de ce guide, veuillez nous le retourner avant le 31 Décembre 2011 avec votre reçu d'achat et nous vous rembourserons. Veuillez, s'il-vous-plaît, nous faire part de la raison de votre insatisfaction.

Est-ce que tous les terrains de camping sont inscrits dans le guide WOODALL'S ?

Non, ce ne sont pas tous les terrains de camping qui sont inscrits. Un terrain doit rencontrer les standards établis par WOODALL'S pour l'entretien du terrain, l'accès au terrain et aux sites et doit offrir un minimum de 20 sites disponibles pour les voyageurs d'un soir afin d'être inscrit dans le guide. Les terrains de camping non-inscrits sont revisités après 3 ans.

Pour quelles raisons WOODALL'S publie un guide à chaque années?

Lors de leur inspection annuelle, nos équipes de représentants suppriment plusieurs centaines d'inscriptions parce qu'elles ne répondent plus à nos standards minimums établis. De plus, des centaines de terrains de camping se rajoutent à chaque année. Ainsi, plus de 300,000 changements sont apportés aux inscriptions de l'édition précédente que ce soit pour les prix, les numéros de téléphone, les dates d'ouverture et de fermeture, les facilités offertes et plus encore. Voici quelques-unes des raisons d'utiliser un guide WOODALL'S actualisé.

Nous voulons connaître votre opinion!

Nous sommes toujours heureux de recevoir vos commentaires, que ce soit une plainte, un compliment ou une suggestion. Utilisez le formulaire fourni à la fin du guide pour nous faire part de vos commentaires; ils nous permettent d'améliorer le guide. Vous pouvez aussi visiter notre site internet à **www.woodalls.com**

Téléphone: (877) 680-6155 Fax: (805) 667-4468

Écrivez-nous à: WOODALL Publications Corporation
Woodall Correspondent
64 Inverness Dr. E.
Englewood, CO 80112, USA

RULES of the ROAD

The following **Rules of the Road** are compiled each year via mailings to state/provincial highway departments and/or police departments. Some changes may have been made since this data was compiled. For additional regulations not addressed in this section, we suggest that you contact the state or provincial agency listed. While every attempt has been made to check this information, the *Woodall's Campground Directory* cannot guarantee its accuracy, and assumes no responsibility for errors and omissions.

ALABAMA: Maximum RV width 102 in.; maximum motorhome length 45 ft.; maximum trailer length 40 ft.; maximum RV height 13.5 ft.; maximum combined length of two vehicles 65 ft. Triple towing is not allowed. Riding allowed in truck campers. Overnight parking in rest areas permitted where posted. **RV Safety Requirements:** At 3,000 lbs.: trailer brakes, flares and breakaway switch. **Driving Laws:** Wipers on/headlights on. Right turn on red permitted unless posted otherwise. All front-seat occupants must use seat belts; children under age 3 must be in child-restraint safety seats; ages 3-6 must wear seat belts. **More Information**: Department of Public Safety, RSA Criminal Justice Center, Bldg. C, 5th Fl., Suite C5-15, 301 S. Ripley St., Montgomery, AL 31604. Emergency number: (334) 242-4395 *HP or *47 on cellular phones.

ALASKA: Maximum RV width 102 in.; maximum motorhome length 45 ft.; maximum trailer length 40 ft.; maximum length of two-vehicle combination 75 ft. Overnight parking in rest areas allowed, unless posted. **RV Safety Requirements:** All RVs: flares or reflective signs, fire extinguisher and gas detector. Over 3,000 lbs.: trailer brakes, breakaway switch and safety chains. **Driving Laws:** Headlight use required on designated highways. Right turn on red permitted, unless posted otherwise. All passengers must wear seat belts; child-restraint safety seats are required for children up to age 4. **More Information:** Alaska State Troopers, 5700 E. Tudor, Anchorage AK 99507. Emergency number: 911, or *273 on cellular phones.

ARIZONA: Maximum RV width 102 in.(some exceptions); maximum motorhome length 45 ft.; maximum trailer length 40 ft.; maximum RV height 13.5 ft.; maximum combined length for two vehicles 65 ft. Triple-towing allowed w/fifth wheel. Riding permitted in travel trailers, fifth-wheel trailers and truck campers. Overnight parking in rest areas allowed unless posted. **RV Safety Requirements:** Over 3,000 lbs.: trailer brakes, breakaway switch and safety chains. **Driving Laws:** Right turn on red permitted, unless posted otherwise. Children under 5 years must be in child-restraint safety seats. **More Information:** Arizona Dept.of Public Safety, Box 6638, Phoenix AZ 85005; (602) 223-2000. Emergency number: 911.

ARKANSAS: Maximum RV width 102 in.; maximum motorhome length 45 ft.; maximum length for single towed trailer 43.5 ft.; maximum length for two-vehicle combination 65 ft. Overnight parking in rest areas allowed unless posted. **RV Safety Requirements:** 3,000 lbs.: trailer brakes, breakaway switches and safety chains. **Driving Laws:** Wipers on/headlights on. Right turn on red permitted unless posted otherwise. **More Information:** Arkansas State Highway and Transportation Department., P.O. Box 2261, Little Rock AR 72203. Emergency number: 911 (in some counties) or *55 on cellular phones.

CALIFORNIA: Maximum RV width 102 in.; maximum motorhome length 40 ft.(45 ft. on some highways); maximum trailer length 40 ft.; maximum RV height 14 ft.; maximum combined length for two-vehicle combination, 65 ft. Riding is allowed in truck campers if passengers are seat-belted; in fifth-wheel trailers with safety glass and an audible or visual device connected with tow vehicle, plus at least one exit must be able to be opened from both outside and inside the trailer. Vehicles towing trailers or dinghies are restricted to the right-hand lane. Overnight parking in rest areas not allowed. **RV Safety Requirements:** Over 1,500 lbs.: trailer brakes, breakaway switch and safety chains. All power-brake systems require breakaway switch. Chains may be required during winter months on mountain roads. **Driving Laws:** Right turn on red permitted, unless posted otherwise (but not on red arrow). At least two/three riders for carpool lane as posted. **More Information:** California Highway Patrol, 444 N. 3rd St., Suite 310, Sacramento CA 95814; (916) 445-1865. www.dot.ca.gov/hq/traffopr/trucks/bus-mh/bus-map.html. Emergency number: 911.

COLORADO: Maximum RV width 102 in.; maximum motor- home length 45 ft.; maximum trailer length not specified; maximum RV height 13 ft.; maximum length of two- or three-vehicle combination 70 ft. Riding in truck campers allowed; in fifth-wheels allowed but not recommended. Overnight parking in rest areas permitted unless posted otherwise. All towed vehicles must stop at ports of entry (only commercial vehicles are required to stop at ports of entry). **RV Safety Requirements**: Chains or snow tires required when posted. Trailers over 3,000 lbs. require trailer brakes and breakaway switch. **Driving Laws:** At least two riders required for carpool lane. Firearms may be transported loaded or unloaded anywhere in a vehicle except on one's person. **More Information:** Colorado State Patrol, 700 Kipling St., Suite 2000, Denver CO 80215; (303) 239-4540. Emergency number: 911; *CSP or *277 on cellular phones.

CONNECTICUT: Maximum RV width 102 in.; maximum motorhome length 45 ft.; maximum trailer length not specified; maximum RV height 13.5 ft.; maximum combined length for two vehicles 60 ft. RVs are not allowed in carpool lanes. Riding allowed in truck campers. Overnight parking in rest areas is permitted, unless posted. **RV Safety Requirements:** Over 3,000 lbs.: safety chains, breakaway switch and trailer brakes. **Driving Laws:** Wipers on/headlights on. Right turn on red allowed unless posted otherwise. Front-seat passengers are required to wear seat belts. **More Information:** Department. of Motor Vehicles, 60 State St., Wethersfield CT 06161. Emergency number: 911.

DELAWARE: Maximum RV width 102 in.; maximum motorhome length 45 ft.; maximum trailer length 40 ft.; maximum RV height 13.5 ft.; maximum combined length for two-vehicle combination 65 ft. Riding allowed in truck campers. Overnight parking in rest areas allowed where posted. **RV Safety Requirements:** Over 4,000 lbs.: trailer brakes and safety chains. **Driving Laws:** Wipers on/headlights on. Right turn on red allowed, unless posted otherwise. Front-seat passengers and all passengers under 16 years are required to wear seat belts. **More Information:** Delaware State Police, P.O. Box 430, Dover DE 19903; (302) 378-5230. Emergency number: 911 or *77 on cellular phones.

DISTRICT OF COLUMBIA: Maximum RV width 96 in.; maximum motorhome length 40 ft.; maximum trailer length not specified; maximum RV height 13.5 ft.; maximum length of two- or three-vehicle combination 55 ft. Riding allowed in truck campers. Overnight parking in rest areas is not allowed. **RV Safety Requirements:** Trailers over 3,000 lbs.: safety chain, breakaway switch, trailer brakes. Emergency number: (202) 727-6161

FLORIDA: Maximum RV width 102 in.; maximum motorhome length 45 ft.; maximum trailer length 40 ft.; maximum RV height 13.5 ft.; maximum combined length for two vehicles 65 ft. Triple towing is illegal. Riding allowed in truck campers. **RV Safety Requirements:** Trailers over 3,000 lbs.: trailer brakes, breakaway switch and safety chains. **Driving Laws:** Wipers on/headlights on. Right turn on red allowed unless posted otherwise. At least two riders for carpool lanes. **More Information:** Florida Highway Patrol, Office of Public Affairs, Room A425, MS44, 2900 Apalachee Pkwy., Tallahassee FL 32399-0553; (850) 617-2381. Emergency number: 911 or *FHP or *347 on cellular phones.

GEORGIA: Maximum RV width 102 in.; maximum motorhome length 45 ft.; maximum trailer length not specified; maximum RV height 13.5 ft.; maximum length for two-vehicle combination 60 ft. Riding allowed in truck campers. Overnight parking in rest areas is not allowed. **RV Safety Requirements:** One mirror required on all RVs. Over 1,500 lbs.: trailer brakes and safety chain. **More Information:** Department of Transportation, Commissioner, 2 Capitol Sq., Atlanta GA 30334. Emergency number: (404) 656-5267, or *GSP on cellular phones.

HAWAII: Maximum RV width 108 in. for both single unit motor vehicles and trailers; maximum height is 14 ft.; maximum single unit motor vehicle length is 45 ft.; maximum trailer length is 48 ft.; maximum combined length for two vehicles is 65 ft.; No triples allowed. Overnight parking in rest areas is not allowed. **RV Safety Requirements:** safety chains. Over 3,000 lbs.: trailer brakes. **Driving Laws**: Right turn on red allowed unless posted otherwise. At least two riders for carpool lanes, three riders for zipper lane. **More Information:** Public Information Office, 869 Punchbowl St., Honolulu, HI, 96813. Emergency number: 911, or *273 on cellular phones.

IDAHO: Maximum RV width 102 in.; maximum motorhome length 45 ft.; maximum trailer length 48 ft.; maximum RV height 14 ft.; maximum combined length for two- or three-vehicle combination 75 ft. Riding is allowed in truck campers. Overnight parking in rest areas is permitted where posted. **RV Safety Requirements:** Over 1,500 lbs.: trailer brakes, breakaway switch and safety chains. **Driving Laws:** Right turn on red is allowed unless posted otherwise. **More Information:** Idaho Transportation Department, P.O. Box 7129, Boise ID 82707-1129. Emergency number: *ISP or *477 on cellular phones.

ILLINOIS: Maximum RV width 102 in. (some roads 96 in.); maximum motorhome length 45 ft.; maximum trailer length 53 ft.; maximum RV height 13.5 ft.; maximum combined length of two- or three-vehicle combination (with fifth-wheel trailer only) 60 ft. Riding is allowed in truck campers. Overnight parking in rest areas only where designated. **RV Safety Requirements:** Safety chains and flares required on all trailers. Trailers over 3,000 lbs.: trailer brakes. Over 5,000 lbs.: brakes on all axles and breakaway switch. **Driving Laws:** Wipers on/headlights on. Right turn on red allowed unless posted otherwise. **More Information:** Illinois State Police Commercial Vehicle Team, 500 Iles Park, Suite 400, Springfield IL 62718; (217) 782-7820. Emergency number: 911 or (217) 786-6677; *999 on cellular phones.

INDIANA: Maximum RV width 102 in.; maximum motorhome length 45 ft.; maximum trailer length 40 ft.; maximum RV height 13.6 ft.; maximum combined length of two-vehicle combination 60 ft.; three-vehicle combination 65 ft. Riding allowed in truck campers, travel trailers and fifth-wheel trailers. Overnight parking in rest areas is not allowed. **RV Safety Requirements:** Trailers over 3,000 lbs.: trailer brakes, breakaway switch and safety chains. **Driving Laws:** Right turn on red allowed if posted. Wipers on/lights on recommended. Mobile police scanners not permitted. **More Information:** Indiana State Police, Commercial Vehicle Enforcement Div., 5252 Decatur Blvd., Suite J, Indianapolis IN 46241; (317) 615-7373 or (800) 523-2261. Emergency number: 911.

IOWA: Maximum RV width 102 in.; maximum motorhome length 45 ft.; maximum trailer length not specified; maximum RV height 13.5 ft.; maximum combined length for two-vehicle combinations 65 ft.; or three-vehicle combinations 70 ft. Riding allowed in truck campers, legal but not recommended in fifth-wheel trailers and travel trailers. Overnight parking allowed if posted. **RV Safety Requirements**: Over 3,000 lbs.: trailer brakes and safety chains. **Driving Laws:** Right turn on red allowed, unless posted otherwise. **More Information:** Iowa Department of Transportation Motor Vehicle Enforcement, P.O. Box 10473, Des Moines IA 50306-0473; (515) 237-3156. Emergency number: 911 or *55 on cellular phones.

KANSAS: Maximum RV width 108 in.; maximum motorhome length 45 ft; maximum RV height 14 ft.; maximum combined length of two- or three-vehicle combination 65 ft. Riding allowed in truck campers and trailers if 14 yrs. or older. Overnight parking in rest areas allowed in designated areas only. **RV Safety Requirements:** All trailers: safety chains. **Driving Laws:** Right turn on red is allowed, unless posted otherwise. **More Information:** Kansas Highway Patrol, 122 SW 7th, Topeka KS 66603; (785) 296-6800. Emergency number: 911, *KTA or *47 on cellular phones.

KENTUCKY: Maximum RV width is 102 in. on any public State maintained highway; maximum RV height is 13 ft 6 inches; Maximum length of two or three vehicle combinations is 65 ft. (RV, motorhome, travel trailer, camping trailer, truck camper). **RV Safety Requirements:** Trailer brakes must be sufficient to stop within legal distance of 40 ft. at 20 mph. **Driving Laws:** Wipers on/headlights on. **More Information:** Kentucky Transportation Cabinet, 200 Mero St., Division of Motor Carriers, 2nd floor, Frankfort KY 40622; (502) 564-4540. Emergency number: 911.

LOUISIANA: Maximum RV width 102 in. (on federal road systems; 96 in. elsewhere); maximum motorhome length 45 ft.; maximum trailer length 40 ft.; maximum length of two- or three-vehicle combination 70 ft. Riding allowed in truck campers. Overnight parking in rest areas is prohibited unless posted otherwise. **RV Safety Requirements:** Over 3,000 lbs.: trailer brakes, breakaway switch. **Driving Laws:** Right turn on red is allowed, unless posted otherwise. Wipers on/lights on. **More Information:** Louisiana State Police, 265 South Foster Dr., Baton Rouge LA 70806; (225) 925-4239. Emergency number: 911 (in metropolitan areas only); *ISP or *911 on cellular phones.

MAINE: Maximum RV width 102 in.; maximum motorhome length 45 ft.; maximum trailer length 48 ft.; maximum RV height 13.5 ft.; maximum combined length for two vehicles 65 ft.; triple-towing not allowed. Riding allowed in truck campers. Overnight parking in rest areas is not allowed. **RV Safety Requirements:** All trailers: 1/4-in. safety chains. Over 3,000 lbs.: brakes on all axles. **Driving Laws:** Right turn on red is allowed, unless posted otherwise. Wipers on/headlights on. **More Information:** Maine State Police, Station 20, Augusta ME 04333; (207) 624-7000. Emergency number: *77 on cellular phones.

MARYLAND: Maximum RV width 102 in.; maximum motorhome length 40 ft; maximum trailer length 40 ft.; maximum RV height 13.6 ft.; maximum combined length for two vehicles 55 ft.; triple-towing allowed unless overall length exceeds 55 feet. Riding allowed in truck campers. Overnight parking in rest areas allowed unless posted otherwise. **RV Safety Requirements:** Over 3,000 lbs.: trailer brakes, breakaway switch and safety chains required. Tunnel Regulations: Trailer hitch must be reinforced or braced to frame of towing vehicle. Safety chains must be attached to frame of towing vehicle and not to pintle hook. No propane tanks in tunnels. **Driving Laws:** Wipers on/headlights on. Right turn on red allowed, unless posted otherwise. At least two riders for carpool lane. **More Information:** State Highway Administration, Motor Carrier Division, 7491 Connelley Dr., Hanover MD 21076. Emergency number: 911; *SP or *77 on cellular phones.

MASSACHUSETTS: Maximum RV width 102 in.; maximum motorhome length 45 ft.; maximum trailer length 40 ft.; maximum RV height 13.5 ft.; maximum two-vehicle combined length 60 ft. Riding is allowed in truck campers. Overnight parking is allowed in rest areas unless posted otherwise. **RV Safety Requirements:** Trailer brakes, chains and wheel chocks. No propane allowed in tunnels (in Boston, I-90, I-93, Rt. 1A; in Newton, I-90). **Driving Laws:** Right turn on red allowed unless posted otherwise. At least two riders for carpool lane. **More Information:** Massachusetts State Police, 760 Elm St., Concord MA 01742; (978) 369-1004. Emergency number: (508) 820-2121; *SP or *77 on cellular phones.

MICHIGAN: Maximum RV width 102 in.; maximum motorhome length 45 ft.; maximum RV height 13.5 ft.; maximum combined length for two-vehicle combination 65 ft.; pickup with fifth-wheel trailer 65 ft. Riding in travel trailers, fifth-wheel trailers and truck campers allowed. Overnight parking in rest areas is not allowed. **RV Safety Requirements:** All trailers: two chains of sufficient strength are required when towing. Over 3,000 lbs.: trailer brakes. **Driving Laws:** Right turn on red allowed, unless otherwise posted. Mobile police scanners not allowed. **More Information:** Michigan State Police, Special Operations Division, Traffic Services Section, 714 Harrison Rd., East Lansing MI 48823; (517) 336-6660. Emergency number: 911.

MINNESOTA: Maximum RV width 102 in.; maximum motorhome length 45 ft; maximum trailer length 45 ft; maximum RV height 13.5 ft.; maximum lengths for two/three combination 75/70 ft. (Three-vehicle combo must be a fifth-wheel trailer, maximum length 28 ft. + watercraft, ATV, motorcycle or snowmobile). Riding allowed in travel trailers, fifth-wheel trailers and truck campers. **RV Safety Requirements:** Over 3,000 lbs.: trailer brakes, two safety chains, glass mirror and hitch to safety stands. Over 6,000 lbs.: breakaway switch also. **Driving Laws:** Headlights on during rain, sleet, snow or hail. Right turn on red is allowed, unless posted otherwise. At least two riders required for carpool lane. Mobile police scanners not allowed. **More Information:** Minnesota State Patrol, 444 Cedar St., Suite 130, St. Paul MN 55101-5130. Emergency number: 911.

MISSISSIPPI: Maximum RV width 102 in.; maximum motorhome length 45 ft; maximum trailer length 40 ft.; maximum RV height 13.5 ft. Triple-towing is allowed. Riding allowed in truck campers, fifth-wheel trailers and travel trailers. Overnight parking in rest areas is not allowed. **RV Safety Requirements:** Trailers over 2,000 lbs.: trailer brakes and safety chains. **More Information:** Mississippi Department of Public Safety, P.O. Box 958, Jackson MS 39205-0958. Emergency number: 911; *HP or *47 on cellular phones.

MISSOURI: Maximum RV width 102 in.; maximum motorhome length 45 ft.; maximum trailer length not specified; maximum RV height 14 ft. (if more than 10 miles from designated highway, width 8 ft.; height 13.5 ft.); maximum combined length for two- or three-vehicle combination 65 ft. (55 ft. if more than 10 miles from a primary or designated highway). Riding allowed in truck campers, fifth-wheel trailers and travel trailers. Overnight parking in rest areas is allowed where posted. **RV Safety Requirements:** Trailers over 3,000 lbs.: trailer brakes and breakaway switch recommended. Safety chains required for bumper hitches. **Driving Laws:** Right turn on red allowed unless posted otherwise. Wipers on/headlights on recommended. **More Information:** Missouri State Highway Patrol, Commercial Vehicle Enforcement Div., P.O. Box 568, Jefferson City MO 65102; (573) 526-6128. Road/highway information (800) 222-6400. Emergency number: 911 or *55 on cellular phones.

MONTANA: Maximum RV width 102 in.; maximum motorhome length 55 ft.; maximum trailer length not specified; maximum RV height 14 ft.; maximum combined length for three vehicles 65 ft. Towing unit must have manufacturer's rated carrying capacity in excess of 2,000 lbs. Riding allowed in truck campers and fifth-wheel trailers. Overnight parking in rest areas is allowed. **RV Safety Requirements:** All RVs should have flares or reflective signs. Trailers under 3,000 lbs.: safety chains minimum 1/4 in. in diameter. Over 3,000 lbs.: trailer brakes, breakaway switch and safety chains. **Driving Laws:** Right turn on red allowed, unless posted otherwise. **More Information:** Montana Highway Patrol, 2550 Prospect Ave., Helena MT 59620-1419. Emergency number: 911.

NEBRASKA: Maximum RV width 102 in.; maximum motorhome length 45 ft.; maximum RV height 14.5 ft.; maximum combined length for two- or three-vehicle combination 65 ft. Riding allowed in travel trailers, fifth-wheel trailers and truck campers. Overnight parking in rest areas is not allowed. **RV Safety Requirements:** All RVs are required to have flares or reflective signs. Trailers over 3,000 lbs.: trailer brakes on each wheel, breakaway switch and safety chains. **Driving Laws:** Right turn on red allowed, unless posted otherwise. **More Information:** Nebraska State Patrol, P.O. Box 94907, Lincoln NE 68509-4907; (402) 471-4545. Emergency number: (800) 525-5555 or *55 on cellular phones.

NEVADA: Maximum RV width 102 in.; maximum motorhome length 45 ft.; maximum length of trailers not specified; maximum length of two- or three-vehicle combination 70 ft. Riding is allowed in truck campers. Overnight parking in rest areas allowed in designated areas only; not to exceed 18 hours in any two-week period. **RV Safety Requirements:** All trailers over 3000 lbs.: chains and brakes on all wheels. **Driving Laws:** It is unlawful for a person to have an open container of an alcoholic beverage within the passenger area of a motor vehicle while on a highway; however, this does not apply to the living quarters of a motorhome or travel trailer. **More Information:** Planning Division Chief, Department of Transportation, 1263 S. Stewart St., Carson City NV 89712. Emergency number: 911, or dial "0" and ask for Zenith 12000 or dial *NHP on cellular phones.

NEW HAMPSHIRE: Maximum RV width 96 in.; maximum motorhome length 45 ft.; maximum trailer length 48 ft.; triple-towing is not allowed. Riding is allowed in truck campers. Overnight parking in rest areas is not allowed. **RV Safety Requirements:** Trailers over 3,000 lbs.: trailer brakes, breakaway switch, safety chains and lights. **Driving Laws:** Right turn on red allowed, unless posted otherwise. **More Information:** Director, Division of Motor Vehicles, 10 Hazen Dr., Concord NH 03305. Emergency number: 911 or *711 on cellular phones.

NEW JERSEY: Maximum RV width 96 in. (102 in. on certain federal roads); maximum motorhome length 40 ft.; maximum RV height 13.5 ft.; maximum combined length 62 ft. Riding is not allowed in truck campers or trailers. **RV Safety Requirements:** Trailers over 3,000 lbs.: trailer brakes, breakaway switch, chains and safety glass. **Driving Laws:** Wipers on/headlights on. Right turn on red is allowed, unless posted otherwise. Seat belts required. At least two riders in carpool lane. Open propane cylinders are not allowed while traveling on open highways. New Jersey Turnpike: Motorhome may tow vehicle as long as all four wheels are on the ground; no tow dollies or piggybacks. Garden State Parkway: Motorhome may tow another vehicle with tow bar, safety chains and emergency tail lights on both vehicles. **More Information:** Department of Transportation, Motor Vehicle Commission, CN-174, Trenton NJ 08666; (609) 292-6500. Emergency number: 911 or (888) SAF-ROAD; *77 on cellular phones.

NEW MEXICO: Maximum RV width 102 in.; maximum motorhome length 45 ft.; maximum trailer length 40 ft; maximum RV height 14 ft.; maximum length of two-vehicle combination 65 ft. Riding is allowed in pickup campers. Overnight parking in rest areas is allowed, but not more than 24 hours in any three-day period in the same area. **RV Safety Requirements:** Trailers over 3,000 lbs.: trailer brakes and chains. **Driving Laws:** Wipers on/headlights on. **More Information:** New Mexico Highway Department, P.O. Box 1149, Santa Fe NM 87504-1149; (505) 827-2241. Emergency number: (505) 827-9000; *911 on cellular phones.

NEW YORK: Maximum RV width 96 in. (102 in. on qualifying or access highways); maximum motorhome length 45 ft.; maximum trailer length 48 ft.; maximum RV height 13.6 ft.; maximum combined length for two-vehicle combination 65 ft. Riding is allowed in truck campers or fifth-wheel trailers. RVs are not allowed in carpool lane, unless posted. Bottled gas is prohibited in tunnels, the lower levels of the George Washington Bridge and the Verrazano-Narrows Bridge, and on I-95 through Manhattan. **RV Safety Requirements:** Trailers over 1,000 lbs. unladen and trailers having a maximum gross weight in excess of 3,000 lbs.: trailer brakes and safety chains. **Driving Laws:** Wipers on/headlights on. Right turn on red allowed, unless posted otherwise; In New York City, right turn on red is not allowed unless posted. Radar detectors and mobile police scanners are not permitted in non-commercial motor vehicles with a gvwr over 18,000 lbs. **More Information:** State of New York Department of Motor Vehicles, Empire State Plaza, Albany NY 12228; (800) CALL-DMV. Emergency number: 911 or *DWI on cellular phones.

NORTH CAROLINA: Maximum RV width 102 in.; maximum motorhome length 45 ft.; maximum trailer length 48 ft.; maximum RV height 13.5 ft.; maximum length for two-vehicle combination 60 ft. Riding allowed in truck campers. Overnight parking is permitted in some rest areas unless otherwise posted. **RV Safety Requirements:** All RVs: safety glass. Trailers over 4,000 lbs.: trailer brakes. **Driving Laws:** Wipers on/lights on. Right turn on red allowed, unless posted otherwise. **More Information**: North Carolina State Highway Patrol, 512 N. Salisbury St., Raleigh NC 27604; (919) 715-8683. Emergency number: 911 or (800) 672-4527; *HP on cellular phones.

NORTH DAKOTA: Maximum RV width 102 in.; maximum motorhome length 50 ft; maximum trailer length 53 ft.; maximum RV height 14 ft.; maximum combined length for two- or three-vehicle combination 75 ft. Riding allowed in fifth-wheel trailers but not in truck campers. Overnight parking in rest areas allowed, unless posted otherwise. **RV Safety Requirements:** All RVs: flares or reflective signs and fire extinguisher. All trailers: trailer brakes, safety chains and breakaway switch. **Driving Laws:** Right turn on red allowed, unless posted otherwise. **More Information:** North Dakota Highway Patrol, 600 E. Boulevard Ave., Bismarck ND 58505-0240. Emergency number: 911.

OHIO: Maximum RV width 102 in; maximum motorhome length 45 ft.; maximum trailer length 40 ft.; maximum length of two- or three-vehicle combination 65 ft. Riding allowed in truck campers. Overnight parking allowed in service areas, no rest areas. Trailers may be barred at any time, or tire chains required, due to hazardous road conditions. **RV Safety Requirements:** Safety chains, turn signals and brake lights. Trailers over 2,000 lbs.: trailer brakes and breakaway switch. Ohio Turnpike: Over 2,000 lbs.: trailer brakes and breakaway switch. **Driving Laws:** Rest area parking allowed for a maximum of three hours. **More Information:** Director, Department of Public Safety, 1970 W. Broad St., Columbus OH 43223. Emergency number: (800) GRAB-DUI, (888) 877-PATROL OR 911; *DUI on cellular phones.

OKLAHOMA: Maximum RV width 102 in.; maximum motorhome length 45 ft.; maximum trailer length 40 ft.; maximum RV height 13.5 ft.; maximum length of two- or three-vehicle combination 65 ft. Riding allowed in truck campers. Overnight parking in rest areas is allowed, unless posted otherwise. **RV Safety Requirements:** All trailers: coupling equipment designed to prevent swerving, trailer brakes, breakaway switch and safety chains. Rubber or fabric aprons behind rear wheels required. **Driving Laws:** Right turn on red allowed unless posted otherwise. **More Information:** Oklahoma Department of Public Safety—Size & Weight Permit Div., 3600 N. Martin Luther King Blvd., Oklahoma City OK 73136; (405) 425-2206. Emergency number: (405) 425-2385 or *55 on cell phone.

OREGON: Maximum RV width 102 in.; maximum motorhome length 45 ft.; maximum trailer length 45 ft.; maximum length of two-vehicle combination 65 ft. Riding in truck campers allowed. Passengers are allowed in fifth-wheel trailers if the trailer is equipped with the following: All windows are made of safety glazing materials; an auditory or visual signaling device that passengers can use to gain the attention of the motor-vehicle driver towing the vehicle; and at least one unobstructed exit capable of being opened from both the interior and exterior of the vehicle. **RV Safety Requirements:** All trailers must have full lighting equipment. Hitches and chains must meet SAE standards and use recommendations. Combinations of vehicles that include a motor vehicle and any other vehicle shall be equipped with a brake system on one or more of the vehicles sufficient to stop both from 20 mph without leaving a 12-foot-wide travel lane. The stopping distance must be within 25 ft. for vehicles under 8,000 GVWR, and within 35 ft. for vehicles weighing 8,000 GVWR and more. Manufacturer's requirements must be followed on towed vehicles. **Driving Laws:** Headlights must be on when limited-visibility conditions exist of 1,000 feet or less. Right turn on red after stopping is allowed unless posted otherwise. **More Information:** Oregon Department of Transportation, Transportation Safety Division, 235 Union St. NE, Salem OR 97301; 511 or (800) 977-ODOT (6368) in state; (503) 588-2941 outside of Oregon. Emergency number: 911.

PENNSYLVANIA: Maximum RV width 102 in.; maximum motorhome length 45 ft.; maximum trailer length not specified; maximum length of two-vehicle combination 60 ft. Riding allowed in fifth-wheel trailers with electronic communications. Overnight parking in rest areas is not allowed. RVs are not allowed in carpool lane. **RV Safety Requirements:** All RVs or motor vehicles towing an RV: flares or reflective signs and fire extinguisher. All trailers: brakes and breakaway system if the gross trailer weight with load exceeds 40 percent of the towing vehicle's gross weight with load; safety chains and lighting equipment (brakes, turn signals, reflectors). **Driving Laws:** Headlights must be on in inclement weather. Right turn on red allowed, unless posted otherwise. **More Information:** Pennsylvania Department of Transportation, Bureau of Highway Safety & Traffic Engineering, 55 Walnut St., Forum Pl., P.O. Box 2047, Harrisburg PA 17105-2047. Emergency number: 911.

RHODE ISLAND: Maximum RV width 102 in.; maximum motorhome length 40 ft; maximum trailer length not specified; maximum length of two-vehicle combination 60 ft. Riding allowed in truck campers. Overnight parking in rest areas allowed unless posted otherwise. **RV Safety Requirements:** Over 4,000 lbs.: trailer brakes, breakaway switch, two safety chains and flares. **Driving Laws:** All passengers must use seat belts. Children under 4 yrs. must be in child-restraint systems; children under 6 yrs. must be properly restrained in the back seat. **More Information:** Rhode Island Division of Motor Vehicles, 100 Main Street, Pawtucket, RI 02860. Emergency number: 911 or *77 on cellular phones.

SOUTH CAROLINA: Maximum RV width 102 in.; maximum motorhome length 45 ft.; maximum trailer length 48 ft.; maximum RV height 13.5 ft. Triple-towing not allowed. Riding is allowed in truck campers. Overnight parking in rest areas is not allowed. **RV Safety**

Requirements: Trailers over 10,001 lbs., other than fifth-wheel trailers: chains, cable, etc. **Driving Laws**: Wipers on/headlights on. Right turn on red (after full stop) is allowed, unless posted otherwise. Front-seat passengers must wear seat belts. Children under 4 yrs. must be in child-restraint safety seats; children 4-6 must use child-restraint safety seats or wear seat belts. **More Information:** South Carolina Department of Public Safety, State Transport Police Div., P. O. Box 1993, Blythewood SC 29016; (803) 896-5500. Emergency number: (803) 896-9621;*HP or *47 on cellular phones.

SOUTH DAKOTA: Maximum RV width 102 in.; maximum motorhome length 45 ft.; maximum trailer length 53 ft.; maximum combined length for a single motor vehicle and two trailers 75 ft. (on Needles Highway 87 in the Black Hills, maximum width 8 ft. 7 in., maximum height 10 ft. 8 in.). Riding allowed in truck campers; in fifth-wheel trailers only with two-way communication. Overnight parking in rest areas is not allowed unless posted otherwise. **RV Safety Requirements:** All RVs: flares or reflective signs. Trailers over 3,000 lbs.: breakaway switch and safety chains. **Driving Laws:** Right turn on red allowed, unless posted otherwise. Weigh-Station Requirements: All towed vehicles, motor trucks or trailers over 8,000 lbs. must stop. **More Information:** South Dakota Highway Patrol, 118 W. Capitol Ave., Pierre SD 57501-2000. (605) 773-4578 or emergency number: 911.

TENNESSEE: Maximum RV width 102 in.; maximum motorhome length 45 ft.; maximum trailer length 40 ft.; maximum RV height 13.5 ft.; maximum combined length for two- or three-vehicle combination 65 ft. Overnight parking in rest areas allowed unless posted. **RV Safety Requirements:** Trailers over 3,000 lbs.: trailer brakes, breakaway switch, safety chains (chains not required on gooseneck fifth-wheel trailers). **Driving Laws:** Wipers on/headlights on. Right turn on red allowed, unless posted otherwise. **More Information:** Tennessee Highway Patrol, 1150 Foster Ave., Nashville TN 37249-1000. Emergency number: 911, (615) 741-2069; *THP or *847 on cellular phones.

TEXAS: Maximum RV width 102 in.; maximum motorhome length 45 ft.; maximum trailer length not specified; maximum RV height 14 ft.; maximum length of two- or three-vehicle combination 65 ft. Speed limit for travel trailers: 60 during the day, 55 at night, unless otherwise posted. Overnight parking in rest areas is allowed (up to 24 hours). **RV Safety Requirements:** All trailers except fifth-wheels: safety chains. Trailers over 4,500 lbs.: trailer brakes, breakaway switch, flares and mirrors. **Driving Laws:** Headlights on 1/2 hour after sunset to 1/2 hour before sunrise. Right turn on red allowed after complete stop. **More Information:** Texas Department of Public Safety, P.O. Box 4087, Austin TX 78773; (512) 424-2000. Emergency number: 911.

UTAH: Maximum RV width 102 in.; maximum motorhome length 45 ft.; maximum trailer length 40 ft.; maximum RV height 14 ft.; maximum combined length for two- or three-vehicle combination 65 ft. or by special permit. Riding in truck campers is allowed. 12-hour maximum parking in rest areas. **RV Safety Requirements:** Trailers over 3,000 lbs.: trailer brakes, safety chains and breakaway switch. **Driving Laws:** Right turn on red is allowed, unless posted otherwise. **More Information:** Utah Department of Transportation, 4501 South 2700 West, Salt Lake City UT 84119-141265; (801) 965-4000. Emergency number: 911 or (801) 965-4219; *911 on cellular phones.

VERMONT: Maximum RV width 102 in.; maximum motorhome length 46 ft.; maximum trailer length 53 ft.; maximum combined length for two-vehicle combinaton 65 ft. Riding is allowed in truck campers. Overnight parking in rest areas is not allowed. **RV Safety Requirements:** Trailers over 3,000 lbs.: trailer brakes on one axle, breakaway switch and safety chains. Trailers over 6,000 lbs.: trailer brakes on all wheels, breakaway switch and safety chains. **Driving Laws:** Right turn on red is allowed, unless posted otherwise. Headlights on from 1/2 hour after sunset to 1/2 hour before sunrise. **More Information:** Department of Motor Vehicles, 120 State St., Montpelier VT 05603-0001; (802) 828-2000. Emergency number: 911.

VIRGINIA: Maximum RV width 102 in.; maximum motorhome length 45 ft.; maximum trailer length 45 ft.; maximum RV height 13.5 ft.; maximum combined length for two-vehicle combination 65 ft. Riding is allowed in truck campers. Overnight parking in rest areas is permitted unless posted otherwise. RVs allowed in the HOV-3 (carpool) lanes if there are three or more occupants. In the Tidewater area, RVs are allowed in the HOV-2 lanes only if there are two or more occupants and the gvw is less than 10,000 lbs. Tunnel Regulations: Maximum height 13 ft 6 in. Maximum of two approved propane gas tanks 20 lbs. each. Tanks must be turned off when going through tunnels. **RV Safety Requirements:** All trailers: safety chains. Trailers over 3,000 lbs.: trailer brakes, breakaway switch. **Driving Laws:** Right turn on red allowed, unless posted otherwise. Wipers on/lights on. Front-seat passengers are required to wear seat belts; children up to 5 yrs. must be in child-restraint safety seats. Radar detectors not permitted. **More Information:** Department of State Police, P.O. Box 27472, Richmond VA 23261-7472; (804) 674-2000. Emergency number: 911 or #77

WASHINGTON: Maximum RV width 102 in.; maximum motorhome length 46 ft.; maximum trailer length 53 ft.; maximum RV height 14 ft.; maximum combined length for two vehicles 60 ft.; triple-towing not allowed. No vehicle towing a trailer, or no vehicle or combination over 10,000 lbs. may be driven in the left-hand lane of a limited-access roadway having three or more lanes for traffic moving in one direction, except when preparing for a left turn. Riding allowed in truck campers. Minimum of two riders required in carpool lane; trailers are not allowed in carpool lanes. Overnight parking in rest areas allowed; 8-hr. maximum suggested. Mountain Pass Regulations: Tire chains are required from November 1-March 31 on RVs over 10,000 lbs. on all passes. **RV Safety Requirements:** All RVs: flares or reflective signs, fire extinguishers and safety chains. Trailers over 3,000 lbs.: trailer brakes, breakaway switch. Vehicles over 10,001 lbs. gvwr and vehicle combinatons are required to obey truck speed limits. **Driving Laws:** Right turn on red allowed, unless posted otherwise. **More Information:** Washington State Patrol, Commercial Vehicle Enforcement Section, P.O. Box 42614, Olympia WA 98504-2614; (360) 753-0350. Road and highway information number: (800) 695-ROAD. Emergency number: 911.

WEST VIRGINIA: Maximum RV width 102 in.; maximum motorhome length 45 ft; maximum trailer length 40 ft.; maximum RV height 13.5 ft.; maximum combined length for two vehicles 65 ft. (major roads)/55 ft. (other routes). Triple-towing is not allowed. Riding allowed in truck campers and fifth-wheel trailers. **RV Safety Requirements:** Safety chains required; trailers over 3,000 lbs. gvwr: trailer brakes required. **Driving Laws:** Wipers on/headlights on. Right turn on red allowed, unless posted otherwise. Overnight parking is not allowed. **More Information:** West Virginia Division of Highways, Maintenance Division, Central Permit Office, Bldg. 5, Room A-337, 1900 Kanawha Blvd. E., Charleston WV 25305-0430; (304) 558-9483. Emergency number: 911; *SP or *77 on cellular phones.

WISCONSIN: Maximum RV width 102 in.; maximum motorhome length 45 ft.; maximum trailer length 48 ft.;maximum RV height 13.5 ft.; maximum combined length for two vehicles 65 ft.; maximum combined length for three vehicles 65 ft (with permit only). Riding is allowed in truck campers. Riding is allowed in fifth-wheel trailers, but no one under age 12 unless accompanied by a person 16 or older; trailer must be equipped with a two-way voice communication between driver and occupant(s). **RV Safety Requirements:** All trailers require safety chains; trailers over 3,000 lbs. require trailer brakes. **Driving Laws:** Right turn on red is allowed, unless posted otherwise. **More Information:** Wisconsin State Patrol, 4802 Sheboygan Ave., Rm. 551, Madison WI 53707-7912; (608) 266-0264. Emergency number: 911.

WYOMING: Maximum RV width 102 in.; maximum motorhome length 60 ft.; maximum trailer length 45 ft.; maximum combined length for two or three vehicles 85 ft. Riding in truck campers is allowed. Overnight parking in rest areas is not allowed unless posted. **RV Safety Requirements:** All house trailers are required to have flares or reflective signs. All vehicles or combinations of vehicles must have sufficient brakes to stop within 40 ft. from an initial speed of 20 mph on a level, dry, smooth, hard surface. **Driving Laws:** Right turn on red is allowed, unless posted otherwise. **More Information:** Wyoming Highway Patrol, 5300 Bishop Blvd., Cheyenne WY 82003-3340; (307) 777-4306. Emergency number: (800) 442-9090 or #HELP on cellular phones.

Canada

Note: 2.6 m. = 8 1/2 ft.
12.5 m. = 41 feet; 16.15 m = 53 ft.

ALBERTA: Maximum RV height 4.0 m.; maximum RV width 2.6 m.; maximum trailer length 12.5 m.; maximum motorhome length 13 m.; combined length for two or three (w/fifth-wheel) vehicles 20 m. **RV Safety Requirements:** Trailers over 2,000 lbs. must have trailer brakes, unless the lead vehicle is twice the weight of the trailer. **Driving Laws:** Right turn on red is allowed, unless posted otherwise. Headlights on when conditions restrict visibility to 150 meters/500 ft. or less; driving with headlights on during all hours of the day is permitted. All passengers are required to wear seat belts; children up to 6 yrs./40 lbs. must be in child safety-restraint seats. **More Information:** Alberta Infrastructure and Transportation, Twin Atria Building, 4999-98 Ave., Edmonton AB T6B 2X3. Emergency number: 911.

BRITISH COLUMBIA: Maximum RV height 4.15 m.; maximum RV width 2.6 m.; maximum trailer length 12.5 m; maximum motorhome length 12.5 m.; maximum length of two-vehicle combination 20 m./65 1/2 ft.; three-vehicle combinations are prohibited. **RV Safety Requirements:** Trailers over 3,000 lbs. must have trailer brakes on all wheels, breakaway switch and safety chains (except fifth-wheel trailers). Motorhomes (only) may tow motor vehicles via a tow bar without brakes hooked up on the towed motor vehicle when the towed motor vehicle's weight is less than 4,409 lbs. and less than 40 percent of the gross vehicle weight rating (gvwr) of the motorhome towing it. **Driving Laws:** Right turn on red is allowed, unless posted otherwise. All passengers must wear seat belts; children up to 40 lbs. must be in child-restraint safety seats. **More Information:** Insurance Corporation of British Columbia, Commercial Transport and Inspection, Box 3750, Victoria BC V8W 3Y5. Emergency number: 911

MANITOBA: Maximum RV height 4.15 m.; maximum RV width 2.6 m.; maximum trailer length 12.5 m.; maximum motorhome length 12.5 m.; maximum combined length for two vehicles 21.5 m.; combined length for three vehicles (fifth-wheel combinations only) 23 m. Riding is allowed in truck campers. Open propane cylinders are not allowed while traveling on open highways. **RV Safety Requirements:** All trailers must have safety chains; trailers over 2,000 lbs. must also have trailer brakes. **Driving Laws:** Right turn on red is allowed, unless posted otherwise. All passengers are required to wear seat belts; children up to age 5 yrs./50 lbs. must be in child-restraint safety seats. Radar detectors and mobile scanners are not permitted. **More Information:** Vehicle Standards and Inspections, 1075 Portage Ave., Winnipeg MB R3G 0S1. Emergency number: (204) 983-5461.

NEW BRUNSWICK: Maximum RV height 4.15 m.; maximum RV width 2.6 m.; maximum trailer length 12.5 m.; maximum motorhome length 12.5 m.; maximum combined length for two-vehicle combination 23 m. Overnight parking is allowed if posted. **RV Safety Requirements:** All RVs are required to have flares or reflective signs and a fire extinguisher. Trailers over 3,000 lbs. must have trailer brakes, breakaway switch and safety chains. **Driving Laws:** Right turn on red is allowed, unless posted otherwise. All occupants must wear seat belts; children up to 40 lbs. (approximately 4 yrs. of age) must be in the appropriate child-restraint safety seat. Radar detectors are not allowed. **More Information:** Department of Public Safety, Licensing Registration Branch, P.O. Box 6000, Fredericton NB E3B 5H1.

NEWFOUNDLAND and LABRADOR: Maximum RV height 4.15 m.; maximum RV width 2.6 m.; maximum trailer length 12.5 m.; maximum motorhome length 12.5 m; maximum combined length for two-vehicle combination 23 m. Riding in truck campers not specified. Overnight parking is not allowed unless posted. **RV Safety Requirements:** All trailers must have safety chains. Trailers with a gvwr in excess of 1,350 kg must also have trailer brakes and breakaway switch. **Driving Laws:** Right turn on red is allowed, unless posted otherwise. All passengers are required to wear seat belts. Radar detectors and mobile police scanners are not permitted. **More Information:** Department of Government Services & Lands, Motor Registration Division, P.O. Box 8710, St. Johns NF A1B 4J5. Emergency numbers: 911 or *RCMP on cellular phones.

NORTHWEST TERRITORIES: Maximum RV height 4.2 m.; maximum RV width 3.2 m.; maximum trailer length not specified; maximum motorhome length 12.5 m.; maximum length of two-vehicle combination not specified. Overnight parking in rest areas is permitted. **RV Safety Requirements:** Brakes are required on trailers over 1,360 kg.; safety chains are required on all trailers except fifth-wheel trailers. **Driving Laws:** Headlights or daytime running lights should be on at all times. Right turn on red allowed after stop and when clear. All passengers must wear seat belts; children up to 40 lbs. must be in child-restraint safety seats. Radar-detection devices are prohibited. **More information:** Department of Transportation, Road Licensing & Safety Division, 4510 Franklin Ave., Yellowknife, NT X1A 2L9. Emergency number: (867) 669-1111.

NOVA SCOTIA: Maximum RV height 4.15 m.; maximum RV width 2.6 m.; maximum trailer length 12.5 m.; maximum motorhome length 12.5 m.; maximum combined length for two-vehicle combination 23 m. Riding in pickup camper is permitted if seats are equipped with safety belts. Open propane cylinders are not allowed while traveling on open highways. Towing mirrors must be attached to vehicle if the load or trailer obscures rear vision; however, it is illegal to drive on the highway with the extra mirrors in place without the load or trailer attached to the vehicle. **RV Safety Requirements:** All RVs are required to have flares. All trailers must have safety chains; trailers over 3,000 lbs. must also have breakaway switch; over 4,000 lbs. must also have trailer brakes. **Driving Laws:** Right turn on red is allowed, unless posted otherwise. All passengers are required to wear seat belts; children up to 40 lbs. must be in child-restraint safety seats. Radar detectors are not allowed. **More Information:** Department of Business & Consumer Services Call Center, 1505 Barrington St. N., 8th Fl., Halifax NS B3J 3E7. Emergency number: 911.

NUNAVUT: Maximum RV height 4.2 m.; maximum RV width 2.6 m.; maximum trailer length not specified; maximum motorhome length 12.0 m.; maximum length of two-vehicle combination 21.0 m. Riding is allowed in truck campers. (Note: Few roadways in Nunavut can accommodate RVs.)

ONTARIO: Maximum RV height 4.15 m.; maximum RV width 2.6 m.; maximum trailer length 12.5 m.; maximum motorhome length 12.5 m.; maximum length of two-vehicle combination 23 m. Riding in truck campers is allowed. Overnight parking is allowed in restricted areas. **RV Safety Requirements:** Over 3,000 lbs./1,360 kg. brakes are required. Safety chains are required unless the trailer is attached by a fifth-wheel attachment. **Driving Laws:** Driver and all passengers are required to wear seat belts. Children up to 9 kg./20 lbs. and under 26 in./66 cm. must be secured in a rearward-facing child-restraint system secured by the seat-belt assembly. Children between 20-40 lbs./9-18 kg. and over 26 in./66 cm. must be secured in a child-restraint system secured by the seat-belt assembly and a tether strap. Children over 40 lbs./18 kg. can use a booster seat secured by the seat-belt assembly. Radar detection and jamming devices are prohibited. **More Information:** Ministry of Transportation Information, 301 St. Paul St., St. Catharines ON L2R 7R4. Emergency number: 911.

PRINCE EDWARD ISLAND: Maximum RV height 4.15 m.; maximum RV width 2.6 m.; maximum trailer length 12.5 m; maximum motorhome length 12.5 m; maximum length for two-vehicle combination 23 m. Riding in truck campers, fifth-wheel trailers not specified. Overnight camping is allowed in rest areas unless posted otherwise. **RV Safety Requirements:** All trailers (except fifth-wheels) must have safety chains. Trailers 1,500 kgs. and over must also have trailer brakes and breakaway switch. **Driving Laws:** Right turn on red is allowed, unless posted otherwise. All passengers must wear seat belts; children up to 40 lbs. must be in child-restraint safety seats. Radar detectors are not allowed. Ferry Regulations: Propane tanks must be shut off. **More Information:** Highway Safety Operations, P.O. Box 2000, Charlottetown, PE C1A 7N8. Emergency numbers: (902) 368-5200 (during business hours); (902) 437-8534 (after hours) or 911.

QUEBEC: Maximum RV height 4.15 m.; maximum RV width 2.6 m.; maximum trailer length 12.5 m.; maximum motorhome length 12.5 m.; maximum length of two-vehicle combination 23 m. Riding is allowed in truck campers, with seat belts. Overnight parking in rest areas is not allowed. **RV Safety Requirements:** All RVs are required to have flares or reflective signs if wider than 2 m./6 1/2 ft. Trailers over 1,300 kg./2,865 lbs. or exceeding 50% of tow-vehicle weight must have trailer brakes, breakaway switch and safety chains. **Driving Laws:** Right turn on red is strictly prohibited except when allowed by an additional green arrow. All occupants are required to wear seat belts; children up to 40 lbs. must be in child-restraint safety seats; children under 8 yrs. should be secured in a booster seat. Radar detectors are not allowed, whether connected or not. **More Information:** Ministere des Transportes, Service de la normalisation technique, 700, boul. Rene Levesque, Est, Quebec PQ G1R 5H1; (418) 643-1345. Emergency number: 911.

SASKATCHEWAN: Maximum RV height 4.15m; maximum RV width 2.6 m.; maximum trailer length 12.5 m.; maximum motorhome length 12.5 m., 14 m with permit; maximum combined length for a two- or three-vehicle combination (only if fifth-wheel combination) 23 m. Triple towing is allowed only with fifth-wheel trailer. Riding is allowed but not recommended in truck campers. **RV Safety Requirements:** Trailers over 3,000 lbs. must have trailer brakes, breakaway switch and double safety chains. **Driving Laws:** Right turn on red is allowed, unless otherwise posted. All passengers are required to wear seat belts; children up to 40 lbs. must be in child-restraint safety seats. **More Information:** Saskatchewan Highways & Transportation, Trucking Policy and Programs, 8th Fl., 1855 Victoria Ave., Regina SK S4P 3T2; (306) 787-5307. Emergency number: 911.

YUKON TERRITORIES: Maximum RV height 4.9 m.; maximum RV width 2.6 m.; maximum trailer length 16.15 m.; maximum motorhome length 16.15 m.; maximum length of two-vehicle combination 25 m. Three-vehicle combinations must be fifth-wheel with one additional trailer on ball hitch connected to fifth-wheel's frame. Overnight parking is allowed unless posted. **RV Safety Requirements:** Trailers over 910 kg. must have trailer brakes and safety chains. **Driving Laws:** Headlights required at all times. Right turn on red is allowed, unless otherwise posted. All passengers are required to wear seat belts; children up to 6 yrs./44 lbs. must be in child-restraint safety seats. **More Information:** Tourism Yukon, P.O. Box 2703, Whitehorse YK Y1A 2C6; (867) 667-5315. Emergency number: 911.

Bridge, Tunnel & Ferry Regulations

RV RESTRICTIONS:

It's wise to check in advance with local authorities before traveling in the following areas, particularly if travel via ferry, bridge or tunnel is planned.

California: Pulling travel trailers may not be allowed in snow areas. Contact the California Highway Patrol before entering a snow area; chains may be required at any time. Trailers may be barred due to high winds, blowing sand, etc. RVs over 20 feet may experience difficulty in negotiating hairpin turns on State Highway 89.

Connecticut: RV size may be limited on the Connecticut River ferry between Chester and Hadlyme; also on Wilbur Cross and Merrit parkways.

Illinois: Trailers are prohibited on boulevards in and around Chicago.

Massachusetts: Trailers are prohibited on Memorial Drive in Cambridge and Storrow Drive in Boston, along the Charles River; and on many other parkways in the Boston area.

Montana: All vehicles over 21 feet long (including bumpers) and 8 feet wide (including mirrors) are not permitted through Logan Pass at the summit of Going-to-the-Sun Road in Glacier National Park. Shuttle service is available between St. Mary and West Glacier. Restriction applies from Avalanche Campground on the south side to Sun Point area on the north side.

New York: Trailers and motorhomes are not permitted on Taconic State Parkway; trailers are not permitted on most parkways.

LP-GAS PROHIBITED:

Maryland/Baltimore: Baltimore Harbor and Fort McHenry (I-95) tunnels. Alternate route for RVs with propane over the Francis Scott Key Bridge is I-695.

Massachusetts/Boston Harbor: All.

New York/East River: Between Manhattan and Brooklyn: Brooklyn Battery Tunnel. Between Manhattan and Queens: Queens Midtown Tunnel.

New York and New Jersey/Hudson River: Between Manhattan and Jersey City: Holland Tunnel. Between Manhattan and Fort Lee: Lower level George Washington Bridge (I-95 South) and George Washington Bridge Expressway. Lower level Verrazano Narrows Bridge. Between Manhattan and Weehawken: Lincoln Tunnel.

LP-GAS RESTRICTIONS:

Virginia/Chesapeake Bay Bridge/Tunnel: RVs equipped with ICC-approved compressed cooking tanks not exceeding two 45-pound capacity tanks (or two permanently mounted containers with maximum total capacity of 200 pounds) may cross the facility provided that, in the opinion of the toll collector or police sergeant after inspection, the tanks are completely shut off and securely attached.

Texas/Houston Ship Channel: Washburn Tunnel between Pasadena and Galena Park: Maximum of two 71/2-gallon containers (30 pounds gas each) or one 10-gallon container (40 pounds gas) of DOT (ICC)-approved type, with shutoff valve at discharge opening. Valve must be closed when in tunnel. LP-gas as vehicle fuel prohibited. 71/2-gallon containers (30 pounds gas each) or one 10-gallon container (40 pounds gas) of DOT (ICC)-approved type, with shutoff valve at discharge opening. Valve must be closed when in tunnel. LP-gas as vehicle fuel prohibited.

TRAVEL SECTION

Alabama

READER SERVICE INFO

The following businesses have placed an ad in the Alabama Travel Section. To receive free information, enter their Reader Service number on the Reader Service Card opposite page 48/Discover Section in the front of this directory:

Advertiser	RS#
Auburn-Opelika Convention & Visitors	4223
Bella Terra of Gulf Shores	4221
Lake Osprey	4304
Noccalula Falls Park & Campground	472
Point Mallard Campground (City Park)	4234

TIME ZONE

Alabama is in the Central Time Zone.

TOPOGRAPHY

The state's terrain is varied; the Appalachian Mountains enter the state from the northeast and gradually spread out into rolling hills and rich farmlands. Alabama has numerous lakes and 53 miles of gulf coastline.

TEMPERATURE

The temperature reaches 60° by March and in summer the average is in the low 80s with periods of 90° and above. Generally, November requires only a sweater or light jacket and snow is rarely found except in the high altitudes of northern Alabama. The average temperature in January is 46°.

TRAVEL & TOURISM INFO

State Agency:
Alabama Tourism Department
401 Adams Ave., Suite 126,
P.O. Box 4927
Montgomery, AL 36103-4927
(800/ALABAMA or 334/242-4169)
www.alabama.travel

Regional Agencies:
Alabama Mountain Lakes Tourist Association
25062 North St., P.O. Box 1075
Mooresville, AL 35649
(800/648-5381)
www.northalabama.org

Metropolitan Lakes Region
1330 Quintard Ave.
Anniston, AL 36202
(256/237-3536 or 800/489-1087)
www.metropolitansregion.com

Southeast Alabama Trails Tourism Association
462 N Oates Street Houston Co.
Admin. Bldg. 4th Fl.
Dothan, AL 36301
(334/794-4093)
www.southeastalabamatrails.com

Tenn-Tom Tourism Association
P.O. Box 671, Columbus, MS 39703
(662/328-3286)
www.tenntom.org

Local Agencies:
For local information, contact the Chamber of Commerce or Convention and Visitor's Bureau for the locality you are interested in.

RECREATIONAL INFO

Biking:
Alabama Dept. of Transportation
1409 Coliseum Blvd.
Montgomery, AL 36130
(334/242-6358).

Fishing & Hunting:
Alabama Dept. of Conservation & Natural Resources
Game & Fish Division
64 N. Union Street
Montgomery, AL 36130

FREE INFO! Enter #4223 on Reader Service Card

FREE INFO! Enter #472 on Reader Service Card

FREE INFO! Enter #4234 on Reader Service Card

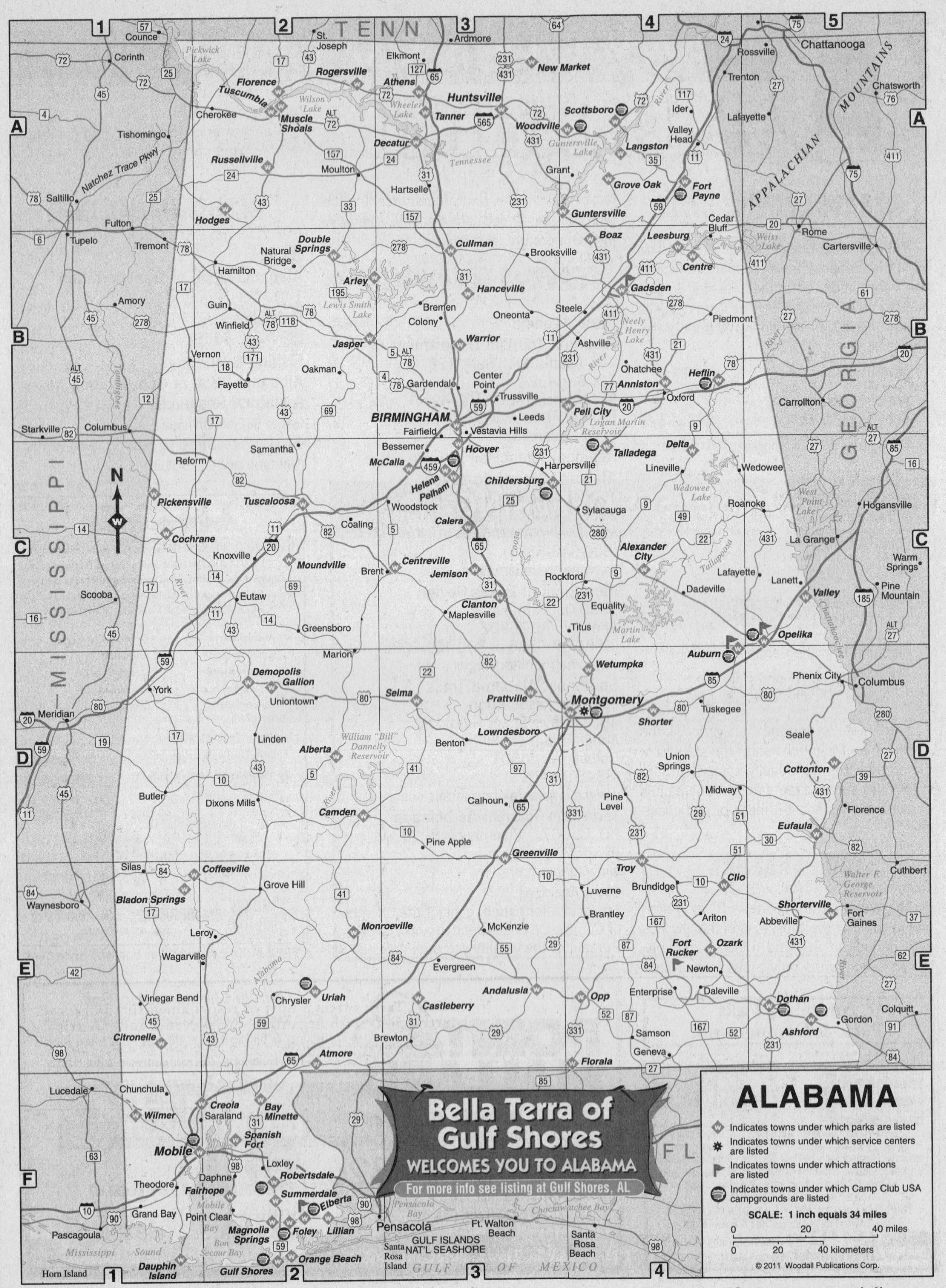
ALABAMA
Indicates towns under which parks are listed
Indicates towns under which service centers are listed
Indicates towns under which attractions are listed
Indicates towns under which Camp Club USA campgrounds are listed
SCALE: 1 inch equals 34 miles
0 20 40 miles
0 20 40 kilometers
© 2011 Woodall Publications Corp.
Bella Terra of Gulf Shores
WELCOMES YOU TO ALABAMA
For more info see listing at Gulf Shores, AL
TENN
MISSISSIPPI
GEORGIA
FL
APPALACHIAN MOUNTAINS
GULF OF MEXICO
BIRMINGHAM
Montgomery
Mobile
Huntsville
Tuscaloosa
Chattanooga
Columbus
Meridian
Pensacola
Dothan
Gulf Shores

(334/242-3465)
www.dcnr.state.al.us.

Golf: For information, call (800/ALABAMA). For information on a complex of 23 courses and 432 holes, which stretches across the state, call **Sunbelt Golf Corporation** (800/949-4444). www.rtj-golf.com

SHOPPING

Mountain Top Flea Market, Attalla, offers 2.6 miles of shopping at 1,500 vendor booths. 11301 US Hwy 278 W, Attalla, AL 35954 (800/535-2286).

Boaz Shopper's Paradise, Boaz. Shop at 140 direct factory outlets and discount retailers. Located one hour from Birmingham or Huntsville, at 306 W Mann Ave, Boaz, AL 35957 (800/SHOP-BOAZ).

Rue's Antique Mall and Deli, Brundidge. You'll find everything from antique bottles and dishes, to comic books and furniture. 123 Main St, Brundidge, AL 36010 (334/735-3125).

UNIQUE FEATURES

The birthplace of Helen Keller, Alabama has a rich history in the Civil Rights Movement, as well as the Civil War. From the mountains and lakes of North and Central Alabama, to the beaches lining the coast, Alabama has much to offer anglers, hunters, or even the most seasoned traveler. Among the many reason to visit Alabama, is to visit Russell Cave National Monument in Bridgeport, and the Indian Mound and Museum in Florence, to see the prehistoric lifestyles of Native Americans. The Jesse Owens Museum Park in Moulton, which pays homage to one of the greatest athletes of the 20th century.

BUSINESSES OFFERING

	Things to See & Do	RV Sales	RV Service
AUBURN			
Auburn University	⚑		
Auburn-Opelika Convention & Visitors Bureau	⚑		
Hodge's Vineyard	⚑		
Jule Collins Smith Museum of Fine Art	⚑		
The Quick Exxon	⚑		
ELBERTA			
Soldiers Creek Golf Course	⚑		
FORT RUCKER			
U.S. Army Aviation Museum	⚑		
GADSDEN			
Noccalula Falls	⚑		
MONTGOMERY			
Prattville Auto & RV Repair Center			✸
OPELIKA			
Robert Trent Jones Grand Nat'l Golf Course	⚑		

CIVIL RIGHTS MUSEUM TRAIL

Travel to Montgomery, Birmingham, Selma and Tuskegee and visit many of the places in Alabama that were battlegrounds from 1955 to 1965.

Montgomery: The Rosa Parks Library and Museum opened on the 45th anniversary of her arrest. Visitors to the city can now ride a replica of the 1953-era bus on which Mrs. Parks was arrested. The modest frame parsonage Dr. King and his young family called home for four years has been authentically restored and opened to the public as the **Dexter Parsonage Museum**. The Interpretive Center next door offers a short video presentation prior to tours of the parsonage. The house is furnished with period furniture, some dating from the residency of the Kings. Dr. King's church, renamed the **Dexter Avenue King Memorial Baptist Church**, is now a National Historic Landmark. A large mural depicts the struggles of the movement and landmark moments in King's life. A block behind the church is the **Civil Rights Memorial** designed by renowned sculptor Maya Lin. Other Montgomery sites include: **Holt Street Baptist Church**, the site of mass meetings leading to the bus boycott; and **The National Center for the Study of Civil Rights & African-American Culture** highlighting the involvement of the local community and Alabama State University students during the boycott and the Civil Rights Movement.

Birmingham: The **Birmingham Civil Rights Institute** is part history lesson, part audience participation and part demonstration of how the city has evolved since the 1960s. Photos, videos, audio recordings and exhibits put visitors inside the integration movement. Visitors can see "white" and "colored" drinking fountains and a 1950s lunch counter that symbolized segregation in public places. A statue of Rev. Fred Shuttlesworth honors the leader of Birmingham's 1963 demonstrations. At the **Sixteenth Street Baptist Church**, photos are on display in the basement showing the damage of a dynamite blast that ripped through the church in 1963. Walk through **Kelly Ingram Park** to see artists' images from the Civil Rights era. Alabama's largest statue of Dr. Martin Luther King Jr. faces the Sixteenth Street Church. Rent an audio wand at the **Civil Rights Institute** that guides visitors through the park.

Selma-to-Montgomery National Historic Trail: Locations along the route (primarily U.S. 80) are indicated by blue signs erected by the National Park Service. It has been designated both a National Scenic Byway and All-American Road. Some of the more prominent sites to see are: **Brown Chapel AME Church** – a bust of Dr. King is in front of the church. **The Voting Rights Trail Interpretive Center** operated by the National Park Service and the State of Alabama at the midpoint of the trail displays photographs and memorabilia from the march. It is between mile markers 105 and 106 in the rural community of White Hall in Lowndes County. Visitors can walk across the **Edmund Pettus Bridge**, one of the most recognized symbols of the Civil Rights Movement. **National Voting Rights Museum** showcases items and participants' stories related to the voting rights movement. Volunteer guides share their recollections of the struggle to gain the right to vote. **Old Depot Museum** is housed in a restored 1891 railway depot. It includes artifacts from the Civil War and voting rights eras, plus rare African-American photography of early 1900s life.

Tuskegee: The university campus offers the following highlights:

Carver Museum features National Park Service exhibits that spotlight the legacy of black scientist George Washington Carver at Tuskegee Institute. His research on peanuts, sweet potatoes and other crops revolutionized Southern agriculture.

The Oaks is the elegant 1899 home of Tuskegee Institute president Booker T. Washington, designed by black architect Robert Taylor and built by students. The National Park Service operates the house museum on the Tuskegee University campus.

Tuskegee Airmen National Historic Site. The site revisits the heroics of the Tuskegee Airmen, who helped end segregation in the Armed Forces after World War II and set the stage for legal challenges to segregation. View exhibits and audiovisual programs and enjoy guided walks to explore this preamble to the Civil Rights Movement. **Moton Field,** where the Tuskegee Airmen trained for flight, includes photos and artifacts depicting the era.

Tuskegee Human & Civil Rights Multi-Cultural Center. The center showcases the student involvement in the Civil Rights Movement.

HANK WILLIAMS TRAIL

The Hank Williams Trail links four museums and additional points of interest important to the life and career of country music's first superstar. Linking sites in Georgiana, Montgomery, Alexander City, Birmingham and Tuscumbia, the trail begins in the rural Mount Olive community off I-65 where young Hank sat on a stool next to the church organ his mother played in the Baptist church. The small church still has services on the second and fourth Sundays of the month and welcomes visitors. The stool is displayed along with other personal mementos nine miles away in Georgiana in the **Hank Williams Boyhood Home**. A stage behind the museum hosts the annual Hank Williams Festival the first weekend of June, reuniting fans, current country musicians and surviving members of his Drifting Cowboys band.

Sixty miles north on I-65, officially named the **Hank Williams Memorial Lost Highway**, is Montgomery, the city where the singer began his career with a live radio show while a teenager. The **Hank Williams Museum** in downtown Montgomery contains the largest collection of costumes, boots, records, photographs and documents related to the careers of Hank and Audrey Williams. The powder blue Cadillac convertible in which the singer died on Jan. 1, 1953, is on loan from his son, singer Hank Williams, Jr. The museum is two blocks from the street where Hank Sr. not only began his radio career and won his first talent contest, but it is also the street where he last performed in public four days before his death

MOUNTAIN REGION

The Mountain Region provides one spellbinding landscape after another. Laden with shimmering lakes, waterfalls, caverns, and forested mountaintops. A myriad of outdoor activities or historic attractions can be enjoyed here.

Cullman is home to the amazing **Ave Maria Grotto**—over 125 miniature reproductions of famous churches, shrines and buildings from all over the world. Scenic pathways lead visitors past the Pantheon in Rome, the Hanging Garden of Babylon, Ave Maria Grotto, the city of Jerusalem and St. Peter's Basilica in Rome. The **North Alabama Museum of History and Fine Arts** is said to have one of the best collections in the world today of porcelain, antiques, bronzes, cut glass and more.

Decatur. Ducks are a big draw at this town on the Tennessee River. The 750-acre **Point Mallard Park** offers hiking and biking trails, picnic facilities, a wave pool, diving pool, duck pond, water slides, wave and kiddie pools and water bubbles. They also have the largest free 4th of July Celebration in North Alabama with family games and live entertainment. Also visit Decatur's **Historic Bank Street** and **Old Decatur and Albany Historic Districts** containing the largest concentration of Victorian homes and bungalows in Alabama. Known as the "Painted Ladies," some date back to the early 1800s. The **Civil War Walking Tour** features 11 historic markers relating events from the four-day battle in 1864. **Cooks Natural Science Museum** contains over 2,000 exhibits and artifacts, science films and live and interactive exhibits. **Wheeler National Wildlife Refuge** is located 1-1/2 miles east of Decatur and is an excellent spot for observing flights of migratory waterfowl from September to May.

Double Springs. Bankhead National Forest's approximately 185,000 acres of natural beauty awaits explorers. Enjoy hiking, biking, canoeing, wildlife watching, swimming, fishing and boating. Trails lead to gorges, canyons, natural bridges, lakes and bluffs. The **Corinth Recreational Area**, part of the **William B Bankhead National Forest,** is located on the banks of beautiful 22,000 acre **Lake Lewis Smith**. Boat launches, a large beach, campgrounds and hiking trails are located in this area of diverse terrain and landscapes. Nearby are many attractions of historic, educational and geological interest.

Fort Payne. Known as the "Grand Canyon of the South," **Little River Canyon** offers scenic views, rafting, rock climbing, camping and nature study. It contains the only stream in the world that has its source and runs its course entirely on the top of a mountain. Also visit the **Depot Museum**, home to a wonderful collection of relics including Native American artifacts, early 20th-century medical equipment and books, the farming tools of early settlers and military uniforms. Adorning the walls are interesting murals.

Huntsville. Housed in one of America's oldest railroad structures, the **Historic Huntsville Depot** invites visitors to enjoy a sight and sound history of Huntsville, original Civil War graffiti and trolley tours of downtown Huntsville. Huntsville has several museums that interpret different time periods, from the early 1800's, when Alabama

QUICK REFERENCE CHART FOR WOODALL'S FEATURED PARKS

	Green Friendly	RV Lots for Sale	Park Models-Onsite Ownership	Park Membership for Sale	Big Rigs Welcome	Internet Friendly	Pets Welcome
ANNISTON							
Country Court RV Park					▲	● (WiFi)	■
ASHFORD							
Shallow Creek RV Park					▲	● (WiFi)	■
AUBURN							
Leisure Time Campgrounds					▲	●	■
BIRMINGHAM							
M & J RV Park					▲		■
CULLMAN							
Cullman Campground					▲	● (WiFi)	■
DAUPHIN ISLAND							
Dauphin Island Campground (City Park)					▲	● (WiFi)	■
DECATUR							
Point Mallard Campground (City Park)					▲	●	■
ELBERTA							
Lake Osprey RV Country Club		✖			▲	● (WiFi)	■
FAIRHOPE							
Driftwood RV Park					▲	● (WiFi)	■
FORT PAYNE							
Wills Creek RV Park					▲	● (WiFi)	■
GADSDEN							
Noccalula Falls Park & Campground (City Park)					▲	● (WiFi)	■
GREENVILLE							
Sherling Lake Park & Campground (City Park)					▲	● (WiFi)	■
GULF SHORES							
Bella Terra of Gulf Shores	🍃	✖			▲	● (WiFi)	■
Gulf Breeze Resort					▲	● (WiFi)	■
GUNTERSVILLE							
Blue Heron Paradise					▲	● (WiFi)	■
HEFLIN							
Cane 9 Creek RV Park & Campground					▲	● (WiFi)	■

Green Friendly 🍃; RV Lots for Sale ✖; Park Models/Onsite Onwership ✱; Park Memberships for Sale ✔; Big Rigs Welcome ▲; Internet Friendly ●; Internet Friendly-WiFi ● (WiFi); Pets Welcome ■

became a state, to the age of American space exploration. Other attractions include:

Alabama Constitution Village. This living history museum portrays a working village including a cabinetmaker's shop, print shop, theater, library and post office. Costumed guides lead the tours.

Burritt on the Mountain – A Living Museum. This unusual architectural landmark (shaped like a Maltese Cross) features historic structures and nature trails, offers panoramic views of the city and provides special events and programs throughout the year.

Huntsville Botanical Garden. One hundred-thirteen acres of woodland paths and grassy meadows include aquatic, herb, annual, perennial, rose and butterfly gardens.

Huntsville Museum of Art offers year-round exhibitions and educational programs.

Twickenham Historic District contains homes dating from 1814. The Weeden House Museum, built in 1819, is noted for its collection of period furnishings.

U.S. Space & Rocket Center. See the past, present and future of space exploration at this center. Take part in hands-on exhibits and demonstrations, including a Mars Mission simulator, **G Force Accelerator**, **Space Shuttle**, **Saturn V** and a bus tour that takes you through the nearby **NASA Marshall Space Flight Center**. It is also home to the **Spacedome IMAX® Theater** and the **US Space Camp**.

Natural Bridge. The Natural Bridge of Alabama is the largest sandstone rock bridge east of the Rockies. At 60-ft. high and 148-ft. long, it spans scenic natural areas, forests and wilderness.

Scottsboro. Located in the middle of Lake Guntersville, **Goose Pond Colony** offers activities such as boating and hiking. In addition to a 126-site campground and golf course, Goose Pond Colony also houses a 1,000-seat meeting facility and a 1,500-seat amphitheater.

Tuscumbia. This historic town offers attractions such as the **Alabama Music Hall of Fame** and the **Tennessee Valley Art Center**. The home of Helen Keller built in 1820 contains many of the original furnishings. In the summer, "The Miracle Worker" is performed live for visitors. The **Belle Mont Mansion** is one of the state's first great plantation houses.

Florence. Follow the Alabama Music Trail to the log cabin where the "Father of the Blues", W. C. Handy, was born.

Valley Head. Located just off I-59 and west of the Georgia border, Valley Head's main attraction is **Sequoyah Caverns**. One of the country's most outstanding show caves, Sequoyah Caverns features fantastic formations, ancient fossils and the famous "Looking Glass Lakes".

METROPOLITAN REGION

The Metropolitan Region is a diverse area, cutting through the midsection of the state.

QUICK REFERENCE CHART FOR WOODALL'S FEATURED PARKS

	Green Friendly	RV Lots for Sale	Park Models-Onsite Ownership	Park Membership for Sale	Big Rigs Welcome	Internet Friendly	Pets Welcome
HELENA							
Cherokee Campground					▲	●	■
HUNTSVILLE							
Mountain Breeze RV Park							■
JASPER							
Sleepy Holler Campground					▲	●	■
LANGSTON							
Little Mountain Marina Camping Resort					▲	●	■
MCCALLA							
McCalla Campground					▲		■
MOBILE							
I-10 Kampground					▲	●	■
Shady Acres Campground					▲	●	■
MONTGOMERY							
Capital City RV Park					▲	●	■
Montgomery Campground							■
OPELIKA							
Lakeside RV Park					▲	●	■
ORANGE BEACH							
Heritage Motorcoach & Marina		✖				●	■
OZARK							
Ozark Travel Park					▲	●	■
PELL CITY							
Lakeside Landing RV Park & Marina					▲	●	■
TUSCALOOSA							
Sunset Travel Park					▲	●	■
WOODVILLE							
Parnell Creek RV Park						●	■

Green Friendly ; RV Lots for Sale ✖; Park Models/Onsite Onwership ✱; Park Memberships for Sale ✔; Big Rigs Welcome ▲; Internet Friendly ●; Internet Friendly-WiFi ●; Pets Welcome ■

Travelers will find the speed they need at Talladega Superpeedway, big city living in Birmingham, juicy peaches in Chilton County, and the roar of water rushing over Noccalula Falls.

Alexander City. Wind Creek State Park is situated on the shores of beautiful Lake Martin and includes camping, a marina, hiking trails and 210-foot fishing pier.

Aliceville Museum. The **Aliceville Museum and Cultural Arts Center** is a unique experience. It is the only one of its kind in the whole world, dedicated to a time when the world was at war. In their center you will find artifacts of German Prisoners of World War II, letters, uniforms, objects of art, statuary, sculpture, photos and books of this fascinating era of world history.

Anniston. See displays of dinosaurs and fossils, a 400 species bird collection, Egyptian mummies and a replica of an Alabama cave at the **Anniston Museum of Natural History**. The **Berman Museum of World History** contains military artifacts from ancient Greece through World War II. Visit the highest point in Alabama at **Cheaha State Park**, 2,407 feet above sea level. A restaurant offers panoramic views and camping is available.

Birmingham. Not-to-be-missed attractions within Birmingham include: **Birmingham Botanical Gardens**; **McWane Center**, an exciting science museum and IMAX Theatre; **Birmingham Zoo**, with more than 700 rare and exotic animals; the **Birmingham Museum of Art**, with Asian, European and American collections; and the **Alabama Sports Hall of Fame**, honoring such greats as Joe Louis, Paul "Bear" Bryant and Jesse Owens. Ride the Rampage wooden roller coaster and other thrill rides at **Magic Adventure Theme Park** or cool off at **Splash Beach Water Park**. Take a self-guided journey through the Civil Rights Movement and human rights struggle at the **Birmingham Civil Rights Institute**. Learn about jazz greats Lionel Hampton, Sun Ra and more at the **Alabama Jazz Hall of Fame**.

Gadsden. Noccalula Falls is the famous site of the Native American legend of the princess who hurled herself from the heights into the river after her lover's death. The park features 90-foot waterfalls, a War Memorial, pioneer homestead, botanical gardens, carpet golf and hiking trails.

Talladega. Auto buffs and racing fans won't want to miss Talladega's automotive attractions. **Talladega Superspeedway** is the world's fastest speedway and the site of numerous racing events. At the **International Motorsports Hall of Fame** you can see record-breaking and special autos, ride the famous "#43" race car simulator and view memorabilia dating back to 1902.

Tuscaloosa. Wonderful old buildings within Tuscaloosa include the **Battle-Friedman House** (1835), Gorgas House (1829) and the Old Tavern Museum (1827). The **Children's Hands-on Museum of Tuscaloosa** features hands-on exhibits, in-depth programs and special events that provide a fun learning experience just for kids. Exhibits include a Choctaw Indian Village, a planetarium, a children's hospital, a bank, a TV studio, **The Wardrobe**, a print shop, a general store and Images (a color and light display). You can view 26 prehistoric platform mounds, a reconstructed Native American village and a museum at **Moundville Archaeological Park**. Nature trails are also available. Public tours are available at the newly opened **Mercedes-Benz U.S. International** assembly plant with museum and gift shop.

Where to Find CCUSA Parks

CAMPCLUB USA

List City	Park Name	Map Coordinates
ASHFORD		
	Shallow Creek RV Park	E-5
AUBURN		
	University Station Motorcoach & RV Resort	D-4
CHILDERSBURG		
	DeSoto Caverns Park Campground	C-3
DOTHAN		
	Pecan Point RV Park	E-5
ELBERTA		
	Lazy Acres	F-2
FOLEY		
	Johnny's Lakeside RV Resort	F-2
	Magnolia Springs RV Hideaway	F-2
FORT PAYNE		
	Wills Creek RV Park	A-4
GULF SHORES		
	Sun-Runners RV Park	F-2
HEFLIN		
	Cane 9 Creek RV Park & Campground	B-4
HELENA		
	Cherokee Campground	C-3
MOBILE		
	Johnny's RV Resort	F-1
MONTGOMERY		
	Montgomery Campground	D-4
	Montgomery South RV Park	D-4
	The Woods RV Park and Campground	D-4
OPELIKA		
	Lakeside RV Park	C-5
ROBERTSDALE		
	Hilltop RV Park	F-2
	Wilderness RV Park	F-2
SCOTTSBORO		
	Crawford RV Park	A-4
TALLADEGA		
	Talladega Creekside Resort	C-4
URIAH		
	Ponderosa RV Park	E-2
WOODVILLE		
	Parnell Creek RV Park	A-4

RIVER HERITAGE REGION

An area full of history and beauty, the River Heritage Region is a must see for any traveler. A few items on the not to miss list include: The Gaineswood Plantation in Demopolis, the Civil Rights landmarks in Selma, the beautiful state Capitol buildings in Montgomery, and Tuskegee, home of the famed Tuskegee Airmen.

Andalusia. Hiking trails at **Conecuh National Forest** lead through holly, dogwoods, longleaf pine and magnolia trees and past scenic cypress ponds and natural springs.

Dothan, Landmark Park. An 1890s farmstead anchors this 100-acre cultural heritage park that also includes nature trails and a planetarium.

Depot Museum. The old railroad museum is home to a wonderful collection of relics including Native American artifacts, early 20th-century medical equipment and books, the farming tools of early settlers and military uniforms. Adorning the walls are interesting murals.

Eufaula. Lake Eufaula, the "Bass Capital of the World," features a lodge, restaurant, camping and marina at Lakepoint Resort State Park. A fabulous historic district in the city provides a chance to visit such landmarks as Shorter Mansion and Fendall Hall.

Fort Rucker. See military airplanes, helicopters and the largest collection of archives on U.S. Army aviation at the **U.S. Army Aviation Museum.**

Gordon. The crystal-clear lake at **Chattahoochee State Park** provides the ideal location for fishing and boating. A picnic along the bank is a perfect way to spend an afternoon.

Montgomery. Attractions include the **Montgomery Zoo**, which features habitats from 5 continents and over 800 animals. Other attractions within Montgomery are:

Dexter Parsonage Museum. Former home of Rev. Dr. Martin Luther King, Jr. family. Interpretive Center chronicles history that led to the Montgomery bus boycott and the Civil Rights Movement.

First White House of the Confederacy. This was the former home of President and Mrs. Jefferson Davis. The home contains many of the family's original furnishings and Civil War memorabilia.

Old Alabama Town. Tour three blocks of houses and landscapes, learning first-hand how people lived in central Alabama from 1800 to 1900. Observe the working craftsmen on-site.

Ozark. This small Southern town almost doubles its size as visitors converge downtown the first Saturday in October. The annual **Claybank Jamboree** features arts and crafts, live music, clogging and line dancing. Anglers may want to stop by **Dale County Public Lake**—92 acres of good bass fishing!

Montgomery Museum of Fine Arts. For seventy years, the Montgomery Museum of Fine Arts has been a showcase for the visual arts in Central Alabama. A primary focus of the Museum's mission is collecting and preserving works by some of history's best known, and some of the region's best loved, artists.

Selma. Historic attractions abound including **Historic Water Avenue**, a 19th century restored commercial district offering scenic views, historic buildings, markers and picnicking areas. **The Old Town Historic District** is one of the largest historic districts in the state including Sturdivant Hall. There are more than 1,200 buildings dating from the 1820s. The "Windshield Tour," with brochures and tapes available from the chamber of commerce, covers 116 historic sites. Take the **Martin Luther King, Jr. Street Historic Walking Tour** and experience the history of Selma's Civil Rights movement.

Tuskegee. Tuskegee has been the site of major achievements by African Americans for more than 100 years. Here, Booker T. Washington founded the Tuskegee Normal School for Colored Teachers, which later became the Tuskegee Institute. One of the most famous teachers at Tuskegee was George Washington Carver, whose name is synonymous with innovative research in southern farming and crops. Today, the university is part of the National Parks Systems, and remains a major center for education.

THE GULF COAST REGION

The most famous attractions in this area are the sugar white sandy beaches of Gulf Shores and Orange Beach. Other points of interest include:

Dauphin Island. Fort Gaines Historic Site was the site of a week-long naval and land battle, which led to the eventual capture by Union forces. Onsite are cannons used in the Civil War battle, soldiers' quarters, tunnels and bastions.

Gulf Shores. The coastal community entices visitors with unsurpassed Gulf vistas and the following attractions:

Gulf Beaches. Enjoy 32 miles of sun and surf on miles of sugar-white sand. Among the facilities at the 6,000-acre **Gulf State Park** is the popular fishing pier, which extends 825 ft. into the Gulf.

Mobile. Founded in 1702, Mobile was the original capital of the Louisiana Territory, and is the oldest city in Alabama. Your first stop in Mobile should be **Fort Conde Museum** with its partially reconstructed 1720s French fort, costumed guides and visitor information center. Also worth seeing in Mobile is the **Cathedral of the Immaculate Conception,** an 1835 Greek revival masterpiece built on old Spanish burial grounds. The **Mobile Museum of Art** has a permanent collection, which spans 2,000 years, and the **Mobile Medical Museum** houses an extensive display of medical memorabilia.

U.S.S. Alabama Battleship Memorial Park. Tour a mighty battleship, inspect aircraft and stroll through the fleet submarine, U.S.S. Drum.

Mobile is not only home of the first known Mardi Gras celebration in 1703, (yes, even before New Orleans!), it still draws a hefty crowd of 200,000+ visitors annually from the state and across the nation, and all within an hours drive of those beautiful Gulf Coast beaches.

Bayou La Batre. Nestled on the Gulf of Mexico, this small picturesque city is steeped in Southern tradition and heritage with a unique French flair. This small little city is the seafood capital of Alabama, which means that not only is it an outstanding place to eat, but also to fish. There are numerous charter pleasure boats to provide accommodations for any sportsman or angler. Special evens are held annually to commemorate the city's fishing industry, such as "Blessing of the Fleet" and "Miss Seafood Contest".

ANNUAL EVENTS

JANUARY

Pancake Day, Fairhope.

FEBRUARY

Mardi Gras (through March), Mobile; Heritage Arts Festival, Monroesville; Mobile Boat Show, Mobile; Black Heritage Festival, Anniston; Mercedes Marathon and Half Marathon, Birmingham.

MARCH

Opp Jaycees Rattlesnake Rodeo, Opp; Bridge Crossing Jubilee, Selma; Arts & Crafts Festival & Outdoor Show, Fairhope; Festival of Flowers, Mobile; German Sausage Festival, Elberta; Colonies of the Gulf Coast, Dauphin Island.

APRIL

Alabama Crawfish Festival, Faunsdale; Birmingham International Festival Salute, Birmingham; Spring Festival of Flowers, Huntsville; Bloomin' Festival Arts and Crafts Fair, Cullman; Chunnenuggee Fair, Union Springs; Magnolia Festival, Gardendale;

MAY

Polk Salat Festival, Arab; Blessing of the Fleet, Bayou La Batre; Alabama Jubilee Hot-Air Balloon Classic, Decatur; Riverfest, Gadsden; Jubilee Cityfest, Montgomery; Whistle Stop Festival & Rocket City BBQ, Huntsville; Catfish Festival, Scottsboro; Buck Creek Festival, Helena.

JUNE

The Miracle Worker Play & Helen Keller Festival (through July), Tuscumbia; Jazz Fest, Alexander City; Miss Alabama Pageant, Birmingham; Alabama Blueberry Festival, Brewton; Masonic Celebration, Florala; Gulf Coast Hot Air Balloon Festival, Foley.

JULY

W. C. Handy Music Festival (through August), Florence & The Shoals Area; World Championship Domino Tournament, Andalusia; Gadsden Art Association Annual Juried Show, Gadsden.

All privately owned campgrounds personally inspected by WOODALL'S Representatives

Lee and Mary Franck

ALBERTA—D-2

(SE) CHILATCHEE CREEK PARK (COE-Alabama River Lakes)—(Wilcox) *From jct Hwy 5 & CR 29: follow signs 9 mi on CR 29.* FACILITIES: 53 sites, 47 W&E, 6 no hkups, tenting, dump, laundry. RECREATION: boating, ramp, dock, river fishing, playground. Partial handicap access. Open all yr. Phone: (334)573-2562.

ALEXANDER CITY—C-4

(S) WIND CREEK SP—(Tallapoosa) *From jct Hwy 63 & Hwy 128: Go 1-1/2 mi E on Hwy 128.* FACILITIES: 636 sites, 245 full hkups, 391 W&E, (30 amps), tenting, dump, laundry, full svc store. RECREATION: lake swim, boating, ramp, dock, lake fishing, playground. Partial handicap access. Open all yr. Phone: (256) 329-0845.

ANDALUSIA—E-3

(S) CONECUH NF (Open Pond Campground)—(Covington) *From jct US-84 & US-29: Go 10 mi S on US-29, then 6 mi S on Hwy-137, then 1/2 mi E on CR-24, then 1 mi SE on FR-336.* FACILITIES: 73 sites, 63 W&E, (20/30 amps), 10 no hkups, tenting, dump, ltd groc. RECREATION: boating, electric motors only, canoeing, ramp, lake/pond fishing. Partial handicap access. Open all yr. Phone: (334)222-2555.

ANNISTON—B-4

(S) COUNTRY COURT RV PARK—(Calhoun) *E'bnd: From jct I-20 (exit 188) & Hwy 78: Go N 300 feet, then 1-1/2 mi E on Hwy 78. (Ent on L). W'bnd: From jct I-20 & Hwy 431/78 (exit 191): Go 2-3/4 mi W on Hwy 431/78 (Ent on R).*

WELCOME

◆◆◆FACILITIES: 68 sites, typical site width 30 ft, accepts full hkup units only, 68 full hkups, (30/50 amps), 25 pull-thrus, cable TV, WiFi Instant Internet at site, picnic tables, patios.

Pets welcome. No tents. Open all yr. No restrooms. Big rigs welcome. Rate in 2010 $22 per vehicle.

Phone: (256)835-2045
Address: 3459 US Hwy 78 E, Anniston, AL 36207
Lat/Lon: 33.61821/-85.76218
Email: countrycourtrvpark@yahoo.com
Web: www.countrycourtrvpark.com

SEE AD THIS PAGE

ARLEY—B-2

(E) Hidden Cove Outdoor Resort—(Winston) *I-65 (Cullman exit 308) & Hwy 278: Go 16 mi W on Hwy 278, then 9 mi S on Hwy 77, then 4 mi E on CR 12/3919. Enter on R.* ◆◆◆◆FACILITIES: 62 sites, 58 full hkups, 4 W&E, (30/50 amps), 30 pull-thrus, tenting, dump, laundry. ◆◆◆◆RECREATION: swim pool, boating, ramp, dock, lake fishing, playground. Pets welcome. Open all yr. Rate in 2010 $32 per vehicle. Phone: (205) 221-7042.

ASHFORD—E-5

(N) SHALLOW CREEK RV PARK—(Houston) *From jct US 431 (Ross Clark Cir) & Hwy 84 E: Go 7 mi E on Hwy 84, then 1-1/2 mi N on Hwy 55. Enter on R.*

WELCOME

◆◆◆FACILITIES: 60 sites, typical site width 30 ft, 60 full hkups, (30/50 amps), 10 pull-thrus, WiFi Instant Internet at site ($), phone/cable on-site Internet (needs activ), tenting, cabins, RV storage, laundry, picnic tables.

◆◆◆RECREATION: rec hall, swim pool, golf nearby, bsktball, play equipment, activities, sports field.

CAMPCLUB USA

Pets welcome. Open all yr. Big rigs welcome. Rate in 2010 $20 for 2 persons. CCUSA 50% Discount. CCUSA reservations Accepted, CCUSA max stay 2 days, Cash only for CCUSA disc.

Phone: (877)586-4920
Address: 1128 N Broadway, Ashford, AL 36312
Lat/Lon: 31.19843/-85.23261

SEE AD DOTHAN PAGE 12

ATHENS—A-3

(N) Northgate RV Travel Park—(Limestone) *From jct I-65 (exit 354) & Hwy 31: Go 500 ft S on Hwy 31. Enter on R.* ◆◆◆FACILITIES: 24 sites, 20 full hkups, 4 W&E, (30/50 amps), 20 pull-thrus. Pets welcome. No tents. Open all yr. Big rigs welcome. Rate in 2010 $24-26 per vehicle. Phone: (256)232-8800.

Alabama State Rock: Marble

ATMORE—E-2

CLAUDE D. KELLEY SP—(Escambia) *From jct I-65 & Hwy 21: Go 12 mi N on Hwy 21.* FACILITIES: 25 sites, 5 full hkups, 20 W&E, (30 amps), tenting. RECREATION: lake swim, boating, canoeing, ramp, dock, lake fishing, playground. Open all yr. Phone: (251)862-2511.

AUBURN—D-4

AUBURN UNIVERSITY—*From I-85 (exit 51) & Hwy 29 (College St): Go 4 mi N on College St. Enter on L.* Auburn is the largest university in Al. Approx 24,000 students from all 50 states & 80 foreign countries. Auburn Univ is committed to offering high quality undergraduate, graduate & professional education to its students. Open all yr.

WELCOME

Address: 23 Samford Hall, Auburn, AL 36849
Lat/Lon: 32.60209/-85.49027
Web: www.auburn.edu

SEE AD TRAVEL SECTION PAGE 1

(C) AUBURN-OPELIKA CONVENTION & VISITORS BUREAU—*From jct I-85 (exit 51) & US 29: Go 4 mi N on US 29, then 4 blocks E on Glenn Ave. Enter on R.* Location for information & brochures on museums, historical homes, Auburn University & parks. Open all yr.

WELCOME

Phone: (334)887-8747
Address: 714 E Glenn Ave, Auburn, AL 36831-2216
Lat/Lon: 32.58387/-85.31023
Email: info@aotourism.com
Web: www.aotourism.com

SEE AD TRAVEL SECTION PAGE 1

AUBURN—Continued on next page

At 2,405 feet, Cheaha Mountain is Alabama's highest point above sea level and mean elevation is 500 feet at its lowest elevation point.

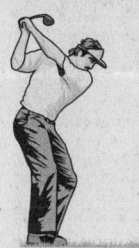

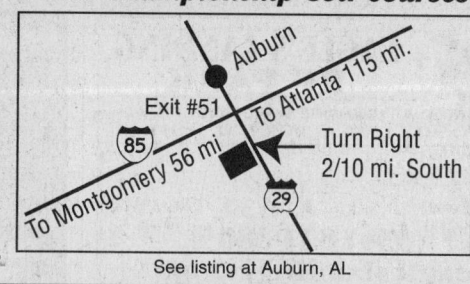

(E) CHEWACLA SP—(Lee) *From jct I-85 (exit 51) & US 29: Go 1/4 mi S on US 29, then 2 mi E on Shell Toomer Pkwy.*

FACILITIES: 31 sites, 16 full hkups, 15 no hkups, 9 pull-thrus, tenting, cabins, dump, laundry, picnic tables, grills.

RECREATION: pavilion, lake swim, boating, electric motors only, canoeing, 2 rowboat/13 canoe/2 pedal boat rentals, lake fishing, playground, tennis, sports field, hiking trails. Rec open to public.

Partial handicap access. Open all yr. MC/VISA/AMEX.

Phone: (334)887-5621
Address: 124 Shell Toomer Pkwy, Auburn, AL 36830
Lat/Lon: 32.55417/-85.48116
Email: chewaclastpk@mindspring.com
Web: www.alapark.com

SEE AD TRAVEL SECTION PAGE 1

EAGLES LANDING RV PARK—(Lee) *From jct I-85 (exit 51) & Hwy 29: Go 1-1/2 mi N on Hwy 29, then 1-1/2 mi W on Hwy 247 (Shug Jordan), then 1 mi S on Wire Rd.*

◊◊◊◊FACILITIES: 60 sites, typical site width 30 ft, 60 full hkups, (20/30/50 amps), some extd stay sites, 21 pull-thrus, cable TV, WiFi Instant Internet at site, family camping, RV's/park model rentals, RV storage, laundry, RV supplies, LP gas by meter, ice, picnic tables, patios, grills, wood.

◊◊◊◊◊RECREATION: rec room/area, putting green, golf nearby, play equipment, activities (wkends), horseshoes, local tours.

Pets welcome, quantity restrict. No tents. Open all yr. Big rigs welcome. Clubs welcome. Rate in 2010 $40-80 for 2 persons. MC/VISA/Debit.

Phone: (334)821-8805
Address: 1900 Wire Rd, Auburn, AL 36832
Email: info@eagleslandingrv.com
Web: www.eagleslandingrv.com

SEE AD THIS PAGE

(W) HODGE'S VINEYARD—*From jct I-85 (exit 51) & College St: Go 1 mi N on college St, then 3 mi W on University Dr, then 1 mi NW on Donahue, then 5 mi W on Farmville Rd (City Rd 72), then left at fork on Cty Rd 71. Enter on R.* Winery open for wine tasting and tours Fri, Sat & Sun. come and enjoy the fruits of our labor. Open all yr. MC/VISA/AMEX.

Address: 230 Lee Road 71, Camp Hill, AL 36850

SEE AD GULF SHORES PAGE 15

Woodall's Tip... If you think Woodall's Ratings mean Good, Better, Best...think again. See the "How to Use" section in the front of this Directory for an explanation of our Rating System.

JULE COLLINS SMITH MUSEUM OF FINE ART—*From jct I-85 (exit 51) & Hwy 29 (College St): Go 2-1/2 mi N. Enter on R.* Located at Auburn University amongst 15 area gardens, walking paths & terraces. You will see traveling exhibitions of international, & regional focus. They also have concerts, films, lectures, childrens programs & many more interesting programs. Open all yr. MC/VISA/AMEX.

Phone: (334)844-1484
Address: 901 S College St, Auburn, AL 36830
Lat/Lon: 32.58854/-85.48479
Web: www.julecollinssmithmuseum.com

SEE AD TRAVEL SECTION PAGE 1

(S) LEISURE TIME CAMPGROUNDS—(Lee) *From jct I-85 (exit 51) & US 29 S: Go 1/10 mi S on US 29 S (end of Hampton Inn). Enter on R.*

◊◊◊◊FACILITIES: 58 sites, typical site width 30 ft, 58 full hkups, (20/30/50 amps), 50 amps ($), some extd stay sites, 28 pull-thrus, cable TV, ($), phone Internet central location, family camping, tenting, laundry, ice, picnic tables, grills.

RECREATION: golf nearby.

Pets welcome. Partial handicap access. Open all yr. Big rigs welcome. Clubs welcome. Rate in 2010 $19-22 per family. MC/VISA/DISC/AMEX/Debit. Member ARVC, ALARVC.

Phone: (334)821-2267
Address: 2670 College St South, Auburn, AL 36832
Lat/Lon: 32.55371/-85.51025

SEE AD PAGE 9

THE QUICK EXXON—*From jct I-85 (exit 51) & Hwy 29: Go 1-1/2 mi N on Hwy 29, then 1-1/2 mi W on Hwy 247 (Shug Jordan), then 3/4 mi S on Wire Rd. Enter on R.* Gas Station, Convenience store and restaurant with country cooking! RV Friendly pumps & parking. Open all yr. MC/VISA/DISC/AMEX/Debit.

Phone: (334)826-1400
Address: 571 Webster Rd, Auburn, AL 36831

SEE AD THIS PAGE

UNIVERSITY STATION MOTORCOACH & RV RESORT—(Lee) *From jct I-85 (exit 51) & US 29: Go 1-1/4 mi N on US 29 (S College St), then 2-1/5 mi W on AL-267/Shug Jordan Pkwy, then 2-1/5 mi SW on AL-14. Enter on R.*

◊◊◊◊FACILITIES: 360 sites, typical site width 30 ft, 300 full hkups, 60 W&E, (20/30/50 amps), some extd stay sites, 9 pull-thrus, WiFi Instant Internet at site ($), family camping, tenting, RV's/park model rentals, RV storage, dump, non-guest dump $, laundry, LP gas by weight/by meter, wood.

Alabama State Gem: Star Blue Quartz

◊◊RECREATION: golf nearby, activities, (wkends), horseshoes, hiking trails, v-ball, local tours.

Pets welcome. Open all yr. Big rigs welcome. Clubs welcome. Rate in 2010 $30-75 for 2 persons. MC/VISA/DISC/AMEX/Debit. CCUSA 50% Discount. CCUSA reservations Required, CCUSA max stay 1 day, Cash only for CCUSA disc., Check only for CCUSA disc. Discount not available Aug 15 thru Nov 30 (Auburn football season).

Phone: (877)828-8968
Address: 3076 AL Hwy 14, Auburn, AL 36832
Lat/Lon: 32.60066/-85.54263
Web: www.universitystationrvpark.com

SEE AD THIS PAGE

BAY MINETTE—F-2

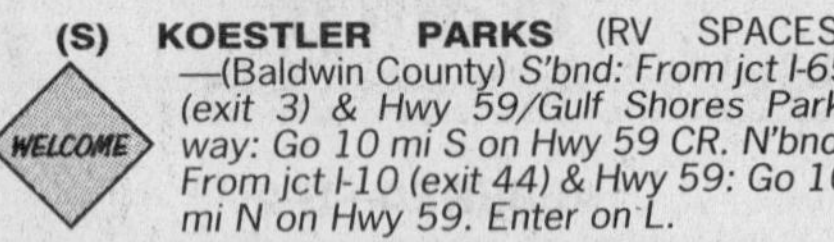

(S) KOESTLER PARKS (RV SPACES) —(Baldwin County) *S'bnd: From jct I-65 (exit 3) & Hwy 59/Gulf Shores Parkway: Go 10 mi S on Hwy 59 CR. N'bnd: From jct I-10 (exit 44) & Hwy 59: Go 10 mi N on Hwy 59. Enter on L.*

FACILITIES: 20 sites, accepts self-contained units only, 20 full hkups, (30/50 amps), cable TV, WiFi Instant Internet at site, laundry, RV supplies, ice, picnic tables, patios.

RECREATION: pavilion, golf nearby.

Pets welcome, breed restrict. No tents. Open all yr. Big rigs welcome. Rate in 2010 $25-30 for 2 persons. MC/VISA/DISC/AMEX/Debit.

Phone: (251)937-4009
Address: 40075 Hwy 59 S, Bay Minette, AL 36507
Email: kevin@kmkoestler.com
Web: www.kmkoestler.com

SEE AD THIS PAGE

BIRMINGHAM—B-3

(NE) Carson Village Mobile Home Community (RV SPACES)—(Jefferson) *From jct I-65 & Walker Chapel Rd (exit 267): Go 6.8 mi E on Walker Chapel Rd/Carson Rd (Cross Red Hollow Rd.). Enter on R.* FACILITIES: 30 sites, typical site width 16 ft, accepts full hkup units only, 30 full hkups, (30/50 amps), laundry. RECREATION: swim pool. Pets welcome, breed restrict. No tents. Open all yr. Big rigs welcome. Rate in 2010 $20 per vehicle. Phone: (205)854-0059.

(S) M & J RV PARK (RV SPACES)—(Jefferson) *S'bnd: From jct I-59/I-20 (exit 118) & Valley Rd: Go 1/2 mi SW on Valley Rd, then 1-1/4 mi SE on Aaron Aronov Dr, then 1/2 mi SW on Hwy 11/State Hwy 5. Enter on L.*

FACILITIES: 72 sites, accepts full hkup units only, 72 full hkups, (15/30/50 amps), 6 pull-thrus, patios.

M & J RV PARK—Continued on next page

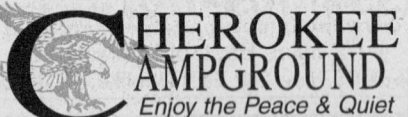

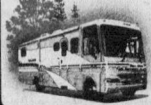

BIRMINGHAM—Continued
M & J RV PARK—Continued

RECREATION: golf nearby, sports field.

Pets welcome, breed restrict. No tents. Open all yr. No restrooms. Big rigs welcome. MC/VISA/DISC/AMEX/Debit. FMCA discount.

Phone: (205)788-2605
Address: 556 Bessemer Super Hwy, Birmingham, AL 35228
Lat/Lon: 33.45496/-86.91906

SEE AD PAGE 10

BLADON SPRINGS—E-1

(E) BLADON SPRINGS STATE PARK—(Choctaw) *From jct US 43 & US 84: Go 25 mi on US 84 E, then turn S on CR 6 traveling approx 4 mi to park.* FACILITIES: 10 sites, 10 full hkups, tenting. RECREATION: Open all yr. Phone: (251)754-9207.

BOAZ—B-4

(E) Barclay RV Parking—(Marshall) *From jct US 431 & Billy Dyar Blvd: Go 3/4 mi W on Billy Dyar Blvd. Enter on L.* ◆◆◆FACILITIES: 22 sites, typical site width 22 ft, accepts full hkup units only, 22 full hkups, (30/50 amps), 50 amps ($), 6 pull-thrus. Pets welcome. No tents. Open all yr. Rate in 2010 $12-15 per vehicle. Phone: (256)593-5913.

CALERA—C-3

(N) Rolling Hills RV Park—(Shelby) *From jct I-65 (exit 231) & US 31: Go 1 blk E to CR 304E, then 1/2 mi S on CR 304E. Enter on L.* ◆◆◆FACILITIES: 60 sites, typical site width 30 ft, 60 full hkups, (30/50 amps), 8 pull-thrus, laundry. ◆◆◆RECREATION: swim pool, boating, no motors, canoeing, lake fishing. Pets welcome. No tents. Open all yr. Rate in 2010 $28 per vehicle. Phone: (205)668-6893.

CAMDEN—D-2

(W) EAST BANK ACCESS AREA (COE-Alabama River Lakes)/Millers Ferry Campground—(Wilcox) *From town: Go 10 mi W on Hwy-28.* FACILITIES: 65 sites, 59 W&E, 6 no hkups, tenting, dump, laundry. RECREATION: lake/river swim, boating, ramp, river fishing, playground. Partial handicap access. Open all yr. Phone: (334)682-4191.

(N) ROLAND COOPER SP—(Wilcox) *From jct Hwy 10 & Hwy 41: Go 6 mi NE on Hwy 41.* FACILITIES: 60 sites, 47 full hkups, 13 no hkups, tenting, dump, laundry, ltd groc. RECREATION: boating, ramp, lake fishing, playground. Pets welcome. Open all yr. Phone: (334)682-4050.

CASTLEBERRY—E-3

(S) Country Sunshine RV Park—(Conecuh) *From jct I-65 (exit 83) & CR 6: Go 3-1/2 mi E on CR 6. Enter on L.* ◆◆FACILITIES: 17 sites, typical site width 20 ft, 17 full hkups, (30/50 amps), 50 amps ($), 11 pull-thrus, tenting, laundry. Pets welcome. Open all yr. Big rigs welcome. Rate in 2010 $21-23.50 for 4 persons. Phone: (251)966-5540.

CENTRE—B-4

(E) John's Campground & Grocery—(Cherokee) *From jct Hwy 9 & US 411: Go 6.1 mi SE on N US 411, then 1-3/4 mi N on CR 31. Enter on R.* ◆◆FACILI-

CENTRE—Continued
John's Campground & Grocery—Continued

TIES: 26 sites, typical site width 26 ft, 32 ft max RV length, 26 full hkups, (30/50 amps), tenting, dump, laundry, full svc store. ◆◆RECREATION: canoeing. Pets welcome. Partial handicap access. Open all yr. Rate in 2010 $25 per family. Phone: (256)475-3234.

CENTREVILLE—C-3

(W) TALLADEGA NF (Payne Lake West Side)—(Hale) *From town: Go 2 mi W on US 82, then 6 mi S on Hwy 5, then 15 mi W on Hwy 25.* FACILITIES: 53 sites, 22 ft max RV length, 7 W&E, 46 no hkups, 3 pull-thrus, tenting, dump. RECREATION: lake swim, boating, electric motors only, canoeing, ramp, lake fishing. Partial handicap access. Open all yr. Phone: (205)926-9765.

CHILDERSBURG—C-3

(E) DeSoto Caverns Park Campground—(Talladega) *From jct US-280 & Hwy-76: Go 5 mi E on Hwy-76. Enter on L.* ◆◆◆◆FACILITIES: 21 sites, typical site width 30 ft, 16 full hkups, (20/30/50 amps), 5 no hkups, WiFi Instant Internet at site, tenting, laundry, ice, picnic tables, grills. ◆◆RECREATION: equipped pavilion, mini-golf, ($), playground, hiking trails. Pets welcome, quantity restrict. Partial handicap access. Open all yr. Rate in 2010 $29.99-34.99 for 4 persons. MC/VISA/DISC/Debit. CCUSA 50% Discount. CCUSA reservations Not Accepted, CCUSA max stay 7 days. Not available Memorial Day, 4th of July, Labor Day or Talladega race weekends.

CAMPCLUB USA

Phone: (800)933-2283
Address: 5181 DeSoto Caverns Pkwy, Childersburg, AL 35044-5663
Lat/Lon: 33.30558/-86.27727
Email: fun@desotocavernspark.com
Web: www.desotocavernspark.com

CITRONELLE—E-1

(W) CITRONELLE LAKEVIEW RV PARK (City Park)—(Mobile) *From jct US 45 & Hwy 96: Go 5 mi W on Hwy 96 to Citronelle Lakeside Park entrance, then 3 mi S. Enter at end.* FACILITIES: 38 sites, 31 full hkups, 7 W&E, (30/50 amps), 7 pull-thrus, tenting, dump, laundry. RECREATION: boating, canoeing, ramp, lake fishing. Partial handicap access. Open all yr. Phone: (251)866-9647.

CLANTON—C-3

(SW) Dandy RV Park (TOO NEW TO RATE)—(Chilton) *I-65 (exit 208) & Cty Rd 28: Go 300' W on Cty Rd 28, then South on Dandy Ln. Enter on L.* FACILITIES: 50 sites, typical site width 30 ft, 50 full hkups, (30/50 amps), 13 pull-thrus, family camping, laundry. RECREATION: lake fishing, playground. Pets welcome. Partial handicap access. No tents. Open all yr. Big rigs welcome. Phone: (205)755-2623.

(E) Peach Park RV Park—(Chilton) *I-65 & Hwy 31 (exit 205): Turn E 300 yds. Enter on L.* ◆◆◆FACILITIES: 14 sites, typical site width 30 ft, accepts full hkup units only, 14 full hkups, (50 amps). ◆RECREATION: playground. Pets welcome. No tents. Open all yr. Big rigs welcome. Rate in 2010 $17 per vehicle. Phone: (205)755-2065.

CLIO—E-4

(E) BLUE SPRINGS SP—(Barbour) *From jct Hwy 51 & Hwy 10: Go 6 mi E on Hwy 10.* FACILITIES: 50 sites, 50 W&E, (30 amps), 7 pull-thrus, tenting, dump. RECREATION: swim pool, river fishing, playground. Partial handicap access. Open all yr. Phone: (334)397-4875.

COCHRANE—C-1

(E) COCHRANE CAMPGROUND (COE-Tennessee/Tombigbee Waterway)—(Pickens) *In town, off Hwy 17, follow signs.* FACILITIES: 60 sites, 60 W&E, (30 amps), dump, laundry. RECREATION: boating, ramp, dock, lake/river fishing, playground. Partial handicap access. Open Mar 1 - Dec 31. Phone: (205)373-8806.

COFFEEVILLE—E-1

(W) SERVICE PARK (COE-Coffeeville Lake)—(Choctaw) *From town: Go 3 mi W on US 84. Enter on R.* FACILITIES: 32 sites, 32 W&E, (50 amps), 11 pull-thrus, tenting, dump, laundry. RECREATION: lake swim, boating, canoeing, ramp, lake/river fishing, playground. Partial handicap access. Open Mar 15 - Dec 15. Phone: (334)754-9338.

COTTONTON—D-5

(W) BLUFF CREEK PARK (COE-Walter F. George Lake)—(Russell) *From Hwy 165 in town: Go 2 mi E on park access road.* FACILITIES: 88 sites, 88 W&E, (30 amps), 6 pull-thrus, tenting, dump, laundry. RECREATION: lake/river swim, boating, ramp, dock, lake/river fishing. Open Mar - Nov. Phone: (334)855-2746.

CREOLA—F-2

(NE) DEAD LAKE MARINA & CG—(Mobile) *From I-65 (exit 22): Go 300 yards W on Sailor Rd, then 1/7-10 mi N on Creola Axis Creek Loop, then 2-1/2 mi E on Dead Lake Rd. Enter on L.* FACILITIES: 42 sites, typical site width 30 ft, 24 full hkups, 13 W&E, 5 E, (50 amps), 50 amps ($), 37 pull-thrus, tenting, dump, laundry, groceries. RECREATION: swim pool, boating, ramp, dock, lake fishing, playground. Partial handicap access. Open all yr. Phone: (251)574-2266.

CULLMAN—B-3

(W) CULLMAN CAMPGROUND—(Cullman) *From jct I-65 (exit 310) & Hwy 157N: Go 1-1/2 mi N on Hwy 157, then 1 mi S on CR 1184 paved road, following signs. Enter on L.*

WELCOME

◆◆◆◆FACILITIES: 75 sites, typical site width 25 ft, 75 full hkups, (20/30/50 amps), 50 amps ($), some extd stay sites, 67 pull-thrus, WiFi Instant Internet at site, phone Internet central location, tenting, RV storage, dump, non-guest dump $, laundry, ltd groc, RV supplies, LP gas by weight/by meter, ice, picnic tables, fire rings, wood.

◆◆RECREATION: pavilion, pond fishing, golf nearby, horseshoes, v-ball.

Pets welcome. Partial handicap access. Open all yr. Big rigs welcome. Escort to site. Clubs welcome. Rate in 2010 $19-21 for 2 persons. MC/VISA/DISC.

Phone: (256)734-5853
Address: 220 County Rd 1185, Cullman, AL 35057
Lat/Lon: 34.21378/-86.90427
Email: campgroundscullm@bellsouth.net

SEE AD THIS PAGE

DAUPHIN ISLAND—F-1

(E) DAUPHIN ISLAND CAMPGROUND (City Park)—(Mobile) *At end of Hwy 193: Turn left & go 2 mi on Bienville Blvd. Enter on R.*

WELCOME

FACILITIES: 152 sites, typical site width 30 ft, 80 full hkups, 72 W&E, (30/50 amps), 8 pull-thrus, WiFi Instant Internet at site ($), family camping, tenting, dump, laundry, groceries, RV supplies, ice, picnic tables, controlled access.

RECREATION: rec hall, equipped pavilion, saltwater swim, boating, ramp, dock, saltwater fishing, golf nearby, bsktball, playground, shuffleboard court shuffleboard court, activities, horseshoes, hiking trails, v-ball.

Pets welcome. Partial handicap access. Open all yr. Big rigs welcome. Clubs welcome. MC/VISA.

DAUPHIN ISLAND CAMPGROUND (City Park)—Continued on next page

DAUPHIN ISLAND—Continued
DAUPHIN ISLAND CAMPGROUND (City Park)—Continued

Phone: (251)861-2742
Address: 109 Bienville Blvd, Dauphin Island, AL 36528
Lat/Lon: 30.24994/-88.08002
Email: dipbb@email.msn.com
Web: www.dauphinisland.org

SEE AD PAGE 11

DECATUR—A-3

(W) MALLARD CREEK (TVA-Wheeler Lake)—(Lawrence) *From town: Go 11-1/2 mi W on US-72A/Hwy-20, then 3-3/4 mi N on Spring Creek Rd.* FACILITIES: 56 sites, 56 W&E, tenting, dump. RECREATION: lake swim, boating, ramp, lake fishing, playground. Open Mar 12 - Nov 4. Phone: (256)386-2560.

(E) POINT MALLARD CAMPGROUND (City Park)—(Morgan) *S'bnd: From jct I-65 (exit 340) & Alt US 72/Hwy 20: Go 3 mi W on Alt US 72/Hwy 20, then 1 mi S on US 31, then 3 mi E on Church St. Enter at end.*

WELCOME

FACILITIES: 217 sites, typical site width 25 ft, 217 full hkups, (20/30/50 amps), 26 pull-thrus, phone Internet central location, family camping, tenting, dump, laundry, ltd groc, RV supplies, ice, picnic tables, grills, wood.

RECREATION: rec hall, equipped pavilion, swim pool, river fishing, putting green, bsktball, playground, tennis, sports field, hiking trails, v-ball. Rec open to public.

Pets welcome. Partial handicap access. Open all yr. No reservations accepted for the months of May, Jun & Jul. Big rigs welcome. Clubs welcome. MC/VISA/Debit.

Phone: (256)341-4826
Address: 2901 Point Mallard Dr, Decatur, AL 35602
Lat/Lon: 34.57715/-86.93295
Web: www.pointmallardpark.com

SEE AD TRAVEL SECTION PAGE 4 AND AD TRAVEL SECTION PAGE 4 AND AD TRAVEL SECTION PAGE 1

DELTA—C-4

CHEAHA SP AND CHEAHA LODGE—(Cleburne) *From jct Hwy 49 & Hwy 281: Go 5 mi N on Hwy 281. Enter on L.* FACILITIES: 73 sites, 73 full hkups, 39 pull-thrus, tenting, laundry, ltd groc. RECREATION: lake swim, boating, canoeing, lake fishing, playground. Pets welcome. Partial handicap access. Open all yr. Phone: (205)488-5111.

DEMOPOLIS—D-2

(N) FORKLAND PARK (COE-Demopolis Lake)—(Greene) *From town: Go 12 mi N on US 43, then 1 mi W on dirt road to pavement. Enter at end.* FACILITIES: 42 sites, 42 W&E, (50 amps), 13 pull-thrus, tenting, dump, laundry. RECREATION: lake/river swim, boating, ramp, dock, lake fishing, playground. Partial handicap access. Open Mar 15 - Dec 15. Phone: (334) 289-5530.

(W) FOSCUE PARK (COE-Demopolis Lake)—(Marengo) *From jct US 43/Hwy 13 & US 80/Hwy 8: Go 2 mi W on US 80/Hwy 8, then 2 mi N on Maria St. Enter on R.* FACILITIES: 54 sites, 49 full hkups, 5 W&E, (50 amps), tenting, dump, laundry. RECREATION: lake swim, boating, canoeing, ramp, dock, lake fishing, playground. Partial handicap access. Open all yr. Phone: (334)289-5535.

DOTHAN—E-5

(S) Pecan Point RV Park—(Henry) *From S jct US 431 (Ross Clark Circle) & US 231 S: Go 1-1/2 mi S on US 231 S/Oates St. Enter on R.* ◇◇◇FACILITIES: 62 sites, typical site width 30 ft, accepts full hkup units only, 62 full hkups, (30/50 amps), 29 pull-thrus, cable TV, WiFi Instant Internet at site, phone Internet central location, dump, non-guest dump $, laundry, picnic tables, patios. ◇RECREATION: pavilion. Pets welcome. No tents. Open all yr. Big rigs welcome. Rate in 2010 $40 for 2 persons. MC/VISA/Debit. Member ARVC, ALARVC. CCUSA 50% Discount. CCUSA reservations Accepted, CCUSA max stay 4 days. Discount available Jun, Jul, Aug & Sept.

CAMPCLUB USA

DOTHAN—Continued
Pecan Point RV Park—Continued

Phone: (334)673-3737
Address: 4100 South Oates St., Dothan, AL 36301
Lat/Lon: 31.16718/-85.40248
Email: pecanpointdhn@aol.com
Web: www.pecanpointrvpark.com

DOUBLE SPRINGS—B-2

(W) BANKHEAD NF (Corinth Rec Area)—(Winston) *From town: Go 5-1/2 mi E on US 278, then 3-1/2 mi S on CR 57.* FACILITIES: 50 sites, 50 full hkups, 5 pull-thrus, dump. RECREATION: lake swim, boating, canoeing, ramp, lake fishing. Partial handicap access. Open Mar 14 - Dec 1. Phone: (205)489-3165.

(E) BANKHEAD NF (Houston Rec Area)—(Winston) *From town: Go 10 mi E on US-278, then 2 mi S on CR-63, then 2 mi SW on CR-64, then 1 mi W on FR-118.* FACILITIES: 57 sites, 30 ft max RV length, 2 full hkups, 55 no hkups, 1 pull-thrus, tenting, dump, ltd groc. RECREATION: lake swim, boating, canoeing, ramp, dock, lake fishing. Partial handicap access. Open Apr 15 - Oct 31. Phone: (205)489-5111.

(W) CORINTH RECREATION AREA—(Winston) *From town: Go 5 mi E on US 278, then go 3 mi S on CR 57 (at church) to entrance. Enter at end.* FACILITIES: 56 sites, 48 full hkups, (30/50 amps), 8 no hkups, tenting, dump. RECREATION: lake swim, boating, ramp, dock, lake/3fishing. Partial handicap access. Open May 16 - Nov 1. Phone: (205)489-3165.

ELBERTA—F-2

(E) LAKE OSPREY RV COUNTRY CLUB (TOO NEW TO RATE)—(Baldwin) *From jct Hwy 59 & Hwy 98: Go 8-1/4 mi E on Hwy 98, then 2-1/2 mi S on CR 95. Enter on L.*

WELCOME

FACILITIES: 194 sites, typical site width 40 ft, 194 full hkups, (30/50 amps), cable TV, WiFi Instant Internet at site, family camping.

RECREATION: rec hall, swim pool, hot tub, boating, electric motors only, canoeing, kayaking, dock, lake fishing, putting green, golf nearby, activities, horseshoes, hiking trails.

Pets welcome, breed restrict, quantity restrict. Partial handicap access. No tents. Open all yr. Big rigs welcome. Clubs welcome. Rate in 2010 $40-55 for 2 persons. MC/VISA/DISC/AMEX/Debit.

Text 107961 to (440)725-8687 to see our Visual Tour.

Phone: (251)986-3800
Address: 12096 B Cty Rd 95, Elberta, AL 36530
Email: austinauner@gmail.com
Web: www.lakeosprey.com

SEE AD TRAVEL SECTION PAGE 4

(E) Lazy Acres—(Baldwin) *From jct Hwy 83 & Hwy 98: Go 9-1/2 mi E on Hwy 98, then 3/4 mi S on Wortel Rd.* ◇◇◇FACILITIES: 56 sites, typical site width 40 ft, 43 full hkups, 8 W&E, (20/30/50 amps), 5 no hkups, 22 pull-thrus, WiFi Instant Internet at site ($), WiFi Internet central location, family camping, tenting, laundry, ice, picnic tables, fire rings, wood. ◇◇◇RECREATION: rec hall, swim pool, pond fishing, fishing supplies, bsktball, playground, activities, horseshoes, v-ball. Pets welcome, breed restrict, quantity restrict. Partial handicap access. Open all yr. Big rigs welcome. Rate in 2010 $30-34 for 2 persons. MC/VISA/Debit. CCUSA 50% Discount. CCUSA reservations Accepted, CCUSA max stay 5 days, CCUSA disc. not avail holidays. Max stay may be extended and/or exception to holiday restriction may be made at discretion of management dependant upon availability. Electricity included up to average of 40 kwts/day 30 amp/58 kwts/day 50 amp. Addl .12/kwt.

CAMPCLUB USA

Phone: (877)986-5266
Address: 12160 Wortel Road, Elberta, AL 36530
Lat/Lon: 30.40356/-87.53029
Email: lazyacres01@hughes.net
Web: www.lazyacrescampground.com

(S) Plantation Harbor RV Resort (Wolf Bay Plantations)—(Baldwin) *From jct Hwy 98 & Hwy 59: Go 2-1/2 mi S on Hwy 59, then 5 mi E on CR 20.* ◇◇◇FACILITIES: 186 sites, typical site width 45 ft, 186 full hkups, (20/30/50 amps), 16 pull-thrus, family

ELBERTA—Continued
Plantation Harbor RV Resort (Wolf Bay Plantations)—Continued

camping, laundry. ◇◇◇◇RECREATION: swim pool, boating, canoeing, ramp, dock, river/pond fishing. Pets welcome. Partial handicap access. No tents. Open all yr. Big rigs welcome. Rate in 2010 $30 for 4 persons. Phone: (251)987-5131.

(E) SOLDIERS CREEK GOLF COURSE—*From jct Hwy 59 & Hwy 98: Go 8-1/4 mi E on Hwy 98, then 2-1/2 mi S on CR 95. Enter on L.* 18-hole golf course adjacent to Gulf Coast Motorcoach Country Club; memberships available. Open all yr. MC/VISA/AMEX.

WELCOME

Phone: (251)986-8633
Address: 12096-A Cty Rd 95, Elberta, AL 36530
Lat/Lon: 30.40077/-87.54722
Web: www.soldierscreekgolf.com

SEE AD TRAVEL SECTION PAGE 4

EUFAULA—D-5

(N) LAKEPOINT RESORT LODGE—(Barbour) *From jct US 82 & US 431: Go 7 mi N on US 431.* FACILITIES: 245 sites, 245 W&E, (30 amps), 57 pull-thrus, tenting, laundry, ltd groc. RECREATION: lake swim, boating, ramp, dock, lake fishing, playground. Open all yr. Phone: (334)687-6676.

(N) LAKEPOINT SP—(Barbour) *From jct US 82 & US 431: Go 7 mi N on US 431.* FACILITIES: 245 sites, 245 W&E, (30 amps), 57 pull-thrus, tenting, dump, laundry, ltd groc. RECREATION: lake swim, boating, ramp, dock, lake fishing, playground. Open all yr. Phone: (334)687-6676.

(S) WHITE OAK CREEK PARK (COE-Walter F. George Lake)—(Barbour) *From jct US-431 & Hwy-95: Go 2 mi S on Hwy-95.* FACILITIES: 130 sites, 130 W&E, tenting, dump, laundry. RECREATION: lake/river swim, boating, ramp, dock, lake/river fishing, playground. Open all yr. Phone: (334)687-3101.

FAIRHOPE—F-2

(S) Coastal Haven RV Park—(Baldwin) *From jct I-10 (exit 38) & Hwy 181/27: Go 12 mi S on Hwy 181/27, then 1/8 mi W on Hwy 32. Enter on L.* ◇◇◇◇FACILITIES: 65 sites, 65 full hkups, (20/30/50 amps), 12 pull-thrus, laundry. Pets welcome, breed restrict. No tents. Open all yr. Big rigs welcome. Rate in 2010 $25 per vehicle. Phone: (251)990-9011.

(SE) DRIFTWOOD RV PARK—(Baldwin) *From jct I-10 (exit 35) & US 98 E: Go 18 miles on US 98 E. Enter on R.*

WELCOME

◇◇◇FACILITIES: 51 sites, typical site width 30 ft, 51 full hkups, (30/50 amps), 51 pull-thrus, cable TV, WiFi Instant Internet at site, phone Internet central location, family camping, laundry, LP gas by weight/by meter.

◇RECREATION: rec hall, pavilion.

Pets welcome. No tents. Open all yr. Big rigs welcome. Rate in 2010 $22 for 2 persons. MC/VISA/Debit.

Phone: (251)928-8233
Address: 9318 US Hwy 98, Fairhope, AL 36532
Lat/Lon: 30.42074/-87.86401
Email: driftwoodrvpark@mchsi.com

SEE AD THIS PAGE

(E) Wales West RV Resort & Light Railway—(Baldwin) *From jct US 98 & CR 48 (near Fairhope): Go 5.6 mi E on CR 48, then 1.4 mi S on CR 9.* ◇◇◇◇FACILITIES: 76 sites, typical site width 40 ft, 76 full hkups, (20/30/50 amps), 37 pull-thrus, family camping, laundry, ltd groc. ◇◇◇◇◇RECREATION: swim pool, lake swim, boating, no motors, dock, lake fishing, playground. Pets welcome. No tents. Open all yr. Big rigs welcome. Rate in 2010 $35 for 2 persons. Phone: (888)569-5337.

FLORALA—E-4

(SE) FLORALA SP—(Covington) *In town off Hwy 9/US 331.* FACILITIES: 28 sites, 28 full hkups, (30 amps), tenting, dump, laundry. RECREATION: lake swim, boating, ramp, dock, lake fishing, playground. Open all yr. Phone: (334)858-6425.

FLORENCE—A-2

(W) MC FARLAND PARK (City Park)—(Lauderdale) *From jct US 43, US 72 & Hwy 120: Go 2 blocks W on Hwy 20. (N of Tennessee River Bridge). Enter on L.* FACILITIES: 60 sites, 60 W&E, 18 pull-thrus, tenting, dump, laundry. RECREATION: boating, ramp, river fishing, playground. Pets welcome. Partial handicap access. Open Apr 1 - Nov 30. Phone: (205)760-6416.

VETERANS MEMORIAL PARK (City Park)—(Lauderdale) *From jct US 43, US 72 & Hwy 133: Go 3 mi S on Hwy 133. (At the N end of Wilson Dam). Enter on L.* FACILITIES: 22 sites, 22 W&E, 10 pull-thrus, tenting, dump, laundry. RECREATION: river fishing, playground. Partial handicap access. Open all yr. Phone: (205)760-6416.

Alabama State Tree: Southern Pine

On December 14, 1819, Alabama became the 22nd state.

FOLEY—F-2

(E) AAA RV Park—(Baldwin) *From jct Hwy 59 & Hwy 20: Go 1/2 mi E on Hwy 20, then N 1/4 mi on Juniper Street. Enter on R.* ◊◊FACILITIES: 24 sites, typical site width 40 ft, accepts full hkup units only, 24 full hkups, (20/30/50 amps), 24 pull-thrus. Pets welcome. No tents. Open all yr. Rate in 2010 $15. Phone: (251)970-1232.

(S) Anchors Aweigh RV Resort—(Baldwin) *From jct Hwy 98 & Hwy 59: Go 3 mi S on Hwy 59, then 1/4 mi W on (2nd) Hwy 20 S.* ◊◊◊◊FACILITIES: 112 sites, typical site width 30 ft, 112 full hkups, (20/30/50 amps), 14 pull-thrus, family camping, laundry, ltd groc. ◊◊◊◊RECREATION: swim pool, playground. Pets welcome, breed restrict, quantity restrict. Partial handicap access. No tents. Open all yr. Big rigs welcome. Green Friendly. Rate in 2010 $33-38 per vehicle. Member ARVC, ALARVC.

Phone: (251)971-6644
Address: 19814 Cty Rd 20S, Foley, AL 36535
Lat/Lon: 30.36268/-87.68556
Email: aarvresort@aol.com
Web: anchorsaweighrvresort.com

Johnny's Lakeside RV Resort—(Baldwin) *From jct I-10 (exit 44) & Hwy 59: Go 14-1/2 mi S on Hwy 59. Enter on L.* ◊◊◊◊FACILITIES: 174 sites, typical site width 30 ft, 174 full hkups, (20/30/50 amps), 90 pull-thrus, cable TV, WiFi Instant Internet at site, phone on-site Internet (needs activ), family camping, RV storage, laundry, LP gas by weight/by meter. ◊◊◊RECREATION: rec hall, 1 swim pools, hot tub, pond fishing, activities, horseshoes. Pets welcome, size restrict, quantity restrict. Partial handicap access. No tents. Open all yr. Big rigs welcome. Rate in 2010 $25 per family. MC/VISA/DISC/Debit. CCUSA 50% Discount. CCUSA reservations Recommended, CCUSA max stay 2 days.

Phone: (251)970-3773
Address: 15810 Hwy 59, FOLEY, AL 36535
Lat/Lon: 30.45568/-87.68735
Email: info@palmlakerv.com
Web: www.johnnyslakesidervresort.com

(W) Magnolia Springs RV Hideaway—(Baldwin) *From jct Hwy 59 and CR 12: Go 5 mi W on CR 12, then 2 mi N on CR 49. Enter on L.* ◊◊◊FACILITIES: 62 sites, typical site width 35 ft, 62 full hkups, (30/50 amps), 2 pull-thrus, WiFi Instant Internet at site, phone Internet central location, laundry, picnic tables, patios. ◊◊RECREATION: rec hall, putting green. Pets welcome, quantity restrict. No tents. Open all yr. Big rigs welcome. Rate in 2010 $28 for 2 persons. MC/VISA. CCUSA 50% Discount. CCUSA reservations Recommended, CCUSA max stay Unlimited.

Phone: (251)965-6777
Address: 10831 Magnolia Springs Hwy, Foley, AL 36535
Lat/Lon: 30.38101/-87.77085
Email: hideaway@gulftel.com
Web: www.magnoliaspringsgolf.com

Reserve Online at Woodalls.com

FORT PAYNE—A-4

(N) DE SOTO SP—(DeKalb) *From jct Hwy 35 & CR 89: Go 5 mi N on CR 89.* FACILITIES: 94 sites, 94 full hkups, (30/50 amps), 10 pull-thrus, tenting, laundry, ltd groc. RECREATION: swim pool, river fishing, playground. Partial handicap access. Open all yr. Phone: (800)760-4089.

(N) DESOTO STATE PARK LODGE—(DeKalb) *From jct Hwy 35 & CR 89: Go 5 mi N on CR 89.* FACILITIES: 94 sites, 94 full hkups, (30/50 amps), tenting, laundry, ltd groc. RECREATION: swim pool, river fishing, playground. Partial handicap access. Open all yr. Phone: (256)845-5380.

Woodall's Tip... To be considered a "Big Rig Friendly" park, the campground must meet the following requirements: minimum of 50 amps, adequate road width, overhead access clearance, site clearance to accommodate the tallest and widest rigs built. Often not every site can accommodate a big rig, so we recommend that you call ahead for availability.

FORT PAYNE—Continued

(N) WILLS CREEK RV PARK—(Dekalb) *From jct I-59 (exit 218) & CR 35: Go 1/8 mi W on CR 35, then 1-1/2 mi N on Airport Rd N. Enter on L.*

◊◊◊FACILITIES: 43 sites, typical site width 30 ft, 43 full hkups, (20/30/50 amps), some extd stay sites, 34 pull-thrus, cable TV, WiFi Instant Internet at site, family camping, tenting, dump, non-guest dump $, laundry, picnic tables, patios, fire rings, wood.

◊RECREATION: equipped pavilion, horseshoes, sports field.

Pets welcome. Open all yr. Big rigs welcome. Clubs welcome. Rate in 2010 $25-27 for 4 persons. MC/VISA. CCUSA 50% Discount. CCUSA reservations Recommended, CCUSA max stay 2 days, Cash only for CCUSA disc., CCUSA disc. not avail S, CCUSA disc. not avail F,Sa, CCUSA disc. not avail holidays. Not accepted during special events. Call for details.

Phone: (256)845-6703
Address: 1310 Airport Rd W, Fort Payne, AL 35968
Lat/Lon: 34.45672/-85.73697
Email: info@willscreekrvpark.com
Web: www.willscreekrvpark.com

SEE AD THIS PAGE

FORT RUCKER—E-4

See listings at Dothan, Ozark & Troy

(N) U.S. ARMY AVIATION MUSEUM—*From jct US 231 & Hwy 249: Go 9.7 mi S on Hwy 249. Enter on L.* Country's largest collection of helicopters in a 87,000 sq foot facility. Many one of a kind aircraft. The aircraft displays trace the history of army aviation. Free admission. Also, gift shop. Open all yr. MC/VISA/DISC/AMEX/Debit.

Phone: (888)ARMY-AVN
Address: Building 6000 Novosel St, Ft Rucker, AL 36362-0610
Lat/Lon: 31.32405/-85.71228
Email: giftshopmanager@armyavnmuseum.org
Web: armyavnmuseum.org

SEE AD THIS PAGE

GADSDEN—B-4

NOCCALULA FALLS—*From jct I-59 (exit 183) & US Hwy 431: Go 4 mi SE on US Hwy 431, then 2 mi N on Hwy 211. Enter on R.* City park featuring 90 foot waterfalls, pioneer village, botanical gardens, petting zoo, train rides & carpet golf. Nature trails & picnic pavilions to seat 2,000. Adjacent to Noccalula Falls Campground. Open all yr.

Phone: (256)549-4663
Address: 1500 Noccalula Rd, Gadsden, AL 35904
Lat/Lon: 34.03585/-86.02450
Web: www.cityofgadsden.com

SEE AD NEXT PAGE AND AD TRAVEL SECTION PAGE 1

(N) NOCCALULA FALLS PARK & CAMPGROUND (City Park)—(Etowah) *From jct I-59 (exit 183) & US Hwy 431: Go 4 mi SE on US Hwy 431, then 2 mi N on Hwy 211. Enter on R.*

FACILITIES: 126 sites, typical site width 25 ft, 75 full hkups, 51 W&E, (30/50 amps), 6 pull-thrus, cable TV, WiFi Instant Internet at site, cable Internet central location, family camping, tenting, cabins, dump, non-guest dump $, laundry, ltd groc, RV supplies, ice, picnic tables, grills, wood.

GADSDEN—Continued
NOCCALULA FALLS PARK & CAMPGROUND (City Park)—Continued

RECREATION: equipped pavilion, swim pool, mini-golf, ($), playground, hiking trails.

Pets welcome. Partial handicap access. Open all yr. Big rigs welcome. Clubs welcome. MC/VISA/Debit.

Phone: (256)543-7412
Address: 1600 Noccalula Rd, Gadsden, AL 35904
Lat/Lon: 34.04206/-86.02017
Web: www.cityofgadsden.com

SEE AD NEXT PAGE AND AD TRAVEL SECTION PAGE 1 AND AD TRAVEL SECTION PAGE 4

GADSDEN—Continued on next page

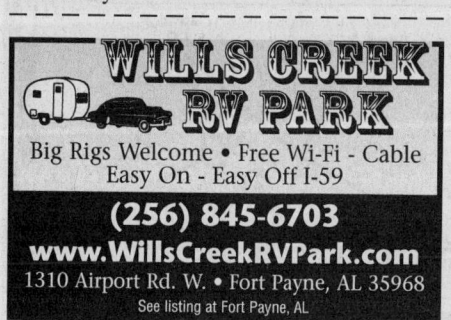

Tell our advertisers you saw them in Woodall's!

GADSDEN, ALABAMA

TEMPORARY DIRECTIONS: FROM I59, EXIT 183 - GO SOUTH ON U.S.HWY 431. TURN LEFT ON TO AL STATE ROAD 211 - GO TO 4TH RED LIGHT FOR CAMPGROUNDS ON THE LEFT.

Search for "THE CITY OF GADSDEN" on FACEBOOK

NOCCALULA FALLS

PARK & CAMPGROUND

Visit us at www.cityofgadsden.com

Known As One of The Old South's Most Beautiful Campgrounds

OPEN 365 DAYS

Discover Alabama's Noccalula Falls Park & Campground. One of Alabama's top attractions. Wake up in the morning to the sound of a rolling brook, dropping 90 feet into a natural gorge. Visit us in April and see the flowers burst into bloom.

RUSTIC ACCOMMODATIONS

Two 2-bedroom Cabins
Enjoy all the comforts of home and the beauty of nature all in one package.

COME, RELAX AND ENJOY THE VERY FINEST IN RV RESORTS FOR A DAY OR WEEK (14 DAY LIMIT)

DELUXE RESORT FACILITIES:

- Paved Roads
- Concrete Sites
- 30 & 50 Amp Service
- Laundry
- 2 Bath Houses
- Country Store
- 24 Hour Security
- Camper Repair (Nearby)
- Restaurants Nearby
- Souvenir Shop
- Wireless Internet

RECREATIONAL FACILITIES:

- Meeting Hall
- Picnic Pavilions
- Swimming Pool
- 90-Ft. Waterfall
- Petting Zoo
- Nature Trail
- Mini-Golf
- Botanical Garden
- Passenger Train
- Pioneer Village
- Wedding Chapel

ANNUAL EVENTS

Gadsden Street Rod Association	June
Coosa Landing Fishing Tournament	May/June
Longest Outdoor Yard Sale	August
Halloween Super Bash	October
Christmas at the Falls	November/December

Wi-Fi

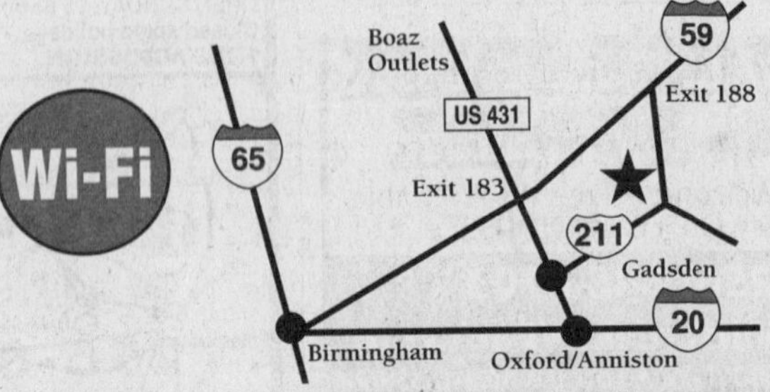

For Reservations, Contact

1600 Noccalula Rd. • Gadsden, AL 35904
Campground Office: 256-543-7412
Park Office: 256-549-4663

GADSDEN—Continued

(E) River Country Campground—(Etowah) *From jct I-59 (exit 182) & I-759: Go 4-1/2 mi E on I-759 to exit 4B, then 1/4 mi N on US 411, then 3/4 mi E on River Rd. Enter at end.* ◇◇◇◇FACILITIES: 235 sites, typical site width 30 ft, 185 full hkups, 50 E, (30/50 amps), 50 amps ($), 98 pull-thrus, laundry, ltd groc. ◇◇◇◇RECREATION: swim pool, boating, ramp, dock, river fishing. Pets welcome. Partial handicap access. No tents. Open all yr. Big rigs welcome. Rate in 2010 $30-34 for 2 persons. Phone: (256)543-7111. FMCA discount.

GALLION—D-2

(N) CHICKASAW SP—(Mobile) *From town: Go 4 mi N on US 43.* FACILITIES: 8 sites, 8 W&E, (30 amps), tenting. RECREATION: playground. Open all yr. Phone: (334)295-8230.

GREENVILLE—D-3

(NW) SHERLING LAKE PARK & CAMPGROUND (City Park)—(Butler) *From I-65 (exit 130) & AL 185: Go 2.5 mi NW on AL 185/AL 263, then 1 mi W on AL 263. Enter on L.*

FACILITIES: 41 sites, typical site width 25 ft, 30 full hkups, 11 W&E, (30/50 amps), some extd stay sites, 20 pull-thrus, WiFi Instant Internet at site, family camping, tenting, dump, ice, picnic tables, patios, fire rings, grills, controlled access.

RECREATION: rec hall, rec room/area, pavilion, boating, electric motors only, canoeing, 4 rowboat rentals, lake fishing, golf nearby, playground, hiking trails. Rec open to public.

Pets welcome. Partial handicap access. Open all yr. Big rigs welcome. Clubs welcome. Member ARVC.

Phone: (800)810-5253
Address: 4397 Braggs Rd, Greenville, AL 36037
Lat/Lon: 31.89655/-86.67077
Email: sherlinglake@cityofgville.com
Web: www.sherlinglake.com

SEE AD THIS PAGE

GROVE OAK—A-4

(N) BUCK'S POCKET SP—(Marshall) *From Hwy 227 in town follow signs N.* FACILITIES: 36 sites, 4 full hkups, 32 W&E, (30/50 amps), 8 pull-thrus, tenting, dump, laundry. RECREATION: boating, ramp, river fishing, playground. Open all yr. Phone: (256) 659-2000.

GULF SHORES—F-2

See listings at Elberta, Fairhope, Foley, Orange Beach, Magnolia Springs, Robertsdale & Summerdale

(W) Bay Breeze RV On the Bay—(Baldwin) *From jct I-10 and Hwy 59 (Loxley Exit #44): Go 29 mi S on Hwy 59, then 6.1 mi W on Hwy 180 W (Ft Morgan Parkway). Enter on R.* ◇◇◇FACILITIES: 30 sites, typical site width 25 ft, 26 full hkups, 4 W&E, (30/50 amps), 50 amps ($), tenting, laundry. ◇◇RECREATION: saltwater swim, boating, canoeing, dock, saltwater fishing. Pets welcome. Partial handicap access. Open all yr. Big rigs welcome. Rate in 2010 $26-45 for 2 persons. Phone: (251)540-2362.

(NE) BELLA TERRA OF GULF SHORES—(Baldwin) *From jct Hwy 59 and Foley Beach Express: Go 9 mi SE on Foley Beach Express, then 1/4 mi W on Brinks Willis Rd. Enter on L.*

◇◇◇◇◇FACILITIES: 176 sites, typical site width 50 ft, 176 full hkups, (30/50 amps), 31 pull-thrus, WiFi Instant Internet at site, family camping, laundry, patios, controlled access.

◇◇◇◇◇RECREATION: rec hall, pavilion, 2 swim pools, wading pool, hot tub, pond fishing, putting green, golf nearby, bsktball, shuffleboard court shuffleboard court, activities, tennis, hiking trails.

Pets welcome, breed restrict, quantity restrict. Partial handicap access. No tents. Open all yr. Class A Motorcoaches only. Big rigs welcome. Escort to site. Clubs welcome. Green Friendly. Rate in 2010 $35-55 per vehicle. MC/VISA/AMEX. Member ARVC, ALARVC. FMCA discount.

Text 81709 to (440)725-8687 to see our Visual Tour.

Alabama State Motto: "We Dare Maintain our Rights."

Phone: (866)880-9522
Address: 101 Via Bella Terra, Foley, AL 36535
Lat/Lon: 30.34823/-87.66010
Email: rentals@bellaterrarvresort.com
Web: www.BTRVWoodalls.com

SEE AD TRAVEL SECTION PAGE 3 AND AD MAP PAGE 2

(W) Doc's RV Park—(Baldwin) *From jct US 98 & Hwy 59: Go 9-1/2 mi S on Hwy 59, then 2-3/10 mi W on Hwy 180. Enter on R.* ◇◇◇FACILITIES: 75 sites, typical site width 30 ft, 75 full hkups, (30/50 amps), dump, laundry. ◇◇◇RECREATION: swim pool, playground. Pets welcome. Partial handicap access. No tents. Open all yr. Big rigs welcome. Rate in 2010 $30 for 2 persons. Phone: (251)968-4511.

(W) Fort Morgan RV Park—(Baldwin) *From jct Hwy 59 & Hwy 180 W: Go 10 mi W on Hwy 180. Enter on R.* ◇◇FACILITIES: 34 sites, typical site width 35 ft, 34 full hkups, (30/50 amps), 2 pull-thrus, family camping, laundry. ◇◇RECREATION: boating, dock, saltwater fishing. Pets welcome. No tents. Open all yr. Big rigs welcome. Rate in 2010 $35-49 for 2 persons. Member ARVC. Phone: (251)540-2416.

GULF SHORES—Continued on next page

Woodall's Tip... Rate information is based on the campground's published rate last year. These rates aren't guaranteed, and you should always call ahead for the most updated rate information.

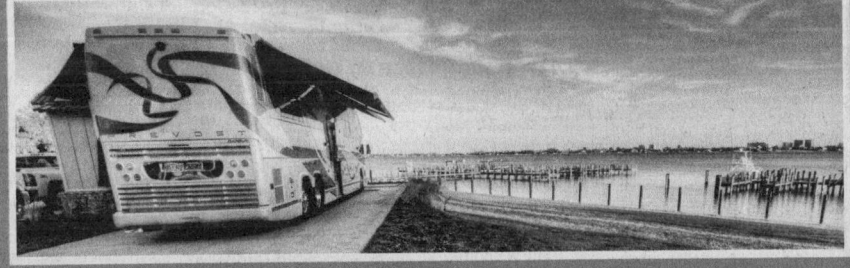

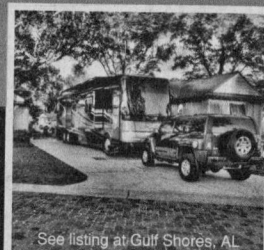

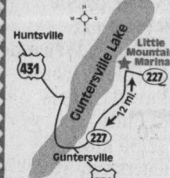

GULF SHORES—Continued

(N) GULF BREEZE RESORT—(Baldwin) *From jct US 98 & Hwy 59: Go 6-1/2 mi S on Hwy 59, then 300 yards on CR 6. Enter on L.*

WELCOME

◆◆◆◆◆FACILITIES: 254 sites, typical site width 45 ft, 254 full hkups, (20/30/50 amps), 50 pull-thrus, cable TV, WiFi Instant Internet at site, phone on-site Internet (needs activ), phone Internet central location, RV's/park model rentals, cabins, RV storage, laundry, LP gas by weight, ice, picnic tables, patios, grills.

◆◆◆◆◆RECREATION: rec hall, rec room/area, equipped pavilion, 2 swim pools, wading pool, hot tub, 5 pedal boat rentals, lake fishing, mini-golf, golf nearby, bsktball, playground, shuffleboard court 4 shuffleboard courts, activities, tennis, v-ball.

Pets welcome. Partial handicap access. No tents. Open all yr. Planned group activities winter only. Big rigs welcome. Clubs welcome. Rate in 2010 $32 for 4 persons. MC/VISA/DISC/AMEX.

Phone: (251)968-8884
Address: 19800 Oak Road West, Gulf Shores, AL 36542
Lat/Lon: 30.31183/-87.68635
Web: www.rvcampresort.com

SEE AD PAGE 15

(E) GULF SP—(Baldwin) *From jct Hwy 59 & Hwy 182: Go 3 mi E on Hwy 182. Enter on L.* FACILITIES: 496 sites, 496 full hkups, (50 amps), 40 pull-thrus, tenting, dump, laundry, ltd groc. RECREATION: saltwater swim, boating, ramp, dock, saltwater fishing, playground. Open all yr. Phone: (251)948-6353.

(W) Island Retreat RV Park—(Baldwin) *From jct I-10 and Hwy 59 (Loxley exit #44): Go 35 mi S on Hwy 59, then 1-1/2 mi W on Hwy 180 W. Enter on R.* ◆◆◆FACILITIES: 174 sites, typical site width 40 ft, 174 full hkups, (20/30/50 amps), 16 pull-thrus, family camping, laundry, ltd groc. ◆◆◆RECREATION: swim pool, playground. Pets welcome, breed restrict. Partial handicap access. No tents. Open all yr. Big rigs welcome. Rate in 2010 $32-35 for 4 persons. Phone: (251)967-1666.

(N) Lazy Lake RV Park—(Baldwin) *From jct Hwy 59 & CR 6: Go 3/4 mi W on CR 6, then 1/4 mi S on Old Plash Island Rd. Enter on L.* ◆◆◆FACILITIES: 40 sites, typical site width 30 ft, 40 full hkups, (30/50 amps), laundry. ◆◆RECREATION: boating, no motors, canoeing, lake fishing, play equipment. Pets welcome. No tents. Open all yr. Big rigs welcome. Rate in 2010 $26.50 for 4 persons. Phone: (251)968-7875.

(S) Luxury RV Resort—(Baldwin) *From jct US 98 & Hwy 59: Go 9 mi S on Hwy 59. Enter on L.* ◆◆◆◆◆FACILITIES: 90 sites, typical site width 35 ft, 90 full hkups, (20/30/50 amps), dump, laundry, ltd groc. ◆◆◆RECREATION: swim pool. Pets welcome, breed restrict. Partial handicap access. No tents. Open all yr. Big rigs welcome. Phone: (800)982-3510.

(N) Southport Campgrounds—(Baldwin) *From jct Hwy 180 & Hwy 59: Go 2 mi N on Hwy 59, then 2/10 mi W on CR 4. Enter at end.* ◆◆FACILITIES: 128 sites,

GULF SHORES—Continued
Southport Campgrounds—Continued

typical site width 25 ft, 78 full hkups, 50 W&E, (20/30/50 amps), 30 pull-thrus, family camping, tenting, dump, laundry. ◆◆◆RECREATION: boating, dock, saltwater fishing. Pets welcome. Partial handicap access. Open all yr. Rate in 2010 $21-25 for 2 persons. Phone: (251)968-6220.

(N) Sun-Runners RV Park—(Baldwin) *From jct US 98 & Hwy 59: Go 5-1/2 mi S on Hwy 59, then 1/2 mi W on CR 8. Enter on L.* ◆◆◆FACILITIES. 60 sites, typical site width 25 ft, 41 full hkups, 19 W&E, (20/30/50 amps), 13 pull-thrus, cable TV, WiFi Instant Internet at site, tenting, RV storage, dump, laundry, ice, picnic tables. ◆◆RECREATION: Pets welcome, breed restrict. Partial handicap access. Open all yr. Rate in 2010 $25 for 2 persons. CCUSA 50% Discount. CCUSA reservations Recommended, CCUSA max stay 1 day, Cash only for CCUSA disc.

CAMPCLUB USA

Phone: (251)955-5257
Address: 19480 Co. Rd 8, Gulf Shores, AL 36542
Lat/Lon: 30.32453/-87.69201
Email: sunrunnersrv@gulftel.com
Web: www.sunrunnersrvpark.com

GUNTERSVILLE—A-4

(N) BLUE HERON PARADISE—(Marshall) *From jct US 431 & Hwy 79: Go 2 mi N on Hwy 79 N. Enter on L.*

◆◆◆◆FACILITIES: 96 sites, typical site width 40 ft, 96 full hkups, (30/50 amps), 5 pull-thrus, WiFi Instant Internet at site ($), family camping, RV storage, laundry, ice, patios.

◆◆◆◆RECREATION: rec hall, swim pool, lake/pond fishing, fishing guides, golf nearby, bsktball, playground, activities, horseshoes.

Pets welcome, breed restrict. Partial handicap access. No tents. Open all yr. Big rigs welcome. Escort to site. Clubs welcome. Rate in 2010 $20-29 per vehicle. MC/VISA/DISC/Debit.

Phone: (256)571-7527
Address: 1727 Convict Camp Rd, Guntersville, AL 35976
Web: www.blueheronparadiserv.com

SEE AD THIS PAGE

(N) LAKE GUNTERSVILLE STATE LODGE AND STATE PARK—(Marshall) *From jct US 431 & Hwy 227: Go 6 mi NE on Hwy 227.* FACILITIES: 321 sites, 143 full hkups, 178 W&E, (30/50 amps), 51 pull-thrus, tenting, laundry, ltd groc. RECREATION: lake swim, boating, ramp, dock, lake fishing, playground. Open all yr. Phone: (205)571-5455.

(N) Seibold Campground—(Marshall) *From jct US 431 & Hwy 79: Go 1 mi N on Hwy 79. Enter on R.* ◆◆◆FACILITIES: 136 sites, typical site width 50 ft, 136 W&E, (20/30/50 amps), family camping, tenting, dump. ◆◆◆◆RECREATION: swim pool, lake swim, boating, canoeing, ramp, dock, lake fishing, playground. Pets welcome. Partial handicap access. Open Mar 1 - Oct 31. Big rigs welcome. Rate in 2010 $22-27 for 5 persons. Member ARVC, ALARVC. Phone: (256) 582-0040.

HANCEVILLE—B-3

(W) Country View RV Park—(Cullman) *From jct I-65 (exit 291) & Hwy 91: Go 1.5 mi N on Hwy 91 N. Enter on L.* ◆◆◆FACILITIES: 33 sites, typical site width 25 ft, 33 full hkups, (30/50 amps), 33 pull-thrus, laundry, ltd groc. ◆RECREATION: play equipment. Pets welcome. No tents. Open all yr. Big rigs welcome. Rate in 2010 $29 for 2 persons. Phone: (256)352-4678.

HEFLIN—B-4

CANE 9 CREEK RV PARK & CAMPGROUND—(Cleburne) *From jct I-20 (exit 205) & Hwy 46: Go 1-3/4 mi NW on Hwy 46. Enter on L.*

WELCOME

◆◆◆FACILITIES: 41 sites, typical site width 35 ft, 34 full hkups, 7 W&E, (20/30/50 amps), 50 amps ($), 12 pull-thrus, WiFi Instant Internet at site, family camping, tenting, RV storage, dump, laundry, picnic tables, fire rings, wood.

◆◆◆RECREATION: rec room/area, canoeing, kayaking, stream fishing, golf nearby, sports field, hiking trails.

CAMPCLUB USA

Pets welcome. Partial handicap access. Open all yr. Big rigs welcome. Escort to site. Clubs welcome. Rate in 2010 $25 for 2 persons. CCUSA 50% Discount. CCUSA reservations Not Accepted, CCUSA max stay 1 day, Cash only for CCUSA disc. Discount available Oct thru Mar. Not available Talledega Race weekends. May call ahead same day for availability. Addl vehicle surcharge $5. No check in prior to 3pm.

Phone: (256)463-2602
Address: 5002 Hwy 46, Heflin, AL 36264
Lat/Lon: 33.65311/-85.53259
Web: www.cane9creekrvpark.com

SEE AD THIS PAGE

(NW) TALLADEGA NF (Coleman Lake)—(Cleburne) *From town: Go 6 mi NE on US 78, then 8-1/2 mi NW on CR 61/FR 553, then 1-1/2 mi N on FR 500. Follow signs.* FACILITIES: 39 sites, 35 ft max RV length, 39 W&E, 1 pull-thrus, tenting, dump. RECREATION: lake swim, boating, no motors, canoeing, ramp. Partial handicap access. Open Apr 15 - Nov 30. Phone: (256)463-2272.

(N) TALLADEGA NF (Pine Glen)—(Cleburne) *From jct Hwy-46 & US-78: Go 2-1/2 mi W on US-78, then 8 mi N on FR-500.* FACILITIES: 23 sites, 22 ft max RV length, 23 no hkups, tenting. RECREATION: Open all yr. Phone: (256)463-2272.

HELENA—C-3

(S) CHEROKEE CAMPGROUND—(Shelby) *From jct I-459 (exit 6) Hwy 52: Go 4 mi SE on Hwy 52/Morgan Rd, then 3/4 mi S on Hwy 93. Enter on L.*

◊◊◊FACILITIES: 100 sites, typical site width 40 ft, 92 full hkups, 8 W&E, (30/50 amps), 50 amps ($), some extd stay sites, 22 pull-thrus, WiFi Instant Internet at site ($), WiFi Internet central location, dump, laundry, ltd groc, LP bottle exch, ice.

◊◊RECREATION: rec room/area, pavilion, lake fishing, golf nearby, bsktball, hiking trails.

Pets welcome, breed restrict. No tents. Open all yr. Big rigs welcome. Escort to site. Clubs welcome. Rate in 2010 $30 for 2 persons. CCUSA 50% Discount. CCUSA reservations Not Accepted, CCUSA max stay Unlimited, Cash only for CCUSA disc. Based on availability, prefer call ahead 1-2 days. No aggressive dog breeds. WiFi available thru 3rd party @ charge.

Phone: (205)428-8339
Address: 2800 Hwy 93, Helena, AL 35080
Lat/Lon: 33.29296/-86.91063
Email: braxenterprises@aol.com
Web: www.cherokeecampground.info

SEE AD BIRMINGHAM PAGE 10 AND AD TRAVEL SECTION PAGE 4

HODGES—A-2

(E) BEAR CREEK DEV AUTH (Horseshoe Bend)—(Franklin) *From jct Hwy 24 & CR 88: Go 2 mi S on CR 88, then 5 mi E on CR 16, then 2 mi W on Horseshoe Bend Rd. Enter on R.* FACILITIES: 26 sites, typical site width 25 ft, 26 W&E, (30 amps), tenting, dump, ltd groc. RECREATION: lake swim, boating, ramp, dock, lake fishing. Partial handicap access. Open Apr - Oct. Phone: (256)332-4392.

HOOVER—C-3

(S) HOOVER RV PARK—(Jefferson) *From W jct I-59 N & I-459 N: Go 10 mi NE on I-459N to exit 10, then 3/10 mi SE on Hwy 150, then 1-1/2 mi W on Stadium Trace Pkwy. Follow RV park signs. Enter on L.* FACILITIES: 144 sites, typical site width 21 ft, 144 full hkups, (20/30/50 amps), 144 pull-thrus, dump. RECREATION: Partial handicap access. No tents. Open all yr. Phone: (866)466-8378.

HUNTSVILLE—A-3

(S) DITTO LANDING MARINA CAMPGROUND (City/County Park)—(Madison) *From jct US 431 & US 231: Go 9 mi S on US 231, then 1 mi E on Hobbs Island Rd. Enter on R.* FACILITIES: 26 sites, 26 W&E, tenting, dump, laundry. RECREATION: boating, canoeing, ramp, river fishing, playground. No pets. Partial handicap access. Open all yr. Phone: (256)882-1057.

(E) MILITARY PARK (Redstone Arsenal Travel Camp)—(Madison) *From I-65: Take Hwy 20 (exit 340 E). On base.* FACILITIES: 23 sites, 23 W&E, tenting, dump. RECREATION: boating. Open Mar 15 - Nov 1. Phone: (256)876-6854.

(E) MONTE SANO SP—(Madison) *From jct I-565 & Hwy 1/US 431: Go E on Hwy 1/US 431 (Governors Dr), then N on Monte Sano Blvd.* FACILITIES: 96 sites, 17 full hkups, 61 W&E, (30/50 amps), 18 no hkups, 4 pull-thrus, tenting, dump, laundry, ltd groc. RECREATION: playground. Partial handicap access. Open all yr. Phone: (256)534-6589.

(S) MOUNTAIN BREEZE RV PARK (RV SPACES)—(Madison) *From jct Hwy 36 & Hwy 231: Go 4-1/2 mi S on Hwy 231 (mm 229). Enter on R.*

FACILITIES: 23 sites, typical site width 30 ft, 23 full hkups, (20/30/50 amps), 8 pull-thrus, tenting, laundry.

RECREATION: rec room/area.

Pets welcome. Open all yr. Big rigs welcome. Rate in 2010 $20 for 2 persons.

Phone: (256)498-2571
Address: 3829 Hwy 231, Laceys Springs, AL 35754
Email: mtnbrzrv@otelco.net

SEE AD THIS PAGE

HUNTSVILLE—Continued

(W) US Space & Rocket Center RV Campground—(Madison) *From jct Hwy 231 & I-565: Go 4-1/2 mi W on I-565 to Space Center exit (exit 15), then 1/4 mi S to Space Center access road, then 1/4 mi W.* ◊◊◊FACILITIES: 27 sites, typical site width 15 ft, 27 full hkups, (20/30 amps), 5 pull-thrus, laundry. Pets welcome. No tents. Open all yr. Rate in 2010 $18-20 per vehicle. Phone: (256)830-4987.

JASPER—B-2

BANKHEAD NF (Clear Creek Rec Area)—(Walker) *From town: Go 5 mi N on Hwy 195, then 8-1/2 mi NE on CR 27.* FACILITIES: 97 sites, 97 W&E, 10 pull-thrus, tenting, dump, ltd groc. RECREATION: lake swim, boating, canoeing, ramp, lake fishing. Partial handicap access. Open Mar 14 - Dec 1. Phone: (205)384-4792.

(E) SLEEPY HOLLER CAMPGROUND—(Walker) *From jct I-22/US 78 (exit 65) & Industrial Blvd: Go approx 2 mi N on Indust Blvd, then 3 mi S on Hwy 5, then 1 mi S(at caution light between mm 165 & 166) on Buttermilk Rd. Enter on L.*

◊◊◊FACILITIES: 130 sites, typical site width 25 ft, 130 full hkups, (15/30/50 amps), 40 pull-thrus, WiFi Instant Internet at site, RV's/park model rentals, cabins, laundry, LP gas by meter, picnic tables.

◊◊RECREATION: rec hall, rec room/area, pavilion, lake fishing, horseshoes, hiking trails.

Pets welcome, breed restrict. No tents. Open all yr. Big rigs welcome. Escort to site. Clubs welcome. Rate in 2010 $25-35 for 2 persons.

Phone: (205)483-7947
Address: 174 Sleepy Holler Circle, Cordova, AL 35550
Lat/Lon: 33.80743/-87.18128
Web: www.sleepyhollercampgroundal.com

SEE AD THIS PAGE

JEMISON—C-3

(E) Peach Queen Campground—(Chilton) *From jct I-65 (Exit 219) & Cty Rd 42: Go 1/2 mi E on Cty Rd 42. Enter on R.* ◊◊◊FACILITIES: 54 sites, typical site width 35 ft, 54 full hkups, (20/30/50 amps), 54 pull-thrus, family camping, tenting, laundry, ltd groc. ◊◊◊RECREATION: swim pool, boating, no motors, lake fishing, play equipment. Pets welcome. Open all yr. Big rigs welcome. Rate in 2010 $25-35 for 2 persons. Member ARVC, ALARVC. Phone: (205)688-2573.

LANGSTON—A-4

(S) LAKESIDE RETREAT RV RESORT (NOT VISITED)—(Marshall) *From jct US 431 & Hwy 227: Go 11-3/4mi S on Hwy 227 (Hwy 227 turns N), then 8-3/4 mi N on S Hwy Rd (City Rd 67). Enter on R.*

FACILITIES: 107 sites, typical site width 40 ft, 107 full hkups, (20/30/50 amps), 4 pull-thrus, cable TV, WiFi Instant Internet at site, family camping, RV storage, laundry, patios, controlled access.

RECREATION: rec hall, swim pool, boating, ramp, dock, lake fishing, putting green, horseshoes, hiking trails, v-ball.

Pets welcome. No tents. Open all yr. Big rigs welcome. Clubs welcome.

Address: 10174 Cty Rd 67, Langston, AL 35755
Lat/Lon: 34.53476/-86.08900
Email: paddyob128@aol.com
Web: www.lakesideretreatrv.com

SEE AD GUNTERSVILLE PAGE 16

The Monarch Butterfly is a native butterfly to Alabama.

LANGSTON—Continued

(S) LITTLE MOUNTAIN MARINA CAMPING RESORT—(Marshall) *From jct US 431 & Hwy 227: Go 12 mi S on Hwy 227 (Hwy 227 turns N), then 1/2 mi N on S Sauty Rd (Hwy 227 goes E at S Sauty Rd) 1/4 mi on Murphy Hill Rd. Enter on L.*

◊◊◊◊◊FACILITIES: 371 sites, typical site width 30 ft, 336 full hkups, 35 W&E, (20/30/50 amps), some extd stay sites, 7 pull-thrus, phone Internet central location, family camping, tenting, cabins, RV storage, dump, laundry, RV supplies, LP gas by weight, LP bottle exch, ice, picnic tables, patios, grills, controlled access.

◊◊◊◊◊RECREATION: rec hall, rec room/area, pavilion, equipped pavilion, coin games, 3 swim pools, wading pool, lake swim, hot tub, boating, canoeing, ramp, dock, lake fishing, mini-golf, bsktball, playground, shuffleboard court 3 shuffleboard courts, activities, tennis, sports field, v-ball.

Pets welcome. Partial handicap access. Open all yr. Big rigs welcome. Clubs welcome. Rate in 2010 $29 for 4 persons. MC/VISA/DISC/AMEX.

Phone: (256)582-8211
Address: 1001 Murphy Hill Rd., Langston, AL 35755
Lat/Lon: 34.45929/-86.18682
Web: www.rvcampresort.com

SEE AD GULF SHORES PAGE 15

(S) Northshore Campground at the Big Rock—(Jackson) *From jct US 431 & Hwy 227: Go 12 mi S on Hwy 227 (Hwy 227 turns N) then 6 1/2 mi N on S Sauty Rd. Enter on R.* ◊◊◊◊FACILITIES: 51 sites, typical site width 30 ft, accepts full hkup units only, 51 full hkups, (20/30/50 amps), full svc store. ◊◊◊RECREATION: swim pool, lake swim, boating, canoeing, ramp, dock, lake fishing. Pets welcome. No tents. Open all yr. Big rigs welcome. Rate in 2010 $27 for 5 persons. Phone: (256) 582-3367.

(S) South Sauty Creek Resort—(Marshall) *From jct US 431 & Hwy 227: Go 12 mi S on Hwy 227 (Hwy 227 turns N), then 6-1/2 mi N on S Sauty Rd. Enter at end.* ◊◊◊FACILITIES: 85 sites, typical site width 30 ft, 85 W&E, (20/30/50 amps), tenting, dump, full svc store. ◊◊◊RECREATION: swim pool, lake swim, boating, canoeing, ramp, dock, lake fishing. Pets welcome. Open all yr. Big rigs welcome. Rate in 2010 $22 for 5 persons. Member ALARVC. Phone: (256)582-3367.

LEESBURG—B-4

(N) Chesnut Bay Campground—(Cherokee) *From jct I-59 (exit 205) & Hwy 68: Go 13 mi S & W on Hwy 68, then 3-3/4 mi E on Cty Rd 44. Enter at end.* ◊◊◊◊FACILITIES: 20 sites, accepts full hkup units only, 20 full hkups, (20/30/50 amps), 2 pull-thrus, family camping, ltd groc. ◊◊◊◊RECREATION: swim pool, lake swim, boating, canoeing, ramp, dock, lake fishing, playground. Pets welcome, size restrict, quantity restrict. No tents. Open all yr. Big rigs welcome. Rate in 2010 $35-45 for 4 persons. Phone: (256)526-7778.

LILLIAN—F-2

(S) Gulf Shores/Pensacola West KOA—(Baldwin) *From jct US-98 & CR-99: Go 1-1/2 mi S on CR-99. Enter on L.* ◊◊◊FACILITIES: 103 sites, typical site width 25 ft, 94 full hkups, 9 W&E, (20/30/50 amps), 103 pull-thrus, family camping, tenting, laundry, groceries. ◊◊◊◊RECREATION: swim pool, saltwater swim, boating, ramp, dock, saltwater fishing, playground. Pets welcome. Open all yr. Big rigs welcome. Green Friendly. Rate in 2010 $28-52 for 2 persons. Phone: (251)961-1717. KOA discount.

LOWNDESBORO—D-3

(N) PRAIRIE CREEK PARK (COE-Alabama River Lakes)—(Lowndes) *From jct US 80 & CR 29: Go N on CR 29. Follow signs.* FACILITIES: 62 sites, 62 W&E, 10 pull-thrus, tenting, dump, laundry. RECREATION: boating, canoeing, ramp, dock, river fishing, playground. Partial handicap access. Open all yr. Phone: (334)418-4919.

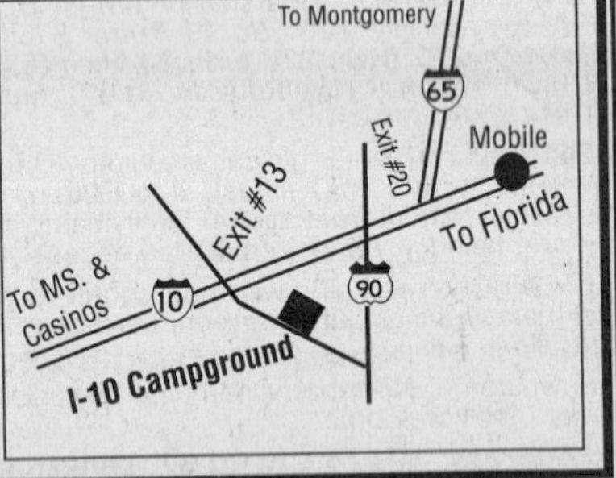

MAGNOLIA SPRINGS—F-2

(W) Southwind RV Park—(Baldwin) *From jct Hwy 59 & US 98: Go 7-1/2 mi W on US 98, then 3/10 mi N on CR 9N. Enter on L.* ◆◆◆FACILITIES: 120 sites, typical site width 35 ft, 120 full hkups, (20/30/50 amps), 105 pull-thrus, laundry. Pets welcome. Partial handicap access. No tents. Age restrict may apply. Open all yr. Big rigs welcome. Rate in 2010 $25 for 2 persons. Phone: (251)988-1216.

MCCALLA—C-3

(S) **MCCALLA CAMPGROUND**—(Tuscaloosa) *From west jct I-459 & I-20/I-59: Go 6 mi SW on I-20/I-59 (exit 100), then 200 yards W on Hwy 216. Enter on L.*

WELCOME

◆◆◆FACILITIES: 46 sites, typical site width 30 ft, 43 full hkups, 3 W&E, (30/50 amps), 50 amps ($), some extd stay sites, 46 pull-thrus, cable TV, phone Internet central location, cabins, RV storage, dump, non-guest dump $, laundry, groceries, RV supplies, LP gas by meter, ice, picnic tables.

◆◆RECREATION: equipped pavilion, swim pool, golf nearby, horseshoes.

Pets welcome. Partial handicap access. No tents. Open all yr. Big rigs welcome. Clubs welcome. Rate in 2010 $24-35 for 2 persons. MC/VISA/DISC/Debit.

Phone: (877)477-4778
Address: 22191 Hwy 216, McCalla, AL 35111
Lat/Lon: 33.27949/-87.09988

SEE AD BIRMINGHAM PAGE 10

(S) TANNEHILL IRONWORKS HISTORICAL STATE PARK—(Tuscaloosa) *From I-59 (exit 100): Go 2-1/2 mi E following signs. Enter on L.* FACILITIES: 300 sites, 43 full hkups, 168 W&E, (50 amps), 89 no hkups, 60 pull-thrus, tenting, dump, laundry, ltd groc. RECREATION: stream fishing. Pets welcome. Partial handicap access. Open all yr. Phone: (205)477-5711.

MOBILE—F-1

See listings at Dauphin Island, Theodore, Creola, & Wilmer

(S) CHICKASABOGUE PARK & CG (Mobile County Pk)—(Mobile) *From I-65 (exit 13) & Hwy 158: Go 2 mi S on Hwy 213, then 3/4 mi SE on Whistler St, then 1 mi N on Aldock Rd. Enter at end.* FACILITIES: 74 sites, typical site width 25 ft, 24 full hkups, 34 W&E, (30/50 amps), 16 no hkups, 30 pull-thrus, tenting, dump, laundry, ltd groc. RECREATION: river swim, boating, canoeing, ramp, river fishing, playground. Partial handicap access. Open all yr. Phone: (251)574-2267.

MOBILE—Continued on next page

The word Alabama means "tribal town" in the Creek Indian language.

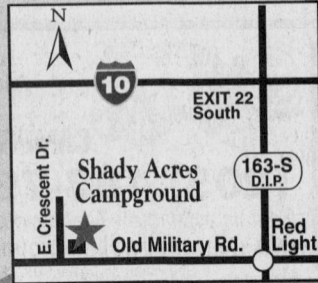

MOBILE—Continued

(W) I-10 KAMPGROUND—(Mobile) *From jct I-10 (exit 13) & Theodore Dawes Rd: Go 1/2 mi S on Theodore Dawes Rd. Enter on L.*

WELCOME

◆◆◆FACILITIES: 165 sites, typical site width 22 ft, 157 full hkups, 8 W&E, (30/50 amps), many extd stay sites, 155 pull-thrus, cable TV, WiFi Internet central location, family camping, dump, non-guest dump $, laundry, ltd groc, RV supplies, LP gas by weight/by meter, ice, picnic tables.

◆◆RECREATION: rec hall, pavilion, swim pool, golf nearby, sports field.

Pets welcome. Partial handicap access. No tents. Open all yr. Big rigs welcome. Clubs welcome. Rate in 2010 $25 for 2 persons. MC/VISA/DISC/AMEX.

Phone: (800)272-1263
Address: 6430 Theodore Dawes Rd, Theodore, AL 36582
Lat/Lon: 30.55776/-88.19196
Email: i10kamp@msn.com

SEE AD PAGE 18

(N) I-65 RV Campground—(Mobile) *From jct I-65 (exit 19) & Hwy 43: Go 1/10 mi N on Hwy 43, then 9/10 mi W on Jackson Rd. Enter on L.* ◆◆◆FACILITIES: 91 sites, typical site width 30 ft, 87 full hkups, (20/30/50 amps), 50 amps ($), 4 no hkups, 16 pull-thrus, tenting, dump, laundry, ltd groc. Pets welcome, breed restrict. Partial handicap access. Open all yr. Big rigs welcome. Rate in 2010 $30 for 2 persons. Phone: (800)287-3208.

(W) Johnny's RV Resort—(Mobile) *From jct I-10 (exit 15A) & US 90: Go 3-1/4 mi SW on US 90. Enter on L.* ◆◆◆◆FACILITIES: 200 sites, typical site width 35 ft, 200 full hkups, (30/50 amps), 13 pull-thrus, cable TV, WiFi Instant Internet at site, WiFi Internet central location, family camping, RV storage, laundry, ltd groc, RV supplies, LP gas by weight, ice, picnic tables.

CAMPCLUB USA

◆◆◆RECREATION: lake swim, boating, no motors, canoeing, kayaking, lake fishing, fishing supplies, bsktball, shuffleboard court shuffleboard court, activities hiking trails. Pets welcome. No tents. Open all yr. Big rigs welcome. Rate in 2010 $27 for 2 persons. MC/VISA/DISC/AMEX. FMCA discount. CCUSA 50% Discount. CCUSA reservations Recommended, CCUSA max stay 7 days. 1998 & newer vehicles only. Reservations for less than 7 days may be made no more than 3 days in advance. Back in sites accomodate 45' unit. Pull thru sites are 70'.

Phone: (251)653-7120
Address: 6171 Hwy 90 W, Theodore, AL 36590
Lat/Lon: 30.53597/-88.18620

(W) PALA VERDE RV PARK (RV SPACES)—(Mobile) *From jct I-10 (exit 15 B) & US 90: Go 2-1/2 mi N on US 90, then 75 yds E on Demetropolis Rd. Enter on L.*

WELCOME

FACILITIES: 19 sites, typical site width 25 ft, accepts full hkup units only, 19 full hkups, (30/50 amps), 5 pull-thrus, phone on-site Internet (needs activ), patios.

Pets welcome, breed restrict. No tents. Open all yr. No restrooms. Rate in 2010 $18-25 for 2 persons.

Phone: (251)660-7148
Address: 3525 Demetropolis Rd, Mobile, AL 36693
Lat/Lon: 30.61712/-88.15608
Email: palaverde@micro-comm.com
Web: palaverderv.com

SEE AD PAGE 18

(S) Payne's RV Park—(Mobile) *From jct I-10 (exit 13) & Theodore Dawes Rd: Go 1-3/4 mi SE, then 1/4 mi S on Hwy 90, then 1-1/2 mi S on Bellingrath Rd. Enter on R.* ◆◆◆◆FACILITIES: 102 sites, typical site width 35 ft, 90 full hkups, 12 W&E, (20/30/50 amps), 62 pull-thrus, tenting, laundry. Pets welcome, breed restrict. Open all yr. Big rigs welcome. Rate in 2010 $25-32 for 2 persons. Phone: (251)653-1034.

MOBILE—Continued

(S) SHADY ACRES CAMPGROUND—(Mobile) *From jct I-10 and Hwy 163/Dauphin Island Parkway (w'bnd exit 22B, E'bnd exit 22): Go 3/4 mi S on Dauphin Island Parkway, then 1/2 mi W on Old Military Rd. Enter on R.*

WELCOME

◆◆◆◆FACILITIES: 92 sites, typical site width 30 ft, 92 full hkups, (30/50 amps), some extd stay sites, 10 pull-thrus, WiFi Instant Internet at site, family camping, tenting, dump, non-guest dump $, laundry, LP gas by weight/by meter, picnic tables, patios.

◆◆◆RECREATION: rec room/area, boating, canoeing, ramp, dock, river fishing, hiking trails.

Pets welcome. Open all yr. Big rigs welcome. Clubs welcome. Rate in 2010 $22 for 2 persons. MC/VISA.

Phone: (251)478-0013
Address: 2500 Old Military Rd, Mobile, AL 36605
Lat/Lon: 30.62783/-88.09518
Email: dogriver13@aol.com
Web: www.shadyacresmobile.com

SEE AD PAGE 18 AND AD TRAVEL SECTION PAGE 4

MONROEVILLE—E-2

(N) ISAAC CREEK PARK (COE - Alabama River Lakes)—(Monroe) *From town: Go 8 mi N on Hwy 41, then follow signs W on CR 17.* FACILITIES: 60 sites, 60 W&E, tenting, dump, laundry, ltd groc. RECREATION: boating, ramp, dock, lake fishing, playground. Partial handicap access. Open all yr. Phone: (251) 282-4254.

MONTGOMERY—D-4

(N) CAPITAL CITY RV PARK—(Pike) *From jct I-85 (exit 6) & East Blvd: Go 4 mi NW on East Blvd; or from jct I-65 (exit 173) & Hwy 152: Go 6-1/4 mi NE on Hwy 152, then 2-1/2 mi N on Hwy 231, then 1 blk E on Old Wetumpka Hwy. Enter on R.*

WELCOME

◆◆◆◆◆FACILITIES: 90 sites, typical site width 35 ft, 90 full hkups, (20/30/50 amps), some extd stay sites, 90 pull-thrus, cable TV, WiFi Instant Internet at site, WiFi Internet central location, family camping, dump, non-guest dump $, laundry, picnic tables.

◆◆◆RECREATION: rec room/area, ramp, pond fishing, golf nearby, playground, horseshoes.

Pets welcome. Partial handicap access. No tents. Open all yr. Big rigs welcome. Escort to site. Clubs welcome. Rate in 2010 $30 for 4 persons. MC/VISA/Debit.

Phone: (877)271-8026
Address: 4655 Old Wetumpka Hwy, Montgomery, AL 36110
Lat/Lon: 32.45290/-86.20614
Email: mjashcraft@bellsouth.net
Web: www.capitalcityrvpark.net

SEE AD THIS PAGE

(W) GUNTER HILL PARK (COE-Alabama River Lakes)—(Montgomery) *From jct I-65 (exit 167) & US 80W: Go 9 mi W on US 80, then 3 mi N on CR 7.* FACILITIES: 146 sites, 146 W&E, 10 pull-thrus, tenting, dump, laundry, ltd groc. RECREATION: boating, ramp, river fishing, playground. Partial handicap access. Open all yr. Phone: (334)872-9554.

(S) MONTGOMERY CAMPGROUND—(Montgomery) *From jct I-65 & US 31 (exit 164): Go 1/4 mi S on US 31. Enter on R.*

WELCOME

◆◆FACILITIES: 96 sites, typical site width 40 ft, 29 full hkups, 67 W&E, (20/30/50 amps), 50 pull-thrus, phone Internet central location, tenting, cabins, RV storage, dump, non-guest dump $, laundry, groceries, RV supplies, LP gas by weight/by meter, ice, picnic tables.

Alabama State Bird: Yellowhammer

MONTGOMERY—Continued
MONTGOMERY CAMPGROUND—Continued

CAMPCLUB USA

◆◆RECREATION: swim pool, lake fishing, golf nearby, bsktball, playground.

Pets welcome. Partial handicap access. Open all yr. Clubs welcome. Rate in 2010 $32-37 for 2 persons. MC/VISA/Debit. CCUSA 50% Discount. CCUSA reservations Recommended, CCUSA max stay 2 days, CCUSA disc. not avail Th,S, CCUSA disc. not avail F,Sa, CCUSA disc. not avail holidays.

Phone: (866)308-3688
Address: 250 Fischer Rd, Hope Hull, AL 36043
Lat/Lon: 32.26009/-86.35528
Email: bcj@mindspring.com
Web: www.montgomerycampground.com

SEE AD THIS PAGE

(S) Montgomery South RV Park—(Montgomery) *From jct I-65 (exit 158) & Tyson/Pintala Rd: Go 1/8 mi E on Tyson Rd, then 1 mi N on Venable Rd. Enter on L.* ◆◆◆◆FACILITIES: 30 sites, typical site width 40 ft, 30 full hkups, (30/50 amps), 22 pull-thrus, cable TV, WiFi Instant Internet at site, family camping, RV storage, laundry, LP gas by weight/by meter, picnic tables, fire rings.

CAMPCLUB USA

◆RECREATION: rec hall. Pets welcome, quantity restrict. Partial handicap access. No tents. Open all yr. Rate in 2010 $25-30 for 2 persons. MC/VISA/DISC/AMEX/Debit. CCUSA 50% Discount. CCUSA reservations Recommended, CCUSA max stay 14 days, Cash only for CCUSA disc., Check only for CCUSA disc., CCUSA disc. not avail Th,S, CCUSA disc. not avail F,Sa.

Phone: (334)284-7006
Address: 731 Venable Road, Hope Hull, AL 36043
Lat/Lon: 32.20502/-86.40802
Email: resv@montgomerysouthrvpark.com
Web: www.montgomerysouthrvpark.com

✻ **(N) PRATTVILLE AUTO & RV REPAIR CENTER**—*N'bnd: From jct I-65 (exit 179) & Hwy 82/W6: Go 1/2 mi W then 2 mi S & W on Hwy 82/W6, then 1 mi N on US 31. (Ent on R). S'bnd: Exit 186 & Hwy 31: Go 10 mi S on Hwy 31 (Ent on L). Enter on R.* SERVICES: full-time mech, engine/chassis repair, RV appliance repair, body work/collision repair, LP gas by weight/by meter, sells parts/accessories. Open all yr. MC/VISA/DISC/AMEX/Debit. FMCA discount.

WELCOME

Phone: (334)365-5085
Address: 1259-C So Memorial Dr., Prattville, AL 36067
Lat/Lon: 32.44884/-86.44022
Email: pvillervrepair@birch.net

SEE AD THIS PAGE

(S) The Woods RV Park and Campground—(Montgomery) *From jct I-65 S (exit 168) and South Blvd: Go 1/8 mi E to Sassafras Cir. Enter on R.* ◆◆◆FACILITIES: 105 sites, typical site width 40 ft, 105 full hkups, (20/30/50 amps), 105 pull-thrus, cable TV, WiFi Instant Internet at site, phone Internet central location, tenting, RV storage, dump, non-guest dump $, laundry, RV supplies, LP gas by weight/by meter, picnic tables, fire rings.

CAMPCLUB USA

◆◆RECREATION: pavilion, lake fishing, bsktball, play equipment, horseshoes, v-ball. Pets welcome. Partial handicap access. Open all yr. Big rigs welcome. Rate in 2010 $25-30 for 2 persons. MC/VISA/DISC/AMEX/Debit. CCUSA 50% Discount. CCUSA reservations Not Accepted, CCUSA max stay 3 days, CCUSA disc. not avail F,Sa, CCUSA disc. not avail holidays.

The Woods RV Park and Campground—Continued on next page

MONTGOMERY—Continued
The Woods RV Park and Campground—Continued

Phone: (334)356-1887
Address: 4350 Sassafras Cir, Montgomery, AL 36105
Lat/Lon: 32.32573/-86.33136
Email: woodsrvpark@knology.net
Web: www.woodsrvpark.com

MOUNDVILLE—C-2

(S) MOUNDVILLE ARCHAEOLOGICAL PARK (Univ of Alabama)—(Hale) *From I20/59 (exit 71A) go 13 miles South on Hwy 69.* FACILITIES: 31 sites, 31 W&E, (30 amps), 6 pull-thrus, tenting, dump. RECREATION: lake/river/pond fishing. No pets. Open all yr. Phone: (205)371-2234.

MUSCLE SHOALS—A-2

(S) WILSON DAM/ROCKPILE (TVA-Wilson Lake)—(Colbert) *From south side of Wilson Dam: Go 1/2 mi W on Hwy 133/TVA Reservation Rd, then 1/2 mi N (follow signs).* FACILITIES: 23 sites, 23 no hkups, tenting, ltd groc. RECREATION: boating, ramp, lake/river fishing. Open all yr. Phone: (256)386-2560.

NEW MARKET—A-3

(N) SHARON JOHNSTON PARK—(Madison) *North on Memorial Parkway, right on Winchester, left on Coleman Rd. Enter on R.* FACILITIES: 33 sites, 33 W&E, tenting, dump. RECREATION: swim pool, lake fishing. Pets welcome. Partial handicap access. Open all yr. Phone: (256)379-2868.

OPELIKA—C-5

(E) LAKESIDE RV PARK—(Lee) *From jct I-85 (exit 62) & US 280: Go 4-1/2 mi E on US 280. Enter on L.*

WELCOME

◆◆◆FACILITIES: 50 sites, typical site width 40 ft, 50 full hkups, (50 amps), some extd stay sites, 36 pull-thrus, cable TV, WiFi Instant Internet at site, phone on-site Internet (needs activ), phone Internet central location, tenting, laundry, picnic tables.

◆RECREATION: pond fishing, golf nearby, play equipment.

CAMPCLUB USA

Pets welcome, breed restrict. Open all yr. Big rigs welcome. Escort to site. Rate in 2010 $30 for 2 persons. CCUSA 50% Discount. CCUSA reservations Not Accepted, CCUSA max stay 1 day, Cash only for CCUSA disc., Check only for CCUSA disc., CCUSA disc. not avail W,Th,S, CCUSA disc. not avail F,Sa, CCUSA disc. not avail holidays. Discount available Jan thru Aug. Discount available 1 day per week.

Phone: (334)705-0701
Address: 5664 US Hwy 280 East, Opelika, AL 36804
Lat/Lon: 32.62680/-85.27988
Web: www.lakesidervparkopelikaal.com

SEE AD AUBURN PAGE 9

(NW) ROBERT TRENT JONES GRAND NAT'L GOLF COURSE—*From jct I-85 (exit 58) & Hwy US 280 W: Go 1/4 mi W on US 280, then 4-1/2 mi NW on Gateway Dr, then 2-1/2 mi N on Shelton Rd. Enter at end.* Rated #1 by Golf Digest and Golf World Magazine as the best public course in the US! Two 18-hole Championship Courses and 1 18-hole short course, plus practice range, putting greens, golf shop, on-site lodging & restaurant. MC/VISA/DISC/AMEX.

WELCOME

Phone: (334)749-9042
Address: 3000 Sunbelt Pkwy, Opelika, AL 36831
Lat/Lon: 32.67606/-85.42649
Web: www.rtjgolf.com

SEE AD TRAVEL SECTION PAGE 1

OPP—E-4

(N) FRANK JACKSON SP—(Covington) *From town: Go 4 mi N on US 331.* FACILITIES: 32 sites, 32 W&E, 26 pull-thrus, tenting, laundry. RECREATION: lake swim, boating, canoeing, ramp, dock, lake fishing, playground. Partial handicap access. Open all yr. Phone: (334)493-6988.

Alabama State Flower: Camellia

ORANGE BEACH—F-2

(E) Beech's Camping MHP—(Baldwin) *From jct Hwy 59 & Hwy 182: Go 7 mi E on Hwy 182, then 1-1/2 mi N on Hwy 161. Enter on R.* ◆FACILITIES: 90 sites, typical site width 30 ft, 65 full hkups, 25 W&E, (20/30/50 amps), 40 pull-thrus, dump, laundry. Pets welcome. No tents. Open all yr. Rate in 2010 $25 for 2 persons. Phone: (251)981-4136.

(E) HERITAGE MOTORCOACH & MARINA—(Baldwin) *From jct Hwy 182 & Hwy 161: Go 1-1/2 mi N on Hwy 161, then 3 mi E on Canal Road. Enter on R.*

WELCOME

◆◆◆◆◆FACILITIES: 79 sites, typical site width 34 ft, 79 full hkups, (30/50 amps), cable TV, WiFi Instant Internet at site, laundry, patios, controlled access.

◆◆◆◆RECREATION: rec hall, swim pool, hot tub, boating, dock, saltwater fishing, putting green, golf nearby, activities.

Pets welcome. Partial handicap access. No tents. Open all yr. Class A motorhomes only. Big rigs welcome. Escort to site. Rate in 2010 $80-120 per vehicle. MC/VISA/DISC/Debit.

Text 107985 to (440)725-8687 to see our Visual Tour.

Phone: (800)730-7032
Address: 28888 Canal Rd, Orange Beach, AL 36561
Lat/Lon: 30.29968/-87.53399
Email: rental@heritageorangebeach.com
Web: www.heritageorangebeach.com

SEE AD GULF SHORES PAGE 15

OZARK—E-4

(S) MILITARY PARK (Fort Rucker Campground)—(Dale) *From US 231 (Fort Rucker Military Res-Ozark Gate exit): Go S to Andrews Ave, then SW on Whittaker Rd, then W on Christian Rd, then N on Johnson Rd. On base. Enter at end.* FACILITIES: 18 sites, 18 W&E, 18 pull-thrus, tenting, dump. RECREATION: lake swim, boating, canoeing, dock, lake fishing, playground. No pets. Open Apr - Oct. Phone: (334)255-4305.

(N) Mr. D's—(Dale) *From jct US 231 & Hwy 27: Go 1/4 mi N on US 231 (45 mile marker). Enter on L.* ◆◆FACILITIES: 50 sites, 50 full hkups, (30/50 amps), 50 pull-thrus, tenting, laundry. Pets welcome. Open all yr. Big rigs welcome. Rate in 2010 $20-25 for 2 persons. Phone: (800)533-0608.

(N) OZARK TRAVEL PARK—(Dale) *From jct US 231 & Hwy 27: Go 3 mi N on US 231 (mile marker 47-east side). Enter on R.*

WELCOME

◆◆◆◆◆FACILITIES: 65 sites, typical site width 30 ft, 65 full hkups, (20/30/50 amps), 47 pull-thrus, cable TV, WiFi Instant Internet at site, WiFi Internet central location, tenting, dump, non-guest dump $, laundry, groceries, RV supplies, LP gas by weight/by meter, ice, picnic tables, patios, fire rings, grills, wood.

◆◆◆◆RECREATION: rec room/area, coin games, swim pool, pond fishing, fishing supplies, golf nearby, playground, horseshoes, v-ball.

Pets welcome. Open all yr. Big rigs welcome. Escort to site. Clubs welcome. Rate in 2010 $32.95 for 2 persons. MC/VISA/DISC/AMEX/Debit. Member ARVC, ALARVC.

Phone: (800)359-3218
Address: 2414 N US 231, Ozark, AL 36360
Lat/Lon: 31.48753/-85.68718
Email: rv@charter.net
Web: www.ozarktravelpark.com

SEE AD THIS PAGE

PELHAM—C-3

(W) Birmingham South Campground—(Shelby) *From jct I-65 (exit 242) & Hwy 52: Go 700 yards W on Hwy 52, then 300 yards N on Hwy 33. Enter on R.* ◆◆◆◆◆FACILITIES: 108 sites, typical site width 50 ft, 102 full hkups, 6 W&E, (30/50 amps), 50 amps ($), 56 pull-thrus, family camping, tenting, dump, laundry,

PELHAM—Continued
Birmingham South Campground—Continued

full svc store. ◆◆◆◆◆RECREATION: swim pool, playground. Pets welcome. Partial handicap access. Open all yr. Big rigs welcome. Rate in 2010 $37-41 for 2 persons. Member ARVC, ALARVC. Phone: (205)664-8832.

(NE) OAK MOUNTAIN SP—(Shelby) *From jct I-65 (exit 246) & Hwy 119: Follow signs.* FACILITIES: 145 sites, 85 full hkups, 60 no hkups, 24 pull-thrus, tenting, dump, laundry, ltd groc. RECREATION: lake swim, boating, electric motors only, canoeing, ramp, dock, lake fishing, playground. Pets welcome. Open all yr. Phone: (205)620-2527.

PELL CITY—B-4

(S) LAKESIDE LANDING RV PARK & MARINA—(St. Clair) *From jct I-20 (Exit 158) & US 231: Go 6 mi S on US 231. Enter on L.*

WELCOME

◆◆◆◆FACILITIES: 193 sites, typical site width 25 ft, 193 full hkups, (15/30/50 amps), some extd stay sites, 164 pull-thrus, cable TV, WiFi Instant Internet at site, family camping, tenting, RV storage, dump, non-guest dump $, laundry, full svc store, RV supplies, LP gas by weight, LP bottle exch, marine gas, ice, picnic tables, patios.

◆◆◆◆RECREATION: rec hall, rec room/area, lake swim, boating, canoeing, kayaking, ramp, dock, lake fishing, fishing supplies, golf nearby. Rec open to public.

Pets welcome. Partial handicap access. Open all yr. Big rigs welcome. Clubs welcome. Rate in 2010 $25-27 for 4 persons. MC/VISA/DISC/AMEX/Debit. ATM.

Phone: (205)525-5701
Address: 4600 Martin St South, Cropwell, AL 35054
Lat/Lon: 33.52875/-86.29173
Web: www.lakeloganmartin.com

SEE AD THIS PAGE

PICKENSVILLE—C-1

(W) PICKENSVILLE CAMPGROUND (COE-Tennessee/Tombigbee Waterway)—(Pickens) *From town: Go 3 mi W on Hwy 86.* FACILITIES: 176 sites, 176 W&E, (30 amps), tenting, dump, laundry. RECREATION: boating, ramp, dock, lake/river/pond fishing, playground. Partial handicap access. Open all yr. Facilities fully operational Jun - Sep. Phone: (205)373-6328.

PRATTVILLE—D-3

(S) Autauga Creek Landing RV Campground—(Autauga) *From jct I-65 (exit 179) & Hwy 82/W 6: Go 1 mi W to Hwy 82, then 2 mi S on Hwy 82, then 1-1/2 mi S on Hwy 31, then 3 mi W on City Rd 4.* ◆◆FACILITIES: 37 sites, typical site width 35 ft, accepts full hkup units only, 37 full hkups, (20/30/50 amps), family camping. ◆◆RECREATION: river swim, canoeing, ramp, pond/stream fishing. Pets welcome. No tents. Open all yr. Big rigs welcome. Rate in 2010 $25 per vehicle. Phone: (334)361-3999.

ROBERTSDALE—F-2

(E) Azalea Acres RV Park—(Baldwin) *From jct I-10 & Hwy 64 S (Exit 53, Wilcox Exit): Go 1/8 mi S to Wilcox Rd, then 1/2 mi S on Wilcox, then 1/2 mi E on Patterson, then 1/2 mi N on Glass Rd. Enter on R.* ◆◆◆FACILITIES: 66 sites, typical site width 43 ft, 58 full hkups, 8 W&E, (20/30/50 amps), 46 pull-thrus, laundry. Pets welcome, breed restrict, quantity restrict. Partial handicap access. No tents. Open all yr. Big rigs welcome. Green Friendly. Rate in 2010 $26 for 2 persons. Phone: (251)947-9530.

(E) Hilltop RV Park—(Baldwin) *From jct Hwy 59 & I-10: Go 8 mi E on I-10 (exit 53), then 1/2 mi S on Hwy 64. Enter on L.* ◆◆◆FACILITIES: 87 sites, typical site width 33 ft, 87 full hkups, (30/50 amps), 50 amps ($), 59 pull-thrus, WiFi Instant Internet at site, tenting, RV storage, laundry, RV supplies, LP gas by weight/by meter, picnic tables. ◆◆RECREATION: rec hall, activities, horseshoes. Pets welcome, breed restrict, quantity restrict. Open all yr. Big rigs welcome. Green Friendly. Rate in 2010 $26-27 for 2 persons. MC/VISA. FMCA discount. CCUSA 50% Discount. CCUSA reservations Recommended, CCUSA max stay Unlimited. Discount does not apply to weekly or monthly rates.

CAMPCLUB USA

Phone: (251)960-1129
Address: 23420 County Rd 64, Robertsdale, AL 36567
Lat/Lon: 30.62593/-87.62504
Web: www.hilltoprvpark.com

(E) Styx River Resort—(Baldwin) *From I-10, take Wilson Rd (exit 53): Go N on service road. At B.P. Station, turn east 1.25 mi. on Waterworld Rd. Enter on L.* ◆◆FACILITIES: 145 sites, typical site width 25 ft, 145 full hkups, (20/30/50 amps), 130 pull-thrus, laun-

Styx River Resort—Continued on next page

dry, ltd groc. ◆◆◆◆◆RECREATION: 2 swim pools, river swim, boating, canoeing, river fishing, playground. Pets welcome. Partial handicap access. No tents. Open all yr. Big rigs welcome. Rate in 2010 $26-30 for 2 persons. Phone: (251)960-1167.

(E) Wilderness RV Park—(Baldwin) *From I-10 (exit 53) & CR 64: Go S 1/4 mi on CR 64, then turn left on Patterson Rd for 1.3 mi.* ◆◆FACILITIES: 74 sites, typical site width 46 ft, 74 full hkups, (30/50 amps), 50 amps ($), 71 pull-thrus, WiFi Internet central location, dump, laundry, RV supplies, LP gas by meter, picnic tables. ◆◆◆RECREATION: rec hall, pavilion, swim pool, lake/pond fishing, activities, horseshoes. Pets welcome, quantity restrict. No tents. Open all yr. Big rigs welcome. Rate in 2010 $28.60 - 33 for 4 persons. MC/VISA. CCUSA 50% Discount. CCUSA reservations Accepted, CCUSA max stay 5 days, Cash only for CCUSA disc., CCUSA disc. not avail holidays. Not available Aug 1-15.

Phone: (251)960-1195
Address: 24280 Patterson Rd, Robertsdale, AL 36567
Lat/Lon: 30.61870/-87.61132
Email: wildernessrv@gulftel.com
Web: www.wildernessrvpark.com

Reserve Online at Woodalls.com

ROGERSVILLE—A-2

(W) JOE WHEELER SP—(Lauderdale) *From town: Go 1 mi W on US-72, then 3 mi S on Park Rd.* FACILITIES: 116 sites, 110 full hkups, 6 W&E, (20/30 amps), 12 pull-thrus, tenting, dump, laundry, ltd groc. RECREATION: lake swim, boating, lake fishing, playground. Partial handicap access. Open all yr. Phone: (256) 247-1184.

(S) JOE WHEELER STATE PARK LODGE—(Lauderdale) *From town: Go 1 mi W on US-72, then 3 mi S on Park Rd.* FACILITIES: 116 sites, 110 full hkups, 6 W&E, (20/30 amps), 12 pull-thrus, tenting, dump, laundry, ltd groc. RECREATION: lake swim, boating, lake fishing, playground. Partial handicap access. Open all yr. Phone: (800)544-5639.

(S) WHEELER RESERVATION CAMPGROUND—(Lauderdale) *From jct US 72 & Hwy 101: Go 3-1/2 mi S on Hwy 101 (just before crossing dam). Enter on L.* FACILITIES: 30 sites, typical site width 35 ft, 30 W&E, (20/30/50 amps), 50 amps ($), tenting, dump. RECREATION: boating, dock, lake/river fishing. Partial handicap access. Open Mar 12 - Nov 4. Phone: (256)386-2560.

RUSSELLVILLE—A-2

(W) BEAR CREEK DEV AUTH (Elliott Branch)—(Franklin) *From town: Go W on Hwy 24, then 1-1/2 mi S on CR 88, then 1/4 mi E on Elliot Branch Rd. Enter at end.* FACILITIES: 30 sites, typical site width 25 ft, 30 W&E, (50 amps), tenting, dump, ltd groc. RECREATION: lake swim, boating, ramp, dock, lake fishing. Partial handicap access. Open Mar - Oct. Phone: (256)332-4392.

(N) BEAR CREEK DEV AUTH (Slickrock)—(Franklin) *From town: Go 9 mi W on Hwy 24, then 6 mi N on CR 33. Enter on L.* FACILITIES: 53 sites, typical site width 25 ft, 53 W&E, (50 amps), tenting, dump, ltd groc. RECREATION: lake swim, boating, ramp, dock, lake fishing. Partial handicap access. Open Mar - Oct. Phone: (256)332-4392.

SCOTTSBORO—A-4

(W) Crawford RV Park—(Jackson) *From jct 72 & Hwy 279: Go 1/2 mi E on Hwy 79. Enter on R.* ◆◆FACILITIES: 18 sites, typical site width 40 ft, accepts self-contained units only, 18 full hkups, (30/50 amps), 4 pull-thrus, cable TV, WiFi Internet at site, phone Internet central location, picnic tables. RECREATION: Pets welcome. No tents. Open all yr. Rate in 2010 $34 for 4 persons. CCUSA 50% Discount. CCUSA reservations Accepted, CCUSA max stay Unlimited, Cash only for CCUSA disc., Check only for CCUSA disc.

Phone: (256)574-5366
Address: 4320 S Broad St, Scottsboro, AL 35769
Lat/Lon: 34.61675/-86.06271
Email: crawford@scottoboro.org
Web: www.crawfordrvpark.com

(W) GOOSE POND COLONY (City Park)—(Jackson) *From jct US 72 & Hwy 79: Go 3 mi S on Hwy 79. Enter on L.* FACILITIES: 117 sites, typical site width 30 ft, 37 full hkups, 80 W&E, (15/30/50 amps), 1 pull-thrus, tenting, dump, ltd groc. RECREATION: swim pool, lake swim, boating, canoeing, ramp, dock, lake fishing, playground. Partial handicap access. Open all yr. Phone: (256)259-1808.

SELMA—D-3

(N) PAUL M. GRIST SP—(Dallas) *From town: Go 15 mi N on Hwy 22.* FACILITIES: 11 sites, 11 full hkups, tenting. RECREATION: lake swim, boating, canoeing, ramp, lake fishing, playground. Partial handicap access. Open all yr. Phone: (334)872-5846.

(S) SIX MILE CREEK (COE-Alabama River Lakes)—(Dallas) *From the bridge in town: Go 1/2 mi E on US 80, then S on CR 77 (Kings Bend Rd).* FACILITIES: 31 sites, 31 W&E, tenting, dump. RECREATION: boating, ramp, river fishing. Partial handicap access. Open all yr. Phone: (334)875-6228.

Alabama's mean elevation is 500 feet at its lowest elevation point.

SHORTER—D-4

(N) Wind Drift Campground—(Macon) *From I-85 (exit 22, Shorter): Go 100 yards S. Enter on R.* ◆◆◆FACILITIES: 33 sites, typical site width 25 ft, 33 full hkups, (20/30/50 amps), 31 pull-thrus, laundry, groceries. ◆◆RECREATION: lake fishing. Pets welcome. No tents. Open all yr. Rate in 2010 $30.44 per family. Phone: (334)724-9428.

SHORTERVILLE—E-5

(N) HARDRIDGE CREEK PARK (COE-Walter F. George Lake)—(Henry) *From jct Hwy 10 & CR 97: Go 6 mi N on CR 97.* FACILITIES: 77 sites, 20 full hkups, 57 W&E, 19 pull-thrus, dump, laundry, ltd groc. RECREATION: lake swim, boating, canoeing, ramp, dock, lake fishing, playground. Partial handicap access. Open all yr. Phone: (334)585-5945.

SPANISH FORT—F-2

(N) BLAKELEY STATE PARK—(Baldwin) *From jct I-10 & US 98: Go N 1 mi on Hwy 98 to Hwy 31, then N 4/5 mi to Hwy 225, follow signs. Enter on L.* FACILITIES: 31 sites, 31 no hkups, dump. RECREATION: river fishing. Open all yr. Phone: (251)626-0798.

MEAHER SP—FACILITIES: 56 sites, 56 W&E, (20/30/50 amps), tenting, laundry. RECREATION: boating, ramp, dock, saltwater/river fishing, playground. Open all yr. Phone: (251)626-5529.

SUMMERDALE—F-2

(W) Escapees Rainbow Plantation—(Baldwin) *From jct Hwy 59 & Cnty Rd 28: Go 5.4 mi W on Cnty Rd 28. Enter on R.* ◆◆◆FACILITIES: 98 sites, typical site width 40 ft, 98 full hkups, (30/50 amps), tenting, dump, laundry. ◆◆◆RECREATION: swim pool. Pets welcome. Partial handicap access. Open all yr. Big rigs welcome. Rate in 2010 $24 for 2 persons. Phone: (251)988-8132.

TALLADEGA—C-4

(NE) Talladega Creekside Resort—(Talladega) *From jct I-20 & Hwy 6 (exit 173): Go 350 yds S to Cty Rd 005, then 4 mi S on Cty Rd 005, then 1/4 mi E on Lake Whitland Dr. Enter on L.* ◆◆◆FACILITIES: 20 sites, typical site width 30 ft, 20 full hkups, (30/50 amps), 2 pull-thrus, WiFi Internet central location, tenting, laundry, ice, picnic tables, wood. ◆◆◆RECREATION: river swim, canoeing, kayaking, float trips, river fishing, horseshoes. Pets welcome, breed restrict. Open all yr. Big rigs welcome. Rate in 2010 $30 for 4 persons. MC/VISA/DISC/Debit. CCUSA 50% Discount. CCUSA reservations Recommended, CCUSA max stay 3 days, CCUSA disc. not avail holidays. Not available weeks of Nascar races at Talladega Super Speedway.

Phone: (256)362-9053
Address: 760 Lake Whitland Rd, Talladega, AL 35160
Lat/Lon: 33.52613/-86.03982
Email: info@talladegacreekside.com
Web: www.talladegacreekside.com

TALLADEGA AREA—C-4

See listings at Pell City, Anniston

TANNER—A-3

(N) Swan Creek Community (RV SPACES)—(Limestone) *From Hwy 65 & Hwy 72 (exit 351): Go 1 mi W on Hwy 72, then 6 mi S on Hwy 31.* FACILITIES: 85 sites, typical site width 30 ft, 85 full hkups, (30/50 amps), 8 pull-thrus, tenting, laundry. RECREATION: playground. Pets welcome. Partial handicap access. Open all yr. Rate in 2010 $24-27 per vehicle. Phone: (256) 355-5392.

TROY—E-4

(W) Deer Run RV Park—(Montgomery) *From jct US 29 & Hwy 231: Go 6-1/2 mi N on US 231 (between mile marker 83 & 84), at Cty Rd 1124. Enter on L.* ◆◆◆◆◆FACILITIES: 86 sites, typical site width 35 ft, 86 full hkups, (20/30/50 amps), 81 pull-thrus, laundry. ◆◆◆◆RECREATION: swim pool, pond fishing. Pets welcome. Partial handicap access. No tents. Open all yr. Big rigs welcome. Rate in 2010 $29 for 2 persons. Phone: (800)552-3036.

TUSCALOOSA—C-2

(NE) DEERLICK CREEK (COE-Holt Lake)—(Tuscaloosa) *From I-20/59 (exit 73): Go 4 mi W on US 82, then 3 mi N on CR 30 (Rice Mine Rd), then 3-1/2 mi E on CR 87, then 3-1/2 mi E on CR 42, then 3-3/4 mi S on CR 89.* FACILITIES: 46 sites, typical site width 15 ft, 40 W&E, (50 amps), 6 no hkups, 11 pull-thrus, tenting, dump, laundry. RECREATION: lake swim, boating, ramp, dock, lake fishing, playground. Partial handicap access. Open Mar 1 - Nov 15. Phone: (205)759-1591.

(NW) LAKE LURLEEN SP—(Tuscaloosa) *From jct US 82 & CR 21: Go 12 mi NW on CR 21.* FACILITIES: 91 sites, 35 full hkups, 56 W&E, (30/50 amps), 34 pull-thrus, tenting, dump, ltd groc. RECREATION: lake swim, boating, ramp, lake fishing, playground. Open all yr. Phone: (205)339-1558.

Helen Keller, author & educator, was from Alabama.

TUSCALOOSA—Continued

(E) SUNSET TRAVEL PARK—(Tuscaloosa) *From jct I-59 (exit 76) & US 11: Go 1/10 mi N on US 11, then 500 feet E on JVC Rd. Enter on R.*

WELCOME

◆◆◆FACILITIES: 93 sites, typical site width 45 ft, accepts full hkup units only, 93 full hkups, (30/50 amps), mostly extd stay sites, 34 pull-thrus, cable TV, WiFi Instant Internet at site, laundry, patios.

RECREATION: golf nearby.

Pets welcome. No tents. Open all yr. Big rigs welcome. Clubs welcome. Rate in 2010 $29-33 per vehicle. MC/VISA/DISC/Debit.

Phone: (205)553-9233
Address: 5001 JVC Rd E, Cottondale, AL 35453
Lat/Lon: 33.17489/-87.46923

SEE AD THIS PAGE

TUSCUMBIA—A-2

(S) Heritage Acres RV Park—(Colbert) *From jct Hwy 43 & Hwy 72: Go 2-1/2 mi W on Hwy 72, then 1/4 mi S on Neil Morris Rd. Enter on L.* ◆◆◆◆FACILITIES: 65 sites, typical site width 30 ft, 65 full hkups, (20/30/50 amps), 2 pull-thrus, tenting, laundry. Pets welcome. Partial handicap access. Open all yr. Big rigs welcome. Rate in 2010 $22.50 for 2 persons. Member ARVC, ALARVC. Phone: (256)383-7368.

URIAH—E-2

(S) Ponderosa RV Park—(Monroe) *From jct 65 & Hwy 21 (exit 57): Go N on Hwy 21 for 12 mi. Enter on L.* ◆◆◆FACILITIES: 16 sites, typical site width 35 ft, accepts full hkup units only, 16 full hkups, (20/30/50 amps), 50 amps ($), 4 pull-thrus, WiFi Instant Internet at site, WiFi Internet central location, laundry, LP gas by meter, picnic tables. RECREATION: swim pool, activities, horseshoes. Pets welcome. No tents. Open all yr. Big rigs welcome. Rate in 2010 $20-25 for 2 persons. CCUSA 50% Discount. CCUSA reservations Accepted, CCUSA max stay 2 days.

Phone: (251)862-2670
Address: 18060 Hwy 21 S, Uriah, AL 36480
Lat/Lon: 31.27148/-87.50120
Email: kennys@frontiernet.net

VALLEY—C-5

(SE) B & B RV Park (RV SPACES)—(Chambers) *From jct I-85 (exit 79) & Hwy 295: Go 5 mi S on Hwy 295, then 1/2 mi E on Cty Rd 279, then 1/5 mi on Hanvey's Rd. Enter on R.* FACILITIES: 23 sites, typical site width 40 ft, accepts full hkup units only, 23 full hkups, (30/50 amps). Pets welcome, breed restrict. No tents. Open all yr. Rate in 2010 $30 for 3 persons. Phone: (334)705-0701.

WARRIOR—B-3

(N) RICKWOOD CAVERNS SP—(Blount) *From I-65 (exit 289): Go 4 mi W.* FACILITIES: 13 sites, 13 full hkups, (30 amps), tenting, dump. RECREATION: swim pool, playground. Open all yr. Phone: (205)647-9692.

WETUMPKA—D-4

(S) FORT TOULOUSE/JACKSON PARK (Ala. State Historical Commission)—(Elmore) *From US 231 (1 mi S of town): Go W on Ft Toulouse Rd.* FACILITIES: 39 sites, 39 W&E, tenting, dump. RECREATION: river swim, boating, canoeing, ramp, river fishing. Open all yr. Phone: (334)567-3002.

WILMER—F-1

(W) Escatawpa Hollow Campground—(Mobile) *Located at the Mississippi/Alabama state line on US 98 W (5 mi W of Wilmer City Limits). Enter on L.* ◆◆◆FACILITIES: 43 sites, typical site width 30 ft, 6 full hkups, 22 W&E, (20/30/50 amps), 15 no hkups, 10 pull-thrus, tenting, dump. ◆◆◆RECREATION: river swim, boating, canoeing, ramp, river fishing. Pets welcome. Open all yr. Rate in 2010 $25 per family. Phone: (251)649-4233.

Alabama was the 22nd state admitted to the Union.

WOODVILLE—A-4

(E) CATHEDRAL CAVERNS SP—(Jackson) *From Huntsville: Take Hwy 72 E to Hwy 63, then right until you see the Cathedral Caverns rock sigh. Turn left & follow signs.* FACILITIES: tenting. RECREATION: Phone: (256)728-8193.

(E) PARNELL CREEK RV PARK—(Jackson) *From jct Hwy 72 and 565 (Huntsville): Go 24 mi E on Hwy 72. From Scotsboro jct 79 and 72: Go 14 mi W on Hwy 72. Enter on R.*

WELCOME

◇◇◇FACILITIES: 34 sites, typical site width 22 ft, 25 full hkups, 9 W&E, (30/50 amps), 50 amps ($), some extd stay sites, 10 pull-thrus, cable TV, ($), WiFi Instant Internet at site, family camping, tenting, cabins, RV storage, dump, non-guest dump $, portable dump, laundry, ltd groc, LP gas by weight/by meter, ice, picnic tables, fire rings, grills.

◇◇◇◇RECREATION: rec hall, rec room/area, pavilion, swim pool, mini-golf, ($), golf nearby, bsktball, playground, activities, (wkends), horseshoes.

Pets welcome. Partial handicap access. Open all yr. Clubs welcome. Rate in 2010 $27-29 MC/VISA. Member ARVC, ALARVC. CCUSA 50% Discount. CCUSA reservations Recommended, CCUSA max stay 3 days. Discount not available Memorial Day, 4th of July, or Labor Day weekends. Fee applies with credit card use.

Phone: (256)776-2348
Address: 115 PARNELL CIRCLE, WOODVILLE, AL 35776
Lat/Lon: 34.61347/-86.23498
Email: parnellcreekrvpark@yahoo.com
Web: www.parnellcreekrvpark.com

Reserve Online at Woodalls.com

SEE AD HUNTSVILLE PAGE 17

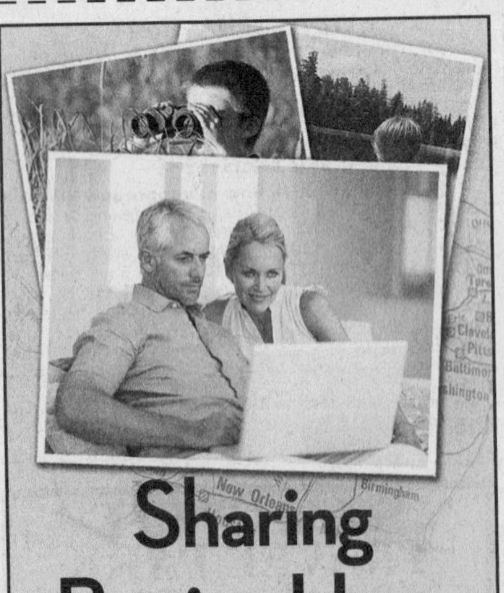

READER SERVICE INFO

The following business has placed an ad in the Arkansas Travel Section. To receive free information, enter the Reader Service number on the Reader Service Card opposite page 48/Discover Section in the front of this directory.

Advertiser	RS#
Fort Smith Visitors Center	3449

TIME ZONE

Arkansas is in the Central Time Zone.

TOPOGRAPHY

Arkansas' altitude ranges from 54 to 2,753 feet above sea level. Arkansas is equally divided between lowlands and highlands, with the Delta and the Gulf Coastal Plain on the east and south and the Interior Highlands (the Ouachitas and the Ozarks) on the west and north.

TEMPERATURE

Springtime temperatures in Arkansas average in the 60s and summer temps in the 80s with occasional periods of 90° and above. Arkansas has an average annual temperature of 61.4°.

TRAVEL & TOURISM INFO

State Agency:

Arkansas Dept of Parks and Tourism
One Capitol Mall
Little Rock, AR 72201
(888/287-2757)
www.arkansas.com

Regional Agencies:

Arkansas' Delta Byways
P.O. Box 2050
State University, AR 72467
(870/972-2803)
www.deltabyways.com

Arkansas' Great Southwest
P.O. Box 1006
Hope, AR 71802-1006
(870/777-7500)
www.agsw.org

Arkansas' Land of Legends Travel Association
P.O. Box 8768
Pine Bluff, AR 71611
(870/536-8742)
www.thelandoflegends.com

Arkansas River Valley Tri-Peaks
101 North Johnson St.
Clarksville, AR 72830
(479/754-6543 or 800/561-6508)
www.arvtripeaks.com

Arkansas South Tourism Association
P.O. Box 10245
El Dorado, AR 71730
(870/814-9676)
www.arkansassouth.com

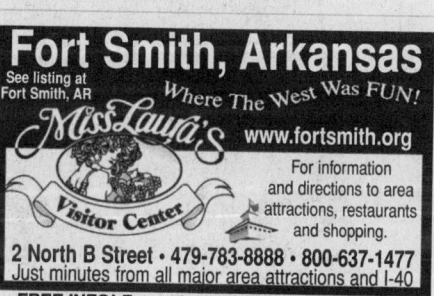

Diamond Lakes Travel Association
P.O. Box 6090
Hot Springs, AR 71902
(501/321-1700)
www.diamondlakes.dina.org

Greers Ferry Lake & Little Red River Association
P.O. Box 1170
Fairfield Bay, AR 72088

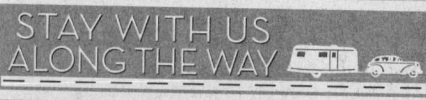

Where to Find CCUSA Parks

List City	Park Name	Map Coordinates
ARKADELPHIA		
	Arkadelphia Campground & RV Park	D-3
BURLINGTON		
	Ozark View RV Park & Campground	A-2
FLIPPIN		
	Blue Heron Campground and Resort	A-3
HAMPTON		
	Silver Eagle RV Campground	E-3
HARRISON		
	Harrison Village Campground & RV Park	A-3
	Parkers RV Park	A-3
	Shady Oaks Campground & RV Park	A-3
MENA		
	Shadow Mountain RV Park	C-2
MOUNTAIN VIEW		
	Arkansas Fiddlers Valley RV Resort	B-4
	Holiday Mountain Resort	B-4
MURFREESBORO		
	Miner's Camping & Rock Shop	D-2
PERRYVILLE		
	Coffee Creek Motel and RV Park	C-3
SHIRLEY		
	Golden Pond RV Park	B-3
WEST MEMPHIS		
	Tom Sawyer's Mississippi River RV Park	B-5

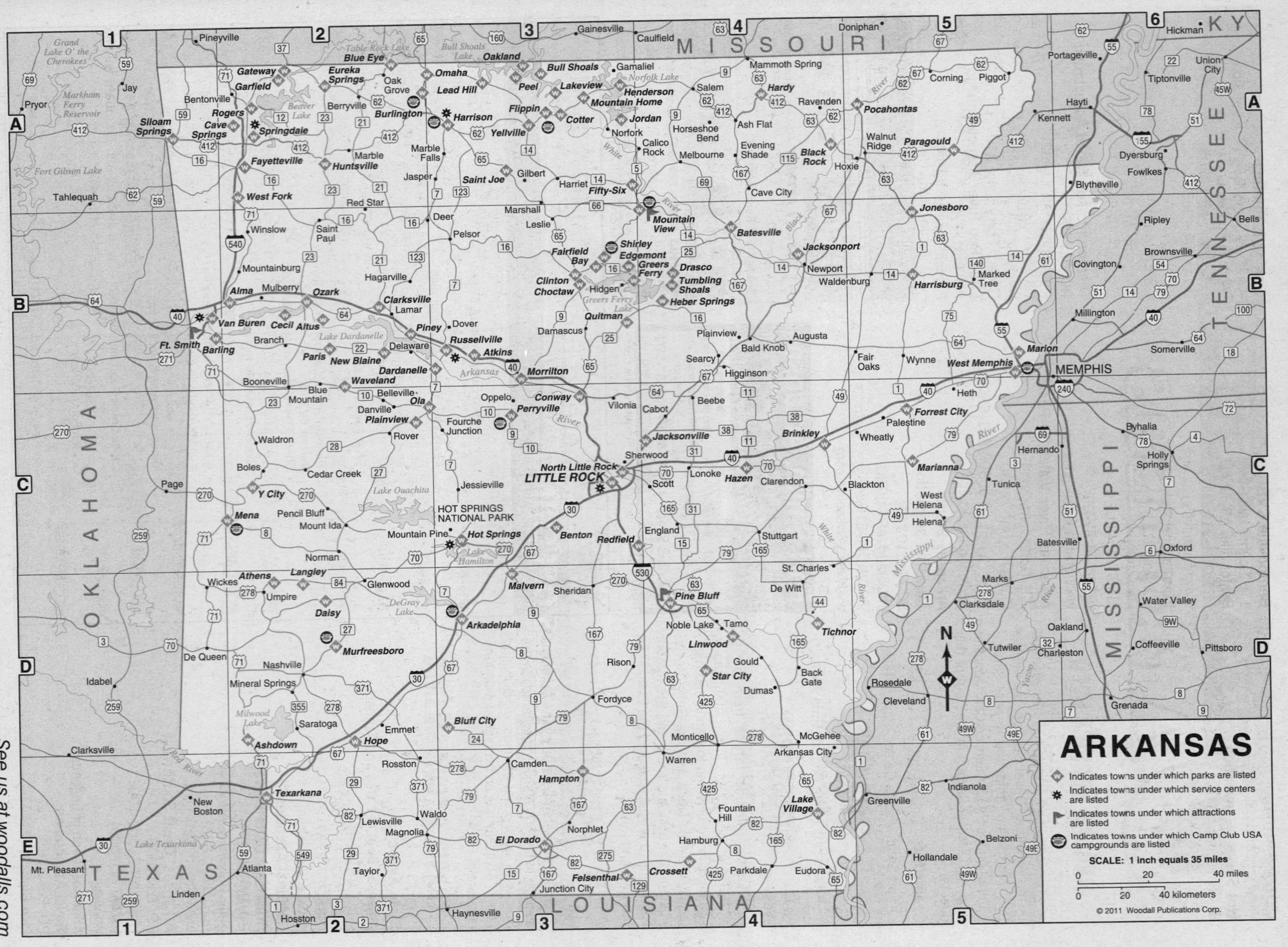
ARKANSAS
Indicates towns under which parks are listed
Indicates towns under which service centers are listed
Indicates towns under which attractions are listed
Indicates towns under which Camp Club USA campgrounds are listed
SCALE: 1 inch equals 35 miles
0 20 40 miles
0 20 40 kilometers
© 2011 Woodall Publications Corp.
MISSOURI
TENNESSEE
MISSISSIPPI
LOUISIANA
TEXAS
OKLAHOMA
KY
LITTLE ROCK
MEMPHIS
HOT SPRINGS NATIONAL PARK

(501/745-6101)
www.greersferrylake.org

Hot Springs Convention & Visitors Bureau
134 Convention Boulevard
P.O. Box 6000
Hot Springs, AR 71902
(501/321-2277 or 800/SPA-CITY)
www.hotsprings.org

Little Rock CVB
P.O. Box 3232
Little Rock, AR 72203
(501/374-2255 or 800/844-4781)
www.littlerock.com

Northwest Arkansas Tourism Association
P.O. Box 5176
Bella Vista, AR 72714
(501/855-1336)

Ozark Mountain Region
P.O. Box 194
Lakeview, AR 72642
(800/544-6867)
www.ozarkmountainregion.com

Sevier County Tourism Commission
P.O. Box 971
De Queen, AR 71832

Western Arkansas' Mountain Frontier Tourism Association
612 Garrison
Fort Smith, AR 72902
(479/783-6118)
www.westarkansastourism.com

Local Agencies:
For local information not listed here, contact the Chamber of Commerce for the locality you are interested in.

Bentonville CVB
116 South Main Street
Bentonville, AR 72712
(479/271-9153)
www.bentonvilleusa.org

Eureka Springs
P.O. Box 522
Eureka Springs, AR 72632
(866/WISH EUREKA)
www.eurekasprings.org

Fort Smith CVB
2 N. B Street
Fort Smith, AR 72901
(800/637-1477)
www.fortsmith.org

Jasper/Newton County Chamber of Commerce
P.O. Box 250
Jasper, AR 72641
(800/670-7792)
http://theozarkmountains.com

Van Buren Chamber of Commerce
510 Main Street
Van Buren, AR 72956
(479/474-2761)
www.vanburenchamber.org

RECREATIONAL INFO

Canoeing:
To receive an Arkansas Adventure Guide, contact Arkansas Parks & Tourism, One Capitol Mall, Little Rock, AR 72201 (800/NATURAL). www.Arkansas.com For information on river levels, float streams and more www.ArkansasCanoeClub.com.

Fishing & Hunting:
Arkansas Game & Fish Commission
#2 Natural Resources Dr.
Little Rock, AR 72205
(800/364-4263).
www.agfc.com

Golf:
(866/2-GOLF-AR)
www.NaturalStateGolfTrail.com

SHOPPING

Arkansas Craft Guild Gallery, 104 East Main St., Mountain View. Headquarters of one of the oldest craft guilds in the mid-south. Handmade, traditional and contemporary crafts by over 300 artists. www.arkansascraftguild.org.

Arlington Mall, Hot Springs. Specialty shops, gifts, collectibles, clothing and accessories. Central Ave. and Fountain St. www.arlingtonhotel.com

Oppelo Flea Market, ARK 9, Perry, AR. 13,000 square feet of shopping with over 70 indoor booths.

Ozark Center Point Place, Springdale. Shop at a discount for popular brand name goods. 5320 West Sunset

River Market, Little Rock. Formerly a nearly abandoned warehouse district, this downtown area is filled with restaurants, shops and a seasonal farmer's market. President Clinton Ave. www.rivermarket.info

DESTINATIONS

There are many diverse communities in Arkansas, each with something unique for traveler to discover. The people and towns in the Delta have been shaped by a tradition in agriculture, and a bit of the "Old South" is still alive there today. Visitors can explore some "Wild West" history on the state's western edge, at Fort Smith. Hot Springs and Eureka, in the Ozark and Ouachita Mountains, are two spa cities that have long drawn travelers in search of healing and relaxation. In the center of the state, the foothills of the Ouachita Mountains begin to rise from the flat farmlands.

OZARKS REGION

This area is comprised of ancient hills, deep valleys, limestone bluffs and more than a million acres of protected hardwood forest. A place of true beauty, where giant clear water lakes feed sparkling mountain rivers, and ancient towering bluffs rise above the rushing waters of the Buffalo River. Underground caverns are preserved here forever. Trout play in streams and abundant wildlife roam the mountain forests.

Caves/Caverns: Onyx Cave, Eureka Springs (radio guided tours). **Bull Shoals Caverns**, Bull Shoals (limestone formations). **Cosmic Cavern**, Berryville (largest under-

BUSINESSES OFFERING

	Things to See & Do	RV Sales	RV Service
FORT SMITH			
Fort Smith Visitors Center	⚑		
HARRISON			
Jordan's RV Service		🚌	✵
HOT SPRINGS			
Razorback Camper Sales		🚌	✵
LITTLE ROCK			
Fred & Jack Trailer Sales		🚌	✵
MOUNTAIN VIEW			
Wild Horse Theatre	⚑		
PINE BLUFF			
Pine Bluff Parks & Recreation	⚑		
RUSSELLVILLE			
Outdoor Living Center		🚌	✵
SPRINGDALE			
Wheels RV		🚌	✵
VAN BUREN			
Outdoor Living Center		🚌	✵

ground lake in Ozarks). **Old Spanish Treasure Cave**, Sulphur Springs (non-strenuous, well-lighted). **War Eagle Cavern**, Rogers (guided tours). **Blanchard Springs Caverns**, Mountain View (among top 10 in country, operated by US Forest Service). **Hurricane River Cave**, Harrison (45-foot waterfall). **Mystic Caverns**, Harrison (calcite draped chambers).

Arkansas Air Museum, Fayetteville is home to many vintage aircraft, including pre-World War II racing planes in flying condition, aeronautical memorabilia and a gift shop housed in a historic hangar at Fayetteville's Drake Field.

Eureka Springs, dubbed "America's Victorian Village," preserves turn-of-the-century architecture amid its winding mountain streets and natural springs. Outdoor performances of **The Great Passion Play** run late April through October. New in 2005 is the **Museum of Earth History**, an interactive museum that includes displays of life-size dinosaur skeletons, life models, fossil plates and high-tech learning stations. View more than 100 life-size dinosaur replicas at **Dinosaur World/Land of Kong.** Tour historical sites in Eureka by rail or trolley, or take a leisurely stroll through the downtown, which is on the National Register of Historic Places. While in Eureka, visit the Ozark's strangest dwelling at **Quigley's Castle**. On the National Register of Historic Places, the dwelling includes two-story tropical plants, birds and fish living naturally indoors plus butterfly, rock and arrowhead collections.

QUICK REFERENCE CHART FOR WOODALL'S FEATURED PARKS

	Green Friendly	RV Lots for Sale	Park Models-Onsite Ownership	Park Membership for Sale	Big Rigs Welcome	Internet Friendly	Pets Welcome
ALMA							
KOA-Fort Smith/Alma					▲	●	■
BENTON							
I-30 Travel Park					▲		■
JB's RV Park & Campground					▲		■
CAVE SPRINGS							
The Creeks RV Resort					▲	●	■
CLINTON							
Whispering Pines RV Park					▲		■
COTTER							
Denton Ferry RV Park Resort					▲	●	■
FAYETTEVILLE							
Southgate RV Park of Fayetteville					▲	●	■
HARRISON							
Harrison Village Campground & RV Park						●	■
Parkers RV Park					▲	●	■
Shady Oaks Campground & RV Park						●	■
HOT SPRINGS							
Cloud Nine RV Park					▲	●	■
Hot Springs National Park - KOA					▲	●	■
Treasure Isle RV Park					▲	●	■
JONESBORO							
Craighead Forest Park (City Park)							■
LAKE VILLAGE							
Pecan Grove RV Park					▲	●	■
MARION							
Memphis KOA	🍃				▲	●	■
MENA							
Shadow Mountain RV Park					▲	●	■
MOUNTAIN VIEW							
Arkansas Fiddlers Valley RV Resort					▲	●	■
Ozark RV Park					▲	●	■
NORTH LITTLE ROCK							
Crystal Hill RV Park							■
PINE BLUFF							
Saracen Trace RV Park (City Park)							■
RUSSELLVILLE							
Ivy's Cove RV Retreat					▲	●	■
Outdoor Living Center RV Park					▲	●	■
VAN BUREN							
Overland RV Park					▲	●	■
WEST MEMPHIS							
Tom Sawyer's Mississippi River RV Park					▲	●	■

Green Friendly 🍃; RV Lots for Sale ✖; Park Models/Onsite Onwership ✱; Park Memberships for Sale ✔; Big Rigs Welcome ▲; Internet Friendly ●; Internet Friendly-WiFi ●; Pets Welcome ■

Ozark Folk Center, Mountain View. "Living museum" state park is dedicated to preserving the heritage and way of life of the Ozark Mountain people. This hands-on, fun-filled center welcomes visitors to toe-tapping mountain music and an opportunity to witness (and often partake in) blacksmithing and pottery making.

Shiloh Museum of Ozark History. Dedicated to the study, interpretation and preservation of the rich history of the Arkansas Ozark Mountains, the museum offers lectures, films, classes, tours and frequently changing exhibits. Beautiful park-like grounds showcase six historical buildings.

War Eagle Mill, Rogers. An authentic reproduction of the 1873 mill using stone burrs to grind wheat and corn. Visitors can watch grain being ground by this water-powered grist mill. Also host to one of the largest craft fairs in the country each spring and fall.

RIVER VALLEY REGION

Running between the Ozarks and the Ouchitas, this area is a combination of flat-topped mountains like those found in the Ozarks, and ridges like the Ouchitas, with the great Arkansas River flowing through its valley. The tallest mountain in the state, Magazine, can be found in this region. The Caddo and Osage inhabited this area before European settlers, like Henri de Tonti, the French explorer who visited the valley in the early 1700's. This wine country area has state parks and an abundance of historic sites.

Wineries: **Cowie Wine Cellar** (also a museum), Paris. **Mount Bethel Winery**, Altus. **Post Familie Winery**, Altus. **Chateau Aux Arc**, Altus. **Wiederkehr Wine Cellars**, Altus.

Arkansas and Missouri Railroad. Take a scenic rail excursion through the Boston Mountains on restored passenger cars. You will travel over high trestles and through the 1882 Winslow tunnel. The trips run from Springdale to Van Buren, Van Buren to Winslow, Fort Smith to Winslow and Springdale to Fort Smith.

Fort Smith. The **Belle Grove Historic District** is a 22-block area of restored homes and buildings featuring Gothic Revival, Neo-Classical, Victorian Renaissance and other period architecture. View remains of two frontier forts and the Federal court for the Western District of Arkansas at the **Fort Smith National Historic Site**. Exhibits include the Trail of Tears and the "Hangin' Judge" Isaac C. Parker's courtroom. Ride from Garrison Ave. to the National Cemetery on a 1926 Birney electric streetcar at the **Fort Smith Trolley Museum** featuring railroad and transportation memorabilia.

North Logan County, Petit Jean State Park. The flagship of the state parks system, this mountaintop retreat has cabins and newly renovated **Mather Lodge**. Enjoy restaurants, swimming pools, campsites, boating and fishing on **Lake Bailey**, hiking trails, spectacular **Cedar Falls** and visitor center exhibits, not to mention twenty miles of hiking trails. 95-foot-high Cedar Falls is the park's focal point.

Potts Inn Museum Historic Stagecoach Station, Pottsville. One of the best preserved stagecoach stations on the Butterfield Overland Mail Route, this restored antebellum home now showcases antiques and a hat museum.

CENTRAL REGION

Little Rock and North Little Rock form the vibrant heart of this region. The two cities and their neighboring towns comprise a metro area of some 500,000 people. Central Arkansas offers a cosmopolitan mix of small town charm, with a big city tempo.

Little Rock. Wander the trails of Pinnacle Mountain State Park and Emerald Park, or visit the Little Rock Zoo or the IMAX Theater in the Aerospace Education Center. A walking tour of the **Quapaw Quarter District** offers a look at handsomely preserved antebellum and Victorian structures. Other attractions include the **William J. Clinton Presidential Center and Park** located on the Arkansas River in the River Market District downtown. Situated on 28 acres, the center contains the largest collection of presidential papers and artifacts in U.S. history. The 20,000 square feet of library and museum space includes an authentic replica of the Oval Office and the Cabinet Room. The **Central High Museum and Visitors Center** has interactive exhibits detailing the events of the 1957 desegregation crisis at the school. The **Central High School National Historic Site** is still a working school. View colorful historic exhibits at the **Old State House Museum**, Arkansas's capitol building from 1836-1911.

North Little Rock. Fish, golf, play tennis or visit the amusement park at the 1,575-acre **Burns Park**. Other attractions at the park include a pre-Civil War log cabin, playground, covered bridge and hiking trails. For some water fun, visit **Wild River Country**, a 26-acre water theme park featuring the "Arkansas Ocean."

The **Arkansas Inland Maritime Museum** is home to the U.S.S Razorback, the longest-serving submarine in the world. Launched in 1944 from the Portsmouth Naval Shipyard in Maine, the U.S.S Razorback entered Tokyo Harbor in 1945 with 11 other submarines to take part in the formal surrender of Japan.

DELTA REGION

The Delta Region has natural wonders, antebellum homes, Civil War sites, blues music and lots of charm. This is the land where Europeans first crossed the Mississippi in 1541. Experience a taste of the civilizations they founded at the Hampson Museum State Park, and at Parkin Archaeological State Park. A highpoint includes the Hemingway-Pfeiffer Museum and Education Center where "Papa" Hemingway penned portions of "A Farewell to Arms".

Scenic Drives: The Great River Road National Scenic Byway through eastern Arkansas runs parallel to the Mississippi River. Other scenic routes are **Crowley's Ridge Parkway National Scenic Byway** and **St. Francis Scenic Byway**. **Sans Souci Landing**, southeast of Osceola and **Barfield**, east of Blytheville, are two scenic overlooks that afford majestic views of the Mississippi.

Helena. Murals greet visitors to this city. The sea wall mural on Cherry St. depicts early Helena culture and blues history. At **Blues Corner** the blues come alive amidst this collection of records, CDs, tapes, books and memorabilia. Take a cultural and musical tour of this Mississippi River town with **Delta Heritage Tours** that feature an authentic gospel church service, a live performance of America's longest running blues radio show and a visit to the **Delta Cultural Center**. The center is a museum in a restored depot and storefront with interactive audio exhibits on the region's heritage of blues and gospel music, natural history and the Civil War battle at Helena. The **Pillow-Thompson House** is an authentically furnished Victorian home open for tours.

Marianna. Located approximately 100 miles east of Little Rock, Marianna was established as a trading post along the L'Anguille River, and serves as the county seat. Marianna's downtown is a National Historic District, and boasts eight listings on the National Register of Historic Places. Marianna is also home to the northern portion of the St. Francis National Forest. At just over 22,000 acres, St. Francis is one of the smallest National Forests, but offers an abundance of outdoor activities.

OUACHITAS REGION

The Ouachita region is one of the two major uplands of Arkansas. It lies in west central Arkansas between the Arkansas River Valley and the West Gulf Coastal Plain. This area contains thermal springs and the only diamond mines open to the public. The mountains of this region are unusual for this continent because they run in an east west alignment and were created by folding and uplifting of the earth's surface.

Hot Springs Area. Named for the 47 thermal springs on Hot Springs Mountain which flow approximately one million gallons daily at a constant temperature of 143° F., Hot Springs is also known for its art galleries.

Listed as one of the 10 best art towns in America, there are an abundance of galleries displaying art from around the world.

Hot Springs. The Greatest Story Ever Told has never been greater than when it is portrayed by this dynamic outdoor musical drama. **The Witness** is the compelling story of the birth, life, death, and resurrection of Jesus of Nazareth as told and sung by the Apostle Peter. Every Friday and Saturday night June 1st – Mid October.

For family fun there is the **Arkansas Alligator Farm and Petting Zoo** with over 200 alligators, feeding shows, petting zoo and museum; **Ducks in the Park Tours**, offering sightseeing on land and water; Magic **Springs Theme Park and Crystal Falls Water Park** with more than 80 attractions including roller coasters, wave pool, waterslides and more; Jungle **Mountain Miniature Golf/Thunder Mountain Speedway** where you can play miniature golf in a rain forest setting complete with animal sounds and waterfall. **Garvan Woodland Gardens** showcase floral landscapes, free-flowing streams and waterfalls on 210 acres of a forested peninsula jutting into Lake Hamilton. **Quartz Crystal Mines/Rock Shops** located in the Hot Springs, Mount Ida and Jessieville areas allow visitors to dig for quartz crystals for a fee.

Hot Springs Mountain Tower is a 216-foot observation tower on top of Hot Springs Mountain.

TIMBERLANDS REGION

Timber, oil, deer hunting, bass fishing. These words are often used when discussing the Timberlands region of Arkansas. A region rich with natural resources that was discovered by pioneers from the eastern U. S. in the early 1800's, and still attracts people today. Each year, thousands of sportsmen descend on the area to hunt deer in what is considered the best deer-hunting region in the state. Anglers come in search of the lunker bass in the area's legendary lakes and rivers. Still, others seek out the legacy of those pioneers from long ago in the log cabins from the 1800's, to the restored Victorian homes and local museums that tell the history of this land.

Arkansas Museum of Natural Resources, Smackover. Films and exhibits tell the history of Arkansas's oil and brine industries and the 1920s oil boom that caused an explosion of population and wealth virtually overnight.

New Rocky Comfort Museum was originally a jail. The 1902 building was constructed in the unusual manner of stacked boards. It is listed on the National Register of Historic Places.

Old Washington Historic State Park, Washington. The birthplace of Sam Houston's plot to liberate Texas in the 1830s and later Arkansas' Confederate capital. Historic, restored buildings depict rugged pioneer days and antebellum Arkansas.

Clinton Center and Hope Visitor Center and Museum in Hope is the restored home where former President Bill Clinton lived as a child offering tours, exhibits on Clinton and railroad memorabilia.

Nevada County Depot Museum in Prescott displays Indian artifacts to railroad memorabilia and Civil War relics. Admission is free.

El Dorado Downtown Historic District. A significant collection of 1920s and 1930s architecture financed by the oil boom of the 1920s can be found here. This historic area also includes boutiques, shops, dining, historic square and the restored art deco **Rialto Theatre**.

Kartways of Arkansas, Warren. Go-kart racing on combination half-mile road course with rentals of beginner and professional level go-carts, race-driving school and sanctioned local, regional and national races.

Murals. Thirteen colorful murals depicting Pine Bluff's past make the downtown area an art gallery. The town of Magnolia has five murals in the city's historic square including one signed by actor Charlton Heston. Texarkana's mural depicts the life of composer Scott Joplin.

CALENDAR OF EVENTS

JANUARY

Warfield Concerts, Helena; Bluegrass Music Showcase, Eureka Springs; Robert Burns Weekend, Eureka Springs; Chateau Aux Arc Amateur Winemaking Competition, Altus; Annual Tri-Lakes Coin Show, Hot Springs; Bull-Riding, Texarkana.

FEBRUARY

Annual Daffodil Days, Hot Springs; Eureka Gras Hookers and Jokers Ball, Eureka Springs; Annual Eureka Gras Extravaganza, Eureka Springs; Annual Winter Bluegrass Show, Hope.

MARCH

Annual Wye Mountain Daffodil Festival, Wye; Depression Era Glass and Pottery Show, Little Rock; Mid-Southern Watercolorists Annual Juried Exhibition, Little Rock; Oaklawn's Live Racing Season, Hot Springs.

APRIL

Young Arkansas Artists Annual Exhibition, Little Rock; FFA Rodeo, Hope; FFA Farm Sale, Piggott; Fayetteville Farmer's Market (thru November), Fayetteville; Annual Hogskin Holidays Festival, Hampton.

MAY

Annual Dinosaur Festival, Nashville; Annual Toad Suck Daze, Conway; Annual Hamburg Armadillo Festival, Hamburg; Annual North Arkansas Woodcarvers Show, Baxter Co. Fairgrounds; Annual Small Business Expo, Pine Bluff; Bald Knob Home Fest, Bald Knob; Annual Old Timers' Day Arts & Crafts Festival, Van Buren; Annual Picklefest, Atkins; Annual Dermott Crawfish Festival, Dermott.

JUNE

Annual Steamboat Days Family Festival, Des Arc; Annual Art Competition, Fort Smith; Annual Portfest 'Rollin' on the River' Festival, Jacksonport; Annual Chicken and Egg Festival, Prescott; Annual Southern Memorial Day, Fayetteville; Annual Lions Club rodeo and Parade, Calico Rock.

JULY

Annual Rodeo of the Ozarks, Springdale; 4th of July Fireworks at Iron Mountain Lodge and Marina, Arkadelphia; Annual Homecoming Picnic, Corning; Freedomfest, Greenwood; Fireworks Extravaganza, Herber Springs; Pops on the River, Little Rock; Annual 4th of July Homecoming and Picnic, Piggott; Annual Sherwood's 4th of July Family Celebration, Sherwood.

AUGUST

Annual Montgomery County Fair, Mount Ida; White Hall Founder's Day, White Hall, Dallas County Fair, Fordyce; Annual Frisco Festival, Rogers; Fulton County Fair, Salem; Annual Tontitown Grape Festival, Tontitown.

SEPTEMBER

Annual Benton County Fair, Bentonville; South Logan County Livestock Show and Fair, Booneville; Annual Johnson County Fair, Clarksville; Flameworked Beadmaking and Wheel Thrown Pottery Demonstrations, Pocahontas; Carroll County Fair, Berryville; Hot Spring County Fair and Rodeo, Malvern.

OCTOBER

Annual Central Arkansas Gem and Mineral Show, Jacksonville; Annual Arkansas Blues and Heritage Festival, Helena; Annual Knights of Columbus Oktoberfest, Fort Smith; Annual Arkansas State Fair, Little Rock; Annual Quartz, Quiltz and Craftz Festival, Mount Ida.

NOVEMBER

Mountain View Bluegrass Festival, Mountain View; Annual Ozark Folk Festival, Eureka Springs; Tinsel and Traditions, Hot Springs; Duck Calling Contest and Wings Over the Prairie Festival, Stuttgart; Annual Hot Springs Chili Cook-Off, Hot Springs.

DECEMBER

Annual Christmas Frolic and Open House, Little Rock; Annual Mountainfest, Mena; Arkansas Winds, Springdale; Ozark Christmas Parade, Ozark; Good Eats, Springdale; Annual Christmas To Share, Hot Springs.

ALMA—B-2

(S) CLEAR CREEK (COE-Ozark Lake)—(Crawford) *From jct US 71 & Hwy 162: Go 5 mi S. Follow signs.* FACILITIES: 41 sites, 25 E, (30 amps), 16 no hkups, 3 pull-thrus, tenting, dump. RECREATION: boating, ramp, dock, river fishing. Partial handicap access. Open all yr. Facilities fully operational Jan 1 - Dec 31. Phone: (479)632-4882.

(N) Crabtree RV Park—(Crawford) *From jct I-40 (exit 13) & US 71: Go 500 ft N on US 71,then 1 block W on Collum Ln, then 1 block SW on Heather Ln. Enter on R.* ◆◆◆FACILITIES: 39 sites, typical site width 14 ft, 39 full hkups, (30/50 amps), 22 pull-thrus, dump, laundry. ◆RECREATION: swim pool. Pets welcome. Partial handicap access. No tents. Open all yr. Big rigs welcome. Rate in 2010 $25-27 for 2 persons. Phone: (479)632-0909. FCRV discount. FMCA discount.

(N) KOA-FORT SMITH/ALMA—(Crawford) *From jct I-40 (exit 13) & US-71: Go 2-1/2 mi N on US-71. Enter on L.*

WELCOME

◆◆◆◆FACILITIES: 60 sites, typical site width 20 ft, 23 full hkups, 37 W&E, (30/50 amps), some extd stay sites, 33 pull-thrus, cable TV, WiFi Instant Internet at site, phone Internet central location, family camping, tenting, cabins, RV storage, dump, non-guest dump $, laundry, ltd groc, RV supplies, LP gas by weight/by meter, ice, picnic tables, patios, fire rings, grills, wood.

◆◆◆RECREATION: rec hall, swim pool, 3 pedal boat rentals, pond fishing, fishing supplies, golf nearby, bsktball, playground, horseshoes, hiking trails, v-ball.

Pets welcome. Open all yr. Big rigs welcome. Escort to site. Clubs welcome. Rate in 2010 $31-39 for 2 persons. MC/VISA/DISC/Debit. KOA discount.

Phone: (479)632-2704
Address: 3539 N US Hwy 71, Alma, AR 72921
Lat/Lon: 35.52190/-94.22170
Email: ftsmithalmakoa@juno.com
Web: www.koa.com

SEE AD FORT SMITH PAGE 31

ALTUS—B-2

(N) Chateau Aux Arc RV Park (RV SPACES) —(Franklin) *From jct I-40 (exit 41) & Hwy 186: Go 2 mi S on Hwy 186. Enter on R.* FACILITIES: 11 sites, 11 full hkups, (20/30/50 amps), family camping, tenting, laundry. Pets welcome. Open all yr. Rate in 2010 $20-22 for 2 persons. Phone: (479)468-4400.

(N) Wiederkehr Wine Cellars RV (RV SPACES) —(Franklin) *From jct I-40 (exit 41) & Hwy 186: Go 5 mi S on Hwy 186. Enter on R.* FACILITIES: 20 sites, typical site width 15 ft, 20 W&E, (20/30 amps), tenting. Pets welcome. Open all yr. Rate in 2010 $15 per vehicle. Phone: (800)622-WINE.

ARKADELPHIA—D-3

(N) Arkadelphia Campground & RV Park—(Clark) *From jct I-30 & Hwy 7 (Exit 78/Caddo Valley): Go 300 yds N on Hwy 7,then 1 mi NE on Frost Rd. Enter on L.* ◆◆◆◆FACILITIES: 70 sites, typical site width 25 ft, 70 full hkups, (20/30/50 amps), 40 pull-thrus, cable TV, WiFi Instant Internet at site, WiFi Internet central location, family camping, tenting, dump, non-guest dump $, laundry, ltd groc, RV supplies, LP gas by weight/by meter, ice, picnic tables, patios. ◆◆◆RECREATION: rec hall, swim pool, pond fishing, fishing supplies, bsktball, playground, activities, horseshoes, hiking trails. Pets welcome. Open all yr. Big rigs welcome. Rate in 2010 $28 for 2 persons. MC/VISA/DISC/Debit. FMCA discount. CCUSA 50% Discount.

CAMPCLUB USA

ARKADELPHIA—Continued
Arkadelphia Campground & RV Park—Continued

CCUSA reservations Required, CCUSA max stay 1 day, Cash only for CCUSA disc., CCUSA disc. not avail F,Sa, CCUSA disc. not avail holidays. Discount available Nov thru Feb.

Phone: (870)246-4922
Address: 221 Frost Rd, Arkadelphia, AR 71923
Lat/Lon: 34.19609/-93.05732
Email: arcampground@iocc.com
Web: www.arkadelphiacampground.com

(NW) DEGRAY LAKE RESORT SP—(Hot Spring) *From jct I-30 (exit 78) & Hwy-7: Go 6 mi N on Hwy-7.* FACILITIES: 113 sites, 113 W&E, tenting, dump, laundry, groceries. RECREATION: lake swim, boating, canoeing, dock, lake fishing. Partial handicap access. Open all yr. Phone: (501)865-2801.

ASHDOWN—D-2

(NE) Bullfrog Marina & RV Park—(Hempstead) *From jct Hwy US 71 & Hwy 32: Go 4-1/2 mi E on Hwy 32, then 2-1/2 mi N on Jacks Isle Rd. Enter at end.* ◆◆FACILITIES: 20 sites, typical site width 20 ft, 40 ft max RV length, accepts self-contained units only, 2 full hkups, 18 W&E, (30/50 amps), family camping, dump, ltd groc. ◆◆RECREATION: lake swim, boating, canoeing, ramp, dock, lake/river fishing. Pets welcome. No tents. Open all yr. Rate in 2010 $15 for 2 persons. Phone: (870)898-8881.

(E) MILLWOOD SP—(Little River) *From jct US-71 & Hwy-32: Go 9 mi E on Hwy-32.* FACILITIES: 115 sites, 2 full hkups, 110 W&E, (30 amps), 3 no hkups, tenting, dump, ltd groc. RECREATION: lake swim, boating, lake fishing, playground. Partial handicap access. Open all yr. Phone: (870)898-2800.

ATHENS—D-2

(W) OUACHITA NATIONAL FOREST (Shady Lake Rec. Area)—(Polk) *From jct Hwy 84 & CR 246: Go 2 mi NW on CR 246, then 2 mi N on FR 38.* FACILITIES: 66 sites, 40 ft max RV length, 1 full hkups, 21 W&E, (30 amps), 44 no hkups, tenting, dump. RECREATION: lake swim, boating, no motors, canoeing, dock, lake/stream fishing, playground. Partial handicap access. Open Mar 1 - Nov 30. Phone: (479)394-2382.

ATKINS—B-3

(SE) SWEEDEN ISLAND (COE-Lake Dardanelle)—(Pope) *From jct I-40 (exit 94) & Hwy 105: Go 8 mi S on Hwy 105 (follow signs).* FACILITIES: 28 sites, 22 W&E, (30 amps), 6 no hkups, tenting, dump. RECREATION: ramp, playground. Partial handicap access. Open all yr. Phone: (479)968-5008.

BARLING—B-1

(N) SPRINGHILL (COE - Ozark Lake)—(Sebastian) *From town: Go 1-1/2 mi N on Hwy-59.* FACILITIES: 45 sites, 32 W&E, 10 E, (30/50 amps), 3 no hkups, tenting, dump. RECREATION: boating, ramp, dock, river/pond fishing, playground. Partial handicap access. Open Mar 1 - Oct 31. Phone: (479)452-4598.

BATESVILLE—B-4

(SW) Speedway RV Park—(Independence) *From jct US 167 & Hwy 25: Go 2 mi S on Hwy 25. Enter on L.* ◆◆◆FACILITIES: 43 sites, typical site width 30 ft, 33 full hkups, 10 E, (20/30/50 amps), 18 pull-thrus, family camping, tenting, dump, laundry. Pets welcome. Partial handicap access. Open all yr. Big rigs welcome. Rate in 2010 $30-35 for 2 persons. Phone: (870)251-1008. FMCA discount.

BENTON—C-3

(N) I-30 TRAVEL PARK—(Saline) *E'bnd from I-30 (exit 118): Go 1-1/2 mi E on service road. W'bnd from I-30 (exit 121): Go 1 mi W on service road, then cross over freeway on Hwy 5 overpass, make loop, then 1/2 mi E on E'bnd service road. Ent on R. Enter on R.*

WELCOME

◆◆◆FACILITIES: 155 sites, typical site width 33 ft, 155 full hkups, (30/50 amps), 50 amps ($), some extd stay sites, 67 pull-thrus, phone Internet central location, family camping, RV storage, dump, non-guest dump $, laundry, ice, picnic tables.

◆RECREATION: rec room/area, pavilion, golf nearby, play equipment.

Pets welcome. Open all yr. Big rigs welcome. Clubs welcome. Rate in 2010 $22.75 for 2 persons. MC/VISA/DISC. FCRV discount. FMCA discount.

Phone: (501)778-1244
Address: 19719 Interstate Highway 30, Benton, AR 72015
Lat/Lon: 34.5992/-92.5492

SEE AD LITTLE ROCK PAGE 35

BENTON—Continued

(SW) JB'S RV PARK & CAMPGROUND—(Saline) *From jct I-30 (exit 106) & Old Military Rd: Go 1/4 mi NE on Old Military Rd, then 600 feet E on J. B. Baxley Rd. Enter on R.*

WELCOME

◆◆◆FACILITIES: 42 sites, typical site width 24 ft, 33 full hkups, 9 W&E, (20/30/50 amps), 50 amps ($), some extd stay sites, 33 pull-thrus, phone Internet central location, tenting, dump, non-guest dump $, laundry, picnic tables.

◆RECREATION: pavilion, pond fishing, hiking trails.

Pets welcome. Open all yr. Big rigs welcome. Rate in 2010 $20-23 for 2 persons.

Phone: (501)778-6050
Address: 8601 J.B. Baxley Rd., Benton, AR 72015
Lat/Lon: 34.48250/-92.72060
Web: www.jbsrvpark.com

SEE AD LITTLE ROCK PAGE 35

BLACK ROCK—A-4

(S) LAKE CHARLES SP—(Lawrence) *From jct US 63 & Hwy 25: Go 6 mi S on Hwy 25.* FACILITIES: 60 sites, 23 full hkups, 37 W&E, (30/50 amps), 5 pull-thrus, tenting, dump, ltd groc. RECREATION: lake swim, boating, ramp, lake fishing, playground. Partial handicap access. Open all yr. Phone: (870)878-6595.

BLUE EYE—A-2

(E) Outdoor Resorts of the Ozarks—(Carroll) *From jct US 62 & Hwy 311 (in Green Forest): Go 16 mi N on Hwy 311, then 1-1/2 mi E on CR 663. Enter at end.* ◆◆◆◆◆FACILITIES: 164 sites, typical site width 43 ft, accepts full hkup units only, 164 full hkups, (30/50 amps), family camping, laundry. ◆◆◆◆◆RECREATION: 2 swim pools, lake swim, boating, canoeing, ramp, dock, lake fishing. Pets welcome, quantity restrict. Partial handicap access. No tents. Open all yr. Big rigs welcome. Rate in 2010 $55 for 4 persons. Phone: (888)749-7396. FMCA discount.

BLUFF CITY—D-3

(S) WHITE OAK SP—(Nevada) *From jct Hwy 24 & 299: Go 100 yards S on Hwy 299, then 2 mi SE on Hwy 387.* FACILITIES: 44 sites, 41 W&E, (20/30 amps), 3 no hkups, 4 pull-thrus, tenting, dump, ltd groc. RECREATION: lake swim, boating, ramp, dock, lake fishing, playground. Partial handicap access. Open all yr. Phone: (870)685-2748.

BRINKLEY—C-4

(N) Heritage Inn and RV Park (RV SPACES) —(Monroe) *From jct I-40 (Exit 216) & US-49: Go 600 feet S on US-49. Enter on R.* FACILITIES: 30 sites, typical site width 20 ft, 18 full hkups, 12 W&E, (30/50 amps), 22 pull-thrus, family camping, tenting, dump. RECREATION: swim pool. Pets welcome. Open all yr. Rate in 2010 $18.50 per vehicle. Member ARVC. Phone: (870)734-2121.

BULL SHOALS—A-3

See listings at Cotter, Flippin, Lakeview, Mountain Home, Yellville & Gamaliel.

(SE) BULL SHOALS SP—(Baxter) *3 mi SE at Bull Shoals Dam on Hwy-178.* FACILITIES: 103 sites, 3 full hkups, 80 W&E, (20/30/50 amps), 20 no hkups, tenting, dump. RECREATION: boating, dock, lake/river fishing, playground. Partial handicap access. Open all yr. Phone: (870)445-3629.

(SE) DAM SITE RECREATION AREA (COE-Bull Shoals Lake)—(Marion) *From town: Go 2 mi SE on Hwy 178.* FACILITIES: 35 sites, 35 E, (30 amps), 4 pull-thrus, tenting, dump. RECREATION: lake swim, boating, ramp, lake fishing, playground. Open Apr 1 - Sep 30. Phone: (870)445-7166.

BURLINGTON—A-2

(N) Ozark View RV Park & Campground—(Boone) *From north jct US 62/US 412 & US 65: Go 7-1/2 mi N on US 65, then 1/4 mi N on Old Hwy 65 (Main St). Enter on R.* ◆◆◆◆FACILITIES: 30 sites, typical site width 32 ft, 29 full hkups, (20/30/50 amps), 1 no hkups, 17 pull-thrus, WiFi Instant Internet at site, WiFi Internet central location, family camping, tenting, RV storage, dump, non-guest dump $, laundry, RV supplies, LP gas by weight/by meter, ice, picnic tables, fire

Ozark View RV Park & Campground—Continued on next page

Arkansas State Tree: Shortleaf Pine

BURLINGTON—Continued
Ozark View RV Park & Campground—Continued

rings, grills, wood. ◆◆RECREATION: equipped pavilion, horseshoes. Pets welcome. Open all yr. Big rigs welcome. Rate in 2010 $28 for 2 persons. MC/VISA/DISC/AMEX/Debit. CCUSA 50% Discount. CCUSA reservations Required, CCUSA max stay 1 day. 25% discount available for any additional nights.

Phone: (870)426-5166
Address: 18412 Old Highway 65, Omaha, AR 72662
Lat/Lon: 36.39287/-93.22131
Email: ozarkvu@omahaweb.net
Web: www.ozarkviewrv.com

CAVE SPRINGS—A-2

(S) THE CREEKS GOLF RESORT—*From jct I-540 & W Monroe Ave/Hwy 264 (exit 78): Go 4-3/4 mi W on Hwy 264, then 1 mi S on AR 112. Enter on R.* 18-hole course nestled along the Spring & Osage Creeks. One of the most scenic and challenging golf venues in NW Arkansas. Pro-Shop. Snack Bar & RV Park. Open all yr. MC/VISA/DISC/AMEX/Debit.

Phone: (479)248-1000
Address: 1499 S Main St, Cave Springs, AR 72718
Lat/Lon: 36.24526/-94.23868
Web: www.creeksrvresort.com

SEE AD FAYETTEVILLE NEXT PAGE

(S) THE CREEKS RV RESORT—(Benton) *From jct I-540 & W Monroe Ave/Hwy 264 (exit 78): Go 4-3/4 mi W on Hwy 264, then 1 mi S on AR 112. Enter on R.*

THE CREEKS GOLF & RV RESORT
Located on 200 acres in the beautiful Osage Valley. The creeks, golf & RV Resort offers an array of ammenities & services. Centrally located. This resort offers fine dining, upscale shopping & much more just minutes away.

◆◆◆◆FACILITIES: 60 sites, typical site width 30 ft, accepts full hkup units only, 60 full hkups, (30/50 amps), some extd stay sites (summer), cable TV, WiFi Instant Internet at site, family camping, dump, non-guest dump $, LP gas by weight/by meter, ice, picnic tables.

◆◆RECREATION: pond fishing, putting green, golf nearby, activities. Rec open to public.

Pets welcome. No tents. Open all yr. Big rigs welcome. Clubs welcome. Rate in 2010 $35 for 2 persons. MC/VISA/DISC/AMEX/Debit. FMCA discount.

Phone: (479)248-1000
Address: 1499 S Main St, Cave Springs, AR 72718
Lat/Lon: 36.24526/-94.23868
Web: www.creeksrvresort.com

SEE AD FAYETTEVILLE NEXT PAGE

CECIL—B-2

(N) CITADEL BLUFF (COE-Ozark Lake)—(Franklin) *From jct Hwy 96 & Hwy 41: Go 2 mi N on Hwy 41. Enter on R.* FACILITIES: 25 sites, 25 no hkups, tenting. RECREATION: boating, ramp, river fishing. Open all yr. Facilities fully operational May 1 - Sep 10. Phone: (479)667-5103.

Arkansas gets its name from the French interpretation of the Sioux word "acansa", meaning "downstream place".

CHOCTAW—B-3

(E) CHOCTAW RECREATION AREA (COE-Greers Ferry Lake)—(Van Buren) *From jct US-65 & Hwy-330: Go 3-1/2 mi E on Hwy-330.* FACILITIES: 146 sites, 78 E, (20/30 amps), 68 no hkups, tenting, dump. RECREATION: lake swim, boating, ramp, dock, playground. Partial handicap access. Open Apr 1 - Oct 31. Phone: (501)362-2416.

CLARKSVILLE—B-2

(E) SPADRA (COE-Lake Dardanelle)—(Johnson) *From town: Go 3 mi S on Hwy-103.* FACILITIES: 29 sites, 24 E, (30 amps), 5 no hkups, tenting, dump. RECREATION: boating, ramp, dock, lake fishing. Partial handicap access. Open all yr. Phone: (479)968-5008.

CLINTON—B-3

(N) WHISPERING PINES RV PARK—(Van Buren) *From jct Hwy-16 & US-65: Go 7-1/4 mi N on US-65. Enter on L.*

◆◆FACILITIES: 34 sites, typical site width 30 ft, 34 full hkups, (20/30/50 amps), 50 amps ($), some extd stay sites, 15 pull-thrus, family camping, tenting, RV's/park model rentals, laundry, picnic tables, grills.

◆RECREATION: rec hall, golf nearby, horseshoes.

Pets welcome, breed restrict. Open all yr. Restrooms closed in winter months. Big rigs welcome. Escort to site. Clubs welcome. Rate in 2010 $18-20 for 2 persons.

Phone: (888)745-4291
Address: 8575 Hwy 65 N, Clinton, AR 72031
Lat/Lon: 35.47905/-92.42403

SEE AD THIS PAGE

CONWAY—C-3

(SW) TOAD SUCK FERRY PARK (COE-Toad Suck Ferry)—(Faulkner) *From jct I-40 (exit 129) & Hwy 286: Go 6 mi W on Hwy 286, then 1 mi W on Hwy 60.* FACILITIES: 48 sites, 48 E, (30/50 amps), tenting, dump. RECREATION: boating, canoeing, ramp, river fishing, playground. Partial handicap access. Open all yr. Phone: (501)329-2986.

(N) WOOLLY HOLLOW SP—(Faulkner) *From jct I-40 (exit 125) & US 65: Go 12 mi N on US 65, then 6 mi E on Hwy 285.* FACILITIES: 30 sites, 20 W&E, (20/30 amps), 10 no hkups, 1 pull-thrus, tenting, dump. RECREATION: lake swim, boating, electric motors only, ramp, dock, lake fishing, playground. Partial handicap access. Open all yr. Phone: (501)679-2098.

COTTER—A-3

(N) DENTON FERRY RV PARK RESORT—(Baxter) *From jct US 62/412 & Denton Ferry Rd: Go 1/2 mi N on Denton Ferry Rd. Enter on L.*

◆◆◆◆FACILITIES: 44 sites, typical site width 30 ft, 44 full hkups, (20/30/50 amps), 27 pull-thrus, WiFi Instant Internet at site, family camping, tenting, laundry, LP gas by weight/by meter, ice, picnic tables, fire rings.

◆◆◆RECREATION: rec room/area, boating, canoeing, river/pond fishing, fishing guides, golf nearby, hiking trails.

Pets welcome. Partial handicap access. Open all yr. Big rigs welcome. Clubs welcome. Rate in 2010 $31-40 per vehicle. MC/VISA/DISC/AMEX/Debit. FMCA discount.

Phone: (870)435-7275
Address: 740 Denton Ferry Road, Cotter, AR 72626
Lat/Lon: 36.29255/-92.52134
Email: info@dentonrv.com
Web: www.dentonrv.com

SEE AD MOUNTAIN HOME PAGE 36

CROSSETT—E-4

(W) CROSSETT RV PARK & CAMPGROUND (Crossett Port Auth)—(Ashley) *From town: Go 8 mi W on US 82. Enter on L.* FACILITIES: 119 sites, 119 W&E, tenting, dump, ltd groc. RECREATION: boating, ramp, dock, river fishing. Partial handicap access. Open all yr. Phone: (870)364-6136.

DAISY—D-2

(S) DAISY SP—(Pike) *From town: Go 1/4 mi S off US 70.* FACILITIES: 103 sites, 82 W&E, (20/30 amps), 21 no hkups, 1 pull-thrus, tenting, dump. RECREATION: boating, ramp, playground. Partial handicap access. Open all yr. Phone: (870)398-4487.

DARDANELLE—B-3

(S) MT. NEBO SP—(Yell) *From jct Hwy 22 & Hwy 155: Go 7 mi W on Hwy 155. CAUTION: Trailers over 15 ft. should not attempt zigzag mountainous climb to park.* FACILITIES: 34 sites, 15 ft max RV length, 24 W&E, (30 amps), 10 no hkups, tenting, ltd groc. RECREATION: swim pool, playground. Open all yr. Phone: (479)229-3655.

Arkansas is officially known as The Natural State.

DRASCO—B-4

(W) CHEROKEE RECREATION AREA (COE-Greers Ferry Lake)—(Cleburne) *From jct Hwy-25 & Hwy-92: Go 7-1/2 mi W on Hwy-92, then 4 mi S on paved access road.* FACILITIES: 33 sites, 16 E, (20/30 amps), 17 no hkups, tenting, dump. RECREATION: lake swim, boating, ramp, playground. Open May 15 - Sep 15. Phone: (501)362-2416.

(W) HILL CREEK PUBLIC USE AREA (COE-Greers Ferry Lake)—(Cleburne) *From jct Hwy-25 & Hwy-92: Go 12 mi W on Hwy-92, then 3 mi NW on Hwy-225, then 1-1/2 mi S on access road.* FACILITIES: 41 sites, 25 E, (20/30 amps), 16 no hkups, tenting, dump. RECREATION: boating, ramp, dock. Open Apr 1 - Sep 5. Phone: (501)362-2416.

EDGEMONT—B-3

(SE) Blue Clouds RV and Cabin Resort—(Lafayette) *From Jct of AR 65 & AR 16: Go 1 3/4 mi E or AR 16. Enter on R.* ◆◆◆FACILITIES: 50 sites, typical site width 60 ft, 40 ft max RV length, 50 full hkups, (30/50 amps), 6 pull-thrus, family camping, tenting, laundry. ◆◆RECREATION: playground. Pets welcome. Partial handicap access. Open all yr. Rate in 2010 $22-24 per family. Phone: (501) 723-4999.

EL DORADO—E-3

(NE) MORO BAY SP—(Bradley) *From jct US 167 & Hwy 15: Go 20 mi NE on Hwy 15.* FACILITIES: 20 sites, 20 W&E, (30/50 amps), 2 pull-thrus, tenting, dump, ltd groc. RECREATION: lake swim, boating, river fishing, playground. Partial handicap access. Open all yr. Phone: (870)463-8555.

EUREKA SPRINGS—A-2

(SW) DAM SITE REC AREA (COE-Beaver Lake)—(Carroll) *From jct Hwy 23 & US 62: Go 7 mi W on US 62, then 2 mi S on Hwy 187.* FACILITIES: 48 sites, 48 E, (30/50 amps), tenting, dump. RECREATION: lake swim, boating, ramp, river fishing, playground. Partial handicap access. Open Apr 1 - Oct 30. Phone: (479)253-9865.

(W) Green Tree Lodge & RV Park—(Carroll) *From west jct Hwy 23 N & US 62: Go 1-1/2 mi W on US 62. Enter on R.* ◆◆FACILITIES: 24 sites, typical site width 28 ft, 24 full hkups, (30/50 amps), 50 amps ($), 9 pull-thrus, family camping. ◆RECREATION: swim pool. Pets welcome. No tents. Open Apr 1 - Mid Nov. Big rigs welcome. Rate in 2010 $23.75-25.75 for 2 persons. Phone: (479)253-8807.

(E) Kettle Campground, Cabins & RV Park—(Carroll) *From jct Hwy 23 & US 62: Go 1-1/2 mi E on US 62. Enter on L.* ◆◆◆FACILITIES: 46 sites, 25 full hkups, 20 W&E, 1 E, (20/30/50 amps), 50 amps ($), 10 pull-thrus, family camping, tenting, dump, laundry. ◆◆RECREATION: swim pool, playground. Pets welcome. Partial handicap access. Open all yr. Big rigs welcome. Rate in 2010 $23-27 for 2 persons. Phone: (479)253-9100.

(W) KOA-Eureka Springs—(Carroll) *From north jct Hwy 23 N & US 62: Go 4-1/4 mi W on US 62, then 1 mi SW on Hwy 187. Enter on L.* ◆◆◆FACILITIES: 89 sites, typical site width 27 ft, 25 full hkups, 46 W&E, (30/50 amps), 50 amps ($), 18 no hkups, 47 pull-thrus, family camping, tenting, dump, laundry, groceries. ◆◆◆RECREATION: swim pool, playground. Pets welcome, breed restrict. Partial handicap access. Open Apr 1 - Oct 31. Big rigs welcome. Rate in 2010 $27-31 for 2 persons. Phone: (479)253-8036. KOA discount.

(N) LAKE LEATHERWOOD CITY PARK—(Carroll) *From north Jct Hwy 23 & US 62: Go 3-1/4 mi NW on US 62, then 1-1/2 mi N on entry road. (Not suitable for Big Rigs). Enter on R.* FACILITIES: 154 sites, 35 ft max RV length, 4 full hkups, 150 no hkups, tenting, ltd groc. RECREATION: lake swim, boating, canoeing, ramp, dock, lake fishing, play equipment. Pets welcome ($). Open all yr. Facilities fully operational Mar 1 - Nov 30. Phone: (479)253-7921.

(SW) STARKEY RECREATION AREA (COE - Beaver Lake)—(Carroll) *From jct Hwy 23 & US 62: Go 4 mi NW on US 62, then SW on Hwy 187 to Mundell Rd to Starkey Park.* FACILITIES: 23 sites, 23 E, (20 amps), tenting, dump. RECREATION: lake swim, boating, ramp, lake fishing, playground. Partial handicap access. Open May 1 - Sep 8. Phone: (479)253-5866.

(E) Wanderlust RV Park—(Carroll) *From jct Hwy-23S & US-62: Go 2 mi E on US-62, then 1/2 mi N on Passion Play Rd. Enter on L.* ◆◆◆◆FACILITIES: 90 sites, typical site width 25 ft, 87 full hkups, 3 W&E, (30/50 amps), 56 pull-thrus, family camping, tenting, dump, laundry. ◆◆◆RECREATION: swim pool. Pets welcome. Partial handicap access. Open all yr. Facilities fully operational Mar 1 - Mid-Nov. Big rigs welcome. Rate in 2010 $25-27.50 for 2 persons. Phone: (800) 253-7385. FMCA discount.

FAIRFIELD BAY—B-3

FAIRFIELD BAY CAMPGROUND—(Van Buren) *From jct Hwy-9 & Hwy-16: Go 2 mi S on Hwy-16, then 4 mi S on Hwy-330.* FACILITIES: 57 sites, 16 E, 41 no hkups, tenting, dump. RECREATION: lake swim, boating, ramp, dock. Partial handicap access. Open Apr 1 - Nov 1. Phone: (501)884-6029.

The state contains six national park sites, two-and-a half million acres of national forests, seven national scenic byways, three state scenic byways, 50 state parks, over 600,000 acres of lakes and 9,700 miles of streams and rivers.

FAYETTEVILLE—A-2

(S) SOUTHGATE RV PARK OF FAYETTEVILLE—(Washington) *North Bound I-540 (exit 60): Go 500 ft S to US 71/Bus 71, then 3/4 mi N on Bus 71B. South Bound I-540 (exit 61): Go 500 ft E on US 71, then 3/4 mi N on 71B. Enter on L.*

◆◆◆FACILITIES: 50 sites, typical site width 30 ft, accepts full hkup units only, 50 full hkups, (30/50 amps), some extd stay sites, 30 pull-thrus, cable TV, WiFi Instant Internet at site, family camping, laundry, patios.

◆RECREATION: pavilion, golf nearby, sports field.

Pets welcome. Partial handicap access. No tents. Open all yr. Big rigs welcome. Escort to site. Clubs welcome. Rate in 2010 $28 for 4 persons.

Phone: (479)442-2021
Address: 2331 S School Ave, Fayetteville, AR 72701
Lat/Lon: 36.03826/-94.16759
Web: www.southgatervpark.com

SEE AD THIS PAGE

FELSENTHAL—E-3

(W) GRAND MARAIS (Union County Park)—(Union) *From jct Hwy 129 & Hwy 129B: Go 1 mi NE on Hwy 129B, then 3-1/2 mi W on CR 30.* FACILITIES: 59 sites, 9 full hkups, 50 W&E, tenting, dump, ltd groc. RECREATION: boating, ramp, river fishing. Open all yr. Phone: (870)943-2930.

FIFTY-SIX—A-3

(N) OZARK NATIONAL FOREST (Blanchard Springs Rec. Area)—(Stone) *From town: Go 1-1/2 mi E on Hwy-14, then 3-1/2 mi N on FR-1110.* FACILITIES: 31 sites, 16 ft max RV length, 31 no hkups, 1 pull-thrus, tenting, dump. RECREATION: Partial handicap access. Open all yr. Phone: (870)269-3228.

(NW) OZARK NATIONAL FOREST (Gunner Pool Rec. Area)—(Stone) *From town: Go 3 mi NW on Hwy 14, then 3 mi NE on gravel, narrow, steep FR 1102.* FACILITIES: 27 sites, 16 ft max RV length, 27 no hkups, tenting. RECREATION: stream fishing. Partial handicap access. Open all yr. Phone: (870)269-3228.

FLIPPIN—A-3

Blue Heron Campground and Resort—(Marion) *From jct Hwy 178 & AR 62: Go 4 mi E on AR 62, then 175 yds N on Bridge View Rd. Enter on L.* ◆◆◆◆FACILITIES: 31 sites, typical site width 35 ft, 6 full hkups, 25 W&E, (30/50 amps), 50 amps ($), 27 pull-thrus, WiFi Instant Internet at site, family camping, tenting, dump, non-guest dump $, portable dump, laundry, ice, picnic tables, wood. ◆◆◆RECREATION: equipped pavilion, river swim, canoeing, kayaking, float trips, river fishing, fishing supplies, fishing guides, horseshoes. Pets welcome. Partial handicap access. Open all yr. Big rigs welcome. Rate in 2010 $25-30 for 4 persons. MC/VISA. CCUSA 50% Discount. CCUSA reservations Recommended, CCUSA max stay 1 day, CCUSA disc. not avail S, CCUSA disc. not avail F,Sa. Discount available Nov thru Feb.

Phone: (870)453-4678
Address: 150 Blue Heron Dr, Flippin, AR 72634
Lat/Lon: 36.28511/-92.53196
Email: blueheron@ozarkmountains.com
Web: www.blueheroncampground.com

Hattie Caraway, senator, was from Arkansas.

FORREST CITY—C-5

(N) VILLAGE CREEK SP—(Cross) *From jct I-40 (exit 242) & Hwy-284: Go 13 mi N on Hwy-284.* FACILITIES: 96 sites, 24 full hkups, 72 W&E, (30/50 amps), tenting, dump, full svc store. RECREATION: lake swim, boating, electric motors only, canoeing, ramp, dock, lake fishing, playground. Partial handicap access. Open all yr. Phone: (870)238-9406.

FORT SMITH—B-1

See listings at Alma & Van Buren

(W) FORT SMITH VISITORS CENTER—*From jct I-40 (exit 1/Dora) & US 64 D: Go 4 mi S on US 64 D, then 1-1/2 mi E on US 64/Hwy 22, then 2 blocks N on 3rd, then 3 blocks W on North B St. Enter on L.* Visitors center is located in "Miss Laura's", a former bordello now restored & listed on the Nat'l Registry. Historic site of Hanging Judge Parker's gallows & courtroom. Tour the Victorian beauties in the Belle Grove District & Chaffer Barber Show Museum. Open all yr.

Phone: (800)637-1477
Address: 2 N. B St., Fort Smith, AR 72901
Lat/Lon: 35.39188/-94.42937
Email: tourism@fortsmith.org
Web: fortsmith.org

SEE AD TRAVEL SECTION PAGE 23

GARFIELD—A-2

(E) LOST BRIDGE PARK (COE-Beaver Lake)—(Benton) *From jct Hwy 127 & US 62: Go 5 mi SE on Hwy 127.* FACILITIES: 48 sites, 48 E, (30 amps), tenting, dump, ltd groc. RECREATION: lake swim, boating, ramp, dock, lake fishing, playground. Partial handicap access. Open Apr 1 - Sep 30. Phone: (779)359-3312.

(NW) Rogers/Pea Ridge Garden RV and Campground—(Benton) *From jct Hwy 94 & US 62: Go 6 mi NE on US 62. Enter on L.* ◆FACILITIES: 61 sites, typical site width 20 ft, 52 full hkups, 9 W&E, (20/30/50 amps), 50 amps ($), 29 pull-thrus, family camping, dump, laundry. ◆RECREATION: swim pool. Pets welcome. No tents. Open all yr. Rate in 2010 $20-25 per vehicle. Phone: (479)451-8566.

GATEWAY—A-2

(S) INDIAN CREEK RECREATION AREA (COE-Beaver Lake)—(Benton) *From jct Hwy 37 & US 62: Go 1-1/2 mi E on US 62, then 5 mi S on Indian Creek Rd.* FACILITIES: 33 sites, 33 E, (20/30 amps), tenting, dump. RECREATION: lake swim, boating, ramp, lake fishing, playground. Partial handicap access. Open May 1 - Sep 8. Phone: (479)656-3145.

GREERS FERRY—B-3

(N) DEVIL'S FORK REC. AREA (COE-Greers Ferry Lake)—(Cleburne) *1/2 mi N at jct Hwy-92 & Hwy-16.* FACILITIES: 55 sites, 55 E, (20/30 amps), tenting, dump. RECREATION: lake swim, boating, ramp, playground. Partial handicap access. Open all yr. Phone: (501)362-2416.

(N) MILL CREEK REC. AREA (COE-Greers Ferry Lake)—(Cleburne) *From jct Hwy 16 & Hwy 92: Go 1/2 mi N on Hwy 92, then 3 mi on paved access road.* FACILITIES: 39 sites, 39 no hkups, tenting. RECREATION: lake swim, boating, ramp, lake fishing. Open May 15 - Sep 15. Phone: (501)362-2416.

(W) NARROWS RECREATION AREA (COE-Greers Ferry Lake)—(Cleburne) *From jct Hwy-92 & Hwy-16: Go 2 mi S on Hwy-16.* FACILITIES: 60 sites, 60 E, (20/30 amps), 2 pull-thrus, tenting, dump. RECREATION: boating, ramp, dock, lake fishing. Partial handicap access. Open Apr 1 - Oct 31. Phone: (501)362-2416.

GREERS FERRY—Continued

(SE) SHILOH RECREATION AREA (COE-Greers Ferry Lake)—(Cleburne) *From jct Hwy-92 & Hwy-110: Go 3 mi S on Hwy-110.* FACILITIES: 116 sites, 60 E, (20/30 amps), 56 no hkups, tenting, dump, ltd groc. RECREATION: lake swim, boating, ramp, dock, lake fishing, playground. Partial handicap access. Open Apr 1 - Nov 1. Phone: (501)362-2416.

(S) SUGAR LOAF REC. AREA (COE-Greers Ferry Lake)—(VanBuren) *4-1/2 mi S on Hwy-16, then 2-1/2 mi SW on Hwy-92 & 337.* FACILITIES: 95 sites, 56 E, (20/30 amps), 39 no hkups, tenting, dump. RECREATION: lake swim, boating, ramp, dock, lake fishing, playground. Partial handicap access. Open Apr 1 - Nov 1. Phone: (501)362-2416.

HAMPTON—E-3

(N) Silver Eagle RV Campground—(Calhoun) *From jct US 167 and US 278: Go 1/2 mi N on US 167. Enter on R.* ◆◆◆FACILITIES: 24 sites, typical site width 25 ft, 24 full hkups, (20/30/50 amps), 13 pull-thrus, cable TV, family camping, laundry. RECREATION: play equipment. Pets welcome. No tents. Open all yr. Big rigs welcome. Rate in 2010 $20 per vehicle. CCUSA 50% Discount. CCUSA reservations Accepted, CCUSA max stay 2 days, Cash only for CCUSA disc.

Phone: (870)798-3798
Address: 473 N Lee, Hampton, AR 71744
Lat/Lon: 32.54390/-92.46780

HARDY—A-4

(E) HARDY CAMPER PARK (City Park)—(Sharp) *From west jct US 62 & US 63: Go 1/4 mi E on US 62/63, then 2 blocks S on Spring St. Enter on R.* FACILITIES: 76 sites, 76 W&E, 14 pull-thrus, tenting, dump, laundry. RECREATION: river swim, boating, canoeing, river fishing. Pets welcome. Open all yr. Phone: (870)856-2356.

HARRISBURG—B-5

(SE) LAKE POINSETT SP—(Pointsett) *From jct Hwy 14 & Hwy 163: Go 3 mi S on Hwy 163.* FACILITIES: 29 sites, 26 W&E, (30/50 amps), 3 no hkups, tenting, dump. RECREATION: boating, canoeing, ramp, lake fishing, playground. Partial handicap access. Open all yr. Phone: (870)578-2064.

HARRISON—A-3

(S) HARRISON VILLAGE CAMPGROUND & RV PARK—(Boone) *S'bnd: From jct Hwy 7 & US 62/65: Go 3-1/2 mi SE on US 65 S. Enter on R. N'bnd: From jct Hwy 412/62E/65 N: Go 1-1/2 mi Non US 65N. Ener on L. Enter on R.*

◆◆◆◆FACILITIES: 79 sites, typical site width 24 ft, 38 full hkups, 41 W&E, (20/30/50 amps), 50 amps ($), some extd stay sites, 72 pull-thrus, cable TV, WiFi Instant Internet at site, phone Internet central location, family camping, tenting, RV storage, dump, non-guest dump $, laundry, RV supplies, LP gas by weight/by meter, ice, picnic tables, fire rings, grills, wood.

HARRISON VILLAGE CAMPGROUND & RV PARK—Continued on next page

The state's highest point is Mount Magazine at 2,753 feet above sea level and the lowest is the southern part of the state, 54 feet above sea level.

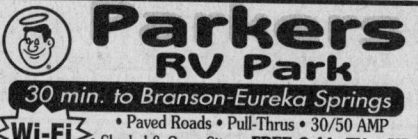

◊◊RECREATION: rec hall, pavilion, swim pool, golf nearby, horseshoes, sports field, v-ball.

Pets welcome. Partial handicap access. Open all yr. Memorial Day - Labor Day. Big rigs welcome. Escort to site. Clubs welcome. Rate in 2010 $24-29 for 2 persons. MC/VISA/Debit. CCUSA 50% Discount. CCUSA reservations Required, CCUSA max stay 1 day, CCUSA disc. not avail S, CCUSA disc. not avail F,Sa, CCUSA disc. not avail holidays. Discount available Dec thru Mar.

Phone: (870)743-3388
Address: 2364 US Highway 65 South, Harrison, AR 72601
Lat/Lon: 36.20554/-93.05982
Email: harrisonvillage@yahoo.com
Web: www.harrisonvillagervpark.com

SEE AD PAGE 31

✲ **(N) JORDAN'S RV SERVICE**—*From jct Hwy 7 & US 62/65: Go 3-1/2 mi N on US 62/65. Enter on L.* SALES: pre-owned unit sales. SERVICES: full-time mech, engine/chassis repair, RV appliance repair, body work/collision repair, bus. hrs emerg rd svc, mobile RV svc, LP gas by weight/by meter, dump station, RV storage, sells parts/accessories, installs hitches. Open all yr. MC/VISA/DISC/AMEX/Debit.

Phone: (870)743-6628
Address: 3629 Hwy 65 N, Harrison, AR 72601
Lat/Lon: 36.28268/-93.16573

SEE AD PAGE 31

(N) PARKERS RV PARK—(Boone) *S'bnd from N jct Hwy 412/US 62: Go 1-1/4 mi S on US 65. Enter on R. N'bnd from S jct Hwy 412/US 65: Go 8 mi N on US 65. Enter on L. Enter on L.*

◊◊◊◊FACILITIES: 41 sites, typical site width 45 ft, 41 full hkups, (20/30/50 amps), 50 amps ($), some extd stay sites, 6 pull-thrus, cable TV, WiFi Instant Internet at site ($), WiFi Internet central location, family camping, RV storage, dump, non-guest dump $, laundry, ltd groc, RV supplies, LP gas by weight/by meter, ice, picnic tables.

Maya Angelou, poet and author, is from Arkansas.

HARRISON—Continued
PARKERS RV PARK—Continued

◊◊RECREATION: rec hall, equipped pavilion, fishing guides, golf nearby, horseshoes.

Pets welcome. Partial handicap access. No tents. Open all yr. Big rigs welcome. Escort to site. Clubs welcome. Rate in 2010 $21.95 for 2 persons. MC/VISA/DISC/AMEX/Debit. FCRV discount. FMCA discount. CCUSA 50% Discount. CCUSA reservations Recommended, CCUSA max stay 1 day, Cash only for CCUSA disc., CCUSA disc. not avail F,Sa, CCUSA disc. not avail holidays. Discount available Dec thru Mar. WiFi surcharge $3.95.

Phone: (870)743-2267
Address: 3629 US Highway 65 N, Harrison, AR 72601
Lat/Lon: 36.28262/-93.16573
Email: parkersrv@eritter.net
Web: www.parkersrvinc.com

Reserve Online at Woodalls.com

SEE AD PAGE 31

(S) Parkway Travel Park—(Boone) *From jct US 62/65 & Hwy 7: Go 7-1/4 mi S on Hwy 7. Enter on L.* ◊◊FACILITIES: 24 sites, typical site width 20 ft, 24 full hkups, (30/50 amps), 50 amps ($), 3 pull-thrus, family camping, tenting, laundry. RECREATION: play equipment. Pets welcome. Open all yr. Rate in 2010 $24-26 for 2 persons. Phone: (870)743-2198.

(S) SHADY OAKS CAMPGROUND & RV PARK—(Boone) *From jct US 62/65 & Hwy 7: Go 7 mi S on Hwy 7, then 1 mi E on Hwy 206. Enter on R.*

◊◊◊FACILITIES: 50 sites, 21 full hkups, 15 W&E, 6 E, (20/30/50 amps), 50 amps ($), 8 no hkups, some extd stay sites, 28 pull-thrus, cable TV, WiFi Instant Internet at site ($), WiFi Internet central location, family camping, tenting, RV's/park model rentals, cabins, dump, non-guest dump $, laundry, ltd groc, RV supplies, ice, picnic tables, fire rings, wood.

◊◊◊RECREATION: equipped pavilion, swim pool, golf nearby, bsktball, playground, horseshoes, v-ball.

Pets welcome. Open all yr. Pool open Memorial Day - Sep. Escort to site. Rate in 2010 $26-28 for 2 persons. MC/VISA/Debit. CCUSA 50% Discount. CCUSA reservations Accepted, CCUSA max stay 1 day, CCUSA disc. not avail holidays. Discount not available May 15-Oct 15. Tent sites not included in discount, electric sites only. WiFi surcharge $2.

HARRISON—Continued
SHADY OAKS CAMPGROUND & RV PARK—Continued

Phone: (870)743-2343
Address: 960 Hwy 206E, Harrison, AR 72601
Lat/Lon: 36.14310/-93.10567
Email: shadyoaks@cox.net
Web: camptheoaks.com

SEE AD PAGE 31

HAZEN—C-4

(N) T Ricks RV Park (RV SPACES)—*(Prairie) From jct I-40 (exit 193) & Hwy 11: Go 100 feet S of overpass on Hwy 11. Enter on L.* FACILITIES: 36 sites, typical site width 24 ft, accepts full hkup units only, 36 full hkups, (20/30/50 amps), 50 amps ($), 30 pull-thrus, dump, ltd groc. Pets welcome. No tents. Open all yr. Big rigs welcome. Rate in 2010 $18 per vehicle. Phone: (870) 255-4914.

HEBER SPRINGS—B-4

(N) DAM SITE RECREATION AREA (COE-Greers Ferry Lake)—(Cleburne) *From town: Go 3 mi N on Hwy 25B.* FACILITIES: 252 sites, 148 E, (20/30/50 amps), 104 no hkups, 5 pull-thrus, tenting, dump. RECREATION: lake swim, boating, ramp, dock, playground. Partial handicap access. Open all yr. Phone: (501)362-2416.

(W) HEBER SPRINGS RECREATION AREA (COE-Greers Ferry Lake)—(Cleburne) *From town: Go 2 mi W on Hwy 110, then 1/2 mi N on access rd.* FACILITIES: 142 sites, 106 E, (20/30 amps), 36 no hkups, tenting, dump, ltd groc. RECREATION: lake swim, boating, ramp, dock, lake fishing, playground. Partial handicap access. Open Apr 1 - Oct 31. Phone: (501)362-2416.

(NE) JOHN F. KENNEDY (COE-Greers Ferry Lake)—(Cleburne) *From town: Go 4 mi N on Hwy 25, cross dam, then right on access road.* FACILITIES: 74 sites, 13 W&E, 61 E, (20/30 amps), tenting, dump. RECREATION: boating, ramp, river fishing, playground. Partial handicap access. Open all yr. Phone: (501)362-2416.

(S) Lindsey's Resort on the Little Red River—(Cleburne) *From jct AR 16 & AR 25: Go 6 mi S on AR 25, then 3 mi E on Rainbow Rd. Enter on R.* ◊◊◊FACILITIES: 24 sites, typical site width 25 ft, 24 full hkups, (20/30/50 amps), family camping, tenting, dump. ◊◊◊RECREATION: swim pool, river swim, boating, ramp, dock, river fishing, play equipment. Pets welcome. Open all yr. Big rigs welcome. Rate in 2010 $28 for 2 persons. Phone: (501)362-3139.

(N) OLD HWY-25 CAMPGROUND (COE-Greers Ferry Lake)—(Cleburne) *From town: Go 6-1/2 mi N on Hwy 25, then 3 mi W on old Hwy 25.* FACILITIES: 125 sites, 89 E, (20/30 amps), 36 no hkups, tenting, dump. RECREATION: boating, ramp, playground. Partial handicap access. Open Apr 1 - Oct 31. Phone: (501)362-2416.

HENDERSON—A-3

(S) HENDERSON REC. AREA (COE-Norfork Lake)—(Baxter) *From jct Hwy-101 & US-62: Go 1/4 mi S off US-62.* FACILITIES: 38 sites, 30 E, 8 no hkups, tenting, dump. RECREATION: lake swim, boating, canoeing, ramp, dock, lake fishing. Pets welcome. Open Apr 1 - Sep 30. Phone: (870)488-5282.

HOPE—D-2

(SW) FAIR PARK RV PARK (City Park)—(Hempstead) *From jct I-30 (exit 30) & Hwy 4: Go 1 mi S on Hwy 4, then 3 blocks W on US 67, then 5 blocks S on Hwy 174, then 3 blocks W on entry road. Enter at end.* FACILITIES: 400 sites, typical site width 25 ft, 400 W&E, (30 amps), 50 pull-thrus, tenting, dump, laundry. RECREATION: swim pool, lake fishing, playground. Open all yr. Phone: (870)777-7500.

HOT SPRINGS—C-3

CATHERINE'S LANDING AT HOT SPRINGS (UNDER CONSTRUCTION)—(Garland) *1700 Shady Grove Rd, Hot Springs, AR 71901. Enter on R.*

LAKESIDE LUXURY

Opening in February 2011, Catherine's Landing at Hot Springs features premier RV sites, custom Cottages & Yurts, community lodge, private boat ramp & pontoon boat rentals & is minutes from the historic downtown Hot Springs.

Text 108000 to (440)725-8687 to see our Visual Tour.

Phone: (501)262-2550
Address: 1700 Shady Grove Rd, Hot Springs, AR 71901
Lat/Lon: 34.45176/-93.00051
Email: catherineslanding@rvcoutdoors.com
Web: www.catherineslandings.rvcoutdoors.com

SEE AD NEXT PAGE

HOT SPRINGS—Continued on next page

Dizzy Dean, baseball player, was from Arkansas.

HOT SPRINGS—Continued

(NE) CLOUD NINE RV PARK—(Garland) *From jct Hwy 7 & US 70B: Go 12 mi E on US 70B/US70. Enter on R.*

WELCOME

◇◇◇◇FACILITIES: 49 sites, typical site width 30 ft, 45 full hkups, 4 E, (20/30/50 amps), 15 pull-thrus, cable TV, WiFi Instant Internet at site, WiFi Internet central location, family camping, tenting, dump, non-guest dump $, laundry, ice, picnic tables, wood.

◇◇◇RECREATION: rec hall, rec room/area, pavilion, horseshoes, hiking trails.

Pets welcome. Partial handicap access. Open all yr. Fire pits available at designated areas. Big rigs welcome. Escort to site. Clubs welcome. Rate in 2010 $28 for 2 persons. MC/VISA/Debit.

Phone: (501)262-1996
Address: 136 Cloud Nine Dr, Hot Springs, AR 71901
Lat/Lon: 34.54310/-92.88280
Email: Cloudninervpark@aol.com
Web: www.cloudninerv.com

SEE AD PAGE 32

(E) HOT SPRINGS NATIONAL PARK - KOA—(Garland) *E'bnd from jct Hwy 7 & US 70B (Grand Ave): Go 3 mi E on US 70B (exit 4), then 100 yds N under overpass, then 200 yds E on Service Rd. Enter on L. W'bnd: Grom jct US 70 & US 70B: Go 1-1/4 mi W on US 70B (exit 4), then 3/4 mi W on Service Rd. Enter on R.*

WELCOME

◇◇◇◇◇FACILITIES: 77 sites, typical site width 25 ft, 68 full hkups, 9 W&E, (20/30/50 amps), 15 pull-thrus, cable TV, WiFi Instant Internet at site, WiFi Internet central location, tenting, RV's/park model rentals, cabins, RV storage, dump, non-guest dump $, laundry, ltd groc, RV supplies, LP gas by weight/by meter, ice, picnic tables, patios, fire rings, grills, wood.

◇◇◇◇◇RECREATION: rec hall, rec room/area, pavilion, equipped pavilion, coin games, swim pool, pond fishing, mini-golf, golf nearby, bsktball, bike rental, playground, activities, sports field, v-ball, local tours.

Pets welcome. Partial handicap access. Open all yr. Pool open mid Mar - end Oct. Big rigs welcome. Escort to site. Clubs welcome. Rate in 2010 $28-70 for 2 persons. MC/VISA/DISC/AMEX/Debit. ATM. KOA discount.

Phone: (501)624-5912
Address: 838 McClendon Rd., Hot Springs, AR 71901
Lat/Lon: 34.50822/-93.00703
Email: agbarrett@aol.com
Web: www.hotspringskoa.com

SEE AD PAGE 32

(E) HOT SPRINGS NP (Gulpha Gorge Campground)—(Garland) *From jct US 70 & US 70B: Go 1/2 mi N on US 70B.* FACILITIES: 43 sites, 43 no hkups, tenting, dump. RECREATION: Pets welcome. Partial handicap access. Open all yr. Phone: (501) 620-6743.

(E) J & J RV Park—(Garland) *E'Bnd: From jct Hwy 7 & US 70B (Grand Ave): Go 3 mi E on US 70B, (exit 4). W'bnd from US 70B (exit 3): Go 200 yds S across overpass, then 1/2 mi E on East Grand. Enter on R.* ◇◇◇◇FACILITIES: 46 sites, typical site width 26 ft,

HOT SPRINGS—Continued
J & J RV Park—Continued

46 full hkups, (30/50 amps), 18 pull-thrus, family camping, laundry. ◇◇RECREATION: river swim, river fishing, play equipment. Pets welcome. Partial handicap access. No tents. Open all yr. Big rigs welcome. Rate in 2010 $29.50 for 2 persons. Phone: (501)321-9852.

(W) Lake Hamilton RV Resort—(Garland) *From west jct US 270B (Albert Pike) & US 270: Go 1 mi W on US 270. Enter on L.* ◇◇◇FACILITIES: 81 sites, typical site width 25 ft, 81 full hkups, (30/50 amps), 11 pull-thrus, family camping, dump, laundry. ◇◇◇RECREATION: swim pool, lake swim, boating, canoeing, ramp, dock, lake fishing. Pets welcome, breed restrict. Partial handicap access. No tents. Open all yr. Big rigs welcome. Rate in 2010 $27.13-37.98 for 2 persons. Phone: (501)767-4400. FCRV discount. FMCA discount.

(N) LAKE OUACHITA SP—(Garland) *From jct US-270 & Hwy-227: Go 12 mi N on Hwy-227.* FACILITIES: 101 sites, 40 full hkups, 25 W&E, (30/50 amps), 36 no hkups, 2 pull-thrus, tenting, dump, ltd groc. RECREATION: lake swim, boating, canoeing, ramp, lake fishing, playground. Open all yr. Phone: (501)767-9366.

HOT SPRINGS—Continued

Leisure Landing RV Park (RV SPACES)—(Garland) *From jct US 270 & Hwy 7: Go 5-1/2 mi S on Hwy 7, then 1/4 mi E on Hwy 290, then 1/4 mi E on Broadview. Enter on L.* FACILITIES: 33 sites, 33 full hkups, (20/30/50 amps), laundry. RECREATION: lake fishing. No tents. Open all yr. Rate in 2010 $25-32 for 2 persons. Phone: (501)525-3289.

(W) OUACHITA NATIONAL FOREST (Charlton Rec. Area)—(Garland) *20 mi W on US-270.* FACILITIES: 57 sites, 22 ft max RV length, 9 full hkups, 48 no hkups, tenting, dump. RECREATION: lake/river swim, lake/stream fishing. Partial handicap access. Open May 1 - Oct 31. Phone: (870)867-2101.

✲ **(W) RAZORBACK CAMPER SALES**—*From jct US 270 (MLK Expwy) & US 270B (Albert Pike): Go 1/4 mi E on US 270 B (Albert Pike). Enter on L.* SALES: travel trailers, 5th wheels, toy hauler, pre-owned unit sales. SERVICES: full-time mech, RV appliance repair, body work/collision repair, LP gas by weight/by meter, sells parts/accessories, installs hitches. Open all yr. MC/VISA/DISC/AMEX/Debit.

WELCOME

RAZORBACK CAMPER SALES—Continued on next page

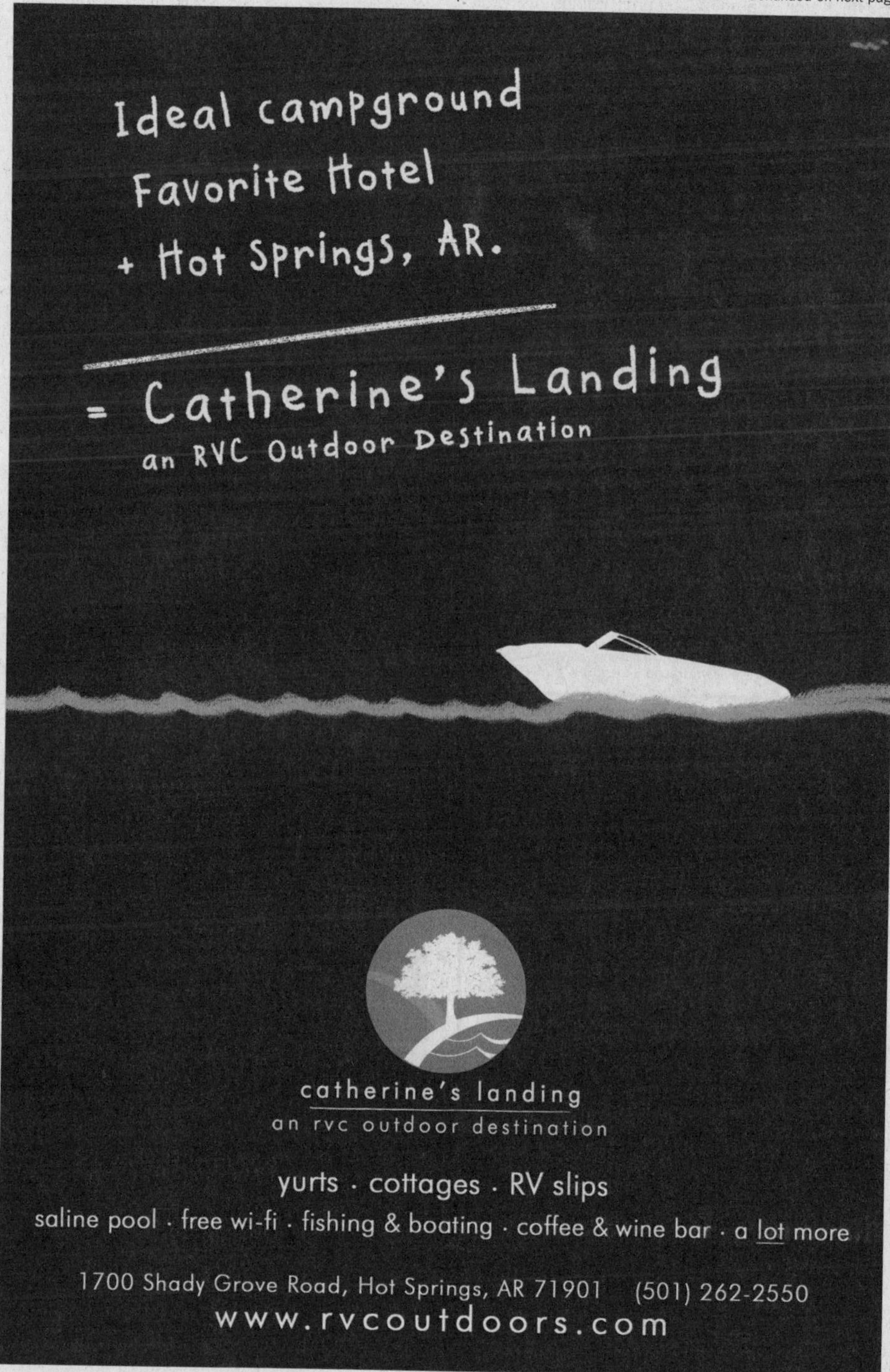

Ideal campground
Favorite Hotel
+ Hot Springs, AR.
= Catherine's Landing
an RVC Outdoor Destination
catherine's landing
an rvc outdoor destination
yurts · cottages · RV slips
saline pool · free wi-fi · fishing & boating · coffee & wine bar · a lot more
1700 Shady Grove Road, Hot Springs, AR 71901 (501) 262-2550
www.rvcoutdoors.com

HOT SPRINGS—Continued
RAZORBACK CAMPER SALES—Continued

Phone: (501)767-3486
Address: 2320 Albert Pike, Hot Springs, AR 71913
Lat/Lon: 34.49226/-93.10836
Email: razorbackcampers@aol.com
Web: www.razorbackcampersales.com

SEE AD PAGE 33

(S) Timbercrest RV & Mobile Home Park (RV SPACES)—(Garland) *From jct US 70B & Hwy 7: Go 3 mi S on Hwy 7. Enter on L.* FACILITIES: 54 sites, typical site width 20 ft, accepts full hkup units only, 54 full hkups, (20/30/50 amps). Pets welcome. No tents. Open all yr. Rate in 2010 $17 for 2 persons. Phone: (501)525-8361.

(W) TREASURE ISLE RV PARK—(Garland) *From W jct US 270 B (Albert Pike) & US 270: Go 4-1/2 mi W on US 270, then 1/4 mi N on Treasure Isle Rd. Enter on L.*

◇◇◇FACILITIES: 64 sites, typical site width 50 ft, 64 full hkups, (20/30/50 amps), some extd stay sites, 45 pull-thrus, WiFi Instant Internet at site, family camping, tenting, cabins, RV storage, laundry, ice, picnic tables, fire rings, grills, wood.

◇◇◇RECREATION: pavilion, equipped pavilion, swim pool, lake swim, boating, canoeing, kayaking, ramp, dock, 2 canoe rentals, lake fishing, golf nearby, bsktball, play equipment, hiking trails.

Pets welcome. Open all yr. Pool open Memorial-Labor Day. Big rigs welcome. Escort to site. Clubs welcome. Rate in 2010 $25-30 for 2 persons. MC/VISA/Debit.

Phone: (501)767-6852
Address: 205 Treasure Isle Rd., Hot Springs, AR 71913
Lat/Lon: 34.51056/-93.17834
Email: treasureislerv@gmail.com
Web: www.treasureisle.com

SEE AD PAGE 33

(W) Young's Lakeshore RV Resort—(Garland) *From jct Hwy 7 & US 270 (MLK Expwy): Go 1-3/4 mi W on US 270/70, then 1000 ft SW on Mc Leod. Enter at end.* ◇◇FACILITIES: 44 sites, typical site width 30 ft, 42 full hkups, 2 W&E, (20/30/50 amps), 16 pull-thrus, family camping, tenting, dump, laundry. ◇◇◇RECREATION: lake swim, boating, canoeing, ramp, dock, lake fishing. Pets welcome. Partial handicap access. Open all yr. Big rigs welcome. Rate in 2010 $26-33 for 2 persons. Phone: (800)470-7875. FCRV discount. FMCA discount.

HUNTSVILLE—A-2

(N) WITHROW SPRINGS SP—(Madison) *From jct US 412 & Hwy 23: Go 5 mi N on Hwy 23.* FACILITIES: 55 sites, 30 full hkups, 17 W&E, (20/30 amps), 8 no hkups, tenting, dump. RECREATION: swim pool, canoeing, river fishing, playground. Partial handicap access. Open all yr. Phone: (479)559-2593.

Good Sam Park
PECAN GROVE
RV PARK
All 70+ Ft. Level Pull-thrus
ON LAKE CHICOT — GREAT FISHING!
• Full Hookups • Laundry • Country Store
• RV Supplies • Gasoline & Diesel • Marine Gas
• Fish Cleaning Station • Historic Cabins
• Boating • Ramp • Dock • Cable TV
www.pecangrove.net
(870) 265-3005
Free WI-FI
LAT. 33.29610
LON. 91.27530
To Little Rock
Lake Chicot
Lake Village
To Texarkana
Pecan Grove
To I-20
To Greenville MS
3768 Highway 82 & 65 South
Lake Village, AR 71653
See listing at Lake Village, AR

JACKSONPORT—B-4

(NW) JACKSONPORT SP—(Jackson) *From jct US 67 & Hwy 69: Go 3 mi N on Hwy 69.* FACILITIES: 20 sites, 20 W&E, (50 amps), tenting. RECREATION: boating, ramp, river fishing, playground. Partial handicap access. Open all yr. Phone: (870)523-2143.

JACKSONVILLE—C-4

(N) MILITARY PARK (Little Rock AFB FAMCAMP)—(Pulaski) *From US 67/167 (exit 11): Go 17 mi N. On base.* FACILITIES: 16 sites, 10 full hkups, 6 W&E, tenting, dump. RECREATION: boating. Open all yr. Phone: (501)987-3365.

JONESBORO—B-5

(S) CRAIGHEAD FOREST PARK (City Park)—(Craighead) *From jct US 63 (exit 44) & Hwy 1B: Go 1 block S on Hwy 1B, then 1 mi W on Parker Rd, then 2 mi S on Culberhouse St (Hwy 141) to Forest Park Dr.*

FACILITIES: 26 sites, 40 ft max RV length, 26 W&E, (30/50 amps), family camping, tenting, dump, non-guest dump $, laundry, picnic tables, patios, fire rings, grills.

RECREATION: pavilion, boating, 5 hp limit, canoeing, ramp, dock, lake fishing, golf nearby, bsktball, playground, horseshoes, sports field, hiking trails, v-ball. Rec open to public.

Pets welcome. Partial handicap access. Open all yr. Facilities fully operational mid Apr - Oct. MC/VISA/DISC/AMEX/Debit.

Phone: (870)933-4604
Address: 4910 S Culberhouse, Jonesboro, AR 72403
Lat/Lon: 35.77919/-90.71394
Email: bwelbourne@jonesboro.org
Web: www.jonesborosports.org

SEE AD THIS PAGE

(SW) Perkins RV Park—(Craighead) *From jct AR 49/Hwy 1 & US 63 (exit 42): Go 1/4 mi W on South Side Service Rd (Parker Rd). Enter on L.* ◇◇◇FACILITIES: 42 sites, typical site width 22 ft, accepts full hkup units only, 42 full hkups, (30/50 amps), 50 amps ($), 11 pull-thrus, dump. Pets welcome. Partial handicap access. No tents. Open all yr. Big rigs welcome. Rate in 2010 $23-26 for 2 persons.

Phone: (870)897-5700
Address: 1821 E Parker Rd, Jonesboro, AR 72404
Lat/Lon: 35.806744/-90.68280

JORDAN—A-3

(N) JORDAN RECREATION AREA (COE-Norfork Lake)—(Baxter) *From jct Hwy 177 & CR 64: Go 3 mi N on CR 64.* FACILITIES: 38 sites, 31 E, (20 amps), 7 no hkups, tenting, dump, ltd groc. RECREATION: lake swim, boating, ramp, dock, lake fishing. Pets welcome. Open Apr 1 - Sep 30. Phone: (870)499-7223.

LAKE VILLAGE—E-4

(NW) LAKE CHICOT COUNTY PARK—(Bowie) *From jct US 65 & US 82: Go 5 mi S on US 82, then 3 blocks W on CR 403, then 1-1/2 mi N on Hwy 144 N, then 7 mi E on Lakehall Rd. Enter on R.* FACILITIES: 80 sites, 80 full hkups, family camping. RECREATION: Phone: (870)265-3500.

(NE) LAKE CHICOT SP—(Chicot) *From jct US-65 & Hwy-144: Go 8 mi NE on Hwy-144.* FACILITIES: 122 sites, 55 full hkups, 67 W&E, (20/30/50 amps), tenting, dump, laundry, ltd groc. RECREATION: swim pool, boating, ramp, dock, lake fishing, playground. Partial handicap access. Open all yr. Phone: (870) 265-5480.

Crater of Diamonds State Park outside of Murfreesboro allows dedicated prospectors to search for diamonds, amethyst, garnet, jasper, agate, and quartz.

LAKE VILLAGE—Continued

(S) PECAN GROVE RV PARK—(Bowie) *From north jct US 82 & US 65: Go 2-3/4 mi S on US 82/65. Entrance on right. From south jct US 82 & US 65: Go 2-1/2 mi N on US 82/65. Entrance on left. Enter on L.*

◇◇◇◇FACILITIES: 114 sites, typical site width 50 ft, 114 full hkups, (30/50 amps), 50 amps ($), many extd stay sites, 108 pull-thrus, cable TV, ($), WiFi Instant Internet at site, WiFi Internet central location, family camping, tenting, cabins, RV storage, laundry, ltd groc, RV supplies, picnic tables, grills, wood.

◇◇◇◇RECREATION: rec hall, pavilion, equipped pavilion, lake swim, boating, canoeing, kayaking, ramp, dock, lake fishing, fishing supplies, golf nearby, bsktball, playground, horseshoes, sports field, hiking trails, v-ball. Rec open to public.

Pets welcome. Open all yr. Big rigs welcome. Clubs welcome. Rate in 2010 $20-25 for 2 persons. FMCA discount.

Phone: (870)265-3005
Address: 3768 Hwy 82 & 65 S, Lake Village, AR 71653
Lat/Lon: 33.29610/-91.27530
Email: deebill@cei.net
Web: www.pecangrove.net

SEE AD THIS PAGE

LAKEVIEW—A-3

(N) LAKEVIEW PUBLIC USE AREA (COE-Bull Shoals Lake)—(Baxter) *1 mi N on Hwy-178.* FACILITIES: 89 sites, 17 W&E, 72 E, (30 amps), tenting, dump. RECREATION: lake swim, boating, ramp, dock, lake fishing, playground. Partial handicap access. Open Apr 1 - Oct 1. Phone: (870)431-8116.

LANGLEY—D-2

(NW) OUACHITA NATIONAL FOREST (Albert Pike Campground)—(Montgomery) *From town: Go 2 mi N on Hwy 369, then 4 mi NW on FR 73.* FACILITIES: 54 sites, 22 ft max RV length, 8 W&E, 46 no hkups, 2 pull-thrus, tenting, dump, laundry, ltd groc. RECREATION: boating, no motors, canoeing. Partial handicap access. Open all yr. Facilities fully operational early Mar - early Nov. Phone: (870)356-4186.

LEAD HILL—A-3

(N) LEAD HILL PUBLIC USE AREA (COE-Bull Shoals Lake)—(Boone) *4 mi N on Hwy-7.* FACILITIES: 75 sites, 75 E, (30 amps), tenting, dump, ltd groc. RECREATION: lake swim, boating, ramp, dock, lake fishing, playground. Partial handicap access. Open Apr 1 - Oct 31. Phone: (870)422-7555.

(NW) TUCKER HOLLOW (COE-Bull Shoals Lake)—(Boone) *From jct Hwy 7 & Hwy 14: Go 7 mi NW on Hwy 14, then 2 mi N on Hwy 281.* FACILITIES: 30 sites, 30 E, (30 amps), tenting, dump, ltd groc. RECREATION: lake swim, boating, canoeing, ramp, dock, lake fishing, playground. Partial handicap access. Open Apr 1 - Oct 31. Phone: (870)436-5622.

LINWOOD—D-4

(NE) RISING STAR (COE-Pine Bluff River Area)—(Jefferson) *From US 65 in town: Go 3-1/2 mi NE on paved county road.* FACILITIES: 24 sites, 24 W&E, tenting, dump. RECREATION: boating, ramp, dock, river fishing, playground. Partial handicap access. Open Mar 1 - Oct 31. Phone: (870)534-0451.

LITTLE ROCK—C-3

FRED & JACK TRAILER SALES—*From jct I-430 & I-30 (exit 129): Go 4 mi W on I-30 (exit 126), then 2 mi W on North Service Rd.* SALES: travel trailers, 5th wheels, Class A motorhomes, Class C motorhomes, Class B motorhomes, pre-owned unit sales. SERVICES: full-time mech, RV appliance repair, body work/collision repair, LP

FRED & JACK TRAILER SALES—Continued on next page

FRED & JACK
TRAILER SALES
EST. 1952
SALES • SERVICE • PARTS
Owned and Operated by the Davie Family Since 1952
1-800-721-9180
ROUTE 66
24218 I-30 West, Bryant, AR
Between Exits 126 & 123
www.FredandJack.com
GPS 34.62893 Lat.
92.47845 Lon.
Dutchmen
EVERGREEN
Four Winds
See listing at Little Rock, AR

LITTLE ROCK—Continued
FRED & JACK TRAILER SALES—Continued

gas by weight/by meter, dump station, RV storage, sells parts/accessories, installs hitches. Open all yr. MC/VISA/DISC.

Phone: (501)847-2617
Address: 24218 I-30, Bryant, AR 72022
Lat/Lon: 34.62870/-92.47860
Web: www.fredandjack.com

SEE AD PAGE 34

I-30 TRAVEL PARK—*From jct I-430 & I-30 (exit 129): Go 8 mi W on I-30 (exit 121), then 1 mi W on Service Rd, then Cross-over freeway on Hwy 5 overpass, make loop, then 1/2 mi E on E'bnd serice road.*

SEE PRIMARY LISTING AT BENTON AND AD THIS PAGE

(NW) MAUMELLE (COE-Toad Suck Ferry)—(Pulaski) *From jct I-430 (exit 2) & Hwy 10: Go 3 mi S on Hwy 10, then 3 mi N on Pinnacle Valley Rd.* FACILITIES: 129 sites, 129 W&E, (30/50 amps), tenting, dump. RECREATION: boating, canoeing, ramp, dock, river fishing, playground. Partial handicap access. Open all yr. Phone: (501)868-9477.

MALVERN—D-3

(N) LAKE CATHERINE SP—(Hot Spring) *From I-30 (exit 97): Go 12 mi N on Hwy-171.* FACILITIES: 70 sites, 44 full hkups, 26 W&E, (20/30/50 amps), tenting, dump, laundry, ltd groc. RECREATION: lake swim, boating, ramp, dock, lake fishing, playground. Partial handicap access. Open all yr. Phone: (501)844-4176.

MARIANNA—C-5

(SE) ST. FRANCIS NATIONAL FOREST (Boundary Campground)—(Lee) *From town: Go 7 mi SE on Hwy 44.* FACILITIES: 41 sites, 22 ft max RV length, 41 no hkups, tenting. RECREATION: lake swim, boating, 10 hp limit, canoeing, ramp, dock, lake fishing. Partial handicap access. Open May - Dec. Phone: (870)295-5278.

MARION—B-5

(NW) MEMPHIS KOA—(Crittenden) *North Bound from jct I-40 & I-55: Go 7 mi N on I-55 (exit 14), then follow camping logo signs to entrance on west service road. South Bound I-55 (exit 14): Continue 500 yards on West Service Road. Enter on R.*

◇◇◇◇FACILITIES: 104 sites, typical site width 25 ft, 78 full hkups, 15 W&E, 8 E, (20/30/50 amps), 50 amps ($), 3 no hkups, some extd stay sites, 51 pull-thrus, WiFi Instant Internet at site,

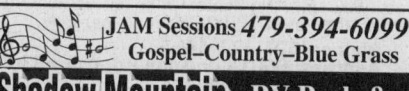

MARION—Continued
MEMPHIS KOA—Continued

WiFi Internet central location, family camping, tenting, cabins, RV storage, dump, non-guest dump $, laundry, ltd groc, RV supplies, LP gas by meter, ice, picnic tables, grills.

◇◇◇◇RECREATION: rec hall, rec room/area, coin games, swim pool, golf nearby, bsktball, 12 bike rentals, playground, activities, horseshoes, sports field.

Pets welcome. Partial handicap access. Open all yr. Big rigs welcome. Clubs welcome. Green Friendly. Rate in 2010 $32-43 for 2 persons. MC/VISA/DISC/AMEX/Debit. Member ARVC, MOARC. KOA discount.

Phone: (800)562-3240
Address: 7037 Interstate 55, Marion, AR 72364
Lat/Lon: 35.26141/-90.22750
Email: info@memphiskoa.com
Web: memphiskoa.com

SEE AD MEMPHIS, TN PAGE 735 AND AD TRAVEL SECTION PAGE 23

MENA—C-2

(W) QUEEN WILHELMINA SP—(Polk) *From jct US-71 & Hwy-88: Go 13 mi NW on Hwy-88.* FACILITIES: 41 sites, 35 W&E, (20/30 amps), 6 no hkups, tenting, dump, laundry, ltd groc. RECREATION: playground. Partial handicap access. Open all yr. Phone: (479)394-2863.

(S) SHADOW MOUNTAIN RV PARK—(Polk) *From mid town Mena: Go 6 mi S on US 71. Enter on R.*

◇◇◇FACILITIES: 65 sites, typical site width 22 ft, 50 full hkups, 15 W&E, (20/30/50 amps), 50 amps ($), 57 pull-thrus, cable TV, WiFi Instant Internet at site, family camping, tenting, cabins, RV storage, dump, non-guest dump $, laundry, ice, picnic tables, fire rings, wood.

◇◇◇RECREATION: rec room/area, swim pool, lake fishing, golf nearby, bsktball, play equipment, activities (wkends), horseshoes, hiking trails.

Pets welcome. Open all yr. Pool open Memorial Day thru Labor Day. Big rigs welcome. Escort to site. Clubs welcome. Rate in 2010 $18-33 for 2 persons. FMCA discount. CCUSA 50% Discount. CCUSA reservations Recommended, CCUSA max stay 1 day, Cash only for CCUSA disc., CCUSA disc. not avail Th, CCUSA disc. not avail F,Sa, CCUSA disc. not avail holidays. Discount available Nov thru Feb.

Woodall's Campground Directory—the best reference for complete campground and RV travel information.

MENA—Continued
SHADOW MOUNTAIN RV PARK—Continued

Phone: (479)394-6099
Address: 3708 Hwy 71 S, Mena, AR 71953
Lat/Lon: 34.53835/-94.31534
Email: ronanddarlene@localnet.com
Web: www.shadowmountaincampground.com

SEE AD THIS PAGE

MORRILTON—B-3

(S) CHEROKEE PARK (COE-Toad Suck Ferry)—(Faulkner) *From jct I-40 (exit 108) & Hwy 9: Go 2 mi S on Hwy 9, then 1 mi W on US 64, then 4 mi S on paved access road.* FACILITIES: 48 sites, 48 W&E, (30 amps), tenting, dump. RECREATION: boating, canoeing, ramp, dock, river fishing, playground. Partial handicap access. Open Mar 1 - Oct 31. Phone: (501)759-2005.

(N) KOA-Morrilton/Conway—(Conway) *From jct I-40 (exit 107) & Hwy 95: Go 100 feet N on Hwy 95, then W on campground entry road. (through gas station). Enter on L.* ◇◇◇FACILITIES: 56 sites, typical site width 20 ft, 56 full hkups, (30/50 amps), 50 amps ($), 52 pull-thrus, family camping, tenting, dump, laundry, ltd groc. ◇◇RECREATION: playground. Pets welcome. Partial handicap access. Open all yr. Big rigs welcome. Rate in 2010 $28.80 for 2 persons. Phone: (501)354-8262. KOA discount.

(W) PETIT JEAN SP—(Conway) *From jct I-40 (exit 108) & Hwy 9: Go 9 mi S on Hwy 9, then 12 mi W on Hwy 154.* FACILITIES: 125 sites, 35 full hkups, 90 W&E, (20/30 amps), 26 pull-thrus, tenting, dump, ltd groc. RECREATION: swim pool, boating, 10 hp limit, canoeing, ramp, dock, lake fishing, playground. Partial handicap access. Open all yr. Phone: (501)727-5441.

MOUNTAIN HOME—A-3

(E) BIDWELL POINT REC. AREA (COE-Norfork Lake)—(Baxter) *From jct Hwy 5 & US 62: Go 8-1/2 mi NE on US 62, then 2 mi N on Hwy 101, across the bridge.* FACILITIES: 48 sites, 46 E, (30 amps), 2 no hkups, 2 pull-thrus, tenting, dump. RECREATION: lake swim, boating, ramp, lake fishing, playground. Pets welcome. Partial handicap access. Open Apr 1 - Sep 30. Phone: (870)467-5375.

(E) CRANFIELD CAMPGROUND (COE-Norfork Lake)—(Baxter) *From jct Hwy 5 & US 62: Go 5-1/2 mi NE on US 62, then 2 mi N on Cranfield Rd.* FACILITIES: 69 sites, 69 E, (20/30 amps), tenting, dump, ltd groc. RECREATION: lake swim, boating, canoeing, ramp, dock, lake fishing, playground. Partial handicap access. Open Apr 1 - Sep 30. Phone: (870)492-4191.

(NW) GAMALIEL RECREATION AREA (COE-Norfork Lake)—(Baxter) *From jct Hwy 5 & US 62: Go 8-1/2 mi NE on US 62, then 5 mi N on Hwy 101, then 3 mi on CR 42.* FACILITIES: 64 sites, 30 E, (20/30 amps), 34 no hkups, 2 pull-thrus, tenting, dump, ltd groc. RECREATION: lake swim, boating, ramp, dock, lake fishing, playground. Partial handicap access. Open Apr 1 - Sep 30. Phone: (870)467-5680.

(E) PANTHER BAY (COE-Norfork Lake)—(Baxter) *From jct Hwy 5 & US 62: Go 8-1/2 mi NE on US 62, then 1 mi N on Hwy 101.* FACILITIES: 28 sites, 15 E, (30 amps), 13 no hkups, tenting, dump. RECREATION: lake swim, boating, ramp, dock, lake fishing, playground. Open Apr 1 - Sep 30. Phone: (870)425-2700.

MOUNTAIN HOME—Continued on next page

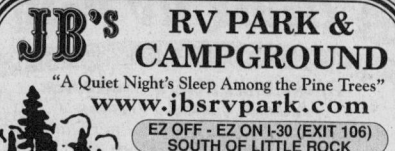

MOUNTAIN HOME—Continued

(SE) QUARRY COVE/DAM PARK (COE - Norfork Lake) —(Baxter) *From jct US 62 & Hwy 5: Go 11 mi SE on Hwy 5 to Salesville, then 2 mi E on Hwy 177 to Norfork Dam.* FACILITIES: 68 sites, 25 W&E, 43 E, (30/50 amps), tenting. RECREATION: lake swim, boating, canoeing, ramp, dock, lake/river fishing, playground. Partial handicap access. Open all yr. Facilities fully operational Apr 1 - Oct 31. Phone: (870)499-7216.

(E) ROBINSON POINT (COE-Norfork Lake)—(Baxter) *From jct Hwy 5 & US 62: Go 8-1/2 mi NE on US 62, then E on CR 279.* FACILITIES: 102 sites, 102 E, (20 amps), tenting, dump. RECREATION: lake swim, boating, ramp, lake fishing, playground. Partial handicap access. Open Apr 1 - Oct 31. Phone: (870)492-6853.

MOUNTAIN VIEW—B-4

(N) ARKANSAS FIDDLERS VALLEY RV RESORT—(Stone) *From jct Hwy 14, 5 & 9 Go: 1/2 mi W on Hwy 9, then 1/2 mi NE on Oak Ave. Enter on L.*

◆◆◆FACILITIES: 70 sites, typical site width 25 ft, 70 full hkups, (30/50 amps), some extd stay sites, cable TV, WiFi Instant Internet at site, family camping, tenting, cabins, laundry, RV supplies.

◆◆RECREATION: rec hall, golf nearby, activities.

Pets welcome. Open all yr. Big rigs welcome. Rate in 2010 $21 for 2 persons. MC/VISA. CCUSA 50% Discount. CCUSA reservations Required, CCUSA max stay 2 days, CCUSA disc. not avail W,T,S, CCUSA disc. not avail F,Sa, CCUSA disc. not avail holidays. Discount available Mon and Tue only.

Phone: (870)269-5700
Address: 324 Oak Ave, Mountain View, AR 72560
Lat/Lon: 35.86959/-92.11404
Email: kboard2play@yahoo.com
Web: www.fiddlersvalleyrv.com

SEE AD THIS PAGE

(N) Blue Sky RV Park—(Stone) *From jct Hwy 66/9/5/14: Go 3-1/4 mi N on Hwy 5/9/14. Enter on L.* ◆FACILITIES: 85 sites, typical site width 25 ft, 85 full hkups, (30/50 amps), 50 amps ($), 48 pull-thrus, tenting, dump. Pets welcome. Partial handicap access. Open Mar 1 - Nov 25. Big rigs welcome. Rate in 2010 $17.75-21.75 for 2 persons. Phone: (800)330-6655.

(N) Green Acres RV Park—(Stone) *From jct Hwys 66/9/5/14: Go 3/4 mi N on Hwy 5/9/14. Enter on L.* ◆◆FACILITIES: 100 sites, typical site width 20 ft, 65 full hkups, 35 W&E, (30 amps), family camping, dump. Pets welcome. Open all yr. Rate in 2010 $19-20 for 2 persons. Phone: (870)269-4404.

(N) Holiday Mountain Resort—(Stone) *From jct Hwy 66/9/5/14: Go 6 mi N on Hwy 5, then 1/4 W on Swinging Bridge Rd. Enter on L.* ◆◆◆FACILITIES: 125 sites, 113 full hkups, (20/30 amps), 12 no hkups, cable TV, ($), WiFi Internet central location, family camping, tenting, RV storage, dump, non-guest dump $, laundry, ltd groc, RV supplies, ice, picnic tables, patios. ◆◆RECREATION: pavilion, swim pool, canoeing, river fishing, fishing supplies, bsktball, play equipment, horseshoes. Pets welcome. Open Apr 1 - Mid Nov. Facilities fully operational Memorial Day - Labor Day. Rate in 2010 $20 per family. MC/VISA/DISC/AMEX/Debit. CCUSA 50% Discount. CCUSA reservations Accepted, CCUSA max stay 7 days. Discount not available Memorial Day, 4th of July, Labor Day weekends or 3rd weekend in Apr & last week of Oct.

Phone: (800)395-7108
Address: 473 Swinging Bridge Rd, Mountain View, AR 72560
Lat/Lon: 35.93515/-92.12070
Email: holidaymountain@mvtel.net
Web: www.holidaymtnresort.com

(NE) Mt. View RV Park/Guest House Motel—(Stone) *From jct Hwys 66/9/5/14: Go 3/4 mi N on Hwy 5/9/14, then 200 ft E on North Bayou Dr. Enter on L.*

MOUNTAIN VIEW—Continued
Mt. View RV Park/Guest House Motel—Continued

◆◆◆◆FACILITIES: 50 sites, typical site width 15 ft, 50 full hkups, (30/50 amps), 16 pull-thrus, family camping, laundry. Pets welcome. Partial handicap access. No tents. Open Mar 1 - Dec 1. Big rigs welcome. Rate in 2010 $22 per vehicle. Phone: (800)793-3161.

(N) OZARK RV PARK—(Stone) *N'bnd jct SR 5/9/14: Go 1/2 mi N on SR 14, then W 7/10 mi on Webb, then N 4/10 mi on Park. S'bnd jct SR 5/9/14 (north of town): S 5 mi on SR 9, then W 2/10 mi on SR 382, then SW 1/2 mi on Roper, then N 500' on park. Enter on L.*

◆◆◆FACILITIES: 73 sites, typical site width 20 ft, 71 full hkups, 2 W&E, (30/50 amps), 50 amps ($), some extd stay sites, 20 pull-thrus, cable TV, WiFi Instant Internet at site, WiFi Internet central location, family camping, tenting, cabins, dump, non-guest dump $, laundry, RV supplies, ice, picnic tables, fire rings, wood.

◆◆RECREATION: rec hall, horseshoes, sports field, hiking trails.

Pets welcome. Open all yr. Big rigs welcome. Clubs welcome. Rate in 2010 $22-26 for 2 persons. MC/VISA/DISC/Debit.

Phone: (870)269-2542
Address: 1022 Park Ave., Mountain View, AR 72560
Lat/Lon: 35.87799/-92.11605
Web: www.ozarkrvpark.com

SEE AD THIS PAGE

(N) Sylamore Creek Camp—(Stone) *From jct Hwy 66/9/5/14: Go 5 mi N on Hwy 5, then 500 ft W on Hwy 14. Enter on R.* ◆◆◆FACILITIES: 46 sites, 12 full hkups, 25 W&E, (30/50 amps), 9 no hkups, 10 pull-thrus, family camping, tenting, dump, laundry, ltd groc. ◆◆◆RECREATION: river swim, boating, canoeing, river fishing, play equipment. Pets welcome. Partial handicap access. Open all yr. Big rigs welcome. Rate in 2010 $18-22 per vehicle. Phone: (877)475-4223.

(W) Whitewater Bluegrass RV Park—(Stone) *From jct Hwys 66/9/5/14: Go 1/2 mi N on Hwy 5/9/14, then 3/4 mi W on Webb St. Enter on R.* ◆◆◆FACILITIES: 64 sites, typical site width 14 ft, 50 full hkups, 1 W&E, 13 E, (20/30 amps), 14 pull-thrus, family camping, tenting, dump, laundry. Pets welcome. Open Mar 15 - 1st wk Nov. Rate in 2010 $17 for 2 persons. Phone: (870)269-8047.

(N) WILD HORSE THEATRE—*From jct Hwy 14, 5 & 9: Go 1/2 mi W on Hwy 9, then 1/2 mi NE on Oak Ave. Enter on L.* Best in Entertainment! Comedy & Music & lots of FUN. Thur - Wild Horse Jam, Fri - 50's at the Hop. Dance & sing-a-long, Sat - Chicken House Opry, Sun - Church & Wild Horse Gospel Opry. Open Mid May - End of Aug.

Address: 324 Oak Ave, Mountain View, AR 72560
Lat/Lon: 35.86959/-92.11404
Email: kboard2play@yahoo.com

SEE AD THIS PAGE

MURFREESBORO—D-2

(SE) CRATER OF DIAMONDS SP—(Pike) *From town: Go 2 mi SE on Hwy-301.* FACILITIES: 59 sites, 59 W&E, (20/30 amps), tenting, dump, laundry. RECREATION: ramp, playground. Partial handicap access. Open all yr. Phone: (870)285-3113.

(SE) Miner's Camping & Rock Shop—(Pike) *From jct Hwy 27/26 & Hwy 301: Go 2 mi S on Hwy 301. Enter on L.* ◆◆◆FACILITIES: 27 sites, typical site width 30 ft, 10 full hkups, 17 W&E, (30/50 amps), 50 amps ($), 3 pull-thrus, WiFi Instant Internet at site, family camping, tenting, dump, picnic tables, fire rings, wood. ◆RECREATION: pavilion, pond fishing, play equipment, horseshoes. Pets welcome. Partial handicap access. Open all yr. Rate in 2010 $20-25 per vehicle. MC/VISA/Debit. CCUSA 50% Discount. CCUSA reservations Required, CCUSA max stay 2 days,

MURFREESBORO—Continued
Miner's Camping & Rock Shop—Continued

CCUSA disc. not avail W,Th,S, CCUSA disc. not avail F,Sa, CCUSA disc. not avail holidays. Discount available Dec and Jan only.

Phone: (870)285-2722
Address: 2235 Hwy 301 S, Murfreesboro, AR 71958
Lat/Lon: 34.04111/-93.67139
Email: jgoodin776@aol.com
Web: minerscamping.com

NEW BLAINE—B-2

(N) SHOAL BAY (COE-Lake Dardanelle)—(Logan) *From town: Go 2 mi NW on Hwy-197.* FACILITIES: 82 sites, 62 W&E, 20 E, (30 amps), tenting, dump. RECREATION: boating, ramp, playground. Partial handicap access. Open all yr. Phone: (479)938-7335.

NORTH LITTLE ROCK—C-3

(N) BURNS PARK (City Park)—(Pulaski) *From jct I-430 & I-40 (exit 147): Go 3 mi E on I-40 (exit 150), then 300 ft S on Championship Dr, then 3/4 mi W on Arlene Laman Dr. Enter on R.*

FACILITIES: 38 sites, 38 W&E, (30/50 amps), tenting, dump, non-guest dump $, picnic tables, fire rings, grills, controlled access.

RECREATION: pavilion, river/pond fishing, putting green, golf nearby, bsktball, playground, tennis, horseshoes, sports field, hiking trails, v-ball. Rec open to public.

Pets welcome. Partial handicap access. Open all yr. Big rigs welcome.

Phone: (501)771-0702
Address: Arlene Layman Drive, AR, AR 72118
Lat/Lon: 34.79733/-92.31395
Email: visitnlr@northlittlerock.org
Web: www.northlittlerock.travel

SEE AD LITTLE ROCK PAGE 35

(NW) CRYSTAL HILL RV PARK (RV SPACES)—(Pulaski) *From jct I-430 & I-40 (exit 147): Go 1 mi SE on I-40 (exit 148) Crystal Hill Rd, then 3/4 mi E on Crystal Hill Rd, then 1 block S on Lumsden Rd. Enter on R.*

FACILITIES: 27 sites, accepts full hkup units only, 27 full hkups, (30/50 amps), 50 amps ($), mostly extd stay sites, 3 pull-thrus, cable TV, ($), family camping.

Pets welcome. No tents. Open all yr. No Restrooms. Rate in 2010 $25-27 for 2 persons.

Phone: (501)771-4496
Address: 6601 Lumsden Rd, North Little Rock, AR 72118
Lat/Lon: 34.82217/-92.34009

SEE AD LITTLE ROCK PAGE 35

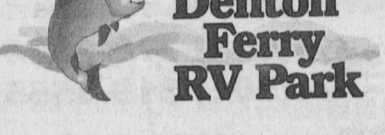

NORTH LITTLE ROCK—Continued on next page

Woodall's RV Owner's Handbook—essential information you need to "get to know" your RV.

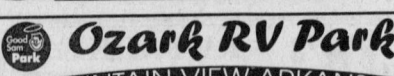

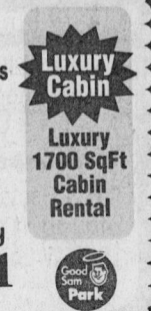

NORTH LITTLE ROCK—Continued

DOWNTOWN RIVERSIDE RV PARK—(Pulaski) *From jct W'bnd I-30 & Broadway (exit 141B): Go 1/4 mi S on Cypress St. to end, then 500 ft E on Riverfront Dr. From jct E'bnd I-30 & Broaday (exit 141B): Go 700 ft W on Broadway, then 1/4 mi S on Cypress, then 500 ft E on Riverside Dr. Enter on R.*

WELCOME

FACILITIES: 72 sites, 42 full hkups, 30 W&E, (30/50 amps), WiFi Instant Internet at site, family camping, dump, laundry, controlled access.

RECREATION: rec hall, equipped pavilion, boating, canoeing, kayaking, ramp, dock, river fishing, golf nearby, hiking trails. Rec open to public.

Pets welcome. Partial handicap access. No tents. Open all yr. Big rigs welcome. Escort to site. Clubs welcome. MC/VISA/DISC/AMEX/Debit. Member ARVC.

Phone: (501)340-5312
Address: 250 S Locust, North Little Rock, AR 72114
Lat/Lon: 34.75208/-92.26174
Email: rvparkriversidenlr@northlittlerock.ar.gov
Web: www.northlittlerockriversidervpark.com

SEE AD LITTLE ROCK PAGE 35

(NW) KOA-Little Rock North—(Pulaski) *From jct I-430 & I-40: Go 1 mi E on I-40 (exit 148), then 1 mi S on Crystal Hill Rd, then 100 yds E on Kampground Way. Enter on R.* ◆◆◆FACILITIES: 84 sites, typical site width 30 ft, 76 full hkups, 7 W&E, (20/30/50 amps), 50 amps ($), 1 no hkups, 50 pull-thrus, family camping, tenting, dump, laundry, ltd groc. ◆◆RECREATION: swim pool, playground. Pets welcome. Open all yr. Big rigs welcome. Rate in 2010 $30-45 for 2 persons. Phone: (501)758-4598. KOA discount.

(NE) NORTH LITTLE ROCK VISITORS BUREAU—*From jct I-430 & I-40 (exit 147): Go 3 mi E on I-40 (exit 150), then 500 ft N on Championship Dr. Enter on L.* Tourism information for North Little Rock and the State of Arkansas. Open all yr.

WELCOME

Phone: (501)758-1424
Address: #1 Eldor Johnson Dr, North Little Rock, AR 72119
Lat/Lon: 34.79885/-92.30307
Email: visitnlr@northlittlerock.org
Web: northlittlerock.travel

SEE AD LITTLE ROCK PAGE 35

(W) Trails End RV Park—(Pulaski) *From jct I-430 & I-40 (exit 147): Go 5 mi NW on I-40 (exit 142) & Hwy 365 (Stricklin Cove Rd), then 1/4 mi S on Hwy 365. Enter on R.* ◆◆FACILITIES: 50 sites, 50 full hkups, (30/50 amps), 50 amps ($), 31 pull-thrus, tenting, dump, laundry. Pets welcome. Open all yr. Big rigs welcome. Rate in 2010 $28-30 for 2 persons. Phone: (501)851-4594.

(E) WILLOW BEACH (Corp of Engineers - Pine Bluff River Area)—(Pulaski) *From jct I-440 & US 165: Go 3-1/2 mi SE on US 165, then 1-3/4 mi S on Baucum-David D. Terry Lock & Dam Rd.* FACILITIES: 21 sites, 21 W&E, (20/30 amps), tenting, dump. RECREATION: boating, ramp, dock, lake/river/pond fishing, playground. Partial handicap access. Open all yr. Phone: (501)961-1332.

OAKLAND—A-3

(W) OAKLAND PUBLIC USE AREA (COE-Bull Shoals Lake)—(Marion) *4 mi W on Hwy-202.* FACILITIES: 32 sites, 32 E, (30 amps), tenting, dump. RECREATION: lake swim, boating, ramp, dock, lake fishing, playground. Partial handicap access. Open Apr 1 - Oct 31. Phone: (870)431-5744.

(SW) OZARK ISLE PARK (COE-Bull Shoals Lake)—(Marion) *From town: Go 4 mi W on Hwy 202 to Oakland Park, then 1-2/10 mi SW on paved park road.* FACILITIES: 63 sites, 14 W&E, (30 amps), 49 no hkups, tenting, dump. RECREATION: lake swim, boating, ramp, lake fishing, playground. Pets welcome. Open May 1 - Oct 31. Phone: (870)431-5744.

OLA—C-2

(SE) QUARRY COVE (COE-Nimrod Lake)—(Perry) *From jct Hwy 10 & Hwy 7: Go 8 mi SE on Hwy 7, then 1/2 mi W on Hwy 60 to access road.* FACILITIES: 31 sites, 31 W&E, tenting, dump. RECREATION: lake swim, boating, ramp, lake fishing, playground. Partial handicap access. Open all yr. Phone: (479)272-4233.

OMAHA—A-3

(N) CRICKET CREEK REC. AREA (COE-Table Rock Lake)—(Boone) *From jct US-65 & Hwy-14: Go 5-1/2 mi W on Hwy-14.* FACILITIES: 35 sites, 16 W&E, 18 E, (30 amps), 1 no hkups, tenting, dump, ltd groc. RECREATION: lake swim, boating, ramp, dock, lake fishing, playground. Pets welcome. Partial handicap access. Open Apr 1 - Sep 15. Phone: (870)426-3331.

OZARK—B-2

(SE) AUX ARC PARK (COE - Ozark Lake)—(Franklin) *From town: Go 1-1/2 mi S on Hwy-23, then l/2 mi E on Hwy-309.* FACILITIES: 60 sites, 48 W&E, 12 E, (20 amps), tenting, dump, groceries. RECREATION: boating, canoeing, ramp, dock, lake fishing, playground. Partial handicap access. Open all yr. Phone: (479)667-1100.

OZARK—Continued

(N) OZARK NATIONAL FOREST (Redding Campground)—(Franklin) *From jct US-64 & Hwy-23: Go 16 mi N on Hwy-23, then 2 mi E on gravel FR-1003.* FACILITIES: 24 sites, 24 no hkups, tenting. RECREATION: canoeing, river fishing. Partial handicap access. Open all yr. Phone: (479)754-2864.

PARAGOULD—A-5

(W) CROWLEY'S RIDGE SP—(Greene) *From town: Go 9 mi W on US 412, then 2 mi S on Hwy 168.* FACILITIES: 26 sites, 18 W&E, 8 no hkups, tenting, dump. RECREATION: lake swim, boating, electric motors only, canoeing, lake fishing, playground. Open all yr. Phone: (870)573-6751.

PARIS—B-2

(S) OZARK NATIONAL FOREST (Cove Lake Campground)—(Logan) *From jct Hwy-109 & Hwy-309: Go 7-1/2 mi SE on Hwy-309, then 1/2 mi SE on FR-1608.* FACILITIES: 29 sites, 22 ft max RV length, 29 no hkups. RECREATION: boating, canoeing, ramp. Open all yr. Phone: (479)963-3067.

PEEL—A-3

(N) BUCK CREEK REC. AREA (COE-Bull Shoals Lake)—(Marion) *5 mi N on Hwy-125 (free ferry).* FACILITIES: 39 sites, 39 E, (30 amps), tenting, dump, ltd groc. RECREATION: lake swim, boating, ramp, dock, playground. Open Apr 1 - Sep 30. Phone: (417)785-4313.

(N) HIGHWAY 125 RECREATION AREA (COE - Bull Shoals Lake)—(Marion) *5 mi N on Hwy-125.* FACILITIES: 38 sites, 38 E, (30 amps), tenting, dump, ltd groc. RECREATION: lake swim, boating, ramp, dock, lake fishing, playground. Pets welcome. Partial handicap access. Open all yr. Phone: (870)436-5711.

PERRYVILLE—C-3

(SE) Coffee Creek Motel and RV Park—(Perry) *From jct Hwy 60 & Hwy 9: Go 2 mi S on Hwy 9, then 1 mi E on Hwy 300. Enter on R.* ◆◆◆FACILITIES: 38 sites, typical site width 25 ft, 26 full hkups, 12 W&E, (30/50 amps), 50 amps ($), 7 pull-thrus, heater not allowed, cable TV, WiFi Instant Internet at site, WiFi Internet central location, family camping, tenting, dump, non-guest dump $, laundry, ltd groc, RV supplies, ice, picnic tables, grills. ◆◆RECREATION: lake swim, boating, canoeing, ramp, dock, lake fishing, fishing supplies, hiking trails. Pets welcome. Partial handicap access. Open all yr. Rate in 2010 $15-25 per vehicle. MC/VISA/Debit. CCUSA 50% Discount. CCUSA reservations Required, CCUSA max stay 3 days, CCUSA disc. not avail holidays. Discount available Mon, Tues, Wed only in Mar, Apr, May, Sep and Oct.

CAMPCLUB USA

Phone: (501)889-2745
Address: 18 Coffee Creek Landing, Perryville, AR 72126
Lat/Lon: 34.98500/-92.78190
Email: coffeecreek@alltel.net
Web: Coffeecreekresort.net

PINE BLUFF—D-4

(NE) PINE BLUFF PARKS & RECREATION—*From E jct US 65 & US 65B: 3-1/2 mi N on US 65B, then 200 ft E on Regional Park Dr, then 1/2 mi N on Lake Saracen Dr. Enter on L.* We've got it ALL - Facilities include: Lake Fishing, boating, swimming, baseball/softball complex, golf course, RV park, amphitheater, Farmers market and Pavilion (on the water) for events - weddings, receptions, concerts, teunions, cook-offs... Open all yr.

WELCOME

Phone: (870)536-0920
Address: 200 Lake Saracen Dr, Pine Bluff, AR 71611
Lat/Lon: 34.23067/-92.00552
Email: parksandrec@att.net
Web: www.saracenlanding.com

SEE AD THIS PAGE

(NE) SARACEN TRACE RV PARK (City Park)—(Jefferson) *From E jct US 65 & US 65 B: Go 3-1/2 mi N on US 65 B, then 2 mi E on Convention Center Dr. Enter at end.*

WELCOME

FACILITIES: 51 sites, accepts self-contained units only, 51 W&E, (30/50 amps), some extd stay sites, 4 pull-thrus, dump, non-guest dump, ice, picnic tables, patios, fire rings, grills, wood, controlled access.

RECREATION: pavilion, lake swim, boating, canoeing, kayaking, ramp, dock, lake fishing, putting green, golf nearby, playground, sports field, hiking trails. Rec open to public.

Pets welcome. No tents. Open all yr. No restrooms. Big rigs welcome.

Phone: (870)534-0711
Address: 3301 Harbor Oaks, Pine Bluff, AR 71601
Lat/Lon: 34.25605/-91.98538
Email: parksandrec@att.net
Web: www.saracenlanding.com

SEE AD THIS PAGE

PINEY—B-2

(N) PINEY BAY (COE - Dardanelle Lake)—(Johnson) *From jct US-64 & Hwy-359: Go 4 mi N on Hwy-359.* FACILITIES: 91 sites, 85 E, (30 amps), 6 no hkups, tenting, dump. RECREATION: boating, ramp, playground. Partial handicap access. Open all yr. Phone: (479)885-3029.

PLAINVIEW—C-2

(E) SUNLIGHT BAY (COE-Nimrod Lake)—(Yell) *From Hwy 28W in town: Go 2-1/2 mi S on Steve Rd, then 1 mi SE on access road.* FACILITIES: 29 sites, 29 W&E, (30 amps), tenting, dump. RECREATION: boating, ramp, lake/river fishing, playground. Partial handicap access. Open all yr. Phone: (479)272-4234.

POCAHONTAS—A-5

(S) OLD DAVIDSONVILLE SP—(Randolph) *From jct US 62 & Hwy 166: Go 9 mi S on Hwy 166.* FACILITIES: 49 sites, 24 W&E, (30/50 amps), 25 no hkups, 4 pull-thrus, tenting, dump, ltd groc. RECREATION: boating, canoeing, dock, lake/river fishing, playground. Partial handicap access. Open all yr. Phone: (870) 892-4708.

QUITMAN—B-3

(NW) COVE CREEK (COE-Greers Ferry Lake)—(Cleburne) *From jct Hwy-124 & Hwy-25: Go 6-1/2 mi NE on Hwy-25, then 3 mi NW on Hwy-16, then 1-1/2 mi on access road.* FACILITIES: 65 sites, 31 E, (20/30 amps), 34 no hkups, tenting, dump. RECREATION: lake swim, boating, ramp, playground. Partial handicap access. Open Apr 1 - Oct 31. Phone: (501)362-2416.

REDFIELD—C-3

(E) TAR CAMP (COE-Pine Bluff River Area)—(Jefferson) *From town: Go 5-3/4 mi E on paved access road.* FACILITIES: 58 sites, 45 W&E, (20/30 amps), 13 no hkups, tenting, dump. RECREATION: boating, ramp, dock, river fishing, playground. Partial handicap access. Open Mar 1 - Oct 31. Phone: (501)397-5101.

ROGERS—A-2

See listings at Garfield & Springdale.

(E) Beaver Lake Hide A Way Campground & RV Park—(Benton) *From jct US 71 & Hwy 12: Go 15 mi E on Hwy 12, then 3-1/4 mi N on Hwy 303. Enter on R.* ◆◆◆FACILITIES: 130 sites, typical site width 25 ft, 60 full hkups, 30 W&E, (20/30/50 amps), 40 no hkups, 20 pull-thrus, family camping, tenting, dump, laundry, ltd groc. ◆◆◆RECREATION: swim pool, lake swim, boating, canoeing, dock, lake fishing, playground. Pets welcome. Partial handicap access. Open all yr. Big rigs welcome. Rate in 2010 $20-22 for 2 persons. Phone: (479)925-1333.

(E) HORSESHOE BEND RECREATION AREA (COE-Beaver Lake)—(Benton) *From jct Business US 71 & Hwy 94: Go 6 mi E on Hwy 94 to Monte Ne, then follow signs 5 mi E.* FACILITIES: 188 sites, 188 E, (30 amps), tenting, dump. RECREATION: lake swim, boating, ramp, dock, lake fishing, playground. Partial handicap access. Open May 1 - Oct 31. Phone: (479)925-2561.

(E) PRAIRIE CREEK RECREATION AREA (COE-Beaver Lake)—(Benton) *4 mi E on Hwy-12, then 1 mi on access road.* FACILITIES: 112 sites, 112 E, (20/30/50 amps), tenting, dump. RECREATION: lake swim, boating, ramp, dock, lake fishing, playground. Pets welcome. Partial handicap access. Open Apr 1 - Oct 31. Phone: (479)925-3957.

(N) ROCKY BRANCH PARK (COE-Beaver Lake)—(Benton) *From town: Go 11 mi E on Hwy-12, then 4-1/2 mi NE on Hwy-303.* FACILITIES: 44 sites, 44 E, (20 amps), tenting, dump. RECREATION: lake swim, boating, ramp, dock, lake fishing, playground. Partial handicap access. Open Apr 1 - Oct 31. Phone: (479)925-2526.

RUSSELLVILLE—B-3

(E) IVY'S COVE RV RETREAT—(Pope) *From jct I-40 (exit 84) & Hwy 331: Go 1/2 mi NE on Hwy 331/Bradley Cove Rd. Enter on R.*

WELCOME

◆◆◆◆FACILITIES: 23 sites, typical site width 30 ft, 23 full hkups, (20/30/50 amps), 14 pull-thrus, cable TV, WiFi Instant Internet at site, WiFi Internet central location, family camping, tenting, RV storage, laundry, RV supplies, ice, picnic tables, fire rings, wood.

◆◆RECREATION: rec room/area, golf nearby, bsktball, playground, horseshoes.

Pets welcome, breed restrict. Partial handicap access. Open all yr. Big rigs welcome. Escort to site.

IVY'S COVE RV RETREAT—Continued on next page

RUSSELLVILLE—Continued
IVY'S COVE RV RETREAT—Continued

Clubs welcome. Rate in 2010 $28-30 for 4 persons. MC/VISA/DISC/Debit. Member ARVC. FCRV discount. FMCA discount.

Phone: (479)747-3561
Address: 321 Bradley Cove Rd, Russellville, AR 72802
Lat/Lon: 35.28411/-93.08372
Email: dmi@ivyscove.com
Web: www.ivyscove.com

SEE AD THIS PAGE AND AD TRAVEL SECTION PAGE 23

(SW) LAKE DARDANELLE SP—(Pope) *From jct I-40 (exit 81) & Hwy 7: Go S on Hwy 7, then immediately 4 mi W on Hwy 326.* FACILITIES: 74 sites, 30 full hkups, 44 W&E, (30/50 amps), tenting, dump. RECREATION: lake swim, boating, ramp, dock, lake fishing, playground. Open all yr. Phone: (479)967-5516.

Mission RV Park—(Pope) *From jct US Hwy 64 & I-40 (exit 78): Go 100 yds S. Enter at end.* ◆◆FACILITIES: 45 sites, typical site width 26 ft, 45 full hkups, (20/30/50 amps), 50 amps ($), 14 pull-thrus, family camping, tenting, dump, laundry. Pets welcome. Partial handicap access. Open all yr. Big rigs welcome. Rate in 2010 $25-27 for 4 persons. Phone: (479)967-3576.

(S) OLD POST ROAD PARK (COE-Lake Dardanelle)—(Pope) *From jct Hwy 7S & Hwy 7S Spur: Go 3 mi W on Hwy 7S Spur.* FACILITIES: 40 sites, 40 W&E, (30 amps), tenting, dump. RECREATION: boating, ramp, lake/river/stream fishing, playground. Partial handicap access. Open Mar 1 - Oct 31. Phone: (479)968-7962.

✽ **(N) OUTDOOR LIVING CENTER**—*From jct I-40 (exit 81) & Hwy 7: Go 500 ft S on Hwy 7, then 1/2 mi W on Lake Front Dr. Enter on R.* SALES: travel trailers, park models, 5th wheels, toy hauler, Class A motorhomes, fold-down camping trailers, pre-owned unit sales. SERVICES: full-time mech, RV appliance repair, body work/collision repair, LP gas by weight/by meter, RV rentals, sells parts/accessories, installs hitches. Open all yr. MC/VISA/DISC/AMEX/Debit.

WELCOME

Phone: (479)968-7706
Address: 300 Lake Front Dr, Russellville, AR 72801
Lat/Lon: 35.35030/-93.14390
Email: mail@olcrv.com
Web: olcrv.com

SEE AD THIS PAGE

(N) OUTDOOR LIVING CENTER RV PARK—(Pope) *From jct I-40 (exit 81) & AR 7: Go 1 mi N on AR 7. Enter on L.*

WELCOME

◆◆◆FACILITIES: 50 sites, typical site width 20 ft, 50 full hkups, (30/50 amps), 50 amps ($), some extd stay sites, 24 pull-thrus, cable TV, WiFi Instant Internet at site, WiFi Internet central location, family camping, RV storage, dump, non-guest dump $, laundry, RV supplies, ice, picnic tables.
◆◆RECREATION: rec hall, pavilion, golf nearby, bsktball.

RUSSELLVILLE—Continued
OUTDOOR LIVING CENTER RV PARK—Continued

Pets welcome. Partial handicap access. No tents. Open all yr. Big rigs welcome. Escort to site. Clubs welcome. Rate in 2010 $27-29 per vehicle. MC/VISA/DISC/Debit.

Phone: (800)828-4307
Address: 10 Outdoor Court, Russellville, AR 72802
Lat/Lon: 35.31104/-93.13808
Email: mail@olcrv.com
Web: olcrv.com

SEE AD THIS PAGE

ST. JOE—A-3

(SW) BUFFALO NATIONAL RIVER (Tyler Bend Campground)—(Searcy) *From town: Go 3 mi S on US 65, then 3 mi W on access road.* FACILITIES: 38 sites, 28 ft max RV length, 38 no hkups, tenting, dump. RECREATION: river swim, boating, 10 hp limit, canoeing, ramp, river/pond/stream fishing. Open all yr. Facilities fully operational Mar 15 - Nov 15. Phone: (870)439-2502.

SHIRLEY—B-3

(S) Golden Pond RV Park—(Van Buren) *From jct US 65 & Hwy 16: Go 2 mi E on Hwy 16 to Fairfield Bay West entrance (Burnt Ridge Rd), then 8 mi S on Burnt Ridge Rd, then 2-1/2 mi N on Hwy 330. Enter on R.* ◆◆◆FACILITIES: 53 sites, typical site width 18 ft, 50 full hkups, 3 W&E, (20/30/50 amps), 50 amps ($), 8 pull-thrus, cable TV, WiFi Instant Internet at site, phone Internet central location, family camping, tenting, RV storage, dump, non-guest dump, laundry, RV supplies, LP gas by weight/by meter, fire rings, wood. ◆◆RECREATION: pavilion, pond fishing, horseshoes, hiking trails. Pets welcome. Partial handicap access. Open all yr. Big rigs welcome. Rate in 2010 $24 for 2 persons. MC/VISA/DISC/Debit. CCUSA 50% Discount. CCUSA reservations Accepted, CCUSA max stay 4 days.

CAMPCLUB USA

Phone: (866)723-1723
Address: 241 Hwy 330 S, Shirley, AR 72153
Lat/Lon: 35.02346/-92.30930
Email: goldenpondrv@artelco.com
Web: www.goldenrv.com

SILOAM SPRINGS—A-1

(W) Greentree RV Park (RV SPACES)—(Benton) *From jct Hwy 59 & US 412: Go 2 mi W on US 412. Enter on L.* FACILITIES: 37 sites, typical site width 25 ft, 37 full hkups, (30/50 amps), 11 pull-thrus, family camping, dump, laundry. RECREATION: swim pool. Pets welcome. No tents. Open all yr. Big rigs welcome. Rate in 2010 $22-32 for 4 persons. Phone: (479)524-8898.

(NE) Wilderness Hills Park & Campground—(Benton) *From jct US 412 & Mt Olive St: Go 1-3/4 mi N on Mt Olive St, then 1-3/4 mi NE on Dawn Hill Rd, then 1-1/4 mi N on Taylor Orchard Rd. Enter on R.* ◆◆FACILITIES: 32 sites, typical site width 20 ft, 32 full hkups, (30/50 amps), 40 pull-thrus, family camping. Pets welcome. Partial handicap access. No tents. Open all yr. Rate in 2010 $25 per vehicle. Phone: (479)524-4955.

SPRINGDALE—A-2

(E) HICKORY CREEK RECREATION AREA (COE-Beaver Lake)—(Benton) *2 mi N on US-71, then 7 mi E on Hwy-264.* FACILITIES: 61 sites, 61 E, (30/50 amps), tenting, dump. RECREATION: lake swim, boating, ramp, dock, lake fishing, playground. Partial handicap access. Open Apr 1 - Oct 31. Phone: (479)750-2943.

(E) Pilgrims's Rest RV Park—(Washington) *From jct Hwy 71 B & US 412: Go 10 mi E on US 412, then 1/4 mi on Hickory Flatt Rd. Enter on L.* ◆◆FACILITIES: 37 sites, typical site width 25 ft, 37 full hkups, (30/50 amps), 30 pull-thrus, family camping, tenting, dump, laundry. ◆RECREATION: play equipment. Pets welcome. Open all yr. Big rigs welcome. Rate in 2010 $22.50 for 2 persons. Phone: (479)789-7152.

(SE) WAR EAGLE PUBLIC USE AREA (COE-Beaver Lake)—(Washington) *From town: Go 10 mi E on US 412, then 3 mi N on Hwy 303.* FACILITIES: 26 sites, 26 E, (20 amps), tenting, dump. RECREATION: lake swim, boating, ramp, dock, lake fishing, playground. Partial handicap access. Open May 1 - Sep 15. Phone: (479)636-1210.

SPRINGDALE—Continued

✽ **(W) Wheels RV**—*From jct I-540 & US 412 (exit 72): Go 4 mi W on US 412. Enter on R.* SALES: travel trailers, 5th wheels, toy hauler, Class A motorhomes, fold-down camping trailers, pre-owned unit sales. SERVICES: full-time mech, RV appliance repair, body work/collision repair, LP gas by weight/by meter, RV rentals, sells parts/accessories, installs hitches. Open all yr. MC/VISA/DISC/AMEX/Debit.

Phone: (479)306-5555
Address: 1358 W Henri De tonti Blvd (Hwy 412W), Springdale, AR 72762
Lat/Lon: 36.17705/-94.25612
Email: info@wheelsmotorrv.com
Web: www.wheelsrv.net

STAR CITY—D-4

(E) CANE CREEK SP—(Lincoln) *From jct US 425 & Hwy 293 (in town): Go 5 mi E on Hwy 293.* FACILITIES: 30 sites, 30 W&E, (20/30 amps), tenting, dump. RECREATION: boating, ramp, dock, lake fishing, playground. Partial handicap access. Open all yr. Phone: (870)628-4714.

TEXARKANA—E-2

(E) Four States Fairgrounds RV Park—(Miller) *From jct I-30 (exit 2) & Loop 245: Go 1 mi S on Loop 245, then 1/4 mi E on Arkansas Blvd, then 1/2 mi N on Fairgrounds Rd. Enter at end.* ◆◆FACILITIES: 100 sites, typical site width 20 ft, 100 full hkups, (20/30/50 amps), 72 pull-thrus, tenting, dump. ◆◆RECREATION: playground. Pets welcome. Open all yr. Big rigs welcome. Rate in 2010 $20 per vehicle. Phone: (870)773-2941. FMCA discount.

(W) Sunrise RV Park—(Miller) *From jct Loop 245 & I-30: Go 4-1/2 mi E on I-30 (exit 7), then 200 yds N on Hwy 108 then 1/4 mi E on North Service Rd. Enter on L.* ◆◆◆◆FACILITIES: 111 sites, typical site width 25 ft, 111 full hkups, (20/30/50 amps), 43 pull-thrus, family camping, tenting, dump, laundry, ltd groc. ◆◆◆RECREATION: swim pool, play equipment. Pets welcome, breed restrict. Partial handicap access. Open all yr. Big rigs welcome. Phone: (870)772-0751.

TICHNOR—D-4

(S) MERRISACH LAKE (COE-Pine Bluff River Area)—(Arkansas) *From town: Go 10 mi S on CR, then 1/4 mi W on paved access road.* FACILITIES: 64 sites, 51 W&E, (30/50 amps), 13 no hkups, tenting, dump. RECREATION: boating, ramp, lake/river fishing, playground. Partial handicap access. Open all yr. Phone: (870)548-2291.

(S) NOTREBES BEND (COE-Arkansas Post River Area)—(Arkansas) *From town: Go 10 mi S on County Road, then follow signs 6-1/2 mi SW & SE on paved access road.* FACILITIES: 50 sites, 16 E, (50 amps), 34 no hkups, tenting, dump. RECREATION: boating, ramp, river fishing. Open Mar 1 - Oct 31. Phone: (870)548-2291.

TUMBLING SHOALS—B-4

(S) Lakeside RV Park—(Cleburne) *From jct Hwy 25 & Hwy 25S: Go 2-7/10 mi W on Hwy 25S. Enter on L.* ◆◆◆FACILITIES: 28 sites, typical site width 20 ft, 25 full hkups, 3 W&E, (20/30/50 amps), 5 pull-thrus, family camping, tenting, dump, ltd groc. Pets welcome. Partial handicap access. Open all yr. Big rigs welcome. Rate in 2010 $20 per vehicle. Phone: (501)362-8872.

VAN BUREN—B-1

✽ **(S) OUTDOOR LIVING CENTER**—*From jct I-40 (exit 5) & Hwy 59: Go 200 ft S on Hwy 59. Enter on L.* SALES: travel trailers, truck campers, 5th wheels, fold-down camping trailers, pre-owned unit sales. SERVICES: full-time mech, RV appliance repair, LP gas by weight/by meter, RV rentals, sells parts/accessories, installs hitches. Open all yr. MC/VISA/DISC/AMEX.

WELCOME

Phone: (800)828-2243
Address: 1716-1/2 Fayetteville Hwy, Van Buren, AR 72956
Lat/Lon: 35.46132/-94.35429
Email: mail@olcrv.com
Web: olcrv.com

SEE AD THIS PAGE

VAN BUREN—Continued on next page

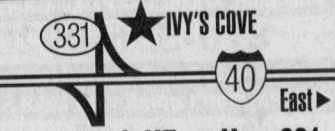

VAN BUREN—Continued

(S) OVERLAND RV PARK—(Crawford) *From jct I-40 (exit 5) & Hwy 59: Go 200 feet S on Hwy 59. Enter on L.*

WELCOME

◆◆◆FACILITIES: 49 sites, typical site width 20 ft, 49 full hkups, (30/50 amps), some extd stay sites, 33 pull-thrus, cable TV, WiFi Instant Internet at site, family camping, RV storage, laundry, RV supplies, LP gas by weight/by meter.

◆RECREATION: rec hall.

Pets welcome. Partial handicap access. No tents. Open all yr. Big rigs welcome. Rate in 2010 $26-28 for 2 persons. MC/VISA/DISC/AMEX/Debit.

Phone: (479)471-5474
Address: 1716-1/2 Fayetteville Rd, Van Buren, AR 72956
Lat/Lon: 35.46074/-94.35342
Email: mail@olcrv.com
Web: olcrv.com

SEE AD PAGE 38

(W) Park Ridge RV Campground—(Crawford) *From jct Hwy 59 & I-40 (exit 5): Go 2 mi W on I-40 (exit 3), then 1/4 mi N on Parkridge, then 1/2 mi E on Rena Rd. Enter on L.* ◆◆FACILITIES: 57 sites, typical site width 25 ft, 57 full hkups, (20/30/50 amps), 50 amps ($), 27 pull-thrus, family camping, tenting, dump, laundry, ltd groc. ◆◆RECREATION: ramp, dock, river fishing, play equipment. Pets welcome. Open all yr. Big rigs welcome. Rate in 2010 $26-29 for 2 persons. Phone: (479)410-4678.

WAVELAND—B-2

(S) OUTLET AREA (COE-Blue Mountain Lake)—(Yell) *From jct Hwy 10 & Hwy 309: Go 1 mi S on Hwy 309, then 1 mi W on access road to the N end of the dam.* FACILITIES: 41 sites, 41 W&E, (20 amps), tenting, dump. RECREATION: river fishing, playground. Partial handicap access. Open Mar 1 - Oct 31. Phone: (479)947-2101.

(W) WAVELAND PARK (COE-Blue Mountain Lake)—(Yell) *From jct Hwy-10 & Hwy-309: Go 1 mi S on Hwy-309, then 1 mi W on paved access road.* FACILITIES: 51 sites, 51 W&E, (30/50 amps), tenting, dump. RECREATION: lake swim, boating, ramp, lake fishing, playground. Partial handicap access. Open Mar 1 - Oct 31. Phone: (479)947-2102.

Arkansas State Bird: Mockingbird

WEST FORK—A-2

(W) DEVIL'S DEN SP—(Washington) *From jct US 71 & Hwy 170: Go 18 mi SW on Hwy 170.* FACILITIES: 144 sites, 77 full hkups, 43 W&E, (20/30 amps), 24 no hkups, tenting, dump, laundry, ltd groc. RECREATION: swim pool, boating, no motors, playground. Partial handicap access. Open all yr. Phone: (479) 761-3325.

WEST MEMPHIS—B-5

(S) TOM SAWYER'S MISSISSIPPI RIVER RV PARK—(Crittenden) *From jct I-40 (exit 280) & M L King Dr: Go 3 mi S on M L King Dr (becomes South Loop). From jct I-55 (exit 4) & M L King Dr: Go 2-1/2 mi S on M L King Dr (becomes South Loop), then 1/2 mi E on 8th St. Enter on L.*

WELCOME

STAY ON THE MIGHTY MISSISSIPPI
Enjoy watching river traffic from your site! Long, level, concrete, full-service pull-thrus on the unspoiled Arkansas banks of the Mississippi River. Minutes from both I-40 and I-55 as well as downtown Memphis.

◆◆◆◆FACILITIES: 100 sites, typical site width 25 ft, 100 full hkups, (20/30/50 amps), 62 pull-thrus, WiFi Instant Internet at site, tenting, laundry, ice, picnic tables, patios, controlled access.

CAMPCLUB USA

◆◆RECREATION: lake swim, lake/river fishing, sports field, hiking trails.

Pets welcome, breed restrict. Open all yr. Facilities fully operational Jan - May. Visit website/NWA Link for river stages. Big rigs welcome. Clubs welcome. Rate in 2010 $27-36 for 4 persons. MC/VISA/DISC/AMEX/Debit. Member ARVC. FMCA discount. CCUSA 50% Discount. CCUSA reservations Recommended, CCUSA max stay Unlimited, Cash only for CCUSA disc. Discount available Nov thru Feb.

Text 108006 to (440)725-8687 to see our Visual Tour.

Arkansas State Gem: Diamond

WEST MEMPHIS—Continued
TOM SAWYER'S MISSISSIPPI RIVER RV PARK—Continued

Phone: (870)735-9770
Address: 1286 South 8th St., West Memphis, AR 72301
Lat/Lon: 35.12690/-90.17030
Email: tomsawyersrvpark@yahoo.com
Web: www.tomsawyersrvpark.com

SEE AD MEMPHIS, TN PAGE 733

Y CITY—C-2

(E) OUACHITA NATIONAL FOREST (Mill Creek Rec. Area)—(Scott) *From town: Go 5 mi E on US 270.* FACILITIES: 15 sites, 15 no hkups. RECREATION: stream fishing. Open Apr 10 - Sep 5. Phone: (479)637-4174.

YELLVILLE—A-3

(S) BUFFALO NATIONAL RIVER (Buffalo Point Campground)—(Marion) *From town: Go 14 mi S on Hwy-14, then 3 mi E on Hwy-268.* FACILITIES: 83 sites, 25 ft max RV length, 83 W&E, (20 amps), tenting, dump. RECREATION: river swim, boating, canoeing, ramp, river fishing. Partial handicap access. Open all yr. Facilities fully operational Mar 15 - Nov 15. Phone: (870) 449-4311.

(S) Sherwood Forest RV Park & Campground—(Marion) *From jct US 62/412 & Hwy 14: Go 5 mi S on Hwy 14. Enter on R.* ◆◆◆FACILITIES: 23 sites, 40 ft max RV length, 11 full hkups, 12 W&E, (20/30/50 amps), 50 amps ($), 4 pull-thrus, family camping, tenting, dump, laundry. ◆RECREATION: swim pool. Pets welcome. Open Mar 1 - Dec 31. Rate in 2010 $25.50 for 2 persons. Phone: (870)449-3452.

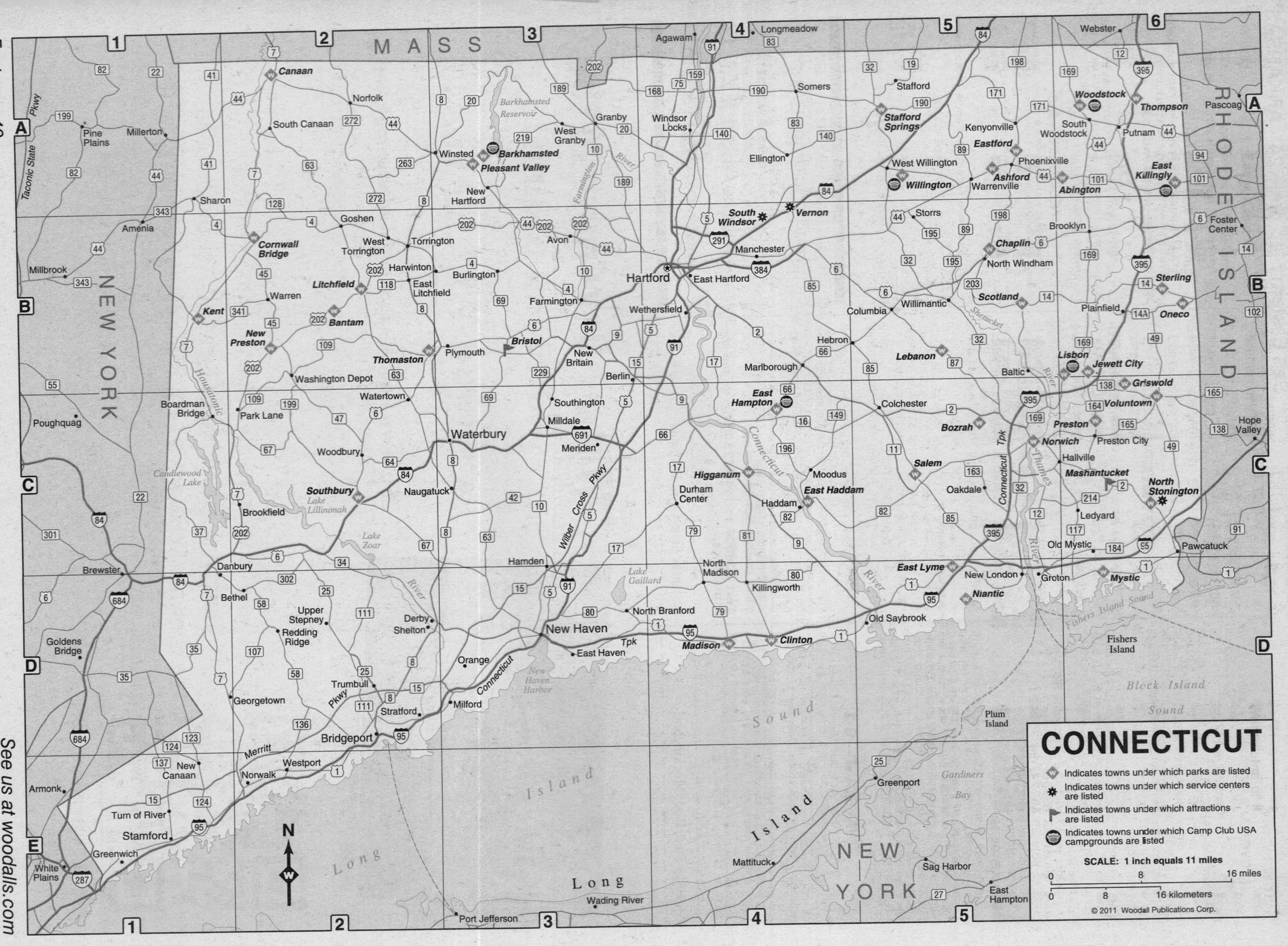

CONNECTICUT
Indicates towns under which parks are listed
Indicates towns under which service centers are listed
Indicates towns under which attractions are listed
Indicates towns under which Camp Club USA campgrounds are listed
SCALE: 1 inch equals 11 miles
0 8 16 miles
0 8 16 kilometers
© 2011 Woodall Publications Corp.
MASS
RHODE ISLAND
NEW YORK
Long Island Sound
Block Island Sound
Fishers Island Sound
Canaan
Norfolk
South Canaan
Pine Plains
Millerton
Taconic State Pkwy
Sharon
Amenia
Millbrook
Cornwall Bridge
Goshen
West Torrington
Torrington
Winsted
Barkhamsted
Pleasant Valley
Barkhamsted Reservoir
New Hartford
West Granby
Granby
Agawam
Longmeadow
Windsor Locks
Somers
Stafford
Stafford Springs
Ellington
Kenyonville
Eastford
Woodstock
South Woodstock
Thompson
Webster
Pascoag
Putnam
East Killingly
Abington
Phoenixville
Ashford
Warrenville
West Willington
Willington
Storrs
Vernon
South Windsor
Manchester
Hartford
East Hartford
Wethersfield
Avon
Farmington
Burlington
Harwinton
East Litchfield
Litchfield
Bantam
Warren
Kent
New Preston
Washington Depot
Thomaston
Plymouth
Bristol
New Britain
Berlin
Southington
Milldale
Meriden
Waterbury
Watertown
Woodbury
Naugatuck
Southbury
Lake Lillinonah
Lake Zoar
Candlewood Lake
Boardman Bridge
Park Lane
Poughquag
Brookfield
Brewster
Danbury
Bethel
Upper Stepney
Redding Ridge
Georgetown
Goldens Bridge
Derby
Shelton
Orange
Trumbull
Stratford
Milford
Bridgeport
Westport
Norwalk
New Canaan
Armonk
Turn of River
Stamford
Greenwich
White Plains
Hamden
New Haven
East Haven
New Haven Harbor
North Branford
Lake Gaillard
North Madison
Madison
Killingworth
Clinton
Durham Center
Higganum
Haddam
East Haddam
Moodus
East Hampton
Marlborough
Hebron
Columbia
Willimantic
Lebanon
Colchester
Bozrah
Salem
Oakdale
East Lyme
Niantic
Old Saybrook
New London
Groton
Mystic
Old Mystic
Ledyard
Mashantucket
North Stonington
Pawcatuck
Hallville
Preston City
Preston
Norwich
Voluntown
Griswold
Jewett City
Lisbon
Baltic
Plainfield
Oneco
Sterling
Scotland
Chaplin
North Windham
Brooklyn
Foster Center
Hope Valley
Fishers Island
Plum Island
Greenport
Gardiners Bay
Sag Harbor
East Hampton
Mattituck
Wading River
Port Jefferson
Wilber Cross Pkwy
Merritt Pkwy
Connecticut Tpk
Housatonic River
Farmington River
Connecticut River
Thames River
Shetucket River

TRAVEL SECTION

Connecticut

READER SERVICE INFO

The following businesses have placed an ad in the Connecticut Travel Section. To receive free information, enter the Reader Service number on the Reader Service Card opposite page 48/Discover Section in the front of this directory.

Advertiser	RS#
Connecticut Campground Owners Assoc	457
Lake Compounce Family Theme Park	4333
Scranton Motors, Inc.	3984

TIME ZONE

Connecticut is in the Eastern Time Zone.

TOPOGRAPHY

Connecticut is the picturesque southern gateway to New England. Split by the Connecticut River, its varied landscape offers travelers a wealth of recreation. Between 2,380-foot Mount Frissell (located in the state's northwest corner) and the 253-mile Atlantic coastline, there are fertile meadows and heavily forested uplands.

TEMPERATURE

Average temperatures in January include highs in the mid 30s and lows in the teens. July temperatures average around 84° for a high, 63° for a low.

TRAVEL & TOURISM INFO

State Agency:

Connecticut Commission on Culture and Tourism
One Financial Plaza
755 Main St.
Hartford, CT 06103
(888/CT VISIT or 860/256-2800)
www.ctvisit.com

Regional Agencies:

Central Regional Tourism
One Constitution Plaza, 2nd Floor
Hartford, CT 06103
(860/787-9640)
www.CentralofCT.com

Eastern Regional Tourism District
27 Coogan Blvd, Bldg 3A
New London, CT 06320
(860/444-2206)
www.mysticcountry.com

Greater New Haven CVB
59 Elm St.
New Haven, CT 06510
(203/777-8550 or 800/332-STAY)
www.newhavencvb.org

Middletown Connecticut Convention and Visitor Bureau
393 Main St.
Middletown, CT 06457
(860/347-0028 or 800/486-3346)
www.ctrivershore.com

Western/Northwest Connecticut CVB
PO Box 968
Litchfield, CT 06759-0968
(860/567-4506)
www.litchfieldhills.com

Norwich Tourism
Norwich, CT 06360
(888/4-NORWICH)
www.norwichct.org

Simsbury Tourism Committee - Visitor Center
P.O. Box 1015
Simsbury, CT 06070
(860/658-4000)

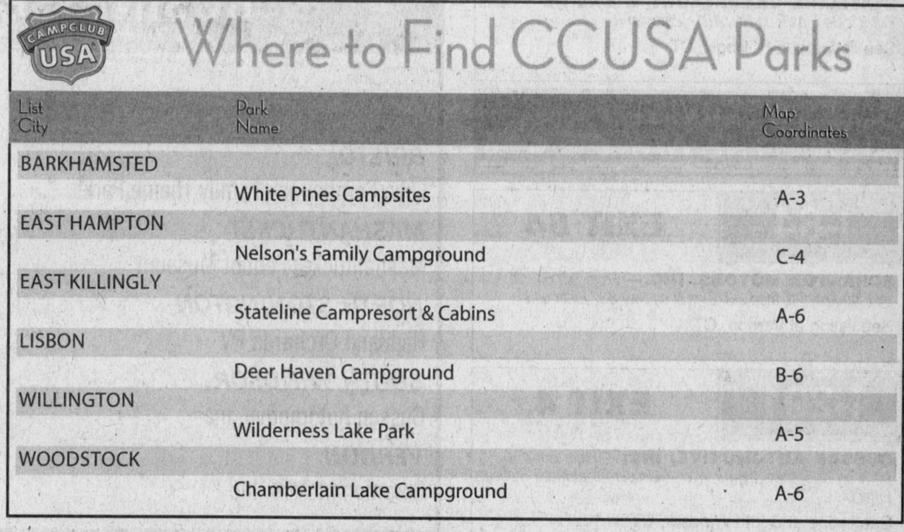

Where to Find CCUSA Parks

List City	Park Name	Map Coordinates
BARKHAMSTED		
	White Pines Campsites	A-3
EAST HAMPTON		
	Nelson's Family Campground	C-4
EAST KILLINGLY		
	Stateline Campresort & Cabins	A-6
LISBON		
	Deer Haven Campground	B-6
WILLINGTON		
	Wilderness Lake Park	A-5
WOODSTOCK		
	Chamberlain Lake Campground	A-6

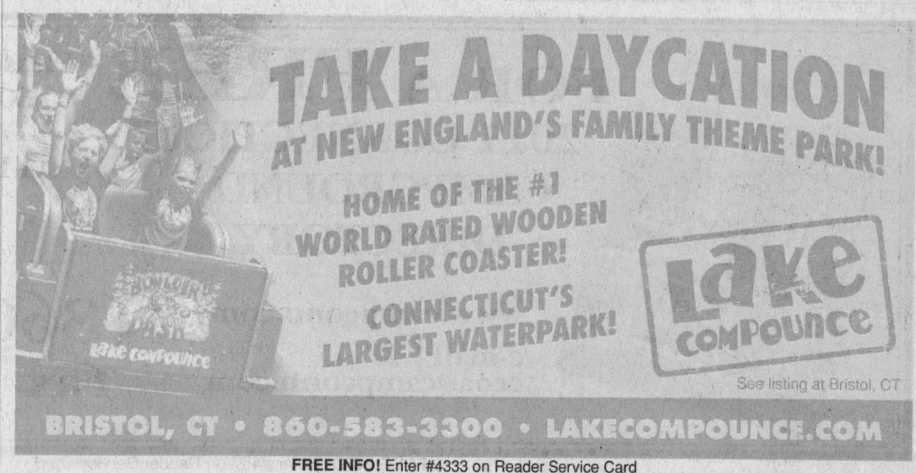

SHOPPING

Cannondale Village, Wilton. New England village with historic buildings offers antiques, arts and crafts.

Clinton Crossing Premium Outlets, Clinton. 70 famous name outlet stores. 20-A Killingworth Tpke. www.premiumoutlets.com/clinton

Crystal Mall, Waterford. Over 125 specialty shops. Located on Rt. 85.

Elephant's Trunk Flea Market, New Milford. Over 300 dealers selling antiques, tools, books, toys, electronics and more. Located on Rte.7.

Olde Mistick Village, Mystic. Over 60 stores and restaurants in a colonial New England setting. At 27 Coogan Blvd.

Stratford Antique Center, Stratford. Antique co-op shop with approx. 200 antique and collectible dealers. Located at 400 Honeyspot Rd.

The Old Carriage Shop Antiques Center, Bantam. Over 20 antique dealers offering furniture, books, glassware, pottery, vintage jewelry and clothing and more. At 920 Bantam Road.

DESTINATIONS

FAIRFIELD COUNTY

Thirty miles of beautiful coastline. A stone's throw from New York City. Rolling hills and picturesque New England countryside. Fairfield County is all of this and more. Travelers looking for a quiet country getaway, or chic hotels, boutique shopping, and first class dining will find all of this, and much, much more.

Bridgeport. Local attractions include the **Connecticut Beardsley Zoo** and **The Discovery Museum**—an interactive art and science museum. See a mummy, Victorian palace, Lilliputian circus and more at the Barnum Museum. Other local museums are the Housatonic Museum of Art and the City Lights Gallery, featuring emerging Connecticut artists.

Fairfield. Connecticut's Audubon Society Birdcraft Museum & Sanctuary, a National Historic Landmark and first nature center in America features wildlife exhibits, children's activity corner, dinosaur footprints and nature trails. The **Ogden House & Gardens** feature an 18th-century saltbox farmhouse furnished to portray the lives of its Revolutionary War-era inhabitants, wildflower trails and herb gardens.

Greenwich. Among the attractions to visit here are the **Audubon Greenwich** wildlife sanctuaries, the **Bruce Museum,** including environmental galleries and a marine touch tank and **Putnam Cottage**, a Revolutionary War era tavern and meeting place.

Norwalk. Located on Long Island Sound, attractions include the Maritime Aquarium at Norwalk, housing a museum, aquarium, IMAX Theater, maritime history hall and interactive exhibits. Or visit the Lockwood-Mathews Mansion Museum, a 62 room Victorian palace dating from 1864. Take a picturesque ferry ride to Sheffield Island, a three-acre park with picnic area and an1868 lighthouse that has four levels and 10 rooms to explore. Other local attractions include the Norwalk Museum, featuring collections and exhibitions that reflect the history, lives and cultures of the local people from its settle-

I-395 EXIT 93

STATELINE CAMPRESORT & CABINS— *From Exit 93: Go 5 mi E on Hwy 101. Enter on R.*
See listing at E. Killingly, CT

I-84 EXIT 64

SCRANTON MOTORS, INC.— *From Exit 64: Go 1/4 mi E on Kelly Rd, then 2-1/2 mi N on Hwy 83. Enter on L.*
See listing at Vernon, CT

I-291 EXIT 4

CUSSON AUTOMOTIVE, INC.— *From Exit 4: Go 1 mi N on US5, then 1/8 mi W on Mascolo Rd at Mobil Station. Enter on L.*
See listing at South Windsor, CT

BUSINESSES OFFERING

	Things to See & Do	RV Sales	RV Service
BRISTOL			
Lake Compounce Family Theme Park	⚑		
MASHANTUCKET			
Mashantucket Pequot Museum	⚑		
NORTH STONINGTON			
Highland Orchards RV		🚌	✱
SOUTH WINDSOR			
Cusson Automotive, Inc			✱
VERNON			
Scranton Motors, Inc			✱

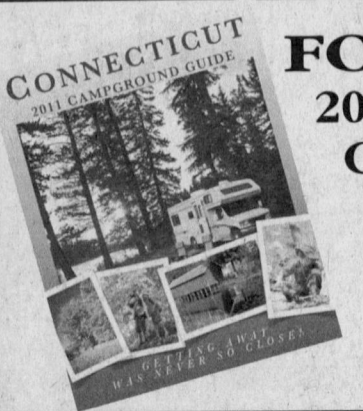

ment to the present; WPA Murals at City Hall and the SoNo Switch Tower Museum. At Stepping Stones Museum for Children, named one of America's Top 50 Children's Museums, children ages ten and under can visit four main galleries, a toddlers-only gallery and more than 100 hands-on activities.

White Memorial Foundation & Conservation Center, Litchfield. Grounds open year-round daily. There are 4,000 acres of nature preserve with 35 miles of trails for hiking, cross-country skiing, birdwatching, picnicking, camping and boating. Nature Museum contains unique exhibits depicting the history and natural resources of the area, as well as a Children's Room and Nature Store. Open year-round.

Institute for American Indian Studies, Washington. The Institute is a museum, and also an education and research center dedicated to the study of the indigenous peoples throughout the western hemisphere, particularly those of the Eastern Woodlands. Longhouse Room with mural depicting village life, permanent exhibit with local artifacts, Connecticut archaeology exhibit, Children's Discovery Room, temporary exhibit gallery featuring art and historical collections, Gift Shop; Outside: 17th century replicated Algonkian Village, simulated Archaeological Site, Healing Plant Garden, Three Sisters Garden, Four Signed Nature Trails. Open year-round.

Naugatuck Railroad, Thomaston. Scenic vintage train ride on the Naugatuck Railroad from the historic 1881 train station in Thomaston. The ride follows the Naugatuck River, passes through state forests, past elements of the regions industrial heritage to the Litchfield Hills. Special events include: Santa Express, Day Out With Thomas, Haight-Brown Vineyard Express, fall foliage events and more.

MYSTIC COUNTRY

People travel from all over the world to explore this region of eastern Connecticut. Yankee heritage abounds in charming villages, scenic farm roads and ancient stonewall, waterfronts, ferries, and yachts. Here, visitors will find a wealth of attractions and events of all sizes.

Coventry. See the **Nathan Hale Homestead** filled with original furnishings.

Groton. Take a trip to the **Naval Submarine Base** and board the **USS Nautilus**, the world's first nuclear-powered submarine. See working periscopes and mini-subs and learn the history of submarines at the **Submarine Force Museum**.

New London. The **Hempsted Houses** include the house of Joshua Hempsted built in 1678, and the adjacent rare 18th-century stone house built by his grandson, Nathaniel. The Joshua Hempsted house is the only Underground Railway stop open to the public on the Connecticut Freedom Trail. The **U.S. Coast Guard Academy** museum spans the 200-year history of America's premier

QUICK REFERENCE CHART FOR WOODALL'S FEATURED PARKS

	Green Friendly	RV Lots for Sale	Park Models-Onsite Ownership	Park Membership for Sale	Big Rigs Welcome	Internet Friendly	Pets Welcome
BOZRAH							
Odetah Camping Resort	🍂				▲	●	■
CANAAN							
Lone Oak Campsites	🍂				▲	●	■
EAST KILLINGLY							
Stateline Campresort & Cabins						●	■
EAST LYME							
Aces High RV Park	🍂				▲	●	■
EASTFORD							
Charlie Brown Campground	🍂				▲	●	■
GRISWOLD							
Countryside RV Park					▲	●	■
HIGGANUM							
Little City Campground							■
LEBANON							
Water's Edge Campground						●	■
LISBON							
Deer Haven Campground						●	■
PRESTON							
Hidden Acres Family Campground					▲	●	■
SALEM							
Salem Farms Campground						●	■
Witch Meadow Lake Campground	🍂					●	■
STAFFORD SPRINGS							
Mineral Springs Family Campground						●	■
WOODSTOCK							
Chamberlain Lake Campground						●	■

Green Friendly 🍂; RV Lots for Sale ✖; Park Models/Onsite Onwership ✱; Park Memberships for Sale ✔; Big Rigs Welcome ▲; Internet Friendly ●; Internet Friendly-WiFi ●; Pets Welcome ■

maritime service. Tall ship Eagle is open when in port.

Mashantucket. Foxwoods Resort Casino is a world-class gaming facility with over 7,000 slots, three hotels, a variety of restaurants and specialty shops. If you're interested in the natural history of southern New England, visit the **Mashantucket Pequot Museum & Research Center,** with extensive permanent exhibits which include a cool descent into a glacial crevasse from 18,000 years ago.

Mystic. Mystic Seaport, a re-created 19th century coastal village. **Mystic Aquarium**, featuring a re-created Louisiana Bayou, Beluga whales and California sea lions.

Old Lyme. The **Florence Griswold Museum**, a national historic landmark, is America's best-known center of Impressionist painting, offering 11 landscaped acres along the Lieutenant River, an education center, restored artist studio, gardens, 1910 Griswold House and the Krieble Gallery for American art.

LITCHFIELD HILLS

West of Harford, and east of New York State lies the charming area known as Litchfield Hills. Here, the Housatonic River provides water to the villages and farms that line its path. No itinerary would be complete without a visit to Kent Falls State Park, and the 250-foot cascade nestled inside it, or the Tapping Reeve House and Law School. This was the first law school in the state, and remains furnished with 18th century pieces.

Bethlehem. Bellamy-Ferriday House & Garden, a 1754 home transformed into a 20th century country estate, includes antiques, a formal garden of historic roses, lilacs and peonies and an orchard.

Bristol. Exhibits at the **New England Carousel Museum** include the finest pieces of antique carousel art in existence. Also houses a fine art gallery with changing shows, a show and sale gallery for reproduction carousel pieces and contemporary woodcarving. **The Museum of Fire History** displays fire department and firehouse memorabilia and collectibles dating back to the mid-1800s. Permanent exhibit at **American Clock & Watch Museum** tells the story of Connecticut clock making and the Industrial Revolution. The largest collection of American production clocks on public display.

RIVER VALLEY

Connecticut's River Valley offers big city sophistication with all the charms and splendors of the New England countryside. There are sparkling rivers and shoreline, centuries of history and culture, and an endless array of sights to be explored and enjoyed.

Hartford. Visit the 1817 **Harriet Beecher Stowe House**. This Victorian cottage was the home of the author of Uncle Tom's Cabin. Grounds include gardens, gift shop and research library. The Mark Twain House, also in Hartford, is an elaborate Victorian (1874) mansion and National Historic Landmark. Visit the Wadsworth Atheneum Museum of Art, the nation's oldest public art museum (1842) and view world-renowned collections including Hudson River School landscapes, Old Master paintings and modernist masterpieces.

New Britain. The 40-foot **National Iwo Jima Memorial Monument** depicts in bronze and granite the sacrifice and courage displayed by Americans in one of the greatest battles in American history. Unique WWII Memorial Eternal Flame. **The New Britain Museum of American Art** has over 10,000 American works of art from colonial times to the present.

GREATER NEW HAVEN

Once the home of the Quinnipiac tribe of Native Americans, Greater New Haven is now home to the prestigious Yale University. Art and architecture abound in this area on an Ivy League scale. Visitors will enjoy Hammonasset Beach State Park, Connecticut's longest saltwater beach, and no one can resist the 80,000 pieces of cartoon art, and theater at the Barker Character, Comic & Cartoon Museum in Chester.

Cheshire. Barker Character, Comic & Cartoon Museum displays over 80,000 items including toys and character collectibles from 1873 to present.

New Haven. Forts from Revolutionary War (Black Rock) and Civil War (Nathan Hale) have spectacular views of New Harbor. At **Yale University** you can visit the **Peabody Museum of Natural History, Yale Collection of Musical Instruments, Art Gallery** and **Center for British Art** – all open to the public.

ANNUAL EVENTS

JANUARY

Hygienic Annual Art Show, New London; The Sun Winefest, Mohegan Sun.

FEBRUARY

Annual Flower and Garden Show, Hartford; Winter Carnival, Chester; Romantic Chocolate Festival, Willimantic.

MARCH

Mystic Irish Parade, Mystic.

APRIL

Earth Day Celebration, New London; Annual Daffodil Festival, Meriden.

MAY

May Day Festival & Bed Race, Mystic; Mystic Annual Dogwood Festival, Fairfield; Seaport's Annual Lobster Days, Mystic; Annual Bluegrass Festival, Preston.

JUNE

Annual Arts & Ideas, New Haven; Farmington Antiques Weekend, Farmington; Annual Blast From the Bayou Festival, Preston; Berlin Blues Festival, East Berlin; Mystic Seaport Sea Music, Mystic; Annual Strawberry Festival & Craft Fair, Unionville.

JULY

Boombox Parade, Willmantic; Riverfest, Hartford/East Hartford; Open House Day Tour of Litchfield, Litchfield; Guilford Handcrafts Exposition, Guilford; Deep River Ancient Muster, Deep River; New England Arts and Crafts Festival, Milford; North Stonington Agricultural Fair, North Stonington; Annual Craft Expo, Guilford; The Midsummer Festival, Old Lyme; Great Connecticut Traditional Jazz Festival, Moodus; Annual Antique & Classic Boat Rendezvous, Mystic Seaport.

AUGUST

Nutmeg State Games, Statewide; Litchfield Jazz Festival, Kent; SoNo Arts Celebration, South Norwalk; Mystic Outdoor Art Festival, Mystic; Grand Band Slam, Hartford; Audubon Festival, Sharon; Annual Milford Oyster Festival, Milford; Bridgewater County Fair, Bridgewater; Wolcott County Fair, Wolcott; Brooklyn Fair, Brooklyn; Chester Fair, Chester; The Terryville Country Fair, Terryville; Haddam Neck Fair, Haddam; Woodstock Fair, Woodstock.

SEPTEMBER

Grecian Fair, Norwich; Bethlehem Fair, Bethlehem; Norwalk Oyster Festival, East Norwalk; Boats Books & Brushes with Taste, New London; Durham Fair, Durham; Chrysanthemum Festival, Bristol; Hebron Harvest Fair, Hebron; North Haven Fair, North Haven; Foxwoods Food & Wine Festival, Ledyard; Annual Apple Harvest Festival, Southington; The Connecticut Renaissance Faire, Hebron (through October).

OCTOBER

Northeast Connecticut Annual Walking Weekend; Greater Hartford Marathon, Hartford; Chowderfest, Mystic; Head of the Connecticut Regatta, Middletown; Portland Fair, Portland.

NOVEMBER

Holiday Craft Exhibition & Sale, Brookfield; Fantasy of Lights, New Haven; Celebration of American Crafts, New Haven; Sugarloaf Crafts Festival, Harford.

DECEMBER

Lantern Light Tours, Mystic; First Night Hartford, Hartford.

All privately owned campgrounds personally inspected by WOODALL'S Representatives

Greg and Maureen Baron

ABINGTON—A-6

(E) MASHAMOQUET BROOK STATE PARK—(Windham) *From jct Hwy-101 & US-44: Go 1 mi E on US-44.* FACILITIES: 55 sites, 35 ft max RV length, 55 no hkups, tenting, dump. RECREATION: lake swim, lake fishing. No pets. Partial handicap access. Open Apr 16 - Oct 11. Phone: (860)928-6121.

ASHFORD—A-5

(N) Brialee RV & Tent Park—(Windham) *From jct US 44 & Hwy 89: Go 1 mi N on Hwy 89, then 1/2 mi W on Perry Hill Rd. then 3/4 mi N on Laurel Lane. Enter at end.* ◊◊◊◊FACILITIES: 267 sites, typical site width 40 ft, 62 full hkups, 199 W&E, (20/30 amps), 6 no hkups, 10 pull-thrus, family camping, tenting, dump, laundry, groceries. ◊◊◊◊◊RECREATION: swim pool, boating, no motors, dock, pond fishing, playground. Pets welcome, quantity restrict. Partial handicap access. Open Mar 15 - Dec 1. Facilities fully operational Apr 1 - Oct 31. Green Friendly. Rate in 2010 $35-55 per family. Member ARVC, CCOA. Phone: (800)303-CAMP.

BANTAM—B-2

(SW) Cozy Hills Campground—(Litchfield) *From jct Hwy 63 & Hwy 202: Go 3-1/2 mi W on Hwy 202. Enter on L.* ◊◊◊FACILITIES: 109 sites, 70 W&E, (30/50 amps), 39 no hkups, family camping, tenting, dump, ltd groc. ◊◊◊◊RECREATION: swim pool, boating, no motors, canoeing, lake/pond fishing, playground. Pets welcome, breed restrict, quantity restrict. Partial handicap access. Open Apr 23 - Oct 15. Big rigs welcome. Rate in 2010 $56 per family. Member ARVC, CCOA. Phone: (860)567-2119.

BARKHAMSTED—A-3

(N) White Pines Campsites—(Litchfield) *From jct US 44 & Hwy 8: Go 1-3/4 mi N on Hwy 8, then 1/4 mi E on Hwy 20, then 3/4 mi S on Old North Rd. Enter on L.* ◊◊◊FACILITIES: 210 sites, typical site width 26 ft, 200 W&E, (20/30/50 amps), 10 no hkups, 32 pull-thrus, cable TV, WiFi Internet central location, family camping, tenting, RV storage, dump, non-guest dump $, portable dump, groceries, RV supplies, LP gas by weight/by meter, ice, picnic tables, fire rings, wood. ◊◊◊RECREATION: rec hall, pavilion, swim pool, no motors, pond fishing, fishing supplies, bsktball, playground, activities, horseshoes, v-ball. Pets welcome, breed restrict. Open Mid Apr - Mid Oct. Rate in 2010 $42-53 per family. MC/VISA/DISC. Member ARVC, CCOA. FMCA discount. CCUSA 50% Discount. CCUSA reservations Recommended, CCUSA max stay 3 days, CCUSA disc. not avail S, Th, CCUSA disc. not avail F,Sa, CCUSA disc. not avail holidays.

Phone: (860)379-0124
Address: 232 Old North Rd., Barkhamsted, CT 06063
Lat/Lon: 41.93814/-73.03909
Email: info@whitepinescamp.com
Web: www.whitepinescamp.com

BOZRAH—C-5

(W) ODETAH CAMPING RESORT—(New London) *N'b from jct I-395 (exit 81W) & Hwy 2: Go 3-1/2 mi W on Hwy 2 (exit 23), then 1/4 mi S on Houghton Rd, straight at intrsctn & stop sign. S'b from jct I-395 (exit 82) & Hwy 2: Go 3-1/2 mi W on Hwy 2, then 100 yds S on Houghton Rd, then straight at intrsc. Enter on R.*

◊◊◊◊◊FACILITIES: 321 sites, typical site width 40 ft, 41 full hkups, 251 W&E, (20/30/50 amps), 29 no hkups, some extd stay sites (summer), 30 pull-thrus, WiFi Instant Internet at site, WiFi Internet central location, family camping, tenting, cabins, RV storage, dump, non-guest dump $, portable dump, laundry, full svc store, RV supplies, LP gas by weight, ice, picnic tables, fire rings, wood, controlled access.

◊◊◊◊◊RECREATION: rec hall, rec room/area, equipped pavilion, coin games, swim pool, lake swim, hot tub, boating, electric motors only, canoeing, kayaking, ramp, 5 rowboat/7 canoe/8 kayak/6 pedal boat rentals, lake fishing, fishing supplies, mini-golf, ($), golf nearby, bsktball, playground, shuffleboard court 5 shuffleboard courts, activities, tennis, horseshoes, sports field, v-ball.

Pets welcome. Partial handicap access. Open May 1 - Oct 31. All water & electric sites have a gray water connection. Big rigs welcome. Escort to site. Clubs welcome. Green Friendly. Rate in 2010 $40-45 for 2 persons. MC/VISA/DISC/AMEX. ATM. Member ARVC, CCOA.

Text 107915 to (440)725-8687 to see our Visual Tour.

Phone: (860)889-4144
Address: 38 Bozrah St Ext, Bozrah, CT 06334
Lat/Lon: 41.55984/-72.15862
Email: info@odetah.com
Web: www.odetah.com

SEE AD NEXT PAGE

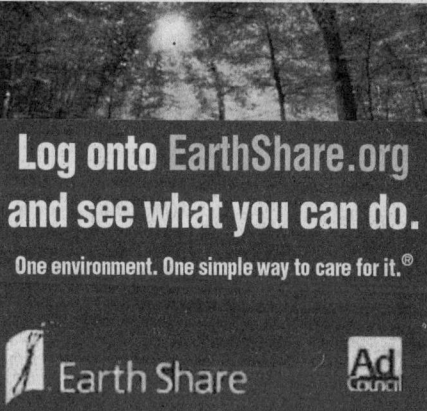

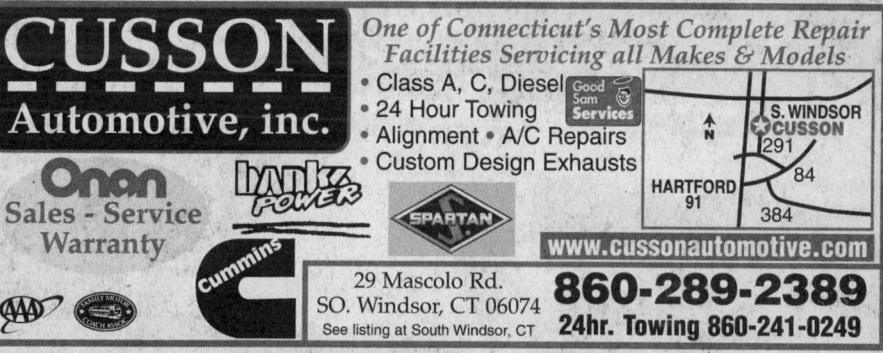

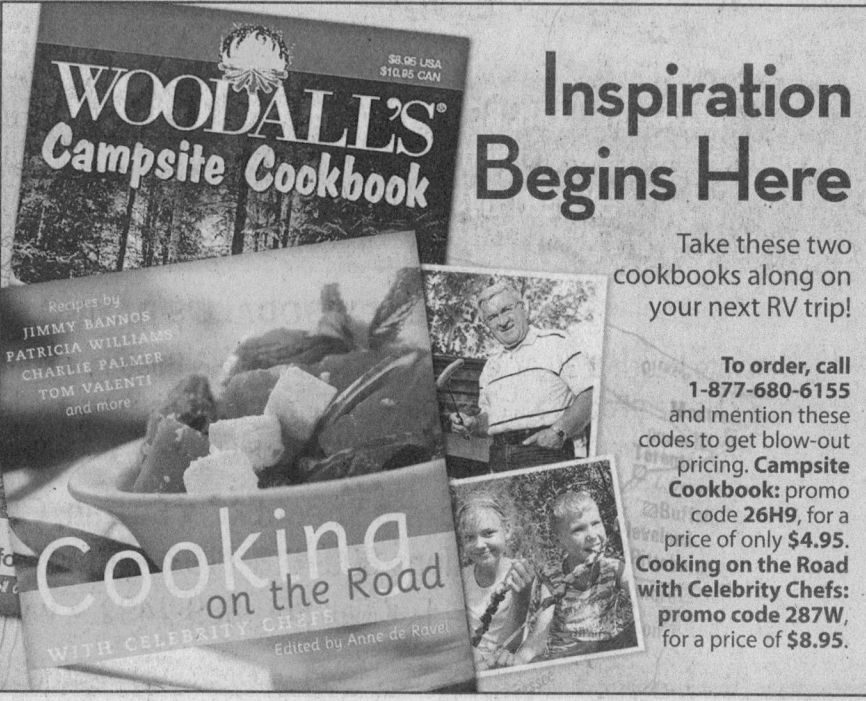

Woodall's Tip... All privately-owned RV parks/campgrounds are personally inspected each year by one of our 25 Representative Teams.

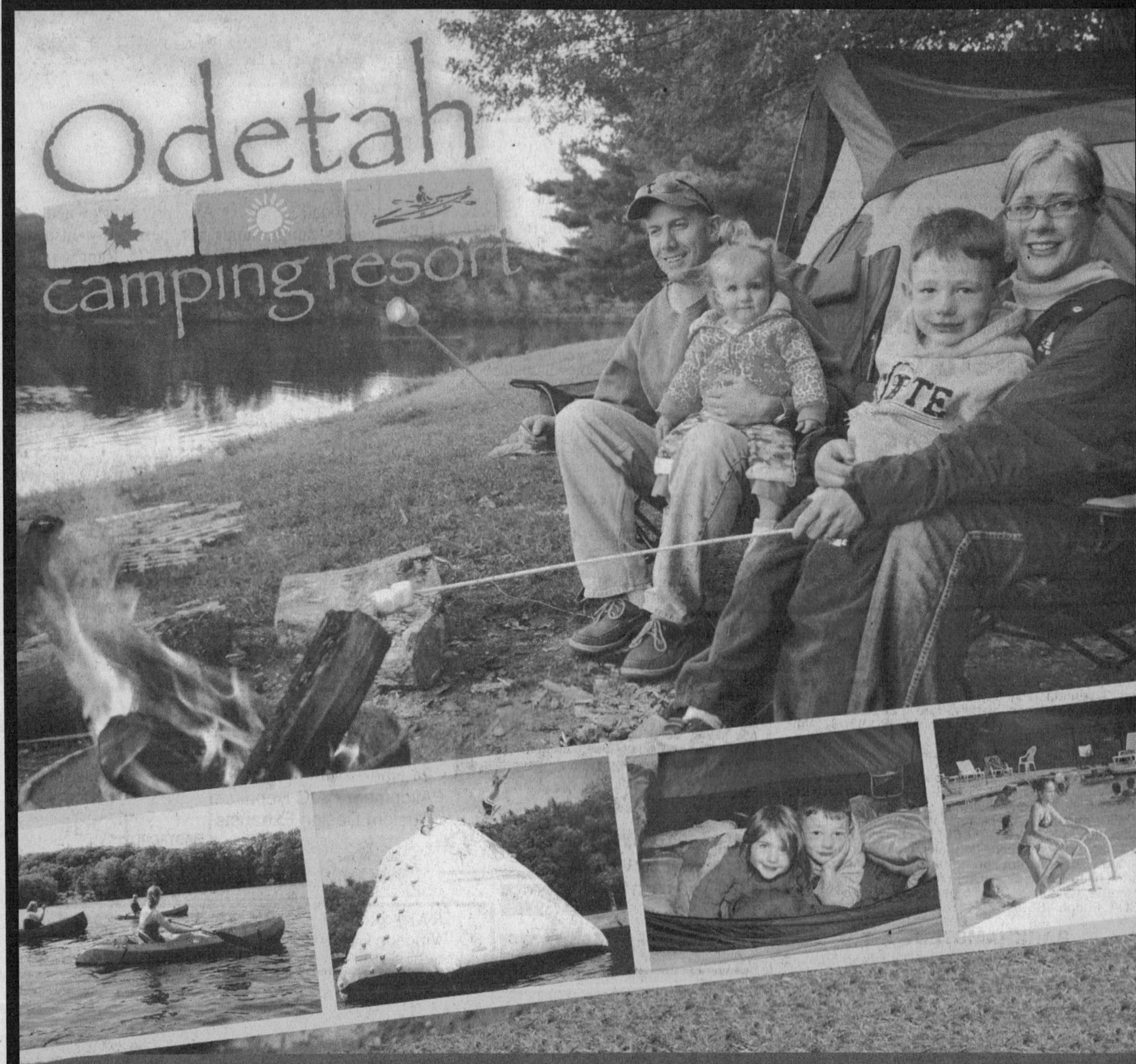
Odetah
camping resort
TE

BRISTOL—B-3

(S) LAKE COMPOUNCE FAMILY THEME PARK—*From jct I-84 (exit 31) & Hwy 229: Go 2 mi N on Hwy 229, then 1 mi W on Welch Rd, then 1 mi N on Mt. Vernon Rd/Lake Avenue. Enter on R.* A 325-acre family theme park including a 23 acre lake. The nation's oldest amusement park and Connecticut's larges water park.

Phone: (860)583-3300
Address: 271 Enterprise Dr, Bristol, CT 06010
Lat/Lon: 41.64747/-72.92351
Web: www.lakecompounce.com

SEE AD TRAVEL SECTION PAGE 41

CANAAN—A-2

(E) LONE OAK CAMPSITES—(Litchfield) *From jct US 7 & US 44: Go 3-1/2 mi E on US 44. Enter on R.*
◊◊◊◊FACILITIES: 480 sites, typical site width 30 ft, 373 full hkups, 64 W&E, (20/30/50 amps), 43 no hkups, many extd stay sites, 25 pull-thrus, cable TV, WiFi Instant Internet at site, family camping, tenting, RV's/park model rentals, cabins, RV storage, shower$, dump, non-guest dump $, laundry, full svc store, RV supplies, LP gas by weight/by meter, ice, picnic tables, fire rings, wood, controlled access.

◊◊◊◊◊RECREATION: rec hall, rec room/area, pavilion, coin games, 2 swim pools, wading pool, hot tub, river/pond/stream fishing, fishing supplies, golf nearby, bsktball, playground, activities, horseshoes, sports field, v-ball.

Pets welcome. Partial handicap access. Open Apr 15 - Oct 15. Big rigs welcome. Clubs welcome. Green Friendly. Rate in 2010 $48-65 for 2 persons. MC/VISA/DISC. Member ARVC, CCOA.

Phone: (800)422-2267
Address: 360 Norfolk Rd, Rte 44, East Canaan, CT 06024
Lat/Lon: 42.00973/-73.26234
Email: info@loneoakcampsites.com
Web: www.loneoakcampsites.com

SEE AD THIS PAGE

CHAPLIN—B-5

(N) Nickerson Park Family Campground—(Windham) *From jct US 6 & Hwy 198: Go 4-1/2 mi N on Hwy 198. Enter on R.* ◊◊FACILITIES: 100 sites, typical site width 45 ft, 36 full hkups, 63 W&E, (20/30 amps), 1 no hkups, 5 pull-thrus, family camping, tenting, dump, ltd groc. ◊◊◊RECREATION: river swim, canoeing, river fishing, playground. Pets welcome. Open all yr. Rate in 2010 $25-27.50 per family. Member ARVC, CCOA. Phone: (860)455-0007.

CLINTON—D-4

(NW) Riverdale Farm Campsite—(Middlesex) *From jct Hwy 81 & I-95: Go 1 mi W on I-95 (exit 62), then 200 feet N on Hammonasett, then 1/2 mi E on Duck Hole Rd, then E over river, then 1-1/2 mi N on River Rd. Enter on L.* ◊◊◊◊FACILITIES: 250 sites, typical site width 45 ft, 150 full hkups, 100 W&E, (20/30/50 amps), 15 pull-thrus, family camping, tenting, dump, laundry, ltd groc. ◊◊◊◊◊RECREATION: river swim, boating, canoeing, river/pond fishing, playground. Pets welcome. Partial handicap access. Open Apr 15 - Nov 1. Rate in 2010 $40-45 for 5 persons. Member ARVC, CCOA. Phone: (860)669-5388.

CORNWALL BRIDGE—B-2

HOUSATONIC MEADOWS STATE PARK—(Litchfield) *From jct US-7 & Hwy-4: Go 1-1/2 mi NE on US-7.* FACILITIES: 95 sites, 35 ft max RV length, 95 no hkups, tenting, dump. RECREATION: canoeing, river fishing. No pets. Open Mid Apr - Dec 31. Phone: (860)672-6772.

EAST HADDAM—C-4

(E) DEVIL'S HOPYARD STATE PARK—(Middlesex) *From town: Go 1 mi E on Hwy 82, then continue 8 mi E. On Hopyard Rd.* FACILITIES: 21 sites, 35 ft max RV length, 21 no hkups, tenting. RECREATION: stream fishing. No pets. Open Mid Apr - Memorial Day Weekend. Phone: (860)526-2336.

(E) Wolf's Den Family Campground—(Middlesex) *From jct Hwy 149 & Hwy 82: Go 3 mi E on Hwy 82. Enter on L.* ◊◊◊FACILITIES: 209 sites, typical site width 30 ft, 209 W&E, (30/50 amps), family camping, tenting, dump, laundry, groceries. ◊◊◊RECREATION: swim pool, pond fishing, playground. Pets welcome. Partial handicap access. Open First weekend in May - Last weekend in Oct. Rate in 2010 $42 per family. Member ARVC, CCOA. Phone: (860)873-9681.

EAST HAMPTON—C-4

(N) Nelson's Family Campground—(Middlesex) *From jct Hwy 2 (exit 13) & Hwy 66: Go 4-1/2 mi W on Hwy 66, then 1-1/2 mi N on North Main St (follow Lake Dr), then 3/4 mi W on Mott Hill Rd. Enter on L.* ◊◊◊FACILITIES: 325 sites, typical site width 45 ft, 325 W&E, (30/50 amps), cable TV, WiFi Internet central location, family camping, tenting, shower$, dump, portable dump, laundry, ltd groc, RV supplies, LP gas by weight/by meter, ice, picnic tables, fire rings, wood. ◊◊◊◊RECREATION: pavilion, swim pool, pond fishing, fishing supplies, mini-golf, ($), bsktball, playground, activities, horseshoes, v-ball. Pets welcome. Partial handicap access. Open Apr 15 - Columbus Day. Big rigs welcome. Rate in 2010 $42 per family. MC/VISA/DISC. Member ARVC, CCOA. CCUSA 50% Discount. CCUSA reservations Recommended, CCUSA max stay 5 days, CCUSA disc. not avail F,Sa, CCUSA disc. not avail holidays.

Phone: (860)267-5300
Address: 71 Mott Hill Rd, East Hampton, CT 06424
Lat/Lon: 41.61079/-72.51245
Email: nelsonsfamilycampground@msn.com
Web: www.nelsonscampground.com

EAST KILLINGLY—A-6

(NE) STATELINE CAMPRESORT & CABINS—(Windham) *From jct I-395 and Hwy 101 (exit 93): Go 5 mi E on Hwy 101. Enter on R.*

FINEST FAMILY CAMPING ON CT/RI LINE
Join us for your best-ever family camping experience. We offer many fun filled activities-rental units-and Spring, Summer and Fall specials. Reservations taken year round. It's always a GREAT time at Stateline!

◊◊◊FACILITIES: 219 sites, typical site width 35 ft, 41 ft max RV length, 7 full hkups, 203 W&E, (15/20/30/50 amps), 50 amps ($), 9 no hkups, some extd stay sites (summer), 5 pull-thrus, heater not allowed, WiFi Instant Internet at site, family camping, tenting, RV's/park model rentals, cabins, dump, portable dump, laundry, ltd groc, RV supplies, LP gas by weight/by meter, ice, picnic tables, fire rings, wood, controlled access.

STATELINE CAMPRESORT & CABINS—Continued on next page

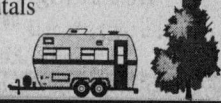

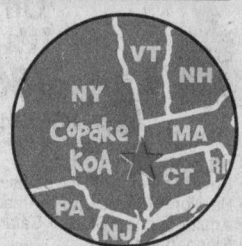

EAST KILLINGLY—Continued
STATELINE CAMPRESORT & CABINS—Continued

◇◇◇◇◇RECREATION: rec room/area, equipped pavilion, coin games, swim pool, boating, dock, 5 rowboat rentals, lake/pond fishing, fishing supplies, golf nearby, bsktball, playground, activities, horseshoes, sports field, v-ball.

Pets welcome ($). Partial handicap access. Open Apr 15 - Oct 31. Reservations taken all year. Clubs welcome. Rate in 2010 $30-40 per family. MC/VISA. Member ARVC, CCOA. CCUSA 50% Discount. CCUSA reservations Required, CCUSA max stay 5 days, CCUSA disc. not avail F,Sa, CCUSA disc. not avail holidays. No drive-ups.

Phone: (860)774-3016
Address: 1639 Hartford Pike, East Killingly, CT 06243
Lat/Lon: 41.84873/-71.79523
Email: camplands@aol.com
Web: www.statelinecampresort.com

SEE AD THIS PAGE AND AD TRAVEL SECTION PAGE 42

EAST LYME—D-5

(N) ACES HIGH RV PARK—(New London) *From jct I-95 (exit 74) & Hwy 161: Go 3 mi N on Hwy 161. Enter on R.*

WELCOME

◇◇◇◇◇FACILITIES: 90 sites, typical site width 45 ft, 90 full hkups, (20/30/50 amps), some extd stay sites (summer), 47 pull-thrus, cable TV, WiFi Instant Internet at site, family camping, cabins, RV storage, shower$, dump, non-guest dump $, laundry, ltd groc, RV supplies, LP gas by meter, ice, picnic tables, fire rings, grills, wood, controlled access.

◇◇◇◇◇RECREATION: rec room/area, coin games, lake swim, boating, canoeing, rowboat/2 canoe/2 pedal boat rentals, pond/stream fishing, fishing supplies, golf nearby, bsktball, 5 bike rentals, playground, activities, horseshoes, sports field, hiking trails, v-ball.

Pets welcome. Partial handicap access. No tents. Open all yr. Big rigs welcome. Clubs welcome. Green Friendly. Rate in 2010 $49-54 for 2 persons. MC/VISA/DISC. Member ARVC, CCOA.

Phone: (860)739-8858
Address: 301 Chesterfield Rd, East Lyme, CT 06333
Lat/Lon: 41.40562/-72.22552
Email: sales@aceshighrvpark.com
Web: www.aceshighrvpark.com

SEE AD MYSTIC NEXT PAGE

EASTFORD—A-5

(S) CHARLIE BROWN CAMPGROUND—(Windham) *From jct US 44 & Hwy 198: Go 1 mi S on Hwy 198. Enter on L.*

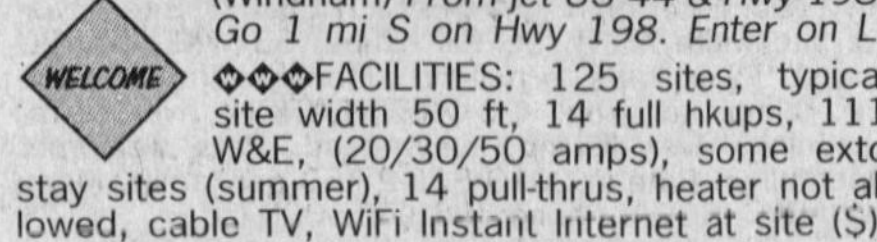

WELCOME

◇◇◇FACILITIES: 125 sites, typical site width 50 ft, 14 full hkups, 111 W&E, (20/30/50 amps), some extd stay sites (summer), 14 pull-thrus, heater not allowed, cable TV, WiFi Instant Internet at site ($), WiFi Internet central location, family camping, tenting, shower$, dump, portable dump, laundry, ltd groc, RV supplies, LP gas by weight/by meter, ice, picnic tables, fire rings, wood.

◇◇◇◇RECREATION: rec room/area, pavilion, coin games, river swim, river fishing, fishing supplies, golf nearby, bsktball, playground, activities, (wkends), horseshoes, sports field, v-ball.

Pets welcome. Partial handicap access. Open Apr 15 - Oct 15. Big rigs welcome. Clubs welcome. Green Friendly. Rate in 2010 $43-60 for 4 persons. MC/VISA. Member ARVC, CCOA.

Phone: (877)974-0142
Address: 98 Chaplin Rd, Eastford, CT 06242
Lat/Lon: 41.84700/-72.09346
Email: info@charliebrowncampground.com
Web: charliebrowncampground.com

SEE AD THIS PAGE

(S) Peppertree Camping—(Windham) *From jct US 44 & Hwy 198: Go 1-1/2 mi S on Hwy 198. Enter on L.* ◇◇◇FACILITIES: 61 sites, typical site width 30 ft, 36 ft max RV length, 41 full hkups, 20 W&E, (20/30 amps), 4 pull-thrus, family camping, tenting, dump, laundry, ltd groc. ◇◇◇RECREATION: river swim, river fishing, playground. Pets welcome. Open Mid Apr - Mid Oct. Rate in 2010 $28-30 per family. Member ARVC, CCOA. Phone: (860)974-1439.

FOXWOODS CASINO-LEDYARD—C-6

ODETAH CAMPING RESORT—*From Foxwoods High Stakes Indian Bingo & Casino: Go 10 mi NW on Hwy 2 (exit 23), then 1/4 mi S on Houghton Rd, then straight at intersection & stop sign. Enter on R.*

WELCOME

SEE PRIMARY LISTING AT BOZRAH AND AD BOZRAH PAGE 46

Connecticut is home to the oldest U.S. newspaper still being published. The Hartford Courant has been in print since its establishment in 1764.

GRISWOLD—C-6

(E) COUNTRYSIDE RV PARK—(New London) *From jct Hwy-138 & Hwy-201: Go 1 mi S on Hwy-201, then 1/3 mi E on Cook Hill Rd. Enter on R.*

WELCOME

YOUR FAMILY'S HOME AWAY FROM HOME!
Our loving, peaceful surroundings calm your soul! Come for a swim or relax on our beach. Our large gathering room and wrap-around porch make for rain or shine events! Large sites with plenty of elbow room & full hookups.

◇◇◇◇FACILITIES: 118 sites, typical site width 50 ft, 118 full hkups, (30/50 amps), many extd stay sites (summer), 7 pull-thrus, heater not allowed, WiFi Internet central location, family camping, RV storage, dump, non-guest dump $, portable dump, laundry, LP gas by meter, ice, picnic tables, fire rings, wood, controlled access.

◇◇◇◇RECREATION: rec room/area, pavilion, lake swim, pond fishing, golf nearby, bsktball, playground, shuffleboard court shuffleboard court, activities (wkends), horseshoes, sports field, hiking trails, v-ball.

Pets welcome. Partial handicap access. No tents. Open May 1 - Oct 9. Big rigs welcome. Clubs welcome. Rate in 2010 $40 per family. MC/VISA/DISC/AMEX. Member ARVC, CCOA.

Phone: (860)376-0029
Address: 75 Cook Hill Rd., Griswold, CT 06351
Lat/Lon: 41.56715/-71.88523
Web: www.countrysidecampground.com

SEE AD THIS PAGE

HIGGANUM—C-4

(SW) LITTLE CITY CAMPGROUND—(Haddam) *From jct Hwy 9 (exit 10) & Hwy 154: Go 2 mi SE on Hwy 154, then 3-1/4 mi SW on Candlewood Hill Rd, then 1 mi SW on Little City Rd.*

WELCOME

◇◇FACILITIES: 55 sites, 8 full hkups, 42 W&E, (30/50 amps), 5 no hkups, many extd stay sites, heater not allowed, family camping, tenting, dump, portable dump, laundry, LP gas by meter, ice, picnic tables, wood.

◇◇◇RECREATION: rec hall, swim pool, pond fishing, bsktball, play equipment, horseshoes, sports field, hiking trails.

Pets welcome. Open May 1 - Oct 1. Rate in 2010 $36-39 per family. Member ARVC, CCOA.

LITTLE CITY CAMPGROUND—Continued on next page

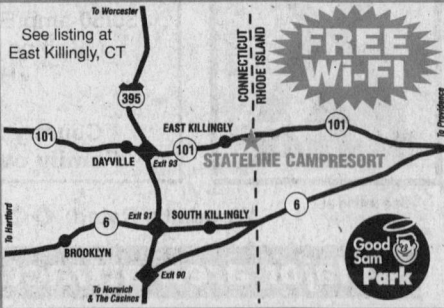

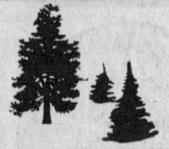

HIGGANUM—Continued
LITTLE CITY CAMPGROUND—Continued

Phone: (860)345-8469
Address: 741 Little City Road, Higganum, CT 06441
Lat/Lon: 41.45590/-72.60303

SEE AD PAGE 48

JEWETT CITY—B-6

(E) HOPEVILLE POND STATE PARK—(New London) *From Connecticut Tpk (exit 86): Go 1 mi E on Hwy 201.* FACILITIES: 80 sites, 80 no hkups, tenting, dump, ltd groc. RECREATION: river swim, boating, canoeing, ramp, river/pond fishing. No pets. Partial handicap access. Open Mid Apr - Sep 30. Phone: (860)376-2920.

KENT—B-1

(W) MACEDONIA BROOK STATE PARK—(Litchfield) *From jct US 7 & Hwy 341: Go 1-1/2 mi NW on Hwy 341, then 2 mi N on Macedonia Brook Rd.* FACILITIES: 51 sites, 51 no hkups, 11 pull-thrus, tenting. RECREATION: river swim, stream fishing. No pets. Open Apr 15 - Sep 30. Phone: (860)927-3238.

LEBANON—B-5

(W) WATER'S EDGE CAMPGROUND—(New London) *From jct Hwy 87 & Hwy 207: Go 5 mi W on Hwy 207, then 3/4 mi N on Leonard's Bridge Rd. Enter on L.*

◊◊◊FACILITIES: 202 sites, typical site width 40 ft, 192 W&E, (20/30 amps), 10 no hkups, many extd stay sites (summer), 5 pull-thrus, cable TV, ($), WiFi Instant Internet at site, WiFi Internet central location, family camping, tenting, RV's/park model rentals, cabins, shower$, dump, portable dump, laundry, groceries, RV supplies, LP gas by weight, ice, picnic tables, fire rings, wood, controlled access.

◊◊◊◊RECREATION: rec hall, rec room/area, pavilion, coin games, swim pool, lake swim, boating, canoeing, 2 rowboat/canoe/6 kayak/3 pedal boat rentals, lake fishing, fishing supplies, bsktball, playground, activities, (wkends), horseshoes, sports field, v-ball.

Pets welcome. Partial handicap access. Open Apr 15 - Oct 15. Clubs welcome. Rate in 2010 $40-45 for 2 persons. MC/VISA/DISC/AMEX. ATM. Member ARVC, CCOA.

Phone: (860)642-7470
Address: 271 Leonard Bridge Rd, Lebanon, CT 06249
Lat/Lon: 41.63806/-72.29315
Email: office@watersedgecampground.com
Web: watersedgecampground.com

SEE AD THIS PAGE

LISBON—B-6

(SW) DEER HAVEN CAMPGROUND—(New London) *From I-395 N (exit 83A) & Hwy 169: Go 1/2 mi N on Hwy 169, then 100 ft W on Kendall Rd Ext., then 1 mi W on Strnad Rd, then 175 yds N on Kenyon Rd. Enter at end.*

◊◊◊FACILITIES: 88 sites, typical site width 45 ft, 40 ft max RV length, 59 full hkups, 21 W&E, (20/30 amps), 8 no hkups, some extd stay sites (summer), WiFi Instant Internet at site, WiFi Internet central location, family camping, tenting, shower$, dump, laundry, ltd groc, RV supplies, LP gas by weight/by meter, ice, picnic tables, fire rings, wood, controlled access.

Connecticut was the fifth state.

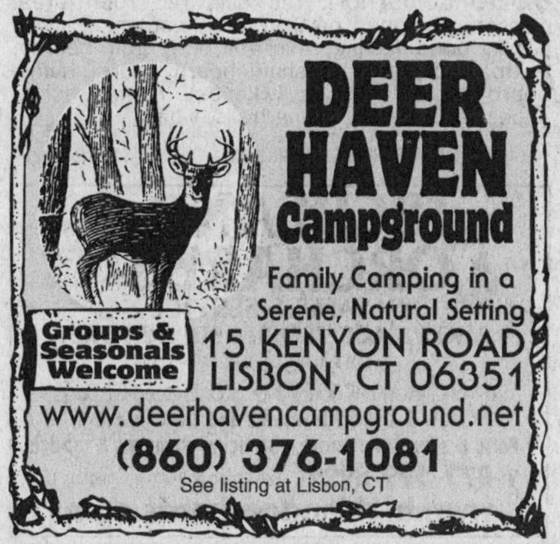

LISBON—Continued
DEER HAVEN CAMPGROUND—Continued

◊◊◊◊RECREATION: rec hall, rec room/area, coin games, lake swim, 5 pedal boat rentals, pond fishing, fishing supplies, mini-golf, golf nearby, bsktball, playground, activities, (wkends), horseshoes, sports field, hiking trails, v-ball.

Pets welcome. Partial handicap access. Open Mid Apr - Mid Oct. Clubs welcome. Rate in 2010 $32-35 per family. MC/VISA/DISC. Member ARVC, CCOA. CCUSA 50% Discount. CCUSA reservations Recommended, CCUSA max stay 3 days, CCUSA disc. not avail S,Th, CCUSA disc. not avail F,Sa, CCUSA disc. not avail holidays. Discount available months of Apr, May, Sep & Oct.

Phone: (860)376-1081
Address: 15 Kenyon Rd, Lisbon, CT 06351
Lat/Lon: 41.59441/-72.02570
Email: deerhavencampground@msn.com
Web: www.deerhavencampground.net

SEE AD THIS PAGE

(NE) Ross Hill Park—(New London) *From jct I-395 (exit 84) & Hwy 12: Go 1/2 mi N on Hwy 12, then 1 mi W on Hwy 138, then 1-1/2 mi N on Hwy 169, then 1 mi E on Ross Hill Rd. Enter on L.* ◊◊◊FACILITIES: 253 sites, typical site width 50 ft, 40 ft max RV length, 115 full hkups, 130 W&E, (20/30/50 amps), 50 amps ($), 8 no hkups, 30 pull-thrus, family camping, tenting, dump, laundry, groceries. ◊◊◊RECREATION: boating, 10 hp limit, canoeing, ramp, river fishing, playground. Pets welcome. Open all yr. Facilities fully operational Apr 1 - Oct 31. Rate in 2010 $43-45 for 2 persons. Member ARVC, CCOA. Phone: (800)308-1089. FCRV discount. FMCA discount.

LITCHFIELD—B-2

(N) Hemlock Hill Camp Resort—(Litchfield) *From jct Hwy 118 & US 202: Go 1 mi W on US 202, then 3 mi N on Milton Rd, then 1-1/2 mi E on Maple, then 1/2 mi S on Hemlock. Enter on L.* ◊◊◊FACILITIES: 134 sites, typical site width 40 ft, 34 ft max RV length, 123 W&E, (20/30/50 amps), 11 no hkups, family camping, tenting, dump, laundry, ltd groc. ◊◊◊◊RECREATION: 2 swim pools, pond fishing, play equipment. Pets welcome, breed restrict, quantity restrict. Open End of Apr - Mid - Oct. Green Friendly. Rate in 2010 $49-59 per family. Member ARVC, CCOA. Phone: (860)567-2267.

(W) WHITE MEMORIAL FAMILY CAMPGROUND (Point Folly)—(Litchfield) *From jct Hwy-63 & US-202: Go 2 mi W on Hwy-202, then 1 mi S on Bissell Rd, then .3 mi W on Whitehall Rd.* FACILITIES: 47 sites, 47 no hkups, tenting, dump, ltd groc. RECREATION: lake swim, boating, canoeing, ramp, dock, lake fishing. Open Early May - Columbus Day. Phone: (860)567-0089.

Located in Mystic, B.F. Clyde's Cider Mill is the only steam-powered Cider Mill in the United States.

MADISON—D-4

(E) HAMMONASSET BEACH STATE PARK—(New Haven) *From jct Hwy-79 & US-1: Go 3 mi E on US-1.* FACILITIES: 552 sites, 552 no hkups, tenting, dump, ltd groc. RECREATION: saltwater swim, boating, canoeing, saltwater fishing, play equipment. No pets. Partial handicap access. Open May 18 - Oct 9. Phone: (203)245-1817.

MASHANTUCKET—C-6

(S) MASHANTUCKET PEQUOT MUSEUM—*From jct I-95 (exit 92) & Hwy 2: Go 7 mi NW on Hwy 2, then 1-1/2 mi SW on Hwy 214. Enter on R.* Life size 16th Century Indian Village. Prehistoric Caribou hunt diorama. 4 acres of interactive exhibits. 18-story observation tower. Gift Shop & restaurant. Open all yr. Tue-Sat 10am-4pm. Closed Sun & Mon.

Phone: (800)411-9671
Address: 110 Pequot Trail, Mashantucket, CT 06338
Lat/Lon: 41.46620/-71.95998
Web: pequotmuseum.org

SEE AD MYSTIC NEXT PAGE

MOHEGAN SUN CASINO-UNCASVILLE—C-5

ODETAH CAMPING RESORT—*From Mohegan Sun Casino: Go 1-3/4 mi W on Hwy 2A, then 4-1/2 mi N on I-395 (exit 81 W), then 3-1/2 mi W on Hwy 2 (exit 23), then 1/4 mi S on Houghton Rd, then straight at intersection & stop sign. Enter on R.*

SEE PRIMARY LISTING AT BOZRAH AND AD BOZRAH PAGE 46

MYSTIC—D-6

ODETAH CAMPING RESORT—*From Mystic at I-95 (exit 90): Go 8 mi S on I-95 (exit 84), then 3-1/2 mi N on Hwy 32, then 8-3/4 mi N on I-395 (exit 81), then 3-1/2 mi W on Hwy 2 (exit 23), then 1/4 mi S on Houghton Rd, then straight at intersection & stop sign. Enter on R.*

SEE PRIMARY LISTING AT BOZRAH AND AD BOZRAH PAGE 46

MYSTIC—Continued on next page

Can you trust the Woodall's ratings? 25 evaluation teams have scoured North American campgrounds to provide you with accurate, up to date information & ratings. Find a rating you don't agree with? Send a letter or email our way, and we'll give it extra attention for 2012.

MYSTIC—Continued

(N) Seaport Campground (Morgan RV Resorts)—(NewLondon) *From jct I-95 & Allyn St/Cow Hill Rd (exit 89): Go 1-1/4 mi N on Allyn St/Cow Hill Rd, then 1-1/2 mi E on Gold Star Hwy (Route 184), then 1/4 mi NW on Campground Rd. Enter at end.* ◆◆◆FACILITIES: 130 sites, typical site width 60 ft, 130 W&E, (30/50 amps), 50 amps ($), 24 pull-thrus, family camping, tenting, dump, laundry, ltd groc. ◆◆◆RECREATION: swim pool, pond fishing, playground. Pets welcome. Partial handicap access. Open Apr 15 - Oct 31. Facilities fully operational May 15 - Sept 15. Big rigs welcome. Green Friendly. Rate in 2010 $36-55 per family. Member ARVC, CCOA. Phone: (860)536-4044. FMCA discount.

NEW PRESTON—B-2

(W) LAKE WARAMAUG STATE PARK—(Litchfield) *From jct US 202 & Hwy 45: Go 1-1/2 mi N on Hwy 45 to Lake Waramaug Rd, then follow signs around the lake.* FACILITIES: 77 sites, 35 ft max RV length, 77 no hkups, tenting, dump, ltd groc. RECREATION: lake swim, boating, canoeing, lake fishing. No pets. Open Weekend prior to Memorial Day - Sep 30. Phone: (860)868-0220.

NIANTIC—D-5

(W) Camp Niantic Family Campground—(New London) *From jct I-95 (exit 72) & Hwy 156: Go 1 mi SE on exit rd, then 1/2 mi SW on Hwy 156. Enter on R.* ◆◆FACILITIES: 135 sites, 135 E, (30 amps), family camping, tenting, dump, laundry. ◆◆RECREATION: play equipment. Pets welcome, breed restrict. Open Apr 15 - Oct 15. Rate in 2010 $35-43 per family. Member ARVC, CCOA. Phone: (860)739-9308.

(W) ROCKY NECK STATE PARK—(New London) *From jct Hwy-161 & Hwy-156: Go 3 mi W on Hwy-156.* FACILITIES: 160 sites, 160 no hkups, tenting, dump, ltd groc. RECREATION: saltwater swim, saltwater fishing. No pets. Partial handicap access. Open May - Sep 30. Phone: (860)739-5471.

NORTH STONINGTON—C-6

✽ **(SE) HIGHLAND ORCHARDS RV**—*S'bnd: From jct I-95 & Hwy 49: Go 1/4 mi N on Hwy 49. N'bnd: From jct I-95 (exit 92) & Hwy 2: Go 1/4 mi W on Hwy 2, then 1 mi NE on Service Rd, then 1/4 mi N on Hwy 49. Enter on R.* SALES: travel trailers, park models, 5th wheels, pre-owned unit sales. SERVICES: full-time mech, RV appliance repair, body work/collision repair, LP gas by weight/by meter, dump station, RV storage, sells parts/accessories, installs hitches. Open all yr. MC/VISA/DISC/AMEX.

NORTH STONINGTON—Continued
HIGHLAND ORCHARDS RV—Continued

Phone: (860)599-8922
Address: 120 Pendleton Hill Rd, North Stonington, CT 06359
Lat/Lon: 41.42525/-71.84274
Email: sales@highlandorchards.com
Web: www.highlandorchards.com

SEE AD THIS PAGE

(SE) Mystic KOA Campground—(New London) *S'bnd: From jct I-95 & Hwy 49: Go 1/4 mi N on Hwy 49. N'bnd: From jct I-95 (exit 92) & Hwy 2: Go 1/4 mi W on Hwy 2, then 1 mi NE on Service Rd, then 1/4 mi N on Hwy 49. Enter on R.* ◆◆◆◆FACILITIES: 270 sites, typical site width 35 ft, 96 full hkups, 167 W&E, (20/30/50 amps), 7 no hkups, 96 pull-thrus, family camping, tenting, dump, laundry, groceries. ◆◆◆◆◆RECREATION: 2 swim pools, pond fishing, playground. Pets welcome. Partial handicap access. Open all yr. Big rigs welcome. Green Friendly. Rate in 2010 $51-86 for 2 persons. Member ARVC, CCOA. Phone: (800)562-3451. KOA discount.

NORWICH—C-5

(W) Acorn Acres Campsites—(New London) *From jct I-395 (exit 80W) & Hwy 82 W: Go 4 mi W on Hwy 82 W, then 1-1/2 mi N on Hwy 163, then 1-1/4 mi W on Lake Rd. Enter on R.* ◆◆◆FACILITIES: 225 sites, typical site width 60 ft, 125 full hkups, 100 W&E, (20/30/50 amps), family camping, tenting, dump, laundry, groceries. ◆◆◆RECREATION: swim pool, lake swim, pond/stream fishing, playground. Pets welcome. Open all yr. Facilities fully operational May 1 - Columbus Day. Big rigs welcome. Rate in 2010 $45-55 per family. Member ARVC, CCOA. Phone: (860)859-1020.

ONECO—B-6

(C) River Bend Campground—(Windham) *From jct I-395 (exit 88) & Hwy 14A: Go 5-1/2 mi E on Hwy 14A, then 1/4 mi S on Pond Street. Enter at end.* ◆◆◆FACILITIES: 160 sites, typical site width 35 ft, 36 ft max RV length, 75 full hkups, 76 W&E, (20/30/50 amps), 9 no hkups, 29 pull-thrus, family camping, tenting, dump, laundry, groceries. ◆◆◆◆RECREATION: swim pool, boating, 3 hp limit, electric motors only, canoeing, ramp, dock, river/pond fishing, playground. Pets welcome. Partial handicap access. Open Mid Apr - Columbus Day. Rate in 2010 $30-46 per family. Member ARVC, CCOA. Phone: (860)564-3440.

PLEASANT VALLEY—A-3

(N) AMERICAN LEGION STATE FOREST (Austin F. Hawes Memorial Campground)—(Litchfield) *From town: Go N on W River Rd.* FACILITIES: 30 sites, 30 no hkups, tenting, dump. RECREATION: river swim, boating, canoeing, river fishing. Pets welcome. Open Apr 15 - Oct 12. Phone: (860)379-0922.

PRESTON—C-6

(N) HIDDEN ACRES FAMILY CAMPGROUND—(New London) *From jct I-395 (exit 85) & Hwy 164: Go 1 mi S on Hwy 164, then 1-1/2 mi S on George Palmer Rd, then 1-1/2 mi W on River Rd. Enter on R.*

HIDDEN ACRES FAMILY CAMPGROUND
Family fun is what you'll find along the Quinebaug River. Relax at our 200 wooded sites, swim in the pool or fish in our pond & river. We have hayrides, craft shop, playground & snack shack. Planned activities, dances, etc.

◆◆◆◆FACILITIES: 190 sites, typical site width 40 ft, 125 full hkups, 50 W&E, (20/30/50 amps), 15 no hkups, many extd stay sites (summer), 2 pull-thrus, WiFi Instant Internet at site, WiFi Internet central location, family camping, tenting, RV's/park model rentals, cabins, shower$, dump, non-guest dump $, laundry, ltd groc, RV supplies, LP gas by weight/by meter, ice, picnic tables, patios, fire rings, wood, controlled access.

◆◆◆◆RECREATION: rec hall, rec room/area, equipped pavilion, coin games, swim pool, river swim, boating, no motors, canoeing, kayaking, river/pond fishing, golf nearby, bsktball, playground, shuffleboard court shuffleboard court, activities, horseshoes, sports field, v-ball.

Pets welcome. Partial handicap access. Open May 1 - Columbus Day. 3 day minimum, on holiday weekends by reservations. Big rigs welcome. Rate in 2010 $35-55 per family. MC/VISA. Member ARVC, CCOA.

Text 107926 to (440)725-8687 to see our Visual Tour.

Phone: (860)887-9633
Address: 47 River Rd, Preston, CT 06365
Lat/Lon: 41.55306/-72.01448
Email: hacampgd@aol.com
Web: www.hiddenacrescamp.com

SEE AD NORWICH NEXT PAGE

(N) Strawberry Park Resort Campground—(New London) *From jct Hwy 164 & Hwy 165: Go 1 mi E on Hwy 165, then 1/2 mi N on Pierce Rd. Enter on R.* ◆◆◆◆◆FACILITIES: 540 sites, typical site width 40 ft, 299 full hkups, 241 W&E, (20/30/50 amps), 6 pull-thrus, family camping, tenting, dump, laundry, groceries. ◆◆◆◆◆RECREATION: 3 swim pools, playground. Pets welcome, breed restrict. Partial handicap access. Open all yr. Facilities fully operational Apr 1 - Oct 31. Big rigs welcome. Rate in 2010 $40-88 per family. Member ARVC, CCOA. Phone: (888)794-7944.

SALEM—C-5

(NW) SALEM FARMS CAMPGROUND—(New London) *From jct I-11 (exit 5) & Witch Meadow Rd: Go 1/2 mi W on Witch Meadow Rd, then 1/4 mi W on Alexander Rd. Enter on L.*

◆◆◆FACILITIES: 191 sites, typical site width 45 ft, 177 W&E, 5 E, (30 amps), 9 no hkups, many extd stay sites (summer), 4 pull-thrus, cable TV, WiFi Instant Internet at site, family camping, tenting, shower$, dump, portable dump, laundry, ltd groc, RV supplies, LP gas by weight, ice, picnic tables, fire rings, wood, controlled access.

◆◆◆◆RECREATION: rec hall, rec room/area, pavilion, equipped pavilion, coin games, 2 swim pools, pond fishing, mini-golf, ($), golf nearby, bsktball, playground, shuffleboard court shuffleboard court, activities (wkends), tennis, horseshoes, sports field, hiking trails, v-ball.

SALEM FARMS CAMPGROUND—Continued on next page

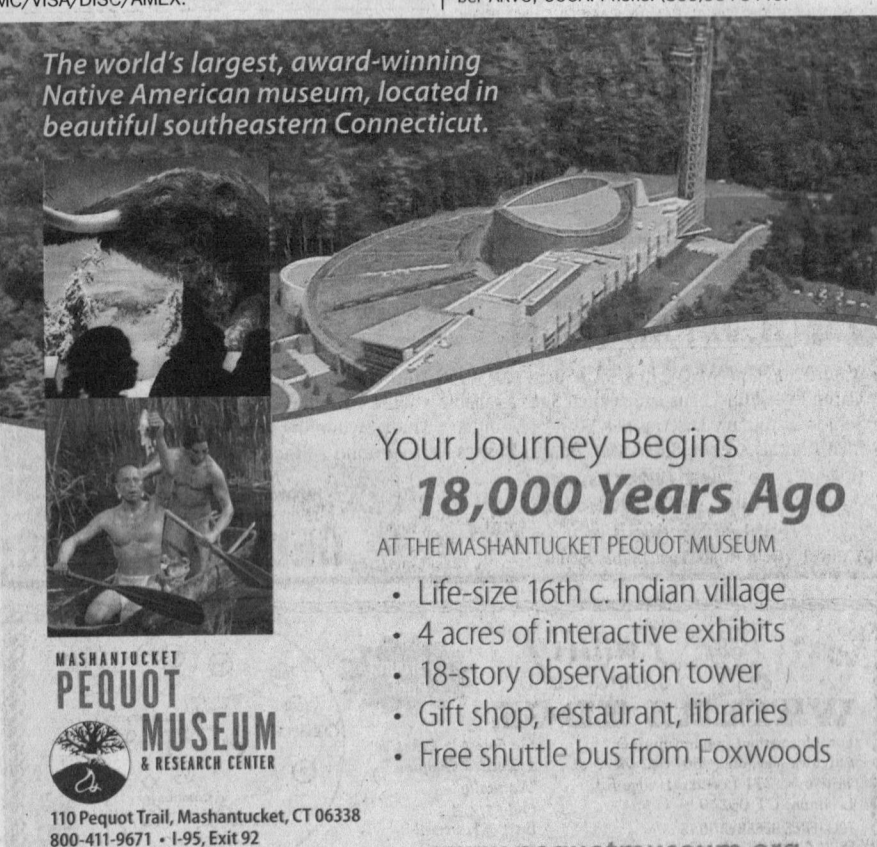

SALEM—Continued
SALEM FARMS CAMPGROUND—Continued

Pets welcome, quantity restrict. Open May 1 - Columbus Day. Escort to site. Clubs welcome. Rate in 2010 $35-45 per family. MC/VISA/DISC. Member ARVC, CCOA.

Phone: (800)479-9238
Address: 39 Alexander Rd, Salem, CT 06420
Lat/Lon: 41.49936/-72.31770
Email: sfcg2003@aol.com
Web: www.salemfarmscampground.com

SEE AD THIS PAGE

(N) WITCH MEADOW LAKE CAMPGROUND—(New London) *From jct Witch Meadow Rd & Hwy 11 (exit 5): Go 1/8 mi SE on Witch Meadow Rd. Enter on R.*

WELCOME

◊◊◊FACILITIES: 280 sites, typical site width 25 ft, 280 W&E, (20/30/50 amps), many extd stay sites (summer), phone Internet central location, family camping, tenting, RV storage, shower$, dump, portable dump, laundry, groceries, RV supplies, LP gas by weight/by meter, ice, picnic tables, fire rings, wood, controlled access.

◊◊◊◊◊RECREATION: rec hall, rec room/area, pavilion, coin games, lake swim, boating, no motors, canoeing, dock, 4 canoe/6 pedal boat rentals, lake fishing, fishing supplies, mini-golf, ($), golf nearby, bsktball, playground, shuffleboard court 2 shuffleboard courts, activities (wkends), tennis, horseshoes, sports field, hiking trails, v-ball.

Pets welcome. Partial handicap access. Open May 1 - Oct 13. Clubs welcome. Green Friendly. Rate in 2010 $40-50 per family. MC/VISA. Member ARVC, CCOA.

Phone: (860)859-1542
Address: 139 Witch Meadow Rd, Salem, CT 06420
Lat/Lon: 41.50034/-72.29655
Email: campwitch@aol.com
Web: www.witchmeadowcampground.com

SEE AD THIS PAGE

Connecticut State Tree: The White Oak

SCOTLAND—B-5

(S) Highland Campground—(Windham) *From jct I-395 (exit 83) & Hwy 97: Go 7-1/2 mi N on Hwy 97, then 200 yards E on Toleration Rd. Enter on L.* ◊◊◊FACILITIES: 150 sites, typical site width 40 ft, 150 W&E, (20/30 amps), 40 pull-thrus, family camping, tenting, dump, laundry, ltd groc. ◊◊◊RECREATION: swim pool, pond fishing, playground. Pets welcome. Partial handicap access. Open all yr. Facilities fully operational May 1 - Oct 31. Rate in 2010 $30 per family. Member ARVC, CCOA. Phone: (860)423-5684.

SOUTH WINDSOR—B-4

✲ **(W) CUSSON AUTOMOTIVE, INC**—*From jct I-291 (exit 4) & US 5: Go 1 mi N on US 5, then 1/8 mi W on Mascolo Rd (at Mobil Station). Enter on L.* SERVICES: full-time mech, engine/chassis repair, RV appliance repair, body work/collision repair, 24-hr emerg rd svc, RV towing, sells parts/accessories, installs hitches. Open all yr. MC/VISA/DISC/AMEX. FMCA discount.

WELCOME

Phone: (860)289-2389
Address: 29 Mascolo Rd, South Windsor, CT 06074
Lat/Lon: 41.82464/-72.60883
Email: don@cussonautomotive.com
Web: www.cussonautomotive.com

SEE AD ABINGTON PAGE 45 AND AD TRAVEL SECTION PAGE 42

SOUTHBURY—C-2

(W) KETTLETOWN STATE PARK—(New Haven) *From jct Hwy 67 & I-84 (exit 15): Go 1/10 mi SE on Hwy 67, then 3-1/2 mi S on Kettletown Rd, then follow sign 3/4 mi W on Georges Hill Rd.* FACILITIES: 68 sites, 28 ft max RV length, 68 no hkups, tenting, dump. RECREATION: lake swim, boating, canoeing, lake fishing. No pets. Partial handicap access. Open May 18 - Oct 1. Phone: (203)264-5169.

Can you trust the Woodall's ratings? 25 evaluation teams have scoured North American campgrounds to provide you with accurate, up to date information & ratings. Find a rating you don't agree with? Send a letter or email our way, and we'll give it extra attention for 2012.

STAFFORD SPRINGS—A-5

(N) MINERAL SPRINGS FAMILY CAMPGROUND—(Tolland) *From jct Hwy 32 & Hwy 190: Go 1/4 mi E on 190, then 2 mi N on Hwy 19, then 2 mi NE on Leonard Rd. Enter on R.*

WELCOME

◊◊◊FACILITIES: 150 sites, typical site width 30 ft, 10 full hkups, 120 W&E, (20/30 amps), 20 no hkups, some extd stay sites (summer), 8 pull-thrus, heater not allowed, WiFi Internet central location, family camping, tenting, cabins, shower$, dump, portable dump, laundry, ltd groc, RV supplies, LP gas by weight/by meter, ice, picnic tables, fire rings, wood.

◊◊◊RECREATION: rec hall, rec room/area, swim pool, pond fishing, bsktball, playground, activities, (wkends), horseshoes.

Pets welcome. Partial handicap access. Open May 1 - Oct 15. 3 day minimum holiday weekends by reservation. Clubs welcome. Rate in 2010 $30-35 per family. Member ARVC, CCOA.

Phone: (860)684-2993
Address: 135 Leonard Rd, Stafford Springs, CT 06076
Lat/Lon: 42.00304/-72.29261
Web: www.mineralspringscampground.com

SEE AD THIS PAGE

STERLING—B-6

(E) KOA - Sterling—(Windham) *From jct I-395 (exit 89) & Hwy 14: Go 6 mi E on Hwy 14, then 1/2 mi N on Gibson Hill Rd. Enter on L.* ◊◊◊FACILITIES: 150 sites, typical site width 25 ft, 120 full hkups, 30 W&E, (30/50 amps), 4 pull-thrus, family camping, tenting, dump, laundry, ltd groc. ◊◊◊RECREATION: playground. Pets welcome. Open Mid Apr - Columbus Day. Rate in 2010 $39 per family. Member ARVC, CCOA. Phone: (860) 564-8777.

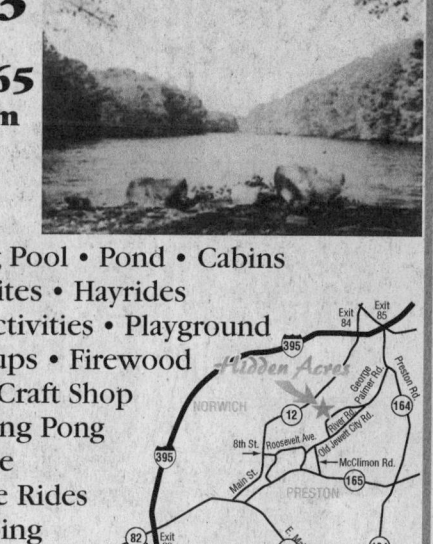

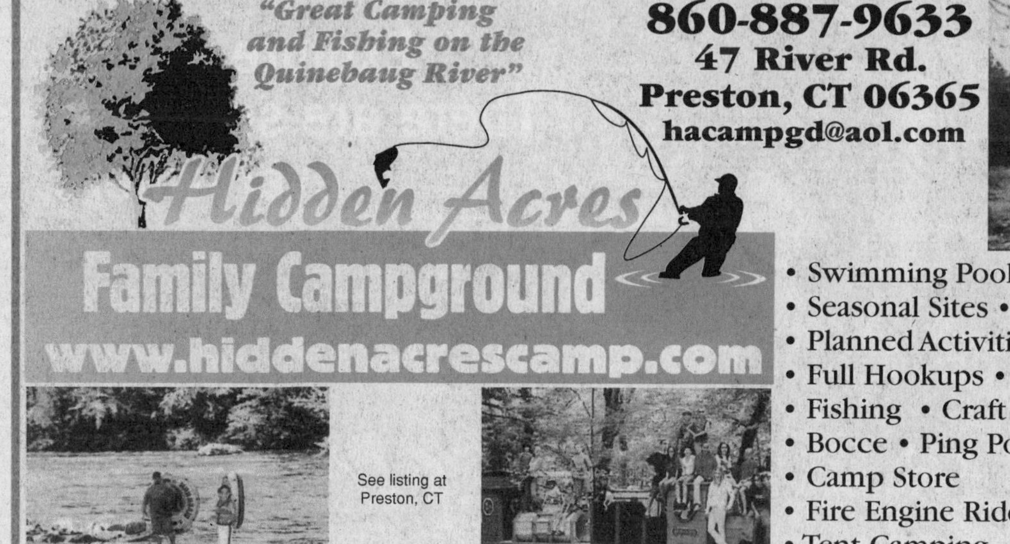

THOMASTON—B-2

(S) BLACK ROCK STATE PARK—(Litchfield) *From jct Hwy 109 & US 6: Go 1/4 mi S on US 6.* FACILITIES: 96 sites, 96 no hkups, tenting, dump, ltd groc. RECREATION: pond/stream fishing. No pets. Partial handicap access. Open Apr 16 - Sep 30. Facilities fully operational Jun - Sep 30. Phone: (860)283-8088.

(W) Branch Brook Campground—(Litchfield) *From jct Hwy 8 (exit 38) & US 6: Go 1 mi W on US 6. Enter on L.* ◆◆◆FACILITIES: 64 sites, typical site width 30 ft, 59 full hkups, 5 W&E, (20/30/50 amps), 2 pull-thrus, family camping, laundry. ◆◆RECREATION: swim pool, pond/stream fishing, playground. Pets welcome. No tents. Open Apr 1 - Nov 1. Big rigs welcome. Rate in 2010 $40 per family. Member ARVC, CCOA. Phone: (860)283-8144.

THOMPSON—A-6

(S) WEST THOMPSON LAKE (COE-West Thompson Lake)—(Windham) *From jct I-395 (exit 99) & Hwy 200: Go 1 mi W on Hwy 200 to Thompson Center, then 2 mi S on Hwy 193, straight across Hwy 12 at traffic light, then 1/4 mi W on Reardon Rd to Campground Rd. Enter on R.* FACILITIES: 22 sites, typical site width 20 ft, 11 W&E, 11 no hkups, tenting, dump. RECREATION: boating, 5 hp limit, canoeing, ramp, lake/river fishing, playground. Partial handicap access. Open Mid May - Mid Sep. Phone: (860)923-3121.

VERNON—B-4

✽ **(C) SCRANTON MOTORS, INC**—*From jct I-84 (exit 64) & Hwy 83: Go 1/4 mi E on Kelly Rd, then 2-1/2 mi N on Hwy 83. Enter on L.* SERVICES: full-time mech, engine/chassis repair, bus. hrs emerg rd svc. Open all yr.

WELCOME

Phone: (860)872-9145
Address: 777 Talcottville Rd (Rte 83), Vernon, CT 06066
Lat/Lon: 41.86332/-72.48212
Web: www.scrantonmotors.com

SEE AD TRAVEL SECTION PAGE 41 AND AD TRAVEL SECTION PAGE 42

VOLUNTOWN—C-6

(NE) Circle C Campground—(New London) *From jct Hwy 138 & Hwy 49: Go 2-1/4 mi N on Hwy 49, then 3 mi NE on Brown Rd, then 1 mi E on Gallup Homestead Rd, then 3/4 mi S on Bailey Pond Rd. Enter on L.* ◆◆◆FACILITIES: 118 sites, typical site width 35 ft, 114 W&E, (20/30/50 amps), 4 no hkups, 10 pull-thrus, family camping, tenting, dump, laundry, ltd groc. ◆◆◆◆RECREATION: lake swim, boating, 10 hp limit, canoeing, ramp, dock, pond fishing, playground. Pets welcome. Open Mid Apr - Mid Oct. Big rigs welcome. Rate in 2010 $39-46 per family. Member ARVC, CCOA. Phone: (800)424-4534.

(NE) Nature's Campsites—(New London) *From jct Hwy-165 & Hwy-49: Go 1/2 mi N on Hwy-49. Enter on R.* ◆◆FACILITIES: 150 sites, typical site width 35 ft, 20 full hkups, 75 W&E, (20/30/50 amps), 55 no hkups, 6 pull-thrus, family camping, tenting, dump, laundry, ltd groc. ◆◆◆RECREATION: 2 swim pools, boating, canoeing, river/pond fishing, playground. Pets welcome. Open May 1 - Oct 15. Rate in 2010 $35-45 per family. Member ARVC, CCOA. Phone: (860)376-4203.

(NE) PACHAUG STATE FOREST (Green Falls Campground)—(New London) *From town: Go 3 mi E on Rt 138.* FACILITIES: 18 sites, 18 no hkups, tenting. RECREATION: river swim, canoeing, ramp, river/pond/stream fishing. Pets welcome. Partial handicap access. Open Apr 20 - Sep 30. Phone: (860)376-4075.

(N) PACHAUG STATE FOREST (Mount Misery Campground)—(New London) *North of town, off Route 49.* FACILITIES: 22 sites, 22 no hkups, tenting. RECREATION: ramp, pond/stream fishing. Pets welcome. Partial handicap access. Open Apr 16 - Dec 31. Phone: (860)376-4075.

WILLINGTON—A-5

(NE) Moosemeadow Camping Resort—(Tolland) *From jct I-84 (exit 69) & Hwy 74: Go 4-1/4 mi E on Hwy 74, then 1-1/4 mi N on Moosemeadow Rd. Enter on L.* ◆◆◆FACILITIES: 150 sites, typical site width 40 ft, 39 full hkups, 54 W&E, 5 E, (20/30/50 amps), 52 no hkups, 26 pull-thrus, family camping, tenting, dump, laundry, groceries. ◆◆◆◆RECREATION: swim pool, pond fishing, playground. Pets welcome. Partial handicap access. Open Apr 23 - Columbus Day. Rate in 2010 $32-52 per family. Phone: (860)429-7451.

(N) Wilderness Lake Park—(Willington) *From jct Hwy 74 & I-84 (exit 69): Go 1-1/2 mi N on I-84 (exit 70), then 1/4 mi N on Hwy 32, then 1-1/2 mi E on Village Hill Rd. Enter on R.* ◆◆◆FACILITIES: 51 sites, 51 W&E, (30 amps), family camping, tenting, portable dump, picnic tables, wood. ◆◆◆RECREATION: rec hall, lake swim, boating, canoeing, lake fishing, mini-golf, playground, horseshoes, v-ball. Pets welcome. Open Apr 1 - Nov 20. Rate in 2010 $45-65 per family. CCUSA 50% Discount. CCUSA reservations Recommended, CCUSA max stay Unlimited, Cash only for CCUSA disc., CCUSA disc. not avail F,Sa, CCUSA disc. not avail holidays. Firewood may not be brought into park.

CAMPCLUB USA

Phone: (860)684-6352
Address: 150 Village Hill Rd, Willington, CT 06279
Lat/Lon: 41.91863/-72.28282
Email: info@wilderness-lake.com
Web: www.wilderness-lake.com

WOODSTOCK—A-6

(W) CHAMBERLAIN LAKE CAMPGROUND—(Windham) *From jct I-84 (exit 73) & Hwy 190: Go 2 mi E on Hwy 190, then 2-1/4 mi E on Hwy 171, then 3-1/2 mi E on Hwy 197. Enter on L.* ◆◆◆FACILITIES: 105 sites, typical site width 30 ft, 100 W&E, (20/30/50 amps), 5 no hkups, some extd stay sites (summer), WiFi Internet central location, family camping, tenting, RV's/park model rentals, shower$, dump, non-guest dump $, portable dump, groceries, RV supplies, LP gas by weight/by meter, ice, picnic tables, fire rings, wood, controlled access.

WELCOME

◆◆◆◆RECREATION: rec room/area, coin games, lake swim, boating, electric motors only, canoeing, kayaking, ramp, dock, 4 rowboat/2 canoe/pedal boat rentals, lake fishing, fishing supplies, golf nearby, bsktball, playground, activities, (wkends), horseshoes, v-ball.

CAMPCLUB USA

Pets welcome. Partial handicap access. Open May 1 - Nov 1. Clubs welcome. Rate in 2010 $40 per family. MC/VISA/AMEX. Member ARVC, CCOA. CCUSA 50% Discount. CCUSA reservations Recommended, CCUSA max stay 5 days, CCUSA disc. not avail F,Sa, CCUSA disc. not avail holidays.

Phone: (860)974-0567
Address: 1379 Rt 197, Woodstock, CT 06281
Lat/Lon: 41.97026/-72.05854
Email: michael.reed@chamberlainlakecampground.net
Web: www.chamberlainlakecampground.net

SEE AD THIS PAGE

Explore nature.
There are surprises
everywhere.
Ad Council
DiscoverTheForest.org
FOREST SERVICE
USDA

TRAVEL SECTION

Delaware

TIME ZONE

Delaware is in the Eastern Time Zone.

TOPOGRAPHY

The state of Delaware is 96 miles long and ranges in width from 9 to 35 miles. It is bordered on the east by the Delaware Bay. The terrain slopes from 442-foot-high rolling hills in the north, to a near-sea-level plain in the south.

TEMPERATURE

Delaware enjoys a moderate year-round climate. The average temperature in the summer months is 76.4°, with lows of about 67° and highs of around 86°. January temperatures range from 22° to 40°.

TRAVEL & TOURISM INFO

State Agency:
Delaware Tourism Office
99 Kings Hwy.
Dover, DE 19901
(866/284-7483)
www.visitdelaware.com

Regional Agencies:
Kent Co. Tourism Corp
435 N. DuPont Hwy.
Dover, DE 19901
(800/233-KENT or 302/734-1736)
www.visitdover.com

Southern Delaware Tourism
PO Box 240
Georgetown, DE 19947
(800/357-1818 or 302/856-1818)
www.visitsoutherndelaware.com

Greater Wilmington CVB
100 W. Tenth St., Ste. 20
Wilmington, DE 19801
(302/295-2210 or 800/489-6664)
www.visitwilmingtonde.com

RECREATIONAL INFO

Fishing/Hunting: Licenses can be purchased online at www.fw.delaware.gov/ or by calling 302/739-4431.

Kayaking/Sailing: Guided kayak eco-tours, kayak rentals, instruction and sailboat rentals by American Canoe Association. (302/539-7999) www.coastalkayak.com

SHOPPING

Bargain Bill's Flea Market, Laurel. It's one of the top 50 flea markets in the U.S. with 15 acres of new and used collectible and antique items. A 46,000-sq.-ft. indoor market, along with 300 outdoor vendor spaces and 160-seat food court. 25 years in business. At Rt 13 & Rt 9. (302/875-9958) www.bargainbill.com

Christiana Mall, Newark. Shop at 130+ tax-free stores. At 715 Christiana Mall Rd. (302/731-9815) www.shopchristianamall.com

Delaware Made General Store, Dover. Delaware gifts, souvenirs and apparel. At 32 W. Loockerman St., Suite 101 B (302/736-1419) www.delawaremade.co

Dover Mall, Macy's JC Penney, Boscov's and more. 1364 N. Dupont Highway, Dover. (302/734-0415) www.dovermall.com

Tanger Outlets and Rehoboth Beach, Delaware Shore, offers 140+ stores of outlet shopping. The ferry offers transportation to and from the outlets. At 36470 Seaside Outlet Dr. (866/665-8682) www.tangeroutlet.com

DESTINATIONS

Delaware's history spans from pre-colonial days to the present. As the first state in the nation, it offers hundreds of exciting and stimulating attractions. Travelers will enjoy discovering the rich history in the museums and monuments that honor the long heritage of this state.

NORTHERN DELAWARE REGION

The Northern region includes the city of Wilmington, and the Brandywine Valley, which is home to a variety of state parks and historic sites. Much of the terrain here is rolling hills and farmlands. At one time, most of the land in this area was owned by

QUICK REFERENCE CHART FOR WOODALL'S FEATURED PARKS

	Green Friendly	RV Lots for Sale	Park Models-Onsite Ownership	Park Membership for Sale	Big Rigs Welcome	Internet Friendly	Pets Welcome
FENWICK ISLAND							
Treasure Beach RV Park					▲	●	■
HARRINGTON							
G & R Campground					▲		■
LEWES							
Tall Pines Campground Resort	🍃				▲	●	■
LINCOLN							
Cedar Creek Landing Campground					▲	●	■
REHOBOTH BEACH							
Big Oaks Family Campground					▲	●	■

Green Friendly 🍃; RV Lots for Sale ✖; Park Models/Onsite Onwership ✱; Park Memberships for Sale ✔; Big Rigs Welcome ▲; Internet Friendly ●; Internet Friendly-WiFi ●; Pets Welcome ■

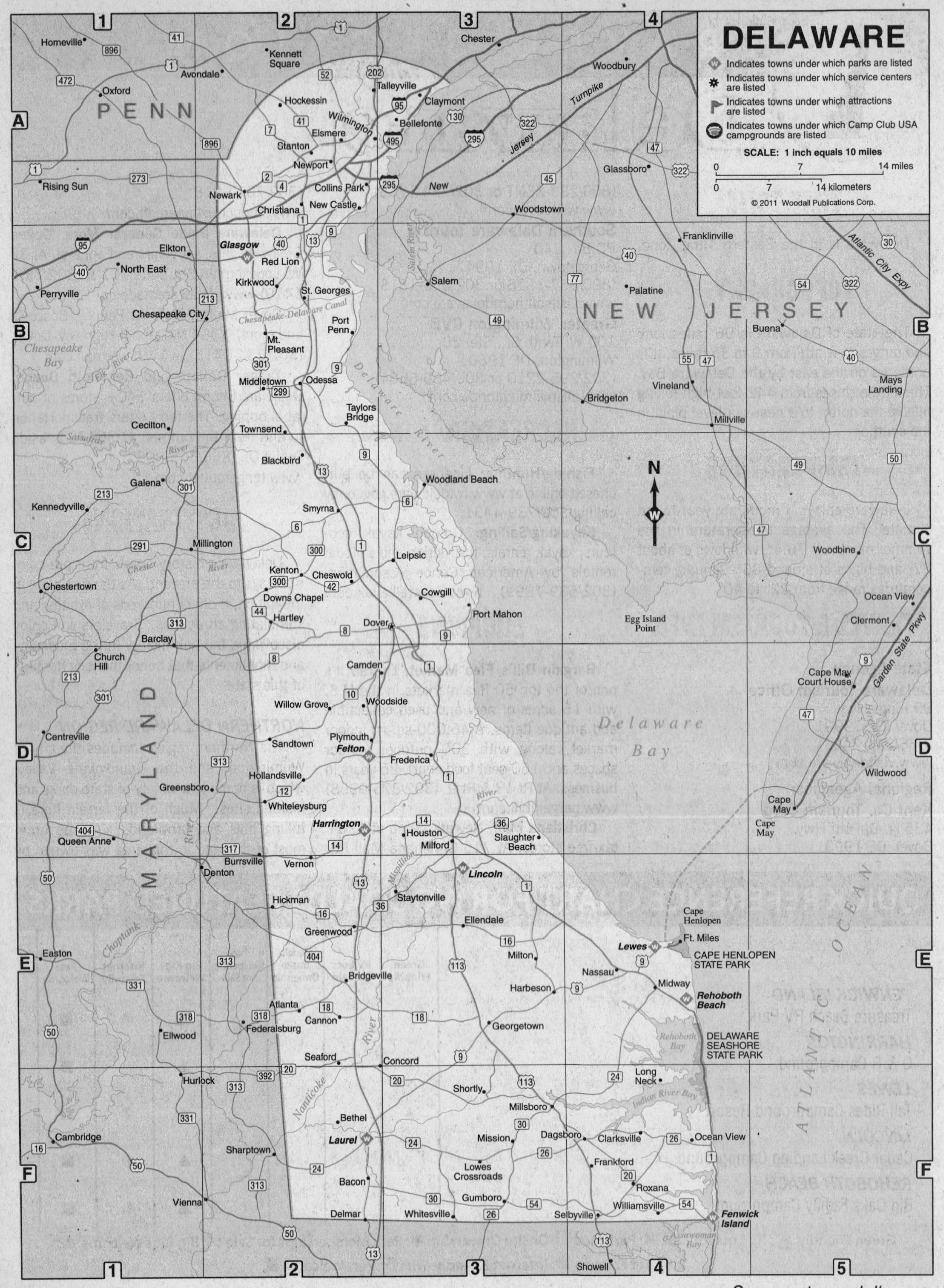
DELAWARE
Indicates towns under which parks are listed
Indicates towns under which service centers are listed
Indicates towns under which attractions are listed
Indicates towns under which Camp Club USA campgrounds are listed
SCALE: 1 inch equals 10 miles
0 7 14 miles
0 7 14 kilometers
© 2011 Woodall Publications Corp.
PENN
NEW JERSEY
MARYLAND
Delaware Bay
ATLANTIC OCEAN
Glasgow
Felton
Harrington
Lincoln
Lewes
Rehoboth Beach
Laurel
Fenwick Island
Dover
Wilmington
CAPE HENLOPEN STATE PARK
DELAWARE SEASHORE STATE PARK
Cape Henlopen
Ft. Miles
Cape May
Chesapeake Bay
Chesapeake-Delaware Canal
Delaware River
Salem River
Rehoboth Bay
Indian River Bay
Assawoman Bay
New Jersey Turnpike
Atlantic City Expy
Garden State Pkwy
Homeville
Oxford
Avondale
Kennett Square
Hockessin
Chester
Talleyville
Claymont
Woodbury
Bellefonte
Elsmere
Stanton
Newport
Newark
Christiana
Collins Park
New Castle
Rising Sun
Elkton
North East
Perryville
Red Lion
Kirkwood
St. Georges
Port Penn
Chesapeake City
Mt. Pleasant
Middletown
Odessa
Taylors Bridge
Townsend
Cecilton
Blackbird
Galena
Kennedyville
Woodland Beach
Smyrna
Millington
Leipsic
Chestertown
Kenton
Cheswold
Downs Chapel
Cowgill
Hartley
Port Mahon
Barclay
Church Hill
Camden
Willow Grove
Woodside
Centreville
Sandtown
Plymouth
Frederica
Hollandsville
Greensboro
Whiteleysburg
Queen Anne
Houston
Milford
Slaughter Beach
Burrsville
Vernon
Denton
Staytonville
Hickman
Ellendale
Greenwood
Easton
Milton
Nassau
Midway
Bridgeville
Harbeson
Atlanta
Cannon
Federalsburg
Georgetown
Ellwood
Seaford
Concord
Hurlock
Long Neck
Shortly
Millsboro
Bethel
Cambridge
Mission
Dagsboro
Clarksville
Ocean View
Sharptown
Frankford
Lowes Crossroads
Bacon
Roxana
Vienna
Gumboro
Williamsville
Delmar
Whitesville
Selbyville
Showell
Glassboro
Woodstown
Franklinville
Salem
Palatine
Buena
Vineland
Bridgeton
Millville
Mays Landing
Woodbine
Egg Island Point
Ocean View
Clermont
Cape May Court House
Wildwood
Cape May
N
1 2 3 4 5
A B C D E F

the DuPont family, as well as many of the parks.

Fort Delaware State Park, Delaware City. Originally a Union military post that held approximately 32,000 prisoners over the course of the war, Fort Delaware is now a museum with living-history interpreters. Witness firsthand cannon fire, cooking demonstrations, the laundry, officers' quarters and military drills. A ferryboat takes you out to the island, which also encompasses a large wading bird sanctuary of herons, egrets and ibis.

Iron Hill Museum. Natural history museum housed in a former one-room schoolhouse is sponsored by Delaware Academy of Science. Collection includes taxidermy, rocks and minerals (fluorescent display), fossils and archaeological artifacts, most indigenous to Delaware. Surrounded by 19 acres of nature trails.

New Castle, southeast of Wilmington. Cobblestone streets and homes date from the colonial era. Visit the **George Read II House & Gardens** built between 1797 and 1804 in high Georgian style.

Wilmington. Delaware's largest city is nestled in the gently rolling hills of the Brandywine Valley. A thriving riverfront district contains shops, restaurants, museums and entertainment. Attractions in and around Wilmington include:

Delaware Art Museum, a brand new facility featuring expanded galleries, unique architecture, revitalized landscaping and the first sculpture park in the Brandywine Valley.

Delaware Museum of Natural History where you can explore an African watering hole or look beneath the seas. Come face to face with a jaguar and encounter life-sized dinosaurs. Enjoy dioramas, exhibits and special programs at this unique destination.

Wilmington & Western Railroad offers steam-train rides from the 107-year-old station through the wooded hills and rolling farmlands of the Red Clay Valley.

Winterthur, the home of Henry Francis du Pont (1880-1969), is one of the greatest surviving country estates of its kind in the nation. Magnificent mansion tours, holiday tours, garden tram tours, new exhibitions, annual events, dining and tax-free shopping.

Medal of Honor. Stop by and see Engine Alley where there is a 28-cylinder engine - 10 times bigger than the biggest NASCAR engines.

Odessa, 23 miles south of Wilmington. Odessa's historic district is on the National Register. "Christmas in Odessa" house tour is held the first weekend in December.

CENTRAL REGION (DOVER AREA)

Bombay Hook National Wildlife Refuge, Smyrna. A 16,000-acre haven for migrating and resident waterfowl. www.fws.gov/northeast/bombayhook/

Dover. Delaware's capital greets visitors with Georgian and Victorian homes, brick sidewalks and many historic buildings. Tour the **State House Museum,** built in 1792 and restored to its original appearance. Other attractions include:

Air Mobility Command Museum. Visitors can sit in the pilot's seat of the C-133 and experience what it's like in the cockpit of the largest Turbo Prop aircraft ever operated. The first C-141 ever built is one of seven aircrafts on display. www.amcmuseum.org

Dover International Speedway. June and September bring NASCAR stock car races to this raceway in Dover. www.doverspeedway.com

SOUTHERN DELAWARE REGION

As the least populated region of the state, its eastern coast contains numerous natural areas and beaches. Inland contains a small patchwork of rural communities, and farmlands lying on sandy soil. Nature lovers will find delight in the miles of trails, beautiful waters and wildlife habitat.

Bethany Beach. Known as one of Delaware's quiet resorts, this beach's boardwalk is a place for summertime fun. It is home to one of the best arts & crafts shows in the region.

Delaware Shore. A 25-mile strand of beach resorts and state parks in the southeast corner of the state.

Nanticoke Indian Museum, Millsboro. Displays demonstrate traditional Nanticoke ways, stone artifacts, carvings, pottery, traditional clothing, tools and implements.

Seaford Museum, Seaford. Depicts life in the days of Native Americans through oystering and fishing, poultry production, DuPont nylon, wars, schools, churches and small businesses.

ANNUAL EVENTS

JANUARY

Live Harness Racing, Dover; Hagley's Invention Convention, Wilmington; Community Day of Celebration, Seaford; Welcome Spring at Longwood Gardens, Chadds Ford.

FEBRUARY

Annual Delaware Antiquarian Book Show/Sale, Wilmington; Merchants Attic I & General Public Garage Sale, Rehoboth Beach; Society Fine Art Show and Sale, Lewes; The Great Railroad Race, Wilmington.

MARCH

Irish Nights, Wilmington; Delaware Home & Garden Expo, Wilmington; Chocolate Festival, Rehoboth Beach; Great Delaware Kite Festival, Cape Henlopen State Park.

APRIL

Ocean to Bay Bike Tour, Bethany-Fenwick Area; Spring Sidewalk Sale, Lewes; Bug & Bud Festival, Milford.

MAY

Annual Antique Truck Show, Delaware City; Wilmington Garden Day, Wilmington; Rocket Day at the Cape, Lewes; Civil War Encampment, Newark; Old Dover Days, Dover; Polish Festival, Wilmington; World Fair Trade Day, Bethany; Craft Show, Rehoboth Beach; Horseshoe Crab Festival, Milton.

JUNE

Separation Day, New Castle; Annual Craft Fair, Wilmington; African-American Festival, Dover; Old Timer's Day, Selbyville; Antique Show, Lewes; Taste of Coastal Delaware, Bethany Beach; Street Rod Show, Delaware City; Greek Festival, Wilmington.

JULY

Beach & Bay Cottage Tour, Bethany/Fenwick Island; Seashore Sandcastle Contest, Rehoboth Beach; Craft Show, Lewes; Delaware State Fair, Harrington; Pennsylvania Guild Fine Craft Fair, Wilmington.

AUGUST

Big Quarterly, Wilmington; Caribbean Festival, Wilmington; Old Tyme Peach Festival, Middletown; Outdoor Fine Art Show, Rehoboth Beach; Peninsula Bluegrass Festival, Georgetown; Riverfront Blues Festival, Wilmington; Annual Sandcastle Contest, Rehoboth Beach; Delmarva Blue Crab Festival, Milton.

SEPTEMBER

Hagley Car Show, Wilmington; Howard Pyle Pirate Festival, Lewes; Nanticoke Indian Pow Wow, Millsboro; Brandywine Arts Festival, Wilmington; Coastal Music & Arts Festival, Ocean View.

OCTOBER

Boast the Coast Maritime Festival, Lewes; Coast Day, Lewes; Fall Surf-Fishing Tournament, Bethany; Sea Witch & Fiddler's Festival, Rehoboth/Dewey Beach; Apple-Scrapple Festival, Bridgeville; Coast Day, Lewes.

NOVEMBER

Delaware Antiques Show, Wilmington; Hagley's Festival of Museum Shopping, Wilmington; Winterthur Nights of Enchanted Lights, Winterthur; World Championship Punkin Chunkin, Millsboro; Delaware Book Festival, Dover.

DECEMBER

Delaware Day, Wilmington; First Night, Dover; A Farmer's Christmas, Dover.

Delaware

FELTON—D-2

(S) KILLENS POND SP—(Kent) *From town: Go 1 mi S on US 13, then 1-1/2 mi E on Paradise Alley Rd.* FACILITIES: 77 sites, 60 W&E, 17 no hkups, family camping, tenting, dump, laundry, ltd groc. RECREATION: swim pool, boating, canoeing, ramp, pond fishing, playground. Pets welcome. Open all yr. Phone: (302)284-4526.

FENWICK ISLAND—F-4

(W) TREASURE BEACH RV PARK—(Sussex) *From jct US 1 & Hwy 54 (Lighthouse Rd): Go 1-1/2 mi W on Hwy 54. From jct US 113 & Hwy 54: Go 11 mi E on Hwy 54. Enter on R.*

WELCOME

◆◆◆◆FACILITIES: 1010 sites, typical site width 25 ft, 1000 full hkups, 10 W&E, (20/30/50 amps), mostly extd stay sites, cable TV, phone/cable on-site Internet (needs activ), WiFi Internet central location, family camping, tenting, dump, laundry, groceries, RV supplies, LP gas by weight/by meter, ice, picnic tables, patios, grills, wood, controlled access.

◆◆◆◆◆RECREATION: rec hall, rec room/area, equipped pavilion, coin games, 2 swim pools, wading pool, boating, canoeing, kayaking, ramp, saltwater/lake fishing, fishing supplies, golf nearby, bsktball, playground, activities, horseshoes, sports field, v-ball.

Pets welcome. Partial handicap access. Open Apr 20 - Oct 15. Family camping by reservation only. Big rigs welcome. Rate in 2010 $60-80 for 2 persons. ATM.

Phone: (302)436-8001
Address: 37291 Lighthouse Rd, Selbyville, DE 19975
Lat/Lon: 38.46273/-78.07951
Email: camping@treasurebeachrvpark.com
Web: treasurebeachrvpark.com

SEE AD THIS PAGE

GLASGOW—B-2

(S) LUMS POND SP—(New Castle) *From town: Go 3 mi S on Hwy 896, then E on Howell School Rd (Hwy 71).* FACILITIES: 68 sites, 6 E, 62 no hkups, tenting, dump. RECREATION: boating, 5 hp limit, canoeing, ramp, pond fishing, playground. Open all yr. Phone: (302)368-6989.

Delaware was the first state to ratify the United States constitution. It did so on December 7, 1787.

HARRINGTON—D-2

(E) G & R CAMPGROUND—(Kent) *From jct US 13 & Hwy 14: Go 2-1/2 mi E on Hwy 14, then 3/4 mi S on Deep Grass Lane, then 1 mi W on Gun & Rod Club Rd. Enter on R.*

WELCOME

◆◆◆FACILITIES: 222 sites, typical site width 24 ft, 55 full hkups, 142 W&E, (30/50 amps), 25 no hkups, 14 pull-thrus, family camping, tenting, cabins, RV storage, dump, non-guest dump $, portable dump, ltd groc, RV supplies, ice, picnic tables, fire rings, wood.

◆◆◆◆RECREATION: rec hall, rec room/area, pavilion, coin games, swim pool, bsktball, playground, activities, (wkends), horseshoes, sports field, hiking trails, v-ball.

Pets welcome, breed restrict. Open all yr. Big rigs welcome. Clubs welcome. Rate in 2010 $35-44 for 2 persons. MC/VISA/DISC.

Phone: (302)398-8108
Address: 4075 Gun and Rod Club Rd, Houston, DE 19954
Lat/Lon: 38.90500/-75.53250
Email: owner@gnrcampground.com
Web: www.gnrcampground.com

SEE AD THIS PAGE

LAUREL—F-2

(E) TRAP POND SP—(Sussex) *From jct US 13 & Hwy 24: Go 4 mi E on Hwy 24, then 1 mi S on CR 449.* FACILITIES: 142 sites, 130 W&E, 12 no hkups, family camping, tenting, dump, laundry, groceries. RECREATION: boating, 5 hp limit, canoeing, ramp, pond fishing, playground. Open Mar 1 - Nov 30. Phone: (302)875-2392.

LEWES—E-4

(E) CAPE HENLOPEN SP—(Sussex) *From jct Hwy 1 & US 9: Go 4 mi NE on US 9.* FACILITIES: 156 sites, 139 W&E, 17 no hkups, tenting, dump, laundry. RECREATION: saltwater swim, saltwater fishing. Open Mar 1 - Nov 30. Phone: (302)645-8983.

(W) TALL PINES CAMPGROUND RESORT—(Sussex) *From jct Hwy 1 & US 9: Go 2-3/4 mi SW on US 9, then 50 feet NW on Sweetbriar Rd, then 3/4 mi SW on Log Cabin Hill Rd. Enter on R.*

WELCOME

◆◆◆◆FACILITIES: 524 sites, typical site width 50 ft, 484 full hkups, 24 W&E, (20/30/50 amps), 16 no hkups, mostly extd stay sites, 5 pull-thrus, WiFi Internet central location, family camping, tenting, cabins, dump, laundry, groceries, LP gas by weight/by meter, ice, picnic tables, fire rings, wood, controlled access.

◆◆◆◆RECREATION: rec room/area, pavilion, coin games, swim pool, golf nearby, bsktball, playground, shuffleboard court 2 shuffleboard courts, activities (wkends), horseshoes, sports field, v-ball.

Pets welcome, breed restrict. Open all yr. Facilities fully operational Memorial Day - Labor Day. Big rigs welcome. Green Friendly. Rate in 2010 $30-60 for 4 persons. MC/VISA. Member DCA.

Phone: (302)684-0300
Address: 29551 Persimmon Rd, Lewes, DE 19958
Lat/Lon: 38.73743/-75.23792
Email: tpinfo@tallpines-del.com
Web: www.tallpines-del.com

SEE AD NEXT PAGE

LINCOLN—E-3

(S) CEDAR CREEK LANDING CAMPGROUND—(Sussex) *From jct US 113 & Hwy 1: Go 6 mi S on Hwy 1, then 1/4 mi W on Brick Granary Rd. Enter on L.*

WELCOME

◆◆◆◆FACILITIES: 277 sites, typical site width 50 ft, 277 full hkups, (20/30/50 amps), 22 pull-thrus, cable TV, WiFi Instant Internet at site, family camping, dump, laundry, ltd groc, RV supplies, ice, picnic tables, patios, fire rings, wood, controlled access.

◆◆◆◆RECREATION: rec hall, rec room/area, equipped pavilion, coin games, swim pool, golf nearby, playground, horseshoes, sports field, hiking trails, v-ball.

Pets welcome. Partial handicap access. No tents. Open Mid Apr - Mid Nov. Big rigs welcome. Escort to site. Clubs welcome. Rate in 2010 $55-65 for 5 persons. MC/VISA/Debit.

Phone: (302)491-6614
Address: 8295 Brick Granary Rd, Lincoln, DE 19960
Lat/Lon: 38.87442/-75.36013
Email: info@cedarcreeklandingcg.com
Web: cedarcreeklandingcg.com

SEE AD THIS PAGE

REHOBOTH BEACH—E-4

(N) BIG OAKS FAMILY CAMPGROUND—(Sussex) *From jct Hwy 1 & Hwy 24: Go 1/2 mi S on Hwy 1, then 1/2 mi E on Munchy Branch Rd, then 1 block E on Wolfe Neck Rd. Enter on L.*

WELCOME

◆◆◆◆FACILITIES: 150 sites, typical site width 30 ft, 125 full hkups, 25 W&E, (20/30/50 amps), many extd stay sites, cable TV, ($), WiFi Instant Internet at site, WiFi Internet central location, family camping, tenting, RV's/park model rentals, cabins, dump, laundry, groceries, RV supplies, ice, picnic tables, fire rings, grills, wood.

◆◆◆◆RECREATION: rec hall, rec room/area, pavilion, equipped pavilion, coin games, swim pool, golf nearby, bsktball, playground, shuffleboard court 2 shuffleboard courts, activities (wkends), horseshoes, hiking trails, local tours.

Pets welcome. Open May 1 - Columbus Day. Minimum 2 day Reservations in Jul & Aug. Big rigs welcome. Clubs welcome. Rate in 2010 $55-62 for 4 persons. Member DCA.

BIG OAKS FAMILY CAMPGROUND—Continued on next page

REHOBOTH BEACH—Continued
BIG OAKS FAMILY CAMPGROUND—Continued

Phone: (302)645-6838
Address: 35567 Big Oaks Ln, Rehoboth Beach, DE 19971
Lat/Lon: 38.73867/-75.13167
Email: campbigoaks@earthlink.net
Web: bigoakscamping.com

SEE AD THIS PAGE

(S) DELAWARE SEASHORE SP—(Sussex) *From town: Go 2 mi S on Hwy 1.* FACILITIES: 182 sites, 145 full hkups, 37 no hkups, tenting, dump, laundry. RECREATION: swim pool, saltwater swim, boating, no motors, ramp, dock, saltwater fishing. Open all yr. Facilities fully operational Apr 1 - Nov 30. Phone: (302)539-7202.

WELCOME **TALL PINES CAMPGROUND RESORT**—*From jct Hwy 1 & US 9: Go 2-3/4 mi SW on US 9, then 50 feet NW on Sweetbriar Rd, then 3/4 mi W on Log Cabin Rd. Enter on R.*

SEE PRIMARY LISTING AT LEWES AND AD THIS PAGE

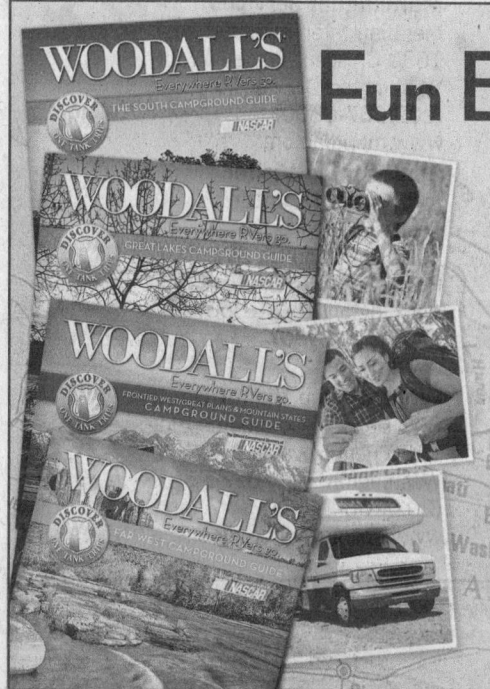

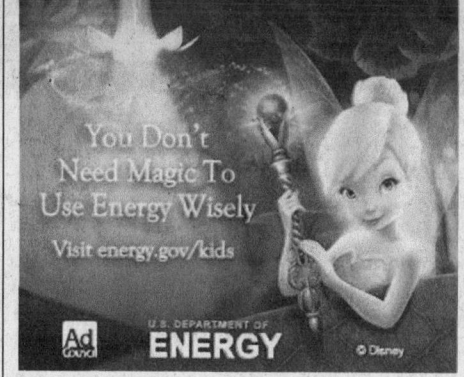

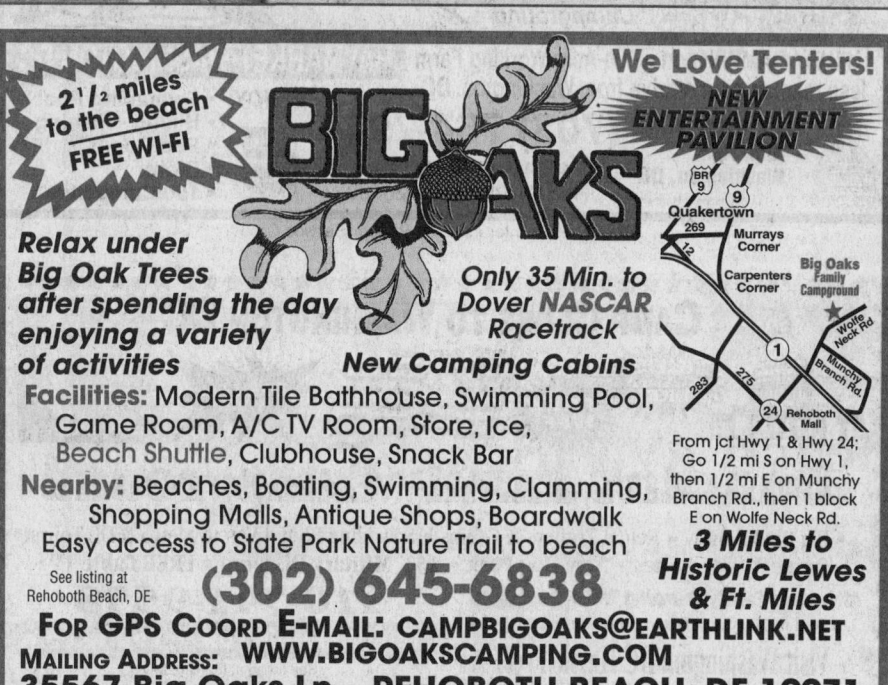

TRAVEL SECTION

Washington DC

READER SERVICE INFO

The following businesses have placed an ad in the Washington, D.C. Travel Section. To receive free information, enter their Reader Service number on the Reader Service Card opposite page 48/Discover Section in the front of this directory:

Advertiser	RS#
Aquia Pines Camp Resort	683
Bethpage Camp Resort	781
Capitol KOA Washington DC NE	3323
Cherry Hill Park	462
Duncan's Family Campground	460
Fredericksburg / Washington DC KOA	565
Greenville Farm Family Campground	562
Travel Trailer Village	564

TIME ZONE

Washington D.C. is in the Eastern Time Zone.

TOPOGRAPHY

Occupying an area of 67 square miles, Washington, D.C. is located at the head of the tidewater of the Potomac River. To the west are the foothills of the Appalachian Mountains and to the east is the coastal plain that stretches to the Atlantic Ocean, some 90 miles away.

TEMPERATURE

Washington, D.C. has a moderate climate, typical of the Eastern Seaboard. Annual precipitation amounts to 38.89 inches. The average high temperature for January is 44° and the average low temperature is 30°. In July, the average high temperature is 87° while the average low temperature is 69°.

TRAVEL & TOURISM INFO

Washington, DC Convention & Tourism Corp.
901 7th St. NW, 4th Floor
Washington, D.C. 20001
(202/789-7000)
www.washington.org

DC Chamber of Commerce
1213 K Street
Washington, DC 20005
(202/347-7201)
www.dcchamber.org

DC Visitor Information Center
1300 Pennsylvania Ave NW
Washington, DC 20004
(202/312-1300)
www.itcdc.com/explore.php?p=2

Cultural Tourism DC
1250 H St. NW, Suite 1000
Washington, DC 20005
(202/661-7581)
www.culturaltourismdc.org

DC Commission on the Arts and Humanities
1371 Harvard Street, NW
Washington, DC 20004
(202/724-5613)
www.dcarts.dc.gov/

Humanities Council of Washington, DC
925 U Street NW
Washington, DC 20001
(202/387-8391)
www.wdchumanities.org

Metro System Guide
600 Fifth St. NW
Washington, DC 20001
(202/962-1234)
www.wmata.com

Multilingual Services
Meridian International Center
1630 Crescent Place NW
Washington DC 20009
(202/667-6800)
www.meridian.org

Smithsonian Visitor Information Center
Castle Building
1000 Jefferson Dr. SW
Room 153 MRC 010
Washington, D.C. 20560
(202/633-1000)
www.si.edu

White House Visitor Center
U.S. Dept. of Commerce Bldg.
1450 Pennsylvania Ave. NW
Washington, DC 20230
(202/208-1631)
www.nps.gov/whho/

Maryland:
Annapolis & Anne Arundel County Conference & Visitors Bureau
26 West St.
Annapolis, MD 21401
(888/302-2852)
www.visit-annapolis.org

Calvert County MD, Dept. of Economic Development & Tourism
Courthouse
Prince Frederick, MD 20678
(800/331-9771)
www.ecalvert.com

Pennsylvania:

Gettysburg CVB
102 Carlisle St.
Gettysburg, PA 17325
(717/334-6274)
www.gettysburgcvb.org

Virginia:

Alexandria Convention & Visitors Assn.
221 King St. Suite 300
Alexandria, VA 22314
(800/388-9119 or 703/838-5005)
www.funside.com

Arlington Visitors Center
1301 South Joyce St.
Arlington, VA 22202
(800/677-6267)
www.stayarlington.com

Fairfax County Visitors Center
8180-A Silverbrook Road
Lorton, VA 22079
(703/550-2450)
www.visitfairfax.org

Fredericksburg Office of Economic Development & Tourism
706 Caroline St.
Fredericksburg, VA 22401
(800/678-4748)
www.fredericksburgva.com

Embassies:
For information on visiting foreign emabb-sie3s on your trip to D.C., visit www.embassy.org

RECREATIONAL INFO

Fishing in DC— Except as otherwise permitted by these rules: a person shall fish only with a rod, hook, and line, not to exceed three lines in number and not having more than two hooks to each line.

Visit the DC website at www.takemefishing.org/state/page/state-fishing/regulations/state/DC for full details.

No license is required for fishing in tidal water, which includes the Potomac as far north as Chain Bridge. Beyond that, a Maryland license is required. For information on recreation within the National Park Service contact:

National Park Service, National Capital Region, 900 Ohio Dr. SW, Washington, DC 20024 (202/426-6841).
www.nps.gov/nacc

GETTING THERE

Baltimore/Washington International Airport. Located approximately 40 minutes from Washington, this airport offers excellent highway access and an elaborate ground transportation system to speed passengers on their way. More than 50 trains between Washington's Union Station and BWI rail station run on weekdays. Ground transportation to 15th & K Sts. runs every 60 minutes with door-to-door service available.

Washington Dulles International Airport is located 26 miles west of Washington, offering a full range of domestic and international flights. Washington Flyer provides bus service to downtown hotels, with departures every 45 minutes.

Ronald Reagan Washington National Airport, located south of the city along the Potomac River, offers a full range of domestic flights on major, regional and commuter carriers. Shuttle bus service to downtown is accessible on Metrorail's yellow and blue lines.

Amtrak, 400 North Capitol St. NW is America's only national passenger railroad system. Tickets may be purchased at Union Station, Amtrak's Travel Center, New Carrollton or Alexandria (800/USARAIL).

Washington Metropolitan Area Transit Authority (202/637-7000). www.wmata.com

Greyhound and Peter Pan-Trailways connects Washington with cities throughout the United States. The bus terminal is located at 1005 1st St. NE, a short walk to Union Station).

Driving: Washington, DC is circled by the Capital Beltway, formed by Interstates I-495 and I-95. Interstate 66 leads from Washington west to Virginia. Interstate 50 heads east to Annapolis, MD, the Chesapeake Bay and the beaches. Interstate 95 heads north to Baltimore, Philadelphia and New York. Interstate 270 heads northwest to Frederick, MD and beyond.

Parking is restricted during rush hours and during some weekend hours as posted on street signs. Read all signs carefully. During rush hour, certain major arteries change in favor of rush hour traffic; be alert to street signs. If your vehicle is towed Friday after 7 p.m. or anytime on weekends, you will not be able to retrieve it until Monday after 9 a.m. For details, call the DC Dept. of Public Works towing information at 202/541-6075.

GETTING AROUND

Getting around Washington, DC is easy, once you understand the ground plan. It's divided into four basic sections: NW, NE, SW and SE, with the U.S. Capitol at the center. Numbered streets run north/south. Lettered streets run east/west (there are no J, X, Y, or Z streets), becoming two-syllable names (Adams, Belmont), then three-syllable names (Allison, Buchanan) as you go farther out from the center. Avenues named for U.S. states run diagonally, often meeting at traffic circles and squares, such as Dupont Circle.

Always check the quadrant indicator (NW, NE, SW and SE) of a local address before setting out. You'll quickly discover that 500 C St. for instance, can be found in the NW, NE, SW and SE quadrants of the nation's capitol.

Train: Metrorail and Metro bus provide an efficient way of getting around Washington, D.C. Five rail lines and an extensive bus system connect the District with the Maryland and Virginia suburbs. Train lines are named for colors: red, yellow, orange, blue and green. Station entrances are marked by brown pylons capped with the letter "M" and colored stripes indicating which lines are available. Route maps are posted at each station and inside each subway car. Metrorail opens weekdays 5:00 a.m. until midnight, weekends 7:00 a.m. until midnight. Friday and Saturday, it stays open until 3:00 a.m. Each train displays the name of its farthest destination. There is a base subway fare and up to two children under four are free. Rail farecards can be purchased at vending machines located inside the stations. Farecards are inserted into the turnstile gates to enter and exit subway platforms. The fare is automatically deducted each time you exit a station. Farecards cannot be shared with another person. To continue your trip by Metrobus, obtain a transfer slip at the turnstile. Buses travel to Georgetown and other areas not serviced by the subway. For additional schedule information regarding connecting Metrobus service and locations to purchase fares, call 202/637-7000.

Taxis: Taxis are readily available in downtown DC and fares are reasonable. DC cabs operate on a zone system instead of meters. By law, basic rates must be posted in every cab. There is a charge for each additional passenger in the party and a surcharge during evening rush hours (4-6:30 p.m). Maryland and Virginia cabs have metered fares and may transport you in and out of the district, but not between points within the district. For inquiries contact the DC Taxicab Commission at 202/727-1000.

SHOPPING

Georgetown Park. Shop in a four-level Victorian setting with nearly 100 stores and galleries. 3222 M St. NW #140, Washington, DC 20007.

National Geographic Store. Globes, maps, travel accessories, books, toys, apparel and more. 1145 17th St. NW, Washington DC 20036.

Shops at National Place features 60 uncommon shops, boutiques and eateries. 1331 Pennsylvania Ave. NW, Washington, DC 20004.

Smithsonian Retail consists of several museum stores carrying everything from freeze dried ice cream to modern art, gifts, books, posters, jewelry, toys and more.

Union Station, 40 Massachusetts Ave. NE. For over 90 years, Union Station has been the gateway to the nation's capital. Every year, 23.4 million visitors enjoy shopping, entertainment and an international variety of food in this Beaux Arts transportation hub.

DESTINATIONS

Ansel Adams Collection, 1400 I St. NW. View a permanent exhibition at the Wilderness Society of Ansel Adams' most important landscape photographs.

Arlington National Cemetery, Arlington, Virginia. Thousands of visitors annually visit Arlington to see the tomb of John F. Kennedy and to watch the **Changing of the Guard** at the **Tomb of the Unknowns.**

Arts & Industries Building, 900 Jefferson Dr. SW. Re-creating the Philadelphia Centennial of 1876, four exhibit halls represent an extensive collection of Victorian Americana. Highlights include working steam engines and other machines of the era; an 1876 Baldwin locomotive and a 51-foot model of the Antietam sloop-of-war.

Bureau of Engraving & Printing, 14th and C streets SW. Self-guided tours show visitors how money and stamps are made and how high speed presses print more than 7,000 sheets of bills each hour. Complimentary tickets are available on a first-come, first-served basis. Calling ahead is recommended as tours can be suspended at any time.

The Capitol Visitor Center was designed to enhance the visitor's experience at the U.S. Capitol Building with an inspiring 13-minute orientation film and informative exhibits that tell the history of the Capitol Building along with the story of representative democracy in the United States. As the largest expansion of the U.S. Capitol, the 580,000 square foot Visitor Center provides numerous amenities including an exhibition gallery, two orientation theaters, a 550-seat cafeteria, two gift shops, and restrooms. The project took 6 years to complete and cost $621 million.

Capital Children's Museum, currently closed for new construction. Scheduled to reopen in 2008.

Civil War Discovery Trail, Arlington, VA. This trail links more than 420 sites in 24 states, allowing visitors to explore battlefields, museums, parks, antebellum plantations and underground railroad station cemeteries.

College Park Aviation Museum, College Park, MD. This 27,000 sq. ft. state-of-the-art museum uses animatronics and interactive exhibits to tell the story of the World's Oldest Operating Airport - the **College Park Airport.** The museum highlights many of the significant achievements in aviation that have occurred since Wilbur Wright taught the first military aviators to fly here in 1909.

Congressional Cemetery. The nation's first national cemetery is the final resting place for many significant Americans, including John Phillip Sousa, Civil War era photographer Matthew Brady, J. Edgar Hoover, senators and many other prominent individuals. Guided tours are available by appointment.

Corcoran Gallery of Art, 17th St. and New York Ave. NW. The city's largest and oldest private gallery houses a comprehensive collection of American art (painting and sculpture), as well as a fine European collection.

DAR Museum, 1776 D St. NW. The museum of the **National Society of the Daughters of the American Revolution** houses 33 period rooms with an impressive collection of pre-1840s furnishings and a gallery with changing exhibits.

Decatur House, 748 Jackson Pl. NW. This elegant Federal-style home of naval hero Commodore Stephen Decatur was designed by Benjamin Henry Latrobe and built in 1819. A National Historic Landmark near the White House, it has been the home of many of the nation's leaders.

Discovery Channel Store: Destination Washington DC, 601 F Street NW. Experience the excitement of the world's largest producer of nonfiction entertainment, through a unique three-story, 25,000 sq. ft. interactive attraction designed to educate and entertain. Start deep beneath the surface of the earth, continue through an exploration of diverse cultures of the planet and wind up in outer space.

Federal Bureau of Investigation Building, 935 Pennsylvania Ave. NW. Tours include explanation of work performed by FBI laboratories, demonstrations of firearms and a brief history of the bureau. Currently closed for renovations. For updated information call 202/324-3447.

Folger Shakespeare Library, 201 Capitol St. SE. The library houses one of the world's finest collections of Renaissance books and manuscripts.

Ford's Theatre & Lincoln Museum, 511 10th St. NW. This 19th-century theater has been newly renovated and features musical and dramatic performances. The Lincoln Museum on the lower level contains more than 400 objects that tell the story of Lincoln's assassination. In February 2009, the theater reopened after an 18-month multi-million-dollar expansion and renovation. A state-of-the-art Center for Education and Leadership will also be built directly across the street from the theater. Six buildings on both sides of 10th Street NW will be linked together to provide a modern museum. Construction of the new education center was expected to begin in 2010.

Frederick Douglass Home, 1411 W St. SE. See the former home of the famous black abolitionist, orator, diplomat, essayist and auditor of the Treasury. A visitor center with film and exhibits is also on-site.

Gallery of Fine Arts (Howard University), 2455 6th St. NW. At the College of Fine Arts you'll see the permanent Alain Locke African collection as well as traveling exhibits.

Georgetown Park, 3222 M St. NW #140. Built in the 1800s, this historic site once housed horse-drawn omnibuses. It was later used for servicing electric streetcars and trolleys. In the 1960s, the site was selected by the White House for location of the Situation Room and housed equipment for the first hotline to Moscow.

Gunston Hall Plantation, Mason Neck, VA. Only 14 miles south of Mount Vernon on the Potomac River lies the former home of George Mason, the father of the Bill of Rights. The grounds include the 1755 Georgia-style mansion, original boxwood gardens, a wooded nature trail and a reconstructed kitchen yard. Take a guided house tour to interpret William Buckland's elaborately designed woodwork and beautiful 18th-century furnishings.

Hirshhorn Museum & Sculpture Garden, 8th and Independence Ave. SW. This modern round building on the mall contains contemporary paintings and sculptures from the collection of Joseph Hirshhorn. With a primary focus on modern American art, the vast collection also contains works by Degas, Rodin, Henry Moore, Picasso, Matisse and many others.

International Child Art Foundation, 1350 Connecticut Ave. NW #905. Join an international festival and exhibition of children's art by participating in a mural creation and activities for children and adults.

International Monetary Fund Visitor's Center, 700 19th Street NW. Visit the permanent exhibit on the International Monetary Fund, temporary cultural and art exhibits of member nations, economic forums and international seminars and varied cultural issues from different countries.

International Spy Museum, 800 F St. NW. Features the largest collection of international espionage-related artifacts open to the public. Test your skills with interactive exhibits.

The International Trade Center and Ronald Reagan Building, 1300 Pennsylvania Ave. NW. Visit one of Washington's newest attractions and home to the Visitor Information Center. See the historic Berlin Wall, The Oscar Strauss Memorial Fountain, the Woodrow Wilson Memorial, and try the diverse food court featuring menus from around the globe.

Islamic Center, 2551 Massachusetts Ave. NW. The minaret above this leading U.S. mosque faces toward Mecca, the birthplace of Mohammed. Inside, visitors will find a lovely courtyard and intricate Islamic designs on the walls.

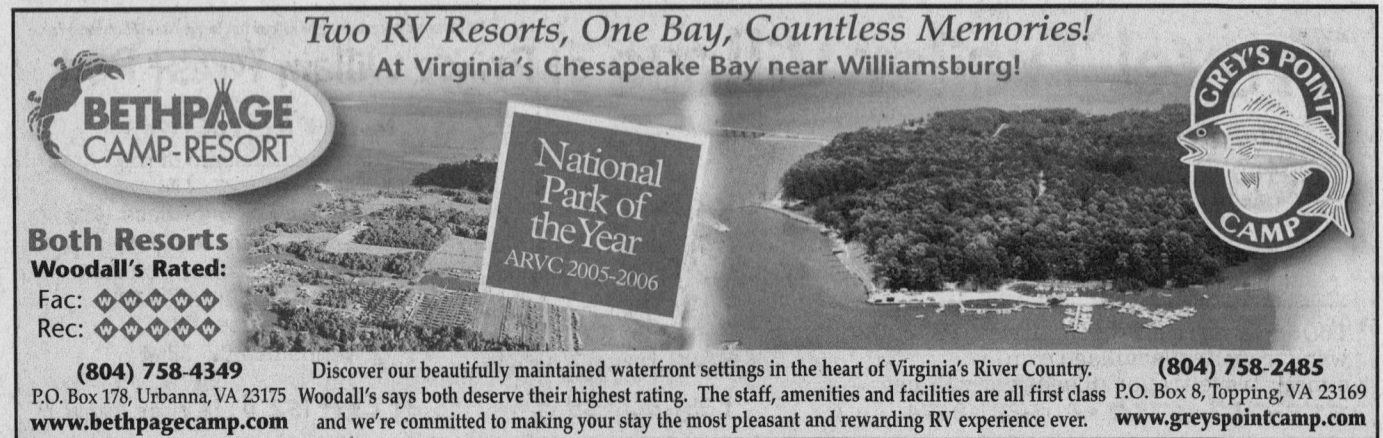

John F. Kennedy Center for the Performing Arts, 2700 F St. NW. The home of the National Symphony Orchestra, Kennedy Center contains a concert hall, an opera house and two theaters.

Library of Congress, 101 Independence Ave. SE. Tour the world's largest library, with almost 110 million items in three buildings. The James Madison Building houses one of the world's three perfect vellum copies of the Gutenberg Bible, as well as changing exhibits. The Main Reading Room and Thomas Jefferson Building can only be seen on the public tour. American Treasures of the Library of Congress is a permanent rotating exhibition.

Martin Luther King Library, 901 G St. NW. This is the main branch of the city's public library system. Of special interest are: the **Washington Division,** with a vast assortment of clippings and photos about the nation's capitol; the **Black Studies Division;** the **Oral History Research Center** and the **Star Library**. Gallery exhibits, along with free film and concert programs, are also available.

Marian Koshland Science Museum of the National Academy of Science. Interactive displays illustrate the role of science in informing national policy and personal decisions impacting people's daily lives. A majority of the museum's exhibits are temporary as the aim is to engage the general public in current scientific issues that impact their lives.

The National Museum of the Marine Corps, A Monument to Honor, Courage and Commitment. The museum is a lasting tribute to U.S. Marines — past, present and future. Situated on a 135-acre site adjacent to the Marine Corps base in Quantico, Virginia, the museum's soaring design evokes the image of the flag raisers of Iwo Jima and beckons visitors to its 100,000 square foot structure. World-class, interactive exhibits using the most innovative technology will surround visitors with irreplaceable artifacts and immerse them in the sights and sounds of Marines in action.

Mount Vernon Estate & Garden, George Washington Parkway, Mount Vernon, Virginia. Visit the Mansion, take a Slave-Life, Landscape and Garden tour, plus view a new pioneer farming site. The estate is also home to seasonal Colonial weekend activities, children's hands-on history activities and a daily wreath-laying graveside ceremony. In addition, there are two museums, archaeology and restoration projects on-site and annual special events. A new $110 million addition features: high tech exhibits, adventure film, wax figures and artifacts of the period and of our first U.S. President.

National Air & Space Museum, 7th and Independence Ave. SW. Be sure to see the most visited museum in the world, with 23 galleries showcasing the evolution of aviation and space technology. Among the 240 aircraft and 50 missiles and rockets are: the original 1903 **Wright Flyer,** Lindbergh's **Spirit of St. Louis**, John Glenn's **Friendship 7,** Apollo 11 command module and a mock-up of a space station. Enjoy exhilarating films in the **Air and Space Theatre** (with its 5-story screen) and watch the planets in the **Spacearium.** Recorded tours in English, French, Spanish, German and Japanese are available for a nominal fee.

National Aquarium, 14th St. and Constitution Ave. NW. The nation's first public aquarium houses rare sea turtles, sharks and alligators, along with a touch tank with hermit crabs and sea urchins. The aquarium is located in the US Dept. of Commerce Building.

National Building Museum, Judiciary Square, F St. between 4th and 5th Streets, NW. Exhibits, lectures, films and family programs and workshops are presented on all aspects of architecture, building and historic preservation.

National Gallery of Art, 4th and Constitution Ave. NW. Visit one of the world's great art museums, with extensive collections of Western European and American works, housed in the West and East Buildings. The West Building, designed by John Russell Pope in 1941, contains works by the Old Masters from the 13th- to the 19th-century. The East Building, designed by architect I.M. Pei in 1978, contains a giant Calder mobile along with other contemporary works.

National Geographic Society, 17th and M Streets, NW. Visit Geographica, an interactive exhibit that teaches about the earth and its geography. **Earth Station One** simulates an orbital flight and features the world's largest unmounted globe.

National Museum of African Art, 950 Independence Ave. SW. The only museum in the U.S. devoted to the art and culture of Africa is housed in what was once the home of abolitionist Frederick Douglass. Permanent and traveling exhibits show the central place of art in many African societies.

National Museum of American History, 14th and Constitution Ave. NW. Newly reopened after an $85 million dollar renovation, the museum has been dramatically transformed with architectural enhancements including a central atrium, a grand staircase and a 10-foot-high artifact wall on both the first and second floors showcasing museum's displays. Nicknamed "The Nation's Attic," this popular museum contains more than 17 million items that represent the heritage of America and her people. Highlights include historical gowns worn by first ladies, George Washington's desk (and his wooden teeth), Ford's original Model T and a priceless instrument collection.

National Museum of Health & Medicine at Walter Reed, 6825-16th St. NW. View exhibits on Civil War medicine, along with the bullet that took Lincoln's life. Also displayed are a seven and a half foot tall skeleton and exhibits on contemporary health issues.

National Museum of Natural History, 10th and Constitution Ave. NW. A collection of more than 60 million items allow visitors to examine humans and their natural environment. Exhibit highlights include huge dinosaur skeletons, displays of early man, giant meteorites, Egyptian mummies, Ice Age mammals, a living coral reef, an insect zoo, the 45.5-carat Hope Diamond and displays of Native North American and Eskimo cultures. The Discovery Room is a hands-on area where you can examine objects and try on costumes from around the world. At the time of this printing, the museum is closed for renovations.

National Museum of the Marine Corps & Marine Corps Heritage Center, Quantico, Virginia. The Museum's soaring design evokes the image of the flag-raisers of Iwo Jima and beckons visitors to its 118,000-square-foot structure. In addition to the central Leatherneck Gallery, there are four permanent galleries and two temporary exhibitions on the first deck. On the mezzanine, check for traveling exhibitions.

National Museum of Women in the Arts, 1250 New York Ave. NW. View this collection of more than 1,500 pieces by 400 female artists from 28 countries, including Cassatt and O'Keeffe.

National Postal Museum, 2 Massachusetts Ave. NE. View a collection of airmail planes, stagecoaches, rare stamps and letters, Owney the Postal Dog, a Pony Express exhibit, rare postage and revenue stamps.

National Theatre, 1321 Pennsylvania Ave. NW. This is one of America's oldest continually operating theaters. Go backstage to see the dressing room, rehearsal hall and fly floor on a one and a half hour-long guided tour.

National Zoological Park, 3001 Connecticut Ave. NW. Home to more than 3,000 exotic animals and Amazonia—a re-creation of the world's largest rain forest. A recently added Kids' Farm features 2 acres of hands-on fun and educational exhibits. Its theme is to better inform our children about animals including grooming and feeding. 62 animals & 52 birds are featured and petting is allowed.

Navy Museum, Washington Navy Yard, 901 M St. SE. Exhibits housed in the old Naval Gun Factory include the foremast of fighting top from the **U.S.S. Constitution,** the bathyscaphe **Trieste,** ship models, uniforms, photos, medals and fine arts.

Newseum, at 6th Street and Pennsylvania Avenue, NW. Highlights of this new facility include a façade featuring a "window on the world," looking out on Pennsylvania Avenue and the Mall. Visitors can explore six levels of displays and experiences, an interactive newsroom, a broadcast studio and a Journalists Memorial. Also includes one of two surviving "Checkpoint Charlie" towers and the largest section of the Berlin Wall outside of Germany, plus an actual news helicopter and front-page newspapers from around the globe.

Octagon Museum, 1799 New York Ave. NW. The first architect of the U.S. Capitol, William Thorton, designed this Federal-style town house for Col. John Taylor III in 1801. After the British burned the White House in 1814, it served as an executive mansion for President James Madison. Today, period furnishings, a museum with changing exhibitions of architecture and allied arts are featured in this historic house.

Old Post Office Pavilion, 1100 Pennsylvania and 12th St. NW. A splendid example of Romanesque architecture, crowned by a 315-ft. clock tower, this former city post office withstood many demolition attempts. Recently restored, it now houses federal offices, restaurants, shops, boutiques and an elegant courtyard. A glass enclosed elevator carries visitors to the Observation Tower for a splendid view of the city.

Old Stone House, 3051 M St. NW. Visit the oldest house in Washington, built in 1765 by a cabinetmaker. Tours are given by park rangers.

Pentagon, Arlington, VA. The world's largest office building (3.7 million sq. ft.) is headquarters for the secretaries of the Defense Department, Army, Navy, Air Force and Coast Guard. Not currently open to public tours at this time. Certain groups are allowed tours. For more information, contact the Tour Office at 703/697-1776.

Phillips Collection, 1600-1612 21st St. NW. American's oldest museum of modern art has a permanent collection that includes masterpieces of European and American art.

Smithsonian Institution is the world's largest museum complex. About 1 percent of the museum's 100 million objects are on display at any one time. The Smithsonian Institution Building, located at 1000 Jefferson Drive, provides a good starting point, where you can obtain brochures about all the Smithsonian buildings as well as find the locations on a model of the National Mall. Popularly known as the "Castle" because of its elaborate design, the building is the oldest of the 12 museums and zoo. All museums are open daily.

Smithsonian Quadrangle was established by the Smithsonian Institution for exhibition, research and education. Located in the area of the National Mall known as the "Quadrangle," the structure is bordered by Independence Avenue, the **Freer Gallery of Art**, the **Smithsonian Institution Building** and the **Arts & Industries Building.** The complex houses two major museums: the **Arthur M. Sackler Gallery of Asian Art** & the **National Museum of African Art,** as well as the **International Center** & the **Education Center. The National Museum of the American Indian is the newest addition to the National Mall.**

Supreme Court, 1st Street and Maryland Ave. NE. Visit the highest court in the land, where the nine presidentially appointed justices rule on constitutional matters. Sit in on courtroom presentations every half-hour, except when court is in session.

Tudor Place, 1644 31st St. NW. This Georgetown mansion and National Historic Landmark set amid five acres of gardens was once the home of Martha Custis Peter, granddaughter of Martha Washington. The grand neo-classical house contains one of the country's most significant collections of objects once belonging to the George Washington family and was designed by William Thornton, first architect of the U.S. Capitol.

Union Station. Washington's historic Union Station was renovated and restored to be Amtrak's "flagship" terminal. It also houses five movie theaters, gourmet restaurants, inexpensive eateries and retail shops. Situated in the Capitol Hill neighborhood, Union Station is convenient to several new hotels and has its own Metro (subway) stop. The building's exterior, a Washington landmark, makes it one of the most beautiful train stations in America.

U.S. Capitol, located at the east end of the Mall. View a gold copy of the **Magna Carta, Statuary Hall, House of Representatives, Senate Chambers** and the original **Supreme Court Chamber**. In order to watch Congress in session, contact your representative's or senator's office a few months in advance for a pass. Visitors must obtain free tickets for tours on a first-come, first-served basis beginning at 9 am each morning at the West front of the Capitol facing the National Mall.

The Washington Design Center, 300 D St. SW #630. Browse through more than 70 showrooms of the world's finest home furnishings, fabrics, floor coverings and accessories to the design trade.

White House, 1600 Pennsylvania Ave. Home of every U.S. president since 1800, this famous "house" is open to tours in groups of ten. Requests should be submitted through your member of Congress at least one month in advance.

Wolf Trap Farm Park is located in Vienna, Virginia. The first national park for the performing arts, Wolf Trap contains an open-air auditorium offering summertime ballet, opera, symphonic music, jazz and drama.

MEMORIALS

African American Civil War Memorial, 10th and U Streets, NW. This new memorial is a sculpture commemorating the more than 208,000 African-American soldiers who fought in the Civil War.

Civil War Memorial, located in the Historic Shaw Neighborhood. This memorial recognizes the heroic efforts of the 185,000 African-American soldiers who fought in the Civil War.

Iwo Jima Statue (Marine Corps Memorial), on Rt. 50 near Arlington National Cemetery, Arlington, Virginia. The largest bronze statue ever cast, this 78-ft. monument commemorates all Marines who have died in battle since 1775. Felix W. de Weldon created the piece from a World War II photograph showing the flag being raised on Mount Suribachi.

Jefferson Memorial. Tidal Basin (South Bank), West Potomac Park. The classical dome and colonnade of this memorial, dedicated in 1943 to the third U.S. president, is in the style Jefferson most preferred. A 19-foot bronze statue stands beneath a simple rotunda. Walls are filled with quotes from the Declaration of Independence and other writings.

Korean War Veterans Memorial, Independence Avenue at the Lincoln Memorial. This new memorial is located on a 2.2-acre site adjacent to the **Lincoln Memorial Reflecting Pool** and features a 19-foot sculptured column of soldiers arrayed for combat with the American flag as their symbolic objective. A 164-foot mural wall is inscribed with the words, "Freedom Is Not Free."

Lincoln Memorial. West Potomac Park at 23rd St. NW. The memorial to Abraham Lincoln is shaped like a Grecian temple and overlooks the broad Reflecting Pool on the National Mall. Inside is a 19-ft. statue of the 16th U.S. president and on the surrounding walls are some of his most famous speeches.

Roosevelt Memorial, Theodore Roosevelt Island, Potomac River between Key and Roosevelt Bridges. This serene island, accessible by footbridge from the parking lot, is a wildlife refuge with nearly two miles of trails. A 17-foot bronze statue of the U.S. president is in Statuary Gardens.

United States Holocaust Memorial Museum, 100 Raoul Wallenberg Pl. NW. Graphic exhibits recount the years of Nazi tyranny from 1933 to 1945. Artifacts, photographs, films and eyewitness testimonies chronicle the persecution and elimination of those deemed racially inferior by the Third Reich. On-site are permanent exhibits, Hall of Remembrance, children's and special exhibitions, the Wexner Learning Center, Oral History Archive, Film and Video Archive and the National Registry of Jewish Holocaust Survivors.

U.S. Air Force Memorial. Across from the Pentagon in Arlington, VA. Featuring three stainless steel spires that soar skyward, the Memorial's design is representative of flight and the flying spirit of the Air Force. The three spires impart a sense of accomplishment in command of the sky, and evoke the image of the precision "bomb burst" maneuver performed by the United States Air Force Thunderbird Demonstration Team. The three spires also represent the three core values of the Air Force - integrity first, service before self, and excellence in all that is done - and the Air Force's total force - active, guard and reserve. Other key elements of the Memorial include a Runway to Glory at the site entrance, a bronze Honor Guard statue developed by the renowned sculptor, Zenos Frudakis, two granite inscription walls located at either end of the central lawn and a Glass Contemplation Wall that honors fallen airmen.

U.S. Navy Memorial, 701 Pennsylvania Avenue. Almost 200 years ago when Pierre L'Enfant designed the nation's capitol, he envisioned a proud and impressive monument to the United States Navy. Today, the **Navy Memorial Complex** (dedicated in 1987) includes an outdoor amphitheater to house all military bands, a commemorative area for official Navy ceremonies, a widescreen movie theater, reception area, Navy Memorial Log and statue of the "Lone Sailor."

Vietnam Veterans Memorial, Constitution Ave. between Henry Bacon Dr. & 21st Street, NW. This modern V-shaped memorial was designed by Maya Ying Lin and is inscribed with the names of the nearly 58,000 people who died in the Vietnam War or remain missing. A new renovation of the lighting system sheds new illumination on The Wall.

Washington Monument, on the National Mall at 15th St. NW. The tallest masonry structure in the world (555 ft.), this majestic obelisk was dedicated in 1885 to the memory of our first president.

WWII Memorial. This moving memorial is located on 17th Street, between Constitution and Independence Avenues and honors the more than sixteen million who served and the more than 400,000 who died in the historic conflict.

PARKS AND GARDENS

Cherry Trees, Tidal Basin, Jefferson Memorial. Hundreds of Yosino and Akebono cherry trees (a gift from Japan in 1912) yield an unforgettable floral display during late March or early April. The famous **National Cherry Blossom Festival** commemorates the event.

Constitution Gardens, between the Washington Monument and Lincoln Memorial, encompassing over 50 acres of rolling, tree-shaded lawns with a six-acre lake in the middle. On an island in the lake is a memorial to the signers of the Declaration of Independence. Immediately adjacent is the **Vietnam Veterans Memorial** and across the street is a statue of Albert Einstein.

Dumbarton Oaks, 1703 32nd St. NW. This splendid 19th-century mansion near Georgetown contains an extensive Byzantine collection, **Garden Library, Rare Book Room** and **Music Room**. The house is surrounded with 10 acres of formal gardens.

Kenilworth Aquatic Gardens, Anacostia Ave. and Douglas St. NE. Thousands of water plants, water lilies, lotuses, water hyacinths and bamboo grow in ponds along the Anacostia River. Watch closely for animals among the plants. Flowers bloom May through early fall. Guided tours are available.

Lafayette Square, Pennsylvania Ave. and 16th St. NW. This meticulously landscaped square is named after Marquis de Lafayette's triumphant visit to America in 1824. In the spring, the equestrian statue of Andrew Jackson is surrounded by tulips.

National Mall, between Constitution and Independence Avenues, SW. This park area extends approximately two miles from the U.S. Capitol to the Washington Monument. Lining either side of the park near the Capitol are 200-year-old American elm trees, several of the **Smithsonian Institution** museums, **National Gallery of Art**, **U.S. Botanic Gardens, National Archives**, featuring the U.S. Constitution, Declaration of Independence and Bill of Rights.

Potomac Park (East & West), north and south of **Jefferson Memorial** & **Tidal Basin**. On the banks of the Potomac River, enjoy many recreational activities including golf, swimming, pedal boating, picnicking and tennis. See the bronze giant called "The Awakening at Hains Point" at the tip of East Potomac Park.

U.S. Botanic Gardens, Maryland Ave. and 1st St. SW. This glass building houses an extraordinary collection of exotic and familiar plants, including orchids, cacti and huge palm trees. The fountain and gardens in front are by Frederic Bartholdi.

U.S. National Arboretum, 3501 New York Ave. NE. The nation's own arboretum offers 444 lovely acres of trees, shrubs, picnic grounds and flowering plants from across the U.S. and around the world. Enjoy the special Japanese bonsai collection and aromatic herb garden. Open daily except on Christmas.

NEIGHBORHOODS

Adams Morgan. Along Columbia Rd. between 18th St. and Kalorama Park NW. Often called the "United Nations," Adams Morgan is a multi-ethnic neighborhood with a number of fine restaurants serving foods from around the world. A collection of art galleries and antique shops can also be found in this colorful section of town.

Anacostia is east from the Anacostia River to Pennsylvania Ave. on the north and Southern Ave. on the south and east. Named after its original Native American inhabitants, Anacostia dates back to the arrival of John Smith in 1607. The **Frederick Douglass Memorial Home** and the **Anacostia Neighborhood Museum** are on Barry's Farm, where African-Americans settled after the Civil War.

Brookland. This Northeast Washington neighborhood features the largest concentration of Catholic institutions outside of the Vatican.

Capitol Hill, streets surrounding the **U.S. Capitol Building**. Presided over by the gleaming white dome of the Capitol, the Capitol Hill area offers visitors a wealth of attractions within just a few blocks.

Chinatown, G and H Streets between 6th and 8th Streets, NW. This area is easily recognized by its spectacular **Friendship Archway** decorated in classical Chinese art. Many of the city's Oriental restaurants and shops are in this historic area. A Chinese Lunar New Year Celebration fills the streets in January or February.

Downtown, from Constitution Avenue to M Street NW between 4th and 7th NW. The downtown area east of the **White House** has undergone massive renovation in recent years and now boasts refurbished hotels, smart shops, wonderful restaurants, **Pavilion at the Old Post Office**, the **Warner Theatre** and the **National Theatre**.

Embassy Row, Massachusetts Ave. between Sheridan and Observatory Circles, NW. Many of the 150 foreign embassies and chanceries established in Washington are located here. Coats of arms and flags identify each diplomatic mission.

Foggy Bottom, the area between Pennsylvania and Virginia Avenues and between 22nd and 25th Streets. Once a foggy swamp along the Potomac River, Foggy Bottom is now a thriving area where visitors can mingle with diplomats from the State Department, as well as students from George Washington University.

Georgetown, west of Rock Creek Park and north of K St. This area has the **Old Stone House,** one of the oldest standing houses in DC, plus shopping boutiques, restaurants and nightclubs in old colonial sections of the city.

Lafayette Square. Surrounding the **White House**, this is an area of historic elegance, refinement and power. Stories of the notable residents can be found in many nearby museums and institutions, including the **Octagon Museum, Decatur House, DAR Museum, American Red Cross Museum** and **St. John's Episcopal Church.**

Mount Pleasant. This neighborhood is home to the newest installment in the city's collection of neighborhood heritage trails. Located north and east of the National Zoo, it's known for its global character. Isolated from downtown by steep hills that were difficult to climb on foot or in carriages, it once served as a retreat for the wealthy elite. Today's visitors are struck by small businesses that service a diverse community in Spanish, Ethiopian, Vietnamese and other languages. The 17-stop trail is outlined at culturaltourismdc.org.

Penn Quarter. This revitalized area on Pennsylvania Ave between 3rd and 12th Streets NW includes eclectic art galleries, numerous new restaurants and several off-the-Mall attractions such as the **National Law Enforcement Officers Memorial, National Portrait Gallery, National Building Museum, U.S. Navy Memorial, Ford's Theatre** and the **Shakespeare Theatre**.

Shaw, north of M Street NW between North Capitol St. and 15th St. This was the business and retail hub of the city's African-American community until the end of segregation in the early 1950s. Landmarks include the **O Street Market, Howard University, Bethune Museum & Archives** and the renovated **Lincoln Theatre**. U Street, from 12th St. to 16th St. NW, is known for its hip nightclubs, restaurants and shops.

Southwest/Waterfront, south of the **National Mall**, east to the Anacostia River. **Home to Arena Stage, Benjamin Banneker Circle and Fountain** and **L'Enfant Plaza**. The scenic Waterfront area runs for several blocks on Maine Ave. SW and features a shimmering array of piers, sailboats, yachts, fishing boats, seafood markets and restaurants.

Upper Northwest, north of Calvert St. NW. An urbane mix of sidewalk cafés, nightclubs, unusual shops and museums. Home to the **National Zoological Park, Washington's National Cathedral** and **Rock Creek Park.**

TOURS

All About Town, Clinton, MD, 301/856-5556. Take one of many regularly scheduled full-day, half-day and evening sightseeing tours of the Capitol, Georgetown, Arlington and Mount Vernon. Board late-model, air-conditioned coaches, including the only glass-topped sightseeing coaches in DC.

Bill Appell's Tech Tours, 235 Chatham Lane, Annapolis, MD 21403. Phone: 301/261-2486. Highly entertaining, six-hour tour aboard a luxury multimedia minibus. Features escorted stops inside the White House, the Vietnam Veterans Memorial and more. For information and a virtual tour, go to http://www.TechToursWashington.com.

Capitol Helicopters Washington National Airport, 703/417-2150. General Aviation Terminal Ste. #210. Soar above it all and experience what makes Washington, DC the most powerful city in the world. You won't miss a single historic monument on this narrated tour aboard these jet helicopters.

Capitol Entertainment Services, 202/636-9203, www.washington-dc-tours.com Regularly scheduled sightseeing tours are given by licensed tour guides. A specialty tour of African-American historical sites is also available.

Capitol River Cruises, Rockville, MD, 301/460-7447, www.capitolrivercruises.com. Discover the most spectacular views of Washington aboard **Nightingale II**, Georgetown's only hourly sightseeing cruise. The 50-minute tours depart daily from Georgetown Harbour.

C&O Canal Barge Rides, Sharpsburg, MD, 301/739-4200. Travel back in time to the 1870s. Experience this one-hour trip on a replica canal boat pulled by mules and narrated by park rangers in period clothing.

Cultural/Heritage Tours, www.dcchamber.org, 202/347-7201. Tour packages of Washington, D.C.'s fascinating and diverse neighborhoods are offered. Lively entertainment and meals are included in these narrated sightseeing tours.

DC Ducks, 202/832-9800, www.historictours.com. See Washington from a different point of view. Tour the Mall by land, then splash into the Potomac River aboard "the boats with wheels." This fully narrated 90-minute tour takes place aboard a re-built World War II amphibious vessel.

Georgetown & Dupont Circle Walking Tours, Silver Spring, MD, 301/588-8999, www.tourdc.com. The romance, history and magic of an earlier time in America come alive in this walking tour of Georgetown—a lovely 18th-century port that lives on as one of Washington's most prestigious and fun neighborhoods. In addition to the stately homes of celebrated residents such as the Kennedys and the Harrimans, you'll see the tiny 18th-century home of a ship captain and the elegant house of a young woman who fled to join the Underground Railroad. You'll hear how the Civil War fiercely divided this town and how the free African-American community struggled to grow even during slavery. www.tourdc.com

Martz Gray Line of Washington, D.C. 800/862-1400, www.graylinedc.com. Specializing in daily, lectured sightseeing tours of Washington, DC including a multilingual city tour, trolley tour and historic day trips to Colonial Williamsburg, Monticello and Gettysburg, PA.

Old Town Trolley Tours, 202/832-9800, www.trolleytours.com. Daily 2-hour narrated tours begin every 30 minutes starting at 9 a.m. Passengers may reboard from 16 sites.

Potomac Riverboat Co., Alexandria, VA, 703/684-0580. View the Capitol city by water and enjoy a 90-minute leisurely cruise that takes you aboard the Matthew Hayes. Sail past the **Lincoln Memorial, Jefferson Memorial, Washington Monument** and the

C & O Canal National Historic Park near D.C. Photo courtesy Maryland Tourism

Kennedy Center aboard this narrated tour. The Admiral Tilp offers a 40-minute narrated sightseeing cruise that allows you to see Alexandria by water as you float down the Potomac River.

SpyDrive, 866/SPY-TREK www.spytrek.com. Intelligence and security experts from the KGB, CIA, FBI and U.S. Military show you where spies lived, worked and operated in the city that is home to more spies than any other city in the world.

Tourmobile Sightseeing, 202/554-5100, www.tourmobile.com. Narrated shuttle tours take you right where you want to go with unlimited free re-boarding. You choose where to stop, stay as long as you want, then re-board and ride to another historic location.

Washington Boat Tours & Shore Shot Cruises, 202/554-6500, www.shoreshot.com. A 50-minute, 10-mile cruise on the Potomac takes you past the **Capitol**, **Washington Monument**, **Lincoln and Jefferson Memorials**, **Kennedy Center**, **Watergate**, **Georgetown**, **National Airport**, **Pentagon** and 30 additional sights.

Washington Walks, 202/484-1565, www.washingtonwalks.com. Two-hour, professionally guided walking tours include Capitol Hauntings, Embassy Row, Foggy Bottom, I've Got A Secret and Washington Waterfront.

CALENDAR OF EVENTS

JANUARY

Chinese New Year Parade; Robert E. Lee's Birthday Celebration; Sugarloaf Crafts Festival.

FEBRUARY

Washington Boat Show; International Wine & Food Festival.

MARCH

National Cherry Blossom Festival; Smithsonian Kite Festival.

APRIL

Filmfest D.C.; Smithsonian Washington Craft Show; White House Spring Garden and House Tours; White House Easter Egg Roll; National Cherry Blossom Festival.

MAY

Arlington Cemetery Memorial Day Ceremony; Georgetown Garden Tour; Vietnam Veterans Memorial Day Ceremony.

JUNE

Jazz Festival; Caribbean Carnival Extravaganza; Marine Band Summer Concert Series; Museum Walk Weekend; Barbecue Battle; Soap Box Derby; WINS Pow Wow.

JULY

Bastille Day; Festival of American Folklife; Latin-American Festival; Fourth of July Celebration.

AUGUST

Asian Festival; Arlington County Fair; Georgia Avenue Day; U.S. Army Band "1812 Overture".

SEPTEMBER

Adams Morgan Festival; Ambassador's Ball; National Black Family Reunion; Kalorama House and Embassy Tour; Kennedy Center Open House.

OCTOBER

Lombardi Gala; Theodore Roosevelt's Birthday Celebration; Apple Harvest Festival; Pumpkin Festival.

NOVEMBER

Marine Corps Marathon; Waterfowl Festival; Bakery Festival; Veterans Day Ceremony.

DECEMBER

Washington Jewish Film Festival; Capital Area Auto Show; Christmas Celebration and Services at Washington National Cathedral; Matzo Ball.

WASHINGTON D.C.

Make The Most Of Your D.C. Trip

BEFORE YOU LEAVE FOR D.C.

At least one month prior to your departure, contact the agencies listed under "Travel Information Sources" on the first page of this travel section. They'll send you free, up-to-date information on all that's happening in our nation's capital.

If you plan on touring the White House, U.S. Capitol or Bureau of Engraving and Printing, contact your congressman or senator's office (six to nine months prior to your departure) for special "VIP" tickets. With these tickets you can avoid long lines and you may be shown attractions not usually seen on regular tours. "VIP" tours are held in the early morning before regular tour hours.

Plan Ahead! While Washington, D.C. seems small enough (67 square miles) it is packed with over 50 museums, more than 70 art galleries, historic homes and neighborhoods... the list goes on! You just can't do it all in one day—better to allow several. By laying out a daily itinerary (before you arrive) you won't be overwhelmed. You'll know exactly what you want to see and when you want to see it. You'll also have a better chance of coming away from your trip realizing you didn't miss a beat!

WHEN YOU GET THERE

Stop in at The Washington D.C. Convention & Tourism Corporation, 1212 New York Avenue NW, Ste. 600. Get information and travel brochures while you are here. The Smithsonian Visitor Information Center is located in the "Castle" building which is the oldest of Smithsonian's 14 museums. Orientation films, scale models of Washington, interactive video information and electronic maps help you find your way around this fantastic complex.

AROUND TOWN

Most museums and attractions offer guided and/or recorded tours. Call the facility ahead of time to find out particulars such as how often the tours run. And while we're talking tours, you might want to consider touring your favorite museum during "off-peak" hours. Check with the museum ahead of time to find out if they offer this service and if it is only on a seasonal basis. And, speaking of "off-peak" hours, photographers might want to catch their favorite memorial or monument during the evening hours when it is bathed in lights. One of the most dramatic photographic shots in the city can be taken at dawn: Go to the hill near the Netherlands Carillon (which is located south of the Iwo Jima Memorial). Look east toward the Lincoln Memorial and wait for the sun to rise behind the Capitol.

TAKE THE METRO

You could waste a lot of time by driving around looking for parking. And if you abuse parking regulations they will ticket or tow your vehicle. The Metro covers not only all parts of downtown, but nearby Virginia and Maryland suburbs as well. Trains operate about every 10 minutes and start at 5:00 a.m. weekdays, 7 a.m. weekends; stop at midnight Sunday - Thursday, 3 a.m. Friday & Saturday.

TAKE YOUR TIME!

While many view "the Mall" as the hub of Washington attractions, set aside some time to venture out and explore the city's neighborhoods or you'll miss an essential part of the city, such as the fun of the Capital Children's Museum and the beauty of the largest Catholic church in the U.S.—The National Shrine of the Immaculate Conception.

Washington DC

WASHINGTON—B-4

WASHINGTON D.C. AREA MAP

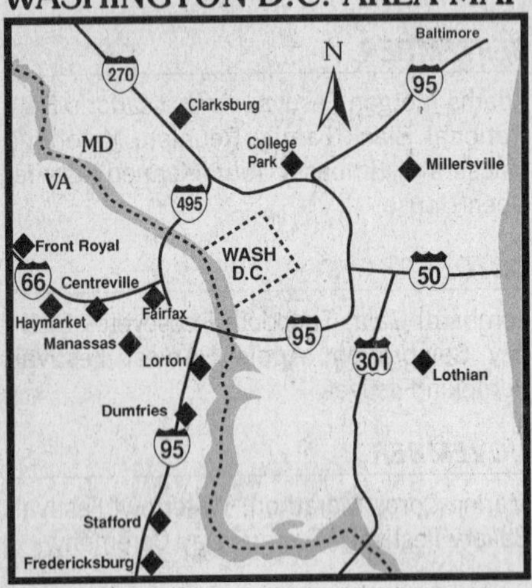

Symbols on map indicate towns within a 30 mi radius of Washington D.C. where campgrounds (diamonds), attractions (flags), & RV service centers & camping supply outlets (gears) are listed. Check listings for more information.

Tell Them Woodall's Sent You!

WELCOME **AQUIA PINES CAMP RESORT**—*From jct I-495 & I-95 (South); Go 26 mi S on I-95 (exit 143A), then 1/2 mi N on US 1. Enter on L.*

SEE PRIMARY LISTING AT STAFFORD, VA AND AD TRAVEL SECTION PAGE 60

WELCOME **BETHPAGE CAMP-RESORT**—*From jct I-495 & I-95: Go 45 mi S on I-95 (exit 126), then 70 mi S on US 17, then 5 mi SE on Hwy 602, then 3/4 mi NE on Brown's Ln. Enter on L.*

SEE PRIMARY LISTING AT URBANNA AND AD URBANNA, VA PAGES 782-783

WELCOME **CHERRY HILL PARK**—*N'bnd from jct I-95 (exit 25) & US 1: Go 175 yds S on US 1, then 1 mi W on Cherry Hill Rd. Enter on left. S'bnd from jct I-95 (exit 29B) & Hwy 212 (Powder Mill Rd): Go 1 mi W on Powder Mill Rd, then 1 mi S on Cherry Hill Rd. Enter on R.*

SEE PRIMARY LISTING AT COLLEGE PARK, MD AND AD MD TRAVEL SECTION PAGE 329

WELCOME **DUNCAN'S FAMILY CAMPGROUND**—*From jct I-495 (exit 11) & Hwy 4: Go 9 mi E on Hwy 4, then 1/2 mi E on Hwy 408, then 1/4 mi N on Sands Rd. Enter on R.*

SEE PRIMARY LISTING AT LOTHIAN, MD AND AD TRAVEL SECTION PAGE 58

WELCOME **TRAVEL TRAILER VILLAGE AT PRINCE WILLIAM FOREST PARK**—*From jct I-495 & I-95: Go 18 mi S on I-95 (exit 152), then 2-1/2 mi NW on Hwy 234. Enter on L.*

SEE PRIMARY LISTING AT DUMFRIES, VA AND AD TRAVEL SECTION PAGE 61

District of Columbia Song: "The Star-Spangled Banner" (Words by Francis Scott Key)

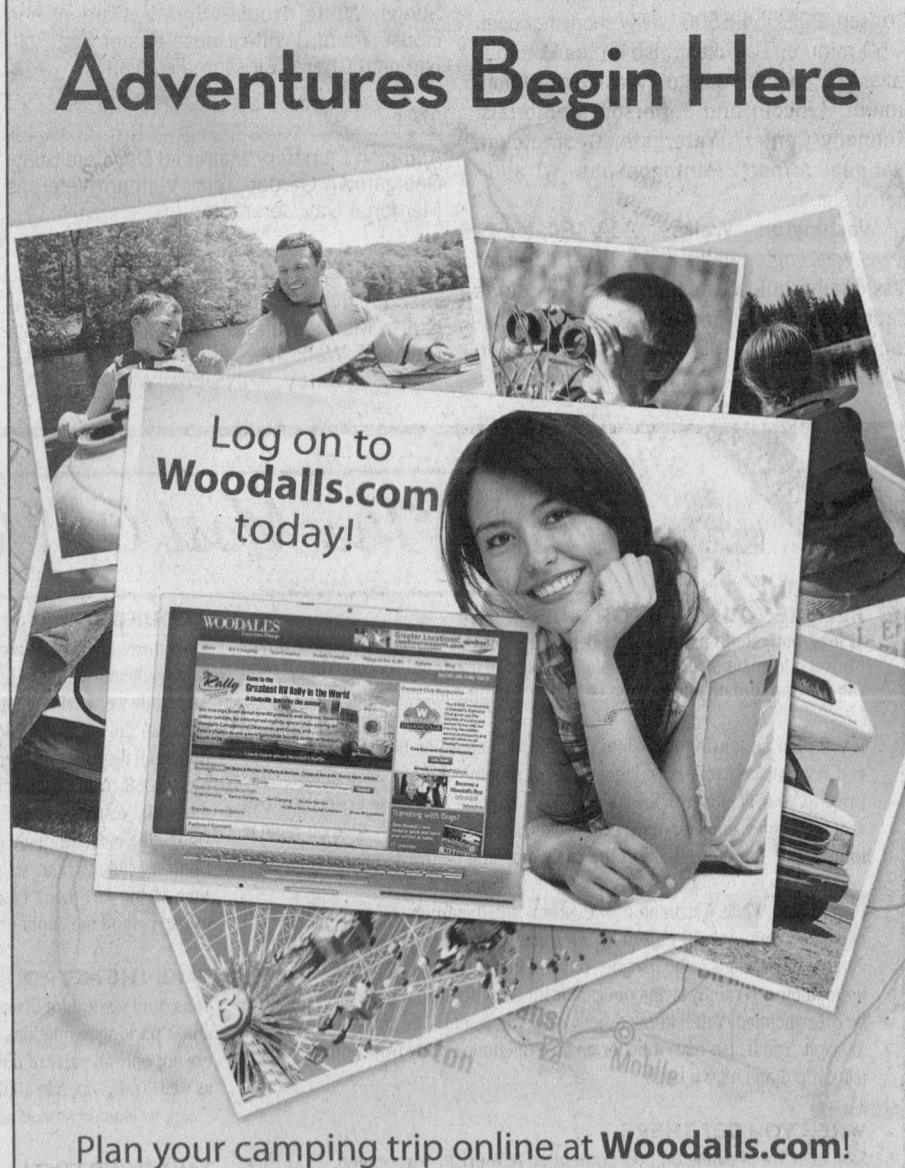

READER SERVICE INFO

The following businesses have placed an ad in the Florida Travel Section. To receive free information, enter their Reader Service number on the Reader Service Card opposite page 48/Discover Section in the front of this directory:

Advertiser	RS#
Aztec RV Resort	4219
Big Cypress RV Resort	3477
Broward County Parks	3784
Broward County Parks	4300
Camping on the Gulf	4263
Como Truck & RV Sales & Service	3671
Disney's Fort Wilderness Resort & Campground	4176
Dunedin RV Resort	671
Emerald Coast RV Beach Resort	4322
Flagler County Chamber of Commerce	3583
Florida Association of RV Parks and Campgrounds	2173
Goethe Trailhead Ranch & RV Park	4265
Hammondell Campsites & RV Sales	4130
Lake Marian Paradise	672
Lazydays RV Campground	4355
Outdoor Resorts at Orlando	4245
Pelican's Landing	4255
Quail Run RV Resort	3666
Rainbow Resort	4270
Revels Nationwide RV Sales	3872
Sarasota Sunny South	3806
Seasons in the Sun RV & Motorcoach Resort	4253
Sonrise Palms Christian RV Park	3374
The Floridian RV Resort	4341
Wilderness RV Park Estates	3670
Zachary Taylor Resort	440

TIME ZONE

Most of Florida is in the Eastern Time Zone; the section west of the Apalachicola River is in the Central Time Zone.

TOPOGRAPHY

The terrain in Florida ranges from farm and pastureland to swampy everglades; flat cattle land to the rolling hills of orange groves. There are more than 1,800 miles of coastline.

TEMPERATURE

In the northern section, summer temperatures average 80.5° and winter temperatures average 53°. The southern areas average 82.7° in summer and 68.5° in winter. Rainfall is fairly even throughout the state and averages 53 inches per year. The heaviest rainfall occurs during June, July, August and September.

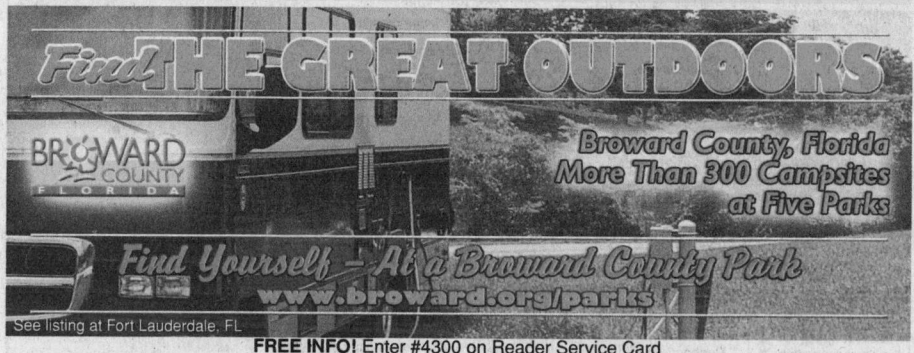

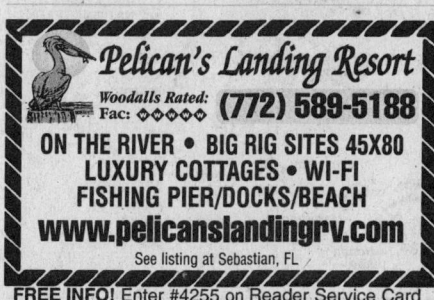

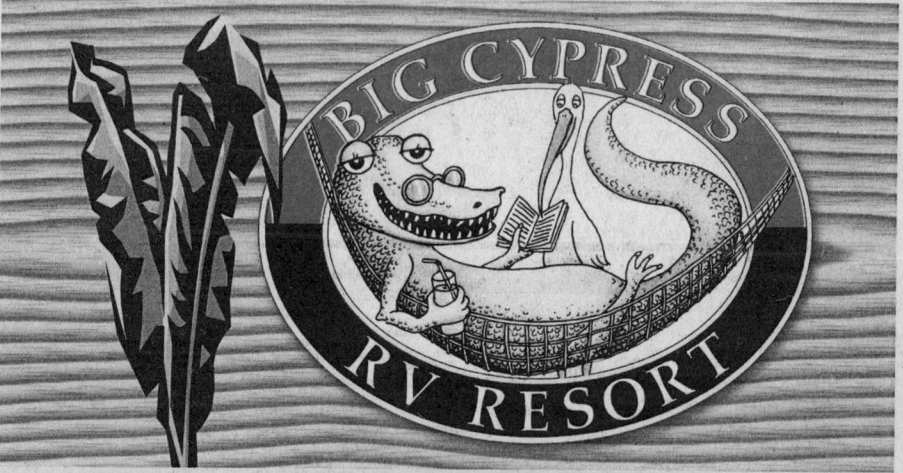

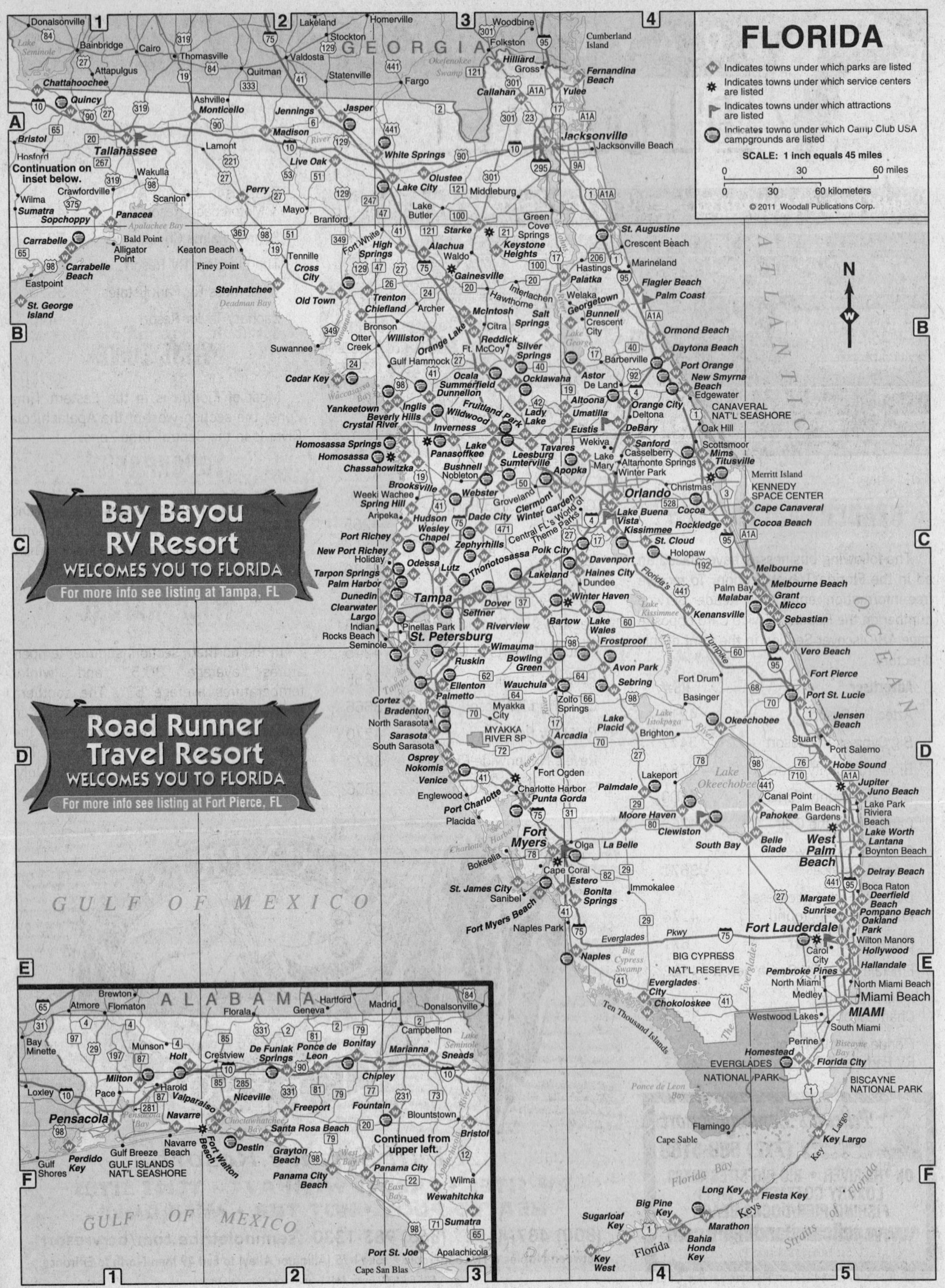

FLORIDA
Indicates towns under which parks are listed
Indicates towns under which service centers are listed
Indicates towns under which attractions are listed
Indicates towns under which Camp Club USA campgrounds are listed
SCALE: 1 inch equals 45 miles
0 30 60 miles
0 30 60 kilometers
© 2011 Woodall Publications Corp.
Bay Bayou RV Resort
WELCOMES YOU TO FLORIDA
For more info see listing at Tampa, FL
Road Runner Travel Resort
WELCOMES YOU TO FLORIDA
For more info see listing at Fort Pierce, FL
Continuation on inset below.
Continued from upper left.
GEORGIA
ALABAMA
ATLANTIC OCEAN
GULF OF MEXICO
Tallahassee
Jacksonville
Orlando
Tampa
St. Petersburg
Fort Myers
West Palm Beach
Fort Lauderdale
MIAMI
Pensacola
Key West
KENNEDY SPACE CENTER
CANAVERAL NAT'L SEASHORE
BIG CYPRESS NAT'L RESERVE
EVERGLADES NATIONAL PARK
BISCAYNE NATIONAL PARK
GULF ISLANDS NAT'L SEASHORE
MYAKKA RIVER SP
Lake Okeechobee
Florida Bay
Straits of Florida
Ten Thousand Islands

Florida is the top travel destination in the world. That's right, the world. And what's not to get excited about? Sun, sand, 663 miles of beaches, home of Disney World, the Florida Keys, and so much more. With so much sun and water, it's no wonder that people keep coming back!

TRAVEL & TOURISM INFO

State Agency:

Visit Florida
2540 W. Executive Center Circle
Suite 200
Tallahassee, FL 32301
(850/488-5607)
www.visitflorida.com

Florida State Chamber of Commerce
136 S. Bronough St.
P.O. Box 11309
Tallahassee, FL 32302
(850/521-1200)
www.flchamber.com

Regional Agencies:

Alachua County Visitors & Convention Bureau
30 East University Ave.
Gainesville, FL 32601
(866/778-5002 or 352/374-5260)
www.visitgainesville.com

Beaches of South Walton
P.O. Box 1248
Santa Rosa Beach, FL 32459-1248
(800/822-6877)
www.beachesofsouthwalton.com

Central Florida VCB
600 N. Broadway, Suite 300
Bartow, FL 33830
(800/828-7655)
www.visitcentralflorida.org

Charlotte Harbor Visitor & Convention Bureau
18501 Murdock Circle, Suite 502
Port Charlotte, FL 33948
(941/743-1900 or 800/652-6090)
www.charlotteharbortravel.com

Citrus County Visitors and Convention Bureau
9225 W. Fishbowl Dr.
Homosassa, FL 34448
(800/587-6667 or 352/628-9305)
www.visitcitrus.com

Cocoa Beach Area Chamber of Commerce
400 Fortenberry Rd.
Merritt Island, FL 32952
(321/459-2200)
www.cocoabeachchamber.com

Emerald Coast CVB
1540 Miracle Strip Parkway
Fort Walton Beach, FL 32548
(800/322-3319 or 850/651-7131)
www.destin-fwb.com

Flagler County Chamber of Commerce
20 Airport Rd, Ste C
Palm Coast, FL 32164
(800/670-2640)
www.visitflagler.org

Florida Keys & Key West Tourist Development Council
1201 White St, Ste 102
Key West, FL 33040
(800/648-5510)
www.fla-keys.com

Florida's Space Coast Office of Tourism
430 Brevard Avenue, Suite 150
Cocoa Village, FL 32922
(877/572-3224)
www.space-coast.com

Highlands County Tourist Development Council
1121 U. S. 27 South
Sebring, FL 33870
(863/386-1316 or 800/545-6021)
www.highlandscvb.com

Lake County Tourism
20763 US Hwy 27
P.O. Box 7800
Groveland, FL 34736
(352/343-3673)
www.lakecountyfl.gov/visitors/

Lee County Visitor & Convention Bureau
12800 University Drive, Suite 550
Fort Myers, FL 33907
(239/338-3500 or 800/237-6444)
www.fortmyerssanibel.com

Nature Coast Business Development Council, Inc.
P.O. Box 1112
Bronson, FL 32621
(352/486-5470)
www.naturecoast.org

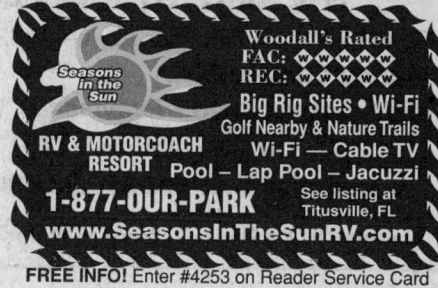

New Smyrna Beach Visitors Bureau
2238 State Road 44
New Smyrna Beach, FL 32168
(800/541-9621)
www.nsbfla.com

North Florida Regional Chamber of Commerce
202 South Walnut Street
P.O. Box 576
Starke, FL 32091
(904/964-5278)
www.bradfordregion.co

Putnam County Chamber of Commerce
P.O. Box 550
1100 Reid Street
Palatka, FL 32178-0550
(386/328-1503)
Fax (386/328 7076)

Seminole County CVB
1230 Douglas Ave. Suite 116
Longwood, FL 32779
(407/665-2900 or 800/800-7832)
www.putnamcountychamber.org

Local Agencies:
Amelia Island Tourist Development
102 Centre Street
Amelia Island, FL 32034
(800/226-3542)
www.ameliaisland.org

Bradenton Area Convention and Visitors Bureau
P.O. Box 1000
Bradenton, FL 34206-1000
(941/729-9177)
www.floridasgulfislands.com

Daytona Beach Area CVB
126 E. Orange Ave.
Daytona Beach, FL 32114
www.daytonabeach.com

Greater Fort Lauderdale CVB
100 E. Broward Blvd., Ste. 200
Fort Lauderdale, FL 33316
(800/22-SUNNY)
www.sunny.org

Jacksonville & the Beaches CVB
550 Water St., Ste 1000
Jacksonville, FL 32202
(800/733-2668)
www.visitjacksonville.com

Kissimmee CVB
1925 E. Irlo Bronson Memorial Hwy
Kissimmee, FL 34744
(407/944-2400)
www.floridakiss.com

Greater Miami CVB
701 Brickell Ave., Ste. 2700
Miami, FL 33131
(800/933-8448)
www.miamiandbeaches.com

Naples, Marco Island, Everglades CVB
3050 N. Horseshoe Dr., Ste. 218
Naples, FL 34104
(800/688-3600)
www.paradisecoast.com

Ocala-Marion County VCB
2102 Southwest 20th Place, Unit 302
Ocala, FL 34474
(888/FL-OCALA or 352/291-9169)
www.ocalamarion.com

Orlando/Orange County CVB
8723 International Dr., Ste. 101
Orlando, FL 32819
(407/363-5872 or 800/972-3304)
www.orlandoinfo.com

Palm Beach County CVB
1555 Palm Beach Lakes Blvd., Ste. 800
West Palm Beach, FL 33401
(800/833-5733)
www.palmbeachfl.com

Panama City Beach CVB
17001 Panama City Beach Pkwy
Panama City Beach, FL 32413
(800/553-1330 or 850/233-5070)
www.thebeachloversbeach.com

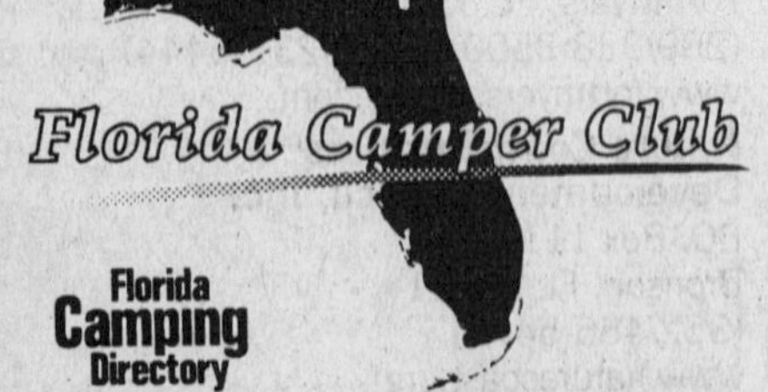

Pensacola Bay Chamber of Commerce
1401 E. Gregory Street
Pensacola, FL 32502
(800/874-1234)
www.visitpensacola.com

Central Pasco Chamber of Commerce
P. O. Box 98
Land O' Lakes, FL 34639
(813/909-2722)

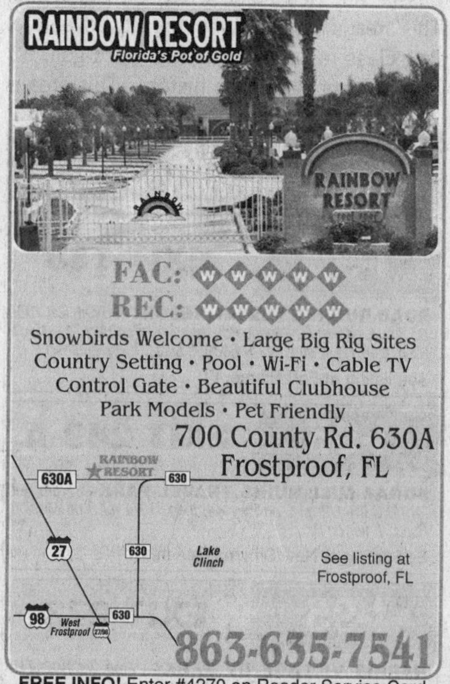

RAINBOW RESORT
Florida's Pot of Gold
RAINBOW RESORT
FAC:
REC:
Snowbirds Welcome • Large Big Rig Sites
Country Setting • Pool • Wi-Fi • Cable TV
Control Gate • Beautiful Clubhouse
Park Models • Pet Friendly
700 County Rd. 630A
Frostproof, FL
630A
RAINBOW RESORT
630
27
630
Lake Clinch
98
West Frostproof
630
See listing at Frostproof, FL
863-635-7541

FREE INFO! Enter #4270 on Reader Service Card

St. Augustine, Ponte Vedra & The Beaches Visitors and Convention Bureau
88 Riberia St., Ste. 400
St. Augustine, FL 32084
(800/653-2489)
www.getaway4florida.com

St. Petersburg/Clearwater Area CVB
13805 - 58th St. N., Ste. 2-200
Clearwater, FL 33760
(877/352-3224 or 727/464-7200)
www.floridasbeach.com

Santa Rosa County Tourism Development Council
8543 Navarre Pkwy.
Navarre, FL 32566
(800/480-7263 or 850/939-2691)
www.floridabeachestorivers.com

Sarasota CVB
701 N. Tamiami Trail
Sarasota, FL 34236

(800/522-9799)
www.sarasotafl.org

Suwannee County Tourist Development Council
816 S. Ohio Ave.
Live Oak, FL 32064
(386/362-3071)
www.suwanneechamber.com

Tallahassee Area CVB/Visitor Information Center
106 E. Jefferson St.
Tallahassee, FL 32301
(800/628-2866)
www.visittallahassee.com

Tampa Bay & Company
401 East Jackson Street, Suite 2100
Tampa, FL 33602
(813/223-1111 or 800/44-TAMPA)
www.visittampabay.com

Sarasota
Sunny South
941-921-4409
FAC:
Daily-Weekly-Monthly-Seasonal-Annual
Big Rigs - 30/50 Amp - Free Wi-Fi - Pool
2100 Doud St., Sarasota, FL
www.srqsunnysouth.com
5 Minutes to Beach and Shopping
Large Quiet Sites & Pool
Over "55" RV Park
See listing at Sarasota, FL

FREE INFO! Enter #3806 on Reader Service Card

RECREATIONAL INFO

Canoeing: Florida Professional Paddlesports Assn. (FPPA), P.O. Box 1764, Arcadia, FL 34265. www.paddleflausa.com

Fishing: Florida Fish and Wildlife Conservation Commission, Division of Freshwater Fisheries, 620 S. Meridian St., Tallahassee, FL 32399 (850/488-4676). www.floridaconservation.org

Golf: Florida Sports Foundation, 2930 Kerry Forest Parkway, Tallahassee, FL 32309. www.flasports.com

Historical Sites: Department of State, Division of Historic Resources, R.A. Gray Bldg., 500 S. Bronough St., Tallahassee, FL 32399. www.flheritage.com

State Parks: Dept. of Environmental Protection, Div. of Rec. & Parks, MS #49, 3900 Commonwealth Blvd., Tallahassee, FL 32399-3000. www.dep.state.fl.us/mainpage

SHOPPING

Aventura Mall, 19501 Biscayne Blvd. & 196th St., Aventura. Florida's largest indoor super-regional mall with 250 stores and six department stores.

Fisherman's Village, 1200 W. Retta

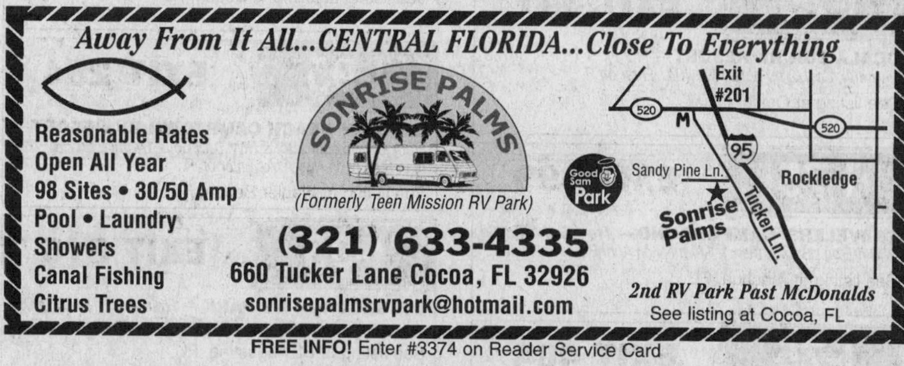

Away From It All...CENTRAL FLORIDA...Close To Everything
Reasonable Rates
Open All Year
98 Sites • 30/50 Amp
Pool • Laundry
Showers
Canal Fishing
Citrus Trees
SONRISE PALMS
(Formerly Teen Mission RV Park)
Good Sam Park
(321) 633-4335
660 Tucker Lane Cocoa, FL 32926
sonrisepalmsrvpark@hotmail.com
Exit #201
520
M
95
520
Sandy Pine Ln.
Rockledge
Sonrise Palms
Tucker Ln.
2nd RV Park Past McDonalds
See listing at Cocoa, FL

FREE INFO! Enter #3374 on Reader Service Card

Luxury and Comfort Await You...
Aztec
R.V. Resort
Visit us now at:
www.aztecrvresort.com
Concierge Service
Pool - Tennis
Fitness Center
Privacy
24 hr. Security
See listing at Margate, FL
Only minutes from the Fort Lauderdale beaches!
Tel: 1-888-493-2856 (Toll-free)

FREE INFO! Enter #4219 on Reader Service Card

Esplanade, Punta Gorda. This waterfront complex features unique shops, restaurants, a marina and museums. While there, visit the Oyster Bar with its beautiful view of Charlotte Harbor.

Orlando Premium Outlets, 8200 Vineland Ave., Orlando. Upscale Mediterranean village style outlet shopping area.

Centro Ybor, 1600 E 8th Ave, Ste A-100, Tampa. These former brick cigar factories were converted into unique shopping, dining and entertainment attractions. Eighth Ave. & 13th St., Tampa, FL.

DESTINATIONS

NORTHWEST REGION

The Northwest Region of Florida lies just south of the Georgia state line along the Atlantic. Stretches southwest, it encompasses America's oldest city, St. Augustine. This area is not only full of big city adventure, first class resorts, and world-class golf, it's also an area steeped in history. This area is

sought out by anglers for the incredible fishing, and golfers, for courses designed by golfing giants like Arnold Palmer and Jack Nicklaus. Amelia Island, with its first class accommodations and Fernandina Beach, a 50 block historic district will have any traveler living in the lap of luxury.

Apalachicola. The name means "friendly people" and the town is the site of Apalachicola Bay, which has over 10,000 acres of oyster beds, producing 90% of Florida's oysters. This is also the home of Fort Gadsden Historic Site. Apalachicola has more antebellum sites than anywhere else in Florida. Upwards of 200 homes and commercial buildings, which hold boutiques, shops, galleries, restaurants, churches and B&Bs, are listed on the National Register of Historic Places. The circa-1912 **Dixie Theatre** hosts a summer repertory group. **John Gorrie Museum State Park** commemorates the 19th-century doctor who invented an ice-making machine, the precursor to modern air conditioning, while searching for a way to make his yellow fever victims more comfortable.

The **St. Vincent National Wildlife Refuge** is an undeveloped barrier island just offshore from the mouth of the Apalachicola River, in the Gulf of Mexico. Ten separate habitat types have been identified. The island is a haven for endangered and threatened species, including bald eagles, sea turtles, indigo snakes and gopher tortoises. Wood storks use the refuge during their migration. In addition, the refuge serves as a breeding area for endangered red wolves. Scuba divers and anglers will enjoy the **Mighty O**, the retired aircraft carrier Oriskany, that was intentionally sunk 24 miles SE of Pensacola to become the world's largest artificial reef.

Falling Waters State Recreation Area, Chipley. One of the most recognized geological features in the state is the 100-ft.-deep sinkhole.

Destin. Known for its incredible fishing, you can also sightsee in glass-bottom boats, snorkel, dive, sail, or partake of almost any water sport you can think of. At **Henderson Beach State Park** or **James W. Lee Park** you'll find amazingly soft and white sand beaches created from pulverized quartz washed, buffeted and delivered by river sweep all the way from the Appalachian Mountains. The sand's quartz origins contribute to the sparkling brightness and to the way it squeaks when you walk on it. **Big Kahuna's Water & Adventure** is a shipwreck-themed water park, with miniature golf, go-karts, food concessions and other kiddie rides.

Fort Walton Beach. The Boardwalk is an energetic center of activity with restaurants, clubs, the town's fishing pier, beach volleyball and the classic Gulfarium, home to animals such as alligators, penguins, tropical birds, otters, grey seals and fresh and saltwater fish. Featured performers are trained dolphins and sea lions. View a panorama of undersea life at the "Living Sea." The **Emerald Coast Science Center** is a hands-on haven for kids. In addition to Destin's annual fishing contests, the area hosts more than 100 festivals each year, many focused on relishing seafood. The annual Billy Bowlegs Pirate Festival celebrates Fort Walton Beach's swashbuckling past during June.

Florida Caverns State Park, Marianna. Explore calcite formations, stalactites, stalagmites and columns.

Panama City Beach offers over 27 miles of unspoiled beaches, with an average water temperature of about 72° and an average air temperature of about 78°—the climate alone is reason enough to visit again and again.

Divers won't want to miss **The Museum of Man in the Sea**, home to interesting displays of diving from the 1500's to the present.

Gulf World Marine Park features four shows, sea lions, dolphins, Penguin Island, performing parrots, underwater show and expert scuba demonstrations.

Shipwreck Island lets you slosh along water canals on inner tubes, zoom down a waterslide at 40 mph, or relax in the shade of gazebos while watching children frolic in the Tadpole Hole.

Pensacola. This thriving resort city is home to several historic districts. The Seville Historic District contains a variety of architecture dating from the 1780s to the late 1800s. North Hill Preservation District was developed between 1870 and 1930 and is on the National Register of Historic Places.

Panhandle Pioneer Settlement, Blountstown. Preserving the artifacts, history and values of the rural Florida Panhandle, the Settlement, located on 47 acres, has 16 buildings dating from 1840 to 1940. They include a general store/post office, four 19th century log homes, a church, an old jail, a country doctor's office, an 1880 two-room school, a farmstead and a dogtrot farmhouse. A blacksmith shop, gristmill and firehouse were built on-site.

Historic Pensacola Village. Museums span 200 years of history. Artifacts and buildings left by early pioneers tell the story of French, Spanish and English rule.

Pensacola Beach. On the western point of Santa Rosa Island, the U.S. built the mammoth Fort Pickens in 1830. Now part of a national park, its well-preserved ruins sit among the pure-white sand dunes of Gulf Islands National Seashore. At Pensacola Beach's east end, more beachscape is pre-

served at a long stretch known as Santa Rosa National Seashore Day Use Area. In between, the town offers seafood restaurants, beach shops, miniature golf and a couple of full-facility beach parks with watersports and fishing piers.

St. George Island. You can reach this island via a bridge from Eastpoint. Here you can enjoy the white dunes and sandy beaches of Florida's Panhandle. St. George Island State Park is a natural area of ghost crabs, salt-dwarfed pines, wild rosemary and reindeer moss. On the beach side, loggerhead and green sea turtles lumber ashore to lay eggs every summer. On the bay side, salt marshes host snakes, turtles and a variety of fish among their reeds.

Vortex Springs, Ponce de Leon. This complete underwater diving resort offers natural springs, swimming, canoeing and paddleboats.

The Zoo, Gulf Breeze. This 50-acre zoo is home to over 700 animals. Also on-site are botanical gardens and the "Safari Line" train ride, which takes passengers through almost a mile of free-roaming animals in their natural habitat.

White Springs. Home to the state's Nature & Heritage Tourism Center and to Stephen Foster Folk Culture Center State Park, which maintains a museum and carillon tower that gongs out his famous compositions. Its village of old-time craftspeople stages candle making, blacksmithing and other demonstrations and every May the park hosts the Florida Folk Festival, along with 15 other annual special events.

NORTH CENTRAL REGION

If you've ever wondered where "way down upon the Suwannee River" is, you'll find it right here in North Central Florida's spring-fed oasis. Sandwiched between the Suwannee and the Santa Fe rivers, this region lays claims to more than 100 springs, pristine wilderness areas, friendly river towns, old-time festivals and intriguing historical sites.

Florida Sports Hall of Fame and Museum of Florida Sports History, Lake City. Florida sports history is preserved with memorabilia from members such as Arnold Palmer, Chris Evert, Steve Spurrier and Ted Williams.

Gainesville. Descend 232 steps into a giant sinkhole at **Devil's Millhopper State Geological Site**. The **Florida Museum of Natural History** is the largest natural history museum in the South. Visit **Paynes Prairie State Preserve** to see wild horses and a herd of bison. View natural history exhibits and archery artifacts dating back to the Stone Age at the **Fred Bear Museum**.

Ginnie Springs. High Springs features 220 acres of wilderness along the beautiful Santa Fe River. Snorkel and swim in crystal clear water, feed fish, discover artifacts, or view awesome springs such as Devil's Eye and Ear. Equipment rental, fishing, tubing, hiking, picnicking, diver training programs, nature trails and camping are also available.

Manatee Springs State Park, Chiefland, comprises over 2,000 acres surrounding a spring that puts out 49,000 gallons of water per minute. Enjoy fishing, hiking and swimming.

Tallahassee. You'll enjoy fragrant magnolia trees and rolling hills in and around Florida's capital city. Among the many attractions are:

The Capitol, offering a panoramic view from the 22nd-floor observatory/art gallery and a tour of the House and Senate.

Maclay State Gardens. This 250-acre display of floral beauty also features nature trails, tours and a museum. View over 200 varieties of plants.

Natural Bridge Battlefield State Historic Site is located just outside Tallahassee. This was the only Confederate capital east of the Mississippi never captured by Union forces. See the 1865 battle re-enacted in March.

Tallahassee Museum of History & Natural Science, a great place for kids, combines a natural-habitat zoo for native animals with a collection of historic structures including a 19th-century farm, one-room schoolhouse and plantation mansion. Cotton plantations dictated much of Tallahassee's history and at one, **Goodwood Museum & Gardens,** you can tour the restored buildings. Or explore Tallahassee's archaeological heritage at **Lake Jackson Mounds Archaeological State Park** and **Mission San Luis**. Its five historic "canopy roads" carry you from capital-city bustle to the tranquility of the Old South.

Nearby is St. Marks, an important harbor for Spanish conquerors and missionaries. **San Marcos de Apalache Historic State Park** preserves a fort site from the era. The lighthouse at **St. Marks National Wildlife Refuge** punctuates the port's import. Birds and butterflies – specifically monarchs during their fall migration – make the refuge a favorite with nature-lovers.

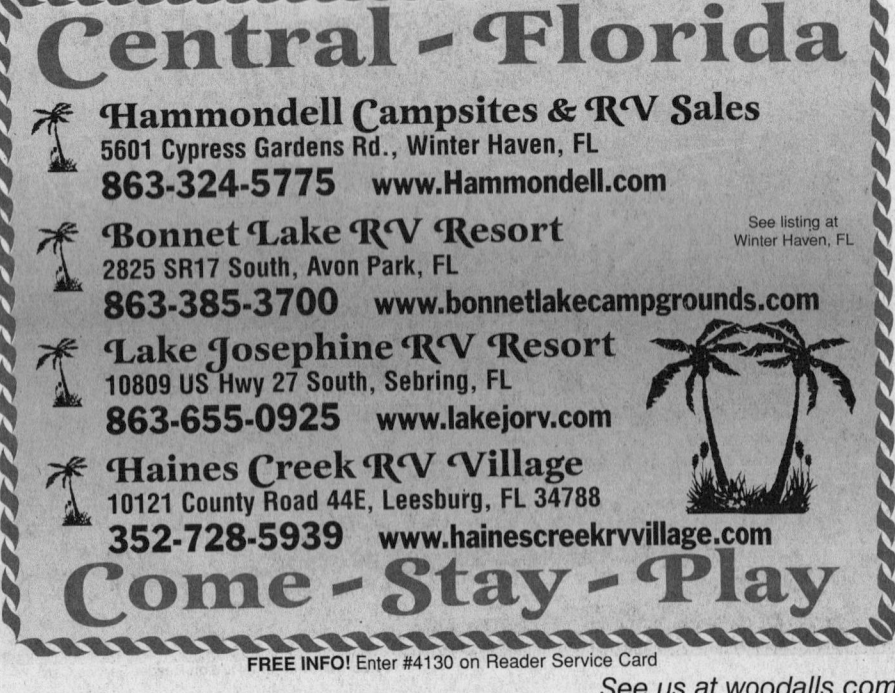

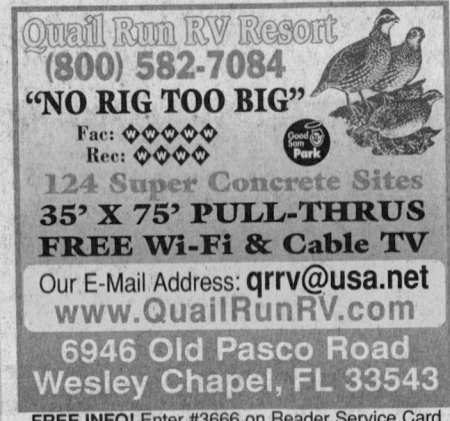

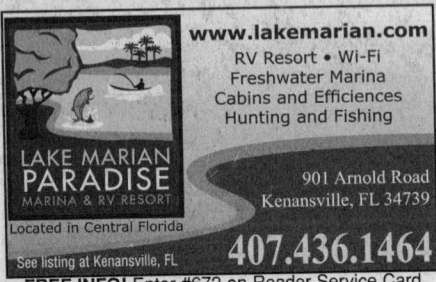

Wakulla Springs State Park. This park has one of the world's deepest freshwater springs and offers glass-bottom boat tours and ranger-led snorkeling program.

NORTHEAST REGION

This area is known as "Florida's First Coast", and offers miles of uncrowded beaches for horseback riding, biking or just relaxing. Here, small towns are the norm and large cities the exception. Tucked off seaside roads and back country rural routs are special hidden places that add to the unique appeal of this region.

Amelia Island. Located off Florida's northeastern-most corner, Amelia Island provides a refreshing change of pace. Fernandina Beach, the island's only town, showcases more than 50 blocks of restored Victorian neighborhoods.

Flagler Beach State Recreation Area. This recreation area is noted for fishing from a long pier and a white sand beach that is sprinkled red from coquina shells. Fishing, hiking and swimming are available.

Flagler County. This county is centrally located between St. Augustine and Daytona Beach, offering 19-miles of scenic, untouched beaches and preserves. Outdoor recreation abounds in this area with fishing, hiking, biking and golfing.

Jacksonville. A continuous stretch of beaches offers fishing from piers, swimming and a carnival-like boardwalk with concessions. The **Museum of Science & History** has a state-of-the-art planetarium and a 1,200-gallon marine aquarium. Observe the brewing and bottling process on a tour of **Anheuser-Busch Brewery.**

Jacksonville Zoological Gardens is home to over 800 birds, reptiles and mammals on 62 acres. On-site is a petting zoo, an African Veldt exhibit with an elevated walkway, a miniature train, the Okavango Trail and the Jax Landing.

St. Augustine Area. St. Augustine, the nation's oldest city, is often called the City of the Centuries because of its antiquity. Founded in 1565, it is the oldest continuously occupied settlement of European origin in the U.S. The city was founded fifty-five years before the Pilgrims landed at Plymouth Rock and was already two centuries old at the time of the American Revolution. "Oldest" structures featuring guided tours include **The Oldest House, Oldest Store Museum** and **Oldest Wooden Schoolhouse.**

While St. Augustine is valued historically, it is also a family resort with a variety of family attractions and 50 miles of hard-packed, white sand. Attractions in the St. Augustine area include:

Ghost Tours of St. Augustine. Candlelight tours of St. Augustine's historic district with licensed professional guides in period attire await you. Meander brick-lined streets while hearing of apparitions past and present. The tour is suitable for all ages.

Marineland of Florida. Newly renovated Dolphin Conservation Center offers interactive and emersion programs with the dolphins. Watch dolphins play and journey beneath the ocean's surface.

Ponce de Leon's Fountain of Youth. The first St. Augustine mission and colony is portrayed through exhibits, foundations and artifacts.

Scenic Cruises aboard the **Victory II** afford visitors a 1-1/4 hour scenic and historical cruise of St. Augustine waterfront and beautiful Matanzas Bay.

St. Augustine Alligator Farm. Founded in 1893, this farm boasts the "Land of crocodiles"—the world's only complete collection of all twenty-two living species. View birds, monkeys, giant tortoises and deer along an elevated nature walk. Visit the futuristic-style World Golf Village, home to the World of Golf Hall of Fame Museum. Browse the PGA Tour Golf Academy, shops and a tee off on a championship, eighteen-hole golf course.

CENTRAL EAST REGION

Spanning the coast form Daytona Beach to Port St. Lucie, the Central East Region is nothing but family friendly fun. From thrills of the Kennedy Space Center on the "Space Coast" to turtle quests along the "Treasure Coast", this area protects the past and embraces the future.

Daytona Beach. Renting a beach cruiser bicycle or moped is a great way to sightsee along Daytona's 23 miles of beaches. Other "toys" for rent include sailboats, jet skis and windsurfers. A boardwalk, amusements, concerts, a gondola skyride and a space needle are great additions to the beach. You won't believe the bargains you'll find at the **World's Largest Flea Market** here in Daytona. Over 1,000 vendors are under one roof and open year-round on Friday, Saturday and Sunday.

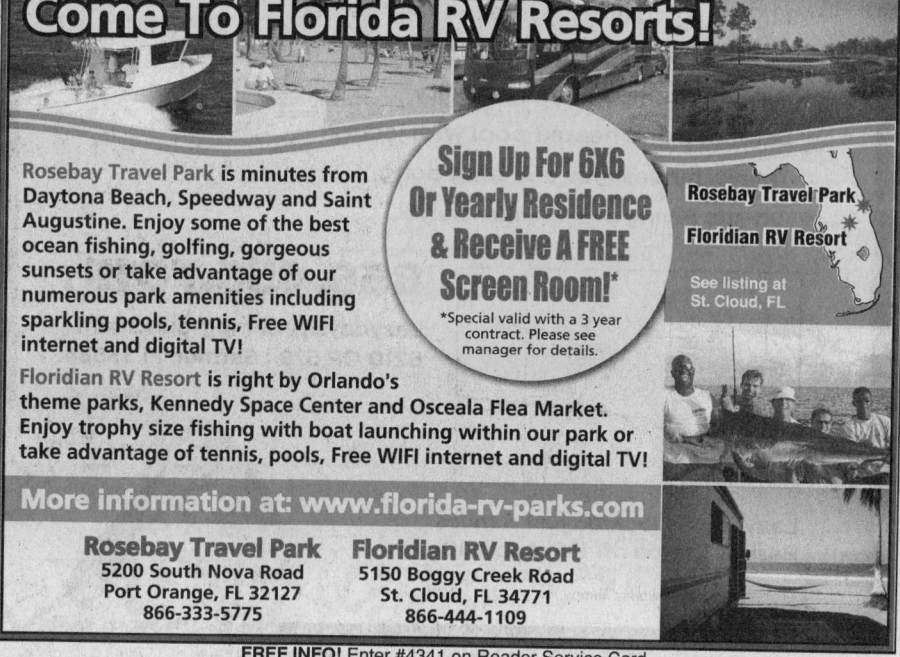

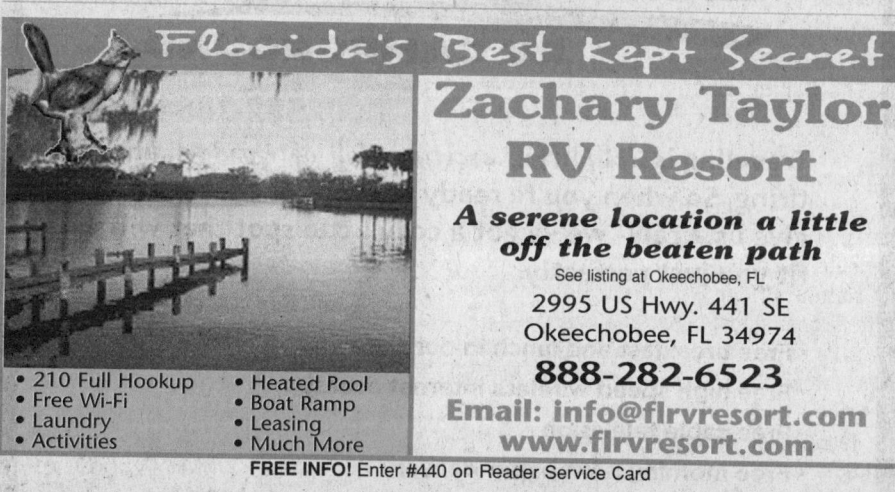

Daytona International Speedway, home of the Daytona USA World Center of Racing, offers displays and audio and visual presentations.

McKee Botanical Garden, Vero Beach. Originally established in 1932, the 18-acre garden had more than 100,000 annual visitors in its heyday. Today the garden has been restored by the Indian River Land Trust.

Merritt Island National Wildlife Refuge, Titusville. Auto routes and foot trails provide access for viewing some 25 mammals, 310 bird species and 117 varieties of fish.

Ponce de Leon Inlet Lighthouse, Ponce Inlet. Located off the Atlantic coast, this 100-year-old structure was still in use until 1970. It is now preserved as a national monument and museum.

Space Coast. Encompassing the cities of Cocoa Beach, Melbourne, Palm Bay and Titusville, the Space Coast area offers attractions such as:

Astronaut Memorial Planetarium & Observatory, Cocoa. Explore the universe through Florida's largest public telescope, planetarium programs and laser light shows.

Space Coast Science Center, Melbourne. Science exhibits allow visitors to experiment with shadows, enter a giant kaleidoscope and experience anti-gravity.

Spaceport USA (Kennedy Space Center). The International Space Station Center and the Launch Complex 39 Observation Gantry provide a new approach to learning about the operational areas of the center. Explore the past, present and future of U.S. space programs. Motion, video and special effects create the Shuttle Launch Experience in a new exhibit at the Visitor Complex.

U.S. Astronaut Hall of Fame, Titusville. View historic artifacts, space hardware, personal mementos and rare video footage. Take a "Shuttle to Tomorrow" in the cargo bay of a full-scale space shuttle mock-up.

Sugar Mill Gardens, Port Orange. These plantation ruins of an old English sugar mill are surrounded by 12 acres of botanical gardens. Enjoy flowering trees, holly, magnolias and other blooming plants.

Turtle Watching, Loggerhead. Green and leatherback sea turtles come ashore to lay eggs in July and August at Jensen Beach, Hutchinson Island, Hobe Sound Wildlife Refuge and Blowing Rocks Preserve.

CENTRAL REGION

This is the most popular destination in Florida, and for good reason. Here is the home of Disney World, the largest amusement park on earth, as well as Sea World, Universal Studios, and other attractions too numerous to mention. Combined, they make up the largest family amusement area on the planet.

Central Florida Zoological Park, Sanford. Explore the world of nature and discover more than 400 animals including cheetahs, leopards, elephants, mandrills, macaws and reptiles.

Cypress Gardens Adventure Park. These lush botanical gardens also feature water ski shows, a butterfly conservatory, ice skating shows, reptile and birds of prey shows and **Nature's Way Zoo.**

Kissimmee is known as the "Gateway to the World" because millions of visitors annually pass through the Kissimmee-St. Cloud area on their way to Walt Disney World®.

A World of Orchids. Exquisite flowering orchids are displayed in a rainforest setting with exotic birds, fish, chameleons and Asian squirrels.

Old Town. This town was re-created to resemble old Florida's brick-lined streets with horse and surrey rides, floral gardens, a fountain, a gazebo and a European antique carrousel.

Wolfman Jack's Rock N' Roll Palace. Relive the fabulous '50s with dining, dancing, saddle shoes, poodle skirts and the stars of the '50s and '60s.

Lake County is aptly named for the area's 1,400 lakes. The largest of these are Lake Harris, Lake Eutis, Lake Yale, Lake Griffin and a large portion of Lake Apopka. Cast your line for shellcrackers, bluegill, speckled perch and bass.

Orlando. Attractions in and around Orlando include:

Discovery Cove. Experience once-in-a-lifetime, up-close encounters with dolphins and other exotic marine animals. Swim with dolphins, rays and thousands of tropical fish.

Gatorland is home to thousands of alligators and crocodiles. A petting zoo, a mini-water park, an eco-tour, a bird sanctuary and wildlife shows are also on-site.

Guinness World Records Experience. You'll experience first-hand what it takes to be a Guinness World Record Holder at this interactive "prototype" attraction.

Meade Botanical Gardens, Winter Park. Enjoy over 50 acres of floral paradise, rockeries, nature trails and picnic pavilions.

Orlando Science Center. Explore hundreds of interactive attractions for all ages in ten themed exhibitions. Surround yourself with images on the eight-story CineDome screen, the world's largest domed theater and planetarium.

SeaWorld Orlando. Try the water coaster and enjoy more than 200 acres of shows, attractions and exhibits.

Titanic—The Exhibition. Experience this major Titanic exhibition with authentic artifacts, historic treasures and full-scale re-creations including the Grand Staircase. Share the stories of her passengers and crew.

Universal Orlando. Set on 444 acres, this motion picture and television studio allows visitors to watch actual shootings and be a part of studio audiences. Enjoy over 40 rides, shows, movie set streets and the new Islands of Adventure.

Wet 'N Wild. This 25-acre water-theme park includes slides, chutes, flumes, floats and plunges. Ride the Bubba Tub (a three-story, triple-dip slide) in a tube big enough for the whole family.

Silver Springs. This nature theme park east of Ocala features Glass Bottom Boats and the World of Bears attraction, plus the Panther Prowl, Big Gator Lagoon, Jungle Cruise, Lost River Voyage, Jeep Safari and live animal shows.

Adjacent to Silver Springs is **Wild Waters**, a family water park located in a grove of oak trees featuring racing flumes, a 450,000-gallon wave pool, miniature golf, volleyball, a video arcade and a picnic area. The water park is open mid-March to September.

Walt Disney World®, Lake Buena Vista, features Magic Kingdom theme park, MGM Studio Tours, resort hotels, a campground resort and championship golf courses. Captain Jack Sparrow joins the cast of the Pirates of the Caribbean ride. Epcot Center is located on the Disney World grounds. This 260-acre entertainment showplace spotlights futuristic ideas and technologies along with the arts, culture, craftsmanship, authentic foods and natural wonders of over 10 nations. Theme areas have exciting (and informative) ride-through attractions, adventure shows and visual experiences. Animal Kingdom combines thrill rides, exotic landscapes and more than a thousand wild animals to view.

CENTRAL WEST REGION

Scenic waterways grace the Central West Region. Meandering fishing and boating waters mixed with year-round sunshine will entice any water sport enthusiast to the region. Here, travelers will find a rich mix of natural and cultural amenities. From Tampa and St. Pete, with its exciting nightlife and first class restaurants, to two of America's best beach destinations, Caladesi Island, and Honeymoon Island state park, there's something here for even the most fickle traveler.

DeSoto Monument, Bradenton. A movie, a tour and nature trails pay tribute to Hernando do Soto and 600 Spaniards who first set foot in the New World.

Dinosaur World, Plant City. View more than 100 life-sized model dinosaurs, reflecting modern scientific theories, displayed in a natural landscape.

Homosassa Springs State Wildlife Park, Homosassa Springs. This display of native Florida wildlife offers unspoiled nature trails,

QUICK REFERENCE CHART FOR WOODALL'S FEATURED PARKS

	Green Friendly	RV Lots for Sale	Park Models-Onsite Ownership	Park Membership for Sale	Big Rigs Welcome	Internet Friendly	Pets Welcome
ALACHUA							
Travelers Campground					▲	●	■
ARCADIA							
Big Tree RV Resort					▲	●	■
Craig's RV Park						●	■
Cross Creek Country Club & RV Resort					▲	●	■
AVON PARK							
Adelaide Shores RV Resort			✱		▲	●	■
BONITA SPRINGS							
Imperial Bonita Estates RV Resort			✱		▲	●	■
BOWLING GREEN							
Orange Blossom Adult RV Park					▲	●	■
BRADENTON							
Holiday Cove RV Resort		✖			▲	●	■
Horseshoe Cove RV Resort			✱		▲	●	■
Pleasant Lake RV Resort			✱		▲	●	■
BROOKSVILLE							
belle parc RV Resort					▲	●	■
Cloverleaf Forest RV Resort						●	■
BUNNELL							
Thunder Gulch Campground						●	■
BUSHNELL							
Paradise Oaks Golf & RV Resort					▲	●	■
Red Oaks RV Resort			✱		▲	●	■
CARRABELLE							
Ho-Hum RV Park					▲	●	■
CARRABELLE BEACH							
Carrabelle Beach Outdoor Destinations					▲	●	■
CEDAR KEY							
Cedar Key RV Resort		✖			▲	●	■
Cedar Key Sunset Isle RV Park						●	■
CHOKOLOSKEE							
Chokoloskee Island Park & Campground						●	■
CLEARWATER							
Clearwater Travel Resort					▲	●	■
CLERMONT							
Outdoor Resorts At Orlando					▲	●	■
CLEWISTON							
Big Cypress RV Resort					▲	●	■
Okeechobee Landings					▲	●	■
COCOA							
Sonrise Palms Christian RV Park					▲	●	■
Sonrise Village RV Resort					▲	●	■
CORTEZ							
Buttonwood Inlet RV Resort (Formerly Key Way)						●	■
CROSS CITY							
Shady Oaks RV & Mobile Home Park, Inc							■
DADE CITY							
Citrus Hill Park & Sales						●	■

Green Friendly 🍃; **RV Lots for Sale** ✖; **Park Models/Onsite Onwership** ✱; **Park Memberships for Sale** ✔; **Big Rigs Welcome** ▲; **Internet Friendly** ●; **Internet Friendly-WiFi** ●; **Pets Welcome** ■

QUICK REFERENCE CHART FOR WOODALL'S FEATURED PARKS

	Green Friendly	RV Lots for Sale	Park Models-Onsite Ownership	Park Membership for Sale	Big Rigs Welcome	Internet Friendly	Pets Welcome
Grove Ridge RV Resort			✱		▲	●	■
Town and Country RV Resort					▲	●	■
Travelers Rest Resort					▲	●	■
DAVENPORT							
Kissimmee South (formerly Three Worlds Resort)			✱			●	■
DAYTONA BEACH							
Nova Family Campground						●	■
DEBARY							
Highbanks Marina & Campresort					▲	●	■
DEERFIELD BEACH							
Quiet Waters Park (Broward County Park)							■
DESTIN							
Camping on the Gulf					▲	●	■
Destin Village RV Resort					▲		■
Geronimo RV Resort					▲	●	■
DUNEDIN							
Dunedin RV Resort					▲	●	■
ELLENTON							
Ellenton Gardens Travel Resort					▲	●	■
FLAGLER BEACH							
Beverly Beach Camptown RV Resort					▲	●	■
Bulow Plantation RV Resort						●	■
Flagler by the Sea Campground							■
FLORIDA CITY							
Florida City Campsite (City Park)					▲	●	■
FORT LAUDERDALE							
Paradise Island					▲	●	■
Twin Lakes Travel Park					▲	●	■
Yacht Haven Park & Marina					▲	●	■
FORT MYERS							
Raintree RV Resort					▲	●	■
Riverbend Motorcoach Resort					▲	●	■
Seminole Campground					▲	●	■
Shady Acres RV Park					▲	●	■
Sunseeker's RV Park						●	■
Upriver RV Resort			✱		▲	●	■
Woodsmoke Camping Resort			✱		▲	●	■
FORT MYERS BEACH							
Gulf Waters RV Resort					▲	●	■
San Carlos Island Resort						●	■
FORT PIERCE							
Road Runner Travel Resort	🍃				▲	●	■
Sunnier Palms (Nudist)					▲	●	■
FORT WALTON BEACH							
Playground RV Park					▲	●	■
FROSTPROOF							
Rainbow Resort					▲	●	■
GRANT							
Orbit RV Park					▲	●	■

Green Friendly 🍃; **RV Lots for Sale** ✖; **Park Models/Onsite Onwership** ✱; **Park Memberships for Sale** ✔; **Big Rigs Welcome** ▲; **Internet Friendly** ●; **Internet Friendly-WiFi** ●; **Pets Welcome** ■

QUICK REFERENCE CHART FOR WOODALL'S FEATURED PARKS

	Green Friendly	RV Lots for Sale	Park Models-Onsite Ownership	Park Membership for Sale	Big Rigs Welcome	Internet Friendly	Pets Welcome
HAINES CITY							
Central Park of Haines City					▲	●	■
HALLANDALE							
Holiday Park						●	■
HIGH SPRINGS							
High Springs Campground					▲	●	■
HOLLYWOOD							
Topeekeegee Yugnee (T.Y.) Park (Broward County Park)					▲	●	■
HOMESTEAD							
Pine Isle Mobile Home Park					▲	●	■
The Boardwalk					▲	●	■
HOMOSASSA							
Nature's Resort & Marina					▲	●	■
HOMOSASSA SPRINGS							
Homosassa Carefree RV Resort(formerly Turtle Creek)			✱			●	■
INVERNESS							
Riverside Lodge					▲	●	■
JACKSONVILLE							
Flamingo Lake RV Resort					▲	●	■
Pecan Park RV Resort					▲	●	■
JENSEN BEACH							
Nettles Island Resort & RV Park					▲	●	■
JUNO BEACH							
Juno Ocean Walk RV Resort	(leaf)				▲	●	■
JUPITER							
West Jupiter Camping Resort					▲	●	■
KENANSVILLE							
Lake Marian Paradise Marina & RV Resort					▲	●	■
KEY LARGO							
Calusa Campground Condominium Association					▲	●	■
KEY WEST							
Bluewater Key RV Resort					▲	●	■
Boyd's Key West Campground					▲	●	■
KISSIMMEE							
East Lake RV Resort Restaurant & Marina						●	■
Mill Creek RV Resort						●	■
Orange Grove Campground					▲	●	■
Tropical Palms Resort					▲	●	■
LA BELLE							
Whisper Creek RV Resort		✖			▲	●	■
LAKE BUENA VISTA							
Disney's Fort Wilderness Resort & Campground					▲	●	■
LAKE CITY							
Inn & Out RV Park					▲	●	■
Lake City Campground					▲	●	■
LAKE PANASOFFKEE							
Turtleback RV Resort					▲	●	■
LAKE PLACID							
Camp Florida Resort		✖	✱		▲	●	■

Green Friendly (leaf); RV Lots for Sale ✖; Park Models/Onsite Onwership ✱; Park Memberships for Sale ✔; Big Rigs Welcome ▲; Internet Friendly ●; Internet Friendly-WiFi ●; Pets Welcome ■

QUICK REFERENCE CHART FOR WOODALL'S FEATURED PARKS

	Green Friendly	RV Lots for Sale	Park Models-Onsite Ownership	Park Membership for Sale	Big Rigs Welcome	Internet Friendly	Pets Welcome
LAKE WALES							
Lake Wales RV & Campsites						● (WiFi)	■
LAKELAND							
Lakeland RV Resort			✱		▲	● (WiFi)	■
Woodall's Mobile Home Village & RV Park						● (WiFi)	
LARGO							
Rainbow Village RV Resort			✱		▲	● (WiFi)	■
Yankee Traveler RV Park						● (WiFi)	■
LEESBURG							
Holiday Travel Resort					▲	● (WiFi)	■
MALABAR							
Camelot RV Park					▲	● (WiFi)	■
MARATHON							
Grassy Key RV Park & Resort					▲	● (WiFi)	■
Jolly Roger Travel Park					▲	● (WiFi)	■
MARGATE							
Aztec RV Resort		✖			▲		■
MARIANNA							
Arrowhead Campsites						● (WiFi)	■
MIAMI							
Larry & Penny Thompson Park & Campground					▲	●	■
MILTON							
Avalon Landing RV Park					▲	● (WiFi)	■
Pelican Palms RV Park					▲	● (WiFi)	■
NAPLES							
Crystal Lake RV Resort	(leaf)				▲	● (WiFi)	■
Marco Naples Hitching Post Travel Resort							■
Neapolitan Cove RV Resort	(leaf)				▲	● (WiFi)	■
Pelican Lake Motorcoach Resort		✖			▲	● (WiFi)	■
Rock Creek RV Resort					▲	● (WiFi)	■
Silver Lakes RV Resort and Golf Club		✖			▲	● (WiFi)	■
NAVARRE							
Emerald Beach RV Park					▲	● (WiFi)	■
NEW SMYRNA BEACH							
New Smyrna Beach RV Park					▲	● (WiFi)	■
Sugar Mill Ruins Travel Park						● (WiFi)	■
OAKLAND PARK							
Easterlin Park (Broward County Park)							■
OCALA							
Holiday Trav-L-Park RV Resort					▲	● (WiFi)	■
Ocala Sun RV Resort					▲	● (WiFi)	■
OKEECHOBEE							
Zachary Taylor RV Resort					▲	● (WiFi)	■
OLD TOWN							
Old Town Campground N' Retreat						● (WiFi)	■
Suwannee River Hideaway Campground, Inc.						● (WiFi)	■
Yellow Jacket Campground Resort					▲	● (WiFi)	■
ORANGE CITY							
Clark Family Campground						● (WiFi)	■
Orange City RV Resort					▲	● (WiFi)	■

Green Friendly (leaf); **RV Lots for Sale** ✖; **Park Models/Onsite Onwership** ✱; **Park Memberships for Sale** ✔; **Big Rigs Welcome** ▲; **Internet Friendly** ●; **Internet Friendly-WiFi** ● (WiFi); **Pets Welcome** ■

QUICK REFERENCE CHART FOR WOODALL'S FEATURED PARKS

	Green Friendly	RV Lots for Sale	Park Models-Onsite Ownership	Park Membership for Sale	Big Rigs Welcome	Internet Friendly	Pets Welcome
ORLANDO							
Bill Frederick Park at Turkey Lake (City Park)					▲		■
Orlando/Lake Whippoorwill KOA Campground					▲	●	■
ORMOND BEACH							
Harris Village RV Park					▲	●	■
PALMDALE							
Sabal Palm RV Resort & Campground					▲	●	■
PALMETTO							
Fiesta Grove RV Resort					▲	●	■
Frog Creek Campground					▲	●	■
Winterset RV Resort						●	■
PANAMA CITY BEACH							
Campers Inn					▲	●	■
Emerald Coast RV Beach Resort					▲	●	■
PEMBROKE PINES							
C.B. Smith Park (Broward County Park)					▲		■
PERDIDO KEY							
Perdido Cove RV Resort & Marina					▲	●	■
POLK CITY							
LeLynn RV Resort					▲	●	■
POMPANO BEACH							
Highland Pines RV Resort							■
PORT CHARLOTTE							
Riverside RV Resort & Campground					▲	●	■
PORT ORANGE							
Daytona Beach RV Resort					▲	●	■
Rose Bay Travel Park						●	■
PORT ST. LUCIE							
Port St. Lucie RV Resort					▲	●	■
PUNTA GORDA							
Punta Gorda RV Resort						●	■
Shell Creek RV Resort						●	■
Sun 'N' Shade Campground						●	■
ROCKLEDGE							
Space Coast RV Resort					▲	●	■
RUSKIN							
Sun Lake RV Resort					▲	●	■
SANFORD							
Twelve Oaks RV Resort					▲	●	■
Wekiva Falls Resort					▲	●	■
SARASOTA							
Sarasota Sunny South RV Park					▲	●	■
Sun-N-Fun RV Resort	🍃		*		▲	●	■
SEBASTIAN							
Pelican's Landing Resort					▲	●	■
Vero Beach Kamp Inc					▲	●	■
SEBRING							
The Outback RV Resort at Tanglewood					▲	●	■
Woody's RV Resort					▲	●	■

Green Friendly 🍃; RV Lots for Sale ✖; Park Models/Onsite Onwership *; Park Memberships for Sale ✔; Big Rigs Welcome ▲; Internet Friendly ●; Internet Friendly-WiFi ●; Pets Welcome ■

QUICK REFERENCE CHART FOR WOODALL'S FEATURED PARKS

	Green Friendly	RV Lots for Sale	Park Models-Onsite Ownership	Park Membership for Sale	Big Rigs Welcome	Internet Friendly	Pets Welcome
SILVER SPRINGS							
Lake Waldena Resort					▲	●	■
Wilderness RV Park Estates						●	■
ST. AUGUSTINE							
North Beach Camp Resort					▲	●	■
Ocean Grove RV Resort					▲	●	■
Stagecoach RV Park					▲	●	■
ST. CLOUD							
The Floridian RV Resort						●	■
SUNRISE							
Markham Park (Broward County Park)					▲		■
TALLAHASSEE							
Big Oak RV Park					▲	●	■
Tallahassee RV Park					▲	●	■
TAMPA							
Bay Bayou RV Resort					▲	●	■
Camp Nebraska					▲	●	■
Lazydays Sale & Service					▲	●	■
TAVARES							
Fisherman's Cove Golf Marina & RV Resort						●	■
THONOTOSASSA							
Happy Traveler RV Park					▲	●	■
Spanish Main RV Resort					▲	●	■
TITUSVILLE							
Seasons in the Sun					▲	●	■
The Great Outdoors RV-Nature & Golf Resort		✖	*		▲	●	■
VENICE							
Florida Pines Mobile Home Court & RV					▲	●	
Myakka RV Resort - KOA					▲	●	■
WESLEY CHAPEL							
Quail Run RV Resort					▲	●	■
WHITE SPRINGS							
Suwannee Valley Campground						●	■
WINTER HAVEN							
Cypress Campground & RV Park					▲	●	■
Hammondell Campsites & RV Sales						●	■
ZEPHYRHILLS							
Baker Acres RV Resort			*			●	■
Forest Lake Estates RV Resort						●	■
Glen Haven RV Resort						●	■
Happy Days RV Park						●	■
Hillcrest RV Resort						●	■
Leisure Days RV Resort					▲	●	■
Majestic Oaks RV Resort						●	■
Rainbow Village RV Resort			*		▲	●	■
Ralph's Travel Park			*		▲	●	■
Southern Charm RV Resort						●	■
Sweetwater RV Park						●	■
Water's Edge RV Resort						●	■

Green Friendly ; RV Lots for Sale ✖; Park Models/Onsite Onwership ✱; Park Memberships for Sale ✔; Big Rigs Welcome ▲; Internet Friendly ●; Internet Friendly-WiFi ●; Pets Welcome ■

guided boat tours, a floating observatory and fascinating nature programs.

Tampa. This city by the bay welcomes visitors with a downtown art district, state-of-the-art museums, festivals and first-class attractions, including the following:

Busch Gardens. This 300-acre African theme park presents song and dance revues, amusement rides and wild animals. A seven-acre area re-creates Egypt in the 1920s, complete with King Tut's tomb and an artifact dig for the children. The largest inverted steel roller coaster in the world, "Montu," also makes its home here. See two big babies born late 2006: a hippo and a white rhinoceros.

The Florida Aquarium. View more than 6,000 aquatic plants and animals native to Florida.

Weeki Wachee Spring, Spring Hill. At this 200-acre nature theme park, guests enjoy underwater performances, along with the Birds of Prey and Exotic Bird Show, Wilderness River Cruise and Animal Forest Petting Zoo.

SOUTHWEST REGION

This is the land of alabaster sand beaches, exotic wildlife, subtropical beauty, and loads of communities with sophistication. High on the list of things to do are shelling and sculpting sandcastles. More than ten thousand islands dot the azure Gulf waters, creating numerous tropical hideaways to be discovered and enjoyed.

Edison & Ford Winter Estates, Fort Myers. Steeped in history, the inventor's charming Old-Florida style home, laboratory and experiment gardens are authentically maintained. Also, visit the home of best friend and next-door neighbor, Henry Ford.

Everglades Wonder Gardens, Bonita Springs. Everglades wildlife in its natural habitat includes bears, otters, wading birds, snakes, the Florida panther and the endangered saltwater crocodile. Alligator feedings and an otter show add to the experience.

Fort Myers. Hop on an old-fashioned trolley for a tour of historic Fort Myers. Visitors can catch the trolley at a variety of downtown locations. Walk the mile-long boardwalk, known as the Six-Mile Cypress Slough, through a 2,000-acre wetland ecosystem filled with subtropical ferns, wild orchids and birds such as herons, egrets, spoonbills and storks.

Calusa Nature Center & Planetarium. View over 100 animals indigenous to Florida—most have been injured and can't return to the wild.

The Shell Factory. Displayed are a huge collection of shells and the exhibit Into Africa, which features taxidermy examples of more than 100 wild animals, including a white Rhino.

J.N. "Ding" Darling National Wildlife Refuge, Sanibel Island. This 6,400-acre refuge is home to otters, raccoons, alligators, brown pelicans, roseate spoonbills and other Florida wildlife. A four-mile auto tour and guided tours led by naturalists are available.

Mote Marine Aquarium, Sarasota. 10 new exhibits, working research labs, a touch tank and interactive Sea Cinema await you. Come face-to-face with a shark or visit with resident manatees and endangered sea turtles. Eco-tours of Sarasota are available.

Pasco County. With more than 30 parks and preserves, there are numerous rivers, trails, shorelines, beaches and recreational areas to see Florida's natural coast. In **New Port Richey, Jay B. Starkey Wilderness Park** offers marked foot trails, horse trails and bicycle paths. You can also take a unique ecotour venturing through pine flatwoods, sand pine ridges and pastureland at the Anclote River Ranch. At **Sims Park**, on the Pithlachascotee River, you can stroll the riverwalk and maybe catch a glimpse of a manatee. Dade City's **Withlacoochee River Park** offers a fishing dock and canoe launch for those interested in exploring the river and its native inhabitants such as river otters, alligators and a variety of fish. **Anclote Key State Preserve** on Anclote Key has a beautiful secluded beach and a recently restored

BUSINESSES OFFERING

	Things to See & Do	RV Sales	RV Service
CLEWISTON			
Ah-Tah-Thi-Ki Museum	X		
DEBARY			
Swamp House Grill	X		
FORT LAUDERDALE			
Broward County Parks & Recreation Division	X		
Dixie Trailer Supply			X
North Trail RV Center		X	X
FORT MYERS			
Lee County Visitor & Convention	X		
North Trail RV		X	X
FORT WALTON BEACH			
Open Road RV Center		X	X
GAINESVILLE			
J. D. Sanders RV Center		X	X
HOMOSASSA			
Como RV & Truck Sales		X	
INVERNESS			
Como RV & Truck Sales, Service & RV Collision Center		X	X
JUPITER			
Land Yachts			X
LAKE BUENA VISTA			
Walt Disney World Resort	X		
PALM COAST			
Flagler County Chamber of Commerce	X		
Princess Place Preserve	X		
PORT CHARLOTTE			
Charlotte RV Center		X	X
STARKE			
Revels Nationwide RV Sales			X
TALLAHASSEE			
Florida Association of RV Parks and Campgrounds	X		
TITUSVILLE			
Eagle's Pride at the Great Outdoors		X	X
WEST PALM BEACH			
Palm Beach RV		X	X
WINTER HAVEN			
Cypress RV Sales		X	

Where to Find CCUSA Parks

List City	Park Name	Map Coordinates
APOPKA		
	Sun Resort	C-4
ARCADIA		
	Big Tree RV Resort	D-3
	Cross Creek Country Club & RV Resort	D-3
	Little Willies RV Resort	D-3
ASTOR		
	Parramore's Campground	B-4
AVON PARK		
	Adelaide Shores RV Resort	D-4
	Bonnet Lake RV Resort	D-4
	Lake Glenada RV Park	D-4
BEVERLY HILLS		
	Sandy Oaks RV Resort	B-3
BONIFAY		
	Florida Springs RV Resort & Campgrounds	E-2
BOWLING GREEN		
	Torrey Oaks RV & Golf Resort	D-3
BRADENTON		
	Arbor Terrace RV Resort	D-3
	Tropical Gardens RV Park	D-3
BROOKSVILLE		
	belle parc RV Resort	C-3
	Campers Holiday	C-3
	Hidden Valley Campground	C-3
BUSHNELL		
	Paradise Oaks Golf & RV Resort	C-3
	Red Oaks RV Resort	C-3
CARRABELLE		
	Sunset Isle RV & Yacht Club Resort	B-1
CEDAR KEY		
	Cedar Key Sunset Isle RV Park	B-2
CLERMONT		
	Bee's RV Resort	C-3
	Rolling Ridge RV Resort	C-3
CLEWISTON		
	Okeechobee Landings	D-4
COCOA		
	Sonrise Palms Christian RV Park	C-4
DADE CITY		
	Citrus Hill Park & Sales	C-3
	Grove Ridge RV Resort	C-3
	Many Mansions RV Park	C-3
	Town and Country RV Resort	C-3
	Travelers Rest Resort	C-3
DAVENPORT		
	Deer Creek Golf & RV Resort	C-4
	Kissimmee South (formerly Three Worlds Resort)	C-4
	Mouse Mountain RV Camping Resort	C-4
	Themeworld RV Resort	C-4
DAYTONA BEACH		
	International RV Park & Campground	B-4
	Nova Family Campground	B-4
DEFUNIAK SPRINGS		
	Sunset King Lake RV Resort	E-2
DESTIN		
	Geronimo RV Resort	F-2
DOVER		
	Tampa East RV Resort	C-3

118-year-old lighthouse. Other attractions include:

Pioneer Florida Museum & Village, which features Lacoochee School, a restored 1930's building; John Overstreet House, a two-story farmhouse built in the 1860's; The Trilby Depot, built in 1896 to haul cypress logs to a sawmill in Lacoochee; Enterprise Church, an 1878 example of rural architecture; and Jack Bromley's Shoe Repair Shop.

Ringling Museum of Art, Sarasota. This complex was willed to the state by circus king John Ringling. It includes art and circus museums, the Asolo State Theatre and the home of John and Mable Ringling.

Sarasota Jungle Gardens, Sarasota. Stroll through acres of beautiful gardens and nature trails. You'll see jungle animal exhibits, reptile encounters and bird shows.

Wooten's Everglades Airboat Tours, Naples. Tours cover the mangrove wilderness—home to 600 varieties of fish, 300 species of birds, countless mammals and 45 indigenous species of plant life found nowhere else.

SOUTHEAST & THE KEYS

The southern tip of Florida consists mostly of jungle and swampland that make up Everglades National Park. The Park covers nearly the entire tip of the peninsula southward from Miami and Naples. This vast wetland is teeming with wild birds, alligators, snakes, and other wildlife. The southeast region also encompasses the beautiful Keys. The Keys make up a 126-mile long archipelago of islands. A 125-mile long series of bridges and causeways connects these islands together. The Keys are a veritable paradise for scuba divers and fishermen. It's easy to understand why "Papa" Hemingway spent so much time here.

Butterfly World, Coconut Creek. Experience a world where thousands of live exotic butterflies and hummingbirds fly around you in tropical flowering gardens.

Conch Tour Train, Key West. Riding the train is the best way to get an overall view of this picturesque island and its varied attractions, which include the homes of Hemingway and Audubon, old Conch architecture and lush tropical foliage.

Dolphin Research Center, Grassy Key. Educational tours give information on these fascinating creatures. The Dolphin Encounter exhibit allows visitors to actually swim with dolphins. Reservations are required.

Everglades National Park. Just 39 miles from Miami, the park encompasses 1.4 million acres of land and water. The visitor center offers a five-minute orientation, brochures and information. Close-up observation of wildlife is accessible through ranger-led hikes. The main entrance can be reached via U.S. Hwy. 1 at Florida City, nine miles along State Hwy. 27. Just outside the main entrance is Everglades Alligator Farm, home to more than 3,000 alligators. Guided airboat tours are available. Live alligator, snake and wildlife shows run continuously during the day. Gator Park offers narrated airboat tours of the Everglades, wildlife shows and alligator wrestling.

Fairchild Tropical Gardens, Coral Gables. This huge 83-acre arboretum is the nation's largest subtropical botanical garden. View the rare plant house, museum, jungle flora and palm display.

Fishermen's Village, Punta Gorda. This area's signature marketplace offers waterfront dining, boutiques, a marina and plenty of entertainment.

Fort Lauderdale is the fabled city of sun and fun. Besides miles of beaches, this city has brick pedestrian promenades lined with sidewalk cafes.

Historical Museum of Southern Florida, Miami. Go back in time 10,000 years with hundreds of artifacts, documents and photos. Get a hands-on look at the past with continuously changing exhibits and multimedia presentations.

The Keys. This 126-mile string of coral islands is connected by the Overseas Highway and together these bodies of land offer a traveler much more than terrific fishing, scuba diving and Key Lime pie!

John Pennekamp Coral Reef State Park, Key Largo. The nation's first underwater preserve covers 75 square miles and is a refuge for dozens of living coral and almost 400 species of fish.

Key West Aquarium. Visit this home to tropical, game and exotic fish, as well as turtles, sharks and birds.

Lake Okeechobee. Excellent bass fishing is offered in the second largest freshwater lake in the continental U.S.

Muscle Car City, Punta Gorda. Private collection of nearly 200 classic cars dating back to the 1920s. The major focus is on "muscle cars" of the 60s to early 70s. Includes a café and gift shop.

Palm Beach County is home to museums that appeal to all ages. The International Museum of Cartoon Art in Boca Raton is the only facility of its kind, displaying masterpieces in every aspect of cartoon art. The Sports Immortals Museum showcases the largest sports memorabilia collection in the world. The Children's Science Explorium and the Children's Museum of Boca Raton at Singing Pines feature exciting and creative hands-on exhibits designed to teach children about everything from electrical fields to recycling.

St. Lucie. St. Lucie offers visitors a real Florida vacation, miles away from the congested freeways and long lines found in

Where to Find CCUSA Parks

List City	Park Name	Map Coordinates
DUNEDIN		
	Dunedin RV Resort	C-3
DUNNELLON		
	Goethe Trailhead Ranch & RV Park	B-3
ELLENTON		
	Ellenton Gardens Travel Resort	D-3
FORT LAUDERDALE		
	Paradise Island	E-5
FORT MYERS		
	Groves RV Resort	D-3
	Seminole Campground	D-3
	Shady Acres RV Park	D-3
	Sunseeker's RV Park	D-3
	Tamiami RV Park	D-3
	Upriver RV Resort	D-3
	Woodsmoke Camping Resort	D-3
FORT MYERS BEACH		
	Indian Creek Resort	E-3
	Siesta Bay RV Resort	E-3
FOUNTAIN		
	Pine Lake RV Park	F-3
FROSTPROOF		
	Lakemont Ridge Home & RV Park	C-4
GRANT		
	Orbit RV Park	C-5
HAINES CITY		
	Central Park of Haines City	C-4
HOLT		
	River's Edge RV Campground	E-1
HOMESTEAD		
	Goldcoaster Mobile Home & RV Resort	E-5
	The Boardwalk	E-5
HOMOSASSA		
	Nature's Resort & Marina	C-3
HOMOSASSA SPRINGS		
	Homosassa Carefree RV Resort(formerly Turtle Creek)	C-3
INGLIS		
	Sunshine Coast Resorts & Retreats	B-3
INVERNESS		
	Riverside Lodge	C-3
JASPER		
	Florida Gateway Resort	A-2
KISSIMMEE		
	East Lake RV Resort Restaurant & Marina	C-4
	Mill Creek RV Resort	C-4
	Orange Grove Campground	C-4
	Ponderosa RV Park	C-4
	Tropical Palms Resort	C-4
LAKE CITY		
	Inn & Out RV Park	A-3
LAKE PANASOFFKEE		
	Turtleback RV Resort	C-3
LAKE WALES		
	Bullock's Landing RV Park & Storage Facility	C-4
	Camp'n Aire RV Resort	C-4
	Lake Wales RV & Campsites	C-4
	The Harbor RV Resort & Marina	C-4
LAKELAND		
	Lakeland RV Resort	C-3

Where to Find CCUSA Parks

List City	Park Name	Map Coordinates
	Woodall's Mobile Home Village & RV Park	C-3
LARGO		
	Lee's Travel Park	C-3
	Rainbow Village RV Resort	C-3
	Yankee Traveler RV Park	C-3
MARATHON		
	Jolly Roger Travel Park	F-4
MILTON		
	Pelican Palms RV Park	F-1
MIMS		
	Crystal Lake RV Park	C-4
MOORE HAVEN		
	M RV Resort	D-4
	Marina RV Resort	D-4
NAPLES		
	Lake San Marino RV Resort	E-4
NEW SMYRNA BEACH		
	New Smyrna Beach RV Park	B-4
	Sugar Mill Ruins Travel Park	B-4
OCALA		
	Holiday Trav-L-Park RV Resort	B-3
	Ocala Sun RV Resort	B-3
	Wild Frontier Rally Park & Campground	B-3
OCKLAWAHA		
	Lake Bryant MH & RV Park	B-3
OKEECHOBEE		
	Gracious RV Park	D-4
	Silver Palms RV Village	D-4
	Zachary Taylor RV Resort	D-4
OLD TOWN		
	Old Town Campground N' Retreat	B-2
	Suwannee River Hideaway Campground, Inc.	B-2
	Yellow Jacket Campground Resort	B-2
ORANGE CITY		
	Orange City RV Resort	B-4
PALM HARBOR		
	Bay Aire Travel Trailer Park	C-3
	Sherwood Forest Travel RV Park	C-3
PALMDALE		
	Sabal Palm RV Resort & Campground	D-4
PALMETTO		
	Fishermans Cove RV Resort	D-3
PORT ORANGE		
	Daytona Beach RV Resort	B-4
	Rose Bay Travel Park	B-4
PORT RICHEY		
	Ja-Mar Travel Park	C-3
	Suncoast RV Resort	C-3
PORT ST. LUCIE		
	Port St. Lucie RV Resort	D-5
PUNTA GORDA		
	Shell Creek RV Resort	D-3
	Sun 'N' Shade Campground	D-3
QUINCY		
	Beaver Lake Campground	A-1
RUSKIN		
	Sun Lake RV Resort	D-3
	Tampa South RV Resort	D-3

bigger tourist destinations. Here you can bask in the golden sunshine surrounded by miles of powder white beaches and see manatees and dolphins frolicking in the Indian River Lagoon.

West Palm Beach. Lion Country Safari, America's First Cageless Zoo. A four-mile drive through the safari with over 900 animals roaming free within inches of your vehicle is a highlight on this adventure. Also included in admission is **Safari World Amusement Park** with animal encounters and demonstrations, rides, games, shopping, food and thrills. Go to www.lioncountry.com for more details.

ANNUAL EVENTS

JANUARY

Winter Music Series, Clermont; Kumquat Festival, Dade City; Sullivan Street Craft Fair, Punta Gorda.

FEBRUARY

African-American Heritage Festival, Tavares; Mount Dora Music Festival, Mount Dora; Pasco County Fair, Dade City; Race for Humanity, Dade City; Celtic Festival & Highland Games, Zephyrhills; Edison Festival of Light, Fort Myers; Lemon Bay Festival, Englewood.

MARCH

Jazz, Wine & Seafood Festival, Clermont; Saturday Downtown Marketplace, Tallahassee; Little Everglades Steeplechase, Dade City; Chasco Fiesta, New Port Richey; Jacksonville Flower Show, Jacksonville; Peace River National Arts Festival, Punta Gorda.

APRIL

Lake County Fair, Eustis; Delray Beach Green Market in the Park, Delray Park; Annual Southern Watercolor Society Exhibit, Panama City Beach.

MAY

FreedomFest, Cape Coral; Annual Pensacola Crawfish Creole Fiesta, Pensacola; Pioneer Craft Day, Dade City; Cajun Zydeco Festival, Deerfield Beach; West Palm Beach Antique & Collectibles Show, West Palm Beach; Annual Children's Festival of the Arts, Davie; Cotee River Seafood Festival & Boat Show, New Port Richey; Florida Estate Winery's Wine Festival, Land O'Lakes.

JUNE

San Juan Festival, Port St. Lucie; Yulee Railroad Days, North Central Florida; San Juan Festival, Port St. Lucie; Fiesta Celebration, Pensacola; Sprint Billy Bowlegs Pirate Festival & Parade, Okaloosa; John Levique Pirate Days, Madeira Beach; World Oceans Day, Fort Pierce; Jazz Jams Uptown, Altamonte Springs; Florida Gulf Coast Outdoor Festival, Bradenton Beach; Boca Grande Silver King

Festival, Englewood; Main Street Blast, New Port Richey; National Hibiscus Festival, Punta Gorda.

JULY

Bradenton Beach Fireworks Celebration, Bradenton Beach; 4th of July on Florida's Gulf Islands, Palmetto; Sertoma's 4th of July Celebration, Pensacola; Florida International Festival, Daytona Beach; Mango Mania Tropical Fruit Fair, Cape Coral; .

SEPTEMBER

Annual Las Olas Art Fair, Fort Lauderdale; Pensacola Seafood Festival, Pensacola; Delray Beach Craft Festival, Delray Beach; Art Festival, Tampa.

OCTOBER

Annual Lake County Folk Festival, Eustis; Arts & Crafts Show, Punta Gorda; Rattlesnake Festival, San Antonio; Amelia Book Island Festival, Amelia Island; Alligator Fest, Lake City; Pensacola Interstate Fair, Pensacola; San Antonio Rattlesnake Festival, San Antonio.

NOVEMBER

Chili Cook-Off, Leesburg; Annual Down Home Days, Trenton; Craft Festival, Gainesville; Pasco Bug Jam, Dade City; Great Gulfcoast Arts Festival, Pensacola; American Indian Arts Celebration, Clewiston; Festival of Lights, Lake City; Greek Festival, Pensacola; American Indian Arts Celebration, Clewiston.

DECEMBER

Country Christmas Stroll, Dade City; Holiday Art & Craft Fair, Cocoa; Annual Fernandina Beach Lighted Holiday Parade, Amelia Island; Skydive City Annual Christmas Boogie, Zephyrhills; Holidays on the Harbor, Charlotte Harbor.

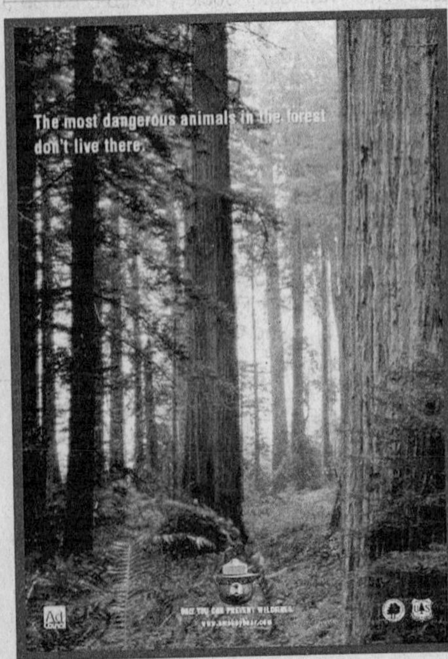

The most dangerous animals in the forest don't live there.

Where to Find CCUSA Parks

List City	Park Name	Map Coordinates
SARASOTA		
	Sun-N-Fun RV Resort	D-3
SEBASTIAN		
	Pelican's Landing Resort	C-5
	Whispering Palms RV Resort	C-5
SEBRING		
	Buttonwood Bay	D-4
	Highland Wheel Estates	D-4
	Lake Josephine RV Resort	D-4
	Woody's RV Resort	D-4
SILVER SPRINGS		
	Lake Waldena Resort	B-3
	Whispering Pines RV Park	B-3
ST. AUGUSTINE		
	Pacetti's Marina RV Park & Fishing Resort	B-4
	St. John's RV Park	B-4
ST. CLOUD		
	Lake Toho RV Resort	C-4
	The Floridian RV Resort	C-4
ST. PETERSBURG		
	Robert's Mobile Home & RV Resort	C-3
TAMPA		
	Bay Bayou RV Resort	C-3
	Camp Nebraska	C-3
TARPON SPRINGS		
	Hickory Point Mobile Home & RV Park	C-3
THONOTOSASSA		
	Spanish Main RV Resort	C-3
TITUSVILLE		
	Seasons in the Sun	C-4
VENICE		
	Florida Pines Mobile Home Court & RV	D-3
	Myakka RV Resort - KOA	D-3
VERO BEACH		
	Sunshine Travel-Encore	D-5
WAUCHULA		
	Crystal Lake Village	D-3
WEBSTER		
	Sunshine Village RV Resort	C-3
WESLEY CHAPEL		
	Quail Run RV Resort	C-3
WHITE SPRINGS		
	Lee's Country Campground	A-3
	Suwannee Valley Campground	A-3
WILDWOOD		
	Thousand Palms RV Resort	B-3
WINTER HAVEN		
	Hammondell Campsites & RV Sales	C-4
ZEPHYRHILLS		
	Baker Acres RV Resort	C-3
	Forest Lake Estates RV Resort	C-3
	Glen Haven RV Resort	C-3
	Happy Days RV Park	C-3
	Jim's RV Park	C-3
	Majestic Oaks RV Resort	C-3
	Rainbow Village RV Resort	C-3
	Ralph's Travel Park	C-3
	Southern Charm RV Resort	C-3
	Sweetwater RV Park	C-3
	Water's Edge RV Resort	C-3

ALACHUA—B-3

(W) TRAVELERS CAMPGROUND—(Alachua) *From jct I-75 (exit 399 old 78) & US 441: Go 200 feet SE on US 441, (turn N at Waffle House), then 1 mi N on April Blvd. Enter on R.*

WELCOME

◆◆◆◆FACILITIES: 142 sites, typical site width 20 ft, 109 full hkups, 33 W&E, (20/30/50 amps), some extd stay sites, 42 pull-thrus, cable TV, WiFi Instant Internet at site, family camping, tenting, RV storage, dump, non-guest dump $, laundry, ltd groc, RV supplies, LP gas by weight/by meter, ice, picnic tables.

◆◆RECREATION: rec room/area, swim pool, golf nearby, bsktball, shuffleboard shuffleboard court, horseshoes, v-ball. Rec open to public.

Pets welcome. Partial handicap access. Open all yr. Big rigs welcome. Escort to site. Clubs welcome. Rate in 2010 $35-38 for 2 persons. Member ARVC, FLARVC. FMCA discount.

Phone: (386)462-2505
Address: 17701 April Blvd, Alachua, FL 32615
Lat/Lon: 29.81767/-82.51527
Email: dreamcamper@juno.com
Web: www.travelerscampground.com

SEE AD GAINESVILLE PAGE 126 AND AD TRAVEL SECTION PAGE 74

ALTOONA—B-4

(NE) OCALA NATIONAL FOREST (Alexander Springs Rec. Area)—(Lake) *From jct Hwy 42 & Hwy 19: Go 3.7 mi N on Hwy 19, then 5.1 mi NE on CR 445.* FACILITIES: 65 sites, typical site width 11 ft, 35 ft max RV length, 1 W&E, 64 no hkups, tenting, dump, ltd groc. RECREATION: lake swim, boating, canoeing, stream fishing. Partial handicap access. Open all yr. Phone: (352)669-3522.

(W) OCALA NATIONAL FOREST (Big Bass Campground)—(Lake) *From jct Hwy 19 & Hwy 42: Go 9.6 mi W on Hwy 42, then 1/4 mi N on FR 588.* FACILITIES: 34 sites, typical site width 19 ft, 32 ft max RV length, 34 no hkups, tenting, dump. RECREATION: Partial handicap access. Open Oct 15 - Apr 15. Phone: (352)669-3153.

(W) OCALA NATIONAL FOREST (Big Scrub Campground)—(Lake) *From town: Go 5-1/2 mi N on Hwy 19, then 7 mi W on FR 573.* FACILITIES: 62 sites, 22 ft max RV length, 62 no hkups, tenting. RECREATION: Open all yr. Phone: (352)625-2520.

APOPKA—C-4

(W) Sun Resort—(Orange) *From Jct US 441 & Hwy 435: Go 2 1/2 mi S on Hwy 435. Enter on R.* ◆◆◆FACILITIES: 104 sites, typical site width 20 ft, 40 ft max RV length, 70 full hkups, 34 W&E, (30/50 amps), 50 amps ($), 45 pull-thrus, cable TV, ($), WiFi Internet central location, family camping, tenting, RV storage, dump, laundry, groceries, LP gas by weight/by meter, ice, picnic tables, patios. ◆◆◆RECREATION: rec hall, swim pool, wading pool, mini-golf, ($), bsktball, playground, shuffleboard court 4 shuffleboard courts, activities, horseshoes, v-ball. Pets welcome. Partial handicap access. Open all yr. Rate in 2010 $30.50 for 2 persons. MC/VISA/DISC/AMEX. Member ARVC, FLARVC. CCUSA 50% Discount. CCUSA reservations Required, CCUSA max stay 7 days, CCUSA disc. not avail holidays.

CAMPCLUB USA

Phone: (407)889-3048
Address: 3000 Clarcona Rd #99, Apopka, FL 32703
Lat/Lon: 28.63494/-81.50135
Email: sunresorts@aol.com
Web: www.sunrvresorts.net

APOPKA—Continued

(NE) WEKIWA SPRINGS STATE PARK—(Orange) *From jct I-4 & Hwy 436: Go 3 mi W on Hwy 436.* FACILITIES: 60 sites, 60 W&E, tenting, dump. RECREATION: lake swim, boating, canoeing, river fishing, playground. Pets welcome. Partial handicap access. Open all yr. Phone: (407)884-2008.

ARCADIA—D-3

(W) Arcadia Peace River Campground—(DeSoto) *From jct US 17 & Hwy 70: Go 2 mi W on Hwy 70. Enter on R.* ◆◆◆FACILITIES: 182 sites, typical site width 25 ft, 182 full hkups, (20/30/50 amps), 110 pull-thrus, family camping, tenting, dump, laundry, groceries. ◆◆◆◆RECREATION: swim pool, river swim, boating, canoeing, ramp, river/pond fishing, playground. Pets welcome. Partial handicap access. Open all yr. Rate in 2010 $15-55 per family. Member ARVC, FLARVC. Phone: (800)559-4011.

ARCADIA—Continued on next page

Florida is larger than England & Wales combined.

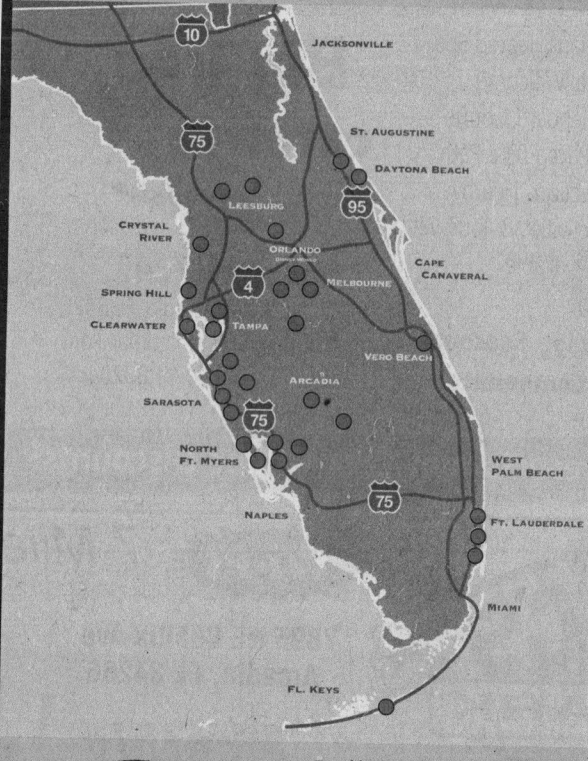

Arcadia • Florida

Soak up the sun and fun.

Beautiful beaches, restaurants, shopping and antiquing nearby

Heated Swimming Pool • Giant Heated Spa
Large Grassy Sites • Pets Welcome
Deluxe Clubhouse • Shuffleboard Courts
Pool Tables • Petanque • Paved Bike Path
Golf, Gambling and Attractions Nearby
Fishing Lake • Planned Activities & Tours
Phone & Cable TV Available
WI-FI Available

Daily • Weekly • Monthly • Seasonal Annual • Senior RV Community

Big Tree

863-494-7247

2626 N.E. Hwy. 70, Arcadia, FL 34266
E-mail: bigtreerv@embarqmail.com
Lat/Lon: 27.21312/-81.83204

www.carefreervresorts.com • For Online Discounts!

ARCADIA—Continued

(E) BIG TREE RV RESORT—(DeSoto) *From jct US-17 & Hwy-70: Go 2-1/2 mi E on Hwy-70. Enter on L.*

WELCOME

WELCOME TO CAREFREE RV RESORTS!
Soak up the sun and fun! Beautiful beaches, shopping, restaurants and antiquing are nearby. Enjoy our lakeside living, pool and lots of fun activites at this 50+ resort. It's a great place to make new friends!

◆◆◆◆FACILITIES: 392 sites, typical site width 40 ft, 392 full hkups, (20/30/50 amps), mostly extd stay sites (winter), WiFi Instant Internet at site ($), dump, laundry, LP gas by weight, picnic tables, patios.

◆◆◆◆RECREATION: rec hall, rec room/area, swim pool, hot tub, golf nearby, shuffleboard court 6 shuffleboard courts, activities, horseshoes, local tours.

Pets welcome, breed restrict. Partial handicap access. No tents. Age restrict may apply. Open all yr. Big rigs welcome. Escort to site. Clubs welcome. Rate in 2010 $32-38 for 2 persons. MC/VISA. Member ARVC, FLARVC. FMCA discount. CCUSA 50% Discount. CCUSA reservations Required, CCUSA max stay 7 days. Discount not available Jan 1-Apr 1. No tents or fire rings allowed. Senior Park. 1 dog under 11 lbs.

Phone: (863)494-7247
Address: 2626 NE Hwy 70, Arcadia, FL 34266
Lat/Lon: 27.20900/-81.83057
Email: bigtreerv@embarqmail.com
Web: www.carefreervresorts.com

SEE AD THIS PAGE

(N) CRAIG'S RV PARK—(DeSoto) *From jct Hwy 70 & US 17 N: Go 7 mi N on US 17 N, then 200 feet SW on Cubitis Ave. Enter on L.*

WELCOME

COUNTRY CAMPING & GREAT BLUEGRASS!
Nestled in the country in SW Florida. Trade the city for quiet country camping. Great rates & home of Bluegrass Jammin' Weekends. Enjoy the climate of Florida's unspoiled heartland & southern hospitality. Come enjoy the fun!

◆◆◆◆FACILITIES: 349 sites, typical site width 35 ft, 40 ft max RV length, 349 full hkups, (20/30/50 amps), many extd stay sites (winter), 64 pull-thrus, WiFi Instant Internet at site ($), RV storage, dump, non-guest dump $, laundry, RV supplies, LP gas by weight/by meter, patios.

◆◆◆◆RECREATION: rec hall, rec room/area, pavilion, swim pool, putting green, golf nearby, bsktball, shuffleboard court 8 shuffleboard courts, activities, horseshoes, hiking trails, local tours.

Pets welcome, quantity restrict. Partial handicap access. No tents. Open all yr. Church services & planned activities during Nov-Apr. Escort to site. Clubs welcome. Rate in 2010 $20-35 for 2 persons. MC/VISA/DISC/Debit. Member ARVC, FLARVC.

Text 107862 to (440)725-8687 to see our Visual Tour.

CRAIG'S RV PARK—Continued on next page

Phone: (863)494-1820
Address: 7895 NE Cubitis Ave., Arcadia, FL 34266
Lat/Lon: 27.30908/-81.81987
Email: craigsrv@desoto.net
Web: www.craigsrv.com

SEE AD PAGE 94

(N) CROSS CREEK COUNTRY CLUB & RV RESORT—(DeSoto) *From jct Hwy 70 & US 17N: Go 5 mi N on US 17, then 1/4 mi W on CR 660, then 1 mi N on Cubitis Ave (Old Hwy 17). Enter on L.*

WELCOME

◆◆◆◆◆FACILITIES: 523 sites, typical site width 40 ft, 523 full hkups, (30/50 amps), mostly extd stay sites (winter), cable TV, phone/WiFi Instant Internet at site ($), RV storage, dump, laundry, LP gas by weight/by meter, ice, picnic tables, patios, controlled access.

CAMPCLUB USA

◆◆◆◆◆RECREATION: rec hall, rec room/area, pavilion, swim pool, hot tub, pond fishing, putting green, golf nearby, bsktball, shuffleboard court 8 shuffleboard courts, activities, tennis, horseshoes, v-ball.

Pets welcome, breed restrict. Partial handicap access. No tents. Open all yr. Big rigs welcome. Escort to site. Clubs welcome. Rate in 2010 $49 for 2 persons. MC/VISA. Member ARVC, FLARVC. CCUSA 50% Discount. CCUSA reservations Required, CCUSA max stay 14 days. Discount not available Dec-Mar.

Phone: (863)494-7300
Address: 6837 Northeast Cubitis Ave, Arcadia, FL 34266
Lat/Lon: 27.29405/-81.82826
Email: info@crosscreekrv.com
Web: www.crosscreekrv.com

Reserve Online at Woodalls.com

SEE AD PAGE 94

(N) Little Willies RV Resort—(DeSoto) *From jct Hwy 70 & US 17N: Go 5 mi N on US 17, then 1/4 mi W on CR 660, then 200 feet S on Cubitus Ave. Enter on R.* ◆◆◆◆FACILITIES: 331 sites, typical site width 30 ft, 331 full hkups, (30/50 amps), 50 pull-thrus, WiFi Internet central location, RV storage, laundry, patios.

CAMPCLUB USA

◆◆◆◆RECREATION: rec hall, equipped pavilion, swim pool, shuffleboard court 6 shuffleboard courts, activities, horseshoes. Pets welcome, size restrict, quantity restrict. Partial handicap access. No tents. Age restrict may apply. Open Sept 15 - May 15. Big rigs welcome. CCUSA 50% Discount. CCUSA reservations Recommended, Cash only for CCUSA disc., Check only for CCUSA disc. Non-aggressive pets only, not over 40 lbs. Surcharge for utilities $4/night.

Phone: (863)494-2717
Address: 5905 NE Cubitis Ave, Arcadia, FL 34266
Lat/Lon: 27.28028/-81.83400
Email: staff@littlewilliesrvresort.com
Web: www.littlewilliesrvresort.com

RIVERSIDE RV RESORT & CAMPGROUND—*From Arcadia: Go 11 mi S on US 17, then 3 mi W on Hwy 761, then 1-1/2 mi S on Hwy 769. Enter on L.*

WELCOME

SEE PRIMARY LISTING AT PORT CHARLOTTE AND AD PORT CHARLOTTE PAGE 158

(E) TOBY'S RV RESORT—(DeSoto) *From jct US 17 & Hwy 70: Go 3 mi E on Hwy 70. Enter on L.*

WELCOME

◆◆◆◆FACILITIES: 408 sites, typical site width 37 ft, 407 full hkups, 1 W&E, (30/50 amps), many extd stay sites (winter), 30 pull-thrus, WiFi Instant Internet at site ($), tenting, RV storage, dump, non-guest dump $, laundry, LP gas by weight/by meter, picnic tables, patios.

◆◆◆◆RECREATION: rec hall, rec room/area, pavilion, swim pool, hot tub, pond fishing, golf nearby, bsktball, shuffleboard court 8 shuffleboard courts, activities, tennis, horseshoes.

Pets welcome, breed restrict, quantity restrict. Partial handicap access. Open all yr. Big rigs welcome. Clubs welcome. Rate in 2010 $29-48 for 2 persons. MC/VISA. Member ARVC, FLARVC.

Phone: (800)307-0768
Address: 3550 NE State Highway 70, Arcadia, FL 34266
Lat/Lon: 27.20893/-81.81493
Email: Tobys_RV_Resort@equitylifestyles.com
Web: www.rvonthego.com

SEE AD ALACHUA PAGE 93

ASTOR—B-4

BLAIR'S JUNGLE DEN (NOT VISITED) —(Volusia) *From jct US 17 & Hwy 40: Go 6-1/4 mi W on Hwy 40, then 1/2 mi N on Riley Pridgeon Rd, then 3/4 mi W on Ormands Jungle Den Rd.*

WELCOME

FACILITIES: 42 sites, 42 full hkups, (50 amps), mostly extd stay sites (winter), 35 pull-thrus, WiFi Internet central location ($), family camping, laundry, ltd groc, marine gas, ice, patios.

RECREATION: boating, canoeing, kayaking, ramp, dock, river fishing, fishing supplies, fishing guides, golf nearby. Rec open to public.

Pets welcome, breed restrict, size restrict. No tents. Open all yr. Escort to site. Rate in 2010 $36 for 2 persons. MC/VISA/DISC/AMEX.

Phone: (386)749-2264
Address: 1820 Ormand's Jungle Den Road, Astor, FL 32102
Email: bassfishing@blairsjungleden.com
Web: www.blairsjungleden.com

SEE AD THIS PAGE

(W) OCALA NATIONAL FOREST (Juniper Springs Rec. Area)—(Marion) *From town: Go 10 mi W on Hwy-40. Enter on R.* FACILITIES: 79 sites, typical site width 11 ft, 35 ft max RV length, 79 no hkups, 17 pull-thrus, tenting, dump, laundry, ltd groc. RECREATION: swim pool, boating, no motors, canoeing, lake fishing. Partial handicap access. Open all yr. Phone: (352)625-3147.

(E) Parramore's Campground—(Volusia) *From US 17 & Hwy 40: Go 6-1/4 mi W on Hwy 40, then 1 mi N on Riley Pridgeon Rd, then 1 mi W on S Moon Rd. Enter on L.* ◆◆◆FACILITIES: 69 sites, typical site width 30 ft, 64 full hkups, 5 W&E, (20/30/50 amps), 3 pull-thrus, cable TV, WiFi Instant Internet at site, cable Internet central location, family camping, tenting, RV storage, dump, non-guest dump $, laundry, RV supplies, ice, picnic tables, fire rings, grills, wood.

CAMPCLUB USA

◆◆◆◆RECREATION: rec hall, pavilion, swim pool, boating, canoeing, ramp, dock, river fishing, fishing supplies, bsktball, playground, activities, tennis, horseshoes. Pets welcome, quantity restrict. Partial handicap access. Open all yr. Big rigs welcome. Rate in 2010 $33.50-36.50 for 2 persons. MC/VISA/DISC. Member ARVC, FLARVC. FMCA discount. CCUSA 50% Discount. CCUSA max stay 2 days, Cash only for CCUSA disc., CCUSA disc. not avail F,Sa, CCUSA disc. not avail holidays. Not available for special events-call for details.

Phone: (800)516-2386
Address: 1675 S Moon Rd, Astor, FL 32102
Lat/Lon: 29.18438/-81.53351
Email: parramores@aol.com
Web: www.parramores.com

AVON PARK—D-4

(W) ADELAIDE SHORES RV RESORT—(Highlands) *N'bnd from jct Hwy 64 & US 27: Go 4 mi N on US 27. Enter on L.*

WELCOME

"CENTRAL FLORIDA'S PREMIER 5W RESORT"

Lakefront RV Community with Big Rig sites & custom park models (Chariot Eagle - Palm Harbor). Full activities & amenities equal a great paradise for the active adult lifestyle your enjoyment is our business.

◆◆◆◆◆FACILITIES: 399 sites, typical site width 45 ft, 399 full hkups, (30/50 amps), mostly extd stay sites (winter), WiFi Instant Internet at site ($), phone/cable on-site Internet (needs activ), WiFi Internet central location, RV's/park model rentals, RV storage, laundry, patios.

CAMPCLUB USA

◆◆◆◆◆RECREATION: rec hall, swim pool, boating, canoeing, dock, lake fishing, golf nearby, shuffleboard court 5 shuffleboard courts, activities, tennis, horseshoes, local tours.

Pets welcome, breed restrict, size restrict, quantity restrict. No tents. Age restrict may apply. Open

all yr. Big rigs welcome. Clubs welcome. Rate in 2010 $33.25 for 2 persons. CCUSA 50% Discount. CCUSA reservations Accepted, CCUSA max stay 7 days, Cash only for CCUSA disc., Check only for CCUSA disc. Age restrictions may apply. Pets accepted up to 40 lbs.

Phone: (800)848-1924
Address: 2881 US 27 North, Avon Park, FL 33825
Lat/Lon: 27.63826/-81.52293
Email: adelaideshores@yahoo.com
Web: www.adelaideshores.com

SEE AD THIS PAGE

(SE) Bonnet Lake RV Resort—(Highlands) *From jct US 27 & Hwy 17 S: Go 6 mi SE on Hwy 17 S. Enter on L.* ◆◆◆FACILITIES: 175 sites, typical site width 22 ft, 175 full hkups, (30/50 amps), 16 pull-thrus, cable TV, WiFi Instant Internet at site, phone on-site Internet (needs activ), WiFi Internet central location, laundry, LP gas by weight/by meter, picnic tables, patios.

Bonnet Lake RV Resort—Continued on next page

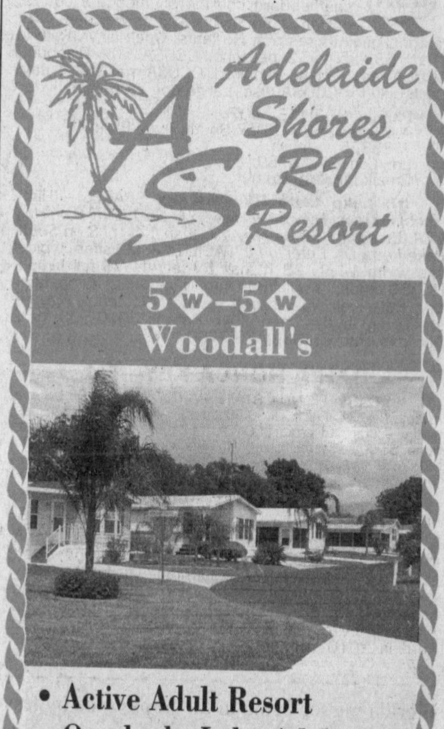

AVON PARK—Continued
Bonnet Lake RV Resort—Continued

◆◆◆◆RECREATION: rec hall, equipped pavilion, swim pool, boating, canoeing, kayaking, ramp, dock, lake fishing, shuffleboard court 3 shuffleboard courts, activities, horseshoes, hiking trails. Pets welcome, breed restrict. No tents. Age restrict may apply. Open all yr. Big rigs welcome. Rate in 2010 $30-35 for 2 persons. MC/VISA/DISC/Debit. CCUSA 50% Discount. CCUSA max stay 4 days, Cash only for CCUSA disc., CCUSA disc. not avail F,Sa,S. Discount available Apr thru Oct.

Phone: (863)385-3700
Address: 2825 SR 17 South, Avon Park, FL 33825
Lat/Lon: 27.54279/-81.45313
Email: info@bonnetlakecampgrounds.com
Web: www.bonnetlakecampgrounds.com

(SW) Lake Glenada RV Park—(Highlands) *From jct Hwy 64 & US 27: Go 2-1/2 mi S on US 27. Enter on L.* ◆◆FACILITIES: 216 sites, typical site width 15 ft, 34 ft max RV length, 216 full hkups, (30/50 amps), phone on-site Internet (needs activ), family camping, RV storage, laundry, picnic tables, patios. ◆◆◆◆RECREATION: rec hall, swim pool, hot tub, boating, ramp, dock, lake fishing, shuffleboard court 4 shuffleboard courts, activities, horseshoes. Pets welcome, size restrict, quantity restrict. No tents. Open all yr. Rate in 2010 $33-35 for 2 persons. CCUSA 50% Discount. CCUSA reservations Required, CCUSA max stay 1 day, Cash only for CCUSA disc. Large dog restriction.

Phone: (863)453-7007
Address: 2525 US 27 South, Avon Park, FL 33825
Lat/Lon: 27.55789/-81.51035
Email: lgrv@strato.net

(N) Lake Letta RV Park (RV SPACES)—(Highlands) *From jct Hwy 64 & Hwy 17A: Go 1/2 mi S on Hwy 17A, then 3 mi SE on Hwy 17, then 1/4 mi S on South Lake Letta Dr. Enter on L.* FACILITIES: 73 sites, typical site width 14 ft, 28 ft max RV length, 73 full hkups, (30/50 amps), 2 pull-thrus, family camping, dump, laundry. Pets welcome, breed restrict. No tents. Age restrict may apply. Open all yr. Rate in 2010 $30 for 2 persons. Phone: (863)453-7700.

BAHIA HONDA KEY—F-4

(S) BAHIA HONDA STATE PARK—(Monroe) *On US 1 at milemarker 37.* FACILITIES: 80 sites, 64 W&E, 16 no hkups, tenting, dump, ltd groc. RECREATION: saltwater swim, boating, ramp, dock, saltwater fishing. No pets. Open all yr. Phone: (305) 872-2353.

BARTOW—C-3

(E) Good Life RV Resort—(Polk) *From jct US 98 & Hwy 60: Go 7 mi E on Hwy 60. Enter on R.* ◆◆◆◆FACILITIES: 397 sites, typical site width 35 ft, 397 full hkups, (30/50 amps), dump, laundry. ◆◆◆◆RECREATION: swim pool. Pets welcome, breed restrict, size restrict, quantity restrict. No tents. Age restrict may apply. Open all yr. Big rigs welcome. Rate in 2010 $35 for 2 persons. Phone: (863)537-1971.

Florida misses being in the tropic zone by less than 100 miles.

BELLE GLADE—D-5

(N) BELLE GLADE CAMPGROUND (City Park)—(Palm Beach) *From jct Hwy 80 & Hwy 715: Go 2-1/4 mi N on Hwy 715, then 2 mi W on Torry Rd. (Turn left immediately after crossing bridge.). Enter at end.* FACILITIES: 380 sites, 240 full hkups, 140 W&E, 20 pull-thrus, tenting, dump, laundry. RECREATION: boating, ramp, dock. Partial handicap access. Open all yr. Phone: (561)996-6322.

BEVERLY HILLS—B-3

(F) Sandy Oaks RV Resort—(Citrus) *From jct US 41 & CR 491: Go 3/4 mi S on CR 491. Enter on R.* ◆◆◆◆FACILITIES: 153 sites, 150 full hkups, (20/30/50 amps), 3 no hkups, 23 pull-thrus, cable TV, WiFi Instant Internet at site, WiFi Internet central location, tenting, RV storage, dump, non-guest dump $, laundry, RV supplies, LP gas by weight/by meter, picnic tables, patios, wood. ◆◆◆RECREATION: rec hall, swim pool, putting green, shuffleboard court shuffleboard court, activities, horseshoes. Pets welcome, breed restrict. Partial handicap access. Open all yr. Rate in 2010 $34 for 2 persons. MC/VISA/DISC/AMEX. Member ARVC, FLARVC. CCUSA 50% Discount.

Phone: (352)465-7233
Address: 6760 N Lecanto Hwy, Beverly Hills, FL 34465
Lat/Lon: 28.96240/-82.43166
Email: info@sandyoaksrvresort.com
Web: www.sandyoaksrvresort.com

BIG PINE KEY—F-4

(S) Breezy Pines RV Estates—(Monroe) *On US 1 at mile marker 29.8. Enter on R.* ◆◆◆FACILITIES: 96 sites, typical site width 25 ft, 38 ft max RV length, 90 full hkups, 6 W&E, (20/30/50 amps), 0 pull-thrus, tenting, laundry. ◆◆◆RECREATION: swim pool. Pets welcome, breed restrict, quantity restrict. Open all yr. Rate in 2010 $33-50 for 2 persons. Phone: (305)872-9041.

(SW) SUNSHINE KEY RESORT—(Monroe) *On US-1 at mile marker 39. Enter on R.* ◆◆◆◆FACILITIES: 400 sites, typical site width 30 ft, 385 full hkups, 15 W&E, (20/30/50 amps), many extd stay sites (winter), 340 pull-thrus, cable TV, WiFi Instant Internet at site ($), family camping, tenting, RV's/park model rentals, RV storage, dump, non-guest dump $, portable dump, laundry, full svc store, RV supplies, LP gas by weight/by meter, marine gas, ice, picnic tables, controlled access.

◆◆◆◆◆RECREATION: rec hall, rec room/area, coin games, swim pool, saltwater swim, boating, canoeing, kayaking, ramp, dock, 3 kayak/4 motorboat rentals, saltwater fishing, fishing supplies, golf nearby, bsktball, shuffleboard court 2 shuffleboard courts, activities, tennis, horseshoes, v-ball.

Pets welcome. Open all yr. Planned activities in winter only. Big rigs welcome. Escort to site. Clubs welcome. Rate in 2010 $67-130 for 6 persons. MC/VISA/DISC/AMEX/Debit. ATM. Member ARVC, FLARVC.

Florida has belonged to five different nations: Spain, England, France, the Confederacy and the U.S.A.

BIG PINE KEY—Continued
SUNSHINE KEY RESORT—Continued

Phone: (800)852-0348
Address: 38801 Overseas Hwy, Big Pine Key, FL 33043
Lat/Lon: 24.67208/-81.24660
Email: sunshine_key@equitylifestyle.com
Web: www.rvonthego.com

SEE AD ALACHUA PAGE 93 AND AD KEY WEST PAGE 134

BONIFAY—E-2

Florida Springs RV Resort & Campgrounds—(Holmes) *From I-10 (exit 112) & Hwy 79: Go 2/10 mi N on Hwy 79, then 600 ft E on Son In Law Rd. Enter on L.* ◆◆◆FACILITIES: 56 sites, 33 full hkups, 18 W&E, (20/30/50 amps), 5 no hkups, 20 pull-thrus, cable TV, ($), WiFi Instant Internet at site, family camping, tenting, RV storage, dump, non-guest dump $, laundry, RV supplies, picnic tables. ◆◆◆RECREATION: rec hall, pavilion, lake swim, pond fishing, play equipment, horseshoes, v-ball. Pets welcome, breed restrict. Open all yr. Rate in 2010 $33 for 2 persons. MC/VISA/DISC/AMEX. Member ARVC, FLARVC. CCUSA 50% Discount. CCUSA reservations Recommended, CCUSA max stay 2 days, Cash only for CCUSA disc., CCUSA disc. not avail F,Sa, CCUSA disc. not avail holidays.

Phone: (850)258-3110
Address: 90 Son In Law Rd, Bonifay, FL 32425
Lat/Lon: 30.76609/-85.68315
Web: www.floridaspringsrv.com

BONITA SPRINGS—E-4

(N) Bonita Lake RV Resort—(Lee) *From jct I-75 (exit 116) & CR 865 (Bonita Beach Rd): Go 1 mi W on Bonita Beach Rd, then 1-1/2 mi N on Old US 41. Enter on R.* ◆◆◆◆FACILITIES: 165 sites, typical site width 30 ft, 165 full hkups, (30/50 amps), family camping, dump, laundry. ◆◆◆RECREATION: swim pool, lake fishing. Pets welcome, breed restrict. Partial handicap access. No tents. Open all yr. Big rigs welcome. Rate in 2010 $39-48 for 2 persons. Member ARVC, FLARVC. Phone: (239)992-2481.

(E) IMPERIAL BONITA ESTATES RV RESORT—(Lee) *From jct I-75 (exit 116) & CR 865 (Bonita Beach Rd): Go 1/2 mi W on Bonita Beach Rd, then 1/4 mi N on Imperial St, then 2 blocks E on Dean St. Enter on L.*

A PARK FULL OF FUN!
Between Naples & Fort Myers on the Imperial River. Pristine beaches, golf, fishing, shopping, dog track & casino within minutes. Calendar full of park activities. You are a stranger here but once.

◆◆◆◆FACILITIES: 312 sites, typical site width 30 ft, 312 full hkups, (20/30/50 amps), many extd stay sites (winter), 30 pull-thrus, WiFi Instant Internet at site, RV storage, dump, non-guest dump $, laundry, LP gas by weight, ice, picnic tables, patios.

◆◆◆◆◆RECREATION: rec hall, rec room/area, pavilion, swim pool, boating, canoeing, kayaking,

IMPERIAL BONITA ESTATES RV RESORT—Continued on next page

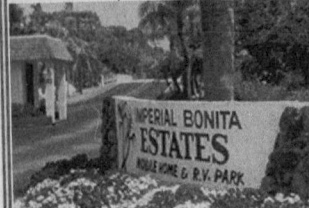

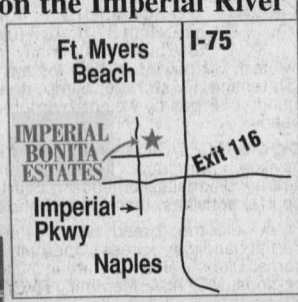

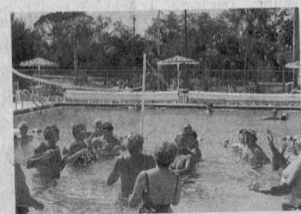

river fishing, putting green, golf nearby, bsktball, shuffleboard court 8 shuffleboard courts, activities, tennis, horseshoes.

Pets welcome. Partial handicap access. No tents. Age restrict may apply. Open all yr. Big rigs welcome. Escort to site. Clubs welcome. Rate in 2010 $40-60 for 2 persons. MC/VISA. Member ARVC, FLARVC.

Text 107864 to (440)725-8687 to see our Visual Tour.

Phone: (239)992-0511
Address: 27700 Bourbonniere Dr, Bonita Springs, FL 34135
Lat/Lon: 26.33512/-81.76079
Email: ibecoop@comcast.net
Web: www.imperialbonitaestates.com

SEE AD PAGE 96 AND AD TRAVEL SECTION PAGE 74

BOWLING GREEN—D-3

(S) ORANGE BLOSSOM ADULT RV PARK —(Hardee) *From jct Hwy 62 & US 17: Go 1/2 mi N on US 17. Enter on L.*

WELCOME

◇◇◇FACILITIES: 170 sites, 170 full hkups, (30/50 amps), mostly extd stay sites (winter), WiFi Instant Internet at site ($), phone/cable on-site Internet (needs activ), phone Internet central location, RV storage, dump, laundry, RV supplies, patios.

◇◇RECREATION: rec hall, rec room/area, swim pool, lake fishing, golf nearby, shuffleboard court 6 shuffleboard courts, activities, horseshoes.

Pets welcome, breed restrict, size restrict. No tents. Age restrict may apply. Open all yr. Group activities in winter only. Big rigs welcome. Rate in 2010 $26.75 for 2 persons.

Phone: (863)773-2282
Address: 2829 US Highway 17 N, Bowling Green, FL 33834
Lat/Lon: 27.60109/-81.82386

SEE AD THIS PAGE

(SW) Torrey Oaks RV & Golf Resort—(Hardee) *From jct Hwy 62 & US 17: Go 1/2 mi N on US 17, then 1/2 mi W on Bostick Rd. Enter on R.* ◇◇◇◇FACILITIES: 231 sites, typical site width 35 ft, accepts full hkup units only, 231 full hkups, (30/50 amps), WiFi Instant Internet at site, phone Internet central location, RV storage, laundry, ice, patios. ◇◇◇◇RECREATION: rec hall, swim pool, pond fishing, putting green, shuffleboard court 6 shuffleboard courts, activities, horseshoes. Pets welcome, quantity restrict. Partial handicap access. No tents. Age restrict may apply. Open all yr. Big rigs welcome. Rate in 2010 $30-40 for 2 persons. MC/VISA/DISC. CCUSA 50% Discount.

CAMPCLUB USA

Phone: (863)773-3157
Address: 2908 Country Club Dr, Bowling Green, FL 33834
Lat/Lon: 27.60250/-81.83100
Email: info@torreyoaksrv.com
Web: torreyoaksrv.com

BRADENTON—D-3

(S) Arbor Terrace RV Resort—(Manatee) *From jct I-75 (exit 217) & Hwy 70: Go 7-1/2 mi W on Hwy 70/53rd Ave, then 1/2 mi S on US 41, then 1/2 mi E on 57 Ave W. Enter on L.* ◇◇◇FACILITIES: 392 sites, typical site width 20 ft, 392 full hkups, (30/50 amps), 62 pull-thrus, WiFi Instant Internet at site ($), phone/cable on-site Internet (needs activ), phone Internet central location ($), dump, non-guest dump $, laundry, patios. ◇◇◇◇RECREATION: rec hall, equipped pavilion, swim pool, shuffleboard court 12 shuffleboard courts, activities, horseshoes. Pets welcome, breed restrict, quantity restrict. No tents. Open all yr. Big rigs welcome. Rate in 2010 $29-43 for 2 persons. MC/VISA/DISC. Member ARVC, FLARVC. CCUSA 50% Discount. CCUSA reservations Required, CCUSA max stay 7 days. Discount not available Nov 30-Apr 30. Additional charges may apply. Electricity metered.

CAMPCLUB USA

Phone: (941)755-6494
Address: 405 - 57th Ave. W., Bradenton, FL 34207
Lat/Lon: 27.44051/-82.56644
Email: sunresv@aol.com
Web: www.arborterracerv.com

(NE) ENCORE MANATEE RV RESORT—(Manatee) *From jct I-75 (exit 220) & Hwy 64: Go 3/4 mi W on Hwy 64, then 1 mi NE on 60th St Ct East. Enter on L.*

WELCOME

◇◇◇◇◇FACILITIES: 415 sites, typical site width 35 ft, 415 full hkups, (30/50 amps), many extd stay sites (winter), 4 pull-thrus, WiFi Instant Internet at site ($), phone/cable on-site Internet (needs activ), phone Internet central location, tenting, RV's/park model rentals, dump, non-guest dump $, laundry, LP gas by weight/by meter, picnic tables, patios, controlled access.

◇◇◇◇◇RECREATION: rec hall, rec room/area, equipped pavilion, 2 swim pools, hot tub, boating, canoeing, canoe/pedal boat rentals, lake fishing, golf nearby, shuffleboard court 5 shuffleboard courts, activities, horseshoes.

Pets welcome. Partial handicap access. Open all yr. Planned activities winter only. Big rigs welcome. Clubs welcome. Rate in 2010 $27-65 for 2 persons. MC/VISA/DISC/AMEX. Member ARVC, FLARVC. FCRV discount. FMCA discount.

Florida's beautiful weather influences almost every part of the state's economy.

Phone: (800)678-2131
Address: 800 Kay Road NE, Bradenton, FL 34212
Lat/Lon: 27.50561/-82.48158
Email: nhcflugm@msn.com
Web: www.rvonthego.com

SEE AD ALACHUA PAGE 93

(NW) HOLIDAY COVE RV RESORT—(Manatee) *From jct I-75 (exit 217) & Hwy 70: Go 12 mi W on Hwy 70 (53rd Ave), then 4 mi W on Cortez Rd. Enter on R.*

WELCOME

◇◇◇◇◇FACILITIES: 97 sites, typical site width 30 ft, 97 full hkups, (20/30/50 amps), mostly extd stay sites (winter), 2 pull-thrus, cable TV, WiFi Instant Internet at site, phone/cable on-site Internet (needs activ), laundry, ice, picnic tables, patios, controlled access.

◇◇◇◇◇RECREATION: rec hall, swim pool, boating, canoeing, kayaking, ramp, dock, saltwater fishing, putting green, golf nearby, bike rental bike rental, shuffleboard court shuffleboard court, activities, horseshoes.

Pets welcome, quantity restrict. Partial handicap access. No tents. Open all yr. Planned activities winter only. Big rigs welcome. Rate in 2010 $50-90 for 2 persons. MC/VISA/DISC. Member ARVC, FLARVC.

Phone: (941)792-1111
Address: 11900 Cortez Rd W, Cortez, FL 34215
Lat/Lon: 27.46911/-82.68213
Email: holidaycoverv@aol.com
Web: www.holidaycoverv.com

SEE AD CORTEZ PAGE 104

(SE) HORSESHOE COVE RV RESORT—(Manatee) *From jct I-75 (exit 217) & Hwy 70: Go 1-1/4 mi W on Hwy 70, then 1/4 mi N on Caruso Rd. Enter on L.*

WELCOME

WELCOME TO CAREFREE RV RESORTS!
Our serene resort offers country living with abundant wildlife, as well as a host of activites. Explore the 12-acre island with well lit docks for the best night fishing year 'round. Beautiful beaches are just minutes away!

◇◇◇◇◇FACILITIES: 476 sites, typical site width 35 ft, accepts full hkup units only, 476 full hkups, (30/50 amps), many extd stay sites (winter), WiFi Instant Internet at site, phone/cable on-site Internet (needs activ), WiFi Internet central location, family camping, RV's/park model rentals, laundry, picnic tables, patios, controlled access.

◇◇◇◇◇RECREATION: rec hall, rec room/area, equipped pavilion, swim pool, hot tub, boating,

HORSESHOE COVE RV RESORT—Continued on next page

BRADENTON—Continued
HORSESHOE COVE RV RESORT—Continued

canoeing, kayaking, dock, river fishing, golf nearby, shuffleboard court 8 shuffleboard courts, activities, horseshoes, hiking trails, local tours.

Pets welcome, quantity restrict. Partial handicap access. No tents. Age restrict may apply. Open all yr. Children's visits 30 days max. Planned activities winter. Big rigs welcome. Clubs welcome. Rate in 2010 $30-60 for 2 persons. MC/VISA.

Phone: (800)291-3446
Address: 5100 60th St. E, Bradenton, FL 34203
Lat/Lon: 27.45006/-82.48574
Email: horseshoerv@tampabay.rr.com
Web: www.carefreervresorts.com

SEE AD SARASOTA PAGE 164

(E) LAKE MANATEE STATE RECREATION AREA—(Manatee) *From jct I-75 (exit 42) & Hwy 64: Go 15 mi E on Hwy 64.* FACILITIES: 60 sites, 60 W&E, tenting, dump. RECREATION: lake swim, boating, 20 hp limit, canoeing, ramp, dock, lake fishing. Open all yr. Phone: (941)741-3028.

(SE) PLEASANT LAKE RV RESORT—(Manatee) *From jct I-75 (exit 217) & Hwy 70: Go 1/2 mi W on Hwy 70. Enter on R.*

WELCOME

WELCOME TO CAREFREE RV RESORTS!
A welcoming retreat near Gulf beaches, shopping and fun! Enjoy our beautiful 25-acre lake with plenty of freshwater fish, wildlife and birds. Our fun and friendly staff will make your stay a carefree experience!

◊◊◊◊FACILITIES: 340 sites, typical site width 20 ft, accepts full hkup units only, 340 full hkups, (30/50 amps), many extd stay sites (winter), 16 pull-thrus, cable TV, WiFi Instant Internet at site, phone/cable on-site Internet (needs activ), phone Internet central location ($), laundry, LP gas by weight/by meter, picnic tables, patios, controlled access.

◊◊◊◊RECREATION: rec hall, swim pool, boating, electric motors only, canoeing, ramp, lake fishing, golf nearby, shuffleboard court 10 shuffleboard courts, activities, horseshoes.

Pets welcome, size restrict, quantity restrict. No tents. Age restrict may apply. Open all yr. Planned activities winter only. Big rigs welcome. Clubs welcome. Rate in 2010 $28-58 for 2 persons. MC/VISA. Member FLARVC.

Phone: (941)756-5076
Address: 6633 SR 70 E, Bradenton, FL 34203
Lat/Lon: 27.44727/-82.47551
Email: pleasantlakerv@newbymanagement.com
Web: www.pleasantlakerv.com

SEE AD SARASOTA PAGE 166

(W) Sarasota Bay RV Park (RV SPACES)—(Manatee) *From jct I-75 (exit 217) & Hwy 70: Go 12 mi W on Hwy 70/53rd Ave, then 3 mi W on Cortez Rd. Enter on L.* FACILITIES: 240 sites, typical site width 25 ft, 40 ft max RV length, accepts full hkup units only, 240 full hkups, (30/50 amps), dump, laundry. RECREATION: swim pool, boating, ramp, saltwater fishing. No pets. No tents. Age restrict may apply. Open all yr. Rate in 2010 $37-45 for 2 persons. Member ARVC, FLARVC. Phone: (941)794-1200.

(SE) Tropical Gardens RV Park—(Manatee) *From jct I-75 (exit 217) & Hwy 70: Go 6 mi W on Hwy 70 (53rd Ave). Enter on L.* ◊◊◊◊FACILITIES: 150 sites, typical site width 18 ft, 38 ft max RV length, 150 full hkups,

BRADENTON—Continued
Tropical Gardens RV Park—Continued

(30/50 amps), 15 pull-thrus, phone/cable on-site Internet (needs activ), dump, non-guest dump $, laundry, patios. ◊◊◊RECREATION: rec hall, swim pool, shuffleboard court 2 shuffleboard courts, activities. Pets welcome, size restrict. No tents. Age restrict may apply. Open all yr. Rate in 2010 $43 for 2 persons. CCUSA 50% Discount. CCUSA reservations Accepted, CCUSA max stay Unlimited, Cash only for CCUSA disc., Check only for CCUSA disc. Discount available May thru Oct. Special Nov & Dec monthly rate $400. Age restrictions may apply. Pets 30 lbs and under accepted.

CAMPCLUB USA

Phone: (941)756-1135
Address: 1120 53rd Ave East (Hwy 70), Bradenton, FL 34203
Lat/Lon: 27.44740/-82.55094
Email: tropicalgardensrv@aol.com
Web: www.tropicalgardensrv.com

BRISTOL—F-3

(N) TORREYA STATE PARK—(Liberty) *From jct Hwy 20 & Hwy 12: Go 4 mi N on Hwy 12, then 7 mi N on CR 270, then 1-1/2 mi N on CR 271.* FACILITIES: 30 sites, 30 ft max RV length, 30 W&E, tenting. RECREATION: playground. No pets. Open all yr. Phone: (850)643-2674.

BROOKSVILLE—C-3

(N) BELLE PARC RV RESORT (TOO NEW TO RATE)—(Hernando) *From jct US 98 & US 41: Go 2-1/4 mi NE on US 41, then 1 block W on Ancient Trail. Enter on L.*

WELCOME

FACILITIES: 100 sites, typical site width 35 ft, 100 full hkups, (20/30/50 amps), many extd stay sites (winter), 9 pull-thrus, WiFi Instant Internet at site, WiFi Internet central location, family camping, RV's/park model rentals, cabins, RV storage, laundry, picnic tables, patios, wood, controlled access.

RECREATION: rec hall, rec room/area, equipped pavilion, swim pool, hot tub, boating, canoeing, kayaking, dock, 2 canoe/2 pedal boat rentals, lake fishing, golf nearby, bike rental 14 bike rentals, activities, horseshoes, hiking trails.

CAMPCLUB USA

Pets welcome, breed restrict, quantity restrict. Partial handicap access. No tents. Open all yr. Big rigs welcome. Escort to site. Clubs welcome. Rate in 2010 $35-60 per family. MC/VISA/Debit. Member ARVC. CCUSA 50% Discount. CCUSA reservations Recommended, CCUSA max stay 3 days, CCUSA disc. not avail F,Sa. Not available Nov thru Mar. 10% discount weekends.

Phone: (352)796-5760
Address: 11089 Ancient Trail, Brooksville, FL 34601
Lat/Lon: 28.58633/-82.37812
Email: don@belleparcrvresorts.com
Web: www.belleparcrvresorts.com

SEE AD THIS PAGE

(S) Campers Holiday—(Hernando) *From jct US 98 & Hwy 581: Go 5-1/2 mi S on Hwy 581. Enter on L.* ◊◊◊◊FACILITIES: 60 sites, 60 full hkups, (30/50 amps), family camping, dump, laundry, picnic tables, patios. ◊◊◊◊RECREATION: rec hall, equipped pavilion, swim pool, bsktball, playground, shuffleboard court 6 shuffleboard courts, horseshoes. Pets welcome, breed restrict, quantity restrict. No tents. Open all yr. Big rigs welcome. Rate in 2010 $28 for 2 persons. CCUSA 50% Discount. CCUSA reservations Accepted, CCUSA max stay 7 days. Discount not available Nov thru Apr. Limit 1 RV & 1 tow vehicle/site; 1 stay/month. Check out time: noon.

CAMPCLUB USA

BROOKSVILLE—Continued
Campers Holiday—Continued

Phone: (352)796-3707
Address: 2092 Culbreath Rd, Brooksville, FL 34602
Lat/Lon: 28.46050/-82.37009

(N) CLOVERLEAF FOREST RV RESORT—(Hernando) *From jct I-75 (exit 301) & US 98 & Hwy 50A: Go 7 mi W on Hwy 50A, then 1 mi N on US 41, then N on Broad St/US 41 for 3/4 mi to Resort - Use RV Entrance only. Enter on R.*

WELCOME

ENJOY A CHARMING COUNTRY SETTING
Beautiful RV resort with access to Florida's BEST attractions. Enjoy our heated indoor Pool & Jacuzzi, Clubhouse, Billiard Rm, Golf Range, and Arts & Crafts Club. Near Golf, Busch Gardens and Sea World. Come, Stay & Play Here!

◊◊◊◊FACILITIES: 277 sites, typical site width 20 ft, 40 ft max RV length, 277 full hkups, (20/30/50 amps), many extd stay sites (winter), 3 pull-thrus, WiFi Internet central location, laundry, picnic tables, patios.

◊◊◊◊RECREATION: rec hall, rec room/area, 2 swim pools, hot tub, golf nearby, shuffleboard court 6 shuffleboard courts, activities, horseshoes, local tours.

Pets welcome, quantity restrict. No tents. Age restrict may apply. Open all yr. Planned activities winter only. Clubs welcome. Rate in 2010 $39 for 2 persons. MC/VISA/DISC/Debit.

Phone: (877)796-5931
Address: 910 N Broad St, Brooksville, FL 34601
Lat/Lon: 28.56570/-82.37525
Email: cloverleafforest@hometownamerica.com
Web: www.cloverleafforest.com

SEE AD THIS PAGE

(E) Hidden Valley Campground (RV SPACES)—(Hernando) *From jct Hwy 50 & US 98: Go 1/2 mi E on US 98. Enter on L.* FACILITIES: 65 sites, typical site width 18 ft, 30 ft max RV length, 65 full hkups, (30/50 amps), phone/cable on-site Internet (needs activ), WiFi Internet central location, RV storage, dump, non-guest dump $, laundry, picnic tables, patios. RECREATION: rec hall, horseshoes. Pets welcome, breed restrict. No tents. Open all yr. Rate in 2010 $22 for 2 persons. MC/VISA/DISC/Debit. Member ARVC. CCUSA 50% Discount. CCUSA reservations Recommended, CCUSA max stay 3 days.

CAMPCLUB USA

Phone: (352)796-8710
Address: 22329 Cortez Blvd, Brooksville, FL 34601
Lat/Lon: 28.54014/-82.35950

BUNNELL—B-4

(SW) BULL CREEK CAMPGROUND & MARINA—(Flager) *From jct US 1 & SR 100: Go 7 mi W on SR 100, then 4 mi S on CR 305, then 4 mi W on CR 2006. Enter at end.*

WELCOME

FACILITIES: 25 sites, 38 ft max RV length, 25 W&E, family camping, dump, laundry, ice, picnic tables.

RECREATION: boating, ramp, dock, lake/river fishing, fishing supplies, golf nearby.

Pets welcome. No tents. Open all yr.

Phone: (386)313-4020
Address: 3861 W CR 2006, Bunnell, FL 32110
Lat/Lon: 29.42290/-81.43507
Web: www.flaglercounty.org

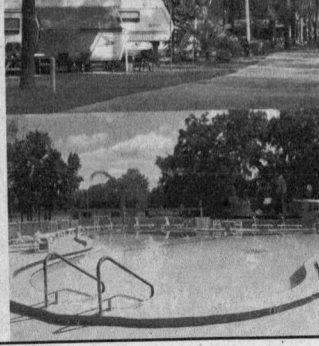

SEE AD TRAVEL SECTION PAGE 81

BUNNELL—Continued on next page

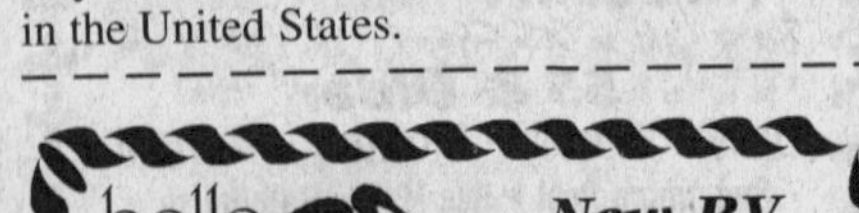

Key West has the highest average temperature in the United States.

BUNNELL—Continued

(N) THUNDER GULCH CAMPGROUND—(Flagler) *From the south on I-95 exit 273, (Old 89): Go N on US 1. From north on I-95 take exit 298 (old 92): Go S on US 1.*

WELCOME

◆◆◆FACILITIES: 67 sites, typical site width 30 ft, 57 full hkups, 10 W&E, (30/50 amps), some extd stay sites (winter), WiFi Instant Internet at site ($), family camping, tenting, RV's/park model rentals, RV storage, dump, non-guest dump $, laundry, LP gas by weight/by meter, ice, picnic tables.

◆◆RECREATION: pond fishing, golf nearby, bsktball, horseshoes.

Pets welcome, quantity restrict. Open all yr. Rates higher during Special Events. Rate in 2010 $31-40 for 2 persons. MC/VISA/DISC/AMEX. Member ARVC, FLARVC.

Phone: (800)714-8388
Address: 2551 N State Street (US 1), Bunnell, FL 32110
Lat/Lon: 29.49279/-81.26579
Email: thundergulchman@aol.com
Web: www.thundergulch-campground.com

SEE AD TRAVEL SECTION PAGE 81

BUSHNELL—C-3

(W) Breezy Oaks RV Park (RV SPACES)—(Sumter) *From jct I-75 & Hwy 673 (exit 309): Go 3/4 mi E on Hwy 673, then 3/4 mi N on Hwy 671. Enter at end.* FACILITIES: 101 sites, typical site width 35 ft, 101 full hkups, (20/30/50 amps), 50 pull-thrus, dump, laundry. RECREATION: swim pool. Pets welcome, breed restrict, quantity restrict. No tents. Open all yr. Big rigs welcome. Rate in 2010 $25 for 2 persons. Member ARVC, FLARVC. Phone: (352)569-0300.

(W) Nascar RV Resorts at Blueberry Hill—(Sumter) *From jct I-75 (exit 314) & Hwy 48: Go 1 block E on Hwy 48. Enter on R.* ◆◆◆◆FACILITIES: 404 sites, typical site width 30 ft, 404 full hkups, (20/30/50 amps), 96 pull-thrus, dump, laundry. ◆◆◆◆RECREATION: swim pool. Pets welcome. Partial handicap access. No tents. Open all yr. Big rigs welcome. Rate in 2010 $39.99 for 2 persons. Phone: (877)793-4112.

(N) PARADISE OAKS GOLF & RV RESORT—(Sumter) *From I-75 & SR 48 (exit 314): Go E on SR 48 for 1.8 mi, then N on CR 475/N Main for 1-1/2 mi. Enter on L.*

WELCOME

WELCOME TO PARADISE IN FLORIDA
Newest RV & Golf Resort in Cen FL! Settle in for the winter & enjoy our Heated Pool & Spa-WiFi-Library-Club House with Stage Exer Rm-Lg TV Rm & Kitchen. Tee time is waiting. Easy day trip to Orlando-Tampa for attractions.

◆◆◆◆FACILITIES: 235 sites, typical site width 25 ft, accepts full hkup units only, 235 full hkups, (30/50 amps), 50 amps ($), mostly extd stay sites (winter), 18 pull-thrus, WiFi Instant Internet at site, WiFi Internet central location, family camping, dump, laundry, patios.

CAMPCLUB USA

◆◆◆◆◆RECREATION: rec hall, rec room/area, pavilion, hot tub, pond fishing, putting green, golf nearby, shuffleboard court 4 shuffleboard courts, activities, horseshoes.

Pets welcome, breed restrict, quantity restrict. Partial handicap access. No tents. Open all yr. Big rigs welcome. Clubs welcome. Rate in 2010 $39 MC/VISA/DISC/Debit. Member ARVC, FLARVC. CCUSA 50% Discount.

Phone: (352)793-1823
Address: 4628 County Road 475, Bushnell, FL 33513
Lat/Lon: 28.68891/-82.11026
Email: myparadiseoaks@yahoo.com
Web: www.theparadiseoaks.com

SEE AD THIS PAGE AND AD TRAVEL SECTION PAGE 74

RED OAKS RV RESORT—(Sumter) *From jct (exit 314) & Hwy 48: Go 1/2 mi E on Hwy 48, then 1/2 mi N on SW 18th Terrace.*

WELCOME

WELCOME TO CAREFREE RV RESORTS!
Let the good times roll...staying at this amazing resort is musc to your ears with weekly jam sessions and sing-a-longs. Double your pleasure with two pools, clubhouses and activities galore! We cater to rallies too!

◆◆◆◆FACILITIES: 994 sites, typical site width 35 ft, 994 full hkups, (20/30/50 amps), many extd stay sites (winter), 335 pull-thrus, cable TV, WiFi Instant Internet at site ($), family camping, RV storage, dump, non-guest dump $, laundry, picnic tables, patios.

CAMPCLUB USA

◆◆◆◆◆RECREATION: rec hall, rec room/area, pavilion, equipped pavilion, 3 swim pools, hot tub, pond fishing, golf nearby, shuffleboard court 22 shuffleboard courts, activities, horseshoes, local tours. Rec open to public.

Pets welcome, breed restrict, quantity restrict. Partial handicap access. Open all yr. Planned activities & church services winter only. Big rigs welcome. Escort to site. Clubs welcome. Rate in 2010 $35-50 for 2 persons. MC/VISA/Debit. CCUSA 50% Discount. CCUSA reservations Recommended, CCUSA max stay 5 days, CCUSA disc. not avail holidays. Discount available May thru Oct. Age Restrictions may apply.

BUSHNELL—Continued
RED OAKS RV RESORT—Continued

Phone: (352)793-7117
Address: 5551 SW 18th Terrace, Bushnell, FL 33513
Lat/Lon: 28.66895/-82.13535
Email: theoaksrv@embarqmail.com
Web: www.carefreervresorts.com

SEE AD THIS PAGE AND AD TRAVEL SECTION PAGE 74

(W) Sumter Oaks RV Park—(Sumter) *From I-75 (exit 309) & Hwy 476B/673: Go 1-1/2 mi E on CR 673. Enter on L.* ◆◆◆FACILITIES: 124 sites, typical site width 35 ft, 124 full hkups, (20/30/50 amps), 14 pull-thrus, family camping, tenting, dump, laundry. ◆◆◆RECREATION: swim pool. Pets welcome. Partial handicap access. Open all yr. Big rigs welcome. Rate in 2010 $26 for 2 persons. Phone: (352)793-1333.

St. Augustine is the oldest European settlement in North America.

CALLAHAN—A-3

(N) Kelly's Countryside RV Park—(Nassau) *From jct US 1 & US 301: Go 7 mi N on US 1/301. Enter on L.* ◆◆◆◆FACILITIES: 67 sites, typical site width 25 ft, 65 full hkups, 2 W&E, (30/50 amps), 15 pull-thrus, family camping, tenting, dump, laundry. Pets welcome, breed restrict. Partial handicap access. Open all yr. Big rigs welcome. Rate in 2010 $30 for 2 persons. Member ARVC, FLARVC. Phone: (904)845-4252.

CAPE CANAVERAL—C-5

(NE) JETTY PARK (Canaveral Port Auth)—(Brevard) *From I95 & SR 528: Go E on 528 to Port Canaveral, then follow signs to Jetty Park.* FACILITIES: 177 sites, 35 ft max RV length, 31 full hkups, 89 W&E, (20/30/50 amps), 57 no hkups, tenting, dump, laundry, full svc store. RECREATION: saltwater swim, boating, ramp, saltwater fishing, playground. Pets welcome ($). Partial handicap access. Open all yr. Phone: (321)783-7111.

Titusville, known as Space City, USA, is located on the west shore of the Indian River directly across from the John F. Kennedy Space Center.

CARRABELLE—B-1

(E) HO-HUM RV PARK—(Franklin) *From jct Hwy 67 & US 98/319: Go 3-1/2 mi E on US 98/319. Enter on R.*

WELCOME

STAY WITH US-RIGHT ON THE BEACH!
On the Gulf's Forgotten Coast, centrally located to Tallahassee & Panama City, come & find a quiet, relaxed adult atmosphere at Ho-Hum! Watch Killer Sunsets from our many BEACH FRONT sites. Experience Great Shelling & Bird Watching!

◆◆◆FACILITIES: 50 sites, typical site width 30 ft, 50 full hkups, (30/50 amps), 50 amps ($), some extd stay sites, 26 pull-thrus, cable TV, WiFi Instant Internet at site, family camping, laundry, RV supplies.

◆◆◆RECREATION: rec hall, saltwater swim, boating, canoeing, kayaking, saltwater fishing.

Pets welcome. Partial handicap access. No tents. Open all yr. Planned group activities in winter only.

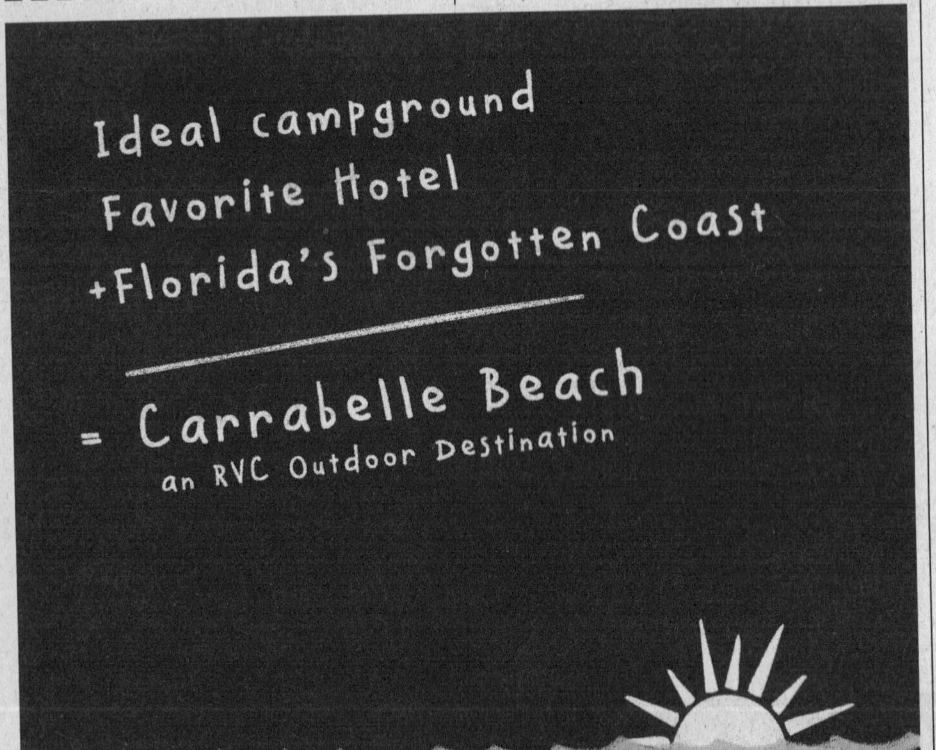

CARRABELLE—Continued
HO-HUM RV PARK—Continued

Big rigs welcome. Clubs welcome. Rate in 2010 $29-33 for 2 persons. MC/VISA/DISC. Member ARVC. FMCA discount.

Phone: (850)697-3926
Address: 2132 US Highway 98 E, Carrabelle, FL 32322
Lat/Lon: 29.87136/-84.60973
Web: www.HOHUMRVPARK.com

SEE AD THIS PAGE

Sunset Isle RV & Yacht Club Resort (TOO NEW TO RATE)—(Franklin) *From Hwy 67 & US 98/319: Go 1-3/10 mi W on US 98, then 3/4 mi E on Timber Island Rd. Enter on R.* FACILITIES: 33 sites, 33 full hkups, (50 amps), WiFi Instant Internet at site, WiFi Internet central location, tenting, dump, non-guest dump, fire rings, wood. RECREATION: swim pool, boating, canoeing, kayaking, ramp, dock, saltwater/river fishing, fishing guides, play equipment, horseshoes, hiking trails. Open all yr. Rate in 2010 $36 for 4 persons. CCUSA 50% Discount. CCUSA reservations Required, CCUSA max stay 4 days, Cash only for CCUSA disc., CCUSA disc. not avail S, CCUSA disc. not avail F,Sa, CCUSA disc. not avail holidays.

CAMPCLUB USA

Phone: (850)370-6223
Address: 260 Timber Island Rd, Carrabelle, FL 32322
Lat/Lon: 29.84578/-84.66843
Email: charlotte@forgottencoastrealestate.com
Web: www.sunsetislervandyachtclubresort.com

CARRABELLE BEACH—B-1

(W) CARRABELLE BEACH OUTDOOR DESTINATIONS (UNDER CONSTRUCTION)—(Franklin) *From jct Hwy 67 & US 98/319: Go 2-3/4 mi W on US 98/319. Enter on R.*

NATURE'S SECRET ON FLORIDA'S COAST
Carabelle Beach is just an hour from Tallahassee and features RV sites, cottages, lofts with ocean views, community lodge, fitness center, free WiFi, boat rentals and charters at our own Carrabelle Beach Boat Club.

FACILITIES: 79 sites, typical site width 34 ft, 79 full hkups, (30/50 amps), many extd stay sites (winter), 51 pull-thrus, cable TV, WiFi Instant Internet at site, family camping, cabins, dump, laundry, RV supplies, ice.

RECREATION: rec hall, swim pool, fishing supplies, golf nearby, playground, horseshoes.

Pets welcome. Partial handicap access. No tents. Open all yr. Big rigs welcome. Clubs welcome. Rate in 2010 $39.50 for 2 persons. MC/VISA/DISC. Member ARVC, FLARVC. FMCA discount.

Text 107999 to (440)725-8687 to see our Visual Tour.

CARRABELLE BEACH OUTDOOR DESTINATIONS—Continued on next page

CARRABELLE BEACH—Continued
CARRABELLE BEACH OUTDOOR DESTINATIONS—Continued

Phone: (850)697-2638
Address: 1843 Hwy 98 W, Carrabelle Beach, FL 32322
Lat/Lon: 29.83054/-84.69133
Email: carrabellebeach@rvcoutdoors.com
Web: www.rvcoutdoors.com

SEE AD PAGE 100

CEDAR KEY—B-2

(E) CEDAR KEY RV RESORT (UNDER CONSTRUCTION)—(Levy) *From jct US 19/98 & Hwy 24: Go 14 mi W on Hwy 24. Enter on R.*

FACILITIES: 83 sites, typical site width 45 ft, 83 full hkups, (20/30/50 amps), 7 pull-thrus, WiFi Instant Internet at site, family camping, non-guest dump $, laundry, ltd groc, RV supplies, ice, picnic tables, patios, wood, controlled access.

RECREATION: rec hall, swim pool, fishing supplies, fishing guides, golf nearby.

Pets welcome. Partial handicap access. No tents. Open all yr. Big rigs welcome. Clubs welcome. MC/VISA/DISC/AMEX.

Phone: (352)543-5097
Address: 11981 SW Shiloh Rd, Cedar Key, FL 32625
Email: cedarkeyrvresort@bellsouth.net
Web: www.cedarkeyrvresort.com

SEE AD THIS PAGE

(N) CEDAR KEY SUNSET ISLE RV PARK—(Levy) *From jct US 19 and SR 24: Go 19 mi W on SR 24. Upon crossing first bridge on the island (Channel 4 Bridge) continue approximately 1 mi. Enter on R.*

◇◇◇FACILITIES: 57 sites, typical site width 30 ft, 55 full hkups, 2 W&E, (20/30/50 amps), 7 pull-thrus, cable TV, WiFi Instant Internet at site, WiFi Internet central location, family camping, tenting, dump, non-guest dump $, ice, picnic tables, wood.

◇◇RECREATION: rec hall, canoeing, kayaking, saltwater fishing.

Pets welcome. Open all yr. Escort to site. Rate in 2010 $25-39 for 2 persons. MC/VISA. Member ARVC, FLARVC. CCUSA 50% Discount. CCUSA reservations Not Accepted, CCUSA max stay 1, CCUSA disc. not avail holidays. Discount available May thru Oct. No discounts island festivals. Reservations accepted with undiscounted nights. $2/night surcharge extra pet.

Phone: (800)810-1103
Address: 11850 S.W. Hwy 24, Cedar Key, FL 32625
Lat/Lon: 29.15413/-83.03049
Email: cedarkeyrv@gmail.com
Web: www.cedarkeyrv.com

SEE AD THIS PAGE

(NE) Rainbow Country RV Campground—(Levy) *From jct US 19/98 & Hwy 24: Go 14 mi SW on Hwy 24. Enter on R.* ◇◇FACILITIES: 65 sites, typical site width 25 ft, 65 full hkups, (30/50 amps), 10 pull-thrus, family camping, tenting, dump, laundry. Pets welcome, quantity restrict. Partial handicap access. Open all yr. Rate in 2010 $21-25 for 2 persons. Member ARVC, FLARVC. Phone: (352)543-6268.

CENTRAL FL'S WORLD OF THEME PARKS—C-4

For facilities near Walt Disney World Vacation Kingdom, Universal Studios & Sea World see listings at Apopka, Kissimmee, Orlando, Winter Garden & Lake Buena Vista

Florida State Gem: Moonstone

CENTRAL FL'S WORLD OF THEME PARKS—Continued

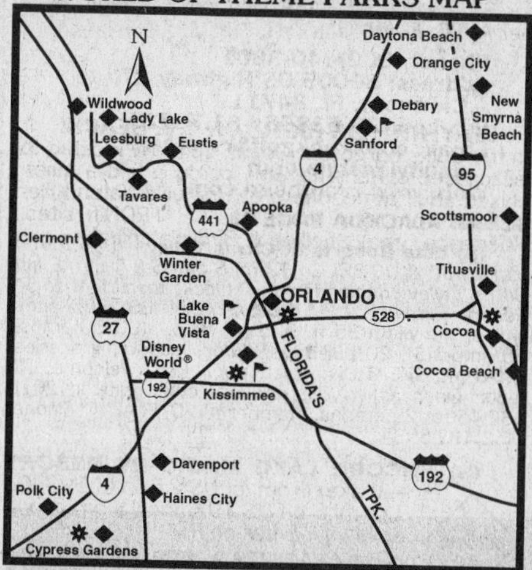

Symbols on map indicate towns within a 45 mi radius of Disney World, Universal Studios, Sea World & Cypress Gardens where campgrounds (diamonds), attractions (flags), & RV service centers & camping supply outlets (gears) are listed. Check listings for more information.
Walt Disney World Vacation Kingdom, Universal Studios, SeaWorld & Cypress Gardens are registered trademarks and/or service marks of their respective owners.

CHASSAHOWITZKA—C-3

(W) CHASSAHOWITZKA RIVER CAMPGROUND (City Park)—(Citrus) *From jct US-19, US-98 & CR-480: Go 1-3/4 mi W on CR-480. Enter on R.* FACILITIES: 88 sites, 88 full hkups, (30/50 amps), 4 pull-thrus, tenting, dump, laundry, groceries. RECREATION: boating, canoeing, ramp, dock, river fishing. Partial handicap access. Open all yr. Phone: (352)382-2200.

CHATTAHOOCHEE—A-1

(S) KOA-Chattahoochee/Tallahassee West—(Gadsden) *From jct I-10 (exit 166) & Hwy 270A: Go 1 mi S on Hwy 270A. Enter on L.* ◇◇◇FACILITIES: 56 sites, typical site width 30 ft, 37 full hkups, 14 W&E, (30/50 amps), 5 no hkups, 45 pull-thrus, family camping, tenting, dump, laundry, ltd groc. ◇◇◇RECREATION: swim pool, playground. Pets welcome. Partial handicap access. Open all yr. Rate in 2010 $30-35 for 2 persons. Phone: (800)KOA-2153. KOA discount.

CHIEFLAND—B-2

(W) MANATEE SPRINGS STATE PARK—(Levy) *From jct US 98/19 & Hwy 320: Go 7 mi W on Hwy 320.* FACILITIES: 92 sites, 92 W&E, (30/50 amps), tenting, dump, groceries. RECREATION: lake swim, boating, canoeing, ramp, lake fishing, playground. Pets welcome, breed restrict. Partial handicap access. Open all yr. Phone: (352)493-6072.

CHOKOLOSKEE ISLAND
IN THE HEART OF THE EVERGLADES
GREAT FISHING YEAR ROUND
★ Efficiencies ★ Bait and Tackle ★ Marina ★ Boat Ramp
· WiFi · Laundry · Full Hookups · Fully Remodeled Rental Units · Cable TV
· RVs Limited to 28' Long In Season · Beautiful New Bathhouse · Office, Store & Rec Hall
P.O. Box 430 • Chokoloskee, FL 34138
(239) 695-2414
www.chokoloskee.com
See listing at Chokoloskee, FL

CHIPLEY—E-2

(S) FALLING WATERS STATE PARK—(Washington) *From town: Go 3 mi S on Hwy 77A.* FACILITIES: 24 sites, 24 W&E, tenting, dump. RECREATION: lake swim, lake fishing, playground. Pets welcome. Open all yr. Phone: (850)638-6130.

CHOKOLOSKEE—E-4

(W) CHOKOLOSKEE ISLAND PARK & CAMPGROUND—(Collier) *From jct US 41 & Hwy 29: Go 8 mi S on CR 29, then 1 block W on Demere Ln, then 1 block W on Hamilton Ln. Enter at end.*

◇◇◇FACILITIES: 54 sites, typical site width 25 ft, 27 ft max RV length, 54 full hkups, (30 amps), many extd stay sites (winter), cable TV, WiFi Instant Internet at site ($), family camping, tenting, dump, laundry, ice, picnic tables.

◇◇◇RECREATION: rec hall, pavilion, boating, canoeing, kayaking, ramp, dock, saltwater/river fishing, fishing supplies, fishing guides, activities.

Pets welcome. Partial handicap access. Open all yr. Planned group activities winter only. Clubs welcome. Rate in 2010 $38-49 for 2 persons. MC/VISA/AMEX. Member ARVC, FLARVC.

Phone: (239)695-2414
Address: 1150 Hamilton Ln, Chokolskee, FL 34138
Lat/Lon: 25.81407/-81.36139
Email: manager@chokoloskee.com
Web: www.chokoloskee.com

SEE AD THIS PAGE

(N) Outdoor Resorts/Chokoloskee Island—(Collier) *From jct US-41 & Hwy-29 (CR 29): Go 8 mi S on CR 29. Enter on L.* ◇◇◇◇◇FACILITIES: 283 sites, typical site width 35 ft, accepts full hkup units only, 283 full hkups, (20/30/50 amps), laundry, groceries. ◇◇◇◇◇RECREATION: 3 swim pools, boating, canoeing, ramp, dock, saltwater fishing, play equipment. Pets welcome, quantity restrict. Partial handicap access. No tents. Open all yr. Big rigs welcome. Rate in 2010 $69-89 for 2 persons. Phone: (239)695-3788. FMCA discount.

CLEARWATER—C-3

(E) CLEARWATER TRAVEL RESORT—(Pinellas) *From jct US-19 & Hwy-60: Go 1/2 mi E on Hwy-60. Enter on L.*

◇◇◇◇FACILITIES: 163 sites, typical site width 40 ft, 163 full hkups, (20/30/50 amps), many extd stay sites (winter), WiFi Instant Internet at site, phone/cable on-site Internet (needs activ), WiFi Internet central location, family camping, RV storage, dump, non-guest dump $, laundry, RV supplies, LP gas by weight/by meter, picnic tables, patios.

◇◇◇RECREATION: rec hall, swim pool, golf nearby, play equipment, 4 shuffleboard courts, activities, horseshoes.

CLEARWATER TRAVEL RESORT—Continued on next page

• Heated Pool • Shuffleboard
• 2 Laundries • Recreation Hall
• Phone & Cable TV
(Through Utility companies)
• Extensive Planned Activities
• Fax, Copies & Notary Service
• FREE Wi-Fi

Phone: (727) 531-7998
Toll Free: 1-866-202-9232
8500 Ulmerton Road
Largo, FL 33771
E-Mail: info@yankeetraveler.net
Visit us on the Web:
www.yankeetraveler.net
See listing at Largo, FL

CLEARWATER—Continued
CLEARWATER TRAVEL RESORT—Continued

Pets welcome. Partial handicap access. No tents. Open all yr. Planned activities winter only. Big rigs welcome. Clubs welcome. MC/VISA/DISC/AMEX/ Debit. Member ARVC.

Phone: (800)831-1204
Address: 2946 Gulf to Bay Blvd, Clearwater, FL 33759
Lat/Lon: 27.96205/-82.71485
Email: clearwatertravel@newbymanagement.com
Web: www.clearwatertravelresort.net

SEE AD THIS PAGE

(SE) Travel World (RV SPACES)—(Pinellas) *From jct I-275 & Hwy 688: Go 4 mi W on Hwy 688, then 1/2 mi S on S'bound frontage road (parallels US 19). Enter on R.* FACILITIES: 320 sites, typical site width 28 ft, 36 ft max RV length, accepts full hkup units only, 320 full hkups, (20/30/50 amps), 6 pull-thrus, dump, laundry. RECREATION: swim pool. Pets welcome. Partial handicap access. No tents. Age restrict may apply. Open all yr. Rate in 2010 $40 for 2 persons. Phone: (727)536-1765. FMCA discount.

CLERMONT—C-3

(NW) Bee's RV Resort—(Lake) *From jct Hwy 50 & US 27: Go 8 mi N on US 27. Enter on R.* ◇◇◇FACILITIES: 245 sites, typical site width 25 ft, 229 full hkups, 16 W&E, (30/50 amps), 100 pull-thrus, cable TV, ($), WiFi Instant Internet at site ($), cable on-site Internet (needs activ), WiFi Internet central location, family camping, tenting, RV storage, dump, laundry, LP gas by meter, ice, picnic tables. ◇◇◇◇RECREATION: rec hall, equipped pavilion, swim pool, pond fishing, mini-golf, play equipment, 4 shuffleboard courts, activities, horseshoes. Pets welcome. Partial handicap access. Open all yr. Big rigs welcome. Rate in 2010 $25-35 for 2 persons. CCUSA 50% Discount. CCUSA reservations Recommended, CCUSA max stay 14 days, Cash only for CCUSA disc., Check only for CCUSA disc. Discount not available Dec thru mid Mar. No credit cards accepted. Rates subject to change without notice. Tent sites available up to 7 nights.

Phone: (352)429-2116
Address: 20260 US Hwy 27, Clermont, FL 34715
Lat/Lon: 28.64096/-81.79653
Email: beesreservations@comcast.net
Web: www.beesrvresort.com

Reserve Online at Woodalls.com

(NW) CLERBROOK GOLF & RV RESORT ENCORE—(Lake) *From jct Hwy 50 & US 27: Go 7-1/2 mi N on US 27. Enter on L.*

◇◇◇◇FACILITIES: 1248 sites, typical site width 30 ft, 40 ft max RV length, 1248 full hkups, (30/50 amps), many extd stay sites (winter), cable TV, ($), WiFi Instant Internet at site ($), phone/cable on-site Internet (needs activ), family camping, tenting, RV's/park model rentals, cabins, RV storage, dump, laundry, LP gas by weight/by meter, ice, picnic tables, patios, controlled access.

◇◇◇◇◇RECREATION: rec hall, pavilion, 3 swim pools, hot tub, pond fishing, putting green, golf nearby, bsktball, play equipment, 20 shuffleboard courts, activities, horseshoes, sports field, local tours.

Pets welcome, breed restrict, size restrict, quantity restrict. Partial handicap access. Open all yr. Tent camping summer months only. Limited to 1

CLERMONT—Continued
CLERBROOK GOLF & RV RESORT ENCORE—Continued

week stay. Clubs welcome. Rate in 2010 $30-46 for 2 persons. MC/VISA/DISC/AMEX/Debit. Member ARVC, FLARVC.

Phone: (800)440-3801
Address: 20005 US Highway 27, Clermont, FL 34711
Lat/Lon: 28.63806/-81.78725
Email: clerbrookgolf&rvresort@equitylifestyle.com
Web: www.rvonthego.com

SEE AD ALACHUA PAGE 93

(S) Elite Resorts at Citrus Valley—(Lake) *From jct Hwy-50 & US-27: Go 12 mi S on US-27, turn E into Citrus Valley Highlands for 1 block, then right to RV Resort. Enter on L.* ◇◇◇◇◇FACILITIES: 305 sites, typical site width 35 ft, 305 full hkups, (30/50 amps), 50 amps ($), 20 pull-thrus, dump, laundry, groceries. ◇◇◇RECREATION: swim pool. Pets welcome. No tents. Open all yr. Big rigs welcome. Rate in 2010 $32-45 for 2 persons. Member ARVC, FLARVC. Phone: (352)432-5934.

(S) ENCORE LAKE MAGIC RV RESORT—(Lake) *From jct US 27 & US 192: Go 1/2 mi E on US 192, then S on to long driveway. Enter on R.*

◇◇◇◇FACILITIES: 469 sites, typical site width 35 ft, 469 full hkups, (30/50 amps), many extd stay sites (winter), 135 pull-thrus, cable TV, WiFi Instant Internet at site ($), phone/cable on-site Internet (needs activ), WiFi Internet central location, family camping, RV storage, dump, non-guest dump $, laundry, picnic tables, patios.

◇◇◇◇◇RECREATION: rec hall, 2 swim pools, wading pool, hot tub, lake fishing, golf nearby, bsktball, shuffleboard court 10 shuffleboard courts, activities, tennis, horseshoes, v-ball.

Pets welcome, breed restrict. Partial handicap access. No tents. Open all yr. Big rigs welcome. Clubs welcome. Rate in 2010 $35-66 for 2 persons. MC/VISA/DISC/AMEX.

Phone: (888)558-5777
Address: 9600 US Highway 192 W, Clermont, FL 34714
Lat/Lon: 28.34338/-81.66436
Email: info@rvonthego.com
Web: www.rvonthego.com

SEE AD ALACHUA PAGE 93 AND AD ORLANDO PAGE 149

(W) OUTDOOR RESORTS AT ORLANDO—(Polk) *From jct I-4 & US-192: Go 6-1/2 mi W on US-192. Enter on L.*

◇◇◇◇◇FACILITIES: 979 sites, typical site width 35 ft, accepts full hkup units only, 979 full hkups, (20/30/50 amps), 50 amps ($), mostly extd stay sites (winter), cable TV, WiFi Internet central location, family camping, RV's/park model rentals, ice, picnic tables, patios, controlled access.

◇◇◇◇◇RECREATION: rec hall, 2 swim pools, wading pool, boating, canoeing, kayaking, ramp, dock, lake fishing, mini-golf, golf nearby, bsktball, playground, shuffleboard court 6 shuffleboard courts, activities, tennis, horseshoes, v-ball.

Pets welcome, breed restrict, size restrict, quantity restrict. Partial handicap access. No tents. Open all yr. Church & planned group activities winter only. No laundry. Big rigs welcome. Rate in 2010 $30 per vehicle. MC/VISA/DISC/Debit. Member ARVC.

CLERMONT—Continued
OUTDOOR RESORTS AT ORLANDO—Continued

Phone: (800)531-3033
Address: 9000 IRLO Broson Hwy (Hwy 192W), Clermont, FL 34711
Lat/Lon: 28.34660/-81.65722
Email: reserve@oro-orlando.com
Web: www.oro-orlando.com

SEE AD TRAVEL SECTION PAGE 72

(NW) Rolling Ridge RV Resort—(Lake) *From jct Hwy 50 & US 27: Go 8 mi N on US 27. Enter on L.* ◇◇◇◇FACILITIES: 154 sites, typical site width 40 ft, 154 full hkups, (20/30/50 amps), WiFi Instant Internet at site, WiFi Internet central location ($), RV storage, dump, laundry, picnic tables, patios. ◇◇◇◇RECREATION: rec hall, equipped pavilion, swim pool, shuffleboard court 2 shuffleboard courts, activities, tennis, horseshoes. Pets welcome, breed restrict, quantity restrict. Partial handicap access. No tents. Age restrict may apply. Open all yr. Big rigs welcome. Rate in 2010 $27.75 for 2 persons. MC/VISA/DISC/AMEX/ Debit. CCUSA 50% Discount. CCUSA reservations Required, CCUSA max stay 7 days. Discount not available Dec thru Apr. High rate is weekly rate which is also discounted.

Phone: (352)429-5003
Address: 20285 Hwy 27 N, Clermont, FL 34715
Lat/Lon: 28.64036/-81.79834
Web: www.rollingridgerv.com

(SE) THOUSAND TRAILS-ORLANDO (CAMP RESORT)—(Lake) *From jct US 192 & US 27(exit 55): Go 2 mi N on US 27, then turn E for 1/4 mi. Enter on R.*

FACILITIES: 734 sites, typical site width 30 ft, 734 full hkups, (20/30/50 amps), some extd stay sites (winter), 75 pull-thrus, WiFi Internet central location, family camping, tenting, RV's/park model rentals, RV storage, laundry, ltd groc, LP gas by weight/by meter, ice, picnic tables, patios, grills, controlled access.

RECREATION: rec hall, equipped pavilion, 2 swim pools, wading pool, hot tub, boating, electric motors only, canoeing, dock, 4 rowboat/6 canoe rentals, lake fishing, mini-golf, bsktball, shuffleboard court 6 shuffleboard courts, activities, tennis, v-ball, local tours.

Pets welcome, quantity restrict. Partial handicap access. Open all yr. Big rigs welcome. Clubs welcome. MC/VISA/DISC/AMEX.

Phone: (800)723-1217
Address: 2110 US Highway 27 S, Clermont, FL 34711
Lat/Lon: 28.37613/-81.67890
Web: www.1000trails.com

SEE AD ALACHUA PAGE 93 AND AD ORLANDO PAGE 149

CLEWISTON—D-4

AH-TAH-THI-KI MUSEUM—*From west jct US 27 & Hwy 80: Go 3 mi W on Hwy 80, then 35-1/2 mi S on CR 833, then 200 feet W on W Boundary Rd. Enter on L.* Museum includes 5,000 sq ft of exhibits on a cypress dome near the Florida Everglades; lifelike displays & rare artifacts from the past. Also, living village, theater and gift shop. Open all yr.

AH-TAH-THI-KI MUSEUM—Continued on next page

Florida is not the southernmost state in the United States.

Phone: (863)902-1113
Address: HC 61, Clewiston, FL 33440
Lat/Lon: 26.32541/-80.99829
Web: www.ahtahthiki.com

SEE AD TRAVEL SECTION PAGE 69

(S) BIG CYPRESS RV RESORT—(Hendry) *From west jct US 27 & Hwy 80: Go 3 mi W on Hwy 80, then 35-1/2 mi S on CR 833. Enter on L.*

WELCOME

◇◇◇◇FACILITIES: 110 sites, typical site width 40 ft, 60 full hkups, 50 W&E, (20/30/50 amps), many extd stay sites (winter), 9 pull-thrus, WiFi Internet central location, family camping, tenting, cabins, RV storage, dump, non-guest dump $, portable dump, laundry, RV supplies, LP gas by weight/by meter, ice, picnic tables, fire rings, grills.

◇◇◇◇RECREATION: rec hall, pavilion, swim pool, hot tub, mini-golf, bsktball, play equipment, 2 shuffleboard courts, activities, horseshoes, sports field.

Pets welcome, breed restrict. Partial handicap access. Open all yr. Big rigs welcome. Escort to site. Clubs welcome. Rate in 2010 $30 for 2 persons. MC/VISA/DISC/AMEX/Debit. Member ARVC, FLARVC.

Text 107967 to (440)725-8687 to see our Visual Tour.

Phone: (800)437-4102
Address: 34950 Halls Rd, Clewiston, Fl 33440
Lat/Lon: 26.32740/-80.99913
Email: bcrvresort@semtribe.com
Web: www.seminoletribe.com/bcrvresort

SEE AD TRAVEL SECTION PAGE 69

(W) Clewiston/Lake Okeechobee KOA Kampground—(Hendry) *From West jct Hwy 80 & US 27: Go 6-1/2 mi S on US 27, then 500 feet N on CR 720. Enter on R.* ◇◇◇◇FACILITIES: 124 sites, typical site width 30 ft, 118 full hkups, 6 W&E, (20/30/50 amps), 90 pull-thrus, family camping, tenting, dump, laundry, ltd groc. ◇◇◇◇RECREATION: swim pool, playground. Pets welcome. Partial handicap access. Open all yr. Big rigs welcome. Rate in 2010 $35-41 for 2 persons. Member ARVC, FLARVC. Phone: (863)983-7078. KOA discount.

(SE) Crooked Hook RV Resort—(Palm Beach) *From west jct Hwy 80 & US 27: Go 12-1/2 mi S on US 27. Enter on R.* ◇◇◇◇FACILITIES: 186 sites, typical site width 30 ft, 186 full hkups, (30/50 amps), 4 pull-thrus, tenting, laundry. ◇◇◇◇RECREATION: swim pool, pond fishing. Pets welcome, breed restrict. Partial handicap access. Age restrict may apply. Open all yr. Big rigs welcome. Rate in 2010 $36 for 2 persons. Member ARVC, FLARVC. Phone: (863)983-7112.

(SE) OKEECHOBEE LANDINGS—(Hendry) *From west jct Hwy 80 & US 27: Go 10 mi S on US 27, then 500 feet S on Holiday Isles Blvd. Enter on L.*

WELCOME

◇◇◇FACILITIES: 270 sites, 270 full hkups, (30/50 amps), some extd stay sites (winter), heater not allowed, WiFi Instant Internet at site ($), tenting, RV storage, laundry, picnic tables, patios.

CAMPCLUB USA

◇◇◇◇RECREATION: rec hall, swim pool, hot tub, lake fishing, golf nearby, bsktball, playground, shuffleboard court 4 shuffleboard courts, activities, tennis, horseshoes, local tours.

Pets welcome, breed restrict, size restrict, quantity restrict. Partial handicap access. Open all yr. Activities in winter season only. Big rigs welcome. Clubs welcome. Rate in 2010 $38.50 for 2 persons. MC/VISA/Debit. Member ARVC, FLARVC. CCUSA 50% Discount. CCUSA reservations Required, CCUSA max stay 7 days. Discount not available Valentine's Day, Thanksgiving, Christmas and week after New Years. Heaters not allowed. Limited to 7 days per year. Discount not available in conjunction w/ any other discounts or special offers.

Phone: (863)983-4144
Address: 420 Holiday Blvd, Clewiston, FL 33440
Lat/Lon: 26.75193/-80.91358
Email: okeechobeelandings@embarqmail.com
Web: www.okeechobeelandingsrv.com

SEE AD THIS PAGE AND AD QC TRAVEL SECTION PAGE 900

Safety Harbor is the home of the historic Espiritu Santo Springs, given in 1539 by the Spanish explorer Hernando de Soto, who was searching for the legendary Fountain of Youth. Known for their curative powers, the natural springs have attracted worldwide attention.

COCOA—C-4

(W) SONRISE PALMS CHRISTIAN RV PARK—(Brevard) *From jct I-95 (exit 201) & Hwy 520: Go 1 block W on Hwy 520, then 3/4 mi S on Tucker Ln. Enter on R.*

WELCOME

◇◇◇◇FACILITIES: 98 sites, typical site width 25 ft, 83 full hkups, 15 W&E, (15/20/30/50 amps), mostly extd stay sites (winter), 5 pull-thrus, WiFi Instant Internet at site ($), phone on-site Internet (needs activ), WiFi Internet central location, family camping, RV's/park model rentals, RV storage, dump, non-guest dump $, laundry, picnic tables, patios.

CAMPCLUB USA

◇◇◇RECREATION: rec hall, swim pool, pond fishing, golf nearby, activities.

Pets welcome, breed restrict, size restrict, quantity restrict. Partial handicap access. No tents. Open all yr. Planned activities winter only. Big rigs welcome. Clubs welcome. Rate in 2010 $45 for 4 persons. MC/VISA/Debit. Member ARVC, FLARVC. CCUSA 50% Discount. CCUSA reservations Recommended, CCUSA max stay Unlimited. Discount available May thru Oct.

Phone: (321)633-4335
Address: 660 Tucker Lane, Cocoa, FL 32926
Lat/Lon: 28.35065/-80.79202
Email: sonrisepalmsrvpark@hotmail.com
Web: www.sonrisepalmsrvpark.com

SEE AD TRAVEL SECTION PAGE 73

(W) SONRISE VILLAGE RV RESORT—(Brevard) *From jct I-95 (exit 201) & Hwy 520: Go 100 yards W on Hwy 520, then 1/2 mi S on Tucker Lane. Enter on R.*

WELCOME

◇◇◇◇FACILITIES: 75 sites, typical site width 32 ft, 75 full hkups, (20/30/50 amps), mostly extd stay sites (winter), 1 pull-thrus, WiFi Instant Internet at site, phone/cable on-site Internet (needs activ), WiFi Internet central location, family camping, RV's/park model rentals, RV storage, laundry, LP gas by weight, picnic tables, patios.

SONRISE VILLAGE RV RESORT—Continued on next page

◆◆◆RECREATION: rec hall, swim pool, golf nearby, activities, horseshoes.

Pets welcome, breed restrict. Partial handicap access. No tents. Open all yr. Big rigs welcome. Clubs welcome. Rate in 2010 $43.25 for 2 persons. MC/VISA/DISC. Member FLARVC.

Phone: (321)631-0305
Address: 245 Flamingo Dr, Cocoa, FL 32926
Lat/Lon: 28.35480/-80.79235
Email: sonrisevillagerv@yahoo.com
Web: www.sonrisevillagervresort.com

SEE AD PAGE 103

COCOA BEACH—C-5

(E) MILITARY PARK (Manatee Cove Campground-Patrick AFB)—(Brevard) *From jct US 1 & Hwy 520: Go E on Hwy 520 to Hwy A1A, then S on Hwy A1A to main gate. On base.* FACILITIES: 80 sites, 46 full hkups, 34 W&E, 5 pull-thrus, tenting, dump, laundry. RECREATION: saltwater swim, boating, canoeing, saltwater fishing, playground. Partial handicap access. Open all yr. Phone: (407)494-4787.

CORTEZ—D-3

(E) BUTTONWOOD INLET RV RESORT (Formerly Key Way)—(Manatee) *From jct US 41 & Hwy 684 (Cortez Rd): Go 7 mi W on Hwy 684 (Cortez Rd). Enter on R.*

WELCOME

NEWEST RV RESORT IN CORTEZ
Nestle into all new RV Sites - just 3/4 mi to Gulf beaches. Enjoy boating - fishing - canoeing behind the Park. Walking to great restaurants - shops - commercial fishing charters & more. Come - Stay & Play with us!

◆◆◆◆FACILITIES: 43 sites, typical site width 18 ft, 40 ft max RV length, 43 full hkups, (30/50 amps), mostly extd stay sites (winter), 1 pull-thrus, WiFi Instant Internet at site, phone/cable on-site Internet (needs activ), phone Internet central location, family camping, RV storage, dump, laundry, picnic tables, patios.

◆◆◆RECREATION: rec room/area, swim pool, boating, canoeing, kayaking, ramp, dock, saltwater fishing, golf nearby, activities, (wkends).

Pets welcome, size restrict. No tents. Open all yr. Rate in 2010 $60 for 2 persons.

Phone: (941)798-3090
Address: 12316 Cortez Rd W, Cortez, FL 34215
Lat/Lon: 27.46927/-82.68637
Email: keywayrv@newbymanagement.com
Web: www.buttonwoodinlet.com

SEE AD BRADENTON PAGE 97

Florida was the 27th state admitted to the Union.

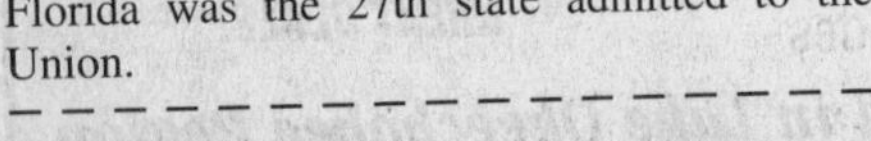

CROSS CITY—B-2

(S) SHADY OAKS RV & MOBILE HOME PARK, INC—(Dixie) *From jct US 27 Alt/US 19 and CR-349. Go 6 mi NW on US 27 - Alt/US 19, then 150 ft E on NE 300th St. Enter on L.*

WELCOME

◆◆◆FACILITIES: 31 sites, typical site width 30 ft, 31 full hkups, (30/50 amps), some extd stay sites (winter), 31 pull-thrus, cable TV, family camping, RV storage, dump, non-guest dump $, laundry, ltd groc, LP gas by weight/by meter, ice, picnic tables.

◆◆RECREATION: rec room/area, swim pool, golf nearby, shuffleboard court 2 shuffleboard courts, horseshoes.

Pets welcome, breed restrict, size restrict, quantity restrict. No tents. Open all yr. Rate in 2010 $18.50-19.50 for 2 persons. MC/VISA.

Phone: (352)498-7276
Address: 153 NE 300th St, Cross City, FL 32628
Lat/Lon: 29.61262/-83.08463

SEE AD THIS PAGE

CRYSTAL RIVER—B-3

(W) CRYSTAL ISLES—(Citrus) *From jct US 19 & Hwy C-44: Go 4 mi W on Hwy C-44. Enter on R.*

WELCOME

◆◆◆◆FACILITIES: 250 sites, typical site width 40 ft, 237 full hkups, 2 W&E, (30/50 amps), 11 no hkups, mostly extd stay sites (winter), 6 pull-thrus, cable TV, WiFi Instant Internet at site ($), phone Internet central location, tenting, cabins, dump, laundry, ltd groc, LP gas by meter, ice, picnic tables, patios, fire rings, wood.

◆◆◆◆◆RECREATION: rec hall, swim pool, wading pool, hot tub, boating, kayaking, ramp, dock, 2 pontoon rentals, lake/river/pond fishing, golf nearby, bsktball, playground, shuffleboard court 2 shuffleboard courts, activities, tennis, horseshoes, v-ball.

Pets welcome, breed restrict. Partial handicap access. Open all yr. Rates adjusted during holiday wknds. Big rigs welcome. Escort to site. Clubs welcome. Rate in 2010 $38-60 for 2 persons. MC/VISA/DISC/AMEX.

Phone: (888)783-6763
Address: 11419 W. Fort Island Trail, Crystal River, FL 34429
Lat/Lon: 28.89888/-82.62527
Email: crystal_isles@mhchomes.com
Web: www.rvonthego.com

SEE AD ALACHUA PAGE 93 AND AD DAYTONA BEACH PAGE 110

(N) Nature Coast Landings Resort—(Citrus) *From jct Hwy 40 & US 19: Go 2-1/4 mi S on US 19. Enter on L.* ◆◆◆◆◆FACILITIES: 239 sites, typical site width 40 ft, 239 full hkups, (20/30/50 amps), 6

CRYSTAL RIVER—Continued
Nature Coast Landings Resort—Continued

pull-thrus, dump, laundry. ◆◆◆RECREATION: swim pool. Pets welcome, breed restrict, quantity restrict. Partial handicap access. No tents. Open all yr. Big rigs welcome. Rate in 2010 $39 for 2 persons. Member ARVC, FLARVC. Phone: (352)447-5820.

(SE) Rock Crusher Canyon RV Park—(Citrus) *From US 19 & SR 44: Go 3-1/2 mi E on SR 44, then 1-1/4 mi S on Rock Crusher Road. Enter on L.* ◆◆◆◆◆FACILITIES: 398 sites, typical site width 35 ft, 398 full hkups, (50 amps), 4 pull-thrus, family camping, laundry. ◆◆◆◆RECREATION: swim pool, playground. Pets welcome, breed restrict, quantity restrict. Partial handicap access. No tents. Open all yr. Big rigs welcome. Rate in 2010 $32-40 for 2 persons. Member ARVC, FLARVC. Phone: (877)722-7875.

CYPRESS GARDENS—C-4

See listings at Bartow, Dundee, Haines City, Lake Wales & Winter Haven

DADE CITY—C-3

(SE) Blue Jay RV Park—(Pasco) *From jct Hwy 301 & US 98: Go 3/4 mi S on US 98. Enter on L.* ◆◆◆FACILITIES: 56 sites, typical site width 20 ft, 38 ft max RV length, 56 full hkups, (20/30/50 amps), laundry. ◆◆◆RECREATION: swim pool. Pets welcome, breed restrict, size restrict, quantity restrict. Partial handicap access. No tents. Age restrict may apply. Open all yr. Rate in 2010 $32 for 2 persons. Phone: (352)567-9678.

(SE) CITRUS HILL PARK & SALES—(Pasco) *From south jct US 301 & US 98: Go 4 mi SE on US 98. Enter on R.*

WELCOME

◆◆◆FACILITIES: 182 sites, typical site width 30 ft, 38 ft max RV length, 182 full hkups, (30/50 amps), mostly extd stay sites (winter), WiFi Instant Internet at site ($), phone/cable on-site Internet (needs activ), WiFi Internet central location, family camping, RV storage, laundry, picnic tables, controlled access.

CAMPCLUB USA

◆◆◆RECREATION: rec hall, golf nearby, shuffleboard court 3 shuffleboard courts, activities, horseshoes.

Pets welcome, breed restrict, size restrict, quantity restrict. Partial handicap access. No tents. Age restrict may apply. Open all yr. Rate in 2010 $32 for 2 persons. CCUSA 50% Discount. CCUSA reservations Recommended, CCUSA max stay 7 days. Discount available May thru Oct.

Phone: (352)567-6045
Address: 9267 US Highway 98 S, Dade City, FL 33525
Lat/Lon: 28.29201/-82.13528
Email: citrushillrv@tampabay.rr.com
Web: www.carefreervresorts.com

SEE AD TAMPA PAGES 170-171

DADE CITY—Continued on next page

DADE CITY—Continued

(SE) GROVE RIDGE RV RESORT—(Pasco) *From jct Hwy 301 & US 98: Go 1 mi S on US 98. Enter on R.*

WELCOME

◊◊◊◊FACILITIES: 247 sites, typical site width 35 ft, accepts full hkup units only, 247 full hkups, (30/50 amps), many extd stay sites (winter), WiFi Instant Internet at site ($), phone/cable on-site Internet (needs activ), WiFi Internet central location, RV's/park model rentals, dump, laundry, picnic tables.

CAMPCLUB USA

◊◊◊◊RECREATION: rec hall, rec room/area, pavilion, swim pool, golf nearby, shuffleboard court 6 shuffleboard courts, activities.

Pets welcome, breed restrict. No tents. Age restrict may apply. Open all yr. No showers. Big rigs welcome. Rate in 2010 $32 for 2 persons. MC/VISA. CCUSA 50% Discount. CCUSA reservations Required, CCUSA max stay 7 days, Cash only for CCUSA disc., CCUSA disc. not avail holidays. Not available Jan 1-Apr 1.

Phone: (352)523-2277
Address: 10721 US Hwy 98, Dade City, FL 33525
Lat/Lon: 28.31358/-82.17383
Email: groveridgerv@tampabay.RR.com
Web: www.carefreervresorts.com

SEE AD TAMPA PAGES 170-171

(SE) Many Mansions RV Park—(Pasco) *From South jct US 301 & US 98: Go 3 mi SE on US 98 (Richland exit), then 1 mi S on Hwy 35A, then 1 block E on Stewart Rd. Enter on L.* ◊◊◊FACILITIES: 235 sites, typical site width 30 ft, accepts full hkup units only, 235 full hkups, (20/30/50 amps), phone/cable on-site Internet (needs activ), WiFi Internet central location, family camping, RV storage, laundry, LP gas by weight/by meter. ◊◊◊RECREATION: rec hall, pavilion, shuffleboard court 4 shuffleboard courts, activities, horseshoes. Pets welcome, quantity restrict. Partial handicap access. No tents. Age restrict may apply. Open all yr. Big rigs welcome. Rate in 2010 $36 for 2 persons. CCUSA 50% Discount. CCUSA reservations Required, CCUSA max stay Unlimited, Cash only for CCUSA disc., Check only for CCUSA disc. Discount on daily rate only. Adult park. Children may visit for 2 week maximum. Cable @ addl charge-call for details.

CAMPCLUB USA

DADE CITY—Continued
Many Mansions RV Park—Continued

Phone: (800)359-0135
Address: 40703 Stewart Rd, Dade City, FL 33525
Lat/Lon: 28.28427/-82.14303
Email: wehavealotforyou@aol.com

(W) TOWN AND COUNTRY RV RESORT—(Pasco) *From jct US 98 & US 301: Go 4-1/4 mi N on US 301. Enter on R.*

WELCOME

◊◊◊◊FACILITIES: 200 sites, typical site width 40 ft, 200 full hkups, (30/50 amps), mostly extd stay sites (winter), phone on-site Internet (needs activ), WiFi Internet central location, family camping, RV storage, laundry, picnic tables, patios.

CAMPCLUB USA

◊◊◊◊RECREATION: rec hall, swim pool, putting green, golf nearby, shuffleboard court 4 shuffleboard courts, activities, horseshoes, local tours.

Pets welcome, breed restrict, size restrict, quantity restrict. Partial handicap access. No tents. Age restrict may apply. Open all yr. Big rigs welcome. Rate in 2010 $34 for 2 persons. Member ARVC, FLARVC. CCUSA 50% Discount. CCUSA reservations Recommended, CCUSA max stay 1 day, Cash only for CCUSA disc. Discount available May thru Sep. Age restrictions may apply.

Phone: (352)567-7707
Address: 18005 US 301 N, Dade City, FL 33523
Lat/Lon: 28.42010/-82.19091
Email: townandcountryrvresortfl@gmail.com
Web: www.townandcountryrvresortfl.com

SEE AD THIS PAGE

Florida is the only state that has 2 rivers with the same name. There is a Withlacoochee in north central Florida (Madison County) and a Withlacoochee in central Florida (Polk County).

DADE CITY—Continued

(W) TRAVELERS REST RESORT—(Pasco) *From jct I-75 (exit 293) & Hwy 41: Go 1/2 mi W on Hwy 41, then 1 mi S on Hwy 577, then 1-1/2 mi W on Johnston Rd. Enter on R.*

WELCOME

◊◊◊◊◊FACILITIES: 647 sites, typical site width 40 ft, accepts full hkup units only, 647 full hkups, (30/50 amps), many extd stay sites, 80 pull-thrus, cable TV, WiFi Instant Internet at site, phone/cable on-site Internet (needs activ), dump, non-guest dump $, laundry, LP gas by weight/by meter, patios.

CAMPCLUB USA

◊◊◊◊◊RECREATION: rec hall, rec room/area, equipped pavilion, swim pool, hot tub, lake fishing, putting green, golf nearby, bsktball, shuffleboard court 8 shuffleboard courts, activities, tennis, horseshoes, local tours.

Pets welcome, quantity restrict. Partial handicap access. No tents. Age restrict may apply. Open all yr. Planned activities only winter season. Big rigs welcome. Escort to site. Clubs welcome. Rate in

TRAVELERS REST RESORT—Continued on next page

DADE CITY—Continued
TRAVELERS REST RESORT—Continued

2010 $34.70 for 2 persons. MC/VISA. Member ARVC, FLARVC. FMCA discount. CCUSA 50% Discount. CCUSA max stay Unlimited. Discount not available Oct 1-Apr 15.

Phone: (800)565-8114
Address: 29129 Johnston Rd, Dade City, FL 33523-6128
Lat/Lon: 28.40615/-82.33370
Email: reservations@travelersrestresort.com
Web: www.travelersrestresort.com

SEE AD TAMPA PAGE 173

DAVENPORT—C-4

(NW) Deer Creek Golf & RV Resort—(Polk) *From jct I-4 (exit 55) & US 27: Go 1 mi S on US 27. Enter on L.* ◇◇◇◇◇FACILITIES: 75 sites, typical site width 45 ft, 75 full hkups, (30/50 amps), cable TV, WiFi Internet central location, dump, non-guest dump $, laundry, picnic tables, patios. ◇◇◇◇◇RECREATION: rec hall, 5 swim pools, hot tub, putting green, bsktball, playground, shuffleboard court 6 shuffleboard courts, activities, tennis. Pets welcome, breed restrict, size restrict. Partial handicap access. No tents. Open all yr. Big rigs welcome. Rate in 2010 $59-65 for 2 persons. MC/VISA/DISC. CCUSA 50% Discount. CCUSA reservations Not Accepted, CCUSA max stay See Rest. Discount available year round, based on site availability. Max stay 7 days Nov thru Apr; unlimited May thru Oct. Drive up accomodations only.

Phone: (800)424-2931
Address: 42749 Hwy 27, Davenport, FL 33837
Lat/Lon: 28.21760/-81.64309
Web: www.crfcommunities.com

(N) Florida Camp Inn (RV SPACES)—(Polk) *From jct I-4 (exit 55) & US 27: Go 4-1/2 mi N on US 27. Enter on L.* FACILITIES: 471 sites, typical site width 20 ft, 36 ft max RV length, 447 full hkups, 24 W&E, (20/30/50 amps), 30 pull-thrus, tenting, dump, laundry, ltd groc. RECREATION: swim pool. Pets welcome. Partial handicap access. Open all yr. Rate in 2010 $25 for 2 persons. Member ARVC, FLARVC. Phone: (863)424-2494.

DAVENPORT—Continued

(NE) KISSIMMEE SOUTH (formerly Three Worlds Resort)—(Polk) *From jct Hwy 547 & US 17-92: Go 3 mi N on US 17-92. Enter on R.*

WELCOME TO CAREFREE RV RESORTS!
The best of both worlds...near all the action...on the quiet side of Disney. You'll never have a shortage of choices for dining, shopping & entertainment. Come summer with us for the winter in this sunny and friendly place!

◇◇◇FACILITIES: 220 sites, typical site width 25 ft, 40 ft max RV length, 220 full hkups, (30/50 amps), many extd stay sites (winter), 5 pull-thrus, WiFi Instant Internet at site ($), phone/cable on-site Internet (needs activ), WiFi Internet central location, family camping, tenting, RV storage, dump, laundry, RV supplies, LP gas by weight, LP bottle exch, ice, picnic tables, patios, controlled access.

◇◇◇RECREATION: rec hall, swim pool, pond fishing, mini-golf, golf nearby, shuffleboard court 8 shuffleboard courts, activities, horseshoes.

Pets welcome, breed restrict, quantity restrict. Partial handicap access. Open all yr. Escort to site. Rate in 2010 $32-45 for 2 persons. MC/VISA. CCUSA 50% Discount. CCUSA reservations Recommended, CCUSA max stay 7 days. Discount available Apr thru Nov.

Phone: (863)424-1286
Address: 3700 US Hwy 17-92 N, Davenport, FL 33837
Lat/Lon: 28.20887/-81.57588
Email: threeworldsrv@tampabay.rr.com
Web: www.carefreervresorts.com

SEE AD ORLANDO PAGE 150

(N) Mouse Mountain RV Camping Resort—(Polk) *From jct I-4 (exit 58) & Hwy 532: Go 2 mi E on Hwy 532, then S on Mini Mountain Rd for 200 ft, then E on Frontage Rd for 1/2 blk. Enter on R.* ◇◇◇◇FACILITIES: 260 sites, typical site width 21 ft, 36 ft max RV length, 260 full hkups, (20/30/50 amps), 12 pull-thrus, cable TV, ($), WiFi Instant Internet at site ($), phone Internet central location, family camping, tenting, RV storage, laundry, LP gas by weight/by meter, picnic tables, patios. ◇◇◇RECREATION: rec hall, swim pool, shuffleboard court 3 shuffleboard courts, activities, horseshoes. Pets welcome, breed restrict, size restrict, quantity restrict. Partial handicap access. Open all yr. Rate in 2010 $32-36 for 2 persons. MC/VISA. Member ARVC. CCUSA 50% Discount. CCUSA reservations Required, CCUSA max stay 4 days. Dogs 35 lbs or less- No Pit Bulls, no Dobermans, no Rottweilers. Discount not available Jan thru Apr.

Phone: (800)347-6388
Address: 7500 Osceola Polk Line Rd, Davenport, FL 33896
Lat/Lon: 28.25902/-81.58576
Email: mousemountain@comcast.com
Web: www.mousemountainrv.com

(SW) Orlando SW - Fort Summit-KOA—(Polk) *From jct I-4 (exit 55) & US 27: Go 1 block S on US 27, then 1/4 mi W on S frontage road. Enter on L.* ◇◇◇◇FACILITIES: 289 sites, typical site width 25 ft, 251 full hkups, 38 W&E, (20/30/50 amps), 100 pull-thrus, family camping, tenting, dump, laundry, ltd groc. ◇◇◇◇RECREATION: swim pool, playground. Pets welcome, breed restrict, quantity restrict. Partial handicap access. Open all yr. Big rigs welcome. Rate in 2010 $55.41-65.41 for 2 persons. Member ARVC, FLARVC. KOA discount.

Phone: (800)424-1880
Address: 2525 Frontage Rd, Davenport, FL 33837
Lat/Lon: 28.22948/-81.65250
Email: fortsummitkoa@aol.com
Web: www.fortsummit.com

(NW) Themeworld RV Resort—(Polk) *From jct I-4 (exit 55) & US 27: Go 1 block S on US 27, then 1/2 mi W on Frontage Rd. Enter on L.* ◇◇◇◇FACILITIES: 282 sites, typical site width 25 ft, 282 full hkups, (30/50 amps), 60 pull-thrus, WiFi Instant Internet at site, cable on-site Internet (needs activ), WiFi Internet central location, family camping, tenting, RV storage, dump, laundry, LP gas by meter, ice, picnic tables, patios. ◇◇◇◇RECREATION: rec hall, swim pool, hot tub, bsktball, playground, shuffleboard court 2 shuffleboard courts, activities, horseshoes. Pets welcome. Partial handicap access. Open all yr. Big rigs welcome. Rate in 2010 $38-48 for 2 persons. MC/VISA/DISC/AMEX/Debit. Member ARVC, FLARVC. FMCA discount. CCUSA 50% Discount. CCUSA reservations Accepted, CCUSA max stay See Rest. Discount available for 1 week stay months of Dec thru Mar. Unlimited stay remainder of year. Both based on availability.

Phone: (863)424-8362
Address: 2727 Frontage Rd, Davenport, FL 33837
Lat/Lon: 28.22718/-81.65606
Email: info@themeworldrv.com
Web: www.themeworldrvresort.com

DAYTONA BEACH—B-4

See listings at Flagler Beach, New Smyrna Beach, Ormond Beach, Palm Coast & Port Orange.

DAYTONA BEACH—Continued on next page

BEVERLY BEACH CAMPTOWN RV RESORT—*From jct I-4 & I-95: Go 23 miles N on I-95, then 3-1/4 mi E on Hwy 100, then 3 mi N on Hwy A1A. Enter on R.*

WELCOME

SEE PRIMARY LISTING AT FLAGLER BEACH AND AD THIS PAGE

(W) Daytona Speedway KOA—(Volusia) *S'bnd from I-95 (exit 261): Go 1 block W on US 92W, then 150 feet S on CR 415 (Tomoka Farms Rd). N'bnd: From I-95 (exit 87): Go 2 blocks W on US 92W, then 150 feet S on CR 415. Enter on R.* ◊◊◊◊FACILITIES: 98 sites, typical site width 20 ft, 98 full hkups, (20/30/50 amps), 4 pull-thrus, family camping, dump, laundry. Pets welcome. No tents. Open all yr. Big rigs welcome. Rate in 2010 $20-45 for 2 persons. Member ARVC, FLARVC. Phone: (386)257-6137. KOA discount.

(W) International RV Park & Campground—(Volusia) *From jct I-95 (exit 261B) & US 92: Go 1-1/3 mi W on US 92. Enter on L.* ◊◊◊◊FACILITIES: 194 sites, typical site width 35 ft, 194 full hkups, (20/30/50 amps), 13 pull-thrus, WiFi Internet central location, family camping, tenting, dump, non-guest dump $, laundry, ltd groc, RV supplies, LP gas by weight/by meter, ice, picnic tables, patios. ◊◊◊RECREATION: rec hall, 2 swim pools, pond fishing, horseshoes. Pets welcome. Partial handicap access. Open all yr. Big rigs welcome. Rate in 2010 $25-40 for 2 persons. MC/VISA/DISC/AMEX. FCRV discount. FMCA discount. CCUSA 50% Discount. CCUSA reservations Required, CCUSA max stay Unlimited. Discount not available Race/bike week-Mar/Jul, Octoberfest/Oct-Nov. Call for details.

CAMPCLUB USA

Phone: (866)261-3698
Address: 3175 West International Speedway Blvd., Daytona Beach, FL 32124
Lat/Lon: 29.15834/-81.09798
Web: www.internationalrvdaytona.com

DAYTONA BEACH—Continued on next page

Woodall's Directory is split, East/West. You can buy a Directory with all of North America, or you can buy only the Eastern or Western editions. Browse our bookstore at www.woodalls.com/shop for more details.

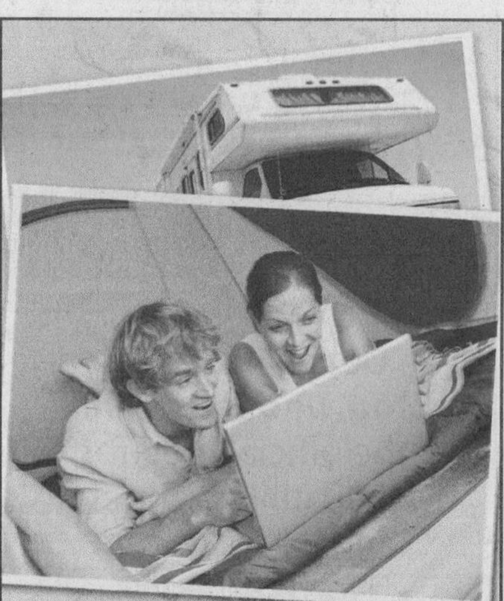

Woodall's Tip... If a park's management welcomes camping clubs, we'll indicate that in the listing.

Woodall's Tip... Time Zone, temperature & topography information is located in the Travel Section in front of each state/province.

Sugar Mill Ruins

"We Pamper the Camper"

• Gated Resort • Pull-Thrus • Laundry • Store • Planned Activities • Cable • Heated Florida Pool • Playground

(386) 427-2284 • 1050 Old Mission Rd. New Smyrna Beach, FL 32168

FREE Wi-Fi

www.sugarmilltravelpark.net

See listing at New Smyrna Beach, FL

NEW SMYRNA BEACH RV PARK

5 miles to World's Finest and Safest "Drive-On Beach"

- Big Rigs Welcome
- Large Shaded Sites
- Free Cable TV
- Full Hookups
- Pull-Thrus
- Free High Speed Internet Computer in Office
- WiFi available throughout Park
- Full RV Repair and Parts available across street from Park
- Propane ❖ Laundry
- RV Storage
- Camping Cabins with A/C and Heat
- Tenting
- Heated Pool

Exit 249A
Daytona Beach
44
2.5 mi.
Turn Right 1-1/2 mi. at Mission Drive
← I-4 20 mi.
N
95
3 mi.
2 mi.
Park Ave.
Stop Light
Indian River
Beach
Exit 244
442
Old Mission Rd.
3/4 mi.
1

High Speed Internet

www.beachcamp.net

(386) 427-3581 • 1-800-928-9962

e-mail: beachcamp@beachcamp.net

1300 Old Mission Rd., New Smyrna Beach, FL 32168

See listing at New Smyrna Beach, FL

Sharing Begins Here

Get new ideas at **blog.woodalls.com** - the official blog for the family camper and RV traveler in North America.

Enjoy daily posts from expert bloggers about great RV and family camping destinations, roads and routes you can't afford to miss, tips for making camping fun and easy, cooking videos, campground reviews and much more!

Visit **blog.woodalls.com** to check it out.

Reserve your copy of Woodall's completely updated RV Owner's Handbook. Written by Gary Bunzer, known throughout the industry as the RV Doctor, the RV Owner's Handbook includes all the information you need to keep your rig running smoothly. Easy-to-follow instructions, diagrams and illustrations cover topics from towing with a motorhome to troubleshooting electrical, water and heating systems. Ideal for both new and older model RVs. To order your copy go to www.woodalls.com/shop.

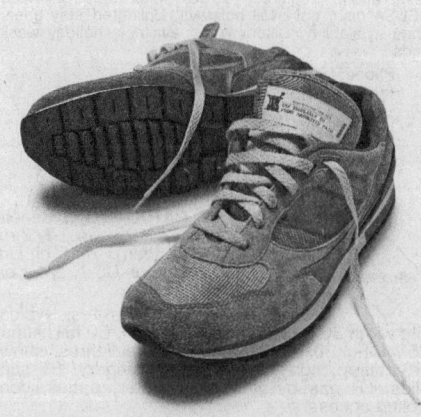

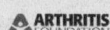

IF YOU THINK WOODALL RATINGS MEAN GOOD, BETTER, BEST....

THINK AGAIN

SEE THE "HOW TO USE" PAGES IN THE FRONT OF THIS DIRECTORY FOR AN EXPLANATION OF OUR RATING SYSTEM

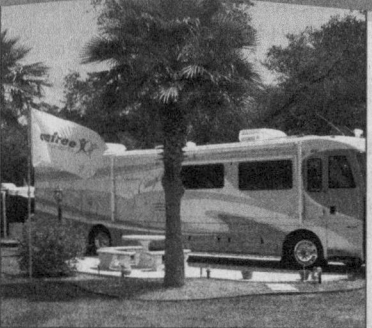

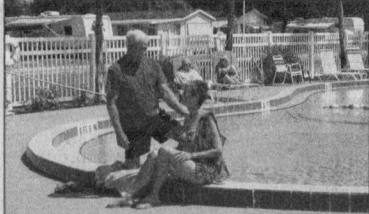

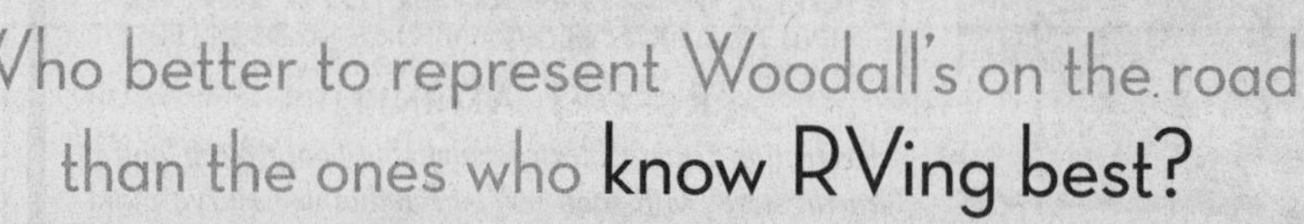

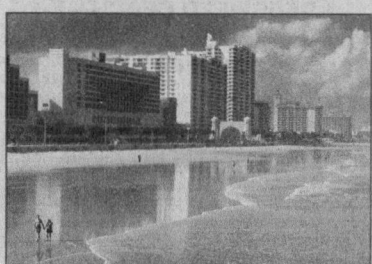

Who better to represent Woodall's on the road than the ones who **know RVing best?**

In an effort to have the industry's finest Sales Rep Teams in the field, Woodall's continually welcomes inquiries from husband and wife couples with RV experience. Several of these couples are selected to represent Woodall's each year. Those selected travel in their own RV throughout assigned territories during spring and summer months. They will make calls on RV Parks/campgrounds, RV dealers and the travel & tourism industry.

If you would like more information, email cdistl@affinitygroup.com.

DAYTONA BEACH—Continued

(S) **NOVA FAMILY CAMPGROUND**—(Volusia) *From I-95 & Hwy 421: Go 1 mi E on Hwy 421, then 1 mi N on Clyde Morris Blvd, then 3/4 mi E on Herbert St. Enter on R.*

◆◆◆FACILITIES: 350 sites, typical site width 30 ft, 117 full hkups, 92 W&E, (20/30/50 amps), 141 no hkups, some extd stay sites (winter), 10 pull-thrus, cable TV, WiFi Instant Internet at site, family camping, tenting, RV's/park model rentals, cabins, RV storage, dump, non-guest dump $, portable dump, laundry, groceries, RV supplies, LP gas by weight/by meter, ice, picnic tables, wood.

◆◆◆◆RECREATION: rec hall, rec room/area, equipped pavilion, coin games, swim pool, golf nearby, shuffleboard court 2 shuffleboard courts, activities, horseshoes, local tours.

Pets welcome ($), breed restrict. Open all yr. RV Storage avail all year, except during Bike Week; No non-guest Big Rig Dmpng drng bke wk. Escort to site. Clubs welcome. Rate in 2010 $25-33.50 for 2 persons. MC/VISA/DISC/AMEX. Member ARVC, FLARVC. FCRV discount. FMCA discount. CCUSA 50% Discount. CCUSA reservations Recommended, CCUSA max stay 2 days. Discount available Apr thru Sep. Discount not available Jul 1-5 or Sep 3-5. Not available on cabins or rv rentals.

Phone: (386)767-0095
Address: 1190 Herbert St, Port Orange, FL 32129
Lat/Lon: 29.13443/-81.01492
Email: friends@novacamp.com
Web: www.novacamp.com

SEE AD PAGE 106

DEBARY—B-4

(W) **HIGHBANKS MARINA & CAMPRESORT**—(Volusia) *From I-4 (exit 108) (circle under cloverleaf): Go 2 mi W on Dirksen Rd, then 1-3/4 mi N on US 17/92, then 2-1/2 mi W on Highbanks Rd. Enter on R.*

◆◆◆◆◆FACILITIES: 218 sites, typical site width 32 ft, 218 full hkups, (30/50 amps), mostly extd stay sites, 10 pull-thrus, cable TV, WiFi Instant Internet at site ($), family camping, tenting, RV's/park model rentals, laundry, ltd groc, RV supplies, LP gas by weight/by meter, marine gas, ice, picnic tables, patios.

◆◆◆◆◆RECREATION: rec hall, rec room/area, equipped pavilion, swim pool, boating, ramp, dock, 10 pontoon rentals, float trips, river/pond fishing, fishing supplies, golf nearby, shuffleboard court 2 shuffleboard courts, activities, horseshoes.

Pets welcome, breed restrict, size restrict, quantity restrict. Partial handicap access. Open all yr.

DEBARY—Continued
HIGHBANKS MARINA & CAMPRESORT—Continued

Tenting May 1 - Sep 30; No pets in tents or pop-ups. Big rigs welcome. Escort to site. Clubs welcome. Rate in 2010 $45-65 for 2 persons. MC/VISA/DISC/AMEX. Member ARVC, FLARVC.

Phone: (386)668-4491
Address: 488 W Highbanks Rd, DeBary, FL 32713
Lat/Lon: 28.89089/-81.35396
Email: info1@campresort.com
Web: www.campresort.com

SEE AD NEXT PAGE

(N) LAKE MONROE PARK (Volusia County Park)—(Volusia) *From jct I-4 (exit 52) & US 17/92N: Go 1/2 mi N on US 17/92N.* FACILITIES: 44 sites, 44 W&E, tenting, dump. RECREATION: boating, ramp, dock, river fishing, playground. Pets welcome. Open all yr. Phone: (386)668-3825.

(W) **SWAMP HOUSE GRILL**—*From I-4 (exit 108) (circle under Cloverleaf): Go 2 mi W on Dirksen Rd, then 1-3/4 mi N on US 17/92, then 2-1/2 mi W on Highbanks Rd. Enter on R.* Open air, riverfront, casual family-oriented restaurant on the beautiful St. John's River. Full bar and menu. Open all yr. Closed on Christmas Day. MC/VISA/DISC/AMEX.

Phone: (386)668-8891
Address: 488 W Highbanks Rd, Debary, FL 32713
Lat/Lon: 28.89089/-81.35396
Email: gm@swamphousegrill.com
Web: www.swamphousegrill.com

SEE AD NEXT PAGE

DEERFIELD BEACH—E-5

(W) **QUIET WATERS PARK (Broward County Park)**—(Broward) *From jct I-95 & SW 10th St: Go 2 mi W on SW 10th St, then 1/2 mi N on Powerline Rd. Enter on L.*

FACILITIES: 27 sites, 27 no hkups, family camping, tenting, tent rentals, ice, picnic tables, fire rings, grills, wood, controlled access.

RECREATION: pavilion, swim pool, boating, electric motors only, canoeing, kayaking, 8 rowboat/16 canoe/2 kayak/15 pedal boat rentals, lake fishing, playground, horseshoes, sports field, hiking trails, v-ball. Rec open to public.

Pets welcome. Partial handicap access. Open all yr. RV sites are not available. MC/VISA/DISC/AMEX.

Phone: (954)360-1315
Address: 401 S Powerline Rd, Deerfield Beach, FL 33442
Email: quietwaterspark@broward.org
Web: www.broward.org/parks/camping

SEE AD TRAVEL SECTION PAGE 75 AND AD DISCOVER SECTION PAGE 33

DEFUNIAK SPRINGS—E-2

(NW) **Sunset King Lake RV Resort**—(Walton) *From jct I-10 (exit 85) & US 331: Go 2 mi N on US 331, then 2 mi W on US 90, then 5-1/2 mi N on US 331, then 1 mi SW on Kings Lake Rd, then 1/4 mi SE on Paradise Island Rd. Enter on R.* ◆◆◆◆◆FACILITIES: 218 sites, typical site width 40 ft, 208 full hkups, (30/50 amps), 10 no hkups, 90 pull-thrus, cable TV, WiFi Instant Internet at site ($), WiFi Internet central location, family camping, tenting, RV storage, dump, non-guest dump $, laundry, groceries, RV supplies, LP gas by weight/by meter, ice, picnic tables, patios, wood. ◆◆◆◆◆RECREATION: rec hall, equipped pavilion, swim pool, hot tub, boating, canoeing, kayaking, ramp, dock, lake fishing, fishing supplies, mini-golf, bsktball, playground, activities, horseshoes, v-ball. Pets welcome. Partial handicap access. Open all yr. Big rigs welcome. Rate in 2010 $32 for 4 persons. MC/VISA/DISC/Debit. Member ARVC, FLARVC. FMCA discount. CCUSA 50% Discount. CCUSA reservations Required, CCUSA max stay Unlimited, CCUSA disc. not avail holidays. Unlimited stay based upon availability. Discount not available holiday weekends.

Phone: (800)774-5454
Address: 366 Paradise Island Dr, DeFuniak Springs, FL 32433
Lat/Lon: 30.78980/-86.19679
Email: reservations@sunsetking.com
Web: www.sunsetking.com

DELRAY BEACH—E-5

(S) **DEL RATON RV PARK**—(Palm Beach) *From jct Hwy 806 & I-95: Go 1-1/2 mi S on I-95 (exit 51), then 1 mi E on Linton Blvd, then 1 mi S on US-1. Enter on R.*

◆◆◆◆FACILITIES: 85 sites, typical site width 30 ft, 36 ft max RV length, 60 full hkups, 25 W&E, (20/30/50 amps), 25 pull-thrus, shower$, dump, non-guest dump $, laundry, RV supplies, LP gas by weight/by meter, patios, controlled access.

◆RECREATION: rec room/area, golf nearby, activities.

No pets. No tents. Open all yr. Planned activities during season. Escort to site. Rate in 2010 $33-39 for 2 persons. MC/VISA/Debit. Member ARVC, FLARVC.

Phone: (561)278-4633
Address: 2998 S Federal Hwy #US-1, Delray Beach, FL 33483
Lat/Lon: 26.42743/-80.07333
Email: delraton@aol.com
Web: www.DelRaton.com

SEE AD NEXT PAGE

DESTIN—F-2

(E) **CAMPING ON THE GULF**—(Walton) *From Destin Mid Bay Bridge (293) & US 98: Go 5 mi E on US 98. Enter on R.*

YOU CAN'T GET ANY CLOSER THAN THIS!
Beachfront camping, designer outlet shopping, gulf fishing, golfing, great seafood, heated pool, Wireless Internet, Deluxe Luxury Cabins. 22 new beautiful family-style bathrooms. 877-CAMPGUL(F) 877-226-7485 WWW.CAMPGULF.COM

◆◆◆◆◆FACILITIES: 201 sites, typical site width 30 ft, 185 full hkups, 16 W&E, (30/50 amps), some extd stay sites (winter), 18 pull-thrus, cable TV, WiFi Instant Internet at site, phone on-site Internet (needs activ), cable Internet central location, family camping, tenting, cabins, RV storage, dump, laundry, ltd groc, RV supplies, LP gas by weight/by meter, ice, picnic tables, patios, controlled access.

◆◆◆◆◆RECREATION: rec hall, rec room/area, equipped pavilion, 2 swim pools, saltwater swim, hot tub, saltwater/lake fishing, fishing supplies, golf nearby, bsktball, playground, shuffleboard court shuffleboard court, activities, horseshoes, v-ball.

Pets welcome. Partial handicap access. Open all yr. Big rigs welcome. Escort to site. Clubs welcome. Rate in 2010 $69-148 for 5 persons. MC/VISA. Member ARVC, FLARVC.

Text 83096 to (440)725-8687 to see our Visual Tour.

CAMPING ON THE GULF—Continued on next page

Charles and John Ringling, circus entrepreneurs, were from Florida.

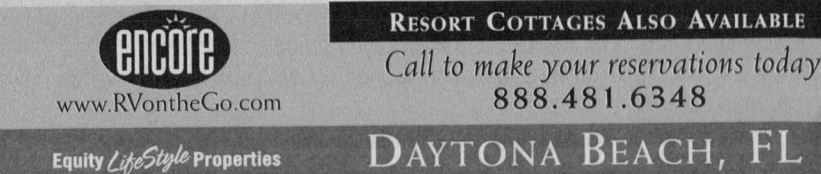

DESTIN—Continued
CAMPING ON THE GULF—Continued

Phone: (877)226-7485
Address: 10005 W Emerald Coast Pkwy (US 98), Miramar Beach, FL 32550
Lat/Lon: 30.37674/-86.34245
Email: camp@campgulf.com
Web: www.campgulf.com

SEE AD PAGES 112-113 AND AD TRAVEL SECTION PAGE 71

(N) DESTIN RECREATION AREA—(Walton) *From jct US 98 & Benning Dr.: Go N on Benning Dr. to the USAIC Reac. Area.* FACILITIES: 170 sites, 170 full hkups, (50 amps), dump, laundry. RECREATION: swim pool, saltwater fishing, playground, play equipment. No tents. Open all yr. Phone: (904)837-6215.

DESTIN—Continued on next page

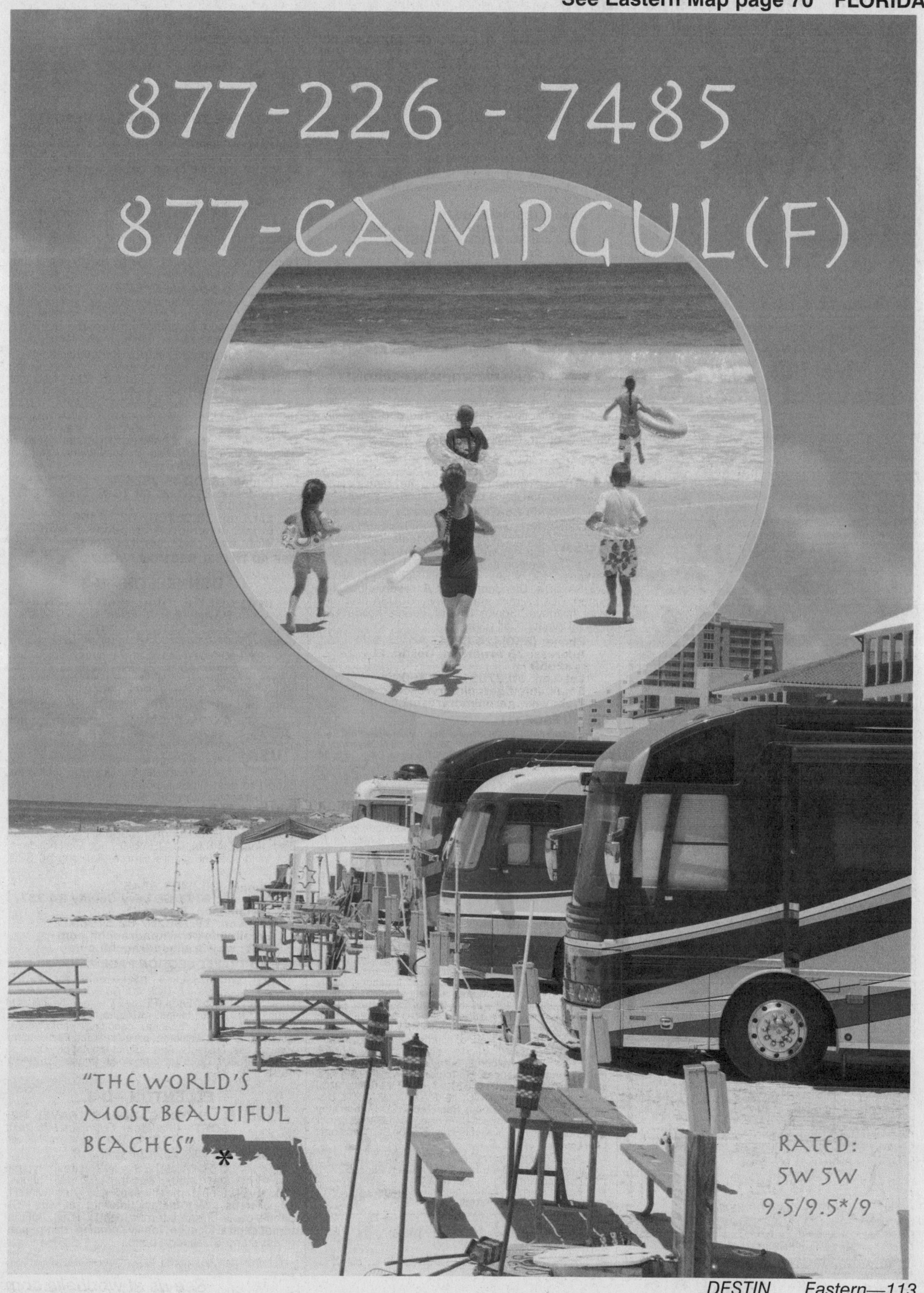
877-226 - 7485
877-CAMPGUL(F)
"THE WORLD'S
MOST BEAUTIFUL
BEACHES" *
RATED:
5W 5W
9.5/9.5*/9

DESTIN—Continued

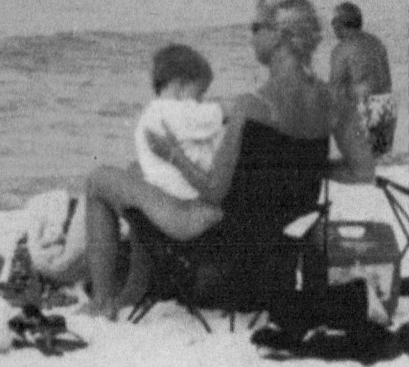

(E) **DESTIN VILLAGE RV RESORT** (RV SPACES)—(Walton) *From jct Hwy 293 (Mid Bay Bridge) and Hwy 98: Go 2-1/4 mi E on Hwy 98 to Driftwood Rd, then 1/4 mi S to Payne St. Enter on R.*

FACILITIES: 27 sites, typical site width 30 ft, accepts full hkup units only, 27 full hkups, (30/50 amps), cable TV, laundry, picnic tables, patios.

RECREATION: rec hall, swim pool, golf nearby.

Pets welcome. Partial handicap access. No tents. Open all yr. Big rigs welcome. Rate in 2010 $55-62 for 4 persons.

Phone: (850)496-6520
Address: 81 Payne St, Destin, FL 32550
Lat/Lon: 30.38121/-86.38766
Email: destinrvresort@aol.com
Web: www.destinvillage.com

SEE AD PAGE 111

(E) **GERONIMO RV RESORT**—(Walton) *From jct US 98 & Hwy 293 (Mid Bay Bridge): Go 4 mi E on US 98, then 1/2 mi S on South Geronimo St, then 500 ft W on Arnett Ln.*

ENJOY YOUR VACATION IN PARADISE!
Fun, Sun, Sand & Surf are just a short walk from our new quiet, secluded Resort, right in the midst of Destin's action! Family oriented & pet friendly, we accommodate any size rig while still leaving you lots of stretching room!

◇◇◇◇◇FACILITIES: 34 sites, 29 full hkups, 5 W&E, (30/50 amps), some extd stay sites (winter), cable TV, WiFi Instant Internet at site, family camping, dump, non-guest dump $, laundry, patios.

RECREATION: golf nearby, sports field.

Pets welcome, breed restrict. Partial handicap access. No tents. Open all yr. Big rigs welcome. Escort to site. Clubs welcome. Rate in 2010 $42-70 for 5 persons. MC/VISA. Member ARVC, FLARVC. CCUSA 50% Discount. CCUSA reservations Required, CCUSA max stay 4 days, CCUSA disc. not avail holidays. Space limited during holidays & special events. Call park.

Phone: (850)424-6801
Address: 75 Arnett Ln, Destin, FL 32550
Lat/Lon: 30.37851/-86.36099
Email: info@geronimorvresort.com
Web: www.geronimorvresort.com

SEE AD PAGE 111

(N) MILITARY PARK (Destin Recreation Area-Fort Benning GA)—(Okaloosa) *Off base. From jct US 98 & Benning Dr in town: Go N on Benning Dr to the USAIC Rec Area.* FACILITIES: 46 sites, 46 full hkups, dump, laundry. RECREATION: swim pool, saltwater swim, ramp, dock, saltwater fishing, play equipment. No pets. No tents. Open all yr. Phone: (706)545-5600.

DOVER—C-3

(SE) **Citrus Hills RV Park**—(Hillsborough) *From jct I-75 & Hwy 60: Go 8 mi E on Hwy 60. Enter on R.* ◇◇◇FACILITIES: 283 sites, typical site width 20 ft, 38 ft max RV length, 283 full hkups, (30/50 amps), family camping, tenting, laundry. Pets welcome, breed restrict, size restrict. Open all yr. Rate in 2010 $28 for 2 persons. Member ARVC, FLARVC. Phone: (813)737-4770.

(N) **Tampa East RV Resort**—(Hillsborough) *From jct I-4 (exit 14) & McIntosh Rd: Go 1 block S on McIntosh Rd. Enter on R.* ◇◇◇◇FACILITIES: 694 sites, typical site width 40 ft, 659 full hkups, 35 W&E, (30/50 amps), WiFi Instant Internet at site ($), phone on-site Internet (needs activ), WiFi Internet central location, family camping, RV storage, dump, non-guest dump $, laundry, RV supplies, LP gas by weight/by meter, picnic tables, patios. ◇◇◇◇◇RECREATION: rec hall, 3 swim pools, hot tub, pond fishing, playground, shuffleboard court 8 shuffleboard courts, activities, horseshoes. Pets welcome, breed restrict, size restrict. Partial handicap access. No tents. Open all yr. Big rigs welcome. Rate in 2010 $31-53 for 2 persons. MC/VISA/DISC. Member ARVC, FLARVC. CCUSA 50% Discount. CCUSA reservations Required, CCUSA max stay 7days, Cash only for CCUSA disc., CCUSA disc. not avail holidays. Not available Nov 30-Apr 30. Additional charges may apply.

Phone: (800)454-7336
Address: 4630 Mc Intosh Rd, Dover, FL 33527
Lat/Lon: 28.01950/-82.24502
Email: sfarnum@suncommunities.com
Web: www.tamparvresort.com

Dwight Gooden, baseball player, is from Florida.

DUNEDIN—C-3

(N) **DUNEDIN RV RESORT**—(Pinellas) *From jct Hwy-586 & Alt US-19 N: Go 3/4 mi N on Alt US-19. Enter on R.*

WELCOME TO CAREFREE RV RESORTS!
Enjoy, explore & experience Clearwater beaches & Honeymoon Island. Walk the Pinellas Trail or jump in the heated pool. Plus, bring your family & friends to stay at the Blue Moon Inn, an on-site Key West style B & B!

◇◇◇◇◇FACILITIES: 233 sites, typical site width 30 ft, 233 full hkups, (20/30/50 amps), mostly extd stay sites, 18 pull-thrus, WiFi Instant Internet at site, WiFi Internet central location, family camping, tenting, RV storage, dump, non-guest dump $, laundry, RV supplies, LP gas by weight/by meter, ice, picnic tables, patios.

◇◇◇◇◇RECREATION: rec hall, swim pool, river fishing, golf nearby, bsktball, playground, shuffleboard court 6 shuffleboard courts, activities, horseshoes, hiking trails, local tours.

Pets welcome, breed restrict. Partial handicap access. Open all yr. Planned group activities winter only. Big rigs welcome. Escort to site. Clubs welcome. Rate in 2010 $38-64 for 2 persons. MC/VISA/DISC/AMEX. Member ARVC, FLARVC. FMCA discount. CCUSA 50% Discount. CCUSA reservations Recommended, CCUSA max stay 4 days, CCUSA disc. not avail holidays. Discount not available Nov thru Apr. Based on availability. Premium sites not discounted.

Phone: (800)345-7504
Address: 2920 US Alt 19 N, Dunedin, FL 34698
Lat/Lon: 28.05706/-82.77468
Email: dunedinrv@tampabay.rr.com
Web: www.carefreervresorts.com

SEE AD TRAVEL SECTION PAGE 76

DUNNELLON—B-3

(NW) **GOETHE TRAILHEAD RANCH & RV PARK**—(Levy) *From US 19 & Hwy 121: Go 5 mi E on Hwy 121, then 1/2 mi S on CR 337. Enter on L.*

◇◇◇FACILITIES: 71 sites, typical site width 45 ft, 71 full hkups, (20/30/50 amps), 6 pull-thrus, WiFi Instant Internet at site, family camping, tenting, RV's/park model rentals, dump, non-guest dump $, ltd groc, RV supplies.

◇◇◇RECREATION: pavilion, golf nearby, bsktball, playground, horseshoes, v-ball.

Pets welcome. Partial handicap access. Open all yr. Big rigs welcome. Escort to site. Clubs welcome. Rate in 2010 $40 for 2 persons. MC/VISA. Member ARVC, FLARVC. CCUSA 50% Discount. CCUSA reservations Recommended, CCUSA max stay 1 day, Cash only for CCUSA disc., CCUSA disc. not avail F,Sa, CCUSA disc. not avail S,M, CCUSA disc. not avail holidays. Not valid special events. Horse stall charge $20, plus shavings.

Phone: (352)489-8545
Address: 9171 SE Levy County Rd 337, Dunnellon, FL 34431
Lat/Lon: 29.19826/-82.57989
Email: info@trailheadranchfl.com
Web: www.trailheadranchfl.com

SEE AD TRAVEL SECTION PAGE 72

(W) **Withlacoochee Backwaters RV Park**—(Levy) *From jct US 41 & CR 40: Go 6 mi W on CR 40. Enter on L.* ◇◇◇FACILITIES: 21 sites, typical site width 30 ft, 21 full hkups, (30/50 amps), 3 pull-thrus. ◇◇◇RECREATION: boating, canoeing, ramp, dock, lake fishing. Pets welcome, breed restrict. Partial handicap access. No tents. Age restrict may apply. Open all yr. Rate in 2010 $25 for 2 persons. Phone: (352)489-6691.

ELLENTON—D-3

(NE) **ELLENTON GARDENS TRAVEL RESORT**—(Manatee) *From jct I-75 (exit 224) & US-301: Go 1-1/4 mi NE on US-301. Enter on L.*

◇◇◇FACILITIES: 192 sites, typical site width 20 ft, 192 full hkups, (20/30/50 amps), mostly extd stay sites (winter), 1 pull-thrus, WiFi Instant Internet at site ($), phone/cable on-site Internet (needs activ), WiFi Internet central location, family camping, dump, non-guest dump $, laundry, patios.

ELLENTON GARDENS TRAVEL RESORT—Continued on next page

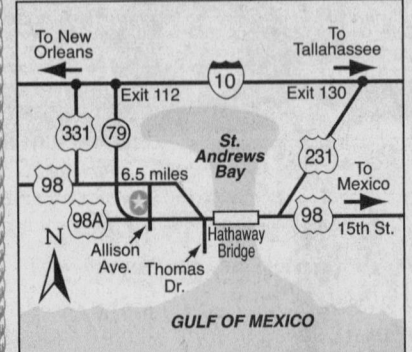

ELLENTON—Continued
ELLENTON GARDENS TRAVEL RESORT—Continued

◊◊◊RECREATION: rec hall, swim pool, pond fishing, golf nearby, shuffleboard court 6 shuffleboard courts, activities, horseshoes.

Pets welcome, breed restrict, size restrict, quantity restrict. Partial handicap access. No tents. Open all yr. Planned activities winter only. Big rigs welcome. Clubs welcome. Rate in 2010 $38 for 2 persons. MC/VISA/Debit. CCUSA 50% Discount. CCUSA reservations Recommended, CCUSA max stay 14 days, Cash only for CCUSA disc. Discount available Apr thru Nov. Cable tv surcharge-call for details.

Phone: (941)722-0341
Address: 7310 Hwy 301 N, Ellenton, FL 34222
Lat/Lon: 27.53757/-82.48847
Email: ellentonrv@tampabay.rr.com
Web: www.carefreervresorts.com

SEE AD SARASOTA PAGE 164

ESTERO—E-3

(W) KORESHAN STATE PARK—(Lee) *From jct I-75 (exit 19) & Corkscrew Rd: Go 2 mi W on Corkscrew Rd to US 41.* FACILITIES: 60 sites, 60 W&E, tenting, dump, laundry. RECREATION: boating, canoeing, ramp, saltwater fishing, playground. Open all yr. Phone: (941)992-0311.

EUSTIS—B-4

(N) SOUTHERN PALMS RV RESORT—(Lake) *From jct US 441 & Hwy 19: Go 3-1/2 mi N on Hwy 19, then 1/2 mi W on CR 44 (not SR 44). Enter on R.*

◊◊◊FACILITIES: 953 sites, typical site width 28 ft, 953 full hkups, (30/50 amps), many extd stay sites, cable TV, WiFi Instant Internet at site ($), phone Internet central location, family camping, RV's/park model rentals, RV storage, dump, non-guest dump $, laundry.

◊◊◊◊◊RECREATION: rec hall, rec room/area, 2 swim pools, hot tub, golf nearby, shuffleboard court 18 shuffleboard courts, activities, horseshoes, local tours.

Pets welcome, quantity restrict. Partial handicap access. No tents. Open all yr. Planned group activities in winter only. Big rigs welcome. Escort to site. Clubs welcome. Rate in 2010 $36-44 for 2 persons. MC/VISA/DISC/AMEX. Member ARVC, FLARVC.

Phone: (866)778-8253
Address: 1 Avocado Lane, Eustis, FL 32726
Lat/Lon: 28.87549/-81.69583
Web: www.rvonthego.com

SEE AD ALACHUA PAGE 93

EVERGLADES CITY—E-4

(N) Everglades Isle Motorcoach Retreat—(Collier) *From jct US 41 & Hwy 29: Go 3 mi S on Hwy 29. Enter on R.* ◊◊◊◊◊FACILITIES: 61 sites, typical site width 38 ft, accepts full hkup units only, 61 full hkups, (20/30/50 amps), laundry. ◊◊◊◊◊RECREATION: swim pool, boating, canoeing, ramp, dock, saltwater/river fishing. Pets welcome. Partial handicap access. No tents. Open all yr. Big rigs welcome. Rate in 2010 $100-150 for 4 persons. Phone: (239)695-2600.

EVERGLADES NATIONAL PARK—F-4

See listings at Chokoloskee, Everglades City, Florida City, Homestead & Maimi

FERNANDINA BEACH—A-4

(E) FORT CLINCH STATE PARK—(Nassau) *From jct Hwy-A1A & Hwy-105: Go 3 mi NE on Hwy-A1A.* FACILITIES: 61 sites, 61 W&E, (20/30 amps), tenting, dump, laundry. RECREATION: saltwater swim, boating, canoeing, ramp, saltwater fishing, playground. Partial handicap access. Open all yr. Phone: (904) 277-7274.

FIESTA KEY—F-5

(W) Fiesta Key RV Resort—(Monroe) *On US 1 at mile marker 70. Enter on R.* ◊◊◊FACILITIES: 319 sites, typical site width 25 ft, 216 full hkups, 72 W&E, (20/30/50 amps), 31 no hkups, 35 pull-thrus, family camping, tenting, dump, laundry, groceries. ◊◊◊RECREATION: swim pool, boating, canoeing, ramp, dock, saltwater fishing, playground. Pets welcome. Partial handicap access. Open all yr. Big rigs welcome. Rate in 2010 $69-119 for 2 persons. Member ARVC, FLARVC. Phone: (305)664-4922.

Woodall's Tip... Find free Tourism Information in the Travel Section

FLAGLER BEACH—B-4

(N) BEVERLY BEACH CAMPTOWN RV RESORT—(Flagler) *From jct I-95 (exit 284) & Hwy 100: Go 3-1/4 mi E on Hwy 100, then 3 mi N on Hwy A1A. Enter on R.*

◊◊◊◊◊FACILITIES: 154 sites, typical site width 25 ft, 150 full hkups, 4 W&E, (30/50 amps), some extd stay sites (winter), cable TV, WiFi Instant Internet at site, family camping, tenting, cabins, dump, non-guest dump $, laundry, groceries, RV supplies, ice, picnic tables.

◊◊◊RECREATION: rec hall, rec room/area, pavilion, saltwater swim, saltwater fishing, fishing supplies.

Pets welcome. Partial handicap access. Open all yr. Big rigs welcome. Clubs welcome. Rate in 2010 $50-130 for 2 persons. MC/VISA/DISC. Member ARVC, FLARVC.

Text 107920 to (440)725-8687 to see our Visual Tour.

Phone: (800)255-2706
Address: 2815 N Ocean Shore Blvd, Flagler Beach, FL 32136
Lat/Lon: 29.52184/-81.14783
Email: beverlybeachcamptown@yahoo.com
Web: www.beverlybeachcamptown.com

SEE AD DAYTONA BEACH PAGE 107 AND AD TRAVEL SECTION PAGE 81 AND AD TRAVEL SECTION PAGE 74

(W) BULOW PLANTATION RV RESORT—(Flagler) *From I-95 (exit 284/Old 91) & Hwy 100: Go 1/4 mi E on Hwy 100, then 3 mi S on Old Kings Rd. Enter on L.*

◊◊◊FACILITIES: 385 sites, typical site width 39 ft, 250 full hkups, (30/50 amps), 135 no hkups, some extd stay sites, 42 pull-thrus, cable TV, WiFi Internet central location ($), family camping, tenting, RV's/park model rentals, cabins, dump, non-guest dump $, laundry, ltd groc, RV supplies, LP gas by weight/by meter, ice, picnic tables, patios, wood.

◊◊◊RECREATION: rec hall, rec room/area, pavilion, coin games, swim pool, boating, dock, lake fishing, golf nearby, shuffleboard court 2 shuffleboard courts, activities, horseshoes, hiking trails, local tours.

Pets welcome, breed restrict. Partial handicap access. Open all yr. Rates higher during special events. Clubs welcome. Rate in 2010 $35-45 for 2 persons. MC/VISA/DISC/AMEX. Member ARVC, FLARVC.

Phone: (386)439-9200
Address: 3345 Old Kings Rd South, Flagler Beach, FL 32136-1328
Lat/Lon: 29.43416/-81.15552
Email: rvinfo@mhchomes.com
Web: www.rvonthego.com

SEE AD ALACHUA PAGE 93 AND AD DAYTONA BEACH PAGE 110 AND AD TRAVEL SECTION PAGE 81

FLAGLER BY THE SEA CAMPGROUND—(Flagler) *From jct I-95 (exit 284) & Hwy 100: Go 3-1/4 mi E on Hwy 100, then 3-1/2 mi N on Hwy A1A. Enter on R.*

◊◊FACILITIES: 31 sites, typical site width 25 ft, 31 full hkups, (30/50 amps), mostly extd stay sites (winter), 13 pull-thrus, cable TV, phone Internet central location, family camping, laundry, RV supplies, ice, picnic tables.

◊◊RECREATION: saltwater swim, saltwater fishing, golf nearby.

Pets welcome, breed restrict. No tents. Open all yr. Rate in 2010 $50-60 for 2 persons. MC/VISA/DISC. Member ARVC, FLARVC.

Phone: (800)434-2124
Address: 2981 N Oceanshore Blvd, Flagler Beach, FL 32136
Lat/Lon: 29.52732/-81.15090

SEE AD TRAVEL SECTION PAGE 81

(S) GAMBLE ROGERS MEMORIAL STATE PARK AT FLAGLER BEACH—(Flagler) *From jct Hwy-100 & Hwy-A1A: Go 2 mi S on Hwy-A1A.*

FACILITIES: 34 sites, 30 ft max RV length, 34 W&E, tenting, dump, picnic tables, grills.

RECREATION: saltwater swim, boating, canoeing, ramp, saltwater fishing, hiking trails.

Pets welcome ($). Open all yr. MC/VISA.

FLAGGER BEACH—Continued
GAMBLE ROGERS MEMORIAL STATE PARK AT FLAGGER BEACH—Continued

Phone: (386)517-2086
Address: 3100 South A1A, Flagler Beach, FL 32136
Lat/Lon: 29.434000/-81.106389
Email: gambler@pfl.net
Web: www.abfla.com/parks/gamblerogers

SEE AD TRAVEL SECTION PAGE 81

FLORIDA CITY—E-5

(E) FLORIDA CITY CAMPSITE (City Park)—(Dade) *From jct Hwy 27, US 1 & Southern Terminus of Florida Tpk: Go 1 block W on Hwy 9336 (Palm Dr), then 1/2 mi N on Hwy 997, then 500 feet W on 336th St, then 500 feet N on 2nd Ave. Enter on R.*

GATEWAY TO THE KEYS
Convenient RV Camping at gateway to FL Keys and the Everglades. Nearby Alligator Farms, Everglades Airboat Rides & Homestead/Miami Speedway. Enjoy the the tropical climate, ocean views & great fishing/boating of S. Florida.

FACILITIES: 310 sites, typical site width 20 ft, 253 full hkups, 27 W&E, (20/30/50 amps), 30 no hkups, some extd stay sites (winter), heater not allowed, WiFi Internet central location, family camping, tenting, dump, non-guest dump $, laundry, LP gas by weight/by meter.

RECREATION: playground, horseshoes.

Pets welcome. Partial handicap access. Open all yr. Big rigs welcome. Clubs welcome. MC/VISA.

Phone: (305)248-7889
Address: 601 NW 3rd Ave, Florida City, FL 33034
Lat/Lon: 25.45690/-80.48080

SEE AD HOMESTEAD PAGE 128

FORT LAUDERDALE—E-5

BROWARD COUNTY PARKS & RECREATION DIVISION—5 County parks: Topeekeegee Yugnee, Easterlin, Markham, C.B. Smith & Quiet Waters. Full hookups to rustic tent camping. Recreation includes water playgrounds, Disc Golf Course, Target Gun Range, Model Airplane field, Raquetball, & a dog park. Open all yr.

Phone: (954)357-8117
Address: 950 NW 38th St, Oakland Park, FL 33309
Lat/Lon: 26.17352/-80.15814
Email: cybaker@broward.org

SEE AD TRAVEL SECTION PAGE 75 AND AD TRAVEL SECTION PAGE 69 AND AD DISCOVER SECTION PAGE 33

DIXIE TRAILER SUPPLY—*From jct I-95 (exit 31) & Hwy 816 (Oakland Blvd): Go 1-3/4 mi E on Hwy 816 (Oakland Blvd), then 3/4 mi N on Hwy 811 (Dixie Hwy). Enter on L.* SERVICES: sells parts/accessories. Boat trailer supplies & sales. Open all yr. MC/VISA/Debit.

Phone: (954)565-9210
Address: 4135 N Dixie Hwy, Ft Lauderdale, FL 33334
Lat/Lon: 26.17748/-80.13418

SEE AD THIS PAGE

(NW) Kozy Kampers RV Park—(Broward) *From jct Hwy 816 (Oakland Park Blvd) & I-95: Go 2 mi N on I-95 (exit 32), then 2-1/2 mi W on Commercial Blvd. Enter on R.* ◊◊◊FACILITIES: 104 sites, typical site

Kozy Kampers RV Park—Continued on next page

FORT LAUDERDALE—Continued
Kozy Kampers RV Park—Continued

width 22 ft, 104 full hkups, (30/50 amps), 13 pull-thrus, dump, laundry. Pets welcome, breed restrict, quantity restrict. No tents. Open all yr. Big rigs welcome. Rate in 2010 $39-49 for 2 persons. Member ARVC, FLARVC. Phone: (954)731-8570.

(S) North Coast RV Park & Marina—(Broward) *From Jct Hwy 816 (Oakland Park Blvd) & I-95: Go 7-3/4 mi S on I-95 (exit 23), then 1/4 mi W on Hwy 818 (Griffin Rd), then 1/4 mi N on Anglers Ave. Enter on R.* ◇◇◇◇FACILITIES: 35 sites, typical site width 35 ft, accepts full hkup units only, 35 full hkups, (20/30/50 amps). ◇◇RECREATION: boating, canoeing, dock, saltwater fishing. Pets welcome, size restrict. No tents. Age restrict may apply. Open all yr. Big rigs welcome. Phone: (954)983-2083.

FORT LAUDERDALE—Continued

✱ NORTH TRAIL RV CENTER—*From jct Hwy 816 (Oakland Park Blvd) & I-95: Go 7-3/4 mi S on I-95 (exit 23), then 1/4 mi W on Hwy 818 (Griffin Rd), then 3/4 mi on Angeles Ave. Enter on R.* SALES: travel trailers, 5th wheels, toy hauler, Class A motorhomes, Class C motorhomes, Class B motorhomes, pre-owned unit sales. SERVICES: full-time mech, RV appliance repair, RV rentals. Open all yr. MC/VISA/DISC/AMEX.

WELCOME

Florida State Flower: Orange Blossom

FORT LAUDERDALE—Continued
NORTH TRAIL RV CENTER—Continued

Phone: (877)289-3127
Address: 4300 Ravenswood Rd, Dania Beach, FL 33312
Lat/Lon: 26.06958/-80.16856
Email: sales@northtrailrv.com
Web: www.northtrailrv.com

SEE AD FORT MYERS PAGE 120

FORT LAUDERDALE—Continued on next page

Florida State Bird: Mockingbird

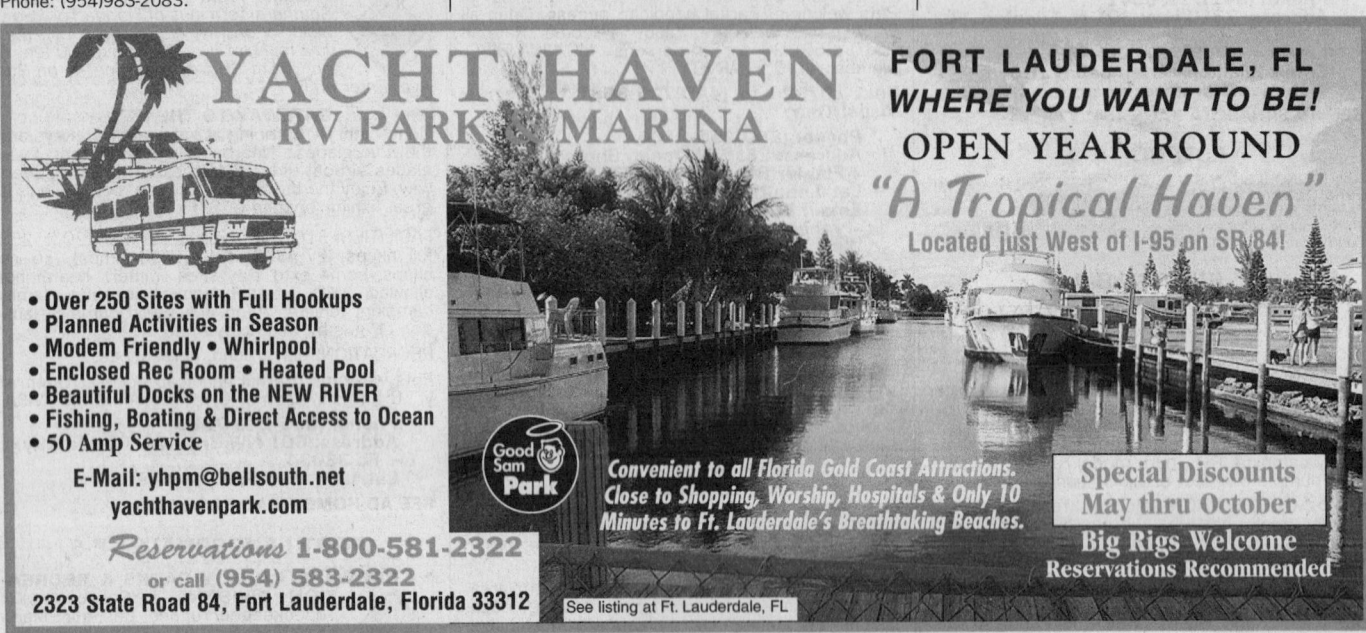

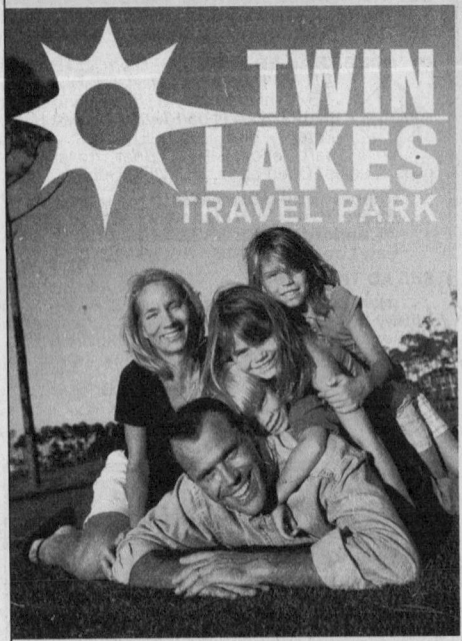

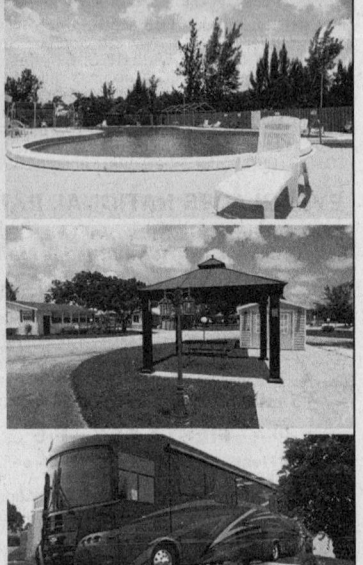

FORT LAUDERDALE—Continued

(NW) PARADISE ISLAND—(Broward) *From jct I-95 (exit 31) & Hwy 816 (Oakland Park Blvd): Go 1/2 mi W on Oakland Park Blvd, then 1 block S on NW 21st Ave. Enter on R.*

SOUTH FLORIDA'S FINEST!

A lush tropical setting in the heart of Ft. Lauderdale. Large shade trees & well kept level sites. Try our busy activity schedule or relax and enjoy the beauty & serenity of Paradise Island. Close to all Florida has to offer!

◊◊◊◊FACILITIES: 232 sites, typical site width 25 ft, 232 full hkups, (20/30/50 amps), some extd stay sites (winter), 25 pull-thrus, WiFi Instant Internet at site ($), family camping, dump, non-guest dump $, laundry, RV supplies, ice, picnic tables, patios.

◊◊◊◊RECREATION: rec hall, rec room/area, equipped pavilion, swim pool, golf nearby, shuffleboard court 2 shuffleboard courts, activities.

Pets welcome, breed restrict, size restrict. Partial handicap access. No tents. Open all yr. Group activities winter only. Big rigs welcome. Escort to site. Clubs welcome. Rate in 2010 $35-45 for 2 persons. MC/VISA/DISC/AMEX/Debit. Member ARVC, FLARVC. FMCA discount. CCUSA 50% Discount. CCUSA reservations Accepted, CCUSA max stay 21 days. Discount not available Nov 1-Mar 31.

Phone: (800)487-7395
Address: 2121 NW 29th Ct., Fort Lauderdale, FL 33311
Lat/Lon: 26.16344/-80.17124
Email: info@paradiserv.com
Web: www.paradiserv.com

SEE AD THIS PAGE AND AD TRAVEL SECTION PAGE 74

Find a park or campground Woodall's does not list? Tell us about it! Use Reader Comment Forms located after the Alphabetical Quick Reference pages.

FORT LAUDERDALE—Continued

(NW) SUNSHINE HOLIDAY RV PARK—(Broward) *From jct I-95 (exit 31) & Hwy 816 (Oakland Park Blvd): Go 1 mi W on Oakland Park Blvd. Enter on L.*

◊◊◊FACILITIES: 133 sites, typical site width 28 ft, 133 full hkups, (30/50 amps), many extd stay sites (winter), 80 pull-thrus, WiFi Instant Internet at site ($), RV storage, laundry, patios, controlled access.

◊◊◊RECREATION: rec hall, pavilion, 2 swim pools, golf nearby, shuffleboard court 2 shuffleboard courts, activities, horseshoes.

Pets welcome, breed restrict. No tents. Open all yr. Big rigs welcome. Clubs welcome. Rate in 2010 $32-50 for 2 persons. MC/VISA/AMEX/Debit. Member ARVC, FLARVC.

Phone: (954)731-1722
Address: 2802 W Oakland Park Blvd, Fort Lauderdale, FL 33311
Lat/Lon: 26.16469/-80.18120
Web: www.rvonthego.com

SEE AD ALACHUA PAGE 93

(SW) TWIN LAKES TRAVEL PARK—(Broward) *From jct Hwy 816 (Oakland Blvd) & I-95 (exit 31): Go 5-1/2 mi S on I-95 (exit 27), then 3-3/4 mi W on Hwy 84, then 1/2 mi S on Hwy 441, then 1/4 mi W on 36th St, then 1/2 mi N on Burris Rd. Enter on L.*

SOUTH FLORIDA'S LUXURY RV RESORT

TWIN LAKES TRAVEL PARK has over 40 acres of land. Paved sites w/electrical & water hookups, lake views, 2 pools and social events in the large Clubhouse. Close to all major highways. Call (800) 327-8182 to book your stay.

◊◊◊◊FACILITIES: 379 sites, 379 full hkups, (20/30/50 amps), many extd stay sites (winter), 300 pull-thrus, WiFi Instant Internet at site, family camping, tenting, RV storage, dump, laundry, ice, picnic tables, patios, controlled access.

◊◊◊◊RECREATION: rec hall, pavilion, swim pool, wading pool, golf nearby, shuffleboard court 3 shuffleboard courts, activities, horseshoes.

FORT LAUDERDALE—Continued
TWIN LAKES TRAVEL PARK—Continued

Pets welcome, breed restrict. Partial handicap access. Open all yr. Big rigs welcome. Escort to site. Clubs welcome. Rate in 2010 $40-85 for 2 persons. MC/VISA/DISC. Member ARVC, FLARVC.

Phone: (800)327-8182
Address: 3055 Burris Rd, Fort Lauderdale, FL 33314
Lat/Lon: 26.08403/-80.20707
Email: twinlakespark@gmail.com
Web: www.twinlakesrvtravelpark.com

SEE AD PAGE 116

(S) YACHT HAVEN PARK & MARINA—(Broward) *From jct Hwy 816 (Oakland Park Blvd) & I-95: Go 5-1/2 mi S on I-95 (exit 25), then 500 feet W on Hwy 84. Enter on R.*

◊◊◊◊FACILITIES: 250 sites, typical site width 35 ft, 250 full hkups, (20/30/50 amps), many extd stay sites (winter), phone Internet central location, family camping, dump, non-guest dump $, laundry, ice, patios, controlled access.

◊◊◊◊RECREATION: rec hall, swim pool, hot tub, boating, dock, saltwater/river fishing, golf nearby, shuffleboard court 2 shuffleboard courts, activities.

Pets welcome, breed restrict, size restrict, quantity restrict. Partial handicap access. No tents. Open all yr. Planned group activities winter only. Big rigs welcome. Clubs welcome. Rate in 2010 $37-71 for 2 persons. MC/VISA/Debit. Member ARVC, FLARVC.

Phone: (954)583-2322
Address: 2323 State Road 84, Ft Lauderdale, FL 33312
Lat/Lon: 26.08794/-80.17229
Email: yhpm@bellsouth.net
Web: www.yachthavenpark.com

SEE AD PAGE 116

FORT MYERS—D-3

(E) Cypress Woods RV Resort—(Lee) *From jct Hwy 82 & I-75: Go 1-1/2 mi N on I-75 (exit 139), then 1/2 mi E on Luckett Rd. Enter on L.* ◊◊◊◊◊FACILI-

Cypress Woods RV Resort—Continued on page 120

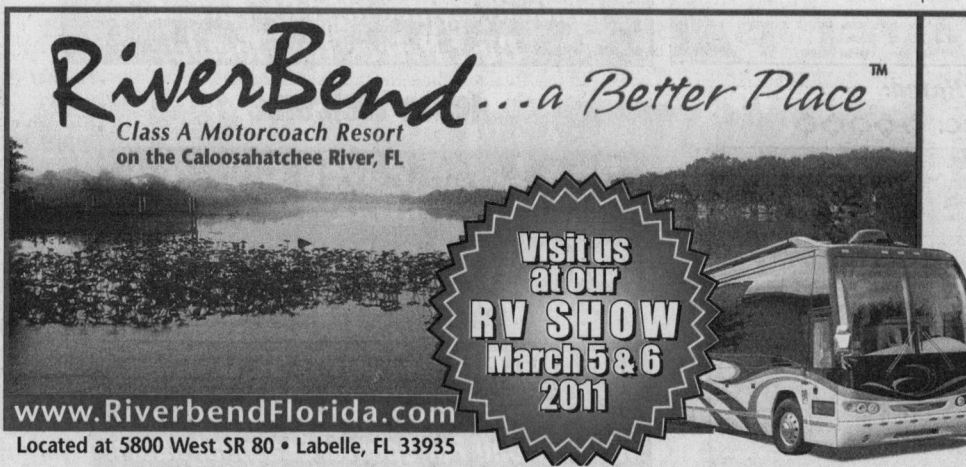

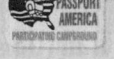

WOODSMOKE CAMPING RESORT

Fort Myers Naples

YES! Everyone from 8 to 80 comes to WOODSMOKE, near Fort Myers in Southwest Florida, because we offer the most beautiful campsites...AND, the friendliest people. In the center of the great gulf beaches, fishing, golf, Sanibel Island, Professional Ice Hockey, Outlet Malls, Edison Home and many other area attractions. Great Restaurants Nearby! Only 4 mi from I-75 (Exit 123).

WHITE SANDY BEACHES NEARBY

- 300 Wooded Campsites with Full Hookups • 75' Concrete Pull-Thrus • Paved Roads
- 4 Clean Bathhouses • Large A/C Rec Hall • Fishing Lake • Giant Heated Pool • Whirlpool
- Nature Trail Boardwalk • Very Easy In & Out • Fitness Center • GREAT ACTIVITIES

Distinctive & Beautiful RV Park Models
Best Prices In Florida

Woodall's Rated:
Fac: ◆◆◆◆ Rec: ◆◆◆◆◆

New Large Paved Concrete Pull-Thru Sites 50 Amp
BIG RIGS WELCOME!

Park Model Sales

BEAUTIFUL WOODED SEASONAL SITES AVAILABLE
Write or Call For Special Seasonal Rates!

We Love Seniors! AAA

On US 41 South

Ft. Myers
Alico Rd
Exit #128
75
Woodsmoke Camping Resort
Exit #123
Gulf of Mexico
41
N
Bonita Beach Rd.
To Naples

Outside 239 Area

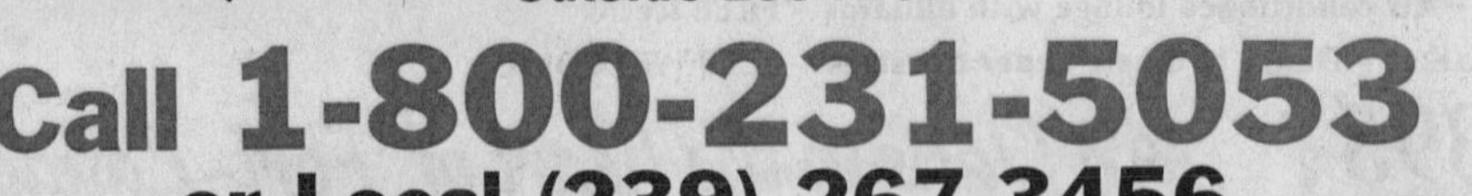

or Local (239) 267-3456

Closest Full Service RV Resort to I-75 (exit 123)

Lat. 26.45625
Long. 81.82414

WebSite: woodsmokecampingresort.com
E-Mail Address: woodsmok@aol.com

WOODSMOKE CAMPING RESORT 19551 S. Tamiami Trail (US 41 S), Ft. Myers, FL 33908

See listing at Fort Myers, FL

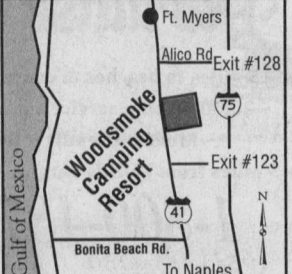

RAINTREE RV RESORT

Family Owned & Operated

WOODALL RATED:
Fac: ◈◈◈◈◈
Rec: ◈◈◈◈◈

TL RATING:
9/9★/10

Fiber-Optics Free Wi-Fi

★ 10% Discount for RVs 27′ or less
- Gated & Fenced • Giant Rec Hall
- Bocci • 50 Amp Available
- Heated Pool (87°) with New Handicap Lift!
- Spa • Large Paved Sites • Billiard Room
- Private Bathrooms • Shuffleboard
- Craft Room • Cable TV
- Many Activities in Season
- Full Time Rec Director

3 Miles N. of Shell Factory on US 41
1/2 mi. Bike Path to Publix Shopping Center

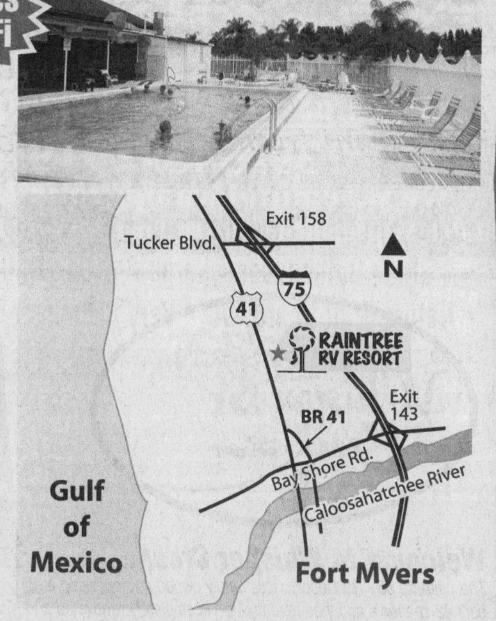

1-800-628-6095 or (239) 731-1441

19250 N. Tamiami Trail, North Ft. Myers, FL 33903

Visit us on the Web: **www.raintreerv.com**

See listing at Fort Myers, FL

Upriver Campground RV Resort

Reservations
1-800-848-1652

Weekend Getaway
Rally Facilities

Good Sam Park

AAA

17021 Upriver Dr.
N. Ft. Myers, FL 33917

Tranquility & Waterfront Fun!

www.upriver.com

See listing at Fort Myers, FL

FORT MYERS—Continued
Cypress Woods RV Resort—Continued

TIES: 423 sites, typical site width 46 ft, accepts full hkup units only, 423 full hkups, (20/30/50 amps), laundry. ◇◇◇◇◇RECREATION: 2 swim pools, boating, no motors, canoeing, lake fishing. Pets welcome, breed restrict, quantity restrict. Partial handicap access. No tents. Open all yr. Big rigs welcome. Rate in 2010 $40-70 for 2 persons. Member ARVC, FLARVC. Phone: (888)299-6637. FMCA discount.

FORT MYERS—Continued

(S) Groves RV Resort—(Lee) *From jct Hwy 82 & I-75: Go 7 mi S on I-75 (exit 131), then 2-1/2 mi W on Daniels Rd, then 8-1/4 mi W on Hwy 865 (Gladiolus Dr), then 2 mi W on Hwy 867 (McGregor Blvd), then 1/2 mi N on John Morris Rd. Enter on R.* ◇◇◇FACILITIES: 284 sites, typical site width 32 ft, 284 full hkups, (30/50 amps), 28 pull-thrus, cable TV, ($), WiFi Instant Internet at site ($), tenting, dump, non-guest dump $,

FORT MYERS—Continued
Groves RV Resort—Continued

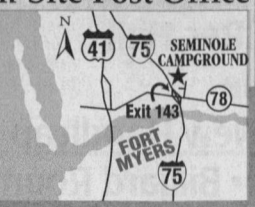

CAMPCLUB USA

laundry, picnic tables, patios. ◇◇◇RECREATION: rec hall, swim pool, shuffleboard court 3 shuffleboard courts, activities, horseshoes. Pets welcome, breed restrict, quantity restrict. Partial handicap access. Open all yr. MC/VISA/DISC/Debit. Member ARVC, FLARVC. CCUSA 50% Discount. CCUSA reservations Required, CCUSA max stay 7 days. Discount not available Nov 30-Apr 30. Additional charges may apply.

Phone: (239)466-4300
Address: 16175 John Morris Rd, Ft Myers, FL 33908
Lat/Lon: 26.50586/-81.96786
Email: sunresv@aol.com
Web: www.grovesrv.com

(N) Labonte's Garden RV Park (RV SPACES) —(Lee) *From jct Hwy 82 & I-75: Go 6 mi N on I-75 (exit 143), then 5-1/4 mi W on Hwy 78 (Ashore Rd), then 1-1/2 mi N on Business 41, then 1/2 mi E on Laurel Dr, then 200 yards N on Garden St. Enter on R.* FACILITIES: 30 sites, typical site width 20 ft, 30 full hkups, (20/30/50 amps), laundry. Pets welcome, size restrict. No tents. Open all yr. Rate in 2010 $35 for 2 persons. Phone: (239)995-7417.

LEE COUNTY VISITOR & CONVENTION

—Welcome to Florida's unspoiled island sanctuary. Reconnect with the person you really are in the unhurried island pace of The Beaches of Fort Myers & Sanibel. Open all yr.

LEE COUNTY VISITOR & CONVENTION—Continued on next page

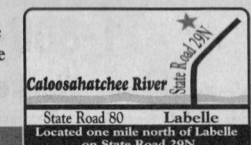

FORT MYERS—Continued
LEE COUNTY VISITOR & CONVENTION—Continued

Phone: (239)338-3500
Address: 12800 University Dr, Ste 550, Fort Myers, FL 33907
Email: leeleads@phasev.com
Web: www.fortmyers-sanibel.com

SEE AD DISCOVER SECTION PAGE 34

✱ **(NE) NORTH TRAIL RV**—*From jct Hwy 82 & I-75: Go 3 mi N on I-75 (exit 141), then 1 block W on Hwy 80, then 1 block S on Orange River Blvd. Enter on L.* SALES: travel trailers, 5th wheels, toy hauler, Class A motorhomes, Class C motorhomes, Class B motorhomes, pre-owned unit sales. SERVICES: full-time mech, engine/chassis repair, RV appliance repair, body work/collision repair, mobile RV svc, LP gas by weight/by meter, RV rentals, RV storage, sells parts/accessories, installs hitches. Open all yr. MC/VISA/DISC/AMEX/Debit.

Phone: (800)741-4383
Address: 5270 Orange River Blvd., Fort Myers, FL 33905
Lat/Lon: 26.68183/-81.80063
Email: sales@northtrailrv.com
Web: www.northtrailrv.com

SEE AD PAGE 120

(NE) Orange Grove Mobile Home & RV Park (RV SPACES)—(Lee) *From jct Hwy 82 & I-75: Go 1-3/4 mi N on I-75 (exit 139), then 1 mi W on Luckett Rd, then 1 mi N on Nuna Ave. Enter on R.* FACILITIES: 72 sites, typical site width 30 ft, accepts full hkup units only, 72 full hkups, (30/50 amps), laundry. RECREATION: swim pool. Pets welcome, breed restrict. Partial handicap access. No tents. Open all yr. Big rigs welcome. Rate in 2010 $55 for 2 persons. Phone: (239)694-5534.

(S) PIONEER VILLAGE RV RESORT (Encore)—(Lee) *From jct Hwy 82 & I-75: Go 6 mi N on I-75 (exit 143), then 1 mi W on Hwy 78 (Bayshore Rd), then 500 feet S on Samville Rd. Enter on L.*

◊◊◊FACILITIES: 543 sites, 543 full hkups, (30/50 amps), many extd stay sites (winter), WiFi Instant Internet at site ($), family camping, tenting, RV's/park model rentals, RV storage, dump, non-guest dump $, laundry, picnic tables, patios.

◊◊◊RECREATION: rec hall, pavilion, swim pool, hot tub, golf nearby, bsktball, shuffleboard court 12 shuffleboard courts, activities, tennis, horseshoes, v-ball.

Pets welcome, breed restrict. Partial handicap access. Open all yr. Escort to site. Clubs welcome. Rate in 2010 $27-53 for 2 persons. MC/VISA/DISC/AMEX. Member ARVC, FLARVC.

Phone: (877)897-2757
Address: 7974 Samville Rd, North Ft. Myers, FL 33917
Lat/Lon: 26.71332/-81.82608
Email: info@rvonthego.com
Web: www.rvonthego.com

SEE AD ALACHUA PAGE 93

(NW) RAINTREE RV RESORT—(Lee) *From jct Hwy 82 & I-75: Go 6 mi N on I-75 (exit 143), then 6-1/4 mi W on Hwy 78 (Bayshore Rd), then 4-1/2 mi N on US 41. Enter on R.*

A PLACE TO COME BACK TO
A beautiful RV Resort located in North Fort Myers full of special activities - dances to hayrides to pool parties & bingo. Free cable TV & Wi-Fi throughout the park. Large pool & renovated clubhouse. Be treated like family!

◊◊◊◊FACILITIES: 340 sites, typical site width 34 ft, 326 full hkups, 14 W&E, (20/30/50 amps), many extd stay sites (winter), 20 pull-thrus, heater not allowed, cable TV, WiFi Instant Internet at site, dump, non-guest dump $, laundry, ice, picnic tables, patios, controlled access.

◊◊◊◊RECREATION: rec hall, rec room/area, swim pool, hot tub, pond fishing, golf nearby, shuffleboard court 8 shuffleboard courts, activities, horseshoes, local tours.

Pets welcome, breed restrict, size restrict, quantity restrict. Partial handicap access. No tents. Age restrict may apply. Open all yr. Planned activities during winter only. Big rigs welcome. Escort to site. Rate in 2010 $52-65 for 2 persons. MC/VISA. Member ARVC, FLARVC.

Text 107881 to (440)725-8687 to see our Visual Tour.

Florida is also knows as the Peninsula State

FORT MYERS—Continued
RAINTREE RV RESORT—Continued

Phone: (800)628-6095
Address: 19250 N Tamiami Trail, North Fort Myers, FL 33903
Lat/Lon: 26.74360/-81.91648
Email: jacquesc500@hotmail.com
Web: www.raintreerv.com

SEE AD PAGE 119

(NE) RIVERBEND MOTORCOACH RESORT—(Hendry) *From jct Hwy 82 & I-75: Go 3 mi N on I-75 (exit 141), then 17 mi E on Hwy 80. Enter on L.*

COME AS A GUEST...LEAVE AS A FRIEND
You're welcome for a night or for a season. Riverbend is the finest Class A Resort in Florida, made beautiful not only by our amenities but by our owners and guests as well. Enjoy wonderful weather and motorcoach living at its best.

◊◊◊◊◊FACILITIES: 315 sites, typical site width 50 ft, accepts full hkup units only, 315 full hkups, (30/50 amps), many extd stay sites (winter), cable TV, WiFi Instant Internet at site, dump, laundry, RV supplies, ice, patios, controlled access.

◊◊◊◊◊RECREATION: rec hall, rec room/area, pavilion, equipped pavilion, swim pool, hot tub, boating, canoeing, kayaking, ramp, dock, river/pond fishing, golf nearby, bsktball, shuffleboard court 4 shuffleboard courts, activities, tennis, horseshoes, hiking trails, v-ball.

Pets welcome, breed restrict, quantity restrict. Partial handicap access. No tents. Open all yr. Planned group activities & restaurant/bar open Jan-Mar. Big rigs welcome. Escort to site. Clubs welcome. Rate in 2010 $40-85 for 2 persons. MC/VISA/Debit. Member ARVC, FLARVC.

Phone: (863)674-0085
Address: 5800 W SR 80, La Belle, FL 33935
Lat/Lon: 26.70988/-81.53117
Email: rental@riverbendflorida.com
Web: www.riverbendflorida.com

SEE AD PAGE 117

RIVERSIDE RV RESORT & CAMPGROUND—*From Fort Myers: Go 31 mi N on I-75 (exit 170), then 4-1/2 mi NE on Hwy 769. Enter on R.*

SEE PRIMARY LISTING AT PORT CHARLOTTE AND AD PORT CHARLOTTE PAGE 158

(NE) SEMINOLE CAMPGROUND—(Lee) *From jct Hwy 82 & I-75: Go 5-1/2 mi N on I-75 (exit 143), then 1/4 mi E on Hwy 78 (Bayshore Rd), then 1/4 mi N on Wells Rd, then 1/4 mi W on Triplett Rd. Enter on R.*

CHARMING "OLD FLORIDA" PARK
Native live Oaks in a natural setting with Pompash Creek adding to the serene landscape. Comforts of Big Rig sites, to tenting & RV rentals. Heated pool & free Wi-Fi. Private & serene but minutes to Fort Myers and Gulf beaches.

◊◊◊◊FACILITIES: 129 sites, typical site width 25 ft, 129 full hkups, (30/50 amps), some extd stay sites (winter), 5 pull-thrus, WiFi Instant Internet at site, family camping, tenting, RV's/park model rentals, RV storage, dump, non-guest dump $, laundry, ltd groc, RV supplies, LP bottle exch, ice, picnic tables, patios, fire rings, wood.

◊◊◊RECREATION: rec hall, rec room/area, swim pool, stream fishing, golf nearby, shuffleboard court 2 shuffleboard courts, activities, horseshoes, sports field, hiking trails, v-ball.

Pets welcome. Partial handicap access. Open all yr. Big rigs welcome. Escort to site. Clubs welcome. Rate in 2010 $35-50 per vehicle. MC/VISA/Debit. Member ARVC, FLARVC. CCUSA 50% Discount. CCUSA reservations Recommended, CCUSA max stay 2 days, Cash only for CCUSA disc. Discount available Jun thru Sep.

Phone: (239)543-2919
Address: 8991 Triplett Rd, N Fort Myers, FL 33917
Lat/Lon: 26.71867/-81.80989
Email: info@seminolecampground.com
Web: www.seminolecampground.com

SEE AD PAGE 120

Florida became a state on March 3, 1845.

FORT MYERS—Continued

(S) SHADY ACRES RV PARK—(Lee) *From jct Hwy 82 & I-75: Go 10 mi S on I-75 (exit 128), then 3 mi W on Alico Rd, then 2-1/4 mi S on US 41 (Tamiami Trail). Enter on R.*

◊◊◊◊FACILITIES: 307 sites, typical site width 33 ft, 299 full hkups, 8 W&E, (20/30/50 amps), many extd stay sites (winter), 2 pull-thrus, WiFi Instant Internet at site, family camping, tenting, RV's/park model rentals, RV storage, dump, non-guest dump $, laundry, ltd groc, RV supplies, LP gas by weight/by meter, ice, picnic tables, patios.

◊◊◊◊RECREATION: rec hall, rec room/area, pavilion, swim pool, golf nearby, shuffleboard court 4 shuffleboard courts, activities, horseshoes.

Pets welcome, breed restrict. Partial handicap access. Open all yr. Group activities winter only. Big rigs welcome. Escort to site. Clubs welcome. Rate in 2010 $37.50 for 2 persons. MC/VISA/DISC/AMEX. Member ARVC, FLARVC. CCUSA 50% Discount. CCUSA reservations Required, CCUSA max stay 21 days. Discount not available Jan-Mar. Discount on daily rate only. Electric surcharge is per day. Cancellation policy. No refunds for early departure.

Phone: (888)634-4080
Address: 19370 S Tamiami Trail, Fort Myers, FL 33908
Lat/Lon: 26.45804/-81.830545
Email: camp@shadyacresfl.com
Web: www.shadyacresfl.com

SEE AD PAGE 120

(NW) SUNSEEKER'S RV PARK—(Lee) *From jct Hwy 82 & I-75: Go 6 mi N on I-75 (exit 143), the 6-1/4 mi W on Hwy 78 (Bayshore Rd), then 5 mi N on US 41. Enter on L.*

◊◊◊FACILITIES: 219 sites, 35 ft max RV length, 204 full hkups, 15 W&E, (20/30 amps), mostly extd stay sites (winter), 8 pull-thrus, WiFi Instant Internet at site, tenting, RV's/park model rentals, dump, laundry, picnic tables, patios, controlled access.

◊◊◊◊RECREATION: rec hall, rec room/area, swim pool, hot tub, golf nearby, shuffleboard court 5 shuffleboard courts, activities, horseshoes.

Pets welcome, breed restrict, quantity restrict. Partial handicap access. Age restrict may apply. Open all yr. Group activities in winter only. Escort to site. Clubs welcome. Rate in 2010 $25-35 for 2 persons. Member ARVC, FLARVC. CCUSA 50% Discount. CCUSA reservations Accepted, CCUSA max stay 3 days, Cash only for CCUSA disc. Discount available May thru Sep.

Phone: (239)731-1303
Address: 19701 N Tamiami Trail, North Fort Myers, FL 33903
Lat/Lon: 26.75040/-81.92062
Email: sunseekrs@aol.com
Web: www.sunseekersrvpark.com

SEE AD PAGE 120

(N) Swan Lake Village Manufactured Homes & RV Resort—(Lee) *From jct Hwy 82 & I-75: Go 6 mi N on I-75 (exit 143), then 5-1/2 mi W on Hwy 78 (Bayshore Rd), then 3/4 mi N on Business 41/Hwy 739. Enter on R.* ◊◊◊FACILITIES: 104 sites, typical site width 22 ft, 104 full hkups, (30/50 amps), laundry. ◊◊◊RECREATION: swim pool, lake fishing. Pets welcome, breed restrict, size restrict. Partial handicap access. No tents. Age restrict may apply. Open all yr. Rate in 2010 $20-35 for 2 persons. Member ARVC, FLARVC. Phone: (239)995-3397.

(NW) Tamiami RV Park—(Lee) *From jct Hwy 82 & I-75: Go 5-1/2 mi N on I-75 (exit 143), then 6-1/4 mi W on Hwy 78 (Bayshore Rd), then 2 mi N on US 41. Enter on L.* ◊◊◊◊FACILITIES: 242 sites, typical site width 27 ft, 242 full hkups, (30/50 amps), WiFi Instant Internet at site, family camping, RV storage, dump, non-guest dump $, laundry, ice, picnic tables, patios. ◊◊◊RECREATION: rec hall, swim pool, shuffleboard court 4 shuffleboard courts, activities. Pets welcome, breed restrict, quantity restrict. Partial handicap access. No tents. Open all yr. Rate in 2010 $27.50-31.50 for 2 persons. MC/VISA/DISC/Debit. CCUSA 50% Discount. CCUSA reservations Recommended, CCUSA max stay 7 days. Discount available May 15-Sep 15. Tenting available May 15-Sep 15 only.

Tamiami RV Park—Continued on next page

Florida has more lakes than any other state.

FORT MYERS—Continued
Tamiami RV Park—Continued

Phone: (239)995-7747
Address: 16555 N Cleveland Ave, North Fort Myers, FL 33903
Lat/Lon: 26.70530/-81.90044
Email: reservationist@tamiamicommunity.com
Web: www.tamiamicommunity.com

(NE) UPRIVER RV RESORT—(Lee) *From jct Hwy 82 & I-75: Go 5-1/2 mi N on I-75 (exit 143), then 1-3/4 mi E on Hwy 78 (Bayshore Rd). Enter on R.*

WELCOME

A PREMIER EXPERIENCE!
An active adult resort on the beautiful Caloosahatchee River near Fort Myers. Enjoy river fishing, boating, heated pool, spa, a non-regulated 9-hole golf course, tennis & more. Spacious sites & luxury facilities. www.upriver.com.

◊◊◊◊FACILITIES: 350 sites, typical site width 35 ft, 350 full hkups, (20/30/50 amps), some extd stay sites (winter), 60 pull-thrus, heater not allowed, cable TV, WiFi Instant Internet at site ($), RV storage, laundry, RV supplies, LP gas by weight/by meter, ice, picnic tables, patios.

CAMPCLUB USA

◊◊◊◊◊RECREATION: rec hall, rec room/area, pavilion, swim pool, hot tub, boating, canoeing, kayaking, ramp, dock, saltwater/river fishing, putting green, golf nearby, bsktball, shuffleboard court 6 shuffleboard courts, activities, tennis, horseshoes, hiking trails, local tours.

FORT MYERS—Continued
UPRIVER RV RESORT—Continued

Pets welcome ($), breed restrict, size restrict, quantity restrict. Partial handicap access. No tents. Age restrict may apply. Open all yr. Group activities during winter season only. Big rigs welcome. Escort to site. Clubs welcome. MC/VISA/DISC/Debit. Member ARVC, FLARVC. FCRV discount. FMCA discount. CCUSA 50% Discount. CCUSA reservations Required, CCUSA max stay 2 days, Cash only for CCUSA disc., CCUSA disc. not avail F, Sa, CCUSA disc. not avail holidays. Discount applies May 1-Oct 1. Maximum stay 2 days at a time-total of 4 days /year. Adult park.

Text 107868 to (440)725-8687 to see our Visual Tour.

Phone: (800)848-1652
Address: 17021 Upriver Dr, North Fort Myers, FL 33917
Lat/Lon: 26.71480/-81.78496
Email: info@upriver.com
Web: www.upriver.com

SEE AD PAGE 119

(S) WOODSMOKE CAMPING RESORT—(Lee) *From jct Hwy 82 & I-75: Go 14 mi S on I-75 (exit 123), then 2 mi W on Corkscrew Rd, then 2 mi N on US 41. Enter on R.*

WELCOME

$10 FREE GAS WITH OVERNIGHT STAY
South Florida's Friendliest and most beautiful RV Resort-300 sites (many wooded) giant heated pool, whirlpool spa, great planned activities, boardwalk nature trail, 5 shuffleboard courts, 75' concrete pull thrus. (800)231-5053.

◊◊◊◊FACILITIES: 300 sites, typical site width 35 ft, 300 full hkups, (20/30/50 amps), many extd stay sites (winter), 16 pull-thrus, WiFi Instant Internet at site, WiFi Internet central location, family camping, tenting, RV's/park model rentals, RV storage, dump, non-guest dump $, laundry, RV supplies, picnic tables, patios.

Home of the Kennedy Space Center

FORT MYERS—Continued
WOODSMOKE CAMPING RESORT—Continued

CAMPCLUB USA

◊◊◊◊◊RECREATION: rec hall, rec room/area, equipped pavilion, swim pool, hot tub, boating, no motors, canoeing, kayaking, lake fishing, golf nearby, bsktball, playground, shuffleboard court 5 shuffleboard courts, activities, horseshoes, hiking trails.

Pets welcome, breed restrict, size restrict, quantity restrict. Partial handicap access. Open all yr. Planned group activities winter only. Big rigs welcome. Clubs welcome. MC/VISA/DISC/Debit. Member ARVC, FLARVC. FCRV discount. FMCA discount. CCUSA 50% Discount. CCUSA reservations Recommended, CCUSA max stay 7 days. Discount not available Jan, Feb, Mar.

Text 107869 to (440)725-8687 to see our Visual Tour.

Phone: (800)231-5053
Address: 19551 S. Tamiami Trail (US 41S), Ft Myers, FL 33908
Lat/Lon: 26.45625/-81.82414
Email: woodsmok@aol.com
Web: www.woodsmokecampingresort.com

SEE AD PAGE 118 AND AD TRAVEL SECTION PAGE 74

FORT MYERS BEACH—E-3

(N) FORT MYERS BEACH RV RESORT—(Lee) *From jct Hwy 82 & I-75: Go 6 mi S on I-75 (exit 131), then 5-3/4 mi W on Daniels Rd, then 5-3/4 mi SW on Summerlin Rd, then 3/4 mi N on San Carlos. Enter on R.*

WELCOME

◊◊◊FACILITIES: 306 sites, typical site width 27 ft, 306 full hkups, (30/50 amps), some extd stay sites (winter), 216 pull-thrus, cable TV, WiFi Instant Internet at site ($), tenting, RV's/park model rentals, laundry, LP gas by weight/by meter, ice, picnic tables, patios.

◊◊◊◊RECREATION: rec hall, rec room/area, swim pool, hot tub, golf nearby, shuffleboard court 4 shuffleboard courts, activities, horseshoes.

FORT MYERS BEACH RV RESORT—Continued on next page

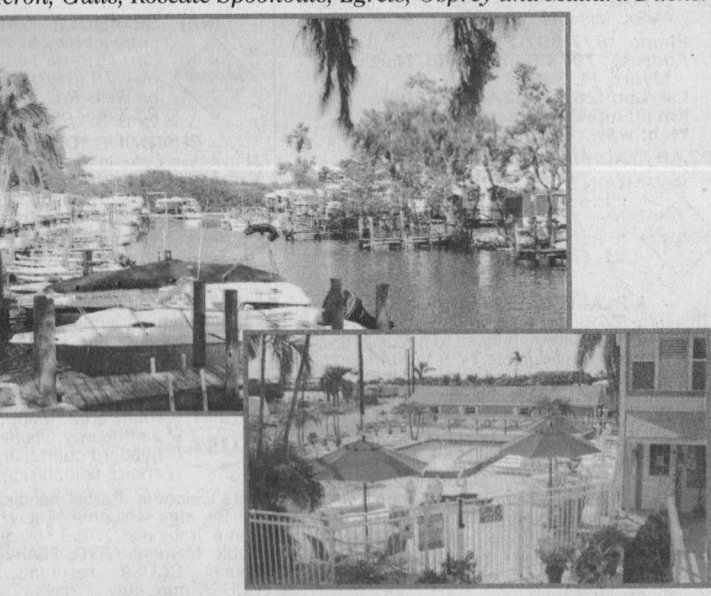

FORT MYERS BEACH—Continued
FORT MYERS BEACH RV RESORT—Continued

Pets welcome, breed restrict, quantity restrict. Partial handicap access. Open all yr. Group activities winter only. Escort to site. Clubs welcome. Rate in 2010 $33-51 for 2 persons. MC/VISA/DISC/AMEX. Member ARVC, FLARVC.

Phone: (800)553-7484
Address: 16299 San Carlos Blvd, Ft Myers, FL 33908
Lat/Lon: 26.50428/-81.94349
Email: info@rvonthego.com
Web: www.rvonthego.com

SEE AD ALACHUA PAGE 93

(N) GULF AIR RV RESORT—(Lee) *From Hwy 82 & I-75: Go 6 mi S on I-75 (exit 131), then 5-3/4 mi W on Daniels Rd, then 5-3/4 mi S on Summerlin Rd, then 1/4 mi S on San Carlos Blvd. Enter on L.*

♦♦♦FACILITIES: 246 sites, typical site width 30 ft, 40 ft max RV length, 246 full hkups, (30/50 amps), many extd stay sites (winter), cable TV, WiFi Instant Internet at site ($), phone Internet central location, tenting, RV's/park model rentals, dump, laundry, LP gas by weight/by meter, picnic tables, patios.

♦♦♦RECREATION: rec hall, swim pool, golf nearby, shuffleboard court 2 shuffleboard courts, activities, horseshoes, local tours.

Pets welcome, size restrict, quantity restrict. Partial handicap access. Open all yr. Escort to site. Clubs welcome. Green Friendly. MC/VISA/DISC/AMEX/Debit. Member ARVC, FLARVC.

Phone: (877)937-2757
Address: 17279 San Carlos Blvd SW, Ft Myers Beach, FL 33931
Lat/Lon: 26.49015/-81.94306
Email: info@RVontheGo.com
Web: www.rvonthego.com

SEE AD ALACHUA PAGE 93

(N) GULF WATERS RV RESORT—(Lee) *From Hwy 82 & I-75: Go 6 mi S on I-75 (exit 131), then 5-3/4 mi W on Daniels Rd/Cypress Lake Dr, then 5-1/2 mi S on Summerlin Rd, then 100 feet E on Pine Ridge Rd, then 500 feet S on Summerlin Sq Dr. Enter on L.*

♦♦♦♦FACILITIES: 319 sites, typical site width 30 ft, 319 full hkups, (20/30/50 amps), many extd stay sites (winter), cable TV, WiFi Instant Internet at site, family camping, dump, non-guest dump $, laundry, ice, picnic tables, patios, controlled access.

♦♦♦RECREATION: rec hall, pavilion, swim pool, hot tub, lake fishing, golf nearby, shuffleboard court 3 shuffleboard courts, activities, tennis, horseshoes.

Pets welcome, size restrict, quantity restrict. Partial handicap access. No tents. Open all yr. Big rigs welcome. Escort to site. Clubs welcome. Rate in 2010 $42-72 for 2 persons. MC/VISA/DISC/Debit.

Phone: (239)437-5888
Address: 11301 Summerlin Sq. Dr, Fort Myers Beach, FL 33931
Lat/Lon: 26.49298/-81.93710
Email: info@gulfwatersrv.com
Web: www.gulfwatersrv.com

SEE AD PAGE 122

(N) Indian Creek Resort—(Lee) *From jct Hwy 82 & I-75: Go 6 mi S on I-75 (exit 131), then 2-1/4 mi W on Daniels Rd, then 3 mi W on Hwy 865, then 4 mi SW on Summerlin Rd, then 1/4 mi S on San Carlos Blvd. Enter on R.* ♦♦♦♦♦FACILITIES: 1148 sites, typical site width 30 ft, 1148 full hkups, (30/50 amps), 60 pull-thrus, cable TV, WiFi Instant Internet at site ($), tenting, RV storage, laundry, ice, picnic tables, patios.

FORT MYERS BEACH—Continued
Indian Creek Resort—Continued

♦♦♦♦♦RECREATION: rec hall, 3 swim pools, hot tub, lake fishing, shuffleboard court 16 shuffleboard courts, activities, tennis, horseshoes, v-ball. Pets welcome, breed restrict, quantity restrict. Partial handicap access. Age restrict may apply. Open all yr. MC/VISA/DISC/Debit. Member ARVC, FLARVC. CCUSA 50% Discount. CCUSA reservations Required, CCUSA max stay 7 days. Discount not available Nov 30-Apr 30. Additional charges may apply.

Phone: (239)466-6060
Address: 17340 San Carlos Blvd, Ft Myers Beach, FL 33931
Lat/Lon: 26.48899/-81.94331
Email: sunresv@aol.com
Web: www.4indiancreek.com

(E) Red Coconut RV Resort on the Beach—(Lee) *From jct Hwy 82 & I-75: Go 6 mi S on I-75 (exit 131), then 5-1/2 mi W on Daniels Rd/Cypress Lake Dr (Hwy 869), then 5-3/4 mi SW on Summerlin Rd/Hwy 869, then 4 mi S on San Carlos Blvd, then 1 mi SE on Estero Blvd. Enter on L.* ♦♦♦FACILITIES: 250 sites, typical site width 28 ft, 250 full hkups, (20/30/50 amps), 13 pull-thrus, family camping, tenting, dump, laundry. ♦♦♦RECREATION: saltwater swim, boating, canoeing, saltwater fishing. Pets welcome ($), breed restrict, quantity restrict. Partial handicap access. Open all yr. Rate in 2010 $48-95 for 2 persons. Member ARVC, FLARVC. Phone: (239)463-7200.

(N) SAN CARLOS ISLAND RESORT—(Lee) *From jct Hwy 82 & I-75: Go 6 mi S on I-75 (exit 131), then 2-1/2 mi W on Daniels Rd, then 4-1/4 mi SW on Six Mile Cypress Pkwy/Gladiolus Rd, then 4 mi SW on Summerlin Rd, then 2 mi S on San Carlos Blvd. Enter on L.*

CAMP ON THE WATER'S EDGE
Waterfront camping and MH rentals. Great wildlife. Planned activities in winter season. Extremely friendly. Family owned & operated. Loyal staff. Customer satisfaction is our main goal! Fee Wi-Fi throughout park.

♦♦♦♦FACILITIES: 142 sites, typical site width 25 ft, 100 full hkups, (20/30/50 amps), some extd stay sites (winter), WiFi Instant Internet at site, family camping, tenting, RV's/park model rentals, dump, laundry, RV supplies, ice, picnic tables, patios, controlled access.

♦♦♦♦RECREATION: rec hall, coin games, swim pool, hot tub, boating, canoeing, kayaking, ramp, dock, 3 kayak rentals, saltwater fishing, golf nearby, shuffleboard court 3 shuffleboard courts, activities, horseshoes.

Pets welcome, breed restrict, quantity restrict. Partial handicap access. Open all yr. Escort to site. Clubs welcome. Rate in 2010 $41-85 for 2 persons. MC/VISA/DISC/Debit. Member ARVC, FLARVC.

Phone: (800)525-7275
Address: 18701 San Carlos Blvd., Fort Myers Beach, FL 33931
Lat/Lon: 26.46817/-81.95087
Email: mail@sancarlosrv.com
Web: www.sancarlosrv.com

SEE AD PAGE 122

(N) Siesta Bay RV Resort—(Lee) *From jct Hwy 82 & I-75: Go 6 mi S on I-75 (exit 131), then 2-1/4 mi W on Daniels Rd, then 4-1/4 mi SW on Six Mile Cypress Pkwy/Gladiolus Rd, then 5 mi W on Summerlin Rd. Enter on L.* ♦♦♦♦♦FACILITIES: 798 sites, typical site width 37 ft, accepts full hkup units only, 798 full hkups, (30/50 amps), WiFi Instant Internet at site ($), RV storage, dump, laundry, ice, patios. ♦♦♦♦♦RECREATION: rec hall, pavilion, 2 swim pools, hot tub, lake fishing, putting green, bsktball, shuffleboard court 12 shuffleboard courts, activities, tennis, horseshoes, v-ball. No pets. Partial handicap access. No tents. Age restrict may apply. Open all yr. Big rigs welcome. Rate in 2010 $32-49 for 2 persons. MC/

FORT MYERS BEACH—Continued
Siesta Bay RV Resort—Continued

VISA/DISC/Debit. Member ARVC, FLARVC. CCUSA 50% Discount. CCUSA reservations Required, CCUSA max stay 7 days. Discount not available Nov 30-Apr 30. Additional charges may apply. Indoor cats only.

Phone: (239)466-8988
Address: 19333 Summerlin Rd, Fort Myers, FL 33908
Lat/Lon: 26.49380/-81.95963
Email: sunresv@aol.com
Web: www.siestabay.com

FORT PIERCE—D-5

(NW) ROAD RUNNER TRAVEL RESORT—(St. Lucie) *From jct Hwy 70 & I-95: Go 9 mi N on I-95 (exit 138), then 3 mi E on Hwy 614 (Indrio Rd), then 3 mi S on Hwy 713 (Kings Hwy), then 1-1/4 mi E on CR 608 (St. Lucie Blvd). Enter on L.*

NESTLED IN A BEAUTIFUL FL HAMMOCK
38 acre 452 site RV Park with 3-hole golf course, tennis, shuffleboard, horseshoes, 2 rec halls & planned activities. 3 miles from the ocean. Good location for travel to all Florida attractions.

♦♦♦♦FACILITIES: 452 sites, typical site width 30 ft, 452 full hkups, (20/30/50 amps), some extd stay sites (winter), 10 pull-thrus, cable TV, WiFi Internet central location, family camping, tenting, cabins, RV storage, dump, non-guest dump $, laundry, full svc store, RV supplies, LP gas by weight/by meter, ice, picnic tables, patios, controlled access.

♦♦♦♦♦RECREATION: rec hall, rec room/area, pavilion, swim pool, pond fishing, fishing supplies, putting green, golf nearby, bsktball, shuffleboard court 4 shuffleboard courts, activities, tennis, horseshoes, v-ball.

Pets welcome, breed restrict, quantity restrict. Partial handicap access. Open all yr. Big rigs welcome. Clubs welcome. Green Friendly. Rate in 2010 $38-42 for 2 persons. MC/VISA/DISC/Debit. ATM. Member ARVC, FLARVC. FMCA discount.

Text 93233 to (440)725-8687 to see our Visual Tour.

Phone: (800)833-7108
Address: 5500 Saint Lucie Blvd., Fort Pierce, FL 34946
Lat/Lon: 27.48413/-80.37983
Email: info@roadrunnerresort.com
Web: www.roadrunnertravelresort.com

SEE AD NEXT PAGE AND AD TRAVEL SECTION PAGE 74 AND AD MAP PAGE 70

(W) SUNNIER PALMS (Nudist) (NUDIST RESORT)—(St. Lucie) *From jct I-95 (exit 129) & Hwy 70: Go 2 mi W on Hwy 70. Enter on R.*

FACILITIES: 53 sites, typical site width 30 ft, 53 full hkups, (20/30/50 amps), some extd stay sites (winter), WiFi Instant Internet at site, family camping, tenting, RV storage, dump, laundry, ice, picnic tables, grills, controlled access.

RECREATION: rec room/area, swim pool, hot tub, golf nearby, bsktball, playground, shuffleboard court shuffleboard court, activities, horseshoes, hiking trails.

Pets welcome, breed restrict, quantity restrict. Partial handicap access. Open all yr. Nudist Resort. Big rigs welcome. Escort to site. Clubs welcome. Rate in 2010 $24-46 per vehicle. MC/VISA/DISC.

SUNNIER PALMS (Nudist)—Continued on next page

Little Richard, singer, is from Florida.

…E—Continued
…ALMS (Nudist)—Continued

Phone: (772)468-8512
Address: 8800 Okeechobee Rd, Fort Pierce, FL 34945
Lat/Lon: 27.41128/-80.41489
Email: sunnierpalms@gmail.com
Web: www.sunnier.com

SEE AD PAGE 123

(SW) Treasure Coast RV Park—(St. Lucie) *From jct I-95 (exit 129) & Hwy 70: Go 1 block W on Hwy 70, then 1/4 mi N on Peters Rd./Crossroads Pkwy. Enter on R.* ◇◇◇◇◇FACILITIES: 165 sites, typical site width 28 ft, 165 full hkups, (20/30/50 amps), 4 pull-thrus, family camping, dump, laundry. ◇◇◇RECREATION: swim pool, pond fishing. Pets welcome, quantity restrict. Partial handicap access. No tents. Open all yr. Big rigs welcome. Rate in 2010 $39-46 per vehicle. Phone: (772)468-2099. FCRV discount. FMCA discount.

FORT WALTON BEACH—F-2

See listings at Destin, Milton & Navarre

Woodall's Tip... Rules of the Road information is located in the front of the Directory.

FORT WALTON BEACH—Continued

(W) OPEN ROAD RV CENTER—*From jct Hwy 189 & US 98: Go 3 mi W on US 98. Enter on L.* SALES: pre-owned unit sales. SERVICES: full-time mech, engine/chassis repair, RV appliance repair, body work/collision repair, sells parts/accessories, installs hitches. Open all yr. MC/VISA/DISC.

WELCOME

Phone: (850)244-4020
Address: 135 E Miracle Strip Parkway, Mary Esther, FL 32569
Lat/Lon: 30.40936/-86.66238
Email: ken@openroad.gccoxmail.com

SEE AD THIS PAGE

(NW) PLAYGROUND RV PARK—(Okaloosa) *From jct US-98 & Hwy-189: Go 4-1/2 mi N on Hwy-189. Enter on R.* ◇◇◇◇FACILITIES: 64 sites, typical site width 20 ft, 64 full hkups, (30/50 amps), mostly extd stay sites, 9 pull-thrus, cable TV, WiFi Instant Internet at site, WiFi Internet central location, family camping, dump, non-guest dump $, laundry, picnic tables, patios.

WELCOME

RECREATION: pavilion.

Pets welcome. Partial handicap access. No tents. Open all yr. Big rigs welcome. Rate in 2010 $35-40 for 2 persons. MC/VISA/DISC/AMEX.

FORT WALTON BEACH—Continued
PLAYGROUND RV PARK—Continued

Phone: (850)862-3513
Address: 777 N Beal Pkwy, Fort Walton Beach, FL 32547
Lat/Lon: 30.44425/-86.63857
Email: playgroundrvpark@aol.com
Web: www.fwbplaygroundrvpark.com

SEE AD THIS PAGE

FOUNTAIN—F-3

(N) Pine Lake RV Park—(Bay) *From I-10 (exit 130): Go 15 mi S on US 231. Enter on L.* ◇◇◇FACILITIES: 131 sites, typical site width 30 ft, 61 full hkups, 20 W&E, (30/50 amps), 50 no hkups, 75 pull-thrus, WiFi Instant Internet at site, phone Internet central location, family camping, tenting, RV storage, dump, non-guest dump $, laundry, RV supplies, LP gas by meter. ◇◇◇RECREATION: rec hall, equipped pavilion, lake fishing, bsktball, horseshoes, hiking trails. Pets welcome, breed restrict. Open all yr. Big rigs welcome. Rate in 2010 $34.95 for 2 persons. MC/VISA/DISC/AMEX. Member ARVC, FLARVC. CCUSA 50% Discount. CCUSA reservations Recommended, CCUSA max stay 6 days. Extra vehicle surcharge $2.

CAMPCLUB USA

Phone: (850)722-1401
Address: 21036 US 231, Fountain, FL 32438
Lat/Lon: 30.53049/-85.39605
Email: pinelakerv@gmail.com
Web: www.pinelakerv.com

Reserve Online at Woodalls.com

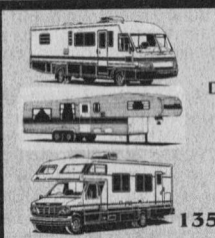

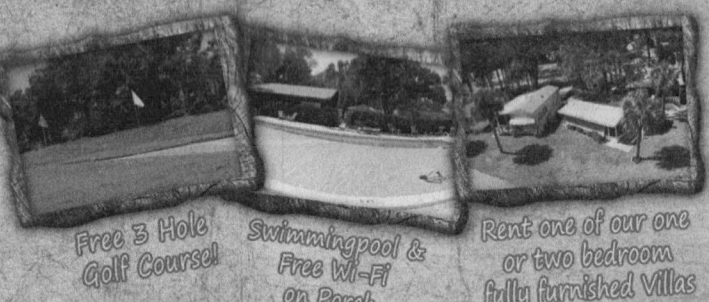

OPEN ROAD INC.
Discount RV Center
Largest RV Parts Store In North Florida
Florida RV trade association
Lat: 30.40935
Lon: 86.66238
See listing at Fort Walton Beach, FL

135 E. Miracle Strip Pkwy (Hwy. 98)
Mary Esther, FL 32569
Stop a Minute ...Save a Mint
(850) 244-4020
RV Sales and Service • Supplies • Consignments

Only Park in Ft. Walton Beach!
• Easy in/out • 50 Amp Pull-Thrus
• Free Cable TV • Close to Super Walmart
Wi-Fi
• Easy Access to Gas, Diesel, & Propane
• Reasonable Daily & Weekly Rates
Hwy 189 - 777 Beal Parkway • Ft. Walton Beach, FL 32547
(850) 862-3513
See listing at Fort Walton Beach, FL

"Nestled in a Beautiful 38 Acre Florida Hammock"

Free 3 Hole Golf Course!
Swimmingpool & Free Wi-Fi on Porch
Rent one of our one or two bedroom fully furnished Villas

Family Owned & Operated!
• 452 Full Hookup Sites with Concrete Patios
• Daily, Weekly & Monthly Rates • LP-Gas • Restaurant
• "Everythung Store" • Clubhouse • Planned Activities
• Laundry • Heated Swimming Pool • RV Storage
• Modem Friendly • Lighted Tennis, Shuffleboard,
• Petanque & Basketball Courts • Great Shopping Nearby
• Extended Cable TV to all Sites (Free) • Special
• Rates for Groups & Reunions • Rustic Cabin Rentals
• **Fully Furnished Villas!**

... close enough to everything but secluded enough to enjoy relaxing with nature!

1-800-833-7108
For Reservations & Information

4 Miles to Beautiful Ocean Beaches & Fishing

Ph: (772) 464-0969 Fax: (772) 464-0987
5500 St. Lucie Blvd., Fort Pierce, FL 34946
Email: info@roadrunnerresort.com
www.roadrunnertravelresort.com

See listing at Ft. Pierce, FL

FREEPORT—F-2

LIVE OAK LANDING (UNDER CONSTRUCTION)—(Walton) *From jct Hwy 20 & US 331: Go 3-1/2 mi S on US 331, then 1 mi E on Black Creek Hwy, then 1 mi N on McDaniels Fish Camp Rd, then 1/4 mi W on Pitts Ave. Enter on L.*

GULF SHORE GETAWAY!

Coming this Fall, Live Oak Landing is within minutes of the Emerald Coast beaches, and features RV sites, beautiful cottages & private boat ramp & dock leading strait to Choctawhatchee Bay, the Gulf, and local rivers & bayous.

FACILITIES: (50 amps), cable TV, family camping.

RECREATION: rec hall, pavilion, boating, ramp, dock.

Partial handicap access. Open all yr. Big rigs welcome. Escort to site.

Text 108003 to (440)725-8687 to see our Visual Tour.

Phone: (901)432-4748
Address: 229 Pitts Ave, Freeport, FL 32439
Email: liveoaklanding@rvcoutdoors.com
Web: www.liveoaklanding.rvcoutdoors.com

SEE AD THIS PAGE

FROSTPROOF—C-4

(NW) Lakemont Ridge Home & RV Park—(Polk) *From jct US 27 US 98 & Hwy 630 (Fort Meade Rd): Go 1/2 mi E on Hwy 630, then continue 1/2 mi on Fort Meade Rd. Enter on R.* ◊◊◊◊FACILITIES: 200 sites, typical site width 35 ft, 200 full hkups, (30/50 amps), WiFi Instant Internet at site, phone/cable on-site Internet (needs activ), phone Internet central location, RV storage, laundry, LP gas by weight/by meter, patios. ◊◊◊◊RECREATION: rec hall, swim pool, hot tub, pond fishing, shuffleboard court 5 shuffleboard courts, activities, horseshoes. Pets welcome. Partial handicap access. No tents. Open all yr. Big rigs welcome. Rate in 2010 $60 for 2 persons. CCUSA 50% Discount. CCUSA reservations Recommended, CCUSA max stay 7 days, Cash only for CCUSA disc., Check only for CCUSA disc. No discount from Jan 15-Mar 15. 55+ park.

Phone: (863)635-4472
Address: 2000 Maine St, Frostproof, FL 33843
Lat/Lon: 27.73339/-81.56099
Email: lakemontridge@aol.com
Web: www.lakemont_ridge.com

(W) RAINBOW RESORT—(Polk) *From jct US 27 & Hwy 630A: Go 1/2 mi E on Hwy 630A. Enter on L.*

◊◊◊◊◊FACILITIES: 499 sites, typical site width 40 ft, 499 full hkups, (50 amps), mostly extd stay sites (winter), 13 pull-thrus, cable TV, ($), WiFi Instant Internet at site ($), phone/cable on-site Internet (needs activ), phone Internet central location, RV storage, laundry, patios, controlled access.

◊◊◊◊◊RECREATION: rec hall, rec room/area, swim pool, hot tub, pond fishing, golf nearby, bsktball, shuffleboard court 6 shuffleboard courts, activities, horseshoes, local tours.

Pets welcome, size restrict, quantity restrict. Partial handicap access. No tents. Age restrict may apply. Open all yr. Planned activities in season only. Big rigs welcome. Clubs welcome. Rate in 2010 $35 for 2 persons.

Sidney Poitier, actor, is from Florida.

FROSTPROOF—Continued
RAINBOW RESORT—Continued

Phone: (863)635-7541
Address: 700 CR 630A, Frostproof, FL 33843
Lat/Lon: 27.75583/-81.57494
Web: www.rainbowresortrv.com

SEE AD TRAVEL SECTION PAGE 73

FRUITLAND PARK—B-3

(N) LAKE GRIFFIN STATE PARK—(Lake) *From jct US-27-441 & Hwy-446A: Go 2 mi S on US-27-441.* FACILITIES: 40 sites, 40 W&E, (50 amps), tenting, dump, laundry. RECREATION: boating, canoeing, ramp, dock, lake fishing, playground. Pets welcome. Partial handicap access. Open all yr. Phone: (352)360-6760.

Woodall's Tip... Is a new Woodall's Directory needed every year? You bet! Each year the Woodall's North American Directory averages over 350,000 changes from the previous year.

GAINESVILLE—B-3

✲ **(NW) J. D. SANDERS RV CENTER**—*From jct I-75 (exit 399) & Hwy 441: Go 6 mi E & SE on Hwy 441. Enter on R.* SALES: travel trailers, park models, 5th wheels, toy hauler, fold-down camping trailers, pre-owned unit sales. SERVICES: full-time mech, RV appliance repair, body work/collision repair, LP gas by weight/by meter, RV storage, sells parts/accessories, installs hitches. Open all yr. MC/VISA/DISC/AMEX.

Phone: (800)541-6439
Address: 12380 NW Hwy 441, Alachua, FL 32615
Lat/Lon: 29.76759/-82.42172
Email: jdsrv@att.net
Web: www.sandersrvs.com

SEE AD THIS PAGE

GAINESVILLE—Continued on next page

Burt Reynolds, actor, is from Florida.

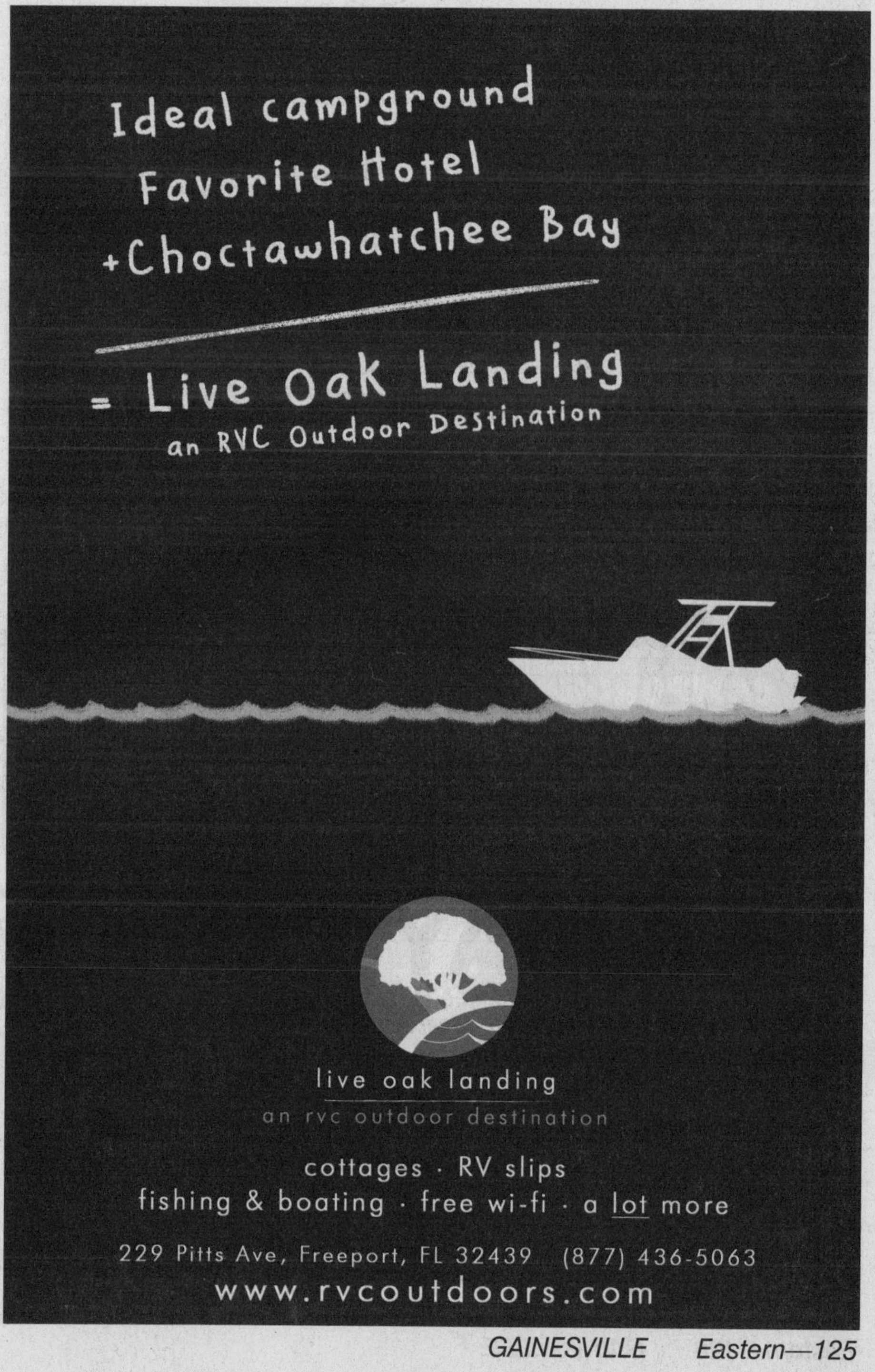

GAINESVILLE—Continued

(S) PAYNES PRAIRIE PRESERVE STATE PARK—(Alachua) *From jct Hwy 121 & US 441: Go 10 mi S on US 441.* FACILITIES: 52 sites, 37 W&E, 15 E, tenting, dump. RECREATION: boating, electric motors only, canoeing, ramp, lake fishing. No pets. Partial handicap access. Open all yr. Phone: (352)466-3397.

TRAVELERS CAMPGROUND—*From jct Hwy 26 & I-75: Go 12 mi N on I-75 to exit 399 (Old 78), then 200 feet E on US 441, then left at Waffle House, then 1 mi N on E Frontage Rd.*

SEE PRIMARY LISTING AT ALACHUA AND AD THIS PAGE

GEORGETOWN—B-4

(W) **Scruftys Riverwood RV Park**—(Putnam) *From Hwy 17 & CR 308: Go 8 mi W on CR 308, then 2 -1/2 mi S on CR 309. Enter on R.* ◆◆◆FACILITIES: 36 sites, typical site width 30 ft, 36 full hkups, (30/50 amps), 2 pull-thrus, tenting, dump, laundry. ◆◆RECREATION: boating, canoeing, dock, river fishing. Pets welcome. Partial handicap access. Open all yr. Big rigs welcome. Rate in 2010 $33.30 for 2 persons. Phone: (386)467-7147.

GRANT—C-5

(N) **ORBIT RV PARK**—(Brevard) *From jct I-95 (exit 173) & Hwy 514: Go 4 mi E on Hwy 514, then 3-1/2 mi S on US 1. Enter on R.*

◆◆◆FACILITIES: 38 sites, typical site width 30 ft, 38 full hkups, (20/30/50 amps), mostly extd stay sites (winter), 4 pull-thrus, cable TV, WiFi Instant Internet at site, WiFi Internet central location, family camping, RV storage, laundry, picnic tables, patios.

◆◆◆RECREATION: rec hall, saltwater fishing, golf nearby, activities, horseshoes.

Pets welcome, breed restrict. No tents. Age restrict may apply. Open all yr. Family camping, Summer only. Big rigs welcome. Clubs welcome. Rate in 2010 $26-38 for 2 persons. FMCA discount. CCUSA 50% Discount. CCUSA reservations Accepted, CCUSA max stay Unlimited, Cash only for CCUSA disc., Check only for CCUSA disc. Discount available May 1- Oct 31. Over 55 park.

Phone: (321)953-2555
Address: 3860 US Hwy 1, Grant, FL 32949
Lat/Lon: 27.95757/-80.53970
Email: info@orbitrv.com
Web: www.orbitrv.com

SEE AD MELBOURNE PAGE 140

GRAYTON BEACH—F-2

(E) GRAYTON BEACH STATE PARK—(Walton) *From jct US-98 & US-331: Go SW on Hwy-30A.* FACILITIES: 37 sites, 37 W&E, (30 amps), tenting, dump. RECREATION: boating, canoeing, ramp, saltwater fishing. Pets welcome. Partial handicap access. Open all yr. Phone: (850)231-4210.

HAINES CITY—C-4

(W) **CENTRAL PARK OF HAINES CITY**—(Polk) *From jct I-4 (exit 55) & US 27: Go 8 mi S on US 27, then 1/4 mi W on Commerce Ave. Enter on L.*

◆◆◆◆FACILITIES: 351 sites, typical site width 30 ft, 351 full hkups, (30/50 amps), mostly extd stay sites (winter), 26 pull-thrus, cable TV, WiFi Instant Internet at site ($), phone/cable on-site Internet (needs activ), WiFi Internet central location, family camping, tenting, RV's/park model rentals, RV storage, dump, laundry, RV supplies, LP gas by weight, picnic tables, patios.

◆◆◆RECREATION: rec hall, swim pool, pond fishing, golf nearby, shuffleboard court 8 shuffleboard courts, activities, horseshoes.

Pets welcome, breed restrict. Partial handicap access. Open all yr. Most activities winter only. Big rigs welcome. Clubs welcome. Rate in 2010 $28-31.50 for 2 persons. MC/VISA/DISC/Debit. CCUSA 50% Discount. CCUSA reservations Recommended, CCUSA max stay 5 days, CCUSA disc. not avail F, Sa. Discount available May thru Oct.

Phone: (863)422-5322
Address: 1501 W Commerce Ave, Haines City, FL 33844
Lat/Lon: 28.11728/-81.64511
Email: centralpark150@yahoo.com
Web: www.centralparkofhainescity.com

SEE AD THIS PAGE

HALLANDALE—E-5

(W) **HOLIDAY PARK**—(Broward) *From jct I-95 (exit 18) & Hwy 858 (Hallandale Bch Blvd): Go 1/4 mi W on W Hallandale Beach Blvd. Enter on L.*

◆◆◆◆FACILITIES: 123 sites, typical site width 24 ft, 123 full hkups, (30/50 amps), many extd stay sites (winter), 113 pull-thrus, WiFi Instant Internet at site, dump, non-guest dump $, laundry, patios.

◆◆◆RECREATION: rec hall, pavilion, swim pool, golf nearby, shuffleboard court 2 shuffleboard courts, activities.

Pets welcome, breed restrict, size restrict. No tents. Open all yr. Planned group activities winter

HALLANDALE—Continued
HOLIDAY PARK—Continued

only. Children on limited basis only. Escort to site. Clubs welcome. Rate in 2010 $35-45 for 2 persons. MC/VISA. Member ARVC, FLARVC.

Phone: (954)981-4414
Address: 3140 W Hallandale Beach Blvd, Hallandale, FL 33009
Lat/Lon: 25.98468/-80.16968
Email: holidayparks@aol.com
Web: www.holidayparksrv.com

SEE AD THIS PAGE

HIGH SPRINGS—B-3

(W) **Ginnie Springs Outdoors LLC**—(Gilchrist) *From jct I-75 (exit 399) & US 441: Go 4 1/2 mi W on US 441, then 1/2 mi S on US 41, then 6 1/2 mi SW on CR 340, then 2 mi N on access road (NE 60th St). Enter at end.* ◆◆◆FACILITIES: 290 sites, typical site width 40 ft, 90 W&E, (20/30/50 amps), 200 no hkups, 5 pull-thrus, family camping, tenting, dump, laundry, ltd groc. ◆◆◆RECREATION: river swim, boating, canoeing, ramp, river fishing, playground. No pets. Open all yr. Rate in 2010 $20.40-27.40 for 1 persons. Member ARVC, FLARVC. Phone: (386)454-7188.

(NE) **HIGH SPRINGS CAMPGROUND**—(Alachua) *From jct I-75 (exit 404) & CR 236: Go 1/4 mi W on CR 236, then 1000 ft N on Old Bellamy Rd. Enter on L.*

◆◆◆FACILITIES: 48 sites, typical site width 30 ft, 47 full hkups, 1 W&E, (30/50 amps), 50 amps ($), some extd stay sites (winter), 17 pull-thrus, WiFi Instant Internet at site, WiFi Internet central location, tenting, laundry, picnic tables, wood.

◆◆RECREATION: swim pool, golf nearby, play equipment, horseshoes.

Pets welcome. Open all yr. Big rigs welcome. Rate in 2010 $28 for 4 persons. Member ARVC, FLARVC. FMCA discount.

Phone: (386)454-1688
Address: 24004 NW Old Bellamy Rd, High Springs, FL 32643
Lat/Lon: 29.87538/-82.54865
Email: camp@highspringscampground.com
Web: www.highspringscampground.com

SEE AD GAINESVILLE THIS PAGE AND AD TRAVEL SECTION PAGE 74

(N) O'LENO STATE PARK/RIVER RISE—(Columbia) *From jct I-10 & US-441-41: Go 20 mi S on US-441-41.* FACILITIES: 61 sites, 61 W&E, (30/50 amps), tenting, dump. RECREATION: river swim, boating, canoeing, dock, playground. No pets. Partial handicap access. Open all yr. Phone: (386)454-1853.

HILLIARD—A-3

(N) St. Mary's River Fish Camp & Campground—(Nassau) *From jct CR 108 & US 301/US 1: Go 6-1/2 mi N on US 301/US 1; then 3/4 mi E on Lake Hampton Rd, then 1/2 mi N on Scotts Landing Rd. Enter at end.* ◆◆FACILITIES: 51 sites, typical site width 25 ft, 49 full hkups, 2 W&E, (20/30/50 amps), 9 pull-thrus, family camping, tenting, dump, laundry, ltd groc. ◆◆◆RECREATION: river swim, boating, canoeing, ramp, river fishing. Pets welcome, breed restrict, size restrict. Partial handicap access. Open all yr. Big rigs welcome. Rate in 2010 $25 for 2 persons. Phone: (866)845-4443. FMCA discount.

HOBE SOUND—D-5

(S) JONATHAN DICKINSON STATE PARK—(Martin) *From I-95 (Hobe Sound exit): Go E to US 1, then S on US 1.* FACILITIES: 135 sites, 35 ft max RV length, 135 W&E, tenting, dump, ltd groc. RECREATION: river swim, boating, canoeing, ramp, saltwater/lake/river fishing, playground. Pets welcome. Open all yr. Phone: (772)546-2771.

HOLLYWOOD—E-5

(W) Lake Trinity Estates—(Broward) *From jct I-95 (exit 19) & Hwy 824 (Pembroke Rd): Go 1/2 mi W on Pembroke Rd. Enter on L.* ◆◆◆◆FACILITIES: 255 sites, typical site width 20 ft, 255 full hkups, (30/50 amps), dump, laundry. ◆◆◆◆RECREATION: 2 swim pools, lake fishing. No pets. Partial handicap access. No tents. Open all yr. Rate in 2010 $32-44 for 2 persons. Phone: (954)962-7400.

Can you trust the Woodall's ratings? 25 evaluation teams have scoured North American campgrounds to provide you with accurate, up to date information & ratings. Find a rating you don't agree with? Send a letter or email our way, and we'll give it extra attention for 2012.

HOLLYWOOD—Continued

(NW) TOPEEKEEGEE YUGNEE (T.Y.) Park (Broward County Park)—(Broward) *From jct I-95 & Sheridan St: Go 1/2 mi W on Sheridan St to N Park Rd. Enter on R.*

WELCOME

FACILITIES: 61 sites, 61 full hkups, (30/50 amps), 61 pull-thrus, WiFi Internet central location, family camping, tenting, dump, non-guest dump, laundry, ice, picnic tables, patios, grills, controlled access.

RECREATION: swim pool, 7 rowboat/24 pedal boat rentals, lake fishing, golf nearby, bsktball, bike rental, playground, tennis, sports field, v-ball. Rec open to public.

Pets welcome. Partial handicap access. Open all yr. Big rigs welcome. Clubs welcome. MC/VISA/DISC/AMEX.

Phone: (954)985-1980
Address: 3300 N Park Rd, Hollywood, FL 33021
Email: typark@broward.org
Web: www.broward.org/parks/camping

SEE AD TRAVEL SECTION PAGE 75 AND AD DISCOVER SECTION PAGE 33

HOLT—E-1

(W) BLACKWATER RIVER STATE PARK—(Santa Rosa) *From US 90: Go 3 mi N.* FACILITIES: 30 sites, 30 W&E, tenting, dump. RECREATION: river swim, boating, canoeing, river fishing. Pets welcome. Partial handicap access. Open all yr. Phone: (850) 983-5363.

(S) River's Edge RV Campground—(Okaloosa) *From jct I-10 (exit 45) & Hwy 189: Go 1-3/4 mi S on Hwy 189. Enter on L.* ◆◆◆FACILITIES: 104 sites, typical site width 45 ft, 83 full hkups, 11 W&E, (30/50 amps), 10 no hkups, 67 pull-thrus, WiFi Instant Internet at site ($), WiFi Internet central location, family camping, RV storage, dump, non-guest dump $, laundry, ltd groc, RV supplies, LP gas by weight/by meter, ice,

HOLT—Continued
River's Edge RV Campground—Continued

CAMPCLUB USA

picnic tables, wood. ◆◆◆RECREATION: pavilion, boating, canoeing, kayaking, ramp, river fishing, playground, activities, horseshoes, hiking trails. Pets welcome, breed restrict. Partial handicap access. No tents. Open all yr. Big rigs welcome. Rate in 2010 $25-37 for 2 persons. Member ARVC, FLARVC. FMCA discount. CCUSA 50% Discount. CCUSA reservations Recommended, CCUSA max stay 3 days, Cash only for CCUSA disc., CCUSA disc. not avail holidays. Discount not available Oct to Mar. Day visitor surcharge $1. River site surcharge $5-12. Call for details.

Phone: (850)537-2267
Address: 4001 Log Lake Rd, Holt, FL 32564
Lat/Lon: 30.67720/-86.74911
Email: riversedgerv@woolcom.net
Web: www.riversedgerv.com

HOMESTEAD—E-5

(SW) EVERGLADES NATIONAL PARK (Long Pine Key)—(Miami-Dade) *From jct US 1 & Palm Dr/SW 344th St: Follow signs for Hwy 9336 (Everglades NP). Campground is 5 mi W from park entrance. Enter on L.* FACILITIES: 108 sites, 35 ft max RV length, 108 no hkups, tenting, dump. RECREATION: pond fishing. Open all yr. Phone: (305)242-7873.

(S) Goldcoaster Mobile Home & RV Resort—(Dade) *From jct US 1 & Hwy 9336 (Palm Dr): Go 1 mi W on Palm Dr, then 1 block S on SW 187th Ave. Enter on R.* ◆◆◆◆◆FACILITIES: 110 sites, typical site width 40 ft, 110 full hkups, (30/50 amps), WiFi Instant Internet at site ($), family camping, laundry, ice, picnic tables, patios. ◆◆◆◆◆RECREATION: rec hall, pavilion, swim pool, hot tub, bsktball, playground, shuffleboard court 6 shuffleboard courts, activities, horseshoes. Pets welcome, breed restrict, quantity restrict. Partial handicap access. No tents. Open all yr. Big rigs welcome. Rate in 2010 $35-50 for 2 persons. MC/VISA/DISC/Debit. CCUSA 50% Discount.

CAMPCLUB USA

Goldcoaster Mobile Home & RV Resort—Continued on next page

HOMESTEAD—Continued
Goldcoaster Mobile Home & RV Resort—Continued

CCUSA reservations Required, CCUSA max stay 7 days. Discount not available Nov 1-May 1. Additional charges may apply.

Phone: (800)828-6992
Address: 34850 SW 187th Ave, Homestead, FL 33034
Lat/Lon: 25.44356/-80.49367
Email: sunresv@aol.com
Web: www.goldcoasterrv.com

Staying close to home next year? Pre-order the 2012 Directory in a smaller regional version. It contains all the great information Woodall's North American Directory contains, but in a handy to-go version, specific to the states or provinces you need.

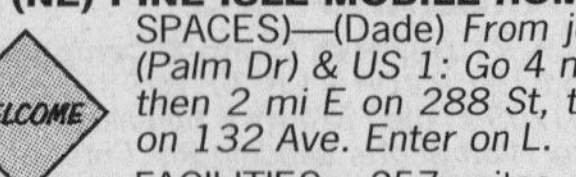

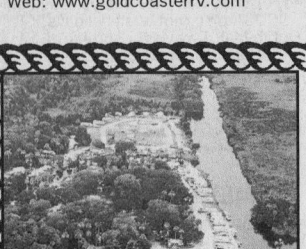

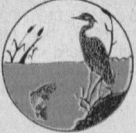

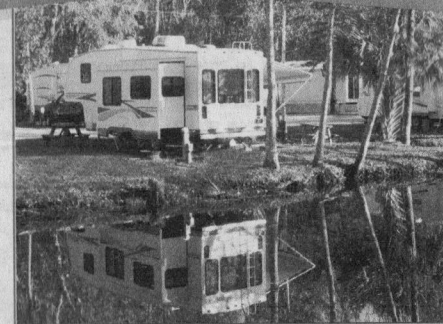

(NE) PINE ISLE MOBILE HOME PARK (RV SPACES)—(Dade) *From jct Hwy 9336 (Palm Dr) & US 1: Go 4 mi N on US 1, then 2 mi E on 288 St, then 500 ft N on 132 Ave. Enter on L.*

FACILITIES: 257 sites, typical site width 50 ft, 257 full hkups, (30/50 amps), mostly extd stay sites (winter), 20 pull-thrus, WiFi Internet central location, laundry, patios.

RECREATION: rec hall, pavilion, swim pool, golf nearby, shuffleboard court 3 shuffleboard courts, activities, horseshoes.

Pets welcome, quantity restrict. No tents. Age restrict may apply. Open all yr. Planned activities in winter only. Big rigs welcome. Clubs welcome. Rate in 2010 $20-25 for 2 persons. MC/VISA.

Phone: (305)248-0783
Address: 28600 SW 132 Ave, Homestead, FL 33033
Lat/Lon: 25.50157/-80.40436
Web: www.pineislepark.com

SEE AD PAGE 127

(E) THE BOARDWALK—(Dade) *From jct Hwy 9336 (Palm Dr) & US 1: Go 2 mi N on US 1, then 1 block E on 328th St, then 200 feet N on 6th Ave. Enter on R.*

EASY ACCESS TO THE KEYS & MIAMI
Gated RV resort located close to shopping and restaurants. Nearby attractions include Biscayne National Park, Everglades National Park, Pennekamp Coral Reef State Park, Homestead-Miami Speedway, and Coral Castle.

◆◆◆◆FACILITIES: 130 sites, typical site width 40 ft, 130 full hkups, (30/50 amps), many extd stay sites (winter), WiFi Internet central location, family camping, RV storage, laundry, picnic tables, patios, controlled access.

◆◆◆◆RECREATION: rec hall, rec room/area, swim pool, golf nearby, playground, shuffleboard court 5 shuffleboard courts, activities, horseshoes, v-ball.

Pets welcome. Partial handicap access. No tents. Open all yr. Big rigs welcome. Escort to site. Clubs welcome. Rate in 2010 $35-45 for 2 persons. MC/VISA/DISC/AMEX/Debit. Member ARVC, FLARVC. CCUSA 50% Discount. CCUSA reservations Recommended, CCUSA max stay 21 days. Discount not available Nov thru Mar.

Phone: (305)248-2487
Address: 100 NE 6th Ave, Homestead, FL 33030
Lat/Lon: 25.47142/-80.46889
Email: boardwalkrv@gmail.com
Web: www.boardwalkrv.com

SEE AD PAGE 127

HOMOSASSA—C-3

See listings at Chassahowitzka & Homosassa Springs, Lecanto, Inversess

✲ **(N) COMO RV & TRUCK SALES**—*From jct Hwy 490A & US 19: Go 3/4 mi N on US 19. Enter on R.* SALES: travel trailers, park models, 5th wheels, Class C motorhomes, Class B motorhomes, fold-down camping trailers, pre-owned unit sales. SERVICES: Open all yr. MC/VISA/DISC/AMEX.

Phone: (352)628-1411
Address: 3335 S Suncoast Blvd (US 19), Homosassa, FL 34448
Lat/Lon: 28.81337/-82.57649
Email: rcomo@tampabay.rr.com
Web: www.comorv.com

SEE AD TRAVEL SECTION PAGE 71

(S) Covered Wagon Campground (RV SPACES)—(Citrus) *From jct Hwy-490 & US-19: Go 3 mi S on US-19. Enter on L.* FACILITIES: 45 sites, typical site width 25 ft, 45 full hkups, (30/50 amps), 30 pull-thrus, family camping, dump. Pets welcome. No tents. Open all yr. Rate in 2010 $27-30 for 2 persons. Phone: (352) 628-4669.

HOMOSASSA—Continued on next page

Prepare gourmet meals in your RV kitchen! Woodall's Cooking on the Road with Celebrity Chefs includes dozens of tips and sidebars that make recipes easier to use while traveling. Go to www.woodalls.com/shop and check it out.

HOMOSASSA—Continued

(NE) NATURE'S RESORT & MARINA—(Citrus) *From jct US 19 & Halls River Rd: Go 2 mi W on Halls River Rd. Enter on R.*

◊◊◊FACILITIES: 310 sites, typical site width 15 ft, 310 full hkups, (20/30/50 amps), many extd stay sites (winter), cable TV, WiFi Instant Internet at site, phone on-site Internet (needs activ), phone Internet central location, family camping, tenting, cabins, RV storage, dump, non-guest dump $, laundry, ltd groc, RV supplies, LP gas by weight/by meter, marine gas, ice, picnic tables, patios, wood.

◊◊◊◊RECREATION: rec hall, rec room/area, swim pool, boating, canoeing, kayaking, ramp, dock, 5 pontoon/4 kayak rentals, saltwater/river fishing, fishing supplies, golf nearby, bsktball, playground, shuffleboard court 2 shuffleboard courts, activities, horseshoes, v-ball.

Pets welcome, quantity restrict. Partial handicap access. Open all yr. Big rigs welcome. Clubs welcome. Rate in 2010 $33-55 per family. MC/VISA/Debit. Member ARVC, FLARVC. CCUSA 50% Discount. CCUSA reservations Recommended, CCUSA max stay 2 days, CCUSA disc. not avail F, Sa, CCUSA disc. not avail holidays. Discount available May thru Oct.

Phone: (800)301-7880
Address: 10359 W Halls River Rd, Homosassa, FL 34448
Lat/Lon: 28.79799/-82.60595
Email: naturesresortFLA@yahoo.com
Web: www.naturesresortfla.com

SEE AD PAGE 128

HOMOSASSA SPRINGS—C-3

(S) HOMOSASSA CAREFREE RV RESORT(formerly Turtle Creek)—(Citrus) *From jct US 19 & Hwy 490A: Go 1/2 mi W on 490A, then 1 mi SW on Fish Bowl Dr. Enter on L.*

WELCOME TO CAREFREE RV RESORTS!
Explore our peaceful river & enjoy nature. Near the Gulf for fun deep-sea fishing or a walk on the beach. A river runs right through the resort for your fishing pleasure! Then enjoy pool-side fun or cookout at sunset!

◊◊◊FACILITIES: 234 sites, typical site width 30 ft, 234 full hkups, (30/50 amps), many extd stay sites (winter), 32 pull-thrus, cable TV, WiFi Instant Internet at site, cable on-site Internet (needs activ), WiFi Internet central location, family camping, tenting, cabins, dump, laundry, RV supplies, LP gas by weight/by meter, ice, picnic tables, patios.

◊◊◊◊RECREATION: rec hall, swim pool, stream fishing, mini-golf, golf nearby, shuffleboard court 2 shuffleboard courts, activities, horseshoes.

Pets welcome, breed restrict. Partial handicap access. Open all yr. Planned acitivities during season only. Big rigs welcome. Clubs welcome. Rate in 2010 $20-35 for 2 persons. MC/VISA/DISC. CCUSA 50% Discount. CCUSA reservations Recommended, CCUSA max stay 2 days, CCUSA disc. not avail F, Sa, CCUSA disc. not avail holidays. Not available Jan thru Mar.

Phone: (800)471-3722
Address: 10200 W Fishbowl Dr, Homosassa Springs, FL 34448
Lat/Lon: 28.79122/-82.60200
Email: turtlecreekrv@embarqmail.com
Web: www.carefreeresorts.com

SEE AD HOMOSASSA PAGE 128

HUDSON—C-3

(E) 7 Oaks RV Park & Sales—(Pasco) *From jct US 19 & Bolton Ave: Go 3/4 mi E on Bolton Ave. Enter on L.* ◊◊FACILITIES: 160 sites, typical site width 18 ft, 36 ft max RV length, 160 full hkups, (30/50 amps), 4 pull-thrus, dump, laundry. ◊◊RECREATION: swim pool. Pets welcome, size restrict, quantity restrict. No tents. Age restrict may apply. Open all yr. Rate in 2010 $20-28 for 2 persons. Phone: (727)862-3016.

(NE) BARRINGTON HILLS RV RESORT—(Pasco) *From jct Hwy 52 & US 19: Go 3-1/2 mi N on US 19, then 1-1/2 mi E on New York Ave. Enter on R.*

◊◊◊FACILITIES: 120 sites, typical site width 30 ft, 40 ft max RV length, accepts full hkup units only, 120 full hkups, (30/50 amps), mostly extd stay sites, WiFi Instant Internet at site ($), phone/cable on-site Internet (needs activ), WiFi Internet central location, RV's/park model rentals, laundry, picnic tables, patios.

HUDSON—Continued
BARRINGTON HILLS RV RESORT—Continued

◊◊◊RECREATION: rec hall, rec room/area, swim pool, golf nearby, shuffleboard court 6 shuffleboard courts, activities, horseshoes.

Pets welcome, breed restrict, size restrict, quantity restrict. Partial handicap access. No tents. Age restrict may apply. Open all yr. Planned activities winter only. Rate in 2010 $31-36 per vehicle. MC/VISA/DISC/AMEX.

Phone: (877)287-2757
Address: 9412 New York Ave, Hudson, FL 34667
Email: barrington_hills@equitylifestyle.com
Web: www.rvonthego.com

SEE AD ALACHUA PAGE 93

(NE) Three Lakes RV Resort (Morgan RV Resorts)—(Pasco) *From jct Hwy 52 & US 19: Go 5 mi N on US 19, then 1 mi E on Denton Ave. Enter on R.* ◊◊◊◊FACILITIES: 308 sites, typical site width 40 ft, 308 full hkups, (20/30/50 amps), laundry. ◊◊◊◊RECREATION: swim pool. Pets welcome, quantity restrict. Partial handicap access. No tents. Age restrict may apply. Open all yr. Big rigs welcome. Rate in 2010 $39.99 for 2 persons. Phone: (727)869-8511.

INGLIS—B-3

(S) RIVER LODGE RV RESORT—(Levy) *From jct US 19 & Hwy 40: Go 3/4 mi S on US 19. Enter on L.*

◊◊◊◊◊FACILITIES: 147 sites, typical site width 45 ft, 147 full hkups, (50 amps), many extd stay sites, 5 pull-thrus, cable TV, WiFi Instant Internet at site, family camping, RV storage, dump, non-guest dump $, laundry, ltd groc, RV supplies, LP gas by weight/by meter, ice, picnic tables, patios, wood.

◊◊◊RECREATION: rec hall, swim pool, golf nearby, bsktball, playground, sports field.

Pets welcome, breed restrict, quantity restrict. Partial handicap access. No tents. Open all yr. Big rigs welcome. Escort to site. Clubs welcome. Rate in 2010 $30 for 4 persons. MC/VISA/DISC/Debit.

Phone: (352)447-2900
Address: 13790 W Foss Groves Path, Ingliss, FL 34449
Lat/Lon: 29.02113/-82.66560
Email: info@riverlodgervresort.com
Web: www.riverlodgervresort.com

SEE AD CRYSTAL RIVER PAGE 105

(S) Sunshine Coast Resorts & Retreats—(Citrus) *From jct US 19 & CR 40: Go 1/4 mi S on US 19. Enter on R.* ◊◊◊FACILITIES: 21 sites, 21 full hkups, (30 amps), 3 pull-thrus, cable TV, family camping, tenting, dump, laundry, LP gas by weight/by meter, ice, picnic tables. ◊◊◊RECREATION: rec hall, swim pool, boating, canoeing, kayaking, ramp, dock, river fishing. Pets welcome, breed restrict, size restrict, quantity restrict. Open all yr. Rate in 2010 $25 for 2 persons. MC/VISA/DISC/AMEX. CCUSA 50% Discount. CCUSA reservations Recommended, CCUSA max stay 3 days, CCUSA disc. not avail S, CCUSA disc. not avail F,Sa.

Phone: (352)447-5333
Address: 14035 W River Rd, Inglis, FL 34449
Lat/Lon: 29.02343/-82.66996
Email: info@sunshinecoastrandr.com
Web: www.sunshinecoastrandr.com

INVERNESS—C-3

✲ **COMO RV & TRUCK SALES, SERVICE & RV COLLISION CENTER**—*From north jct US 41 & Hwy 44: Go 1/2 mi W on Hwy 44. Enter on L.* SALES: travel trailers, park models, 5th wheels, toy hauler, Class C motorhomes, Class B motorhomes, fold-down camping trailers, pre-owned unit sales. SERVICES: full-time mech, engine/chassis repair, RV appliance repair, body work/collision repair, LP gas by weight/by meter, sells parts/accessories. Open all yr. MC/VISA/DISC/AMEX.

Phone: (866)344-1411
Address: 1601 W Main St, Inverness, FL 34450
Lat/Lon: 28.83573/-82.34949
Email: rcomo@tampabay.rr.com
Web: comorv.com

SEE AD TRAVEL SECTION PAGE 71

Woodall's Tip... Looking for a particular campground? Use our Alphabetical Quick Reference in the middle & near the end of this Directory.

INVERNESS—Continued

(E) RIVERSIDE LODGE—(Citrus) *From north jct Hwy 41 & Hwy 44: Go 7 mi E on Hwy 44. Enter on L.*

◊◊◊◊FACILITIES: 24 sites, typical site width 20 ft, 16 full hkups, 8 W&E, (30/50 amps), some extd stay sites, cable TV, WiFi Instant Internet at site, family camping, tenting, dump, laundry, picnic tables, patios.

◊◊◊RECREATION: rec hall, boating, canoeing, kayaking, dock, rowboat/2 canoe rentals, river fishing, golf nearby, activities, (wkends).

Pets welcome ($), quantity restrict. Open all yr. Big rigs welcome. Rate in 2010 $40 for 2 persons. MC/VISA. Member ARVC, FLARVC. CCUSA 50% Discount. CCUSA reservations Recommended, CCUSA max stay Unlimited. Discount valid May thru Dec. 2 day minimum stay required. Not valid holiday weekends & special events. Shower surcharge includes up to 2 persons.

Phone: (888)404-8332
Address: 12561 E Gulf to Lake Hwy (SR 44), Inverness, FL 34450
Lat/Lon: 28.85147/-82.22517
Email: info@riversidelodgerv.com
Web: www.riversidelodgerv.com

SEE AD CRYSTAL RIVER PAGE 104

JACKSONVILLE—A-3

COUNTRY OAKS CAMPGROUND & RV PARK—*From north jct I-295 & I-95: Go 19 mi N on I-95 (GA exit 1), then 1/4 mi W on St. Mary's Rd. Enter on L.*

SEE PRIMARY LISTING AT KINGSLAND, GA AND AD THIS PAGE

(N) FLAMINGO LAKE RV RESORT—(Duval) *From jct I-95 & I-295: Go 3 mi S on I-295 (exit 32), then 200 yds N on Hwy 115 (Lem Turner Blvd), then 200 yds SE on Newcomb Rd. Enter on L.*

◊◊◊◊◊FACILITIES: 286 sites, typical site width 40 ft, 286 full hkups, (20/30/50 amps), many extd stay sites, 118 pull-thrus, cable TV, WiFi Instant Internet at site, WiFi Internet central location, family camping, cabins, dump, non-guest dump $, laundry, ltd groc, RV supplies, LP gas by weight/by meter, ice, picnic tables, patios, controlled access.

◊◊◊◊◊RECREATION: rec hall, rec room/area, pavilion, equipped pavilion, swim pool, lake swim, boating, electric motors only, canoeing, kayaking, dock, canoe/2 pedal boat rentals, lake fishing, fishing supplies, golf nearby, bsktball, playground, activities, (wkends), horseshoes, v-ball.

Pets welcome, breed restrict. Partial handicap access. No tents. Open all yr. Big rigs welcome. Escort to site. Clubs welcome. Rate in 2010 $42-65 for 2 persons. MC/VISA. ATM. Member ARVC, FLARVC.

Text 86098 to (440)725-8687 to see our Visual Tour.

Phone: (800)782-4323
Address: 3640 Newcomb Rd, Jacksonville, FL 32218
Lat/Lon: 30.45696/-81.70771
Email: customer.service@flamingolake.com
Web: www.flamingolake.com

SEE AD PAGE 131

JACKSONVILLE—Continued on next page

JACKSONVILLE—Continued

(E) HANNA PARK (City Park)—(Duval) *From jct Hwy 10 & Hwy A1A: Go 2-1/4 mi N on Hwy A1A, then 1 mi NE on Mayport Rd/Hwy 101, then 1 block E on Wonderwood Rd. Enter at end.* FACILITIES: 293 sites, typical site width 19 ft, 293 full hkups, (20/30/50 amps), 53 pull-thrus, family camping, tenting, dump, laundry, ltd groc. RECREATION: saltwater swim, boating, no motors, canoeing, dock, saltwater/lake fishing, playground. Pets welcome, quantity restrict. Partial handicap access. Open all yr. Big rigs welcome. Member ARVC, FLARVC. Phone: (904)249-4700.

(E) LITTLE TALBOT ISLAND STATE PARK—(Duval) *From jct I-95 & Hwy 105: Go 14 mi E on Hwy 105, then 3 mi N on Hwy A1A.* FACILITIES: 40 sites, 30 ft max RV length, 40 W&E, tenting, dump. RECREATION: saltwater swim, boating, canoeing, saltwater fishing. Pets welcome. Open all yr. Phone: (904)251-2320.

(N) MILITARY PARK (Jacksonville NAS)—(Duval) *Off base. US 95S & US 295N: Go N on US 17.* FACILITIES: 43 sites, 28 full hkups, 9 W&E, 6 no hkups, tenting. RECREATION: Open all yr. Phone: (904)542-3227.

WELCOME

(N) PECAN PARK RV RESORT—(Duval) *From I-95 (exit 366) and Pecan Park Rd: Go 200 yds W on Pecan Park Rd. Enter on L.*

******FROM ORLANDO TO SAVANNAH******
Stay with us at Jacksonville's Newest, Finest Resort! Min's to Alltel Stadium, Airport, Mayo Clinic, & Attractions from Orlando to Savannah, & adjacent to Flea & Farmers Market, we offer 183 FHU Luxury Sites incl. Cable & WIFI.

◆◆◆◆◆FACILITIES: 183 sites, typical site width 40 ft, 183 full hkups, (20/30/50 amps), some extd stay sites, 183 pull-thrus, cable TV, WiFi Instant Internet at site, family camping, RV storage, dump, non-guest dump, laundry, ltd groc, RV supplies, LP gas by weight/by meter, ice, picnic tables, patios.

◆◆◆RECREATION: rec hall, swim pool, lake fishing, bsktball, horseshoes, sports field.

CAMPCLUB USA

Pets welcome. Partial handicap access. No tents. Open all yr. Big rigs welcome. Clubs welcome. Rate in 2010 $40 for 2 persons. MC/VISA/DISC. Member ARVC, FLARVC. FMCA discount. CCUSA 50% Discount. CCUSA reservations Not Accepted, CCUSA max stay 2 days, CCUSA disc. not avail F,Sa. Discount not available when park @ 75% occupancy.

Text 87167 to (440)725-8687 to see our Visual Tour.

Phone: (888)604-6770
Address: 650 Pecan Park Rd, Jacksonville, FL 32218
Lat/Lon: 30.51618/-81.63883
Email: mrkt723@bellsouth.net
Web: www.pecanparkrvresort.com

SEE AD PAGE 130 AND AD TRAVEL SECTION PAGE 74

JASPER—A-2

(SE) Florida Gateway Resort (TOO NEW TO RATE)—(Hamilton) *From jct I-75 & US 129 (exit 451): Go 3/4 mi S on US 129, then 1-1/4 mi W on SE 113th Blvd. Enter on L.* FACILITIES: 82 sites, typical site width 35 ft, 70 full hkups, 1 E, (30/50 amps), 11 no hkups, 70 pull-thrus, cable TV, WiFi Instant Internet at site, family camping, tenting, RV storage, dump, non-guest dump $, laundry, ice, picnic tables, fire rings, wood. RECREATION: rec hall, pavilion, swim pool, pond fishing, mini-golf, bike rental 6 bike rentals, playground, shuffleboard court 2 shuffleboard courts, horseshoes, hiking trails, v-ball. Pets welcome. Partial handicap access. Open all yr. Rate in 2010 $36.36 per vehicle. MC/VISA/DISC. Member ARVC, FLARVC. CCUSA 50%

CAMPCLUB USA

JASPER—Continued
Florida Gateway Resort—Continued

Discount. CCUSA reservations Recommended, CCUSA max stay 5 days, CCUSA disc. not avail F,Sa. Not valid special events.

Phone: (877)253-0114
Address: 7516 SE 113th Blvd, Jasper, FL 32052
Email: info@gatewayfl.com
Web: www.gatewayfl.com

Reserve Online at Woodalls.com

JENNINGS—A-2

(W) Jennings Outdoor Resort Campground—(Hamilton) *From jct I-75 (exit 467) & Hwy 143: Go 500 feet W on Hwy 143. Enter on R.* ◆◆◆◆FACILITIES: 102 sites, typical site width 25 ft, 102 full hkups, (30/50 amps), 102 pull-thrus, family camping, tenting, laundry, full svc store. ◆◆◆◆RECREATION: swim pool, boating, no motors, canoeing, lake fishing, playground. Pets welcome. Partial handicap access. Open all yr. Big rigs welcome. Rate in 2010 $25.95 for 2 persons. Member ARVC, FLARVC. Phone: (386)938-3321. FMCA discount.

JENSEN BEACH—D-5

WELCOME

(N) NETTLES ISLAND RESORT & RV PARK—(St. Lucie) *From jct Hwy 716 & US 1: Go 2 mi S on US 1, then 3 mi E on Jensen Beach Blvd, then 1/2 mi N on Indian River, then 2 mi E on Hwy 732, then 2-1/4 mi N on A-1-A. Enter on L.*

◆◆◆◆◆FACILITIES: 100 sites, typical site width 35 ft, accepts full hkup units only, 100 full hkups, (30/50 amps), cable TV, WiFi Instant Internet at site ($), family camping, RV's/park model rentals, full svc store, LP gas by weight/by meter, ice, patios, controlled access.

◆◆◆◆◆RECREATION: rec hall, rec room/area, coin games, 2 swim pools, saltwater swim, hot tub, boating, canoeing, kayaking, ramp, dock, saltwater/river fishing, fishing supplies, mini-golf, golf nearby, bsktball, playground, shuffleboard court 6 shuffleboard courts, activities, tennis, horseshoes, v-ball.

Pets welcome ($), breed restrict, size restrict, quantity restrict. Partial handicap access. No

JENSEN BEACH—Continued
NETTLES ISLAND RESORT & RV PARK—Continued

tents. Open all yr. Big rigs welcome. Clubs welcome. Rate in 2010 $37-64 for 4 persons. MC/VISA/Debit.

Phone: (866)229-1518
Address: 9803 S Ocean Dr, Jensen Beach, FL 34957
Lat/Lon: 27.28665/-80.21276
Email: info@nettlescoastalrealty.com
Web: www.nettlescoastalrealty.com

SEE AD THIS PAGE

JUNO BEACH—D-5

WELCOME

(N) JUNO OCEAN WALK RV RESORT—(Palm Beach) *From jct Hwy 786 (PGA Blvd) & I-95: Go 3 mi N on I-95 (exit 83), then 4-1/2 mi E on Donald Ross Rd, then 3/4 mi N on US 1, then 1/4 mi W on Juno Ocean Walk. Enter at end.*

WALK TO THE OCEAN!
A vacation retreat in beautiful Palm Beach County. Miles of sandy beaches & St Louis Cardinal Spring Training nearby. Large heated pool with jacuzzi. First rate clubhouse. Free Wi-FI & Cable TV. Enjoy the carefree FL lifestyle!

◆◆◆◆◆FACILITIES: 246 sites, typical site width 30 ft, 246 full hkups, (30/50 amps), some extd stay sites (winter), cable TV, WiFi Instant Internet at site, RV's/park model rentals, dump, non-guest dump $, laundry, picnic tables, patios.

◆◆◆◆RECREATION: rec hall, rec room/area, swim pool, hot tub, golf nearby, playground, shuffleboard court 2 shuffleboard courts, activities, v-ball.

Pets welcome, quantity restrict. Partial handicap access. No tents. Open all yr. Big rigs welcome. Escort to site. Clubs welcome. Green Friendly. Rate in 2010 $32-75 for 2 persons. MC/VISA/DISC/Debit. Member ARVC, FLARVC.

JUNO OCEAN WALK RV RESORT—Continued on next page

Butterfly McQueen, actor, is from Florida.

Phone: (561)622-7500
Address: 900 Juno Ocean Walk, Juno Beach, FL 33408
Lat/Lon: 26.89278/-80.06237
Email: Junorvresort@comcast.net
Web: www.junooceanwalkrvresort.com

SEE AD THIS PAGE

JUPITER—D-5

✲ **(W) Land Yachts**—*From jct I-95 (exit 87) & Hwy 706 (Indian Town Rd): Go 1-1/4 mi E on Hwy 706, then 1/4 mi S on Maplewood Dr, then 1/4 mi E on Commerce Ln. Enter on R.* SERVICES: full-time mech, engine/chassis repair, RV appliance repair, body work/collision repair, RV storage, sells parts/accessories, installs hitches. Warranty Work. Open all yr. MC/VISA/DISC/AMEX/Debit.

Phone: (561)745-0242
Address: 1414 Commerce Ln, Jupiter, FL 33458
Lat/Lon: 26.93012/-80.12061
Email: landyachtsinc@bellsouth.net
Web: www.landyachtsinc.com

WELCOME

(W) WEST JUPITER CAMPING RESORT—(Palm Beach) *From jct I-95 (exit 87B) & Hwy 706 (Indiantown Rd): Go 5 mi W on Hwy 706, then 500 ft S on 130th Ave. Enter on R.*

◊◊◊FACILITIES: 84 sites, typical site width 30 ft, 84 full hkups, (20/30/50 amps), many extd stay sites (winter), cable TV, ($), WiFi Instant Internet at site ($), family camping, RV's/park model rentals, RV storage, dump, non-guest dump $, laundry, full svc store, RV supplies, LP bottle exch, ice, picnic tables, patios, fire rings, wood, controlled access.

◊◊◊◊RECREATION: rec room/area, pavilion, swim pool, pond fishing, fishing supplies, golf nearby, bsktball, playground, shuffleboard court 2 shuffleboard courts, activities, horseshoes, v-ball, local tours.

Pets welcome, breed restrict. Partial handicap access. No tents. Open all yr. Big rigs welcome. Escort to site. Clubs welcome. Rate in 2010 $25-47 for 2 persons. MC/VISA/DISC/Debit. Member ARVC, FLARVC. FMCA discount.

Phone: (888)746-6073
Address: 17801 130th Ave N, Jupiter, FL 33478
Lat/Lon: 26.93963/-80.23931
Email: wjcr@bellsouth.net
Web: www.westjupitercampingresort.com

SEE AD WEST PALM BEACH PAGE 177

KENANSVILLE—C-4

WELCOME

(W) LAKE MARIAN PARADISE MARINA & RV RESORT—(Osceola) *From jct US 441 & Hwy 523: Go 3-1/4 mi W on Hwy 523, then 1/2 mi S on Arnold Rd. Enter at end.*

◊◊◊FACILITIES: 59 sites, typical site width 35 ft, 59 full hkups, (30/50 amps), mostly extd stay sites (winter), 5 pull-thrus, WiFi Instant Internet at site, family camping, cabins, RV storage, dump, laundry, ltd groc, RV supplies, ice, picnic tables, patios.

◊◊◊◊RECREATION: rec hall, equipped pavilion, boating, canoeing, kayaking, pontoon rentals, lake fishing, fishing supplies, golf nearby, shuffleboard court 2 shuffleboard courts, activities, horseshoes.

Pets welcome, breed restrict. No tents. Open all yr. Big rigs welcome. Clubs welcome. Rate in 2010 $28-37 per vehicle. MC/VISA. Member ARVC.

Phone: (407)436-1464
Address: 901 Arnold Rd, Kenansville, FL 34739
Lat/Lon: 27.86992/-81.04379
Email: info@lakemarian.com
Web: www.lakemarian.com

SEE AD TRAVEL SECTION PAGE 78

KEY LARGO—F-5

WELCOME

(SW) CALUSA CAMPGROUND CONDOMINIUM ASSOCIATION—(Monroe) *On US 1 at milepost 101-1/2(Bayside). Enter on R.*

◊◊◊◊FACILITIES: 367 sites, typical site width 35 ft, 367 full hkups, (30/50 amps), mostly extd stay sites (winter), 15 pull-thrus, cable TV, WiFi Instant Internet at site ($), family camping, RV's/park model rentals, laundry, LP bottle exch, ice, picnic tables, patios, controlled access.

◊◊◊◊RECREATION: rec hall, pavilion, swim pool, boating, canoeing, kayaking, ramp, dock, saltwater fishing, bsktball, playground, activities, tennis, horseshoes.

Pets welcome ($). Partial handicap access. Open all yr. Planned group activities in winter only. Big rigs welcome. Escort to site. Clubs welcome. Rate in 2010 $53-120 for 2 persons. MC/VISA/DISC. Member ARVC, FLARVC.

Phone: (305)451-0232
Address: 325 Calusa, Key Largo, FL 33037
Lat/Lon: 25.11168/-80.42458
Email: office@calusacampground.com
Web: www.calusacampground.com

SEE AD THIS PAGE

(N) JOHN PENNEKAMP CORAL REEF STATE PARK—(Monroe) *From jct Hwy 905 & US 1: Go 8 mi S on US 1 to milepost 102.5.* FACILITIES: 47 sites, 30 ft max RV length, 47 W&E, tenting, dump. RECREATION: saltwater swim, boating, canoeing, ramp, dock, saltwater fishing. No pets. Partial handicap access. Open all yr. Phone: (800)326-3521.

(NE) Kings Kamp, RV, Tent & Marina—(Monroe) *On US 1 at milepost 103-1/2. Enter on R.* ◊◊◊FACILITIES: 60 sites, typical site width 25 ft, 35 ft max RV length, 52 full hkups, 8 W&E, (15/30/50 amps), family camping, tenting, dump, laundry. ◊◊RECREATION: saltwater swim, boating, canoeing, ramp, dock, saltwater fishing. Pets welcome, size restrict. Open all yr. Rate in 2010 $50-60 for 2 persons. Phone: (305)451-0010.

WELCOME

QUAIL RUN RV RESORT—*From FL-5/ N/US 1N: Go 28 mi N on FL-5/US 1N, then N on Florida 821 Toll N for 38 mi, then N on I-75 for 275 mi, then 1 mi W on Wesley Chapel Blvd, then 2.1 mi N on Old Paseo Rd. Enter on R.*

SEE PRIMARY LISTING AT WESLEY CHAPEL AND AD WESLEY CHAPEL PAGE 177

KEY WEST—F-4

WELCOME

⚑ **BIG PINE KEY & FLORIDA'S LOWER KEYS**—

DOESN'T GET MORE LOW KEY THAN THIS
Talk about truth in advertising. No crowds. No Noise. And unlimited biking, hiking, camping and kayaking. Big Pine Key and The Lower Keys is exactly as the name implies.

Florida Keys campgrounds & RV facilities range from small properties w/basic amentities to waterfront campground resorts, incl heated swimming

BIG PINE KEY & FLORIDA'S LOWER KEYS—Continued on next page

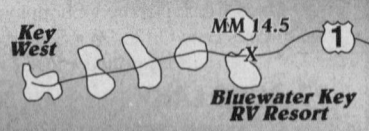

pools, hot tubs, onsite laundries, gift/conv stores, marina/dock facilties & restaurants. Busy each winter. Open all yr.

Phone: (800)USA-ESCAPE
Address: 31020 Overseas Hwy, Big Pine Key, FL 33043
Email: webeditor@fla-keys.com
Web: www.fla-keys.com/lowerkeys

SEE AD DISCOVER SECTION PAGE 35

(NE) BLUEWATER KEY RV RESORT—(Monroe) *On US 1 at mile marker 14-1/2. Enter on L.*

WELCOME

LUXURY OCEAN WATERFRONT RESORT
Enjoy paradise in the Florida Keys. Beautifully-landscaped exclusive ownership RV Resort only 10 mi from Key West. Lot rentals on large, private sites avail with Tiki Huts. Pool. Boating & fishing. www.bluewaterkey.com. Free Wi-Fi.

◇◇◇◇◇FACILITIES: 81 sites, typical site width 35 ft, accepts full hkup units only, 81 full hkups, (30/50 amps), many extd stay sites (winter), cable TV, WiFi Instant Internet at site, laundry, ice, picnic tables, patios, controlled access.

◇◇◇RECREATION: rec room/area, pavilion, swim pool, saltwater swim, boating, canoeing, kayaking, ramp, dock, saltwater fishing, golf nearby, horseshoes, hiking trails.

Pets welcome, quantity restrict. Partial handicap access. No tents. Open all yr. RV minimum length 26'. Big rigs welcome. Escort to site. Clubs welcome. MC/VISA/DISC/Debit. Member ARVC, FLARVC.

Text 107872 to (440)725-8687 to see our Visual Tour.

Phone: (305)745-2494
Address: 2950 US Highway 1, Key West, FL 33040
Lat/Lon: 24.62390/-81.60059
Email: bluekeyrv@aol.com
Web: www.bluewaterkey.com

SEE AD PAGE 132

(NE) BOYD'S KEY WEST CAMPGROUND—(Monroe) *From US 1 at milepost 5:Go 1 block S on 3rd St, then 1/4 mi E on Maloney (MacDonald) Ave. Enter on L.*

WELCOME

KEY WEST CAMPING
Our family owned and operated park is surrounded by the enchanting ocean on one side and exciting Key West on the other! Waterfront sites, marina with boat ramp and docks, heated pool, and wonderful tropical weather all year.

◇◇◇◇FACILITIES: 263 sites, typical site width 30 ft, 203 full hkups, 28 W&E, (20/30/50 amps), 32 no hkups, some extd stay sites (winter), cable TV, WiFi Instant Internet at site, family camping,

tenting, RV storage, dump, non-guest dump $, laundry, groceries, RV supplies, ice, picnic tables, patios, grills, wood, controlled access.

◇◇◇◇RECREATION: rec room/area, pavilion, equipped pavilion, coin games, swim pool, boating, canoeing, kayaking, ramp, dock, saltwater fishing, fishing supplies, golf nearby, activities.

Pets welcome, breed restrict. Partial handicap access. Open all yr. Storage available Apr 1 to Dec 1. Big rigs welcome. Clubs welcome. Rate in 2010 $60-120 for 2 persons. MC/VISA/Debit. ATM. Member ARVC, FLARVC.

Text 107873 to (440)725-8687 to see our Visual Tour.

Phone: (305)294-1465
Address: Stock Island, 6401 Maloney Ave, Key West, FL 33040
Lat/Lon: 24.57102/-81.73397
Email: info@boydscampground.com
Web: www.boydscampground.com

SEE AD THIS PAGE

KEY WEST—Continued on next page

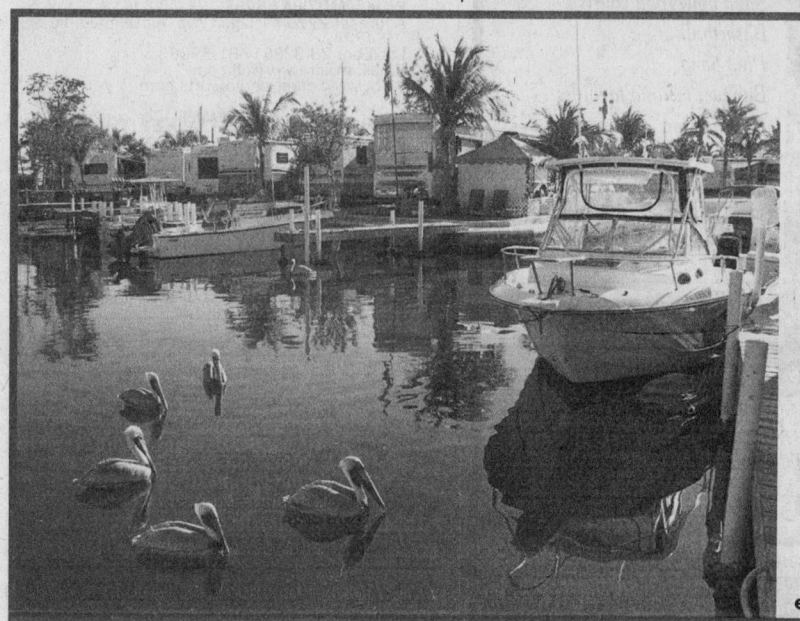

KEY WEST—Continued

MILITARY PARK (Key West NAS-Sigsbee Park)—(Monroe) *On US 1. On base.* FACILITIES: 70 sites, 70 full hkups, tenting, dump, laundry. RECREATION: boating, ramp, saltwater fishing, playground. Open all yr. Phone: (888)539-7697.

KEYSTONE HEIGHTS—B-3

(NE) MIKE ROESS GOLD HEAD BRANCH STATE PARK—(Clay) *From jct Hwy-21 & Hwy-100: Go 6 mi NE on Hwy-21.* FACILITIES: 76 sites, 30 ft max RV length, 64 W&E, (30/50 amps), 12 no hkups, tenting, dump. RECREATION: lake swim, boating, canoeing, ramp, dock, lake fishing. Pets welcome. Partial handicap access. Open all yr. Phone: (352)473-4701.

The 10,000 islands of mangrove trees off the coast of Marco Island and the Everglades are formed from bits of shell, driftwood and seaweed that get trapped in the roots. As the trees mature and topple into the water, more trees take root. New islands are constantly being formed this way, so they are impossible to count. There may be as many as 20,000.

KISSIMMEE—C-4

(NE) EAST LAKE RV RESORT RESTAURANT & MARINA—(Osceola) *From jct US 192 & Boggy Creek Rd: Go 6 mi NE on Boggy Creek Rd, then continue 1-1/2 SE on Boggy Creek Rd, the 1/2 mi S on Fish Camp Rd. Enter on L.*

AN RVER'S DREAM COME TRUE

Fabulous Championship Bass Fishing Resort with RV Sites & Cabin Rentals. A full Service Marina & Restaurant (Great Prime Rib). Easy drive to the Atlantic Ocean Beaches and all of Orlando Fun Attractions. Come - Stay - Play!

◊◊◊FACILITIES: 243 sites, typical site width 14 ft, 36 ft max RV length, 243 full hkups, (30/50 amps), some extd stay sites (winter), 25 pull-thrus, cable TV, phone/cable on-site Internet (needs activ), WiFi Internet central location, family camping, tenting, cabins, dump, laundry, ltd groc, RV supplies, LP gas by weight, marine gas, ice, picnic tables, patios.

Norman Thargard, astronaut, is from Florida.

KISSIMMEE—Continued

EAST LAKE RV RESORT RESTAURANT & MARINA—Continued

◊◊◊◊◊RECREATION: rec room/area, equipped pavilion, coin games, swim pool, boating, canoeing, kayaking, ramp, dock, 5 motorboat rentals, lake fishing, fishing supplies, golf nearby, bsktball, playground, shuffleboard court 2 shuffleboard courts, activities, tennis, horseshoes, v-ball.

Pets welcome. Partial handicap access. Open all yr. Rate in 2010 $40-45 for 2 persons. MC/VISA/DISC/AMEX/Debit. CCUSA 50% Discount. CCUSA reservations Not Accepted, CCUSA max stay 1 day, Cash only for CCUSA disc., CCUSA disc. not avail holidays. Discount available May thru Oct.

Phone: (407)348-2040
Address: 3705 Big Bass Rd, Kissimmee, FL 34744
Lat/Lon: 28.32718/-81.29290
Email: info@eastlakefishcamp.com
Web: www.eastlakefishcamp.net

SEE AD ORLANDO PAGE 149

(N) Great Oak Campgrounds—(Osceola) *From jct US-17/441 & US-192: Go 3-1/2 mi W on US-192, then 3/4 mi S on Bass Rd, then 500 feet W on Yowell Rd. Enter on L.* ◊◊◊FACILITIES: 196 sites, typical site width 20 ft, 38 ft max RV length, 196 full hkups, (30/50 amps), 10 pull-thrus, family camping, tenting, laundry. ◊◊◊RECREATION: swim pool. Pets welcome, breed restrict. Partial handicap access. Open all yr. Rate in 2010 $32 for 2 persons. Phone: (407)396-9092.

KOA Orlando/Kissimmee—(Osceola) *From jct I-4 & US 192: Go 4-3/4 mi E on US 192, then left on Seven Dwarfs Lane (at Sam's Warehouse.). Enter on L.* ◊◊◊◊◊FACILITIES: 102 sites, 102 full hkups, (20/30/50 amps), 46 pull-thrus, family camping, tenting, dump, laundry, ltd groc. ◊◊◊RECREATION: swim pool, playground. Pets welcome. Partial handicap access. Open all yr. Big rigs welcome. Rate in 2010 $58-80 for 2 persons. Phone: (407)396-2400. KOA discount.

(S) Merry "D" RV Sanctuary—(Orange) *From jct US 17/92/441 (John Young Parkway) & US 192: Go 3-1/2 mi S on US 17/92, then 7 mi S on Hwy 531, (Pleasant Hill Rd). Enter on L.* ◊◊◊FACILITIES: 133 sites, typical site width 40 ft, 121 full hkups, 5 W&E, (20/30/50 amps), 7 no hkups, 33 pull-thrus, family camping, tenting, dump, laundry. ◊◊◊RECREATION: pond fishing, playground. Pets welcome. Partial handicap access. Open all yr. Big rigs welcome. Rate in 2010 $35-38 for 2 persons. Phone: (407)870-0719.

(W) Mill Creek RV Resort—(Osceola) *From jct US 17/92 & US 192: Go 3/4 mi E on US 192, then 1-1/2 mi N on Hwy 531 (Michigan Ave). Enter on R.* ◊◊FACILITIES: 157 sites, typical site width 22 ft, 36 ft max RV length, 157 full hkups, (20/30/50 amps), phone/cable on-site Internet (needs activ), WiFi Internet central location, family camping, laundry, LP gas by weight/by meter, picnic tables, patios. ◊◊◊RECREATION: rec hall, swim pool, shuffleboard court 4 shuffleboard courts, activities, horseshoes. Pets welcome, breed restrict, quantity restrict. No tents. Open all yr. Rate in 2010 $32 for 2 persons. MC/VISA. Member ARVC, FLARVC. CCUSA 50% Discount. CCUSA reservations Recommended, CCUSA max stay 1 day. Discount not available Jan thru Mar.

Phone: (407)847-6288
Address: 2775 Michigan Ave, Kissimmee, FL 34744
Lat/Lon: 28.32881/-81.39083
Email: millcreekrv@cfl.com
Web: www.carefreervresorts.com

KISSIMMEE—Continued on next page

Woodall's Tip... 100% Money Back Guarantee... If for any reason you're not satisfied with this Directory, please return it to us by December 31, 2011 along with your sales receipt, and we'll reimburse you for the amount you paid for the Directory.

KISSIMMEE—Continued

(N) ORANGE GROVE CAMPGROUND—(Osceola) *From jct I-4 (exit 62) & US 192: Go 6-3/4 mi E on US 192, then 1-1/4 mi NW on Old Vineland Rd. Enter on R.*

◆◆◆FACILITIES: 200 sites, typical site width 25 ft, 176 full hkups, 24 W&E, (20/30/50 amps), many extd stay sites (winter), 3 pull-thrus, phone/WiFi Instant Internet at site ($), WiFi Internet central location ($), family camping, tenting, RV storage, dump, non-guest dump $, portable dump, laundry, RV supplies, LP gas by meter, ice, picnic tables, patios.

◆◆◆◆RECREATION: rec hall, swim pool, mini-golf, golf nearby, playground, shuffleboard court 2 shuffleboard courts, activities, horseshoes.

Pets welcome, breed restrict, quantity restrict. Open all yr. Planned group activities winter only. Big rigs welcome. Clubs welcome. Rate in 2010 $34-39 for 2 persons. MC/VISA/DISC/Debit. Member ARVC, FLARVC. CCUSA 50% Discount. CCUSA reservations Recommended, CCUSA max stay 1 day. Discount available Apr thru Oct.

Phone: (407)396-6655
Address: 2425 Old Vineland Rd, Kissimmee, FL 34746
Lat/Lon: 28.31703/-81.46438
Email: info@ogcrvpark.com
Web: www.ogcrvpark.com

SEE AD PAGE 134

Ponderosa RV Park—(Osceola) *From jct US 17/92/441 & US 192: Go 1-1/2 mi E on US 192 & 441, then 1 mi NE on Hwy C-530 (Boggy Creek Rd). Enter on L.* ◆◆◆FACILITIES: 210 sites, typical site width 30 ft, 40 ft max RV length, 200 full hkups, 10 W&E, (30/50 amps), 2 pull-thrus, WiFi Instant Internet at site ($), phone/cable on-site Internet (needs activ), WiFi Internet central location, family camping, tenting, RV storage, dump, laundry, portable dump, laundry, picnic tables, patios. ◆◆◆RECREATION: rec hall, swim pool, bsktball, play equipment, 3 shuffleboard courts, activities, horseshoes. Pets welcome, breed restrict, size restrict, quantity restrict. Open all yr. Rate in 2010 $30 for 2 persons. MC/VISA/DISC. CCUSA 50% Discount. CCUSA reservations Recommended, CCUSA max stay Unlimited. Discount not available Jan thru Apr. All pets must be under 40 lbs, no bulldogs, no animals considered dangerous. Persons 14 and up are considered adults for surcharge purposes.

Phone: (407)847-6002
Address: 1983 Boggy Creek Rd, Kissimmee, FL 34744
Lat/Lon: 28.30466/-81.36457
Web: www.ponderosarvpark.com

SHERWOOD FOREST RV RESORT—(Osceola) *From jct I-4 & US-192: Go 3 mi E on US-192. Enter on R.*

◆◆◆◆FACILITIES: 512 sites, typical site width 25 ft, 512 full hkups, (30/50 amps), mostly extd stay sites (winter), 450 pull-thrus, heater not allowed, WiFi Instant Internet at site ($), phone on-site Internet (needs activ), WiFi Internet central location, family camping, RV storage, laundry, ice, picnic tables.

◆◆◆◆◆RECREATION: rec hall, rec room/area, pavilion, swim pool, hot tub, lake fishing, mini-golf, golf nearby, bsktball, playground, shuffleboard court 14 shuffleboard courts, activities, tennis, horseshoes, v-ball, local tours.

Pets welcome, breed restrict, size restrict, quantity restrict. Partial handicap access. No tents. Open all yr. Planned activities winter only. Big rigs welcome. Clubs welcome. MC/VISA/DISC/AMEX. Member ARVC, FLARVC.

Phone: (407)396-7431
Address: 5300 W. Irlo Bronson (Hwy US 192), Kissimmee, FL 34746
Lat/Lon: 28.32769/-81.49460
Email: sherwood_forest_rv@equitylifestyles.com
Web: www.equitylifestyles.com

SEE AD ALACHUA PAGE 93 AND AD ORLANDO PAGE 149

Can you trust the Woodall's ratings? 25 evaluation teams have scoured North American campgrounds to provide you with accurate, up to date information & ratings. Find a rating you don't agree with? Send a letter or email our way, and we'll give it extra attention for 2012.

KISSIMMEE—Continued

TROPICAL PALMS RESORT—(Osceola) *From jct I-4 & US 192: Go 1-1/2 mi E on US 192, then 1/2 mi S on Holiday Trail. Enter on R.*

FAR FROM ORDINARY, CLOSE TO THE MAGIC

Tropical Palms located within 5 miles of the world's most popular theme parks, water parks can accommodate anything from a tent trailer to the biggest RV. Kick back and relax in our heated pool, playground, fishing and more.

◆◆◆◆◆FACILITIES: 335 sites, typical site width 35 ft, 275 full hkups, 60 W&E, (20/30/50 amps), mostly extd stay sites (winter), 270 pull-thrus, cable TV, ($), WiFi Instant Internet at site, WiFi Internet central location, family camping, tenting, cabins, RV storage, dump, laundry, ltd groc, RV supplies, LP gas by weight, ice, picnic tables, patios, controlled access.

◆◆◆◆◆RECREATION: rec hall, rec room/area, swim pool, wading pool, pond fishing, fishing supplies, mini-golf, golf nearby, bsktball, playground, shuffleboard court 2 shuffleboard courts, activities, horseshoes, v-ball, local tours.

Pets welcome, quantity restrict. Partial handicap access. Open all yr. Church services during season. Big rigs welcome. Escort to site. Clubs welcome. MC/VISA/DISC/AMEX. Member ARVC, FLARVC. CCUSA 50% Discount. CCUSA reservations Recommended, CCUSA max stay Unlimited. Discount available May thru Oct but not holiday weekends.

Phone: (800)647-2567
Address: 2650 Holiday Trail, Kissimmee, FL 34746
Lat/Lon: 28.32545/-81.51674
Email: reservations@tropicalpalmsresortfl.com
Web: www.tropicalpalmsresortfl.com

SEE AD ALACHUA PAGE 93 AND AD ORLANDO PAGE 148

LA BELLE—D-4

(W) Aqua Isles Mobile Home & RV Resort (Morgan RV Resorts)—(Hendry) *From jct Hwy 29 & Hwy 80: Go 1/2 mi W on Hwy 80, then 1/4 mi W on Shady Oaks Ave. Enter on R.* ◆◆◆◆FACILITIES: 140 sites, 140 full hkups, (30/50 amps), dump, laundry. ◆◆◆◆RECREATION: swim pool, boating, canoeing, ramp, dock, lake/river fishing. Pets welcome. Partial handicap access. No tents. Open all yr. Big rigs welcome. Rate in 2010 $34.99 for 2 persons. Member ARVC, FLARVC. Phone: (863)675-2331.

(E) The Glades RV, Golf & Marina Resort—(Glades) *From jct Hwy 29 & Hwy 80: Go 13 mi E on Hwy 80. Enter on L.* ◆◆◆◆FACILITIES: 327 sites, typical site width 35 ft, 327 full hkups, (30/50 amps), family camping, tenting, dump, laundry. ◆◆◆◆◆RECREATION: swim pool, boating, canoeing, ramp, dock, river/pond fishing. Pets welcome, breed restrict. Partial handicap access. Open all yr. Big rigs welcome. Rate in 2010 $35-40 for 2 persons. Member ARVC, FLARVC. Phone: (863)983-8070.

(N) WHISPER CREEK RV RESORT—(Glades) *From jct Hwy 80 & Hwy 29: Go 1.5 mi N on Hwy 29. Enter on L.*

THE ULTIMATE 55+ RV RESORT

Our Family Owned and Operated Resort is 1 mile N of the Historic town of LaBelle. Celebrating over 20 Seasons in our completely renovated Resort. Stay on one of our 393 Rental sites or Buy one of the 73 deeded Super sites.

◆◆◆◆◆FACILITIES: 445 sites, typical site width 40 ft, 445 full hkups, (30/50 amps), mostly extd stay sites (winter), cable TV, WiFi Instant Internet at site, RV storage, dump, laundry, patios.

◆◆◆◆◆RECREATION: rec hall, rec room/area, equipped pavilion, swim pool, golf nearby, bsktball, shuffleboard court 5 shuffleboard courts, activities, horseshoes, local tours.

Pets welcome, quantity restrict. Partial handicap access. No tents. Age restrict may apply. Open all yr. Planned group activities winter only. Big rigs welcome. Escort to site. Clubs welcome. Rate in 2010 $40 for 2 persons. Member ARVC, FLARVC.

Woodall's. The name that's trusted for over 75 years.

LA BELLE—Continued
WHISPER CREEK RV RESORT—Continued

Phone: (863)675-6888
Address: 1887 N State Road 29, La Belle, FL 33935
Lat/Lon: 26.78713/-81.43482
Email: whispercreek@whispercreek.com
Web: www.whispercreek.com

SEE AD FORT MYERS PAGE 120

LADY LAKE—B-3

(W) The Recreation Plantation RV Resort—(Lake) *From jct US 27/441 & CR 466: Go 3/4 mi W on CR 466. Enter on R.* ◆◆◆◆FACILITIES: 850 sites, typical site width 35 ft, 850 full hkups, (20/30/50 amps), tenting, dump, laundry. ◆◆◆◆◆RECREATION: swim pool. Pets welcome, breed restrict, quantity restrict. Partial handicap access. Age restrict may apply. Open all yr. Big rigs welcome. Rate in 2010 $41 for 2 persons. Member ARVC, FLARVC. Phone: (800) 448-5646.

LAKE BUENA VISTA—C-4

LAKE BUENA VISTA AREA MAP

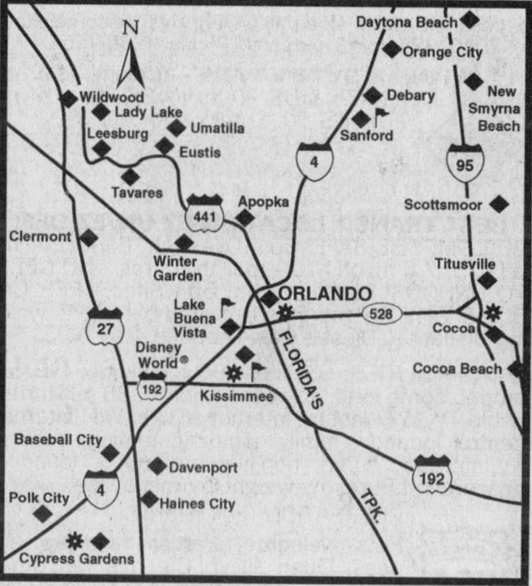

Symbols on map indicate towns within a 45 mi radius of Lake Buena Vista where campgrounds (diamonds), attractions (flags), & RV service centers & camping supply outlets (gears) are listed. Check listings for more information.

Tell Them Woodall's Sent You!

(W) DISNEY'S FORT WILDERNESS RESORT & CAMPGROUND—(Orange) *From jct I-4 & US 192: Go 1 mi W on US 192, then 1 mi N on World Dr. Enter on R.*

◆◆◆◆◆FACILITIES: 799 sites, typical site width 40 ft, 709 full hkups, 90 W&E, (20/30/50 amps), many extd stay sites, cable TV, phone/cable Instant Internet at site, WiFi Internet central location, family camping, tenting, cabins, laundry, full svc store, RV supplies, LP gas by weight/by meter, ice, picnic tables, patios, grills, controlled access.

◆◆◆◆◆RECREATION: rec hall, rec room/area, equipped pavilion, coin games, 2 swim pools, spray ground, hot tub, boating, canoeing, dock, 8 pontoon/20 canoe/10 kayak/60 motorboat rentals, lake fishing, fishing supplies, fishing guides, mini-golf, putting green, golf nearby, bsktball, 300 bike rentals, playground, shuffleboard court 2 shuffleboard courts, activities, tennis, horseshoes, sports field, hiking trails, v-ball, local tours.

Pets welcome. Partial handicap access. Open all yr. Big rigs welcome. Clubs welcome. Rate in 2010 $59-121 per family. MC/VISA/DISC/AMEX/Debit. ATM. Member ARVC, FLARVC.

Text 81188 to (440)725-8687 to see our Visual Tour.

Phone: (407)WDWCAMP (939-2267)
Address: 4510 N. Fort Wilderness Trail, Lake Buena Vista, FL 32830
Lat/Lon: 28.39361/-81.55528
Web: wdwcamp.com

SEE AD TRAVEL SECTION PAGE 77

LAKE BUENA VISTA—Continued on next page

LAKE BUENA VISTA—Continued

(W) **WALT DISNEY WORLD RESORT**—*From jct I-4 & US-192: Go 1 mi W on US-192, then N to the park admission gate. Enter on R.* Walt Disney World Resort includes Magic Kingdom Park, Disney's Animal Kingdom Theme Park, Epcot, Disney MGM Studios, 2 Water Parks, 19 Disney owned Hotels, 5 Championship Golf Courses. Downtown Disney Marketplace and Pleasure Island Nightime entertainment. Open all yr. MC/VISA/DISC/AMEX. ATM.

Phone: (407)WDISNEY
Address: 3111 World Dr, Lake Buena Vista, FL 32830
Lat/Lon: 28.39361/-81.39361

SEE AD TRAVEL SECTION PAGE 77

LAKE CITY—A-3

(SE) **Casey Jones' RV Park**—(Columbia) *From jct I-75 (exit 423) & Hwy 47: Go 200 ydsi W on Hwy 47, then 200 yds N on CR 242. Enter on R.* ◇◇◇FACILITIES: 130 sites, typical site width 32 ft, 130 full hkups, (30/50 amps), 50 amps ($), 90 pull-thrus, family camping, laundry. ◇◇RECREATION: play equipment. Pets welcome, breed restrict, size restrict. Partial handicap access. No tents. Open all yr. Big rigs welcome. Rate in 2010 $27 for 2 persons. Phone: (386)755-0471.

(W) **INN & OUT RV PARK**—(Columbia) *From jct I-75 & US 90 (exit 427): Go 1/4 mi E on US 90. Enter on R.*

BEST TRANSIT LOCATION-EZ ON/EZ OFF!
BE COMFY-BE SAFE! Best Overnight Park (1/4 mi off I-75, 7.5 mi off I-10)—pull thru sites—NO NEED TO UNHOOK! Big Rig Sites. 50A Sites, FREE CABLE & WI-FI! Restaurants to suit ANY taste in walking distiance. Diesel, Gas, Propane.

◇◇◇FACILITIES: 95 sites, 95 full hkups, (30/50 amps), some extd stay sites (winter), 80 pull-thrus, cable TV, WiFi Instant Internet at site, WiFi Internet central location, family camping, tenting, cabins, RV storage, dump, non-guest dump $, laundry, groceries, LP gas by weight/by meter, ice.

RECREATION: golf nearby.

Pets welcome. Partial handicap access. Open all yr. Big rigs welcome. Clubs welcome. Rate in 2010 $29.95 for 4 persons. MC/VISA/DISC/AMEX. ATM. CCUSA 50% Discount. CCUSA reservations Required, CCUSA max stay 2 days. Discount available May thru Sep. 2 night stay required.

LAKE CITY—Continued
INN & OUT RV PARK—Continued

Phone: (386)752-1648
Address: 3010 US Hwy 90 West, Lake City, FL 32055
Lat/Lon: 30.17959/-82.68179
Email: Jrs929@hotmail.com
Web: www.inandoutrvpark.com

SEE AD THIS PAGE AND AD TRAVEL SECTION PAGE 74

(N) **LAKE CITY CAMPGROUND**—(Columbia) *From I-10 (exit 303) & Hwy 441: Go 1 mi N on Hwy 441. Enter on R.*

◇◇◇◇FACILITIES: 52 sites, typical site width 30 ft, 40 full hkups, 12 W&E, (30/50 amps), some extd stay sites, 40 pull-thrus, cable TV, WiFi Instant Internet at site, phone Internet central location, family camping, tenting, RV's/park model rentals, cabins, RV storage, dump, non-guest dump $, laundry, groceries, RV supplies, LP gas by weight/by meter, ice, picnic tables, fire rings, wood.

◇◇◇◇RECREATION: rec hall, rec room/area, coin games, swim pool, pond fishing, fishing supplies, golf nearby, playground, shuffleboard court shuffleboard court, horseshoes, hiking trails, v-ball.

Pets welcome. Partial handicap access. Open all yr. Pool open during Spring & Summer. Big rigs welcome. Escort to site. Clubs welcome. Rate in 2010 $32-34 for 2 persons. MC/VISA. Member ARVC, FLARVC. FMCA discount.

Phone: (386)752-9131
Address: 4743 N US Hwy 441, Lake City, FL 32055
Lat/Lon: 29.99644/-82.59883
Email: lakecitycampground@yahoo.com
Web: www.lakecitycampground.com

SEE AD THIS PAGE AND AD TRAVEL SECTION PAGE 74

(N) **Oaks 'N Pines RV Campground**—(Columbia) *From I-10 (exit 303) & Hwy 441: Go 1/4 mi N on Hwy 441. Enter on L.* ◇◇◇◇FACILITIES: 67 sites, typical site width 30 ft, 67 full hkups, (20/30/50 amps), 67 pull-thrus, family camping, dump, laundry. ◇◇RECREATION: pond fishing. Pets welcome, breed restrict, quantity restrict. Partial handicap access. No tents. Open all yr. Big rigs welcome. Rate in 2010 $33-36 for 2 persons. Member ARVC, FLARVC. Phone: (386)752-0830. FMCA discount.

LAKE PANASOFFKEE—C-3

(W) **Countryside RV Park** (RV SPACES)—(Sumter) *From jct I-75 (exit 321) & Hwy 470: Go 1/4 mi W on Hwy 470, then 1/2 mi W on Hwy 489. Enter on L.* FACILITIES: 66 sites, typical site width 45 ft, 62 full hkups, 4 W&E, (20/30/50 amps), 50 amps ($), 10 pull-thrus, tenting, dump, laundry. Pets welcome, breed restrict, size restrict, quantity restrict. Open all yr. Big rigs welcome. Rate in 2010 $29 for 2 persons. Phone: (352)793-8103.

TURTLEBACK RV RESORT—(Sumter) *From jct I-75 (exit 321) & Hwy 470: Go 1/4 mi W on Hwy 470, turn onto CR 488 Rd. Enter on R.*

◇◇◇◇FACILITIES: 141 sites, typical site width 35 ft, 131 full hkups, 10 W&E, (20/30/50 amps), many extd stay sites, cable TV, ($), WiFi Instant Internet at site, WiFi Internet central location, family camping, RV's/park model rentals, cabins, RV storage, dump, non-guest dump $, laundry, RV supplies, LP gas by weight/by meter, ice, picnic tables, patios, wood.

◇◇◇◇RECREATION: rec hall, swim pool, boating, canoeing, kayaking, ramp, dock, 2 canoe/motorboat rentals, lake fishing, golf nearby, shuffleboard court 2 shuffleboard courts, activities, horseshoes.

Pets welcome, breed restrict, quantity restrict. No tents. Open all yr. Big rigs welcome. Rate in 2010 $30 per vehicle. MC/VISA/Debit. Member ARVC. CCUSA 50% Discount. CCUSA max stay 4 days. Discount available Mar 1-Dec 31.

Phone: (800)887-8525
Address: 190 CR 488, Lake Panasoffkee, FL 33538
Lat/Lon: 28.75644/-82.10776
Email: diane@turtlebackrvresort.com
Web: www.turtlebackrvresort.com

SEE AD THIS PAGE

LAKE PLACID—D-4

(S) **CAMP FLORIDA RESORT**—(Highlands) *From jct Hwy 70 & US 27: Go 4-1/2 mi N on US 27. Enter on R.*

◇◇◇◇◇FACILITIES: 397 sites, typical site width 40 ft, 397 full hkups, (30/50 amps), mostly extd stay sites (winter), WiFi Instant Internet at site ($), phone/cable on-site Internet (needs activ), phone Internet central location, family camping, RV's/park model rentals, RV storage, dump, non-guest dump $, laundry, patios, controlled access.

◇◇◇◇◇RECREATION: rec hall, rec room/area, swim pool, boating, canoeing, kayaking, ramp,

CAMP FLORIDA RESORT—Continued on next page

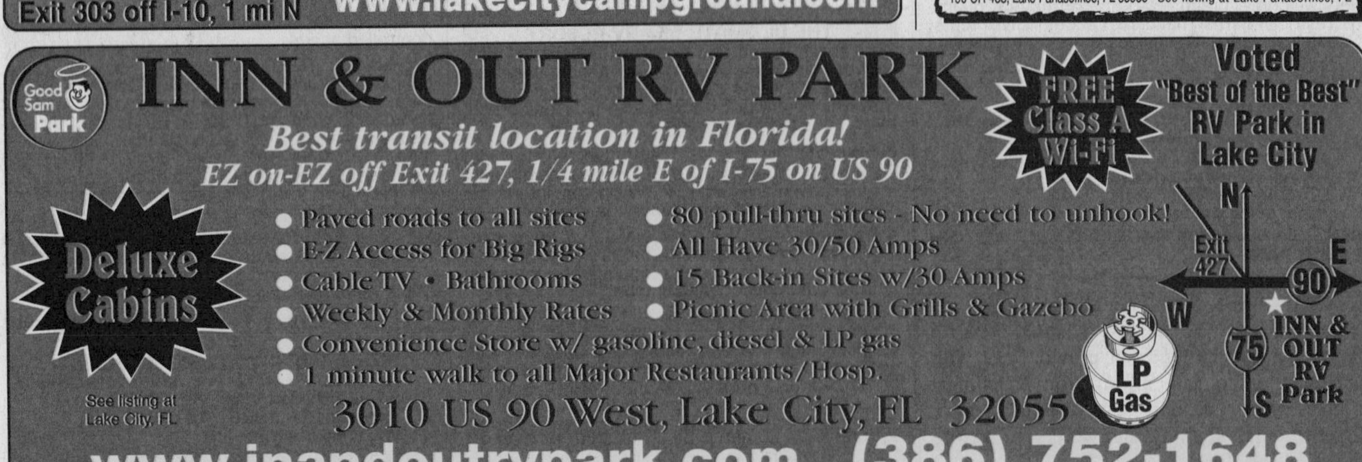

LAKE PLACID—Continued
CAMP FLORIDA RESORT—Continued

dock, lake fishing, golf nearby, shuffleboard court 8 shuffleboard courts, activities, tennis, horseshoes, local tours.

Pets welcome, breed restrict, size restrict, quantity restrict. Partial handicap access. No tents. Open all yr. Big rigs welcome. Clubs welcome. Rate in 2010 $40 per vehicle. MC/VISA/DISC/AMEX/Debit. Member ARVC, FLARVC.

Phone: (863)699-1991
Address: 100 Shoreline Dr, Lake Placid, FL 33852
Lat/Lon: 27.26533/-81.34639
Email: campflorida@hotmail.com
Web: www.campflaresort.com

SEE AD THIS PAGE

(E) Cypress Isle RV Park & Marina (RV SPACES)—(Highlands) *From jct of US 27 & Hwy 621: Go 7-1/2 mi E on Hwy 621, then 1/2 mi W on Cypress Isle Rd (gravel rd). Enter on R.* FACILITIES: 30 sites, 34 ft max RV length, 30 full hkups, (30 amps), tenting, laundry. RECREATION: boating, saltwater fishing. Pets welcome. Open all yr. Rate in 2010 $30 for 2 persons. Phone: (863)465-5241.

(S) Sunshine RV Resort—(Highland) *From jct US 27S & Hwy 70: Go 1/4 mi E on Hwy 70. Enter on R.* ◊◊◊FACILITIES: 325 sites, typical site width 15 ft, 325 full hkups, (30/50 amps), 30 pull-thrus, laundry. ◊◊◊◊RECREATION: swim pool, lake fishing. Pets welcome, breed restrict. Partial handicap access. No tents. Open all yr. Big rigs welcome. Rate in 2010 $30-35 for 2 persons. Member ARVC, FLARVC. Phone: (800)760-7270.

LAKE WALES—C-4

(NW) Bullock's Landing RV Park & Storage Facility (RV SPACES)—(Polk) *From jct US 27 & Hwy 540A: Go 1/2 mi W on Hwy 540A. Enter on L.* FACILITIES: 50 sites, 36 ft max RV length, 50 full hkups, (20/30/50 amps), 44 pull-thrus, phone on-site Internet (needs activ), family camping, tenting, RV storage, dump, laundry, picnic tables, patios. RECREATION: activities. Pets welcome. Age restrict may apply. Open all yr. Rate in 2010 $28 for 2 persons. CCUSA 50% Discount. CCUSA reservations Accepted, CCUSA max stay 6 days, Cash only for CCUSA disc. Discount available Apr thru Oct.

Phone: (863)676-0000
Address: 2041 Thompson Nursery Rd, Lake Wales, FL 33853
Lat/Lon: 27.95690/-81.62465

(E) Camp Macks River Resort—(Polk) *From jct US 27 & Hwy 60: Go 10 mi E on Hwy 60, then 3-1/2 mi N on Boy Scout Rd, then 6 mi E on Camp Mack Rd. Enter on L.* ◊◊◊FACILITIES: 200 sites, typical site width 50 ft, 200 full hkups, (30/50 amps), family camping, tenting, dump, laundry, ltd groc. ◊◊◊◊RECREATION: swim pool, boating, ramp, dock, lake/river fishing. Pets welcome. Open all yr. Big rigs welcome. Rate in 2010 $36 for 4 persons. Phone: (863)696-1108.

(S) Camp'n Aire RV Resort—(Polk) *From jct Hwy 60 & US 27: Go 3 mi S on US 27. Enter on R.* ◊◊◊◊FACILITIES: 102 sites, typical site width 20 ft, 40 ft max RV length, 102 full hkups, (20/30/50 amps), 40 pull-thrus, heater not allowed, WiFi Instant Internet at site, phone on-site Internet (needs activ), WiFi Internet central location, family camping, dump, non-guest dump $, laundry, LP gas by weight/by meter, ice, picnic tables, patios. ◊◊◊◊RECREATION: rec hall, swim pool, stream fishing, bsktball, shuffleboard court 2 shuffleboard courts, activities, horseshoes, hiking trails, v-ball. Pets welcome, breed restrict, size restrict, quantity restrict. No tents. Age restrict may apply. Open all yr. Rate in 2010 $40 for 2 persons. MC/VISA/DISC. CCUSA 50% Discount. CCUSA reservations Required, CCUSA max stay 5 days. Discount available May thru Oct. Seniors park. No loud or vicious pets or pets over 40 lbs.

Phone: (863)638-1015
Address: 15860 Hwy 27, Lake Wales, FL 33859
Lat/Lon: 27.85057/-81.58583
Email: info@campnaire.com
Web: www.campnaire.com

LAKE WALES—Continued

(E) LAKE KISSIMMEE STATE PARK—(Polk) *From town: Go 15 mi E on Hwy 60, then N on Camo Mack Rd.* FACILITIES: 60 sites, 60 W&E, tenting, dump. RECREATION: boating, canoeing, ramp, lake fishing. No pets. Open all yr. Phone: (863)696-1112.

(S) LAKE WALES RV & CAMPSITES—(Polk) *From jct Hwy 60 & US 27: Go 3 mi S on US 27. Enter on R.*

◊◊◊◊FACILITIES: 118 sites, typical site width 22 ft, 28 ft max RV length, 116 full hkups, (30/50 amps), 50 amps ($), 2 no hkups, 50 pull-thrus, heater not allowed, WiFi Instant Internet at site, phone on-site Internet (needs activ), WiFi Internet central location, family camping, tenting, RV storage, dump, non-guest dump $, laundry, RV supplies, ice, picnic tables, fire rings, grills, wood.

◊◊◊◊RECREATION: rec hall, rec room/area, swim pool, hot tub, pond fishing, golf nearby, bsktball, shuffleboard court 2 shuffleboard courts, activities, local tours.

Pets welcome, breed restrict. Partial handicap access. Open all yr. Planned activities winter only. Rate in 2010 $32-35 per vehicle. MC/VISA. CCUSA 50% Discount. CCUSA reservations Recommended, CCUSA max stay 1 day, Cash only for CCUSA disc. Discount available Apr thru Oct. $1 surcharge for greater than 1 pet/site.

Phone: (863)638-9011
Address: 15898 Hwy 27, Lake Wales, FL 33859
Lat/Lon: 27.85185/-81.58603
Email: lwcgfl@yahoo.com
Web: www.lakewalescampgroundrvresort.com

SEE AD THIS PAGE

The Harbor RV Resort & Marina—(Polk) *From jct of US 27 & Hwy 60: Go 10 mi E on Hwy 60, then 3-1/2 mi N on Boy Scout Rd, then 1-3/4 mi E on Camp Marina, then 1/4 mi SE on Kentucky, then 1/4 mi SE on N Marina Park Way, then 1 blk S on Monroe Ct. Enter at end.* ◊◊◊FACILITIES: 91 sites, typical site width 25 ft, 91 full hkups, (20/30/50 amps), WiFi Instant Internet at site ($), WiFi Internet central location, family camping, tenting, dump, laundry, picnic tables, patios. ◊◊◊RECREATION: rec hall, equipped pavilion, swim pool, hot tub, boating, canoeing, ramp, dock, lake fishing, shuffleboard court 2 shuffleboard courts, activities, horseshoes. Pets welcome. Open all yr. Big rigs welcome. Rate in 2010 $21-42 for 2 persons. Member ARVC, FLARVC. FMCA discount. CCUSA 50% Discount. CCUSA reservations Accepted, CCUSA max stay Unlimited. Discount not available Jan 1 thru Mar 31. Seasonal surcharge $3/day Oct thru Apr.

Phone: (863)696-1194
Address: 10511 Monroe Ct, Lake Wales, FL 33898
Lat/Lon: 27.94051/-81.42263
Email: harborrv@harbor-rv-marina.com
Web: harbor-rv-marina.com

LAKE WORTH—D-5

(S) JOHN PRINCE MEMORIAL PARK (Palm Beach County Park)—(Palm Beach) *From jct Hwy 812 & I-95: Go 2 mi N on I-95 (exit 63), then 1-1/4 mi W on 6th Ave, then 1/2 mi S on Congress Ave. Enter on L.* FACILITIES: 297 sites, typical site

LAKE WORTH—Continued
JOHN PRINCE MEMORIAL PARK (Palm Beach County Park)—Continued

width 25 ft, 111 full hkups, 186 W&E, (30/50 amps), 18 pull-thrus, family camping, tenting, dump. RECREATION: boating, canoeing, ramp, dock, lake fishing, playground. Pets welcome, quantity restrict. Partial handicap access. Open all yr. Big rigs welcome. Member ARVC, FLARVC. Phone: (877)992-9925.

LAKELAND—C-3

(N) LAKELAND RV RESORT—(Polk) *From I-4 (exit 33 & Hwy 582): Go 1/4 mi NE on Hwy 582, then 1/4 mi E on Old Combee Rd. Enter on L.*

WELCOME TO CAREFREE RV RESORTS!
An extraordinary getaway with all the extras! This prime location is only 30 minutes to the fun and excitement of Orlando or Tampa with easy access to I-4. It's your beautiful oasis amid all the great fun of Central Florida.

◊◊◊◊FACILITIES: 230 sites, typical site width 35 ft, 230 full hkups, (20/30/50 amps), mostly

LAKELAND RV RESORT—Continued on next page

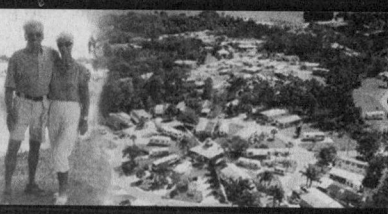

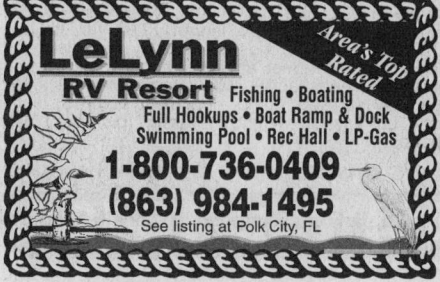

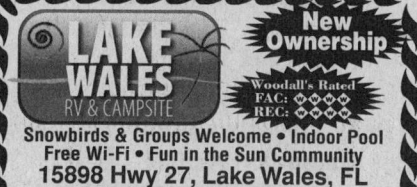

LAKELAND—Continued
LAKELAND RV RESORT—Continued

extd stay sites (winter), 100 pull-thrus, WiFi Instant Internet at site ($), phone on-site Internet (needs activ), WiFi Internet central location ($), family camping, tenting, cabins, RV storage, dump, non-guest dump $, laundry, RV supplies, LP gas by weight/by meter, ice, picnic tables, patios, controlled access.

◆◆◆◆◆RECREATION: rec hall, rec room/area, swim pool, wading pool, hot tub, boating, 2 pedal boat rentals, pond fishing, mini-golf, golf nearby, bsktball, playground, shuffleboard court 3 shuffleboard courts, activities, horseshoes, v-ball.

Pets welcome, breed restrict, quantity restrict. Open all yr. Church service & planned activities winter only. Discounts Apr - Dec. Big rigs welcome. Clubs welcome. Rate in 2010 $28-40 for 2 persons. MC/VISA. Member ARVC, FLARVC. FMCA discount. CCUSA 50% Discount. CCUSA reservations Required, CCUSA max stay 7 days. Discount available Apr thru Dec.

Phone: (888)622-4115
Address: 900 Old Combee Rd, Lakeland, FL 33805
Lat/Lon: 28.10979/-81.93968
Email: lakelandrv@tampabay.rr.com
Web: www.carefreervresorts.com

SEE AD THIS PAGE

(N) Lazy Dazy Retreat (RV SPACES)—(Polk) *From jct I-4 & US-98: Go 3 mi N on US-98. Enter on R.* FACILITIES: 86 sites, typical site width 20 ft, 34 ft max RV length, 86 full hkups, (15/20/30/50 amps), 30 pull-thrus, family camping, dump, laundry. Pets welcome. No tents. Open all yr. Rate in 2010 $30 for 2 persons. Phone: (863)858-2026.

(S) Sanlan RV Park—(Polk) *From jct Polk Pkwy (570)(exit 10) & US 98: Go 1/2 mi S on US 98. Enter on R.* ◆◆◆◆FACILITIES: 531 sites, typical site width 40 ft, 531 full hkups, (20/30/50 amps), 84 pull-thrus, family camping, tenting, dump, laundry. ◆◆◆◆◆RECREATION: 2 swim pools, boating, canoeing, lake fishing, playground. Pets welcome ($), quantity restrict. Partial handicap access. Open all yr. Big rigs welcome. Rate in 2010 $20-44 for 2 persons. Member ARVC, FLARVC. Phone: (863)665-1726.

(W) WOODALL'S MOBILE HOME VILLAGE & RV PARK—(Polk) *From jct I-4 & Memorial Blvd: Go 2 mi E on Memorial Blvd, then 1 mi S on Wabash Ave, then 1 block W on New Tampa Hwy. Enter on R.*

PARK THE RV HERE!
Enjoy many beautiful RV sites, fun activities, and superb amenities, in a park close to many Central Florida attractions! Experience a quality vacation at Woodall's Mobile Home Village.

◆◆◆FACILITIES: 120 sites, typical site width 30 ft, 40 ft max RV length, accepts self-contained units only, 120 full hkups, (30/50 amps), some extd stay sites (winter), 6 pull-thrus, phone/cable on-site Internet (needs activ), WiFi Internet central location, RV's/park model rentals, RV storage, dump, non-guest dump $, laundry, patios, controlled access.

LAKELAND—Continued
WOODALL'S MOBILE HOME VILLAGE & RV PARK—Continued

◆◆◆RECREATION: rec hall, swim pool, golf nearby, shuffleboard court 6 shuffleboard courts, activities, horseshoes, local tours.

No pets. Partial handicap access. No tents. Open all yr. Group activities winter season only. Rate in 2010 $30-45 for 2 persons. CCUSA 50% Discount. CCUSA reservations Recommended, CCUSA max stay 4 days, Cash only for CCUSA disc. No restrooms or shower facilities. No pets. $10 non-guest dump surcharge.

Phone: (863)686-7462
Address: 2121 New Tampa Hwy, Lakeland, FL 33815-7303
Lat/Lon: 28.04143/-81.99204
Email: woodalls@newbymanagement.com
Web: www.woodallsvillage.com

SEE AD PAGE 137

LANTANA—D-5

(W) Palm Beach Traveler Park—(Palm Beach) *From jct Hwy 802 (Lake Worth Rd) & Hwy 809 (Military Trail): Go 2 mi S on Military Trail, then 1/2 mi E on Lantana, then 1 block S on Lawrence Rd. Enter on R.* ◆◆◆◆FACILITIES: 104 sites, typical site width 30 ft, 104 full hkups, (20/30/50 amps), 50 amps ($), dump, laundry. ◆◆RECREATION: swim pool. Pets welcome, breed restrict. Partial handicap access. No tents. Open all yr. Rate in 2010 $38-59 for 2 persons. Member ARVC, FLARVC. Phone: (561)967-3139.

LARGO—C-3

(S) Lee's Travel Park—(Pinellas) *From jct US 19 & Hwy 688 (Ulmerton): Go 1 mi W on Hwy 688, then 1/2 mi N on Belcher Rd. Enter on L.* ◆◆◆FACILITIES: 155 sites, typical site width 18 ft, accepts full hkup units only, 155 full hkups, (20/30/50 amps), WiFi Instant Internet at site, WiFi Internet central location, family camping, laundry, picnic tables, patios. ◆◆◆RECREATION: rec hall, swim pool, shuffleboard court 3 shuffleboard courts, activities, horseshoes. Pets welcome, size restrict, quantity restrict. No tents. Open all yr. Rate in 2010 $40 for 2 persons. MC/VISA/Debit. CCUSA 50% Discount. CCUSA reservations Recommended, CCUSA max stay See Rest., Cash only for CCUSA disc. Max stay unlimited Apr 1 thru Dec 15. Max stay 2 days Dec 15-Apr 1. Part of park is No Smoking. Limited hours on restrooms. 20 lb pet limit. Limited 50 amp sites. Cable is locally contracted.

LARGO—Continued
Lee's Travel Park—Continued

Phone: (888)510-8900
Address: 1610 S Belcher Rd, Largo, FL 33771
Lat/Lon: 27.90080/-82.74601
Email: info@leestravelpark.com
Web: www.leestravelpark.com

(S) RAINBOW VILLAGE RV RESORT—(Pinellas) *From jct I-275 & Hwy 688 (Ulmerton): Go 4 mi W on Hwy 688, then 3/4 mi S on 66th St N. Enter on L.*

WELCOME TO CAREFREE RV RESORTS!
Where carefree vacations are beachy keen! This resort borders the Gulf on Florida's West Coast with easy access to I-75. Great shopping and restaurants in nearby St. Petersburg. Make a lifetime of memories & friends!

◆◆◆◆FACILITIES: 307 sites, typical site width 35 ft, accepts full hkup units only, 307 full hkups, (20/30/50 amps), mostly extd stay sites (winter), WiFi Instant Internet at site ($), phone/cable on-site Internet (needs activ), shower$, laundry, patios.

◆◆◆◆RECREATION: rec hall, rec room/area, equipped pavilion, swim pool, golf nearby, shuffleboard court 6 shuffleboard courts, activities.

Pets welcome, breed restrict, size restrict, quantity restrict. Partial handicap access. No tents. Age restrict may apply. Open all yr. Big rigs welcome. Rate in 2010 $40 for 2 persons. CCUSA 50% Discount. CCUSA reservations Required, CCUSA max stay 7 days, Cash only for CCUSA disc., CCUSA disc. not avail holidays. Discount not available Jan 1-Apr 1.

Phone: (800)348-9607
Address: 11911 66th St N, Largo, FL 33773
Lat/Lon: 27.88082/-82.72871
Email: rainbowlargo@tampabay.rr.com
Web: www.carefreeresorts.com

SEE AD ST. PETERSBURG PAGE 163

(E) VACATION VILLAGE (Formerly Sunburst RV Park)—(Pinellas) *From jct I-275 (exit 18) & Ulmerton Rd: Go 3 mi W on Ulmerton Rd. Enter on L.*

◆◆◆FACILITIES: 281 sites, typical site width 24 ft, 38 ft max RV length, 281 full hkups, (30/50 amps), mostly extd stay sites (winter), WiFi Instant Internet at site ($), phone/cable on-site Internet (needs activ), WiFi Internet central location ($), family camping, tenting, dump, non-guest dump $, laundry, patios.

◆◆◆RECREATION: rec hall, swim pool, golf nearby, shuffleboard court 4 shuffleboard courts, activities, horseshoes, v-ball.

Pets welcome, breed restrict, quantity restrict. Partial handicap access. Open all yr. Planned activities winter only. Clubs welcome. Rate in 2010 $32-43 for 2 persons. MC/VISA/DISC/AMEX.

Phone: (877)297-2757
Address: 6900 Ulmerton Rd, Largo, FL 33771
Lat/Lon: 27.89345/-82.73373
Email: linda_Rich@equitylifestyle.com
Web: www.rvonthego.com/Vacation-Village-RV-Resort-CL36-8.htm

SEE AD ALACHUA PAGE 93

(S) YANKEE TRAVELER RV PARK—(Pinellas) *From jct US 19 & Hwy 688 (Ulmerton Rd): Go 2 mi W on Hwy 688. Enter on L.*

BEST RV PARK IN CENTRAL FLORIDA
Centrally located between Clearwater - St Petersburg - Tampa and minutes to the Beaches. Beautiful Landscaping, Heated Pool, WiFi and Extensive Activites. Perfect any time of the year... Bring Family & Friends...Come Stay & Play!

◆◆◆◆FACILITIES: 210 sites, typical site width 30 ft, 40 ft max RV length, 210 full hkups, (20/30/50 amps), mostly extd stay sites (winter), WiFi Instant Internet at site, phone/cable on-site Internet (needs activ), WiFi Internet central location, RV storage, dump, non-guest dump $, laundry, LP gas by weight/by meter, picnic tables, patios.

YANKEE TRAVELER RV PARK—Continued on next page

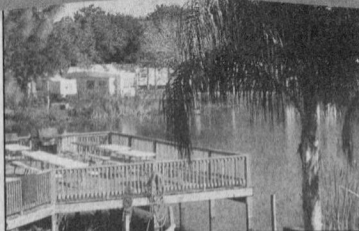

LARGO—Continued
YANKEE TRAVELER RV PARK—Continued

◆◆◆◆RECREATION: rec hall, rec room/area, swim pool, golf nearby, shuffleboard court 7 shuffleboard courts, activities, horseshoes.

Pets welcome, size restrict, quantity restrict. No tents. Age restrict may apply. Open all yr. Planned activities season only. Rate in 2010 $30-38 for 2 persons. MC/VISA. Member ARVC, FLARVC. CCUSA 50% Discount. CCUSA reservations Recommended, CCUSA max stay See Rest. Max stay unlimited (nightly rates) May thru Oct. Max stay 1 night Nov, Dec & Apr. Discount not available Jan, Feb, Mar. Limited pet area, call for details. Age restrictions may apply.

Phone: (866)202-9232
Address: 8500 Ulmerton Rd (SR 688), Largo, FL 33771
Lat/Lon: 27.89392/-82.75705
Email: info@yankeetraveler.net
Web: www.yankeetraveler.net

SEE AD CLEARWATER PAGE 101

LEESBURG—C-3

Haines Creek RV Village—(Lake) *From jct US 441 & CR 44: Go 1/4 mi N on CR 44. Enter on L.* ◆◆FACILITIES: 86 sites, typical site width 30 ft, 86 full hkups, (30/50 amps), 2 pull-thrus, tenting, dump, laundry. ◆◆RECREATION: boating, canoeing, ramp, dock, river fishing. Pets welcome, breed restrict, size restrict. Partial handicap access. Open all yr. Big rigs welcome. Rate in 2010 $30 for 2 persons. Phone: (352)728-5939.

HOLIDAY TRAVEL RESORT—(Lake) *From jct FL Turnpike (exit 296) & CR 470: Go 3 mi E on CR 470, then 1 mi E on CR 33. Enter on L.*

◆◆◆◆◆FACILITIES: 935 sites, typical site width 50 ft, 935 full hkups, (30/50 amps), mostly extd stay sites (winter), 935 pull-thrus, cable TV, ($), WiFi Internet central location, tenting, dump, non-guest dump $, laundry, LP gas by weight/by meter, marine gas, ice, picnic tables, controlled access.

◆◆◆◆◆RECREATION: rec hall, rec room/area, equipped pavilion, 2 swim pools, hot tub, boating, canoeing, kayaking, ramp, dock, lake fishing, fishing supplies, mini-golf, golf nearby, bsktball, playground, shuffleboard court 15 shuffleboard courts, activities, tennis, horseshoes, sports field, v-ball, local tours.

Pets welcome. Partial handicap access. Open all yr. Tenting in summer only. Non-guest dumping summer only. Big rigs welcome. Escort to site. Clubs welcome. Rate in 2010 $39 for 2 persons. MC/VISA/DISC. Member ARVC, FLARVC.

Phone: (800)428-5334
Address: 28229 CR 33, Leesburg, FL 34748-8999
Lat/Lon: 28.75682/-81.88594
Web: www.holidaytravelresort.com

SEE AD THIS PAGE

LEESBURG—Continued

(E) Ridgecrest RV & Mobile Home Resort—(Lake) *From jct CR 48 & US 27: Go 1-1/2 mi S on US 27. Enter on R.* ◆◆◆FACILITIES: 145 sites, typical site width 25 ft, 139 full hkups, 6 W&E, (30/50 amps), dump, laundry. ◆◆◆RECREATION: swim pool. Pets welcome, breed restrict, size restrict, quantity restrict. Partial handicap access. No tents. Age restrict may apply. Open all yr. Big rigs welcome. Rate in 2010 $29-31 for 2 persons. Member ARVC, FLARVC. Phone: (352)787-1504.

LIVE OAK—A-2

(W) SUWANNEE RIVER STATE PARK—(Suwannee) *From town: Go 13 mi W on US 90.* FACILITIES: 30 sites, 32 ft max RV length, 30 full hkups, (30/50 amps), tenting, dump, laundry. RECREATION: boating, canoeing, ramp, river fishing, playground. Pets welcome. Open all yr. Phone: (386)362-2746.

LONG KEY—F-4

(W) LONG KEY STATE PARK—(Monroe) *From town: Go 1 mi W on US 1. Milepost 67.5.* FACILITIES: 60 sites, 28 ft max RV length, 60 W&E, tenting, dump. RECREATION: saltwater swim, boating, canoeing, saltwater fishing. No pets. Open all yr. Phone: (305)664-4815.

LUTZ—C-3

(N) ENCORE WINTER QUARTERS-PASCO RV PARK—(Pasco) *From jct I-75 (exit 275) & Hwy 56: Go 5 mi W on Hwy 54/56. Enter on L.*

◆◆◆FACILITIES: 255 sites, typical site width 25 ft, 255 full hkups, (30/50 amps), many extd stay sites (winter), WiFi Instant Internet at site ($), phone on-site Internet (needs activ), phone Internet central location, family camping, tenting, dump, non-guest dump $, laundry, LP gas by weight/by meter, ice, picnic tables, patios.

◆◆◆◆RECREATION: rec hall, swim pool, hot tub, lake fishing, golf nearby, shuffleboard court 4 shuffleboard courts, activities, horseshoes.

Pets welcome, breed restrict, size restrict, quantity restrict. Partial handicap access. Open all yr. Planned activities winter only. Big rigs welcome. Clubs welcome. Rate in 2010 $32-43 for 2 persons. MC/VISA/DISC/AMEX. Member ARVC, FLARVC.

Phone: (800)879-2131
Address: 21632 State Road 54, Lutz, FL 33549
Lat/Lon: 28.18895/-82.45859
Email: info@rvonthego.com
Web: www.rvonthego.com/Winter-Quarters-Pasco-RV-Resort-CL18-8.htm

SEE AD ALACHUA PAGE 93

MADISON—A-2

(S) Deerwood Madison Campground & Motel—(Madison) *From jct I-10 (exit 258) & Hwy 53: Go 1/4 mi S on Hwy 53, then 500 ft W on SW Old St. Augustine Rd. Enter on L.* ◆◆FACILITIES: 75 sites, typical site width 35 ft, 38 full hkups, 37 W&E, (20/30/50 amps), 75 pull-thrus, family camping, tenting, dump, laundry. ◆◆RECREATION: swim pool, playground. Pets welcome. Partial handicap access. Open all yr. Rate in 2010 $25-28 per family. Phone: (850)973-2504.

MADISON—Continued

(S) Yogi Bear's Jellystone Park Camp Resort—(Madison) *From I-10 (exit 258) & Hwy 53: Go 1/4 mi S on Hwy 53, then 1/2 mi W on Ragans Lake Rd. Enter on L.* ◆◆◆◆FACILITIES: 166 sites, typical site width 25 ft, 124 full hkups, 34 W&E, (20/30/50 amps), 50 amps ($), 8 no hkups, 89 pull-thrus, family camping, tenting, dump, laundry, ltd groc. ◆◆◆◆◆RECREATION: swim pool, lake swim, boating, no motors, canoeing, lake fishing, playground. Pets welcome, quantity restrict. Partial handicap access. Open all yr. Big rigs welcome. Rate in 2010 $35-45 for 2 persons. Member ARVC, FLARVC. Phone: (800)347-0174.

MALABAR—C-5

(SE) CAMELOT RV PARK—(Brevard) *From jct I-95 (exit 173) & Hwy 514 (Malabar/Palm Bay exit): Go 4-1/2 mi E on Hwy 514, then 2 blocks S on US 1 (5 mi S of Melbourne on US 1). Enter on R.*

E. CENTRAL FL - MELB./PALM BAY AREA
15 minutes to the Ocean! Our area has much to See & Do! Come Have Fun! Camelot has a variety of activities so you can meet New Friends. Whether you want to Relax or Be Busy - It's Here! Come Enjoy your Stay at Camelot!

◆◆◆◆FACILITIES: 130 sites, typical site width 35 ft, 130 full hkups, (30/50 amps), mostly extd stay sites (winter), 25 pull-thrus, heater not allowed, cable TV, WiFi Instant Internet at site, phone/cable on-site Internet (needs activ), WiFi Internet central location, RV storage, laundry, LP gas by weight/by meter, ice, picnic tables, patios, controlled access.

◆◆◆RECREATION: rec hall, saltwater/river fishing, golf nearby, bsktball, shuffleboard court 2 shuffleboard courts, activities, horseshoes.

Pets welcome, breed restrict. Partial handicap access. No tents. Open all yr. Planned group activities winter only. Big rigs welcome. Escort to site. Clubs welcome. Rate in 2010 $36-40 for 2 persons. MC/VISA/DISC/Debit.

Phone: (321)724-5396
Address: 1600 US Hwy 1, Malabar, FL 32950
Lat/Lon: 27.99983/-80.56152
Email: camelot@camelotrvpark.com
Web: www.camelotrvpark.com

SEE AD MELBOURNE NEXT PAGE

Woodall's Tip... To be considered a "Big Rig Friendly" park, the campground must meet the following requirements: minimum of 50 amps, adequate road width, overhead access clearance, site clearance to accommodate the tallest and widest rigs built. Often not every site can accommodate a big rig, so we recommend that you call ahead for availability.

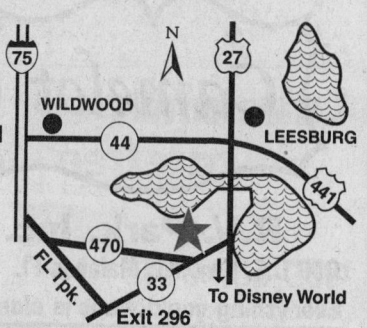

MARATHON—F-4

(NE) GRASSY KEY RV PARK & RESORT —(Monroe) *On US 1 at mile marker 58-3/4. Enter on R.*

WELCOME

◇◇◇◇◇FACILITIES: 38 sites, typical site width 24 ft, accepts full hkup units only, 38 full hkups, (20/30/50 amps), some extd stay sites (winter), 10 pull-thrus, cable TV, WiFi Instant Internet at site, family camping, laundry, RV supplies, picnic tables.

◇◇◇◇RECREATION: rec hall, pavilion, swim pool, boating, canoeing, kayaking, dock, saltwater fishing, golf nearby, activities, horseshoes, hiking trails.

Pets welcome. No tents. Open all yr. No restrooms. Big rigs welcome. Escort to site. Clubs welcome. Rate in 2010 $40-110 for 6 persons. MC/VISA/DISC. Member ARVC, FLARVC.

Phone: (305)289-1606
Address: 58671 Overseas Hwy, Marathon, FL 33050
Lat/Lon: 24.76474/-80.94800
Email: paradise@grassykeyrvpark.com
Web: www.grassykeyrvpark.com

SEE AD THIS PAGE

(NE) JOLLY ROGER TRAVEL PARK—(Monroe) *On US 1 at mile marker 59-1/2. Enter on R.*

WELCOME

◇◇◇FACILITIES: 162 sites, typical site width 24 ft, 162 full hkups, (20/30/50 amps), 21 pull-thrus, cable TV, WiFi Instant Internet at site, family camping, tenting, laundry, ice, picnic tables, patios.

CAMPCLUB USA

◇◇RECREATION: pavilion, saltwater swim, boating, canoeing, kayaking, ramp, dock, saltwater fishing, golf nearby, activities.

Pets welcome, quantity restrict. Open all yr. Planned Activities winter only. Big rigs welcome. Escort to site. Clubs welcome. Rate in 2010 $45-77 for 2 persons. MC/VISA/DISC/Debit. Member ARVC, FLARVC. CCUSA 50% Discount. CCUSA reservations Required, CCUSA max stay 5 days. Limited # of discount sites available. Discount honored 5 night max stay/6 mo period & may not be combined with other discount or special offers.

Woodall's Tip... Understand our ratings—Turn to the "How to Use" pages in the front of this Directory.

MARATHON—Continued
JOLLY ROGER TRAVEL PARK—Continued

Phone: (800)995-1525
Address: 59275 Overseas Highway, Marathon, FL 33050
Lat/Lon: 24.76932/-80.94199
Email: email@jrtp.com
Web: www.jrtp.com

SEE AD KEY WEST PAGE 132

(SW) Key RV Park—(Monroe) *On US 1 at mile marker 50-1/2. Enter on L.* ◇◇◇FACILITIES: 210 sites, typical site width 30 ft, 201 full hkups, 9 W&E, (20/30/50 amps), dump, laundry. ◇◇◇RECREATION: boating, canoeing, ramp, dock, saltwater fishing. Pets welcome, breed restrict. No tents. Open all yr. Rate in 2010 $45-80 for 2 persons. Phone: (305)743-5164.

MARGATE—E-5

(SE) AZTEC RV RESORT (UNDER CONSTRUCTION)—(Broward) *From jct Hwy 814 & US 441: Go 1/2 mi S on US 441. Enter on L.*

WELCOME

FACILITIES: 646 sites, typical site width 30 ft, accepts full hkup units only, 646 full hkups, (50 amps), RV storage, laundry, ltd groc, ice, patios, controlled access.

RECREATION: rec hall, rec room/area, 2 swim pools, hot tub, boating, ramp, golf nearby, activities, tennis.

Pets welcome. Partial handicap access. No tents. Open all yr. Big rigs welcome. Escort to site. Clubs welcome. MC/VISA.

Phone: (954)975-6411
Address: 1-A Sundial Circle, Margate, FL 33068
Lat/Lon: 26.22594/-80.20424
Web: www.aztecrvresort.com

SEE AD TRAVEL SECTION PAGE 73

MARIANNA—E-3

(E) ARROWHEAD CAMPSITES—(Jackson) *From jct I-10 (exit 142) & Hwy 71: Go 2 mi N on Hwy 71, then 1/2 mi W on US 90. Enter on R.*

WELCOME

◇◇◇FACILITIES: 245 sites, typical site width 30 ft, 175 full hkups, 45 W&E, (20/30/50 amps), some extd stay sites, 175 pull-thrus, cable TV, WiFi Internet central location, family camping, tenting, cabins, dump, non-guest dump $, laundry, groceries, RV supplies, LP gas by weight/by meter, ice, picnic tables, controlled access.

MARIANNA—Continued
ARROWHEAD CAMPSITES—Continued

◇◇◇◇RECREATION: pavilion, swim pool, boating, canoeing, kayaking, ramp, dock, lake fishing, fishing supplies, golf nearby, bsktball, playground.

Pets welcome. Partial handicap access. Open all yr. Escort to site. Rate in 2010 $26-39 for 2 persons. MC/VISA/DISC/AMEX. ATM. Member ARVC, FLARVC.

Phone: (800)643-9166
Address: 4820 Hwy 90 E, Marianna, FL 32446
Lat/Lon: 30.75512/-85.19437
Email: arrowhead@phonl.com
Web: www.arrowheadcamp.com

SEE AD THIS PAGE

✽ **(E) ARROWHEAD RV SALES**—*From jct I-10 (exit 142) & Hwy 71: Go 2 mi N on Hwy 71, then 1/2 mi W on US 90. Enter on R.* SALES: travel trailers, truck campers, 5th wheels, toy hauler, fold-down camping trailers, pre-owned unit sales.

WELCOME

SERVICES: full-time mech, RV appliance repair, body work/collision repair, LP gas by weight/by meter, dump station, sells parts/accessories, installs hitches. Open all yr. MC/VISA/DISC/AMEX. ATM.

Phone: (866)277-6978
Address: 4820 Hwy 90 E, Marianna, FL 32446
Lat/Lon: 30.75512/-85.19410
Email: arrowhead@phonl.com
Web: www.arrowheadcamp.com

SEE AD THIS PAGE

(SE) Dove Rest RV Park & Campground—(Jackson) *From jct I-10 (exit 142) & Hwy-71: Go 1/2 mi S on Hwy-71. Enter on R.* ◇◇◇FACILITIES: 24 sites, typical site width 35 ft, 10 full hkups, 14 W&E, (20/30/50 amps), tenting, dump, laundry. Pets welcome. Open all yr. Rate in 2010 $23-34 for 2 persons. Phone: (850)482-5313.

(N) FLORIDA CAVERNS STATE PARK—(Jackson) *From jct US 90 & Hwy 166: Go 3 mi N on Hwy 166.* FACILITIES: 35 sites, 30 ft max RV length, 35 W&E, tenting, dump. RECREATION: lake swim, boating, canoeing, ramp, lake fishing, playground. Pets welcome. Open all yr. Phone: (850)482-1228.

MCINTOSH—B-3

(E) Sportsman's Cove Resort—(Marion) *From jct Hwy 320 & US 441: Go 1 block N on US 441, then 1/2 mi E on Avenue F. Enter at end.* ◇◇◇FACILITIES: 36 sites, typical site width 30 ft, 36 full hkups, (30/50 amps), family camping, tenting, dump, laundry. ◇◇RECREATION: boating, canoeing, ramp, dock, lake fishing. Pets welcome. Open all yr. Big rigs welcome. Rate in 2010 $22 for 2 persons. Member ARVC, FLARVC. Phone: (352)591-1435.

MELBOURNE—C-5

(SE) Breezy Palms RV Park (RV SPACES)—(Brevard) *From I-95 (exit 173): Go 4 mi E on Hwy 514, then 1/2 mi N on US 1. Enter on L.* FACILITIES: 65 sites, typical site width 15 ft, 36 ft max RV length, 65 full hkups, (30/50 amps), laundry. Pets welcome. No tents. Open all yr. Rate in 2010 $35 for 2 persons. Phone: (321)724-1639.

MELBOURNE—Continued on next page

MELBOURNE—Continued

(NW) WICKHAM PARK (Brevard County Park)—(Brevard) *From US 192 & US-1: Go 7 mi N on US-1, then 1-1/2 mi W on Parkway Dr.* FACILITIES: 87 sites, 31 ft max RV length, 87 W&E, tenting, dump, laundry. RECREATION: lake swim, pond fishing, playground. Pets welcome. Open all yr. Phone: (321)255-4307.

MELBOURNE BEACH—C-5

(S) Melbourne Beach Mobile Park (RV SPACES) —(Brevard) *From jct US-192 & Hwy-A1A: Go 3-1/2 mi S on Hwy-A1A. Enter on R.* FACILITIES: 75 sites, typical site width 25 ft, 36 ft max RV length, 75 full hkups, (20/30/50 amps), 15 pull-thrus, family camping, dump, laundry. RECREATION: saltwater swim, saltwater/river fishing. No pets. No tents. Open all yr. Phone: (321) 723-4947.

(S) Outdoor Resorts/Melbourne Beach—(Brevard) *From jct US 192 & Hwy A1A: Go 4 mi S on Hwy A1A. Enter on R.* ◆◆◆◆FACILITIES: 75 sites, typical site width 34 ft, accepts full hkup units only, 75 full hkups, (20/30/50 amps), laundry. ◆◆◆◆RECREATION: 3 swim pools, saltwater swim, boating, ramp, saltwater/river fishing. Pets welcome. No tents. Open all yr. Big rigs welcome. Phone: (321)724-2600.

MIAMI—E-5

(W) Gator Park (RV SPACES)—(Dade) *From jct Hwy 997 & US 41: Go 6 mi W on US 41. Enter on L.* FACILITIES: 60 sites, typical site width 20 ft, accepts self-contained units only, 15 full hkups, 15 W&E, (30/50 amps), 30 no hkups, dump. Pets welcome, breed restrict, size restrict. No tents. Open all yr. Rate in 2010 $30 per vehicle. Phone: (800)559-2205.

WELCOME

(W) LARRY & PENNY THOMPSON PARK & CAMPGROUND—(Dade) *From jct US 41 & Hwy 997: Go 11-1/2 mi S on Hwy 997, then 5 mi E on 184th St. Enter on R.*

FACILITIES: 240 sites, typical site width 35 ft, 240 full hkups, (20/30/50 amps), some extd stay sites (winter), 10 pull-thrus, phone Internet central location, family camping, tenting, dump, non-guest dump $, laundry, ice, picnic tables, fire rings.

RECREATION: rec hall, equipped pavilion, swim pool, lake fishing, golf nearby, playground, activities, horseshoes, sports field, hiking trails, v-ball.

Pets welcome, size restrict. Partial handicap access. Open all yr. Big rigs welcome. Escort to site. Clubs welcome. MC/VISA/AMEX. Member ARVC, FLARVC.

Phone: (305)232-1049
Address: 12451 SW 184 St, Miami, FL 33177
Lat/Lon: 25.59738/-80.39510
Email: L&PCampground@miamidade.gov
Web: www.miamidade.gov/parks

SEE AD THIS PAGE

(SW) Miami Everglades Campground—(Dade) *From jct US 41 & Hwy 997: Go 12-1/2 mi S on Hwy 997, then 1-1/2 mi E on Quail Roost Dr, then 1/4 mi S on Farm Life School Rd. Enter on L.* ◆◆◆◆FACILITIES: 327 sites, typical site width 22 ft, 234 full hkups, 79 W&E, (30/50 amps), 50 amps ($), 14 no hkups, 229 pull-thrus, family camping, tenting, dump, laundry, full svc store. ◆◆◆◆◆RECREATION: swim pool, playground. Pets welcome. Partial handicap access. Open all yr. Big rigs welcome. Rate in 2010 $35-65 for 2 persons. Member ARVC, FLARVC. Phone: (800)917-4923.

WELCOME

THE BOARDWALK—*From Miami: Go 31 mi S on US 1, then 1 block E on 328th St, then 200 ft N on 6th Ave. Enter on R.*
SEE PRIMARY LISTING AT HOMESTEAD AND AD HOMESTEAD PAGE 127

MICCO—C-5

(N) Indian River Shores Mobile Home Park (RV SPACES)—(Brevard) *From jct Micco Rd & US 1: Go 1 mi N on US 1. Enter on L.* FACILITIES: 48 sites, typical site width 12 ft, 34 ft max RV length, 48 full hkups, (30/50 amps), 2 pull-thrus, dump, laundry. RECREATION: river swim, boating, canoeing, dock, saltwater fishing. Pets welcome, breed restrict. No tents. Open all yr. Rate in 2010 $35 for 2 persons. Phone: (772) 664-9888.

Can you trust the Woodall's ratings? 25 evaluation teams have scoured North American campgrounds to provide you with accurate, up to date information & ratings. Find a rating you don't agree with? Send a letter or email our way, and we'll give it extra attention for 2012.

MILTON—F-1

WELCOME

(S) AVALON LANDING RV PARK—(Santa Rosa) *From jct I-10 (exit 22) & Hwy 281 (Avalon Blvd): Go 1/2 mi S on Hwy 281. Enter on L.*

◆◆◆◆◆FACILITIES: 37 sites, typical site width 30 ft, 37 full hkups, (20/30/50 amps), some extd stay sites, cable TV, WiFi Instant Internet at site, WiFi Internet central location, family camping, dump, non-guest dump $, laundry, RV supplies, LP gas by weight/by meter, ice, picnic tables.

◆◆◆◆RECREATION: rec hall, swim pool, boating, canoeing, kayaking, ramp, canoe/pedal boat rentals, saltwater fishing, fishing supplies, golf nearby, activities, horseshoes, v-ball.

Pets welcome, breed restrict, quantity restrict. Partial handicap access. No tents. Open all yr. Planned group activities during Fall/Winter season only. Big rigs welcome. Escort to site. Clubs welcome. Rate in 2010 $35-39 for 2 persons. MC/VISA/DISC. Member ARVC, FLARVC.

Phone: (850)995-5898
Address: 2444 Avalon Blvd, Milton, FL 32583
Lat/Lon: 30.52622/-87.08715
Email: contact@avalonlandingrvpark.com
Web: www.avalonlandingrvpark.com

SEE AD PENSACOLA PAGE 156 AND AD TRAVEL SECTION PAGE 74

(N) Cedar Pines Campground—(Santa Rosa) *From jct US 90 & Hwy 87: Go 4-1/2 mi N on Hwy 87. Enter on R.* ◆◆◆FACILITIES: 40 sites, typical site width 30 ft, 40 full hkups, (30/50 amps), 33 pull-thrus, tenting, dump, laundry. ◆RECREATION: swim pool. Pets welcome, breed restrict, size restrict, quantity restrict. Open all yr. Rate in 2010 $30-32 for 2 persons. Member ARVC, FLARVC. Phone: (850)623-8869.

(E) Gulf Pines KOA—(Santa Rosa) *From jct I-10 (exit 31) & Hwy 87: Go 1 block N on Hwy 87, then 200 feet E on Gulf Pines Dr. Enter on R.* ◆◆◆◆FACILITIES: 122 sites, typical site width 30 ft, 100 full hkups, 11 W&E, (30/50 amps), 11 no hkups, 100 pull-thrus, family camping, tenting, dump, laundry, ltd groc. ◆◆◆◆RECREATION: swim pool, playground. Pets welcome, breed restrict, quantity restrict. Partial handicap access. Open all yr. Big rigs welcome. Rate in 2010 $34-52 for 2 persons. Member ARVC, FLARVC. Phone: (850)623-0808. KOA discount.

WELCOME

(S) PELICAN PALMS RV PARK—(Santa Rosa) *From jct I-10 (exit 26) & Hwy 191: Go 200 yds S on Hwy 191. Enter on L.*

COUNTRY COMFORT - CITY CONVENIENCE! Location, Environment, Proximity - we've got it all! 1/10 mi off I-10 & close to Emerald Coast Gulf Beaches. Large, level, full-hookup sites. Swim or relax in our sunny pool after a day of driving or sightseeing. Enjoy us soon!

◆◆◆◆FACILITIES: 51 sites, typical site width 30 ft, 49 full hkups, 2 E, (30/50 amps), many extd stay sites, 29 pull-thrus, WiFi Instant Internet at site, family camping, tenting, dump, non-guest dump $, laundry, RV supplies, LP gas by weight/by meter, ice.

CAMPCLUB USA

◆◆RECREATION: rec room/area, equipped pavilion, swim pool, horseshoes, hiking trails.

Pets welcome. Open all yr. Big rigs welcome. Escort to site. Clubs welcome. Rate in 2010 $31 for 2 persons. MC/VISA/DISC/AMEX. Member ARVC, FLARVC. CCUSA 50% Discount. CCUSA reservations Recommended, CCUSA max stay 1 day, Cash only for CCUSA disc. Space limited during holidays & special events. Call park.

Phone: (850)623-0576
Address: 3700 Garcon Point Rd, Milton, FL 32583
Lat/Lon: 30.56753/-87.03125
Email: pprvp@aol.com
Web: www.pelicanpalmsrvpark.com

SEE AD PENSACOLA PAGE 156 AND AD TRAVEL SECTION PAGE 74

MIMS—C-4

(W) Crystal Lake RV Park—(Brevard) *From jct I-95 (exit 231) & Stuckway Rd (formerly CR 5A): Go 200 yds on Stuckway Rd. Enter on L.* ◆◆◆FACILITIES: 62 sites, typical site width 25 ft, 60 full hkups, (20/30/50 amps), 2 no hkups, 44 pull-thrus, heater not allowed, WiFi Instant Internet at site ($), family camping, tenting, RV storage, laundry, RV supplies, picnic tables.

MIMS—Continued
Crystal Lake RV Park—Continued

CAMPCLUB USA

◆◆RECREATION: rec hall, swim pool, lake fishing, shuffleboard court 2 shuffleboard courts. Pets welcome, quantity restrict. Open all yr. Rate in 2010 $26-36 for 2 persons. MC/VISA/DISC. Member ARVC, FLARVC. CCUSA 50% Discount. CCUSA reservations Recommended, CCUSA max stay Unlimited. Discount not available Feb 1-Mar13.

Phone: (321)268-8555
Address: 4240 Stuckway Rd, Mims, FL 32754
Lat/Lon: 28.77359/-80.89280
Email: crystallakepark1@bellsouth.net
Web: www.crystallakervpark.com

MONTICELLO—A-2

(S) KOA-Tallahassee East/Monticello—(Jefferson) *From jct I-10 (exit 225) & US 19: Go 1/4 mi S on US 19, then 2 mi W on CR 158B, then 1/2 mi N on CR 259, then 1/4 mi E on KOA Rd. Enter on R.* ◆◆◆FACILITIES: 77 sites, typical site width 35 ft, 72 full hkups, 5 W&E, (30/50 amps), 66 pull-thrus, family camping, tenting, dump, laundry, ltd groc. ◆◆◆RECREATION: swim pool, lake fishing, playground. Pets welcome. Partial handicap access. Open all yr. Rate in 2010 $35-40 for 2 persons. Phone: (800)562-3890. KOA discount.

MOORE HAVEN—D-4

(E) Aruba RV Park—(Glades) *From east jct US 27 & Hwy 78: Go 9 mi N on Hwy 78, then 200 ft W on Old Lakeport Rd. Enter on L.* ◆◆◆FACILITIES: 137 sites, typical site width 40 ft, 137 full hkups, (30/50 amps), 6 pull-thrus, laundry. ◆◆◆◆RECREATION: swim pool, boating, ramp, dock, lake/river fishing. Pets welcome. Partial handicap access. No tents. Open all yr. Big rigs welcome. Rate in 2010 $30 for 2 persons. Member ARVC, FLARVC. Phone: (863)946-1324.

(NW) M RV Resort—(Glades) *From E jct Hwy 78 & US 27: Go 6-1/2 mi N on US 27. Enter on L.* ◆◆◆FACILITIES: 243 sites, typical site width 30 ft, 243 full hkups, (30/50 amps), 2 pull-thrus, WiFi Instant Internet at site ($), WiFi Internet central location, RV storage, dump, laundry, picnic tables, patios.

CAMPCLUB USA

◆◆◆RECREATION: rec hall, swim pool, pond fishing, shuffleboard court 3 shuffleboard courts, activities, horseshoes. Pets welcome, breed restrict. Partial handicap access. No tents. Open all yr. Big rigs welcome. Rate in 2010 $27.50 for 2 persons. MC/VISA/DISC. Member ARVC, FLARVC. CCUSA 50% Discount. CCUSA reservations Recommended, CCUSA max stay 14 days, Cash only for CCUSA disc. Discount available Apr thru Dec. Jan thru Mar-call for same day availability.

Phone: (863)946-6616
Address: 17192 Hwy 27, Moore Haven, FL 33471
Lat/Lon: 26.86186/-81.21289
Email: mrvresort@earthlink.net
Web: www.mrvresort.com

(E) Marina RV Resort—(Glades) *From east jct Hwy 78 & US 27: Go 1-1/2 mi S on US 27, then 1/2 mi N on 6th St, then 1/2 mi E on CR 720 NW (Tobias Ave). Enter at end.* ◆◆◆FACILITIES: 139 sites, typical site width 30 ft, 133 full hkups, 6 W&E, (20/30/50 amps), WiFi Instant Internet at site ($), tenting, RV storage, laundry, picnic tables, patios.

CAMPCLUB USA

◆◆◆◆RECREATION: rec hall, swim pool, boating, canoeing, kayaking, ramp, dock, lake/river fishing, shuffleboard court 2 shuffleboard courts, activities, horseshoes, hiking trails. Pets welcome. Partial handicap access. Open all yr. Big rigs welcome. Rate in 2010 $27.25-32.70 for 2 persons. MC/VISA/Debit. CCUSA 50% Discount. CCUSA reservations Recommended, CCUSA max stay 14 days, Cash only for CCUSA disc.

Phone: (863)946-1587
Address: 900 CR 720 NW/Tobias Ave, Moore Haven, FL 33471
Lat/Lon: 26.84096/-81.08910

(N) North Lake Estates RV Resort (Morgan RV Resorts)—(Glades) *From east jct US 27 & Hwy 78: Go 10 mi N on Hwy 78. Enter on R.* ◆◆◆◆FACILITIES:

North Lake Estates RV Resort (Morgan RV Resorts)—Continued on next page

MOORE HAVEN—Continued
North Lake Estates RV Resort (Morgan RV Resorts)—Continued

300 sites, 300 full hkups, (30/50 amps), laundry. ◊◊◊◊RECREATION: swim pool, lake fishing. Pets welcome. Partial handicap access. No tents. Open all yr. Big rigs welcome. Rate in 2010 $35 for 2 persons. Member ARVC, FLARVC. Phone: (863)946-0700.

NAPLES—E-4

(E) Club Naples RV Resort (Morgan RV Resorts)—(Collier) *From jct I-75 (exit 101) & Hwy 951: Go 1/4 mi S on Hwy 951, then 1 mi E on Old Hwy 84 (Alligator Alley). Enter on R.* ◊◊◊◊FACILITIES: 305 sites, typical site width 33 ft, 305 full hkups, (30/50 amps), 12 pull-thrus, tenting, dump, laundry. ◊◊◊◊RECREATION: swim pool. Pets welcome. Partial handicap access. Open all yr. Big rigs welcome. Rate in 2010 $45-50 for 2 persons. Member ARVC, FLARVC. Phone: (888)795-2780.

Say you saw it in Woodall's!

NAPLES—Continued

(SE) COLLIER-SEMINOLE STATE PARK—(Collier) *From jct Hwy-84 & US-41: Go 15 mi S on US-41.* FACILITIES: 120 sites, 120 W&E, tenting, dump. RECREATION: boating, canoeing, ramp, dock, saltwater fishing, playground. Partial handicap access. Open all yr. Phone: (941)394-3397.

(NE) CRYSTAL LAKE RV RESORT—(Collier) *From jct I-75 (exit 101) & Hwy 951: Go 7 mi N on Hwy 951. Enter on R.*

WELCOME

◊◊◊◊◊FACILITIES: 490 sites, typical site width 40 ft, accepts full hkup units only, 490 full hkups, (30/50 amps), mostly extd stay sites (winter), cable TV, WiFi Internet central location, RV's/park model rentals, RV storage, dump, laundry, picnic tables, patios, controlled access.

◊◊◊◊◊RECREATION: rec hall, rec room/area, equipped pavilion, 2 swim pools, hot tub, boating, electric motors only, canoeing, kayaking, ramp, dock, lake fishing, putting green, golf nearby, bsktball, shuffleboard court 8 shuffleboard courts, activities, tennis, horseshoes, hiking trails, local tours.

NAPLES—Continued
CRYSTAL LAKE RV RESORT—Continued

Pets welcome, quantity restrict. Partial handicap access. No tents. Open all yr. Big rigs welcome. Escort to site. Green Friendly.

Phone: (239)348-0017
Address: 14960 Collier Blvd, Naples, FL 34119
Lat/Lon: 26.26518/-81.68892
Email: crystalrealty@mindspring.com
Web: www.crystallakervresort.com

SEE AD NEXT PAGE

(E) Endless Summer RV Park—(Collier) *From jct I-75 (exit 101) & Hwy 951: Go 1/4 mi S on Hwy 951 (Collier Blvd), then 1/2 mi W on Hwy 84 (Davis Blvd), then 2 mi W on CR 856 (Radio Rd). Enter on R.* ◊◊◊FACILITIES: 120 sites, typical site width 24 ft, 120 full hkups, (20/30/50 amps), tenting, dump, laundry. ◊◊RECREATION: swim pool. Pets welcome, size restrict. Open all yr. Rate in 2010 $40-50 for 2 persons. Phone: (239)643-1511.

(SE) KOA Naples—(Collier) *From jct I-75 (exit 101) & Hwy 951: Go 7-3/4 mi S on Hwy 951, then 1/2 mi W on TV Tower Rd., then 500 feet S on Barefoot Williams Rd. Enter on L.* ◊◊◊◊FACILITIES: 187 sites, typical site width 20 ft, 150 full hkups, 25 W&E, (30/50 amps), 12 no hkups, 75 pull-thrus, family camping, tenting, dump, laundry, groceries. ◊◊◊◊◊RECREATION: swim pool, boating, canoeing, ramp, saltwater/river fishing, playground. Pets welcome. Partial handicap access. Open all yr. Rate in 2010 $45-84.50 for 2 persons. Member ARVC, FLARVC. Phone: (800)562-7734. KOA discount.

(N) Lake San Marino RV Resort—(Collier) *From jct Hwy 951 & I-75: Go 10 mi N on I-75 (exit 111), then 3-1/2 mi W on CR 846, then 1-1/2 mi N on US 41, then*

Lake San Marino RV Resort—Continued on next page

NAPLES—Continued
Lake San Marino RV Resort—Continued

1/4 mi E on Wiggins Pass Rd. Enter on R. ◆◆◆◆FACILITIES: 410 sites, typical site width 35 ft, accepts full hkup units only, 410 full hkups, (30/50 amps), WiFi Instant Internet at site ($), RV storage, dump, non-guest dump $, laundry, picnic tables, patios. ◆◆◆◆RECREATION: rec hall, swim pool, boating, no motors, canoeing, kayaking, dock, lake fishing, shuffleboard court 8 shuffleboard courts, activities, horseshoes. Pets welcome, breed restrict, quantity restrict. Partial handicap access. No tents. Age restrict may apply. Open all yr. Rate in 2010 $35-48 for 2 persons. MC/VISA/DISC/Debit. Member ARVC, FLARVC. CCUSA 50% Discount. CCUSA reservations Required, CCUSA max stay 7 days. Discount not available Nov 30-Apr 30. Additional charges may apply.

Phone: (239)597-4202
Address: 1000 Wiggins Pass Rd East, Naples, FL 34110
Lat/Lon: 26.29426/-81.79828
Email: sunresv@aol.com
Web: www.lakesanmarino.com

(SE) MARCO NAPLES HITCHING POST TRAVEL RESORT—(Collier) *From jct I-75 (exit 101) & Hwy 951: Go 7 mi S on 951 (Collier Blvd), then 1-1/4 mi N on US 41. Enter on L.*

◆◆◆FACILITIES: 305 sites, typical site width 30 ft, 295 full hkups, 10 W&E, (20/30 amps), mostly extd stay sites (winter), 295 pull-thrus, heater not allowed, dump, non-guest dump $, picnic tables, patios.

◆◆◆◆RECREATION: rec hall, swim pool, golf nearby, shuffleboard court 4 shuffleboard courts, activities, horseshoes.

Pets welcome. Partial handicap access. No tents. Age restrict may apply. Open Oct 1 - Apr 30. Planned group activities winter only. Clubs welcome. Rate in 2010 $46 for 2 persons.

Phone: (800)362-8968
Address: 100 Barefoot Williams Rd, Naples, FL 34113
Lat/Lon: 26.07314/-81.71697
Email: hprvresort@aol.com

SEE AD PAGE 142

(SE) Naples Gardens - Morgan RV Resorts (formerly Kountree Kampinn)—(Collier) *From jct I-75 (exit 101) & Hwy 951: Go 4-1/4 mi S on Hwy 951. Enter on L.* ◆◆◆◆FACILITIES: 161 sites, typical site width 32 ft, 161 full hkups, (30/50 amps), 15 pull-thrus, family camping, tenting, dump, laundry. ◆◆◆RECREATION: swim pool. Pets welcome. Partial handicap access. Open all yr. Rate in 2010 $45-60 for 2 persons. Member ARVC, FLARVC. Phone: (239)775-4340.

(SE) NEAPOLITAN COVE RV RESORT—(Collier) *From jct I-75 (exit 101) & Hwy 951: Go 1/4 mi S on Hwy 951, then 5 mi W on Hwy 84, then 3/4 mi S on Airport Rd, then 1/2 mi SE on US 41. Enter on R.*

NEW LUXURIOUS RV RESORT
Beautiful landscaped RV Resort on Florida's West Coast. All the amenities of Naples within 2-1/2 miles. Located near some of Florida's most beautiful beaches. New clubhouse, laundry & pool. Enjoy fun & relax in a sunny paradise.

◆◆◆◆◆FACILITIES: 60 sites, typical site width 25 ft, accepts full hkup units only, 60 full hkups, (20/50 amps), many extd stay sites (winter), 18 pull-thrus, cable TV, WiFi Instant Internet at site, RV storage, dump, non-guest dump $, laundry, ice, picnic tables, patios.

◆◆◆RECREATION: rec hall, pavilion, swim pool, golf nearby, activities.

Pets welcome, quantity restrict. Partial handicap access. No tents. Open all yr. Big rigs welcome. Escort to site. Clubs welcome. Green Friendly. MC/VISA. Member ARVC, FLARVC.

Phone: (239)793-0091
Address: 3790 Tamiami Trail E, Naples, FL 34112
Lat/Lon: 26.12007/-81.76003
Email: info@neapolitancoverv.com
Web: www.neapolitancoverv.com

SEE AD PAGE 142

(SE) Paradise Pointe Luxury RV Resort—(Collier) *From jct I-75 (exit 101) & Hwy 951: Go 7 mi S on Hwy 951 (Collier Blvd), then 2-1/2 mi E on US 41. Enter on R.* ◆◆◆◆FACILITIES: 383 sites, typical site width 40 ft, 383 full hkups, (30/50 amps), dump, laundry. ◆◆◆◆RECREATION: swim pool, pond fishing. Pets welcome. Partial handicap access. No tents. Age restrict may apply. Open all yr. Big rigs welcome. Rate in 2010 $45-50 for 2 persons. Phone: (877)462-7537.

NAPLES—Continued on next page

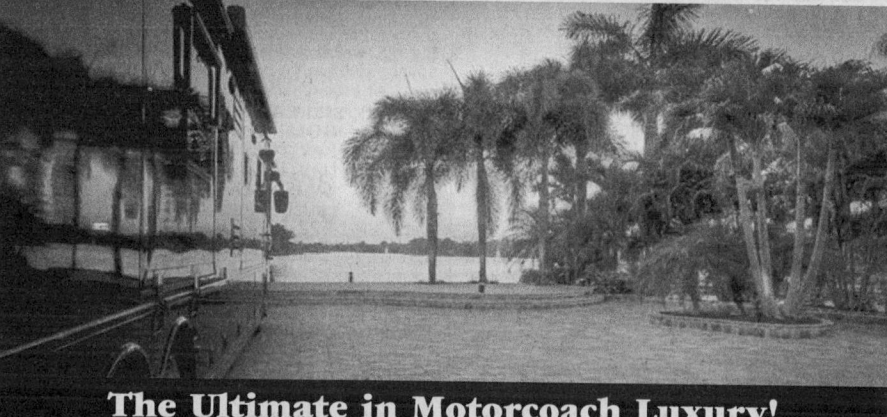

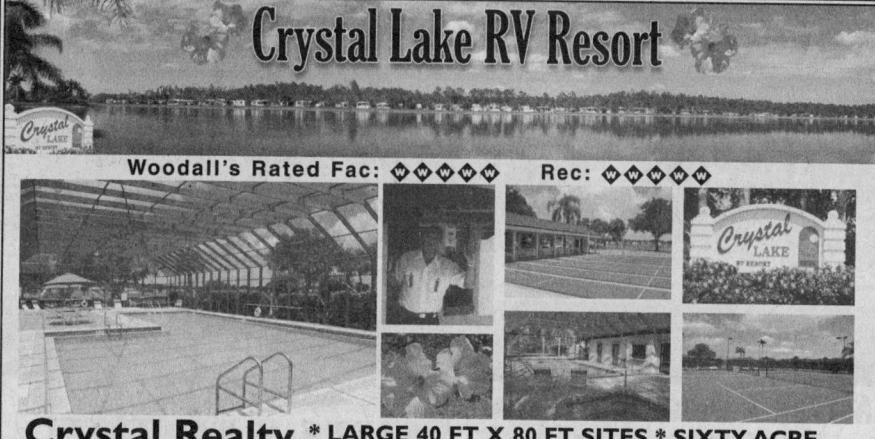

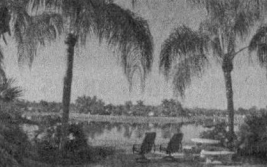

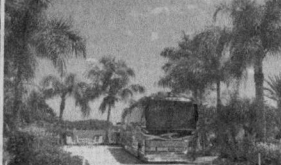

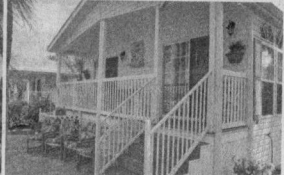

NAPLES—Continued

(SE) PELICAN LAKE MOTORCOACH RESORT—(Collier) *From jct I-75 (exit 101) & Hwy 951: Go 9 mi S on Hwy 951. Enter on L.*

WELCOME

◊◊◊◊◊FACILITIES: 289 sites, typical site width 55 ft, accepts full hkup units only, 289 full hkups, (20/50 amps), some extd stay sites (winter), cable TV, WiFi Instant Internet at site, laundry, picnic tables, patios, controlled access.

◊◊◊◊◊RECREATION: rec hall, equipped pavilion, swim pool, hot tub, boating, electric motors only, canoeing, kayaking, dock, lake fishing, golf nearby, shuffleboard court 4 shuffleboard courts, activities, tennis.

Pets welcome, quantity restrict. Partial handicap access. No tents. Open all yr. Class A Motor Coaches only 26-ft minimum. Big rigs welcome. Escort to site. Clubs welcome. Rate in 2010 $60-125 for 6 persons. MC/VISA/DISC.

Phone: (800)835-4389
Address: 4555 Southern Breeze Dr, Naples, FL 34114
Lat/Lon: 26.03265/-81.69612
Email: pelicanlakeinfo@aol.com
Web: www.pelicanlake.com

SEE AD PAGE 143

(E) ROCK CREEK RV RESORT—(Collier) *From jct I-75 (exit 101) & Hwy 951: Go 1/4 mi S on Hwy 951, then 1/2 mi W on Hwy 84, then 4-1/4 mi W on CR 856 (Radio Rd), then 1/2 mi S on CR 31 (Airport/Pulling Rd), then 500 feet W on North Rd. Enter on L.*

WELCOME

ROCK CREEK TROPICAL PARADISE

2.5 miles to Naples' exquisite beaches, downtown Historic District, & mall. A private family owned friendly business. Beautiful tropical setting of lush foilage, oaks, palms & a creek that flows to the Gulf. www.rockcreekrv.com

◊◊◊◊FACILITIES: 230 sites, typical site width 25 ft, 230 full hkups, (30/50 amps), some extd stay sites (winter), 3 pull-thrus, cable TV, WiFi Internet central location, tenting, dump, non-guest dump $, laundry, RV supplies, ice, picnic tables, patios.

NAPLES—Continued
ROCK CREEK RV RESORT—Continued

◊◊◊◊RECREATION: rec hall, rec room/area, pavilion, swim pool, boating, canoeing, kayaking, ramp, dock, saltwater fishing, golf nearby, shuffleboard court 2 shuffleboard courts, activities.

Pets welcome. Partial handicap access. Age restrict may apply. Open all yr. Children limited stay only. Group activities winter only. Big rigs welcome. Escort to site. Clubs welcome. Rate in 2010 $45-60 for 2 persons. MC/VISA. Member ARVC, FLARVC.

Phone: (239)643-3100
Address: 3100 North Rd, Naples, FL 34104
Lat/Lon: 26.14573/-81.76864
Email: rc@rockcreekrv.com
Web: www.rockcreekrv.com

SEE AD PAGE 142

(SE) Signature Motorcoach Resort at Naples—(Collier) *From jct I-75 (exit 101) & Hwy 951: Go 7 mi S on Hwy 951, then 1/2 mi E on US 41. Enter on R.* ◊◊◊◊◊FACILITIES: 184 sites, accepts full hkup units only, 184 full hkups, (50 amps), laundry. ◊◊◊◊◊RECREATION: 3 swim pools, boating, canoeing, ramp, saltwater fishing. Pets welcome, quantity restrict. Partial handicap access. No tents. Open all yr. Big rigs welcome. Phone: (239)530-0153. FMCA discount.

(SE) SILVER LAKES RV RESORT AND GOLF CLUB—(Collier) *From jct I-75 (exit 101) & Hwy 951: Go 9 mi S on Hwy 951. Enter on L.*

WELCOME

◊◊◊◊◊FACILITIES: 522 sites, typical site width 40 ft, accepts full hkup units only, 522 full hkups, (30/50 amps), many extd stay sites (winter), 13 pull-thrus, cable TV, WiFi Internet central location, laundry, ice, picnic tables, patios, controlled access.

◊◊◊◊◊RECREATION: rec hall, rec room/area, 2 swim pools, hot tub, boating, electric motors only, canoeing, kayaking, lake fishing, golf nearby, shuffleboard court 8 shuffleboard courts, activities, tennis, horseshoes.

Pets welcome, breed restrict, quantity restrict. Partial handicap access. No tents. Open all yr. 25

NAPLES—Continued
SILVER LAKES RV RESORT AND GOLF CLUB—Continued

ft min RV. Big rigs welcome. Escort to site. Clubs welcome. Rate in 2010 $45-79 for 6 persons. MC/VISA/DISC.

Phone: (800)843-2836
Address: 1001 Silver Lakes Blvd, Naples, FL 34114
Lat/Lon: 26.03893/-81.70010
Email: silverlkes@aol.com
Web: www.silverlakesrvresort.com

SEE AD THIS PAGE

NAVARRE—F-1

(E) EMERALD BEACH RV PARK—(Santa Rosa) *From jct Hwy 87 & US 98: Go 1 mi E on US 98. (Big Rigs coming from east-turn on Navarre Sound Circle to make right turn into park.). Enter on R.*

WELCOME

◊◊◊◊◊FACILITIES: 76 sites, typical site width 25 ft, 76 full hkups, (30/50 amps), some extd stay sites (winter), 37 pull-thrus, cable TV, WiFi Instant Internet at site ($), family camping, cabins, dump, non-guest dump $, laundry, RV supplies, LP gas by weight/by meter, ice, picnic tables, patios.

◊◊◊◊RECREATION: rec hall, equipped pavilion, swim pool, saltwater swim, kayaking, 2 kayak rentals, saltwater fishing, activities.

Pets welcome, breed restrict, quantity restrict. No tents. Open all yr. Planned group activities winter only. Big rigs welcome. Escort to site. Clubs welcome. Rate in 2010 $40-65 for 2 persons. MC/VISA/DISC. Member ARVC, FLARVC.

Phone: (866)939-3431
Address: 8885 Navarre Pkwy, Navarre, FL 32566
Lat/Lon: 30.40448/-86.85135
Email: emrldbch1@aol.com
Web: www.emeraldbeachrvpark.com

SEE AD THIS PAGE

(E) Navarre Beach Campground—(Santa Rosa) *From jct Hwy 87 & US 98: Go 2 mi E on US 98. Enter on R.* ◊◊◊◊◊FACILITIES: 144 sites, typical site width 32 ft, 144 full hkups, (30/50 amps), 41 pull-thrus, family camping, tenting, dump, laundry, ltd groc. ◊◊◊◊RECREATION: swim pool, saltwater swim, saltwater fishing, playground. Pets welcome. Partial handicap access. Open all yr. Big rigs welcome. Rate in 2010 $45-80 for 2 persons. Member ARVC, FLARVC. Phone: (888)639-2188.

NEW PORT RICHEY—C-3

(E) Orchid Lake RV Resort (RV SPACES)—(Pasco) *From jct US 19 & Hwy 587A (Ridge Rd): Go 2-1/2 mi E on Hwy 587A, then 3/4 mi S on Little Rd, then 1/4 mi W on Arevee Dr. Enter at end.* FACILITIES: 67 sites, typical site width 18 ft, 35 ft max RV length, accepts full hkup units only, 67 full hkups, (20/30/50 amps), laundry. RECREATION: swim pool, lake fishing. No pets. No tents. Age restrict may apply. Open all yr. Rate in 2010 $38 for 2 persons. Phone: (727)847-1925.

(SE) Seven Springs Travel Park—(Pasco) *From jct US 19 & Hwy 54: Go 3-1/2 mi E on Hwy 54, then 1 block E on Old County Rd 54. Enter on L.* ◊◊◊FACILITIES: 120 sites, typical site width 32 ft, accepts full hkup units only, 120 full hkups, (30/50 amps), 50 amps ($), family camping, laundry. ◊◊◊RECREATION: swim pool. No pets. Partial handicap access. No tents. Age restrict may apply. Open all yr. Big rigs welcome. Rate in 2010 $28 for 2 persons.

Phone: (727)376-0000
Address: 8039 Old County Rd 54, New Port Richey, FL 34653
Lat/Lon: 28.21771/-82.68106
Email: joe@sevenspringstravelpark.com
Web: www.sevenspringstravelpark.com

Woodall's Tip... For details on how to read the listings, turn to the "How to Use" pages in the front of the Directory.

NEW SMYRNA BEACH—B-4

(SW) NEW SMYRNA BEACH RV PARK—(Volusia) *S'bnd from jct I-95 (exit 249A) & Hwy 44: Go 2-1/2 mi E on Hwy 44, then 2 mi S on Mission Dr. Entrance on right. N'bnd from jct I-95 (exit 244) & Hwy 442: Go 3/4 mi E on Hwy 442, then 3 mi N on Old Mission Dr. Entrance on left.*

◊◊◊◊◊FACILITIES: 250 sites, typical site width 30 ft, 193 full hkups, 9 W&E, (30/50 amps), 48 no hkups, many extd stay sites (winter), 86 pull-thrus, cable TV, WiFi Instant Internet at site, cable Internet central location, family camping, tenting, cabins, RV storage, dump, non-guest dump $, laundry, LP gas by weight/by meter, ice, picnic tables.

◊◊◊◊◊RECREATION: rec hall, rec room/area, equipped pavilion, swim pool, mini-golf, ($), golf nearby, bsktball, playground, shuffleboard court shuffleboard court, activities, horseshoes, v-ball.

Pets welcome, quantity restrict. Partial handicap access. Open all yr. Rates adjusted during special events. Big rigs welcome. Escort to site. Clubs welcome. Rate in 2010 $30 for 2 persons. MC/VISA/DISC. Member ARVC, FLARVC. FCRV discount. FMCA discount. CCUSA 50% Discount. CCUSA reservations Accepted, CCUSA max stay 2 days, CCUSA disc. not avail F,Sa, CCUSA disc. not avail holidays. Discount available May-Sep, not valid during special events, may not be combined w/other discounts.

Phone: (800)928-9962
Address: 1300 Old Mission Rd., New Smyrna Beach, FL 32168
Lat/Lon: 28.99635/-80.94336
Email: beachcamp@beachcamp.net
Web: www.beachcamp.net

SEE AD DAYTONA BEACH PAGE 108

(W) SUGAR MILL RUINS TRAVEL PARK—(Volusia) *From jct I-95 (exit 249A) & Hwy 44: Go 3-1/2 mi E on Hwy 44, then 1-3/4 mi S on Mission Rd. Enter on R.*

◊◊◊◊FACILITIES: 180 sites, typical site width 25 ft, 176 full hkups, (30/50 amps), 4 no hkups, many extd stay sites (winter), 100 pull-thrus, cable TV, WiFi Instant Internet at site, WiFi Internet central location, family camping, tenting, cabins, dump, laundry, ltd groc, RV supplies, LP gas by weight/by meter, ice, picnic tables, controlled access.

◊◊◊◊RECREATION: rec hall, rec room/area, pavilion, coin games, swim pool, canoeing, kayaking, 2 canoe rentals, lake fishing, golf nearby, bsktball, playground, shuffleboard court 3 shuffleboard courts, activities, horseshoes, sports field, hiking trails, v-ball.

Pets welcome. Partial handicap access. Open all yr. Escort to site. Clubs welcome. Rate in 2010 $27.95-36.95 for 2 persons. MC/VISA/DISC. Member ARVC, FLARVC. CCUSA 50% Discount. CCUSA reservations Recommended, CCUSA max stay 3 days, CCUSA disc. not avail F,Sa, CCUSA disc. not avail holidays. Not valid Nov thru Apr & special events. Anyone over 12 considered adult for surcharge purposes.

Phone: (386)427-2284
Address: 1050 Old Mission Rd, New Smyrna Beach, FL 32168
Lat/Lon: 29.00152/-80.94036
Email: sugarmillruinstravelpark@gmail.com
Web: www.sugarmilltravelpark.net

SEE AD DAYTONA BEACH PAGE 108 AND AD TRAVEL SECTION PAGE 74

NICEVILLE—F-2

(E) FRED GANNON ROCKY BAYOU STATE RECREATION AREA—(Okaloosa) *From jct Hwy-20 & Hwy-285: Go 3 mi E on Hwy-20.* FACILITIES: 42 sites, 30 ft max RV length, 42 W&E, tenting, dump. RECREATION: boating, ramp, dock, saltwater fishing, playground. Pets welcome. Open all yr. Phone: (850)833-9144.

MILITARY PARK (Lake Pippin Rec Area-Maxwell/Gunter AFB AL)—(Okaloosa) *Off base. Off I-10 on Choctawhatchee Bay.* FACILITIES: 80 sites, 46 full hkups, 34 W&E, tenting, dump. RECREATION: boating. No pets. Open all yr. Phone: (334)953-3509.

NOKOMIS—D-3

(NW) ENCORE ROYAL COACHMAN—(Sarasota) *From jct I-75 (exit 195) & Laurel Rd: Go 2-1/4 mi W on Laurel Rd. Enter on L.*

◊◊◊◊◊FACILITIES: 551 sites, typical site width 30 ft, 551 full hkups, (20/30/50 amps), some extd stay sites (winter), 5 pull-thrus, cable TV, phone/cable on-site Internet (needs activ), WiFi Internet central location ($), family camping, RV's/park model rentals, RV storage, dump, non-guest dump $, laundry, RV supplies, ice, picnic tables, controlled access.

◊◊◊◊◊RECREATION: rec hall, rec room/area, equipped pavilion, swim pool, boating, canoeing, kayaking, saltwater fishing, mini-golf, putting green, golf nearby, bsktball, 50 bike rentals, playground, shuffleboard court 6 shuffleboard courts, activities, tennis, horseshoes, sports field, v-ball, local tours.

Pets welcome. Partial handicap access. Open all yr. Big rigs welcome. Clubs welcome. Rate in 2010 $43-88 for 2 persons. MC/VISA/DISC/AMEX. Member ARVC, FLARVC.

Phone: (941)488-9674
Address: 1070 Laurel Rd E, Nokomis, FL 34275
Lat/Lon: 27.13455/-82.44168
Email: royal_coachman@mhchomes.com
Web: www.rvonthego.com/Royal-Coachman-RV-Resort

SEE AD ALACHUA PAGE 93

OAKLAND PARK—E-5

(W) EASTERLIN PARK (Broward County Park)—(Broward) *From jct I-95 (exit 32) & Commerical Blvd: Go 1 block W on Commercial Blvd, then 3/4 mi S on Powerline Rd, then 1/2 mi W on NW 38th St. Enter on L.*

FACILITIES: 55 sites, 46 full hkups, 9 W&E, (20/30/50 amps), 7 pull-thrus, family camping, tenting, dump, non-guest dump $, ice, picnic tables, grills.

RECREATION: pavilion, bsktball, playground, horseshoes, hiking trails, v-ball. Rec open to public.

Pets welcome. Partial handicap access. Open all yr. Clubs welcome. MC/VISA/DISC/AMEX.

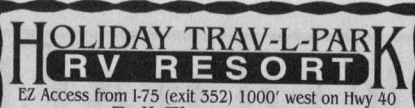

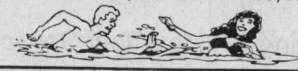

OAKLAND PARK—Continued
EASTERLIN PARK (Broward County Park)—Continued

Phone: (954)938-0610
Address: 1000 NW 38th St, Oakland Park, FL 33309
Lat/Lon: 26.17363/-80.16007
Email: easterlinpark@broward.org
Web: www.broward.org/parks/camping

SEE AD TRAVEL SECTION PAGE 75 AND AD DISCOVER SECTION PAGE 33

OCALA—B-3

See listings at Dunnellon, McIntosh, Orange Lake, Ocklawaha, & Silver Springs

(S) Camper Village—(Marion) *From jct I-75 (exit 350) & Hwy 200: Go 1/4 mi SW on Hwy 200. Enter on R.* ◊◊◊FACILITIES: 250 sites, typical site width 25 ft, 250 full hkups, (30/50 amps), 150 pull-thrus, dump, laundry. Pets welcome, breed restrict, quantity restrict. Partial handicap access. No tents. Age restrict may apply. Open all yr. Big rigs welcome. Rate in 2010 $39 for 2 persons. Member ARVC, FLARVC. Phone: (352) 237-3236.

(SW) HOLIDAY TRAV-L-PARK RV RESORT—(Marion) *From jct I-75 (exit 352) & Hwy 40: Go 1000 feet W on Hwy 40. Enter on R.*

◊◊◊FACILITIES: 110 sites, typical site width 35 ft, 105 full hkups, 5 W&E, (30/50 amps), many extd stay sites (winter), 103 pull-thrus, heater not allowed, cable TV, WiFi Internet central location, family camping, tenting, dump, non-guest dump $, laundry, RV supplies, LP gas by weight/by meter, ice, picnic tables.

◊◊◊RECREATION: rec room/area, pavilion, swim pool, bsktball, play equipment, shuffleboard court, activities, local tours.

Pets welcome, breed restrict, size restrict, quantity restrict. Partial handicap access. Open all yr. Big rigs welcome. Clubs welcome. Rate in 2010 $23.95-29.95 for 2 persons. MC/VISA/DISC. Member ARVC, FLARVC. CCUSA 50% Discount. CCUSA reservations Recommended, CCUSA max stay Unlimited.

HOLIDAY TRAV-L-PARK RV RESORT—Continued on next page

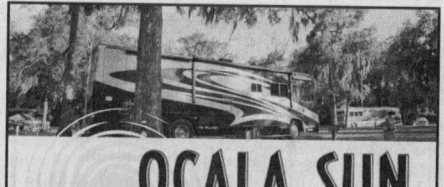

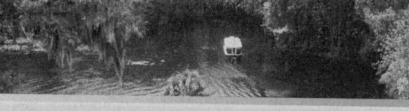

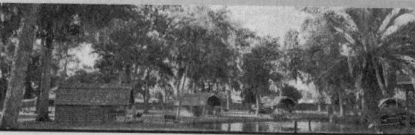

OCALA—Continued
HOLIDAY TRAV-L-PARK RV RESORT—Continued

Phone: (800)833-2164
Address: 4001 W Silver Springs Blvd, Ocala, FL 34482
Lat/Lon: 29.18681/-82.18813
SEE AD PAGE 145

Oak Tree Village Campground—(Marion) *From jct I-75 (exit 354) & US 27: Go 1/8 mi W on US 27, then 1/4 mi N on Blitchton Rd. Enter on R.* ◆◆FACILITIES: 137 sites, typical site width 20 ft, 70 full hkups, 67 W&E, (20/30/50 amps), 137 pull-thrus, dump, laundry. ◆◆◆RECREATION: swim pool, playground. Pets welcome, breed restrict, size restrict, quantity restrict. Partial handicap access. No tents. Open all yr. Rate in 2010 $22-25 for 2 persons. Phone: (352)629-1569.

(S) Ocala RV Camp Resort—(Marion) *From jct I-75, (exit 350) & HWY 200: Go 200 feet W on Hwy 200, then 1/2 mi N on SW 38th Ave. Enter on L.* ◆◆◆◆FACILITIES: 176 sites, typical site width 35 ft, 164 full hkups, 6 W&E, (20/30/50 amps), 6 no hkups, 146 pull-thrus, family camping, tenting, dump, laundry. ◆◆◆◆◆RECREATION: swim pool, pond fishing, playground. Pets welcome, breed restrict, quantity restrict. Partial handicap access. Open all yr. Big rigs welcome. Rate in 2010 $28-39 for 2 persons. Member ARVC, FLARVC. Phone: (866)858-3400.

(S) OCALA SUN RV RESORT—(Marion) *From jct I-75 (exit 341) & Hwy 484: Go 1/2 mi W on Hwy 484. Enter on R.* ◆◆◆◆FACILITIES: 170 sites, typical site width 35 ft, 170 full hkups, (30/50 amps), many extd stay sites, 47 pull-thrus, WiFi Instant Internet at site ($), WiFi Internet central location, RV storage, laundry, LP gas by weight/by meter, controlled access.

◆◆◆RECREATION: rec hall, swim pool, activities, horseshoes.

Pets welcome, quantity restrict. Partial handicap access. No tents. Open all yr. Planned group activities winter only. Big rigs welcome. Escort to site. Clubs welcome. Rate in 2010 $31-37 for 2 persons. MC/VISA/DISC. Member ARVC, FLARVC. CCUSA 50% Discount. CCUSA reservations Accepted, CCUSA max stay 7 days.

Tell them Woodall's sent you!

OCALA—Continued
OCALA SUN RV RESORT—Continued

Phone: (877)809-1100
Address: 2559 SW Hwy 484, Ocala, FL 34473
Lat/Lon: 29.02587/-82.16738
Email: info@ocalasunrvresort.com
Web: www.ocalasunrvresort.com
SEE AD PAGE 145 AND AD TRAVEL SECTION PAGE 74

(N) Wild Frontier Rally Park & Campground—(Marion) *From jct I-75 (exit 358) & SR 326: Go 1 mi E on SR 326, then 4 mi S on CR 25A. Enter on R.* ◆◆◆◆FACILITIES: 100 sites, typical site width 25 ft, 100 full hkups, (20/30/50 amps), cable TV, WiFi Instant Internet at site, WiFi Internet central location, dump, non-guest dump $, laundry, RV supplies, LP gas by weight/by meter, ice, picnic tables, patios. ◆◆RECREATION: rec hall, swim pool, horseshoes. Pets welcome. Partial handicap access. No tents. Open all yr. Big rigs welcome. Rate in 2010 $29-34 for 2 persons. MC/VISA/DISC/AMEX. CCUSA 50% Discount. CCUSA reservations Recommended, CCUSA max stay See Rest. Max stay 1 night Nov thru Mar; 2 nights remainder of year. Child surcharge is for those 4-17 yrs.

Phone: (352)629-3540
Address: 3040 NW Gainesville Rd, Ocala, FL 34475
Lat/Lon: 29.21894/-82.14751
Email: ocalawildfrontier@gmail.com
Web: www.wildfrontiercampground.com

OCKLAWAHA—B-3

(NE) Lake Bryant MH & RV Park—(Marion) *From jct I-75 (exit 352) & SR 40: Go 22 mi E on SR 40, then 2-1/2 mi S on SE 183rd Ave Rd.* ◆◆◆FACILITIES: 147 sites, typical site width 35 ft, 147 full hkups, (30/50 amps), 15 pull-thrus, WiFi Internet central location, family camping, tenting, laundry, ice, picnic tables, patios. ◆◆◆◆RECREATION: rec hall, lake swim, boating, canoeing, kayaking, ramp, dock, lake fishing, bsktball, shuffleboard court shuffleboard court, activities, horseshoes, v-ball. Pets welcome, breed restrict, quantity restrict. Partial handicap access. Open all yr. Big rigs welcome. Rate in 2010 $30-35 for 4 persons. MC/VISA. Member ARVC, FLARVC. CCUSA 50% Discount. CCUSA reservations Recommended, CCUSA max stay 1 day, Cash only for CCUSA disc. Discount available Apr thru Sep.

Phone: (352)625-2376
Address: 5000 SE 183rd Ave Rd (Levy Hemmock Rd), Ocklawaha, FL 32179
Lat/Lon: 29.13753/-81.84656
Email: floridianman@aol.com
Web: www.lakebryant.com

Reserve Online at Woodalls.com

Woodall's Tip... If you are camping in bear country, be sure to cook at least 300 feet downwind of your sleeping area. Use baking soda to rid your clothes and hands of cooking odors.

ODESSA—C-3

(SW) SILVER DOLLAR RV AND GOLF RESORT—(Hillsborough) *From jct Hwy 587 & Hwy 582: Go 3-1/2 mi W on Hwy 582, then 1-3/4 mi S on Patterson Rd. Enter on R.*

◆◆◆FACILITIES: 113 sites, typical site width 20 ft, 37 ft max RV length, 35 full hkups, 78 W&E, (30/50 amps), mostly extd stay sites (winter), WiFi Instant Internet at site, phone on-site Internet (needs activ), WiFi Internet central location, family camping, dump, non-guest dump $, laundry, patios.

◆◆◆RECREATION: rec hall, rec room/area, swim pool, putting green, golf nearby, activities.

Pets welcome. No tents. Open all yr. Clubs welcome. Rate in 2010 $26-58 for 2 persons. MC/VISA/DISC/AMEX. Member ARVC, FLARVC.

Phone: (813)920-4185
Address: 12515 Silver Dollar Dr., Odessa, FL 33556
Lat/Lon: 28.11667/-82.64226
Web: www.rvonthego.com/encore-unique-park-silver-dollar-8.htm
SEE AD ALACHUA PAGE 93

OKEECHOBEE—D-4

See listings at Belle Glade, Clewiston, Moore Haven, Palmdale & South Bay.

(SW) Buckhead Ridge Marina Resort—(Glades) *From jct Hwy 70 & US 441/98: Go 3 mi S on US 441/US 98, then 8 mi W on Hwy 78, then 1 mi S on Hunter Rd. Enter on L.* ◆◆◆FACILITIES: 102 sites, typical site width 25 ft, 102 full hkups, (30/50 amps), laundry. ◆◆◆◆RECREATION: swim pool, boating, canoeing, ramp, dock, lake/river fishing. Pets welcome. Partial handicap access. No tents. Open all yr. Rate in 2010 $29-34 per vehicle. Phone: (863)763-2826.

(SE) Gracious RV Park—(Okeechobee) *From jct Hwy 78 & US 441/98: Go 5-3/4 mi SE on US 441/98. Enter on R.* ◆◆◆FACILITIES: 78 sites, typical site width 20 ft, 78 full hkups, (30/50 amps), WiFi Instant Internet at site, family camping, tenting, laundry, ice, picnic tables, patios. ◆◆◆RECREATION: rec hall, boating, ramp, dock, lake/river fishing, activities, horseshoes, hiking trails. Pets welcome. Open all yr. Rate in 2010 $36-37 for 2 persons. MC/VISA/DISC. Member ARVC, FLARVC. CCUSA 50% Discount. CCUSA reservations Recommended, CCUSA max stay 3 days, CCUSA disc. not avail holidays.

Phone: (863)763-6200
Address: 6500 Highway 441 SE, Okeechobee, FL 34974
Lat/Lon: 27.19049/-80.75372
Email: admin@graciousrvpark.com
Web: www.graciousrvpark.com

OKEECHOBEE—Continued on next page

Woodall's Tip... Turn to the Travel Section for a list of the RV Parks & Campgrounds that Welcome Big Rigs.

OKEECHOBEE—Continued

(N) OKEECHOBEE COUNTY TOURISM DEVELOPMENT COUNCIL—Okeechobee Counry is centrally located on the North Shore of Lake Okeechobee, 2nd largest fresh waterlake in USA. There are over 5000 campsites throughout the county. Local events include annual festivals, PRCA rodeos & an outdoor sportman's paradise.

Phone: (863)763-3959
Address: 2800 NW 20th Trail, Okeechobee, FL 34972
Lat/Lon: 27.26574/-80.85575
Email: tourism@co.okeechobee.fl.us
Web: www.okeechobee-tdc.com

SEE AD PAGE 146

(S) Okeechobee Resort KOA—(Okeechobee) *From jct Hwy-78 & US-441/98: Go 1/4 mi N on US 441/98. Enter on R.* ◊◊◊◊FACILITIES: 750 sites, typical site width 20 ft, 750 full hkups, (20/30/50 amps), 14 pull-thrus, family camping, tenting, laundry, full svc store. ◊◊◊◊◊RECREATION: 2 swim pools, pond fishing, playground. Pets welcome, breed restrict. Partial handicap access. Open all yr. Big rigs welcome. Rate in 2010 $50-70 for 2 persons. Member ARVC, FLARVC. Phone: (800)562-7748. KOA discount.

(S) Silver Palms RV Village—(Okeechobee) *From jct Hwy 70 & Hwy 441: Go 2-1/2 mi S on Hwy 441. Enter on R.* ◊◊◊◊◊FACILITIES: 167 sites, typical site width 42 ft, accepts full hkup units only, 167 full hkups, (30/50 amps), 8 pull-thrus, WiFi Instant Internet at site ($), RV storage, laundry, LP gas by weight/by meter, picnic tables, patios. ◊◊◊◊◊RECREATION: rec hall, swim pool, hot tub, lake fishing, bsktball, shuffleboard court 8 shuffleboard courts, activities, tennis, horseshoes, v-ball. Pets welcome. Partial handicap access. No tents. Open all yr. Big rigs welcome. Rate in 2010 $50-70 MC/VISA/DISC. Member ARVC, FLARVC. CCUSA 50% Discount. CCUSA reservations Recommended, CCUSA max stay 7 days. Discount not available Dec thru Mar. Space avilable basis.

Phone: (863)467-5800
Address: 4143 Hwy 441 S, Okeechobee, FL 34974
Lat/Lon: 27.20630/-80.83005
Email: sales@silverpalmsrv.com
Web: www.silverpalmsrv.com

OKEECHOBEE—Continued

(SE) ZACHARY TAYLOR RV RESORT—(Okeechobee) *From jct Hwy 78 & US 441/98: Go 2-1/4 mi SE on US 441/98, then 500 feet on 30th St. Enter on L.*

◊◊◊◊FACILITIES: 210 sites, typical site width 30 ft, 210 full hkups, (30/50 amps), 50 amps ($), many extd stay sites (winter), 14 pull-thrus, WiFi Instant Internet at site, cabins, RV storage, laundry, RV supplies, ice, picnic tables, patios.

◊◊◊◊RECREATION: rec hall, swim pool, boating, canoeing, kayaking, ramp, dock, lake/river fishing, fishing supplies, fishing guides, golf nearby, shuffleboard court 3 shuffleboard courts, activities, horseshoes, hiking trails.

Pets welcome ($), breed restrict, quantity restrict. Partial handicap access. No tents. Age restrict may apply. Open all yr. Big rigs welcome. Escort to site. Clubs welcome. Rate in 2010 $47-55 for 2 persons. MC/VISA/DISC/Debit. Member ARVC, FLARVC. CCUSA 50% Discount. CCUSA reservations Recommended, CCUSA max stay Unlimited. Discount available Apr thru Nov.

Phone: (888)282-6523
Address: 2995 US Hwy 441 SE, Okeechobee, FL 34974
Lat/Lon: 27.21194/-80.79736
Email: info@flrvresort.com
Web: www.flrvresort.com

SEE AD TRAVEL SECTION PAGE 79

OKEECHOBEE LAKE—D-4

OKEECHOBEE LAKE AREA MAP

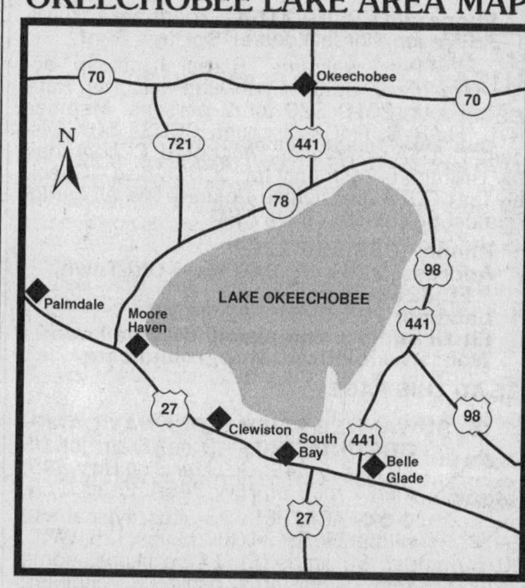

Symbols on map indicate towns within a 30 mi radius of Lake Okeechobee where campgrounds (diamonds), attractions (flags), & RV service centers & camping supply outlets (gears) are listed. Check listings for more information.

OLD TOWN—B-2

(S) OLD TOWN CAMPGROUND N' RETREAT—(Dixie) *From jct US 19N & Hwy 349S: Go 2 mi S on Hwy 349S. Enter on L.*

◊◊◊FACILITIES: 46 sites, typical site width 40 ft, 18 full hkups, 28 W&E, (30/50 amps), 50 amps ($), some extd stay sites, 14 pull-thrus, cable TV, WiFi Instant Internet at site, WiFi Internet central location, family camping, tenting, RV's/park model rentals, RV storage, dump, non-guest dump $, laundry, LP bottle exch, ice, picnic tables, fire rings, wood.

OLD TOWN CAMPGROUND N' RETREAT—Continued on next page

OLD TOWN—Continued
OLD TOWN CAMPGROUND N' RETREAT—Continued

◆RECREATION: rec room/area, pavilion, horseshoes.

Pets welcome. Partial handicap access. Open all yr. Clubs welcome. Rate in 2010 $20 for 2 persons. Member ARVC, FLARVC. FMCA discount. CCUSA 50% Discount. CCUSA reservations Accepted, CCUSA max stay Unlimited, Cash only for CCUSA disc., Check only for CCUSA disc. Office closes 7 PM. All campers must be registered by 7 PM.

Phone: (888)950-2267
Address: 2241 SE 349 Hwy, Old Town, FL 32680
Lat/Lon: 29.56951/-82.98572
Email: oldtowncampground@gmail.com
Web: www.oldtowncampground.com

SEE AD THIS PAGE

(S) SUWANNEE RIVER HIDEAWAY CAMPGROUND, INC.—(Dixie) *From jct US 19 & Hwy 349: Go 3 mi S on Hwy 349, then 1 mi E on Hwy 346A. Enter on R.*

◆◆◆FACILITIES: 73 sites, typical site width 35 ft, 34 full hkups, 25 W&E, (30/50 amps), 50 amps ($), 14 no hkups, some extd stay sites, 19 pull-thrus, cable TV, WiFi Internet central location, family camping, tenting, dump, laundry, RV supplies, ice, picnic tables, wood.

◆◆◆RECREATION: rec hall, swim pool, river swim, boating, canoeing, kayaking, dock, river fishing, fishing supplies, golf nearby, horseshoes.

Pets welcome. Partial handicap access. Open Week before Labor Day - Mid July. Escort to site. Clubs welcome. Rate in 2010 $30-34 for 2 persons. MC/VISA/DISC. Member ARVC, FLARVC. FMCA discount. CCUSA 50% Discount. CCUSA reservations Recommended, CCUSA max stay 7 days, Cash only for CCUSA disc., CCUSA disc. not avail holidays. Not available month of Aug & special events. Call for details.

Phone: (352)542-7800
Address: 1218 SE 346 Hwy, Old Town, FL 32680
Lat/Lon: 29.56146/-82.96807
Email: camping@riverhideaway.com
Web: www.riverhideaway.com

SEE AD THIS PAGE

(SW) YELLOW JACKET CAMPGROUND RESORT—(Dixie) *From jct US 19 & SR 349: Go 10 mi S on SR 349, then 1 mi E on SE 477 Rd. Enter at end.*

◆◆◆◆FACILITIES: 95 sites, typical site width 35 ft, 77 full hkups, 18 W&E, (30/50 amps), some extd stay sites (winter), 10 pull-thrus, cable TV, WiFi Instant Internet at site, family camping, tenting, cabins, RV storage, dump, laundry, ice, picnic tables, fire rings, grills, wood.

◆◆◆◆RECREATION: rec hall, equipped pavilion, swim pool, hot tub, boating, canoeing, kayaking, ramp, dock, 4 pontoon/3 motorboat rentals, river fishing, golf nearby, bsktball, playground, activities, hiking trails.

Pets welcome ($), breed restrict, quantity restrict. Partial handicap access. Open all yr. Big rigs welcome. Escort to site. Clubs welcome. Rate in 2010 $31.78-45.79 for 2 persons. MC/VISA. Member ARVC, FLARVC. CCUSA 50% Discount. CCUSA reservations Required, CCUSA max stay 1

OLD TOWN—Continued
YELLOW JACKET CAMPGROUND RESORT—Continued

day, Cash only for CCUSA disc., CCUSA disc. not avail holidays. Not available on riverfront or riverview sites.

Phone: (352)542-8365
Address: 55-SE 503rd Ave, Old Town, FL 32680
Lat/Lon: 29.46443/-83.00155
Email: star1@svic.net
Web: www.yellowjacketcampground.com

SEE AD PAGE 147

OLUSTEE—A-3

(N) OSCEOLA NATIONAL FOREST (Ocean Pond Campground)—(Baker) *From jct Hwy 231 & US 90: Go 1 mi E on US 90, then 4 mi N on CR 250A, then 1 mi S on FR 268.* FACILITIES: 67 sites, typical site width 18 ft, 22 ft max RV length, 19 W&E, 48 no hkups, tenting, dump. RECREATION: lake swim, boating, canoeing, ramp, lake fishing, playground. Open all yr. Phone: (904)752-2577.

ORANGE CITY—B-4

(W) BLUE SPRING STATE PARK—(Volusia) *2 mi W of Orange City - off US-17-92.* FACILITIES: 57 sites, 57 W&E, tenting, dump, groceries. RECREATION: boating, canoeing, ramp, dock, river fishing. Partial handicap access. Open all yr. Phone: (386)775-3663.

(N) CLARK FAMILY CAMPGROUND—(Volusia) *From jct I-4 (exit 114) & Hwy 472: Go 1 1/2 mi NW on Hwy 472, then 1/3 mi W on Minnesota Ave. Enter on L.*

◆◆◆FACILITIES: 160 sites, typical site width 20 ft, 120 full hkups, 30 W&E, (20/30/50 amps), 10 no hkups, many extd stay sites, 50 pull-thrus, WiFi Instant Internet at site ($), family camping, tenting, cabins, dump, non-guest dump $, laundry, ltd groc, RV supplies, LP gas by weight/by meter, ice, picnic tables, patios, fire rings, grills, wood.

◆◆◆RECREATION: rec hall, rec room/area, coin games, swim pool, golf nearby, bsktball, playground, shuffleboard court 2 shuffleboard courts, activities, horseshoes. Rec open to public.

Pets welcome, breed restrict. Open all yr. Planned group activities winter season only. Escort to site. Rate in 2010 $27-45 for 2 persons. MC/VISA/DISC. FCRV discount. FMCA discount.

Phone: (386)775-3996
Address: 1440 E Minnesota Ave, Orange City, FL 32763
Lat/Lon: 28.96963/-81.28757
Email: info@clarkfamilycampground.com
Web: www.clarkfamilycampground.com

SEE AD DAYTONA BEACH PAGE 106

(NE) ORANGE CITY RV RESORT—(Volusia) *From I-4 (exit 114) & Hwy 472: Go 3/4 mi W on Hwy 472, then 3/4 mi S on CR 4101, then 1 block E on Graves. Enter on R.*

◆◆◆◆FACILITIES: 525 sites, typical site width 30 ft, 525 full hkups, (30/50 amps), some extd stay sites, 20 pull-thrus, cable TV, WiFi Instant Internet at site, WiFi Internet central location, family camping, tenting, dump, non-guest dump $, laundry, LP gas by weight/by meter, ice, picnic tables, patios.

◆◆◆◆RECREATION: rec hall, equipped pavilion, swim pool, wading pool, hot tub, mini-golf, golf nearby, shuffleboard court 4 shuffleboard courts, activities, horseshoes.

Pets welcome, breed restrict, size restrict, quantity restrict. Partial handicap access. Open all yr.

ORANGE CITY—Continued
ORANGE CITY RV RESORT—Continued

Big rigs welcome. Escort to site. Clubs welcome. Rate in 2010 $33-39 for 2 persons. MC/VISA/DISC. Member ARVC, FLARVC. CCUSA 50% Discount. CCUSA reservations Accepted, CCUSA max stay 7 days. Discount not available Jan 1-Mar 31.

Phone: (800)545-7354
Address: 2300 East Graves Ave, Orange City, FL 32763
Lat/Lon: 28.94771/-81.26370
Email: orangecityrv@newbymanagement.com
Web: www.orangecityrvresort.com

SEE AD ORLANDO NEXT PAGE

ORANGE LAKE—B-3

(N) Grand Lake RV & Golf Resort (Morgan RV Resorts)—(Marion) *From jct I-75 (exit 368) & Hwy 318: Go 2-3/4 mi E on Hwy 318. Enter on L.* ◆◆◆◆◆FACILITIES: 423 sites, typical site width 40 ft, 423 full hkups, (30/50 amps), 270 pull-thrus, family camping, dump, laundry, groceries. ◆◆◆◆◆RECREATION: swim pool, boating, canoeing, dock, lake fishing. Pets welcome. Partial handicap access. No tents. Open all yr. Big rigs welcome. Rate in 2010 $24.99-39.99 for 2 persons. Member ARVC, FLARVC. Phone: (800)435-2291.

ORLANDO—C-4

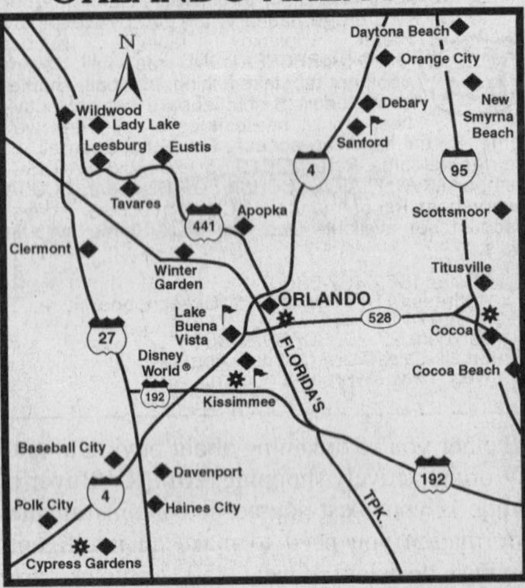

Symbols on map indicate towns within a 45 mi radius of Orlando where campgrounds (dia-monds), attractions (flags), & RV service centers & camping supply outlets (gears) are listed. Check listings for more information.

Tell Them Woodall's Sent You!

ORLANDO—Continued on next page

Read interesting travel facts in the front of every state/province.

ORLANDO—Continued

(W) BILL FREDERICK PARK AT TURKEY LAKE (City Park)—(Orange) *From jct I-4 & Hwy 435: Go 1-1/2 mi N on Hwy 435 (Conroy Rd): Go 1-1/2 mi N on Hwy 435, then 1 mi N on Hiawassee Rd. Enter on R.*

FACILITIES: 136 sites, typical site width 40 ft, 14 full hkups, 22 W&E, (20/30/50 amps), 100 no hkups, family camping, tenting, cabins, dump, laundry, picnic tables, controlled access.

RECREATION: pavilion, swim pool, boating, 5 rowboat rentals, lake fishing, mini-golf, golf nearby, playground, horseshoes, sports field, hiking trails, v-ball.

Pets welcome. Open all yr. Pool open May thru Sep. Big rigs welcome. Clubs welcome. MC/VISA/AMEX/Debit.

BILL FREDERICK PARK AT TURKEY LAKE (City Park)—Continued on next page

Located 15 mi from International Speedway and 23 mi from Daytona Beach
Heated Pool & Spa • Mini Golf
Shuffleboard • Bocce Ball • Billiard Room
Rec Hall • Activities • Laundry
Close to Shopping, Restaurants • 7 Miles from Blue Springs State Park
Toll Free Reservations 1-800-545-7354
2300 East Graves Ave. Orange City, FL 32763
See listing at Orange City, FL

Relax and enjoy.
Bill Frederick Park at Turkey Lake

Open year-round with 36 sites on 175 acres, Bill Frederick Park at Turkey Lake is the place to be for family fun! Located 2 miles from Universal Studios, we offer a wide variety of recreational activities, including picnicking, fishing, hiking, bicycling, roller blading/skating, and frisbee golf. There's a swimming pool available for all guests. Rent a fishing boat for the day, a cabin for evening comfort, or a pavilion for your family gathering!

3401 S. Hiawassee Rd.
Orlando, FL 32835
407-299-5581
See listing at Orlando, FL

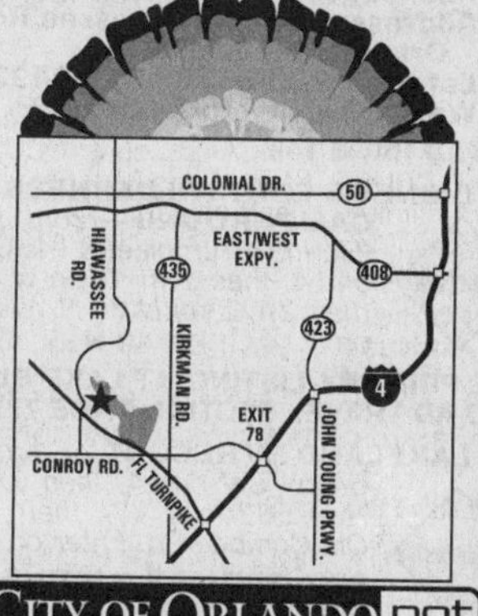

EXPLORE ORLANDO
WITH encore RV RESORTS!

RESORT AMENITIES
Close to all your favorite Orlando attractions, including Walt Disney World® and Universal Studios®
Spectacular clubhouses • Heated swimming pools
Whirlpool/spas • Exciting on-site activities and events
RESORT COTTAGES ALSO AVAILABLE

CLERBROOK GOLF & RV RESORT
20005 U.S. Highway 27
Clermont, FL

LAKE MAGIC RV RESORT
9600 Highway 192 W.
Clermont, FL

SHERWOOD FOREST RV RESORT
5300 W. Irlo Bronson Hwy.
Kissimmee, FL

THOUSAND TRAILS ORLANDO
2110 U.S. Highway 27 S.
Clermont, FL

WINTER GARDEN RV RESORT
13905 W. Colonial Dr.
Winter Garden, FL

See listing at Kissimmee, FL

www.RVontheGo.com

Call to make your reservations today!
888.481.6348

ANNUAL & SEASONAL SITES
Equity *LifeStyle* Properties

ORLANDO—Continued
BILL FREDERICK PARK AT TURKEY LAKE (City Park)—Continued

Phone: (407)299-5581
Address: 3401 S Hiawassee Rd, Orlando, FL 32835
Lat/Lon: 28.50678/-81.48493
Web: www.cityoforlando.net

SEE AD PAGE 149

DISNEY'S FORT WILDERNESS RESORT & CAMPGROUND—*From jct Hwy 91 (Florida's Turnpike) & I-4: Go 10 mi SW on I-4, then 2 mi W on W Ocala Pkwy, then 2-1/2 mi N on N World Dr. Enter on R.*

SEE PRIMARY LISTING AT LAKE BUENA VISTA AND AD TRAVEL SECTION PAGE 77

LAKELAND RV RESORT—*From Orlando: Go 54 mi SW on I-4, then 1/2 mi NE on Hwy 582 (exit 33), then 1/2 mi E on Old Combee Rd. Enter on R.*

SEE PRIMARY LISTING AT LAKELAND AND AD LAKELAND PAGE 138

MYAKKA RV RESORT - KOA—*W'bnd from Orlando at Jct I-4 & Toll Rd 408: Go S on I-4 for 24 mi, take exit 9 on I-75, then S on I-75 for 71 mi to exit 191, then W on North River Rd for 6 mi to US 41, then E on US 41/SR 45 for 3/4 mi to Park. Enter on R.*

SEE AD PRIMARY LISTING AT VENICE AND SARASOTA PAGE 165

(E) ORLANDO/LAKE WHIPPOORWILL KOA CAMPGROUND—(Orange) *From jct Hwy 528 (Bee Line Exwy)& SR 15 (Narcoosee Rd): Go 5 mi S on SR 15 (Narcoosee Rd) (1/2 mi S of Greeneway Toll Rd 417). Enter on L.*

◆◆◆◆FACILITIES: 124 sites, typical site width 25 ft, 119 full hkups, 5 W&E, (20/30/50 amps), some extd stay sites (winter), 30 pull-thrus, cable TV, WiFi Instant Internet at site, phone/cable on-site Internet (needs activ), phone Internet central location, family camping, tenting, cabins, RV storage, dump, non-guest dump $, laundry, ltd groc, RV supplies, LP gas by weight/by meter, ice, picnic tables.

◆◆◆◆◆RECREATION: rec hall, rec room/area, pavilion, swim pool, hot tub, boating, canoeing, kayaking, ramp, dock, 2 canoe rentals, lake fishing, fishing supplies, golf nearby, bike rental 3 bike rentals, playground, shuffleboard court 2 shuffleboard courts, activities, horseshoes, sports field, v-ball.

Pets welcome, breed restrict, quantity restrict. Partial handicap access. Open all yr. Planned activities winter & holidays. Big rigs welcome. Clubs welcome. Rate in 2010 $38-55 for 2 persons. MC/VISA/DISC/AMEX/Debit. Member ARVC, FLARVC. KOA discount.

ORLANDO—Continued
ORLANDO/LAKE WHIPPOORWILL KOA CAMPGROUND—Continued

Phone: (800)999-5267
Address: 12345 Narcoossee Rd, Orlando, FL 32832
Lat/Lon: 28.38833/-81.24417
Email: whippoorwillkoa@orlandoteam.com
Web: www.orlandokoa.com

SEE AD PAGE 149

THE GREAT OUTDOORS RV-NATURE & GOLF RESORT—*From jct Hwy 417 (Central Florida Greeneway) & Hwy 50: Go 25 mi E on Hwy 50. Enter on R.*

SEE PRIMARY LISTING IN TITUSVILLE AND AD TITUSVILLE PAGE 175

ORMOND BEACH—B-4

(N) HARRIS VILLAGE RV PARK—(Volusia) *From jct I-95 (exit 273) (old exit 89) & US 1: Go 2-1/2 mi S on US 1. Enter on R.*

◆◆◆◆FACILITIES: 25 sites, typical site width 25 ft, 25 full hkups, (20/30/50 amps), 4 pull-thrus, cable TV, WiFi Instant Internet at site, RV's/park model rentals, cabins, laundry, ice, picnic tables, patios.

RECREATION: rec room/area.

Pets welcome, breed restrict, size restrict, quantity restrict. Partial handicap access. No tents. Age restrict may apply. Open Oct 1 - Apr 30. Big rigs welcome. Escort to site. Rate in 2010 $32-42.50 for 2 persons. MC/VISA/DISC. Member ARVC, FLARVC. FMCA discount.

Phone: (386)673-0494
Address: 1080 N US Highway 1, Ormond Beach, FL 32174
Lat/Lon: 29.31104/-81.10076
Email: harrisvillage@aol.com
Web: www.harrisvillage.com

SEE AD DAYTONA BEACH PAGE 106 AND AD TRAVEL SECTION PAGE 74

(N) SUNSHINE HOLIDAY RV PARK—(Volusia) *From jct I-95 (exit 273) & US-1: Go 1/2 mi NW on US-1. Enter on R.*

◆◆◆◆FACILITIES: 336 sites, typical site width 45 ft, 250 full hkups, 86 W&E, (20/30/50 amps), many extd stay sites, 219 pull-thrus, cable TV, ($), WiFi Instant Internet at site ($), phone Internet central location, family camping, tenting, cabins, dump, portable dump, laundry, ltd groc, RV supplies, LP gas by weight/by meter, ice, picnic tables, patios.

◆◆◆◆◆RECREATION: rec hall, equipped pavilion, swim pool, pond fishing, fishing supplies, mini-golf, golf nearby, bsktball, playground, shuffleboard court 2 shuffleboard courts, activities, tennis, horseshoes, v-ball.

ORMOND BEACH—Continued
SUNSHINE HOLIDAY RV PARK—Continued

Pets welcome, quantity restrict. Partial handicap access. Open all yr. Rates higher during special events. Big rigs welcome. Escort to site. Clubs welcome. Rate in 2010 $38-53 per vehicle. MC/VISA/DISC/AMEX. Member ARVC, FLARVC.

Phone: (386)672-3045
Address: 1701 N US Highway 1, Ormond Beach, FL 32174
Lat/Lon: 29.34179/-81.13883
Email: info@RVontheGO.com
Web: www.rvonthego.com

SEE AD ALACHUA PAGE 93 AND AD DAYTONA BEACH PAGE 110

(N) TOMOKA STATE PARK—(Volusia) *From jct US 1 & Hwy 40: Go 1/2 mi E on Hwy 40, then 3 mi N on North Beach St.* FACILITIES: 100 sites, 100 W&E, tenting, dump, groceries. RECREATION: boating, canoeing, ramp, dock, saltwater fishing, playground. Pets welcome. Partial handicap access. Open all yr. Phone: (386)676-4050.

OSPREY—D-3

(S) OSCAR SCHERER STATE PARK—(Sarasota) *From US-41 & Hwy-72: Go S 4 mi on US-41.* FACILITIES: 104 sites, 104 W&E, tenting, dump. RECREATION: lake swim, boating, canoeing, ramp, dock, saltwater fishing, playground. Partial handicap access. Open all yr. Phone: (941)483-5956.

PAHOKEE—D-5

(W) LAKE OKEECHOBEE OUTPOST KOA—(Palm Beach) *From jct S Hwy 715 & N US 441: Go 100 ft N on US 441, then 1 blk W on S Lake Ave. Enter at end.*

◆◆◆◆FACILITIES: 96 sites, 96 full hkups, (30/50 amps), some extd stay sites (winter), WiFi Internet central location, family camping, tenting, cabins, dump, laundry, picnic tables.

◆◆◆◆RECREATION: rec hall, pavilion, swim pool, boating, ramp, dock, pontoon rentals, lake fishing, fishing supplies, golf nearby, hiking trails.

Pets welcome, size restrict. Partial handicap access. Open all yr. Clubs welcome. Rate in 2010 $30-35 MC/VISA/DISC/AMEX. KOA discount.

Phone: (561)924-7832
Address: 190 North Lake Avenue, Pahokee, FL 33476
Lat/Lon: 26.82502/-80.66639
Web: www.lakeokeechobeeoutpost.com

SEE AD OKEECHOBEE PAGE 146

PALATKA—B-4

(S) RODMAN (COE - Lake Ocklawaha)—(Putnam) *From jct Hwy 20 & Hwy 19: Go 12 mi S on Hwy 19, then 2 mi W on Rodman Dam Rd.* FACILITIES: 67 sites, 28 full hkups, 13 W&E, (30/50 amps), 26 no hkups, tenting, dump. RECREATION: boating, canoeing, ramp, lake/river fishing. Partial handicap access. Open all yr. Phone: (386)326-2846.

PALM COAST—B-4

(N) FLAGLER COUNTY CHAMBER OF COMMERCE—*From jct I-95 & Hwy 100 (exit 284): Go 1-1/2 mi W on Hwy 100. Enter on L.* The Tourist Development Council & Chamber of Commerce provide information & brochures about activities, campgrounds & RV Parks available in the Flagler County area. Open all yr.

Phone: (800)670-2640
Address: 20 Airport Road, Palm Coast, FL 32164
Lat/Lon: 29.47481/-81.20890
Email: peggy@flaglerchamber.org
Web: www.visitflagler.org

SEE AD TRAVEL SECTION PAGE 81

(N) PRINCESS PLACE PRESERVE—*From I-95 & US 1 (exit 298): Go 1-1/2 mi S on US 1. Then 1-1/2 mi E on Old Kings Rd. Enter on L.* The crown jewel in Flagler County's setting of Parks, this 1500 acre preserve features the oldest standing homesite in Flagler Co. & Florida's first in ground pool. Open all yr.

Phone: (386)313-4020
Address: 2500 Princess Place Rd, Palm Coast, FL 32137
Email: hpetito@flaglercounty.org
Web: www.flaglerparks.com

SEE AD TRAVEL SECTION PAGE 81

PALM HARBOR—C-3

(NW) Bay Aire Travel Trailer Park (RV SPACES) —(Pinellas) *From jct US 19 & Hwy 752: Go 2 mi W on Hwy 752, then 1-1/2 mi N on Alt US 19. Enter on R.* FACILITIES: 152 sites, typical site width 18 ft, 36 ft max RV length, 152 full hkups, (20/30/50 amps), 50 amps

Bay Aire Travel Trailer Park—Continued on next page

PALM HARBOR—Continued
Bay Aire Travel Trailer Park—Continued

($), WiFi Instant Internet at site, phone/cable on-site Internet (needs activ), phone Internet central location, family camping, tenting, laundry, RV supplies, LP gas by weight/by meter, ice, picnic tables, patios. RECREATION: rec hall, swim pool, shuffleboard court 3 shuffleboard courts, activities, horseshoes. Pets welcome. Partial handicap access. Open all yr. Rate in 2010 $55 for 2 persons. MC/VISA. Member ARVC, FLARVC. CCUSA 50% Discount. CCUSA reservations Recommended, CCUSA max stay See Rest., CCUSA disc. not avail holidays. Max stay: Nov & Dec-1 week: Jan thru Mar-3/4 days; remainder of year-based on availability. Church & planned activities winter only. Tenting summer only.

Phone: (727)784-4082
Address: 2242 US Hwy Alt 19 North, Palm Harbor, FL 34683
Lat/Lon: 28.08839/-82.77128
Email: bayairervpark@gmail.com
Web: www.bayairervpark.com

(NW) Caladesi RV Park (RV SPACES)—(Pinellas) *From jct US 19 & Hwy 752: Go 3 mi W on Hwy 752, then 1 block N on Dempsy Rd. Enter on L.* FACILITIES: 86 sites, typical site width 30 ft, 38 ft max RV length, 86 full hkups, (20/30/50 amps), family camping, dump, laundry. RECREATION: swim pool. Pets welcome, quantity restrict. No tents. Open all yr. Rate in 2010 $30-40 for 2 persons. Phone: (727)784-3622.

(N) Clearwater-Tarpon Springs RV Campground—(Pinellas) *From jct Hwy 584 & US 19: Go 4 mi N on US 19. Enter on R.* ◆◆◆FACILITIES: 116 sites, typical site width 18 ft, 36 ft max RV length, 84 full hkups, 32 W&E, (20/30/50 amps), family camping, tenting, dump, laundry. ◆◆◆RECREATION: swim pool, play equipment. Pets welcome, size restrict, quantity restrict. Open all yr. Rate in 2010 $37.95-42.95 for 2 persons. Member ARVC, FLARVC. Phone: (727)937-8412.

(N) Sherwood Forest Travel RV Park—(Pinellas) *From jct US 19 & Hwy 752: Go 2 mi W on Hwy 752, then 1 block S on Alt US 19. Enter on R.* ◆◆◆FACILITIES: 108 sites, typical site width 20 ft, 104 full hkups, (20/30/50 amps), 4 no hkups, WiFi Instant Internet at site, phone/cable on-site Internet (needs activ), WiFi Internet central location, tenting, laundry, picnic tables. ◆◆◆RECREATION: rec hall, swim pool, pond fishing, activities, horseshoes. Pets welcome, breed restrict, size restrict, quantity restrict. Partial handicap access. Open all yr. Big rigs welcome. Rate in 2010 $35-54 for 2 persons. MC/VISA/DISC/AMEX/Debit. Member ARVC, FLARVC. CCUSA 50% Discount. CCUSA reservations Recommended, CCUSA max stay 4 days, Cash only for CCUSA disc. Discount available Apr 15-Dec 15.

Phone: (727)784-4582
Address: 175 Alt US Highway 19, Palm Harbor, FL 34683
Lat/Lon: 28.06702/-82.77017
Email: sherwoodRV@aol.com
Web: www.meetrobinhood.com

PALMDALE—D-4

(S) FISHEATING CREEK CAMPGROUND—(Glades) *From jct Hwy 29 & US 27: Go 1 mi N on US 27. Enter on L.* FACILITIES: 156 sites, 52 full hkups, 10 W&E, 4 E, (20/30/50 amps), 90 no hkups, family camping, tenting, dump, laundry, ltd groc. RECREATION: lake swim, boating, canoeing, ramp, dock, lake/stream fishing. Pets welcome. Partial handicap access. Open all yr. Phone: (863)675-5999.

(NE) SABAL PALM RV RESORT & CAMPGROUND—(Glades) *From jct Hwy 29 & US 27: Go 2 mi N on US 27, then 1/2 mi E on Flemming Dr, then 1-1/2 mi N on Main Ave. Enter on L.*

◆◆◆FACILITIES: 110 sites, typical site width 35 ft, 80 full hkups, (30/50 amps), 30 no hkups, some extd stay sites (winter), 30 pull-thrus, WiFi Instant Internet at site, family camping, tenting, RV's/park model rentals, RV storage, dump, laundry, groceries, RV supplies, ice, picnic tables, patios, fire rings, wood, controlled access.

Visit Woodall's Attractions

PALMDALE—Continued
SABAL PALM RV RESORT & CAMPGROUND—Continued

◆◆◆RECREATION: rec hall, rec room/area, pavilion, canoe/2 pedal boat rentals, pond fishing, fishing supplies, golf nearby, bsktball, 3 bike rentals, shuffleboard court 2 shuffleboard courts, activities, horseshoes.

Pets welcome, quantity restrict. Partial handicap access. Open all yr. Big rigs welcome. Escort to site. Clubs welcome. Rate in 2010 $25 for 2 persons. MC/VISA/DISC/AMEX/Debit. CCUSA 50% Discount. CCUSA reservations Recommended, CCUSA max stay 3 days, CCUSA disc. not avail holidays. Discount available May thru Sep.

Phone: (863)675-1778
Address: 1947 Main St, Palmdale, FL 33944
Lat/Lon: 26.96577/-81.30853
Email: sales@sabalpalmrv.com
Web: www.sabalpalmrv.com

SEE AD THIS PAGE

PALMETTO—D-3

(NE) FIESTA GROVE RV RESORT—(Manatee) *From jct I-75 (exit 228) & I-275: Go 1 mi W on I-275 (exit 1), then 3/4 mi N on US-41, then 1/4 mi SW on Bayshore Rd. Enter on R.*

◆◆◆◆FACILITIES: 220 sites, typical site width 40 ft, 205 full hkups, 15 W&E, (30/50 amps), many extd stay sites (winter), cable TV, ($), phone/cable on-site Internet (needs activ), WiFi Internet central location, family camping, RV storage, shower$, dump, non-guest dump $, laundry, picnic tables, patios.

◆◆◆◆RECREATION: rec hall, swim pool, golf nearby, bsktball, shuffleboard court 4 shuffleboard courts, activities, horseshoes, v-ball, local tours.

Pets welcome, breed restrict, quantity restrict. No tents. Age restrict may apply. Open all yr. Planned activities winter only. Big rigs welcome. Clubs welcome. Rate in 2010 $30-38 for 2 persons. Member ARVC, FLARVC.

Phone: (941)722-7661
Address: 8615 Bayshore Rd, Palmetto, FL 34221
Lat/Lon: 27.5920/-82.54430
Email: fiestagrovervresort@gmail.com
Web: www.fiestagroverv.com

SEE AD BRADENTON PAGE 97

(N) Fishermans Cove RV Resort—(Manatee) *From jct I-275 & US 41: Go 2-1/2 mi SE on US 41, then 1 mi N on US 19. Enter on R.* ◆◆◆FACILITIES: 75 sites, typical site width 24 ft, 36 ft max RV length, 75 full hkups, (30/50 amps), phone/cable on-site Internet (needs activ), WiFi Internet central location, dump, laundry, picnic tables, patios. ◆◆◆◆RECREATION: rec hall, equipped pavilion, swim pool, hot tub, boating, canoeing, kayaking, ramp, dock, saltwater fishing, bsktball, shuffleboard court 2 shuffleboard courts, activities, tennis, horseshoes, v-ball. Pets welcome, breed restrict. No tents. Open all yr. Rate in 2010 $30-55 for 2 persons. MC/VISA/Debit. CCUSA 50% Discount. CCUSA reservations Recommended, CCUSA max stay 2 days, Cash only for CCUSA disc. Discount available May thru Oct.

Phone: (941)729-3685
Address: 100 Palmview Rd, Palmetto, FL 34221
Lat/Lon: 27.56682/-82.56492
Email: sales@myfishermanscove.com
Web: www.myfishermanscove.com

Woodall's Tip... Turn to the Travel Section for a list of the RV Parks & Campgrounds that Welcome Pets.

PALMETTO—Continued

(N) FROG CREEK CAMPGROUND—(Manatee) *From jct I-75 (exit 228) & I-275: Go 1 mi W on I-275 (exit 1), then 3/4 mi N on US 41, then 1/4 mi SW on Bayshore Rd. Enter on R.*

◆◆◆◆◆FACILITIES: 188 sites, typical site width 30 ft, 173 full hkups, 15 W&E, (30/50 amps), many extd stay sites (winter), WiFi Instant Internet at site, phone on-site Internet (needs activ), WiFi Internet central location, family camping, RV's/park model rentals, RV storage, dump, non-guest dump $, laundry, ice, picnic tables, patios.

◆◆◆◆RECREATION: rec hall, equipped pavilion, swim pool, boating, canoeing, kayaking, 2 canoe rentals, stream fishing, golf nearby, shuffleboard court 2 shuffleboard courts, activities, horseshoes.

Pets welcome, breed restrict, size restrict, quantity restrict. Partial handicap access. No tents. Open all yr. Planned activities Jan/Feb/March only. Big rigs welcome. Clubs welcome. Rate in 2010 $35-48 for 2 persons. MC/VISA. Member ARVC, FLARVC.

Phone: (941)722-6154
Address: 8515 Bayshore Rd, Palmetto, FL 34221
Lat/Lon: 27.59017/-82.54585
Email: info@frogcreek.us.com
Web: www.frogcreek.us.com

SEE AD THIS PAGE

(NE) TERRA CEIA VILLAGE—(Manatee) *From jct I-75 (exit 228) & I-275: Go 1 mi W on I-275 (exit 1), then 3/4 mi N on US 41. Enter on R.*

◆◆◆FACILITIES: 203 sites, typical site width 30 ft, accepts full hkup units only, 203 full hkups, (30/50 amps), many extd stay sites (winter), WiFi Instant Internet at site ($), phone/cable on-site Internet (needs activ), WiFi Internet central location, dump, laundry, patios.

◆◆◆RECREATION: rec hall, swim pool, golf nearby, shuffleboard court 4 shuffleboard courts, activities, horseshoes.

Pets welcome. No tents. Age restrict may apply. Open all yr. Planned activities winter only. Big rigs welcome. Rate in 2010 $28-38 for 2 persons. MC/VISA.

Phone: (941)729-4422
Address: 9303 Bayshore Rd, Palmetto, FL 34221
Lat/Lon: 27.59617/-82.54112
Email: terra_ceia@MHChomes.com
Web: www.rvonthego.com/Terra-Ceia-Village-RV-Resort-8.htm

SEE AD ALACHUA PAGE 93

(N) WINTERSET RV RESORT—(Manatee) *From jct I-275 (exit 2) & US 41: Go 1/4 mi E on US 41.*

◆◆◆◆FACILITIES: 237 sites, typical site width 30 ft, 221 full hkups, 16 W&E, (30/50 amps), mostly extd stay sites (winter), WiFi Instant Internet at site, cable on-site Internet (needs activ), WiFi Internet central location, RV storage, dump, laundry, LP gas by weight, picnic tables, patios.

◆◆◆◆RECREATION: rec hall, swim pool, boating, canoeing, kayaking, stream fishing, golf nearby, bsktball, shuffleboard court 8 shuffleboard courts, activities, tennis, horseshoes.

Pets welcome, breed restrict, size restrict, quantity restrict. Partial handicap access. No tents. Age

WINTERSET RV RESORT—Continued on next page

PALMETTO—Continued
WINTERSET RV RESORT—Continued

restrict may apply. Open all yr. Big rigs welcome. Rate in 2010 $30-39 for 2 persons. Member ARVC.

Phone: (941)722-4884
Address: 8515 US 41 N, Palmetto, FL 34221
Lat/Lon: 27.59046/-82.54034
Email: winterset@newbymanagement.com
Web: www.wintersetrvresort.com

SEE AD TAMPA PAGE 173

PANACEA—A-1

(W) Holiday Campground—(Wakulla) *From S jct US 98 & US 319: Go 7 mi S on US 98. Enter on R.* ◆◆◆FACILITIES: 77 sites, typical site width 20 ft, 75 full hkups, 2 W&E, (30/50 amps), 4 pull-thrus, family camping, tenting, dump, laundry. ◆◆◆RECREATION: swim pool, boating, saltwater fishing, playground. Pets welcome, breed restrict, size restrict. Open all yr. Big rigs welcome. Rate in 2010 $34.75-37.75 for 2 persons. Phone: (850)984-5757.

PANAMA CITY—F-2

MILITARY PARK (Tyndall AFB FAMCAMP)—(Bay) *On US 98. On base.* FACILITIES: 90 sites, 59 full hkups, 31 W&E, tenting, dump, laundry. RECREATION: boating. Open all yr. Phone: (850)283-2798.

PANAMA CITY BEACH—F-2

(SW) CAMPERS INN—(Bay) *From east jct US 98 & Alt 98 (Scenic 98): Go 1-1/2 mi SW on Alt 98 (Scenic 98), then 1 mi S on Joan Ave, then 1/4 mi W on Thomas Dr (Hwy 392).*

WELCOME

◆◆◆FACILITIES: 115 sites, typical site width 40 ft, 105 full hkups, (30/50 amps), 10 no hkups, many extd stay sites (winter), 10 pull-thrus, cable TV, ($), WiFi Instant Internet at site, WiFi Internet central location, family camping, tenting, cabins, RV storage, dump, non-guest dump $, laundry, full svc store, RV supplies, LP gas by weight/by meter, ice, picnic tables, patios, controlled access.

◆◆◆◆RECREATION: rec hall, equipped pavilion, swim pool, wading pool, pond fishing, bsktball, playground, shuffleboard court 4 shuffleboard courts, activities, horseshoes, v-ball.

Pets welcome. Partial handicap access. Open all yr. Planned group activities winter season only. Big rigs welcome. Escort to site. Clubs welcome. Rate in 2010 $32.95-54.95 for 2 persons. MC/VISA/DISC. ATM. Member ARVC, FLARVC.

Text 83099 to (440)725-8687 to see our Visual Tour.

Phone: (866)872-2267
Address: 8800 Thomas Dr, Panama City Beach, FL 32408
Lat/Lon: 30.17101/-85.79354
Email: manager@campersinn.net
Web: www.campersinn.net

SEE AD THIS PAGE

CAMPING ON THE GULF—*From East jct US 98 & Alt US 98 (Scenic 98): Go 39 mi W on US 98. Enter on L.*

WELCOME

SEE PRIMARY LISTING AT DESTIN AND AD DESTIN PAGES 112-113

Can you trust the Woodall's ratings? 25 evaluation teams have scoured North American campgrounds to provide you with accurate, up to date information & ratings. Find a rating you don't agree with? Send a letter or email our way, and we'll give it extra attention for 2012.

Campers Inn Inc.
Home of the World's Most Beautiful Beaches!
866-872-2267
www.campersinn.net
See listing at Panama City Beach, FL

PANAMA CITY BEACH—Continued

(NW) EMERALD COAST RV BEACH RESORT—(Bay) *From Hathaway Bridge on Alt US 98: Go 2-1/4 mi W on Alt US 98, then 100 feet S on Allison Ave. Enter on L.*

WELCOME

A BEAUTIFUL TROPICAL ELEGANT RESORT!
A Paradise RV Resort Nestled in the Heart Of Panama City Beach, "The Worlds Most Beautiful Beaches". Lush Landscaping, Concrete Pads, Paved Streets, Heated Pool, Spa, Clubhouse, ETC. 1-800-BEACHRV, 1-800-232-2478
WWW.RVRESORT.COM

◆◆◆◆◆FACILITIES: 138 sites, typical site width 35 ft, accepts full hkup units only, 138 full hkups, (20/30/50 amps), many extd stay sites (winter), 35 pull-thrus, cable TV, ($), WiFi Instant Internet at site ($), WiFi Internet central location, family camping, RV storage, laundry, RV supplies, LP gas by weight/by meter, ice, picnic tables, patios, controlled access.

◆◆◆◆◆RECREATION: rec hall, swim pool, hot tub, 2 pedal boat rentals, pond fishing, fishing supplies, golf nearby, bsktball, 15 bike rentals, playground, shuffleboard court 2 shuffleboard courts, activities, horseshoes, sports field, v-ball.

Pets welcome, breed restrict. Partial handicap access. No tents. Open all yr. Big rigs welcome. Escort to site. Clubs welcome. Rate in 2010 $50-70 for 2 persons. MC/VISA/DISC. Member ARVC, FLARVC.

Text 81704 to (440)725-8687 to see our Visual Tour.

Phone: (800)BEACHRV (232-2478)
Address: 1957 Allison Ave, Panama City Beach, FL 32407
Lat/Lon: 30.18386/-85.78675
Email: rvinfo@rvresort.com
Web: www.rvresort.com

SEE AD PAGES 154-155 AND AD DESTIN PAGE 114 AND AD TRAVEL SECTION PAGE 76

(E) Panama City Beach RV Resort—(Bay) *From jct US 98 & Thomas Rd: Go 3-1/2 mi S on Thomas Rd, then 1/4 mi SE on CR-392. Enter on L.* ◆◆◆◆◆FACILITIES: 69 sites, typical site width 30 ft, 69 full hkups, (30/50 amps), 14 pull-thrus, family camping, dump, laundry. ◆◆RECREATION: swim pool. Pets welcome, quantity restrict. Partial handicap access. No tents. Open all yr. Big rigs welcome. Rate in 2010 $54-74 for 2 persons. Member ARVC, FLARVC. Phone: (866)637-3529.

(N) Pineglen RV Park—(Bay) *From jct Hwy 79 & US 98: Go 4 mi E on US 98. Enter on L.* ◆◆◆◆FACILITIES: 60 sites, typical site width 25 ft, 60 full hkups, (30/50 amps), 23 pull-thrus, dump, laundry. ◆◆RECREATION: swim pool, pond fishing. Pets welcome, breed restrict, size restrict, quantity restrict. Partial handicap access. No tents. Open all yr. Big rigs welcome. Rate in 2010 $31.25-39.28 for 2 persons. Member ARVC, FLARVC. Phone: (850)230-8535.

(N) Raccoon River Campground—(Bay) *From US 98A (Scenic Rt 98) & Hwy 392: Go 2-3/4 mi NW on Hwy 392 (Middle Beach Rd/Hutchinson Blvd). Enter on L.* ◆◆◆FACILITIES: 171 sites, typical site width 25 ft, 141 full hkups, (30/50 amps), 30 no hkups, 50 pull-thrus, family camping, tenting, dump, laundry, groceries. ◆◆◆◆RECREATION: 2 swim pools, lake fishing, playground. Pets welcome ($), breed restrict. Partial handicap access. Open all yr. Big rigs welcome. Rate in 2010 $38-60 for 4 persons. Phone: (877)234-0181.

PANAMA CITY BEACH—Continued on next page

LIVE UNITED
GIVE. ADVOCATE. VOLUNTEER.
LIVE UNITED.
United Way
Ad Council
Want to make a difference? Find out how at LIVEUNITED.ORG.

Fun Begins Here

Call 1-877-680-6155 and mention the promotion codes to get each 2011 Woodall's Regional Guide at a low price of $4.50. Choose from: **28D4** for the **Far West**, **28D5** for **Frontier West/Great Plains and Mountain Region**, **28D6** for **The Great Lakes**, **28D9** for the **South**, **28D7** for the **Mid-Atlantic**, **28D8** for **New York/New England and Eastern Canada**, and **28DA** for **Canada**.

WOODALL'S
Everywhere RVers go.
DISCOVER ONE TANK TRIPS
FAR WEST CAMPGROUND GUIDE
NASCAR
NEW FOR 2011!

See us at woodalls.com

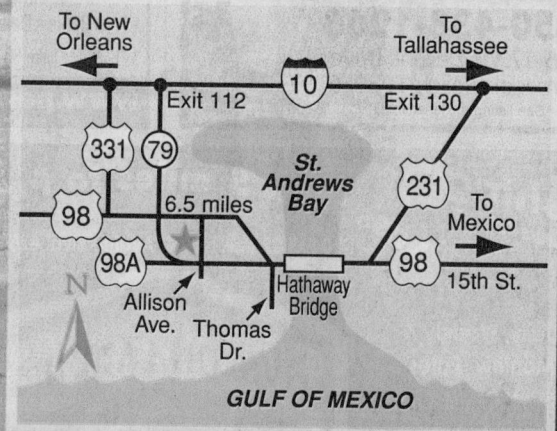

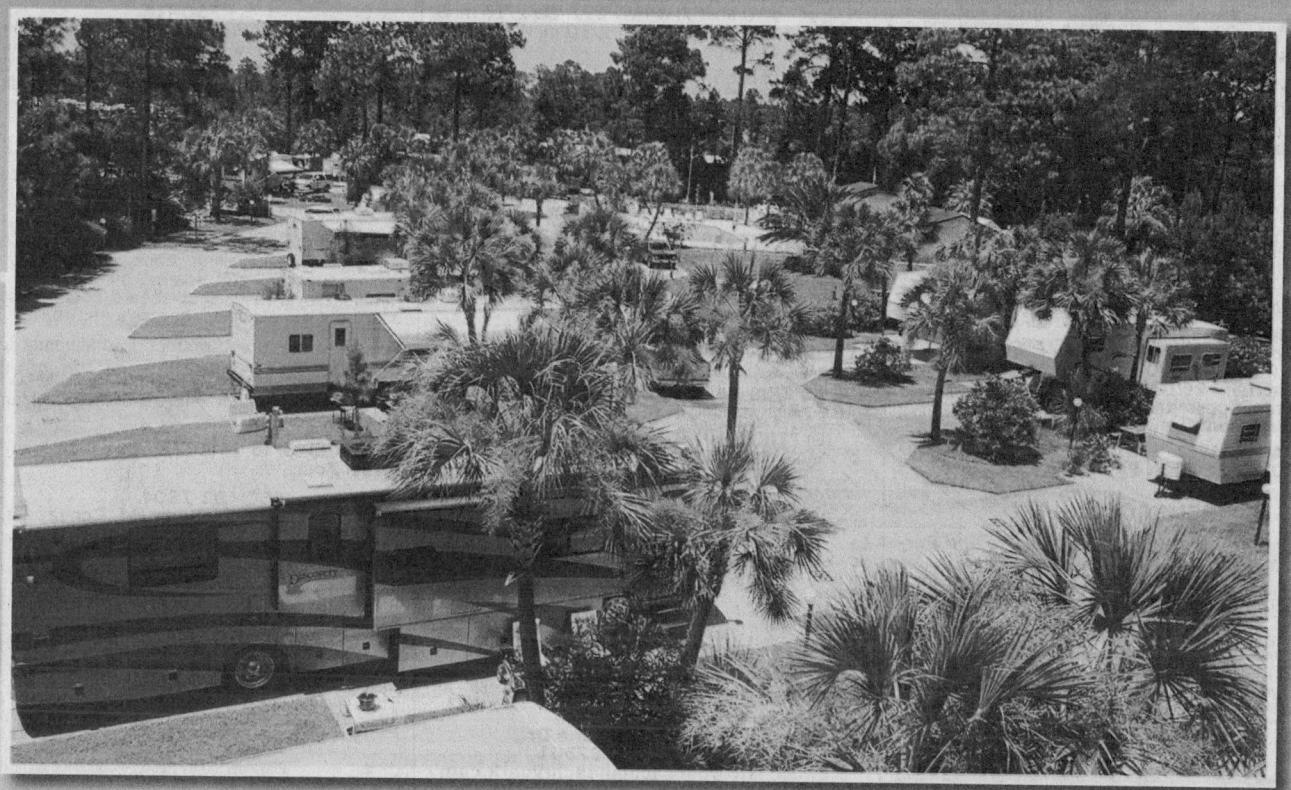

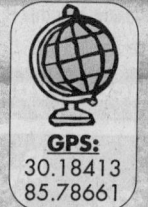

PANAMA CITY BEACH—Continued

(E) ST. ANDREWS STATE RECREATION AREA—(Bay) *From jct US 98 & SR 392 (Thomas Drive): Go 3-1/2 mi S on SR 392 (Thomas Drive), then 1/4 mi SE on SR 392 (Thomas Drive).* FACILITIES: 176 sites, 176 W&E, tenting, dump, laundry, groceries. RECREATION: saltwater swim, boating, canoeing, ramp, dock, saltwater fishing, playground. Pets welcome. Open all yr. Phone: (850)233-5140.

PEMBROKE PINES—E-5

(W) C.B. SMITH PARK (Broward County Park)—(Broward) *From jct I-95 (exit 20) & Hwy 820 (Hollywood Blvd): Go 9 mi W on Hollywood Blvd, then 1/2 mi N on Flamingo Rd. Enter on L.*

FACILITIES: 71 sites, 71 full hkups, (20/30/50 amps), 30 pull-thrus, family camping, tenting, dump, non-guest dump $, laundry, ice, picnic tables, patios, fire rings, grills, controlled access.

RECREATION: pavilion, swim pool, kayaking, 10 canoe/25 pedal boat rentals, lake fishing, bsktball, playground, tennis, horseshoes, sports field, hiking trails, v-ball. Rec open to public.

Pets welcome. Partial handicap access. Open all yr. Big rigs welcome. Clubs welcome. MC/VISA/DISC/AMEX.

Phone: (954)437-2650
Address: 900 N Flamingo Rd, Pembroke Pines, FL 33028
Lat/Lon: 26.014306/-80.312194
Email: cbsmithpark@broward.org
Web: www.broward.org/parks/camping

SEE AD TRAVEL SECTION PAGE 75 AND AD DISCOVER SECTION PAGE 33

PENSACOLA—F-1

See listings at Holt, Milton, Navarre and Perdido Key, FL & Lillian AL

(E) BIG LAGOON STATE PARK—(Escambia) *From jct Hwy 292 & Hwy 292A: Go 2 mi E on Hwy 292A.* FACILITIES: 75 sites, 75 W&E, tenting, dump. RECREATION: saltwater swim, boating, canoeing, ramp, dock, saltwater/pond fishing, playground. Open all yr. Phone: (904)492-1595.

GULF ISLANDS NATIONAL SEASHORE (Fort Pickens) —(Escambia) *From jct US-98 & Hwy-399: Go 15 mi SW on Hwy-399 & Ft. Pickens Rd.* FACILITIES: 200 sites, 136 E, 64 no hkups, tenting, dump, laundry, ltd groc. RECREATION: saltwater swim, boating, saltwater fishing. Open all yr. Phone: (850)934-2621.

PENSACOLA—Continued

(W) MILITARY PARK (Oak Grove Fam-Camp-Pensacola NAS)—(Escambia) *From I-10 (exit 2): Go 2 mi S on Pine Forest Rd (Hwy 297), then 15 mi W & S on Hwy 297, which becomes Hwy 173 (Blue Angel Pkwy). On base.* FACILITIES: 59 sites, 51 full hkups, 8 no hkups, 10 pull-thrus, tenting, dump. RECREATION: saltwater swim, saltwater fishing, play equipment. Open all yr. Phone: (850)452-2535.

PENSACOLA RV PARK—(Escambia) *E'bnd from jct I-10 (exit 7A) & Hwy 297: Go 100 yds S on Hwy 297, then 7/10 mi W on Wilde Lake Blvd. W'bnd from jct I-10 (exit 7) & Hwy 297: Go 2/10 mi S on Hwy 297, then 7/10 mi W on Wilde Lake Blvd. Enter on L.*

◊◊◊◊FACILITIES: 51 sites, typical site width 34 ft, 51 full hkups, (30/50 amps), some extd stay sites, 17 pull-thrus, heater not allowed, cable TV, WiFi Instant Internet at site, laundry, ice, picnic tables.

RECREATION: rec hall, golf nearby.

Pets welcome, breed restrict, quantity restrict. Partial handicap access. No tents. Open all yr. Big rigs welcome. Escort to site. Clubs welcome. Rate in 2010 $32 MC/VISA/DISC.

Phone: (850)944-1734
Address: 3117 Wilde Lake Blvd, Pensacola, FL 32526
Lat/Lon: 30.51972/-87.32581
Email: info@pensacolarvpark.com
Web: www.pensacolarvpark.com

SEE AD THIS PAGE AND AD TRAVEL SECTION PAGE 74

(S) TIKI HOUSE RV PARK ON PENSACOLA BEACH (UNDER CONSTRUCTION)—(Escambia) *From I-110 (Exit 1) & US 98; Go 5-3/4 mi E on US 98, then 2-1/2 mi E on CR 399. Enter on L.*

FACILITIES: 60 sites, typical site width 30 ft, 60 full hkups, (20/30/50 amps), cable TV, WiFi Instant Internet at site, family camping, laundry, ltd groc, RV supplies, ice, picnic tables, patios.

RECREATION: rec hall, swim pool, saltwater swim, kayaking, saltwater fishing, golf nearby.

Pets welcome. Partial handicap access. No tents. Open all yr. Clubs welcome. MC/DISC.

Phone: (850)438-1266
Address: 15-17 Via De Luna Dr., Pensacola Beach, FL 32561
Email: info@pensacolabeachrvpark.com
Web: www.pensacolabeachrvpark.com

SEE AD THIS PAGE

Visit our website www.woodalls.com

PERDIDO KEY—F-1

(N) PERDIDO COVE RV RESORT & MARINA—(Escambia) *From jct I-10 (exit 7) & Hwy 297: Go 2-1/2 mi S on Hwy 297, then 10 mi SW on Hwy 173 (Blue Angle Pkwy), then 6 mi W on 292, then 350 ft E on Gongora Dr, then 1/10 mi N on Don Carlos Dr, then 1/10 mi W on River Rd. Enter on R.*

PERDIDO KEY'S NEW LUXURY RV RESORT

A NEW Luxury RV Resort & Marina, located on the Intracoastal Waterway, minutes from the Gulf of Mexico on Perdido Key, FL. Paved Streets, Clubhouse, Free WiFi at all sites, Pool, Store, Fishing, (877)402-7873, (850)492-7304.

◊◊◊◊◊FACILITIES: 56 sites, typical site width 30 ft, 56 full hkups, (30/50 amps), 13 pull-thrus, cable TV, WiFi Instant Internet at site, family camping, laundry, RV supplies, LP gas by weight/by meter, ice, picnic tables, patios.

◊◊◊◊RECREATION: rec hall, swim pool, boating, canoeing, kayaking, dock, saltwater fishing, fishing supplies, golf nearby, bike rental 6 bike rentals, playground, shuffleboard court 2 shuffleboard courts, activities, horseshoes, v-ball.

Pets welcome, breed restrict. Partial handicap access. No tents. Open all yr. Big rigs welcome. Escort to site. Clubs welcome. Rate in 2010 $45-85 for 2 persons. MC/VISA/DISC/AMEX. Member ARVC, FLARVC.

Text 83045 to (440)725-8687 to see our Visual Tour.

Phone: (850)492-7304
Address: 13770 River Rd, Pensacola, FL 32507
Lat/Lon: 30.31128/-87.42747
Email: perdidocoverv@innisfree.com
Web: www.perdidocove.com

SEE AD PENSACOLA THIS PAGE

(W) Playa del Rio RV Resort—(Escambia) *From jct I-10 (exit 7) & Hwy 297: Go 2-1/2 mi S on Hwy 297, then 10 mi SW on Hwy 173 (Blue Angel Pkwy), then 10-1/4 mi W on Hwy 292. Enter on R.* ◊◊◊FACILITIES: 30 sites, typical site width 30 ft, 30 full hkups, (30/50 amps), family camping, dump, laundry.

Playa del Rio RV Resort—Continued on next page

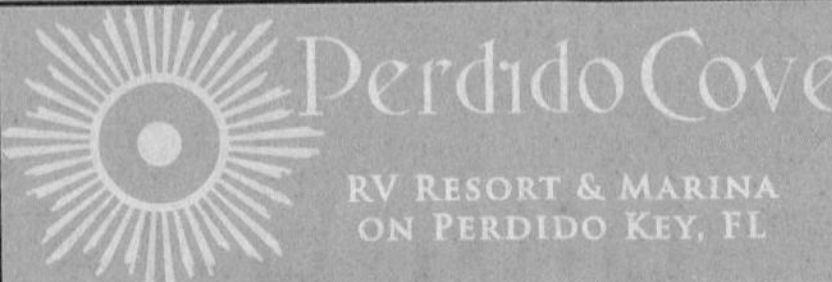

◊◊◊◊RECREATION: saltwater swim, boating, canoeing, dock, saltwater fishing. Pets welcome, breed restrict. Partial handicap access. No tents. Open all yr. Big rigs welcome. Rate in 2010 $40-71 per family. Phone: (888)200-0904.

PERRY—A-2

(S) Perry KOA—(Taylor) *From jct US 98/19/27 & US 98/19/27A: Go 3 mi S on US 98/19/27A. Enter on R.* ◊◊◊◊FACILITIES: 72 sites, typical site width 25 ft, 68 full hkups, 4 W&E, (30/50 amps), 49 pull-thrus, family camping, tenting, laundry, ltd groc. ◊◊◊◊RECREATION: swim pool, playground. Pets welcome. Partial handicap access. Open all yr. Big rigs welcome. Rate in 2010 $27-36 for 2 persons. Member ARVC, FLARVC. Phone: (850)584-3221. KOA discount.

POLK CITY—C-3

(S) LELYNN RV RESORT—(Polk) *From jct I-4 (exit 44) & SR 559: Go 1 block N on SR 559. Enter on L.*

◊◊◊◊FACILITIES: 360 sites, typical site width 35 ft, 360 full hkups, (30/50 amps), mostly extd stay sites (winter), 10 pull-thrus, WiFi Instant Internet at site ($), phone on-site Internet (needs activ), WiFi Internet central location, family camping, RV storage, dump, non-guest dump $, laundry, LP gas by weight/by meter, picnic tables, patios.

◊◊◊◊RECREATION: rec hall, rec room/area, swim pool, boating, canoeing, kayaking, ramp, dock, lake fishing, golf nearby, shuffleboard court 4 shuffleboard courts, activities, horseshoes, local tours.

Pets welcome, breed restrict, size restrict, quantity restrict. Partial handicap access. No tents. Open all yr. Big rigs welcome. Clubs welcome. Member ARVC, FLARVC.

Phone: (800)736-0409
Address: 1513 State Rd 559, Polk City, FL 33868
Lat/Lon: 28.16348/-81.80222

SEE AD LAKELAND PAGE 137 AND AD TRAVEL SECTION PAGE 74

POMPANO BEACH—E-5

(N) BREEZY HILL RV RESORT—(Broward) *From jct I-95 (exit 39) & Hwy 834 (Sample Rd): Go 1/4 mi E on Hwy 834, then 1 mi N on 3rd Ave, then 2 blocks E on 48th St. Enter on R.*

◊◊◊◊FACILITIES: 594 sites, typical site width 20 ft, accepts full hkup units only, 594 full hkups, (30/50 amps), some extd stay sites (winter), 7 pull-thrus, WiFi Instant Internet at site ($), laundry, patios, controlled access.

◊◊◊RECREATION: rec hall, rec room/area, pavilion, 2 swim pools, golf nearby, shuffleboard court 11 shuffleboard courts, activities, horseshoes.

Pets welcome, size restrict. Partial handicap access. No tents. Open all yr. Planned activities during winter season only. Clubs welcome. Rate in 2010 $33-66 for 2 persons. MC/VISA. Member ARVC, FLARVC.

Phone: (954)942-8688
Address: 800 NE 48th St., Pompano Beach, FL 33064
Lat/Lon: 26.28978/-80.11274
Email: breezy_hill_gm@equitylifestyle.com
Web: www.equitylifestyle.com

SEE AD ALACHUA PAGE 93

(N) HIGHLAND PINES RV RESORT—(Broward) *From jct I-95 (exit 39) & Hwy 834 (Sample Rd): Go 3/4 mi E on Hwy 834, then 1 mi N on Hwy 811 (Dixie Hwy), then 1 block W on 48th St. Enter on R.*

◊◊◊◊FACILITIES: 421 sites, typical site width 20 ft, 40 ft max RV length, accepts full hkup units only, 421 full hkups, (20/30/50 amps), many extd stay sites (winter), RV storage, dump, laundry, patios.

◊◊◊◊RECREATION: rec hall, rec room/area, pavilion, swim pool, golf nearby, shuffleboard court 3 shuffleboard courts, activities, horseshoes, local tours.

Pets welcome, breed restrict, size restrict, quantity restrict. Partial handicap access. No tents. Open all yr. Escort to site. Clubs welcome. Rate in 2010 $45-50 for 2 persons.

Phone: (954)421-5372
Address: 875 N E 48th Street, Pompano Beach, FL 33064
Lat/Lon: 26.29010/-80.11221
Email: highlandpines@bellsouth.net
Web: www.floridarvparks.net

SEE AD THIS PAGE

(N) HIGHLAND WOODS—(Broward) *From jct I-95 (exit 39) & Hwy 834 (Sample Rd): Go 3/4 mi E on Hwy 834, then 1 mi N on Hwy 811 (Dixie Hwy), then 1 block W on 48th St. Enter on L.*

◊◊◊◊FACILITIES: 147 sites, typical site width 20 ft, accepts full hkup units only, 147 full hkups, (30/50 amps), some extd stay sites (winter), 5 pull-thrus, WiFi Instant Internet at site ($), family camping, dump, non-guest dump $, laundry, patios.

◊◊◊RECREATION: rec hall, rec room/area, pavilion, swim pool, golf nearby, activities.

Pets welcome, size restrict. No tents. Open all yr. Planned activities during winter season only. Clubs welcome. Rate in 2010 $33-63 for 2 persons. MC/VISA. Member ARVC, FLARVC.

Phone: (954)942-8688
Address: 900 NE 48th St, Pompano Beach, FL 33064
Lat/Lon: 26.28979/-80.11212
Email: breezy_hill_gm@equitylifestyle.com
Web: www.equitylifestyle.com

SEE AD ALACHUA PAGE 93

PONCE DE LEON—E-2

(N) Vortex Spring Camping and Diving Resort—(Holmes) *From jct I-10 (exit 96) & Hwy 81: Go 5 mi N on Hwy 81. Enter on R.* ◊◊◊FACILITIES: 24 sites, typical site width 50 ft, 5 full hkups, 19 W&E, (30/50 amps), 50 amps ($), 9 pull-thrus, family camping, tenting, dump, ltd groc. ◊◊◊RECREATION: lake swim, canoeing, playground. Pets welcome, size restrict. Partial handicap access. Open all yr. Rate in 2010 $17.50-25 for 2 persons. Phone: (800)342-0640.

PORT CHARLOTTE—D-3

✱ **(SE) CHARLOTTE RV CENTER**—*From jct Hwy 769 (Kings Hwy) & I 75: Go 6 mi S on Hwy I-75 (exit 164), then 2 mi S on US 17, then 2 mi N on US 41, then 1 block E on Harper Ave. Enter on L.* SALES: fold-down camping trailers, pre-owned unit sales. SERVICES: full-time mech, engine/chassis repair, RV appliance repair, body work/collision repair, sells parts/accessories, installs hitches. Open all yr. MC/VISA/DISC/AMEX/Debit.

Phone: (941)883-5555
Address: 4628 Tamiami Trail (US 41), Port Charlotte, FL 33980
Lat/Lon: 26.96129/-82.06804
Email: info@charlottervcenter.com
Web: www.charlottervcenter.com

SEE AD THIS PAGE

CROSS CREEK COUNTRY CLUB & RV RESORT—*From Port Charlotte: Go 6 mi N on Hwy 769, then 3 mi E on Hwy 761, then 17 mi N on US 17, then 1/4 mi W on CR 660, then 1 mi N on Cubitus Ave (Old Hwy 17). Enter on L.*

SEE PRIMARY LISTING AT ARCADIA AND AD ARCADIA PAGE 94

(W) HARBOR LAKES—(Charlotte) *From jct I-75 (exit 170) & Hwy 769 (Kings Hwy): Go 500 ft S on Hwy 769, then 10-1/2 mi W on Hwy 776. Enter on R.*

◊◊◊◊◊FACILITIES: 528 sites, typical site width 45 ft, 528 full hkups, (20/30/50 amps), mostly extd stay sites (winter), WiFi Internet central location, RV storage, dump, non-guest dump $, laundry, ice, picnic tables, patios.

◊◊◊◊◊RECREATION: rec hall, rec room/area, equipped pavilion, swim pool, hot tub, golf nearby, bsktball, shuffleboard court 8 shuffleboard courts, activities, tennis, horseshoes, v-ball.

Pets welcome. Partial handicap access. No tents. Open all yr. Planned group activities, winter season only. Big rigs welcome. Clubs welcome. Rate in 2010 $33-63 for 2 persons. MC/VISA/DISC/AMEX. Member ARVC, FLARVC.

Phone: (800)468-5022
Address: 3737 El Jobean Rd, Port Charlotte, FL 33953
Lat/Lon: 26.98172/-82.20735
Email: harbor_lakes@equitylifestyle.com
Web: www.rvonthego.com

SEE AD ALACHUA PAGE 93

(NE) Lettuce Lake Travel Resort—(DeSoto) *From jct I-75 (exit 170) & Hwy 769: Go 6 mi N on Hwy 769, then 2 mi E on Hwy 761, then 1/2 mi S on Lettuce Lake Rd. Enter on R.* ◊◊◊◊FACILITIES: 255 sites, typical site width 25 ft, 40 ft max RV length, 255 full hkups, (30/50 amps), 6 pull-thrus, laundry. ◊◊◊◊RECREATION: swim pool, boating, canoeing, saltwater/lake/river fishing. Pets welcome, breed restrict, size restrict, quantity restrict. Partial handicap access. No tents. Age restrict may apply. Open all yr. Rate in 2010 $40 for 2 persons. Member ARVC, FLARVC. Phone: (863)494-6057.

(NE) Oak Haven MH & RV Park—(DeSoto) *From jct I-75 (exit 170) & Hwy 769 (Kings Hwy): Go 6 mi N on Hwy 769 (Kings Hwy), then 2 mi E on Hwy 761, then 1/4 S mi on Lettuce Lake Ave. Enter on L.* ◊◊◊◊FACILITIES: 89 sites, typical site width 30 ft, 89 full hkups, (30/50 amps), 22 pull-thrus, laundry. ◊◊◊RECREATION: swim pool. Pets welcome, breed restrict, quantity restrict. Partial handicap access. No tents. Age restrict may apply. Open all yr. Rate in 2010 $34 for 2 persons. Member ARVC, FLARVC. Phone: (888)611-4678.

PORT CHARLOTTE—Continued on next page

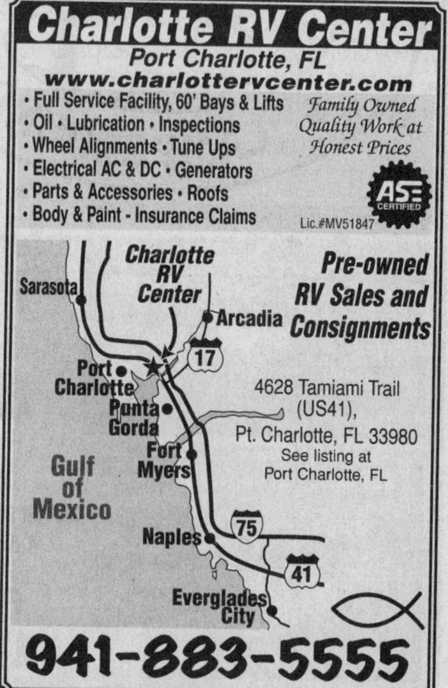

PORT CHARLOTTE—Continued

(NE) RIVERSIDE RV RESORT & CAMPGROUND—(DeSoto) *From jct I-75 (exit 170) & Hwy 769 (Kings Hwy): Go 4-1/2 mi NE on Hwy 769. Enter on R.*

A TRUE RV RESORT ON THE PEACE RIVER

You will love our quiet country setting, friendly helpful staff, sparkling facilities & outstanding planned activities! Enjoy our 2 heated pools, riverfront piers & boat ramp. Big rig & pet friendly. Nearby new Super Walmart!

◆◆◆◆◆FACILITIES: 350 sites, typical site width 35 ft, 350 full hkups, (30/50 amps), 50 amps ($), many extd stay sites (winter), 4 pull-thrus, WiFi Instant Internet at site ($), family camping, tenting, RV's/park model rentals, RV storage, dump, non-guest dump $, laundry, groceries, RV supplies, LP gas by weight/by meter, ice, picnic tables, patios, fire rings, wood, controlled access.

◆◆◆◆◆RECREATION: rec hall, rec room/area, equipped pavilion, coin games, 2 swim pools, hot tub, boating, canoeing, kayaking, ramp, dock, 6 canoe rentals, river fishing, fishing supplies, golf nearby, bsktball, playground, shuffleboard court 4 shuffleboard courts, activities, horseshoes, v-ball, local tours.

Pets welcome. Partial handicap access. Open all yr. Big rigs welcome. Escort to site. Clubs welcome. MC/VISA/DISC/AMEX/Debit. Member ARVC, FLARVC.

Phone: (800)795-9733
Address: 9770 SW County Rd 769 Kings Hwy, Arcadia, FL 34269
Lat/Lon: 27.07961/-82.01331
Email: riverside@desoto.net
Web: www.riversidervresort.com

SEE AD THIS PAGE

PORT ORANGE—B-4

(N) Daytona Beach KOA—(Volusia) *From jct I-95 (exit 261) & US 92: Go 3-1/4 mi E on US 92, then 4-1/2 mi S on Hwy 5A (Nova Rd). Enter on R.* ◆◆◆FACILITIES: 350 sites, typical site width 30 ft, 160 full hkups, 119 W&E, (20/30/50 amps), 71 no hkups, family camping, tenting, dump, laundry. ◆◆RECREATION: swim pool, playground. Pets welcome. Partial handicap access. Open all yr. Big rigs welcome. Rate in 2010 $20-45 for 2 persons. Member ARVC, FLARVC. Phone: (386)767-9170. KOA discount. FMCA discount.

(S) DAYTONA BEACH RV RESORT—(Volusia) *From I-95 (exit 256) & Hwy 421: Go 3/4 mi E on Hwy 421, then 1-1/4 N on Clyde Morris Blvd. Enter on R.*

WELCOME TO CAREFREE RV RESORTS!

The world's most famous beach, International Speedway with Orlando attractions nearby-it's what great vacations are made of! Enjoy all the excitement and then relax in a peaceful, family-friendly resort.

◆◆◆◆FACILITIES: 225 sites, typical site width 30 ft, 190 full hkups, 35 W&E, (20/30/50 amps), some extd stay sites (winter), 16 pull-thrus, cable TV, WiFi Instant Internet at site, WiFi Internet central location, family camping, tenting, RV's/park model rentals, dump, non-guest dump $, laundry, ltd groc, RV supplies, LP gas by weight/by meter, ice, picnic tables, patios.

◆◆◆◆RECREATION: rec hall, rec room/area, pavilion, swim pool, wading pool, golf nearby, shuffleboard court 2 shuffleboard courts, activities, horseshoes.

Pets welcome, breed restrict. Partial handicap access. Open all yr. Planned group activities winter only. Big rigs welcome. Escort to site. Clubs welcome. Rate in 2010 $40-45 for 2 persons. MC/VISA. Member ARVC, FLARVC. FMCA discount. CCUSA 50% Discount. CCUSA reservations Recommended, CCUSA max stay 2 days. Not valid during special events, call park for details. Call park regarding surcharge for children.

Phone: (386)761-2663
Address: 4601 Clyde Morris Blvd, Port Orange, FL 32129
Lat/Lon: 29.13212/-81.02786
Email: dbcampground@cfl.rr.com
Web: www.carefreeresorts.com

SEE AD DAYTONA BEACH PAGE 109

PORT ORANGE—Continued

(S) ROSE BAY TRAVEL PARK—(Volusia) *From I-95 (exit 256) & Hwy 421: Go 2-1/4 mi E on Hwy 421, then 1-1/2 mi S on Hwy 5-A. Enter on R.*

OCEAN FISHING - BEST BEACH - DAYTONA 500

Right by the white gleaming beaches, Rosebay offers surf, sand and sun! Bring your own boat/catch a deep sea charter for ocean fishing, hop on over to see Daytona Speedway and more. A full amenity park.

◆◆◆FACILITIES: 311 sites, typical site width 24 ft, 306 full hkups, 5 W&E, (30/50 amps), mostly extd stay sites, cable TV, WiFi Instant Internet at site, tenting, RV's/park model rentals, dump, non-guest dump $, portable dump, laundry, LP gas by weight/by meter, picnic tables, patios.

◆◆◆◆RECREATION: rec hall, swim pool, hot tub, boating, ramp, dock, saltwater fishing, golf nearby, shuffleboard court 3 shuffleboard courts, activities, horseshoes.

Pets welcome, size restrict. Partial handicap access. Open all yr. MC/VISA/DISC/AMEX. CCUSA 50% Discount. CCUSA reservations Recommended, CCUSA max stay 1 day, CCUSA disc. not avail F,Sa, CCUSA disc. not avail holidays. Discount not available Race Week or Bike Week.

Phone: (386)767-4308
Address: 5200 S Nova Rd, Port Orange, FL 32127
Lat/Lon: 29.11469/-80.98518
Web: www.florida-rv-resorts.com/rose_bay.html

SEE AD TRAVEL SECTION PAGE 79

PORT RICHEY—C-3

(N) Ja-Mar North Travel Park (RV SPACES)—(Pasco) *From jct Hwy 52 & US-19: Go 1 mi S on US 19, then 1 block W on San Marco Dr. Enter on R.* FACILITIES: 353 sites, typical site width 30 ft, 38 ft max RV length, accepts full hkup units only, 353 full hkups,

Ja-Mar North Travel Park—Continued on next page

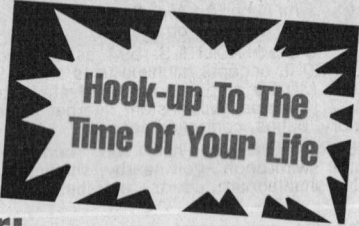

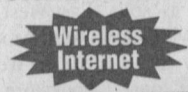

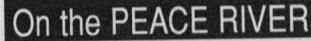

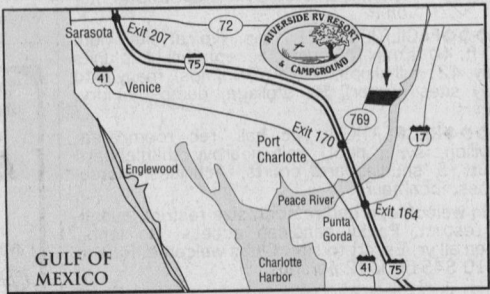

PORT RICHEY—Continued
Ja-Mar North Travel Park—Continued

(30/50 amps), 50 amps ($), laundry. RECREATION: swim pool, pond fishing. Pets welcome, breed restrict. No tents. Age restrict may apply. Open all yr. Rate in 2010 $30-31.50 for 2 persons. Phone: (727)862-8882.

(N) Ja-Mar Travel Park—(Pasco) *From jct Hwy 52 & US 19: Go 1-1/4 mi S on US 19. Enter on R.* ◆◆◆FACILITIES: 396 sites, typical site width 22 ft, 38 ft max RV length, 396 full hkups, (30/50 amps), 50 amps ($), phone/cable on-site Internet (needs activ), WiFi Internet central location, RV storage, laundry, patios. ◆◆◆RECREATION: rec hall, pavilion, swim pool, pond fishing, shuffleboard court 8 shuffleboard courts, activities, horseshoes. Pets welcome, breed restrict. No tents. Age restrict may apply. Open all yr. Rate in 2010 $37 for 2 persons. FMCA discount. CCUSA 50% Discount. CCUSA reservations Recommended, CCUSA max stay Unlimited, Cash only for CCUSA disc. 1 week minimum stay required.

Phone: (727)863-2040
Address: 11203 US 19 N, Port Richey, FL 34668
Lat/Lon: 28.31983/-82.69968
Web: www.ja-mar-travelpark.com

(N) Suncoast RV Resort—(Pasco) *From jct Hwy 52 & US 19: Go 3 mi S on US 19. Enter on R.* ◆◆◆FACILITIES: 154 sites, typical site width 18 ft, 35 ft max RV length, 154 full hkups, (20/30/50 amps), cable TV, ($), WiFi Instant Internet at site, WiFi Internet central location, family camping, RV storage, dump, non-guest dump $, laundry, picnic tables, patios. ◆◆◆RECREATION: rec hall, swim pool, shuffleboard court shuffleboard court, activities, horseshoes. Pets welcome, breed restrict, size restrict, quantity restrict. No tents. Open all yr. Rate in 2010 $37.02 for 2 persons. MC/VISA/DISC/AMEX/Debit. Member FLARVC. CCUSA 50% Discount. CCUSA reservations Recommended, CCUSA max stay 2 days, Cash only for CCUSA disc. Discount available May thru Oct. Pet restrictions include breed, size & quantity. Call for details.

Phone: (888)922-5603
Address: 9029 US Hwy 19, Port Richey, FL 34668
Lat/Lon: 28.28877/-82.71344
Email: rvparks@aol.com
Web: www.suncoastrvresort.com

(N) Sundance Lakes RV Resort—(Pasco) *From Jct Hwy 52 & US 19: Go 1/2 mi S on US 19, then 1 block W on Hachem Dr. Enter on R.* ◆◆◆FACILITIES:

PORT RICHEY—Continued
Sundance Lakes RV Resort—Continued

523 sites, typical site width 28 ft, 40 ft max RV length, 523 full hkups, (30/50 amps), laundry. ◆◆◆◆RECREATION: swim pool. Pets welcome, breed restrict, size restrict, quantity restrict. No tents. Age restrict may apply. Open all yr. Rate in 2010 $31 for 2 persons. Phone: (727)862-3565.

(N) Tropic Breeze (RV SPACES)—(Pasco) *From jct Hwy 52 & US 19: Go 1 mi S on US 19. Enter on L.* FACILITIES: 44 sites, typical site width 35 ft, 35 ft max RV length, 44 full hkups, (30/50 amps). Pets welcome. No tents. Age restrict may apply. Open all yr. Rate in 2010 $31 for 2 persons. Phone: (727)868-1629.

PORT ST. JOE—F-3

(S) ST. JOSEPH PENINSULA STATE PARK—(Gulf) *From jct Hwy 71 & US 98: Go 9 mi S on US 98 & paved road, then 4 mi W on Hwy 30, then 9 mi N on Hwy C-30 (Cape San Blas Rd).* FACILITIES: 119 sites, 28 ft max RV length, 119 W&E, tenting, dump, groceries. RECREATION: saltwater swim, boating, canoeing, ramp, dock, saltwater fishing, playground. No pets. Open all yr. Phone: (904)227-1327.

PORT ST. LUCIE—D-5

Outdoor Resorts St. Lucie West Motorcoach Resort—(St. Lucie) *From jct I-95 (exit 121) & St. Lucie W Blvd: Go 1 block E on St. Lucie W Blvd, then 1-1/2 mi N on NW Peacock Rd. Enter on L.* ◆◆◆◆◆FACILITIES: 401 sites, typical site width 40 ft, accepts full hkup units only, 401 full hkups, (20/30/50 amps), laundry. ◆◆◆◆RECREATION: 3 swim pools, lake fishing. Pets welcome, quantity restrict. Partial handicap access. No tents. Open all yr. Big rigs welcome. Green Friendly. Rate in 2010 $65 for 4 persons. Member ARVC, FLARVC. Phone: (866)456-2303. FMCA discount.

Woodall's Tip... To be considered a "Big Rig Friendly" park, the campground must meet the following requirements: minimum of 50 amps, adequate road width, overhead access clearance, site clearance to accommodate the tallest and widest rigs built. Often not every site can accommodate a big rig, so we recommend that you call ahead for availability.

PORT ST. LUCIE—Continued

(SE) PORT ST. LUCIE RV RESORT—(St. Lucie) *From jct Hwy 716 (W. Port St. Lucie Blvd) & I-95: Go 3 mi S on I-95 (exit 118), then 2-1/2 mi E on Gatlin Blvd, then 5-1/2 mi E on Port St. Lucie Blvd, then 1/2 mi N on US 1, then 1 block E on Jennings Rd. Enter on R.*

WE'RE NEAR EVERYTHING!
We offer a heated pool & sites with cable access. Seasonal & Summer specials. Top-of-the-Season Party, a favorite among campers. Great summer ocean breezes - a perfect get-away! www.portstluciervresort.com

◆◆◆◆FACILITIES: 117 sites, typical site width 35 ft, 117 full hkups, (20/30/50 amps), 50 amps ($), some extd stay sites (winter), 4 pull-thrus, cable TV, ($), WiFi Instant Internet at site, family camping, laundry, ice, picnic tables, patios.

◆◆◆RECREATION: rec hall, pavilion, swim pool, golf nearby, activities, horseshoes.

Pets welcome, quantity restrict. Partial handicap access. No tents. Open all yr. Big rigs welcome. Clubs welcome. Rate in 2010 $36.50-46.50 for 2 persons. MC/VISA/DISC/Debit. Member ARVC, FLARVC. FMCA discount. CCUSA 50% Discount. CCUSA reservations Recommended, CCUSA max stay. See rest. Discount not available Dec 15 to Apr 15 (Peak Season). 21 day max stay Apr 15-Nov 1. 14 day max stay Nov 1-Dec 15 & Apr 1-15.

Phone: (877)405-2333
Address: 3703 SE Jennings Rd, Port St Lucie, FL 34952
Lat/Lon: 27.27822/-80.28780
Email: portstluciervresort@juno.com
Web: www.portstluciervresort.com

SEE AD THIS PAGE

PUNTA GORDA—D-3

(SE) Alligator Park—(Charlotte) *From jct US 17 & I-75: Go 3-1/4 mi S on I-75 (exit 161), then 500 feet W on CR 768 (Jones Loop Rd), then 1 mi S on CR 765A (Taylor Rd). Enter on L.* ◆◆◆◆FACILITIES: 166 sites,

Alligator Park—Continued on next page

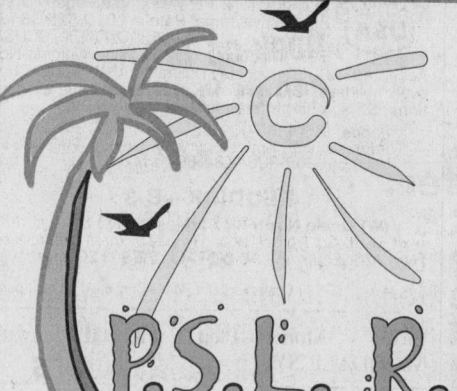

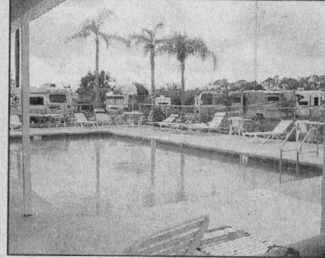

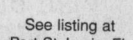

PUNTA GORDA—Continued
Alligator Park—Continued

typical site width 30 ft, 166 full hkups, (30/50 amps), dump, laundry. ◊◊◊◊RECREATION: swim pool, boating, no motors, canoeing, lake fishing. Pets welcome, breed restrict, size restrict, quantity restrict. Partial handicap access. No tents. Age restrict may apply. Open all yr. Rate in 2010 $25-39.70 for 2 persons. Member ARVC, FLARVC. Phone: (941)639-7000. FMCA discount.

(S) GULF VIEW RV RESORT—(Charlotte) *From jct US 17 & I-75: Go 3 mi S on I-75 (exit 161), then 1-1/2 mi W on Hwy 768 (Jones Loop Rd), then 1/2 mi S on Burnt Store Rd. Enter on R.*

WELCOME

◊◊◊◊FACILITIES: 204 sites, typical site width 35 ft, 204 full hkups, (20/30/50 amps), many extd stay sites (winter), 138 pull-thrus, WiFi Instant Internet at site ($), tenting, RV's/park model rentals, laundry, picnic tables, patios.

◊◊◊◊RECREATION: rec hall, swim pool, hot tub, boating, canoeing, kayaking, ramp, dock, saltwater/river fishing, golf nearby, shuffleboard court 4 shuffleboard courts, activities, horseshoes.

Pets welcome. Partial handicap access. Open all yr. Group activities winter only. Big rigs welcome. Clubs welcome. Rate in 2010 $30-45 for 2 persons. MC/VISA/DISC/AMEX. Member ARVC, FLARVC.

Phone: (877)237-2757
Address: 10205 Burnt Store Rd, Punta Gorda, FL 33950
Lat/Lon: 26.88276/-82.02359
Email: info@rvonthego.com
Web: www.rvonthego.com

SEE AD ALACHUA PAGE 93

(S) PUNTA GORDA RV RESORT—(Charlotte) *S'bnd: From I-75 (exit 164) & US 17: Go 2 mi S on US 17, then 2 mi S on US 41, then 500 ft W on Rio Villa Dr. Enter on L.*

WELCOME

◊◊◊◊FACILITIES: 223 sites, typical site width 25 ft, 40 ft max RV length, 223 full hkups, (30/50 amps), many extd stay sites (winter), cable TV, WiFi Instant Internet at site ($), laundry, RV supplies, picnic tables.

◊◊◊◊RECREATION: rec hall, rec room/area, swim pool, hot tub, boating, canoeing, kayaking, ramp, dock, saltwater fishing, golf nearby, shuffleboard court 2 shuffleboard courts, activities, horseshoes.

PUNTA GORDA—Continued
PUNTA GORDA RV RESORT—Continued

Pets welcome. Partial handicap access. No tents. Open all yr. Clubs welcome. Rate in 2010 $30-45 for 2 persons. MC/VISA/Debit. Member ARVC, FLARVC.

Phone: (941)639-2010
Address: 3701 Baynard Dr, Punta Gorda, FL 33950
Lat/Lon: 26.90529/-82.03950
Email: puntagordarv@earthlink.net
Web: www.pgrvresort.com

SEE AD THIS PAGE AND AD TRAVEL SECTION PAGE 74

(NE) SHELL CREEK RV RESORT—(Charlotte) *From jct I-75 (exit 164) & US 17: Go 4 mi N on US 17, then 4-1/4 mi E on Washington Loop Rd. Enter on L.*

WELCOME

◊◊◊◊FACILITIES: 239 sites, typical site width 30 ft, 239 full hkups, (30/50 amps), mostly extd stay sites (winter), WiFi Instant Internet at site ($), RV storage, laundry, ltd groc, RV supplies, LP gas by weight/by meter, ice, patios.

CAMPCLUB USA

◊◊◊◊RECREATION: rec hall, rec room/area, swim pool, hot tub, boating, canoeing, kayaking, ramp, dock, saltwater/river fishing, fishing supplies, golf nearby, shuffleboard court 8 shuffleboard courts, activities, horseshoes.

Pets welcome, breed restrict. Partial handicap access. No tents. Age restrict may apply. Open all yr. Escort to site. Clubs welcome. Rate in 2010 $28-35 for 2 persons. MC/VISA/Debit. CCUSA 50% Discount. CCUSA reservations Recommended, CCUSA max stay 7 days, CCUSA disc. not avail holidays. Not available Jan 15-Mar 15. A/C surcharge $5-10, depending upon time of year.

Phone: (941)639-4234
Address: 35711 Washington Loop Rd, Punta Gorda, FL 33982
Lat/Lon: 26.97252/-81.89539
Email: shellcreek@nhcmgt.com
Web: www.carefreervresorts.com

SEE AD FORT MYERS BEACH PAGE 123

Woodall's Tip... If you think Woodall's Ratings mean Good, Better, Best...think again. See the "How to Use" section in the front of this Directory for an explanation of our Rating System.

PUNTA GORDA—Continued

(SE) SUN 'N' SHADE CAMPGROUND—(Charlotte) *From jct US 17 & I-75: Go 6-1/2 mi S on I-75 (exit 158), then 1 mi W on Tucker Grade Rd, then 3-1/2 mi S on US 41. Enter on L.*

WELCOME

◊◊◊◊FACILITIES: 191 sites, typical site width 30 ft, 191 full hkups, (20/30/50 amps), many extd stay sites (winter), heater not allowed, WiFi Instant Internet at site ($), family camping, RV storage, dump, non-guest dump $, laundry, RV supplies, ice, picnic tables, patios.

CAMPCLUB USA

◊◊◊RECREATION: rec hall, swim pool, pond fishing, golf nearby, shuffleboard court 2 shuffleboard courts, activities, horseshoes, hiking trails.

Pets welcome, breed restrict. Partial handicap access. No tents. Open all yr. Escort to site. Clubs welcome. Rate in 2010 $30-35 for 2 persons. MC/VISA/DISC/AMEX/Debit. Member ARVC, FLARVC. FMCA discount. CCUSA 50% Discount. CCUSA reservations Recommended, CCUSA max stay 21 days. Discount not available Dec 21 thru Mar.

Text 107902 to (440)725-8687 to see our Visual Tour.

Phone: (941)639-5388
Address: 14880 Tamiami Trail (Hwy 41), Punta Gorda, FL 33955
Lat/Lon: 26.81369/-81.95905
Email: parkinfo@sunnshade.com
Web: www.sunnshade.com

SEE AD THIS PAGE AND AD TRAVEL SECTION PAGE 74

(E) Water's Edge RV Resort of Punta Gorda—(Charlotte) *From jct US 17 & I-75: Go 3 mi S on I-75 (exit 161), then 500 feet E on Jones Loop Rd, then 2-3/4 mi N on Piper Rd. Enter on R.* ◊◊◊◊FACILITIES: 187 sites, typical site width 30 ft, 171 full hkups, 16 W&E, (20/30/50 amps), 37 pull-thrus, dump, laundry. ◊◊◊RECREATION: swim pool, boating, electric motors only, dock, lake fishing. Pets welcome. Partial handicap access. No tents. Age restrict may apply. Open all yr. Big rigs welcome. Rate in 2010 $38-42 for 2 persons. Phone: (800)637-9224.

QUINCY—A-1

(S) Beaver Lake Campground—(Gadsden) *From jct I-10 (exit 174) & Hwy 12: Go 1/4 mi N on Hwy 12. Enter on R.* ◊◊FACILITIES: 30 sites, typical site width 32 ft, 30 full hkups, (30/50 amps), 30 pull-thrus, family camping, tenting, RV storage, dump, non-guest dump $, laundry, groceries, ice, picnic tables. RECREATION: Pets welcome. Open all yr. Big rigs welcome. Rate in 2010 $29-38 for 2 persons. MC/VISA/DISC/AMEX. CCUSA 50% Discount. CCUSA reservations Not Accepted, CCUSA max stay Unlimited, CCUSA disc. not avail holidays. Discount not available during evacuations. $2 surcharge for washer & dryer in RV.

CAMPCLUB USA

Phone: (850)856-9095
Address: 133 Kneeology Way, Quincy, FL 32351
Lat/Lon: 30.58064/-84.69704

REDDICK—B-3

(W) Ocala North RV Park—(Athens) *From jct I-75 (exit 368). Go 1 block W on Hwy 318, then 1/2 mi S on Hwy 225. Enter on L.* ◊◊◊FACILITIES: 126 sites, typi-

Ocala North RV Park—Continued on next page

Save Money—Plan Ahead with WOODALL'S!

REDDICK—Continued
Ocala North RV Park—Continued

cal site width 30 ft, 126 full hkups, (30/50 amps), 47 pull-thrus, tenting, dump, laundry. ◊◊◊RECREATION: swim pool. Pets welcome, breed restrict. Open all yr. Big rigs welcome. Rate in 2010 $31-35 for 2 persons. Member ARVC, FLARVC. Phone: (877)267-8737.

RIVERVIEW—C-3

(S) Hidden River Travel Resort—(Hillsborough) *From I-75 (exit 250) & Gibsonton Rd: Go 1-1/2 mi E on Gibsonton Rd, then 1-1/2 mi E on Boyette, then 3/4 mi NE McMullen Rd, then 2/3 mi E on McMullen Loop to the end. Enter at end.* ◊◊◊FACILITIES: 320 sites, typical site width 25 ft, 320 full hkups, (20/30/50 amps), family camping, dump, laundry. ◊◊◊◊RECREATION: swim pool, boating, canoeing, ramp, river/pond fishing. Pets welcome, breed restrict, size restrict, quantity restrict. Partial handicap access. No tents. Open all yr. Big rigs welcome. Rate in 2010 $36-45 for 2 persons. Member ARVC. Phone: (813)677-1515.

ROCKLEDGE—C-4

(S) SPACE COAST RV RESORT—(Brevard) *S'bound from I-95 (exit 195): Go 200 yards N on Fiske Blvd, then 200 yards E on Barnes Blvd. N'bound from I-95 (exit 195): Go 300 yards straight ahead from light. Enter on L.*

WELCOME

◊◊◊◊◊FACILITIES: 267 sites, typical site width 35 ft, 267 full hkups, (20/30/50 amps), mostly extd stay sites (winter), 85 pull-thrus, phone/cable on-site Internet (needs activ), WiFi Internet central location, family camping, tenting, RV storage, dump, non-guest dump $, laundry, RV supplies, LP gas by weight/by meter, ice, picnic tables, patios.

◊◊◊◊RECREATION: rec hall, rec room/area, equipped pavilion, swim pool, wading pool, pond fishing, golf nearby, shuffleboard court 4 shuffleboard courts, activities, horseshoes.

Pets welcome, breed restrict, size restrict, quantity restrict. Partial handicap access. Open all yr. Planned group activities winter only. Big rigs welcome. Escort to site. Clubs welcome. Rate in 2010 $40-55 for 2 persons. MC/VISA/DISC/Debit. Member FLARVC.

Text 107904 to (440)725-8687 to see our Visual Tour.

Phone: (800)982-4233
Address: 820 Barnes Blvd., Rockledge, FL 32955
Lat/Lon: 28.29569/-80.73898
Email: scrv@spacecoastrv.com
Web: www.spacecoastrv.com

SEE AD COCOA PAGE 103

RUSKIN—D-3

(S) Hide-A-Way RV Resort—(Hillsborough) *From jct I-75 (exit 240) & Hwy 674: Go 3 mi W on Hwy 674, then 2-1/2 mi S on US 41, then 3/4 mi E on Chaney Dr. Enter on L.* ◊◊◊FACILITIES: 384 sites, typical site width 35 ft, 384 full hkups, (30/50 amps), 12 pull-thrus, family camping, dump, laundry. ◊◊◊◊RECREATION: swim pool, boating, canoeing, ramp, dock, saltwater/river fishing. Pets welcome, size restrict, quantity restrict. Partial handicap access. No tents. Open all yr. Big rigs welcome. Rate in 2010 $32-37 for 2 persons. Member ARVC, FLARVC. Phone: (800)607-2532.

(S) SUN LAKE RV RESORT—(Hillsborough) *From jct I-75 (exit 240B) & Hwy 674: Go 1/4 mi W on Hwy 674, then 3/4 mi S on 33rd St SE. N'bnd: Use exit 240. Enter on R.*

WELCOME

◊◊◊◊FACILITIES: 47 sites, typical site width 40 ft, 47 full hkups, (30/50 amps), 18 pull-thrus, cable TV, ($), WiFi Instant Internet at site, phone/cable on-site Internet (needs activ), phone Internet central location, family camping, tenting, RV storage, dump, non-guest dump $, laundry, picnic tables, patios.

CAMPCLUB USA

◊◊◊RECREATION: rec hall, swim pool, boating, dock, lake fishing, putting green, golf nearby, shuffleboard court shuffleboard court, activities.

Pets welcome. Open all yr. Planned activities winter only. Big rigs welcome. Clubs welcome. Rate in 2010 $30 for 2 persons. MC/VISA/DISC. CCUSA 50% Discount. CCUSA reservations Required, CCUSA max stay 5 days. Discount available Apr thru Nov. No refunds on deposits.

Phone: (800)856-2105
Address: 3006 14th Ave SE, Ruskin, FL 33570
Lat/Lon: 27.70594/-82.39389
Email: sunlakerv@aol.com

SEE AD THIS PAGE

(S) Tampa South RV Resort—(Hillsborough) *From jct I-75 (exit 240) & Hwy 674: Go 3 mi W on Hwy 674,then 2 mi S on US 41. Enter on L.* ◊◊◊◊FACILITIES: 121 sites, typical site width 30 ft, 121 full hkups, (20/30/50 amps), 70 pull-thrus, WiFi Instant Internet at site, WiFi Internet central location, family camping, RV storage, dump, non-guest dump $, laundry, picnic tables, patios. ◊◊◊◊RECREATION: swim pool, boating, canoeing, kayaking, dock, saltwater fishing, shuffleboard court 4 shuffleboard courts, activities, horseshoes. Pets welcome, breed restrict. No tents. Open all yr. Big rigs welcome. Rate in 2010 $35-45 for 2 persons. MC/VISA/DISC/AMEX. Member FLARVC. CCUSA 50% Discount. CCUSA reservations Recommended, CCUSA max stay 5 days.

CAMPCLUB USA

Phone: (813)645-1202
Address: 2900 So. US Hwy 41, Ruskin, FL 33570
Lat/Lon: 27.69648/-82.45942
Email: tampasouthrv@yahoo.com
Web: www.tampasouthrvresort.com

ST. AUGUSTINE—B-4

(S) ANASTASIA STATE PARK—(St. Johns) *From jct US 1 & Hwy A1A: Go 3 mi S on Hwy A1A at Hwy 3 (St. Augustine Beach). Enter on R.* FACILITIES: 139 sites, 30 ft max RV length, 139 W&E, tenting, dump, laundry, ltd groc. RECREATION: saltwater swim, boating, canoeing, saltwater fishing, playground. Open all yr. Phone: (904)461-2033.

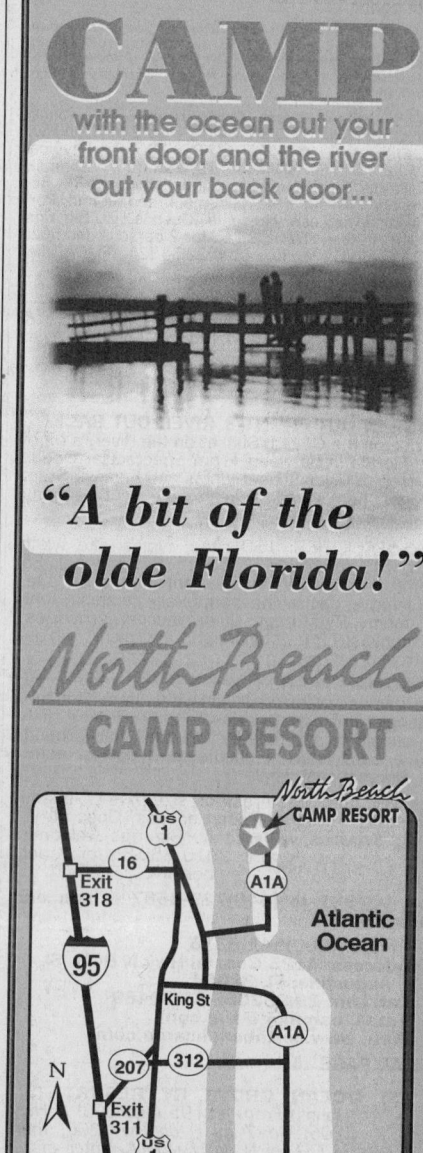

ST. AUGUSTINE—Continued on next page

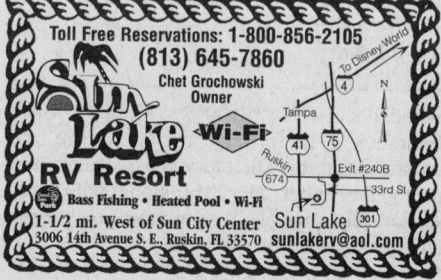

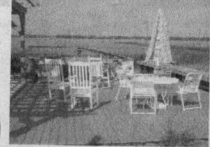

ST. AUGUSTINE—Continued

(S) FAVER-DYKES STATE PARK—(St. Johns) *From town: Go 15 mi S on US-1.* FACILITIES: 30 sites, 30 ft max RV length, 30 W&E, tenting, dump. RECREATION: boating, canoeing, ramp, dock, saltwater fishing, playground. No pets. Open all yr. Phone: (904)794-0997.

(W) Indian Forest Campground—(St. Johns) *From jct I-95 (exit 311) & Hwy 207: Go 2 mi E on Hwy 207. Enter on L.* ◆◆◆FACILITIES: 105 sites, typical site width 30 ft, 86 full hkups, 19 W&E, (30/50 amps), 40 pull-thrus, family camping, dump, laundry. ◆RECREATION: pond fishing. Pets welcome, breed restrict. Partial handicap access. No tents. Open all yr. Big rigs welcome. Rate in 2010 $33-43 for 2 persons. Member ARVC, FLARVC. Phone: (800)223-4324. FMCA discount.

(NE) NORTH BEACH CAMP RESORT—(St. Johns) *From jct Business US 1 & Hwy A1A: Go 4-1/4 mi N on Hwy A1A. Enter on L.*

OCEAN OUT FRONT & RIVER OUT BACK!

Sunrise on the Ocean, Sunset on the River, a bit of Olde Florida In Between! From Spectacular Ocean Sunrises to River Sunset Vistas and Endless Stars at Night, here's your ticket to the best camping vacation ever!

◆◆◆FACILITIES: 150 sites, typical site width 40 ft, 143 full hkups, 7 W&E, (30/50 amps), 35 pull-thrus, cable TV, WiFi Instant Internet at site, WiFi Internet central location, family camping, tenting, cabins, RV storage, dump, laundry, groceries, RV supplies, LP gas by weight, ice, picnic tables, controlled access.

◆◆◆◆◆RECREATION: rec hall, rec room/area, coin games, swim pool, saltwater swim, hot tub, boating, ramp, dock, saltwater/river fishing, fishing supplies, golf nearby, bsktball, playground, shuffleboard court 4 shuffleboard courts, activities, horseshoes, v-ball.

Pets welcome, breed restrict, size restrict, quantity restrict. Partial handicap access. Open all yr. Group activities winter only. Big rigs welcome. Clubs welcome. Rate in 2010 $50-85 for 2 persons. MC/VISA/DISC. Member ARVC, FLARVC.

Text 107921 to (440)725-8687 to see our Visual Tour.

Phone: (800)542-8316
Address: 4125 Coastal Hwy N BCH, St Augustine, FL 32084
Lat/Lon: 29.95206/-81.30489
Email: camping@aug.com
Web: www.northbeachcamp.com

SEE AD PAGE 161

(S) OCEAN GROVE RV RESORT—(St. Johns) *From jct I-95 (exit 305) & Hwy 206: Go 7 mi E on Hwy 206, then 3-1/2 mi N on Hwy A1A. Enter on L.* ◆◆◆FACILITIES: 198 sites, typical site width 41 ft, 198 full hkups, (20/30/50 amps), some extd stay sites, 50 pull-thrus, cable TV, WiFi Internet central location, family camping, tenting, RV storage, laundry, LP gas by weight/by meter, ice, picnic tables, patios, controlled access.

◆◆◆◆◆RECREATION: rec hall, pavilion, equipped pavilion, swim pool, wading pool, hot tub, boating, canoeing, kayaking, ramp, dock, saltwater fishing, golf nearby, bsktball, 2 bike rentals, playground, shuffleboard court shuffleboard court, activities, horseshoes, v-ball.

Pets welcome, breed restrict. Partial handicap access. Open all yr. Planned Group Activities during Winter months. Big rigs welcome. Clubs welcome. Rate in 2010 $60-70 for 4 persons. MC/VISA/DISC/AMEX. Member ARVC, FLARVC.

ST. AUGUSTINE—Continued
OCEAN GROVE RV RESORT—Continued

Phone: (800)342-4007
Address: 4225 Hwy A1A S, St Augustine, FL 32080
Lat/Lon: 29.81781/-81.26973
Email: debbie@oceangroveresort.com
Web: www.oceangroveresort.com

SEE AD PAGE 161

(W) PACETTI'S MARINA RV PARK & FISHING RESORT—(St. Johns) *From I-95 (exit 318) & Hwy 16: Go 9 mi W on Hwy 16, then 2-1/4 mi W on Hwy 13 N/Hwy 16. Enter on R.*

◆◆◆FACILITIES: 147 sites, 147 full hkups, (30/50 amps), some extd stay sites, 40 pull-thrus, WiFi Internet central location, family camping, tenting, cabins, dump, laundry, ltd groc, RV supplies, marine gas, ice, picnic tables.

◆◆◆RECREATION: rec hall, pavilion, coin games, boating, canoeing, kayaking, ramp, dock, river fishing, fishing supplies, golf nearby, play equipment, horseshoes, v-ball.

Pets welcome, size restrict. Open all yr. Escort to site. Rate in 2010 $30-35 for 4 persons. MC/VISA. Member ARVC, FLARVC. CCUSA 50% Discount. CCUSA reservations Recommended, CCUSA max stay Unlimited.

Phone: (904)522-1374
Address: 6550 State Road 13N, St. Augustine, FL 32092
Lat/Lon: 29.98590/-81.56781
Email: pacetti@myexcel.com
Web: www.pacettirv.com

SEE AD PAGE 161

(S) St. Augustine Beach KOA Kampground Resort—(St. Johns) *From jct I-95 (exit 311-Old 94) & Hwy 207: Go 4 mi E on Hwy 207, then 4 mi E on Hwy 312, then 1/4 mi S on Hwy A1A, then 50 feet W on Pope Rd. Enter on L.* ◆◆◆◆FACILITIES: 119 sites, typical site width 40 ft, 84 full hkups, 35 W&E, (20/30/50 amps), 61 pull-thrus, family camping, tenting, dump, laundry, ltd groc. ◆◆◆◆RECREATION: swim pool, boating, dock, lake fishing, playground. Pets welcome. Partial handicap access. Open all yr. Big rigs welcome. Rate in 2010 $51.95-98.95 for 2 persons. Member ARVC, FLARVC. KOA discount.

Phone: (800)562-4022
Address: 525 W Pope Rd, St Augustine, FL 32080
Lat/Lon: 29.85873/-81.28239
Email: staugkoa@aol.com
Web: www.koa.com/where/fl/09205/

(SW) St. John's RV Park—(St. Johns) *From I-95 (exit 311) & Hwy 207: Go 1/4 mi E on Hwy 207. Enter on L.* ◆◆◆FACILITIES: 78 sites, 57 full hkups, 9 W&E, (20/30/50 amps), 50 amps ($), 16 pull-thrus, cable TV, WiFi Instant Internet at site, family camping, RV storage, dump, non-guest dump $, laundry, picnic tables. RECREATION: lake fishing, horseshoes. Pets welcome, breed restrict. Partial handicap access. No tents. Open all yr. Big rigs welcome. Rate in 2010 $28-33 for 2 persons. MC/VISA. CCUSA 50% Discount. CCUSA reservations Recommended, CCUSA max stay 14 days. No tenting.

Phone: (904)824-9840
Address: 2493 SR 207, St. Augustine, FL 32086
Lat/Lon: 29.82913/-81.37713

Woodall's Tip... 100% Money Back Guarantee... If for any reason you're not satisfied with this Directory, please return it to us by December 31, 2011 along with your sales receipt, and we'll reimburse you for the amount you paid for the Directory.

ST. AUGUSTINE—Continued

(W) STAGECOACH RV PARK—(St. Johns) *From jct I-95 (exit 318) & Hwy 16: Go 3/10 mi W on Hwy 16, then 1 block S on Toms Rd, then 3/10 mi W on CR 208. Enter on L.*

◆◆◆◆FACILITIES: 80 sites, typical site width 45 ft, 80 full hkups, (30/50 amps), many extd stay sites (winter), 60 pull-thrus, WiFi Instant Internet at site, family camping, RV storage, dump, non-guest dump $, laundry, RV supplies, LP gas by weight/by meter, ice, picnic tables.

◆◆RECREATION: rec hall, rec room/area, golf nearby, bsktball, play equipment, horseshoes.

Pets welcome, breed restrict. Partial handicap access. No tents. Open all yr. Big rigs welcome. Clubs welcome. Rate in 2010 $38-41 for 2 persons. MC/VISA/DISC. Member ARVC, FLARVC. FMCA discount.

Phone: (877)824-2319
Address: 2711 CR 208, St. Augustine, FL 32092
Lat/Lon: 29.91930/-81.42239
Email: stagecoachrvpark@bellsouth.net
Web: www.stagecoachrv.net

SEE AD THIS PAGE AND AD TRAVEL SECTION PAGE 74

ST. CLOUD—C-4

(SW) Lake Toho RV Resort (RV SPACES)—(Osceola) *From jct US 192 & Kissimmee Park Rd: Go 4 mi S, then 4 mi E on Kissimmee Park Rd. Enter on L.* FACILITIES: 200 sites, 36 ft max RV length, 200 full hkups, (30/50 amps), phone on-site Internet (needs activ), dump, laundry, picnic tables, patios. RECREATION: pavilion, boating, canoeing, kayaking, ramp, lake fishing, fishing supplies. Pets welcome, breed restrict, size restrict, quantity restrict. No tents. Open all yr. Rate in 2010 $25-30 for 2 persons. CCUSA 50% Discount. CCUSA reservations Recommended, CCUSA max stay 4 days, Cash only for CCUSA disc. Discount not available Jan thru Mar.

Phone: (407)892-8795
Address: 4715 Kissimmee Park Rd, St Cloud, FL 34772
Lat/Lon: 28.202228/-81.37548

THE FLORIDIAN RV RESORT—(Osceola) *From jct Florida Tnpk (exit 254) & Hwy 528A/528: Go 12 mi E on Hwy 528A/528 (Bee Line Expwy), then 7 mi S on Hwy 15 to jct Hwy 530. Enter on L.*

BEST BASS FISHING +DISNEY PARKS & MORE

On Kissimmee's beautiful chain of lakes, boat launching right from our facilities for some of the best big bass fishing, minutes from Disney & other theme parks. A full amenity park +Free WIFI Internet and Digital TV.

◆◆◆FACILITIES: 488 sites, typical site width 20 ft, 38 ft max RV length, 388 full hkups, 100 W&E, (30/50 amps), some extd stay sites (winter), 75 pull-thrus, cable TV, WiFi Instant Internet at site, phone Internet central location, family camping, tenting, RV storage, dump, non-guest dump $, laundry, picnic tables, patios, controlled access.

◆◆◆RECREATION: rec hall, rec room/area, 2 swim pools, hot tub, boating, ramp, lake fishing, golf nearby, play equipment, 4 shuffleboard courts, activities, tennis, horseshoes.

Pets welcome, breed restrict, size restrict, quantity restrict. Partial handicap access. Open all yr. Planned activities & church services, winter only. Clubs welcome. Rate in 2010 $37.29 for 2 persons. MC/VISA/DISC/AMEX/Debit. CCUSA 50% Discount. CCUSA reservations Recommended, CCUSA max stay 7 days, CCUSA disc. not avail holidays. Discount available May thru Oct.

Phone: (866)444-1109
Address: 5150 Boggy Creek Rd, St. Cloud, FL 34771
Lat/Lon: 28.33917/-81.23500
Email: floridian1@leasco.net
Web: www.florida-rv-parks.com/floridian.html

SEE AD TRAVEL SECTION PAGE 79

ST. GEORGE ISLAND—B-1

(E) ST. GEORGE ISLAND STATE PARK—(Franklin) *Cross the bridge to St George Island & go East.* FACILITIES: 60 sites, 33 ft max RV length, 60 W&E, tenting, dump. RECREATION: saltwater swim, boating, canoeing, ramp, saltwater fishing, playground. Pets welcome. Open all yr. Phone: (904)927-2111.

ST. JAMES CITY—E-3

(N) PINE ISLAND RESORT—(Lee) *From jct Hwy 78 & Hwy 767: Go 5-1/2 mi S on Hwy 767. Enter on L.*

WELCOME

◊◊◊◊FACILITIES: 364 sites, typical site width 35 ft, 364 full hkups, (20/30/50 amps), some extd stay sites (winter), cable TV, WiFi Instant Internet at site ($), family camping, tenting, RV's/park model rentals, cabins, dump, non-guest dump $, laundry, ltd groc, RV supplies, LP gas by weight/by meter, ice, picnic tables, patios.

◊◊◊◊RECREATION: rec hall, rec room/area, swim pool, saltwater swim, hot tub, lake fishing, golf nearby, bsktball, 15 bike rentals, playground, shuffleboard court 2 shuffleboard courts, activities, tennis, horseshoes, sports field.

Pets welcome, breed restrict. Partial handicap access. Open all yr. Local tours & group activities winter only. Big rigs welcome. Escort to site. Clubs welcome. Rate in 2010 $25-52 for 2 persons. MC/VISA/DISC/AMEX/Debit. Member ARVC, FLARVC. KOA discount.

Phone: (800)562-8505
Address: 5120 Stringfellow Rd, St James City, FL 33956
Lat/Lon: 26.53486/-82.08831
Email: pineisland@mhchomes.com
Web: www.rvonthego.com

SEE AD ALACHUA PAGE 93

ST. PETERSBURG—C-3

(W) KOA-St. Petersburg—(Pinellas) *From jct I-275 (exit 25) & 38th Ave N: Go 5-1/2 mi N on 38th Ave, then 1-1/2 mi N on Tyrone (Bay Pines), then 1/2 mi N on 95th St. Enter at end.* ◊◊◊◊FACILITIES: 398 sites, typical site width 25 ft, 40 ft max RV length, 341 full hkups, 40 W&E, (20/30/50 amps), 50 amps ($), 17 no hkups, 75 pull-thrus, family camping, tenting, dump, laundry, full svc store. ◊◊◊◊◊RECREATION: swim pool, boating, canoeing, ramp, dock, saltwater fishing, playground. Pets welcome, breed restrict, quantity restrict. Partial handicap access. Open all yr. Rate in 2010 $59-95 for 2 persons. Member ARVC, FLARVC. Phone: (800)562-7714. KOA discount.

(N) Robert's Mobile Home & RV Resort—(Pinellas) *From jct I-275 & Hwy 694: Go 1 mi W on Hwy 694. Enter on L.* ◊◊◊◊FACILITIES: 450 sites, typical site width 35 ft, 450 full hkups, (20/30/50 amps), WiFi Instant Internet at site ($), phone/cable on-site Internet (needs activ), WiFi Internet central location, family camping, RV storage, dump, non-guest dump $, laundry, ice, picnic tables, patios.

CAMPCLUB USA

◊◊◊◊RECREATION: rec hall, equipped pavilion, swim pool, hot tub, minigolf, bsktball, shuffleboard court 12 shuffleboard courts, activities, tennis, horseshoes, v-ball. Pets welcome, breed restrict, size restrict. No tents. Open all yr. Big rigs welcome. Rate

ST. PETERSBURG—Continued
Robert's Mobile Home & RV Resort—Continued

in 2010 $30-35 for 2 persons. MC/VISA. CCUSA 50% Discount. CCUSA reservations Recommended, CCUSA max stay Unlimited. Discount available Apr thru Oct. Cable can be arranged for longer stays $. Secure high speed WiFi $.

Phone: (727)577-6820
Address: 3390 Gandy Blvd, St Petersburg, FL 33702
Lat/Lon: 27.84267/-82.67924
Email: robertsresort@aol.com
Web: www.robertsrv.com

(N) Treasure Village MH/RV Park (RV SPACES)—(Pinellas) *From jct I-275 & 54th St: Go 1-1/2 mi E on 54th St, then 1 block S on Hwy 92. Enter on L.* FACILITIES: 37 sites, typical site width 18 ft, 36 ft max RV length, 37 full hkups, (20/30 amps), laundry. No tents. Open all yr. Rate in 2010 $31 for 2 persons. Phone: (727)527-1701.

SALT SPRINGS—B-3

(N) Elite Resorts At Salt Springs—(Marion) *From jct CR 314 & Hwy 19: Go 1 mi N on Hwy 19, then 200 yds W on CR 316. Enter on L.* ◊◊◊◊FACILITIES: 475 sites, typical site width 50 ft, 475 full hkups, (20/30/50 amps), 25 pull-thrus, family camping. ◊◊◊◊◊RECREATION: 2 swim pools, lake swim, boating, canoeing, ramp, dock, lake fishing, playground. Pets welcome, breed restrict, quantity restrict. Partial handicap access. No tents. Open all yr. Big rigs welcome. Rate in 2010 $32 for 2 persons. Member ARVC, FLARVC. Phone: (800)356-2460.

(N) OCALA NATIONAL FOREST (Salt Springs Rec. Area)—(Marion) *From jct Hwy-314 & Hwy-19: Go 1 mi N on Hwy-19.* FACILITIES: 160 sites, typical site width 14 ft, 32 ft max RV length, 160 full hkups, tenting, dump. RECREATION: lake swim, boating, canoeing, ramp, lake fishing. Partial handicap access. Open all yr. Phone: (352)685-2048.

SALT SPRINGS—Continued

(N) Salt Springs Resort—(Marion) *From CR 314 & Hwy 19: Go 1 mi N on Hwy 19, then 200 yds W on CR 316. Enter on L.* ◊◊◊◊FACILITIES: 100 sites, typical site width 50 ft, 100 full hkups, (20/30/50 amps), family camping, laundry, ltd groc. ◊◊◊◊◊RECREATION: 2 swim pools, lake swim, boating, canoeing, ramp, dock, lake fishing, playground. Pets welcome, quantity restrict. Partial handicap access. No tents. Age restrict may apply. Open all yr. Big rigs welcome.

SANFORD—C-4

(W) TWELVE OAKS RV RESORT—(Seminole) *From Jct I-4 (exit 101C) & Hwy 46: Go 2 mi W on Hwy 46. Enter on R.*

WELCOME

FUNZONE BETWEEN DAYTONA AND DISNEY
Twelve Oaks is a pristine park in a shady country setting but close to all the goodies. Full facilities and activities. Near mall shopping, restaurants, golfing, gambling, fishing, canoeing, beaches and Disney minutes away.

◊◊◊◊FACILITIES: 247 sites, typical site width 30 ft, 247 full hkups, (20/30/50 amps), many extd stay sites, 34 pull-thrus, WiFi Instant Internet at site, WiFi Internet central location, family camping, RV storage, dump, laundry, RV supplies, LP gas by weight/by meter, picnic tables, patios.

TWELVE OAKS RV RESORT—Continued on next page

Woodall's Tip... Turn to the Travel Section for a list of the RV Parks & Campgrounds that are Internet Friendly and have Wifi.

Woodall's Tip... Gear symbols on maps indicate towns under which Dealer Locations are listed.

◆◆◆◆RECREATION: rec hall, rec room/area, swim pool, golf nearby, shuffleboard court 2 shuffleboard courts, activities, horseshoes, local tours.

Pets welcome, breed restrict, size restrict, quantity restrict. Partial handicap access. No tents. Open all yr. Big rigs welcome. Escort to site. Clubs welcome. Rate in 2010 $32 for 2 persons. MC/VISA. Member ARVC, FLARVC.

Phone: (800)633-9529
Address: 6300 State Rd 46 West, Sanford, FL 32771
Lat/Lon: 28.81206/-81.37150
Email: info@twelveoaksrvresort.com
Web: www.twelveoaksrvresort.com

SEE AD PAGE 163

(N) WEKIVA FALLS RESORT—(Lake) *From jct I-4 & State Road 46 (exit 101C): Go 7 mi W on SR 46, then left on Wekiva River Rd. Enter on L.*

WELCOME

◆◆◆◆FACILITIES: 817 sites, typical site width 40 ft, 817 full hkups, (20/30/50 amps), some extd stay sites (winter), cable TV, ($), WiFi Instant Internet at site ($), phone/cable on-site Internet (needs activ), WiFi Internet central location, family camping, tenting, RV storage, laundry, ltd groc, RV supplies, LP gas by weight, ice, picnic tables, patios, controlled access.

◆◆◆◆◆RECREATION: rec hall, pavilion, equipped pavilion, swim pool, river swim, boating, canoeing, kayaking, ramp, dock, 15 canoe/11 kayak rentals, float trips, river fishing, fishing supplies, golf nearby, activities, horseshoes, sports field, hiking trails, v-ball. Rec open to public.

Pets welcome, breed restrict. Partial handicap access. Open all yr. Big rigs welcome. Escort to site. Clubs welcome. Rate in 2010 $34-40 for 2 persons. MC/VISA/AMEX/Debit. Member ARVC.

Phone: (888)4 WEKIVA
Address: 30700 Wekiva River Rd, Sorrento, FL 32776
Lat/Lon: 28.79476/-81.42580
Email: info@wekivafallsresort.com
Web: www.wekivafallsresort.com

SEE AD PAGE 163

SANTA ROSA BEACH—F-2

(W) TOPSAIL HILL PRESERVE STATE PARK—(Walton) *Eastbound from Destin City limits: Go 8 mi E on US 98, then 1/4 mi S on Hwy 30A. Westbound from jct US 331 & US 98: Go 5 mi W on US 98, then 1/4 mi S on Hwy 30A. Enter on R.* FACILITIES: 178 sites, typical site width 45 ft, 156 full hkups, 22 W&E, (30/50 amps), 20 pull-thrus, family camping, tenting, laundry. RECREATION: swim pool, saltwater swim, saltwater/lake fishing. Pets welcome. Partial handicap access. Open all yr. Big rigs welcome. Phone: (850)267-8330.

SARASOTA—D-3

(SE) MYAKKA RIVER STATE PARK—(Sarasota) *From jct US 41 & Hwy 72: Go 12 mi E on Hwy 72.* FACILITIES: 76 sites, 35 ft max RV length, 76 W&E, tenting, dump, groceries. RECREATION: boating, canoeing, ramp, dock, lake/river fishing, playground. No pets. Open all yr. Phone: (941)361-6511.

(NW) Sarasota Lakes Camping Resort (RV SPACES)—(Sarasota) *From jct I-75 (exit 213) & University Prkwy: Go 5 1/2 mi W on University Prkwy. Enter on L.* FACILITIES: 420 sites, typical site width 20 ft, 420 full hkups, (20/30/50 amps), dump, laundry. RECREATION: swim pool, play equipment. Pets welcome, quantity restrict. No tents. Open all yr. Big rigs welcome. Phone: (941)355-8585.

SARASOTA—Continued on next page

(S) SARASOTA SUNNY SOUTH RV PARK —(Sarasota) *From jct I-75 & Hwy 72 (exit 205): Go 3 mi W on Hwy 72 to US 41, then S on US 41 for 1.5 mi, then E on Doud St 1 blk. Enter on R.*

WELCOME

◇◇◇◇FACILITIES: 43 sites, typical site width 35 ft, 43 full hkups, (20/30/50 amps), many extd stay sites (winter), cable TV, ($), WiFi Instant Internet at site, RV's/park model rentals, laundry, picnic tables, patios.

◇◇◇RECREATION: rec hall, swim pool, golf nearby, activities.

Pets welcome. Partial handicap access. No tents. Age restrict may apply. Open all yr. Big rigs welcome. Rate in 2010 $32.50-36 for 2 persons. MC/VISA/DISC/Debit.

Phone: (941)921-4409
Address: 2100 Doud St, Sarasota, FL 34231
Lat/Lon: 27.24231/-82.50391
Email: info@srqsunnysouth.com
Web: www.srqsunnysouth.com

SEE AD PAGE 164 AND AD TRAVEL SECTION PAGE 73

(E) SUN-N-FUN RV RESORT—(Manatee) *From jct I-75 (exit 210) & Hwy 780 (Fruitville Rd): Go 1 mi E on Hwy 780. Enter on L.*

WELCOME

◇◇◇◇◇FACILITIES: 1491 sites, typical site width 35 ft, 1491 full hkups, (30/50 amps), many extd stay sites (winter), 50 pull-thrus, cable TV, WiFi Instant Internet at site, phone/cable on-site Internet (needs activ), WiFi Internet central location, family camping, tenting, RV's/park model rentals, RV storage, dump, non-guest dump $, laundry, RV supplies, LP gas by weight/by meter, picnic tables, patios, controlled access.

CAMPCLUB USA

◇◇◇◇◇RECREATION: rec hall, rec room/area, equipped pavilion, swim pool, wading pool, hot tub, boating, no motors, canoeing, kayaking, lake fishing, mini-golf, golf nearby, bsktball, 75 bike rentals, playground, shuffleboard court 18 shuffleboard courts, activities, tennis, horseshoes, v-ball.

Pets welcome, quantity restrict. Partial handicap access. Open all yr. Group activities winter season only. Big rigs welcome. Clubs welcome. Green Friendly. Rate in 2010 $34-75 per vehicle. MC/VISA/DISC/AMEX. Member ARVC, FLARVC. FMCA discount. CCUSA 50% Discount. CCUSA reservations Accepted, CCUSA max stay 2 days. Discount not available Jan 15 to Mar 15.

Phone: (800)843-2421
Address: 7125 Fruitville Rd., Sarasota, FL 34240
Lat/Lon: 27.339349/-82.426901
Email: gweir@sunnfunfl.com
Web: www.sunnfunfl.com

SEE AD THIS PAGE

SARASOTA—Continued on next page

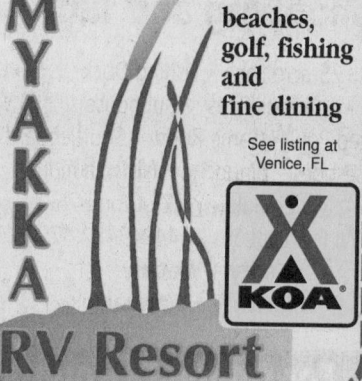

SARASOTA—Continued

(W) Turtle Beach Campground at Turtle Beach Park—(Sarasota) *From jct I-75 & exit 205 (Clark Rd): Go W on Clark Rd/Hwy 72 for 6 mi to Siest Key to Midnight Pass Rd, then S on Midnight Pass Rd for 2.5 mi to Park. Enter on R.* FACILITIES: 50 sites, typical site width 20 ft, 50 full hkups, (30/50 amps), 50 amps ($), family camping, tenting, laundry. RECREATION: saltwater swim, canoeing, saltwater fishing, playground. No pets. Open all yr. Rate in 2010 $32-60 for 2 persons. Member ARVC, FLARVC. Phone: (941)349-3839.

SEBASTIAN—C-5

(N) LONG POINT PARK (Brevard County Park)—(Brevard) *From town: Go 7 mi N on Hwy-A1A.* FACILITIES: 170 sites, 15 full hkups, 155 W&E, (20/30 amps), tenting, dump, laundry, ltd groc. RECREATION: ramp, dock, saltwater fishing, playground. Open all yr. Phone: (321)952-4532.

(E) PELICAN'S LANDING RESORT—(Indian River) *From jct I-95 (exit 156) & Hwy 512: Go 6-1/4 mi E on Hwy 512, then 1 mi S on Indian River Dr. Enter on L.*

BOUTIQUE WATERFRONT RV RESORT
Breathtaking Premium 5-W Big Rig Sites (46X80) with fabulous Salt Water/River Fishing-a ramp/pier/docks. Enjoy our new Boat House Pavilion with friends to watch a glorious sunrise. Limited number of sites-Reserve Today!

◇◇◇◇◇FACILITIES: 17 sites, typical site width 46 ft, accepts self-contained units only, 17 full hkups, (20/30/50 amps), mostly extd stay sites, phone/WiFi/cable Instant Internet at site, phone/cable on-site Internet (needs activ), family camping, cabins, laundry, RV supplies, picnic tables, patios, grills.

SEBASTIAN—Continued
PELICAN'S LANDING RESORT—Continued

◇◇◇◇RECREATION: rec hall, equipped pavilion, boating, ramp, dock, saltwater fishing, golf nearby, shuffleboard court shuffleboard court, activities.

Pets welcome, breed restrict. No tents. Open all yr. No restrooms. No showers. Reservations needed. Big rigs welcome. Rate in 2010 $40-60 for 2 persons. MC/VISA/DISC. Member FLARVC. CCUSA 50% Discount. CCUSA reservations Required, CCUSA max stay 3 days, Cash only for CCUSA disc., CCUSA disc. not avail F,Sa, CCUSA disc. not avail holidays. Discount available May thru Oct on standard sites. No restrooms, no showers. Pet breed restrictions-call for details.

Text 107906 to (440)725-8687 to see our Visual Tour.

Phone: (772)589-5188
Address: 11330 Indian River Dr., Sebastian, FL 32958
Lat/Lon: 27.80042/-80.46086
Email: info@pelicanslandingresort.com
Web: pelicanslandingrv.com

SEE AD TRAVEL SECTION PAGE 69

(S) SEBASTIAN INLET STATE PARK—(Brevard) *From jct Hwy-510 & Hwy-A1A: Go 7 mi N on Hwy-A1A.* FACILITIES: 51 sites, 32 ft max RV length, 51 W&E, (30 amps), tenting, dump, laundry. RECREATION: saltwater swim, boating, ramp, dock, saltwater fishing, playground. Partial handicap access. Open all yr. Phone: (772)589-9659.

Where Will You Camp Tonight? Stay With a Campground in Woodall's.

SEBASTIAN—Continued

(SE) VERO BEACH KAMP INC—(Indian River) *From jct I-95 (exit 156) & Hwy 512: Go 6 mi E on Hwy 512, then 4-1/4 mi S on US 1. Enter on L.*

◇◇◇FACILITIES: 140 sites, typical site width 30 ft, 120 full hkups, 20 W&E, (20/30/50 amps), many extd stay sites (winter), cable TV, phone/cable on-site Internet (needs activ), WiFi Internet central location, family camping, tenting, cabins, RV storage, dump, laundry, RV supplies, LP gas by weight/by meter, ice, picnic tables, patios, grills.

◇◇◇RECREATION: rec hall, rec room/area, swim pool, golf nearby, bsktball, playground, shuffleboard court shuffleboard court, activities, horseshoes.

Pets welcome. Open all yr. Group activities winter only. Big rigs welcome. Rate in 2010 $37-49 for 2 persons. MC/VISA/DISC/AMEX. Member ARVC, FLARVC.

Phone: (877)589-5643
Address: 8850 N US 1-Wabasso, Sebastian, FL 32970
Lat/Lon: 27.75474/-80.43611
Web: www.verobeachkamp.com

SEE AD VERO BEACH PAGE 176

(S) Whispering Palms RV Resort—(Indian River) *From jct I-95 (exit 156) & Hwy 512: Go 6 mi E on Hwy 512, then 2-1/4 mi S on US 1. Enter on R.* ◇◇◇◇FACILITIES: 250 sites, typical site width 28 ft, 250 full hkups, (30/50 amps), 15 pull-thrus, cable TV, WiFi Instant Internet at site, phone/cable on-site Internet (needs activ), WiFi Internet central location, family camping, RV storage, dump, non-guest dump $, laundry, LP gas by weight/by meter, picnic tables, patios. ◇◇◇◇RECREATION: rec hall, 2 swim pools, lake fishing, shuffleboard court 8 shuffleboard courts, activities, tennis, horseshoes. Pets welcome. No tents. Open all yr. Big rigs welcome. Rate in 2010 $40 for 2 persons. MC/VISA/DISC/AMEX. Member ARVC, FLARVC. CCUSA 50% Discount. CCUSA reservations Accepted, CCUSA max stay 7 days, CCUSA disc. not avail holidays. Not available Oct 1- Apr 1. 55+ Park. No tents or pop-ups. Cable TV some sites.

Phone: (800)414-0814
Address: 10305 US Hwy 1 S, Sebastian, FL 32958
Lat/Lon: 27.78203/-80.45251
Email: whisperingpalms@bellsouth.net
Web: www.whisperingpinesresort.com

SEBRING—D-4

(SW) Buttonwood Bay—(Highlands) *From jct Hwy 17 & US 27 & 98: Go 5 mi S on US 27. Enter on R.* ◇◇◇◇FACILITIES: 534 sites, typical site width 40 ft, 534 full hkups, (30/50 amps), cable TV, ($), WiFi Instant Internet at site ($), phone/cable on-site Internet (needs activ), cable Internet central location, family camping, RV storage, dump, laundry, ice, picnic tables, patios. ◇◇◇◇◇RECREATION: rec hall, 2 swim pools, boating, ramp, dock, lake fishing, mini-golf, bsktball, shuffleboard court 16 shuffleboard courts, activities, tennis, horseshoes, hiking trails. Pets welcome, breed restrict, quantity restrict. Partial handicap access. No tents. Age restrict may apply. Open all yr. Big rigs welcome. Rate in 2010 $28-40 for 2 persons. MC/VISA/DISC/Debit. Member FLARVC. CCUSA 50% Discount. CCUSA reservations Required, CCUSA max stay 7 days. Discount not available Nov 30-Apr 30. Additional charges may apply.

Phone: (866)655-5565
Address: 10001 US 27 S, Sebring, FL 33876
Lat/Lon: 27.40710/-81.41693
Email: sunresv@aol.com
Web: www.buttonwoodbay.com

(SE) Highland Oaks RV Resort (RV SPACES)—(Highlands) *From jct US 27 & US 98: Go 1/4 mi E on US 98, then 1/2 mi N on CR 17, then 1 blk W on Tartan St, then S on Old Plantation Ave (stay on pavement).*

Highland Oaks RV Resort—Continued on next page

SEBRING—Continued
Highland Oaks RV Resort—Continued

Enter on R. FACILITIES: 106 sites, typical site width 20 ft, 38 ft max RV length, 106 full hkups, (30/50 amps), 3 pull-thrus, laundry. Pets welcome, breed restrict. No tents. Open all yr. Rate in 2010 $25 for 2 persons. Phone: (863)655-1685.

(NW) Highland Wheel Estates (RV SPACES)—(Highlands) *From jct US 27 & Hwy 634 (Hammock Rd): Go 1 block W on Hwy 634. Enter on R.* FACILITIES: 120 sites, typical site width 15 ft, 30 ft max RV length, 120 full hkups, (30/50 amps), 8 pull-thrus, WiFi Instant Internet at site, WiFi Internet central location, family camping, tenting, RV storage, dump, non-guest dump $, laundry, patios. RECREATION: rec hall, swim pool, shuffleboard court 4 shuffleboard courts, activities, horseshoes. Pets welcome, breed restrict, quantity restrict. Age restrict may apply. Open all yr. Rate in 2010 $17.50-35 for 2 persons. CCUSA 50% Discount. CCUSA reservations Required, CCUSA max stay Unlimited, Cash only for CCUSA disc. Discount available May 1-Sep 30.

Phone: (863)385-6232
Address: 1004 Hammock Rd, Sebring, FL 33872
Lat/Lon: 27.47499/-81.47503
Web: www.hwepark.com

(W) HIGHLANDS HAMMOCK STATE PARK—(Highlands) *From jct US-98 & US-27: Go 6 mi NW on US-27, exit Hwy-634.* FACILITIES: 143 sites, 30 ft max RV length, 143 W&E, tenting, dump, laundry. RECREATION: playground. Partial handicap access. Open all yr. Phone: (941)386-6094.

(S) Lake Josephine RV Resort—(Highlands) *From jct US 98 & US 27: Go 3 mi S on US 27. Enter on R.* ◆◆◆FACILITIES: 180 sites, typical site width 22 ft, 38 ft max RV length, 180 full hkups, (30/50 amps), 20 pull-thrus, phone/cable on-site Internet (needs activ), WiFi Internet central location, laundry, LP gas by weight/by meter, ice, picnic tables, patios. ◆◆◆◆RECREATION: rec hall, swim pool, boating, canoeing, kayaking, ramp, dock, lake fishing, shuffleboard court 3 shuffleboard courts, activities, tennis, horseshoes. Pets welcome, breed restrict. Partial handicap access. No tents. Open all yr. Rate in 2010 $22-32 for 2 persons. MC/VISA/DISC. CCUSA 50% Discount. CCUSA reservations Required, CCUSA max stay 4 days, CCUSA disc. not avail F,Sa,S, CCUSA disc. not avail holidays. Discount available Apr thru Oct.

Phone: (877)503-4141
Address: 10809 US Hwy 27 S, Sebring, FL 33876
Lat/Lon: 27.40230/-81.41685
Email: lakeJORV@yahoo.com
Web: www.lakejorv.com

(S) Sebring Grove RV Resort—(Highlands) *From jct Hwy-17 & US-27/98: Go 1 mi S on US-27. Enter on R.* ◆◆◆FACILITIES: 114 sites, typical site width 15 ft, 38 ft max RV length, 114 full hkups, (30/50 amps), 8 pull-thrus, laundry. ◆◆◆RECREATION: swim pool. Pets welcome, breed restrict. No tents. Age restrict may apply. Open all yr. Rate in 2010 $38 for 2 persons. Phone: (863)382-1660.

(NW) Sunny Pines (RV SPACES)—(Highlands) *From jct Hwy 634A & US 27: Go 1-1/2 mi S on US 27. Enter on L.* FACILITIES: 134 sites, typical site width 20 ft, 134 full hkups, (30/50 amps), laundry. RECREATION: swim pool. Pets welcome, breed restrict, size restrict, quantity restrict. No tents. Open all yr. Rate in 2010 $30 for 2 persons. Phone: (863)385-4144. FMCA discount.

(NW) THE OUTBACK RV RESORT AT TANGLEWOOD—(Highlands) *From jct Hwy 634A & US 27: Go 3/4 mi N on US 27. Enter on L.*

CENTRAL FLORIDA PREMIER 5W RV RESORT
Live the Florida Lifestyle at our 40+ RV resort-Chipping & putting greens, 2 clubhouses, billiards, laundry, tennis, pickleball, pitanque & more at this gated resort with big rig sites, WiFi, Cable & central to FL attractions.

◆◆◆◆◆FACILITIES: 272 sites, typical site width 50 ft, 272 full hkups, (20/30/50 amps), mostly extd stay sites (winter), cable TV, phone/cable on-site Internet (needs activ), WiFi Internet central location, RV storage, dump, laundry, ice, picnic tables, patios, controlled access.

◆◆◆◆◆RECREATION: rec hall, rec room/area, swim pool, pond fishing, putting green, golf nearby, bsktball, shuffleboard court 8 shuffleboard courts, activities, tennis, horseshoes, v-ball, local tours.

Pets welcome, breed restrict. Partial handicap access. No tents. Age restrict may apply. Open all yr. Big rigs welcome. Escort to site. Clubs welcome. MC/VISA/DISC/Debit.

SEBRING—Continued
THE OUTBACK RV RESORT AT TANGLEWOOD—Continued

Phone: (888)402-1501
Address: 3000 Tanglewood Pkwy, Sebring, FL 33872
Lat/Lon: 27.52378/-81.49957
Email: rvinfo@tanglerv.com
Web: www.tanglerv.com

SEE AD PAGE 166

Whispering Pines Village—(Highlands) *From jct US 27/98 & Hwy 634 (Hammock Rd): Go 3/4 mi W on Hwy 634, then 3/4 mi N on Brunns Rd. Enter on L.* ◆◆◆FACILITIES: 154 sites, typical site width 22 ft, 154 full hkups, (30/50 amps), family camping, tenting, laundry. ◆◆◆RECREATION: swim pool. Pets welcome. Age restrict may apply. Open all yr. Big rigs welcome. Rate in 2010 $45 per vehicle. Phone: (863)385-8806.

(S) WOODY'S RV RESORT—(Highlands) *From jct Hwy 17 & US 27/98: Go 1 mi S on Hwy 27.*

◆◆◆◆FACILITIES: 110 sites, typical site width 20 ft, 110 full hkups, (30/50 amps), mostly extd stay sites (winter), 15 pull-thrus, WiFi Instant Internet at site ($), WiFi Internet central location, family camping, RV storage, laundry, LP gas by weight, picnic tables, patios.

◆◆◆RECREATION: rec hall, pavilion, swim pool, golf nearby, shuffleboard court 2 shuffleboard courts, activities, horseshoes.

Pets welcome. Partial handicap access. No tents. Open all yr. Big rigs welcome. Clubs welcome. Rate in 2010 $30-35 for 2 persons. CCUSA 50% Discount. CCUSA reservations Recommended, CCUSA max stay 7 days, Cash only for CCUSA disc., CCUSA disc. not avail holidays. Discount available May thru Oct.

Phone: (863)385-0500
Address: 4414 US 27 South, Sebring, FL 33870
Lat/Lon: 27.46006/-81.42741
Email: cww4003@earthlink.net
Web: www.woodysrvresort.com

SEE AD PAGE 166

SILVER SPRINGS—B-3

(E) LAKE WALDENA RESORT—(Marion) *From jct Hwy-35 & Hwy-40: Go 8 mi E on Hwy-40. Enter on R.*

◆◆◆FACILITIES: 104 sites, typical site width 30 ft, 100 full hkups, 4 W&E, (20/30/50 amps), 50 amps ($), mostly extd stay sites (winter), cable TV, WiFi Instant Internet at site, family camping, tenting, dump, non-guest dump $, laundry, ltd groc, RV supplies, ice, picnic tables, patios, wood.

◆◆◆◆RECREATION: rec hall, pavilion, lake swim, boating, electric motors only, canoeing, kayaking, dock, 5 rowboat rentals, lake fishing, fishing supplies, golf nearby, bsktball, playground, shuffleboard court 4 shuffleboard courts, activities, horseshoes.

Pets welcome, breed restrict. Open all yr. Closed Christmas, New Year's & Thanksgiving day. Big rigs welcome. Escort to site. Rate in 2010 $22-25 for 4 persons. MC/VISA/DISC. Member ARVC, FLARVC. CCUSA 50% Discount. CCUSA reservations Accepted, CCUSA max stay 7 days. Discount not available Oct 31st-May 1 & Memorial Day weekend.

Phone: (800)748-7898
Address: 13582 E Highway 40, Silver Springs, FL 34488
Lat/Lon: 29.19872/-81.92867
Email: lwaldenaresort@earthlink.net
Web: www.lakewaldena.com

SEE AD OCALA PAGE 145

(E) OCALA NATIONAL FOREST (Fore Lake Campground)—(Marion) *From town: Go 11.8 mi E on Hwy 40, then 6 mi NE on Hwy 314. Enter on L.* FACILITIES: 31 sites, typical site width 12 ft, 35 ft max RV length, 31 no hkups, tenting. RECREATION: lake swim, boating, no motors, lake fishing. Open all yr. Phone: (352)625-2520.

(E) Whispering Pines RV Park—(Marion) *From jct Hwy 314 & Hwy 40: Go 1 mi E on Hwy 40, then 1/2 mi S on NE 118th Ave, then 1/4 mi W on NE 19th St, then 200 yds S on NE 115th Ave. Enter on R.* ◆◆◆FACILITIES: 65 sites, typical site width 30 ft, 62 full hkups, 3 W&E, (30/50 amps), 50 amps ($), 19 pull-thrus, cable TV, cable Internet central location, family camping, dump, laundry, RV supplies, picnic tables, wood. ◆◆RECREATION: rec hall, shuffleboard court shuffleboard court, activities, horseshoes. Pets welcome, quantity restrict. No tents. Open all yr. Rate in 2010 $28 for 2 persons. Member ARVC, FLARVC. CCUSA 50% Discount. CCUSA reservations Recommended, CCUSA max stay 14 days, Cash only for CCUSA disc. Discount available Apr 1- Oct 31. Pets must be friendly, leashed when outdoors & picked up after.

SILVER SPRINGS—Continued
Whispering Pines RV Park—Continued

Phone: (352)625-1295
Address: 1700 NE 115th Ave, Silver Springs, FL 34488
Lat/Lon: 29.20443/-81.96307
Email: whisperingpinesrvpark@yahoo.com
Web: www.wprvp.com

(E) WILDERNESS RV PARK ESTATES—(Marion) *From jct I-75 (exit 358) & Hwy 326: Go 9 mi E on Hwy 326, then 3 mi E on Hwy 40 (Just over bridge). Enter on L.*

WILDERNESS RV RESORT SELLS RV LOTS!
Own & enjoy one of our 412 deeded 55+ RV lots at the Ocklawaha River along the Greenway. One section features DELUXE big rig RV lots, & other park models. Enjoy nearby shopping convenience & nature in a serene setting. 877-900-9399.

◆◆◆◆◆FACILITIES: 278 sites, 40 ft max RV length, 278 full hkups, (30/50 amps), mostly extd stay sites, 48 pull-thrus, cable TV, WiFi Instant Internet at site ($), WiFi Internet central location, RV's/park model rentals, RV storage, dump, non-guest dump $, laundry, ltd groc, RV supplies, LP gas by weight/by meter, ice, controlled access.

◆◆◆◆◆RECREATION: rec hall, pavilion, 3 swim pools, hot tub, boating, canoeing, kayaking, pontoon/11 canoe/8 kayak rentals, river fishing, fishing supplies, golf nearby, shuffleboard court 2 shuffleboard courts, activities, horseshoes.

Pets welcome, breed restrict, size restrict, quantity restrict. Partial handicap access. No tents. Age restrict may apply. Open all yr. Escort to site. Clubs welcome. Rate in 2010 $36.50-39.50 for 2 persons. MC/VISA/DISC. Member ARVC, FLARVC.

Phone: (352)625-1122
Address: 2771 NE 102nd Ave Rd, Silver Springs, FL 34488
Lat/Lon: 29.21446/-81.98204
Email: reservations@wildernessrvparkestates.com
Web: www.wildernessrvparkestates.com

SEE AD TRAVEL SECTION PAGE 71

SNEADS—E-3

(N) THREE RIVERS STATE PARK—(Jackson) *From jct US-90 & Hwy-271: Go 1 mi N on Hwy-271.* FACILITIES: 30 sites, 20 ft max RV length, 30 W&E, tenting, dump. RECREATION: boating, canoeing, ramp, lake fishing, playground. Open all yr. Phone: (850)482-9006.

SOPCHOPPY—A-1

(S) OCHLOCKONEE RIVER STATE PARK—(Wakulla) *From jct Hwy-375 & US-319: Go 4 mi S on US-319.* FACILITIES: 30 sites, 30 W&E, tenting, dump. RECREATION: river swim, boating, canoeing, ramp, river fishing. Pets welcome. Open all yr. Phone: (904)962-2771.

SOUTH BAY—D-4

(N) SOUTH BAY RV CAMPGROUND (Palm Beach County Park)—(Palm Beach) *From jct Hwy 80 & US 27: Go 2 mi N on US 27. Enter on R.* FACILITIES: 72 sites, 72 W&E, (30/50 amps), 3 pull-thrus, tenting, dump, laundry. RECREATION: boating, ramp, lake fishing, playground. Partial handicap access. Open all yr. Phone: (561)992-9045.

SPRING HILL—C-3

(E) TOPICS RV COMMUNITY—(Hernando) *From jct US 19 & Hwy 578 (County Line Rd): Go 7 mi E on Hwy 578. Enter on L.*

◆◆◆FACILITIES: 233 sites, typical site width 40 ft, accepts full hkup units only, 233 full hkups, (30/50 amps), mostly extd stay sites (winter), WiFi Internet central location, RV storage, laundry, picnic tables, patios.

◆◆◆RECREATION: rec hall, swim pool, golf nearby, shuffleboard court 4 shuffleboard courts, activities, horseshoes.

Pets welcome, size restrict, quantity restrict. Partial handicap access. No tents. Age restrict may apply. Open all yr. Big rigs welcome. Rate in 2010 $34-40 for 2 persons. MC/VISA.

Phone: (352)796-0625
Address: 13063 County Line Rd, Spring Hill, FL 34609
Lat/Lon: 28.43395/-82.51286
Email: topicsrv@mhchomes.com
Web: www.rvonthego.com

SEE AD ALACHUA PAGE 93

STARKE—B-3

✽ **(S) REVELS NATIONWIDE RV SALES**—*From jct Hwy 100 & US 301: Go 200 yds E on Hwy 100. Enter on R.* SERVICES: sells parts/accessories. Open all yr. MC/VISA/DISC.

WELCOME

Phone: (800)473-8357
Address: 206 W Madison St, Starke, FL 32091
Lat/Lon: 29.94346/-82.11108

SEE AD TRAVEL SECTION PAGE 72 AND AD TRAVEL SECTION PAGE 74

(S) Starke/Gainesville NE KOA—(Bradford) *From jct Hwy 100 & US 301: Go 1 mi S on US 301. Enter on R.* ◇◇◇◇FACILITIES: 138 sites, typical site width 50 ft, 133 full hkups, 5 W&E, (30/50 amps), 80 pull-thrus, family camping, dump, laundry, groceries. ◇◇◇◇RECREATION: swim pool, pond fishing, playground. Pets welcome, breed restrict, size restrict, quantity restrict. Partial handicap access. No tents. Open all yr. Big rigs welcome. Rate in 2010 $33-46 for 2 persons. Member ARVC, FLARVC. Phone: (800)562-8498. KOA discount.

STEINHATCHEE—B-2

(E) Redfish RV Park—(Dixie) *From jct US 19 & Hwy 51: Go 8-1/4 mi S on Hwy 51, then 1/4 mi W on 1st Ave, then 1/4 mi N on 12th St E. Enter on L.* ◇◇◇FACILITIES: 33 sites, typical site width 25 ft, 31 full hkups, 2 W&E, (50 amps), 50 amps ($), 16 pull-thrus, tenting, dump. Pets welcome. Open all yr. Big rigs welcome. Rate in 2010 $30-35 per vehicle. Phone: (352)498-1188.

SUGARLOAF KEY—F-4

See listings at Bahia Honda Key, Big Pine Key & Key West

(S) KOA-Sugarloaf Key West—(Monroe) *On US-1 at mile marker 20. Enter on L.* ◇◇◇◇FACILITIES: 346 sites, typical site width 25 ft, 160 full hkups, 36 W&E, (30/50 amps), 150 no hkups, family camping, tenting, dump, laundry, full svc store. ◇◇◇◇◇RECREATION: swim pool, saltwater swim, boating, canoeing, ramp, dock, saltwater fishing, playground. Pets welcome. Partial handicap access. Open all yr. Big rigs welcome. Rate in 2010 $77-125 for 2 persons. Member ARVC, FLARVC. Phone: (305)745-3549. KOA discount.

(S) Lazy Lakes RV Resort—(Monroe) *On US 1 at mile marker 19-3/4. Enter on L.* ◇◇◇◇FACILITIES: 122 sites, typical site width 35 ft, 40 ft max RV length, 97 full hkups, (20/30/50 amps), 25 no hkups, 14 pull-thrus, family camping, tenting, dump, laundry. ◇◇◇RECREATION: swim pool, canoeing, lake fishing. Pets welcome, breed restrict, quantity restrict. Open all yr. Rate in 2010 $40-115 for 2 persons. Phone: (305) 745-1079.

SUMATRA—F-3

(S) APALACHICOLA NATIONAL FOREST (Wright Lake Campground)—(Liberty) *From jct CR 379 & Hwy 65: Go 2 mi S on Hwy 65, then 2 mi W on FR 101. Enter on R.* FACILITIES: 25 sites, typical site width 19 ft, 25 no hkups, tenting, dump. RECREATION: lake swim, boating, no motors, lake fishing. Partial handicap access. Open all yr. Phone: (850)643-2282.

SUMMERFIELD—B-3

(E) SOUTHERN OAKS RV RESORT (NOT VISITED)—(Marion) *From jct I-75 (exit 341) & CR 484: Go 8 mi E on CR 484, then stay straight on 132nd St to US 441, then 1/2 mi S on US 441. Enter on R.*

WELCOME

FACILITIES: 138 sites, typical site width 36 ft, 138 full hkups, (50 amps), 20 pull-thrus, WiFi Instant Internet at site, family camping, tenting, RV's/park model rentals, RV storage, dump, non-guest dump $, laundry.

SUMMERFIELD—Continued
SOUTHERN OAKS RV RESORT—Continued

RECREATION: rec hall, swim pool, golf nearby, activities, horseshoes.

Pets welcome ($), breed restrict. Partial handicap access. Open all yr. Big rigs welcome. Escort to site. Clubs welcome. Rate in 2010 $25-35 for 2 persons. MC/VISA/DISC.

Phone: (352)347-2550
Address: 14140 SE US Hwy 441, Summerfield, FL 34491
Lat/Lon: 29.01680/-82.01300
Email: rich@southernoaksrv.com
Web: www.southernoaksrv.com

SEE AD THIS PAGE

SUMTERVILLE—C-3

(NW) Shady Brook Golf & RV Resort (RV SPACES)—(Sumter) *From jct I-75 (exit 321) & Hwy 470: Go 2-1/2 mi E on Hwy 470, then 3/4 mi N on US 301. Enter on L.* FACILITIES: 170 sites, typical site width 25 ft, 170 full hkups, (30/50 amps), 3 pull-thrus, tenting, dump, laundry. RECREATION: lake fishing. Pets welcome. Partial handicap access. Age restrict may apply. Open all yr. Big rigs welcome. Rate in 2010 $35 for 2 persons. Phone: (352)568-2244.

SUNRISE—E-5

(SW) MARKHAM PARK (Broward County Park)—(Broward) *From jct I-95 & I-595: Go W on I-595 (Weston Rd exit), then continue W on Hwy 84 to second traffic light. Enter on R.*

WELCOME

FACILITIES: 88 sites, 88 full hkups, (20/30/50 amps), 8 pull-thrus, family camping, dump, non-guest dump $, ice, picnic tables, fire rings, grills, wood.

RECREATION: pavilion, swim pool, boating, canoeing, kayaking, ramp, 6 rowboat/18 canoe/8 kayak/8 pedal boat rentals, lake fishing, playground, tennis, horseshoes, sports field, hiking trails, v-ball. Rec open to public.

Pets welcome. Age restrict may apply. Open all yr. Big rigs welcome. Clubs welcome. MC/VISA/DISC/AMEX.

Phone: (954)389-2000
Address: 16001 W SR 84, Sunrise, FL 33326
Lat/Lon: 26.126278/-80.360750
Email: markhampark@broward.org
Web: www.broward.org/parks/camping

SEE AD TRAVEL SECTION PAGE 75 AND AD DISCOVER SECTION PAGE 33

SUNSHINE KEY—F-4

See listing at Marathon.

SUWANNEE RIVER—B-2

See listings at Cross City & Old Town

TALLAHASSEE—A-1

(N) BIG OAK RV PARK—(Leon) *From jct I-10 (exit 199) & US 27: Go 2-1/2 mi N on US 27. Enter on L.*

WELCOME

◇◇◇◇FACILITIES: 117 sites, accepts full hkup units only, 117 full hkups, (30/50 amps), some extd stay sites, 37 pull-thrus, cable TV, WiFi Instant Internet at site, dump, non-guest dump $, laundry, ice, picnic tables.

Pets welcome. No tents. Open all yr. Big rigs welcome. Escort to site. Rate in 2010 $36 for 2 persons. MC/VISA. Member ARVC, FLARVC. FMCA discount.

Woodall's Tip... Flag symbols on maps indicate towns under which Travel & Tourism Locations are listed.

TALLAHASSEE—Continued
BIG OAK RV PARK—Continued

Phone: (850)562-4660
Address: 4024 N Monroe St, Tallahassee, FL 32303
Lat/Lon: 30.50796/-84.33808
Email: manager@bigoakrvpark.com
Web: www.bigoakrvpark.com

SEE AD THIS PAGE AND AD TRAVEL SECTION PAGE 74

⚑ **FLORIDA ASSOCIATION OF RV PARKS AND CAMPGROUNDS**—Campground owner's association.

WELCOME

Phone: (850)562-7151
Address: 1340 Vickers Rd, Tallahassee, FL 32303

SEE AD TRAVEL SECTION PAGE 72

(E) TALLAHASSEE RV PARK—(Leon) *From jct I-10 (exit 209A) & US 90: Go 1/2 mi W on US 90. Enter on R.*

WELCOME

SOUTHERN HOSPITALITY AT ITS FINEST!
A Country Setting Convenient to Tallahassee's Dining and Entertainment off I-10. Big Rig 50 AMP, X-Long Pull-Thrus, Beautiful Flowers, Pool, FREE WI-FI & CABLE, Sparkling Restrooms. (850)878-7641. WWW.TALLAHASSEERVPARK.COM

◇◇◇◇FACILITIES: 66 sites, typical site width 25 ft, 66 full hkups, (30/50 amps), many extd stay sites, 59 pull-thrus, cable TV, WiFi Instant Internet at site, dump, non-guest dump $, laundry, picnic tables.

◇◇RECREATION: rec hall, swim pool, golf nearby, horseshoes.

Pets welcome, breed restrict, quantity restrict. Partial handicap access. No tents. Open all yr. Big rigs welcome. Escort to site. Clubs welcome. Rate in 2010 $40 per vehicle. MC/VISA/DISC. Member ARVC, FLARVC.

Phone: (850)878-7641
Address: 6504 Mahan Dr, Tallahassee, FL 32308
Lat/Lon: 30.43414/-84.30636
Email: manager@tallahasseervpark.com
Web: www.tallahasseervpark.com

SEE AD NEXT PAGE

TAMPA—C-3

TAMPA—Continued on next page

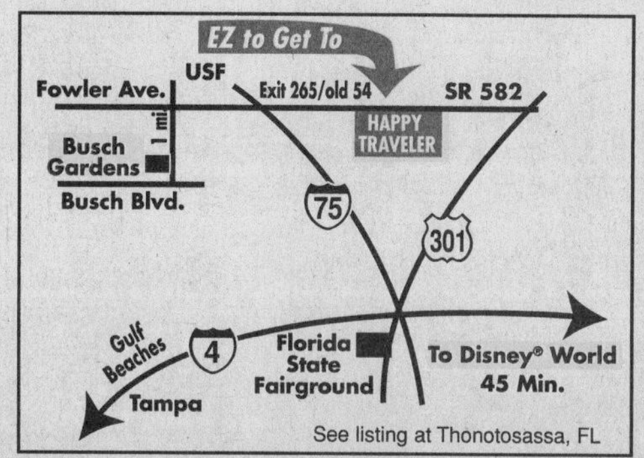

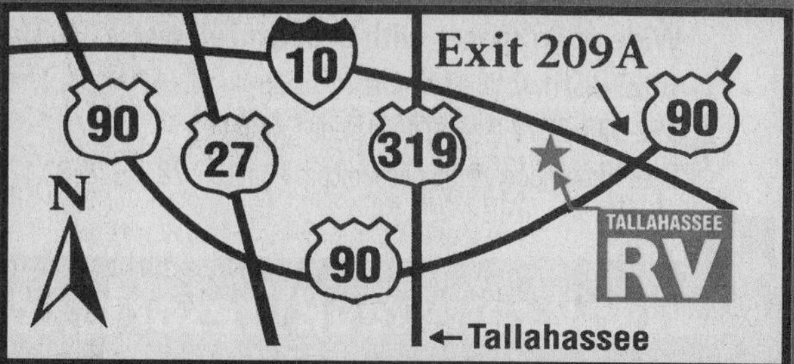

Carefree RV Resorts in Florida's Fabulous Tampa Area.

carefree rv resorts

The experiences are countless. Visit the fabulous Salvador Dali Museum. Then eat fried catfish and hush puppies with your fingers at a dockside café while you watch boats sail by. Or, just stay in your neighborhood and enjoy all of the fun activities, the friendly community spirit, and the attention of a professional staff.

Each Tampa area resort has its own distinctive array of amenities and a clubhouse for spending time with friends.

Splash around in the sparkling pool or soak up the sun and read a good book on a lounge chair. Join in the fun and games such as shuffleboard, horseshoes, Bocce ball, Petanque, cards or bingo.

Whatever you want to do, we'll make sure your vacation experience is carefree!

Sweetwater Carefree RV Resort

Where life couldn't be sweeter

37647 Chancey Rd., Zephyrhills, FL 33541

813-788-7513 (See listing in Zephyrhills, FL)

Email: sweetwaterrv@tampabay.rr.com • Lat/Lon: 28.20841/-82.19347

Waters Edge Carefree RV Resort

Friends and fun waiting for you to dive right in

39146 Otis Allen Rd., Zephyrhills, FL 33540

813-783-2708 (See listing in Zephyrhills, FL)

Email: watersedgerv@tampabay.rr.com • Lat/Lon: 28.27097/-82.16862

Daily • Weekly • Monthly • Seasonal • Annual
Pet Friendly • Wi-Fi Available at All RV Resorts
Rentals* Available • Homes for Sale

*Not available at Southern Charm, Majestic Oaks, Glen Haven and Blue Jay.

Manufactured Home Communities

Blue Jay RV & MH Park

Fun and the good life all year-round

38511 Wilds Rd., Dade City, FL 33525

352-567-9678 (See listing in Dade City, FL)

Email: bluejayrv@tampabay.rr.com • Lat/Lon: 28.317519/-82.178267

Citrus Hill RV Resort

A sunny place with smiling faces

9267 U.S. Hwy 98, Dade City, FL 33525

352-567-6045 (See listing in Dade City, FL)

Email: citrushillrv@tampabay.rr.com • Lat/Lon: 28.29221/-82.13500

Spanish Main RV Park

Your shady retreat with a sparkling lake

12110 Spanish Main Resort Trail, Thonotasassa, FL 33592

813-986-2415 (See listing in Thonotasassa, FL)

Email: spanishmainrv@tampabay.rr.com • Lat/Lon: 28.06399/-82.30539

www.carefreeRVresorts.com • For Reservations!

Tampa Bay's Finest RV Resort

In a setting of Beautiful, Ancient Oaks, Bay Bayou is where you want to be:

- **5W/5W** Woodall's highest rating in 2010-11 - One of 40 RV Parks in Florida with highest rating
- Rated in the top 100 Parks in the USA, 2008-9 by Trailer Life - Good Sam rating: 9/10★/9
- 272 Oversized Sites with patio, picnic table - sewer, water, 30/50 amp, telephone, Free Cable with HBO
- Large, Heated Pool with Jacuzzi & Tiki Hut
- Wi-Fi access throughout the Park, Clubhouse + DSL to all sites
- Docks for fishing & viewing, located on beautiful Double Branch Creek
- Kayaking from our riverfront, Shuffleboard, Horseshoes, Bocce Ball, Fire Pit + more
- Fenced dog run with hot water bath
- 6,000 sq. ft. Clubhouse: lending library, big screen TV, pool tables plus exercise equipment
- Year-round activities including line dancing, karaoke, bingo & dinner dances with live music

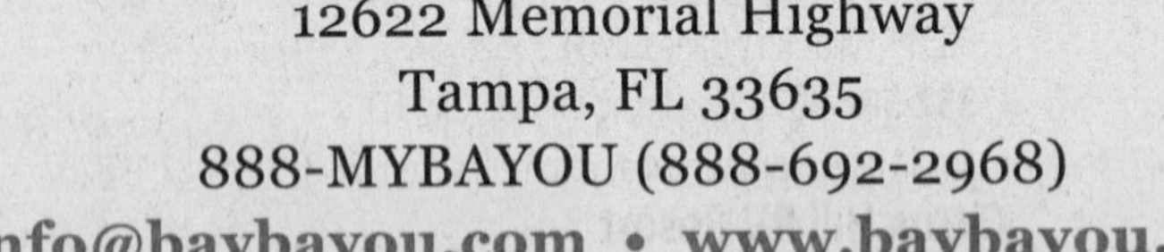

info@baybayou.com • www.baybayou.com

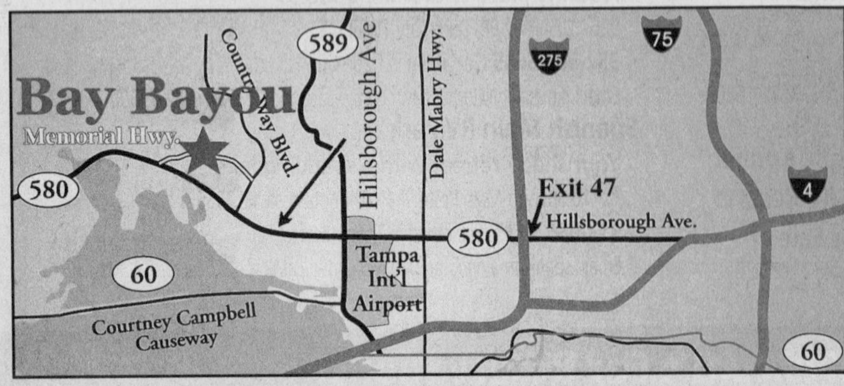

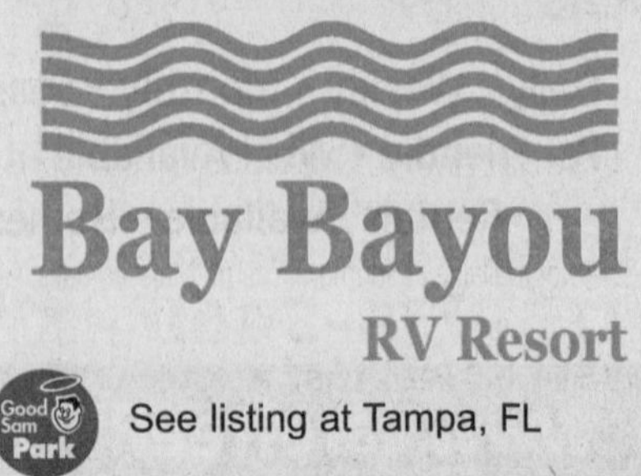

Good Sam Park See listing at Tampa, FL

TAMPA—Continued

(NW) BAY BAYOU RV RESORT—(Hillsborough) *N'bnd from jct I-275 (exit 47) & Hillsborough Ave (SR 580): Go 10-1/2 mi W on Hillsborough Ave (SR 580), then 1/2 mi N on Countryway Blvd, then 3/4 mi W on Memorial Hwy. Enter on L.*

5W - 5W WATERFRONT CAMPING IN TAMPA
Spacious heavily wooded sites in a rural setting yet only minutes from the beach and all Tampa, St. Petersburg, Clearwater area attractions. A full amenity park with a friendly staff to help you enjoy your stay.

◆◆◆◆◆FACILITIES: 275 sites, typical site width 50 ft, 275 full hkups, (30/50 amps), many extd stay sites (winter), cable TV, WiFi Instant Internet at site, phone/cable on-site Internet (needs activ), WiFi Internet central location, family camping, RV storage, dump, non-guest dump $, laundry, RV supplies, LP gas by weight/by meter, picnic tables, patios, controlled access.

◆◆◆◆◆RECREATION: rec hall, rec room/area, equipped pavilion, swim pool, hot tub, boating, canoeing, kayaking, 2 kayak rentals, saltwater/pond fishing, golf nearby, bike rental 4 bike rentals, shuffleboard court 2 shuffleboard courts, activities, horseshoes.

Pets welcome, breed restrict, quantity restrict. Partial handicap access. No tents. Open all yr. Children accepted, 21 day limit. Big rigs welcome. Clubs welcome. Rate in 2010 $39-62 for 2 persons. MC/VISA/DISC/Debit. Member ARVC, FLARVC. FMCA discount. CCUSA 50% Discount. CCUSA reservations Recommended, CCUSA max stay Unlimited. Discount not available Nov thru Apr. No tents, pop-ups or truck campers.

Text 87755 to (440)725-8687 to see our Visual Tour.

Phone: (813)855-1000
Address: 12622 Memorial Hwy, Tampa, FL 33635
Lat/Lon: 28.02982/-82.63058
Email: info@baybayou.com
Web: www.baybayou.com

SEE AD PAGE 172 AND AD MAP PAGE 70

(NE) CAMP NEBRASKA—(Hillsborough) *From jct I-4 & I-275: Go 5-1/2 mi N on I-275 (exit 51), then 1 block E on Fowler Ave, then 3/4 mi S on US 41, then 1 block W on Bouganvillea Ave. Enter on L.*

◆◆◆FACILITIES: 86 sites, typical site width 25 ft, 86 full hkups, (20/30/50 amps), mostly extd stay sites (winter), 40 pull-thrus, WiFi Instant Internet at site, phone/cable on-site Internet (needs activ), family camping, laundry, picnic tables.

TAMPA—Continued
CAMP NEBRASKA—Continued

◆RECREATION: golf nearby.

Pets welcome, breed restrict, size restrict, quantity restrict. No tents. Open all yr. Big rigs welcome. Rate in 2010 $30 for 2 persons. MC/VISA/Debit. Member ARVC, FLARVC. CCUSA 50% Discount. CCUSA reservations Recommended, CCUSA max stay 4 days. Discount available Apr thru Sep. No discount on tent sites.

Phone: (877)971-6990
Address: 10314 North Nebraska Ave, Tampa, FL 33612
Lat/Lon: 28.04343/-82.45216

SEE AD THIS PAGE

HORSESHOE COVE RV RESORT—*From jct I-4 & I-75: Go 39 mi S on I-75 (exit 41), then 1-1/4 mi W on Hwy 70.*

SEE PRIMARY LISTING AT BRADENTON AND AD SARASOTA PAGE 164

LAZYDAYS RV CAMPGROUND—(Hillsborough) *From jct I-75 & I-4: Go 1 mi E on I-4 (exit 10), then1/4 mi N on Hwy 579. Enter on L.*

◆◆◆◆◆FACILITIES: 299 sites, typical site width 28 ft, 299 full hkups, (30/50 amps), mostly extd stay sites (winter), cable TV, WiFi Instant Internet at site, WiFi Internet central location ($), dump, non-guest dump, laundry, RV supplies, LP gas by weight/by meter, ice, picnic tables, patios.

◆◆◆◆RECREATION: rec hall, rec room/area, swim pool, hot tub, golf nearby, play equipment, 4 shuffleboard courts, tennis, horseshoes.

Pets welcome. Partial handicap access. No tents. Open all yr. Maximum stay two weeks winter. Big rigs welcome. Clubs welcome. Rate in 2010 $24.99-34.99 per vehicle. MC/VISA/DISC/AMEX/Debit. Member ARVC, FLARVC.

Phone: (866)456-7015
Address: 6210 Cty Rd. 579, Seffner, FL 33584
Lat/Lon: 28.01266/-82.30298
Email: campground@lazydays.com
Web: www.lazydays.com

SEE AD TRAVEL SECTION PAGE 80 AND AD DISCOVER SECTION PAGE 32

✲ (NW) LAZYDAYS SALES & SERVICE—*From jct I-75 & I-4: Go 1 mi E on I-4 (exit 10), then 1/4 mi N on Hwy 579, then 1/2 mi W on Sligh Ave, then 1/2 mi S & W on Lazy Days Blvd. Enter on R.*
SALES: travel trailers, 5th wheels, toy hauler, Class A motorhomes, Class C motorhomes, Class B motorhomes, pre-owned unit sales. SERVICES: engine/chassis repair, RV appliance repair, LP gas by weight/by meter, sells

TAMPA—Continued
LAZYDAYS SALES & SERVICE—Continued

parts/accessories, installs hitches. Open all yr. MC/VISA/DISC/AMEX. ATM.

Phone: (813)246-4333
Address: 6130 Lazydays Blvd, Seffner, FL 33584-2968
Lat/Lon: 28.00638/-82.30848
Web: www.lazydays.com

SEE AD TRAVEL SECTION PAGE 80 AND AD DISCOVER SECTION PAGE 32

QUAIL RUN RV RESORT—*From Tampa N'Bnd: Go N on I-75 for 25 mi to exit 279, & SR 54, then W on SR 54 for 1/2 mi, then N on Old Paseo Road for 2 mi to Park. Enter on R.*

SEE PRIMARY LISTING AT WESLEY CHAPEL AND AD WESLEY CHAPEL PAGE 177

TARPON SPRINGS—C-3

(NW) Hickory Point Mobile Home & RV Park (RV SPACES)—(Pinelas) *From N jct US 19 & US 19A: Go 1 mi SW, then 2 mi W on Anclote Blvd, then 1 blk SE on Anclote Rd (Seminole St). Enter on R.* FACILITIES: 33 sites, typical site width 20 ft, 40 ft max RV length, 33 full hkups, (30/50 amps), cable TV, family camping, tenting, dump, non-guest dump $, laundry, picnic tables, patios. RECREATION: rec hall, boating, canoeing, kayaking, ramp, dock, saltwater fishing, bsktball, shuffleboard court shuffleboard court, activities. Pets welcome, breed restrict, size restrict, quantity restrict. Open all yr. Rate in 2010 $40 for 2 persons. CCUSA 50% Discount. CCUSA reservations Required, CCUSA max stay 4 days, Cash only for CCUSA disc. Discount available May 1-Sep 1. Does not apply to waterfront sites.

Phone: (727)937-7357
Address: 1181 Anclote Rd, Tarpon Springs, FL 34689
Lat/Lon: 28.17063/-82.78138
Email: info@hickorypointmhp.com
Web: www.hickorypointmhp.com

TAVARES—C-3

(S) FISHERMAN'S COVE GOLF MARINA & RV RESORT—(Lake) *From jct US-441 & Hwy-19: Go 3-1/4 mi SW on Hwy-19. Enter on R.*

◆◆◆◆FACILITIES: 333 sites, typical site width 40 ft, 333 full hkups, (30/50 amps), cable TV, WiFi Internet central location, family camping, RV's/park model rentals, dump, non-guest dump $, laundry, LP gas by weight, ice, controlled access.

◆◆◆◆RECREATION: rec hall, swim pool, hot tub, boating, canoeing, kayaking, ramp, dock, 3 kayak rentals, stream fishing, putting green, golf nearby, shuffleboard court 4 shuffleboard courts, horseshoes.

FISHERMAN'S COVE GOLF MARINA & RV RESORT—Continued on next page

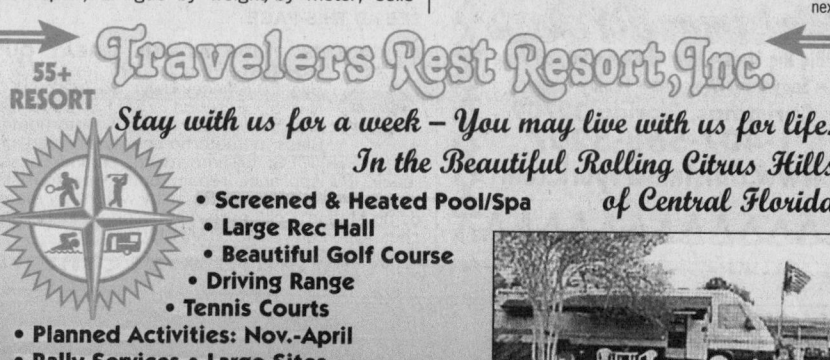

Pets welcome, breed restrict. Partial handicap access. No tents. Age restrict may apply. Open all yr. Escort to site. Clubs welcome. Rate in 2010 $39 for 2 persons. MC/VISA.

Phone: (800)254-9993
Address: 29115 Eichelberger Rd, Tavares, FL 32778
Lat/Lon: 28.76526/-81.75427
Email: info@lakeharrisresort.com
Web: www.lakeharrisresort.com

SEE AD THIS PAGE

THE VILLAGES—B-3

See listings at Eustis, Leesburg & Tavares.

THONOTOSASSA—C-3

(NE) Camp Lemora RV Park—(Hillsborough) *From jct I-75 (exit 265) & US 301: Go 8 mi NE on US 301, then 1 block N on Dead River Rd. Enter on L.* ◇◇◇◇FACILITIES: 298 sites, typical site width 40 ft, 298 full hkups, (20/30 amps), family camping, laundry, groceries. ◇◇◇◇RECREATION: swim pool. Pets welcome, breed restrict. No tents. Open all yr. Rate in 2010 $31 for 2 persons. Phone: (813)986-4456.

(W) HAPPY TRAVELER RV PARK—(Hillsborough) *From jct I-75 (exit 265) & Fowler Ave: Go 1/2 mi E on Fowler Ave. Enter on R.*

◇◇◇FACILITIES: 224 sites, typical site width 35 ft, 224 full hkups, (20/30/50 amps), some extd stay sites (winter), 10 pull-thrus, cable TV, ($), WiFi Instant Internet at site ($), phone/cable on-site Internet (needs activ), WiFi Internet central location, family camping, RV's/park model rentals, cabins, RV storage, dump, non-guest dump $, laundry, LP gas by meter, ice, picnic tables, patios.

◇◇◇RECREATION: rec hall, swim pool, golf nearby, shuffleboard court 2 shuffleboard courts, activities, horseshoes.

Pets welcome, quantity restrict. No tents. Age restrict may apply. Open all yr. Children allowed for max 2 weeks stay. Planned activities winter season only. Big rigs welcome. Clubs welcome. Rate in 2010 $26-36 for 2 persons. MC/VISA/DISC. FMCA discount.

Text 107934 to (440)725-8687 to see our Visual Tour.

Phone: (800)758-2795
Address: 9401 E Fowler Ave, Thonotosassa, FL 33592
Lat/Lon: 28.05383/-82.33939
Email: htrvpk@aol.com
Web: www.happytravelerrvpark.com

SEE AD TAMPA PAGE 169

(N) SPANISH MAIN RV RESORT—(Hillsborough) *From jct Hwy-582 E & I-75 (exit 265 Temple Terrace-Hwy-582 E): Go 1/2 mi E on Fowler, then 1-1/2 mi N on US-301. Enter on R.*

◇◇◇FACILITIES: 280 sites, typical site width 18 ft, 280 full hkups, (30/50 amps), many extd stay sites (winter), 7 pull-thrus, phone/cable on site Internet (needs activ), WiFi Internet central location, family camping, RV storage, laundry, picnic tables, patios.

◇◇◇◇RECREATION: rec hall, rec room/area, swim pool, pond fishing, golf nearby, bsktball, playground, shuffleboard court 6 shuffleboard courts, activities, horseshoes.

Pets welcome, breed restrict. No tents. Open all yr. Planned activities winter only. Big rigs welcome. Rate in 2010 $33 for 2 persons. MC/VISA. Member ARVC, FLARVC. CCUSA 50% Discount. CCUSA reservations Required, CCUSA max stay 7 days, Cash only for CCUSA disc., CCUSA disc. not avail holidays. Not available Jan 1-Apr 1.

Phone: (813)986-2415
Address: 12110 Spanish Main Resort Trail, Thonotosassa, FL 33592
Lat/Lon: 28.06528/-82.30482
Email: spanishmainrv@tampabay.rr.com
Web: www.carefreervresorts.com

SEE AD TAMPA PAGES 170-171

TITUSVILLE—C-4

CHRISTMAS RV PARK—(Orange) *From jct of I-95 & SR 50 (exit 215): Go W for 8-1/2 mi on SR 50 to Park. Enter on R.*

◇◇◇FACILITIES: 167 sites, 164 full hkups, 3 W&E, (20/30/50 amps), many extd stay sites (winter), 127 pull-thrus, WiFi Instant Internet at site, phone on-site Internet (needs activ), WiFi Internet central location, family camping, RV's/park model rentals, RV storage, dump, non-guest dump $, RV supplies, picnic tables, patios.

◇◇◇◇RECREATION: rec hall, rec room/area, equipped pavilion, swim pool, golf nearby, play equipment, shuffleboard court, activities, horseshoes, hiking trails.

Pets welcome, breed restrict, quantity restrict. Partial handicap access. No tents. Open all yr. Big rigs welcome. Escort to site. Clubs welcome. Rate in 2010 $35-50 for 2 persons. MC/VISA/DISC.

Phone: (407)568-5207
Address: 25525 E Colonial Dr, Christmas, FL 32709
Lat/Lon: 28.53767/-80.98771
Email: christmasrvpark@yahoo.com
Web: christmasrvpark.com

SEE AD THIS PAGE

✱ **EAGLE'S PRIDE AT THE GREAT OUTDOORS**—*From jct I-95 (exit 215) & Hwy 50 (Cheney Hwy): Go 1/2 mi W on Hwy 50. Enter on L.* SALES: travel trailers, 5th wheels, Class A motorhomes, Class C motorhomes, pre-owned unit sales. SERVICES: full-time mech, engine/chassis repair, RV appliance repair, body work/collision repair, mobile RV svc, LP gas by weight/by meter, dump station, sells parts/accessories, installs hitches. Open all yr. MC/VISA/DISC.

Phone: (800)552-3555
Address: 108 C Plantation Dr, Titusville, FL 32780
Lat/Lon: 28.32456/-80.86426
Web: www.tgoresort.com/about/services.asp

SEE AD NEXT PAGE

(NW) KOA-Cape Kennedy—(Brevard) *From jct I-95 (exit 223) & Hwy 46: Go 1/4 mi W on Hwy 46. Enter on L.* ◇◇◇FACILITIES: 147 sites, typical site width 25 ft, 125 full hkups, 22 W&E, (15/20/30/50 amps), 5 pull-thrus, family camping, tenting, dump, laundry, ltd groc. ◇◇◇◇RECREATION: swim pool, playground. Pets welcome, breed restrict. Open all yr. Big rigs welcome. Rate in 2010 $33-44 for 2 persons. Member ARVC, FLARVC. Phone: (321)269-7361. KOA discount.

(S) MANATEE HAMMOCK PARK (Brevard County Park) —(Brevard) *From jct Hwy 50 & US 1: Go 3 mi S on US 1 to 7275 S US 1 (Bellwood).* FACILITIES: 182 sites, 147 full hkups, 35 W&E, (30/50 amps), tenting, dump, laundry. RECREATION: swim pool, saltwater/river swim, saltwater/river fishing. Open all yr. Phone: (321)264-5083.

SEASONS IN THE SUN—(Brevard) *From jct I-95 (exit 223) & Hwy 46: Go 1/2 mi W on Hwy 46. Enter on L.*

◇◇◇◇◇FACILITIES: 232 sites, typical site width 40 ft, 232 full hkups, (20/30/50 amps), mostly extd stay sites (winter), cable TV, WiFi Instant Internet at site ($), phone/cable on-site Internet (needs activ), WiFi Internet central location, RV storage, dump, non-guest dump $, laundry, LP gas by meter, picnic tables, patios, controlled access.

◇◇◇◇◇RECREATION: rec hall, rec room/area, 2 swim pools, hot tub, pond fishing, golf nearby, shuffleboard court 2 shuffleboard courts, activities, tennis, horseshoes.

Pets welcome. Partial handicap access. No tents. Age restrict may apply. Open all yr. Big rigs welcome. Clubs welcome. Rate in 2010 $33.07-41.85 for 2 persons. MC/VISA/DISC/AMEX. CCUSA 50% Discount. CCUSA reservations Recommended, CCUSA max stay 5 days, Cash only for CCUSA disc. Discount available Apr thru Nov.

Phone: (877)687-7275
Address: 2400 Seasons in the Sun Blvd., Titusville, FL 32754
Lat/Lon: 28.66583/-80.87778
Email: seasonsinthesunrv@aol.com
Web: www.seasonsinthesunrvresort.com

SEE AD TRAVEL SECTION PAGE 71

(SW) THE GREAT OUTDOORS RV-NATURE & GOLF RESORT—(Brevard) *From jct I-95 (exit 215) & Hwy 50 (Cheney Hwy): Go 1/2 mi W on Hwy 50 (Cheney Hwy) to entrance. Enter on L.*

STAY A NIGHT OR A LIFETIME!

Conveniently located near Florida's premier attractions-Kennedy Space Center, Orlando, Daytona & miles of beaches-or enjoy our resort's own amenities: golf, fishing, tennis, swimming & more w/RV service facility on site.

◇◇◇◇◇FACILITIES: 626 sites, typical site width 40 ft, accepts full hkup units only, 626 full hkups, (30/50 amps), some extd stay sites (winter), cable TV, phone/WiFi/cable Instant Internet at site ($), phone/cable on-site Internet (needs activ), WiFi In-

THE GREAT OUTDOORS RV-NATURE & GOLF RESORT—Continued on next page

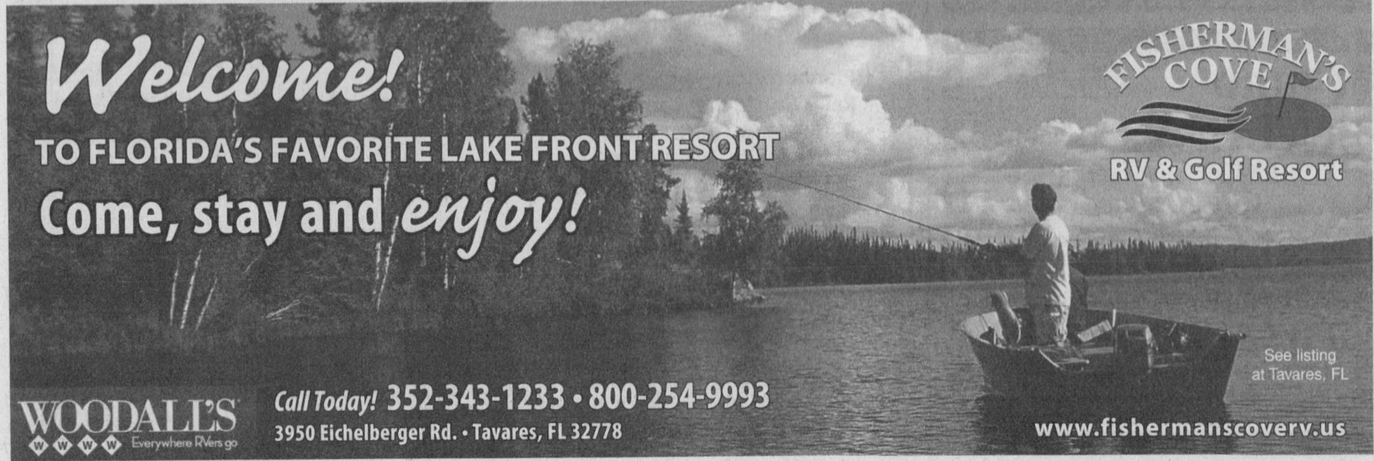

TITUSVILLE—Continued
THE GREAT OUTDOORS RV-NATURE & GOLF RESORT—Continued

ternet central location, RV storage, dump, laundry, RV supplies, LP gas by weight/by meter, ice, picnic tables, patios, controlled access.

◆◆◆◆◆RECREATION: rec hall, rec room/area, equipped pavilion, 2 swim pools, hot tub, lake fishing, putting green, golf nearby, shuffleboard court 8 shuffleboard courts, activities, tennis, horseshoes, hiking trails, local tours.

Pets welcome, quantity restrict. Partial handicap access. No tents. Open all yr. Water & electric sites for rallies. Big rigs welcome. Clubs welcome. Rate in 2010 $40-65 for 2 persons. MC/VISA/DISC/AMEX. ATM.

Text 81438 to (440)725-8687 to see our Visual Tour.

Phone: (800)621-2267
Address: 125 Plantation Dr, Titusville, FL 32780
Lat/Lon: 28.52456/-80.86426
Email: info@tgoresort.com
Web: www.tgoresort.com

SEE AD THIS PAGE

TRENTON—B-2

(N) Otter Springs Park & Campground—(Gilchrist) *From jct US 19/US 27 Alt & Hwy 26: Go 1-1/4 mi N on Hwy 26, then 1-3/4 mi N on CR 232, then 1 mi W on SW 70th St, then 1/2 mi N on SW 80th Ave. Enter on R.* ◆◆◆FACILITIES: 110 sites, 100 full hkups, 10 W&E, (20/30/50 amps), 99 pull-thrus, tenting, dump, laundry, ltd groc. ◆◆RECREATION: swim pool, boating, canoeing, river fishing. Pets welcome, breed restrict. Partial handicap access. Open all yr. Big rigs welcome. Rate in 2010 $24 for 2 persons. Phone: (352)463-0800.

UMATILLA—B-4

(E) OCALA NATIONAL FOREST (Clearwater Lake Campground)—(Lake) *From jct Hwy 19 & 42: Go 6.6 mi E on Hwy 42. Enter on L.* FACILITIES: 42 sites, typical site width 8 ft, 22 ft max RV length, 42 no hkups, tenting, dump. RECREATION: lake swim, boating, no motors, canoeing, lake fishing. Open all yr. Phone: (352)669-3153.

(N) OCALA NATIONAL FOREST (Lake Dorr Campground)—(Lake) *From jct Hwy 42 & Hwy 19: Go 3 mi N on Hwy 19.* FACILITIES: 34 sites, typical site width 11 ft, 22 ft max RV length, 34 no hkups, tenting. RECREATION: lake swim, boating, ramp, lake fishing. Open all yr. Phone: (352)669-3153.

VALPARAISO—F-2

(S) MILITARY PARK (FAMCAMP-Eglin AFB)—(Okaloosa) *From jct I-10 & Hwy 85: Go S on Hwy 85 to Hwy 20 (John Sims Pkwy), then follow signs to Eglin AFB.* FACILITIES: 22 sites, 22 W&E, 22 pull-thrus, tenting, dump, laundry, ltd groc. RECREATION: swim pool, saltwater swim, boating, canoeing, ramp, dock, saltwater/lake/river fishing, playground. Open all yr. Phone: (850) 883-1243.

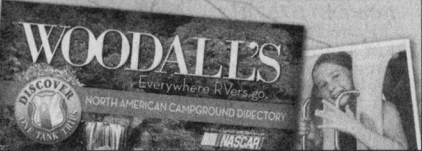

VENICE—D-3

(E) FLORIDA PINES MOBILE HOME COURT & RV—(Sarasota) *From jct I-75 (exit 193) & Jacaranda Blvd: Go 5-1/2 mi S on Jacaranda Blvd, then 1/4 mi NW on Hwy 776. Enter on R.*

◆◆◆FACILITIES: 30 sites, typical site width 35 ft, accepts full hkup units only, 30 full hkups, (20/30/50 amps), mostly extd stay sites, cable TV, phone/cable on-site Internet (needs activ), WiFi Internet central location, RV storage, dump, laundry, patios.

◆◆◆RECREATION: rec hall, lake fishing, golf nearby, shuffleboard court 3 shuffleboard courts, activities, horseshoes, local tours.

No pets. No tents. Age restrict may apply. Open all yr. Planned group activities winter only. Big rigs welcome. Clubs welcome. Rate in 2010 $32-46 for 2 persons. CCUSA 50% Discount. CCUSA reservations Recommended, CCUSA max stay Unlimited, Cash only for CCUSA disc. Discount available Apr 15- Nov 15. Accepts full hookup units only. No pets. Age restrictions may apply.

Phone: (941)493-0019
Address: 150 Satulah Circle, Venice, FL 34293
Lat/Lon: 27.04830/-82.40497

SEE AD THIS PAGE

(SE) MYAKKA RV RESORT - KOA—(Sarasota) *From jct I-75 (exit 191) & River Rd: Go 5-1/2 mi SE on River Rd, then 3/4 mi E on US 41. Enter on R.*

A KOA RESORT WITH ITS OWN ISLAND
Convenient location & minutes from Gulf beaches, golf courses or local dining. Tropical setting with 77 sites all with full hook up. Relax in a full amenity park where our friendly staff will make your stay one to repeat.

◆◆◆◆FACILITIES: 78 sites, typical site width 35 ft, 78 full hkups, (30/50 amps), mostly extd stay sites, 2 pull-thrus, WiFi Instant Internet at site, phone/cable on-site Internet (needs activ), WiFi Internet central location, family camping, tenting, dump, non-guest dump $, laundry, LP gas by weight/by meter, ice, picnic tables, patios.

◆◆◆◆RECREATION: rec room/area, pavilion, swim pool, saltwater fishing, golf nearby, shuffleboard court 2 shuffleboard courts, activities (wkends), horseshoes.

Pets welcome, breed restrict. Partial handicap access. Open all yr. Big rigs welcome. Rate in 2010 $39-67 for 2 persons. MC/VISA/DISC/Debit. Member ARVC. KOA discount. CCUSA 50% Discount. CCUSA reservations Recommended, CCUSA max stay Unlimited. Discount not available Dec thru Apr.

Text 84839 to (440)725-8687 to see our Visual Tour.

Phone: (800)562-9166
Address: 10400 Tamiami Trail S, Venice, FL 34287
Lat/Lon: 27.04699/-82.28872
Email: myakkariverrv@hotmail.com
Web: www.myakkarv.com

SEE AD SARASOTA PAGE 165

VENICE—Continued on next page

Woodall's Tip... Get FREE Information—Use the Reader Service card.

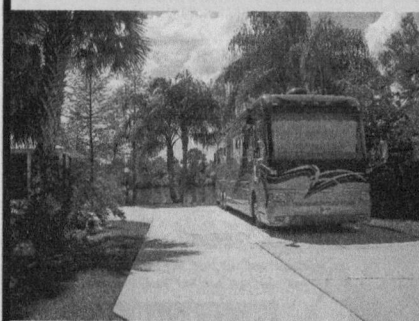

VENICE—Continued

(SE) RAMBLERS REST RESORT CAMPGROUND—(Sarasota) *From jct I-75 (exit 191) & River Rd: Go 3 mi S on River Rd. Enter on L.*

◊◊◊FACILITIES: 655 sites, typical site width 30 ft, 620 full hkups, 16 W&E, (20/30/50 amps), 50 amps ($), mostly extd stay sites (winter), 12 pull-thrus, WiFi Instant Internet at site ($), phone/cable on-site Internet (needs activ), WiFi Internet central location, family camping, tenting, RV storage, laundry, LP gas by weight/by meter, ice, picnic tables.

◊◊◊◊RECREATION: rec hall, rec room/area, equipped pavilion, swim pool, hot tub, boating, canoeing, kayaking, ramp, river fishing, golf nearby, bsktball, shuffleboard court 12 shuffleboard courts, activities, horseshoes, v-ball, local tours.

Pets welcome, breed restrict, quantity restrict. Partial handicap access. Open all yr. Group activities winter only. Big rigs welcome. Clubs welcome. Rate in 2010 $39-72 for 2 persons. MC/VISA/DISC/AMEX/Debit. Member ARVC, FLARVC.

Phone: (941)493-4354
Address: 1300 N River Rd, Venice, FL 34293
Lat/Lon: 27.06837/-82.32164
Email: ramblersrestrv@mhchomes.com
Web: www.ramblersrestrv.com

SEE AD ALACHUA PAGE 93

VERO BEACH—D-5

(NW) SUNSHINE TRAVEL-ENCORE—(Indian River) *From jct I-95 (exit 156) & Hwy 512: Go 1 block E on Hwy 512, then 1/2 block S on 108th St. Enter at end.*

◊◊◊◊FACILITIES: 304 sites, typical site width 20 ft, 304 full hkups, (30/50 amps), mostly extd stay sites (winter), 10 pull-thrus, cable TV, WiFi Instant Internet at site ($), phone/cable on-site Internet (needs activ), WiFi Internet central location, family camping, tenting, RV storage, dump, non-guest dump $, laundry, LP gas by meter, ice, picnic tables, controlled access.

◊◊◊RECREATION: rec hall, rec room/area, swim pool, mini-golf, golf nearby, shuffleboard court 4 shuffleboard courts, activities, horseshoes.

Pets welcome. Partial handicap access. Open all yr. Big rigs welcome. Escort to site. Clubs welcome. Rate in 2010 $36-55 for 2 persons. MC/VISA/DISC/AMEX/Debit. Member ARVC. CCUSA 50% Discount.

Phone: (800)628-7081
Address: 9455 108th Ave, Vero Beach, FL 32967
Lat/Lon: 27.76694/-80.54750
Web: www.rvonthego.com

SEE AD ALACHUA PAGE 93

WAUCHULA—D-3

(N) Crystal Lake Village (RV SPACES)—(Hardee) *From jct Hwy 62 & US 17: Go 1/4 mi S on US 17. Enter on L.* FACILITIES: 401 sites, typical site width 34 ft, accepts full hkup units only, 401 full hkups, (30/50 amps), 5 pull-thrus, phone/cable on-site Internet (needs activ), WiFi Internet central location, RV storage, laundry, LP gas by weight, patios. RECREATION: rec hall, swim pool, hot tub, pond fishing, shuffleboard court 6 shuffleboard courts, activities, horseshoes. Pets welcome, breed restrict. Partial handicap access. No tents. Age restrict may apply. Open all yr. Big rigs welcome. Rate in 2010 $25-27.50 for 2 persons. MC/VISA/DISC/AMEX. CCUSA 50% Discount. CCUSA reservations Accepted, CCUSA max stay 2 days, Cash only for CCUSA disc. Discount available May thru Oct.

Phone: (800)661-3582
Address: 237 Maxwell Dr, Wauchula, FL 33873
Lat/Lon: 27.58667/-81.81701
Email: clrv@vistanet.net
Web: www.crystallakevillage.com

(N) Little Charlie Creek RV Park—(Hardee) *From jct Hwy 62 & US 17: Go 1-1/4 mi S on US 17, then 1/2 mi E on Rea Rd, then 3/4 mi NE on Heard Bridge Rd. Enter on R.* ◊◊◊FACILITIES: 188 sites, typical site width 32 ft, 188 full hkups, (30/50 amps), laundry. ◊◊◊RECREATION: river/pond fishing. Pets welcome, breed restrict. No tents. Age restrict may apply. Open all yr. Big rigs welcome. Rate in 2010 $25 for 2 persons. Phone: (863)773-0088.

(E) PEACE RIVER - THOUSAND TRAILS (CAMP RESORT)—(Hardee) *Sbnd: From I-17 S & Hwy 64: Go E on Hwy 64 for 12 mi, turn on US 64 towards ZOLFO Springs for 7 mi, then S on US 17 S for 3/4 mi, cross Peace River Bridge to Park. Enter on R.*

FACILITIES: 400 sites, 40 ft max RV length, 200 full hkups, 200 W&E, (20/30 amps), WiFi Internet central location, family camping, tenting, cabins, dump, laundry, ltd groc, picnic tables, controlled access.

RECREATION: rec hall, rec room/area, swim pool, hot tub, boating, canoeing, ramp, dock, river fishing, golf nearby, bike rental bike rental, playground, shuffleboard court 3 shuffleboard courts, activities, horseshoes, hiking trails.

Pets welcome. Partial handicap access. Open all yr. No mail delivery - Honey Wagon Dec thru Mar.

Phone: (863)735-8888
Address: 2555 US Hwy 17 South, Wauchula, FL 33873
Lat/Lon: 27.30509/-81.48127

SEE AD ALACHUA PAGE 93

WEBSTER—C-3

(E) Florida Grande Motor Coach Resort—(Sumter) *From I-75 & exit 301: Go E on US 50 for 13-1/2 then N on CR 471 for 4 mi to Webster, then East on SE 1st Ave/CR 478 for 2 miles. Enter on L.* ◊◊◊◊FACILITIES: 215 sites, typical site width 30 ft, accepts full hkup units only, 215 full hkups, (30/50 amps), laundry. ◊◊◊RECREATION: swim pool. Pets welcome, quantity restrict. Partial handicap access. No tents. Open all yr. Big rigs welcome. Rate in 2010 $27-35 per vehicle. Phone: (352)569-1169.

(W) Sunshine Village RV Resort—(Sumter) *From jct Hwy 471 & Hwy 740 (W Central Ave): Go 3/4 mi W on Hwy 740. Enter on R.* ◊◊◊FACILITIES: 80 sites, typical site width 25 ft, 80 full hkups, (20/30/50 amps), WiFi Instant Internet at site ($), phone/cable on-site Internet (needs activ), family camping, dump, laundry. ◊◊◊RECREATION: rec hall, equipped pavilion, swim pool, shuffleboard court 4 shuffleboard courts, activities, horseshoes. Pets welcome, quantity restrict. No tents. Open all yr. Rate in 2010 $40 for 2 persons. Member ARVC. CCUSA 50% Discount. CCUSA reservations Accepted, CCUSA max stay Unlimited, Cash only for CCUSA disc. Discount available May thru Sep.

Phone: (352)793-8626
Address: 10129 SE 22nd Path, Webster, FL 33597
Lat/Lon: 28.60991/-82.06717
Email: sunshinevillage33597@yahoo.com
Web: www.sushinevillageflorida.com

(W) Webster Travel Park (RV SPACES)—(Sumter) *From jct Hwy 471 & Hwy 740 (W Central Ave): Go 1 mi W on Hwy 740. Enter on L.* FACILITIES: 249 sites, typical site width 35 ft, 240 full hkups, 9 W&E, (30/50 amps), dump, laundry. RECREATION: swim pool, pond fishing. Pets welcome ($), breed restrict, size restrict, quantity restrict. Partial handicap access. No tents. Open all yr. Big rigs welcome. Rate in 2010 $35 for 2 persons. Member ARVC. Phone: (352)793-6765.

Woodall's Tip... Turn to the Travel Section for "at-a-glance" RV Sales & Service Locations.

WESLEY CHAPEL—C-3

(W) QUAIL RUN RV RESORT—(Pasco) *From jct I-75 (Zepher Hills exit 279) & SR 54: Go 1/2 mi W on SR 54, then 2 mi N on Old Pasco Rd. Enter on R.*

◊◊◊◊◊FACILITIES: 291 sites, typical site width 35 ft, 291 full hkups, (20/30/50 amps), many extd stay sites (winter), 53 pull-thrus, cable TV, WiFi Instant Internet at site, WiFi Internet central location, family camping, dump, non-guest dump $, laundry, full svc store, RV supplies, LP gas by weight/by meter, ice, picnic tables, patios, controlled access.

◊◊◊◊RECREATION: rec hall, rec room/area, equipped pavilion, swim pool, golf nearby, play equipment, 4 shuffleboard courts, activities, horseshoes.

Pets welcome, breed restrict. Partial handicap access. No tents. Open all yr. Planned activities winter only. Big rigs welcome. Escort to site. Clubs welcome. Rate in 2010 $38-44 for 2 persons. MC/VISA/DISC/Debit. Member ARVC, FLARVC. FMCA discount. CCUSA 50% Discount. CCUSA reservations Recommended, CCUSA max stay 3 days. Discount available Apr thru Sep.

Text 81345 to (440)725-8687 to see our Visual Tour.

Phone: (800)582-7084
Address: 6946 Old Pasco Rd., Wesley Chapel, FL 33544
Lat/Lon: 28.25846/-82.34200
Email: qrrv@usa.net
Web: www.quailrunrv.com

SEE AD PAGE 178 AND AD TRAVEL SECTION PAGE 78 AND AD TRAVEL SECTION PAGE 74

WEST PALM BEACH—D-5

JUNO OCEAN WALK RV RESORT—*From West Palm Beach: Go 12-1/4 mi N on I-95 (exit 83), then 4-1/2 mi E on Donald Ross Rd, then 3/4 mi N on US 1, then 1/4 mi W on Juno Ocean Walk. Enter at end.*

SEE PRIMARY LISTING AT JUNO BEACH AND AD JUNO BEACH PAGE 132

(NW) Lion Country Safari KOA—(Palm Beach) *From jct I-95 (exit 68) & US 98/80 (Southern Blvd): Go 15 1/2 mi W on Southern Blvd. Enter on R.* ◊◊◊FACILITIES: 233 sites, typical site width 30 ft, 40 ft max RV length, 211 full hkups, 22 W&E, (20/30/50 amps), 50 amps ($), 160 pull-thrus, family camping, tenting, dump, laundry, full svc store. ◊◊◊RECREATION: swim pool, playground. Pets welcome, breed restrict, quantity restrict. Partial handicap access. Open all yr. Rate in 2010 $49-56 for 2 persons. Member ARVC, FLARVC. Phone: (800)562-9115. KOA discount. FMCA discount.

✱ **(NW) PALM BEACH RV**—*From jct US 98/80 (Southern Blvd) & I-95: Go 8 mi N on I-95 (exit 76), then 1/2 mi W on Hwy 708 (Blue Heron Blvd), then 1-1/4 mi S on Hwy 809 (Military Tr). Enter on L.*
SALES: travel trailers, park models, 5th wheels, toy hauler, pre-owned unit sales. SERVICES: full-time mech, RV appliance repair, body work/collision repair, LP gas by weight/by meter, sells parts/accessories, installs hitches. Open all yr. MC/VISA/DISC/AMEX/Debit.

Phone: (561)689-5788
Address: 5757 N Military Trail, West Palm Beach, FL 33407
Lat/Lon: 26.76335/-80.10851
Email: palmbeachrv@aol.com
Web: www.palmbeachrv.com

SEE AD NEXT PAGE

(NW) VACATION INN RESORT (CAMP RESORT)—(Palm Beach) *From jct US 98/80 (Southern Blvd) & I-95: Go 8 mi N on I-95 (exit 76), then 1/2 mi W on Hwy 708 (Blue Heron Blvd), then 3/4 mi S on Hwy 809 (Military Rd). Enter on L.*

PARADISE FOUND IN WEST PALM BEACH

Winter/Summer, Vacation Inn offers luxury RVing for most selective customer. Rated 5W. Member of Best Parks in America. The only luxury Resort in Palm Beach Cty. Only admit units 10 yrs old or newer. $45/70 per night. Reserv, only.

FACILITIES: 400 sites, typical site width 35 ft, accepts full hkup units only, 400 full hkups, (30/50 amps), mostly extd stay sites (winter), cable TV, WiFi Instant Internet at site, laundry, picnic tables, patios, controlled access.

VACATION INN RESORT—Continued on page 178

WEST PALM BEACH—Continued
VACATION INN RESORT—Continued

RECREATION: rec hall, rec room/area, 2 swim pools, hot tub, lake fishing, golf nearby, playground, shuffleboard court 6 shuffleboard courts, activities, tennis.

Pets welcome, breed restrict. Partial handicap access. No tents. Open all yr. Big rigs welcome. Escort to site. Rate in 2010 $55-70 for 2 persons. MC/VISA/DISC/AMEX/Debit. Member ARVC, FLARVC.

Phone: (561)848-6170
Address: 6500 N. Military Trl, Office, W Palm Beach, FL 33407
Lat/Lon: 26.77150/-80.10601
Email: virrentals@comcast.net
Web: www.vacationinnrvpark.com

SEE AD THIS PAGE

WEWAHITCHKA—F-3

(N) DEAD LAKES STATE RECREATION AREA—(Gulf) *From jct Hwy-71 & Hwy-22: Go 4 mi N on Hwy-71.* FACILITIES: 20 sites, 35 ft max RV length, 10 E, 10 no hkups, tenting, dump. RECREATION: boating, canoeing, ramp, lake fishing. Open all yr. Phone: (850)639-2702.

WHITE SPRINGS—A-3

(SW) Lee's Country Campground—(Columbia) *From jct I-75 (exit 439) & Hwy 136: Go 3/4 mi E on Hwy 136. Enter on R.* ◇◇◇FACILITIES: 38 sites, typical site width 30 ft, 21 full hkups, 17 W&E, (20/30/50 amps), 30 pull-thrus, WiFi Instant Internet at site, tenting, dump, non-guest dump $, laundry, ice. ◇RECREATION: rec hall, pavilion, horseshoes. Pets welcome, breed restrict, quantity restrict. Partial handicap access. Open all yr. Big rigs welcome. Rate in 2010 $28-30 for 2 persons. CCUSA 50% Discount. CCUSA reservations Accepted, CCUSA max stay 14 days. Dependant upon availability, pet restrictions, cash only, discount not available Memorial weekend,.

Phone: (386)397-4132
Address: 2264 NW Thunder St (SR 136), White Springs, FL 32096
Lat/Lon: 30.31976/-82.79367
Web: www.leescountrycampground.com

(NW) STEPHEN FOSTER FOLK CULTURE CENTER STATE PARK—(Hamilton) *From jct I-75 (exit 439) & Hwy 136: Go 3 mi E on Hwy 136, then 1/4 mi N on US 41 N. From I-10 (exit*

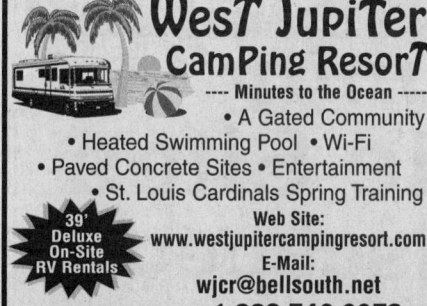

WHITE SPRINGS—Continued
STEPHEN FOSTER FOLK CULTURE CENTER STATE PARK—Continued

301) & US 41 N: Go 9 mi on US 41 N. Enter on L. FACILITIES: 45 sites, 45 W&E, (30/50 amps), 14 pull-thrus, family camping, tenting, dump, laundry. RECREATION: canoeing, river fishing, playground. Pets welcome. Partial handicap access. Open all yr. Big rigs welcome. Phone: (386)397-2733.

(W) SUWANNEE VALLEY CAMPGROUND—(Columbia) *From jct I-75 (exit 439) & Hwy 136: Go 2-1/2 mi E on Hwy 136, then 1/10 mi S on White Springs Rd, then 1/2 mi SE on Stephen Foster Rd. Enter at end.*

◇◇FACILITIES: 219 sites, typical site width 35 ft, 119 full hkups, (30/50 amps), 100 no hkups, 119 pull-thrus, WiFi Instant Internet at site, WiFi Internet central location, family camping, tenting, RV's/park model rentals, cabins, RV storage, dump, non-guest dump $, laundry, ltd groc, RV supplies, LP gas by weight/by meter, ice, picnic tables, fire rings, wood.

◇◇◇RECREATION: rec hall, rec room/area, equipped pavilion, swim pool, wading pool, boating, no motors, canoeing, kayaking, dock, 5 canoe/4 kayak rentals, river fishing, golf nearby, bsktball, play equipment, 2 shuffleboard courts, horseshoes, hiking trails, v-ball.

Pets welcome. Partial handicap access. Open all yr. Planned group activities & church services winter only. Clubs welcome. Rate in 2010 $30-32 for 2 persons. MC/VISA/DISC/AMEX. CCUSA 50% Discount. CCUSA reservations Recommended, CCUSA max stay 7 days. Discount not available Memorial Day weekend.

Phone: (386)397-1667
Address: 786 NW Stephen Foster Dr, White Springs, FL 32096
Lat/Lon: 30.31954/-82.75524
Email: svcg01@gmail.com
Web: www.suwanneevalleycampground.net

SEE AD THIS PAGE

WILDWOOD—B-3

(W) KOA-Wildwood—(Sumter) *From jct I-75 (exit 329 - old 66) & Hwy 44: Go 100 feet E on Hwy 44. Enter on L.* ◇◇◇FACILITIES: 125 sites, typical site width 30 ft, 108 full hkups, 2 E, (30/50 amps), 15 no hkups, 88 pull-thrus, family camping, tenting, dump, laundry, ltd groc. ◇◇◇RECREATION: swim pool, playground. Pets welcome, breed restrict. Partial handicap access. Open all yr. Rate in 2010 $39-63 for 2 persons. Phone: (352) 748-2774. KOA discount.

(E) Thousand Palms RV Resort—(Sumter) *From north jct Hwy 41 & Hwy 44: Go 7-1/2 mi on Hwy 44. Enter on R.* ◇◇◇◇FACILITIES: 105 sites, typical site width 80 ft, 85 full hkups, 20 W&E, (30/50 amps), 14

WILDWOOD—Continued
Thousand Palms RV Resort—Continued

pull-thrus, WiFi Instant Internet at site ($), WiFi Internet central location, family camping, tenting, RV storage, dump, laundry, RV supplies, ice, picnic tables, patios. ◇◇◇RECREATION: rec hall, swim pool, pond fishing, putting green, shuffleboard court 2 shuffleboard courts, activities, horseshoes, hiking trails. Pets welcome. Partial handicap access. Open all yr. Big rigs welcome. Rate in 2010 $30-55 per family. MC/VISA. Member ARVC, FLARVC. CCUSA 50% Discount. CCUSA reservations Required, CCUSA max stay 7 days, Cash only for CCUSA disc. Discount available 12 mos/yr, 2 night minimum stay/7 night maximum at discounted rate. Reservations limited to 30 days in advance for CCUSA discount.

Phone: (321)284-4910
Address: 6545 W State Rt 44, Lake Panasoffkee, FL 33538
Lat/Lon: 28.85297/-82.21244
Email: reservations@thousandpalmsresort.com
Web: www.thousandpalmsresort.com

(W) THREE FLAGS RV RESORT (CAMP RESORT)—(Sumter) *From jct I-75 (exit 329) & Hwy 44: Go 1 mi E on Hwy 44. Enter on R.*

FACILITIES: 216 sites, typical site width 25 ft, 216 full hkups, (20/30/50 amps), some extd stay sites (winter), 95 pull-thrus, WiFi Instant Internet at site ($), family camping, tenting, RV's/park model rentals, dump, non-guest dump $, laundry, picnic tables.

RECREATION: rec hall, swim pool, mini-golf, putting green, golf nearby, bsktball, play equipment, 2 shuffleboard courts, activities, horseshoes.

Pets welcome. Partial handicap access. Open Nov 1 - May 1. Big rigs welcome. Escort to site. Clubs welcome. Rate in 2010 $32 per vehicle. MC/VISA/AMEX.

Phone: (352)748-3870
Address: 1755 E SR 44, Wildwood, FL 34785
Lat/Lon: 28.85994/-82.07457

SEE AD ALACHUA PAGE 93 AND AD ORLANDO PAGE 149

WILLISTON—B-3

(NW) Devil's Den Springs Resort—(Levy) *From jct US 41 & US 27A: Go 1 mi W on US 27A, then 1 mi N on NE 180th Ave. Enter on L.* ◇◇◇FACILITIES: 42 sites, typical site width 30 ft, 30 full hkups, 6 W&E, (20/30/50 amps), 6 no hkups, 20 pull-thrus, tenting, dump. ◇◇RECREATION: swim pool. No pets. Partial handicap access. Open all yr. Rate in 2010 $22 for 2 persons. Phone: (352)528-3344.

WILLISTON—Continued on page 179

WILLISTON—Continued

(NE) Williston Crossings RV Resort—(Iguy) *From W jct US 41 & Us 27A: Go 1 mi E on US 27A, then 300 ft N on NE 5th St. Enter on R.* ◊◊◊◊◊FACILITIES: 149 sites, typical site width 45 ft, 149 full hkups, (30/50 amps), 16 pull-thrus, dump, laundry. ◊◊◊RECREATION: lake fishing. Pets welcome, breed restrict, size restrict, quantity restrict. Partial handicap access. No tents. Open all yr. Big rigs welcome. Rate in 2010 $33.95-38.95 for 2 persons. Member ARVC, FLARVC. Phone: (800)615-5774.

WIMAUMA—D-3

(S) LITTLE MANATEE RIVER STATE RECREATION AREA—(Hillsborough) *From jct Hwy 674 & US 301: Go 5 mi S on US 301, then W on Lightfoot Rd.* FACILITIES: 34 sites, 34 W&E, tenting, dump. RECREATION: boating, 5 hp limit, canoeing, river fishing, playground. Partial handicap access. Open all yr. Phone: (813)671-5005.

WINTER GARDEN—C-4

(W) Stage Stop Campground—(Orange) *From jct Florida Tpk (exit 267) & Hwy 50: Go 2-1/2 mi W on Hwy 50. Enter on L.* ◊◊◊FACILITIES: 248 sites, typical site width 35 ft, 248 full hkups, (20/30/50 amps), 25 pull-thrus, family camping, tenting, dump, laundry, ltd groc. ◊◊◊RECREATION: swim pool, pond fishing, play equipment. Pets welcome, quantity restrict. Open all yr. Big rigs welcome. Rate in 2010 $32 for 2 persons. Phone: (407)656-8000.

(W) WINTER GARDEN RV RESORT - ENCORE—(Orange) *From Florida Turnpike (exit 267): Go 2 mi W on Hwy 50. Enter on R.*

WELCOME

◊◊◊◊FACILITIES: 377 sites, typical site width 25 ft, 377 full hkups, (20/30/50 amps), 50 amps ($), many extd stay sites (winter), 50 pull-thrus, cable TV, phone/cable Instant Internet at site, WiFi Internet central location, family camping, tenting, RV storage, dump, laundry, LP gas by weight/by meter, picnic tables, patios.

◊◊◊◊RECREATION: rec hall, equipped pavilion, 2 swim pools, wading pool, golf nearby, bsktball, playground, shuffleboard court 4 shuffleboard courts, activities, horseshoes.

Pets welcome, breed restrict. Partial handicap access. Open all yr. Church & planned activities winter only. Big rigs welcome. Clubs welcome. Rate in 2010 $36-47 for 2 persons. MC/VISA/DISC. Member ARVC, FLARVC.

Phone: (407)656-1415
Address: 13905 W Colonial Dr, Winter Garden, FL 34787
Lat/Lon: 28.55112/-81.59062
Email: wintergarden@mhchomes.com

SEE AD ALACHUA PAGE 93 AND AD ORLANDO PAGE 149

WINTER HAVEN—C-4

(E) CYPRESS CAMPGROUND & RV PARK—(Polk) *From jct Hwy-540 & US-27: Go 1-1/2 mi W on Hwy-540. Enter on L.*

WELCOME

OLD FAVORITE, NEW LOOK

www.cypresscampground.com, Florida's best attractions nearby. We offer cable, Wi-Fi, clean bathhouses, laundry, heated pool & many activities. RV dealership with consignment sales. (863)324-7400.

◊◊◊◊FACILITIES: 191 sites, typical site width 32 ft, 191 full hkups, (20/30/50 amps), many extd stay sites (winter), 120 pull-thrus, heater not allowed, cable TV, WiFi Instant Internet at site, phone/cable on-site Internet (needs activ), WiFi Internet central location, family camping, tenting, RV storage, dump, laundry, LP gas by weight/by meter, picnic tables, patios.

◊◊◊◊RECREATION: rec hall, rec room/area, swim pool, mini-golf, golf nearby, shuffleboard court 2 shuffleboard courts, activities, horseshoes.

Pets welcome, breed restrict. Partial handicap access. Open all yr. Big rigs welcome. Clubs welcome. Rate in 2010 $24.95-37.95 for 2 persons. MC/VISA/DISC/Debit. Member ARVC.

Phone: (863)324-7400
Address: 7400 Cypress Gardens Blvd, Winter Haven, FL 33884
Lat/Lon: 27.97805/-81.65082
Email: info@cypresscampgorund.com
Web: www.cypresscampground.com

SEE AD THIS PAGE

Check out our web site www.woodalls.com

WINTER HAVEN—Continued

CYPRESS RV SALES—*From jct Hwy 540 & US 27: Go 1-1/2 mi W on Hwy 540. Enter on L.* SALES: park models, preowned unit sales. SERVICES: Open all yr. MC/VISA/Debit.

WELCOME

Phone: (800)858-7275
Address: 7400 Cypress Garden Blvd, Winter Haven, FL 33884
Email: info@cypressgardensrvsales.com
Web: cypressgardensrvsales.com

SEE AD THIS PAGE

(E) East Haven RV Park (RV SPACES)—(DeSoto) *From jct US 27 & Hwy 542 W: Go 1-1/2 mi W on Hwy 542 W. Enter on L.* FACILITIES: 73 sites, typical site width 15 ft, 36 ft max RV length, 73 full hkups, (30/50 amps), 12 pull-thrus, family camping, laundry. RECREATION: swim pool. Pets welcome. No tents. Age restrict may apply. Open all yr. Rate in 2010 $40-45 for 2 persons. Phone: (863)324-2624.

(SE) HAMMONDELL CAMPSITES & RV SALES—(Polk) *From jct US 27 & Hwy 540: Go 1-3/4 mi W on Hwy 540, then 1/2 mi N on Cypress Gardens Rd. Enter on L.*

WELCOME

◊◊◊FACILITIES: 163 sites, typical site width 22 ft, 40 ft max RV length, 163 full hkups, (30/50 amps), some extd stay sites (winter), 40 pull-thrus, WiFi Instant Internet at site, phone/cable on-site Internet (needs activ), WiFi Internet central location, family camping, cabins, dump, non-guest dump $, laundry, LP gas by weight/by meter, picnic tables, patios.

CAMPCLUB USA

◊◊◊RECREATION: rec hall, pavilion, swim pool, golf nearby, shuffleboard court 4 shuffleboard courts, activities.

Pets welcome. No tents. Open all yr. Planned activities in winter only. Security System. Rate in 2010 $30 for 2 persons. MC/VISA/DISC/AMEX/Debit. CCUSA 50% Discount. CCUSA reservations Required, CCUSA max stay 4 days, Cash only for CCUSA disc., CCUSA disc. not avail S, CCUSA disc. not avail F,Sa, CCUSA disc. not avail holidays. Discount available Apr thru Oct. No tents.

Phone: (863)324-5775
Address: 5601 Cypress Gardens Rd, Winter Haven, FL 33884
Lat/Lon: 27.98581/-81.66103
Email: hammondell@verizon.net
Web: www.hammondell.com

SEE AD TRAVEL SECTION PAGE 78

YANKEETOWN—B-3

(W) Cattail Creek RV Park—(Levy) *From jct Hwy 19 & Hwy 40: Go 3 mi W on Hwy 40. Enter on L.* ◊◊FACILITIES: 82 sites, typical site width 40 ft, 72 full hkups, (30/50 amps), 10 no hkups, 5 pull-thrus, family camping, tenting, dump, laundry. ◊◊RECREATION: swim pool. Pets welcome. Partial handicap access. Open all yr. Rate in 2010 $30 for 2 persons. Phone: (352)447-3050.

YULEE—A-3

(N) Osprey First In Florida RV Park—(Nassau) *From jct I-95 & US 17 (exit 380): Go 100 yards E on US 17, then 1 block N on Hance's Pkwy. Enter on L.* ◊◊◊FACILITIES: 73 sites, typical site width 25 ft, 73 full hkups, (30/50 amps), 72 pull-thrus, family camping, dump, laundry. ◊◊◊RECREATION: swim pool, pond fishing, playground. Pets welcome, breed restrict. Partial handicap access. No tents. Open all yr. Big rigs welcome. Rate in 2010 $35 for 2 persons. Phone: (904)225-2080. FMCA discount.

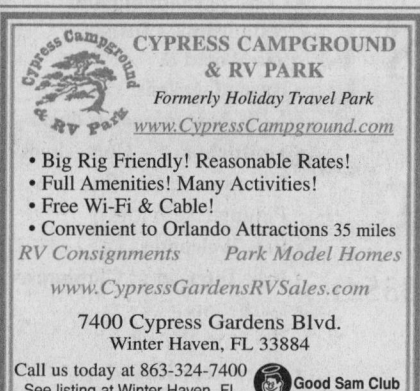

ZEPHYRHILLS—C-3

(NE) BAKER ACRES RV RESORT—(Pasco) *From N jct US 301 & Hwy 54 West: Go 1/4 mi E on Hwy 54, then 1-1/2 mi N on Wire Rd. Enter on R.*

WELCOME

WELCOME TO CAREFREE RV RESORTS!

A charming country setting you will love! This adult resort is just minutes from shopping, great golf, restaurants & medical facilities, plus all the attractions in Tampa. Always something fun to do & great people to meet!

◊◊◊◊FACILITIES: 353 sites, typical site width 30 ft, 40 ft max RV length, accepts full hkup units only, 353 full hkups, (20/30/50 amps), mostly extd stay sites (winter), WiFi Instant Internet at site ($), phone/cable on-site Internet (needs activ), phone Internet central location, RV storage, dump, non-guest dump $, laundry, picnic tables, patios.

BAKER ACRES RV RESORT—Continued on next page

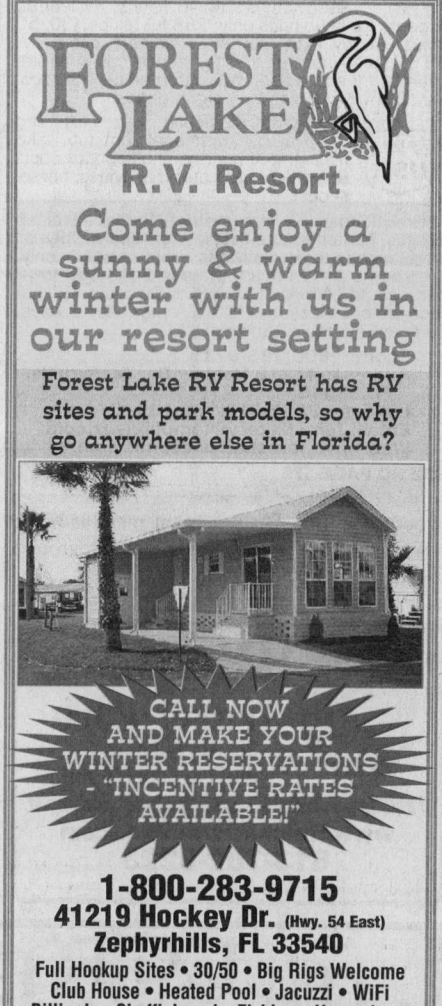

ZEPHYRHILLS—Continued
BAKER ACRES RV RESORT—Continued

◊◊◊◊RECREATION: rec hall, rec room/area, swim pool, golf nearby, shuffleboard court 12 shuffleboard courts, activities, horseshoes.

Pets welcome ($), breed restrict. No tents. Age restrict may apply. Open all yr. Church services winter only. No showers. Member ARVC, FLARVC. CCUSA 50% Discount. CCUSA reservations Required, CCUSA max stay 3 days, Cash only for CCUSA disc., CCUSA disc. not avail holidays. Not available Jan 1-Apr 1.

Phone: (813)782-3950
Address: 7820 Wire Rd, Zephyrhills, FL 33540
Lat/Lon: 28.27113/-82.17962
Email: bakeracresrv@tampabay.rr.com
Web: www.carefreervresorts.com

SEE AD TAMPA PAGES 170-171

FOREST LAKE ESTATES RV RESORT—(Pasco) *From north jct US 301 & SR 54: Go 3 mi E on SR 54-East. Enter on R.*

◊◊◊◊FACILITIES: 268 sites, typical site width 35 ft, 40 ft max RV length, accepts full hkup units only, 268 full hkups, (30/50 amps), many extd stay sites (winter), cable TV, WiFi Instant Internet at site, phone/cable on-site Internet (needs activ), WiFi Internet central location, laundry, LP gas by weight, patios.

◊◊◊◊RECREATION: rec hall, rec room/area, swim pool, hot tub, lake fishing, golf nearby, shuffleboard court 6 shuffleboard courts, activities, horseshoes.

Pets welcome ($), size restrict. Partial handicap access. No tents. Age restrict may apply. Open all yr. Planned group activities winter season only. Restrooms limited hours. Rate in 2010 $30 for 2 persons. MC/VISA. CCUSA 50% Discount. CCUSA reservations Accepted, CCUSA max stay 2 days. Discount available Apr thru Oct.

Phone: (800)283-9715
Address: 41219 Hockey Dr, Zephyrhills, FL 33540
Lat/Lon: 28.25312/-82.13520
Email: forestlakerv@tampabay.rr.com
Web: www.forestlakes-estates.com/rv

SEE AD PAGE 179

Woodall's Tip... Diamonds on maps indicate towns under which RV Park & Campground locations are listed.

ZEPHYRHILLS—Continued

(SW) GLEN HAVEN RV RESORT—(Pasco) *From S jct SR 54 West & US 301: Go 2 mi S on US 301, then 1/2 mi W on Chancey Rd. Enter on R.*

◊◊◊◊FACILITIES: 218 sites, typical site width 25 ft, 40 ft max RV length, 218 full hkups, (30/50 amps), mostly extd stay sites (winter), WiFi Instant Internet at site ($), phone/cable on-site Internet (needs activ), phone Internet central location, dump, laundry, picnic tables, patios.

◊◊◊◊RECREATION: rec hall, rec room/area, swim pool, hot tub, golf nearby, shuffleboard court 12 shuffleboard courts, activities, horseshoes.

Pets welcome, breed restrict, size restrict, quantity restrict. Partial handicap access. No tents. Age restrict may apply. Open all yr. Rate in 2010 $32 for 2 persons. MC/VISA. CCUSA 50% Discount. CCUSA reservations Required, CCUSA max stay 7 days, Cash only for CCUSA disc., CCUSA disc. not avail holidays. Not available Jan 1-Apr 1.

Phone: (813)782-1856
Address: 37251 Chancey Rd., Zephyrhills, FL 33541
Lat/Lon: 28.20828/-82.20000
Email: glenhavenrv@tampabay.rr.com
Web: www.carefreervresorts.com

SEE AD TAMPA PAGES 170-171

(SW) HAPPY DAYS RV PARK—(Pasco) *From jct I-75 (exit 58) & SR 54: Go 8 mi E on SR 54, then 2 blocks S on Allen Rd. Enter on R.*

◊◊◊FACILITIES: 300 sites, typical site width 30 ft, 38 ft max RV length, 300 full hkups, (20/30/50 amps), many extd stay sites (winter), phone/cable on-site Internet (needs activ), WiFi Internet central location, family camping, RV's/park model rentals, RV storage, dump, non-guest dump $, laundry.

◊◊◊RECREATION: rec hall, rec room/area, swim pool, golf nearby, shuffleboard court 4 shuffleboard courts, activities, horseshoes.

Pets welcome, breed restrict, size restrict. No tents. Open all yr. Church services during winter only. Rate in 2010 $32 for 2 persons. MC/VISA. Member ARVC, FLARVC. CCUSA 50% Discount. CCUSA reservations Recommended, CCUSA max stay 4 days. Discount available Apr thru Sept. Age restrictions may apply.

Visit a Dealer/Service Location in Woodall's.

ZEPHYRHILLS—Continued
HAPPY DAYS RV PARK—Continued

Phone: (813)788-4858
Address: 4603 Allen Rd, Zephyrhills, FL 33541
Lat/Lon: 28.22388/-82.20522
Email: happydaysrv@hotmail.com

SEE AD THIS PAGE

(SW) HILLCREST RV RESORT—(Pasco) *From jct US 301 & Hwy 54 West: Go 1 mi W on Hwy 54 West, then 1/2 mi S on Lane Rd. Enter on R.*

◊◊◊FACILITIES: 502 sites, typical site width 35 ft, 502 full hkups, (30/50 amps), mostly extd stay sites (winter), phone on-site Internet (needs activ), WiFi Internet central location, RV storage, dump, laundry.

◊◊◊◊RECREATION: rec hall, rec room/area, swim pool, hot tub, golf nearby, shuffleboard court 10 shuffleboard courts, activities, horseshoes.

Pets welcome, breed restrict, size restrict, quantity restrict. Partial handicap access. No tents. Age restrict may apply. Open all yr. Big rigs welcome. Rate in 2010 $31 for 2 persons. MC/VISA.

Phone: (813)782-1947
Address: 4421 Lane Rd, Zephyrhills, FL 33541
Lat/Lon: 28.22139/-82.19694
Email: hillcrestrv@verizon.net

SEE AD THIS PAGE

(SW) Hunter's Run RV Resort—(Pasco) *From south jct SR 54 West & US 301: Go 2 mi S on US 301, then 1-1/2 mi W on Chancey Rd. Enter on R.* ◊◊◊FACILITIES: 309 sites, typical site width 20 ft, 40 ft max RV length, 309 full hkups, (20/30/50 amps), dump, laundry. ◊◊◊◊RECREATION: swim pool. Pets welcome, breed restrict, size restrict, quantity restrict. Partial handicap access. No tents. Age restrict may apply. Open all yr. Rate in 2010 $31 per vehicle. Member FLARVC. Phone: (813)783-1133.

(W) Jim's RV Park—(Pasco) *From south jct US 301 & SR 54 West: Go 3 mi W on SR 54 West. Enter on L.* ◊◊◊FACILITIES: 155 sites, 40 ft max RV length, 147 full hkups, 8 W&E, (20/30/50 amps), 25 pull-thrus, phone on-site Internet (needs activ), WiFi Internet central location, RV storage, dump, laundry. ◊◊◊RECREATION: rec hall, swim pool, shuffleboard court 2 shuffleboard courts, activities, horseshoes. Pets welcome, breed restrict, size restrict, quantity restrict. No tents. Age restrict may apply. Open all yr. Rate in 2010 $28-30 for 2 persons. CCUSA 50% Discount. CCUSA reservations Not Accepted, Cash only for CCUSA disc. Discount available Apr thru Oct. 55+ park.

Phone: (813)782-5610
Address: 35120 SR 54 W, Zephyrhills, FL 33541
Lat/Lon: 28.22304/-82.23558

ZEPHYRHILLS—Continued on next page

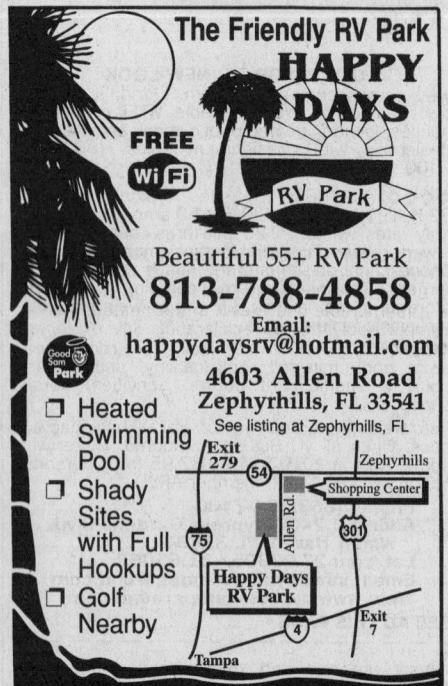

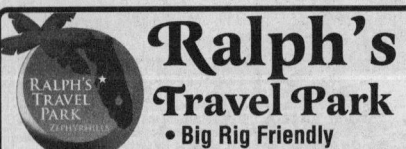

ZEPHYRHILLS—Continued

(W) LEISURE DAYS RV RESORT—(Pasco) *From jct I-75 (exit 279) & Hwy 54 West: Go 6-3/4 mi E on Hwy 54, then 1 block S on Hwy 579. Enter on R.*

◆◆◆FACILITIES: 44 sites, typical site width 27 ft, 36 ft max RV length, 44 full hkups, (30/50 amps), mostly extd stay sites (winter), phone/cable on-site Internet (needs activ), phone Internet central location, family camping, RV's/park model rentals, dump, laundry, LP gas by weight, patios.

◆◆◆RECREATION: rec hall, swim pool, golf nearby, shuffleboard court 4 shuffleboard courts, activities, horseshoes.

Pets welcome, breed restrict, size restrict, quantity restrict. Partial handicap access. No tents. Open all yr. Rate in 2010 $30-36 for 2 persons.

Phone: (813)788-2631
Address: 34533 Leisure Days Dr, Zephyrhills, FL 33541
Lat/Lon: 28.21599/-82.24536
Email: leisuredays@newbymanagement.com
Web: www.Leisuredaysrvresort.com

SEE AD PAGE 180

(SE) MAJESTIC OAKS RV RESORT—(Pasco) *From jct SR 54 West & US 301: Go 2 mi S on US 301, then 1-1/2 mi E on Chancey Rd. Enter on L.*

WELCOME TO CAREFREE RV RESORTS!
Enjoy a relaxing lifestyle in a majestic setting for active adults! Near Tampa, Busch Gardens, Gulf beaches and Orlando theme parks. Our friendly staff will help make your stay with us everything you dreamed it could be!

◆◆◆◆FACILITIES: 252 sites, typical site width 40 ft, 252 full hkups, (30/50 amps), many extd stay sites (winter), WiFi Instant Internet at site ($), phone/cable on-site Internet (needs activ), phone Internet central location, RV storage, laundry, patios.

◆◆◆◆RECREATION: rec hall, pavilion, swim pool, golf nearby, shuffleboard court 8 shuffleboard courts, activities, tennis, horseshoes.

Pets welcome, breed restrict. Partial handicap access. No tents. Age restrict may apply. Open all yr. Planned activities in winter only. Big rigs welcome. Escort to site. Rate in 2010 $32 for 2 persons. MC/VISA/Debit. Member ARVC, FLARVC. CCUSA 50% Discount. CCUSA reservations Required, CCUSA max stay 7 days, Cash only for CCUSA disc., CCUSA disc. not avail holidays. Not available Jan 1-Apr 1.

Phone: (813)783-7518
Address: 3751 Laurel Valley Blvd, Zephyrhills, FL 33542
Lat/Lon: 28.21004/-82.16135
Email: majesticoaksrv@tampabay.rr.com
Web: www.carefreervresorts.com

SEE AD TAMPA PAGES 170-171

(SW) RAINBOW VILLAGE RV RESORT—(Pasco) *From jct US 301 & Hwy 54 West: Go 1 mi W on Hwy 54 West, then 1 mi S on Lane Rd. Enter on L.*

WELCOME TO CAREFREE RV RESORTS!
A friendly place for the fun at heart! This resort is full of fun things to do that will make your stay with us a memorable one. Relax in the heated, indoor Olympic pool after an exhilarating day exploring Tampa!

◆◆◆◆FACILITIES: 382 sites, typical site width 35 ft, accepts full hkup units only, 382 full hkups, (20/30/50 amps), mostly extd stay sites (winter), WiFi Instant Internet at site ($), phone/cable on-site Internet (needs activ), WiFi Internet central location, RV's/park model rentals, laundry, picnic tables, patios.

◆◆◆◆RECREATION: rec hall, rec room/area, swim pool, golf nearby, bsktball, shuffleboard court 6 shuffleboard courts, activities, horseshoes, v-ball.

Pets welcome, breed restrict. Partial handicap access. No tents. Age restrict may apply. Open all yr. Planned activities winter only. Free cable for summer only. Big rigs welcome. Rate in 2010 $32 for 2 persons. MC/VISA. CCUSA 50% Discount.

ZEPHYRHILLS—Continued
RAINBOW VILLAGE RV RESORT—Continued

CCUSA reservations Recommended, CCUSA max stay 7 days. Based on availability. No aggressive breed pets. Metered electric.

Phone: (813)782-5075
Address: 4150 Lane Rd, Zephyrhills, FL 33541
Lat/Lon: 28.21822/-82.19641
Email: rainbowrv@tampabay.rr.com
Web: www.carefreervresorts.com

SEE AD TAMPA PAGES 170-171

(W) RALPH'S TRAVEL PARK—(Pasco) *From jct US 301 & Hwy 54 West: Go 2-1/2 mi W on Hwy 54. Enter on L.*

◆◆◆FACILITIES: 410 sites, typical site width 25 ft, 40 ft max RV length, 410 full hkups, (30/50 amps), mostly extd stay sites (winter), phone/cable on-site Internet (needs activ), WiFi Internet central location, RV storage, dump, non-guest dump $, laundry, patios.

◆◆◆RECREATION: rec hall, rec room/area, swim pool, golf nearby, shuffleboard court 8 shuffleboard courts, activities, horseshoes.

Pets welcome, breed restrict, size restrict, quantity restrict. No tents. Age restrict may apply. Open all yr. Rate in 2010 $31 for 2 persons. Member FLARVC. CCUSA 50% Discount. CCUSA reservations Recommended, CCUSA max stay 3 days, Cash only for CCUSA disc. Discount available May thru Sep.

Phone: (813)782-8223
Address: 34408 Hwy 54 W, Zephyrhills, FL 33543
Lat/Lon: 28.21859/-82.24739
Email: info@ralphstravelpark.com
Web: www.ralphstravelpark.com

SEE AD PAGE 180

(SW) Settlers Rest RV Park—(Pasco) *From S jct SR 54 West & US 301: Go 2 mi S on US 301, then 1/2 mi W on Chancey Rd. Enter on R.* ◆◆◆FACILITIES: 379 sites, typical site width 30 ft, 36 ft max RV length, accepts full hkup units only, 379 full hkups, (20/30/50 amps), laundry. Pets welcome, breed restrict. No tents. Age restrict may apply. Open all yr. Rate in 2010 $42 for 2 persons. Phone: (813)782-2003.

(SW) SOUTHERN CHARM RV RESORT—(Pasco) *From S jct Hwy 54 West & US 301: Go 2 mi S on US 301, then 1/4 mi W on Chancey Rd. Enter on R.*

WELCOME TO CAREFREE RV RESORTS!
Southern hospitality at it's best, all waiting for your arrival! Whether you like to relax by the pool, golf at one of the nearby courses or meet up with friends, we have it all for you. Ya'll come see us soon!

◆◆◆◆FACILITIES: 497 sites, typical site width 30 ft, 40 ft max RV length, accepts full hkup units only, 497 full hkups, (20/30/50 amps), many extd stay sites (winter), WiFi Instant Internet at site ($), phone/cable on-site Internet (needs activ), phone Internet central location, RV storage, dump, laundry, picnic tables, patios.

◆◆◆◆RECREATION: rec hall, swim pool, hot tub, golf nearby, shuffleboard court 8 shuffleboard courts, activities, horseshoes, v-ball.

Pets welcome, breed restrict, size restrict. Partial handicap access. No tents. Age restrict may apply. Open all yr. Planned activities winter only. MC/VISA. CCUSA 50% Discount. CCUSA reservations Required, CCUSA max stay 7 days, Cash only for CCUSA disc., CCUSA disc. not avail holidays. Not available Jan 1-Apr 1.

Phone: (813)783-3477
Address: 37811 Chancey Rd, Zephyrhills, FL 33541
Lat/Lon: 28.20848/-82.19115
Email: southerncharmrv@tampabay.rr.com
Web: www.carefreervresorts.com

SEE AD TAMPA PAGES 170-171

ZEPHYRHILLS—Continued

(SW) SWEETWATER RV PARK—(Pasco) *From south jct Hwy 54 West & US 301: Go 2 mi S on US 301, then 1/4 mi W on Chancey Rd. Enter on R.*

WELCOME TO CAREFREE RESORTS!
Where life couldn't be sweeter! Your home away from home welcomes you to a quiet, friendly park. Enjoy our new, heated pool & much more! Tampa's tourist attractions, great golf & fabulous shopping nearby.

◆◆◆FACILITIES: 289 sites, typical site width 30 ft, 38 ft max RV length, 289 full hkups, (30/50 amps), mostly extd stay sites (winter), WiFi Instant Internet at site ($), phone/cable on-site Internet (needs activ), phone Internet central location, laundry, picnic tables.

◆◆◆RECREATION: rec hall, swim pool, golf nearby, shuffleboard court 6 shuffleboard courts, activities, horseshoes.

Pets welcome, size restrict, quantity restrict. Partial handicap access. No tents. Age restrict may apply. Open all yr. MC/VISA. CCUSA 50% Discount. CCUSA reservations Required, CCUSA max stay Unlimited, Cash only for CCUSA disc., CCUSA disc. not avail holidays. Not available Feb 1-Mar 15. Cable tv available for long term use at fee.

Phone: (813)788-7513
Address: 37647 Chancey Rd, Zephyrhills, FL 33541
Lat/Lon: 28.20831/-82.19348
Email: sweetwaterrv@tampabay.RR.com
Web: www.carefreervresorts.com

SEE AD TAMPA PAGES 170-171

(NE) WATER'S EDGE RV RESORT—(Pasco) *From north jct US 301 & Hwy 54 W: Go 1 block E on Hwy 54, then 2 mi N on Wire Rd, then 2 mi E on Otis Allen Rd. Enter on R.*

WELCOME TO CAREFREE RV RESORTS!
A cozy, quiet resort, the perfect location to spend the winter. Close to all of Tampa's attractions, shopping & restaurants, plus lots of great amenities for your enjoyment. Come stay for a day, week, month or the season!

◆◆◆◆FACILITIES: 217 sites, typical site width 35 ft, 40 ft max RV length, accepts full hkup units only, 217 full hkups, (30/50 amps), mostly extd stay sites (winter), cable TV, ($), WiFi Instant Internet at site ($), phone/cable on-site Internet (needs activ), phone Internet central location, dump, laundry, picnic tables.

◆◆◆RECREATION: rec hall, swim pool, golf nearby, shuffleboard court 8 shuffleboard courts, activities.

Pets welcome, breed restrict. Partial handicap access. No tents. Age restrict may apply. Open all yr. CCUSA 50% Discount. CCUSA reservations Required, CCUSA max stay 7 days, Cash only for CCUSA disc., CCUSA disc. not avail holidays. Not available Jan 1-Apr 1. Cable tv available for long term only. Electricity metered.

Phone: (813)783-2708
Address: 39146 Otis Allen Rd, Zephyrhills, FL 33540
Lat/Lon: 28.27353/-82.16810
Email: watersedgerv@tampabay.rr.com
Web: www.carefreervresorts.com

SEE AD TAMPA PAGES 170-171

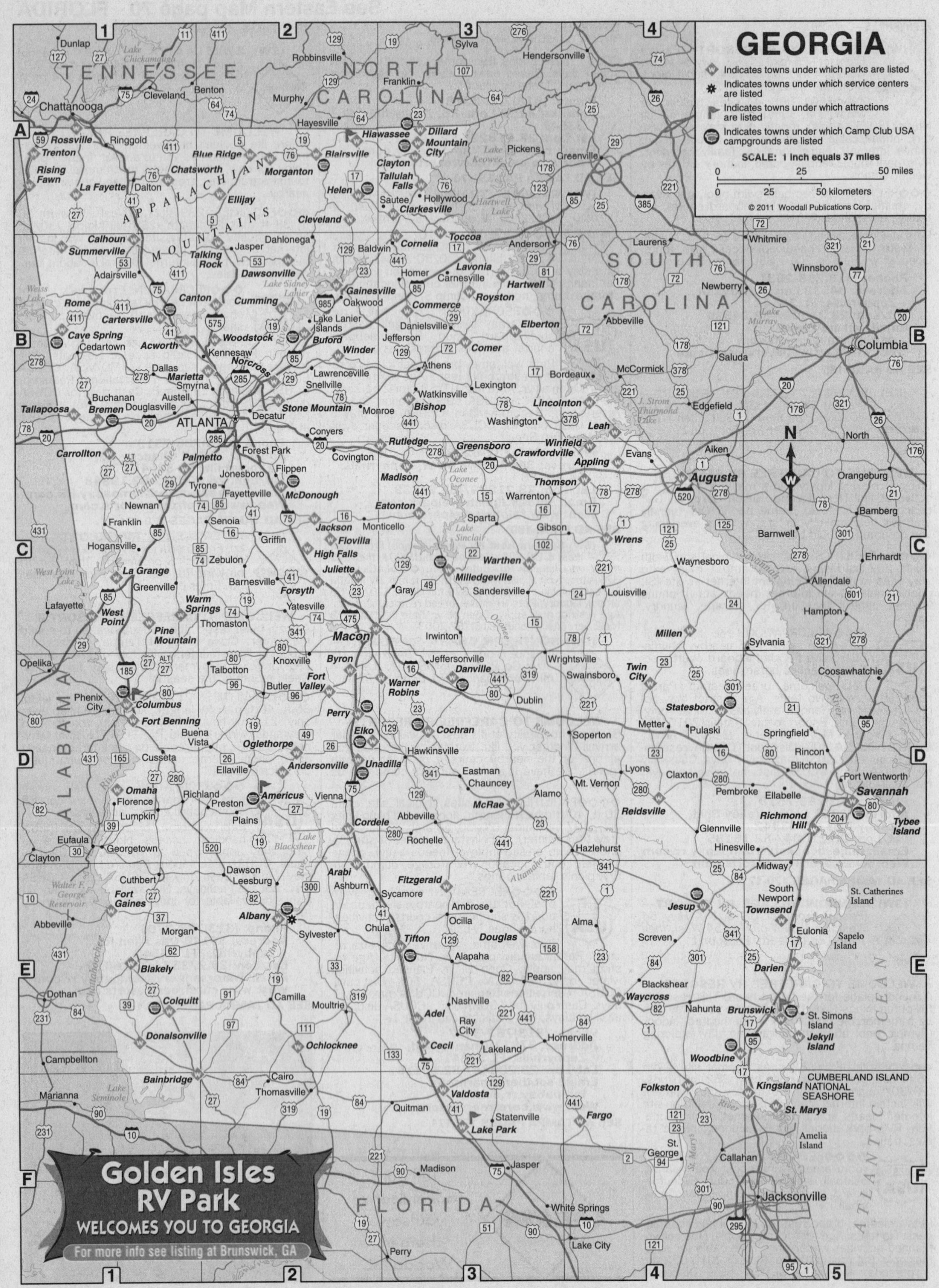

GEORGIA
Indicates towns under which parks are listed
Indicates towns under which service centers are listed
Indicates towns under which attractions are listed
Indicates towns under which Camp Club USA campgrounds are listed
SCALE: 1 inch equals 37 miles
0 25 50 miles
0 25 50 kilometers
© 2011 Woodall Publications Corp.
TENNESSEE
NORTH CAROLINA
SOUTH CAROLINA
ALABAMA
FLORIDA
ATLANTIC OCEAN
APPALACHIAN MOUNTAINS
Dunlap
Lake Chickamauga
Chattanooga
Cleveland
Benton
Robbinsville
Franklin
Murphy
Hayesville
Sylva
Hendersonville
Rossville
Ringgold
Trenton
Rising Fawn
La Fayette
Dalton
Chatsworth
Blue Ridge
Morganton
Blairsville
Hiawassee
Dillard
Mountain City
Clayton
Tallulah Falls
Helen
Hollywood
Sautee
Clarkesville
Lake Keowee
Pickens
Greenville
Hartwell Lake
Ellijay
Cleveland
Dahlonega
Jasper
Talking Rock
Calhoun
Summerville
Adairsville
Weiss Lake
Rome
Cartersville
Cave Spring
Cedartown
Canton
Cumming
Dawsonville
Lake Sidney Lanier
Gainesville
Oakwood
Cornelia
Baldwin
Toccoa
Homer
Carnesville
Lavonia
Hartwell
Royston
Anderson
Laurens
Whitmire
Winnsboro
Newberry
Lake Murray
Columbia
Abbeville
Saluda
Commerce
Danielsville
Elberton
Acworth
Woodstock
Lake Lanier Islands
Buford
Winder
Jefferson
Comer
Kennesaw
Norcross
Dallas
Marietta
Smyrna
Lawrenceville
Snellville
Athens
Watkinsville
Bishop
Lexington
Bordeaux
McCormick
Buchanan
Austell
Douglasville
Tallapoosa
Bremen
ATLANTA
Decatur
Stone Mountain
Monroe
Washington
Lincolnton
J. Strom Thurmond Lake
Edgefield
Leah
Carrollton
Forest Park
Conyers
Covington
Rutledge
Greensboro
Crawfordville
Winfield
Appling
Evans
Aiken
North
N
Palmetto
Jonesboro
Flippen
McDonough
Madison
Lake Oconee
Thomson
Augusta
Orangeburg
Tyrone
Fayetteville
Newnan
Warrenton
Eatonton
Bamberg
Franklin
Senoia
Griffin
Jackson
Monticello
Sparta
Gibson
Wrens
Barnwell
Hogansville
Flovilla
High Falls
Lake Sinclair
Waynesboro
Savannah River
Ehrhardt
Zebulon
Juliette
Warthen
Allendale
West Point Lake
La Grange
Greenville
Barnesville
Forsyth
Milledgeville
Gray
Sandersville
Louisville
Lafayette
West Point
Warm Springs
Yatesville
Hampton
Thomaston
Pine Mountain
Macon
Irwinton
Oconee River
Millen
Sylvania
Wrightsville
Opelika
Talbotton
Knoxville
Byron
Jeffersonville
Danville
Twin City
Coosawhatchie
Phenix City
Columbus
Butler
Fort Valley
Warner Robins
Swainsboro
Dublin
Statesboro
Fort Benning
Buena Vista
Perry
Cochran
Metter
Pulaski
Springfield
Elko
Oglethorpe
Hawkinsville
Soperton
Cusseta
Andersonville
Ellaville
Unadilla
Eastman
Chauncey
Lyons
Claxton
Rincon
Blitchton
Mt. Vernon
Alamo
Pembroke
Ellabelle
Port Wentworth
Savannah
Omaha
Florence
Richland
Preston
Americus
Vienna
McRae
Reidsville
Richmond Hill
Tybee Island
Lumpkin
Plains
Cordele
Abbeville
Lake Blackshear
Rochelle
Glennville
Hinesville
Eufaula
Georgetown
Clayton
Hazlehurst
Altamaha River
Midway
Cuthbert
Dawson
Leesburg
Arabi
Ashburn
Sycamore
Fitzgerald
South Newport
St. Catherines Island
Walter F. George Reservoir
Fort Gaines
Albany
Ambrose
Ocilla
Alma
Jesup
Townsend
Abbeville
Morgan
Sylvester
Chula
Tifton
Douglas
Screven
Eulonia
Sapelo Island
Blakely
Alapaha
Pearson
Blackshear
Darien
Dothan
Camilla
Nashville
Waycross
Nahunta
Brunswick
St. Simons Island
Colquitt
Moultrie
Adel
Ray City
Homerville
Jekyll Island
Donalsonville
Ochlocknee
Cecil
Lakeland
Woodbine
Campbellton
Bainbridge
Cairo
Thomasville
Valdosta
Folkston
Kingsland
CUMBERLAND ISLAND NATIONAL SEASHORE
Marianna
Lake Seminole
Quitman
Lake Park
Statenville
Fargo
St. Marys
Amelia Island
St. George
Callahan
Madison
Jasper
Jacksonville
White Springs
Lake City
Perry
Golden Isles RV Park
WELCOMES YOU TO GEORGIA
For more info see listing at Brunswick, GA

READER SERVICE INFO

The following businesses have placed an ad in the Georgia Travel Section. To receive free information, enter their Reader Service number on the Reader Service Card opposite page 48/Discover Section in the front of this directory:

Advertiser	RS#
Brickyard Plantation RV Park	4251
Cedar Creek RV Park & Outdoor Center	3696
Flynn's Inn Camping Village	3221
Georgia Mountain Fairgrounds Campground	473
Georgia Power Company Parks	849

TIME ZONE

Georgia is in the Eastern Time Zone.

TOPOGRAPHY

Georgia's terrain ranges from mountains in the north to rolling hills in the central part; plains in the southwest and the coast in the southeast.

TEMPERATURE

Average yearly rainfall in Georgia ranges from 38 inches in the east-central area to 48 inches in the southwest. Average temperatures in January range from lows between 30° and 43° and highs between 34° and 46°. July temperatures vary from lows between 78° and 80° and highs from 80° to 83°.

If you're looking for a taste of history, charm, and southern hospitality, Georgia should be the first stop on your list! Visit historic cities like Savannah, enjoy pristine beaches along the coast, and the beautiful north Georgia mountains. Whatever the adventure you're looking for, Georgia has you covered!

TRAVEL & TOURISM INFO

State Agency:
Georgia Dept. of Economic Development
75 Fifth St., NW, Suite 1200
Atlanta, GA 30308
(404/962-4000)
www.georgiaonmymind.org

Local Agencies:
For local agencies not listed here, contact the Convention and Visitor's Bureau for the locality you are interested in.

Albany Area Chamber of Commerce
225 W. Broad Ave.
Albany, GA 31701
(800/475-8700 or 229/434-8700)
www.albanyga.com

Athens CVB
300 N. Thomas St.
Athens, GA 30601
(800/653-0603 or 706/357-4430)
www.visitathensga.com

Atlanta CVB
233 Peachtree St. NE Suite 1400
Atlanta, GA 30303
(404/521-6600)
www.atlanta.net

Augusta Metropolitan CVB
PO Box 1331
Augusta, GA 30903
(800/726-0243)
www.augustaga.org

Brunswick-Golden Isles Chamber of Commerce
4 Glynn Ave.
Brunswick, GA 31520
(912/265-0620 or 800/933-COAST)
www.bgivb.com

Columbus CVB
900 Front Ave.
Columbus, GA 31902
(706/322-1613 or 800/999-1613)
www.columbusga.com

Jekyll Island Welcome Center
901 Downing Musgrove Causeway
(912/635-3636)
www.jekyllisland.com

Macon CVB
450 Martin Luther King Jr. Blvd.
Macon, GA 31201
www.maconga.org

Savannah CVB
101 East Bay St.
Savannah, GA 31401

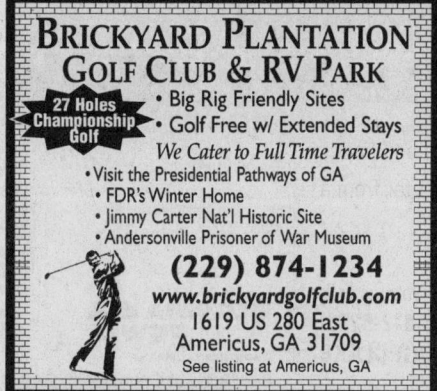

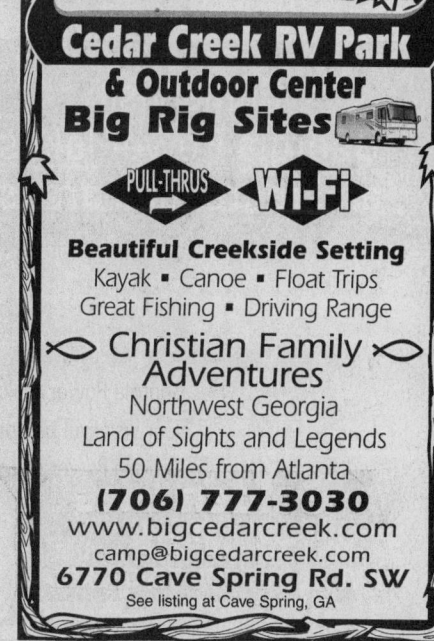

(877-savannah)
www.savannahvisit.com

RECREATIONAL INFO

Georgia Dept. of Natural Resources Martin Luther King, Jr. Dr. S.E., Suite 1252 East Tower, Atlanta, GA 30334 (404/656-3500) www.gadnr.org

Golf: Visit www.georgia.org/Travel/Rejuvenate/Golf.htm or www.golfgeorgia.org

History: Georgia State Parks & Historic Sites, 2 MLK Jr. Dr., Suite 1352, East Atlanta, GA 30334 (404/656-2770). www.gastateparks.org

SHOPPING

Antiques & Crafts Unlimited Mall, Warm Springs. Shop indoors at 114 antique, collectible and craft shops.

Lane Packing, Fort Valley. Find culinary treats with a unique Georgia flavor from Vidalia onions to Georgia peaches and pecans. Cafe, gift shop and roadside market. At 50 Lane Rd.

North Georgia Premium Outlets, Dawsonville. Impressive savings at 140 outlet stores. At 800 Hwy 400 South.

Lenox Square, Atlanta. Over 240 specialty and designer shops. 3393 Peachtree Rd., Atlanta, GA 30303.

Tanger Outlet Centers, Commerce. Over 120 name brand outlet stores. Commerce, GA 30529. At 800 Steven B. Tanger Blvd. just off I-85.

DESTINATIONS

HISTORIC HIGH COUNTRY

Known as "the enchanted land" of the Cherokee Indians, this region has numerous driving, walking, pedaling or riding trails that lead you through the area's Native American roots, historic districts and homegrown attractions, from Civil War sites to national forests.

Cartersville. Featured attractions include: **The Bartow History Center**, portraying the workshops, farmsteads and mercantiles of north Georgian pioneers; **Allatoona Dam & Lake** with over 270 miles of shoreline and the **Red Top Mountain State Park & Lodge**, home to a variety of wildlife. **Barnsley Gardens** has over 30 acres of English-style gardens and dramatic ruins.

Etowah Indian Mounds, on the banks of the Etowah River, was home to several thousand Native Americans between 1000 A.D. and 1500 A.D. Today, 54 acres protect six earthen mounds, a village area and a museum housing beads, ornaments, stone effigies, pots and other artifacts. The **Booth Western Art Museum** features six main galleries housing a permanent collection and a special "Cowboys and Indians" exhibit.

Chickamauga & Chattanooga National Military Park, located partially in Georgia at Fort Oglethorpe and partially in Tennessee.

This is the site of the last major Confederate victory in the War Between the States. The oldest and largest military park in the country also offers 50 miles of hiking trails, a slide program, a bookstore and a 355-piece weapon collection of military shoulder arms.

Lookout Mountain. At the **Lookout Mountain Flight Park**, hang gliders launch from McCarty's Bluff in Dade County and soar 1,000 feet over the ridge. Lessons and training are available. Lush gardens, unique rock formations and a view of seven states from legendary Lover's Leap await visitors at **Rock City Gardens**. **Cloudland Canyon,** one of Georgia's most scenic areas, is located on the western edge of Lookout Mountain. Enjoy rugged canyons, waterfalls and beautiful views.

New Echota. Once the capital of the Cherokee Nation, it is now a State Historic Site in Calhoun. Before the treaty was signed in 1835, it was the seat of government for an independent Native American Nation that covered Georgia and four southeastern states. Buildings on-site include the Supreme Court House, Council House, Vann's Tavern, a missionary school and the print shop that published the bilingual Cherokee Phoenix, the only Native American language newspaper ever printed in North America.

Tunnel Hill Heritage Center and Battlefield Park, Tunnel Hill. Walk the 1,477-foot Western and Atlantic Railroad Tunnel, the oldest railroad tunnel south of the Mason-Dixon line and explore the Native American and other local and Civil War artifacts and memorabilia at the nearby museum. The 1850 Clisby Austin House, where Sherman spent six days making his final plans for the Atlanta campaign, still stands.

NORTHEAST GEORGIA MOUNTAINS

The Mountain region is an area of breathtaking scenery and dramatic extremes. The villages and towns are filled with friendly, picturesque retreats, snow-capped in the winter and warm in the summer. Its foothills and mountains serve as the gateway to the Appalachian Mountains and the birthplace of the Chattahoochee River.

Anna Ruby Falls, located one and a half miles north of Unicoi State Park (near Helen), features fishing, hiking, picnicking, a visitor center and Braille trail. The waterfall is accessible via a half-mile trail from a public use area.

Appalachian Trail. This famous hiking trail begins at Springer Mountain (Dawsonville) and runs 78 miles through Georgia and continues to Maine.

Dahlonega. Authentic 19th century buildings circle the courthouse museum, many of which are listed on the National Register of Historic Places. Try your luck at finding gold, or hike the Appalachian Trail, fish, or take a scenic drive. Visit the **Appalachian Outfitters** downtown to arrange canoe, kayak and tube trips on the nearby Chestatee and Etowah Rivers. Stroll through the **Annual Wildflower Festival of the Arts** that takes place on the third weekend in May or Gold Rush Days, the third weekend in October.

De Soto Falls Scenic Area, 13 miles outside of Dahlonega. Visitors enjoy rugged mountainous country, exceptional views, beautiful waterfalls, hiking, fishing and wading in clear streams.

Helen. Bavarian Alpine architecture is depicted throughout this town in the North Georgia Mountains. The town has stone streets, unique shops, crafts, mountain music, specialty foods, Old World taverns and German restaurants. Visitors enjoy Oktoberfest in the fall, with live Bavarian music, German food and beverage and dancing.

Duke's Creek Mines, Helen. Visit the site of the first major discovery of gold in the U.S. Pan for gold and browse through gems, jewelry and rocks at the gift shop.

Russel-Brasstown Scenic Byway, just north of Helen. Take GA 348, one of two U.S. Forest Service-designated Scenic Byways in Georgia. This route will then take you close to Brasstown Bald, the highest mountain in Georgia at 4,784 ft. The interpretive center here offers a film, exhibits and an observation deck with a panoramic view of four states.

Hiawassee is home to the **Fred Hamilton Rhododendron Gardens**, displaying over 2,000 rhododendron and azalea plants plus native wildflowers and lakeside walking paths. In nearby **Young Harris** is "The Reach of Song," a summer epic musical celebration of the Appalachian Mountains. Attend the **Georgia Mountain Fair** in August.

Lake Lanier Islands, Buford/Gainesville, is home to a 1,200-acre family recreation resort with two hotels and a 300-site campground, located on the lake. The resort has facilities for golfing, swimming, sailing, houseboating and fishing. Also featured are an amphitheater and a 430-ft. waterslide.

Tallulah Gorge, Tallulah Falls. Tallulah Gorge is believed to be the oldest natural gorge in North America—two miles long and 2,000 ft. deep, with five waterfalls, overlooks and an interpretive center.

ATLANTA METRO

This international city and surrounding area offers a unique blend of urban style and community charm. Around the city you'll find charming neighborhoods like Buckhead, Virginia-Highlands and College Park, each branching off from the city's center. Explore the magnificent architecture of downtown while walking through the tree-shaded streets that are so common throughout Atlanta. A short drive out of Atlanta provides you with charming communities and parks.

Atlanta. Visit the state capital in April for the week-long Dogwood Festival through Lenox Square and Phipps Plaza, located in Buckhead where you can visit the Governor's Mansion. While in Atlanta, don't miss the **Atlanta Botanical Gardens** or the **Atlanta History Center**. **Imagine It! Children's Museum of Atlanta** features hands-on colorful exhibits and activities. Visit the **Jimmy Carter Library & Museum** and see his Nobel Peace Prize on display. **Fernbank Science Center** is home to an exhibit hall, forest and planetarium. Check out **Underground Atlanta** and the **World of Coca-Cola,** then visit **CNN Center**, featuring studio tours of live news coverage. The **High Museum of Art, Folk Art and Photography** is located at the **Woodruff Arts Center**, also the home of the Atlanta Symphony Orchestra. A must see is the **Zoo Atlanta**, known for its panda and gorilla habitats, where almost 1,000 animals reside in lush, naturalistic environments.

Atlanta Cyclorama. Visit one of the city's most beloved art treasures and learn the poignant tale of one of the pivotal events in Civil War history—the Battle of Atlanta (July 22, 1864). All the action of that terrible day is captured in a three-dimensional, 358-foot painting-in-the-round. Illustrations are made vivid by sound effects and narration of each facet of the battle. Setting the scene is an introductory film. See the Museum of Civil War artifacts and the 1862 steam locomotive Texas.

The **Georgia Aquarium** has over eight million gallons of fresh and marine water and 100,000 animals representing 500 species from around the globe. With over 505,000 sq. ft of total space, it is the largest aquarium in the world. The different areas to explore include Cold Water Quest, Georgia Explorer, Ocean Voyager, River Scout and Tropical Diver. Also includes 4-D Theater, a cafe and gift shops.

The **Martin Luther King, Jr. National Historic Site** unveiled its **International Civil Rights Walk of Fame** in September 2004. The Walk of Fame was created to "pay homage to the brave warriors of justice who sacrificed and struggled to make equality a reality for all."

Georgia's Stone Mountain Park, Dekalb/Decatur. Experience the world's largest exposed granite monolith—a geological marvel featuring carvings of Confederate war heroes Jefferson Davis, Stonewall Jackson and Robert E. Lee on horseback on the side of the mountain. This 3,200-acre park offers a wide variety of attractions including the Stone Mountain Railroad, Paddlewheel Riverboat, Mountain Top Skylift, authentic Antebellum Plantation, Discovering Stone Mountain Museum, Antique Auto and Treasures Museum, Wildlife Preserve and Petting Zoo, a beach and waterslides, row boats, pedal boats, hydro-bikes, mini-golf, tennis, hiking trails, fishing, a 36-hole golf course, lodging, dining and shopping. The park also holds events and festivals throughout the year and features a laser show May—October.

Kennesaw Mountain National Battlefield Park, Kennesaw. This historic mountaintop re-creates the fiercely contested battle where General Johnston's Confederate troops temporarily halted General Sherman's Union Army and their march to Atlanta. Visitors center open daily year-round.

Marietta Gone With the Wind Museum: Scarlett on the Square. Large collection of GWTW movie memorabilia including the bengaline gown worn by Scarlett in the honeymoon scene and a section dedicated to the African-American cast members.

Six Flags Over Georgia, Austell. Located on Riverside Pkwy, Six Flags is a 331-acre amusement park with more than 100 rides, several shows and various attractions. Ride BATMAN The Ride®, a suspended, outside looping themed roller coaster and visit Gotham City®.

Smith Plantation House. Built in 1845 with about 13 outbuildings about a mile north of Roswell in 1845, this home was kept in the family for generations and preserved in its original state. The plantation opened to the public in 1991 and is an accurate portrayal of the lifestyle of a mid-19th-century southern cotton planter.

Southeastern Railway Museum, Duluth. Georgia's largest railway museum displays over 90 pieces of railway equipment, including a WWII troop kitchen, steam locomotives and wooden freight cars.

BUSINESSES OFFERING

	Things to See & Do	RV Sales	
ALBANY			
Team RV Inc		🚌	✱
AMERICUS			
Brickyard Plantation Golf Club	⚑		
BRUNSWICK			
Fran's Place Restaurant	⚑		
Three Oaks Farm	⚑		
COLUMBUS			
Lake Pines Event Center	⚑		
HIAWASSEE			
Georgia Mountain Fairgrounds & Music Hall	⚑		
LAKE PARK			
Bargainville Flea Market	⚑		

QUICK REFERENCE CHART FOR WOODALL'S FEATURED PARKS

	Green Friendly	RV Lots for Sale	Park Models-Onsite Ownership	Park Membership for Sale	Big Rigs Welcome	Internet Friendly	Pets Welcome
ALBANY							
Albany RV Resort					▲	●	■
AMERICUS							
Brickyard Plantation RV Park					▲	●	■
AUGUSTA							
Flynn's Inn Camping Village					▲		■
BREMEN							
Yogi Bear's Jellystone Park of Georgia					▲	●	■
BRUNSWICK							
Blythe Island Regional Park Campground					▲	●	■
Coastal Georgia RV Resort					▲	●	■
Golden Isles RV Park					▲	●	■
CARTERSVILLE							
Allatoona Landing Marine Resort & Campground					▲	●	■
CAVE SPRING							
Cedar Creek RV Park & Outdoor Center					▲	●	■
CECIL							
Cecil Bay RV Park					▲	●	■
COLUMBUS							
Blanton Creek Park (Georgia Power)					▲		■
Lake Pines RV Park & Campground					▲	●	■
CUMMING							
Twin Lakes RV Park					▲	●	■
DARIEN							
Cat Head Creek RV Park					▲	●	■
DILLARD							
River Vista Mountain Village		✖			▲	●	■
EATONTON							
Lawrence Shoals Park (Georgia Power)					▲		■
ELLIJAY							
Plum Nelly Campground					▲	●	■
FORSYTH							
Forsyth KOA					▲	●	■
GREENSBORO							
Old Salem Park (Georgia Power)					▲		■
Parks Ferry Park (Georgia Power)					▲		■
HELEN							
Enota Mountain Retreat					▲	●	■
HIAWASSEE							
Bald Mountain Camping Resort					▲	●	■
Georgia Mountain Fairgrounds Campground (County Park)					▲	●	■
JULLIETTE							
Dames Ferry Park (Georgia Power)					▲		■

Green Friendly ; RV Lots for Sale ✖; Park Models/Onsite Onwership ✱; Park Memberships for Sale ✔; Big Rigs Welcome ▲; Internet Friendly ●; Internet Friendly-WiFi ●; Pets Welcome ■

QUICK REFERENCE CHART FOR WOODALL'S FEATURED PARKS

	Green Friendly	RV Lots for Sale	Park Models-Onsite Ownership	Park Membership for Sale	Big Rigs Welcome	Internet Friendly	Pets Welcome
KINGSLAND							
Country Oaks Campground & RV Park					▲	●	■
LAKE PARK							
Eagles Roost RV Resort					▲	●	■
MACON							
Lake Tobesofkee Recreation Area (Bibb Co.)					▲		■
MARIETTA							
Atlanta-Marietta RV Resort					▲	●	■
MCDONOUGH							
Atlanta South RV Resort					▲	●	■
MILLEDGEVILLE							
Scenic Mountain RV Park					▲	●	■
MOUNTAIN CITY							
Cross Creek Campground					▲	●	■
NORCROSS							
Jones RV Park					▲	●	■
PERRY							
Crossroads Holiday Trav-L-Park					▲	●	■
Fair Harbor RV Park & Campground					▲	●	■
PINE MOUNTAIN							
Pine Mountain RV Resort					▲	●	■
ROSSVILLE							
Best Holiday Trav-L-Park					▲	●	■
SAVANNAH							
Biltmore Gardens RV Park					▲	●	■
Red Gate CG & RV Resort					▲	●	■
Savannah Oaks RV Resort					▲	●	■
TOCCOA							
Toccoa RV Park							■
TOWNSEND							
Lake Harmony RV Park & Campground					▲	●	■
TYBEE ISLAND							
River's End Campground & RV Park					▲	●	■
VALDOSTA							
River Park RV Park					▲	●	■
WARM SPRINGS							
Ramsey RV Park					▲		■
WRENS							
Boss's RV Park					▲	●	■

Green Friendly ; RV Lots for Sale ✖; Park Models/Onsite Onwership ✱; Park Memberships for Sale ✔; Big Rigs Welcome ▲; Internet Friendly ●; Internet Friendly-WiFi ●; Pets Welcome ■

Southern Museum of Civil War and Locomotive History, Kennesaw. Formerly the Civil War Museum, this newly renovated Smithsonian-affiliated museum features a reproduction of a turn-of-the-century locomotive factory and a glimpse into the daily lives of Americans during the Civil War.

MAGNOLIA MIDLANDS

Located in southeastern Georgia, this region provides a backdrop of beautiful scenery for any adventure you might seek, from outdoor sports to local festivals, from great food to a rich agricultural history.

Averitt Center for the Arts, Statesboro. Housed in two historic buildings, The Old Bank of Statesboro and The Springer Opera House, the center features the 362-seat Emma Kelly Theater and six small studios.

Douglas. Visit this Georgia Main Street City and find several interesting attractions such as the **Coffee County Bank**, which is listed on the National Historic Register. Also along the way are the **Coffee Art Walk** and **Heritage Art Walk**. Other stops to make include:

General Coffee State Park. Take advantage of the pool, nature trails, group shelters and group tours. Also on-site are a pioneer village and agricultural museum.

Lott's Grist Mill, Willacoochee. This working gristmill is more than a century old. See corn become grits and participate in hands-on activities.

Gordonia-Altamaha State Park & Golf Course, Reidsville. This 280-acre park has a swimming pool, boat dock, fishing, miniature golf, paddle boats and nine-hole golf course.

McRae is a hub of the Georgia pecan industry. Nature lovers will delight in the beautiful, old, spreading pecan trees, while pecan lovers can savor a variety of pecan products sold locally.

PRESIDENTIAL PATHWAYS

This west central Georgia region is deeply rooted in American history. Soak up reflections from the antebellum era, Civil War years, two U.S. presidents and the birth of the modern South.

Andersonville National Historic Site. National cemetery, Confederate prison site, museum, monuments, reconstructed portion of the stockade and special programs are available for viewing at the site where over 12,900 Union prisoners perished.

Georgia Veterans Memorial State Park & Golf Course, Cordele. An 18-hole golf course, camping, a swimming pool, a boat ramp and dock, a museum, water skiing and fishing are activities available at the park.

Habitat for Humanity Global Village & Discover Center, Americus. A multimedia museum and town dedicated to educating

Where to Find CCUSA Parks

List City	Park Name	Map Coordinates
ALBANY		
	Creekside Plantation RV Campground	E-2
AMERICUS		
	Brickyard Plantation RV Park	D-2
ATLANTA		
	Atlanta South RV Resort	B-2
BLAIRSVILLE		
	Trackrock Campground & Cabins	A-2
BREMEN		
	Yogi Bear's Jellystone Park of Georgia	B-1
BRUNSWICK		
	Golden Isles RV Park	E-5
BUFORD		
	Lake Lanier Islands Campground	B-2
CARTERSVILLE		
	Allatoona Landing Marine Resort & Campground	B-1
CAVE SPRING		
	Cedar Creek RV Park & Outdoor Center	B-1
COCHRAN		
	Hillside Bluegrass RV Park	D-3
COLQUITT		
	Emerald Lake RV Park	E-1
COLUMBUS		
	Lake Pines RV Park & Campground	D-1
DANVILLE		
	Back to Nature Campground	D-3
DILLARD		
	River Vista Mountain Village	A-3
ELKO		
	Twin Oaks RV Park	D-2
HELEN		
	Creekwood Resort Campground & Cabins	A-2
JESUP		
	Mossy Oaks RV Park & Campground (Not visited)	E-4
MCDONOUGH		
	Atlanta South RV Resort	C-2
MILLEDGEVILLE		
	Little River Park Campground & Marina	C-3
	Scenic Mountain RV Park	C-3
MOUNTAIN CITY		
	Cross Creek Campground	A-3
PERRY		
	Fair Harbor RV Park & Campground	D-2
SAVANNAH		
	Biltmore Gardens RV Park	D-5
STATESBORO		
	Parkwood RV Park & Cottages	D-4
TIFTON		
	Agrirama RV Park	E-3
UNADILLA		
	Southern Trails RV Resort	D-2
WOODBINE		
	King George RV Resort	E-4

people about the worldwide need for adequate housing.

LaGrange. The historic 31-acre **Hills and Dales Estate** includes Ferrell Gardens, which date to 1832 and consist of an elaborate blend of extensive boxwood plantings, fountains, descending terraces, a greenhouse and more. The centerpiece is the Italian-villa style house.

Warm Springs invites you to step back in time as you stroll down one sq. mile of shops and restaurants. Visit Roosevelt's **Little White House & Museum**, also in Warm Springs. It was built in 1932 by President Franklin Delano Roosevelt, so he could be close to Warm Springs for polio therapy. The house remains exactly the way it was the day he died there in 1945.

Westville. Visit the town where it's always 1850. Realistically depicting Georgia's pre-industrial lifestyle and culture, this living history village allows you to try your hand at making crafts such as candles, syrups and soaps.

HISTORIC HEARTLAND

Enjoy true Southern hospitality in Georgia's Historic Heartland, just south of Atlanta. Step back in time in this region of quaint towns, antiques, scenic byways and local festivals.

Athens. Known as the "Classic City" in Georgia's Historic Heartland. **The Antebellum Trail** recaptures the romance and mystery of the Old South through glorious plantations and quaint town squares. Shop in picturesque downtown and lunch at a sidewalk cafe. Attractions within Athens include the **State Botanical Gardens of Georgia**, **Georgia Museum of Art** and **Founders Memorial Garden**. Stop by the **Athens Welcome Center** for information on easy-to-follow self-guided tours of local historic sites. The **Lyndon House Arts Center** contains galleries, a children's wing, artists' workshops, gift shop and more. The 1856 **Lyndon House** features authentic period furniture.

Macon. Home to six National Historic Districts with thousands of buildings dating to the 1830s. **The Hay House/Georgia Trust for Historic Preservation** features priceless furniture, a secret room and 18 hand-carved marble mantels. Also in Macon is **The Georgia Music Hall of Fame** dedicated to nurturing the cultural climate for music—its creators and those who enjoy it. Among the many artists featured are Toni Braxton, Otis Redding, Gladys Knight, Alan Jackson, Trisha Yearwood, Jimi Hendrix and many more, all with a connection to Georgia. **Museum of Arts & Sciences** has changing art and science exhibits, along with daily star shows. The **Georgia Sports Hall of Fame** includes Olympic champions, legendary coaches and professional superstars.

Museum of Aviation, Inc., Warner Robins. 90 historic aircraft plus 100,000 sq. ft. of indoor aviation exhibits, from WWII, Korea and Desert Storm.

Rum Creek Wildlife Management Area, Forsyth, contains 8,100 acres of rolling hills, lakes, camping, hunting, hiking and habitat of one of the most varied bird populations in the southeast.

PLANTATION TRACE

Located in rural southwestern Georgia, this region is full of plantations and historic farms that allow you to re-live Georgia's historic past.

Fort Valley features the **Blue Bird Body Company**, offering tours of their school bus and luxury RV building plant (by appointment). Also within Fort Valley is the **Historic Massee Lane Gardens**, complete with arboretum, lake, gazebo, rose garden, educational museum and extensive porcelain collection.

Albany. Explore the wildlife of the Apalachicola, Chattahoochee and Flint River basins at the **Flint Riverquarium**, featuring an open-air, 175,000-gallon Blue Hole freshwater spring aquarium with scores of fish, reptiles, amphibians and regional plants as well as many high-tech, interactive educational exhibits, a big-screen, three-story IWERKS movie theater and more.

Blue & Gray Museum, Fitzgerald. Home to a rare collection of Union and Confederate relics, this museum interprets Fitzgerald's beginning as a Union Soldiers' colony in former Confederate territory where Yank and Rebel met and formed the first Blue & Gray in America.

The Parks at Chehaw, Albany. Protective trails, elevated walkways and swinging suspension bridges wind through this 200-acre wildlife preserve.

Georgia Agrirama, Tifton. This living history town depicts rural Georgia prior to 1900. More than 35 authentic restorations including a gristmill, a sawmill, a cotton gin and farmhouses are displayed here.

Kolomoki Mounds State Park, Blakely. On-site are hiking trails, an interpretive museum, seven Native American mounds, fishing facilities, swimming, mini-golf and camping.

Lake Seminole, Bainbridge/ Donalsonville. Contained in these 37,500 acres is boating, swimming, water skiing, camping and great fishing. Anglers can expect to hook into largemouth, striper and hybrid bass.

Splash Island, Valdosta. This newly opened water park features the Rain Fortress, Paradise River, the Double Dip Zip and Cathawave Bay.

CLASSIC SOUTH

This region is considered Georgia's heart and soul. Offering a rich cultural heritage of music and literature along with its bountiful agriculture and entertaining festivals throughout the year, the Classic South has many restored antebellum homes and museums.

Augusta. A classic southern city, Augusta is known for its combination of beauty, elegance and tradition. The city is also home of six National Register districts and host to great sporting events such as the Masters Golf Tournament and the Southern National Dragboat Races. Also in Augusta is **The Morris Museum of Art**, featuring a unique collection of southern art as well as traveling exhibitions. **Riverwalk Augusta** is a beautiful outdoor walking path, set on the banks of the Savannah River. Tree-lined paths loaded with seasonal flowers provide the perfect backdrop for a charming array of restaurants, unique shops, museums and special events.

Callaway Plantation, located five miles west of Washington. This restored working plantation contains seven historic outbuildings, including a log cabin and a schoolhouse.

Dublin, located along I-16, is aptly called "The Emerald City." The whole town of Dublin goes all-out during the annual St. Patrick's Day Festival. This 10-day celebration features a grand parade, beauty pageant, food, entertainment, arts and crafts, dances, 10K road race, century bike race and a leprechaun contest.

Hazelhurst. Stroll through the 1890 Farmstead. Restored buildings illustrate the lifestyles of that bygone era. Bring your own corn to grind or take home a bag of already-ground grits or meal at the **Frogbottom Grist Mill**.

Hickory Hill, Thomson. The historic home of Georgia's populist statesman, senator and author Thomas E. Watson, is a museum depicting the senator's life and political career. Restored to its 1920 incarnation featuring original furnishings throughout.

Juliette. Taste some fried green tomatoes at the famous Whistle Stop Cafe, shop for antiques or spend a leisurely afternoon fishing at Lake Juliette.

Kettle Creek Battlefield, Washington. Visit this Revolutionary War Battlefield, cemetery, historic markers and monuments.

Lake Oconee, Greensboro. This 19,000-acre lake was formerly Native American territory and is still a hunting ground for Creek and Cherokee artifacts. Fishing, swimming, water skiing and sailing are available.

Madison. 19th century homes and buildings line the streets of this town recently voted "No. 1 Small Town in America." Museums dating back to the early 1800s include Heritage Hall, Madison-Morgan Cultural Center, Morgan County African American Museum and Rogers House/Rose Cottage.

Milledgeville. The Old Governor's Mansion in Milledgeville was recently reopened after a historic restoration. The Mansion, originally built in 1839, was home to eight of Georgia's governors until 1868 when the capital moved to Atlanta. It is considered one of the finest examples of High Greek Revival architecture in the country.

Reynolds Plantation, located midway between Atlanta and Augusta. Nestled against the banks of Lake Oconee, Reynolds Plantation has 32 miles of shoreline along this fabulous 19,000-acre lake.

COAST

Here you will find beauty and serenity in the coastal towns. Soak up the warm sea air as you walk among the moss-draped oaks of the coastal communities. Explore beyond the city streets and roam the lands of Georgia's pristine barrier islands, quiet swamps, unspoiled beaches and marshes – all thriving with wildlife. A variety of birds, fish, snakes, alligators, otters and sea turtles live within the lush vegetation of the area. Take an outdoor expedition through the trails of **Blackbeard Island** or **Okefenokee National Wildlife Refuge** and witness creatures in their natural habitat. This region also offers world-class golf courses, tennis, canoe trips along the waterways of the Atlantic and a variety of other recreational sports.

Brunswick. The Gateway to the Golden Isles also features many wildlife management areas, historic buildings, a 900-year-old oak tree and the **Mary Miller Doll Museum**, housing over 3,000 dolls.

Okefenokee Swamp. The swamp is a wilderness area accessible through Fargo, Folkston and Waycross. Guided boat tours take passengers through the swamp for views of wildlife and plant life. Also available are hiking trails, fishing, canoeing and camping.

Savannah. Savannah's Historic District is the largest registered urban landmark district in the nation. **Riverfront Plaza** provides a nine-block concourse dotted with fountains, benches, plantings, museums, pubs, restaurants, artists' galleries and boutiques. Tours of a former whaling vessel are also available. Railroad buffs will enjoy the **Central of Georgia Railroad Roundhouse Complex**. Guided tours are plentiful throughout Savannah. Aside from the usual walking/driving tours, visitors can also tour via horse-drawn carriage or riverboat. Before you begin, stop by the Savannah Visitor Center (301 Martin Luther King Blvd.).

St. Simons, Sea Island, Jekyll Island and **Little St. Simons Island**. Each of these beach resort areas is accessible only from Brunswick. Features of the islands include historical sites, crabbing, horseback riding, shelling, swimming, golf, tennis and fishing.

ANNUAL EVENTS

JANUARY

Polar Bear Swim, Gainesville; Arts for the Parks, Cartersville; Storytelling at Roswell, Roswell; Valdosta National, Valdosta; Island Treasures, Jekyll Island (through February); New Year's Bluegrass Festival, Jekyll Island; Atlanta Boat Show, Atlanta; Annual Augusta Futurity, Augusta; Southern Gardening Symposium, Pine Mountain; Southeastern Flower Show, Atlanta.

FEBRUARY

Festival of Camellias, Fort Valley; Augusta Arsenal Spring Shootout, Augusta; Madison Antique Show, Madison; Georgia National Rodeo, Perry.

MARCH

Golden Corral 500 Event Weekend, Hampton; Forsythia Festival, Forsyth; Cherry Blossom Festival, Macon; Savannah Music Festival, Savannah; Peaches to the Beaches Yard Sale, Culloden; Savannah Tour of Homes and Gardens, Savannah; Blessing of the Fleet, Darien; Conyers Cherry Blossom Festival, Conyers; Annual Rattlesnake Roundup, Claxton.

APRIL

Historic Buford Spring Festival, Buford; Twilight Festival, Athens; Annual Riverfest Weekend, Columbus; Macon Gardens, Mansions and Moonlight, Macon; Plantation Ball, Thomasville; Human Rights Festival, Athens; Crawfish Festival, Woodbine; Atlanta Dogwood Festival, Atlanta; Masters Tournament, Augusta; Georgia Renaissance Festival, Fairburn (through June); Tour de Georgia; Annual Rose Show and Festival, Thomasville; Georgia Strawberry Festival, Reynolds; Vidalia Onion Festival, Vidalia; Inman Park Spring Festival and Tour of Homes, Atlanta; Atlanta Film Festival, Atlanta; Mossy Creek Barnyard Festival, Perry; National Mayhaw Festival, Colquitt.

MAY

Mayfest, Augusta; Peacock Festival, Pavo; Cotton Pickin' Fair, Gay; Winefest, Helen; Pine Tree Festival, Swainsboro; Blueberry Festival, Alma; 1890's Day Jamboree, Atlanta; Stars, Cars & Bar-B-Q, Dawsonville; Art in the Park, Helen; Red, White and Blue Celebration, Evans; Apple Blossom Auto Show, East Ellijay; American Indian Festival, Lawrenceville; Antique Show and Sale, St. Simons Island; Fiesta Atlanta, Atlanta; Sweet Auburn Springfest, Atlanta; Atlanta Jazz Festival, Atlanta.

JUNE

Mid Summer Music Fest, Atlanta; Mountain Top Rodeo, Dahlonega; Georgia Wine Country Festival, Dahlonega; Georgia Peach Festival, Byron; Echota Cultural Arts Festival, Sautee.

JULY

Lazy Daze Festival, Winder; Lake Country Freedom Festival, Eatonton; Georgia Mountain Fair, Hiawassee; Butternut Creek Festival, Blairsville; Folk Life Festival, Helen; National Black Arts Festival, Atlanta; Sunflower Farm Festival, Rutledge; Summer Redneck Games, East Dublin.

AUGUST

Tom Watson Watermelon Festival, Thomson; Summer Shade Festival, Atlanta; Appalachian Regional Fair, East Ellijay; Vineyard Fest, Braselton.

SEPTEMBER

Pepper Festival, Omega; Jug Tavern Festival, Winder; Annual Yellow Daisy Festival, Stone Mountain Park; Georgia State Fair, Macon; Ocmulgee Indian Celebration, Macon; JapanFest, Stone Mountain Park; Big Pig Jig, Vienna; The Wild Georgia Shrimp Festival, Jekyll Island; Savannah Jazz Festival, Savannah; Annual Wine South Festival Atlanta, Atlanta; North Georgia State Fair, Marietta; Rockdale County Fair, Conyers; Native American Festival, Flovilla.

OCTOBER

Georgia Peanut Festival, Sylvester; Georgia National Fair, Perry; Georgia Mountain Fall Festival, Hiawassee; Sorghum Festival, Blairsville; Lake Oconee Jazz & Balloon Festival, Lake Oconee; Taste of Atlanta, Atlanta; North Georgia Folk Festival, Athens; Sweetwater Festival, Milledgeville.

NOVEMBER

Swine Time Festival, Climax; A Southern Christmas at Stone Mountain Park, Stone Mountain; Rock City's Enchanted Garden of Lights, Lookout Mountain; Magical Nights of Lights, Lake Lanier Islands; National BBQ Festival, Douglas.

DECEMBER

Victorian Christmas Festival, Thomasville; Marietta Pilgrimage Christmas Home Tour, Marietta; Old Fashioned Christmas, Dahlonega.

Woodall's listings for public campgrounds are based upon information supplied by the appropriate government agency.

Unless otherwise noted all listed campgrounds have hot showers & flush toilets.

All privately owned campgrounds personally inspected by WOODALL'S Representatives
Chip and Pat Dennis

ACWORTH—B-1

(W) CLARK CREEK NORTH (Allatoona Lake COE)—(Bartow) *From I-75 (exit 121/278) & Glade Rd: Go 3 mi NE on Glade Rd.* FACILITIES: 40 sites, typical site width 20 ft, 24 W&E, (30/50 amps), 16 no hkups, tenting, dump, laundry. RECREATION: lake swim, boating, ramp, dock, lake fishing. Partial handicap access. Phone: (678)721-6700.

(N) Holiday Harbor Marina & Resort—(Bartow) *From jct I-75 (exit 278) & Glade Rd: Go 3/4 mi E on Glade Rd, then 1 mi N on Tanyard Creek Rd, then 3/4 mi E on Groovers Landing Rd. Enter at end.* ◇◇◇FACILITIES: 24 sites, typical site width 30 ft, 24 W&E, (20/30/50 amps), 6 pull-thrus, family camping, laundry, ltd groc. ◇◇◇RECREATION: boating, canoeing, ramp, dock, lake fishing. Pets welcome. Partial handicap access. No tents. Open all yr. Big rigs welcome. Rate in 2010 $30 per family. Phone: (770)974-2575.

(W) MCKINNEY CAMPGROUND (Allatoona Lake COE)—(Bartow) *From jct I-75 (exit 121/278) & Glade Rd: Go 4 mi NE on Glade Rd, then 3/4 mi W on King's Camp Rd & follow signs.* FACILITIES: 150 sites, typical site width 8 ft, 150 W&E, (50 amps), 25 pull-thrus, tenting, dump, laundry. RECREATION: lake swim, boating, ramp, dock, lake fishing. Pets welcome, quantity restrict. Partial handicap access. Open all yr. Facilities fully operational Apr 1 - Oct 31. Phone: (678)721-6700.

(S) MILITARY PARK (World Famous Navy Lake Site-Atlanta NAS)—(Bartow) *From I-75 (exit 122/283-Emerson): Go 4 mi S on Sandtown Rd. Off base.* FACILITIES: 12 sites, typical site width 14 ft, 12 W&E, (30 amps), 1 pull-thrus, tenting, dump, laundry, ltd groc. RECREATION: lake swim, boating, canoeing, ramp, dock, lake fishing, playground. No pets. Open all yr. Phone: (770)974-6309.

(N) OLD 41 NO. 3 CAMPGROUND (COE Allatoona Lake)—(Bartow) *From town: Go 2-1/2 mi N on Hwy-293.* FACILITIES: 44 sites, typical site width 20 ft, 44 W&E, (50 amps), 4 pull-thrus, tenting, dump, laundry. RECREATION: lake swim, boating, ramp, dock, lake fishing, playground. Pets welcome, quantity restrict. Partial handicap access. Open Apr 30 - Sep 7. Phone: (678)721-6700.

(NW) PAYNE CAMPGROUND (COE-Allatoona Lake)—(Cherokee) *From jct I-75 (exit 120/277) & Hwy 92: Go 1 mi N on Hwy 92, then 2-3/4 mi W on Kellogg Creek Rd. Enter on R.* FACILITIES: 60 sites, typical site width 20 ft, 2 full hkups, 39 W&E, (30/50 amps), 19 no hkups, 3 pull-thrus, tenting, dump, laundry. RECREATION: lake swim, boating, ramp, dock, lake fishing, playground. Pets welcome, quantity restrict. Partial handicap access. Open Mar 27 - Sep 8. Phone: (678)721-6700.

ADEL—E-3

(W) REED BINGHAM STATE PARK—(Colquitt) *From jct I-75 (exit 39) & Hwy 37: Go 5-3/4 mi W on Hwy 37, then 3/4 mi N on Reed Bingham Rd. Enter at end.* FACILITIES: 46 sites, 46 W&E, (20/30/50 amps), 8 pull-thrus, family camping, tenting, dump, laundry. RECREATION: lake swim, boating, canoeing, ramp, dock, lake/river fishing, playground. Pets welcome. Partial handicap access. Open all yr. Phone: (800) 864-7275.

ALBANY—E-2

(S) ALBANY RV RESORT—(Dougherty) *From jct US 82 & US 19/Hwy 300: Go 4-1/2 mi S on US 19/Hwy 300. Enter on L.*

WELCOME

◇◇◇◇◇FACILITIES: 82 sites, typical site width 40 ft, 82 full hkups, (20/30/50 amps), some extd stay sites, 42 pull-thrus, cable TV, WiFi Instant Internet at site, phone on-site Internet (needs activ), WiFi Internet central location, family camping, tenting, RV storage, laundry, RV supplies, picnic tables, patios.

◇◇RECREATION: rec hall, pavilion, pond fishing, horseshoes.

Pets welcome. Partial handicap access. Open all yr. Big rigs welcome. Clubs welcome. Rate in 2010 $34-36 for 2 persons. MC/VISA/DISC/AMEX.

Phone: (866)792-1481
Address: 1202 Liberty Expwy SE, Albany, GA 31705
Lat/Lon: 31.52048/-84.11515
Email: info@albanyrvresort.com
Web: www.albanyrvresort.com

SEE AD THIS PAGE

(S) Creekside Plantation RV Campground—(Dougherty) *From jct US 82 & US 19/Hwy 300: Go 8 mi S on US 19/Hwy 300, then 1 block E on Hancock Rd. Enter on L.* ◇◇◇FACILITIES: 75 sites, typical site width 40 ft, 75 full hkups, (30/50 amps), 50 amps ($), 24 pull-thrus, cable TV, WiFi Instant Internet at site, phone/cable on-site Internet (needs activ), WiFi Internet central location, family camping, tenting, RV storage, laundry, LP gas by weight/by meter, ice, picnic tables, patios. ◇RECREATION: pavilion, river swim, pond fishing. Pets welcome. Partial handicap access. Open all yr. Big rigs welcome. Rate in 2010 $25 per vehicle. MC/VISA/DISC. CCUSA 50% Discount. CCUSA reservations Required, CCUSA max stay Unlimited. Discounts available on daily rates only, does not apply to weekly or monthly rates.

CAMPCLUB USA

Phone: (229)886-0504
Address: 1437 Hancock Rd., Albany, GA 31705
Lat/Lon: 31.45264/-84.11607
Email: info@creeksidervparkcampground.com
Web: www.creeksidervparkcampground.com

(S) TEAM RV INC—*From jct US 82 & US 19/Hwy 300: Go 4-1/2 mi S on US 19/Hwy 300. Enter on L.* SALES: travel trailers, 5th wheels, toy hauler, pre-owned unit sales. SERVICES: full-time mech, RV appliance repair, body work/collision repair, LP gas by weight/by meter, dump station, RV storage, sells parts/accessories, installs hitches. Open all yr. MC/VISA/AMEX/Debit.

WELCOME

Phone: (800)424-6301
Address: 1218 Liberty Expwy SE, Albany, GA 31705
Lat/Lon: 31.51873/-84.11514
Email: sales@teamrvinc.com
Web: www.teamrvinc.com

SEE AD THIS PAGE

(N) THE PARKS AT CHEHAW CAMPGROUND (City Park)—(Dougherty) *From jct US 19 & Hwy 91: Go 1-1/4 mi NE on Hwy 91. Enter on L.* FACILITIES: 50 sites, typical site width 25 ft, 50 W&E, (20/30/50 amps), 14 pull-thrus, family camping, tenting, dump, laundry. RECREATION: boating, canoeing, ramp, dock, lake/pond fishing, playground. Pets welcome. Partial handicap access. Open all yr. Big rigs welcome. Phone: (229)430-5277.

AMERICUS—D-2

(E) BRICKYARD PLANTATION GOLF CLUB—*From east jct Hwy 27 & US 280: Go 7 mi E on US 280. From jct I-75 (exit 101) & US 280: Go 24 mi W on US 280. Enter on L.* 27-hole championship golf course, 2 PGA pros, driving range, senior activities Wed & Fri. Snack Bar. Open to public all year. M-Sat 8-6, Sun 12:30-6 except Thanksgiving & Christmas, Golf clinics & lessons. Open all yr. MC/VISA/DISC/AMEX/Debit.

WELCOME

Phone: (229)874-1234
Address: 1619 US 280 East, Americus, GA 31709
Lat/Lon: 32.00536/-84.11317
Email: bpgcdeb@sowega.net
Web: www.brickyardgolfclub.com

SEE AD TRAVEL SECTION PAGE 183

(E) BRICKYARD PLANTATION RV PARK—(Sumter) *From jct Hwy 27 & US 280: Go 7 mi E on US 280, then 1/2 mi S on Parkers Crossing. Enter on L.*

WELCOME

◇◇◇FACILITIES: 48 sites, typical site width 30 ft, 48 full hkups, (30/50 amps), 32 pull-thrus, WiFi Instant Internet at site, WiFi Internet central location, family camping, laundry, picnic tables, patios.

◇◇RECREATION: rec hall, pond fishing, golf nearby, activities.

CAMPCLUB USA

Pets welcome, breed restrict, quantity restrict. Partial handicap access. No tents. Open all yr. Big rigs welcome. Escort to site. Clubs welcome. Rate in 2010 $30 per vehicle. MC/VISA/DISC/AMEX. CCUSA 50% Discount. CCUSA reservations Required, CCUSA max stay Unlimited.

Phone: (229)874-1234
Address: 224 Parkers Crossing, Americus, GA 31709
Lat/Lon: 31.99779/-84.11437
Email: bpgcdeb@sowega.net
Web: www.brickyardgolfclub.com

SEE AD TRAVEL SECTION PAGE 183

ANDERSONVILLE—D-2

BRICKYARD PLANTATION RV PARK—*From jct Hwy 228 & Hwy 49: Go S 6 mi on Hwy 49, then bear left and go S 5-1/2 mi on District Line Rd, then W 1/2 mi on Lamar Rd, then 4-1/2 mi SE on US 280, then 1/2 mi S on Parkers Crossing. Enter on L.*

SEE PRIMARY LISTING AT AMERICUS, GA AND AD TRAVEL SECTION PAGE 183

(W) CITY CAMPGROUND—(Sumter) *From jct Hwy 49 & Hwy 228: Go 1/4 mi W on Hwy 228, then 1 block S to Monument, then 1 block W (follow signs).* FACILITIES: 40 sites, 12 full hkups, 18 W&E, 10 no hkups, 12 pull-thrus, tenting, ltd groc. RECREATION: Open all yr. Phone: (229)924-2558.

APPLING—C-4

(N) MISTLETOE STATE PARK—(Columbia) *From jct I-20 (exit 175) & Hwy 150: Go 7 3/4 mi NE on Hwy 150, then 3 mi NW on Mistletoe Rd. Enter at end.* FACILITIES: 96 sites, 96 W&E, (20/30/50 amps), 26 pull-thrus, family camping, tenting, dump, laundry. RECREATION: lake swim, boating, canoeing, ramp, dock, lake fishing, playground. Pets welcome. Partial handicap access. Open all yr. Phone: (800)864-7275.

(E) WILDWOOD PARK (Columbia County Park)—(Columbia) *From jct I-20 (exit 183) & US 221: Go 8 mi N on US 221, then 2 mi NW on Hwy 104, then 1 mi E on Holloway Rd. Enter at end.* FACILITIES: 61 sites, typical site width 24 ft, 61 W&E, (20/30/50 amps), 7 pull-thrus, tenting, dump. RECREATION: lake swim, boating, ramp, dock, lake fishing, playground. Pets welcome ($). Open all yr. Phone: (706)541-0586.

It is illegal to eat chicken with a fork in Gainesville, the "Chicken Capital of the World".

ARABI—E-2

(E) Southern Gates RV Park & Campground—(Crisp) *From I-75 (Exit 92) & First St: Go 1/4 mi W on First St, then 1/4 mi N on Campsite Rd. Enter on R.* ◆◆FACILITIES: 44 sites, typical site width 25 ft, 26 full hkups, 18 W&E, (20/30/50 amps), 23 pull-thrus, family camping, tenting, dump, laundry, ltd groc. ◆◆RECREATION: swim pool, pond fishing, playground. Pets welcome. Open all yr. Big rigs welcome. Rate in 2010 $44-50 per family. Phone: (229)273-6464. FMCA discount.

ATHENS—B-3

See listings at Comer, Commerce, Elberton, Royston, Rutledge, & Winder.

ATLANTA—B-2

ATLANTA AREA MAP

Symbols on map indicate towns within a 40 mi radius of Atlanta where campgrounds (diamonds), attractions (flags), & RV service centers & camping supply outlets (gears) are listed. Check listings for more information.

Tell Them Woodall's Sent You!

ALLATOONA LANDING MARINE RESORT & CAMPGROUND—*From jct I-285 (exit 20) & I-75: Go 24 mi N on I-75 to exit 283, then 2 mi E on Allatoona Landing Road. Enter on L.*

WELCOME

SEE LISTING IN CARTERSVILLE AND AD THIS PAGE

Whether you're dreaming about buying a new RV or are actively shopping, 2011 RV Buyer's Guide is your best source. It contains all the information you need to make an intelligent buying decision. Over 450 vehicles are profiled with complete information about construction features, dimensions, popular options, and more, making comparing models easy. To order your copy go to www.woodalls.com/shop.

ATLANTA—Continued

(NW) ATLANTA - MARIETTA RV RESORT —*From jct I-285 & I-75: Go 2-3/4 mi N on I-75 (exit 261), then 3/4 mi W on Hwy 280, then 1/2 mi N on US 41, then 1 block W on Wylie Rd. Enter on R.*

WELCOME

◆◆◆FACILITIES: 70 sites, typical site width 25 ft, 70 full hkups, (30/50 amps), many extd stay sites, cable TV, WiFi Instant Internet at site, cable Internet central location, laundry, LP gas by weight/by meter, ice, picnic tables, patios.

◆RECREATION: swim pool, golf nearby.

Pets welcome, breed restrict. Partial handicap access. No tents. Open all yr. Big rigs welcome. Clubs welcome. Rate in 2010 $49.99 per vehicle. MC/VISA/DISC/AMEX. Member ARVC, GARVC. FMCA discount.

Phone: (877)727-5787
Address: 1031 Wylie Rd SE, Marietta, GA 30067
Lat/Lon: 33.92826/-84.50668
Email: information@amrvresort.com
Web: www.amrvresort.com

SEE PRIMARY LISTING IN MARIETTA AND AD PAGE 193

ATLANTA—Continued

ATLANTA SOUTH RV RESORT—*From jct I-285 & I-75: Go 16 mi S on I-75 (exit 222), then 1/2 block W on Jodeco Rd, then 1/4 mi S on Mt. Olive Rd.*

WELCOME

SEE PRIMARY LISTING AT MC DONOUGH AND AD THIS PAGE

JONES RV PARK—*From jct I-285 (exit 33B) & I-85: Go 5-1/2 mi NE on I-85 (exit 101), then 400 feet E on Indian Trail, then 1 block S on Willowtrail Pkwy. Enter at end.*

WELCOME

SEE PRIMARY LISTING AT NORCROSS AND AD THIS PAGE

YOGI BEAR'S JELLYSTONE PARK OF GEORGIA—*From jct I-285 (exit 10) & I-20: Go 41 mi W on I-20 to exit 9, then 1 mi N on Waco Rd/Atlantc Ave, then 1/4 mi S on King. Enter on L.*

WELCOME

SEE PRIMARY LISTING IN BREMEN AND AD PAGE 193

AUGUSTA—C-4

(S) FLYNN'S INN CAMPING VILLAGE—(Richmond) *From jct I-20 (exit 196 A) & I-520 (Bobby Jones Expressway): Go 7 mi S on I-520 (exit 7), then 3-1/2 mi S on US 25 (Peach Orchard Rd). Enter on L.*

WELCOME

THE PLACE TO STAY IN AUGUSTA
Make us your base camp for golfing, attending the Masters or Futurity, boat racing in the Savannah River or tour our historic city. We're close to the Medical College and hospitals, plus shopping.

◆◆◆FACILITIES: 71 sites, typical site width 30 ft, 62 full hkups, (30/50 amps), 9 no hkups, some extd stay sites, 30 pull-thrus, family camping, laundry.

AUGUSTA—Continued
FLYNN'S INN CAMPING VILLAGE—Continued

RECREATION: golf nearby.

Pets welcome. No tents. Open all yr. Big rigs welcome. Clubs welcome. Rate in 2010 $25-30 for 2 persons.

Phone: (706)798-6912
Address: 3746 Peach Orchard Rd, Augusta, GA 30906
Lat/Lon: 33.35861/-82.04316

SEE AD TRAVEL SECTION PAGE 184

BAINBRIDGE—F-1

(S) Flint River KOA—(Decatur) *From jct US 27 & US 84 Bypass: Go 1-1/2 mi W on US 84 Byp, then 1/4 mi S on Shotwell St. Enter on L.* ◆◆◆FACILITIES: 85 sites, typical site width 30 ft, 85 full hkups, (20/30/50 amps), 34 pull-thrus, family camping, tenting, dump, laundry, ltd groc. ◆◆◆RECREATION: swim pool, boating, play equipment. Pets welcome. Open all yr. Big rigs welcome. Rate in 2010 $29-33 for 2 persons. Member ARVC. Phone: (229)246-5802. KOA discount.

BISHOP—B-3

(W) Pine Lake RV Campground—(Oconee) *From jct US 441 & Hwy 186: Go 1-1/4 mi W on Hwy 186. Enter on L.* ◆◆◆FACILITIES: 34 sites, typical site width 25 ft, 27 full hkups, 7 W&E, (20/30/50 amps), 10 pull-thrus, family camping, tenting, laundry, ltd groc. ◆◆RECREATION: pond fishing, playground. Pets welcome. Open all yr. Rate in 2010 $28-30 for 2 persons. Phone: (706)769-5486.

BLAIRSVILLE—A-2

(S) CHATTAHOOCHEE NATIONAL FOREST (Lake Winfield Scott Campground)—(Union) *From town: Go 10-1/4 mi S on US-19, then 6-1/2 mi W on Hwy-180.* FACILITIES: 32 sites, typical site width 15 ft, 22 ft max RV length, 32 no hkups, 6 pull-thrus, tenting. RECREATION: lake swim, boating, electric motors only, ramp, lake fishing, playground. Open all yr. Phone: (706)745-6928.

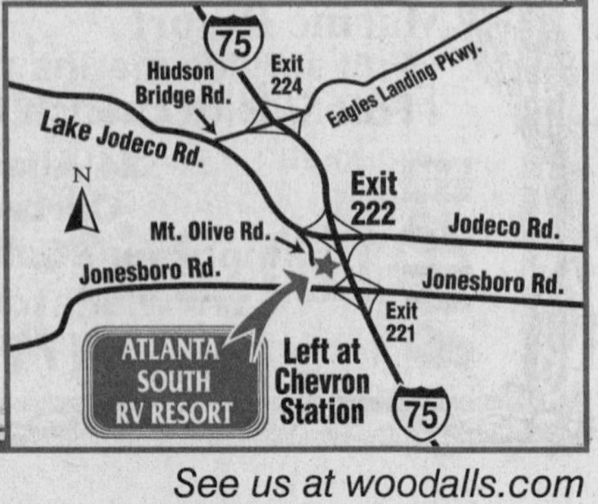

BLAIRSVILLE—Continued on next page

BLAIRSVILLE—Continued

(W) POTEETE CREEK (Union County Park)—(Union) *From jct US-19/129 & Hwy-325: Go 3-1/2 mi W on Hwy-325, then follow signs 1 mi E on county road.* FACILITIES: 59 sites, 59 E, tenting, dump, laundry, ltd groc. RECREATION: lake swim, boating, ramp, lake fishing. Open Apr 1 - Oct 15. Phone: (706)439-6103.

(E) **Trackrock Campground & Cabins**—(Union) *From jct US 19/129 & US-76: Go 6-1/2 mi E on US-76, then 2-3/4 mi S on Trackrock Gap Rd, then 1 mi S on Trackrock Church Rd. Enter on L.* ◆◆◆◆FACILITIES: 97 sites, typical site width 25 ft, 40 ft max RV length, 74 full hkups, 23 W&E, (30/50 amps), 26 pull-thrus, WiFi Instant Internet at site, family camping, tenting, RV storage, laundry, LP gas by weight, ice, picnic tables, fire rings, wood. ◆◆◆◆RECREATION: rec hall, pavilion, lake swim, lake fishing, bsktball, playground, horseshoes, hiking trails, v-ball. Pets welcome. Partial handicap access. Open all yr. Facilities fully operational Apr 1 - Nov 1. Rate in 2010 $25-37 per family. MC/VISA/Debit. Member ARVC. CCUSA 50% Discount. CCUSA reservations Recommended, CCUSA max stay 7 days. Discount is valid max of 7 days on any stay. Discount is valid Sun thru Thurs only during May, Aug & Sep. Discount not valid Jun, Jul, or Oct. Discount not valid during holiday periods. Call for availability, reservations strongly suggested.

Phone: (706)745-2420
Address: 4887 Trackrock Camp Rd, Blairsville, GA 30512
Lat/Lon: 34.85677/-83.87397
Email: trackroc@windstream.net
Web: www.trackrock.com

(S) VOGEL STATE PARK—(Union) *From jct US 76 & US 129/19: Go 11 mi S on US 129/19. Enter on R.* FACILITIES: 103 sites, 85 W&E, (30/50 amps), 18 no hkups, 20 pull-thrus, family camping, tenting, dump, laundry, ltd groc. RECREATION: lake swim, lake fishing, playground. Pets welcome. Partial handicap access. Open all yr. Big rigs welcome. Phone: (800)864-7275.

BLAKELY—E-1

(N) KOLOMOKI MOUNDS STATE PARK—(Early) *From jct Hwy 62, Hwy 39 & US 27: Go 1-1/2 mi N on US 27, then 6-1/2 mi N on SR 1940. Enter on R.* FACILITIES: 24 sites, typical site width 30 ft, 24 W&E, (30/50 amps), 12 pull-thrus, family camping, tenting, dump, laundry. RECREATION: swim pool, boating, 10 hp limit, canoeing, ramp, dock, lake/stream fishing, playground. Pets welcome. Partial handicap access. Open all yr. Big rigs welcome. Phone: (800) 864-7275.

BLUE RIDGE—A-2

(SW) CHATTAHOOCHE NATIONAL FOREST (Mulky) —(Union) *From town: Go E 4.5 mi on Hwy 76 to Hwy 60, then S 16 mi to FR.4, then NE 4.9 mi on FR-4. Enter at end.* FACILITIES: 11 sites, typical site width 15 ft, 20 ft max RV length, 11 no hkups, tenting. RECREATION: stream fishing. Open all yr. Facilities fully operational Mar 26 - Oct 31. Phone: (706)632-3031.

We all know that one of the best parts about camping is the food! Woodall's Campsite Cookbook is a classic cookbook containing such fun campsite and RV recipes as Roadside Spuds, The Fastest Sauce in the West, and Hairy Squares (which taste a lot better than they sound!) To order your copy go to www.woodalls.com/shop.

BREMEN—B-1

(W) YOGI BEAR'S JELLYSTONE PARK OF GEORGIA—(Haralson) *From jct I-20 (exit 9) & Waco Rd: Go 1 mi N on Waco Rd/Atlantic Ave, then 1/2 mi W on US 78, then 1/4 mi S on King. Enter on L.*

◆◆◆◆FACILITIES: 91 sites, 91 full hkups, (30/50 amps), 50 amps ($), some extd stay sites, 83 pull-thrus, cable TV, ($), WiFi Instant Internet at site, family camping, tenting, cabins, laundry, LP gas by meter, ice, picnic tables, fire rings, grills, wood.

◆◆◆◆RECREATION: rec room/area, pavilion, coin games, swim pool, spray ground, mini-golf, ($), golf nearby, playground, activities, (wkends), horseshoes. Rec open to public.

Pets welcome. Partial handicap access. Open all yr. Big rigs welcome. Escort to site. Clubs welcome. Rate in 2010 $28-30 for 2 persons. MC/VISA/DISC/AMEX/Debit. CCUSA 50% Discount. CCUSA reservations Recommended, CCUSA max stay Unlimited, CCUSA disc. not avail F,Sa. Not available for rallies, groups or special events, Memorial Day, 4th of July & Labor Day weekends.

Text 107874 to (440)725-8687 to see our Visual Tour.

Phone: (770)537-3140
Address: 106 King St, Bremen, GA 30110
Lat/Lon: 33.70309/-85.19537
Email: info@georgiajellystone.com
Web: georgiajellystone.com

SEE AD ATLANTA PAGE 193 AND AD TRAVEL SECTION PAGE 185

Georgia State Name: Named in honor of King George II

BRUNSWICK—E-5

(W) BLYTHE ISLAND REGIONAL PARK CAMPGROUND—(Glynn) *From jct I-95 (exit 29) & US 17: Go 1/2 mi W on US 17, then 2-3/4 mi NE on Hwy 303. Enter on R.*

FACILITIES: 97 sites, typical site width 28 ft, 97 full hkups, (30/50 amps), some extd stay sites, 32 pull-thrus, cable TV, WiFi Instant Internet at site, WiFi Internet central location, family camping, RV storage, dump, non-guest dump $, laundry, LP gas by weight/by meter, ice, picnic tables, fire rings, wood, controlled access.

RECREATION: pavilion, lake swim, boating, electric motors only, canoeing, kayaking, ramp, dock, 3 rowboat/6 canoe/6 kayak rentals, saltwater/lake fishing, golf nearby, playground, hiking trails, v-ball. Rec open to public.

Pets welcome. Partial handicap access. No tents. Open all yr. Big rigs welcome. Clubs welcome. MC/VISA/AMEX/Debit.

Phone: (800)343-7855
Address: Sam Coffer Rd, Brunswick, GA 31523
Lat/Lon: 31.16739/-81.54951
Email: blytheisland@glynncounty-ga.gov
Web: www.glynncounty.org

SEE AD THIS PAGE AND AD TRAVEL SECTION PAGE 185

BRUNSWICK—Continued on next page

The pirate Edward "Blackbeard" Teach made a home on Blackbeard Island. The United States Congress designated the Blackbeard Island Wilderness Reserve in 1975 and it now has a total of 3,000 acres.

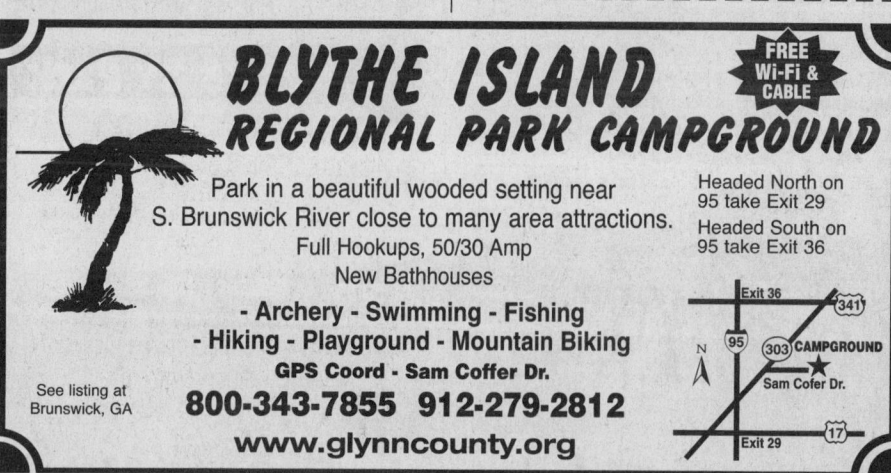

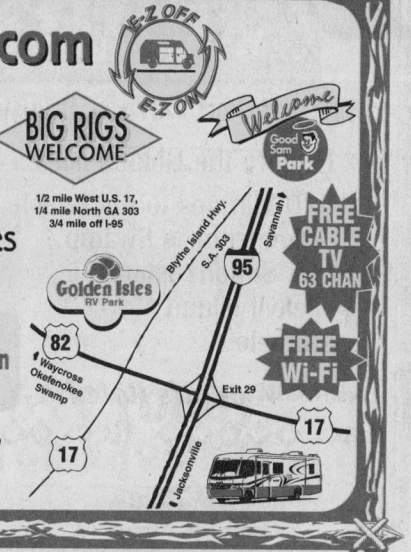

BRUNSWICK—Continued

(SW) COASTAL GEORGIA RV RESORT—(Glynn) *From jct I-95 (exit 29) & US 17: Go 1/2 mi W on US 17, then 1/4 mi S on US 17, then 1/2 mi E on Martin Palmer Dr. Enter at end.*

NEWEST RV RESORT NEAR SOUTH GA COAST!
Bring the family and enjoy our amenities! Only minutes from Golf, Beaches, Historical Sites & Shopping. Have a Cookout at the Pavilion, enjoy fun in the sun at our Pool, cruise the lake in Paddleboats or do some Fishing.

◆◆◆◆◆FACILITIES: 105 sites, typical site width 35 ft, 105 full hkups, (30/50 amps), 83 pull-thrus, cable TV, WiFi Instant Internet at site, WiFi Internet central location, family camping, laundry, ltd groc, RV supplies, LP gas by weight, ice, picnic tables, grills, wood.

◆◆◆RECREATION: rec room/area, pavilion, swim pool, dock, 4 pedal boat rentals, lake fishing, golf nearby, play equipment, shuffleboard court, horseshoes.

Pets welcome, breed restrict, quantity restrict. Partial handicap access. No tents. Open all yr. Big rigs welcome. Clubs welcome. Rate in 2010 $40 for 2 persons. MC/VISA/DISC.

Text 81940 to (440)725-8687 to see our Visual Tour.

Phone: (912)264-3869
Address: 287 South Port Pkwy, Brunswick, GA 31523
Lat/Lon: 31.13385/-81.58251
Email: coastalgarv@att.net
Web: www.coastalGARVResort.com

SEE AD THIS PAGE AND AD TRAVEL SECTION PAGE 185

(W) FRAN'S PLACE RESTAURANT—*From jct I-95 (exit 29) & US 17: Go 1/2 mi W on US 17, then 1/4 mi N on Hwy 303. Enter on L.* Full Service restaurant serving breakfast and lunch featuring country cooking & special menu items. Hrs 8am-2pm weekdays. Friday seafood buffet 5:30pm - 8pm. Open all yr. MC/VISA/DISC/AMEX/Debit.

Phone: (912)262-9663
Address: 7445 Blythe Island Hwy, Brunswick, GA 31523
Lat/Lon: 31.14438/-81.57933
Email: goldenislesrv@bellsouth.net
Web: www.goldenislesrvpark.com

SEE AD PAGE 195

WELCOME **(W) GOLDEN ISLES RV PARK**—(Glynn) *From jct I-95 (exit 29) & US 17: Go 1/2 mi W on US 17, then 1/4 mi N on Hwy 303. Enter on L.*

ENJOY BRUNSWICK & THE GOLDEN ISLES!
Fresh local seafood prepared at Fran's Place. Beautiful beaches, historic sites, waterpark & cruise ship. Golf, fish & sightsee. Affordable family fun! Come relax by the pool or a campfire! Free WIFI! and 63 ch cable TV.

◆◆◆◆FACILITIES: 160 sites, typical site width 26 ft, 149 full hkups, 11 W&E, (20/30/50 amps), some extd stay sites, 102 pull-thrus, cable TV, WiFi Instant Internet at site, phone on-site Internet (needs activ), cable Internet central location, family camping, tenting, cabins, RV storage, dump, non-guest dump $, laundry, LP gas by weight/by meter, ice, picnic tables, wood.

CAMPCLUB USA ◆◆RECREATION: pavilion, swim pool, golf nearby, playground, horseshoes.

Pets welcome. Partial handicap access. Open all yr. AAA & Passport Discounts. Big rigs welcome. Clubs welcome. Rate in 2010 $30-32 for 2 persons. MC/VISA/DISC/AMEX/Debit. CCUSA 50% Discount. CCUSA reservations Accepted, CCUSA max stay 3 days. Discount not available holiday weekends, during area special events. Call for details. Discount not valid on dry camping or tent sites.

Text 80161 to (440)725-8687 to see our Visual Tour.

GOLDEN ISLES RV PARK—Continued on next page

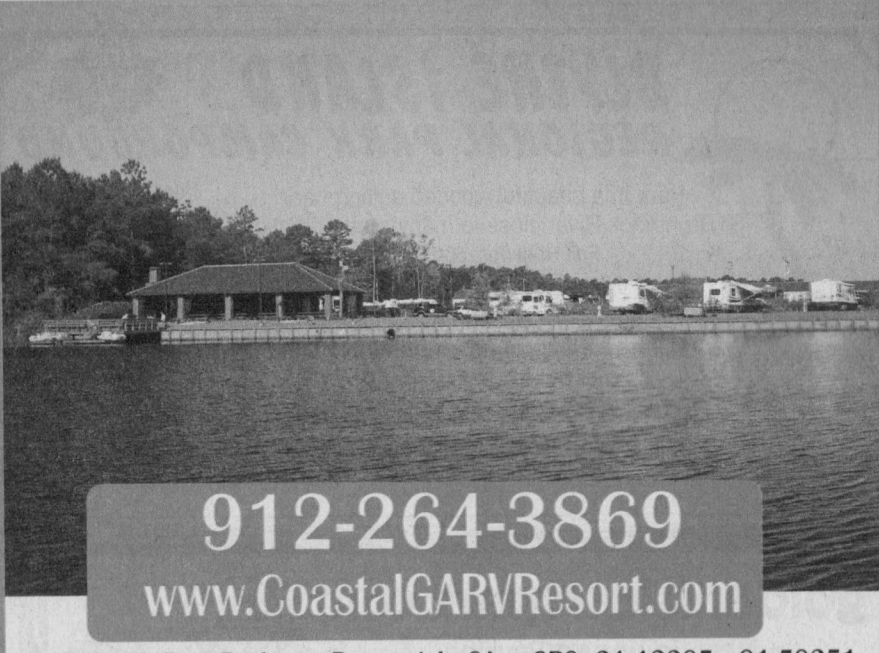

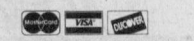

The name of the famous south Georgia swamp, the Okeefenokee, is derived from an Indian word meaning "the trembling earth".

BRUNSWICK—Continued
GOLDEN ISLES RV PARK—Continued

Phone: (912)261-1025
Address: 7445 Blythe Island Hwy, Brunswick, GA 31523
Lat/Lon: 31.14438/-81.57933
Email: goldenislesrv@bellsouth.net
Web: goldenislesrvpark.com

SEE AD PAGE 195 AND AD TRAVEL SECTION PAGE 185 AND AD MAP PAGE 182

(W) THREE OAKS FARM—*From jct I-95 (exit 29) & US 17/82: Go 2 mi W on US 82, then 1/4 mi N on Emanuel Church Rd, then 1 block E on Fish Hall Rd, then 1/2 mi N on Oyster Rd to entrance at Oyster Rd Extn. Enter on R.* 50 acre equine facility. Boarding, lessons, horseback riding, horse sales & leasing. Specializing in Hunter Jumpers, Dressage & Western Trail rides on beach & Forest. Carriage rides. Horseback riding on Jekyll & St. Simons Beaches. Open all yr.

Phone: (912)269-0623
Address: 332 Oyster Rd, Brunswick, GA 31523
Lat/Lon: 31.17022/-81.58803
Email: tlcrum1@aol.com
Web: www.three-oaks.com

SEE AD PAGE 195

BUFORD—B-2

(NW) CHESTNUT RIDGE PARK (COE-Lake Sidney Lanier)—(Forsyth) *From jct I-985 (exit 1/4) & Hwy 20: Go 2 mi W on Hwy 20, then 2-1/2 mi N on Peachtree Industrial Blvd, then 3/4 mi W on Gaines Ferry Rd, then N on Chestnut Ridge Rd. Enter at end.* FACILITIES: 84 sites, typical site width 12 ft, 51 W&E, (30 amps), 33 no hkups, 4 pull-thrus, tenting, dump, laundry, ltd groc. RECREATION: lake swim, boating, canoeing, ramp, dock, lake fishing, playground. Partial handicap access. Open Mar 31 - Sep 6. Phone: (770)967-6710.

(N) Lake Lanier Islands Campground—(Forsyth) *From jct I-985 (exit 8) & Hwy 347: Go 4-1/2 mi NW on Hwy 347. Enter at end.* ◆◆◆FACILITIES: 135 sites, typical site width 25 ft, 28 full hkups, 95 W&E, (20/30 amps), 12 no hkups, 11 pull-thrus, family camping, tenting, dump, laundry, marine gas, ice, picnic tables, fire rings, grills, wood. ◆◆◆RECREATION: lake swim, boating, canoeing, kayaking, ramp, dock, lake fishing, fishing supplies, bike rental 30 bike rentals. Pets welcome. Open all yr. Rate in 2010 $38-42 for 2 persons. MC/VISA/DISC/AMEX/Debit. CCUSA 50% Discount. CCUSA reservations Recommended, CCUSA max stay Unlimited. Minimum 2 nights/stay. Only 1 stay per 30 day period. Discount not available Memorial Day, 4th of July or Labor Day weekends.

Phone: (770)932-7270
Address: 7000 Holiday Rd (Attn: Campgrounds), Buford, GA 30518
Lat/Lon: 34.17455/-84.03655
Email: campgrounds@LLImail.com
Web: lakelanierislands.com

BYRON—D-2

(E) Interstate RV Campground—(Peach) *From jct I-75 (exit 149) & Hwy 49: Go 500 ft W on Hwy 49, then 1/2 mi N on Chapman Rd. Enter on L.* ◆◆FACILITIES: 105 sites, typical site width 25 ft, 105 full hkups, (30/50 amps), 53 pull-thrus, family camping, laundry. ◆RECREATION: swim pool. Pets welcome. No tents. Open all yr. Big rigs welcome. Rate in 2010 $25 for 2 persons. Phone: (888)817-0906.

CALHOUN—B-1

(E) KOA-Calhoun—(Gordon) *From jct I-75 (exit 315) & Hwy 156: Go 1 3/4 mi E on Hwy 156. Enter on R.* ◆◆◆FACILITIES: 89 sites, typical site width 25 ft, 27 full hkups, 62 W&E, (30/50 amps), 50 pull-thrus, family camping, tenting, dump, laundry, ltd groc. ◆◆◆◆RECREATION: swim pool, pond fishing, playground. Pets welcome. Partial handicap access. Open all yr. Big rigs welcome. Rate in 2010 $30-45 for 2 persons. Phone: (800)562-7512. KOA discount.

CANTON—B-2

(W) SWEETWATER CAMPGROUND (Allatoona Lake COE)—(Cherokee) *From town: Go 5-1/2 mi W on Hwy-20, then 2 mi S at Sweetwater Corner Store.* FACILITIES: 151 sites, typical site width 20 ft, 2 full hkups, 118 W&E, (50 amps), 31 no hkups, 10 pull-thrus, tenting, dump, laundry. RECREATION: lake swim, boating, ramp, dock, lake fishing, playground. Partial handicap access. Open Mar 26 - Sep 7. Phone: (678)721-6700.

CARROLLTON—C-1

(W) JOHN TANNER STATE PARK—(Carroll) *From jct US 27 & Hwy 16: Go 6 mi W on Hwy 16, then 1/2 mi S on Tanner Beach Rd. Enter at end.* FACILITIES: 31 sites, typical site width 25 ft, 31 W&E, (20/30 amps), 6 pull-thrus, family camping, tenting, dump, laundry. RECREATION: lake swim, boating, electric motors only, canoeing, lake fishing, playground. Pets welcome. Partial handicap access. Open all yr. Phone: (800) 864-7275.

Georgia State Gem: Quartz

CARTERSVILLE—B-1

(S) ALLATOONA LANDING MARINE RESORT & CAMPGROUND—(Bartow) *From jct I-75 (exit 283) & Emerson/Allatoona Rd: Go 2 mi E on Allatoona Landing Rd. Enter on L.*

◆◆◆◆FACILITIES: 120 sites, typical site width 25 ft, 17 full hkups, 103 W&E, (30/50 amps), some extd stay sites, 16 pull-thrus, cable TV, WiFi Instant Internet at site, family camping, tenting, RV's/park model rentals, RV storage, dump, non-guest dump $, portable dump, laundry, ltd groc, RV supplies, LP gas by weight/by meter, marine gas, ice, picnic tables, fire rings, wood, controlled access.

◆◆◆RECREATION: rec hall, swim pool, lake swim, boating, canoeing, kayaking, ramp, dock, lake fishing, fishing supplies, golf nearby, bsktball, playground, horseshoes, hiking trails, v-ball.

Pets welcome, breed restrict. Partial handicap access. Open all yr. Big rigs welcome. Clubs welcome. Rate in 2010 $26-39 for 6 persons. MC/VISA/DISC/AMEX/Debit. CCUSA 50% Discount. CCUSA reservations Recommended, CCUSA max stay 6 days. Not available May 1 thru Labor Day. Discount applies to partial hook-up sites only.

Phone: (770)974-6089
Address: 24 Allatoona Landing Rd SE, Cartersville, GA 30121
Lat/Lon: 34.10886/-84.71202
Email: campground@allatoonalandingmarina.com
Web: www.allatoonalandingmarina.com

SEE AD ATLANTA PAGE 193

(N) Cartersville KOA—(Bartow) *From jct I-75 (exit 296) & Cass-White Rd: Go 1/4 mi W on Cass-White Rd. Enter on L.* ◆◆◆◆FACILITIES: 101 sites, typical site width 25 ft, 62 full hkups, 39 W&E, (30/50 amps), 101 pull-thrus, family camping, tenting, dump, laundry. ◆◆RECREATION: swim pool, play equipment. Pets welcome, breed restrict. Open all yr. Big rigs welcome. Rate in 2010 $28-37 for 2 persons. Phone: (770)382-7330. KOA discount.

(E) MCKASKEY CAMPGROUND (COE-Allatoona Lake)—(Bartow) *From jct I-75 (exit 125/290) & Hwy 20 Spur: Go 2 mi S on Hwy 20 Spur, then E on access road.* FACILITIES: 51 sites, typical site width 20 ft, 32 W&E, (30/50 amps), 19 no hkups, 2 pull-thrus, tenting, dump, laundry. RECREATION: lake swim, boating, ramp, dock, lake fishing, playground. Pets welcome, quantity restrict. Partial handicap access. Open Mar 26 - Sep 7. Phone: (678)721-6700.

(N) MILITARY PARK (Ft. McPherson-Lk Allatoona Army Rec Area)—(Bartow) *From I-75 (exit 122/283): Go 2-3/4 mi E off exit, then 1 block S on Old Sandtown Rd, then bear left and follow signs to office. Off Base: 45 mi N of Ft. McPherson.* FACILITIES: 25 sites, 12 full hkups, 8 W&E, 5 no hkups, tenting, dump, laundry. RECREATION: lake swim, boating, ramp, dock, lake fishing, playground. No pets. Open all yr. Phone: (770)974-3413.

(E) RED TOP MOUNTAIN STATE PARK—(Bartow) *From I-75 (exit 285) & Red Top Mountain Rd: Go 3 mi E on Red Top Mountain Rd. Enter on L.* FACILITIES: 92 sites, 68 W&E, (20/30/50 amps), 24 no hkups, 12 pull-thrus, family camping, tenting, dump. RECREATION: swim pool, lake swim, boating, canoeing, ramp, dock, lake fishing, playground. Pets welcome. Partial handicap access. Open all yr. Big rigs welcome. Phone: (800) 864-7275.

CAVE SPRING—B-1

(N) CEDAR CREEK RV PARK & OUTDOOR CENTER—(Floyd) *From jct US 411 & US 27: Go 7 mi S on US 411. Enter on R.*

◆◆◆◆FACILITIES: 62 sites, typical site width 30 ft, 62 full hkups, (20/30/50 amps), some extd stay sites, 10 pull-thrus, WiFi Instant Internet at site, WiFi Internet central location, family camping, tenting, RV's/park model rentals, RV storage, laundry, ltd groc, RV supplies, LP gas by weight/by meter, LP bottle exch, ice, picnic tables, fire rings, grills, wood.

◆◆◆RECREATION: pavilion, river swim, boating, canoeing, kayaking, 5 canoe/5 kayak rentals, float trips, river fishing, fishing supplies, golf nearby, bsktball, activities, (wkends), horseshoes, sports field, v-ball.

Pets welcome. Partial handicap access. Open all yr. Big rigs welcome. Escort to site. Clubs welcome. Rate in 2010 $18-35 for 5 persons. MC/VISA/DISC/AMEX/Debit. Member ARVC. CCUSA 50% Discount. CCUSA reservations Recommended, CCUSA max stay 4 days, CCUSA disc. not avail F,Sa, CCUSA disc. not avail holidays.

Georgia State Motto: "Wisdom, Justice & Moderation"

CAVE SPRING—Continued
CEDAR CREEK RV PARK & OUTDOOR CENTER—Continued

Phone: (706)777-3030
Address: 6770 Cave Spring Rd SW, Cave Spring, GA 30124
Lat/Lon: 34.13332/-85.30839
Email: camp@bigcedarcreek.com
Web: bigcedarcreek.com

SEE AD TRAVEL SECTION PAGE 183

CECIL—E-3

(W) CECIL BAY RV PARK—(Cook) *From jct I-75 (exit 32) & Old Coffee Rd: Go 150 yds W on Old Coffee Rd. Enter on R.*

BEST STOP TO & FROM FLORIDA
Nestled among 42 acres of beautiful trees that are over 40' tall is a RV Park for todays Big Rigs. All pull thru sites with cable tv and wi-fi. Come once for a visit - you'll come back as a friend.

◆◆◆FACILITIES: 104 sites, typical site width 30 ft, 98 full hkups, 6 W&E, (30/50 amps), 104 pull-thrus, cable TV, WiFi Instant Internet at site, tenting, RV storage, dump, non-guest dump $, laundry.

◆RECREATION: rec hall, pond fishing.

Pets welcome. Open all yr. Big rigs welcome. Clubs welcome. Rate in 2010 $28 for 4 persons. MC/VISA/DISC/AMEX.

Phone: (229)794-1484
Address: 1787 Old Coffee Rd, Cecil, GA 31627
Lat/Lon: 31.04415/-83.39865
Web: www.cecilbayrv.com

SEE AD VALDOSTA PAGE 209 AND AD TRAVEL SECTION PAGE 185

CHATSWORTH—A-1

(NE) CHATTAHOOCHEE NATIONAL FOREST (Lake Conasauga Campground)—(Murray) *From town: Go 4 mi N on US 411 to Eton, then 10 mi E on FR 18, then 10 mi NE on FR 68.* FACILITIES: 34 sites, 22 ft max RV length, 34 no hkups, 2 pull-thrus, tenting. RECREATION: lake swim, boating, electric motors only, ramp, lake fishing. Partial handicap access. Open Apr 14 - Oct 29. Phone: (706)695-6736.

(S) FORT MOUNTAIN STATE PARK—(Murray) *From jct US 411 & Hwy 52/2 (in town): Go 7-1/4 mi E on Hwy 52/2.* FACILITIES: 74 sites, 70 W&E, (30/50 amps), 4 no hkups, 35 pull-thrus, family camping, tenting, dump, laundry. RECREATION: lake swim, canoeing, lake fishing, playground. Pets welcome. Partial handicap access. Open all yr. Big rigs welcome. Phone: (800) 864-7275.

(SE) WOODRING BRANCH PUBLIC USE AREA (COE-Carters Lake)—(Gilmer) *From town: Go 20 mi S on US 411 & follow signs.* FACILITIES: 42 sites, typical site width 20 ft, 31 W&E, (20/30 amps), 11 no hkups, tenting, dump, laundry. RECREATION: boating, ramp, dock, lake fishing, playground. Partial handicap access. Open Apr 7 - Oct 28. Phone: (706)276-6050.

CLARKESVILLE—A-3

(N) MOCCASIN CREEK STATE PARK—(Rabun) *From jct Hwy 197 & US 441/23: Go 25 mi N on Hwy 197. Enter on R.* FACILITIES: 55 sites, 55 W&E, (30 amps), 12 pull-thrus, family camping, tenting, dump, laundry. RECREATION: boating, canoeing, ramp, dock, lake/stream fishing, playground. Pets welcome. Partial handicap access. Open all yr. Phone: (800) 864-7275.

CLAYTON—A-3

(NW) CHATTAHOOCHE-OCONEE NATIONAL FOREST-TALLULAH RIVER—(Rabun) *From town: Go 8 mi W on US 76 to County Rd, then 4 mi N to FS-70, then 1 mi NW. Enter on L.* FACILITIES: 17 sites, typical site width 20 ft, 35 ft max RV length, 17 no hkups, 3 pull-thrus, tenting. RECREATION: river fishing. Partial handicap access. Open Mar 28 - Nov 3. Phone: (706)782-3320.

(S) CHATTAHOOCHEE NATIONAL FOREST (Rabun Beach Campground)—(Rabun) *From town: Go 7 mi S on US 441/23, then 1/10 mi W on county road, then 2 mi S on Hwy 15, then 5 mi W on CR 10.* FACILITIES: 80 sites, typical site width 20 ft, 35 ft max RV length, 26 W&E, (20 amps), 54 no hkups, 3 pull-thrus, tenting, dump, ltd groc. RECREATION: lake swim, boating, ramp, lake fishing. Partial handicap access. Open Apr 25 - Nov 3. Phone: (706)782-3320.

(NW) CHATTAHOOCHEE-OCONEE NATIONAL FOREST-SANDY BOTTOM—(Rabun) *From town: Go 8 mi W on US 76 to County Rd, then 4 mi N to FS 70, then 5 mi Nw. Enter on L.* FACILITIES: 12 sites, typical site width 20 ft, 35 ft max RV length, 12 no hkups. RECREATION: river fishing. Open Mar 25 - Nov 8. Phone: (706)782-3320.

(NW) CHATTAHOOCHEE-OCONEE NATIONAL FOREST-TATE BRANCH—(Rabun) *From town: Go 8 mi W on US 76 to County Rd, then 4 mi W to FS 70, then 5 mi NW. Enter on R.* FACILITIES: 18 sites, typical site width 10 ft, 18 no hkups, tenting. RECREATION: river fishing. Open all yr. Phone: (706)782-3320.

CLEVELAND—A-2

(S) Leisure Acres Campground—(White) *From jct Hwy 75 & US 129: Go 4 mi S on US 129, then 1/2 mi W on Westmoreland. Enter on L.* ◆◆◆FACILITIES:

Leisure Acres Campground—Continued on next page

CLEVELAND—Continued
Leisure Acres Campground—Continued

93 sites, typical site width 25 ft, 88 full hkups, 5 W&E, (30/50 amps), 38 pull-thrus, family camping, tenting, laundry, ltd groc. ◆◆◆RECREATION: swim pool, pond fishing, playground. Pets welcome, breed restrict. Open all yr. Big rigs welcome. Rate in 2010 $32 per family. Member ARVC, GARVC. Phone: (706)865-6466.

COCHRAN—D-3

(S) Hillside Bluegrass RV Park—(Bleckley) *From jct Alt US 129 & Bus US 23/Bus Ga Hwy 87: Go 2-1/2 mi S on GA Hwy 87. Enter on R.* ◆◆◆FACILITIES: 343 sites, typical site width 25 ft, 43 full hkups, 300 W&E, (30/50 amps), 50 pull-thrus, WiFi Instant Internet at site ($), family camping, tenting, RV storage, dump, non-guest dump $, laundry, LP gas by weight/by meter, ice, picnic tables, fire rings, wood. ◆◆RECREATION: rec hall, pavilion, pond fishing, bike rental 3 bike rentals, playground, horseshoes, hiking trails, v-ball. Pets welcome. Partial handicap access. Open all yr. Big rigs welcome. Rate in 2010 $25-35 per family. MC/VISA/DISC/Debit. FMCA discount. CCUSA 50% Discount. CCUSA reservations Required, CCUSA max stay 2 days, CCUSA disc. not avail F,Sa. Not available Memorial Day, 4th of July & special events. Call for details.

Phone: (478)934-6694
Address: 592 GA Hwy 87 S, Cochran, GA 31014
Lat/Lon: 32.36216/-83.34330
Email: hillsidervpark@bellsouth.net
Web: www.hillsidervpark.com

COLQUITT—E-1

(S) Emerald Lake RV Park—(Miller) *From jct US 27 & Hwy 91: Go 5-1/2 mi S on Hwy 91. Enter on L.* ◆◆◆◆FACILITIES: 35 sites, typical site width 30 ft, 28 full hkups, 7 W&E, (20/30/50 amps), 50 amps ($), 18 pull-thrus, WiFi Instant Internet at site, WiFi Internet central location, family camping, tenting, RV storage, laundry, RV supplies, ice, picnic tables, patios, grills. ◆◆RECREATION: rec hall, equipped pavilion, swim pool, canoeing, pond fishing, fishing supplies, mini-golf, ($), play equipment, horseshoes. Pets welcome. Partial handicap access. Open all yr. Big rigs welcome. Rate in 2010 $35 for 2 persons. MC/VISA. CCUSA 50% Discount. CCUSA reservations Recommended, CCUSA max stay Unlimited, Cash only for CCUSA disc., Check only for CCUSA disc. Discount not available during Blue Grass Festival-Call for details.

Phone: (229)758-9929
Address: 698 Enterprise Rd, Colquitt, GA 39837
Lat/Lon: 31.12228/-84.82530
Email: dcmathis@hughes.net
Web: www.emeraldlakervpark.com

Georgia's State Nicknames: Peach State; Empire State of the South

COLUMBUS—D-1

(N) BLANTON CREEK PARK (Georgia Power)—(Harris) *From jct I-185 (exit 25) & Hwy 116: Go 1,000 feet W on Hwy 116, then 3-1/2 mi W on Hwy 103, then 3/4 mi S on Lickskillet Rd. Enter on R.*

◆◆◆FACILITIES: 51 sites, typical site width 40 ft, 43 W&E, 8 E, (20/30/50 amps), 2 pull-thrus, family camping, tenting, dump, laundry, ice, picnic tables, fire rings, grills, controlled access.

◆◆◆RECREATION: pavilion, lake swim, boating, canoeing, kayaking, ramp, dock, lake fishing, golf nearby, playground, horseshoes, v-ball. Rec open to public.

Pets welcome, breed restrict, quantity restrict. Partial handicap access. Open Mar - Sep. Big rigs welcome. Clubs welcome. Rate in 2010 $18 per vehicle.

Phone: (706)643-7737
Address: 1001 Lick Skillet Rd, Hamilton, GA 31811
Lat/Lon: 32.73932/-85.102276
Web: georgiapower.com/lakes

SEE AD TRAVEL SECTION PAGE 184

(E) LAKE PINES EVENT CENTER—*From jct I-185 & US 80: Go 9-1/2 mi E on US 80 (between milepost 12 & 13), then 1/4 mi S on Garrett Rd. Enter on L.* Specializing in weddings, family reunions, clubs, special meetings & gatherings. Open all yr.

Phone: (706)561-9675
Address: 6404 Garrett Rd, Midland, GA 31820
Lat/Lon: 32.53812/-84.82727
Email: info@lakepineseventcenter.com
Web: www.lakepine.net

SEE AD THIS PAGE

(E) LAKE PINES RV PARK & CAMPGROUND—(Muscogee) *From jct I-185 & US 80: Go 9-1/2 mi E on US 80, between milepost 12 & 13, then 1/4 mi S on Garrett Rd. Enter on L.*

SOUTHERN HOSPITALITY AT IT'S FINEST
Come for a night & you'll want to stay for a week or more! Rent our event Center for groups, weddings or private events. Near Columbus area attractions & a short drive to Roosevelt's Little White House & Callaway Gardens.

◆◆◆◆FACILITIES: 85 sites, typical site width 25 ft, 76 full hkups, 9 W&E, (20/30/50 amps), some extd stay sites, 37 pull-thrus, WiFi Instant Internet at site, phone on-site Internet (needs activ), cable Internet central location, family camping, tenting, RV's/park model rentals, cabins, RV storage, dump, non-guest dump $, laundry, LP gas by weight/by meter, picnic tables, patios, wood.

COLUMBUS—Continued
LAKE PINES RV PARK & CAMPGROUND—Continued

◆◆◆RECREATION: rec hall, swim pool, pond fishing, golf nearby, bike rental 8 bike rentals, playground, horseshoes, hiking trails.

Pets welcome, breed restrict, quantity restrict. Open all yr. Big rigs welcome. Escort to site. Clubs welcome. Rate in 2010 $32 for 2 persons. MC/VISA/Debit. Member ARVC. CCUSA 50% Discount. CCUSA reservations Accepted, CCUSA max stay 2 days.

Text 107896 to (440)725-8687 to see our Visual Tour.

Phone: (706)561-9675
Address: 6404 Garrett Rd, Midland, GA 31820
Lat/Lon: 32.53812/-84.82727
Email: info@lakepines.net
Web: www.lakepines.net

SEE AD THIS PAGE AND AD TRAVEL SECTION PAGE 185

COMER—B-3

(S) WATSON MILL BRIDGE STATE PARK—(Oglethorpe) *From jct Hwy 72 & Hwy 22: Go 2-3/4 mi S on Hwy 22, then 3-1/2 mi E on Watson Mill Rd. Enter at end.* FACILITIES: 32 sites, 21 W&E, (30 amps), 11 no hkups, 18 pull-thrus, family camping, tenting, dump, laundry. RECREATION: river swim, canoeing, river fishing, playground. Pets welcome. Partial handicap access. Open all yr. Phone: (800)864-7275.

COMMERCE—B-3

(S) Country Boy's RV Park—(Jackson) *From jct I-85 (exit 149) & US 441: Go 1-1/2 mi S on US 441, then 1/4 mi W on Mt. Olive Rd. Enter on R.* ◆◆FACILITIES: 69 sites, typical site width 20 ft, 60 full hkups, 9 W&E, (20/30/50 amps), 50 amps ($), 35 pull-thrus, family camping, tenting, laundry. ◆◆RECREATION: swim pool, playground. Pets welcome. Open all yr. Big rigs welcome. Rate in 2010 $23-25 for 2 persons. Phone: (706)335-5535.

CORDELE—D-2

(S) Cordele KOA—(Crisp) *From jct I-75 (exit 97) & Hwy 33 Conn: Go 1/4 mi W on Hwy 33 Conn. Enter on R.* ◆◆◆◆FACILITIES: 67 sites, typical site width 35 ft, 31 full hkups, 29 W&E, (20/30/50 amps), 50 amps ($), 7 no hkups, 51 pull-thrus, family camping, tenting, dump, laundry, groceries. ◆◆◆RECREATION: swim pool, playground. Pets welcome, breed restrict. Partial handicap access. Open all yr. Big rigs welcome. Rate in 2010 $30-34 for 2 persons. Phone: (229)273-5454. KOA discount.

(W) GEORGIA VETERANS MEMORIAL STATE PARK —(Crisp) *From jct I-75 (exit 101) & US 280/Hwy 30: Go 9 mi W on US 280/Hwy 30. Enter on L.* FACILITIES: 77 sites, 77 W&E, (30/50 amps), 43 pull-thrus, family camping, tenting, dump, laundry. RECREATION: swim pool, lake swim, boating, canoeing, ramp, dock, lake fishing, playground. Pets welcome. Partial handicap access. Open all yr. Big rigs welcome. Phone: (229)276-2371.

CORNELIA—B-3

(E) CHATTAHOOCHEE NATIONAL FOREST (Lake Russell Campground)—(Habersham) *From town: Go 1-1/2 mi N on US 123, then 2 mi E on FR 59 (Lake Russell Rd).* FACILITIES: 42 sites, typical site width 12 ft, 35 ft max RV length, 42 no hkups, tenting, dump. RECREATION: lake swim, boating, electric motors only, canoeing, ramp, lake fishing. Partial handicap access. Open May 1 - Nov 10. Phone: (706)754-6221.

CRAWFORDVILLE—C-3

(N) ALEXANDER H. STEPHENS STATE HISTORIC PARK—(Taliaferro) *From jct I-20 (exit 148) & Hwy 22: Go 2 mi N on Hwy 22, then 3/4 mi E on US 278. Enter on R.* FACILITIES: 25 sites, typical site width 20 ft, 25 W&E, (20/30/50 amps), 6 pull-thrus, family camping, tenting, dump, laundry. RECREATION: boating, electric motors only, canoeing, ramp, lake/pond fishing, playground. Pets welcome. Partial handicap access. Open all yr. Phone: (800)864-7275.

CUMMING—B-2

(E) BALD RIDGE CREEK CAMPGROUND (COE-Lake Sidney Lanier)—(Forsyth) *From US 19/Hwy 400 (exit 16): Go 1 mi E and 1 mi S on Pilgrim Mill Rd, then 1/2 mi SW on Sinclair Shoals Rd, then E on Bald Ridge Rd. Enter at end.* FACILITIES: 82 sites, typical site width 25 ft, 82 W&E, (30 amps), 15 pull-thrus, tenting, dump, laundry, ltd groc. RECREATION: lake swim, boating, canoeing, ramp, dock, lake fishing, playground. Partial handicap access. Open Mar 29 - Oct 28. Phone: (770)889-1591.

(E) BOLDING MILL (COE-Lake Sidney Lanier)—(Hall) *From US 19/Hwy 400 (exit 17): Go 6 mi E on Hwy 306, then 4-1/2 mi NE on Hwy 53, then 1/2 mi N on Sardis Rd, then 3-1/2 mi W on Chestatee Rd. Enter at end.* FACILITIES: 97 sites, typical site width 12 ft, 88 W&E, (30 amps), 9 no hkups, 5 pull-thrus, tenting, dump, laundry. RECREATION: lake swim, boating, ramp, lake fishing, playground. Partial handicap access. Open Apr 26 - Sep 10. Phone: (770)534-6960.

(SE) SAWNEE CAMPGROUND (COE-Lake Sidney Lanier)—(Forsyth) *From US 19/Hwy 400 (exit 14): Go 1/2 mi E on Hwy 20, then 1/2 mi N on Sanders Rd, then 2-1/2 mi E on Buford*

SAWNEE CAMPGROUND (COE-Lake Sidney Lanier)—Continued on next page

CUMMING—Continued
SAWNEE CAMPGROUND (COE-Lake Sidney Lanier)—Continued

Dam Rd. Enter on L. FACILITIES: 55 sites, typical site width 12 ft, 44 W&E, (30 amps), 11 no hkups, 6 pull-thrus, tenting, dump, laundry. RECREATION: lake swim, boating, canoeing, ramp, dock, lake fishing, playground. Partial handicap access. Open Apr 20 - Sep 11. Phone: (770)887-0592.

(NE) SHADY GROVE PARK (COE-Lake Sidney Lanier) —(Forsyth) *From jct US 19/Hwy 400 & Hwy 369: Go 1 mi E on Hwy 369, then 2-1/2 mi SE on Shady Grove Rd. Enter at end.* FACILITIES: 126 sites, typical site width 12 ft, 76 W&E, (30 amps), 50 no hkups, tenting, dump, laundry. RECREATION: lake swim, boating, canoeing, ramp, dock, lake fishing, playground. Partial handicap access. Open Apr 2 - Nov 7. Phone: (770)205-6849.

(S) TWIN LAKES RV PARK—(Forsyth) *From jct US 19/Hwy 400 (exit 13) & Hwy 141: Go 500 ft N on Hwy 141, then 1 mi W on Hwy 9, then 1/4 mi N on Lake Rd. Enter at end.*

WELCOME

◆◆◆◆FACILITIES: 120 sites, typical site width 25 ft, accepts self-contained units only, 100 full hkups, 20 W&E, (30/50 amps), many extd stay sites, 6 pull-thrus, WiFi Instant Internet at site, phone on-site Internet (needs activ), phone Internet central location, family camping, dump, non-guest dump $, LP gas by weight/by meter, picnic tables.

◆RECREATION: lake fishing, golf nearby, horseshoes.

Pets welcome. No tents. Open all yr. No restrooms. Big rigs welcome. Rate in 2010 $25-30 for 2 persons.

Phone: (770)887-4400
Address: 3300 Shore Dr, Cumming, GA 30040
Lat/Lon: 34.16304/-84.19442
Web: twinlakes-rvpark.com

SEE AD ATLANTA PAGE 194

DANVILLE—D-3

Back to Nature Campground—*From jct I-16 & Hwy 358 (exit 27): E on Hwy 358 2-1/2 mi, L on Hwy 80 7/10 mi. Enter on L.* FACILITIES: 148 sites, 18 full hkups, 12 W&E, (30/50 amps), 118 no hkups, 17 pull-thrus, tenting, dump, laundry, fire rings, grills, wood.

CAMPCLUB USA

RECREATION: lake fishing, bsktball, playground, horseshoes, hiking trails, v-ball. Pets welcome. Partial handicap access. Open all yr. Rate in 2010 $15-45 for 4 persons. MC/VISA/Debit. CCUSA 50% Discount. CCUSA reservations Accepted, CCUSA max stay 4 days.

Phone: (478)442-1862
Address: 20044 US Highway 80, Danville, GA 31017
Lat/Lon: 32.6146/-83.2839
Email: info@backtonaturecampground.com
Web: www.backtonaturecampground.com

DARIEN—E-5

(W) CAT HEAD CREEK RV PARK—(McIntosh) *From jct I-95 (exit 49) & Hwy 251: Go 3 mi W on Hwy 251. Enter on R.*

WELCOME

◆◆◆◆FACILITIES: 24 sites, typical site width 25 ft, 23 full hkups, 1 W&E, (30/50 amps), 17 pull-thrus, cable TV, WiFi Internet central location, family camping, RV storage, dump, laundry, ltd groc, ice, picnic tables, fire rings, grills, wood.

◆◆RECREATION: equipped pavilion, boating, electric motors only, 2 rowboat rentals, pond fishing, hiking trails.

Pets welcome, quantity restrict. Partial handicap access. No tents. Open all yr. Big rigs welcome. Clubs welcome. Rate in 2010 $25-28 for 2 persons. MC/VISA/DISC.

DARIEN—Continued
CAT HEAD CREEK RV PARK—Continued

Phone: (912)437-2441
Address: 1288 Cox Rd SW, Townsend, GA 31331
Lat/Lon: 31.42452/-81.48861
Email: info@catheadcreekrvpark.com
Web: www.catheadcreekrvpark.com

SEE AD THIS PAGE AND AD TRAVEL SECTION PAGE 185

(W) Inland Harbor RV Park—(McIntosh) *From SE jct I-95 (exit 49) & Hwy 251: Go 1/4 mi E on Hwy 251. Enter on R.* ◆◆◆FACILITIES: 60 sites, typical site width 28 ft, 50 full hkups, 10 E, (30/50 amps), 40 pull-thrus, laundry. Pets welcome, breed restrict, size restrict, quantity restrict. Partial handicap access. No tents. Open all yr. Big rigs welcome. Rate in 2010 $27-30 for 2 persons. Phone: (912)437-6172.

DAWSONVILLE—B-2

(N) AMICALOLA FALLS STATE PARK & LODGE—(Dawson) *From jct Hwy 9 & Hwy 53: Go 3 mi W on Hwy 53, then 11 mi NW on Hwy 183, then 2 mi E on Hwy 52. (Steep mtn. grade - trailers over 16 ft not recommended). Enter on L.* FACILITIES: 24 sites, 24 W&E, (20/30/50 amps), 2 pull-thrus, family camping, tenting, dump, laundry. RECREATION: pond/stream fishing. Pets welcome. Partial handicap access. Open all yr. Phone: (800)864-7275.

DILLARD—A-3

(N) RIVER VISTA MOUNTAIN VILLAGE—(Rabun) *From jct US 441/23 & Hwy 246: Go 1 mi E on Hwy 246. Enter on R.*

WELCOME

A RESORT PARK CLOSE TO HIGHLANDS, NC

Everything here is first class and the setting is not to be missed-a beautiful valley surrounded by the Smoky and Blue Ridge Mountains. Come visit or buy your own lot. You'll find everything here you want, including peace and quiet.

◆◆◆◆◆FACILITIES: 144 sites, typical site width 35 ft, 144 full hkups, (20/30/50 amps), some extd stay sites, 27 pull-thrus, cable TV, WiFi Instant Internet at site, WiFi Internet central location, family camping, cabins, laundry, ltd groc, LP gas by weight/by meter, ice, picnic tables, grills.

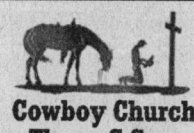

DILLARD—Continued
RIVER VISTA MOUNTAIN VILLAGE—Continued

◆◆◆RECREATION: rec hall, pavilion, 2 swim pools, hot tub, pond fishing, golf nearby, bsktball, play equipment, activities, horseshoes.

Pets welcome. Partial handicap access. No tents. Open all yr. Big rigs welcome. Escort to site. Clubs welcome. Rate in 2010 $24-49 per vehicle. MC/VISA/DISC/AMEX/Debit. Member GARVC. FMCA discount. CCUSA 50% Discount. CCUSA reservations Recommended, CCUSA max stay 2 days, CCUSA disc. not avail F,Sa, CCUSA disc. not avail holidays.

Phone: (888) 850-7275
Address: 20 River Vista Dr, Dillard, GA 30537
Lat/Lon: 34.98600/-83.36850
Email: relax@rvmountainvillage.com
Web: www.rvmountainvillage.com

SEE AD THIS PAGE AND AD FRANKLIN, NC PAGE 590

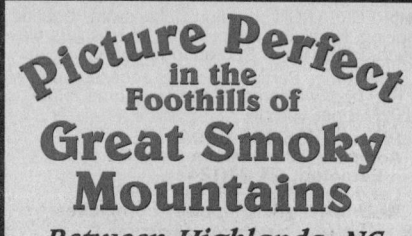

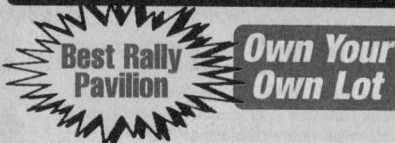

Woodall's Tip... Is a new Woodall's Directory needed every year? You bet! Each year the Woodall's North American Directory averages over 350,000 changes from the previous year.

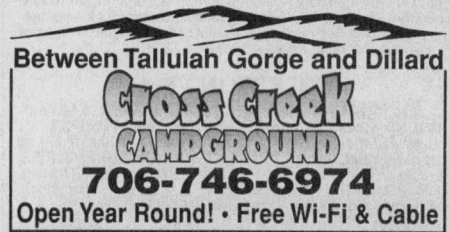

DONALSONVILLE—E-1

(S) SEMINOLE STATE PARK—(Seminole) *From jct US 84 & Hwy 39: Go 16 mi S on Hwy 39, then 1/4 mi E on Hwy 253. Enter on R.* FACILITIES: 50 sites, 50 W&E, (30/50 amps), 43 pull-thrus, family camping, tenting, dump, laundry. RECREATION: lake swim, boating, canoeing, ramp, dock, lake/pond fishing. Pets welcome. Open all yr. Big rigs welcome. Phone: (800)864-7275.

DOUGLAS—E-3

(N) GENERAL COFFEE STATE PARK—(Coffee) *From jct US 441 & Hwy 32: Go 6 mi E on Hwy 32. Enter on L.* FACILITIES: 50 sites, 50 W&E, (20/30 amps), family camping, tenting, dump, laundry. RECREATION: canoeing, river/pond fishing, playground. Pets welcome. Partial handicap access. Open all yr. Phone: (800) 864-7275.

EATONTON—C-3

(E) LAWRENCE SHOALS PARK (Georgia Power)—(Putnam) *From jct US 129/441 & Hwy 16: Go 12 mi E on Hwy 16, then 150 yds N on Wallace Dam Rd, then 1-1/2 mi W. Enter at end.*

WELCOME

◆◆◆FACILITIES: 49 sites, typical site width 30 ft, 49 W&E, (20/30/50 amps), family camping, tenting, RV storage, dump, non-guest dump $, laundry, ice, picnic tables, fire rings, grills, controlled access.

◆◆◆RECREATION: pavilion, lake swim, boating, canoeing, kayaking, ramp, dock, lake fishing, playground, hiking trails. Rec open to public.

Pets welcome. Partial handicap access. Open all yr. Big rigs welcome. Clubs welcome. Rate in 2010 $18 per vehicle.

Phone: (706)485-5494
Address: 123 Wallace Dam Rd, Eatonton, GA 31024
Lat/Lon: 33.35143/-83.16981
Web: www.georgiapower.com/lakes

SEE AD TRAVEL SECTION PAGE 184

(S) OCONEE NATIONAL FOREST (Lake Sinclair Campground)—(Putnam) *From town: Go 10 mi S on US 129, then 1 mi E on Hwy 212, then 2 mi N on FR 1062, follow signs.* FACILITIES: 44 sites, 22 ft max RV length, 6 full hkups, 38 no hkups, tenting, dump. RECREATION: lake swim, boating, ramp, lake fishing, playground. Open Mar 15 - Dec 4. Phone: (706)485-7110.

(E) OCONEE SPRINGS PARK (Putnam County Park) —(Putnam) *From jct US 129/441 & Hwy 16: Go 10 mi E on Hwy 16, then 1-1/2 mi S on Oconee Springs Rd, then 1-3/4 mi SE on Rockville Rd, then continue 1-3/4 mi on S Spring Rd. Enter on L.* FACILITIES: 43 sites, 6 full hkups, 37 W&E, (30 amps), dump, laundry, ltd groc. RECREATION: lake swim, boating, canoeing, ramp, dock, lake fishing, playground. Partial handicap access. No tents. Open all yr. Phone: (706)485-8423.

ELBERTON—B-3

(S) BOBBY BROWN STATE PARK—(Elbert) *From jct Hwy 17 & Hwy 72: Go 12-1/2 mi E on Hwy 72, then 6-1/2 mi S on Bobby Brown Park Rd. Enter at end.* FACILITIES: 61 sites, 61 W&E, (30/50 amps), 7 pull-thrus, family camping, tenting, dump, laundry. RECREATION: swim pool, boating, canoeing, ramp, dock, lake fishing, playground. Pets welcome. Partial handicap access. Open all yr. Big rigs welcome. Phone: (800)864-7275.

(N) RICHARD B RUSSELL STATE PARK—(Elbert) *From jct Hwy 17/72 & Hwy 77: Go 2 mi N on Hwy 77, then 8 mi NE on Ruckersville Rd. Enter on R.* FACILITIES: 28 sites, 28 W&E, (20/30 amps), 4 pull-thrus, family camping, tenting, dump, laundry. RECREATION: lake swim, boating, canoeing, ramp, dock, lake fishing, play equipment. Pets welcome. Partial handicap access. Open all yr. Phone: (800) 864-7275.

ELKO—D-2

(S) Twin Oaks RV Park—(Houston) *From jct I-75 (exit 127) & Hwy 26: Go 1000 ft E on Hwy 26. Enter on L.* ◆◆◆◆FACILITIES: 64 sites, typical site width 40 ft, 64 full hkups, (30/50 amps), 40 pull-thrus, WiFi Instant Internet at site, phone on-site Internet (needs activ), WiFi Internet central location, family camping, tenting, RV storage, laundry, ltd groc, RV supplies, LP gas by weight/by meter, ice, picnic tables, patios, fire rings.

CAMPCLUB USA

◆◆◆RECREATION: rec hall, equipped pavilion, swim pool, hot tub, horseshoes. Pets welcome. Partial handicap access. Open all yr. Big rigs welcome. Rate in 2010 $36 for 2 persons. MC/VISA/DISC/Debit. Member ARVC. FMCA discount. CCUSA 50% Discount. CCUSA reservations Accepted, CCUSA max stay Unlimited. Discount not available during special area events-call for details.

ELKO—Continued
Twin Oaks RV Park—Continued

Phone: (478)987-9361
Address: 305 Highway 26 East, Elko, GA 31025
Lat/Lon: 32.33614/-83.76479
Email: info@twinoaksrvpark.com
Web: www.twinoaksrvpark.com

ELLIJAY—A-2

(W) DOLL MOUNTAIN CAMPGROUND (COE-Carters Lake)—(Gilmer) *From town: Go 5 mi S on Hwy-5, then 10 mi W on Hwy-382 to Doll Mountainsign, then 1 mi N.* FACILITIES: 65 sites, typical site width 20 ft, 4 full hkups, 35 W&E, (30/50 amps), 26 no hkups, 5 pull-thrus, tenting, dump, laundry, ltd groc. RECREATION: lake swim, boating, ramp, lake fishing, playground. Pets welcome. Partial handicap access. Open Apr 2 - Oct 24. Phone: (706)276-4413.

(S) PLUM NELLY CAMPGROUND—(Gilmer) *From jct US 76 & Hwy 515: Go 3-1/2 mi S on Hwy 515. Enter on R.*

WELCOME

◆◆FACILITIES: 32 sites, 32 full hkups, (20/30/50 amps), 28 pull-thrus, cable TV, WiFi Instant Internet at site, WiFi Internet central location, family camping, tenting, cabins, RV storage, laundry, LP bottle exch, ice, picnic tables, wood.

◆RECREATION: pavilion, hot tub, pond fishing, golf nearby, bsktball, play equipment.

Pets welcome. Open all yr. Big rigs welcome. Rate in 2010 $24-32 per vehicle. MC/VISA.

Phone: (706)698-7586
Address: 15828 Highway 515 S, Ellijay, GA 30540
Lat/Lon: 34.63994/-84.50109
Email: plumnellycampground@yahoo.com
Web: www.plumnellycampground

SEE AD THIS PAGE

FARGO—F-4

(E) STEPHEN C. FOSTER STATE PARK—(Charlton) *From jct Hwy-177 & Hwy-94: Go 18 mi NE on Hwy-177. Enter at end.* FACILITIES: 66 sites, 66 W&E, (30/50 amps), 8 pull-thrus, family camping, tenting, dump, laundry, ltd groc. RECREATION: boating, 10 hp limit, canoeing, ramp, dock, lake fishing, playground. Pets welcome. Partial handicap access. Open all yr. Big rigs welcome. Phone: (800)864-7275.

FITZGERALD—E-3

(S) PAULK PARK RV PARK & CAMPGROUND—(Ben Hill) *From jct I-75 (exit 82) & Hwy 107: Go 28 mi E on Hwy 107. Enter on L.* FACILITIES: 25 sites, typical site width 25 ft, 25 full hkups, (30/50 amps), 25 pull-thrus, family camping, dump, laundry. RECREATION: boating, electric motors only, canoeing, pond fishing. Pets welcome. No tents. Open all yr. Phone: (229)426-5033.

FLOVILLA—C-2

(S) INDIAN SPRINGS STATE PARK—(Butts) *From jct I-75 (exit 205) & Hwy 16: Go 7-3/4 mi NE on Hwy 16, then 7 mi SE on Hwy 42. Enter on R.* FACILITIES: 88 sites, 88 W&E, (30/50 amps), family camping, tenting, dump, laundry. RECREATION: lake swim, boating, 10 hp limit, canoeing, ramp, dock, lake fishing, playground. Pets welcome. Partial handicap access. Open all yr. Big rigs welcome. Phone: (800) 864-7275.

FOLKSTON—F-4

(S) TRADERS HILL RECREATION AREA & CAMPGROUND (Charlton County)—(Charlton) *From jct US 1/23/301 & Hwys 23/40/121: Go 3 mi S on Hwys 23/121, then 1-1/4 mi E on paved road, then 1,000 feet N to park entrance.* FACILITIES: 38 sites, 12 full hkups, (20/30 amps), 26 no hkups, tenting, dump. RECREATION: river swim, boating, canoeing, ramp, dock, river fishing. Open all yr. Phone: (912)496-3412.

FORSYTH—C-2

(E) FORSYTH KOA—(Monroe) *From jct I-75 (exit 186) & Juliette Rd: Go 100 feet E on Juliette Rd, then 1/4 mi N on Frontage Rd. Enter on R.*

WELCOME

◆◆◆◆FACILITIES: 141 sites, typical site width 18 ft, 117 full hkups, 14 W&E, (20/30/50 amps), 10 no hkups, some extd stay sites, 97 pull-thrus, cable TV, ($), WiFi Instant Internet at site ($), phone on-site Internet (needs activ), WiFi Internet central location, family camping, tenting, cabins, dump, non-guest dump $, laundry, groceries, RV supplies, LP gas by weight/by meter, ice, picnic tables, wood.

◆◆◆RECREATION: rec hall, pavilion, swim pool, 2 pedal boat rentals, pond fishing, fishing supplies, golf nearby, bsktball, 6 bike rentals, playground, horseshoes, v-ball.

Pets welcome. Partial handicap access. Open all yr. Big rigs welcome. Escort to site. Clubs welcome. Rate in 2010 $29-31 for 2 persons. MC/VISA/DISC/AMEX/Debit. ATM. KOA discount.

The "Little White House" in Warm Springs, is where Franklin D. Roosevelt died.

FORSYTH—Continued
FORSYTH KOA—Continued

Phone: (800)562-8614
Address: 414 S Frontage Rd, Forsyth, GA 31029
Lat/Lon: 33.03776/-83.92599
Email: ke123@msn.com
Web: www.koa.com/where/ga/10101.htm

SEE AD NEXT PAGE AND AD TRAVEL SECTION PAGE 185

FORT BENNING—D-1

MILITARY PARK (Uchee Creek Army Campground/Marina)—(Muscogee) *From I-185 (exit 1): Go 1-1/4 mi S on I-185 to Fort Benning entrance, then continue 2 mi S to jct of Dixie Rd & Firt Division Rd, then continue 3-3/4 mi SW on Dixie Rd., then follow signs. Enter at end.* FACILITIES: 103 sites, typical site width 40 ft, 85 full hkups, (30/50 amps), 18 no hkups, 11 pull-thrus, tenting, dump, laundry, ltd groc. RECREATION: swim pool, boating, canoeing, ramp, dock, lake/river fishing, playground. Partial handicap access. Open all yr. Phone: (706)545-3060 x200.

FORT GAINES—E-1

(N) COTTON HILL PARK (COE-Walter F George Lake) —(Clay) *From jct Hwy 37 & Hwy 39: Go 7 mi N on Hwy 39, then 1-1/2 mi SW on access roads.* FACILITIES: 104 sites, typical site width 40 ft, 94 W&E, (20/30 amps), 10 no hkups, 10 pull-thrus, tenting, dump, laundry. RECREATION: lake/river swim, boating, ramp, dock, lake/river fishing, playground. Partial handicap access. Open all yr. Phone: (229)768-3061.

FORT VALLEY—D-2

(E) Ponderosa Park Campground—(Peach) *From jct I-75 (exit 142) & Hwy 96: Go 1/4 mi E on Hwy 96. Enter on L.* ◆◆◆FACILITIES: 65 sites, typical site width 25 ft, 65 full hkups, (30/50 amps), 65 pull-thrus, family camping, laundry. ◆RECREATION: playground. Pets welcome. No tents. Open all yr. Big rigs welcome. Phone: (478)825-8030.

GAINESVILLE—B-2

(W) DUCKETT MILL (COE - Lake Sidney Lanier)—(Hall) *From US 19/Hwy 400 (exit 17): Go E on Hwy 53, then 1-1/2 mi S on Duckett Mill Rd. Follow signs.* FACILITIES: 111 sites, typical site width 12 ft, 97 W&E, (30 amps), 14 no hkups, 9 pull-thrus, tenting, dump, laundry, ltd groc. RECREATION: lake swim, boating, canoeing, ramp, dock, lake fishing, playground. Partial handicap access. Open Apr 28 - Sep 9. Phone: (770)532-9802.

(S) OLD FEDERAL ROAD PARK (COE-Lake Sidney Lanier)—(Hall) *From jct Hwy 369 & Hwy 53: Go 2 mi S on Hwy 53/McEver Rd, then 1/2 mi S on McEver Rd, then 2 mi S on Stephens Rd, then 1 mi W on Old Federal Rd.* FACILITIES: 83 sites, typical site width 12 ft, 59 W&E, (30 amps), 24 no hkups, 10 pull-thrus, tenting, dump, laundry, ltd groc. RECREATION: lake swim, boating, canoeing, ramp, dock, lake fishing, playground. Open Mar 29 - Nov. Phone: (770)967-6757.

(W) RIVER FORKS PARK AND CAMPGROUND—(Hall) *From jct of Hwy 369 & Hwy 53: Go 1 mi W on Hwy 369, then 1/4 mi N on Keith Bridge Rd. Enter at end.* FACILITIES: 63 sites, typical site width 25 ft, 63 W&E, (30/50 amps), 8 pull-thrus, tenting, dump. RECREATION: lake swim, boating, ramp, dock, lake fishing, playground. Pets welcome. Partial handicap access. Open Mar 1 - Dec 31. Phone: (770)531-3952.

GREENSBORO—C-3

(S) OLD SALEM PARK (Georgia Power) —(Greene) *From jct I-20 (exit 130) & Hwy 44: Go 7 mi SW on Hwy 44, then 3/4 mi SE on Linger Longer Rd, then 1 mi SW on Old Salem Rd. Enter at end.*

WELCOME

◆◆◆FACILITIES: 92 sites, typical site width 30 ft, 92 W&E, (30/50 amps), 20 pull-thrus, family camping, tenting, RV storage, dump, non-guest dump $, laundry, ice, picnic tables, fire rings, grills, wood, controlled access.

◆◆◆RECREATION: pavilion, lake swim, boating, canoeing, kayaking, ramp, dock, lake fishing, golf nearby, playground, sports field. Rec open to public.

Pets welcome. Partial handicap access. Open Early Apr - Mid Sep. Big rigs welcome. Clubs welcome. Rate in 2010 $18 per vehicle.

Phone: (706)467-2850
Address: 1530 Old Salem Rd., Greensboro, GA 30642
Lat/Lon: 33.43749/-83.24563
Web: www.georgiapower.com/lakes

SEE AD TRAVEL SECTION PAGE 184

(S) PARKS FERRY PARK (Georgia Power) —(Greene) *From jct I-20 (exit 130) & Hwy 44: Go 5-1/2 mi SW on Hwy 44, then 3-1/2 mi N on Carey Station Rd., then 1 mi W on Parks Mill Rd. Enter on R.*

WELCOME

◆◆◆FACILITIES: 53 sites, typical site width 30 ft, 53 W&E, (20/30/50 amps), 9 pull-thrus, family

PARKS FERRY PARK (Georgia Power)—Continued on next page

GREENSBORO—Continued
PARKS FERRY PARK (Georgia Power)—Continued

camping, tenting, RV storage, dump, non-guest dump $, laundry, ice, picnic tables, grills, wood, controlled access.

◆◆◆RECREATION: pavilion, lake swim, boating, canoeing, kayaking, ramp, dock, lake fishing, golf nearby, playground, sports field. Rec open to public.

Pets welcome. Partial handicap access. Open Early Summer - Labor Day. Big rigs welcome. Clubs welcome. Rate in 2010 $18 per vehicle.

Phone: (706)453-4308
Address: 1491 Parks Mill Rd NE, Greensboro, GA 30642
Lat/Lon: 33.52009/-83.26450
Web: www.georgiapower.com/lakes

SEE AD TRAVEL SECTION PAGE 184

HARTWELL—B-3

(N) HART STATE PARK—(Hart) *From town: Go 1 mi E on US 29N, then 1-1/2 mi N on Ridge Rd, then follow signs. Enter at end.* FACILITIES: 78 sites, 62 W&E, (20/30 amps), 16 no hkups, 33 pull-thrus, family camping, tenting, dump, laundry. RECREATION: lake swim, boating, canoeing, ramp, dock, lake fishing, playground. Pets welcome. Partial handicap access. Open all yr. Phone: (800) 864-7275.

(N) MILLTOWN CAMPGROUND (COE - Hartwell Lake) —(Hart) *From town: Go 5 mi N on Hwy 51, then 6 mi E on CR 319 (New Prospect Rd), then 4 mi S on CR 310 to end.* FACILITIES: 25 sites, typical site width 20 ft, 25 no hkups, tenting, dump. RECREATION: lake swim, boating, ramp, lake fishing, playground. Open May 1 - Sep 6. Phone: (888)893-0678.

(N) PAYNES CREEK CAMPGROUND (COE - Hartwell Lake)—(Hart) *From town: Go 12 mi N on Hwy-51, then 4 mi W on Cr-301, then 2 mi N onCR-279 to end.* FACILITIES: 44 sites, typical site width 20 ft, 44 W&E, (50 amps), 31 pull-thrus, tenting, dump. RECREATION: lake swim, boating, ramp, lake fishing, playground. Pets welcome. Open May 1 - Sep 6. Phone: (888)893-0678.

(SE) WATSADLER CAMPGROUND (COE - Hartwell Lake)—(Hart) *From town: Go 5 mi E on US-29.* FACILITIES: 51 sites, typical site width 20 ft, 51 W&E, (50 amps), 18 pull-thrus, tenting, dump. RECREATION: lake swim, boating, ramp, dock, lake fishing, playground. Open all yr. Phone: (888)893-0678.

HELEN—A-2

(N) Cherokee Campground—(White) *From jct Hwy 17/75 & Hwy 356: Go 5 mi NE on Hwy 356. Enter on R.* ◆◆◆FACILITIES: 47 sites, typical site width 35 ft, 41 full hkups, (20/30/50 amps), 50 amps ($), 6 no hkups, 8 pull-thrus, family camping, tenting, laundry. ◆◆RECREATION: play equipment. Pets welcome. Partial handicap access. Open all yr. Big rigs welcome. Rate in 2010 $22 for 2 persons. Member ARVC, GARVC. Phone: (888)878-2268.

(N) Creekwood Resort Campground & Cabins —(White) *From jct Hwy 75/17 & Hwy 356: Go 5-3/4 mi NE on Hwy 356. Enter on R.* ◆◆◆◆FACILITIES: 18 sites, typical site width 30 ft, 18 full hkups, (20/30/50 amps), cable TV, WiFi Instant Internet at site, family camping, laundry, picnic tables, patios, fire rings, wood. ◆RECREATION: horseshoes, hiking trails. Pets welcome, breed restrict, quantity restrict. No tents. Open all yr. Big rigs welcome. Rate in 2010 $25-35 for 4 persons. MC/VISA/DISC/Debit. Member ARVC, GARVC. CCUSA 50% Discount. CCUSA reservations Required, CCUSA max stay 2 days, Cash only for CCUSA disc., Check only for CCUSA disc., CCUSA disc. not avail S, CCUSA disc. not avail F,Sa. Not available holidays, days surrounding holidays or months of Jun, Jul & Oct. Discount does not include premier sites.

Phone: (706)878-2164
Lat/Lon: 34.74933/-83.66824
Email: creekwoodresort@alltell.net
Web: www.creekwoodresort.com

(N) ENOTA MOUNTAIN RETREAT—(Towns) *From jct Hwy 75/17 & Hwy 356: Go 10-3/4 mi N on Hwy 75/17, then 2-1/2 mi W on Hwy 180. Enter on L.*

◆◆◆◆◆FACILITIES: 145 sites, typical site width 32 ft, 35 full hkups, 10 W&E, (30/50 amps), 100 no hkups, 3 pull-thrus, WiFi Instant Internet at site, phone Internet central location, family camping, tenting, cabins, laundry, full svc store, RV supplies, ice, picnic tables, patios, fire rings, grills, wood.

◆◆◆◆◆RECREATION: rec hall, rec room/area, pavilion, equipped pavilion, river swim, hot tub,

ENOTA MOUNTAIN RETREAT—Continued on next page

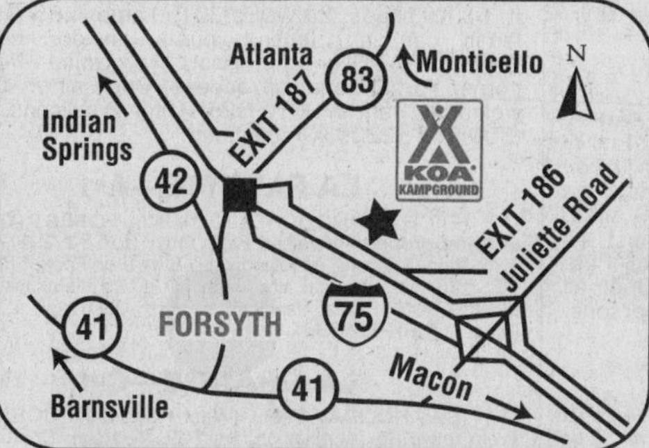

HELEN—Continued
ENOTA MOUNTAIN RETREAT—Continued

pond fishing, fishing supplies, fishing guides, playground, activities, horseshoes, sports field, hiking trails, v-ball. Rec open to public.

Pets welcome ($). Partial handicap access. Open all yr. Big rigs welcome. Escort to site. Clubs welcome. Rate in 2010 $30-34 for 2 persons. MC/VISA/Debit.

Phone: (800)990-8869
Address: 1000 Highway 180, Hiawassee, GA 30546
Lat/Lon: 34.83772/-83.77018
Email: enota@enota.com
Web: www.enota.com

SEE AD PAGE 201

(N) UNICOI STATE PARK—(White) *From jct Hwy 17/75 & Hwy 356: Go 1 mi E on Hwy 356. Enter on R.* FACILITIES: 115 sites, 82 W&E, (20/30/50 amps), 33 no hkups, family camping, tenting, dump, laundry, ltd groc. RECREATION: lake swim, lake/stream fishing, playground. Pets welcome. Partial handicap access. Open all yr. Big rigs welcome. Phone: (800)864-7275.

HIAWASSEE—A-2

(S) BALD MOUNTAIN CAMPING RESORT—(Towns) *From east jct US 76 & Hwys 75/17: Go 1/4 mi NW on US 76/Hwys 75/17, then 1/4 mi W on Hwy 288, then 3-1/2 mi S on Fodder Creek Rd, then on Gander Gap Rd. Enter on L.*

WELCOME

ENJOY GREAT GA MOUNTAIN CAMPING!

A little slice of heaven in the GA Mountains! Your base camp for trips to Alpine Helen, the Appalachian Trail, Brasstown Bald, Georgia Mountain Fairgrounds & Lake Chatuge. Come experience an exceptional vacation destination!

◆◆◆◆◆FACILITIES: 293 sites, typical site width 30 ft, 286 full hkups, 7 W&E, (20/30/50 amps), some extd stay sites, 49 pull-thrus, cable TV, WiFi Instant Internet at site, family camping, tenting, cabins, RV storage, dump, non-guest dump $, laundry, ltd groc, RV supplies, LP gas by weight/by meter, ice, picnic tables, patios, fire rings, grills, wood.

◆◆◆◆◆RECREATION: rec hall, rec room/area, pavilion, equipped pavilion, coin games, swim pool, boating, kayaking, 4 kayak/3 pedal boat rentals, pond fishing, fishing supplies, mini-golf, golf nearby, bsktball, playground, shuffleboard court 2 shuffleboard courts, activities, horseshoes, sports field, hiking trails, v-ball.

Pets welcome, breed restrict. Partial handicap access. Open Apr 1 - Oct 31. Big rigs welcome. Escort to site. Clubs welcome. Rate in 2010 $28-30 per vehicle. MC/VISA/DISC/Debit. Member ARVC, GARVC. FMCA discount.

Phone: (706)896-8896
Address: 751 Gander Gap Rd., Hiawassee, GA 30546
Lat/Lon: 34.88954/-83.76836
Web: www.baldmountainpark.com

SEE AD THIS PAGE

(W) GEORGIA MOUNTAIN FAIRGROUNDS CAMPGROUND (County Park)—(Towns) *From west jct Hwy 75 & US 76/Hwy 17: Go 1 mi W on US 76/Hwy 17. Enter on R.*

WELCOME

FACILITIES: 189 sites, typical site width 30 ft, 97 full hkups, 92 W&E, (30/50 amps), some extd stay sites (summer), cable TV, WiFi Instant Internet at site, WiFi Internet central location, family camping, tenting, dump, non-guest dump $, ice, picnic tables, controlled access.

RECREATION: pavilion, lake swim, boating, canoeing, kayaking, ramp, lake fishing, golf nearby, bsktball, playground, tennis, sports field, hiking trails, v-ball. Rec open to public.

Pets welcome. Open all yr. Big rigs welcome. Clubs welcome. MC/VISA/DISC/AMEX/Debit.

Phone: (706)896-4191
Address: 1311 Music Hall Rd, Hiawassee, GA 30546
Lat/Lon: 34.96438/-83.77169
Email: gamtfair@windstream.net
Web: georgiamountainfairgrounds.com

SEE AD TRAVEL SECTION PAGE 183

(W) GEORGIA MOUNTAIN FAIRGROUNDS & MUSIC HALL—*From west jct Hwy 75 & US 76/Hwy 17: Go 1 mi W on US 76/Hwy 17. Enter on R.* Fair held each Aug in 2,900-seat music hall; music festivals-May thru Oct; mountain fiddlers convention in Oct. Open May 1 - Oct 31. MC/VISA/DISC/AMEX.

WELCOME

Phone: (706)896-4191
Address: 1311 Music Hall Rd, Hiawassee, GA 30506
Lat/Lon: 34.96390/-83.77132
Email: gamtfair@windsteam.net
Web: georgiamountainfairgrounds.com

SEE AD TRAVEL SECTION PAGE 183

(S) River Bend Campground—(Towns) *From E jct Hwy 17/75: Go 3/4 mi S on Hwy 75, then 1 mi E on Streak Hill Rd. Enter on R.* ◆◆◆FACILITIES: 85 sites, typical site width 30 ft, 68 full hkups, 17 W&E, (30/50 amps), 3 pull-thrus, family camping, tenting, dump. ◆◆◆RECREATION: swim pool, canoeing, river fishing, playground. Pets welcome, breed restrict. Partial handicap access. Open all yr. Big rigs welcome. Rate in 2010 $28-30 per vehicle. Phone: (706)896-1415. FMCA discount.

HIGH FALLS—C-2

(S) HIGH FALLS STATE PARK—(Monroe) *From I-75 (exit 198) & Moreland Rd: Go 1-3/4 mi E on Moreland Rd. Enter on L.* FACILITIES: 103 sites, 103 W&E, (30/50 amps), 6 pull-thrus, family camping, tenting, dump, laundry. RECREATION: swim pool, boating, 10 hp limit, canoeing, ramp, dock, lake/river fishing, playground. Pets welcome. Partial handicap access. Open all yr. Big rigs welcome. Phone: (800) 864-7275.

JACKSON—C-2

(W) Forest Glen Mobile Home & RV Park—(Butts) *From jct I-75 (exit 205) & Hwy 16: Go 1/4 mi W on Hwy 16, then 150 yds S on Windy Lane, then 1/4 mi E on un-named paved road continuing 150 yds S on Glade Rd. Enter at end.* ◆◆◆◆FACILITIES: 83 sites, typical site width 30 ft, 83 full hkups, (30/50 amps), 41 pull-thrus, laundry. ◆◆RECREATION: swim pool. Pets welcome. Partial handicap access. No tents. Open all yr. Big rigs welcome. Rate in 2010 $30 for 2 persons. Phone: (770)228-3399.

JEKYLL ISLAND—E-5

(N) JEKYLL ISLAND CAMPGROUND—(Glynn) *From jct I-95 (exit 29) & US 17N: Go 5 mi E on US 17N, then 6 mi SE on Hwy 520 (Jekyll Island Causeway), then 4-1/2 mi N on Beachview Dr. Enter on L.* FACILITIES: 206 sites, typical site width 20 ft, 162 full hkups, 2 W&E, (30/50 amps), 42 no hkups, 50 pull-thrus, family camping, tenting, dump, laundry, ltd groc. RECREATION: saltwater swim, saltwater/lake fishing. Pets welcome ($). Partial handicap access. Open all yr. Big rigs welcome. Phone: (866) 658-3021.

Georgia State Flower: Cherokee Rose

JESUP—E-4

(E) Mossy Oaks RV Park & Campground (Not visited)—(Wayne) *From jct US 301 & US 341/US 25: Go 4 mi SE on US 25/US 341, then 1-1/2 mi NE on Odessa Rd, then 3/4 mi N on Bethlehem Rd, then 2-1/4 mi NE on Whaley Rd. Enter on L.* FACILITIES: 30 sites, 21 full hkups, 9 W&E, (30/50 amps), 21 pull-thrus, laundry, picnic tables. RECREATION: pavilion. Rate in 2010 $25. CCUSA 50% Discount. CCUSA reservations Recommended, CCUSA max stay 2 days, Cash only for CCUSA disc., Check only for CCUSA disc. Pets on leash when outside rv. Tent sites $15. Limited rentals & monthly rates available. Neither discounted.

CAMPCLUB USA

Phone: (912)427-4452
Address: 1162 Whaley Rd, Jesup, GA 31546
Web: mossyoaksrvpark.com

JULLIETTE—C-2

(N) DAMES FERRY PARK (Georgia Power)—(Monroe) *From jct I-75 (exit 171) & US 23/Hwy 87: Go 9-1/4 mi N on US 23/Hwy 87. Enter on L.*

WELCOME

◆◆◆FACILITIES: 50 sites, typical site width 35 ft, 45 W&E, (20/30/50 amps), 5 no hkups, 6 pull-thrus, family camping, tenting, dump, non-guest dump $, ice, picnic tables, fire rings, grills, wood, controlled access.

◆◆◆RECREATION: pavilion, lake swim, boating, 25 hp limit, canoeing, kayaking, ramp, dock, lake fishing, golf nearby, hiking trails. Rec open to public.

Pets welcome, quantity restrict. Partial handicap access. Open Mar 1 - Oct 31. Big rigs welcome. Clubs welcome. Rate in 2010 $18 per vehicle.

Phone: (478)994-7945
Address: 180 Dam Rd, Jackson, GA 30233
Lat/Lon: 33.04424/-83.75785
Web: www.georgiapower.com/lakes

SEE AD TRAVEL SECTION PAGE 184

KINGSLAND—F-5

(E) COUNTRY OAKS CAMPGROUND & RV PARK—(Camden) *From I-95 (exit 1) & St. Mary's Rd.: Go 1/4 mi W on St. Mary's Rd. Enter on L.*

WELCOME

◆◆◆◆FACILITIES: 43 sites, typical site width 30 ft, 42 full hkups, 1 W&E, (30/50 amps), some extd stay sites (winter), 18 pull-thrus, WiFi Instant Internet at site, family camping, RV storage, laundry, LP gas by weight/by meter, ice, picnic tables, fire rings, wood.

◆RECREATION: rec room/area, pond fishing, golf nearby, horseshoes.

Pets welcome. Partial handicap access. No tents. Open all yr. Big rigs welcome. Clubs welcome. Rate in 2010 $30 for 2 persons. MC/VISA/DISC/Debit. Member ARVC.

Phone: (912)729-6212
Address: 6 Carlton Cemetery Rd, Kingsland, GA 31548
Lat/Lon: 30.76087/-81.65839
Web: www.countryoaksrv.com

SEE AD JACKSONVILLE, FL PAGE 129 AND AD TRAVEL SECTION PAGE 185

(E) Jacksonville North/Kingsland KOA—(Camden) *From I-95 (exit 1) & St Mary's Rd: Go 500 ft W on St Mary's Rd, then 1/4 mi S on Scrubby Bluff Rd. Enter on R.* ◆◆◆FACILITIES: 85 sites, typical site width 25 ft, 61 full hkups, 24 W&E, (30/50 amps), 85 pull-thrus, family camping, tenting, dump, laundry, ltd groc. ◆◆RECREATION: swim pool, playground. Pets welcome. Partial handicap access. Open all yr. Big rigs welcome. Rate in 2010 $28-40 for 2 persons. Phone: (800)562-5220. KOA discount.

LA FAYETTE—A-1

(E) CHATTAHOOCHEE NATIONAL FOREST (The Pocket Campground)—(Walker) *From town: Go 13-1/2 mi E on Hwy 136, then (1/2 mi E of Villanow) go 8 mi S on Pocket Rd.* FACILITIES: 26 sites, typical site width 10 ft, 26 no hkups, tenting. RECREATION: Partial handicap access. Open Apr 4 - Nov 3. Phone: (706)695-6736.

LA GRANGE—C-1

(SW) HOLIDAY PARK (West Point Lake COE)—(Troup) *From town: Go 10 mi W on Hwy-109, then over Chattahoochee River & follow signs.* FACILITIES: 143 sites, 92 W&E, (30 amps), 51 no hkups, tenting, dump, laundry. RECREATION: lake swim, boating, ramp, dock, lake fishing, playground. Partial handicap access. Open Feb 25 - Sep 24. Phone: (706)884-6818.

(N) RINGER PARK (COE - West Point Lake)—(Troup) *From town: Go 10 mi N on US-27, follow signs.* FACILITIES: 37 sites, typical site width 15 ft, 37 no hkups, tenting. RECREATION: boating, ramp, dock, lake fishing. Open all yr. Phone: (706)645-2937.

LA GRANGE—Continued on next page

LA GRANGE—Continued

(SW) STATE LINE PARK (COE - West Point Lake)—(Troup) *From town: Go 14 mi W on Hwy-109 to Hwy-109 spur, then follow signs.* FACILITIES: 122 sites, typical site width 20 ft, 56 W&E, (20/30 amps), 66 no hkups, tenting, dump, laundry. RECREATION: lake swim, boating, ramp, dock, lake fishing, playground. Partial handicap access. Open Mar 1 - Sep 30. Phone: (706)882-5439.

(SW) WHITETAIL RIDGE (COE - West Point Lake)—(Troup) *From town: Go 10 mi W on Hwy 109, then over Chattahoochee River and follow signs.* FACILITIES: 58 sites, typical site width 20 ft, 58 W&E, (20/30 amps), 8 pull-thrus, tenting, dump, laundry, ltd groc. RECREATION: boating, ramp, lake fishing, playground. Partial handicap access. Open Mar 19 - Nov 28. Phone: (706)884-8972.

LAKE PARK—F-3

(W) BARGAINVILLE FLEA MARKET—*From jct I-75 (exit 5) & Hwy 376: Go 150 yds E, then 1/2 mi S on Mill Store Road. Enter on L.* New, old & used collectable merchandise. Over 150 dealers under cover adjoining Eagles Roost RV Resort. Open all yr. Open Sat & Sun only, 9 a.m.-5 p.m.

Phone: (229)559-5192
Address: 5465 Mill Store Rd, Lake Park, GA 31636
Lat/Lon: 30.66900/-83.21149
Email: camp@eaglesroostresort.com
Web: www.eaglesroostresort.com

SEE AD VALDOSTA PAGE 210

(W) EAGLES ROOST RV RESORT—(Lowndes) *From jct I-75 (exit 5) & Hwy 376: Go 150 yds E on Hwy 376, then 1/2 mi S on Mill Store Rd. Enter on L.*

◆◆◆◆FACILITIES: 140 sites, typical site width 25 ft, 116 full hkups, 24 W&E, (30/50 amps), 140 pull-thrus, cable TV, ($), WiFi Instant Internet at site, cable Internet central location, family camping, tenting, RV storage, dump, non-guest dump $, laundry, RV supplies, LP gas by weight/by meter, ice, picnic tables.

◆◆◆RECREATION: rec hall, rec room/area, pavilion, swim pool, golf nearby, bsktball, playground, shuffleboard court 4 shuffleboard courts, horseshoes.

Pets welcome. Open all yr. Big rigs welcome. Clubs welcome. Rate in 2010 $31-43 for 4 persons. MC/VISA/DISC. Member ARVC. FMCA discount.

Phone: (229)559-5192
Address: 5465 Mill Store Rd, Lake Park, GA 31636
Lat/Lon: 30.66959/-83.21267
Email: camp@EaglesRoostResort.com
Web: www.EaglesRoostResort.com

SEE AD VALDOSTA PAGE 210 AND AD TRAVEL SECTION PAGE 185

(S) MILITARY PARK (Grassy Pond Rec. Area)—(Lowndes) *Offbase, 25 mi S on Moody AFB. From jct I-75 (exit 2/5) & Hwy 376: Go W on Hwy 376, then S on Loch Laurel Rd. Follow signs.* FACILITIES: 42 sites, 42 full hkups, (30/50 amps), 2 pull-thrus, tenting, dump, laundry, ltd groc. RECREATION: boating, ramp, pond fishing, playground. Open all yr. Phone: (912) 559-5840.

(W) Valdosta/Lake Park KOA—(Lowndes) *From jct I-75 (exit 5) & Hwy 376: Go 500 feet W on Hwy 376, then 1/2 mi S on Jewell Futch Rd. Enter at end.* ◆◆◆◆FACILITIES: 127 sites, typical site width 35 ft, 127 full hkups, (30/50 amps), 67 pull-thrus, family camping, tenting, dump, laundry, ltd groc. ◆◆◆RECREATION: swim pool, pond fishing, playground. Pets welcome. Partial handicap access. Open all yr. Big rigs welcome. Rate in 2010 $39 for 2 persons. Phone: (800)562-2124. KOA discount.

LAVONIA—B-3

(N) TUGALOO STATE PARK—(Franklin) *From jct Hwy 59 & Hwy 328: Go 4 mi N on Hwy 328, then 1-3/4 mi E on Tugaloo State Park Rd. Enter at end.* FACILITIES: 110 sites, 35 ft max RV length, 105 W&E, (20/30 amps), 5 no hkups, 30 pull-thrus, family camping, tenting, dump, laundry. RECREATION: lake swim, boating, canoeing, ramp, dock, lake fishing. Pets welcome. Partial handicap access. Open all yr. Phone: (800)864-7275.

LEAH—B-4

(N) MILITARY PARK (Fort Gordon Rec. Area)—*Off base, 23 mi N of Fort Gordon Military Reservation. From jct I-20 & Hwy 47/US 221: Go N on Hwy 47/Ray Owens Rd (Leah).* FACILITIES: 117 sites, 52 full hkups, 20 E, (30/50 amps), 45 no hkups, tenting, laundry, ltd groc. RECREATION: lake swim, boating, canoeing, ramp, dock, lake fishing, playground. Pets welcome. Open all yr. Phone: (706)541-1057.

(SE) PETERSBURG CAMP AREA (COE - J. Strom Thurmond Lake)—(Columbia) *From town: Go 5 mi SE on Hwy-104, then 2 mi N on US-221.* FACILITIES: 93 sites, typical site width 20 ft, 85 W&E, (50 amps), 8 no hkups, 55 pull-thrus, tenting, dump, laundry. RECREATION: lake swim, boating, ramp, dock, lake fishing, playground. Pets welcome. Open all yr. Phone: (706)541-9464.

LEAH—Continued

(E) RIDGE ROAD CAMP AREA (COE-J. Strom Thurmond Lake)—(Columbia) *From town: Go 2 mi S on Hwy-104, then follow signs on paved county road.* FACILITIES: 69 sites, typical site width 20 ft, 27 ft max RV length, 63 W&E, (30/50 amps), 6 no hkups, 20 pull-thrus, tenting, dump, laundry. RECREATION: lake swim, boating, ramp, dock, lake fishing, playground. Open Apr 1 - Sep 30. Phone: (706)541-0282.

LINCOLNTON—B-4

(E) ELIJAH CLARK STATE PARK—(Lincoln) *From jct US 378 & Hwy 47: Go 6 mi NE on US 378. Enter on L.* FACILITIES: 165 sites, 165 W&E, (20/30 amps), 68 pull-thrus, family camping, tenting, dump, laundry. RECREATION: lake swim, boating, canoeing, ramp, dock, lake fishing, playground. Pets welcome. Partial handicap access. Open all yr. Phone: (800) 864-7275.

(N) HESTERS FERRY CAMP AREA (COE - J. Strom Thurmond Lake)—(Lincoln) *From town: Go 12 mi N on Hwy 79, then 3 mi E on Hwy 44.* FACILITIES: 26 sites, typical site width 20 ft, 27 ft max RV length, 16 W&E, (30 amps), 10 no hkups, 6 pull-thrus, tenting, dump. RECREATION: lake swim, boating, ramp, lake fishing, playground. Open Apr 1 - Sep 29. Phone: (706)359-2746.

MACON—C-2

(W) LAKE TOBESOFKEE RECREATION AREA (Bibb Co.)—(Bibb) *From jct I-475 (exit 5) & Hwy 74: Go 3/4 mi SW on Hwy 74,then 1-3/4 mi SW on Mosley Dixon Rd. Enter on L.*

◆◆◆FACILITIES: 103 sites, typical site width 35 ft, 22 full hkups, 81 W&E, (30/50 amps), 23 pull-thrus, cable TV, family camping, tenting, dump, non-guest dump $, laundry, marine gas, ice, picnic tables, fire rings, grills, controlled access.

◆◆◆RECREATION: pavilion, lake swim, boating, canoeing, kayaking, ramp, dock, lake fishing, golf nearby, playground, v-ball. Rec open to public.

Pets welcome. Partial handicap access. Open all yr. Big rigs welcome. Clubs welcome. Rate in 2010 $22-25 for 4 persons. MC/VISA/DISC.

Phone: (478)474-8770
Address: 6600 Mosley Dixon Rd, Macon, GA 31220
Lat/Lon: 32.83124/-83.77744
Email: wbennett@co.bibb.ga.us
Web: www.laketobo.com

SEE AD THIS PAGE AND AD TRAVEL SECTION PAGE 185

MADISON—C-3

(S) Country Boy's RV Park—(Morgan) *From jct I-20 (exit 114) & US 441/129: Go 1-1/2 mi S on US 441/129. Enter on L.* ◆◆FACILITIES: 106 sites, typical site width 25 ft, 106 full hkups, (30/50 amps), 100 pull-thrus, family camping, dump, laundry. ◆RECREATION: playground. Pets welcome. No tents. Open all yr. Big rigs welcome. Rate in 2010 $25 for 2 persons. Phone: (706)342-1799. FCRV discount. FMCA discount.

MARIETTA—B-2

(S) ATLANTA-MARIETTA RV RESORT—(Cobb) *From N'bnd jct I-75 (exit 261) & Hwy 280: Go 3/4 mi W on Hwy 280, then 1/2 mi N on US 41, then 1 block E on Wylie Rd. Enter on right. From S'bnd jct I-75 (exit 263) & Hwy 120: Go 1-1/2 mi W on Hwy 120, then 1 mi S on Wylie Rd. Enter on L.*

◆◆◆FACILITIES: 70 sites, typical site width 25 ft, 70 full hkups, (30/50 amps), many extd stay sites, cable TV, WiFi Instant Internet at site, cable Internet central location, laundry, LP gas by weight/by meter, ice, picnic tables, patios.

◆RECREATION: swim pool, golf nearby.

Pets welcome, breed restrict. Partial handicap access. No tents. Open all yr. Big rigs welcome. Clubs welcome. Rate in 2010 $49.99 per vehicle. MC/VISA/DISC/AMEX. Member ARVC, GARVC. FMCA discount.

Phone: (877)727-5787
Address: 1031 Wylie Rd SE, Marietta, GA 30067
Lat/Lon: 33.92826/-84.50668
Email: information@amrvresort.com
Web: www.amrvresort.com

SEE AD ATLANTA PAGE 193

(W) MILITARY PARK (Dobbins ARB Family Campground)—(Cobb) *From jct I-75 & Delk Rd/Hwy 280: Go 2 mi W on Delk Rd, then S on US 41 to 1st light. On base.* FACILITIES: 18 sites, 35 ft max RV length, 18 W&E, (30 amps), tenting, dump, laundry. RECREATION: playground. Open all yr. Phone: (678)655-4870.

MCDONOUGH—C-2

(N) ATLANTA SOUTH RV RESORT—(Henry) *From jct I-75 (exit 222) & Jodeco Rd: Go 1/2 block W on Jodeco Rd, then 1/4 mi S on Mt. Olive Rd. Enter at end.*

ONE OF THE SOUTH'S FINEST RESORTS!
Easy on/off I-75 just 30 min from downtown Atlanta. Many of Georgia's most popular attractions are nearby. After sightseeing, relax by the pool, enjoy our resort amenities or sit by a fire. A fun and friendly place to stay!

◆◆◆◆FACILITIES: 170 sites, typical site width 25 ft, 170 full hkups, (30/50 amps), mostly extd stay sites, 80 pull-thrus, WiFi Instant Internet at site, phone Internet central location, family camping, tenting, cabins, RV storage, dump, laundry, RV supplies, LP gas by meter, ice, picnic tables, fire rings.

ATLANTA SOUTH RV RESORT—Continued on next page

Georgia is the nation's number one producer of the three P's: peanuts, pecans, and peaches.

MCDONOUGH—Continued
ATLANTA SOUTH RV RESORT—Continued

◆◆RECREATION: rec hall, rec room/area, pavilion, swim pool, pond fishing, golf nearby, bsktball, playground.

Pets welcome. Partial handicap access. Open all yr. Big rigs welcome. Escort to site. Clubs welcome. Rate in 2010 $36 for 2 persons. MC/VISA/DISC/AMEX/Debit. ATM. CCUSA 50% Discount. CCUSA reservations Required, CCUSA max stay 1 day, Cash only for CCUSA disc., CCUSA disc. not avail holidays. Not available special events. Call for details.

Phone: (800)778-0668
Address: 281 Mt Olive Rd, McDonough, GA 30253
Lat/Lon: 33.47482/-84.21613
Email: atlrvresort@gmail.com
Web: atlantasouthrvresort.com

SEE AD ATLANTA PAGE 194 AND AD TRAVEL SECTION PAGE 185

MCRAE—D-3

(N) LITTLE OCMULGEE STATE PARK—(Telfair) *From jct US 441 & US 280: Go 1 mi N on US 441/319. Enter on L.* FACILITIES: 54 sites, 54 W&E, (30/50 amps), 12 pull-thrus, family camping, tenting, dump, laundry. RECREATION: swim pool, lake swim, boating, canoeing, ramp, dock, lake fishing, playground. Pets welcome. Partial handicap access. Open all yr. Big rigs welcome. Phone: (800) 864-7275.

MILLEDGEVILLE—C-3

(N) Little River Park Campground & Marina—(Baldwin) *From jct Hwy 49/22 & US 441: Go 9 mi N on US 441. Enter on R.* ◆◆◆FACILITIES: 130 sites, typical site width 25 ft, 130 full hkups, (30/50 amps), 27 pull-thrus, cable TV, phone on-site Internet (needs activ), WiFi Internet central location, family camping, tenting, dump, non-guest dump $, laundry, ltd groc, RV supplies, LP gas by meter, marine gas, ice, picnic tables. ◆◆◆RECREATION: pavilion, lake swim, boating, canoeing, kayaking, ramp, dock, lake fishing, fishing supplies, fishing guides, bsktball, playground, horseshoes. Pets welcome, breed restrict. Partial handicap access. Open all yr. Big rigs welcome. Rate in 2010 $30-45 for 4 persons. MC/VISA/DISC/AMEX/Debit. CCUSA 50% Discount. CCUSA reservations Accepted, CCUSA max stay 2 days, CCUSA disc. not avail F,Sa, CCUSA disc. not avail holidays. Not valid special events-call for details.

Phone: (478)452-1605
Address: 3069 N Columbia St, Milledgeville, GA 31061
Lat/Lon: 33.18544/-83.29065
Email: littleriverpark@windstream.net
Web: www.littleriverpark.com

(S) SCENIC MOUNTAIN RV PARK—(Baldwin) *From jct Hwy 49/22 & US-441: Go 4 mi S on US-441, then 1/4 mi N on US-441 Bus/Hwy 243. Enter on R.*

◆◆◆◆FACILITIES: 72 sites, typical site width 25 ft, 72 full hkups, (50 amps), mostly extd stay sites, 7 pull-thrus, cable TV, WiFi Instant Internet at site, phone on-site Internet (needs activ), family camping, tenting, RV's/park model rentals, cabins, RV storage, laundry, ltd groc, RV supplies, LP gas by weight/by meter, LP bottle exch, ice, picnic tables, patios, fire rings, grills, wood.

With an elevation of 4,784 feet, Brasstown Bald Mountain is the highest point in Georgia.

MILLEDGEVILLE—Continued
SCENIC MOUNTAIN RV PARK—Continued

◆◆◆RECREATION: rec room/area, pavilion, swim pool, pond fishing, golf nearby, horseshoes, hiking trails.

Pets welcome, breed restrict. Open all yr. Big rigs welcome. Escort to site. Clubs welcome. Rate in 2010 $35 for 2 persons. MC/VISA/DISC/Debit. CCUSA 50% Discount. CCUSA reservations Recommended, CCUSA max stay 3 days, Cash only for CCUSA disc., Check only for CCUSA disc. Discount not available during Bluegrass Festival.

Phone: (800)716-3015
Address: 2686 Irwinton Rd, Milledgeville, GA 31061
Lat/Lon: 33.02898/-83.23576
Email: scenicmountainrv@windstream.net
Web: scenicmountainrv.com

SEE AD THIS PAGE

MILLEN—C-4

(N) MAGNOLIA SPRINGS STATE PARK—(Jenkins) *From jct US-25 & Hwy-23: Go 5 mi N on US-25. Enter on R.* FACILITIES: 26 sites, 39 ft max RV length, 26 W&E, (20/30/50 amps), 5 pull-thrus, family camping, tenting, dump, laundry. RECREATION: swim pool, boating, 10 hp limit, canoeing, ramp, dock, lake fishing, playground. Pets welcome. Partial handicap access. Open all yr. Phone: (800) 864-7275.

MORGANTON—A-2

(W) CHATTAHOOCHEE NATIONAL FOREST (Morganton Point Campground)—(Fannin) *From jct Hwy 60 & CR 616: Go 1 mi SW on CR 616.* FACILITIES: 42 sites, typical site width 15 ft, 30 ft max RV length, 42 no hkups, 2 pull-thrus, tenting, ltd groc. RECREATION: lake swim, boating, ramp, lake fishing. Partial handicap access. Open Apr 11 - Nov 2. Phone: (706)745-6928.

MOUNTAIN CITY—A-3

(W) BLACK ROCK MOUNTAIN STATE PARK—(Rabun) *From jct US 76 & US 441/23: Go 3 mi N on US 441/23 (Mountain City), then 3 mi W on Black Rock Mountain Pkwy. (Caution: steep grade). Enter at end.* FACILITIES: 60 sites, 48 W&E, (20/30 amps), 12 no hkups, 1 pull-thrus, family camping, tenting, dump, laundry, ltd groc. RECREATION: lake fishing, playground. Pets welcome. Partial handicap access. Open all yr. Phone: (800)864-7275.

CROSS CREEK CAMPGROUND—(Rabun) *From jct US 76 & US 44/123: Go 2-1/2 mi N on US 441/23. Enter on R.*

◆◆◆FACILITIES: 24 sites, typical site width 25 ft, 24 full hkups, (20/30/50 amps), some extd stay sites (summer), 3 pull-thrus, cable TV, WiFi Instant Internet at site, family camping, tenting, RV storage, dump, non-guest dump $, laundry, RV supplies, LP gas by weight, ice, picnic tables, fire rings, grills, wood, controlled access.

RECREATION: pavilion, horseshoes.

Pets welcome. Open all yr. Big rigs welcome. Clubs welcome. Rate in 2010 $24-28 for 2 persons. MC/VISA. CCUSA 50% Discount. CCUSA reservations Accepted, CCUSA max stay 7 days. Must identify as Camp Club mbr when making reservation & present card upon arrival. No electric heaters. Dump & shower surcharges are for non-guests only.

Martin Luther King, Jr., civil rights activist, was from Georgia.

MOUNTAIN CITY—Continued
CROSS CREEK CAMPGROUND—Continued

Phone: (706)746-6974
Address: 618 File Street, Mountain City, GA 30562
Lat/Lon: 34.91146/-83.38699
Email: cccgc1@windstream.net
Web: crosscreekcampground.com

SEE AD DILLARD PAGE 199

NORCROSS—B-2

(E) JONES RV PARK—(Gwinnett) *From jct I-85 (exit 101) & Indian Trl/Lilburn Rd: Go 400 ft E on Indian Trl/Lilburn Rd, then 1 block S on Willowtrail Pkwy. Enter at end.*

◆◆◆FACILITIES: 173 sites, typical site width 24 ft, 173 full hkups, (20/30/50 amps), many extd stay sites, 55 pull-thrus, WiFi Instant Internet at site ($), RV storage, dump, non-guest dump $, laundry, LP gas by weight/by meter.

RECREATION: golf nearby.

Pets welcome, breed restrict. Partial handicap access. No tents. Open all yr. Big rigs welcome. Clubs welcome. Rate in 2010 $30 per vehicle. MC/VISA/AMEX/Debit.

Phone: (770)923-0911
Address: 2200 Willowtrail Pkwy., Norcross, GA 30093
Lat/Lon: 33.92555/-84.17652
Email: info@jonesrvpark.com
Web: www.jonesrvpark.com

SEE AD ATLANTA PAGE 194

OCHLOCKNEE—E-2

(N) Sugar Mill Plantation RV Park—(Thomas) *From N jct US 84 & US 19: Go 7 mi N on US 19, then 500 feet W on McMillan Rd. Enter on R.* ◆◆◆◆FACILITIES: 131 sites, typical site width 35 ft, 131 full hkups, (20/30/50 amps), 25 pull-thrus, family camping, tenting, laundry. ◆◆RECREATION: pond fishing. Pets welcome. Partial handicap access. Open all yr. Big rigs welcome. Rate in 2010 $28 per vehicle. Member ARVC. Phone: (229)227-1451.

OGLETHORPE—D-2

(N) WHITEWATER CREEK PARK (Macon County Park)—(Oglethorpe) *From jct Hwy 26 & Hwy 49/128: Go 6-1/4 mi N on Hwy 128 or Hwy 128 Bypass.* FACILITIES: 72 sites, 16 full hkups, 56 W&E, tenting, dump. RECREATION: lake swim, boating, 10 hp limit, canoeing, ramp, dock, lake fishing, playground. Partial handicap access. Open all yr. Phone: (478)472-8171.

OMAHA—D-1

(S) FLORENCE MARINA STATE PARK—(Stewart) *At jct Hwy 39C & Hwy 39.* FACILITIES: 43 sites, 43 full hkups, (30/50 amps), 20 pull-thrus, family camping, tenting, laundry, ltd groc. RECREATION: swim pool, boating, canoeing, ramp, dock, lake fishing, playground. Pets welcome. Partial handicap access. Open all yr. Big rigs welcome. Phone: (800) 864-7275.

PALMETTO—C-1

(E) South Oaks Mobile Home & RV Community (RV SPACES)—(Coweta) *From jct I-85 (exit 56) & Collingsworth Rd: Go 100 yds W on Collingsworth Rd, then 1/2 mi N on Tingle Ln. Enter at end.* FACILITIES: 150 sites, accepts full hkup units only, 150 full hkups, (30/50 amps), 3 pull-thrus, family camping. RECREATION: playground. Pets welcome. No tents. Open all yr. Big rigs welcome. Phone: (770)463-3070.

PERRY—D-2

(E) Boland's RV Park—(Houston) *From jct of I-75 (exit 136) & US 341: Go 1/4 mi E on US 341, then 1/4 mi N on Perimeter Rd. Enter on L.* ◆◆◆FACILITIES: 65 sites, typical site width 20 ft, 65 full hkups, (20/30/50 amps), 64 pull-thrus, family camping, tenting, laundry. ◆◆RECREATION: swim pool, playground. Pets welcome. Open all yr. Rate in 2010 $27 for 2 persons. Phone: (478)987-3371. FCRV discount.

PERRY—Continued on next page

PERRY—Continued

(N) **CROSSROADS HOLIDAY TRAV-L-PARK**—(Houston) *From I-75 (exit 136) & US 341: Go 500 ft W on US 341. Enter on L.*

WELCOME

◇◇◇FACILITIES: 64 sites, typical site width 28 ft, 58 full hkups, 6 W&E, (20/30/50 amps), some extd stay sites (winter), 34 pull-thrus, cable TV, phone on-site Internet (needs activ), phone Internet central location, family camping, tenting, RV storage, laundry, ltd groc, RV supplies, LP gas by weight/by meter, ice, picnic tables.

◇RECREATION: pavilion, swim pool, golf nearby, bsktball, play equipment.

Pets welcome. Open all yr. Big rigs welcome. Clubs welcome. Rate in 2010 $24-29 for 2 persons. MC/VISA/DISC/AMEX/Debit. FCRV discount. FMCA discount.

Phone: (478)987-3141
Address: 1513 Sam Nunn Blvd, Perry, GA 31069
Lat/Lon: 32.47374/-83.74644
Email: crossroadscampground@windstream.net

SEE AD THIS PAGE AND AD TRAVEL SECTION PAGE 185

(W) **FAIR HARBOR RV PARK & CAMPGROUND**—(Houston) *From jct I-75 (exit 135) & Hwy 127/224: Go 150 yds W on Hwy 127/224. Enter on R.*

WELCOME

WONDERFUL FAMILY OWNED & OPERATED PARK!

Enjoy a peaceful "state park environment" with full service campsites quietly nestled around a stocked fishing lake. Amenities include FREE Cable TV, WiFi, and seasonal Breakfast on - Sat. Fair Harbor... You're almost home!

◇◇◇◇FACILITIES: 153 sites, typical site width 30 ft, 153 full hkups, (30/50 amps), some extd stay sites, 101 pull-thrus, cable TV, WiFi Instant Internet at site, WiFi Internet central location, family camping, RV storage, dump, non-guest dump $, laundry, RV supplies, LP gas by weight/by meter, ice, picnic tables.

◇◇RECREATION: rec hall, rec room/area, pavilion, pond fishing, golf nearby, activities, horseshoes, hiking trails.

CAMPCLUB USA

Pets welcome. Partial handicap access. No tents. Open all yr. Big rigs welcome. Clubs welcome. Rate in 2010 $34 for 4 persons. MC/VISA/Debit. Member ARVC. FMCA discount. CCUSA 50% Discount. CCUSA reservations Not Accepted, CCUSA max stay 6 days. Not valid for or during rallies, groups, conventions or special events. Not valid GA Natl Fair or 1 week before, during & 1 week after FMCA rally Mar 14-18. CCUSA discount does not apply if reservations are made. Call 877 988-8844 with any questions.

Phone: (877)988-8844
Address: 515 Marshallville Rd, Perry, GA 31069
Lat/Lon: 32.44717/-83.75838
Email: fairharbor@yahoo.com
Web: www.fairharborrvpark.com

Reserve Online at Woodalls.com

SEE AD PAGE 204 AND AD TRAVEL SECTION PAGE 185

Ray Charles, singer, was from Georgia.

PINE MOUNTAIN—C-1

(E) F. D. ROOSEVELT STATE PARK—(Harris) *From jct US 27 & Hwy 354: Go 3 mi E on Hwy 354 to Hwy 190. Enter on R.* FACILITIES: 140 sites, 140 W&E, (20/30/50 amps), 30 pull-thrus, family camping, tenting, dump, laundry, ltd groc. RECREATION: swim pool, boating, electric motors only, canoeing, dock, lake fishing, playground. Pets welcome. Partial handicap access. Open all yr. Big rigs welcome. Phone: (800) 864-7275.

(N) **PINE MOUNTAIN RV RESORT**—(Troup) *From jct I-185 (exit 42) & US 27: Go 8 mi S on US 27. Enter on R.*

WELCOME

WE'RE IN THE HEART OF IT ALL Y'ALL!

Your resort destination in the Georgia countryside! Near Callaway Gardens, Roosevelt's Little White House, Wild Animal Safari & National POW Museum. Ideal for golfers, antique collectors, history buffs & gardening fans.

◇◇◇◇FACILITIES: 200 sites, typical site width 30 ft, 188 full hkups, 12 W&E, (30/50 amps), some extd stay sites, 161 pull-thrus, cable TV, WiFi Instant Internet at site, WiFi Internet central location, family camping, tenting, cabins, RV storage,

PINE MOUNTAIN—Continued
PINE MOUNTAIN RV RESORT—Continued

dump, non-guest dump $, laundry, RV supplies, LP gas by weight/by meter, ice, picnic tables, fire rings, wood, controlled access.

◇◇◇◇RECREATION: rec room/area, pavilion, coin games, swim pool, hot tub, golf nearby, bike rental 5 bike rentals, playground, horseshoes, sports field.

Pets welcome. Partial handicap access. Open all yr. Big rigs welcome. Escort to site. Clubs welcome. Rate in 2010 $32-50 for 2 persons. MC/VISA/Debit. Member ARVC. FMCA discount.

Text 86062 to (440)725-8687 to see our Visual Tour.

Phone: (706)663-4329
Address: 8804 Hamilton Rd, Hwy 27 N, Pine Mountain, GA 31822
Lat/Lon: 32.87444/-84.87069
Email: info@pinemountainrvc.com
Web: www.pinemountainrvc.com

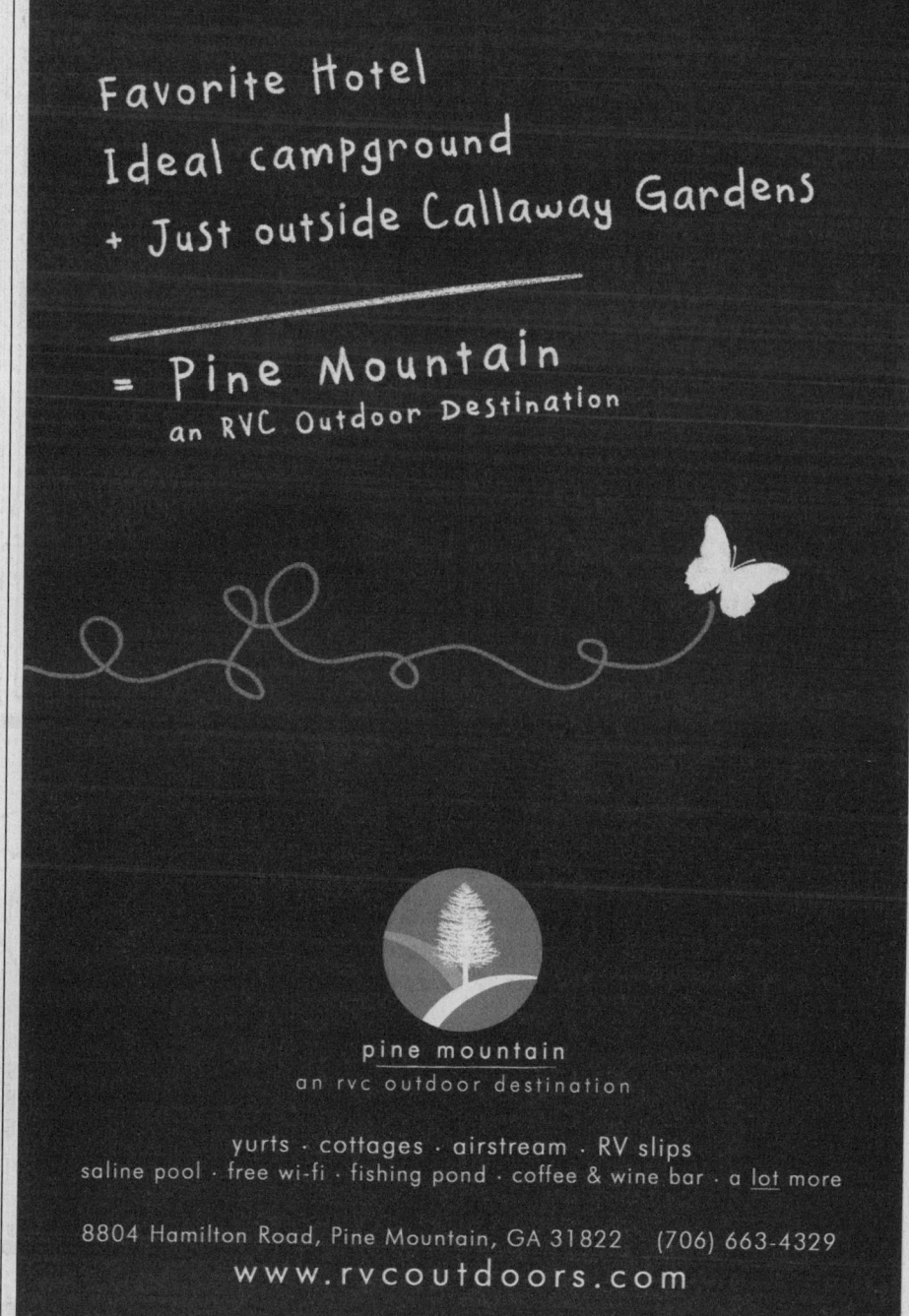

SEE AD THIS PAGE

REIDSVILLE—D-4

(C) GORDONIA-ALATAMAHA STATE PARK—(Tattnall) *In city limits at Jct US 280 & Park St.* FACILITIES: 29 sites, 29 W&E, (30/50 amps), 3 pull-thrus, family camping, tenting, dump, laundry. RECREATION: boating, electric motors only, canoeing, dock, lake fishing. Pets welcome. Partial handicap access. Open all yr. Big rigs welcome. Phone: (800) 864-7275.

RICHMOND HILL—D-5

(SE) FORT MCALLISTER STATE HISTORIC PARK—*From jct I-95 (exit 15/90) & Hwy 144: Go 6-1/2 mi SE on Hwy 144, then E on Spur 144 to the end.* FACILITIES: 65 sites, 65 W&E, (30/50 amps), 57 pull-thrus, family camping, tenting, dump, laundry. RECREATION: boating, canoeing, ramp, dock, saltwater/river fishing, playground. Pets welcome. Partial handicap access. Open all yr. Big rigs welcome. Phone: (800) 864-7275.

RICHMOND HILL—Continued

(W) KOA-Savannah South—(Bryan) *From jct I-95 (exit 87) & US 17: Go 3/4 mi S on US 17. Enter on L.*
◆◆◆FACILITIES: 125 sites, typical site width 24 ft, 105 full hkups, 20 W&E, (30/50 amps), 100 pull-thrus, family camping, tenting, dump, laundry, groceries.
◆◆◆RECREATION: swim pool, boating, electric motors only, canoeing, lake fishing, playground. Pets welcome, breed restrict, quantity restrict. Open all yr. Big rigs welcome. Phone: (912)756-3396. KOA discount.

RISING FAWN—A-1

(N) CLOUDLAND CANYON STATE PARK—(Dade) *From I-59 (exit 11) & Hwy 136: Go 7 mi E on Hwy 136. Enter on L.* FACILITIES: 114 sites, 73 W&E, (20/30 amps), 41 no hkups, 24 pull-thrus, family camping, tenting, dump, laundry, ltd groc. RECREATION: swim pool, playground. Pets welcome. Partial handicap access. Open all yr. Phone: (800)864-7275.

ROME—B-1

(S) COOSA RIVER CAMPGROUND (Rome-Floyd County Park) & Nature Center—(Floyd) *From Rome jct US 411 & US 27: Go 3 1/2 mi S on US 27/US 411 then 3 1/2 mi W on Walker Mountain Rd, then 1/2 mi N on Lock & Dam Rd. Enter at end.* FACILITIES: 33 sites, typical site width 30 ft, 33 full hkups, (30/50 amps), tenting, dump, laundry, ltd groc. RECREATION: boating, canoeing, ramp, dock, river fishing, playground. Partial handicap access. Open all yr. Phone: (706)234-5001.

ROSSVILLE—A-1

BEST HOLIDAY TRAV-L-PARK—(Walker) *From jct I-24 & I-75: Go 1/2 mi S on I-75 (S'bnd exit 1; N'bnd 1B), then 1/4 mi W on US 41N, then 1/2 mi S on Mack Smith Rd. Enter on R.*

WELCOME

◆◆◆◆FACILITIES: 171 sites, typical site width 30 ft, 131 full hkups, 22 W&E, (20/30/50 amps), 18 no hkups, some extd stay sites, 130 pull-thrus, cable TV, WiFi Instant Internet at site, phone on-site Internet (needs activ), cable Internet central location, family camping, tenting, cabins, RV storage, dump, non-guest dump $, laundry, ltd groc, RV supplies, LP gas by weight/by meter, ice, picnic tables, patios, fire rings, wood.

ROSSVILLE—Continued
BEST HOLIDAY TRAV-L-PARK—Continued

◆◆◆◆RECREATION: rec hall, rec room/area, pavilion, swim pool, golf nearby, bsktball, playground, shuffleboard court 2 shuffleboard courts, horseshoes, sports field, v-ball.

Pets welcome, breed restrict. Partial handicap access. Open all yr. Big rigs welcome. Clubs welcome. Rate in 2010 $35-37 for 2 persons. MC/VISA/Debit. Member ARVC, TNARVC. FCRV discount. FMCA discount.

Phone: (800)693-2877
Address: 1623 Mack Smith Rd, Rossville, GA 30741
Lat/Lon: 34.97932/-85.2124
Email: campmail@chattacamp.com
Web: www.chattacamp.com

SEE AD CHATTANOOGA, TN PAGE 721

ROYSTON—B-3

(W) VICTORIA BRYANT STATE PARK—(Franklin) *From jct Hwy 17 & US 29: Go 3 mi W on US 29S, then 1 mi N on Hwy 327. Enter on L.* FACILITIES: 35 sites, 27 W&E, (30/50 amps), 8 no hkups, family camping, tenting, dump, laundry. RECREATION: swim pool, river swim, lake fishing, playground. Pets welcome. Partial handicap access. Open all yr. Phone: (800)864-7275.

RUTLEDGE—C-3

(W) HARD LABOR CREEK STATE PARK—(Morgan) *From I-20 (exit 105) & Newborn Rd: Go 2-3/4 mi N on Newborn Rd, then 2 mi NE on Fairplay St. Enter on R.* FACILITIES: 63 sites, typical site width 30 ft, 63 W&E, (30/50 amps), 8 pull-thrus, family camping, tenting, dump, laundry, ltd groc. RECREATION: lake swim, boating, 10 hp limit, canoeing, ramp, dock, lake fishing, playground. Pets welcome. Partial handicap access. Open all yr. Big rigs welcome. Phone: (800) 864-7275.

ST. MARYS—F-5

(N) CROOKED RIVER STATE PARK—(Camden) *From jct I-95 (exit 3) & Hwy 40: Go 2-1/4 mi SE on Hwy 40, then 3 mi E on Kings Bay Rd, then 3-1/2 mi N on Spur 40. Enter on R.* FACILITIES: 62 sites, 62 W&E, (30/50 amps), family camping, tenting, dump, laundry. RECREATION: swim pool, boating, canoeing, ramp, dock, saltwater fishing, playground. Pets welcome. Partial handicap access. Open all yr. Phone: (800) 864-7275.

SAVANNAH—D-5

(SW) BILTMORE GARDENS RV PARK—(Chatham) *From jct I-95 & I-16: Go 5 mi E on I-16 (exit 162), then 1-1/2 mi S on Chatham Pkwy, then 1/2 mi SW on US 17 (Ogeechee Rd). Enter on L.*

WELCOME

◆◆◆FACILITIES: 38 sites, typical site width 25 ft, accepts full hkup units only, 38 full hkups, (20/30/50 amps), some extd stay sites, 5 pull-thrus, cable TV, WiFi Internet central location, family camping, patios.

RECREATION: local tours.

CAMPCLUB USA

Pets welcome. No tents. Open all yr. Big rigs welcome. MC/VISA. CCUSA 50% Discount. CCUSA reservations Not Accepted, CCUSA max stay 2 days, Cash only for CCUSA disc., CCUSA disc. not avail F, Sa, CCUSA disc. not avail holidays. Not available Feb thru Apr or special events. Must

BILTMORE GARDENS RV PARK—Continued on next page

present card upon arrival & identify as CCUSA when calling. Do not park after closing without prior arrangement. Accepts drive up only on first come basis. Min stay 2 days.

Phone: (912)236-4065
Address: 4707 Ogeechee Rd, Savannah, GA 31405
Lat/Lon: 32.04464/-81.17995
Web: www.biltmorervpark.com/index.html

SEE AD NEXT PAGE

WELCOME **HARDEEVILLE RV-THOMAS' PARKS AND SITES**—*From jct I-95 & I-16: Go 8-1/2 mi E on I-16 (exit 166), then 9 mi N on US 17, then 4 mi NE on 170-Alt. Enter on R.*

SEE PRMIARY LISTING AT HARDEEVILLE, SC AND AD PAGE 206

(E) MILITARY PARK (Hunter Army Airfield Trailer Camp)—(Chatham) *From jct I-95 & Hwy 204: Go 13 mi E on Hwy 204, then W on Stevenson Ave.* FACILITIES: 15 sites, 15 no hkups, tenting. RECREATION: Pets welcome. Open all yr. Phone: (912) 315-9554.

WELCOME **(SW) RED GATE CG & RV RESORT** (TOO NEW TO RATE)—(Chatham) *From jct I-95 (exit 99) & I-16: Go 5 mi E on I-16 (exit 162), then 2-1/2 mi S on Chatham Pkwy.*

8 MIN FROM HISTORIC DOWNTOWN SAVANNAH
Nestled within 200 acres of the most beautiful old country scenery, we can accommodate the largest RVs with comfort and privacy. We're the newest RV park in the area and the BEST. Come see why!

FACILITIES: 40 sites, 35 full hkups, 5 W&E, (30/50 amps), 10 pull-thrus, WiFi Instant Internet at site, family camping, dump, laundry, picnic tables.

RECREATION: rec hall, pavilion, swim pool, lake swim, pond fishing, fishing supplies, golf nearby, bsktball, playground, horseshoes, sports field, v-ball.

Pets welcome. No tents. Open all yr. Big rigs welcome. Clubs welcome. Rate in 2010 $40-50 per vehicle. MC/VISA/DISC/AMEX. FMCA discount.

Phone: (912)232-3246
Address: 105 Red Gate Farms Trail, Savannah, GA 31405
Lat/Lon: 32.04060/-81.16563
Email: redgaterv@gmail.com
Web: www.redgatecampground.com

SEE AD PAGE 206

WELCOME **(E) RIVER'S END CAMPGROUND & RV PARK**—*From jct I-95 & I 16: Go 9 mi E on I-16 to exit 167A, then 3/4 mi N on MLK Jr Blvd, then 1 mi E on Bay St (stay in left lane), then 15 mi E on President St (becomes Island Expy, then US 80), then 2 blks N on Plk St. Enter on L.*

◆◆◆FACILITIES: 150 sites, typical site width 20 ft, 91 full hkups, 19 W&E, (30/50 amps), 40 no hkups, some extd stay sites (winter), 44 pull-thrus, cable TV, WiFi Instant Internet at site, cable Internet central location, family camping, tenting, cabins, dump, non-guest dump $, laundry, ltd groc, RV supplies, LP gas by weight/by meter, ice, picnic tables, wood.

◆◆◆RECREATION: rec hall, rec room/area, pavilion, swim pool, golf nearby, bike rental 7 bike rentals, activities, horseshoes, hiking trails.

Pets welcome, breed restrict, size restrict, quantity restrict. Partial handicap access. Open all yr. Big rigs welcome. Escort to site. Clubs welcome. Rate in 2010 $34-50 for 2 persons. MC/VISA/DISC/AMEX/Debit. Member ARVC.

Phone: (800)786-1016
Address: Five Fort Ave, Tybee Island, GA 31328
Lat/Lon: 32.02313/-80.85165
Email: riversend1@aol.com
Web: www.riversendcampground.com

SEE PRIMARY LISTING AT TYBEE ISLAND AND AD PAGE 206

SAVANNAH—Continued on next page

Woodall's Tip... If you are camping in bear country, be sure to cook at least 300 feet downwind of your sleeping area. Use baking soda to rid your clothes and hands of cooking odors.

SAVANNAH—Continued

(W) SAVANNAH OAKS RV RESORT—(Chatham) *From jct I-95 (exit 94) & Hwy 204: Go 2 1/2 mi W on Hwy 204. (Fort Argyle Rd). Enter on L.*

WELCOME

◆◆◆FACILITIES: 139 sites, typical site width 30 ft, 111 full hkups, 28 W&E, (30/50 amps), some extd stay sites, 76 pull-thrus, cable TV, WiFi Instant Internet at site, WiFi Internet central location, family camping, cabins, dump, non-guest dump $, laundry, groceries, RV supplies, LP gas by weight/by meter, marine gas, ice, picnic tables, grills, controlled access.

◆◆◆RECREATION: rec room/area, pavilion, coin games, swim pool, boating, canoeing, kayaking, ramp, dock, 2 kayak rentals, lake fishing, golf nearby, playground, local tours.

Pets welcome. Partial handicap access. No tents. Open all yr. Big rigs welcome. Escort to site. Clubs welcome. Rate in 2010 $39-44 for 2 persons. MC/VISA/DISC. Member ARVC. FMCA discount.

Phone: (800)851-0717
Address: 805 Fort Argyle Rd., Savannah, GA 31419
Lat/Lon: 32.02647/-81.31989
Email: campinginsavannah@yahoo.com
Web: www.savannahoaks.net

SEE AD PAGE 207

(S) SKIDAWAY ISLAND STATE PARK—(Chatham) *From jct I-16 (exit 34A/164A) & Hwy 21: Go 5 mi SE on Hwy 21, then 2-1/2 mi S on Waters Ave, then 2-1/2 mi E on Diamond Causeway. Enter on L.* FACILITIES: 87 sites, 87 W&E, (30/50 amps), 88 pull-thrus, family camping, tenting, dump, laundry. RECREATION: swim pool, playground. Pets welcome. Partial handicap access. Open all yr. Big rigs welcome. Phone: (800)864-7275.

STATESBORO—D-4

(S) Parkwood RV Park & Cottages—(Bulloch) *From jct I-16 (exit 116) & US 301: Go 8-1/2 mi N on US 301. Enter on R.* ◆◆◆FACILITIES: 48 sites, typical site width 30 ft, 48 full hkups, (20/30/50 amps), 41 pull-thrus, cable TV, WiFi Instant Internet at site, family camping, laundry, ice, picnic tables. ◆RECREATION: rec hall, swim pool, activities. Pets welcome, breed restrict. No tents. Open all yr. Big rigs welcome. Rate in 2010 $29 for 2 persons. MC/VISA/DISC/AMEX. CCUSA 50% Discount. CCUSA reservations Recommended, CCUSA max stay 1 day, Cash only for CCUSA disc., CCUSA disc. not avail holidays. Discount available May thru Aug, not available special events.

CAMPCLUB USA

Phone: (912)681-3105
Address: 12188 US Highway 301 S, Statesboro, GA 30458
Lat/Lon: 32.41186/-81.80377
Email: parkwood@parkwoodrv.com
Web: www.parkwoodrv.com

Jackie Robinson, baseball player, was from Georgia.

STONE MOUNTAIN—B-2

(N) STONE MOUNTAIN FAMILY CAMPGROUND—(DeKalb) *From east jct I-285 (exit 39B) & US 78: Go 7-1/2 mi E on US 78 (Stone Mountain Fwy), to exit 8, then 500 ft S to East Gate. Enter at end.*

WELCOME

◆◆◆◆◆FACILITIES: 449 sites, typical site width 30 ft, 202 full hkups, 191 W&E, (20/30/50 amps), 56 no hkups, some extd stay sites (winter), 17 pull-thrus, WiFi Instant Internet at site, WiFi Internet central location, family camping, tenting, dump, non-guest dump $, laundry, groceries, RV supplies, LP gas by weight/by meter, ice, picnic tables, fire rings, grills, wood, controlled access.

◆◆◆◆◆RECREATION: equipped pavilion, swim pool, boating, 10 hp limit, canoeing, kayaking, ramp, dock, 12 rowboat/50 pedal boat rentals, lake fishing, mini-golf, ($), golf nearby, playground, activities, horseshoes, sports field, hiking trails, v-ball. Rec open to public.

Pets welcome. Partial handicap access. Open all yr. 14 day max stay Apr 1-Oct 31. 3 day min reservation Mem Day, 4th of July & Lab Day wknds. Big rigs welcome. Clubs welcome. Rate in 2010 $33-58 per family. MC/VISA/DISC/AMEX/Debit. ATM.

Text 84837 to (440)725-8687 to see our Visual Tour.

Phone: (800)385-9807
Address: 1900 Stonewall Jackson Dr, Stone Mountain, GA 30086
Lat/Lon: 33.80251/-84.12354
Email: campground@stonemountainpark.com
Web: www.stonemountainpark.com

SEE AD THIS PAGE

SUMMERVILLE—B-1

(S) JAMES H. FLOYD STATE PARK—(Chattooga) *From jct US 27 & Sloppy Floyd Lake Rd: Go 3 mi SW on Sloppy Floyd Lake Rd. Enter at end.* FACILITIES: 25 sites, 25 W&E, (20/30/50 amps), 8 pull-thrus, family camping, tenting, dump, laundry. RECREATION: boating, electric motors only, canoeing, ramp, dock, lake fishing, playground. Pets welcome. Partial handicap access. Open all yr. Big rigs welcome. Phone: (800) 864-7275.

TALKING ROCK—B-2

(N) Talona Creek Campground—(Gilmer) *From jct US 76 & Hwy 515: Go 11-1/2 mi S on 515, then 1/2 mi E on Carns Mill Rd. Enter on R.* ◆◆◆FACILITIES: 46 sites, typical site width 25 ft, 21 full hkups, 25 W&E, (30/50 amps), 4 pull-thrus, family camping, dump, laundry, ltd groc. ◆◆RECREATION: river fishing, playground. Pets welcome. Partial handicap access. Open all yr. Big rigs welcome. Rate in 2010 $25 per family. Phone: (888)835-1266.

TALLAPOOSA—B-1

(S) Big Oak RV Park—(Haralson) *From jct I-20 (exit 5) & Hwy 100: Go 1/4 mi N on Hwy 100. Enter on R.* ◆◆◆FACILITIES: 50 sites, typical site width 25 ft, 50 full hkups, (20/30/50 amps), 26 pull-thrus, family camping, tenting, dump, laundry. Pets welcome. Open all yr. Rate in 2010 $18-20 for 2 persons. Phone: (770) 574-5522.

TALLULAH FALLS—A-3

(C) TALLULAH GORGE STATE PARK—(Rabun) *From Jct Tallulah Gorge Bridge & US 441: Go 1/2 mi N on US 441, then 1/2 mi SE on Jane Hurt Yarn Rd. Enter on R.* FACILITIES: 50 sites, typical site width 30 ft, 50 W&E, (20/30 amps), 10 pull-thrus, family camping, tenting, dump, laundry. RECREATION: lake swim, boating, electric motors only, canoeing, lake/river fishing, playground. Pets welcome. Partial handicap access. Open all yr. Phone: (706)754-7979.

Oliver Hardy, comedian, was from Georgia.

THOMSON—C-4

(W) BIG HART CAMP AREA (COE - J. Strom Thurmond Lake)—(McDuffie) *From town: Go 8 mi N on US 78, then 4 mi E on Russell Landing Rd.* FACILITIES: 31 sites, typical site width 20 ft, 30 ft max RV length, 31 W&E, (30/50 amps), 15 pull-thrus, tenting, dump. RECREATION: lake swim, boating, ramp, dock, lake fishing, playground. Open Apr 1 - Oct 31. Phone: (706)595-8613.

(W) RAYSVILLE BRIDGE CAMP AREA (COE - J. Strom Thurmond Lake)—(McDuffie) *From jct US-78 & Hwy-43: Go 7 mi N on Hwy 43.* FACILITIES: 55 sites, typical site width 20 ft, 30 ft max RV length, 55 W&E, (50 amps), 4 pull-thrus, tenting, dump. RECREATION: lake swim, boating, ramp, lake fishing, playground. Pets welcome. Partial handicap access. Open Mar 1 - Oct 30. Phone: (706)595-6759.

TIFTON—E-3

(W) Agrirama RV Park—(Tifton) *From jct I-75 (exit 63B) & Whiddon Mill Rd: Go 1/4 mi W on Whiddon Mill Rd. Enter on R.* ◆◆◆FACILITIES: 42 sites, typical site width 24 ft, accepts full hkup units only, 42 full hkups, (20/30/50 amps), 42 pull-thrus, WiFi Internet central location, family camping. RECREATION: pavilion. Pets welcome. No tents. Open all yr. Big rigs welcome. Rate in 2010 $20 per vehicle. DISC/AMEX. ATM. CCUSA 50% Discount. CCUSA reservations Recommended, CCUSA max stay 1 day, CCUSA disc. not avail Th,S, CCUSA disc. not avail F,Sa. Accepts full hook-up units only.

CAMPCLUB USA

Phone: (800)767-1875
Address: 1392 Whiddon Mill Rd, Tifton, GA 31793
Lat/Lon: 31.46832/-83.52987
Email: market@agrirama.com
Web: www.agrirama.com

(W) Amy's South Georgia RV Park—(Tift) *From jct I-75 (exit 60) & South Central Ave: Go 1 mi W on South Central Ave. Enter on R.* ◆◆◆FACILITIES: 90 sites, typical site width 30 ft, 84 full hkups, 6 W&E, (30/50 amps), 58 pull-thrus, family camping, tenting, dump, laundry, ltd groc. ◆◆RECREATION: swim pool, pond fishing, play equipment. Pets welcome. Partial handicap access. Open all yr. Big rigs welcome. Rate in 2010 $33-35 for 2 persons. Phone: (229)386-8441.

(S) The Pines Campground—(Tift) *From jct I-75 (exit 61) & Omega Rd: Go 500 ft W on Omega Rd, then 300 feet S on Casseta Rd. Enter on R.* ◆◆◆FACILITIES: 34 sites, typical site width 25 ft, 34 full hkups, (20/30/50 amps), 30 pull-thrus, family camping, tenting, laundry. Pets welcome. Partial handicap access. Open all yr. Big rigs welcome. Rate in 2010 $22 per vehicle. Phone: (229)382-3500.

TOCCOA—B-3

(S) TOCCOA RV PARK—(Stephens) *From jct I-85 (exit 173) & Hwy 17: Go 13 mi N on Hwy 17A, then 3-1/4 mi E on Oak Valley Rd. Enter on R.*

WELCOME

◆◆FACILITIES: 46 sites, typical site width 28 ft, 30 full hkups, 1 W&E, (30/50 amps), 50 amps ($), 15 no hkups, some extd stay sites, 20 pull-thrus, phone on-site Internet (needs activ), family camping, tenting, dump, non-guest dump $, laundry, picnic tables.

◆RECREATION: pavilion, golf nearby.

Pets welcome. Open all yr. Clubs welcome.

Phone: (706)886-2654
Address: 3494 Oak Valley Rd, Toccoa, GA 30577
Lat/Lon: 34.58060/-83.24039

SEE AD THIS PAGE

Woodall's Tip... FREE Additional Information! Use the Reader Service card opposite page 48 in the front of the book.

TOWNSEND—E-5

(E) LAKE HARMONY RV PARK & CAMPGROUND—(McIntosh) *From jct I-95 (exit 58) & Hwy 57: Go 1/4 mi W on Hwy 57. Enter on L.*

WELCOME

◇◇◇FACILITIES: 50 sites, typical site width 25 ft, 50 full hkups, (30/50 amps), some extd stay sites, 50 pull-thrus, cable TV, WiFi Internet at site, family camping, tenting, RV storage, laundry, RV supplies, LP gas by weight/by meter, ice, picnic tables, fire rings, wood.

◇◇◇RECREATION: rec hall, lake swim, boating, electric motors only, canoeing, kayaking, 3 rowboat/4 kayak/pedal boat rentals, lake fishing, fishing supplies, golf nearby, bsktball, shuffleboard court 2 shuffleboard courts, horseshoes, sports field.

Pets welcome. Partial handicap access. Open all yr. Big rigs welcome. Escort to site. Clubs welcome. Rate in 2010 $27-31 for 2 persons. MC/VISA/Debit. Member GARVC. FMCA discount.

Phone: (888)767-7864
Address: 1088 Lake Harmony Dr SVV, Townsend, GA 31331
Lat/Lon: 31.53708/-81.45530
Email: info@lakeharmonypark.com
Web: www.lakeharmonypark.com

SEE AD THIS PAGE

(W) McIntosh Lake RV Park—(McIntosh) *From jct I-95 (exit 58) & Hwy 57: Go 1/2 mi W on Hwy 57. Enter on L.* ◇◇FACILITIES: 38 sites, typical site width 24 ft, 34 full hkups, 4 W&E, (30/50 amps), 22 pull-thrus, family camping, laundry. ◇◇RECREATION: lake swim, lake fishing. Pets welcome. No tents. Open all yr. Big rigs welcome. Rate in 2010 $22 per vehicle. Phone: (912)832-6215.

TRENTON—A-1

(W) Lookout Mountain KOA-Chattanooga West—(Dade) *From jct I-24 (exit 167) & I-59: Go 2 mi S on I-59 (exit 17/ Slygo Rd), then 1/2 mi W on Slygo Rd, then 1-1/4 mi S on Hales Gap, then 3/4 mi W on Mountain Shadows Rd. Enter at end.* ◇◇◇◇FACILITIES: 74 sites, typical site width 25 ft, 33 full hkups, 41 W&E, (20/30/50 amps), 14 pull-thrus, family camping, tenting, dump, laundry, ltd groc. ◇◇◇◇RECREATION: swim pool, playground. Pets welcome, breed restrict. Open all yr. Big rigs welcome. Rate in 2010 $29-45 for 2 persons. Member ARVC. Phone: (800)562-1239. KOA discount.

TWIN CITY—D-4

(E) GEORGE L. SMITH STATE PARK—(Emanuel) *From jct US 80 & Hwy 23: Go 3-1/2 mi SE on Hwy 23, then 1-3/4 mi E on George L Smith State Park Rd. Enter at end.* FACILITIES: 25 sites, 25 W&E, (20/30/50 amps), 5 pull-thrus, family camping, tenting, dump, laundry. RECREATION: boating, 10 hp limit, canoeing, ramp, dock, lake/stream fishing, playground. Pets welcome. Partial handicap access. Open all yr. Big rigs welcome. Phone: (800) 864-7275.

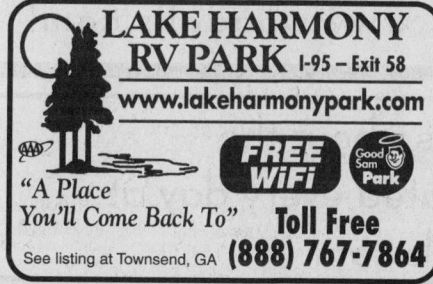

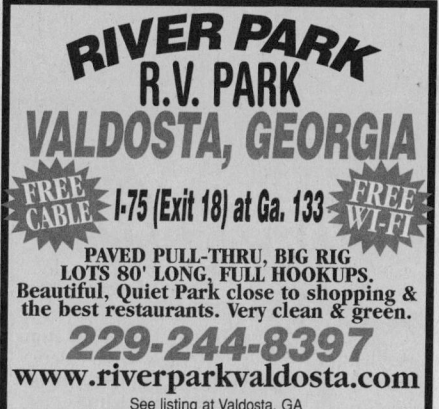

TYBEE ISLAND—D-5

(W) RIVER'S END CAMPGROUND & RV PARK—(Chatham) *From jct I-95 & I-16: Go 9 mi E on I-16 to(exit 167A), then 3/4 mi N on MLK Jr Blvd, then 1 mi E on Bay St (stay in left hand lane), then 15 mi E on President St (Becomes Island Expwy then into US 80 to Tybee Island), then 2 blks N on Polk St. Enter on L.*

WELCOME

WHERE THE RIVER MEETS THE SEA!
A place for all seasons. Sandy beaches, great fishing & history at every turn. Only 1.5 blocks from beach & 12 mi to historic Savannah. Enjoy Tybee Time under our live oak canopy. www.riversendcampground.com

FACILITIES: 150 sites, typical site width 20 ft, 91 full hkups, 19 W&E, (30/50 amps), 40 no hkups, some extd stay sites (winter), 44 pull-thrus, cable TV, WiFi Instant Internet at site, cable Internet central location, family camping, tenting, cabins, dump, non-guest dump $, laundry, ltd groc, RV supplies, LP gas by weight/by meter, ice, picnic tables, wood.

RECREATION: rec hall, rec room/area, pavilion, swim pool, golf nearby, bike rental 7 bike rentals, activities, horseshoes, hiking trails.

Pets welcome, breed restrict, size restrict, quantity restrict. Partial handicap access. Open all yr. Big rigs welcome. Escort to site. Clubs welcome. MC/VISA/DISC/AMEX/Debit. Member ARVC.

Text 81245 to (440)725-8687 to see our Visual Tour.

Phone: (800)786-1016
Address: Five Fort Ave, Tybee Island, GA 31328
Lat/Lon: 32.02313/-80.85165
Email: riversend1@aol.com
Web: www.riversendcampground.com

SEE AD SAVANNAH PAGE 206

UNADILLA—D-2

(S) Southern Trails RV Resort—(Dooly) *From jct I-75 (exit 121) & US 41: Go 1/4 mi E on US 41, then 500 ft E on Speeg Rd, then 1/2 mi S on E Railroad St/Arena Rd. Enter on L.* ◇◇◇FACILITIES: 230 sites, typical site width 30 ft, 170 full hkups, 60 W&E, (30/50 amps), 50 amps ($), 180 pull-thrus, cable TV, ($), WiFi Internet central location, family camping, tenting, RV

UNADILLA—Continued
Southern Trails RV Resort—Continued

storage, dump, laundry, LP gas by weight/by meter, ice, picnic tables. ◇◇◇◇RECREATION: rec hall, swim pool, pond fishing, mini-golf, bsktball, playground, activities, horseshoes. Pets welcome. Open all yr. Big rigs welcome. Rate in 2010 $30 for 2 persons. MC/VISA/DISC/AMEX. FMCA discount. CCUSA 50% Discount. CCUSA reservations Not Accepted, Cash only for CCUSA disc., Check only for CCUSA disc., CCUSA disc. not avail holidays.

Phone: (478)627-3255
Address: 2690 Arena Rd, Unadilla, GA 31091
Lat/Lon: 32.24037/-83.73928
Email: sttrails@windstream.net
Web: www.southerntrailsrvresort.com

VALDOSTA—F-3

EAGLES ROOST RV RESORT—*From jct US 84 & I-75 (exit 16): Go 11 mi S on I-75 (exit 5), then 500 ft E on Hwy 376, then 1/2 mi S on Mill Store Rd. Enter on L.*

WELCOME

SEE PRIMARY LISTING AT LAKE PARK AND AD NEXT PAGE

VALDOSTA—Continued on next page

IF YOU THINK WOODALL RATINGS MEAN GOOD, BETTER, BEST....

THINK AGAIN

SEE THE "HOW TO USE" PAGES IN THE FRONT OF THIS DIRECTORY FOR AN EXPLANATION OF OUR RATING SYSTEM

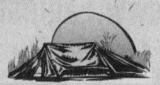

VALDOSTA—Continued

(W) RIVER PARK RV PARK—(Lowndes) *From jct I-75 (exit 18) & Hwy 133: Go 300 yds W on Hwy 133. Enter on R.*

WELCOME

◆◆◆FACILITIES: 118 sites, typical site width 25 ft, 118 full hkups, (30/50 amps), many extd stay sites, 57 pull-thrus, cable TV, WiFi Instant Internet at site, phone on-site Internet (needs activ), family camping, dump, non-guest dump $, laundry, picnic tables, patios.

RECREATION: golf nearby.

Pets welcome. No tents. Open all yr. Big rigs welcome. Escort to site. Clubs welcome. MC/VISA/Debit.

Phone: (229)244-8397
Address: 1 Suwanee Dr., Valdosta, GA 31602
Lat/Lon: 30.84756/-83.33459
Email: info@riverparkvaldosta.com
Web: www.riverparkvaldosta.com

SEE AD PAGE 209 AND AD TRAVEL SECTION PAGE 185

WARM SPRINGS—C-1

(N) RAMSEY RV PARK—(Meriwether) *From jct Alt US 27/Hwy 41 & Alt Hwy 85: Go 1-1/4 mi N on Alt Hwy 85. (White House Pkwy). Enter on L.*

WELCOME

◆◆FACILITIES: 27 sites, typical site width 24 ft, 27 full hkups, (30/50 amps), 50 amps ($), some extd stay sites, 17 pull-thrus, family camping, tenting, laundry, picnic tables.

◆RECREATION: swim pool, golf nearby.

Pets welcome. Partial handicap access. Open all yr. Big rigs welcome. Clubs welcome. Rate in 2010 $19-23 for 2 persons.

Phone: (706)655-2480
Address: 5153 White House Pkwy, Warm Springs, GA 31830
Lat/Lon: 32.90831/-84.67735

SEE AD THIS PAGE

WARNER ROBINS—D-3

MILITARY PARK (Robins AFB FAMCAMP)—(Houston) *On I-75. On base.* FACILITIES: 21 sites, 18 W&E, (20/30/50 amps), 3 no hkups, tenting, dump, laundry, ltd groc. RECREATION: canoeing. Pets welcome. Open all yr. Phone: (912)926-0918.

WARTHEN—C-3

(N) HAMBURG STATE PARK—(Washington) *From jct Hwy 15 & Hwy 102: Go 1 mi N on Hwy 102, then 5 mi N on Hamburg Rd.* FACILITIES: 30 sites, 30 W&E, (30 amps), 7 pull-thrus, family camping, tenting, dump, laundry, ltd groc. RECREATION: boating, 10 hp limit, canoeing, ramp, dock, lake/river fishing, playground. Pets welcome. Partial handicap access. Open all yr. Phone: (800) 864-7275.

WAYCROSS—E-4

(S) LAURA S. WALKER STATE PARK—(Ware) *From jct US 1 & US 82: Go 10 mi SE on US 82, then 2 mi E on Hwy 177. Enter on L.* FACILITIES: 44 sites, 44 W&E, (20/30/50 amps), 4 pull-thrus, family camping, tenting, dump, laundry. RECREATION: boating, canoeing, ramp, dock, lake fishing, playground. Pets welcome. Open all yr. Big rigs welcome. Phone: (800) 864-7275.

WEST POINT—C-1

(N) AMITY PARK (West Point Lake COE)—(Troup) *From town: Go 7 mi N on State Line Rd (crossing Georgia/Alabama border), then 1 mi E on CR 393. Park is in Alabama & Georgia.* FACILITIES: 96 sites, 93 W&E, 3 no hkups, tenting, dump, laundry. RECREATION: boating, ramp, dock, lake fishing, playground. Open Mar 18 - Sep 10. Phone: (334)499-2404.

(N) R. SHAEFER HEARD (COE - West Point Lake)—(Troup) *From town: Go 3 mi N on US-29 & follow signs.* FACILITIES: 117 sites, typical site width 20 ft, 117 W&E, (20/30 amps), tenting, dump, laundry. RECREATION: lake swim, boating, ramp, dock, lake fishing, playground. Partial handicap access. Open Jan 1 - Sep 26. Phone: (706)645-2404.

WINDER—B-2

(W) FORT YARGO STATE PARK—(Barrow) *From jct Hwy 8 & Hwy 81: Go 1 mi S on Hwy 81. Enter on L.* FACILITIES: 47 sites, 40 W&E, (20/30/50 amps), 7 no hkups, 4 pull-thrus, family camping, tenting, dump, laundry. RECREATION: lake swim, boating, 10 hp limit, canoeing, ramp, dock, lake fishing. Pets welcome. Partial handicap access. Open all yr. Big rigs welcome. Phone: (800) 864-7275.

WINFIELD—C-4

(N) WINFIELD CAMP AREA (COE - J. Strom Thurmond Lake)—(Mc Duffie) *From Hwy 150: Follow signs 4 mi N on Winfield Rd.* FACILITIES: 80 sites, typical site width 20 ft, 35 ft max RV length, 80 W&E, (50 amps), tenting, dump. RECREATION: lake swim, boating, ramp, lake fishing, playground. Open Mar 1 - Oct 31. Phone: (706)541-0147.

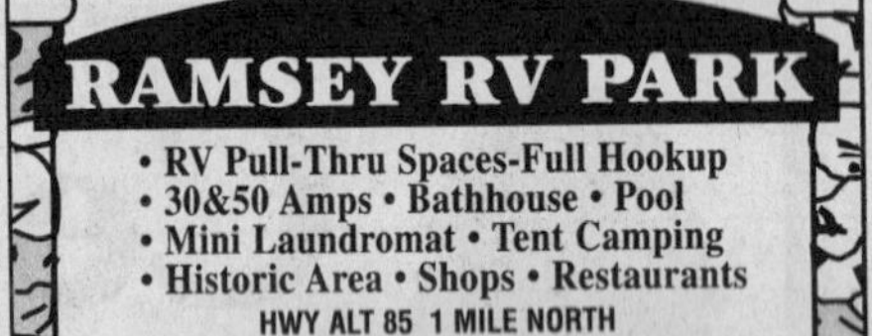

WOODBINE—E-4

(E) King George RV Resort—(Camden) *From jct I-95 (exit 7) & Harriets Bluff Rd Go: 1/4 mi W on Harriets Bluff Rd, then 1/2 mi S on Old Still Rd. Enter on L.*

◆◆◆FACILITIES: 40 sites, typical site width 25 ft, 40 full hkups, (30/50 amps), 40 pull-thrus, WiFi Instant Internet at site, phone/cable on-site Internet (needs activ), family camping, RV storage, dump, laundry, LP gas by weight/by meter, picnic tables.

CAMPCLUB USA

◆◆RECREATION: rec hall, pavilion, swim pool. Pets welcome. No tents. Open all yr. Big rigs welcome. Rate in 2010 $32-36 for 2 persons. CCUSA 50% Discount. CCUSA reservations Accepted, CCUSA max stay 3 days, CCUSA disc. not avail holidays. Not available Aug. 1-15.

Phone: (912)729-4110
Address: 5200 Old Still Rd, Woodbine, GA 31569
Lat/Lon: 30.84059/-81.67691
Email: kinggeorgerv@hotmail.com

WOODSTOCK—B-2

(S) VICTORIA CAMPGROUND (Allatoona Lake COE) —(Cherokee) *From town: Go S on Hwy 5, then 6 mi W on Hwy 92, then 2 mi N on Bells Ferry Rd, then 2-1/2 mi W. Enter on L.* FACILITIES: 74 sites, typical site width 20 ft, 74 W&E, 8 pull-thrus, tenting, dump, laundry. RECREATION: lake swim, boating, ramp, dock, lake fishing, playground. Partial handicap access. Open Mar 26 - Oct 10. Phone: (678)721-6700.

WRENS—C-4

(S) BOSS'S RV PARK—(Jefferson) *From Hwy 17 & US 1: Go 1-1/2 mi S on US1/Hwy 17. Enter on L.*

WELCOME

◆◆◆◆FACILITIES: 77 sites, typical site width 25 ft, 77 full hkups, (20/30/50 amps), some extd stay sites, WiFi Instant Internet at site, family camping, tenting, RV storage, laundry, picnic tables.

◆RECREATION: equipped pavilion, golf nearby, horseshoes.

Pets welcome. Open all yr. Big rigs welcome. Clubs welcome.

Phone: (706)547-0402
Address: 2801 Hoyt Braswell Rd, Wrens, GA 30833
Lat/Lon: 33.17757/-82.39713
Email: bossrvpark@gmail.com
Web: www.bossrv.bestparkview.com

SEE AD AUGUSTA PAGE 194

TIME ZONE

Illinois is in the Central Time Zone.

TOPOGRAPHY

The state has the lowest overall elevation of all the north-central states, with an average elevation of 600 feet above sea level.

TEMPERATURE

Due to its elongated north-south dimensions, Illinois experiences a significant climactic diversity.

Illinois is a magnificent destination catering to every kind of traveler. Visitors searching for a city break with a laid back feel, with an uptown tempo will find the best of both worlds in Chicago. Traveling beyond Chicago, travelers will soon learn why Illinois is considered the "most American state".

TRAVEL & TOURISM INFO

State Agency:
Illinois Office of Tourism
100 W. Randolph St., Ste. 3-400
Chicago, IL 60601
(800/2-CONNECT)
www.enjoyillinois.com

Regional Agencies:
Central Illinois Tourism Dev. Office
700 East Adams
Springfield, IL 62701
(217/525-7980)
www.visitcentralillinois.com

Chicago Convention and Tourism Bureau
2301 S. Lake Shore Drive
Chicago, IL 60616
(312/567-8500)
www.choosechicago.com

Northern Illinois Tourism Development Office
200 South State St.
Belvidere, IL 61108
(815/547-3740)
www.visitnorthernillinois.com

Southernmost Illinois Tourism Bureau
PO Box 378
Anna, IL 62906
(618/833-9928 or 800/248-4373)
www.southernmostillinois.com

The Tourism Bureau of Southwestern Illinois
10950 Lincoln Trail
Fairview Heights, IL 62208
(618/397-1488 or 800/442-1488)
www.thetourismbureau.org

Western Illinois Tourism Dev. Office
581 South Deere Rd.
Macomb, IL 61455
(309/837-7460)
www.visitwesternillinois.info

Local Agencies:
Contact the Chamber of Commerce or Tourism Bureau for the locality you are interested in.

RECREATIONAL INFO

Fishing & Hunting: Illinois Dept. of Natural Resources, One Natural Resources Way, Springfield, IL 62702 For fishing and hunting licenses, call 217/782-6302. To apply online: http://dnr.state.il.us/Sh

SHOPPING

In Chicago: **The Antiquarians Building**, 159 W. Kinzie St. Five floors showcase 30 dealers who specialize in a host of decorative furnishings. **Antiques Row** on Belmont Avenue features shops carrying everything from sports memorabilia to fine Victorian antiques. Nearby on Lincoln Ave. is **Lincoln Antique Mall**, 3141 N. Lincoln Ave., 11,000 square feet of estate jewelry, mid-century modern pieces and a large collection of furniture. **Uncle Fun**, 1338 W. Belmont Ave., offers affordably priced nostalgic toys and gag gifts.

The **Gurnee Antique Center**, 5742 Northridge Dr., furniture and collectibles from 200 dealers.

Emporium of Antiques, 227 Robert Parker Coffin Rd., Long Grove, offering the wares of more than 15 different dealers.

Antique Markets I, 11 N. Third St., **II**, 303 W. Main St. and **III**, 413 W. Main St. are all in St. Charles. **Kane County Flea Market** is held on the first Sunday and preceding Saturday of every month at the Kane County Fairgrounds. You can call the St. Charles Convention & Visitors Bureau at 800/777-4373 for a free copy of its Antiques Guide.

DJ's Antiques, 326 E. Lena St., Lena, specializes in vintage license plates and unusual collectibles.

Galena Antique Mall, 8201 Rte. 20 W., houses 60 dealers specializing in everything from 1800s lamps to Hall pottery.

Barrel Antique Mall, 5850 S. 6th Rd., Springfield, a 27,000-square-foot center rep-

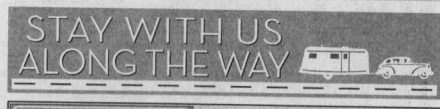

BUSINESSES OFFERING

	Things to See & Do	RV Sales	RV Service
ANNAPOLIS			
Crossties Christian Ministries	⚑		
CAHOKIA			
Sawmill BBQ	⚑		
MARION			
Kamper's Supply		🚌	✵
SPRINGFIELD			
Double J RV Sales & Service		🚌	✵
WOODSTOCK			
Bigfoot Construction Equipment			✵

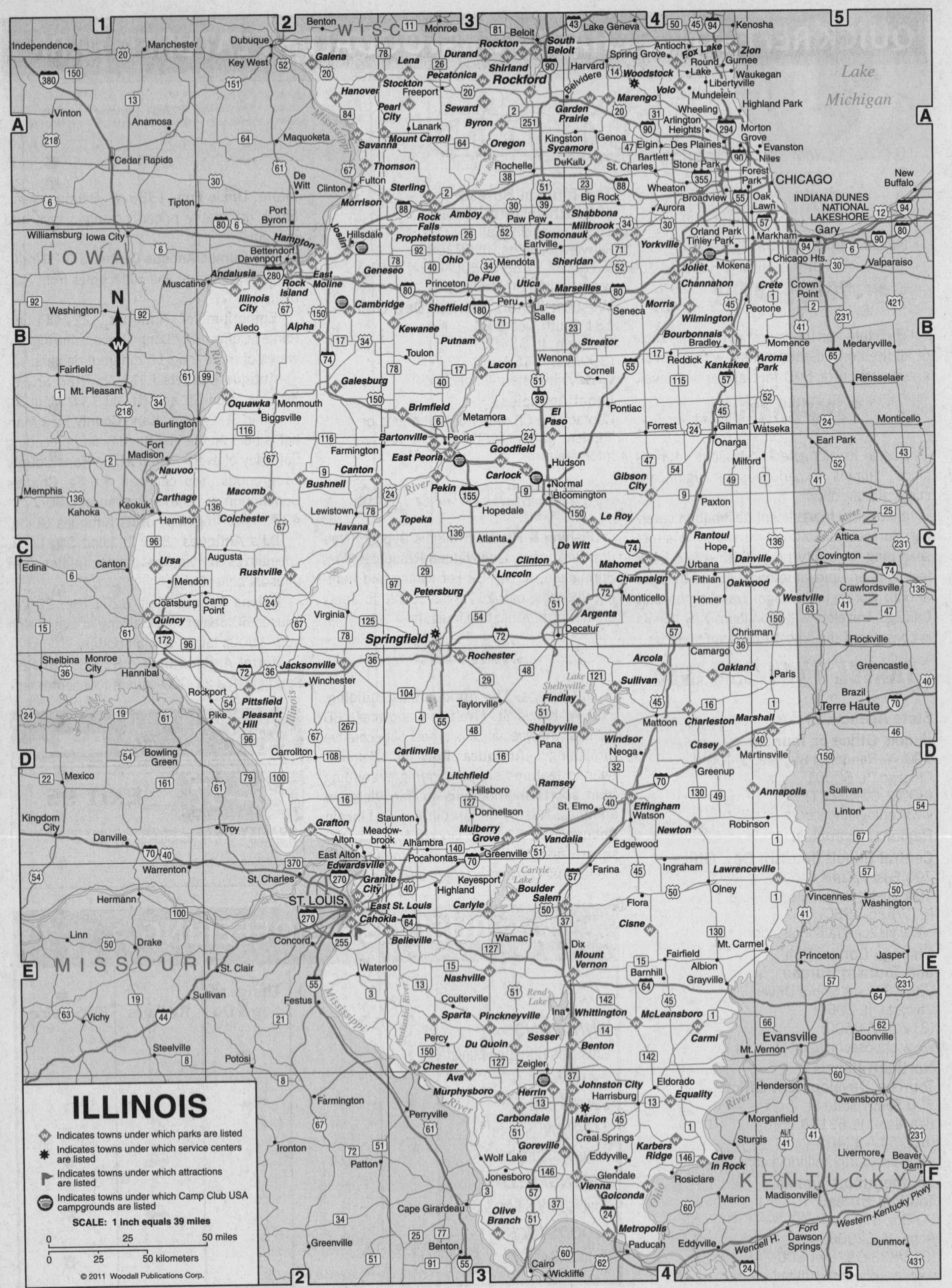

ILLINOIS
Indicates towns under which parks are listed
Indicates towns under which service centers are listed
Indicates towns under which attractions are listed
Indicates towns under which Camp Club USA campgrounds are listed
SCALE: 1 inch equals 39 miles
0 25 50 miles
0 25 50 kilometers
© 2011 Woodall Publications Corp.
IOWA
MISSOURI
KENTUCKY
INDIANA
WISC
Lake Michigan
INDIANA DUNES NATIONAL LAKESHORE
Mississippi River
Illinois River
Ohio River
Wabash River
CHICAGO
Rockford
Springfield
ST. LOUIS
Peoria
Evansville
Terre Haute
Western Kentucky Pkwy

QUICK REFERENCE CHART FOR WOODALL'S FEATURED PARKS

	Green Friendly	RV Lots for Sale	Park Models-Onsite Ownership	Park Membership for Sale	Big Rigs Welcome	Internet Friendly	Pets Welcome
AMBOY							
O'Connell's Yogi Bear's Jellystone Park Camp-Resort					▲	●	■
Pine View Campground							■
ANNAPOLIS							
Hickory Holler Campground							■
AROMA PARK							
Twin River Campground & Retreat Center							■
BARTONVILLE							
Leisure Oaks Park							■
BYRON							
Lake Louise Campground					▲		■
CAHOKIA							
Cahokia RV Parque					▲		■
CAMBRIDGE							
The Old Timber RV Park						●	■
CARLOCK							
Kamp Komfort					▲	●	■
EAST PEORIA							
Millpoint Park							■
EFFINGHAM							
Camp Lakewood					▲	●	■
EL PASO							
Hickory Hill Campground							■
GALENA							
Palace Campground					▲	●	■
GALESBURG							
Galesburg East Best Holiday Trav-L-Park					▲	●	■
GENESEO							
Geneseo Campground					▲	●	■
GIBSON CITY							
South Park Municipal Campground							■
MT VERNON							
Quality Times					▲	●	■
MULBERRY GROVE							
Timber Trails Campground					▲	●	■
ROCK ISLAND							
Rock Island/Quad Cities-KOA					▲	●	■
SHERIDAN							
Rolling Oaks Campground							■
SPRINGFIELD							
The Double J Campground & RV Park					▲	●	■
UTICA							
KOA-LaSalle/Peru					▲	●	■
VANDALIA							
Okaw Valley Kampground							■
WHITTINGTON							
Whittington Woods Campground					▲	●	■
WILMINGTON							
Fossil Rock Recreation Area					▲		■

Green Friendly 🍃; RV Lots for Sale ✖; Park Models/Onsite Onwership ✱; Park Memberships for Sale ✔; Big Rigs Welcome ▲; Internet Friendly ●; Internet Friendly-WiFi ●; Pets Welcome ■

resenting more than 100 dealers from across the state.

Wonderland Antiques, 217 S. Main St., Palestine, showcases 6,000 square feet of fine and primitive pieces displayed in interesting themed rooms.

Hoffman's Patterns of the Past, 513 S. Main St., Princeton, offers more than 100,000 varieties of discontinued china, crystal, stoneware and flatware dating back to the 1800s.

DESTINATIONS

NORTHERN ILLINOIS REGION

DeKalb. To view a premier example of Egyptian/Art Deco architecture, visit the Egyptian Theater, a fully restored movie palace. Or tour the Gurler House, an 1875 mansion built in the Greek Revival style. Other attractions in this college town include the Altgeld Art Gallery and the Ellwood House Museum.

Dixon. Take a tour of the **Ronald Reagan Home and Visitor Center** restored to its 1920 appearance and complete with period furniture.

Franklin Grove. See a functioning ecosystem at work at the Nachusa Grasslands. Over 1,000 acres of native Illinois prairie, sandstone buttes, oak savannas, wetlands and original species of plants and animals.

Freeport offers visitors over 500 acres of parks including two 18-hole golf courses. The statue at the corner of Douglas and State Streets marks the spot of one of the historic Lincoln-Douglas debates.

Galena. Enjoy at least 60 antique shops, 20 art galleries, charming restaurants and pubs, excellent golf and downhill skiing. Among the historic sites and architecture are the **City Brewery Museum**, **The Galena/Jo Daviess County History Museum**, the **Galena Wax Museum** and the **Old General Store Museum**.

Geneva. Return to the past in this quaint town with over 100 specialty shops nestled in historic storefronts and charming Victorian style homes.

Rock Cut State Park, Caledonia. A super getaway place, especially in winter, this park welcomes campers with two lakes (one is 162 acres), miles of hiking trails, ice fishing and cross-country skiing.

Rockford. One of the finest and most extensive collections of timekeeping devices can be found at **The Time Museum**. Rockford has over 160 parks for biking, fishing, hiking and camping. There are a dozen championship golf courses, fourteen museums and two indoor antique malls. The **Anderson Japanese Gardens** includes waterfalls, formal gardens, koi ponds and a teahouse. Also visit the largest wave pool in Illinois at **Magic Waters**, a 35-acre water theme park.

Union. Train buffs will enjoy the **Illinois Railway Museum.** With more than 250 railcars and locomotives including the Burlington Zephyr Streamliner, it is the largest railway museum in the country.

Utica offers two beautiful state parks. At **Matthiesen State Park**, you'll see bluffs, canyons and waterfalls. **Starved Rock State Park** contains eighteen canyons that dominate the landscape. Both parks offer hiking, hunting and horseback riding.

Woodstock. In the Victorian town square, complete with bandstand and gazebo, shop at many unique antique and collectible stores or enjoy a summer ice cream social. **Woodstock Opera House**, where Orson Welles and Paul Newman began their careers, was built in 1889 and still hosts musicals, dramas and dance entertainment.

CHICAGOLAND

Baha'i House of Worship, Wilmette. This nine-sided, domed structure reflects the Baha'i belief in the unity of religions. It is surrounded by nine beautiful flower gardens and fountains.

Brookfield Zoo, Brookfield. Follow the paths through Tropic World, an immense rain forest filled with gorillas, monkeys, exotic birds and more.

Chicago Botanic Garden, Glenview. Explore 26 beautifully landscaped botanical gardens covering 385 acres, including lakes and islands featuring Japanese, rose, sensory and children's garden.

Cuneo Museum, in Vernon Hills, is a historic mansion, dating from 1914, nestled on 75 acres of formal gardens.

Frank Lloyd Wright Home and Studio, Oak Park. Restored to its 1909 appearance, the home is open for viewing along with 25 Wright buildings in the surrounding Oak Park neighborhood.

Ernest Hemingway Birthplace and Museum, Oak Park. Hemingway's first 20 years are captured in a collection of memorabilia.

Jurica Nature Museum, Lisle. Located at Benedictine University, this museum has one of the largest bird collections in the Midwest. Also includes a North Woods habitat and a Northern Illinois diorama.

Morton Arboretum, Lisle. 1,700 acres of spectacular gardens, world-renowned plant collections and unique natural areas can be viewed by car, foot, or the open-air Acorn Express tram.

Six Flags Great America, Gurnee. The Midwest's premier theme park features spectacular roller coasters, stage shows and a variety of attractions. Don't forget to visit **Six Flags Hurricane Harbor** with 25 major water slides and a wave pool in a Caribbean-themed waterpark.

The Tempel Lipizzans, Wadsworth. Majestic white stallions prance and dance as they perform a centuries-old tradition of classical dressage at Tempel Farms.

CHICAGO

A delightful mix of everything, Chicago offers visitors unlimited excitement. Electric theatre, outstanding music, scores of museums, international restaurants, tours, sports, zoos and of course, a lakefront and skyline that can't be beat.

Adler Planetarium. Explore three floors of exhibits on astronomy, space exploration, telescopes and navigation.

Art Institute of Chicago. Visit one of the world's leading art museums. This site is home to one of the largest collections of French Impressionist masterpieces.

Blues Clubs. From Blue Chicago to Buddy Guy's Legends to the House of Blues to

CAMPCLUB USA

Where to Find CCUSA Parks

List City	Park Name	Map Coordinates
CAMBRIDGE		
	The Old Timber RV Park	B-2
CARLOCK		
	Kamp Komfort	C-3
CARLYLE		
	Hickory Shores Resort	E-3
EAST PEORIA		
	Millpoint Park	C-3
HERRIN		
	Four Seasons Campground	F-3
JOLIET		
	Leisure Lake Membership Resort	B-4
JOSLIN		
	Sunset Lakes Resort	B-2

Kingston Mines to Rosa's Lounge, there is no shortage of blues music clubs in Chicago. Whether you're looking to experience the history of blues giants like Muddy Waters and Howlin' Wolf, or just want to enjoy some great music, you'll find (and hear) it all over the city.

Hancock Observatory. You'll get one of the best views of Chicago and Lake Michigan from the 94th floor Hancock Observatory. Take a self-guided audio Sky Tour, then step onto the Skywalk, an open-air viewing deck located 1,000 feet above the Magnificent Mile.

Magnificent Mile. Power shoppers grab their wallets and head for North Michigan Avenue, one of the ritziest retail stretches in the world. A unique urban experience awaits you with world-class shopping, dining and leisure entertainment throughout the Magnificent Mile area. There are four outdoor festivals—once each season.

Millennium Park. A wonderful Chicago attraction that showcases the Jay Pritzker Pavilion, designed by architect Frank Gehry and Great Lawn featuring free summer concerts; Harris Theater, a music and dance theater; restaurant, ice-skating, exhibits, the cutting-edge **Lurie Garden** and a stainless steel reflective sculpture by Anish Kapoor called **Cloud Gate** (known as "the Bean" by locals). **Crown Fountain** features projected images of Chicagoans who playfully spurt water. Millennium Park is an award-winning center for art, music, architecture and landscape design. The result of a unique partnership between the City of Chicago and the philanthropic community, the 24.5-acre Park features the work of world-renowned architects, planners, artists and designers.

CENTRAL ILLINOIS REGION

Historic Amish Country, Arcola & Arthur. Journey back in time to the years following the Civil War. Things aren't that much different for the Amish here right now. You can uncover exquisitely crafted wood furniture, handmade quilts and great home cooking.

Lake Shelbyville. This 11,000-acre lake is a popular vacation destination. Enjoy boating, fishing, camping and swimming.

Macon County Historical Museum Complex, Decatur. Stroll through historical buildings, including the 1830s log courthouse where Lincoln tried several cases, a train depot, a one-room schoolhouse, a blacksmith shop, and a print shop.

Miller Park Zoo, Bloomington. Home to a variety of exotic and domestic animals, including the rare and endangered Sumatran tigers and red wolves, this zoo has the only walk-through tropical rain forest exhibit in Illinois.

Springfield. The state capital and former home of Abraham Lincoln features the following attractions: **Governor's Mansion, Illinois State Historical Library, The Lincoln Home National Historic Site** and **Lincoln Tomb State Historic Site** (resting place of Lincoln, his wife Mary Todd and 3 of their 4 sons). The **Air Combat Museum** has a variety of operational military aircraft on display.

SOUTHERN ILLINOIS REGION

Cahokia Mounds State Historic Site, Collinsville. See the largest known historic Native American city north of Mexico.

Carlyle Lake is the largest manmade lake in Illinois, known as one of the best and most challenging in the state for sailboats. You'll also find sandy swimming beaches, fishing, hunting, hiking and golfing.

Fort Massac State Park overlooks the Ohio River. The historic site is a replica of the 1802 American fort that was originally located on the site. On-site interpreters answer questions and explain the Native American artifacts and military items on display, representing the period when the French occupied the fort.

WESTERN ILLINOIS REGION

Bishop Hill is a historic country village that honors its Swedish heritage. Home to descendants of the original founders, Bishop Hill offers museums, restored colony buildings, craft and antiques shops and restaurants that serve up authentic Swedish cuisine.

Galesburg. This town has combined history, tradition and culture in its preservation of local attractions: The **Galesburg Railroad Museum** is where you can experience railroading of the 1900s through memorabilia housed in a Pullman parlor car. At **Carl Sandburg Historic Site** you can visit the birthplace of this Pulitzer Prize-winning writer, poet, Lincoln biographer, folk singer and one-time hobo. Tour the Visitors' Center and pay your respects in the perennial garden where the author's ashes are buried beneath Remembrance Rock.

Peoria. See the world's largest solar system model and other exhibits in the **Lakeview Museum of Arts and Sciences. Wheels O'Time Museum** is a hands-on museum featuring vintage and classic automobiles, gasoline engines, real and model trains and a miniature circus. Other attractions include the **Flanagan House Museum** and Peoria's **RiverFront**, a complex of shops, restaurants, galleries and entertainment on the banks of the Illinois River. Don't miss a ride on the Spirit of Peoria, an old-fashioned paddlewheel boat. At the **Wildlife Prairie Park,** discover the animals native to Illinois in a unique 2,000-acre zoological park, home to wolves, bison, black bear, cougar, otter, elk and much more.

Rock Island. The Black Hawk State Historic Site pays homage to the Sauk and Mesquakie Indian tribes that occupied it as far back as 12,000 years ago. Also the home of the John Hauberg Indian Museum, located in a 1930s lodge, which exhibits important collections of Sauk and Fox Indian artifacts. Many of the pieces came directly from the family of Black Hawk, the famed Sauk warrior.

ANNUAL EVENTS

JANUARY

Northern Illinois Farm Show, DeKalb.

FEBRUARY

Midwestern Herb and Garden Show, Vernon; Annual Antiques Show, Loves Park.

MARCH

Tours of Ronald Reagan's Boyhood Home, Dixon (through October); Annual Sci-Fi Convention and Show, Metropolis.

APRIL

Long Grove Chocolate Fest, Long Grove; Southern Illinois Irish Festival, Carbondale; Heartland International Tattoo, Hoffman Estates.

MAY

Skokie Festival of Cultures, Skokie; Belmont-Sheffield Music Festival, Chicago; Fulton Dutch Days Festival, Fulton; Fair Diddley Craft Show, Woodstock; Rare Breeds Livestock and Poultry Show, Geneva; Young at Heart Festival, Loves Park; Wamac Spring Festival, Centralia; Randolph County Pig Party, Steeleville; Strawberry Festival, Belleville.

JUNE

The Raven Festival, Chicago; Strawberry Festival, Long Grove; Taste of Chicago, Chicago; Belmont Music Festival, Chicago; Annual Old Town Art Fair, Chicago; Wells Street Art Festival, Chicago; Rhubarb Fest, Rockton; Chicago Blues Festival, Chicago; Harvard Milk Days, Harvard; Prairiefest, Oswego; 1900 American Chatauqua, Rockford; Fields Project Arts Festival, Oregon; Annual Midsommar Festival, Geneva; Chicago Gospel Festival, Chicago; Garden Farir, Rockford; 57th Street Hyde Park Art Fair, Chicago; 40 Mile Long Garage Sale, Rockton; Woodstock Music Fest, Woodstock; River Front Festival, Savanna; Strawberry Festival, Richmond; Superman Celebration, Metropolis.

JULY

Chinatown Summer Fair, Chicago; Annual Midwest Heritage Quilt Show, Danville; Sheffield Garden Walk, Chicago; Italian Style, Chicago; Lakeside Music and Arts Festival, Decatur.

ALPHA—B-2

(SW) Shady Lakes Camping & Recreation—(Mercer) *From jct I-74 (exit 32) & Hwy 17: Go 2-1/2 mi W on Hwy 17, then 1/2 mi S on Hwy 150, then 3-3/4 mi W on Oxford Rd. Enter on L.* ◇◇◇FACILITIES: 328 sites, typical site width 30 ft, 328 full hkups, (30/50 amps), 50 amps ($), 64 pull-thrus, family camping, tenting, dump, laundry, ltd groc. ◇◇◇◇◇RECREATION: swim pool, boating, electric motors only, canoeing, ramp, dock, lake/pond fishing, playground. Pets welcome. Partial handicap access. Open mid Apr - late Oct. Big rigs welcome. Rate in 2010 $26 per family. Member ARVC, ICA. Phone: (309)667-2709. FCRV discount. FMCA discount.

AMBOY—A-3

(SW) Green River Oaks Camping Resort—(Lee) *From jct US 30 & US 52: Go 1 mi S on US 52, then 3/4 mi W on Main St, then 1-3/4 mi SW on Rockyford Rd, then 1/2 mi W on Sleepy Hollow Rd. Enter on R.* ◇◇◇FACILITIES: 225 sites, typical site width 35 ft, 115 full hkups, 110 W&E, (20/30 amps), family camping, tenting, dump, laundry, ltd groc. ◇◇◇◇RECREATION: 2 swim pools, lake/river fishing, playground. Pets welcome. Partial handicap access. Open Apr 27 - Oct 15. Rate in 2010 $25-40 per family. Phone: (815)857-2815.

(SE) Mendota Hills Campground—(Lee) *From jct US 30 & US 52: Go 6-1/2 mi S on US 52. Enter on L.* ◇◇FACILITIES: 250 sites, typical site width 28 ft, 110 full hkups, 90 W&E, (20/30/50 amps), 50 no hkups, 7 pull-thrus, family camping, tenting, dump, laundry, ltd groc. ◇◇◇◇RECREATION: lake swim, lake fishing, playground. Pets welcome. Open all yr. Facilities fully operational mid Apr - mid Oct. Rate in 2010 $26-35 per family. Member ARVC, ICA. Phone: (815)849-5930.

WELCOME **(E) O'CONNELL'S YOGI BEAR'S JELLYSTONE PARK CAMP-RESORT**—(Lee) *From jct US 30 & US 52: Go 1 mi S on US 52, then 1-1/2 mi E on Main St, then 2-1/2 mi SE on Shaw Rd, then 1 mi N on Green Wing Rd. Enter on R.*

◇◇◇◇◇FACILITIES: 747 sites, typical site width 40 ft, 493 full hkups, 154 W&E, (20/30/50 amps), 100 no hkups, some extd stay sites, 173 pull-thrus, WiFi Instant Internet at site ($), family camping, tenting, RV's/park model rentals, cabins, RV storage, dump, non-guest dump $, portable dump, laundry, groceries, RV supplies, LP gas by weight/by meter, ice, picnic tables, fire rings, wood, controlled access.

◇◇◇◇◇RECREATION: rec hall, rec room/area, pavilion, equipped pavilion, coin games, 3 swim pools, wading pool, lake swim, hot tub, electric motors only, canoeing, kayaking, 6 kayak/21 pedal boat rentals, lake/river fishing, fishing supplies, mini-golf, ($), golf nearby, bsktball, playground, activities, horseshoes, sports field, hiking trails, v-ball. Rec open to public.

Pets welcome. Facilities fully operational Apr 1 - Oct 30. Big rigs welcome. Clubs welcome. Rate in 2010 $41-56 per family. MC/VISA/DISC/AMEX/Debit. Member ARVC, ICA.

Phone: (815)857-3860
Address: 970 Green Wing Rd, Amboy, IL 61310-0200
Lat/Lon: 41.72436/-89.26620
Email: oconnells@equitylifestyle.com
Web: www.jellystoneamboy.com

SEE AD THIS PAGE

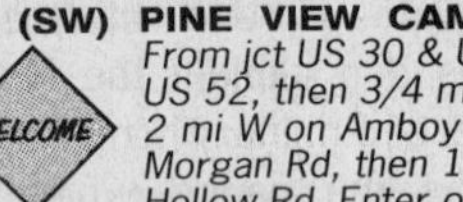

(SW) PINE VIEW CAMPGROUND—(Lee) *From jct US 30 & Us 52: Go 1 mi S on US 52, then 3/4 mi W on Main St, then 2 mi W on Amboy Rd, then 3 mi S on Morgan Rd, then 100 yds W on Sleepy Hollow Rd. Enter on L.*

◇◇◇FACILITIES: 130 sites, typical site width 30 ft, 113 full hkups, 17 W&E, (20/30/50 amps), many extd stay sites, family camping, tenting, RV's/park model rentals, dump, non-guest dump $, ltd groc, RV supplies, LP gas by weight, ice, picnic tables, fire rings, wood.

◇◇◇RECREATION: rec hall, lake swim, lake fishing, golf nearby, bsktball, playground, shuffleboard court shuffleboard court, activities (wkends), horseshoes, sports field, v-ball.

Pets welcome. Partial handicap access. Open Apr 15 - Oct 15. Clubs welcome. Rate in 2010 $25-27 for 7 persons. MC/VISA. Member ARVC, ICA.

Phone: (815)857-3964
Address: 1273 Sleepy Hollow Rd, Amboy, IL 61310
Lat/Lon: 41.67142/-89.38741
Web: www.pineviewcampgrounds.com

SEE AD THIS PAGE

ANDALUSIA—B-2

(W) ANDALUSIA SLOUGH (COE-Mississippi River Rec Areas-Muscatine Area)—(Rock Island) *From town: Go 4 mi W on Hwy 92 (follow signs).* FACILITIES: 25 sites, 25 no hkups. RECREATION: boating, canoeing, ramp, dock, river fishing. Open all yr. Facilities fully operational May 1 - Oct 31. Phone: (563)263-7913.

ANNAPOLIS—D-5

WELCOME **(E) CROSSTIES CHRISTIAN MINISTRIES**—*From jct I-70 (exit 147) and Hwy 1: Go 21 mi S on Hwy 1, then 4-1/2 mi W on Annapolis Rd. Enter on R.* A family Retreat Center providing recreational facilities, education, camping, gospel singing and Christian activities for families. Open all yr.

With a collection of more than 2 million books, the Chicago Public Library is the world's largest public library.

Phone: (618)563-4992
Address: 9876 E 2000th Ave, West York, IL 62478
Lat/Lon: 39.14555/-87.76318
Email: tj3dguyer@gmail.com
Web: www.crosstiescm.org

SEE AD NEXT PAGE

WELCOME **(E) HICKORY HOLLER CAMPGROUND**—(Crawford) *From jct I-70 (exit 147) and Hwy 1: Go 21 mi S on Hwy 1, then 4-1/4 mi W on Annapolis Rd. Enter on R.*

◇◇◇FACILITIES: 100 sites, typical site width 40 ft, 42 full hkups, 58 W&E, (30/50 amps), 50 amps ($), some extd stay sites, 20 pull-thrus, tenting, RV storage, portable dump, laundry, LP gas by weight, ice, picnic tables, fire rings, wood.

◇◇◇RECREATION: rec hall, coin games, lake swim, boating, electric motors only, 2 pedal boat rentals, lake/pond fishing, mini-golf, ($), golf nearby, bsktball, playground, shuffleboard court shuffleboard court, activities (wkends), horseshoes, sports field, v-ball.

Pets welcome. Open all yr. Clubs welcome. Rate in 2010 $15-19 for 4 persons.

Phone: (618)563-4779
Address: 9876 E 2000th Ave, West York, IL 62478
Lat/Lon: 39.14911/-87.76308
Email: tj3dguyer@gmail.com

SEE AD NEXT PAGE

ARCOLA—D-4

(C) Arcola Camper Stop—(Douglas) *From jct I-57 (exit 203) & Hwy 133: Go 1/4 mi W on Hwy-133, then 1 block N on Sheldon St. Enter on L.* ◇◇FACILITIES: 30 sites, typical site width 50 ft, 28 W&E, 2 E, (20/30/50 amps), 20 pull-thrus, tenting, dump. Pets welcome. Open all yr. Facilities fully operational Apr 15 - Oct 31. Rate in 2010 $18 for 2 persons. Phone: (217)268-4616.

ARGENTA—C-4

(NE) FRIENDS CREEK REGIONAL PARK (Macon County Park)—(Macon) *From jct I-72 (Argenta exit) & CR 25: Go 2 mi N on CR 25, then 2-1/2 mi NE on Hwy 48, then 2 mi N on County Park Rd.* FACILITIES: 36 sites, typical site width 30 ft, 36 E, (30 amps), tenting, dump. RECREATION: stream fishing, playground. Open May 1 - Nov 1. Phone: (217)795-2031.

AROMA PARK—B-5

WELCOME **(S) TWIN RIVER CAMPGROUND & RETREAT CENTER**—(Kankakee) *From jct I-57 (exit 312) & Hwy 17: Go 1-1/4 mi E on Hwy 17, then 2-3/4 mi S on Lowe Rd, then 1/4 mi E on 3rd St, then 1 mi S on Bridge St, then 1/4 mi W on Youth Camp Rd. Enter on R.*

◇◇◇FACILITIES: 70 sites, 54 full hkups, 16 W&E, (20/30/50 amps), 30 pull-thrus, family camping, tenting, LP gas by weight/by meter.

◇◇◇◇RECREATION: rec hall, rec room/area, pavilion, boating, 8 canoe rentals, river fishing, golf nearby, playground, horseshoes, sports field, hiking trails.

TWIN RIVER CAMPGROUND & RETREAT CENTER—Continued on next page

AROMA PARK—Continued
TWIN RIVER CAMPGROUND & RETREAT CENTER—Continued

Pets welcome. Partial handicap access. Open Apr 1 - Nov 15. Big rigs welcome. Clubs welcome. Rate in 2010 $22.50-34.50 for 6 persons. MC/VISA/DISC.

Phone: (815)937-1181
Address: 4112 S Youth Camp Rd, Saint Anne, IL 60964
Lat/Lon: 41.06315/-87.81062
Email: twinriversrcc@yahoo.com
Web: twinriverscamp.com

SEE AD KANKAKEE PAGE 222

AVA—F-3

(S) SHAWNEE NATIONAL FOREST (Johnson Creek Campground)—(Jackson) *From town: Go 4 mi S on Hwy-151.* FACILITIES: 20 sites, 20 no hkups, tenting, dump. RECREATION: lake swim, boating, canoeing, ramp, lake fishing, playground. Partial handicap access. Open Mar 16 - Dec 15. Phone: (618) 687-1731.

BARTONVILLE—C-3

(S) LEISURE OAKS PARK—(Peoria) *From jct I-474 & Hwy 24 (exit 64): Go 1-1/2 mi W on Hwy 24, then 1-1/4 mi W on Pfeifer Rd, then 1-1/2 mi S on Lafayette St. Enter on R.*

WELCOME

◆◆FACILITIES: 40 sites, typical site width 25 ft, 40 full hkups, (30/50 amps), mostly extd stay sites, family camping, tenting, RV storage, laundry, picnic tables, fire rings, wood.

◆◆RECREATION: rec hall, pavilion, pond fishing, golf nearby, playground, sports field, v-ball.

Pets welcome. Open Apr 15 - Oct 31. Rate in 2010 $30 for 4 persons.

Phone: (309)697-4871
Address: 5805 S Lafayette Ave, Bartonville, IL 61607
Lat/Lon: 40.61765/-89.67230
Web: www.leisureoakspark.com

SEE AD THIS PAGE

BELLEVILLE—E-3

(E) MILITARY PARK (Scott AFB FAMCAMP)—(St. Clair) *From town: Go 6 mi E on Hwy 158. On base.* FACILITIES: 22 sites, 22 W&E, (50 amps), dump. RECREATION: Partial handicap access. Open all yr. Phone: (618)256-2067.

BENTON—E-4

(N) Benton KOA—(Franklin) *From jct I-57 (exit 71) & Hwy 14: Go 1/2 mi E on Hwy 14, then 1-1/4 mi N on DuQuoin St. Enter on R.* ◆◆◆FACILITIES: 59 sites, 27 full hkups, 18 W&E, 4 E, (30/50 amps), 50 amps ($), 13 pull-thrus, tenting, dump, laundry, ltd groc. ◆◆◆RECREATION: swim pool, pond fishing, playground. Pets welcome, breed restrict. Open all yr. Big rigs welcome. Rate in 2010 $25-37 for 2 persons. Member ARVC. Phone: (800)562-8619. KOA discount.

(N) GUN CREEK RECREATION AREA (COE - Rend Lake)—(Franklin) *From jct I-57 (exit 77) & Hwy 154: Go 1/4 mi W on Hwy 154, then 1/2 mi S on CR 1210E, then W. Enter at end.* FACILITIES: 100 sites, typical site width 15 ft, 25 ft max RV length, 100 E, (30 amps), tenting, dump, laundry. RECREATION: lake swim, boating, canoeing, ramp, dock, lake fishing, playground. Partial handicap access. Open Mar 18 - Nov 28. Phone: (618)724-2493.

(W) NORTH SANDUSKY CREEK REC. AREA (COE - Rend Lake)—(Franklin) *From jct I-57 (exit 77) & Hwy 154: Go 6 mi W on Hwy 154, then 1-1/2 mi S on Rend City Rd.* FACILITIES: 118 sites, typical site width 15 ft, 15 full hkups, 103 E, (50 amps), 50 amps ($), tenting, dump. RECREATION: lake swim, boating, ramp, dock, lake/river/pond/stream fishing, playground. Partial handicap access. Open Apr 1 - Oct 30. Phone: (618)724-2493.

BENTON—Continued

(N) SOUTH MARCUM RECREATION AREA (COE - Rend Lake)—(Franklin) *From jct Hwy 37 & Hwy 14: Go 1/2 mi N on Hwy 37, then 3/4 mi W on Petroff Rd, then 3 mi N & W, then N to E end of main dam.* FACILITIES: 160 sites, typical site width 15 ft, 146 E, (50 amps), 14 no hkups, tenting, dump. RECREATION: lake swim, boating, ramp, dock, lake/pond fishing, playground. Partial handicap access. Open Apr 1 - Oct 30. Phone: (618)724-2493.

(W) SOUTH SANDUSKY CREEK REC. AREA (COE - Rend Lake)—(Franklin) *From jct I-57 (exit 77) & Hwy 154: Go 6 mi W on Hwy 154, then 3-1/2 mi S on Rend City Rd.* FACILITIES: 147 sites, typical site width 15 ft, 18 full hkups, 121 E, (30/50 amps), 8 no hkups, 4 pull-thrus, tenting, dump. RECREATION: lake swim, boating, ramp, lake fishing, playground. Partial handicap access. Open Apr 1 - Oct 30. Phone: (618)625-3011.

BLOOMINGTON—C-3

See listings at Carlock, El Paso and Goodfield

BOULDER—E-3

(W) BOULDER ACCESS AREA (Lake Carlyle-Corp of Engineers)—(Clinton) *From jct US 50 & US 51: Go 7 mi W on US 50, then 6 mi N on Boulder Rd.* FACILITIES: 84 sites, typical site width 20 ft, 9 full hkups, 75 W&E, (30/50 amps), tenting, dump, laundry. RECREATION: lake swim, boating, ramp, dock, lake fishing, playground. Partial handicap access. Open Apr 14 - Oct 14. Phone: (618)594-5253.

(W) COLES CREEK RECREATION AREA (Lake Carlyle - COE)—(Clinton) *From jct US 50 & US 51: Go 7 mi W on US 50, then 4 mi N on Boulder Rd, then 2 mi W on Coles Creek Rd.* FACILITIES: 121 sites, typical site width 20 ft, 121 W&E, (30/50 amps), 1 pull-thrus, tenting, dump, laundry. RECREATION: lake swim, boating, ramp, dock, lake fishing, playground. Open May 11 - Sep 30. Phone: (618)594-5253.

BOURBONNAIS—B-4

(NW) KANKAKEE RIVER STATE PARK—(Kankakee) *From jct US-45-52 & Hwy-102: Go 6 mi NW on Hwy-102.* FACILITIES: 213 sites, typical site width 15 ft, 35 ft max RV length, 167 E, (30/50 amps), 46 no hkups, tenting, dump. RECREATION: boating, 10 hp limit, canoeing, ramp, river/stream fishing, playground. Pets welcome. Partial handicap access. Open all yr. Phone: (815)933-1383.

BRIMFIELD—B-3

(E) JUBILEE COLLEGE STATE PARK—(Peoria) *From jct Hwy-91 & US-150: Go 7 mi W on US-150.* FACILITIES: 167 sites, typical site width 12 ft, 35 ft max RV length, 107 E, (30 amps), 60 no hkups, tenting, dump. RECREATION: pond fishing, playground. Partial handicap access. Open Apr 15 - Nov 1. Phone: (309)446-3758.

BUSHNELL—C-2

(NE) Timberview Lakes Campground—(McDonough) *From jct Hwy 9 & Hwy 41: Go 1-3/4 mi N on Hwy 41, then 1-3/4 mi E on 2000 N. Enter on L.* ◆◆◆FACILITIES: 86 sites, typical site width 30 ft, 62 full hkups, 21 W&E, 3 E, (20/30/50 amps), 50 amps ($), 11 pull-thrus, phone Internet central location, tenting, RV storage, dump, non-guest dump $, portable dump, laundry, ltd groc, LP gas by weight/by meter, ice, picnic tables, fire rings, wood. ◆◆◆RECREATION: rec hall, pavilion, lake swim, boating, no motors, lake fishing, fishing supplies, bsktball, playground, v-ball. Pets welcome. Open Apr 15 - Oct 15. Big rigs welcome. Rate in 2010 $26 per family. Member ARVC, ICA. CCUSA 50% Discount. CCUSA reservations Accepted, CCUSA max stay 7 days, CCUSA disc. not avail holidays. May stay longer than 7 days if space available. Pull-thru surcharge $5. $1 surcharge for credit card usage.

CAMPCLUB USA

Phone: (309)772-3609
Lat/Lon: 40.56996/-90.46227
Email: entLc1@comcast.net

Illinois State Tree: White Oak

BYRON—A-3

(NE) LAKE LOUISE CAMPGROUND—(Ogle) *From jct Hwy 72 & Hwy 2: Go 3 mi N on Hwy 2. Enter on L.*

WELCOME

◆◆◆FACILITIES: 317 sites, typical site width 40 ft, 164 full hkups, 150 W&E, (20/30/50 amps), 3 no hkups, many extd stay sites, 5 pull-thrus, family camping, tenting, cabins, shower$, dump, non-guest dump $, portable dump, laundry, ltd groc, RV supplies, LP gas by weight/by meter, ice, picnic tables, patios, fire rings, wood, controlled access.

◆◆◆◆RECREATION: rec room/area, pavilion, coin games, swim pool, lake swim, hot tub, boating, electric motors only, canoeing, kayaking, 6 rowboat/7 kayak/5 pedal boat rentals, lake/pond fishing, fishing supplies, golf nearby, bsktball, playground, activities, (wkends), horseshoes, sports field, hiking trails, v-ball. Rec open to public.

Pets welcome. Open Apr 1 - Oct 31. Facilities fully operational Memorial Day - Labor Day. Big rigs welcome. Clubs welcome. Rate in 2010 $35-45 for 4 persons. MC/VISA/Debit. Member ARVC, ICA.

Phone: (815)234-8483
Address: 8840 IL Rte 2N, Byron, IL 61010
Lat/Lon: 42.14034/-89.24677
Email: info@lakelouisellc.com
Web: www.lakelouisellc.com

SEE AD CHICAGO PAGE 219

CAHOKIA—E-2

(C) CAHOKIA RV PARQUE—(St. Clair) *From jct I-255 (exit 13) & Hwy 157: Go 2 mi W on Hwy 157, then 500 feet N on Hwy 3. Enter on L.*

WELCOME

◆◆◆◆FACILITIES: 121 sites, typical site width 25 ft, 103 full hkups, 12 W&E, (20/30/50 amps), 50 amps ($), 6 no hkups, some extd stay sites, 24 pull-thrus, family camping, tenting, RV's/park model rentals, cabins, laundry, ltd groc, RV supplies, LP gas by weight/by meter, ice, picnic tables, patios, fire rings, wood.

◆RECREATION: rec room/area, swim pool, golf nearby, playground, local tours.

Pets welcome. Partial handicap access. Open all yr. Big rigs welcome. Clubs welcome. Rate in 2010 $30-32 for 2 persons. MC/VISA/DISC/AMEX. Member ARVC, ICA. FCRV discount. FMCA discount.

CAHOKIA RV PARQUE—Continued on next page

CAHOKIA—Continued
CAHOKIA RV PARQUE—Continued

Phone: (618)332-7700
Address: 4060 Mississippi Ave (Rt 3), Cahokia, IL 62206
Lat/Lon: 38.57366/-90.18671
Email: cahokiarv@cahokiarv.com
Web: www.cahokiarv.com

SEE AD THIS PAGE

SAWMILL BBQ—*From jct I-255 (exit 13) & Hwy 157: Go 2 mi W on Hwy 157, then 500 ft on Hwy 31. Enter on R.* Rated #2 BBQ restaurant in the St. Louis area. Located next to Cahokia RV Parque. Open all yr. MC/VISA/Debit.

Phone: (618)332-3000
Address: 4060 Mississippi Ave (Rt 3), Cahokia, IL 62206
Lat/Lon: 38.57366/-90.18671

SEE AD THIS PAGE

CAMBRIDGE—B-2

(SE) THE OLD TIMBER RV PARK—(Henry) *From jct I-80 (exit 19) & Hwy 82: Go 10 mi S on Hwy 82, then 2 mi E on Hwy 81, then 3/4 mi N on County Rd 1600. Enter on R.*

◆◆FACILITIES: 157 sites, typical site width 30 ft, 117 W&E, (20/30/50 amps), 40 no hkups, some extd stay sites, 4 pull-thrus, WiFi Internet central location, family camping, tenting, RV storage, dump, non-guest dump $, portable dump, laundry, ltd groc, RV supplies, LP gas by weight, ice, picnic tables, fire rings, grills, wood.

◆◆◆◆RECREATION: rec room/area, pavilion, coin games, lake swim, boating, electric motors only, canoeing, dock, rowboat/canoe/2 pedal boat rentals, lake fishing, fishing supplies, golf nearby, bsktball, playground, activities, (wkends), horseshoes, sports field, v-ball. Rec open to public.

Pets welcome. Partial handicap access. Open Apr 15 - Oct 15. Clubs welcome. Rate in 2010 $20-25 for 2 persons. MC/VISA/DISC/AMEX/Debit. Member ARVC, ICA. CCUSA 50% Discount. CCUSA reservations Recommended, CCUSA max stay 2 days, CCUSA disc. not avail S, CCUSA disc. not avail F,Sa, CCUSA disc. not avail holidays.

Phone: (309)937-2314
Address: 10768 E 1600 St, Cambridge, IL 61238
Lat/Lon: 41.30652/-90.12476
Email: info@theoldtimber.com
Web: www.theoldtimber.com

SEE AD THIS PAGE

CANTON—C-2

(E) RICE LAKE (State Cons Area)—(Fulton) *From jct Hwy-78 & Hwy-9: Go 10 mi E on Hwy-9, then 3 mi SW on US-24.* FACILITIES: 34 sites, typical site width 12 ft, 35 ft max RV length, 34 E, (30/50 amps), tenting, dump. RECREATION: boating, canoeing, ramp, dock, lake fishing. Open all yr. Phone: (309)647-9184.

CARBONDALE—F-3

(E) CRAB ORCHARD CAMPGROUND—(Williamson) *From jct US 51 & Hwy 13: Go 4 mi E on Hwy 13 (over bridge), then 1/2 mi S on Campground Rd (at large marina). Enter on R.* FACILITIES: 55 sites, typical site width 24 ft, 35 W&E, (30 amps), 20 no hkups, tenting, dump, ltd groc. RECREATION: lake swim, boating, canoeing, ramp, dock, lake fishing. Pets welcome. Open Apr 1 - Oct 31. Phone: (618)985-4983.

(S) GIANT CITY STATE PARK—(Jackson) *From jct Hwy 13 & US 51: Go 8 mi S on US 51, then 3 mi E (Makanda).* FACILITIES: 99 sites, typical site width 12 ft, 85 W&E, (30 amps), 14 no hkups, 75 pull-thrus, tenting, dump. RECREATION: boating, 10 hp limit, canoeing, ramp, pond fishing, playground. Partial handicap access. Open all yr. Phone: (618)457-4836.

(SE) LITTLE GRASSY LAKE CAMPGROUND & MARINA—(Williamson) *From jct Hwy 51 & Hwy 13: Go 1-3/4 mi E on Hwy 13, then 6 mi S on Giant City Rd, then 1/2 mi E on Grassy Rd, then 1/2 mi S on Hidden Bay. Enter at end.* FACILITIES: 105 sites, typical site width 24 ft, 14 full hkups, 54 W&E, (30/50 amps), 37 no hkups, tenting, dump, ltd groc. RECREATION: lake swim, boating, 10 hp limit, canoeing, ramp, dock, lake fishing. Pets welcome. Open Apr 1 - Oct 31. Phone: (618)457-6655.

Reserve Online at Woodalls.com

CARLINVILLE—D-3

(SW) BEAVER DAM STATE PARK—(Macoupin) *From jct Hwy-4 & Hwy-108: Go 7 mi SW on blacktop road.* FACILITIES: 77 sites, typical site width 15 ft, 59 E, (30 amps), 18 no hkups, 5 pull-thrus, tenting, dump, ltd groc. RECREATION: boating, electric motors only, canoeing, ramp, dock, lake fishing, play equipment. Partial handicap access. Open all yr. Phone: (217)854-8020.

CARLOCK—C-3

(NW) KAMP KOMFORT—(McClean) *From jct I-55 & I-74: Go 7 mi NW on I-74 (exit 120), then 1/2 mi W on 2050 Rd N, then 1 mi N on N 600 E Rd. Enter on L.*

◆◆◆◆FACILITIES: 116 sites, typical site width 30 ft, 28 full hkups, 27 W&E, 11 E, (30/50 amps), 50 amps ($), 50 no hkups, 61 pull-thrus, WiFi Instant Internet at site, family camping, tenting, dump, ltd groc, RV supplies, picnic tables, patios, fire rings, wood.

◆◆◆RECREATION: pavilion, swim pool, golf nearby, bsktball, playground, horseshoes, sports field, v-ball.

Pets welcome. Open Apr 1 - Nov 1. Big rigs welcome. Clubs welcome. Rate in 2010 $24-28 per family. FMCA discount. CCUSA 50% Discount. CCUSA max stay Unlimited, Cash only for CCUSA disc., CCUSA disc. not avail S, CCUSA disc. not avail F,Sa, CCUSA disc. not avail holidays. Wi-Fi surcharge $2 per day.

Phone: (309)376-4411
Address: 21408 North 600 E Rd, Carlock, IL 61725
Lat/Lon: 40.59549/-89.15659

SEE AD THIS PAGE

CARLYLE—E-3

(N) DAM WEST RECREATION AREA (Lake Carlyle-COE)—(Clinton) *From jct US 50 & Hwy 127: Go 1/2 mi N on Hwy 127, then 1 mi E on William Rd.* FACILITIES: 113 sites, typical site width 20 ft, 26 full hkups, 87 E, (50 amps), 10 pull-thrus, tenting, dump, laundry. RECREATION: lake swim, boating, ramp, dock, lake fishing, playground. Partial handicap access. Open Apr 1 - Oct 31. Phone: (618)594-4410.

(NE) ELDON HAZLET STATE PARK—(Clinton) *From jct US-50 & Hwy-127: Go 2 mi N on Hwy-127.* FACILITIES: 364 sites, 328 E, (30/50 amps), 36 no hkups, tenting, dump, laundry, ltd groc. RECREATION: swim pool, boating, ramp, dock, lake/pond fishing, playground. Open all yr. Phone: (618)594-3015.

(NE) Hickory Shores Resort—(Clinton) *From jct I-70 (exit 45) & Hwy 127: Go 9 mi S on Hwy 127, then 4 mi E On Keyesport Rd, then 1-1/4 mi S on Emerald Dr. Enter on R.* ◆◆◆FACILITIES: 167 sites, typical site width 25 ft, 86 full hkups, 75 W&E, 6 E, (20/30/50 amps), 30 no hkups, 11 pull-thrus, WiFi Internet central location, family camping, tenting, RV storage, dump, non-guest dump $, laundry, ltd groc, RV supplies, LP gas by meter, ice, picnic tables, fire rings, wood.

◆◆◆◆RECREATION: rec hall, pavilion, 2 swim pools, boating, canoeing, kayaking, lake/pond fishing, mini-golf, bsktball, playground, shuffleboard court 2 shuffleboard courts, activities tennis, horseshoes, v-ball. Pets welcome. Partial handicap access. Open all yr. Rate in 2010 $20-29 for 4 persons. MC/VISA/DISC/AMEX/Debit. CCUSA 50% Discount. CCUSA reservations Not Accepted, CCUSA max stay Unlimited. Discount not available Memorial Day, 4th of July, Labor Day weekends.

Phone: (618)749-5288
Address: 21925 Dove Ln, Carlyle, IL 62231
Lat/Lon: 38.72143/-89.29391
Email: camping@hickoryshoresresort.com
Web: www.hickoryshoresresort.com

(E) MCNAIR CAMPGROUND (Lake Carlyle-Corp of Engineers)—(Clinton) *From jct Hwy-127 & US-50: Go 1 mi E on US-50.* FACILITIES: 25 sites, 25 W&E. RECREATION: lake swim, boating, ramp, lake fishing, playground. Open May 1 - Sep 30. Phone: (618)594-5253.

CARLYLE—Continued

(SE) SOUTH SHORE STATE PARK—(Clinton) *From jct Hwy 127 & US 50: Go 5 mi E on US 50.* FACILITIES: 33 sites, typical site width 12 ft, 33 no hkups, tenting, dump. RECREATION: boating, canoeing, ramp, lake fishing. Open all yr. Phone: (618)594-3015.

CARMI—E-4

(W) BURRELL PARK CAMPGROUND (City Park)—(White) *From jct Hwy 14 & Hwy 1: Go N on Third St, then 2 mi N on Stewart St.* FACILITIES: 35 sites, 25 full hkups, (50 amps), 10 no hkups, tenting, dump. RECREATION: lake/pond fishing, playground. Partial handicap access. Open Apr 15 - Oct 15. Phone: (618)382-2693.

CARTHAGE—C-1

(S) Circle G Campground—(Hancock) *From Jct Hwy 136 and Hwy 94: Go 11 mi S on Hwy 336. Enter on R.* ◆FACILITIES: 80 sites, typical site width 30 ft, 80 W&E, (20/30/50 amps), 60 pull-thrus, family camping, tenting, dump, laundry, ltd groc. ◆◆◆RECREATION: swim pool, boating, canoeing, lake/stream fishing, play equipment. Pets welcome. Open Apr 1 - Oct 31. Rate in 2010 $25 for 4 persons. Member ARVC, ICA. Phone: (217)743-9933.

CASEY—D-4

(N) Casey KOA Kampground & RV Service—(Clark) *From jct I-70 (exit 129) & Hwy-49: Go 1/4 mi N on Hwy-49, then 1/4 mi W on 1250 Rd. Enter on L.* ◆◆◆◆FACILITIES: 78 sites, typical site width 30 ft, 21 full hkups, 57 W&E, (30/50 amps), 50 amps ($), 47 pull-thrus, tenting, dump, laundry, ltd groc. ◆◆◆◆RECREATION: swim pool, boating, no motors, lake fishing, playground. Pets welcome, breed restrict. Open Mar 1 - Oct 31. Rate in 2010 $32.77-41.25 for 2 persons. Phone: (800)562-9113. KOA discount.

CAVE IN ROCK—F-4

(S) CAVE-IN-ROCK STATE PARK—(Hardin) *From jct Hwy-146 & Hwy-1: Go 2 mi S on Hwy-1.* FACILITIES: 59 sites, typical site width 15 ft, 34 E, (30 amps), 25 no hkups, tenting, dump, ltd groc. RECREATION: river swim, boating, ramp, dock, river/pond fishing, playground. Partial handicap access. Open all yr. Phone: (618)289-4325.

(W) SHAWNEE NATIONAL FOREST (Tower Rock Campground)—(Hardin) *From jct Hwy-1 & Hwy-146: Go 4 mi W on Hwy-146, then 1 mi S on FR-101.* FACILITIES: 25 sites, typical site width 16 ft, 25 no hkups, 1 pull-thrus, tenting. RECREATION: boating, ramp, river fishing, playground. Open May 1 - Dec 15. Phone: (618)253-7114.

CHAMPAIGN—C-4

(N) D & W Lake Camping and RV Park—(Champaign) *From jct I-74 & I-57: Go 3 mi N on I-57 (exit 240), then 1/2 mi W on Market St, then 1/4 mi S on Hensley Rd. Enter on L.* ◆◆◆FACILITIES: 45 sites, typical site width 28 ft, 34 full hkups, 6 W&E, (30/50 amps), 5 no hkups, 34 pull-thrus, tenting, dump, laundry, ltd groc. ◆◆RECREATION: lake fishing, play equipment. Pets welcome. Open all yr. Big rigs welcome. Rate in 2010 $20-25 per family. Member ARVC. Phone: (217)356-3732.

CHANNAHON—B-4

(W) CHANNAHON STATE PARK—(Will) *From jct I-55 & US 6: Go 3 mi W on US 6, then 4 blocks S on Canal St.* FACILITIES: 25 sites, 25 no hkups, tenting. RECREATION: canoeing, river fishing, playground. Open all yr. Phone: (815)467-4271.

CHARLESTON—D-4

(S) FOX RIDGE STATE PARK—(Coles) *From jct Hwy-16 & Hwy-130: Go 8 mi S on Hwy-130.* FACILITIES: 43 sites, typical site width 12 ft, 35 ft max RV length, 43 E, tenting, dump, ltd groc. RECREATION: canoeing, lake/river fishing, playground. Partial handicap access. Open all yr. Phone: (217)345-6416.

CHESTER—E-3

(N) RANDOLPH COUNTY STATE FISH & WILDLIFE AREA—(Randolph) *From jct Hwy 3 & Hwy 150: Go 6 mi NE on Hwy 150 to CR DD.* FACILITIES: 95 sites, typical site width 12 ft, 95 no hkups, 40 pull-thrus, tenting, dump. RECREATION: boating, 10 hp limit, canoeing, ramp, dock, lake fishing, playground. Partial handicap access. Open all yr. Phone: (618)826-2706.

Illinois State Nicknames: Land of Lincoln, The Prairie State

CHICAGO—A-5

CHICAGO AREA MAP

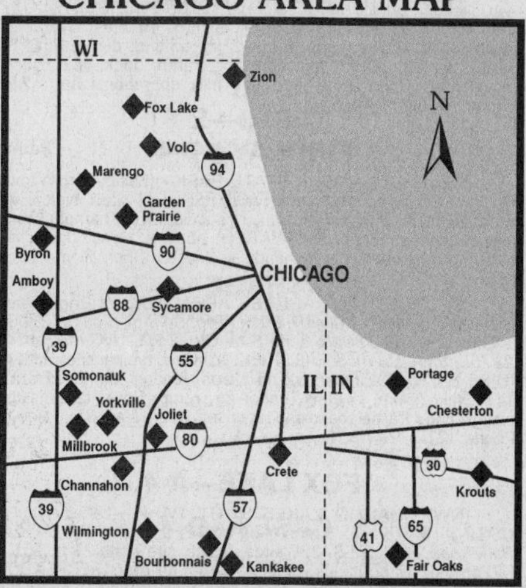

Symbols on map indicate towns within a 50 mi radius of Chicago where campgrounds (diamonds), attractions (flags), & RV service centers & camping supply outlets (gears) are listed. Check listings for more information.

Tell Them Woodall's Sent You!

CISNE—E-4

(W) SAM DALE LAKE (State Cons Area)—(Wayne) *From town: Go 9 mi W on Hwy-161.* FACILITIES: 93 sites, typical site width 10 ft, 68 E, (20/50 amps), 25 no hkups, tenting, dump. RECREATION: lake swim, boating, 10 hp limit, canoeing, ramp, dock, lake fishing, playground. Partial handicap access. Open all yr. Phone: (618)835-2292.

CLINTON—C-3

(SE) WELDON SPRINGS STATE PARK—(De Witt) *From town: Go 2 mi S on US-51, then follow sign 2 mi E.* FACILITIES: 75 sites, typical site width 12 ft, 75 E, (30 amps), tenting, dump, ltd groc. RECREATION: boating, electric motors only, canoeing, ramp, dock, pond/stream fishing, playground. Partial handicap access. Open all yr. Facilities fully operational Mar - Oct. Phone: (217)935-2644.

COLCHESTER—C-2

(NW) ARGYLE LAKE STATE PARK—(McDonough) *From jct Hwy-136 & Hwy-67: Go 8 mi NW off Hwy-136.* FACILITIES: 159 sites, typical site width 12 ft, 35 ft max RV length, 86 full hkups, 24 W&E, 18 E, (30 amps), 31 no hkups, tenting, dump. RECREATION: boating, 10 hp limit, canoeing, ramp, dock, lake fishing, playground. Open all yr. Phone: (309)776-3422.

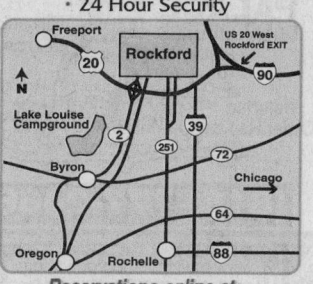

CRETE—B-5

(SE) Emerald Trails Campground—(Will) *From jct I-80 & Hwy 394: Go 10 mi S on Hwy 394, then 2 mi E on Exchange Ave, then 3 mi S on Klemme Rd, then 1/4 mi E on Goodenow Rd. Enter on L.* ◇◇◇FACILITIES: 105 sites, typical site width 20 ft, 75 full hkups, 30 W&E, (30/50 amps), 50 amps ($), 10 pull-thrus, tenting, dump, laundry, ltd groc. ◇◇◇RECREATION: boating, lake fishing. Pets welcome. Open Apr 15 - Oct 15. Rate in 2010 $30-35 per family. Member ICA. Phone: (800)870-8357.

DANVILLE—C-5

(W) KICKAPOO STATE PARK—(Vermilion) *From jct Hwy-150 & I-74: Go 4 mi W on Hwy-150, then 2 mi N, then 1/2 mi E.* FACILITIES: 184 sites, typical site width 12 ft, 35 ft max RV length, 90 E, (20 amps), 94 no hkups, 7 pull-thrus, tenting, dump, ltd groc. RECREATION: boating, electric motors only, canoeing, ramp, dock, river fishing, playground. Partial handicap access. Open all yr. Phone: (217)442-4915.

DE PUE—B-3

(S) LAKE DE PUE CITY PARK—(Bureau) *From center of town: Go 2 blocks S on Lake St.* FACILITIES: 25 sites, 6 E, 19 no hkups, tenting. RECREATION: lake fishing, playground. Open Apr 15 - Oct 31. Facilities fully operational May 1 - Oct 31. Phone: (815)447-2177.

DE WITT—C-4

(S) CLINTON LAKE-MASCOUTIN STATE RECREATION COMPLEX—(De Witt) *From jct Hwy-54 & CR-14: Go 2 mi S on CR-14.* FACILITIES: 308 sites, 17 full hkups, 286 E, 5 no hkups, dump, ltd groc. RECREATION: lake swim, boating, canoeing, ramp, dock, lake fishing, playground. Partial handicap access. Open all yr. Facilities fully operational Apr - Oct. Phone: (217)935-8722.

DU QUOIN—E-3

(S) DU QUOIN STATE FAIR CAMPGROUND—(Perry) *From jct Hwy-152 & US-51: Go 2-1/4 mi S on US-51.* FACILITIES: 300 sites, 300 W&E, (30 amps), tenting, dump. RECREATION: lake fishing. Open all yr. Phone: (618)542-9373.

DURAND—A-3

(W) Sugar Shores RV Resort—(Winnebago) *From jct I-90 (Rockton Rd exit) & CR 9: Go 12 mi W on Rockton Rd, then 1-1/2 mi W on Shirland Rd, then 1 mi W on Winslow Rd. Enter on L.* ◇◇◇◇FACILITIES: 90 sites, 90 full hkups, (20/30/50 amps), 4 pull-thrus, family camping, dump, laundry, ltd groc. ◇◇◇◇REC-

DURAND—Continued
Sugar Shores RV Resort—Continued

REATION: swim pool, river swim, boating, river/pond fishing, playground. Pets welcome. Partial handicap access. No tents. Open Apr 15 - Oct 15. Rate in 2010 $32 for 4 persons. Member ARVC, ICA. Phone: (815)629-2568.

EAST MOLINE—B-2

(NE) Lundeen's Landing—(Rock Island) *From jct I-80 (exit 4A) & Hwy 5: Go 1/2 mi W on Hwy 5, then 3 mi E & S on 193 St N, then 1 mi E on Barstow Rd. CALL FOR ALTERNATE ROUTE TO AVOID 12' 2" CLEARANCE. Enter on R.* ◇◇◇FACILITIES: 60 sites, typical site width 30 ft, 60 W&E, (30/50 amps), 21 pull-thrus, family camping, tenting, dump, ltd groc. ◇◇RECREATION: boating, canoeing, ramp, dock, river fishing, play equipment. Pets welcome. Open Apr 1 - Oct 31. Rate in 2010 $20 per family. Member ARVC, ICA. Phone: (309) 781-9766.

EAST PEORIA—C-3

MILLPOINT PARK—(Woodford) *From jct I-74 (exit 95) & Hwy 116: Go 5 mi N on Hwy 116, then 3-1/2 mi N on Hwy 26, then 3/4 mi W on Millpoint Rd. Enter at end.*

WELCOME

◇◇◇FACILITIES: 80 sites, accepts full hkup units only, 80 full hkups, (30/50 amps), 5 pull-thrus, family camping, wood.

◇◇◇RECREATION: river swim, boating, river fishing, hiking trails.

CAMPCLUB USA

Pets welcome. No tents. Open Mar 1 - Nov 30. No restrooms. Rate in 2010 $23 for 2 persons. MC/VISA/DISC/AMEX/Debit. Member ICA. CCUSA 50% Discount. CCUSA reservations Accepted, CCUSA max stay Unlimited.

Phone: (309)231-6497
Address: 310 Ash Lane, East Peoria, IL 61611
Lat/Lon: 40.78089/-89.53795
Email: millpointpark@mchsi.com

SEE AD NEXT PAGE

Abraham Lincoln lived and studied in Springfield, where his house can be seen.

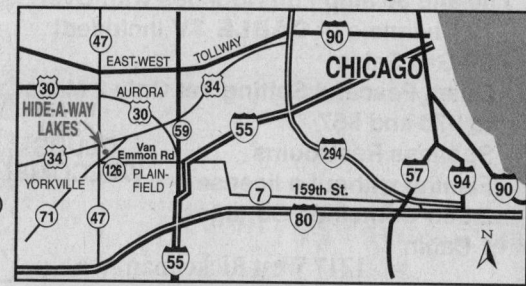

EAST ST. LOUIS—E-2

(W) **Casino Queen RV Park**—(Saint Clair) *From jct I-55/70/40 & US 3/64 (exit 2A): Go 1/2 mi SW on Third St., then 3/4 mi W on River Park Dr., then 3/4 mi S on Front St. Enter on L.* ◇◇◇◇FACILITIES: 132 sites, typical site width 30 ft, 132 full hkups, (30/50 amps), 132 pull-thrus, dump, laundry, ltd groc. ◇◇RECREATION: swim pool, playground. Pets welcome. Partial handicap access. No tents. Open all yr. Big rigs welcome. Rate in 2010 $25.25-36.25 per vehicle. Member ARVC, ICA. Phone: (800)777-0777. FMCA discount.

EDWARDSVILLE—E-3

(E) **Red Barn Rendezvous RV Park**—(Madison) *From I-55 (exit 23) & Hwy 143: Go 1/4 mi W on Hwy 143,then 3/4 mi NE on W Frontage Road. (Blackburn Rd). Enter on L.* ◇◇◇◇FACILITIES: 30 sites, typical site width 30 ft, 30 full hkups, (20/30/50 amps), 23 pull-thrus, family camping, dump, laundry. Pets welcome. Partial handicap access. No tents. Open Apr 1 - Oct 31. Big rigs welcome. Rate in 2010 $28-30 per vehicle. Member ARVC, ICA. Phone: (618)692-9015.

EFFINGHAM—D-4

(N) **CAMP LAKEWOOD**—(Effingham) *From jct I-70/I-57 (exit 160) & Hwy 32/33: Go 1/2 mi N on Hwy 32/33, then 1/2 mi E on Ford Ave, then 1/2 mi N on Raney St, then 1/4 mi W on Rickelman Ave. Enter at end.*

WELCOME

◇◇◇◇FACILITIES: 62 sites, typical site width 25 ft, 55 full hkups, 4 W&E, 3 E, (30/50 amps), 44 pull-thrus, cable TV, WiFi Instant Internet at site, WiFi Internet central location, family camping, tenting, cabins, dump, non-guest dump $, laundry, ltd groc, RV supplies, LP gas by weight, ice, picnic tables, fire rings, grills, wood.

◇◇◇◇RECREATION: rec room/area, coin games, boating, ramp, rowboat/canoe rentals, lake fishing, fishing supplies, golf nearby, playground, horseshoes.

Pets welcome. Partial handicap access. Open Mar - Dec 29. Big rigs welcome. Escort to site. Clubs welcome. Rate in 2010 $25-30 for 2 persons. MC/VISA/DISC/Debit. Member ARVC, ICA. FMCA discount.

EFFINGHAM—Continued
CAMP LAKEWOOD—Continued

Phone: (217)342-6233
Address: 1217 W Rickelman Ave, Effingham, IL 62401
Lat/Lon: 39.14715/-88.56680
Email: camp@camplakewoodcampground.com
Web: www.camplakewoodcampground.com

SEE AD THIS PAGE

EL PASO—B-3

(W) **HICKORY HILL CAMPGROUND**—(Woodford) *From jct I-39 (exit 14) & US 24: Go 4 mi W on US 24, then 1/4 mi S on 2250 E. Enter on R.*

WELCOME

◇◇◇FACILITIES: 289 sites, typical site width 25 ft, 194 full hkups, 70 W&E, (20/30/50 amps), 25 no hkups, many extd stay sites, 29 pull-thrus, family camping, tenting, dump, non-guest dump $, laundry, ltd groc, RV supplies, LP gas by weight, ice, picnic tables, fire rings, wood.

◇◇◇◇RECREATION: rec hall, coin games, swim pool, no motors, canoeing, kayaking, stream fishing, mini-golf, golf nearby, bsktball, play equipment, shuffleboard court, activities (wkends), horseshoes, sports field, hiking trails, v-ball. Rec open to public.

Pets welcome. Open all yr. Facilities fully operational Apr 1 - Nov 1. Big rigs welcome. Clubs welcome. Rate in 2010 $20-31 per family. MC/VISA. Member ARVC, ICA.

Phone: (309)744-2407
Address: 973 CR 2250 E, Secor, IL 61771
Lat/Lon: 40.73177/-89.11124
Email: hickoryh@route24.net

SEE AD THIS PAGE

The world's first skyscraper was built in Chicago, 1885.

EQUALITY—F-4

(S) SALINE COUNTY STATE CONSERVATION AREA—(Gallatin) *From jct Hwy-13 & Hwy-142: Go 1 mi SE on Hwy-142, then 4 mi S on blacktop road.* FACILITIES: 45 sites, typical site width 12 ft, 45 no hkups, 8 pull-thrus, tenting, dump. RECREATION: boating, 10 hp limit, canoeing, ramp, dock, lake fishing, playground. Open all yr. Facilities fully operational Apr - Sep. Phone: (618)276-4405.

FINDLAY—D-4

(SE) EAGLE CREEK STATE PARK—(Shelby) *From town: Go 3 mi SE on county roads.* FACILITIES: 174 sites, typical site width 12 ft, 35 ft max RV length, 148 W&E, (30/50 amps), 26 no hkups, tenting, dump. RECREATION: boating, ramp, dock, lake fishing, playground. Partial handicap access. Open all yr. Phone: (217)756-8260.

(S) LONE POINT ACCESS AREA (Corp of Engineers - Lake Shelbyville)—(Shelby) *From town: Go 3 mi S on CR 2100E, 1/2 mi E on CR 1800N, 1 mi S on CR 2150E, 1/3 mi E on CR 2175E, then 2/3 mi S.* FACILITIES: 95 sites, typical site width 45 ft, 63 E, (20/30 amps), 32 no hkups, tenting, dump. RECREATION: lake swim, boating, canoeing, ramp, dock, lake fishing, playground. Partial handicap access. Open May 21 - Sep 8. Phone: (217)774-3951.

FOX LAKE—A-4

(NW) CHAIN O' LAKES STATE PARK—(Lake) *From jct US-12 & Hwy-59: Go 3 mi NW on US-12, then 2 mi NE on State Park Road.* FACILITIES: 238 sites, typical site width 25 ft, 151 E, (30 amps), 87 no hkups, tenting, dump, ltd groc. RECREATION: boating, canoeing, ramp, dock, lake/river fishing, playground. Partial handicap access. Age restrict may apply. Open Jan - Oct. Phone: (847)587-5512.

GALENA—A-2

(NW) **PALACE CAMPGROUND**—(Jo Daviess) *From N jct Hwy 84 & Hwy 20: Go 2 mi E on Hwy 20. Enter on L.*

WELCOME

◇◇◇◇FACILITIES: 182 sites, typical site width 28 ft, 50 full hkups, 50 W&E, 32 E, (15/30/50 amps), 50 no hkups, some extd stay sites, 8 pull-thrus, WiFi Internet central location, family camping, tenting, cabins, RV storage, dump, non-guest dump $, laundry, ice, picnic tables, fire rings, wood, controlled access.

◇◇◇◇RECREATION: rec room/area, coin games, swim pool, wading pool, mini-golf, ($), bsktball, playground, activities, (wkends), horseshoes, sports field. Rec open to public.

Pets welcome. Age restrict may apply. Open Apr 1 - Nov 1. Big rigs welcome. Clubs welcome. Rate in 2010 $27-31 for 4 persons.

Phone: (815)777-2466
Address: 11357 Highway 20 W, Galena, IL 61036
Lat/Lon: 42.43490/-90.44917
Web: www.palacecampground.com

SEE AD THIS PAGE

The highest point in Illinois is Charles Mound at 1,235 feet above sea level.

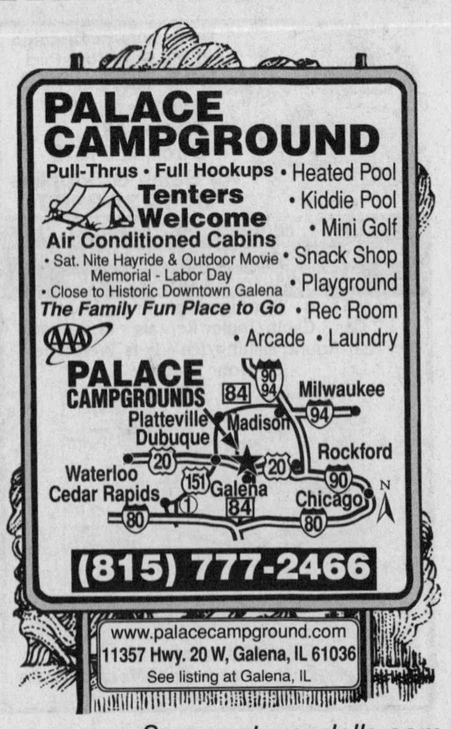

GALESBURG—B-2

(E) GALESBURG EAST BEST HOLIDAY TRAV-L-PARK—(Knox) *From jct I-74 & Hwy-150 (Exit 54): Go 1 mi E on Hwy-150. Enter on L.*

WELCOME

◆◆◆◆FACILITIES: 68 sites, typical site width 30 ft, 58 full hkups, (20/30/50 amps), 50 amps ($), 10 no hkups, 48 pull-thrus, WiFi Instant Internet at site, phone Internet central location, family camping, tenting, cabins, RV storage, dump, non-guest dump $, laundry, ltd groc, RV supplies, LP gas by meter, ice, picnic tables, fire rings, wood.

◆◆◆RECREATION: rec hall, rec room/area, coin games, swim pool, pond fishing, golf nearby, playground, horseshoes, sports field, hiking trails.

Pets welcome. Open Apr 1 - Oct 31. Big rigs welcome. Escort to site. Clubs welcome. Rate in 2010 $28-33 for 2 persons. MC/VISA. Member ARVC, ICA. FCRV discount. FMCA discount.

Phone: (309)289-2267
Address: 1081 US Hwy 150E, Knoxville, IL 61448-9405
Lat/Lon: 40.90820/-90.23588
Email: galesburgcamp@galesburg.net
Web: www.galesburgeastrvpark.com

SEE AD THIS PAGE

GARDEN PRAIRIE—A-4

(W) Holiday Acres Camping Resort—(Boone) *From jct Hwy 23 & I-90: Go 6 mi NW on I-90, then 1/2 mi N on Belvidere-Genoa Rd, then 3 mi E on Hwy 20, then 1/4 mi N on Epworth Rd. Enter on L.* ◆◆◆FACILITIES: 610 sites, typical site width 50 ft, 10 full hkups, 500 W&E, (20/30/50 amps), 100 no hkups, 14 pull-thrus, family camping, tenting, dump, laundry, ltd groc. ◆◆◆◆◆RECREATION: swim pool, boating, canoeing, river fishing, playground. Pets welcome. Partial handicap access. Open all yr. Facilities fully operational Apr 15 - Oct 15. Big rigs welcome. Rate in 2010 $40 per family. Member ARVC. Phone: (815)547-7846.

GENESEO—B-2

(N) GENESEO CAMPGROUND—(Henry) *From jct I-80 (exit 19) & Hwy 82: Go 4 mi N on Hwy 82. Follow blue camping signs. Enter on R.*

WELCOME

◆◆◆◆FACILITIES: 74 sites, typical site width 24 ft, 40 full hkups, 23 W&E, 11 E, (20/30/50 amps), 59 pull-thrus, WiFi Instant Internet at site, family camping, tenting, cabins, dump, non-guest dump $, laundry, ltd groc, RV supplies, LP gas by weight/by meter, ice, picnic tables, patios, fire rings, grills, wood.

◆◆◆RECREATION: rec hall, rec room/area, boating, 10 hp limit, canoeing, kayaking, ramp, 2 canoe/6 kayak rentals, stream fishing, fishing supplies, golf nearby, playground, horseshoes, sports field, hiking trails, v-ball.

Pets welcome. Open Apr 1 - Oct 31. Big rigs welcome. Clubs welcome. Rate in 2010 $22-27 per family. MC/VISA/DISC/Debit. Member ARVC, ICA.

Phone: (309)944-6465
Address: 22978 Illinois Hwy 82, Geneseo, IL 61254-8319
Lat/Lon: 41.48358/-90.15704
Email: w6465@geneseo.net
Web: www.campingfriend.com/geneseocampground

SEE AD THIS PAGE

GIBSON CITY—C-4

SOUTH PARK MUNICIPAL CAMPGROUND—(Ford) *From jct IL47/54/9: Go E one block. Enter on L.*

WELCOME

FACILITIES: 9 sites, typical site width 24 ft, 40 ft max RV length, 9 W&E, (20/50 amps), 1 pull-thrus, family camping, tenting, dump, picnic tables, fire rings, grills.

RECREATION: pavilion, golf nearby, bsktball, playground. Rec open to public.

Pets welcome ($). Partial handicap access. Open all yr. Facilities fully operational Apr 1 - Oct 31. Clubs welcome.

Phone: (217)784-5872
Address: E 1st St, Gibson City, IL 60936
Lat/Lon: 40.45788/-88.37265
Email: mayor@gibsoncityillinois.com
Web: www.gibsoncityillinois.com

SEE AD THIS PAGE

GOLCONDA—F-4

(W) DIXON SPRINGS STATE PARK—(Pope) *From jct Hwy-145 & Hwy-146: Go 2 mi E on Hwy-146.* FACILITIES: 49 sites, typical site width 15 ft, 35 ft max RV length, 39 E, (30/50 amps), 10 no hkups, 2 pull-thrus, tenting, dump. RECREATION: swim pool, playground. Open all yr. Phone: (618)949-3394.

GOODFIELD—C-3

(NE) Yogi Bear Jellystone/Goodfield—(Woodford) *From jct I-74 (exit 112) & Hwy 117: Go 1 mi N on Hwy 117, then 3/4 mi E on Timberline Rd. Enter at end.* ◆◆◆◆FACILITIES: 330 sites, typical site width 30 ft, 187 full hkups, 119 W&E, (30/50 amps), 24 no hkups, 16 pull-thrus, family camping, tenting, dump, laundry, groceries. ◆◆◆◆◆RECREATION: swim pool, dock, lake fishing, playground. Pets welcome. Open all yr. Big rigs welcome. Rate in 2010 $28-43 per family. Member ARVC, ICA. Phone: (309)965-2224.

GOREVILLE—F-3

(S) FERNE CLYFFE STATE PARK—(Johnson) *From town: Go 1/4 mi S on Hwy 37.* FACILITIES: 109 sites, typical site width 50 ft, 56 E, (30 amps), 53 no hkups, tenting, dump. RECREATION: lake fishing, playground. Partial handicap access. Open all yr. Phone: (618)995-2411.

(W) Hilltop Campgrounds—(Johnson) *From jct I-24 & I-57: Go 4 mi S on I-57 (exit 40), then 150 feet E on Goreville Rd, then 1/8 mi S on Baker Lane. Enter on L.* ◆◆FACILITIES: 52 sites, typical site width 55 ft, 34 full hkups, (20/30/50 amps), 18 no hkups, 14 pull-thrus, tenting. ◆RECREATION: play equipment. Pets welcome. Partial handicap access. Open all yr. Big rigs welcome. Rate in 2010 $17-20 for 2 persons. Phone: (618)995-2189.

GRAFTON—D-2

(W) PERE MARQUETTE STATE PARK—(Jersey) *From jct Hwy-100 & US-67: Go 25 mi W on Hwy-100.* FACILITIES: 80 sites, 80 E, (30/50 amps), tenting, dump. RECREATION: boating, ramp, dock, river fishing, playground. Partial handicap access. Open all yr. Phone: (618)786-3323.

GRANITE CITY—E-2

(S) HORSESHOE LAKE STATE PARK—(Madison) *From jct I-270 & Hwy 111: Go 4 mi S on Hwy 111.* FACILITIES: 48 sites, 48 no hkups, tenting, dump, ltd groc. RECREATION: boating, 25 hp limit, canoeing, ramp, lake fishing, playground. Open May 1 - Oct 31. Phone: (618)931-0270.

(N) KOA-St. Louis Area—(Madison) *From jct I-270 (exit 3A) & Hwy 3: Go 1/4 mi S on Hwy 3, then 1/2 mi E on Chain of Rocks Rd, then 1/4 mi S on Dial Dr. Enter on R.* ◆◆◆FACILITIES: 70 sites, typical site width 35 ft, 70 full hkups, (20/30/50 amps), 50 amps ($), 70 pull-thrus, family camping, tenting, laundry, ltd groc. ◆◆◆RECREATION: swim pool, play equipment. Pets welcome. Open Mar 15 - Nov 1. Big rigs welcome. Rate in 2010 $35-44 for 2 persons. Phone: (800)KOA-5861. KOA discount.

(N) MGM Campground—(Madison) *From jct I-270 (exit 3A) & Hwy 3: Go 1/4 mi S on Hwy 3, then 3/4 mi E on Chain of Rocks Rd. Enter on R.* ◆◆FACILITIES: 30 sites, 26 full hkups, 4 W&E, (30/50 amps), tenting, dump, laundry. ◆RECREATION: lake fishing, playground. Pets welcome. Open all yr. Rate in 2010 $20-24 for 4 persons. Phone: (618)797-2820.

HAMPTON—B-2

(S) FISHERMENS CORNER REC. AREA (COE-Thomson Park)—(Rock Island) *From jct I-80 & Hwy 84: Go 1-1/2 mi S on Hwy 84.* FACILITIES: 56 sites, typical site width 12 ft, 32 ft max RV length, 51 E, (30 amps), 5 no hkups, tenting, dump. RECREATION: boating, canoeing, river fishing, playground. Partial handicap access. Open Apr 9 - Oct 24. Phone: (800)645-0248.

HANOVER—A-2

(W) BLANDING LANDING (COE - Lock & Dam 11)—(Jo Daviess) *From Hwy-84 in town: Go 7 mi W on Blanding Rd, follow signs.* FACILITIES: 37 sites, 30 E, (50 amps), 7 no hkups, dump. RECREATION: boating, canoeing, ramp, river fishing, playground. Partial handicap access. Open May 14 - Oct 23. Phone: (563)582-0881.

HAVANA—C-2

(S) ANDERSON LAKE STATE CONSERVATION AREA —(Mason) *From jct US 136 & Hwy 100: Go 9 mi S on Hwy 100.* FACILITIES: 100 sites, typical site width 15 ft, 35 ft max RV length, 100 no hkups, tenting, dump. RECREATION: boating, canoeing, ramp, dock, river fishing. Open all yr. Phone: (309)759-4484.

HERRIN—F-3

(N) Four Seasons Campground—(Williamson) *From jct Hwy 13 & Hwy 148: Go 6 mi N on Hwy 148, then 1-1/2 mi E on Carroll. Enter on L.* ◆◆◆◆FACILITIES: 33 sites, typical site width 45 ft, 30 full hkups, 3 W&E, (30/50 amps), 50 amps ($), 12 pull-thrus, WiFi Instant Internet at site, dump, non-guest dump $, laundry, LP gas by weight/by meter, picnic tables, fire rings. ◆RECREATION: pond fishing. Pets welcome. Partial handicap access. No tents. Open all yr. Big rigs welcome. CCUSA 50% Discount.

CAMPCLUB USA

Phone: (618)942-2069
Address: 721 E Carroll, Herrin, IL 62948
Lat/Lon: 37.81921/-89.01628
Email: 11k63@verizon.net
Web: www.rvparkfourseasons.com

ILLINOIS CITY—B-2

(W) BLANCHARD ISLAND (COE-Mississippi River Rec Areas-Muscatine Area)—(Rock Island) *From town: Go 6 mi W on Hwy 92/New Boston Rd, follow signs.* FACILITIES: 34 sites, 34 no hkups, dump. RECREATION: boating, canoeing, ramp, river fishing. Open May 14 - Oct 22. Phone: (563)263-7913.

JACKSONVILLE—D-2

(NE) Crazy Horse Campground—(Morgan) *From jct I-72 (exit 64) & US 67: Go 4 mi E on I-72 (exit 68): Go 3/4 mi W on E Morton Rd: Go 4-1/4 mi N on Mobile Rd, then 100 yds W on Hacker, then 3-1/4 mi N on Spaulding (name changes to Crazy Horse Rd). Enter on L.* ◆◆◆◆FACILITIES: 119 sites, typical site width 50 ft, 101 full hkups, (20/30/50 amps), 18 no hkups, 13 pull-thrus, family camping, tenting, dump, laundry, ltd groc. ◆◆◆RECREATION: lake swim, canoeing, pond/stream fishing, playground. Pets welcome. Partial handicap access. Open Apr 1 - Oct 31. Big rigs welcome. Rate in 2010 $34 for 6 persons. Member ARVC. Phone: (217)886-2089.

JOHNSTON CITY—F-4

(E) ARROWHEAD LAKE CAMPGROUND (City Park)—(Williamson) *From jct I-57 (exit 59) & CR 2E/Broadway: Go 2 mi E on CR 2. Follow signs.* FACILITIES: 53 sites, typical site width 40 ft, 53 W&E, (20/30 amps), 2 pull-thrus, tenting, dump, laundry, ltd groc. RECREATION: lake swim, boating, electric motors only, canoeing, lake fishing. Pets welcome. Partial handicap access. Open all yr. Facilities fully operational Feb - Nov. Phone: (618)983-3535.

JOLIET—B-4

(W) Leisure Lake Membership Resort—(Will) *From jct I-55 & Hwy 52 (exit 253): Go 1/2 mi W on Hwy 52, then 1 mi S on Hwy 59, then 2 mi W on Frontage Rd. Enter on R.* ◇◇◇◇FACILITIES: 231 sites, typical site width 30 ft, 162 full hkups, 69 W&E, (30/50 amps), 50 amps ($), 24 pull-thrus, WiFi Internet central location, family camping, RV storage, dump, non-guest dump $, laundry, LP gas by weight/by meter, ice, picnic tables, patios, fire rings, wood. ◇◇◇◇RECREATION: rec hall, equipped pavilion, swim pool, lake swim, boating, electric motors only, dock, lake fishing, fishing supplies, mini-golf, bsktball, playground, shuffleboard court shuffleboard court, activities tennis, horseshoes, hiking trails, v-ball. Pets welcome. No tents. Open all yr. Facilities fully operational Mar 1 - Nov 30. Big rigs welcome. Member ARVC, ICA. CCUSA 50% Discount. CCUSA reservations Recommended, CCUSA max stay Unlimited, Cash only for CCUSA disc., CCUSA disc. not avail holidays. No dirt bikes or fireworks.

Phone: (815)741-9405
Address: 21900 SW Frontage Rd, Joliet, IL 60404
Lat/Lon: 41.48457/-88.20167
Email: info@leisurelakeresort.com
Web: www.leisurelakeresort.com

(E) Martin Campground—(Will) *From Hwy 52 & I-55 (exit 253): Go 2 mi S on I-55, then 8 mi E on I-80 (exit 134), then 1 block S on Briggs St, then 1 mi E on New Lenox Rd. Enter on L.* ◇◇FACILITIES: 110 sites, typical site width 23 ft, 40 full hkups, 52 W&E, (30/50 amps), 50 amps ($), 18 no hkups, 47 pull-thrus, family camping, tenting, dump. Pets welcome. Open Mar 15 - Nov 1. Big rigs welcome. Rate in 2010 $28-32 for 2 persons. Phone: (815)726-3173.

(S) Oasis RV Park—(Will) *From Hwy 52 & I-55 (exit 253): Go 2 mi S on I-55, then 1 mi E on I-80 (exit 127), then 3/4 mi S on Empress Rd, then 1/2 mi E on Hwy 6. Enter on R.* ◇◇◇◇FACILITIES: 80 sites, typical site width 40 ft, 1 full hkups, 79 W&E, (30/50 amps), 17 pull-thrus, dump, laundry. Pets welcome. Partial handicap access. No tents. Open all yr. Facilities fully operational Apr 16 - Oct 15. Big rigs welcome. Rate in 2010 $24-30 per vehicle. Phone: (815)744-9400.

JOSLIN—B-2

(E) Sunset Lakes Resort—(Rock Island) *From jct I-88 (exit 6) & Hwy 92 : Go 1 mi E on Hwy 92, then 1/2 mi S on 290th St. Enter on L.* ◇◇◇◇◇FACILITIES: 275 sites, typical site width 30 ft, 175 full hkups, 100 W&E, (20/30/50 amps), 31 pull-thrus, WiFi Instant Internet at site, family camping, tenting, RV storage, dump, laundry, ltd groc, ice, picnic tables, patios, fire rings, grills, wood. ◇◇◇◇◇RECREATION: rec hall, pavilion, swim pool, boating, electric motors only, canoeing, ramp, lake/river fishing, mini-golf, ($), bsktball, playground, shuffleboard court shuffleboard court, activities, tennis, horseshoes, hiking trails, v-ball. Pets welcome. Partial handicap access. Open Apr 15 - Oct 15. Big rigs welcome. MC/VISA/DISC/AMEX/Debit. Member ARVC, ICA. CCUSA 50% Discount. CCUSA reservations Recommended, CCUSA max stay 7 days, CCUSA disc. not avail S, CCUSA disc. not avail F,Sa.

Phone: (800)747-5253
Address: 2700-290th St N, Hillsdale, IL 61257
Lat/Lon: 41.54878/-90.21590
Email: info@sunsetlakesresort.com
Web: www.sunsetlakesresort.com

Reserve Online at Woodalls.com

KANKAKEE—B-4

(S) KOA-Kankakee South—(Kankakee) *From jct I-57 (exit 308) & US 45/52: Go 3 mi S on US 45/52, then 1/2 mi E on CR 6000. Enter on L.* ◇◇◇FACILITIES: 84 sites, typical site width 30 ft, 34 full hkups, 33

KANKAKEE—Continued
KOA-Kankakee South—Continued

W&E, (20/30 amps), 17 no hkups, 46 pull-thrus, family camping, tenting, dump, laundry, ltd groc. ◇◇◇RECREATION: swim pool, playground. Pets welcome, breed restrict. Open Apr 1 - Oct 31. Rate in 2010 $27-35 for 2 persons. Phone: (800)KOA-4192. KOA discount.

KARBERS RIDGE—F-4

(NE) SHAWNEE NATIONAL FOREST (Pine Ridge-Pounds Hollow Recreation Area)—(Gallatin) *From jct Hwy 1 & CR 13 (Karbers Ridge Blacktop): Go 2 mi W on CR 13.* FACILITIES: 35 sites, typical site width 10 ft, 35 no hkups, tenting. RECREATION: lake swim, boating, electric motors only, canoeing, lake fishing. Open Apr 1 - Dec 15. Phone: (618)253-7114.

KEWANEE—B-3

(E) FRANCIS PARK (City Park)—(Henry) *From jct Hwy 78/34 & Hwy 34: Go 3 mi E on Hwy 34, then 1/2 mi N on CR.* FACILITIES: 60 sites, typical site width 60 ft, 60 E, (20/30 amps), 20 pull-thrus, tenting, dump. RECREATION: playground. Open Apr 15 - Oct 15. Phone: (309)852-2611.

(N) JOHNSON SAUK TRAIL STATE PARK—(Henry) *From jct US-34 & Hwy-78: Go 7 mi N on Hwy-78.* FACILITIES: 95 sites, typical site width 12 ft, 35 ft max RV length, 70 E, (30 amps), 25 no hkups, tenting, dump, ltd groc. RECREATION: lake swim, boating, electric motors only, canoeing, ramp, dock, lake/pond fishing, playground. Partial handicap access. Open all yr. Phone: (309)853-5589.

LACON—B-3

(S) MARSHALL STATE FISH & WILDLIFE AREA—(Marshall) *From jct Hwy 17 & Hwy 26: Go 4 mi S on Hwy 26.* FACILITIES: 28 sites, typical site width 30 ft, 22 W&E, (20/30 amps), 6 no hkups, tenting, dump. RECREATION: boating, canoeing, ramp, dock, lake/river fishing. Open all yr. Phone: (309)246-8351.

LAWRENCEVILLE—E-5

(W) RED HILLS LAKE STATE PARK—(Lawrence) *From jct Hwy 1 & US 50: Go 9 mi W on US 50.* FACILITIES: 129 sites, typical site width 12 ft, 104 E, (30/50 amps), 25 no hkups, 5 pull-thrus, tenting, dump. RECREATION: boating, electric motors only, canoeing, ramp, dock, lake fishing, playground. Partial handicap access. Open Apr - Nov. Phone: (618)936-2469.

LE ROY—C-4

(NE) MORAINE VIEW STATE PARK—(McLean) *From town: Go 5 mi N on blacktop road, then 2 mi E on Leroy-Levington Rd.* FACILITIES: 199 sites, typical site width 12 ft, 137 full hkups, 30 W&E, (20/50 amps), 32 no hkups, tenting, dump. RECREATION: lake swim, boating, 10 hp limit, canoeing, ramp, dock, lake fishing, playground. Partial handicap access. Open all yr. Phone: (309)724-8032.

LENA—A-3

(C) KOA-Lena—(Stephenson) *From jct Hwy 73 & US 20: Go 1/4 mi E on US 20. Enter on L.* ◇◇◇FACILITIES: 88 sites, typical site width 27 ft, 67 full hkups, 21 W&E, (30/50 amps), 33 pull-thrus, family camping, tenting, dump, laundry, ltd groc. ◇◇◇◇RECREATION: swim pool, playground. Pets welcome, breed restrict. Partial handicap access. Open Apr 1 - Nov 1. Big rigs welcome. Rate in 2010 $27-46 per family. Member ARVC, ICA. Phone: (800)562-5361. KOA discount.

(N) LAKE LE-AQUA-NA STATE PARK—(Stephenson) *From jct US-20 & Hwy-73: Go 5 mi N on Hwy-73 & Lake Park Road.* FACILITIES: 171 sites, 141 E, 30 no hkups, tenting, dump, groceries. RECREATION: lake swim, boating, electric motors only, canoeing, ramp, dock, lake fishing, playground. Pets welcome. Partial handicap access. Open all yr. Facilities fully operational May 1 - Nov 1. Phone: (815)369-4282.

LINCOLN—C-3

(NE) McMillen's Camp-A-While—(Logan) *From jct I-55 & I-155 (exit 133): Go 6 mi E on I-55, then 3/4 mi S on Business I-55, then 2 mi W on CR 1800 N, then 1/4 mi S on CR 1250 E (Nicholson Rd). Enter on R.* ◇◇◇FACILITIES: 34 sites, typical site width 25 ft, 8 full hkups, 23 W&E, 3 E, (15/20/30/50 amps), 3 pull-thrus, family camping, tenting, dump, laundry. Pets welcome. Open all yr. Rate in 2010 $30 for 2 persons. Phone: (217)732-8840. FMCA discount.

LITCHFIELD—D-3

(N) Kamper Kompanion Campground—(Montgomery) *From jct I-55 & SR 108 (exit 60): Go E on SR 108 to East Frontage Rd SE 500 ft (L). Enter on L.* ◇◇◇◇FACILITIES: 28 sites, typical site width 25 ft, 28 full hkups, (20/30/50 amps), 25 pull-thrus, family camping, tenting, laundry, ltd groc. ◇RECREATION: playground. Pets welcome. Open all yr. Big rigs welcome. Rate in 2010 $20-22 for 2 persons. Member ARVC. Phone: (217)324-4747.

(SW) Lankels Lazy Days Campground—(Montgomery) *From jct I-55 & Hwy 16 (exit 52): Go 1 mi W on Hwy 16, then 1/2 mi S on West County Line Rd, then 1 mi W on S Hornsby Rd, then 1/2 mi S on Litchfield Rd, then 3/10 mi W on White Park Ln. Enter on R.* ◇◇◇FACILITIES: 116 sites, typical site width 25 ft, 39 ft max RV length, 16 full hkups, 100 W&E, (30/50 amps), 8 pull-thrus, family camping, tenting, dump, ltd groc. ◇◇◇RECREATION: lake swim, lake fishing, playground. Pets welcome. Open Apr 1 - Oct 31. Rate in 2010 $23 for 6 persons. Phone: (217)324-3233.

MACOMB—C-2

(NW) SPRING LAKE PARK CAMPGROUND (City Park)—(McDonough) *From west jct US 136 & US 67: Go 4 mi N on US 67, then 2 mi W on CR N1500. (Spring Lake Park Rd). Enter on R.* FACILITIES: 120 sites, 120 E, (20/30 amps), tenting, dump. RECREATION: boating, 10 hp limit, canoeing, ramp, dock, lake/stream fishing, playground. Pets welcome. Open all yr. Facilities fully operational Apr 1 - Sep 30. Phone: (309)833-2052.

MAHOMET—C-4

(E) Champaign Sportsmen's Club—(Champaign) *From jct I-57 & I-74: Go 5 mi NW on I-74 (exit 174), then 1/2 mi N on Prairie View Rd, then 1 mi W on Tincup Rd, then 500 ft N on Lake of the Woods Rd. Enter on R.* ◇◇◇FACILITIES: 158 sites, typical site width 25 ft, 19 full hkups, 139 E, (20/30/50 amps), 10 pull-thrus, tenting, dump. ◇◇◇RECREATION: boating, electric motors only, canoeing, pond fishing, playground. Pets welcome. Open all yr. Big rigs welcome. Rate in 2010 $15-21 per vehicle. Phone: (217)586-9951.

(W) Tincup RV Park—(Champaign) *From jct I-57 & I-74: Go 5 mi NW on I-74 (exit 174), then 1/2 mi N on Prairie View Rd, then 1/2 mi W on Tincup Rd. Enter on L.* ◇◇◇FACILITIES: 70 sites, typical site width 30 ft, 50 full hkups, 20 W&E, (20/30/50 amps), 26 pull-thrus, family camping, tenting, dump, ltd groc. ◇RECREATION: playground. Pets welcome. Open all yr. Big rigs welcome. Rate in 2010 $17.50-28.50 for 2 persons. Member ARVC, ICA. Phone: (217)586-3011.

MARENGO—A-4

(S) BEST HOLIDAY LEHMAN'S LAKESIDE RV RESORT—(McHenry) *From jct I-90 (Marengo exit) & US 20: Go 1 mi NW on US 20, then 3 mi W on Harmony Rd. Enter on L.*

WELCOME

◇◇◇◇FACILITIES: 295 sites, typical site width 60 ft, 105 full hkups, 190 W&E, (30/50 amps), some extd stay sites, 20 pull-thrus, cable TV, WiFi Instant Internet at site, WiFi Internet central location, family camping, tenting, RV storage, dump, portable dump, laundry, ltd groc, RV supplies, LP gas by weight/by meter, ice, picnic tables, patios, fire rings, wood.

◇◇◇◇RECREATION: rec hall, coin games, lake swim, boating, electric motors only, canoeing, dock, rowboat/3 canoe/4 pedal boat rentals, lake/pond fishing, golf nearby, bsktball, playground, activities, (wkends), horseshoes, sports field, hiking trails, v-ball.

Pets welcome. Open all yr. Reservations preferred. Big rigs welcome. Escort to site. Clubs welcome. Rate in 2010 $39-43 for 4 persons. MC/VISA/Debit.

Phone: (877)242-8533
Address: 19609 Harmony Rd, Marengo, IL 60152
Lat/Lon: 42.17264/-88.57859
Web: www.lehmansrv.com

SEE AD NEXT PAGE

(SE) KOA-Chicago Northwest—(McHenry) *From jct I-90 (Marengo exit) & US-20: Go 4-1/2 mi NW on US-20, then 500 feet N on S Union Rd. Enter on R.* ◇◇◇◇FACILITIES: 141 sites, typical site width 28 ft, 36 full hkups, 76 W&E, (20/30/50 amps), 50 amps ($), 29 no hkups, 82 pull-thrus, family camping, tenting, dump, laundry, ltd groc. ◇◇◇RECREATION: swim pool, playground. Pets welcome, breed restrict. Partial handicap access. Open Mid Apr - Mid Oct. Big rigs welcome. Rate in 2010 $26-49 for 2 persons. Member ARVC, ICA. Phone: (800)KOA-2827. KOA discount.

MARION—F-4

(W) KAMPER'S SUPPLY—*From jct I-57 (exit 54B) & Hwy-13: Go 7 mi W on Hwy 13, then 50 yds N on Division St, then 1/4 mi W on frontage road (Plaza). Enter on R.* SALES: travel trailers, 5th wheels, pre-owned unit sales. SERVICES: full-time mech, RV appliance repair, body work/collision repair, RV storage, sells parts/accessories, installs hitches. Open all yr. MC/VISA/DISC.

WELCOME

Phone: (618)985-6959
Address: 400 W Plaza Dr (Hwy 13), Carterville, IL 62918
Lat/Lon: 37.74617/-89.08362
Email: shirley@kampersupply.com
Web: www.kamperssupply.com

SEE AD NEXT PAGE

(W) Marion Campground & RV Park—(Williamson) *From jct Hwy 13 & I-57: Go 1 mi S on I-57 (exit 53), then 300 yds E on Main St, then 1/4 mi N on 7th St. Enter on R.* ◇◇◇◇FACILITIES: 58 sites, typical site width 30 ft, 58 full hkups, (20/30/50 amps), 27 pull-

Marion Campground & RV Park—Continued on next page

MARION—Continued
Marion Campground & RV Park—Continued

thrus, laundry. ◆RECREATION: playground. Pets welcome. Partial handicap access. No tents. Open all yr. Big rigs welcome. Rate in 2010 $29-31 per vehicle. Member ARVC. Phone: (618)997-3484. FMCA discount.

MARSEILLES—B-4

(E) Four Star Campground—(La Salle) *From jct Hwy 71 & I-80 (exit 93): Go 4 mi E on I-80, then 1/2 mi S on CR 15, then 1-1/2 mi E on N 30th Rd, then 2 mi S on 2575th Rd, then 1/2 mi E on 28th Rd, then 1/4 mi S on E 2625th Rd. Enter on L.* ◆◆◆FACILITIES: 400 sites, typical site width 40 ft, 350 full hkups, 50 W&E, (30/50 amps), 40 pull-thrus, family camping, tenting, dump, laundry, ltd groc. ◆◆◆RECREATION: swim pool, boating, no motors, canoeing, lake fishing, playground. Pets welcome. Open all yr. Big rigs welcome. Rate in 2010 $25-35 per family. Phone: (815)795-5720.

MARSHALL—D-5

(S) LINCOLN TRAIL STATE PARK—(Clark) *From jct US-40 & Hwy-1: Go 5 mi S on Hwy-1, then 1 mi W on blacktop road.* FACILITIES: 242 sites, typical site width 12 ft, 35 ft max RV length, 208 E, (30 amps), 34 no hkups, 23 pull-thrus, tenting, dump. RECREATION: lake swim, boating, 10 hp limit, canoeing, ramp, dock, lake fishing, playground. Partial handicap access. Open Apr 15 - Nov 15. Phone: (217)826-2222.

(NW) MILL CREEK PARK CAMPGROUND (Clark County Park)—(Clark) *From jct I-70 (exit 147) & Hwy 1: Go 1 mi S on Hwy 1, then 3/4 mi W on US 40, then 7 mi NW on Lincoln Heritage Tr. Enter on L.* FACILITIES: 148 sites, 139 E, 9 no hkups, tenting, dump. RECREATION: lake swim, boating, canoeing, ramp, dock, lake fishing, playground. Open Apr 1 - Nov 1. Phone: (217)889-3601.

MCLEANSBORO—E-4

(E) HAMILTON COUNTY STATE CONSERVATION AREA—(Hamilton) *From town: Go 14 mi E on Hwy-14, then 1 mi S on entrance road.* FACILITIES: 71 sites, typical site width 10 ft, 61 E, (20/30 amps), 10 no hkups, tenting, dump, ltd groc. RECREATION: lake swim, boating, 10 hp limit, canoeing, ramp, dock, lake fishing, playground. Partial handicap access. Open all yr. Phone: (618)773-4340.

METROPOLIS—F-4

(E) FORT MASSAC STATE PARK—(Massac) *From jct I-24 & US 45: Go 2-1/2 mi W on US 45.* FACILITIES: 50 sites, typical site width 10 ft, 50 E, (30/50 amps), tenting, dump. RECREATION: boating, canoeing, ramp, river fishing, playground. Partial handicap access. Open all yr. Phone: (618)524-4712.

MILLBROOK—B-4

(SE) Yogi Bear Jellystone Camp-Resort Chicago-Millbrook—(Kendall) *From jct Hwy 47 & Hwy 71: Go 6 mi SW on Hwy 71, then 1 mi W on Millbrook Rd. Enter on R.* ◆◆◆◆FACILITIES: 391 sites, typical site width 40 ft, 224 full hkups, 161 W&E, (20/30/50 amps), 2 pull-thrus, tenting, dump, laundry, groceries. ◆◆◆◆RECREATION: 2 swim pools, pond/stream fishing, playground. Pets welcome. Open all yr. Big rigs welcome. Rate in 2010 $46-58 per family. Member ARVC, ICA. Phone: (800)438-9644.

MOLINE—B-3

See listing at Rock Island

MORRIS—B-4

(SW) GEBHARD WOODS STATE TRAIL ACCESS—(Grundy) *From jct I-80 & Hwy 47: Go 1 mi S on Hwy 47, then W on US 6 (follow signs).* FACILITIES: 25 sites, 25 no hkups, tenting. RECREATION: boating, canoeing, river/pond fishing, playground. Pets welcome. Open all yr. Phone: (815)942-0796.

The state motto is "State Sovereignty, National Union".

MORRISON—A-3

(NW) MORRISON-ROCKWOOD STATE PARK—(Whiteside) *From jct US 30 & Hwy 78: Go 2-1/2 mi N on Hwy 78.* FACILITIES: 92 sites, typical site width 15 ft, 35 ft max RV length, 92 E, (30 amps), 4 pull-thrus, tenting, dump, ltd groc. RECREATION: lake swim, boating, 10 hp limit, canoeing, ramp, dock, lake fishing, playground. Partial handicap access. Open May 1 - Oct 31. Phone: (815)772-4708.

MT. CARROLL—A-3

(SE) Timber Lake Resort & Campground—(Carroll) *From jct Hwy 64 & Hwy 78: Go 2 mi S on Hwy 78, then 2 mi E on Timber Lake Rd, then 1/4 mi N on Black Oak Rd. Enter on L.* ◆◆◆FACILITIES: 133 sites, typical site width 30 ft, 102 full hkups, 25 W&E, (30/50 amps), 6 no hkups, 10 pull-thrus, tenting, dump, ltd groc. ◆◆◆◆RECREATION: swim pool, canoeing, lake fishing, playground. Pets welcome. Partial handicap access. Open Apr 15 - Nov 1. Rate in 2010 $36-38 for 6 persons. Member ARVC, ICA. Phone: (800)485-0145.

Wild Bill Hickock, U.S. Marshal, was from Illinois.

MT VERNON—E-4

(W) QUALITY TIMES—(Jefferson) *From jct I-57/I-64 (exit 95) & Hwy 15: Go 3/4 mi W on Hwy 15. Enter on R.*

WELCOME

◆◆FACILITIES: 43 sites, typical site width 22 ft, 37 full hkups, 6 W&E, (20/30/50 amps), 50 amps ($), some extd stay sites, 43 pull-thrus, cable TV, WiFi Instant Internet at site, phone Internet central location, tenting, dump, non-guest dump $, laundry, RV supplies, LP gas by weight/by meter, ice, picnic tables, fire rings, grills, wood.

◆RECREATION: pond fishing, bsktball, play equipment, sports field.

Pets welcome. Partial handicap access. Open all yr. Big rigs welcome. Clubs welcome. Rate in 2010 $20-25 per vehicle. MC/VISA/DISC/Debit. Member ARVC, ICA.

QUALITY TIMES—Continued on next page

Bill Murray, actor, is from Illinois.

MT VERNON—Continued
QUALITY TIMES—Continued

Phone: (618)244-0399
Address: 9746 E IL Highway 15, Mt Vernon, IL 62864
Lat/Lon: 38.31191/-88.96544
SEE AD TRAVEL SECTION PAGE 211

MULBERRY GROVE—D-3

(SW) Cedarbrook RV Park and Campground—(Bond) *From jct US 127 & I-70: Go 7 mi E on I-70 (exit 52), then 1 mi S on Mulberry Grove Rd. Enter on R.* ◇◇◇◇FACILITIES: 70 sites, typical site width 25 ft, 59 full hkups, 18 W&E, (30/50 amps), 6 no hkups, 16 pull-thrus, tenting, dump, laundry, ltd groc. ◇◇◇RECREATION: swim pool, boating, dock, lake fishing, playground. Pets welcome. Open Apr 1 - Oct 31. Big rigs welcome. Rate in 2010 $23-27 for 4 persons. Phone: (618)326-8865.

(W) TIMBER TRAILS CAMPGROUND—(Bond) *From jct US 127 & I-70: Go 7 mi E on I-70 (exit 52), then 3/4 mi N on Maple St, then 1 mi W on Hwy 140 (Wall St.). Enter on R.*

WELCOME

◇◇◇FACILITIES: 155 sites, typical site width 25 ft, 70 full hkups, 85 W&E, (30/50 amps), many extd stay sites, 27 pull-thrus, WiFi Internet central location, non-guest dump $, portable dump, laundry, LP gas by weight/by meter, ice, picnic tables, fire rings, wood.

◇◇◇RECREATION: rec room/area, pavilion, coin games, swim pool, lake fishing, bsktball, playground, activities, (wkends), horseshoes, sports field, v-ball.

Pets welcome. Open Apr 15 - Nov 15. Facilities fully operational Apr 1 - Nov 15. Water reduced to 4 hydrants Nov 16-Mar 31. Big rigs welcome. Clubs welcome. Rate in 2010 $17-34 per family. FMCA discount.

Phone: (618)326-8264
Address: 1276 Matts Lane, Mulberry Grove, IL 62262
Lat/Lon: 38.92286/-89.28816
Email: rbroad@frontiernet.net
Web: www.timbertrails.itgo.com
SEE AD THIS PAGE

MURPHYSBORO—F-3

(W) LAKE MURPHYSBORO STATE PARK—(Jackson) *From jct Hwy-127 & Hwy-149: Go 4 mi W on Hwy-149.* FACILITIES: 74 sites, typical site width 12 ft, 35 ft max RV length, 54 E, (30/50 amps), 20 no hkups, 18 pull-thrus, tenting, dump. RECREATION: boating, 10 hp limit, canoeing, ramp, dock, lake fishing, playground. Partial handicap access. Open all yr. Phone: (618)684-2867.

NASHVILLE—E-3

(S) WASHINGTON COUNTY LAKE (State Cons Area)—(Washington) *From jct Hwy-127 & Hwy-15: Go 4 mi S on Hwy-127.* FACILITIES: 150 sites, typical site width 12 ft, 50 E, (30 amps), 100 no hkups, tenting, dump. RECREATION: boating, 10 hp limit, canoeing, ramp, dock, lake fishing, playground. Partial handicap access. Open all yr. Phone: (618)327-3137.

NAUVOO—C-1

(S) NAUVOO STATE PARK—(Hancock) *From jct Hwy-96 & US-136: Go 12 mi N on Hwy-96.* FACILITIES: 150 sites, typical site width 12 ft, 75 E, (30 amps), 75 no hkups, 25 pull-thrus, tenting, dump. RECREATION: boating, electric motors only, canoeing, ramp, lake fishing, playground. Partial handicap access. Open all yr. Phone: (217)453-2512.

NEWTON—D-4

(NE) SAM PARR STATE PARK—(Jasper) *From jct Hwy-33 & Hwy-130: Go 3 mi N on Hwy-130.* FACILITIES: 80 sites, typical site width 12 ft, 35 ft max RV length, 10 E, (30 amps), 70 no hkups, tenting, dump. RECREATION: boating, 10 hp limit, canoeing, ramp, dock, lake fishing, playground. Open all yr. Phone: (618)783-2661.

OAKLAND—D-4

(S) Hebron Hills Camping—(Coles) *From jct Hwy 130 & Hwy 133: Go 7 mi E on Hwy 133, then 3-1/2 mi S on CR 2400E. (Ashmore Rd), then 1/2 mi W on CR 1470, then 1 mi S on CR 2350E, then 1/2 mi W on CR 1430N. Enter at end.* ◇◇◇FACILITIES: 45 sites, typical site width 40 ft, 18 full hkups, 15 W&E, 4 E, (20/30/50 amps), 8 no hkups, 11 pull-thrus, tenting. ◇◇◇RECREATION: lake swim, boating, no motors, dock, lake/pond fishing, play equipment. Pets welcome. Open May 15 - Oct 15. Rate in 2010 $16-22 for 4 persons. Member ARVC, ICA. Phone: (217)346-3385.

(N) WALNUT POINT STATE PARK—(Coles) *From jct Hwy-133 & Hwy-130: Go 8 mi E on Hwy-133, then 3-1/2 mi N on county road, then 1/4 mi W on county road.* FACILITIES: 60 sites, typical site width 12 ft, 34 E, (30 amps), 26 no hkups, tenting, dump. RECREATION: lake swim, boating, electric motors only, canoeing, ramp, dock, lake fishing, playground. Partial handicap access. Open Mar - Nov. Phone: (217)346-3336.

OAKWOOD—C-4

(NE) MIDDLE FORK STATE FISH & WILDLIFE AREA—(Vermilion) *From I-74 (exit 206 Oakwood): Go 8 mi NW on blacktop road.* FACILITIES: 45 sites, typical site width 12 ft, 35 ft max RV length, 45 no hkups, tenting, ltd groc. RECREATION: canoeing, river fishing, playground. Partial handicap access. Open May - Nov. Phone: (217)442-4915.

OHIO—B-3

(NW) GREEN RIVER STATE WILDLIFE AREA—(Bureau) *From town: Go 6 mi N on hwy 26, then follow signs W on blacktop road.* FACILITIES: 50 sites, 50 no hkups, tenting, dump. RECREATION: Open all yr. Phone: (815)379-2324.

OLIVE BRANCH—F-3

(SE) HORSESHOE LAKE STATE CONSERVATION AREA—(Alexander) *From town: Go 3 mi S on Hwy-3, then 3 mi W on Miller City Rd.* FACILITIES: 88 sites, 78 E, (30 amps), 10 no hkups, tenting, dump. RECREATION: lake swim, boating, 10 hp limit, canoeing, ramp, dock, lake fishing, playground. Pets welcome. Partial handicap access. Open May 1 - Oct 31. Phone: (618)776-5689.

OQUAWKA—B-2

(N) BIG RIVER STATE FOREST—(Mercer) *From town: Go 1 mi E on Hwy 164, then 8 mi N on Oquawka-Keithsburg blacktop road.* FACILITIES: 104 sites, typical site width 40 ft, 104 no hkups, tenting, dump. RECREATION: boating, canoeing, ramp, river fishing, playground. Open all yr. Phone: (309)374-2496.

(N) DELABAR STATE PARK—(Henderson) *From town: Go 1 mi E on Hwy 164, then 2 mi N on Keithsburg blacktop road.* FACILITIES: 56 sites, typical site width 22 ft, 56 E, (30 amps), tenting, dump. RECREATION: boating, canoeing, ramp, dock, river fishing, playground. Partial handicap access. Open all yr. Phone: (309)374-2496.

(S) HENDERSON COUNTY STATE CONSERVATION AREA.—(Henderson) *From town: Go 4 mi S on Hwy 164.* FACILITIES: 35 sites, 35 no hkups, tenting. RECREATION: boating, no motors, canoeing, ramp, lake fishing. Open all yr. Phone: (309) 374-2496.

OREGON—A-3

(SW) Hansen's Hide Away Ranch & Family Campground—(Ogle) *From jct Hwy 64 & Hwy 2: Go 3/4 mi S on Hwy 2, then 3-1/2 mi W on Pines Rd, then 1-1/2 mi S on Ridge Rd, then 3/4 mi W on Harmony Rd. Enter on L.* ◇◇FACILITIES: 123 sites, 3 full hkups, 60 W&E, 60 E, (20/30 amps), 18 pull-thrus, family camping, tenting, dump. ◇◇RECREATION: play equipment. Pets welcome. Partial handicap access. Open Apr 15 - Nov 1. Rate in 2010 $23-25 per family. Phone: (815) 732-6489.

(NW) Lake LaDonna Family Campground—(Ogle) *From jct Hwy 64 & Hwy 2: Go 3/4 mi S on Hwy 2, then 3-1/2 mi W on Pines Rd, then 1/2 mi N on Ridge Rd, then 1 mi W on Raccoon Rd (dirt road), the 3/4 mi S on Harmony Rd. Enter on R.* ◇◇FACILITIES: 205 sites, typical site width 28 ft, 205 W&E, (20/30 amps), 20 pull-thrus, family camping, tenting, dump, ltd groc. ◇◇◇RECREATION: lake swim, playground. Pets welcome. Open Apr 15 - Oct 15. Rate in 2010 $27-30 per family. Phone: (815)732-6804.

(N) LOWDEN MEMORIAL STATE PARK—(Ogle) *From jct Hwy-64 & Hwy-2: Go 1/2 mi E on Hwy-64, then 1-1/2 mi N on East River Road.* FACILITIES: 130 sites, typical site width 15 ft, 30 ft max RV length, 80 E, (20 amps), 50 no hkups, tenting, dump. RECREATION: boating, canoeing, ramp, dock, river fishing, playground. Partial handicap access. Open May 1 - Feb 28. Phone: (815)732-6828.

(W) WHITE PINES FOREST STATE PARK—(Ogle) *From jct Hwy-64 & Hwy-2: Go 3/4 mi S on Hwy-2, then 7 mi SW on Pines Road.* FACILITIES: 103 sites, typical site width 15 ft, 35 ft max RV length, 3 E, (30 amps), 100 no hkups, 42 pull-thrus, tenting, dump. RECREATION: stream fishing, playground. Partial handicap access. Open May - Oct. Phone: (815)946-3717.

PEARL CITY—A-3

(SE) Emerald Acres Campground—(Stephenson) *From jct US 20 & Hwy 73: Go 7 mi S on Hwy 73, then 3.2 mi E on Pearl City Rd, then 1.3 mi S on Block Rd. Enter on L.* ◇◇FACILITIES: 136 sites, typical site width 25 ft, 90 full hkups, 46 W&E, (20/30 amps), family camping, tenting, dump. ◇◇RECREATION: pond fishing, playground. Pets welcome. Partial handicap access. Open May 1 - Oct 15. Rate in 2010 $19 for 2 persons. Member ARVC, ICA. Phone: (815)443-2550.

Walt Disney, film animator and producer, was from Illinois.

PECATONICA—A-3

(W) PECATONICA RIVER FOREST PRESERVE (Winnebago County)—(Winnebago) *From jct US 20 & CR 18: Go N on CR 18 to CR 83, follow signs.* FACILITIES: 50 sites, typical site width 15 ft, 30 ft max RV length, 50 E, (20 amps), tenting, dump. RECREATION: boating, canoeing, ramp, river fishing. Open Apr - Nov. Phone: (815)877-6100.

PEKIN—C-3

(SW) SPRING LAKE (State Cons Area)—(Tazewell) *From jct Hwy 9 & Hwy 29: Go 2 mi S on Hwy 29, then 8 mi SW on Manito Blacktop Rd, then 3 mi W.* FACILITIES: 70 sites, typical site width 30 ft, 30 ft max RV length, 70 no hkups, tenting, dump. RECREATION: boating, 25 hp limit, canoeing, ramp, dock, lake fishing, playground. Open all yr. Phone: (309)968-7135.

PEORIA—C-3

See listings at Bartonville, Carlock, East Peoria, El Paso, Goodfield & Hopedale

PETERSBURG—C-3

(S) LINCOLN'S NEW SALEM PARK (IL Historic Preservation Agency)—(Menard) *From jct Hwy-123 & Hwy-97: Go 2 mi S on Hwy-97.* FACILITIES: 200 sites, 100 E, 100 no hkups, tenting, dump. RECREATION: playground. Partial handicap access. Open all yr. Facilities fully operational Mar 16 - Nov 30. Phone: (217)632-4003.

PINCKNEYVILLE—E-3

(S) PYRAMID STATE PARK—(Perry) *From jct Hwy 154 & Hwy 127/13: Go 6 mi S on Hwy 127/13.* FACILITIES: 54 sites, typical site width 20 ft, 35 ft max RV length, 54 no hkups, tenting, dump. RECREATION: boating, 10 hp limit, canoeing, ramp, lake fishing. Open all yr. Phone: (618)357-2574.

PITTSFIELD—D-2

(N) Pine Lakes Resort—(Pike) *From jct I-72 (exit 35) & US 54: Go 5 mi S on US 54, then 1/4 mi W on Benson St, then 3/4 mi N on Memorial. Enter on L.* ◇◇◇FACILITIES: 158 sites, typical site width 35 ft, 83 full hkups, 75 W&E, (20/30/50 amps), 15 pull-thrus, family camping, tenting, laundry, ltd groc. ◇◇◇◇RECREATION: lake swim, boating, canoeing, dock, lake/pond fishing, playground. Pets welcome. Open Apr 10 - Dec 15. Facilities fully operational Apr - Oct. Big rigs welcome. Rate in 2010 $33-43 per family. Member ARVC, ICA. Phone: (877)808-7463.

PLEASANT HILL—D-2

(S) GREAT RIVER ROAD CAMPGROUND (City Park)—(Pike) *From Hwy 96 & S Main St: Go 1/2 mi S on S Main St. Enter on R.* FACILITIES: 59 sites, typical site width 20 ft, 24 full hkups, 35 W&E, 40 pull-thrus, tenting, dump. RECREATION: Open Apr 1 - Oct 31. Phone: (217)734-9006.

PROPHETSTOWN—B-3

(E) PROPHETSTOWN STATE PARK—(Whiteside) *From jct Hwy 92 & Hwy 78: Go 7 mi N on Hwy 78.* FACILITIES: 119 sites, typical site width 20 ft, 44 E, (30 amps), 75 no hkups, tenting, dump. RECREATION: boating, canoeing, ramp, river fishing, play equipment. Open May 1 - Oct 30. Phone: (815)537-2926.

PUTNAM—B-3

(N) Condit's Ranch—(Putnam) *From jct I-80 & I-180: Go 8 mi S on I-180, then 4 mi S on Hwy 29, then 3/4 mi W on Log Cabin Rd. Enter on L.* ◇◇FACILITIES: 355 sites, 300 full hkups, 20 W&E, 5 E, (30/50 amps), 50 amps ($), 30 no hkups, 20 pull-thrus, family camping, tenting, dump, ltd groc. ◇◇◇RECREATION: lake swim, lake fishing, playground. Pets welcome. Open Apr 15 - Oct 15. Rate in 2010 $24-30 for 4 persons. Member ARVC, ICA. Phone: (815)437-2226. FCRV discount.

QUINCY—C-1

(N) Driftwood Campground—(Adams) *From jct I-172 (exit 19) & US 24: Go 5 mi W on US 24, then 50 ft N on 5th St, then 1 mi W on Valley View. Enter on R.* ◇◇◇FACILITIES: 55 sites, typical site width 30 ft, 20 full hkups, 15 W&E, (20/30/50 amps), 20 no hkups, family camping, tenting, dump, laundry. ◇◇RECREATION: swim pool, playground. Pets welcome. Open all yr. Big rigs welcome. Rate in 2010 $18-25 for 2 persons. Member ARVC, ICA. Phone: (217)222-7229.

(E) SILOAM SPRINGS STATE PARK—(Adams) *From jct Hwy-96 & Hwy-104: Go 27 mi E on Hwy-104, then 5 mi N on Kellerville Road.* FACILITIES: 182 sites, typical site width 12 ft, 98 E, (30 amps), 84 no hkups, 1 pull-thrus, tenting, dump. RECREATION: boating, electric motors only, canoeing, ramp, dock, lake fishing, play equipment. Partial handicap access. Open Apr - Dec. Phone: (217)894-6205.

RAMSEY—D-3

(NW) RAMSEY LAKE STATE PARK—(Fayette) *From town: Go 1 mi N on US-51, then 1 mi W on local road.* FACILITIES: 159 sites, typical site width 12 ft, 114 E, (30/50 amps), 45 no hkups, 4 pull-thrus, tenting, dump, ltd groc. RECREATION: boating, electric motors only, canoeing, ramp, dock, lake/pond fishing, playground. Partial handicap access. Open all yr. Phone: (618)423-2215.

Jimmy Connors, tennis champion, is from Illinois.

RANTOUL—C-4

(S) PRAIRIE PINES CAMPGROUND (City Park)—(Champaign) *From jct I-57 (exit 250) & US 136: Go 1-1/4 mi E on US 136, then 1-1/4 mi S on US 45, then 1/2 mi E on Chandler Rd. Enter on L.* FACILITIES: 95 sites, 95 full hkups, (20/30 amps), 50 pull-thrus, tenting, dump, laundry. RECREATION: playground. Partial handicap access. Open all yr. Facilities fully operational Apr - Nov. Phone: (217)893-0438.

ROCHESTER—D-3

(S) SANGCHRIS LAKE STATE PARK—(Sangamon) *From jct Hwy-29 & county road: Go 5 mi S on county road to New City, then 3 mi E on county road.* FACILITIES: 185 sites, typical site width 12 ft, 135 E, (30 amps), 50 no hkups, tenting, dump. RECREATION: boating, 25 hp limit, canoeing, ramp, dock, lake fishing, playground. Pets welcome. Partial handicap access. Open Apr 1 - Jun 15. Phone: (217)498-9208.

ROCK FALLS—A-3

(S) Leisure Lake Campground—(Whiteside) *From jct I-88 (exit 44) & US 30: Go 1 mi W on US 30, then 1/4 mi S on Spruce St, then 100 yards E on French St. Enter on R.* ◊◊◊FACILITIES: 68 sites, typical site width 50 ft, 68 full hkups, (20/30/50 amps), 32 pull-thrus, family camping, dump, laundry. ◊◊◊RECREATION: lake swim, boating, electric motors only, canoeing, lake fishing, play equipment. Pets welcome. No tents. Open Apr 1 - Oct 15. Big rigs welcome. Rate in 2010 $25-27 for 2 persons. Phone: (815)626-0005.

ROCK ISLAND—B-2

(S) ROCK ISLAND/QUAD CITIES-KOA—(Rock Island) *From jct I-280 (exit 11A) & Hwy 92: Go 1-1/2 mi S on Hwy 92, then 1 mi E on Andalusia Rd (78th Ave W). Enter on L.*

WELCOME

◊◊◊FACILITIES: 150 sites, typical site width 25 ft, 78 full hkups, 72 W&E, (20/30/50 amps), some extd stay sites, 15 pull-thrus, cable TV, WiFi Instant Internet at site, phone Internet central location, family camping, tenting, cabins, RV storage, dump, non-guest dump $, portable dump, laundry, ltd groc, RV supplies, LP gas by weight/by meter, ice, picnic tables, patios, fire rings, wood.

◊◊◊◊◊RECREATION: rec room/area, equipped pavilion, swim pool, spray ground, hot tub, boating, electric motors only, canoeing, ramp, dock, 2 canoe/4 pedal boat rentals, lake fishing, fishing supplies, mini-golf, golf nearby, bsktball, 14 bike rentals, playground, activities, (wkends), horseshoes, sports field, hiking trails, v-ball. Rec open to public.

Pets welcome. Open all yr. Big rigs welcome. Clubs welcome. Rate in 2010 $20-45 per family. MC/VISA/DISC/AMEX/Debit. Member ARVC, ICA. KOA discount.

Phone: (309)787-0665
Address: 2311 78th Ave W, Rock Island, IL 61201
Lat/Lon: 41.44352/-90.59829
Email: koa@rigckoa.com
Web: www.rockislandkoa.com

SEE AD MOLINE PAGE 223

ROCKFORD—A-3

(S) Black Hawk Valley Campground—(Winnebago) *From jct Hwy 20 & Hwy 251: Go 2-1/2 mi S on Hwy 251, then 1-1/4 mi E on Blackhawk Rd, then 3/4 mi S on Valley Trail Rd. Enter at end.* ◊◊◊FACILITIES: 162 sites, typical site width 30 ft, 115 full hkups, 47 W&E, (30/50 amps), 37 pull-thrus, family camping, tenting, dump, laundry, ltd groc. ◊◊◊RECREATION: boating, canoeing, river/pond fishing, playground. Pets welcome. Open mid Apr - mid Oct. Big rigs welcome. Rate in 2010 $29-33 for 6 persons. Member ARVC, ICA. Phone: (815)874-9767.

(W) ROCK-CUT STATE PARK—(Winnebago) *From jct US 51 & Hwy 173: Go 3 mi W on Hwy 173.* FACILITIES: 268 sites, typical site width 12 ft, 268 E, (20/50 amps), tenting, dump, ltd groc. RECREATION: lake swim, boating, 10 hp limit, canoeing, ramp, dock, lake fishing, playground. Partial handicap access. Open all yr. Phone: (815)885-3311.

Willow Creek Resort (Not Visited)—(Winnebago) *From jct Hwy 20 & Hwy 251: Go 5 mi S on Hwy 251, then 1/2 mi W on Baxter Rd (which becomes S Bend Rd). Enter on R.* FACILITIES: 120 sites, 20 full hkups, 100 W&E, (20/30 amps). RECREATION: stream fishing. No tents. Open Apr 1 - Nov 1. Rate in 2010 $20-28 per family. Phone: (815)874-4737.

ROCKTON—A-3

(N) HONONEGAH FOREST PRESERVE (Winnebago County)—(Winnebago) *From jct I-90 & CR 9: Go W on CR 9, then S on CR 58, follow signs.* FACILITIES: 60 sites, typical site width 15 ft, 30 ft max RV length, 60 E, (20/30 amps), tenting, dump. RECREATION: boating, canoeing, ramp, river fishing, playground. Open Apr 16 - Nov 19. Phone: (815)877-6100.

(W) Riversedge Campground and Restaurant—(Winnebago) *From jct Hwy 251 & Hwy 173: Go 6 mi W on Hwy 173, then 5 mi N on Meridian Rd. Enter on L.* ◊◊FACILITIES: 111 sites, 100 W&E, (30 amps), 11 no hkups, 5 pull-thrus, family camping, tenting, dump, laundry. ◊◊RECREATION: river/pond fishing, playground. Pets welcome. Open Apr 15 - Oct 15. Rate in 2010 $20 per family. Member ARVC, ICA. Phone: (815) 629-2526.

RUSHVILLE—C-2

(S) SCHUY-RUSH PARK—(Schuyler) *Jct of Hwy 24 & Hwy 67: Go 2 mi S on Hwy 67, turn W on CR 190 E.* FACILITIES: 77 sites, 77 W&E, (20/30 amps), tenting, dump, ltd groc. RECREATION: boating, canoeing, ramp, dock, lake fishing, play equipment. Open all yr. Facilities fully operational Apr 1 - Nov 1. Phone: (217)322-6628.

SALEM—E-3

(NE) STEPHEN A. FORBES STATE PARK—(Marion) *From jct I-57 (exit 116) & US-50: Go 8 mi E on US-50, then 7 mi N on Omega Rd, follow signs.* FACILITIES: 136 sites, typical site width 12 ft, 115 E, 21 no hkups, 4 pull-thrus, tenting, dump, ltd groc. RECREATION: lake swim, boating, canoeing, ramp, dock, lake fishing, playground. Open all yr. Phone: (618)547-3381.

SAVANNA—A-2

(N) MISSISSIPPI PALISADES STATE PARK—(Stevenson) *From jct Hwy-84 & Hwy-64: Go 2 mi N on Hwy-84.* FACILITIES: 241 sites, typical site width 12 ft, 35 ft max RV length, 110 E, (30 amps), 131 no hkups, 12 pull-thrus, tenting, dump, ltd groc. RECREATION: boating, canoeing, ramp, dock, river fishing, playground. Partial handicap access. Open May 1 - Oct 31. Phone: (815)273-2731.

SESSER—E-3

(E) WAYNE FITZGERRELL STATE PARK—(Jefferson) *From town: Go 6 mi E on Hwy-154.* FACILITIES: 283 sites, 243 E, (30/50 amps), 40 no hkups, tenting, dump, ltd groc. RECREATION: lake swim, boating, ramp, lake fishing, playground. Partial handicap access. Open all yr. Phone: (618)629-2320.

SEWARD—A-3

(S) SEWARD BLUFFS FOREST PRESERVE (Winnebago County)—(Winnebago) *From jct US 20 & CR 18: Go S on CR 18, then 1/4 mi W on Comly Rd.* FACILITIES: 60 sites, typical site width 15 ft, 30 ft max RV length, 60 E, (20 amps), tenting, dump. RECREATION: stream fishing, playground. Open Apr 16 - Nov 19. Phone: (815)877-6100.

SHABBONA—A-4

(S) SHABBONA LAKE STATE PARK—(DeKalb) *From town: Go 1/2 mi S on US 30, then 1/4 mi E on Preserve Rd.* FACILITIES: 150 sites, typical site width 15 ft, 35 ft max RV length, 150 E, (30 amps), tenting, dump. RECREATION: boating, 10 hp limit, canoeing, ramp, dock, lake fishing, playground. Partial handicap access. Open all yr. Phone: (815)824-2106.

SHEFFIELD—B-3

(N) Hickory Grove Campground—(Bureau) *From jct I-80 (exit 45) & Hwy 40: Go 1 mi N on Hwy 40, then 1-1/2 mi W on 1745 Ave N. Enter on L.* ◊◊FACILITIES: 200 sites, typical site width 30 ft, 14 full hkups, 120 W&E, (15/30/50 amps), 66 no hkups, 10 pull-thrus, tenting, dump. ◊RECREATION: river fishing. Pets welcome. Open Apr 1 - Oct 31. Rate in 2010 $30 per vehicle. Phone: (815)866-4557.

SHELBYVILLE—D-4

(NE) COON CREEK (COE-Shelbyville Lake)—(Shelby) *From jct Hwy 128 & Hwy 16: Go 4-1/2 mi N on Hwy 128, 1 mi E on CR 1750N, 1/2 mi N on CR 1900E, 1-3/4 mi E on CR 1785N, then 1-1/2 mi S on CR 2075E.* FACILITIES: 229 sites, typical site width 20 ft, 30 ft max RV length, 207 E, (20/50 amps), 22 no hkups, tenting, dump, laundry. RECREATION: lake swim, boating, canoeing, ramp, lake fishing, playground. Partial handicap access. Open May 6 - Oct 11. Phone: (217)774-3951.

(E) LITHIA SPRINGS ACCESS AREA (COE-Shelbyville Lake)—(Shelby) *From jct Hwy 128 & Hwy 16: Go 4-1/2 mi E on Hwy 16, then 2 mi N on CR 2200E, then 1-1/2 mi W on CR 1500N.* FACILITIES: 122 sites, typical site width 20 ft, 30 ft max RV length, 113 E, (20/30 amps), 9 no hkups, tenting, dump, laundry, ltd groc. RECREATION: lake swim, boating, canoeing, ramp, lake fishing, playground. Partial handicap access. Open Apr 16 - Oct 29. Phone: (217)774-3951.

(N) OPOSSUM CREEK REC. AREA (COE - Lake Shelbyville)—(Shelby) *From town: Go 3-1/2 mi N on Hwy 128, 1 mi E on CR 1650N, 1/2 mi S on CR 1880E, then 3/4 mi E on CR 1600N.* FACILITIES: 79 sites, typical site width 20 ft, 30 ft max RV length, 51 E, (20/30 amps), 28 no hkups, tenting, dump. RECREATION: lake swim, boating, canoeing, ramp, lake fishing, playground. Partial handicap access. Open May 20 - Sep 5. Phone: (217)774-3951.

(E) Robin Hood Woods Campground & Resort—(Shelby) *From jct Hwy 128 & Hwy 16: Go 4-1/2 mi E on Hwy 16. Enter on L.* ◊◊◊FACILITIES: 246 sites, typical site width 35 ft, 116 full hkups, 130 W&E, (20/30/50 amps), 26 pull-thrus, tenting, dump, laundry, ltd groc. ◊◊◊RECREATION: swim pool, pond fishing, playground. Pets welcome. Open Apr 1 - Nov 1. Big rigs welcome. Rate in 2010 $20-28 per family. Member ARVC. Phone: (217)774-4222.

SHERIDAN—B-4

(NE) Mallard Bend Campground & RV Park—(La Salle) *From jct Hwy 47 & Hwy 71: Go 9 mi SW on Hwy 71, then 3 mi W on 41st St, then 1 mi N on Robinson St, then 2-3/4 mi E on 42nd St, then 1 mi NE on N 4351st Rd. Enter on R.* ◊◊◊FACILITIES: 168 sites, typical site width 50 ft, 127 full hkups, 14 W&E, (20/30 amps), 27 no hkups, family camping, tenting, dump, laundry, ltd groc. ◊◊◊RECREATION: swim pool, boating, canoeing, dock, river fishing, playground. Pets welcome. Partial handicap access. Open May 1 - Oct 8. Rate in 2010 $38 for 4 persons. Member ARVC. Phone: (815)496-2496.

(NE) ROLLING OAKS CAMPGROUND—(La Salle) *From jct Hwy 47 & Hwy 71: Go 9 mi SW on Hwy 71, then 3 mi W on 41st St, then 1 mi N on Robinson St, then 2-1/2 mi E on 42nd Rd. Enter on R.*

WELCOME

◊◊FACILITIES: 520 sites, typical site width 28 ft, 400 full hkups, 100 W&E, (20/30/50 amps), 20 no hkups, many extd stay sites, family camping, tenting, shower$, dump, non-guest dump $, portable dump, ltd groc, LP gas by weight/by meter, ice, picnic tables, wood.

◊◊◊RECREATION: rec hall, rec room/area, pavilion, coin games, lake swim, boating, electric motors only, canoeing, river fishing, bsktball, playground, activities, (wkends), horseshoes, sports field, v-ball. Rec open to public.

Pets welcome. Open Apr 15 - mid Oct. Clubs welcome. Rate in 2010 $20-30 per family. MC/VISA/DISC/Debit. Member ICA.

Phone: (815)496-2334
Address: 2743 N 4251 1st Rd, Sheridan, IL 60551
Lat/Lon: 41.55225/-88.64799

SEE AD THIS PAGE

SHIRLAND—A-3

(NW) SUGAR RIVER FOREST PRESERVE (Winnebago County)—(Winnebago) *From town: Go N on Boswell Rd, then W on Forest Preserve Rd to the end.* FACILITIES: 82 sites, typical site width 15 ft, 30 ft max RV length, 82 E, (30 amps), tenting, dump. RECREATION: boating, canoeing, ramp, river fishing, playground. Partial handicap access. Open all yr. Facilities fully operational Apr 15 - Nov 19. Phone: (815)877-6100.

SOMONAUK—B-4

(SW) Hi-Tide Recreation—(La Salle) *From east jct US 34 & Hwy 23/E 22nd Rd: Go 1 mi S on E 22nd Rd. Enter on R.* ◊◊◊FACILITIES: 144 sites, typical site width 35 ft, 81 full hkups, 38 W&E, (20/30/50 amps), 25 no hkups, 3 pull-thrus, family camping, tenting, dump, laundry, ltd groc. ◊◊◊◊◊RECREATION: swim pool, lake swim, stream fishing, playground. Pets welcome. Open Apr 15 - Oct 15. Big rigs welcome. Rate in 2010 $33-38 per family. Member ARVC, ICA. Phone: (815)495-9032.

SOUTH BELOIT—A-3

(S) Pearl Lake Campground—(Winnebago) *From jct I-90 & Hwy 75: Go 1 mi W on Hwy 75, then 1/2 mi S on Hwy 251, then 100 yds W on Prairie Hill Rd, then 1/4 mi N on Dearborn. Enter on L.* ◊◊◊FACILITIES: 200 sites, typical site width 29 ft, 150 full hkups, 50 W&E, (20/30/50 amps), 6 pull-thrus, family camping, tenting, dump, ltd groc. ◊◊◊RECREATION: lake swim, lake fishing, playground. Pets welcome. Open May 1 - Oct 15. Rate in 2010 $45 for 4 persons. Phone: (815) 389-1479.

SPARTA—E-3

(NW) WORLD SHOOTING & RECREATIONAL COMPLEX—(Randolph) *From jct Hwy 154 & Hwy 4: Go 4-1/2 mi N on Hwy 4, then 3 mi W on CR 18. Enter on L.* FACILITIES: 1001 sites, typical site width 25 ft, 341 full hkups, 350 W&E, 310 E, (50 amps), 600 pull-thrus, family camping, tenting, dump. RECREATION: lake fishing, playground. Pets welcome. Open all yr. Big rigs welcome. Phone: (618)295-2700.

Did you know... Chicago is one of the busiest ports in the world? Ships reach the Atlantic Ocean through the Great Lakes & St. Lawrence Seaway. By using the Illinois and Mississippi Rivers, ships can travel from Chicago to the Gulf of Mexico.

SPRINGFIELD—C-3

✻ **(S) DOUBLE J RV SALES & SERVICE**—*From S jct I-72 & I-55 (exit 92): Go 4 mi S on I-55 (exit 88), then 2 mi S on Frontage Rd. Enter on R.* SALES: travel trailers, 5th wheels, pre-owned unit sales. SERVICES: full-time mech, RV appliance repair, LP gas by weight/by meter, dump station, RV storage, sells parts/accessories, installs hitches. Open all yr. MC/VISA/DISC.

Phone: (217)483-5900
Address: 9683 Palm Rd, Chatham, IL 62629
Lat/Lon: 39.65712/-89.64841

SEE AD THIS PAGE

(N) ILLINOIS STATE FAIR GROUNDS—*From jct I-55 & I-72: Go 2 mi W on SR 97, then 1 mi N on 5th St, then 1/4 mi E on Taintor Rd, then 1/8 mi N on Natural Resources Way. Enter on L.* FACILITIES: 300 sites, 84 full hkups, 216 W&E, (30/50 amps), dump. RECREATION: Pets welcome. Partial handicap access. Open April 1 - Nov 1.

(SE) KOA-Springfield—(Sangamon) *From S jct I-72 & I-55 (exit 92): Go 2 mi N on I-55 (exit 94), then 4 mi SE on East Lake Shore Dr, then 1-1/2 mi S on Lake Services Rd, then 1 mi E on KOA Rd. Enter on R.* ◇◇◇◇FACILITIES: 93 sites, typical site width 30 ft, 48 full hkups, 25 W&E, (20/30/50 amps), 50 amps ($), 20 no hkups, 23 pull-thrus, family camping, tenting, dump, laundry, groceries. ◇◇◇RECREATION: swim pool, playground. Pets welcome. Open Apr 1 - Nov 1. Rate in 2010 $27-40 for 2 persons. Member ARVC, ICA. Phone: (800)562-7212. KOA discount.

(S) THE DOUBLE J CAMPGROUND & RV PARK—(Sangamon) *From S jct I-72 & I-55 (exit 92): Go 4 mi S on I-55 (exit 88), then 2 mi S on Palm Rd. Enter on R.*

◇◇◇◇FACILITIES: 141 sites, typical site width 30 ft, 78 full hkups, 63 W&E, (20/30/50 amps), some extd stay sites, 70 pull-thrus, cable TV, WiFi Instant Internet at site, phone Internet central location, family camping, RV storage, dump, laundry, ltd groc, RV supplies, LP gas by weight/by meter, ice, picnic tables, fire rings, grills, wood.

◇◇◇◇RECREATION: rec room/area, pavilion, coin games, swim pool, mini-golf, ($), golf nearby, bsktball, playground, shuffleboard court shuffleboard court, activities (wkends), tennis, horseshoes, sports field, v-ball.

Pets welcome. No tents. Open Apr 1 - Oct 31. Big rigs welcome. Escort to site. Clubs welcome. Rate in 2010 $35 for 2 persons. MC/VISA/DISC. Member ARVC, ICA.

Phone: (888)483-9998
Address: 9683 Palm Rd, Chatham, IL 62629
Lat/Lon: 39.65825/-89.64902
Email: doublejcampground@msn.com
Web: www.doublejcampground.com

SEE AD THIS PAGE

STERLING—A-3

(SW) Crow Valley Campground—(Whiteside) *From jct I-88 (exit 36) & Hwy 30: Go 1/2 mi N on ramp, then 1/2 mi W on Moline Rd. Enter on L.* ◇◇FACILITIES: 100 sites, typical site width 28 ft, 80 W&E, (20/30 amps), 20 no hkups, family camping, tenting, dump, ltd groc. ◇◇◇◇RECREATION: swim pool, boating, ramp, river fishing, play equipment. Pets welcome. Open Apr 15 - Oct 15. Rate in 2010 $24 for 6 persons. Member ARVC. Phone: (815)626-5376.

(SW) Ruffit Park—(Whiteside) *From jct I-88 (exit 36) & Hwy 30: Go 1/4 mi E on Hwy 30. Enter on L.* ◇◇◇FACILITIES: 120 sites, typical site width 28 ft, 95

W&E, (30/50 amps), 25 no hkups, 50 pull-thrus, family camping, tenting, dump, laundry, ltd groc. ◇◇◇RECREATION: swim pool, stream fishing, playground. Pets welcome. Open May 1 - Oct 1. Rate in 2010 $20-22 for 2 persons. Phone: (815)626-0221.

STOCKTON—A-3

(N) APPLE RIVER CANYON STATE PARK—(Jo Daviess) *From jct Hwy-78 & US-20: Go 6 mi N on Hwy-78, then 3 mi W on access road.* FACILITIES: 47 sites, typical site width 12 ft, 30 ft max RV length, 47 no hkups, tenting, dump. RECREATION: river fishing, playground. Partial handicap access. Open May 1 - Nov 1. Phone: (815)745-3302.

STREATOR—B-4

(S) Katchewan Lakes RV Resort—(Livingston) *From jct Hwy 18 & Hwy 23: Go 1-1/2 mi S on Hwy 23, then 1 mi E on 3246N Rd, then 1 bl S on 541E (IL St), then 1 bl W on 3244N Rd, then 1 mi S on Barr St. Enter at end.* ◇◇FACILITIES: 74 sites, typical site width 25 ft, 30 full hkups, 26 W&E, (30 amps), 18 no hkups, 8 pull-thrus, family camping, tenting, dump. ◇◇◇RECREATION: river/pond fishing, playground. Pets welcome. Open May 1 - Oct 1. Rate in 2010 $30 for 6 persons. Phone: (815)672-9098.

SULLIVAN—D-4

(S) FORREST W. BO WOODS RECREATION AREA (COE-Lake Shelbyville)—(Moultrie) *From jct Hwy 121 & Hwy 32: Go 2-2/3 mi S on Hwy 32, then 1/2 mi W.* FACILITIES: 77 sites, typical site width 20 ft, 30 ft max RV length, 77 E, (20/30 amps), 3 pull-thrus, tenting, dump, laundry. RECREATION: lake swim, boating, canoeing, ramp, lake fishing, playground. Partial handicap access. Open Apr 15 - Oct 28. Phone: (217)774-3951.

(S) Sullivan Marina & Campgrounds Resort—(Moultrie) *From Sullivan jct IL 121 & Hwy 32: Go 4 mi S on Hwy 32. Enter on L.* ◇◇FACILITIES: 255 sites, typical site width 20 ft, 142 full hkups, 90 W&E, (15/30/50 amps), 23 no hkups, 104 pull-thrus, tenting, dump, laundry, ltd groc. ◇◇◇RECREATION: swim pool, boating, ramp, dock, lake fishing, play equipment. Pets welcome. Partial handicap access. Open all yr. Rate in 2010 $23-33 per vehicle. Phone: (217)728-7338.

(SW) WHITLEY CREEK RECREATION AREA (COE - Lake Shelbyville)—(Moultrie) *From jct Hwy 121 & Hwy 32: Go 5 mi S on Hwy 32, then 1 mi W on CR 2100N (Findlay Rd), then 1 mi N.* FACILITIES: 84 sites, typical site width 20 ft, 30 ft max RV length, 84 no hkups, tenting, dump, laundry. RECREATION: boating, canoeing, ramp, lake fishing, playground. Partial handicap access. Open May 5 - Sep 4. Phone: (217)774-3951.

SYCAMORE—A-4

(NW) Sycamore RV Resort—(DeKalb) *From Hwy 64 & Hwy 23: Go 1/2 mi N on Hwy 23, then 200 yards E on East North Ave. Enter at end.* ◇◇◇FACILITIES: 86 sites, typical site width 30 ft, 83 full hkups, 3 W&E, (30/50 amps), 14 pull-thrus, family camping, dump, laundry, ltd groc. ◇◇◇◇RECREATION: swim pool, lake swim, boating, electric motors only, canoeing, lake fishing. Pets welcome. No tents. Open all yr. Facilities fully operational Apr 1 - Nov 1. Big rigs welcome. Rate in 2010 $32-36 for 4 persons. Member ARVC, ICA. Phone: (815)895-5590.

THOMSON—A-2

(E) THOMSON CAUSEWAY (COE-Thomson Park)—(Carroll) *From jct Hwy 84 & Main St: Go 3 blocks W on Main St, then follow signs S on Lewis Ave.* FACILITIES: 103 sites, typical site width 12 ft, 32 ft max RV length, 98 E, (50 amps), 5 no hkups, tenting, dump. RECREATION: boating, ramp, dock, river fishing, playground. Partial handicap access. Open Apr 8 - Oct 23. Phone: (815)259-2353.

TOPEKA—C-3

(E) Evening Star Camping Resort—(Mason) *From jct Hwy 97 & US 136: Go 7 mi E on US 136. Enter on R.* ◇◇◇FACILITIES: 336 sites, typical site width 35

ft, 186 full hkups, 100 W&E, (20/30/50 amps), 50 no hkups, 42 pull-thrus, tenting, dump, laundry, ltd groc. ◇◇◇◇RECREATION: swim pool, pond fishing, playground. Pets welcome. Open Apr 1 - Oct 31. Rate in 2010 $23-33 per family. Member ARVC, ICA. Phone: (309)562-7590.

URSA—C-1

(W) BEAR CREEK (COE - Lock & Dam 21)—(Adams) *From jct Hwy 96 & CR 2150: Go 3 mi W on CR 2150, then 2-1/2 mi N on CR 500E, then 2-1/2 mi W on CR 2400N, then 1 mi W over levee on gravel road.* FACILITIES: 30 sites, 30 no hkups. RECREATION: boating, canoeing, ramp, river fishing. Open May 1 - Oct 31. Phone: (217)222-0918.

UTICA—B-3

(N) Hickory Hollow Campground—(La Salle) *From jct I-80 (exit 81) & Hwy 178: Go 1/4 mi N on Hwy 178, then 1/2 mi W on 3029th Rd. Enter on R.* ◇◇◇◇FACILITIES: 124 sites, typical site width 30 ft, 57 full hkups, 27 W&E, (20/30/50 amps), 40 no hkups, 35 pull-thrus, family camping, tenting, dump, laundry, ltd groc. ◇◇◇RECREATION: swim pool, playground. Pets welcome. Partial handicap access. Open Apr 1 - Nov 1. Big rigs welcome. Rate in 2010 $30-32 per family. Phone: (815)667-4996.

(N) KOA-LASALLE/PERU—(LaSalle) *From jct I-80 (exit 81) & Hwy 178: Go 1-1/2 mi N on Hwy 178, then 1/2 mi W on N 3150th Rd. Enter on L.*

◇◇◇◇FACILITIES: 120 sites, typical site width 30 ft, 20 full hkups, 60 W&E, (30/50 amps), 50 amps ($), 40 no hkups, 40 pull-thrus, WiFi Instant Internet at site, family camping, tenting, cabins, dump, laundry, groceries, RV supplies, LP gas by weight/by meter, ice, picnic tables, fire rings, grills, wood.

◇◇◇◇RECREATION: rec room/area, pavilion, coin games, swim pool, stream fishing, golf nearby, bsktball, 4 bike rentals, playground, activities (wkends), horseshoes.

Pets welcome, breed restrict. Open Apr 1 - Nov 1. Big rigs welcome. Escort to site. Clubs welcome. Rate in 2010 $30-39 for 2 persons. MC/VISA/DISC/Debit. Member ARVC, ICA. KOA discount.

Phone: (800)KOA-9498
Address: 756 N 3150th Rd, Utica, IL 61373
Lat/Lon: 41.38940/-89.01923
Web: koa.com

SEE AD THIS PAGE

(SE) STARVED ROCK STATE PARK—(La Salle) *From jct Hwy-178 & Hwy-71: Go 2 mi E on Hwy-71.* FACILITIES: 133 sites, typical site width 20 ft, 133 E, (20/30 amps), tenting, dump. RECREATION: boating, canoeing, ramp, dock, river fishing, playground. Partial handicap access. Open all yr. Phone: (815)667-4726.

VANDALIA—D-3

(W) OKAW VALLEY KAMPGROUND—(Fayette) *From jct I-70 (exit 68) & US 40: Go 1/4 mi N on US 40, then 1/4 mi W on Boley Dr. Enter on R.*

◇◇FACILITIES: 118 sites, typical site width 30 ft, 14 full hkups, 31 W&E, 3 E, (20/30/50 amps), 70 no hkups, some extd stay sites, 23 pull-thrus, phone Internet central location, tenting, cabins, RV storage, dump, non-guest dump $, laundry, groceries, RV supplies, ice, picnic tables, fire rings, grills, wood.

◇◇◇RECREATION: rec room/area, pavilion, equipped pavilion, coin games, swim pool, boating, dock, 2 rowboat/2 pedal boat rentals, lake fishing, bsktball, play equipment, sports field, v-ball. Rec open to public.

Pets welcome. Open all yr. Facilities fully operational Apr 1 - Oct 31. Clubs welcome. Rate in 2010 $22-28 for 4 persons. MC/VISA.

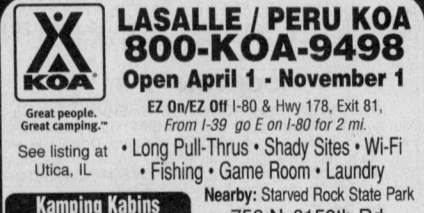

OKAW VALLEY KAMPGROUND—Continued on next page

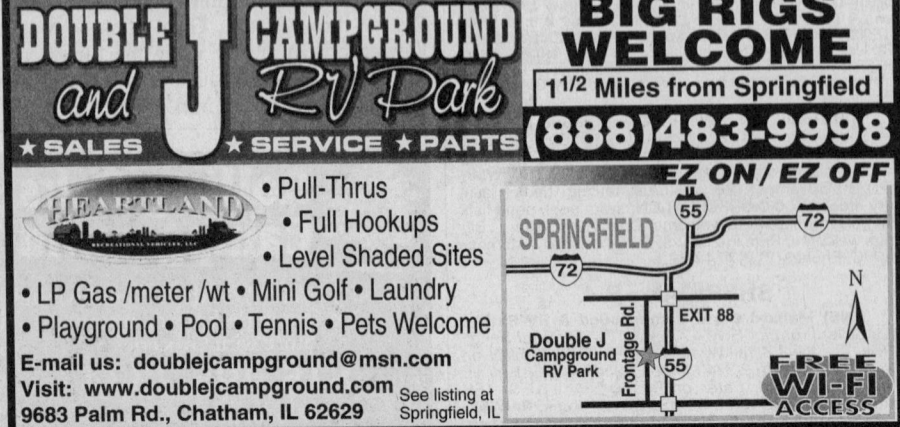

VANDALIA—Continued
OKAW VALLEY KAMPGROUND—Continued

Phone: (888)470-3968
Address: RR 2, Box 55A, Brownstown, IL 62418
Lat/Lon: 38.97699/-89.00301
Web: www.okawvalley.com

SEE AD THIS PAGE

VIENNA—F-4

(NW) SHAWNEE NATIONAL FOREST (Buck Ridge Campground)—(Johnson) *From town: Go 7 mi NW on I-24, then 3 mi E on Tunnel Hill Blacktop. Follow signs.* FACILITIES: 37 sites, 32 ft max RV length, 37 no hkups, 2 pull-thrus, tenting. RECREATION: boating, ramp, lake fishing. Partial handicap access. Open Mar 15 - Dec 15. Phone: (618)253-7114.

(E) SHAWNEE NATIONAL FOREST (Lake Glendale-Oak Point Campground)—(Johnson) *From town: Go 12 mi E on Hwy 146, then 2 mi N on Hwy 145.* FACILITIES: 56 sites, 32 ft max RV length, 31 E, 25 no hkups, tenting, dump. RECREATION: lake swim, boating, no motors, ramp, lake fishing, playground. Open Mar 10 - Dec 10. Phone: (618)253-7114.

VOLO—A-4

(E) Fish Lake Beach Camping Resort—(Lake) *From jct Hwy 120 & US 12: Go 2 blocks N on US 12. Enter on R.* ◆◆◆FACILITIES: 635 sites, typical site width 30 ft, 593 full hkups, 42 W&E, (30/50 amps), 15 pull-thrus, family camping, tenting, dump, laundry, ltd groc. ◆◆◆◆◆RECREATION: swim pool, lake swim, boating, electric motors only, dock, lake fishing, playground. Pets welcome. Open May 1 - Oct 15. Rate in 2010 $35-37 for 4 persons. Member ARVC, ICA. Phone: (847)546-2228.

WATSON—D-4

Percival Springs Airport Campground—(Effingham) *From jct I-57 (exit 51) & SR 37: Go 4 mi E on SR 37, then 12 mi S on US 45.* ◆FACILITIES: 26 sites, typical site width 30 ft, 26 full hkups, (50 amps), 5 pull-thrus, tenting. ◆RECREATION: pond fishing. Open all yr. Rate in 2010 $20 per vehicle. Phone: (888)536-5352.

WESTVILLE—C-5

(E) FOREST GLEN PRESERVE (Vermilion County Park)—(Vermilion) *From jct I-74 & Hwy 1: Go 5 mi S on Hwy 1, then 7 mi E on CR 5.* FACILITIES: 42 sites, 34 E, (20/30/50 amps), 8 no hkups, tenting, dump, ltd groc. RECREATION: boating, electric motors only, canoeing, ramp, lake/river/pond fishing, playground. Open all yr. Phone: (217)662-2142.

WHITTINGTON—E-4

(SW) WHITTINGTON WOODS CAMPGROUND—(Franklin) *From jct I-57 (exit 77) & Hwy 154: Go 1/2 mi E on Hwy 154, then 1/2 mi S on Hwy 37. Enter on R.*

WELCOME

◆◆◆FACILITIES: 112 sites, typical site width 25 ft, 65 full hkups, 32 W&E, (20/30/50 amps), 15 no hkups, 21 pull-thrus, cable TV, WiFi Instant Internet at site, tenting, cabins, RV storage, dump, non-guest dump $, laundry, groceries, RV supplies, LP gas by meter, ice, picnic tables, fire rings, grills, wood.

◆◆◆RECREATION: rec room/area, pavilion, coin games, swim pool, golf nearby, bsktball, playground, shuffleboard court 2 shuffleboard courts, activities (wkends), horseshoes, sports field, v-ball.

Pets welcome. Partial handicap access. Open all yr. Big rigs welcome. Clubs welcome. Rate in 2010 $30-34 for 2 persons. Member ARVC, ICA. FCRV discount. FMCA discount.

Phone: (618)435-3401
Address: 14297 State Hwy 37, Whittington, IL 62897
Lat/Lon: 38.07055/-88.91521
Email: whittingtonwoodscampground@gmail.com
Web: www.whittingtonwoodscampground.com

SEE AD THIS PAGE

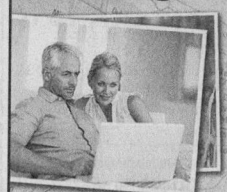

WILMINGTON—B-4

(W) DES PLAINES STATE FISH & WILDLIFE AREA—(Will) *From I-55 (exit 241): Go 1 mi W.* FACILITIES: 22 sites, 22 no hkups, tenting, dump. RECREATION: boating, 10 hp limit, canoeing, ramp, lake/river/pond fishing, playground. Open Jan - Oct. Phone: (815)423-5326.

(W) FOSSIL ROCK RECREATION AREA—(Will) *From jct I-80 & I-55: Go 10 mi S on I-55, then 1 mi S on Hwy 129, then 1/2 mi W on Strip Mine Rd. Enter on L.*

WELCOME

◆◆FACILITIES: 290 sites, 215 full hkups, 10 E, (20/30/50 amps), 65 no hkups, some extd stay sites, 10 pull-thrus, family camping, tenting, RV's/park model rentals, cabins, dump, ice, picnic tables, patios, fire rings, controlled access.

◆◆RECREATION: pavilion, lake swim, boating, electric motors only, canoeing, lake fishing, golf nearby, bsktball, playground, activities, (wkends), horseshoes, sports field, hiking trails, v-ball.

Pets welcome. Open all yr. Facilities fully operational Apr 1 - Oct 31. Clubs welcome. Rate in 2010 $35 for 4 persons. MC/VISA/Debit. Member ARVC, ICA.

Phone: (815)476-6784
Address: 24615 W Strip Mine Rd, Wilmington, IL 60481
Lat/Lon: 41.30366/-88.20519
Web: www.gahnet.com

SEE AD THIS PAGE

WINDSOR—D-4

(NW) WOLF CREEK STATE PARK—(Shelby) *From jct Hwy 16 & Hwy 32: Go 8 mi NW on Hwy 32 and blacktop road.* FACILITIES: 382 sites, typical site width 12 ft, 304 W&E, (30 amps), 78 no hkups, tenting, dump. RECREATION: lake swim, boating, ramp, dock, lake fishing, playground. Partial handicap access. Open all yr. Phone: (217)459-2831.

WOODSTOCK—A-4

✲ **(NW) BIGFOOT CONSTRUCTION EQUIPMENT**—*From jct US 20 & SR 47: Go N on SR 47 11.5 mi, then E on SR 176 for 2.5 mi, then L(NW) onto Briarwood Dr 1/2 mi. Enter on L.* SERVICES: sells parts/accessories. Manufactures Jack Pads for RVs. Open all yr. MC/VISA/DISC/Debit.

Phone: (888)743-7320
Address: 5119 Briarwood Rd, Woodstock, IL 60098
Lat/Lon: 42.25373/-88.38190
Email: bigfoot@outriggerpads.com
Web: outriggerpads.com

SEE AD DISCOVER SECTION PAGE 55

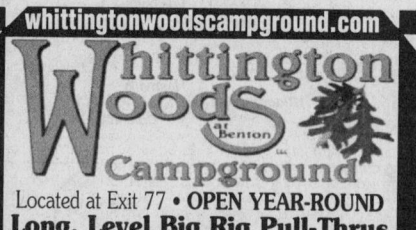

YORKVILLE—B-4

(SE) HIDE-A-WAY LAKES (NOT VISITED)—(Kendall) *From jct US 34 & Hwy 47: Go 1/4 mi S on Hwy 47, then 2 mi E on Van Emmon Rd. Enter on R.*

WELCOME

FACILITIES: 480 sites, 280 full hkups, 100 W&E, (30/50 amps), 100 no hkups, some extd stay sites, 40 pull-thrus, WiFi Internet central location, family camping, tenting, RV's/park model rentals, RV storage, dump, non-guest dump $, laundry, ltd groc, RV supplies, LP bottle exch, ice, picnic tables, fire rings, grills, wood, controlled access.

RECREATION: rec hall, pavilion, lake/river swim, canoeing, kayaking, 4 rowboat/6 pedal boat rentals, float trips, lake/river fishing, fishing supplies, playground, activities, (wkends), horseshoes, v-ball.

Pets welcome. Open all yr. Big rigs welcome. Escort to site. Clubs welcome. Rate in 2010 $25-33 for 4 persons. MC/VISA/DISC/AMEX/Debit. Member ICA. FMCA discount.

Phone: (630)553-6323
Address: 8045 Van Emmon Rd, Yorkville, IL 60560
Web: hide-away-lakes.com

SEE AD CHICAGO PAGE 219

ZION—A-4

(SE) ILLINOIS BEACH STATE PARK—(Lake) *From jct Hwy-173 & Sheridan Road: Go 2 mi S on Sheridan Road.* FACILITIES: 244 sites, typical site width 10 ft, 30 ft max RV length, 244 E, (30/50 amps), tenting, dump, ltd groc. RECREATION: lake swim, boating, canoeing, lake/pond fishing, playground. Partial handicap access. Open May 15 - Oct 15. Phone: (847)662-6433.

Ray Bradbury, author, is from Illinois.

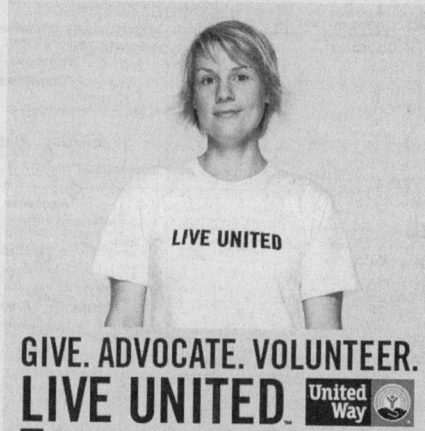

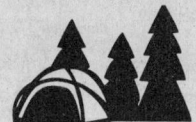

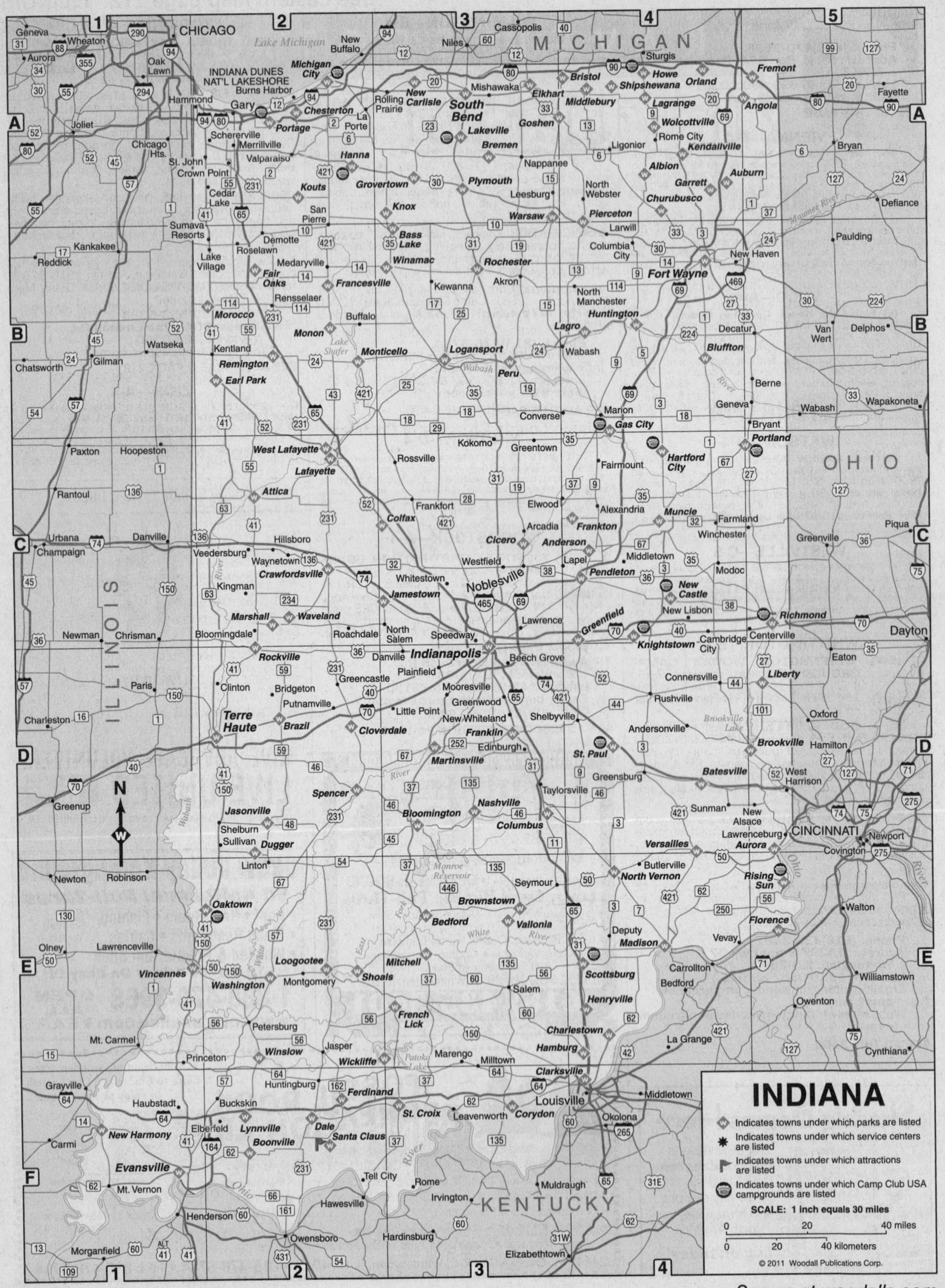
INDIANA
Indicates towns under which parks are listed
Indicates towns under which service centers are listed
Indicates towns under which attractions are listed
Indicates towns under which Camp Club USA campgrounds are listed
SCALE: 1 inch equals 30 miles
0 20 40 miles
0 20 40 kilometers
© 2011 Woodall Publications Corp.
MICHIGAN
OHIO
ILLINOIS
KENTUCKY
CHICAGO
Lake Michigan
INDIANA DUNES NAT'L LAKESHORE
CINCINNATI
N
Geneva
Wheaton
Aurora
Oak Lawn
Hammond
Gary
Joliet
Chicago Hts.
Michigan City
New Buffalo
Burns Harbor
Chesterton
Portage
La Porte
Rolling Prairie
New Carlisle
South Bend
Mishawaka
Niles
Cassopolis
Elkhart
Bristol
Goshen
Middlebury
Lakeville
Bremen
Sturgis
Howe
Shipshewana
Orland
Fremont
Lagrange
Angola
Wolcottville
Rome City
Kendallville
Ligonier
Fayette
Bryan
Defiance
Schererville
Merrillville
St. John
Crown Point
Valparaiso
Cedar Lake
Hanna
Kouts
Grovertown
Plymouth
Nappanee
North Webster
Leesburg
Albion
Garrett
Auburn
Churubusco
Sumava Resorts
Lake Village
Roselawn
Demotte
San Pierre
Knox
Bass Lake
Warsaw
Pierceton
Larwill
Columbia City
New Haven
Fort Wayne
Pauling
Kankakee
Reddick
Fair Oaks
Medaryville
Winamac
Francesville
Rochester
Akron
Kewanna
North Manchester
Huntington
Rensselaer
Morocco
Buffalo
Monon
Lake Shafer
Monticello
Logansport
Peru
Wabash
Lagro
Bluffton
Decatur
Van Wert
Delphos
Watseka
Kentland
Remington
Earl Park
Chatsworth
Gilman
Berne
Geneva
Wabash
Wapakoneta
Marion
Gas City
Converse
Bryant
Portland
Paxton
Hoopeston
West Lafayette
Lafayette
Kokomo
Greentown
Rossville
Fairmount
Hartford City
Rantoul
Attica
Frankfort
Elwood
Alexandria
Muncie
Farmland
Winchester
Colfax
Arcadia
Frankton
Cicero
Anderson
Urbana
Champaign
Danville
Veedersburg
Hillsboro
Waynetown
Crawfordsville
Westfield
Lapel
Middletown
Greenville
Piqua
Whitestown
Noblesville
Pendleton
Modoc
New Castle
Kingman
Jamestown
New Lisbon
Richmond
Marshall
Waveland
Bloomingdale
Roachdale
North Salem
Speedway
Lawrence
Greenfield
Knightstown
Cambridge City
Centerville
Dayton
Newman
Chrisman
Rockville
Danville
Indianapolis
Beech Grove
Eaton
Paris
Clinton
Bridgeton
Greencastle
Plainfield
Mooresville
Greenwood
Connersville
Liberty
Charleston
Terre Haute
Brazil
Putnamville
Little Point
New Whiteland
Shelbyville
Rushville
Oxford
Cloverdale
Franklin
Edinburgh
Andersonville
Brookville Lake
Brookville
Hamilton
Martinsville
St. Paul
Greensburg
Batesville
West Harrison
Greenup
Spencer
Taylorsville
Jasonville
Bloomington
Nashville
Columbus
Sunman
New Alsace
Lawrenceburg
Aurora
Newport
Covington
Shelburn
Sullivan
Dugger
Linton
Versailles
Monroe Reservoir
Butlerville
North Vernon
Rising Sun
Newton
Robinson
Seymour
Brownstown
Vallonia
Oaktown
Bedford
Deputy
Madison
Walton
Florence
Vevay
Olney
Lawrenceville
Loogootee
Mitchell
Carrollton
Williamstown
Vincennes
Washington
Montgomery
Shoals
Salem
Scottsburg
Bedford
Henryville
Owenton
French Lick
Mt. Carmel
Petersburg
Charlestown
La Grange
Hamburg
Winslow
Jasper
Marengo
Milltown
Cynthiana
Princeton
Wickliffe
Patoka Lake
Clarksville
Grayville
Huntingburg
Ferdinand
Louisville
Middletown
Haubstadt
Buckskin
St. Croix
Leavenworth
Corydon
Okolona
Elberfeld
Lynnville
Boonville
Dale
Santa Claus
New Harmony
Carmi
Evansville
Tell City
Rome
Muldraugh
Mt. Vernon
Hawesville
Irvington
Henderson
Owensboro
Hardinsburg
Morganfield
Elizabethtown

TIME ZONE

Most of Indiana is in the Eastern Standard Time Zone. These counties are on Central Time: Daviess, Dubois, Gibson, Jasper, Knox, Lake, LaPorte, Martin, Newton, Perry, Pike, Porter, Posey, Pulaski, Spencer, Starke, Vanderburgh and Warrick. All of Indiana observes Daylight Savings Time.

TOPOGRAPHY

Northern Indiana contains hundreds of small inland lakes and dozens of sandy beaches along the shoreline of Lake Michigan. Southern Indiana is rolling and forested and has numerous caves and interesting river towns.

TEMPERATURE

Indiana's average January temperature is 26° and in July, it's a balmy 82°. Snowfall averages 6.2 inches in January and July averages 9.2 days of precipitation.

TRAVEL & TOURISM INFO

State Agency:
Indiana Office of Tourism Development
One North Capitol, Suite 600
Indianapolis, IN 46204
(800/677-9800)
www.VisitIndiana.com

Local Agencies:
For a complete list of local tourism offices, chambers of commerce and convention and visitors bureaus, see the Indiana State Travel Guide available from the above agency.

Amish Country/Elkhart County CVB
219 Caravan Dr.
Elkhart, IN 46514
(800/250-4827)
www.AmishCountry.org

Anderson/Madison County VCB
6335 S. Scatterfield Rd.
Anderson, IN 46013
(765/643-5633 or 800/533-6569)
www.heartlandspirit.com

Bloomington/Monroe County CVB
Bloomington, IN 47404
(812/334-8900 or 888/333-0088)
www.visitbloomington.com

Brown County Convention & Visitors Bureau
10 North Van Buren Street
Nashville, IN 47448
(800/313-0842)
www.browncounty.com

Clark/Floyd Counties CVB
Southern Indiana Visitor Center
315 Southern Indiana Ave.
Jeffersonville, IN 47130-3218
(812/282-6654 or 800/552-3842),
www.sunnysideoflouisville.org

Clinton County Chamber of Commerce
259 E. Walnut St.
Frankfort, IN 46041
(765/654-5507)
www.ccinchamber.org

Covered Bridge Country (Parke County)
PO Box 165
Rockville, IN 47872
(765/569-5226)
www.parkecounty.com

Covered Bridge Country (Putnam County)
12 West Washington St.
Greencastle, IN 46135
(765/653-8743 or 800/829-4639)
www.coveredbridgecountry.com

Crawford County Tourism Information Center
6225 E. Industrial Lane
Leavenworth, IN 47137
(812/739-2246 or 888/846-5397)
www.crawfordcountyindiana.com

Daviess County Visitors Bureau
1 Train Depot St.
Washington, IN 47501
(812/254-5262 or 800/449-5262)
www.daviesscounty.net

Dearborn County Convention, Visitor & Tourism Bureau
320 Walnut St.
Lawrenceburg, IN 47025
(812/537-0814 or 800/322-8198)
www.visitsoutheastindiana.com

Decatur Chamber of Commerce (Adams County)
125 E. Monroe St.
Decatur, IN 46733
(260/724-2604)
www.decaturchamber.org

Franklin County Convention, Recreation, Visitors Commission
P.O. Box 97
Brookville, IN 47012
(765/647-6522 or 866/647-6555)
www.franklincountyin.com

Fort Wayne/Allen County CVB
1021 S. Calhoun St.
Fort Wayne, IN 46802
(260/424-3700 or 800/767-7752)
www.visitfortwayne.com

Harrison County CVB
310 N. Elm Street
Corydon, IN 47112
(888/738-2137)
www.thisisindiana.org

Huntington County VCB
407 N. Jefferson St.
PO Box 212
Huntington, IN 46750
(260/359-8687 or 800/848-4282)
www.visithuntington.org

Kokomo/Howard County CVB
1504 N. Reed Rd.
Kokomo, IN 46901
(765/457-6802 or 800/837-0971)
www.visitkokomo.org

LaPorte County CVB
1503 S. Meer Rd.
Michigan City, IN 46360
(800/634-2650)
www.visitlaportecounty.com

Lawrence County Tourism Commission
(812/849-1090 or 800/798-0769)
www.limestonecountry.com

Marion/Grant Co. CVB
428 S. Washington St., Ste. 261
Marion, IN 46953
(765/668-5435 or 800/662-9474)
www.showmegrantcounty.com

Marshall County CVB
220 N. Center St.
PO Box 669

BUSINESSES OFFERING

	Things to See & Do	RV Sales	RV Service
SANTA CLAUS Holiday World & Splashin' Safari	►		

Plymouth, IN 46563
(574/936-1882 or 800/626-5353)
www.marshallcountytourism.org

Montgomery County VCB
218 E. Pike St.
Crawfordsville, IN 47933
(765/362-5200 or 800/866-3973)
www.crawfordsville.org

Muncie Visitors Bureau (Delaware County)
425 N. High Street, Ste. 5
Muncie, IN 47305
(765/284-2700 or 800/568-6862)
www.munciecvb.org

Perry County CVB
PO Box 721
Tell City, IN 47586
(888/343-6262)
www.perrycountyindiana.org

Peru/Miami Co. Chamber of Commerce
13 E. Main
Peru, IN 46970
(765/472-1923)
www.miamicochamber.com

Porter County Convention, Recreation & Visitor Commission
Dorothy Buell Memorial Visitor Center
1420 Munson Road
Porter, IN 46304
(219/926-2255 or 800/283-8687)
www.indianadunes.com

Richmond/Wayne Co. CVB
5701 National Rd. E
Richmond, IN 47374
(765/935-8687 or 800/828-8414)
www.visitrichmond.org

Spencer County Visitors Bureau
PO Box 131
Dale, IN 47523-0131
(888/444-9252 or 812/937-4199)
www.LegendaryPlaces.org

South Bend/Mishawaka CVB (St. Joseph County)
401 E. Colfax #310
South Bend, IN 46634-1677
(800/519-0577)
www.exploresouthbend.org

Steuben County Tourism Bureau
207 S. Wayne
Angola, IN 46703
(260/665-5386 or 800/525-3101)
www.lakes101.org

Terre Haute CVB (Vigo County)
2155 State Road 46
Terre Haute, IN 47803
(812/234-5555 or 800/366-3043)
www.terrehaute.com

Where to Find CCUSA Parks

List City	Park Name	Map Coordinates
GAS CITY		
	Sports Lake Campground	B-4
HANNA		
	Last Resort Campground	A-2
HARTFORD CITY		
	Wildwood Acres Campground	C-4
HOWE		
	Grand View Bend	A-4
	Twin Mills Camping Resort	A-4
KNIGHTSTOWN		
	Yogi Bear's Jellystone Park-Knightstown	C-4
LAKEVILLE		
	Beaver Ridge Family Camping Inc.	A-3
MICHIGAN CITY		
	Michigan City Campground	A-2
NEW CASTLE		
	Walnut Ridge Campground	C-4
OAKTOWN		
	New Vision RV Park, LLC	E-2
PORTAGE		
	Yogi Bear's Jellystone Park Camp-Resort	A-2
PORTLAND		
	Hickory Grove Lakes Campground	C-5
RICHMOND		
	Deer Ridge Camping Resort	C-5
RISING SUN		
	Little Farm on the River Camping Resort	E-5
SCOTTSBURG		
	Yogi Bear Jellystone at Raintree Lake	E-4
ST. PAUL		
	Hidden Paradise Campground	D-4

Vincennes/Knox County CVB
102 N. 3rd St.
PO Box 602
Vincennes, IN 47591
(812/886-0400 or 800/886-6443)
www.vincennescvb.org

Wabash County CVB
PO Box 746
Wabash, IN 46992
(260/563-7171 or 800/563-1169)
www.wabashcountycvb.com

Washington County Tourism Bureau
210 E. Market St., Ste. 104
Salem, IN 47167
(812/883-4303)
www.washingtoncountytourism.org

RECREATIONAL INFO

Birding Guide: www.indianaaudubon.org

Canoeing/Hiking/Fishing/Hunting: Indiana Dept. of Natural Resources, 402 W. Washington St., Indianapolis, IN 46204 (317/232-4080) www.in.gov/dnr

Canoe Trails: www.hoosier.canoeclub.org

Golf: Indiana Golf & Travel Guide, www.VisitIndianaGolf.com

Hiking Trails: Hoosier Sierra Club Chapter Office, 1915 W. 18th St., Ste. D, Indianapolis, IN 46202 (317/822-3750) www.hoosier.sierraclub.org

Indoor Rock Climbing: Climb Time Indy, 8750 Corporation Drive, Indianapolis, IN (317/596-3330) www.climbtimeindy.com/

Mountain Biking Trails: www.indianaoutfitters.com/mtn_biking

Snowboarding: (812/723-4696) www.paolipeaks.com

Snowmobiling: Indiana Snowmobilers Assoc, 2114 E. Boulevard #214, Kokomo, IN 46902; www.indianasnowmobilers.com

SHOPPING

Amish Backroads, Michigan City. (260/768-4008) www.backroads.org

Borkholder Dutch Village, Nappanee. Nation's largest antiques, crafts and collectibles mall. Auction every Tuesday. On CR101, one mile north of US 6. (574/773-3144) www.borkholder.com

Edinburgh Premium Outlets, Edinburgh. 85 stores. I-65 at U.S. 31, Exit 76B. (812/526-9764). www.premiumoutlets.com/edinburgh

Prime Outlets, Fremont. Extraordinary values are what you'll find at this brand name outlet mall. www.primeoutlets.com

DESTINATIONS

Many of the natural treasures of this state can be discovered while touring the caverns, traveling the covered bridges, or checking out the Indiana Dunes. The Indianapolis 500 is a

QUICK REFERENCE CHART FOR WOODALL'S FEATURED PARKS

	Green Friendly	RV Lots for Sale	Park Models-Onsite Ownership	Park Membership for Sale	Big Rigs Welcome	Internet Friendly	Pets Welcome
ANGOLA							
Camp Sack-In							■
BREMEN							
Rupert's Resort Campground							■
CHESTERTON							
Sand Creek Campground							■
CLARKSVILLE							
KOA-Louisville Metro Campground						●	■
COLUMBUS							
Columbus Woods-N-Waters					▲	●	■
ELKHART							
Elkhart Campground					▲	●	■
FLORENCE							
Follow the River RV Resort					▲	●	■
FRANKTON							
Miami Camp						●	■
GAS CITY							
Mar-Brook Campground						●	■
GREENFIELD							
Heartland Resort					▲	●	■
S & H Campground						●	■
GROVERTOWN							
EZ Kamp							■
HARTFORD CITY							
Wildwood Acres Campground						●	■
INDIANAPOLIS							
Indiana State Fairgrounds Campground							■
Lake Haven Retreat					▲	●	■
KNIGHTSTOWN							
Yogi Bear's Jellystone Park-Knightstown						●	■
MIDDLEBURY							
Elkhart County, Middlebury Exit KOA					▲	●	■
NASHVILLE							
The Last Resort RV Park & Campground					▲	●	■
Westward Ho Campground							■
ORLAND							
Manapogo Park					▲	●	■
PENDLETON							
Glo Wood Campground					▲		■
PERU							
Honey Bear Hollow Family Campground						●	■
REMINGTON							
Caboose Lake Campground					▲	●	■
RICHMOND							
KOA-Indiana Ohio Kampground					▲	●	■
RISING SUN							
Little Farm on the River Camping Resort					▲	●	■
SANTA CLAUS							
Lake Rudolph Campground & RV Resort					▲	●	■
WARSAW							
Hoffman Lake Camp					▲		■

Green Friendly 🍂; **RV Lots for Sale** ✖; **Park Models/Onsite Onwership** ✱; **Park Memberships for Sale** ✔; **Big Rigs Welcome** ▲;
Internet Friendly ●; **Internet Friendly-WiFi** ●; **Pets Welcome** ■

hot spot each year for those with a need for speed. There's something here for those that need to slow it down a bit, with horseback riding, hiking, bicycling, and many other outdoor activities.

NORTHERN REGION

Travelers will discover simple pleasures, friendly folk, well-known sights and hidden treasures. This area is home to a football hall of fame, sandy dunes, a huge flea market, a whitewater raceway, and a place where visitors can experience life in the "past lane" in Amish Country.

Amish Acres, Nappanee. Visit this 80-acre living history farm listed on the National Register of Historic Places. Guided house and farm tours, craft demonstrations, horse drawn buggy rides, award-winning dining, live professional Broadway theatre, craft and antique shopping are awaiting you. Open March through December.

Angola. Home of the **Fun Spot Amusement Park & Zoo** featuring rides, a huge arcade, and a zoo. Take a scenic train ride departing from downtown Angola on the **Lake Central Railroad.**

Crown Point. For a wet and wild time, spend the day at **Deep River Waterpark**, which includes the Dragon, a slide that drops straight down and hits speeds of up to 35 mph.

Elkhart. Experience premier museums and audio tours celebrating RV manufacturing, railroads, art and history at **Amish Country/Elkhart County Museum.** The **Midwest Museum of American Art** showcases 19th and 20th century American art including a collection of Norman Rockwell lithographs. **RV/MH Hall of Fame** is also located in Elkhart. Visit the **National Hall of Fame,** museum and archival library for the recreational vehicle and manufactured housing industry. Buy locally grown produce and related products at the new **American Countryside Farmer's Market** with 493 vendors.

Fremont. Tour the 400-acre **Wild Winds Buffalo Preserve** via vehicle and horseback.

Howe. Visit a 1903 hand-carved chapel, an 1846 flour mill, or explore nature along the Pigeon River at **Amish Backroads.**

Indiana Dunes National Lakeshore, located on Lake Michigan, at U.S. Rte. 12. Fine, white, sandy beaches and magnificent dunes. Enjoy 15 miles of hiking trails, swimming, fishing, horseback riding and water skiing.

LaPorte. Door Prairie Auto Museum offers three floors of classic automobiles, airplanes, antique toys and historic facades spanning 100 years of automotive history. The exhibit includes the world's first car, an 1886 Benz Motor Wagon.

Michigan City. Barker Mansion, circa 1900, houses a museum with original furnishings and art objects. A turn-of-the century architectural garden is on the grounds.

Pierceton is home to the **Pisgah Marsh** whose interpretive signs highlight nature features and area history. An accessible boardwalk offers excellent wildlife viewing.

South Bend. Take a tour of **Notre Dame's** historic campus. Its **Sacred Heart Church** contains priceless artwork, frescoes, murals, sculptures and 19th-century French stained glass windows. Or visit the **College Football Hall of Fame** showing the history and heroes of college football. The interactive displays, exhibits, photo galleries, artifacts and mementos bring the game to life.

Also in South Bend is the **Studebaker National Museum** with its world-class collection of cars, trucks, carriages and wagons. See the carriage that brought Abraham Lincoln to Ford's Theatre in 1865. Be sure to visit the **Potawatomi Zoo**, housing more than 400 mammals and plenty of reptiles, as well as friendly animals at the petting zoo. If you have a sweet tooth, don't miss the **South Bend Chocolate Company Factory and Museum**. Tour the factory and museum and see one of the world's largest chocolate collections.

EASTERN REGION

"Diverse" is the word that best describes Eastern Indiana. Small towns, urban areas, lakes, prairies and wooden retreats blend together to provide visitors with an unforgettable experience.

Anderson. Mounds State Park offers a fascinating look at ten mounds and earthworks that are believed to have been constructed by the Adena and Hopewell mound builders about 150 B.C. Scenic trails, canoeing, fishing, hiking, swimming and cross-country skiing are available. Anderson is also home to the **Historic Military Armor Museum**. Collection includes vehicles from World War I to the present.

Fort Wayne. Visit **Old City Hall Historical Museum** and see an 1886 doll house, window shop in the 1880s, marvel at the 20th-century inventions and feel the turmoil of settlers and Native Americans clashing over land in the 1700s in this century-old "castle." **Science Central** is where the laws of physics were made to be broken. Bend a rainbow or create an earthquake! Over 120 hands-on math, science and technology exhibits for kids. Wander among the indoor tropical and desert gardens at the **Foellinger-Freimann Botanical Conservatory**. Outdoor terrace and exploration gardens. The **Lincoln Museum** includes 11 galleries featuring hundreds of artifacts from Lincoln's era. Explore Fort Wayne's history at **The History Center**, offering three floors of interactive exhibits and galleries.

Kendallville. At the **Mid-America Windmill Museum** you'll see forty acres of grounds displaying restored windmills and hear the story of windpower.

Kokomo. Attractions include the **City of Firsts Automotive Heritage Museum**, displaying approximately 100 automobiles chronologically from 1895. The **Elwood Hayes Museum** offers memorabilia, furnishings, classic cars and industrial displays of this famous inventor. While you're in Kokomo, did you know that it's the first city to turn a giant sycamore tree stump into a monument and encase it in glass. In fact, it's the **World's Largest Sycamore Stump**, 57 feet in circumference and 12 feet high. It was over 800 years old when a storm demolished it. The stump survived and for many years, a telephone booth, large enough to hold more than a dozen people at a time, was housed inside it.

Muncie. Stroll through the downtown **Muncie Arts District** and visit the numerous galleries featuring arts, crafts and collectibles. The **Muncie Children's Museum** offers 15 interactive exhibits.

Peru offers the **Circus Hall of Fame** where you can view colorful wagons, posters and circus stars. Or let your imagination take flight at the **Grissom Air Museum State Historic Site.** View more than 20 historic aircraft, climb the observation tower and visit indoor displays.

WESTERN REGION

Covered Bridges: Parke County has 30 covered bridges amid beautiful scenery. www.coveredbridges.com.

Crawfordsville. Old Jail Museum, built in 1882, was the last operating rotary jail in America. The Sheriff's residence has also been restored for viewing.

Cutler. Adams Mill is a grist mill with pioneer life antiques displayed. Most of the original mill equipment is running.

Fair Oaks Dairy Adventure, Fair Oaks. An interactive, working dairy farm with live birthing center (almost always guaranteed to see a live birth), exhibits and dairy processing plants where you can see cheese and ice cream made. 27,000 cows on 17,000 acres.

Lafayette. The Red Crown Mini-Museum is a 1930s-era Standard Oil filling station that was restored in 1991 and turned into a "walk-by" museum; it is located at the corner of 6th and South Streets. It features restored antique cars in the auto bays, a 1931 Ford Model B tow truck in the parking lot and random gas-station memorabilia inside.

Monticello. Indiana Beach Resort is on 1,400-acre Lake Shafer in the center of Indiana vacationland. A ferry brings guests to the Boardwalk, a wide promenade with a half-mile of family attractions, almost 20 adult rides, 6 kiddie rides, mini-golf, ski shows and shops.

Terre Haute offers the **Children's Science and Technology Museum of Terre Haute** and **Inland Aquatics**, housing more than 35,000 gallons of saltwater production tanks and America's largest public coral reef display. Or view the works of American artists and sculptors at the **Swope Art Museum.**

CENTRAL REGION

Indianapolis. Visit the **Indianapolis Children's Museum**. The kids will enjoy 5 floors of interactive fun and an incredible "put-you-in-the-action" 5-story theater. There are more than 105,000 artifacts, 10 galleries, 356,000 sq. ft. of hands-on activities and a round, giant screen film theater at the Cine-Dome™ Theater.

Indianapolis Motor Speedway & Museum. Take a ride around the world-famous 500-mile racetrack, site of the world's largest one-day sporting event; or leisurely browse through the museum and **Auto Racing Hall of Fame**.

White River State Park. In addition to beautiful waterways, grassy expanses and tree-lined boulevards, the park also houses the **Indiana State Museum** where you'll find Indiana's only IMAX® 3D Theater.

White River Gardens at the Indianapolis Zoo features a 5,000 square foot glass conservatory, 18 garden designs, water gardens and more.

SOUTH CENTRAL REGION

The magnificent landscape of this region will take even the seasoned traveler's breath away. From the majestic hills of Brown County to the banks of the mighty Ohio River, this diverse landscape will amaze.

Amish Country Tours, Montgomery. Guided tours to Amish stores, harness makers, quilt shops, farms and homes.

Bedford. Antique Auto & Race Car Museum, where over 100 race and antique cars are on display.

The Big Peach, Bruceville. The famous landmark is really a country stand that is family owned and has been around for over 50 years. They offer peaches and other fine produce.

Clifty Falls State Park, Madison. A breathtaking view of the Ohio River, atop a 400-foot bluff, is worth the drive. A 178-acre nature preserve and nature center are on-site.

Vincennes. The Old Cathedral Complex, Indiana's oldest Catholic church (founded in 1732), has parish records dating to 1749. The library houses rare volumes dating to 1319

SOUTHERN REGION

Angel Mounds State Historic Site, Evansville. This 500-acre site was inhabited by Mississippian Indians from 1100 - 1450. You'll find 11 platform mounds, trails, exhibits, a picnic area and a gift shop.

Indiana Caves. Some of America's most beautiful caves can be found in Indiana's southern region. Stop by **Wyandotte Caves** in Leavenworth or visit **Squire Boone Caverns** in Corydon.

ANNUAL EVENTS

JANUARY

The Week of Chocolate, Bloomington; North Webster Winter Festival, North Webster.

FEBRUARY

Maple Syrup Festival, Salem; Parke County Maple Syrup Fair, Parke County.

MARCH

Indiana Flower and Patio Show, Indianapolis; Southern Indiana's Spring Draft Horse, Carriage and Machine Auction, Cannelburg; Spring Eggstravaganza, Vevay.

APRIL

Bridgeton Mountain Man Rendezvous, Bridgeton; Dogwood Tour, Tell City; Mansfield Village Mushroom Festival & Car Show, Parke County; Wakarusa Maple Syrup Festival, Wakarusa.

MAY

Daviess County Rail Fest, Washington; Fairbanks Park Arts and Music Festival, Terre Haute; The Great Race Sports Festival, Elkhart; Madison in Bloom, Madison; Ohio River Valley Folk Festival, Madison; Round the Fountain Art Fair, Lafayette; Spirit of Vincennes, Vincennes; Taste of Noble County Ethnic Festival, Ligonier; Tri-State Antique Market, Lawrenceburg.

JUNE

All American Country Hoe Down, Campbellsburg; Billie Creek Village Civil War Days, Rockville; Friendship Flea Market, Friendship; Indy Jazz Fest, Indianapolis; Junque Jubilee, Vevay; Livonia Summerfest Festival, Livonia; Masterworks Performing Arts Festival, Winona Lake; Monon Food Fest, Monon; Pennsy Trail Art Fair & Music Festival, Greenfield; Pioneer Days, Royal Center.

JULY

American Countryside Midsummer Fair, Elkhart; Carmelfest, Carmel; Cedar Valley Bluegrass Festival, Derby; Circus City Festival, Peru; Three Rivers Festival, Fort Wayne; Jasper Strassenfest, Jasper; Lapel Village Fair, Lapel; Pekin 4th of July Festival, Pekin; Pierogi Fest, Whiting; Quilter's Celebration, Marion; Spirit of Monticello Festival, Monticello; St. Joseph County 4-H Fair, South Bend.

AUGUST

Auburn Cord Duesenberg Festival, Auburn; Billie Creek Village Harvest Days, Rockville; Daviess County Amish Quilt Auction, Cannelburg; Derby Riverfest, Derby; Annual National Toy Truck 'N Construction Show & Auction, Indianapolis; Elwood Glass Festival, Elwood; Farmer's Pike Antique Arts & Crafts Festival, New Castle; Indiana State Fair, Indianapolis; Lakefront Art Festival, Michigan City; Ligonier Marshmallow Festival, Ligonier; Little Italy Festival, Clinton; Madison Ribberfest, Madison

SEPTEMBER

American Countryside Harvest Celebration, Elkhart; Atlanta New Earth Festival, Atlanta; Bear Hollow Fall Fest & Das Holz Fest, Saint Croix; Cambridge City Canal Days, Cambridge City; Columbus Scottish Festival, Columbus; Daviess County Amish Quilt Auction, Cannelburg; Cory Apple Festival, Cory; Fairmount Museum Days/Remembering James Dean Festival, Fairmont; Family Arts Festival, Logansport; Feast of the Hunter's Moon, West Lafayette; Forks of the Wabash Pioneer Festival, Huntington; Farncesville Fall Festival, Francesville; Golden Heritage Days Festival, Princeton; Grabill County Fair, Grabill; Herbstfest, Huntingburg. Lawrenceburg Fall Fest, Lawrenceburg; Madison Chatauqua Festival of Art, Madison

OCTOBER

Apple Festival of Kendalville, Kendalville; Aurora Farmers Fair, Aurora; Bloomfield Apple Festival, Bloomfield; Civil War Days and Living History, Hartford City; Fort Vallonia Days, Vallonia; Four Rivers Arts & Crafts Harvest Home Show, Jasper; Grape Harvest Festival, Plainfield; Harvest Moon Festival, Sheridan; Hoosier Heritage Fall Tour, Tell City; Hoosier Storytelling Festival, Indianapolis; Mansfield Covered Bridge Festival, Mansfield; Mississinewa 1812, Marion; Mooresville Subway Grand Prix, Mooresville; Navy Bean Festival, Rising Sun; Newport Antique Auto Hill Climb, Newport; Annual Feast of the Hunter's Moon, Lafayette; Parke County Covered Bridge Festival, Rockville.

NOVEMBER

Christmas Gift and Hobby Show, Indianapolis; Christmas in Brown County, Brown County; El Dia de los Muertos/Day of the Dead Celebration, Indianapolis; Ferdinand Christkindlmarkt, Ferdinand; Huntingburg Christmas Stroll, Huntingburg; International Festival, Indianapolis; Metamora Old Fashioned Christmas Walk, Metamora; Nights Before Christmas Candlelight Tour, Madison.

DECEMBER

Christmas in Brown County, Brown County; Dickens of a Christmas, Lafayette; Jasper O' Tannenbaum Days, Jasper; Purdue Christmas Show, Lafayette.

Indiana

ALBION—A-4

(S) CHAIN O'LAKES SP—(Noble) *From business center: Go 5 mi SE on Hwy-9.* FACILITIES: 413 sites, 331 E, (30/50 amps), 82 no hkups, tenting, dump, ltd groc. RECREATION: lake swim, boating, electric motors only, canoeing, ramp, lake fishing, playground. Pets welcome. Partial handicap access. Open all yr. Phone: (260)636-2654.

ANDERSON—C-4

(E) MOUNDS SP—(Madison) *From business center: Go 3 mi NE on Hwy-232.* FACILITIES: 75 sites, 75 E, (30 amps), tenting, dump, ltd groc. RECREATION: swim pool, river fishing, playground. Open all yr. Phone: (765)642-6627.

ANGOLA—A-5

(E) CAMP SACK-IN—(Steuben) *From jct I-69 & US 20: Go 11 mi E on US 20, then 1/2 mi N on Old Rd 1, then 1/2 mi E on CR 40-S. Enter on L.*

WELCOME

◆◆FACILITIES: 140 sites, typical site width 38 ft, 120 W&E, 13 E, (20/30/50 amps), 7 no hkups, many extd stay sites (summer), 5 pull-thrus, family camping, tenting, RV storage, dump, non-guest dump $, portable dump, ltd groc, RV supplies, ice, picnic tables, fire rings, wood.

◆◆◆RECREATION: pavilion, lake swim, pond fishing, fishing supplies, mini-golf, ($), golf nearby, bsktball, playground, shuffleboard court shuffleboard court, activities (wkends), horseshoes, sports field, hiking trails, v-ball.

Pets welcome. Open mid Apr - mid Oct. Escort to site. Clubs welcome. Rate in 2010 $18-25 per family. MC/VISA. Member ARVC, ICOA.

ANGOLA—Continued
CAMP SACK-IN—Continued

Phone: (260)665-5166
Address: 8740 East 40 S, Angola, IN 46703
Lat/Lon: 41.63960/-84.82511
Email: campsackin@hotmail.com
Web: www.campsackin.com

SEE AD THIS PAGE

(W) Captain Carl's Famous Buck Lake Ranch—(Steuben) *From jct I-69 & US 20: Go 1-1/2 mi E on US 20, then 1 mi N on S 200 W, then 1/2 mi W on Buck Lake Rd. Enter on L.* ◆◆FACILITIES: 120 sites, 70 full hkups, 20 W&E, (20/30 amps), 30 no hkups, 1 pull-thrus, family camping, tenting, dump, ltd groc. ◆◆◆RECREATION: lake swim, boating, electric motors only, canoeing, ramp, dock, lake fishing, playground. Pets welcome. Partial handicap access. Open Apr 15 - Oct 15. Rate in 2010 $25-30 per family. Member ARVC. Phone: (260)665-6699.

(W) Circle B Park—(Steuben) *From jct I-69 (Exit 148) & US 20: Go 2-1/2 mi W on US 20. Enter on L.* ◆◆◆◆FACILITIES: 300 sites, typical site width 30 ft, 250 full hkups, 50 W&E, (30/50 amps), 45 pull-thrus, family camping, tenting, dump, laundry, groceries. ◆◆◆◆RECREATION: lake swim, boating, 10 hp limit, canoeing, ramp, dock, lake/pond fishing, playground. Pets welcome. Partial handicap access. Open all yr. Facilities fully operational Apr 15 - Oct 15. Big rigs welcome. Rate in 2010 $31-37 per family. Member ARVC, ICOA. Phone: (260)665-5353.

(N) POKAGON SP—(Steuben) *From I-69 (exit 154): Go W on Hwy 727 & follow signs. Entrance fee required.* FACILITIES: 273 sites, 200 E, (20/30 amps), 73 no hkups, tenting, dump, ltd groc. RECREATION: lake swim, boating, dock, lake fishing, playground. Open all yr. Phone: (219)833-2012.

ATTICA—C-2

(NW) Summers-Carroll Campground—(Warren) *From jct US 41/SR 28 & SR 55: Go 6 mi N on SR 55, then 1 mi W on CR E 500 N (gravel road), then 1/2 mi N on CR N 200 E (gravel road). Enter on R.* ◆◆FACILITIES: 152 sites, typical site width 40 ft, 40 full hkups, 90 W&E, (30/50 amps), 22 no hkups, 10 pull-thrus, family camping, tenting, dump, laundry, ltd groc. ◆◆◆RECREATION: swim pool, pond fishing, playground. Pets welcome. Partial handicap access. Open Apr 20 - Oct 20. Facilities fully operational Memorial Day - Labor Day. Rate in 2010 $25 for 4 persons. Phone: (765)762-2832.

AUBURN—A-4

(SW) Fireside Resort at Kruse Park—(DeKalb) *At jct I-69 (exit 126) & CR 11A: Go 300 yds W. Enter on R.* ◆◆◆FACILITIES: 61 sites, typical site width 32 ft, 49 full hkups, 6 W&E, (30/50 amps), 6 no hkups, 36 pull-thrus, family camping, tenting, dump, laundry, ltd groc. ◆◆RECREATION: swim pool, playground. Pets welcome. Partial handicap access. Open all yr. Big rigs welcome. Rate in 2010 $28-33 for 2 persons. Phone: (260)925-6747.

AURORA—D-5

(S) Camp Shore Campground—(Ohio) *From jct US 50 & Hwy 56: Go 4 mi W on Hwy 56. Enter on L.* ◆◆◆FACILITIES: 260 sites, typical site width 28 ft, 70 full hkups, 190 W&E, (15 amps), 64 pull-thrus, family camping, tenting, dump, ltd groc. ◆◆◆RECREATION: swim pool, boating, ramp, river fishing, playground. Open all yr. Facilities fully operational Apr 1 - Nov 1. Rate in 2010 $18 for 4 persons. Phone: (812)438-2135.

BASS LAKE—B-3

(N) Hickory Hills Campground at Bass Lake—(Starke) *From US 30 & US 35: Go 10 mi S on US 35, then 1-1/2 mi E on CR E 400 S, then 200 yds S on S 550 E. Enter on L.* ◆◆FACILITIES: 325 sites, typical site width 40 ft, 65 full hkups, 200 W&E, (30/50 amps), 60 no hkups, 3 pull-thrus, family camping, tenting, dump, ltd groc. ◆◆RECREATION: pond fishing, play equipment. Pets welcome. Open all yr. Facilities fully operational May 1 - End of Oct. Phone: (574)772-4817.

(S) Rising Sun Campground—(Starke) *From US 30 to US 35: Go 15-3/4 mi S, then go 2 mi E on CR W 900 S, then 1/2 mi S on CR 200 E, then 400 yds E on CR E750 N. Enter on R.* ◆FACILITIES: 114 sites, typical site width 40 ft, 84 W&E, (30 amps), 30 no hkups, family camping, tenting, dump, laundry, groceries. ◆◆◆RECREATION: swim pool, boating, canoeing, ramp, river fishing, playground. Pets welcome. Partial handicap access. Open April 15 - Oct 15. Facilities fully operational Memorial Day - Labor Day. Member ICOA. Phone: (866)542-0055.

BATESVILLE—D-4

INDIAN LAKES-NACO—(Ripley) *7234 E State Rd, Batesville, IN 47006.*

FACILITIES: tenting.

Open all yr. Rate in 2010 $32 for 2 persons.

INDIAN LAKES-NACO—Continued on next page

Indiana was the 19th state admitted to the Union.

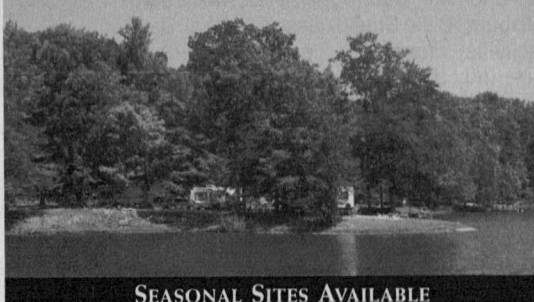

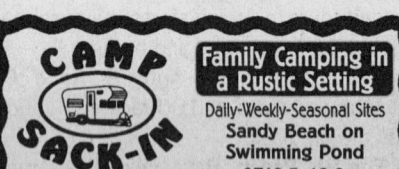

BATESVILLE—Continued
INDIAN LAKES-NACO—Continued

Phone: (800)405-6188
Address: 7234 E State Rd, Batesville, IN 47006
Email: tripexpert@1000trails.com

SEE AD ALBION PAGE 234

BEDFORD—E-3

(E) Free Spirit RV Resort—(Lawrence) *From jct Hwy 37 & US 50: Go 10 mi E on US 50 then 1 mi N on SR 446, then 1 blck W on Erie Church Rd. Enter on L.* ◇◇FACILITIES: 40 sites, typical site width 24 ft, 26 full hkups, 14 W&E, (20/30/50 amps), 20 no hkups, 22 pull-thrus, family camping, tenting, dump, laundry. ◇◇◇RECREATION: swim pool, playground. Pets welcome. Open all yr. Facilities fully operational Memorial Day - Labor Day. Rate in 2010 $22-27 for 5 persons. Member ARVC, ICOA. Phone: (812)834-6164.

BLOOMINGTON—D-3

(S) HOOSIER NF (Hardin Ridge Rec. Area)—(Monroe) *From jct Hwy 46 & Hwy 446: Go 13 mi S on Hwy 446, then 2 mi W on Chapel Hill Rd.* FACILITIES: 200 sites, 10 ft max RV length, 87 E, 113 no hkups, tenting, dump. RECREATION: lake swim, boating, ramp, lake fishing, playground. Partial handicap access. Open all yr. Facilities fully operational Apr 12 - Oct 13. Phone: (812)837-9453.

(S) Lake Monroe Village—(Monroe) *From jct SR 37 & Smithville Rd: Go 2 mi E on Smithville Rd, then 1-1/2 mi S on Fairfax Rd. Enter on L.* ◇◇◇◇◇FACILITIES: 425 sites, typical site width 33 ft, 115 full hkups, 25 W&E, (20/30/50 amps), 50 amps ($), 285 no hkups, 20 pull-thrus, family camping, tenting, dump, laundry, groceries. ◇◇◇◇◇RECREATION: swim pool, canoeing, lake fishing, playground. Pets welcome. Partial handicap access. Open all yr. Big rigs welcome. Rate in 2010 $35-55 for 2 persons. Member ARVC, ICOA. Phone: (812)824-2267. FMCA discount.

(S) MONROE LAKE SRA—(Monroe) *From business center: Go 1 mi E on Hwy-46, then 7 mi S on Hwy-446.* FACILITIES: 320 sites, 226 E, 94 no hkups, tenting, dump. RECREATION: lake swim, boating, ramp, lake/river fishing, playground. Open all yr. Facilities fully operational Apr 1 - Oct 31. Phone: (812)837-9546.

BLUFFTON—B-4

(E) Mendenhall's RV/Mobile Park (RV SPACES) —(Wells) *From jct SR 1 & SR 124: Go 1/2 mi E on SR 124. Enter on L.* FACILITIES: 14 sites, typical site width 30 ft, accepts self-contained units only, 12 full hkups, 2 W&E, (30/50 amps), 8 pull-thrus. Pets welcome. No tents. Open all yr. Big rigs welcome. Rate in 2010 $28 for 2 persons. Phone: (260)827-8719.

(E) OUABACHE SP—(Wells) *From jct Hwy 124 & Hwy 201/CR 450E: Go 3/4 mi S on Hwy 201/CR 450S, then 1 mi E on CR 100.* FACILITIES: 124 sites, 77 E, (30 amps), 47 no hkups, tenting, dump. RECREATION: swim pool, boating, no motors, ramp, dock, lake fishing, playground. Open all yr. Phone: (260) 824-0926.

BOONVILLE—F-2

(E) SCALES LAKE PARK (Warrick County Park)—(Warrick) *From jct I-64 (exit 39) & Hwy 61: Go 10 mi S on Hwy 61, (Town Square) then 1/2 mi E on Hwy 62 (Locust St.): then 1/4 mi E on Walnut St., then 1/2 mi N on Park Lane Dr. Enter on L.* FACILITIES: 141 sites, 141 W&E, (30/50 amps), 14 pull-thrus, tenting, dump, laundry. RECREATION: lake swim, boating, electric motors only, ramp, dock, lake fishing, playground. Partial handicap access. Open all yr. Facilities fully operational Memorial Day - mid Aug. Phone: (812)897-6200.

BRAZIL—D-2

(N) Fallen Rock Park Campground—(Parke) *From jct I-70 & SR 59: Go 13-3/4 mi N on SR 59, then 2-3/4 mi E on CR 900 S. Enter on L.* ◇◇FACILITIES: 83 sites, typical site width 50 ft, 52 full hkups, 5 W&E, 6 E, (20/30/50 amps), 50 amps ($), 20 no hkups, 6 pull-thrus, family camping, tenting, dump, ltd groc. ◇◇RECREATION: dock, stream fishing, playground. Pets welcome. Partial handicap access. Open March 1 - Nov 1. Facilities fully operational Memorial Day - Labor Day. Member ARVC, ICOA. Phone: (765)672-4301.

BREMEN—A-3

(E) Pla-Mor Campground—(Marshall) *From jct SR 331 & US 6: Go 3-1/2 mi E on US 6. Enter on L.* ◇◇◇FACILITIES: 565 sites, typical site width 40 ft, 225 full hkups, 340 W&E, (30/50 amps), 150 pull-thrus, family camping, tenting, dump, laundry, ltd groc. ◇◇◇◇RECREATION: pond fishing, playground. Pets welcome, breed restrict. Partial handicap access. Open Mid Apr - Mid Oct. Big rigs welcome. Rate in 2010 $23-30 per family. Phone: (574)546-3665.

(SW) RUPERT'S RESORT CAMPGROUND —(Marshall) *From jct SR 331 & US 6: Go 5-1/2 mi W on US 6, then 1 mi S on Kenilworth Rd, then 1 mi E on 3rd Rd, then 1/4 mi S on W Shore Dr. Enter on L.*

◇◇FACILITIES: 120 sites, typical site width 40 ft, 32 full hkups, 68 W&E, (30/50 amps), 20 no hkups, many extd stay sites, 4 pull-thrus, family camping, tenting, RV storage, dump, non-guest dump $, ice, picnic tables, fire rings, wood.

BREMEN—Continued
RUPERT'S RESORT CAMPGROUND—Continued

◇◇◇RECREATION: rec hall, coin games, lake swim, boating, canoeing, kayaking, ramp, dock, 4 pontoon/5 rowboat/4 pedal boat rentals, lake fishing, fishing supplies, golf nearby, bsktball, play equipment, activities (wkends), horseshoes, sports field, v-ball. Rec open to public.

Pets welcome. Partial handicap access. Open May 1 - Sep 30. Clubs welcome. Rate in 2010 $24-26.50 per family. MC/VISA. Member ARVC, ICOA.

Phone: (574)546-2657
Address: 3408 W Shore Dr, Bremen, IN 46506
Lat/Lon: 41.42941/-86.23534

SEE AD THIS PAGE

BRISTOL—A-4

(E) Eby's Pines RV Park & Campground—(Elkhart) *From jct I-80/90 (Indiana Turnpike exit 101) & SR 15: Go 1 mi S on SR 15, then 3 mi E on SR 120. Enter on R.* ◇◇◇FACILITIES: 320 sites, typical site width 40 ft, 90 full hkups, 230 W&E, (30/50 amps), 65 pull-thrus, family camping, tenting, dump, laundry, groceries. ◇◇◇◇RECREATION: 2 swim pools, river/pond fishing, playground. Pets welcome. Partial handicap access. Open all yr. Facilities fully operational Apr 15 - Nov 1. Big rigs welcome. Rate in 2010 $33-39.75 per family. Phone: (574)848-4583.

BROOKVILLE—D-5

(N) BROOKVILLE LAKE (State Lake)—(Franklin) *From business center: Go 5 mi N on Hwy-101.* FACILITIES: 450 sites, 62 full hkups, 388 E, tenting, dump, full svc store. RECREATION: lake swim, boating, ramp, dock, lake fishing, playground. No pets. Partial handicap access. Open all yr. Facilities fully operational Apr 1 - Nov 1. Phone: (765)647-2657.

BROWNSTOWN—E-3

(SE) JACKSON-WASHINGTON SF—(Vanderburgh) *From Business Center: Go 2.5 mi SE of Brownstown.* FACILITIES: 56 sites, 56 no hkups, tenting. RECREATION: boating, electric motors only, ramp, dock, lake fishing, playground. Partial handicap access. Open all yr. Facilities fully operational Apr - Nov. Phone: (812)358-2160.

CHARLESTOWN—E-4

(E) CHARLESTOWN STATE PARK—(Clark) *7 miles East on Hwy 62, straight through stoplight, one more mile-gate is on the right. Enter on R.* FACILITIES: 192 sites, 60 full hkups, 132 E, tenting, dump. RECREATION: lake fishing, play equipment. Partial handicap access. Open all yr. Facilities fully operational Apr - Oct 31. Phone: (812)256-5600.

CHESTERTON—A-2

(N) INDIANA DUNES SP—(Porter) *From business center: Go 3 mi N on Hwy 49.* FACILITIES: 140 sites, 140 E, (50 amps), tenting, dump, ltd groc. RECREATION: lake swim, lake fishing, playground. Open all yr. Phone: (219)926-1952.

(SE) SAND CREEK CAMPGROUND—(Porter) *From jct I-80/90 (exit 31) & SR 49: Go 3/4 mi N on SR 49, then 2-1/4 mi E on CR 1050N, then 1/2 mi S on CR 350E. Enter on R.*

WELCOME

◇◇FACILITIES: 195 sites, typical site width 35 ft, 32 full hkups, 65 W&E, 8 E, (30/50 amps), 90 no hkups, 8 pull-thrus, family camping, tenting, cabins, RV storage, dump, non-guest dump $, portable dump, laundry, ltd groc, ice, picnic tables, fire rings, wood.

◇◇RECREATION: rec room/area, pavilion, coin games, swim pool, golf nearby, bsktball, playground, sports field, hiking trails, v-ball.

Pets welcome. Open Apr 15 - Oct 15. Clubs welcome. Rate in 2010 $27-33 per family. MC/VISA.

Phone: (219)926-7482
Address: 1000 N CR 350 E, Chesterton, IN 46304
Lat/Lon: 41.57852/-86.99939
Email: jilee@sandcreekcampground.com
Web: www.sandcreekcampground.com

SEE AD MICHIGAN CITY PAGE 240

CHURUBUSCO—A-4

(NW) Blue Lake Resort Campground—(Whitley) *From jct US 33 & Blue Lake Rd: Go 3/4 mi S on Blue Lake Rd. Enter on R.* ◇FACILITIES: 75 sites, typical site width 35 ft, 75 W&E, (20/30/50 amps), 2 pull-thrus, family camping, tenting, dump, laundry, ltd groc. ◇◇◇RECREATION: lake swim, boating, canoeing, ramp, dock, lake fishing, playground. Pets welcome. Partial handicap access. Open Apr - Oct. Rate in 2010 $25 per family. Member ARVC, RVIC. Phone: (260)693-2265.

CICERO—C-3

(E) WHITE RIVER CAMPGROUND—(Hamilton) *From jct US 31 & SR 47/E 236th St: Go 7 mi E on SR 47/E 236th St. Enter on R.* FACILITIES: 106 sites, typical site width 33 ft, 62 full hkups, 38 W&E, (30/50 amps), 6 no hkups, 2 pull-thrus, tenting, dump, laundry, ltd groc. RECREATION: boating, canoeing, ramp, dock, river/pond fishing, playground. Pets welcome. Partial handicap access. Open Apr 15 - Oct 31. Big rigs welcome. Phone: (317) 984-2705.

CLARKSVILLE—F-4

(N) Add-More RV Park—(Clark) *From jct I-65 & exit 5: Go 1/4 mi W on Veterans Pkwy, then 1/4 mi N on Giltner Ln, then 1/4 mi E on Progress Way, then 1/4 mi N on Add-More Ln. Enter on L.* ◇◇◇FACILITIES: 100 sites, typical site width 25 ft, 100 full hkups, (30/50 amps), family camping, laundry. ◇RECREATION: lake fishing. Pets welcome, size restrict. Partial handicap access. No tents. Open all yr. Facilities fully operational Apr 1 - Dec 1. Big rigs welcome. Rate in 2010 $30 for 2 persons. Member ARVC, ICOA. Phone: (812)283-4321.

(SW) KOA-LOUISVILLE METRO CAMPGROUND—(Clark) *From jct I-65 (exit 1) & Stansifer Ave: Go 50 ft W on Stansifer Ave, then 1/4 mi S on Marriott Dr. Enter on L.*

WELCOME

◇◇◇◇FACILITIES: 115 sites, typical site width 28 ft, 82 full hkups, 8 W&E, (30/50 amps), 50 amps ($), 25 no hkups, some extd stay sites, 28 pull-thrus, cable TV, ($), WiFi Instant Internet at site, WiFi Internet central location, family camping, tenting, cabins, dump, non-guest dump $, laundry, full svc store, RV supplies, LP gas by weight/by meter, ice, picnic tables, fire rings, grills.

◇◇◇RECREATION: coin games, swim pool, mini-golf, golf nearby, bsktball, playground, horseshoes. Rec open to public.

Pets welcome. Partial handicap access. Open all yr. Escort to site. Clubs welcome. Rate in 2010 $33.50-43 for 2 persons. MC/VISA/DISC/Debit. Member ARVC, ICOA. KOA discount.

Phone: (812)282-4474
Address: 900 Marriott Dr, Clarksville, IN 47129
Lat/Lon: 38.27959/-85.75421

SEE AD LOUISVILLE, KY PAGE 272

CLINTON—D-2

HORSESHOE LAKES (CAMP RESORT) —(Vermillion) *12962 S 225 W., Clinton, IN 47842.*

WELCOME

FACILITIES: 123 sites.
RECREATION: rec hall, swim pool.

Phone: (800)579-4987
Address: 12962 S 225 W, Clinton, IN 47842
Web: www.oneparkmembership.com

SEE AD ALBION PAGE 234

CLOVERDALE—D-2

(N) Blackhawk Campground—(Putnam) *From jct US 231 & I-70: Go 4 mi W on I-70 (exit 37), then 1-1/2 mi S on SR 243, then 1 mi W on CR 1050 S. Enter on L.* ◇◇FACILITIES: 167 sites, typical site width 25 ft, 20

Blackhawk Campground—Continued on next page

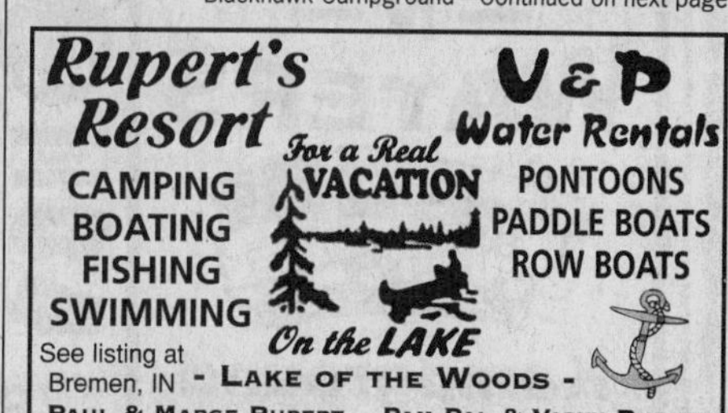

CLOVERDALE—Continued
Blackhawk Campground—Continued

full hkups, 97 W&E, (30/50 amps), 50 no hkups, 20 pull-thrus, family camping, tenting, dump, laundry, groceries. ◆◆RECREATION: pond fishing, playground. Pets welcome. Open all yr. Rate in 2010 $20-25 for 6 persons. Phone: (765)795-4795.

CLOVERDALE RV PARK—(Putnam) *From jct I-70 (exit 41) & US 231: Go 1/2 mi N on US 231, then 1/4 mi E on CR 800 S. Enter on L.*

WELCOME

◆◆◆FACILITIES: 72 sites, typical site width 25 ft, 26 full hkups, 24 W&E, (30 amps), 22 no hkups, some extd stay sites, 60 pull-thrus, WiFi Instant Internet at site, family camping, tenting, RV storage, dump, non-guest dump $, laundry, ltd groc, RV supplies, ice, picnic tables, fire rings, wood.

◆◆RECREATION: rec hall, pond fishing, fishing supplies, bsktball, play equipment, horseshoes, sports field, hiking trails, v-ball.

Pets welcome. Open all yr. Facilities fully operational Apr 1 - Nov 1. Clubs welcome. Rate in 2010 $26-28 for 4 persons. MC/VISA/DISC/Debit. Member ARVC, ICOA.

Phone: (765)795-3294
Address: 2789 E County Rd 800 S, Cloverdale, IN 46120
Lat/Lon: 39.54426/-86.79923
Email: cdalervp@ccrtc.com
Web: www.cloverdalervpark.com

SEE AD PAGE 235

(SW) LIEBER SRA (Cagles Mill Lake)—(Putnam) *From business center: Go 5 mi SW on Hwy-42, then 1 mi N on Hwy-243.* FACILITIES: 252 sites, 150 E, (30 amps), 102 no hkups, tenting, dump, ltd groc. RECREATION: swim pool, boating, ramp, dock, lake fishing, playground. Partial handicap access. Open all yr. Facilities fully operational Apr 1 - Nov 1. Phone: (765)795-4576.

(SW) Misty Morning Campground—(Owen) *From jct US 231 & I-70: Go 4 mi W on I-70 (exit 37), then 4-1/2 mi S on SR 243. Enter on L.* ◆FACILITIES: 122 sites, 4 full hkups, 18 W&E, 100 E, (30 amps), 5 pull-thrus, tenting, ltd groc. ◆◆RECREATION: pond fishing, play equipment. Pets welcome. Open all yr. Facilities fully operational Apr 15 - Oct 15. Rate in 2010 $20-25. Phone: (812)239-7884.

COLFAX—C-3

(N) Broadview Lake and Campground—(Clinton) *From jct I-65 (exit 158) & SR 28: Go 2-1/2 mi W on SR 28, then 3 mi S on US 52, then 1/4 mi W on*

COLFAX—Continued
Broadview Lake and Campground—Continued

Broadview Rd/CR 800 W. Enter on R. ◆◆◆FACILITIES: 167 sites, typical site width 30 ft, 48 full hkups, 119 W&E, (30/50 amps), 2 pull-thrus, family camping, tenting, dump, ltd groc. ◆◆◆RECREATION: swim pool, pond fishing, playground. Pets welcome. Open Apr 15 - Oct 15. Facilities fully operational Memorial Day - Labor Day. Rate in 2010 $21-22 for 4 persons. Member ICOA. Phone: (765)324-2622.

COLUMBUS—D-3

(S) COLUMBUS WOODS-N-WATERS—(Bartholomew) *From jct I-65 (exit 64) & SR 58 (Ogilville): Go 1/2 mi W on SR 58, then 1 mi S on CR S 300 W. Enter on L.*

WELCOME

◆◆◆◆FACILITIES: 108 sites, typical site width 35 ft, 21 full hkups, 87 W&E, (30/50 amps), 50 amps ($), some extd stay sites, 16 pull-thrus, WiFi Instant Internet at site, family camping, tenting, RV storage, dump, non-guest dump $, portable dump, laundry, groceries, RV supplies, LP gas by weight/by meter, ice, picnic tables, fire rings, wood.

◆◆◆◆RECREATION: rec room/area, equipped pavilion, coin games, swim pool, lake fishing, fishing supplies, golf nearby, bsktball, playground, activities, (wkends), horseshoes, sports field, hiking trails, v-ball.

Pets welcome. Partial handicap access. Open all yr. Big rigs welcome. Escort to site. Clubs welcome. Rate in 2010 $29-31 for 2 persons. MC/VISA/DISC/Debit. Member ARVC, ICOA. FCRV discount. FMCA discount.

Phone: (800)799-3928
Address: 8855 S 300 W., Columbus, IN 47201
Lat/Lon: 39.12051/-85.96658
Email: woodnwaters@bcremc.net
Web: www.woodsnwaters.com

SEE AD THIS PAGE

CORYDON—F-3

(S) Grand Trails RV Park (Not Visited)—(Harrison) *From jct I-64 (exit 105) & SR 135: Go 1-3/4 mi S on SR 135, then 1-1/4 mi E on SR 62, then 300 yds S on Mulberry St. Enter on R.* ◆◆FACILITIES: 37 sites, typical site width 22 ft, 22 full hkups, 15 W&E, (20/30/50 amps), 4 pull-thrus, tenting, laundry. ◆RECREATION: swim pool, river fishing. Pets welcome. Open all yr. Big rigs welcome. Rate in 2010 $32.90-35.90 for 2 persons. Phone: (812)738-9077.

(W) HARRISON-CRAWFORD SF—(Harrison) *From jct I-64: Go 7 mi W on Hwy 62, then 3 mi S on Hwy 462.* FACILITIES: 306 sites, 281 E, 25 no hkups, tenting, dump. RECREATION: ramp, lake fishing, playground. Open all yr. Phone: (812)738-8232.

(W) WYANDOTTE WOODS SF REC AREA—(Harrison) *From jct Hwy-135 & Hwy-62: Go 7 mi W on Hwy-62, then 1 mi S on Hwy-462.* FACILITIES: 281 sites, 281 E, tenting, dump. RECREATION: boating, canoeing, ramp, lake/river/pond fishing, playground. Partial handicap access. Open all yr. Facilities fully operational Spring - Fall. Phone: (812)738-8232.

CRAWFORDSVILLE—C-2

(N) KOA-Crawfordsville—(Montgomery) *From jct US 136 & US 231: Go 1-1/4 mi N on US 231. Enter on R.* ◆◆◆FACILITIES: 70 sites, typical site width 48 ft, 38 ft max RV length, 28 full hkups, 32 W&E, (30/50 amps), 10 no hkups, 55 pull-thrus, family camping, tenting, dump, laundry, ltd groc. ◆◆◆RECREATION: swim pool, playground. Pets welcome. Open Mar 15 - Nov 15. Facilities fully operational Jun 1 - Labor Day. Rate in 2010 $27-38 for 2 persons. Member ARVC, RVIC. Phone: (800)562-4191. KOA discount.

CRAWFORDSVILLE—Continued

(W) Sugar Creek Campground of Crawfordsville—(Montgomery) *From jct US 231 & US 136: Go 1-1/2 mi W on US 136. Enter on R.* ◆◆◆FACILITIES: 64 sites, typical site width 25 ft, 44 full hkups, 16 W&E, (30/50 amps), 15 no hkups, 14 pull-thrus, family camping, tenting, dump. ◆◆◆RECREATION: boating, canoeing, river/pond fishing, playground. Pets welcome, breed restrict. Open all yr. Big rigs welcome. Rate in 2010 $25-30 for 2 persons. Phone: (765)414-3971.

DALE—F-2

(S) LINCOLN SP—(Spencer) *From south city limits: Go 1/4 mi S on US 231.* FACILITIES: 270 sites, 150 E, 120 no hkups, tenting, dump, groceries. RECREATION: lake swim, boating, electric motors only, ramp, dock, lake fishing, playground. Open all yr. Phone: (812)937-4710.

DUGGER—D-2

(S) GREENE-SULLIVAN SF—(Sullivan) *From town: Go 2 mi S on Hwy-159.* FACILITIES: 100 sites, 100 no hkups, tenting, dump. RECREATION: boating, electric motors only, ramp, lake/pond fishing, playground. Open all yr. Facilities fully operational Apr - Nov. Phone: (812)648-2810.

EARL PARK—B-2

(W) EARL PARK REST AREA (City Park)—(Benton) *From jct US-41/52 & Seventh St (550N): Go 1/2 mi W on Seventh St.* FACILITIES: 30 sites, 20 W&E, 10 no hkups, tenting. RECREATION: playground. Open all yr. Facilities fully operational Apr 1 - Oct 1. Phone: (219)474-6108.

ELKHART—A-3

(N) ELKHART CAMPGROUND—(Elkhart) *From jct I-80/90 (Exit 92) & SR 19: Go 1/4 mi N on SR 19, then 3/4 mi E on CR-4. Enter on R.*

WELCOME

◆◆◆◆FACILITIES: 320 sites, typical site width 30 ft, 195 full hkups, 125 W&E, (30/50 amps), 50 amps ($), some extd stay sites (summer), 280 pull-thrus, WiFi Instant Internet at site, WiFi Internet central location, family camping, tenting, cabins, RV storage, dump, non-guest dump $, laundry, ltd groc, RV supplies, LP gas by weight/by meter, ice, picnic tables, fire rings, wood.

◆◆◆◆RECREATION: rec hall, rec room/area, pavilion, coin games, swim pool, mini-golf, ($), golf nearby, bsktball, playground, tennis, horseshoes, sports field, v-ball.

Pets welcome. Partial handicap access. Open Apr 1 - Nov 1. Facilities fully operational Memorial Day - Nov 1. Big rigs welcome. Escort to site. Clubs welcome. Rate in 2010 $37-38 for 2 persons. MC/VISA/DISC/Debit. Member ARVC, RVIC. FMCA discount.

Phone: (574)264-2914
Address: 25608 CR 4 E, Elkhart, IN 46514
Lat/Lon: 41.73814/-85.95878
Web: www.elkhartcampground.com

SEE AD THIS PAGE

EVANSVILLE—F-1

See listings at Boonville & Selvin

(S) VANDERBURGH 4H CENTER CAMPGROUND (Vanderburgh County Park)—(Vanderburgh) *From jct I-64 & US 41: Go 5 mi S on US 41, then 1-1/4 mi W on Boonville-New Harmony Rd. Enter on L.* FACILITIES: 67 sites, 31 full hkups, 36 W&E, (50 amps), tenting, dump. RECREATION: pond fishing, playground. Partial handicap access. Open all yr. Phone: (812)867-6217.

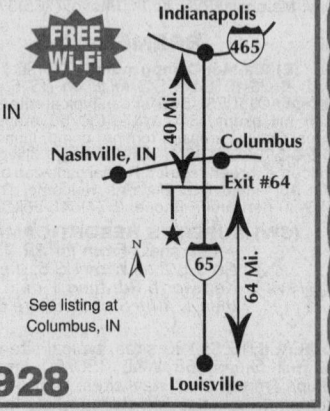

FAIR OAKS—B-2

(W) OAK LAKE FAMILY CAMPGROUND —(Newton) *From jct I-65 & SR 10 (exit 230): Go 1/2 mi W on SR 10, then 1 mi S on 600 E, then 1/2 mi W on CR E 900 N. Enter on R.*

WELCOME

◆◆◆FACILITIES: 325 sites, typical site width 35 ft, 295 full hkups, 30 W&E, (30/50 amps), 50 amps ($), many extd stay sites, 20 pull-thrus, WiFi Instant Internet at site, family camping, tenting, cabins, RV storage, dump, laundry, groceries, RV supplies, ice, picnic tables, fire rings, wood, controlled access.

◆◆RECREATION: rec hall, pavilion, coin games, lake swim, lake fishing, fishing supplies, bsktball, playground, activities, (wkends), horseshoes, sports field, hiking trails, v-ball.

Pets welcome, breed restrict, quantity restrict. Partial handicap access. Open Apr 15 - Oct 15. Clubs welcome. Rate in 2010 $25-30 per family. MC/VISA/DISC/Debit. Member ARVC, ICOA.

Phone: (219)345-3153
Address: 5310 E 900 N, Fair Oaks, IN 47943
Lat/Lon: 41.13015/-87.28941
Email: oaklakecampground@netnitco.net
Web: www.oaklakefamilycampground.com

SEE AD THIS PAGE

FERDINAND—F-2

(NE) FERDINAND SF—(Dubois) *From jct Hwy-162 & Hwy-264: Go 5 mi NE on Hwy-264.* FACILITIES: 69 sites, 69 no hkups, tenting, dump. RECREATION: lake swim, boating, electric motors only, ramp, dock, lake fishing, playground. Open all yr. Facilities fully operational Apr 15 - Sep 15. Phone: (812)367-1524.

FLORENCE—E-5

FOLLOW THE RIVER RV RESORT—(Switzerland) *From jct of Hwy 101 Markland Locks/Dam Rd & SR 156: Go 1 mi S on Hwy 156. Enter on R.*

WELCOME

◆◆◆◆◆FACILITIES: 160 sites, accepts self-contained units only, 160 full hkups, (20/30/50 amps), 20 pull-thrus, cable TV, WiFi Instant Internet at site, WiFi Internet central location, family camping, dump, non-guest dump $, laundry, ltd groc, RV supplies, LP gas by weight/by meter, ice, picnic tables, patios, fire rings, wood.

◆◆◆RECREATION: rec hall, rec room/area, swim pool, lake fishing, playground, activities, (wkends), hiking trails, v-ball.

Pets welcome, breed restrict. Partial handicap access. No tents. Open all yr. Big rigs welcome. Clubs welcome. Rate in 2010 $34-44 for 2 persons. MC/VISA/DISC/Debit.

Text 83052 to (440)725-8687 to see our Visual Tour.

Phone: (812)427-3330
Address: 12273 Markland Town Rd, Florence, IN 47020
Email: info@followtheriverrvresort.com
Web: www.followtheriverrvresort.com

SEE AD THIS PAGE

FORT WAYNE—B-4

(N) JOHNNY APPLESEED PARK (Municipal Park)—(Allen) *From jct I-69 & Coldwater Rd, S 1.4 mi on Coldwater Rd to Coliseum Blvd, E 0.5 mi on Coliseum Blvd to Parnell Ave, S 0.25 mi (L).* FACILITIES: 36 sites, 36 E, tenting, dump. RECREATION: canoeing, ramp, dock, river fishing, playground. No pets. Partial handicap access. Open Apr 1 - Oct 30. Phone: (219)427-6720.

FRANCESVILLE—B-2

(S) Acorn Oaks Campground—(Pulaski) *From I-65 & SR 114 (exit 215): Go 15-3/4 mi E on SR 114. Enter on L.* ◆◆FACILITIES: 108 sites, typical site width 30 ft, 52 full hkups, 36 W&E, (20/30/50 amps), 20 no hkups, family camping, tenting, dump, ltd groc. ◆◆RECREATION: pond fishing, playground. Pets welcome. Open Mid April - Mid Oct. Phone: (219)567-2524.

FRANKLIN—D-3

(S) JOHNSON COUNTY PARK & RECREATION AREA —(Johnson) *From jct Hwy 144/Hwy 44 & US 31: Go 3 mi S on US 31, then 3-1/2 mi W on Hwy 252, then 2-1/2 mi S on Schoolhouse Rd (CR 550S), follow signs. Enter on R.* FACILITIES: 80 sites, typical site width 40 ft, 50 W&E, (30 amps), 30 no hkups, 82 pull-thrus, tenting, dump. RECREATION: lake swim, playground. Open Apr 1 - Oct 31. Member ARVC. Phone: (812)526-6809.

FRANKTON—C-4

(SW) MIAMI CAMP—(Madison) *From south jct SR 13/SR 37 & CR W 400 N: Go 1-1/4 mi E on CR W 400 N. Enter on R.*

WELCOME

◆◆FACILITIES: 109 sites, 42 full hkups, 17 W&E, (30/50 amps), 50 no hkups, 2 pull-thrus, WiFi Internet central location, family camping, tenting, RV storage, dump, non-guest dump $, ice, picnic tables, fire rings, wood.

◆◆◆RECREATION: pavilion, swim pool, canoeing, kayaking, stream fishing, golf nearby, bsktball, play equipment, horseshoes, v-ball.

Pets welcome. Partial handicap access. Open all yr. Facilities fully operational Apr 15 - Oct 15. Winter months call first. Clubs welcome. Rate in 2010 $25-30 for 4 persons. Member ICOA.

Phone: (765)734-1365
Address: 8851 W 400 N, Frankton, IN 46044-9684
Lat/Lon: 40.16348/-85.84029
Email: info@miamicamp.org
Web: www.miamicamp.org

SEE AD ANDERSON PAGE 234

FREMONT—A-5

(W) Yogi Bear's Jellystone Park at Barton Lake —(Steuben) *From I-80/90 (Indiana Turnpike) exit 144: Take exit to SR 120, then go 3-1/4 mi W on SR 120, then 1/2 mi N on CR N 300W. Enter on L.* ◆◆◆◆◆FACILITIES: 540 sites, typical site width 40 ft, 237 full hkups, 283 W&E, (30/50 amps), 20 no hkups, 110 pull-thrus, family camping, tenting, dump, laundry, groceries. ◆◆◆◆◆RECREATION: 3 swim pools, lake swim, boating, 7 hp limit, canoeing, ramp, dock, lake fishing, playground. Pets welcome, quantity restrict. Partial handicap access. Open Apr 1 - Nov 1. Facilities fully operational Mid Apr - Mid Oct. Big rigs welcome. Rate in 2010 $21-60 per family. Member ARVC, RVIC. Phone: (800)375-6063.

FRENCH LICK—E-3

Lane Motel (RV SPACES)—(Orange) *From jct SR 145 & Hwy 56: Go 1/2 mi N on SR 56. Enter on R.* FACILITIES: 18 sites, typical site width 20 ft, 18 full hkups, (20/30 amps), 6 pull-thrus, tenting. RECREATION: swim pool. Pets welcome. Open Apr 1 - Nov 1. Facilities fully operational Memorial Day - Labor Day. Phone: (812)936-9919.

GARRETT—A-4

(S) Indian Springs Campground—(DeKalb) *From jct I-69 (exit 129) & SR 8: Go 3 mi W on SR 8, then 5 mi S on SR 327/Coldwater Rd, then 1/2 mi W on CR*

GARRETT—Continued
Indian Springs Campground—Continued

64. Enter on R. ◆◆◆FACILITIES: 365 sites, typical site width 35 ft, 300 full hkups, 50 W&E, (30/50 amps), 15 no hkups, 5 pull-thrus, family camping, tenting, dump, laundry, ltd groc. ◆◆◆◆◆RECREATION: lake swim, boating, electric motors only, canoeing, lake fishing, playground. Pets welcome, quantity restrict. Open Apr - Oct. Rate in 2010 $30 per family. Phone: (260)357-5572.

GAS CITY—B-4

(E) MAR-BROOK CAMPGROUND—(Grant) *From jct I-69 (exit 59) & SR 22: Go 1/4 mi E on SR 22, then 1 mi S on CRS 700E, then 1 mi W on CR E 600 S. Enter at end.*

WELCOME

◆◆◆FACILITIES: 221 sites, typical site width 25 ft, 122 full hkups, 99 W&E, (30 amps), mostly extd stay sites (summer), 10 pull-thrus, WiFi Internet central location, family camping, tenting, dump, non-guest dump $, laundry, ltd groc, RV supplies, LP gas by weight, ice, picnic tables, patios, fire rings, wood.

◆◆◆RECREATION: rec hall, pavilion, coin games, swim pool, river fishing, mini-golf, ($), golf nearby, bsktball, playground, activities, (wkends), horseshoes, sports field, hiking trails, v-ball.

Pets welcome, breed restrict. Open Apr 1 - Oct 31. Facilities fully operational Memorial Day - Labor Day. Escort to site. Clubs welcome. Rate in 2010 $23-25 per family. MC/VISA/DISC. Member ARVC.

Phone: (765)674-4383
Address: 6690 E 600 S, Gas City, IN 46933
Lat/Lon: 40.45853/-85.55077
Email: mike1slattery@yahoo.com
Web: www.marbrookcampground.com

SEE AD THIS PAGE

(SE) Sports Lake Campground—(Grant) *From jct I-69 (exit 59) & SR 22: Go 1/2 mi E on SR 22, then 1 mi N on CR-S 700 E, then 1/4 mi E on CR-E 400 S. Enter on R.* ◆◆◆FACILITIES: 163 sites, typical site width 30 ft, 49 full hkups, 114 W&E, (30/50 amps), 16 pull-thrus, WiFi Internet central location, family camping, tenting, dump, portable dump, ltd groc, RV supplies, picnic tables, fire rings, wood. ◆◆◆RECREATION: rec hall, pavilion, swim pool, boating, electric motors only, canoeing, kayaking, dock, lake fishing, fishing supplies, mini-golf, bsktball, playground, shuffleboard court 2 shuffleboard courts, horseshoes, hiking trails, v-ball. Pets welcome. Open Apr 15 - Oct 15. Rate in 2010 $24-30 for 4 persons. Member RVIC. CCUSA 50% Discount. CCUSA reservations Accepted, CCUSA max stay 1 day, Cash only for CCUSA disc., Check only for CCUSA disc., CCUSA disc. not avail F,Sa, CCUSA disc. not avail holidays.

CAMPCLUB USA

Phone: (765)998-2558
Address: 7230 E 400 S, Marion, IN 46953
Lat/Lon: 40.49502/-85.53422
Email: zoerichards@aol.com
Web: www.sportslakecampground.com

GOSHEN—A-3

(E) ELKHART CO. 4-H & AGRICULTURE EXPOSITION, INC.—(Elkhart) *From jct US 33 & Monroe St (CR 34): Go 1/2 mi E on Monroe St (CR 34) to gate 2. Enter on R.* FACILITIES: 235 sites, typical site width 30 ft, 135 full hkups, 100 W&E, (30/50 amps), 18 pull-thrus, tenting, dump. RECREATION: Pets welcome. Partial handicap access. Open Apr 1 - Nov 1. Big rigs welcome. Phone: (574)533-3247.

GREENFIELD—C-4

(E) HEARTLAND RESORT—(Hancock) *From I-70 (exit 96) & Mt Comfort Rd: Go 1/4 mi N on Mt Comfort Rd, then 4-1/2 mi E on CR W 300 N. Enter on R.*

WELCOME

◆◆◆FACILITIES: 285 sites, typical site width 30 ft, 211 full hkups, 64 W&E, (30/50 amps), 50 amps ($), 10 no hkups, some extd stay sites, 55 pull-thrus, WiFi Instant Internet at site ($), family camping, tenting, RV storage, dump, non-guest dump $, laundry, ltd groc, RV supplies, LP gas by weight/by meter, ice, picnic tables, fire rings, wood.

◆◆◆◆RECREATION: rec hall, rec room/area, pavilion, equipped pavilion, coin games, swim pool, lake swim, lake fishing, fishing supplies, mini-golf, ($), putting green, golf nearby, bsktball, playground, activities, (wkends), horseshoes, sports field, v-ball. Rec open to public.

Pets welcome. Partial handicap access. Open all yr. Facilities fully operational Memorial Day - Labor Day. Indoor pool open Memorial to Labor Day. Big rigs welcome. Clubs welcome. Rate in 2010 $29-33 for 4 persons. MC/VISA/DISC/Debit. Member ICOA.

Phone: (317)326-3181
Address: 1613 W 300 N, Greenfield, IN 46140
Lat/Lon: 39.82767/-85.83337
Email: information@heartlandresort.com
Web: www.heartlandresort.com

SEE AD INDIANAPOLIS NEXT PAGE

(NE) KOA-Indianapolis—(Hancock) *From jct I-70 (exit 96) & Mt Comfort Rd: Go 1/8 mi S on Mt Comfort Rd (600 N), then 1/8 mi E on 200 N. Enter on L.* ◆◆◆FACILITIES: 205 sites, typical site width 35 ft, 135 full hkups, 40 W&E, (30/50 amps), 50 amps ($), 30 no hkups, 200 pull-thrus, family camping, tenting, dump, laundry, groceries. ◆◆◆◆RECREATION: swim pool, playground. Pets welcome, breed restrict. Partial handicap access. Open Mar 1 - Nov 15. Facilities fully operational Memorial Day - Labor Day. Big rigs welcome. Rate in 2010 $35.35-67.63 for 2 persons. Member ARVC, ICOA. Phone: (317)894-1397. KOA discount.

S & H CAMPGROUND—(Hancock) *From jct I-70 (exit 96) & Mt Comfort Rd: Go 1-1/4 mi S on Mt Comfort Rd, then 3-1/2 mi E on McKenzie Rd (CR 100 N). Enter on R.*

WELCOME

◆◆◆FACILITIES: 350 sites, typical site width 36 ft, 225 full hkups, 100 W&E, (30/50 amps), 50 amps ($), 25 no hkups, many extd stay sites (summer), 35 pull-thrus, WiFi Instant Internet at site, family camping, tenting, RV's/park model rentals, cabins, RV storage, dump, portable dump, laundry, groceries, RV supplies, LP gas by weight/by meter, ice, picnic tables, fire rings, wood.

◆◆◆◆RECREATION: rec hall, rec room/area, equipped pavilion, coin games, swim pool, canoeing, pond/stream fishing, fishing supplies, mini-golf, ($), golf nearby, bsktball, bike rental, playground, shuffleboard court shuffleboard court, activities (wkends), horseshoes, sports field, hiking trails, v-ball. Rec open to public.

Pets welcome. Partial handicap access. Open all yr. Facilities fully operational Apr 1 - Nov 1. Pool open Memorial Day to Labor Day. Big rigs welcome. Escort to site. Clubs welcome. Rate in 2010 $30-38 for 4 persons. MC/VISA/Debit. Member ARVC.

Phone: (317)326-3208
Address: 2573 W 100N, Greenfield, IN 46140
Lat/Lon: 39.79845/-85.85065
Email: reservations@shcampground.com
Web: www.shcampground.com

SEE AD THIS PAGE

GROVERTOWN—A-3

(W) EZ KAMP—(Stark) *From jct US 30 & SR 23: Go 25 ft N on SR 23. Enter on L.*

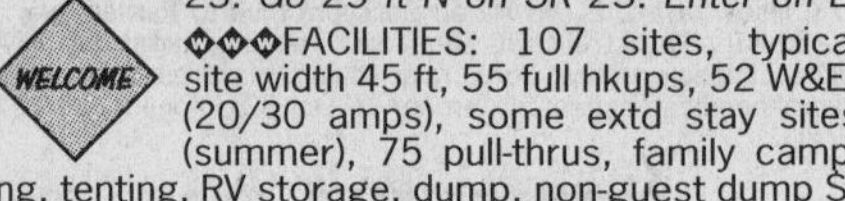

WELCOME

◆◆◆FACILITIES: 107 sites, typical site width 45 ft, 55 full hkups, 52 W&E, (20/30 amps), some extd stay sites (summer), 75 pull-thrus, family camping, tenting, RV storage, dump, non-guest dump $, laundry, ice, picnic tables, fire rings, wood.

◆◆RECREATION: rec room/area, pavilion, pond fishing, golf nearby, horseshoes.

Pets welcome. Open all yr. Limited water in winter. Clubs welcome. Rate in 2010 $19.95-22.95 for 2 persons. Member ARVC, RVIC.

Phone: (574)867-2022
Address: 9415 E 500 N Rd, Grovertown, IN 46531
Lat/Lon: 41.37206/-86.50854

SEE AD THIS PAGE

HAMBURG—E-4

(NW) DEAM LAKE SF REC AREA—(Clark) *From jct I-65 & Hwy-60: Go 10 mi NW on Hwy-60.* FACILITIES: 184 sites, 116 full hkups, 68 W&E, tenting, dump. RECREATION: lake swim, boating, electric motors only, canoeing, ramp, dock, lake fishing, playground. Partial handicap access. Open all yr. Phone: (812)246-5421.

HANNA—A-2

(N) Last Resort Campground—(LaPorte) *From jct US 421 & US 30: Go 6 mi E on US 30, then 1/2 mi NW on 1300 S. Enter at end.* ◆◆◆FACILITIES: 86 sites, typical site width 35 ft, 45 full hkups, 36 W&E, (30 amps), 5 no hkups, 6 pull-thrus, WiFi Instant Internet at site, WiFi Internet central location, family camping, tenting, dump, non-guest dump $, laundry, ltd groc, RV supplies, LP gas by weight/by meter, ice, picnic tables, fire rings, wood. ◆◆◆◆RECREATION: pavilion, swim pool, pond fishing, fishing supplies, bsktball, 7 bike rentals, playground, activities, horseshoes, v-ball. Pets welcome. Partial handicap access. Open Apr 1 - Nov 1. Facilities fully operational Memorial Day - Labor Day. Rate in 2010 $27-35 for 2 persons. MC/VISA/DISC/Debit. CCUSA 50% Discount. CCUSA reservations Required, CCUSA max stay 4 days, Cash only for CCUSA disc. Discount not available Jun thru Aug. Discount available any day in month of Apr: available Mon thru Thu months of May, Sep & Oct. Fully operational Memorial Day-Labor Day.

CAMPCLUB USA

Phone: (219)797-2267
Address: 4707 W 1300 S, Hanna, IN 46340
Lat/Lon: 41.42132/-86.78685
Email: lastresortcamp@aol.com
Web: www.lastresortcampground.com

HARTFORD CITY—C-4

(N) WILDWOOD ACRES CAMPGROUND—(Blackford) *From jct SR 18 & SR 3: Go 4 mi S on SR 3, then 1/2 mi W on CR 300N. Enter on L.*

WELCOME

◆◆◆FACILITIES: 228 sites, typical site width 28 ft, 63 full hkups, 120 W&E, 15 E, (20/30/50 amps), 50 amps ($), 30 no hkups, some extd stay sites (summer), 17 pull-thrus, WiFi Instant Internet at site, family camping, tenting, dump, non-guest dump $, portable dump, laundry, ltd groc, RV supplies, LP gas by weight, ice, picnic tables, fire rings, wood.

◆◆◆◆RECREATION: rec hall, rec room/area, pavilion, coin games, pond fishing, mini-golf, ($), golf nearby, bsktball, playground, activities, horseshoes, sports field, v-ball. Rec open to public.

CAMPCLUB USA

Pets welcome. Open Apr 15 - Oct 15. Full hookups @ ext. stay sites only. Big rigs welcome. Clubs welcome. Rate in 2010 $25-29 per family. MC/VISA. FCRV discount. CCUSA 50% Discount. CCUSA reservations Accepted, CCUSA disc. not avail F,Sa, CCUSA disc. not avail holidays.

HARTFORD CITY—Continued
WILDWOOD ACRES CAMPGROUND—Continued

Phone: (765)348-2100
Address: 0520 W 300N, Hartford City, IN 47348
Lat/Lon: 40.49404/-85.38039
Web: www.campindiana.com/wildwood

SEE AD MARION PAGE 240

HENRYVILLE—E-4

(N) CLARK SF—(Clark) *From town: Go 1 mi N on US-31.* FACILITIES: 45 sites, 45 no hkups, tenting, dump. RECREATION: boating, electric motors only, ramp, lake fishing, playground. Open all yr. Phone: (812)294-4306.

HOWE—A-4

(SE) Grand View Bend—(Lima) *From jct SR 120 & SR 9: Go 1 mi E on SR 120, then 1/2 mi S on CR N100E. Enter on R.* ◆◆◆FACILITIES: 344 sites, typical site width 20 ft, 344 W&E, (30/50 amps), phone Internet central location, family camping, tenting, dump, ice, picnic tables. ◆◆◆RECREATION: pavilion, swim pool, wading pool, boating, canoeing, kayaking, ramp, river/pond fishing, mini-golf, bsktball, playground, activities, tennis, horseshoes, v-ball. Pets welcome. Partial handicap access. Open Mid Apr - Mid Oct. Facilities fully operational Memorial Day - Labor Day. Big rigs welcome. Rate in 2010 $20 per vehicle. CCUSA 50% Discount. CCUSA reservations Not Accepted, CCUSA max stay 2 days, Cash only for CCUSA disc., CCUSA disc. not avail holidays.

CAMPCLUB USA

Phone: (574)220-9554
Address: 4630 N 100 E, Howe, IN 46746
Lat/Lon: 41.70881/-85.40799
Email: mecoyne8@verizon.net

(W) TWIN MILLS CAMPING RESORT—(LaGrange) *From jct SR 9 & SR 120: Go 1-1/2 mi W on SR 120. Enter on R.*

WELCOME

◆◆◆FACILITIES: 540 sites, typical site width 35 ft, 285 full hkups, 245 W&E, (30/50 amps), 10 no hkups, many extd stay sites (summer), 19 pull-thrus, WiFi Internet central location ($), family camping, tenting, RV's/park model rentals, cabins, RV storage, dump, non-guest dump $, portable dump, laundry, groceries, RV supplies, LP gas by weight/by meter, ice, picnic tables, fire rings, wood, controlled access.

◆◆◆◆RECREATION: rec hall, rec room/area, pavilion, coin games, swim pool, wading pool, lake/river swim, boating, 10 hp limit, canoeing, kayaking, ramp, dock, 2 rowboat/4 canoe rentals, lake/river/pond fishing, fishing supplies, mini-golf, ($), golf nearby, bsktball, 10 bike rentals, playground, shuffleboard court 4 shuffleboard courts, activities (wkends), horseshoes, sports field, hiking trails, v-ball.

CAMPCLUB USA

Pets welcome, breed restrict. Partial handicap access. Open Apr 15 - Nov 1. Facilities fully operational Memorial Day - Labor Day. Clubs welcome. Rate in 2010 $36-44 per family. MC/VISA/Debit. Member ARVC, ICOA. CCUSA 50% Discount. CCUSA max stay 5 days, CCUSA disc. not avail F,Sa, CCUSA disc. not avail holidays. Discount not available Memorial Day thru Labor Day. Some sites have grills. Float trips available sometimes. RV repair facility is limited. Honey wagon surcharge $12 pump out, $15 wand service. $8 dump surcharge if not staying in park.

Phone: (866)562-3212
Address: 1675 W SR 120, Howe, IN 46746
Lat/Lon: 41.71918/-85.45860
Email: twinmillsrv@equitylifestyle.com
Web: www.twinmills.net

Reserve Online at Woodalls.com

SEE AD ALBION PAGE 234

The first co-ed classroom in the U.S.A. was in New Harmony, Indiana over 150 years ago.

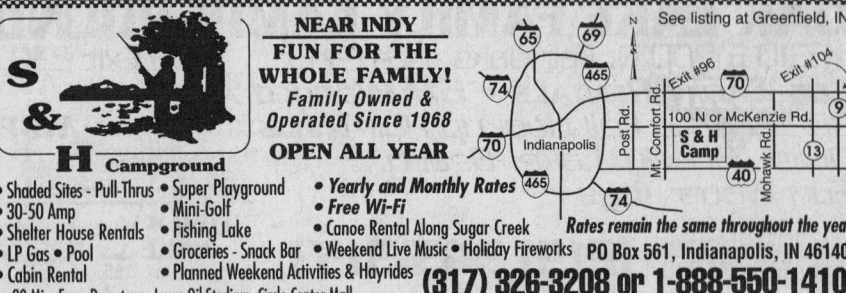

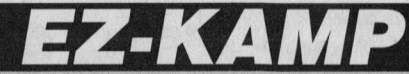

HUNTINGTON—B-4

(S) HUNTINGTON STATE LAKE—(Huntington) *From town: Go 1-1/2 mi S on Hwy-5.* FACILITIES: 130 sites, 130 no hkups, tenting. RECREATION: lake swim, boating, ramp, lake fishing, playground. Open all yr. Facilities fully operational Apr 1 - Oct 31. Phone: (260)468-2165.

(S) SALAMONIE LAKE (State Lake)—(Huntington) *From jct US-24 & Hwy-105: Go 9 mi S on Hwy-105.* FACILITIES: 376 sites, 245 E, 131 no hkups, dump, ltd groc. RECREATION: lake swim, boating, ramp, lake/river fishing, playground. Open all yr. Facilities fully operational Apr 1 - Oct 31. Phone: (260)468-2124.

INDIANAPOLIS—D-3

See listings at Greenfield.

(N) INDIANA STATE FAIRGROUNDS CAMPGROUND—(Marion) *From jct US 40 & US 31: Go 4 mi N on US 31, then 1 mi E on W 38th St. Enter on L.*

WELCOME

FACILITIES: 170 sites, 170 full hkups, (30 amps), family camping, tenting, dump.

Pets welcome. Open all yr. Reservations needed in August-Fair time. Clubs welcome. ATM.

Phone: (317)927-7510
Address: 1202 E 38th St, Indianapolis, IN 46205
Lat/Lon: 39.82656/-86.13476
Email: jraymann@indianastatefair.com
Web: www.indianastatefair.com

SEE AD THIS PAGE

(S) LAKE HAVEN RETREAT—(Marion) *From jct I-465 (exit 4) & SR-37: Go 1-1/2 mi S on SR-37. Enter on L.*

WELCOME

◆◆◆◆FACILITIES: 110 sites, typical site width 30 ft, 110 full hkups, (30/50 amps), many extd stay sites, 62 pull-thrus, cable TV, WiFi Instant Internet at site, family camping, tenting, RV storage, dump, non-guest dump $, laundry, picnic tables, fire rings, wood.

◆◆◆RECREATION: rec hall, pavilion, lake swim, 2 pedal boat rentals, lake fishing, golf nearby.

Pets welcome. Open all yr. Big rigs welcome. Rate in 2010 $29 per family. MC/VISA/Debit. Member ARVC, ICOA.

Phone: (317)783-5267
Address: 1951 W Edgewood Ave, Indianapolis, IN 46217
Lat/Lon: 39.67790/-86.19491
Email: info@lakehavenretreat.com
Web: www.lakehavenretreat.com

SEE AD THIS PAGE

JAMESTOWN—C-3

(S) Hillside Camp Grounds—(Hendricks) *From jct I-74 (exit 52) & SR 75: Go 2-1/2 mi S on SR 75. Enter on R.* ◆◆FACILITIES: 27 sites, typical site width 25 ft, 10 full hkups, 17 W&E, (20/30/50 amps), 6 pull-thrus, tenting. Pets welcome. Open May 1 - Oct 31. Big rigs welcome. Phone: (765)676-5075.

JASONVILLE—D-2

(W) SHAKAMAK SP—(Sullivan) *From business center: Go 3-1/2 mi NW on Hwy-48.* FACILITIES: 174 sites, 122 E, (20/30 amps), 52 no hkups, tenting, dump. RECREATION: swim pool, lake swim, boating, electric motors only, ramp, lake fishing, playground. Partial handicap access. Open all yr. Facilities fully operational Apr - Oct. Phone: (812)665-2158.

KENDALLVILLE—A-4

(E) BIXLER LAKE CAMPGROUND (City Park)—(Noble) *From business center: Go 3/4 mi E off Hwy-6 at Fairgrounds.* FACILITIES: 103 sites, 78 E, 25 no hkups, tenting, dump. RECREATION: lake swim, boating, electric motors only, ramp, lake fishing, playground. Partial handicap access. Open May 15 - Oct 15. Phone: (260)347-1064.

KNIGHTSTOWN—C-4

(NE) YOGI BEAR'S JELLYSTONE PARK-KNIGHTSTOWN—(Henry) *From jct I-70 (exit 115) & SR 109: Go 1/2 mi N on SR 109. Enter on R.*

WELCOME

◆◆◆FACILITIES: 135 sites, typical site width 40 ft, 10 full hkups, 125 W&E, (30/50 amps), many extd stay sites, 25 pull-thrus, WiFi Internet central location, family camping, tenting, cabins, RV storage, dump, portable dump, laundry, groceries, RV supplies, LP gas by weight/by meter, ice, picnic tables, patios, fire rings, wood.

◆◆◆◆RECREATION: rec room/area, pavilion, swim pool, 5 pedal boat rentals, lake/river fishing, fishing supplies, bsktball, playground, activities, horseshoes, v-ball.

Pets welcome, breed restrict. Partial handicap access. Open Apr 1 - Nov 1. Escort to site. Clubs welcome. Rate in 2010 $35-47 for 6 persons. MC/VISA/DISC. Member ARVC, RVIC. CCUSA 50% Discount. CCUSA reservations Not Accepted, CCUSA max stay 5 days, CCUSA disc. not avail F,Sa, CCUSA disc. not avail holidays.

Historic Parke County, the Covered Bridge Capital of the world, has 32 covered bridges.

KNIGHTSTOWN—Continued
YOGI BEAR'S JELLYSTONE PARK-KNIGHTSTOWN—Continued

Phone: (800)446-9644
Address: 5964 S SR 109, Knightstown, IN 46148
Lat/Lon: 39.84591/-85.56149
Email: smoll@sonicwave.net
Web: www.jellystoneindy.com

SEE AD THIS PAGE

KNOX—A-3

(SE) BASS LAKE STATE BEACH—(Starke) *From business center: Go 5 mi S on US 35, then 2 mi E on Hwy 10.* FACILITIES: 60 sites, 60 E, tenting, dump. RECREATION: lake swim, boating, canoeing, dock, lake fishing, playground. Open May 23 - Sep 1. Phone: (574)772-3382.

KOUTS—A-2

(S) Donna Jo Camping & Recreation Area—(Porter) *From jct Hwy 8 & Hwy 49: Go 3-1/4 mi S on Hwy 49, then 1-1/2 mi E on CR 1125 S, then 1-1/2 mi S on CR 350 E. Enter on L.* ◆◆FACILITIES: 75 sites, typical site width 30 ft, 32 ft max RV length, 35 full hkups, 40 W&E, (20/30 amps), 14 pull-thrus, family camping, tenting, dump, laundry. ◆◆RECREATION: lake swim, lake fishing, playground. Pets welcome. Partial handicap access. Open May 1 - Nov 1. Rate in 2010 $32.50 for 2 persons. Member ARVC. Phone: (219) 766-2186.

LAFAYETTE—C-2

(NE) Wolfe's Leisure Time Campground—(Tippecanoe) *From jct I-65 & SR 26: Go 3 mi N on I-65 (exit 175), then 7 mi N on SR 25. Enter on L.* ◆◆FACILITIES: 135 sites, typical site width 25 ft, 48 full hkups, 28 W&E, 16 E, (30/50 amps), 43 no hkups, 12 pull-thrus, family camping, tenting, dump, laundry. ◆◆◆RECREATION: swim pool, boating, ramp, river fishing, playground. Pets welcome, breed restrict. Open all yr. Facilities fully operational Memorial Day - Labor Day. Rate in 2010 $18-26 per family. Member ICOA. Phone: (765)589-8089.

The first professional baseball game was played in Fort Wayne on May 4, 1871.

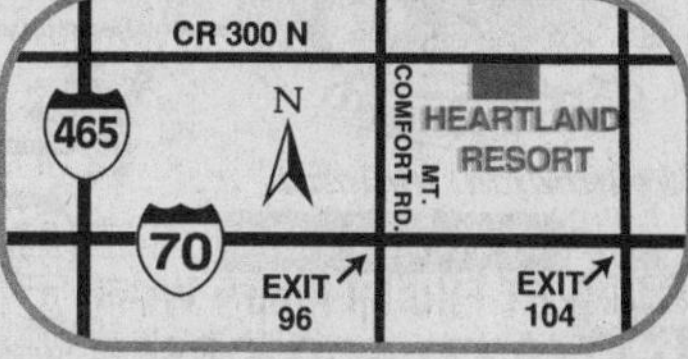

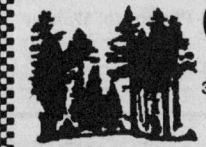

LAGRANGE—A-4

(E) PIGEON RIVER STATE FISH & WILDLIFE AREA—(La Grange) *From jct Hwy-9 & US-20: Go 7-1/4 mi E on US-20, then 3 mi N on Hwy-3, then 1/2 mi E on CR-300N (Mongo).* FACILITIES: 44 sites, 44 no hkups, tenting. RECREATION: canoeing, pond fishing. Open all yr. Phone: (260)367-2164.

LAGRO—B-4

(SE) SALAMONIE RIVER SF—(Penellas) *From jct US-24 & Hwy-524: Go 3 mi SE on Hwy-524.* FACILITIES: 37 sites, 37 no hkups, tenting, dump. RECREATION: boating, electric motors only, ramp, lake fishing, playground. Open all yr. Facilities fully operational Apr - Sep. Phone: (219)468-2125.

LAKEVILLE—A-3

(NW) Beaver Ridge Family Camping Inc.—(St. Joseph) *From jct US 6 & US 31: Go 6-1/2 mi N on US 31, then 1 mi W on SR 4, then 1/4 mi N on Maple Rd. Enter on L.* ◊◊◊FACILITIES: 113 sites, typical site width 30 ft, 102 W&E, (30/50 amps), 11 no hkups, 19 pull-thrus, WiFi Instant Internet at site, WiFi Internet central location, family camping, tenting, RV storage, dump, non-guest dump $, portable dump, ltd groc, ice, picnic tables, fire rings, wood. ◊◊◊RECREATION: pavilion, swim pool, bsktball, playground, activities, horseshoes, hiking trails, v-ball. Pets welcome. Open Apr 15 - Oct 15. Facilities fully operational Memorial Day - Labor Day. Rate in 2010 $28.04 for 4 persons. MC/VISA/Debit. CCUSA 50% Discount. CCUSA reservations Accepted, CCUSA max stay 3 days, CCUSA disc. not avail F,Sa, CCUSA disc. not avail holidays.

Phone: (574)784-8532
Address: 65777 Maple Rd, Lakeville, IN 46536
Lat/Lon: 41.53967/-86.29232
Email: rmf@go-camping.com
Web: www.go-camping.com

(W) POTATO CREEK SP—(St. Joseph) *From jct US-31 & Hwy-4: Go 4 mi W on Hwy-4.* FACILITIES: 287 sites, 287 E, (20 amps), tenting, dump, full svc store. RECREATION: lake swim, boating, electric motors only, canoeing, ramp, dock, lake fishing, playground. Open all yr. Phone: (574)656-8186.

LIBERTY—D-5

(S) WHITEWATER MEMORIAL SP—(Union) *From business center: Go 2 mi S on Hwy-101.* FACILITIES: 281 sites, 236 E, 45 no hkups, tenting, dump, ltd groc. RECREATION: lake swim, boating, electric motors only, canoeing, ramp, lake fishing, playground. Open all yr. Phone: (765)458-5565.

LOGANSPORT—B-3

(W) FRANCE PARK (Cass County Park)—(Cass) *From business center: Go 4 mi W on US-24.* FACILITIES: 200 sites, 130 W&E, (30 amps), 70 no hkups, tenting, dump, ltd groc. RECREATION: lake swim, boating, electric motors only, canoeing, lake fishing, playground. Pets welcome. Partial handicap access. Open all yr. Facilities fully operational May - Sep. Phone: (574) 753-2928.

LOOGOOTEE—E-2

(N) WEST BOGGS PARK (Daviess-Martin County)—(Daviess-Martin) *From jct US 50 & Hwy 231: Go 4 mi N on Hwy 231.* FACILITIES: 222 sites, typical site width 30 ft, 12 full hkups, 210 W&E, tenting, dump, laundry. RECREATION: lake swim, boating, canoeing, ramp, dock, lake fishing, playground. Open all yr. Facilities fully operational Mar 15 - Oct 15. Phone: (812)295-3421.

LYNNVILLE—F-2

(W) LYNNVILLE PARK (City Park)—(Warrick) *From jct I-64 (exit 39) & Hwy 61: Go 1/4 mi N on Hwy 61, then 2 mi W on Hwy 68. Enter on R.* FACILITIES: 69 sites, 24 full hkups, 6 W&E, 39 E, (30/50 amps), tenting, dump. RECREATION: boating, canoeing, ramp, lake fishing, playground. Partial handicap access. Open all yr. Phone: (812)922-5144.

MADISON—E-4

(W) CLIFTY FALLS SP—(Jefferson) *From business center: Go 1 mi W on Hwy 56/62.* FACILITIES: 165 sites, 106 E, 59 no hkups, tenting, dump, ltd groc. RECREATION: swim pool, playground. Open all yr. Facilities fully operational Apr 15 - Oct 15. Phone: (812)273-8885.

MARION—B-4

See listings at Gas City & Hartford City

James R. Hoffa, labor leader, was from Indiana.

MARSHALL—C-2

(N) TURKEY RUN STATE PARK—(Parke) *From jct US 41 & Hwy 47: Go 2 mi E on Hwy 47. Enter on L.* FACILITIES: 213 sites, 213 E, tenting, dump, ltd groc. RECREATION: swim pool, boating, no motors, stream fishing, playground. Open all yr. Phone: (317)597-2635.

MARTINSVILLE—D-3

(SE) MORGAN-MONROE SF—(Monroe) *From town: Go 5 mi S on Hwys-39 & 37, then follow signs.* FACILITIES: 29 sites, 29 no hkups, tenting, dump. RECREATION: boating, electric motors only, ramp, lake fishing, playground. Open all yr. Phone: (765)342-4026.

MICHIGAN CITY—A-2

(S) Michigan City Campground—(LaPorte) *From jct I-94 (exit 34A) & US 421: Go 1-3/4 mi S on US 421. Enter on L.* ◊◊◊FACILITIES: 153 sites, typical site width 30 ft, 114 full hkups, 14 W&E, (30/50 amps), 25 no hkups, 53 pull-thrus, heater not allowed, WiFi Instant Internet at site, family camping, tenting, RV storage, dump, non-guest dump $, portable dump, laundry, groceries, RV supplies, LP gas by weight/by meter, ice, picnic tables, patios, fire rings, wood. ◊◊◊RECREATION: rec hall, swim pool, pond fishing, fishing supplies, bsktball, playground, horseshoes, hiking trails, v-ball. Pets welcome. Open all yr. Facilities fully operational Memorial Day - Labor Day. Big rigs welcome. Rate in 2010 $32-36 per family. MC/VISA/DISC. Member ARVC, ICOA. CCUSA 50% Discount. CCUSA reservations Accepted, CCUSA max stay 2 days, Cash only for CCUSA disc., CCUSA disc. not avail F,Sa. Not valid Jun-Aug or any holiday weekends.

Phone: (800)813-2267
Address: 1601 N US 421, Michigan City, IN 46360
Lat/Lon: 41.63190/-86.89397
Email: info@michigancitycampground.com
Web: www.michigancitycampground.com

MIDDLEBURY—A-4

(NE) ELKHART COUNTY, MIDDLEBURY EXIT KOA—(Elkhart) *From jct I-80/90 (exit 107-Middlebury) & SR 13: Go 1-1/4 mi S on SR 13. Enter on R.*

◊◊◊FACILITIES: 120 sites, typical site width 35 ft, 50 full hkups, 58 W&E, 12 E, (30/50 amps), 50 amps ($), 58 pull-thrus, cable TV, WiFi Instant Internet at site, WiFi Internet central location, family camping, tenting, RV's/park model rentals, cabins, RV storage, dump, non-guest dump $, laundry, groceries, RV supplies, LP gas by weight/by meter, ice, picnic tables, fire rings, wood.

◊◊◊◊RECREATION: rec hall, rec room/area, coin games, swim pool, 2 pedal boat rentals, pond fishing, fishing supplies, mini-golf, ($), golf nearby, bsktball, 10 bike rentals, playground, activities, (wkends), horseshoes, sports field, hiking trails, v-ball, local tours.

Pets welcome. Partial handicap access. Open Apr 1 - Oct 31. Facilities fully operational Memorial Day - Labor Day. Big rigs welcome. Escort to site. Clubs welcome. Rate in 2010 $30-50 per family. MC/VISA/DISC/AMEX/Debit. Member ARVC, RVIC. KOA discount.

Phone: (800)562-5892
Address: 52867 St. Rd. 13, Middlebury, IN 46540
Lat/Lon: 41.72750/-85.68391
Email: kamp@middleburykoa.com
Web: www.middleburykoa.com

SEE AD SHIPSHEWANA PAGE 243

MITCHELL—E-3

(E) SPRING MILL SP—(Lawrence) *From jct US 37 S & Hwy 60 E: Go 3 mi E on Hwy 60 E.* FACILITIES: 224 sites, 187 E, (30/50 amps), 37 no hkups, tenting, dump. RECREATION: swim pool, boating, electric motors only, canoeing, dock, lake fishing, playground. Partial handicap access. Open all yr. Facilities fully operational May - Oct. Phone: (812)849-4129.

MONON—B-2

(E) Thrasher's Woods—(White) *From jct US 421 & SR 16: Go 3 mi E on SR 16. Enter on R.* ◊◊FACILITIES: 150 sites, typical site width 28 ft, 100 W&E, (30 amps), 50 no hkups, 25 pull-thrus, family camping, tenting, dump. ◊◊◊RECREATION: swim pool, pond fishing, playground. Pets welcome. Open Apr 15 - Oct 15. Facilities fully operational Memorial Day - Labor Day. Phone: (219)253-8224.

MONTICELLO—B-2

(N) Indiana Beach Camp Resort (Morgan RV Resorts)—(White) *From jct US 24 & US 421: Go 3/4 mi W on US 421/US 24, then 3-1/4 mi N on N Sixth St. Enter on L.* ◊◊◊FACILITIES: 1030 sites, typical site width 35 ft, 371 full hkups, 424 W&E, (20/30/50 amps), 235 no hkups, 532 pull-thrus, tenting, dump, laundry, full svc store. ◊◊◊◊◊RECREATION: swim pool, lake swim, boating, canoeing, ramp, dock, lake fishing, playground. Pets welcome. Partial handicap access. Open May 1 - Oct 12. Big rigs welcome. Rate in 2010 $38-50 per family. Member ARVC. Phone: (800) 583-5306.

(N) Jellystone Park Camp Resort (Morgan RV Resorts)—(White) *From jct US 24 & US 421: Go 3/4 mi W on US 421/US 24, then 3-1/2 mi N on N Sixth St. Enter on L.* ◊◊◊◊FACILITIES: 137 sites, typical site width 40 ft, 68 full hkups, 69 W&E, (30/50 amps), 131 pull-thrus, family camping, tenting, dump, laundry, groceries. ◊◊◊◊RECREATION: swim pool, playground. Pets welcome. Partial handicap access. Open May 15 - Sep 1. Facilities fully operational Memorial Day - Sep 1. Big rigs welcome. Rate in 2010 $40-45 per family. Phone: (574)583-8646.

(N) Lost Acres RV Park—(White) *From jct US 421 & US 24: Go 3/4 mi W on US 421/US 24, then 3-3/4 mi N on N Sixth St, then 3/4 mi W on Arrowhead Rd, then 200 yds N on CR N 400 E. Enter on L.* ◊◊◊FACILITIES: 330 sites, typical site width 40 ft, 250 full hkups, 80 W&E, (20/30/50 amps), family camping, dump, laundry, ltd groc. ◊◊◊◊RECREATION: swim pool, pond fishing, playground. Pets welcome. Partial handicap access. No tents. Open all yr. Facilities fully operational Apr 15 - Oct 15. Big rigs welcome. Rate in 2010 $30 per vehicle. Phone: (574) 583-5198.

(N) Norway Campground—(White) *From jct US 24 & US 421: Go 1 mi E on US 24, then 2.5 mi N on SR 39, then 200 yards N on E Shafer. Enter on R.* ◊◊FACILITIES: 119 sites, typical site width 20 ft, 89 full hkups, 30 W&E, (30 amps), 3 pull-thrus, tenting, laundry, groceries. ◊◊RECREATION: stream fishing, playground. Pets welcome. Open Mar 1 - Nov 1. Rate in 2010 $24-27 per family. Phone: (574)583-9300.

(S) White Oaks On the Lake A Western Horizon Property—(White) *From jct US 24 & US 421: Go 4-1/2 mi S on US 421, then 1 mi W on CR-W 950 N. Enter at end.* ◊◊◊FACILITIES: 123 sites, typical site width 40 ft, 77 full hkups, 46 W&E, (30/50 amps), 50 amps ($), 14 pull-thrus, family camping, tenting, dump, laundry. ◊◊◊◊RECREATION: swim pool, lake swim, boating, canoeing, ramp, dock, lake fishing, playground. Pets welcome. Partial handicap access. Open Apr - Oct. Facilities fully operational Memorial Day - Labor Day. Big rigs welcome. Phone: (219)207-5081.

MOROCCO—B-2

(W) WILLOW SLOUGH STATE FISH & WILDLIFE AREA—(Newton) *From jct US-41 & CR-275S: Go 2 mi W on CR-275S.* FACILITIES: 75 sites, 75 E, tenting. RECREATION: boating, electric motors only, ramp, lake fishing. Open all yr. - May 1. Facilities fully operational Oct 31. Phone: (219)285-2704.

MUNCIE—C-4

(W) Big Oak Park—(Delaware) *From I-69 (exit 45): Go 4 mi E on SR 28, then 300 yds S on N 500 W. Enter on R.* ◊◊FACILITIES: 70 sites, typical site width 20 ft, 60 full hkups, (30/50 amps), 50 amps ($), 10 no hkups, 14 pull-thrus, tenting. ◊RECREATION: pond fishing. Pets welcome. Open all yr. Facilities fully operational Apr - Nov. Rate in 2010 $17-18 per family. Phone: (765)358-3208.

NAPPANEE—A-3

See listings at Bremen, Plymouth, Warsaw

Indiana State Tree: Tulip Tree

NASHVILLE—D-3

(NE) Bill Monroe Memorial Music Park & Campground—(Brown) *From jct SR 135 & SR 46: Go 5-1/2 mi N on SR 135. Enter on R.* ◆◆◆FACILITIES: 700 sites, typical site width 35 ft, 300 W&E, (30/50 amps), 400 no hkups, 8 pull-thrus, family camping, tenting, dump, laundry, ltd groc. ◆◆RECREATION: lake fishing, play equipment. Pets welcome. Partial handicap access. Open May 1 - Nov 1. Rate in 2010 $26.75-32.10 for 2 persons. Member ARVC, RVIC. Phone: (812)988-6422.

(SW) BROWN COUNTY SP—(Brown) *From town: Go 2 mi W on Hwy 46. Entrance fee required.* FACILITIES: 489 sites, 401 E, (30 amps), 88 no hkups, tenting, dump, ltd groc. RECREATION: swim pool, lake fishing, playground. Open all yr. Facilities fully operational Apr - Nov. Phone: (812)988-6406.

(W) Ski World (RV SPACES)—(Brown) *From jct SR 135 & SR 46: Go 5 mi W on SR 46. Enter on L.* FACILITIES: 23 sites, typical site width 25 ft, accepts full hkup units only, 23 full hkups, (30 amps). RECREATION: lake fishing. Pets welcome. No tents. Open all yr.

(SE) THE LAST RESORT RV PARK & CAMPGROUND—(Brown) *From jct of I-65 & SR 46 (exit 68): Go 14 mi W on SR 46. Enter on R.*

WELCOME

◆◆◆◆FACILITIES: 110 sites, typical site width 35 ft, 73 full hkups, 37 W&E, (30/50 amps), some extd stay sites (summer), 18 pull-thrus, cable TV, ($), WiFi Instant Internet at site, family camping, tenting, cabins, dump, laundry, groceries, RV supplies, LP gas by weight/by meter, ice, picnic tables, patios, fire rings, wood.

◆◆◆RECREATION: rec hall, rec room/area, pavilion, coin games, swim pool, golf nearby, bsktball, playground, activities, (wkends), horseshoes, hiking trails.

Pets welcome. Partial handicap access. Open Apr 1 - Nov 1. Facilities fully operational Apr 1 - Nov 1. Big rigs welcome. Clubs welcome. Rate in 2010 $24-30 for 2 persons. MC/VISA/DISC/Debit. Member ARVC, ICOA.

Phone: (812)988-4675
Address: 2248 East State Rd 46, Nashville, IN 47448
Lat/Lon: 39.19869/-86.20531
Email: tlrofbc@aol.com
Web: www.lastresortrvpark.com

SEE AD THIS PAGE

(SE) WESTWARD HO CAMPGROUND—(Brown) *From jct I-65 & SR-46 (exit 68): Go 11-1/2 W on 54 46/35. Enter on L.*

WELCOME

◆◆◆FACILITIES: 92 sites, typical site width 24 ft, 92 full hkups, (30/50 amps), some extd stay sites (summer), 40 pull-thrus, phone Internet central location, family camping, cabins, dump, RV supplies, ice, picnic tables, patios, fire rings, wood.

◆◆RECREATION: rec hall, swim pool, lake fishing, golf nearby.

Pets welcome. Partial handicap access. No tents. Open Apr 1 - Nov 1. Clubs welcome. Rate in 2010 $28-33 for 2 persons. MC/VISA/Debit. Member ARVC, ICOA. FCRV discount. FMCA discount.

Indiana State Nickname: The Hoosier State

NASHVILLE—Continued
WESTWARD HO CAMPGROUND—Continued

Phone: (812)988-0008
Address: 4557 E State Rd. 46, Nashville, IN 47448
Lat/Lon: 39.18985/-86.16420
Web: www.gowestwardho.com

SEE AD THIS PAGE

(W) YELLOWWOOD SF—(Brown) *From business center: Go 7 mi W on Hwy-46.* FACILITIES: 80 sites, 80 no hkups, tenting. RECREATION: boating, electric motors only, ramp, dock, lake/stream fishing, playground. Open all yr. Facilities fully operational Apr - Nov. Phone: (812)988-7945.

NEW CARLISLE—A-3

(W) LAKESIDE RV RESORT (CAMP RESORT)—(St. Joseph) *From jct SR 2 & US 20: Go 4 mi E on US 20, then 1/4 mi N on N 900 E, then 1/2 mi W on E700N. Enter on R.*

WELCOME

FACILITIES: 90 sites, typical site width 35 ft, 38 ft max RV length, 90 full hkups, (30/50 amps), many extd stay sites (summer), 5 pull-thrus, WiFi Instant Internet at site ($), family camping, tenting, RV's/park model rentals, LP gas by weight/by meter, ice, picnic tables, patios, fire rings.

RECREATION: rec hall, rec room/area, swim pool, lake swim, boating, canoeing, kayaking, ramp, dock, lake fishing, golf nearby, playground, activities, (wkends), horseshoes, v-ball.

Pets welcome, breed restrict. Open Apr 1 - Nov 1. Facilities fully operational Memorial Day - Labor Day. Escort to site. Rate in 2010 $38 per family. MC/VISA/DISC/AMEX/Debit.

Phone: (574)654-3260
Address: 7089 N Chicago Rd, New Carlisle, IN 46552
Lat/Lon: 41.71009/-86.53734
Email: lakeside@mhchomes.com
Web: www.rvonthego.com

Reserve Online at Woodalls.com

SEE AD ALBION PAGE 234

(S) Mini Mountain Campground—(St. Joseph) *From jct US 20 & SR 2: Go 4-3/4 mi E on SR 2. Enter on L.* ◆◆◆FACILITIES: 272 sites, typical site width 28 ft, 215 full hkups, 17 W&E, (30/50 amps), 40 no hkups, 16 pull-thrus, family camping, tenting, dump, laundry, ltd groc. ◆◆◆◆RECREATION: swim pool, pond fishing, playground. Pets welcome. Partial handicap access. Open all yr. Facilities fully operational Apr 1 - Nov 1. Big rigs welcome. Rate in 2010 $26-29 per family. Member ARVC, ICOA. Phone: (574)654-3307.

NEW CASTLE—C-4

(SE) New Lisbon Family Campground LLC—(Henry) *From jct I-70 (exit 131) & Wilbur Wright Rd: Go 1/4 mi S on Wilbur Wright Rd, then 1/4 mi E on CR 600. Enter on L.* ◆◆FACILITIES: 160 sites, typical site width 30 ft, 160 full hkups, (30 amps), 20 pull-thrus, family camping, dump, laundry, ltd groc. ◆◆◆RECREATION: boating, electric motors only, ramp, dock, lake fishing, playground. Pets welcome. Partial handicap access. No tents. Open Mar 1 - Nov 30. Rate in 2010 $25 for 2 persons. Member ICOA. Phone: (765)332-2948.

(NE) SUMMIT LAKE SP—(Henry) *From jct Hwy 3 & Hwy 38: Go 2-3/4 mi W on Hwy 38, then 2 mi S on CR 275. Enter on R.* FACILITIES: 125 sites, 125 E, (30/50 amps), 2 pull-thrus, tenting, dump. RECREATION: lake swim, boating, canoeing, ramp, dock, lake fishing. Open all yr. Facilities fully operational Apr 1 - Nov 1. Phone: (765)766-5873.

(W) Walnut Ridge Campground—(Henry) *From jct I-70 & SR 3: Go 5-1/2 mi N on SR 3, then 3 mi W on SR 38, then 1/4 mi N on CR 300 W. Enter on R.* ◆◆◆◆FACILITIES: 171 sites, typical site width 25 ft, 166 W&E, (30/50 amps), 5 no hkups, 20 pull-thrus, WiFi Internet central location, family camping, tenting, RV storage, dump, non-guest dump $, portable dump, laundry, groceries, RV supplies, LP gas by weight/by meter, ice, picnic tables, patios, fire rings, grills, wood.

NEW CASTLE—Continued
Walnut Ridge Campground—Continued

CAMPCLUB USA

◆◆◆◆RECREATION: rec hall, equipped pavilion, swim pool, mini-golf, ($), bsktball, playground, hiking trails, v-ball. Pets welcome. Partial handicap access. Open Apr 15 - Oct 15. Facilities fully operational Memorial Day - Labor Day. Rate in 2010 $30-35 for 4 persons. MC/VISA/DISC. Member ARVC, ICOA. CCUSA 50% Discount. CCUSA reservations Accepted, CCUSA max stay 7 days, CCUSA disc. not avail F,Sa, CCUSA disc. not avail holidays.

Phone: (765)533-6611
Address: 408 N County Rd 300 W, New Castle, IN 47362
Lat/Lon: 39.93784/-85.44479
Email: information@walnutridgecampground.com
Web: www.walnutridgecampground.com

(W) WESTWOOD PARK (Big Blue River Conservancy Dist.)—(Henry) *From jct Hwy 38 & CR 275W: Go 2-1/4 mi S on CR 275W.* FACILITIES: 46 sites, 46 W&E, (30/50 amps), 4 pull-thrus, tenting, dump. RECREATION: lake swim, boating, electric motors only, canoeing, ramp, dock, lake fishing, playground. Partial handicap access. Open all yr. Facilities fully operational May - Oct. Phone: (765)987-1232.

NEW HARMONY—F-1

(SW) HARMONIE SP—(Posey) *From business center: Go S on Hwy-69.* FACILITIES: 200 sites, 200 E, (30 amps), tenting, dump. RECREATION: swim pool, boating, ramp, dock, river fishing, playground. Open all yr. Phone: (812)682-4821.

NORTH VERNON—E-4

(S) MUSCATATUCK (Jennings County Park)—(Jennings) *From jct US 50 & Hwy 7/3: Go 2 mi S on Hwy 7/3. Enter on R.* FACILITIES: 135 sites, 35 ft max RV length, 35 W&E, (20/30 amps), 100 no hkups, 3 pull-thrus, tenting, dump. RECREATION: canoeing, river fishing, playground. Partial handicap access. Open all yr. Facilities fully operational Apr 1 - Nov 4. Phone: (812)346-2953.

OAKTOWN—E-2

New Vision RV Park, LLC—(Knox) *From US 150 & US 50: Go 13 mi N on US 150/US 41 N. Enter on R.* ◆◆◆FACILITIES: 45 sites, typical site width 20 ft, 39 full hkups, (20/30/50 amps), 6 no hkups, 16 pull-thrus, WiFi Instant Internet at site ($), family camping, tenting, laundry, LP gas by weight/by meter, ice, picnic tables, fire rings, grills, wood. ◆◆RECREATION: pavilion, boating, electric motors only, lake fishing, fishing supplies, playground. Pets welcome. Open all yr. Big rigs welcome. Rate in 2010 $24.66-26.88 per family. MC/VISA/DISC/Debit. Member ARVC, ICOA. FCRV discount. FMCA discount. CCUSA 50% Discount. CCUSA reservations Accepted, CCUSA max stay Unlimited. Pull thru sites are always $2 more than back-in. Visitors entering park: $2/vehicle/day.

CAMPCLUB USA

Phone: (812)745-2125
Address: 13552 N US Hwy 41, Oaktown, IN 47561
Lat/Lon: 38.87162/-87.43103
Email: thorrall@peoplepc.com
Web: www.newvisionrvpark.com

ORLAND—A-4

(NE) MANAPOGO PARK—(Steuben) *From jct SR 327 & SR 120: Go 3-1/4 mi E on SR 120, then 3/4 mi N on CR-650 W, then 1 mi E on CR-W 760 N. Enter on R.*

WELCOME

◆◆◆◆FACILITIES: 300 sites, typical site width 50 ft, 182 full hkups, 118 W&E, (30/50 amps), mostly extd stay sites (summer), WiFi Instant Internet at site ($), family camping, tenting, cabins, RV storage, shower$, dump, non-guest dump $, portable dump, laundry, groceries, RV supplies, LP gas by weight, ice, picnic tables, fire rings, wood, controlled access.

◆◆◆◆RECREATION: rec hall, rec room/area, coin games, lake swim, boating, canoeing, kayaking, ramp, dock, 4 rowboat/2 canoe/pedal boat rentals, lake fishing, fishing supplies, golf nearby,

MANAPOGO PARK—Continued on next page

ORLAND—Continued
MANAPOGO PARK—Continued

bsktball, 6 bike rentals, playground, shuffleboard court 2 shuffleboard courts, activities (wkends), horseshoes, sports field, v-ball.

Pets welcome. Partial handicap access. Open Mid Apr - Mid Oct. Big rigs welcome. Escort to site. Clubs welcome. Rate in 2010 $35-38 for 5 persons. MC/VISA/DISC. Member ARVC, RVIC.

Phone: (260)833-3902
Address: 5495 W 760 N, Orland, IN 46776
Lat/Lon: 41.75423/-85.09735
Email: questions@manapogo.com
Web: www.manapogo.com

SEE AD PAGE 241

PENDLETON—C-4

(W) GLO WOOD CAMPGROUND—(Madison) *From jct I-69 (exit 14) & SR 13: Go 1/2 mi N on SR 13, then 1/2 mi W on CR W 700 S. Enter on R.*

◇◇◇FACILITIES: 60 sites, typical site width 25 ft, 10 full hkups, 25 W&E, (30/50 amps), 25 no hkups, 25 pull-thrus, family camping, tenting, RV storage, dump, non-guest dump $, ltd groc, ice, picnic tables, wood.

◇◇RECREATION: rec hall, play equipment, sports field.

Pets welcome. Partial handicap access. Open all yr. Facilities fully operational Apr - Oct. Big rigs welcome. Clubs welcome. Rate in 2010 $24-27 for 2 persons. Member ARVC, ICOA.

Phone: (317)485-5239
Address: 9384 W 700 S, Pendleton, IN 46064
Lat/Lon: 40.00279/-85.85099
Email: glowoodcamp@embarqmail.com
Web: www.glowoodcamp.com

SEE AD INDIANAPOLIS PAGE 239

(W) Pine Lakes Camping and Fishing—(Madison) *From jct I 69 (exit 19) & SR 38: Go 200 yds W on SR 38. Enter on L.* ◇◇◇FACILITIES: 100 sites, typical site width 30 ft, 100 full hkups, (30/50 amps), 16 pull-thrus, family camping, tenting, dump, ltd groc. ◇◇RECREATION: lake/pond fishing, playground. Pets welcome, breed restrict. Open all yr. Rate in 2010 $25 per family. Phone: 765-778-7878.

PERU—B-3

(NE) HONEY BEAR HOLLOW FAMILY CAMPGROUND—(Miami) *From jct US 31 & US 24 (north jct): Go 1-1/4 mi N on US 31, then 1-1/4 mi W on CR 200. Enter on R.*

◇◇◇◇FACILITIES: 103 sites, typical site width 30 ft, 12 full hkups, 87 W&E, (30/50 amps), 50 amps ($), 4 no hkups, some extd stay sites, 20 pull-thrus, WiFi Internet central location, family camping, tenting, cabins, RV storage, dump, non-guest dump $, portable dump, laundry, groceries, RV supplies, LP gas by meter, ice, picnic tables, fire rings, wood.

◇◇◇◇RECREATION: rec room/area, pavilion, coin games, swim pool, pond fishing, fishing supplies, golf nearby, bsktball, 3 bike rentals, playground, activities, (wkends), horseshoes, sports field, hiking trails, v-ball. Rec open to public.

Pets welcome. Open all yr. Facilities fully operational Apr 15 - Oct 15. Escort to site. Clubs welcome. Rate in 2010 $24-28 per family. MC/VISA/DISC. Member ARVC, ICOA. FMCA discount.

Phone: (765)473-4342
Address: 4252 W 200N, Peru, IN 46970
Lat/Lon: 40.79338/-86.15380
Email: tylewr@yahoo.com

SEE AD THIS PAGE

PERU—Continued

(S) MISSISSINEWA LAKE (State Lake)—(Miami) *From business center: Go 7 mi S on Hwy 19, then 3 mi E on CR 500 S, then 1/4 mi N on CR 625E.* FACILITIES: 431 sites, 39 full hkups, 335 E, (30 amps), 57 no hkups, 10 pull-thrus, tenting, dump. RECREATION: lake swim, boating, ramp, dock, lake fishing, playground. Open all yr. Facilities fully operational Apr 1 - Oct 31. Phone: (765)473-6528.

PIERCETON—A-4

(N) Yogi Bear's Jellystone Park—(Kosciusko) *From jct US 30 & SR 13: Go 4 mi N on SR 13, then 1 mi E on CR E 200 N. Enter at end.* ◇◇◇◇FACILITIES: 108 sites, typical site width 60 ft, 100 full hkups, 8 W&E, (20/30 amps), 6 pull-thrus, family camping, tenting, dump, laundry, groceries. ◇◇◇◇◇RECREATION: 2 swim pools, lake swim, boating, canoeing, ramp, dock, lake/river fishing, playground. Pets welcome. Partial handicap access. Open mid May - mid Sept. Rate in 2010 $37.95-59.95 per family. Member ARVC. Phone: (574)594-2124.

PLYMOUTH—A-3

(NW) Yogi Bear's Jellystone Park Camp Resort—(Marshall) *From jct US 31 & US-30: Go 6-1/2 mi W on US-30. Enter on R.* ◇◇◇◇FACILITIES: 165 sites, typical site width 40 ft, 150 full hkups, (20/30/50 amps), 15 no hkups, 10 pull-thrus, family camping, tenting, dump, laundry, groceries. ◇◇◇◇◇RECREATION: 2 swim pools, lake swim, boating, canoeing, dock, lake/pond fishing, playground. Pets welcome. Partial handicap access. Open May 15 - Oct 1. Facilities fully operational Memorial Day - Labor Day. Rate in 2010 $39-42 for 4 persons. Member ARVC, ICOA. Phone: (574)936-7851.

PORTAGE—A-2

(W) Yogi Bear's Jellystone Park Camp-Resort—(Porter) *From jct I-94 (exit 19) & SR 249: Go 400 yds S on SR 249, then 1 mi W on US 20, then 200 yds N on Marine Dr, then 1/2 mi W on Old Porter Rd. Enter at end.* ◇◇◇FACILITIES: 926 sites, typical site width 35 ft, 40 ft max RV length, 926 full hkups, (30 amps), 8 pull-thrus, WiFi Internet central location ($), family camping, tenting, RV storage, dump, non-guest dump $, laundry, groceries, RV supplies, LP gas by weight/by meter, ice, picnic tables, patios, fire rings, wood. ◇◇◇◇◇RECREATION: rec hall, pavilion, equipped pavilion, 3 swim pools, wading pool, lake swim, hot tub, boating, electric motors only, canoeing, kayaking, dock, lake fishing, fishing supplies, mini-golf, ($), bsktball, 4 bike rentals, playground, shuffleboard court shuffleboard court, activities, tennis, v-ball. Pets welcome. Partial handicap access. Open all yr. Facilities fully operational Memorial Day - Labor Day. Rate in 2010 $45-56 per family. MC/VISA/DISC/AMEX/Debit. Member ARVC. CCUSA 50% Discount. CCUSA reservations Required, CCUSA max stay 5 days, CCUSA disc. not avail F,Sa, CCUSA disc. not avail holidays. $4 entertainment surcharge. $1 maintenance fee surcharge. 4 pools +spa.

Phone: (219)762-7757
Address: 5300 Old Porter Rd, Portage, IN 46368
Lat/Lon: 41.59408/-87.20248
Email: reservations@campjellystone-portage.com
Web: www.campjellystone-portage.com

PORTLAND—C-5

(SE) Hickory Grove Lakes Campground—(Jay) *From jct SR 26 & US 27: Go 7 mi S on US 27, then 3 mi E on CR 800 S, then 1/2 mi N on CR 300E. Enter on L.* ◇◇FACILITIES: 95 sites, typical site width 35 ft, 61 full hkups, 12 W&E, 22 E, (20/30/50 amps), 50 amps ($), 18 pull-thrus, family camping, tenting, RV storage, dump, non-guest dump $, portable dump, RV supplies, ice, picnic tables, fire rings, wood. ◇◇◇RECREATION: pavilion, lake fishing, fishing supplies, mini-golf, bsktball, playground, activities, horseshoes, hiking trails, v-ball. Pets welcome. Open all yr. Facilities fully operational Apr 15 - Oct 15. Big rigs welcome. Member ARVC, ICOA. FCRV discount. FMCA discount. CCUSA 50% Discount. CCUSA reservations Accepted, CCUSA max stay Unlimited, Cash only for CCUSA disc.,

PORTLAND—Continued
Hickory Grove Lakes Campground—Continued

Check only for CCUSA disc. 3rd week/Aug-Antique Tractor & Gas Engine Show, Memorial, 4th of July & Labor Day weekends-10 % discount at those times. $10 dump surcharge for non-campers. .10 kwh including tax metered electric for 50 amp.

Phone: (260)335-2639
Address: 7424 S 300 E, Portland, IN 47371
Lat/Lon: 40.33241/-84.91934
Email: jmacnut@yahoo.com

REMINGTON—B-2

(E) CABOOSE LAKE CAMPGROUND—(Jasper) *From jct I-65 (exit 201) & US 24E: Go 500 feet E on US 24. Enter on R.*

◇◇◇◇FACILITIES: 115 sites, typical site width 30 ft, 115 full hkups, (30/50 amps), some extd stay sites, 43 pull-thrus, WiFi Instant Internet at site, family camping, tenting, RV's/park model rentals, cabins, dump, non-guest dump $, portable dump, laundry, ltd groc, RV supplies, LP gas by weight/by meter, ice, picnic tables, fire rings, wood.

◇◇◇◇RECREATION: rec hall, pavilion, lake swim, boating, electric motors only, ramp, 2 rowboat/4 pedal boat rentals, lake fishing, fishing supplies, golf nearby, playground, activities, (wkends), horseshoes, sports field, v-ball.

Pets welcome. Partial handicap access. Open all yr. Big rigs welcome. Clubs welcome. Rate in 2010 $25 per family. MC/VISA/Debit. Member ICOA.

Phone: (219)261-3828
Address: 3657 W US 24, Remington, IN 47977
Lat/Lon: 40.76547/-87.11524
Email: info@cabooselake.com
Web: www.cabooselake.com

SEE AD LAFAYETTE PAGE 240

RICHMOND—C-5

(E) Deer Ridge Camping Resort—(Wayne) *From jct I-70 & US 27: Go 2 mi E on I-70 (exit 153), then 300 yds S on SR 227, then 1/2 mi E on Smyrna Rd. Enter on L.* ◇◇◇FACILITIES: 65 sites, typical site width 35 ft, 65 full hkups, (30/50 amps), 6 pull-thrus, WiFi Instant Internet at site, family camping, tenting, laundry, ltd groc, RV supplies, LP gas by weight/by meter, ice, picnic tables, fire rings, wood. ◇◇◇RECREATION: rec hall, pavilion, swim pool, no motors, river/pond fishing, mini-golf, ($), bsktball, playground, activities, horseshoes, v-ball. Pets welcome. Partial handicap access. Open Mid Apr 15 - Nov 1. Facilities fully operational Memorial Day - Labor Day. Rate in 2010 $28-38 per family. MC/VISA/Debit. Member ARVC, RVIC. FCRV discount. FMCA discount. CCUSA 50% Discount. CCUSA max stay 2 days, Cash only for CCUSA disc., Check only for CCUSA disc. No discount on tent sites. Discount applies to back-in sites only. No babies or toddlers in pool. Adult surcharge $5 Memorial Day-Labor Day-$2 remainder of season. (Due to pool).

Deer Ridge Camping Resort—Continued on next page

RICHMOND—Continued
Deer Ridge Camping Resort—Continued

Phone: (765)939-0888
Address: 3696 Smyrna Rd, Richmond, IN 47374
Lat/Lon: 39.86788/-84.85114
Email: deerridg@aol.com
Web: www.deerridgecampingresort.com

(N) Grandpa's Farm—(Wayne) *From jct I-70 & US 27: Go 2 mi E on I-70/(exit 153), then 1-1/2 mi N on SR 227. Enter on L.* ◆◆◆FACILITIES: 96 sites, typical site width 30 ft, 50 full hkups, 46 W&E, (30/50 amps), 13 pull-thrus, family camping, tenting, dump, laundry, ltd groc. ◆◆◆◆RECREATION: swim pool, river fishing, playground. Pets welcome. Open Apr 1 - Nov 1. Big rigs welcome. Rate in 2010 $22-30 per family. Member ARVC. Phone: (765)962-7907. FMCA discount.

(SE) KOA-INDIANA OHIO KAMPGROUND—(Wayne) *From jct I-70 (exit 151) & US 27: Go 50 ft N on US 27, then 1 mi E on Highland Rd, then 1/4 mi S on Cart Rd. Enter at end.*

WELCOME

◆◆◆FACILITIES: 70 sites, typical site width 36 ft, 17 full hkups, 41 W&E, 12 E, (30/50 amps), 25 pull-thrus, WiFi Instant Internet at site, family camping, tenting, cabins, dump, non-guest dump $, laundry, groceries, RV supplies, LP gas by weight/by meter, ice, picnic tables, fire rings, grills, wood.

◆◆◆RECREATION: rec hall, pavilion, coin games, swim pool, dock, 2 pedal boat rentals, lake fishing, mini-golf, golf nearby, bsktball, playground, horseshoes, sports field, hiking trails, v-ball.

Pets welcome. Partial handicap access. Open Mar 15 - Nov 1. Big rigs welcome. Clubs welcome. Rate in 2010 $26-50 for 2 persons. MC/VISA/DISC/AMEX/Debit. Member ARVC. KOA discount.

Phone: (765)962-1219
Address: 3101 Cart Rd, Richmond, IN 47374
Lat/Lon: 39.86983/-84.86454
Email: richmondin@mykoa.com
Web: www.richmondinkoa.com

SEE AD PAGE 242

RISING SUN—E-5

(S) LITTLE FARM ON THE RIVER CAMPING RESORT—(Ohio) *From jct SR 262 & SR 56: Go 1-3/4 mi N on SR 56, then 1/4 mi E on E Bellview Ln. Enter on R.*

WELCOME

◆◆◆◆FACILITIES: 186 sites, typical site width 40 ft, 158 full hkups, 28 W&E, (30/50 amps), some extd stay sites (summer), 55 pull-thrus, WiFi Instant Internet at site, WiFi Internet central location, family camping, tenting, RV's/park model rentals, cabins, RV storage, dump, non-guest dump $, laundry, full svc store, RV supplies, LP gas by weight/by meter, ice, picnic tables, fire rings, wood.

CAMPCLUB USA

◆◆◆◆RECREATION: rec hall, equipped pavilion, coin games, swim pool, boating, river/pond fishing, fishing supplies, mini-golf, ($), golf nearby, bsktball, playground, shuffleboard court 2 shuffleboard courts, activities (wkends), horseshoes, sports field, local tours. Rec open to public.

Pets welcome. Partial handicap access. Open all yr. Big rigs welcome. Clubs welcome. Rate in 2010 $31-38 for 4 persons. MC/VISA/DISC/AMEX/Debit. Member ARVC. CCUSA 50% Discount. CCUSA reservations Accepted, CCUSA max stay 3 days, CCUSA disc. not avail S,Th, CCUSA disc. not avail F,Sa.

Phone: (812)438-4500
Address: 1343 E Bellview Lane, Rising Sun, IN 47040
Lat/Lon: 38.97356/-84.84466
Email: littlefarmrv@hotmail.com
Web: www.littlefarmresort.com

SEE AD CINCINNATI, OH PAGE 619

ROCHESTER—B-3

(NE) Lakeview Campground—(Fulton) *From jct US 31 & SR 14: Go 6-1/2 mi E on SR 14, then 3 mi N on CR 650E, then 1 mi E on CR 300N. Enter on R.* ◆◆◆FACILITIES: 103 sites, typical site width 30 ft, 10 full hkups, 68 W&E, (30 amps), 25 no hkups, 10 pull-thrus, family camping, tenting, dump, ltd groc. ◆◆◆◆RECREATION: lake swim, boating, canoeing, ramp, dock, lake fishing, playground. Pets welcome. Open Apr 15 - Oct 15. Rate in 2010 $29-32 per family. Phone: (800)838-9760.

Explorers Lewis and Clark set out from Fort Vincennes on their exploration of the Northwest Territory.

ROCKVILLE—D-2

(E) RACCOON SRA (Cecil M Hardin Lake)—(Parke) *From business center: Go 8 mi E on US 36.* FACILITIES: 310 sites, 235 E, (20 amps), 75 no hkups, tenting, dump, ltd groc. RECREATION: lake swim, boating, ramp, dock, lake fishing, playground. Open all yr. Facilities fully operational Apr 1 - Oct 31. Phone: (765)344-1412.

ST. CROIX—F-3

(S) HOOSIER NF (Celina Campground)—(Spencer) *From jct I-64 & Hwy 37: Go 2 mi S on Hwy 37, then W into recreation area.* FACILITIES: 60 sites, 26 E, (20 amps), 34 no hkups, tenting. RECREATION: boating, electric motors only, canoeing, ramp, lake fishing, playground. Partial handicap access. Open Apr 1 - Oct 15. Phone: (812)843-4891.

(S) HOOSIER NF (Tipsaw Lake Campground)—(Spencer) *From jct I-64 & Hwy 37: Go 4 mi S on Hwy 37, then 2 mi W. Follow recreation area signs.* FACILITIES: 35 sites, 35 E, tenting, dump, ltd groc. RECREATION: lake swim, boating, electric motors only, ramp, lake fishing. Open Apr 1 - Oct 14. Phone: (812) 843-4890.

ST. PAUL—D-4

(S) HIDDEN PARADISE CAMPGROUND—(Decatur) *From jct I-74 (exit 123) & N CR 800E: Go 2 mi S on N CR 800E, then 1/2 mi E on Jefferson St. Enter on L.*

WELCOME

◆◆◆◆FACILITIES: 168 sites, typical site width 34 ft, 30 full hkups, 138 W&E, (30/50 amps), some extd stay sites, 53 pull-thrus, WiFi Instant Internet at site, family camping, tenting, cabins, RV storage, dump, non-guest dump $, portable dump, laundry, ltd groc, RV supplies, LP gas by weight, ice, picnic tables, fire rings, grills, wood, controlled access.

CAMPCLUB USA

◆◆◆◆◆RECREATION: rec hall, rec room/area, pavilion, equipped pavilion, coin games, lake/river swim, boating, canoeing, kayaking, 6 canoe/11 kayak/6 pedal boat rentals, float trips, river fishing, fishing supplies, bsktball, playground, activities, horseshoes, sports field, hiking trails, v-ball. Rec open to public.

Pets welcome. Partial handicap access. Open all yr. Limited water Nov to Mar. Big rigs welcome. Escort to site. Clubs welcome. Rate in 2010 $28-32 per family. MC/VISA/DISC. ATM. Member ARVC, ICOA. CCUSA 50% Discount. CCUSA reservations Required, CCUSA max stay 5 days, CCUSA disc. not avail F,Sa, CCUSA disc. not avail holidays.

Phone: (765)525-6582
Address: 802 East Jefferson St, St Paul, IN 47272
Lat/Lon: 39.42310/-85.62455
Email: hpcamp@tds.net
Web: www.hiddenparadise.info

SEE AD INDIANAPOLIS PAGE 239

SANTA CLAUS—F-2

(E) HOLIDAY WORLD & SPLASHIN' SAFARI—*From jct I-64 & US 162 (exit 63): Go 7 mi S on 162, then 1/4 mi N on 245. Enter on L.* Theme Park with three of the top rated wooden roller coasters in the world. Two wave pools and some of the worlds top rated water rides. Pilgrims Plunge - World's Tallest Water Ride! Open May - mid Oct. Wkends May, Sep, Oct & Lbr day. Ph 877-Go-Family for hrs. MC/VISA/Debit. ATM.

WELCOME

Phone: (877)-GO-FAMILY
Address: 452 East Christmas Blvd, Santa Claus, IN 47579
Lat/Lon: 38.12131/-86.92150
Web: www.holidayworld.com

SEE AD THIS PAGE

Knute Rockne, football coach, was from Indiana.

SANTA CLAUS—Continued

(E) LAKE RUDOLPH CAMPGROUND & RV RESORT—(Spencer) *From jct I-64 & US 162 (exit 63): Go 7 mi S on US 162, then 1/4 mi N on Hwy 245/Holiday Blvd. Enter on R.*

WELCOME

◆◆◆◆◆FACILITIES: 234 sites, typical site width 30 ft, 189 full hkups, 45 W&E, (30/50 amps), 2 pull-thrus, WiFi Instant Internet at site, family camping, tenting, RV's/park model rentals, cabins, RV storage, dump, non-guest dump $, laundry, groceries, RV supplies, LP gas by weight/by meter, ice, picnic tables, patios, fire rings, grills, wood, controlled access.

◆◆◆◆◆RECREATION: rec hall, rec room/area, pavilion, equipped pavilion, coin games, 1 swim pools, wading pool, no motors, 2 rowboat/2 kayak/8 pedal boat rentals, lake fishing, fishing supplies, mini-golf, golf nearby, bsktball, playground, activities, horseshoes, hiking trails, v-ball, local tours. Rec open to public.

Pets welcome. Partial handicap access. Open Apr 1 - Oct 31. Facilities fully operational Memorial Day - Labor Day. Apr-wknds only, May thru Oct-daily. Big rigs welcome. Escort to site. Clubs welcome. Rate in 2010 $30-52 for 8 persons. MC/VISA/DISC/Debit. ATM. Member ARVC, ICOA.

Phone: (877)478-3657
Address: 78 North Holiday Blvd, Santa Claus, IN 47579
Lat/Lon: 38.12133/-86.92265
Email: info@lakerudolph.com
Web: www.lakerudolph.com

SEE AD THIS PAGE

SCOTTSBURG—E-4

(N) HARDY LAKE (State Lake)—(Scott) *From jct Hwy 56 & Hwy 203: Go 3 mi N on Hwy 203, then 2-1/4 mi N on CR 350/N Hardy Lake Rd.* FACILITIES: 168 sites, 149 E, (30 amps), 19 no hkups, tenting, dump. RECREATION: lake swim, boating, ramp, dock, lake/river fishing, playground. Partial handicap access. Open all yr. Phone: (812)794-3800.

(W) Yogi Bear Jellystone at Raintree Lake—(Scott) *From jct I-65 (exit 29B) & SR 56: Go 4 mi W on SR 56. Enter on L.* ◆◆◆◆FACILITIES: 93 sites, typical site width 30 ft, 56 full hkups, 35 W&E, (20/30/50 amps), 50 amps ($), 2 no hkups, 66 pull-thrus, WiFi Instant Internet at site ($), family camping, tenting, RV storage, dump, non-guest dump $, laundry, groceries, RV supplies, LP gas by weight/by meter, ice, picnic tables, patios, fire rings, grills, wood. ◆◆◆◆◆RECREATION: rec hall, pavilion, swim pool, boating, electric motors only, dock, lake fishing, fishing supplies, mini-golf, ($), bsktball, playground, activities, horseshoes, v-ball. Pets welcome. Partial handicap access. Open all yr. Facilities fully operational Memorial Day - Labor Day. Rate in 2010 $34-50 for 4 persons. MC/VISA/DISC/Debit. Member ARVC. FMCA discount. CCUSA 50% Discount. CCUSA reservations Recommended, CCUSA max stay Unlimited, Cash only for CCUSA disc., CCUSA disc. not avail F,Sa, CCUSA disc. not avail holidays. Fully operational Memorial Day thru Labor Day. Wifi surcharge $3/day.

CAMPCLUB USA

Phone: (800)437-0566
Address: 4577 W State Rd 56, Scottsburg, IN 47170
Lat/Lon: 38.68109/-85.86116
Email: yogisburg@gmail.com
Web: www.yogibearatraintreelake.com

SHIPSHEWANA—A-4

See listings at Bristol, Howe, Middlebury & Wolcottville

(NE) Riverside Campground—(LaGrange) *From jct SR 5 & SR 120: Go 3-1/2 mi E on SR 120, then 1/4 mi N on N450W. Enter on L.* ◆◆◆FACILITIES: 30 sites, typical site width 25 ft, 28 ft max RV length, 30 W&E, (30 amps), 2 pull-thrus, family camping, tenting, dump. ◆◆RECREATION: river swim, boating, canoeing, river fishing. Pets welcome. Open May 15 - Oct 15. Rate in 2010 $23 for 4 persons. Member ARVC, RVIC. Phone: (260)562-3742.

SHIPSHEWANA—Continued on next page

SHIPSHEWANA—Continued

(N) Shipshewana Campground-North—(LaGrange) *At intersection of SR 5 & SR 120 (Southwest corner).* ◊◊◊FACILITIES: 63 sites, typical site width 30 ft, 17 full hkups, 43 W&E, (30/50 amps), 3 no hkups, 10 pull-thrus, family camping, tenting, dump. Pets welcome. Partial handicap access. Open Apr 1 - Oct 30. Big rigs welcome. Rate in 2010 $30-37 for 4 persons. Member ARVC, RVIC. Phone: (260)768-7770.

(S) Shipshewana Campground-South—(LaGrange) *From jct SR 120 & SR 5: Go 4-1/2 mi S on SR 5. Enter on L.* ◊◊◊◊FACILITIES: 165 sites, typical site width 35 ft, 110 full hkups, 26 W&E, 29 E, (30/50 amps), 107 pull-thrus, family camping, tenting, dump, laundry. Pets welcome. Partial handicap access. Open Apr 15 - Oct 15. Big rigs welcome. Rate in 2010 $30-37 for 4 persons. Member ARVC, RVIC. Phone: (260) 768-4669.

(N) Shipshewana Trading Place RV Park (RV SPACES)—(La Grange) *From jct US 20 & IN 5: Go 1-1/4 mi N on IN 5, then 500 ft E on Farver St. Enter on L.* FACILITIES: 70 sites, accepts self-contained units only, 70 full hkups, (30/50 amps), 55 pull-thrus, family camping. Pets welcome. No tents. Open Apr 15 - Nov 15. Big rigs welcome. Rate in 2010 $27-33 per vehicle. Phone: (260)768-4129.

SHOALS—E-2

(E) MARTIN SF—(Martin) *From business center: Go 4 mi E on US-50.* FACILITIES: 26 sites, 26 no hkups, tenting. RECREATION: boating, electric motors only, lake fishing. Open all yr. Phone: (812)247-3491.

SOUTH BEND—A-3

See listings at Buchanan, Elkhart, Lakeville, Nappanee, New Carlisle & Niles, MI

FULLER'S RESORT & CAMPGROUND ON CLEAR LAKE—*From South Bend: Go 6-1/4 mi N on US 933/Hwy 51, then 7-1/2 W on US 12, then 1-1/2 mi N on Baker Town Rd, then 3/4 m W on Elm Valley Rd, then 1 mi NW on East Clear Lake Rd. Enter at end.*

WELCOME

SEE PRIMARY LISTING AT BUCHANAN, MI AND AD BUCHANAN, MI PAGE 375

(NE) KOA-South Bend East—(St. Joseph) *From jct SR 331 (Capital Ave) & SR 23: Go 2 mi N on SR 23, then 300 yds E on Adams Rd, then 400 yds N on Princess Way. Enter on L.* ◊◊◊◊FACILITIES: 80 sites, typical site width 30 ft, 45 full hkups, 25 W&E, (30/50 amps), 10 no hkups, 40 pull-thrus, family camping, tenting, dump, laundry, groceries. ◊◊◊RECREATION: swim pool, playground. Pets welcome. Partial handicap access. Open Apr 1 - Nov 14. Facilities fully operational Memorial Day - Labor Day. Big rigs welcome. Rate in 2010 $25-63 per family. Member ARVC, RVIC. Phone: (574)277-1335. KOA discount.

SPAULDING LAKE CAMPGROUND—*From Indiana Toll Rd (I-80 & I-90) (exit 77): Go 6 mi N on Hwy 933/51, then 2 mi E on Bell Rd. Enter on L.*

WELCOME

SEE PRIMARY LISTING AT NILES, MI AND AD THIS PAGE

SPENCER—D-2

(E) MCCORMICK'S CREEK SP—(Owen) *From business center: Go 2 mi E on Hwy-46.* FACILITIES: 221 sites, 189 E, (30 amps), 32 no hkups, tenting, dump. RECREATION: swim pool, playground. Open all yr. Facilities fully operational Apr - Oct. Phone: (812)829-2235.

(W) OWEN-PUTNAM SF—(Spencer) *From town: Go 5 miles W on Hwy 46, then 1 mile N on Fish Creek Rd.* FACILITIES: 40 sites, 40 no hkups, tenting. RECREATION: pond fishing. Open all yr. Facilities fully operational Apr - Dec. Phone: (812)829-2462.

TERRE HAUTE—D-2

(S) FOWLER PARK (Vigo County)—(Vigo) *From jct I-70 & US 41: Go 7 mi S on US 41.* FACILITIES: 77 sites, 62 E, 15 no hkups, tenting, dump. RECREATION: lake swim, boating, ramp, lake fishing, playground. Partial handicap access. Open May 1 - Oct 31. Phone: (812)462-3392.

TERRE HAUTE—Continued

(E) Terre Haute KOA—(Vigo) *From jct I-70 (exit 11) & SR 46: Go 300 yds S on SR 46, then 400 yds E on E Sony Dr. Enter at end.* ◊◊◊◊FACILITIES: 80 sites, typical site width 30 ft, 31 full hkups, 46 W&E, (30/50 amps), 50 amps ($), 3 no hkups, 61 pull-thrus, family camping, tenting, dump, laundry, groceries. ◊◊◊◊RECREATION: swim pool, playground. Pets welcome, breed restrict. Partial handicap access. Open all yr. Facilities fully operational Memorial Day - Labor Day. Big rigs welcome. Member ARVC. Phone: (800)KOA-4179. KOA discount.

VALLONIA—E-3

(SE) STARVE HOLLOW LAKE SF—(Jackson) *From town: Go 2-1/2 mi E on CR-250.* FACILITIES: 163 sites, 53 full hkups, 87 E, 23 no hkups, tenting, dump. RECREATION: lake swim, boating, electric motors only, ramp, lake fishing, playground. Partial handicap access. Open all yr. Facilities fully operational Apr - Nov. Phone: (812)358-3464.

VERSAILLES—D-4

(E) VERSAILLES SP—(Ripley) *From business center: Go 2-1/2 mi E on US 50.* FACILITIES: 226 sites, 226 E, (20 amps), tenting, dump, ltd groc. RECREATION: swim pool, lake swim, boating, electric motors only, canoeing, ramp, lake/river fishing, playground. Partial handicap access. Open all yr. Facilities fully operational Apr - Oct. Phone: (812)689-6424.

VINCENNES—E-1

(NE) OUABACHE (Wabash) Trails Park (Knox County Park)—(Knox) *From Rte 41 or Rte 50 take Vincennes 6th St exit, turn right at Executive Inn. Follow signs to park, 2-1/2 mi.* FACILITIES: 44 sites, 35 W&E, 9 no hkups, tenting, dump. RECREATION: river fishing, playground. Partial handicap access. Open Apr 15 - Oct 15. Facilities fully operational Apr - Nov. Phone: (812)882-4316.

WARSAW—A-3

(NW) HOFFMAN LAKE CAMP—(Kosciusko) *From jct SR 15 & US 30: Go 8 mi W on US 30, then 1/2 mi N on CR 800 W, then 1/2 mi E on CR 300 N. Enter on L.*

WELCOME

◊◊◊◊FACILITIES: 200 sites, typical site width 30 ft, 73 full hkups, 107 W&E, (20/30/50 amps), 20 no hkups, many extd stay sites (summer), 5 pull-thrus, family camping, tenting, cabins, dump, non-guest dump $, portable dump, laundry, ltd groc, RV supplies, LP gas by weight/by meter, ice, picnic tables, patios, fire rings, wood, controlled access.

◊◊◊◊◊RECREATION: rec hall, pavilion, coin games, swim pool, lake swim, boating, canoeing, kayaking, ramp, dock, 5 rowboat/2 pedal boat rentals, lake fishing, fishing supplies, mini-golf, ($), golf nearby, bsktball, 8 bike rentals, playground, activities, (wkends), horseshoes, v-ball.

Pets welcome. Partial handicap access. Open Apr 15 - Sep 30. Big rigs welcome. Escort to site. Clubs welcome. Rate in 2010 $24-28 per family. MC/VISA. Member ARVC, RVIC.

Phone: (574)858-9628
Address: 7638 West 300 N, Warsaw, IN 46582
Lat/Lon: 41.27516/-85.99160
Email: hoffmanlakecamp@msn.com
Web: www.campindiana.com/hoffmanlake

SEE AD THIS PAGE

(NE) Pic-A-Spot Campground—(Kosciusko) *From jct SR 30 & SR 13: Go 2-1/4 mi N on SR 13, then 1/4 mi W on Old US 30, then 3 1/2 mi N on 650E, then 100 yds W on McKenna Rd. Enter on R.* ◊◊FACILITIES: 168 sites, typical site width 25 ft, 162 W&E, (30 amps), 6 no hkups, 2 pull-thrus, family camping, tenting, dump, ltd groc. ◊◊◊RECREATION: lake swim, boating, canoeing, ramp, lake fishing, play equipment. Pets welcome. Open Apr 15 - Oct 15. Rate in 2010 $22 for 5 persons. Member ARVC. Phone: (574)594-2635.

WASHINGTON—E-2

(SE) GLENDALE STATE FISH & WILDLIFE AREA CAMP GROUND—(Daviess) *From business center: Go 12 mi SE on Hwy-257, then 3 mi E on CR.* FACILITIES: 121 sites, 67 E, (20/30 amps), 54 no hkups, tenting, dump. RECREATION: boating, 10 hp limit, ramp, dock, lake fishing. Open all yr. Facilities fully operational Apr - Oct. Phone: (812)644-7711.

WAVELAND—C-2

(NW) SHADES STATE PARK—(Montgomery) *From jct Hwy 47 & Hwy 234: Go 4-1/2 mi W on Hwy 234.* FACILITIES: 105 sites, 105 no hkups, tenting, dump. RECREATION: canoeing, river fishing, playground. Partial handicap access. Open all yr. Phone: (765)435-2810.

WEST LAFAYETTE—C-2

(NE) PROPHETSTOWN STATE PARK—(Tippecanoe) *From I-65, take exit 178 (St Rd 43), south on State Road 43 to Burnett Road, (1/4 mi), left on Burnett Rd to 9th St Road (3/4 mi), right on 9th St Road to Swisher Road (3/4 mi), left on Swisher Road to park entrance (1-1/2 mi). Enter on R.* FACILITIES: 110 sites, 55 full hkups, 55 E, (20/30/50 amps), tenting, dump. RECREATION: river fishing, playground. Pets welcome. Open all yr. Facilities fully operational May 1 - Nov 1. Phone: (765)567-4919.

WICKLIFFE—E-2

(N) PATOKA LAKE SRA—(Orange) *From Hwy-164 in town: Go 3 mi N on service road.* FACILITIES: 500 sites, 455 E, 45 no hkups, tenting, dump, ltd groc. RECREATION: lake swim, boating, ramp, dock, lake/river/pond fishing. Open all yr. Facilities fully operational Apr 1 - Oct 31. Phone: (812)685-2464.

WINAMAC—B-3

(N) Broken Arrow Campground—(Pulaski) *From jct SR 14 & US 35: Go 3 mi N on US 35. Enter on L.* ◊FACILITIES: 1030 sites, typical site width 36 ft, 450 full hkups, 540 W&E, (30/50 amps), 40 no hkups, 600 pull-thrus, family camping, tenting, dump, laundry. ◊◊RECREATION: swim pool, lake fishing, playground. Pets welcome. Open Apr 1 - Nov 1. Facilities fully operational Memorial Day - Labor Day. Big rigs welcome. Member ICOA. Phone: (574)946-4566.

(N) TIPPECANOE RIVER SP—(Pulaski) *From business center: Go 5 mi N on US 35.* FACILITIES: 178 sites, 112 E, (30/50 amps), 66 no hkups, tenting, dump. RECREATION: boating, canoeing, ramp, river/pond fishing, playground. Open all yr. Phone: (574)946-3213.

WINSLOW—E-2

(E) PIKE SF—(Pike) *From jct Hwy-61 & Hwy-364: Go 3 mi E on Hwy-364.* FACILITIES: 36 sites, 36 no hkups, tenting. RECREATION: river fishing. Open all yr. Phone: (812)367-1524.

WOLCOTTVILLE—A-4

(W) Atwood Lake Campground—(La Grange) *From jct Hwy 9 & CR E 1200 N: Go 1-1/2 mi W on CR E 1200 N. Enter on R.* ◊◊FACILITIES: 220 sites, typical site width 40 ft, 220 W&E, (30 amps), 5 pull-thrus, family camping, tenting, dump, laundry, groceries. ◊◊◊RECREATION: lake swim, boating, 10 hp limit, canoeing, ramp, dock, lake fishing, playground. Pets welcome. Open May 1 - Oct 15. Rate in 2010 $25 per family. Member ARVC, RVIC. Phone: (260)854-3079.

(E) Gordon's Camping—(LaGrange) *From jct SR 3 & E 600S: Go 1-1/4 mi E on E 600S. Enter on R.* ◊◊FACILITIES: 321 sites, typical site width 50 ft, 321 W&E, (20/30/50 amps), 30 pull-thrus, family camping, tenting, dump, laundry, groceries. ◊◊◊RECREATION: swim pool, pond fishing, playground. Pets welcome. Partial handicap access. Open Apr 15 - Oct 15. Facilities fully operational Memorial Day - Labor Day. Rate in 2010 $30 per family. Member ARVC, ICOA. Phone: (260)351-3383.

(W) Indian Lakes Campground—(La Grange) *From jct Hwy 9 & CR 700S: Go 5 mi W on CR 700S, then 1-1/4 mi N on CR 75W. Enter on L.* ◊◊◊◊FACILITIES: 250 sites, typical site width 30 ft, 250 full hkups, (30/50 amps), family camping, laundry, ltd groc. ◊◊◊RECREATION: swim pool, lake swim, boating, canoeing, ramp, dock, lake fishing, playground. Pets welcome ($), breed restrict, quantity restrict. Partial handicap access. No tents. Open Apr 15 - Oct 15. Rate in 2010 $29.95-37.95 per family. Member ARVC, RVIC. Phone: (260)854-4215.

Indiana State Rock: Limestone

WOODALL'S®
Everywhere RVers go
www.woodalls.com
Scan me! I'm a QR Code! Be sure to install a FREE QR Reader app on your smartphone. Then, point it at the code above and give it a try!

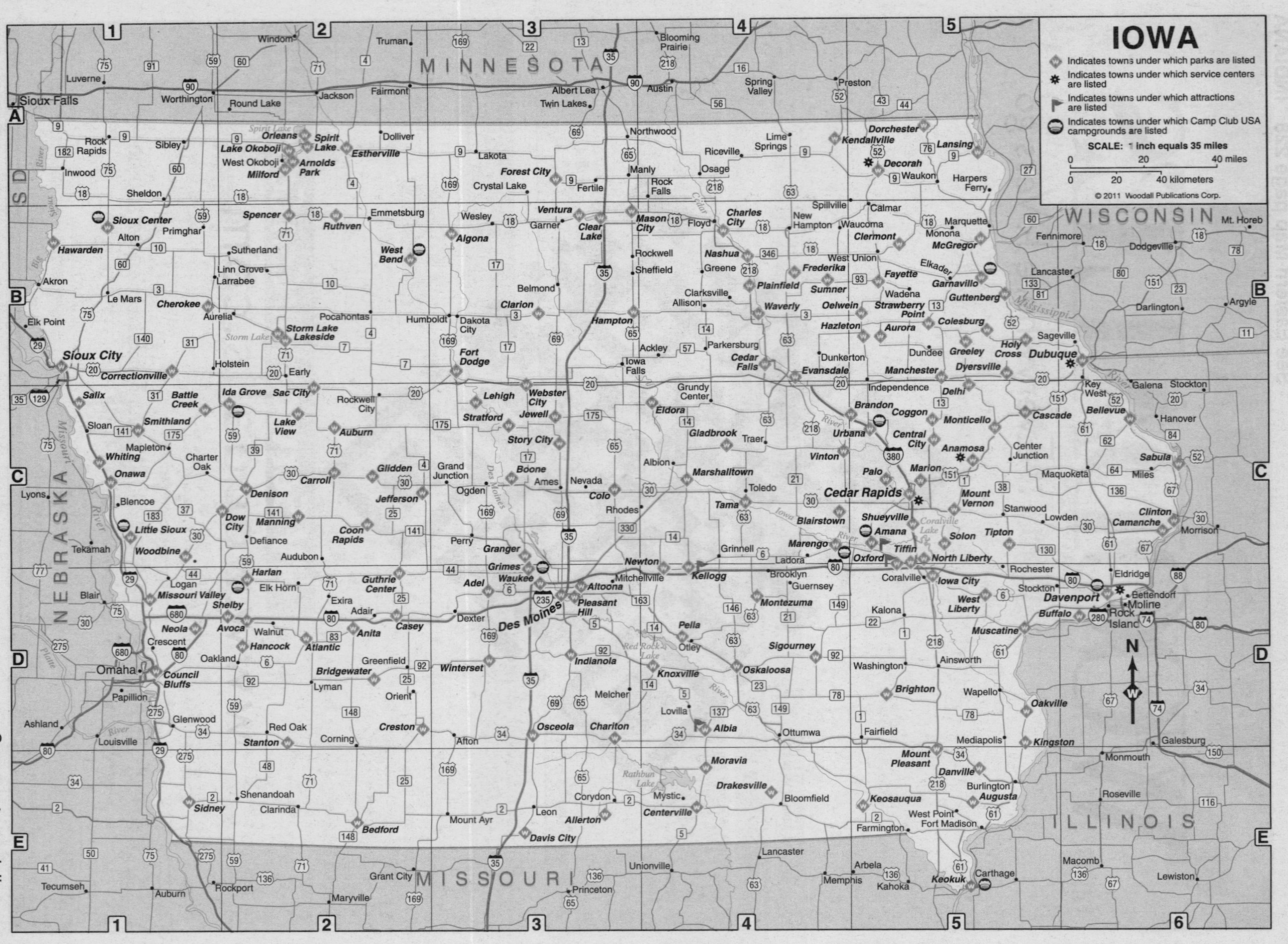
IOWA
Indicates towns under which parks are listed
Indicates towns under which service centers are listed
Indicates towns under which attractions are listed
Indicates towns under which Camp Club USA campgrounds are listed
SCALE: 1 inch equals 35 miles
0 20 40 miles
0 20 40 kilometers
© 2011 Woodall Publications Corp.
MINNESOTA
WISCONSIN
ILLINOIS
MISSOURI
NEBRASKA
S D
N
Des Moines
Cedar Rapids
Davenport
Dubuque
Iowa City
Sioux City
Council Bluffs
Omaha
Mississippi River
Missouri River
Des Moines River
Cedar River
Iowa River

TRAVEL SECTION

Iowa

READER SERVICE INFO

The following businesses have placed an ad in the Iowa Travel Section. To receive free information, enter their Reader Service number on the Reader Service Card opposite page 48/Discover Section in the front of this directory:

Advertiser	RS#
Amana Colonies Visitors Center	4000
Iowa ARVC	3276
Truck Country	3458

TIME ZONE

Iowa is in the Central Time Zone.

TOPOGRAPHY

Located between the upper Mississippi and Missouri Rivers, the state of Iowa comprises 56,000 square miles, primarily rolling prairie. Elevation ranges from 480 feet to 1,670 feet.

TEMPERATURE

Iowa's 4 distinct seasons provide a climate that is classified as "humid continental." The average January temperature is 17.3°; April averages 49.3°; July averages 74.3° and November averages 37.2°. A typical year brings 166 days of sunshine, 100 partly cloudy days, 99 cloudy days, 32" of rainfall and 30" of snowfall.

Located in the Midwest region of the U.S., Iowa is bordered by two great American rivers. Iowa's cultural heritage can be found in pockets all over the state. World-class museums, including the Danish Immigrant Museum and the National Czech and Slovak Museum can be found here. And thousands still make the pilgrimage to see the Field of Dreams every year.

TRAVEL & TOURISM INFO

State Agency:
Iowa Dept of Economic Development
200 E. Grand Ave.
Des Moines, IA 50309
(800/345-IOWA or 515/725-33083)
www.iowalifechanging.com or www.traveliowa.com

Regional Agencies:
Central Iowa Tourism Region
PO Box 454
Webster City, IA 50595
(515/832-4808 or 800/285-5842)
www.iowatourism.com

Eastern Iowa Tourism Assoc.
PO Box 189
Dyersville, IA 52040
(563/875-7269 or 800/891-3482)
www.easterniowatourism.org

Western Iowa Tourism Region
103 N. Third St.
Red Oak, IA 51566
(888/623-4232 or 712/623-4232)
www.visitwesterniowa.com

Local Agencies:
For local agencies not listed here, contact the Convention and Visitors Bureau for the locality you are interested in.

RECREATIONAL INFO

Biking, Recreation Trails: Iowa Natural Heritage Foundation, 505 Fifth Ave., Ste. 444, Des Moines, IA 50309 (515/288-1846). www.inhf.gov

Fishing & Hunting: Iowa Department of Natural Resources, 502 E. 9th St., Des Moines, IA 50319 (515/281-5918). www.iowadnr.com

Historic Sites: Historical Society of Iowa, State Historical Bldg., 600 E. Locust, Des Moines, IA 50319 (515/281-6258). www.iowahistory.com

SHOPPING

Factory Stores of America Outlet Center, Story City. Shop for bargains at this outlet center. 324 Factory Outlet Dr., Story City, Iowa.

Tanger Outlet Center, Williamsburg. Over 55 authentic brand-name manufacturer and designer outlet stores. I-80, Exit 220, 150 Tanger Dr. www.tangeroutlet.com

Walnut. Antique and gift shops in 1900s storefronts line the brick streets of this town located in West Central Iowa.

DESTINATIONS

NORTHWEST REGION

LeMars is recognized as "The Ice Cream Capital of the World" because more ice cream is made there by a single company

(Wells Blue Bunny) than in any other city in the world – more than 120 million gallons. **The Ice Cream Capital of the World Visitor Center** has a family-friendly museum that provides a look at the history of ice cream and a 1920s-style ice cream parlor that serves up tasty treats.

Okoboji. Iowa's resort region offers year-round recreation with water sports in the summer sunshine and cold-weather activities such as the University of Okoboji Winter Games. **Arnolds Park Amusement Park** boasts one of the top 10 wooden rollers coasters in the country.

Orange City. Tour Dutch sites and historic buildings such as **The Old Mill – Vogel Windmill**, the historic courthouse and **Old Factory** (which offers demonstrations on wooden shoe making).

Sioux City. This Missouri River city where explorers Lewis & Clark left their mark is making a splash of its own with a revitalized downtown, beautiful riverfront and new attractions and events. Don't miss **Trinity Heights**, the restored **Orpheum Theatre** and the **Lewis & Clark Interpretive Center**. The **Sioux City Art Center** is a three-story glass atrium, hands-on gallery for children, 900-piece permanent collection, traveling exhibitions and gift gallery. Annual outdoor art festival, **ARTSPLASH**, is held Labor Day weekend. At the **Sioux City Public Museum**, built from pink-colored Sioux Falls quartzite in the early 1890s, the Peirce Mansion exhibits artifacts from American Indian life and early settlement of the region to the present.

Storm Lake. Home to **King's Pointe** Resort, one of the most spectacular indoor/outdoor waterpark resorts in the Midwest featuring adventure slide technology.

West Bend. The **Grotto of Redemption** is a composite of nine separate grottos portraying scenes from the life of Christ using stones and gems from around the world. Sometimes called the "Eighth Wonder of the World."

BUSINESSES OFFERING

	Things to See & Do	RV Sales	RV Service
ALBIA			
Indian Hills Inn	⚑		
The White Buffalo Restaurant & Lounge	⚑		
AMANA			
Amana Colonies Visitors Center	⚑		
ANAMOSA			
Lasso E RV		🚌	✱
Lasso E RV		🚌	✱
CEDAR RAPIDS			
Truck Country			✱
DAVENPORT			
Truck Country			✱
DECORAH			
Truck Country			✱
DUBUQUE			
Truck Country			✱
KELLOGG			
Iowa's Best Burger Cafe	⚑		
OXFORD			
Sleepy Hollow Pizza and Ice Cream	⚑		

WEST CENTRAL REGION

Travelers will find the beauty of Iowa's western prairie in this region. Travelers don't want to miss the picturesque beauty of Loess Hills, or a travel to the past with the many heritage celebrations.

Council Bluffs. Explore the **Loess Hills National Scenic Byway**, discover history at the **Western Historic Trails Center, General Dodge House, Union Pacific Railroad Museum** or the **RailsWest Railroad Museum.** Unique **Squirrel Cage Jail** is one of three remaining examples of rotary jails.

Denison. The **Donna Reed Center for the Performing Arts** honors hometown Academy-award winner Donna Reed. It houses the Donna Reed Heritage Museum, Donna Reed

Theatre and Reiney's Soda Fountain. Reed's Oscar can be found in the **W.A. McHenry House.**

Elk Horn/Kimballton. Two miles apart and an ocean away from their Danish homeland, these twin villages celebrate their heritage on a daily basis. Elk Horn is home to an authentic **Danish Windmill** originally built in Denmark in 1848 and transported to Elk Horn in 1975. The **Danish Immigrant Museum** offers self-guided exhibits tracing the immigration of the Danes to America. Kimballton features a replica of **"The Little Mermaid"** statue of Copenhagen Harbor.

Lewis. The **Hitchcock House** is a restored station on the Underground Railroad and a designated National Historical Landmark.

SOUTHWEST REGION

Clarinda. The **Glenn Miller Birthplace Home** honors the king of swing and native son with period furnishings and family photographs.

Greenfield. Each year a young artist paints a new patriotic theme on **Patriotic Rock** as a tribute to the armed forces serving our country. The **Henry A. Wallace Country Life Center** is a 40-acre outdoor interpretive site featuring the philosophies, ideas and achievements of Henry A. Wallace.

Stanton. This town of all painted white houses gets its water from the world's largest Swedish coffeepot – a water tower honoring its immigrant heritage and a local actress who became "Mrs. Olson" of coffee commercial fame.

NORTH CENTRAL REGION

Clear Lake/Mason City. In Clear Lake, visit the legendary **Surf Ballroom** where Buddy Holly, Ritchie Valens and the Big Bopper played their last concert. **Fort Custer Maze** challenges visitors to conquer eight stations on the way to completing the maze, which depicts the early west with animal mounts, pictures and history. Mason City boasts an array of attractions including the **Meredith Willson Boyhood Home** (author of The Music Man), **The Music Man Square** and Frank Lloyd Wright architecture.

Iowa Falls. Walk across the Iowa River on the **Swinging Bridge**. Drink in the Art Deco atmosphere at the **Princess Café and Sweet Shoppe**. Take a ride on the **Scenic City Empress Boat Club**; a double-deck riverboat that offers chartered or catered cruises on the Iowa River.

CENTRAL REGION

Ames. Home of **Iowa State University**, one of the most beautiful campuses in the nation. **Reiman Gardens**, the state's largest public garden, features a 5000-square-foot

QUICK REFERENCE CHART FOR WOODALL'S FEATURED PARKS

	Green Friendly	RV Lots for Sale	Park Models-Onsite Ownership	Park Membership for Sale	Big Rigs Welcome	Internet Friendly	Pets Welcome
ADEL Des Moines West KOA	🍂				▲	●	■
ALBIA Indian Hills RV Park					▲	●	■
ALTOONA Griffs Valley View RV	🍂				▲	●	■
AMANA Amana Colonies RV Park	🍂				▲	●	■
DAVENPORT Interstate RV Park					▲	●	■
KELLOGG Kellogg RV Park & Campground-Interstate 80					▲	●	■
MOUNT PLEASANT Crossroads RV Campground	🍂				▲	●	■
NEWTON Newton KOA					▲	●	■
NORTH LIBERTY Colony Country Campground	🍂				▲	●	■
ONAWA On-Ur-Wa RV Park	🍂				▲	●	■
OXFORD Sleepy Hollow RV Park & Campground	🍂				▲	●	■
TIPTON Hunts Cedar River Campground					▲	●	■
URBANA Lazy Acres RV Park	🍂				▲	●	■
WAUKEE Timberline Campground	🍂				▲	●	■
WEST LIBERTY West Liberty RV Park					▲		■

Green Friendly 🍂; RV Lots for Sale ✖; Park Models/Onsite Onwership ✱; Park Memberships for Sale ✔; Big Rigs Welcome ▲; Internet Friendly ●; Internet Friendly-WiFi ●; Pets Welcome ■

indoor conservatory with changing displays and a butterfly flight house with more than 50 exotic and native butterflies.

Boone. The **Boone and Scenic Valley Railroad** offers a 15-mile round trip through the beautiful Des Moines River Valley over two great bridges. The **Mamie Doud Eisenhower Birthplace** includes furniture from Mamie's family, photos of Mamie and Ike plus other memorabilia.

Des Moines. Iowa's capital city includes the **Blank Park Zoo; Des Moines Art Center** (designed in stages by three internationally-renowned architects); **Historic Valley Junction,** featuring more than 120 specialty stores, art galleries, fashion boutiques, restaurants and antique shops; **Iowa Hall of Pride**, highlighting Iowa's educational system, extracurricular activities and history through games, trivia and more; 275-foot gold-leafed **Iowa State Capitol** and 110,000-square-foot **Science Center of Iowa and Blank IMAX Dome Theater.**

Newton. NASCAR legend Rusty Wallace designed the 7/8-mile track at the **Iowa Speedway.** Word-famous Maytag Blue Cheese is made at the **Maytag Dairy Farms.**

SOUTH CENTRAL REGION

Centerville. Iowa's first destination state park, the 850-acre Honey Creek Resort boasts a lodge, outdoor patio, 105-room hotel, indoor waterpark, conference center, 18-hole golf course and more outdoor recreation options.

Eldon. In 1930, Iowa artist Grant Wood sketched an Eldon home on a visit to the area. The home would later appear as the background to his famous "American Gothic" painting. The **American Gothic House,** listed on the National Register of Historic Places, now has a visitor center.

Knoxville. The "Sprint Car Capital of the World" hosts weekly sprint car racing and the Nationals each August at the **Knoxville Raceway**. Fans of the sport won't want to miss the **National Sprint Car Hall of Fame and Museum**, the only museum dedicated to preserving the history of "big car" and sprint car racing.

Pella. Looks, tastes and sounds just like Holland. The **Vermeer Windmill** is the nation's tallest working windmill. The **Klokkenspel**, designed and created just for Pella, is a carillon clock with eight four-foot mechanical figures and 147 bell chimes that perform at regular intervals through the day. The **Cordova Park Observation Tower**, a converted 106-foot water tower and the tallest observation tower in the Midwest, provides an unparalleled view of the Des Moines River Valley and Lake Red Rock.

· **Winterset**. Home to the world-famous **Covered Bridges of Madison County**. The birthplace of John Wayne pays tribute to the nation's most favorite cowboy with rare photographs and memorabilia from his career.

Where to Find CCUSA Parks

List City	Park Name	Map Coordinates
AMANA		
	Amana Colonies RV Park	C-5
DAVENPORT		
	Lakeside RV Park & Campground	D-6
GARNAVILLO		
	Clayton Hills Campground	B-5
GRIMES		
	Cutty's Des Moines Camping Club	D-3
HARLAN		
	Nielsen RV Park	D-2
IDA GROVE		
	Cobb Park & Campground	C-2
KEOKUK		
	Hickory Haven Campground	E-5
LITTLE SIOUX		
	Woodland Campground	C-1
MARENGO		
	Sudbury Court Motel & RV Park	C-4
SIOUX CENTER		
	Country Home Campground & Motel	B-1
URBANA		
	Lazy Acres RV Park	C-5
WEST BEND		
	The Grotto of the Redemption RV Park	B-2

NORTHEAST REGION

Decorah. Seed Savers Exchange/Heritage Farm comprises 2000 heirloom vegetable varieties, more than 800 old-time apple trees and a gift shop selling heirloom seeds. The immigrant story comes alive at the **Vesterheim Norwegian-American Museum**, one of America's oldest and largest museums devoted to an immigrant group. Displays feature costumes, homes, room settings, colorful folk arts, church altars and a 25-foot boat.

Independence. The Heartland Acres Agribition Center is an interactive salute to agriculture and displays featuring livestock, renewable energy, farm machinery, classic cars and other historical items.

McGregor/Marquette. Three miles north of Marquette, you'll find **Effigy Mounds National Monument**, prehistoric American Indian burial and ceremonial grounds dating from 500 B.C. to 1300 A.D. and located on more than 2500 acres of forested land along the Mississippi River. In McGregor, climb aboard and get a 35-minute guided tour of **Spook Cave** by boat (the only way to see it).

Quasqueton. Cedar Rock, a Frank Lloyd Wright designed and signed home, was completed in 1950. The original home site includes the Usonian style home, a river pavilion, council fire and entrance gate, all designed by Wright.

Waterloo. Make a splash at **Lost Island Adventure Park**, which features nine major water slides. The **Dan Gable International Wrestling Institute and Museum** showcases Olympic, collegiate and pro wrestling history, including a display on Dan Gable, Iowa's Olympic champion. The **Phelps Youth Pavilion** launches a world of wonder, discover and learning throughout.

EAST CENTRAL REGION

Amana Colonies. These seven historic villages were founded by German immigrants as a religious communal society in 1855 and have been collectively named a National Historic Landmark. Purchase antiques, hand-woven baskets, furniture and clocks, plus locally made wine and beer.

Iowa City. The **Old Capitol Museum** is a National Historic Landmark restored to reflect the years it served as the last capitol of the Iowa Territory (1842-1846), the first state capitol (1846-1857) and The University of Iowa's first building. At the **Devonian Fossil Gorge** visitors can walk over acres of Devonian age sea floor and get a firsthand look at fossils normally hidden from view.

Cedar Rapids. Attractions include **Brucemore**, one of 25 properties of the National Historic Trust for Historic Preservation; the

National Czech and Slovak Museum and Library, the nation's foremost institution interpreting Czech and Slovak history and culture; the **Cedar Rapids Museum of Art**, boasting the world's largest collection of works by Cedar Rapids native Grant Wood; and the **Grant Wood Studio and Visitor Center**, where Wood lived and worked from 1924 to 1934 and where he painted "American Gothic" and many other famous works.

Wilton. Housed in an 1856 building listed on the National Register for Historic Places, the **Wilton Candy Kitchen** is considered the oldest ongoing ice cream parlor/soda fountain/confectionery in the world. Founded in 1860, it serves homemade ice cream, phosphates, lunches and candy.

EAST REGION

Anamosa. Tour the **Anamosa Penitentiary Museum** displaying artifacts and historical information about Iowa's largest correctional facility. The **National Motorcycle Museum** showcases more than 200 rare and vintage motorcycles dating back to 1903 as well as the original Captain America bike from the 1969 movie "Easy Rider."

Dubuque. Attractions include the **Fenelon Place Elevator,** the world's shortest, steepest scenic railway; **Grand Harbor Resort and Waterpark**, a Mississippi River-themed indoor waterpark with 25,000 square feet of family fun; **Dubuque River Boats**, sightseeing cruises on the Mississippi River; and the **National Mississippi River Museum and Aquarium**, which features five large aquariums and other interactive exhibits regarding the mighty Mississippi.

Dyersville. Run the bases at the legendary **Field of Dreams Movie Site** or browse 30,000 farm toys and trucks on display at the **National Farm Toy Museum**.

Davenport. Attractions include the **Channel Cat Water Taxi** which lets you see the Mississippi River and Quad Cities from a unique point of view aboard a 47-passenger ferry boat operating between two docks in Iowa and three docks in Illinois; the **Family Museum**, a hands-on museum with interactive exhibits for children and families; **Figge Art Museum**, housed in a dramatic facility overlooking the Mississippi River and boasting Regionalist, Haitian, Mexican Colonial, American and contemporary art collections, along with an extensive traveling exhibit schedule.

SOUTHEAST REGION

Burlington. Attractions include **Fun City**, a family entertainment facility offering indoor/outdoor waterparks, 24 lanes of bowling, electric go-karts, casino and spa; **Snake Alley**, named the "Crookedest Street in the World" by Ripley's Believe it or Not, is perhaps Burlington's most famous landmark. Test your driving, walking or biking skills on the five half-curves and two quarter-curves that drop 58 feet over a distance of 275 feet.

Fort Madison. At **Old Fort Madison**, watch living history demonstrations and visit with costumed interpreters at this reconstructed military fort on the banks of the Mississippi. Built in 1808, the original structure was destroyed in 1813 when abandoned by U.S. military soldiers.

Keokuk. The **Keokuk National Cemetery** is Iowa's only national cemetery, designated by Congress at the same time as Arlington National Cemetery. Union and Confederate soldiers, as well as members of the military representing all conflicts since the Civil War, are buried here. Get a great Mississippi River view from the **Observation Deck**, a historic swing span bridge that is now a lighted observation deck with picnic tables.

Maharishi Vedic City. Incorporated on July 21, 2001, as a model of ideal city life. Every building is designed according to Maharishi Sthapatya Veda design to promote health, happiness and good fortune. Each building faces east and has a central silent space called a Brahmasthan and a golden roof ornament called a kalash. The **Raj Hotel and Resort** was named one of the top five health spas of the new millennium by Town & Country magazine.

ANNUAL EVENTS

JANUARY

Cherokee Jazz and Blues Festival, Cherokee; Ice Fest, Dubuque; Winter Games, Okoboji; Eagle Watch, Bellevue/Guttenberg/Keokuk/Quad Cities; Winterfest, Amana Colonies.

FEBRUARY

Color the Wind Kite Festival, Clear Lake; Frostbite Olympics, Algona; Winter Dance Party, Clear Lake; Northeast Iowa Steel Guitar Jam, Waterloo.

MARCH

Maple Syrup Festival, Cedar Falls; Culture Fest, Waterloo; Maple Syrup Festival, Cedar Falls; St. Pat's Celebration, Emmetsburg.

APRIL

Kalona Quilt Show, Kalona; River Fest, Iowa City; Earthfest Celebration, Sioux City; Civil War Re-Enactment: Battle of Pea Ridge, Keokuk.

MAY

Maifest, Amana Colonies; Tulip Time Festival, Pella/Orange City; Syttende Mai, Decorah; Snake Alley Criterium, Burlington; Tivoli Fest, Elk Horn; North Iowa Band Festival, Mason City.

JUNE

Cherokee PRCA Rodeo, Cherokee; Frontier Days, Fort Dodge; Scandinavian Days, Story City; Glenn Miller Festival, Clarinda; Lewis & Clark Festival, Onawa; Flight Breakfast, Audubon; Grant Wood Art Festival, Stone City/Anamosa; Des Moines Arts Festival, Des Moines; Wapello County Fair, Eldon; Kalona Days, Kalona.

JULY

Register's Annual Great Bike Ride Across Iowa; Iowa Games, Ames; Water Carnival, Lake View; Nordic Fest, Decorah; Bix Beiderbecke Memorial Jazz Festival, Davenport; Rodeo, Leon; Corn Carnival, Gladbrook; Croatian Fest, Centerville.

AUGUST

Iowa Championship Rodeo, Sidney; Hooverfest, West Branch; Balloon Classic, Indianola; Knoxville Nationals, Knoxville; National Hobo Convention, Britt; Meskwaki Pow Wow, Tama; Iowa State Fair, Des Moines; Festival of the Arts, Amana Colonies; Czech Days, Protivin; Bike Van Buren; Bridgefest, Ottumwa; Bluegrass Festival, Oskaloosa.

SEPTEMBER

Old Threshers Reunion, Mt. Pleasant; Britt Draft Horse Show, Britt; ARTSPLASH Festival of the Arts, Sioux City; Pufferbilly Days, Boone; Kalona Fall Festival, Kalona; Pancake Day, Centerville; Renaissance Faire, Des Moines; Pioneer Farm Festival, Oskaloosa; Davis County Old Time Music Festival, Bloomfield.

OCTOBER

Heritage Days, Elkader; Madison Co. Covered Bridge Festival, Winterset; Rocktober Geode Fest & Hunt, Keokuk; Night Eyes at the Blank Park Zoo, Des Moines.

NOVEMBER

Festival of Trees, Davenport; Julefest, Elk Horn; National Farm Toy Show, Dyersville; Julefest, Elk Horn/Kimballton; Dickens of a Christmas, Indianola; De Kerstdagen, Pella.

DECEMBER

Victorian Stroll, Albia; Sinterklaas Day, Orange City; Sv. Mikulas (St. Nicholas Day), Cedar Rapids; Festival of Lights, Wayland; POW Nativity Scene, Algona.

All privately owned campgrounds personally inspected by WOODALL'S Representatives
Dave and Kate Reikofski

ADEL—D-3

(N) DALLAS COUNTY FAIR CAMPGROUNDS—(Dallas) *From jct I-80 (exit 110) & US 169: Go 5 mi N on US 169.* FACILITIES: 110 sites, 20 full hkups, 35 E, 55 no hkups, tenting, dump. RECREATION: boating, river fishing. Open Apr 1 - Oct 31. Phone: (515)993-4984.

(SW) DES MOINES WEST KOA—(Dallas) *From jct I-80 & CR P58 (exit 106): Go 1-1/2 mi N on CR P58. Enter on R.*

WELCOME

QUIET COUNTRY CHARM!
After the noise and fast pace on the road or in the city, relax beside your RV, Lodge, Kabin, or tent, and listen to the birds. Then take a swim in the pool, fish in the pond, and enjoy a peaceful rural setting. Families are welcome!

◆◆◆◆FACILITIES: 67 sites, typical site width 25 ft, 67 full hkups, (20/30/50 amps), 67 pull-thrus, WiFi Instant Internet at site, WiFi Internet central location, family camping, tenting, cabins, laundry, ltd groc, RV supplies, LP gas by weight/by meter, ice, picnic tables, fire rings, wood.

◆◆◆RECREATION: swim pool, pond fishing, fishing supplies, bsktball, playground, sports field.

Pets welcome. Open Apr 1 - Oct 31. No water to sites in winter. Big rigs welcome. Clubs welcome. Green Friendly. Rate in 2010 $31.45-38.45 for 2 persons. MC/VISA/DISC/AMEX/Debit. KOA discount.

Phone: (800)562-2181
Address: 34308 L Ave, Adel, IA 50003-8136
Lat/Lon: 41.54173/-94.07995
Email: drnwkoa@iowatelecom.net
Web: www.koa.com/where/ia/15103

SEE AD DES MOINES PAGE 256

ALBIA—D-4

(S) INDIAN HILLS INN—*From jct SR 5 & US 34: Go 26 blks E on US 34. Enter on R.* 60 guest rooms with full amenities, indoor pool, hot tub, sauna, free high-speed wireless Internet, and welcome cocktails. Restaurant on site. Aquatics Center nearby. Open all yr. MC/VISA/DISC/AMEX/Debit.

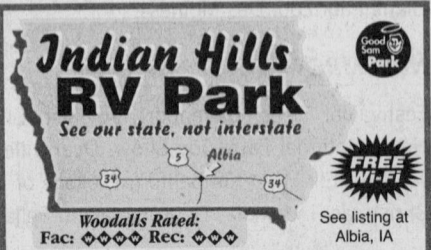

ALBIA—Continued
INDIAN HILLS INN—Continued

Phone: (800)728-4286
Address: 100 Hwy 34 E, Albia, IA 52531
Lat/Lon: 41.01574/-92.80457
Email: indianhillsinn@iowatelecom.net
Web: www.indianhillsinn.com

SEE AD THIS PAGE

(S) INDIAN HILLS RV PARK—(Monroe) *From jct SR 5 & US 34 & SR 5: Go 2 Blks E on US 34. Enter on L.*

WELCOME

◆◆◆◆FACILITIES: 20 sites, typical site width 36 ft, 20 full hkups, (20/30/50 amps), some extd stay sites, 20 pull-thrus, cable TV, WiFi Instant Internet at site, WiFi Internet central location, dump, non-guest dump $, laundry, ltd groc, LP gas by meter, ice.

◆◆◆RECREATION: rec room/area, swim pool, hot tub, golf nearby, sports field, hiking trails.

Pets welcome. Partial handicap access. No tents. Open all yr. subject to snow conditions. Big rigs welcome. Clubs welcome. Rate in 2010 $29 for 2 persons. MC/VISA/DISC/AMEX/Debit.

Phone: (800)728-4286
Address: 100 Hwy 34 E, Albia, IA 52531
Lat/Lon: 41.01574/-92.80457
Email: indianhillsinn@iowatelecom.net
Web: www.indianhillsinn.com

SEE AD THIS PAGE

(N) MIAMI PARK—(Monroe) *From jct SR 34 & SR 137: Go 3 mi N on SR 137, then 1-1/2 mi W on 160th St, then 2 mi N on 640th Ave, then 1/2 mi W on 140th St., then 1-1/4 mi N on 635 Ave. Enter on R.* FACILITIES: 43 sites, typical site width 50 ft, 16 full hkups, 27 E, (30/50 amps), tenting, dump. RECREATION: lake swim, boating, ramp, lake fishing, playground. Open all yr. Phone: (641)946-8112.

(S) THE WHITE BUFFALO RESTAURANT & LOUNGE—*From jct SR 5 & US 34 & SR 5: Go 2 Blks E on US 34. Enter on L.* Full breakfast, lunch & dinner menu. 40 choices, soup & salad bar. Lounge features, late night pizza. Open all yr. MC/VISA/DISC/AMEX/Debit.

WELCOME

Phone: (641)932-7181
Address: 100 Hwy 34 E, Albia, IA 52531
Lat/Lon: 41.01574/-92.80457
Web: www.indianhillsinn.com

SEE AD THIS PAGE

ALGONA—B-3

(SW) AMBROSE A. CALL SP—(Kossuth) *From jct US 18 & US 169: Go 2 mi S on US 169, then 2 mi W on Hwy 274.* FACILITIES: 16 sites, 30 ft max RV length, 13 E, 3 no hkups, tenting. RECREATION: playground. Open all yr. Phone: (641)581-4835.

(N) SMITH LAKE PARK (Kossuth County Park)—(Kossuth) *From jct US-18 & US-169: Go 3 mi N on US-169.* FACILITIES: 49 sites, typical site width 20 ft, 49 E, (30 amps), tenting, dump. RECREATION: lake swim, boating, electric motors only, canoeing, ramp, dock, lake fishing, playground. Partial handicap access. Open Apr 1 - Oct 31. Phone: (515)295-2138.

ALLERTON—E-3

(W) BOBWHITE SP—(Wayne) *From jct Hwy 40 & Main St (CR J46): Go 1-1/2 mi W on CR J46.* FACILITIES: 32 sites, 19 E, 13 no hkups, tenting. RECREATION: lake swim, boating, ramp, lake fishing. Open all yr. Facilities fully operational Apr 15 - Nov 1. Phone: (641)873-4670.

ALTOONA—D-3

(N) Adventureland Campground—(Polk) *From jct I 80 & US 6(NE Hubbell Ave): Go 400 yds on US 6(NE Hubbell Ave) then 350 yds E on Adventureland Dr. Enter on R.* ◆◆◆◆FACILITIES: 310 sites, typical site width 30 ft, 310 full hkups, (30/50 amps), 98 pull-thrus, family camping, tenting, laundry, ltd groc. ◆◆◆◆RECREATION: swim pool, pond fishing. Pets welcome. Partial handicap access. Open Apr 1 - Oct 31. Big rigs welcome. Rate in 2010 $35-45 for 2 persons. Phone: (515)265-7384.

Woodall's Tip... All privately-owned RV parks/campgrounds are personally inspected each year by one of our 25 Representative Teams.

ALTOONA—Continued

GRIFFS VALLEY VIEW RV—(Polk) *From jct I-35 & Corporate Woods Dr becomes 62nd,(exit 89): Go 2-3/4 mi E on Corporate Woods Dr, then 1/4 mi N on NE 46th St. (sign in at office W 1/2 mi on 62nd). Enter on R.*

◆◆◆◆FACILITIES: 142 sites, 142 full hkups, (30/50 amps), 21 pull-thrus, WiFi Instant Internet at site ($), WiFi Internet central location, laundry, LP gas by weight/by meter.

◆◆◆RECREATION: rec hall, rec room/area, equipped pavilion, coin games, pond fishing, golf nearby, play equipment, sports field.

Pets welcome. Partial handicap access. No tents. Open all yr. Big rigs welcome. Green Friendly. Rate in 2010 $27.50 per vehicle. MC/VISA/DISC/AMEX/Debit.

Phone: (515)967-5474
Address: 6429 NE 46th St, Altoona, IA 50009
Lat/Lon: 41.67717/-93.52215
Email: griffieon@msn.com
Web: www.griffs.biz

SEE AD DES MOINES PAGE 255

AMANA—C-5

(NW) AMANA COLONIES RV PARK—(Iowa) *From jct US 151 & I-80 (exit 225): Go 12 mi N on US 151 cross SR 220, then 1/2 mi N on US 151, then 1/4 mi W on C St. Enter on L.*

WELCOME

◆◆◆◆FACILITIES: 478 sites, typical site width 30 ft, 148 full hkups, 330 W&E, (20/30/50 amps), 30 pull-thrus, WiFi Instant Internet at site, family camping, tenting, RV storage, dump, non-guest dump $, laundry, ltd groc, RV supplies, LP gas by weight/by meter, ice, picnic tables, fire rings, wood.

◆◆RECREATION: rec hall, rec room/area, pavilion, play equipment, horseshoes, sports field.

CAMPCLUB USA

Pets welcome. Partial handicap access. Open Apr 15 - Oct 31. Big rigs welcome. Escort to site. Clubs welcome. Green Friendly. Rate in 2010 $29-32 per family. MC/VISA/DISC/Debit. Member ARVC, IAARVC. CCUSA 50% Discount. CCUSA reservations Recommended, CCUSA max stay 2 days. Discount not available during special events & rallies.

Phone: (800)471-7616
Address: 3890 C St, Amana, IA 52203
Lat/Lon: 41.81411/-91.87828
Email: amanarvhost@amanas.net
Web: www.amanarvpark.com

SEE AD TRAVEL SECTION PAGE 248

(NE) AMANA COLONIES VISITORS CENTER—*From jct US 151 & I-80 (exit 225): Go 12 mi N on 151, then 1/2 mi E on SR 220. Enter on L.* Seven Old World villages featuring museums, restaurants, wineries, a brewery, Iowa's only woolen mill, furniture factories, antique, gift & specialty shops, RV Park & more. Local tours are available - food tours & village tours. Open all yr.

WELCOME

Phone: (319)622-7622
Address: 622 46th Ave, Amana, IA 52203
Lat/Lon: 41.79978/-91.86785
Email: info@amanacolonies.com
Web: www.amanacolonies.com

SEE AD TRAVEL SECTION PAGE 248

AMANA COLONIES—C-5

See listings at Amana, Marengo, Oxford, North Liberty, Tipton, West Liberty

AMES—C-3

See listings at Boone, Colo, Jefferson, Marshalltown & Story City

---

Iowa State Bird: Eastern Goldfinch, also known as the Wild Canary

---

ANAMOSA—C-5

✽ **(E) LASSO E RV**—*From jct Hwy 64 & US 151: Go 2-1/2 mi N on US 151, then 3-1/2 mi E on CR E 23, then 1/2 mi S on CR X-44. Enter on L.* SALES: travel trailers, truck campers, 5th wheels, Class A motorhomes, Class C motorhomes, fold-down camping trailers, SERVICES: full-time mech, RV appliance repair, body work/collision repair. NUWA, Coachman, Salem, Sierra. 51 yrs experience. Open all yr.

WELCOME

Phone: (319)462-6750
Address: 12942 CO RD X-44, Anamosa, IA 52205
Lat/Lon: 42.12138/-91.17426
Email: lassoerv@inavia.net
Web: www.lassoerv.com

SEE AD CEDAR RAPIDS NEXT PAGE

✽ **(SW) LASSO E RV**—*From jct US 151 & SR 1: Go 100 yds N on SR 1. Enter on L.* SALES: travel trailers, truck campers, 5th wheels, Class A motorhomes, Class C motorhomes, fold-down camping trailers, pre-owned unit sales. SERVICES: full-time mech, RV appliance repair, body work/collision repair, sells parts/accessories, installs hitches. NuWa, Coachman, Salem, Sierra, 51 yrs experience. Open all yr.

WELCOME

Phone: (319)462-6750
Address: 23486 Co Rd E-34, Anamosa, IA 52205
Lat/Lon: 42.07282/-91.33433
Email: lassoerv@1navia.net
Web: www.lassoerv.com

SEE AD CEDAR RAPIDS NEXT PAGE

(SW) WAPSIPINICON SP—(Jones) *In town off US-151.* FACILITIES: 26 sites, 14 E, (30 amps), 12 no hkups, 22 pull-thrus, tenting, dump. RECREATION: boating, ramp, dock, stream fishing, playground. Partial handicap access. Open May 1 - Sep 30. Phone: (319)462-2761.

ANITA—D-2

(S) LAKE ANITA SP—(Cass) *From jct I-80 & Hwy-148: Go 4 mi S on Hwy-148.* FACILITIES: 161 sites, typical site width 20 ft, 35 ft max RV length, 40 full hkups, 52 E, (20 amps), 69 no hkups, tenting, dump. RECREATION: lake swim, boating, canoeing, ramp, dock, lake fishing, playground. Partial handicap access. Open all yr. Open Apr 15 - Oc 15. Phone: (712)762-3564.

ARNOLDS PARK—A-2

(S) ARNOLDS PARK (City Park)—(Dickinson) *From jct Hwy 9 & US 71: Go 4 mi S on US 71.* FACILITIES: 52 sites, 24 E, 28 no hkups, tenting. RECREATION: boating, ramp, dock, lake fishing, playground. Open May 15 - Sep 15. Phone: (712)332-2341.

(S) Fieldstone RV Park—(Dickinson) *From jct US 71 & 202nd St: Go 1/2 mi E on 202nd St. Enter on R.* ◆◆◆FACILITIES: 106 sites, typical site width 36 ft, 106 full hkups, (30/50 amps), 6 pull-thrus, laundry. Pets welcome. Partial handicap access. No tents. Open May 15 - Oct 15. Big rigs welcome. Rate in 2010 $25 per vehicle. Phone: (712)332-7631.

ATLANTIC—D-2

(S) CASS COUNTY FAIRGROUNDS CAMPGROUND—(Cass) *From I 80 & US 71/US 6 (Exit 60): Go 6-1/4 mi S on US 71/US 6, then 5 mi W on US 6. Enter on L.* FACILITIES: 30 sites, typical site width 30 ft, 30 W&E, (30 amps), 8 pull-thrus, tenting, dump. RECREATION: Pets welcome. Open Apr 1 - Oct 31. Phone: (712)243-1132.

AUBURN—C-2

(W) GRANT PARK (Sac County Park)—(Sac) *From jct US-71 & Hwy-175: Go W on US-71/Hwy-175, then 1/2 mi N on CR-D54, then 1/4 mi W.* FACILITIES: 46 sites, 25 full hkups, (30/50 amps), 21 no hkups, tenting, dump. RECREATION: canoeing, river fishing, playground. Open Apr - Mid Oct. Phone: (712) 662-4530.

AUGUSTA—E-5

(E) LOWER SKUNK RIVER ACCESS (Des Moines County Park)—(Des Moines) *From town: Go 1/2 mi E on Skunk River Rd.* FACILITIES: 41 sites, 24 E, 17 no hkups, tenting, dump. RECREATION: river fishing. Open all yr. Phone: (319)753-8260.

AURORA—B-5

(S) JAKWAY AREA (Buchanan County Park)—(Buchanan) *From town: Go 1-1/2 mi S on CR W45. Enter on R.* FACILITIES: 75 sites, 40 E, 35 no hkups, tenting, dump. RECREATION: stream fishing, play equipment. Partial handicap access. Open Apr 15 - Nov 30. Phone: (319)636-3378.

AVOCA—D-2

(S) E. POTT CO. FAIRGROUNDS CAMPGROUND—(Pottawattamie) *From jct I-80 (exit 40) & US 59: Go 1-3/4 mi S on US 59, then 200 yds W on West Lincoln. Enter on L.* FACILITIES: 334 sites, typical site width 40 ft, 34 full hkups, 300 E, (20/30 amps), 100 pull-thrus, tenting, dump. RECREATION: play equipment. Pets welcome. Partial handicap access. Open Apr 1 - Nov 1. Phone: (712)343-2377.

Dubuque is the state's oldest city.

BATTLE CREEK—C-1

(S) CRAWFORD CREEK RECREATION AREA (Ida County Park)—(Ida) *From jct Hwy 175 & CR L51: Go 3 mi S on CR L51/Dodge Ave, then 1/4 mi W. Enter on R.* FACILITIES: 37 sites, typical site width 45 ft, 37 E, tenting, dump. RECREATION: lake swim, boating, canoeing, ramp, dock, lake fishing. Partial handicap access. Open all yr. Facilities fully operational May - Oct. Phone: (712)364-3300.

BEDFORD—E-2

(N) LAKE OF THREE FIRES SP—(Taylor) *From jct Hwy-49 & Hwy-2: Go 3 mi NE on Hwy-49.* FACILITIES: 140 sites, 30 E, (30 amps), 110 no hkups, tenting, dump, ltd groc. RECREATION: lake swim, boating, ramp, dock, lake fishing, playground. Partial handicap access. Open Apr 15 - Oct 15. Phone: (712)523-2700.

BELLEVUE—C-6

(S) BELLEVUE SP—(Jackson) *From jct Hwy 62 & US 52: Go 2 mi S on US 52.* FACILITIES: 46 sites, 31 E, (30 amps), 15 no hkups, 12 pull-thrus, tenting, dump. RECREATION: boating, ramp, stream fishing, playground. Partial handicap access. Open May 1 - Oct 15. Phone: (563)872-4019.

(S) PLEASANT CREEK (COE - Lock & Dam 11)—(Dubuque) *From jct US-52 & Hwy-62: Go 3-1/2 mi S on US-52.* FACILITIES: 55 sites, 55 no hkups, tenting, dump. RECREATION: river swim, boating, canoeing, ramp, river fishing, playground. Open May 15 - Oct 15. Phone: (563)582-0881.

(N) SPRUCE CREEK (Jackson County Park)—(Jackson) *From jct Hwy 62 & US 52: Go 3 mi N on US 52, then 1/2 mi NE on 396th Ave. Enter on R.* FACILITIES: 85 sites, 85 E, (20/30 amps), tenting, dump. RECREATION: river swim, boating, ramp, dock, river fishing, playground. Partial handicap access. Open Apr 1 - Nov 1. Phone: (563)652-3783.

BLAIRSTOWN—C-4

(SE) HANNEN PARK (Benton County Park)—(Benton) *From town: Go 1 mi S on CR-V56, then 3 mi SE on blacktop road.* FACILITIES: 85 sites, 80 E, 5 no hkups, tenting, dump. RECREATION: boating, electric motors only, canoeing, ramp, lake fishing, playground. Partial handicap access. Open all yr. Phone: (319) 454-6382.

BOONE—C-3

(S) LEDGES SP—(Boone) *From jct US 30 (exit 137) & Hwy 17: Go 3 mi S on Hwy 17, then 3 mi W on CR E 52. Enter on R.* FACILITIES: 95 sites, typical site width 14 ft, 26 ft max RV length, 40 E, (30 amps), 55 no hkups, 10 pull-thrus, tenting, dump. RECREATION: stream fishing, playground. Partial handicap access. Open Apr 15 - Oct 15. Phone: (515)432-1852.

BRANDON—C-5

(W) LIME CREEK AREA (Buchanan County Park)—(Buchanan) *From jct Hwy 150 & Hwy 283: Go 5 mi W on Hwy 283, then 1-1/2 mi NE on CR W17. Enter on L.* FACILITIES: 32 sites, 12 E, 20 no hkups, tenting. RECREATION: lake/river fishing, playground. Partial handicap access. Open Apr 15 - Sep 30. Phone: (319)636-2617.

BRIDGEWATER—D-2

(S) MORMAN TRAIL PARK (Adair County Park)—(Adair) *From jct CR N51 & Hwy 92: Go 1 mi E on Hwy 92, then 1-1/2 mi S on gravel road.* FACILITIES: 20 sites, 15 E, 5 no hkups, tenting. RECREATION: boating, electric motors only, ramp, dock, lake fishing, playground. Open Apr 15 - Oct 31. Phone: (641)743-6450.

BRIGHTON—D-5

(W) LAKE DARLING SP—(Washington) *From jct Hwy-1 & Hwy-78: Go 3 mi W on Hwy-1 & Hwy-78.* FACILITIES: 118 sites, typical site width 20 ft, 35 ft max RV length, 81 E, (30 amps), 37 no hkups, tenting, dump, ltd groc. RECREATION: lake swim, boating, canoeing, ramp, dock, lake fishing, playground. Partial handicap access. Open all yr. Facilities fully operational Apr 15 - Oct 15. Phone: (319)694-2323.

BUFFALO—D-6

(W) BUFFALO SHORES (Scott County Park)—(Scott) *From jct I-280 (exit 8) & Hwy 22: Go 6 mi W on Hwy 22. Enter on L.* FACILITIES: 65 sites, 65 W&E, (50 amps), tenting, dump. RECREATION: river swim, boating, canoeing, ramp, river fishing, playground. Open all yr. Phone: (563)328-3281.

CAMANCHE—C-6

(N) ROCK CREEK MARINA & CAMPGROUND (Clinton County Park)—(Clinton) *From jct I-80 (exit 306) & US 67: Go 14 mi N on US 67, then 1 mi E on 291st St (gravel road).* FACILITIES: 77 sites, typical site width 30 ft, 30 ft max RV length, 66 E, 11 no hkups, tenting, dump, laundry, ltd groc. RECREATION: river swim, boating, canoeing, ramp, dock, river fishing, playground. Open all yr. Phone: (563)847-7202.

CARROLL—C-2

(SE) SWAN LAKE STATE PARK—(Carroll) *From jct SR 30 & SR 71: Go 2 mi S on SR 71, then go 1-1/2 mi E on 220th. Enter at end.* FACILITIES: 125 sites, typical site width 19 ft, 46 full hkups, 54 W&E, 25 E, (30 amps), 20 pull-thrus, tenting, dump. RECREATION: lake swim, canoeing, lake fishing. Pets welcome. Partial handicap access. Open May 1 - Oct 31. Phone: (712)792-4614.

CASCADE—C-5

(E) FILLMORE RECREATION AREA (Dubuque County Park)—(Dubuque) *From town: Go 5 mi E on Hwy 151.* FACILITIES: 29 sites, 30 ft max RV length, 4 E, 25 no hkups, tenting. RECREATION: playground. Partial handicap access. Open Apr 15 - Nov 1. Phone: (563)556-6745.

CASEY—D-2

(W) CASEY CITY PARK—(Guthrie) *From jct Hwy-25 & I-80: Go 2 mi W on I-80.* FACILITIES: 50 sites, 25 E, 25 no hkups, tenting. RECREATION: playground. Open May 1 - Oct 1. Phone: (641)746-3315.

CEDAR FALLS—B-4

(E) GEORGE WYTH MEMORIAL SP—(Black Hawk) *From jct Hwy 57 & US 218: Go 2-1/4 mi E on US 218, then S on Airport Blvd. Enter on R.* FACILITIES: 69 sites, typical site width 12 ft, 35 ft max RV length, 46 E, (30 amps), 23 no hkups, tenting, dump. RECREATION: lake swim, boating, ramp, dock, lake/stream fishing, playground. Partial handicap access. Open all yr. Facilities fully operational Apr 15 - Nov 1. Phone: (319)232-5505.

CEDAR RAPIDS—C-5

(N) MORGAN CREEK CAMPGROUND (Linn County Park)—(Linn) *From jct 16th Ave SW & Stoney Point Rd at W edge of town: Go 2 mi N on Stoney Point Rd, then 1/2 mi W on Worcester Rd.* FACILITIES: 36 sites, 36 W&E, (50 amps), tenting, dump. RECREATION: stream fishing, playground. Partial handicap access. Open Apr 15 - Oct 15. Phone: (319)892-3505.

CEDAR RAPIDS—Continued on next page

CEDAR RAPIDS—Continued

✽ **(NW) TRUCK COUNTRY**—*From jct US 151 & I-380: Go 1-1/4 mi N on I-380, then 1/4 mi W on 33rd Ave, then 1/4 mi N on 6th St, then 100 yds W on 29th Ave. Enter at end.* SERVICES: full-time mech, engine/chassis repair, body work/collision repair, RV towing. Front end, transmissions & DYNO Diagnostics. Open all yr. MC/VISA/DISC/AMEX/Debit.

WELCOME

Phone: (800)332-6158
Address: 700 29th Ave SW, Cedar Rapids, IA 52406
Lat/Lon: 41.94911/-91.68015
Web: www.truckcountry.com

SEE AD TRAVEL SECTION PAGE 247 AND AD WI TRAVEL SECTION PAGE 798

CENTERVILLE—E-4

(NW) ISLAND VIEW (COE - Rathbun Lake)—(Appanoose) *From jct Hwy-5 & CR-J29: Go 3 mi NW on CR-J29.* FACILITIES: 194 sites, 194 E, (30/50 amps), tenting, dump. RECREATION: lake swim, boating, canoeing, ramp, dock, lake fishing, playground. Partial handicap access. Open May 1 - Sep 29. Phone: (641)647-2464.

(NW) ROLLING COVE (COE - Rathbun Lake)—(Appanoose) *From jct Hwy-5 & CR-J29: Go 3 mi NW on CR-J29, then 4 mi W on CR-J5T, then 2 mi N on county road.* FACILITIES: 32 sites, 32 no hkups, tenting, dump. RECREATION: boating, canoeing, ramp, dock, lake fishing. Partial handicap access. Open May 1 - Sep 29. Phone: (641)647-2464.

CENTRAL CITY—C-5

(N) PINICON RIDGE FLYING SQUIRREL CAMPGROUND (Linn county Park)—(Linn) *From town: Go 1 mi N on Hwy 13, then 1/4 mi W on county road.* FACILITIES: 90 sites, 35 ft max RV length, 76 W&E, (20/30/50 amps), 14 no hkups, 32 pull-thrus, tenting, dump. RECREATION: boating, canoeing, ramp, river fishing, playground. Open Apr 15 - Oct 15. Phone: (319)892-6450.

CHARITON—D-3

(E) RED HAW SP—(Lucas) *From south jct Hwy 14 & US 34: Go 1 mi E on US 34.* FACILITIES: 80 sites, typical site width 12 ft, 35 ft max RV length, 60 E, (30 amps), 20 no hkups, 17 pull-thrus, tenting, dump, ltd groc. RECREATION: lake swim, boating, electric motors only, canoeing, ramp, dock, lake fishing, playground. Partial handicap access. Open all yr. Facilities fully operational Apr 15 - Nov 1. Phone: (641)774-5632.

CHARLES CITY—B-4

(SE) R Campground—(Floyd) *From jct US 218 (exit 212) & BUS 218: Go 2 mi SE on BUS 218, then 1/4 mi on Hwy 18E, then 1 mi SE on Clark St. Enter on R.* ◇◇◇FACILITIES: 70 sites, typical site width 30 ft, 54 full hkups, 8 E, (20/30/50 amps), 8 no hkups, 40 pull-thrus, family camping, tenting, dump, laundry. ◇◇RECREATION: river swim, canoeing, river/pond fishing, play equipment. Pets welcome. Partial handicap access. Open all yr. Facilities fully operational Apr - Nov 1. Big rigs welcome. Rate in 2010 $18-24 per vehicle. Phone: (641)257-0549.

CHEROKEE—B-1

(S) CHEROKEE CITY PARK—(Cherokee) *From jct Hwy 3 & US 59: Go 3-1/2 mi S on US 59, past Little Sioux River bridge, then 2 blocks W.* FACILITIES: 40 sites, typical site width 20 ft, 16 full hkups, 24 W&E, dump. RECREATION: lake fishing, playground. Open all yr. Facilities fully operational Apr 15 - Nov 15. Phone: (712)225-2715.

CLARION—B-3

(NE) LAKE CORNELIA PARK (Wright County Park)—(Wright) *From town: Go 5 mi N on CR-R45.* FACILITIES: 84 sites, 14 full hkups, 52 E, (30 amps), 18 no hkups, tenting, dump. RECREATION: lake swim, boating, canoeing, ramp, dock, lake fishing, playground. Partial handicap access. Open Apr 15 - Oct 15. Phone: (515)532-3185.

CLEAR LAKE—B-3

(S) CLEAR LAKE SP—(Cerro Gordo) *From jct US-18 & Hwy-107: Go 2 mi S on Hwy-107.* FACILITIES: 200 sites, 95 E, 105 no hkups, tenting, dump. RECREATION: lake swim, boating, ramp, lake fishing, playground. Open all yr. Facilities fully operational Apr 15 - Nov 1. Phone: (641)357-4212.

CLEAR LAKE—Continued

(S) Deer Valley Lodge CG—(Cerro Gordo) *From jct US 35 & US 18 (exit 194): Go 6-1/4 mi W on US 18, then 1-1/4 mi S on Main, then 1/4 mi E on 242nd St. Enter on R.* ◇◇◇FACILITIES: 54 sites, typical site width 20 ft, 54 full hkups, (20/30/50 amps). ◇◇◇RECREATION: swim pool, boating, dock, lake fishing, playground. Pets welcome. Open Apr 15 - Oct 15. Big rigs welcome. Rate in 2010 $23 for 2 persons. Phone: (641)829-4433.

(SW) Oakwood RV Park—(Cerro Gordo) *From jct I-35 (exit 193) & 4th Ave: Go 1 mi W on 4th Ave, then 1/2 mi S on 8th St (Hwy 107), then 1/2 mi W on 27th Ave, (follow signs) then 1-1/4 mi S on South Shore Dr, then left on 240th. Enter on L.* ◇◇◇FACILITIES: 90 sites, typical site width 40 ft, 90 full hkups, (30/50 amps), 58 pull-thrus, family camping, dump, laundry. ◇RECREATION: play equipment. Pets welcome, breed restrict. No tents. Open Apr 15 - Oct 15. Big rigs welcome. Rate in 2010 $25 for 2 persons. Member ARVC, IAARVC. Phone: (641)357-4019.

CLERMONT—B-5

(SW) Skip-A-Way RV Park & Campground—(Fayette) *On US 18 at west end of Clermont at bottom of hill - south side. (3825 Harding Rd US Hwy 18).* ◇◇◇◇FACILITIES: 198 sites, typical site width 30 ft, 160 full hkups, 38 W&E, (20/30/50 amps), 10 pull-thrus, family camping, tenting, dump, laundry, ltd groc. ◇◇◇◇RECREATION: lake/river/boating, canoeing, lake/river fishing, playground. Pets welcome. Partial handicap access. Open all yr. Facilities fully operational Apr 15 - Oct 15. Big rigs welcome. Rate in 2010 $28 per vehicle. Member ARVC, IAARVC.

Phone: (800)728-1167
Address: 3825 Harding Rd (US Hwy 18), Clermont, IA 52135
Lat/Lon: 42.99487/-92.66057
Web: www.skipawayresort.com

CLINTON—C-6

(NE) BULGERS HOLLOW REC AREA (COE-Thomson Park)—(Clinton) *From town: Go 5 mi N on US 67, then E at Bulgers Hollow sign.* FACILITIES: 26 sites, 26 no hkups, tenting, dump. RECREATION: boating, canoeing, ramp, river fishing, playground. Open May 10 - Sep 15. Phone: (815)259-3628.

COGGON—C-5

(W) BUFFALO CREEK PARK-WALNUT GROVE CAMPGROUND (Linn County Park)—(Linn) *From town: Go 1/2 mi W on CR-D62.* FACILITIES: 18 sites, 18 W&E, (20/30/50 amps), tenting, dump. RECREATION: canoeing, stream fishing, playground. Open Apr 15 - Oct 15. Phone: (319)892-6450.

COLESBURG—B-5

(W) TWIN BRIDGES (Delaware County Park)—(Delaware) *From town: Go 5 mi W on Hwy 3.* FACILITIES: 44 sites, 15 E, 29 no hkups, tenting, dump. RECREATION: stream fishing, playground. Partial handicap access. Open May 1 - Nov 1. Phone: (563)927-3410.

COLO—C-3

(SW) HICKORY GROVE BREEZY BAY (Story County Park)—(Story) *From jct US-30 & US-65: Go 2 mi W on US-30, then 2 mi SW on CR.* FACILITIES: 52 sites, typical site width 10 ft, 26 ft max RV length, 42 E, (30/50 amps), 10 no hkups, tenting, dump. RECREATION: lake swim, boating, electric motors only, canoeing, ramp, dock, lake fishing, playground. Partial handicap access. Open Apr 1 - Nov 30. Phone: (515)232-2516.

(SW) Twin Anchors Campground—(Story) *From jct US-65 & US-30: Go 1-1/2 mi W on US-30. Enter on L.* ◇◇FACILITIES: 205 sites, typical site width 25 ft, 125 full hkups, 25 W&E, 55 E, (30/50 amps), 15 pull-thrus, tenting, dump, laundry, ltd groc. ◇◇◇RECREATION: lake swim, lake fishing, playground. Pets welcome. Open all yr. Facilities fully operational Apr - Oct. Rate in 2010 $16.50-21 for 4 persons. Phone: (641) 377-2243.

COON RAPIDS

(NE) RIVERSIDE PARK—(Carroll) *From jct SR 141 & 330th St: Go 1 mi E on 330th, then 1/2 mi N on Walnut St. Enter on L.* FACILITIES: 12 sites, typical site width 20 ft, 12 W&E, (30 amps), 12 pull-thrus, tenting. RECREATION: river fishing. Pets welcome. Open Apr 1 - Nov 1. Phone: (712)792-4614.

CORRECTIONVILLE—B-1

(SW) LITTLE SIOUX PARK (Woodbury County Park)—(Woodbury) *From jct Hwy-31 & US-20: Go 2 mi SW.* FACILITIES: 192 sites, 30 ft max RV length, 42 E, (30 amps), 150 no hkups, tenting, dump. RECREATION: boating, no motors, canoeing, ramp, lake/stream fishing, playground. Partial handicap access. Open May 1 - Oct 31. Phone: (712)372-4984.

COUNCIL BLUFFS—D-1

(SW) Bluffs Run RV Park—(Pottawattamie) *From jct I-29/I-80 & S 24th St: Go 1/2 mi N on 24th St, then 1/2 mi W on 23rd Ave. Enter on R.* ◇◇◇FACILITIES: 44 sites, typical site width 16 ft, 44 W&E, (20/30/50 amps), dump, laundry. No tents. Open all yr. Rate in 2010 $30-40 per vehicle. Phone: (800)238-2946.

(S) LAKE MANAWA SP—(Mills) *From town: Go 1 mi S on Hwy-192.* FACILITIES: 72 sites, typical site width 10 ft, 25 ft max RV length, 37 E, (20/30 amps), 35 no hkups, 12 pull-thrus, tenting, dump. RECREATION: lake swim, boating, ramp, lake fishing, playground. Partial handicap access. Open all yr. Facilities fully operational Apr 15 - Oct 15. Phone: (712)366-0220.

(S) Tomes RV Park—(Pottawattamie) *From jct I 80/I 29 & 24th St: Go 1 mi S on 24th St, then 1/4 mi E on US 275. Enter on L.* ◇◇◇FACILITIES: 25 sites, typical site width 35 ft, accepts full hkup units only, 25 full hkups, (30/50 amps). Pets welcome. No tents. Open Apr 1 - Nov 1. Big rigs welcome. Phone: (712) 366-0363.

CRESTON—D-2

(W) Country Court RV Park (RV SPACES)—(Union) *From jct US 34 & SR 25: Go 1/2 mi W on US 34, then 300 yds S. on Smith St., then 50 yds E on Patt St. Enter on R.* FACILITIES: 12 sites, typical site width 22 ft, accepts full hkup units only, 12 full hkups, (20/30/50 amps). Pets welcome. No tents. Open all yr. Rate in 2010 $20 for 2 persons. Phone: (800)398-9646.

(N) GREEN VALLEY SP—(Union) *From jct US 34 & Hwy 25: Go 3 mi N on Hwy 25, then 3 mi E on CR H24, then 1 mi N on Hwy 186, then 1/4 mi W on 130th St.* FACILITIES: 100 sites, typical site width 35 ft, 18 full hkups, 65 E, (30/50 amps), 17 no hkups, 50 pull-thrus, tenting, dump, ltd groc. RECREATION: boating, ramp, lake fishing, playground. Partial handicap access. Open all yr. Facilities fully operational May 1 - Sep 30. Phone: (641)782-5131.

DANVILLE—E-5

(SW) GEODE SP—(Henry) *From jct US 34 & Hwy 79: Go 4 mi W on Hwy 79, then 1 mi SW on CR J20 (Geode Rd). Enter on R.* FACILITIES: 168 sites, 87 E, (30 amps), 81 no hkups, 16 pull-thrus, tenting, dump, ltd groc. RECREATION: lake swim, boating, ramp, dock, lake fishing, playground. Partial handicap access. Open all yr. Facilities fully operational Apr 15 - Nov 1. Phone: (319)392-4601.

DAVENPORT—D-6

(SW) CLARK'S FERRY (COE-Mississippi River Rec Areas-Muscatine)—(Muscatine) *From town: Go 15 mi SW on Hwy 22 (Montpelier).* FACILITIES: 45 sites, 45 E, (30/50 amps), tenting, dump. RECREATION: boating, canoeing, ramp, dock, river fishing, playground. Partial handicap access. Open Apr 14 - Oct 9. Phone: (563)381-4043.

DAVENPORT—Continued on next page

Woodall's Tip... Looking for a place to stay for an extended period of time? Check out our Extended Stay Guide (the yellow pages in the middle of this Directory).

DAVENPORT—Continued

(NW) INTERSTATE RV PARK—(Scott) *From jct I-80 & SR 130 (exit 292): Go 1/2 mi N on SR 130, then 150 yds W on Fairmount Rd. Enter on R.*

◆◆◆◆FACILITIES: 97 sites, typical site width 27 ft, 90 full hkups, 7 W&E, (20/30/50 amps), some extd stay sites, 49 pull-thrus, WiFi Instant Internet at site, WiFi Internet central location, family camping, RV storage, dump, non-guest dump $, laundry, ltd groc, RV supplies, LP gas by weight/by meter, ice, picnic tables, patios, fire rings, wood.

◆◆◆RECREATION: rec room/area, pavilion, swim pool, wading pool, golf nearby, playground, horseshoes, v-ball. Rec open to public.

Pets welcome, breed restrict. No tents. Open all yr. Big rigs welcome. Escort to site. Clubs welcome. Rate in 2010 $28.97-38.32 for 2A persons. MC/VISA/DISC/Debit. Member ARVC, IAARVC. FMCA discount.

Phone: (563)386-7292
Address: 8448 N Fairmount, Davenport, IA 52806
Lat/Lon: 41.60518/-90.62986

SEE AD PAGE 254

(W) Lakeside RV Park & Campground—(Scott) *From jct I-280 & US 61 (exit 6): Go 1/2 mi W on US 61. Enter on L.* ◆◆◆FACILITIES: 20 sites, typical site width 35 ft, 20 full hkups, (30/50 amps), 3 pull-thrus, cable TV, WiFi Instant Internet at site, cable on-site Internet (needs activ), WiFi Internet central location, tenting, picnic tables, fire rings, wood. RECREATION: pond fishing. Pets welcome. Open all yr. Big rigs welcome. Rate in 2010 $25 for 2 persons. MC/VISA/Debit. CCUSA 50% Discount. CCUSA reservations Recommended, CCUSA max stay 2 days, CCUSA disc. not avail F,Sa, CCUSA disc. not avail holidays.

Phone: (563)381-3413
Address: 11279 140th St, Davenport, IA 52804
Lat/Lon: 41.50710/-90.68218

(N) SCOTT COUNTY PARK—(Scott) *From jct I-80 (exit 295) & US 61: Go 7 mi N on US 61 (exit 129), then 3/4 mi E on 267th St, then 1/4 mi N on Scott Park Rd, then 1-1/4 mi E on 270th St. Enter on L.* FACILITIES: 398 sites, typical site width 15 ft, 30 ft max RV length, 48 W&E, 37 E, (30 amps), 313 no hkups, tenting, dump. RECREATION: swim pool, playground. Partial handicap access. Open all yr. Facilities fully operational Apr - Oct. Phone: (563)328-3282.

(NW) TRUCK COUNTRY—*From jct I-80 & SR 130: Go 300 yds S on SR 130, then 150 yds E on 76th St. Enter on L.* SERVICES: full-time mech, engine/chassis repair, 24-hr emerg rd svc, mobile RV svc. 24 hr service bays. Open all yr. MC/VISA/DISC/AMEX/Debit.

Phone: (563)445-5870
Address: 2350 West 76th Street, Davenport, IA 52806
Lat/Lon: 41.59705/-90.61370
Web: www.truckcountry.com

SEE AD TRAVEL SECTION PAGE 247 AND AD WI TRAVEL SECTION PAGE 798

DAVENPORT—Continued

(W) WEST LAKE PARK (Scott County Park)—(Scott) *From jct I-280 (exit 6) & US 61: Go 1/2 mi W on US 61, then 3/4 mi N on CR Y48. Enter on R.* FACILITIES: 127 sites, 74 full hkups, 48 W&E, 3 E, (30 amps), 2 no hkups, 48 pull-thrus, tenting, dump. RECREATION: lake swim, boating, electric motors only, canoeing, ramp, dock, lake fishing, playground. Partial handicap access. Open Apr 15 - Oct 15. Phone: (563)328-3281.

DAVIS CITY—E-3

(SE) NINE EAGLES SP—(Decatur) *From jct US-69 & CR-J66: Go 6 mi SE on CR-J66.* FACILITIES: 68 sites, typical site width 12 ft, 35 ft max RV length, 28 E, (20 amps), 40 no hkups, 20 pull-thrus, tenting, dump, ltd groc. RECREATION: lake swim, boating, electric motors only, canoeing, ramp, dock, lake fishing, playground. Partial handicap access. Open Apr 15 - Oct 15. Phone: (641)442-2855.

DECORAH—A-5

(N) PULPIT ROCK CAMPGROUND (City Park)—(Winneshiek) *From jct US 52 & Hwy 9: Go 3/4 mi N on US 52, exit Pulpit Rock Rd.* FACILITIES: 200 sites, 120 E, (20/30/50 amps), 80 no hkups, 15 pull-thrus, tenting, dump. RECREATION: river swim, canoeing, river/stream fishing, playground. Partial handicap access. Open Apr 1 - Nov 1. Phone: (563)382-9551.

(E) TRUCK COUNTRY—*From jct US 52 & SR 9: Go 4-1/2 mi E on SR 9. Enter on R.* SERVICES: full-time mech, engine/chassis repair, RV appliance repair, 24-hr emerg rd svc, mobile RV svc. Open all yr. MC/VISA/DISC/AMEX/Debit.

Phone: (563)382-6551
Address: 1653 State Hwy 9, Decorah, IA 52101
Lat/Lon: 43.27124/-91.72681
Email: darinbohr@truckcountry.com
Web: www.truckcountry.com

SEE AD TRAVEL SECTION PAGE 247 AND AD WI TRAVEL SECTION PAGE 798

DELHI—C-5

(SE) TURTLE CREEK RIVER ACCESS (Delaware County Park)—(Delaware) *From jct US-20 & CR-D-5X: Go 4 mi SE on CR-D-5X, then 4 mi S on CR-X21, then 3 mi E.* FACILITIES: 29 sites, 24 E, 5 no hkups, tenting. RECREATION: boating, canoeing, ramp, lake/river fishing. Partial handicap access. Open May 1 - Nov 1. Phone: (563)927-3410.

DENISON—C-2

(E) YELLOW SMOKE PARK (Crawford County Park)—(Crawford) *From town: Go 1 mi E on US 30, then 3/4 mi N on paved road.* FACILITIES: 61 sites, 61 W&E, (30 amps), tenting, dump. RECREATION: lake swim, boating, electric motors only, canoeing, ramp, dock, lake fishing, playground. Partial handicap access. Open May 1 - Sep 30. Phone: (712)263-2748.

DES MOINES—D-3

DES MOINES AREA MAP

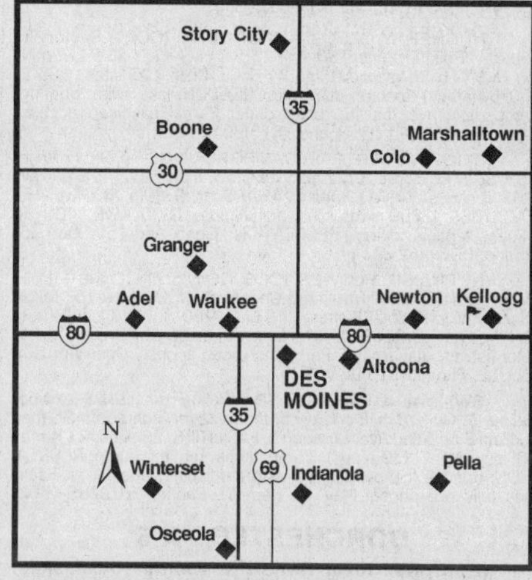

Symbols on map indicate towns within a 50 mi radius of Des Moines where campgrounds (diamonds), attractions (flags), & RV service centers & camping supply outlets (gears) are listed. Check listings for more information.

Tell Them Woodall's Sent You!

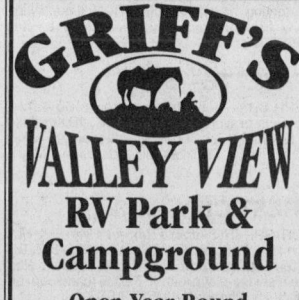

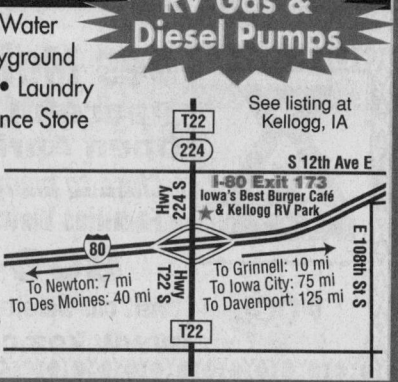

DES MOINES—Continued

(N) ACORN VALLEY (COE - Saylorville Lake)—(Polk) *From I-35/80 (exit 131): Go 5 mi N on Hwy-401 to NW Beaver Dr.* FACILITIES: 108 sites, 29 E, (30/50 amps), 79 no hkups, tenting, dump. RECREATION: boating, ramp, lake/pond fishing, playground. Partial handicap access. Open Apr 28 - Sep 30. Phone: (515)276-0429.

(N) BOB SHETLER CAMPGROUND (COE - Saylorville Lake)—(Polk) *From I-35/80 (Merle Hay Rd exit): Go 4 mi N on Merle Hay Rd to NW Beaver Dr.* FACILITIES: 69 sites, 69 E, (30 amps), 6 pull-thrus, tenting. RECREATION: river swim, boating, ramp, river fishing, playground. Partial handicap access. Open Apr 28 - Sep 30. Phone: (515)276-4656.

(N) CHERRY GLEN CAMPGROUND (COE - Saylorville Lake)—(Polk) *From jct I-80 (exit 136) & Hwy-415: Go 6-1/2 mi N on Hwy-415, then follow sign W.* FACILITIES: 125 sites, 125 E, (30/50 amps), tenting, dump. RECREATION: lake swim, boating, ramp, lake/river fishing, playground. Partial handicap access. Open Apr 15 - Oct 13. Phone: (515)964-8792.

(S) IOWA STATE FAIR CAMPGROUNDS—(Polk) *From jct I-35/80 & I-235: Go 3-1/2 mi S on I-235, then 1-1/2 mi E on Hwy 163 (University Ave.), then 1/4 mi S on E 30th St (Hwy 46).* FACILITIES: 2800 sites, 600 full hkups, 1800 W&E, 400 no hkups, tenting, dump. RECREATION: Open Apr 15 - Oct 15. Phone: (515)262-3111.

(N) PRAIRIE FLOWER (COE - Saylorville Lake)—(Polk) *From jct I-80/35 & Hwy-415: Go 19 mi N on Hwy-415, follow signs.* FACILITIES: 248 sites, 248 E, (30/50 amps), 11 pull-thrus, tenting, dump. RECREATION: lake swim, boating, ramp, dock, lake fishing, playground. Partial handicap access. Open Apr 30 - Oct 12. Phone: (515)984-6925.

(SW) WALNUT WOODS SP—(Polk) *From jct I-35 (exit 68) & Hwy 5: Go 1/2 mi E on Hwy 5, then 1/2 mi N on 105th St, then 1/2 mi E on 52nd Ave. Enter on L.* FACILITIES: 23 sites, 21 ft max RV length, 8 E, (30 amps), 15 no hkups, tenting, dump. RECREATION: boating, canoeing, ramp, stream fishing. Open all yr. Facilities fully operational May 1 - Sep 30. Phone: (515)285-4502.

DORCHESTER—A-5

(S) Upper Iowa Resort & Rental—(Allamakee) *From jct Hwy 76 & Hwy 9: Go 15 mi N on Hwy 76, then 1/4 mi W on Lonnings Dr (just before Upper Iowa Bridge). Enter at end.* ◆◆FACILITIES: 114 sites, typical site width 45 ft, 0 full hkups, 108 W&E, 6 E, (30/50 amps), tenting, dump, ltd groc. ◆◆◆◆RECREATION: swim pool, canoeing, river fishing, playground. Pets welcome. Partial handicap access. Facilities fully operational Apr 1 - Oct 31. Rate in 2010 $26 for 4 persons. Member ARVC, IAARVC. Phone: (563)568-3263.

DOW CITY—C-2

(SW) NELSON PARK (Crawford County Park)—(Crawford) *From town: Go 1-1/2 mi SW on US 30, then 4 mi NW on Nelson Park Rd.* FACILITIES: 90 sites, 35 ft max RV length, 50 E, (30 amps), 40 no hkups, tenting, dump. RECREATION: lake swim, boating, electric motors only, ramp, lake fishing, playground. Partial handicap access. Open May 15 - Oct 15. Phone: (712)643-5426.

DRAKESVILLE—E-4

(W) LAKE WAPELLO SP—(Davis) *From jct US-63 & Hwy-273: Go 6 mi W on Hwy-273.* FACILITIES: 80 sites, 42 E, (30 amps), 38 no hkups, tenting, dump. RECREATION: boating, ramp, lake fishing, playground. Partial handicap access. Open Apr 15 - Oct 15. Phone: (641)722-3371.

DUBUQUE—B-6

(N) FINLEY'S LANDING (Dubuque County Park)—(Dubuque) *From town: Go 5 mi NW on Hwy 3/US 52, then 15 mi on Great River Rd (Sherill Blacktop Rd), then 3 mi NE on Finley's Landing Rd.* FACILITIES: 32 sites, typical site width 15 ft, 25 ft max RV length, 32 E, (20/30 amps), 1 pull-thrus, tenting, dump. RECREATION: boating, canoeing, ramp, dock, river fishing, playground. Partial handicap access. Open Apr 15 - Nov 1. Phone: (563)552-1571.

(E) MASSEY MARINA (Dubuque County Park)—(Dubuque) *From town: Go 4 mi SE on US 52, then 7 mi E on Massey Station Rd.* FACILITIES: 60 sites, 42 W&E, 4 E, 14 no hkups, 40 pull-thrus, tenting, dump, laundry, ltd groc. RECREATION: boating, canoeing, ramp, dock, river/stream fishing, playground. Partial handicap access. Open Apr 15 - Nov 1. Phone: (563)556-6745.

(N) MUD LAKE CAMPGROUND (Dubuque County Park)—(Dubuque) *From jct US 20 & Hwy 52: Go 5 mi NW on Hwy 52, then 1/8 mi N on Sageville Rd, then 3 mi E on Mud Lake Rd.* FACILITIES: 76 sites, 18 W&E, 26 E, (20/30 amps), 32 no hkups, tenting, dump. RECREATION: boating, canoeing, ramp, dock, river fishing, playground. Partial handicap access. Open Apr 15 - Oct 31. Phone: (563)552-2746.

DUBUQUE—Continued

(SW) SWISS VALLEY CAMPGROUND (Dubuque County Park)—(Dubuque) *From town: Go 6 mi W on US 20, then 5 mi S on Swiss Valley Rd, then 1/2 mi E on Whitetop Rd.* FACILITIES: 96 sites, 26 W&E, 60 E, (20/30 amps), 10 no hkups, 1 pull-thrus, tenting, dump. RECREATION: stream fishing, playground. Partial handicap access. Open Apr 15 - Oct 15. Phone: (563)556-6745.

✲ **(S) TRUCK COUNTRY**—*From jct US 61/US 151 S & US 52: Go 1/2 mi S on US 61/US 151. Enter on R.* SERVICES: full-time mech, engine/chassis repair, body work/collision repair, 24-hr emerg rd svc, RV towing. Front end alignment, DYNO Diagnostics. Open all yr. MC/VISA/DISC/AMEX/Debit.

WELCOME

Phone: (800)553-3642
Address: 10785 Rt 61 South, Dubuque, IA 52003
Lat/Lon: 42.45211/-90.67967
Web: www.truckcountry.com

SEE AD TRAVEL SECTION PAGE 247 AND AD WI TRAVEL SECTION PAGE 798

DYERSVILLE—B-5

(NW) NEW WINE PARK (Dubuque County Park)—(Dubuque) *From town: Go 4 mi N on Hwy 136, then 2 mi W on New Wine Park Lane.* FACILITIES: 36 sites, 21 W&E, 5 E, (20/30 amps), 10 no hkups, 1 pull-thrus, tenting, dump. RECREATION: stream fishing, playground. Pets welcome. Partial handicap access. Open Apr 15 - Nov 1. Phone: (563)921-3475.

ELDORA—C-4

(NE) PINE LAKE SP—(Hardin) *From jct Hwy-175 & Hwy-118: Go 1/2 mi NE on Hwy-118.* FACILITIES: 124 sites, 124 E, (30/50 amps), 40 pull-thrus, tenting, dump, ltd groc. RECREATION: lake swim, boating, electric motors only, canoeing, ramp, dock, lake fishing, playground. Partial handicap access. Open Apr 15 - Oct 15. Phone: (641)858-5832.

ESTHERVILLE—A-2

(SW) FORT DEFIANCE SP—(Emmet) *From jct Hwy-9 & Hwy-4: Go 1 mi W on Hwy-9.* FACILITIES: 16 sites, 8 E, (20 amps), 8 no hkups, tenting. RECREATION: Open all yr. Facilities fully operational Apr 15 - Nov 1. Phone: (712)337-3211.

EVANSDALE—B-4

(N) DEERWOOD PARK (City Park)—(To River) *From jct I-380 (exit 70) & River Forest Rd: Go 1 block N on River Forest Rd, then 1/4 mi W on campground road.* FACILITIES: 118 sites, 94 E, 24 no hkups, tenting, dump. RECREATION: lake swim, boating, canoeing, river fishing, playground. Open May 1 - Sep 30. Phone: (319)232-6683.

FAYETTE—B-5

(N) VOLGA RIVER SRA—(Fayette) *From town: Go 4 mi N on Hwy-150, then 2 mi E on gravel road.* FACILITIES: 49 sites, 49 no hkups, tenting. RECREATION: boating, canoeing, ramp, lake/stream fishing. Open all yr. Facilities fully operational May 1 - Sep 30. Phone: (563)425-4161.

FOREST CITY—A-3

(E) PILOT KNOB SP—(Hancock) *From jct Hwy 9 & Hwy 332: Go 1-1/4 mi S on Hwy 332.* FACILITIES: 60 sites, 48 E, (20 amps), 12 no hkups, tenting, dump. RECREATION: boating, electric motors only, lake fishing, playground. Partial handicap access. Open Apr 15 - Oct 15. Phone: (641)581-4835.

FORT DODGE—B-3

(N) JOHN F. KENNEDY MEMORIAL PARK (Webster County Park)—(Webster) *From jct US 20 & US 169: Go 7 mi N on US 169, then 3 mi E on CR D14, then 3 mi N on CR P56.* FACILITIES: 129 sites, 32 ft max RV length, 29 full hkups, 100 no hkups, 29 pull-thrus, tenting, dump. RECREATION: lake swim, boating, electric motors only, canoeing, ramp, dock, lake fishing, playground. Partial handicap access. Open Apr 15 - Oct 15. Phone: (515)576-4258.

FREDERIKA—B-4

(W) ALCOCK PARK (Bremer County Park)—(Bremer) *From jct US 63 & CR C16: Go 1 mi E on CR C16, follow signs.* FACILITIES: 50 sites, 50 E, (20/30 amps), 45 pull-thrus, tenting, dump. RECREATION: boating, canoeing, ramp, river fishing, playground. Open May 1 - Oct 30. Phone: (319)882-4742.

GARNAVILLO—B-5

(NE) Clayton Hills Campground—(Clayton) *From jct US 52 & CR C17: Go 4-1/2 mi N on CR C17 (at jct CR X56 & CR 17). Enter on R.* ◆◆◆FACILITIES: 97 sites, 60 full hkups, 37 W&E, (20/30/50 amps), family camping, tenting, dump, ice, picnic tables, fire rings, wood. ◆RECREATION: rec hall, play equipment, hiking trails, v-ball. Pets welcome. Partial handicap access. Open Mid Apr - Oct 31. Rate in 2010 $20 per vehicle. CCUSA 50% Discount. CCUSA reservations Recommended, CCUSA max stay 3 days, CCUSA disc. not avail F,Sa, CCUSA disc. not avail holidays.

CAMPCLUB USA

Phone: (563)964-2236
Address: 31848 Clayton Rd, Garnavillo, IA 52049
Lat/Lon: 42.90334/-91.17471

GLADBROOK—C-4

(SW) UNION GROVE SP—(Tama) *From jct Hwy 96 & CR T47: Go 5 mi S on CR T47.* FACILITIES: 26 sites, 7 E, 19 no hkups, 3 pull-thrus, tenting. RECREATION: lake swim, boating, canoeing, ramp, dock, lake fishing. Partial handicap access. Open May 1 - Sep 30. Phone: (641)473-2556.

GLIDDEN—C-2

(NE) DICKSON TIMBER—(Carroll) *From jct SR 30 & CR N 50: Go 3-1/2 mi N on CRN 50. Enter on L.* FACILITIES: 50 sites, typical site width 20 ft, 16 W&E, (20/30 amps), 34 no hkups, tenting. RECREATION: Pets welcome. Open all yr. Phone: (712) 792-4614.

(NE) RICHEY PARK—(Carroll) *From jct SR 30 & CR N58: Go 3 mi N on CR N58. Enter on L.* FACILITIES: 12 sites, typical site width 20 ft, 12 E, (30 amps), 6 pull-thrus, tenting. RECREATION: river swim, river fishing. Pets welcome. Open Apr 1 - Nov 1. Phone: (712)792-4614.

GRANGER—C-3

(W) JESTER PARK (Polk County Park)—(Polk) *From jct I-80/35 (exit 127) & Hwy 141: Go 7-1/2 mi W on Hwy 141, then 3 mi N on NW 121st St, then 1/2 mi E on NW 118th Ave. Enter on L.* FACILITIES: 252 sites, 52 E, 200 no hkups, tenting, dump. RECREATION: boating, ramp, pond fishing, playground. Partial handicap access. Open all yr. Facilities fully operational mid Apr - mid Oct. Phone: (515)323-5300.

GREELEY—B-5

(NE) FOUNTAIN SPRINGS (Delaware County Park)—(Delaware) *From town: Go 3 mi NE on gravel county roads, follow signs.* FACILITIES: 25 sites, 25 no hkups, tenting. RECREATION: stream fishing. Open May 1 - Nov 1. Phone: (563)927-3410.

GRIMES—D-3

(SE) Cutty's Des Moines Camping Club—(Polk) *From jct I-80/I-35 & SR 141 (Exit 127): Go 1/2 mi N on SR 141, then 1/2 mi E on SE 37th St. Enter on R.* ◆◆◆◆FACILITIES: 448 sites, typical site width 30 ft, 330 full hkups, 118 W&E, (30/50 amps), 50 amps ($), 408 pull-thrus, WiFi Internet central location, family camping, tenting, RV storage, dump, portable dump, laundry, groceries, RV supplies, LP gas by weight/by meter, ice, picnic tables, patios, fire rings, grills, wood. ◆◆◆◆RECREATION: rec hall, pavilion, 2 swim pools, wading pool, hot tub, boating, electric motors only, canoeing, dock, lake fishing, fishing supplies, mini-golf, putting green, bsktball, playground, shuffleboard court 2 shuffleboard courts, activities, tennis, horseshoes, hiking trails, v-ball. Pets welcome. Partial handicap access. Open all yr. Facilities fully operational April 15 - Oct 15. Big rigs welcome. MC/VISA/DISC/Debit. CCUSA 50% Discount. CCUSA reservations Not Accepted, CCUSA max stay 3 days, CCUSA disc. not avail holidays. Sep 1-May 15 no arrivals after 5 pm. Fully operational Apr 15-Oct 15. Check in by 6 pm.

CAMPCLUB USA

Phone: (515)986-3929
Address: 2350 SE 37th St, Grimes, IA 50111
Lat/Lon: 41.65821/-93.76434
Web: www.cuttys.com

GUTHRIE CENTER—D-2

(N) SPRINGBROOK SP—(Guthrie) *From jct Hwy 44 & Hwy 25: Go 7 mi N on Hwy 25, then 1 mi SE on Hwy 384.* FACILITIES: 120 sites, 32 ft max RV length, 81 E, (20/50 amps), 39 no hkups, tenting, dump, ltd groc. RECREATION: lake swim, boating, electric motors only, ramp, lake fishing, playground. Partial handicap access. Open May 1 - Sep 30. Phone: (641)747-3591.

GUTTENBERG—B-5

(N) BOY SCOUT CAMPGROUND—(Clayton) *From jct US 52 & Hayden: Go 3 blocks E on Hayden, then 4 blocks N on Third St to the Mississippi River.* FACILITIES: 40 sites, 25 W&E, 15 no hkups, tenting. RECREATION: swim pool, boating, ramp, dock, river fishing. Open Apr 1 - First freeze.

HAMPTON—B-3

(NW) BEEDS LAKE SP—(Franklin) *From jct US 65 & Hwy 3: Go 1-1/2 mi W on Hwy 3, then 1-1/2 mi N on Olive/Hwy 134. Enter at end.* FACILITIES: 144 sites, 99 E, 45 no hkups, tenting, dump, ltd groc. RECREATION: lake swim, boating, ramp, dock, lake fishing, playground. Open May 1 - Oct 15. Phone: (641)456-2047.

HANCOCK—D-2

(W) BOTNA BEND PARK (Pottawattamie County Park) —(Pottawattamie) *From jct I-80 (exit 40) & US 59: Go 8 mi S on US 59.* FACILITIES: 40 sites, 40 E, (30 amps), 60 pull-thrus, tenting, dump. RECREATION: canoeing, ramp, river fishing, playground. Partial handicap access. Open all yr. Facilities fully operational Apr 15 - Oct 1. Phone: (712)741-5465.

HARLAN—D-2

(N) Nielsen RV Park—(Shelby) *From jct I-80 (exit 40) & US 59: Go 16 mi N on US 59, then 1 mi E on CR F32. Enter on L.* ◇◇◇FACILITIES: 18 sites, typical site width 35 ft, 12 full hkups, 6 E, (30/50 amps), phone on-site Internet (needs activ), tenting, dump, non-guest dump $, laundry, picnic tables, fire rings, wood. ◇RECREATION: horseshoes. Pets welcome. Partial handicap access. Open May 15 - Labor Day. Rate in 2010 $20 for 2 persons. CCUSA 50% Discount. CCUSA reservations Required, CCUSA max stay 1 day, Cash only for CCUSA disc., CCUSA disc. not avail holidays.

Phone: (712)627-4640
Address: 1244 F32, Harlan, IA 51537
Lat/Lon: 41.73255/-95.32757

(SE) PRAIRIE ROSE SP—(Shelby) *From town: Go 4-1/2 mi E on Hwy 44, then 2 mi S on Prairie Rose Rd (CR M47).* FACILITIES: 95 sites, 31 ft max RV length, 77 E, (20/30 amps), 18 no hkups, tenting, ltd groc. RECREATION: lake swim, boating, ramp, dock, lake fishing, playground. Partial handicap access. Open all yr. Facilities fully operational May 1 - Sep 30. Phone: (712)773-2701.

HAWARDEN—B-1

(NE) OAK GROVE COUNTY PARK (Sioux County Park) —(Sioux) *From jct Hwy-10 & CR-K18 at East city limits: Go 5-1/2 mi N on CR-K18.* FACILITIES: 58 sites, 32 ft max RV length, 52 E, (30 amps), 6 no hkups, tenting, dump. RECREATION: boating, canoeing, river/stream fishing, playground. Partial handicap access. Open May 15 - Oct 15. Phone: (712)552-1047.

HAZLETON—B-5

(SW) FONTANA PARK (Buchanan County Park)—(Buchanan) *From jct CR C-57 & Hwy 150: Go 1-1/2 mi SW on Hwy 150. Enter on R.* FACILITIES: 54 sites, 54 E, tenting, dump. RECREATION: boating, electric motors only, canoeing, lake/river fishing, play equipment. Partial handicap access. Open Apr 15 - Nov 1. Phone: (319)636-2617.

(S) Morwood Campground & Resort—(Buchanan) *From jct US 20 & SR 150: Go 8 mi N on SR 150, then 1/4 mi W on 150th St. Enter on R.* ◇◇◇FACILITIES: 114 sites, 60 full hkups, 54 W&E, (30/50 amps), 24 pull-thrus, family camping, tenting, dump, laundry, ltd groc. ◇◇◇RECREATION: swim pool, river fishing, playground. Pets welcome. Open Apr - Oct. Facilities fully operational Memorial Day - Labor Day. Big rigs welcome. Rate in 2010 $22-30 per family. Member ARVC, IAARVC. Phone: (319)636-2422.

HOLY CROSS—B-5

(E) BANKSTON PARK (Dubuque County Park)—(Dubuque) *From town: Go 2 mi E on US 52, then 1-1/2 mi S on Bankston Park Rd.* FACILITIES: 50 sites, 50 no hkups, tenting. RECREATION: stream fishing, playground. Open Apr 15 - Nov 1. Phone: (563)556-6745.

IDA GROVE—C-2

(NW) Cobb Park & Campground—(Ida) *From jct US 20 & US 59E: Go 9 mi S on US 59, then 1 mi E on US 159/SR175. Enter on R.* ◇◇◇FACILITIES: 45 sites, typical site width 25 ft, 45 W&E, (30 amps), 25 pull-thrus, family camping, tenting, dump, picnic tables, fire rings. ◇◇RECREATION: rec hall, pavilion, pond fishing, playground. Pets welcome. Open all yr. Facilities fully operational mid Apr - mid Oct. Rate in 2010 $14 per vehicle. CCUSA 50% Discount. CCUSA reservations Accepted, CCUSA max stay 1 day, Cash only for CCUSA disc., Check only for CCUSA disc.

Phone: (712)364-2686
Address: 801 W. SR 175 & US 59, Ida Grove, IA 51445
Lat/Lon: 42.35201/-95.47391

INDIANOLA—D-3

(S) LAKE AHQUABI SP—(Warren) *From jct Hwy-92 & US-65-69: Go 5-1/2 mi S on US-65-69, then 2 mi W on Hwy-349.* FACILITIES: 141 sites, 35 ft max RV length, 85 E, 56 no hkups, tenting, dump, ltd groc. RECREATION: lake swim, boating, canoeing, ramp, dock, lake fishing, playground. Partial handicap access. Open Apr 15 - Nov 1. Phone: (515)961-7101.

IOWA CITY—D-5

(N) LINDER POINT (COE - Coralville Lake)—(Johnson) *From I-80 (exit 244): Go 3 mi N, then follow sign 1 mi E.* FACILITIES: 28 sites, 8 full hkups, 6 E, 14 no hkups, tenting. RECREATION: lake swim, boating, lake fishing, playground. Partial handicap access. Open Apr 15 - Oct 14. Phone: (319)338-3543.

(N) TAILWATER WEST (COE - Coralville Lake)—(Johnson) *From I-80 (exit 244): Go 3 mi N, then follow signs 1-1/2 mi E.* FACILITIES: 30 sites, 30 no hkups, tenting. RECREATION: lake swim, boating, river fishing. Partial handicap access. Open Apr 15 - Oct 14. Phone: (319)338-3543.

(N) WEST OVERLOOK (COE - Coralville Lake)—(Johnson) *From I-80 (exit 244): Go 3 mi N, then follow sign 1-1/2 mi E.* FACILITIES: 89 sites, 89 E, tenting. RECREATION: lake swim, boating, ramp, dock, lake fishing, playground. Partial handicap access. Open Apr 15 - Oct 14. Phone: (319)338-3543.

JEFFERSON—C-2

(NE) SPRING LAKE (Greene County Park)—(Greene) *From jct US-30 & CR-P33: Go 2-1/2 mi N on CR-P33, then 1/2 mi W.* FACILITIES: 124 sites, 30 ft max RV length, 124 E, tenting, dump. RECREATION: lake swim, boating, electric motors only, canoeing, ramp, dock, lake fishing, playground. Partial handicap access. Open all yr. Phone: (515)738-5069.

JEWELL—C-3

(S) LITTLE WALL LAKE CAMPGROUND (Hamilton County Park)—(Hamilton) *From jct I-35 & Hwy 175: Go 3 mi W to jct Hwy 175 & US 69, then 2 mi S on US 69.* FACILITIES: 104 sites, 32 ft max RV length, 104 E, (30 amps), 104 pull-thrus, tenting, dump. RECREATION: lake swim, boating, canoeing, ramp, dock, lake fishing, playground. Partial handicap access. Open Apr 15 - Oct 15. Phone: (515)832-9570.

KELLOGG—D-4

(S) IOWA'S BEST BURGER CAFE—*From jct I-80 (exit 173) & SR 224: Go 200 yds N on SR 224. Enter on R.* A cafe open 7 days a week from 11am to 10pm serving full meals, great burgers and sandwiches. Also featuring 16 flavors of ice cream. Open all yr. MC/VISA/DISC/AMEX/Debit. ATM.

Phone: (641)526-8535
Address: 1570 Hwy 224 S, Kellogg, IA 50135
Lat/Lon: 41.68518/-92.90253
Email: dew@partnercom.net
Web: iowasbestburgercafe.com

SEE AD DES MOINES PAGE 255

(S) KELLOGG RV PARK & CAMPGROUND-INTERSTATE 80—(Jasper) *From jct I-80 (exit 173) & SR 224: Go 200 yds N on SR 224. Enter on R.* ◇◇◇◇FACILITIES: 38 sites, typical site width 25 ft, 15 full hkups, 23 W&E, (20/30/50 amps), 38 pull-thrus, WiFi Internet central location, tenting, dump, laundry, ltd groc, ice, picnic tables, grills.

◇◇RECREATION: playground, sports field.

Pets welcome, breed restrict. Partial handicap access. Facilities fully operational Apr 15 - Nov 15. Open weather permitting - call for information. Big

rigs welcome. Clubs welcome. Rate in 2010 $19.95-24.95 per vehicle. MC/VISA/DISC/AMEX/Debit. ATM. Member ARVC, IAARVC.

Phone: (641)526-8535
Address: 1570 Hwy 224 S., Kellogg, IA 50135
Lat/Lon: 41.68518/-92.90253
Email: dew@partnercom.net
Web: iowasbestburgercafe.com

SEE AD DES MOINES PAGE 255

(NE) ROCK CREEK SP—(Jasper) *From jct US 6 & Hwy 224: Go 2 mi N on Hwy 224, then 2-1/4 mi E on CR F27. Enter on R.* FACILITIES: 200 sites, typical site width 12 ft, 35 ft max RV length, 101 E, (30/50 amps), 99 no hkups, 20 pull-thrus, tenting, dump, laundry. RECREATION: lake swim, boating, ramp, dock, lake fishing, playground. Partial handicap access. Open Apr 15 - Oct 15. Phone: (641)236-3722.

KENDALLVILLE—A-4

(N) Harvest Farm Campground—(Winneshiek) *From jct SR 9 & SR 139: Go 8 1/2 mi N n SR 139, then 1 1/4 mi W on 366th St. (gravel), then 1/2 mi N on 318th Ave (gravel). Enter on R.* ◇◇◇FACILITIES: 125 sites, typical site width 48 ft, 53 full hkups, 32 W&E, 28 E, (20/30/50 amps), 12 no hkups, 32 pull-thrus, family camping, tenting, dump, groceries. ◇◇◇RECREATION: river swim, canoeing, river fishing, playground. Pets welcome. Partial handicap access. Age restrict may apply. Open Apr 1 - Oct 31. Big rigs welcome. Rate in 2010 $25 per vehicle. Phone: (563) 883-8562.

KEOKUK—E-5

(NE) Hickory Haven Campground—(Lee) *From south jct US 218 & US 61: Go 1 mi N on US 218/61, then 3/4 mi W on 353 St. Enter on R.* ◇◇◇FACILITIES: 46 sites, typical site width 22 ft, 33 full hkups, 8 W&E, 5 E, (30/50 amps), 50 amps ($), 21 pull-thrus, family camping, tenting, RV storage, dump, non-guest dump $, laundry, RV supplies, ice, picnic tables, fire rings, wood. ◇◇RECREATION: pavilion, pond fishing, play equipment, hiking trails, v-ball. Pets welcome. Open all yr. Rate in 2010 $18-23 for 2 persons. MC/VISA/Debit. Member IACO. CCUSA 50% Discount. CCUSA reservations Recommended, CCUSA max stay 3 days, CCUSA disc. not avail holidays.

Phone: (800)890-8459
Address: 2413 353rd St, Keokuk, IA 52632
Lat/Lon: 40.44490/-91.45055

VICTORY PARK & HUBINGER LANDING CAMPING (City Parks)—(Lee) *From jct US 136 & S 2nd St (Iowa end of Miss. River bridge): Go 1 block W on S 2nd St, then 2 blocks S on Johnson St, then 1/2 block E on Water St, then 100 feet S across RR tracks (under bridge), then 1 block W on frontage road (past museum). Enter on L.* FACILITIES: 21 sites, typical site width 20 ft, 21 W&E, dump. RECREATION: playground. No tents. Open Apr 1 - Oct 31. Phone: (319)524-7122.

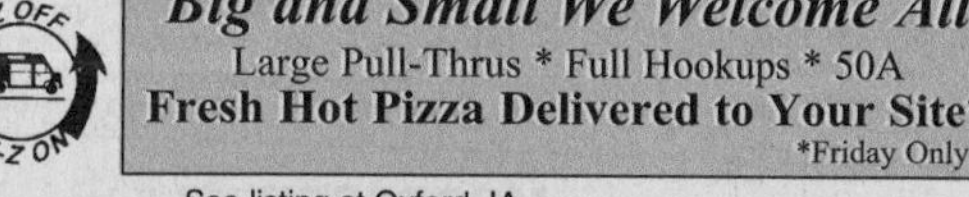

KEOSAUQUA—E-5

(S) LACEY-KEOSAUQUA SP—(Van Buren) *From Hwy 1 just S of Des Moines River bridge: Go 1-1/2 mi SW on park road.* FACILITIES: 113 sites, 45 E, (30 amps), 68 no hkups, 15 pull-thrus, tenting, dump, ltd groc. RECREATION: lake swim, boating, electric motors only, ramp, dock, lake/stream fishing, playground. Partial handicap access. Open Apr 10 - Nov 1. Phone: (319)293-3502.

KINGSTON—D-5

(N) 4TH PUMPING PLANT RECREATION PARK (Des Moines County Park)—(Des Moines) *From town: Go 6 mi N on Hwy 99, then 5 mi E on Pumping Station Rd.* FACILITIES: 46 sites, 22 E, 24 no hkups, tenting, dump. RECREATION: boating, lake fishing. Partial handicap access. Open all yr. Phone: (319)753-8260.

KNOXVILLE—D-4

(N) ELK ROCK SP—(Marion) *From town: Go 7 mi N on Hwy-14. Enter on R.* FACILITIES: 30 sites, 21 E, (20/30 amps), 9 no hkups, 30 pull-thrus, tenting, dump. RECREATION: boating, ramp, lake fishing, playground. Open all yr. Phone: (641)842-6008.

(N) WHITEBREAST (COE-Red Rock Lake)—(Marion) *From jct Hwy-92 & CR T15: Go 2 mi N on CR T15, then 3 mi N on CR S71.* FACILITIES: 132 sites, 128 E, (20/50 amps), 4 no hkups, tenting, dump. RECREATION: lake swim, boating, canoeing, ramp, lake fishing, playground. Partial handicap access. Open Apr 22 - Sep 27. Phone: (641)828-7522.

LAKE OKOBOJI—A-2

ELINOR BEDELL SP—(Dickinson) FACILITIES: 8 sites, 8 full hkups, (30 amps), tenting. RECREATION: playground. Open all yr. Facilities fully operational Apr 15 - Nov 1. Phone: (712)337-3211.

LAKE VIEW—C-2

(E) BLACK HAWK SP—(Sac) *From jct US-71 & Hwy-175: Go 1/2 mi E on US-71 & Hwy-175.* FACILITIES: 128 sites, 89 E, (20/30 amps), 39 no hkups, tenting, dump, laundry. RECREATION: lake swim, boating, ramp, dock, lake fishing, playground. Partial handicap access. Open Jun - Sep. Phone: (712)657-8712.

(NE) CAMP CRESCENT (Municipal Park)—(Sac) *From jct Hwy 196 & US 71/Hwy 175: Go 4-1/4 mi W on US 71/Hwy 175, then 1/4 mi SW on paved road & 3rd St. Follow signs. Enter on L.* FACILITIES: 181 sites, 73 full hkups, 70 W&E, (20/50 amps), 38 no hkups, 118 pull-thrus, tenting, dump, laundry. RECREATION: lake swim, boating, canoeing, ramp, dock, lake fishing, playground. Open Apr 15 - Oct 1. Phone: (712)657-2189.

LAKESIDE—B-2

Lakeside Marina and Campground—(Buena Vista) *From jct US 71 & Hwy 7B: Go 1-1/2 mi W on Hwy 7/71B (at lighthouse), then 1/2 mi S on Sunrise Park Rd. Enter on R.* ◆◆◆FACILITIES: 30 sites, typical site width 40 ft, accepts self-contained units only, 30 full hkups, (30/50 amps), ltd groc. ◆◆RECREATION: lake swim, boating, canoeing, ramp, dock, lake fishing. Pets welcome. Partial handicap access. No tents. Open Apr 4 - Oct 15. Facilities fully operational Memorial Day - Labor Day. Big rigs welcome. Rate in 2010 $20.75-22.20 per vehicle. Phone: (712)732-7465.

LANSING—A-5

(W) Red Barn Resort—(Allamakee) *From jct west end Mississippi River bridge & Hwy 9: Go 2 mi W on Hwy 9. Enter on L.* ◆◆◆FACILITIES: 117 sites, typical site width 45 ft, 82 full hkups, 7 W&E, 28 E, (30/50 amps), 10 pull-thrus, tenting, dump, laundry. ◆◆◆RECREATION: stream fishing, playground. Pets welcome. Open Apr 15 - Oct 15. Rate in 2010 $20-28 for 2 persons. Member ARVC, IAARVC. Phone: (563)538-4956.

LEHIGH—C-3

(E) BRUSHY CREEK SRA—(Webster) *From jct US-169 & Hwy-50: Go 7 mi E on Hwy-50, then 5 mi NE on CR-D46.* FACILITIES: 181 sites, 8 full hkups, 151 E, 22 no hkups, tenting, dump. RECREATION: lake swim, ramp, stream fishing, playground. Open all yr. Facilities fully operational May 15 - Nov 1. Phone: (515)543-8298.

(W) DOLLIVER MEMORIAL SP—(Webster) *From town: Go 1-1/4 mi W on Hwy 50, then 1 mi N on CR D33.* FACILITIES: 33 sites, 33 E, tenting, dump. RECREATION: boating, canoeing, ramp, river/stream fishing, playground. Open all yr. Facilities fully operational Apr 15 - Nov 1. Phone: (515)359-2539.

LITTLE SIOUX—C-1

(W) Woodland Campground—(Harrison) *From jct I-29 (exit 95) & CR F20: Go 200 yds W on CR F20. Enter at end.* ◆◆FACILITIES: 21 sites, typical site width 25 ft, 21 W&E, (15/20/30 amps), 20 pull-thrus, family

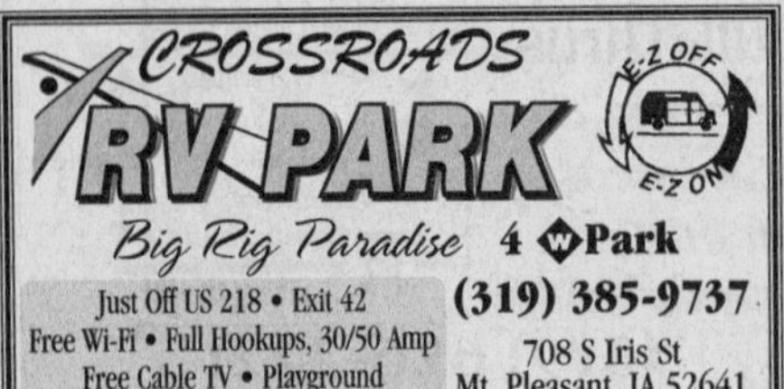

LITTLE SIOUX—Continued
Woodland Campground—Continued

camping, tenting, dump, LP gas by weight/by meter, ice. ◆◆RECREATION: rec hall, swim pool, bsktball, playground, shuffleboard court 2 shuffleboard courts, tennis, horseshoes, v-ball. Pets welcome. Partial handicap access. Open Apr 15 - Oct 15. Facilities fully operational Memorial Day - Labor Day. Rate in 2010 $20 for 4 persons. CCUSA 50% Discount. CCUSA reservations Recommended, CCUSA max stay Unlimited, Cash only for CCUSA disc. Reservations required for holiday weekends. 6-8 PM call 712 420-1516.

Phone: (712)649-2594
Address: 1449 Benton Ln, Little Sioux, IA 51545
Lat/Lon: 41.80013/-96.05932

MANCHESTER—B-5

(SE) BAILEY FORD (Delaware County Park)—(Delaware) *From jct US-20 & CR-D-5X: Go 3 mi SE on CR-D-5X.* FACILITIES: 50 sites, 24 E, 26 no hkups, tenting, dump. RECREATION: boating, canoeing, ramp, river/stream fishing, playground. Partial handicap access. Open May 1 - Oct 30. Phone: (563)927-3410.

(W) COFFINS GROVE (Delaware County Park)—(Delaware) *From jct Hwy 13 & CR D-22: Go 2-1/2 mi W on CR D-22, then 1/2 mi W on gravel CR W-69.* FACILITIES: 25 sites, 25 E, tenting, dump. RECREATION: stream fishing, playground. Partial handicap access. Open May 1 - Oct 30. Phone: (563)927-3410.

MANNING—C-2

(SW) GREAT WESTERN PARK—(Carroll) *From jct SR 141 & CR M66: Go 1/4 mi S on M66. Enter on R.* FACILITIES: 8 sites, typical site width 20 ft, 8 W&E, (30 amps), 8 pull-thrus, tenting, dump. RECREATION: lake swim, boating, electric motors only, lake/pond fishing. Pets welcome. Open Apr 1 - Nov 1. Phone: (712)792-4614.

MARENGO—C-4

Sudbury Court Motel & RV Park—(Iowa) *From jct I-80 & V66 (exit 216): Go 7 mi N then 50 yds E on Rte 6. Enter on L.* ◆◆◆◆FACILITIES: 18 sites, typical site width 30 ft, 18 full hkups, (20/30/50 amps), 6 pull-thrus, WiFi Instant Internet at site, tenting, laundry, RV supplies, picnic tables, fire rings, wood. ◆RECREATION: pond fishing. Pets welcome. Partial handicap access. Open all yr. Big rigs welcome. Rate in 2010 $24.50 for 4 persons. MC/VISA/DISC/Debit. FMCA discount. CCUSA 50% Discount. CCUSA reservations Recommended, CCUSA max stay 2 days, Cash only for CCUSA disc., Check only for CCUSA disc., CCUSA disc. not avail Th, CCUSA disc. not avail F,Sa, CCUSA disc. not avail holidays. Discount not available during State Fair.

Phone: (319)642-5411
Address: 2211 Hwy 6 Trail, Marengo, IA 52301
Lat/Lon: 41.78955/-92.06303
Web: www.sudburymotelandrv.com

MARION—C-5

(E) SQUAW CREEK PARK (Linn County Park)—(Linn) *From jct US-151 & Hwy-13: Go 1 mi S on Hwy-13, then 1/4 mi W on CR-E45.* FACILITIES: 61 sites, 47 W&E, (50 amps), 14 no hkups, tenting, dump. RECREATION: playground. Partial handicap access. Open Apr 15 - Oct 15. Phone: (319)892-6450.

MARSHALLTOWN—C-4

(E) Shady Oaks Camping—(Marshall) *From jct SR 14 & US 30: Go 3 mi E on US 30, then 1/4 mi N on Shady Oaks Rd. Enter on R.* ◆◆◆FACILITIES: 15 sites, typical site width 25 ft, 13 full hkups, 2 E, (30/50 amps), family camping, tenting. Pets welcome. Open Apr 1 - Oct 31. Rate in 2010 $22-24 for 4 persons. Phone: (641)752-2946.

MASON CITY—B-3

(N) M. MACNIDER PARK (Municipal Park)—(Cerro Gordo) *From jct US 18 & Kentucky Ave: Go 6 blocks N on Kentucky Ave, then 1 block W on Birch Dr.* FACILITIES: 136 sites, 30 ft max RV length, 85 full hkups, 31 E, 20 no hkups, tenting, dump. RECREATION: swim pool, river fishing, playground. No pets. Partial handicap access. Open Apr 20 - Oct 20. Phone: (641)421-3679.

MCGREGOR—B-5

(S) PIKES PEAK SP—(Clayton) *From jct Hwy 76 & Hwy 340: Go 2 mi S on Hwy 340. Enter at end.* FACILITIES: 77 sites, 60 E, (30/50 amps), 17 no hkups, 16 pull-thrus, tenting, dump, ltd groc. RECREATION: playground. Partial handicap access. Open all yr. Facilities fully operational Apr 15 - Oct 15. Phone: (563)873-2341.

(W) Spook Cave and Campground—(Clayton) *From jct of Business 18 & US 18 at McGregor: Go 4 mi W on US 18, then 2 mi N on Spook Cave Rd. Enter on L.* ◆◆◆FACILITIES: 72 sites, typical site width 30 ft, 38 full hkups, 21 W&E, 7 E, (30/50 amps), 6 no hkups, family camping, tenting, dump, laundry. ◆◆◆◆RECREATION: lake swim, lake/stream fishing, playground. Pets welcome. Open May 1 - Oct 31. Big rigs welcome. Rate in 2010 $18-25 for 3 persons. Member ARVC, IAARVC. Phone: (563)873-2144.

Iowa State Motto: "Our liberties we prize and our rights we will maintain"

MILFORD—A-2

(N) EMERSON BAY SRA—(Dickinson) *From town: Go 2-1/2 mi N on Hwy 86.* FACILITIES: 117 sites, 57 E, 60 no hkups, tenting, dump. RECREATION: lake swim, boating, ramp, lake fishing, playground. Open all yr. Facilities fully operational Apr 15 - Nov 1. Phone: (712)337-3211.

(N) GULL POINT SP—(Dickinson) *From town: Go 3-1/2 mi N on Hwy 86.* FACILITIES: 112 sites, 31 ft max RV length, 60 E, (30 amps), 52 no hkups, tenting, dump. RECREATION: lake swim, boating, canoeing, ramp, dock, lake fishing, playground. Partial handicap access. Open all yr. Facilities fully operational Apr 15 - Nov 1. Phone: (712)337-3211.

MISSOURI VALLEY—D-1

(SW) WILSON ISLAND SRA—(Harrison) *From jct I-29 (exit 72) & Hwy 362: Go 5-1/2 mi W on Hwy 362, then 1/4 mi S.* FACILITIES: 135 sites, 63 E, (30 amps), 72 no hkups, tenting, dump. RECREATION: boating, ramp, dock, stream fishing, playground. Partial handicap access. Open all yr. Facilities fully operational May 1 - Sep 30. Phone: (712)642-2069.

MONTEZUMA—D-4

(NW) DIAMOND LAKE PARK (Poweshiek County Park)—(Marion) *From jct US-63 & F-57: Go 1 mi N on US-63.* FACILITIES: 100 sites, 50 E, (30 amps), 50 no hkups, tenting, dump. RECREATION: boating, electric motors only, ramp, lake fishing, playground. Partial handicap access. Open May 1 - Oct 15. Phone: (641)623-3191.

MONTICELLO—C-5

(N) Walnut Acres Campground—(Jones) *From E jct US Bus 151 & Hwy 38N: Go 1 1/2 mi N on Hwy 38 N. Enter on R.* ◆◆◆◆FACILITIES: 266 sites, typical site width 30 ft, 144 full hkups, 37 W&E, 72 E, (20/30/50 amps), 13 no hkups, 46 pull-thrus, family camping, tenting, dump, laundry. ◆◆◆◆RECREATION: river swim, canoeing, lake/river fishing, playground. Pets welcome, breed restrict. Open mid Apr - mid Oct. Big rigs welcome. Rate in 2010 $22-26 per family. Member ARVC, IAARVC. Phone: (319)465-4665. FMCA discount.

MORAVIA—E-4

(W) BRIDGE VIEW (COE - Rathbun Lake)—(Appanoose) *From town: Go 8 mi W on Hwy-142, then 1 mi S.* FACILITIES: 114 sites, 103 E, (30 amps), 11 no hkups, tenting, dump. RECREATION: boating, canoeing, ramp, dock, lake fishing, playground. Partial handicap access. Open May 1 - Sep 29. Phone: (641)647-2464.

(S) BUCK CREEK (COE - Rathbun Lake)—(Appanoose) *From jct Hwy-142 & CR-J5T: Go 3 mi S on CR-J5T.* FACILITIES: 42 sites, 42 E, (30/50 amps), tenting, dump. RECREATION: lake swim, boating, canoeing, ramp, dock, lake fishing, playground. Partial handicap access. Open May 1 - Sep 29. Phone: (641)647-2464.

(W) Doggs RV Park—(Appanoose) *From jct SR-5 & CRJ18: Go 7 mi W on CRJ18. Enter on L.* ◆◆◆FACILITIES: 75 sites, typical site width 30 ft, 75 full hkups, (30/50 amps), 50 amps ($), 27 pull-thrus, family camping, tenting, dump, laundry. ◆◆◆RECREATION: swim pool, pond fishing, playground. Pets welcome. Partial handicap access. Open all yr. Facilities fully operational Memorial Day - Labor Day. Big rigs welcome. Rate in 2010 $20 per vehicle. Member ARVC, IAARVC. Phone: (641)724-3762.

(W) HONEY CREEK SP—(Appanoose) *From jct Hwy-5 & CR-J-18: Go 9 mi W on J-18, then 4 mi SE on CR.* FACILITIES: 149 sites, 28 full hkups, 75 E, (30 amps), 46 no hkups, 30 pull-thrus, tenting, dump. RECREATION: lake swim, boating, canoeing, ramp, dock, lake fishing. Partial handicap access. Open all yr. Phone: (641)724-3739.

(W) PRAIRIE RIDGE (COE - Rathbun Lake)—(Appanoose) *From town: Go 4 mi W on Hwy-142, then 3 mi S on county road.* FACILITIES: 54 sites, 54 E, tenting, dump. RECREATION: lake swim, boating, canoeing, ramp, dock, lake fishing, playground. Partial handicap access. Open May 1 - Sep 29. Phone: (641)724-3103.

MOUNT PLEASANT—E-5

CROSSROADS RV CAMPGROUND—(Henry) *From jct US 218 & (Business) US 34 (exit 42): Go 300 yards W on (Business) US 34, then 200 yards S on Iris St. Enter on L.*

◆◆◆◆FACILITIES: 34 sites, typical site width 25 ft, 34 full hkups, (30/50 amps), 34 pull-thrus, cable TV, WiFi Instant Internet at site, cable Internet central location, family camping, tenting, dump, non-guest dump $, laundry, RV supplies, ice, picnic tables.

◆◆RECREATION: rec room/area, golf nearby, bsktball, 3 bike rentals, playground, horseshoes, sports field, hiking trails, v-ball.

Pets welcome, breed restrict. Partial handicap access. Open all yr. Big rigs welcome. Green Friendly. Rate in 2010 $32 for 2 persons. MC/VISA/DISC/Debit. Member ARVC, IAARVC.

CROSSROADS RV CAMPGROUND—Continued on next page

Statehood: Iowa became the 29th state on December 28, 1846.

MOUNT PLEASANT—Continued
CROSSROADS RV CAMPGROUND—Continued

Phone: (319)385-9737
Address: 708 S Iris St, Mt Pleasant, IA 52641
Lat/Lon: 40.95809/-91.52522
Email: office@xrdsrv.com
Web: www.xrdsrv.com

SEE AD PAGE 258

MOUNT VERNON—C-5

(W) PALISADES-KEPLER SP—(Linn) *From jct US-30 & Hwy-1: Go 4 mi W on US-30.* FACILITIES: 44 sites, 26 E, (30/50 amps), 18 no hkups, 10 pull-thrus, tenting, dump. RECREATION: boating, ramp, dock, river fishing. Partial handicap access. Open all yr. Facilities fully operational May 1 - Sep 30. Phone: (319)895-6039.

MUSCATINE—D-5

(E) FAIRPORT SRA/WILDCAT DEN STATE PARK—(Muscatine) *From jct US-61 & Hwy-22: Go 5 mi E on Hwy-22. Enter on R.* FACILITIES: 42 sites, 42 E, (30 amps), tenting, dump. RECREATION: boating, ramp, dock, river fishing, playground. Open all yr. Facilities fully operational Apr 15 - Nov 1. Phone: (563)263-4337.

(E) SHADY CREEK (COE-Mississippi River Rec Areas-Muscatine)—(Rock Island) *From east city limits: Go 10 mi E on Hwy 22, then follow signs.* FACILITIES: 53 sites, typical site width 20 ft, 53 E, (30/50 amps), tenting, dump. RECREATION: boating, canoeing, ramp, dock, river fishing, playground. Partial handicap access. Open May 7 - Oct 24. Phone: (563)262-8090.

(NE) WILDCAT DEN SP—(Muscatine) *From jct US-61 & Hwy-22: Go 11 mi NE on Hwy-22.* FACILITIES: 28 sites, 30 ft max RV length, 28 no hkups, tenting, ltd groc. RECREATION: stream fishing. Open all yr. Facilities fully operational May 1 - Sep 30. Phone: (563)263-4337.

NASHUA—B-4

(N) CEDAR VIEW PARK (Municipal Park)—(Chickasaw) *From jct Hwy-346 & US-218: Go 1/2 mi N on US-218, then 1 block E on Charles City Rd.* FACILITIES: 39 sites, 37 W&E, (30 amps), 2 no hkups, tenting, dump, ltd groc. RECREATION: lake/river swim, boating, canoeing, ramp, dock, lake/river fishing, playground. Partial handicap access. Open Apr 15 - Nov 15. Facilities fully operational May 1 - Nov 1. Phone: (641)435-4156.

(NE) River Ranch Camping—(Chickasaw) *From jct US 218 & Hwy 346 (exit 220): Go 3 mi E on Hwy 346 (thru town following signs to Little Brown Church), then 1 mi N on Cheyenne Ave. (Gravel). Enter on L.* ◊◊◊FACILITIES: 122 sites, 20 full hkups, 87 W&E, (20/30/50 amps), 15 no hkups, 20 pull-thrus, family camping, tenting, dump. ◊◊◊RECREATION: river swim, canoeing, river/pond fishing, play equipment. Pets welcome. Open May 1 - Oct 31. Big rigs welcome. Rate in 2010 $16.50-20 for 2 persons. Phone: (641) 435-2108.

NEOLA—D-1

(SW) ARROWHEAD PARK (Pottawattamie County Park)—(Pottawattamie) *From I-80 (exit 23): Go 1/2 mi SE on CR-L55.* FACILITIES: 60 sites, 54 E, (30/50 amps), 6 no hkups, 6 pull-thrus, tenting, dump. RECREATION: boating, electric motors only, canoeing, ramp, lake fishing, playground. Partial handicap access. Open all yr. Facilities fully operational May 1 - Oct 1. Phone: (712)485-2295.

NEWTON—D-4

(E) NEWTON KOA—(Jasper) *From jct I-80 & Iowa Speedway Dr (exit 168): Go 1 mi N on Iowa Speedway Dr, then 1/4 mi W on E 36th St S (hard left turn past the water tower in front of entrace sign). Enter at end.*

◊◊◊◊FACILITIES: 68 sites, 37 full hkups, 31 W&E, (20/30/50 amps), 50 amps ($), some extd stay sites, 36 pull-thrus, WiFi Instant Internet at site, WiFi Internet central location, family camping, tenting, RV storage, dump, non-guest dump $, laundry, ltd groc, RV supplies, LP gas by weight/by meter, ice, picnic tables, fire rings, wood.

◊◊◊◊RECREATION: rec hall, rec room/area, coin games, swim pool, pond fishing, fishing supplies, bsktball, playground, shuffleboard court shuffleboard court, horseshoes, sports field, hiking trails, v-ball.

Pets welcome, breed restrict. Partial handicap access. Open Apr 1 - Oct 31. Facilities fully operational Memorial Day - Labor Day. Rates may change on

NEWTON—Continued
NEWTON KOA—Continued

race events, holidays & off season. Big rigs welcome. Clubs welcome. Rate in 2010 $24.39-36.39 for 2 persons. MC/VISA/DISC/Debit. Member ARVC, IAARVC. KOA discount.

Phone: (877)792-2428
Address: 1601 E 36th St South, Newton, IA 50208
Lat/Lon: 41.68830/-93.00962
Email: rollingacres@iowatelecom.net
Web: www.koa.com/where/ia/15131

Reserve Online at Woodalls.com

SEE AD THIS PAGE

NORTH LIBERTY—C-5

(SW) COLONY COUNTRY CAMPGROUND—(Johnson) *From I-80 & Coral Ridge Rd (exit 240): Go 2 mi N on Coral Ridge Rd, then 1/2 mi W on Forevergreen Rd. Enter on L.*

◊◊◊◊FACILITIES: 38 sites, typical site width 30 ft, 22 full hkups, 16 W&E, (30/50 amps), some extd stay sites, 4 pull-thrus, WiFi Instant Internet at site, dump, non-guest dump $, laundry, ltd groc, RV supplies, ice, picnic tables, fire rings, wood.

◊◊RECREATION: bsktball, playground, sports field.

Pets welcome. Partial handicap access. No tents. Open Apr 1 - Nov 30. Call ahead early season. Big rigs welcome. Green Friendly. Rate in 2010 $26-33 for 4 persons. MC/VISA/DISC. Member ARVC, IAARVC.

Phone: (319)626-2221
Address: 1275 W Forevergreen Rd, North Liberty, IA 52317
Lat/Lon: 41.72315/-91.61920
Email: colonycc@southslope.net
Web: colonycountry.com

SEE AD IOWA CITY PAGE 257 AND AD TRAVEL SECTION PAGE 247

(N) Scales Pointe Camping and Boating—(Johnson) *From Jct I-80 & Coral Ridge Rd (SR 965)(Exit 240): Go 3 mi N on Coral Ridge Rd.; then 3 mi E on Scales Bend Rd. Enter at end.* ◊◊◊◊FACILITIES: 92 sites, typical site width 25 ft, 64 full hkups, 28 W&E, (30/50 amps), 1 pull-thrus, tenting, dump, ltd groc. ◊◊◊◊◊RECREATION: boating, ramp, dock, lake fishing, play equipment. Pets welcome. Open Mar 1 - Oct 31. Big rigs welcome. Rate in 2010 $28-30 per family. Phone: (319)665-3474.

(NE) SUGAR BOTTOM (COE - Coralville Lake)—(Johnson) *From town: Go 4 mi N on CR-F28.* FACILITIES: 255 sites, 238 E, (30/50 amps), 17 no hkups, 5 pull-thrus, tenting, dump. RECREATION: lake swim, boating, ramp, lake fishing, playground. Partial handicap access. Open May 1 - Sep 29. Phone: (319)338-3543.

OAKVILLE—D-5

(E) FERRY LANDING (COE-Mississippi River Rec Areas-Muscatine)—(Louisa) *From jct Hwy 99 & CR 51: Go 5 mi E on CR 51.* FACILITIES: 50 sites, 50 no hkups, 40 pull-thrus, tenting, dump. RECREATION: boating, canoeing, ramp, river fishing. Open all yr. Facilities fully operational May 1 - Oct 31. Phone: (563)263-7913.

OELWEIN—B-5

(S) OELWEIN CITY PARK CAMPGROUND—(Fayette) *From jct Hwy 150 & Hwy 281: Go 1/8 mi W on Hwy 281. Enter on R.* FACILITIES: 30 sites, typical site width 25 ft, 30 W&E, tenting, dump. RECREATION: boating, canoeing, ramp, dock, lake fishing, playground. Open all yr. Facilities fully operational Apr - Nov. Phone: (319)283-5440.

OKOBOJI—A-2

See listings at Arnolds Park, Orleans, Spirit Lake

ONAWA—C-1

(W) KOA-Onawa/Blue Lake—(Monona) *From jct I-29 (exit 112) & SR 175: Go 1 mi W on SR 175, then 1-1/2 mi N on Dogwood Ave. Enter on L.* ◊◊◊◊FACILITIES: 110 sites, typical site width 25 ft, 52 full hkups, 39 W&E, 5 E, (30/50 amps), 50 amps ($), 14 no hkups, 50 pull-thrus, tenting, dump, laundry, groceries. ◊◊◊◊RECREATION: swim pool, boating, dock, lake fishing, playground. Pets welcome. Partial handicap access. Open Apr 15 - Oct 15. Facilities fully operational Memorial Day - Labor Day. Rate in 2010 $28-35 for 2 persons. Phone: (712)423-1633. KOA discount.

(W) LEWIS & CLARK SP—(Monona) *From jct I-29 & Hwy-175: Go 1 mi W on Hwy-175, then 1 mi N on Hwy-324.* FACILITIES: 112 sites, typical site width 12 ft, 30 ft max RV length, 12 full hkups, 100 E, (20/30 amps), 9 pull-thrus, tenting, dump, ltd groc. RECREATION: lake swim, boating, canoeing, ramp, dock, lake fishing, playground. Partial handicap access. Open Apr 15 - Oct 15. Phone: (712)423-2829.

(W) ON-UR-WA RV PARK—(Monona) *From jct I-29 (exit 112) & SR 175: Go 250 yds E on SR 175, then 100 yds S on 28th St. Enter on L.*

◊◊◊◊FACILITIES: 44 sites, typical site width 35 ft, 44 full hkups, (30/50 amps), 50 amps ($), some extd stay sites (summer), 34 pull-thrus, WiFi Instant Internet at site, WiFi Internet central location, laundry, RV supplies, LP gas by weight/by meter, ice, picnic tables.

◊RECREATION: rec room/area, horseshoes, sports field, v-ball.

Pets welcome. Partial handicap access. No tents. Open Apr 1 - Oct 15. Call for off season availability/Group Rally Meeting Hall. Big rigs welcome. Escort to site. Clubs welcome. Green Friendly. Rate in 2010 $27-29 for 2 persons. MC/VISA. Member ARVC, IAARVC.

Phone: (712)423-1387
Address: 1111 28 St, Onawa, IA 51040
Lat/Lon: 42.02564/-96.12650
Email: onurwarv@onawave.net
Web: www.onurwarvpark.com

SEE AD THIS PAGE

ORLEANS—A-2

(N) MARBLE BEACH SRA—(Dickinson) *From town: Go 2 mi NW on Hwy-276.* FACILITIES: 112 sites, 30 ft max RV length, 60 E, (20/30 amps), 52 no hkups, tenting, dump. RECREATION: lake swim, boating, ramp, dock, lake fishing, playground. Partial handicap access. Open all yr. Phone: (712)337-3211.

OSCEOLA—D-3

(W) Terrible's Lakeside Casino RV Park Osceola, IA—(Clarke) *From jct US 34 & I-35: Go 1 mi N on I 35 (exit 34), then 1/2 mi W on Clay St.(Delivery Truck Entrance). Enter on L.* ◊◊◊FACILITIES: 47 sites, typical site width 30 ft, accepts full hkup units only, 47 full hkups, (30/50 amps), 47 pull-thrus, ltd groc. ◊◊◊RECREATION: swim pool, lake swim, boating, ramp, dock, lake/pond fishing. Pets welcome. Partial handicap access. No tents. Open all yr. Big rigs welcome. Rate in 2010 $20 per vehicle. Phone: (641) 342-9511.

OSKALOOSA—D-4

(E) LAKE KEOMAH SP—(Mahaska) *From east jct US 63 & Hwy 92: Go 3 mi E on Hwy 92, then 1/2 mi S on Hwy 371. Enter on L.* FACILITIES: 65 sites, 41 E, (30 amps), 24 no hkups, tenting, dump, ltd groc. RECREATION: lake swim, boating, electric motors only, ramp, dock, lake fishing. Partial handicap access. Open Apr 15 - Oct 15. Phone: (641)673-6975.

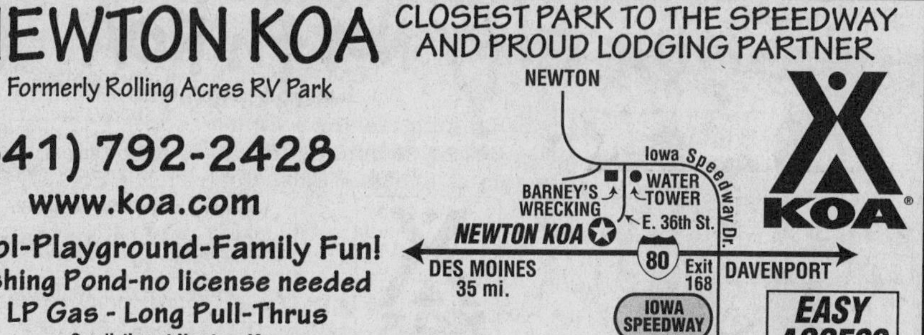

OXFORD—C-5

(S) SLEEPY HOLLOW PIZZA AND ICE CREAM—*From jct I-80 & SR 109 (exit 230): Go 200 yds N on SR 109. Enter on R.* Fri evening pizza delivery or take-out. Ice cream, coffee, and snacks 7 days a week! Open all yr. MC/VISA/DISC/Debit.

Phone: (319)828-4900
Address: 3340 Black Hawk Ave NW, Oxford, IA 52322
Lat/Lon: 41.69070/-91.80379
Email: shcamping@southslope.net
Web: sleepyhollowia.com

SEE AD IOWA CITY PAGE 257

(S) SLEEPY HOLLOW RV PARK & CAMPGROUND—(Johnson) *From jct I-80 & SR 109 (exit 230): Go 200 yds N on SR 109. Enter on R.*

◆◆◆◆FACILITIES: 110 sites, typical site width 35 ft, 67 full hkups, 43 W&E, (20/30/50 amps), 50 amps ($), some extd stay sites (summer), 61 pull-thrus, WiFi Instant Internet at site, WiFi Internet central location, family camping, tenting, dump, non-guest dump $, laundry, groceries, RV supplies, LP gas by weight/by meter, ice, picnic tables, fire rings, wood.

◆◆◆◆RECREATION: rec room/area, equipped pavilion, coin games, swim pool, lake fishing, fishing supplies, bsktball, 6 bike rentals, playground, activities, (wkends), horseshoes, sports field, v-ball. Rec open to public.

Pets welcome, breed restrict. Partial handicap access. Open all yr. Facilities fully operational Apr 1 - Nov 1. Big rigs welcome. Clubs welcome. Green Friendly. Rate in 2010 $26-34 per family. MC/VISA/DISC/Debit. Member ARVC, IAARVC.

Phone: (319)828-4900
Address: 3340 Black Hawk Ave NW, Oxford, IA 52322
Lat/Lon: 41.69070/-91.80379
Email: shcamping@southslope.net
Web: www.sleepyhollowia.com

SEE AD IOWA CITY PAGE 257

PALO—C-5

(N) PLEASANT CREEK SRA—(Linn) *From town: Go 4 mi N on CR-W36.* FACILITIES: 69 sites, 43 E, 26 no hkups, tenting, dump. RECREATION: lake swim, boating, canoeing, ramp, dock, lake fishing, playground. Phone: (319)436-7716.

PELLA—D-4

(SW) HOWELL STATION (COE - Red Rock Lake)—(Marion) *From jct CR G28 & CR T15: Go 5 mi SW on CR T15, then E on Idaho Drive, then S on 198th Place, then follow signs.* FACILITIES: 143 sites, typical site width 15 ft, 32 ft max RV length, 143 E, (20/50 amps), tenting, dump. RECREATION: boating, ramp, river fishing, playground. Partial handicap access. Open Mar 30 - Oct 27. Phone: (641)828-7522.

(SW) NORTH OVERLOOK (COE - Red Rock Lake)—(Marion) *From jct CR-G28 & CR-T15: Go 4 mi S on CR-T15.* FACILITIES: 55 sites, 51 E, (20/30 amps), 4 no hkups, tenting, dump. RECREATION: lake swim, lake fishing, playground. Partial handicap access. Open Apr 20 - Sep 25. Phone: (641)828-7522.

(W) WALLASHUCK (COE - Red Rock Lake)—(Marion) *From town: Go 3-1/2 mi W on CR G28.* FACILITIES: 83 sites, 69 E, (20/50 amps), 14 no hkups, tenting, dump. RECREATION: boating, ramp, lake fishing, playground. Open Apr 22 - Oct 11. Phone: (641)828-7522.

PLAINFIELD—B-4

(E) NORTH CEDAR PARK (Bremer County Park)—(Bremer) *From jct US 218 & Hwy 188: Go 1 mi E on Hwy 188. Enter on L.* FACILITIES: 48 sites, 48 E, (20/30 amps), 40 pull-thrus, tenting, dump. RECREATION: boating, canoeing, ramp, river fishing, playground. Partial handicap access. Open May 1 - Oct 31. Phone: (319)882-4742.

Imes Bridge is the oldest of Madison County's six bridges.

PLEASANT HILL—D-3

(SE) YELLOW BANKS PARK (Polk County Park)—(Polk) *From jct US 65 & Vandalia Rd: Go 3 mi E on Vandalia Rd, then turn S on SE 68th St. Follow signs. Enter at end.* FACILITIES: 60 sites, 48 E, 12 no hkups, tenting, dump. RECREATION: boating, ramp, river/pond fishing, play equipment. Partial handicap access. Open all yr. Facilities fully operational mid Apr - mid Oct. Phone: (515)266-1563.

RUTHVEN—B-2

(NE) LOST ISLAND-HUSTON PARK (Palo Alto County Park)—(Palo Alto) *From jct US 18 & 350th Ave: Go 2 mi N on 350th Ave, then 1/2 mi E on CR B25, then 2 mi N on CR N26, then 1/2 mi W on paved road.* FACILITIES: 40 sites, 30 ft max RV length, 35 E, (20/30 amps), 5 no hkups, tenting, dump. RECREATION: lake swim, boating, canoeing, ramp, dock, lake fishing. Partial handicap access. Open Apr 15 - Oct 15. Phone: (712)837-4866.

SABULA—C-6

(S) SOUTH SABULA LAKES PARK (Jackson County Park)—(Jackson) *From jct Hwy 64 & US 52: Go 1 mi S on Broad St.* FACILITIES: 41 sites, 41 E, (20/30 amps), tenting, dump. RECREATION: lake/river swim, boating, canoeing, dock, lake/river/stream fishing, playground. Partial handicap access. Open Apr 1 - Nov 1. Phone: (563)652-3783.

SAC CITY—C-2

(S) HAGGE PARK (Sac County Park)—(Sac) *From town: Go 2-1/2 mi S on CR-M54, then 1/4 mi E on CR-D42.* FACILITIES: 15 sites, 15 full hkups, (30 amps), 8 pull-thrus, tenting, dump. RECREATION: boating, ramp, river fishing, playground. Partial handicap access. Open Apr 1 - Oct 31. Phone: (712)662-4530.

(W) SAC CITY PARK—(Sac) *From jct Hwy-196 & US-20: Go 1-3/4 mi W on US-20.* FACILITIES: 30 sites, 25 ft max RV length, 8 W&E, 22 no hkups, tenting. RECREATION: playground. Open May 15 - Oct 15. Phone: (712)662-4295.

SALIX—C-1

(W) BROWN'S LAKE BIGELOW PARK (Woodbury County Park)—(Woodbury) *From I-29 (Salix exit): Go 2 mi W on county road.* FACILITIES: 42 sites, 30 ft max RV length, 42 E, (50 amps), tenting, dump. RECREATION: lake swim, boating, canoeing, ramp, dock, lake fishing, play equipment. Open May 1 - Oct 31. Phone: (712)946-7114.

(SW) SNYDER BEND PARK (Woodbury County Park)—(Woodbury) *From I-29 (Salix exit): Go 2-1/2 mi W on county road, then 1-1/2 mi SW on park road.* FACILITIES: 50 sites, 30 ft max RV length, 35 E, (30 amps), 15 no hkups, tenting, dump. RECREATION: boating, ramp, dock, lake fishing, playground. Partial handicap access. Open May 1 - Oct 31. Phone: (712)946-5622.

SHELBY—D-2

(S) Shelby Country Inn and RV Park—(Pottawattamie) *From jct I 80(exit 34) & CR-M16 (385th St): Go 100 yds N on CR-M16 (385th St). Enter on R.* ◆◆◆FACILITIES: 125 sites, 125 full hkups, (20/30/50 amps), 50 amps ($), 100 pull-thrus, tenting, laundry. ◆RECREATION: play equipment. Pets welcome. Open all yr. Big rigs welcome. Rate in 2010 $20-30 per vehicle. Phone: (712)544-2766.

SHUEYVILLE—C-5

(E) SANDY BEACH (COE - Coralville Lake)—(Johnson) *From jct I-380 (Swisher/Shueyville exit) & CR F12: Go 1 mi E on CR F12, then follow signs 4 mi.* FACILITIES: 60 sites, 50 E, 10 no hkups, tenting, dump. RECREATION: lake swim, boating, ramp, lake fishing, playground. Open May 1 - Sep 29. Phone: (319)338-3543.

SIDNEY—E-1

(SW) WAUBONSIE SP—(Fremont) *From jct Hwy-2 & US-275: Go 4 mi S on US-275-Hwy-2, then 2 mi W on Hwy-2, then 1/2 mi S on Hwy-239.* FACILITIES: 40 sites, 24 E, (20 amps), 16 no hkups, tenting, dump, ltd groc. RECREATION: Open all yr. Facilities fully operational May 1 - Sep 30. Phone: (712)382-2786.

SIGOURNEY—D-4

(N) Bridgeport Campground (RV SPACES)—(Keokula) *From jct SR 92 & SR 149 (Main Street): Go 1/2 mi N on Main St. Enter on R.* FACILITIES: 12 sites, 12 full hkups, (30/50 amps), tenting, dump, laundry. Pets welcome. Open all yr. Big rigs welcome. Rate in 2010 $16 for 6 persons. Phone: (641)622-2306.

SIOUX CENTER—B-1

(N) Country Home Campground & Motel—(Sioux) *From jct W CR-B-40 & US 75: Go 1-1/4 mi N on US 75. Enter on L.* ◆◆◆FACILITIES: 12 sites, 10 full hkups, 2 W&E, (30/50 amps), 4 pull-thrus, WiFi Instant Internet at site, WiFi Internet central location, family camping, tenting, laundry, fire rings, grills, wood. ◆◆RECREATION: playground, horseshoes, v-ball. Pets welcome. Partial handicap access. Open all yr. Rate in 2010 $16 for 4 persons. MC/VISA/DISC/AMEX/Debit. CCUSA 50% Discount. CCUSA reservations Not Accepted, CCUSA max stay 1 day, Cash only for CCUSA disc., CCUSA disc. not avail holidays.

Phone: (800)919-2309
Address: 3741 US 75th Ave., Sioux Center, IA 51250
Lat/Lon: 43.10830/-96.17625
Email: nancy@mtcnet.net

SIOUX CITY—B-1

(NW) STONE SP—(Plymouth) *From jct I-29 (exit 151) & Hwy 12: Go 5 mi N on Hwy 12.* FACILITIES: 30 sites, 30 ft max RV length, 10 E, (20/30 amps), 20 no hkups, tenting. RECREATION: lake/stream fishing, playground. Open Apr 15 - Nov 1. Phone: (712)255-4698.

SMITHLAND—C-1

(W) SOUTHWOOD CONSERVATION AREA (Woodbury County Park)—(Woodbury) *From jct Hwy 31 & US 141: Go 1-1/2 mi W on US 141, then 3/4 mi S & E on gravel road.* FACILITIES: 30 sites, 30 ft max RV length, 10 E, 20 no hkups, tenting. RECREATION: boating, electric motors only, canoeing, ramp, dock, pond fishing. Partial handicap access. Open May 1 - Oct 31. Phone: (712)889-2215.

SOLON—C-5

(W) LAKE MACBRIDE SP—(Johnson) *From jct Hwy-382 & Hwy-1: Go 4 mi W on Hwy-382.* FACILITIES: 108 sites, typical site width 14 ft, 30 ft max RV length, 10 full hkups, 38 E, (30 amps), 60 no hkups, tenting, dump, ltd groc. RECREATION: lake swim, boating, 10 hp limit, canoeing, ramp, dock, lake fishing, playground. Partial handicap access. Open Apr 15 - Oct 15. Phone: (319)624-2200.

SPENCER—B-2

(SE) LEACH PARK CAMPGROUND—(Clay) *From south jct US 18 & US 71: Go N to 4th St, then 3 blocks E.* FACILITIES: 200 sites, 100 W&E, 100 E, (30 amps), 10 pull-thrus, tenting, dump. RECREATION: river swim, canoeing, ramp, river fishing, playground. Partial handicap access. Open Apr 15 - Oct 15. Phone: (712)264-7265.

SPIRIT LAKE—A-2

(SW) Cen La RV Park—(Dickinson) *From jct SR 9 & US-71: Go 1 mi S on US-71. Enter on R.* ◆◆◆◆FACILITIES: 152 sites, typical site width 40 ft, 142 full hkups, 9 W&E, 1 E, (30/50 amps), 35 pull-thrus, family camping, tenting, dump, laundry, ltd groc. ◆◆◆◆RECREATION: swim pool, dock, lake fishing, playground. Pets welcome, breed restrict. Partial handicap access. Open Apr 15 - Oct 15. Facilities fully operational Memorial Day - Labor Day. Big rigs welcome. Rate in 2010 $26.50-32.50 for 2 persons. Member ARVC, IAARVC. Phone: (712)336-2925.

(W) Vick's Corner—(Dickinson) *From jct SR-9 & SR-86: at NW corner. Enter on R.* ◆FACILITIES: 72 sites, typical site width 20 ft, accepts self-contained units only, 6 full hkups, 66 E, (20/30 amps), dump, ltd groc. Pets welcome. No tents. Open all yr. Rate in 2010 $20 per vehicle. Phone: (712)336-5602.

STANTON—D-2

(SE) VIKING LAKE SP—(Montgomery) *From town: Go 1-1/2 mi E on US 34, then 1/2 mi S on CR M65. Enter on L.* FACILITIES: 120 sites, 22 full hkups, 72 E, (20/30 amps), 26 no hkups, 15 pull-thrus, tenting, dump, ltd groc. RECREATION: lake swim, boating, canoeing, ramp, dock, lake fishing, playground. Partial handicap access. Open May 1 - Sep 30. Phone: (712)829-2235.

STORM LAKE—B-2

(SE) SUNRISE CAMPGROUND—(Buena Vista) *From jct US Hwy 71 & Hwy 7/Bus 71: Go 1.5 mi W on Hwy 7/Bus 71 (at lighthouse), then S on Sunrise Rd 1/4 mi. Enter on L.*

FACILITIES: 164 sites, typical site width 25 ft, 80 full hkups, 84 E, (30/50 amps), 2 pull-thrus, WiFi Instant Internet at site, WiFi Internet central location, family camping, tenting, dump, non-guest dump $, laundry, ice, picnic tables, patios, fire rings, grills, wood.

RECREATION: lake swim, boating, canoeing, kayaking, ramp, dock, lake fishing, golf nearby, playground, sports field, hiking trails. Rec open to public.

Pets welcome. Partial handicap access. Open Apr 1 - Oct 1. Big rigs welcome. Escort to site. Clubs welcome. MC/VISA/DISC/AMEX/Debit.

SUNRISE CAMPGROUND—Continued on next page

STORM LAKE—Continued
SUNRISE CAMPGROUND—Continued

Phone: (712)732-8023
Address: 1001 Sunrise Park Rd, Storm Lake, IA 50588
Lat/Lon: 42.62776/-95.17544
Email: campground@stormlake.org
Web: www.sunrisecampgrounds.com

SEE AD ARNOLDS PARK PAGE 253

STORY CITY—C-3

(NE) Whispering Oaks RV Park & Campground—(Story) *From jct I-35 (exit 124) & Broad Rd: Go 300 yds W on Broad Rd, then 1/4 mi N on Timberland Dr. Enter on L.* ◆◆◆◆FACILITIES: 75 sites, typical site width 30 ft, 11 full hkups, 64 W&E, (30/50 amps), 50 amps ($), 18 pull-thrus, family camping, tenting, dump, laundry, ltd groc. ◆◆RECREATION: canoeing, river fishing, playground. Pets welcome, breed restrict. Open all yr. Big rigs welcome. Rate in 2010 $25-29 for 4 persons. Phone: (515)733-4663.

STRATFORD—C-3

(NE) BELLS MILL PARK (Hamilton County Park)—(Hamilton) *From jct Hwy 175 & CR R21: Go 3 mi N on CR R21, then 1 mi E on CR D56, then follow signs 2 mi N on a gravel road.* FACILITIES: 60 sites, 32 ft max RV length, 60 E, (20/30 amps), tenting, dump. RECREATION: river swim, boating, canoeing, ramp, river fishing, playground. Partial handicap access. Open all yr. Phone: (515)832-9570.

STRAWBERRY POINT—B-5

(S) BACKBONE SP—(Delaware) *From jct Hwy 13 & Hwy 3: Go 2 mi S on Hwy 3, then 3/4 mi W & 3/4 mi S on Hwy 410.* FACILITIES: 125 sites, 49 E, (30 amps), 76 no hkups, 20 pull-thrus, tenting, dump, ltd groc. RECREATION: lake swim, boating, ramp, dock, lake/stream fishing, playground. Partial handicap access. Open Apr 1 - Oct 15. Phone: (563)924-2000.

SUMNER—B-4

(N) NORTH WOODS PARK (Bremer County Park)—(Bremer) *From jct US 63 & Hwy 93: Go 15 mi E on Hwy 93, then 2 mi N on CR V62. Enter on R.* FACILITIES: 30 sites, 30 E, 20 pull-thrus, tenting. RECREATION: playground. Open May 1 - Oct 31. Phone: (319)882-4742.

TAMA—C-4

Meskwaki Casino RV Park—(Tama) *From jct US 63 & US 30: Go 4-3/4 mi W on US 30 (behind casino). Enter on L.* ◆◆◆◆FACILITIES: 50 sites, accepts self-contained units only, 50 E, (30/50 amps), 50 pull-thrus, dump, laundry. ◆◆RECREATION: swim pool. Pets welcome, breed restrict. No tents. Open all yr. Big rigs welcome. Rate in 2010 $15 per vehicle. Phone: (641) 484-1439.

TIFFIN—C-5

(W) F.W. KENT PARK (Johnson County Park)—(Johnson) *From I-80 (exit 237): Go 1 mi N, then 3-1/2 mi W on US-6.* FACILITIES: 86 sites, 38 E, 48 no hkups, tenting, dump. RECREATION: lake swim, boating, electric motors only, ramp, lake fishing. Partial handicap access. Open Apr 17 - Nov 4. Phone: (319)645-2315.

TIPTON—C-5

(S) HUNTS CEDAR RIVER CAMPGROUND—(Cedar) *From jct I-80 (exit 267) & SR 38: Go 200 yds N on SR 38, then 1 mi W on 306th St. Enter on L.*

◆◆◆FACILITIES: 168 sites, typical site width 30 ft, 103 full hkups, 65 W&E, (20/30/50 amps), many extd stay sites, 40 pull-thrus, WiFi Instant Internet at site, phone on-site Internet (needs activ), WiFi Internet central location, family camping, tenting, RV storage, dump, non-guest dump $, laundry, ltd groc, LP gas by weight/by meter, ice, picnic tables, fire rings, wood.

◆◆◆◆RECREATION: rec room/area, pavilion, coin games, swim pool, boating, canoeing, dock, 8 canoe rentals, river fishing, mini-golf, ($), bsktball, playground, activities, (wkends), horseshoes, sports field, v-ball.

Pets welcome, breed restrict. Partial handicap access. Open Apr 15 - Oct 15. Facilities fully operational Memorial Day - Labor Day. Big rigs welcome. Escort to site. Clubs welcome. Rate in 2010 $23-26 for 4 persons. MC/VISA/Debit. Member ARVC, IAARVC.

Phone: (563)946-2431
Address: 1231 306th St, Tipton, IA 52772
Lat/Lon: 41.64580/-91.12701
Email: hcrcg95@msn.com
Web: www.campingfriend.com

SEE AD DAVENPORT PAGE 254

The state's lowest elevation point (at 480 feet) is in Lee County.

URBANA—C-5

(E) LAZY ACRES RV PARK—(Benton) *From jct SR-150 & I-380: Go 1-1/2 mi S on I-380 (exit 41), then 100 yds E on 54th St Trail, then 100 yds NW on 32nd Ave. Enter on R.*

◆◆◆◆FACILITIES: 46 sites, typical site width 75 ft, 22 full hkups, 24 W&E, (20/30/50 amps), some extd stay sites, 46 pull-thrus, WiFi Instant Internet at site, WiFi Internet central location, family camping, tenting, RV's/park model rentals, cabins, RV storage, dump, non-guest dump $, laundry, ltd groc, RV supplies, picnic tables, fire rings, wood.

◆◆◆◆RECREATION: rec hall, pavilion, coin games, dock, 2 pedal boat rentals, pond fishing, mini-golf, bsktball, 3 bike rentals, playground, horseshoes, sports field, v-ball. Rec open to public.

Pets welcome. Partial handicap access. Open Apr 1 - Oct 30. Big rigs welcome. Escort to site. Clubs welcome. Green Friendly. Rate in 2010 $22-25 for 2 persons. MC/VISA. Member ARVC, IAARVC. CCUSA 50% Discount. CCUSA reservations Recommended, CCUSA max stay 1 day, CCUSA disc. not avail S,W,Th, CCUSA disc. not avail F,Sa, CCUSA disc. not avail holidays. Discount not available during special events & rallies.

Phone: (319)443-4000
Address: 5486 32 nd Ave, Center Point, IA 52213
Lat/Lon: 42.23056/-91.86591
Email: office@lazyacresrv.com
Web: www.lazyacresrv.com

SEE AD CEDAR RAPIDS PAGE 253

(SE) WILDCAT BLUFF (Benton County Park)—(Benton) *From jct Hwy 150 & Hwy 363: Go 1 mi E on Hwy 363 into Urbana, then S on CR W28.* FACILITIES: 23 sites, 23 E, tenting. RECREATION: boating, canoeing. Open all yr. Phone: (319)472-3318.

VENTURA—B-3

(E) MCINTOSH WOODS SP—(Hancock) *From town: Go 3/4 mi E on US 18, then 1/2 mi S on McIntosh Rd.* FACILITIES: 49 sites, 45 E, 4 no hkups, tenting, dump. RECREATION: lake swim, boating, ramp, lake fishing, playground. Open all yr. Facilities fully operational Spring thaw - Fall freeze. Phone: (641)829-3847.

VINTON—C-4

(E) BENTON CITY-FRY CAMPGROUND (Benton County Park)—(Benton) *From Hwy 150 & 13th St: Go 4-1/2 mi E on 13th St, then follow signs.* FACILITIES: 21 sites, 30 ft max RV length, 16 E, 5 no hkups, tenting. RECREATION: river swim, boating, canoeing, ramp, river fishing, playground. Open all yr. Phone: (319)472-3318.

(N) MINNE ESTEMA CAMPGROUND (Benton County Park)—(Benton) *From jct US 218 & Hwy 150: Go 3-1/2 mi N on Hwy 150, then follow signs.* FACILITIES: 30 sites, 25 ft max RV length, 20 E, 10 no hkups, tenting. RECREATION: river swim, boating, canoeing, river fishing. Open all yr. Phone: (563)472-3318.

(W) RODGERS PARK (Benton County Park)—(Benton) *From town: Go 3 mi W on US-218, then 1 mi N on CR-V61, then 1/4 mi E.* FACILITIES: 53 sites, 25 ft max RV length, 53 E, tenting, dump. RECREATION: lake swim, boating, electric motors only, canoeing, ramp, lake fishing, playground. Partial handicap access. Open all yr. Phone: (319)472-4942.

WAUKEE—D-3

(S) TIMBERLINE CAMPGROUND—(Dallas) *From jct I-80 & CR R22 (Ute Ave) exit 117: Go 1 mi N on Ute Ave, then 1/2 mi E on Ashworth Rd (CR F 64). Enter on L.*

◆◆◆◆FACILITIES: 112 sites, typical site width 25 ft, 38 full hkups, 67 W&E, (30/50 amps), 7 no hkups, some extd stay sites (summer), 76 pull-thrus, WiFi Instant Internet at site, phone on-site Internet (needs activ), WiFi Internet central location, family camping, tenting, cabins, RV storage, dump, non-guest dump $, laundry, ltd groc, RV supplies, LP gas by weight/by meter, ice, picnic tables, patios, fire rings, grills, wood.

◆◆◆◆RECREATION: rec hall, rec room/area, pavilion, coin games, swim pool, bsktball, playground, horseshoes, sports field, hiking trails, v-ball.

Pets welcome, breed restrict. Partial handicap access. Open Apr 1 - Nov 1. Facilities fully operational Memorial day - Labor day. Big rigs welcome. Clubs welcome. Green Friendly. Rate in 2010 $31.50-34 for 2 persons. MC/VISA/DISC/Debit. Member ARVC, IAARVC.

Phone: (515)987-1714
Address: 31635 Ashworth Rd., Waukee, IA 50263
Lat/Lon: 41.57730/-93.87336
Email: timberrv@aol.com
Web: www.timberlineiowa.com

SEE AD DES MOINES PAGE 256

WAVERLY—B-4

(NW) CEDAR BEND PARK (Bremer County Park)—(Bremer) *From jct US 218 & Co. Blacktop C-33: Go E 1 mi, then S on Co road T77 for 1-1/2 mi, then E on T77 1/2 mile. Enter on L.* FACILITIES: 86 sites, 86 E, (30/50 amps), 50 pull-thrus, tenting, dump. RECREATION: canoeing, river fishing, playground. Partial handicap access. Open May 1 - Oct 31. Phone: (319)882-4742.

WEBSTER CITY—C-3

(S) BRIGGS WOODS PARK (Hamilton County Park)—(Hamilton) *From jct US 20 & Hwy 17: Go 2 mi S on Hwy 17.* FACILITIES: 81 sites, 30 ft max RV length, 30 full hkups, 51 E, (20/30/50 amps), tenting, dump. RECREATION: lake/river swim, boating, electric motors only, canoeing, ramp, dock, lake/river fishing, playground. Partial handicap access. Phone: (515)832-9570.

WEST BEND—B-2

(N) The Grotto of the Redemption RV Park—(Palo Alto) *From jct CR-B63 & Hwy-15: Go 1 mi N on Hwy-15, then 3 blocks W on 4th St, then 1 blk on 1 Ave NW. Enter on L.* ◆◆◆FACILITIES: 53 sites, 33 E, (30 amps), 20 no hkups, WiFi Internet central location, family camping, tenting, dump, non-guest dump $, ice, picnic tables, fire rings, grills, wood. ◆◆RECREATION: bsktball, playground. Pets welcome. Open all yr. Facilities fully operational Apr 1 - Oct 30. Rate in 2010 $15 per vehicle. MC/VISA/DISC/Debit. CCUSA 50% Discount.

Phone: (800)868-3641
Address: 300 N. Broadway, West Bend, IA 50597
Lat/Lon: 42.96398/-94.44661
Email: info@westbendgrotto.com
Web: www.westbendgrotto.com

WEST LIBERTY—D-5

(N) WEST LIBERTY RV PARK—(Cedar) *From jct I-80 (exit 259) & Garfield Ave: Go 1/4 mi S on Garfield Ave. On asphalt (behind BP Station). Enter on R.*

◆◆◆◆FACILITIES: 51 sites, typical site width 30 ft, 45 full hkups, (20/30/50 amps), 6 no hkups, some extd stay sites, 45 pull-thrus, tenting, cabins, dump, non-guest dump $, laundry, ltd groc, RV supplies, ice, picnic tables, fire rings, grills, wood.

◆◆RECREATION: pavilion, swim pool, playground, sports field.

Pets welcome. Partial handicap access. Open all yr. Facilities fully operational Memorial Day - Labor Day. Big rigs welcome. Clubs welcome. Rate in 2010 $26 for 2 persons. MC/VISA/DISC/Debit. Member IACO.

Phone: (319)627-2676
Address: 1961 Garfield Ave., West Liberty, IA 52776
Lat/Lon: 41.66094/-91.25146

SEE AD THIS PAGE

WHITING—C-1

(SW) Hildreth Lighthouse Campground—(Monona) *From I-29 & 160th St (K-42): Go 2 mi W, then 1 mi S on Berry Ave, then 3/4 mi W on 170th St. Enter at end.* ◆◆◆FACILITIES: 51 sites, typical site width 40 ft, 40 full hkups, 10 W&E, 1 E, (30/50 amps), 6 pull-thrus, family camping, tenting, laundry. ◆◆◆RECREATION: river swim, boating, canoeing, ramp, dock, river fishing, play equipment. Pets welcome. Open all yr. Big rigs welcome. Rate in 2010 $22 per vehicle. Phone: (712)420-1103.

WINTERSET—D-3

(SE) WINTERSET CITY PARK CAMPGROUND—(Madison) *From north jct US 169 & Hwy 92: Go 1/2 mi E on Hwy 92, then 9 blocks S on 10th St. Enter at end.* FACILITIES: 34 sites, 22 full hkups, 5 W&E, 7 E, (15/30/50 amps), 6 pull-thrus, tenting, dump. RECREATION: playground. Partial handicap access. Open Apr 1 - Nov 1. Phone: (515)462-3258.

Quaker Oats, in Cedar Rapids, is the largest cereal company in the world.

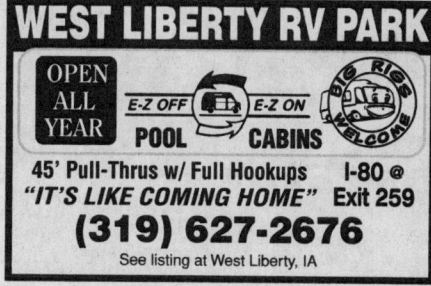

WOODBINE—C-1

(W) WILLOW LAKE (Harrison County Park)—(Harrison) *From jct US 30 & CR F20L (Easton Trail): Go 6 mi W on CR F20L (Easton Trail). Enter on R.* FACILITIES: 26 sites, typical site width 15 ft, 35 ft max RV length, 26 E, tenting. RECREATION: lake swim, boating, electric motors only, canoeing, ramp, dock, lake fishing, playground. Partial handicap access. Open Apr 1 - Oct 31. Phone: (712)647-2785.

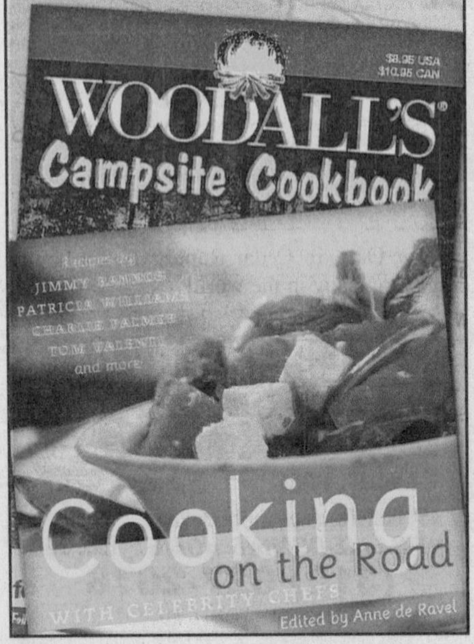

TIME ZONE

North central and eastern Kentucky are in the Eastern Time Zone and the south central and western part of the state are in the Central Time Zone.

TOPOGRAPHY

Kentucky's topography ranges from mountains in the east to uplands in the central portion to plains in the west. Elevation ranges from 260 feet along the Mississippi River to 4,145 feet at Black Mountain.

The southern hospitality and charm of Kentucky are found everywhere visitors travel through the state. Kentucky's wealth of natural wonders is punctuated with history, heritage, and two major metropolitan cities.

TRAVEL & TOURISM INFO

State Agency:
Kentucky Department of Travel
Capital Plaza Tower, 22nd Floor
500 Mero Street
Frankfort, KY 40601
(800/225-8747 or 502/564-4930)
www.kentuckytourism.com

Regional Agencies:
Ashland Area CVB
1509 Winchester Ave.
Ashland, KY 41101
(800/377-6249 or 606/329-1007)
www.visitashlandky.com

Bardstown/Nelson County Tourist & Convention Commission
One Court Square
Bardstown, KY 40004
(502/348-4877 or 800/638-4877)

Bell County Tourism Commission
2215 Cumberland Ave.
Middlesboro, KY 40965
(800/988-1075 or 606/248-2482)
www.MountainGateway.com

Bowling Green Area CVB
352 Three Springs Road
Bowling Green, KY 42104
(800/326-7465 or 270/782-0800)
www.visitbgky.com

Cave City Tourist & Convention Commission
P.O. Box 518
Cave City, KY 42127
(270/773-3131 or 800/346-8908)

Columbia/Adair County Tourism
P.O. Box 116
201 Burkesville St.
Columbia, KY 42728
(270/384-6020)
www.columbia-adaircounty.com

Cumberland County Tourism Commission
7951 Glasgow Road
Burkesville, KY 42717
(270/864-2256)

Frankfort/Franklin Co Tourism
100 Capital Avenue
Frankfort, KY 40601
(502/875-8687)
www.visitfrankfort.com

Henderson County Tourist Commission
101 N. Water Street, Suite B
Henderson, KY 42420
(800/648-3128 or 270/826-3128)
www.hendersonky.org

Louisville CVB
401 W. Main St., Suite 2300
Louisville, KY 40202
(888/LOUISVILLE or 800/626-5646)
www.gotolouisville.com

Northern Kentucky CVB
50 E. Rivercenter Blvd., Suite 200
Covington, KY 41011
(800/STAY-NKY)
www.staynky.com

Where to Find CCUSA Parks

List City	Park Name	Map Coordinates
BEREA		
	Walnut Meadow RV Park	D-4
CAVE CITY		
	Singing Hills Campground and RV Park	D-3
ELIZABETHTOWN		
	Glendale Campground	D-3
FRANKLIN		
	Bluegrass Music RV Park	E-2
GRAND RIVERS		
	Exit 31 RV Park	B-2
HARTFORD		
	Ohio County Park	D-2
OWENSBORO		
	Windy Hollow Campground & Recreation Area (Not Visited)	D-2
PARKERS LAKE		
	Eagle Falls Lodge	E-4

I-24 EXIT 3

FERN LAKE CAMPGROUND— *From Exit #3 (SR 305): Go 1/2 mi W on 305. Enter on R.*
See listing at Paducah, KY

I-24 EXIT 11

DUCK CREEK RV PARK— *From Exit 11: Go 1/2 mi N on John Puryear Dr. Enter on R.*
See listing at Paducah, KY

I-24 EXIT 31

EXIT 31 RV PARK— *From Exit 31: Go 1/10 mi S on Hwy 453. Enter on R.*
See listing at Grand Rivers, KY

I-24 EXIT 45

OUTBACK RV RESORT— *From Exit 45: Go 400 yds W on SR 293, then 1 mi S on SR 293. Enter on L.*
See listing at Eddyville, KY

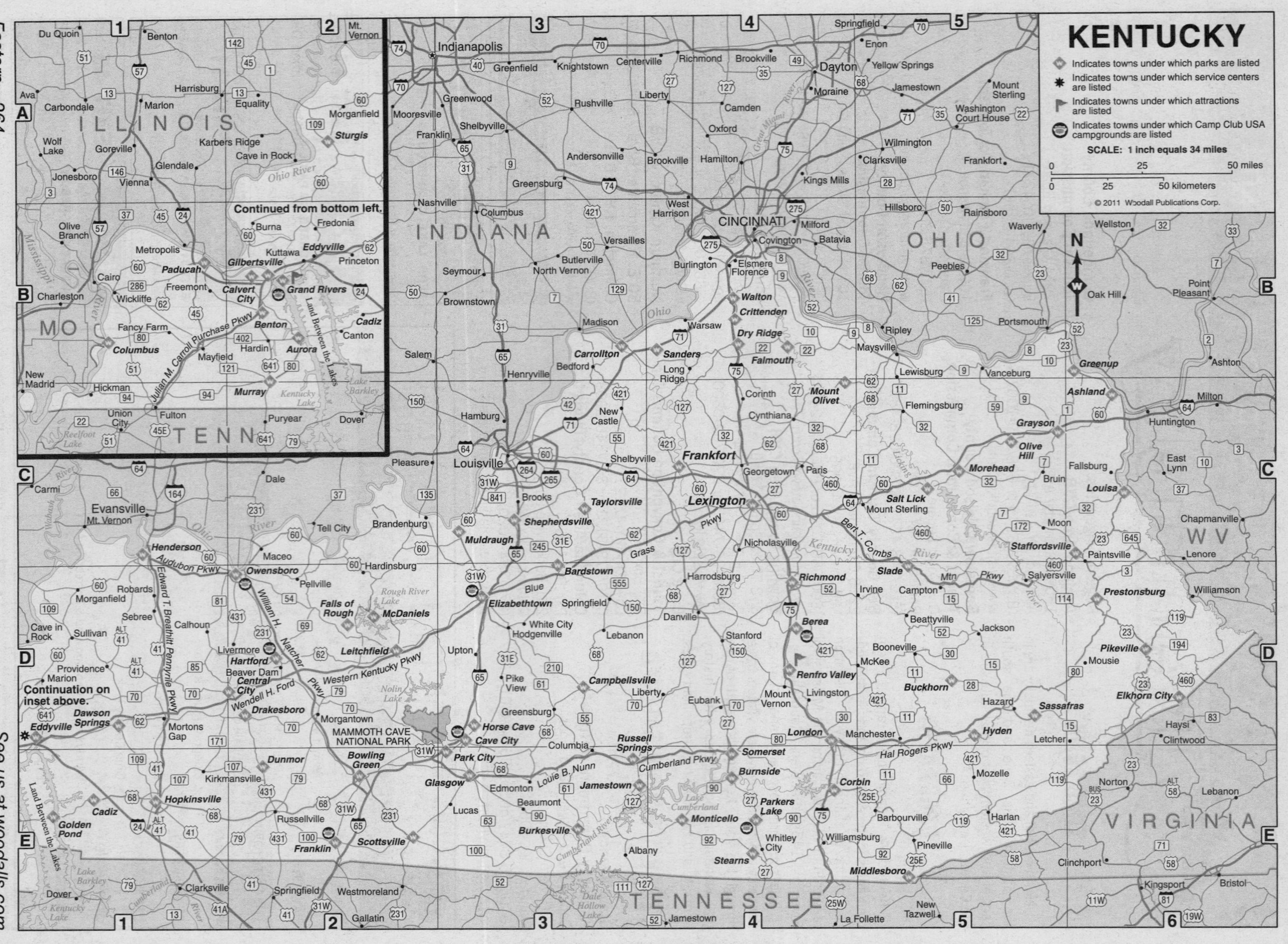

KENTUCKY
Indicates towns under which parks are listed
Indicates towns under which service centers are listed
Indicates towns under which attractions are listed
Indicates towns under which Camp Club USA campgrounds are listed
SCALE: 1 inch equals 34 miles
0 25 50 miles
0 25 50 kilometers
© 2011 Woodall Publications Corp.
ILLINOIS
INDIANA
OHIO
WV
VIRGINIA
TENNESSEE
MO
TENN
Continued from bottom left.
Continuation on inset above.
MAMMOTH CAVE NATIONAL PARK
Land Between the Lakes
Louisville
Lexington
Frankfort
CINCINNATI
Indianapolis
Dayton
Evansville

Paducah CVB
128 Broadway
Paducah, KY 42001
(800/PADUCAH or 270/443-8783)
www.paducah-tourism.org

Local Agencies:

Check with the Chamber of Commerce or Tourism Bureau for the locality you are interested in. Check with the state or regional agencies for phone numbers and addresses. Also visit the Kentucky Dept. of Tourism website for links to communities at www.kentuckytourism.com

SHOPPING

Factory Stores of America Outlet Center, Georgetown. Located off I-75 at exit 126, this outlet center includes Carolina Pottery and Levi's. (502/868-0682).

Flea Land of Bowling Green/Antique Mall at Flea Land. Kentucky's largest indoor, climate controlled flea market. Over 85,000 square feet with antiques, collectibles, crafts, clothing and specialty items. www.flealand.com

Hamburg Place, Lexington, KY. Located off I-75 at Exit 108, this shopping center was once a horse farm. Includes everything from sporting goods to fine dining. http://hamburgplace-lexington-ky.com/default.aspx

RECREATIONAL INFO

Hunting/Fishing/Boating Regulations & Licenses: Kentucky Dept. of Fish and Wildlife Resources, #1 Sportsman's Lane, Frankfort, KY 40601 (800/858-1549) www.fw.ky.gov

Golf: Kentucky State Parks http://parks.ky.gov

UNIQUE FEATURES

EXPERIENCE KENTUCKY.

Plan a trip any time of the year to experience Kentucky firsthand. Make sure to include a trip to the Kentucky Horse Park on your itinerary. Hands-on, family-friendly activities draw people in, and learning activities abound at this working horse farm. In addition, the park includes two museums, the international Museum of the Horse, a Smithsonian affiliate, and the American Saddlebred Museum. The Hall of Champions serves as the retirement home for several world-class champions and the Parade of Breeds showcases the more than 50 breeds of horses at the park. But horses are not all Kentucky has to offer. From Barbecue and Bluegrass music, to zip lines and breathtaking scenery, wonderful adventures abound in Kentucky. Round out your trip with shopping, dining and sampling Kentucky bourbon. For more information, visit www.kentuckytourism.com

LINCOLN HERITAGE TRAIL

Comprised of the main sites that relate to President Lincoln's Kentucky roots, the trail takes you on an historic journey that explores the key people, places and events in Lincoln's Kentucky story. In Hodgenville, visit Abe's birthplace, boyhood home and the **Lincoln Museum**. The museum's main exhibit includes twelve dioramas showing pivotal times in Abraham Lincoln's life from his boyhood to his assassination. Rare newspaper clippings, campaign posters and memorabilia are also on display. Other highlights include the **Mary Todd Lincoln House** in Lexington and **Lincoln Homestead State Park** in Springfield. The park features the home of Lincoln's mother, Nancy Hanks and historic building replicas. **Perryville Battlefield State Historic Site** is one of the most unaltered Civil War sites in the nation. Vistas visible today are virtually those soldiers saw in 1862 when one of the most destructive Civil War battles took place. Many more historic sites, homes and memorials are included on the trail. For more information, visit www.heritage.ky.gov.

DESTINATIONS

BLUEGRASS REGION

Berea. See working studios of woodworkers, potters, quilters, jewelers, photographers, weavers and furniture makers in the "Folk Arts & Crafts Capital of Kentucky." **The Kentucky Artisan Center**, at Exit 77 on I-75, celebrates the accomplishments of Kentucky's artisans. Free admittance, shopping, demonstrations and restaurants.

Danville. History abounds in this picturesque community. Ten constitutional conventions took place at Danville's **Constitution Square State Historic Site** between 1784 and 1792.

Frankfort. It was here in the valley of the Kentucky River that Vice President Aaron Burr was first charged with treason. Today, Frankfort pays tribute to its past with museums such as the **Kentucky History Center** and the **Kentucky Military History Museum**. The **Frankfort Cemetery** contains the gravesites of Daniel and Rebecca Boone. Free tours of **Buffalo Trace Distillery** are offered. The **Old Governor's Mansion,** built in 1798, was once referred to as the "Palace," hosting many presidents, officials of state and visiting dignitaries. Both the Kentucky Military Museum and the Old Governor's Mansion are closed for renovation this year, and are expected to reopen in 2010.

Located next to the State Capitol Building, the Governor's Mansion is open for tours Tuesday & Thursday 9 am to 11 am, excluding state and some federal holidays. Twenty-four Kentucky governors have lived in this house since it's completion in 1914. This magnificent building is on the National Register of Historic Places. 502/564-3449.

Harrodsburg. At **Old Fort Harrod State Park**, costumed interpreters guide visitors through the fort's daily activities. Also on-site are a pioneer cemetery, a cabin (believed to be where Abraham Lincoln's parents were married) and an 1830 Mansion Museum containing Native American and Civil War artifacts.

Kentucky Horse Park. Self-guided tours feature wide-screen films, horse-drawn trolley rides, pony rides, the Parade of Breeds, and the Hall of Champions. The American Saddlebred Museum and the International Museum of the Horse feature interactive exhibits. A campground is also available.

Lawrenceburg. Wild Turkey Bourbon Distillery allows you to experience all the sights, sounds and smells of a real working distillery, located on the top of a scenic 300-foot Kentucky River gorge.

The Explorium of Kentucky has 9 discovery zones and 90 exhibits that can be touched and explored by children of all ages. There are experiment stations, traveling exhibits and workshops.

Perryville. Kentucky's most important Civil War battle took place at **Perryville Battlefield State Historic Site** in October 1862. Perryville's downtown **Merchant's Row** buildings appear much as they did during the Civil War.

BUSINESSES OFFERING

	Things to See & Do	RV Sales	RV Service
EDDYVILLE			
Murphy's RV's		●	●
GRAND RIVERS			
Miss Scarlett's Restaurant	●		
RENFRO VALLEY			
Mt. Vernon-Rock Castle County Tourist Commission	●		

Shaker Village of Pleasant Hill contains 34 buildings on 3000 acres of farmland with over 20 miles of restored stone fencing.

BLUEGRASS, BLUES AND BARBECUE REGION

Henderson. Founded and mapped with the guidance of Daniel Boone, Henderson has a wide array of 19th century homes. John James Audubon created many of his bird paintings while living here, many of which are on view at the **John James Audubon Museum** where visitors can also watch birds in a circular observation room and purchase limited edition prints.

Owensboro. The state's third largest city is home to the **International Bluegrass Music Museum.** Two floors of the state-of-the-art exhibits include a history of bluegrass, instruments used by well-known musicians and listening stations equipped with audio domes. The **Owensboro Area Museum of Science and History** houses exhibits on astronomy, geology, paleontology, archaeology, biology and a hands-on physical science area.

CAVES, LAKES AND CORVETTES REGION

Bowling Green. Stop by the **Kentucky Museum,** which preserves Kentucky's cultural heritage with a variety of photographs, manuscripts, artifacts and permanent and rotating exhibits. Also visit the **National Corvette Museum, just across the street from the GM Plant,** the only place in the world where this classic American car is made. The **L & N Depot and Railpark** is home to one of the most beautiful depots built in 1925. View a historic Pullman dining car, a presidential office car and Chessie Class caboose.

Cave City. In the heart of Cave Country, the city boasts many famous area caves as well as activities for the whole family. Attractions include: Big Mike's Mystery House; Dinosaur World, an outdoor museum; Guntown Mountain with live entertainment, saloon shows, carnival rides and more; Kentucky Action Park with go-carts, bumper boats and shops; several museums and water activities on the Green River. The many area caves include:

Mammoth Cave National Park. A World Heritage Site and International Biosphere Reserve, Mammoth Cave's history stretches back 4,000 years. The longest cave system in the world holds over 350 miles of mapped corridors. Geologists estimate that there could be as many as 600 miles of undiscovered passageways. The 379 feet deep cave contains vast subterranean chambers. Several underground rivers, including Echo River and the River Styx, flow through the deepest chambers. Over 10 guided tours are available ranging from one and a half to six hours long. Above ground, enjoy a myriad of outdoor activities including hiking, camping, boat rides, fishing and wildlife viewing as you explore the 53,000 acres of scenic beauty.

Horse Cave. Visit the **American Cave Museum** and learn of the adventures of early cavers. Exhibits include lifelike models of cave animals, modern cave exploration, history of Horse Cave and Mammoth Cave and groundwater science and conservation. Then visit **Hidden River Cave**, known as the greatest cave restoration in the U.S. Closed for 50 years due to pollution, the cave was revived due to conservation efforts and reopened a decade ago. At **Kentucky Down Under**, you can interact with Australian wildlife such as kangaroos, wallabies, Blue Tongued Skinks and Bearded Dragons; or learn to play a didgeridoo or throw a boomerang.

DANIEL BOONE COUNTRY

Cumberland Gap. One of America's most important historical sites is located in Kentucky's far southeast corner. Walk in the footsteps of Daniel Boone at the **Cumberland Gap National Historic Park,** the largest National Historic Park in the country.

QUICK REFERENCE CHART FOR WOODALL'S FEATURED PARKS

	Green Friendly	RV Lots for Sale	Park Models-Onsite Ownership	Park Membership for Sale	Big Rigs Welcome	Internet Friendly	Pets Welcome
BEREA							
Oh Kentucky Campground					▲	●	■
CAVE CITY							
Cave Country RV Campground					▲	●	■
EDDYVILLE							
Outback RV Resort					▲	●	■
FRANKFORT							
Elkhorn Campground					▲	●	■
GRAND RIVERS							
Exit 31 RV Park					▲	●	■
LONDON							
Westgate RV Camping					▲	●	■
PADUCAH							
Duck Creek RV Park					▲	●	■
Fern Lake Campground					▲		■
SHEPHERDSVILLE							
Grandma's RV Park					▲	●	■
WALTON							
Oak Creek Campground						●	■

Green Friendly ; RV Lots for Sale ✖; Park Models/Onsite Onwership ✱; Park Memberships for Sale ✔; Big Rigs Welcome ▲; Internet Friendly ●; Internet Friendly-WiFi ●; Pets Welcome ■

Daniel Boone National Forest. Canoe and whitewater raft on the Cumberland, Rockcastle and Red rivers or hike on the **Sheltowee Trace National Recreation Trail.**

Natural Bridge, Slade. Located in the midst of the Daniel Boone National Forest, near the Red River Gorge Geological Area, the natural sandstone arch was formed over million of years. The arch spans 78 feet in length and 65 feet in height.

Renfro Valley. Travel the rhythm of the road in eastern Kentucky, where you'll find the Commonwealth's musical roots. Visit the **Renfro Valley Entertainment Center,** "Kentucky's Country Music Capital," for toe-tappin' tunes of the Bluegrass. Nearby, the **Kentucky Music Hall of Fame and Museum** showcases Kentucky's Musical Heritage.

KENTUCKY'S APPALACHIANS REGION

Carter Cave State Resort Park, located 38 miles west of Ashland. An underground waterfall 30 feet high is featured. Take a tour through **Saltpetre Cave, Cascade Cave** and **Bat Cave**.

Paintsville. The U.S. 23 Country Music Highway Museum opened in the spring of '05. It is dedicated to the country music entertainers that are listed on the brown state signs along U.S. 23. Entertainers featured in the museum are: Billy Ray Cyrus, The Judds, Ricky Skaggs, Hylo Brown, Loretta Lynn, Crystal Gayle, Dwight Yoakam, Patty Loveless, Tom T. Hall, Keith Whitley, Gary Stewart and Rebecca Lynn Howard.

Van Lear. The **Coal Miners' Museum** is located in the building that originally housed the headquarters of the Miller's Creek Division of the Consolidation Coal Company. Displays include: coal mining tools, a restored "company" doctor's office, a post office, a 1950's snack bar, a diorama of the town as it was in the 1930's, the old town jail, a Van Lear Schools collection and much more.

KENTUCKY'S DERBY REGION

Bardstown. A trolley or driving tour includes attractions such as **Heaven Hill Distilleries**, offering guided tours; and **My Old Kentucky Home State Park,** which features "The Stephen Foster Story" outdoor musical during the summer months. **Federal Hill** is a Georgian-style mansion and formal gardens. **The Civil War Museum** contains rare artifacts, photos, uniforms, cannons, flags, battle wagons, medical equipment, weapons and personal items. The museum focuses on the western states involved in the war.

Elizabethtown. Walking tours are led by characters such as Carrie Nation, George Armstrong Custer, Sara Bush Lincoln, P.T. Barnum and Jenny Lind.

Louisville. Hop the **Toonerville II Trolley** or opt for a leisurely carriage ride on the **Louisville Horse Trams**. Cruise the Ohio River aboard the **Belle of Louisville**, or the **Star of Louisville. Louisville Zoo** offers seasonal camel and elephant rides. If it's a thrill you're looking for, check out **Six Flags Kentucky Kingdom.** Art enthusiasts won't want to miss the **Kentucky Center** with its 3 stages of entertainment, the **Speed Art Museum and GlassWorks**. For an all-star experience admire the world's largest baseball bat at the **Louisville Slugger Museum and Factory.** The **Kentucky Derby Festival** and the **Thunder Over Louisville** fireworks extravaganza is the prelude to the one and only **Kentucky Derby**. Visit the **Kentucky Derby Museum** next to Churchill Downs. It features exhibits, computerized hands-on displays, memorabilia and a multimedia show that captures the thrill of the race.

NORTHERN KENTUCKY RIVER REGION

Covington Landing, Covington. This riverfront showcase offers outstanding views of the Cincinnati skyline and entertainment. **Newport on the Levee** is an entertainment center housing the Newport Aquarium and numerous restaurants and shops. 'Ride the Ducks' takes you on a splashing sightseeing tour of the Newport area and the Ohio River in an amphibious vehicle.

SOUTHERN LAKES REGION

Big South Fork National River and Recreation Area offers a variety of natural and historical sights and activities. Aboard the **Big South Fork Scenic Railway** take the 16-mile round-trip tour and ride next to spectacular gorges along the river. The train also includes visits to the **McCreary County Museum** and the **Blue Heron Coal Mining Camp**.

See some of the most pristine lakes in the country and be sure not to miss **Cumberland Falls** - the only place to see a moonbow during a full moon in the Northern Hemisphere.

WESTERN WATERLANDS REGION

Hopkinsville. The 19.7-acre **Trail of Tears Commemorative Park** is one of the few documented campsites along the 1,200-mile trail.

Fort Campbell, 15 miles south of Hopkinsville, is the headquarters of the 101st Airborne "Screaming Eagles" Division. Exhibits can be seen at the **Don F. Pratt Memorial Museum**, which displays historic aircraft including WWII cargo gliders and those of the C-119 and C-47 series.

Great River Road. A 40-mile portion of this scenic car and bike route passes through western Kentucky's Reelfoot National Wildlife Refuge to Columbus-Belmont State Park. **Reelfoot Lake** was formed by earthquakes in the early 1800s. The national wildlife refuge has a vast cypress swamp that is home to many wetland plants and animals.

Land Between the Lakes. Located between Kentucky Lake and Lake Barkley, this 40-mile-long peninsula offers unlimited opportunities for camping, swimming, fishing, boating and hiking. Also on-site is the **Golden Pond Visitor Center** for maps and a list of attractions, nature center, planetarium and living history farm. In January, guides lead visitors to nesting sites of Bald and Golden eagles during the **Gathering of Eagles** weekend.

Paducah. Known as "Quilt City USA," visit the **National Quilt Museum** located in this historic town. Various exhibits are on display in three galleries. The lobby features a quality museum shop and sunlit stained glass windows based on quilt patterns. Also see Paducah's colorful history depicted in over 30 spectacular murals painted on the city's floodwall. The 1905 brick **Market House** is home to the **Yeiser Art Center**, the **William Clark Market House Museum** and the **Market House Theatre.**

Venture River Water Park, Eddyville. This waterpark is home to such rides as Hurricane Bay, Dueling Demons and Old Man River.

The Woods and Wetlands Wildlife Center, west of Cadiz. See the huge 12,000-gallon aquarium, home to native fish, reptiles and amphibians. A walk through the park features birds of prey and wild mammals.

ANNUAL EVENTS

JANUARY

Kentucky Opry Talent Show, Benton; Elk Viewing Tours, Prestonsburg/Buckhorn/Pineville; Eagle Watch, Burkesville/Gilbertsville/Cadiz; Annual Civil War Battle Observance, Nancy.

FEBRUARY

Edison Birthday Celebration, Louisville; Eagle Watch, Aurora/Burkesville; Elk Tours, Buckhorn/Prestonsburg; Great Backyard Bird Count, Henderson; Sandhill Crane Weekend, Lucas.

MARCH

Humana Festival of New American Plays, Louisville; Bluegrass Series, Renfro Valley; Battle of Paducah, Paducah; Kentucky Crafted the Market, Louisville.

APRIL

Chocolate Festival, Maysville; Thunder Over Louisville, Louisville; Kentucky Derby Festival, Louisville; Rolex Three Day Event, Lexington; Hillbilly Days, Pikeville; AQS National Quilt Show & Contest, Paducah.

ASHLAND—C-6

KOA Ashland/West Huntington—(Greenup) *From jct I-64 (exit 179) & Hwy 67: Go 3/4 mi N on Hwy 67, then 500 ft W on Longtown Rd, then 500 ft N on E Park Dr. Enter on L.* ◆◆◆FACILITIES: 92 sites, 92 full hkups, (30/50 amps), 62 pull-thrus, family camping, tenting, dump, laundry, ltd groc. ◆◆◆◆RECREATION: swim pool, pond fishing, playground. Pets welcome, breed restrict. Partial handicap access. Open all yr. Facilities fully operational May 15 - Sep 30. Big rigs welcome. Rate in 2010 $32.76-42.76 for 5 persons. Phone: (606)929-5504. KOA discount.

AURORA—B-2

(W) Aurora Oaks Campground—(Marshall) *From jct US 68 & SR 80: Go 250 yds E on US 68/SR 80, then 500 yds N on KOA Ln. Enter at end.* ◆◆FACILITIES: 59 sites, typical site width 25 ft, accepts full hkup units only, 59 full hkups, (30/50 amps), 7 pull-thrus, family camping, laundry. ◆RECREATION: swim pool, pond fishing, play equipment. Pets welcome. No tents. Open Mar 15 - Nov 15. Rate in 2010 $24-26 for 2 persons. Phone: (888)886-8704.

(E) KENLAKE STATE RESORT PARK—(Marshall) *From jct Hwy 80 & Hwy 94: Go 1/10 mi N on Hwy 94. Enter on R.* FACILITIES: 90 sites, 90 W&E, tenting, dump, laundry. RECREATION: swim pool, boating, ramp, dock, lake fishing, playground. Pets welcome. Open Mar 31 - Oct 31. Phone: (800)325-0143.

(W) Lakeside Campground & Marina—(Marshall) *From jct SR 80 & US 68: Go 3-3/4 mi N on US 68. Enter on R.* ◆◆◆FACILITIES: 135 sites, typical site width 20 ft, 50 full hkups, 85 W&E, (30 amps), 1 pull-thrus, family camping, tenting, dump. ◆◆◆RECREATION: swim pool, boating, ramp, dock, lake fishing, playground. Pets welcome. Open 3rd wknd in Mar. - Oct 31. Facilities fully operational Memorial Day - Labor Day. Rate in 2010 $26-28 for 2 persons. Phone: (270) 354-8157.

BARDSTOWN—D-3

(NW) Holt's Campground (Not Visited)—(Nelson) *From jct Blue Grass Pky & US 31E: Go 2 mi N on US 31E, then 1/4 mi E on US 62, then 1-1/4 mi W on US 150, then 1-3/4 mi W on SR 245, then 100 yards S on SR 1430. Enter on R.* ◆◆FACILITIES: 60 sites, typical site width 30 ft, 8 full hkups, 32 W&E, (30/50 amps), 20 no hkups, 32 pull-thrus, tenting, dump. RECREATION: lake fishing. Pets welcome. Open all yr. Big rigs welcome. Rate in 2010 $20 for 2 persons. Phone: (502)348-6717. FCRV discount. FMCA discount.

(E) MY OLD KENTUCKY HOME SP—(Nelson) *From jct Blue-Grass Pky & US 31E: Go 2 mi N on US 31E, then 1/4 mi E on US 62, then 3/4 mi E on US 150, then 1/2 mi S on SR 49.* FACILITIES: 39 sites, 39 W&E, tenting, dump. RECREATION: playground. Pets welcome. Open Mar 17 - Nov 17. Phone: (502)348-3502.

(W) White Acres Campground (Not Visited)—(Nelson) *From jct Blue Grass Pky & US 31E: Go 2 mi N on US 31E, then 2-1/4 mi W on US 62. Enter on R.* ◆◆FACILITIES: 82 sites, typical site width 35 ft, 12 full

BARDSTOWN—Continued
White Acres Campground (Not Visited)—Continued

hkups, 50 W&E, (30/50 amps), 20 no hkups, 40 pull-thrus, family camping, tenting, dump. ◆◆RECREATION: pond fishing, play equipment. Pets welcome. Open all yr. Big rigs welcome. Rate in 2010 $26 for 2 persons. Phone: (502)348-9677. FCRV discount. FMCA discount.

BENTON—B-2

(NE) Big Bear Resort—(Marshall) *From jct Purchase Pkwy & US 68: Go 4-1/2 mi S on US 68, then 3-1/2 mi E on Big Bear Hwy/SR 58. Enter on L.* ◆◆◆FACILITIES: 75 sites, typical site width 24 ft, 15 full hkups, 57 W&E, (30 amps), 3 no hkups, 10 pull-thrus, family camping, tenting, dump, groceries. ◆◆RECREATION: swim pool, lake swim, boating, ramp, dock, lake fishing, play equipment. No pets. Open Apr 1 - Oct 31. Facilities fully operational Memorial Day - Labor Day. Rate in 2010 $27-38 for 2 persons. Phone: (800)922-BEAR.

Reserve Online at Woodalls.com

BEREA—D-4

OH KENTUCKY CAMPGROUND—(Madison) *From jct I-75 (exit 76) & SR 21: Go 1/2 mi W on SR 21. Enter on R.*

WELCOME

◆◆◆FACILITIES: 80 sites, typical site width 20 ft, 42 full hkups, 29 W&E, (30/50 amps), 9 no hkups, many extd stay sites, 71 pull-thrus, WiFi Instant Internet at site, family camping, tenting, RV storage, dump, non-guest dump $, laundry, groceries, RV supplies, LP gas by weight/by meter, ice, picnic tables, fire rings, wood.

◆◆RECREATION: rec hall, swim pool, playground, horseshoes, v-ball.

Pets welcome. Partial handicap access. Open all yr. Pools open Memorial Day to Labor Day. Big rigs welcome. Clubs welcome. Rate in 2010 $20-22 for 2 persons. MC/VISA/DISC/AMEX/Debit.

Phone: (859)986-1150
Address: 562 Paint Lick Rd, Berea, KY 40403
Lat/Lon: 37.56683/-84.32235
Email: dbowman@gmail.com
Web: www.ohkentuckycampground.com

SEE AD THIS PAGE

Walnut Meadow RV Park—(Madison) *From jct I-75 (exit 76) & SR 21: Go 3/4 mi W on SR 21. Enter on L.* ◆◆◆FACILITIES: 105 sites, typical site width 25 ft, 61 full hkups, 44 W&E, (20/30/50 amps), 59 pull-thrus, WiFi Instant Internet at site, family camping, tenting, RV storage, dump, non-guest dump $, laundry, LP gas by weight/by meter, ice, picnic tables, fire rings, wood. ◆◆RECREATION: bsktball, playground, activities, horseshoes, hiking trails, v-ball. Pets welcome. Partial handicap access. Open all yr. Big rigs welcome. Rate in 2010 $24-26 for 2 persons. MC/VISA/DISC/AMEX/Debit. CCUSA 50% Discount. CCUSA max stay 1 day. Discount available on water & electric sites. Sewer $3 addl, if available.Reservations recommended 1 week prior to stay.

CAMPCLUB USA

Phone: (859)986-6180
Address: 711 Paint Lick Rd, Berea, KY 40403
Lat/Lon: 37.56490/-84.32368
Web: www.walnutmeadowcampground.com

BOWLING GREEN—E-2

(SE) KOA-Bowling Green—(Warren) From jct I-65 & US 231: Go 1/2 mi N on US 231, then 1-1/2 mi S on Three Springs Rd. Enter on R. ◆◆◆FACILITIES: 148 sites, typical site width 30 ft, 82 full hkups, 37 W&E, (30/50 amps), 29 no hkups, 78 pull-thrus, family camping, tenting, dump, laundry, groceries. ◆◆◆RECREATION: swim pool, lake fishing, playground. Pets welcome. Partial handicap access. Open all yr. Big rigs welcome. Rate in 2010 $28.87-53.17 for 2 persons. Phone: (270)843-1919. KOA discount.

BUCKHORN—D-5

(S) BUCKHORN DAM RECREATION AREA (COE-Buckhorn Lake)—(Perry) *From town: Go 1/2 mi S on Buckhorn Dam Rd.* FACILITIES: 33 sites, 29 W&E, 4 no hkups, tenting, dump, laundry. RECREATION: lake swim, boating, canoeing, ramp, dock, lake/river fishing, playground. Pets welcome. Open April - Sep 30. Phone: (606)398-7251.

BUCKHORN—Continued

(S) TAILWATER CAMPGROUND (COE-Buckhorn Lake)—(Leslie) *From jct Hwy 28 & Old Hwy 28: Go 1/2 mi S on Old Hwy 28 (follow signs).* FACILITIES: 30 sites, 30 W&E, tenting, dump, laundry. RECREATION: ramp, lake/river fishing, playground. Pets welcome. Open Mid Apr - Mid Oct. Phone: (606)398-7220.

BURKESVILLE—E-3

(S) DALE HOLLOW LAKE STATE PARK—(Cumberland) *From town: Go 5 mi E on Hwy 90, then 5 mi SW on Hwy 449, then 3 mi S on Hwy 1206.* FACILITIES: 145 sites, 145 W&E, tenting, dump, laundry. RECREATION: swim pool, boating, ramp, dock, lake fishing, playground. Pets welcome. Open all yr. Phone: (270) 433-7431.

(S) Sulphur Creek Resort (Not Visited)—(Cumberland) *From jct SR 90 & SR 61: Go 6-1/4 mi S on SR 61, then 1/2 mi E on Hwy 449, then 3-1/2 mi S on SR 485. Enter at end.* ◆◆◆FACILITIES: 22 sites, typical site width 22 ft, 9 full hkups, 13 W&E, (30 amps), 2 pull-thrus, tenting, dump, laundry, groceries. ◆◆◆RECREATION: lake swim, boating, canoeing, ramp, dock, lake fishing, playground. Pets welcome. Open Apr 1 - Oct 31. Rate in 2010 $25 for 2 persons. Member COAK. Phone: (270)433-7200.

BURNSIDE—E-4

(S) GENERAL BURNSIDE STATE PARK—(Pulaski) *From jct US 27 & Hwy 90: Go 2 mi S on US 27.* FACILITIES: 94 sites, 94 W&E, tenting, dump, laundry. RECREATION: swim pool, lake swim, boating, ramp, lake fishing, playground. Pets welcome. Open Apr 1 - Oct 31. Phone: (606)561-4104.

(SW) Lake Cumberland RV Park—(Pulaski) *From jct US 27 & Hwy 90: Go 1-1/2 mi W on Hwy 90, then 1/4 mi N on Gibson Ln. Enter on L.* ◆◆◆◆FACILITIES: 102 sites, typical site width 35 ft, 102 full hkups, (30/50 amps), 16 pull-thrus, family camping, tenting, laundry. ◆◆◆RECREATION: swim pool, play equipment. Pets welcome, breed restrict. Partial handicap access. Open all yr. Facilities fully operational May 1 - Nov 1. Big rigs welcome. Rate in 2010 $20-22 per family. Phone: (606)561-8222.

CADIZ—E-1

(NW) HURRICANE CREEK RECREATIONAL AREA (COE-Lake Barkley)—(Trigg) *From jct US 68 & Hwy 139: Go 6-1/2 mi N on Hwy 139, then 7 mi W on Hwy 276, then 1/2 mi N on Hwy 274.* FACILITIES: 51 sites, 51 W&E, (20/30 amps), tenting, dump, laundry, ltd groc. RECREATION: lake swim, boating, ramp, lake fishing, playground. Pets welcome. Open Apr 29 - Sep 5. Phone: (270)522-8821.

(NW) Kentucky Lakes KOA at Prizer Point—(Trigg) *From jct I-24 (exit 56) & Hwy 139: Go 1-1/2 mi S on Hwy 139, then 6 mi W on Hwy 276, then 1/4 mi S on Hwy 274, then 1 mi W on Prizer Point Rd. Enter on R.* ◆◆◆◆FACILITIES: 112 sites, typical site width 40 ft, 73 full hkups, 29 W&E, (30/50 amps), 50 amps ($), 10 no hkups, 52 pull-thrus, family camping, tenting, dump, laundry, full svc store. ◆◆◆◆◆RECREATION: 2 swim pools, lake swim, boating, canoeing, ramp, dock, lake/river fishing, playground. Pets welcome. Partial handicap access. Open Mid Mar - Nov 30. Big rigs welcome. Rate in 2010 $36-85 for 6 persons. Member ARVC. Phone: (270)522-3762. KOA discount.

(W) LAKE BARKLEY STATE RESORT PARK—(Trigg) *From jct Hwy 80 & US 68: Go 7 mi W on Hwy 80, then 2 mi N on Hwy 1489.* FACILITIES: 78 sites, 78 W&E, tenting, dump, laundry. RECREATION: lake swim, boating, ramp, dock, lake fishing, playground. Pets welcome. Open April - October. Phone: (800)325-1708.

CALVERT CITY—B-2

(S) Cypress Lakes RV Park—(Marshall) *From jct I-24 (exit 27) & US 62: Go 1/2 mi W on US 62. Enter on R.* ◆◆◆FACILITIES: 130 sites, typical site width 30 ft, 122 full hkups, 8 W&E, (30/50 amps), 11 pull-thrus, family camping, tenting, dump, laundry. ◆◆RECREATION: swim pool, lake fishing, playground. Pets welcome. Open all yr. Big rigs welcome. Rate in 2010 $21-23 for 2 persons. Phone: (270)395-4267.

(S) KOA-KY Lake Dam/Paducah—(Marshall) *From jct I-24 (exit 27) & US 62: Go 1-1/2 mi W on US 62. Enter on L.* ◆◆◆FACILITIES: 85 sites, typical site width 24 ft, 25 full hkups, 40 W&E, (20/30/50 amps), 20 no hkups, 55 pull-thrus, family camping, tenting, dump, laundry, groceries. ◆◆◆RECREATION: swim pool, pond fishing, playground. Pets welcome, breed restrict. Open Mar 15 - Nov 15. Big rigs welcome. Rate in 2010 $30-40 for 2 persons. Phone: (270)395-5841. KOA discount.

Farmers in Kentucky grow large crops of tobacco, corn and hay.

CAMPBELLSVILLE—D-3

(S) GREEN RIVER LAKE STATE PARK—(Taylor) *From jct Hwy 70 & Hwy 55: Go 8 mi S on Hwy 55.* FACILITIES: 157 sites, 157 W&E, tenting, dump, laundry, groceries. RECREATION: lake swim, boating, ramp, dock, river fishing, playground. Pets welcome. Open Mar 1 - Nov 30. Phone: (270)465-8255.

(S) HOLMES BEND RECREATION AREA (COE-Green River Lake)—(Adair) *From jct Hwy 55 & Hwy 70: Go 12 mi S on Hwy 55, then 6 mi N on Holmes Bend Road, follow signs.* FACILITIES: 125 sites, 42 W&E, 60 E, 23 no hkups, tenting, dump, groceries. RECREATION: lake swim, boating, ramp, dock, lake fishing, playground. Pets welcome. Open Apr 15 - Oct 22. Phone: (270)465-4463.

(S) Indian Ridge Campground—(Taylor) *From jct US 68 & SR 55: Go 10 Mi S on SR 55. Enter on R.* ◆◆◆FACILITIES: 86 sites, 20 full hkups, 66 W&E, (20/30/50 amps), 39 pull-thrus, family camping, tenting, dump, laundry, ltd groc. ◆◆◆RECREATION: swim pool, river fishing, playground. Pets welcome. Open all yr. Big rigs welcome. Rate in 2010 $25-30 for 4 persons. Phone: (270)465-7697.

(SW) PIKE RIDGE (COE-Green River Lake)—(Taylor) *From jct Hwy 55 & Hwy 70: Go 3 mi E on Hwy 70, then 3 mi SE on Hwy 76, then S at sign.* FACILITIES: 60 sites, 60 no hkups, tenting, dump, ltd groc. RECREATION: lake swim, boating, canoeing, ramp, lake/river/stream fishing, playground. Pets welcome. Partial handicap access. Open Mid Apr - Mid Sep. Phone: (270) 465-6488.

(SE) SMITH RIDGE (COE - Green River Lake)—(Taylor) *From jct Hwy 55 & Hwy 70: Go 1 mi E on Hwy 70, then 4 mi S on Hwy 372.* FACILITIES: 80 sites, 31 W&E, 31 E, 18 no hkups, 1 pull-thrus, tenting, dump, ltd groc. RECREATION: lake/river swim, boating, ramp, lake/river/stream fishing, playground. Pets welcome. Open Apr 18 - Sep 27. Phone: (270)789-2743.

CARROLLTON—B-3

(S) GENERAL BUTLER STATE RESORT PARK—(Carroll) *From town: Go 1 mi S on US 227.* FACILITIES: 111 sites, 111 W&E, tenting, dump, laundry. RECREATION: boating, no motors, canoeing, ramp, dock, lake fishing, playground. Pets welcome. Open all yr. Phone: (866)462-8853.

CAVE CITY—D-3

(E) CAVE COUNTRY RV CAMPGROUND —(Barren) *From jct I-65 & SR 70/90 (exit 53): Go 1/2 mi E on SR 90, then 350 yds N on Sanders St., then 350 yds E on Gaunce Dr. Enter at end.*

WELCOME

◆◆◆FACILITIES: 51 sites, typical site width 40 ft, 51 full hkups, (30/50 amps), some extd stay sites, 51 pull-thrus, cable TV, WiFi Instant Internet at site, family camping, RV storage, laundry, RV supplies, LP gas by weight/by meter, ice, picnic tables, fire rings, wood.

◆◆RECREATION: rec hall, rec room/area, pavilion, golf nearby, horseshoes.

Pets welcome. Partial handicap access. Open all yr. Big rigs welcome. Clubs welcome. Rate in 2010 $32-34 for 2 persons. MC/VISA/Debit. Member ARVC. FMCA discount.

Phone: (270)773-4678
Address: 216 Gaunce Dr, Cave City, KY 42127
Lat/Lon: 37.13427/-85.96801
Email: office@cavecountryrv.com
Web: www.cavecountryrv.com

SEE AD THIS PAGE

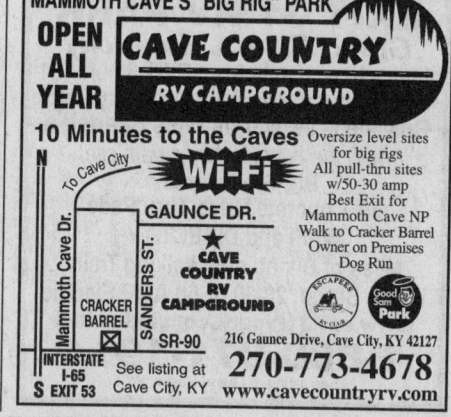

(W) Mammoth Cave Jellystone Park Camp Resort—(Barren) *From jct I-65 (Exit 53) & SR-70: Go 1 mi W on SR 70. Enter on R.* ◆◆◆◆FACILITIES: 181 sites, typical site width 30 ft, 89 full hkups, 42 W&E, (30/50 amps), 50 no hkups, 100 pull-thrus, family camping, tenting, dump, laundry, groceries. ◆◆◆◆◆RECREATION: swim pool, pond fishing, playground. Pets welcome, breed restrict, quantity restrict. Partial handicap access. Open all yr. Big rigs welcome. Rate in 2010 $25-55 per family. Member ARVC. Phone: (800)523-1854.

(W) Singing Hills Campground and RV Park—(Barren) *From jct I-65 (exit 53) & SR 70: Go 2-1/2 mi W on SR 70. Enter on R.* ◆◆◆FACILITIES: 31 sites, 17 full hkups, 14 W&E, (20/30/50 amps), 22 pull-thrus, WiFi Instant Internet at site, WiFi Internet central location, family camping, tenting, dump, non-guest dump $, LP gas by weight/by meter, ice, picnic tables, fire rings, grills, wood. RECREATION: pond fishing, play equipment. Pets welcome. Partial handicap access. Open all yr. Big rigs welcome. Rate in 2010 $28-32 for 5 persons. MC/VISA. FMCA discount. CCUSA 50% Discount. CCUSA reservations Recommended, CCUSA max stay 2 days. Unlimited stay at 25% discount.

CAMPCLUB USA

Phone: (270)773-3789
Address: 4110 Mammoth Cave Rd, Cave City, KY 42127
Lat/Lon: 37.13311/-86.02228
Email: ebrown@outdrs.net
Web: www.singinghillsrvpark.com

CENTRAL CITY—D-2

(S) Western Kentucky RV Park (Not Visited)—(Muhlenberg) *From jct Western Ky Pkwy & Hwy 431: Go 1/4 mi S on Hwy 431, then 1/4 mi E on Youngstown Rd. Enter on L.* ◆◆FACILITIES: 50 sites, typical site

CENTRAL CITY—Continued
Western Kentucky RV Park (Not Visited)—Continued

width 30 ft, accepts full hkup units only, 50 full hkups, (30/50 amps), 50 pull-thrus, family camping. ◆RECREATION: playground. Pets welcome. No tents. Open all yr. Big rigs welcome. Rate in 2010 $20 per vehicle. Phone: (270)757-0345.

COLUMBUS—B-1

(N) COLUMBUS - BELMONT STATE PARK—(Hickman) *From town: Take Hwy 80 & follow signs.* FACILITIES: 38 sites, 38 W&E, tenting, dump, laundry. RECREATION: river swim, boating, ramp, playground. Pets welcome. Open all yr. Phone: (270)677-2327.

CORBIN—E-4

(NE) Corbin-KOA—(Laurel) *From jct I-75 (exit 29) & US 25 E: Go 1/2 mi W, then first left hand turn after passing Love's Station. Enter on L.* ◆◆◆◆FACILITIES: 40 sites, typical site width 18 ft, 25 full hkups, 15 W&E, (20/30/50 amps), 36 pull-thrus, family camping, tenting, dump, laundry, groceries. ◆◆◆RECREATION: swim pool, playground. Pets welcome, breed restrict. Open all yr. Big rigs welcome. Rate in 2010 $36-48 for 2 persons. Phone: (606)528-1534. KOA discount.

(SW) CUMBERLAND FALLS STATE RESORT PARK—(Whitley) *From I-75 (Corbin exit): Go 8 mi S on US 25W, then 8 mi W on Hwy 90.* FACILITIES: 50 sites, 50 full hkups, tenting, dump, laundry, groceries. RECREATION: swim pool, river fishing, playground. Pets welcome. Open Apr 1 - Oct 31. Phone: (800)325-0063.

(W) DANIEL BOONE NATIONAL FOREST (Grove Boat-In Campground)—(Whitley) *From town: Go 5 mi SW on US 25, then 2 mi N on Hwy 1193, then 3-1/2 mi NE on FR 558 to boat ramp. Then 1 mi by private boat on the Laurel River Lake.* FACILITIES: 31 sites, 31 no hkups, tenting, dump. RECREATION: lake swim, boating, canoeing, ramp, lake fishing. Pets welcome. Partial handicap access. Open all yr. Phone: (606)528-6156.

(W) DANIEL BOONE NATIONAL FOREST (Grove Campground)—(Whitley) *From town: Go 5 mi W on US 25, then 2 mi N on Hwy 1193, then 3 mi NE on FR 558.* FACILITIES: 54 sites, 32 ft max RV length, 54 W&E, (20/30 amps), tenting, dump. RECREATION: lake swim, boating, canoeing, ramp, dock, lake fishing. Pets welcome. Partial handicap access. Open Apr 11 - Oct 12. Phone: (606)864-4163.

CRITTENDEN—B-4

(S) Cincinnati South Rose Garden Resort—(Grant) *From jct I-75 (exit 166) & US 25: Go 1/4 mi E on Hwy 491, then 2-1/2 mi S on US 25. Enter on R.* ◆◆◆◆FACILITIES: 101 sites, typical site width 35 ft, 27 full hkups, 66 W&E, (30/50 amps), 50 amps ($), 62 pull-thrus, family camping, tenting, dump, laundry, groceries. ◆◆◆◆RECREATION: swim pool, boating, dock, lake fishing, playground. Pets welcome. Partial handicap access. Open Mar 1 - Dec 1. Big rigs welcome. Rate in 2010 $23-33 for 2 persons. Member ARVC, OCOA. Phone: (866)477-0024.

DAWSON SPRINGS—D-1

(S) PENNYRILE FOREST STATE RESORT PARK—(Christian) *From jct US-62 & Hwy-109: Go 5 mi S on Hwy-109.* FACILITIES: 68 sites, 68 W&E, tenting, dump, laundry, groceries. RECREATION: lake swim, boating, no motors, canoeing, dock, lake fishing, playground. Pets welcome. Open Mar 15 - Oct 31. Phone: (800)325-1711.

DRAKESBORO—D-2

(W) Gregory Lake RV Park—(Muhlenberg) *From US 431 & SR 176: Go 1-1/2 mi W on SR 176. Enter on L.* ◆◆FACILITIES: 117 sites, typical site width 50 ft, 84 full hkups, 33 W&E, (30/50 amps), 50 pull-thrus, family camping, tenting, dump, laundry, groceries. ◆◆◆◆RECREATION: boating, electric motors only, canoeing, ramp, lake fishing, playground. Pets welcome. Partial handicap access. Open all yr. Big rigs welcome. Rate in 2010 $20-25 for 2 persons. Phone: (270)476-9223.

DRY RIDGE—B-4

(NW) I-75 Camper Village—(Grant) *From jct I-75 (exit 159) & Hwy 22: Go 50 yards W on Hwy 22, then 1 mi N on service road. Enter at end.* ◆◆FACILITIES: 55 sites, typical site width 30 ft, 45 full hkups, (20/30/50 amps), 10 no hkups, 13 pull-thrus, family camping, tenting, dump, laundry. ◆◆RECREATION: boating, 10 hp limit, ramp, dock, lake fishing, play equipment. Pets welcome. Open all yr. Rate in 2010 $21.60-25 for 2 persons. Phone: (859)824-5836.

DUNMOR—E-2

(E) Dogwood Lakes Camping & Resort (Not Visited)—(Muhlenberg) *From jct US 431 & SR 973: Go 1 mi E on SR 973. Enter on R.* ◆◆FACILITIES: 160 sites, typical site width 25 ft, 110 full hkups, 50 W&E, (30 amps), 40 pull-thrus, family camping, tenting, dump, ltd groc. ◆◆◆◆RECREATION: lake swim, pond fishing, playground. Pets welcome ($). Partial handicap access. Open all yr. Facilities fully operational Mar 15 - Oct 15. Rate in 2010 $25-29. Phone: (270)657-8380.

(W) LAKE MALONE STATE PARK—(Muhlenberg) *From jct US 431 & 973: Go 3-1/4 mi W & N.* FACILITIES: 55 sites, 25 W&E, 30 no hkups, tenting, dump, laundry. RECREATION: lake swim, boating, ramp, dock, lake fishing, playground. Pets welcome. Open Mid Mar - Mid Dec. Phone: (270)657-2111.

EDDYVILLE—D-1

(SE) Holiday Hills Resort—(Lyon) *From jct I-24 (exit 45) & SR 293: Go 100 yards W on SR 293, then 2 mi S on SR 93. Enter on L.* ◆◆◆◆FACILITIES: 125 sites, typical site width 22 ft, 34 ft max RV length, 90 full hkups, 35 W&E, (30/50 amps), 30 pull-thrus, family camping, tenting, dump, laundry, groceries. ◆◆◆◆RECREATION: swim pool, lake swim, boating, canoeing, ramp, dock, lake fishing, playground. Pets welcome. Open Mid Mar - Oct 31. Rate in 2010 $34-38 for 4 persons. Phone: (800)337-8550.

✱ **(S) MURPHY'S RV'S**—*From jct I-24 (exit 45) & SR 293: Go 400 yds W on SR 293, then 1 mi S on SR 293. Enter on L.* SALES: travel trailers, park models, 5th wheels, pre-owned unit sales. SERVICES: full-time mech, RV appliance repair, RV storage, sells parts/accessories, installs hitches. Open Mar 1 - Nov 1. MC/VISA/DISC/Debit.

WELCOME

Phone: (800)910-7275
Address: 4481 State Road 93S, Eddyville, KY 42038
Lat/Lon: 37.12181/-87.85461
Email: murphysrv@bellsouth.net
Web: www.murphysrv.com

SEE AD THIS PAGE

(S) OUTBACK RV RESORT—(Lyon) *From jct I-24 (exit 45) & SR 293: Go 400 yards W on SR 293, then 1 mi S on SR 93. Enter on L.*

WELCOME

◆◆◆◆FACILITIES: 95 sites, typical site width 30 ft, 95 full hkups, (30/50 amps), many extd stay sites (summer), 75 pull-thrus, WiFi Instant Internet at site, phone Internet central location, laundry, picnic tables, fire rings.

◆◆RECREATION: equipped pavilion, swim pool, golf nearby, playground, activities, (wkends), horseshoes, hiking trails.

Pets welcome. Partial handicap access. No tents. Open Apr 1 - Nov 1. Pool open Memorial Day to Labor Day. Big rigs welcome. Escort to site. Clubs welcome. Rate in 2010 $32 for 2 persons. MC/VISA/DISC/Debit.

Phone: (800)910-7275
Address: 4481 State Route 93 S, Eddyville, KY 42038
Lat/Lon: 37.04356/-88.03175
Email: murphysrv2@bellsouth.net
Web: www.murphysrv.com

SEE AD THIS PAGE AND AD TRAVEL SECTION PAGE 263

ELIZABETHTOWN—D-3

(NE) Elizabethtown Crossroads Campground—(Hardin) *From jct I-65 (Exit 94) & US-62: Go 1 mi E on US-62, then 1/4 mi N on Tunnel Hill Rd. Enter on L.* ◆◆FACILITIES: 50 sites, typical site width 30 ft, 23

Elizabethtown Crossroads Campground—Continued on next page

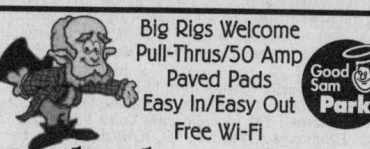

ELIZABETHTOWN—Continued
Elizabethtown Crossroads Campground—Continued

full hkups, 27 W&E, (30/50 amps), 22 pull-thrus, family camping, tenting, dump, laundry, ltd groc. ◇◇◇RECREATION: swim pool, play equipment. Pets welcome, breed restrict. Open all yr. Big rigs welcome. Rate in 2010 $28-30 for 2 persons. Phone: (800)975-6521.

(S) Glendale Campground—(Hardin) *From jct I-65 & SR 222: Go 1/2 mi E on SR 222 until T in road, then left 3/4 mi N on Sportsman Lake Rd. Enter on R.* ◇◇FACILITIES: 72 sites, typical site width 33 ft, 17 full hkups, 55 W&E, (20/30/50 amps), 30 pull-thrus, cable TV, ($), WiFi Instant Internet at site, phone on-site Internet (needs activ), phone Internet central location, RV storage, dump, laundry, ltd groc, RV supplies, ice, picnic tables, fire rings, wood. ◇◇◇RECREATION: rec hall, pavilion, swim pool, lake fishing, bsktball, playground, activities, horseshoes, hiking trails, v-ball. Pets welcome. Partial handicap access. Open all yr. Facilities fully operational Memorial Day - Oct 31. Big rigs welcome. Rate in 2010 $25-31 for 6 persons. MC/VISA/Debit. CCUSA 50% Discount. CCUSA reservations Required, CCUSA max stay 2 days, CCUSA disc. not avail F,Sa, CCUSA disc. not avail holidays. Nov-Apr: 6 back in, 30/50 amp, no water sites; 3 pull thru 30 amp, 2 full hookup w/cable/wireless. May-Sep 30 same sites have water. No site availability in Oct.

Phone: (270)369-7755
Address: 4566 Sportsman Lake Rd, Elizabethtown, KY 42701
Lat/Lon: 37.60389/-85.85612
Web: www.glendalecampground.com

ELKHORN CITY—D-6

(S) BREAKS INTERSTATE PARK—(Pike) *From town: Go 8 mi S on Hwy 80, then 2 mi NW on Park Rd. Enter on R.* FACILITIES: 122 sites, 34 ft max RV length, 37 full hkups, 58 W&E, 14 E, 13 no hkups, 20 pull-thrus, tenting, dump. RECREATION: swim pool, boating, electric motors only, canoeing, ramp, lake/river/pond fishing, playground. Pets welcome. Open Apr 1 - Oct 31. Phone: (800)982-5122.

FALLS OF ROUGH—D-2

(S) CAVE CREEK (COE-Rough River Lake)—(Grayson) *From jct Hwy 79 & Hwy 736: Go 1 mi E on Hwy 736.* FACILITIES: 86 sites, 16 E, 70 no hkups, tenting, dump. RECREATION: boating, canoeing, ramp, lake fishing, playground. Pets welcome. Open 3rd Fri in Apr - 3rd Sun in Sep. Phone: (270)879-4304.

(W) ROUGH RIVER DAM STATE RESORT PARK—(Grayson) *From jct Hwy 110 & Hwy 79: Go 3 mi NE on Hwy 79.* FACILITIES: 64 sites, 33 W&E, 31 E, (50 amps), 6 pull-thrus, tenting, dump, laundry. RECREATION: lake swim, boating, ramp, dock, lake fishing, playground. Pets welcome. Open Mid Mar - Mid Nov. Phone: (606)636-6450.

FALMOUTH—B-4

(E) KINCAID LAKE STATE PARK—(Pendleton) *From jct Hwy 22 & US 27: Go 4 mi N on Hwy 22 & Hwy 159.* FACILITIES: 84 sites, 84 W&E, (30/50 amps), tenting, dump, laundry, groceries. RECREATION: swim pool, boating, 10 hp limit, ramp, dock, lake fishing, playground. Pets welcome. Open Mid Mar - Mid Nov. Phone: (859)654-3531.

FRANKFORT—C-4

(E) ELKHORN CAMPGROUND—(Franklin) *From I-64 (exit 58) & US 60: Go 2-1/2 mi N on US 60, then 2-1/4 mi E on US 460, then 1/4 mi S on N Scruggs Ln. Enter on R.*

WELCOME

◇◇◇◇FACILITIES: 125 sites, typical site width 30 ft, 71 full hkups, 54 W&E, (30/50 amps), 50 amps ($), some extd stay sites, 30 pull-thrus, cable TV, WiFi Instant Internet at site, phone/cable on-site Internet (needs activ), WiFi Internet central location, family camping, tenting, RV storage, dump, non-guest dump $, laundry, ltd groc, RV supplies, LP gas by weight/by meter, ice, picnic tables, patios, fire rings, wood.

◇◇◇◇RECREATION: rec room/area, equipped pavilion, coin games, swim pool, stream fishing,

FRANKFORT—Continued
ELKHORN CAMPGROUND—Continued

fishing supplies, mini-golf, ($), golf nearby, bsktball, playground, shuffleboard court shuffleboard court, activities (wkends), horseshoes, v-ball.

Pets welcome, breed restrict. Partial handicap access. Open all yr. Facilities fully operational Apr 1 - Oct 31. Pool open Memorial Day to Labor Day. Big rigs welcome. Clubs welcome. Rate in 2010 $24-27 for 2 persons. MC/VISA/DISC/Debit.

Phone: (502)695-9154
Address: 165 No Scruggs Lane, Frankfort, KY 40601
Lat/Lon: 38.21059/-84.80096
Web: www.elkhorncampground.com

SEE AD LEXINGTON NEXT PAGE

(NE) Still Waters Campground—(Franklin) *From jct I-64 & US 60: Go 3 mi N on US 60, then 1-1/2 mi W on US 421 (Wilkenson Blvd), then 7-1/2 mi N on US 127, then 1/4 mi W on Strohmeier Rd. Enter at end.* ◇◇FACILITIES: 110 sites, typical site width 45 ft, 50 full hkups, 32 W&E, (20/30/50 amps), 28 no hkups, family camping, tenting, dump, ltd groc. ◇◇◇RECREATION: river swim, boating, canoeing, ramp, river fishing, playground. Pets welcome. Open all yr. Facilities fully operational Apr 1 - Oct 31. Rate in 2010 $20-26 per family. Phone: (502)223-8896.

FRANKLIN—E-2

(E) Bluegrass Music RV Park—(Simpson) *From jct I-65 (exit 6) & Hwy 100: Go 1/4 mi W on Hwy 100. Enter on L.* ◇◇◇◇FACILITIES: 120 sites, typical site width 30 ft, 88 full hkups, 8 E, (30/50 amps), 50 amps ($), 24 no hkups, 91 pull-thrus, WiFi Instant Internet at site, family camping, tenting, RV storage, dump, non-guest dump $, laundry, ltd groc, RV supplies, LP gas by weight/by meter, ice, picnic tables, fire rings, grills, wood. ◇◇◇◇RECREATION: rec hall, pavilion, swim pool, lake fishing, fishing supplies, playground, shuffleboard court shuffleboard court, activities, horseshoes, hiking trails, v-ball. Pets welcome. Open all yr. Big rigs welcome. Rate in 2010 $33.50-37.50 for 2 persons. MC/VISA/DISC. CCUSA 50% Discount. CCUSA max stay Unlimited. Reservations accepted for 3 or more days only.

Phone: (270)586-5622
Address: KOA Lane, Franklin, KY 42135
Lat/Lon: 36.71490/-86.52679
Email: bluegrassrv@gmail.com
Web: www.bluegrassmusicrvpark.com

GILBERTSVILLE—B-2

(SW) KENTUCKY DAM VILLAGE STATE RESORT PARK—(Marshall) *At jct US 62 & US 641.* FACILITIES: 219 sites, 219 W&E, (50 amps), tenting, dump, laundry, groceries. RECREATION: lake swim, boating, ramp, dock, lake fishing, playground. Pets welcome. Open all yr. Phone: (800)325-0146.

GLASGOW—E-3

(S) BARREN RIVER LAKE STATE RESORT PARK—(Barren) *From jct Hwy 90 & US 31E: Go 12 mi S on US 31E.* FACILITIES: 99 sites, 99 W&E, (30 amps), tenting, dump, laundry. RECREATION: lake swim, boating, ramp, dock, playground. Pets welcome. Open Apr 1 - Oct 31. Phone: (800)325-0057.

(SW) THE NARROWS (COE-Barren River Lake)—(Barren) *From jct Cumberland Pkwy & US 31E: Go 11 mi SW on US 31E, then W on CR (Lucas).* FACILITIES: 92 sites, 85 W&E, 7 no hkups, tenting, dump, laundry. RECREATION: lake swim, boating, canoeing, ramp, lake fishing, playground. Pets welcome. Open Apr 11 - Sep 13. Phone: (270)646-3094.

GOLDEN POND—E-1

(N) ENERGY LAKE (LBL) National Recreation Area—(Trigg) *From jct US 68 & Hwy 453 (The Trace): Go 6-1/2 mi N on The Trace, then 5 mi E on Mulberry Flat Rd, then 2 mi S on Energy Lake Rd.* FACILITIES: 48 sites, 35 E, (50 amps), 13 no hkups, 5 pull-thrus, tenting, laundry. RECREATION: lake swim, boating, canoeing, lake fishing, playground. Partial handicap access. Open Mar 1 - Nov 30. Phone: (270)924-2000.

(W) FENTON (LBL) National Recreation Area—(Trigg) *From jct The Trace (Hwy 453) & US 68: Go 3 mi W on US 68.* FACILITIES: 29 sites, 13 E, 16 no hkups, 9 pull-thrus, tenting. RECREATION: boating, canoeing, ramp, lake fishing. Open all yr. Phone: (270)924-2000.

(NE) HILLMAN FERRY CAMPGROUND (LBL)—(Lyon) *From jct Hwy 94/80/68: Go 5 mi E on Hwy 80/68, then 17 mi N on The Trace Rd, then 1/2 mi W on Rd 110. Enter at end.* FACILITIES: 379 sites, 88 full hkups, 143 W&E, 48 E, (30/50 amps), 100 no hkups, tenting. RECREATION: boating, ramp, dock, lake fishing, playground. Open Mar 1 - Nov 30. Phone: (270)362-8030.

(S) RUSHING CREEK (LBL) National Recreation Area—(Stewart) *From jct US-68 & The Trace (Hwy-453): Go 8 mi S on The Trace, then 1-1/2 mi on Rushing Creek Rd.* FACILITIES: 56 sites, 1 E, 55 no hkups, tenting. RECREATION: boating, canoeing, ramp, dock, lake fishing, playground. Open all yr. Facilities fully operational mid Mar - mid Oct. Phone: (270)924-2000.

WRANGLER (LBL) National Recreation Area—(Trigg) *From jct US 68/Hwy 80 & Hwy 453 (The Trace): Go 1/4 mi S on the Trace, then 6 mi E on CR 165. Enter on R.* FACILITIES: 168 sites, 18 full hkups, 2 W&E, 125 E, (50 amps), 23 no hkups, 7 pull-thrus, tenting, dump, laundry, ltd groc. RECREATION: playground. Partial handicap access. Open all yr. Phone: (270)924-2000.

GOLDEN POND—Continued

(SE) WRANGLERS CAMPGROUND (LBL)—(Trigg) *From jct Hwy 94/80/68: Go 5 mi E on Hwy 80/68, then 1 mi S on The Trace Rd, then 5 mi W on Rd 168. Enter on R.* FACILITIES: 184 sites, 18 full hkups, 2 W&E, 137 E, (30 amps), 27 no hkups, tenting, dump. RECREATION: playground. Open all yr. Phone: (270)924-2000.

GRAND RIVERS—B-2

(S) BIRMINGHAM FERRY (LBL) National Recreation Area—(Livingston) *From jct I-24 & The Trace (Hwy 453): Go 9 mi S on The Trace, then 3 mi W on Rd 114 (Old Ferry Rd).* FACILITIES: 26 sites, 26 no hkups, 1 pull-thrus, tenting. RECREATION: boating, canoeing, ramp, lake fishing. Partial handicap access. Open all yr. Phone: (502)924-2000.

(S) CANAL RECREATION AREA (COE-Lake Barkley)—(Livingston) *From town: Go 1 mi S on The Trace (Hwy-453).* FACILITIES: 110 sites, 110 W&E, tenting, dump, laundry. RECREATION: lake swim, boating, canoeing, ramp, lake fishing, playground. Pets welcome. Open Apr 5 - Oct 29. Phone: (270)362-4840.

(E) CRAVENS BAY (LBL) National Recreation Area—(Livingston) *From jct I-24 & The Trace (Hwy 453): Go 9 mi S on The Trace, then 5 mi E on Craven Bay Rd.* FACILITIES: 30 sites, 30 no hkups, tenting. RECREATION: boating, canoeing, ramp, lake fishing. Open all yr. Phone: (270)924-2000.

Crockett Frontier Campground—(Livingston) *Jct I-24 & SR 453 (exit 31): Take SR 453 S 3.2 mi, then L on W Commerce Ave, then L on SR 952, then .1 mi & turn L on Maxwell Dr. Enter on L.* ◇◇FACILITIES: 53 sites, typical site width 15 ft, 53 full hkups, (30/50 amps), 6 pull-thrus, family camping, tenting, laundry. ◇RECREATION: play equipment. Pets welcome. Partial handicap access. Open all yr. Big rigs welcome. Rate in 2010 $25 for 4 persons. Phone: (270)217-3432.

(N) EXIT 31 RV PARK—(Livingston) *From jct I-24 and Hwy 453 (exit 31): Go 1/10 mi S on Hwy 453. Enter on R.*

WELCOME

◇◇◇◇FACILITIES: 32 sites, accepts full hkup units only, 32 full hkups, (20/30/50 amps), some extd stay sites, 12 pull-thrus, cable TV, WiFi Instant Internet at site, WiFi Internet central location, family camping, laundry, picnic tables.

RECREATION: golf nearby, hiking trails.

Pets welcome, size restrict. No tents. Open all yr. No restrooms. Big rigs welcome. Rate in 2010 $22.50-35 per vehicle. MC/VISA/DISC/AMEX/Debit. CCUSA 50% Discount. CCUSA reservations Recommended, CCUSA max stay 7 days, CCUSA disc. not avail holidays. Accepts full hook-up units only.

Phone: (800)971-1914
Address: 708 Complex Dr, Grand Rivers, KY 42045
Lat/Lon: 37.03790/-88.26842
Email: exit31_rv_park@yahoo.com
Web: www.exit31rvpark.com/index.htm

SEE AD THIS PAGE AND AD TRAVEL SECTION PAGE 263

(S) HILLMAN FERRY (LBL) National Recreation Area—(Livingston) *From jct I-24 & The Trace (Hwy-453): Go 5 mi S on The Trace, then 1 mi W on Hillman Ferry Rd. Enter at end.* FACILITIES: 366 sites, typical site width 28 ft, 65 full hkups, 157 W&E, 45 E, (20/30/50 amps), 99 no hkups, 80 pull-thrus, tenting, dump, laundry, ltd groc. RECREATION: lake swim, boating, canoeing, ramp, dock, lake fishing, playground. Pets welcome. Partial handicap access. Open Mar 1 - Nov 30. Big rigs welcome. Phone: (270)924-2000.

(N) MISS SCARLETT'S RESTAURANT—*From jct I-24 & Hwy 453 (exit 31): Go 1/10 mi S on Hwy 453. Enter on R.* Restaurant at Exit 31 RV Park. Open all yr. MC/VISA/DISC/AMEX/Debit.

WELCOME

Phone: (800)971-1914
Address: 708 Complex Dr, Grand Rivers, KY 42045
Lat/Lon: 37.03790/-88.26842

SEE AD THIS PAGE

GRAYSON—C-5

(SW) GRAYSON LAKE STATE PARK—(Carter) *From jct US 60 & Hwy 7: Go 10 mi S on Hwy 7.* FACILITIES: 71 sites, 71 W&E, tenting, dump, laundry. RECREATION: lake swim, boating, ramp, dock, lake fishing, playground. Pets welcome. Open Apr 1 - Oct 31. Phone: (606)474-9727.

(S) Valley Breeze RV Campground (RV SPACES)—(Carter) *From jct I-64 (exit 172) & SR 7: Go 150 feet N on SR 7, then 3/4 mi W on Hwy 1947. Enter on R.* FACILITIES: 16 sites, typical site width 30 ft, accepts full hkup units only, 16 full hkups, (30/50 amps), 50 amps ($), 5 pull-thrus, family camping. Pets welcome. No tents. Open all yr. Big rigs welcome. Rate in 2010 $24-27 for 2 persons. Phone: (606)474-6779.

The Kentucky Derby is the oldest continuously-held horse race in the country. It is held at Churchill Downs in Louisville on the first Saturday in May.

GREENUP—B-6

(S) GREENBO LAKE STATE RESORT PARK—(Greenup) *From jct US 23 & Hwy 1: Go 8 mi SE on Hwy 1.* FACILITIES: 98 sites, 63 W&E, (20/30 amps), 35 no hkups, tenting, dump, laundry, groceries. RECREATION: swim pool, boating, 10 hp limit, canoeing, ramp, dock, lake fishing, playground. Pets welcome. Open Apr 1 - Oct 31. Phone: (800)325-0083.

HARTFORD—D-2

(E) OHIO COUNTY PARK—(Ohio) *From jct William Natcher Pkwy & Hwy 69: Go 1/2 mi N on Hwy 69. Enter on R.* FACILITIES: 75 sites, typical site width 24 ft, 75 W&E, (30/50 amps), 7 pull-thrus, tenting, dump, laundry. RECREATION: ramp, pond fishing, playground. Pets welcome. Partial handicap access. Open all yr. Phone: (270)298-4466.

HENDERSON—C-1

(N) JOHN JAMES AUDUBON STATE PARK—(Henderson) *From jct US 60 & US 41: Go 3 mi N on US 41.* FACILITIES: 69 sites, 69 W&E, (30 amps), tenting, dump, laundry. RECREATION: boating, no motors, canoeing, lake fishing, playground. Pets welcome. Partial handicap access. Open Mar 16 - Nov 30. Phone: (270)826-2247.

HOPKINSVILLE—E-1

MILITARY PARK (Eagle's Rest Army Travel Camp-Fort Campbell)—(Christian) *Off US 41A. On base.* FACILITIES: 41 sites, 16 full hkups, 25 W&E, tenting, dump, laundry, ltd groc. RECREATION: boating, lake fishing, playground. Pets welcome. Open all yr. Phone: (270)798-3126.

HORSE CAVE—D-3

(W) KOA-Horse Cave (Not Visited)—(Hart) *From jct I-65 (exit 58) & SR 218: Go 100 yards W on SR 218. Enter on L.* ◆◆FACILITIES: 45 sites, typical site width 25 ft, 11 full hkups, 29 W&E, 4 E, (20/30 amps), 1 no hkups, 30 pull-thrus, family camping, tenting, dump, laundry, groceries. ◆◆RECREATION: swim pool, pond fishing, playground. Pets welcome. Open all yr. Facilities fully operational Memorial Day - Labor Day. Rate in 2010 $22-29 for 2 persons. Phone: (270)786-2819. KOA discount.

HYDEN—D-5

(N) TRACE BRANCH (COE-Buckhorn Lake)—(Leslie) *From town: Go 6 mi N on Hwy 257, after passing under Daniel Boone Pkwy, turn E and cross Dry Hill Bridge, then 6 mi N on Grassy Branch Rd.* FACILITIES: 14 sites, 25 ft max RV length, 14 W&E, tenting, dump, laundry. RECREATION: lake swim, boating, canoeing, ramp, dock, lake fishing, playground. Pets welcome. Open May 1 - Sep 30. Facilities fully operational Memorial Day - Labor Day. Phone: (606)672-3670.

JAMESTOWN—E-3

(SW) KENDALL RECREATION AREA (COE-Lake Cumberland)—(Russell) *From jct US 127 & Hwy 92: Go 12 mi S on US 127.* FACILITIES: 108 sites, 108 W&E, tenting, dump, laundry, ltd groc. RECREATION: boating, canoeing, ramp, lake fishing, playground. Pets welcome. Open all yr. Phone: (270)343-4660.

(S) LAKE CUMBERLAND STATE RESORT PARK—(Russell) *From jct Hwy 92 & US 127: Go 14 mi S on US 127, then 5 mi E on Hwy 1370.* FACILITIES: 129 sites, 35 ft max RV length, 129 W&E, (30/50 amps), tenting, dump, laundry, groceries. RECREATION: swim pool, boating, dock, lake fishing, playground. Pets welcome. Open Mar 14 - Nov 29. Phone: (800)325-1709.

LAND BETWEEN THE LAKES—B-2

See listings at Aurora, Cadiz, Golden Pond & Grand Rivers

LEITCHFIELD—D-2

(S) DOG CREEK (COE - Nolin River Lake)—(Grayson) *From jct Hwy-259 & US-62: Go 4 mi E on US-62, then 11 mi S on Hwy-88, then 1 mi W on Hwy-1015.* FACILITIES: 70 sites, 24 W&E, 46 no hkups, tenting, dump. RECREATION: lake swim, boating, ramp, lake fishing, playground. Partial handicap access. Open Mid Apr - Late Sep. Phone: (270)524-5454.

(S) MOUTARDIER (COE-Nolin River Lake)—(Edmonson) *From jct US-62 & Hwy-259: Go 10 mi S on Hwy-259, then E.* FACILITIES: 167 sites, 81 W&E, 86 no hkups, tenting, dump, ltd groc. RECREATION: lake swim, boating, canoeing, ramp, dock, lake fishing, playground. Partial handicap access. Open Mid Apr - Late Oct. Phone: (270)286-4230.

(S) NOLIN LAKE STATE PARK—(Edmonson) *From jct US 62 & Hwy 259: Go 17 mi S on Hwy 259, then E and follow signs.* FACILITIES: 52 sites, 32 W&E, 20 no hkups, tenting, dump, laundry, groceries. RECREATION: lake swim, boating, ramp, lake fishing, playground. Pets welcome. Partial handicap access. Open Mid Mar - Mid Nov. Phone: (270)286-4240.

LEITCHFIELD—Continued

(W) WAX SITE (COE-Nolin River Lake)—(Edmonson) *From jct US 62 & Hwy 259: Go 4 mi E on US 62, then 14 mi S on Hwy 88.* FACILITIES: 110 sites, 56 W&E, 54 no hkups, tenting, dump, groceries. RECREATION: lake swim, boating, ramp, dock, lake fishing, playground. Pets welcome. Partial handicap access. Open Apr 18 - Sep 21. Phone: (270)242-7578.

LEXINGTON—C-4

KENTUCKY HORSE PARK (SP)—(Fayette) *From jct I-75 & US 27: Go 6-1/2 mi N on I-75, then 2 mi E on Ironworks Pike. Enter on L.* FACILITIES: 260 sites, typical site width 15 ft, 260 W&E, (50 amps), tenting, dump, laundry, full svc store. RECREATION: swim pool, pond fishing, playground. Pets welcome. Partial handicap access. Open all yr. Big rigs welcome. Phone: (859) 233-4303.

LONDON—D-4

(W) DANIEL BOONE NATIONAL FOREST (Holly Bay Rec. Area)—(Laurel) *From town: Go 20 mi SW on Hwy-192, then 2 mi SW on Hwy-1193, then 1 mi S on Hwy-770, then 1-1/2 mi E on FR-611.* FACILITIES: 94 sites, 32 ft max RV length, 75 W&E, 19 no hkups, tenting, dump. RECREATION: lake swim, boating, canoeing, ramp, dock, lake fishing. Pets welcome. Open Apr 9 - Oct 17. Phone: (606)864-4163.

(SW) DANIEL BOONE NATIONAL FOREST (White Oak Boat-In Campground)—(Laurel) *From town: Go 10 mi SW on Hwy 192, then 2 mi S on FR 774, then 1 mi S by private boat on the Laurel River Lake.* FACILITIES: 51 sites, 51 no hkups, tenting. RECREATION: lake swim, boating, ramp, lake fishing. Open all yr. Phone: (606)864-4163.

(S) LEVI JACKSON WILDERNESS ROAD STATE PARK—(Laurel) *From jct Hwy 80 & US 25: Go 3 mi S on US 25.* FACILITIES: 146 sites, 146 W&E, tenting, dump, laundry, groceries. RECREATION: swim pool, playground. Pets welcome. Open all yr. Phone: (606)878-8000.

(NW) WESTGATE RV CAMPING (RV SPACES)—(Laurel) *From jct I-75 (exit 41) & Hwy 80: Go 100 yards W on Hwy 80. Enter on R.*

FACILITIES: 14 sites, typical site width 18 ft, 14 full hkups, (30/50 amps), some extd stay sites, 4 pull-thrus, cable TV, WiFi Instant Internet at site, family camping, tenting, ice, picnic tables, grills.

RECREATION: pavilion, swim pool, playground.

Pets welcome. Open all yr. Facilities fully operational Memorial Day - Labor Day. Dump station at tourism office next door. Big rigs welcome. Rate in 2010 $25.25 for 2 persons. MC/VISA/DISC/AMEX/Debit.

Phone: (606)878-7330
Address: 254 Russell Dyche Memoral Hwy, London, KY 40741
Lat/Lon: 37.14896/-84.11603
Web: www.hikercentral.com/campgrounds/105295.htm

SEE AD THIS PAGE

LOUISA—C-6

(NW) The Falls Campground—(Lawrence) *From jct US 23 & Hwy 3: Go 5-1/2 mi N on Hwy 3. Enter on R.* ◆◆◆FACILITIES: 93 sites, 7 full hkups, 86 W&E, (30/50 amps), 50 amps ($), 12 pull-thrus, tenting, dump, laundry. ◆◆◆RECREATION: river swim, river fishing, playground. Pets welcome. Partial handicap access. Open May 1 - Nov 1. Rate in 2010 $25-29 for 4 persons. Phone: (606)686-3398.

(W) YATESVILLE LAKE SP—(Lawrence) *From jct US 23 & Hwy 32W: Go 7 mi SW on Hwy 32 to Hwy 1325. Enter on R.* FACILITIES: 47 sites, 27 full hkups, 20 no hkups, tenting, dump, laundry, groceries. RECREATION: lake swim, boating, ramp, lake fishing, playground. Pets welcome. Open Apr 1 - Nov 15. Phone: (606)673-1492.

LOUISVILLE—C-3

LOUISVILLE AREA MAP

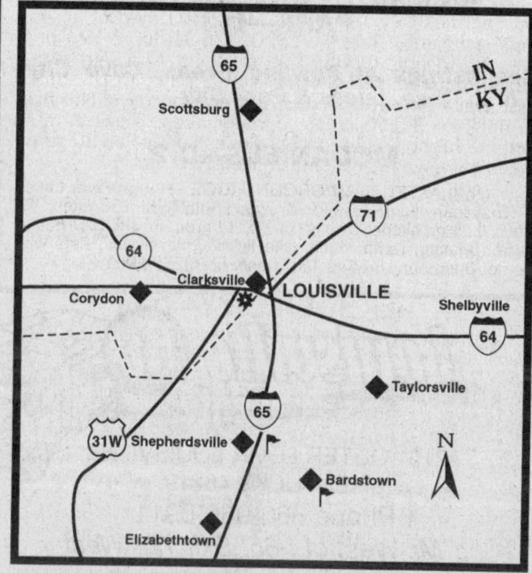

Symbols on map indicate towns within a 40 mi radius of Louisville where campgrounds (diamonds), attractions (flags), & RV service centers & camping supply outlets (gears) are listed. Check listings for more information.

Tell Them Woodall's Sent You!

LOUISVILLE—Continued on next page

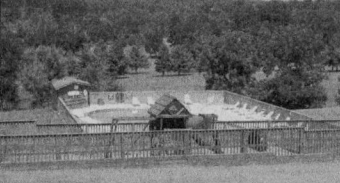

(SW) **LOUISVILLE RV CENTER**—*From jct I-65 & (exit 127): Go 1 mi W on Outer Loop. Enter on R.* SALES: travel trailers, 5th wheels, Class A motorhomes, pre-owned unit sales. SERVICES: full-time mech, engine/chassis repair, RV appliance repair, body work/collision repair, LP gas by weight/by meter, RV rentals, RV storage, sells parts/accessories, installs hitches. Open all yr. MC/VISA/DISC/AMEX/Debit.

Phone: (502)966-0911
Lat/Lon: 38.13292/-85.72820
Web: www.louisvillerv.com

SEE AD THIS PAGE

MAMMOTH CAVE NATIONAL PARK—D-3

See listings at Bowling Green, Cave City, Horse Cave, Lucas & Park City

MCDANIELS—D-2

(NW) AXTEL CAMPGROUND (COE - Rough River Lake) —(Grayson) *At jct Hwys-79 & 259.* FACILITIES: 158 sites, 43 W&E, 115 no hkups, tenting, dump, ltd groc. RECREATION: lake swim, boating, ramp, dock, lake fishing, playground. Pets welcome. Open Apr 18 - Sep 13. Phone: (270)257-2061.

MCDANIELS—Continued

(N) LAUREL BRANCH CAMPGROUND (COE- Rough River Lake)—(Breckinridge) *From jct Hwy 79 & Hwy 259: Go 1/2 mi SE on Hwy 259, then 1/2 mi S on Hwy 110.* FACILITIES: 77 sites, 25 W&E, 52 no hkups, tenting, dump. RECREATION: lake swim, boating, ramp, lake fishing, playground. Pets welcome. Facilities fully operational Mar 26 - Nov 1. Phone: (270)257-8839.

(N) NORTH FORK (Corps of Enigneers-Rough River Lake)—(Grayson) *From jct Hwy 79 & Hwy 259: Go W on Hwy 259 (follow signs).* FACILITIES: 107 sites, 81 W&E, (50 amps), 26 no hkups, tenting, dump, ltd groc. RECREATION: lake swim, boating, ramp, dock, lake fishing, playground. Pets welcome. Open May 1 - Mid Sep. Phone: (270)257-8139.

MIDDLESBORO—E-5

(SE) CUMBERLAND GAP NATIONAL HISTORICAL PARK (Wilderness Road Campground)—(Bell) *From jct US 25E & Hwy 74: Go 3 mi S on US 25E, then 1 mi E on US 58.* FACILITIES: 160 sites, 41 full hkups, 119 no hkups, tenting, dump. RECREATION: Partial handicap access. Open all yr. Phone: (606)248-2817.

MONTICELLO—E-4

(N) FALL CREEK CAMPGROUND (Corps of Engineers) —(Wayne) *From jct SR 90 & SR 1275: Go 5 mi N on SR 1275 (Follow signs). Enter on L.* FACILITIES: 10 sites, 10 E, tenting, dump. RECREATION: lake swim, boating, ramp, dock, playground. Open Apr 4 - Oct 28. Phone: (606)348-6042.

Kentucky and neighboring Tennessee have enough coal to mine for thousands of years.

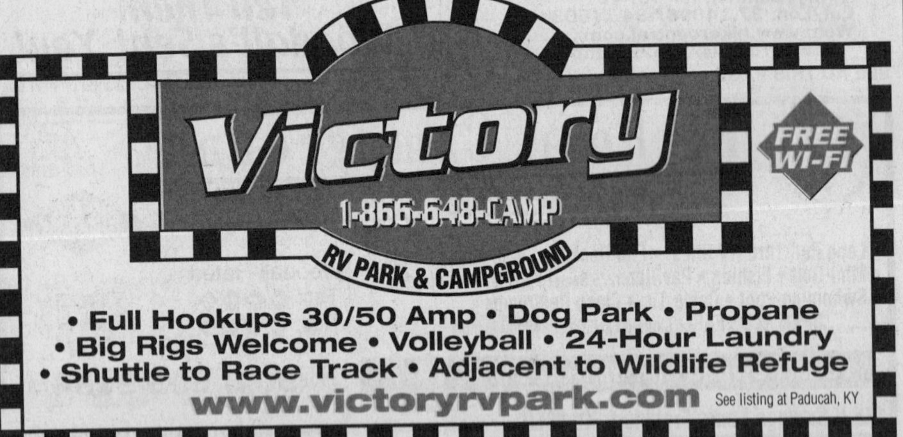

MOREHEAD—C-5

(SW) DANIEL BOONE NATIONAL FOREST (Twin Knobs Rec. Area)—(Rowan) *From jct US-60 & Hwy-801: Go 5-1/2 mi SE on Hwy-801, then 1 mi W on FR-1017.* FACILITIES: 216 sites, 24 full hkups, 102 E, 90 no hkups, tenting, dump. RECREATION: lake swim, boating, ramp, dock, lake fishing. Partial handicap access. Open Mar 13 - Nov 3. Phone: (606)784-8816.

MOUNT OLIVET—C-4

(SE) BLUE LICKS BATTLEFIELD STATE PARK—(Nicholas) *From jct US 62 & Hwy 65: Go 12 mi SE on Hwy 165.* FACILITIES: 51 sites, 51 W&E, tenting, dump, laundry. RECREATION: swim pool, ramp, river fishing, playground. Pets welcome. Open all yr. Facilities fully operational Apr - Mid Nov. Phone: (800)443-7008.

MULDRAUGH—C-3

(W) MILITARY PARK (Camp Carlson Army Travel Camp) —(Meade) *From jct US 31W & US 60: Go 2-1/2 mi W on US 60. On base at Fort Knox Military Reservation.* FACILITIES: 83 sites, 40 full hkups, 18 W&E, 25 no hkups, 9 pull-thrus, tenting, dump, laundry. RECREATION: boating, electric motors only, lake/stream fishing, playground. Pets welcome. Open all yr. Phone: (502)624-4836.

MURRAY—C-2

(E) WILDCAT CREEK REC AREA—(Calloway) *From jct Hwy 94 & Hwy 280 E of town: Go 5-1/4 mi E on Hwy 280, then 2.1 mi NE on Hwy 614E. Follow signs. Enter on R.* FACILITIES: 54 sites, 54 W&E, (30/50 amps), 6 pull-thrus, tenting, dump, laundry. RECREATION: lake swim, boating, ramp, lake fishing. Partial handicap access. Open all yr. Open Mar 15 - Oct 31. Phone: (270)436-5628.

OLIVE HILL—C-5

(NE) CARTER CAVES STATE RESORT PARK—(Carter) *From jct Hwy 2 & US 60: Go 5 mi E on US 60, then 3 mi N on Hwy 182.* FACILITIES: 89 sites, 89 W&E, tenting, dump, laundry. RECREATION: boating, no motors, canoeing, ramp, lake fishing, playground. Pets welcome. Open Apr - Nov 15. Phone: (800)325-0059.

OWENSBORO—D-2

(SW) Diamond Lake Resort Campground (Not Visited)—(Davies) *From jct SR 56 & US 60 bypass: Go 10 mi W on SR 56, then 100 yds S on SR 815, then 500 yds S on Hobbs Rd. Enter on L.* ◇◇◇FACILITIES: 270 sites, typical site width 40 ft, 240 full hkups, 30 W&E, (30/50 amps), 10 pull-thrus, dump, laundry, ltd groc. ◇◇◇◇RECREATION: swim pool, lake swim, lake/pond fishing, playground. Pets welcome. Partial handicap access. No tents. Open all yr. Big rigs welcome. Rate in 2010 $26-28 per family. Phone: (270) 229-4900.

(SW) Windy Hollow Campground & Recreation Area (Not Visited)—(Daviess) *From jct SR 56/81 & US 60 bypass: Go 3/4 mi W on SR 56/81, then 6 mi S on SR 81, then 3/4 mi S on Old SR 81, then 2 mi W on Windy Hollow Rd. Enter on R.* ◇◇◇FACILITIES: 170 sites, typical site width 35 ft, 28 ft max RV length, 100 full hkups, 70 W&E, (30/50 amps), 14 pull-thrus, tenting, dump, non-guest dump $, laundry, ltd groc, picnic tables, fire rings, wood. ◇◇◇RECREATION: pavilion, equipped pavilion, lake/pond fishing, fishing supplies, mini-golf, ($), bsktball, playground, activities, horseshoes, hiking trails, v-ball. Pets welcome. Partial handicap access. Open all yr. Facilities fully operational Apr 1 - Oct 31. Rate in 2010 $25-28 for 2 persons. CCUSA 50% Discount. CCUSA max stay 1 day, Cash only for CCUSA disc. Discount not available Jun & Jul.

Phone: (270)785-4150
Address: 5141 Windy Hollow Rd., OWENSBORO, KY 42301
Lat/Lon: 37.66268/-87.23415
Web: www.windyhollowcampground.com

PADUCAH—B-1

(SE) **DUCK CREEK RV PARK**—(McCracken) *From jct I-24 (exit 11) & Hwy 1954: Go 1/2 mi N on John Puryear Dr. Enter on R.*

◇◇◇◇FACILITIES: 99 sites, typical site width 30 ft, 93 full hkups, 6 W&E, (30/50 amps), 50 amps ($), some extd stay sites, 51 pull-thrus, WiFi Instant Internet at site, family camping, tenting, RV's/park model rentals, RV storage, dump, non-guest dump $, laundry, groceries, RV supplies, LP gas by weight/by meter, ice, picnic tables, wood.

◇◇RECREATION: rec room/area, pavilion, equipped pavilion, swim pool, pond fishing, bsktball, horseshoes, sports field.

Pets welcome, breed restrict. Partial handicap access. Open all yr. Big rigs welcome. Escort to site. Clubs welcome. Rate in 2010 $25.50-27.50 for 2 persons. MC/VISA/DISC/Debit.

DUCK CREEK RV PARK—Continued on next page

The Bluegrass Country around Lexington is home to some of the world's finest racehorses.

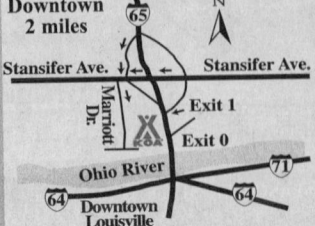

PADUCAH—Continued
DUCK CREEK RV PARK—Continued

Phone: (800)728-5109
Address: 2540 John Puryear Dr, Paducah, KY 42003
Lat/Lon: 37.02099/-88.58735
Email: info@duckcreekrvpark.com
Web: www.duckcreekrvpark.com

SEE AD THIS PAGE AND AD TRAVEL SECTION PAGE 263

(SW) FERN LAKE CAMPGROUND—(McCracken) *From jct I-24 and SR 305 (exit 3) 1/2 mi W on 305, then park on right. Enter on R.*

WELCOME

◆◆◆FACILITIES: 90 sites, typical site width 30 ft, 50 full hkups, 30 W&E, (30/50 amps), 10 no hkups, some extd stay sites, 40 pull-thrus, phone Internet central location, family camping, tenting, dump, non-guest dump $, laundry, ice, picnic tables, grills, wood.

◆RECREATION: pavilion, lake fishing, bsktball, play equipment, v-ball.

Pets welcome. Open all yr. Big rigs welcome. Clubs welcome. Rate in 2010 $27-29 for 2 persons. MC/VISA.

Phone: (270)444-7939
Address: 5535 Caro Rd, Paducah, KY 42001
Lat/Lon: 37.09595/-88.69523

SEE AD THIS PAGE AND AD TRAVEL SECTION PAGE 263

(SE) VICTORY RV PARK & CAMPGROUND, INC—(McCracken) *From jct I-24 (exit 11) & Hwy I-954: Go 1/4 mi S on Hwy I-954, then 2 mi E on KY Hwy 3075, then 1-1/2 mi SE on Hwy 450, then 1/2 mi S on Shemwell Ln. Enter on L.*

◆◆◆FACILITIES: 39 sites, typical site width 30 ft, 39 full hkups, (30/50 amps), 18 pull-thrus, WiFi Instant Internet at site, family camping, tenting, RV supplies, ice, picnic tables, wood.

◆◆RECREATION: equipped pavilion, pond fishing, fishing supplies, golf nearby, bsktball, horseshoes, sports field, v-ball.

Pets welcome. Open all yr. Big rigs welcome. Rate in 2010 $20-23 for 2 persons. MC/VISA/DISC/Debit.

Phone: (866)648-CAMP
Address: 4300 Shemwell Ln, Paducah, KY 42003
Lat/Lon: 36.96902/-88.56086
Web: www.victoryrvpark.com

SEE AD PAGE 272

Kentucky is known as "the Bluegrass State". Bluegrass is not really blue—it's green—but in the spring bluegrass produces bluish purple buds that when seen in large fields give a blue cast to the grass.

PARK CITY—E-3

(NW) DIAMOND CAVERNS RESORT & GOLF CLUB—(Barren) *From jct I 65 & SR 255: Go 1-1/4 mi N on SR 255.*

WELCOME

◆◆◆FACILITIES: 82 sites, typical site width 30 ft, 76 full hkups, 6 W&E, (30/50 amps), some extd stay sites, 37 pull-thrus, WiFi Internet central location, family camping, tenting, cabins, dump, non-guest dump, laundry, ltd groc, RV supplies, LP gas by weight/by meter, ice, picnic tables, patios, fire rings, wood.

◆◆◆◆RECREATION: rec hall, rec room/area, pavilion, equipped pavilion, coin games, 2 swim pools, mini-golf, golf nearby, bsktball, playground, activities, horseshoes, sports field, hiking trails, v-ball.

Pets welcome. Open all yr. Facilities fully operational Mar 1 - Nov 1. Swimming Memorial Day to Labor Day. Big rigs welcome. Clubs welcome. Rate in 2010 $30-33 for 2 persons. MC/VISA/DISC/AMEX/Debit.

Phone: (270)749-2891
Address: 1878 Mammoth Cave Parkway, Park City, KY 42160
Lat/Lon: 37.11556/-86.06141
Web: www.1000trails.com

SEE AD LOUISVILLE PAGE 271

(W) MAMMOTH CAVE NP (Headquarters Campground) —(Edmonson) *N'bound from jct I-65 (exit 48) & Hwy 255: Go 8 mi NW on Hwy 255. S'bound from jct I-65 (exit 53) & Hwy 70: Go 9 mi W on Hwy 70.* FACILITIES: 109 sites, 28 ft max RV length, 109 no hkups, tenting, dump, laundry, ltd groc, full svc store. RECREATION: boating, ramp. Facilities fully operational Sep 16 - May 15. Phone: (270)758-2181.

PARKERS LAKE—E-4

(E) Eagle Falls Lodge—(McCreary) *From jct US 27 & Hwy 90: Go 10 mi E on Hwy 90. Enter on L.* ◆◆◆FACILITIES: 56 sites, typical site width 20 ft, 41 W&E, (20/30/50 amps), 15 no hkups, family camping, tenting, dump, laundry, groceries, ice, picnic tables, fire rings, grills, wood. ◆◆◆RECREATION: pavilion, swim pool, pond fishing, fishing supplies, bsktball, playground, horseshoes, hiking trails. Pets welcome. Partial handicap access. Open all yr. Facilities fully operational Apr 1 - Nov 1. Rate in 2010 $25 per vehicle. MC/VISA/DISC/AMEX/Debit. CCUSA 50% Discount. CCUSA reservations Accepted, CCUSA max stay Unlimited.

CAMPCLUB USA

Phone: (888)318-2658
Address: 11251 Hwy 90, Parkers Lake, KY 42634
Lat/Lon: 36.83442/-84.35107
Email: eaglefalls@highland.net
Web: www.stayateaglefalls.com

PIKEVILLE—D-6

(S) (COE-Fishtrap Lake) Fish Trap Lake Shelters—(Pike) *From jct Hwy 80 & US 119: Go 9-1/2 mi E on US 119 to Meta, then 16 mi S on Hwy 194.* FACILITIES: 28 sites, 10 W&E, 18 no hkups, tenting, dump, laundry, groceries. RECREATION: lake swim, boating, canoeing, ramp, lake fishing, playground. Pets welcome. Open Memorial Day - Labor Day. Phone: (606)437-7496.

PRESTONSBURG—D-6

(E) GERMAN BRIDGE CAMPING AREA—(Floyd) *From town: Go 6 mi S on Hwy-1428, then 7 mi on Hwy-194.* FACILITIES: 40 sites, 40 no hkups, tenting, dump, laundry. RECREATION: boating, canoeing, ramp, lake fishing, playground. Open Memorial Day Wkend - Labor Day Wkend. Phone: (606)886-2371.

Diane Sawyer, broadcast journalist, is from Kentucky.

PRESTONSBURG—Continued

(E) JENNY WILEY STATE RESORT PARK—(Floyd) *From jct US 23-460 & Hwy 80: Go 3 mi N on US 23-460, then 2 mi E on Hwy 3, then S on Hwy 302.* FACILITIES: 121 sites, 30 ft max RV length, 121 E, (30/50 amps), tenting, dump, laundry, groceries. RECREATION: swim pool, boating, ramp, dock, lake fishing, playground. Pets welcome. Open Apr 1 - Oct 31. Phone: (800) 325-0142.

RENFRO VALLEY—D-4

(N) KOA-Renfro Valley—(Rockcastle) *From jct I-75 (exit 62) & US 25: Go 1-1/2 mi N on US 25. Enter on R.* ◆◆◆◆FACILITIES: 133 sites, typical site width 30 ft, 68 full hkups, 35 W&E, (30/50 amps), 30 no hkups, 77 pull-thrus, family camping, tenting, dump, laundry, full svc store. ◆◆◆◆◆RECREATION: swim pool, playground. Pets welcome. Open all yr. Big rigs welcome. Rate in 2010 $26-42 for 2 persons. Member ARVC, COAK. Phone: (800)KOA-2475. KOA discount.

(N) MT. VERNON-ROCK CASTLE COUNTY TOURIST COMMISSION—*From jct I-75 (exit 62) & US 25: Go 1/4 mi N on US 25.* Just off I-75 at exit 62 is Rockcastle County, "Kentucky's Country Music Capital" since 1939. Home to the World Famous Renfro Valley Barn Dance, The KY Music Hall of Fame, Appalachian history, quilt blocks, festivals, premier camping and much more. Open all yr.

WELCOME

Address: 2325 Richmond St, Mt. Vernon, KY 40456
Lat/Lon: 37.38718/-84.33175
Email: tourism@snapp.net

SEE AD THIS PAGE

(N) Renfro Valley RV Park—(Rockcastle) *From I-75 (exit 62) & US 25: Go 1/4 mi N on US 25. Enter on R.* ◆◆◆◆FACILITIES: 234 sites, typical site width 25 ft, 97 full hkups, 17 W&E, 120 E, (30/50 amps), 50 pull-thrus, family camping, dump, laundry. ◆◆◆RECREATION: lake/stream fishing, play equipment. Pets welcome. Partial handicap access. No tents. Open all yr. Facilities fully operational Mar - Dec. Big rigs welcome. Rate in 2010 $29.68-34.95 per vehicle. Phone: (800)765-7464.

RICHMOND—D-4

(N) FORT BOONESBOROUGH STATE PARK—(Madison) *From jct Hwy 338 & Hwy 627: Go 1/2 mi S on Hwy 338.* FACILITIES: 167 sites, 167 W&E, tenting, dump, laundry, ltd groc. RECREATION: swim pool, boating, ramp, river fishing, playground. Pets welcome. Open all yr. Phone: (859)527-3131.

RUSSELL SPRINGS—E-3

(SE) KOA-Indian Hills—(Russell) *From jct US 127 & Hwy 80: Go 2-1/2 mi E on Hwy 80, then 2-1/2 mi S on Hwy 910, then 4-1/2 mi S on Hwy 76, then 1-1/2 mi S on Hwy 1383. Enter on L.* ◆◆◆FACILITIES: 156 sites, typical site width 24 ft, 32 full hkups, 118 W&E, (30/50 amps), 6 no hkups, 22 pull-thrus, family camping, tenting, dump, laundry, groceries. ◆◆◆RECREATION: swim pool, playground. Pets welcome. Open Apr 1 - Nov 1. Facilities fully operational Memorial Day - Labor Day. Rate in 2010 $31-36 for 2 persons. Phone: (270)866-5616. KOA discount.

SALT LICK—C-5

(S) DANIEL BOONE NATIONAL FOREST (Zilpo Recreation Area)—(Bath) *From jct I-64 (exit 123) & US 60: Go 6-1/2 mi E on US 60, then 4 mi S on 211, then 3 mi E on FDR 129, then 9 mi N on FDR 918 (Nat'l Scenic Byway).* FACILITIES: 164 sites, 40 E, 124 no hkups, tenting, dump, groceries. RECREATION: lake swim, boating, ramp, dock, lake fishing. Partial handicap access. Open Apr 10 - Oct 20. Phone: (606)768-2722.

Jefferson Davis, President of the Confederacy, was from Kentucky.

SANDERS—B-4

(SW) Eagle Valley Camping Resort—(Owen) *From jct I-71 & Hwy 35 (exit 57): Go 2 mi S on Hwy 35, then 6-1/2 mi W on Hwy 467, then 1-1/2 mi S on Stephanus Rd. Enter on R.* ◆◆FACILITIES: 269 sites, typical site width 20 ft, 17 full hkups, 252 W&E, (30/50 amps), 1 pull-thrus, family camping, tenting, dump, laundry, groceries. ◆◆RECREATION: swim pool, boating, electric motors only, ramp, dock, lake fishing, playground. Pets welcome. Partial handicap access. Open all yr. Facilities fully operational Apr 1 - Nov 1. Rate in 2010 $25 for 4 persons. Phone: (502)347-9361.

SASSAFRAS—D-5

(E) CARR CREEK STATE PARK—(Knott) *From town: Go E on Hwy 15.* FACILITIES: 39 sites, 39 W&E, tenting, dump, laundry. RECREATION: lake swim, boating, ramp, dock, lake fishing, playground. Pets welcome. Partial handicap access. Open Mar 31 - Oct 31. Phone: (606)642-4050.

SCOTTSVILLE—E-2

(N) BAILEY'S POINT CAMPGROUND (COE-Barren River Lake)—(Allen) *From jct US 231 & US 31E: Go 9 mi N on US 31E, then 1 mi W on Hwy 252, then 4 mi N on Hwy 517.* FACILITIES: 215 sites, 114 E, 101 no hkups, tenting, dump, laundry, ltd groc. RECREATION: lake swim, boating, canoeing, ramp, lake fishing, playground. Pets welcome. Open Mid Apr - 3rd Sat in Oct. Phone: (270)622-6959.

(N) THE TAILWATER BELOW DAM (COE-Barren River Lake)—(Allen) *From jct US 231 & US 31E: Go 9 mi N on US 31E, then 8 mi W on Hwy 252.* FACILITIES: 48 sites, 48 no hkups, tenting. RECREATION: lake swim, boating, canoeing, ramp, lake/river fishing, playground. Pets welcome. Open all yr. Facilities fully operational mid Apr - mid Sep. Phone: (270)622-7732.

SHEPHERDSVILLE—C-3

(S) GRANDMA'S RV PARK—(Bullitt) *From jct SR 44 & I-65: Go 1 mi S on I -65, then 200 yds W on SR 480. Enter on R.*

WELCOME

◆◆◆◆◆FACILITIES: 65 sites, typical site width 25 ft, 64 full hkups, 1 E, (30/50 amps), many extd stay sites, 30 pull-thrus, WiFi Instant Internet at site, family camping, cabins, RV storage, laundry, patios.

RECREATION: pavilion.

Pets welcome. Partial handicap access. No tents. Open all yr. Big rigs welcome. Clubs welcome. Rate in 2010 $27 for 2 persons. MC/VISA/DISC/Debit.

Phone: (502)543-7023
Address: 159 Dawson Drive, Shepherdsville, KY 40165
Lat/Lon: 37.97947/-85.70148
Email: bink222@hotmail.com
Web: www.grandmasrvcamping.net

SEE AD THIS PAGE

SHEPHERDSVILLE—Continued

(E) Louisville South KOA (Not Visited)—(Bullitt) *From jct I-65 (exit 117) & Hwy-44: Go 1-1/2 mi E on Hwy-44. Enter on R.* ◆◆◆◆FACILITIES: 216 sites, typical site width 30 ft, 114 full hkups, 65 W&E, (30/50 amps), 50 amps ($), 37 no hkups, 68 pull-thrus, family camping, tenting, dump, laundry, groceries. ◆◆◆◆◆RECREATION: swim pool, river/pond fishing, playground. Pets welcome. Open all yr. Big rigs welcome. Rate in 2010 $42-92.50 for 2 persons. Member ARVC. Phone: (800)KOA-1880. KOA discount.

SLADE—D-5

(E) DANIEL BOONE NATIONAL FOREST (Koomer Ridge Campground)—(Wolfe) *From jct Mountain Parkway & Hwy-15: Go 3-1/2 mi SE on Hwy-15.* FACILITIES: 54 sites, 22 ft max RV length, 54 no hkups, tenting. RECREATION: Pets welcome. Partial handicap access. Open Apr 10 - Oct 30. Phone: (606)668-7939.

(S) NATURAL BRIDGE STATE RESORT PARK—(Powell) *From jct Mountain Parkway & Hwy 11: Go 2-1/2 mi S on Hwy 11.* FACILITIES: 94 sites, 82 W&E, (20/30/50 amps), 12 no hkups, tenting, dump, laundry. RECREATION: swim pool, boating, dock, lake fishing, playground. Pets welcome. Open Apr 15 - Oct 31. Phone: (800)325-1710.

SOMERSET—E-4

(W) CUMBERLAND POINT PUBLIC USE AREA (COE-Lake Cumberland)—(Wayne) *From jct Hwy 80 & US 27: Go 8 mi SW on Hwy 80, then 1 mi S on Hwy 235, then 10 mi E on Hwy 761.* FACILITIES: 30 sites, 30 W&E, tenting, dump, laundry. RECREATION: lake swim, boating, ramp, lake fishing, playground. Pets welcome. Open May 4 - Sep 24. Phone: (606)871-7886.

(W) FISHING CREEK PUBLIC USE AREA (COE-Lake Cumberland)—(Pulaski) *From jct Hwy 80 & US 27: Go 5 mi W on Hwy 80, then 3 mi N on Hwy 1248.* FACILITIES: 46 sites, 46 W&E, (30/50 amps), tenting, dump, laundry, ltd groc. RECREATION: lake swim, boating, ramp, lake fishing, playground. Pets welcome. Open Apr 18 - Sep 24. Phone: (606)679-5174.

(S) WAITSBORO REC AREA (COE-Lake Cumberland)—(Pulaski) *From town: Go 5 mi S on US 27, then 1 mi W on Waitsboro Rd. Enter at end.* FACILITIES: 25 sites, 25 W&E, tenting, dump, laundry. RECREATION: lake swim, boating, canoeing, ramp, dock, lake fishing, playground. Pets welcome. Open Apr 4 - Oct 13. Phone: (606)561-5513.

STAFFORDSVILLE—C-6

(W) PAINTSVILLE LAKE STATE PARK—(Johnson) *From jct US 23 & SR 40: Go 1-1/4 mi W on SR 40, then 1 mi N on Rt 2275. Enter at end.* FACILITIES: 42 sites, typical site width 35 ft, 32 full hkups, (15/30/50 amps), 10 no hkups, 12 pull-thrus, tenting, laundry. RECREATION: boating, ramp, lake fishing, playground. Pets welcome. Partial handicap access. Open all yr. Big rigs welcome. Phone: (606)297-8486.

Can you trust the Woodall's ratings? 25 evaluation teams have scoured North American campgrounds to provide you with accurate, up to date information & ratings. Find a rating you don't agree with? Send a letter or email our way, and we'll give it extra attention for 2012.

STEARNS—E-4

(S) BIG SOUTH FORK NAT'L RIVER & REC. AREA (Blue Heron Campground)—(McCreary) *From jct US 27 & Hwy 92: Go 1 mi W on Hwy 92, then 1 mi S on Hwy 1651, then 9 mi S on Hwy 741. Enter on R.* FACILITIES: 45 sites, 33 ft max RV length, 45 W&E, tenting, dump. RECREATION: canoeing, river fishing, play equipment. Open Apr - Nov. Phone: (606)376-5073.

STURGIS—A-2

(E) UNION COUNTY FAIR & EXPO CENTER—(Union) *From jct SR-109 & US-60: Go 1 mi E on US-60. Enter on L.* FACILITIES: 45 sites, typical site width 35 ft, accepts self-contained units only, 30 W&E, 15 E, (20/30/50 amps), 20 pull-thrus. RECREATION: boating, electric motors only, ramp, lake fishing. Pets welcome. No tents. Open all yr. Big rigs welcome. Phone: (270)333-4107.

TAYLORSVILLE—C-3

(E) TAYLORSVILLE LAKE STATE PARK—(Spencer) *From jct Hwy 155 & Hwy 44: Go 3 mi E on Hwy 44. Enter on R.* FACILITIES: 42 sites, 42 W&E, tenting, dump, laundry, ltd groc. RECREATION: boating, canoeing, ramp, dock, lake fishing, playground. Pets welcome. Partial handicap access. Open Apr 1 - Dec 15. Phone: (502)477-8713.

WALTON—B-4

(W) BIG BONE LICK STATE PARK—(Boone) *From jct I-75 & Hwy-1292: Go 4-1/2 mi W on Hwy-1292, then 3 mi on Hwy-338.* FACILITIES: 62 sites, 62 W&E, tenting, dump, laundry, groceries. RECREATION: swim pool, stream fishing, playground. Pets welcome. Open all yr. Phone: (859)384-3522.

OAK CREEK CAMPGROUND—(Boone) *From jct I-75 (exit 171) & SR 16 (exit 171): Go 1 mi S on SR 16. Enter on R.*

WELCOME

◆◆◆FACILITIES: 105 sites, typical site width 30 ft, 100 W&E, (30/50 amps), 50 amps ($), 5 no hkups, some extd stay sites, 6 pull-thrus, cable TV, WiFi Instant Internet at site, WiFi Internet central location, family camping, tenting, RV storage, dump, non-guest dump $, portable dump, laundry, groceries, RV supplies, ice, picnic tables, fire rings, wood.

◆◆◆RECREATION: rec room/area, equipped pavilion, coin games, swim pool, stream fishing, bsktball, playground, activities, (wkends), horseshoes, hiking trails.

Pets welcome. Open all yr. Pool open Memorial Day - Labor Day. Limited facilities in winter months. Big rigs welcome. Clubs welcome. Rate in 2010 $29-30 for 2 persons. MC/VISA/DISC/AMEX. FCRV discount. FMCA discount.

Phone: (859)485-9131
Address: 13333 Oak Creek Rd, Walton, KY 41094
Lat/Lon: 38.84908/-84.62879
Email: oakcreek@fuse.net
Web: www.oakcreekcampground.com

SEE AD CINCINNATI, OH PAGE 620

Woodall's Tip... Read travel information at the beginning of each state's / province's Travel Section.

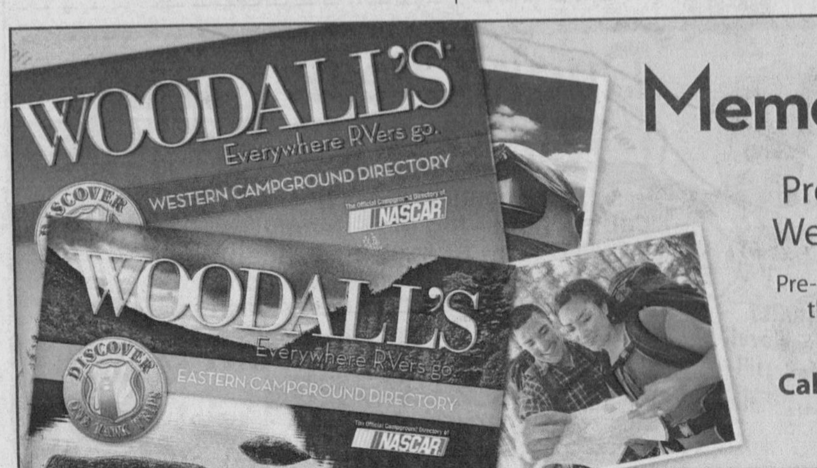

WOODALL'S
Everywhere RVers go.
CANADA CAMPGROUND GUIDE
WOODALL'S
Everywhere RVers go.
NEW YORK/NEW ENGLAND & EASTERN CANADA
WOODALL'S
Everywhere RVers go.
MID ATLANTIC CAMPGROUND GUIDE
WOODALL'S
Everywhere RVers go.
THE SOUTH CAMPGROUND GUIDE
WOODALL'S
Everywhere RVers go.
GREAT LAKES CAMPGROUND GUIDE
WOODALL'S
Everywhere RVers go.
FRONTIER WEST/GREAT PLAINS & MOUNTAIN STATES
CAMPGROUND GUIDE
WOODALL'S
Everywhere RVers go.
DISCOVER
ONE TANK TRIPS
FAR WEST CAMPGROUND GUIDE
NASCAR
NEW FOR 2011!
INCLUDES ALL NEW UPDATES:

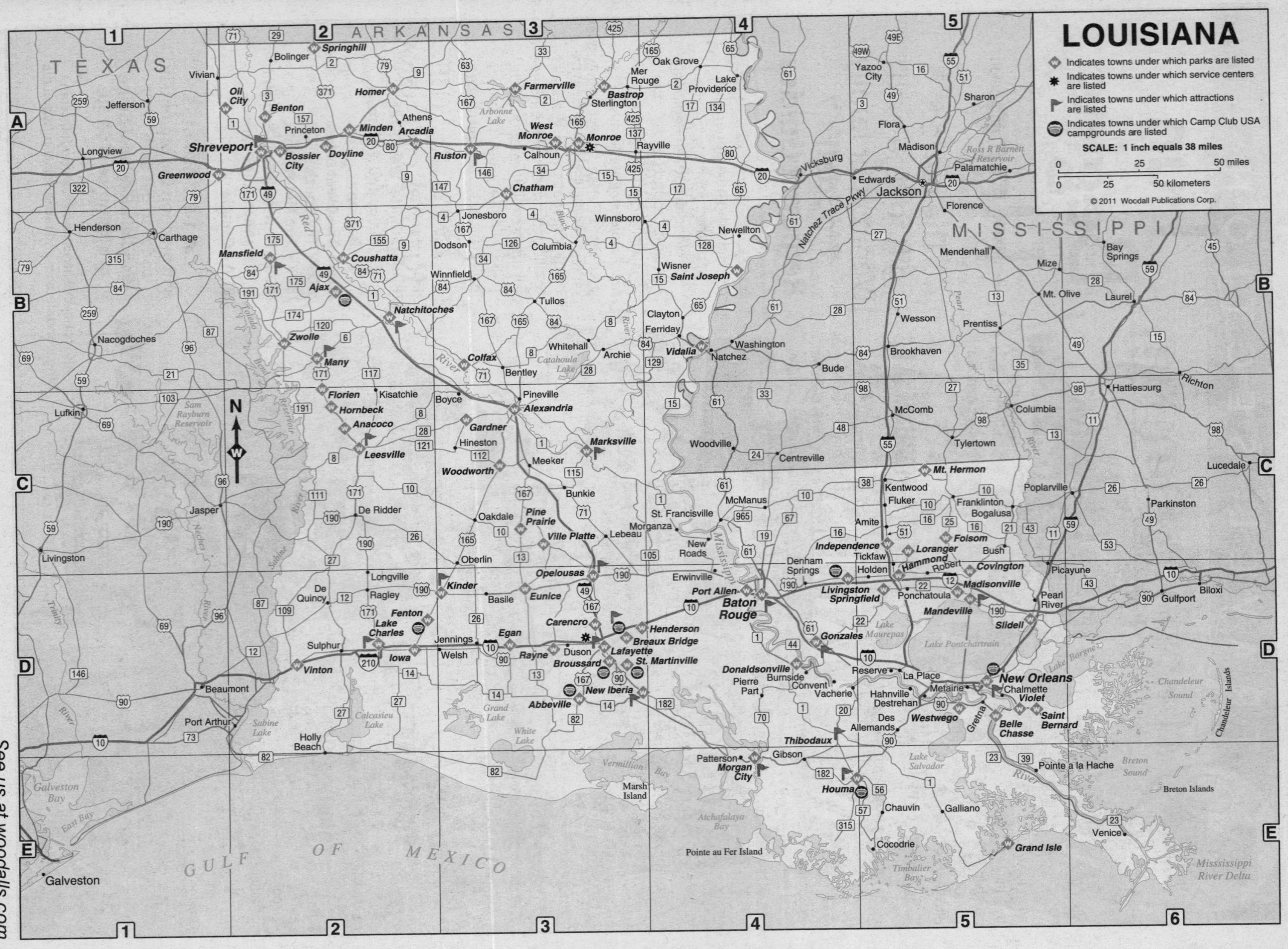
LOUISIANA
Indicates towns under which parks are listed
Indicates towns under which service centers are listed
Indicates towns under which attractions are listed
Indicates towns under which Camp Club USA campgrounds are listed
SCALE: 1 inch equals 38 miles
0 25 50 miles
0 25 50 kilometers
© 2011 Woodall Publications Corp.
TEXAS
ARKANSAS
MISSISSIPPI
GULF OF MEXICO
Shreveport
Bossier City
Monroe
Alexandria
Baton Rouge
Lafayette
Lake Charles
New Orleans
Jackson
Houma

READER SERVICE INFO

The following businesses have placed an ad in the Louisiana Travel Section. To receive free information, enter their Reader Service number on the Reader Service Card opposite page 48/Discover Section in the front of this directory:

Advertiser	RS#
Bayou LaFourche Area CVB	4256
Cajun Coast Visitors & Convention Bureau	2687
Coushatta Luxury RV Resort at Red Shoes Park	4065
Houma Area Convention & Visitors Bureau	396
Lafayette Convention & Visitors Commission	2843
Lake Charles/SW Louisiana Convention & Visitors Bureau	3013
Louisiana Campground Owners Assoc	3255
Louisiana Travel Promotion Association	3767
Mississippi State Parks	4314
Paragon Casino RV Resort	2589
St. Tammany Parish Tourist & Convention Commission	153

TIME ZONE

Louisiana is in the Central Time Zone.

TOPOGRAPHY

Louisiana's varied terrain encompasses rich alluvial plains, rolling hills, river bluffs, coastal marches, rivers and bayous.

TEMPERATURE

Snow rarely falls in the southern sections, with only light snowfall recorded in the northern regions. January's low/high temperatures are 25°/59° and July's low/high temperatures are 71°/92°.

TRAVEL & TOURISM INFO

Although the Louisiana coast was devastated by Hurricane Katrina, there is much that was untouched or has been reconstructed. The following bureaus can give you up-to-date information on the area you are visiting:

State Agency:
Louisiana Office of Tourism
1051 N. Third Street
Baton Rouge, LA 70804
(225/342-8119)
www.louisianatravel.com

Local Agencies:
Acadia Parish Tourist Commission
P.O. Box 1342
Crowley, LA 70527
(337/783-2108)
www.acadiatourism.org

Alexandria-Pineville Area CVB
707 Main St.
Alexandria, LA 71309
(800/551-9546 or 318/442-9546)
www.louisianafromhere.com

Allen Parish Tourist Commission
Box 1280
Oberlin, LA 70655
(888/639-4868 or 318/639-4884)
www.allenparish.com

Ascension Parish Tourist Commission
6967 Hwy. 22
Sorrento, LA 70778
(888/775-7990)
www.ascensiontourism.com

Avoyelles Parish Commission of Tourism Office
208 South Main St, P.O. Box 24
Marksville, LA 71351
(800/833-4195 or 318/253-0585)
www.travelavoyelles.com

Baton Rouge Area Convention & Visitors Bureau
359 Third St.
Baton Rouge, LA 70801
(800/LA-ROUGE)
www.visitbatonrouge.com

Beauregard Parish Tourist Commission
P.O.Box 1174
104 Port Street
DeRidder, LA 70634
(318/463-5534 or 800/738-5534)
www.beau.lib.la.us

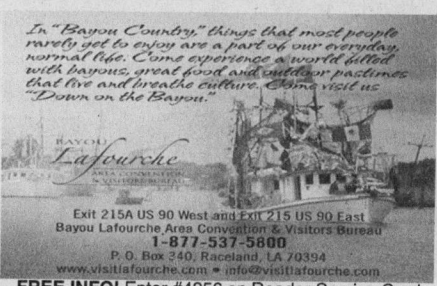

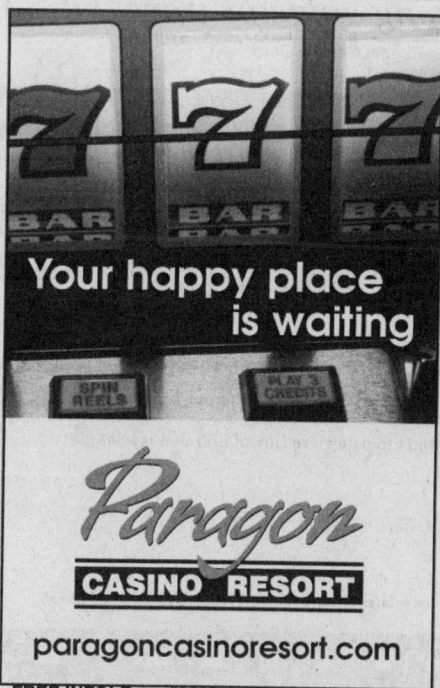

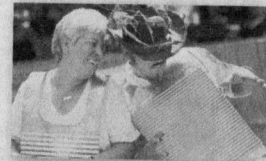

Bayou Teche Visitors Center (City of Breaux Bridge)
314 E. Bridge Street
Breaux Bridge, LA 70517
(337/332-8500 or 888/565-5939)
www.breauxbridgelive.net

Caldwell Parish Chamber of Commerce
P.O. Box 726
Columbia, LA 71418
(318/649-0726)

Cameron Parish Tourist Commission
P.O. Box 388
Cameron, LA 70631

Claiborne Parish-Homer Tourist Commission
P.O.Box 449
Homer, LA 71040
(318/927-3271)

Concordia Parish
C/o Vidalia Welcome Center
1401 Carter St., Vidalia LA 71373
(318/336-7008)

DeSoto Parish Tourist Bureau
P.O.Box 1327, Mansfield LA 71052
101 N. Washington
Mansfield LA 71052
(318/872-1177)
www.discoverdesoto.com

East Carroll Parish (Byerley House Visitor & Community Center, Doorway to Louisiana, Inc.)
600 Lake St.
Lake Providence, LA 71254
(318/559-5125)

East Feliciana Tourist Commission
P.O. Box 667
Jackson, LA 70748
(225/634-7155)
www.felicianatourism.org

Evangeline Parish Tourism Commission
P.O. Box 412
126 E. Main Street
Ville Platte, LA 70586
(337/363-1878)
www.EvangelineTourism.com

Franklin Parish Tourist Commission
P.O.Box 351
Winnsboro, LA 71295
721 Prairie St, 71295
(318/435-7607)

Grant Parish Chamber
305 Main St.
Colfax, LA 71467
(318/627-3019)

Gretna (City of) Office of Tourism & Visitor Center
Jefferson Parish
P.O. Box 404
4th Street @ Huey P. Long Ave.
Gretna, LA 70053
(504/363-1580)
www.gretnala.com

Houma-Terrebonne Tourist Commission
P.O. Box 2792
Houma, LA 70361
(800/688-2732 or 985/868-2732)
www.houmatourism.com

Iberia Parish CVB
2513 Hwy. 14
New Iberia, LA 70560
(888/942-3742 or 337/365-1540)
www.iberiatravel.com

Jefferson Davis Parish Tourist Commission
100 Rue de l'Acadie
Jennings, LA 70546
(800/264-5521 or 337/821-5521)
www.jeffdavis.org

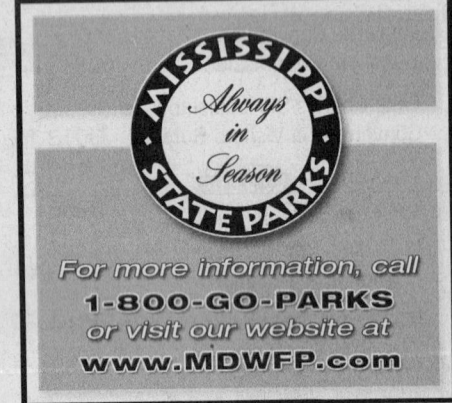

Jefferson Convention & Visitors Bureau
Jefferson Parish Yenni Building
1221 Elmwood Park Blvd, Ste. 300
Jefferson, LA 70123
(877/572-7474 or 504/731-7083)
www.neworleansgateway.com

Kenner Convention and Visitors Bureau
2100 3rd St, Suite 10
Kenner, LA 70062
(504/464-9494 or 800/231-5282)
www.kennercvb.com

Lafayette Convention and Visitors Center
1400 N. W. Evangeline Throughway
Lafayette, LA 70501
(800/346-1958 U.S. or 800/543-5340 Canada)
www.lafayettetravel.com

Lafourche Parish Visitor Welcome Center
4484 LA Hwy. 1, P.O. Box 340
Raceland, LA 70394
(877/537-5800 or 985/537-5800)
www.visitlafourche.com

Livingston Parish CVB
P.O. Box 864
Livingston, LA 70754

Madison Parish Tourist Commission
305 Dabney St.
Tallulah, LA 71282
(888/775-2987)

Monroe-West Monroe CVB
P.O. Box 1436
601 Constitution Drive
West Monroe, LA 71294
(800/843-1872 or 318/387-5691)
www.monroe-westmonroe.org

Morgan City (City of) Tourist Center
St. Mary Parish
725 Myrtle St.
Morgan City LA 70380
(985/384-3343)

Natchitoches CVB
781 Front St.
Natchitoches, LA 71457
(800/259-1714 or 318/352-8072)
www.natchitoches.net

New Orleans Metropolitan Convention & Visitors Bureau
2020 St. Charles Ave.
New Orleans, LA 70130
(800/672-6124 or 504/566-5011)
www.neworleanscvb.com

Plaquemines Parish Office of Tourism
P.O.Box 937
104 New Orleans St.
Belle Chasse LA 70037
(504/394-0018)
www.plaqueminesparish.com

Pointe Coupee Parish Office of Tourism
500 W. Main St, P.O. Box 733
New Roads, LA 70760
(225/638-3998)
www.pctourism.org

Ruston-Lincoln Chamber
104 E. Mississippi St
Ruston, LA 71270
(800/392-9032 or 318/255-2031)
www.rustonlincoln.org

Sabine Parish Tourism Commission
1601 Texas Hwy.
Many, LA 71449
(318/256-5880)
www.SabineParish.com

St. Bernard Parish Tourist Commission
8201 W. Judge Perez Dr.
Chalmette, LA 70043
(504/278-4242)
www.st-bernard.la.us

St. Charles Parish Economic Development Dept.
P.O.Box 302
14996 River Rd,
Hahnville, LA 70057
(985/783-5140)
visitor center (985/783-5145)
www.st.charlesgov.net

St. James Parish Tourist Commission
P.O. Box 629
Gramercy, LA 70052
(225/869-1717)
www.stjamesla.com

St. John the Baptist Parish Economic Development Department
1801 W. Airline Hwy.
LaPlace, LA 70068
(985/652-9569)
www.stjohnla.org

St. Landry Parish Tourist Commission
P.O. Box 1415
Opelousas, LA 70571-1415
(877/948-8004)
www.cajuntravel.com

St. Martin Parish Tourist Commission
P.O. Box 9
St. Martinville, LA 70582
(337/298-3556)
www.CajunCountry.org

St. Martinville Tourist Commission
215 Evangeline Blvd., P.O.Box 379
St. Martinville LA 70582
(337/394-2233)
www.CityOfStMartinville.com

St. Mary Parish/Cajun Coast Visitors & Convention Bureau
P.O.Box 2332
Morgan City LA 70381
(985/395-4905 or 800/256-2931)
www.cajuncoast.com

St. Tammany West Chamber
68099 Highway 59
Mandeville LA 70471
(985/892-0520)
www.neworleansnorthshore.com

Shreveport-Bossier Convention & Tourist Bureau
629 Spring St, P.O. Box 1761
Shreveport, LA 71101
(800/551-8682)
www.shreveport-bossier.org

Southwest Louisiana CVB
1205 N. Lakeshore Dr.
Lake Charles, LA 70601

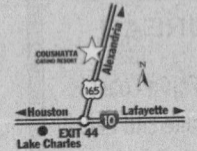

(800/456-7952 or 337/436-9588)
www.visitlakecharles.org

Tangipahoa Parish CVB
42271 S. Morrison Blvd.
Hammond, LA 70403
(800/542-7520)
www.tangi-cvb.org

Vermilion Parish Tourist Commission
P.O. Box 1106
Abbeville, LA 70511
(337/898-6600)
www.vermilion.org

West Feliciana Parish Tourist Commission
P.O. Box 1548
St Francisville, LA 70775
(225/635-4224 or 800/789-4221)
www.stfrancisville.us

RECREATIONAL INFO

Louisiana Office of State Parks: P.O. Box 44426, Baton Rouge, LA 70804 (888/677-1400 or 225/342-8111). www.LaStateParks.com

Biking: For an official highway travel map or Parish road map, contact: Department of Transportation & Development, P.O. Box 94245, Baton Rouge, LA 70804-9245 (225/379-1232).

Hunting & Fishing Info: Louisiana Dept. of Wildlife and Fisheries, 2000 Quail Drive, Baton Rouge, LA 70808 (225/765-2800). www.wlf.state.la.us.

River Cruising: River Barge Excursion Lines (888/GO-BARGE) or visit www.river-barge.com.

SHOPPING

America's Antique City, Ponchatoula. Historic District renovated in 1920-1930s featuring over 40 antique stores representing 200 dealers.

The Shop at the Top, Ponchatoula. Located on the top floor of the Louisiana State Capitol, The Shop at the Top offers fantastic views and heritage souvenirs. Operated by Foundation for Historical Louisiana. LA State Capitol, 27th Floor, Baton Rouge, LA 70802.

Historic District and Antique Village, Denham Springs. Antique shops, apparel, fine gifts, ice cream parlor and more in a 3-block area. 133 Hummell St., Denham Springs, LA 70726.

Magazine Street, New Orleans. Six miles of antique shops, art galleries and specialty shops. Call for free map (866/679-4764 or 504/342-4435) www.magazinestreet.com

Maskarade, New Orleans. Handmade masks by local, national & international artists. Feather, ceramic, wood, tribal masks and more. 630 Ann St. www.themask-store.com

BUSINESSES OFFERING

	Things to See & Do	RV Sales	RV Service
BATON ROUGE			
Louisiana Culinary Trails	✓		
Louisiana Travel Promotion Association	✓		
BREAUX BRIDGE			
Poche's Market, Restaurant & Smokehouse	✓		
GONZALES			
Poche Plantation	✓		
HOUMA			
Houma Area Convention & Visitors Bureau	✓		
KINDER			
Coushatta Casino Resort	✓		
Koasati Pines At Coushatta	✓		
LAFAYETTE			
G & J Mobile Home & RV Supplies			✓
Gauthier's RV Service Center		✓	✓
Lafayette Convention & Visitors Commission	✓		
LAKE CHARLES			
Lake Charles/Southwest Louisiana Convention & Visitors Bureau	✓		
LEESVILLE			
Vernon Parish Tourist Information Center	✓		
MANDEVILLE			
St. Tammany Parish Tourist & Convention Commission	✓		
MANSFIELD			
New Rockdale Radio Shop LLC	✓		
MANY			
Sabine Parish	✓		
MARKSVILLE			
Avoyelles Parish Tourism Commission	✓		
Paragon Casino	✓		
MONROE			
Hope's Camper Corner RV Center		✓	✓
MORGAN CITY			
Cajun Coast Visitors & Convention Bureau	✓		
NATCHITOCHES			
Natchitoches Parish Tourist Commission	✓		
NEW IBERIA			
Iberia Parish Convention & Visitors Bureau	✓		
NEW ORLEANS			
New Orleans Plantation Country	✓		
OPELOUSAS			
St. Landry Parish Tourist Commission	✓		
RUSTON			
Ruston/Lincoln Convention & Visitors Bureau	✓		
SHREVEPORT			
Shreveport/Bossier Convention & Tourist Bureau	✓		
THIBODAUX			
Bayou LaFourche Area CVB	✓		

QUICK REFERENCE CHART FOR WOODALL'S FEATURED PARKS

	Green Friendly	RV Lots for Sale	Park Models-Onsite Ownership	Park Membership for Sale	Big Rigs Welcome	Internet Friendly	Pets Welcome
BATON ROUGE							
Baton Rouge KOA					▲	●	■
BREAUX BRIDGE							
Poche's Fish-N-Camp					▲	●	■
CARENCRO							
Bayou Wilderness RV Resort					▲	●	■
DONALDSONVILLE							
B & B RV Park					▲		■
GONZALES							
Poche Plantation RV Resort					▲	●	■
KINDER							
Coushatta Luxury RV Resort At Red Shoes Park					▲	●	■
LAFAYETTE							
KOA-Lafayette					▲	●	■
LAKE CHARLES							
Hidden Ponds RV Park					▲	●	■
Whispering Meadow RV Park					▲	●	■
LIVINGSTON							
Lakeside RV Park					▲	●	■
MANSFIELD							
New Rockdale RV Park/Radioshop LLC					▲		■
MARKSVILLE							
Paragon Casino RV Resort					▲	●	■
MINDEN							
Cinnamon Creek RV Park					▲	●	■
MONROE							
Shiloh Campground & RV Resort					▲	●	■
MT. HERMON							
Silver Creek Campground					▲		■
NATCHITOCHES							
Nakatosh Campground					▲	●	■
NEW IBERIA							
KOC Kampground					▲	●	■
NEW ORLEANS							
French Quarter RV Resort					▲	●	■
Pontchartrain Landing					▲	●	■
Riverboat RV Park					▲	●	■
SHREVEPORT							
Tall Pines RV Park					▲	●	■
SLIDELL							
New Orleans East Kampground					▲	●	■
Pine Crest RV Park					▲	●	■
ST. BERNARD							
Fanz RV Park						●	■
VIDALIA							
River View RV Park					▲	●	■

Green Friendly ; RV Lots for Sale ✖; Park Models/Onsite Onwership ✱; Park Memberships for Sale ✔; Big Rigs Welcome ▲; Internet Friendly ●; Internet Friendly-WiFi ●; Pets Welcome ■

Riverwalk Marketplace, New Orleans. Shop 140 stores plus food court with river views for a true taste of New Orleans. On the riverfront between Aquarium & Convention Center. www.riverwalkmarketplace.com

UNIQUE FEATURES

CAJUN AND CREOLE CULTURES

Creole in its broadest sense can refer to a variety of combinations of French culture with Spanish, African and Caribbean cultures in colonial Louisiana. In early 19th century New Orleans, the term Creole was a way that these "born in the colony" cultural groups differentiated themselves from the many Americans who settled in the city after the Louisiana Purchase and from the waves of German and other immigrants arriving in the area. In rural Southwestern Louisiana, a blending of French, African and Caribbean cultures was considered Creole.

Cajun culture sprang from the Acadians who settled in South Louisiana following their expulsion from Acadia, or Nova Scotia, in the 1700s. This French colonial culture melded with mainland French immigrant cultures and with Haitian, Spanish, English, German and Native American cultures as it evolved to form the distinctive and unique Cajun culture found today in South Louisiana.

FISHERMAN'S CASTLE ON THE IRISH BAYOU, SLIDELL.

Simon Villemarrette built Fisherman's Castle in 1981 and he based it upon a fourteenth-century French castle. The original plan was for it to be a secondary tourist attraction for the 1984 World's Fair in New Orleans. However, the location of the castle was far from the center of town, and the plans to get the tour buses and boats to stop by fell through.

The castle was purposely built with round turrets and enough concrete to withstand 140 mile-an-hour winds and is one of the only structures that withstood Hurricane Katrina in 2005. It appears to look somewhat neglected but word has it, a renovation may be on the way in the future. It is located on US 11 along the east shore of Lake Pontchartrain at Irish Bayou. This dwelling gives new meaning to the old adage of a "man's home is a man's castle".

MARDI GRAS

People all over the world may be starting their usual Tuesday routines, but in Louisiana it's Carnival Time! Every year locals outdo themselves in fun, fantasy and creativity. You can find Zulu warriors handing out gilded coconuts; a pregnant woman dressed like a Faberge egg; and a butterfly with wings as wide as the street. Be prepared for nonstop fun and frivolity on Mardi Gras day.

Mardi Gras is an ancient tradition, with origins in Greece and Rome, that celebrates food and fun just before the 40 days of Lent, the Catholic time of prayer and sacrifice. Brought to Louisiana by the French, it evolved from a simple celebration into the "Largest Free Show on Earth" with a healthy dose of irreverence for its own traditions of pomp and circumstance.

The season begins on Twelfth Night in the New Orleans area with more than 60 parades rolling during the two weeks before Fat Tuesday. But the parade route doesn't end in the Crescent City. Slidell and Madisonville celebrate with colorful boat parades. Monroe-West Monroe and Houma have lighted float parades, Shreveport-Bossier City boasts a citywide Mardi Gras tradition with a focus on family activities and the Alexandria Pineville area celebrates the season with family fun during the weekend before Fat Tuesday. Lake Charles celebrates with the Krewe of Barkus (a costumed dog parade). Lafayette has a unique tradition of naming the king and queen of festivities after their legendary Acadian lovers Gabriel and Evangeline. And in Church Point, Eunice, Mamou and other towns, men on horseback roam the countryside from farm to farm on a "Mardi Gras Ride," gathering the ingredients for their towns' communal gumbos.

From north to south, east to west, Mardi Gras is celebrated. A few parade organizations (krewes) even allow visitors to ride on floats. For more information, call the tourist bureau in the city you will be visiting. Or, if you can't attend Mardi Gras, check out the year-round Mardi Gras exhibit in the Louisiana State Museum's Presbytere in New Orleans.

SCENIC DRIVES

With so much to see and do in such an interesting state, the following are some of the more scenic drives through Louisiana:

Acadiana Trail, U.S. 190 from Baton Rouge to the Texas border. Paralleling I-10, this route leads past many of the scenic, recreational and historic attractions of Cajun Country.

Bayou Lafourche Tour. Shrimp fleets, quaint towns and fine plantations line Bayou Lafourche as it flows south to the Gulf. For a map, contact the Lafourche Parish Tourist Commission.

Bayou Teche Corridor. Follow Bayou Teche (a Native American word meaning snake), starting at Hwy. 31 & Hwy. 345 in St. Martinville, home of Longfellows Evangeline and continue on Hwy. 182 through New Iberia, home to Tabasco® & Konriko rice mill, to Franklin with over 400 historic properties listed on the National Register of Historic Places.

Longleaf Trail Scenic Byway. One of the most scenic drives in the state is in **Kisatchie National Forest** near Natchitoches. This 17-mile drive through rugged terrain with unique vistas includes mesas, buttes and sandstone outcrops among long leaf pine.

Creole Nature Trail. Loop tour from I-10 in Sulphur via Hwy. 27 to I-10 in Lake Charles, passing the **Sabine and Rockefeller Wildlife Refuges** and other bird and wildlife watching opportunities in the marshland along the Gulf Coast.

CAMPCLUB USA

Where to Find CCUSA Parks

List City	Park Name	Map Coordinates
ABBEVILLE		
	Betty's RV Park	D-3
AJAX		
	Ajax Country Livin' at I-49 Rv Park, LLC	B-2
BREAUX BRIDGE		
	Poche's Fish-N-Camp	D-3
BROUSSARD		
	Maxie's Campground	D-3
FENTON		
	Quiet Oaks RV Park	D-2
HOUMA		
	Capri Court MHP	E-4
LIVINGSTON		
	Lakeside RV Park	D-4
NEW ORLEANS		
	French Quarter RV Resort	D-5
ST. MARTINVILLE		
	Catfish Heaven Agua Farm & Campground	D-3

Old Spanish Trail. Drive this historic trail through Calcasieu Parish, via US 90 and Hwy. 109, passing historic landmarks, Delta Downs Racetrack and much natural beauty.

SCENIC BYWAYS

Louisiana's Scenic Byways are marked by distinctive signs throughout the state leading you through historic and cultural towns and past beautiful natural landscapes. For a map of all the scenic byways call (800/926-3758) or visit:
www.louisianatravel.com/explorela/outdoors/scenicbyways/

The **Atchafalaya Trace Heritage Area**. America's largest freshwater swamp and the 14 parishes in and around the Atchafalaya Basin form the Atchafalaya Trace Heritage Area. Experience Louisiana culture through the stories, traditions, music and cuisine of the area.

Acadiana Trail. First used by Indians as a path that connected water routes, the Acadiana Trail now follows U.S. 190 from Baton Rouge to the Texas border. Paralleling I-10, this route leads past many of the scenic, recreational and historic attractions of Cajun Country.

Creole Nature Trail. One of only 20 All-American Roads—the highest ranking for a scenic byway in the United States—the trail travels through areas of breathtaking beauty. Loop tour from I-10 in Sulphur via Hwy. 27 to I-10 in Lake Charles, passing the Sabine and Rockefeller Wildlife Refuges and other bird and wildlife watching opportunities in the marshland along the Gulf Coast. Traversing Louisiana's outback, the 180-mile Creole Trail will lead you past where the notorious pirate Jean Lafitte hid treasure and where French traders did business with the Attakapas Indians. Prairie, marshland, thousands of acres of untouched wetlands and two national wildlife refuges are along the Byway. Wildlife abounds, especially alligators and waterfowl. Running along the Gulf of Mexico and up to Lake Charles, there are ample recreational opportunities including surf fishing, boating, hunting and swimming.

Mississippi River Road Corridor. A portion of the Great River Road runs through Louisiana between New Orleans and Baton Rouge. Passing through eight parishes, it is a historic stretch of road that affords views of romantic plantations, ancient cemeteries, quaint river towns and Civil War sites that take you back in time. There are numerous National Historic Districts, National Historic Landmarks, structures listed on the National Register of Historic Places and museums interpreting local history and river life. River outlooks along the way provide magnificent views of the Mississippi.

Longleaf Trail Scenic Byway. One of the most scenic drives in the state is in Kisatchie National Forest near Natchitoches. This 17-mile drive through rugged terrain with unique vistas includes mesas, buttes and sandstone outcrops among long leaf pine.

Louisiana Colonial Trails. This trail is comprised of the prehistoric and pioneer trail from Natchez to Natchitoches and into the Spanish Southwest. It begins at US 84 and Hwy. 6.

Louisiana's Western Corridor. This area transcends several regions along the western border of the state. Travel US 171 from I-10 to I-20, passing **Hodges Gardens, Kisatchie National Forest** and much more.

Old Spanish Trail. Drive this historic trail through Calcasieu Parish, via US 90 and Hwy. 109, passing historic landmarks, Delta Downs Racetrack and much natural beauty. For a map, contact the Southwest Convention & Visitors Bureau.

Promised Land Scenic Byway. So named because of a promise for land made to the exiled Acadians by the Spanish Governor of the Louisiana territory, the Byway borders the Henderson side of the Atchafalaya Basin.

DESTINATIONS

ANCIENT MOUNDS

Louisiana has more than 700 known earthen mound sites built hundreds to thousands of years ago. Prehistoric Native American cultures built them to serve as homes for tribal leaders, ceremonial sites and even burial sites. They can range in size from a few feet to over 70 feet tall. The Louisiana Ancient Mounds Trail is a current ongoing project to link the mounds in a trail with maps and interpretive guides. The first phase covering parts of northeast and central Louisiana links 40 mound sites and is interpreted in a 50 page map and interpretive guide. To order a copy visit www.louisianatravel.com/explorela/outdoors/ancientmounds/order.cfm.

SPORTSMAN'S PARADISE REGION

With its thick, piney woods, rolling hills, and sparkling lakes filled with mouth bass and trout, it's no wonder this area is called Sportsman's Paradise. This area is a haven for bird watchers, campers, anglers, and nature photographers alike. This region is also alive with history that goes back long before Greece and Rome were on the map, to a time when the Native Americans who roamed this land traded pottery and trapped deer. It's here that brave soldiers in blue and gray fought and fell at the Battle of Mansfield. And right outside of Arcadia, travelers will find a chipped little monument that marks the spot where Bonnie and Clyde took their last ride.

This area of northern Louisiana is filled with museums, parks, sporting and cultural events and is known for its fishing, hunting and outdoor recreation.

Arcadia. This peaceful town is located midway between Shreveport and Monroe and is surrounded by rolling hills and beautiful lakes. Visit Louisiana's largest flea market, Bonnie & Clyde Trade Days.

Mansfield State Historic Site. Located four miles south of Mansfield, this is the site of the most important Civil War battle fought west of the Mississippi. This 44-acre park includes a museum noted for its variety of military artifacts.

Monroe/West Monroe is located on the scenic **Ouachita River**. Visitors can enjoy diverse cultural experiences, along with riverboats, southern cuisine, festivals by the river and antique shopping. This area also offers a multitude of attractions including the **Emy-Lou Biedenharn Home**, built by Joseph Biedenharn, the first bottler of Coca-Cola. The **Louisiana Purchase Gardens & Zoo** houses 850 rare and exotic animals. Formal gardens, winding paths and waterways and huge live oaks provide a relaxing atmosphere. The **Masur Museum of Art** is the two-story English Tudor home of the Masur family.

Shreveport/Bossier City. Come experience roses, racing, riverboats and world class museums. Enjoy the Riverfront with year-round festivals and dining, entertainment and shopping at the **Louisiana Boardwalk.**

CROSSROADS REGION

Crossroads aptly gets its name by being right in the center of Louisiana. Here, travelers will want to visit Natchitoches, the inspiration for the movie, "Steel Magnolias". Follow the Red River that winds its way through town, and you will reach Alexandria, this region's largest city, surrounded by natural beauty and wildlife. Travelers looking for a bigger slice of Mother Nature shouldn't miss the 800,000-acre Kisatchie National Forest that is teeming with wildlife. Crossroads is alive with the plantations of the past, Native American culture and mounds, and a natural beauty hard to find anywhere else.

Arna Bontemps African-American Museum is the boyhood home of the noted author/poet, scholar, and librarian, Arna W. Bontemps. A great selection of his works along with many historical photos and artifacts are on display.

Kent House is the oldest remaining "Crossroads" plantation, built circa 1800. The house, outbuildings and herb gardens reflect the early 1800s.

Marksville is located in the southeastern section of the region. Marksville is home to the Marksville State Historic Site, an area of

Indian culture and earthen mounds dating from 1,400 A.D. The **Tunica-Biloxi Regional Indian Center and Museum** houses the world's largest collection of Native American/European artifacts from Louisiana's colonial period. Located on the reservation is **Paragon Casino**, featuring live entertainment, more than 1,500 slot machines and 60 table games, a poker room, four restaurants and Kids Quest.

DeRidder. Parish attractions include a Gothic jail with hanging tower, the **Beauregard Museum**, a pioneer village and the first building built for the USO in World War II.

Many. While in the beautiful **Toledo Bend** country area, experience Louisiana's "Garden in the Forest," **Hodges Gardens**, featuring 4,700 acres of woodlands, waterfalls and multi-level botanical gardens, an old-fashioned rose garden, as well as hiking and nature trails.

Natchitoches. Points of interest in Natchitoches include the first French Settlement, **Fort St. Jean Baptists State Historic Site**, a National Historic Landmark District, the **American Cemetery**, the **Center for the History of Louisiana Education** and the **Louisiana Sports Hall of Fame**. Tours of the Landmark District are available aboard the trolley **"City Belle." Magnolia Plantation Home** is a National Bicentennial farm dating from 1753. View the extensive collection of Southern Empire and Louisiana furniture.

CAJUN COUNTRY

This southern area, full of lush, mysterious swamps and bayous has a time-honored tradition of cultural and spiritual richness. The first French Canadians settled here, and forever changed the landscape and culture of this great state. These were the people that turned soup into gumbo, washboards into musical instruments, and made this swampy region a mystical paradise.

Kinder. Located on the **Coushatta Indian Reservation, Grand Casino Coushatta** offers more than 1,200 slot machines, 50 table games, a buffet, restaurant and lounge and Kids Quest— a supervised children's activity center.

Lafayette. The Capital of Cajun Country, Lafayette offers horse racing, boat tours of the **Atchafalaya Basin Swamp**, an authentically restored Acadian Village, nearby plantation homes, natural history, as well as contemporary and traditional art museums.

Lake Charles. Cajunland City, located in southwestern Louisiana, features freshwater, saltwater and deep-sea fishing access. The city also offers duck hunting views of alligators in their natural habitat along the **Creole Nature Trail Scenic Byway** and the 1,000-acre **Sam Houston Jones State Park**. Enjoy the Historic "Charpentier" District, museums, palm beaches, quarter horse and thoroughbred racing, off-track betting, video poker and many casinos, including the Isle of Capri Casino.

New Iberia/Avery Island. Known as Cajun paradise, New Iberia offers everything from historic homes and gardens to fishing, golfing and is home of the world's most famous hot sauce—Tabasco®! In touring **McIlhenny Company's Tabasco® Factory**, you'll view an 8-minute film about the history of Tabasco® sauce, observe the bottling line and end the tour in the Tabasco® Country Store.

Avery Island's Jungle Gardens is southwest of New Iberia. In addition to the garden's lush plant life, the great number of egrets and herons are of special interest.

Jefferson Island. The Victorian home of actor Joseph Jefferson features 25 acres of gardens in bloom year-round, **Café Jefferson**, a gift shop, a conference center and boat excursions.

Shadows-on-the-Teche. Built in 1834 for sugar planter David Weeks, the Shadows exhibits the lifestyle of the antebellum South through its 9 rooms.

PLANTATION COUNTRY

Visitors to Plantation Country get a glimpse back in time. Plantations dot this area, and open their doors to tours of gardens and homes. Many offer overnight stays, including The Myrtles, which has been called "the most haunted house in America". These homes are the crown jewels of Louisiana, giving visitors an up close and intimate look into the daily lives of a truly fascinating period in history.

Convent. Poche Plantation Bed and Breakfast and Guided Tours. Located less than an hour from New Orleans, on the majestic River Road, the Poche Plantation hosts a bed and breakfast and guided tours at this Louisiana plantation home that has been beautifully restored to its original splendor.

Baton Rouge. Attractions include old and new state capitals, the **LSU Rural Life Museum** and a zoo with more than 500 animals from 6 continents, plus plantation and river tours.

U.S.S. Kidd. A national historic landmark, the Kidd is a restored World War II destroyer that was awarded 8 battle stars. A detailed tour takes you to over 50 inner spaces. The adjacent **Historic Center** contains a collection of ship models and a P-40 fighter plane.

GREATER NEW ORLEANS REGION

This area of Louisiana is undoubtedly the most talked about, and widely known. This area is so deeply connected to its French and Spanish roots, visitors can't help but see the influence everywhere, from the Creole cottages, with their lacy iron balconies, to the gothic spires of St. Louis Cathedral. It's said that jazz was born in New Orleans, because words just wouldn't do this city justice.

Destrehan Plantation. Built in 1787, Destrehan is the oldest plantation left intact in the lower Mississippi Valley. It is located on the Great River Road. Daily tours are offered and a gift shop is located on the grounds.

New Orleans. The city boasts magnificent food, music, attractions and fun. Cruise on an authentic paddlewheeler through one of America's busiest ports to **Chalmette Battlefield**, the site of the Battle of New Orleans. Or, enjoy a dinner/jazz cruise, complete with a Creole buffet, a Dixieland jazz band and a sparkling city skyline. If you're interested in wildlife, take a swamp tour at **Jean Lafitte Swamp Tours**. See the gators jump, the owl's hoot and moss-draped bayous. The **New Orleans Steamboat Company** offers an aquarium/zoo cruise on the riverboat John James Audubon that transports you to the **Audubon Zoo** and the **Aquarium of the Americas**. Ride on the only authentic steam powered sternwheeler, the Steamboat Natchez, on a 2-hour harbor cruise with live jazz music. Have your coffee at **Cafe Du Monde,** since 1862 the original French Market Coffee Stand, or dine at **Mulate's—The World's Most Famous Cajun Restaurant** and have a memorable time dancing to a Cajun band and savoring Cajun cuisine. Enjoy the comfort of your own recreational vehicle on board the deck of the "Cruising Campground" with **RV River Charters** and experience the ever-changing scenery as you cruise America's inland waters. If you would rather stay on land, **Gray Line of New Orleans** offers a variety of daily tours to suit your interest: city, plantations and French Quarter walking tours. Get a glimpse of where Mardi Gras is made at **Blaine Kern's Mardi Gras World**. Try on costumes worn by Mardi Gras Royalty and marvel at figures of dinosaurs, monsters and more. **French Quarter (Vieux Carre)**. The Quarter sets New Orleans apart from any other place in the world. Wander down any of the narrow streets and be drawn into the romance of the past and present. The French Market is 5 blocks of festive shopping in the French Quarter. Enjoy famous cafe au lait and beignets 24 hours a day, a flea market, Pirate's Alley with free music, entertainment, history and life-sized sculptures. **Jackson Square**. The hub of New Orleans is also the heart of the French Quarter. Surrounded on 3 sides by buildings and fronted by the Mississippi River, the square's landscaped tranquility belies the turbulent history it has witnessed. **LA Superdome**. The world's largest domed stadium is home to the New Orleans Saints and the Sugar Bowl. There are guided tours daily. **New Orleans Riverwalk.** Stroll along this half-mile festival marketplace filled with live entertainment.

ABBEVILLE—D-3

(W) Abbeville RV Park (RV SPACES)—(Vermilion) *From jct US 167 & Bus. Hwy 14: Go 1/2 mi W on Bus. Hwy 14. Enter on L.* FACILITIES: 54 sites, 49 full hkups, 5 W&E, (15/30/50 amps), 50 amps ($), family camping, dump. Pets welcome. Partial handicap access. No tents. Open all yr. Big rigs welcome. Rate in 2010 $20-22 for 4 persons. Member ARVC, LCOA. Phone: (337)898-4042.

(S) Betty's RV Park—(Vermillion) *From jct US 167 & Bus Hwy 14: Go 1/2 mi on Bus Hwy 14, then 1-1/2 mi S on State St. Enter on R.* ◆◆◆FACILITIES: 15 sites, accepts full hkup units only, 15 full hkups, (20/30/50 amps), 50 amps ($), cable TV, WiFi Instant Internet at site, WiFi Internet central location, picnic tables. RECREATION: Pets welcome, breed restrict. No tents. Open all yr. Rate in 2010 $18-20 for 2 persons. CCUSA 50% Discount. CCUSA reservations Recommended, CCUSA max stay See Rest., Cash only for CCUSA disc., CCUSA disc. not avail holidays. Discount available May-Sep. Discount not available during Mardi Gras. Max stay unlimited but only 1 night in a 7 day time period. Adults only.

ABBEVILLE—Continued
Betty's RV Park—Continued

Phone: (337)893-7057
Address: 2118 S State St, Abbeville, LA 70510
Lat/Lon: 29.95296/-92.14272
Email: bettybernard@cox.net
Web: www.bettysrvpark.com

AJAX—B-2

(C) Ajax Country Livin' at I-49 Rv Park, LLC—(Natchitoches) *From jct I-49 (exit 155) & Hwy 174: Go 1/4 mi W on Hwy 174. Enter on L.* ◆◆◆FACILITIES: 27 sites, typical site width 25 ft, 27 full hkups, (20/30/50 amps), 50 amps ($), 22 pull-thrus, phone Internet central location, family camping, tenting, RV storage, laundry, RV supplies, LP gas by weight/by meter, picnic tables, wood. ◆RECREATION: pond fishing, horseshoes, hiking trails. Pets welcome. Open all yr. Big rigs welcome. Rate in 2010 $24-27 for 2 persons. CCUSA 50% Discount. CCUSA reservations Recommended, CCUSA max stay 5 days, Cash only for CCUSA disc., Check only for CCUSA disc., CCUSA disc. not avail holidays. Based on availability. No discount available 1st & 2nd weekends of Dec.

Phone: (318)796-2543
Address: 1115 Highway 174, Marthaville, LA 71450
Lat/Lon: 31.88253/-93.37479
Email: countrylivin@cp-tel.net

ALEXANDRIA—C-3

(W) RAPIDES COLISEUM (Parish Park)—(Rapides) *From jct US 71/US 165 & Hwy 28 W: Go 1 mi W on Hwy 28. Enter on R.* FACILITIES: 216 sites, accepts self-contained units only, 16 full hkups, 200 E, (30 amps). RECREATION: Pets welcome. No tents. Open all yr. Phone: (318)442-1272.

ANACOCO—C-2

(W) SOUTH TOLEDO BEND STATE PARK—(Vernon) *From jct US 171 & Hwy 111/392: Go 10-1/2 mi W on Hwy 111/392, then 1 mi N on Hwy 191, then 1/2 mi W on Bald Eagle Rd. Enter on L.* FACILITIES: 60 sites, 55 W&E, (20/30 amps), 5 no hkups, 4 pull-thrus, family camping, tenting, dump, laundry. RECREATION: lake swim, boating, canoeing, ramp, lake/river fishing, playground. Pets welcome. Open all yr. Phone: (888)398-4770.

ARCADIA—A-2

(S) Bonnie & Clyde Trade Days & Campground—(Bienville) *From jct I-20 (exit 69) & Hwy 151: Go 1 mi S on Hwy 151, then continue S (straight ahead) 2-1/2 mi on Hwy 9. Enter on R.* ◆◆◆FACILITIES: 72 sites, typical site width 24 ft, 44 full hkups, 28 W&E, (20/30/50 amps), 50 amps ($), 25 pull-thrus, family camping, tenting, dump, laundry. ◆◆RECREATION: pond fishing. Pets welcome, breed restrict. Open all yr. Big rigs welcome. Rate in 2010 $22-26 per vehicle. Phone: (318)263-2437. FMCA discount.

BASTROP—A-3

(N) CHEMIN-A-HAUT STATE PARK—(Morehouse) *From jct US 165 & US 425: Go 10 mi N on US 425, then 1/2 mi E on Loop Park Rd/SR 2229.* FACILITIES: 26 sites, 26 W&E, (30 amps), tenting, dump, laundry. RECREATION: swim pool, ramp, lake fishing, playground. Pets welcome. Open all yr. Phone: (888) 677-2436.

BATON ROUGE—D-4

(SW) BATON ROUGE KOA—(Livingston) *From jct I-12 (exit 10) & Hwy 3002: Go 1/2 mi S on Hwy 3002, then 1/2 mi W on Hwy 1034. Enter on L.*

◆◆◆◆FACILITIES: 112 sites, typical site width 35 ft, 106 full hkups, (30/50 amps), 6 no hkups, some extd stay sites, 67 pull-thrus, cable TV, WiFi Instant Internet at site, phone Internet central location, family camping, tenting, cabins, dump, non-guest dump $, laundry, groceries, RV supplies, LP gas by weight/by meter, ice, picnic tables, patios, fire rings, grills.

◆◆◆◆RECREATION: rec hall, rec room/area, pavilion, coin games, swim pool, wading pool, hot tub, mini-golf, ($), golf nearby, bsktball, playground, activities, sports field.

Pets welcome, breed restrict. Partial handicap access. Open all yr. Big rigs welcome. Escort to site. Clubs welcome. Rate in 2010 $35-40 for 2 persons. MC/VISA/DISC/AMEX/Debit. Member ARVC, LCOA. KOA discount.

Phone: (225)664-7281
Address: 7628 Vincent Rd., Denham Springs, LA 70726
Lat/Lon: 30.45460/-90.96376
Email: gbacot@ix.netcom.com
Web: www.batonrougekoa.com

SEE AD THIS PAGE

(SW) FARR PARK CAMPGROUND & HORSE ACTIVITY CENTER—(East Baton Rouge) *From jct I-10 (exit 158) & College Dr: Go 5-1/2 mi S on College (which becomes Lee Dr, then becomes Brightside Lane), then 1/2 mi S on River Rd. Enter on L.* FACILITIES: 79 sites, typical site width 15 ft, 79 W&E, (20/30 amps), 79 pull-thrus, dump, laundry. RECREATION: playground. Pets welcome. Partial handicap access. No tents. Open all yr. Phone: (225)769-7805.

LAKESIDE RV PARK—*From Baton Rouge (jct I-10 & I-12): Go 22 mi E on I-12, then 1-1/4 mi S on Hwy 63 (exit 22). Enter on R.*

SEE PRIMARY LISTING AT LIVINGSTON AND AD THIS PAGE

LOUISIANA CULINARY TRAILS—Discover seven delicious road trips designed to make you drool on one or all seven of Louisiana's Culinary Trails. Start your journey today!.

Phone: (225)346-1857
Address: 1165 S Foster Dr, Baton Rouge, LA 70806
Web: www.louisianaculinarytrails.com

SEE AD TRAVEL SECTION PAGE 280

BATON ROUGE—Continued on next page

The fantastic floats of New Orleans' Mardi Gras are constructed and named by societies known as "Krewes".

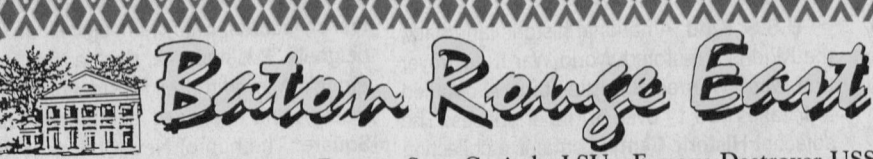

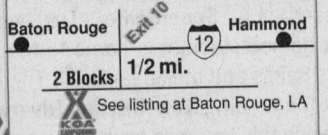

BATON ROUGE—Continued

(E) LOUISIANA TRAVEL PROMOTION ASSOCIATION—Explore the many regions of Louisiana and discover the diversity of its many cultures-from casinos to plantations to restaurants and museums. Open all yr.

Phone: (225)346-1857
Address: 1165 S Foster Dr, Baton Rouge, LA 70806
Lat/Lon: 30.43866/-91.13295
Email: tschultz@ltpa.org
Web: www.ltpa.org

SEE AD TRAVEL SECTION PAGE 280-281

POCHE PLANTATION RV RESORT—*From Baton Rouge jct I-12 & I-10: Go 20 mi S on I-10 (exit 179), then 15-3/4 mi S on Hwy 44. Enter on L.*

SEE PRIMARY LISTING AT GONZALES AND AD NEXT PAGE

BELLE CHASSE—D-5

(SE) MILITARY PARK (New Orleans NAS Travel Camp)—(PlaqueMines) *From I-10: Cross E over Miss. River to Business US 90/Westbank Expwy, then 9 mi SE on Hwy 23 (Lafayette St/Belle-Chase Hwy. On base. Enter on R.* FACILITIES: 30 sites, 30 full hkups, 2 pull-thrus, tenting, dump, laundry. RECREATION: swim pool. Open Campground has been closed. Phone: (504) 678-3142.

BENTON—A-2

(N) CYPRESS BLACK BAYOU RECREATION AREA—(Bossier) *From jct I-220 & Airline Dr (Exit 12): Go 5-1/2 mi N on Airline Dr, then 4-1/4 mi E on Linton Rd. Enter on R.* FACILITIES: 73 sites, typical site width 25 ft, 73 W&E, (30/50 amps), 21 pull-thrus, family camping, tenting, dump. RECREATION: lake swim, boating, canoeing, ramp, dock, lake fishing, playground. Pets welcome. Partial handicap access. Open all yr. Big rigs welcome. Phone: (318)965-0007.

BOSSIER CITY—A-2

(N) Cash Point Landing—(Bossier) *From jct I-220 (exit 11) & LA 3: Go 3-3/4 mi N on LA 3. Enter on L.* ◊◊FACILITIES: 102 sites, typical site width 35 ft, 102 full hkups, (20/30/50 amps), 42 pull-thrus, family camping, laundry, ltd groc. ◊◊RECREATION: boating, ramp, river fishing. Pets welcome. No tents. Open all yr. Big rigs welcome. Rate in 2010 $25 per vehicle. Phone: (318)742-4999.

(C) Diamond Jacks RV Park—(Bossier) *From jct I-20 (exit 20A) & Diamond Jacks Blvd: Go 1 block S on Diamond Jacks Blvd. Enter at end.* ◊◊◊◊FACILITIES: 32 sites, 32 full hkups, (30/50 amps), 20 pull-thrus, family camping, laundry. ◊◊RECREATION: swim pool. Pets welcome. Partial handicap access. No tents. Open all yr. Big rigs welcome. Rate in 2010 $34.05-45.40 v. Phone: (318)678-7661.

MILITARY PARK (Barksdale AFB FAMCAMP)—(Caddo) *Off I-20 & US 71. On base.* FACILITIES: 42 sites, 42 full hkups, (20/30/50 amps), family camping, tenting, dump, laundry, ltd groc. RECREATION: boating. Pets welcome. Open all yr. Big rigs welcome. Phone: (318)456-2679.

BREAUX BRIDGE—D-3

(N) POCHE'S FISH-N-CAMP—(St. Martin) *From jct I-10 (exit 109) & Hwy 328: Go 1-3/4 mi NW on Hwy 328, then 1/4 mi N on Posche Bridge Rd, then 1/4 mi E on Hwy 31, then N 1-3/4 mi on Hwy 341, then 1/2 mi W on Hwy 354. Enter on R.*

◊◊◊◊FACILITIES: 88 sites, typical site width 32 ft, 88 full hkups, (20/30/50 amps), 3 pull-thrus, WiFi Instant Internet at site ($), WiFi Internet central location ($), family camping, tenting, cabins, laundry, ltd groc, ice, picnic tables, fire rings, wood.

◊◊◊RECREATION: rec hall, equipped pavilion, swim pool, pond fishing, fishing supplies, golf nearby, play equipment.

Pets welcome. Open all yr. Big rigs welcome. Clubs welcome. Rate in 2010 $30 for 2 persons. MC/VISA/DISC/AMEX/Debit. CCUSA 50% Discount. CCUSA reservations Recommended, CCUSA max stay 5 days, CCUSA disc. not avail F,Sa.

Phone: (337)332-0326
Address: 1080 Sawmill Hwy, Breaux Bridge, LA 70517
Lat/Lon: 30.33464/-91.92549
Email: camp@pochesrvpark.com
Web: www.pochesrvpark.com

SEE AD LAFAYETTE PAGE 291

Louisiana is the only state in the union that does not have counties. Its political subdivisions are called parishes.

BREAUX BRIDGE—Continued

(N) POCHE'S MARKET, RESTAURANT & SMOKEHOUSE—*From jct I-10 (exit 109) & Hwy 328: Go 1-3/4 mi NW on Hwy 328, then 1/4 mi N on Poche Bridge Rd, then 100 ft W on Hwy 31.* Specialty meats, market,restaurant and smokehouse. Many cajun specialties. Daily lunches served. Most items available for shipping. USDA inspected. Open all yr. MC/VISA/DISC/AMEX.

Phone: (337)332-2108
Address: 3015 A Main Hwy, Breaux Bridge, LA 70517
Lat/Lon: 30.29569/-91.91116
Email: reservations@pochesmarket.com
Web: www.poches.com

SEE AD LAFAYETTE PAGE 291

BROUSSARD—D-3

(S) LaBoulaie RV Park & Campground (RV SPACES)—(St. Martin) *From Jct Hwy 182 & Hwy 90: Go 3 mi S on Hwy 90 (Evangeline Hwy). Enter on R.* FACILITIES: 47 sites, typical site width 30 ft, 47 full hkups, (20/30/50 amps), family camping, laundry. Pets welcome, breed restrict. No tents. Open all yr. Member LCOA. Phone: (337)856-0555. FMCA discount.

(N) Maxie's Campground—(Lafeyette) *From jct Hwy 182 & Hwy 90: Go 1 m N on Hwy 90 (Evangaline Hwy). Enter on R.* ◊◊◊FACILITIES: 64 sites, typical site width 20 ft, 64 full hkups, (20/30/50 amps), 50 amps ($), WiFi Instant Internet at site ($), phone Internet central location, family camping, tenting, laundry, picnic tables. RECREATION: Pets welcome. Open all yr. Big rigs welcome. Rate in 2010 $24.64 for 2 persons. Member ARVC, LCOA. CCUSA 50% Discount. CCUSA reservations Recommended, CCUSA max stay Unlimied, Cash only for CCUSA disc., Check only for CCUSA disc. Discount not available during Mardi Gras. Cable tv available for long term use only.WiFi available thru Tengo internet for a fee.

Phone: (337)837-6200
Address: 4350 Hwy 90 E, Broussard, LA 70518
Lat/Lon: 33.14963/-91.95119
Email: jason@maxiescampground.com
Web: www.maxiescampground.com

CARENCRO—D-3

(E) BAYOU WILDERNESS RV RESORT—(Lafayette) *From jct I-10 (exit 103B) & US 167/I-49N: Go 2-1/2 mi N on US 167/I-49, then 2-1/4 mi E on Gloria Switch (exit 2), then 3/4 mi N on North Wilderness Trail. Enter on R.*

◊◊◊◊FACILITIES: 120 sites, typical site width 25 ft, accepts full hkup units only, 120 full hkups, (20/30/50 amps), 50 amps ($), some extd stay sites, 120 pull-thrus, cable TV, WiFi Instant Internet at site ($), WiFi Internet central location, family camping, RV storage, dump, non-guest dump $, laundry, ltd groc, RV supplies, LP gas by weight/by meter, ice, picnic tables.

◊◊◊◊RECREATION: rec hall, rec room/area, swim pool, hot tub, lake fishing, golf nearby, playground, shuffleboard court, activities (wkends), tennis, sports field, v-ball.

Pets welcome. Partial handicap access. No tents. Open all yr. Big rigs welcome. Clubs welcome. Rate in 2010 $43-46 for 4 persons. MC/VISA/DISC/Debit. Member ARVC, LCOA. FMCA discount.

Phone: (337)896-0598
Address: 201 St Clair Rd, Carencro, LA 70520
Lat/Lon: 30.30512/-91.98447
Email: bayouwilderness@bellsouth.net
Web: www.bwrvr.com

SEE AD LAFAYETTE PAGE 292

CHATHAM—A-3

(C) JIMMY DAVIS STATE PARK—(Jackson) *From jct US 167 & Hwy 4: Go 4 mi E on Hwy 4, exit on N Lakeshore Dr, then right on State Parks Rd.* FACILITIES: 73 sites, 73 W&E, (30/50 amps), tenting, dump, laundry. RECREATION: lake swim, boating, ramp, lake fishing, playground. Pets welcome. Open all yr. Phone: (888)677-2263.

COLFAX—B-3

(NW) COLFAX RECREATION AREA RV PARK & CAMPGROUND—(Grant) *From jct I-49 (exit 99) & LA-8: Go 11-1/4 mi E on Hwy 8, then E on Main St 1/2 mi, then W on LA-158 1 mi to Lock & Dam sign, then 1/4 mi W to Area. Enter on R.* FACILITIES: 25 sites, 25 full hkups, (30/50 amps), tenting, dump, laundry. RECREATION: boating, ramp, dock, river fishing, playground. Pets welcome. Partial handicap access. Open all yr. Big rigs welcome. Phone: (318)627-2640.

COUSHATTA—B-2

(SE) GRAND BAYOU RESORT—(Red River) *From jct I-49 (exit 162) & LA 177: Go 6 mi NE on LA 177, then 7-1/2 mi SE on US 84, then 1-1/4 mi E on Hwy 784. Enter on R.* FACILITIES:

COUSHATTA—Continued
GRAND BAYOU RESORT—Continued

59 sites, 49 W&E, (30/50 amps), 50 amps ($), 10 no hkups, 11 pull-thrus, tenting, dump, laundry, groceries. RECREATION: lake swim, boating, ramp, dock, lake fishing, playground. Pets welcome. Partial handicap access. Open all yr. Phone: (877)932-3821.

COVINGTON—D-5

(N) Land-O-Pines Family Campground—(St. Tammany) *From jct US 190 & Hwy 25: Go 4-1/2 mi NW on Hwy 25, then 2 mi E & N on Million Dollar Rd. Enter on L.* ◊◊◊FACILITIES: 270 sites, typical site width 35 ft, 185 full hkups, 85 W&E, (20/30/50 amps), 1 pull-thrus, family camping, tenting, dump, laundry, groceries. ◊◊◊◊RECREATION: swim pool, river swim, river/pond fishing, playground. Pets welcome, breed restrict. Partial handicap access. Open all yr. Facilities fully operational April - Sep. Big rigs welcome. Rate in 2010 $36-60 for 5 persons. Member ARVC, LCOA. Phone: (985)892-6023.

DONALDSONVILLE—D-4

(C) B & B RV PARK (RV SPACES)—(Ascension) *From jct Hwy 18 & Hwy 1: Go 1 1/2 mi SW on Hwy 1, then 1 block N on Bellina Dr. Enter on R.*

FACILITIES: 48 sites, typical site width 25 ft, accepts full hkup units only, 48 full hkups, (30/50 amps), some extd stay sites, cable on-site Internet (needs activ), laundry, patios.

Pets welcome. No tents. Open all yr. No restrooms. Big rigs welcome. Rate in 2010 $20 per vehicle.

Phone: (225)473-4744
Address: 100 Bellina Dr, Donaldsonville, LA 70346
Lat/Lon: 30.09764/-91.01288
Email: cjbellina@cox.net

SEE AD THIS PAGE

DOYLINE—A-2

(S) LAKE BISTINEAU STATE PARK—(Webster) *From jct I-20 (exit 47) & Hwy 7: Go 3-1/2 mi S on Hwy 7, then 6-1/2 mi W on Hwy 164, then 7 mi S on Hwy 163. Enter on L.* FACILITIES: 67 sites, 67 W&E, (30/50 amps), 5 pull-thrus, tenting, dump, laundry. RECREATION: 2 swim pools, boating, canoeing, ramp, lake fishing, playground. Pets welcome. Open all yr. Phone: (888) 677-2478.

EGAN—D-3

(S) Cajun Haven RV Park—(Acadia) *From jct I-10 & Egan Hwy (exit 72): Go 1/4 mi N on Egan Hwy (Trumps Rd). Enter on R.* ◊◊◊FACILITIES: 63 sites, 54 full hkups, 9 W&E, (30/50 amps), 50 amps ($), 63 pull-thrus, family camping, tenting, dump, laundry. ◊◊RECREATION: pond fishing, playground. Pets welcome. Open all yr. Big rigs welcome. Rate in 2010 $20 for 2 persons.

EUNICE—D-3

(N) LAKEVIEW RV PARK (TOO NEW TO RATE)—(Evangeline Parish) *From jct US 190 & SR 13: Go 3-1/2 mi N on SR 13. Enter on R.*

FACILITIES: 80 sites, typical site width 40 ft, 80 full hkups, (20/30/50 amps), 65 pull-thrus, cable TV, WiFi Instant Internet at site, WiFi Internet central location, family camping, tenting, cabins, laundry, LP gas by weight, ice, fire rings, wood.

RECREATION: pavilion, 2 canoe rentals, lake fishing, golf nearby, bsktball, playground, activities (wkends), horseshoes, v-ball.

LAKEVIEW RV PARK—Continued on next page

EUNICE—Continued
LAKEVIEW RV PARK—Continued

Pets welcome. Partial handicap access. Open all yr. Big rigs welcome. Clubs welcome. Rate in 2010 $27 for 4 persons. MC/VISA/Debit. Member ARVC, LCOA.

Phone: (337)457-2881
Address: 1717 Veteran Memorial Highway, Eunice, LA 70535
Lat/Lon: 30.32523/-92.25605
Email: bonnie@lvpark.com
Web: www.lvpark.com

SEE AD THIS PAGE

FARMERVILLE—A-3

(E) LAKE D'ARBONNE STATE PARK—(Union) *From town: Go 5 mi W on Hwy 2, then 1/4 mi S on Evergreen Rd. Enter on R.* FACILITIES: 58 sites, 58 W&E, (20/30 amps), tenting, dump, laundry. RECREATION: swim pool, boating, ramp, dock, lake fishing, play equipment. Pets welcome. Open all yr. Phone: (888)677-5200.

FENTON—D-2

(S) Quiet Oaks RV Park—(Jefferson) *From jct I-10 (exit 44) & US 165: Go 10 mi N on US 165, then 1/4 mi W on TV Tower Rd. Enter on L.* ◆◆◆FACILITIES: 57 sites, typical site width 20 ft, 57 full hkups, (20/30/50 amps), 23 pull-thrus, WiFi Internet central location, family camping, tenting, laundry, wood. RECREATION: pond fishing, horseshoes. Pets welcome, breed restrict. Open all yr. Rate in 2010 $24 for 2 persons. MC/VISA/DISC/Debit. FCRV discount. FMCA discount. CCUSA 50% Discount. CCUSA reservations Recommended, CCUSA max stay 14 days, Cash only for CCUSA disc., Check only for CCUSA disc. 2 night minimum stay.

CAMPCLUB USA

Phone: (888)755-2230
Address: 18159 TV Tower Rd, Kinder, LA 70648
Lat/Lon: 30.37955/-92.91416
Email: quietoak@quietoaks.com
Web: www.quietoaks.com

Reserve Online at Woodalls.com

FLORIEN—C-2

(S) HODGES GARDENS—(Sabine) *From jct Hwy 6 & US 171: Go 14-1/2 mi S on US 171. Enter on L.* RECREATION: Open all yr. Phone: (318)586-3523.

FOLSOM—C-5

(W) Tchefuncte Campground—(Tangipahoa) *From jct Hwy 25 & Hwy 40: Go 4-1/2 mi W on Hwy 40, then 2-1/4 mi N on Campground Rd. Enter at end.* ◆◆◆FACILITIES: 109 sites, typical site width 25 ft, 43 full hkups, 66 W&E, (20/30/50 amps), 50 amps ($), 8 pull-thrus, family camping, tenting, dump, laundry, ltd groc. ◆◆◆RECREATION: swim pool, river/river/pond fishing, play equipment. Pets welcome, breed restrict. Open all yr. Rate in 2010 $30 for 5 persons. Member LCOA.

The capital of Louisiana is Baton Rouge.

FOLSOM—Continued
Tchefuncte Campground—Continued

Phone: (985)796-3654
Address: 54492 Campground Rd, Folsom, LA 70437
Lat/Lon: 30.6170/-90.2533
Email: tchefuncte@hughes.net
Web: www.tchefunctecampground.com

GARDNER—C-3

(S) KISATCHIE NATIONAL FOREST (Kincaid Rec. Site) —(Rapides) *From jct Hwy 28 & Hwy 121: Go 1/4 mi SW on Hwy 121, then 5 mi S on FR 279, then 2 mi NE on FR 205.* FACILITIES: 40 sites, typical site width 10 ft, 40 W&E, 1 pull-thrus, tenting, dump. RECREATION: lake swim, boating, canoeing, ramp, lake fishing. Pets welcome. Partial handicap access. Open all yr. Phone: (318)445-9396.

GONZALES—D-4

(S) LAMAR DIXON EXPO CENTER RV PARK—(Ascension) *From jct I-10 & LA 30 (exit 177): Go 1/2 mi W on LA Hwy 30, then 1 mi S on St Landry Rd. Enter on R.* FACILITIES: 284 sites, 284 full hkups, (20/30/50 amps), 50 amps ($), 100 pull-thrus, family camping. RECREATION: Pets welcome. No tents. Open all yr. Big rigs welcome. Phone: (225)621-1700.

(C) POCHE PLANTATION—*From jct I-10 (exit 179) & Hwy 44: Go 15-3/4 mi S on Hwy 44. Enter on L.* Bed & Breakfast and guided tours, Poche Plantation listed on the National Register of historic places. Guided tours & museum. Post Office on site. Open all yr. MC/VISA/DISC/AMEX.

WELCOME

Phone: (225)562-7728
Address: 6554 Hwy 44 River Rd, Convent, LA 70723
Lat/Lon: 30.01268/-90.82761
Email: innkeeper@pocheplantation.com
Web: www.pocheplantation.com

SEE AD THIS PAGE

(C) POCHE PLANTATION RV RESORT—(St. James) *From jct I-10 (exit 179) & Hwy 44: Go 15-3/4 mi S on Hwy 44. Enter on L.*

WELCOME

◆◆◆◆◆FACILITIES: 85 sites, typical site width 30 ft, 85 full hkups, (20/30/50 amps), many extd stay sites, 21 pull-thrus, cable TV, WiFi Instant Internet at site, phone on-site Internet (needs activ), WiFi Internet central location, cabins, laundry, picnic tables, patios.

◆◆◆RECREATION: rec hall, rec room/area, swim pool, hot tub, golf nearby, bsktball, activities, sports field, hiking trails.

Pets welcome. No tents. Open all yr. Big rigs welcome. Escort to site. Clubs welcome. Rate in 2010 $18-38 for 2 persons. MC/VISA/DISC/AMEX. Member ARVC, LCOA. FMCA discount.

Text 108012 to (440)725-8687 to see our Visual Tour.

Louisiana State Bird: Brown Pelican

GONZALES—Continued
POCHE PLANTATION RV RESORT—Continued

Phone: (225)715-9510
Address: 6554 Hwy 44 River Rd, Convent, LA 70723
Lat/Lon: 30.01268/-90.82761
Email: innkeeper@pocheplantation.com
Web: www.pocheplantation.com

SEE AD THIS PAGE

(W) Sugar Hill RV Park (TOO NEW TO RATE) —(Ascension) *From jct I-10 (exit 179) & Hwy 44: Go 7-3/4 mi S on Hwy 44. Enter on L.* FACILITIES: 161 sites, typical site width 45 ft, 161 full hkups, (20/30/50 amps), 24 pull-thrus, family camping, laundry, groceries. RECREATION: swim pool. Pets welcome. Partial handicap access. No tents. Open all yr. Big rigs welcome. Rate in 2010 $15-31 for 2 persons. Phone: (225)715-9510.

GRAND ISLE—E-5

(SW) GRAND ISLE STATE PARK—(Jefferson) *From town: Go E on Hwy 1 to the end of the island. Enter at end.* FACILITIES: 49 sites, typical site width 30 ft, 49 W&E, (20/30/50 amps), 49 pull-thrus, tenting, dump. RECREATION: saltwater swim, saltwater fishing. Pets welcome. Open all yr. Phone: (888)787-2559.

GREENWOOD—A-1

(C) Travel America's RV Park—(Caddo) *E'bound from jct I-20 (exit 5) & Hwy 80: Go 50 yards N on Hwy 80, then 200 yards W on service road. W'bound: Continue straight across Hwy 80, then 200 yards W on service road. Enter on R.* ◆◆◆FACILITIES: 44 sites, typical site width 25 ft, 44 full hkups, (20/30/50 amps), 10 pull-thrus, family camping, laundry, groceries. ◆RECREATION: swim pool. Pets welcome. No tents. Open all yr. Big rigs welcome. Rate in 2010 $22 per vehicle. Phone: (318)938-6360.

HAMMOND—D-5

(S) Calloway RV & Campground—(Tangipahoa) *From jct I-12 & I-55 (Exit 28): Go 1 mi S on I-55, then 1/2 mi N on US 51, then 3/4 mi W on Club Deluxe Rd. Enter on L.* ◆◆◆◆FACILITIES: 60 sites, typical site width 20 ft, 60 full hkups, (30/50 amps), 50 amps ($), 49 pull-thrus, tenting, dump, laundry. ◆◆◆RECREATION: swim pool, lake fishing, play equipment. Pets welcome, breed restrict. Open all yr. Big rigs welcome. Rate in 2010 $30-33 for 2 persons. Member ARVC, LCOA. Phone: (985)542-8094.

(E) Hidden Oaks Family Campground—(Tangipahoa) *From jct I-12 (exit 47) & Hwy-445: Go 2 mi N on Hwy-445, then 1-1/4 mi W on US-190. Enter on L.* ◆◆FACILITIES: 225 sites, typical site width 25 ft, 225 full hkups, (30/50 amps), 30 pull-thrus, family camping, tenting, dump, laundry, ltd groc. ◆◆◆◆RECREATION: swim pool, river swim, boating, canoeing, lake/river fishing, playground. Pets welcome, breed restrict. Open all yr. Big rigs welcome. Rate in 2010 $35-40 for 5 persons. Phone: (800)359-0940.

(W) Punkin Park Campground—(Tangipahoa) *From jct I-55 & I-12: Go 3 mi W on I-12 (exit 35), then 1/2 mi N on CR 17, then 1/2 mi E on Hwy 1040, then 1/2 mi S on N Billville Rd. Enter on R.* ◆◆◆FACILITIES: 52 sites, typical site width 30 ft, 52 full hkups, (20/30/50 amps), 10 pull-thrus, family camping, tenting, dump, laundry. ◆◆RECREATION: swim pool, lake fishing. Pets welcome. Open all yr. Big rigs welcome. Rate in 2010 $34.35 for 4 persons. Phone: (225)567-3418.

(N) Yogi Bear's Jellystone Park Camp Resort —(Tangipahoa) *From jct I-12 (exit 47) & Hwy 445: Go 3 mi N on Hwy 445. Enter on L.* ◆◆◆◆FACILITIES: 366 sites, typical site width 35 ft, 311 full hkups, 55 W&E, (20/30/50 amps), 60 pull-thrus, family camping, tenting, dump, laundry, groceries. ◆◆◆◆◆RECREATION: 6 swim pools, boating, no motors, canoeing, lake/pond fishing, playground. Pets welcome, breed restrict. Partial handicap access. Open all yr. Big rigs welcome. Rate in 2010 $30-65 for 5 persons. Member ARVC, LCOA. Phone: (985)542-1507.

Because Covington is in a region referred to as the Ozone Belt, it has long been known for its clean air and water.

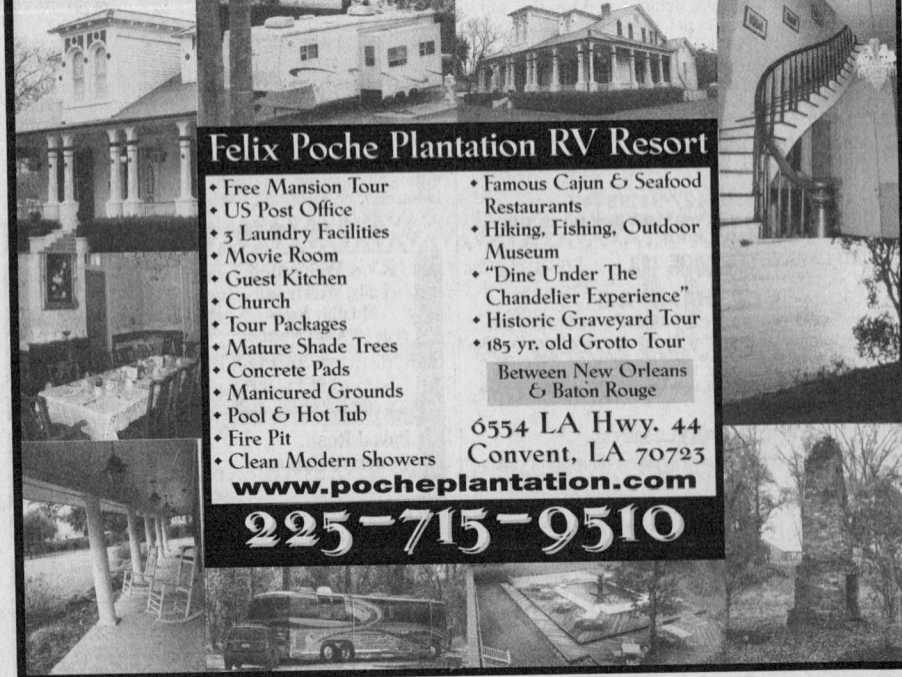

HENDERSON—D-3

(E) Frenchman's Wilderness—(St. Martin) *From jct I-10 (exit 121) & Hwy-3177: Go 3/4 mi S on Hwy-3177. Enter on R.* ◆◆◆FACILITIES: 140 sites, typical site width 50 ft, 140 full hkups, (30/50 amps), 50 amps ($), 2 pull-thrus, family camping, tenting, laundry, ltd groc. ◆◆◆◆RECREATION: swim pool, boating, ramp, lake fishing, playground. Pets welcome, breed restrict, size restrict. Open all yr. Big rigs welcome. Rate in 2010 $26.50 for 4 persons. Phone: (337)228-2616.

HOMER—A-2

(SE) LAKE CLAIBORNE STATE PARK—(Claiborne) *From jct I-20 (exit 61) & Hwy 154: Go 7 mi N on Hwy 154, then 8-1/2 mi NE on Hwy 518, then 1 mi S on Hwy 146.* FACILITIES: 89 sites, 87 W&E, (30/50 amps), 2 no hkups, 12 pull-thrus, tenting, dump, laundry. RECREATION: lake swim, boating, ramp, lake fishing, playground. Pets welcome. Open all yr. Phone: (888)677-2524.

HORNBECK—C-2

(SW) PLEASURE POINT/TOLEDO BEND LAKE (Sabine River Auth. Site 15)—(Sabine) *From jct US 171 & Hwy 473: Go 8 mi W on Hwy 473, then 10 mi S on Hwy 191, then W on access road. Enter on L.* FACILITIES: 124 sites, typical site width 25 ft, 50 full hkups, 74 W&E, (30 amps), tenting, dump. RECREATION: lake swim, boating, ramp, dock, lake fishing, playground. Pets welcome. Partial handicap access. Open all yr. Member ARVC, LCOA. Phone: (318)565-4810.

HOUMA—E-4

(E) Capri Court MHP—(Terrebonne) *From jct US 90 (exit 204) and Bayou Blue Rd: Go 2 mi S on Bayou Blue Rd. Enter on R.* ◆◆FACILITIES: 50 sites, typical site width 30 ft, 45 full hkups, 5 W&E, (15/30/50 amps), 5 pull-thrus, WiFi Internet central location, family camping, tenting, RV storage, dump, non-guest dump $, laundry, RV supplies, picnic tables, patios, fire rings.

◆◆RECREATION: pavilion, boating, ramp, dock, stream fishing. Pets welcome, breed restrict, size restrict. Partial handicap access. Open all yr. Big rigs welcome. Rate in 2010 $29.80-33.40 for 2 persons. MC/VISA. Member ARVC, LCOA. FMCA discount. CCUSA 50% Discount. CCUSA reservations Accepted, CCUSA max stay Unlimited, Cash only for CCUSA disc. Sat & Sun by reservation only.

Phone: (800)428-8026
Address: 101 Capri Court, Houma, LA 70364
Lat/Lon: 29.67173/-90.72352
Email: capricrt@bellsouth.net
Web: www.houmanet.com/capri

(N) HOUMA AREA CONVENTION & VISITORS BUREAU—*From jct US 90 & Hwy 24: Go 1 block mi S on Hwy 24, then 1/4 mi W on W. Frontage Rd, then S on Tourist Dr. Enter on L.* Visit Houma, the Heart of America's WETLAND. Area info on camping, fresh & salt water fishing, swamp tours, gardens, museums, festivals, special events, attractions, Mardi Gras Parades, Cajun food & music. On site: dump station. Open all yr.

Text 107903 to (440)725-8687 to see our Visual Tour.

Phone: (800)688-2732
Address: 114 Tourist Dr, Gray, LA 70359
Lat/Lon: 29.67763/-90.78653
Email: info@houmatourism.com
Web: www.houmatravel.com

SEE AD TRAVEL SECTION PAGE 281 AND AD TRAVEL SECTION PAGE 282

INDEPENDENCE—C-5

(W) Indian Creek Campground & RV Park—(Tangipahoa) *From jct I-55 (exit 40) & Hwy 40: Go 1000 feet W on Hwy 40, then 1-1/2 mi S on Fontana Rd. Enter on R.* ◆◆◆FACILITIES: 184 sites, typical site width 25 ft, 60 full hkups, 124 W&E, (20/30/50 amps), 50 amps ($), 20 pull-thrus, family camping, dump, laundry, ltd groc. ◆◆◆RECREATION: swim pool, canoeing, river/pond fishing, playground. Pets welcome. No tents. Open all yr. Rate in 2010 $30-39 for 5 persons. Member ARVC, LCOA. Phone: (985)878-6567.

IOWA—D-2

(N) CYPRESS BEND RV PARK—(Calcasieu) *From jct I-10 (exit 43): on southwest corner, turn at Conoco & McDonald's.*

◆◆◆◆FACILITIES: 80 sites, typical site width 30 ft, 80 full hkups, (30/50 amps), some extd stay sites, 40 pull-thrus, cable TV, WiFi Instant Internet at site, family camping, RV's/park model rentals, shower$, laundry, groceries, controlled access.

RECREATION: play equipment.

Pets welcome. Partial handicap access. No tents. Open all yr. Big rigs welcome. Rate in 2010 $30 for 2 persons. MC/VISA/DISC/Debit.

Phone: (877)409-2784
Address: 717 N Thompson Blvd, Iowa, LA 70647
Lat/Lon: 30.24702/-93.01362
Email: cypressbendrv@aol.com
Web: www.toledo-bend.com/toledo-bend/index.asp?request=sra_11

SEE AD LAKE CHARLES PAGE 293

KINDER—D-3

(N) COUSHATTA CASINO RESORT—*From jct US 190 & US 165: Go 3 mi N on US 165. Enter on L.* Louisiana's premier casino resort. 2800 slots, 70 tables, 6 restaurants, 500 luxurious rooms, RV Resort, supervised childcare, teen arcade, award-winning championship golf course & more. Open all yr. MC/VISA/DISC/AMEX. ATM.

Phone: (800)584-7263
Address: 777 Coushatta, Kinder, LA 70648
Lat/Lon: 30.54296/-92.81664
Web: www.coushattacasinoresort.com

SEE AD TRAVEL SECTION PAGE 282

(N) COUSHATTA LUXURY RV RESORT AT RED SHOES PARK—(Allen) *From jct US 190 & US 165: Go 3 mi N on US 165. Enter on L.*

◆◆◆◆◆FACILITIES: 107 sites, typical site width 30 ft, 107 full hkups, (20/30/50 amps), 105 pull-thrus, cable TV, WiFi Instant Internet at site, phone Internet central location, family camping, dump, non-guest dump, laundry, full svc store, RV supplies, ice, picnic tables, patios.

◆◆◆◆RECREATION: rec room/area, swim pool, pond fishing, golf nearby, bsktball, playground, shuffleboard court 2 shuffleboard courts, tennis, v-ball.

Pets welcome. Partial handicap access. No tents. Open all yr. Limited stay is 14 days. Big rigs welcome. Clubs welcome. Rate in 2010 $19-24 per vehicle. MC/VISA/DISC/AMEX. ATM. Member ARVC, LCOA. FMCA discount.

Phone: (800)584-7263
Address: 777 Coushatta Dr, Kinder, LA 70648
Lat/Lon: 30.54127/-92.81400
Email: rmaggard@coushattacasinoresort.com
Web: www.coushattacasinoresort.com/accomodations/red-shoes-rv-park/

SEE AD TRAVEL SECTION PAGE 282

(N) KOASATI PINES AT COUSHATTA—*From jct US 190 & US 165: Go 4 mi N on US 165. Enter on L.* 18-hole, Par 72 layout. Clubhouse with bar & grill, 12 acre practice facility. PGA instruction staff, golf shop.

Phone: (800)584-7263
Address: 300 Koasati Dr, Kinder, LA 70648
Lat/Lon: 30.55450/-92.80516
Web: www.koasatipines.com

SEE AD TRAVEL SECTION PAGE 282

LAFAYETTE—D-3

(SE) G & J MOBILE HOME & RV SUPPLIES—*From jct US 90 & Pinhook Rd: Go 2-1/2 mi S on W Pinhook Rd, then 1 mi W on Verot School Rd (Hwy 339), then 100 yards N on John Wayne Dr. Enter on R.* SERVICES: sells parts/accessories. Complete Mobile Home Supplies too!. Open all yr. MC/VISA/DISC/AMEX.

G & J MOBILE HOME & RV SUPPLIES—Continued on next page

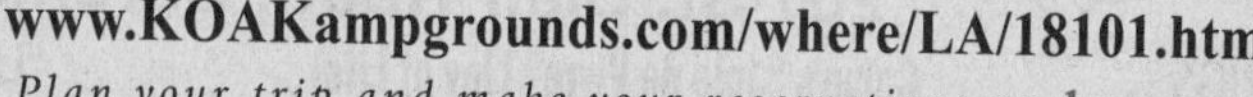

LAFAYETTE—Continued
G & J MOBILE HOME & RV SUPPLIES—Continued

Phone: (337)234-6585
Address: 280 John Wayne Dr, Lafayette, LA 70508
Lat/Lon: 30.17220/-92.01857
Email: gjmobilehome@bellsouth.net
Web: www.gjmobilehomervsuppplies.com

SEE AD THIS PAGE

(NW) GAUTHIER'S RV SERVICE CENTER —*From jct I-10 (exit 100): Go 200 ft N on Ambassador Caffery Pkwy. Enter on R.* SALES: travel trailers, park models, 5th wheels, toy hauler, pre-owned unit sales. SERVICES: full-time mech, RV appliance repair, body work/collision repair, LP gas by weight/by meter, sells parts/accessories, installs hitches. Open all yr. MC/VISA/DISC/AMEX/Debit.

LAFAYETTE—Continued
GAUTHIER'S RV SERVICE CENTER—Continued

Phone: (800)235-8547
Address: 124 N Ambassador, Lafayette, LA 70583
Lat/Lon: 30.24875/-92.06475
Email: sales@gauthiersrv.com
Web: www.Gauthiersrv.com

SEE AD THIS PAGE

(W) KOA-LAFAYETTE—(Lafayette) *From jct US-167 & I-10: Go 5-1/4 mi W on I-10 (exit 97), then 100 feet S on Hwy 93, then 1/4 mi W on entry road. Enter at end.*

◆◆◆◆◆FACILITIES: 185 sites, typical site width 25 ft, 150 full hkups, 35 W&E, (15/20/30/50 amps), 50 amps ($), some extd stay sites, 100 pull-thrus, cable TV, ($), WiFi Instant Internet at site, cable Internet central location, family camping, tenting, cabins, RV storage, dump, non-guest dump $, laundry, full svc store, RV supplies, LP gas by weight/by meter, ice, picnic tables, patios, fire rings, wood.

◆◆◆◆◆RECREATION: rec hall, rec room/area, pavilion, coin games, 2 swim pools, boating, kayaking, 7 kayak/8 pedal boat rentals, lake fishing, fishing supplies, mini-golf, ($), golf nearby, bsktball, playground, activities, v-ball, local tours. Rec open to public.

Pets welcome, breed restrict. Open all yr. Big rigs welcome. Clubs welcome. Rate in 2010 $37.29-47.39 for 4 persons. MC/VISA/DISC/Debit. Member ARVC, LCOA. KOA discount.

LAFAYETTE—Continued
KOA-LAFAYETTE—Continued

Phone: (800)562-0809
Address: 537 Apollo Rd, Scott, LA 70583
Lat/Lon: 30.24645/-92.11150
Email: twosonskoa@aol.com
Web: www.koa.com

SEE AD PAGE 291

(N) LAFAYETTE CONVENTION & VISITORS COMMISSION—*From jct I-49/I-10 (exit 103A) & US 167: Go 1 mi S on US 167. Enter on L.* The Lafayette Visitor Center is situated on an area surrounded by flora and fauna. Start your Cajun Country tour in Lafayette with real Cajun food, Cajun & Zydeco music and fun! Free Wi-Fi. Open all yr.

Text 83714 to (440)725-8687 to see our Visual Tour.

Phone: (800)346-1958
Address: 1400 NW Evangeline Thruway, Lafayette, LA 70505
Lat/Lon: 30.24235/-92.01279
Email: info@lafayettetravel.com
Web: www.lafayette.travel

SEE AD TRAVEL SECTION PAGE 278

LAKE CHARLES—D-2

(S) A +Motel & RV Park—(Calcasieu) *From jct I-10 (exit 20) & Hwy 27: Go 2 mi S on Hwy 27. Enter on L.*
◆◆◆◆FACILITIES: 78 sites, typical site width 32 ft,

A +Motel & RV Park—Continued on next page

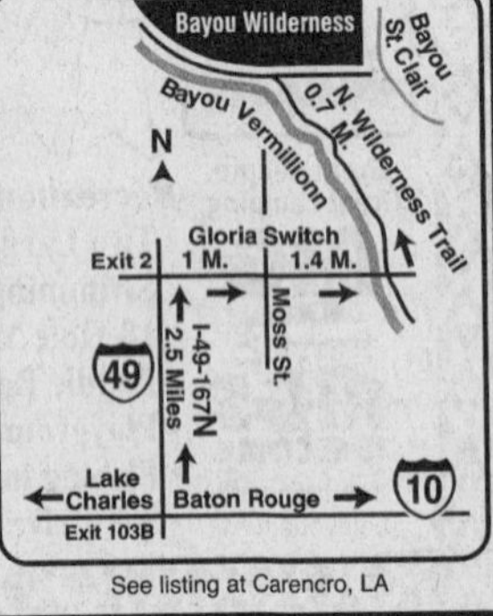

See listing at Carencro, LA

LAKE CHARLES—Continued
A +Motel & RV Park—Continued

78 full hkups, (30/50 amps), 50 amps ($), 41 pull-thrus, family camping, laundry. ◆◆RECREATION: lake swim, boating. Pets welcome, breed restrict, quantity restrict. Partial handicap access. No tents. Open all yr. Big rigs welcome. Rate in 2010 $25.20-30 for 2 persons. Member ARVC, LCOA. Phone: (337)583-2631.

(S) HIDDEN PONDS RV PARK—(Calcasieu) *From I-10 (DeQuincy, exit 21): Go 1 mi S. Enter on L.*

WELCOME

◆◆◆FACILITIES: 159 sites, typical site width 35 ft, 159 full hkups, (30/50 amps), mostly extd stay sites, 104 pull-thrus, WiFi Instant Internet at site, WiFi Internet central location, family camping, cabins, dump, non-guest dump $, laundry, fire rings.

◆RECREATION: pond fishing.

Pets welcome. Partial handicap access. No tents. Open all yr. Big rigs welcome. Escort to site. Rate in 2010 $27 for 2 persons. MC/VISA/DISC/Debit. Member ARVC, LCOA. FCRV discount. FMCA discount.

Phone: (800)440-4709
Address: 1201 Ravia Rd, Sulphur, LA 70665
Lat/Lon: 30.11607/-93.21512
Email: hiddenponds@camtel.net
Web: www.travelingusa.com

SEE AD PAGE 292

(E) I-10 Mobile Village & RV Campground—(Calcasieu) *From east jct I-210 Bypass & I-10: Go 2-1/2 mi E on I-10 (exit 36), then 1 mi N on Pojol Rd., then 3 mi E on Mark Le Bleu Rd, then 3/4 mi S on Mobile Village Rd. Enter on L.* ◆◆FACILITIES: 58 sites, 58 full hkups, (20/30/50 amps), 50 amps ($), 6 pull-thrus, family camping, dump, laundry. ◆RECREATION: swim pool, pond fishing. Pets welcome, breed restrict. No tents. Open all yr. Rate in 2010 $25-30 for 2 persons. Phone: (337)433-2077.

(SW) LAKE CHARLES/SOUTHWEST LOUISIANA CONVENTION & VISITORS BUREAU—*Eastbound: From jct I-10 (exit 29) & Lakeshore Dr: Go 50 feet E on Lakeshore Dr. Westbound: From jct I-10 (exit 30A) & Lakeshore Dr: Go 1 mi W on Lakeshore Dr (making U-turn under I-10), then 1/2 mi E on Lakeshore Dr. Enter on R.* Lake Charles/Southwest Louisiana is the Festival Capital of Louisiana w/Cajun food & culture around every corner! You can bet on the bayou at our casino complexes and then explore the Creole Nature Trail All-American Road. Open all yr.

WELCOME

Text 107955 to (440)725-8687 to see our Visual Tour.

Phone: (800)456-7952
Address: 1205 N Lakeshore Dr, Lake Charles, LA 70601
Lat/Lon: 30.23656/-93.22896
Email: info@visitlakecharles.org
Web: www.visitlakecharles.org

SEE AD TRAVEL SECTION PAGE 282

RAYFORD CROSSING RV RESORT—*From Lake Charles LA—W'bnd: Go W on I-10 for 135 mi, then NW onto I-610 for 7 mi to I-45 N, then N on I-45 for 1-1/2 mi to Exit 73, then E for 1-1/2 mi on Rayford Rd, then 1/2 mi S on Geneva Dr, turn E on Plum Creek Dr for 1/4 mi into the Resort.*

WELCOME

SEE PRIMARY LISTING AT THE WOODLANDS AND AD HOUSTON, TX PAGE 492

(N) SAM HOUSTON JONES STATE PARK—(Calcasieu) *From jct I-10 & US 171: Go 4 mi N on US 171, then 3 mi W on Hwy 378, then 1 mi NW on a blacktop road, then 1/2 mi W on State Park Rd. Enter at end.* FACILITIES: 82 sites, 20 full hkups, 62 W&E, (30/50 amps), 7 pull-thrus, tenting, dump. RECREATION: boating, canoeing, ramp, river/stream fishing, playground. Pets welcome. Open all yr. Phone: (888)677-7264.

TWELVE OAKS RV PARK (NOT VISITED) —(Calcasieu) *From jct I-10 (exit 33) & US Hwy 171: Go 1 mi N on US Hwy 171, then 1/4 mi E on Conoco St. Enter at end.*

WELCOME

FACILITIES: 19 sites, typical site width 30 ft, 19 full hkups, (20/30/50 amps), 6 pull-thrus, WiFi Instant Internet at site, picnic tables.

Pets welcome, breed restrict. No tents. Open all yr. Big rigs welcome. Rate in 2010 $30 for 4 persons. MC/VISA. FMCA discount.

Phone: (337)439-2916
Address: 2736 Conoco St, Lake Charles, LA 70601

SEE AD PAGE 292

Louisiana State Gem: Agate

LAKE CHARLES—Continued

(W) WHISPERING MEADOW RV PARK—(Calcasieu) *From jct I-10 (exit 27): Go 3 mi N on Sampson/Westwood Rd. Enter on R.*

WELCOME

◆◆◆◆FACILITIES: 50 sites, typical site width 40 ft, 50 full hkups, (30/50 amps), 50 amps ($), many extd stay sites, 32 pull-thrus, WiFi Instant Internet at site, family camping, RV's/park model rentals, laundry, picnic tables, patios, wood.

◆RECREATION: rec hall, golf nearby.

Pets welcome, breed restrict. No tents. Open all yr. Big rigs welcome. Escort to site. Clubs welcome. Rate in 2010 $29 for 2 persons. MC/VISA. Member ARVC, LCOA.

Phone: (337)433-8188
Address: 3210 Westwood Rd, Westlake, LA 70669
Lat/Lon: 30.10854/-99.22547
Email: whisperingmeadow@bellsouth.net
Web: www.whisperingmeadowrvpark.com

SEE AD PAGE 292

(NE) Yogi Bear's Jellystone Park Camp-Resort—(Calcasieu) *From east jct I-210 Bypass & I-10: Go 2-1/2 mi E on I-10 (exit 36), then 2 mi N on Pujol Rd, then 1 mi W & 1/4 mi N on Luke Powers Rd. Enter on R.* ◆◆◆FACILITIES: 63 sites, typical site width 25 ft, 63 full hkups, (20/30/50 amps), 20 pull-thrus, family camping, tenting, dump, laundry, ltd groc. ◆◆◆◆RECREATION: swim pool, canoeing, lake fishing, playground. Pets welcome, breed restrict. Partial handicap access. Open all yr. Big rigs welcome. Rate in 2010 $35-55 for 4 persons. Phone: (877)433-2400.

LEESVILLE—C-2

MILITARY PARK (Toledo Bend Rec Site-Fort Polk)—(Vernon) *Off base, on US 171 or Hwy 10.* FACILITIES: 13 sites, 35 ft max RV length, 13 W&E, (30/50 amps), tenting, dump, groceries. RECREATION: lake swim, boating, lake fishing. Pets welcome. Open all yr. Phone: (318)545-4235.

(C) VERNON PARISH TOURIST INFORMATION CENTER—*From S jct Hwy 171 & Hwy 8: Go 1/4 mi E on Texas St, then right on 3rd St. - In Court House. Enter on L.* Venture into Vernon Parish, the Heart of Nature's Wonderland, Festivals, Historic Cemetaries & Churches, History, Museums and Outdoor Recreation. Open all yr.

WELCOME

Phone: (800)349-6287
Address: 9261 Hwy 171 N, Leesville, LA 71446
Lat/Lon: 31.14181/-93.26009
Email: vernontourism@bellsouth.net

SEE AD TRAVEL SECTION PAGE 280

LIVINGSTON—D-4

(N) LAKESIDE RV PARK—(Livingston) *From jct of I-12 & Hwy 63 (exit 22): Go 1 1/4 mi S on Hwy 63. Enter on L.*

WELCOME

◆◆◆◆FACILITIES: 139 sites, 139 full hkups, (20/30/50 amps), some extd stay sites, 13 pull-thrus, WiFi Instant Internet at site, phone Internet central location, family camping, cabins, laundry, ltd groc, RV supplies, LP gas by weight/by meter, ice, picnic tables, patios, fire rings, wood.

CAMPCLUB USA

◆◆◆◆RECREATION: rec hall, rec room/area, swim pool, boating, electric motors only, lake fishing, fishing supplies, golf nearby, bsktball, playground, activities, horseshoes, sports field, v-ball.

Pets welcome, breed restrict. Partial handicap access. No tents. Open all yr. Big rigs welcome. Escort to site. Clubs welcome. Rate in 2010 $28-35 per family. MC/VISA/DISC/Debit. Member ARVC, LCOA. CCUSA 50% Discount. CCUSA max

LIVINGSTON—Continued
LAKESIDE RV PARK—Continued

stay 2 days, Cash only for CCUSA disc., CCUSA disc. not avail F,Sa, CCUSA disc. not avail holidays. Reservations not accepted for 1 night stays. Discount available on back-in sites only, subject to availability, not valid with other discounts. Cash only. No tents or 4 wheelers. Pets must be leashed & cleaned up after.

Phone: (225)686-7676
Address: 28370 South Frost Rd, Livingston, LA 70754
Lat/Lon: 30.45454/-90.74415
Email: info@lakeside-rvpark.com
Web: www.lakeside-rvpark.com

SEE AD BATON ROUGE PAGE 288 AND AD TRAVEL SECTION PAGE 279

LORANGER—C-5

(N) Sweetwater Campground & RV Park—(Tangipahoa) *From jct Hwy 40 & Hwy 1054: Go 200 yds N on Hwy 1054, then 4-1/2 mi E on Cooper Rd. Enter on R.* ◆◆◆FACILITIES: 225 sites, 185 full hkups, 40 W&E, (30/50 amps), family camping, tenting, dump, laundry, groceries. ◆◆◆◆RECREATION: swim pool, pond fishing, playground. Pets welcome. Open all yr. Rate in 2010 $28-55 for 5 persons. Member ARVC, LCOA. Phone: (985)878-6868.

MADISONVILLE—D-5

(NE) FAIRVIEW-RIVERSIDE STATE PARK—(St. Tammany) *From jct Hwy 21 & Hwy 22: Go 1 mi E on Hwy 22. Enter on L.* FACILITIES: 101 sites, typical site width 30 ft, 81 W&E, (30/50 amps), 20 no hkups, tenting, dump, laundry. RECREATION: river swim, boating, canoeing, ramp, river fishing, playground. Pets welcome. Partial handicap access. Open all yr. Phone: (888)677-3247.

MANDEVILLE—D-5

(SE) FOUNTAINEBLEAU STATE PARK—(St. Tammany) *From jct Hwy 59 & US 190: Go 4 mi E on US 190. Enter on R.* FACILITIES: 163 sites, 23 full hkups, 103 W&E, (30/50 amps), 37 no hkups, 55 pull-thrus, tenting, dump, laundry. RECREATION: swim pool, lake swim, boating, canoeing, lake fishing, playground. Pets welcome. Open all yr. Phone: (888)677-3668.

(N) ST. TAMMANY PARISH TOURIST & CONVENTION COMMISSION—*From jct I-12 (exit 65) & US 59: Go 1/4 mi N on US 59. Enter on L.* Tourism office for information on camping, attractions and special events. Brochures & quarterly newspaper detailing local festivals, shopping, restaurants & activities. Boardwalk nature trail on site. Open all yr.

WELCOME

Phone: (800)634-9443
Address: 68099 Hwy 59, Mandeville, LA 70471
Lat/Lon: 30.41655/-90.04100
Email: ladana@louisiananorthshore.com
Web: www.louisiananorthshore.com

SEE AD TRAVEL SECTION PAGE 279

MANSFIELD—B-2

(E) NEW ROCKDALE RADIO SHOP LLC—*From jct I-49 (exit 172) & US 84: Go 4-1/4 mi W on US 84, then 1/4 mi S on Hwy 522. Enter on L.* Complete CB Radio Sales, installation & repair. Parts & accessories on site with RV Park. Open all yr. MC/VISA/DISC/AMEX.

WELCOME

Phone: (318)871-9918
Address: 103 Henry Cir, Mansfield, LA 71052
Lat/Lon: 32.04929/-93.63609
Email: zeslott@cmaaccess.com

SEE AD NEXT PAGE

MANSFIELD—Continued on next page

MANSFIELD—Continued

(E) **NEW ROCKDALE RV PARK/ RADIOSHOP LLC**—(De Soto) *From jct I-49 (exit 172) & US 84: Go 4-1/4 mi W on US 84, then 1/4 mi S on Hwy 522. Enter on L.*

WELCOME

◆◆◆FACILITIES: 150 sites, typical site width 40 ft, 150 full hkups, (20/30/50 amps), 50 amps ($), 17 pull-thrus, cable on-site Internet (needs activ), family camping, laundry, LP gas by weight/by meter.

◆RECREATION: pond fishing.

Pets welcome. Partial handicap access. No tents. Open all yr. Big rigs welcome. Rate in 2010 $20-26 for 2 persons. MC/VISA/DISC/AMEX.

Phone: (318)871-9918
Address: 103 Henry Cir, Mansfield, LA 71052
Lat/Lon: 32.04929/-93.63609
Email: zeslott@cmaaccess.com

SEE AD THIS PAGE

MANY—B-2

(SW) CYPRESS BEND PARK/TOLEDO BEND LAKE (Sabine River Auth. Site 11)—(Sabine) *From jct US 171 & Hwy 6: Go 12 mi W on Hwy 6, then 3 mi S on Hwy 191. Enter on R.* FACILITIES: 67 sites, typical site width 20 ft, 26 full hkups, 41 W&E, (30 amps), tenting, dump, laundry. RECREATION: lake swim, boating, ramp, dock, lake fishing, playground. Pets welcome. Partial handicap access. Open all yr. Member ARVC, LCOA. Phone: (318)256-4118.

(S) HODGES WILDERNESS CAMP GROUND—(Sabine) *From jct Hwy 6 & US 171: Go 14-1/2 mi S on US 171. Enter on L.* FACILITIES: 27 sites, typical site width 35 ft, 9 full hkups, 8 W&E, (20/30/50 amps), 10 no hkups, tenting. RECREATION: boating, canoeing, lake fishing. Pets welcome. Open all yr. Phone: (318)586-3523.

SABINE PARISH—*From jct US 171 & Hwy 6: Go W on Hwy 6 thru Many. Enter on L.* Toledo Bend Lake Country: Enjoy the largest man-made lake in the South. On the Louisiana - Texas line. Twenty-one lakeside accomodations offering 750 RV pads, 1-800-259-5253; 1-800-358-7802. Open all yr.

WELCOME

Phone: (318)256-5880
Address: 1601 Texas Hwy, Many, LA 71449
Email: director@toledobendlakecountry.com
Web: www.toledobendlakecountry.com

SEE AD TRAVEL SECTION PAGE 280

MARKSVILLE—C-3

(W) **AVOYELLES PARISH TOURISM COMMISSION**—*From jct Hwy 107 & Hwy 1: Go 3 mi S on Hwy 1. Enter on R.* Historic home tours, museums, French Acadian Culture, festivals, parades, casinos, agricultural attractions, hunting and fishing. Open all yr.

WELCOME

Phone: (318)964-2025
Address: 8592 Hwy 1 Ste 3, Mansura, LA 71350
Lat/Lon: 31.12552/-92.0686
Web: www.travelavoyelles.com

SEE AD TRAVEL SECTION PAGE 280

(S) **PARAGON CASINO**—*From jct LA 452 & Hwy 1: Go 3/4 mi S on Hwy 1. Enter on L.* Spacious, land based casino with supervised kids activity center, new 18 hole golf course, four restaurants & buffet. Over 2,000 slot machines. Table games and poker room. Great entertainment. Open 7 days a week, 24 hours. Open all yr. MC/VISA/DISC/AMEX. ATM.

WELCOME

Text 83715 to (440)725-8687 to see our Visual Tour.

Louisiana Nickname: Pelican State; Creole State; Sportsman's Paradise; Sugar State

MARKSVILLE—Continued
PARAGON CASINO—Continued

Phone: (800)946-1946
Address: 711 Grand Blvd, Marksville, LA 71351
Lat/Lon: 31.10587/-92.06265
Web: www.paragoncasinoresort.com

SEE AD TRAVEL SECTION PAGE 277 AND AD DISCOVER SECTION PAGE 38

(S) **PARAGON CASINO RV RESORT**—(Avoyelles) *From jct LA 452 & Hwy 1: Go 1 mi S on Hwy 1, then 1/4 mi E on Slim Lemoine Rd. Enter on L.*

WELCOME

◆◆◆◆◆FACILITIES: 185 sites, typical site width 35 ft, 185 full hkups, (20/30/50 amps), 166 pull-thrus, cable TV, WiFi Instant Internet at site ($), phone Internet central location, family camping, cabins, dump, non-guest dump, laundry, ice, picnic tables, patios.

◆◆◆◆RECREATION: rec room/area, equipped pavilion, 1 swim pools, golf nearby, playground, shuffleboard court 4 shuffleboard courts, activities, horseshoes, sports field, v-ball. Rec open to public.

Pets welcome. Partial handicap access. No tents. Open all yr. Big rigs welcome. Clubs welcome. Rate in 2010 $17-32 per vehicle. MC/VISA/DISC/AMEX/Debit. ATM.

Phone: (800)946-1946
Address: 124 Earl Barbry Sr Blvd, Marksville, LA 71351
Lat/Lon: 31.10547/-92.05825
Email: avomjw@paragoncasinoresort.com
Web: www.paragoncasinoresort.com

SEE AD TRAVEL SECTION PAGE 277 AND AD DISCOVER SECTION PAGE 38

MINDEN—A-2

(S) **CINNAMON CREEK RV PARK**—(Webster Parish) *From jct I-20 (exit 44) & Hwy 371: Go 1/2 mi N on Hwy 371. Enter on L.*

WELCOME

◆◆◆◆FACILITIES: 69 sites, typical site width 24 ft, 69 full hkups, (20/30/50 amps), 7 pull-thrus, WiFi Instant Internet at site, family camping, tenting, laundry, picnic tables.

RECREATION: golf nearby.

Pets welcome. Partial handicap access. Open all yr. Big rigs welcome. Escort to site. Clubs welcome. Rate in 2010 $30 for 2 persons. MC/VISA/Debit.

Phone: (318)371-5111
Address: 12996 Hwy 371, Minden, LA 71055
Lat/Lon: 32.35710/-93.20366
Email: trishstanley@suddenlink.net
Web: www.cinnamoncreekrvpark.com

SEE AD SHREVEPORT PAGE 299

MONROE—A-3

See listings at Bastrop & West Monroe

(E) **HOPE'S CAMPER CORNER RV CENTER**—*From jct I-20 (exit 120) & Garrett Rd: Go 1 block S on Garrett Rd, then 3/4 mi E on Frontage. Enter on R.* SALES: travel trailers, 5th wheels, Class A motorhomes, Class C motorhomes, pre-owned unit sales. SERVICES: full-time mech, RV appliance repair, LP gas by weight/by meter, sells parts/accessories. Open all yr. MC/VISA/DISC/AMEX/Debit.

WELCOME

Phone: (318)345-1691
Address: 6120 Frontage Rd E, Monroe, LA 71202
Lat/Lon: 32.49312/-92.04414
Email: hopes@hopescampers.com
Web: www.hopescampers.com

SEE AD THIS PAGE

MONROE—Continued

(E) **SHILOH CAMPGROUND & RV RESORT**—(Ouachita) *From jct I-20 (exit 120) & Garrett Rd: Go 1 block S on Garrett, then 1-1/2 mi E on Frontage Rd. Enter on R.*

WELCOME

◆◆◆FACILITIES: 91 sites, typical site width 30 ft, 80 full hkups, 11 W&E, (30/50 amps), 50 amps ($), 50 pull-thrus, WiFi Instant Internet at site, WiFi Internet central location, family camping, tenting, cabins, RV storage, dump, non-guest dump $, laundry, RV supplies, ice, picnic tables.

◆◆◆RECREATION: rec room/area, swim pool, lake fishing, bsktball, playground, shuffleboard court shuffleboard court, horseshoes, v-ball.

Pets welcome. Open all yr. Big rigs welcome. Rate in 2010 $26.95-29.95 for 2 persons. MC/VISA/DISC/AMEX/Debit.

Phone: (318)343-6098
Address: 7300 Frontage Rd, Monroe, LA 71202
Lat/Lon: 32.49216/-92.03229
Email: happycamping10@aol.com
Web: www.shilohrvresorts.com

Reserve Online at Woodalls.com

SEE AD THIS PAGE

MORGAN CITY—E-4

(N) **CAJUN COAST VISITORS & CONVENTION BUREAU**—*From jct Hwy 70 & US 90: Go 5-3/4 mi W on US 90. Enter on R.* Located Midway between New Orleans & Lafayette on the banks of Bayou Teche, Atchafalaya National Heritage Area, Bayon Teche Scenic Byway an Audubon Go. Swamp tours, plantation homes, festivals, casinos, golf course, eagle tours & more. Open all yr.

WELCOME

Text 108014 to (440)725-8687 to see our Visual Tour.

Phone: (800)256-2931
Address: 112 Main St, Patterson, LA 70392
Lat/Lon: 29.67911/-91.29239
Email: info@cajuncoast.com
Web: www.cajuncoast.com

SEE AD TRAVEL SECTION PAGE 281 AND AD TRAVEL SECTION PAGE 277

(W) KEMPER WILLIAMS PARK (St. Mary Parish Park)—(St Mary) *From jct Hwy 70 & US 90: Go 5-3/4 mi W on US 90, then 1/2 mi S on Parish Rd 133. Enter on R.* FACILITIES: 209 sites, typical site width 16 ft, 44 full hkups, 165 W&E, (30/50 amps), 50 amps ($), 4 pull-thrus, tenting, dump. RECREATION: pond fishing, playground. Pets welcome. Partial handicap access. Open all yr. Big rigs welcome. Member ARVC, LCOA. Phone: (985)395-2298.

(N) LAKE END RV CAMPGROUND (Municipal Park)—(St. Mary) *From jct US 90 & Hwy 70: Go 1-1/2 mi N on Hwy 70. Enter on R.* FACILITIES: 94 sites, typical site width 36 ft, 74 full hkups, (30/50 amps), 20 no hkups, 9 pull-thrus, tenting, dump, laundry. RECREATION: boating, ramp, dock, lake fishing, playground. Pets welcome. Partial handicap access. Open all yr. Big rigs welcome. Member ARVC, LCOA. Phone: (985)380-4623.

MT. HERMON—C-5

(E) **SILVER CREEK CAMPGROUND**—(Washington) *From jct I-55 (exit 61) & Hwy 38: Go 15 mi E on Hwy 38, then 1-1/4 mi E on Hwy 1055. Enter on L.*

WELCOME

◆◆◆FACILITIES: 297 sites, typical site width 35 ft, 111 full hkups, 186 W&E, (30/50 amps), 187 pull-thrus, phone Internet central location, family camping, tenting, cabins, RV storage, dump, non-guest dump $, laundry, ltd groc, RV supplies, ice, picnic tables, wood.

◆◆◆◆RECREATION: rec room/area, pavilion, swim pool, pond/stream fishing, fishing supplies, golf nearby, bsktball, playground, activities, horseshoes, hiking trails, v-ball, local tours.

SILVER CREEK CAMPGROUND—Continued on next page

MT. HERMON—Continued
SILVER CREEK CAMPGROUND—Continued

Pets welcome. Partial handicap access. Open all yr. Big rigs welcome. Clubs welcome. Rate in 2010 $38-40 for 4 persons. MC/VISA/DISC/AMEX/Debit. Member ARVC, LCOA.

Phone: (985)877-4256
Address: 37567 Hwy 1055, Mt. Hermon, LA 70450
Lat/Lon: 30.957665/-90.270292
Email: silvercreekcamp@bellsouth.net
Web: www.silvercreekcamp.com

SEE AD THIS PAGE

NATCHITOCHES—B-2

(S) NAKATOSH CAMPGROUND—(Natchitoches) *From jct I-49 (exit 138) & Hwy 6: Go 1/4 mi W on Hwy 6. Enter on R.*

WELCOME

◆◆◆FACILITIES: 41 sites, typical site width 30 ft, 41 full hkups, (20/30/50 amps), mostly extd stay sites, 22 pull-thrus, cable TV, WiFi Instant Internet at site, WiFi Internet central location, family camping, tenting, dump, non-guest dump, laundry, groceries, ice.

◆RECREATION: rec hall, horseshoes.

Pets welcome. Partial handicap access. Open all yr. Big rigs welcome. Clubs welcome. Rate in 2010 $30 for 2 persons. MC/VISA/DISC/AMEX. ATM.

Phone: (318)352-0911
Address: 5428 Hwy 6, Natchitoches, LA 71457
Lat/Lon: 31.72473/-93.16378
Email: cwarner@cp.tel.net
Web: www.nakatoshcamp.com

SEE AD THIS PAGE

(C) NATCHITOCHES PARISH TOURIST COMMISSION—*From jct I-49 (exit 138) & Hwy 6: Go 3-1/4 mi E on Hwy 6 to Business Hwy 6, then go 2 mi E. Enter on R.* The oldest permanent settlement in the Louisiana Purchase. Visitors Center on Front St provides information on accommodations, restaurants & area attractions. Open all yr.

WELCOME

Phone: (800)259-1714
Address: 781 Front St, Natchitoches, LA 71458
Lat/Lon: 31.76315/-93.08573
Email: est1714@natchitoches.net
Web: www.natchitoches.net

SEE AD TRAVEL SECTION PAGE 280

NEW IBERIA—D-3

Chase's RV Park—(Iberia) *From jct US 90 & Hwy 83 (exit 130): Go 1/4 mi S on Hwy 83. Enter on R.* ◆◆◆FACILITIES: 91 sites, 91 full hkups, (15/30/50 amps), 50 amps ($), 8 pull-thrus, laundry. Pets welcome. No tents. Open all yr. Big rigs welcome. Rate in 2010 $24-25 for 2 persons. Phone: (337)365-9865.

The Eastern Brown Pelican is Louisiana's official state bird.

NEW IBERIA—Continued

(C) IBERIA PARISH CONVENTION & VISITORS BUREAU—*From jct US 90 (New Iberia exit) & Hwy 14: Go 1/2 mi E on Hwy 14. Enter on R.* Tourist information office for Iberia Parish that assists with itinerary planning, touring maps, brochures, tips on dining coupons and accommodations. Travel the HOT side of Cajun Country. Open all yr.

WELCOME

Phone: (337)365-1540
Address: 2513 Hwy 14, New Iberia, LA 70560
Lat/Lon: 29.98478/-91.85001
Email: info@iberiatravel.com
Web: www.iberiatravel.com

SEE AD TRAVEL SECTION PAGE 280

(S) KOC KAMPGROUND—(Iberia) *From US 90 (exit 129) & Lewis St: Go 500 ft S on Lewis St, then 3/4 mi NW (right turn) on Frontage Road. Enter on L.*

WELCOME

◆◆◆◆FACILITIES: 200 sites, typical site width 30 ft, 200 full hkups, (30/50 amps), 50 amps ($), many extd stay sites, cable TV, WiFi Instant Internet at site, WiFi Internet central location, family camping, RV storage, dump, non-guest dump $, portable dump, laundry, ltd groc, RV supplies, ice, patios, fire rings.

◆◆RECREATION: pavilion, swim pool, lake fishing, golf nearby, play equipment, sports field.

Pets welcome. Partial handicap access. No tents. Open all yr. Big rigs welcome. Escort to site. Clubs welcome. Rate in 2010 $25-27.50 for 2 persons. MC/VISA/DISC. Member ARVC, LCOA.

Phone: (866)902-5267
Address: 3104 Curtis Ln, New Iberia, LA 70560
Lat/Lon: 29.97387/-91.84502
Email: kockampground@aol.com
Web: www.kockampground.com

SEE AD THIS PAGE

NEW ORLEANS—D-5

NEW ORLEANS AREA MAP

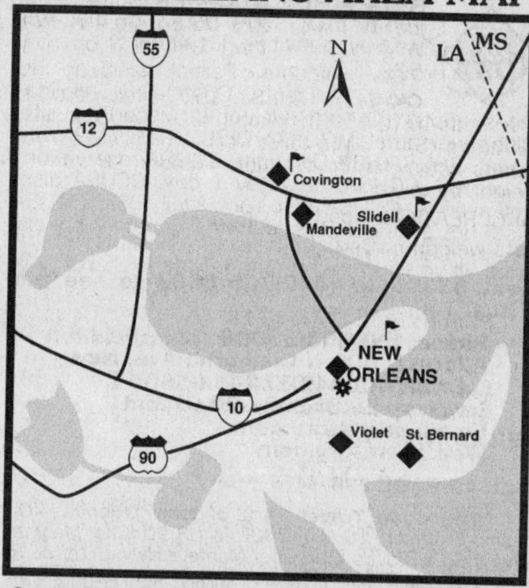

Symbols on map indicate towns within a 30 mi radius of New Orleans where campgrounds (diamonds), attractions (flags), & RV service centers & camping supply outlets (gears) are listed. Check listings for more information.

(C) FRENCH QUARTER RV RESORT—*(Orleans) From jct I-10 (exit 235A) (Orleans St/Vieux Carre) & Basin St: Go 1/4 mi S on Basin St, then 100 ft W on Crozat St (follow signs), then S through parking lot to entrance. Enter on L.*

WELCOME

◆◆◆◆◆FACILITIES: 52 sites, typical site width 30 ft, 52 full hkups, (50 amps), cable TV, WiFi Instant Internet at site, WiFi Internet central location, family camping, laundry, ice, patios, controlled access.

FRENCH QUARTER RV RESORT—Continued on next page

Louisiana was named in honor of King Louis XIV.

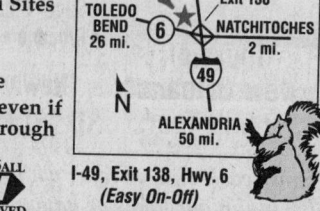

NEW ORLEANS—Continued
FRENCH QUARTER RV RESORT—Continued

◆◆◆◆RECREATION: rec hall, rec room/area, swim pool, hot tub, golf nearby, activities, local tours.

CAMPCLUB USA

Pets welcome. Partial handicap access. No tents. Open all yr. Holiday rates apply. Big rigs welcome. Escort to site. Clubs welcome. MC/VISA/DISC. ATM. FMCA discount. CCUSA 50% Discount. CCUSA reservations Accepted, CCUSA max stay 1 day, CCUSA disc. not avail S, CCUSA disc. not avail F,Sa, CCUSA disc. not avail holidays. Mardi Gras, other special events. Call for details.

Text 83396 to (440)725-8687 to see our Visual Tour.

Phone: (504)586-3000
Address: 500 N Claiborne Ave, New Orleans, LA 70112
Lat/Lon: 29.96200/-90.07253
Email: stay@fqrv.com
Web: www.fqrv.com

SEE AD PAGE 298

(NE) Jude Travel Park of New Orleans—(Orleans) *From jct I-10 (exit 240B) & US 90 (Chef Menteur Hwy): Go 8 blocks E on Chef Menteur Hwy. Enter on R.* ◆◆◆◆FACILITIES: 47 sites, typical site width 20 ft, 47 full hkups, (20/30/50 amps), 50 amps ($), family camping, tenting, laundry. ◆◆RECREATION: swim pool. Pets welcome. Open all yr. Big rigs welcome. Rate in 2010 $30 for 2 persons. Member ARVC, LCOA. Phone: (800)523-2196.

NEW ORLEANS—Continued

(W) KOA-New Orleans West—(Jefferson) *From jct I-10 (exit 223A) & Hwy 49 (Williams Blvd): Go 3 mi S on Hwy 49 (Williams Blvd), then 3/4 mi E on Jefferson Hwy. Enter on L.* ◆◆◆◆FACILITIES: 97 sites, typical site width 30 ft, 97 full hkups, (20/30/50 amps), 50 amps ($), family camping, tenting, laundry, groceries. ◆◆◆RECREATION: swim pool, playground. Pets welcome. Partial handicap access. Open all yr. Big rigs welcome. Rate in 2010 $35-55 for 2 persons. Member ARVC, LCOA. Phone: (504)467-1792. KOA discount.

WELCOME

LAKESIDE RV PARK—*From New Orleans West jct of I-610 & I-10: Go 20 mi W on I-10 (exit 210), then 30 mi N on I-55, then 16 mi W on I-12 (exit 22), then 1-1/4 mi S on Hwy 63. Enter on L.*
SEE PRIMARY LISTING AT LIVINGSTON AND AD BATON ROUGE PAGE 288

WELCOME

NEW ORLEANS EAST KAMPGROUND—*From jct I-510 & I-10 in New Orleans: Go 21 mi NE on I-10 to exit 263, then 3/4 mi E on Hwy 433. Enter on R.*
SEE PRIMARY LISTING AT SLIDELL AND AD NEXT PAGE

WELCOME

NEW ORLEANS PLANTATION COUNTRY—Open all yr. MC/VISA.

NEW ORLEANS—Continued
NEW ORLEANS PLANTATION COUNTRY—Continued

Phone: (985)359-2562 X3
Address: 2900 Hwy 51, La Place, LA 70068
Web: www.neworleansplantationcountry.com

SEE AD TRAVEL SECTION PAGE 281

WELCOME

PINE CREST RV PARK—*From jct I-510 & I-10: Go 21 mi E on I-10, then 1/4 mi E on Hwy 433 (exit 263).*
SEE PRIMARY LISTING AT SLIDELL AND AD THIS PAGE

WELCOME

POCHE PLANTATION RV RESORT—*From New Orleans jct Lake Pontchartrain Causeway & I-10: Go 34 mi W & N on I-10 (exit 199), then 5 mi S on 641 before Gramercy Bridge, then 12 mi N on Hwy 44. Enter on R.*
SEE PRIMARY LISTING AT GONZALES AND AD GONZALES PAGE 290

NEW ORLEANS—Continued on next page

The town of Jean Lafitte was named after the famous pirate of the same name. The area in which it is located was once a hideaway for pirates.

NEW ORLEANS—Continued

(N) PONTCHARTRAIN LANDING—(Orleans) *W'bnd: I-10 (exit 240B) & Chef Menteur Hwy/US 90: Go 1 mi W on Chef Menteur Hwy, then 1 mi N on France Rd. E'bnd: I-10 (exit 239B) & Louisa St: Go 250 yards N on Louisa St, then 1/4 mi E on Chef Menteur Hwy (stay right for France Rd), then 1-1/4 mi N. Enter on R.*

◆◆◆◆FACILITIES: 107 sites, typical site width 30 ft, 107 full hkups, (20/30/50 amps), some extd stay sites, 17 pull-thrus, cable TV, WiFi Instant Internet at site, WiFi Internet central location, family camping, tenting, RV's/park model rentals, cabins, dump, non-guest dump $, laundry, LP gas by weight/by meter, picnic tables, patios.

◆◆◆RECREATION: swim pool, hot tub, boating, ramp, dock, river fishing, golf nearby, local tours.

Pets welcome. Partial handicap access. Open all yr. Big rigs welcome. Escort to site. Clubs welcome. Rate in 2010 $43-95 for 6 persons. MC/VISA/DISC/AMEX. Member ARVC, LCOA. FMCA discount.

Phone: (504)286-8155
Address: 6001 France Rd, New Orleans, LA 70126
Lat/Lon: 30.02314/-90.03460
Email: request@pontchartrainlanding.com
Web: www.pontchartrainlanding.com

SEE AD NEXT PAGE

(NE) RIVERBOAT RV PARK—(Orleans) *W-bnd from jct I-10 (exit 240B) & US 90 (Chef Menteur Hwy): Go 50 yards W on Chef Menteur Hwy. Entrance on left. E-bnd from I-10 (exit 240A) & Downman Rd: Go 1/4 mi N on Downman Rd, then 1/4 mi E on US 90E (Chef Hwy). Enter on R.*

◆◆◆FACILITIES: 67 sites, typical site width 20 ft, 67 full hkups, (20/30/50 amps), some extd stay sites, cable TV, WiFi Instant Internet at site, WiFi

Famous Louisianan: Jazz musician Louis Armstrong—born in New Orleans

NEW ORLEANS—Continued
RIVERBOAT RV PARK—Continued

Internet central location, family camping, tenting, laundry, ltd groc, RV supplies, ice, picnic tables, controlled access.

◆◆RECREATION: swim pool, golf nearby, local tours.

Pets welcome. Partial handicap access. Open all yr. Big rigs welcome. Escort to site. Clubs welcome. Rate in 2010 $30 for 2 persons. MC/VISA/DISC. ATM.

Phone: (504)246-2628
Address: 6232 Chef Menteur Hwy, New Orleans, LA 70126
Lat/Lon: 30.01036/-90.01486
Web: www.riverboattravelpark.com

SEE AD PAGE 296

Jerry Lee Lewis is from Louisiana.

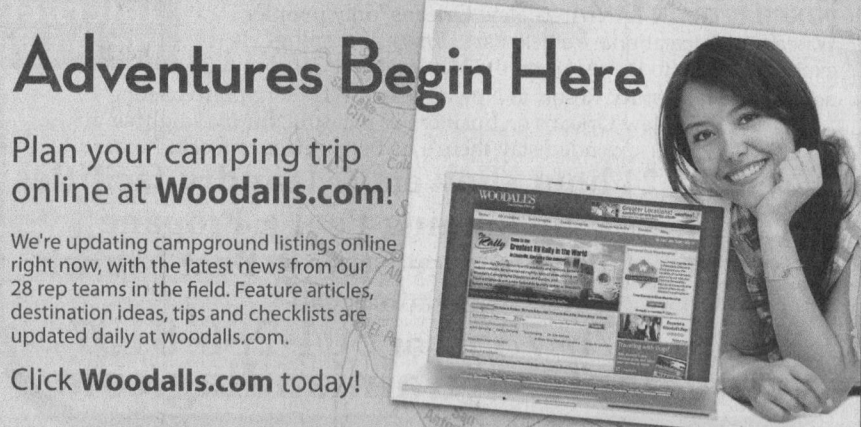

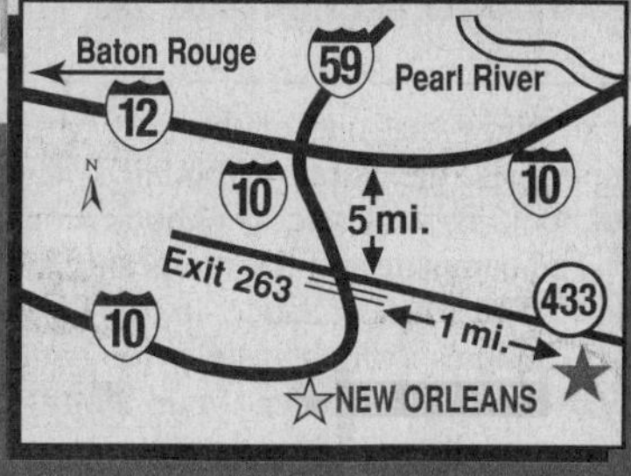

OIL CITY—A-2

(N) EARL WILLIAMSON PARK/CADDO LAKE PARK (Caddo Parish)—(Caddo) *From jct Hwy 220 & Hwy 1 (N Market): Go 18 mi N on Hwy 1.* FACILITIES: 25 sites, 10 W&E, 15 no hkups, tenting, dump. RECREATION: lake swim, boating, canoeing, ramp, dock, lake fishing, playground. Pets welcome. Open all yr. Phone: (318)995-7139.

OPELOUSAS—D-3

(S) OPELOUSAS CITY PARK—(St. Landry) *From jct I-49 & US 190: Go 2 mi W on Hwy 190 (Landry), then 1/2 mi S on S Market St. Enter at end.* FACILITIES: 68 sites, typical site width 20 ft, 68 W&E, (20/30 amps), 30 pull-thrus, family camping, tenting, dump. RECREATION: swim pool, playground. Pets welcome. Open all yr. Facilities fully operational mid May - mid Aug. Phone: (337)948-2562.

(C) ST. LANDRY PARISH TOURIST COMMISSION—*In town on Market St at Town Square. Enter on L.* St. Landry Parish captures the spirit of the people of Acadiana. Rich in historic structures, majestic oaks and noted as "the birthplace of Zydeco Music!" Open all yr.

WELCOME

Phone: (877)948-8004
Address: 131 Market St, Opelousas, LA 70570
Lat/Lon: 30.53110/-92.07388
Email: stlandry@cajuntravel.com
Web: www.cajuntravel.com

SEE AD TRAVEL SECTION PAGE 280

PINE PRAIRIE—C-3

(NW) CROOKED CREEK REC. AREA—(Evangeline) *From jct Hwy 106 & Hwy 13 & Hwy 3187 (1 mi N of Pine Prairie): Go 4-1/2 mi W on Hwy 3187 to Entrance Rd, then 1/2 mi N on Entrance Rd. Enter at end.* FACILITIES: 150 sites, 150 W&E, (50 amps), family camping, tenting, dump. RECREATION: lake swim, boating, canoeing, ramp, dock, lake fishing, playground. Pets welcome. Partial handicap access. Open Feb - Nov. Phone: (337)599-2661.

PORT ALLEN—D-4

(W) Cajun Country Campground—(West Baton Rouge) *From jct I-10 (exit 151) & Hwy 415: Go 3/4 mi N on Hwy 415, then 1/2 mi W on Hwy 76 (Rosedale Rd), then 1/2 mi W on Rebelle Lane. Enter on L.* ◆◆◆FACILITIES: 77 sites, typical site width 35 ft, 77 full hkups, (20/30/50 amps), 54 pull-thrus, family camping, laundry, ltd groc. ◆◆RECREATION: swim pool, play equipment. Pets welcome, breed restrict. No tents. Open all yr. Big rigs welcome. Rate in 2010 $27.72 per vehicle. Member ARVC, LCOA. Phone: (800)264-8554. FCRV discount. FMCA discount.

RAYNE—D-3

(C) CITY OF RAYNE RV PARK—(Acadia) *From jct I-10 (exit 87) & Hwy 98/35: Go 1/4 mi S on Hwy 98/35, then 200 yards W on Oak St, then NW on Gossen Memorial Dr to Frog Festival Blvd. Enter at end.* FACILITIES: 737 sites, typical site width 22 ft, 737 W&E, (20/30/50 amps), family camping, dump. RECREATION: swim pool. Pets welcome. Partial handicap access. No tents. Open all yr. Big rigs welcome. Phone: (337)334-6607.

RUSTON—A-3

(N) LINCOLN PARISH PARK—(Lincoln) *From jct I-20 (exit 86) & Hwy 33: Go 3-1/4 mi N on Hwy 33. Enter on L.* FACILITIES: 45 sites, 33 full hkups, (20/30/50 amps), 12 no hkups, 4 pull-thrus, tenting. RECREATION: lake swim, boating, electric motors only, canoeing, ramp, dock, lake fishing, playground. Pets welcome. Partial handicap access. Open all yr. Phone: (318)251-5156.

(C) RUSTON/LINCOLN CONVENTION & VISITORS BUREAU—*From jct I-20 (exit 85) & US 167: Go 1-1/2 mi N on US 167. Enter on L.* Area information on the MANY & VARIED attractions & activities including: 4 yearly festivals, museums, special events, Nat' mountain bike races, antique & specialty shops, over 100 craftsmen & artists, hunting & fishing. Mon-Thurs 8:30-5, Fri 8-4. Open all yr.

WELCOME

Phone: (800)392-9032
Address: 2111 N Trenton St, Ruston, LA 71270
Lat/Lon: 32.56123/-92.63729
Email: tbush@rustonlincoln.com
Web: www.experiencerustonlincoln.com

SEE AD TRAVEL SECTION PAGE 280

ST. BERNARD—D-5

(E) FANZ RV PARK (RV SPACES)—(St. Bernard) *From I-10 (exit 236) & Hwy 39: Go 15 mi S on Hwy 39 to Hwy 46, then 2 mi E on Hwy 46, then 1/4 mi S on West Fanz Rd. Enter at end.*

WELCOME

FACILITIES: 154 sites, typical site width 35 ft, accepts full hkup units only, 154 full hkups, (30/50 amps), some extd stay sites, cable TV, ($), WiFi Instant Internet at site ($), WiFi Internet central location, family camping, RV's/park model rentals, RV storage, laundry.

RECREATION: boating, river fishing.

Pets welcome, breed restrict. No tents. Open all yr. Please call for holiday rates. Big rigs welcome. Rate in 2010 $25-35 per family. Member ARVC, LCOA.

Phone: (504)682-4900
Address: 2100 West Fanz Rd, St. Bernard, LA 70085
Lat/Lon: 29.86985/-89.83447
Email: cfanz@cox.net
Web: www.campneworleans.com

SEE AD NEW ORLEANS PAGE 295

ST. FRANCISVILLE—C-4

(SE) PEACEFUL PINES RV PARK—(West Feliciana) *From jct US 61 & Hwy 965: Go 3 mi E on Hwy 965. Enter on L.*

WELCOME

◊◊◊FACILITIES: typical site width 30 ft, 46 full hkups, (30/50 amps), 50 amps ($), 2 no hkups, 6 pull-thrus, WiFi Instant Internet at site, WiFi Internet central location, family camping, tenting, laundry, ice, picnic tables, wood.

◊◊RECREATION: rec hall, equipped pavilion, swim pool, pond fishing.

Pets welcome, breed restrict. Open all yr. Big rigs welcome. Escort to site. Rate in 2010 $30 for 2 persons. MC/VISA/DISC/Debit.

Phone: (225)635-4903
Address: 11907 LA Highway 965, St. Francisville, LA 70775
Lat/Lon: 30.80275/-91.30421
Email: peacefulpinesrv@aol.com
Web: www.peacefulpinesrvpark.com

SEE AD THIS PAGE

ST. JOSEPH—B-4

(E) LAKE BRUIN STATE PARK—(Tensas) *From jct US 65 & Hwy 607: Go 1 mi E on Hwy 607, then 1/2 mi N on Hwy 605, then 7 mi E on Hwy 604, then 1/2 mi SW on Lake Bruin St. Enter on L.* FACILITIES: 48 sites, 35 ft max RV length, 48 W&E, (30 amps), 5 pull-thrus, tenting, dump, laundry. RECREATION: lake swim, boating, ramp, lake fishing, playground. Pets welcome. Partial handicap access. Open all yr. Phone: (888)677-2784.

ST. MARTINVILLE—D-3

(N) Catfish Heaven Aqua Farm & Campground—(IBERIA) *From jct I-10 (exit 109) & Hwy 328: Go 1-3/4 mi S on Hwy 328, then 1/4 mi W on Hwy 336, then 4 mi S on Hwy 31, then 2-3/4 mi SW on Hwy 314, then 1/4 mi E on Hwy 353. Enter on R.* ◊◊◊◊FACILITIES: 60 sites, typical site width 25 ft, 60 full hkups, (20/30/50 amps), 22 pull-thrus, WiFi Instant Internet at site, tenting, shower$, dump, laundry, ice, picnic tables. ◊◊◊◊RECREATION: rec hall, equipped pavilion, swim pool, pond fishing, fishing supplies, bsktball, playground, v-ball. Pets welcome. Partial handicap access. Open all yr. Big rigs welcome. Rate in 2010 $19.50-25 for 2 persons. CCUSA 50% Discount. CCUSA reservations Recommended, CCUSA max stay 4 days, CCUSA disc. not avail F,Sa, CCUSA disc. not avail holidays.

CAMPCLUB USA

ST. MARTINVILLE—Continued
Catfish Heaven Aqua Farm & Campground—Continued

Phone: (337)394-9087
Address: 1554 Cypress Island Hwy, St. Martinville, LA 70582
Lat/Lon: 30.19044/-91.88213
Email: catfishheaven@aol.com
Web: www.catfishheaven.com

(E) LAKE FAUSSE POINTE STATE PARK—(Iberia) *From jct Hwy 96 & Hwy 679: Go 4 mi E on Hwy 679, then 4 mi E on Hwy 3083, then 7-1/2 mi S on W Atchafalaya protection levee road.* FACILITIES: 55 sites, 35 ft max RV length, 50 W&E, (20/30/50 amps), 5 no hkups, tenting, dump, laundry. RECREATION: boating, canoeing, ramp, dock, lake/stream fishing, playground. Pets welcome. Open all yr. Phone: (888)677-7200.

SHREVEPORT—A-2

(C) SHREVEPORT/BOSSIER CONVENTION & TOURIST BUREAU—*From jct I-20 (exit 19A) & Spring St: Go 2 blocks N on Spring St. Enter on R.* Contact for information on camping, dining, entertainment & attractions in the Shreveport-Bossier City area. Open all yr.

WELCOME

Phone: (800)551-8682
Address: 629 Spring St, Shreveport, LA 71166
Lat/Lon: 32.51362/-93.74492
Email: info@sbctb.org
Web: www.shreveport-bossier.org

SEE AD TRAVEL SECTION PAGE 280

(W) TALL PINES RV PARK—(Caddo) *From I-20 (exit 8): Go 2 blocks S on Hwy 526, then 1 mi E on W 70th St (Hwy 511). Enter on R.*

WELCOME

◊◊◊◊FACILITIES: 93 sites, typical site width 25 ft, 83 full hkups, 10 E, (15/20/30/50 amps), some extd stay sites, 60 pull-thrus, cable TV, WiFi Instant Internet at site, phone Internet central location, cabins, laundry, ltd groc, RV supplies, LP gas by weight/by meter, ice, picnic tables, patios, grills.

◊◊◊RECREATION: rec hall, swim pool, golf nearby, horseshoes.

Pets welcome, breed restrict. Partial handicap access. No tents. Age restrict may apply. Open all yr. Pool open May 15. Big rigs welcome. Clubs welcome. Rate in 2010 $28-36 for 2 persons. MC/VISA/DISC/AMEX/Debit. ATM. FCRV discount. FMCA discount.

Phone: (318)687-1010
Address: 6510 W 70th St, Shreveport, LA 71129
Lat/Lon: 32.44234/-93.87814
Email: info@tallpinesrvpark.com
Web: www.tallpinesrvpark.com

SEE AD THIS PAGE

SLIDELL—D-5

(S) NEW ORLEANS EAST KAMPGROUND—(St.Tammany) *From jct I-59/I-12 & I-10: Go 4 mi SW on I-10 (exit 263), then 3/4 mi E on Hwy 433. Enter on R.*

WELCOME

◊◊◊◊FACILITIES: 107 sites, typical site width 20 ft, 84 full hkups, 23 W&E, (15/20/30/50 amps), some extd stay sites, 92 pull-thrus, WiFi Instant Internet at site, family camping, tenting, cabins, dump, non-guest dump $, laundry, ltd groc, RV supplies, LP gas by weight/by meter, ice, picnic tables.

◊◊◊RECREATION: swim pool, stream fishing, mini-golf, golf nearby, bsktball, playground, horseshoes, v-ball, local tours.

Pets welcome. Partial handicap access. Open all yr. Tent campers limited stay 1 week. Big rigs welcome. Clubs welcome. Rate in 2010 $34-65 for 4 persons. MC/VISA/DISC/Debit. Member ARVC, LCOA.

SLIDELL—Continued
NEW ORLEANS EAST KAMPGROUND—Continued

Phone: (800)562-2128
Address: 56009 Hwy 433, Slidell, LA 70461
Lat/Lon: 30.23988/-89.75339
Email: noeast@sonic.net
Web: www.neworleanseastkampground.com

SEE AD NEW ORLEANS PAGE 297

(S) PINE CREST RV PARK—(St. Tammany) *From jct I-59/I-12 & I-10: Go 4 mi SW on I-10 (exit 263), then 1/4 mi E on 433. Enter on R.*

WELCOME

◊◊◊◊FACILITIES: 160 sites, typical site width 30 ft, 160 full hkups, (20/30/50 amps), some extd stay sites, 130 pull-thrus, WiFi Instant Internet at site, phone Internet central location, family camping, tenting, RV storage, dump, laundry, RV supplies, LP gas by weight/by meter, ice, picnic tables, patios.

◊◊◊RECREATION: rec hall, rec room/area, pavilion, lake fishing, golf nearby, play equipment, local tours.

Pets welcome, breed restrict. Partial handicap access. Open all yr. Big rigs welcome. Clubs welcome. Rate in 2010 $30 for 2 persons. MC/VISA.

Phone: (800)879-5936
Address: 2601 Old Spanish Trail, Slidell, LA 70461
Lat/Lon: 30.24205/-89.75796
Email: pinecrestrvpark@gmail.com
Web: www.pinecrestrv.com

SEE AD NEW ORLEANS PAGE 296 AND AD TRAVEL SECTION PAGE 279

SPRINGFIELD—D-5

(E) TICKFAW STATE PARK—(Livingston) *From jct I-12 & Hwy 43: Go 3 mi S on Hwy 43, then 1 mi E on Hwy 42, then 6 mi W on Hwy 1037, then 1-1/4 mi E on Patterson Rd. Enter at end.* FACILITIES: 50 sites, 30 W&E, (20/30/50 amps), 20 no hkups, tenting, dump, laundry. RECREATION: canoeing, river fishing, playground. Pets welcome. Partial handicap access. Open all yr. Phone: (888)981-2020.

SPRINGHILL—A-2

(E) SPRINGHILL RV PARK (City Park)—(Webster) *From jct Hwy 157 & US 371: Go 1 block S on US 371, then 2 blocks E on West Church St. Enter on R.* FACILITIES: 30 sites, accepts full hkup units only, 30 full hkups, (50 amps), dump. RECREATION: Pets welcome. No tents. Open all yr. Phone: (318)539-5681.

Can you trust the Woodall's ratings? 25 evaluation teams have scoured North American campgrounds to provide you with accurate, up to date information & ratings. Find a rating you don't agree with? Send a letter or email our way, and we'll give it extra attention for 2012.

THIBODAUX—D-4

(E) **BAYOU LAFOURCHE AREA CVB**—*At jct US 90 (Lockport/Thibodaux exit) & Hwy 1: Follow signs on Hwy 1. (Southeast Corner). Enter on L.* Visit for information on camping, special events and attractions in Cajun Bayou country. Its Cajun heritage gives the area a unique appeal. Restaurants, festivals and great outdoor recreation. Open all yr.

Text 107898 to (440)725-8687 to see our Visual Tour.

Phone: (877)537-5800
Address: 4484 Hwy 1, Raceland, LA 70394
Lat/Lon: 29.70665/-90.57236
Email: info@visitlafourche.com
Web: www.visitlafourche.com

SEE AD TRAVEL SECTION PAGE 277

TOLEDO BEND LAKE—B-2

See listings at Hornbeck, Many and Zwolle.

VIDALIA—B-4

(S) **RIVER VIEW RV PARK**—(Concordia) *From jct US Hwy 65/84 & SR 131: Go 1 mi S on SR 131. Enter on L.*

◆◆◆◆FACILITIES: 197 sites, typical site width 35 ft, 192 full hkups, 5 W&E, (15/20/30/50 amps), 50 amps ($), 120 pull-thrus, WiFi Instant Internet at site, WiFi Internet central location, family camping, tenting, laundry, ltd groc, RV supplies, LP gas by weight/by meter, ice.

◆◆◆◆RECREATION: rec room/area, pavilion, swim pool, hot tub, golf nearby, playground, hiking trails, local tours.

Pets welcome, breed restrict. Partial handicap access. Open all yr. Big rigs welcome. Clubs wel-

VIDALIA—Continued
RIVER VIEW RV PARK—Continued

come. Rate in 2010 $25-39 for 2 persons. MC/VISA/DISC/Debit. Member ARVC, LCOA. FCRV discount. FMCA discount.

Phone: (318)336-1400
Address: 100 River View Pkwy, Vidalia, LA 71373
Lat/Lon: 31.55719/-91.43672
Email: info@riverviewrvpark.com
Web: www.riverviewrvpark.com

SEE AD NATCHEZ, MS PAGE 445

VILLE PLATTE—C-3

(N) CHICOT STATE PARK—(Evangeline) *From jct Hwy 29 & US 167: Go 3 mi W on US 167, then 7 mi N on Hwy 3042. Enter on R.* FACILITIES: 208 sites, 208 W&E, (20/30/50 amps), 7 pull-thrus, tenting, dump, laundry. RECREATION: swim pool, boating, canoeing, ramp, dock, lake fishing, playground. Pets welcome. Open all yr. Phone: (888)677-2442.

VINTON—D-2

(SE) V RV Park-Lake Charles/Vinton—(Calcasieu) *From jct I-10 (exit 8 Vinton) & Hwy-108: Go 200 yds N on Hwy-108, then 200 yds W on Goodwin St. Enter on L.* ◆◆◆FACILITIES: 141 sites, typical site width 30 ft, 141 full hkups, (20/30/50 amps), 50 amps ($), 67 pull-thrus, family camping, tenting, laundry, ltd groc. ◆RECREATION: swim pool, play equipment. Pets welcome, breed restrict, quantity restrict. Open all yr. Big rigs welcome. Rate in 2010 $28.31-33.98 for 2 persons. Phone: (337)589-2300.

VIOLET—D-5

(E) SAINT BERNARD STATE PARK—(St. Bernard) *From jct I-510/10 & Hwy 47: Go 8 mi S on Hwy 47, then 10-1/2 mi SE on Hwy 39. Enter on L.* FACILITIES: 51 sites, 51 W&E, (30/50 amps), tenting, dump, laundry. RECREATION: swim pool, playground. Pets welcome. Partial handicap access. Open all yr. Phone: (888)677-7823.

WEST MONROE—A-3

(SW) Pavilion RV Park—(Ouachita) *From jct I-20 (exit 112) & Well Rd: Go 1/4 mi S on Well Rd. Enter on L.* ◆◆◆◆FACILITIES: 104 sites, typical site width 32 ft, 104 full hkups, (15/20/30/50 amps), 29 pull-thrus, family camping, laundry, ltd groc. ◆◆◆RECREATION: 2 swim pools, lake fishing, playground. Pets welcome, breed restrict, size restrict. Partial handicap access. No tents. Open all yr. Big rigs welcome. Rate in 2010 $38 for 4 persons. Member ARVC, LCOA. Phone: (888)322-4216. FCRV discount. FMCA discount.

Reserve Online at Woodalls.com

WESTWEGO—D-5

(W) BAYOU SEGNETTE STATE PARK—(Jefferson) *In town at jct Drake Ave & the Westbank Expy (US 90).* FACILITIES: 98 sites, 98 W&E, (30/50 amps), family camping, tenting, dump, laundry. RECREATION: swim pool, boating, canoeing, ramp, saltwater/river/stream fishing, playground. Pets welcome. Open all yr. Phone: (888)677-2296.

WOODWORTH—C-3

(SE) INDIAN CREEK RECREATION AREA (Alexander SF)—(Rapides) *From town: Follow signs E off US-165.* FACILITIES: 109 sites, typical site width 20 ft, 101 W&E, (30/50 amps), 8 no hkups, 17 pull-thrus, tenting, dump. RECREATION: lake swim, boating, canoeing, ramp, dock, lake fishing, playground. Pets welcome. Partial handicap access. Open all yr. Phone: (318) 487-5058.

ZWOLLE—B-2

(W) NORTH TOLEDO BEND STATE PARK—(Sabine) *From jct Hwy 482 & Hwy 3229: Go 4 mi SW on Hwy 3229. Enter at end.* FACILITIES: 63 sites, 63 W&E, (20/30 amps), family camping, tenting, dump, laundry. RECREATION: swim pool, boating, canoeing, ramp, lake fishing, playground. Pets welcome. Partial handicap access. Open all yr. Phone: (888)677-6400.

(SW) SAN MIGUEL PARK/TOLEDO BEND LAKE (Sabine River Auth. Site 7-A)—(Sabine) *From jct Hwy 191 & Carter Ferry Rd: Go 2 mi W on Carter Ferry Rd. Enter on R.* FACILITIES: 40 sites, typical site width 25 ft, 20 full hkups, 20 W&E, (20/30/50 amps), tenting, dump. RECREATION: lake swim, boating, ramp, dock, lake fishing, playground. Pets welcome. Open all yr. Member ARVC, LCOA. Phone: (318)645-6748.

The Eastern Brown Pelican is Louisiana's official state bird.

Louisiana was named in honor of King Louis XIV.

Louisiana's State Motto: "Union, justice and confidence"

READER SERVICE INFO

The following businesses have placed an ad in the Maine Travel Section. To receive free information, enter their Reader Service number on the Reader Service Card opposite page 48/Discover Section in the front of this directory:

Advertiser	RS#
Libby's Oceanside Camp	2613
Maine Campground Owner Association	709
Point Sebago Golf & Beach RV Resort	716

TIME ZONE

Maine is in the Eastern Time Zone.

TOPOGRAPHY

Known as the Pine Tree State, Maine has more than 17 million acres of forestland, extending over 87% of the state's total land area. One-tenth of the state's total area is water, including about 6,000 inland lakes and ponds.

TEMPERATURE

Maine is recognized as one of the most healthful states in the nation. Summer temperatures average around 70° and winter temperatures average around 20°.

Average snowfall in Maine is 50-70 inches annually in the Coastal area, 60-90 inches in the Southern Interior and 90-110 inches in the Northern Interior.

TRAVEL & TOURISM INFO

State Agency:
Maine Office of Tourism
59 State House Station
Augusta, ME 04333
(888/624-6345)
www.visitmaine.com

Statewide information:
Maine Office of Tourism
59 State House Station
Augusta, ME 04333
(888/624-6345)
www.visitmaine.com

Road Conditions & Traffic Information:
(207/624-3595) or 511 from any phone within the state.

Regional Agencies:

DownEast Acadia Regional Tourism
87 Milbridge Road
Cherryfield, ME 04622
(888/665-3278)
www.downeastacadia.com

Aroostook County Tourism
(888/216-2463)
www.visitaroostook.com

Kennebec & Moose River Valley Tourism
(800/393-8629 or 207/623-4883)
www.kennebecvalley.org

The Maine Beaches Association
P.O. Box 388
York, ME 03909
www.mainebeachesassociation.com

The Maine Highlands
P.O. Box 1938
Bangor, ME 04402
(800/91-MOOSE)
www.themainehighlands.com

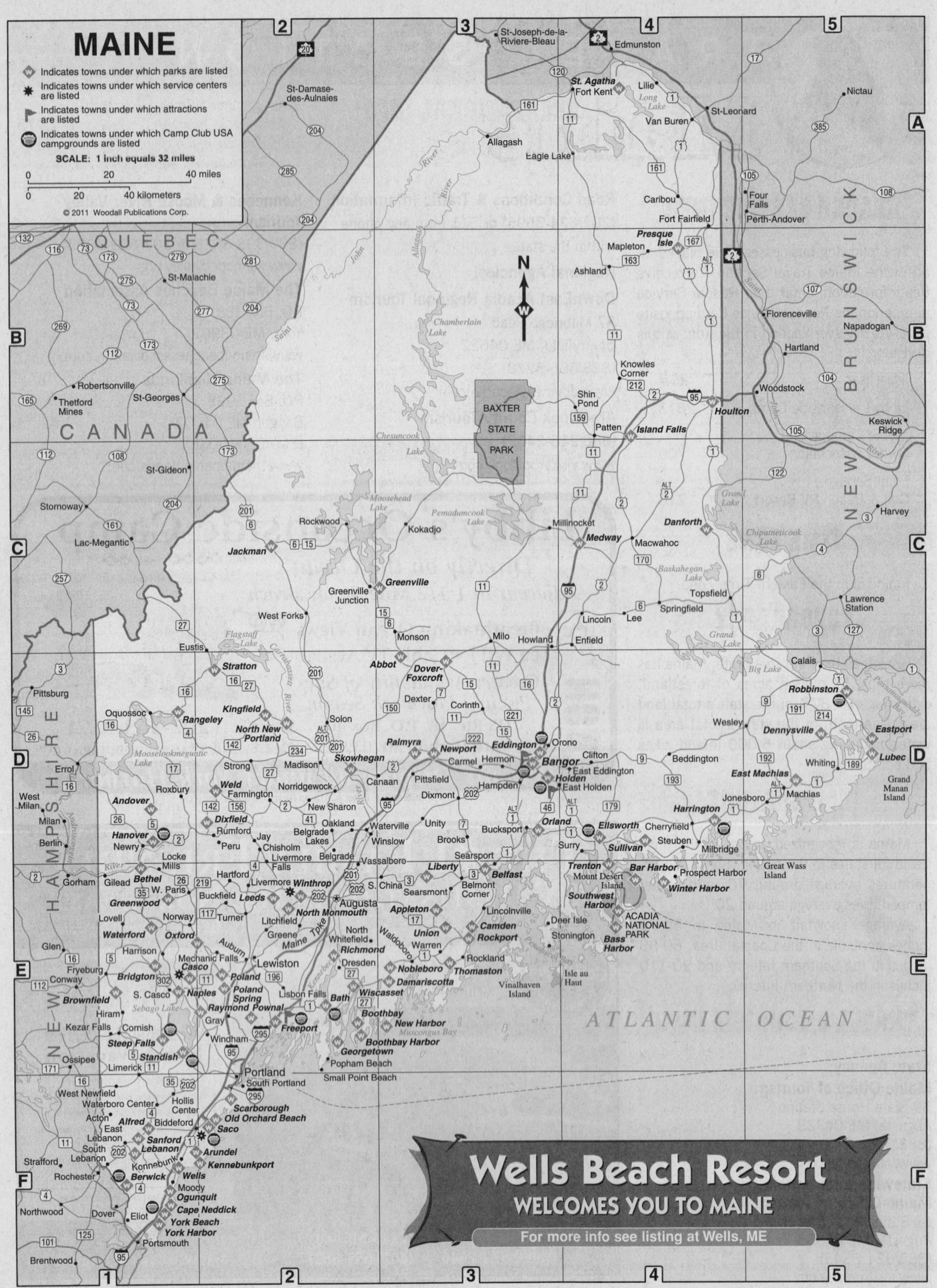
MAINE
Indicates towns under which parks are listed
Indicates towns under which service centers are listed
Indicates towns under which attractions are listed
Indicates towns under which Camp Club USA campgrounds are listed
SCALE: 1 inch equals 32 miles
0 20 40 miles
0 20 40 kilometers
© 2011 Woodall Publications Corp.
QUEBEC
CANADA
NEW BRUNSWICK
NEW HAMPSHIRE
ATLANTIC OCEAN
BAXTER STATE PARK
ACADIA NATIONAL PARK
Wells Beach Resort
WELCOMES YOU TO MAINE
For more info see listing at Wells, ME

Maine Lakes & Mountains Tourism Council
125 Manley Road
Auburn, ME 04210
(888/688-0099)
www.westernmaine.org

MidCoast Chamber Council
(800/872-6246)
www.mainesmidcoast.com

Convention & Visitors Bureau of Greater Portland
94 Commercial Street Suite 300
Portland, ME 04101
(207/772-5800)
www.visitportland.com

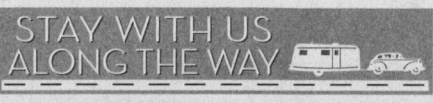

Local Agencies:
Contact the Chamber of Commerce or Tourism Bureau for the locality you are interested in.

RECREATIONAL INFO

Ferry Information: For general schedule of Maine State Ferry Service, call 800/491-4883 or visit www.state.me.us/mdot/opt/ferry /ferry.htm Ruckland 207/596-2202

Fishing: Maine Department of Inland Fisheries and Wildlife. Licensing applications, fishing locations and tournament information.
(207/287-8000)
www.maine.gov/ifw

Golf: Maine State Golf Association, www.mesga.org (207/846-3800); Golf Maine, www.golfme.com (877/553-4653).

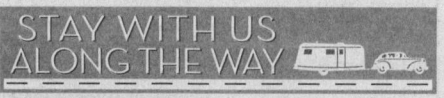

Kayaking: Maine Association of Sea Kayak Guides and Instructors, www.maine-seakayakguides.com

Scenic Byways: (207/624-3250) www.exploremaine.org/ byways/

Skiing: Ski Maine Association (207/773-7669). www.skimaine.com

Snowmobiling: Maine Snowmobile Association, (207/622-6983). www.mesnow.com

State Parks: Maine Bureau of Parks and Lands. (207/287-3821) www.maine.gov/doc/parks

Whitewater Rafting: Raft Maine, P.O. Box 78, West Forks, ME 04985 (800/723-8633). www.raftmaine.com

Wildlife Viewing, Hunting, Fishing: Maine Department of Inland Fisheries & Wildlife, (207/287-8000). www.state.me.us/ifw/fishing/index.htm

Wineries: Maine Wines & Wineries, www.mainewines.com

Winter Sports: Maine Winter Sports Center, 552 Main St., Caribou, ME 04736 (207/492-1444). www.mainewsc.org

SHOPPING

Bangor Mall, Bangor. Enclosed regional mall boasting 80 + stores. 663 Stillwater Ave., (207/947-7333).
www.simon.com/mall/find

Freeport Merchants Association. The town of Freeport has more than 170 outlet stores and specialty shops. 23 Depot Street, (207/865-1212). www.freeportusa.com

Kittery Outlets, Kittery. Visit America's Maine Street for shopping. Exit 3 off I-95 to Rt. 1, Kittery, ME (888/KITTERY). Web: www.thekitteryoutlets.com

Maine Mall, South Portland. Visit Maine's largest retail shopping center with over 140 shops & restaurants. Don't miss "The

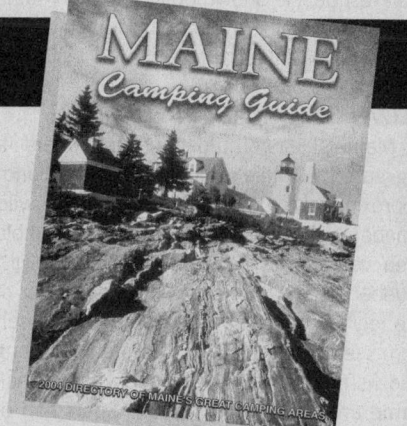

Uncommon Market" featuring unique local & regional products. 364 Maine Mall Rd. (207/774-0303). www.mainemall.com

Native Arts, Woolwich. Arts and crafts made by Native people. Items such as baskets, carvings, turquoise jewelry, kachinas, pottery, fetishes, sand paintings, musical instruments and more. From the different nations such as Navajo, Hopi, Zuni, Penobscot, Passamaquoddy, Mic Mac, Iroquois, Huichol, Lakota, Acoma, Jemez, as well as many other tribes. 813 Route 1. (207/442-8399 or 866/862-8483).

Salt River Artisans Gallery, Boothbay. Representing exclusively Maine Made furnishings. 473 Wiscasset Rd. (877/725-8748 or 207/633-0770). www.saltrivergallery.com

United Maine Craftsmen, Inc., Manchester. Organization of over 700 crafts people. Website offers information on members and craft shows. 16 Old Winthrop Road #2 (207/621-2818). www.unitedmainecraftsmen.com

DESTINATIONS

AROOSTOOK REGION

With more than 6,400 square miles of forest, fields and freshwater, Aroostook County is adventure waiting to happen. Anglers cast their lines into over 2,000 lakes, streams, rivers and ponds for landlocked salmon, trout, deep fighting squaretail, black bass, brook trout, togue and lake whitefish.

Ashland, south of Portage. One of the largest lumbering communities in Aroostook is home to the **Ashland Logging Museum**, containing tools and photos recounting the state's lumber industry.

Presque Isle. Numerous sparkling clean lakes and streams offer the perfect opportunity for swimming, boating and fishing. Presque Isle has also become a popular snowmobiling area. Situated along Maine's 2,000-mile Interconnected Trail System, the natural setting offers great fun. In addition, the Presque Isle Snowmobile Club maintains 75 miles of trails. In the summer, enjoy the 4-mile paved bike trail.

DOWN EAST/ACADIA REGION

Maine's easternmost border offers a rugged 1,000-mile coastline. Moving inland, approximately 80 percent of the nation's wild blueberry crop is grown here and the whole area celebrates the August harvests with blueberry fairs and festivals. The interior of the region contains vast areas of nature seldom seen by humans. It is a notable hunting and fishing territory, with deer, bear, small game and birds in profusion. Sport fish of unusual size (including Atlantic salmon) can be found in numerous lakes and streams.

Acadia National Park. Donated by the Rockefeller family in 1916, this unique park encompasses 40,000 acres of Mount Desert Island and Schoodic Point. Hulls Cove Visitor Center, located off Rt. 3 at the start of the Park Loop Road, offers a 15-minute film on the history of Acadia, a scale model of the park and an opportunity to sign up for programs and ranger-led activities. Well-marked trails vary in degrees of difficulty. This park, the oldest national park east of the Mississippi River, is a geological wonder. Ice-age glaciers cut through its existing mountains, carving valleys and fjord-like inlets, leaving the area with islands, bays and peninsulas. Ocean Drive scenic route follows the park's

Where to Find CCUSA Parks

List City	Park Name	Map Coordinates
BANGOR		
	Pumpkin Patch RV Resort	D-3
BATH		
	Meadowbrook Camping	E-2
BERWICK		
	Beaver Dam Campground	F-1
EDDINGTON		
	The Waltons Campground	D-3
ELLSWORTH		
	Hospitality Woods RV Park	D-4
FREEPORT		
	Blueberry Pond Campground	E-2
HANOVER		
	Stony Brook Recreation	D-1
HARRINGTON		
	Sunset Point Campground	D-4
HOLDEN		
	Red Barn Campground	D-3
ROBBINSTON		
	Hilltop Campground	D-5
SACO		
	Silver Springs Campground	F-2
STANDISH		
	Family and Friends Campground	E-1
STEEP FALLS		
	Acres of Wildlife	E-1
YORK BEACH		
	York Beach Camper Park	F-1

BUSINESSES OFFERING

	Things to See & Do	RV Sales	RV Service
BANGOR			
Hermon Family Resaurant	⚑		
CASCO			
Point Sebago		🚌	✱
FREEPORT			
Desert of Maine	⚑		
HOLDEN			
Red Barn Diner	⚑		
SACO			
Seacoast RV's		🚌	✱
WINTHROP			
Augusta-West Lakeside RV Sales & Service		🚌	✱

entire eastern perimeter. Sights range from sheer rising cliffs to pounding surf to beaches formed of minute shells as fine as sand. Take the road to the top of **Cadillac Mountain** (1,530 ft.) for an incredible overlook of the surrounding ocean, islands and countryside. Schoodic Point lies on the Gouldsboro Peninsula and can be reached from the town of Winter Harbor.

Bangor is a farming, industrial and recreational region bisected by the Penobscot River. Bangor was once an important Native American rendezvous point before Champlain landed here in 1604, in his search for the fabled city of Norumbega. Today the city features boutiques, shopping centers, stately residences and scenic parks, such as the beautiful **Grotto Cascade Park** (opposite the Bangor Salmon Pool), home to a 45-foot cascade. Sporting, cultural and political events are held at the Bangor Municipal Auditorium and Civic Center. The **Maine Air Museum**, located at Bangor International Airport, presents aviation history through dioramas, historical artifacts and aircraft. Bangor is also the home of Paul Bunyan — there is a birth certificate to prove it. The Paul Bunyan statue was made from scratch and refurbished years ago and when the city wanted to dismantle it; the community fought to keep it standing.

Bar Harbor. Visit the **Oceanarium**, a marine education center and home to live marine mammals, a salt marsh and a Marine Lobster museum. Bay Ferries are available for day trips to Nova Scotia.

Calais is situated in the beautiful St. Croix River Valley, with an international bridge across the river to St. Stephen, New Brunswick.

Moosehorn National Wildlife Refuge was established for the protection and study of all species of wildlife in the area. Located on 23,000 acres of woods, fields, streams and ponds, you'll find deer, shrew, mole, bear, moose, beaver, mink, geese and eagles. With 190 species of birds recorded, the refuge is a bird watchers paradise. The terrain shows the effects of glaciation with a landscape of rolling hills, large ledge outcroppings, valleys, streams, lakes, bogs and marshes.

MID-COAST REGION

Bath is known as the "City of Ships" because of its vast shipbuilding industries. Located near the mouth of the Kennebec River, the city is rich in maritime history. The downtown area looks much the same as it did 100 years ago—period lighting, original

QUICK REFERENCE CHART FOR WOODALL'S FEATURED PARKS

	Green Friendly	RV Lots for Sale	Park Models-Onsite Ownership	Park Membership for Sale	Big Rigs Welcome	Internet Friendly	Pets Welcome
ABBOT							
Balsam Woods Campground						●	■
ALFRED							
Walnut Grove Campground						●	■
ANDOVER							
South Arm Campground	🍃						■
BANGOR							
Paul Bunyan Campground					▲	●	■
Pleasant Hill RV Park & Campground					▲	●	■
Pumpkin Patch RV Resort					▲	●	■
BAR HARBOR							
Hadley's Point Campground						●	■
BOOTHBAY							
Shore Hills Campground & RV Park					▲	●	■
CASCO							
Point Sebago Golf and Beach RV Resort	🍃				▲	●	■
DAMARISCOTTA							
Lake Pemaquid Camping	🍃					●	■
EDDINGTON							
The Waltons Campground						●	■
FREEPORT							
Blueberry Pond Campground						●	■
Desert Dunes of Maine Campground						●	■
Freeport Village Campground					▲	●	■
HARRINGTON							
Sunset Point Campground					▲	●	■
HOLDEN							
Holden Family Campground					▲	●	■
Red Barn Campground						●	■
HOULTON							
My Brothers Place Campground					▲	●	■
JACKMAN							
Moose River Campground & Cabins						●	■
KENNEBUNKPORT							
Red Apple Campground	🍃				▲	●	■

Green Friendly 🍃; RV Lots for Sale ✖; Park Models/Onsite Onwership ✱; Park Memberships for Sale ✔; Big Rigs Welcome ▲; Internet Friendly ●; Internet Friendly-WiFi ●; Pets Welcome ■

storefronts and brick sidewalks add to the atmosphere.

Boothbay Harbor Area. This busy summer resort region has excellent facilities for fishing, swimming, antique shows, art exhibits, band concerts, dinner theaters, yachting and boat trips. The **Coastal Maine Botanical Gardens**, a 128-acre botanical garden has over two miles of trails along the shorefront and woodlands. During the summer, over 30 excursion boats operate from the harbor. Secluded resort communities include **Spruce Point, Southport, West Southport and Newagen**. The islands are connected by a short drawbridge.

Boothbay Railway Village. Browse through 24 exhibit buildings, housing artifacts, trains and antique cars. Hop aboard the Boothbay Central for a ride around the turn-of-the-century New England village.

Brunswick Area. Situated along the Androscoggin River, Brunswick was once a thriving lumber and shipbuilding community. It is now the site of **Bowdoin College**, and the newly renovated **Bowdoin College Museum of Art**. **Harpswell, Great Island, Orrs Island** and **Bailey Island** can be reached by highway from Brunswick.

Bailey Island Bridge is a 1,200-foot bridge connecting Orrs and Bailey islands across Will's gut. Built in 1928 of cribstone, no metal or cement was used. It is believed to be the only one of its kind.

Bowdoin College Museum of Art, Brunswick. This museum contains a permanent collection of Colonial, Federal, and American 19th-century paintings, European Old Master drawings, Renaissance and 17th-century paintings.

Camden is one of the mid-coast's most popular yachting centers and is known as the town "Where mountains meet the sea." **Camden Hills State Park** provides panoramic views of Penobscot Bay and islands miles out into the Gulf of Maine. Windjammer cruises range from 2 hours to 3 or 6 days. Rent a bicycle for a leisurely Sunday afternoon or take to the coast on a mountain bike tour. View the islands of Penobscot Bay, lighthouses, harbor seals and shorefront mansions. Fall foliage is beautiful and winter brings skiing and tobogganing enthusiasts to Camden Snow Bowl.

Penobscot Bay is 40 miles long and 15 miles wide, encompassing more than 200 islands, including Isleboro, accessible by car ferry; Warren Island, which has a state park; Matinicus Island and a fishing village.

QUICK REFERENCE CHART FOR WOODALL'S FEATURED PARKS

	Green Friendly	RV Lots for Sale	Park Models-Onsite Ownership	Park Membership for Sale	Big Rigs Welcome	Internet Friendly	Pets Welcome
ORLAND							
Shady Oaks Campground and Cabins	🍃				▲	●	■
POLAND SPRING							
Poland Spring Campground						●	■
PRESQUE ISLE							
Arndt's Aroostook River Lodge & Campground	🍃					●	■
RAYMOND							
Kokatosi Campground						●	■
SACO							
Saco/Old Orchard Beach KOA	🍃				▲	●	■
SCARBOROUGH							
Bayley's Camping Resort	🍃				▲	●	■
Wassamki Springs Campground					▲	●	■
Wild Duck Adult Campground	🍃				▲	●	■
SKOWHEGAN							
Two Rivers Campground					▲	●	■
THOMASTON							
Saltwater Farm Campground	🍃				▲	●	■
TRENTON							
Timberland Acres RV Park					▲	●	■
WELLS							
Beach Acres Campground					▲		
Sea Vu Campground					▲	●	■
Wells Beach Resort					▲	●	■
WINTHROP							
Augusta-West Lakeside Resort Kampground						●	■
YORK HARBOR							
Libby's Oceanside Camp	🍃				▲	●	■

Green Friendly 🍃; RV Lots for Sale ✖; Park Models/Onsite Onwership ✱; Park Memberships for Sale ✔; Big Rigs Welcome ▲; Internet Friendly ●; Internet Friendly-WiFi ●; Pets Welcome ■

Monhegan Island offers some of the best scenery in Maine, with its painted dramatic cliffs—the highest on the New England coast. A wildlife sanctuary containing more than 600 varieties of wildflowers and 200 kinds of birds and a peaceful area of spruce trees make Monhegan a popular place for naturalists and hikers to visit. It also contains 17 miles of trails, inns, a lighthouse, a museum and a swimming beach.

Searsport. The town is known as "the home of the famous sea captains" and the "Antique Capital of Maine." Over 360 sailing vessels have been built in Searsport, once home to 280 sea captains. **The Penobscot Marine Museum** houses one of the finest collections of marine paintings and artifacts in the country, including historical boat exhibits.

MAINE BEACHES REGION

Freeport is often referred to as the "birthplace of Maine." It was here the state became a member of the Union in 1820. Today, the area is known for its distinctive outlet and specialty stores. Hike along the trails at **Wolfe's Neck Woods State Park**. From the fishing harbor of South Freeport, you'll find bay cruises to Eagle Island.

Desert of Maine. Nature trails wind through 40 acres of once fertile land. Beautiful forests surround sand dunes that continue to engulf tall trees and small buildings. Peak touring times are during spring's wildflower season and during autumn's fall foliage changes.

Kennebunk. Kennebunk Beach, Kennebunk and Kennebunkport have long catered to summer residents. Once a shipbuilding town, Kennebunk now provides visitors and residents with a relaxed atmosphere, miles of beautiful beaches and fantastic scenes of rocky coastlines. Fish for striped bass at the mouth of the Kennebunk and Mousam rivers. Consider taking a reflective walk through the **Shrine of St. Anthony** (Franciscan Monastery). It is within walking distance of the Lower Village and features paths through woods and gardens, past small shrines and statues of saints.

Seashore Trolley Museum. Ride an antique electric trolley and view over 225 trolleys at the oldest and largest transit museum in the world.

Kittery. Boasting a long and prestigious history of shipbuilding, Kittery is Maine's southern-most town and also the state's oldest (settled in 1623). Captain John Paul Jones' sloop **Ranger** and the **U.S.S. Raleigh** had their keels laid in Kittery. America's first submarine was launched from Kittery in 1917. Through displays, models, dioramas, paintings, artifacts and photographs, the **Kittery Historical & Naval Museum** preserves and interprets the history of the Naval Shipyard in Kittery.

Portland. The town has been destroyed by fire four times and each time rebuilt. Hence their motto resurgam which means, "I shall rise again." With over 200 stores and 100 restaurants, Portland greets visitors with everything from crafts, antiques and imported goods to lobsters, clams, Indian, Afghani and Vietnamese cuisine. The **Portland Observatory** was built in 1807 and alerted merchants when their ships entered the harbor. The **Narrow Gauge Railroad Museum** offers free admission to its displays of narrow-gauge railcars and model trains.

Casco Bay. The picturesque islands of Casco Bay extend 20 miles east of Portland and can be reached by ferryboat from Portland Harbor. One of the more popular islands to visit is **Peaks Island**—a resort area offering sandy beaches, a Civil War Museum and the STAR (Solar Technology and Applied Research) facility.

Scarborough Marsh is located in Scarborough off Pine Point Road. Three thousand acres of nature are operated by the Maine Audubon Society. Contact the Scarborough Marsh Nature Center for information on canoe tours through the area. Special programs include Dawn Birding and Full Moon Canoe Tours.

WESTERN LAKES & MOUNTAINS REGION

Carrabassett Valley is an area rich in forests, outdoor recreation, agriculture and scenery. A marvelous view of Mount Abraham, Saddleback, Spaulding, Sugarloaf and Crocker mountains can be seen from the town of Kingfield. Sugarloaf is Maine's second highest mountain and offers 18 holes of golf at one of Maine's best courses during summer and fall and 54 miles of skiing on 134 trails during the winter.

Rangeley Lakes. This area is made up of seven lakes in the Longfellow Mountains, bordered to the west by the White Mountains of New Hampshire.

Maine Wildlife Park, Gray. The park serves as a permanent home for wildlife no longer able to survive in the wild. See a Maine Black Bear, Bald Eagle, Moose, Lynx, and many other animals.

KENNEBEC VALLEY/ MOOSE RIVER VALLEY REGION

Augusta is the state capital of Maine. The dome of the capitol building can be seen for miles up and down the Kennebec River. Visitors can tour the **State House**, with its Hall of Flags; the **Blaine House**, which is the governor's residence; and the **Maine State Library, Museum** and **Archive Building.** Also within Augusta is **Fort Western**, which contains the original barracks of 20 rooms, built by the Plymouth Company in 1754 during the French and Indian War. Trails traversing over 200 acres at the **Pine Tree State Arboretum** are open year-round.

Jackman/Moose River, located along Hwy. 201. Surrounded by 250,000 acres of natural, unspoiled wilderness, you'll find salmon, brook trout, togue and smelt in the 60 lakes and ponds. Boating, swimming, mountain climbing, backpacking, bicycling and canoeing are also popular during the summer months. Winter tourists enjoy over 200 miles of groomed snowmobile trails, ice fishing, cross-country skiing and snowshoeing.

MAINE HIGHLAND REGION

Appalachian Trail. Beginning at Mount Katahdin in Maine and extending to Springer Mountain in Georgia, this 2,158-mile wilderness trail crosses some of Maine's finest peaks through 280 miles of breathtaking scenery. This region has a history of paper making and lumbering and there are several museums that illustrate its past. The **Ambajejus Boom House** on Ambajejus Lake in Millinocket provides insight into the old days of papermaking. It is accessible by snowmobile or boat. **Baxter State Park** is a 204,733-acre wilderness and wildlife sanctuary offering mountain climbing, camping, hiking and canoeing opportunities. Mountain trails and shelters harmonize with the unspoiled surroundings. The 5,267-foot **Katahdin Mountain** and the northern terminus of the **Appalachian Trail** are located here.

Grand Canyon of the East, nickname for Gulf Hagas Reserve, is located on the west branch of the Pleasant River near Brownville and Brownville Junction. Accessible only by trail, this secluded area is the site of waterfalls, sheer walls, fantastic shapes and unusual rock formations.

Moosehead Lake Region is a centrally-located unspoiled wilderness, with over 20,000 free-roaming moose. The lake itself, surrounded by rugged mountains and dense forests, is 40 miles long and 10 miles wide and contains several large islands and many bays and inlets.

ANNUAL EVENTS

JANUARY

Annual Maine Bridal Show, Portland; Bath Antiques Show, Bath; Mushers Bowl Winter Carnival, Bridgton; Wyman Lake Ice Fishing Derby, Moscow; Annual Snowfest, Norway.

FEBRUARY

Chocolate Extravaganza, Kennebunk; US National Toboggan Championships, Camden; International Snowmobilers Festival, Madawaska; Winter Carnival & Snow Mobile Festival, Caribou; Moosehead Lake Snofest, Greenville; Family Fest, Bridgton.

ABBOT—D-3

(NW) BALSAM WOODS CAMPGROUND—(Piscataquis) *From jct Hwy 16 & Hwy 15: Go 1 mi N on Hwy 15, then 3 mi W on Pond Rd. Enter on L.*

◇◇◇FACILITIES: 64 sites, typical site width 40 ft, 21 full hkups, 42 W&E, (20/30/50 amps), 1 no hkups, some extd stay sites, 4 pull-thrus, WiFi Instant Internet at site, WiFi Internet central location, family camping, tenting, RV's/park model rentals, cabins, RV storage, dump, non-guest dump $, portable dump, laundry, groceries, RV supplies, LP gas by meter, ice, picnic tables, fire rings, wood.

◇◇◇◇RECREATION: rec room/area, pavilion, coin games, swim pool, canoeing, kayaking, canoe/3 kayak rentals, golf nearby, bsktball, playground, activities, (wkends), horseshoes, sports field, hiking trails, v-ball.

Pets welcome. Open mid May - mid Oct. Clubs welcome. Rate in 2010 $29-32 for 4 persons. MC/VISA/DISC/AMEX/Debit. Member ARVC, MECOA.

Phone: (207)876-2731
Address: 112 Pond Rd, Abbot, ME 04406
Lat/Lon: 45.21758/-69.51479
Email: info@balsamwoods.com
Web: www.balsamwoods.com

SEE AD THIS PAGE

ACADIA NATIONAL PARK—E-4

See listings at Bar Harbor, Bass Harbor, Ellsworth, Mt. Desert Southwest Harbor & Trenton.

ALFRED—F-1

(NE) Scott's Cove Camping Area—(York) *From jct Hwy 111 & Hwy 202/4: Go 2-1/2 mi N on Hwy 202/4, then 1/2 mi E on Brock Rd. Enter on R.* ◇◇◇FACILITIES: 50 sites, typical site width 34 ft, 8 full hkups, 42 W&E, (30 amps), 5 pull-thrus, family camping, tenting, dump, laundry, ltd groc. ◇◇◇RECREATION: lake/boating, canoeing, ramp, dock, lake fishing, play equipment. No pets. Open May 1 - Columbus Day. Rate in 2010 $35-47 per family. Member ARVC, MECOA.

ALFRED—Continued
Scott's Cove Camping Area—Continued

Phone: (207)324-6594
Address: 356 Brock Rd, Alfred, ME 04002
Lat/Lon: 43.51369/-70.70975
Email: scottscove@roadrunner.com
Web: www.scottscovecamping.com

(NW) WALNUT GROVE CAMPGROUND—(York) *From jct Hwy 111 & Hwy 202/4: Go 1 mi N on Hwy 202/4, then 1 mi NW on Gore Rd, then continue 1-3/4 mi W on Gore Rd. Enter on R.*

◇◇◇◇FACILITIES: 93 sites, typical site width 40 ft, 32 full hkups, 61 W&E, (20/30/50 amps), many extd stay sites, 3 pull-thrus, heater not allowed, cable TV, WiFi Instant Internet at site, family camping, tenting, cabins, shower$, dump, non-guest dump $, portable dump, laundry, groceries, RV supplies, LP gas by weight/by meter, ice, picnic tables, fire rings, wood, controlled access.

◇◇◇◇RECREATION: rec hall, coin games, swim pool, golf nearby, bsktball, playground, activities, (wkends), horseshoes, sports field, hiking trails, v-ball.

Pets welcome, quantity restrict. Open May 1 - Columbus Day. Clubs welcome. Rate in 2010 $30-39 for 4 persons. MC/VISA/Debit. Member ARVC, MECOA.

Phone: (207)324-1207
Address: 599 Gore Rd, Alfred, ME 04002
Lat/Lon: 43.51764/-70.75147
Email: walnutgrove@roadrunner.com
Web: www.walnutgrovecampground.net

SEE AD THIS PAGE

ANDOVER—D-1

(N) SOUTH ARM CAMPGROUND—(Oxford) *From jct Hwy 5 & Hwy 120: Go 1/2 mi E on Hwy 120, then 11 mi N on South Arm Rd (no street sign-watch for Hwy sign). Enter on L.*

◇◇◇FACILITIES: 103 sites, typical site width 50 ft, 65 W&E, (20/30/50 amps), 38 no hkups, 4 pull-thrus, family camping, tenting, cabins, shower$, dump, portable dump, laundry, groceries, LP gas by meter, marine gas, ice, picnic tables, fire rings, wood, controlled access.

◇◇◇◇RECREATION: rec room/area, lake swim, boating, canoeing, kayaking, ramp, dock, 14 canoe/9 kayak/7 motorboat rentals, lake/river/pond/stream fishing, fishing supplies, fishing guides, bsktball, activities, horseshoes, sports field, hiking trails, v-ball.

ANDOVER—Continued
SOUTH ARM CAMPGROUND—Continued

Pets welcome. Open Early May - Late Sep. Generated electricity 6:30 am -10 pm. Clubs welcome. Green Friendly. Rate in 2010 $24-32 for 2 persons. Member ARVC, MECOA.

Phone: (207)364-5155
Address: 62 Kennett Dr, Andover, ME 04216
Lat/Lon: 44.74833/-70.83830
Email: camp@southarm.com
Web: www.southarm.com

SEE AD THIS PAGE

APPLETON—E-3

(S) Sennebec Lake Campground—(Knox) *From west jct Hwy-17 & Hwy-131: Go 3 mi N on Hwy-131. Enter on R.* ◇◇◇FACILITIES: 106 sites, typical site width 28 ft, 35 ft max RV length, 11 full hkups, 85 W&E, (20/30 amps), 10 no hkups, family camping, tenting, dump, laundry, ltd groc. ◇◇◇◇RECREATION: lake swim, boating, canoeing, ramp, dock, lake fishing, playground. Pets welcome. Open May 1 - Nov 1. Rate in 2010 $35-42 per family. Member ARVC, MECOA. Phone: (207)785-4250.

ARUNDEL—F-1

(NW) Hemlock Grove Campground—(York) *From jct I-95 (exit 32) & Biddeford Spur: Go 7/8 mi E on Biddeford Spur, then 4-1/2 mi S on US 1 (Portland Rd). Enter on R.* ◇◇◇◇FACILITIES: 73 sites, typical site width 40 ft, 56 full hkups, 12 W&E, (20/30/50 amps), 5 no hkups, family camping, tenting, dump, laundry, ltd groc. ◇◇◇RECREATION: playground. Pets welcome, quantity restrict. Partial handicap access. Open May 15 - Oct 15. Big rigs welcome. Rate in 2010 $48 per family. Member ARVC, MECOA. Phone: (207) 985-0398.

AUBURN—E-2

POLAND SPRING CAMPGROUND—*From jct I-95 (exit 63) S of Auburn & Hwy 26: Go 12 mi N on Hwy 26, then 1/2 mi E on Connor Ln. Enter at end.*

SEE PRIMARY LISTING AT POLAND SPRING AND AD THIS PAGE

AUGUSTA—E-2

See listings at Litchfield, North Monmouth, Richmond & Winthrop

BANGOR—D-3

(W) HERMON FAMILY RESAURANT—*From jct I-95 (exit 180) & Cold Brook Rd: Go 2-1/2 mi W on Cold Brook Rd, then 1-1/2 mi W (left) on Rte 2, then 1/2 mi N on Billings Rd. Enter on R.* Serving breakfast, lunch & dinner 7 days a week plus a to go menu. Featuring seafood, pasta, sandwiches, omelets & more. 10% discount for campground guests. Open all yr. MC/VISA.

Phone: (207)848-5088
Address: 151 Billings Rd, Hermon, ME 04401

SEE AD NEXT PAGE

BANGOR—Continued on next page

Maine State Flower: White Pine cone and tassel.

BANGOR—Continued

(W) PAUL BUNYAN CAMPGROUND—(Penobscot) *From jct I-95 (exit 184) & Hwy 222: Go 2-1/2 mi W on Hwy 222. Enter on L.*

WELCOME

◆◆◆FACILITIES: 52 sites, typical site width 30 ft, 12 full hkups, 40 W&E, (20/30/50 amps), 50 amps ($), some extd stay sites, 20 pull-thrus, WiFi Instant Internet at site, family camping, tenting, RV storage, dump, non-guest dump $, portable dump, laundry, ltd groc, RV supplies, ice, picnic tables, fire rings, wood.

◆◆◆◆RECREATION: rec room/area, equipped pavilion, coin games, swim pool, boating, 2 pedal boat rentals, pond fishing, fishing supplies, golf nearby, bsktball, playground, activities, (wkends), horseshoes, sports field, hiking trails, v-ball.

Pets welcome, breed restrict. Open Apr 15 - Oct 15. Big rigs welcome. Clubs welcome. Rate in 2010 $27-38 for 4 persons. MC/VISA/DISC/Debit. Member ARVC, MECOA.

Phone: (207)941-1177
Address: 1862 Union St, Bangor, ME 04401
Lat/Lon: 44.83113/-68.83974
Email: paulbunyancg@aol.com
Web: www.paulbunyancampground.com

SEE AD THIS PAGE

Eastport is the most eastern city in the United States, and is considered the first place in the United States to receive the rays of the morning sun.

BANGOR—Continued

(W) PLEASANT HILL RV PARK & CAMPGROUND—(Penobscot) *From jct I-95 (exit 184) & Hwy 222: Go 5 mi W on Hwy 222. Enter on L.*

WELCOME

◆◆◆◆FACILITIES: 105 sites, typical site width 35 ft, 34 full hkups, 61 W&E, (20/30/50 amps), 50 amps ($), 10 no hkups, some extd stay sites, 40 pull-thrus, cable TV, WiFi Instant Internet at site ($), phone Internet central location, family camping, tenting, RV's/park model rentals, RV storage, dump, non-guest dump $, portable dump, laundry, ltd groc, RV supplies, LP gas by weight/by meter, ice, picnic tables, fire rings, wood.

◆◆◆◆RECREATION: rec room/area, pavilion, coin games, swim pool, mini-golf, ($), golf nearby, bsktball, playground, activities, (wkends), horseshoes, sports field, hiking trails, v-ball.

Pets welcome. Open May 1 - Columbus Day. Big rigs welcome. Clubs welcome. Rate in 2010 $36-41 for 2 persons. MC/VISA/DISC/Debit. Member ARVC, MECOA.

Phone: (207)848-5127
Address: 45 Mansell Rd, Hermon, ME 04401
Lat/Lon: 44.84815/-68.87788
Email: info@pleasanthillcampground.com
Web: www.pleasanthillcampground.com

SEE AD THIS PAGE

(W) PUMPKIN PATCH RV RESORT—(Penobscot) *From jct I-95 (exit 180) & Cold Brook Rd: Go 2-1/2 mi W on Cold Brook Rd, then 1-1/2 mi W on Rt 2, then 1/2 mi N on Billings Rd. Enter on R.*

FRIENDLIEST RV PARK IN NEW ENGLAND
Quiet & relaxing country atmosphere in central Maine-Suburb of Bangor-Many interesting places to visit nearby including museums & Stephen Kings home. Sports enthusiasts enjoy Golfing, Stock Car & harness racing, fishing...

◆◆◆◆◆FACILITIES: 75 sites, typical site width 38 ft, 65 full hkups, 10 W&E, (20/30/50 amps), some extd stay sites, 44 pull-thrus, cable TV, WiFi

PUMPKIN PATCH RV RESORT—Continued on next page

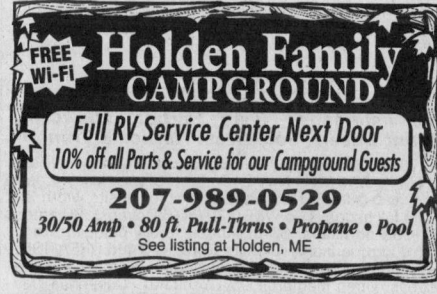

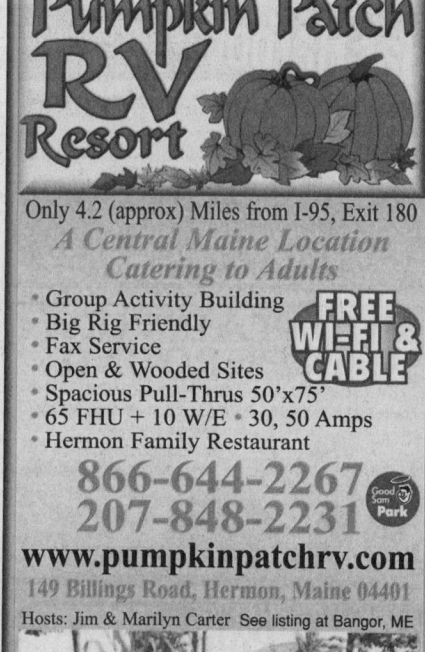

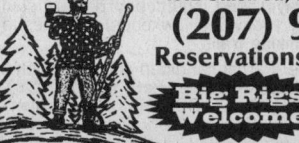

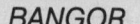

BANGOR—Continued
PUMPKIN PATCH RV RESORT—Continued

Instant Internet at site, WiFi Internet central location, RV storage, dump, non-guest dump $, laundry, ice, picnic tables.

◇◇◇RECREATION: rec hall, golf nearby, activities, horseshoes, sports field. Pets welcome, breed restrict. Partial handicap access. No tents. Open May 1 - Oct 15. Big rigs welcome. Escort to site. Clubs welcome. Rate in 2010 $30-32 for 4 persons. MC/VISA/Debit. Member ARVC, MECOA. CCUSA 50% Discount. CCUSA reservations Accepted, CCUSA max stay 5 days. Discount not available Fri & Sat during Jul, Aug, Sep or any holidays or holiday weekends. Discount may be extended depending upon availability. Pet surcharge is for over 2 pets. No pit bulls or Rottweilers. All pets must be leashed & picked up after.

Phone: (866)644-2267
Address: 149 Billings Rd, Hermon, ME 04401
Lat/Lon: 44.81655/-68.90237
Email: rvoffice@pumpkinpatchrv.com
Web: www.pumpkinpatchrv.com

SEE AD PAGE 309 AND AD TRAVEL SECTION PAGE 303

(W) Wheeler Stream Campground—(Penobscot) *From jct I-95 (exit 180) & Coldbrook Rd: Go 2 mi W on Coldbrook Rd, then 500 ft W on US 2. Enter on R.* ◇◇FACILITIES: 25 sites, typical site width 35 ft, 25 W&E, (20/30/50 amps), 50 amps ($), 11 pull-thrus, family camping, tenting, dump, laundry. ◇◇RECREATION: swim pool, boating, no motors, canoeing, dock, stream fishing. Pets welcome. Open Memorial Wknd - Sep 15. Rate in 2010 $23-27 for 4 persons. Member ARVC, MECOA. Phone: (207)848-7877.

BAR HARBOR—E-4

See listings at Bass Harbor, Ellsworth, Mount Desert, Southwest Harbor & Trenton

(NW) Bar Harbor Campground—(Hancock) *From jct Hwy-102/198 & Hwy-3: Go 5 mi SE on Hwy-3. Enter on L.* ◇◇◇FACILITIES: 308 sites, typical site width 24 ft, 70 full hkups, 105 W&E, (20/30/50 amps), 50 amps ($), 133 no hkups, 60 pull-thrus, family camping, tenting, dump, laundry, full svc store. ◇◇◇RECREATION: swim pool, playground. Pets welcome. Partial handicap access. Open Memorial Day Weekend - Columbus Day Weekend. Rate in 2010 $36-40 for 4 persons. Member ARVC, MECOA. Phone: (207)288-5185.

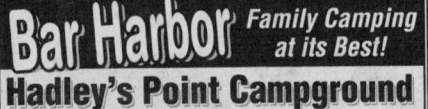

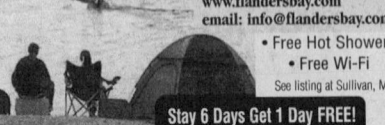

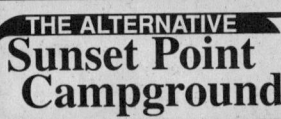

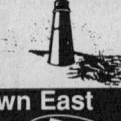

BAR HARBOR—Continued

(W) Bar Harbor KOA—(Hancock) *At jct Hwy 3 & Hwy 102 at head of island. Enter on R.* ◇◇◇FACILITIES: 200 sites, typical site width 28 ft, 38 full hkups, 137 W&E, (30/50 amps), 25 no hkups, 75 pull-thrus, family camping, tenting, dump, laundry, groceries. ◇◇◇RECREATION: saltwater swim, boating, canoeing, ramp, saltwater fishing, playground. Pets welcome. Partial handicap access. Open early May - mid Oct. Rate in 2010 $46-95 for 2 persons. Member ARVC, MECOA. Phone: (888)562-5605. KOA discount.

(W) Bar Harbor Woodlands KOA—(Hancock) *From jct Hwy-3 & Hwy-102: Go 1-1/2 mi S on Hwy-102. Enter on L.* ◇◇◇FACILITIES: 102 sites, typical site width 35 ft, 20 full hkups, 28 W&E, (20/30/50 amps), 54 no hkups, 5 pull-thrus, family camping, tenting, dump, laundry, ltd groc. ◇◇◇◇RECREATION: swim pool, playground. Pets welcome. Partial handicap access. Open Memorial Day - Late Sept. Rate in 2010 $43-68 for 2 persons. Member ARVC, MECOA. Phone: (207)288-5139. KOA discount.

(NW) HADLEY'S POINT CAMPGROUND—(Hancock) *From jct Hwy 102/198 & Hwy 3: Go 3 mi SE on Hwy 3, then 1/4 mi N on Hadley Point Rd. Enter on R.*

WELCOME

◇◇◇FACILITIES: 180 sites, typical site width 26 ft, 15 full hkups, 117 W&E, (20/30 amps), 48 no hkups, 9 pull-thrus, WiFi Instant Internet at site, WiFi Internet central location, family camping, tenting, RV storage, shower$, dump, portable dump, laundry, ltd groc, RV supplies, LP gas by meter, ice, picnic tables, fire rings, wood.

◇◇◇RECREATION: swim pool, golf nearby, bsktball, playground, shuffleboard court 2 shuffleboard courts, horseshoes, sports field, local tours.

Pets welcome. Open May 15 - Oct 15. Clubs welcome. Rate in 2010 $35-40 for 4 persons. MC/VISA/DISC/Debit. Member ARVC, MECOA.

Phone: (207)288-4808
Address: 33 Hadley Point Rd, Bar Harbor, ME 04609
Lat/Lon: 44.43767/-68.31528
Web: www.hadleyspoint.com

SEE AD THIS PAGE

(NW) MT. DESERT NARROWS CAMPING RESORT—(Hancock) *From jct Hwy 102/198 & Hwy 3: Go 1-1/2 mi SE on Hwy 3. Enter on L.*

WELCOME

◇◇◇FACILITIES: 235 sites, typical site width 24 ft, 62 full hkups, 120 W&E, (20/30/50 amps), 53 no hkups, 64 pull-thrus, cable TV, WiFi Instant Internet at site ($), phone Internet central location, family camping, tenting, RV's/park model rentals, dump, portable dump, laundry, full svc store, RV supplies, LP gas by meter, ice, picnic tables, fire rings, wood.

◇◇◇◇◇RECREATION: rec hall, rec room/area, coin games, swim pool, boating, canoeing, kayaking, 2 canoe/2 kayak rentals, saltwater fishing, golf nearby, bsktball, playground, activities, horseshoes, sports field, local tours.

Pets welcome. Open May 15 - Columbus Day. Big rigs welcome. Clubs welcome. Rate in 2010 $45-80 per family. MC/VISA/DISC/Debit. Member ARVC, MECOA.

Phone: (866)917-4300
Address: 1219 St Hwy 3, Bar Harbor, ME 04609
Lat/Lon: 44.41982/-68.33678
Web: www.barharborcampingresorts.com

Reserve Online at Woodalls.com

SEE AD NEXT PAGE

BAR HARBOR—Continued

(NW) NARROWS TOO CAMPING RESORT—(Hancock) *From jct Hwy 102/198 & Hwy 3: Go 1-1/4 mi W on Hwy 3. Enter on R.*

WELCOME

◇◇◇◇FACILITIES: 200 sites, typical site width 24 ft, 200 full hkups, (20/30/50 amps), 41 pull-thrus, cable TV, WiFi Instant Internet at site ($), phone Internet central location, family camping, RV's/park model rentals, cabins, dump, non-guest dump $, portable dump, laundry, full svc store, RV supplies, LP gas by meter, ice, picnic tables, fire rings, wood.

◇◇◇RECREATION: rec hall, coin games, swim pool, canoeing, kayaking, 2 canoe/2 kayak rentals, saltwater fishing, golf nearby, activities, horseshoes, v-ball, local tours.

Pets welcome. No tents. Open May 1 - Oct 25. Big rigs welcome. Clubs welcome. MC/VISA/DISC/Debit. Member ARVC, MECOA.

Phone: (866)917-4300
Address: 1150 Bar Harbor Rd, Trenton, ME 04605
Lat/Lon: 44.43929/-68.36985
Web: www.barharborcampingresorts.com

Reserve Online at Woodalls.com

SEE AD NEXT PAGE

TIMBERLAND ACRES RV PARK—*From jct Hwy 102 & Hwy 3: Go 6-1/2 mi N on Hwy 3.*

WELCOME

SEE PRIMARY LISTING AT TRENTON AND AD THIS PAGE

BASS HARBOR—E-4

(SE) Bass Harbor Campground—(Hancock) *From jct Hwy 102 & Hwy 102A: Go 5 mi S on Hwy 102A. Enter on L.* ◇◇◇FACILITIES: 117 sites, typical site width 28 ft, 29 full hkups, 33 W&E, (20/30/50 amps), 50 amps ($), 55 no hkups, 9 pull-thrus, family camping, tenting, dump, laundry. ◇◇◇RECREATION: swim pool, play equipment. Pets welcome. Partial handicap access. Open mid May - mid Oct. Facilities fully operational mid June - mid Oct. Rate in 2010 $35-50 for 2 persons. Member ARVC, MECOA. Phone: (207)244-5857.

BATH—E-2

(S) MEADOWBROOK CAMPING—(Sagadahoc) *From jct US 1 & Hwy 209: Go 2-1/2 mi S on Hwy 209, then 3 mi W on High St/Campbells Pond Rd/Meadowbrook Rd (stay left). Enter on R.*

◇◇◇FACILITIES: 139 sites, typical site width 30 ft, 48 full hkups, 49 W&E, (20/30/50 amps), 50 amps ($), 42 no hkups, some extd stay sites, 15 pull-thrus, WiFi Instant Internet at site, family camping, tenting, cabins, RV storage, dump, portable dump, laundry, groceries, RV supplies, LP gas by weight/by meter, ice, picnic tables, fire rings, wood.

◇◇◇◇RECREATION: rec hall, rec room/area, coin games, swim pool, boating, canoeing, kayaking, dock, 2 canoe/3 kayak rentals, golf nearby, playground, shuffleboard court shuffleboard court, activities (wkends), horseshoes, sports field, hiking trails.

Pets welcome. Partial handicap access. Open May 1 - Oct 1. Clubs welcome. Rate in 2010 $31-40 per family. MC/VISA/DISC/AMEX/Debit. Member ARVC, MECOA. CCUSA 50% Discount. CCUSA reservations Accepted, CCUSA max stay Unlimited, CCUSA disc. not avail holidays. Discount available May, Jun, Sep after Labor Day. Rates are 50% off 30 amp electric site. Add $4 for sewer & $4 for 50 amp. Discounts cannot be taken after site is paid for. Please identify as Camp Club member when making reservation.

Phone: (207)443-4967
Address: 33 Meadowbrook Rd, Phippsburg, ME 04562
Lat/Lon: 43.84290/-69.83723
Email: mbcamp@meadowbrookme.com
Web: www.meadowbrookme.com

SEE AD PAGE 112

See the highest tides off the U.S. mainland at Passamaquoddy Bay.

BELFAST—E-3

(E) **The Moorings**—(Waldo) *From jct Hwy 3 & US 1: Go 2-1/2 mi NE on US 1. Enter on R.* ◆◆◆FACILITIES: 44 sites, typical site width 26 ft, 44 W&E, (20/30/50 amps), 8 pull-thrus, dump, laundry. ◆◆RECREATION: saltwater swim, canoeing, saltwater fishing, playground. Pets welcome, quantity restrict. Partial handicap access. No tents. Open May 1 - Oct 24. Rate in 2010 $48-60 for 2 persons. Member ARVC, MECOA. Phone: (207)338-6860.

BERWICK—F-1

(NE) **Beaver Dam Campground**—(York) *From jct Hwy 236 & Hwy 9: Go 4 mi NE on Hwy 9. Enter on L.* ◆◆◆FACILITIES: 66 sites, typical site width 30 ft, 23 full hkups, 43 W&E, (20/30/50 amps), 50 amps ($), 6 pull-thrus, WiFi Instant Internet at site, WiFi Internet central location, family camping, tenting, RV storage, shower$, dump, non-guest dump $, portable dump, laundry, ltd groc, RV supplies, ice, picnic tables, fire rings, wood. ◆◆◆◆RECREATION: swim pool, lake swim, boating, no motors, canoeing, kayaking, dock, pond fishing, fishing supplies, mini-golf, ($), bsktball, playground, activities, horseshoes, v-ball. Pets welcome, breed restrict. Open Mid May - Columbus Day. Big rigs welcome. Rate in 2010 $31-45 for 2 persons. MC/VISA/Debit. Member ARVC, MECOA. CCUSA 50% Discount. CCUSA reservations Recommended, CCUSA max stay 7 days, CCUSA disc. not avail holidays. Discount available May 15-Jun 18 & Aug 30-Sep 30.

Phone: (207)698-2267
Address: 551 School St, Berwick, ME 03901
Lat/Lon: 43.29014/-70.78773
Email: camp@beaverdamcampground.com
Web: www.beaverdamcampground.com

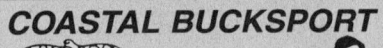

BETHEL—E-1

(N) **Bethel Outdoor Adventure and Campground**—(Oxford) *From jct Hwy 26 & US 2 (in Bethel): Go 3/4 mi N on US 2.* ◆◆FACILITIES: 39 sites, typical site width 25 ft, 20 full hkups, 7 W&E, (20/30/50 amps), 50 amps ($), 12 no hkups, 27 pull-thrus, family camping, tenting, dump, laundry. ◆◆◆RECREATION: canoeing, river fishing. Pets welcome. Open Mid May - Late Oct. Rate in 2010 $32-35 per family. Member ARVC, MECOA. Phone: (800)533-3607. FMCA discount.

(W) **Pleasant River Campground**—(Oxford) *From jct Hwy 26 & US 2 (in Bethel): Go 5 mi W on US 2. Enter on L.* ◆◆◆FACILITIES: 75 sites, typical site width 40 ft, 3 full hkups, 35 W&E, (20/30/50 amps), 37 no hkups, 8 pull-thrus, family camping, tenting, dump, ltd groc. ◆◆◆RECREATION: swim pool, boating, canoeing, river fishing, playground. Pets welcome. Open May 1 - Oct 31. Rate in 2010 $28-30 for 2 persons. Member ARVC, MECOA. Phone: (207)836-2000.

BOOTHBAY—E-2

(N) **SHORE HILLS CAMPGROUND & RV PARK**—(Lincoln) *From jct US-1 & Hwy-27: Go 7-1/2 mi S on Hwy-27. Enter on R.*

◆◆◆◆FACILITIES: 150 sites, typical site width 30 ft, 83 full hkups, 52 W&E, (20/30/50 amps), 15 no hkups, some extd stay sites, 15 pull-thrus, cable TV, WiFi Internet central location, family camping, tenting, cabins, RV storage, shower$, dump, non-guest dump $, laundry, ltd groc, RV supplies, LP gas by weight/by meter, ice, picnic tables, fire rings, wood, controlled access.

◆◆RECREATION: rec hall, boating, canoeing, kayaking, 2 canoe rentals, saltwater/river fishing, golf nearby, playground, horseshoes.

Pets welcome. Open May 1 - Columbus Day. Big rigs welcome. Clubs welcome. Rate in 2010 $38-45 per family. Member ARVC, MECOA. FMCA discount.

Phone: (207)633-4782
Address: 553 Wiscasset Rd, Boothbay, ME 04537
Lat/Lon: 43.90518/-69.62020
Web: www.shorehills.com

SEE AD THIS PAGE

BOOTHBAY HARBOR—E-2

(S) **Gray Homestead Oceanfront Camping**—(Lincoln) *From jct Hwy 27 & Hwy 238: Go 2 mi S on Hwy 238. Enter on L.* ◆◆◆FACILITIES: 40 sites, typical site width 22 ft, 22 full hkups, 8 W&E, (20/30/50 amps), 10 no hkups, family camping, tenting, dump, laundry.

Maine State Bird: Chickadee

BOOTHBAY HARBOR—Continued
Gray Homestead Oceanfront Camping—Continued

◆◆◆RECREATION: saltwater swim, boating, canoeing, saltwater fishing. Pets welcome, quantity restrict. Open May 14 - Columbus Day. Rate in 2010 $38-48 for 2 persons. Member ARVC, MECOA. Phone: (207)633-4612.

BRIDGTON—E-1

(N) **Lakeside Pines Campground**—(Cumberland) *From jct US-302 & Hwy-117: Go 2 mi N on Hwy-117. Enter on R.* ◆◆◆FACILITIES: 185 sites, typical site width 24 ft, 175 full hkups, 10 W&E, (20/30/50 amps), family camping, tenting, dump, laundry, ltd groc. ◆◆◆◆RECREATION: lake swim, boating, canoeing, ramp, dock, lake/stream fishing, play equipment. Pets welcome. Partial handicap access. Open Memorial Day - Sep 15. Rate in 2010 $42 per family. Member ARVC, MECOA. Phone: (207)647-3935.

BROWNFIELD—E-1

(E) **Shannons Sanctuary**—(Oxford) *From jct Hwy 5/113 & Hwy 160: Go 2 mi E on Hwy 160. Enter on R.* ◆◆FACILITIES: 44 sites, typical site width 30 ft, 28 full hkups, (30/50 amps), 16 no hkups, 28 pull-thrus, family camping, tenting, dump, laundry, ltd groc. ◆◆◆RECREATION: river swim, boating, canoeing, dock, river fishing, play equipment. Pets welcome, breed restrict, quantity restrict. Open May 15 - Columbus Day. Rate in 2010 $24-30 for 2 persons. Member ARVC, MECOA. Phone: (207)452-2274.

(E) **Woodland Acres Campground & Canoe**—(Oxford) *From jct Hwy 5/113 & Hwy 160: Go 1/2 mi E on Hwy 160. Enter on L.* ◆◆◆FACILITIES: 104 sites, typical site width 50 ft, 39 full hkups, 45 W&E, (30/50 amps), 20 no hkups, 5 pull-thrus, family camping, tenting, dump, laundry, groceries. ◆◆◆◆RECREATION: river swim, boating, canoeing, ramp, dock, river fishing, playground. Pets welcome, quantity restrict. Partial handicap access. Open mid May - mid Oct. Rate in 2010 $34-42 per family. Member ARVC, MECOA. Phone: (207)935-2529.

BUCKSPORT—D-3

See listing at Orland

CAMDEN—E-3

(N) CAMDEN HILLS STATE PARK—(Waldo) *From jct Hwy-105 & US-1: Go 2 mi NE on US-1.* FACILITIES: 107 sites, 107 no hkups, tenting, dump. RECREATION: saltwater/lake fishing, playground. Open May 15 - Oct 15. Phone: (207)236-3109.

CAPE NEDDICK—F-1

(S) **Dixon's Coastal Maine Campground**—(York) *From jct I-95 (exit 7) & US Rte 1: Go 5 mi N on US Rte 1. Enter on L.* ◆◆◆FACILITIES: 126 sites, 31 ft max RV length, 65 W&E, (20/30/50 amps), 61 no hkups, family camping, tenting, dump, ltd groc. ◆◆RECREATION: swim pool, playground. Pets welcome. Open May 15 - Mid Sep. Rate in 2010 $40-44 for 2 persons. Phone: (207)363-3626.

CASCO—E-1

✽ (S) **POINT SEBAGO**—*From jct Hwy 85 & US 302: Go 5 mi N on US 302, then 1 mi W at Casco Alliance Church (Pt Sebago Rd). Enter on R.* SALES: travel trailers, park models, pre-owned unit sales. SERVICES: full-time mech, RV appliance repair, bus. hrs emerg rd svc, LP gas by weight/by meter, dump station, RV storage. Open May 1 - Oct 31. MC/VISA/DISC.

POINT SEBAGO—Continued on next page

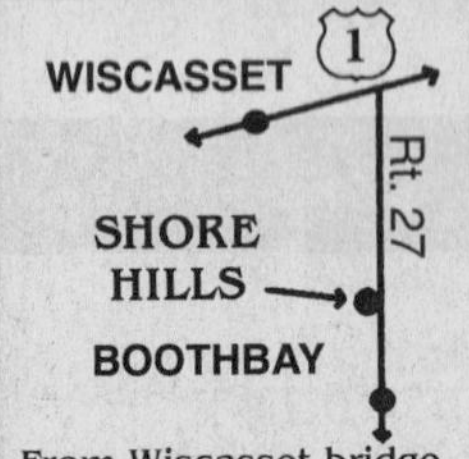

CASCO—Continued
POINT SEBAGO—Continued

Phone: (207)655-3821
Address: RR 1, Casco, ME 04015
Lat/Lon: 43.93726/-70.54436

SEE AD TRAVEL SECTION PAGE 301

(S) POINT SEBAGO GOLF AND BEACH RV RESORT—(Cumberland) *From jct Hwy 85 & US 302: Go 5 mi N on US 302, then 1 mi W at Casco Alliance Church (Pt. Sebago Rd). Enter on R.*

◊◊◊◊◊FACILITIES: 95 sites, typical site width 30 ft, 82 full hkups, 13 W&E, (20/30/50 amps), 10 pull-thrus, cable TV, WiFi Instant Internet at site, phone Internet central location, family camping, tenting, cabins, RV storage, dump, portable dump, laundry, full svc store, RV supplies, LP gas by weight/by meter, LP bottle exch, marine gas, ice, picnic tables, fire rings, grills, wood, controlled access.

◊◊◊◊◊RECREATION: rec hall, rec room/area, equipped pavilion, coin games, lake swim, boating, canoeing, kayaking, ramp, dock, 15 pontoon/15 canoe/20 kayak/20 pedal boat/15 motorboat rentals, lake fishing, fishing supplies, mini-golf, ($), putting green, golf nearby, bsktball, playground, shuffleboard court 12 shuffleboard courts, activities, tennis, horseshoes, sports field, hiking trails, v-ball.

Pets welcome, size restrict. Open May 1 - Oct 31. Big rigs welcome. Clubs welcome. Green Friendly. Rate in 2010 $35-90 per family. MC/VISA/DISC/Debit. ATM. Member ARVC, MECOA.

Text 108005 to (440)725-8687 to see our Visual Tour.

Phone: (800)872-7646
Address: 261 Point Sebago Rd, Casco, ME 04015
Lat/Lon: 43.91939/-70.55000
Email: dtoms@pointsebago.com
Web: www.pointsebago.com

SEE AD TRAVEL SECTION PAGE 301

DAMARISCOTTA—E-3

(NE) LAKE PEMAQUID CAMPING—(Lincoln) *From jct Hwy 130 & Business US 1: Go 1 mi NE on Business US 1, then 2 mi S on Biscay Rd, then 1/4 mi E on Egypt Rd, then E on Twin Cove Lane. Enter at end.*

◊◊◊◊FACILITIES: 300 sites, typical site width 28 ft, 145 full hkups, 155 W&E, (20/30/50 amps), some extd stay sites, 10 pull-thrus, WiFi Internet central location, family camping, tenting, cabins, RV storage, shower$, dump, non-guest dump $, laundry, ltd groc, RV supplies, LP bottle exch, marine gas, ice, picnic tables, fire rings, wood, controlled access.

◊◊◊◊◊RECREATION: rec hall, rec room/area, equipped pavilion, coin games, swim pool, lake swim, hot tub, boating, canoeing, kayaking, ramp, dock, 4 rowboat/12 canoe/12 kayak/6 pedal boat/10 motorboat rentals, lake fishing, fishing supplies, mini-golf, ($), golf nearby, bsktball, playground, activities, tennis, horseshoes, sports field, v-ball.

Pets welcome. Partial handicap access. Age restrict may apply. Open Memorial Day - Sep 30. Clubs welcome. Green Friendly. Rate in 2010 $24-44 per family. MC/VISA/DISC/AMEX/Debit. ATM. Member ARVC, MECOA.

Phone: (207)563-5202
Address: 100 Twincove Ln, Damariscotta, ME 04543
Lat/Lon: 44.03315/-69.46839
Email: lakepem@tidewater.net
Web: www.lakepemaquid.com

SEE AD THIS PAGE

DANFORTH—C-4

(E) Greenland Cove Campground—(Washington) *From jct Hwy 169 & US 1: Go 2-1/2 mi S on US 1, then 2-1/2 mi SE on Greenland Cove Rd, then 1/2 mi E on Brown Rd. Enter at end.* ◊◊◊FACILITIES: 69 sites, 3 full hkups, 60 W&E, 6 E, (30/50 amps), 15 pull-thrus, tenting, dump, laundry, groceries. ◊◊◊◊RECREATION: swim pool, lake swim, boating, canoeing, ramp, dock, lake fishing, play equipment. Pets welcome. Partial handicap access. Open Mid May - Oct 1st. Rate in 2010 $28 per family. Member ARVC, MECOA. Phone: (207)448-2863.

Maine is the single largest producer of blueberries in the United States producing 99 percent of all the blueberries in the country.

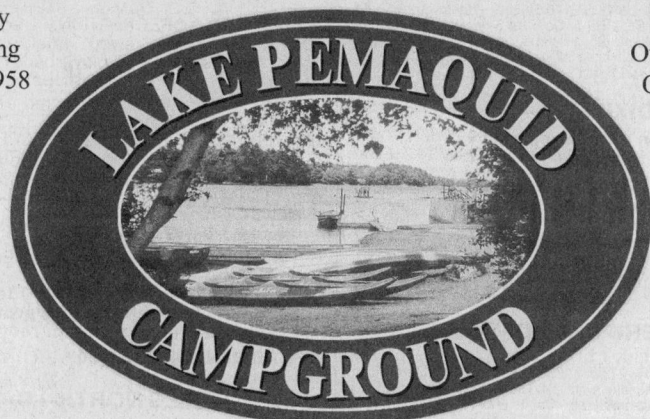

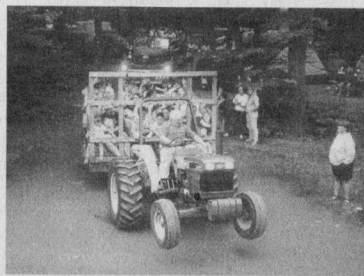

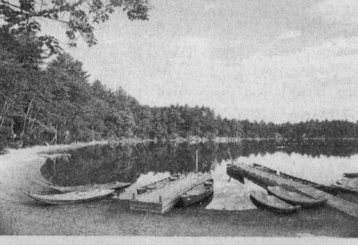

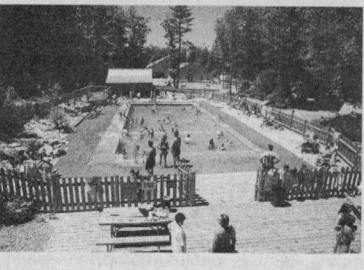

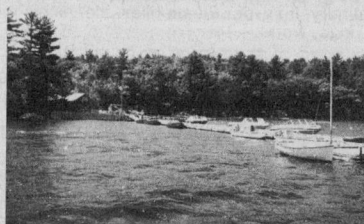

DENNYSVILLE—D-5

(S) COBSCOOK BAY STATE PARK—(Washington) *Southbound, from jct Hwy-86 & US-1: Go 6 mi S on US-1.* FACILITIES: 106 sites, 106 no hkups, 25 pull-thrus, tenting, dump. RECREATION: boating, ramp, saltwater fishing, playground. Open May 15 - Oct 15. Phone: (207)726-4412.

DIXFIELD—D-2

(N) Mountain View Campground—(Oxford) *From jct US 2 & Hwy 142: Go 1-1/4 mi N on Hwy 142. Enter on L.* ◆◆◆FACILITIES: 62 sites, typical site width 28 ft, 46 full hkups, 6 W&E, (20/30 amps), 12 no hkups, 20 pull-thrus, family camping, tenting, dump, laundry, ltd groc. ◆◆◆◆RECREATION: swim pool, boating, canoeing, dock, river fishing, play equipment. Pets welcome. Partial handicap access. Open May 1 - Oct 30. Facilities fully operational May 15 - Oct 15. Rate in 2010 $24-26 per family. Phone: (207)562-8285.

DOVER-FOXCROFT—D-3

(N) PEAKS-KENNY STATE PARK—(Piscataquis) *From town: Go 6 mi N on Hwy-153.* FACILITIES: 56 sites, 56 no hkups, tenting. RECREATION: lake swim, lake fishing, playground. Partial handicap access. Open May 15 - Oct 1. Phone: (207)564-2003.

EAST MACHIAS—D-5

(S) MILITARY PARK (Sprague Neck Campsites)—(Washington) *From jct US 1 & Hwy 191: Go 7 mi S on Hwy 191 to NCTS Cutler Admin. Area, then 6 mi. On base.* FACILITIES: 10 sites, typical site width 20 ft, 10 no hkups, 5 pull-thrus, tenting, ltd groc. RECREATION: boating, canoeing, saltwater/lake/pond fishing. Open May 15 - Oct 30. Phone: (207)259-8284.

EASTPORT—D-5

(N) Seaview Campground—(Washington) *From jct US 1 & Hwy 190: Go 5-1/2 mi E on Hwy 190. Enter on L.* ◆◆◆◆FACILITIES: 92 sites, typical site width 25 ft, 82 full hkups, (20/30/50 amps), 10 no hkups, 6 pull-thrus, family camping, tenting, dump, laundry. ◆◆◆◆RECREATION: swim pool, saltwater swim, boating, canoeing, ramp, dock, saltwater fishing, playground. Pets welcome. Open May 15 - Oct 15. Big rigs welcome. Rate in 2010 $38-53 for 4 persons. Member ARVC, MECOA. Phone: (207)853-4471.

EDDINGTON—D-3

(W) THE WALTONS CAMPGROUND—(Penobscot) *From jct Hwy 9 & Hwy 178: Go 1 mi N on Hwy 178. Enter on R.*

◆◆◆FACILITIES: 62 sites, typical site width 30 ft, 43 full hkups, (20/30 amps), 19 no hkups, some extd stay sites, 13 pull-thrus, cable TV, WiFi Instant Internet at site, family camping, tenting, cabins, RV storage, dump, non-guest dump $, laundry, ltd groc, RV supplies, LP gas by weight/by meter, ice, picnic tables, fire rings, wood.

See the highest tides off the U.S. mainland at Passamaquoddy Bay.

EDDINGTON—Continued
THE WALTONS CAMPGROUND—Continued

◆◆◆RECREATION: rec hall, coin games, swim pool, golf nearby, bsktball, playground, activities, (wkends), horseshoes, sports field.

Pets welcome, breed restrict. Open May 1 - Oct 15. Rate in 2010 $32.50 per family. MC/VISA/DISC. FMCA discount. CCUSA 50% Discount. CCUSA reservations Recommended, CCUSA max stay 2 days, Cash only for CCUSA disc., CCUSA disc. not avail F,Sa, CCUSA disc. not avail holidays.

Phone: (207)989-8898
Address: 211 Riverside Dr, Eddington, ME 04428
Lat/Lon: 44.83858/-68.69341
Email: info@waltonscampground.com
Web: www.waltonscampground.com

SEE AD BANGOR PAGE 309

ELLSWORTH—D-4

(SE) LAMOINE STATE PARK—(Ellsworth) *From jct US-1 & Hwy-184: Go 10 mi SE on Hwy-184.* FACILITIES: 61 sites, 20 ft max RV length, 61 no hkups, tenting. RECREATION: boating, ramp, dock, saltwater fishing, playground. Open May 15 - Oct 15. Phone: (207)667-4778.

(W) PATTEN POND CAMPING RESORT—(Hancock) *From jct US 1A/US 1 & Hwy 3: Go 7-1/4 mi W on US 1/Hwy 3. Enter on L.*

◆◆◆FACILITIES: 155 sites, typical site width 32 ft, 102 full hkups, 20 W&E, (20/30/50 amps), 33 no hkups, some extd stay sites, 38 pull-thrus, cable TV, WiFi Instant Internet at site ($), phone Internet central location, family camping, tenting, RV's/park model rentals, cabins, dump, portable dump, laundry, full svc store, RV supplies, LP gas by meter, ice, picnic tables, fire rings, wood.

◆◆◆◆◆RECREATION: rec hall, rec room/area, pavilion, coin games, lake swim, boating, canoeing, kayaking, dock, 2 canoe/4 kayak/4 pedal boat/2 motorboat rentals, lake fishing, fishing supplies, golf nearby, bsktball, 12 bike rentals, playground, activities, horseshoes, sports field, hiking trails, v-ball.

Pets welcome. Open May 15 - Columbus Day. Big rigs welcome. Clubs welcome. MC/VISA/DISC/AMEX/Debit. Member ARVC, MECOA.

Phone: (866)917-4300
Address: 1470 Bucksport Rd, Ellsworth, ME 04605
Lat/Lon: 44.55716/-68.56492
Web: www.barharborcampingresorts.com

Reserve Online at Woodalls.com

SEE AD BAR HARBOR PAGE 311

FREEPORT—E-2

(NW) BLUEBERRY POND CAMPGROUND—(Cumberland) *From I-295 (exit 22) & Hwy 125/136: Go 2-1/2 mi N on Hwy 136, then 1-1/2 mi W on Poland Rd. Enter on L.*

◆◆◆FACILITIES: 43 sites, typical site width 46 ft, 14 full hkups, 14 W&E, (20/30/50 amps), 15 no hkups, 3 pull-thrus, WiFi Instant Internet at site, phone Internet central location, family camping, tenting, cabins, dump, non-guest dump $, laundry, ltd groc, RV supplies, ice, picnic tables, fire rings, wood.

Numerous lighthouses dot the Maine coast including Fort Point Lighthouse at Fort Point State Park in Stockton Springs and Grindle Point Lighthouse on Isleboro.

FREEPORT—Continued
BLUEBERRY POND CAMPGROUND—Continued

◆◆◆RECREATION: swim pool, golf nearby, bsktball, playground, activities, (wkends), horseshoes, hiking trails, v-ball.

Pets welcome. Partial handicap access. Open Mid May - Oct 31. Rate in 2010 $35-40 per family. MC/VISA/Debit. Member ARVC, MECOA. CCUSA 50% Discount. CCUSA reservations Required, CCUSA max stay 2 days, Cash only for CCUSA disc., CCUSA disc. not avail holidays. Not available months of Jul & Aug.

Phone: (877)290-1381
Address: 218 Poland Range Rd, Pownal, ME 04069
Lat/Lon: 43.90990/-70.14292
Email: fun@blueberrycampground.com
Web: www.blueberrycampground.com

SEE AD THIS PAGE

(SW) DESERT DUNES OF MAINE CAMPGROUND—(Cumberland) *From jct I-295 (exit 20) & Desert Rd: Go 2 mi W on Desert Rd. Enter at end.*

◆◆◆FACILITIES: 50 sites, typical site width 22 ft, 12 full hkups, 29 W&E, (20/30 amps), 9 no hkups, 7 pull-thrus, WiFi Internet central location, family camping, tenting, shower$, dump, non-guest dump $, laundry, ltd groc, RV supplies, LP gas by weight/by meter, ice, picnic tables, fire rings, wood.

◆◆◆RECREATION: swim pool, golf nearby, bsktball, horseshoes, sports field, hiking trails, v-ball, local tours. Rec open to public.

Pets welcome, quantity restrict. Partial handicap access. Open early May - mid Oct. Clubs welcome. Rate in 2010 $35-39 for 2 persons. MC/VISA/DISC/Debit. Member ARVC, MECOA. FMCA discount.

Phone: (207)865-6962
Address: 95 Desert Rd, Freeport, ME 04032
Lat/Lon: 43.85944/-70.15533
Email: info@desertofmaine.com
Web: www.desertofmaine.com

SEE AD THIS PAGE

(SW) DESERT OF MAINE—*From jct I-295 (exit 20) & Desert Rd: Go 2 mi W on Desert Rd. Enter at end.* Maine's famous natural phenomenon- A natural desert surrounded by natural forest. Narrated tours, walking tours, nature trails, museum and gift shop on site. Walk through our new butterfly room. Open early May - mid Oct. MC/VISA/DISC.

Phone: (207)865-6962
Address: 95 Desert Rd, Freeport, ME 04032
Lat/Lon: 43.85958/-70.15530
Email: info@desertofmaine.com
Web: www.desertofmaine.com

SEE AD THIS PAGE

(W) FREEPORT VILLAGE CAMPGROUND—(Cumberland) *From I-295 (exit 22) & Rt 136: Go 500 ft W on Durnam, then 1- 1/2 mi W on Pownal Rd, then 100 ft N on Doten's Ln. Enter on R.*

◆◆◆FACILITIES: 33 sites, typical site width 50 ft, 33 full hkups, (20/30/50 amps), many extd stay sites, 3 pull-thrus, cable TV, WiFi Internet central location, dump, laundry, ice, picnic tables, fire rings.

◆◆◆RECREATION: rec room/area, pavilion, swim pool, golf nearby, activities.

Pets welcome. Partial handicap access. No tents. Open May 1 - Oct 31. Minimum Stay 2 nights. Big rigs welcome. Clubs welcome. Rate in 2010 $40 for 2 persons. MC/VISA. Member ARVC, MECOA.

FREEPORT VILLAGE CAMPGROUND—Continued on next page

FREEPORT—Continued
FREEPORT VILLAGE CAMPGROUND—Continued

Phone: (207)865-9227
Address: 11 Doten's Ln, Freeport, ME 04032
Lat/Lon: 43.87002/-70.13440

SEE AD PAGE 314

(N) Freeport/Durham KOA—(Cumberland) *From jct I-295 (exit 22) & Hwy 125/136: Go 3 mi N on Hwy 136, then 3 mi W on Brown Rd, then 1/2 mi NE on Hwy 9. Enter on R.* ◇◇◇FACILITIES: 96 sites, typical site width 50 ft, 32 full hkups, 64 W&E, (20/30/50 amps), 16 pull-thrus, family camping, tenting, dump, laundry, ltd groc. ◇◇◇◇RECREATION: swim pool, playground. Pets welcome. Open May 2 - Mid Oct. Facilities fully operational Memorial Day - Labor Day. Big rigs welcome. Rate in 2010 $33-45 for 2 persons. Member ARVC, MECOA. Phone: (888)562-5609. KOA discount.

GEORGETOWN—E-2

(S) Sagadahoc Bay Campground—(Sagadahoc) *From jct US 1 & Hwy 127; Go 9 mi S on Hwy 127, then 2 mi SW on Bay Point Rd, then 1/2 mi S on Sagadahoc Rd. Enter on R.* ◇◇FACILITIES: 50 sites, typical site width 25 ft, 9 full hkups, 30 W&E, (20/30/50 amps), 11 no hkups, 11 pull-thrus, tenting, dump. ◇◇RECREATION: saltwater swim, boating, canoeing, saltwater fishing. Pets welcome. Partial handicap access. Open May 1 - Nov 1. Big rigs welcome. Rate in 2010 $47-50 for 4 persons. Member ARVC, MECOA. Phone: (207)371-2014.

Reserve Online at Woodalls.com

GREENVILLE—C-3

(N) LILY BAY STATE PARK (Moosehead Lake)—(Piscataquis) *From town: Go 9 mi NE on county road.* FACILITIES: 91 sites, 91 no hkups, tenting, dump. RECREATION: lake swim, boating, canoeing, ramp, dock, lake fishing, playground. Open May 1 - Oct 15. Facilities fully operational Labor Day - Columbus Day. Phone: (207)695-2700.

(S) Moosehead Family Campground—(Piscataquis) *From town jct Pritham Ave (Rte 6/15) & Moosehead Lake Rd (Rte 6/15): Go 1 mi S on Hwy 6/15 (Moosehead Lake Rd). Enter on L.* ◇◇◇FACILITIES: 33 sites, typical site width 50 ft, 26 W&E, 2 E, (20/30/50 amps), 50 amps ($), 5 no hkups, 7 pull-thrus, tenting, dump. ◇RECREATION: play equipment. Pets welcome. Open May 1 - Oct. Big rigs welcome. Rate in 2010 $25-32 for 2 persons. Member ARVC, MECOA. Phone: (207)695-2210.

GREENWOOD—E-1

(S) Littlefield Beaches Lakeside Campground—(Oxford) *From jct Rte 2, 5 & 26: Go 6 mi S on Rte 26. Enter on R.* ◇◇◇◇FACILITIES: 130 sites, typical site width 30 ft, 90 full hkups, 40 W&E, (20/30 amps), 11 pull-thrus, family camping, tenting, dump, laundry, ltd groc. ◇◇◇◇RECREATION: lake swim, boating, canoeing, ramp, dock, lake fishing, playground. Pets welcome. Open Mid May - End of Sep. Rate in 2010 $32-38 for 2 persons. Member ARVC, MECOA. Phone: (207) 875-3290.

HANOVER—D-1

(W) Stony Brook Recreation—(Oxford) *From jct Hwy 26 & US 2 (in Newry): Go 3/4 mi E on US 2. Enter on L.* ◇◇◇FACILITIES: 60 sites, typical site width 30 ft, 30 full hkups, 14 W&E, (20/30/50 amps), 16 no hkups, 22 pull-thrus, cable TV, WiFi Instant Internet at site, WiFi Internet central location, tenting, RV storage, dump, non-guest dump $, laundry, ltd groc, RV supplies, LP gas by meter, ice, picnic tables, fire rings, wood. ◇◇◇◇RECREATION: rec hall, pavilion, swim pool, boating, canoeing, kayaking, float trips, river fishing, mini-golf, bsktball, playground, shuffleboard court 2 shuffleboard courts, horseshoes, hiking trails, v-ball. Pets welcome, breed restrict. Partial handicap access. Open all yr. Facilities fully operational Mid Apr - Mid Oct. Big rigs welcome. Rate in 2010 $25-32 per family. MC/VISA/DISC/Debit. Member ARVC, MECOA. FCRV discount. FMCA discount. CCUSA 50% Discount. CCUSA reservations Accepted, CCUSA max stay Unlimited, CCUSA disc. not avail holidays.

Phone: (207)824-2836
Address: 42 Powell Pl, Hanover, ME 04237
Lat/Lon: 44.48874/-70.77547
Email: camping@stonybrookrec.com
Web: www.stonybrookrec.com

Woodall's Tip... To be considered a "Big Rig Friendly" park, the campground must meet the following requirements: minimum of 50 amps, adequate road width, overhead access clearance, site clearance to accommodate the tallest and widest rigs built. Often not every site can accommodate a big rig, so we recommend that you call ahead for availability.

HARRINGTON—D-4

(S) SUNSET POINT CAMPGROUND—(Washington) *From the north jct of US 1A & US 1: Go 3/4 mi N on US 1, then 3 mi E on Marshville Rd. Enter on R.*

◇◇◇FACILITIES: 30 sites, typical site width 22 ft, 13 full hkups, 8 W&E, (20/30/50 amps), 9 no hkups, 4 pull-thrus, WiFi Instant Internet at site, WiFi Internet central location, tenting, cabins, dump, non-guest dump $, laundry, ice, picnic tables, fire rings, wood.

◇◇RECREATION: saltwater swim, canoeing, kayaking, dock, golf nearby, bsktball, playground, horseshoes, sports field.

Pets welcome. Open May 15 - Oct 15. Big rigs welcome. Rate in 2010 $24-32 for 4 persons. MC/VISA. Member ARVC, MECOA. CCUSA 50% Discount. CCUSA reservations Accepted, CCUSA max stay Unlimited. Discount available May 15 thru Jun 30 & Sep 1 thru Oct 15-designated sites. Discount not available Jul & Aug.

Phone: (207)483-4412
Address: 24 Sunset Point Rd., Harrington, ME 04643
Lat/Lon: 44.58967/-67.78300
Email: kurt0347@aol.com
Web: www.sunsetpointcampground.com

SEE AD BAR HARBOR PAGE 310

HOLDEN—D-3

(W) HOLDEN FAMILY CAMPGROUND—(Penobscot) *From jct I-395 & US-1A: Go 1 mi E on US-1A. Enter on L.*

◇◇◇FACILITIES: 40 sites, typical site width 30 ft, 40 full hkups, (30/50 amps), some extd stay sites, 10 pull-thrus, WiFi Instant Internet at site, family camping, RV storage, dump, non-guest dump $, laundry, RV supplies, LP gas by weight/by meter, picnic tables, fire rings, wood.

◇RECREATION: swim pool, golf nearby, playground, horseshoes.

Pets welcome, breed restrict. No tents. Open May 15 - Oct 15. Big rigs welcome. Rate in 2010 $29 for 4 persons. MC/VISA/DISC/AMEX/Debit.

Phone: (207)989-0529
Address: 108 Main Rd, Holden, ME 04429
Lat/Lon: 44.45500/-68.42130
Email: holdenfamilycampground@roadrunner.com
Web: holdenfamilycampground.com

SEE AD BANGOR PAGE 309

(E) RED BARN CAMPGROUND—(Penobscot) *From jct I-395 & US-1A: Go 3 mi SE on US-1A. Enter on L.*

◇◇◇FACILITIES: 120 sites, typical site width 24 ft, 52 full hkups, 64 W&E, (20/30/50 amps), 50 amps ($), 4 no hkups, some extd stay sites, 6 pull-thrus, cable TV, WiFi Instant Internet at site, family camping, tenting, RV storage, shower$, dump, non-guest dump $, laundry, ltd groc, RV supplies, LP gas by weight/by meter, ice, picnic tables, fire rings, wood.

◇◇◇◇RECREATION: rec hall, rec room/area, pavilion, coin games, swim pool, golf nearby, bsktball, play equipment, activities (wkends), horseshoes, sports field, v-ball.

Pets welcome, quantity restrict. Open May 7 - mid Oct. Big rigs welcome. Clubs welcome. Rate in 2010 $32-42 for 4 persons. MC/VISA/Debit. Member ARVC, MECOA. FMCA discount. CCUSA 50% Discount. CCUSA reservations Recommended, CCUSA max stay 3 days, CCUSA disc. not avail S, CCUSA disc. not avail F,Sa, CCUSA disc. not avail holidays.

HOLDEN—Continued
RED BARN CAMPGROUND—Continued

Phone: (207)843-6011
Address: 602 Main Rd, Holden, ME 04429
Lat/Lon: 44.75459/-68.65969
Email: info@redbarnmaine.com
Web: www.redbarnmaine.com

SEE AD BANGOR PAGE 309

(E) RED BARN DINER—*From jct I-395 & US-1A: Go 3 mi SE on US-1A. Enter on L.* Serving breakfast, lunch & dinner 7 days a week. Open 7am to 7 pm Sun-Thur, and Friday & Saturday 7am-8pm. Featuring omelets,burgers, sandwiches, salads & more. Open all yr. MC/VISA/Debit.

Phone: (207)843-6011
Address: 602 Main Rd, Holden, ME 04429
Lat/Lon: 44.75459/-68.6569
Email: info@redbarnmaine.com
Web: www.redbarnmaine.com

SEE AD BANGOR PAGE 309

HOULTON—B-4

(N) MY BROTHERS PLACE CAMPGROUND—(Aroostook) *From jct I-95 (exit 302) & US 1: Go 2 mi N on US 1. Enter on R.*

◇◇◇◇FACILITIES: 75 sites, typical site width 30 ft, 50 full hkups, 25 W&E, (30/50 amps), 50 amps ($), 70 pull-thrus, heater not allowed, WiFi Instant Internet at site, phone Internet central location, family camping, tenting, RV's/park model rentals, cabins, shower$, dump, non-guest dump $, laundry, ltd groc, RV supplies, ice, picnic tables, fire rings, wood.

◇◇◇◇RECREATION: rec hall, rec room/area, coin games, boating, no motors, canoeing, rowboat/2 pedal boat rentals, pond fishing, fishing supplies, golf nearby, bsktball, play equipment, activities, horseshoes, sports field, hiking trails, v-ball.

Pets welcome. Partial handicap access. Open May 10 - Oct 20. Big rigs welcome. Clubs welcome. Rate in 2010 $25-34 per family. MC/VISA/Debit. Member ARVC, MECOA.

Phone: (207)532-6739
Address: 659 North St, Houlton, ME 04730
Lat/Lon: 46.17065/-67.84052
Email: mybrotherspl@aol.com
Web: www.mainerec.com/mybro.html

SEE AD THIS PAGE

ISLAND FALLS—B-4

(NE) Birch Point Lodge Campground & Cottage Resort—(Aroostook) *From jct I-95 & Hwy 159: Go 1/2 mi E on Hwy 159 (exit 276), then 3 mi E on US 2, then 1-1/2 mi E on Pond Rd. Enter on R.* ◇◇◇FACILITIES: 64 sites, typical site width 18 ft, 7 full hkups, 57 W&E, (20/30 amps), 6 pull-thrus, tenting, dump, laundry, ltd groc. ◇◇◇◇RECREATION: lake swim, boating, canoeing, ramp, dock, lake fishing, play equipment. Pets welcome. Open all yr. Facilities fully operational May 14 - Oct 15. Rate in 2010 $26-32 per family. Member ARVC, MECOA. Phone: (207)463-2515.

JACKMAN—C-2

(NE) MOOSE RIVER CAMPGROUND & CABINS—(Somerset) *From jct Hwy 6/15 & US 201: Go 2 mi N on US 201/Hwy 6, then 1-1/2 mi E on Heald Stream Rd. Enter on R.*

◇◇◇FACILITIES: 52 sites, typical site width 22 ft, 7 full hkups, 26 W&E, 2 E, (20/30 amps), 17 no hkups, some extd stay sites, 7 pull-thrus, cable TV, ($), WiFi Internet central location, family camping, tenting, cabins, RV storage, dump, portable dump, ltd groc, RV supplies, ice, picnic tables, fire rings, grills, wood.

MOOSE RIVER CAMPGROUND & CABINS—Continued on next page

JACKMAN—Continued
MOOSE RIVER CAMPGROUND & CABINS—Continued

◇◇◇◇RECREATION: rec hall, rec room/area, coin games, swim pool, boating, no motors, canoeing, kayaking, 4 canoe/pedal boat rentals, pond/stream fishing, fishing supplies, fishing guides, golf nearby, playground, horseshoes, sports field, v-ball.

Pets welcome. Partial handicap access. Open all yr. Facilities fully operational Mid May - Nov. Cabins open all year. Clubs welcome. Rate in 2010 $28-30 per family. MC/VISA/DISC/Debit. Member ARVC, MECOA.

Phone: (207)668-3341
Address: 107 Heald Stream Rd, Jackman, ME 04945
Lat/Lon: 45.65034/-70.24519
Email: mooserivercampground@gmail.com
Web: www.mooserivercampground.net

SEE AD PAGE 315

KENNEBUNKPORT—F-2

(NE) RED APPLE CAMPGROUND—(York) *From jct I-95 (exit 25) & Hwy 35: Go 1/2 mi E on Hwy 35, then 1-1/2 mi N on Ross Rd, then 1/4 mi N on US 1, then 2-1/4 mi E on Old Post Rd. Enter on L.*

WELCOME

"CLEAN, QUIET & RELAXING-
"The Way Camping Should Be!" Located only 5 minutes from the ocean, beaches, fabulous lobster & seafood, deep sea fishing & great shopping. Simply put - Wicked Good Camping - we treat you like family & sometimes even better!

◇◇◇◇◇FACILITIES: 140 sites, typical site width 35 ft, 120 full hkups, 20 W&E, (20/30/50 amps), many extd stay sites, 9 pull-thrus, cable TV, WiFi Instant Internet at site, family camping, tenting, RV's/park model rentals, cabins, dump, non-guest dump $, laundry, ltd groc, RV supplies, ice, picnic tables, fire rings, grills, wood.

◇◇◇RECREATION: rec hall, rec room/area, golf nearby, bsktball, playground, shuffleboard court shuffleboard court, activities, horseshoes, sports field, v-ball.

KENNEBUNKPORT—Continued
RED APPLE CAMPGROUND—Continued

Pets welcome, quantity restrict. Partial handicap access. Open May 6 - Columbus Day. Big rigs welcome. Escort to site. Clubs welcome. Green Friendly. Rate in 2010 $44.86-49.53 for 4 persons. Member ARVC, MECOA.

Text 81429 to (440)725-8687 to see our Visual Tour.

Phone: (207)967-4927
Address: 111 Sinnott Rd, Kennebunkport, ME 04046
Lat/Lon: 43.39092/-70.49306
Email: redapple@roadrunner.com
Web: www.redapplecampground.com

SEE AD THIS PAGE AND AD TRAVEL SECTION PAGE 303

(NE) Salty Acres Campground—(York) *From jct I-95 (exit 25) & Hwy 35: Go 5 mi SE on Hwy 35, then 5 mi NE on Hwy 9. Enter on R.* ◇◇FACILITIES: 274 sites, typical site width 25 ft, 20 W&E, 34 E, (20/30 amps), 220 no hkups, family camping, tenting, dump, laundry, groceries. ◇◇RECREATION: swim pool. Pets welcome. Open Mid May - Columbus Day. Rate in 2010 $33-55 per family. Member MECOA. Phone: (207)967-2483.

KINGFIELD—D-2

(NW) Deer Farm Camps & Campground—(Franklin) *From jct Hwy 27 & Hwy 16: Go 1 mi N on Hwy 16, then 2-1/2 mi W on Tufts Pond Rd. Enter on R.* ◇◇FACILITIES: 47 sites, typical site width 30 ft, 47 W&E, (20/30 amps), 1 pull-thrus, family camping, tenting, dump, laundry, ltd groc. ◇◇◇RECREATION: pond fishing, playground. Pets welcome. Open mid May - Columbus Day. Rate in 2010 $22 per family. Member ARVC, MECOA. Phone: (207)265-4599.

LEBANON—F-1

(W) Flat Rock Bridge Family Resort—(York) *From jct Hwy 109 & US 202 (in Sanford): Go 12 mi S on US 202, then 1-1/2 mi N on River Rd, then 1/4 mi W on Flat Rock Bridge Rd. Enter on L.* ◇◇◇FACILITIES: 350 sites, typical site width 34 ft, 200 full hkups, 150 W&E, (20/30/50 amps), 10 pull-thrus, family camping, tenting, dump, laundry, full svc store. ◇◇◇◇◇RECREATION: 2 swim pools, river swim, boating, canoeing,

LEBANON—Continued
Flat Rock Bridge Family Resort—Continued

river fishing, playground. Pets welcome, breed restrict. Partial handicap access. Open mid May - Oct 1. Facilities fully operational Father's Day - Labor Day. Big rigs welcome. Rate in 2010 $40-59 per family. Member ARVC, MECOA. Phone: (207)339-9465.

(N) Salmon Falls River Camping Resort (REBUILDING)—(York) *From jct Spaulding Turnpike (exit 16) & Rt 202: Go 3 mi E on Rt 202. Enter on R.* FACILITIES: 219 sites, typical site width 35 ft, 99 full hkups, 120 W&E, (20/30/50 amps), 48 pull-thrus, family camping, tenting, dump, laundry, ltd groc. RECREATION: 2 swim pools, canoeing, river/pond fishing, playground. Pets welcome, breed restrict. Partial handicap access. Open May 1 - Oct 31. Big rigs welcome. Rate in 2010 $33-50 for 4 persons. Member ARVC, MECOA. Phone: (207) 339-8888.

LEEDS—E-2

(N) Riverbend Campground—(Androscoggin) *From jct US 202 & Hwy 106: Go 7-1/2 mi N on Hwy 106. Enter on L.* ◇◇◇FACILITIES: 100 sites, typical site width 30 ft, 98 W&E, (20/30/50 amps), 2 no hkups, 12 pull-thrus, family camping, tenting, dump, laundry, groceries. ◇◇◇◇RECREATION: swim pool, boating, canoeing, ramp, dock, river fishing, playground. Pets welcome. Open May 1 - Mid Oct. Rate in 2010 $27-34 per family. Member ARVC, MECOA.

Phone: (207)524-5711
Address: 1540 ME - 106, Leeds, ME 04263-3328
Lat/Lon: 44.31960/-70.12228
Email: inquiries@riverbendcampgroundmaine.com
Web: www.riverbendcampgroundmaine.com

LIBERTY—E-3

LAKE ST. GEORGE STATE PARK—(Waldo) *In town on Hwy-3.* FACILITIES: 38 sites, 38 no hkups, 18 pull-thrus, tenting, dump. RECREATION: lake swim, boating, ramp, lake fishing, playground. Open May 15 - Oct 1. Phone: (207)589-4255.

LUBEC—D-5

(C) Sunset Point RV Trailer Park—(Washington) *From jct US-1 & Hwy-189: Go 9 mi NE on Hwy-189. Enter on L.* ◇◇◇FACILITIES: 40 sites, typical site width 18 ft, 30 W&E, (20/30 amps), 10 no hkups, 12

Sunset Point RV Trailer Park—Continued on next page

LUBEC—Continued
Sunset Point RV Trailer Park—Continued

pull-thrus, tenting, dump, laundry. ◆◆RECREATION: boating, canoeing, ramp, saltwater fishing. Pets welcome. Open May 20 - mid Oct. Rate in 2010 $28-31 for 4 persons. Member ARVC, MECOA. Phone: (207)733-2272.

MEDWAY—C-4

(W) Katahdin Shadows Campground & Cabins—(Penobscot) *From jct I-95 (exit 244) & Hwy-157: Go 1-1/2 mi W on Hwy-157. Enter on R.* ◆◆◆◆FACILITIES: 149 sites, typical site width 26 ft, 50 full hkups, 68 W&E, (20/30/50 amps), 31 no hkups, 13 pull-thrus, family camping, tenting, dump, laundry, groceries. ◆◆◆◆RECREATION: swim pool, playground. Pets welcome. Partial handicap access. Open all yr. Facilities fully operational Memorial Day - Oct 15. Big rigs welcome. Rate in 2010 $29-31 for 2 persons. Member ARVC, MECOA. Phone: (800)794-5267.

(NW) PINE GROVE CAMPGROUND & COTTAGES—(Penobscot) *From jct I-95 & Hwy 157 (exit 244): Go 3/4 mi W on Hwy 157, then 4 mi N on Hwy 11/Grindstone Rd. Enter on L.*

WELCOME

◆◆FACILITIES: 43 sites, typical site width 35 ft, 4 full hkups, 24 W&E, (20/30 amps), 15 no hkups, 3 pull-thrus, tenting, cabins, dump, non-guest dump $, laundry, ice, picnic tables, fire rings, wood.

◆◆RECREATION: rec room/area, river swim, canoeing, kayaking, 3 canoe/kayak rentals, river fishing, fishing supplies, golf nearby, play equipment.

Pets welcome. Open all yr. Facilities fully operational Mid May - Oct 4. Rate in 2010 $25.68 for 2 persons. MC/VISA. Member ARVC, MECOA.

Phone: (207)746-5172
Address: HCR 86, Medway, ME 04460
Lat/Lon: 45.66502/-68.56230
Email: pinegrovecampgroundandcottages@.com
Web: www.pinegrovecamping.com

SEE AD THIS PAGE

NAPLES—E-1

(NE) Colonial Mast Campground—(Cumberland) *From jct Hwy 11/114 & US 302: Go 2-3/4 mi NW on US 302, then 1/4 mi NE on Kansas Rd, then 1/2 mi E on Campground Rd. Enter on R.* ◆◆◆FACILITIES: 110 sites, typical site width 25 ft, 70 full hkups, 40 W&E, (30/50 amps), tenting, dump, laundry, ltd groc. ◆◆◆◆◆RECREATION: swim pool, lake swim, boating, canoeing, ramp, dock, lake fishing, playground. Pets welcome. Partial handicap access. Open all yr. Rate in 2010 $29-49 per family. Member ARVC, MECOA. Phone: (207)693-6652.

(W) Four Seasons Camping Area—(Cumberland) *From jct Hwy 11/114 & US 302: Go 2-1/2 mi NW on US 302. Enter on R.* ◆◆◆FACILITIES: 115 sites, typical site width 20 ft, 11 full hkups, 104 W&E, (20/30 amps), family camping, tenting, dump, ltd groc. ◆◆◆◆RECREATION: lake swim, boating, canoeing, ramp, dock, lake fishing, playground. Pets welcome. Open Mid May - Columbus Weekend. Rate in 2010 $39-59 per family. Member ARVC, MECOA. Phone: (207) 693-6797.

(S) Loon's Haven Family Campground—(Cumberland) *From jct US-302 & Hwy-11/114: Go 1 mi S on Hwy-11/114, then 1/4 mi W on Campground Rd. Enter on R.* ◆◆◆FACILITIES: 150 sites, typical site width 30 ft, 41 full hkups, 109 W&E, (20/30 amps), tenting,

Maine State Gem: Tourmaline

NAPLES—Continued
Loon's Haven Family Campground—Continued

dump, laundry, ltd groc. ◆◆◆◆RECREATION: lake swim, boating, canoeing, ramp, dock, lake fishing, playground. Pets welcome. Open Memorial Day - Columbus Day. Rate in 2010 $25-55 per family. Member ARVC, MECOA. Phone: (207)693-6881.

(S) Naples Campground—(Cumberland) *From jct US 302 & Hwy 11/114: Go 1-1/2 mi S on Hwy 11/114. Enter on R.* ◆◆◆◆FACILITIES: 113 sites, typical site width 40 ft, 113 full hkups, (20/30/50 amps), 1 pull-thrus, tenting, dump, laundry, ltd groc. ◆◆◆◆RECREATION: swim pool, canoeing, playground. Pets welcome, breed restrict. Open May 1 - Oct 15. Big rigs welcome. Rate in 2010 $40-55 per family. Member ARVC, MECOA. Phone: (207)693-5267.

(S) SEBAGO LAKE STATE PARK—(Cumberland) *From jct US-302E & Hwy-11/114: Go 4 mi S on US-302E, then 2-1/2 mi W.* FACILITIES: 250 sites, 30 ft max RV length, 250 no hkups, tenting, dump, ltd groc. RECREATION: lake swim, boating, canoeing, ramp, lake fishing. No pets. Partial handicap access. Open May 1 - Oct 15. Phone: (207)693-6613.

NEW HARBOR—E-3

(W) Sherwood Forest Campsite & Cabins—(Lincoln) *From US Business Rt 1 & Hwy 130, (in Damariscotta): Go 12 mi S on Hwy 130, then go 3/4 mi W on Snowball Hill Rd, (at Hanna's) then 800 feet S on Pemaquid Trail. Enter on L.* ◆◆◆FACILITIES: 80 sites, typical site width 24 ft, 64 W&E, (20/30 amps), 16 no hkups, 4 pull-thrus, tenting, dump, laundry, ltd groc. ◆◆RECREATION: swim pool, playground. Pets welcome. Open mid May - mid Oct. Rate in 2010 $33-43 per family. Member ARVC, MECOA. Phone: (800)274-1593.

NEWPORT—D-3

(E) Christie's Campground & Cottages—(Penobscot) *N'bound from jct I-95 (exit 157) & US 2: Go 3 mi E on US 2. Entrance on left. S'bound from jct I-95 (exit 161) & Hwy 7: Go 1 mi N on Hwy 7, then 1/2 mi W on US 2. Entrance on right.* ◆◆◆FACILITIES: 50 sites, typical site width 22 ft, 16 full hkups, 34 W&E, (30/50 amps), 10 pull-thrus, dump, laundry, ltd groc. ◆◆◆◆RECREATION: lake swim, boating, canoeing, ramp, dock, lake fishing, playground. Pets welcome. No tents. Open May 1 - Nov 30. Rate in 2010 $25-27 for 4 persons. Member ARVC, MECOA. Phone: (800) 688-5141.

(E) Sebasticook Lake Campground—(Penobscot) *N'bound from jct I-95 (exit 157) & US 2: Go 3-1/2 mi E on US 2. Entrance on left. S'bound from jct I-95 (exit 161) & Hwy 7: Go 1 mi N on Hwy 7, then 1/4 mi W on US 2. Entrance on right.* ◆◆◆FACILITIES: 60 sites, typical site width 22 ft, 3 full hkups, 51 W&E, (20/30 amps), 6 no hkups, 16 pull-thrus, family camping, tenting, dump, laundry, ltd groc. ◆◆◆◆RECREATION: swim pool, lake/boating, canoeing, ramp, dock, lake fishing, playground. Pets welcome ($). Partial handicap access. Open Mid May - Columbus Day. Rate in 2010 $26-29 for 4 persons. Member ARVC, MECOA. FMCA discount.

Phone: (800)319-9333
Address: 52 Tent Village Rd, Newport, ME 04953
Lat/Lon: 44.82473/-69.23326
Email: info@mainervpark.com
Web: www.mainervpark.com

NOBLEBORO—E-3

(NE) Duck Puddle Family Campground—(Lincoln) *From south jct US 1 & Business US 1: Go 6-1/4 mi N on US 1, then 1-1/4 mi E on Winslow Rd/Duck Puddle Rd. Enter on R.* ◆◆◆FACILITIES: 135 sites, typical site width 24 ft, 80 full hkups, 45 W&E, (20/30/50 amps), 50 amps ($), 10 no hkups, 2 pull-

NOBLEBORO—Continued
Duck Puddle Family Campground—Continued

thrus, family camping, tenting, dump, laundry, ltd groc. ◆◆◆◆RECREATION: lake swim, boating, canoeing, ramp, dock, lake fishing, playground. Pets welcome. Open May 1 - Columbus Day. Rate in 2010 $27-41 per family. Member ARVC, MECOA. Phone: (207)563-5608.

NORTH MONMOUTH—E-2

(NW) Beaver Brook Campground—(Kennebec) *From jct Hwy 106 & US 202/Hwy 11/100: Go 2-1/2 mi E on US 202/Hwy 11/100, then 1-1/2 mi NW on Back St., then 1-1/2 mi SW on Wilson Pond Rd. Enter at end.* ◆◆◆FACILITIES: 191 sites, typical site width 50 ft, 18 full hkups, 173 W&E, (20/30/50 amps), 13 pull-thrus, family camping, tenting, dump, laundry, groceries. ◆◆◆◆◆RECREATION: swim pool, lake swim, boating, canoeing, ramp, dock, lake fishing, playground. Pets welcome. Partial handicap access. Open May 7 - Columbus Day weekend. Rate in 2010 $34-48 per family. Member ARVC, MECOA.

NORTH NEW PORTLAND—D-2

(N) Happy Horseshoe Campground—(Somerset) *From jct US Rt 16 & Long Falls Dam Rd: Go 5-1/2 mi N on Long Falls Dam Rd. Enter on L.* ◆◆◆FACILITIES: 91 sites, typical site width 40 ft, 88 W&E, (30/50 amps), 3 no hkups, 8 pull-thrus, family camping, tenting, dump, laundry, ltd groc. ◆◆◆◆RECREATION: swim pool, playground. Pets welcome. Partial handicap access. Open Memorial Day - Labor Day. Rate in 2010 $30 for 7 persons. Phone: (207)628-3471.

OGUNQUIT—F-1

(NW) Pinederosa Camping Area—(York) *From Ogunquit town center: Go 1 mi N on US 1, then 1-1/2 mi W on Captain Thomas Rd. Enter on R.* ◆◆◆FACILITIES: 186 sites, typical site width 50 ft, 58 full hkups, 63 W&E, (20/30/50 amps), 65 no hkups, tenting, dump, laundry, ltd groc. ◆RECREATION: swim pool, river fishing. Pets welcome. Open Jun - Labor Day. Big rigs welcome. Rate in 2010 $30-40 for 2 persons. Member ARVC, MECOA. Phone: (207)646-2492.

OLD ORCHARD BEACH—F-2

(S) BAYLEY'S CAMPING RESORT—*From jct I-95 & I-195 (exit 36): Go 1-3/4 mi E on I-195, then 6 mi N on US 1, then 3 mi E on Hwy 9 to Pine Point. Enter on R.*

WELCOME

◆◆◆◆◆FACILITIES: 745 sites, typical site width 35 ft, 600 full hkups, 65 W&E, (20/30/50 amps), 80 no hkups, 60 pull-thrus, cable TV, WiFi Instant Internet at site, WiFi Internet central location, family camping, tenting, RV's/park model rentals, RV storage, dump, non-guest dump $, laundry, full svc store, RV supplies, LP gas by weight/by meter, ice, picnic tables, fire rings, grills, wood, controlled access.

BAYLEY'S CAMPING RESORT—Continued on next page

OLD ORCHARD BEACH—Continued
BAYLEY'S CAMPING RESORT—Continued

◆◆◆◆◆RECREATION: rec hall, rec room/area, pavilion, equipped pavilion, coin games, 3 swim pools, hot tub, kayaking, 14 kayak/6 pedal boat rentals, pond fishing, fishing supplies, mini-golf, ($), golf nearby, bsktball, 33 bike rentals, playground, activities, horseshoes, sports field, hiking trails, v-ball, local tours.

Pets welcome. Open End of April - Mid Oct. Big rigs welcome. Clubs welcome. Rate in 2010 $30-86 for 2 persons. MC/VISA/Debit. ATM. Member ARVC, MECOA.

Phone: (207)883-6043
Address: 275 Pine Point Rd, Scarborough, ME 04074
Lat/Lon: 43.54751/-70.35676
Email: info@bayleys-camping.com
Web: www.baleys-camping.com

SEE PRIMARY LISTING AT SCARBOROUGH AND AD SCARBOROUGH PAGE 322

(W) Hid'n Pines Family Campground—(York) *From jct I-95 & I-195 (exit 36): Go 1-3/4 mi E on I-195 (exit 2B), then 2-1/2 mi N on US 1, then 2 mi E on Hwy 98. Enter on L.* ◆◆◆FACILITIES: 279 sites, typical site width 30 ft, 35 ft max RV length, 132 full hkups, 105 W&E, (20/30/50 amps), 42 no hkups, 7 pull-thrus, family camping, tenting, dump, laundry, ltd groc. ◆◆◆RECREATION: swim pool, playground. Pets welcome. Partial handicap access. Open Mid May - Labor Day. Rate in 2010 $30-55 for 2 persons. Member ARVC, MECOA. Phone: (207)934-2352.

(SE) NASCAR RV Resort at Virginia Park (Morgan RV Resorts)—(York) *From jct I-95 & I-195 (exit 36): Go 2-1/2 mi E on I-195, then 1/2 mi E on Hwy 5, then 1/2 mi straight on Temple Ave, then 300 ft N on Williams. Enter on L.* ◆◆◆FACILITIES: 132 sites, typical site width 30 ft, 89 full hkups, 28 W&E, (20/30/50 amps), 50 amps ($), 15 no hkups, 8 pull-thrus, tenting, dump, laundry, ltd groc. ◆◆◆RECREATION: swim pool, playground. Pets welcome. Open Memorial Day - Columbus Day. Rate in 2010 $46-49 for 3 persons. Member ARVC, MECOA. Phone: (207)934-4791.

(S) Nascar RV Resort at Wagon Wheel (Morgan RV Resorts)—(York) *From jct I-95 & I-195 (exit 36): Go 2-1/2 mi E on I-195, then 1/2 mi E on Hwy 5, then 600 ft S on Old Orchard Rd. Enter on L.* ◆◆◆FACILITIES: 283 sites, typical site width 32 ft, 238 full hkups, 45 W&E, (20/30/50 amps), 50 amps ($), family camping, tenting, dump, laundry, ltd groc. ◆◆◆RECREATION: 2 swim pools, playground. Pets welcome. Open May 1 - Mid Oct. Rate in 2010 $36.99-45.99 for 2 persons. Member ARVC, MECOA. Phone: (207)934-2160.

(S) Nascar RV Resort at Wild Acres (Morgan RV Resorts)—(York) *From jct I-95 & I-195 (exit 36): Go 2-1/2 mi E on I-195, then 3/4 mi E on Hwy 5. Enter on R.* ◆◆◆◆FACILITIES: 510 sites, typical site width 30 ft, 370 full hkups, 99 W&E, (20/30/50 amps), 41 no hkups, 65 pull-thrus, family camping, tenting, dump, laundry, groceries. ◆◆◆◆◆RECREATION: 3 swim pools, pond fishing, playground. Pets welcome. Partial handicap access. Open May 1 - Mid Oct. Rate in 2010 $34-62 for 2 persons. Member ARVC, MECOA. Phone: (207)934-2535.

(C) NE'RE Beach Family Campground—(York) *From jct I-95 (exit 36) & I-95: Go 2-1/2 mi E on I-195, then 1-3/4 mi E on Hwy 5. Enter on L.* ◆◆FACILITIES: 46 sites, typical site width 22 ft, 20 full hkups, 20 W&E, (20/30/50 amps), 6 no hkups, tenting, laundry. ◆RECREATION: swim pool. Pets welcome, breed restrict. Open mid May - Oct 1. Rate in 2010 $45-50 for 2 persons. Member ARVC, MECOA. Phone: (207)934-7614.

(C) Paradise Park Resort Campground—(York) *From jct I-95 & I-195 (exit 36): Go 2-1/2 mi E on I-195, then continue on 2 mi E on Hwy 5, then 1/4 mi N on Adelaide St. Enter at end.* ◆◆◆◆FACILITIES: 230 sites, typical site width 35 ft, 172 full hkups, 54

OLD ORCHARD BEACH—Continued
Paradise Park Resort Campground—Continued

W&E, (20/30/50 amps), 4 no hkups, family camping, tenting, dump, laundry, ltd groc. ◆◆◆◆RECREATION: 2 swim pools, boating, no motors, dock, pond fishing, playground. Pets welcome. Partial handicap access. Open May 15 - Columbus Day. Big rigs welcome. Rate in 2010 $46-56 for 2 persons. Member ARVC, MECOA. Phone: (207)934-4633.

(NE) Pinehirst RV Resort—(York) *From jct I-95 & I-195 (exit 36): Go 2-1/2 mi E on I-195, then 3/4 mi E on Hwy 5, then 1/4 mi W on Oregon Ave. Enter at end.* ◆◆◆FACILITIES: 537 sites, typical site width 30 ft, 537 full hkups, (30 amps), family camping, laundry, groceries. ◆◆◆◆RECREATION: 3 swim pools, pond fishing, playground. Pets welcome, quantity restrict. Partial handicap access. No tents. Open Mid Apr - Mid Oct. Rate in 2010 $55 for 2 persons. Phone: (207)934-5526.

Reserve Online at Woodalls.com

(W) Powder Horn Family Camping Resort—(York) *From jct I-95 & I-195 (exit 36): Go 1-3/4 mi E on I-195 (exit 2B), then 2-1/2 mi N on US 1, then 1-3/4 mi E on Hwy 98. Enter on L.* ◆◆◆◆◆FACILITIES: 482 sites, typical site width 35 ft, 385 full hkups, 97 W&E, (30/50 amps), 22 pull-thrus, family camping, tenting, dump, laundry, full svc store. ◆◆◆◆◆RECREATION: 4 swim pools, playground. Pets welcome. Partial handicap access. Open Mid May - Mid Oct. Big rigs welcome. Rate in 2010 $30-65 for 2 persons. Member ARVC, MECOA. Phone: (207)934-4733.

WASSAMKI SPRINGS CAMPGROUND—*From jct I-95 (exit 46) & Hwy 22: Go 3 mi W on Hwy 22, then 1/4 mi N on Saco St.*
WELCOME
SEE PRIMARY LISTING AT SCARBOROUGH AND AD PORTLAND PAGE 320

ORLAND—D-3

(S) Balsam Cove Campground—(Hancock) *From S jct Hwy 15 & US 1: Go 7 mi N on US 1, then 1-1/2 mi E on Backridge Rd. Follow signs. Enter on L.* ◆◆◆FACILITIES: 85 sites, typical site width 30 ft, 77 full hkups, (20/30/50 amps), 8 no hkups, 15 pull-thrus, family camping, tenting, laundry, ltd groc. ◆◆◆◆RECREATION: lake swim, boating, canoeing, ramp, dock, lake fishing, playground. Pets welcome. Open May 15 - Sep 28. Big rigs welcome. Rate in 2010 $33-44 per family. Member ARVC, MECOA. Phone: (800)469-7771.

(E) SHADY OAKS CAMPGROUND AND CABINS—(Hancock) *From jct Hwy 15 & US 1 (Bucksport): Go 2 mi E on US 1, then at intersection of Hwy 1 & 175 turn 1/8 mi S on Leaches Point Rd. Enter on L.*
WELCOME

◆◆◆◆FACILITIES: 70 sites, typical site width 24 ft, 68 full hkups, 2 W&E, (20/30/50 amps), many extd stay sites, 13 pull-thrus, WiFi Instant Internet at site, WiFi Internet central location, family camping, tenting, cabins, RV storage, dump, non-guest dump $, laundry, ltd groc, RV supplies, LP gas by weight/by meter, ice, picnic tables, patios, fire rings, wood, controlled access.

◆◆◆◆RECREATION: rec room/area, swim pool, golf nearby, bsktball, playground, activities, horseshoes, sports field, hiking trails, v-ball.

Pets welcome. Partial handicap access. Open May 1 - Sep 30. No dogs. Big rigs welcome. Escort to site. Clubs welcome. Green Friendly. Rate in 2010 $30-32 for 2 persons. MC/VISA/Debit. Member ARVC, MECOA.

Phone: (207)469-7739
Address: 32 Leaches Point Rd, Orland, ME 04472
Lat/Lon: 44.56973/-68.75269
Email: cuatsorvpk@aol.com
Web: www.shadyoakscampground.com

SEE AD BUCKSPORT PAGE 312

OXFORD—E-1

(SE) Two Lakes Camping Area—(Oxford) *From south jct Hwy 121 & Hwy 26: Go 1/2 mi S on Hwy 26. Enter on R.* ◆◆FACILITIES: 60 sites, typical site width 28 ft, 16 full hkups, 39 W&E, (20/30/50 amps), 5 no hkups, 3 pull-thrus, family camping, tenting, dump, laundry, groceries. ◆◆◆◆RECREATION: lake swim, boating, canoeing, ramp, dock, lake/river fishing, playground. Pets welcome. Partial handicap access. Open May 1 - Oct 1. Rate in 2010 $30-38 per family. Member ARVC, MECOA. Phone: (207)539-4851.

PALMYRA—D-3

(W) Palmyra Golf Course & Campground—(Somerset) *From jct I-95 (exit 157) & US 2: Go 3 mi W on US 2, then 1/2 mi N on Lang Hill Rd. Enter on R.* ◆◆◆◆FACILITIES: 91 sites, typical site width 40 ft, 34 full hkups, 57 W&E, (20/30/50 amps), 2 pull-thrus,

PALMYRA—Continued
Palmyra Golf Course & Campground—Continued

tenting, dump, laundry, ltd groc. ◆◆◆RECREATION: swim pool. Pets welcome. Open Mid May - Oct 15. Big rigs welcome. Rate in 2010 $25-27.50 per family. Member ARVC, MECOA. Phone: (207)938-5677. KOA discount. FMCA discount.

POLAND—E-2

(E) Rango Pond Campground—(Androscoggin) *From jct Hwy-26 & Hwy-122: Go 1-3/10 mi E on Hwy-122, then 1-2/10 mi N on Empire Rd, then 1/2 mi W on Plains Rd. Enter on R.* ◆◆◆FACILITIES: 115 sites, typical site width 24 ft, 91 full hkups, 17 W&E, (20/30 amps), 7 no hkups, 28 pull-thrus, family camping, tenting, dump, laundry, groceries. ◆◆◆◆RECREATION: swim pool, play equipment. Pets welcome. Partial handicap access. Open mid Apr - mid Oct. Rate in 2010 $28-40 per family. Member ARVC, MECOA.

Phone: (207)998-2624
Address: 94 Plains Rd, Poland, ME 04274
Lat/Lon: 44.04280/-70.34485
Email: rpcg88@aol.com
Web: www.rangepondcamp.com

POLAND SPRING—E-2

(N) POLAND SPRING CAMPGROUND—(Androscoggin) *From I-95 (exit 63) & Hwy 26: Go 12 mi N on Hwy 26, then 1/2 mi E on Connor Lane. Enter at end.*
WELCOME

◆◆◆FACILITIES: 132 sites, typical site width 35 ft, 66 full hkups, 53 W&E, (20/30/50 amps), 50 amps ($), 13 no hkups, some extd stay sites, 4 pull-thrus, heater not allowed, WiFi Instant Internet at site, family camping, tenting, RV's/park model rentals, shower$, dump, non-guest dump $, portable dump, laundry, groceries, RV supplies, LP gas by weight/by meter, ice, picnic tables, fire rings, wood, controlled access.

◆◆◆◆◆RECREATION: rec hall, rec room/area, coin games, swim pool, lake swim, boating, 9.9 hp limit, canoeing, kayaking, ramp, dock, 2 rowboat/2 canoe/8 kayak/pedal boat rentals, lake fishing, fishing supplies, golf nearby, bsktball, playground, activities, horseshoes, sports field, hiking trails, v-ball.

Pets welcome. Partial handicap access. Open May 1 - Columbus Day. Rate in 2010 $24-38 per family. MC/VISA/DISC/Debit. Member ARVC, MECOA.

Phone: (207)998-2151
Address: 128 Connor Ln, Poland Spring, ME 04274
Lat/Lon: 44.04389/-70.37498
Email: info@polandspringcamp.com
Web: www.polandspringcamp.com

SEE AD AUBURN PAGE 308

PORTLAND—F-2

WASSAMKI SPRINGS CAMPGROUND—*From jct I-95 (exit 46) & Hwy 22: Go 3 mi W on Hwy 22, then 1/4 mi N on Saco St. Enter on L.*
WELCOME
SEE PRIMARY LISTING AT SCARBOROUGH AND AD PAGE 320

Lobstering is a lucrative occupation in Maine.

West Quoddy Head is the most easterly point in the United States.

POWNAL—E-2

(E) BRADBURY MOUNTAIN STATE PARK—(Cumberland) *From town center: Go 1 mi E on Hwy-9.* FACILITIES: 35 sites, 30 ft max RV length, 35 no hkups, tenting. RECREATION: playground. Open all yr. Phone: (207)688-4712.

PRESQUE ISLE—B-4

(NE) ARNDT'S AROOSTOOK RIVER LODGE & CAMPGROUND—(Aroostook) *From jct Hwy 1 & Hwy 167: Go 3-1/2 mi E on Hwy 167, then 3/4 mi N on Hwy 205. Enter on R.*

WELCOME

◆◆◆FACILITIES: 75 sites, typical site width 40 ft, 26 full hkups, 29 W&E, (30/50 amps), 50 amps ($), 20 no hkups, 7 pull-thrus, WiFi Internet central location, family camping, tenting, cabins, dump, non-guest dump $, laundry, ltd groc, RV supplies, ice, picnic tables, fire rings, wood.

◆◆◆◆RECREATION: rec room/area, swim pool, river swim, canoeing, kayaking, 4 canoe/10 kayak rentals, float trips, river fishing, fishing guides, golf nearby, bsktball, play equipment, horseshoes, sports field, hiking trails.

Pets welcome. Open May 15 - Oct 15. Clubs welcome. Green Friendly. Rate in 2010 $26-32 for 4 persons. MC/VISA/DISC. Member ARVC, MECOA. FMCA discount.

Phone: (207)764-8677
Address: 95 Parkhurst Siding Rd, Presque Isle, ME 04769
Lat/Lon: 46.72278/-67.95066
Email: clare@arndtscamp.com
Web: www.arndtscamp.com

SEE AD THIS PAGE

(SW) AROOSTOOK STATE PARK—(Aroostook) *From jct Hwy-163 & US-1: Go 3-3/4 mi S on US-1, then 2 mi SW on Spragueville Rd.* FACILITIES: 30 sites, 30 no hkups, tenting. RECREATION: lake swim, boating, ramp, dock, lake fishing. Open all yr. Phone: (207)768-8341.

(S) Neil E Michaud Campground—(Aroostook) *From jct Hwy 167 & US 1: Go 2-1/2 mi S on US 1. Enter on L.* ◆◆◆FACILITIES: 45 sites, typical site width 28 ft, 8 full hkups, 37 W&E, (20/30 amps), 45 pull-thrus, tenting, dump, laundry. ◆RECREATION: play equipment. Pets welcome. Open all yr. Facilities fully operational May 1 - Oct 15. Rate in 2010 $22-25 for 4 persons. Member ARVC, MECOA. Phone: (207)769-1951.

RANGELEY—D-1

(SE) RANGELEY (Lake) State Park—(Franklin) *From jct Hwy-16 & Hwy-4: Go 4 mi S on Hwy-4, then 5 mi W on S Shore Drive, then 1 mi N.* FACILITIES: 50 sites, 50 no hkups, tenting. RECREATION: lake swim, boating, canoeing, ramp, dock, lake fishing, playground. Open May 15 - Oct 1. Phone: (207)864-3858.

RAYMOND—E-2

(N) KOKATOSI CAMPGROUND—(Cumberland) *From jct US-302 & Hwy-85: Go 6 mi NE on Hwy-85. Enter on R.*

WELCOME

◆◆◆FACILITIES: 162 sites, typical site width 30 ft, 148 full hkups, 14 W&E, (20/30 amps), some extd stay sites, cable TV, WiFi Instant Internet at site, family camping, tenting, RV's/park model rentals, RV storage, dump, non-guest dump $, portable dump, laundry, groceries, RV supplies, LP gas by weight/by meter, marine gas, ice, picnic tables, patios, fire rings, wood, controlled access.

◆◆◆◆◆RECREATION: rec hall, rec room/area, coin games, lake swim, boating, canoeing, kayaking, dock, pontoon/7 canoe/4 kayak/2 motorboat rentals, lake fishing, fishing supplies, golf nearby, bsktball, playground, activities, horseshoes, sports field, hiking trails, v-ball.

Pets welcome. Partial handicap access. Open mid May - mid Oct. Clubs welcome. Rate in 2010 $36-44 per family. MC/VISA/Debit. Member ARVC, MECOA.

Phone: (207)627-4642
Address: 635 Webbs Mills Rd, Raymond, ME 04071
Lat/Lon: 43.95941/-70.46422
Email: kokatosi@fairpoint.net
Web: www.kokatosicampground.com

SEE AD THIS PAGE

RICHMOND—E-2

(NW) KOA-Augusta/Gardiner—(Sagadahoc) *From jct I-295 (exit 49) & US 201: Go 2-1/4 mi S on US 201. Enter on R.* ◇◇◇FACILITIES: 80 sites, typical site width 28 ft, 27 full hkups, 43 W&E, (20/30/50 amps), 50 amps ($), 10 no hkups, 63 pull-thrus, family camping, tenting, dump, laundry, groceries. ◇◇◇◇RECREATION: swim pool, boating, canoeing, dock, pond fishing, playground. Pets welcome, breed restrict. Open Mid May - Mid Oct. Rate in 2010 $29-37 for 2 persons. Member ARVC, MECOA. Phone: (800)562-1496. KOA discount.

ROBBINSTON—D-5

(SW) Hilltop Campground—(Washington) *From South town limits: Go 6 mi S on US-1, then 1-1/2 mi W on Ridge Rd. Enter on L.* ◇◇◇FACILITIES: 86 sites, typical site width 24 ft, 36 full hkups, 50 W&E, (20/30/50 amps), 30 pull-thrus, WiFi Instant Internet at site, phone Internet central location, family camping, tenting, dump, non-guest dump $, portable dump, laundry, ltd groc, LP gas by meter, ice, picnic tables, fire rings, wood. ◇◇◇◇RECREATION: rec hall, swim pool, pond fishing, bsktball, playground, activities, horseshoes, hiking trails, v-ball. Pets welcome. Open Mid May - mid Oct. Facilities fully operational Mid May - Labor Day. Rate in 2010 $24-36 per family. MC/VISA. CCUSA 50% Discount. CCUSA reservations Not Accepted, CCUSA max stay 3 days, Cash only for CCUSA disc., CCUSA disc. not avail F,Sa, CCUSA disc. not avail holidays. Electric heater surcharge $3.

Phone: (207)454-3985
Address: 317 Ridge Rd, Robbinston, ME 04671
Lat/Lon: 45.04619/-67.14521
Email: dmhenn@wwsisp.com
Web: www.hilltopcampgroundmaine.com

ROCKPORT—E-3

(SW) Camden Hills RV Resort (Morgan RV Resorts)—(Knox) *From jct US-1 & Hwy-90: Go 2 mi SW on Hwy-90. Enter on L.* ◇◇◇FACILITIES: 62 sites, 52 full hkups, (20/30/50 amps), 10 no hkups, 14 pull-thrus, family camping, tenting, dump, laundry. ◇◇◇RECREATION: swim pool, play equipment. Pets welcome. Open May 15 - Oct 15. Big rigs welcome. Rate in 2010 $34-44 per family. Member ARVC, MECOA. Phone: (888) 842-0592.

(S) Nascar RV Resort at Megunticook (Morgan RV Resorts)—(Knox) *From jct Hwy 90 & US 1 (in Rockport): Go 2 mi S on US 1. Enter on L.* ◇◇◇◇FACILITIES: 87 sites, typical site width 26 ft, 45 full hkups, 17 W&E, (20/30/50 amps), 25 no hkups, 13 pull-thrus, family camping, tenting, dump, laundry. ◇◇◇◇RECREATION: swim pool, saltwater fishing, playground. Pets welcome. Open May 15 - Columbus Day. Rate in 2010 $28-45 per family. Member ARVC, MECOA. Phone: (800)884-2428.

SACO—F-2

(N) Cascadia Park—(York) *From jct I-95 (exit 36) & I-195: Go 1-1/4 mi E on I-195 (exit 2B), then 2-1/2 mi N on US 1. Enter on R.* ◇◇FACILITIES: 92 sites, 32 ft max RV length, 49 full hkups, 18 W&E, 3 E, (20/30 amps), 22 no hkups, 10 pull-thrus, tenting, laundry. Pets welcome, quantity restrict. Open May 1 - Nov 1. Rate in 2010 $26-35 for 2 persons. Phone: (207)282-1666.

Maine has over 400 coastal islands.

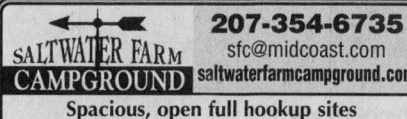

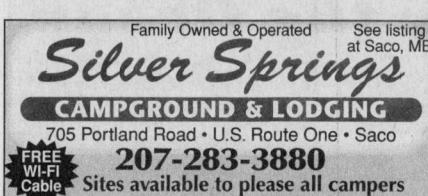

SACO—Continued

(N) SACO/OLD ORCHARD BEACH KOA—(York) *From jct I-95 & I-195 (exit 36): Go 1-3/4 mi E on I-195,(exit 2B), then 1-1/2 mi N on US 1. Enter on L.*

◇◇◇◇FACILITIES: 95 sites, typical site width 30 ft, 50 full hkups, 30 W&E, (20/30/50 amps), 50 amps ($), 15 no hkups, 55 pull-thrus, cable TV, WiFi Instant Internet at site, family camping, tenting, RV's/park model rentals, cabins, dump, non-guest dump $, laundry, groceries, RV supplies, LP gas by weight/by meter, ice, picnic tables, fire rings, wood, controlled access.

◇◇◇◇RECREATION: rec room/area, equipped pavilion, coin games, swim pool, golf nearby, bsktball, playground, activities, horseshoes, v-ball, local tours.

Pets welcome, breed restrict. Partial handicap access. Open Late Apr - Mid Oct. Big rigs welcome. Escort to site. Clubs welcome. Green Friendly. Rate in 2010 $33-62 for 2 persons. MC/VISA/DISC/Debit. Member ARVC, MECOA. KOA discount.

Phone: (800)562-1886
Address: 814 Portland Rd, Saco, ME 04072
Lat/Lon: 43.53445/-70.42713
Email: sacokoa@aol.com
Web: www.sacokoa.com

SEE AD OLD ORCHARD BEACH PAGE 318 AND AD TRAVEL SECTION PAGE 303

(NE) SEACOAST RV'S—*From jct I-95 (exit 36) & I-195: Go 1-3/4 mi E on I-195 (exit 2B), then 1-1/4 mi N on US 1. Enter on R.* SALES: travel trailers, park models, 5th wheels, Class C motorhomes, pre-owned unit sales. SERVICES: full-time mech, RV appliance repair, body work/collision repair, bus. hrs emerg rd svc, mobile RV svc, LP gas by meter, RV rentals, RV storage, sells parts/accessories, installs hitches. Open all yr. MC/VISA/DISC/Debit.

Phone: (207)282-3511
Address: 729 Portland Rd., Saco, ME 04072
Lat/Lon: 43.52114/-70.42743
Web: www.seacoastrv.com

SEE AD OLD ORCHARD BEACH PAGE 317

(N) SILVER SPRINGS CAMPGROUND—(York) *From jct I-95 (exit 36) & I-195: Go 1-1/4 mi E on I-195, (exit 2B)then 1/2 mi N on US 1. Enter on R.*

◇◇◇FACILITIES: 135 sites, typical site width 25 ft, 135 full hkups, (20/30/50 amps), many extd stay sites, 8 pull-thrus, cable TV, WiFi Instant Internet at site, WiFi Internet central location, family camping, tenting, cabins, RV storage, shower$, dump, non-guest dump $, laundry, ltd groc, RV supplies, ice, picnic tables, fire rings, wood.

◇◇◇◇RECREATION: rec hall, rec room/area, coin games, 2 swim pools, golf nearby, bsktball, playground, shuffleboard court shuffleboard court, activities (wkends), horseshoes, hiking trails, v-ball.

Pets welcome, quantity restrict. Open May 1 - Oct 15. Clubs welcome. Rate in 2010 $35-48 per family. MC/VISA/DISC/Debit. Member ARVC, MECOA. CCUSA 50% Discount. CCUSA max stay Unlimited. Discount not available Memorial Day weekend, Jul & Aug.

SACO—Continued
SILVER SPRINGS CAMPGROUND—Continued

Phone: (207)283-3880
Address: 705 Portland Rd (US Hwy 1), Saco, ME 04072
Lat/Lon: 43.51883/-70.42715
Email: silver-springs@earthlink.net
Web: www.silverspringscampgroundandcottages.com

SEE AD THIS PAGE

ST. AGATHA—A-4

(C) Lakeview Camping Resort—(Aroostook) *From jct Hwy 161 & Hwy 162: Go 12-3/4 mi NE on Hwy 162, then 1/4 mi SW on Flat Mountain Rd. Enter on L.* ◇◇◇FACILITIES: 80 sites, typical site width 28 ft, 55 full hkups, 25 W&E, (20/30/50 amps), family camping, tenting, dump, laundry, ltd groc. ◇◇RECREATION: playground. Pets welcome. Partial handicap access. Open May 1 - Oct 1. Rate in 2010 $27.95-32.95 for 2 persons. Member ARVC, MECOA. Phone: (207)543-6331.

SANFORD—F-1

(S) Yellowstone Park—(York) *From jct I-95 (exit 19) & Rte 19: Go 5 mi W on Rte 109. Enter on L.* ◇◇◇FACILITIES: 131 sites, typical site width 40 ft, 35 ft max RV length, 100 full hkups, 10 W&E, (20/30/50 amps), 21 no hkups, 6 pull-thrus, family camping, tenting, dump, laundry. ◇◇◇RECREATION: swim pool, playground. Pets welcome, breed restrict. Partial handicap access. Open May 15 - Sep 15. Rate in 2010 $26-34 per family. Member ARVC, MECOA.

SCARBOROUGH—F-2

(S) BAYLEY'S CAMPING RESORT—(Cumberland) *From jct I-95 Maine Tpk (exit 42) & Scarborough (US 1): Go 1-1/2 mi S on US 1, then 3 mi E on Hwy 9 West to Pine Point. Enter on R.*

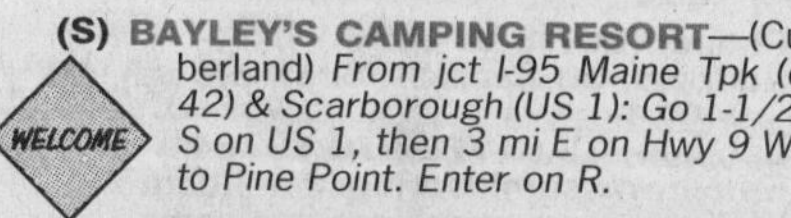

Ultimate family camping for all...from the largest of rigs to the purest wanting wilderness tenting. All the comforts you expect, all the amenities you hope for...located only 1/2 mile from 7 miles of pristine ocean beach.

◇◇◇◇◇FACILITIES: 745 sites, typical site width 35 ft, 600 full hkups, 65 W&E, (20/30/50 amps), 50 amps ($), 80 no hkups, 60 pull-thrus, cable TV, WiFi Instant Internet at site, WiFi Internet central location, family camping, tenting, RV's/park model rentals, cabins, RV storage, dump, non-guest dump $, laundry, full svc store, RV supplies, LP gas by weight/by meter, ice, picnic tables, fire rings, grills, wood, controlled access.

◇◇◇◇◇RECREATION: rec hall, rec room/area, pavilion, equipped pavilion, coin games, 3 swim pools, hot tub, kayaking, 14 kayak/6 pedal boat rentals, pond fishing, fishing supplies, mini-golf, ($), golf nearby, bsktball, 33 bike rentals, playground, activities, horseshoes, sports field, hiking trails, v-ball, local tours.

Pets welcome. Open End of April - Mid Oct. Big rigs welcome. Clubs welcome. Green Friendly. Rate in 2010 $30-86 for 2 persons. MC/VISA/DISC/AMEX/Debit. ATM. Member ARVC, MECOA.

Text 83383 to (440)725-8687 to see our Visual Tour.

BAYLEY'S CAMPING RESORT—Continued on next page

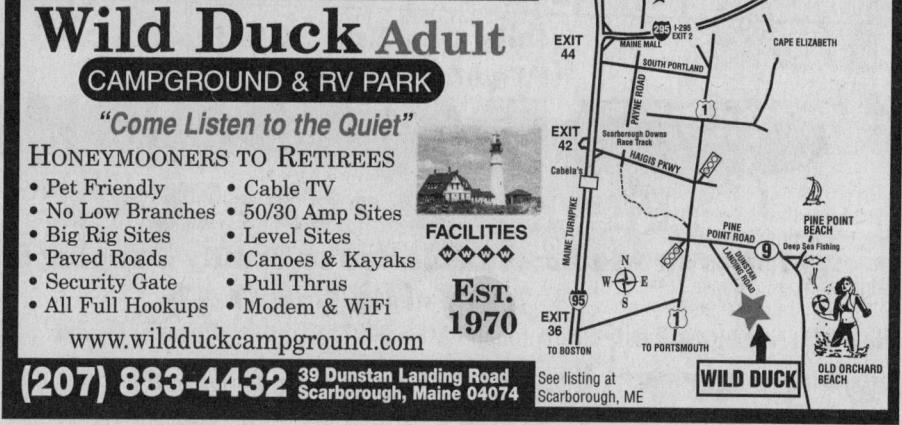

SCARBOROUGH—Continued
BAYLEY'S CAMPING RESORT—Continued

Phone: (207)883-6043
Address: 275 Pine Point Rd, Scarborough, ME 04074
Lat/Lon: 43.54776/-70.35515
Email: info@bayleys-camping.com
Web: www.bayleys-camping.com

SEE AD THIS PAGE AND AD TRAVEL SECTION PAGE 303

(NW) WASSAMKI SPRINGS CAMPGROUND—(Cumberland) *From jct I-95 (exit 46) & Hwy 22: Go 3 mi W on Hwy 22, then 1/4 mi N on Saco St. Enter on L.*

WELCOME

◇◇◇FACILITIES: 170 sites, typical site width 30 ft, 150 full hkups, 20 W&E, (20/30/50 amps), 50 amps ($), many extd stay sites, 30 pull-thrus, WiFi Instant Internet at site, phone Internet central location, family camping, tenting, RV storage, dump, non-guest dump $, laundry, ltd groc, RV supplies, LP gas by weight/by meter, ice, picnic tables, fire rings, wood, controlled access.

◇◇◇◇◇RECREATION: rec hall, rec room/area, coin games, lake swim, boating, canoeing, kayaking, 5 pedal boat rentals, lake fishing, fishing supplies, golf nearby, bsktball, playground, activities, horseshoes, sports field, v-ball. Rec open to public.

Pets welcome, breed restrict. Open May 1 - Oct 15. Big rigs welcome. Clubs welcome. Rate in 2010 $26-53 for 2 persons. MC/VISA/Debit. Member ARVC, MECOA.

Text 107939 to (440)725-8687 to see our Visual Tour.

Phone: (207)839-4276
Address: 56 Saco St, Scarborough, ME 04074
Lat/Lon: 43.64722/-70.39864
Email: wassamkisprings@aol.com
Web: www.wassamkisprings.com

SEE AD PORTLAND PAGE 320 AND AD TRAVEL SECTION PAGE 303

America's first chartered city, (in 1641) was York.

SCARBOROUGH—Continued

(W) WILD DUCK ADULT CAMPGROUND—(Cumberland) *From jct I-95 (exit 42) & Scarborough (US 1): Go 1-1/2 mi E on Haiais Pkwy, then 1-1/2 mi S on US 1, then 1/4 mi E on Hwy 9 (Pine Point Rd), then 1/4 mi SE on Dunstan Landing Rd. Enter at end.*

WELCOME

◇◇◇◇FACILITIES: 70 sites, typical site width 28 ft, 56 full hkups, 4 W&E, (20/30/50 amps), 10 no hkups, some extd stay sites, 8 pull-thrus, cable TV, WiFi Instant Internet at site, phone Internet central location, tenting, RV's/park model rentals, dump, non-guest dump $, laundry, ltd groc, RV supplies, ice, picnic tables, fire rings, wood, controlled access.

◇◇RECREATION: boating, no motors, canoeing, kayaking, dock, 2 canoe/2 kayak rentals, river fishing, fishing supplies, golf nearby, hiking trails.

Pets welcome, breed restrict. Open Apr 30 - Oct 20. Big rigs welcome. Escort to site. Clubs welcome. Green Friendly. Rate in 2010 $27-54 for 2 persons. MC/VISA/DISC/Debit. Member ARVC, MECOA. FCRV discount. FMCA discount.

Phone: (207)883-4432
Address: 39 Dunstan Landing Rd, Scarborough, ME 04074
Lat/Lon: 43.56614/-70.38047
Email: info@wildduckcampground.com
Web: www.wildduckcampground.com

SEE AD PAGE 321

SKOWHEGAN—D-2

(E) KOA-Skowhegan-Canaan—(Somerset) *From jct US 201 & US 2: Go 9 mi E on US 2. Enter on R.* ◇◇◇FACILITIES: 108 sites, typical site width 26 ft, 78 full hkups, (20/30/50 amps), 30 no hkups, 60 pull-thrus, family camping, tenting, dump, laundry, groceries. ◇◇◇◇◇RECREATION: swim pool, canoeing, playground. Pets welcome. Partial handicap access. Open mid May - mid Oct. Big rigs welcome. Rate in 2010 $35-48 for 4 persons. Member ARVC, MECOA. Phone: (207)474-2858. KOA discount.

(E) TWO RIVERS CAMPGROUND—(Somerset) *From jct US-201 & US-2: Go 2-1/2 mi E on US-2. Enter on R.*

WELCOME

◇◇◇FACILITIES: 69 sites, typical site width 30 ft, 44 full hkups, 12 W&E, (20/30/50 amps), 50 amps ($), 13 no hkups, some extd stay sites, 25 pull-thrus, cable TV, WiFi Instant Internet at site, family camping, tenting, dump, non-guest dump $, laundry, ltd groc, RV supplies, LP gas by weight/by meter, ice, picnic tables, fire rings, wood.

◇◇◇RECREATION: pavilion, swim pool, river swim, boating, canoeing, kayaking, dock, 2 canoe/2 kayak/2 pedal boat rentals, river/stream fishing, fishing supplies, golf nearby, playground, horseshoes, sports field, v-ball.

Pets welcome. Open May 15 - Oct 15. Big rigs welcome. Clubs welcome. Rate in 2010 $33 per family. Member ARVC, MECOA.

SKOWHEGAN—Continued
TWO RIVERS CAMPGROUND—Continued

Phone: (207)474-6482
Address: 327 Canaan Rd, Skowhegan, ME 04976
Lat/Lon: 44.77141/-69.67651
Email: info@tworvrs.com
Web: www.tworvrs.com

SEE AD THIS PAGE

(N) Yogi Bear's Jellystone Park—(Somerset) *From jct US-2 & US-201: Go 3-1/2 mi N on US-201. Enter on R.* ◇◇◇FACILITIES: 127 sites, typical site width 26 ft, 105 full hkups, 22 W&E, (20/30/50 amps), 4 pull-thrus, tenting, dump, laundry, ltd groc. ◇◇◇◇RECREATION: swim pool, pond fishing, playground. Pets welcome, size restrict. Open May 15 - Oct 15. Rate in 2010 $32-42 for 2 persons. Member ARVC, MECOA. Phone: (207)474-7353.

SOUTHWEST HARBOR—E-4

(S) ACADIA NATIONAL PARK (Seawall Campground) —(Hancock) *Southbound, from jct Hwy-102 & Hwy-102A: Go 5 mi S on Hwy-102A.* FACILITIES: 214 sites, 35 ft max RV length, 214 no hkups, 42 pull-thrus, tenting, dump. RECREATION: Pets welcome. Open Late May - Sep 30. Phone: (207)288-3338.

(N) Smuggler's Den Campground—(Hancock) *From jct Hwy-198 & Hwy-102: Go 5 mi S on Hwy-102. Enter on R.* ◇◇◇FACILITIES: 106 sites, typical site width 30 ft, 57 full hkups, 18 W&E, (20/30/50 amps), 31 no hkups, 3 pull-thrus, family camping, tenting, dump, laundry, ltd groc. ◇◇◇RECREATION: swim pool, playground. Pets welcome. Open Memorial Day Wknd - mid Oct. Rate in 2010 $35-51 for 4 persons. Member ARVC, MECOA. Phone: (207)244-3944.

STANDISH—E-1

(NW) Family and Friends Campground—(Cumberland) *From jct Hwy 35 & Hwy 114: Go 3/4 mi NW on Hwy 114. Enter on L.* ◇◇◇FACILITIES: 68 sites, typical site width 28 ft, 41 full hkups, 27 W&E, (20/30 amps), 1 pull-thrus, cable TV, WiFi Instant Internet at site, WiFi Internet central location, family camping, tenting, dump, non-guest dump $, laundry, RV supplies, LP gas by meter, ice, picnic tables, fire rings, wood.

CAMPCLUB USA

◇◇◇◇RECREATION: rec hall, swim pool, hot tub, pond fishing, fishing supplies, play equipment, activities horseshoes, v-ball. Pets welcome. Open Mid Apr - Mid Oct. Rate in 2010 $29-44 per family. MC/VISA/DISC/AMEX. Member ARVC, MECOA. CCUSA 50% Discount. CCUSA reservations Accepted, CCUSA max stay 7 days, Cash only for CCUSA disc., Check only for CCUSA disc., CCUSA disc. not avail F,Sa, CCUSA disc. not avail holidays.

Phone: (207)642-2200
Address: 140 Richville Rd., Standish, ME 04084
Lat/Lon: 43.76776/-70.53538
Email: info@familynfriends.com
Web: www.familynfriends.com

STEEP FALLS—E-1

(NE) Acres of Wildlife—(Cumberland) *From jct Hwy-113 & Hwy-11: Go 1/2 mi W on Hwy-113/Hwy-11, then 3 mi N on campground road. Enter at end.* ◇◇◇FACILITIES: 205 sites, typical site width 50 ft, 80 full hkups, 110 W&E, (20/30/50 amps), 15 no hkups,

Acres of Wildlife—Continued on next page

STEEP FALLS—Continued
Acres of Wildlife—Continued

6 pull-thrus, WiFi Instant Internet at site, WiFi Internet central location, family camping, tenting, dump, non-guest dump $, portable dump, laundry, groceries, RV supplies, LP gas by weight/by meter, ice, picnic tables, fire rings, grills, wood. ◆◆◆◆◆RECREATION: rec hall, equipped pavilion, lake swim, boating, electric motors only, canoeing, kayaking, dock, lake/pond fishing, fishing supplies, mini-golf, ($), bsktball, playground, activities, horseshoes, hiking trails, v-ball. Pets welcome ($). Partial handicap access. Open May 1 - Oct 18. Rate in 2010 $26-48 per family. MC/VISA/DISC/AMEX/Debit. ATM. Member ARVC, MECOA. CCUSA 50% Discount. CCUSA reservations Recommended, CCUSA max stay 4 days, CCUSA disc. not avail F,Sa, CCUSA disc. not avail holidays. Discount available May 1-Father's Day and Labor Day-Columbus Day weekend. Peak season discount: $10 drop in fee discounted. CCUSA rate includes all site types.

Phone: (207)675-CAMP
Address: Rte 11/113-60 Acres of Wildlife Rd, Steep Falls, ME 04085
Lat/Lon: 43.81792/-70.63383
Email: office@acresofwildlife.com
Web: www.acresofwildlife.com

STRATTON—D-2

(N) CATHEDRAL PINES (Stratton-Eustis Dev. Corp.)—(Franklin) *From jct Hwy-16 & Hwy-27: Go 4 mi N on Hwy-27.* FACILITIES: 115 sites, 2 full hkups, 96 W&E, (30 amps), 17 no hkups, tenting, dump, laundry. RECREATION: lake swim, boating, canoeing, ramp, dock, lake fishing, playground. Partial handicap access. Open May 15 - Oct 1. Phone: (207)246-3491.

SULLIVAN—D-4

(SE) MOUNTAINVIEW CAMPGROUND—(Hancock) *From jct Hwy 183 & US 1: Go 1/4 mi N on US 1. Enter on R.*

◆◆◆FACILITIES: 47 sites, typical site width 30 ft, 8 full hkups, 39 W&E, (20/30/50 amps), 11 pull-thrus, WiFi Instant Internet at site, WiFi Internet central location, tenting, cabins, dump, ice, picnic tables, fire rings, wood.

◆◆RECREATION: saltwater swim, canoeing, kayaking, saltwater fishing, golf nearby.

Pets welcome. Open Mid May - Oct 15. Rate in 2010 $30-38 for 2 persons. Member ARVC, MECOA.

Phone: (207)422-6408
Address: 2695 Hwy Rt 1 (Campground Rd), East Sullivan, ME 04664
Lat/Lon: 44.50102/-68.14899
Email: info@flandersbay.com
Web: www.flandersbay.com

SEE AD BAR HARBOR PAGE 310

THOMASTON—E-3

(S) SALTWATER FARM CAMPGROUND—(Knox) *From jct Hwy 97 & US 1: Go 1-3/4 mi N on US 1, then 1-1/2 mi E on Wadsworth St. Enter on L.*

◆◆◆FACILITIES: 47 sites, typical site width 30 ft, 35 full hkups, 12 W&E, (20/30/50 amps), some extd stay sites, WiFi Instant Internet at site, phone Internet central location, tenting, cabins, dump, non-guest dump $, laundry, ltd groc, RV supplies, ice, picnic tables, fire rings, wood.

◆◆◆RECREATION: rec room/area, swim pool, hot tub, saltwater fishing, golf nearby, play equipment, horseshoes, sports field, hiking trails.

THOMASTON—Continued
SALTWATER FARM CAMPGROUND—Continued

Pets welcome, quantity restrict. Open May 15 - Oct 15. Big rigs welcome. Clubs welcome. Green Friendly. Rate in 2010 $40-45 per family. MC/VISA/DISC/Debit. Member ARVC, MECOA. FMCA discount.

Phone: (207)354-6735
Address: 47 Kalloch Ln, Cushing, ME 04563
Lat/Lon: 44.06202/-69.20084
Email: sfc@midcoast.com
Web: www.saltwaterfarmcampground.com

SEE AD ROCKPORT PAGE 321

TRENTON—E-4

(E) TIMBERLAND ACRES RV PARK—(Hancock) *From jct US-1A/US-1 & Hwy-3: Go 3 mi E on Hwy-3. Enter on R.*

◆◆◆◆FACILITIES: 246 sites, typical site width 30 ft, 173 full hkups, 61 W&E, (20/30/50 amps), 12 no hkups, some extd stay sites, 75 pull-thrus, WiFi Internet central location, family camping, tenting, RV storage, dump, laundry, ltd groc, RV supplies, LP gas by weight/by meter, ice, picnic tables, fire rings, wood.

◆◆◆◆RECREATION: rec hall, rec room/area, pavilion, coin games, swim pool, golf nearby, bsktball, playground, shuffleboard court 2 shuffleboard courts, activities, horseshoes, sports field, v-ball.

Pets welcome. Open Mid May - Mid Oct. Big rigs welcome. Clubs welcome. Rate in 2010 $34-37 for 4 persons. MC/VISA/Debit. Member ARVC, MECOA.

Phone: (207)667-3600
Address: 57 Bar Harbor Rd, Trenton, ME 04605
Lat/Lon: 44.50672/-68.38857
Email: info@timberlandacresrvpark.com
Web: www.timberlandacresrvpark.com

SEE AD BAR HARBOR PAGE 310

UNION—E-3

(E) Mic Mac Cove—(Knox) *From west jct Hwy-131 & Hwy-17: Go 1-3/4 mi E on Hwy-17. Enter on R.* ◆◆FACILITIES: 96 sites, typical site width 24 ft, 9 full hkups, 79 W&E, (20/30/50 amps), 8 no hkups, 1 pull-thrus, family camping, tenting, dump, ltd groc. ◆◆◆RECREATION: lake swim, boating, canoeing, ramp, dock, lake fishing, play equipment. Pets welcome. Open May 1 - Columbus Day. Rate in 2010 $35-40 per family. Member ARVC, MECOA. Phone: (207) 785-4100.

WATERFORD—E-1

(NW) Papoose Pond Resort & Campground—(Oxford) *From downtown Norway: Go 9 mi W on Hwy 118. Enter on R.* ◆◆◆◆FACILITIES: 173 sites, typical site width 75 ft, 78 full hkups, 82 W&E, (20/30 amps), 12 no hkups, family camping, tenting, dump, laundry, full svc store. ◆◆◆◆RECREATION: swim pool, lake swim, boating, no motors, canoeing, dock, river/pond fishing, playground. Pets welcome. Open mid May - Columbus Day. Rate in 2010 $27-80 per family. Member ARVC, MECOA. Phone: (207)583-4470.

Maine was the 23rd state admitted to the Union.

WELD—D-2

(W) MOUNT BLUE STATE PARK—(Franklin) *From jct Hwy-156 & Hwy-142: Go 2-1/4 mi N on Hwy-156, then 4 mi W on Shore Road, then 1 mi S.* FACILITIES: 136 sites, 136 no hkups, tenting, dump. RECREATION: lake swim, boating, canoeing, ramp, dock, lake fishing, playground. Open all yr. Phone: (207) 585-2347.

WELLS—F-1

(S) BEACH ACRES CAMPGROUND—(York) *From jct I 95 (exit 19) & Hwy 109: Go 1-1/2 mi E on Hwy 109, then 2 mi S on US 1, then 1 block E on Eldridge Rd. Enter on L.*

◆◆◆FACILITIES: 400 sites, typical site width 40 ft, 320 full hkups, 20 W&E, 11 E, (20/30/50 amps), 49 no hkups, mostly extd stay sites, cable on-site Internet (needs activ), family camping, tenting, RV storage, shower$, dump, non-guest dump $, laundry, ice, picnic tables, fire rings, wood, controlled access.

◆◆◆RECREATION: swim pool, golf nearby, bsktball, playground, shuffleboard court shuffleboard court, activities (wkends), horseshoes, sports field.

No pets. Open late May - mid Sep. Big rigs welcome. Clubs welcome. Rate in 2010 $40-54 for 2 persons. Member ARVC, MECOA.

Text 107941 to (440)725-8687 to see our Visual Tour.

Phone: (207)646-5612
Address: 76 Eldridge, Wells, ME 04090
Lat/Lon: 43.29105/-70.58719
Email: beachacres@beachacres.com
Web: www.beachacres.com

SEE AD THIS PAGE

(NE) Ocean View Cottages & Camping—(York) *From jct I-95 (exit 19) & Hwy 109: Go 1-1/2 mi E on Hwy 109, then 100 feet N on US 1, then 1/4 mi E on Harbor Rd. Enter on L.* ◆◆FACILITIES: 108 sites, typical site width 40 ft, 32 ft max RV length, 60 full hkups, 30 W&E, 5 E, (20/30 amps), 13 no hkups, family camping, tenting, dump, laundry. ◆◆◆RECREATION: swim pool, saltwater fishing, playground. Pets welcome. Open May 1 - Columbus Day. Rate in 2010 $24-35 for 4 persons. Member ARVC. Phone: (207)646-3308.

(N) Riverside Park Campground—(York) *From jct I-95 (exit 19) & Hwy 109: Go 1-1/2 mi E on Hwy 109, then 1-3/4 mi N on US 1. Enter on R.* ◆◆◆FACILITIES: 127 sites, typical site width 26 ft, 35 ft max RV length, 93 full hkups, 26 W&E, (20/30/50 amps), 8 no hkups, family camping, tenting, laundry, ltd groc. ◆◆RECREATION: swim pool, river fishing, play equipment. Pets welcome. Partial handicap access. Open May 12 - Oct 15. Facilities fully operational Jun 30 - Labor Day. Rate in 2010 $35-55 for 2 persons. Member ARVC, MECOA. Phone: (207)646-3145. FMCA discount.

WELLS—Continued on next page

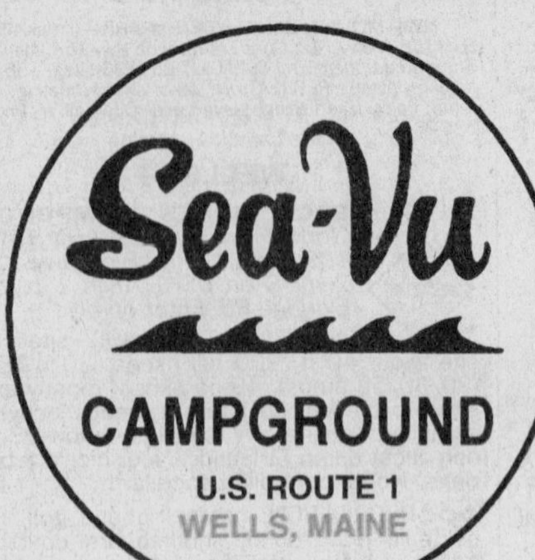

COASTAL WELLS

Overlooking the Ocean

Picturesque View of Wells Harbor and the Atlantic Ocean

Miles of Beautiful Sandy Beaches

5 Miles to Ogunquit or Kennebunkport

Sea Vu Features

50 Amp • Cable TV
Wireless Internet

Pool with Patio • Kiddie Pool
Mini Golf • Playground
Recreation Hall/Function Room
Large Entertainment Room
Aerobic Dance Classes
Basketball
Horseshoes • Bocce
Recreation Field
Large Store • LP Gas
Pets Welcome on Leash

BIG RIGS WELCOME

Open May 15 - Columbus Day
Discounted Spring & Fall Rates
Senior Citizen Discount

Locally Owned & Operated

1733 Post Road, PO Box 67 • Wells, ME 04090
(207) 646-7732

www.sea-vucampground.com

seavu@maine.rr.com
Contact us for additional information

Within Immediate Area

Miles of Beautiful Sandy Beaches
Boat Launching • Boat Rentals
Deep Sea Fishing
Excursion Boats • Sailing
Playland • Funtown • Aquaboggan
Lobster Pounds • Fine Restaurants
Antique Car Museum • Area Shops
Factory Outlets • Flea Markets
Auctions • Fairs • Historic Sites
Famous Ogunquit Playhouse
Movie Theatre (multi-screen)
Summer Stock Theatres

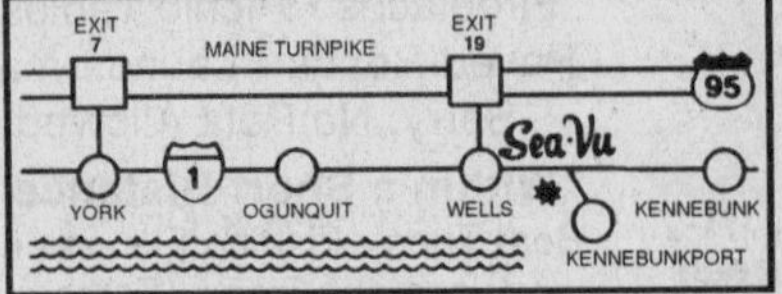

Leave Maine Turnpike (Interstate 95) at Exit 19-Wells, Maine. Turn left onto Route 109 and 9 and go 1 1/2 miles to intersection. Turn left onto Route 1. Campground is 4/10's miles from the intersection on the right hand side of Route 1 next to a church. 43 19 00.0 N; 70 34 00.0 W

LOW OFF SEASON RATES

(N) SEA VU CAMPGROUND—(York) *From jct I-95 (exit 19) & Hwy 109: Go 1-1/2 mi E on Hwy 109, then 1/2 mi N on US 1. Enter on R.*

WELCOME

◊◊◊◊FACILITIES: 225 sites, typical site width 40 ft, 218 full hkups, (20/30/50 amps), 7 no hkups, many extd stay sites, cable TV, WiFi/cable Instant Internet at site, WiFi Internet central location, family camping, tenting, RV storage, dump, non-guest dump $, laundry, groceries, RV supplies, LP gas by weight/by meter, ice, picnic tables, fire rings, wood, controlled access.

◊◊◊◊◊RECREATION: rec hall, rec room/area, coin games, swim pool, wading pool, mini-golf, ($), golf nearby, bsktball, playground, activities, horseshoes, sports field, local tours.

Pets welcome. Partial handicap access. Open May 8 - Columbus Day. Big rigs welcome. Clubs welcome. Rate in 2010 $36-60 for 2 persons. MC/VISA/DISC/Debit. Member ARVC, MECOA.

Phone: (207)646-7732
Address: 1733 Post Rd, Wells, ME 04090
Lat/Lon: 43.32699/-70.57687
Email: seavucampground@maine.rr.com
Web: www.SEA-VUCAMPGROUND.com

SEE AD PAGE 324 AND AD TRAVEL SECTION PAGE 303

(N) The Casey's Stadig Campground—(York) *From jct I-95 (exit 19) & Hwy 109: Go 1-1/2 mi E on Hwy 109, then 2 mi N on US 1. Enter on R.* ◊◊FACILITIES: 150 sites, typical site width 26 ft, 37 full hkups, 5 W&E, 11 E, (20/30 amps), 97 no hkups, 22 pull-thrus, family camping, tenting, dump, laundry. ◊◊RECREATION: play equipment. Pets welcome. Open Memorial Day wkend - Oct 15. Rate in 2010 $30-35 for 4 persons. Member ARVC, MECOA. Phone: (207)646-2298.

(S) WELLS BEACH RESORT—(York) *From jct I-95 (exit 19) & Hwy 109: Go 1-1/2 mi E on Hwy 109, then 1-1/4 mi S on US 1. Enter on R.*

WELCOME

◊◊◊◊◊FACILITIES: 231 sites, typical site width 33 ft, 215 full hkups, (20/30/50 amps), 16 no hkups, some extd stay sites, 100 pull-thrus, cable TV, WiFi Instant Internet at site, WiFi Internet central location, family camping, tenting, RV's/park model rentals, RV storage, dump, non-guest dump $, laundry, groceries, RV supplies, ice, picnic tables, patios, fire rings, wood, controlled access.

◊◊◊◊◊RECREATION: rec room/area, pavilion, coin games, swim pool, mini-golf, ($), golf nearby, bsktball, playground, shuffleboard court 2 shuffleboard courts, activities (wkends), horseshoes, v-ball, local tours.

Pets welcome, quantity restrict. Open May 15 - Oct 15. Big rigs welcome. Clubs welcome. Rate in 2010 $49-77 for 2 persons. MC/VISA/DISC/Debit. Member ARVC, MECOA.

Text 86099 to (440)725-8687 to see our Visual Tour.

Phone: (207)646-7570
Address: 1000 Post Rd, Wells, ME 04090
Lat/Lon: 43.30360/-70.58575
Web: www.wellsbeach.com

SEE AD PORTLAND PAGE 319 AND AD MAP PAGE 302

WINTER HARBOR—E-4

(S) MILITARY PARK (Winter Harbor Rec Area)—(Hancock) *From jct US 1 & Hwy 186: Go 6 mi S on Hwy 186, then at the end of the road at the water turn left 1 mi, then right 3 mi at entr. to Schoodic Pk Rd. On base.* FACILITIES: 9 sites, 5 W&E, 4 no hkups, tenting, dump, laundry, groceries. RECREATION: saltwater swim, boating, canoeing, saltwater fishing, playground. Open Apr 15 - Oct 15.

WINTHROP—E-2

(S) AUGUSTA-WEST LAKESIDE RESORT KAMPGROUND—(Kennebec) *From jct I-95 (exit 109) & US 202: Go 8 mi W on US 202, then 1/2 mi S on Highland Ave, then 3/4 mi W (right) on Holmes Brook Rd. Enter at end.*

WELCOME

◊◊◊FACILITIES: 81 sites, typical site width 30 ft, 17 full hkups, 64 W&E, (20/30 amps), many extd stay sites, 20 pull-thrus, WiFi Instant Internet at site, family camping, tenting, RV's/park model rentals, RV storage, dump, non-guest dump $, portable dump, laundry, groceries, RV supplies, LP gas by weight/by meter, marine gas, ice, picnic tables, fire rings, wood, controlled access.

◊◊◊◊RECREATION: rec room/area, equipped pavilion, coin games, swim pool, lake swim, boating, canoeing, kayaking, ramp, dock, 2 rowboat/2 canoe/2 kayak/4 pedal boat/2 motorboat rentals, lake fishing, fishing supplies, fishing guides, golf nearby, bsktball, playground, activities, (wkends), horseshoes, sports field, v-ball.

Pets welcome, breed restrict. Open May 15 - Sep 30. Clubs welcome. Rate in 2010 $26-38 for 2 persons. MC/VISA/DISC/Debit. Member ARVC, MECOA.

Phone: (207)377-9993
Address: 183 Holmes Brook Lane, Winthrop, ME 04364
Lat/Lon: 44.28101/-69.97176
Email: augustawest@fairpoint.net
Web: www.augustawestkampground.com

SEE AD AUGUSTA PAGE 309

✲ **(S) AUGUSTA-WEST LAKESIDE RV SALES & SERVICE**—*From jct I-95 (exit 109) & US 202: Go 8 mi W on US 202, then 1/2 mi S on Highland Ave, then 3/4 mi W on access road. Enter at end.* SALES: travel trailers, 5th wheels, pre-owned unit sales. SERVICES: LP gas by weight/by meter, dump station, RV storage, sells parts/accessories. Open all yr. MC/VISA/DISC.

WELCOME

Phone: (207)377-9993
Address: 183 Holmes Brooke Ln, Winthrop, ME 04364
Lat/Lon: 44.28101/-69.97176
Email: augustawest@fairpoint.net
Web: www.augustawestkampground.com

SEE AD AUGUSTA PAGE 309

(W) More to Life Family Campground—(Kennebec) *From jct I-95 (exit 109) & US 202: Go 6 mi W on US 202, then 2-1/2 mi S on Hwy 135. Enter on R.* ◊◊FACILITIES: 70 sites, typical site width 30 ft, 10 full hkups, 60 W&E, (15/30 amps), 9 pull-thrus, tenting, dump, laundry, ltd groc. ◊◊◊◊RECREATION: lake swim, canoeing, dock, lake fishing, playground. Pets welcome. Open Mid May - Mid Oct. Rate in 2010 $25-35 per family. Member ARVC, MECOA. Phone: (207)395-4908.

West Quoddy Head is the most easterly point in the United States.

WISCASSET—E-2

(SW) Chewonki Campgrounds—(Lincoln) *From jct Hwy 27 & US 1: Go 3-1/2 mi S on US 1, then 1/4 mi SE on Hwy 144, then 1 mi S on Chewonki Rd. Enter on R.* ◊◊◊FACILITIES: 48 sites, typical site width 30 ft, 12 full hkups, 27 W&E, (20/30 amps), 9 no hkups, 5 pull-thrus, family camping, tenting, dump, ltd groc. ◊◊◊◊RECREATION: swim pool, boating, canoeing, dock, saltwater fishing, play equipment. Pets welcome. Partial handicap access. Open mid May - mid Oct. Rate in 2010 $35-61 per family. Member ARVC, MECOA. Phone: (207)882-7426.

YORK BEACH—F-1

(N) York Beach Camper Park—(York) *From jct I-95 (exit 7) & US 1: Go 3.3 mi N on US 1, then 1.1 mi E on US 1A, then 100 feet S on Cappy's Lane. Enter on R.* ◊◊◊FACILITIES: 51 sites, typical site width 25 ft, 39 full hkups, 5 W&E, (20/30/50 amps), 7 no hkups, 2 pull-thrus, WiFi Internet central location, family camping, tenting, RV storage, dump, non-guest dump $, laundry, ltd groc, ice, picnic tables, fire rings, grills, wood. ◊RECREATION: bsktball, play equipment, horseshoes, hiking trails. Pets welcome. Partial handicap access. Open Memorial Wknd - mid Oct. Rate in 2010 $43.70 for 2 persons. Member ARVC, MECOA.

CAMPCLUB USA

CCUSA 50% Discount. CCUSA reservations Recommended, CCUSA max stay 1 day, Cash only for CCUSA disc., CCUSA disc. not avail S,Th, CCUSA disc. not avail F,Sa, CCUSA disc. not avail holidays. Discount available Jun & Sep.

Phone: (207)363-1343
Address: 11 Cappy's Ln, York Beach, ME 03910
Lat/Lon: 43.18003/-70.61102
Web: www.yorkbeachcamping.com

YORK HARBOR—F-1

(NE) Camp Eaton—(York) *From I-95 (exit 7): Go 1/4 mi S on US 1, then 3 mi NE on US 1A. Enter on L.* ◊◊◊FACILITIES: 256 sites, typical site width 25 ft, 256 full hkups, (20/30/50 amps), 2 pull-thrus, family camping, dump, ltd groc. ◊◊◊◊RECREATION: saltwater swim, saltwater fishing, playground. Pets welcome. Partial handicap access. No tents. Open May 1 - Oct 15. Rate in 2010 $40-68 for 2 persons. Member ARVC, MECOA. Phone: (207)363-3424.

(NE) LIBBY'S OCEANSIDE CAMP—(York) *From I-95 (exit 7): Go 1/4 mi S on US 1, then 3 mi NE on US 1A. Enter on R.*

WELCOME

◊◊◊◊FACILITIES: 95 sites, typical site width 20 ft, 88 full hkups, 7 W&E, (20/30/50 amps), 50 amps ($), many extd stay sites, 8 pull-thrus, cable TV, WiFi Instant Internet at site, WiFi Internet central location, tenting, laundry, ltd groc, RV supplies, ice, picnic tables, fire rings, wood.

◊◊RECREATION: saltwater swim, saltwater fishing, golf nearby, local tours.

Pets welcome, quantity restrict. Partial handicap access. Open Mid May - Mid Oct. Big rigs welcome. Clubs welcome. Green Friendly. Rate in 2010 $75-87 for 3 persons. MC/VISA/DISC/Debit. Member ARVC, MECOA.

Phone: (207)363-4171
Address: 725 York St, York Harbor, ME 03911-0040
Lat/Lon: 43.14701/-70.62632
Email: ndavidson@main.rr.com
Web: www.libbysoceancamping.com

SEE AD NEXT PAGE AND AD TRAVEL SECTION PAGE 301 AND AD TRAVEL SECTION PAGE 303

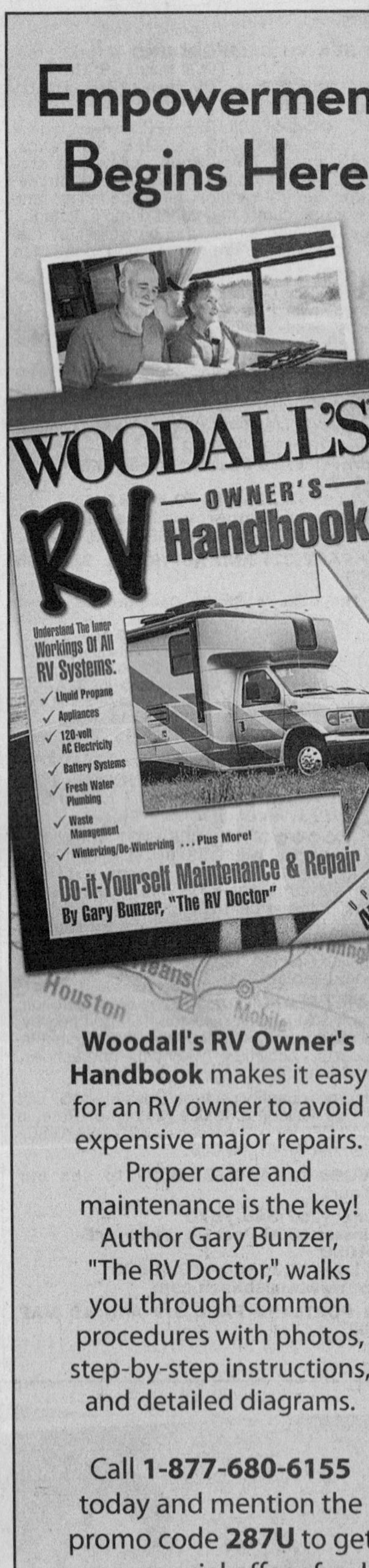

Woodall's RV Owner's Handbook makes it easy for an RV owner to avoid expensive major repairs. Proper care and maintenance is the key! Author Gary Bunzer, "The RV Doctor," walks you through common procedures with photos, step-by-step instructions, and detailed diagrams.

Call **1-877-680-6155** today and mention the promo code **287U** to get a very special offer of only **$12**! (Psst… that's over 50% off the cover price.)

CELEBRATING 75 YEARS 1936 W 2011

READER SERVICE INFO

The following businesses have placed an ad in the Maryland Travel Section. To receive free information, enter their Reader Service number on the Reader Service Card opposite page 48/Discover Section in the front of this directory:

Advertiser	RS#
Cherry Hill Park	461
Cherrystone Family Camping Resort	4106
Yogi Bear's Jellystone Camp Resort Williamsport	3482

TIME ZONE

Maryland is in the Eastern Time Zone.

TOPOGRAPHY

The Chesapeake Bay divides Maryland into 2 parts. The area east of the bay is comprised of farmlands, pine forests and marshes. The area west of the bay contains low, rolling hills, fertile river valleys and mountainous ridges.

TEMPERATURE

Maryland has a humid climate, with hot summers and generally mild winters.

Maryland is a state steeped in Civil and Revolutionary War history, some of the best seafood in the country, and miles of beaches and grasslands. Tourist destinations range from the 10 miles of white, sandy beaches at Ocean City, to Chesapeake Bay's 4,000 miles of shoreline, which is the busiest sailing destination on the Eastern Seaboard.

TRAVEL & TOURISM INFO

State Agency:
Maryland Office of Tourism Development
401 East Pratt St., 14th Floor
Baltimore, MD 21202
(800/543-1036 or 410/767-3400)
www.visitmaryland.org

Local Agencies:
For information on an area not listed here, contact the State Agency or the Chamber of Commerce or Tourism Bureau for the locality you are interested in.

Alleghany County Dept. of Tourism
13 Canal Place, Rm 306
Cumberland, MD 21502
(301/777-5134 or 800/425-2067)
www.mdmountainside.com

Annapolis/Anne Arundel County CVB
26 West Street
Annapolis, MD 21401
(410/280-0445)
www.visitannapolis.org

Baltimore Area Convention & Visitors Association
100 Light St., 12th Floor
Baltimore, MD 21202
(410/659-7131)
www.baltimore.org

Baltimore County CVB
P.O. Box 5426
Lutherville, MD 21094
(410/296-4886 or 800/570-2836)
www.visitbacomd.com

Calvert County Department of Economic Development & Tourism
205 Main St., 2nd Floor
Prince Frederick, MD 20678
(410/535-4583 or 800/331-9771)
www.ecalvert.com

Caroline Economic Development Corp.
15 S. Third St., Suite B
Denton, MD 21629
(410/479-2730)
www.tourcaroline.com

Carroll Co. Office of Tourism
210 E. Main St.
Westminster, MD 21157
(800/272-1933 or 410/848-1388)
www.carrollcountytourism.com

Cecil County Tourism
Perryville Outlet Center
68 Heather Lane, Suite #43
Perryville, MD 21903-2554
(410/996-6290 or 800/CECIL-95)
www.seececil.org

Charles County Economic Development & Tourism
103 Centennial St., Suite C
La Plata, MD 20646

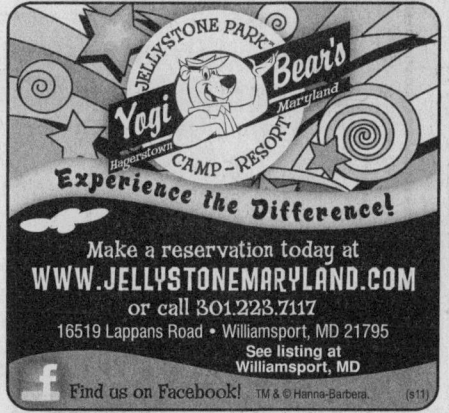

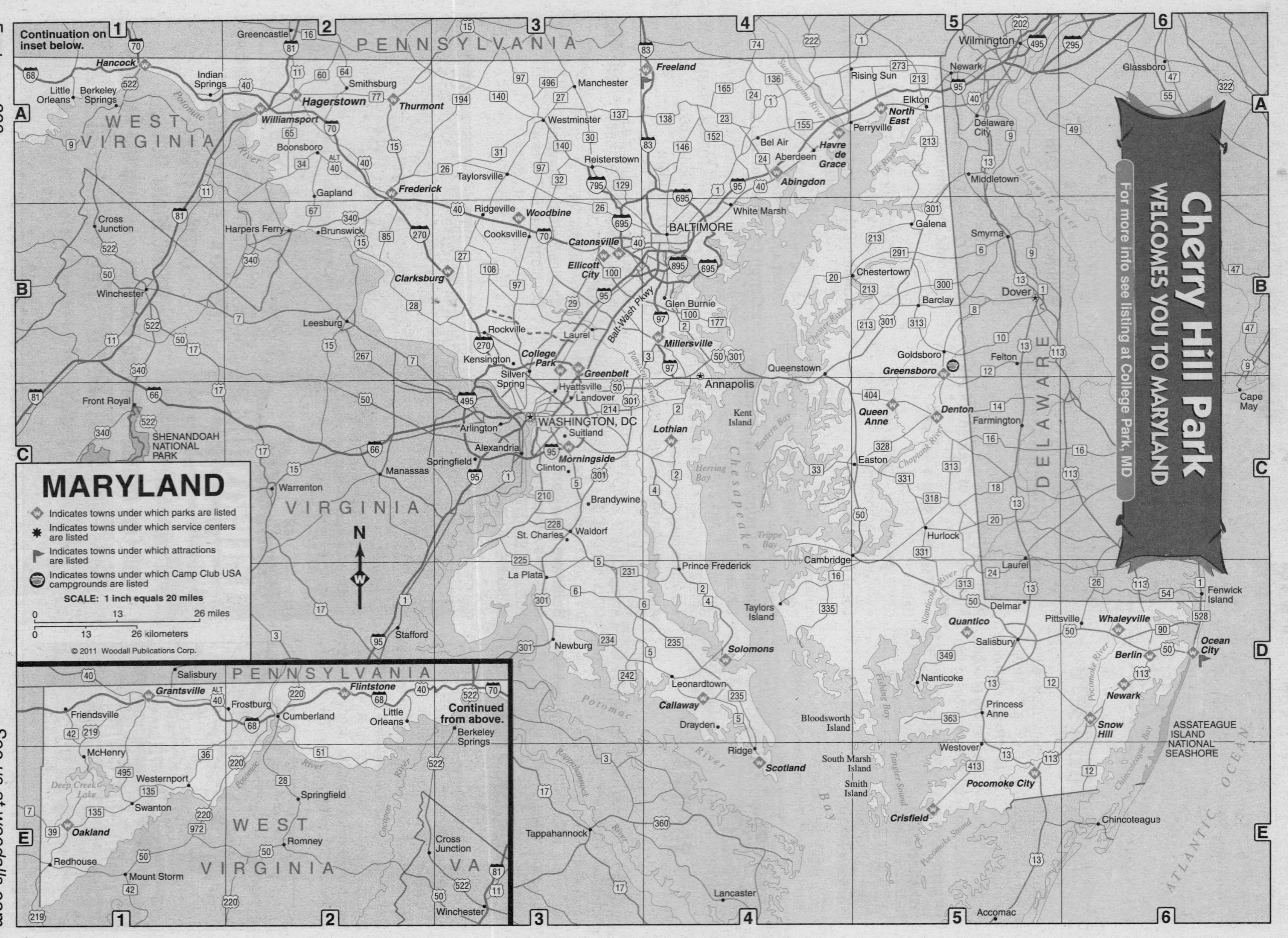
Cherry Hill Park
WELCOMES YOU TO MARYLAND
For more info see listing at College Park, MD
MARYLAND
Indicates towns under which parks are listed
Indicates towns under which service centers are listed
Indicates towns under which attractions are listed
Indicates towns under which Camp Club USA campgrounds are listed
SCALE: 1 inch equals 20 miles
0 13 26 miles
0 13 26 kilometers
© 2011 Woodall Publications Corp.
Continuation on inset below.
Continued from above.
PENNSYLVANIA
DELAWARE
VIRGINIA
WEST VIRGINIA
VA
ATLANTIC OCEAN
Chesapeake Bay
BALTIMORE
WASHINGTON, DC
Annapolis
Dover
Wilmington
Cape May
Ocean City
Hagerstown
Frederick
Cumberland
Salisbury
ASSATEAGUE ISLAND NATIONAL SEASHORE
SHENANDOAH NATIONAL PARK

(301/645-0558 or 800/766-3386)
www.thenationsbackyard.com

CVB of Montgomery, MD, Inc.
111 Rockville Pike, Ste 800
Rockville, MD 20852
(240/777-2060 or 877/789-6904)
www.visitmontgomery.com

Dorchester Co. Tourism
2 Rose Hill Place
Cambridge, MD 21613
(410/228-1000)
www.tourdorchester.org

St. Mary's County Dept. of Econ. & Community Dev.
23115 Leonard Hall Dr.
Leonardtown, MD 20650
(301/475-4200)
www.stmarysmd.com/tourism

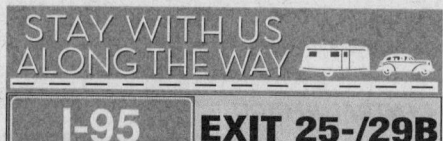

Somerset County Tourism
11440 Ocean Hwy.
Princess Anne, MD 21853
(410/651-2968 or 800/521-9189)
www.visitsomerset.com

Tourism Council of Frederick Co., Inc.
19 E. Church St.
Frederick, MD 21701
(800/999-3613 or 301/600-2888)
www.fredericktourism.org

Garrett Co. Chamber of Commerce, Inc.
15 Visitors Center Drive
McHenry, MD 21541
(301/387-4386)
www.visitdeepcreek.com

Hagerstown/Wash. Co. CVB
Elizabeth Hager Center
16 Public Square
Hagerstown, MD 21740
(301/791-3246)
www.marylandmemories.org

Harford Co. Office of Tourism
220 S. Main St.
Bel Air, MD 21014
(410/638-3327 or 888/544-4695)
www.harfordmd.com

Howard County Tourism, Inc.
P.O. Box 9
Ellicott City, MD 21043
(410/313-1900 or 800/288-8747)
www.visithowardcounty.com

Kent Co. Tourism
400 High St. 2nd Flr.
Chestertown, MD 21620
(410/778-0416)
www.kentcounty.com

Ocean City CVB
4001 Coastal Hwy
Ocean City, MD 21842
(410/723-8600 or 800/626-2326)
www.ococean.com

Prince George's Co. CVB
9200 Basil Court, Suite 101
Largo, MD 20774
(301/925-8300)
www.visitprincegeorges.com

Queen Anne's Co. Office of Tourism
425 Piney Narrows Rd.
Chester, MD 21619
(410/604-2100)
www.discoverqueenannes.com

Talbot Co. Office of Tourism
11 South Harrison Street
Easton, MD 21601
(410/770-8000)
www.tourtalbot.org

Wicomico County CVB
8480 Ocean Highway
Delmar, MD 21875
(410/548-4914 or 800/332-TOUR)
www.wicomicotourism.org

Worcester County Tourism
104 West Market Street
Snow Hill, MD 21863
(410/632-3110 or 800/852-0335)

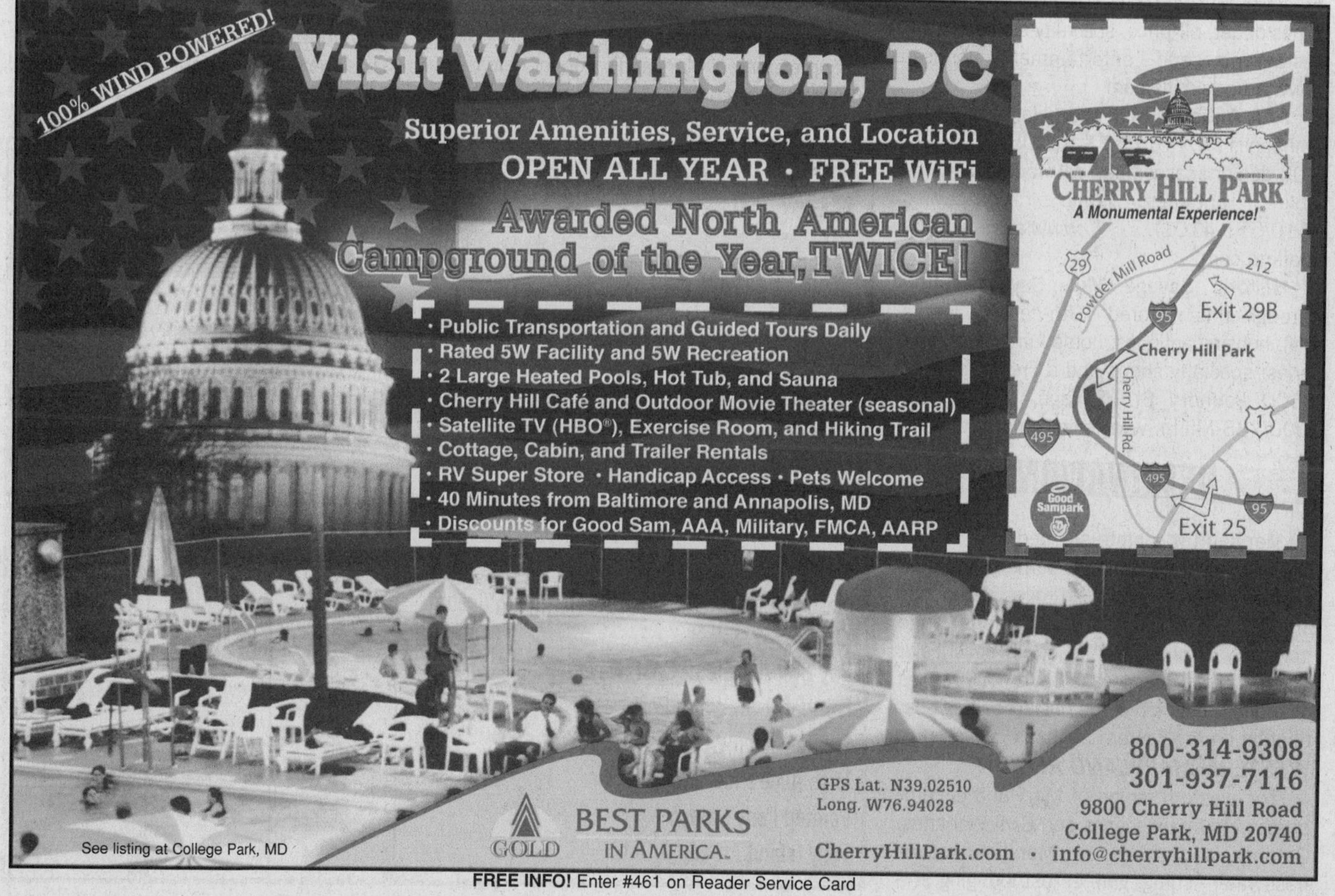

FREE INFO! Enter #461 on Reader Service Card

www.visitworcester.org

RECREATIONAL INFO

Bicycling: DNR Cycling Trail Maps: (800/830-3974) www.dnr.state.md.us/outdoors/biking.html; Maryland Bicycle Map: (410/545-5656)

Birding: Maryland Ornithological Society (800/823-0050) www.mdbirds.org

Fall Foliage Hotline: (800/532-8371)

Fishing: U.S. Fish & Wildlife Service, Maryland Fishery Resources Office: (410/263-2604) http://marylandfisheries.fw.gov; Maryland Saltwater Sportfishermen's Association: (410/255-5535) www.mssa.net

Hunting: Licenses: (800/918-2870) General Information: www.dnr.state.md.us/wildlife/hntgp.asp; Guide to Hunting & Trapping: (410/260-8540) www.dnr.state.md.us/huntersguide/index.asp

SHOPPING

Arts at Canal Place, 16 Howard St., Cumberland. Located in the Canal Place Heritage Area, this cooperative gallery features art and crafts by more than 30 area artists. (301/777-8199)

Arundel Mills, 7000 Arundel Mills Circle, Hanover, MD 21076 (410/540-5100). Combines outlet, off-price, specialty stores, theme restaurants and entertainment venues. www.arundelmills.com

AAA Antiques Mall Inc., Hanover. 2659 Annapolis Rd, Rt 175 E & Rt 295. More than 400 dealer spaces filled with quality, affordable antiques and collectibles (410/551-4101). www.aaaantiquesmallmd.com

Historic Savage Mill, Savage. Stroll through this restored 19th-century textile mill, housing antiques, home furnishings, galleries, specialty shops and a French bakery. 8600 Foundry St., Savage, MD 20763 (800/788-MILL). www.savagemill.com

DESTINATIONS

Maryland is a state steeped in Civil and Revolutionary War history, some of the best seafood in the country, and miles of beaches and grasslands. Tourist destinations range from the 10 miles of white, sandy beaches at Ocean City, to Chesapeake Bay's 4,000 miles of shoreline, which is the busiest sailing destination on the Eastern Seaboard.

WESTERN MARYLAND REGION

The western region of Maryland encompasses mountain scenes and Civil War sites. Getting away to Western Maryland means freshwater fishing, golf, or just lounging at a lakeside cabin and enjoying the majestic view.

Antietam National Battlefield, Sharpsburg. Visit the Civil War battle site of the bloodiest single-day battle in American history. One can explore the museum exhibits in the visitor center or take the self-guided 8 ½-mile auto tour through the battlefield in just a couple of hours. The tour has 11 stops and begins at the Dunker Church.

Boonsborough Museum of History, Boonsboro. Extensive Civil War collection, displays of ceramics, glassware, early lighting, weapons and ancient artifacts. Reconstructions of cabinetmaker's shop and old-time country store.

Cumberland C&O Canal National Historical Park Visitor Center, Cumberland. A 3,200-exhibit center tells the story of the C&O Canal. Exhibits on boat building, coal industry and Cumberland as a transportation crossroads.

Cranesville Subartic Swamp, Oakland. A boardwalk crosses this swamp, left after the Ice Age and now home to unique species of plants and animals.

Crystal Grottoes Caverns, Boonsboro. Take a 30-minute tour through brilliantly lighted chambers.

Deep Creek Lake State Park. Enjoy water sports on a six-square mile man-made lake. Visit the many exhibits at the Discovery Center.

Fort Frederick State Park, Big Pool. Visit the cornerstone of Maryland's frontier defense during the French and Indian War.

Hagerstown. Located in the heart of Washington County, Hagerstown welcomes visitors with a variety of attractions. For rail fans, there's the **Hagerstown Roundhouse Museum**; for historians, there's the **Miller House & Historical Society** and **Hager House & Museum**. Craft and gift shops provide ample shopping opportunities. Other Hagerstown attractions include:

Discovery Station at Hagerstown, Inc. provides a hands-on environment, in association with the Maryland Science Center. Visit the Betty Clopper Early Childhood Gallery, Dinosaur Gallery, Vault Gallery and more.

Western Maryland Scenic Railroad. Baldwin 1916 steam locomotive makes a three-hour round trip from Cumberland to Frostburg. Dinner and murder mystery excursions are available.

CENTRAL REGION

In one day, visitors can see where Francis Scott Key wrote the National Anthem, have awesome seafood, then drive to Annapolis and stroll cobblestone streets.

Annapolis. Once the capital of the U.S., the city continues to reflect its Colonial beginnings. Enjoy theatre, boat cruises, tours, museums, art galleries and festivals.

Highlights of the Annapolis area include the Maryland State House, U.S. Naval Academy, Annapolis Maritime Museum and Watermark Tours, offering tours by guides in Colonial dress.

Baltimore. Maritime atmosphere and historical appeal are evident in this National Anthem city. A promenade around the

Where to Find CCUSA Parks

List City	Park Name	Map Coordinates
GREENSBORO		
	Holiday Park Campground	B-5

BUSINESSES OFFERING

	Things to See & Do	RV Sales	RV Service
FREELAND			
Morris Meadows Historic Preservation Museum	⚑		
OCEAN CITY			
Bay Breeze Cafe at Castaways	⚑		
Frontier Town Water Park	⚑		
Frontier Town Western Theme Park	⚑		
Miss Alice's Ice Cream Parlor	⚑		
Painted Pony Saloon	⚑		
Pony Island Arcade & Gifts	⚑		

water's edge leads past the city's major attractions. Some of the many highlights include **Fort McHenry**, cruise boat rides, **World Trade Center Observation Level & Museum, Star-Spangled Banner Flag House Museum, Baltimore & Ohio Railroad Museum, Harborplace & the Gallery** and the **National Aquarium** in Baltimore. The Walters Art Museum features 39 galleries and many technical upgrades including a 300-stop audio tour. The **Babe Ruth Birthplace & Museum** showcases "The Babe" through photos and film. View Francis Scott Key's original manuscript of The Star Spangled Banner at the **Maryland Historical Society**. At the **Maryland Science Center** you can visit three floors of hands-on exhibits, IMAX® and IMAX® 3D movies, laser theater and more. Or walk through the No. 1-rated **Children's Zoo at the Maryland Zoo** in Baltimore. A new feeding station will enable visitors to feed giraffes by holding out branches from a platform built to the same height as the giraffe's neck.

SOUTHERN MARYLAND

Amid the natural beauty of thick woods, wildflower fields and the magnificent estuary formed by the Potomac and Patuxent rivers, the settlers established a vibrant community that reflected freedom and tolerance, known as Southern Maryland. This area is a tidewater wonderland. Visitors can gaze out at lighthouses, search for fossils, stroll through waterfront villages, hike along woodland, riverside and cypress-swamp trails, or bike across the wide-open spaces.

Historic St. Mary's City. This outdoor history museum is at the site of Maryland's 17th-century capital. Places of interest include: **Chancellor's Point Natural History Area,** with 66 acres of woodland, marsh, gardens, beaches and bluffs; the re-constructed **State House of 1676**; and **Margaret Brent Memorial Garden & Gazebo**. In 2009, St. Mary's City will celebrate its 375th anniversary.

Jefferson Patterson Park & Museum, St. Leonard. Located on **Patuxent River**, this archaeological and environmental preserve features nature trails, wagon tours and archaeological sites.

Piney Point. This town is home to the first lighthouse built along the Potomac River. **The Piney Point Lighthouse** is now the only accessible lighthouse in its original location. The German World War II submarine, **Black Panther**, was sunk in the Potomac River, after U.S. testing was completed. In 1994, the area was designated as Maryland's first historic shipwreck preserve.

Point Lookout State Park, Scotland. Civil War buffs will enjoy exhibits depicting Point Lookout's role in the Civil War. Stop by the **Visitor's Center**, **Civil War Museum**, **Confederate Cemetery** and an earthen fort, all built by Confederate prisoners.

Solomons, Drum Point Lighthouse. Visit the 1883 screwpile cottage-type lighthouse, one of three remaining on the Chesapeake Bay. It's located at the **Calvert Marine Museum**. Explore the history, culture and lighthouses of the Chesapeake Bay and Patuxent River all in one place.

QUICK REFERENCE CHART FOR WOODALL'S FEATURED PARKS

	Green Friendly	RV Lots for Sale	Park Models-Onsite Ownership	Park Membership for Sale	Big Rigs Welcome	Internet Friendly	Pets Welcome
ABINGDON							
Bar Harbor RV Park & Marina						◍	■
COLLEGE PARK							
Cherry Hill Park					▲	◍	■
FLINTSTONE							
Hidden Springs Campground					▲		■
FREELAND							
Morris Meadows Recreation Farm					▲	●	■
GREENSBORO							
Holiday Park Campground	🍃					◍	■
LOTHIAN							
Duncan's Family Campground	🍃				▲	◍	■
MILLERSVILLE							
Capitol KOA/Washington D.C. Northeast						◍	■
OCEAN CITY							
Castaways RV Resort & Campground					▲	◍	■
Frontier Town Campground					▲	◍	■
QUANTICO							
Sandy Hill Family Camp							■
WHALEYVILLE							
Fort Whaley Campground					▲	◍	■
WILLIAMSPORT							
Yogi Bear's Jellystone Park Camp-Resort-Williamsport-Hagerstown	🍃				▲	◍	■
WOODBINE							
Ramblin' Pines Family Campground & RV Park					▲	◍	■

Green Friendly 🍃; RV Lots for Sale ✖; Park Models/Onsite Onwership ✱; Park Memberships for Sale ✔; Big Rigs Welcome ▲; Internet Friendly ●; Internet Friendly-WiFi ◍; Pets Welcome ■

CAPITAL REGION

Here in the Capital Region, like the rest of Maryland, history is everywhere. Walk where Civil War troops clashed in "The Battle That Saved Washington", see attractions that feature the author of the National Anthem, the founder of the American Red Cross, or the first U.S. born saint.

Andrews Air Force Base, Camp Springs. Toured by appointment only, the base is home to individual units of the Air Force, Navy and Marine Corps, including the 89th Military Airlift Wing, which provides air transportation for the president and other high-ranking U.S. officials.

Audubon Naturalist Society, Chevy Chase. Forty-acre nature preserve and headquarters of the organization founded in 1897.

Emmitsburg. Site of two national shrines. **National Shrine Grotto of Lourdes** is the oldest replica of the Grotto of Lourdes in the western hemisphere. **National Shrine of St. Elizabeth Ann Seton** honoring the first native-born American saint, has a museum and video, gorgeous Basilica with saint's tomb and restored period buildings.

Frederick. Guides conduct walking tours of the outstanding historic district. Fifty blocks of historic homes and mansions including federal-period townhouses are part of the tour. Or take a driving tour of the many covered bridges (maps available from Tourism Council of Frederick County). Also in Frederick: **Mount Olivet Cemetery**, the final resting place of Francis Scott Key, the **Barbara Fritchie House and Museum** and the **National Museum of Civil War Medicine**. A 1950's dairy barn is the unusual home of the **Monocacy National Battlefield** visitor center. The facility has a view of much of the battlefield, bookstore, and several hands-on experiences for visitors.

Montpelier Mansion, Laurel. One of the finest examples of 18th-century Georgian architecture in Maryland. The grounds boast a reproduction kitchen and an original 18th-century summer house, one of only two surviving in the country.

NASA/Goddard Space Flight Center/Museum, Greenbelt. Ultra-modern, interactive Earth Gallery provides information about our knowledge of Earth's systems.

Six Flags America, Largo, south of Baltimore. Featuring more than 50 rides, attractions and shows, this theme park is also home to a giant wave pool and 13 water flumes.

EASTERN SHORE

The Maryland Eastern Shore, a peninsula extending hundreds of miles between the Chesapeake Bay and the Atlantic Ocean, offers endless recreational opportunities and is a popular summer vacation destination. Visitors flock to the Eastern Shore to explore the historic towns, beaches and beautiful natural areas and enjoy activities such as boating, swimming, fishing, bird watching, biking and golf. The communities along the Eastern Shore host wonderful annual events including waterfront festivals, seafood festivals, boating regattas and races, fishing tournaments, boat shows, museum events, arts and crafts shows, and more.

Maryland's Atlantic coastline stretches just 31 miles, but when you factor in all of the river and bay shores, the total mileage of shoreline climbs to more than 3,000 miles. In this region, blue crabs are harvested on the shore, and are often the center of traditional get-togethers.

Assateague State & National Seashore Parks. A barrier island off the Eastern Shore, Assateague is a Mecca for campers, swimmers, surfers, bird watchers, fishermen, canoeists and beachcombers. A special feature of the island is the unique, shaggy-haired, wild ponies that roam freely over the area

Cambridge. The main attraction here is the Blackwater National Wildlife Refuge, a 27,000-acre resting and feeding area for migrating waterfowl and home to 250 species of birds, 35 species of reptiles and amphibians, 165 species of threatened and endangered plants, and numerous mammals. Richardson Maritime Museum & Boatworks displays ship models and boatbuilding artifacts.

Ocean City. Known as the white marlin capital of the world, this seashore has 10 miles of white sand beaches along the Atlantic Ocean filled with first-class restaurants, many sightseeing attractions and excellent fishing in the ocean and bay. **Ocean City Pier Rides & Amusements** offers rides, games and food along the three-mile boardwalk.

ANNUAL EVENTS

JANUARY

Baltimore Bay Boat Show, Baltimore City; Bethesda Art Walk, Bethesda; Historic Annapolis, Antique Show.

FEBRUARY

Seaside Boat Show, Ocean City; Hunt Valley Antiques Show, Timonium; Maryland Recreational Vehicle Show, Timonium.

MARCH

Maple Sugarin' Festival, Westminster; All Militaria Show, Pikesville; Eagle Festival, Cambridge; Maryland Day Celebration, Annapolis/Baltimore City/St. Mary's City; Garrett Lakes Arts Festival, McHenry.

APRIL

Bay Bridge Boat Show, Stevensville; Cavalcade of Trolleys, Colesville; Maryland International Kite Festival, Ocean City; Pork in the Park, Salisbury; Shad Festival, Vienna; Sugarloaf Craft Festival, Gaithersburg/Timonium; Milltown Quilters Quilt Show; Pork in the Park, Eastern Shore.

MAY

Harlem Renaissance Festival, Landover; Chesapeake Bay Blues Festival, Annapolis; Tea Party Festival, Chestertown; Preakness, Baltimore City; Blacksmith Days, Westminster; Blue Angels Demonstration, Annapolis; Maryland Brewer's Spring Beer Fest, Frederick; Solomons Maritime Festival, Solomons; Garlic Mustard Challenge, Elkridge and Relay; Preakness Celebration, Baltimore.

JUNE

Cypress Festival, Pocomoke; Delmarva Chicken Festival, Salisbury; Strawberry Festival, Sandy Spring/Sykesville; Blues Festival, Havre de Grace; Catfish Derby, Thurmont; Pirates of the Chesapeake, Annapolis; Blue and Gray Days, Scotland; Antique and Classic Boat Festival, St. Michaels.

JULY

Lawnmower Races, Havre de Grace; Sharkfest, Solomons; Potomac Jazz and Seafood Festival, Colon's Point; Reggae Wine Festival, Mt. Airy; Surf and Turf Festival, Westminster; Old-Fashioned Corn Roast Festival, Union Mills; Artscape, Baltimore.

AUGUST

Seafood Festival, Havre de Grace; Peach Festival, Westminster; Bayou Wine Festival, Mt. Airy; State Fair, Timonium; Beach Bayfest, North Beach; Renaissance Festival, Annapolis; Augustoberfest, Hagerstown; Maryland State Fair, Timonium.

SEPTEMBER

Maryland Seafood Festival, Annapolis; Maryland Wine Festival, Westminster; Russian Festival, Baltimore; Duck Fair, Havre de Grace; Shaker Forest Festival, Gaithersburg; RV Show, Timonium; Baltimore Summer Antiques Fair, Baltimore City.

OCTOBER

Multi-Cultural Fall Festival, Columbia; Apple Festival, Darlington; Powerboat Show, Annapolis; Autumn Glory Festival, Oakland; Fiddle Contest, Oakland; Chocolate Festival, Baltimore; Fell's Point Fun Festival, Baltimore.

NOVEMBER

Lighthouse Open House, Scotland; Oysterfest, St. Michaels; Amish Quilt Auction, Mechanicsville.

DECEMBER

Christmas on the Beach, North Beach; Holiday Trolleyfest, Colesville; Festival of Wreaths, Westminister; Festival of Trees, Hagerstown; Museums By Candlelight, Frederick; First Night Talbot, Easton.

Maryland

All privately owned campgrounds personally inspected by
WOODALL'S
Representatives
Dave and Jaynie Carlson

ABINGDON—A-4

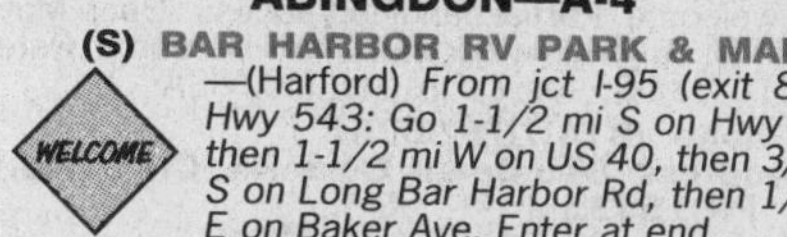

(S) **BAR HARBOR RV PARK & MARINA** —(Harford) *From jct I-95 (exit 80) & Hwy 543: Go 1-1/2 mi S on Hwy 543, then 1-1/2 mi W on US 40, then 3/4 mi S on Long Bar Harbor Rd, then 1/2 mi E on Baker Ave. Enter at end.*

WE CATER TO WATER-LOVERS!
In addition to our waterfront sites, we offer waterfront and floating house rentals with screened porches, gorgeous views and all amenities.

◇◇◇◇FACILITIES: 93 sites, typical site width 30 ft, 93 full hkups, (30/50 amps), some extd stay

ABINGDON—Continued
BAR HARBOR RV PARK & MARINA—Continued

sites, 7 pull-thrus, cable TV, WiFi Instant Internet at site, phone/cable on-site Internet (needs activ), WiFi Internet central location, family camping, RV's/park model rentals, dump, non-guest dump $, laundry, ltd groc, RV supplies, LP gas by weight/by meter, ice, picnic tables, patios, fire rings, grills, wood, controlled access.

◇◇◇◇RECREATION: rec hall, rec room/area, coin games, swim pool, boating, canoeing, kayaking, ramp, dock, 2 kayak/pedal boat rentals, saltwater/river fishing, fishing supplies, golf nearby, playground.

Pets welcome. No tents. Open all yr. Facilities fully operational Mar 1 - Dec 31. Dec 31 thru Mar 1, self-contained units only. Rate in 2010 $47-50 for 2 persons. MC/VISA. ATM. Member ARVC, MAC.

Phone: (800)351-2267
Address: 4228 Birch Ave, Abingdon, MD 21009
Lat/Lon: 39.46075/-76.24387
Web: barharborrvpark.com

SEE AD THIS PAGE

ANNAPOLIS—B-4

See listings at Gambrills, Glen Burnie, Millersville & Lothian.

BALTIMORE—B-4

See listings at Abingdon, College Park, Freeland, Gambrills, Glen Burnie, Millersville & Woodbine.

IF YOU THINK WOODALL RATINGS MEAN GOOD, BETTER, BEST....
THINK AGAIN
SEE THE "HOW TO USE" PAGES IN THE FRONT OF THIS DIRECTORY FOR AN EXPLANATION OF OUR RATING SYSTEM

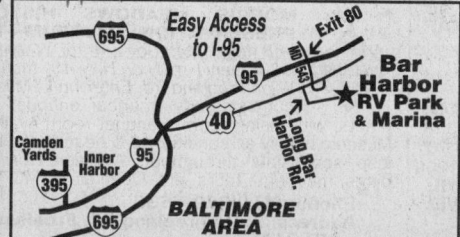

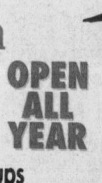

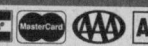

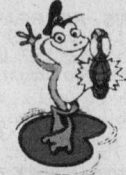

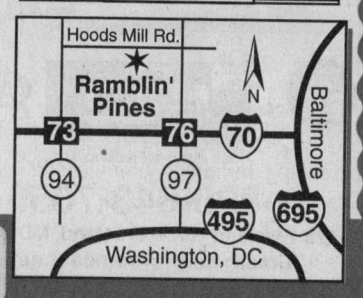

BERLIN—D-6

(SE) ASSATEAGUE ISLAND NATIONAL SEASHORE (Bayside Campground)—(Worcester) *From jct Hwy 376 & Hwy 611: Go 4 mi SE on Hwy 611, then after bridge, 2 mi S on Bayberry Dr.* FACILITIES: 49 sites, 49 no hkups, 22 pull-thrus, family camping, tenting, dump. RECREATION: saltwater swim, boating, no motors, canoeing, saltwater fishing. Open all yr. Phone: (410)641-3030.

(SE) ASSATEGUE ISLAND NATIONAL SEASHORE (Oceanside Campground)—(Worcester) *From jct Hwy 376 & Hwy 611: Go 4 mi SE on Hwy 611, then after crossing bridge continue S on Bayberry Dr.* FACILITIES: 104 sites, 104 no hkups, family camping, tenting, dump. RECREATION: saltwater swim, boating, no motors, canoeing, saltwater fishing. Partial handicap access. Open all yr. Facilities fully operational May 15 - Oct 1. Phone: (410)641-3030.

CALLAWAY—D-4

(S) Take-It-Easy Campground—(St. Mary's) *From jct Rt 5 & Rt 249: Go 3/4 mi S on Rt 249. Enter on L.* ◊◊◊FACILITIES: 242 sites, 196 full hkups, 46 W&E, (15/20/30/50 amps), 5 pull-thrus, family camping, tenting, dump, laundry. ◊◊◊RECREATION: swim pool, pond fishing, playground. Pets welcome. Open all yr. Big rigs welcome. Rate in 2010 $40-50 for 2 persons. Member ARVC, MAC. Phone: (877)994-0494.

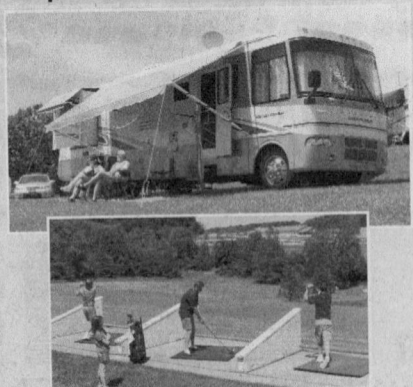

CATONSVILLE—B-3

(S) PATAPSCO VALLEY SP (Hilton Area)—(Baltimore) *From jct I-695 (exit 13) & Hwy 144 (Frederick Rd): Go 3/4 mi W on Hwy 144, then 2 mi S on Hilton Ave.* FACILITIES: 14 sites, 29 ft max RV length, 14 no hkups, family camping, tenting. RECREATION: canoeing, river/stream fishing, playground. No pets. Partial handicap access. Open Mar - Oct. Phone: (410)461-5005.

CLARKSBURG—B-3

(N) LITTLE BENNETT REGIONAL PARK (Montgomery County Park)—(Montgomery) *From jct I-270 (exit 18) & Hwy 121: Go 1/2 mi NE on Hwy 121, then 1/2 mi N on Hwy 355. Follow signs. Enter on R.* FACILITIES: 91 sites, typical site width 60 ft, 25 E, (20/30 amps), 66 no hkups, family camping, tenting, dump, laundry, ltd groc. RECREATION: playground. Pets welcome. Partial handicap access. Open Apr 1 - Oct 31. Phone: (301)528-3430.

COLLEGE PARK—B-3

(N) CHERRY HILL PARK—(Prince George's) *N'bound from jct I-95 (exit 25) & US 1: Go 175 yds S on US 1, then 1 mi W on Cherry Hill Rd. Enter on left. S'bound from jct I-95 (exit 29B) & Hwy 212 (Powder Mill Rd): Go 1 mi W on Powder Mill Rd, then 1 mi S on Cherry Hill Rd. Enter on R.*

WELCOME

◊◊◊◊◊FACILITIES: 400 sites, typical site width 30 ft, 350 full hkups, 50 E, (30/50 amps), 33 pull-thrus, cable TV, WiFi Instant Internet at site, WiFi Internet central location, family camping, tenting, RV's/park model rentals, cabins, RV storage, dump, non-guest dump $, laundry, ltd groc, RV supplies, LP gas by weight/by meter, ice, picnic tables, fire rings, wood, controlled access.

◊◊◊◊◊RECREATION: rec hall, rec room/area, pavilion, equipped pavilion, coin games, 2 swim pools, wading pool, hot tub, pond fishing, mini-golf, ($), golf nearby, bsktball, playground, activities, hiking trails, local tours.

Pets welcome. Partial handicap access. Open all yr. Big rigs welcome. Clubs welcome. Rate in 2010 $58-68 for 2 persons. MC/VISA/DISC/AMEX/Debit. ATM. Member ARVC, MAC. FCRV discount. FMCA discount.

Text 81825 to (440)725-8687 to see our Visual Tour.

Phone: (800)314-9308
Address: 9800 Cherry Hill Rd, College Park, MD 20740
Lat/Lon: 39.02515/-76.94049
Email: info@cherryhillpark.com
Web: www.cherryhillpark.com

SEE AD TRAVEL SECTION PAGE 329 AND AD DC TRAVEL SECTION PAGE 59 AND AD MAP PAGE 328

COLUMBIA—B-3

KOA-WILLIAMSBURG—*From Columbia, MD: Go 175 mi S on I-95/I-64, then at I-64 (exit 234B) go 1 mi NE on Hwy 199 (becomes Newman Rd).*

WELCOME

SEE PRIMARY LISTING AT WILLIAMSBURG, VA AND AD VA TRAVEL SECTION PAGE 762

CRISFIELD—E-5

(S) JANES ISLAND SP—(Somerset) *From business center: Go 1-1/2 mi NE on CR-358.* FACILITIES: 104 sites, 29 ft max RV length, 49 E, (30 amps), 55 no hkups, 6 pull-thrus, family camping, tenting, dump, laundry, ltd groc. RECREATION: saltwater swim, boating, canoeing, ramp, dock, saltwater/river fishing, playground. Pets welcome. Partial handicap access. Open Apr 25 - Oct 27. Phone: (410)968-1565.

DENTON—C-5

(E) MARTINAK SP—(Caroline) *From business center: Go 1 mi S on Hwy 404, then 3/4 mi on Deep Shore Rd. Enter on L.* FACILITIES: 63 sites, 30 ft max RV length, 30 E, 33 no hkups, family camping, tenting, dump. RECREATION: boating, canoeing, ramp, dock, saltwater/river fishing, playground. Pets welcome. Partial handicap access. Open Mar 21 - Oct 27. Phone: (410)820-1668.

Maryland State Tree: White Oak

ELLICOTT CITY—B-3

(W) PATAPSCO VALLEY SP (Hollofield Area)—(Howard) *From jct I-695W (exit 15) & US 40: Go 3 mi W on US 40.* FACILITIES: 73 sites, 29 ft max RV length, 30 E, 43 no hkups, 5 pull-thrus, family camping, tenting, dump, groceries. RECREATION: canoeing, river fishing, playground. Open Mar - Oct. Phone: (410)461-5005.

FLINTSTONE—D-2

(N) HIDDEN SPRINGS CAMPGROUND—(Allegheny) *From I-68 (exit 50): Go 3-1/2 mi N on Pleasant Valley Rd. (Turn right at Rocky Gap State Park sign). Park physically located 1-1/2 mi inside Pennsylvania (road name changes to Beans Cove Rd). Enter on L.*

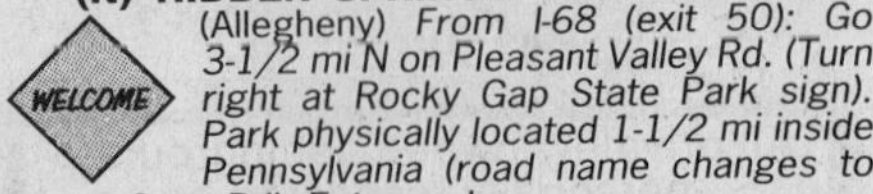

◊◊◊FACILITIES: 127 sites, typical site width 35 ft, 75 full hkups, 17 W&E, (20/30/50 amps), 35 no hkups, some extd stay sites, 8 pull-thrus, family camping, tenting, cabins, dump, non-guest dump $, laundry, groceries, LP gas by weight/by meter, ice, picnic tables, fire rings, wood, controlled access.

◊◊◊RECREATION: rec room/area, pavilion, coin games, swim pool, pond fishing, mini-golf, ($), golf nearby, bsktball, playground, shuffleboard court shuffleboard court, horseshoes, v-ball. Rec open to public.

Pets welcome. Partial handicap access. Open May 1 - Oct 31. Big rigs welcome. Clubs welcome. Rate in 2010 $33-35 for 4 persons. MC/VISA.

Phone: (814)767-9676
Address: 815 Beans Cove Rd, Clearville, PA 15535
Lat/Lon: 39.74157/-78.62291
Web: www.hiddenspringscampground.com

SEE AD THIS PAGE

(E) ROCKY GAP SP—(Allegany) *From jct I-68 (exit 50) & US 40: Go 1 block N on Pleasant Valley Rd. Enter on L.* FACILITIES: 278 sites, 29 ft max RV length, 30 E, 248 no hkups, 35 pull-thrus, family camping, tenting, dump, laundry, groceries. RECREATION: lake swim, boating, electric motors only, canoeing, ramp, dock, lake fishing, playground. Pets welcome. Open all yr. Facilities fully operational Apr - Dec. Phone: (301)722-1480.

FREDERICK—A-2

(NW) GAMBRILL SP—(Frederick) *From town: Go 6 mi W on I-70.* FACILITIES: 34 sites, 34 no hkups, 2 pull-thrus, family camping, tenting, dump. RECREATION: playground. Pets welcome. Partial handicap access. Open Apr - Oct. Phone: (301)271-7574.

FREELAND—A-4

(W) MORRIS MEADOWS HISTORIC PRESERVATION MUSEUM—*From I-83 (exit 36): Go 1/4 mi W on Hwy 439, then 1 mi N on Hwy 45, then 3 mi W on Freeland Rd. Enter on L.* Museum contains early American antiques & artifacts, with dining room. Banquet room available. Museum is fully air-conditioned & heated and handicap accessible throughout. Available for weddings, meetings, tours, etc. Open all yr. MC/VISA.

Phone: (410)329-6636
Address: 1523 Freeland Rd, Freeland, MD 21053
Lat/Lon: 39.69507/-76.69897
Email: mmrf@comcast.net
Web: www.morrismeadows.us

SEE AD THIS PAGE

(W) MORRIS MEADOWS RECREATION FARM—(Baltimore) *From I-83 (exit 36): Go 1/4 mi W on Hwy 439, then 1 mi N on Hwy 45, then 3 mi W on Freeland Rd. Enter on L.*

WELCOME

◊◊◊◊◊FACILITIES: 300 sites, typical site width 50 ft, 300 full hkups, (20/30/50 amps), many extd stay sites, 75 pull-thrus, cable TV, phone/cable on-site Internet (needs activ), phone Internet central location, family camping, tenting, cabins, RV storage, laundry, groceries, RV supplies, LP gas by weight/by meter, ice, picnic tables, patios, fire rings, wood, controlled access.

◊◊◊◊◊RECREATION: rec hall, rec room/area, pavilion, coin games, swim pool, pond fishing, mini-golf, ($), bsktball, playground, shuffleboard court 4 shuffleboard courts, activities, tennis, horseshoes, sports field, hiking trails, v-ball.

Pets welcome. Partial handicap access. Open all yr. Big rigs welcome. Clubs welcome. Rate in 2010 $41-56 for 2 persons. MC/VISA. Member ARVC, MAC. FCRV discount. FMCA discount.

MORRIS MEADOWS RECREATION FARM—Continued on next page

"The Star-Spangled Banner" was written during the War of 1812 while the British attacked Baltimore's Fort McHenry.

FREELAND—Continued
MORRIS MEADOWS RECREATION FARM—Continued

Phone: (800)643-7056
Address: 1523 Freeland Rd, Freeland, MD 21053
Lat/Lon: 39.69507/-76.69897
Email: mmrf@comcast.net
Web: www.morrismeadows.us

SEE AD BALTIMORE PAGE 334

GRANTSVILLE—D-1

(S) BIG RUN SP—(Garrett) *From I-68 (exit 22): Go S on Chestnut Ridge Rd to New Germany Rd to Big Run Rd.* FACILITIES: 30 sites, 29 ft max RV length, 30 no hkups, family camping, tenting. RECREATION: boating, electric motors only, canoeing, ramp, lake/stream fishing, playground. Partial handicap access. Open all yr. Phone: (301)895-5453.

(S) NEW GERMANY SP—(Garrett) *From I-68 (exit 22): Go S on Chestnut Ridge Rd to New Germany Rd.* FACILITIES: 39 sites, 29 ft max RV length, 39 no hkups, family camping, tenting, dump, ltd groc. RECREATION: lake swim, boating, no motors, canoeing, ramp, dock, lake fishing, playground. Pets welcome. Partial handicap access. Open Apr - Oct. Phone: (301)895-5453.

GREENBELT—B-3

(SE) GREENBELT NP (Greenbelt Campground)—(Prince George's) *From jct I-495 (exit 23) & Kenilworth Ave: Go S on Kenilworth Ave, then E on Greenbelt Rd.* FACILITIES: 174 sites, 35 ft max RV length, 174 no hkups, family camping, tenting, dump. RECREATION: playground. Pets welcome. Open all yr. Phone: (301)344-3948.

GREENSBORO—B-5

(E) HOLIDAY PARK CAMPGROUND—(Caroline) *From jct Hwy 313 & Hwy 314: Go 1/4 mi E on Hwy 314, then 500 ft. N on Wothers Rd, then 3/4 mi E on Boyce Mill Rd, then 2 mi N on Drapers Mill Rd. Enter on L.*

◊◊◊FACILITIES: 200 sites, typical site width 40 ft, 200 W&E, (20/30/50 amps), 50 amps ($), some extd stay sites, 30 pull-thrus, cable TV, WiFi Internet central location, family camping, tenting, RV's/park model rentals, RV storage, dump, portable dump, laundry, groceries, RV supplies, LP gas by meter, ice, picnic tables, fire rings, grills, wood, controlled access.

◊◊◊◊RECREATION: rec hall, rec room/area, pavilion, equipped pavilion, coin games, swim pool, boating, no motors, canoeing, kayaking, river fishing, mini-golf, ($), golf nearby, bsktball, playground, shuffleboard court 2 shuffleboard courts, activities (wkends), tennis, horseshoes, sports field, hiking trails, v-ball.

Pets welcome, breed restrict. Partial handicap access. Open Apr 1 - Nov 15. Facilities fully operational Memorial Day - Labor Day. Self-contained units only Mar 15 - Apr 1 & Nov 15 - Dec 1. Clubs welcome. Green Friendly. Rate in 2010 $38-50 for 2 persons. MC/VISA. Member ARVC, MAC. FCRV discount. FMCA discount. CCUSA 50% Discount. CCUSA reservations Accepted, CCUSA max stay 1 day, Cash only for CCUSA disc., CCUSA disc. not avail F,Sa. Not available any holiday weekends.

Phone: (410)482-6797
Address: 14620 Drapers Mill Rd, Greensboro, MD 21639
Lat/Lon: 39.00793/-75.76472
Email: holiday@dmv.com
Web: www.holidaypark.com

SEE AD THIS PAGE

HAGERSTOWN—A-2

(W) FORT FREDERICK SP—(Washington) *From town: Go 18 mi W on I-70 to exit 12, then 1 mi S on Hwy 56.* FACILITIES: 29 sites, 29 ft max RV length, 29 no hkups, family camping, tenting, ltd groc. RECREATION: boating, electric motors only, canoeing, ramp, lake fishing, playground. No pets. Partial handicap access. Open May - Oct. Phone: (301)842-2155.

(SE) GREENBRIER SP—(Washington) *From town: Go 8 mi E on US 40.* FACILITIES: 165 sites, 29 ft max RV length, 40 E, 125 no hkups, 4 pull-thrus, family camping, tenting, dump, groceries. RECREATION: lake swim, boating, electric motors only, canoeing, ramp, dock, lake fishing, playground. Pets welcome. Partial handicap access. Open Apr - Oct. Phone: (301)791-4767.

HANCOCK—A-1

(S) Happy Hills Campground—(Washington) *From jct I-70 (exit 1-B) & Hwy 522: Go 1/4 mi S on Hwy 522, then 2-1/2 mi W on Hwy 144, then 2-1/2 mi S on Willow Rd, then 1/4 mi S on Seavolt Rd. Enter on L.* ◊◊◊FACILITIES: 205 sites, typical site width 40 ft, 170 full hkups, 15 W&E, (20/30/50 amps), 20 no hkups, 37 pull-thrus, family camping, tenting, dump, laundry, groceries. ◊◊◊RECREATION: swim pool, playground. Pets welcome. Partial handicap access. Open all yr. Rate in 2010 $35-38 for 2 persons. Phone: (301)678-7760.

The capital of Maryland is Annapolis.

HAVRE DE GRACE—A-4

(W) SUSQUEHANNA SP—(Harford) *From town: Go 3 mi N on Hwy-155.* FACILITIES: 69 sites, 29 ft max RV length, 6 E, 63 no hkups, family camping, tenting. RECREATION: boating, canoeing, ramp, saltwater/river/pond fishing, playground. Pets welcome. Open May - Sep 30. Phone: (410)557-7794.

LOTHIAN—C-4

(W) DUNCAN'S FAMILY CAMPGROUND—(Anne Arundel) *From jct US 301 & Hwy 4: Go 2 mi SE on Hwy 4, then 1/2 mi E on Hwy 408, then 1/4 mi N on Sands Rd. Enter on R.*

WE CATER TO WASHINGTON DC TOURISTS!
Affordable family camping while touring DC! Kids camp FREE! We love military families - 15% Discount, FREE WIFI & Cable TV. Van to Metro Station & DC tours Available. Big Rig Friendly. Sparkling pool. Visit DC Hassle Free!

◊◊◊FACILITIES: 270 sites, typical site width 30 ft, 152 full hkups, 70 W&E, (20/30/50 amps), 48 no hkups, some extd stay sites, 152 pull-thrus, cable TV, WiFi Instant Internet at site, family camping, tenting, RV's/park model rentals, cabins, dump, non-guest dump $, laundry, groceries, RV supplies, LP gas by weight/by meter, ice, picnic tables, fire rings, wood.

◊◊◊◊RECREATION: rec room/area, pavilion, swim pool, wading pool, mini-golf, ($), golf nearby, bsktball, playground, shuffleboard court shuffleboard court, activities (wkends), horseshoes, hiking trails, v-ball, local tours.

Pets welcome. Open all yr. Activities fully operational Memorial Day thru Labor Day. Big rigs welcome. Clubs welcome. Green Friendly. Rate in 2010 $36.75-56.75 for 2 persons. MC/VISA/DISC. Member ARVC, MAC. FMCA discount.

Phone: (800)222-2086
Address: 5381 Sands Rd, Lothian, MD 20711
Lat/Lon: 38.81467/-76.69167
Email: go2duncans@aol.com
Web: www.duncansfamilycampground.com

SEE AD DC TRAVEL SECTION PAGE 58

MILLERSVILLE—B-4

(S) CAPITOL KOA/WASHINGTON D.C. NORTHEAST—(Anne Arundel) *N'bound from jct Hwy 32/I-97/Hwy 3: Go 1/2 mi N on Veterans Hwy, then follow blue campground signs. S'bound from jct I-695 & I-97 (exit 4): Go 8-1/2 mi S on I-97 (exit 10A), then S on Veterans Hwy & follow blue campground signs. Enter on R.*

◊◊◊◊FACILITIES: 156 sites, typical site width 40 ft, 68 full hkups, 56 W&E, (20/30/50 amps), 32 no hkups, 69 pull-thrus, WiFi Instant Internet at site, family camping, tenting, cabins, RV storage, dump, laundry, groceries, RV supplies, LP gas by meter, ice, picnic tables, fire rings, grills, wood.

◊◊◊RECREATION: equipped pavilion, swim pool, golf nearby, bsktball, playground, activities, horseshoes, sports field, hiking trails, v-ball, local tours.

Pets welcome, breed restrict. Partial handicap access. Open Mar 1 - Nov 15. Clubs welcome. Rate in 2010 $57-65 for 2 persons. MC/VISA/DISC. Member ARVC, MAC. KOA discount.

Phone: (800)562-0248
Address: 768 Cecil Ave North, Millersville, MD 21108
Lat/Lon: 39.06986/-76.64315
Email: capitolkoacampground@att.net
Web: www.capitolkoa.com

SEE AD TRAVEL SECTION PAGE 329 AND AD DC TRAVEL SECTION PAGE 60

MORNINGSIDE—C-3

(S) MILITARY PARK (FAMCAMP-Andrews AFB)—(Prince George's) *From I-95/495 (exit 11): Go S to Andrews AFB. On base (Delivery gate).* FACILITIES: 47 sites, 30 full hkups, 14 E, (50 amps), 3 no hkups, dump, laundry. RECREATION: playground. No tents. Open all yr. Big rigs welcome. Phone: (301) 981-4109.

NEWARK—D-6

(N) Island Resort Campground—(Worcester) *From jct US 50 & US 113: Go 6-1/4 mi SW on US 113, then 1 mi SE on Cropper Island Rd. Enter on L.* ◊◊◊◊FACILITIES: 93 sites, typical site width 49 ft, 93 full hkups, (20/30/50 amps), 10 pull-thrus, family camping, laundry, ltd groc. ◊◊◊RECREATION: swim pool, boating, canoeing, pond fishing, playground. Pets welcome. Partial handicap access. No tents. Open Apr 1 - Oct 31. Big rigs welcome. Rate in 2010 $35-55 per family. Member ARVC, MAC. Phone: (410)641-9838.

NORTH EAST—A-5

(S) ELK NECK SP—(Cecil) *From business center: Go 9 mi S on Hwy-272.* FACILITIES: 268 sites, 29 ft max RV length, 31 full hkups, 237 no hkups, family camping, tenting, dump, groceries. RECREATION: river swim, boating, canoeing, ramp, dock, saltwater/river fishing, playground. Open all yr. Facilities fully operational Mar - Oct. Phone: (410)287-5333.

OAKLAND—E-1

(N) DEEP CREEK LAKE SP—(Garrett) *From town: Go 10 mi N on US-219, then 2 mi NE on Glendale Bridge Rd.* FACILITIES: 112 sites, 29 ft max RV length, 26 E, 86 no hkups, family camping, tenting, dump. RECREATION: lake swim, boating, canoeing, ramp, dock, lake fishing, playground. Pets welcome. Partial handicap access. Open Apr - Sep. Phone: (301)387-4111.

OCEAN CITY—D-6

(E) BAY BREEZE CAFE AT CASTAWAYS—*From jct US 50 & Hwy 611: Go 5 mi S on Hwy 611, then 1-1/2 mi E on Eagles Nest Rd. Enter at end.* Open daily 8am - 10pm Memorial Day to Labor Day. Featuring Breakfast, Lunch & Dinner. Sunday Buffet 8am - 11am. Catering & Delivery available. Open Apr 1 - Oct 31. MC/VISA/DISC/Debit.

Phone: (410)213-2030
Address: 12652 Eagles Nest Rd, Berlin, MD 21811
Lat/Lon: 38.30441/-75.11943

SEE AD PAGE 337

(E) CASTAWAYS RV RESORT & CAMPGROUND—(Worcestor) *From jct US 50 & Hwy 611: Go 5 mi S on Hwy 611, then 1-1/2 mi E on Eagles Nest Rd. Enter at end.*

CLOSEST CAMPGROUND TO OCEAN CITY, MD!
Simply Remarkable Camping! On the shores of beautiful Sinepuxent Bay overlooking storied Assateague Island. Spend a day on our private bay front beach or ride the free shuttle into Ocean City. Luxury camping at nature's doorstep!

◊◊◊◊◊FACILITIES: 354 sites, typical site width 40 ft, 347 full hkups, 7 W&E, (20/30/50 amps), cable TV, WiFi Instant Internet at site, family camping, tenting, RV's/park model rentals, cabins, RV storage, laundry, groceries, RV supplies, LP gas by weight/by meter, ice, picnic tables, fire rings, grills, wood, controlled access.

◊◊◊◊◊RECREATION: rec hall, rec room/area, pavilion, equipped pavilion, coin games, 2 swim pools, saltwater swim, boating, canoeing, kayaking, ramp, dock, 12 kayak/11 motorboat rentals, saltwater fishing, fishing supplies, golf nearby, bsktball, playground, activities, horseshoes, sports field, hiking trails, v-ball, local tours.

Pets welcome, breed restrict, quantity restrict. Partial handicap access. Open Apr 1 - Oct 31. Advance reservations peak season-minimum 3 nights. Big rigs welcome. Escort to site. Clubs welcome. Rate in 2010 $42-73 for 2 persons. MC/VISA/DISC. ATM. Member ARVC, MAC.

Text 81711 to (440)725-8687 to see our Visual Tour.

Phone: (410)213-0097
Address: 12550 Eagles Nest Rd, Berlin, MD 21811
Lat/Lon: 38.30441/-75.11943
Email: info@castawaysrvoc.com
Web: www.castawaysrvoc.com

SEE AD THIS PAGE

OCEAN CITY—Continued

(S) FRONTIER TOWN CAMPGROUND—(Worcester) *From jct Hwy-528 & US-50: Go 1 mi W on US-50, then 3-3/4 mi S on Hwy-611. Enter on L.*

◊◊◊◊◊FACILITIES: 542 sites, typical site width 40 ft, 313 full hkups, 190 W&E, (20/30/50 amps), 39 no hkups, cable TV, WiFi Instant Internet at site, phone/cable on-site Internet (needs activ), WiFi Internet central location, family camping, tenting, RV's/park model rentals, cabins, RV storage, dump, laundry, full svc store, RV supplies, LP gas by weight, ice, picnic tables, fire rings, wood, controlled access.

◊◊◊◊◊RECREATION: rec hall, rec room/area, pavilion, coin games, 2 swim pools, wading pool, boating, canoeing, kayaking, ramp, dock, 6 kayak rentals, saltwater fishing, fishing supplies, fishing guides, mini-golf ($), golf nearby, bsktball, playground, shuffleboard court 2 shuffleboard courts, activities, horseshoes, hiking trails, v-ball.

Pets welcome. Partial handicap access. Open Mid Apr - Mid Oct. Big rigs welcome. Clubs welcome. Rate in 2010 $38-92 for 2 persons. MC/VISA. ATM. Member ARVC, MAC.

Text 108002 to (440)725-8687 to see our Visual Tour.

Phone: (800)228-5590
Address: 8428 Stephen Decatur Rd, Ocean City, MD 21843
Lat/Lon: 38.29045/-75.15119
Email: info@frontiertown.com
Web: frontiertown.com

SEE AD PAGE 336

We all know that one of the best parts about camping is the food! Woodall's Campsite Cookbook is a classic cookbook containing such fun campsite and RV recipes as Roadside Spuds, The Fastest Sauce in the West, and Hairy Squares (which taste a lot better than they sound!) To order your copy go to www.woodalls.com/shop.

OCEAN CITY—Continued

(S) FRONTIER TOWN WATER PARK—*From jct Hwy 528 & US 50: Go 1 mi W on US 50, then 3-3/4 mi S on Hwy 611. Enter on L.* 3 Flume waterslides, large, full service family restaurant; beautifully landscaped miniature golf course, recreation pool & arcade. New 1000 foot Lazy River Ride. Free to Frontier Town & Whaley Campers. Open Memorial Day - Labor Day. MC/VISA.

Phone: (410)289-7877
Address: 8428 Stephen Decatur Hwy, Ocean City, MD 21843
Lat/Lon: 38.28933/-75.01462
Email: info@frontiertown.com
Web: frontiertown.com

SEE AD PAGE 336

(S) FRONTIER TOWN WESTERN THEME PARK—*From jct Hwy-528 & US-50: Go 1 mi W on US-50, then 3-3/4 mi S on Hwy-611. Enter on L.* Western theme park with Can-Can Show, Indian Ceremonial dancing, Gunfight at OK Corral, Bank Robberies, Steam Train Rides, Stagecoach rides, Western Gift Shops, Cowboy Store & Leather Shop, Hold ups, Horseback Rides & Rodeo. Open Mid Jun - Labor Day. MC/VISA.

Phone: (410)641-0057
Address: 8426 Stephen Decatur Hwy, Ocean City, MD 21843
Lat/Lon: 38.28933/-75.01462
Email: info@frontiertown.com
Web: frontiertown.com

SEE AD PAGE 336

(S) MISS ALICE'S ICE CREAM PARLOR—*From jct Hwy 528 and US 50: Go 1 mi W on US 50, then 3 3/4 mi S on Hwy 611. Enter on L.* Turn of the century ice cream parlor adjoining, Frontier Town Campground. Open May - Sep. Weekends, Spring & Fall. MC/VISA.

Phone: (410)629-0013
Address: 8426 Stephen Decatur Hwy, Ocean City, MD 21843
Lat/Lon: 38.28933/-75.01462
Email: info@frontiertown.com
Web: frontiertown.com

SEE AD PAGE 336

OCEAN CITY—Continued

(S) PAINTED PONY SALOON—*From jct Hwy 58 & US 50: Go 1 mi W on US 50, then 3-3/4 mi S on Hwy 611. Enter on L.* Specializing in seafood, pizza & family dining. Open Mid Apr - Mid Oct. MC/VISA.

Phone: (410)629-0909
Address: 8428 Stephen Decatur Rd, Ocean City, MD 21843
Lat/Lon: 38.29045/-75.15119
Email: info@frontiertown.com
Web: frontiertown.com

SEE AD PAGE 336

(S) PONY ISLAND ARCADE & GIFTS—*From jct Hwy 528 & US 50: Go 1 mi W on US 50, then 3-3/4 mi S on Hwy 611. Enter on L.* Complete array of nautical treasures available for purchase and arcade. Open Mid Apr - Mid Oct. Weekend only in spring & fall. MC/VISA.

Phone: (410)629-1301
Address: 8426 Stephen Decatur Hwy, Ocean City, MD 21843
Lat/Lon: 38.28933/-75.01462
Email: info@frontiertown.com
Web: frontiertown.com

SEE AD PAGE 336

POCOMOKE CITY—E-5

(NE) POCOMOKE RIVER SP (Milburn Landing Area)—(Worcester) *From town: Go 7 mi NE on Hwy-364.* FACILITIES: 32 sites, 29 ft max RV length, 10 E, 22 no hkups, family camping, tenting, dump. RECREATION: boating, canoeing, ramp, dock, saltwater/river fishing, playground. Pets welcome. Open Apr 29 - Dec 12. Phone: (410)632-2566.

Woodall's Camping Life magazine is the perfect family camping companion to any of Woodall's Directories and Guides. With 7 monthly issues per year, containing camping stories, destination articles, buyer's guides and more, Camping Life is a valuable resource for any family camper. Visit www.campinglife.com for more info.

QUANTICO—D-5

(W) SANDY HILL FAMILY CAMP—(Wicomico) *From jct US 50 (Bus) & Hwy 349: Go 10 mi W on Hwy 349, then 3-1/2 mi N on Royal Oak Rd, then 3/4 mi E on Sandy Hill Rd. Enter at end.*

◇◇◇FACILITIES: 99 sites, typical site width 25 ft, 99 W&E, (20/30 amps), mostly extd stay sites, 3 pull-thrus, family camping, tenting, dump, portable dump, laundry, ltd groc, RV supplies, LP gas by weight, ice, picnic tables, fire rings, wood.

◇◇◇RECREATION: rec hall, river swim, boating, ramp, dock, river fishing, fishing supplies, golf nearby, playground, activities, (wkends), hiking trails.

Pets welcome. Partial handicap access. Open Mar 1 - Dec 15. Clubs welcome. Rate in 2010 $25 for 4 persons. MC/VISA. Member ARVC, MAC.

Phone: (410)873-2471
Address: 5752 Sandy Hill Rd, Quantico, MD 21856
Lat/Lon: 38.35385/-75.85321
Email: sandyhill@sandyhillfamilycamp.com
Web: www.sandyhillfamilycamp.com

SEE AD THIS PAGE

QUEEN ANNE—C-5

(N) TUCKAHOE SP—(Caroline) *From jct Hwy 404 & Hwy 480: Go 1/10 mi N, then 5 mi N on Eveland Rd.* FACILITIES: 51 sites, 30 ft max RV length, 33 E, 18 no hkups, family camping, tenting, dump. RECREATION: boating, canoeing, ramp, lake/stream fishing, playground. Pets welcome. Partial handicap access. Open Mar 21 - Oct 27. Phone: (410)820-1668.

SCOTLAND—E-4

(S) POINT LOOKOUT SP—(St. Mary's) *From business center: Go 4 mi S on Hwy-5.* FACILITIES: 143 sites, 34 ft max RV length, 26 full hkups, 31 E, (20/30 amps), 86 no hkups, family camping, tenting, dump, ltd groc. RECREATION: river swim, boating, canoeing, ramp, dock, saltwater/lake/river fishing, playground. Pets welcome. Open all yr. Facilities fully operational Apr - Oct. Phone: (301)872-5688.

SNOW HILL—D-6

(SW) POCOMOKE RIVER SP (Shad Landing Area)—(Worcester) *From business center: Go 4 mi SW on Hwy-113.* FACILITIES: 191 sites, 24 ft max RV length, 59 E, 132 no hkups, family camping, tenting, dump, groceries. RECREATION: swim pool, boating, canoeing, ramp, dock, saltwater/river/pond fishing, playground. No pets. Open Mar 24 - Sep 26. Phone: (410) 632-2566.

SOLOMONS—D-4

MILITARY CAMPGROUND (Solomons Navy Rec Center)—(Calvert) *Off base. Located on Hwy 4 outside of front gate. Check in at Bldg 411.* FACILITIES: 208 sites, typical site width 16 ft, 39 ft max RV length, 146 full hkups, 6 W&E, (20/30/50 amps), 56 no hkups, tenting, dump, laundry. RECREATION: 4 swim pools, saltwater/river swim, boating, 20 hp limit, canoeing, ramp, dock, saltwater/river fishing, playground. Open all yr. Facilities fully operational Apr 1 - Oct 15. Phone: (410)326-5202.

THURMONT—A-2

(W) CATOCTIN MOUNTAIN NP (Owens Creek)—(Frederick) *From jct US 15 & Hwy 77: Go 3 mi W on Hwy 77, then 5 mi N on Park Central Rd, then 1 mi NE on Foxville-Deerfield Rd.* FACILITIES: 51 sites, 22 ft max RV length, 51 no hkups, 3 pull-thrus, family camping, tenting. RECREATION: stream fishing. Open Apr 15 - Nov 20. Phone: (301)663-9388.

(W) CUNNINGHAM FALLS SP (Houck Area)—(Frederick) *From town: Go 3 mi W on Hwy 77.* FACILITIES: 140 sites, typical site width 23 ft, 33 E, (30 amps), 107 no hkups, family camping, tenting, dump, groceries. RECREATION: lake swim, boating, electric motors only, canoeing, ramp, lake/stream fishing, playground. Pets welcome. Partial handicap access. Open Apr - Oct 24. Phone: (301)271-7574.

(S) CUNNINGHAM FALLS SP (Manor Area)—(Frederick) *From town: Go 3 mi S on US 15.* FACILITIES: 31 sites, 10 E, 21 no hkups, family camping, tenting. RECREATION: canoeing, lake/stream fishing, playground. No pets. Open May 23 - Sep 1. Phone: (301)271-7574.

WHALEYVILLE—D-6

(S) FORT WHALEY CAMPGROUND—(Worcester) *From jct US 50 & Hwy 610: Go 1/4 mi S on Hwy 610. Enter on L.*

◇◇◇◇◇FACILITIES: 169 sites, typical site width 40 ft, 66 full hkups, 70 W&E, (20/30/50 amps), 33 no hkups, 19 pull-thrus, cable TV, WiFi Instant Internet at site, family camping, tenting, cabins, RV storage, dump, laundry, full svc store, RV supplies, LP gas by weight/by meter, ice, picnic tables, fire rings, wood, controlled access.

◇◇◇◇◇RECREATION: rec hall, equipped pavilion, coin games, swim pool, boating, 3 pedal boat rentals, lake fishing, fishing supplies, mini-golf, golf nearby, bsktball, 10 bike rentals, playground, shuffleboard court 2 shuffleboard courts, activities, horseshoes, sports field, v-ball.

Pets welcome. Partial handicap access. Open Mar 1 - Dec 1. Big rigs welcome. Clubs welcome. Rate in 2010 $30-75 for 2 persons. MC/VISA. Member ARVC, MAC.

Phone: (410)641-9785
Address: 11224 Dale Rd, Whaleyville, MD 21872
Lat/Lon: 38.38500/-75.31233
Email: info@fortwhaley.com
Web: fortwhaley.com

SEE AD OCEAN CITY PAGE 336

WILLIAMSPORT—A-2

(N) Hagerstown/Antietam Battlefield-KOA—(Washington) *From jct I-70 & I-81: Go 1-1/2 mi W on I-70 (exit 24), then 1/4 mi S on Hwy 63, then 2-1/2 mi W on Kemps Mill Rd. Follow printed directions - Do not use GPS. Enter on R.* ◇◇◇◇FACILITIES: 96 sites, typical site width 25 ft, 48 full hkups, 48 W&E, (20/30/50 amps), 20 pull-thrus, family camping, tenting, dump, laundry, groceries. ◇◇◇◇RECREATION: swim pool, boating, canoeing, dock, river fishing, playground. Pets welcome. Partial handicap access. Open Mar 23 - Nov 30. Big rigs welcome. Rate in 2010 $39.50-58.50 for 2 persons. Member ARVC, MAC. Phone: (800)562-7607. KOA discount.

(S) YOGI BEAR'S JELLYSTONE PARK CAMP-RESORT-WILLIAMSPORT-HAGERSTOWN

—(Washington) *From jct I-81 (exit 1) & Hwy 68: Go 1-1/4 mi E on Hwy 68. (Cappans Rd). Enter on L.*

◇◇◇◇◇FACILITIES: 180 sites, typical site width 40 ft, 133 full hkups, 41 W&E, (20/30/50 amps), 50 amps ($), 6 no hkups, 109 pull-thrus, cable TV, WiFi Instant Internet at site, family camping, tenting, cabins, dump, laundry, groceries, RV supplies, LP gas by weight/by meter, ice, picnic tables, fire rings, wood.

◇◇◇◇◇RECREATION: rec hall, rec room/area, pavilion, equipped pavilion, coin games, 2 swim pools, wading pool, mini-golf, ($), golf nearby, bsktball, 26 bike rentals, playground, activities, horseshoes, sports field, hiking trails, v-ball, local tours.

Pets welcome. Partial handicap access. Open Mar 1 - Nov 30. Big rigs welcome. Escort to site. Clubs welcome. Green Friendly. Rate in 2010 $30-72 for 2 persons. MC/VISA/DISC. ATM. Member ARVC, MAC.

Text 84896 to (440)725-8687 to see our Visual Tour.

Phone: (800)421-7116
Address: 16519 Lappans Rd, Williamsport, MD 21795
Lat/Lon: 39.58084/-77.79617
Email: vicki@jellystonemaryland.com
Web: jellystonemaryland.com

SEE AD TRAVEL SECTION PAGE 327

WOODBINE—B-3

(E) RAMBLIN' PINES FAMILY CAMPGROUND & RV PARK—(Carroll) *From jct I-70 (exit 76) & Hwy-97: Go 2-1/2 mi N on Hwy-97, then 1/2 mi NW on Hoods Mill Rd. (Do not turn right on first Hoods Mill Rd; go across railroad tracks & up hill, then turn left on Hoods Mill Rd). Enter on L.*

◇◇◇◇◇FACILITIES: 200 sites, typical site width 42 ft, 200 full hkups, (20/30/50 amps), some extd stay sites, 15 pull-thrus, WiFi Instant Internet at site, phone on-site Internet (needs activ), family camping, tenting, cabins, RV storage, dump, non-guest dump $, laundry, groceries, RV supplies, LP gas by weight/by meter, ice, picnic tables, patios, fire rings, grills, wood, controlled access.

◇◇◇◇◇RECREATION: rec hall, rec room/area, equipped pavilion, coin games, swim pool, pond fishing, fishing supplies, mini-golf, ($), golf nearby, bsktball, playground, shuffleboard court 2 shuffleboard courts, activities (wkends), horseshoes, sports field, hiking trails, v-ball.

Pets welcome, breed restrict. Partial handicap access. Open all yr. Discounts not available on Holiday weekends. Big rigs welcome. Escort to site. Clubs welcome. Rate in 2010 $50 for 2 persons. MC/VISA. ATM. Member ARVC, MAC. FCRV discount. FMCA discount.

Phone: (800)550-8733
Address: 801 Hoods Mill Rd, Woodbine, MD 21797
Lat/Lon: 39.36704/-77.02533
Email: rpines@qis.net
Web: www.ramblinpines.com

SEE AD BALTIMORE PAGE 333

TRAVEL SECTION

Massachusetts

READER SERVICE INFO

The following business has placed an ad in the Massachusetts Travel Section. To receive free information, enter their Reader Service number on the Reader Service Card opposite page 48/Discover Section in the front of this directory:

Advertiser	RS#
Massachusetts Association of Campground Owners	2222

TIME ZONE

Massachusetts is in the Eastern Time Zone.

TOPOGRAPHY

The varied terrain of Massachusetts comprises beaches, farmland, forests and mountains.

TEMPERATURE

High and low temperature extremes occur occasionally in certain portions of the state, but temperatures are generally moderate. January averages range from 23° to 36° and July averages 65° to 81°. Annual precipitation ranges from 40 to 48 inches.

TRAVEL & TOURISM INFO

State Agency:

Massachusetts Office of Travel & Tourism
10 Park Plaza, Ste. 4510
Boston, MA 02116
(800/227-MASS or 617/973-8500)
www.massvacation.com

Regional Agencies:

Greater Boston CVB
2 Copley Place, Ste., 105
Boston, MA 02116
(888/SEE-BOSTON)
www.bostonusa.com

North of Boston Convention & Visitors Bureau
17 Peabody Square
Peabody, MA 01960
(978/977-7760)
www.northofboston.org

Central Massachusetts Convention and Visitors Bureau
30 Elm Street (2nd floor)
Worcester, MA 01609
(508/755-7400 or 866/755-7439)
www.centralmass.org

Southeastern Massachusetts CVB
70 North Second St., PO Box 976
New Bedford, MA 02741
(800/288-6263 or 508/997-1250)
www.bristol-county.org

The Berkshire Visitors Bureau
3 Hoosac Street
Adams, MA 01220
(413/743-4500 or 800/237-5747)
www.berkshires.org

Cape Cod Chamber of Commerce
Junction of Route 6 and Route 132
Hyannis, MA
(888/33-CAPECOD or 888/332-2732)
www.capecodchamber.org

Martha's Vineyard Chamber of Commerce
PO Box 1698
Vineyard Haven, MA 02568
(508/693-0085 or 800/505-4815)
www.mvy.com

Greater Merrimack Valley CVB
9 Central St., Suite 201
Lowell, MA 01852
(800/443-3332 or 978/250-9704)
www.merrimackvalley.org

Mohawk Trail Association
P.O. Box 1044
North Adams, MA 01247
(866/743-8127 or 413/743-8127)
www.mohawktrail.com

Nantucket Island Chamber of Commerce
Zero Main St. 2nd Floor
Nantucket, MA 02554
(508/228-1700)
www.nantucketchamber.org

Plymouth County Development Council Convention & Visitors Bureau
170 Water Street, Suite 24
Plymouth, MA 02360
(508/747-0100 or 800/231-1620)
www.seeplymouth.com

Greater Springfield Convention and Visitors Bureau
1441 Main St.
Springfield, MA 01103
(413/787-1548 or 800/723-1548)
www.valleyvisitor.com

Ferry Service:

Most ferries are seasonal. Only the Steamship Authority transports vehicles (www.islandferry.com). Space for vehicles to Martha's Vineyard and Nantucket Island is limited; reservations are required and should be made far in advance. If you plan to leave your car on Cape Cod, parking is available, for a fee, at the Steamship Authority docks.

Commuter Boat Service

Long Wharf, Boston to the Charlestown Navy Yard; Charlestown Navy Yard to Lovejoy Wharf, North Station. Lovejoy Wharf to John Joseph Moakley United States Courthouse and the World Trade Center.

Rowes Wharf, Boston to Hewitt's Cove, Hingham; Hingham Shipyard, Hingham to Rowes Wharf, Boston; Pemberton Pier, Hull to Long Wharf, Boston. **Boston Harbor Cruises**, 617/227-4321

STAY WITH US ALONG THE WAY

HWY-28 **EXIT -THOMAS B. LANDERS**

CAPE COD CAMP RESORT & CABINS— *From Thomas B Landers Exit: Go 2-1/2 mi E on Thomas B Landers. Enter on R.*

See listing at East Falmouth, MA

I-495 **EXIT 18**

CIRCLE CG FARM ADULT RV PARK— *From Exit 18: Go 1 mi S on Hwy 126. Enter on L.*

See listing at Bellingham, MA

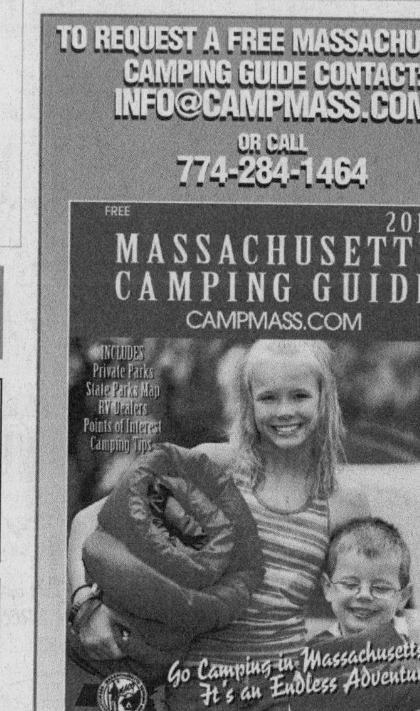
TO REQUEST A FREE MASSACHUSETTS CAMPING GUIDE CONTACT:
INFO@CAMPMASS.COM
OR CALL
774-284-1464
FREE
2011
MASSACHUSETTS CAMPING GUIDE
CAMPMASS.COM
Go Camping in Massachusetts—It's an Endless Adventure!

FREE INFO! Enter #2222 on Reader Service Card

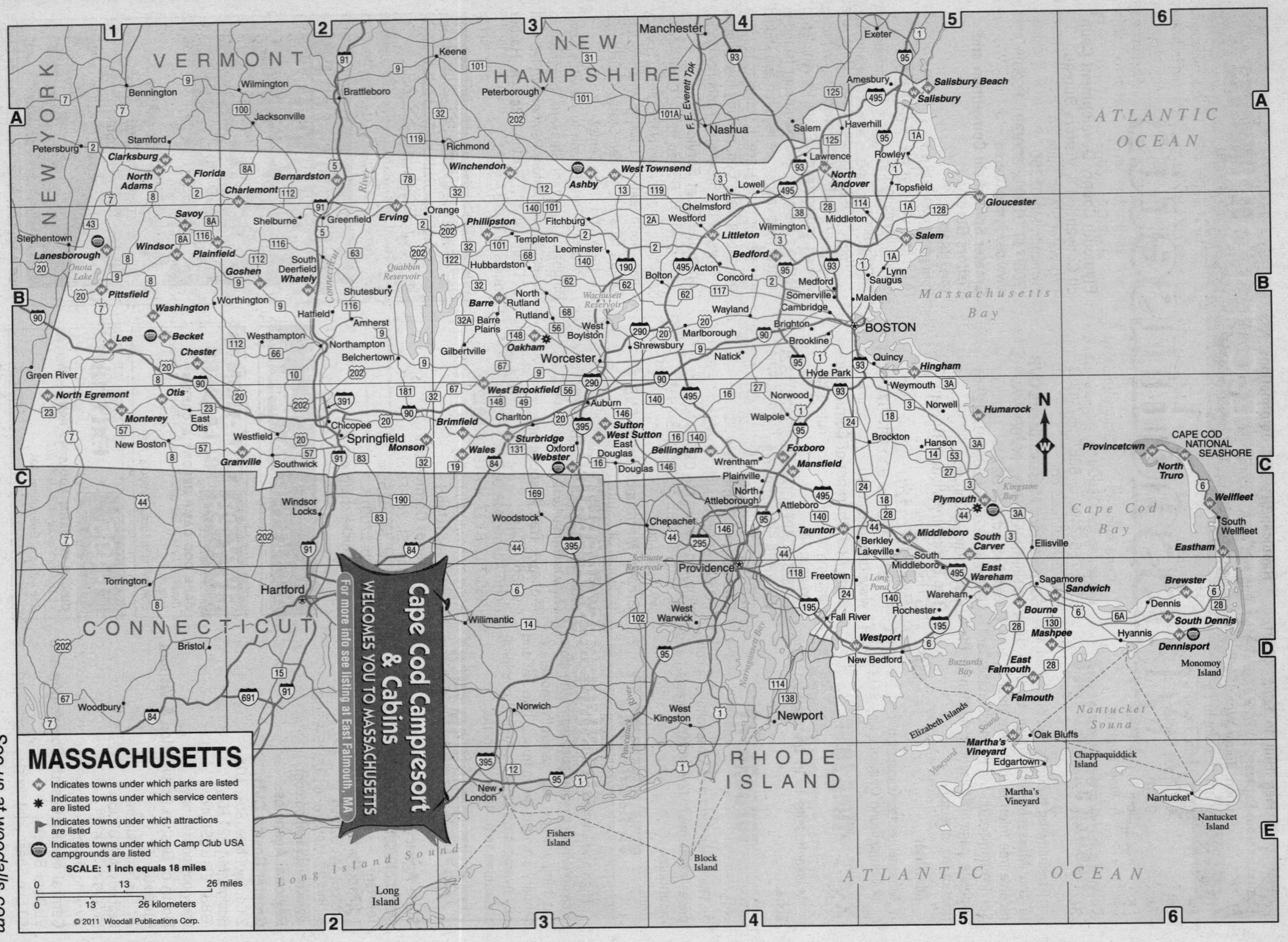
MASSACHUSETTS
Indicates towns under which parks are listed
Indicates towns under which service centers are listed
Indicates towns under which attractions are listed
Indicates towns under which Camp Club USA campgrounds are listed
SCALE: 1 inch equals 18 miles
0 13 26 miles
0 13 26 kilometers
© 2011 Woodall Publications Corp.
Cape Cod Campresort & Cabins
WELCOMES YOU TO MASSACHUSETTS
For more info see listing at East Falmouth, MA
ATLANTIC OCEAN
NEW HAMPSHIRE
VERMONT
NEW YORK
CONNECTICUT
RHODE ISLAND
Massachusetts Bay
Cape Cod Bay
Nantucket Sound
Long Island Sound
CAPE COD NATIONAL SEASHORE
BOSTON
Worcester
Springfield
Providence
Hartford

Pemberton Pier, Hull to Long Wharf, Boston. **Harbor Express**, 617/222-6999

USS Constitution, Tudor Wharf, Lovejoy Wharf, Lewis Wharf, Christopher Columbus Park, Rowes Wharf, John Joseph Moakley Courthouse, World Trade Center; **City Water Taxi**, 617/633-9240

From New Bedford to Oak Bluffs and Vineyard Haven (YR); **New England Fast Ferry Company** 866/453-6800, 617/748-1428

Seasonal Ferry Service

Salem Ferry, Blaney St., Salem MA 01970

617/741-0220; Salemferry.com

Seasonal round-trip ferry service between Central Wharf, Boston and Bloaney Street Dock in Salem.

Long Wharf, Boston to Boston Harbor Islands.

Boston Harbor Cruises, 617/227-4321

Quonset Point, RI to Oak Bluffs, Martha's Vineyard.

RECREATIONAL INFO

Fishing & Hunting: For licenses visit www.mass.gov/massoutdoors or call (508/389-6300). For information on Saltwater Fishing call the Division of Marine Fisheries at (617/626-1520).

Ski Conditions: For up-to-date ski conditions, visit snocountry.com.

Handicap/Disabled Information: New England ADA Technical Assistance Center (800/949-4232) V/TTY www.newenglandada.org

SHOPPING

Cape Ann Artisans, Gloucester. Visit 17 studios, meet the artisans and see their work in the places where it is created. On Washington St. www.capeannartisans.com

Cape Cod Crafters of New England, locations in Avon, Hyannis, Lynnfield, North Attleboro, Shrewsbury and Pembroke. Browse through handcrafted pottery, woodcrafts, quilts, baskets and folk art. www.capecodcrafters.com

Colony Place, Plymouth. The largest outdoor shopping and entertainment in the Plymouth region. Exceptionally designed lifestyle destination for the entire family. Special events, specialty retail, restaurants, shopping and services. More of what you want, all in one place. www.colonyplace.com

Wrentham Village Premium Outlets, Wrentham. Savings at 170 outlet stores. One Premium Outlets Blvd., Wrentham. (508/384-0600).

BUSINESSES OFFERING

	Things to See & Do	RV Sales	RV Service
OAKHAM			
Oakham Trailer Sales & Service		🚌	✱
PLYMOUTH			
Pinewood Lodge RV Service		🚌	✱

Where to Find CCUSA Parks

List City	Park Name	Map Coordinates
ASHBY		
	The Pines Campground	A-3
BECKET		
	Bonny Rigg Camping Club	B-1
DENNISPORT		
	Camper's Haven RV Resort	D-6
LANESBOROUGH		
	Hidden Valley Campground	B-1
PLYMOUTH		
	Pinewood Lodge Campground	C-5
WEBSTER		
	Indian Ranch Campground	C-3
	Webster/Sturbridge Family Camp	C-3

DESTINATIONS

For such a little state, Massachusetts has a lot to offer any traveler. Steeped in history, Massachusetts was the epicenter of several major chapters of Colonial and Revolutionary War history. Visitors can see the rock where the Mayflower supposedly landed in Plymouth, examine sites of the 1692 witch trials in Salem, see where David Thoreau developed his ideas about living close to nature in Walden, and walk the paths where the first shots of the Revolutionary War were fired.

BERKSHIRES, CONNECTICUT RIVER VALLEY & CENTRAL MASSACHUSETTS

The heart of the state offers mountains and meadows, cultural attractions and New England's second largest city, Worcester.

Amherst, the home of Emily Dickinson and the site of the University of Massachusetts and Amherst and Hampshire colleges.

Hancock Shaker Village, Pittsfield. A restored Shaker settlement dating from 1790 interprets the life and industries of the sect. Contains 20 buildings, all furnished with Shaker artifacts, exhibits on the sect's culture, history and philosophy and shops selling herbs and baked goods. Craft demonstrations and special programs run daily from April to November. Guests can also participate in Shaker candlelight dinners on Saturday evenings, July through October.

Higgins Armory, Worcester. Collection of Medieval and Renaissance armor.

Mohawk Trail follows Rt. 2 from Williams Town east to Orange. This 63-mile Native American footpath has nearly 100 attractions and more than 50,000 acres for recreational enjoyment. The trail moves through woodlands, gorges and mountain peaks.

Norman Rockwell Museum, Stockbridge. View original works of art by one of America's most beloved illustrators and artists. See the studio, easel, palette, paints and other personal belongings used by the legendary painter.

Historic Deerfield. Early settlers first arrived in 1669 and then again in 1682. Both times their village was destroyed by raids. In 1707, Deerfield was finally settled permanently. Today, it is a mile-long National Historic Landmark. Twelve homes have been turned into museums that relate a vivid tale of courage, heartache and determination.

Mohawk Trail, along State Route 2 from Orange to Williamstown, began as a Native American trail and was later developed as America's first scenic automobile route. Today the trail links villages, covered bridges and many beautiful views.

QUICK REFERENCE CHART FOR WOODALL'S FEATURED PARKS

	Green Friendly	RV Lots for Sale	Park Models-Onsite Ownership	Park Membership for Sale	Big Rigs Welcome	Internet Friendly	Pets Welcome
ASHBY							
The Pines Campground						●	■
BELLINGHAM							
Circle CG Farm Family Camping & RV Park					▲	●	■
BOURNE							
Bay View Campgrounds						●	■
Bourne Scenic Park (Municipal Park)						●	■
BREWSTER							
Shady Knoll Campground						●	■
CHARLEMONT							
Country Aire Campground					▲	●	■
DENNISPORT							
Camper's Haven RV Resort					▲	●	■
EAST FALMOUTH							
Cape Cod Campresort & Cabins					▲	●	■
EASTHAM							
Atlantic Oaks					▲	●	■
FOXBORO							
Normandy Farms Family Camping Resort						●	■
GLOUCESTER							
Cape Ann Camp Site						●	■
LITTLETON							
Boston Minuteman Campground					▲	●	■
MANSFIELD							
Canoe River Campground						●	■
MARTHA'S VINEYARD							
Martha's Vineyard Family Campground						●	
MONSON							
Sunsetview Farm Camping Area					▲	●	■
OAKHAM							
Pine Acres Family Camping Resort					▲	●	■
PLYMOUTH							
Pinewood Lodge Campground					▲	●	■
SALISBURY							
Black Bear Campground					▲	●	■
Rusnik Family Campground							■
SALISBURY BEACH							
Beach Rose RV Park					▲	●	■
SANDWICH							
Dunroamin' Cottages & Trailer Park						●	■
STURBRIDGE							
Yogi Bear's Jellystone Park-Sturbridge						●	■
WEBSTER							
Webster/Sturbridge Family Camp					▲	●	■
WEST BROOKFIELD							
The Old Sawmill Campground							■

Green Friendly 🍃; **RV Lots for Sale** ✖; **Park Models/Onsite Onwership** ✱; **Park Memberships for Sale** ✔; **Big Rigs Welcome** ▲; **Internet Friendly** ●; **Internet Friendly-WiFi** ●; **Pets Welcome** ■

Old Sturbridge Village, Sturbridge. This re-created New England country town of homes, shops, mills, schools, meeting houses and general stores illustrates American rural life in the 1830s.

Quadrangle, Springfield. This cultural center consists of the **Museum of Fine Arts**, the **Science Museum**, the **Connecticut Valley Historical Museum** and the **George Walter Vincent Smith Art Museum**.

Six Flags, Agawam. New England's largest theme park and water park with rides for all ages. Ten coasters include Mr. Six's Pandemonium, Typhoon water coaster and Superman- Ride of Steel.

NORTHEAST

Travelers will find an astonishing array of pleasures, from whale watching, fine arts and colonial history, to the incomparable New England seafood, and a wealth of fascinating tours. Like the rest of Massachusetts, this region will delight history buffs who visit Salem, not only the site of the witch trials, but also home to Nathaniel Hawthorn, who penned his classics, "The Scarlet Letter", and "House of Seven Gables" here.

Danvers. Putnam House circa 1648 is open by appointment only. Joseph Putnam lived here in 1692 during the witch trials. Major General Israel Putnam was born here in 1718, famous for his command "Don't fire until you see the whites of their eyes." Also in Danvers is the **Rebecca Nurse Homestead**, a colonial farmstead and meeting house. Originally owned in 1636 by Townsend Bishop and occupied by Francis Nurse whose wife, Rebecca was accused of witchcraft and executed in 1692.

Gloucester, a fishing port made famous by "The Perfect Storm." Local seafood restaurants and artists' studios dot the wharves of Rocky Neck. The **Gloucester Maritime Heritage Center** is on Gloucester's working waterfront. Aquarium, exhibits, historic marine railway and gift shop.

Marblehead is one of the East Coast's premier sailing centers. Surrounding the harbor are hundreds of 18th and 19th-century homes.

Peabody. One of the few remaining federal-style farmhouses is now the **George Peabody House & Museum**. The birthplace of George Peabody, the family occupied the house from 1793 to 1832. Also of interest is the **Nathaniel Felton, Jr. House.** On the National Register of Historical Places circa 1683, the house is the oldest surviving of the early settlers and is furnished with period antiques and furniture.

Salem. Among the most popular of Salem's many attractions are the **House of Seven Gables** (built in 1668 and made famous by Nathaniel Hawthorne), the newly renovated **Peabody Essex Museum** and the **Salem Witch Museum.** The museum examines witches from pagan times to the present. And at the **Witch History Museum,** the stories of 1692 are told through a historically accurate live presentation followed by a guided tour downstairs. The unique and little known history of New England sea-robbers comes alive at the **Pirate Museum**. Roam a colonial seaport, board a pirate ship and stroll through an eighty-foot cave.

GREATER BOSTON

Every year, Boston welcomes thousands of visitors, a city brimming with urban and cultural pleasures, natural beauty, and many sites of Colonial and Revolutionary history. Visitors needing to sharpen up on their Revolutionary history should start on the Freedom trail, and walk their way back through time. This is also home to the Boston Symphony Pops, the Boston Symphony Orchestra, the Museum of Fine Arts, the Isabella Stewart Gardner Museum, as well as some of the nation's top colleges.

Boston. The capital holds many varied attractions for tourists. Among the most popular is the Freedom Trail, a self-guided, 2.5-mile walk that begins at the Boston Common where hordes of red-clad British troops once trained. The redbrick Freedom Trail connects 16 of Boston's most storied landmarks that changed America's history forever. Wind your way through the same narrow streets Ben Franklin once walked. Relive the mayhem of the Boston Tea Party. Listen closely and you'll still hear the shouts of protest reverberating through **Faneuil Hall**. See the **USS Constitution**, the oldest commissioned war ship afloat in the world. Visitors can view over 60 miles of breathtaking panorama atop the **Prudential-Skywalk Observatory Deck.**

While in Boston, make sure to take your pick of performing arts and museums to visit. The **Boston Symphony Orchestra** and the **Boston Ballet** are among the fine choices. The **Boston Opera House** has just completed a multi-million dollar restoration to this 76-year old landmark building.

History comes to life at the **Boston Tea Party Ship and Museum**—a replica of the ship where the notorious tea party took place on December 16, 1773.

John F. Kennedy Library and Museum. See the life, leadership and legacy of President Kennedy portrayed through exhibits, video presentations and period settings.

Cambridge. Tour the **Longfellow National Historic Site**, a grand mansion that served as George Washington's Revolutionary War headquarters.

See advanced levels of holography, high technology, mathematics and dimensions of science demonstrated at the **MIT Museum.**

Minuteman National Historic Park, Concord. This 750-acre park is the site of Battle-Road Visitor Center. Featured are the Minuteman Statue and North Bridge—where the "shot heard around the world" was fired.

SOUTHEAST

Nantucket and Martha's Vineyard are two island jewels off the coast of Cape Cod. Travelers will find beautiful beaches, elegant towns and some incredible dining and shopping. Both Islands are accessible by ferry and air. Cape Cod boasts warm sea breezes, and 560 miles of unspoiled coastline that make for spectacular views of wide dune fields, and sandy bluffs. Add the charm of quaint villages and harbors, and any visitor is sure to understand the lure of Cape Cod.

Adams National Historic Site, Quincy. Built in 1731, this structure was home to four generations of the Adams' family including presidents John and John Quincy Adams. View family furnishings, portraits and mementos.

Cape Cod. Featured on this island are many historic homes, lighthouses and museums.

Martha's Vineyard. Accessible by ferry, this popular picturesque resort island features sandy beaches, moors, a lighthouse, gray-shingled houses, flower-covered cottages and quaint little fishing villages. Ferries leave from Falmouth, Hyannis, New Bedford and Woods Hole.

Nantucket Island. A small, crescent-shaped island that was one of the busiest and most prosperous whaling ports in the world, Nantucket is now known as "the little grey lady of the sea."

New Bedford Whaling Museum, New Bedford. New Bedford was once heralded as the whaling capital of the world. This museum brings to life the often dangerous lives of fishermen who spent long months at sea.

Plymouth. Landing place of the Pilgrims in 1620 and home to Plymouth Rock and 400 years of history, telling America's Story in America's Hometown.

The Sarcophagus. This tomb contains bones of the first settlers, which were washed out of the hillside by rainstorms before the streets were paved and the hill landscaped. The area was an Indian cornfield in 1620.

Pilgrim Hall. This stately museum is the headquarters of the Pilgrim Society, built in 1824 it houses the actual possessions of the Pilgrims.

Visit the **Mayflower II**, a full-scale reproduction of the ship that carried the Pilgrims to the New World in 1620. Open daily April through November.

Massachusetts

All privately owned campgrounds personally inspected by WOODALL'S® Representatives

John and Carla Skolburg

ASHBY—A-3

(NE) THE PINES CAMPGROUND—(North Middlesex) *From jct Hwy 119 & Hwy 31: Go 3 mi N on Hwy 31, then 200 yds E on Davis Rd. Enter on R.*

WELCOME

◆◆◆FACILITIES: 58 sites, typical site width 30 ft, 43 full hkups, 9 W&E, (20/30/50 amps), 6 no hkups, many extd stay sites, heater not allowed, cable TV, WiFi Instant Internet at site, WiFi Internet central location, family camping, tenting, shower$, dump, non-guest dump $, portable dump, laundry, ltd groc, LP gas by weight/by meter, ice, picnic tables, fire rings, grills, wood.

◆◆◆RECREATION: rec room/area, coin games, swim pool, stream fishing, golf nearby, bsktball, playground, activities, (wkends), horseshoes, sports field, hiking trails.

Pets welcome ($). Partial handicap access. Open all yr. Facilities fully operational May 1 - Oct 15. Escort to site. Clubs welcome. Rate in 2010 $38 per family. MC/VISA/Debit. Member ARVC, MACO. CCUSA 50% Discount. CCUSA reservations Required, CCUSA max stay 3 days, CCUSA disc. not avail S,Th, CCUSA disc. not avail F,Sa, CCUSA disc. not avail holidays. Not available Jul & Aug. Fully operational May 1-Oct 15. Electric heater not allowed.

Massachusetts State Rock: Roxbury Puddingstone

ASHBY—Continued
THE PINES CAMPGROUND—Continued

Phone: (978)386-7702
Address: 39 Davis Rd, Ashby, MA 01431
Lat/Lon: 42.69678/-71.78583
Email: camping@thepines-campground.com
Web: www.thepines-campground.com

SEE AD THIS PAGE

(E) WILLARD BROOK STATE FOREST—(Middlesex) *From town: Go E on Hwy 119. Follow signs.* FACILITIES: 21 sites, 20 ft max RV length, 21 no hkups, tenting. RECREATION: lake swim, lake fishing. Partial handicap access. Open May 25 - Sep 3. Phone: (978)386-7146.

BARRE—B-3

(SE) Camp Coldbrook RV Resort (Morgan RV Resort)—(Worcester) *From jct Hwy 122 & Hwy 148: Go 2-3/4 mi N on Hwy 122, then 1-1/2 mi N on Old Coldbrook Rd. Enter on R.* ◆◆◆FACILITIES: 330 sites, 280 full hkups, 30 W&E, (30 amps), 20 no hkups, family camping, tenting, dump, laundry, ltd groc. ◆◆◆◆RECREATION: 2 swim pools, pond fishing, playground. Pets welcome ($), breed restrict. Partial handicap access. Open Mid Apr - Mid Oct. Rate in 2010 $40-45 per family. Member ARVC, MACO. Phone: (978) 355-2090.

BECKET—B-1

(S) Bonny Rigg Camping Club—(Berkshire) *From jct US 20 & Hwy 8: Go 200 ft N on Hwy 8. Enter on L.* ◆◆◆FACILITIES: 206 sites, 200 W&E, (30/50 amps), 6 no hkups, WiFi Instant Internet at site ($), family camping, tenting, dump, non-guest dump $, portable dump, laundry, ltd groc, RV supplies, LP gas by meter, ice, picnic tables, fire rings, wood. ◆◆◆RECREATION: rec hall, pavilion, swim pool, playground, shuffleboard court shuffleboard court, activities horseshoes, hiking trails, v-ball. Pets welcome, quantity restrict. Partial handicap access. Open all yr. Facilities fully operational May - Oct. Big rigs welcome. Rate in 2010 $30-35 for 6 persons. MC/VISA. Member ARVC, MACO. CCUSA 50% Discount. CCUSA reservations Recommended, CCUSA max stay 7 days. Fully operational May-Oct.

Phone: (413)623-5366
Address: 59 Main St., Becket, MA 01223
Lat/Lon: 42.26529/-73.05153
Email: brcc14@aol.com
Web: www.bonnyriggcampground.com

BEDFORD—B-4

(W) MILITARY PARK (Hanscom AFB FAMCAMP)—(Middlesex) *From jct Hwy 128/I-95 (exit 31) & Hwy 4/225: Go NW on Hwy 4/225, then SW on Hartwell Ave, then W on Magyuire Rd, then continue W on Sumner St. Off base.* FACILITIES: 78 sites, typical site width 30 ft, 47 full hkups, 21 W&E, (20/30/50 amps), 10 no hkups, 20 pull-thrus, tenting, dump, laundry. RECREATION: boating, 15 hp limit, canoeing, river/pond fishing, playground. Open May 1 - Oct 30. Phone: (781)377-4670.

BELLINGHAM—C-4

(N) CIRCLE CG FARM FAMILY CAMPING & RV PARK—(Norfolk) *From jct Hwy-495 & Hwy-126 (exit 18): Go 1 mi S on Hwy-126. Enter on L.*

WELCOME

◆◆◆◆FACILITIES: 150 sites, typical site width 30 ft, 90 full hkups, 60 W&E, (20/30/50 amps), 50 amps ($), some extd stay sites, 20 pull-thrus, cable TV, WiFi Instant Internet at site, WiFi Internet central location, family camping, tenting, RV storage, dump, laundry, groceries, RV supplies, LP gas by weight/by meter, ice, picnic tables, fire rings, wood, controlled access.

◆◆◆◆◆RECREATION: rec hall, rec room/area, equipped pavilion, coin games, 2 swim pools, pond fishing, mini-golf, ($), golf nearby, bsktball, shuffleboard court shuffleboard court, activities (wkends), tennis, horseshoes, v-ball.

Pets welcome, breed restrict, quantity restrict. Partial handicap access. Open all yr. Facilities fully operational Apr 15 - Oct 15. Big rigs welcome. Escort to site. Clubs welcome. Rate in 2010 $45-50 for 4 persons. MC/VISA/DISC. Member ARVC, MACO. FCRV discount. FMCA discount.

Phone: (508)966-1136
Address: 131 N Main St, Bellingham, MA 02019
Lat/Lon: 42.10085/-71.47293
Email: info@circlecgfarm.com
Web: www.circlecgfarm.com

SEE AD THIS PAGE AND AD TRAVEL SECTION PAGE 339 AND AD DISCOVER SECTION PAGE 15

BERNARDSTON—A-2

(S) Travelers Woods of New England—(Franklin) *From jct I-91 (exit 28B N'bound, exit 28 S'bound) & Hwy 10: Go 1/2 mi W on Hwy 10, then 1/2 mi S on Hwy 5/10, then 3/4 mi E on Cross St, then 1/8 mi S on River St. Enter on L.* ◆◆◆FACILITIES: 78 sites, 8 full hkups, 58 W&E, (20/30/50 amps), 12 no hkups, 3 pull-thrus, tenting, dump, laundry. ◆◆◆RECREATION: stream fishing, playground. Pets welcome. Open May 1 - Oct 15. Big rigs welcome. Rate in 2010 $24-27 for 2 persons. Member ARVC, MACO. Phone: (413)648-9105.

BOSTON—B-5

See listings at Bellingham, Foxboro, Gloucester, Littleton, Mansfield, Middleboro, Plymouth & Salisbury

BOSTON MINUTEMAN CAMPGROUND—*30 miles NW of Boston at jct I-495 (exit 30) & Hwy 2A: Go 2-3/4 mi W on Hwy 2A.*

SEE PRIMARY LISTING AT LITTLETON AND AD NEXT PAGE

BOSTON—Continued on next page

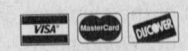

BOSTON—Continued

CIRCLE CG FARM FAMILY CAMPING & RV PARK—*From jct I-95 & I-90, Mass. Pike (west of Boston): Go 17 mi W on I-90, then 14 mi SE on I-495, then 1 mi S on Hwy 126.*

SEE PRIMARY LISTING AT BELLINGHAM AND AD BELLINGHAM PAGE 344

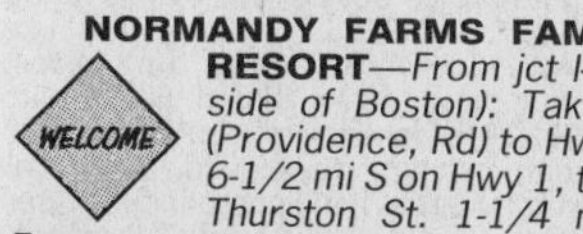

NORMANDY FARMS FAMILY CAMPING RESORT—*From jct I-93 & I-95 (south side of Boston): Take exit 95 South (Providence, Rd) to Hwy 1 (exit 9), then 6-1/2 mi S on Hwy 1, then turn left onto Thurston St. 1-1/4 mi to Normandy Farm.*

SEE PRIMARY LISTING AT FOXBORO AND AD THIS PAGE

BOURNE—D-5

(S) BAY VIEW CAMPGROUNDS—(Barnstable) *From jct I-495/Hwy 25 & Bourne Bridge: Cross Bourne Bridge to rotary, then 1 mi S on Hwy 28. Enter on R.*

CAPE COD'S DOUBLE 5W CAMPGROUND
Family Camping at its best! Immaculate restrooms; cable and WiFi, 3 pools, playgrounds, rec-hall, tennis, basketball. In-season: activities, entertainment, ice-cream parlor, snack bar, Big Rigs & pets welcome. Reserve online.

◇◇◇◇◇FACILITIES: 418 sites, typical site width 40 ft, 379 full hkups, 39 W&E, (20/30/50 amps), many extd stay sites (summer), 7 pull-thrus, cable TV, WiFi Instant Internet at site, WiFi Internet central location, family camping, tenting, RV storage, dump, non-guest dump $, laundry, ltd groc, RV supplies, LP gas by weight, ice, picnic tables, fire rings, wood.

◇◇◇◇◇RECREATION: rec hall, rec room/area, pavilion, coin games, 3 swim pools, golf nearby, bsktball, playground, shuffleboard court 2 shuffleboard courts, activities, tennis, horseshoes, sports field, hiking trails, v-ball.

Pets welcome. Partial handicap access. Open May 1 - Oct 15. Pools open Mem Day-Mid Sep, weather permitting. Planned activities start Mid Jun & Mem Day. Escort to site. Clubs welcome. Rate in 2010 $43-59 for 2 persons. MC/VISA. Member ARVC, MACO.

Text 107968 to (440)725-8687 to see our Visual Tour.

Phone: (508)759-7610
Address: 260 MacArthur Blvd, Rte 28, Bourne, MA 02532
Lat/Lon: 41.72541/-70.58505
Email: info@bayviewcampground.com
Web: www.bayviewcampground.com

SEE AD PAGE 346

BOURNE—Continued on next page

Boston Minuteman Campground
See listing at Littleton, MA
(978) 772-0042
264 Ayer Road
Littleton, Massachusetts
MinutemanCampground.com

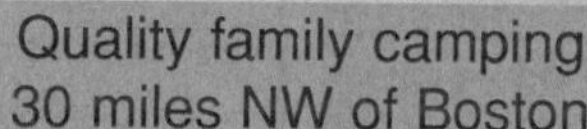

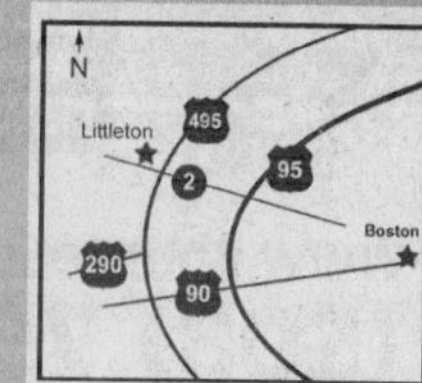

See listing at Foxboro, MA

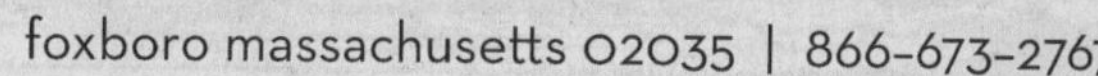

BOURNE—Continued

(C) **BOURNE SCENIC PARK (Municipal Park)**—(Barnstable) *From jct I-495/Hwy 25 & US 6 (exit 2): Go around rotary. Stay on N US 6 300 ft (Beneath North end of Bourne Bridge). Enter on R.*

FACILITIES: 455 sites, typical site width 40 ft, 417 W&E, (30 amps), 38 no hkups, some extd stay sites, WiFi Internet central location, family camping, tenting, cabins, dump, non-guest dump $, ltd groc, RV supplies, LP gas by weight, ice, picnic tables, fire rings, wood.

RECREATION: rec hall, pavilion, coin games, swim pool, saltwater fishing, fishing supplies, golf nearby, bsktball, playground, activities, horseshoes, sports field, hiking trails.

Pets welcome. Partial handicap access. Open End of Mar - End of Oct. Clubs welcome. MC/VISA. Member ARVC, MACO.

Phone: (508)759-7873
Address: 370 Scenic Hwy, Bourne, MA 02532
Lat/Lon: 41.75124/-70.59106
Email: scenicpark@capecod.net
Web: www.bournescenicpark.com

SEE AD THIS PAGE

BREWSTER—D-6

(E) NICKERSON SP—(Barnstable) *From jct US 6 (exit 12) & Hwy 6A: Go 3 mi W on Hwy 6A.* FACILITIES: 420 sites, 420 no hkups, tenting, dump. RECREATION: lake swim, boating, electric motors only, canoeing, ramp, lake fishing. Partial handicap access. Facilities fully operational Apr - Oct. Phone: (508)896-3491.

BREWSTER—Continued

(W) **SHADY KNOLL CAMPGROUND**—(Barnstable) *From jct US 6 (exit 11) & Hwy 137: Go 4 mi N on Hwy 137 to jct with US 6 A. Enter at end.*

◆◆◆FACILITIES: 100 sites, typical site width 25 ft, 34 ft max RV length, 49 full hkups, 31 W&E, (20/30/50 amps), 50 amps ($), 20 no hkups, some extd stay sites (summer), 7 pull-thrus, cable TV, WiFi Instant Internet at site, WiFi Internet central location, family camping, tenting, RV storage, dump, laundry, ltd groc, RV supplies, ice, picnic tables, fire rings, grills, wood.

◆◆◆RECREATION: rec hall, rec room/area, coin games, golf nearby, bsktball, playground.

Pets welcome ($), quantity restrict. Partial handicap access. Open May 15 - Columbus Day. Clubs welcome. Rate in 2010 $35-54 for 2 persons. MC/VISA/DISC. Member ARVC, MACO.

Phone: (508)896-3002
Address: 1709 Main St (Rt 6A), Brewster, MA 02631
Lat/Lon: 41.75757/-70.08868
Email: shady_knoll@capecamping.com
Web: www.capecamping.com

SEE AD CAPE COD PAGE 348

(S) **Sweetwater Forest Family Camping Resort**—(Barnstable) *From jct US 6 (exit 10) & Hwy 124: Go 3 mi N on Hwy 124. Enter on L.* ◆◆◆FACILITIES: 248 sites, typical site width 30 ft, 73 full hkups, 113 W&E, (30/50 amps), 62 no hkups, 2 pull-thrus, family camping, tenting, dump, groceries. ◆◆◆◆RECREATION: boating, 3 hp limit, canoeing, lake fishing, playground. Pets welcome ($). Partial handicap access. Open Apr 1 - Nov 1. Rate in 2010 $34-46 for 4 persons. Member ARVC, MACO. Phone: (508)896-3773.

BRIMFIELD—C-3

(E) **Quinebaug Cove Campground**—(Hampden) *From jct I-84 & US 20: Go 3-1/2 mi W on US 20, then 1/4 mi S on E Brimfield/Holland Rd. Enter on L.* ◆◆◆FACILITIES: 121 sites, typical site width 40 ft, 45 full hkups, 65 W&E, (20/30 amps), 11 no hkups, family camping, tenting, dump, laundry, ltd groc. ◆◆◆◆RECREATION: swim pool, lake swim, boating,

Massachusetts State Mineral: Babingtonite

BRIMFIELD—Continued
Quinebaug Cove Campground—Continued

canoeing, ramp, lake fishing, playground. Pets welcome. Partial handicap access. Open all yr. Facilities fully operational Apr 15 - Oct 15. Rate in 2010 $25-40 per family. Member ARVC, MACO. Phone: (413)245-9525.

(E) **Village Green Family Campground**—(Hampden) *From jct I-84 & US 20: Go 4-3/4 mi W on US 20. Enter on L.* ◆◆◆FACILITIES: 175 sites, typical site width 50 ft, 170 W&E, (15/20/30 amps), 5 no hkups, 5 pull-thrus, family camping, tenting, dump, laundry, ltd groc. ◆◆◆◆RECREATION: lake swim, boating, no motors, canoeing, pond fishing, playground. Pets welcome, quantity restrict. Partial handicap access. Open May 1 - Oct 30. Rate in 2010 $30 for 2 persons. Member ARVC, MACO. Phone: (413)245-3504.

CAPE COD—D-6

See listings at Bourne, Brewster, Dennisport, Eastham, East Falmouth, Martha's Vineyard, North Truro, Plymouth, Provincetown, Sandwich & South Dennis

ATLANTIC OAKS—*From National Seashore Main Visitors Center & Hwy 6: Go 1/2 mi E on Hwy 6.*

SEE PRIMARY LISTING AT EASTHAM AND AD PAGE 348

BAY VIEW CAMPGROUNDS—*From jct I-495/Hwy 25 & Bourne Bridge: Cross Bourne Bridge to rotary, then go 1 mi S on Hwy 28. Enter on R.*

SEE PRIMARY LISTING AT BOURNE AND AD THIS PAGE

CAPE COD CAMPRESORT & CABINS—*From jct Hwy 28 & Thomas B Landers Rd: Go 2-1/2 mi E on Thomas B Landers Rd. Enter on R.*

SEE PRIMARY LISTING AT EAST FALMOUTH AND AD NEXT PAGE

CAPE COD—Continued on next page

The Boston Tea Party reenactment takes place in Boston Harbor every December 16th.

CAPE COD—Continued

DUNROAMIN' COTTAGES & TRAILER PARK—*From jct US 6 (exit 2) & Hwy 130: Go 3-1/10 mi S on Hwy 130, then 3/4 mi E on Quaker Meeting House Rd, then 1-1/10 mi S on Cotuit Rd, then 1/10 mi W on John Ewer Rd. Enter on R.*

WELCOME

SEE PRIMARY LISTING AT SANDWICH AND AD SANDWICH PAGE 353

SHADY KNOLL CAMPGROUND—*From jct US 6 (exit 11) & Hwy 137: Go 4 mi N on Hwy 137 to jct US 6A. Enter at end.*

WELCOME

SEE PRIMARY LISTING AT BREWSTER AND AD THIS PAGE

CHARLEMONT—A-2

(E) COUNTRY AIRE CAMPGROUND—(Franklin) *From jct I-91 (exit 26) & Hwy 2: Go 12-1/2 mi W on Hwy 2 (between mileposts 35 & 36). Enter on R.*

WELCOME

◆◆◆FACILITIES: 171 sites, 93 full hkups, 43 W&E, (20/30/50 amps), 35 no hkups, some extd stay sites, 48 pull-thrus, WiFi Instant Internet at site, family camping, tenting, RV storage, shower$, dump, non-guest dump $, portable dump, laundry, ltd groc, RV supplies, LP gas by weight/by meter, ice, picnic tables, fire rings, wood, controlled access.

◆◆◆RECREATION: rec hall, rec room/area, pavilion, coin games, swim pool, stream fishing, fishing supplies, putting green, golf nearby, bsktball, playground, activities, (wkends), horseshoes, sports field, hiking trails, v-ball.

Pets welcome, breed restrict, quantity restrict. Open May 1 - Oct 31. Big rigs welcome. Escort to site. Clubs welcome. Rate in 2010 $29-32 for 2 persons. MC/VISA. Member ARVC, MACO.

Phone: (413)625-2996
Address: 1753 Mohawk Trail (Rt 2), Shelburne Falls, MA 01370
Lat/Lon: 42.62136/-72.79211
Email: countryairecampground@verizon.net
Web: www.countryairecampground.com

SEE AD SHELBURNE FALLS PAGE 354

(W) MOHAWK TRAIL STATE FOREST—(Franklin) *From town: Go 4 mi W on Hwy 2.* FACILITIES: 56 sites, 56 no hkups, tenting. RECREATION: river swim, canoeing, river fishing. Partial handicap access. Open May - Oct. Phone: (413)339-5504.

CHESTER—B-1

(W) Walker Island Family Camping—(Hamden) *From east jct Hwy 8 & US 20: Go 2-1/4 mi E on US 20. Enter on R.* ◆◆FACILITIES: 86 sites, typical site width 35 ft, 30 ft max RV length, 25 full hkups, 48 W&E, (20/30 amps), 13 no hkups, family camping, tenting, dump, laundry, ltd groc. ◆◆◆RECREATION: swim pool, stream fishing, playground. Pets welcome. Open May 1 - Oct 15. Rate in 2010 $33-35 for 2 persons. Member ARVC, MACO. Phone: (413)354-2295.

CLARKSBURG—A-1

(N) CLARKSBURG STATE PARK—(Berkshire) *From town: Go N on Hwy 8, then follow signs on Middle Rd.* FACILITIES: 45 sites, 16 ft max RV length, 45 no hkups, tenting. RECREATION: boating, no motors, canoeing. Partial handicap access. Open all yr. Facilities fully operational May - Oct. Phone: (413)664-8345.

DENNISPORT—D-6

(E) CAMPER'S HAVEN RV RESORT—(Barnstable) *From jct US 6 (exit 9A) & Hwy 134: Go 2 mi S on Hwy 134 across Hwy 28, then 1 mi SW on Swan River Rd, then 1/3 mi E on Lower County Rd, then 3/4 mi SE on Old Wharf Rd. Enter on L.*

WELCOME TO CAREFREE RV RESORTS!
Oceanfront family fun on beautiful Cape Cod! Our mid-Cape location is close to Martha's Vineyard & Nantucket ferries, golf courses, shopping, dining & more! Enjoy our private beach and lots of great activities for all.

◆◆◆◆FACILITIES: 244 sites, typical site width 25 ft, 244 full hkups, (20/30/50 amps), mostly extd stay sites (summer), 10 pull-thrus, cable TV, WiFi Instant Internet at site, WiFi Internet central location, family camping, tenting, dump, portable dump, laundry, ltd groc, RV supplies, ice, picnic tables, patios, grills, controlled access.

◆◆◆◆RECREATION: rec room/area, equipped pavilion, coin games, saltwater swim, saltwater fishing, fishing supplies, mini-golf, ($), golf nearby, bsktball, playground, shuffleboard court shuffleboard court, activities, horseshoes.

Pets welcome, breed restrict. Partial handicap access. Open May 1 - Columbus Day. No pets allowed June 25 thru Labor Day. Rates higher on Holiday weekends. Big rigs welcome. Escort to site. Rate in 2010 $44-64 per family. MC/VISA. Member ARVC, MACO. CCUSA 50% Discount. CCUSA reservations Recommended, CCUSA max stay 5 days, CCUSA disc. not avail F,Sa, CCUSA disc. not avail holidays. Not available Jun 13-Sep 1.

Phone: (508)398-2811
Address: 184 Old Wharf Rd, Dennisport, MA 02639
Lat/Lon: 41.65152/-70.14172
Email: campershaven@comcast.net
Web: www.carefreervresorts.com

SEE AD CAPE COD PAGE 348

EAST FALMOUTH—D-5

(N) CAPE COD CAMPRESORT & CABINS—(Barnstable) *From jct Hwy 28 & Thomas B. Landers Rd: Go 2-1/2 mi E on Thomas B. Landers Rd. Enter on R.*

CAPE COD'S NEWEST 5W/5W BIG RIG PARK
Central to Cape Cod's Beaches, Ferries & Attractions, you'll love our Luxury Resort w/ Superior Amenities to suit Your Style! All Paved Super Sites, Superb Rustic Sites, Cottages & Cabins—we offer THE perfect Cape Cod Vacation!

◆◆◆◆◆FACILITIES: 195 sites, typical site width 50 ft, 165 full hkups, (30/50 amps), 30 no hkups, some extd stay sites (summer), 8 pull-thrus, cable TV, WiFi Instant Internet at site, WiFi Internet central location, family camping, tenting, cabins, dump, portable dump, laundry, ltd groc, RV supplies, ice, picnic tables, fire rings, grills, wood, controlled access.

◆◆◆◆◆RECREATION: rec hall, rec room/area, equipped pavilion, coin games, 2 swim pools, wading pool, spray ground, lake swim, hot tub, boating, no motors, dock, 6 rowboat/6 pedal boat rentals, lake fishing, fishing supplies, golf nearby, bsktball, playground, activities, horseshoes, sports field, hiking trails, v-ball.

Pets welcome ($), breed restrict. Partial handicap access. Open May 1 - Late Oct. Pools (inc heated) weather permitting. Rates adjusted on holiday wknds. Min stay Jun-Jul. Big rigs welcome. Escort to site. Clubs welcome. Rate in 2010 $34-87 for 2 persons. MC/VISA/AMEX. Member ARVC, MACO.

Text 86112 to (440)725-8687 to see our Visual Tour.

Phone: (508)548-1458
Address: 176 Thomas B. Landers Rd, East Falmouth, MA 02536
Lat/Lon: 41.60658/-70.57581
Email: camp@capecampresort.com
Web: www.capecampresort.com

SEE AD CAPE COD PAGE 347 AND AD TRAVEL SECTION PAGE 339 AND AD MAP PAGE 340

EAST WAREHAM—D-5

(E) Yogi Bear's Jellystone Park Cape Cod at Maple Park—(Plymouth) *From jct Hwy 6 & Glen Charlie Rd: Go 2 mi N on Glen Charlie Rd. Enter on L.* ◆◆◆FACILITIES: 451 sites, typical site width 24 ft, 324 full hkups, 50 W&E, 17 E, (20/30/50 amps), 50

EAST WAREHAM—Continued
Yogi Bear's Jellystone Park Cape Cod at Maple Park—Continued

amps ($), 60 no hkups, family camping, tenting, dump, ltd groc. ◆◆◆◆RECREATION: lake swim, boating, no motors, canoeing, lake/pond fishing. Pets welcome ($), breed restrict, quantity restrict. Partial handicap access. Open May 1 - Mid Oct. Rate in 2010 $30-61 for 4 persons. Member ARVC, MACO. Phone: (888)295-4945.

EASTHAM—C-6

(N) ATLANTIC OAKS—(Barnstable) *From National Seashore Main Visitors Center and Hwy-6: Go 1/2 mi E on Hwy-6. Enter on R.*

◆◆◆◆FACILITIES: 110 sites, typical site width 35 ft, 100 full hkups, (30/50 amps), 10 no hkups, some extd stay sites, 81 pull-thrus, cable TV, WiFi Instant Internet at site, WiFi Internet central location, family camping, tenting, RV's/park model rentals, laundry, ltd groc, RV supplies, LP gas by weight/by meter, ice, picnic tables, fire rings, grills, wood.

◆◆◆RECREATION: rec hall, rec room/area, coin games, golf nearby, bsktball, playground, horseshoes, hiking trails.

Pets welcome ($), breed restrict, quantity restrict. Partial handicap access. Open May 1 - Nov 1. Jul & Aug weekends may require minimum length of stay. Winter by reservation. Big rigs welcome. Clubs welcome. Rate in 2010 $47-63 for 2 persons. MC/VISA/DISC. Member ARVC, MACO.

Phone: (508)255-1437
Address: 3700 State Hwy (Hwy 6), Eastham, MA 02642
Lat/Lon: 41.84562/-69.98426
Email: atlanticoaks3700@capecamping.com
Web: www.capecamping.com

SEE AD CAPE COD PAGE 348

ERVING—B-2

(E) ERVING STATE FOREST—(Franklin) *From town: Go E on Hwy 2, then turn at firestation & follow signs.* FACILITIES: 29 sites, 16 ft max RV length, 29 no hkups, tenting. RECREATION: lake swim, boating, 10 hp limit, canoeing, ramp, lake fishing. Open May 25 - Oct 8. Phone: (978)544-3939.

FALMOUTH—D-5

(N) Sippewissett Cabins & Campground—(Barnstable) *From jct Hwy 28 & Sippewissett Cutoff: Go 200 yards W, then 1/2 mi S on Palmer Ave. Enter on R.* ◆◆◆FACILITIES: 100 sites, typical site width 30 ft, 34 ft max RV length, 70 W&E, (20/30 amps), 30 no hkups, family camping, tenting, dump, laundry, ltd groc. ◆◆RECREATION: playground. No pets. Open May 15 - Oct 15. Rate in 2010 $34-45 for 2 persons. Member ARVC, MACO. Phone: (508)548-2542.

(E) WAQUOIT BAY NAT'L. ESTUARINE RESERVE (SP)—(Barnstable) *Private boat access only. From US 6 (exit 2): Go E on Hwy 130 to Great Neck Rd to Mashpee rotary, then 3-1/2 mi N on Hwy 28.* FACILITIES: 11 sites, 11 no hkups, tenting. RECREATION: boating, no motors, canoeing, saltwater fishing. Partial handicap access. Open May 12 - Oct 8. Phone: (508)457-0495.

FLORIDA—A-1

(S) SAVOY MOUNTAIN SF—(Berkshire) *From town: Go 1 mi W on Hwy 2, then 4 mi S on Central Shaft Rd.* FACILITIES: 45 sites, 16 ft max RV length, 45 no hkups, tenting. RECREATION: boating, no motors, canoeing, ramp. Partial handicap access. Open May 15 - Oct 15. Phone: (413)663-8469.

FOXBORO—C-4

(SW) NORMANDY FARMS FAMILY CAMPING RESORT—(Norfolk) *From jct I-495 (exit 14A) & US 1: Go 1 mi N on US 1, then 1-1/2 mi E on Thurston-West Sts. Enter on R.*

◆◆◆◆◆FACILITIES: 379 sites, typical site width 35 ft, 232 full hkups, 134 W&E, (20/30/50 amps), 13 no hkups, 225 pull-thrus, cable TV, WiFi Instant Internet at site, WiFi Internet central location, family camping, tenting, cabins, RV storage, dump, non-guest dump $, portable dump, laundry, full svc store, RV supplies, LP gas by weight/by meter, ice, picnic tables, patios, fire rings, grills, wood, controlled access.

◆◆◆◆◆RECREATION: rec hall, rec room/area, pavilion, coin games, 4 swim pools, hot tub, pond fishing, fishing supplies, golf nearby, bsktball, playground, shuffleboard court 2 shuffleboard courts, activities, horseshoes, sports field, hiking trails, v-ball.

Pets welcome. Partial handicap access. Open all yr. Park fully operational all year. Big rigs welcome. Escort to site. Clubs welcome. Rate in 2010 $30-76 for 2 persons. MC/VISA/DISC. ATM. Member ARVC, MACO.

FOXBORO—Continued
NORMANDY FARMS FAMILY CAMPING RESORT—Continued

Phone: (866)673-2767
Address: 72 West Street, Foxboro, MA 02035
Lat/Lon: 42.04141/-71.28137
Email: camp@normandyfarms.com
Web: www.NORMANDYFARMS.com

SEE AD BOSTON PAGE 345

GLOUCESTER—B-5

(NW) CAPE ANN CAMP SITE—(Essex) *From jct Hwy 128 & Concord St (exit 13): Go 3/4 mi N on Concord St, then 1/2 mi NE on Atlantic St (Wingaersheek Beach Rd). Enter on L.*

◆◆◆FACILITIES: 230 sites, typical site width 40 ft, 40 full hkups, 90 W&E, (20/30/50 amps), 100 no hkups, some extd stay sites, WiFi Instant Internet at site, WiFi Internet central location, family camping, tenting, shower$, dump, non-guest dump $, groceries, RV supplies, ice, picnic tables, fire rings, wood.

Pets welcome. Open Mid May - Mid Oct. Mid June-Labor Day: 3 day minimum Friday arrivals, 2 day minimum Saturday arrivals. Big rigs welcome. Rate in 2010 $36-52 for 2 persons. MC/VISA. Member ARVC, MACO.

Phone: (978)283-8683
Address: 80 Atlantic St, Gloucester, MA 01930
Lat/Lon: 42.63959/-70.70061
Email: info@capeanncampsite.com
Web: www.capeanncampsite.com

SEE AD BOSTON PAGE 345

GOSHEN—B-2

(NE) D.A.R. STATE FOREST—(Hampshire) *From jct Hwy 9 & Hwy 112: Follow signs N on Hwy 112.* FACILITIES: 52 sites, 52 no hkups, tenting, dump. RECREATION: lake swim, boating, no motors, canoeing, ramp, lake fishing. Partial handicap access. Open all yr. Phone: (413)268-7098.

GRANVILLE—C-2

(W) GRANVILLE STATE FOREST—(Hampden) *From town: Go 7 mi W on Hwy-57, then 2 mi S on W Hartland Rd.* FACILITIES: 22 sites, 31 ft max RV length, 22 no hkups, tenting. RECREATION: river swim, river fishing. Partial handicap access. Open May 25 - Oct 8. Phone: (413)357-6611.

(W) Prospect Mountain Campground & RV Park—(Hampden) *From jct Hwy 189 & Hwy 57: Go 4-1/2 mi W on Hwy 57. Enter on L.* ◆◆◆FACILITIES: 205 sites, 23 full hkups, 170 W&E, (20/30/50 amps), 12 no hkups, 21 pull-thrus, family camping, tenting, dump, laundry, ltd groc. ◆◆◆◆RECREATION: swim pool, boating, no motors, pond fishing, playground. Pets welcome. Open Late Apr - Mid Oct. Big rigs welcome. Rate in 2010 $34-46 per family. Member ARVC, MACO. Phone: (413)357-6494.

HINGHAM—B-5

BOSTON HARBOR ISLANDS STATE PARK—(Norfolk) *From Hingham Shipyard at 349 Lincoln St./Hwy 3A: Ferry to campsites on 4 islands. (Apply for permit prior to date of camping trip). Ferry #617-227-4321.* FACILITIES: 20 sites, 20 no hkups, tenting. RECREATION: saltwater swim, boating, canoeing, saltwater fishing. No pets. Open May 25 - Sep 3. Phone: (781)740-1605.

(N) WOMPATUCK STATE PARK—(Norfolk) *From jct Hwy 3 (exit 14) & Hwy 228: Go N on Hwy 228. Follow signs.* FACILITIES: 260 sites, 30 ft max RV length, 138 E, (20 amps), 122 no hkups, tenting, dump. RECREATION: boating, no motors, ramp. Partial handicap access. Open Apr 14 - Oct 28. Phone: (781)749-7160.

HUMAROCK—C-5

(E) MILITARY PARK (Fourth Cliff Rec. Area-Hanscom AFB)—(Plymouth) *Off base, 30 mi S of Boston. From jct Hwy 139: Go 1-1/2 mi SE on Hwy 139, then continue E on Furnace, then NE on Ferry St, then E on Sea, then N on Central.* FACILITIES: 11 sites, 11 full hkups, (30/50 amps), tenting, dump, laundry. RECREATION: saltwater swim, saltwater fishing. Open all yr. Phone: (781)837-6785.

LANESBOROUGH—B-1

(NW) Hidden Valley Campground—(Berkshire) *From jct US 7 and N Main St.: Go 3/4 mi N on N Main St., then 4 blocks N on Scott Rd. Enter on L.* ◆◆◆FACILITIES: 104 sites, typical site width 35 ft, 85 W&E, (20/30/50 amps), 19 no hkups, heater not allowed, WiFi Internet central location, family camping, tenting, shower$, dump, non-guest dump $, portable dump, laundry, ltd groc, RV supplies, LP gas by weight/by meter, ice, picnic tables, fire rings, wood. ◆◆◆RECREATION: rec hall, swim pool, pond fishing, fishing supplies, bsktball, play equipment, activities horseshoes, v-ball. Pets welcome, breed restrict, quantity restrict. Open all yr. Facilities fully operational May 15 - Columbus Day. Big rigs welcome. Rate in 2010 $28 per family. MC/VISA/DISC/Debit. Member

Hidden Valley Campground—Continued on next page

LANESBOROUGH—Continued
Hidden Valley Campground—Continued

ARVC, MACO. CCUSA 50% Discount. CCUSA reservations Recommended, CCUSA max stay 1 day, CCUSA disc. not avail F,Sa, CCUSA disc. not avail holidays. Fully operational May 15-Columbus Day. No electric heater allowed.

Phone: (877)392-2267
Address: 15 Scott Rd, Lanesborough, MA 01237
Lat/Lon: 42.55123/-73.22948
Email: hdnvaly@bcn.net
Web: www.hiddenvalleycg.com

LEE—B-1

(W) OCTOBER MOUNTAIN STATE FOREST—(Berkshire) *From jct I-90 (exit 2) & US 20: Go N on US 20W, then E on Center St. Follow signs.* FACILITIES: 46 sites, 30 ft max RV length, 46 no hkups, 7 pull-thrus, tenting, dump. RECREATION: boating, no motors, canoeing, lake/stream fishing. Partial handicap access. Open May 12 - Oct 8. Phone: (413)243-1778.

LENOX—B-1

WOODLAND HILLS CAMPGROUND—*About 15 minutes from Lenox: Go W on Hwy 183 to Hwy 102, then turn right on Hwy 102 to Hwy 22, then left on Hwy 22 to Middle Rd, then 1/2 mi W on Middle Rd, then 3/4 mi N on Fog Hill Rd. Enter on L.*

SEE PRIMARY LISTING AT AUSTERLITZ, NY AND AD AUSTERLITZ, NY PAGE 538

LITTLETON—B-4

(W) BOSTON MINUTEMAN CAMPGROUND—(Middlesex) *From jct I-495 (exit 30) & Hwy 2A: Go 2-3/4 mi W on Hwy 2A. Enter on L.*

◊◊◊◊FACILITIES: 93 sites, typical site width 40 ft, 45 full hkups, 48 W&E, (20/30/50 amps), 20 pull-thrus, cable TV, WiFi Instant Internet at site, WiFi Internet central location, family camping, tenting, cabins, dump, laundry, groceries, RV supplies, LP gas by weight/by meter, ice, picnic tables, fire rings, wood.

◊◊◊RECREATION: rec hall, rec room/area, coin games, swim pool, golf nearby, bsktball, playground, horseshoes, sports field, v-ball.

Pets welcome. Partial handicap access. Open May 1 - 3rd week of Oct. Pool open Memorial Day - Labor Day. Big rigs welcome. Escort to site. Clubs welcome. Rate in 2010 $40-51 for 2 persons. MC/VISA. Member ARVC, MACO.

Phone: (978)772-0042
Address: 264 Ayer Rd (Rte. 2A), Littleton, MA 01460
Lat/Lon: 42.55128/-71.53767
Email: info@minutemancampground.com
Web: www.minutemancampground.com

SEE AD BOSTON PAGE 345

MANSFIELD—C-4

(E) CANOE RIVER CAMPGROUND—(Bristol) *From jct I-495 (exit 10) & Hwy 123: Go 1 mi E on Hwy 123, then 2-1/4 mi N on Newland St/Mill St. Enter on L.*

◊◊◊FACILITIES: 280 sites, typical site width 24 ft, 250 full hkups, (30/50 amps), 30 no hkups, some extd stay sites, 23 pull-thrus, WiFi Instant Internet at site ($), family camping, tenting, shower$, dump, non-guest dump $, portable dump, laundry, groceries, RV supplies, LP gas by weight/by meter, ice, picnic tables, wood, controlled access.

◊◊◊◊RECREATION: rec hall, rec room/area, coin games, 2 swim pools, boating, no motors, canoeing, kayaking, dock, 4 canoe/10 pedal boat rentals, pond fishing, fishing supplies, golf nearby, bsktball, playground, activities, horseshoes, sports field.

Pets welcome, breed restrict, quantity restrict. Partial handicap access. Open all yr. Facilities fully operational Apr 15 - Oct 15. Limited facilities Mid Oct-Mid Apr. Escort to site. Clubs welcome. Rate in 2010 $33-40 per family. MC/VISA/DISC/AMEX/Debit. Member ARVC, MACO.

Phone: (508)339-6462
Address: 137 Mill St, Mansfield, MA 02048
Lat/Lon: 42.01925/-71.18028
Email: joe@canoeriver.com
Web: www.canoeriver.com

SEE AD THIS PAGE

MARTHA'S VINEYARD—D-5

See listings at Vineyard Haven

(S) MARTHA'S VINEYARD FAMILY CAMPGROUND—(Dukes) *From the Steamship Authority in Vineyard Haven: At the 1st intersection past Stop & Shop, then 1/4 mi W (uphill away from the ocean), then 1-1/4 mi S on Edgartown Rd. (Follow large blue signs). Enter on R.*

◊◊◊FACILITIES: 157 sites, 50 full hkups, 87 W&E, (20/30/50 amps), 20 no hkups, some extd stay sites (summer), cable TV, ($), WiFi Internet central location, family camping, tenting, cabins, dump, non-guest dump $, laundry, groceries, RV supplies, ice, picnic tables, fire rings, wood.

◊◊◊RECREATION: rec room/area, coin games, golf nearby, bsktball, 25 bike rentals, playground, sports field, hiking trails, v-ball.

No pets. Partial handicap access. Open Mid May - Oct 15. Clubs welcome. Rate in 2010 $55 for 2 persons. MC/VISA/DISC. Member ARVC, MACO.

Phone: (508)693-3772
Address: 569 Edgartown Rd, Vineyard Haven, MA 02568
Lat/Lon: 41.43565/-70.61008
Email: info@campmv.com
Web: www.campmv.com

SEE AD THIS PAGE

MASHPEE—D-5

(N) John's Pond Campground/Otis Trailer Village—(Barnstable) *From west jct Hwy 28 & Hwy 151: Go 3-1/2 mi E on Hwy 151, then 2-1/4 mi N on Sandwich Rd. Enter on R.* ◊◊FACILITIES: 144 sites, typical site width 25 ft, 32 ft max RV length, 90 full hkups, (20/30 amps), 54 no hkups, family camping, tenting. ◊◊RECREATION: lake swim, boating, canoeing, lake fishing. Pets welcome. Partial handicap access. Open Apr 15 - Oct 15. Rate in 2010 $45 for 4 persons. Member ARVC, MACO. Phone: (508)477-0444.

MIDDLEBORO—C-5

(N) Boston/Cape Cod KOA—(Plymouth) *From jct I-495 (exit 6) & US 44: Go 2-3/4 mi E on US 44. Enter on L.* ◊◊◊◊FACILITIES: 238 sites, typical site width 30 ft, 115 full hkups, 118 W&E, (20/30/50 amps), 5 no hkups, 50 pull-thrus, family camping, tenting, dump, laundry, ltd groc. ◊◊◊◊◊RECREATION: swim pool, playground. Pets welcome, breed restrict. Partial handicap access. Open Mar 1 - Nov 30. Big rigs welcome. Rate in 2010 $33-69 for 2 persons. Member ARVC, MACO. Phone: (800)562-3046. KOA discount.

MONSON—C-2

(S) Partridge Hollow Camping Area—(Hampden) *From jct I-90 (exit 8) & Hwy 32: Go 3/4 mi S on Hwy 32, then 5-4/10 mi E on US 20, then 3/4 mi SW on Monson Rd, then at Brimfield State Park sign go 2-1/2 mi SE on Dean Pond Rd. Enter on R.* ◊◊◊◊FACILITIES: 244 sites, typical site width 35 ft, 125 full hkups, 101 W&E, (20/30/50 amps), 50 amps ($), 18 no hkups, 3 pull-thrus, family camping, tenting, dump, laundry, ltd groc. ◊◊◊◊RECREATION: swim pool, playground. Pets welcome, breed restrict, quantity restrict. Open mid Apr - Columbus Day Weekend. Big rigs welcome. Rate in 2010 $30-36 for 2 persons. Member ARVC, MACO. Phone: (413)267-5122.

(NE) SUNSETVIEW FARM CAMPING AREA—(Hampden) *From jct I-90 (exit 8) & Hwy 32: Go 2-1/4 mi S on Hwy 32, then left 1/2 mi on Fenton Rd. (Big Rigs phone ahead for alternate route.). Enter on L.*

◊◊◊◊FACILITIES: 200 sites, typical site width 28 ft, 180 full hkups, 20 W&E, (20/30/50 amps), 50 amps ($), many extd stay sites, 18 pull-thrus, WiFi Internet central location, family camping, tenting, shower$, dump, portable dump, laundry, ltd groc, RV supplies, ice, picnic tables, fire rings, wood, controlled access.

◊◊◊◊RECREATION: rec hall, equipped pavilion, coin games, swim pool, lake swim, golf nearby, bsktball, playground, shuffleboard court shuffleboard court, activities (wkends), horseshoes, sports field, hiking trails, v-ball.

Pets welcome, quantity restrict. Partial handicap access. Open Apr 15 - Oct 15. Rates higher during holidays & special events. Big rigs welcome. Escort to site. Clubs welcome. Rate in 2010 $32-36 for 2 persons. MC/VISA/DISC. Member ARVC, MACO.

Phone: (413)267-9269
Address: 57 Town Farm Rd, Monson, MA 01057
Lat/Lon: 42.12167/-72.29433
Email: camp@sunsetview.com
Web: www.sunsetview.com

SEE AD SPRINGFIELD PAGE 354

MONTEREY—C-1

(E) BEARTOWN SF—(Berkshire) *From jct US 7 & Hwy 23: Go E on Hwy 23 to Blue Hill Rd. Follow signs.* FACILITIES: 12 sites, 12 no hkups, tenting. RECREATION: boating, no motors, canoeing, ramp. Pets welcome. Partial handicap access. Open all yr. Facilities fully operational mid May - Columbus Day. Phone: (413) 528-0904.

NORTH ADAMS—A-1

(E) HISTORIC VALLEY CAMPGROUND (Municipal Park) —(Berkshire) *From jct Hwy 2 & E Main St: Go 1/4 mi S on E Main St, then 3/4 mi SE on Kemp Ave. Enter at end.* FACILITIES: 100 sites, 80 W&E, (20/30 amps), 20 no hkups, tenting, dump, laundry. RECREATION: lake swim, boating, no motors, canoeing, ramp, dock, lake fishing, playground. Open all yr. Phone: (413) 662-3198.

NORTH ANDOVER—A-4

(W) HAROLD PARKER STATE FOREST—(Middlesex) *From jct I-95 & Hwy 114: Go 10 mi W on Hwy 114. Follow signs.* FACILITIES: 91 sites, 20 ft max RV length, 91 no hkups, tenting, dump. RECREATION: lake swim, boating, no motors, canoeing, playground. Partial handicap access. Open mid Apr - Columbus Day. Phone: (978)686-3391.

NORTH EGREMONT—C-1

(SW) Prospect Lake Park—(Berkshire) *From jct Hwy-23 & Hwy-71: Go 3 mi W on Hwy-71, then 3/4 mi SW on Prospect Lake Rd. Enter on R.* ◊◊FACILITIES: 129 sites, typical site width 40 ft, 36 ft max RV length, 25 full hkups, 104 W&E, (20/30 amps), 30 pull-thrus, family camping, tenting, dump, laundry, ltd groc.

Prospect Lake Park—Continued on next page

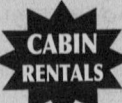

NORTH EGREMONT—Continued
Prospect Lake Park—Continued

◆◆◆RECREATION: lake swim, boating, 9.9 hp limit, canoeing, ramp, dock, lake fishing, playground. Pets welcome ($). Open 1st weekend in May - Oct 15. Rate in 2010 $28-32 for 2 persons. Member ARVC, MACO. Phone: (877)860-4757.

NORTH TRURO—C-6

(NE) Adventure Bound Camping Resorts - Cape Cod (Formerly North Truro Camping Area)—(Barnstable) *From Jct Hwy 6 & Highland Rd: Go 1/4 mi E on Highland Rd. Enter on L.* ◆◆◆FACILITIES: 332 sites, 107 full hkups, 125 W&E, (30 amps), 100 no hkups, family camping, tenting, dump, laundry, ltd groc. ◆◆◆RECREATION: playground. Pets welcome, breed restrict. Open Early Apr - End Oct. Rate in 2010 $25-54 for 2 persons. Member ARVC, MACO. Phone: (508)487-1847.

OAKHAM—B-3

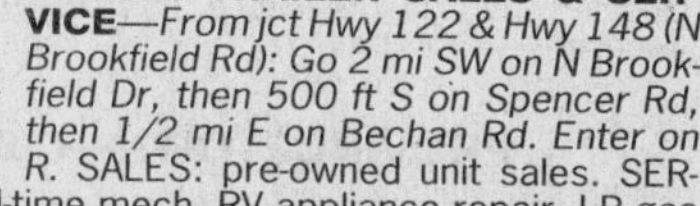

✲ **(SE) OAKHAM TRAILER SALES & SERVICE**—*From jct Hwy 122 & Hwy 148 (N Brookfield Rd): Go 2 mi SW on N Brookfield Dr, then 500 ft S on Spencer Rd, then 1/2 mi E on Bechan Rd. Enter on R.* SALES: pre-owned unit sales. SERVICES: full-time mech, RV appliance repair, LP gas by weight/by meter, dump station, RV storage, sells parts/accessories. Open all yr. MC/VISA/DISC. ATM.

Phone: (508)882-9511
Address: 204 Bechan Road, Oakham, MA 01068
Lat/Lon: 42.34032/-72.02761
Email: service@pineacresresort.com
Web: www.oakhamtrailersales.com

SEE AD THIS PAGE

(SE) PINE ACRES FAMILY CAMPING RESORT—(Worcester) *From jct Hwy 122 & Hwy 148 (N Brookfield Rd): Go 2 mi SW on N Brookfield Rd, then 500 ft S on Spencer Rd, then 1/2 mi E on Bechan Rd. Enter on L.*

YOUR PERFECT NEW ENGLAND GETAWAY! Resort Pool, Kids Fun Splash Zone, Adult Spa. WI-FI Gem Mine, ATM, Family Fun Arcade, Fun Boat Marina, Cabin/RV Rentals Lakeside, Country Store & Cafe, Mini-Golf, Dog Park, Big Rigs Welcome, and Many Resort Amenities!

◆◆◆◆◆FACILITIES: 350 sites, typical site width 40 ft, 300 full hkups, 15 W&E, (20/30/50 amps), 35 no hkups, some extd stay sites, 5 pull-thrus, cable TV, WiFi Instant Internet at site ($), family camping, tenting, RV's/park model rentals, cabins, RV storage, dump, portable dump, laundry, groceries, RV supplies, LP gas by weight/by meter, ice, picnic tables, fire rings, grills, wood, controlled access.

◆◆◆◆◆RECREATION: rec hall, rec room/area, pavilion, coin games, swim pool, spray ground, lake swim, hot tub, boating, canoeing, kayaking, ramp, dock, 4 rowboat/6 canoe/6 kayak/6 pedal boat/2 motorboat rentals, lake fishing, fishing supplies, mini-golf, ($), golf nearby, bsktball, 4 bike rentals, playground, activities, tennis, horseshoes, sports field, hiking trails, v-ball.

Pets welcome ($), breed restrict, quantity restrict. Partial handicap access. Open all yr. Recreational facilities limited in winter months. Big rigs welcome. Escort to site. Clubs welcome. Rate in 2010 $41-75 for 2 persons. MC/VISA/DISC. ATM. Member ARVC, MACO.

Text 81929 to (440)725-8687 to see our Visual Tour.

Phone: (508)882-9509
Address: 203 Bechan Rd, Oakham, MA 01068
Lat/Lon: 42.34032/-72.02761
Email: camp@pineacresresort.com
Web: www.pineacresresort.com

SEE AD THIS PAGE

OTIS—C-1

(SE) Camp Overflow Campground & Marina—(Berkshire) *From jct Hwy 8 & Hwy 23: Go 3 mi E on Hwy 23, then 2 mi S on Westshore Rd/Reservoir Rd/Tolland Rd (follow signs). Enter on R.* ◆◆◆FACILITIES: 225 sites, 35 ft max RV length, 200 W&E, (20/30/50 amps), 25 no hkups, family camping, tenting, dump, laundry, ltd groc. ◆◆◆RECREATION: lake swim, boating, canoeing, ramp, dock, lake fishing, playground. Pets welcome, quantity restrict. Open May 15 - Oct 1. Rate in 2010 $40 for 2 persons. Member ARVC, MACO. Phone: (413)269-4036.

Visit Woodall's blog at blog.woodalls.com

OTIS—Continued

(E) TOLLAND STATE FOREST—(Berkshire) *From town: Go S on Hwy 8, then E on Reservoir Rd.* FACILITIES: 92 sites, 24 ft max RV length, 92 no hkups, tenting, dump. RECREATION: boating, canoeing, ramp. Partial handicap access. Open May 15 - Oct 15. Phone: (413)269-6002.

PHILLIPSTON—B-3

(N) Lamb City Campground—(Worcester) *From jct US 2 (exit 19) & Hwy 2A: Go 400 feet on Hwy 2A, then 1/2 mi on Royalston Rd. Follow camping signs. Enter on L.* ◆◆◆FACILITIES: 241 sites, typical site width 44 ft, 224 full hkups, 17 W&E, (20/30/50 amps), 6 pull-thrus, family camping, tenting, dump, laundry, full svc store. ◆◆◆◆◆RECREATION: 2 swim pools, boating, electric motors only, canoeing, dock, pond fishing, playground. Pets welcome, breed restrict, quantity restrict. Partial handicap access. Open all yr. Facilities fully operational Mid May - Mid Oct. Rate in 2010 $28-44 per family. Member ARVC, MACO. Phone: (800)292-5262.

There is a house in Rockport built entirely of newspaper.

PITTSFIELD—B-1

(W) PITTSFIELD STATE FOREST—(Berkshire) *From jct US 7/20 & US 20: Go W on US 20. Follow signs.* FACILITIES: 33 sites, 16 ft max RV length, 33 no hkups, tenting. RECREATION: river swim, boating, no motors, canoeing, river fishing. Partial handicap access. Open May 12 - Oct 8. Phone: (413)442-8992.

PLAINFIELD—B-1

(NE) Peppermint Park Camping Resort—(Hampshire) *From jct Hwys-8A/116: Go 4 mi SE on Hwy-116, then 1 mi NE on Bow St. Enter on R.* ◆◆◆FACILITIES: 200 sites, 125 full hkups, 25 W&E, (20/30/50 amps), 50 no hkups, family camping, tenting, dump, laundry, ltd groc. ◆◆◆◆RECREATION: swim pool, playground. Pets welcome. Open all yr. Facilities fully operational May 15 - Nov 1. Rate in 2010 $34-38 per family. Member ARVC, MACO. Phone: (413) 634-5385.

PLYMOUTH—C-5

See listings at Bourne, Middleboro & Sandwich

PLYMOUTH—Continued on next page

PLYMOUTH—Continued

(SW) Ellis Haven Campground—(Plymouth) *From jct Hwy 3 & Hwy 44 (exit 6): Go 1 mi W on Hwy 44, then 2-1/2 mi SW on Seven Hills & Federal Furnace Rd. Enter on R.* ◆◆◆FACILITIES: 642 sites, typical site width 40 ft, 64 full hkups, 538 W&E, (30/50 amps), 40 no hkups, 10 pull-thrus, family camping, tenting, dump, laundry. ◆◆◆RECREATION: lake swim, boating, no motors, canoeing, lake fishing, playground. Pets welcome ($), quantity restrict. Partial handicap access. Open May 1 - Oct 1. Rate in 2010 $52-57 for 4 persons. Member ARVC, MACO. Phone: (508)746-0803.

(S) Indianhead Resort—(Plymouth) *From jct Hwy 44 & Hwy 3 (exit 6): Go 15 mi S on Hwy 3 (exit 2), then 2 mi N on Hwy 3A. Enter on L.* ◆◆◆FACILITIES: 200 sites, typical site width 40 ft, 200 W&E, (20/30/50 amps), family camping, tenting, dump, laundry, groceries. ◆◆RECREATION: boating, no motors, canoeing, pond fishing, playground. Pets welcome, breed restrict. Open mid Apr - Columbus Day. Rate in 2010 $35-40 for 4 persons. Member ARVC, MACO. Phone: (508)888-3688.

(W) PINEWOOD LODGE CAMPGROUND—(Plymouth) *S'bnd from jct Hwy 3 & Samoset/Carver Rd (exit 6B): Go 3 mi W on Samoset/Carver Rd, then 1/2 mi S on Pinewood Rd; N'bnd from jct Hwy 3 & Samoset/Carver Rd (exit 6): Go 3 mi W on Samoset/Carver Rd, then 1/2 mi S on Pinewood Rd. Enter at end.*

PLYMOUTH-BETWEEN BOSTON & CAPE COD

Nestled on over 200 acres of white pine forest are 275 beautifully spaced sites. Some in secluded tenting areas, others with full facilities for any size rig. So come gather around the campfire and enjoy the great outdoors.

◆◆◆◆FACILITIES: 279 sites, 109 full hkups, 150 W&E, (20/30/50 amps), 20 no hkups, some extd stay sites (summer), 18 pull-thrus, cable TV, WiFi Instant Internet at site ($), WiFi Internet central location ($), family camping, tenting, RV's/park model rentals, cabins, RV storage, shower$, dump, non-guest dump $, portable dump, laundry, ltd groc, RV supplies, LP gas by weight/by meter, ice, picnic tables, fire rings, wood, controlled access.

PLYMOUTH—Continued
PINEWOOD LODGE CAMPGROUND—Continued

◆◆◆◆◆RECREATION: rec hall, rec room/area, pavilion, coin games, lake swim, boating, electric motors only, canoeing, kayaking, ramp, dock, 5 rowboat/2 canoe/5 kayak rentals, lake fishing, fishing supplies, golf nearby, bsktball, playground, activities, (wkends), horseshoes, sports field, hiking trails, v-ball

Pets welcome ($), breed restrict, size restrict, quantity restrict. Partial handicap access. Open May 1 - Oct 30. Facilities fully operational May 15 - Oct 15. Call for Holiday & special event rates. Big rigs welcome. Escort to site. Clubs welcome. Rate in 2010 $25-51 for 2 persons. MC/VISA/Debit. Member ARVC, MACO. FCRV discount. FMCA discount. CCUSA 50% Discount. CCUSA reservations Recommended, CCUSA max stay 2 days, CCUSA disc. not avail S, CCUSA disc. not avail F'Sa, CCUSA disc. not avail holidays. Not available Jun 30 thru Aug 15. Pet breed & weight restrictions, refer to pet policy on park website or call for details.

Text 83385 to (440)725-8687 to see our Visual Tour.

Phone: (508)746-3548
Address: 190 Pinewood Rd, Plymouth, MA 02360
Lat/Lon: 41.92663/-70.73402
Email: camp@pinewoodlodge.com
Web: www.pinewoodlodge.com

SEE AD THIS PAGE

(W) PINEWOOD LODGE RV SERVICE—*S'bnd from jct Hwy 3 & Samoset/Carver Rd (exit 6B): Go 3 mi W on Samoset/Carver Rd, then 1/2 mi S on Pinewood Rd. N'bnd from jct Hwy 3 & Samoset/Carver Rd (exit 6): Go 3 mi W on Samoset/Carver Rd, then 1/2 mi S on Pinewood Rd. Enter at end.* SALES: pre-owned unit sales. SERVICES: full-time mech, RV appliance repair, LP gas by weight/by meter, dump station, RV storage, sells parts/accessories. Open May 1 - Oct 30. MC/VISA/Debit.

Woodall's — Trusted for Over 75 Years.

PLYMOUTH—Continued
PINEWOOD LODGE RV SERVICE—Continued

Phone: (508)746-3548
Address: 190 Pinewood Rd, Plymouth, MA 02360
Lat/Lon: 41.92663/-70.73402
Email: camp@pinewoodlodge.com
Web: www.pinewoodlodge.com

SEE AD THIS PAGE

(SW) Sandy Pond Campground—(Plymouth) *From jct I-195 & I-495: Go 12 mi SE on Hwy 25 (exit 3/ Bourne-Sagamore), then 1st right at Rotary, then 1-1/2 mi NW on Head of Bay Rd, then 1-3/4 mi N on Plymouth Lane (Bourne Rd). Enter on R.* ◆◆◆FACILITIES: 217 sites, typical site width 40 ft, 101 full hkups, 89 W&E, (30/50 amps), 27 no hkups, 13 pull-thrus, family camping, tenting, dump, laundry. ◆◆◆◆RECREATION: swim pool, boating, electric motors only, canoeing, pond fishing, playground. Pets welcome ($), breed restrict. Partial handicap access. Open Mid Apr - Mid Oct. Big rigs welcome. Rate in 2010 $35-42 for 2 persons. Member ARVC, MACO. Phone: (508)759-9336. FMCA discount.

PROVINCETOWN—C-6

(NW) Coastal Acres Camping Court—(Barnstable) *From jct US 6 & Hwy 6A: Go 1/2 mi N on Hwy 6A, then 1/2 mi W on West Vine. Enter at end.* ◆◆◆FACILITIES: 114 sites, typical site width 50 ft, 80 W&E, (20/30 amps), 34 no hkups, family camping, tenting, dump, ltd groc. Pets welcome ($), quantity restrict. Partial handicap access. Open Apr 1 - Nov 1. Rate in 2010 $32-56 for 2 persons. Member ARVC, MACO. Phone: (508)487-1700.

(N) Dunes' Edge Campground—(Barnstable) *From sign "Entering Provincetown": Go 2 mi E on Hwy 6 (After milepost 116). Enter on R.* ◆◆◆FACILITIES: 100 sites, typical site width 50 ft, 32 ft max RV length, 15 W&E, 8 E, (20/30 amps), 77 no hkups, family camping, tenting, dump, laundry, ltd groc. Pets welcome, breed restrict, quantity restrict. Partial handicap access. Open early May - late Sep. Rate in 2010 $38-50 for 2 persons. Member ARVC, MACO. Phone: (508)487-9815.

In 1634, Boston Common became the first public park in America.

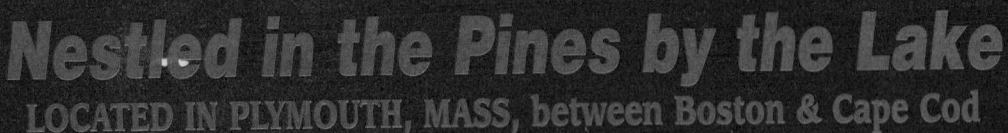

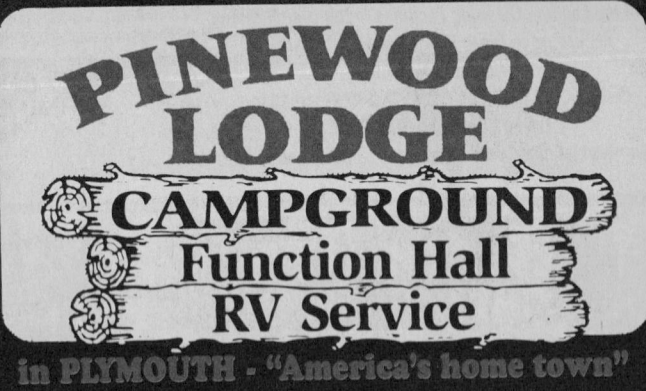

SALEM—B-5

(NE) WINTER ISLAND PARK (City Park)—(Essex) *From jct Derby St & Fort Ave in town: Go 3/4 mi NE on Fort Ave, then 1/2 mi E on Winter Island Rd. Enter at end.* FACILITIES: 57 sites, typical site width 15 ft, 30 W&E, 27 no hkups, tenting, dump, ltd groc. RECREATION: saltwater swim, boating, canoeing, ramp, dock, saltwater/pond fishing. Open May 1 - Oct 31. Phone: (978) 745-9430.

SALISBURY—A-5

(N) BLACK BEAR CAMPGROUND—(Essex) *From jct I-95 (exit 60) & Hwy 286: Go down ramp to first traffic light, then 200 feet E on Main St. Enter on L.*

WELCOME

◊◊◊◊◊FACILITIES: 285 sites, typical site width 30 ft, 200 full hkups, 35 W&E, (20/30/50 amps), 50 no hkups, some extd stay sites (summer), 20 pull-thrus, heater not allowed, cable TV, WiFi Instant Internet at site, WiFi Internet central location, family camping, tenting, shower$, dump, laundry, ice, picnic tables, fire rings, wood, controlled access.

◊◊◊◊RECREATION: rec hall, rec room/area, coin games, 2 swim pools, golf nearby, bsktball, playground, shuffleboard court shuffleboard court, horseshoes, sports field, v-ball.

Pets welcome, size restrict. Partial handicap access. Open May 15 - Sep 30. Big rigs welcome. Escort to site. Clubs welcome. Rate in 2010 $40-45 for 2 persons. MC/VISA. Member ARVC, MACO.

Phone: (978)462-3183
Address: 54 Main St, Salisbury, MA 01952
Lat/Lon: 42.87049/-70.88141
Email: bbcamping@aol.com
Web: www.blackbearcamping.com

SEE AD THIS PAGE

(E) Pines Camping Area—(Essex) *From jct I-95 (exit 58) & Hwy 110: Go 2-1/4 mi E on Hwy 110, then 500 ft N on US 1/US 1A, then 1/2 mi E on US 1A, then 50 ft S on Glenwood, then 1/2 m SE on CCC Rd.* ◊◊◊FACILITIES: 210 sites, 22 full hkups, 165 W&E, (20/30/50 amps), 23 no hkups, 6 pull-thrus, family camping, tenting, dump, laundry, ltd groc. ◊◊◊RECREATION: swim pool, playground. Pets welcome. Partial handicap access. Open Early Apr - Late Oct. Rate in 2010 $37-42 for 2 persons. Member ARVC, MACO. Phone: (978)465-0013.

(N) RUSNIK FAMILY CAMPGROUND—(Essex) *From jct I-495 (exit 55) & Hwy 110: Go 3-1/2 mi E on Hwy 110, then 1 mi N on US 1. Enter on L.*

WELCOME

◊◊◊FACILITIES: 150 sites, typical site width 40 ft, 150 W&E, (30 amps), many extd stay sites, heater not allowed, family camping, tenting, RV's/park model rentals, shower$, dump, portable dump, laundry, RV supplies, ice, picnic tables, fire rings, wood, controlled access.

SALISBURY—Continued
RUSNIK FAMILY CAMPGROUND—Continued

◊◊◊◊RECREATION: rec room/area, pavilion, coin games, swim pool, mini-golf, ($), golf nearby, bsktball, playground, shuffleboard court 2 shuffleboard courts, horseshoes, sports field, v-ball.

Pets welcome. Partial handicap access. Open May 15 - Columbus Day. Clubs welcome. Rate in 2010 $32-40 for 2 persons. MC/VISA. Member ARVC, MACO. FMCA discount.

Phone: (978)462-9551
Address: 115 Lafayette Rd, Salisbury, MA 01952
Lat/Lon: 42.85520/-70.87163
Email: rusnik2001@aol.com
Web: www.rusnik.com

SEE AD BOSTON PAGE 345

(N) SALISBURY BEACH STATE RESERVATION—(Essex) *From jct I-95 & Hwy 110: Go E on Hwy 110 to Hwy 1AN. Follow signs.* FACILITIES: 484 sites, 31 ft max RV length, 484 W&E, (20 amps), tenting, dump. RECREATION: boating, canoeing, ramp, playground. Partial handicap access. Facilities fully operational Apr 15 - Oct 15. Phone: (877)422-6762.

SALISBURY BEACH—A-5

(E) BEACH ROSE RV PARK—(Essex) *From jct I-95 (exit 58) & Hwy 110: Go 2-1/2 mi E on Hwy110, then 500 ft N on US 1/US 1A, then 1-1/4 mi E on US 1A. Enter on L.*

WELCOME

◊◊◊◊◊FACILITIES: 50 sites, typical site width 40 ft, 50 full hkups, (20/30/50 amps), some extd stay sites, cable TV, WiFi Instant Internet at site, family camping, shower$, dump, non-guest dump $, laundry, LP gas by weight/by meter, ice, picnic tables, fire rings, wood, controlled access.

◊◊◊RECREATION: rec room/area, coin games, swim pool, golf nearby, bsktball, shuffleboard court shuffleboard court, activities (wkends), horseshoes.

Pets welcome ($). No tents. Open Apr 1 - Nov 15. Big rigs welcome. Clubs welcome. Rate in 2010 $37-56 for 2 persons. MC/VISA/DISC.

Phone: (800)382-2230
Address: 147 Beach Rd (SR 1A), Salisbury Beach, MA 01952
Lat/Lon: 42.83998/-70.83551
Email: info@beachroservpark.com
Web: www.beachroservpark.com

SEE AD THIS PAGE

552 original documents pertaining to the Salem witch trials of 1692 have been preserved and are still stored by the Peabody Essex Museum.

SANDWICH—D-5

(S) DUNROAMIN' COTTAGES & TRAILER PARK—(Barnstable) *From jct US 6 (exit 2) & Hwy 130: Go 3 mi S on Hwy 130, then 3/4 mi E on Quaker Meeting House Rd, then 1 mi S on Cotuit Rd, then 500 ft W on John Ewer Rd. Enter on R.*

WELCOME

◊◊◊FACILITIES: 66 sites, typical site width 50 ft, accepts full hkup units only, 66 full hkups, (20/30/50 amps), 50 amps ($), many extd stay sites, 66 pull-thrus, WiFi Internet central location, family camping, cabins, laundry, picnic tables.

◊◊◊RECREATION: lake swim, boating, canoeing, kayaking, 4 rowboat/pedal boat rentals, pond fishing, golf nearby, bsktball, playground, activities, horseshoes, hiking trails, v-ball.

Pets welcome, breed restrict. No tents. Open mid Apr - mid Oct. No restrooms. Escort to site. Rate in 2010 $35 for 4 persons. MC/VISA/DISC. Member ARVC, MACO.

Phone: (508)477-0541
Address: 5 John Ewer Rd, Sandwich, MA 02563-2668
Lat/Lon: 41.68347/-70.48008
Email: dunroamintrailer@aol.com
Web: www.dunroamintrailerpark.com

SEE AD THIS PAGE

(S) Peters Pond RV Resort (Morgan RV Resorts)—(Barnstable) *From jct US 6 (exit 2) & Hwy 130: Go 3 mi S on Hwy 130, then 3/4 mi E on Quaker Meeting House Rd, then 3/4 mi S on Cotuit Rd. Enter on R.* ◊◊◊◊FACILITIES: 418 sites, typical site width 40 ft, 400 full hkups, 17 W&E, (30/50 amps), 1 no hkups, 3 pull-thrus, family camping, tenting, dump, laundry, groceries. ◊◊◊◊◊RECREATION: lake swim, boating, canoeing, ramp, dock, lake fishing, playground. Pets welcome, breed restrict, quantity restrict. Partial handicap access. Open Mid Apr - Mid Oct. Big rigs welcome. Rate in 2010 $35.99-74.99 for 4 persons. Member ARVC, MACO. Phone: (508)477-1775.

SANDWICH—Continued on next page

SANDWICH—Continued

(NE) SCUSSET BEACH STATE PARK—(Plymouth) *From town: Go N over Sagamore Bridge, then E on Scusset Rd.* FACILITIES: 98 sites, 98 W&E, tenting, dump. RECREATION: saltwater swim, saltwater fishing. Partial handicap access. Open all yr. Phone: (508)888-0859.

(E) SHAWME CROWELL STATE FOREST—(Barnstable) *From town: Go 1-1/2 mi N on Hwy-6A, then 1-1/2 mi on Hwy-130.* FACILITIES: 285 sites, 30 ft max RV length, 285 no hkups, tenting, dump. RECREATION: Partial handicap access. Open all yr. Facilities fully operational mid Apr - mid Oct. Phone: (508)888-0351.

SAVOY—B-1

(E) Shady Pines Campground—(Berkshire) *From west jct Hwy 8A & Hwy 116: Go 3 mi SE on Hwy 116, then 1/4 mi N on Loop Rd. Enter on R.* ◇◇◇FACILITIES: 150 sites, typical site width 35 ft, 38 full hkups, 112 W&E, (20 amps), 12 pull-thrus, tenting, dump, laundry, ltd groc. ◇◇◇◇RECREATION: swim pool, playground. Pets welcome, quantity restrict. Partial handicap access. Open all yr. Facilities fully operational May 1 - Nov 1. Rate in 2010 $35-38 for 2 persons. Member ARVC, MACO. Phone: (413)743-2694.

SHELBURNE FALLS—B-2

See listing at Charlemont

SOUTH CARVER—C-5

(E) MYLES STANDISH STATE FOREST—(Plymouth) *From I-495 (exit 2) & Hwy 58: Go N on Hwy 58 to Cranberry Rd. Follow signs.* FACILITIES: 475 sites, 32 ft max RV length, 475 no hkups, tenting, dump. RECREATION: boating, electric motors only, canoeing, ramp. Partial handicap access. Open Apr 15 - Oct 15. Phone: (508)866-2526.

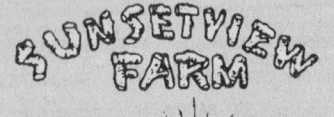

SOUTH DENNIS—D-6

(S) Old Chatham Road RV Resort—(Barnstable) *From Jct US 6 & Hwy 134: Go 1/2 mi N on Hwy 134, then 1/4 mi NE on Airline, then 1/4 mi SW on Old Chatham Rd. Enter on L.* ◇◇◇FACILITIES: 307 sites, typical site width 30 ft, 303 full hkups, 4 W&E, (15/20/30/50 amps), family camping, dump. ◇◇◇◇RECREATION: swim pool, playground. Pets welcome, breed restrict. No tents. Open Apr 15 - Oct 31. Rate in 2010 $34-65 for 2 persons. Phone: (508) 385-3616.

Reserve Online at Woodalls.com

SPRINGFIELD—C-2

See listings at Monson & Wales

STURBRIDGE—C-3

THE OLD SAWMILL CAMPGROUND—*From jct US 20 & Hwy 148: Go 8 mi N on Hwy 148, then 3 mi W on Hwy 9 to West Brookfield Center, then 1/2 mi S on Central St, then 200 yds W on Front St, then 3/4 mi S on Long Hill Rd. Enter on R.*

WELCOME

SEE PRIMARY LISTING AT WEST BROOKFIELD AND AD THIS PAGE

(E) WELLS STATE PARK—(Worcester) *From jct US-20 & Hwy-49: Go 2-1/4 mi N on Hwy-49 (Podnak Pike).* FACILITIES: 60 sites, 60 no hkups, tenting, dump. RECREATION: lake swim, boating, canoeing, ramp. Partial handicap access. Open May 1 - mid Oct. Phone: (508)347-9257.

(W) YOGI BEAR'S JELLYSTONE PARK-STURBRIDGE—(Worcester) *From jct US 20 & I-84: Go 1 mi W on I-84 to exit 2, then 3/4 mi E on River Rd (follow signs). Enter on R.*

WELCOME

JELLYSTONE PARK - MORE FUN THAN EVER

Come & Enjoy our Friendly Staff & Fun Activities - Lots to do with Never a Dull Moment, 2 Pools - Aquacenter & Waterslide, Lake with Sandy Beach - Boat Rentals & Fishing. Nightly Entertainment & Planned Recreational Activities.

◇◇◇FACILITIES: 358 sites, typical site width 28 ft, 55 full hkups, 277 W&E, (20/30/50 amps), 26 no hkups, some extd stay sites, 36 pull-thrus, cable TV, WiFi Instant Internet at site, WiFi Internet central location, family camping, tenting, RV's/park model rentals, cabins, dump, non-guest dump $, portable dump, laundry, groceries, RV supplies, LP gas by weight/by meter, ice, picnic tables, fire rings, wood, controlled access.

◇◇◇◇◇RECREATION: rec hall, rec room/area, coin games, 2 swim pools, lake swim, hot tub, boating, no motors, canoeing, kayaking, 2 rowboat/2 canoe/10 pedal boat rentals, lake fishing,

YOGI BEAR'S JELLYSTONE PARKSTURBRIDGE—Continued on next page

STURBRIDGE—Continued
YOGI BEAR'S JELLYSTONE PARKSTURBRIDGE—Continued

fishing supplies, mini-golf, ($), golf nearby, bsktball, playground, shuffleboard court 2 shuffleboard courts, activities, horseshoes, hiking trails, v-ball.

Pets welcome. Partial handicap access. Open all yr. Facilities fully operational Mid June - Labor Day. Escort to site. Clubs welcome. Rate in 2010 $30-67 for 2 persons. MC/VISA/DISC/AMEX. Member ARVC, MACO.

Phone: (508)347-9570
Address: 30 River Rd, Sturbridge, MA 01566
Lat/Lon: 42.08962/-72.08188
Email: rsmith@jellystonesturbridge.com
Web: www.jellystonesturbridge.com

SEE AD PAGE 354

SUTTON—C-3

(S) King's Family Campground—(Worcester) *From jct I-395 (exit 4A) & Sutton Ave: Go 3-1/4 mi E on Sutton Ave, then 2-1/2 mi SE on Manchaug, then 1/4 mi SW on Holt Rd. Enter on R.* ◊◊◊FACILITIES: 100 sites, typical site width 25 ft, 100 full hkups, (30/50 amps), family camping, tenting, dump, laundry, ltd groc. ◊◊◊RECREATION: lake swim, boating, canoeing, lake fishing, playground. Pets welcome, breed restrict, quantity restrict. Partial handicap access. Open May 1 - Oct 15. Rate in 2010 $45-55 per family. Member MACO. Phone: (877)279-3206.

TAUNTON—C-4

(E) MASSASOIT STATE PARK—(Bristol) *From jct Hwy 24 (exit 13) & US 44: Follow signs E on US 44.* FACILITIES: 126 sites, 21 ft max RV length, 24 W&E, 77 E, (30 amps), 25 no hkups, tenting, dump. RECREATION: lake swim, boating, no motors, canoeing, ramp. Partial handicap access. Open Apr 21 - Oct 8. Phone: (508)822-7405.

WALES—C-3

(C) Oak Haven Family Campground—(Hampden) *From jct US 20 & Hwy 19: Go 4-1/2 mi S on Hwy 19. Enter on L.* ◊◊◊◊FACILITIES: 140 sites, typical site width 32 ft, 96 full hkups, 44 W&E, (20/30/50 amps), 50 amps ($), 19 pull-thrus, family camping, tenting, dump, laundry, ltd groc. ◊◊◊◊RECREATION: swim pool, playground. Pets welcome, quantity restrict. Partial handicap access. Open May 1 - Columbus Day Weekend. Rate in 2010 $34-36 for 2 persons. Member ARVC, MACO. Phone: (413)245-7148. FCRV discount. FMCA discount.

WASHINGTON—B-1

(NE) Summit Hill Campground—(Berkshire) *From jct US 20 & Hwy 8: Go 11 mi N on Hwy 8, then 1-3/4 mi E on Summit Hill Rd. Enter on R.* ◊◊◊FACILITIES: 89 sites, typical site width 24 ft, 38 full hkups, 26 W&E, (15/30 amps), 25 no hkups, 1 pull-thrus, family camping, tenting, dump, laundry, ltd groc. ◊◊◊◊RECREATION: swim pool, playground. Pets welcome. Partial handicap access. Open May 1 - Oct 1. Rate in 2010 $40 per family. Member ARVC, MACO. Phone: (413)623-5761.

WEBSTER—C-3

(E) Indian Ranch Campground—(Worcester) *From jct I-395 (exit 2) & Hwy 16: Go 1-1/4 mi E on Hwy 16. Enter on R.* ◊◊◊◊FACILITIES: 200 sites, accepts full hkup units only, 200 full hkups, (20/30/50 amps), cable TV, WiFi Instant Internet at site, WiFi Internet central location, family camping, dump, portable dump, laundry, ice, picnic tables, fire rings, wood.

WEBSTER—Continued
Indian Ranch Campground—Continued

◊◊◊RECREATION: rec hall, equipped pavilion, lake swim, boating, dock, lake fishing, activities, horseshoes. Pets welcome, breed restrict, size restrict, quantity restrict. Partial handicap access. No tents. Open May 1 - Oct 15. Big rigs welcome. Rate in 2010 $35-70 for 2 persons. MC/VISA/DISC/AMEX. ATM. Member ARVC, MACO. CCUSA 50% Discount. CCUSA reservations Recommended, CCUSA max stay 3 days, CCUSA disc. not avail S, CCUSA disc. not avail F,Sa, CCUSA disc. not avail holidays. Not available Jun thru Aug.

Phone: (508)943-3871
Address: 200 Gore Rd (Rt 16), Webster, MA 01570
Lat/Lon: 42.05304/-71.83935
Email: camping@indianranch.com
Web: www.indianranch.com/camping

(E) WEBSTER/STURBRIDGE FAMILY CAMP—(Worcester) *From jct I-395 (exit 2) & Hwy 16: Go 2-1/2 mi E on Hwy 16. Enter on R.*

WELCOME

◊◊◊FACILITIES: 104 sites, typical site width 25 ft, 65 full hkups, 39 W&E, (30/50 amps), some extd stay sites, 29 pull-thrus, heater not allowed, cable TV, WiFi Instant Internet at site, family camping, tenting, RV storage, dump, non-guest dump $, portable dump, laundry, ltd groc, RV supplies, LP gas by weight/by meter, ice, picnic tables, fire rings, wood.

CAMPCLUB USA

◊◊◊RECREATION: rec room/area, coin games, swim pool, golf nearby, bsktball, playground, horseshoes, sports field, v-ball.

Pets welcome, breed restrict. Partial handicap access. Open all yr. Facilities fully operational Mid Apr - Mid Oct. Limited facilities during winter. Big rigs welcome. Escort to site. Clubs welcome. Rate in 2010 $32-36 for 2 persons. MC/VISA. CCUSA 50% Discount. CCUSA reservations Recommended, CCUSA max stay 4 days, CCUSA disc. not avail S, CCUSA disc. not avail F,Sa, CCUSA disc. not avail holidays. Electric heater not allowed.

Phone: (866)562-1895
Address: 106 Douglas Rd (Rt 16), Webster, MA 01570
Lat/Lon: 42.05841/-71.82224
Email: wbcamp_1@msn.com
Web: www.webstercamp.com

SEE AD STURBRIDGE PAGE 354

WELLFLEET—C-6

(N) Maurice's Campground—(Barnstable) *From jct US-6 & Entrance to National Seashore Visitors Center: Go 2-1/2 mi N on US-6 (Enter Park at Eastham-Wellfleet Town Line). Enter on R.* ◊◊◊FACILITIES: 237 sites, typical site width 50 ft, 32 ft max RV length, 168 full hkups, 53 W&E, (20/30 amps), 16 no hkups, family camping, tenting, dump, full svc store. ◊RECREATION: playground. No pets. Open Memorial Day Weekend - Columbus Day. Rate in 2010 $42-45 for 2 persons. Member ARVC, MACO. Phone: (508)349-2029.

WEST BROOKFIELD—C-3

(S) THE OLD SAWMILL CAMPGROUND—(Worcester) *From jct Hwy 148 & Hwy 9: Go 3 mi W on Hwy 9 to W Brookfield Center, then 1/2 mi S on Central St, then 200 yds W on Front St, then 3/4 mi S on Long Hill Rd. Enter on R.*

WELCOME

◊◊◊FACILITIES: 99 sites, typical site width 28 ft, 51 full hkups, 48 W&E, (15/20/30 amps), some extd stay sites, family camping, tenting, shower$, dump, laundry, ltd groc, RV supplies, LP gas by weight, ice, picnic tables, fire rings, wood.

WEST BROOKFIELD—Continued
THE OLD SAWMILL CAMPGROUND—Continued

◊◊◊◊RECREATION: rec hall, rec room/area, coin games, swim pool, wading pool, stream fishing, golf nearby, bsktball, playground, activities, (wkends), horseshoes.

Pets welcome, quantity restrict. Partial handicap access. Open May 1 - Columbus Day. Facilities fully operational Memorial Day - Labor Day. Escort to site. Clubs welcome. Rate in 2010 $24-26 for 2 persons. Member ARVC, MACO.

Phone: (508)867-2427
Address: 75 Long Hill Rd, West Brookfield, MA 01585
Lat/Lon: 42.22195/-72.15263
Web: www.oldsawmillcampground.com

SEE AD STURBRIDGE PAGE 354

WEST SUTTON—C-3

(E) The Old Holbrook Place—(Worcester) *From jct I-395 (exit 4A) & Sutton Ave: Go 3-1/2 mi E on Sutton Ave, then 1 mi SE on Manchaug Rd. Enter on R.* ◊◊◊FACILITIES: 66 sites, typical site width 30 ft, 32 ft max RV length, 35 full hkups, 31 W&E, (20 amps), family camping, dump, ltd groc. ◊◊RECREATION: lake swim, boating, canoeing, ramp, dock, lake fishing. Pets welcome. No tents. Open Memorial Day - Labor Day. Rate in 2010 $23-31 per family. Member ARVC, MACO. Phone: (508)865-5050.

WEST TOWNSEND—A-3

(S) PEARL HILL STATE PARK—(Middlesex) *From Hwy 119: Go 6 mi S on New Fitchburg Rd.* FACILITIES: 51 sites, 20 ft max RV length, 51 no hkups, tenting. RECREATION: Partial handicap access. Open Memorial Day - Columbus Day. Phone: (978)597-8802.

WESTPORT—D-5

(S) HORSENECK BEACH STATE RESERVATION—(Bristol) *From jct I-195 & Hwy 88: Go 10 mi S on Hwy 88.* FACILITIES: 100 sites, 100 no hkups, 100 pull-thrus, tenting, dump. RECREATION: saltwater swim, boating, canoeing, ramp, playground. Partial handicap access. Open May 5 - Oct 8. Phone: (508)636-8817.

WHATELY—B-2

(N) White Birch Campground—(Franklin) *From jct I-91 (exit 24) & Hwy 116: Go 1/4 mi N on Hwy 116, then 2 mi SW on Whately Rd. Enter on L.* ◊◊FACILITIES: 80 sites, typical site width 35 ft, 65 W&E, (20/30/50 amps), 15 no hkups, 16 pull-thrus, family camping, tenting, dump, laundry. ◊◊RECREATION: swim pool, play equipment. Pets welcome, breed restrict. Partial handicap access. Open May 1 - Oct 31. Facilities fully operational Memorial Day - Columbus Day. Rate in 2010 $32-33 for 2 persons. Member ARVC, MACO. Phone: (413)665-4941.

WINCHENDON—A-3

(N) LAKE DENNISON STATE RECREATION AREA—(Worcester) *From town: Go 6 mi S on US-202.* FACILITIES: 150 sites, 150 no hkups, tenting, dump. RECREATION: lake swim, boating, no motors, canoeing, ramp. Partial handicap access. Open May 25 - Sep 3. Phone: (978)939-8962.

(S) OTTER RIVER STATE FOREST—(Worcester) *From town: Go 7 mi S on US-202.* FACILITIES: 89 sites, 89 no hkups, tenting. RECREATION: lake swim, stream fishing. Partial handicap access. Open May - Sep. Phone: (978)939-8962.

WINDSOR—B-1

(E) WINDSOR STATE FOREST—(Berkshire) *From town: Go E on Hwy 9, then N on River Rd.* FACILITIES: 24 sites, 24 no hkups, tenting. RECREATION: river swim. Open May 25 - Sep 3. Phone: (413)684-0948.

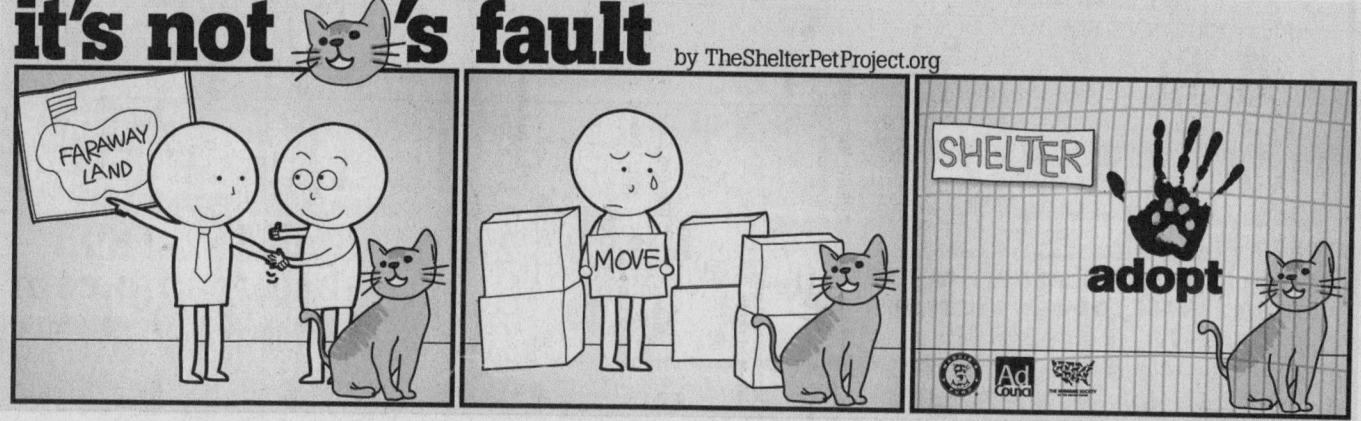

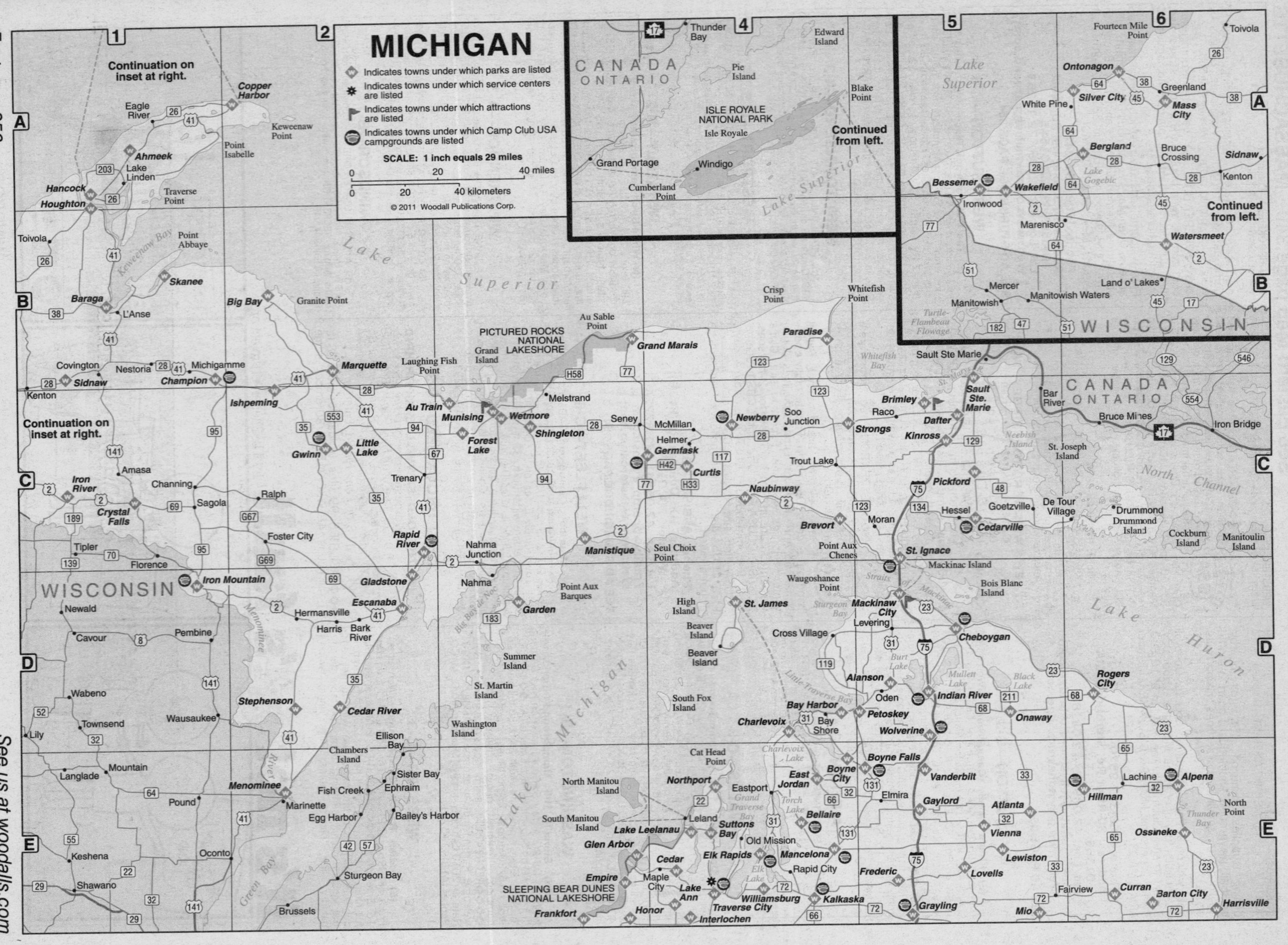
MICHIGAN
Indicates towns under which parks are listed
Indicates towns under which service centers are listed
Indicates towns under which attractions are listed
Indicates towns under which Camp Club USA campgrounds are listed
SCALE: 1 inch equals 29 miles
0 20 40 miles
0 20 40 kilometers
© 2011 Woodall Publications Corp.
Continuation on inset at right.
Continued from left.
CANADA ONTARIO
ISLE ROYALE NATIONAL PARK
Isle Royale
Windigo
Grand Portage
Cumberland Point
Thunder Bay
Pie Island
Edward Island
Blake Point
Lake Superior
Ontonagon
Silver City
White Pine
Greenland
Mass City
Fourteen Mile Point
Toivola
Bergland
Lake Gogebic
Bruce Crossing
Sidnaw
Kenton
Bessemer
Wakefield
Ironwood
Marenisco
Watersmeet
Land o' Lakes
Mercer
Manitowish
Manitowish Waters
Turtle-Flambeau Flowage
WISCONSIN
Copper Harbor
Eagle River
Ahmeek
Lake Linden
Hancock
Houghton
Keweenaw Point
Point Isabelle
Traverse Point
Point Abbaye
Keweenaw Bay
Skanee
Baraga
L'Anse
Big Bay
Granite Point
Covington
Nestoria
Michigamme
Sidnaw
Champion
Marquette
Ishpeming
Gwinn
Little Lake
Amasa
Channing
Sagola
Ralph
Iron River
Crystal Falls
Tipler
Florence
Foster City
Iron Mountain
Newald
Cavour
Pembine
Wabeno
Townsend
Lily
Wausaukee
Langlade
Mountain
Pound
Keshena
Shawano
Oconto
Brussels
Green Bay
Menominee
Marinette
Stephenson
Cedar River
Menominee River
Hermansville
Harris
Bark River
Escanaba
Gladstone
Rapid River
Trenary
Nahma Junction
Nahma
Big Bay de Noc
Garden
Point Aux Barques
Summer Island
St. Martin Island
Washington Island
Ellison Bay
Chambers Island
Sister Bay
Ephraim
Fish Creek
Egg Harbor
Bailey's Harbor
Sturgeon Bay
Laughing Fish Point
Au Train
Munising
Grand Island
Wetmore
Forest Lake
Shingleton
Melstrand
PICTURED ROCKS NATIONAL LAKESHORE
Au Sable Point
Grand Marais
Seney
McMillan
Helmer
Germfask
Curtis
Manistique
Seul Choix Point
Newberry
Soo Junction
Crisp Point
Whitefish Point
Paradise
Whitefish Bay
Trout Lake
Naubinway
Brevort
Strongs
Raco
Brimley
Dafter
Kinross
Sault Ste Marie
Sault Ste. Marie
Bar River
Bruce Mines
Iron Bridge
Neebish Island
St. Joseph Island
North Channel
Pickford
Hessel
Cedarville
Goetzville
De Tour Village
Drummond
Drummond Island
Cockburn Island
Manitoulin Island
Moran
St. Ignace
Point Aux Chenes
Mackinac Island
Bois Blanc Island
Straits of Mackinac
Waugoshance Point
Mackinaw City
Levering
Cheboygan
High Island
St. James
Beaver Island
Sturgeon Bay
Cross Village
Burt Lake
Mullen Lake
Black Lake
Alanson
Oden
Indian River
Rogers City
Onaway
Lake Huron
Little Traverse Bay
Bay Harbor
Bay Shore
Petoskey
Charlevoix
Wolverine
South Fox Island
Charlevoix Lake
Boyne Falls
Boyne City
East Jordan
Vanderbilt
Cat Head Point
Northport
Eastport
Grand Traverse Bay
Torch Lake
Elmira
Gaylord
Atlanta
Hillman
Lachine
Alpena
North Point
Thunder Bay
Ossineke
North Manitou Island
South Manitou Island
Leland
Suttons Bay
Bellaire
Lake Leelanau
Glen Arbor
Old Mission
Elk Rapids
Mancelona
Rapid City
Elk Lake
Vienna
Lewiston
Empire
Cedar
Maple City
Lake Ann
Williamsburg
Kalkaska
Frederic
Lovells
Fairview
Curran
Barton City
Harrisville
SLEEPING BEAR DUNES NATIONAL LAKESHORE
Frankfort
Honor
Traverse City
Interlochen
Grayling
Mio
Lake Michigan

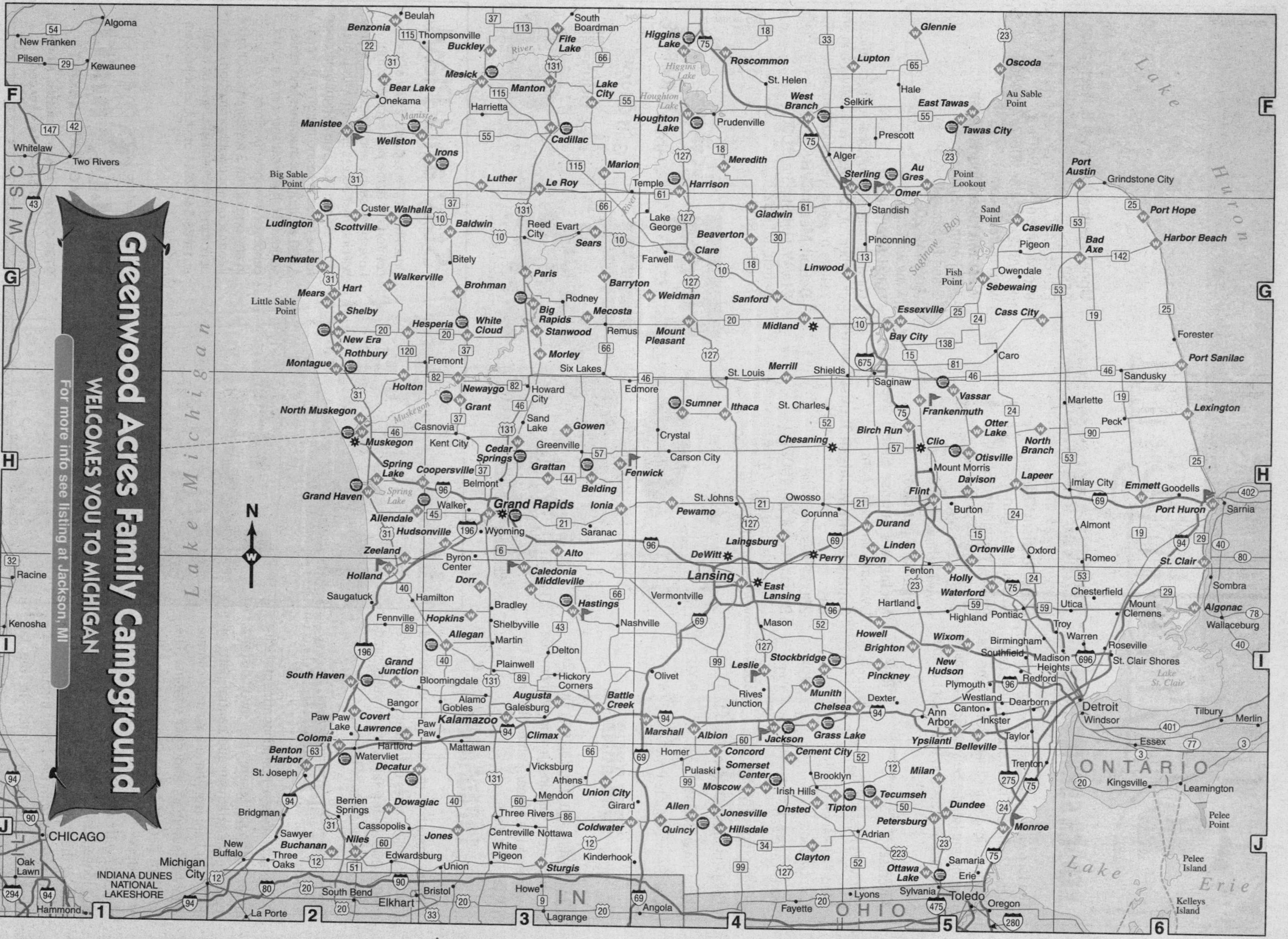
Greenwood Acres Family Campground
WELCOMES YOU TO MICHIGAN
For more info see listing at Jackson, MI
Lake Michigan
Lake Huron
Lake Erie
Saginaw Bay
Lake St. Clair
WISC
IN
OHIO
ONTARIO
CHICAGO
INDIANA DUNES NATIONAL LAKESHORE
Michigan City
Detroit
Windsor
Lansing
East Lansing
Grand Rapids
Kalamazoo
Jackson
Battle Creek
Flint
Saginaw
Bay City
Midland
Toledo
Ann Arbor
Ypsilanti
Muskegon
North Muskegon
Holland
Grand Haven
South Haven
Benton Harbor
St. Joseph
Port Huron
Sarnia
Monroe
Mount Pleasant
Cadillac
Ludington
Manistee
Higgins Lake
Houghton Lake
Roscommon
West Branch
Oscoda
Tawas City
East Tawas
Port Austin
Port Hope
Harbor Beach
Port Sanilac
Lexington
Caseville
Sebewaing
Frankenmuth
Birch Run
Clio
Holly
Brighton
Howell
Hastings
Coldwater
Sturgis
Niles
South Bend
Elkhart
F
G
H
I
J
1
2
3
4
5
6

READER SERVICE INFO

The following businesses have placed an ad in the Michigan Travel Section. To receive free information, enter their Reader Service number on the Reader Service Card opposite page 48/Discover Section in the front of this directory:

Advertiser	RS#
Bay Mills Resort & Casino	4332
Cran-Hill Ranch Family Campground	469
Haas Lake Park	4282
Hidden Ridge RV Resort	3804
Lake Chemung Outdoor Resort	4179
Little River Casino	3022
Oak Beach County Park	4057

TIME ZONE

Michigan is in the Eastern Time Zone. Gogebic, Iron, Dickinson and Menominee counties of the Upper Peninsula are in the Central Time Zone.

TOPOGRAPHY

More than half of Michigan is covered with 18 million acres of forested land. There are 11,000 inland lakes, freshwater sand dunes and hundreds of islands.

TEMPERATURE

Michigan has a humid continental climate, although there are two distinct regions. The southern and central parts of the Lower Peninsula have a warmer climate with hot summers and cold winters. The northern part of Lower Peninsula and the entire Upper Peninsula has a more severe climate, with warm, but shorter summers and longer, cold to freezing winters. Some parts of the state average high temperatures below freezing from December through February, and into early March in the far northern parts.

TRAVEL & TOURISM INFO

State Tourism Office:
Travel Michigan
300 N. Washington Sq.
Lansing, MI 48913
(888/784-7328)
www.michigan.org

Regional Agencies:

Michigan's Sunrise Side Travel Assn.
www.misunriseside.com

Southwestern Michigan Tourist Council
2300 Pipestone Road
Benton Harbor, MI 49022
(269/925-6301)
www.swmichigan.org

Upper Peninsula Travel & Recreation Assn.
P.O. Box 400
Iron Mountain, MI 49801
(800/562-7134 or 906/774-5480)
www.uptravel.com

West Michigan Tourist Assn.
741 Kenmoor Suite E
Grand Rapids, MI 49546
(800/442-2084)
www.wmta.org

Local Agencies:
For a complete list of local tourism offices, chambers of commerce and convention and visitors bureaus, visit Michigan.org.

Detroit Metro CVB
211 W. Fort St., Ste. 1000
Detroit, MI 48226
(800/DETROIT)

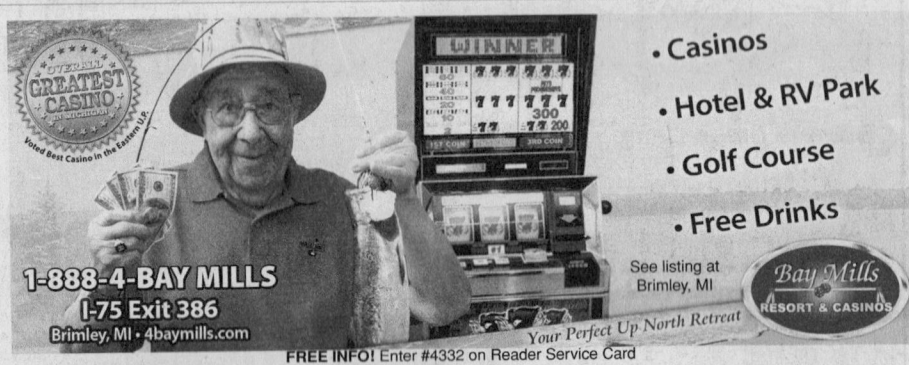

www.visitdetroit.com

Frankenmuth CVB
635 S. Main St., Frankenmuth, MI 48734
(800/FUN-TOWN)
www.frankenmuth.org

Grand Rapids/Kent County CVB
171 Monroe NW, Ste. 700
Grand Rapids, MI 49503
(800/678-9859 or 616/459-8287)
www.visitgrandrapids.org

Holland Area CVB
76 E. Eighth St.
Holland, MI 49423
(616/394-0000)
www.holland.org

Indian River Area Tourist Bureau
3435 S. Straits Hwy, PO Box 57
Indian River, MI 49749
(231/238-9325)
www.irtourism.com

Jackson Convention & Tourist Bureau
PO Box 889
Jackson, MI 49204
(800/245-5282 or 517/764-4440)
www.jackson-mich.org

Kalamazoo County CVB
141 E. Michigan Ave., Ste 100
Kalamazoo, MI 49007
(800/888-0509 or 269/488-9000)
www.discoverkalamazoo.com

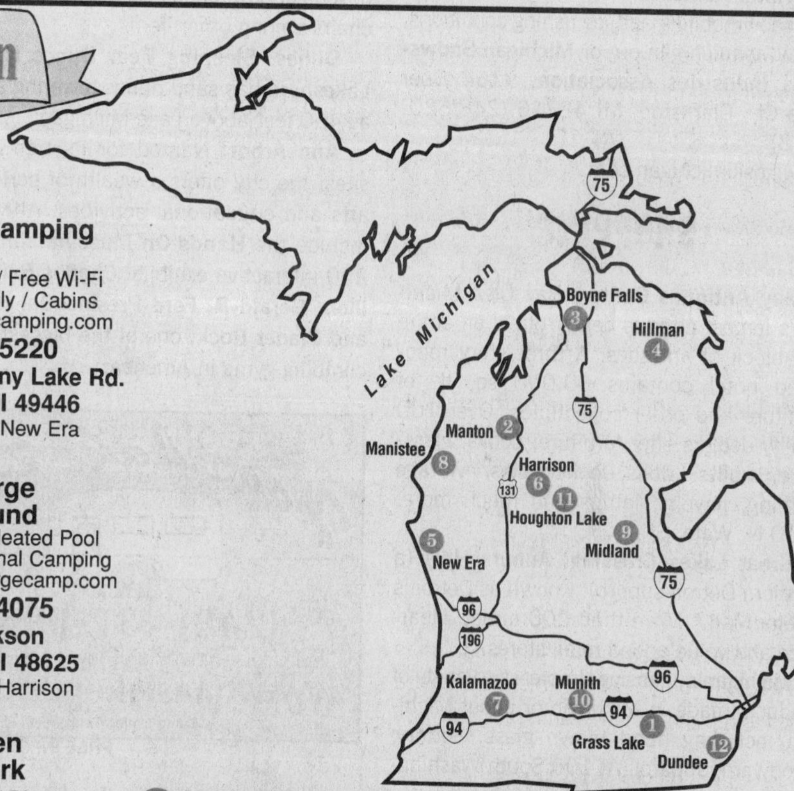

Greater Lansing CVB
1223 Turner St., Ste. 200
Lansing, MI 48906
(888/2LANSING)
www.lansing.org

Mackinaw Area Visitors Bureau
10800 W. US 23
Mackinaw City, MI 49701
(800/666-0160 or 231/436-5664)
www.mackinawcity.com

St. Ignace Chamber of Commerce
560 N. State St.
St. Ignace, MI 49781
(800/970-8717)
www.stignace.com

Traverse City CVB
101 W. Grandview Pky.
Traverse City, MI 49684
(800/940-1120 or 231/947-1120)
www.visittraversecity.com

RECREATIONAL INFO

Bicycling: MDOT Biking information: (517/373-9815); League of Michigan Bicyclists: (517/334-9100); for regional or county bike maps, see www.michigan.gov

Boating: To locate and map boating access sites, harbors, and marinas, see www.mcgi.state.mi.us/MRBIS/

Boat Charters: (fishing, duck hunting, diving, cruises and excursions): Michigan

Charter Boat Assn. (800/MCBA-971. www.micharterboats.com

Marine Business Info: Michigan Boating Industries Association, 32398 Five Mile Road, Livonia, MI 48154-6109 (800/932-2628). www.mbia.org

Canoeing: Michigan Assn. of Paddle Sport Providers, www.michigancanoe.com

Golf: The Golf Association of Michigan, 24116 Research Dr., Farmington Hills, MI 48335 (248/478-9242). www.gam.org

Hunting & Fishing: MI Dept. of Natural Resources, License Control Division, PO Box 30446, Lansing, MI 48909 (517/373-1280).
www.mdnr-elicense.com/welcome.asp

Wineries: For more information contact Michigan Department of Agriculture, MI Grape & Wine Industry Council, PO Box 30017, Lansing, MI 48909 (517/241-4468). www.michiganwines.com

Winter Activities: For information on skiing, snowmobiling and ice fishing conditions, see www.michigan.org or **Michigan Snowsports Industries Association**, 7164 Deer Lake Ct., Clarkston, MI 48346 (248/620-4448)
www.goskimichigan.com

SHOPPING

Bay Antiques Center, Bay City. Michigan's largest antique center offers an entire city block of antiques. A three-story renovated hotel contains 60,000 sq. ft. of furniture and other collectibles. Over 100 quality dealers offer furniture, books, glassware, quilts, dolls, collectibles, vintage clothing, jewelry, lamps and much more. 1010 N. Water St.

Great Lakes Crossing, Auburn Hills (a northern Detroit suburb). Known as Detroit's "Mega Mall." More than 200 outlet, clearance and value added retail stores.

Michigania, Lansing. Impressive variety of products made in Michigan or about Michigan including hand blown glass, pottery, woodware, apparel. At 100 South Washington Square.

Monroe Factory Shops, Monroe. Discounted merchandise at over 40 designer outlets. Off I-75, exit 11.

Prime Outlets at Birch Run, Birch Run. The Midwest's largest outlet shopping center. With 150 outlet stores with discounts from 25-65% off retail. 12240 S. Beyer Road.

Tanger Outlet Center Howell, Howell. Over 80 stores supplied direct from the factories with savings of up to 70% over retail. 1475 North Burkhart Rd.

Tanger Outlet Center, West Branch. Features brand name manufacturers with an average of 40% off retail prices. 2990 Cook Road.

DESTINATIONS

Michigan is affectionately known as the "mitten-shaped state", and provides 3,200 miles of freshwater shoreline, 3.9 million acres of managed land, and dozens of cultured cites. Visitors have everything from fishing, boating, snowmobiling, skiing, hiking, and much, much more.

LOWER PENINSULA

The Lower Peninsula is bounded on the south by Ohio and Indiana, sharing land and water boundaries with both, the rest of the area is bound by water. Because of Michigan's "mitten" shape, there are several folkloric tales of it being the handprint of Paul Bunyan.

Amish areas: Clare offers a bakery, woodworking and buggy-making shops. Mio has dozens of craft shops selling hickory rocking chairs among other items.

Dunes: **Sleeping Bear Dunes National Lakeshore** has sand dunes towering as high as 460 feet above Lake Michigan.

Ann Arbor. Named for its tree-shaded sites, the city offers a wealth of performing arts and educational activities. Attractions include the **Hands-On Museum** containing 250 interactive exhibits; **Charles Baird Carillon; Gerald R. Ford Presidential Library;** and **Planet Rock,** one of the biggest indoor climbing gyms in America.

Auburn Hills. This suburb of Detroit is home to the **Walter P. Chrysler Museum**, showcasing 70 cars and exhibits.

Bay City. One of Michigan's busiest ports was born during the 1800's lumber boom. A trolley takes you through the downtown area and past mansions built by lumber magnates.

Beaver Island. Located northwest of Charlevoix in Lake Michigan, Beaver Island is the most remote, inhabited island in the Great Lakes.

Benton Harbor. Mary's City of David Museum opened in 1997 for the public. Tour sites include a print shop, powerhouse, carpentry shop, cannery, mechanic garage, Shiloh gardens and the nature trail to the famous Eastman Springs. Open weekends June - September.

Betsie River. One of the state's best canoeing rivers, this 49-mile stretch has no rapids and moves at a steady, relaxed pace. A state designated Wild and Scenic River, it provides a view of nature at its best.

Bloomfield Hills. At **Cranbrook Institute of Science** you can visit a T-Rex skeleton cast, explore exhibits and view the stars at their planetarium and observatory.

Dearborn. The Henry Ford is the nation's largest indoor-outdoor museum complex. The museum covers 12 acres and focuses on America's industrial development between 1800 and 1950. The **Ford Rouge Factory Tour** is a cross between an interactive video game, an amusement park ride, an old-fashioned movie, a cool museum exhibit and a short course about gardening. Besides the plant's history, the tour showcases its newest addition, a revolutionary, environmentally friendly new F-150 truck plant. Greenfield Village is a 240-acre living history site celebrating three centuries of Americana. At the **Spirit of Ford Visitors Center**, hands-on exhibits will show you a car assembly line and take you to a re-created Ford design studio.

Detroit. The Detroit People Mover, one of the most technologically advanced transportation systems in the world, affords travelers a breathtaking view of the city. Or see Detroit from a different angle—climb aboard the **Trolley Line** for a unique open-air city tour. The **Renaissance Center**, a symbol of Detroit's rebirth, is a complex comprised of offices, shops, restaurants and an eight-story atrium lobby filled with exotic plants, reflecting pools and observation ponds. **The New Detroit Science Center** entertains guests with 5 hands-on laboratories, live science stage shows, Michigan's only IMAX® Dome Theatre, and state-of-the-art Dassault Systèmes Planetarium. Detroit has dozens of unique museums including the **Motown Historical Museum, Dossin Great Lakes Museum** and **The Henry Ford**, which includes museum, IMAX theater, Ford Rouge factory tours and Greenfield Village where you can take an authentic Model-T ride or climb aboard a steam-powered train for a tour of the village.

Flint. Take a tour of **Durand Union Station,** home of the Michigan Railroad History Museum, a 1905 Victorian-style railroad depot. At the **Sloan Museum** you can explore the birth of General Motors and visit their gallery, which includes rare antique automobiles, colorful neon signs, period clothing, household furnishings, commercial goods, and original film footage. **Buick Gallery & Research Center** houses the world's largest collection of vintage Buicks, automotive memorabilia, and research archives.

Crossroads Village & Huckleberry Railroad is an assemblage of century-old buildings brought from surrounding Genesee County. At the railroad depot visitors can board a train and take a 10-mile trip on a narrow-gauge track.

Frankenmuth. Known for its restaurants including the **Bavarian Inn Restaurant** and **Zehnders of Frankenmuth**, Christmas stores, wineries and breweries, this town boasts more than 100 Bavarian themed shops and attractions such as **Frankenmuth Clock Company**, which houses one of the largest collections of Black Forest Clocks. This authentic shop offers hundreds of hand-carved clocks, German steins, Swiss music boxes and beautiful glass items.

Bronner's Christmas Wonderland invites you to come to the world's largest Christmas store, where every day is Christmas day. This incredible sensation is the size of four football fields and a Christmas lover's dream! More than 50,000 gifts and trims from all over the globe come together under one roof. You'll browse through thousands and thousands of ornaments, lights and Christmas trees. Bronner's also has a great selection of trees, Nativities and collectibles. A giant Santa, a snowman and hundreds of decorations are arranged outside. Don't miss their welcome sign, written in more than 60 languages.

Grand Rapids. Located on the banks of the Grand River, the second largest city in Michigan offers a variety of attractions including:

Frederik Meijer Gardens and Sculpture Park Experience beautiful gardens, a world-class sculpture park, a children's garden and the state's largest tropical conservatory.

Grand Rapids Art Museum. Opened in 2007, this is the world's first newly built LEED certified art museum.

Heritage Hill. Nearly 100 historical homes are showcased, including the **Meyer May House** designed by Frank Lloyd Wright.

Grand Rapids Children's Museum. Let your kids' imaginations run free as they build Lego® structures in the Funstruction Zone and translucent structures in the bubble-making area. Also in Grand Rapids is the **Gerald R. Ford Museum** honoring former President Ford.

Hart-Montague Trail State Park. Cyclists, hikers and horseback riders delight in panoramic beauty through nearly 22 miles of varied terrain (orchards, forests, farmland, residential and commercial areas). It winds through west central and southern Oceana County and northern Muskegon County.

Holland. DeKlomp Wooden Shoe & Delftware Factory. Dutch craftsmen create traditional wooden shoes and artists hand-paint delftware at the only delft pottery factory in the U.S. Free factory tours are available. At **Dutch Village**, you'll experience a re-created Dutch town of 100 years in the past featuring 15 acres of quaint shops, Dutch architecture and colorful gardens. You can watch craftsmen carve wooden shoes on machines brought over from the Netherlands.

Windmill Island. More than flowers... there are the colors of costumes and candles, ice cream fudge, shops and flags, a carousel and canal. Beyond the dike and garden pathways, you can cross the drawbridge to another place in time and tour the majestic *DeZwaan*. More than 230 years old, this graceful giant is the only authentic Dutch windmill operating in the United States. Witness the power of the wind as you climb inside and watch the gears turn.

Gilmore Car Museum, Hickory Corners. This unique rural facility houses nearly 200 vintage cars along with restored historic barns and period buildings. See the Tucker Historical Collection and Library, the Pierce-Arrow Museum and other classic cars.

Jackson. Enjoy 19th-century architecture and championship golf courses or spend a day at the races at the **Jackson Harness Raceway. Cascades** is a spectacular display of illuminated cascading water accompanied by music and color. **Jennison Nature Center & Tobico Marsh** in Bay City features an interpretive area with hiking trails, observation towers and a boardwalk for viewing migrating waterfowl.

Kalamazoo. Air Zoo. View an airplane display including WWII originals and authentic restorations. The "flying feline foursome," also known as the Wildcat, Hellcat, Tigercat and Bearcat are on display along with the pioneering Wright Flyer. Every afternoon from May to September you can see the "Flight of the Day" or purchase a ride on the "Tin Goose." **Kalamazoo Public Museum & Hans Baldauf Planetarium**. Exhibits deal with science, history and technology. The planetarium presents programs for children and adults.

Kellogg Bird Sanctuary, Augusta. Experience waterfront viewing and feeding of waterfowl on Wintergreen Lake. Birds of prey are in large flight pens and white-tailed deer roam in a natural setting enclosure.

Lansing. Michigan's capital city offers riverboat cruises on the **Grand River** and the **Woldumar Nature Center**. You can also see the **Carl G. Fenner Arboretum**, with easy hiking trails, nature center, trailside exhibits, herb garden, buffalo, and waterfowl pond. The **Michigan Historical Museum** recounts the state's history from the Ice Age through the mining and lumber eras and into the late 20th-century. Housed in a 100-year-old building is the **Impression 5 Science Museum** with interactive exhibits for the whole family. Experience over 5,000 years of artistic development at **The Art Museum at Michigan State University**. Other attractions include **Michigan International Speedway**, located outside of Jackson. **Meridian Historical Village, MSU Museum** and the **Nokomis Learning Center**, focusing on the woodland Indians of the Great Lakes.

Leelanau Peninsula. Hike to the crest of 480-foot Sleeping Bear for an outstanding view of the dunes.

Ludington welcomes visitors with year-round recreation and attractions. At the **Historic White Pine Village**, re-discover small town Michigan life in the late 1800s. Twenty restored buildings overlook Lake Michigan.

Lake Michigan Car Ferry. The S.S. Badger will transport you and your vehicle from Ludington, Michigan to Manitowoc, Wisconsin in four hours. On-board services include dining, activities and historical displays.

Mackinaw City. Located at the northernmost tip of Lower Michigan, Mackinaw City is noted for its historic landmarks, museums, shops and water activities. Tour **Colonial Michilimackinac & Mackinac Maritime Museum**, a reconstructed fort with a 40-ft. lighthouse. The 5-mile long **Mackinac Bridge** connects the Upper Peninsula with the Lower Peninsula.

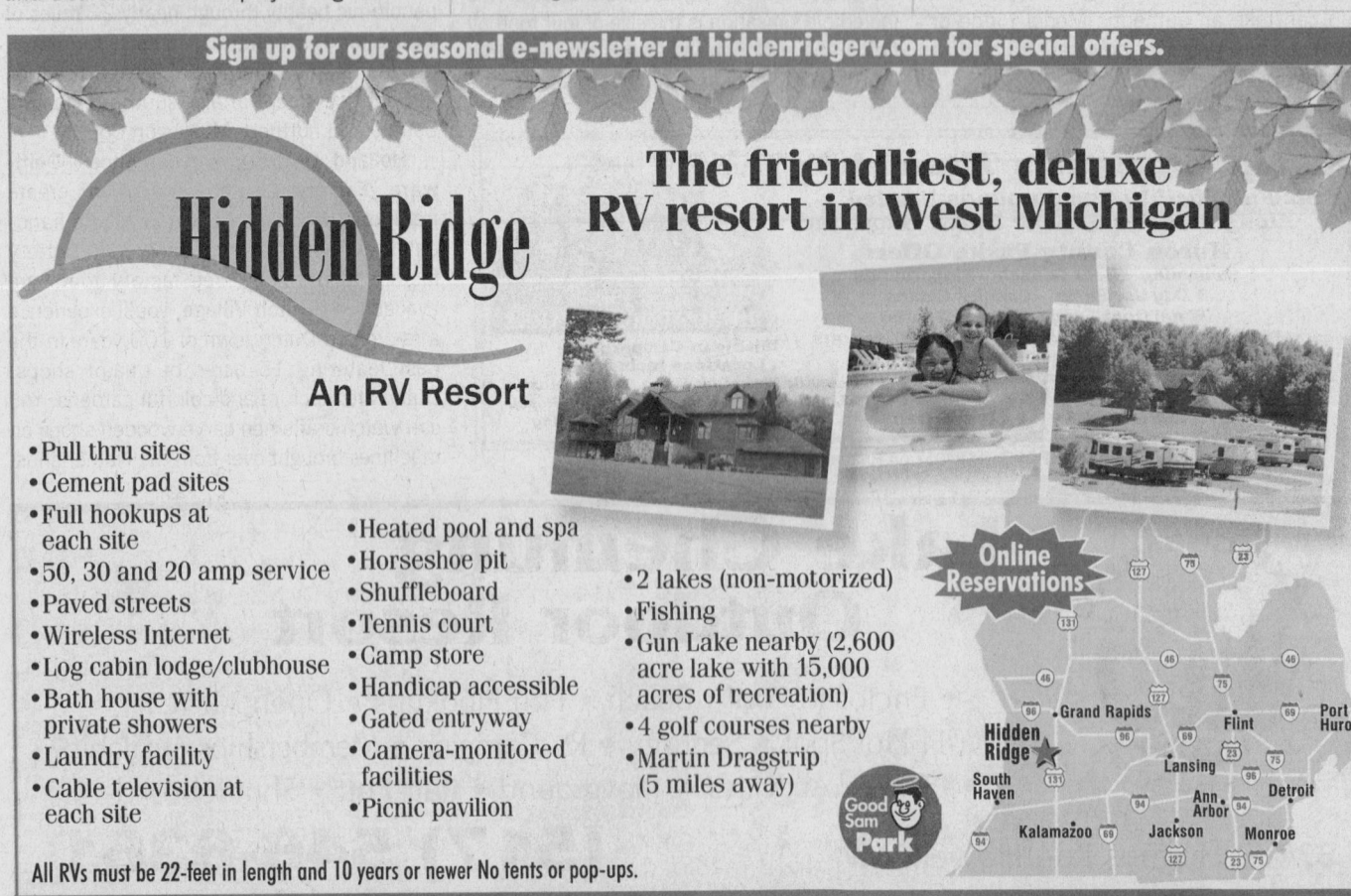

Manistee. Manistee is famous for salmon and steelhead fishing. You can spend a day on Lake Michigan or go kayaking, and canoeing on the Manistee River. During your stay you can choose from swimming or sunbathing on Lake Michigan, shopping in many local shops along the Riverwalk, golfing on the multiple area courses or try your luck at the Little River Casino Resort.

Visit historic **Marshall**, 12 miles southeast of Battle Creek, to take a trip deep into the 19th century. Most of the town's more than 800 buildings are listed with the National Register of Historic Places.

At **Midland**, tour the home and studio of Albert Dow, noted architect and son of the Dow company founder. The 100-acre Dow Gardens are also open to the public.

Mount Pleasant attractions include **Loafer's Glory-Village of Yesteryear**, a restored historical 1800's store featuring handmade crafts from the local Amish settlement and collections of folk art.

Muskegon. Located on the shores of Lake Michigan, this city offers charter boat fishing, canoeing, cruises on the lake, amusement parks, golf courses and art galleries. At the dual-themed **Michigan's Adventure Amusement Park and WildWater Adventure Waterpark**, you can enjoy breathtaking rides including six roller coasters at Shivering Timbers or cool off at WildWater Adventure on waterslides and other water rides.

Ocqueoc Falls, Onaway. Enjoy the beauty of the largest waterfall in the Lower Peninsula.

Portage. In association with the Smithsonian Institution, Air Zoo offers a multi-sensory experience with 4D theatres and over 80 rare aircraft. Celebrate the Wright Brothers' first flight, tour the International Space Station or take the controls of a military jet plane.

Romeo. At the **Farm Wool Shop**, you can mingle with the sheep as you pick out your wool, patterns and clothing, all completely hand made.

Saginaw. Take in the **Saginaw Art Museum** with its changing exhibits, beautiful gardens and hands-on exhibits. Or experience Far Eastern culture at the **Japanese Cultural Center & Tea House**.

St. Ignace. Gateway to the Upper Peninsula. **Mighty Mac** is the five-mile long bridge spanning the straits. Area Attractions are educational, historical and best of all fun! Choose from tours, museums, natural wonders like **Castle Rock** and the **Mystery Spot**, to historic places like **Mackinac Island** and the **Soo Locks**.

Saint Joseph. One of Michigan's featured Beach towns; brick streets welcome visitors in this resort town. Shops display art, antiques, collectibles and lighthouse memorabilia. The **Krasl Art Center,** featuring a Chihuly glass sculpture, hosts traveling exhibits, but may be best known for its art fair the second weekend of July. Silver Beach stretches 1600 feet along the lake and claims title as one of the best US beaches, as reported in Parents magazine. In July, the Venetian Festival sets up volleyball and sand sculpture competitions, a carnival and musical entertainment near the shore.

Saugatuck. Rolling grassy dunes and white sand beaches typify this area known as "The Art Coast of Michigan." Each summer since 1910, The Art Institute of Chicago has conducted a summer school called Ox Bow just north of the city. Over the years many artists have stayed here and the area is dotted with studios, galleries, quaint and unique shops, fine dining and many attractions like golfing, dune rides, boat cruises, hiking, swimming and professional summer theater, jazz and chamber music.

Silver Lake Sand Dunes & Mac Wood's Dune Rides, Mears. Located between Lake Michigan and Silver Lake, these huge, windswept open-sand mountains can be enjoyed through Mac Wood's thrilling dune rides. You'll climb to the summit, then glide down the sweeps into valleys, drive past sparkling Silver Lake and splash along Lake Michigan's scenic beach.

Sleeping Bear Dunes National Lakeshore Park, Honor. Enjoy a trip down the Platte River on a canoe, kayak, tube, raft, motorboat, or rowboat. Rentals and group trips are available at **Riverside Canoe Trips**.

South Haven. On the shores of Lake Michigan is the **Michigan Maritime Museum**

featuring historical watercrafts, maritime art, photographs and more.

Traverse City prides itself on being the "Cherry Capital of the World." Orchards line Lake Michigan in the Traverse area and everyone turns out for the annual **National Cherry Festival** held in July. Exhibits at the **Grand Traverse Lighthouse & Museum** chronicle the lives and experiences of those who sailed the Great Lakes. Visitors are welcome at the campus of **The Interlochen Center for the Arts** a premier training center for young musicians for over 70 years. Take an astounding 20-mile drive in a pastoral setting from Traverse City to the tip of the Old Mission Peninsula; featuring beautiful farms, orchards, wineries, beaches, Old Mission Point Lighthouse and Old Mission and Bowers Harbor.

At **The Music House**, located northeast of Traverse City in Acme, you'll view an extensive collection of automatic musical instruments.

Wolf Lake State Fish Hatchery & Michigan Fisheries Interpretive Center, Mattawan. Learn about fish life and fishing at a myriad of exhibits: showcases of record catches, fish in underwater habitats, anatomical fish models, 100 kinds of fishing gear, old sport tackle, AV programs and fish display pond.

Ypsilanti, a former French trading post turned railroad center. Historic district known as **Depot Town** is dotted with specialty shops and antique stores in historic buildings. **Automotive Heritage Museum** traces the city's role in the car industry.

UPPER PENINSULA

If you're planning a trip to the Upper Peninsula, the best time to go is the Golden Season. By early September, chilly nights and shorter days trigger bursts of color from Drummond Island at the peninsula's eastern tip; west about 380 miles to the Wisconsin line. During this time, millions of acres of forest, most protected within state parks and national preserves, are cascades to Tahquamenon Falls; more than 150 waterfalls rush through woodlands engulfed in a rainbow of colors.

Castle Rock, St. Ignace. Once used as a lookout by Algonquin Native Americans, this 200-ft. high rock formation offers magnificent views.

Cross in the Woods, Indian River. The centerpiece for an outdoor sanctuary, the cross was made from a 55-foot redwood tree with a bronze 7-ton image of Jesus mounted on it. Grounds include unique statuary and a doll museum.

Copper Harbor. Located at the tip of the Keweenaw Peninsula, Copper Harbor is surrounded by beautiful hills and waters loaded with trout.

BUSINESSES OFFERING

	Things to See & Do	RV Sales	RV Service
BRIMLEY			
Bay Mills Resort & Casinos	X		
CALEDONIA			
Indian Valley Canoe Livery & Campground	X		
CHELSEA			
Lloyd Bridges Traveland		X	X
CHESANING			
Parshallburg Campers		X	X
CLIO			
Leisure Days Travel Trailer Sales		X	X
DEWITT			
Annie Rae RV		X	X
EAST LANSING			
Gillette's Interstate RV		X	X
FENWICK			
Snow Lake Kampground & Restaurant	X		
FRANKENMUTH			
Bronner's Christmas Wonderland	X		
Frankenmuth Bavarian Inn Restaurant	X		
GRAND RAPIDS			
Terry Town Travel Center		X	X
HASTINGS			
Whispering Waters Kayak Rental	X		
HOLLAND			
Beachside Bike Rentals	X		
JACKSON			
Greenwood Acres Golf	X		
LESLIE			
Whitetail Acres Archery	X		
MACKINAW CITY			
Mackinaw Club Golf Course	X		
MANISTEE			
Insta-Launch Marina & Campground	X		
Little River Casino	X		
Manistee Paddlesport Adventures	X		
MIDLAND			
Midland RV Sales		X	X
MONROE			
Go Karts Plus	X		
MUNISING			
Pictured Rocks Cruises	X		
MUSKEGON			
Lakeshore RV Center		X	X
OMER			
Big Bend Canoe Livery	X		
PERRY			
Signature Ford of Perry			X
PORT HURON			
Sawmill City	X		
STERLING			
River View Canoe Livery	X		
TRAVERSE CITY			
Just Trucks		X	X

QUICK REFERENCE CHART FOR WOODALL'S FEATURED PARKS

	Green Friendly	RV Lots for Sale	Park Models-Onsite Ownership	Park Membership for Sale	Big Rigs Welcome	Internet Friendly	Pets Welcome
AU GRES							
Au Gres City Riverfront Park & Campground						●	■
BATTLE CREEK							
Creek Valley						● (WiFi)	■
BIG RAPIDS							
Cran-Hill Ranch Family Campground						● (WiFi)	■
BOYNE FALLS							
Chandler Hill Campground	🍃						■
BRIMLEY							
Bay Mills RV Campground					▲	● (WiFi)	■
BUCKLEY							
Traverse City KOA					▲	● (WiFi)	■
BYRON							
Myers Lake Campground	🍃					● (WiFi)	■
CADILLAC							
Camp Cadillac					▲	● (WiFi)	■
CALEDONIA							
Indian Valley Campground Canoe Livery					▲	● (WiFi)	■
CASEVILLE							
Caseville County Park					▲	● (WiFi)	■
CEDAR SPRINGS							
Duke Creek Campground						● (WiFi)	■
Lakeside Camp Park						● (WiFi)	■
CEDARVILLE							
Cedarville RV Park		✖			▲	● (WiFi)	■
CHAMPION							
Michigamme Shores Campground Resort					▲	● (WiFi)	■
CHEBOYGAN							
Waterways Campground						● (WiFi)	■
CLIMAX							
Cold Brook County Park							■
COLDWATER							
Waffle Farm Camp					▲	● (WiFi)	■
DORR							
Hungry Horse Campground					▲	● (WiFi)	■
DUNDEE							
Wilderness Campground							■
EMMETT							
Emmett KOA						● (WiFi)	■
FENWICK							
Snow Lake Kampground					▲	● (WiFi)	■
FRANKENMUTH							
Frankenmuth Jellystone Park Camp-Resort					▲	● (WiFi)	■

Green Friendly 🍃; RV Lots for Sale ✖; Park Models/Onsite Onwership ✱; Park Memberships for Sale ✔; Big Rigs Welcome ▲; Internet Friendly ●; Internet Friendly-WiFi ● (WiFi); Pets Welcome ■

QUICK REFERENCE CHART FOR WOODALL'S FEATURED PARKS

	Green Friendly	RV Lots for Sale	Park Models-Onsite Ownership	Park Membership for Sale	Big Rigs Welcome	Internet Friendly	Pets Welcome
GAYLORD							
Gaylord KOA					▲	●	■
GRAND RAPIDS							
Woodchip Campground						●	■
GRASS LAKE							
Apple Creek Campground & RV Park						●	■
GRAYLING							
Yogi Bear's Jellystone Camp Resort						●	■
GWINN							
Horseshoe Lake Campground & RV Park							■
HARBOR BEACH							
Wagener County Park					▲		■
HARRISON							
Countryside Campground					▲	●	■
Lake George Campground						●	■
HASTINGS							
Michawana Campground						●	■
Whispering Waters Campground and Kayak Rental							■
HILLMAN							
Emerick Park							■
HILLSDALE							
Gateway Park Campground	🍃				▲	●	■
HOLLAND							
Oak Grove Campground Resort					▲	●	■
HOPKINS							
Hidden Ridge RV Resort					▲	●	■
HOUGHTON LAKE							
Houghton Lake Travel Park					▲	●	■
West Houghton Lake Campground	🍃					●	■
HOWELL							
Lake Chemung Outdoor Resort					▲	●	■
Taylor's Beach Campground						●	■
IRON MOUNTAIN							
Summer Breeze Campground & RV Park					▲	●	■
JACKSON							
Greenwood Acres Family Campground						●	■
KALAMAZOO							
Markin Glen County Park							■
KALKASKA							
Kalkaska RV Park & Campground						●	■
KINROSS							
Kinross RV Park East						●	■
LANSING							
Lansing Cottonwood Campground					▲	●	■

Green Friendly 🍃; RV Lots for Sale ✖; Park Models/Onsite Onwership ✱; Park Memberships for Sale ✔; Big Rigs Welcome ▲; Internet Friendly ●; Internet Friendly-WiFi ●; Pets Welcome ■

QUICK REFERENCE CHART FOR WOODALL'S FEATURED PARKS

	Green Friendly	RV Lots for Sale	Park Models-Onsite Ownership	Park Membership for Sale	Big Rigs Welcome	Internet Friendly	Pets Welcome
LAWRENCE							
Yoreplace RV Resort						◉	■
LESLIE							
Wheel Inn Campground and White Tail Acres Archery						●	■
LUDINGTON							
Kibby Creek Campground						◉	■
MACKINAW CITY							
KOA-Mackinaw City/Mackinac Island						◉	■
Tee Pee Campground						◉	■
MANISTEE							
Insta-Launch Campground & Marina						◉	■
Little River Resort					▲	◉	■
Matson's Big Manistee River Campground							■
MANISTIQUE							
Indian Lake Travel Resort						◉	■
MANTON							
The Campground					▲	◉	■
MILAN							
K C Campground						◉	■
MIO							
Mio Pine Acres Campground					▲	◉	■
MONROE							
Harbortown RV Resort					▲	◉	■
MOSCOW							
Moscow Maples RV Park						◉	■
MUNISING							
Munising Tourist Park Campground					▲	◉	■
MUNITH							
The Oaks Resort							■
NEW ERA							
Holiday Camping Resort					▲	◉	■
NEW HUDSON							
Haas Lake Park					▲	◉	■
NILES							
Spaulding Lake Campground					▲	◉	■
NORTH BRANCH							
Washakie Campground & Golf						◉	■
OMER							
Big Bend Family Campground						◉	■
ONTONAGON							
River Road RV Park & Campground					▲	◉	■
ORTONVILLE							
Clearwater Campground					▲	◉	■

Green Friendly (leaf); **RV Lots for Sale ✖; Park Models/Onsite Onwership ✱; Park Memberships for Sale ✔; Big Rigs Welcome ▲; Internet Friendly ●; Internet Friendly-WiFi ◉; Pets Welcome ■**

QUICK REFERENCE CHART FOR WOODALL'S FEATURED PARKS

	Green Friendly	RV Lots for Sale	Park Models-Onsite Ownership	Park Membership for Sale	Big Rigs Welcome	Internet Friendly	Pets Welcome
OTISVILLE							
Covenant Hills Camp					▲	●	■
OTTAWA LAKE							
Covered Wagon Camp Resort						●	■
PETERSBURG							
Totem Pole Park					▲	●	■
PETOSKEY							
Magnus Municipal Park							■
PORT AUSTIN							
Oak Beach County Park					▲		■
PORT HOPE							
Lighthouse County Parks					▲		■
Stafford County Park					▲		■
PORT HURON							
KOA-Port Huron					▲	●	■
RAPID RIVER							
Whitefish Hill RV Park					▲	●	■
SAULT STE. MARIE							
Aune-Osborn RV Park						●	■
SEBEWAING							
Sebewaing County Park					▲		■
SOMERSET CENTER							
Somerset Beach Campground						●	■
SOUTH HAVEN							
South Haven Family Campground	🍃				▲	●	■
Sunny Brook RV Resort		✖			▲	●	■
ST. IGNACE							
Castle Rock Lakefront Campark						●	■
Lake Shore Park Campground					▲	●	■
St. Ignace/Mackinac Island KOA					▲	●	■
Tiki RV Park & Campground					▲	●	■
STERLING							
River View Campground & Canoe Livery	🍃				▲	●	■
SUMNER							
Leisure Lake Family Campground					▲	●	■
TRAVERSE CITY							
Holiday Park Campground					▲	●	■
Traverse Bay RV Resort					▲	●	■
VASSAR							
Ber-Wa-Ga-Na Campground						●	■
WAKEFIELD							
Sunday Lake Campground					▲		■
YPSILANTI							
Detroit/Greenfield RV Park						●	■
ZEELAND							
Dutch Treat Camping & Recreation					▲	●	■

Green Friendly 🍃; RV Lots for Sale ✖; Park Models/Onsite Onwership ✱; Park Memberships for Sale ✔; Big Rigs Welcome ▲; Internet Friendly ●; Internet Friendly-WiFi ●; Pets Welcome ■

Where to Find CCUSA Parks

List City	Park Name	Map Coordinates
ALLEGAN		
	Tri Ponds Family Camp Resort	I-3
ALLEN		
	Marble Springs Campground	J-4
ALLENDALE		
	Allendale/Grand Rapids West KOA	H-2
ALPENA		
	Campers Cove RV Park & Canoe Livery	E-6
BELDING		
	Double R Ranch Resort	H-3
BELLAIRE		
	Chain O'Lakes Campground	E-4
BESSEMER		
	Alpine Campground	A-5
BIG RAPIDS		
	Cran-Hill Ranch Family Campground	G-3
BOYNE FALLS		
	Chandler Hill Campground	E-5
CADILLAC		
	Cadillac Woods Campground	F-3
CEDAR SPRINGS		
	Lakeside Camp Park	H-3
CEDARVILLE		
	Cedarville RV Park	C-5
CHAMPION		
	Michigamme Shores Campground Resort	B-1
CHEBOYGAN		
	Waterways Campground	D-5
COLOMA		
	Dune Lake Campground	J-2
DECATUR		
	Leisure Valley RV Resort & Campground	J-2
	Oak Shores Campground	J-2
	Timber Trails RV Park	J-2
ELK RAPIDS		
	Honcho Rest Campground	E-4
GERMFASK		
	Big Cedar Campground & Canoe Livery	C-4
GRAND HAVEN		
	Campers Paradise, Inc.	H-2
GRAND RAPIDS		
	Woodchip Campground	H-3
GRANT		
	Salmon Run Campground and Vic's Canoes	H-3
GRASS LAKE		
	Apple Creek Campground & RV Park	I-4
GRAYLING		
	Yogi Bear's Jellystone Camp Resort	E-5
GWINN		
	Horseshoe Lake Campground & RV Park	C-2
HARRISON		
	Downhour's Shady Acres Campground	F-4
HASTINGS		
	Welcome Woods Campground	I-3
HIGGINS LAKE		
	Great Circle Campground	F-4
HILLMAN		
	Thunder Bay RV & Golf Resort	E-6

Drummond Island, located to the east of the U.P., is an explorer's paradise. Fishing, hiking, hunting and 110 miles of groomed snowmobile trails await you.

Fayette. A once thriving iron-smelting town is now a ghost town with free guided tours and displays.

Isle Royale National Park. Famous for its population of moose and wolves, Isle Royale has a striking combination of wildlife and clear blue waters.

Keweenaw National Historical Park. Take a ride on a "cog" railway, down the side of a mountain to the Quincy copper mine. Then board tractor-drawn wagons for the half-mile trip into the mountain. Once inside (400 ft. beneath the surface), you'll see methods and working conditions in the mine's pre-Civil War heyday.

Mackinac Island, located in the Straits of Mackinac, allows no modern transportation vehicles. **Mackinac Island Carriage Tours** picks up visitors near the dockside for a horse drawn tour of the town. The restored 18th- and 19th-century military outpost Fort Mackinac features 14 original buildings, musket and cannon-firing exhibitions, craft demonstrations and re-enactments of historic events.

Mill Creek State Historic Park. Northern Michigan's first industrial complex (1780-1839) is brought to life by lively demonstrations of saw milling and other crafts. Authentically reconstructed buildings, hiking trails and scenic overlooks are located throughout the 625-acre park.

Manistique. The home of the Siphon Bridge and legendary springs also features the **Water Tower**.

Kitch-iti-kipi. See swirling and bubbling formations clearly at 40 ft. below water surface. More than 10,000 gallons of water gush every minute from fissures in the underlying limestone.

Siphon Bridge. This bridge is supported by water, which is atmospherically forced under it. The roadway itself is approximately four feet below water level, 399 feet long, 66 feet wide and has a depth of 20 feet. The feed flume is 3,000 feet long, 200 feet wide and has a flow of 650,000 gallons per hour.

Marquette. Attractions within this historic port city include the **Shiras Planetarium**, the **Moose Trail**, **Sugarloaf Mountain**, **Mount Marquette Lookouts**, the **Marquette State Fish Hatchery** and the 328-acre **Presque Isle Park** with its hiking and cross-country trails.

Paradise. Attractions near Paradise include the **Great Lakes Shipwreck Historical Museum** featuring exhibits of the Edmund Fitzgerald and other vessels shipwrecked on Lake Superior. **Whitefish Point** is the oldest active light on Lake Superior. The Keepers Quarters Dwelling attached to the light has been fully restored and is open for tours. Recreational activities in the area include rockhounding, skiing, snowshoeing, snowmobiling, camping, fishing and swimming. Hiking trails provide access to beautiful **Tahquamenon Falls**, located in **Tahquamenon Falls State Park**.

Sault Ste. Marie. The oldest town in Michigan has attractions such as the **Tower of History**, offering a bird's eye view of the Soo locks and a 20 mile complete spectrum view; the **Shipwreck Museum** where you can learn about the **Edmund Fitzgerald**; **Twilight Walking Tours** complete with stories of ghost ships and hidden graveyards; and **Point Iroquois Light House**, offering a museum and bookstore.

Soo Locks Boat Tours offers narrated tours through the Soo Locks and around Sugar Island, as well as dinner cruises.

Landlubbers will enjoy **Soo Locks Train Tours**, providing a historical tour of the city and a stopover in Sault Ste. Marie, Ontario, Canada.

Seney National Wildlife Refuge, Seney. There are several ways to view this extensive wildlife area: self-guided auto tours, a 1.4-mile hiking trail, 70 miles of roads designed for bicycles and groomed cross-country skiing and snowshoeing trails are provided. Canoeing is permitted on the Manistique, Driggs and Creighton Rivers and Walsh Creek. Parts of the refuge are open for picking morel mushrooms, blueberries and other wild foods. Nearly 250 species of birds and nearly 50 species of mammals can be seen within the area. Best viewing seasons are spring, late summer and fall. The best viewing times are early morning and evening.

ANNUAL EVENTS

JANUARY

Metro Blues Festival, Ferndale; Tip-Up Town U.S.A., Houghton Lake; North American Snowmobile Festival, Cadillac; Ice Sculpture Spectacular, Plymouth; Zehnder's Snowfest, Frankenmuth; White Lake Perch Festival, Whitehall; Hunter Ice Festival, Niles; Mackinaw City Winterfest, Mackinaw City.

FEBRUARY

Detroit Boat Show, Detroit; North American Snow Festival, Cadillac; Winter Beer Festival, Grand Rapids; International 500 Snowmobile Race, Sault Ste. Marie; Winter Carnival, Houghton; Snowfest, Cedarville; Cherry Capital Winterfest, Traverse City; Ice Breaker, South Haven; Outhoouse 500, Coopersville; Pine Mountain Continental Cup Ski Jumping Tournament, Iron Mountain; UP 200 /Midnight Run Sled Dog Races, Marquette.

MARCH

Butterflies are Blooming, Grand Rapids;

Where to Find CCUSA Parks

List City	Park Name	Map Coordinates
HILLSDALE		
	Gateway Park Campground	J-4
	Sugar Bush Campground	J-4
HOUGHTON LAKE		
	Houghton Lake Travel Park	F-4
	West Houghton Lake Campground	F-4
INDIAN RIVER		
	Yogi Bear's Jellystone Park Indian River	D-5
IRON MOUNTAIN		
	Summer Breeze Campground & RV Park	D-1
IRONS		
	Leisure Time Campground	F-3
JACKSON		
	Greenwood Acres Family Campground	I-4
KALKASKA		
	Kalkaska RV Park & Campground	E-4
LUDINGTON		
	Kibby Creek Campground	G-2
MANCELONA		
	Whispering Pines Family Campground	E-4
MANISTEE		
	Matson's Big Manistee River Campground	F-2
MESICK		
	Northern Exposure Campground	F-3
MONTAGUE		
	Trailway Campground	G-2
MUNITH		
	The Oaks Resort	I-4
MUSKEGON		
	Lake Sch-Nepp-A-Ho Campground	H-2
NEW ERA		
	Stony Haven Campground & Cabins	G-2
NEWBERRY		
	Clementz's Northcountry Campground and Cabins	C-4
OMER		
	Rippling Waters Campground	F-5
OTISVILLE		
	Covenant Hills Camp	H-5
OTTAWA LAKE		
	Covered Wagon Camp Resort	J-5
RAPID RIVER		
	Vagabond Resort	C-2
SOMERSET CENTER		
	Somerset Beach Campground	J-4
SOUTH HAVEN		
	South Haven Family Campground	I-2
ST. IGNACE		
	Tiki RV Park & Campground	C-5
STERLING		
	River View Campground & Canoe Livery	F-5
STOCKBRIDGE		
	Heartland Woods Family RV	I-4
SUMNER		
	Leisure Lake Family Campground	H-4
TAWAS CITY		
	East Branch River RV Park	F-5
TECUMSEH		
	Indian Creek Camp & Conference Center	J-5

Celtic Fest, Port Huron; Kalamazoo Living History Show, Kalamazoo; Ultimate Sport & RV Show, Grand Rapids; St. Patrick's Day Festival, Downtown Saginaw; Irish Festival, Clare; Klondike Challenge, Oscoda.

APRIL

Blossomtime Festival, Benton Harbor-St. Joseph; National Trout Festival, Kalkaska; Maple Syrup Festival, Vermontville; Troutfest, Newaygo.

MAY

Downtown Hoedown, Detroit; Tulip Time Festival, Holland; Jackson Storyfest, Jackson; National Morel Mushroom Festival, Boyne City; World Expo of Beer, Frankenmuth; East Lansing Art Festival, East Lansing; Highland Festival, Alma; Electronic Music Festival, Detroit; Dogwood Fin Arts Festival, Dowagiac; Alma Highland Festival & Games, Alma College; Morel Mushroom Festival, Boyne City; Mayfaire Renaissance Festival, Marshall.

JUNE

Island Festival, Kalamazoo; Bavarian Festival, Frankenmuth; Annual Lilac Festival, Mackinac Island; International Freedom Festival, Detroit; Michigan Antique & Collectibles Festival, Midland; St. Ignace Car Show, St. Ignace; Summer Celebration, Muskegon; Michigan Challenge Balloonfest, Howell; Log Cabin Day, various locations; Festival of the Arts, Grand Rapids; Leland Wine & Food Festival, Leland; Arts & Crafts Festival, Whitehall; National Asparagus Festival, Shelby; Three Rivers Water Festival, Three Rivers; Waterfront Film Festival, Saugatuck; Harborfest, South Haven.

JULY

Venetian Festival, St. Joseph; Sand Lakes Blues Fest, National City; National Baby Food Festival, Fremont; National Cherry Festival, Traverse City; US Coast Guard Festival, Grand Haven; Common Ground Festival, Lansing; Showboat Festival, Chesaning; Upper Peninsula Championship Rodeo, Iron River; Manitou Music Festival, Glen Arbor/Leland; Little Traverse Bay Regatta, Petoskey; Idlewild Music Festival, Idlewild; Riverwalk Festival, Lowell; Muskegon Bike Time, Muskegon; National Forest Festival, Manistee; Taste of Kalamazoo, Kalamazoo; Air Show & Balloon Fest, Battle Creek; Indian River Summer Fest, Indian River; National Baby Food Festival, Fremont.

AUGUST

Great Lakes Irish Festival, Comstock Park; The Roots Jamboree, Ypsilanti; Great Lakes Folk Festival, East Lansing; National Blueberry Festival, South Haven; Michigan Renaissance Festival, Holly; Les Cheneaux Islands Antique Wooden Boat Show & Festival of Arts, Hessel. Leelanau Peninsula Wine & Food Festival, Northport; Coopersville Summerfest, Coopersville; Ludington Gold Coast Celebration, Ludington; Shoreline Spectacular, Muskegon; Polish Festival, Boyne Falls; Festival on the Bay, Petoskey; Grant Frontier Festival, Grant; Michigan Fiber Festival, Allegan County Fairgrounds.

SEPTEMBER

Art & Apples Festival, Rochester; Mackinac Bridge Walk, Mackinaw City/St. Ignace; Frankenmuth Oktoberfest, Frankenmuth; Wine and Harvest Festival, Paw Paw; Celebration on the Grand, Grand Rapids; Annual Labor Day Bridge Walk, Mackinaw City; White Lake Fall Fest, White Lake; Bangor Harvest Festival, Bangor; Logging Festival, Newaygo.

OCTOBER

Custer Week Celebration, Monroe; Great Lakes Lighthouse Festival, Alpena; Apple Harvest Festival, Bangor; Fremont Harvest Festival, Celebration, Fremont; Pumpkinfest, Montague.

NOVEMBER

International Festival of Lights, Battle Creek; Dutch Winterfest, Holland; Evergreen Festival, Read City; Silver Bells in the City, Lansing; Dutch Winterfest, Holland; Holidays in the Village, South Haven.

DECEMBER

Christmas Pickle Festival, Berrien Springs; Victorian Sleighbell Parade, Manistee; Holiday Balloon Fest, Battle Creek; Eve on the Ave, Jackson.

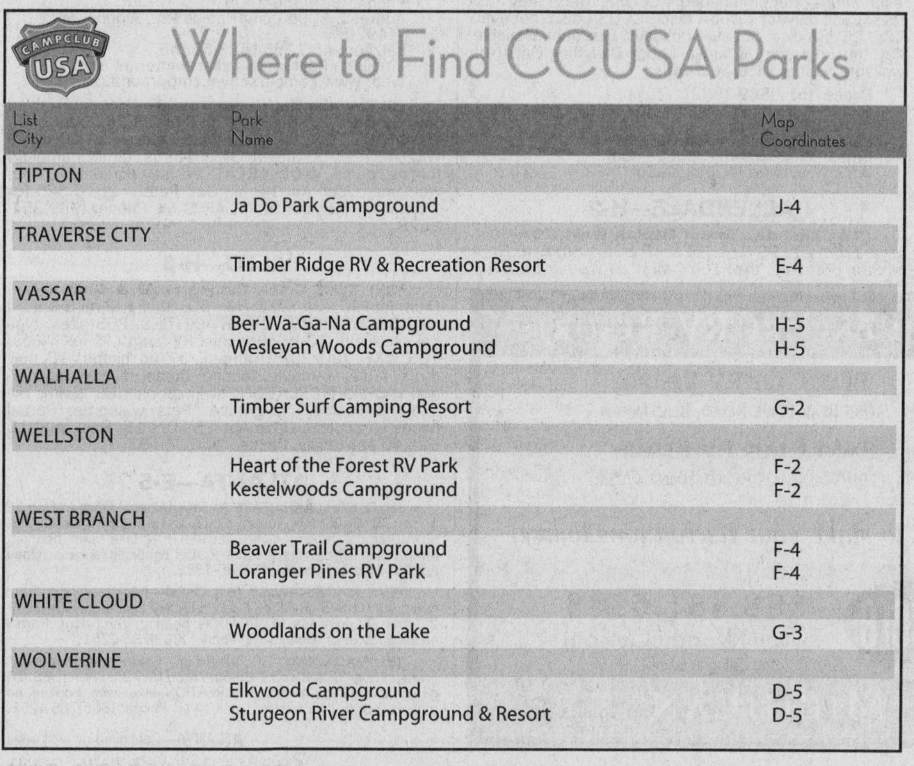

Where to Find CCUSA Parks

List City	Park Name	Map Coordinates
TIPTON		
	Ja Do Park Campground	J-4
TRAVERSE CITY		
	Timber Ridge RV & Recreation Resort	E-4
VASSAR		
	Ber-Wa-Ga-Na Campground	H-5
	Wesleyan Woods Campground	H-5
WALHALLA		
	Timber Surf Camping Resort	G-2
WELLSTON		
	Heart of the Forest RV Park	F-2
	Kestelwoods Campground	F-2
WEST BRANCH		
	Beaver Trail Campground	F-4
	Loranger Pines RV Park	F-4
WHITE CLOUD		
	Woodlands on the Lake	G-3
WOLVERINE		
	Elkwood Campground	D-5
	Sturgeon River Campground & Resort	D-5

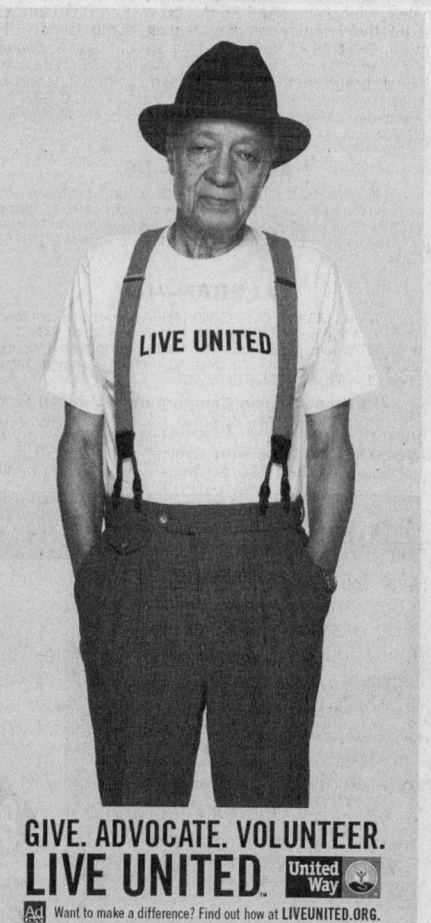

AHMEEK—A-1

(N) Sunset Bay Campground & RV Resort—(Keweenaw) *From north jct Hwy 203 & US 41: Go 4 mi N on US 41, then 1/4 mi W on Wright St, then 5 mi N on Vivian St/5 Mile Point Rd, then 1 mi W on Sunset Bay Beach Rd. Enter on L.* ◆◆◆FACILITIES: 30 sites, 6 full hkups, 14 W&E, (30 amps), 10 no hkups, 2 pull-thrus, family camping, tenting, dump, laundry, ltd groc. ◆◆RECREATION: lake swim, boating, canoeing, lake fishing. Pets welcome. Open May 15 - Oct 3. Rate in 2010 $22-30 for 4 persons. Phone: (906)337-2494.

ALANSON—D-5

(E) MACKINAW SF (Maple Bay)—(Cheboygan) *From town: Go 3-1/2 mi E on Brutus, then 1/2 mi S, on Burt Lake.* FACILITIES: 38 sites, 38 no hkups, tenting. RECREATION: lake swim, boating, ramp, lake fishing. Open all yr. Phone: (989)732-3541.

ALBION—I-4

(N) Rockeys Campground—(Calhoun) *From jct Hwy 99 & I-94: Go 2 mi W on I-94 (exit 121), then 7 mi N on 28 Mile Rd. Enter on R.* ◆◆◆FACILITIES: 100 sites, typical site width 35 ft, 100 W&E, (20/30 amps), 1 pull-thrus, family camping, tenting, dump, laundry, ltd groc. ◆◆◆◆RECREATION: lake swim, boating, canoeing, ramp, dock, lake fishing, playground. Pets welcome, breed restrict, quantity restrict. Partial handicap access. Open Early May - Oct 1. Rate in 2010 $28 for 2 persons. Member ARVC, ARVC MI. Phone: (877)762-5397.

ALGONAC—I-6

(N) ALGONAC STATE PARK—(St. Clair) *From town: Go 2 mi N on Hwy 29.* FACILITIES: 296 sites, 296 E, tenting, dump. RECREATION: boating, ramp, river fishing, playground. Open all yr. Facilities fully operational Apr 3 - Nov 29. Phone: (810)765-5605.

ALLEGAN—I-3

(W) ALLEGAN STATE GAME AREA—(Allegan) *From town: Go 6 mi W on Monroe Road, then 1 mi S on 48th St, then 1 mi W on 116th Ave.* FACILITIES: 113 sites, 113 no hkups, tenting. RECREATION: lake swim, boating, no motors, canoeing, ramp. Open all yr. Phone: (616)673-0378.

(N) Dumont Lake Campground—(Allegan) *From jct Hwy 40/89 & Hwy 222: Go 1/2 mi E on Hwy 222, then 5 mi N on CR A 37 (Main St). Enter on R.* ◆◆◆FACILITIES: 86 sites, typical site width 30 ft, 3 full hkups, 64 W&E, (20/30 amps), 19 no hkups, family

ALLEGAN—Continued
Dumont Lake Campground—Continued

camping, tenting, dump, laundry, ltd groc. ◆◆◆RECREATION: lake swim, boating, canoeing, ramp, dock, lake/pond fishing, playground. Pets welcome ($), quantity restrict. Partial handicap access. Open May 1 - Oct 15. Rate in 2010 $28 for 2 persons. Member ARVC, ARVC MI. Phone: (269)673-6065.

(NW) Tri Ponds Family Camp Resort—(Allegan) *From jct Hwy 222 & Hwy 40/89: Go 3 mi NW on Hwy 40/89, then 1-3/4 mi N on 36th St, then 1/2 mi W on Dumont Rd. Enter on R.* ◆◆◆FACILITIES: 129 sites, typical site width 35 ft, 53 full hkups, 72 W&E, (20/30 amps), 4 no hkups, 8 pull-thrus, WiFi Internet central location ($), family camping, tenting, RV storage, dump, non-guest dump $, laundry, ltd groc, RV supplies, ice, picnic tables, fire rings, wood. ◆◆◆◆RECREATION: rec hall, swim pool, lake swim, pond fishing, fishing supplies, bsktball, playground, activities, horseshoes, hiking trails, v-ball. Pets welcome ($), breed restrict. Partial handicap access. Open May 1 - Oct 31. Rate in 2010 $25-35 per family. MC/VISA/DISC/AMEX/Debit. Member ARVC, ARVCMI. CCUSA 50% Discount. CCUSA reservations Required, CCUSA max stay 3 days, Cash only for CCUSA disc., CCUSA disc. not avail F,Sa, CCUSA disc. not avail holidays. Not available Jul & Aug. $2 electric heater surcharge.

Phone: (269)673-4740
Address: 3687 Dumont Road, Allegan, MI 49010
Lat/Lon: 42.59180/-85.90741
Email: info@triponds.com
Web: www.triponds.com

ALLEN—J-4

Marble Springs Campground—(Hillsdale) *From jct I-69 & US 12: Go 11 mi E on US 12. Enter on R.* ◆◆◆FACILITIES: 80 sites, typical site width 30 ft, 80 W&E, (20/30 amps), 3 pull-thrus, family camping, tenting, RV storage, dump, non-guest dump $, portable dump, laundry, ltd groc, RV supplies, LP gas by weight/by meter, ice, picnic tables, fire rings, wood. ◆◆◆◆RECREATION: pavilion, swim pool, lake swim, pond fishing, fishing supplies, bsktball, playground, activities, horseshoes, hiking trails, v-ball. Pets welcome, breed restrict, quantity restrict. Partial handicap access. Open all yr. Facilities fully operational Early May - Mid Oct. Rate in 2010 $30 per family. MC/VISA/DISC/Debit. CCUSA 50% Discount. CCUSA reservations Recommended, CCUSA max stay 21 days, Cash only for CCUSA disc., CCUSA disc. not avail F,Sa, CCUSA disc. not avail holidays. Discount available May thru mid June & again Labor Day thru Oct. Not available Nascar race weekends.

Phone: (517)869-2522
Address: 9411 W Chicago Rd/ US 12, Allen, MI 49227
Lat/Lon: 41.95174/-84.79546
Email: office@marblesprings.com
Web: www.marblesprings.com

ALLENDALE—H-2

(NW) Allendale/Grand Rapids West KOA—(Ottawa) *From jct I-96 (exit 16) & CR B35/68th Ave: Go 4 mi S on 68th Ave, then 1-3/4 mi W on Warner St. Enter*

ALLENDALE—Continued
Allendale/Grand Rapids West KOA—Continued

on R. ◆◆◆FACILITIES: 150 sites, typical site width 40 ft, 89 full hkups, 36 W&E, (20/30/50 amps), 25 no hkups, cable TV, ($), WiFi Internet central location, family camping, tenting, RV storage, dump, non-guest dump $, laundry, ltd groc, RV supplies, ice, picnic tables, fire rings, wood. ◆◆◆◆RECREATION: pavilion, swim pool, boating, canoeing, kayaking, river/pond fishing, fishing supplies, bsktball, 10 bike rentals, playground, activities, horseshoes, hiking trails, v-ball. Pets welcome. Partial handicap access. Open all yr. Facilities fully operational Memorial Day - Oct 31. Big rigs welcome. Rate in 2010 $30-44 for 2 persons. MC/VISA/DISC/AMEX/Debit. Member ARVC, ARVC MI. KOA discount. CCUSA 50% Discount. CCUSA reservations Required, CCUSA max stay 3 days, CCUSA disc. not avail F,Sa, CCUSA disc. not avail holidays. Not available Jul & Aug. Fully operational May thru Oct.

Phone: (616)895-6601
Address: 8275 Warner St., Allendale, MI 49401
Lat/Lon: 42.99419/-85.99163
Email: info@allendalekoa.com
Web: www.koa.com

ALPENA—E-6

(NW) Campers Cove RV Park & Canoe Livery—(Alpena) *From jct Hwy 32 & US 23: Go 1-1/2 mi N on US 23, then 6 mi W on Long Rapids Rd. Enter on L.* ◆◆◆◆FACILITIES: 95 sites, typical site width 30 ft, 18 full hkups, 65 W&E, (20/30/50 amps), 12 no hkups, 8 pull-thrus, heater not allowed, cable TV, WiFi Internet central location, family camping, tenting, RV storage, dump, non-guest dump $, portable dump, laundry, ltd groc, RV supplies, LP gas by weight/by meter, ice, picnic tables, fire rings, wood. ◆◆◆◆◆RECREATION: pavilion, swim pool, lake/river swim, boating, canoeing, kayaking, ramp, dock, float trips, lake/river/pond fishing, fishing supplies, mini-golf, ($), bsktball, 20 bike rentals, playground, shuffleboard court 2 shuffleboard courts, activities, horseshoes, v-ball. Pets welcome. Partial handicap access. Open May 1 - mid Oct. Rate in 2010 $23-35 per family. MC/VISA/DISC/Debit. Member ARVC, ARVC MI. CCUSA 50% Discount. CCUSA reservations Accepted, CCUSA max stay 14 days, Cash only for CCUSA disc., Check only for CCUSA disc., CCUSA disc. not avail F,Sa, CCUSA disc. not avail holidays.

Phone: (989)356-3708
Address: 5005 Long Rapids Rd., Alpena, MI 49707
Lat/Lon: 45.11554/-83.55646
Email: camperscove@charterinternet.com
Web: www.camperscovecampground.com

(S) Thunder Bay Campground—(Alpena) *From jct Hwy 32 & US 23: Go 3-1/4 mi S on US 23. Enter on R.* ◆◆◆FACILITIES: 59 sites, typical site width 50 ft, 59 W&E, (20/30/50 amps), 34 pull-thrus, family camping, tenting, dump. ◆◆RECREATION: play equipment. Pets welcome. Open Apr 1 - mid Oct. Rate in 2010 $25 for 2 persons. Member ARVC, ARVC MI. Phone: (989)354-2528.

ALTO—H-3

(SE) Tyler Creek Campground & Golf—(Kent) *From jct I-96 (exit 52) & Hwy 50: Go 6-1/2 mi S & E on Hwy 50. Enter on L.* ◆◆◆FACILITIES: 203 sites, typical site width 30 ft, 40 ft max RV length, 3 full hkups, 163 W&E, (20/30/50 amps), 37 no hkups, 10 pull-thrus, family camping, tenting, dump, laundry, groceries. ◆◆◆◆RECREATION: swim pool, river swim, river/pond fishing, playground. Pets welcome. Partial handicap access. Open Apr 15 - Oct 15. Rate in 2010 $25-40 per family. Phone: (616)868-6751.

ATLANTA—E-5

(N) CLEAR LAKE STATE PARK—(Alpena) *From jct Hwy 32 & Hwy 33: Go 8 mi N on Hwy 33.* FACILITIES: 200 sites, 200 E, (20/30 amps), tenting, dump. RECREATION: lake swim, boating, ramp, lake fishing, playground. Partial handicap access. Open Apr 15 - Dec 1. Phone: (989)785-4388.

(SW) MACKINAW SF (Big Oaks)—(Montmorency) *From town: Go 10 mi S on CR 487 & W on Avery Lake Rd.* FACILITIES: 27 sites, 27 no hkups. RECREATION: boating, lake fishing. Partial handicap access. Open all yr. Phone: (989)785-4251.

(E) MACKINAW SF (Jackson Lake)—(Montmorency) *From jct Hwy-32 & Hwy-33: Go 6 mi N on Hwy-33.* FACILITIES: 18 sites, 18 no hkups, tenting. RECREATION: lake swim, boating, no motors, ramp, lake fishing. Open all yr. Phone: (805)785-4251.

ATLANTA—Continued on next page

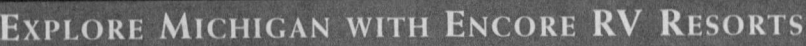

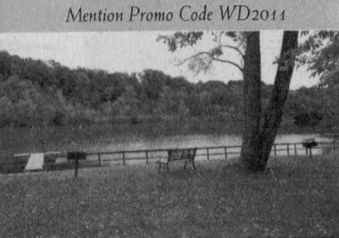

ATLANTA—Continued

(N) MACKINAW SF (Tomahawk Creek Flooding)—(Presque Isle) *From town: Go 13 mi N on Hwy 33, then 1 mi E on Tomahawk Lake Rd. Enter on R.* FACILITIES: 36 sites, 36 no hkups, tenting. RECREATION: boating, canoeing, ramp, lake/river fishing. Open all yr. Phone: (989)785-4251.

AU GRES—F-5

(N) AU GRES CITY RIVERFRONT PARK & CAMPGROUND—(Arenac) *From jct Hwy 65 & US 23: Go 6 mi N on US 23, then 500 feet N on Main St. Enter on L.*

WELCOME

FACILITIES: 109 sites, 25 full hkups, 84 W&E, (20/30 amps), some extd stay sites (summer), 12 pull-thrus, cable TV, phone Internet central location, family camping, tenting, RV storage, dump, non-guest dump $, picnic tables, fire rings, grills.

RECREATION: pavilion, boating, canoeing, kayaking, ramp, lake/river fishing, golf nearby, bsktball, playground, shuffleboard court shuffleboard court, tennis, horseshoes, sports field, hiking trails, v-ball. Rec open to public.

Pets welcome. Partial handicap access. Open Apr 15 - Oct 15. Clubs welcome. MC/VISA/DISC.

Phone: (989)876-8310
Address: 522 Park St, Au Gres, MI 48703
Lat/Lon: 44.05104/-83.68599
Email: cityofaugres@centurytel.net
Web: www.cityofau-gres-mi.org

SEE AD THIS PAGE

(S) Pt Au Gres Marina & Campground—(Arenac) *From jct Hwy 65 & US 23: Go 5 mi N on US 23, then 2-1/2 mi S on Santiago Rd, then 1 mi E on Gordon Rd, then 1/4 mi N on Green Dr. Enter on R.* ◆◆◆FACILITIES: 75 sites, typical site width 30 ft, 42 full hkups, 4 W&E, 15 E, (30/50 amps), 14 no hkups, family camping, tenting, dump, ltd groc. ◆◆◆RECREATION: lake swim, boating, canoeing, ramp, dock, lake fishing, play equipment. Pets welcome. Open May 1 - Sep 15. Rate in 2010 $18-26 per family. Member ARVC, ARVCMI. Phone: (989)876-7314.

AU TRAIN—C-3

(S) HIAWATHA NATIONAL FOREST (Au Train Lake Campground)—(Alger) *From town: Go 4-1/2 mi S on FR 2278, then 1/2 mi E on FR 2276, then 1-1/2 mi N on FR 2596.* FACILITIES: 36 sites, 36 no hkups, tenting. RECREATION: lake swim, boating, canoeing, ramp, lake fishing. Open May 15 - Sep 30. Phone: (906)387-2512.

AUGUSTA—I-3

(NE) Shady Bend Campground and Canoe Livery—(Kalamazoo) *From jct Hwy 37 & Hwy 89: Go 3-3/4 mi W on Hwy 89, then 2 mi W on Augusta Dr. Enter on L.* ◆◆FACILITIES: 80 sites, typical site width 35 ft, 62 W&E, 18 E, (20/30 amps), family camping, tenting, dump, laundry, ltd groc. ◆◆◆RECREATION: river swim, boating, 5 hp limit, canoeing, river/pond fishing, playground. Pets welcome, breed restrict, size restrict. Open May 15 - Oct 1. Rate in 2010 $28 for 2 persons. Phone: (269)731-4503.

BAD AXE—G-6

(SW) Camper's Haven Family Campground—(Huron) *From jct Hwy 142 & Hwy 53: Go 5-1/2 mi SW on Hwy 53. Enter on R.* ◆◆◆FACILITIES: 130 sites, typical site width 45 ft, 105 W&E, (30 amps), 25 no hkups, 25 pull-thrus, family camping, tenting, dump, laundry, ltd groc. ◆◆◆◆RECREATION: swim pool, lake swim, boating, no motors, canoeing, dock, lake fishing, playground. Pets welcome, breed restrict, quantity restrict. Partial handicap access. Open May 1 - Mid Oct. Rate in 2010 $29-33 for 6 persons. Member ARVC, ARVCMI. Phone: (989)269-7989.

BALDWIN—G-3

(S) Whispering Oaks Campground & Cabins—(Lake) *From south jct US 10 & Hwy 37: Go 2-1/2 mi S on Hwy 37. Enter on L.* ◆◆◆FACILITIES: 39 sites, typical site width 35 ft, 39 W&E, (20/30/50 amps), 3 pull-thrus, family camping, tenting, dump, laundry, ltd groc. ◆◆RECREATION: playground. Pets welcome, quantity restrict. Partial handicap access. Open Mar 1 - Oct 31. Rate in 2010 $20-35 for 6 persons. Phone: (231)745-7152.

BARAGA—B-1

(S) BARAGA STATE PARK—(Baraga) *From jct Hwy 38 & US 41: Go 1 mi S on US 41.* FACILITIES: 118 sites, 108 E, (20/30 amps), 10 no hkups, 50 pull-thrus, tenting, dump. RECREATION: lake swim, boating, ramp, lake/stream fishing, playground. Open Apr 15 - Nov 15. Facilities fully operational May 1 - Oct 15. Phone: (906)353-6558.

Ojibwa RV Park (RV SPACES)—(Baraga) *From jct Hwy 41 & Hwy 38: Go 1 mi W on Hwy 38. Enter on R.* FACILITIES: 12 sites, 12 full hkups, (20/30/50 amps). RECREATION: swim pool. Pets welcome. Partial handicap access. No tents. Open May - Mld Nov. Big rigs welcome. Rate in 2010 $15 per vehicle. Phone: (800)323-8045.

BARRYTON—G-3

(N) MERRILL LAKE PARK (Mecosta County)—(Missaukee) *From jct Hwy-66 & US-10: Go 7 mi S on Hwy-66.* FACILITIES: 147 sites, 30 ft max RV length, 123 W&E, (20 amps), 24 no hkups, tenting, dump. RECREATION: lake swim, boating, 10 hp limit, canoeing, ramp, lake fishing, playground. Open May 1 - Oct 1. Phone: (989)382-7158.

BARTON CITY—E-6

(W) HURON NATIONAL FOREST (Jewell Lake Campground)—(Alcona) *From town: Go 1/2 mi E on Trask Lake Rd, then 1/2 mi S on FR-4601.* FACILITIES: 32 sites, 22 ft max RV length, 32 no hkups, tenting, ltd groc. RECREATION: lake swim, boating, canoeing, ramp, lake fishing. Open Memorial Day - Labor Day. Phone: (989)739 -0728.

BATTLE CREEK—I-3

(NW) Battle Creek Michigan Campground—(Calhoun) *From jct Hwy 37 & I-94: Go 3 mi E on I-94 (exit 95), then 6 mi N on Helmer Rd/Bedford Rd, then 1-1/2 mi W on Hwy 89, then 2-1/2 mi N on Collier Ave, then 1 block W on Sunshine Ln. Enter on L.* ◆◆◆FACILITIES: 60 sites, 26 full hkups, 34 W&E, (20/30 amps), 22 pull-thrus, family camping, tenting, dump. ◆◆◆◆RECREATION: swim pool, lake swim, boating, no motors, dock, pond fishing, playground. No pets. Partial handicap access. Open May 1 - Labor Day. Rate in 2010 $20-35 per vehicle. Phone: (269)962-1600.

(N) Creek Valley (RV SPACES)—(Calhoun) *From jct I-94 (exit 95) & Hwy 37: Go 8-1/2 mi N on Hwy 37. Enter on L.* FACILITIES: 22 sites, typical site width 25 ft, accepts full hkup units only, 22 full hkups, (20/30 amps), 1 pull-thrus, family camping. Pets welcome, breed restrict. No tents. Open all yr. Rate in 2010 $30 for 2 persons. Phone: (269)964-9577.

(W) FORT CUSTER STATE RECREATION AREA—(Kalamazoo) *From town: Go 6 mi W on Hwy 96.* FACILITIES: 219 sites, 219 E, tenting, dump. RECREATION: lake swim, boating, 3 hp limit, ramp, lake/river fishing, playground. Partial handicap access. Open all yr. Facilities fully operational Mar 22 - Dec 1. Phone: (269)731-4200.

BAY CITY—G-5

(E) BAY CITY STATE RECREATION AREA—(Bay) *From jct US 10 & Hwy 247: Go 5 mi N on Hwy 247.* FACILITIES: 193 sites, 193 E, tenting, dump. RECREATION: lake swim, boating, lake fishing, playground. Partial handicap access. Open all yr. Phone: (989)684-3020.

BAY HARBOR—D-4

(W) Signature Motorcoach Resort at Bay Harbor—(Emmett) *From jct US 131 & US 31: Go 4-1/4 mi S on US 31. Enter on L.* ◆◆◆◆◆FACILITIES: 78 sites, typical site width 40 ft, accepts full hkup units only, 78 full hkups, (50 amps), laundry. ◆◆◆◆◆RECREATION: swim pool. Pets welcome, quantity restrict. Partial handicap access. No tents. Open May 1 - Nov 1. Big rigs welcome. Rate in 2010 $59-79 for 4 persons. Phone: (877)348-2401. FMCA discount.

BEAR LAKE—F-2

(N) HOPKINS PARK CAMPGROUND (City Park)—(Manistee) *From jct Hwy-22 & US-31: Go 12 mi N on US-31.* FACILITIES: 30 sites, 30 ft max RV length, 30 E, (30 amps), tenting, dump. RECREATION: lake swim, boating, ramp, lake fishing, playground. Open Apr 15 - Nov. Phone: (231)864-4300.

(N) Kampvilla RV Park & Family Campground—(Manistee) *From south jct Hwy 115 & US 31: Go 7-1/4 mi S on US 31. Enter on R.* ◆◆◆◆FACILITIES: 92 sites, typical site width 30 ft, 67 full hkups, (20/30/50 amps), 50 amps ($), 25 no hkups, 34 pull-thrus, family camping, tenting, dump, laundry, ltd groc. ◆◆◆RECREATION: swim pool, pond fishing, playground. Pets welcome. Partial handicap access. Open Apr 1 - Nov 1. Rate in 2010 $30 for 2 persons. Member ARVC, ARVC MI. Phone: (800)968-0027.

BEAVERTON—G-4

(W) CALHOUN CAMPGROUND (City Park)—(Gladwin) *From town: Go 1/2 mi S on Hwy 18, then 2 mi W on Brown, then 200 yards S on Roehrs Rd.* FACILITIES: 92 sites, typical site width 30 ft, 43 full hkups, 24 W&E, 25 no hkups, 10 pull-thrus, tenting, dump. RECREATION: lake swim, boating, canoeing, ramp, dock, lake/river fishing, playground. Partial handicap access. Open May 1 - Nov 1. Facilities fully operational May - Oct. Phone: (989)435-2100.

BEAVERTON—Continued

(SW) Lost Haven Campground—(Gladwin) *From jct US-10 & Hwy-18: Go 7 mi N on Hwy-18, then 3 mi W on Lyle Rd, then 1/4 mi N on Townhall Rd. Enter on L.* ◆◆◆FACILITIES: 100 sites, typical site width 30 ft, 100 W&E, (20/30/50 amps), family camping, dump, laundry, ltd groc. ◆◆◆RECREATION: lake swim, pond fishing, playground. Pets welcome. No tents. Open May 1 - Oct 1. Rate in 2010 $25 per family. Member ARVC, ARVCMI. Phone: (989)435-7623.

BELDING—H-3

(SW) Double R Ranch Resort—(Ionia) *From jct Hwy 91 & Hwy 44: Go 100 yards W on Hwy 44, then 3 mi S on White Bridge Rd. Enter on L.* ◆◆◆FACILITIES: 100 sites, typical site width 40 ft, 24 full hkups, 76 W&E, (20/30 amps), 10 pull-thrus, WiFi Internet central location, family camping, tenting, RV storage, dump, non-guest dump $, portable dump, laundry, ltd groc, RV supplies, LP gas by weight/by meter, ice, picnic tables, fire rings, wood. ◆◆◆RECREATION: rec hall, 2 swim pools, river swim, boating, canoeing, kayaking, ramp, float trips, river fishing, fishing supplies, putting green, bsktball, playground, activities, horseshoes, hiking trails, v-ball. Pets welcome, quantity restrict. Open May 1 - Oct 1. Rate in 2010 $32-35 for 2 persons. MC/VISA/DISC/AMEX/Debit. Member ARVC, ARVC MI. CCUSA 50% Discount. CCUSA reservations Required, CCUSA max stay 5 days, CCUSA disc. not avail F,Sa, CCUSA disc. not avail holidays. Not available Jul & Aug.

CAMPCLUB USA

Phone: (877)794-0520
Address: 4424 N Whites Bridge Rd, Belding, MI 48809
Lat/Lon: 43.05006/-85.26964
Email: info@doublerranch.com
Web: www.doublerranch.com

BELLAIRE—E-4

(SE) Chain O'Lakes Campground—(Antrim) *From jct US 131 & Hwy 88: Go 7 mi W on Hwy 88. Enter on R.* ◆◆◆FACILITIES: 89 sites, typical site width 30 ft, 55 full hkups, 34 W&E, (20/30/50 amps), 7 pull-thrus, heater not allowed, WiFi Instant Internet at site, family camping, tenting, RV storage, dump, non-guest dump $, laundry, ltd groc, RV supplies, ice, picnic tables, fire rings, wood. ◆◆◆RECREATION: pavilion, swim pool, bsktball, playground, activities, horseshoes, hiking trails, v-ball. Pets welcome. Open all yr. Facilities fully operational Memorial Day - Labor Day. Big rigs welcome. Rate in 2010 $30-36 for 2 persons. MC/VISA/DISC. CCUSA 50% Discount. CCUSA max stay 4 days, CCUSA disc. not avail S, CCUSA disc. not avail F,Sa, CCUSA disc. not avail holidays. Reservations accepted within 1 week of stay only.

CAMPCLUB USA

Phone: (231)533-8432
Address: 7231 S M 88, Bellaire, MI 49615
Lat/Lon: 44.92464/-85.18591
Email: reserve@chainolakescamp.com
Web: www.chainolakescamp.com

BELLEVILLE—I-5

(NW) WAYNE COUNTY FAIRGROUNDS & RV PARK—(Wayne) *From jct I-275 & I-94: Go 4 mi W on I-94 (exit 190/Belleville Rd), then 1/2 mi W on N Service Rd, then 1/4 mi N on Quirk Rd. Enter on R.* FACILITIES: 110 sites, typical site width 35 ft, 100 W&E, (20/30/50 amps), 10 no hkups, 99 pull-thrus, family camping, tenting, dump, laundry. RECREATION: Pets welcome. Partial handicap access. Open Apr 1 - Oct 31. Phone: (734)697-7002.

BENTON HARBOR—J-2

(E) Eden Springs Park & Campground (formerly House of Davids)—(Berrien) *From jct I-196 & I-94: Go 5-1/2 mi S on I-94 (exit 28), then 2-1/2 mi N on Hwy 139. Enter on R.* ◆◆◆FACILITIES: 100 sites, typical site width 40 ft, 50 full hkups, 50 W&E, (30/50 amps), 100 pull-thrus, family camping, tenting, dump, laundry. RECREATION: play equipment. Pets welcome. Open all yr. Rate in 2010 $30 per family. Phone: (269)927-3302.

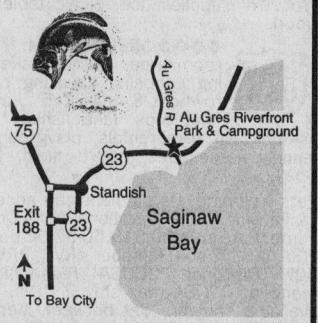

BENZONIA—F-2

(S) Timberline Campground—(Benzie) *From south jct US 31 & Hwy 115: Go 1/4 mi N on US 31/Hwy 115. Enter on L.* ◆◆◆FACILITIES: 206 sites, typical site width 35 ft, 144 full hkups, 45 W&E, (20/30 amps), 17 no hkups, 18 pull-thrus, family camping, tenting, dump. ◆◆◆RECREATION: swim pool, playground. Pets welcome. Partial handicap access. Open Apr 1 - Dec 1. Rate in 2010 $25-27 for 2 persons. Member ARVC, ARVC MI. Phone: (231)882-9548.

(S) Vacation Trailer Park—(Benzie) *From south jct Hwy 115 & US 31: Go 1 mi N on US 31. Enter on L.* ◆◆◆FACILITIES: 100 sites, typical site width 30 ft, 30 full hkups, 70 W&E, (20/30/50 amps), 2 pull-thrus, family camping, tenting, dump, laundry, ltd groc. ◆◆◆◆RECREATION: swim pool, canoeing, dock, river fishing, playground. Pets welcome. Open all yr. Facilities fully operational late Mar - Late Nov. Rate in 2010 $29.50-35 for 4 persons. Member ARVC, ARVC MI. Phone: (231)882-5101.

BERGLAND—A-6

(S) LAKE GOGEBIC STATE PARK—(Gogebic) *From town: Go 11 mi S on Hwy 64.* FACILITIES: 127 sites, 93 E, (20/30 amps), 34 no hkups, 2 pull-thrus, tenting, dump. RECREATION: lake swim, boating, canoeing, ramp, dock, lake fishing, playground. Partial handicap access. Open Apr 15 - Nov 15. Phone: (906)842-3341.

BESSEMER—A-5

(E) Alpine Campground—(Gogebic) *From jct Hwy 28 & US 2: Go 2-1/2 mi W on US 2. Enter on R.* ◆◆◆FACILITIES: 41 sites, typical site width 30 ft, 16 full hkups, 25 W&E, (20/30 amps), 39 pull-thrus, cable TV, ($), family camping, tenting, RV storage, shower$, dump, non-guest dump $, laundry, picnic tables, fire rings, grills, wood. ◆RECREATION: lake fishing, mini-golf, ($), playground. Pets welcome. Open all yr. Facilities fully operational Memorial Day - Labor Day. Rate in 2010 $29.50 for 2 persons. CCUSA 50% Discount. CCUSA reservations Accepted, CCUSA max stay 3 days, Cash only for CCUSA disc. Fully operational Memorial Day-Labor Day. Electric heater surcharge: $3.50.

Phone: (906)667-0737
Address: E8072 US 2, Bessemer, MI 49911
Lat/Lon: 46.48284/-90.00175

(N) OTTAWA NATIONAL FOREST (Black River Harbor Campground)—(Gogebic) *From jct US-2 & CR-513: Go 15 mi N on CR-513.* FACILITIES: 39 sites, 39 no hkups, tenting, dump, ltd groc. RECREATION: lake swim, boating, ramp, dock, lake/river fishing, playground. Partial handicap access. Open May 25 - Sep 30. Phone: (906)932-7250.

BIG BAY—B-2

(N) PERKINS PARK (Marquette County Park)—(Marquette) *In town on CR-550.* FACILITIES: 83 sites, typical site width 15 ft, 37 full hkups, 14 E, (20/50 amps), 32 no hkups, tenting, dump. RECREATION: lake swim, boating, canoeing, ramp, lake fishing, play equipment. Partial handicap access. Open May 15 - Sep 15. Phone: (906)345-9353.

BIG RAPIDS—G-3

(E) CRAN-HILL RANCH FAMILY CAMPGROUND—(Mecosta) *From jct US 131 (exit 139) & Hwy 20: Go 3-1/4 mi E on Hwy 20, then 3-1/4 mi E on Colburn Ave/16 Mile Rd, then 1 mi N on 160th Ave, then 1-3/4 mi E on 17 Mile Rd. Enter on L.*

CHRISTIAN FAMILY CAMPING EXPERIENCE
10 min East of Big Rapids - 300 acres, 2 lakes (1 all-sports), fun, safe, convenient, full week programming Jun-Aug, year-round activities/events. Truly Michigan's best kept secret where families rest, play & grow together.

◆◆◆FACILITIES: 150 sites, typical site width 30 ft, 6 full hkups, 114 W&E, (30 amps), 30 no hkups, WiFi Instant Internet at site, WiFi Internet central location, family camping, tenting, cabins, RV storage, dump, non-guest dump $, laundry, ltd groc, RV supplies, ice, picnic tables, fire rings, wood.

◆◆◆◆◆RECREATION: rec hall, rec room/area, pavilion, lake swim, boating, canoeing, kayaking, ramp, dock, 5 rowboat/8 canoe/5 kayak rentals, float trips, lake fishing, golf nearby, bsktball, 24 bike rentals, playground, activities, tennis, horseshoes, sports field, hiking trails, v-ball.

Pets welcome. Partial handicap access. Open all yr. Facilities fully operational Apr - Oct. Clubs welcome. Rate in 2010 $16.50-37.50 per family. MC/VISA/DISC/Debit. Member ARVC, ARVCMI. CCUSA 50% Discount. CCUSA reservations Recommended, CCUSA max stay 2 days. Discount not available Thu thru Sat between Memorial Day & Labor Day only. Fully operational Apr thru Oct.

BIG RAPIDS—Continued
CRAN-HILL RANCH FAMILY CAMPGROUND—Continued

Phone: (231)796-7669
Address: 14444 17 Mile Rd, Rodney, MI 49342
Lat/Lon: 43.71669/-85.37400
Email: info@cranhillranch.com
Web: www.cranhillranch.com

SEE AD TRAVEL SECTION PAGE 360

BIRCH RUN—H-5

(S) Pine Ridge RV Campground—(Saginaw) *From jct I-75 (exit 136) & Hwy 83: Go 2 mi E on Birch Run Rd, then 1/4 mi N on Hwy 83 (Gera Rd). Enter on L.* ◆◆◆◆FACILITIES: 207 sites, typical site width 40 ft, 207 full hkups, (20/30/50 amps), 147 pull-thrus, family camping, laundry. ◆◆RECREATION: playground. Pets welcome, quantity restrict. Partial handicap access. No tents. Open Apr 1 - Nov 15. Big rigs welcome. Rate in 2010 $34 for 4 persons. Phone: (989)624-9029.

BOYNE CITY—E-4

(NW) YOUNG STATE PARK—(Charlevoix) *From jct hwy 75 & CR 56: Go 2 mi NW on CR 56.* FACILITIES: 240 sites, 240 E, tenting, dump, groceries. RECREATION: lake swim, boating, ramp, lake/pond fishing, playground. Partial handicap access. Open Apr 1 - Dec 1. Phone: (231)582-7523.

BOYNE FALLS—E-5

(NE) CHANDLER HILL CAMPGROUND—(Charlevoix) *From jct Hwy 75 & US 131: Go 1/2 mi N on US 131, then 8-3/4 mi E on Thumb Lake Rd, then 4-1/4 mi N on Magee Rd. Enter on R.*

◆◆◆FACILITIES: 76 sites, typical site width 30 ft, 17 full hkups, 53 W&E, (20/30/50 amps), 6 no hkups, 4 pull-thrus, family camping, tenting, dump, non-guest dump $, laundry, ltd groc, RV supplies, LP gas by weight/by meter, ice, picnic tables, fire rings, wood.

◆◆◆RECREATION: swim pool, 3 canoe/2 kayak rentals, golf nearby, playground, activities, (wkends), horseshoes, sports field, hiking trails, v-ball, local tours. Rec open to public.

Pets welcome. Partial handicap access. Open all yr. Facilities fully operational May 1 - Nov 1. Clubs welcome. Green Friendly. Rate in 2010 $18-25 for 5 persons. MC/VISA/DISC/Debit. Member ARVC, ARVCMI. CCUSA 50% Discount. CCUSA reservations Required, CCUSA max stay 2 days, CCUSA disc. not avail F,Sa, CCUSA disc. not avail holidays. 2 tents/site. Discount not available on rustic sites. Fully operational May 1-Nov 1.

Phone: (231)549-7878
Address: 02930 Magee Rd, Boyne Falls, MI 49713
Lat/Lon: 45.24492/-84.75415
Email: camping@chandlerhillcampground.com
Web: www.chandlerhillcampground.com

SEE AD TRAVEL SECTION PAGE 359

BREVORT—C-4

(NE) LAKE SUPERIOR SF (Little Brevport Lk-North Unit)—(Mackinac) *From US 2 in town: Go 2 mi NE on Carp River Rd & Worth Rd. Enter on L.* FACILITIES: 20 sites, 20 no hkups. RECREATION: lake swim, boating, ramp, lake/stream fishing. Open all yr. Phone: (906)635-5281.

BRIGHTON—I-5

(SW) BRIGHTON RECREATION AREA (SP)—(Livingston) *From jct US 23 & I-96: Go 1/2 mi W on I-96 to exit 147, then W 6 mi to Chilson Rd, then S 1-1/2 mi to Bishop Lake Rd to park.* FACILITIES: 194 sites, 144 E, 50 no hkups, tenting, dump, groceries. RECREATION: lake swim, boating, canoeing, ramp, lake fishing, playground. Partial handicap access. Open Apr 1 - Dec 1. Facilities fully operational Apr 15 - Oct 15. Phone: (810)229-6566.

BRIMLEY—C-5

(NW) BAY MILLS RESORT & CASINOS—*From jct Hwy 28 & Hwy 221: Go 2-1/2 mi N on Hwy 221, then 1-3/4 mi W on Lakeshore Dr. Enter on R.* Resort including 2 casinos, a 144 room hotel, restaurants, and a conference center. Open 24 hrs. Open all yr. MC/VISA/DISC/AMEX/Debit. ATM.

Phone: (888)422-9645
Address: 11386 W Lakeshore Dr, Brimley, MI 49715
Lat/Lon: 46.42287/-84.60357
Email: kperron@4baymills.com
Web: www.4baymills.com

SEE AD TRAVEL SECTION PAGE 358

Michigan State Bird: Robin

BRIMLEY—Continued

(NW) BAY MILLS RV CAMPGROUND—(Chippewa) *From jct Hwy 28 & Hwy 221: Go 2-1/2 mi N on Hwy 221, then 2 mi W on Lakeshore Dr. Enter on L.*

◆◆◆◆FACILITIES: 76 sites, typical site width 30 ft, 30 full hkups, 46 W&E, (20/30/50 amps), 76 pull-thrus, cable TV, WiFi Internet central location, family camping, tenting, dump, non-guest dump $, laundry, ice, picnic tables, fire rings, grills, wood.

◆◆◆◆RECREATION: coin games, boating, ramp, dock, lake fishing, putting green, golf nearby. Rec open to public.

Pets welcome. Partial handicap access. Open May 1 - Nov 1. Open May 1st weather permitting. Big rigs welcome. Clubs welcome. Rate in 2010 $17-25 per vehicle. MC/VISA/DISC/AMEX/Debit. ATM.

Phone: (888)422-9645
Address: 11386 W Lakeshore Dr, Brimley, MI 49715
Lat/Lon: 46.42392/-84.60389
Email: kperron@4baymills.com
Web: www.4baymills.com

SEE AD TRAVEL SECTION PAGE 358

(E) BRIMLEY STATE PARK—(Mackinac) *From jct I-75 & Hwy 28: Go 8 mi W on Hwy 28, then 2 mi N on Hwy 221, then 1 mi E on Lakeshore Dr.* FACILITIES: 237 sites, 237 E, (20 amps), tenting, dump. RECREATION: lake swim, boating, ramp, lake fishing, playground. Partial handicap access. Open Apr 15 - Dec 1. Phone: (906)248-3422.

(NW) Chippewa Landing of Bay Mills—(Chippewa) *From jct Hwy 28 & Hwy 221: Go 2-1/2 mi N on Hwy 221, then 4 mi N & W on Lakeshore Dr, then 1/4 mi SE on Bay Mills Pt Rd. Enter on L.* ◆◆FACILITIES: 21 sites, typical site width 30 ft, 32 ft max RV length, 5 full hkups, 7 W&E, 9 E, (20/30 amps), family camping, tenting, dump. ◆◆◆RECREATION: lake swim, boating, canoeing, ramp, dock, lake fishing. Pets welcome. Open May 15 - Nov 1. Rate in 2010 $12-28 for 4 persons. Phone: (906)248-5278.

(NW) HIAWATHA NATIONAL FOREST (Monocle Lake Campground)—(Chippewa) *From jct Hwy 28 & Hwy 221: Go 3 mi N on Hwy 221, then 6-1/3 mi NW on CR-3150, then 2/3 mi W on FH-3699.* FACILITIES: 39 sites, 32 ft max RV length, 39 no hkups, 3 pull-thrus, tenting. RECREATION: lake swim, boating, ramp, lake fishing. Partial handicap access. Open May 15 - Oct 15. Phone: (906)248-3431.

(E) Minnow Lake Campground—(Chippewa) *From jct Hwy 28 & Hwy 221: Go 2-1/2 mi N on Hwy 221, then 3 mi E on Lakeshore Dr/6 Mile Rd. Enter on R.* ◆◆FACILITIES: 30 sites, typical site width 25 ft, 38 ft max RV length, 4 full hkups, 26 E, (20/30 amps), 5 pull-thrus, tenting, dump. ◆RECREATION: boating, no motors, river/pond fishing. Pets welcome. Open Mid May - Sep 30. Rate in 2010 $15-20 for 4 persons. Phone: (906)632-6980.

(NW) WILD BLUFF GOLF COURSE—*From jct Hwy 28 & Hwy 221: Go 2-1/2 mi N on Hwy 221 mi N on Hwy 221, then 1-3/4 mi W on Lakeshore Dr.* 18-hole golf course surrounded by views of Lake Superior. Restaurant on site. Open May 1 - Oct 31. Weather permitting. MC/VISA/DISC/AMEX/Debit. ATM.

Phone: (888)422-9645
Address: 11335 W. Lakeshore Dr, Brimley, MI 49715
Lat/Lon: 46.42073/-84.60387
Web: www.wildbluff.com

SEE AD TRAVEL SECTION PAGE 358

BROHMAN—G-3

(SW) MANISTEE NATIONAL FOREST (Nichols Lake Campground)—(Lake) *From town: Go 2 mi N on Hwy 37, then 4-1/2 mi W on 11 Mile Rd, then 3/4 mi N on FR 5140.* FACILITIES: 29 sites, 29 no hkups, tenting. RECREATION: lake swim, boating, canoeing, ramp, lake fishing. Partial handicap access. Open May 13 - Sep 27. Phone: (231)723-2211.

BUCHANAN—J-2

(N) BEAR CAVE RESORT (CAMP RESORT)—(Berrien) *From jct US 31 (exit 72) & US 12: Go 2 mi W on US 12, then 5-1/2 mi N on Red Bud Trail. Enter on R.*

FACILITIES: 120 sites, typical site width 35 ft, 35 full hkups, 85 W&E, (30/50 amps), family camping, tenting, cabins, RV storage, dump, portable dump, laundry, ltd groc, RV supplies, ice, picnic tables, patios, fire rings, wood, controlled access.

RECREATION: rec hall, rec room/area, equipped pavilion, coin games, swim pool, hot tub, boating, canoeing, kayaking, ramp, dock, 2 rowboat/3 canoe rentals, river fishing, fishing supplies, golf nearby, bsktball, playground, shuffleboard court 2 shuffleboard courts, activities, horseshoes, sports field, hiking trails, v-ball.

BEAR CAVE RESORT—Continued on next page

BUCHANAN—Continued
BEAR CAVE RESORT—Continued

Pets welcome, breed restrict. Partial handicap access. Open May 1 - Oct 1. Clubs welcome. Rate in 2010 $39 for 2 persons. MC/VISA/DISC/AMEX/Debit.

Phone: (269)695-3050
Address: 4085 Bear Cave Rd, Buchanan, MI 49107
Lat/Lon: 41.88121/-86.36321
Email: bcmgr@mhchomes.com
Web: www.1000trails.com

SEE AD ADRIAN PAGE 372

(W) FULLER'S RESORT & CAMPGROUND ON CLEAR LAKE—(Berrien) *From jct US 31 (exit 72) & US 12: Go 3-1/2 mi W on US 12, then 1-1/2 mi N on Bakertown Rd, then 3/4 mi W on Elm Valley Rd, then 1 mi NW on East Clear Lake Rd. Enter at end.*

◊◊◊FACILITIES: 176 sites, typical site width 30 ft, 76 full hkups, 64 W&E, (20/30/50 amps), 36 no hkups, some extd stay sites (summer), 7 pull-thrus, WiFi Instant Internet at site, family camping, tenting, RV's/park model rentals, cabins, RV storage, dump, non-guest dump $, portable dump, laundry, ltd groc, RV supplies, LP gas by weight/by meter, ice, picnic tables, fire rings, wood.

◊◊◊◊RECREATION: rec hall, rec room/area, coin games, lake swim, boating, 10 hp limit, canoeing, kayaking, ramp, dock, pontoon/6 rowboat/3 canoe/12 kayak/4 pedal boat/motorboat rentals, lake fishing, fishing supplies, golf nearby, bsktball, playground, activities, (wkends), horseshoes, sports field, v-ball. Rec open to public.

Pets welcome, breed restrict, quantity restrict. Partial handicap access. Open mid Apr - Nov 1. Clubs welcome. Rate in 2010 $20-55 for 2 persons. MC/VISA/DISC/AMEX/Debit.

Phone: (269)695-3785
Address: 1622 E Clear Lake Rd, Buchanan, MI 49107
Lat/Lon: 41.83435/-86.41824
Email: info@fullersresort.com
Web: www.fullersresort.com

SEE AD THIS PAGE

BUCKLEY—F-3

(N) TRAVERSE CITY KOA—(Grand Traverse) *From jct Hwy 113 & Hwy 37: Go 3-1/2 mi S on Hwy 37. Enter on R.*

◊◊◊◊FACILITIES: 110 sites, typical site width 30 ft, 60 full hkups, 29 W&E, 10 E, (20/30/50 amps), 11 no hkups, some extd stay sites (summer), 18 pull-thrus, cable TV, WiFi Instant Internet at site, family camping, tenting, cabins, RV storage, dump, non-guest dump $, portable dump, laundry, groceries, RV supplies, LP gas by weight/by meter, ice, picnic tables, fire rings, wood.

◊◊◊◊RECREATION: rec room/area, pavilion, coin games, swim pool, mini-golf, ($), golf nearby, bsktball, 14 bike rentals, playground, activities, horseshoes, sports field, v-ball.

Pets welcome, breed restrict. Partial handicap access. Open May 1 - Oct 15. Big rigs welcome. Escort to site. Clubs welcome. Rate in 2010 $25-52 per family. MC/VISA/DISC/Debit. Member ARVC, ARVC MI. KOA discount.

Phone: (800)249-3203
Address: 9700 M37, Buckley, MI 49620
Lat/Lon: 44.54593/-85.67634
Email: info@traversecitykoa.com
Web: www.traversecitykoa.com

SEE AD TRAVERSE CITY PAGE 405

BYRON—H-5

(SE) MYERS LAKE CAMPGROUND—(Genesee) *From south jct I-75 & US 23: Go 10 mi S on US 23 (exit 79), then 10 mi W on Silver Lake Rd, then 100 ft S on Murray Rd. Enter on R.*

◊◊◊FACILITIES: 126 sites, typical site width 30 ft, 35 W&E, 91 E, (20/30/50 amps), some extd stay sites (summer), WiFi Instant Internet at site, WiFi Internet central location, family camping, tenting, cabins, RV storage, dump, non-guest dump $, portable dump, laundry, ltd groc, RV supplies, LP gas by weight/by meter, ice, picnic tables, fire rings, wood.

◊◊◊◊◊RECREATION: rec hall, pavilion, coin games, lake swim, boating, 75 hp limit, canoeing, kayaking, ramp, dock, 6 rowboat/5 kayak/6 pedal boat rentals, lake fishing, fishing supplies, golf nearby, bsktball, 12 bike rentals, playground, activities, (wkends), horseshoes, sports field, v-ball.

BYRON—Continued
MYERS LAKE CAMPGROUND—Continued

Pets welcome, quantity restrict. Partial handicap access. Open May 1 - Oct 15. No alcohol allowed. Clubs welcome. Green Friendly. Rate in 2010 $27-38 per family. MC/VISA/DISC. Member ARVC, ARVC MI. FCRV discount. FMCA discount.

Text 81830 to (440)725-8687 to see our Visual Tour.

Phone: (800)994-5050
Address: 10575 W Silver Lake Rd, Byron, MI 48418
Lat/Lon: 42.80623/-83.88175
Email: mlinfo@umccamps.org
Web: www.myerslake.org

SEE AD FENTON PAGE 380

CADILLAC—F-3

(SE) Cadillac Woods Campground—(Osceola) *From jct US-131 & Hwy 115: Go 6 mi SE on Hwy 115. Enter on R.* ◊◊◊FACILITIES: 50 sites, typical site width 30 ft, 35 ft max RV length, 42 W&E, 8 E, (20/30/50 amps), 15 pull-thrus, family camping, tenting, RV storage, dump, non-guest dump $, portable dump, laundry, ltd groc, RV supplies, ice, picnic tables, fire rings, wood. ◊◊RECREATION: pavilion, swim pool, mini-golf, bsktball, playground, horseshoes, hiking trails, v-ball. Pets welcome. Partial handicap access. Open May 1 - Oct 31. Rate in 2010 $23-29 per family. MC/VISA/DISC/Debit. Member ARVC, ARVC MI. CCUSA 50% Discount. CCUSA reservations Recommended, CCUSA max stay Unlimited, CCUSA disc. not avail holidays.

Phone: (231)825-2012
Address: 23163 M-115, Tustin, MI 49688
Lat/Lon: 44.14921/-85.32369
Email: albarnhart3@netzero.com
Web: www.cadillacwoodscampground.com

(NE) CAMP CADILLAC—(Wexford) *From jct Hwy 115 & US 131: Go 6-1/2 mi N on US 131 (exit 183), then 1 mi E on 34 Rd/Boon Rd. Enter on L.*

◊◊◊◊FACILITIES: 115 sites, typical site width 45 ft, 30 full hkups, 69 W&E, 7 E, (20/30/50 amps), 9 no hkups, some extd stay sites (summer), 9 pull-thrus, WiFi Instant Internet at site, family camping, tenting, cabins, RV storage, dump, non-guest dump $, portable dump, laundry, ltd groc, RV supplies, LP gas by weight/by meter, ice, picnic tables, fire rings, grills, wood.

◊◊◊◊RECREATION: rec hall, rec room/area, coin games, swim pool, pond/stream fishing, fishing supplies, golf nearby, bsktball, 17 bike rentals, playground, activities, (wkends), horseshoes, sports field, hiking trails, v-ball. Rec open to public.

Pets welcome. Partial handicap access. Open Apr 15 - Oct 15. Big rigs welcome. Clubs welcome. Rate in 2010 $26-36 for 2 persons. MC/VISA/DISC/Debit. Member ARVC, ARVC MI.

Phone: (231)775-9724
Address: 10621 E 34 Rd, Cadillac, MI 49601
Lat/Lon: 44.28143/-85.36600
Email: campcadillac2009@yahoo.com
Web: www.campcadillac.com

Reserve Online at Woodalls.com

SEE AD THIS PAGE

(NW) WILLIAM MITCHELL STATE PARK—(Wexford) *From jct US-131 & Hwy-115: Go 3-1/2 mi NW on Hwy-115.* FACILITIES: 215 sites, 215 E, tenting, dump. RECREATION: lake swim, boating, ramp, dock, lake fishing, playground. Partial handicap access. Open all yr. Phone: (231)775-7911.

CALEDONIA—I-3

(SE) INDIAN VALLEY CAMPGROUND CANOE LIVERY—(Barry) *From jct Hwy 6 & Hwy 37: Go 6 mi S on Hwy 37, then 2 mi E on 108th St. Enter on R.*

◊◊◊FACILITIES: 143 sites, typical site width 30 ft, 22 full hkups, 88 W&E, (20/30/50 amps), 33 no hkups, some extd stay sites (summer), 20 pull-thrus, WiFi Instant Internet at site, WiFi Internet central location, family camping, tenting, RV's/park model rentals, cabins, RV storage, dump, non-guest dump $, portable dump, laundry, ltd groc, RV supplies, LP gas by weight/by meter, ice, picnic tables, fire rings, wood, controlled access.

◊◊◊◊RECREATION: rec room/area, pavilion, coin games, swim pool, river swim, boating, canoeing, kayaking, ramp, dock, 4 rowboat/55 canoe/24 kayak/4 pedal boat rentals, float trips, river/pond fishing, fishing supplies, mini-golf, ($), golf nearby, bsktball, playground, activities, (wkends), horseshoes, v-ball. Rec open to public.

Pets welcome, quantity restrict. Partial handicap access. Open all yr. Facilities fully operational Apr 1 - Nov 1. Winter camping by appt. only. Big rigs welcome. Escort to site. Clubs welcome. Rate in 2010 $25-33 per family. MC/VISA/DISC/Debit. Member ARVC, ARVC MI.

Phone: (616)891-8579
Address: 8200 108th St SE, Middleville, MI 49333
Lat/Lon: 42.76888/-85.46333
Web: www.indianvalleycampgroundandcanoe.com

SEE AD GRAND RAPIDS PAGE 383

(SE) INDIAN VALLEY CANOE LIVERY & CAMPGROUND—*From jct Hwy 6 & Hwy 37: Go 6 mi S on Hwy 37, then 2 mi E on 108th St. Enter on R.* Canoe, kayak, raft & tube trips lasting 2 to 6 hours. Relaxing float trips or paddle the beginner level scenic Coldwater & Thornapple Rivers. Adjacent modern & rustic sites at campground. Open Apr 1 - Nov 1. MC/VISA/DISC/Debit.

Phone: (616)891-8579
Address: 8200 108th St SE, Middleville, MI 49333
Lat/Lon: 42.76888/-85.46333
Web: www.indianvalleycampgroundandcanoe.com

SEE AD GRAND RAPIDS PAGE 383

CASEVILLE—G-5

(NE) ALBERT E. SLEEPER STATE PARK—(Huron) *From town: Go 5 mi NE on Hwy 25.* FACILITIES: 223 sites, 223 E, tenting, dump, groceries. RECREATION: lake swim, boating, ramp, playground. Partial handicap access. Open all yr. Facilities fully operational Apr 1 - Nov 1. Phone: (989)856-4411.

CASEVILLE—Continued on next page

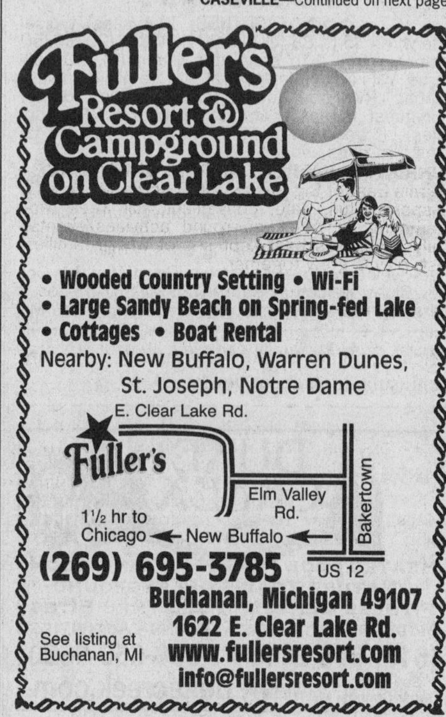

CASEVILLE—Continued

(N) CASEVILLE COUNTY PARK—(Huron) *In town on M-25.*

WELCOME

FACILITIES: 132 sites, typical site width 35 ft, 67 full hkups, 65 W&E, (30/50 amps), some extd stay sites (summer), 25 pull-thrus, heater not allowed, WiFi Instant Internet at site, family camping, tenting, shower$, dump, non-guest dump $, ice, picnic tables, fire rings, wood.

RECREATION: pavilion, lake swim, lake fishing, golf nearby, playground, horseshoes, v-ball.

Pets welcome. Partial handicap access. Open Apr 15 - Oct 31. Big rigs welcome. Clubs welcome. MC/VISA/Debit.

Phone: (877)404-7447
Address: 6400 Main St., Caseville, MI 48725
Lat/Lon: 43.94711/-83.27117
Email: huronpks@comcast.net
Web: www.huroncountyparks.com

SEE AD TRAVEL SECTION PAGE 361

CASS CITY—G-5

(N) EVERGREEN PARK—(Sanilac) *From jct Hwy 46 & Hwy 53: Go 9 mi N on Hwy 53. Enter on L.* FACILITIES: 147 sites, 42 full hkups, 59 W&E, (20/30/50 amps), 50 amps ($), 46 no hkups, 12 pull-thrus, tenting, dump. RECREATION: canoeing, river fishing, playground. Pets welcome. Partial handicap access. Open May 1 - Dec 1. Phone: (989)872-6600.

CEDAR—E-4

(NE) Leelanau Pines Campground—(Leelanau) *From jct CR-651 & CR-645: Go 1/2 mi E & N on CR-645, then 3 mi E & N on CR-643. Enter on R.* ◊◊◊FACILITIES: 181 sites, typical site width 30 ft, 122 full hkups, 40 W&E, 19 E, (20/30/50 amps), family camping, tenting, dump, laundry, groceries. ◊◊◊◊RECREATION: lake swim, boating, canoeing, ramp, lake/stream fishing, playground. Pets welcome, quantity restrict. Partial handicap access. Open May 1 - Oct 15. Rate in 2010 $33-49 per family. Phone: (231) 228-5742.

CEDAR RIVER—D-2

(S) J. W. WELLS STATE PARK—(Menominee) *From jct CR-G 12 & Hwy 35: Go 1 mi S on Hwy35.* FACILITIES: 150 sites, 150 E, (20 amps), tenting, dump, ltd groc. RECREATION: lake swim, boating, ramp, lake fishing, playground. Partial handicap access. Open Apr 15 - Oct 15. Phone: (906)863-9747.

(S) KLEINKE PARK (Menominee County Park)—(Gladwin) *From jct CR G-12 & Hwy 35: Go 6 mi S on Hwy 35. Enter on L.* FACILITIES: 25 sites, typical site width 40 ft, 34 ft max RV length, 20 E, (50 amps), 5 no hkups, tenting. RECREATION: lake swim, boating, canoeing, ramp, lake fishing, playground. Open May - Nov. Phone: (906)863-7255.

CEDAR SPRINGS—H-3

(W) DUKE CREEK CAMPGROUND—(Kent) *From jct US 131 (exit 104) & west Hwy 46 (17 Mile Rd): Go 500 ft E on Hwy 46, then 1-1/2 mi N on White Creek Ave. Enter on R.*

WELCOME

◊◊◊◊FACILITIES: 114 sites, typical site width 35 ft, 88 full hkups, 26 W&E, (20/30/50 amps), many extd stay sites (summer), 10 pull-thrus, WiFi Instant Internet at site, family camping, tenting, RV's/park model rentals, cabins, dump, non-guest dump $, laundry, groceries, RV supplies, LP gas by weight/by meter, ice, picnic tables, fire rings, wood.

◊◊◊◊RECREATION: rec hall, rec room/area, coin games, swim pool, stream fishing, fishing supplies, golf nearby, bsktball, playground, shuffleboard court 2 shuffleboard courts, activities (wkends), horseshoes, hiking trails, v-ball.

Pets welcome, breed restrict. Open May 1 - Oct 15. Clubs welcome. Rate in 2010 $31-33 for 5 persons. MC/VISA/Debit. Member ARVC, ARVC MI.

Michigan State Motto: "If you seek a pleasant peninsula, look about you."

CEDAR SPRINGS—Continued
DUKE CREEK CAMPGROUND—Continued

Phone: (888)656-5620
Address: 15190 White Creek Ave, Cedar Springs, MI 49319
Lat/Lon: 43.24141/-85.57121
Email: info@dukecreek.com
Web: www.dukecreek.com

SEE AD THIS PAGE

(SW) LAKESIDE CAMP PARK—(Kent) *From jct US 131 (exit 104) & West Hwy 46 (17 Mile Rd): Go 100 yds E on 17 Mile Rd, then 1/4 mi S on White Creek Ave. Enter on R.*

WELCOME

◊◊◊◊FACILITIES: 146 sites, typical site width 30 ft, 92 full hkups, 54 W&E, (20/30 amps), some extd stay sites (summer), 15 pull-thrus, WiFi Instant Internet at site, family camping, tenting, RV storage, dump, non-guest dump $, laundry, groceries, RV supplies, ice, picnic tables, fire rings, wood.

CAMPCLUB USA

◊◊◊◊RECREATION: rec hall, pavilion, coin games, lake swim, boating, electric motors only, canoeing, kayaking, dock, 2 rowboat/10 kayak/3 pedal boat rentals, lake/stream fishing, fishing supplies, golf nearby, bsktball, playground, activities, (wkends), horseshoes, sports field, hiking trails, v-ball.

Pets welcome, breed restrict. Open Apr 22 - Oct 9. Escort to site. Clubs welcome. Rate in 2010 $28-31 per family. MC/VISA/DISC/Debit. Member ARVC, ARVC MI. CCUSA 50% Discount. CCUSA reservations Recommended, CCUSA max stay 3 days, CCUSA disc. not avail F,Sa, CCUSA disc. not avail holidays. Not available Jun 15 thru Labor Day.

Phone: (616)696-1735
Address: 13677 White Creek Ave, Cedar Springs, MI 49319
Lat/Lon: 43.21347/-85.57125
Web: www.lakesidecamppark.com

SEE AD GRAND RAPIDS PAGE 383

CEDARVILLE—C-5

(E) CEDARVILLE RV PARK—(Mackinac) *From jct Hwy 129 & Hwy 134: Go 3/4 mi E on Hwy 134. Enter on R.*

WELCOME

◊◊◊◊FACILITIES: 55 sites, typical site width 32 ft, 55 full hkups, (20/30/50 amps), some extd stay sites (summer), WiFi Instant Internet at site, family camping, laundry, RV supplies, ice, picnic tables, fire rings, wood.

CAMPCLUB USA

◊◊◊RECREATION: rec hall, lake swim, boating, canoeing, kayaking, dock, 2 rowboat/4 kayak rentals, lake fishing, golf nearby, activities.

Pets welcome, quantity restrict. Open May 1 - Oct 15. Facilities fully operational May 1 - Oct 1. Big rigs welcome. Clubs welcome. Rate in 2010 $29-36 for 4 persons. MC/VISA/Debit. Member ARVC, ARVC MI. FMCA discount. CCUSA 50% Discount. CCUSA reservations Required, CCUSA max stay 7 days, CCUSA disc. not avail holidays. Not available Thu-Sat in Jun, Jul, Aug.

Phone: (906)484-3351
Address: 634 Grove St, Cedarville, MI 49719
Lat/Lon: 45.99719/-84.34984
Email: info@cedarvillervpark.com
Web: www.cedarvillervpark.com

SEE AD THIS PAGE

(E) Loons Point RV Park & Campground—(Mackinac) *From jct Hwy-129 & Hwy-134: Go 1-1/4 mi E on Hwy-134. Enter on R.* ◊◊◊FACILITIES: 65 sites, typical site width 22 ft, 37 full hkups, 20 W&E, (30/50 amps), 8 no hkups, family camping, tenting, dump, laundry. ◊◊RECREATION: lake swim, boating, canoeing, dock, lake fishing. Pets welcome. Partial handicap access. Open May 15 - Oct 1. Rate in 2010 $28-37 per vehicle. Member ARVC, ARVC MI. Phone: (906)484-2881.

CEMENT CITY—J-4

(SE) Irish Hills Kampground—(Lenawee) *From jct Hwy 50 & US 12: Go 5 mi W on US 12. Enter on R.* ◊◊◊FACILITIES: 138 sites, typical site width 33 ft, 100 W&E, (20/30 amps), 38 no hkups, 14 pull-thrus, family camping, tenting, dump, laundry, ltd groc. ◊◊◊RECREATION: swim pool, boating, no motors, dock, lake/pond fishing, playground. Pets welcome, breed restrict, quantity restrict. Partial handicap access. Open Late Apr - Early Oct. Facilities fully operational Memorial Day - Early Oct. Rate in 2010 $28-30 per family. Member ARVC, ARVC MI. Phone: (517)592-6751.

CHAMPION—B-1

(W) MICHIGAMME SHORES CAMPGROUND RESORT—(Marquette) *From jct Hwy 95 & US 41/Hwy 28: Go 5-1/2 mi W on US 41/Hwy 28. Enter on L.*

WELCOME

◊◊◊◊FACILITIES: 80 sites, typical site width 30 ft, 58 full hkups, 22 E, (20/30/50 amps), 10 pull-thrus, WiFi Internet central location, family camping, tenting, cabins, dump, non-guest dump $, laundry, ltd groc, RV supplies, LP gas by weight/by meter, ice, picnic tables, fire rings, wood.

CAMPCLUB USA

◊◊◊◊RECREATION: lake swim, boating, canoeing, kayaking, ramp, dock, 2 pontoon/rowboat/3 canoe/4 kayak/2 pedal boat/4 motorboat rentals, lake/river fishing, fishing supplies, golf nearby, bsktball, 8 bike rentals, playground, tennis, horseshoes, sports field, hiking trails, v-ball. Rec open to public.

Pets welcome, quantity restrict. Partial handicap access. Open May - Oct 15. Big rigs welcome. Escort to site. Clubs welcome. Rate in 2010 $29-42 for 2 persons. MC/VISA/Debit. Member ARVC, ARVC MI. CCUSA 50% Discount. CCUSA reservations Recommended, CCUSA max stay 3 days, CCUSA disc. not avail holidays. Discount available May & Sep. Pull thru sites not available.

Phone: (906)339-2116
Address: 64 Purple Rd, Michigamme, MI 49861
Lat/Lon: 46.53195/-88.00743
Web: www.michigammeshores.com

SEE AD MARQUETTE PAGE 393

(W) VAN RIPER STATE PARK—(Marquette) *From jct US-41 & Hwy-95: Go 5 mi W on US-41.* FACILITIES: 147 sites, 99 E, 48 no hkups, tenting, dump, ltd groc. RECREATION: lake swim, boating, ramp, lake fishing, playground. Partial handicap access. Open Apr 15 - Nov 1. Facilities fully operational May 15 - Oct 15. Phone: (906)339-4461.

CHARLEVOIX—D-4

(S) FISHERMAN'S ISLAND STATE PARK—(Charlevoix) *From town: Go 5 mi S on US 31, turn right on Bell Bay Rd, then go 2-1/2 mi on Bell Bay Rd to posted entrance.* FACILITIES: 81 sites, 81 no hkups, tenting. RECREATION: lake swim, boating, stream fishing. Open May - Nov. Phone: (231)547-6641.

(NE) Uhricks Motel & RV Park—(Charlevoix) *From jct Hwy 66 & US 31: Go 2-1/2 mi N on US 31. Enter on L.* ◊◊FACILITIES: 30 sites, typical site width 25 ft, 4 full hkups, 21 W&E, (20/30/50 amps), 5 no hkups, 20 pull-thrus, tenting, dump. Pets welcome. Open Apr 1 - Nov 15. Rate in 2010 $27-40 for 2 persons. Phone: (231)547-4881.

CHEBOYGAN—D-5

(S) ALOHA STATE PARK—(Cheboygan) *From jct Hwy 33 & US 23: Go 9 mi S on Hwy 33, then W on Hwy 212.* FACILITIES: 285 sites, 35 ft max RV length, 285 E, tenting, dump. RECREATION: lake swim, boating, ramp, lake fishing, playground. Open Jun 20 - Oct 28. Facilities fully operational May 1 - Oct 15. Phone: (231)625-2522.

(SE) CHEBOYGAN STATE PARK—(Cheboygan) *From jct Hwy 33 & US 23: Go 4 mi E on US 23, then 2 mi W on park road.* FACILITIES: 76 sites, 76 E, tenting, ltd groc. RECREATION: lake swim, stream fishing, playground. Open all yr. Facilities fully operational May 1 - Oct 15. Phone: (231)627-2811.

CHEBOYGAN—Continued on next page

CHEBOYGAN—Continued

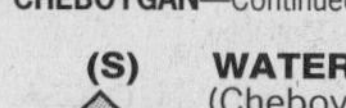

(S) WATERWAYS CAMPGROUND—(Cheboygan) *From jct Hwy 27 & Hwy 33: Go 1/4 mi S on Hwy 33. Enter on R.*

THE BEST OF NORTHERN MICHIGAN

Located on the 42 mile inland waterway & 62 mile hike/bike trail. Launch and docks to make your boating and fishing convenient. Just minutes to parks, beaches, Mackinaw attractions. A great spot for a great vacation.

◊◊◊◊FACILITIES: 50 sites, typical site width 30 ft, 38 full hkups, 8 W&E, 4 E, (30/50 amps), some extd stay sites (summer), 9 pull-thrus, cable TV, WiFi Instant Internet at site, family camping, tenting, tent rentals, RV storage, dump, ltd groc, RV supplies, ice, picnic tables, fire rings, wood.

◊◊◊RECREATION: rec hall, coin games, boating, canoeing, kayaking, ramp, dock, rowboat/pedal boat/motorboat rentals, river fishing, fishing supplies, golf nearby, bsktball, playground, activities, (wkends), horseshoes, hiking trails, v-ball.

Pets welcome. Partial handicap access. Open May 1 - Oct 15. Escort to site. Clubs welcome. Rate in 2010 $30-35 per family. MC/VISA/DISC/Debit. Member ARVC, ARVC MI. CCUSA 50% Discount. CCUSA reservations Recommended, CCUSA max stay 7 days, CCUSA disc. not avail holidays. Discount not available June 15-Sep 15 or any holiday weekends. Pull thru sites not available for discount.

Phone: (888)882-7066
Address: 9575 M-33 Hwy, Cheboygan, MI 49721
Lat/Lon: 45.59620/-84.47442
Email: waterwayscampground@gmail.com
Web: www.waterwayscampground.com

SEE AD MACKINAW CITY PAGE 392

CHELSEA—I-5

✲ (SW) LLOYD BRIDGES TRAVELAND—*From jct I-94 & Hwy-52 (exit 159): Go 1 block N. Enter on R.* SALES: travel trailers, park models, truck campers, 5th wheels, toy hauler, Class A motorhomes, Class C motorhomes, Class B motorhomes, fold-down camping trailers, pre-owned unit sales. SERVICES: full-time mech, engine/chassis repair, RV appliance repair, body work/collision repair, LP gas by weight/by meter, RV rentals, sells parts/accessories, installs hitches. Open all yr. MC/VISA/DISC.

Phone: (800)475-1347
Address: 1603 S Main, Chelsea, MI 48118
Lat/Lon: 42.29723/-84.02558
Email: sales@funrving.com
Web: www.funrving.com

SEE AD THIS PAGE

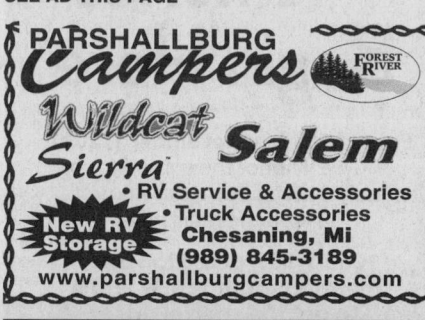

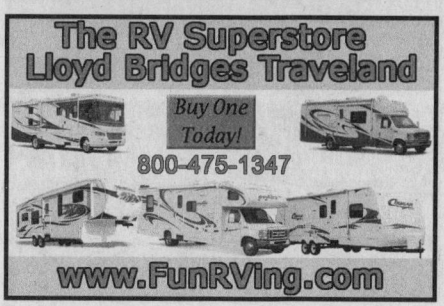

CHELSEA—Continued

(N) WATERLOO STATE REC. AREA (Green Lake Unit)—(Washtenaw) *From jct I-94 & Hwy-52: Go 6-1/2 mi N on Hwy-52.* FACILITIES: 25 sites, 32 ft max RV length, 25 no hkups, tenting, ltd groc. RECREATION: lake swim, boating, ramp, lake fishing, playground. Partial handicap access. Open May 15 - Dec 1. Phone: (734)475-8307.

(N) WATERLOO STATE REC. AREA (Portage Unit)—(Washtenaw) *From I-94 (exit 147): Go 2-1/2 mi N on Race Rd, then 1-1/2 mi E on Seymour Rd.* FACILITIES: 136 sites, 136 E, tenting, dump, groceries. RECREATION: lake swim, boating, ramp, dock, lake fishing, playground. Partial handicap access. Open all yr. Facilities fully operational Apr 15 - Dec 1. Phone: (734)475-8307.

(NW) WATERLOO STATE REC. AREA (Sugarloaf Lake Unit)—(Washtenaw) *From jct I-94 & Hwy-52: Go 6 mi W on I-94 to Exit 153, then 6 mi N on Clearlake Rd, then 1-1/2 mi SE on Loveland Rd.* FACILITIES: 164 sites, 164 E, tenting, dump, ltd groc. RECREATION: lake swim, boating, ramp, lake fishing, playground. Open May 15 - Sep 15. Phone: (734)475-8307.

CHESANING—H-4

✲ (W) PARSHALLBURG CAMPERS—*From jct Hwy 57 & Hwy 52: Go 900 ft N on Hwy 52. Enter on R.* SALES: travel trailers, park models, 5th wheels, toy hauler, pre-owned unit sales. SERVICES: full-time mech, RV appliance repair, body work/collision repair, LP gas by weight/by meter, RV storage, sells parts/accessories, installs hitches. Open all yr. MC/VISA/DISC/Debit.

Phone: (989)845-3189
Address: 15775 South Oakley (M-52), Chesaning, MI 48616
Lat/Lon: 43.18943/-84.16891
Email: parshcamper@centurytel.net
Web: www.parshallburgcampers.com

SEE AD THIS PAGE

CLARE—G-4

(SE) HERRICK RECREATION AREA (Isabella County)—(Isabella) *From jct Business US 27 & Business US 10: Go 2-1/4 mi E on Business US 10, then 3/4 mi S on Summerton Rd, then 1/3 mi E on Herrick Rd.* FACILITIES: 73 sites, 73 E, (20/30 amps), tenting, dump. RECREATION: boating, electric motors only, ramp, pond fishing, playground. Partial handicap access. Open May 1 - Sep 30. Phone: (989)772-0911.

CLAYTON—J-4

LAKE HUDSON STATE RECREATION AREA—(Adrian) *From jct US 127 & Hwy 34: Go 6-1/2 mi E on Hwy 34, then 1-1/2 mi S on Hwy 156.* FACILITIES: 50 sites, 50 E. RECREATION: lake swim, boating, ramp, lake fishing. Open Apr 18 - Nov 30. Phone: (517)445-2265.

CLIMAX—I-3

(W) COLD BROOK COUNTY PARK—(Kalamazoo) *From jct US 131 & I-94: Go 11 mi E on I-94 (exit 85), then 1-1/2 S on 35th St, then 3/4 mi E on MN Ave. Enter on L.* FACILITIES: 44 sites, 29 W&E, (30/50 amps), 15 no hkups, family camping, tenting, dump. RECREATION: lake swim, boating, canoeing, ramp, dock, lake fishing, playground. Pets welcome. Partial handicap access. Open Late Apr - Oct. Phone: (269)383-8778.

CLIO—H-5

✲ (E) LEISURE DAYS TRAVEL TRAILER SALES—*From jct I-75 & Hwy 57 (exit 131): Go 4-1/2 mi E on Hwy 57. Enter on R.* SALES: travel trailers, truck campers, 5th wheels, toy hauler, fold-down camping trailers, pre-owned unit sales. SERVICES: full-time mech, RV appliance repair, body work/collision repair, LP gas by weight/by meter, dump station, RV storage, sells parts/accessories, installs hitches. Open Feb 1 - Christmas. MC/VISA/DISC/Debit.

CLIO—Continued
LEISURE DAYS TRAVEL TRAILER SALES—Continued

Phone: (810)686-2090
Address: 1354 E Vienna Rd, Clio, MI 48420
Lat/Lon: 43.17844/-83.68188
Email: leisuredaysrv@aol.com
Web: www.LeisureDays-RV.com

SEE AD THIS PAGE

COLDWATER—J-3

(NW) ANGEL COVE (Branch County)—(Branch) *From jct I-69 & US 12: Go 3-3/4 mi W on US 12, then 4-3/4 mi N on River Rd.* FACILITIES: 130 sites, 110 W&E, (20/30 amps), 20 no hkups, 30 pull-thrus, tenting, dump, ltd groc. RECREATION: boating, ramp, dock, lake fishing, playground. Open Apr 15 - Oct 15. Phone: (517)278-8541.

(W) BRANCH COUNTY MEMORIAL PARK—(Branch) *From jct I-69 & US-12: Go 3 mi W on US-12, then 1/2 mi S on Behnke Rd.* FACILITIES: 50 sites, 20 E, 30 no hkups, tenting. RECREATION: lake swim, boating, ramp, dock, playground. Open Memorial Day - Labor Day. Phone: (517)278-4820.

(NW) WAFFLE FARM CAMP—(Branch) *From jct I-69 & US-12: Go 3-1/2 mi N on I-69 (Exit 16), then 2-3/4 mi W on Jonesville Rd, then 3/4 mi N on Union City Rd. Enter on L.*

◊◊◊◊FACILITIES: 376 sites, typical site width 28 ft, 189 full hkups, 162 W&E, (20/30/50 amps), 25 no hkups, many extd stay sites (summer), 30 pull-thrus, cable TV, WiFi Internet central location, family camping, tenting, RV storage, dump, non-guest dump $, groceries, RV supplies, LP gas by weight, marine gas, ice, picnic tables, wood.

◊◊◊◊RECREATION: rec room/area, pavilion, coin games, lake swim, boating, canoeing, kayaking, ramp, 8 rowboat/6 pedal boat rentals, lake fishing, fishing supplies, mini-golf, ($), golf nearby, playground, sports field, hiking trails. Rec open to public.

Pets welcome. Partial handicap access. Open Mid Apr - Mid Oct. 16 FHU & 95 W & E available for overnighters. Big rigs welcome. Clubs welcome. Rate in 2010 $28-36 for 2 persons. ATM. Member ARVC, ARVC MI.

Phone: (517)278-4315
Address: 790 N Union City Rd, Coldwater, MI 49036
Lat/Lon: 41.99689/-85.02065
Email: info@wafflefarm.com
Web: www.wafflefarm.com

SEE AD THIS PAGE

Detroit is known as the "Car Capital of the World".

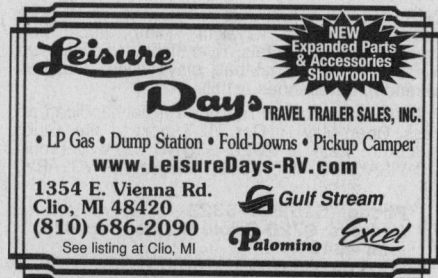

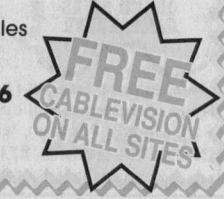

COLOMA—J-2

(N) Dune Lake Campground—(Van Buren) *From jct I-94 & I-196: Go 7 mi N on I-196 (exit 7), then 1/4 mi W on Hager Shore Rd, then 2-1/4 mi N on Blue Star Hwy, then 1 mi E on CR 376. Enter on R.* ◆◆◆FACILITIES: 80 sites, typical site width 30 ft, 59 W&E, (20/30 amps), 21 no hkups, 3 pull-thrus, WiFi Internet central location, family camping, tenting, RV storage, dump, non-guest dump $, ltd groc, RV supplies, ice, picnic tables, fire rings, wood. ◆◆◆RECREATION: pavilion, lake swim, mini-golf, ($), bsktball, playground, shuffleboard court shuffleboard court, activities horseshoes, hiking trails, v-ball. Pets welcome, breed restrict, quantity restrict. Open May - Sep. Rate in 2010 $29 for 2 persons. MC/VISA/DISC. CCUSA 50% Discount. CCUSA reservations Accepted, CCUSA max stay 7 days, CCUSA disc. not avail holidays.

Phone: (269)764-8941
Address: 80855 CR 376, Coloma, MI 49038
Lat/Lon: 42.25766/-86.32909
Email: info@dunelakecampground.com
Web: www.dunelakecampground.com

(W) KOA-Coloma/St. Joseph—(Berrien) *From jct I-94 & I-196: Go 4 mi N on I-196 (exit 4), then 1 block E on Coloma/Riverside Rd. Enter on L.* ◆◆◆◆FACILITIES: 123 sites, typical site width 40 ft, 40 full hkups, 65 W&E, (20/30/50 amps), 18 no hkups, 19 pull-thrus, family camping, tenting, dump, laundry, groceries. ◆◆◆◆◆RECREATION: swim pool, pond fishing, playground. Pets welcome, breed restrict. Partial handicap access. Open Apr 15 - Oct 15. Facilities fully operational Memorial Day - Labor Day. Rate in 2010 $29-49 for 2 persons. Member ARVC, ARVCMI. Phone: (269)849-3333. KOA discount.

CONCORD—J-4

(SW) Twin Pines Campground & Canoe Livery—(Jackson) *From east jct Hwy 99 & Hwy 60: Go 3 mi E on Hwy 60, then 3-1/2 mi S on Wheeler Rd. Enter on L.* ◆◆FACILITIES: 79 sites, typical site width 30 ft, 49 W&E, (20/30 amps), 30 no hkups, family camping, tenting, dump, laundry, ltd groc. ◆◆◆RECREATION: river swim, boating, no motors, canoeing, river fishing, playground. Pets welcome. Open May 1 - Mid Oct. Rate in 2010 $25 per family. Phone: (517)524-6298.

COOPERSVILLE—H-2

(SW) CONESTOGA GRAND RIVER CAMPGROUND—(Ottawa) *From jct I-96 (exit 16) & CR B 35/68th Ave: Go 3 mi S on 68th Ave, then 4 mi W on Leonard St, then 3/4 mi S on 96th Ave, then 1/4 mi W on Oriole Dr. Enter on L.*

WELCOME

◆◆◆FACILITIES: 92 sites, typical site width 35 ft, 25 full hkups, 67 W&E, (30/50 amps), some extd stay sites (summer), 3 pull-thrus, WiFi Instant Internet at site, family camping, tenting, RV's/park model rentals, RV storage, dump, non-guest dump $, portable dump, laundry, ltd groc, RV supplies, ice, picnic tables, patios, fire rings, wood.

◆◆◆◆RECREATION: rec room/area, swim pool, boating, canoeing, kayaking, ramp, dock, pontoon/motorboat rentals, river fishing, fishing supplies, golf nearby, bsktball, playground, activities, (wkends), horseshoes, v-ball.

Pets welcome, breed restrict. Partial handicap access. Open May 1 - Oct 31. Escort to site. Clubs welcome. Rate in 2010 $38-46 for 4 persons. MC/VISA/DISC/AMEX/Debit. Member ARVC, ARVC MI.

Phone: (616)837-6323
Address: 9720 Oriole Dr, Coopersville, MI 49404
Lat/Lon: 43.03001/-86.03262
Email: conestoga@mapleisland.net
Web: www.conestogacampground.com

SEE AD THIS PAGE

COPPER HARBOR—A-2

(E) FORT WILKINS STATE PARK—(Keweena) *From jct US 41 & Hwy 26: Go 1 mi E on US 41.* FACILITIES: 159 sites, 159 E, (30 amps), tenting, dump, ltd groc. RECREATION: boating, ramp, lake fishing, playground. Partial handicap access. Open Apr 15 - Nov 1. Phone: (906)289-4215.

COPPER HARBOR—Continued

(S) Lake Fanny Hooe Resort & Campground—(Keweenaw) *From jct Hwy 26 & US 41 in Copper Harbor: Go 2 blocks E on US 41, then 1 block S on 2nd St. Enter on R.* ◆◆◆FACILITIES: 64 sites, 40 ft max RV length, 10 full hkups, 54 W&E, (20/30 amps), family camping, tenting, dump, laundry. ◆◆◆◆RECREATION: lake swim, boating, canoeing, dock, lake/stream fishing, playground. Pets welcome. Open May 15 - Oct 15. Rate in 2010 $28-40 for 2 persons. Phone: (800) 426-4451.

COVERT—I-2

COVERT PARK BEACH & CAMPGROUND—(Newaygo) *From I-196 exit 13 (Covert): Go W 1 mile to park. Enter at end.* FACILITIES: 62 sites, 54 W&E, (15/30/50 amps), 8 no hkups, tenting, dump. RECREATION: lake swim, lake fishing, playground. Pets welcome ($). Open Mid May - Mid Oct. Phone: (269)764-1421.

(S) South Haven KOA RV Resort—(Van Buren) *From jct I-196 (exit 18) & Hwy 140: Go 6-1/4 mi S on Hwy 140. Enter on L.* ◆◆◆◆FACILITIES: 100 sites, typical site width 50 ft, 73 full hkups, 27 W&E, (20/30/50 amps), 70 pull-thrus, family camping, tenting, dump, laundry, ltd groc. ◆◆◆◆RECREATION: swim pool, pond fishing, playground. Pets welcome. Partial handicap access. Open Apr 15 - Oct 15. Big rigs welcome. Rate in 2010 $34-48 for 2 persons. Member ARVC, ARVCMI. Phone: (269)764-0818. KOA discount.

CRYSTAL FALLS—C-1

(W) BEWABIC STATE PARK—(Iron) *From jct US 2 & Hwy 141: Go 4 mi W on US 2.* FACILITIES: 137 sites, 137 E, (20 amps), tenting, dump, groceries. RECREATION: lake swim, boating, ramp, dock, lake fishing, playground. Partial handicap access. Open Apr 15 - Nov 15. Phone: (906)875-3324.

(SE) COPPER COUNTRY SF (Glidden Lake)—(Iron) *From town: Go 5 mi E on Hwy 69 & 1 mi S on Lake Mary Rd. Enter on R.* FACILITIES: 23 sites, 23 no hkups, tenting. RECREATION: lake swim, boating, canoeing, ramp, lake/stream fishing. Open all yr. Phone: (906)875-6622.

CURRAN—E-6

(NW) AU SABLE SF (McCollum Lake)—(Oscoda) *From town: Go 6 mi N on Hwy 65, then 2-1/2 mi W on McCollum Lake Rd. Enter on R.* FACILITIES: 32 sites, 32 no hkups, tenting. RECREATION: lake swim, boating, ramp, lake fishing. Open all yr. Phone: (989)348-6371.

CURTIS—C-4

(W) LAKE SUPERIOR SF (South Manistique Lake)—(Mackinac) *From town: Go 3 mi W on S Curtis Rd, then 2 mi S on Long Point Rd, then 1/2 mi SE, on West side of lake.* FACILITIES: 29 sites, 29 no hkups, tenting. RECREATION: lake swim, boating, ramp, lake fishing. Open May - Dec. Phone: (906)635-5281.

(NW) Log Cabin Resort & Campground—(Mackinac) *From jct Hwy 77 & US 2: Go 9 mi E on US 2, then 8-1/2 mi N on H33, then 3 mi NW on H42. Enter on R.* ◆◆◆FACILITIES: 53 sites, typical site width 30 ft, 34 full hkups, 5 W&E, 14 E, (20/30/50 amps), 12 pull-thrus, family camping, tenting, dump, laundry, ltd groc. ◆◆◆◆RECREATION: lake swim, boating, canoeing, ramp, dock, lake fishing, playground. Pets welcome. Open May 15 - Oct 15. Big rigs welcome. Rate in 2010 $21-34 for 4 persons. Member ARVC, ARVC MI. Phone: (906)586-9732.

DAFTER—C-5

(SW) Clear Lake Campground—(Chippewa) *From jct Hwy 80 & I-75: Go 1 mi N on I-75 (exit 379), then 1-1/2 mi N on CR-H 63. Enter on R.* ◆◆◆FACILITIES: 80 sites, typical site width 30 ft, 60 W&E, 20 E, (20/30 amps), 25 pull-thrus, family camping, tenting, dump, laundry, ltd groc. ◆◆RECREATION: lake swim, boating, no motors, lake fishing, play equipment. Pets welcome. Open May 15 - Oct 1. Rate in 2010 $23 for 2 persons. Phone: (906)635-0201.

DAVISON—H-5

(NE) WOLVERINE CAMPGROUND (Genesee County Park)—(Genesee) *From jct Hwy 57 & Hwy 15: Go 3-3/4 mi S on Hwy 15, then 2-1/2 mi E on Mt Morris Rd, then 1/2 mi S on Baxter Rd. Enter at end.* FACILITIES: 194 sites, 163 E, (20/30/50 amps), 31 no hkups, 70 pull-thrus, family camping, tenting, dump, ltd groc. RECREATION: lake swim, boating, canoeing, ramp, lake fishing, playground. Pets welcome. Partial handicap access. Open Memorial Wknd - Labor Day. Big rigs welcome. Member ARVC, ARVCMI. Phone: (800)648-7275.

DECATUR—J-2

(S) Leisure Valley RV Resort & Campground—(Van Buren) *From jct I-94 & Hwy 51: Go 6-1/4 mi S on Hwy 51, then 3 mi S on George St. then 1/4 mi W on Valley Rd (CR 669). Enter on L.* ◆◆◆FACILITIES: 106 sites, typical site width 30 ft, 92 full hkups, 14 W&E, (20/30 amps), 1 pull-thrus, WiFi Internet central location, family camping, tenting, RV storage, dump, non-guest dump $, laundry, ltd groc, RV supplies, LP gas by weight, ice, picnic tables, fire rings, wood. ◆◆◆RECREATION: rec hall, pavilion, swim pool, lake swim, boating, no motors, canoeing, kayaking, dock, lake fishing, mini-golf, ($), bsktball, playground, shuffleboard court 2 shuffleboard courts, activities horseshoes, hiking trails, v-ball. Pets welcome. Partial handicap access. Open Apr 15 - Oct 15. Rate in 2010 $27-30 for 4 persons. MC/VISA/DISC/AMEX.

DECATUR—Continued
Leisure Valley RV Resort & Campground—Continued

Member ARVC, ARVC MI. CCUSA 50% Discount. CCUSA reservations Recommended, CCUSA max stay 5 days, CCUSA disc. not avail F,Sa, CCUSA disc. not avail holidays.

Phone: (269)423-7122
Address: 40851 CR 669, Decatur, MI 49045
Lat/Lon: 42.07557/-85.94384
Email: leisure@i2k.com
Web: www.leisurevalley.com

(W) Oak Shores Campground—(Van Buren) *From jct I-94 (exit 56) & Hwy 51: Go 10-1/2 mi SW on Hwy 51, then 1/4 mi N on CR 215. Enter on L.* ◆◆◆◆FACILITIES: 248 sites, typical site width 30 ft, 222 full hkups, 26 W&E, (20/30/50 amps), 13 pull-thrus, WiFi Instant Internet at site ($), family camping, tenting, RV storage, dump, non-guest dump $, laundry, ltd groc, RV supplies, LP gas by weight/by meter, ice, picnic tables, fire rings, wood. ◆◆◆◆◆RECREATION: rec hall, pavilion, swim pool, lake swim, hot tub, boating, 5 hp limit, canoeing, kayaking, lake fishing, fishing supplies, bsktball, playground, shuffleboard court 2 shuffleboard courts, activities, tennis, horseshoes, v-ball. Pets welcome. Partial handicap access. Open Apr 15 - Oct 15. Facilities fully operational Memorial Day - Labor Day. Rate in 2010 $31-36 for 4 persons. MC/VISA/DISC/AMEX/Debit. Member ARVC, ARVC MI. CCUSA 50% Discount. CCUSA reservations Recommended, CCUSA max stay 3 days, CCUSA disc. not avail F,Sa. Discount available Apr 15 -6 days prior to Memorial Day & 3 days after Labor Day-Oct 15. May not be combined with other offers.

Phone: (269)423-7370
Address: 86232 County Rd 215, Decatur, MI 49045
Lat/Lon: 42.10598/-86.05035
Web: www.oakshorescampground.com

(W) Timber Trails RV Park—(Van Buren) *From jct I-94 (exit 56) & Hwy 51: Go 8 mi S on Hwy 51 (through Decatur), then 3/4 mi N on 47-1/2 St. Enter on R.* ◆◆◆FACILITIES: 162 sites, typical site width 33 ft, 162 full hkups, (30/50 amps), 16 pull-thrus, WiFi Internet central location, family camping, tenting, RV storage, shower$, dump, non-guest dump $, laundry, RV supplies, LP gas by weight/by meter, ice, picnic tables, fire rings, wood. ◆◆◆◆RECREATION: lake swim, boating, canoeing, kayaking, dock, lake fishing, fishing supplies, bsktball, playground, shuffleboard court shuffleboard court, horseshoes, v-ball. Pets welcome. Open May 1 - Sep 30. Rate in 2010 $30 for 2 persons. MC/VISA/Debit. Member ARVC, ARVCMI. FMCA discount. CCUSA 50% Discount. CCUSA max stay Unlimited, CCUSA disc. not avail F,Sa, CCUSA disc. not avail holidays. 8 sites for pets.

Phone: (269)423-7311
Address: 84981 47 1/2 St, Decatur, MI 49045
Lat/Lon: 42.10980/-86.00657
Email: timbertrailsrvpark@hotmail.com
Web: www.michcampgrounds/timbertrails

Della Reese, singer, is from Michigan.

DETROIT—I-6

DETROIT AREA MAP

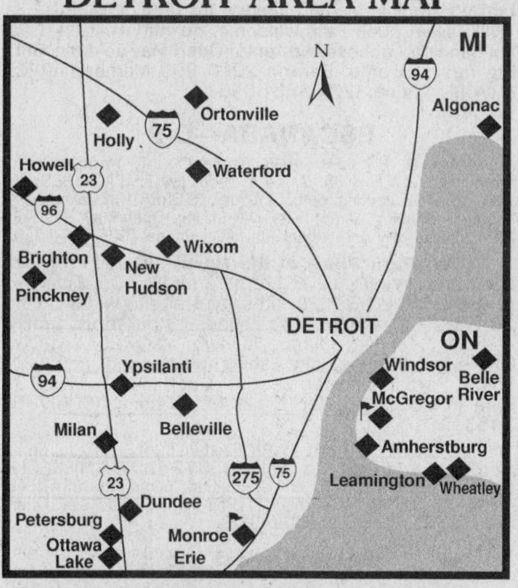

Symbols on map indicate towns within a 45 mi radius of Detroit where campgrounds (diamonds), attractions (flags), & RV service centers & camping supply outlets (gears) are listed. Check listings for more information.

Tell Them Woodall's Sent You!

DETROIT/GREENFIELD RV PARK—*From Detroit: Go 23 mi W on I-94 (exit 187), then 1 mi S on Rawsonville Rd, then 1 mi W on Textile Rd, then 1/2 mi S on Bunton Rd. Enter on R.*

SEE PRIMARY LISTING AT YPSILANTI AND AD THIS PAGE

DEWITT—H-4

(E) ANNIE RAE RV—*From jct US 127 & I-69: Go 1-3/4 mi W on I-69 (exit 87), then 1/2 mi N on Old Hwy 27. Enter on R.* SALES: travel trailers, park models, truck campers, 5th wheels, fold-down camping trailers, pre-owned unit sales. SERVICES: full-time mech, engine/chassis repair, RV appliance repair, body work/collision repair, LP gas by weight/by meter, RV rentals, sells parts/accessories, installs hitches. Open all yr. MC/VISA/DISC/AMEX/Debit.

Phone: (800)328-0158
Address: 12909 US 27 North, DeWitt, MI 48820
Lat/Lon: 42.82884/-84.54277
Email: jeffevery@annieraerv.com
Web: www.annieraerv.com

SEE AD THIS PAGE

DORR—I-3

(W) HUNGRY HORSE CAMPGROUND—*(Allegan) From jct Hwy 179 & US 131: Go 7 mi N on US 131 (exit 68), then 4 mi W on 142nd Ave. Enter on L.*

◇◇◇◇FACILITIES: 85 sites, typical site width 30 ft, 31 full hkups, 54 W&E, (20/30/50 amps), some extd stay sites (summer), 31 pull-thrus, WiFi Instant Internet at site, family camping, tenting, cabins, RV storage, dump, non-guest dump $, portable dump, laundry, ltd groc, RV supplies, ice, picnic tables, fire rings, wood.

◇◇◇◇RECREATION: rec room/area, pavilion, coin games, swim pool, wading pool, golf nearby,

DORR—Continued
HUNGRY HORSE CAMPGROUND—Continued

bsktball, playground, shuffleboard court 2 shuffleboard courts, activities (wkends), horseshoes, sports field, hiking trails, v-ball.

annieRaeRV.com
Parts • Sales • Service • Rentals
Main: (517) 669-2755
Toll Free: (800) 328-0158
Fax: (517) 669-0525
12909 US 27 North • DeWitt, MI 48820 See listing at DeWitt, MI

Pets welcome, breed restrict. Partial handicap access. Open May 1 - Oct 15. Big rigs welcome. Clubs welcome. Rate in 2010 $31-36 for 4 persons. MC/VISA/Debit. Member ARVC, ARVC MI.

Phone: (616)681-9843
Address: 2016 142nd Ave, Dorr, MI 49323
Lat/Lon: 42.72513/-85.74095
Email: hungryhorsecampground@gmail.com
Web: www.hungryhorsecampground.com

SEE AD GRAND RAPIDS PAGE 382

DUNDEE—J-5

(SE) WILDERNESS CAMPGROUND—*(Monroe) From jct US-23 & Hwy-50: Go 3 mi E on Hwy-50, then 1 mi S on Meanwell Rd. Enter on R.*

◇◇◇FACILITIES: 100 sites, typical site width 30 ft, 92 W&E, (20/30/50 amps), 8 no hkups, many extd stay sites (summer), 12 pull-thrus, cable TV, ($), family camping, tenting, cabins, RV storage, dump, non-guest dump $, portable dump, ltd groc, RV supplies, ice, picnic tables, fire rings, wood.

◇◇◇RECREATION: rec room/area, pavilion, coin games, lake swim, boating, no motors, canoeing, 2 pedal boat rentals, lake fishing, fishing supplies, golf nearby, bsktball, playground, activities, (wkends), horseshoes, sports field, v-ball. Rec open to public.

Pets welcome, breed restrict. Partial handicap access. Open Late Apr - Nov 1. Escort to site. Clubs welcome. Rate in 2010 $25-33 for 2 persons. MC/VISA. Member ARVC, ARVCMI.

DUNDEE—Continued
WILDERNESS CAMPGROUND—Continued

Phone: (734)529-5122
Address: 1350 Meanwell, Dundee, MI 48131
Lat/Lon: 41.93602/-83.61392
Email: wildernesscampgroundindundee@yahoo.com
Web: www.wildernesscampgroundinmi.com

SEE AD TRAVEL SECTION PAGE 359

DURAND—H-5

(NE) Holiday Shores—*(Shiawassee) From jct Hwy 71 & I-69: Go 5 mi E on I-69 (exit 123), then 1 mi S on Hwy 13, then 1 mi W on Goodall Rd. Enter on R.* ◇◇◇◇FACILITIES: 585 sites, typical site width 35 ft, accepts full hkup units only, 585 full hkups, (20/30/50 amps), family camping. ◇◇◇RECREATION: lake swim, boating, electric motors only, canoeing, lake fishing, playground. Pets welcome. No tents. Open May 1 - Oct 31. Big rigs welcome. Rate in 2010 $30-35 per family. Phone: (989)288-4444.

EAST JORDAN—E-4

(N) EAST JORDAN TOURIST PARK (City of East Jordan)—(Charlevoix) *From jct Hwy 32 & Hwy 66: Go 500 feet N on Hwy 66. Enter on R.* FACILITIES: 92 sites, typical site width 30 ft, 70 full hkups, 6 E, (20/30/50 amps), 16 no hkups, family camping, tenting, dump. RECREATION: lake swim, boating, canoeing, ramp, dock, lake/river fishing, playground. Pets welcome. Partial handicap access. Open Apr 15 - Oct 15. Facilities fully operational May 1 - Oct 15. Big rigs welcome. Member ARVC, ARVCMI. Phone: (231)536-2561.

(W) WOODEN SHOE PARK (Village Park)—(Charlevoix) *From jct Hwy-66 & East Jordan-Ellsworth Rd: Go 7 mi W on East Jordan-Ellsworth Rd, follow signs.* FACILITIES: 55 sites, 55 no hkups, tenting, dump. RECREATION: lake swim, lake fishing, playground. Open May 13 - Oct 1. Phone: (231)588-6382.

The only state bordered by four of the five Great Lakes.

EAST LANSING—I-4

(NE) **GILLETTE'S INTERSTATE RV**—*From jct I-69 (exit 94) & Business 69 (E Saginaw): Go 1/2 mi W on E Saginaw. Enter on L.* SALES: travel trailers, park models, 5th wheels, toy hauler, Class A motorhomes, Class C motorhomes, Class B motorhomes, fold-down camping trailers, pre-owned unit sales. SERVICES: full-time mech, RV appliance repair, body work/collision repair, LP gas by weight/by meter, dump station, sells parts/accessories, installs hitches. Open all yr. MC/VISA/DISC/Debit.

Phone: (517)339-8271
Address: 7210 E Saginaw, East Lansing, MI 48823
Lat/Lon: 42.77119/-84.41707
Email: Sales@gilletesinterstaterv.com
Web: www.gillettesinterstaterv.com

SEE AD GRAND RAPIDS PAGE 383

EAST TAWAS—F-5

(S) EAST TAWAS CITY PARK—(Iosco) *From jct Hwy 55 & US 23: Go 1 mi N on US 23.* FACILITIES: 174 sites, 35 ft max RV length, 174 full hkups, (30 amps), dump, laundry. RECREATION: lake swim, boating, ramp, dock, lake fishing, playground. Open all yr. Phone: (989)362-5562.

(SE) TAWAS POINT STATE PARK—(Iosco) *From jct US-23 & Hwy-55: Go 3 mi S on US-23 to Tawas Point Lighthouse Rd.* FACILITIES: 193 sites, 35 ft max RV length, 193 E, tenting, dump. RECREATION: lake swim, boating, lake fishing, playground. Partial handicap access. Open Apr 15 - Oct 30. Phone: (989)362-5041.

ELK RAPIDS—E-4

(S) Honcho Rest Campground—(Antrim) *From jct Hwy 72 & US 31: Go 10 mi N on US 31, then 1-1/4 mi SE on Ames St. Enter on L.* ◊◊◊FACILITIES: 110 sites, typical site width 30 ft, 95 full hkups, 15 W&E, (20/30/50 amps), 4 pull-thrus, cable TV, WiFi Instant Internet at site, family camping, RV storage, dump, non-guest dump $, laundry, RV supplies, LP gas by weight/by meter, ice, picnic tables, patios, fire rings, grills, wood. ◊◊◊RECREATION: pavilion, lake swim, boating, canoeing, kayaking, dock, lake fishing, fishing supplies, bsktball, playground, activities, horseshoes, v-ball. Pets welcome. Partial handicap access. No tents. Open May 1 - Oct 8. Big rigs welcome. Rate in 2010 $35-45 per family. MC/VISA/DISC/Debit. Member ARVC, ARVC MI. FMCA discount. CCUSA 50% Discount. CCUSA reservations Recommended, CCUSA max stay 3 days, CCUSA disc. not avail S, CCUSA disc. not avail F,Sa, CCUSA disc. not avail holidays. Discount available May 1 - Jun 1 & Sep 15 thru Oct 1.

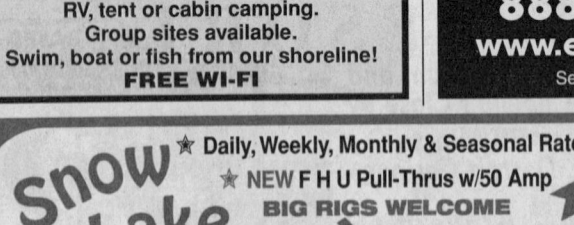

Phone: (231)264-8548
Address: 8988 Cairn Hwy, Elk Rapids, MI 49629
Lat/Lon: 44.90499/-85.39066
Email: info@honchorestcampground.com
Web: www.honchorestcampground.com

EMMETT—H-6

(NW) **EMMETT KOA**—(St. Clair) *From jct Hwy 19 & I-69: Go 4 mi W on I-69 (exit 180), then 1/4 mi N on Riley Center Rd, then 1/4 mi W on Burt Rd, then 1-1/2 mi N on Breen Rd. Enter on R.*

◊◊◊◊FACILITIES: 108 sites, typical site width 30 ft, 23 full hkups, 80 W&E, (20/30/50 amps), 50 amps ($), 5 no hkups, 26 pull-thrus, WiFi Instant Internet at site, family camping, tenting, RV's/park model rentals, cabins, dump, non-guest dump $, portable dump, laundry, groceries, RV supplies, LP gas by weight/by meter, ice, picnic tables, fire rings, wood, controlled access.

◊◊◊◊RECREATION: rec hall, pavilion, coin games, lake swim, lake fishing, fishing supplies, mini-golf, ($), golf nearby, bsktball, 30 bike rentals, playground, shuffleboard court shuffleboard court, activities (wkends), horseshoes, sports field, hiking trails, v-ball.

Pets welcome, quantity restrict. Partial handicap access. Open Mid Apr - Mid Oct. Escort to site. Clubs welcome. Rate in 2010 $36-54 for 2 persons. MC/VISA/DISC/AMEX/Debit. Member ARVC, ARVCMI. KOA discount.

Phone: (810)395-7042
Address: 3864 Breen Rd, Emmett, MI 48022
Lat/Lon: 43.00805/-82.84924
Email: emmettkoa@hotmail.com
Web: www.emmettkoa.com

SEE AD THIS PAGE

EMPIRE—E-3

(E) Indigo Bluffs Rally Park (Formerly Sleepy Bear Campground)—(Leelanau) *From jct Hwy 22 & Hwy 72: Go 3-1/2 mi E on Hwy 72. Enter on L.* ◊◊◊FACILITIES: 119 sites, 26 full hkups, 93 W&E, (20/30 amps), 8 pull-thrus, family camping, dump, laundry, ltd groc. ◊◊◊RECREATION: swim pool, playground. Pets welcome. Partial handicap access. No tents. Open May 1 - Late Oct. Rate in 2010 $36-48 for 4 persons. Member ARVC, ARVCMI. Phone: (231)326-5566.

(E) Indigo Bluffs Resort—(Leelanau) *From jct Hwy 22 & Hwy 72: Go 3-1/2 mi E on Hwy 72. Enter on L.* ◊◊◊◊◊FACILITIES: 23 sites, typical site width 60 ft, accepts full hkup units only, 23 full hkups, (50 amps), family camping, dump, laundry, ltd groc. ◊◊RECREATION: swim pool. Pets welcome, quantity restrict. Partial handicap access. No tents. Open May 1 - Late Oct. Big rigs welcome. Rate in 2010 $55 Member ARVC, ARVCMI. Phone: (231)326-5050.

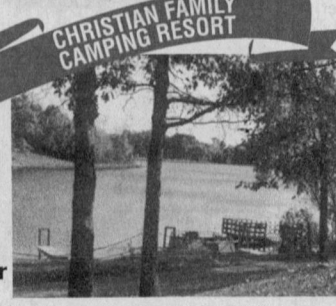

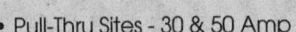

ESCANABA—D-2

(S) O.B. FULLER PARK (Delta County Park)—(Delta) *From jct US 2 & Hwy 35: Go 14 mi S on Hwy 35.* FACILITIES: 25 sites, 25 W&E, tenting, dump, laundry. RECREATION: lake swim, boating, canoeing, ramp, lake/river fishing. Open May 20 - Sep 20. Facilities fully operational Jun - Aug. Phone: (906)786-1020.

(SW) Park Place of the North—(Delta) *From jct US 2 and Hwy 35: Go 6 1/2 mi S on Hwy 35. Enter on L.* ◊◊◊FACILITIES: 25 sites, typical site width 30 ft, 20 W&E, (30 amps), 5 no hkups, 13 pull-thrus, family camping, tenting, dump, laundry. ◊◊RECREATION: lake swim, boating, lake fishing, playground. Pets welcome. Partial handicap access. Open May 1 - Oct 15. Rate in 2010 $22 for 2 persons. Phone: (906)786-8453.

(N) PIONEER TRAIL PARK (Delta County)—(Delta) *From jct Hwy-35 & US-2-41: Go 3 mi N on US-2-41.* FACILITIES: 213 sites, 213 W&E, (20/30 amps), tenting, dump. RECREATION: ramp, river fishing, playground. Partial handicap access. Open May - Oct 15. Phone: (906)786-1020.

ESSEXVILLE—G-5

(E) FINN ROAD CAMPGROUND & BOAT LAUNCH (Hampton Township)—(Bay) *From jct Hwy 15 & Hwy 25: Go 5 mi E on Hwy 25, then 2 mi N on Finn Rd.* FACILITIES: 50 sites, typical site width 30 ft, 50 full hkups, tenting, dump. RECREATION: boating, ramp, dock, lake fishing, playground. Partial handicap access. Open May 1 - Oct 31. Phone: (989)894-0055.

FENTON—H-5

See listing at Byron

FENWICK—H-3

(SE) **SNOW LAKE KAMPGROUND**—(Montcalm) *From jct Hwy 57 & Hwy 66: Go 3 mi S on Hwy 66, then 3/4 mi E (left) on Snows Lake Rd. Enter on R.*

◊◊◊◊FACILITIES: 309 sites, typical site width 30 ft, 288 full hkups, 21 W&E, (20/30/50 amps), many extd stay sites (summer), 53 pull-thrus, WiFi Instant Internet at site ($), family camping, tenting, cabins, dump, non-guest dump $, portable dump, laundry, groceries, RV supplies, LP gas by weight/by meter, ice, picnic tables, fire rings, grills, wood, controlled access.

◊◊◊◊◊RECREATION: rec hall, rec room/area, equipped pavilion, coin games, swim pool, wading pool, hot tub, boating, canoeing, kayaking, ramp, dock, 5 rowboat/2 canoe/6 kayak/2 pedal boat

SNOW LAKE KAMPGROUND—Continued on next page

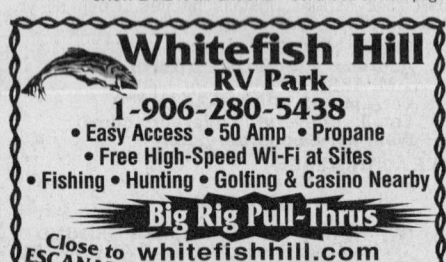

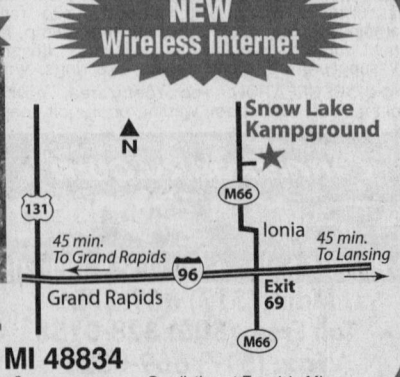

FENWICK—Continued
SNOW LAKE KAMPGROUND—Continued

rentals, lake fishing, fishing supplies, mini-golf, golf nearby, bsktball, playground, shuffleboard court 3 shuffleboard courts, activities (wkends), horseshoes, sports field, v-ball.

Pets welcome, breed restrict. Partial handicap access. Open May 1 - Oct 1. Big rigs welcome. Escort to site. Clubs welcome. Rate in 2010 $32-36 for 4 persons. MC/VISA/Debit. Member ARVC, ARVC MI.

Phone: (989)248-3224
Address: 644 E Snows Lake Rd, Fenwick, MI 48834
Lat/Lon: 43.13463/-85.05782
Email: snowlake@pathwaynet.com
Web: www.snowlakekampground.com

SEE AD PAGE 380

WELCOME

(SE) SNOW LAKE KAMPGROUND & RESTAURANT—*From jct Hwy 57 & Hwy 66: Go 3 mi S on Hwy 66, then 3/4 mi E (left) on Snows Lake Rd. Enter on R.* Full Service Restaurant serving campers and local residents. Buffets available for holidays & groups of 50. Occasional all-you-can-eat dinners. Open early May - mid Sep. Open weekends May thru early June. Open daily early June thru Labor Day. MC/VISA/Debit.

Phone: (989)248-3224
Address: 644 E Snows Lake Rd, Fenwick, MI 48834
Lat/Lon: 43.13379/-85.05799
Email: snowlake@pathwaynet.com
Web: www.snowlakekampground.com

SEE AD PAGE 380

FIFE LAKE—F-3

(SW) PERE MARQUETTE SF (Spring Lake)—(Grand Traverse) *From jct Hwy-186 & US-131: Go 1 mi S on US-131.* FACILITIES: 32 sites, 30 ft max RV length, 32 no hkups, tenting. RECREATION: lake swim, boating, ramp, lake fishing. Open all yr. Phone: (231)775-9727.

FLINT—H-5

(NE) Holt's RV Sites & Mobile Home Court (RV SPACES)—(Genesee) *From jct I-75 & I-69: Go 4 mi E on I-69 (exit 137), then 5 mi N on I-475 (exit 11), then 1/4 mi E on Carpenter Rd, then 1/4 mi S on Dort Rd (Hwy 54). Enter on L.* FACILITIES: 20 sites, typical site width 33 ft, 20 full hkups, (20/30/50 amps), 3 pull-thrus, dump, laundry. Pets welcome ($). No tents. Open all yr. Big rigs welcome. Rate in 2010 $30-35 for 2 persons. Phone: (810)787-5289.

FOREST LAKE—C-3

(S) ESCANABA RIVER SF (Forest Lake)—(Alger) *From town: Go 1/4 mi W on Hwy 94, then 2 mi S on Campground Rd. Enter at end.* FACILITIES: 23 sites, 23 no hkups, tenting, laundry. RECREATION: lake/river swim, boating, lake fishing. Open all yr. Phone: (906)346-9201.

FRANKENMUTH—H-5

WELCOME

(S) BRONNER'S CHRISTMAS WONDERLAND—*From jct I-75 (exit 136) & Hwy 83: Go 2 mi E on Birch Run Rd, then 4-1/2 mi N on Hwy 83. Enter on R.* A dazzling fantasyland acclaimed to have the world's largest year-round display of Christmas decorations. Over 50,000 trims & gifts. Open all yr. MC/VISA/DISC/AMEX/Debit. ATM.

Phone: (989)652-9931
Address: 25 Christmas Lane, Frankenmuth, MI 48734
Lat/Lon: 43.31686/-83.74039
Email: customerservice@bronner.com
Web: www.bronners.com

SEE AD THIS PAGE

The Peninsulas of Michigan were inaccessible to each other until 1957 when the Mackinac Bridge connected them.

FRANKENMUTH—Continued

WELCOME

(E) FRANKENMUTH BAVARIAN INN RESTAURANT—*From jct I-75 (exit 136) & Hwy 83: Go 2 mi E on Birch Run Rd, then 5-1/2 mi N on Hwy 83. Enter on R.* Bavarian-themed restaurant featuring world famous chicken. Glockenspiel bell tower, free outdoor entertainment and 9 unique shops. Open all yr. MC/VISA/DISC/AMEX/Debit. ATM.

Phone: (800)228-2742
Address: 713 S Main, Frankenmuth, MI 48734
Lat/Lon: 43.32570/-83.73991
Email: diningreservations@bavarianinn.com
Web: www.bavarianinn.com

SEE AD THIS PAGE

FRANKENMUTH—Continued on next page

FRANKENMUTH—Continued

(SE) FRANKENMUTH JELLYSTONE PARK CAMP-RESORT—(Saginaw) *From jct I-75 (exit 136) & Hwy 83: Go 2 mi E on Birch Run Rd, then 4-1/2 mi N on Hwy 83, then 1/4 mi N on Weiss St. Enter on R.*

◆◆◆◆◆FACILITIES: 244 sites, typical site width 30 ft, 176 full hkups, 68 W&E, (20/30/50 amps), 48 pull-thrus, WiFi Instant Internet at site, family camping, tenting, RV's/park model rentals, cabins, dump, non-guest dump $, laundry, groceries, RV supplies, LP gas by weight/by meter, ice, picnic tables, patios, wood, controlled access.

◆◆◆◆◆RECREATION: rec hall, rec room/area, pavilion, coin games, swim pool, hot tub, mini-golf, ($), golf nearby, bsktball, 8 bike rentals, playground, activities, sports field, v-ball.

Pets welcome. Partial handicap access. Open all yr. Facilities fully operational Apr 1 - Nov 1. Big rigs welcome. Clubs welcome. Rate in 2010 $45-67 per family. MC/VISA/Debit. ATM. Member ARVC, ARVC MI.

Phone: (989)652-6668
Address: 1339 Weiss St, Frankenmuth, MI 48734
Lat/Lon: 43.31715/-83.73472
Email: reservations@frankenmuthjellystone.com
Web: www.frankenmuthjellystone.com

SEE AD PAGE 381

FRANKFORT—E-3

(SE) Betsie River Campsite—(Benzie) *From south jct Hwy 115 & N US 31: Go 2 mi N on US 31, then 5 mi W on Traverse Ave/River Rd/Hwy 608. Enter on L.* ◆◆◆FACILITIES: 100 sites, typical site width 40 ft, 78 W&E, 22 E, (20 amps), 32 pull-thrus, family camping, tenting, dump, ltd groc. ◆◆RECREATION: river fishing, playground. Pets welcome, quantity restrict. Partial handicap access. Open May 1 - Oct 1. Rate in 2010 $26-29.50 for 2 persons. Member ARVC, ARVC MI. Phone: (231)352-9535.

FREDERIC—E-5

(E) AU SABLE SF (Jones Lake)—(Crawford) *From town: Go 9 mi E on CR 612.* FACILITIES: 42 sites, 30 ft max RV length, 42 no hkups, tenting. RECREATION: lake swim, boating, ramp, lake fishing. Open all yr. Phone: (989)348-6371.

(W) AU SABLE SF (Upper Manistee River)—(Crawford) *From town: Go 6-1/2 mi W on CR 612, then S on Manistee Rd. Enter on R.* FACILITIES: 40 sites, 40 no hkups, tenting. RECREATION: canoeing, river fishing. Open all yr. Phone: (989)348-6371.

(S) Happi Days Campground & Diner—(Crawford) *From jct I-75 (exit 259) & Hwy 93: Go 1-1/2 mi W on Hwy 93, then 4 mi N on Old 27, then 1 block W on Batterson Rd. Enter on R.* ◆◆◆FACILITIES: 40 sites, 30 W&E, 10 E, (20/30 amps), 30 pull-thrus, family camping, tenting, dump, laundry, ltd groc. ◆◆RECREATION: play equipment. Pets welcome. Partial handicap access. Open all yr. Facilities fully operational May - Oct. Rate in 2010 $23-25 for 2 persons. Phone: (989) 348-8172.

GARDEN—D-3

(S) FAYETTE HISTORIC STATE PARK—(Delta) *From jct of US 2 & M-183: Go 17 mi Sw on M-183.* FACILITIES: 61 sites, 61 E, (20 amps), 4 pull-thrus, tenting. RECREATION: lake swim, boating, ramp, dock, lake fishing, playground. Open Apr 15 - Nov 15. Phone: (906)644-2603.

Father Jacques Marquette founded Sault Ste. Marie, the third-oldest remaining settlement in the United States in 1668.

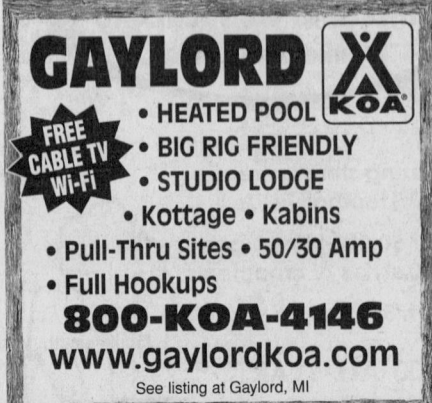

GAYLORD—E-5

(S) GAYLORD KOA—(Otsego) *From jct Hwy 32 & I-75: Go 3 mi S on I-75 (exit 279), then 2 mi S on Old 27, then 3/4 mi E on Charles Brink Rd. Enter on R.*

◆◆◆◆FACILITIES: 104 sites, typical site width 35 ft, 50 full hkups, 49 W&E, (20/30/50 amps), 5 no hkups, 40 pull-thrus, cable TV, WiFi Instant Internet at site, family camping, tenting, cabins, RV storage, dump, non-guest dump $, portable dump, laundry, groceries, RV supplies, LP gas by weight/by meter, ice, picnic tables, fire rings, wood, controlled access.

◆◆◆◆RECREATION: rec hall, rec room/area, coin games, swim pool, mini-golf, ($), golf nearby, bsktball, 10 bike rentals, playground, shuffleboard court shuffleboard court, activities (wkends), horseshoes, hiking trails, v-ball.

Pets welcome. Partial handicap access. Open Apr 29 - Oct 16. Big rigs welcome. Escort to site. Clubs welcome. Rate in 2010 $31-50 for 4 persons. MC/VISA/Debit. Member ARVC, ARVCMI. KOA discount.

Phone: (800)562-4146
Address: 5101 Campfires Pkwy, Gaylord, MI 49735
Lat/Lon: 44.95844/-84.66066
Email: gaylordkoa@gmail.com
Web: www.gaylordkoa.com

SEE AD THIS PAGE

(S) OTSEGO LAKE STATE PARK—(Otsego) *From jct I-75 & Old US 27: Go 5 mi N on Old US 27.* FACILITIES: 155 sites, 155 E, tenting, dump, laundry, groceries. RECREATION: lake swim, boating, ramp, lake fishing, playground. Partial handicap access. Open Apr 27 - Dec 1. Phone: (989)732-5485.

GERMFASK—C-4

(S) Big Cedar Campground & Canoe Livery—(Schoolcraft) *From jct US 2 & Hwy 77: Go 10 mi N on Hwy 77. Enter on R.* ◆◆◆FACILITIES: 50 sites, typical site width 25 ft, 9 full hkups, 41 W&E, (20/30 amps), 9 pull-thrus, family camping, tenting, RV storage, dump, laundry, ice, picnic tables, fire rings, wood. ◆◆◆RECREATION: pavilion, river swim, boating, canoeing, kayaking, float trips, river fishing, fishing supplies, bsktball, play equipment, horseshoes, v-ball. Pets welcome, breed restrict. Open May 1 - Oct 15. Rate in 2010 $18-26 for 2 persons. MC/VISA/DISC/Debit. Member ARVC, ARVC MI. CCUSA 50% Discount. CCUSA reservations Recommended, CCUSA max stay 2 days, Cash only for CCUSA disc., Check only for CCUSA disc., CCUSA disc. not avail F,Sa, CCUSA disc. not avail holidays. Electric heat surcharge $3.

Phone: (906)586-6684
Address: 7936 Hwy 77, Germfask, MI 49836
Lat/Lon: 46.24289/-85.92653
Email: bigcedar_up@yahooo.com
Web: www.bigcedarcampground.com

GLADSTONE—D-2

(E) GLADSTONE BAY CAMPGROUND (City Park)—(Delta) *From N jct Hwy 35 & US 2/41: Go 1/2 mi S on US 2/41, then 1 mi E on Delta Ave. Enter at end.* FACILITIES: 62 sites, typical site width 25 ft, 25 full hkups, 25 E, (20/30 amps), 12 no hkups, 12 pull-thrus, family camping, tenting, dump. RECREATION: lake swim, boating, canoeing, lake fishing, playground. Pets welcome. Partial handicap access. Open May 1 - Oct 15. Phone: (906)428-1211.

GLADWIN—G-4

(S) GLADWIN CITY PARK & CAMPGROUND—(Gladwin) *From east jct Hwy 18 & Hwy 61: Go 4 blocks W on Hwy 61.* FACILITIES: 59 sites, 59 W&E, (20 amps), 17 pull-thrus, tenting, dump. RECREATION: river swim, canoeing, river fishing, playground. Partial handicap access. Open May 1 - Nov 30. Phone: (989)426-8126.

(SW) River Valley RV Park—(Clare) *From west jct Hwy 18 & Hwy 61: Go 7 mi W on Hwy 61, then 2-1/2 mi S on Bailey Lake Ave. Enter on L.* ◆◆◆FACILITIES: 149 sites, typical site width 45 ft, 149 W&E, (20/30 amps), 2 pull-thrus, family camping, tenting, dump, laundry, groceries. ◆◆◆◆RECREATION: lake swim, canoeing, lake/river fishing, playground. Pets welcome. Partial handicap access. Open May 1 - Oct 1. Rate in 2010 $27-31 per family. Member ARVC, ARVC MI. Phone: (989)386-7844.

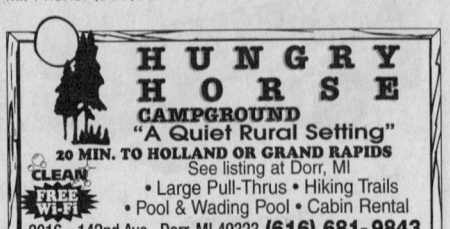

GLEN ARBOR—E-3

(W) SLEEPING BEAR DUNES NATIONAL LAKESHORE (D.H. Day Campground)—(Leelanau) *From jct Hwy-22 & Hwy-109: Go 1 mi W on Hwy-109. Enter on L.* FACILITIES: 88 sites, 88 no hkups, tenting, dump. RECREATION: lake swim, lake fishing. Partial handicap access. Open Apr 1 - Nov 26. Phone: (231)334-4634.

GLENNIE—F-5

(SW) ALCONA COUNTY PARK—(Alcona) *From jct Hwy 72 & Hwy 65: Go 7 mi S on Hwy 65, then 3 mi W on Bamfield Rd, then 1-1/2 mi N on Au Sable Rd.* FACILITIES: 502 sites, 48 full hkups, 104 E, (20/30/50 amps), 350 no hkups, tenting, dump, laundry. RECREATION: lake swim, boating, canoeing, ramp, lake/river/stream fishing, playground. Open Apr 1 - Dec 1. Phone: (989)735-3881.

GOWEN—H-3

Lincoln Pines Resort—(Kent) *From jct Hwy 91 & Hwy 57: Go 5 mi W on Hwy 57, then 5-1/4 mi N on Lincoln Lake Rd/19 Mile. Enter on L.* ◆◆◆◆FACILITIES: 339 sites, 335 full hkups, 4 W&E, (30/50 amps), 4 pull-thrus, family camping, tenting, dump, laundry, ltd groc. ◆◆◆◆RECREATION: lake swim, boating, canoeing, ramp, dock, lake fishing, playground. Pets welcome, quantity restrict. Partial handicap access. Open Apr 15 - Oct 15. Rate in 2010 $30-40 per family. Member ARVC, ARVCMI. Phone: (616)984-2100.

GRAND HAVEN—H-2

(S) Campers Paradise, Inc.—(Ottawa) *From jct Hwy 45 & US 31: Go 5 mi N on US 31, then 100 yards W on Robbins Rd. Enter on L.* ◆◆◆FACILITIES: 107 sites, 107 W&E, (15/30 amps), family camping, tenting, dump, non-guest dump $, portable dump, laundry, ice, picnic tables, fire rings, wood. ◆◆RECREATION: pavilion, bike rental 8 bike rentals, playground, shuffleboard court shuffleboard court, activities horseshoes. Pets welcome. Partial handicap access. Open May 15 - Oct 15. Rate in 2010 $25-35 for 4 persons. MC/VISA/Debit. CCUSA 50% Discount. CCUSA reservations Recommended, CCUSA max stay 14 days. Discount not available 4th of July week, last weekend of Jul thru first weekend of Aug. Surcharge of $2 only for extra family members.

Phone: (616)846-1460
Address: 800 Robbins Rd, Grand Haven, MI 49417
Lat/Lon: 43.04438/-86.22243
Email: campgroundmgr@aol.com
Web: www.campersparadiseinc.com

(W) GRAND HAVEN STATE PARK—(Ottawa) *From US 31 in Grand Haven: Follow the "waterfront" signs, then go S at the waterfront to park entrance.* FACILITIES: 174 sites, 174 E, tenting, groceries. RECREATION: lake swim, lake fishing, playground. Partial handicap access. Open Apr 1 - Nov 1. Facilities fully operational May 1 - Oct 15. Phone: (616)798-3711.

(S) Yogi Bear's Jellystone Park Grand Haven (Morgan RV Resorts)—(Ottawa) *From jct Hwy 45 & US 31: Go 1/4 mi S on US 31. Enter on L.* ◆◆◆◆FACILITIES: 284 sites, typical site width 45 ft, 97 full hkups, 159 W&E, (15/30/50 amps), 28 no hkups, 37 pull-thrus, family camping, tenting, dump, laundry, groceries. ◆◆◆◆◆RECREATION: swim pool, playground. Pets welcome. Partial handicap access. Open May 1 - Oct 15. Big rigs welcome. Rate in 2010 $45-65 for 2 persons. Member ARVC, ARVC MI. Phone: (800)828-1453.

GRAND JUNCTION—I-2

(N) Warner Camp RV Park—(Allegan) *From jct Hwy 140 & I-96/US 31: Go 2 mi N on I-196 (exit 20), then 9 mi E on CR 388, then 1 mi N on CR 215, then 1/4 mi E on Baseline Rd, then 1/4 mi N on 55th St. Enter on L.* ◆◆◆FACILITIES: 91 sites, typical site width 35 ft, 84 W&E, (20/30 amps), 7 no hkups, family camping, tenting, dump, laundry. ◆◆◆◆RECREATION: lake swim, boating, canoeing, ramp, dock, lake fishing, playground. Pets welcome, quantity restrict. Partial handicap access. Open May 1 - Oct 1. Rate in 2010 $27 for 6 persons. Member ARVC, ARVCMI. Phone: (269)434-6844.

GRAND MARAIS—B-3

(E) LAKE SUPERIOR SF (Blind Sucker No. 2)—(Luce) *From town: Go 16 mi E on Grand Marais Truck Trail.* FACILITIES: 32 sites, 32 no hkups, tenting. RECREATION: boating, ramp, lake fishing. Open all yr. Phone: (906)293-3293.

(NW) WOODLAND PARK (Burt Twp Park)—(Alger) *From Hwy-77 in town: Go 4 blocks W on Braziel St.* FACILITIES: 125 sites, 110 W&E, 15 no hkups, tenting, dump, laundry. RECREATION: lake swim, boating, canoeing, ramp, dock, lake fishing, playground. Open May 1 - Oct 15. Phone: (906)494-2381.

GRAND RAPIDS—H-3

See listings at Allendale, Alto, Belding, Caledonia, Cedar Springs, Coopersville, Dorr, Gowen, Hopkins, Hudsonville, Middleville & Zeeland

(NE) Grand Rogue Campgrounds and Paddlesports—(Kent) *From north jct I-96 & US 131: Go 1-1/2 mi N on US 131 (exit 91), then 4 mi E (left) on West River Dr(entrance on right). From West bound I-96 (exit*

Grand Rogue Campgrounds and Paddlesports—Continued on next page

GRAND RAPIDS—Continued
Grand Rogue Campgrounds and Paddlesports—Continued

38): Go 6-1/2 mi N on Hwy 44, then 3/4 mi W on W. River Dr(entrance on left). ◊◊◊FACILITIES: 110 sites, typical site width 40 ft, 86 W&E, (20/30 amps), 24 no hkups, 5 pull-thrus, family camping, tenting, dump, laundry, groceries. ◊◊◊◊RECREATION: lake swim, boating, canoeing, ramp, lake/river/stream fishing, playground. Pets welcome, quantity restrict. Partial handicap access. Open Late Apr - Late Sep. Rate in 2010 $20-33.50 for 4 persons. Member ARVC, ARVC MI. Phone: (616)361-1053. FCRV discount. FMCA discount.

✽ **(S) TERRY TOWN TRAVEL CENTER**—*From jct US-131 & Hwy-11 (28th St): Go 1/2 mi E on Hwy-11, then 6 mi S on S Division Ave. Enter on R.* SALES: travel trailers, park models, truck campers, 5th wheels, toy hauler, Class A motorhomes, Class C motorhomes, Class B motorhomes, fold-down camping trailers, pre-owned unit sales. SERVICES: full-time mech, RV appliance repair, body work/collision repair, LP gas by weight/by meter, sells parts/accessories, installs hitches. Open all yr. MC/VISA/DISC/Debit.

Phone: (616)455-5590
Address: 7145 S Division Ave, Grand Rapids, MI 49548
Lat/Lon: 42.83460/-85.66381
Email: sales@terrytownrv.com
Web: www.terrytownrv.com

SEE AD THIS PAGE

(S) WOODCHIP CAMPGROUND—(Kent) *From jct Hwy 11 (28th St) & US 131: Go 6 mi S on US 131 (exit 75), then 1-3/4 mi W on 76th St, then 100 yds N on Burlingame SW. Enter on L.*

◊◊◊FACILITIES: 122 sites, typical site width 25 ft, 17 full hkups, 90 W&E, (20/30/50 amps), 15 no hkups, some extd stay sites (summer), WiFi Instant Internet at site, family camping, tenting, RV's/park model rentals, RV storage, dump, portable dump, laundry, RV supplies, ice, picnic tables, fire rings, wood.

◊◊◊RECREATION: rec hall, pavilion, swim pool, golf nearby, bsktball, playground, shuffleboard court shuffleboard court, activities (wkends), sports field, v-ball.

Pets welcome. Partial handicap access. Open all yr. Facilities fully operational May 1 - mid Oct. Clubs welcome. Rate in 2010 $30-37 for 4 persons. MC/VISA/DISC/Debit. Member ARVC, ARVC MI. CCUSA 50% Discount. CCUSA reservations Recommended, CCUSA max stay 3 days. Fully operational May 1-mid Oct.

Phone: (616)878-9050
Address: 7501 Burlingame S W, Byron Center, MI 49315
Lat/Lon: 42.82804/-85.70345
Email: info@woodchipcampground.com
Web: www.woodchipcampground.com

SEE AD THIS PAGE

Michigan State Rock: Petoskey Stone

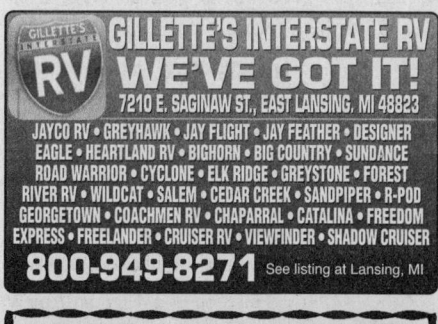

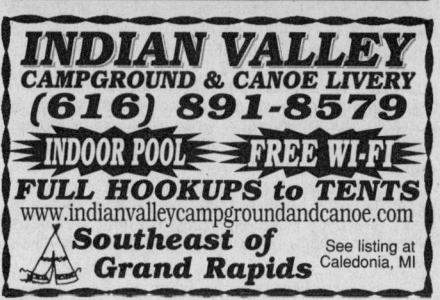

GRANT—H-3

(W) Chinook Camping—(Newaygo) *From south jct Hwy 82 & Hwy 37: Go 3-3/4 mi S on Hwy 37, then 6 mi W on 112th St. Enter on R.* ◊◊◊FACILITIES: 120 sites, typical site width 40 ft, 120 W&E, (20/30 amps), family camping, tenting, dump, laundry, groceries. ◊◊◊◊RECREATION: swim pool, boating, canoeing, ramp, river fishing, playground. Pets welcome. Partial handicap access. Open Mid Apr - Mid Oct. Rate in 2010 $25 per family. Phone: (231)834-7505.

(NW) Salmon Run Campground and Vic's Canoes—(Newaygo) *From south jct Hwy 82 & Hwy 37: Go 3-3/4 mi S on Hwy 37, then 1/2 mi W on 112th St, then 1 mi N on Gordon St, then 1/2 mi W on 104th St, then 2-1/4 mi N on Felch Rd. Enter at end.* ◊◊◊FACILITIES: 80 sites, typical site width 35 ft, 72 W&E, (20/30 amps), 8 no hkups, 5 pull-thrus, family camping, tenting, dump, non-guest dump $, laundry, ltd groc, RV supplies, ice, picnic tables, fire rings, wood. ◊◊◊RECREATION: swim pool, boating, canoeing, kayaking, ramp, float trips, river fishing, fishing supplies, bsktball, playground, horseshoes, v-ball. Pets welcome. Partial handicap access. Open May 1 - mid Oct. Rate in 2010 $26-36 for 2 persons. MC/VISA/DISC. Member ARVC, ARVC MI. CCUSA 50% Discount. CCUSA reservations Recommended, CCUSA max stay 4 days, CCUSA disc. not avail F,Sa, CCUSA disc. not avail holidays. Not available Jun 16-Sep 1.

Phone: (231)834-5494
Address: 8845 Felch Ave, Grant, MI 49327
Lat/Lon: 43.39072/-85.83216
Email: info@salmonrunmi.com
Web: www.salmonrunmi.com

GRASS LAKE—I-4

(S) APPLE CREEK CAMPGROUND & RV PARK—(Jackson) *From jct US 127S & I-94: Go 8 mi E on I-94 (exit 150), then 2-3/4 mi S on Mt Hope Rd, then 3/4 mi W on Michigan, then 4 mi S on Wolf Lake Rd, then 1/2 mi E on Orban Rd. Enter on R.*

◊◊◊FACILITIES: 170 sites, typical site width 50 ft, 168 W&E, (20/30 amps), 2 no hkups, many extd stay sites (summer), 10 pull-thrus, WiFi Instant Internet at site, family camping, tenting, RV's/park model rentals, cabins, RV storage, dump, portable dump, laundry, groceries, RV supplies, LP gas by weight/by meter, ice, picnic tables, fire rings, wood, controlled access.

◊◊◊◊RECREATION: rec hall, rec room/area, pavilion, coin games, swim pool, boating, 4 pedal boat rentals, pond fishing, fishing supplies, mini-golf, ($), golf nearby, bsktball, 4 bike rentals, playground, activities, (wkends), horseshoes, sports field, hiking trails, v-ball.

Pets welcome, breed restrict. Open Apr 15 - Nov 30. Holiday weekends 3-nite minimum, race 3-nite minimum. Escort to site. Clubs welcome. Rate in 2010 $25-28 for 4 persons. MC/VISA/DISC/Debit. Member ARVC, ARVC MI. CCUSA 50% Discount. CCUSA reservations Recommended, CCUSA max stay 7 days, CCUSA disc. not avail

GRASS LAKE—Continued
APPLE CREEK CAMPGROUND & RV PARK—Continued

F,Sa, CCUSA disc. not avail holidays. Weekends available before Memorial Day & after Labor Day weekends.

Phone: (517)522-3467
Address: 11185 Orban Rd, Grass Lake, MI 49240
Lat/Lon: 42.19688/-84.20737
Email: mbrennan@modempool.com
Web: www.applecreekrv.com

SEE AD TRAVEL SECTION PAGE 359

GRATTAN—H-3

(SE) Scalley Lake Park—(Kent) *From jct Hwy 91 & Hwy 44: Go 5 mi W on Hwy 44, then 3/4 mi S on Lincoln Lake Ave, then 1/2 mi W on 7 Mile Rd, then 1/4 mi S on Scalley Ave. Enter on R.* ◊◊◊FACILITIES: 43 sites, typical site width 40 ft, 12 full hkups, 23 W&E, (20/30 amps), 8 no hkups, 6 pull-thrus, family camping, tenting, dump, laundry, ltd groc. ◊◊◊RECREATION: lake swim, boating, electric motors only, canoeing, ramp, dock, lake fishing, playground. Pets welcome, breed restrict. Partial handicap access. Open May 1 - Oct 1. Rate in 2010 $30 per family. Member ARVC, ARVC MI. Phone: (616)691-8534.

GRAYLING—E-5

(E) HURON NATIONAL FOREST (Kneff Lake Campground)—(Crawford) *From jct Business I-75 & Hwy 72: Go 6-1/2 mi E on Hwy 72, then 1-1/2 mi S on Stephan Bridge Rd, then 1 mi E on FR 4003.* FACILITIES: 26 sites, 22 ft max RV length, 26 no hkups, tenting. RECREATION: lake swim, boating, no motors, lake fishing. Partial handicap access. Open May 15 - Sep 10. Phone: (989)826-3252.

(NE) River Park Campground—(Crawford) *From jct US 27 & I-75: Go 10 mi N on I-75 (exit 259), then 3 mi NE on Hwy 93, then 2 mi S on Bobcat Trail. Enter on R.* ◊◊◊FACILITIES: 97 sites, typical site width 40 ft, 43 W&E, 24 E, (20/30 amps), 30 no hkups, family camping, tenting, dump, laundry, ltd groc. ◊◊RECREATION: river fishing, playground. Pets welcome. Partial handicap access. Open all yr. Facilities fully operational May 15 - Oct 15. Rate in 2010 $27-29 per family. Member ARVC, ARVC MI. Phone: (888)517-9092.

GRAYLING—Continued on next page

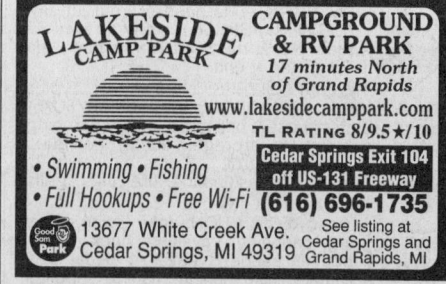

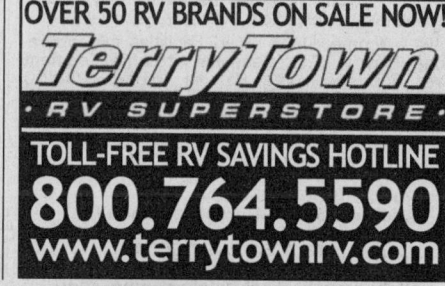

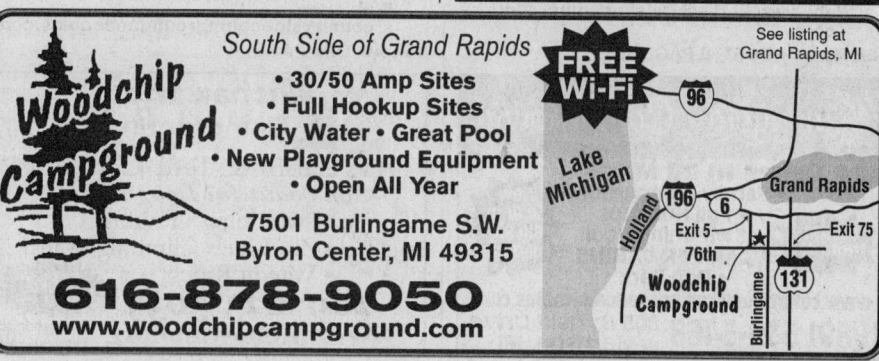

GRAYLING—Continued

(NE) Sno-Trac Camper Village—(Crawford) *From jct US 27 & I-75: Go 5 mi N on I-75(exit 254), then 15 mi E on Hwy 72, then 7 mi N on McMasters Bridge Rd/F-97, then 3/4 mi E on North Down River Rd, then 1 mi N on Lovells Rd. Enter on R.* ◆◆◆FACILITIES: 66 sites, typical site width 35 ft, 11 full hkups, 55 W&E, (20/30/50 amps), 50 amps ($), 20 pull-thrus, tenting, dump, ltd groc. ◆◆◆RECREATION: river swim, canoeing, river fishing. Pets welcome. Open all yr. Rate in 2010 $32-42 per family. Phone: (989)348-9494.

(SE) YOGI BEAR'S JELLYSTONE CAMP RESORT—(Crawford) *From jct US 27 & I-75: Go 2 mi N on I-75 (exit 251), then 4-1/2 mi E on Four Mile Rd. Enter on L.*

◆◆◆FACILITIES: 218 sites, typical site width 45 ft, 52 full hkups, 166 W&E, (20/30/50 amps), some extd stay sites (summer), WiFi Instant Internet at site, WiFi Internet central location, family camping, tenting, RV's/park model rentals, cabins, RV storage, dump, non-guest dump $, portable dump, laundry, groceries, RV supplies, LP gas by weight/by meter, LP bottle exch, ice, picnic tables, fire rings, wood.

◆◆◆◆RECREATION: rec room/area, pavilion, coin games, swim pool, mini-golf, ($), golf nearby, bsktball, 17 bike rentals, playground, shuffleboard court 2 shuffleboard courts, activities, horseshoes, sports field, hiking trails, v-ball.

Pets welcome. Partial handicap access. Open May 1 - Oct 15. Clubs welcome. Rate in 2010 $25-45 for 4 persons. MC/VISA/DISC/Debit. ATM. Member ARVC, ARVCMI. CCUSA 50% Discount. CCUSA reservations Recommended, CCUSA max stay 4 days, CCUSA disc. not avail S, CCUSA disc. not avail F,Sa, CCUSA disc. not avail holidays.

Phone: (989)348-2157
Address: 370 W Four Mile Rd, Grayling, MI 49738
Lat/Lon: 44.59919/-84.61549
Email: campjellystonegrayling@yahoo.com
Web: www.graylingjellystone.com

SEE AD PAGE 383

GWINN—C-2

(W) HORSESHOE LAKE CAMPGROUND & RV PARK—(Marquette) *From jct Hwy 553 & Hwy-35: Go 7 mi W on Hwy-35, then 1-1/2 mi S on Horseshoe Lake Rd. Enter at end.*

◆◆◆FACILITIES: 125 sites, typical site width 30 ft, 13 full hkups, 90 W&E, (20/30/50 amps), 22 no hkups, 4 pull-thrus, family camping, tenting, cabins, RV storage, dump, non-guest dump $, laundry, ltd groc, LP gas by weight/by meter, ice, picnic tables, patios, fire rings, grills, wood.

◆◆◆RECREATION: lake swim, boating, canoeing, kayaking, dock, 6 row-boat/2 canoe/8 kayak/4 pedal boat rentals, lake fishing, fishing supplies, golf nearby, bsktball, playground, horseshoes, sports field, hiking trails, v-ball.

Pets welcome. Open all yr. Facilities fully operational May 1 - Oct. Seasonal sites have cement pads. Clubs welcome. Rate in 2010 $30.31.50 per family. MC/VISA/Debit. CCUSA 50% Discount. CCUSA reservations Required, CCUSA max stay 3 days, Cash only for CCUSA disc., CCUSA disc. not avail holidays. Fully operational May 1-Oct. Discount not available Jun thru Aug.

Phone: (906)346-9937
Address: 840 N Horseshoe Lake Rd., Gwinn, MI 49841
Lat/Lon: 46.30577/-87.55048
Email: omnibillboards@yahoo.com
Web: www.horseshoelakecampground.com

SEE AD MARQUETTE PAGE 393

HANCOCK—A-1

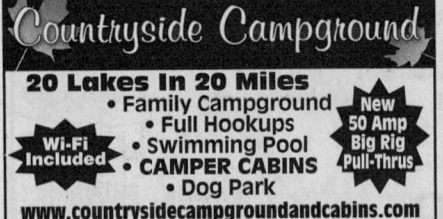

(N) F.J. MCLAIN STATE PARK—(Houghton) *From town: Go 10 mi N on Hwy 203.* FACILITIES: 103 sites, 103 E, (20/30 amps), tenting, dump, ltd groc. RECREATION: lake swim, lake fishing, playground. Partial handicap access. Open May 14 - Oct 17. Phone: (906)482-0278.

(W) HANCOCK RECREATION AREA (City Park)—(Houghton) *From jct US-41 & Hwy-203: Go 2 mi W on Hwy-203. Enter on L.* FACILITIES: 71 sites, typical site width 14 ft, 56 E, (20/30 amps), 15 no hkups, 2 pull-thrus, tenting, dump, laundry. RECREATION: lake swim, boating, canoeing, ramp, dock, lake fishing, playground. Partial handicap access. Open May 15 - Oct 15. Phone: (906)482-7413.

HARBOR BEACH—G-6

(N) NORTH PARK CAMPGROUND (City Park)—(Huron) *From jct Hwy 142 & Hwy 25: Go 1/2 mi N on Hwy 25.* FACILITIES: 184 sites, 184 full hkups, (50 amps), 50 amps ($), 30 pull-thrus, tenting, dump. RECREATION: stream fishing, playground. Open all yr. Phone: (989)479-9554.

(S) WAGENER COUNTY PARK—(Huron) *From jct Hwy 142 & Hwy 25: Go 5 mi S on Hwy 25. Enter on L.*

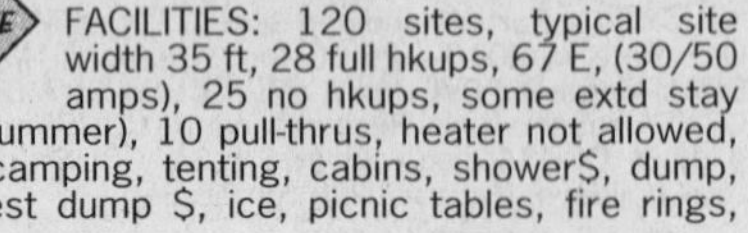

FACILITIES: 120 sites, typical site width 35 ft, 28 full hkups, 67 E, (30/50 amps), 25 no hkups, some extd stay sites (summer), 10 pull-thrus, heater not allowed, family camping, tenting, cabins, shower$, dump, non-guest dump $, ice, picnic tables, fire rings, wood.

RECREATION: pavilion, lake swim, boating, ramp, lake fishing, golf nearby, playground, horseshoes, hiking trails, v-ball.

Pets welcome. Partial handicap access. Open May 1 - Oct 15. Big rigs welcome. Clubs welcome. MC/VISA/Debit.

Phone: (877)404-7447
Address: 2671 S Lakeshore Rd, Harbor Beach, MI 48441
Lat/Lon: 43.77196/-82.62311
Email: huronpks@comcast.net
Web: www.huroncountyparks.com

SEE AD TRAVEL SECTION PAGE 361

HARRISON—F-4

(N) Camp Withii—(Clare) *From jct Hwy-61 & Business US-127: Go 1-1/4 mi N on Business US-127, then 200 yards W on Hampton Rd. Enter on L.* ◆◆◆FACILITIES: 100 sites, typical site width 40 ft, 60 full hkups, 4 W&E, 36 E, (20/30/50 amps), 50 amps ($), 8 pull-thrus, family camping, tenting, dump. ◆RECREATION: play equipment. Pets welcome, breed restrict, quantity restrict. Open Apr 15 - Oct 8. Rate in 2010 $23-27 for 2 persons. Phone: (989)539-3128.

(W) COUNTRYSIDE CAMPGROUND—(Clare) *From jct Business 127 & Hwy 61 (in town): Go 3/4 mi W on Hwy 61/Main St, then 1/4 mi N on Byfield Dr. Enter on L.*

◆◆◆◆FACILITIES: 73 sites, typical site width 35 ft, 59 full hkups, 14 W&E, (20/30/50 amps), some extd stay sites (summer), 37 pull-thrus, WiFi Instant Internet at site, family camping, tenting, cabins, RV storage, dump, non-guest dump $, laundry, ltd groc, RV supplies, ice, picnic tables, fire rings, wood.

◆◆◆RECREATION: rec hall, pavilion, swim pool, golf nearby, bsktball, 8 bike rentals, playground, activities, (wkends), horseshoes, sports field, hiking trails, v-ball.

Pets welcome. Open May 1 - Early Oct. Big rigs welcome. Clubs welcome. Rate in 2010 $29-35 per family. MC/VISA/Debit. Member ARVC, ARVC MI.

Phone: (989)539-5468
Address: 805 Byfield Dr, Harrison, MI 48625
Lat/Lon: 44.02098/-84.81308
Email: info@countrysidecampgroundandcabins.com
Web: www.countrysidecampgroundandcabins.com

SEE AD THIS PAGE

HARRISON—Continued

(N) Downhour's Shady Acres Campground—(Clare) *From jct Hwy 61 & Bus US 127: Go 6 mi N on Bus 127 (Clare Ave), then 500 ft E on Long Lake Rd, then 1/4 mi S on Jack's Rd. Enter on L.* ◆◆◆FACILITIES: 46 sites, typical site width 30 ft, 18 full hkups, 28 W&E, (20/30/50 amps), family camping, tenting, RV storage, dump, non-guest dump $, portable dump, laundry, picnic tables, fire rings, wood. ◆RECREATION: pavilion, play equipment, 2 shuffleboard courts, horseshoes. Pets welcome. Open Apr 15 - Nov 15. Facilities fully operational May 1 - Oct 15. Rate in 2010 $25 for 6 persons. CCUSA 50% Discount. CCUSA reservations Recommended, CCUSA max stay Unlimited, CCUSA disc. not avail F,Sa, CCUSA disc. not avail holidays.

Phone: (989)539-3111
Address: 7785 Jack's Rd, Harrison, MI 48625
Lat/Lon: 44.10015/-84.78610

(S) Hidden Hill Family Campground—(Clare) *From jct US 127 & Hwy 61: Go 1 block W on Hwy 61/Bus US 127. Enter on R.* ◆◆◆FACILITIES: 55 sites, typical site width 30 ft, 35 full hkups, 10 W&E, (20/30/50 amps), 10 no hkups, 10 pull-thrus, family camping, tenting, dump, laundry. ◆◆RECREATION: playground. Pets welcome, breed restrict. Open Apr 15 - Oct 31. Rate in 2010 $28-32 per family. Member ARVC, ARVCMI. Phone: (989)539-9372. FMCA discount.

LAKE GEORGE CAMPGROUND—(Clare) *From jct Bus US 127 & Hwy 61: Go 7-1/2 mi W on Hwy 61, then 5-3/4 mi S on Bringold/Arthur/S Jackson. Enter on L.*

◆◆◆FACILITIES: 65 sites, typical site width 45 ft, 40 ft max RV length, 52 W&E, 13 E, (20/30/50 amps), some extd stay sites (summer), 7 pull-thrus, WiFi Instant Internet at site, family camping, tenting, RV's/park model rentals, cabins, RV storage, dump, non-guest dump $, portable dump, laundry, groceries, RV supplies, LP gas by weight/by meter, ice, picnic tables, fire rings, wood.

◆◆◆RECREATION: rec hall, rec room/area, pavilion, swim pool, golf nearby, bsktball, playground, shuffleboard court shuffleboard court, activities (wkends), horseshoes, sports field, hiking trails, v-ball.

Pets welcome, quantity restrict. Open May 1 - Oct 31. Escort to site. Clubs welcome. Rate in 2010 $22-25 for 6 persons. MC/VISA. Member ARVC, ARVCMI.

Phone: (989)588-4075
Address: 1935 S Jackson, Harrison, MI 48625
Lat/Lon: 43.95944/-84.92882
Email: info@lakegeorgecamp.com
Web: www.lakegeorgecamp.com

SEE AD TRAVEL SECTION PAGE 359

(N) WILSON STATE PARK—(Clare) *From US 27 (Harrison exit): Go 3-1/2 mi W.* FACILITIES: 160 sites, 160 E, 5 pull-thrus, tenting, dump. RECREATION: lake swim, boating, ramp, lake fishing, playground. Open Apr 1 - Dec 1. Phone: (989)539-3021.

HARRISVILLE—E-6

(SE) HARRISVILLE STATE PARK—(Alcona) *From jct Hwy 72 & US 23: Go 1/2 mi S on US 23.* FACILITIES: 195 sites, 195 E, tenting, dump. RECREATION: lake swim, playground. Open May 9 - Oct 26. Phone: (989)724-5126.

HART—G-2

(E) JOHN GURNEY PARK (Municipal)—(Oceana) *From jct US 31 & Polk Rd: Go 2 mi E on Polk Rd, then 1 mi N on Oceana Dr, then 1 block W on E Main into park. Enter at end.* FACILITIES: 85 sites, 85 full hkups, (20 amps), 2 pull-thrus, tenting, dump. RECREATION: lake swim, boating, canoeing, ramp, dock, lake fishing. Open Apr 15 - Oct 15. Member ARVC. Phone: (231)873-4959.

HASTINGS—I-3

(SW) MICHAWANA CAMPGROUND—(Barry) *From west jct Hwy 37 & Hwy 43: Go 6 mi S on Hwy 43, then 1 mi W on Head Lake Rd. Enter on L.*

◆◆◆FACILITIES: 52 sites, 10 full hkups, 42 W&E, (20/30/50 amps), 5 pull-thrus, WiFi Instant Internet at site, family camping, tenting, cabins, dump, non-guest dump $, portable dump, laundry, groceries, RV supplies, ice, picnic tables, patios, fire rings, wood.

◆◆◆◆◆RECREATION: rec hall, lake swim, boating, canoeing, kayaking, dock, 10 canoe/4 kayak/8 pedal boat rentals, lake fishing, mini-golf, golf nearby, bsktball, playground, activities, (wkends), tennis, horseshoes, sports field, hiking trails, v-ball.

MICHAWANA CAMPGROUND—Continued on next page

Pets welcome, quantity restrict. Partial handicap access. Open Apr 30 - Oct 2. Clubs welcome. Rate in 2010 $24-29 per family. MC/VISA/DISC.

Phone: (269)623-3035
Address: 5800 Head Lake Rd, Hastings, MI 49058
Lat/Lon: 42.56618/-85.36996
Email: rvcampground.michawana@gmail.com
Web: www.michawana.org

SEE AD PAGE 384

(N) Welcome Woods Campground—(Barry) *From west jct Hwy 37 & Hwy 43: Go 2 mi E on Hwy 37/Hwy 43, then 3-1/2 mi N on Hwy 43, then 1/2 mi E on Welcome Rd. Enter on R.* ◆◆◆FACILITIES: 75 sites, 50 W&E, (30/50 amps), 25 no hkups, WiFi Internet central location, family camping, tenting, dump, non-guest dump $, portable dump, laundry, ltd groc, RV supplies, ice, picnic tables, fire rings, wood. ◆◆◆RECREATION: pavilion, lake swim, boating, canoeing, kayaking, ramp, dock, lake fishing, fishing supplies, bsktball, playground, activities, horseshoes, hiking trails, v-ball. Pets welcome. Partial handicap access. Open April - Oct 15. Rate in 2010 $26-28 per family. MC/VISA/DISC/AMEX. Member ARVC, ARVCMI. CCUSA 50% Discount. CCUSA reservations Accepted, CCUSA max stay 4 days, CCUSA disc. not avail S, CCUSA disc. not avail F,Sa.

Phone: (269)945-2803
Address: 522 Welcome Rd, Hastings, MI 49058
Lat/Lon: 42.70034/-85.27978
Email: welcomewoods@yahoo.com
Web: www.welcomewoods.com

(NW) WHISPERING WATERS CAMPGROUND AND KAYAK RENTAL—(Barry) *From west jct Hwy 43 & Hwy 37: Go 3 mi N on Hwy 37, then 1/4 mi N on Irving Rd. Enter on L.*

◆◆◆FACILITIES: 88 sites, typical site width 35 ft, 47 full hkups, 13 W&E, 15 E, (20/30/50 amps), 13 no hkups, some extd stay sites (summer), 20 pull-thrus, family camping, tenting, RV storage, dump, portable dump, laundry, groceries, RV supplies, LP gas by weight/by meter, ice, picnic tables, fire rings, wood.

◆◆◆◆RECREATION: rec room/area, equipped pavilion, swim pool, canoeing, kayaking, 28 canoe/70 kayak rentals, float trips, river fishing, fishing supplies, golf nearby, playground, activities, (wkends), horseshoes, sports field, hiking trails, v-ball. Rec open to public.

Pets welcome, breed restrict. Partial handicap access. Open Apr (last) - Sep (last). Clubs welcome. Rate in 2010 $28-40 per family. MC/VISA/Debit. Member ARVC, ARVC MI.

Phone: (269)945-5166
Address: 1805 Irving Rd, Hastings, MI 49058
Lat/Lon: 42.67656/-85.38380
Email: whisper1805@gmail.com
Web: www.whisperingwatersonline.com

SEE AD THIS PAGE

(NW) WHISPERING WATERS KAYAK RENTAL—*From west jct Hwy 43 & Hwy 37: Go 3 mi N on Hwy 37, then 1/4 mi N on Irving Rd. Enter on L.* 1-1/4 to 8 hr kayak/canoe float trips down the Thornapple River. Family friendly river & livery. Free kayak lessons. Whispering Waters Campground is endpoint of all trips. Open Apr (last) - Sep (last). MC/VISA/Debit.

Phone: (269)945-5166
Address: 1805 Irving Rd, Hastings, MI 49058
Lat/Lon: 42.67656/-85.38380
Email: whisper1805@gmail.com
Web: www.whisperingwatersonline.com

SEE AD THIS PAGE

HESPERIA—G-2

(SW) MANISTEE NATIONAL FOREST (Pines Point Campground)—(Lake) *From town: Go 2 mi W on Hwy 20, then 1 mi S on 192nd Ave, then 3 mi W on Garfield, then 2-1/2 mi S on 168th Ave (FR 5118).* FACILITIES: 12 sites, 22 ft max RV length, 12 no hkups, 3 pull-thrus, tenting. RECREATION: boating, river fishing. Partial handicap access. Open May 7 - Sep 19. Phone: (231)723-2211.

HIGGINS LAKE—F-4

(SW) Great Circle Campground—(Roscommon) *From jct Hwy 55 & US 127: Go 7 mi N on US 127, then 4-1/4 mi E on Higgins Lake Rd/CR 104. Enter on L.* ◆◆◆FACILITIES: 57 sites, typical site width 45 ft, 12 full hkups, 36 W&E, (20/30/50 amps), 9 no hkups, 45 pull-thrus, WiFi Instant Internet at site, family camping, tenting, RV storage, dump, non-guest dump $, portable dump, laundry, ltd groc, RV supplies, ice, picnic tables,

fire rings, wood. ◆◆RECREATION: bsktball, playground, activities, horseshoes, hiking trails, v-ball. Pets welcome. Partial handicap access. Open May 1 - Oct 14. Rate in 2010 $22-30 for 4 persons. MC/VISA/DISC/Debit. CCUSA 50% Discount. CCUSA reservations Recommended, CCUSA max stay Unlimited, CCUSA disc. not avail S,Th, CCUSA disc. not avail F,Sa, CCUSA disc. not avail holidays.

Phone: (800)272-5428
Address: 5370 West Marl Lake Rd, Roscommon, MI 48653
Lat/Lon: 44.42129/-84.72150
Email: greatcirclecampground@gmail.com
Web: www.greatcirclecampground.net

(NE) Higgins Lake KOA—(Crawford) *From jct Hwy 18 & I-75: Go 5 mi N on I-75 (exit 244), then 1-1/4mi W on Federal Hwy. Enter on R.* ◆◆◆◆FACILITIES: 106 sites, typical site width 30 ft, 84 full hkups, 8 W&E, 2 E, (30/50 amps), 12 no hkups, 36 pull-thrus, family camping, tenting, dump, laundry, groceries. ◆◆◆◆RECREATION: playground. Pets welcome. Partial handicap access. Open May 1 - Nov 1. Rate in 2010 $28-56 for 2 persons. Member ARVC, ARVC MI. Phone: (800)562-3351. KOA discount.

HILLMAN—E-6

(S) EMERICK PARK—(Montmorency) *From jct Hwy 65S & Hwy 32: Go 7-1/2 mi W on Hwy 32, then 1/2 mi N on State St/CR F-21. Enter on L.*

FACILITIES: 22 sites, 11 full hkups, 9 W&E, (30/50 amps), 2 no hkups, family camping, tenting, dump, non-guest dump $, picnic tables, fire rings, grills.

RECREATION: pavilion, lake swim, boating, canoeing, kayaking, ramp, dock, lake/river fishing, golf nearby, playground, v-ball.

Pets welcome. Partial handicap access. Open May 1 - Oct 31. Clubs welcome.

Phone: (989)733-0613
Address: 351 S State St, Hillman, MI 49746
Lat/Lon: 45.06013/-83.90102
Email: hillman@freeway.net
Web: www.hillmanmichigan.org

SEE AD TRAVEL SECTION PAGE 359

(SE) Jack's Landing Resort—(Alpena) *From jct Hwy 65 & Hwy 32: Go 5-1/4 mi W on Hwy 32, then 4-1/2 mi S on Jack's Landing Rd, then 1/4 mi W on Palmateer Rd, then 1/2 mi S on Fishing Site Rd, then 3/4 mi W on Tennis Rd. Enter at end.* ◆◆◆FACILITIES: 30 sites, typical site width 30 ft, 9 W&E, 9 E, (20/30/50 amps), 12 no hkups, 1 pull-thrus, family camping, tenting, dump, ltd groc. ◆◆◆RECREATION: lake swim, boating, ramp, dock, lake fishing, playground. Pets welcome. Open all yr. Facilities fully operational May 1 - Oct 1. Rate in 2010 $25-30 for 4 persons. Phone: (989)742-4370.

(S) Lyons' Landing & Travel Trailer Park—(Alpena) *From east jct Hwy 33 & Hwy 32: Go 5-3/4 mi E on Hwy 32, then 3 mi S on Farrier Rd, then 1 mi E on Landing Rd. Enter on R.* ◆◆◆FACILITIES: 75 sites, typical site width 35 ft, 60 E, (20/30 amps), 15 no hkups, 20 pull-thrus, family camping, tenting, dump, ltd groc. ◆◆◆RECREATION: boating, ramp, dock, lake fishing, play equipment. Pets welcome. Partial handicap access. Open Mid May - Oct 31. Rate in 2010 $15-17 for 2 persons. Phone: (989)742-4756.

(E) Thunder Bay RV & Golf Resort—(Montmorency) *From jct Hwy 65 & Hwy 32: Go 6-1/2 mi W on Hwy 32. Enter on R.* ◆◆◆◆◆FACILITIES: 23 sites, typical site width 33 ft, accepts full hkup units only, 23 full hkups, (20/30/50 amps), 23 pull-thrus, cable TV, WiFi Instant Internet at site, picnic tables, patios, wood. ◆◆◆◆RECREATION: rec hall, pavilion, hot tub, float trips, river fishing, putting green, activities, tennis, horseshoes, hiking trails. Pets welcome. No tents. Open Apr 1 - Nov 1. Big rigs welcome. Rate in 2010 $24-39 for 4 persons. MC/VISA/DISC/AMEX/Debit. Member ARVC, ARVC MI. FMCA discount. CCUSA

50% Discount. CCUSA reservations Recommended, CCUSA max stay 2 days, CCUSA disc. not avail S, CCUSA disc. not avail F,Sa.

Phone: (800)729-9375
Address: 27800 M-32, Hillman, MI 49746
Lat/Lon: 45.05907/-83.88428
Email: tbg@thunderbaygolf.com
Web: www.thunderbayresort.com

HILLSDALE—J-4

(SE) 6 Lakes Campground—(Hillsdale) *From US 12 & Hwy 99: Go 7-1/2 mi S on Hwy 99. Enter on R.* ◆◆◆FACILITIES: 108 sites, typical site width 30 ft, 60 full hkups, 45 W&E, (20/30/50 amps), 3 no hkups, 10 pull-thrus, family camping, tenting, dump. ◆◆◆RECREATION: boating, ramp, dock, lake fishing, play equipment. Pets welcome, breed restrict, quantity restrict. Partial handicap access. Open May 1 - Nov 30. Rate in 2010 $26-30 for 2 persons. Member ARVC, ARVCMI. Phone: (517)439-5660.

(W) GATEWAY PARK CAMPGROUND—(Hillsdale) *From jct US 12 & Hwy 99: Go 1-1/4 mi S on Hwy 99, then 3-1/2 mi S on Lake Wilson Rd, then 1 mi W on Hallett Rd. Enter on L.*

ENJOY DELUXE FAMILY RESORT
Beautiful campground with 130 wooded acres located on South Sand Lake. Heated 50' pool. Free Wi-Fi & cable. Rental log Cabins & rental full-hookup trailers. Night/week/seasonal rates. www.gatewayparkcampground.com.

◆◆◆◆FACILITIES: 99 sites, typical site width 30 ft, 83 full hkups, 6 W&E, 10 E, (20/30/50 amps), many extd stay sites (summer), 9 pull-thrus, cable TV, WiFi Instant Internet at site, family camping, tenting, RV's/park model rentals, cabins, dump, non-guest dump $, portable dump, laundry, ltd groc, RV supplies, LP gas by weight/by meter, ice, picnic tables, patios, fire rings, wood, controlled access.

◆◆◆◆RECREATION: rec hall, coin games, swim pool, boating, canoeing, kayaking, ramp, dock, pontoon/rowboat/2 kayak/3 pedal boat rentals, lake fishing, fishing supplies, golf nearby, bsktball, 8 bike rentals, playground, activities, (wkends), horseshoes, v-ball.

Pets welcome. Partial handicap access. Open Apr 15 - Oct 15. Big rigs welcome. Escort to site. Clubs welcome. Green Friendly. Rate in 2010 $32-44 for 3 persons. MC/VISA/DISC. Member ARVC, ARVC MI. CCUSA 50% Discount. CCUSA reservations Recommended, CCUSA max stay 4 days, CCUSA disc. not avail F,Sa, CCUSA disc. not avail holidays.

Phone: (517)437-7005
Address: 4111 W Hallett Rd, Hillsdale, MI 49242
Lat/Lon: 41.91175/-84.69057
Email: gatecamp@modempool.com
Web: www.gatewayparkcampground.com

SEE AD THIS PAGE

(SW) Sugar Bush Campground—(Hillsdale) *From jct US 12 & Hwy 99: Go 1-1/4 mi S on Hwy 99, then 4-1/2 mi S on Lake Wilson Rd, then 2 mi W on Bankers/Cole Rd, then 1/2 mi S on Sand Lake Rd. Enter on L.* ◆◆◆FACILITIES: 45 sites, 45 W&E, (30 amps), 6 pull-thrus, WiFi Internet central location, family camping, tenting, dump, non-guest dump $, portable dump, ltd groc, RV supplies, ice, picnic tables, fire rings, wood. ◆◆◆RECREATION: pavilion, lake swim, pond fishing, bsktball, playground, activities, hiking trails, v-ball. Pets welcome, breed restrict. Partial handicap access. Open May 15 - Oct 15. Rate in 2010 $26 per family. MC/VISA. CCUSA 50% Discount. CCUSA

Sugar Bush Campground—Continued on next page

HILLSDALE—Continued
Sugar Bush Campground—Continued

reservations Required, CCUSA max stay 30 days, CCUSA disc. not avail holidays. All visitors $3/day. Honey wagon charge $7.

Phone: (517)439-9525
Address: 2571 South Sand Lake Rd, Hillsdale, MI 49242
Lat/Lon: 41.89050/-84.70923
Email: camp@sugarbushcampground.com
Web: www.sugarbushcampground.com

HOLLAND—I-2

See listings at Allegan, Allendale, Coopersville, Dorr, Grand Haven, Hopkins, Hudsonville, Spring Lake & Zeeland

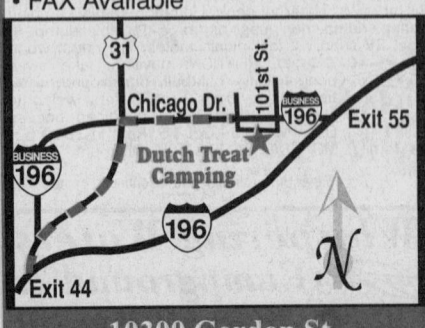

WELCOME (W) **BEACHSIDE BIKE RENTALS**—*From N jct Bus I-96 & US 31: Go 1/2 mi N on US 31, then 1-1/2 mi W on Lakewood Blvd, then 1-1/2 mi W on Douglas, then 3 mi W on Ottawa Beach Rd. Enter on R.* Single & 21 speed, kids' bikes, tandems, children's pull behind and baby seats. Hourly, daily or weekly rentals. Bike helmets provided with each bike rental. Bike to Holland State Park, downtown Holland, Grand Haven, Veldheer Tulip Gardens & more. Open Apr 25 - Early Oct. MC/VISA/DISC/Debit.

Phone: (616)399-9230
Address: 2011 Ottawa Beach Rd, Holland, MI 49424
Email: oakgrovecampground@yahoo.com
Web: www.oakgroveresort.com

SEE AD THIS PAGE

HOLLAND—Continued
BEACHSIDE BIKE RENTALS—Continued

(N) **Drews Country Camping**—(Ottawa) *From north jct Bus I-196 & US 31: Go 3-1/2 mi N on US 31. Enter on R.* ◆◆FACILITIES: 86 sites, 86 W&E, (20/30/50 amps), 13 pull-thrus, family camping, tenting, dump, laundry. ◆◆RECREATION: swim pool, playground. Pets welcome. Open Apr 15 - Nov 1. Facilities fully operational Memorial Day - Labor Day. Rate in 2010 $27-30 for 2 persons. Phone: (616)399-1886.

WELCOME **DUTCH TREAT CAMPING & RECREATION**—*From Holland: Go 2-1/4 mi E on Bus I-196, then 1/4 mi E on Gordon Ave (Service Rd). Enter on R.*

SEE PRIMARY LISTING AT ZEELAND AND AD THIS PAGE

(W) HOLLAND STATE PARK—(Ottawa) *From town: Go 8 mi W on Ottawa Beach Rd.* FACILITIES: 309 sites, 31 full hkups, 211 E, (50 amps), 67 no hkups, 5 pull-thrus, tenting, dump, laundry, ltd groc. RECREATION: lake swim, boating, ramp, lake fishing, playground. Partial handicap access. Open Apr 1 - Nov 1. Facilities fully operational Apr 15 - Oct 15. Phone: (616)399-9390.

WELCOME (W) **OAK GROVE CAMPGROUND RESORT**—(Ottawa) *From north jct Bus I-96 & US 31: Go 2 mi N on US 31, then 1-1/2 mi W on Lakewood Blvd, then 1-1/2 mi W on Douglas, then 3 mi W on Ottawa Beach Rd. Enter on R.*

◆◆◆◆◆FACILITIES: 135 sites, typical site width 35 ft, 135 full hkups, (20/30/50 amps), some extd stay sites (summer), cable TV, WiFi Instant Internet at site, family camping, RV's/park model rentals, cabins, laundry, groceries, RV supplies, LP gas by weight/by meter, ice, picnic tables, patios, fire rings, wood, controlled access.

◆◆◆◆RECREATION: rec hall, rec room/area, swim pool, hot tub, golf nearby, bsktball, 20 bike rentals, playground, activities, (wkends), hiking trails.

Pets welcome ($). Partial handicap access. No tents. Open Apr 25 - Early Oct. Big rigs welcome. Clubs welcome. Rate in 2010 $35-48 for 2 persons. MC/VISA/DISC/Debit. Member ARVC, ARVC MI.

Rogers City boasts the world's largest limestone quarry.

HOLLAND—Continued
OAK GROVE CAMPGROUND RESORT—Continued

Phone: (616)399-9230
Address: 2011 Ottawa Beach Rd, Holland, MI 49424
Lat/Lon: 42.78355/-86.19228
Email: oakgrovecampground@yahoo.com
Web: www.oakgroveresort.com

SEE AD THIS PAGE

HOLLY—I-5

(NE) **Holly KOA Fun Park**—(Oakland) *From jct Hwy 15 & I-75: Go 11 mi N on I-75 (exit 101), then 100 yds E on Grange Hall Rd. Enter on R.* ◆◆◆FACILITIES: 121 sites, typical site width 30 ft, 6 full hkups, 90 W&E, 25 E, (20/30/50 amps), 47 pull-thrus, family camping, tenting, dump, laundry, groceries. ◆◆◆◆◆RECREATION: swim pool, playground. Pets welcome. Partial handicap access. Open Apr 1 - Dec 31. Facilities fully operational Memorial Day - Oct 1. Rate in 2010 $30-52 for 2 persons. Member ARVC, ARVC MI. Phone: (800) 562-3962. KOA discount.

(E) HOLLY STATE RECREATION AREA—(Oakland) *From I-75 (exit 101): Go 1 mi E on Grange Hall Rd, then 3/4 mi on McGinais Rd to park entrance.* FACILITIES: 159 sites, 144 E, 15 no hkups, tenting. RECREATION: lake swim, boating, electric motors only, canoeing, ramp, lake fishing, playground. Partial handicap access. Open Apr 4 - Nov 3. Phone: (248)634-8811.

(SW) SEVEN LAKES STATE PARK—(Oakland) *From I-75 (exit 101): Go 4-7/10 mi SW on Grange Hall Rd, then 1/10 mi N on Fagan Rd, then bear left on Quick Rd 2 mi, then N 1/2 mi on Fish Lake Rd, then E 1-3/5 mi on Tinsman Rd.* FACILITIES: 70 sites, 70 E, tenting, dump, ltd groc. RECREATION: lake swim, boating, canoeing, ramp, lake fishing, playground. Partial handicap access. Open Apr 1 - Nov 1. Phone: (248)634-7271.

HOLTON—H-2

(N) BLUE LAKE COUNTY PARK (Muskegon County Park)—(Muskegon) *From jct Hwy 120 & US 31 (Russell Rd exit): Go 10-1/4 mi N on Russell Rd (CR B23), then 1 mi E on Owassippi Rd, then 1/4 mi N on Nichols Rd.* FACILITIES: 25 sites, 25 W&E, tenting, dump. RECREATION: lake swim, boating, ramp, lake fishing, playground. Open May 15 - Sep 15. Phone: (231)744-3580.

(NW) **Oak Knoll Family Campground**—(Muskegon) *From jct US 31 & CR B-86/Fruitvale Rd: Go 10 mi E on Fruitvale Rd (CR B-86). Enter on L.* ◆◆◆FACILITIES: 60 sites, typical site width 30 ft, 5 full hkups, 17 W&E, 20 E, (20/30 amps), 18 no hkups, 1 pull-thrus, family camping, tenting, dump, laundry, ltd groc. ◆◆RECREATION: playground. Pets welcome. Open May - mid Oct. Rate in 2010 $23-37 for 4 persons. Phone: (231)894-6063.

HONOR—E-3

(SE) PERE MARQUETTE SF (Platte River)—(Benzie) *From town: Go 2-1/2 mi SE on US 31, then S on Goose Rd. Enter on R.* FACILITIES: 26 sites, 26 no hkups, tenting. RECREATION: river swim, canoeing, ramp, river fishing. Open all yr. Phone: (231)922-5280.

(E) PERE MARQUETTE SF (Veteran's Memorial)—(Benzie) *From town: Go 3-1/2 mi E on US 31. Enter on R.* FACILITIES: 24 sites, 24 no hkups, tenting. RECREATION: canoeing, ramp, river fishing. Open all yr. Phone: (231)922-5280.

(NW) SLEEPING BEAR DUNES NATIONAL LAKESHORE (Platte River Campground)—(Benzie) *From jct US 31 & Hwy 708: Go 5 mi NW on Hwy 708, then 3/4 mi W on Hwy 22, then 1/4 mi NW on Lake Michigan Rd. Enter on R.* FACILITIES: 179 sites, 96 W&E, (30 amps), 83 no hkups, tenting, dump. RECREATION: river swim, boating, ramp, dock, lake/river fishing. Partial handicap access. Open all yr. Phone: (231)325-5881.

HOPKINS—I-3

(N) **East Lake Camping**—(Allegan) *From jct Hwy 179 & US 131: Go 3 mi N on US 131 (exit 64), then 3 mi W on 135th Ave, then 2-1/2 mi S on 18th St, then 2-1/2 mi W on 130th Ave, then 1/4 mi N on Weick Dr. Enter on R.* ◆◆◆FACILITIES: 110 sites, typical site width 25 ft, 13 full hkups, 82 W&E, (20/30/50 amps), 15 no hkups, 3 pull-thrus, family camping, tenting, dump, laundry, groceries. ◆◆◆◆RECREATION: lake swim, boating, canoeing, ramp, dock, lake fishing, playground. Pets welcome, breed restrict. Partial handicap access. Open May 1 - Oct 1. Rate in 2010 $34-37 per family. Member ARVC, ARVC MI. Phone: (269)793-7177.

WELCOME (SE) **HIDDEN RIDGE RV RESORT**—(Allegan) *From jct Hwy 179 & US 131: Go 2 mi S on US 131 (exit 59), then 1/4 mi S on 12th St. Enter on R.*

DELUXE RV RESORT IN WEST MICHIGAN
Located in the beautiful countryside of West Michigan, Hidden Ridge resort provides the rustic environment you desire, along with activities and amenities to make your camping experience memorable. come find out for yourself!

◆◆◆◆◆FACILITIES: 277 sites, typical site width 40 ft, 277 full hkups, (20/30/50 amps), some extd stay sites (summer), 12 pull-thrus, cable TV, WiFi Instant Internet at site, WiFi Internet central

HIDDEN RIDGE RV RESORT—Continued on next page

HOPKINS—Continued
HIDDEN RIDGE RV RESORT—Continued

location, family camping, RV storage, dump, non-guest dump $, laundry, ltd groc, RV supplies, LP gas by weight/by meter, ice, picnic tables, patios, fire rings, wood, controlled access.

◇◇◇◇◇RECREATION: rec hall, rec room/area, pavilion, coin games, swim pool, hot tub, boating, no motors, dock, 2 rowboat/2 pedal boat rentals, lake fishing, fishing supplies, golf nearby, bsktball, playground, shuffleboard court 2 shuffleboard courts, activities, tennis, horseshoes, hiking trails, v-ball.

Pets welcome, breed restrict, quantity restrict. Partial handicap access. No tents. Open Apr 1 - Oct 31. Big rigs welcome. Escort to site. Clubs welcome. Rate in 2010 $39-49 per family. MC/VISA. ATM. Member ARVC, ARVCMI.

Text 108019 to (440)725-8687 to see our Visual Tour.

Phone: (877)RV STAYS
Address: 2306 12th St, Hopkins, MI 49328
Lat/Lon: 42.59039/-85.66360
Email: manager@hiddenridgerv.com
Web: www.hiddenridgerv.com

SEE AD TRAVEL SECTION PAGE 362

(SE) Miller Lake Campground—(Allegan) *From jct Hwy 179 & US 131: Go 2 mi S on US 131 (exit 59), then 1 mi S on 12th St, then 1/4 mi S on Entrance Rd. Enter at end.* ◇◇◇FACILITIES: 73 sites, typical site width 25 ft, 34 full hkups, 39 W&E, (20/30/50 amps), family camping, tenting, dump, laundry, ltd groc. ◇◇◇RECREATION: lake swim, boating, 25 hp limit, canoeing, ramp, dock, lake fishing, playground. Pets welcome, breed restrict. Open May 1 - Oct 1. Rate in 2010 $28-30 for 4 persons. Member ARVC, ARVC MI. Phone: (269)672-7139.

(NW) Sandy Pines RV Resort & Campground—(Allegan) *From jct Hwy 179 & US 131: Go 7 mi N on US 131 (exit 68), then 9 mi W on 142nd, then 2 mi S on A 37, then 1 mi E on 138th, then 1 mi S on 12th St. Enter on L.* ◇◇◇◇FACILITIES: 65 sites, typical site width 40 ft, 65 W&E, (30/50 amps), family camping, tenting, dump, laundry, groceries. ◇◇◇◇◇RECREATION: 5 swim pools, lake swim, boating, ramp, dock, lake fishing, playground. Pets welcome. Partial handicap access. Open Apr 15 - Oct 15. Rate in 2010 $42 per family. Member ARVC, MIARVC. Phone: (616)896-8315.

HOUGHTON—A-1

(W) HOUGHTON RV PARK (City Park)—(Hougton) *From jct US 41 & Hwy 26: Go 1/2 mi W, then 2/10 mi N on Lake Ave. Enter on L.* FACILITIES: 22 sites, typical site width 24 ft, accepts full hkup units only, 22 full hkups, (20/30/50 amps). RECREATION: lake swim, boating, canoeing, ramp, dock, lake fishing, play equipment. Pets welcome. No tents. Open May 1 - Oct 7. Phone: (906)482-8745.

HOUGHTON LAKE—F-4

(N) AU SABLE SF (Houghton Lake)—(Roscommon) *From jct US 27 & Hwy 55: Go 6 mi E on Hwy 55, then 6 mi N on West Shore Dr, then E on CR-300.* FACILITIES: 50 sites, 36 ft max RV length, 50 no hkups, tenting. RECREATION: lake swim, boating, ramp, lake fishing. Open all yr. Facilities fully operational Apr 20 - Sep 15. Phone: (989)275-4622.

(NW) AU SABLE SF (Reedsburg Dam)—(Roscommon) *From jct US 27 & Hwy 55: Go 1 mi E on Hwy 55, then 2 mi N on CR 300.* FACILITIES: 42 sites, 42 no hkups, tenting. RECREATION: lake swim, boating, canoeing, ramp, lake fishing. Open all yr. Phone: (989)275-4622.

(NW) HOUGHTON LAKE TRAVEL PARK—(Roscommon) *From jct US 127 & Hwy 55: Go 200 yards E on Hwy 55, then 1/4 mi S on Cloverleaf Lane. Enter on R.*

◇◇FACILITIES: 85 sites, 27 full hkups, 45 W&E, (20/30/50 amps), 13 no hkups, some extd stay sites (summer), 72 pull-thrus, cable TV, WiFi Instant Internet at site, family camping, tenting, cabins, RV storage, dump, non-guest dump $, portable dump, laundry, ltd groc, RV supplies, LP gas by weight/by meter, ice, picnic tables, fire rings, wood.

◇◇RECREATION: rec room/area, coin games, swim pool, golf nearby, bsktball, playground, horseshoes, sports field, v-ball. Rec open to public.

Pets welcome. Open Apr 1 - Oct 1. Big rigs welcome. Clubs welcome. Rate in 2010 $30-43 for 3 persons. MC/VISA/Debit. Member ARVC, ARVC MI. CCUSA 50% Discount. CCUSA reservations Recommended, CCUSA max stay 5 days, CCUSA disc. not avail Th, CCUSA disc. not avail F,Sa, CCUSA disc. not avail holidays. Discount not available month of Jul.

Michigan Nickname: Wolverine State

HOUGHTON LAKE—Continued
HOUGHTON LAKE TRAVEL PARK—Continued

Phone: (800)659-9379
Address: 370 Cloverleaf Lane, Houghton Lake, MI 48629
Lat/Lon: 44.32919/-84.80350
Email: hltp89@charter.net
Web: www.houghtonlaketravelpark.com

SEE AD THIS PAGE

(W) WEST HOUGHTON LAKE CAMPGROUND—(Roscommon) *From jct US-127 & Hwy-55: Go 1/2 mi E on Hwy-55, then 1/4 mi N on Old Hwy-127. Enter on L.*

◇◇◇FACILITIES: 127 sites, typical site width 28 ft, 46 full hkups, 28 W&E, 40 E, (30/50 amps), 7 no hkups, many extd stay sites (summer), 2 pull-thrus, WiFi Instant Internet at site, family camping, tenting, RV's/park model rentals, cabins, RV storage, dump, non-guest dump $, laundry, ltd groc, RV supplies, LP gas by weight/by meter, ice, picnic tables, fire rings, wood.

◇◇RECREATION: rec room/area, pavilion, coin games, golf nearby, bsktball, playground, shuffleboard court shuffleboard court, activities (wkends), horseshoes, sports field, hiking trails, v-ball.

Pets welcome. Open all yr. Facilities fully operational mid Apr - mid Oct. Clubs welcome. Green Friendly. Rate in 2010 $25-33 for 4 persons. MC/VISA/DISC/Debit. Member ARVC, ARVCMI. CCUSA 50% Discount. CCUSA reservations Not Accepted, CCUSA max stay 5 days, CCUSA disc. not avail F,Sa, CCUSA disc. not avail holidays. No water to sites Oct 15-Apr 15.

Phone: (989)422-5130
Address: 9371 W. Houghton Lake Dr, Houghton Lake, MI 48629
Lat/Lon: 44.34029/-84.79360
Email: whlc_2003@verizon.net
Web: www.westhoughtonlakecampground.com

SEE AD TRAVEL SECTION PAGE 359

(W) Wooded Acres Campground—(Roscommon) *From jct US 127 & Hwy 55: Go 2 mi E on Hwy 55, then 1 mi S on Loxley. Enter on L.* ◇◇◇FACILITIES: 88 sites, typical site width 30 ft, 40 ft max RV length, 12 full hkups, 46 W&E, 25 E, (20/30/50 amps), 5 no hkups, 18 pull-thrus, family camping, tenting, dump, laundry, ltd groc. ◇◇◇RECREATION: swim pool, pond fishing, playground. Pets welcome. Open all yr. Facilities fully operational May 15 - Oct 15. Rate in 2010 $23-38 for 4 persons. Member ARVC, ARVC MI. Phone: (989)422-3413.

HOWELL—I-5

(SE) LAKE CHEMUNG OUTDOOR RESORT—(Livingston) *From jct US 23 & I-96: Go 3 mi W on I-96 (exit 145), then 3 mi NW on Grand River Ave, then 2 mi N on Hughes Rd. Enter on L.*

◇◇◇◇FACILITIES: 340 sites, typical site width 30 ft, 340 full hkups, (30/50 amps), mostly extd stay sites, WiFi Internet central location, family camping, laundry, groceries, LP bottle exch, ice, picnic tables, patios, fire rings, wood, controlled access.

◇◇◇◇◇RECREATION: rec hall, rec room/area, pavilion, swim pool, lake swim, boating, canoeing, kayaking, lake/pond fishing, fishing supplies, mini-golf, golf nearby, bsktball, playground, shuffleboard court 2 shuffleboard courts, activities, tennis, horseshoes, sports field, v-ball.

Pets welcome, quantity restrict. Partial handicap access. No tents. Open all yr. Facilities fully operational Memorial Day - Labor Day. Mid May thru mid Sep daily rates apply. Big rigs welcome. Escort to site. Member ARVC, ARVCMI.

Michigan State Flower: Apple Blossom

HOWELL—Continued
LAKE CHEMUNG OUTDOOR RESORT—Continued

Phone: (517)546-6361
Address: 320 S Hughes Rd, Howell, MI 48843
Lat/Lon: 42.59304/-83.85342
Email: lcori@comcast.net
Web: www.lcori.com

SEE AD TRAVEL SECTION PAGE 361

(NW) TAYLOR'S BEACH CAMPGROUND—(Livingston) *From jct I-96 & Hwy 59 (exit 133): Go 500 ft NE on Hwy 59, then 5-1/4 mi N on Burkhart Rd. Enter on L.*

◇◇◇FACILITIES: 193 sites, typical site width 35 ft, 48 full hkups, 145 W&E, (20/30/50 amps), mostly extd stay sites (summer), heater not allowed, cable TV, WiFi Instant Internet at site, family camping, tenting, RV's/park model rentals, RV storage, dump, non-guest dump $, portable dump, laundry, ltd groc, RV supplies, LP bottle exch, ice, picnic tables, fire rings, wood, controlled access.

◇◇◇◇RECREATION: rec room/area, pavilion, coin games, lake swim, boating, 10 hp limit, dock, 8 rowboat/2 kayak/3 pedal boat rentals, lake/pond fishing, fishing supplies, golf nearby, bsktball, 6 bike rentals, playground, activities, (wkends), horseshoes, sports field, hiking trails, v-ball.

Pets welcome, breed restrict. Open Apr 1 - Nov 1. Facilities fully operational Memorial Day - Labor Day. Clubs welcome. Rate in 2010 $36-48 for 4 persons. MC/VISA/DISC/AMEX/Debit.

Phone: (517)546-2679
Address: 6197 N Burkhart, Howell, MI 48855
Lat/Lon: 42.68829/-83.99641
Email: info@taylorsbeachcampground.com
Web: www.taylorsbeachcampground.com

Reserve Online at Woodalls.com

SEE AD THIS PAGE

HUDSONVILLE—H-3

(NW) Baldwin Oaks Campground—(Ottawa) *From jct I-196 (exit 62) & CR A 37/32nd Ave: Go 4-1/2 mi N on 32nd Ave/Balsam/28th Ave, then 3 mi W on Baldwin St. Enter on L.* ◇◇◇FACILITIES: 126 sites, typical site width 35 ft, 126 W&E, (20/30/50 amps), 2 pull-thrus, family camping, tenting, dump, laundry. ◇◇◇RECREATION: swim pool, playground. Pets welcome, breed restrict. Partial handicap access. Open May 1 - Oct 1. Rate in 2010 $30 for 4 persons. Phone: (616)669-1600.

(NW) Chapel in the Pines Campground—(Ottawa) *From jct I-196 (exit 62) & CR A 37/32nd Ave: Go 3 mi N on 32nd Ave, then 4-1/2 mi W on Port Sheldon Rd, then 1/2 mi N on 64th Ave. Enter on L.* ◇◇◇FACILITIES: 100 sites, typical site width 30 ft, 74 W&E, 26 E, (20/30 amps), 1 pull-thrus, family camping, tenting, dump, laundry. ◇◇◇RECREATION: lake/boating, 10 hp limit, pond fishing, playground. Pets welcome, breed restrict. Partial handicap access. Open May 1 - Sep 30. Rate in 2010 $25-35 for 4 persons.

Phone: (616)875-8928
Address: 6881 64th Ave, Hudsonville, MI 49426
Lat/Lon: 42.89373/-85.94122
Web: www.chapelinthepinescampground.com

Michigan has the longest freshwater shoreline in the world.

INDIAN RIVER—D-5

(SW) BURT LAKE STATE PARK—(Cheboygan) *From I-75 (exit 310): Go 1/4 mi W.* FACILITIES: 306 sites, 306 E, (20/30 amps), tenting, dump, ltd groc. RECREATION: lake swim, boating, ramp, lake/river fishing, playground. Partial handicap access. Open Apr - Nov. Phone: (231)238-9392.

(N) Indian River RV Resort & Campground—(Cheboygan) *From jct Hwy 68 & I-75: Go 3 mi N on I-75 (exit 313), then 1-1/2 mi N on Hwy 27. Enter on L.* ◊◊◊◊FACILITIES: 150 sites, typical site width 35 ft, 97 full hkups, 43 W&E, (30/50 amps), 10 no hkups, 97 pull-thrus, family camping, tenting, dump, laundry, groceries. ◊◊◊RECREATION: swim pool, playground. Pets welcome. Partial handicap access. Open Apr - Oct. Rate in 2010 $27-41 per family. Member ARVC, ARVC MI. Phone: (888)792-CAMP.

(SE) Yogi Bear's Jellystone Park Indian River—(Cheboygan) *From jct I-75 (exit 310) & Hwy 68: Go 4 mi E on Hwy 68. Enter on R.* ◊◊◊FACILITIES: 164 sites, typical site width 30 ft, 31 full hkups, 56 W&E, 57 E, (20/30/50 amps), 20 no hkups, 36 pull-thrus, family camping, tenting, RV storage, dump, non-guest dump $, laundry, groceries, RV supplies, LP gas by weight/by meter, ice, picnic tables, fire rings, wood. ◊◊◊◊RECREATION: pavilion, swim pool, mini-golf, ($), bsktball, playground, shuffleboard court 2 shuffleboard courts, activities, horseshoes, hiking trails, v-ball. Pets welcome, breed restrict, quantity restrict. Partial handicap access. Open May 15 - Sep 30. Rate in 2010 $30-45 for 4 persons. MC/VISA/DISC/Debit. Member ARVC, ARVC MI. CCUSA 50% Discount. CCUSA reservations Accepted, CCUSA max stay 4 days, CCUSA disc. not avail S, CCUSA disc. not avail F,Sa, CCUSA disc. not avail holidays.

Phone: (231)238-8259
Address: 2201 E. M-68, Indian River, MI 49749
Lat/Lon: 45.37440/-84.53180
Email: ybear183@hughes.net
Web: www.jellystoneindianriver.com

INTERLOCHEN—E-4

(S) INTERLOCHEN STATE PARK—(Manistee) *From jct US 31 & Hwy 137: Go 2 mi S on Hwy 137.* FACILITIES: 480 sites, 30 ft max RV length, 418 E, 62 no hkups, tenting, dump, groceries. RECREATION: lake swim, boating, ramp, dock, lake fishing, playground. Partial handicap access. Open Apr 15 - Dec 1. Phone: (231)276-9511.

IONIA—H-3

(S) Alice Springs RV Park & Resort—(Ionia) *From jct I-96 & Hwy 66: Go 2 mi N on Hwy 66. Enter on R.* ◊◊◊◊FACILITIES: 140 sites, 140 full hkups, (30/50 amps), family camping, tenting, dump, laundry, groceries. ◊◊◊◊RECREATION: swim pool, no motors, canoeing, pond fishing, playground. Pets welcome. Partial handicap access. Open May - Nov 1. Big rigs welcome. Rate in 2010 $37 for 2 persons. Member ARVC, ARVCMI. Phone: (616)527-1608.

(SW) IONIA STATE RECREATION AREA—(Ionia) *From jct Hwy 66 & I-96: Go 3 mi W on I-96, then 3-1/2 mi N on Jordan Lake Rd.* FACILITIES: 100 sites, 100 E, tenting, dump. RECREATION: lake swim, boating, canoeing, ramp, lake/river/stream fishing. Open Apr 1 - Dec 1. Facilities fully operational May 1 - Oct 15. Phone: (616)527-3750.

IRISH HILLS—J-4

See listings at Cement City, Chelsea, Clayton, Concord, Grass Lake, Hillsdale, Jackson, Jonesville, Moscow, Onsted, Somerset Center, Tecumseh & Tipton

IRON MOUNTAIN—D-1

(N) Rivers Bend Campground—(Dickinson) *From west jct US 2 & Hwy 95 (north side of Iron Mountain): Go 1/2 mi W on US 2, then 1/2 mi SW on Pine Mountain Rd. Enter on R.* ◊◊◊FACILITIES: 155 sites, typical site width 35 ft, 48 full hkups, 107 W&E, (20/30/50 amps), 30 pull-thrus, family camping, tenting, dump, laundry. ◊◊◊RECREATION: lake swim, boating, canoeing, ramp, dock, river fishing, playground. Pets welcome. Open Apr 15 - Oct 15. Big rigs welcome. Rate in 2010 $23-25 per vehicle. Phone: (906)779-1171.

(N) SUMMER BREEZE CAMPGROUND & RV PARK—(Dickinson) *From west jct US 2 & Hwy 95: Go 1-1/4 mi N on Hwy 95, then 1/4 mi W on Twin Falls Rd. Enter on R.*

◊◊◊FACILITIES: 69 sites, typical site width 40 ft, 28 full hkups, 41 W&E, (20/30/50 amps), 50 amps ($), 40 pull-thrus, WiFi Instant Internet at site, WiFi Internet central location, family camping, tenting, RV storage, dump, non-guest dump $, laundry, ltd groc, RV supplies, ice, picnic tables, fire rings, wood.

◊◊RECREATION: swim pool, golf nearby, bsktball, playground, activities, (wkends), horseshoes, sports field, hiking trails, v-ball.

Pets welcome. Partial handicap access. Open May 1 - Oct 15. Big rigs welcome. Escort to site. Clubs welcome. Rate in 2010 $18-26 for 4 persons. MC/VISA/Debit. Member ARVC, ARVC MI. CCUSA 50% Discount. CCUSA reservations Recommended, CCUSA max stay 3 days, Cash only for CCUSA disc., CCUSA disc. not avail F,Sa, CCUSA disc. not avail holidays. Not available on full hookup sites.

Phone: (906)774-7701
Address: W 8576 Twin Falls Rd., Iron Mountain, MI 49801
Lat/Lon: 45.88155/-88.05643
Email: sbreeze@charter.net
Web: www.summerbreezecampground.com

SEE AD THIS PAGE

IRON RIVER—C-1

IRON RIVER RV PARK (City Park)—(Iron) *In town at E end of Genesee St (US 2).* FACILITIES: 32 sites, 18 full hkups, 14 W&E, tenting, dump. RECREATION: canoeing, river fishing. Partial handicap access. Open all yr. Facilities fully operational May 1 - Oct 31. Phone: (906)265-3822.

(SW) OTTAWA NATIONAL FOREST (Lake Ottawa Campground)—(Iron) *From jct Hwy-189 & US-2: Go 1-1/3 mi W on US-2, then 1/2 mi SW on Hwy-73, then 4 mi W on FR-101.* FACILITIES: 31 sites, 22 ft max RV length, 31 no hkups, tenting, dump. RECREATION: lake swim, boating, ramp, lake fishing, playground. Partial handicap access. Open May 26 - Oct 1. Phone: (906)265-5139.

IRONS—F-3

(SW) Leisure Time Campground—(Lake) *From north jct US 10 & Hwy 37: Go 8 mi N on Hwy 37, then 7-1/2 mi W on 4 Mile Rd/5 Mile Rd. Enter on R.* ◊◊◊FACILITIES: 90 sites, typical site width 35 ft, 6 full hkups, 56 W&E, (20/30/50 amps), 28 no hkups, 2 pull-thrus, cable TV, WiFi Instant Internet at site, WiFi Internet central location, family camping, tenting, RV storage, dump, non-guest dump $, portable dump, laundry, ltd groc, RV supplies, LP gas by weight/by meter, ice, picnic tables, fire rings, wood. ◊◊◊RECREATION: pavilion, swim pool, lake swim, boating, electric motors only, canoeing, kayaking, dock, lake fishing, fishing supplies, bsktball, 6 bike rentals, playground, horseshoes, hiking trails, v-ball. Pets welcome. Partial handicap access. Open Apr 1 - Nov 30. Rate in 2010 $24-30 per vehicle. MC/VISA/Debit. Member ARVC, ARVC MI. CCUSA 50% Discount. CCUSA reservations Recommended, CCUSA max stay 3 days, CCUSA disc. not avail F,Sa, CCUSA disc. not avail holidays.

Phone: (800)266-8214
Address: 9214 W Five Mile, Irons, MI 49644
Lat/Lon: 44.05991/-85.98139
Email: ltc@leisuretimecampground.com
Web: www.leisuretimecampground.com

Michigan State Tree: White Pine

ISHPEMING—C-2

(N) Country Village RV Park—(Marquette) *From jct Hwy 35 & US 41/Hwy 28: Go 7 mi W on US 41/Hwy 28, then 1/4 mi N on Country Lane. Enter at end.* ◊◊◊◊FACILITIES: 105 sites, typical site width 60 ft, 48 full hkups, 47 W&E, (20/30/50 amps), 10 no hkups, 24 pull-thrus, family camping, tenting, dump, laundry, ltd groc. ◊◊◊RECREATION: swim pool, playground. Pets welcome. Partial handicap access. Open May 15 - Oct 15. Rate in 2010 $23.99-38.99 for 5 persons. Member ARVC, ARVCMI. Phone: (906)486-0300.

ITHACA—H-4

(SE) Just-In-Time Campground—(Gratiot) *From jct Hwy 57 & US 127: Go 8 mi N on US 127, then 7 mi E on Washington Rd, then 2 mi S on Ransom, then 1/2 mi E on Pierce Rd. Enter on L.* ◊◊◊FACILITIES: 63 sites, typical site width 30 ft, 31 full hkups, 29 W&E, (20/30/50 amps), 3 no hkups, family camping, tenting, dump, laundry, ltd groc. ◊◊◊RECREATION: lake swim, boating, electric motors only, canoeing, lake fishing, playground. Pets welcome, quantity restrict. Partial handicap access. Open May 1 - Oct 15. Rate in 2010 $30 for 4 persons. Member ARVC, ARVC MI. Phone: (989)875-2865.

JACKSON—I-4

(E) GREENWOOD ACRES FAMILY CAMPGROUND—(Jackson) *From jct US 127 S & I-94: Go 5 mi E on I-94 (exit 147), then 1 block S on Race Rd, then 3/4 mi W on Ann Arbor Rd, then 1-1/4 mi S on Portage Rd, then 1/2 mi E on Greenwood Rd, then N on Hilton. Enter on L.*

AN UNFORGETTABLE CAMPING EXPERIENCE

Large RVs to tents welcome. Join our campers that come from all parts of the country to relax and have fun at the pool, beach, golf course, rec center, cafe, and store. Enjoy visiting or take part in an activity or two.

◊◊◊FACILITIES: 1080 sites, typical site width 40 ft, 500 full hkups, 580 W&E, (20/30/50 amps), many extd stay sites (summer), 35 pull-thrus, heater not allowed, WiFi Instant Internet at site, WiFi Internet central location, family camping, tenting, dump, portable dump, laundry, ltd groc, RV supplies, LP gas by weight/by meter, ice, picnic tables, fire rings, wood, controlled access.

◊◊◊◊RECREATION: rec hall, rec room/area, pavilion, coin games, swim pool, lake swim, boating, 5 hp limit, canoeing, kayaking, ramp, dock, lake fishing, fishing supplies, mini-golf, golf nearby, bsktball, playground, activities, (wkends), tennis, horseshoes, sports field, hiking trails, v-ball.

Pets welcome. Partial handicap access. Open April 1 - Oct 31. Facilities fully operational Memorial Day - Labor Day. Clubs welcome. Rate in 2010 $31-40 per family. MC/VISA/Debit. ATM. Member ARVC, ARVC MI. CCUSA 50% Discount. CCUSA reservations Required, CCUSA max stay 4 days, CCUSA disc. not avail S, CCUSA disc. not avail F,Sa, CCUSA disc. not avail holidays. Not available on seasonal stays. Motorcycles must park in visitor lot-call for questions.

Text 83413 to (440)725-8687 to see our Visual Tour.

Phone: (517)522-8600
Address: 2401 Hilton Rd, Jackson, MI 49201
Lat/Lon: 42.26571/-84.26070
Email: office@greenwoodacrescampground.com
Web: www.greenwoodacrescampground.com

SEE AD NEXT PAGE AND AD MAP PAGE 357

(E) GREENWOOD ACRES GOLF—*From jct US 127 S & I-94: Go 5 mi E on I-94 (exit 147), then 1 block S on Race Rd, then 3/4 mi W on Ann Arbor Rd, then 1-1/4 mi S on Portage Rd, then 1/2 mi E on Greenwood Rd, then N on Hilton to entrance. Enter on L.* 9-hole golf course adjacent to an RV CAMPGROUND, golf included only when camping at Greenwood Acres, must have own equipment, artificial greens. Open Apr 1 - Oct 31. MC/VISA/Debit.

Phone: (517)522-8600
Address: 2401 Hilton Rd, Jackson, MI 49201
Lat/Lon: 42.26571/-84.26070
Web: www.greenwoodacrescampground.com

SEE AD NEXT PAGE

JACKSON—Continued on next page

JACKSON—Continued

(NE) Hideaway RV Park—(Jackson) *From jct US 127 S & I-94: Go 3 mi E on I-94 (exit 145), then 1/4 mi S on Sargent Rd, then 1-1/4 mi E on Ann Arbor, then 1/4 mi N on Whipple, then 1/2 mi E on Updyke. Enter on L.* ◇◇◇FACILITIES: 55 sites, typical site width 35 ft, 55 full hkups, (20/30/50 amps), 20 pull-thrus, family camping, dump. ◇◇RECREATION: lake swim, boating, electric motors only, pond fishing, playground. Pets welcome, breed restrict. Partial handicap access. No tents. Open Apr 15 - Oct 15. Big rigs welcome. Rate in 2010 $30 per family. Phone: (517)522-5858.

JONES—J-3

(W) Camelot Campground—(Cass) *From jct Hwy-40 & Hwy-60: Go 2-1/2 mi W on Hwy-60. Enter on R.* ◇◇FACILITIES: 141 sites, typical site width 50 ft, 66 full hkups, 75 W&E, (20/30/50 amps), 4 pull-thrus, family camping, tenting, dump, laundry, ltd groc. ◇◇◇RECREATION: swim pool, lake swim, boating, canoeing, ramp, dock, lake fishing, playground. Pets welcome. Partial handicap access. Open Apr 15 - Oct 15. Rate in 2010 $25-33 for 2 persons. Member ARVC, ARVC MI. Phone: (269)476-2473.

JONESVILLE—J-4

(N) Wildwood Acres—(Hillsdale) *From jct US-12 & Hwy-99: Go 1/2 mi E on US-12, then 6 mi N on Concord Rd, then 2 mi W on Goose Lake Rd. Enter at end.* ◇◇◇FACILITIES: 125 sites, typical site width 25 ft, 100 W&E, (20/30 amps), 25 no hkups, 4 pull-thrus, family camping, tenting, dump, ltd groc. ◇◇◇RECREATION: lake swim, boating, electric motors only, canoeing, ramp, dock, lake fishing, playground. Pets welcome, breed restrict. Open May 1 - Sep 15. Rate in 2010 $25 for 4 persons. Phone: (517)524-7149.

KALAMAZOO—I-3

See listings at Allegan, Augusta, Battle Creek, Decatur, Grand Junction & Lawrence

(N) MARKIN GLEN COUNTY PARK—(Kalamazoo) *From jct I-94 & US 131: Go 7-1/2 mi N on US 131 (exit 44), then 3-1/2 mi E on D Ave, then 2-3/4 mi S on N Westnedge Ave.*

FACILITIES: 38 sites, 38 full hkups, (30/50 amps), 7 pull-thrus, family camping, tenting, dump, non-guest dump $, picnic tables, patios, fire rings, wood.

RECREATION: pavilion, lake swim, canoeing, kayaking, lake fishing, golf nearby, playground, tennis, sports field, hiking trails, v-ball. Rec open to public.

Pets welcome. Partial handicap access. Open Late Apr - Oct. Clubs welcome. Rate in 2010 $25 for 4 persons. MC/VISA/DISC.

Phone: (269)383-8778
Address: 5300 N Westnedge Ave, Kalamazoo, MI 49004
Lat/Lon: 42.33532/-85.58974
Email: parks@kalcounty.com

SEE AD TRAVEL SECTION PAGE 359

Book your reservation online at woodalls.com

KALKASKA—E-4

(SE) KALKASKA RV PARK & CAMPGROUND—(Kalkaska) *From south jct US-131 & Hwy-72: Go 1 mi E on Hwy-72. Enter on R.*

◇◇◇FACILITIES: 105 sites, typical site width 45 ft, 15 full hkups, 50 W&E, 5 E, (20/30/50 amps), 35 no hkups, 23 pull-thrus, cable TV, ($), WiFi Instant Internet at site, family camping, tenting, cabins, RV storage, dump, non-guest dump $, portable dump, laundry, ltd groc, RV supplies, ice, picnic tables, fire rings, wood.

◇◇◇RECREATION: rec hall, rec room/area, pavilion, coin games, swim pool, golf nearby, bike rental 14 bike rentals, playground, activities, (wkends), horseshoes, sports field, hiking trails, v-ball. Rec open to public.

Pets welcome, quantity restrict. Open Apr 1 - Dec 1. Escort to site. Clubs welcome. Rate in 2010 $25-37 for 4 persons. MC/VISA/DISC/Debit. Member ARVC, ARVC MI. CCUSA 50% Discount. CCUSA reservations Recommended, CCUSA max stay 5 days, Cash only for CCUSA disc., CCUSA disc. not avail S, CCUSA disc. not avail F,Sa, CCUSA disc. not avail holidays. No group or on-line reservations. Discount not available Jun 29-12, 2011. Fully operational Apr 15-Dec 1.

Phone: (231)258-9863
Address: 580 M 72 SE, Kalkaska, MI 49646
Lat/Lon: 44.71377/-85.16331
Email: gclark53@gmail.com
Web: www.kalkaskacampground.com

SEE AD THIS PAGE

(SE) PERE MARQUETTE SF (CCC Bridge)—(Kalkaska) *From town: Go 10 mi SE on Hwy 72 & Sunset Trail Rd.* FACILITIES: 32 sites, 32 no hkups, tenting. RECREATION: canoeing, ramp, river fishing. Open all yr. Phone: (231)922-5280.

(SW) PERE MARQUETTE SF (Guernsey Lake)—(Kalkaska) *From town: Go 8 mi W on Island Lake Rd & Campground Rd. Enter at end.* FACILITIES: 36 sites, 30 ft max RV length, 36 no hkups, tenting. RECREATION: lake swim, boating, canoeing, ramp, lake fishing. Partial handicap access. Open all yr. Phone: (231)922-5280.

Robin Williams, actor and comedian, is from Michigan.

KINROSS—C-5

(E) KINROSS RV PARK EAST—(Chippewa) *From jct I-75 (exit 378) & Hwy 80: Go 2-3/4 mi E on Hwy 80, then 1 blk N on Riley St. Enter on R.*

FACILITIES: 64 sites, 64 full hkups, (20/30 amps), WiFi Instant Internet at site ($), family camping, tenting, RV storage, picnic tables, fire rings.

RECREATION: rec hall, golf nearby.

Pets welcome. Partial handicap access. Open May 1 - Oct 15. Clubs welcome.

Phone: (906)495-3023
Address: 16768 S Armstrong Loop, Kinross, MI 49788
Lat/Lon: 46.26070/-84.46210
Web: www.kinross.net

SEE AD THIS PAGE

(E) KINROSS RV PARK EAST (Township Park)—(Chippewa) *From I-75 (exit 378): Go 2-3/4 mi E on Tone Rd, then 1 block N on Riley. Enter on L.* FACILITIES: 64 sites, 64 full hkups, tenting, dump. RECREATION: Open May 15 - Oct 15. Phone: (906)495-3023.

(NE) KINROSS RV PARK WEST (Township Park)—(Chippewa) *From I-75 (exit 378): Go 1/2 mi E on Tone Rd, then 1/2 mi N on Fair Rd. Enter on L.* FACILITIES: 52 sites, 52 W&E, tenting, dump. RECREATION: playground. Open May 15 - Oct 15. Phone: (906)495-5381.

LAINGSBURG—H-4

(W) SLEEPY HOLLOW STATE PARK—(Shiawassee) *From jct US 27 & Price Rd: Go 7-1/2 mi E on Price Rd. Follow signs.* FACILITIES: 181 sites, 181 E, tenting, dump, ltd groc. RECREATION: lake swim, boating, canoeing, ramp, dock, lake fishing, play equipment. Partial handicap access. Open Apr 26 - Nov 4. Phone: (517)651-6217.

Lily Tomlin, actress and comedienne, is from Michigan.

LAKE ANN—E-4

(N) PERE MARQUETTE SF (Lake Ann)—(Benzie) *From town: Go 3 mi W on CR (Maple), then 1 mi S on Reynolds Rd.* FACILITIES: 30 sites, 35 ft max RV length, 30 no hkups, tenting. RECREATION: boating, no motors, canoeing, ramp, lake fishing. Open all yr. Phone: (231)922-5280.

LAKE CITY—F-3

(W) CROOKED LAKE PARK (Missaukee County Park) —(Missaukee) *From jct Hwy 66 & Jennings Rd: Go 4 mi W on Jennings Rd, then 1 mi N on LaChonce Rd.* FACILITIES: 52 sites, 15 E, 37 no hkups, tenting, dump. RECREATION: lake swim, boating, ramp, lake fishing, playground. Open May 15 - Oct 15. Phone: (231)839-4945.

(N) MISSAUKEE LAKE PARK (Missaukee County Park) —(Haughton) *From jct Hwy-55 & 66: Go 1/4 mi W on Park St.* FACILITIES: 170 sites, 96 full hkups, 21 E, (30 amps), 53 no hkups, tenting, dump. RECREATION: lake swim, boating, ramp, dock, lake fishing, playground. Partial handicap access. Open May 15 - Oct 15. Phone: (231)839-4945.

(N) PERE MARQUETTE SF (Goose Lake)—(Missaukee) *From jct Hwy-55 & Hwy-66: Go 1/2 mi N on Hwy-66, then 2 mi W on Goose Lake Rd.* FACILITIES: 54 sites, 54 no hkups, 3 pull-thrus, tenting. RECREATION: lake swim, boating, ramp, lake fishing. Open all yr. Phone: (231)775-9727.

(NW) PERE MARQUETTE SF (Long Lake)—(Missaukee) *From town: Go 3-1/2 mi NW on Hwy 66 & Goose Lake Rd. Enter on L.* FACILITIES: 20 sites, 20 no hkups, tenting. RECREATION: boating, ramp, lake fishing. Open all yr. Phone: (231) 775-9727.

LAKE LEELANAU—E-4

(S) Lake Leelanau RV Park—(Leelanau) *From jct Hwy 22 & Hwy 204: Go 4 mi W on Hwy 204, then 3-1/2 mi S on CR 643. Enter on L.* ◊◊◊◊FACILITIES: 196 sites, typical site width 40 ft, 196 full hkups, (20/30/50 amps), 25 pull-thrus, family camping, tenting, laundry. ◊◊◊◊RECREATION: lake swim, boating, canoeing, ramp, dock, lake fishing, playground. Pets welcome, quantity restrict. Partial handicap access. Open May 1 - Oct 31. Big rigs welcome. Rate in 2010 $49-59 per family. Member ARVC, ARVC MI. Phone: (231)256-7236.

LANSING—I-4

(SE) LANSING COTTONWOOD CAMPGROUND—(Ingham) *From jct US 127 & I-96: Go 2 mi W on I-96 (Cedar St exit 104), then 1/4 mi N on exit Rd, then 1/4 mi N on Pennsylvania Ave, then 3/4 mi E on Miller Rd, then 3/4 mi N on Aurelius Rd. Enter on R.*

WELCOME

◊◊◊FACILITIES: 135 sites, typical site width 30 ft, 11 full hkups, 99 W&E, (20/30/50 amps), 25 no hkups, 11 pull-thrus, WiFi Instant Internet at site, family camping, tenting, RV storage, dump, non-guest dump $, portable dump, laundry, groceries, RV supplies, ice, picnic tables, fire rings, wood.

◊◊◊◊RECREATION: rec hall, rec room/area, coin games, swim pool, boating, electric motors only, canoeing, kayaking, rowboat/6 kayak/4 pedal boat rentals, pond fishing, fishing supplies, golf nearby, playground, horseshoes, sports field, hiking trails, v-ball.

Pets welcome. Partial handicap access. Open May 1 - Oct 29. Big rigs welcome. Clubs welcome. Rate in 2010 $23-30 for 2 persons. MC/VISA/DISC/Debit. Member ARVC, ARVC MI.

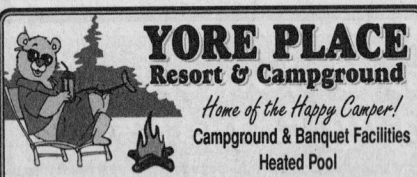

LANSING—Continued
LANSING COTTONWOOD CAMPGROUND—Continued

Phone: (517)393-3200
Address: 5339 Aurelius Rd, Lansing, MI 48911
Lat/Lon: 42.67870/-84.52333
Email: cottoncamp@aol.com
Web: www.lansingcottonwoodcampground.com

SEE AD THIS PAGE

LAPEER—H-5

(SW) Hilltop Campground—(Lapeer) *From jct Hwy 244 & I-69: Go 2 mi W on I-69 (exit 153), then 1/2 mi S on Lake Nepessing Rd, then 1/4 mi W on Piper Dr. Enter at end.* ◊◊◊FACILITIES: 60 sites, typical site width 45 ft, 60 W&E, (20/30/50 amps), family camping, tenting, dump, laundry, groceries. ◊◊◊RECREATION: lake swim, boating, canoeing, ramp, dock, lake fishing, playground. Pets welcome. Partial handicap access. Open May 1 - Oct 1. Rate in 2010 $25-30 per family. Member ARVC, ARVCMI. Phone: (810)664-2782.

(S) METAMORA-HADLEY STATE RECREATION AREA —(Oakland) *From jct Hwy 21 & Hwy 24: Go 6-1/2 mi S on Hwy 24, then 2-1/2 mi W on Pratt Rd, then 2/3 mi S on Hurd Rd.* FACILITIES: 214 sites, 214 E, tenting, dump, laundry, ltd groc. RECREATION: lake swim, boating, no motors, canoeing, ramp, playground. Open Apr 1 - Dec 1. Facilities fully operational Apr 15 - Nov 1. Phone: (810)797-4439.

(N) WATER TOWER TRAVEL TRAILER PARK (City Park) —(Lapeer) *From jct Hwy 21 & Hwy 24: Go 1-1/4 mi N on Hwy 24.* FACILITIES: 30 sites, typical site width 30 ft, 30 full hkups, 30 pull-thrus, tenting, dump. RECREATION: lake fishing. Open May 1 - Oct 31. Phone: (810)664-4296.

LAWRENCE—I-2

(NW) YOREPLACE RV RESORT—(Van Buren) *From jct Hwy 51 & I-94: Go 4 mi W on I-94 (exit 52), then 1 mi N on Paw Paw St, then 3 W on Red Arrow Hwy, then 2-3/4 mi N on Hwy 681, then 1 mi W on 44th Ave. Enter on L.*

◊◊◊FACILITIES: 91 sites, 91 W&E, (30 amps), 8 pull-thrus, WiFi Instant Internet at site, family camping, tenting, RV's/park model rentals, cabins, dump, portable dump, laundry, ice, picnic tables, fire rings, grills, wood.

◊◊◊RECREATION: rec room/area, pavilion, coin games, swim pool, boating, no motors, canoeing, kayaking, dock, 2 rowboat/3 pedal boat rentals, lake fishing, golf nearby, bsktball, playground, shuffleboard court shuffleboard court, activities (wkends), horseshoes, hiking trails, v-ball.

Pets welcome. Partial handicap access. Open Apr 15 - Oct 31. Clubs welcome. Rate in 2010 $25 per family. MC/VISA/DISC.

Phone: (269)427-7908
Address: 59381 44th Ave, Lawrence, MI 49064
Lat/Lon: 42.25685/-86.12497
Email: yoreplace@bciwildblue.com
Web: www.yoreplacervresort.com

SEE AD THIS PAGE

LE ROY—F-3

(E) ROSE LAKE PARK (Osceola County Park)—(Osceola) *From town: Go 2 mi N on Old US 131, then 4 mi E on 18 Mile Rd.* FACILITIES: 160 sites, 160 W&E, tenting, dump, laundry, groceries. RECREATION: lake swim, boating, ramp, lake fishing, playground. Open May 2 - Sep 15. Phone: (231)768-4923.

Michigan includes 56,954 square miles of land area; 11,000 inland lakes and 36,000 miles of streams making up 1,194 square miles of inland waters; and 38,575 square miles of Great Lakes water area.

LESLIE—I-4

(NE) WHEEL INN CAMPGROUND AND WHITE TAIL ACRES ARCHERY—(Ingham) *From jct Hwy 36 & US 127: Go 5 mi S on US 127, then 4-1/2 mi E on Barnes Rd, then 3-1/2 mi S on Meridian Rd, then 1/2 mi E on Fogg Rd. Enter on R.*

◊◊◊FACILITIES: 180 sites, typical site width 35 ft, 52 full hkups, 114 W&E, 14 E, (20/30 amps), some extd stay sites (summer), 60 pull-thrus, phone Internet central location, family camping, tenting, dump, non-guest dump $, portable dump, ice, picnic tables, fire rings, wood.

◊◊◊RECREATION: rec hall, pond fishing, golf nearby, bsktball, playground, activities, horseshoes, sports field, hiking trails, v-ball. Rec open to public.

Pets welcome, breed restrict. Open all yr. Clubs welcome. Rate in 2010 $25 for 2 persons. MC/VISA/DISC/Debit.

Phone: (517)589-8097
Address: 240 Fogg Rd, Leslie, MI 49251
Lat/Lon: 42.47150/-84.34505
Email: ataylor3d@aol.com
Web: www.whitetailacresarchery.com

SEE AD THIS PAGE

(NE) WHITETAIL ACRES ARCHERY—*From jct Hwy 36 & US 127: Go 5 mi S on US 127, then 4-1/2 mi E on Barnes Rd, then 3-1/2 mi S on Meridian Rd, then 1/2 mi E on Fogg Rd. Enter on R.* Range with 30 3-D targets, two tree stands and competition archery shoots. Archery supplies, service & repair. Open Dec - Sep. MC/VISA/DISC/Debit.

Phone: (517)589-0133
Address: 240 Fogg Rd, Leslie, MI 49251
Lat/Lon: 42.47150/-84.34505
Email: ataylor3d@aol.com
Web: www.whitetailacresarchery.com

SEE AD THIS PAGE

LEWISTON—E-5

(SE) MACKINAW SF (Little Wolf Lake)—(Montmorency) *From town: Go 3 mi SE on CR 489 & Wolf Lake Rd.* FACILITIES: 24 sites, 24 no hkups, tenting. RECREATION: lake swim, boating, ramp, lake fishing. Open May 1 - Labor Day. Phone: (989)785-4251.

LEXINGTON—H-6

(N) LEXINGTON PARK—(Sanilac) *From jct Hwy 90 & Hwy 25: Go 3 mi N on Hwy 25. Enter on R.* FACILITIES: 43 sites, 26 E, (20/30 amps), 17 no hkups, tenting, dump. RECREATION: lake swim, boating, canoeing, lake fishing, playground. Pets welcome. Open May 1 - Oct 31. Phone: (810)359-7473.

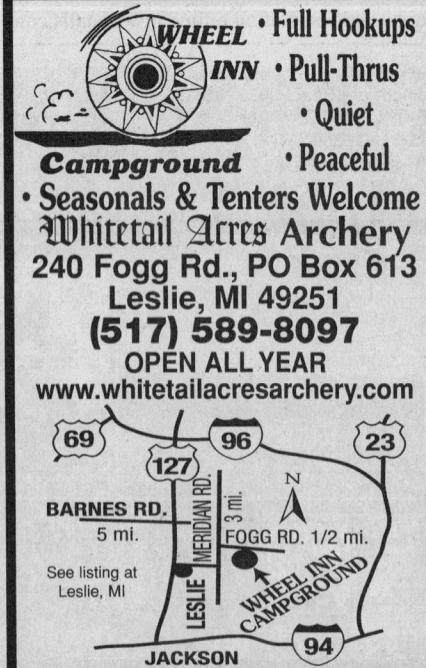

LINDEN—H-5

(SW) Hide Away Park—(Livingston) *From jct Hwy 59 & US 23: Go 3 mi N on US 23 (exit 70), then 4 mi W on Clyde Rd, then 5 mi N on Argentine Rd, then 1/2 mi W on Hogan Rd. Enter on L.* ◇◇◇FACILITIES: 163 sites, typical site width 30 ft, 32 full hkups, 121 W&E, (15/20/30/50 amps), 10 no hkups, 25 pull-thrus, family camping, tenting, dump. ◇◇◇RECREATION: boating, 10 hp limit, canoeing, ramp, dock, lake fishing, playground. Pets welcome, quantity restrict. Open Apr 15 - Oct 15. Rate in 2010 $23-28 per family. Phone: (810)735-7666.

LINWOOD—G-4

(E) Linwood Beach Marina & Campground—(Bay) *From jct I-75 (exit 173) & Linwood: Go 4 mi E on Linwood. Enter on R.* ◇◇◇◇FACILITIES: 135 sites, typical site width 30 ft, 86 full hkups, 40 W&E, (20/30/50 amps), 9 no hkups, 10 pull-thrus, family camping, tenting, dump, laundry, groceries. ◇◇◇RECREATION: boating, canoeing, ramp, dock, lake/pond fishing, playground. Pets welcome. Partial handicap access. Open May 1 - Nov 1. Big rigs welcome. Rate in 2010 $26-38 per vehicle. Phone: (989) 697-4415.

LITTLE LAKE—C-2

(SE) ESCANABA SF (Little Lake)—(Marquette) *From town: Go 1 mi SE on Hwy 35.* FACILITIES: 26 sites, 26 no hkups, tenting. RECREATION: lake swim, boating, ramp, lake fishing. Open all yr. Phone: (906)346-9201.

LOVELLS—E-5

(NE) AU SABLE SF (Shupac Lake)—(Crawford) *From town: Go 2 mi N on Twin Bridge Rd. Enter on R.* FACILITIES: 30 sites, 30 ft max RV length, 30 no hkups. RECREATION: lake swim, boating, lake fishing. Open all yr. Phone: (989)348-6371.

LUDINGTON—G-2

(S) KIBBY CREEK CAMPGROUND—(Mason) *From west jct US 10 & US 31: Go 2-1/2 mi S on US 31, then 4-1/2 mi S on Pere Marquette Dr (Old US 31), then 200 yards W on Deren Rd. Enter on R.*

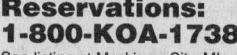

FAMILY FUN CAMPING MEMORIES

KIBBY CREEK is near beautiful Lake Michigan beaches. Great family camping with heated pool, modern playground, mini-golf, game room, and fishing in our ponds. General Store, Laundry and propane are available. www.kibbycreek.com

◇◇◇FACILITIES: 240 sites, typical site width 50 ft, 163 full hkups, 77 W&E, (20/30/50 amps), many extd stay sites (summer), 10 pull-thrus, WiFi Internet central location ($), family camping, tenting, RV's/park model rentals, dump, non-guest dump $, portable dump, laundry, groceries, RV supplies, LP gas by weight/by meter, ice, picnic tables, fire rings, wood.

LUDINGTON—Continued
KIBBY CREEK CAMPGROUND—Continued

◇◇◇◇RECREATION: rec hall, rec room/area, pavilion, coin games, swim pool, pond fishing, fishing supplies, mini-golf, ($), golf nearby, bsktball, playground, shuffleboard court 2 shuffleboard courts, activities (wkends), horseshoes, sports field, v-ball.

Pets welcome. Partial handicap access. Open Apr 15 - Oct 15. Clubs welcome. Rate in 2010 $34-36 per family. MC/VISA/DISC/Debit. Member ARVC, ARVC MI. CCUSA 50% Discount.

Phone: (800)574-3995
Address: 4900 W Deren Rd, Ludington, MI 49431
Lat/Lon: 43.85571/-86.40138
Email: kibby_creek@yahoo.com
Web: www.kibbycreek.com

SEE AD THIS PAGE

(N) LUDINGTON STATE PARK—(Mason) *From jct US-31-10 & Hwy-116: Go 8 mi N on Hwy-116.* FACILITIES: 362 sites, 352 E, (50 amps), 10 no hkups, tenting, dump, groceries. RECREATION: lake swim, boating, canoeing, ramp, lake fishing, playground. Partial handicap access. Open all yr. Facilities fully operational Apr 15 - Nov 1. Phone: (231)843-2423.

(S) MASON COUNTY CAMPGROUND & PICNIC AREA—(Mason) *From jct US 10/31 & US 31: Go 4 mi S on US 31, then 1/2 mi S on Old US 31, then 1-1/2 mi W on Chauvez Rd.* FACILITIES: 50 sites, 50 E, tenting, dump. RECREATION: boating, canoeing, ramp, dock, lake fishing, playground. Open Memorial Day - Labor Day. Phone: (231)845-7609.

(E) Poncho's Pond—(Mason) *From west jct US 31 & US 10: Go 2 mi W on US 10, then 1 block south on Marquette St, then 1 block E on Wallace Rd. Enter on R.* ◇◇◇◇◇FACILITIES: 251 sites, typical site width 35 ft, 243 full hkups, 8 W&E, (20/30/50 amps), 76 pull-thrus, family camping, tenting, laundry, ltd groc. ◇◇◇◇◇RECREATION: 3 swim pools, pond fishing, playground. Pets welcome, quantity restrict. Partial handicap access. Open Apr 1 - Oct 31. Big rigs welcome. Rate in 2010 $37-49 per family. Member ARVC, ARVC MI. Phone: (888)308-6602.

Vacation Station RV Resort—(Mason) *From west jct US 31 & US 10: Go 1 mi W on US 10. Enter on L.* ◇◇◇◇◇FACILITIES: 150 sites, typical site width 40 ft, 150 full hkups, (20/30/50 amps), 14 pull-thrus, family camping, tenting, laundry, groceries. ◇◇◇RECREATION: swim pool, pond fishing, playground. Pets welcome, quantity restrict. Partial handicap access. Open Apr 1 - Oct 31. Big rigs welcome. Rate in 2010 $20-50 per family. Member ARVC, ARVC MI. Phone: (231)845-0130.

LUPTON—F-5

(E) RIFLE RIVER STATE RECREATION AREA—(Alcona) *From town: Go 1 mi SE on Rose City Rd.* FACILITIES: 175 sites, 75 E, 100 no hkups, tenting, dump. RECREATION: lake swim, boating, no motors, canoeing, ramp, lake fishing, playground. Open all yr. Phone: (989)473-2258.

LUTHER—F-3

(N) PERE MARQUETTE SF (Silver Creek)—(Lake) *From town: Go 5-1/2 mi N on State road.* FACILITIES: 26 sites, 26 no hkups, tenting. RECREATION: boating, no motors, canoeing, ramp, river fishing. Open all yr. Phone: (231)775-9727.

MACKINAW CITY—D-5

(SW) KOA-MACKINAW CITY/MACKINAC ISLAND—(Emmet) *N'bound: From jct I-75 (exit 337) & Hwy 108: Go 1/4 mi S on Hwy 108 (Nicolet St), then 1/2 mi W on Trailsend Rd. S'bound: From jct I-75 (exit 338) & US 23: Go 1/4 mi S on US 23, then 3/4 mi S on Hwy 108, then 1/2 mi W on Trailsend Rd. Enter on R.*

◇◇◇◇FACILITIES: 109 sites, typical site width 35 ft, 33 full hkups, 57 W&E, (20/30/50 amps), 19 no hkups, 63 pull-thrus, WiFi Instant Internet at site, family camping, tenting, cabins, dump, non-guest dump $, laundry, groceries, RV supplies, LP gas by weight/by meter, ice, picnic tables, fire rings, wood.

◇◇◇RECREATION: rec room/area, coin games, swim pool, golf nearby, playground, horseshoes, hiking trails, local tours.

Pets welcome, breed restrict. Partial handicap access. Open May 1 - Oct 15. Clubs welcome. Rate in 2010 $25-42 for 2 persons. MC/VISA/DISC/Debit. Member ARVC, ARVCMI. KOA discount.

KOA-MACKINAW CITY/MACKINAC ISLAND—Continued on next page

Charles A. Lindbergh, aviator, was from Michigan.

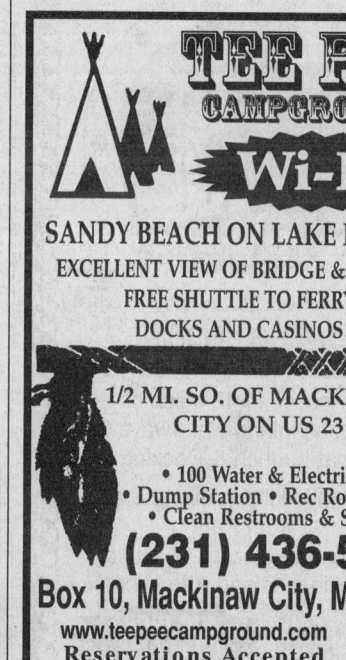

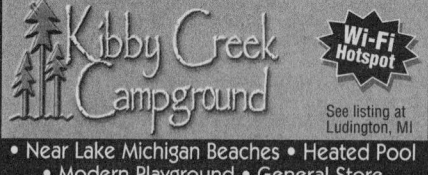

MACKINAW CITY—Continued
KOA-MACKINAW CITY/MACKINAC ISLAND—Continued

Phone: (800)KOA-1738
Address: 566 Trailsend Rd, Mackinaw City, MI 49701
Lat/Lon: 45.76732/-84.74014
Email: mackinawcitykoa@freeway.net
Web: www.koa.com/where/mi/22211

SEE AD PAGE 391

(S) MACKINAW CLUB GOLF COURSE *From jct I-75 (exit 337) & Hwy 108 (Nicolet St): Go 2-3/4 mi S on Hwy 108 (Nicolet St). Enter on R.* 18-hole par 72 Jerry Matthews' designed golf course. Over 310 acres of wooded & open terrain. 3 miles S of Mackinaw City's dining & shopping district. Club rental available. Stay-and-Play Packages with Mackinaw Creek Camping. Open Early May - Late Oct. MC/VISA/DISC/AMEX/Debit.

Woodall's Tip... Find free Tourism Information in the Travel Section

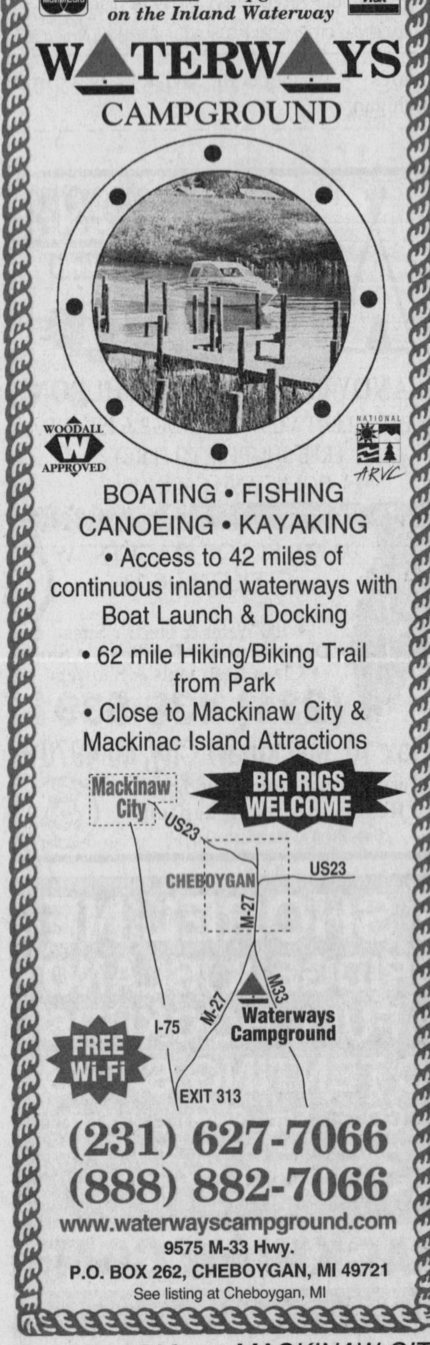

NEWEST Campground on the Inland Waterway
WATERWAYS
CAMPGROUND
WOODALL W APPROVED
NATIONAL ARVC
BOATING • FISHING
CANOEING • KAYAKING
• Access to 42 miles of continuous inland waterways with Boat Launch & Docking
• 62 mile Hiking/Biking Trail from Park
• Close to Mackinaw City & Mackinac Island Attractions
Mackinaw City
US23
BIG RIGS WELCOME
CHEBOYGAN
US23
M-27
M33
M-27
Waterways Campground
I-75
FREE Wi-Fi
EXIT 313
(231) 627-7066
(888) 882-7066
www.waterwayscampground.com
9575 M-33 Hwy.
P.O. BOX 262, CHEBOYGAN, MI 49721
See listing at Cheboygan, MI

MACKINAW CITY—Continued
MACKINAW CLUB GOLF COURSE—Continued

Phone: (231)537-4955
Address: 8700 Mackinaw Club Dr, Mackinaw City, MI 49701
Lat/Lon: 45.72292/-84.73203
Email: info@mackinawclub.com
Web: www.mackinawclub.com

SEE AD PAGE 391

(SE) MACKINAW MILL CREEK CAMPING—(Cheboygan) *N'bound: From jct I-75 (exit 337) & Hwy 108 (Nicolet St): Go 1/2 mi N on Nicolet St, then 4 mi SE on US 23. S'bound: From jct I-75 (exit 338) & US 23: Go 4-1/4 mi SE on US 23. Enter on L.*

SHORELINE, CABINS AND RV SITES
Our beautiful mile of Lake Huron shoreline and 200 acre park makes our camping experience unique. We offer a variety of campsites and cabin settings where you will be sure to find your own special site.

◆◆◆◆FACILITIES: 600 sites, typical site width 35 ft, 300 full hkups, 100 W&E, 150 E, (20/30/50 amps), 50 no hkups, 10 pull-thrus, WiFi Instant Internet at site ($), WiFi Internet central location, family camping, tenting, cabins, RV storage, dump, non-guest dump $, groceries, RV supplies, LP gas by weight/by meter, ice, picnic tables, fire rings, wood, controlled access.

◆◆◆◆RECREATION: rec hall, rec room/area, pavilion, coin games, swim pool, lake swim, canoeing, kayaking, lake fishing, fishing supplies, mini-golf, golf nearby, bsktball, 6 bike rentals, playground, activities, sports field, hiking trails, local tours.

Pets welcome, breed restrict, quantity restrict. Partial handicap access. Open Early May - Late Oct. Pool operational early Jun to early Sep. Store open thru late Sep. Big rigs welcome. Clubs welcome. Rate in 2010 $15-45 for 3 persons. MC/VISA/DISC/AMEX/Debit. Member ARVC, ARVC MI.

Text 83418 to (440)725-8687 to see our Visual Tour.

Phone: (231)436-5584
Address: 9730 US 23, Mackinaw City, MI 49701
Lat/Lon: 45.75069/-84.68655
Email: office@campmackinaw.com
Web: www.campmackinaw.com

SEE AD PAGE 391

(SE) TEE PEE CAMPGROUND—(Cheboygan) *From jct I-75 & Hwy 108 (Nicolet St.): Go 1/2 mi N on Nicolet St., then 1 mi SE on US 23. Enter on L.*

◆◆◆FACILITIES: 100 sites, typical site width 25 ft, 100 W&E, (20/30/50 amps), 6 pull-thrus, WiFi Instant Internet at site ($), WiFi Internet central location, family camping, tenting, dump, non-guest dump $, portable dump, groceries, RV supplies, ice, picnic tables, fire rings, wood.

◆◆◆RECREATION: rec room/area, coin games, lake swim, canoeing, kayaking, lake fishing, fishing supplies, golf nearby, bsktball, playground, horseshoes, v-ball, local tours.

Pets welcome. Partial handicap access. Open May 15 - Oct 15. Clubs welcome. Rate in 2010 $28-35 for 4 persons. MC/VISA/DISC/AMEX/Debit.

Woodall's Tip... Before you decide where to stay, check out Woodalls.com

Insta Launch
Campground & Marina
On the Big Manistee River
• Manistee Paddlesport Adventures (canoe, kayak, tube trips)
• Boat Rentals • Close to Lake Michigan & Casino
FREE Wi-Fi
866-452-8642
See listing at Manistee, MI
www.instalaunch.com
King Salmon & Steelhead Fishing at its Best!

MACKINAW CITY—Continued
TEE PEE CAMPGROUND—Continued

Phone: (231)436-5391
Address: 11262 W US 23, Mackinaw City, MI 49701
Lat/Lon: 45.76332/-84.71587
Email: teepee@mstraits.com
Web: www.teepeecampground.com

SEE AD PAGE 391

WATERWAYS CAMPGROUND—*From Mackinaw City: Go 16 mi SE on US 23, then 3-1/2 mi S on Hwy 27, then 1/4 mi S on Hwy 33. Enter on R.*

SEE PRIMARY LISTING AT CHEBOYGAN AND AD THIS PAGE

(W) WILDERNESS STATE PARK—(Emmet) *From town: Go 11 mi W on Wilderness Park Rd.* FACILITIES: 250 sites, 250 E, tenting, dump. RECREATION: lake swim, boating, ramp, lake fishing, playground. Open Apr 1 - Dec 1. Phone: (231)436-5381.

MANCELONA—E-4

(S) Antrim 131 RV Campground—(Antrim) *From jct Hwy 88 & US 131: Go 1 mi S on US 131, then 50 feet W on Elder Rd. Enter on L.* ◆◆FACILITIES: 23 sites, typical site width 30 ft, 7 full hkups, 16 W&E, (20/30 amps), 11 pull-thrus, tenting, dump, laundry. Pets welcome. Open Apr 15 - Oct 31. Rate in 2010 $17-20 for 2 persons. Phone: (231)587-5665.

(E) Whispering Pines Family Campground—(Antrim) *From jct US 131 & Hwy 88: Go 1-1/2 mi E on CR 38 (E State St). Enter on R.* ◆◆◆FACILITIES: 98 sites, typical site width 50 ft, 48 full hkups, 26 W&E, (20/30/50 amps), 24 no hkups, 5 pull-thrus, heater not allowed, WiFi Internet central location, family camping, tenting, RV storage, dump, non-guest dump $, laundry, ltd groc, RV supplies, ice, picnic tables, fire rings, wood. ◆◆◆◆RECREATION: rec hall, pavilion, swim pool, wading pool, putting green, bsktball, playground, activities, horseshoes, hiking trails, v-ball. Pets welcome. Partial handicap access. Open all yr. Facilities fully operational Apr - Oct. Big rigs welcome. Rate in 2010 $30-35 per family. MC/VISA/Debit. Member ARVC, ARVC MI. CCUSA 50% Discount. CCUSA reservations Accepted, CCUSA max stay 7 days, CCUSA disc. not avail F,Sa, CCUSA disc. not avail holidays.

Phone: (231)587-5122
Address: 3060 Mancelona Rd, Mancelona, MI 49659
Lat/Lon: 44.89961/-85.03052
Email: whisperingpinemi@aol.com
Web: www.whisperingpinesmi.com

MANISTEE—F-2

(N) INSTA-LAUNCH CAMPGROUND & MARINA—(Manistee) *From jct Hwy 55 & US 31: Go 1/4 mi S on US 31, then 1/4 mi E on Park Ave. Enter on R.*

◆◆◆FACILITIES: 174 sites, typical site width 35 ft, 70 full hkups, 19 W&E, 75 E, (20/30/50 amps), 10 no hkups, some extd stay sites (summer), 6 pull-thrus, cable TV, WiFi Instant Internet at site, family camping, tenting, RV's/park model rentals, cabins, RV storage, shower$, dump, non-guest dump $, laundry, groceries, RV supplies, LP bottle exch, ice, picnic tables, fire rings, grills, wood.

◆◆◆◆RECREATION: rec hall, pavilion, lake swim, boating, canoeing, kayaking, ramp, dock, 2 pontoon/10 canoe/14 kayak/3 motorboat rentals, float trips, lake/river fishing, fishing supplies, fishing guides, golf nearby, playground, activities, (wkends), horseshoes, v-ball, local tours. Rec open to public.

Pets welcome, quantity restrict. Partial handicap access. Open Apr 15 - Nov 15. Facilities fully operational mid Apr - Nov 1. Clubs welcome. Rate in 2010 $21-33 for 4 persons. MC/VISA/DISC/Debit. Member ARVC, ARVC MI.

Phone: (866)452-8642
Address: 20 Park Ave, Manistee, MI 49660
Lat/Lon: 44.26502/-86.30502
Email: jim@instalaunch.com
Web: www.instalaunch.com

Reserve Online at Woodalls.com

SEE AD THIS PAGE

(N) INSTA-LAUNCH MARINA & CAMPGROUND—*From jct Hwy 55 & US 31: Go 1/4 mi S on US 31, then 1/4 mi E on Park Ave. Enter on R.* 108 boat slips, a campground, kayak, canoe, pontoon, & fishing boat rentals located on Big Manistee River with access to Manistee Lake & Lake Michigan. Float trips on the river. King

INSTA-LAUNCH MARINA & CAMPGROUND—Continued on next page

MANISTEE—Continued
INSTA-LAUNCH MARINA & CAMPGROUND—Continued

Salmon, Pan & Steelhead fishing at it's best! Open Apr 15 - Nov 15. Weather permitting. MC/VISA/DISC/Debit.

Phone: (866)452-8642
Address: 20 Park Ave, Manistee, MI 49660
Lat/Lon: 44.26502/-86.30502
Email: jim@instalaunch.com
Web: www.instalaunch.com

SEE AD PAGE 392

(NE) LITTLE RIVER CASINO—*From jct Hwy 55 & US 31: Go 4 mi N o Us 31, then 500 ft W on Hwy 22. Enter on L.* Free shuttle service from the RV Park to Little River Casino where you will find over 1300 slots, also craps, blackjack, roulette & let-it-ride bonus. The Rapids Deli is open 24 hours. Open all yr. MC/VISA/DISC/AMEX/Debit. ATM.

WELCOME

Phone: (866)466-7338
Address: 2700 Orchard Hwy, Manistee, MI 49660
Lat/Lon: 44.28663/-86.24329
Email: fun@lrcr.com
Web: www.lrcr.com

SEE AD TRAVEL SECTION PAGE 358

(NE) LITTLE RIVER RESORT—(Manistee) *From jct Hwy 55 & US 31: Go 4 mi N on US 31, then 500 ft W o Hwy 22. Enter on L.*

WELCOME

◆◆◆◆◆FACILITIES: 95 sites, 45 full hkups, 50 W&E, (20/30/50 amps), some extd stay sites (summer), 44 pull-thrus, cable TV, WiFi Instant Internet at site, family camping, dump, non-guest dump, laundry, LP bottle exch, ice, picnic tables, patios.

◆◆◆RECREATION: rec room/area, pavilion, coin games, swim pool, hot tub, golf nearby, playground. Rec open to public.

Pets welcome. Partial handicap access. No tents. Open Apr 1 - Nov 30. As weather permits. Big rigs welcome. Clubs welcome. Rate in 2010 $18-38 per vehicle. MC/VISA/DISC/AMEX/Debit. ATM.

Phone: (866)572-4386
Address: 2700 Orchard Highway, Manistee, MI 49660
Lat/Lon: 44.28663/-86.24329
Email: fun@lrcr.com
Web: www.lrcr.com

SEE AD TRAVEL SECTION PAGE 358

(S) MANISTEE NATIONAL FOREST (Lake Michigan Rec. Area)—(Manistee) *From jct Hwy 55 & US 31: Go 10 mi S on US 31, then 8 mi W on Forest Trail (FR 5629).* FACILITIES: 99 sites, 99 no hkups, tenting. RECREATION: lake swim. Partial handicap access. Open May 13 - Oct 3. Phone: (231)723-2211.

(N) MANISTEE PADDLESPORT ADVENTURES—*From jct Hwy 55 & US 31: Go 1/2 mi S on US 31. Enter on L.* Family-oriented canoe, kayak & tube trips on the Big Manistee River—a designated wild & scenic river. Excellent river for beginner and intermediate paddlers, and families with children. Open Apr 15 - Nov 15. MC/VISA/DISC/Debit.

WELCOME

Phone: (888)408-8850
Address: 231 Parkdale Ave, Manistee, MI 49660
Lat/Lon: 44.26616/-86.30883
Web: www.manisteepaddlesports.com

SEE AD PAGE 392

(NE) MATSON'S BIG MANISTEE RIVER CAMPGROUND—(Manistee) *From jct US 31 & Hwy 55: Go 9 mi E on Hwy 55, then 3 mi N on Skocelas Rd, then 3/4 mi W on Becker Rd, then 3/4 mi N on Bialik Rd. Enter at end.*

WELCOME

◆◆◆FACILITIES: 71 sites, typical site width 30 ft, 38 ft max RV length, 28 full hkups, 28 W&E, (20/30 amps), 15 no hkups, some extd stay sites

MANISTEE—Continued
MATSON'S BIG MANISTEE RIVER CAMPGROUND—Continued

(summer), family camping, tenting, RV's/park model rentals, cabins, RV storage, dump, non-guest dump $, portable dump, laundry, groceries, RV supplies, ice, picnic tables, fire rings, wood.

◆◆◆RECREATION: river swim, boating, canoeing, kayaking, ramp, dock, 6 motorboat rentals, float trips, river fishing, fishing supplies, fishing guides, golf nearby, hiking trails.

Pets welcome. Partial handicap access. Open Apr 1 - Dec 1. Clubs welcome. Rate in 2010 $23-29 per vehicle. MC/VISA/Debit. Member ARVC, ARVC MI. CCUSA 50% Discount. CCUSA reservations Required, CCUSA max stay See rest. July thru Oct discount not available weekends or holidays. Apr thru Jun discount available any day other than Memorial Day weekend. $1.50 surcharges for A/C, electric heater & electricity on rustic sites.

Phone: (888)556-2424
Address: 2680 Bialik Rd, Manistee, MI 49660
Lat/Lon: 44.28243/-86.15961
Email: cmatson@manistee.org
Web: www.matsonscampground.com

SEE AD TRAVEL SECTION PAGE 359

(N) ORCHARD BEACH STATE PARK—(Mason) *From jct US-31 & Hwy-110: Go 2 mi N on Hwy-110.* FACILITIES: 166 sites, 166 E, tenting, dump, laundry. RECREATION: lake swim, playground. Open Apr 1 - Dec 1. Facilities fully operational Apr 15 - Nov 1. Phone: (231)723-7422.

MANISTIQUE—C-3

(W) HIAWATHA NATIONAL FOREST (Camp Seven Lake)—(Schoolcraft) *From town: Go 9-1/2 mi W on CR-442, then 7-1/2 mi N on CR-437, then 4 mi W on CR-443, then 1/4 mi N on FR-2218.* FACILITIES: 41 sites, 32 ft max RV length, 41 no hkups, tenting. RECREATION: lake swim, boating, ramp, lake fishing. Partial handicap access. Open May 15 - Oct 7. Phone: (906) 341-5666.

(NE) INDIAN LAKE STATE PARK (South Shore)—(Schoolcraft) *From jct Hwy 94 & US 2: Go 5 mi W on US 2 & Hwy 149.* FACILITIES: 145 sites, 145 E, (20 amps), 7 pull-thrus, tenting, dump, laundry. RECREATION: lake swim, boating, ramp, dock, lake fishing, playground. Partial handicap access. Open Apr 15 - Nov 1. Phone: (906)341-2355.

(W) INDIAN LAKE STATE PARK (West Shore)—(Schoolcraft) *From jct US 2 & Hwy-94: Go 6 mi W on US 2, then 8 mi NW on Hwy 149.* FACILITIES: 72 sites, 72 E, (20 amps), tenting. RECREATION: lake swim, boating, ramp, lake fishing, playground. Partial handicap access. Open Apr 15 - Nov 1. Phone: (906)341-2355.

(W) INDIAN LAKE TRAVEL RESORT—(Schoolcraft) *From jct US-2 & Hwy-149: Go 3-3/4 mi NW on Hwy-149, then 1/2 mi N on CR-455. Enter on R.*

WELCOME

◆◆◆FACILITIES: 62 sites, typical site width 35 ft, 41 full hkups, 17 W&E, (20/30/50 amps), 50 amps ($), 4 no hkups, some extd stay sites (summer), 4 pull-thrus, WiFi Instant Internet at site ($), family camping, tenting, RV storage, dump, laundry, ltd groc, RV supplies, LP gas by weight, ice, picnic tables, fire rings, wood.

◆◆◆◆RECREATION: rec hall, lake swim, boating, canoeing, kayaking, ramp, dock, lake fishing, fishing supplies, golf nearby, bsktball, playground, activities, (wkends), horseshoes, sports field, hiking trails, v-ball.

Pets welcome. Partial handicap access. Open May 1 - Sep 30. Clubs welcome. Rate in 2010 $22 for 2 persons. Member ARVC, ARVC MI.

Phone: (906)341-2807
Address: 202 S County Rd 455, Manistique, MI 49854
Lat/Lon: 45.94735/-86.36437

SEE AD THIS PAGE

(E) Manistique KOA—(Schoolcraft) *From jct Hwy 149 & US 2: Go 8 mi E on US 2. Enter on L.* ◆◆◆FACILITIES: 40 sites, 4 full hkups, 36 W&E, (30/50 amps), 4 pull-thrus, family camping, tenting, dump, laundry, ltd groc. ◆◆RECREATION: swim pool, play equipment. Pets welcome, breed restrict. Open Apr 15 - Oct 31. Rate in 2010 $25-38 per vehicle. Phone: (906)341-6911. KOA discount.

MANISTIQUE—Continued

(SW) Woodstar Beach Campground—(Schoolcraft) *From jct US-2 & Hwy-149: Go 1-1/4 mi S on Little Harbor Rd. Enter on L.* ◆◆FACILITIES: 45 sites, typical site width 30 ft, 40 ft max RV length, 31 W&E, 4 E, (20/30 amps), 10 no hkups, family camping, tenting, dump, laundry. ◆◆RECREATION: lake swim, canoeing, play equipment. Pets welcome. Open Mid May - Oct 1. Rate in 2010 $19-24 for 2 persons. Phone: (906)341-6514.

MANTON—F-3

(N) Chippewa Landing Campground—(Wexford) *From jct US 131 & Bus US 131: Go 1 mi S on Bus US 131, then 3/4 mi E on 10 Rd, then 2 mi N on 43-1/4 Rd, then 1/2 mi W (left) on Chippewa Landing Trail. Enter on R.* ◆FACILITIES: 25 sites, 25 no hkups, family camping, tenting. ◆◆◆RECREATION: river swim, boating, canoeing, river fishing. Pets welcome. Open Apr - Oct. Rate in 2010 $5 for 1 persons. Phone: (231)313-0832.

(NE) LAKE BILLINGS CAMPGROUND (Municipal Park)—(Wexford) *From jct US 131 & E Main St: Go 2 blocks E on E Main St, then 1 block N on Park St.* FACILITIES: 85 sites, 37 full hkups, 48 W&E, tenting, dump, laundry. RECREATION: lake swim, boating, no motors, canoeing, lake/stream fishing, playground. Open Apr 15 - Oct 15. Phone: (231)824-6454.

(NW) PERE MARQUETTE SF (Baxter Bridge)—(Wexford) *From town: Go 6 mi W on Hwy 42, then 6 mi N on Rd 31. Enter on L.* FACILITIES: 25 sites, 25 no hkups, tenting. RECREATION: canoeing, river fishing. Open all yr. Phone: (231)775-9727.

(N) PERE MARQUETTE SF (Old US 131)—(Wexford) *From town: Go 6 mi N on US 131 & Old US 131. Enter on L.* FACILITIES: 25 sites, 25 no hkups, tenting. RECREATION: canoeing, river fishing. Open all yr. Phone: (231)775-9727.

(E) THE CAMPGROUND—(Wexford) *From jct US 131 & Hwy 42: Go 1/2 mi E on Hwy 42. Enter on R.*

WELCOME

◆◆◆FACILITIES: 30 sites, typical site width 36 ft, 22 full hkups, 8 W&E, (15/30/50 amps), some extd stay sites (summer), 15 pull-thrus, WiFi Instant Internet at site, family camping, tenting, dump, non-guest dump $, laundry, picnic tables, fire rings, wood.

◆◆RECREATION: equipped pavilion, golf nearby, playground, horseshoes, sports field, hiking trails, v-ball.

Pets welcome. Partial handicap access. Open Apr 1 - Late Nov. Big rigs welcome. Clubs welcome. Rate in 2010 $20 for 2 persons. Member ARVC, ARVCMI.

Phone: (231)824-9111
Address: 10330 E M-42, Manton, MI 49663
Lat/Lon: 44.40371/-85.37086
Email: thecampground@att.net

SEE AD TRAVEL SECTION PAGE 359

MARION—F-3

(N) VETERANS MEMORIAL PARK (Village Park)—(Osceola) *From jct Hwy 115 & Hwy 66: Go 5 mi N on Hwy 66. Enter on L.* FACILITIES: 38 sites, 12 full hkups, 26 W&E, (30/50 amps), family camping, tenting, dump. RECREATION: stream fishing, playground. Pets welcome. Partial handicap access. Open Apr 15 - Dec 1. Big rigs welcome. Phone: (231)667-0100.

MARQUETTE—B-2

See listings at Autrain, Big Bay, Champion, Gwinn, Ishpeming & Little Lake

(E) Gitche Gumee RV Park & Campground—(Marquette) *From jct US 41 & Hwy 28: go 5-3/4 mi E on Hwy 28. Enter on R.* ◆◆◆FACILITIES: 74 sites, 30

Gitche Gumee RV Park & Campground—Continued on next page

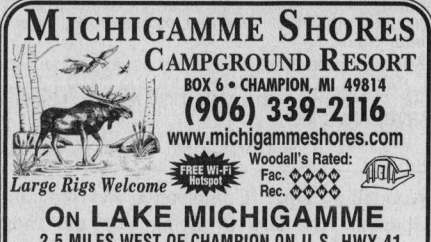

MARQUETTE—Continued
Gitche Gumee RV Park & Campground—Continued

full hkups, 30 W&E, (20/30/50 amps), 14 no hkups, 20 pull-thrus, family camping, tenting, dump, laundry. Pets welcome. Partial handicap access. Open April 15 - Nov 15. Big rigs welcome. Rate in 2010 $25-39 for 4 persons. Phone: (866)447-8727.

HORSESHOE LAKE CAMPGROUND & RV PARK—*From Marquette: Go 6 mi W on US 41/Hwy 28, then 21 mi S on Hwy 35, then 1-1/2 mi S on Horse Shoe Lake Rd. Enter at end.*

SEE PRIMARY LISTING AT GWINN MI AND AD PAGE 393

(N) MARQUETTE TOURIST PARK (City Park)—(Marquette) *From east jct Hwy 28 & US 41/Hwy 28: Go 7-1/2 mi N on US 41/Hwy 28, then 3 mi N on Wright St, then 1/4 mi N on Sugarloaf Ave (CR 550). Enter on L.* FACILITIES: 110 sites, typical site width 30 ft, 39 full hkups, 4 W&E, 57 E, (20/30/50 amps), 10 no hkups, 42 pull-thrus, family camping, tenting, dump. RECREATION: canoeing, river fishing, playground. Pets welcome. Partial handicap access. Open Memorial Day - mid Oct. Phone: (906) 228-0465.

MICHIGAMME SHORES CAMPGROUND RESORT—*From Marquette: Go 33 mi W on US 41/Hwy 28. Enter on L.*

SEE PRIMARY LISTING AT CHAMPION AND AD PAGE 393

(SE) Ojibwa Casino RV Park (RV SPACES) —(Marquette) *From US 41 & Hwy 28: Go 5 mi E on Hwy 28.* FACILITIES: 7 sites, 7 E, (20/30/50 amps). Pets welcome. Partial handicap access. No tents. Open May - Mid Nov. Big rigs welcome. Phone: (888)560-9905.

MARSHALL—I-4

(S) Tri Lake Trails Campground—(Calhoun) *From jct I-94 & I-69: Go 5-3/4 mi S on I-69 (exit 32), then 1-1/4 mi E on "F" Drive South, then 1/4 mi S on Old US-27, then 3/4 mi W on Lyon Lake Rd. Enter on R.* ◆◆◆FACILITIES: 272 sites, typical site width 40 ft, 272 W&E, (20/30 amps), family camping, tenting, dump. ◆◆◆◆RECREATION: lake swim, boating, 5 hp limit, lake fishing, playground. Pets welcome, breed restrict. Partial handicap access. Open May 1 - Oct 1. Rate in 2010 $29 for 2 persons. Phone: (269)781-2297.

MASS CITY—A-6

(N) TWIN LAKES STATE PARK—(Houghton) *From jct Hwy 26 & Hwy 38: Go 20 mi N on Hwy 26. Entrance fee required.* FACILITIES: 62 sites, 62 E, (20 amps), tenting, dump. RECREATION: lake swim, boating, ramp, lake fishing, playground. Open Apr 15 - Oct 15. Phone: (906)288-3321.

MEARS—G-2

(SW) Hideaway Campground & Resort—(Oceana) *From jct Hwy 20 & US 31: Go 3-1/2 mi N on US 31, then 5 mi W on Shelby Rd., then 4-1/2 mi N on Scenic Dr (CR B-15). Enter on L.* ◆◆◆FACILITIES: 213 sites, typical site width 30 ft, 175 W&E, (20/30/50 amps), 38 no hkups, 19 pull-thrus, family camping, tenting, dump, laundry, groceries. ◆◆RECREATION: swim pool, playground. Pets welcome. Partial handicap access. Open May 1 - Oct 1. Rate in 2010 $40 for 2 persons. Member ARVC, ARVC MI. Phone: (231)873-4428.

(SW) Sandy Shores Campground—(Oceana) *From jct Hwy 20 & US 31: Go 3-1/2 mi N on US 31, then 5 mi W on Shelby Rd, then 4 mi N on Scenic Dr (CR B-15), then 1/2 mi E on Silver Lake Rd. Enter on R.* ◆◆◆◆FACILITIES: 212 sites, typical site width 40 ft, 156 full hkups, 56 W&E, (20/30/50 amps), 11 pull-thrus, family camping, tenting, dump, laundry. ◆◆◆RECREATION: swim pool, lake swim, boating, canoeing, dock, lake fishing, playground. Pets welcome. Partial handicap access. Open May 1 - Sep 30. Rate in 2010 $37-44 per family. Member ARVC, ARVC MI. Phone: (231)873-3003.

(SW) Silver Creek RV Resort—(Oceana) *From jct Hwy 20 & US 31: Go 9 mi N on US 31 (exit 149), then 5 mi W on Polk Rd/56th Ave/Fox Rd. Enter on R.* ◆◆◆◆◆FACILITIES: 258 sites, typical site width 50 ft, 258 full hkups, (20/30/50 amps), 20 pull-thrus, family camping, laundry, ltd groc. ◆◆◆◆RECREATION: swim pool, playground. Pets welcome, quantity

MEARS—Continued
Silver Creek RV Resort—Continued

restrict. Partial handicap access. No tents. Open Apr - Oct 31. Facilities fully operational Memorial Day - Labor Day. Big rigs welcome. Rate in 2010 $20-60 per vehicle. Member ARVC, ARVC MI. Phone: (866)258-2541. FMCA discount.

(SW) Silver Hills Camp Resort—(Oceana) *From jct Hwy 20 & US 31: Go 9 mi N on US 31, then 5 mi W on Polk Rd/56th St/Fox Rd/34th Ave, then 1/4 mi E on Hazel Rd. Enter on L.* ◆◆◆FACILITIES: 105 sites, typical site width 30 ft, 22 W&E, (20/30 amps), 83 no hkups, 12 pull-thrus, family camping, tenting, dump. ◆RECREATION: swim pool, pond fishing, playground. Pets welcome, breed restrict. Partial handicap access. Open Mid May - Mid Sep. Rate in 2010 $40-45 for 2 persons. Phone: (800)637-3976.

(SW) Silver Lake Resort & Campground—(Oceana) *From jct Hwy 20 & US 31: Go 9 mi N on US 31, then 1-1/4 mi W on Polk Rd, then 1/2 mi S on 56th St, then 2-1/2 mi W on Fox Rd, then 1/2 mi S on 34th Ave.. Enter on L.* ◆◆◆◆FACILITIES: 199 sites, typical site width 35 ft, 89 full hkups, 76 W&E, 6 E, (20/30/50 amps), 28 no hkups, 24 pull-thrus, family camping, tenting, dump, laundry, groceries. ◆◆◆RECREATION: swim pool, pond fishing, playground. Pets welcome. Partial handicap access. Open May 1 - Sep 30. Rate in 2010 $30-45 for 2 persons. Member ARVC, ARVC MI. Phone: (231)873-7199.

(SW) Yogi Bear's Jellystone Park Silver Lake —(Oceana) *From jct Hwy 20 & US 31: Go 9 mi N on US 31, then 5-1/2 mi W on Polk Rd/56th Ave/Fox Rd, then 1/2 mi W on Hazel Rd. Enter on L.* ◆◆◆FACILITIES: 202 sites, typical site width 40 ft, 82 full hkups, 120 W&E, (20/30/50 amps), 2 pull-thrus, family camping, tenting, dump, laundry, groceries. ◆◆◆◆RECREATION: swim pool, pond fishing, playground. Pets welcome. Partial handicap access. Open Apr 15 - Oct 15. Facilities fully operational Memorial Day - Labor Day. Rate in 2010 $20-52 per family. Member ARVC, ARVC MI. Phone: (231)873-4502.

MECOSTA—G-3

(N) Lighthouse Family Camping Resort—(Mecosta) *From jct Hwy 66 & Hwy 20: Go 6-1/2 mi W on Hwy 20, then 4-1/2 mi N on 80th Ave, then 1/2 mi E on Taft Rd, then 1/2 mi N on Pretty Lake Dr. Enter on R.* ◆◆◆FACILITIES: 100 sites, 100 W&E, (20/30/50 amps), 1 pull-thrus, family camping, tenting, dump, ltd groc. ◆◆◆RECREATION: lake swim, boating, electric motors only, canoeing, ramp, dock, lake fishing, playground. Pets welcome. Open Apr 15 - Oct 15. Rate in 2010 $30 per family. Member ARVC, ARVCMI. Phone: (231)972-2112.

(SW) SCHOOL SECTION LAKE (Mecosta County)—(Mecosta) *From jct Hwy-66 & Hwy-20: Go 4 mi W on Hwy-20, then 2 mi S on 70th Ave, then 2 mi W on 9-Mile Rd.* FACILITIES: 166 sites, 166 W&E, tenting, dump. RECREATION: lake swim, boating, 10 hp limit, canoeing, lake fishing, playground. No pets. Open May 1 - Oct 1. Phone: (231)972-7450.

MENOMINEE—E-2

(S) RIVER PARK CAMPGROUND (City Park)—(Menominee) *In town on US 41.* FACILITIES: 69 sites, 54 full hkups, 15 E, (20/30 amps), 9 pull-thrus, tenting, dump, laundry. RECREATION: boating, ramp, dock, lake/river fishing, playground. Partial handicap access. Open May 15 - Oct 15. Phone: (906)863-5101.

MEREDITH—F-4

(NE) AU SABLE SF (House Lake)—(Gladwin) *From town: Go 2-1/2 mi NE on Meredith Grade Rd.* FACILITIES: 41 sites, 41 no hkups, tenting. RECREATION: lake swim, boating, ramp, lake fishing. Open all yr. Phone: (989)426-9205.

(N) AU SABLE SF (Trout Lake)—(Gladwin) *From town: Go 3 mi N on Meredith Grade Rd.* FACILITIES: 35 sites, 35 no hkups, tenting. RECREATION: lake swim, boating, canoeing, ramp, lake fishing. Open all yr. Phone: (989)426-9205.

MERRILL—G-4

(SW) Lake of Dreams Campground—(Saginaw) *From jct Hwy 52 & Hwy 46: Go 11 mi W on Hwy 46, then 1/2 mi S on Fenmore Rd. Enter on R.* ◆◆◆FACILITIES: 197 sites, typical site width 50 ft, 197 W&E, (30/50 amps), family camping, tenting, dump, ltd groc. ◆◆◆◆RECREATION: lake swim, lake fishing, playground. Pets welcome, quantity restrict. Partial handicap access. Open Apr 15 - Oct 15. Rate in 2010 $27.50 per family. Member ARVC, ARVCMI. Phone: (989)643-0403.

MESICK—F-3

(SW) Northern Exposure Campground—(Wexford) *From west jct Hwy 37 & Hwy 115: Go 1-1/4 mi W on Hwy 115, then 2-1/2 mi SW on Hodenpyle Rd, then 1/4 mi S on N 3-1/2 Rd. Enter at end.* ◆◆◆FACILITIES: 262 sites, typical site width 30 ft, 220 W&E, (30/50 amps), 42 no hkups, 22 pull-thrus, WiFi Instant Internet at site, WiFi Internet central location, family camping, tenting, dump, non-guest dump $, ice, picnic tables, fire rings, wood. ◆◆◆RECREATION: pavilion, lake swim, boating, canoeing, kayaking, ramp, dock, lake fishing, fishing supplies, bsktball, playground, activities, horseshoes, hiking trails, v-ball. Pets welcome. Partial handicap access. Open May 1 - Oct 15. Rate in 2010 $25-40 per vehicle. MC/VISA/

MESICK—Continued
Northern Exposure Campground—Continued

DISC. CCUSA 50% Discount. CCUSA reservations Recommended, CCUSA max stay 4 days, CCUSA disc. not avail Th, CCUSA disc. not avail F,Sa, CCUSA disc. not avail holidays.

Phone: (800)563-7425
Address: 285 Manistee River Dr, Mesick, MI 49668
Lat/Lon: 44.38096/-85.78988
Email: northernexposure@acegroup.cc
Web: www.northernexposureinc.com

MICHIGAMME—B-1

See listings at Baraga, Big Bay, Champion, Gwinn, Ishpeming, Marquette, Sidnaw & Skanee

MIDDLEVILLE—I-3

(N) YANKEE SPRINGS STATE REC. AREA (Deep Lake Campground)—(Barry) *From jct Hwy-43 & Hwy-37: Go 6-1/2 mi N on Hwy-37, then 4-1/2 mi S on CR-611 (Yankee Springs Rd).* FACILITIES: 120 sites, 35 ft max RV length, 120 no hkups, tenting, ltd groc. RECREATION: lake swim, boating, ramp, lake fishing, playground. Partial handicap access. Open Apr 1 - Dec 1. Phone: (269)795-9081.

(SW) YANKEE SPRINGS STATE REC AREA (Gun Lake Campground)—(Barry) *From jct Hwy 43 & Hwy 37: Go 9-1/2 mi W on Gun Lake Rd.* FACILITIES: 200 sites, 200 E, tenting, dump. RECREATION: lake swim, boating, canoeing, ramp, lake fishing, playground. Open Apr 1 - Nov 30. Phone: (269)795-9081.

MIDLAND—G-4

(NE) MIDLAND RV SALES—*From jct US 10 & Bus US 10/Eastman Rd: Go 1 mi S on Eastman Rd, then 2 mi SE on Saginaw Rd. Enter on L.* SALES: travel trailers, 5th wheels, fold-down camping trailers, pre-owned unit sales. SERVICES: full-time mech, RV appliance repair, body work/collision repair, RV rentals, sells parts/accessories, installs hitches. Open all yr. MC/VISA/DISC.

Phone: (989)631-1231
Address: 607 South Saginaw, Midland, MI 48640
Lat/Lon: 43.62210/-84.22205
Web: www.midlandrv.com

SEE AD TRAVEL SECTION PAGE 359

(SW) River Ridge Campground—(Midland) *From jct US 10 & Business US 10/Eastman Rd: Go 2-3/4 mi S on Eastman Rd, then 6-1/4 mi W on Hwy 20, then 3 mi S on Meridian Rd, then 4-1/2 mi W on Pine River Rd. Enter on L.* ◆◆◆◆FACILITIES: 150 sites, typical site width 30 ft, 84 full hkups, 54 W&E, (20/30/50 amps), 12 no hkups, 10 pull-thrus, family camping, tenting, dump, laundry, groceries. ◆◆◆◆RECREATION: swim pool, river swim, canoeing, pond/stream fishing, playground. Pets welcome, breed restrict. Partial handicap access. Open May 1 - Oct 15. Big rigs welcome. Rate in 2010 $30-36 for 4 persons. Member ARVC, ARVC MI. Phone: (800)647-2267.

(SE) Valley Plaza Resort RV Park—(Bay) *From jct Business US 10/Eastman Rd & US 10: Go 6-1/4 mi E on US 10, then 1/4 mi W on Bay City Rd, then 500 feet N on Rockwell Dr. Enter on R.* ◆◆◆◆FACILITIES: 77 sites, typical site width 30 ft, 77 full hkups, (30/50 amps), 46 pull-thrus, family camping. ◆◆◆◆◆RECREATION: swim pool, lake swim, canoeing, lake fishing, playground. Pets welcome. Partial handicap access. No tents. Open Apr 1 - Nov 10. Big rigs welcome. Rate in 2010 $39-50 per vehicle. Member ARVC, ARVC MI. Phone: (989)496-2159.

MILAN—J-5

(SE) K C CAMPGROUND—(Monroe) *From jct Hwy 50 & US 23: Go 8 mi N on US 23 (exit 25), then 1-1/2 mi SE on Plank Rd, then 1/2 mi E on Sherman Rd. Enter on R.*

◆◆◆FACILITIES: 129 sites, typical site width 30 ft, 100 W&E, 29 E, (20/30 amps), 30 pull-thrus, WiFi Instant Internet at site, family camping, tenting, dump, non-guest dump $, portable dump, ltd groc, LP gas by weight/by meter, ice, picnic tables, fire rings, wood.

◆◆◆RECREATION: rec hall, pavilion, coin games, lake swim, golf nearby, bsktball, playground, activities, (wkends), horseshoes, sports field, v-ball.

Pets welcome. Partial handicap access. Open Apr 1 - Mid Nov. Clubs welcome. Rate in 2010 $25-28 for 2 persons. MC/VISA/DISC/Debit. Member ARVC, ARVC MI.

K C CAMPGROUND—Continued on next page

Woodall's Tip... Completely Revised and Updated Annually to Bring you the most update information available

MILAN—Continued
K C CAMPGROUND—Continued

Phone: (734)439-1076
Address: 14048 Sherman Rd, Milan, MI 48160
Lat/Lon: 42.06319/-83.63790
Email: kccampground@aol.com
Web: www.kccampgroundmilan.com

SEE AD PAGE 394

MIO—E-5

(N) AU SABLE SF (Mio Pond)—(Oscoda) *From town: Go 3 mi N on Hwy 72 & W on Popps Rd. Enter on L.* FACILITIES: 24 sites, 24 no hkups. RECREATION: canoeing, ramp, pond fishing. Open all yr. Phone: (989)348-6371.

HURON NATIONAL FOREST (Mack Lake Campground) —(Oscoda) *From jct Hwy-72 & Hwy-33: Go 3-2/3 mi S on Hwy-33, then 4-1/3 mi E on CR-489.* FACILITIES: 42 sites, 30 ft max RV length, 42 no hkups, tenting. RECREATION: boating, no motors, lake fishing. Open Apr 15 - Sep 15. Phone: (989)826-3252.

(W) MIO PINE ACRES CAMPGROUND—(Oscoda) *From jct Hwy-33 & Hwy-72: Go 1 mi W on Hwy-72. Enter on L.*

◊◊◊FACILITIES: 75 sites, typical site width 30 ft, 40 W&E, 35 E, (20/30/50 amps), some extd stay sites (summer), 12 pull-thrus, heater not allowed, WiFi Instant Internet at site, family camping, tenting, cabins, dump, non-guest dump $, laundry, groceries, RV supplies, LP gas by weight/by meter, ice, picnic tables, fire rings, grills, wood.

◊◊RECREATION: mini-golf, ($), golf nearby, bike rental 20 bike rentals, playground, activities, (wkends), horseshoes, v-ball.

Pets welcome, breed restrict. Open Apr 1 - Dec 1. Facilities fully operational May 1 - Nov 1. Big rigs welcome. Escort to site. Clubs welcome. Rate in 2010 $28-30 per family. MC/VISA/DISC/AMEX/Debit. Member ARVC, ARVC MI. FCRV discount. FMCA discount.

Phone: (800)289-2845
Address: 1215 W 8th St (M-72), Mio, MI 48647
Lat/Lon: 44.65216/-84.14591
Email: info@miopineacres.com
Web: www.miopineacres.com

SEE AD THIS PAGE

(N) OSCODA COUNTY PARK—(Oscoda) *In town, off northbound jct Hwy-33 & Hwy-72 on the S side of Mio Dam impoundment of the Au Sable River.* FACILITIES: 138 sites, 35 ft max RV length, 50 W&E, (20/30 amps), 88 no hkups, tenting, dump. RECREATION: river swim, boating, canoeing, lake/river fishing, playground. Partial handicap access. Open Apr 1 - Nov 30. Facilities fully operational May 15 - Sep 15. Phone: (989)826-5114.

MONROE—J-5

(N) Camp Lord Willing Management RV Park & Campground—(Monroe) *From jct I-275 & I-75: Go 2 mi S on I-75 (exit 18), then 1 mi W on Nadeau Rd, then 1 mi N on Hwy 125, then 1 mi W on Stumpmier Rd. Enter on R.* ◊◊◊◊FACILITIES: 100 sites, typical site width 40 ft, 100 full hkups, (20/30/50 amps), 6 pull-thrus, family camping, tenting, laundry. ◊◊◊RECREATION: lake swim, boating, electric motors only, ramp, pond fishing, playground. Pets welcome. Partial handicap access. Open all yr. Big rigs welcome. Rate in 2010 $28-42 per family. Phone: (877)210-8700.

(S) GO KARTS PLUS—*From jct I-275 & I-75: Go 9 mi S on I-75 (exit 11), then 3/4 mi NW on La Plaisance Rd. Enter on L.* Large arcade, birthday party packages, 18 hole miniature golf, grand prix go-cart track, batting cages, company picnics and family reunions. Open Apr 1 - Oct. MC/VISA/Debit.

Phone: (734)384-kart
Address: 14999 Laplaisance Rd, Monroe, MI 48161
Lat/Lon: 41.88903/-83.39619
Email: harbortown@harbortownrv.com
Web: www.harbortownrv.com

SEE AD DETROIT PAGE 379

E—Continued

(S) HARBORTOWN RV RESORT—(Monroe) *From jct I-275 & I-75: Go 9 mi S on I-75 (exit 11, then 3/4 mi NW on La Plaisance Rd. Enter on L.*

◊◊◊◊◊FACILITIES: 250 sites, typical site width 30 ft, 143 full hkups, 107 W&E, (30/50 amps), some extd stay sites (summer), 81 pull-thrus, cable TV, WiFi Instant Internet at site, family camping, tenting, cabins, dump, non-guest dump $, laundry, ltd groc, RV supplies, ice, picnic tables, fire rings, grills, wood.

◊◊◊◊◊RECREATION: rec hall, pavilion, coin games, swim pool, mini-golf, ($), golf nearby, bsktball, playground, activities, (wkends), horseshoes, sports field, v-ball.

Pets welcome. Partial handicap access. Open all yr. Facilities fully operational Easter - Halloween. Big rigs welcome. Clubs welcome. Rate in 2010 $36-52 per family. MC/VISA/DISC/AMEX/Debit. Member ARVC, ARVC MI.

Text 107932 to (440)725-8687 to see our Visual Tour.

Phone: (734)384-4700
Address: 14931 Laplaisance Rd, Monroe, MI 48161
Lat/Lon: 41.88731/-83.39587
Email: harbortown@harbortownrv.com
Web: www.harbortownrv.com

SEE AD DETROIT PAGE 379

(NE) STERLING STATE PARK—(Monroe) *From town: Go 5 mi N on N Dixie Hwy.* FACILITIES: 256 sites, 256 E, tenting, dump, ltd groc. RECREATION: boating, ramp, dock, lake fishing, playground. Partial handicap access. Open July 11 - Dec 1. Facilities fully operational Apr 15 - Nov 1. Phone: (734)289-2715.

MONTAGUE—G-2

(E) TRAILWAY CAMPGROUND—(Muskegon) *From jct US 31 (exit Whitehall-Montague) & Business 31: Go 2-1/4 mi W on Business 31. Enter on R.* FACILITIES: 55 sites, typical site width 30 ft, 16 full hkups, 3 W&E, 36 no hkups, 21 pull-thrus, tenting, dump. RECREATION: play equipment. Open late Apr - mid Oct. Member ARVC, ARVC MI. Phone: (231)894-4903.

(NE) White River RV Park & Campground—(Muskegon) *From jct Hwy 120 & US 31: Go 12 mi on N on US 31, then 5 mi E on CR B-86/Fruitvale Rd. Enter on R.* ◊◊◊◊FACILITIES: 229 sites, typical site width 40 ft, 56 full hkups, 130 W&E, (20/30/50 amps), 43 no hkups, 65 pull-thrus, family camping, tenting, dump, laundry, groceries. ◊◊◊◊RECREATION: swim pool, canoeing, lake/river fishing, playground. Pets welcome. Partial handicap access. Open May 1 - Oct 15. Facilities fully operational Memorial Day - mid Sep. Big rigs welcome. Rate in 2010 $28-44 per family. Member ARVC, ARVC MI. Phone: (231)894-4708.

MORLEY—G-3

(SW) Mecosta Pines Campground—(Mecosta) *From jct west Hwy 20 & US 131: Go 6 mi S on US 131 (exit 125), then 1-1/2 mi E on Jefferson Rd. Enter on R.* ◊◊◊FACILITIES: 62 sites, typical site width 30 ft, 10 full hkups, 40 W&E, (20/30/50 amps), 50 amps ($), 12 no hkups, family camping, tenting, dump, laundry, ltd groc. ◊◊◊RECREATION: swim pool, river swim, river fishing, playground. Pets welcome, breed restrict. Partial handicap access. Open Mar 1 - Nov 15. Facilities fully operational Memorial Day - Labor Day. Big rigs welcome. Member ARVC, ARVC MI. Phone: (231)856-4556.

MOSCOW—J-4

(E) MOSCOW MAPLES RV PARK—(Hillsdale) *From jct US 127 & US 12: Go 7 mi W on US 12. Enter on L.*

◊◊◊FACILITIES: 185 sites, typical site width 25 ft, 100 full hkups, 65 W&E, 20 E, (20/30 amps), some extd stay sites (summer), WiFi Instant Internet at site, family camping, tenting, RV storage, dump, non-guest dump $, laundry, ltd groc, RV supplies, LP gas by weight/by meter, ice, picnic tables, fire rings, wood.

◊◊◊RECREATION: rec hall, rec room/area, coin games, swim pool, mini-golf, ($), golf nearby, bsktball, playground, activities, (wkends), horseshoes, v-ball.

Pets welcome. Partial handicap access. Open May 1 - Oct 1. Clubs welcome. Rate in 2010 $25-40 per family. MC/VISA/DISC/Debit. Member ARVC, ARVCMI.

Phone: (517)688-9853
Address: 8291 E Chicago Rd, Moscow, MI 49257
Lat/Lon: 42.05536/-84.49111
Email: camping@moscowmaples.com
Web: www.moscowmaples.com

SEE AD THIS PAGE

MOUNT PLEASANT—G-4

DEERFIELD NATURE PARK—(Isabella) *From jct US 10 & US 127: Go 13 mi South on US 127 (to Lansing), then .7 mi to US 127 Bus exit toward Mt. Pleasant, then 1.4 mi on N Mission St/US 127 BR, then 6.4 mi on E High St/ M-20 to park.* FACILITIES: 10 sites, 10 no hkups, tenting. RECREATION: river swim, boating, ramp, river fishing. Pets welcome. Open all yr. Phone: (989)772-0911.

MUNISING—C-3

(NW) HIAWATHA NATIONAL FOREST (Bay Furnace Campground)—(Alger) *From jct Hwy 94 & Hwy 28: Go 4-3/4 mi NW on Hwy 28.* FACILITIES: 50 sites, 50 no hkups, tenting, dump. RECREATION: lake swim, boating, lake fishing. Partial handicap access. Open May 15 - Sep 30. Phone: (906)387-2512.

(W) MUNISING TOURIST PARK CAMPGROUND—(Alger) *From jct Hwy 94 & Hw 28: Go 4-3/4 mi W on Hwy 28. Enter on R.*

FACILITIES: 99 sites, typical site width 30 ft, 69 W&E, 8 E, (20/30/50 amps), 22 no hkups, 9 pull-thrus, WiFi Instant Internet at site, family camping, tenting, dump, non-guest dump $, RV supplies, ice, picnic tables, fire rings, grills, wood.

RECREATION: pavilion, lake swim, boating, canoeing, kayaking, ramp, dock, lake fishing, golf nearby, bsktball, playground, horseshoes, sports field, hiking trails, v-ball. Rec open to public.

MUNISING TOURIST PARK CAMPGROUND—Continued on next page

MUNISING—Continued
MUNISING TOURIST PARK CAMPGROUND—Continued

Pets welcome. Partial handicap access. Open May - Oct. Big rigs welcome. Clubs welcome. MC/VISA/DISC/Debit.

Phone: (906)387-3145
Address: E 8518 M-28 W, Munising, MI 49862
Lat/Lon: 46.44005/-86.67741
Email: cityofm@jamadots.com
Web: www.munisingtouristpark.com

SEE AD PAGE 395

(SW) Otter Lake Campground—(Alger) *From jct Hwy 28 & Hwy 94: Go 6 mi W on Hwy 94, then 2-1/2 mi SE on Buckhorn Rd. Enter on R.* ◇◇◇FACILITIES: 70 sites, typical site width 25 ft, 52 E, (20/30 amps), 18 no hkups, 3 pull-thrus, family camping, tenting, dump, laundry, ltd groc. ◇◇◇RECREATION: lake swim, boating, 5 hp limit, canoeing, ramp, dock, lake fishing, playground. Pets welcome. Open May - Nov. Rate in 2010 $20 for 4 persons. Phone: (906)387-4648.

(N) PICTURED ROCKS CRUISES—*From jct Hwy 94 & Hwy 28: Go 1-1/2 mi W on Hwy 28, then 1/2 block N on Elm Ave. Enter on L.* From 2-1/2 hours to 2 hours & 40 minute cruises covering more than 37 miles of breathtaking beauty of the Pictured Rocks National lakeshore located along the south shore of Lake Superior. Open May 15 - Oct 17. MC/VISA/Debit.

Phone: (800)650-2379
Address: 100 City Park Dr, Munising, MI 49862
Lat/Lon: 46.41241/-86.65464
Email: pictrocks@jamadots.com
Web: www.picturedrocks.com

SEE AD PAGE 395

(SE) Wandering Wheels Campground—(Alger) *From town: Go 3-1/2 mi E on Hwy-28. Enter on L.* ◇◇◇FACILITIES: 97 sites, typical site width 40 ft, 26 full hkups, 31 W&E, 30 E, (20/30/50 amps), 10 no hkups, 41 pull-thrus, family camping, tenting, dump, laundry, ltd groc. ◇◇◇RECREATION: swim pool, playground. Pets welcome. Open May 15 - Oct 15. Rate in 2010 $24.95-45.95 for 4 persons. Member ARVC, ARVC MI. Phone: (906)387-3315.

MUNITH—I-4

(SW) THE OAKS RESORT—(Jackson) *From jct Hwy 52 & Hwy 106: Go 7 mi S on Hwy 106, then 2 mi S on Sayers Rd, then 3/4 mi E on Coon Hill Rd, then 2 mi S on Duhn Rd, thend 3/4 mi W on Cutler Rd. Enter at end.*

◇◇◇FACILITIES: typical site width 40 ft, 40 ft max RV length, 186 W&E, (20/30 amps), 29 no hkups, 10 pull-thrus, family camping, tenting, dump, non-guest dump $, portable dump, laundry, ltd groc, RV supplies, LP gas by weight/by meter, ice, picnic tables, fire rings, wood.

◇◇◇RECREATION: rec hall, rec room/area, pavilion, coin games, lake swim, pond fishing, fishing supplies, mini-golf, ($), golf nearby, bsktball, playground, activities, (wkends), horseshoes, sports field, hiking trails, v-ball. Rec open to public.

Pets welcome, breed restrict. Partial handicap access. Open all yr. Facilities fully operational Apr 15 - Oct 15. Clubs welcome. Rate in 2010 $20-25 for 2 persons. MC/VISA/DISC/Debit. CCUSA 50% Discount. CCUSA reservations Recommended, CCUSA max stay Unlimited, CCUSA disc. not avail F,Sa, CCUSA disc. not avail holidays. Fully operational Apr 15-Oct 15. No aggressive breed dogs.

Woodall's Tip... Learn what's essential to know about RVing in Canada by reading the Crossing Into Canada Information.

MUNITH—Continued
THE OAKS RESORT—Continued

Phone: (517)596-2747
Address: 7800 Cutler Rd, Munith, MI 49259
Lat/Lon: 42.33910/-84.27032
Email: oakscamping@yahoo.com
Web: www.oakscamping.com

Reserve Online at Woodalls.com

SEE AD TRAVEL SECTION PAGE 359

MUSKEGON—H-2

(S) ALL SEASONS RV SUPERCENTER—*From jct US 31 & I-96: Go 1/4 mi E on I-96 (exit 2), then 1/4 mi N on Hile Rd, then 500 ft E on Airline Rd. Enter on R.* SALES: travel trailers, park models, truck campers, 5th wheels, toy hauler, Class A motorhomes, Class C motorhomes, Class B motorhomes, fold-down camping trailers, pre-owned unit sales. SERVICES: full-time mech, RV appliance repair, LP gas by weight/by meter, dump station, sells parts/accessories, installs hitches. Open all yr. MC/VISA/Debit.

Phone: (231)739-5269
Address: 4701 Airline Rd, Muskegon, MI 49444
Lat/Lon: 43.16736/-86.19913
Email: ted@allseasonsrv.com
Web: www.allseasonsrv.com

SEE AD THIS PAGE

(N) Duck Creek RV Resort—(Muskegon) *From jct Hwy 46 & US 31: Go 6-1/2 mi N on US 31, then 2 mi N on Russell Rd, then 3 mi W on Riley Thompson Rd. Enter on L.* ◇◇◇◇◇FACILITIES: 157 sites, typical site width 50 ft, 157 full hkups, (20/30/50 amps), family camping, laundry, ltd groc. ◇◇◇◇RECREATION: swim pool, playground. Pets welcome. Partial handicap access. No tents. Open May 1 - Oct 15. Big rigs welcome. Rate in 2010 $35-50 for 8 persons. Member ARVC, ARVCMI. Phone: (231)766-3646.

(N) Lake Sch-Nepp-A-Ho Campground—(Muskegon) *From jct Hwy 46 & US 31: Go 6-1/2 mi N on US 31, then 1/4 mi S on Russell Rd, then 100 yds E on Tyler Rd. Enter on L.* ◇◇◇FACILITIES: 100 sites, typical site width 30 ft, 70 W&E, 12 E, (20/30/50 amps), 18 no hkups, 9 pull-thrus, heater not allowed, WiFi Internet central location, family camping, tenting, RV storage, dump, non-guest dump $, portable dump, laundry, ltd groc, RV supplies, LP gas by weight/by meter, ice, picnic tables, fire rings, wood. ◇◇◇RECREATION: lake swim, boating, electric motors only, lake fishing, fishing supplies, bsktball, playground, horseshoes, v-ball. Pets welcome ($), breed restrict. Partial handicap access. Open May 1 - Oct 1. Rate in 2010 $26-40 for 4 persons. MC/VISA/DISC/Debit. ATM. CCUSA 50% Discount.

Phone: (231)766-2209
Address: 390 E Tyler Rd, Muskegon, MI 49445
Lat/Lon: 43.31763/-86.23517
Email: campmaster@michigan-campgrounds.com
Web: www.michigan-campgrounds.com

(E) LAKESHORE RV CENTER—*From jct US 31 & Hwy 46 (Apple Ave): Go 4 mi E on Hwy 46 (Apple Ave). Enter on L.* SALES: travel trailers, park models, 5th wheels, toy hauler, Class A motorhomes, Class C motorhomes, Class B motorhomes, fold-down camping trailers, pre-owned unit sales. SERVICES: full-time mech, RV appliance repair, body work/collision repair, bus. hrs emerg rd svc, mobile RV svc, RV towing, LP gas by weight/by meter, RV rentals, RV storage, sells parts/accessories, installs hitches. Open all yr. MC/VISA/DISC/AMEX/Debit.

Phone: (231)788-2040
Address: 4500 Apple Ave, Muskegon, MI 49442
Lat/Lon: 43.23483/-86.13335
Email: info@lakeshore-rv.com
Web: www.lakeshore-rv.com

SEE AD THIS PAGE

SKEGON—Continued

(N) Muskegon-KOA—(Muskegon) *From jct Hwy 46 & US 31: Go 6-1/2 mi on US 31, then 50 yards N on Russell Rd, then 1/4 mi E on Bard, then 1/4 mi S on Strand. Enter on L.* ◇◇◇FACILITIES: 91 sites, typical site width 38 ft, 35 ft max RV length, 42 full hkups, 37 W&E, 12 E, (20/30 amps), family camping, tenting, dump, laundry, groceries. ◇◇◇◇RECREATION: lake swim, boating, no motors, lake fishing, playground. Pets welcome, breed restrict. Partial handicap access. Open May 1 - Mid Oct. Rate in 2010 $25-45 for 2 persons. Phone: (800)562-3902. KOA discount.

(S) P.J. HOFFMASTER STATE PARK—(Muskegon) *From jct I-96 & US-31: Go 5 mi S on US-31, then 2-1/2 mi W on Pontaluna Rd to 6585 Lake Harbor Rd.* FACILITIES: 293 sites, 293 E, tenting, dump, ltd groc. RECREATION: lake swim, lake fishing, playground. Partial handicap access. Open Apr 11 - Oct 27. Phone: (231)798-3711.

NAUBINWAY—C-4

(SW) LAKE SUPERIOR SF (Big Knob)—(Mackinac) *From town: Go 14 mi SW on US 2 & Big Knob Rd. Enter on R.* FACILITIES: 23 sites, 23 no hkups, tenting. RECREATION: lake swim, canoeing, ramp, lake fishing. Open all yr. Phone: (906)635-5281.

(E) LAKE SUPERIOR SF (Hog Island Point)—(Mackinac) *From jct Hwy 117 & US 2: Go 13 mi E on US 2.* FACILITIES: 59 sites, 59 no hkups, tenting. RECREATION: lake swim, boating, canoeing, ramp, lake fishing. Open May - Dec. Phone: (906)635-5281.

(W) LAKE SUPERIOR SF (Milakokia Lake)—(Mackinac) *From jct Hwy 117 & US 2: Go 11-1/2 mi W on US 2, then 1-1/2 mi S on Pike Lake Grade.* FACILITIES: 35 sites, 35 no hkups, tenting. RECREATION: lake swim, boating, ramp, lake fishing. Open May - Dec. Phone: (906)635-5281.

NEW ERA—G-2

(W) HOLIDAY CAMPING RESORT—(Oceana) *From jct US 31 (exit 140) & Hwy 20/Stony Lake Rd: Go 1 mi W on Stony Lake Rd. Enter on L.*

◇◇◇FACILITIES: 111 sites, typical site width 35 ft, 80 full hkups, 23 W&E, 8 E, (20/30/50 amps), some extd stay sites (summer), 8 pull-thrus, WiFi Instant Internet at site, family camping, tenting, cabins, RV storage, dump, laundry, ltd groc, RV supplies, ice, picnic tables, fire rings, wood.

◇◇◇RECREATION: rec room/area, pavilion, coin games, swim pool, golf nearby, bsktball, playground, activities, (wkends), horseshoes, sports field, hiking trails, v-ball.

Pets welcome. Partial handicap access. Open May 1 - Oct 1. Big rigs welcome. Clubs welcome. Rate in 2010 $30-35 per family. MC/VISA/Debit. Member ARVC, ARVC MI.

Phone: (231)861-5220
Address: 5483 W Stony Lake Rd, New Era, MI 49446
Lat/Lon: 43.55869/-86.41483
Email: holidaycamping@hughes.net
Web: www.holidaycamping.com

SEE AD TRAVEL SECTION PAGE 359

(W) Stony Haven Campground & Cabins—(Oceana) *From jct US 31 & Hwy 20/Stony Lake Rd: Go 4-1/4 mi W on Stony Lake Rd. Enter on L.* ◇◇FACILITIES: 64 sites, typical site width 30 ft, 38 full hkups, 10 W&E, (20/30/50 amps), 16 no hkups, 2 pull-thrus, phone Internet central location, family camping, tenting, RV storage, dump, non-guest dump $, laundry, RV supplies, ice, picnic tables, fire rings, wood. ◇◇◇RECREATION: pavilion, canoeing, kayaking, float trips, pond fishing, bsktball, 19 bike rentals, playground, shuffleboard court shuffleboard court, horseshoes, hiking trails, v-ball. Pets welcome. Partial handicap access. Open May 1 - Sep 30. Rate in 2010 $20-35 per family. MC/VISA/Debit. Member ARVC, ARVC MI. CCUSA 50% Discount. CCUSA reservations Recommended, CCUSA max stay Unlimited, CCUSA disc. not avail F,Sa, CCUSA disc. not avail holidays.

Phone: (231)861-5201
Address: 8079 W Stony Lake Rd, New Era, MI 49446
Lat/Lon: 43.55531/-86.47870
Email: stonyhaven@oceana.net
Web: www.campingfriend.com/stonyhavencampground

Whether you're dreaming about buying a new RV or are actively shopping, 2011 RV Buyer's Guide is your best source. It contains all the information you need to make an intelligent buying decision. Over 450 vehicles are profiled with complete information about construction features, dimensions, popular options, and more, making comparing models easy. To order your copy go to www.woodalls.com/shop.

NEW HUDSON—I-5

(SE) HAAS LAKE PARK—(Oakland) *From jct US 23 & I-96: Go 8 mi E on I-96 (exit 155), then 1/2 mi S on Milford Rd, then 2 mi E on Grand River Ave, then 1-3/4 mi S on Haas Rd. Enter at end.*

♦♦♦FACILITIES: 494 sites, typical site width 35 ft, 252 full hkups, 242 W&E, (30/50 amps), many extd stay sites (summer), 69 pull-thrus, WiFi Instant Internet at site, family camping, RV storage, dump, non-guest dump $, portable dump, laundry, ltd groc, RV supplies, LP gas by weight/by meter, ice, picnic tables, fire rings, wood, controlled access.

♦♦♦♦RECREATION: rec room/area, pavilion, coin games, lake swim, boating, 5 hp limit, canoeing, kayaking, ramp, lake fishing, fishing supplies, golf nearby, bsktball, playground, activities, horseshoes, sports field, v-ball.

Pets welcome, breed restrict, quantity restrict. Partial handicap access. No tents. Open Mid March - Mid Nov. Big rigs welcome. Clubs welcome. Rate in 2010 $28-38 per family. MC/VISA/DISC/Debit. Member ARVC, ARVC MI.

Phone: (248)437-0900
Address: 25800 Haas Rd, New Hudson, MI 48165
Lat/Lon: 42.48192/-83.57930
Email: service@haaslakepark.com
Web: www.haaslakepark.com

SEE AD TRAVEL SECTION PAGE 360

NEWAYGO—H-3

(NW) CROTON TOWNSHIP PARK—(Newaygo) *From jct Hwy 37 & Hwy 82: Go 8 mi E on CR to the E side of Muskegon River at Croton Dam.* FACILITIES: 150 sites, 36 ft max RV length, 150 E, (20 amps), tenting, dump. RECREATION: lake swim, boating, ramp, lake fishing. Open Apr 15 - Oct 15. Phone: (231)652-4642.

(E) ED HENNING PARK (Newaygo County Park)—(Newaygo) *From town: Go 1/4 mi E on Croton Drive.* FACILITIES: 60 sites, 60 E, tenting, dump. RECREATION: river swim, boating, canoeing, ramp, dock, river fishing, playground. Open Apr 27 - Oct 21. Phone: (231)652-1202.

(W) NEWAYGO STATE PARK—(Newaygo) *Take US-131 to exit 125, then go 5 mi W to Beech St, then N on Beech St to park entrance.* FACILITIES: 99 sites, 99 no hkups, tenting, dump. RECREATION: river swim, boating, ramp, river fishing, playground. Partial handicap access. Open Apr 25 - Nov 2. Phone: (231)856-4452.

NEWBERRY—C-4

(N) Clementz's Northcountry Campground and Cabins—(Luce) *From west jct Hwy 28 & Hwy 123: Go 8-1/2 mi N on Hwy 123. Enter on L.* ♦♦♦FACILITIES: 50 sites, typical site width 30 ft, 8 full hkups, 24 W&E, 8 E, (20/30/50 amps), 10 no hkups, 40 pull-thrus, cable TV, ($), WiFi Internet central location, family camping, tenting, dump, non-guest dump $, laundry, ice, picnic tables, fire rings, wood. ♦♦RECREATION: pavilion, bsktball, playground, horseshoes, hiking trails, v-ball. Pets welcome. Open May 15 - Oct 15. Rate in 2010 $18-24 for 4 persons. MC/VISA/DISC/Debit. Member ARVC, ARVC MI. CCUSA 50% Discount. CCUSA reservations Not Accepted, CCUSA max stay 2 days, Cash only for CCUSA disc., CCUSA disc. not avail holidays. Discount available on dry & rustic sites only. Not available on special event weekends or on full sites at any time. Full site rate is $26, partial rate is $24. Drive-ups only.

Phone: (906)293-8562
Address: 13209 State Hwy M-123, Newberry, MI 49868
Lat/Lon: 46.42403/-85.51028
Email: cclementz@lighthouse.net
Web: www.northcountrycampground.com

(SE) KOA Newberry/Tahquamenon—(Luce) *From west jct Hwy 123 & Hwy 28: Go 1/4 mi E on Hwy 28. Enter on L.* ♦♦♦FACILITIES: 99 sites, typical site width 35 ft, 9 full hkups, 72 W&E, (20/30/50 amps), 18 no hkups, 40 pull-thrus, family camping, tenting, dump, laundry, ltd groc. ♦♦♦RECREATION: swim pool, playground. Pets welcome. Partial handicap access. Open Mid May - Mid Oct. Rate in 2010 $38 for 2 persons. Phone: (800)562-5853. KOA discount.

(NW) LAKE SUPERIOR SF (Mouth of Two Hearted River)—(Luce) *From jct Hwy-28 & Hwy-123: Go 7-1/2 mi N on Hwy-123, then 15 mi NW on CR-407, then 10 mi NE on CR-412, then 3 mi NW on CR-423.* FACILITIES: 39 sites, 39 no hkups, tenting. RECREATION: lake swim, boating, canoeing, ramp, lake fishing. Open all yr. Phone: (906)293-3293.

(NW) LAKE SUPERIOR SF (Perch Lake)—(Luce) *From jct Hwy-28 & Hwy-123: Go 7-1/2 mi N on Hwy-123, then 19 mi NW on CR-407.* FACILITIES: 35 sites, 35 no hkups, tenting. RECREATION: lake swim, boating, ramp, lake fishing. Open all yr. Phone: (906)293-3293.

(NW) MUSKALLONGE LAKE STATE PARK—(Luce) *From jct Hwy-28 & Hwy-123: Go 33 mi N on Hwy-123 & CR-407.* FACILITIES: 159 sites, 159 E, tenting, dump. RECREATION: lake swim, boating, ramp, lake fishing, playground. Open Apr 15 - Nov 1. Facilities fully operational May 3 - Oct 30. Phone: (906)658-3338.

NILES—J-2

(SE) SPAULDING LAKE CAMPGROUND—(Cass) *From jct US 12 & Hwy 51: Go 1/4 mi S on Hwy 51, then 2 mi E on Bell Rd. Enter on L.*

♦♦♦♦FACILITIES: 120 sites, typical site width 30 ft, 120 full hkups, (20/30/50 amps), 44 pull-thrus, WiFi Instant Internet at site, family camping, tenting, RV storage, laundry, RV supplies, ice, picnic tables, fire rings, wood.

♦♦♦♦RECREATION: rec hall, lake swim, lake/stream fishing, fishing supplies, golf nearby, bsktball, playground, shuffleboard court shuffleboard court, horseshoes, sports field, hiking trails, v-ball.

Pets welcome. Partial handicap access. Open Apr 1 - Oct 31. Big rigs welcome. Clubs welcome. Rate in 2010 $28 for 2 persons.

Phone: (269)684-1393
Address: 33524 Bell St, Niles, MI 49120
Lat/Lon: 41.79395/-86.21503
Email: spauldingcampground@yahoo.com
Web: www.spauldinglake.com

SEE AD SOUTH BEND, IN PAGE 244

NORTH BRANCH—H-5

(W) Sutter's Recreation Area—(Lapeer) *From jct Hwy-24 & Hwy-90: Go 1-3/4 mi E on Hwy-90, then 1/2 mi S on McKibben Rd, then 1/2 mi W on Tozer Rd. Enter on R.* ♦♦♦FACILITIES: 220 sites, typical site width 35 ft, 127 full hkups, 93 W&E, (20/30 amps), 3 pull-thrus, family camping, tenting, dump, laundry, ltd groc. ♦♦♦RECREATION: lake swim, lake fishing, playground. Pets welcome ($), breed restrict. Partial handicap access. Open Apr 15 - Nov 1. Rate in 2010 $26-29 per family. Member ARVC, ARVC MI. Phone: (810)688-3761.

(SW) WASHAKIE CAMPGROUND & GOLF—(Lapeer) *From jct Hwy 90 & Hwy 24: Go 1 mi S on Hwy 24, then 4-3/4 mi E on Burnside Rd. Enter on L.*

♦♦♦♦FACILITIES: 96 sites, typical site width 30 ft, 96 W&E, (30 amps), mostly extd stay sites (summer), heater not allowed, cable TV, WiFi Internet central location, family camping, RV storage, dump, non-guest dump $, laundry, ltd groc, RV supplies, LP bottle exch, ice, picnic tables, wood.

♦♦♦♦RECREATION: rec hall, pavilion, lake swim, boating, electric motors only, lake fishing, fishing supplies, putting green, golf nearby, playground, horseshoes, hiking trails.

Pets welcome. Partial handicap access. No tents. Open May 1 - Nov 1. Clubs welcome. Rate in 2010 $27 per family. Member ARVC, ARVCMI.

Phone: (810)688-3235
Address: 3461 Burnside Rd, North Branch, MI 48461
Lat/Lon: 43.20694/-83.22051
Email: sales@washakiegolfrv.com
Web: www.washakiegolfrv.com

SEE AD THIS PAGE

NORTH MUSKEGON—H-2

(W) MUSKEGON STATE PARK—(Muskegan) *From town: Go 5 mi W on Giles Rd.* FACILITIES: 247 sites, 247 E, tenting, laundry, groceries. RECREATION: lake swim, boating, ramp, lake fishing, playground. Partial handicap access. Open May 2 - Oct 27. Phone: (231)744-3480.

(W) PIONEER PARK (Muskegon County)—(Muskegon) *From jct US-31 & Hwy-120: Go 2 mi SW on Hwy-120 (Holton Rd), then 7 mi W on Giles Rd, then 1/4 mi N on Scenic Drive to park entrance on Lake Michigan.* FACILITIES: 235 sites, 235 W&E, tenting, dump. RECREATION: lake swim, lake fishing, playground. Open May - Sep. Phone: (231)744-3480.

NORTHPORT—E-4

(NE) LEELANAU STATE PARK—(Grand Traverse) *From jct Hwy 201 & Hwy 22: Go 8 mi N on Hwy 201.* FACILITIES: 52 sites, 52 no hkups, tenting. RECREATION: lake swim, canoeing, lake fishing, playground. Partial handicap access. Open May 3 - Nov 3. Phone: (231)386-5422.

OMER—F-5

(SE) BIG BEND CANOE LIVERY—*From jct US 23 & Hwy 65: Go 1-1/2 mi S on Hale Rd, then 1 mi W on Conrad Rd. Enter on L.* Canoe, kayak & tube (single, family & double) trips on Rifle River ranging from 2-1/2 to 6 hours. Bussed upriver and all trips end at campground. MC/VISA/Debit.

Phone: (989)653-2267
Address: 513 Conrad Rd, Standish, MI 48658
Lat/Lon: 44.02594/-83.82697
Email: bigbendfamilycampground@hotmail.com
Web: www.bigbendcamp.com

SEE AD THIS PAGE

(SE) BIG BEND FAMILY CAMPGROUND—(Arenac) *From jct US 23 & Hwy 65: Go 1-1/2 mi S on Hale Rd, then 1 mi W on Conrad Rd. Enter on L.*

♦♦♦FACILITIES: 172 sites, typical site width 40 ft, 132 W&E, (20/30/50 amps), 40 no hkups, some extd stay sites (summer), WiFi Instant Internet at site, family camping, tenting, RV's/park model rentals, RV storage, dump, non-guest dump $, portable dump, laundry, ltd groc, RV supplies, LP gas by weight/by meter, LP bottle exch, ice, picnic tables, fire rings, wood.

♦♦♦♦RECREATION: rec hall, rec room/area, pavilion, coin games, swim pool, lake/river swim, canoeing, kayaking, 58 canoe/25 kayak rentals, float trips, lake/river fishing, fishing supplies, golf nearby, bsktball, playground, activities, (wkends), horseshoes, sports field, v-ball. Rec open to public.

Pets welcome. Partial handicap access. Open Late Mar - Mid Oct. Escort to site. Clubs welcome. Rate in 2010 $22-30 for 4 persons. MC/VISA/DISC/Debit. Member ARVC, ARVC MI.

Phone: (989)653-2267
Address: 513 Conrad Rd, Standish, MI 48658
Lat/Lon: 44.02594/-83.82697
Email: bigbendfamilycampground@hotmail.com
Web: www.BIGBENDCAMP.com

SEE AD THIS PAGE

(NW) Rippling Waters Campground—(Arenac) *From jct I-75 (exit 188) & US 23: Go 8 mi NE on US 23, then 3/4 mi N on Main St. Enter on L.* ♦♦♦FACILITIES: 100 sites, typical site width 30 ft, 13 full hkups, 46 W&E, 37 E, (20/30 amps), 4 no hkups, WiFi Internet central location, family camping, tenting, RV storage, dump, ltd groc, RV supplies, ice, picnic tables, fire rings, wood. ♦♦♦RECREATION: pavilion, river swim, float trips, river fishing, playground, activities, horseshoes, hiking trails, v-ball. Pets welcome. Partial handicap access. Open May 1 - Nov 30. Rate in 2010 $26-40 per family. MC/VISA/DISC. CCUSA 50% Discount. CCUSA reservations Recommended, CCUSA max stay 5 days, Cash only for CCUSA disc. Discount not available Memorial Day weekend thru Labor Day.

Phone: (989)653-2200
Address: 864 Main St Rd, Omer, MI 48749
Lat/Lon: 44.05856/-83.85734
Email: contact@ripplingwaterscamping.com
Web: www.ripplingwaterscamping.com

ONAWAY—D-5

(NE) MACKINAW SF (Black Lake)—(Presque Isle) *From town: Go 11 mi NE on Hwy 211, CR 489, Black Mtn Rd, then Doriva Beach Rd.* FACILITIES: 50 sites, 50 no hkups, tenting. RECREATION: lake swim, boating, canoeing, ramp, lake fishing. Partial handicap access. Open all yr. Phone: (989)785-4251.

(S) MACKINAW SF (Shoepac Lake)—(Presque Isle) *From jct Hwy-68 & Hwy-33: Go 10-1/2 mi S on Hwy-33, then 2 mi E on Tomahawk Lake Hwy, then 1 mi N on access road.* FACILITIES: 28 sites, 28 no hkups, tenting. RECREATION: lake swim, boating, ramp, lake fishing. Partial handicap access. Open all yr. Phone: (989)785-4251.

ONAWAY—Continued on next page

ONAWAY—Continued

(N) ONAWAY STATE PARK—(Presque Isle) *From jct Hwy-68 & Hwy-211: Go 5-1/2 mi N on Hwy-211.* FACILITIES: 96 sites, 96 E, (30 amps), tenting, dump. RECREATION: lake swim, boating, ramp, dock, lake fishing, playground. Partial handicap access. Open Apr 11 - Nov 2. Phone: (989)733-8279.

ONSTED—J-4

(N) W. J. HAYES STATE PARK—(Lenawee) *From jct US 12 & Hwy 124: Go 1/2 mi N on Hwy 124.* FACILITIES: 185 sites, 185 E, tenting, dump, ltd groc. RECREATION: lake swim, boating, canoeing, ramp, lake fishing, playground. Partial handicap access. Open Apr 12 - Nov 1. Facilities fully operational Apr 11 - Nov 2. Phone: (517)467-7401.

ONTONAGON—A-6

(S) RIVER ROAD RV PARK & CAMPGROUND—(Ontonagon) *From jct US 45 & Hwy 64: Go 1/2 mi W on Hwy 64, then 3/4 mi N on North River Rd. Enter on R.*

WELCOME

◆◆◆FACILITIES: 42 sites, typical site width 35 ft, 30 full hkups, 6 E, (30/50 amps), 6 no hkups, 36 pull-thrus, cable TV, WiFi Instant Internet at site, family camping, tenting, RV storage, dump, non-guest dump $, laundry, ice, picnic tables, fire rings, wood.

◆◆◆RECREATION: river swim, boating, canoeing, kayaking, dock, lake/river fishing, golf nearby, bsktball, playground, horseshoes, sports field, v-ball, local tours.

Pets welcome. Partial handicap access. Open all yr. Facilities fully operational May - Oct. Big rigs welcome. Clubs welcome. Rate in 2010 $25-35 for 2 persons. MC/VISA/DISC/Debit.

Phone: (906)884-4600
Address: 600 River Rd, Ontonagon, MI 49953
Lat/Lon: 46.86390/-89.31804
Email: riverrd@jamadots.com
Web: www.riverroadrvpark.net

SEE AD THIS PAGE

ORTONVILLE—H-5

(SW) CLEARWATER CAMPGROUND—(Oakland) *From jct I-75 (exit 91) & Hwy 15: Go 6-1/4 mi N on Hwy 15. Enter on L.*

WELCOME

◆◆◆◆FACILITIES: 114 sites, typical site width 25 ft, 114 full hkups, (20/30/50 amps), some extd stay sites (summer), 12 pull-thrus, WiFi Internet central location, family camping, tenting, RV's/park model rentals, cabins, RV storage, dump, non-guest dump $, laundry, ltd groc, RV supplies, ice, picnic tables, patios, fire rings, wood, controlled access.

◆◆◆RECREATION: rec hall, pavilion, lake swim, boating, electric motors only, canoeing,

ORTONVILLE—Continued
CLEARWATER CAMPGROUND—Continued

kayaking, 3 rowboat rentals, lake fishing, fishing supplies, golf nearby, bsktball, playground, activities, (wkends), horseshoes, hiking trails, v-ball.

Pets welcome, breed restrict. Partial handicap access. Open Apr 15 - Oct 15. No credit cards. Big rigs welcome. Clubs welcome. Rate in 2010 $35-50 per family.

Phone: (248)627-3820
Address: 1140 S Ortonville Rd (Hwy 15), Ortonville, MI 48462
Lat/Lon: 42.83638/-83.44762
Email: clearwatercampground1140@yahoo.com
Web: www.campsmore.com

SEE AD THIS PAGE

OSCODA—F-5

(NW) AU SABLE SF (Van Etten Lake)—(Iosco) *From town: Go 4-1/2 mi NW on US 23 & CR F41 (Old Hwy 171).* FACILITIES: 58 sites, 58 no hkups, tenting. RECREATION: lake swim, boating, ramp, lake fishing. Open all yr. Phone: (989)348-6371.

(W) OLD ORCHARD PARK (Iosco County Park)—(Alcona) *From jct US-23 & River Rd (at stop light in Oscoda): Go 8 mi W on River Rd.* FACILITIES: 525 sites, 38 ft max RV length, 200 W&E, (30 amps), 325 no hkups, 4 pull-thrus, tenting, dump, groceries. RECREATION: river swim, boating, ramp, river fishing, playground. Open all yr. Facilities fully operational May 1 - Oct 31. Phone: (989)739-7814.

(SW) Oscoda KOA—(Iosco) *From jct Hwy 55 & US 23: Go 14 mi N on US 23, then 3/4 mi W on Johnson Rd, then 3/4 mi S on Forest Ave. Enter at end.* ◆◆◆◆FACILITIES: 146 sites, typical site width 35 ft, 43 full hkups, 68 W&E, (20/30/50 amps), 35 no hkups, 65 pull-thrus, family camping, tenting, dump, laundry, groceries. ◆◆◆◆RECREATION: swim pool, playground. Pets welcome, breed restrict. Partial handicap access. Open mid Apr - mid Oct. Big rigs welcome. Rate in 2010 $34-54 for 2 persons. Member ARVC, ARVC MI. Phone: (800)562-9667. KOA discount.

OSSINEKE—E-6

(NE) MACKINAW SF (Ossineke)—(Alpena) *From town: Go 1 mi E off US-23.* FACILITIES: 42 sites, 42 no hkups, tenting. RECREATION: lake swim, boating, ramp, lake fishing. Partial handicap access. Open all yr. Phone: (989)785-4251.

(S) Paul Bunyan Family Kamp—(Alcona) *From jct Hwy 32 & US 23: go 15 mi S on US 23, then 50 feet W on Hubert Rd. Enter on L.* ◆◆FACILITIES: 80 sites, 19 full hkups, 50 W&E, (20/30 amps), 11 no hkups, 52 pull-thrus, family camping, tenting, dump, laundry, ltd groc. ◆◆RECREATION: swim pool, play equipment. Pets welcome. Open mid May - Dec 1. Rate in 2010 $22.50-24 for 4 persons. Phone: (989)471-2921.

Woodall's Tip... Spray your garbage and trash with ammonia to keep the animals away.

OTISVILLE—H-5

(N) COVENANT HILLS CAMP—(Genesee) *From jct Hwy 57 & Hwy 15: Go 1 mi N on Hwy 15, then 3/4 mi E on Farrand Rd. Enter on L.*

WELCOME

◆◆◆◆FACILITIES: 333 sites, typical site width 30 ft, 321 full hkups, (20/30/50 amps), 12 no hkups, 55 pull-thrus, WiFi Internet central location, family camping, tenting, cabins, RV storage, dump, non-guest dump $, portable dump, ltd groc, RV supplies, ice, picnic tables, fire rings, wood.

CAMPCLUB USA

◆◆◆◆◆RECREATION: rec hall, rec room/area, pavilion, lake swim, boating, no motors, canoeing, kayaking, 10 rowboat/16 canoe/8 kayak/6 pedal boat rentals, lake fishing, golf nearby, bsktball, playground, activities, (wkends), horseshoes, sports field, hiking trails, v-ball. Rec open to public.

Pets welcome. Partial handicap access. Open all yr. Facilities fully operational Apr 1 - Oct 31. Big rigs welcome. Clubs welcome. Rate in 2010 $32 per family. MC/VISA/DISC/Debit. CCUSA 50% Discount. CCUSA reservations Recommended, CCUSA max stay Unlimited. Not available Memorial Day or Labor Day weekends or 3rd thru 4th weekends of Jul. Fully operational Apr thru Oct.

Phone: (810)631-4531
Address: 10359 E. Farrand Rd, Otisville, MI 48463
Lat/Lon: 43.19498/-83.50576
Email: camp@CovenantHills.org
Web: www.CovenantHills.org

SEE AD THIS PAGE

OTTAWA LAKE—J-5

(NE) COVERED WAGON CAMP RESORT—(Monroe) *From jct US 23 & US 223 (exit 5): Go 1/4 mi E on CR 151 (St. Anthony Rd). Enter on R.*

WELCOME

◆◆◆FACILITIES: 140 sites, typical site width 35 ft, 14 full hkups, 100 W&E, 12 E, (20/30/50 amps), 50 amps ($), 14 no hkups, some extd stay sites (summer), 34 pull-thrus, WiFi Instant Internet at site ($), family camping, tenting, RV's/park model rentals, cabins, RV storage, dump, non-guest dump $, portable dump, laundry, ltd groc, RV supplies, ice, picnic tables, fire rings, wood, controlled access.

CAMPCLUB USA

◆◆◆RECREATION: rec room/area, pavilion, coin games, swim pool, lake swim, 2 pedal boat rentals, pond fishing, fishing supplies, mini-golf, ($), golf nearby, bsktball, 5 bike rentals, playground, activities, horseshoes, sports field, v-ball. Rec open to public.

Pets welcome, breed restrict. Partial handicap access. Open Apr 15 - Nov 1. Facilities fully operational Late May - Nov 1. Clubs welcome. Rate in 2010 $28-33 for 2 persons. MC/VISA/DISC/Debit. Member ARVC, ARVC MI. FMCA discount. CCUSA 50% Discount. CCUSA reservations Recommended, CCUSA max stay 3 days, Cash only for CCUSA disc., CCUSA disc. not avail F,Sa, CCUSA disc. not avail holidays. Discount available Sep 10-Nov 1. Fully operational Memorial Day-Nov 1.

COVERED WAGON CAMP RESORT—Continued on next page

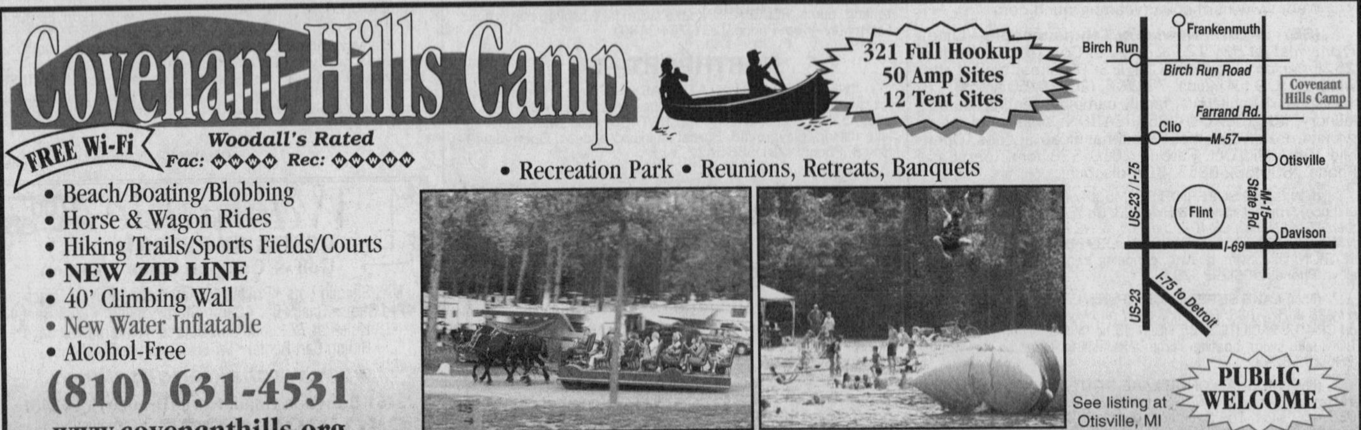

OTTAWA LAKE—Continued
COVERED WAGON CAMP RESORT—Continued

Phone: (734)856-3058
Address: 5639 St Anthony Rd, Ottawa Lake, MI 49267
Lat/Lon: 41.79833/-83.68237
Email: wagon10@bex.net
Web: www.coveredwagoncamp.com

SEE AD TOLEDO, OH PAGE 634

OTTER LAKE—H-5

(NE) OTTER LAKE CAMPGROUND (Village Park)—(Genesee) *From jct Eleventh & Genesee in center of town: Go 1 block W on Genesee.* FACILITIES: 39 sites, 30 W&E, 9 no hkups, tenting, laundry, ltd groc. RECREATION: lake swim, boating, canoeing, ramp, lake fishing, playground. Open Apr 15 - Oct 15. Phone: (810)793-4258.

PARADISE—B-4

(NW) LAKE SUPERIOR SF (Andrus Lake)—(Chippewa) *From town: Go 6 mi N on Wire Rd & Vermillion Rd. Enter on L.* FACILITIES: 25 sites, 25 no hkups, tenting. RECREATION: lake swim, boating, ramp, lake fishing. Partial handicap access. Open all yr. Phone: (906)293-3293.

(W) LAKE SUPERIOR SF (Bodi Lake)—(Luce) *From town: Go 17 mi W on Hwy 123, then N on CR 500 & CR 437. Enter on R.* FACILITIES: 20 sites, 20 no hkups, tenting. RECREATION: lake swim, boating, ramp, lake fishing. Phone: (906)293-3293.

(W) LAKE SUPERIOR SF (Culhane Lake)—(Luce) *From town: Go 17 mi W on Hwy 123, then N on CR 500 (Northwestern Rd N). Enter on R.* FACILITIES: 22 sites, 22 no hkups, tenting. RECREATION: lake swim, boating, canoeing, ramp, lake fishing. Open all yr. Phone: (906)293-3293.

(W) LAKE SUPERIOR SF (Pike Lake)—(Luce) *From town: Go 17 mi W on Hwy 123, then N on CR 500, then W on CR 414. Enter on R.* FACILITIES: 23 sites, 23 no hkups, tenting. RECREATION: lake swim, ramp, lake fishing. Open all yr. Phone: (906)293-3293.

(SW) TAHQUAMENON FALLS STATE PARK—(Luce) *From town: Go 4-1/2 mi S on Hwy-123.* FACILITIES: 296 sites, 296 E, (30 amps), tenting, dump, ltd groc. RECREATION: boating, canoeing, river fishing, playground. Partial handicap access. Open all yr. Phone: (906)492-3415.

PARIS—G-3

(N) PARIS PARK (Mecosta County)—(Mecosta) *From jct Hwy-20 & US-131: Go 6 mi N on US-131..* FACILITIES: 68 sites, 68 full hkups, (20/50 amps), tenting, dump. RECREATION: canoeing, river fishing, playground. Open Apr 20 - Sep 30. Phone: (231)796-3420.

PENTWATER—G-2

(W) CHARLES MEARS STATE PARK—(Oceana) *At north edge of town off US 31: Take the Pentwater exit, then W on Lowell St.* FACILITIES: 175 sites, 175 E, tenting, dump, ltd groc. RECREATION: lake swim, lake fishing, playground. Open Apr 4 - Nov 9. Facilities fully operational Apr 15 - Nov 1. Phone: (231)869-2051.

(N) Hill and Hollow Campground—(Oceana) *From north jct US 31 & Business US 31: Go 1-1/4 mi S on Business US 31. Enter on R.* ◊◊◊FACILITIES: 200 sites, typical site width 45 ft, 73 full hkups, 116 W&E, 5 E, (20/30/50 amps), 6 no hkups, 8 pull-thrus, family camping, tenting, dump, groceries. ◊◊◊◊RECREATION: 2 swim pools, playground. Pets welcome ($). Partial handicap access. Open May 1 - Oct 18. Big rigs welcome. Rate in 2010 $40-42 per family. Phone: (231)869-5811.

(N) Whispering Surf Camping Resort—(Mason) *From north jct US 31 & Business US 31: Go 3/4 mi W on Business US 31, then 1 mi N on Lake Shore Dr. Enter on R.* ◊◊◊FACILITIES: 79 sites, typical site width 35 ft, 40 ft max RV length, 70 full hkups, 1 W&E, 1 E, (20/30/50 amps), 7 no hkups, family camping, tenting, dump. ◊◊◊RECREATION: lake swim, boating, canoeing, dock, lake fishing, playground. Pets welcome ($). Partial handicap access. Open May 1 - Oct 31. Rate in 2010 $33-34 for 2 persons. Member ARVC, ARVCMI. Phone: (231)869-5050.

Say you saw it in Woodall's!

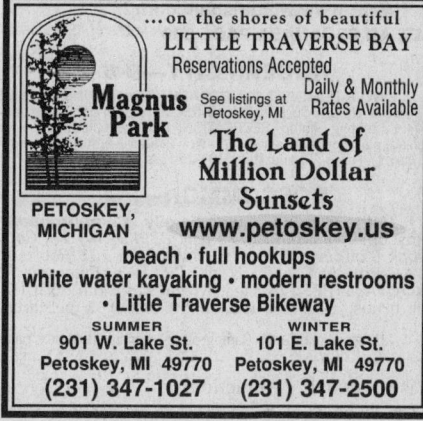

PERRY—H-4

✱ **(NW) SIGNATURE FORD OF PERRY**—*From jct I-69 (exit 105) & Hwy-52: Go 500 ft S on Hwy Hwy 52, then 1 mi W on Old Hwy 78/Lansing Rd. Enter on R.* SERVICES: full-time mech, engine/chassis repair. Open all yr. MC/VISA/DISC/AMEX/Debit.

Phone: (800)393-6202
Address: 3942 W. Old Lansing Rd., Perry, MI 48872
Lat/Lon: 42.83189/-84.23781
Email: rwitgen@signatureautogroup.com
Web: www.sigautogroup.com

SEE AD THIS PAGE

PETERSBURG—J-5

(SE) Monroe County KOA—(Monroe) *From jct US-23 & Hwy-50: Go 9 mi S on US-23 (exit 9), then 200 yards SE on Summerfield Rd, then 100 yards E on Tunnicliffe Rd. Enter on L.* ◊◊◊◊FACILITIES: 249 sites, typical site width 35 ft, 48 full hkups, 149 W&E, 49 E, (20/30/50 amps), 3 no hkups, 56 pull-thrus, family camping, tenting, dump, laundry, groceries. ◊◊◊◊RECREATION: lake swim, boating, no motors, canoeing, lake fishing, playground. Pets welcome ($), breed restrict. Partial handicap access. Open Mid Apr - Oct 31. Green Friendly. Rate in 2010 $30-55 for 2 persons. Member ARVC, ARVC MI. Phone: (800)KOA-7646. KOA discount.

(S) Pirolli Park RV Resort—(Monroe) *From jct Hwy 50 & US 23: Go 9 mi S on US 23 (exit 9), then 1/4 mi N on Summerfield Rd, then 1-1/2 mi W on Teal Rd, then 1-1/2 mi SW on Ida Center Rd, then 1/4 mi S on Sylvania-Petersburg Rd. Enter on R.* ◊◊◊FACILITIES: 185 sites, typical site width 30 ft, 10 full hkups, 100 W&E, 50 E, (30/50 amps), 25 no hkups, family camping, tenting, dump, laundry, groceries. ◊◊◊RECREATION: lake swim, lake fishing, playground. Pets welcome ($), breed restrict. Partial handicap access. Open all yr. Facilities fully operational Apr 15 - Oct 15. Rate in 2010 $29-37 for 2 persons. Phone: (734)279-1487.

WELCOME

(SE) TOTEM POLE PARK—(Monroe) *From jct Hwy 50 & US 23: Go 9 mi S on US 23 (exit 9), then 2-1/2 mi N on Summerfield Rd, then 1/4 mi W on Lulu Rd. Enter on L.*

◊◊◊◊FACILITIES: 130 sites, typical site width 35 ft, 35 full hkups, 95 W&E, (20/30/50 amps), some extd stay sites (summer), 32 pull-thrus, WiFi Instant Internet at site, WiFi Internet central location, family camping, tenting, cabins, RV storage, dump, non-guest dump $, ltd groc, RV supplies, ice, picnic tables, fire rings, wood.

◊◊◊RECREATION: pavilion, lake swim, lake fishing, fishing supplies, golf nearby, bsktball, 9 bike rentals, playground, shuffleboard court shuffleboard court, activities (wkends), horseshoes, sports field, v-ball. Rec open to public.

Pets welcome, quantity restrict. Partial handicap access. Open Apr 15 - Oct 15. Big rigs welcome. Clubs welcome. Rate in 2010 $30-35 per family. MC/VISA. Member ARVC, ARVC MI.

Phone: (800)227-2110
Address: 16333 Lulu Road, Petersburg, MI 49270
Lat/Lon: 41.88047/-83.67808
Email: camping@totempolepark.com
Web: www.totempolepark.com

SEE AD TOLEDO, OH PAGE 634

PETOSKEY—D-5

(NE) Hearthside Grove Luxury Motorcoach Resort—(Emmet) *From jct US 131 & US 31: Go 5-1/2 mi N on US 31. Enter on R.* ◊◊◊◊FACILITIES: 101 sites, typical site width 58 ft, accepts full hkup units only, 101 full hkups, (30/50 amps), laundry. ◊◊◊◊RECREATION: swim pool. Pets welcome,

PETOSKEY—Continued
Hearthside Grove Luxury Motorcoach Resort—Continued

breed restrict, quantity restrict. Partial handicap access. No tents. Open all yr. Facilities fully operational Apr - Oct. Big rigs welcome. Rate in 2010 $49-150 for 2 persons. Member ARVC, ARVCMI. Phone: (231)347-0905. FMCA discount.

WELCOME

(W) MAGNUS MUNICIPAL PARK—(Emmet) *From jct US 131 & US 31: Go 1 mi N on US 31, then 4 blocks W on Lake St. Enter at end.*

FACILITIES: 78 sites, typical site width 30 ft, 36 full hkups, 30 W&E, (20/30/50 amps), 12 no hkups, some extd stay sites (summer), 18 pull-thrus, family camping, tenting, dump, non-guest dump $, picnic tables, fire rings.

RECREATION: lake swim, boating, canoeing, kayaking, ramp, dock, lake fishing, golf nearby, playground, hiking trails.

Pets welcome. Partial handicap access. Open May 1 - Mid Oct. Clubs welcome. MC/VISA/Debit.

Phone: (231)347-1027
Address: 901 W Lake St, Petoskey, MI 49770
Lat/Lon: 45.37391/-84.97243
Email: magnus@petoskey.us
Web: www.petoskey.us

SEE AD THIS PAGE

(NE) Petoskey KOA—(Emmet) *From jct US 131 & US 31: Go 4-1/2 mi N on US 31. Enter on R.* ◊◊◊◊◊FACILITIES: 174 sites, typical site width 30 ft, 144 full hkups, 30 W&E, (20/30/50 amps), 3 no hkups, 29 pull-thrus, family camping, tenting, dump, laundry, groceries. ◊◊◊◊◊RECREATION: swim pool, playground. Pets welcome. Partial handicap access. Open May 9 - Oct 11. Big rigs welcome. Rate in 2010 $25-69 for 2 persons. Member ARVC, ARVC MI. Phone: (231)347-0005. KOA discount.

(N) PETOSKEY STATE PARK—(Emmet) *From town: Go 3 mi NE on US-31, then 1-1/2 mi W on M-119.* FACILITIES: 168 sites, 168 E, tenting, dump, groceries. RECREATION: lake swim, playground. Open Apr 11 - Nov 2. Facilities fully operational May 1 - Nov 1. Phone: (231)347-2311.

PEWAMO—H-4

(N) Maple River Campground—(Clinton) *From jct Hwy 66 & Hwy 21: Go 12 1/2 mi E on Hwy 21, then 5 mi N on Hubbardston Rd, then 1/4 mi E on French Rd. Enter on L.* ◊◊FACILITIES: 63 sites, 50 W&E, (20/30/50 amps), 13 no hkups, family camping, tenting, dump. ◊◊◊RECREATION: river swim, boating, canoeing, ramp, river fishing, playground. Pets welcome. Open May 1 - Dec 1. Rate in 2010 $24 per family. Member ARVC, ARVCMI. Phone: (989)981-6792.

PICKFORD—C-5

(NE) LAKE SUPERIOR SF (Munuscong River)—(Chippewa) *From jct Hwy 48 & Hwy 129: Go 8 mi E & N on Sterlingville Rd.* FACILITIES: 50 sites, 50 no hkups, tenting. RECREATION: boating, canoeing, ramp, river fishing. Phone: (906)635-5281.

PINCKNEY—I-5

(NE) PINCKNEY STATE REC. AREA (Bruin Lake Campground)—(Washtenaw) *From jct US-23 & Hwy-36: Go 16-1/2 mi W on Hwy-36, then 1 mi S on Livermore, then 1/2 mi W on Doyle, then 1-1/4 mi S on Unadilla, then 1 mi E on Kaiser.* FACILITIES: 221 sites, 186 E, 35 no hkups, tenting, dump, ltd groc. RECREATION: lake swim, boating, ramp, lake fishing, playground. Partial handicap access. Open Mar 28 - Dec 1. Facilities fully operational Apr 15 - Nov 1. Phone: (734)426-4913.

PORT AUSTIN—F-6

(SW) Duggan's Campground—(Huron) *From jct Hwy 53 & Hwy 25: Go 7-3/4 mi SW on Hwy 25. Enter on L.* ◊◊◊FACILITIES: 327 sites, typical site width 40 ft, 308 W&E, (15/20/30 amps), 19 no hkups, 5 pull-

Duggan's Campground—Continued on next page

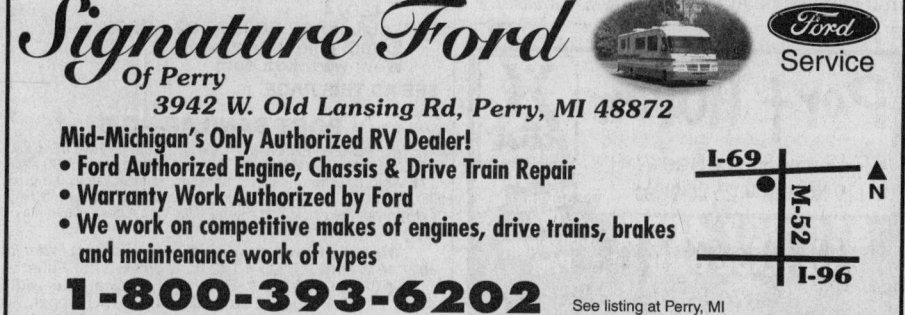

PORT AUSTIN—Continued
Duggan's Campground—Continued

thrus, family camping, tenting, dump, laundry, groceries. ◇◇◇RECREATION: swim pool, lake swim, playground. Pets welcome. Partial handicap access. Open April 15 - Oct 15. Rate in 2010 $30 per family. Phone: (989)738-5160.

(SW) OAK BEACH COUNTY PARK—(Huron) *From jct Hwy 53 & Hwy 25: Go 8-1/2 mi SW on Hwy 25.*

WELCOME

FACILITIES: 55 sites, typical site width 30 ft, 55 full hkups, (30/50 amps), some extd stay sites (summer), heater not allowed, family camping, tenting, shower$, dump, non-guest dump $, laundry, ice, picnic tables, fire rings, wood.

RECREATION: pavilion, lake swim, boating, canoeing, kayaking, lake fishing, golf nearby, playground, horseshoes, hiking trails. Rec open to public.

Pets welcome. Partial handicap access. Open May 1 - Oct 15. Big rigs welcome. Clubs welcome. MC/VISA/Debit.

Phone: (877)404-7447
Address: 3356 Port Austin Rd, Port Austin, MI 48467
Lat/Lon: 43.99363/-83.12626
Email: huronpks@comcast.net
Web: www.huroncountyparks.com

SEE AD TRAVEL SECTION PAGE 361

(SW) PORT CRESCENT STATE PARK—(Huron) *From jct Hwy-53 & Hwy-25: Go 4-1/2 mi SW on US-25.* FACILITIES: 137 sites, 137 E, tenting, dump. RECREATION: lake swim, boating, lake fishing, playground. Partial handicap access. Open May 17 - Oct 13. Facilities fully operational Apr 1 - Nov 1. Phone: (989) 738-8663.

PORT HOPE—G-6

(N) LIGHTHOUSE COUNTY PARKS—(Huron) *From Town: Go 5 mi N on M-25, then 1 mi E on Lighthouse Rd.*

WELCOME

FACILITIES: 103 sites, typical site width 35 ft, 73 full hkups, 30 E, (30/50 amps), many extd stay sites (summer), heater not allowed, family camping, tenting, cabins, shower$, dump, non-guest dump $, ice, picnic tables, fire rings, wood.

RECREATION: rec hall, pavilion, lake swim, boating, canoeing, kayaking, ramp, lake fishing, golf nearby, playground, horseshoes, sports field, hiking trails.

Pets welcome. Partial handicap access. Open May 1 - Oct 15. Big rigs welcome. Clubs welcome. MC/VISA/Debit.

Phone: (877)404-7447
Address: 7320 Lighthouse Rd, Port Hope, MI 48468
Lat/Lon: 44.01873/-82.79852
Email: huronpks@comcast.net
Web: www.huroncountyparks.com

SEE AD TRAVEL SECTION PAGE 361

(E) STAFFORD COUNTY PARK—(Huron) *In town.*

WELCOME

FACILITIES: 100 sites, typical site width 35 ft, 50 full hkups, 25 E, (30/50 amps), 25 no hkups, some extd stay sites (summer), 4 pull-thrus, heater not allowed, family camping, tenting, cabins, shower$, dump, non-guest dump $, ice, picnic tables, fire rings, wood.

RECREATION: pavilion, lake swim, boating, canoeing, kayaking, lake fishing, golf nearby, playground, shuffleboard court shuffleboard court, tennis, horseshoes, sports field, v-ball. Rec open to public.

Pets welcome. Partial handicap access. Open May 1 - Oct 15. Big rigs welcome. Clubs welcome. MC/VISA/Debit.

PORT HOPE—Continued
STAFFORD COUNTY PARK—Continued

Phone: (877)404-7447
Address: 4451 West Huron Street, PORT HOPE, MI 48468
Lat/Lon: 43.94360/-82.70929
Email: huronpks@comcast.net
Web: www.huroncountyparks.com

SEE AD TRAVEL SECTION PAGE 361

PORT HURON—H-6

(W) KOA-PORT HURON—(St. Clair) *From jct I-94 & I-69: Go 2-1/2 mi W on I-69 (exit 196), then 1/2 mi N on Wadhams Rd, then 1/4 mi E on Lapeer Rd. Enter on R.*

WELCOME

IT'S A GREAT DAY AT PORT HURON KOA!
70 fun filled acres w/RV & Tent sites, Kabin & Kottage rentals, 2 pools, free Wi-Fi, ice cream parlor, snack bars, waterslide, Go-Karts, Bumper Boats, Roller Hockey, Mini-Golf & More! A "Top Kid Friendly" park for a perfect vacation!

◇◇◇◇◇FACILITIES: 306 sites, typical site width 42 ft, 124 full hkups, 172 W&E, (20/30/50 amps), 10 no hkups, 68 pull-thrus, cable TV, WiFi Instant Internet at site, family camping, tenting, cabins, RV storage, dump, non-guest dump $, portable dump, laundry, groceries, RV supplies, ice, picnic tables, patios, fire rings, grills, wood, controlled access.

◇◇◇◇◇RECREATION: rec hall, rec room/area, equipped pavilion, coin games, 2 swim pools, mini-golf, ($), golf nearby, bsktball, 200 bike rentals, playground, shuffleboard court 3 shuffleboard courts, activities, tennis, horseshoes, sports field, hiking trails, v-ball.

Pets welcome. Partial handicap access. Open Apr 30 - Oct 31. Big rigs welcome. Escort to site. Clubs welcome. Rate in 2010 $30-80 for 2 persons. MC/VISA/DISC/AMEX/Debit. ATM. Member ARVC, ARVC MI. KOA discount.

Text 81436 to (440)725-8687 to see our Visual Tour.

Phone: (810)987-4070
Address: 5111 Lapeer Rd, Kimball, MI 48074
Lat/Lon: 42.98439/-82.52881
Email: phkoa@aol.com
Web: www.koa.com

SEE AD THIS PAGE

(N) LAKEPORT STATE PARK—(Saint Clair) *From jct I-94 & Hwy-25: Go 12 mi N on Hwy-25.* FACILITIES: 250 sites, 250 E, tenting, dump, groceries. RECREATION: lake swim, boating, playground. Open Apr 11 - Nov 3. Phone: (810)327-6224.

(NW) Ruby Campground—(St. Clair) *From jct I-94 & I-69: Go 4-1/2 mi W on I-69 (exit 194), then 500 ft N on Barth Rd, then 2-1/2 mi W on Lapeer Rd, then 3 mi N on Cribbins Rd, then 1/2 mi W on Imlay City Rd. Enter on R.* ◇◇◇FACILITIES: 68 sites, typical site width 30 ft, 19 full hkups, 29 E, (20/30 amps), 20 no hkups, 2 pull-thrus, family camping, tenting, dump, ltd groc. ◇◇◇RECREATION: lake/boating, no motors, canoeing, dock, pond/stream fishing, playground. Pets welcome. Partial handicap access. Open May 15 - Oct 15. Rate in 2010 $25-30 per family.

Phone: (810)324-2766
Address: 7700 Imlay City Rd, Avoca, MI 48006
Lat/Lon: 43.03429/-82.64212
Email: rubyfamilycampground@live.com
Web: www.rubycampground.com

(W) SAWMILL CITY—*From jct I-94 & I-69: Go 2-1/2 mi W on I-69 (exit 196), then 1/2 mi N on Wadhams Rd, then 1/4 mi E on Lapeer Rd. Enter on R.* Miniature Western town featuring train rides, adventure golf, batting cages, bumper boats, bankshot basketball, water wars go-carts, & water slide. Open Apr 30 - Oct 31. MC/VISA/DISC/AMEX/Debit. ATM.

WELCOME

Phone: (810)982-5090
Address: 5055 Lapeer Rd, Kimball, MI 48074
Lat/Lon: 42.98390/-82.52662
Email: phkoa@aol.com
Web: www.koa.com

SEE AD THIS PAGE

PORT SANILAC—G-6

(N) FORESTER PARK—(Sanilac) *From jct Hwy 46 & Hwy 25: Go 6 1/2 mi N on Hwy 25. Enter on R.* FACILITIES: 190 sites, 171 W&E, (20/30 amps), 19 no hkups, tenting, dump, ltd groc. RECREATION: lake swim, boating, canoeing, ramp, lake fishing, playground. Pets welcome. Partial handicap access. Open May 1 - Oct 31. Phone: (810)622-8715.

(N) Lake Huron Campground—(Sanilac) *From jct Hwy 46 & Hwy 25; Go 4-1/2 mi N on Hwy 25. Enter on L.* ◇◇◇◇◇FACILITIES: 395 sites, typical site width 40 ft, 275 full hkups, 100 W&E, (20/30/50 amps), 20 no hkups, 229 pull-thrus, family camping, tenting,

PORT SANILAC—Continued
Lake Huron Campground—Continued

dump, laundry, groceries. ◇◇◇◇◇RECREATION: swim pool, lake swim, lake fishing, playground. Pets welcome, breed restrict, quantity restrict. Partial handicap access. Open Apr 15 - Oct 31. Facilities fully operational Mid May - Sep 15. Big rigs welcome. Rate in 2010 $21-68 for 2 persons. Member ARVC, ARVCMI. Phone: (866)360-CAMP.

QUINCY—J-4

(E) QUINCY MARBLE LAKE (Branch County Park)—(Branch) *From jct I-69 & US-12: Go 5 mi E on US-12, then 1/4 S on Lake Blvd.* FACILITIES: 100 sites, 100 W&E, tenting, dump. RECREATION: boating, ramp, dock, playground. Open Memorial Day - Labor Day. Phone: (517)639-4414.

RAPID RIVER—C-2

(E) HIAWATHA NATIONAL FOREST (Little Bay de Noc Rec. Area)—(Delta) *From jct US 2 & US 41: Go 3 mi E on US 2, then 6 mi S on CR 513.* FACILITIES: 38 sites, 38 no hkups, tenting. RECREATION: lake swim, boating, no motors, lake fishing. Partial handicap access. Open May 15 - Oct 7. Phone: (906) 474-6442.

(SE) Vagabond Resort—(Delta) *From jct US 2 & US 41: Go 3 mi E on US 2, then 3 mi S on CR 513. Enter on R.* ◇◇◇FACILITIES: 61 sites, typical site width 30 ft, 10 full hkups, 26 W&E, 10 E, (20/30/50 amps), 15 no hkups, 4 pull-thrus, WiFi Internet central location, family camping, tenting, RV storage, dump, non-guest dump $, laundry, ice, picnic tables, fire rings, grills, wood. ◇◇◇RECREATION: rec hall, lake swim, boating, canoeing, kayaking, dock, lake fishing, fishing supplies, bsktball, playground, shuffleboard court shuffleboard court, horseshoes, hiking trails, v-ball. Pets welcome. Partial handicap access. Open all yr. Facilities fully operational May 1 - Dec 1. Rate in 2010 $20-26 for 4 persons. MC/VISA/DISC/Debit. CCUSA 50% Discount. CCUSA reservations Recommended, CCUSA max stay Unlimited, CCUSA disc. not avail F,Sa, CCUSA disc. not avail holidays.

CAMPCLUB USA

Phone: (906)474-6122
Address: 8935 County 513T Rd, Rapid River, MI 49878
Lat/Lon: 45.86950/-86.94823
Email: vagabondresort@charter.net
Web: www.vagabondresort.com

(E) Whispering Valley Campground & RV Park—(Delta) *From jct US 2 & US 41: Go 2-1/4 mi E on US 2. Enter on L.* ◇◇◇◇FACILITIES: 26 sites, typical site width 40 ft, 26 full hkups, (20/30/50 amps), 26 pull-thrus, family camping, dump, laundry. ◇RECREATION: pond fishing. Pets welcome. Partial handicap access. No tents. Open all yr. Facilities fully operational Apr 1 - Nov 30. Rate in 2010 $30-34 for 2 persons. Phone: (800)664-7044.

(E) WHITEFISH HILL RV PARK—(Delta) *From jct US 2 & US 41: Go 2-1/2 mi E on US 2. Enter on R.*

WELCOME

◇◇◇FACILITIES: 24 sites, typical site width 30 ft, 24 full hkups, (20/30/50 amps), some extd stay sites (summer), 7 pull-thrus, cable TV, ($), WiFi Instant Internet at site, family camping, tenting, RV's/park model rentals, RV storage, dump, non-guest dump $, laundry, RV supplies, LP gas by weight/by meter, ice, picnic tables, fire rings, grills, wood.

◇◇RECREATION: rec room/area, golf nearby, bsktball, playground, horseshoes, v-ball.

Pets welcome. Partial handicap access. Open Early Apr - Nov 30. Big rigs welcome. Clubs welcome. Rate in 2010 $28-35 for 2 persons. MC/VISA. FMCA discount.

Phone: (906)280-5438
Address: 8455 US 2, Rapid River, MI 49878
Lat/Lon: 45.92325/-86.93819
Email: pviolette5438@charter.net
Web: www.whitefishhill.com

SEE AD ESCANABA PAGE 380

ROGERS CITY—D-6

(NW) P.H. HOEFT STATE PARK—(Presque Isle) *From jct Hwy-68 & US-23: Go 5 mi NW on US-23.* FACILITIES: 144 sites, 144 E, tenting, dump. RECREATION: lake swim, boating, lake fishing, playground. Open Apr 11 - Nov 2. Facilities fully operational May 1 - Nov 1. Phone: (989)734-2543.

ROSCOMMON—F-4

(SW) Higgins Lake Family Campground—(Roscommon) *From jct I-75 (exit 239) & Hwy 18: Go 1 block S on Hwy 18, then 3 mi W on CR 103/Robinson Lake Rd, then 1 mi N on CR 100. Enter on R.* ◇◇◇FACILITIES: 74 sites, typical site width 35 ft, 14 full hkups, 60 W&E, (20/30/50 amps), 1 pull-thrus,

Higgins Lake Family Campground—Continued on next page

ROSCOMMON—Continued
Higgins Lake Family Campground—Continued

family camping, tenting, dump, ltd groc. ◇◇RECREATION: playground. Pets welcome. Partial handicap access. Open Early May - mid Oct. Rate in 2010 $28-37 per family. Member ARVC, ARVC MI. Phone: (989)821-6891.

(W) NORTH HIGGINS LAKE STATE PARK—(Crawford) *From jct I-75 & Hwy-76: Go 5-1/2 mi W on Hwy-76, then 3 mi W on CR-203.* FACILITIES: 174 sites, 174 E, tenting, dump. RECREATION: lake swim, boating, ramp, lake fishing, play equipment. Partial handicap access. Open May 23 - Nov 24. Phone: (989)821-6125.

(N) Paddle Brave Canoe & Campground Resort—(Crawford) *From jct I-75 (exit 239) & Hwy-18: Go 3-1/4 mi NE on Hwy-18, then 2 mi N on Lancewood/Steckert Bridge Rd. Enter on L.* ◇◇FACILITIES: 43 sites, typical site width 25 ft, 40 ft max RV length, 33 E, (20/30 amps), 10 no hkups, family camping, tenting, dump, ltd groc. ◇◇◇RECREATION: river swim, canoeing, dock, river fishing, play equipment. Pets welcome, breed restrict. Open all yr. Rate in 2010 $24 for 4 persons. Phone: (800)681-7092.

(SW) SOUTH HIGGINS LAKE STATE PARK—(Crawford) *From jct I-75 & Hwy-76: Go 10 mi SW on Hwy-76 & CR-100.* FACILITIES: 400 sites, 400 E, tenting, dump, groceries. RECREATION: lake swim, boating, ramp, lake fishing, playground. Partial handicap access. Open Apr 15 - Nov 30. Phone: (989)821-6374.

ROTHBURY—G-2

(NW) Back Forty RV Park—(Oceana) *From jct Hwy 20 & US 31: Go 3 mi S on US 31, then 1/2 mi E on Winston Rd, then 3/4 mi N on Water Rd. Enter on R.* ◇◇◇FACILITIES: 58 sites, 21 full hkups, 17 W&E, 2 E, (20/30/50 amps), 18 no hkups, 2 pull-thrus, family camping, tenting, dump, laundry, groceries. ◇◇◇◇◇RECREATION: swim pool, canoeing, lake fishing, playground. Pets welcome. Partial handicap access. Open Apr - Nov 1. Big rigs welcome. Rate in 2010 $45-65 for 2 persons. Phone: (800)368-2535.

SAINT CLAIR—H-6

(NW) THOUSAND TRAILS SAINT CLAIR CAMPGROUND—(Saint Clair) *From jct I-69/I-94 & I-94: Go 10 mi S on I-94 (exit 262), then 100 yrds N on S Wadhams Rd. Enter on R.*

WELCOME

◇◇◇FACILITIES: 224 sites, typical site width 28 ft, 142 full hkups, 82 W&E, (20/30/50 amps), 21 pull-thrus, WiFi Internet central location, family camping, RV storage, dump, portable dump, laundry, ltd groc, RV supplies, LP gas by meter, picnic tables, fire rings, wood, controlled access.

◇◇◇◇RECREATION: rec hall, pavilion, coin games, swim pool, river fishing, mini-golf, golf nearby, bsktball, playground, shuffleboard court shuffleboard court, activities, horseshoes, v-ball.

Pets welcome. Partial handicap access. No tents. Open May 1 - Oct 17. Reservations Required. Big rigs welcome. MC/VISA/DISC/AMEX.

Visit our website www.woodalls.com

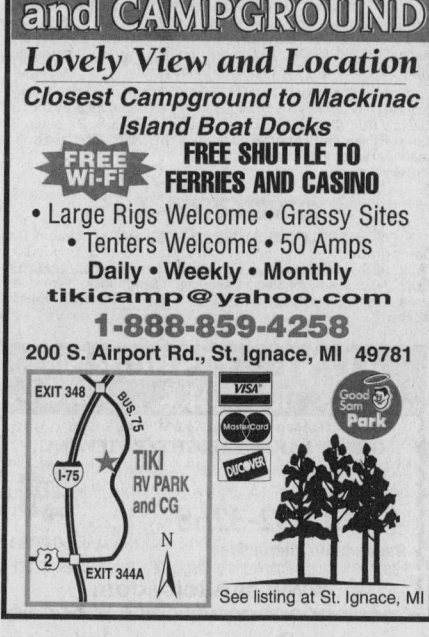

SAINT CLAIR—Continued
THOUSAND TRAILS SAINT CLAIR CAMPGROUND—Continued

Phone: (800)905-CAMP
Address: 1299 Wadhams Rd, Saint Clair, MI 48079
Lat/Lon: 42.86619/-82.55710
Web: www.1000trails.com

SEE AD ADRIAN PAGE 372

ST. IGNACE—C-5

(N) CASTLE ROCK LAKEFRONT CAMPARK—(Mackinac) *From jct US 2 & I-75: Go 4 mi N on I-75 (exit 348), then 1/4 mi S on Business I-75, then 1/4 mi N on Mackinac Trail. Enter on R.*

WELCOME

◇◇◇FACILITIES: 95 sites, typical site width 30 ft, 20 full hkups, 60 W&E, (20/30 amps), 15 no hkups, 7 pull-thrus, WiFi Instant Internet at site, family camping, tenting, dump, non-guest dump $, laundry, ltd groc, RV supplies, ice, picnic tables, fire rings, wood.

◇◇◇RECREATION: rec room/area, coin games, lake swim, boating, canoeing, kayaking, ramp, dock, lake fishing, golf nearby, playground, horseshoes, v-ball, local tours.

Pets welcome. Open May 15 - Oct 10. Clubs welcome. Rate in 2010 $22-30 per family. MC/VISA/Debit.

Phone: (800)333-8754
Address: 2811 Mackinac Trail, St Ignace, MI 49781
Lat/Lon: 45.90945/-84.73915
Web: www.castlerockcampark.com

SEE AD THIS PAGE

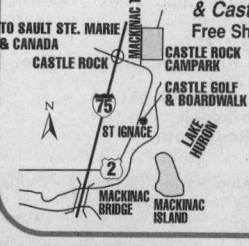

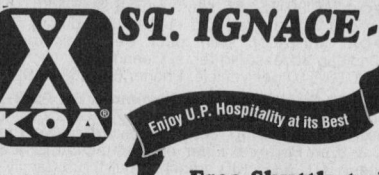

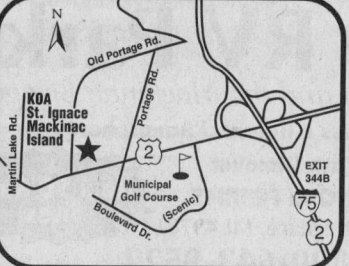

ST. IGNACE—Continued

(NW) HIAWATHA NATIONAL FOREST (Brevoort Lake Campground)—(Mackinac) *From jct I-75 & US 2: Go 17 mi NW on US 2, then 1-1/2 mi N on FH-3108, then 1/2 mi NE on FH-3473.* FACILITIES: 70 sites, 35 ft max RV length, 70 no hkups, 5 pull-thrus, tenting, dump, ltd groc. RECREATION: lake swim, boating, canoeing, ramp, lake fishing, playground. Partial handicap access. Open May 7 - Sep 13. Phone: (906)643-7900.

(N) HIAWATHA NATIONAL FOREST (Carp River Campground)—(Mackinac) *From jct US 2 & I-75: Go 7-2/3 mi N on I-75, then 5 mi N on CR-412.* FACILITIES: 38 sites, 32 ft max RV length, 38 no hkups, 11 pull-thrus, tenting. RECREATION: river fishing. Partial handicap access. Open May 7 - Oct 15. Phone: (906)643-7900.

(N) HIAWATHA NATIONAL FOREST (Foley Creek Campground)—(Mackinac) *From jct US 2 & I-75: Go 4 mi N on I-75, then 2-1/3 mi N on CR-412.* FACILITIES: 53 sites, 32 ft max RV length, 53 no hkups, 1 pull-thrus, tenting. RECREATION: lake swim. Partial handicap access. Open May 12 - Oct 2. Phone: (906)643-7900.

(NW) HIAWATHA NATIONAL FOREST (Lake Michigan Campground)—(Mackinac) *From jct US 2 & I-75: Go 16-1/2 mi NW on US 2.* FACILITIES: 35 sites, 32 ft max RV length, 35 no hkups, 1 pull-thrus, tenting, ltd groc. RECREATION: lake swim, lake fishing. Partial handicap access. Open May 7 - Sep 13. Phone: (906)643-7900.

ST. IGNACE—Continued on next page

Can you trust the Woodall's ratings? 25 evaluation teams have scoured North American campgrounds to provide you with accurate, up to date information & ratings. Find a rating you don't agree with? Send a letter or email our way, and we'll give it extra attention for 2012.

ST. IGNACE—Continued

LAKE SHORE PARK CAMPGROUND—(Mackinac) *From jct I-75 & US 2: Go 2 mi W on US 2, then 1-1/2 mi SW on CR 405 (Point La Barbe Rd). Enter on R.*

WELCOME

◆◆◆FACILITIES: 80 sites, typical site width 28 ft, 53 full hkups, 7 W&E, (20/30/50 amps), 20 no hkups, 34 pull-thrus, WiFi Instant Internet at site, family camping, tenting, RV storage, dump, laundry, RV supplies, ice, picnic tables, fire rings, wood.

◆RECREATION: golf nearby, activities, local tours.

Pets welcome. Partial handicap access. Open May 1 - Oct 15. Off season reservation number: (810) 523-7530. Big rigs welcome. Escort to site. Clubs welcome. Rate in 2010 $33-35 for 2 persons. MC/VISA/DISC/Debit. Member ARVC, ARVC MI. FMCA discount.

Phone: (906)643-9522
Address: W1234 Pte La Barbe Rd, St Ignace, MI 49781
Lat/Lon: 45.85448/-84.78208
Email: lakeshoreparkcampground@yahoo.com
Web: www.lakeshoreparkcampground.com

SEE AD THIS PAGE

(W) ST. IGNACE/MACKINAC ISLAND KOA—(Mackinac) *From jct I-75 & US-2: Go 2 mi W on US-2. Enter on R.*

WELCOME

◆◆◆◆FACILITIES: 200 sites, typical site width 50 ft, 46 full hkups, 94 W&E, (20/30/50 amps), 60 no hkups, 82 pull-thrus, cable TV, WiFi Instant Internet at site, family camping, tenting, cabins, dump, non-guest dump $, portable dump, laundry, groceries, RV supplies, ice, picnic tables, fire rings, wood.

◆◆◆◆RECREATION: rec room/area, coin games, swim pool, mini-golf, ($), golf nearby, playground, sports field, local tours. Rec open to public.

Pets welcome. Partial handicap access. Open May 1 - Oct 31. Big rigs welcome. Clubs welcome. Rate in 2010 $28-52 for 2 persons. MC/VISA/DISC/AMEX/Debit. Member ARVC, ARVC MI. KOA discount.

Phone: (800)562-0534
Address: W1118 US 2, St Ignace, MI 49781
Lat/Lon: 45.85397/-84.77389
Email: simikoa@charterinternet.com
Web: www.simikoa.com

SEE AD PAGE 401

(E) STRAITS STATE PARK—(Mackinac) *From jct US-2 & I-75: Go 500 feet E on Bus I-75.* FACILITIES: 273 sites, 255 E, 18 no hkups, tenting, dump, laundry. RECREATION: lake swim, playground. Open Apr 15 - Nov 15. Phone: (906)643-8620.

(N) TIKI RV PARK & CAMPGROUND—(Mackinac) *From jct I-75 & Bus I-75: Go 3 mi N on Bus I-75, then 400 feet W on S Airport Rd. Enter on L.*

WELCOME

BIG RIGS AND SMALL TENTS WELCOME!
26 acres of relaxing woods and open spaces. Close to Mackinac Island ferries, restaurants, and shops. 50 amp pull-thurs and Free Wi-Fi. A great location for a vacation.

◆◆◆◆FACILITIES: 115 sites, typical site width 30 ft, 31 full hkups, 34 W&E, 10 E, (20/30/50 amps), 50 amps ($), 40 no hkups, 27 pull-thrus, WiFi Internet central location, family camping, tenting, RV storage, dump, non-guest dump $, portable dump, laundry, ltd groc, RV supplies, ice, picnic tables, fire rings, wood.

ST. IGNACE—Continued
TIKI RV PARK & CAMPGROUND—Continued

CAMPCLUB USA

◆◆RECREATION: rec room/area, coin games, golf nearby, playground, sports field, local tours.

Pets welcome. Partial handicap access. Open May 15 - Oct. Big rigs welcome. Escort to site. Clubs welcome. Rate in 2010 $22-32 for 2 persons. MC/VISA/Debit. CCUSA 50% Discount.

Phone: (888)859-4258
Address: 200 S Airport Rd, St. Ignace, MI 49781
Lat/Lon: 45.88263/-84.72790
Email: tikicamp@yahoo.com

SEE AD PAGE 401

ST. JAMES—D-4

(S) MACKINAW SF (Beaver Island)—(Charlevoix) *From Charlevois: Take ferry to St. James on Beaver Island, then go 7 mi S on East Side Rd.* FACILITIES: 25 sites, 25 no hkups, tenting. RECREATION: lake swim, boating, ramp, lake fishing. Open all yr. Phone: (989)732-3541.

ST. JOSEPH—J-2

See listings at Benton Harbor, Buchanan, Coloma, Covert, Decatur, Grand Junction, Lawrence, Niles & South Haven.

SANFORD—G-4

(NW) AU SABLE SF (Black Creek)—(Midland) *From town: Go 3 mi NW on Saginaw Rd & W River Rd. Enter on R.* FACILITIES: 23 sites, 23 no hkups, tenting. RECREATION: ramp, stream fishing. Open all yr. Phone: (989)426-9205.

SAULT STE. MARIE—C-5

(NE) AUNE-OSBORN RV PARK—(Chippewa) *From jct Bus I-75 & I-75: Go 2 mi N on I-75 (exit 394), then 1 block W on Easterday Rd, then 3-3/4 mi N & E on Portage Rd (Riverside Dr). Enter on L.*

WELCOME

FACILITIES: 100 sites, typical site width 42 ft, 100 W&E, (30/50 amps), 50 pull-thrus, WiFi Instant Internet at site, family camping, tenting, dump, non-guest dump $, ice, picnic tables, fire rings.

RECREATION: boating, ramp, river fishing, golf nearby, playground, sports field, local tours.

Pets welcome. Partial handicap access. Open May 15 - Oct 15.

Phone: (906)632-3268
Address: 1225 Riverside Dr, Sault Ste. Marie, MI 49783
Lat/Lon: 46.48849/-84.31034
Email: auneosb@sault.com
Web: www.saultcity.com

SEE AD THIS PAGE

(S) Kewadin Casino Park—(Chippewa) *From jct I-75 (exit 392) & Business I-75: Go 1-3/4 mi N on Business I-75 (Ashmun St), then 3/4 mi E on Marquette Ave, then 1/2 mi S on Shunk Rd. Enter on R.* ◆◆◆FACILITIES: 65 sites, typical site width 35 ft, 65 E, (20/30 amps), 25 pull-thrus, dump, laundry. ◆◆RECREATION: swim pool. Pets welcome. Partial handicap access. No tents. Open May 1 - Oct 15. Rate in 2010 $10 per vehicle. Phone: (906)635-4926.

(E) Soo Locks Campground & RV Park—(Chippewa) *From jct Business I-75 & I-75: Go 2 mi N on I-75 (exit 394), then 500 feet W on Easterday Ave, then 3 mi N & E on Portage. Enter on L.* ◆◆◆FACILITIES: 101 sites, 101 W&E, (30 amps), 9 pull-thrus, family camping, tenting, dump, laundry, ltd groc. ◆◆RECREATION: boating, dock, river fishing, play equipment. Pets welcome. Open May 1 - Oct 20. Rate in 2010 $24-28 per vehicle. Phone: (906)632-3191.

SCOTTVILLE—G-2

(NE) Crystal Lake Campground—(Mason) *From east jct US 10 & US 31: Go 3 mi W on US 31, then 1-1/2 mi N on Stiles Rd, then 1/2 mi E on Hansen Rd.*

SCOTTVILLE—Continued
Crystal Lake Campground—Continued

Enter on L. ◆◆◆FACILITIES: 160 sites, typical site width 30 ft, 38 ft max RV length, 60 full hkups, 100 W&E, (20/30 amps), family camping, tenting, dump, laundry, groceries. ◆◆◆◆RECREATION: lake swim, boating, canoeing, dock, lake fishing, playground. Pets welcome, quantity restrict. Partial handicap access. Open May 1 - Oct 15. Rate in 2010 $34-37 per family. Member ARVC, ARVCMI. Phone: (231)757-4510.

(S) SCOTTVILLE RIVERSIDE PARK (City Park)—(Mason) *From jct US-10 & Main St (in town): Go 1/2 mi S on Main St. Enter on L.* FACILITIES: 52 sites, 52 W&E, tenting, dump, laundry. RECREATION: swim pool, boating, canoeing, ramp, river fishing, playground. Partial handicap access. Open May 1 - Oct 31. Phone: (231)757-2429.

SEARS—G-3

(E) CRITTENDEN PARK (Osceola County Park)—(Osceola) *From jct US 131 & US 10: Go 13 mi E on US 10, then 5 mi SE on Big Lake.* FACILITIES: 90 sites, 70 W&E, 20 no hkups, tenting, dump, ltd groc. RECREATION: lake swim, boating, ramp, lake fishing, playground. Partial handicap access. Open May 14 - Sep 26. Phone: (231)734-2588.

SEBEWAING—G-5

(SW) SEBEWAING COUNTY PARK—(Huron) *From jct Hwy 25 & Pine St: Go W on Pine St, then S on Miller, then W on Union St.*

WELCOME

FACILITIES: 64 sites, typical site width 35 ft, 54 full hkups, (30/50 amps), 10 no hkups, some extd stay sites (summer), heater not allowed, family camping, tenting, cabins, shower$, dump, non-guest dump $, picnic tables, fire rings.

RECREATION: lake swim, boating, canoeing, kayaking, lake/river fishing, golf nearby, playground, hiking trails. Rec open to public.

Pets welcome. Partial handicap access. Open May 1 - Oct 15. Big rigs welcome. Clubs welcome. MC/VISA/Debit.

Phone: (877)404-7447
Address: 759 Union Street, Sebewaing, MI 48759
Lat/Lon: 43.73755/-83.45919
Email: huronpks@comcast.net
Web: www.huroncountyparks.com

SEE AD TRAVEL SECTION PAGE 361

SHELBY—G-2

(W) SILVER LAKE STATE PARK—(Oceana) *From jct US 31 & Shelby Rd: Go 8 mi W on Shelby Rd, then follow signs N on CR B15.* FACILITIES: 200 sites, 200 E, tenting, dump. RECREATION: lake swim, boating, canoeing, ramp, lake fishing, playground. Open Apr 20 - Oct 31. Phone: (231)873-3083.

SHINGLETON—C-3

(S) HIAWATHA NATIONAL FOREST (Colwell Lake Campground)—(Alger) *From jct Hwy 28 & Hwy 94: Go 10 mi S on Hwy 94, then 1/2 mi E on CR-2246.* FACILITIES: 34 sites, 5 E, (30 amps), 29 no hkups, 2 pull-thrus, tenting, dump. RECREATION: lake swim, boating, ramp, lake fishing. Partial handicap access. Open May 15 - Oct 7. Phone: (906)341-5666.

SIDNAW—B-1

(S) OTTAWA NATIONAL FOREST (Lake Ste. Kathryn Campground)—(Iron) *From jct Hwy-28 & CR-137: Go 8 mi S on CR-137.* FACILITIES: 23 sites, 22 ft max RV length, 23 no hkups, tenting. RECREATION: lake swim, boating, ramp, lake fishing. Open May 15 - Oct 15. Phone: (906)852-3501.

(S) OTTAWA NATIONAL FOREST (Norway Lake Campground)—(Iron) *From jct Hwy 28 & CR 137: Go 6 mi S on CR 137 (Sidnaw Rd), then 2 mi E on FR 2400.* FACILITIES: 27 sites, 22 ft max RV length, 27 no hkups, tenting. RECREATION: lake swim, boating, ramp, lake fishing. Open May 15 - Oct 15. Phone: (906) 852-3501.

SILVER CITY—A-6

(W) PORCUPINE MTNS. STATE PARK (Union Bay Campground)—(Ontonogan) *From town: Go 3 mi W on Hwy 107.* FACILITIES: 100 sites, 100 E, tenting, dump, laundry. RECREATION: lake swim, boating, canoeing, ramp, dock, lake/river/stream fishing, playground. Open Apr 5 - Nov 3. Phone: (906)885-5275.

SKANEE—B-1

(E) COPPER COUNTRY SF (Big Eric's Bridge)—(Baraga) *From town: Go 6 mi E on Skanee-Big Bay Rd. Enter on L.* FACILITIES: 20 sites, 20 no hkups, tenting. RECREATION: canoeing, river/stream fishing. Open all yr. Phone: (906)353-6651.

(NW) Witz's Marina & Campground—(Baraga) *From US 41/Hwy 28/US 141 & US 41: Go 12 mi N on US 41, then 3/4 mi N on Broad St, then 15 mi NE on Skanee Rd, then 1 mi N on Town Rd, then 1/2 mi N on Witz Rd. Enter at end.* ◊◊FACILITIES: 50 sites, 50 W&E, (20/30/50 amps), 5 pull-thrus, family camping, tenting, dump, ltd groc. ◊◊◊RECREATION: lake swim, boating, canoeing, ramp, dock, lake fishing, playground. Pets welcome. Open May - Oct. Big rigs welcome. Rate in 2010 $25 for 4 persons. Phone: (906) 524-7795.

SOMERSET CENTER—J-4

(SW) SOMERSET BEACH CAMPGROUND—(Hillsdale) *From jct Hwy127 & US12: Go 4 mi W on US 12, then 1/2 mi S on Fairway Dr/Heatherway Dr, then 1/4 mi SW on Brooklawn Ct. Enter on L.*

◊◊◊FACILITIES: 250 sites, typical site width 30 ft, 200 E, (20/30 amps), 50 no hkups, some extd stay sites (summer), WiFi Internet central location, family camping, tenting, RV's/park model rentals, cabins, RV storage, dump, non-guest dump $, portable dump, laundry, RV supplies, LP bottle exch, ice, picnic tables, fire rings, wood.

CAMPCLUB USA ◊◊◊◊◊RECREATION: rec hall, rec room/area, pavilion, lake swim, boating, electric motors only, canoeing, kayaking, ramp, dock, 6 rowboat/5 canoe/5 kayak/6 pedal boat rentals, lake fishing, golf nearby, bsktball, playground, activities, (wkends), tennis, horseshoes, sports field, hiking trails, v-ball. Rec open to public.

Pets welcome. Partial handicap access. Open all yr. Facilities fully operational May 1 - Nov 1. Clubs welcome. Rate in 2010 $27 per family. MC/VISA/DISC. CCUSA 50% Discount. CCUSA reservations Recommended, CCUSA max stay 14 days, CCUSA disc. not avail holidays. Discount available May 1 thru Jun 30 & Aug 1 thru Oct 31. Not available with other discounts.

Phone: (517)688-3783
Address: 9822 Brooklawn Ct, Somerset Center, MI 49282
Lat/Lon: 42.04226/-84.43029
Email: info@somersetbeach.org
Web: www.somersetbeach.org

SEE AD THIS PAGE

SOUTH HAVEN—I-2

(E) SOUTH HAVEN FAMILY CAMPGROUND—(Van Buren) *From north jct Bus I-196 & I-196 (exit 20): Go 5 mi E on Phoenix Rd (CR 388), then 1/4 mi N on 64 St. Enter on R.*

WELCOME ◊◊◊◊FACILITIES: 37 sites, typical site width 50 ft, 7 full hkups, 19 W&E, (20/30/50 amps), 11 no hkups, 8 pull-thrus, WiFi Instant Internet at site, family camping, tenting, cabins, RV storage, dump, non-guest dump $, portable dump, laundry, ltd groc, RV supplies, LP gas by weight/by meter, ice, picnic tables, fire rings, wood.

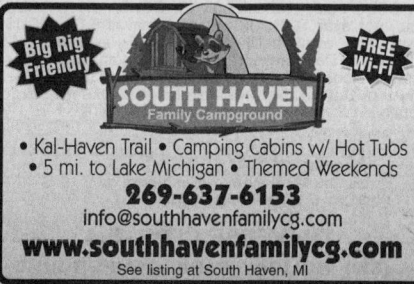

SOUTH HAVEN—Continued
SOUTH HAVEN FAMILY CAMPGROUND—Continued

◊◊◊RECREATION: rec room/area, coin games, golf nearby, bike rental 4 bike rentals, playground, activities, (wkends), horseshoes, sports field, v-ball.

Pets welcome. Partial handicap access. Open Apr 15 - Oct 30. Big rigs welcome. Clubs welcome. Green Friendly. Rate in 2010 $22-61 for 2 persons. MC/VISA/Debit. Member ARVC, ARVCMI. CCUSA 50% Discount. CCUSA reservations Required, CCUSA max stay 14 days, CCUSA disc. not avail Th, CCUSA disc. not avail F,Sa, CCUSA disc. not avail holidays. Not available Jul & Aug.

Phone: (269)637-6153
Address: 03403 64th St, South Haven, MI 49090
Lat/Lon: 42.40725/-86.16830
Email: info@southhavenfamilycg.com
Web: www.southhavenfamilycg.com

SEE AD THIS PAGE

(E) SUNNY BROOK RV RESORT—(Van Buren) *From north jct Bus I-196 & I-196 (exit 20): Go 3 mi E on Phoenix Rd (CR 388). Enter on L.*

WELCOME ◊◊◊◊◊FACILITIES: 123 sites, typical site width 45 ft, accepts full hkup units only, 123 full hkups, (20/30/50 amps), some extd stay sites (summer), WiFi Instant Internet at site, family camping, laundry, picnic tables, patios, fire rings, wood, controlled access.

◊◊◊◊RECREATION: rec hall, rec room/area, coin games, swim pool, hot tub, boating, no motors, canoeing, kayaking, dock, 2 kayak/pedal boat rentals, pond fishing, golf nearby, playground, shuffleboard court 2 shuffleboard courts, activities (wkends), horseshoes, hiking trails, v-ball.

Pets welcome, breed restrict, quantity restrict. Partial handicap access. No tents. Open Apr 15 - Oct 31. Big rigs welcome. Escort to site. Clubs welcome. Rate in 2010 $39-54 per family. MC/VISA/DISC/AMEX/Debit. Member ARVC, ARVCMI.

Phone: (888)499-5253
Address: 68300 CR 388, South Haven, MI 49090
Lat/Lon: 42.40402/-86.21011
Email: info@sunnybrookrvresort.com
Web: www.sunnybrookrvresort.com

SEE AD THIS PAGE

(NE) VAN BUREN STATE PARK—(Allegan) *From town: Go 5 mi S on BR-196 to exit 13, then go N 5 mi.* FACILITIES: 220 sites, 220 E, tenting, dump, groceries. RECREATION: lake swim, playground. Open Apr 1 - Dec 1. Facilities fully operational Apr 15 - Nov 1. Phone: (269)637-2788.

Visit Woodall's on Facebook at www.Facebook.com/Woodalls

SPRING LAKE—H-2

(E) SPRING LAKE TOURIST PARK (Municipal Park)—(Ottawa) *From jct US-31 & Hwy-104: Go 3/4 mi E on Hwy-104, then 2 blocks S on Park St.* FACILITIES: 38 sites, 38 full hkups, laundry. RECREATION: playground. No pets. No tents. Open Apr 15 - Oct 15. Phone: (616)842-5230.

STANWOOD—G-3

(W) BROWER PARK (Mecosta County)—(Mecosta) *From jct Hwy-46 & US-131: Go 10 mi N, then 3/4 mi on US-131, then 2-1/4 mi W on Eight Mile Rd, then 2-1/4 mi SW on Old State Rd, then 1-1/2 mi W on Polk Rd.* FACILITIES: 230 sites, 230 W&E, (30/50 amps), tenting, dump. RECREATION: river swim, boating, ramp, dock, river fishing, playground. No pets. Open Apr 15 - Oct 31. Phone: (231)823-2561.

(W) River Ridge RV Resort—(Mecosta) *From jct US 131 & Hwy 20 (exit 131): Go 2 mi W on Hwy 20, then 1/4 mi S on Elder Rd. Enter on L.* ◊◊◊◊◊FACILITIES: 231 sites, typical site width 40 ft, 231 full hkups, (20/30/50 amps), family camping, laundry, groceries. ◊◊◊◊◊RECREATION: swim pool, boating, canoeing, ramp, dock, river fishing, playground. Pets welcome ($), quantity restrict. Partial handicap access. No tents. Open Apr 15 - Oct 31. Big rigs welcome. Rate in 2010 $42-50 per family. Member ARVC, ARVC MI. Phone: (877)287-4837. FMCA discount.

STEPHENSON—D-2

(W) SHAKEY LAKES PARK (Menominee County Park)—(Menominee) *From jct US 41 & CR G-12: Go 12 mi W on CR G-12. Follow signs. Enter on R.* FACILITIES: 103 sites, typical site width 40 ft, 36 ft max RV length, 74 E, (15/30 amps), 29 no hkups, 8 pull-thrus, tenting, dump, laundry, ltd groc. RECREATION: lake swim, boating, canoeing, ramp, dock, lake fishing, playground. Partial handicap access. Open all yr. Phone: (906) 753-4582.

STERLING—F-5

(N) RIVER VIEW CAMPGROUND & CANOE LIVERY—(Arenac) *From jct US 23 & I-75: Go 7 mi N on I-75 (exit 195), then 1-1/2 mi E on Sterling Rd, then 3-1/4 mi N on School Rd (Melita Rd), then 2 mi W on Townline Rd. Enter at end.*

WELCOME ◊◊◊◊FACILITIES: 290 sites, typical site width 35 ft, 86 full hkups, 144 W&E, (20/30/50 amps), 60 no hkups, some extd stay sites (summer), 44 pull-thrus, WiFi Instant Internet at site ($), family camping, tenting, cabins, RV storage, dump, non-guest dump $, laundry, groceries, RV supplies, LP bottle exch, ice, picnic tables, fire rings, grills, wood.

CAMPCLUB USA ◊◊◊◊RECREATION: rec room/area, pavilion, coin games, river swim, canoeing, kayaking, 340 canoe/120 kayak rentals, float trips, river fishing, fishing supplies, golf nearby, bsktball, playground, activities, (wkends), horseshoes, hiking trails, v-ball. Rec open to public.

Pets welcome, breed restrict. Partial handicap access. Open May 1 - Oct 15. Big rigs welcome.

RIVER VIEW CAMPGROUND & CANOE LIVERY—Continued on next page

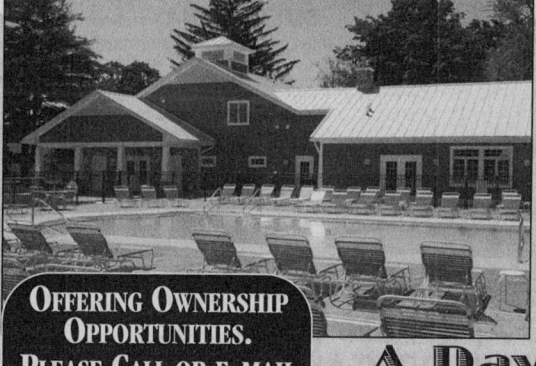

STERLING—Continued
RIVER VIEW CAMPGROUND & CANOE LIVERY—Continued

Clubs welcome. Green Friendly. Rate in 2010 $32-36 for 2 persons. MC/VISA/DISC/Debit. Member ARVC, ARVC MI. CCUSA 50% Discount. CCUSA reservations Required, CCUSA max stay Unlimited, CCUSA disc. not avail S, CCUSA disc. not avail F,Sa, CCUSA disc. not avail holidays. Not available Jun 29 thru Jul 8. Discount available May 1-Jun 29 & Jul 8 to Labor Day weekend weekdays only. Discount available anyday after Labor Day thru Oct 30. 10% off seasonal rates May 1-Oct 30.

Phone: (989)654-2447
Address: 5755 N Townline Rd, Sterling, MI 48659
Lat/Lon: 44.08352/-84.03491
Email: rvc@riverviewcampground.com
Web: www.riverviewcampground.com

SEE AD THIS PAGE

(N) RIVER VIEW CANOE LIVERY—*From jct US 23 & I-75: Go 7 mi N on I-75 (exit 195), then 1-1/2 mi E on Sterling Rd, then 3-1/4 mi N on School Rd (Melita Rd), then 2 mi W on Townline Rd. Enter at end.* Canoe, tube & kayak trips ranging from 1 hr to 6 hours on the Rifle River, accommodating families & groups. Open May 1 - Oct 15. MC/VISA/DISC/Debit.

Phone: (989)654-2447
Address: 5755 N Townline Rd, Sterling, MI 48659
Lat/Lon: 44.08352/-84.03491
Email: rvc@riverviewcampground.com
Web: www.riverviewcampground.com

SEE AD THIS PAGE

STOCKBRIDGE—I-4

(SW) Heartland Woods Family RV—(Ingham) *From South jct Hwy 52 & Hwy 106: Go 4-1/4 mi SW on Hwy 106, then 1-3/4 mi W on Territorial Rd, then 1-1/4 mi N on Fitchburg Rd, then 1/2 mi W on Baseline Rd, then 1/2 mi N on Freiermuth Rd. Enter on L.* ◇◇◇FACILITIES: 223 sites, 220 W&E, (20/30/50 amps), 3 no hkups, WiFi Internet central location, family camping, tenting, RV storage, dump, portable dump, laundry, groceries, RV supplies, ice, picnic tables, fire rings, wood. ◇◇◇◇RECREATION: rec hall, 2 swim pools, pond fishing, fishing supplies, mini-golf, putting green, bsktball, playground, shuffleboard court 4 shuffleboard courts, activities, horseshoes, hiking trails, v-ball. Pets welcome, quantity restrict. Partial handicap access. Open May 15 - Oct 15. Rate in 2010 $32-45 per family. MC/VISA/DISC/Debit. Member ARVC, ARVCMI. CCUSA 50% Discount. CCUSA reservations Recommended, CCUSA max stay 14 days, CCUSA disc. not avail holidays. Not available Heartland Haunting.

Phone: (517)565-3500 Address: 5120 Freiermuth Rd.
Lat/Lon: 42.43565/-84.27797
Email: heartlandwoodsrv@comcast.net
Web: www.heartlandwoodsrv.com

(W) PJ's Family Campground—(Ingham) *From jct I-94 (exit 139) & Hwy 106: Go 9 mi N on Hwy 106, then 2 mi N on Bunker Hill Rd, then 1/4 mi W on Baseline Rd, then 1/2 mi N on Williamston Rd. Enter on L.* ◇◇◇FACILITIES: 145 sites, typical site width 40 ft, 4 full hkups, 130 W&E, (30 amps), 11 no hkups, 26 pull-thrus, tenting, dump, laundry. ◇◇RECREATION: pond fishing, play equipment. Pets welcome. Open Late Apr - Late Oct. Rate in 2010 $22 for 2 persons. Phone: (517)565-3044. FCRV discount. FMCA discount.

STRONGS—C-4

(W) HIAWATHA NATIONAL FOREST (Soldier Lake Campground)—(Chippewa) *From town: Go 5-4/10 mi E on Hwy 28.* FACILITIES: 44 sites, 32 ft max RV length, 44 no hkups, 1 pull-thrus, tenting. RECREATION: lake swim, boating, no motors, canoeing, lake fishing. Open May 15 - Oct 15. Phone: (906)635-5311.

STRONGS—Continued

(S) HIAWATHA NATIONAL FOREST (Three Lakes Campground)—(Chippewa) *From town: Go 2 mi S on Forest Rt 3142.* FACILITIES: 28 sites, 32 ft max RV length, 28 no hkups, tenting. RECREATION: boating, no motors, canoeing, lake fishing. Open May 15 - Oct 15. Phone: (906)635-5311.

STURGIS—J-3

(SW) Green Valley Campground—(St. Joseph) *From West jct US-12 & Hwy-66: Go 1-1/4 mi S on Hwy-66, then 1-1/2 mi W on Fawn River Rd, then 1/2 mi S on entry road. Enter at end.* ◇◇◇FACILITIES: 220 sites, typical site width 40 ft, 220 W&E, (20/30 amps), 5 pull-thrus, family camping, tenting, dump, laundry, ltd groc. ◇◇◇◇RECREATION: swim pool, pond fishing, playground. Pets welcome. Open May 1 - Oct 15. Rate in 2010 $21-23 per family. Member ARVC, ARVC MI. Phone: (269)651-8760.

(E) Sweet Lake Resort Community (RV SPACES)—(St.Joseph) *From jct Hwy 66 & US 12: Go 3-3/4 mi E on US 12. Enter on L.* FACILITIES: 48 sites, typical site width 25 ft, 47 W&E, 1 E, (20/30 amps), family camping, tenting, dump, laundry. RECREATION: lake swim, boating, 10 hp limit, ramp, dock, lake fishing, playground. Pets welcome. Open May 1 - Oct 1. Rate in 2010 $15-25 for 2 persons. Phone: (269)651-8149.

SUMNER—H-4

(SE) LEISURE LAKE FAMILY CAMPGROUND—(Gratiot) *From jct US 127 & Washington Rd (exit 117): Go 10 mi W on Washington Rd, then 1/2 mi S on Warner Rd. Enter on L.*

◇◇◇◇FACILITIES: 137 sites, typical site width 40 ft, 84 full hkups, 53 W&E, (20/30/50 amps), some extd stay sites (summer), 7 pull-thrus, WiFi Instant Internet at site, WiFi Internet central location, family camping, tenting, cabins, RV storage, dump, non-guest dump $, portable dump, laundry, ltd groc, RV supplies, LP gas by weight/by meter, ice, picnic tables, patios, fire rings, wood, controlled access.

◇◇◇◇RECREATION: pavilion, coin games, lake swim, boating, electric motors only, canoeing, kayaking, ramp, 8 rowboat/6 kayak/6 pedal boat rentals, lake fishing, fishing supplies, mini-golf, ($), golf nearby, bsktball, 11 bike rentals, playground, activities, (wkends), horseshoes, sports field, v-ball.

Pets welcome, breed restrict. Partial handicap access. Open May 1 - Oct 1. Big rigs welcome. Escort to site. Clubs welcome. Rate in 2010 $29-35 for 4 persons. MC/VISA/Debit. Member ARVC, ARVC MI. CCUSA 50% Discount. CCUSA reservations Required, CCUSA max stay 2 days, Cash only for CCUSA disc., Check only for CCUSA disc., CCUSA disc. not avail S, CCUSA disc. not avail F,Sa, CCUSA disc. not avail holidays.

Phone: (877)975-4689
Address: 505 S. Warner Rd, Sumner, MI 48889
Lat/Lon: 43.28194/-84.77715
Email: pat@leisurelakefamilycampground.com
Web: www.leisurelakefamilycampground.com

SEE AD ITHACA PAGE 388

SUTTONS BAY—E-4

(NW) Wild Cherry RV Resort—(Leelanau) *From jct Hwy 22 & Hwy 204: Go 2 mi W on Hwy 204, then 1/2 mi NW on Horn Rd. Enter on R.* ◇◇◇◇FACILITIES: 76 sites, typical site width 45 ft, 66 full hkups, (20/30/50 amps), 10 no hkups, 1 pull-thrus, family camping, tenting. Pets welcome, quantity restrict. Open May 1 - Oct 31. Big rigs welcome. Rate in 2010 $36-55 for 4 persons. Member ARVC, ARVC MI. Phone: (231)271-5550. FMCA discount.

TAWAS CITY—F-5

(W) East Branch River RV Park—(Iosco) *From jct US 23 & Hwy 55: Go 10 mi W on Hwy 55. Enter on L.* ◇◇◇◇FACILITIES: 125 sites, typical site width 40 ft, 33 full hkups, (20/30/50 amps), 92 no hkups, family camping, tenting, dump, non-guest dump $, laundry, ice, picnic tables, fire rings, wood. ◇RECREATION: river fishing, playground, horseshoes, hiking trails. Pets welcome. Partial handicap access. Open May 1 - Oct 31. Big rigs welcome. Rate in 2010 $26 for 4 persons. CCUSA 50% Discount. CCUSA reservations Accepted, CCUSA max stay 7 days, Cash only for CCUSA disc. Fully operational May thru Oct.

Phone: (989)362-8000
Address: 4793 M-55, Tawas City, MI 48763
Lat/Lon: 44.27784/-83.71533
Email: eastbranchrvpark@m33access.com
Web: www.eastbranchriverrvpark.com

(NW) HURON NATIONAL FOREST (Round Lake Campground)—(Arenac) *From jct Hwy 55 & Plank Rd: Go 7 mi W on Plank Rd, then 1 mi S on Indian Lake Rd, then 1/2 mi W on Latham Rd.* FACILITIES: 33 sites, 22 ft max RV length, 33 no hkups, tenting, ltd groc. RECREATION: lake swim, boating, canoeing, ramp, lake fishing. Partial handicap access. Open Memorial Day - Labor Day. Phone: (989)739-0728.

TECUMSEH—J-5

(NE) Indian Creek Camp & Conference Center—(Lenawee) *From jct Hwy 52 & Hwy 50: Go 7 mi E on Hwy 50, then 2-1/2 mi N on Ford Hwy. Enter on R.* ◇◇◇◇FACILITIES: 47 sites, typical site width 30 ft, 42 full hkups, 5 W&E, (20/30 amps), 13 pull-thrus, WiFi Instant Internet at site, family camping, tenting, RV storage, dump, non-guest dump $, portable dump, laundry, ice, picnic tables, fire rings, wood. ◇◇◇◇RECREATION: rec hall, pavilion, swim pool, boating, kayaking, lake fishing, fishing supplies, mini-golf, ($), bsktball, playground, activities, horseshoes, hiking trails, v-ball. Pets welcome. Partial handicap access. Open Apr 15 - Oct 15. Rate in 2010 $31-39 per family. MC/VISA/Debit. Member ARVC, ARVC MI. CCUSA 50% Discount. CCUSA reservations Accepted, CCUSA max stay 4 days, CCUSA disc. not avail S, CCUSA disc. not avail F,Sa, CCUSA disc. not avail holidays. Discount available Mon thru Thu only. No Exceptions. Cancellation policy: must use credit card to guarantee reservation. If cancelled $30 fee applies No exceptions. Not available on Race weeks or holiday weekends Thurs thru Mon.

Phone: (517)423-5659
Address: 9415 Tangent Hwy, Tecumseh, MI 49286
Lat/Lon: 42.03189/-83.86924
Email: rdorman@tecumsehteamquest.com
Web: www.indiancreekcamping.com

TIPTON—J-4

(NW) Ja Do Park Campground—(Lenawee) *From jct US-12 & Hwy-52: Go 4-1/2 mi W on US-12. Enter on L.* ◇◇◇FACILITIES: 60 sites, typical site width 50 ft, 60 W&E, (20/30 amps), family camping, tenting, RV storage, dump, non-guest dump $, portable dump, ltd groc, RV supplies, ice, picnic tables, fire rings, wood. ◇◇◇RECREATION: pond fishing, fishing supplies, bsktball, playground, activities, horseshoes, hiking trails, v-ball. Pets welcome, quantity restrict. Partial handicap access. Open May 1 - Oct 15. Rate in 2010 $22-27 for 2 persons. MC/VISA/Debit. Member ARVC, ARVC MI. CCUSA 50% Discount. CCUSA reservations Recommended, CCUSA max stay Unlimited, Cash only for CCUSA disc., Check only for CCUSA disc., CCUSA disc. not avail S, CCUSA disc. not avail F,Sa, CCUSA disc. not avail holidays. Discount available May 1-Memorial Day weekend anytime (including weekends). Discount not available weekends Memorial Day Weekend thru Oct 15. Not available Race Weekends-call for details.

Phone: (517)431-2111
Address: 5603 US Hwy 12, Tipton, MI 49287
Lat/Lon: 42.06748/-84.09866
Email: info@jadocampground.com
Web: www.jadocampground.com

TRAVERSE CITY—E-4

(SW) HOLIDAY PARK CAMPGROUND—(Grand Traverse) *From west jct Hwy 72 & US 31/Hwy 37: Go 6-3/4 mi S on US 31/Hwy 37, then 1 mi SW on US 31. Enter on R.*

ON SHORES OF SILVER LAKE

Quiet spacious RV sites - Enjoy fishing, boating, the sandy beach, & playgrounds in the park, or try the nearby shopping, restaurants, casinos, horseback riding, and wineries near Traverse City.

◇◇◇◇◇FACILITIES: 214 sites, typical site width 35 ft, 169 full hkups, 45 W&E, (20/30/50 amps), some extd stay sites (summer), 65 pull-thrus, cable TV, WiFi Instant Internet at site, WiFi Internet

HOLIDAY PARK CAMPGROUND—Continued on next page

TRAVERSE CITY—Continued
HOLIDAY PARK CAMPGROUND—Continued

central location, family camping, tenting, RV storage, dump, non-guest dump $, laundry, ltd groc, RV supplies, LP gas by weight/by meter, ice, picnic tables, fire rings, grills, wood.

◆◆◆RECREATION: lake swim, boating, canoeing, kayaking, ramp, dock, 4 rowboat/2 canoe/6 kayak/4 pedal boat rentals, lake fishing, fishing supplies, golf nearby, bsktball, playground, horseshoes, sports field, v-ball.

Pets welcome. Partial handicap access. Open Mid Apr - mid Nov. No camping motorcyclists. Big rigs welcome. Clubs welcome. Rate in 2010 $36-53 for 4 persons. MC/VISA/DISC/Debit. Member ARVC, ARVC MI.

Text 107958 to (440)725-8687 to see our Visual Tour.

Phone: (231)943-4410
Address: 4860 US 31 South, Traverse City, MI 49685
Lat/Lon: 44.67077/-85.67347
Web: www.michcampgrounds.com/holidaypark

SEE AD THIS PAGE

(SW) JUST TRUCKS—*From west jct Hwy 72 & US 31/Hwy 37: Go 6-3/4 mi S on US 31/Hwy 37, then 3 mi SW on US 31. Enter on R.* SALES: pre-owned unit sales. SERVICES: engine/chassis repair, RV appliance repair, 24-hr emerg rd svc, mobile RV svc, sells parts/accessories, installs hitches. Complete RV Service Center. Open all yr. MC/VISA/DISC/AMEX/Debit.

Phone: (231)276-5158
Address: 7030 US 31, Grawn, MI 49637
Lat/Lon: 44.66359/-85.71809
Email: justtrucks2@att.net
Web: www.justtrucksrepair.com

SEE AD THIS PAGE

(SE) PERE MARQUETTE SF (Arbutus No. 4)—(Grand Traverse) *From town: Go 5-1/2 mi SE on CR 611 (Garfield Rd), then 2-1/2 mi E on Potter Rd, then 1/2 mi S on 4 Mile Rd, then 1/2 mi E on N Arbutus Rd.* FACILITIES: 30 sites, 30 no hkups, tenting. RECREATION: lake swim, boating, ramp, lake fishing. Partial handicap access. Open Memorial Day - Labor Day. Phone: (231)922-5280.

(SE) Timber Ridge RV & Recreation Resort—(Grand Traverse) *From West jct HWY 72 & US 31/Hwy 37: Go 5 mi E on US31/Hwy 72, then 2 mi S on 4 Mile Rd, then 2 mi E on Hammond Rd. Enter on L.* ◆◆◆◆FACILITIES: 218 sites, typical site width 30 ft, 144 full hkups, 74 W&E, (30/50 amps), 95 pull-thrus, cable TV, WiFi Instant Internet at site, WiFi Internet central location, family camping, tenting, RV storage, shower$, dump, non-guest dump $, portable dump, laundry, groceries, RV supplies, LP gas by weight/by meter, ice,

Woodall's. The name that's trusted for over 75 years.

TRAVERSE CITY—Continued
Timber Ridge RV & Recreation Resort—Continued

picnic tables, fire rings, wood. ◆◆◆◆RECREATION: rec hall, pavilion, swim pool, mini-golf, ($), bsktball, 22 bike rentals, playground, shuffleboard court 2 shuffleboard courts, activities, horseshoes, hiking trails, v-ball. Pets welcome. Partial handicap access. Open May 1 - Oct 31. Rate in 2010 $40-52 per family. MC/VISA/Debit. Member ARVC, ARVC MI. CCUSA 50% Discount. CCUSA reservations Required, CCUSA max stay Unlimited, CCUSA disc. not avail F,Sa, CCUSA disc. not avail holidays. Not available Jun 27-July 15.

Save time! Plan ahead with WOODALL'S!

TRAVERSE CITY—Continued
Timber Ridge RV & Recreation Resort—Continued

Phone: (877)9-RVFUNN
Address: 4050 Hammond Road, Traverse City, MI 49686
Lat/Lon: 44.71430/-85.49586
Email: info@timberridgeresort.net
Web: www.timberridgeresort.net

TRAVERSE CITY—Continued on next page

Woodall's Tip... The North American Edition is split into Eastern and Western sections; each organized alphabetically starting with Alabama in the East and Alaska in the West.

(NE) TRAVERSE BAY RV RESORT—(Grand Traverse) *From north jct US 31 & Hwy 72: Go 1-1/2 mi E on Hwy 72. Enter on L.*

NORTHERN MICHIGANS'S PREMIER RV RESORT

Traverse Bay offers beautiful scenery and world-class amenities. 150 acres of rolling hills, scenic woods, and shimmering ponds. An adult-oriented RV Resort, with something for everyone. Join the lifestyle at Traverse Bay!

◊◊◊◊◊FACILITIES: 217 sites, typical site width 48 ft, accepts full hkup units only, 217 full hkups, (20/30/50 amps), cable TV, WiFi Instant Internet at site, laundry, LP gas by weight/by meter, ice, picnic tables, patios.

◊◊◊◊RECREATION: rec hall, rec room/area, swim pool, hot tub, golf nearby, bike rental 6 bike rentals, activities, tennis, horseshoes, sports field, hiking trails, local tours.

Pets welcome, breed restrict, quantity restrict. Partial handicap access. No tents. Open May 1 - Oct 31. Big rigs welcome. Escort to site. Clubs welcome. Rate in 2010 $45-65 for 2 persons. MC/VISA/DISC/Debit. Member ARVC, ARVC MI.

Phone: (231)938-5800
Address: 5555 M 72 E, Williamsburg, MI 49690
Lat/Lon: 44.77282/-85.46464
Email: info@traversebayrv.com
Web: www.traversebayrv.com

SEE AD PAGE 405

(E) TRAVERSE CITY STATE PARK—*From East city limits: Go 1 mi N on US 31.* FACILITIES: 343 sites, 343 E, (20/30 amps), tenting, dump, ltd groc. RECREATION: lake swim, boating, lake fishing, playground. Open all yr. Phone: (231)922-5270.

UNION CITY—J-3

(SE) Potawatomie Recreation Area—(Branch) *From jct Hwy 60 & I-69: Go 2 mi S on I-69 (exit 23), then 1/4 mi S on Marshall Rd/Old 27, then 1-1/2 mi W on County Line Rd, then 1-3/4 mi S on Bell Rd. Enter on L.* ◊◊◊FACILITIES: 176 sites, typical site width 30 ft, 39 ft max RV length, 56 full hkups, 110 W&E, (20/30/50 amps), 10 no hkups, 6 pull-thrus, family camping, tenting, dump, laundry, ltd groc. ◊◊◊◊RECREATION: lake swim, boating, electric motors only, canoeing, lake fishing, playground. Pets welcome. Open Apr 15 - Oct 15. Rate in 2010 $24-27 for 2 persons. Member ARVC, ARVC MI. Phone: (517)278-4289.

VANDERBILT—E-5

(NE) MACKINAW SF (Pickerel Lake)—(Otsego) *From Old US 27 in town: Go 10 mi E on Sturgeon Valley Rd & Pickerel Lake Rd.* FACILITIES: 39 sites, 39 no hkups, tenting. RECREATION: lake swim, boating, no motors, canoeing, ramp, lake fishing. Partial handicap access. Open all yr. Phone: (989)983-4101.

VASSAR—H-5

(NE) BER-WA-GA-NA CAMPGROUND—(Tuscola) *From jct Hwy 15 & Hwy 46: Go 11 mi E on Hwy 46. Enter on R.*

◊◊◊FACILITIES: 150 sites, typical site width 30 ft, 120 full hkups, 30 W&E, (20/30 amps), many extd stay sites (summer), 7 pull-thrus, heater not allowed, WiFi Instant Internet at site, family camping, tenting, RV's/park model rentals, RV storage, dump, non-guest dump $, laundry, ltd groc, RV supplies, LP gas by weight/by meter, ice, picnic tables, fire rings, wood.

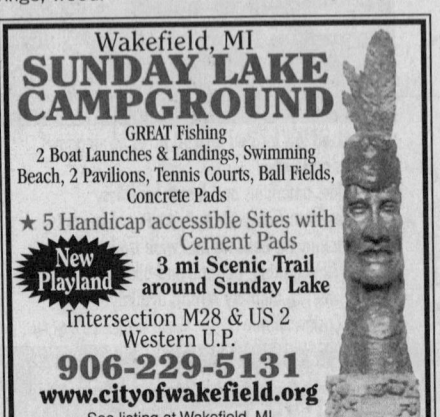

◊◊◊◊RECREATION: rec hall, rec room/area, pavilion, coin games, lake swim, 7 kayak/2 pedal boat rentals, pond fishing, fishing supplies, mini-golf, ($), golf nearby, bsktball, 24 bike rentals, playground, shuffleboard court 2 shuffleboard courts, activities (wkends), horseshoes, sports field, hiking trails, v-ball. Rec open to public.

Pets welcome. Partial handicap access. Open May 1 - Nov 1. Escort to site. Clubs welcome. Rate in 2010 $20-32 for 4 persons. MC/VISA/DISC. Member ARVC, ARVC MI. CCUSA 50% Discount. CCUSA reservations Required, CCUSA max stay 5 days, CCUSA disc. not avail F,Sa, CCUSA disc. not avail holidays. Electric heater not allowed.

Phone: (989)673-7125
Address: 2601 W Sanilac Rd (M46), Vassar, MI 48768
Lat/Lon: 43.40805/-83.44435
Email: berwagana@hotmail.com
Web: www.berwaganacampground.com

SEE AD FRANKENMUTH PAGE 381

Krystal Lake Campground—(Tuscola) *From jct Hwy 15 & Hwy 46: Go 10 mi E on Hwy 46, then 3-3/4 mi S on Washburn Rd. Enter on L.* ◊◊◊FACILITIES: 208 sites, typical site width 30 ft, 21 full hkups, 162 W&E, (20/30/50 amps), 25 no hkups, 50 pull-thrus, family camping, tenting, dump, laundry, ltd groc. ◊◊◊◊RECREATION: swim pool, lake swim, boating, electric motors only, ramp, lake fishing, playground. Pets welcome. Partial handicap access. Open Apr 15 - Oct 15. Big rigs welcome. Rate in 2010 $22-34 for 2 persons. Member ARVC, ARVCMI. Phone: (989)843-0591.

(NE) Wesleyan Woods Campground—(Tuscola) *From jct Hwy 15 & Hwy 46: Go 7 mi E on Hwy 46, then 1 mi S on Ringle Rd, then 100 ft W on Waterman Rd, then 1/2 mi S on Caine Rd. Enter on R.* ◊◊◊FACILITIES: 225 sites, 50 full hkups, 146 W&E, (30/50 amps), 29 no hkups, 150 pull-thrus, family camping, tenting, RV storage, dump, non-guest dump $, portable dump, ice, picnic tables, fire rings, wood. ◊◊◊RECREATION: rec hall, pavilion, lake swim, canoeing, lake/river fishing, mini-golf, bsktball, playground, activities, horseshoes, v-ball. Pets welcome, quantity restrict. Partial handicap access. Open Apr 15 - Oct 15. Rate in 2010 $25-29 per family. MC/VISA. CCUSA 50% Discount. CCUSA reservations Recommended, CCUSA max stay See rest., CCUSA disc. not avail F,Sa, CCUSA disc. not avail holidays. No Discount first & second week of July. Max stay dependant upon availability. Please call office.

Phone: (989)823-8840
Address: 4320 Caine Rd, Vassar, MI 48768
Lat/Lon: 43.38622/-83.52245
Email: camping@wesleyanwoods.org
Web: www.wesleyanwoods.org

VIENNA—E-5

(SW) MACKINAW SF (Big Bear Lake)—(Otsego) *From town: Go 1-1/2 mi SW on Principal Meridian Rd & Little Bear Lake Rd.* FACILITIES: 30 sites, 30 no hkups, tenting. RECREATION: lake swim, boating, no motors, canoeing, ramp, lake fishing. Partial handicap access. Open May 1 - Labor Day. Phone: (989) 732-3541.

WAKEFIELD—A-5

(N) PORCUPINE MTNS. STATE PARK (Presque Isle Unit)—(Gogebic) *From town: Go 16 mi N on CR-519.* FACILITIES: 50 sites, 50 no hkups, tenting. RECREATION: boating, canoeing, ramp, dock, lake/river/stream fishing, playground. Pets welcome. Open Apr 5 - Nov 3. Phone: (906)885-5275.

(SW) SUNDAY LAKE CAMPGROUND—(Gogebic) *From jct Hwy 28 & US 2: Go 1 mi W on US 2, then 1 mi NE on Lakeshore Dr. Enter on R.*

WELCOME

FACILITIES: 71 sites, 18 full hkups, 46 W&E, (20/30/50 amps), 7 no hkups, some extd stay sites (summer), 10 pull-thrus, family camping, tenting, shower$, dump, non-guest dump $, picnic tables, fire rings.

RECREATION: pavilion, lake swim, boating, canoeing, kayaking, ramp, dock, lake fishing, golf nearby, bsktball, playground, tennis, sports field, hiking trails, v-ball. Rec open to public.

Pets welcome. Partial handicap access. Open Memorial Day - Oct 1. Reservations after Memorial Day (906)224-4481. Big rigs welcome. Clubs welcome.

Phone: (906)229-5131
Address: 300 Eddy Park Rd, Wakefield, MI 49968
Lat/Lon: 46.48394/-89.95081
Email: citymanager@cityofwakefield.org
Web: www.cityofwakefield.org

SEE AD THIS PAGE

WALHALLA—G-2

(N) Timber Surf Camping Resort—(Mason) *From east jct US 31 & US 10: Go 9 mi E on US 10, then 3-1/2 mi N on Benson Rd, then 1/2 mi W on Sugar Grove Rd, then 1 mi N on Morse Rd, then 3/4 mi E on Dewey Rd. Enter on R.* ◊◊◊FACILITIES: 70 sites, typical site width 30 ft, 21 full hkups, 49 W&E, (20/30/50 amps), 2 pull-thrus, phone Internet central location, family camping, tenting, dump, non-guest dump $, portable dump, laundry, groceries, RV supplies, ice, picnic tables, fire rings, wood. ◊◊◊◊RECREATION: lake swim, boating, canoeing, kayaking, ramp, dock, lake fishing, fishing supplies, bsktball, playground, activities, horseshoes, v-ball. Pets welcome. Partial handicap access. Open Apr 1 - Nov 30. Facilities fully operational May 1 - Oct 15. Rate in 2010 $24-26 for 4 persons. Member ARVC, ARVC MI. CCUSA 50% Discount. CCUSA reservations Accepted, CCUSA max stay 4 days, CCUSA disc. not avail S, CCUSA disc. not avail F,Sa, CCUSA disc. not avail holidays.

CAMPCLUB USA

Phone: (231)462-3468
Address: 6575 Dewey Rd, Fountain, MI 49410
Lat/Lon: 44.01860/-86.11633
Email: info@timbersurfresort.com
Web: www.timbersurfresort.com

WALKERVILLE—G-2

(NE) Pine Haven Campground—(Oceana) *From south jct US 31 & Business US 31/Monroe Rd: Go 7 mi E on Monroe Rd, then 1 mi N on 126th, then 6 mi E on Madison, then 2 mi N & E on 176th, then 1/4 mi S on 186th Ave. Enter on L.* ◊◊FACILITIES: 72 sites, typical site width 30 ft, 35 ft max RV length, 48 full hkups, 12 W&E, (20/30 amps), 12 no hkups, tenting, dump, groceries. ◊◊◊RECREATION: lake swim, boating, canoeing, dock, lake fishing, playground. Pets welcome. Open all yr. Facilities fully operational Apr - Nov. Rate in 2010 $18-25 for 4 persons. Phone: (231)898-2722.

WATERFORD—I-5

(E) PONTIAC LAKE STATE RECREATION AREA—(Oakland) *From jct US 23 & Hwy 59: Go 13 mi E on Hwy 59, then 2-1/2 mi N on Teggerdine Rd.* FACILITIES: 176 sites, 176 E, (20/30 amps), tenting, dump, ltd groc. RECREATION: lake swim, boating, ramp, lake fishing, playground. Partial handicap access. Open May 1 - Oct 31. Phone: (248)666-1020.

WATERSMEET—B-6

(SW) OTTAWA NATIONAL FOREST (Clark Lake Campground)—(Gogebic) *From jct US 45 & US 2: Go 4 mi W on US 2, then 5-1/2 mi SW on CR 535, then 1/2 mi SW on FR 6360.* FACILITIES: 47 sites, 22 ft max RV length, 47 no hkups, tenting, dump. RECREATION: lake swim, boating, no motors, canoeing, ramp, lake fishing, playground. Partial handicap access. Open all yr. Facilities fully operational May 22 - Sep 15. Phone: (906)358-4551.

(E) OTTAWA NATIONAL FOREST (Marion Lake Campground)—(Gogebic) *From jct US 45 & US 2: Go 3-3/4 mi E on US 2, then 1-1/2 mi N on FR 3980.* FACILITIES: 38 sites, 22 ft max RV length, 38 no hkups, 5 pull-thrus, tenting. RECREATION: lake swim, boating, ramp, lake fishing. Open all yr. Facilities fully operational May 15 - Sep 15. Phone: (906)358-4551.

WEIDMAN—G-4

(NW) COLDWATER LAKE FAMILY PARK (Isabella County)—(Isabella) *From jct Business US 27 & Hwy 20: Go 7 mi W on Hwy 20, then 5 mi N on Winn Rd, then 2 mi W on Beal City Rd, then 1/4 mi S on Littlefield Rd.* FACILITIES: 95 sites, 95 W&E, (20/30 amps), 8 pull-thrus, tenting, dump. RECREATION: lake swim, boating, ramp, dock, lake fishing, playground. Partial handicap access. Open May 1 - Sep 30. Phone: (989)772-0911.

(S) Gammy Woods Campground—(Isabella) *From jct Hwy 66 & Hwy 20: Go 8 mi E on Hwy 20, then 5 mi N on Coldwater Rd. Enter on L.* ◊◊◊FACILITIES: 83 sites, typical site width 30 ft, 78 W&E, (20/30/50 amps), 5 no hkups, 5 pull-thrus, family camping, tenting, dump. ◊◊◊RECREATION: lake swim, playground. Pets welcome, quantity restrict. Partial handicap access. Open May 1 - Oct 1. Rate in 2010 $24 per family. Member ARVC, ARVCMI. Phone: (989)506-8005.

WELLSTON—F-2

(W) Heart of the Forest RV Park—(Manistee) *From jct Hwy 37 & Hwy 55: Go 7-1/2 mi W on Hwy 55. Enter on R.* ◊◊◊FACILITIES: 65 sites, typical site width 35 ft, 20 full hkups, 45 E, (20/30/50 amps), 9 pull-thrus, family camping, tenting, RV storage, dump, non-guest dump $, laundry, groceries, RV supplies, ice, picnic tables, fire rings, wood. RECREATION: playground, horseshoes. Pets welcome. Open Apr 1 - Nov 30. Big rigs welcome. Rate in 2010 $20-27 for 2 persons. MC/VISA/DISC/AMEX/Debit. ATM. Member ARVC, ARVCMI. CCUSA 50% Discount. CCUSA reservations Recommended, CCUSA max stay 5 days, CCUSA disc. not avail F,Sa, CCUSA disc. not avail holidays. Not available Aug 31-Oct 14.

CAMPCLUB USA

Phone: (231)848-4161
Address: 16992 Caberfae Hwy (M-55), Wellston, MI 49689
Lat/Lon: 44.22555/-85.96196
Email: urcamping@jackpine.com
Web: www.heartoftheforestrvpark.com

WELLSTON—Continued on next page

WELLSTON—Continued

(E) Kestelwoods Campground—(Manistee) *From jct Hwy-55 & Hwy-37: Go 2-1/2 mi S on Hwy-37, then 1/8 mi E on 48-1/2 Mile Rd. Enter on L.* ◆◆◆FACILITIES: 96 sites, typical site width 30 ft, 96 W&E, (20/30 amps), 24 pull-thrus, WiFi Instant Internet at site, family camping, tenting, RV storage, dump, non-guest dump $, groceries, RV supplies, ice, picnic tables, fire rings, wood. ◆◆RECREATION: pavilion, swim pool, bsktball, playground, shuffleboard court 4 shuffleboard courts, horseshoes, v-ball. Pets welcome. Open Apr 22 - Oct 30. Rate in 2010 $34 for 2 persons. Member ARVC, ARVCMI. CCUSA 50% Discount.

Phone: (231)862-3476
Address: 10860 W 48-1/2 Rd, Wellston, MI 49689
Lat/Lon: 44.18630/-85.79749
Email: info@kestelwoodscampground.com
Web: www.kestelwoods.com

(S) MANISTEE NATIONAL FOREST (Sand Lake Campground)—(Manistee) *From jct Hwy 55 & Snyder Rd: Go 3 mi S on Snyder Rd to Dublin, then 1/4 mi S on Seaman Rd, then 1/2 mi W on FR 5728. For reservations call (877)444-6777.* FACILITIES: 47 sites, 47 no hkups, tenting. RECREATION: lake swim, boating, canoeing, ramp, lake fishing. Partial handicap access. Open May 1 - Sep 10. Phone: (616)723-2211.

(E) Pine River Paddlesport Center and Campground—(Wexford) *From jct Hwy 55 & Hwy 37: Go 1-1/2 mi S on Hwy 37. Enter on R.* ◆◆FACILITIES: 43 sites, typical site width 40 ft, 43 no hkups, family camping, tenting. ◆◆RECREATION: river swim, canoeing, river fishing. No pets. Partial handicap access. Open Apr 1 - Nov 1. Rate in 2010 $22 for 2 persons. Phone: (231)862-3471.

WEST BRANCH—F-4

(N) AU SABLE SF (Ambrose Lake)—(Ogemaw) *From town: Go 11 mi N on CR 15 & CR 20.* FACILITIES: 19 sites, 19 no hkups, tenting. RECREATION: lake swim, boating, ramp, lake fishing. Open May - Dec 1. Phone: (989)275-4622.

(NW) Beaver Trail Campground—(Ogemaw) *From jct I-75 & Bus I-75 (exit 212): Go 2-1/4 mi N on Bus I-75, then 5 mi N on Fairview Rd/CR F7, then 7 mi NW on Clear Lake Rd/Grass Lake Rd. Enter on R.* ◆◆FACILITIES: 28 sites, 40 ft max RV length, 10 W&E, 10 E, (20/30 amps), 8 no hkups, 8 pull-thrus, family camping, tenting, RV storage, dump, non-guest dump $, picnic tables, fire rings, wood. ◆◆RECREATION: lake swim, pond fishing, bsktball, 3 bike rentals, playground, horseshoes, v-ball. Pets welcome, quantity restrict. Partial handicap access. Open all yr. Facilities fully operational May 1 - Nov 1. Rate in 2010 $22-25 for 4 persons. MC/VISA. Member ARVC, ARVCMI. CCUSA 50% Discount. CCUSA reservations Recommended, CCUSA max stay 4 days, CCUSA disc. not avail holidays. Not available Nov 15-30. Fully operational May 1-Nov 1.

Phone: (989)345-7745
Address: 4408 Grass Lake Rd, West Branch, MI 48661
Lat/Lon: 44.39938/-84.30305
Email: yedinak@hotmail.com
Web: www.beavertrailcampground.com

(SE) Loranger Pines RV Park—(Ogemaw) *From jct I-75 (exit 212) & Bus I-75: Go 1-1/4 mi N on Bus I-75, then 3-3/4 mi S on Old Hwy 76/CR F9. Enter on R.* ◆◆◆FACILITIES: 84 sites, typical site width 50 ft, 33 full hkups, (30/50 amps), 51 no hkups, heater not allowed, WiFi Instant Internet at site, family camping, tenting, RV storage, dump, non-guest dump $, LP gas by weight/by meter, ice, picnic tables, fire rings, wood. ◆RECREATION: pavilion, hiking trails. Pets welcome, breed restrict. Partial handicap access. Open Apr 1 - Nov 30. Rate in 2010 $27 for 2 persons. CCUSA 50% Discount. CCUSA reservations Recommended, CCUSA max stay 2 days, CCUSA disc. not avail S,Th, CCUSA disc. not avail F,Sa, CCUSA disc. not avail holidays. No rottweilers, pit-bulls or doberman breeds.

Phone: (989)343-0261
Address: 1700 Crawford Ln, West Branch, Mi 48661
Lat/Lon: 44.21718/-84.18586
Email: lorangerpinesrvpark@gmail.com
Web: www.loranterpinesrvpark.com

(E) Troll Landing Canoe Livery & Campground—(Ogemaw) *From jct I-75 (exit 202) & Hwy 33: Go 10 mi N on Hwy 33, then 2-1/2 mi E on Hwy 55, then 1-1/2 mi S on Rifle River Trail. Enter on R.* ◆FACILITIES: 25 sites, typical site width 30 ft, 5 E, (20/30 amps), 20 no hkups, family camping, tenting, ltd groc. ◆◆RECREATION: river swim, canoeing, river fishing, play equipment. Pets welcome ($). Open Apr 1 - Nov 30. Rate in 2010 $10 for 1 persons. Member ARVC, ARVC MI. Phone: (989)345-7260.

(N) WEST BRANCH RV PARK (Ogemaw County Pk)—(Ogemaw) *From I-75 (exit 212): Go 1-1/2 mi N. Enter on L.* FACILITIES: 53 sites, typical site width 25 ft, 41 W&E, 12 no hkups, 6 pull-thrus, tenting, dump. RECREATION: lake fishing, playground. Partial handicap access. Open Apr 1 - Oct 15. Phone: (989)345-3295.

WETMORE—C-3

(S) HIAWATHA NATIONAL FOREST (Island Lake Campground)—(Alger) *From jct Hwy 28 & Hwy 94: Go 6-1/2 mi SW on Hwy 94, then 6-1/3 mi SE on CR-2254, then 1/3 mi S on FR-2557.* FACILITIES: 44 sites, 22 ft max RV length, 44 no hkups, tenting. RECREATION: boating, no motors, canoeing, lake fishing. Open May 13 - Sep 7. Phone: (906)387-2512.

(S) HIAWATHA NATIONAL FOREST (Petes Lake Campground)—(Alger) *From jct Hwy 94 & CR H13: Go 10 mi S on CR H13, then 1/2 mi E on CR 2173, then 1/2 mi S on FR 2256.* FACILITIES: 47 sites, 24 ft max RV length, 47 no hkups, tenting. RECREATION: lake swim, boating, ramp, lake fishing. Partial handicap access. Open May 15 - Sep 30. Phone: (906)387-2512.

(S) HIAWATHA NATIONAL FOREST (Widewaters Campground)—(Alger) *From jct Hwy 94 & FH-13: Go 11-2/3 mi S on FH-13, then 1/3 mi NW on FR-2262.* FACILITIES: 34 sites, 22 ft max RV length, 34 no hkups, tenting, ltd groc. RECREATION: river swim, boating, canoeing, ramp, river fishing. Partial handicap access. Open May 15 - Sep 30. Phone: (906)387-2512.

WHITE CLOUD—G-3

(E) BIG BEND PARK (Big Prairie Township)—(Oceana) *From US 131 (exit 131 N): Go 6 mi W to Beech, then 3 mi S to Park. Enter on L.* FACILITIES: 230 sites, typical site width 20 ft, 35 ft max RV length, 100 W&E, 130 E, tenting, dump. RECREATION: swim pool, river swim, boating, ramp, river fishing, playground. Open all yr. Facilities fully operational Apr 15 - Oct 15. Phone: (231)689-6325.

(W) OXBOW PARK (Big Prairie Township)—(Newaygo) *From US 131 (exit 125): Go 8 mi W on Jefferson, then N on Chestnut. Enter at end.* FACILITIES: 197 sites, typical site width 30 ft, 35 ft max RV length, 197 W&E, (30 amps), 44 pull-thrus, tenting, dump. RECREATION: river swim, boating, canoeing, ramp, dock, river fishing, playground. Open all yr. Facilities fully operational Apr 15 - Oct 15. Phone: (231)856-4279.

(S) SANDY BEACH (Newaygo County Park)—(Newaygo) *From jct US 131 (exit 125) & Jefferson Rd: Go 9 mi W on Jefferson Rd, then 1 mi W on 36th St across dam, then 3/4 mi N on Elm, then 3/4 mi E on 30th. Enter at end.* FACILITIES: 200 sites, typical site width 30 ft, 72 W&E, 28 E, (30 amps), 100 no hkups, tenting, dump. RECREATION: lake swim, boating, canoeing, ramp, lake/river/stream fishing, playground. Partial handicap access. Open May 15 - Sep 15. Phone: (231)689-7281.

(SE) Woodlands on the Lake—(Newaygo) *From north jct Hwy 82 & Hwy 37: Go 4 mi N on Hwy 37, then 1-1/2 mi E on 40th St, then 1/2 mi S on Spruce Ave. Enter on R.* ◆◆◆FACILITIES: 260 sites, 40 ft max RV length, 50 full hkups, 210 W&E, (30/50 amps), 50 amps ($), 19 pull-thrus, WiFi Internet central location ($), family camping, tenting, RV storage, dump, non-guest dump $, portable dump, laundry, LP gas by weight/by meter, ice, picnic tables, fire rings, grills, wood. ◆◆◆◆RECREATION: rec hall, pavilion, swim pool, hot tub, boating, electric motors only, canoeing, kayaking, dock, lake fishing, mini-golf, bsktball, playground, shuffleboard court 4 shuffleboard courts, tennis, horseshoes, hiking trails, v-ball. Pets welcome. Partial handicap access. Open May 1 - Oct 15. Rate in 2010 $35 per vehicle. MC/VISA/DISC. CCUSA 50% Discount. CCUSA reservations Required, CCUSA max stay 3 days.

Phone: (231)689-6685
Address: 4495 S. Spruce, White Cloud, MI 49349
Lat/Lon: 43.47319/-85.74303
Web: www.westernhorizonresorts.com

WILLIAMSBURG—E-4

(W) Everflowing Waters Campground—(Grand Traverse) *From north jct Hwy. 72 & US 31: Go 1 mi N on US 31, then go 1 mi E on Brackett Rd. Enter on L.* ◆◆FACILITIES: 52 sites, typical site width 25 ft, 8 W&E, 28 E, (20/30/50 amps), 16 no hkups, 6 pull-thrus, tenting. RECREATION: stream fishing. Pets welcome. Open Apr 15 - Oct 31. Rate in 2010 $25-32 per family. Phone: (231)938-0933.

(S) PERE MARQUETTE SF (Scheck's Place)—(Grand Traverse) *From town: Go 7 mi S on Williamsburg Rd/CR 605, then 6 mi W on Supply Rd/CR 660 & Brown Bridge Rd.* FACILITIES: 30 sites, 30 no hkups, tenting. RECREATION: canoeing, river fishing. Open May 1 - Oct 15. Phone: (231)922-5280.

WIXOM—I-5

(N) PROUD LAKE STATE RECREATION AREA—(Oakland) *From town: Go 4-1/2 mi N on Wixom Rd.* FACILITIES: 130 sites, 130 E, tenting, dump, ltd groc. RECREATION: boating, canoeing, ramp, lake fishing, playground. Open all yr. Facilities fully operational Apr 16 - Oct 16. Phone: (248)685-2433.

WOLVERINE—D-5

(SE) Elkwood Campground—(Cheboygan) *From jct Hwy 68 & I-75: Go 9 mi S on I-75 (exit 301), then 1 mi E on Webb Rd, then 4-1/2 mi S on Molineaux/Lance Lake Rd. Enter on R.* ◆◆◆FACILITIES: 66 sites, 12 full hkups, 30 W&E, 22 E, (20/30/50 amps), 2 no hkups, 17 pull-thrus, family camping, tenting, RV storage, dump, non-guest dump $, portable dump, laundry, ltd groc, RV supplies, LP gas by weight/by meter, ice, picnic tables, fire rings, wood. ◆◆◆RECREATION: pavilion, swim pool, fishing supplies, bsktball, playground, activities, horseshoes, hiking trails, v-ball. Pets welcome. Partial handicap access. Open May 1 - Dec 31. Rate in 2010 $19-32 per family. MC/VISA/DISC/Debit. CCUSA 50% Discount. CCUSA reservations Recommended, CCUSA max stay 4 days, CCUSA disc. not avail holidays. Honey wagon surcharge $6.

WOLVERINE—Continued
Elkwood Campground—Continued

Phone: (877)355-9663
Address: 2733 Lance Lake Rd., Wolverine, MI 49799
Lat/Lon: 45.22887/-84.54342
Email: elkwoodcamp@yahoo.com
Web: www.elkwoodcamp.com

(S) Sturgeon River Campground & Resort—(Cheboygan) *From jct Hwy 68 & I-75: Go 9 mi S on I-75 (exit 301), then 1/2 mi W on Webb Rd, then (through villagepark) 2-1/2 mi S on Trowbridge Rd. Enter on L.* ◆◆◆FACILITIES: 63 sites, typical site width 50 ft, 63 W&E, (20/30 amps), WiFi Internet central location, family camping, tenting, RV storage, dump, non-guest dump $, portable dump, laundry, ltd groc, RV supplies, ice, picnic tables, fire rings, wood. ◆◆◆RECREATION: pavilion, lake swim, canoeing, kayaking, float trips, river/pond fishing, fishing supplies, bsktball, 8 bike rentals, playground, activities, horseshoes, hiking trails, v-ball. Pets welcome. Partial handicap access. Open all yr. Facilities fully operational early Apr - mid Nov. Rate in 2010 $28 for 2 persons. MC/VISA. FMCA discount. CCUSA 50% Discount. CCUSA reservations Recommended, CCUSA max stay 14 days, Cash only for CCUSA disc., Check only for CCUSA disc., CCUSA disc. not avail S, CCUSA disc. not avail F,Sa, CCUSA disc. not avail holidays. Discount available May thru Sept, Mon thru Thu.

Phone: (231)525-8300 Address: 15247 Trowbridge Rd.
Lat/Lon: 45.24084/-84.59190
Email: camp@srivercamp.com
Web: www.srivercamp.com

YPSILANTI—I-5

(S) DETROIT/GREENFIELD RV PARK—(Washtenaw) *From jct US 23 & I-94: Go 7 mi E on I-94 (exit 187), then 1 mi S on Rawsonville Rd, then 1 mi W on Textile Rd, then 1/2 mi S on Bunton Rd. Enter on R.*

DETROIT GREENFIELD CAMPGROUND
Come and visit our private spring-fed lake and scenic forest setting. Campers receive 3 free rides on our BRAND NEW water slide! We offer boat, bike rentals and mini-golf.

◆◆◆◆FACILITIES: 207 sites, typical site width 35 ft, 119 full hkups, 65 W&E, (20/30/50 amps), 23 no hkups, some extd stay sites (summer), 110 pull-thrus, WiFi Instant Internet at site, family camping, tenting, RV's/park model rentals, cabins, RV storage, dump, non-guest dump $, laundry, groceries, RV supplies, LP gas by weight/by meter, ice, picnic tables, fire rings, wood.

◆◆◆◆RECREATION: rec room/area, pavilion, coin games, lake swim, boating, no motors, 3 rowboat/2 canoe/3 pedal boat rentals, lake fishing, fishing supplies, mini-golf, ($), golf nearby, bsktball, 11 bike rentals, playground, activities, (wkends), horseshoes, sports field, hiking trails, v-ball. Rec open to public.

Pets welcome, breed restrict. Partial handicap access. Open Apr 1 - Oct 31. Clubs welcome. Rate in 2010 $36-42 for 2 persons. MC/VISA/DISC/Debit. Member ARVC, ARVC MI.

Phone: (734)482-7722
Address: 6680 Bunton Rd, Ypsilanti, MI 48197
Lat/Lon: 42.19249/-83.56226
Email: information@detroitgreenfield.com
Web: www.detroitgreenfield.com

SEE AD DETROIT PAGE 379

ZEELAND—H-2

(SW) DUTCH TREAT CAMPING & RECREATION—(Ottawa) *From N jct Hwy 31 & Bus I-96/Chicago Dr: Go 2-1/4 mi E on Bus I-196, then S on 104th, then E on Gordon (Service Rd). Ent on R. From Bus I-196 & I-196 (exit 55): Go 2-3/4 mi W on E/W Bus I-196, then S on 101st & W on Gordon (Service Rd). Enter on L.*

◆◆◆◆FACILITIES: 130 sites, typical site width 35 ft, 90 full hkups, 30 W&E, (20/30/50 amps), 10 no hkups, some extd stay sites (summer), 44 pull-thrus, heater not allowed, WiFi Internet central location, family camping, tenting, RV storage, dump, non-guest dump $, laundry, ltd groc, RV supplies, ice, picnic tables, fire rings, wood.

◆◆◆◆RECREATION: rec hall, rec room/area, coin games, swim pool, kayaking, 2 kayak/3 pedal boat rentals, pond fishing, fishing supplies, golf nearby, bsktball, playground, activities, (wkends), horseshoes, sports field, v-ball.

DUTCH TREAT CAMPING & RECREATION—Continued on next page

ZEELAND—Continued
DUTCH TREAT CAMPING & RECREATION—Continued

Pets welcome. Partial handicap access. Open Apr 1 - Nov 1. Big rigs welcome. Clubs welcome. Rate in 2010 $25-34 for 2 persons. MC/VISA/DISC. Member ARVC, ARVCMI.

Phone: (616)772-4303
Address: 10300 Gordon Ave, Zeeland, MI 49464
Lat/Lon: 42.80482/-86.03553
Web: www.dutchtreatcamping.com

SEE AD HOLLAND PAGE 386

Woodall's Tip... Rate information is based on the campground's published rate last year. These rates aren't guaranteed, and you should always call ahead for the most updated rate information.

Subscribe to Woodall's Camping Life... a magazine dedicated to providing readers with articles, destinations, products and activities for the Family Camper. This magazine also has a special edition in April that includes a Guide to Select Locations for Family Camping and Tenting. This special edition provides readers with accurate up-to-date information that can be used to make decisions about where to go camping, types of facilities that can be found there and what activities are available once they've arrived at their campsites. Woodall's Camping Life for the Active Family and Tent Camper. Visit www.campinglife.com to subscribe.

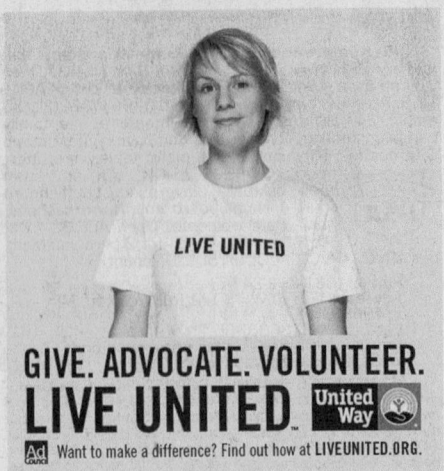

Who better to represent Woodall's on the road than the ones who know RVing best?

In an effort to have the industry's finest Sales Rep Teams in the field, Woodall's continually welcomes inquiries from husband and wife couples with RV experience. Several of these couples are selected to represent Woodall's each year. Those selected travel in their own RV throughout assigned territories during spring and summer months. They will make calls on RV Parks/campgrounds, RV dealers and the travel & tourism industry.

If you would like more information, email cdistl@affinitygroup.com.

Win a 7-Day Cruise to the Hawaiian Islands!

Compliments of WOODALL'S
Everywhere RVers go

Visit **www.woodalls.com/myfavoritecampground** for official rules and sweepstakes details.

Vote for your favorite RV park or campground in North America and you, a friend, and the campground owners could win a 7-day cruise of the Hawaiian Islands!

* Scan me! I'm a QR Code! Be sure to install a FREE QR Reader app on your smartphone. Then, point it at the code above and give it a try!

READER SERVICE INFO

The following business has placed an ad in the Minnesota Travel Section. To receive free information, enter their Reader Service number on the Reader Service Card opposite page 48/Discover Section in the front of this directory:

Advertiser	RS#
Fortune Bay Resort Casino & RV Park	4174
Grand Casino Hinckley RV Resort	3298
Lebanon Hills Campground (Formerly Lake Byllesby Campground (Dakota County Park)	647
Minnesota Resort Campground Association	3420
Prairie View RV Park & Campground	3560
Treasure Island Resort & Casino	4315

TIME ZONE

Minnesota is in the Central Time Zone.

TOPOGRAPHY

Minnesota encompasses 79,289 square miles of land and 4,779 square miles of inland water.

TEMPERATURE

The four seasons in Minnesota are very distinct. Summer temps can reach the 90s although they usually stay in the 70-80 degree range. Winters are cold with an average snowfall of 53 inches.

TRAVEL & TOURISM INFO

State Agency:

Explore Minnesota Tourism
100 Metro Square Bldg.
121 7th Place E.
St. Paul, MN 55101
(888/TOURISM)
in the Twin Cities, call (651/296-5029)
www.exploreminnesota.com

Local Agencies:

For information on an area not listed here, contact the Chamber of Commerce or Tourism Bureau for the locality you are interested in visiting.

Bemidji Area Chamber of Commerce and CVB
300 Bemidji Ave.
Bemidji, MN 56601
(800/458-2223)
www.bemidji.org

Southeastern Minnesota Bluff Country Regional CVB
15 2nd Street NW
P. O. Box 609
Harmony, MN 55939
(507/886-2230 or 800/428-2030)
www.bluffcountry.com

Brainerd Lakes Area Chamber of Commerce & CVB
7393 State Hwy 371 S
Brainerd, MN 56401
(800/450-2838)
www.explorebrainerdlakes.com

Detroit Lakes Regional Chamber of Commerce
700 Summit Ave
P.O. Box 348
Detroit Lakes, MN 56502
(800/542-3992)
www.visitdetroitlakes.com

Duluth Area Chamber of Commerce
21 West Superior St., Ste 100
Duluth, MN 55802
(800/438-5884 or 218/722-4011)
www.visitduluth.com

Ely Chamber of Commerce
1600 E. Sheridan St.
Ely, MN 55731
(800/777-7281 or 218/365-6123)
www.ely.org

Greater Grand Forks CVB
4251 Gateway Drive
Grand Forks, ND 58203
(800/866-4566 or 701/746-0444)
www.visitgrandforks.com

Visit Grand Rapids
501 S Pokegama Ave., Ste 3
Grand Rapids, MN 55744
(800/355-9740 or 218/326-9607)
www.visitgrandrapids.com

International Falls & Rainy Lake CVB
301 2nd Ave
International Falls, MN 56649
(218/283-9400 or 800/325-5766)
www.rainylake.org

Lake of the Woods Tourism Bureau
P.O. Box 518
Baudette, MN 56623
(800/382-3474)
www.lakeofthewoodsmn.com

Meet Minneapolis
250 Marquette Ave. S, Ste 1300
Minneapolis, MN 55401
(1-888/676-MPLS)
www.minneapolis.org

Rochester Convention & Visitors Bureau
30 Civic Center Drive SE, Suite 200
Rochester, MN 55904
(800/634-8277 or 507/288-9144)
www.visitrochestermn.com

St. Cloud Area CVB
525 Highway 10 S, Ste 1
St. Cloud, MN 56304
(320/251-4170 or 800/264-2940)
www.granitecountry.com

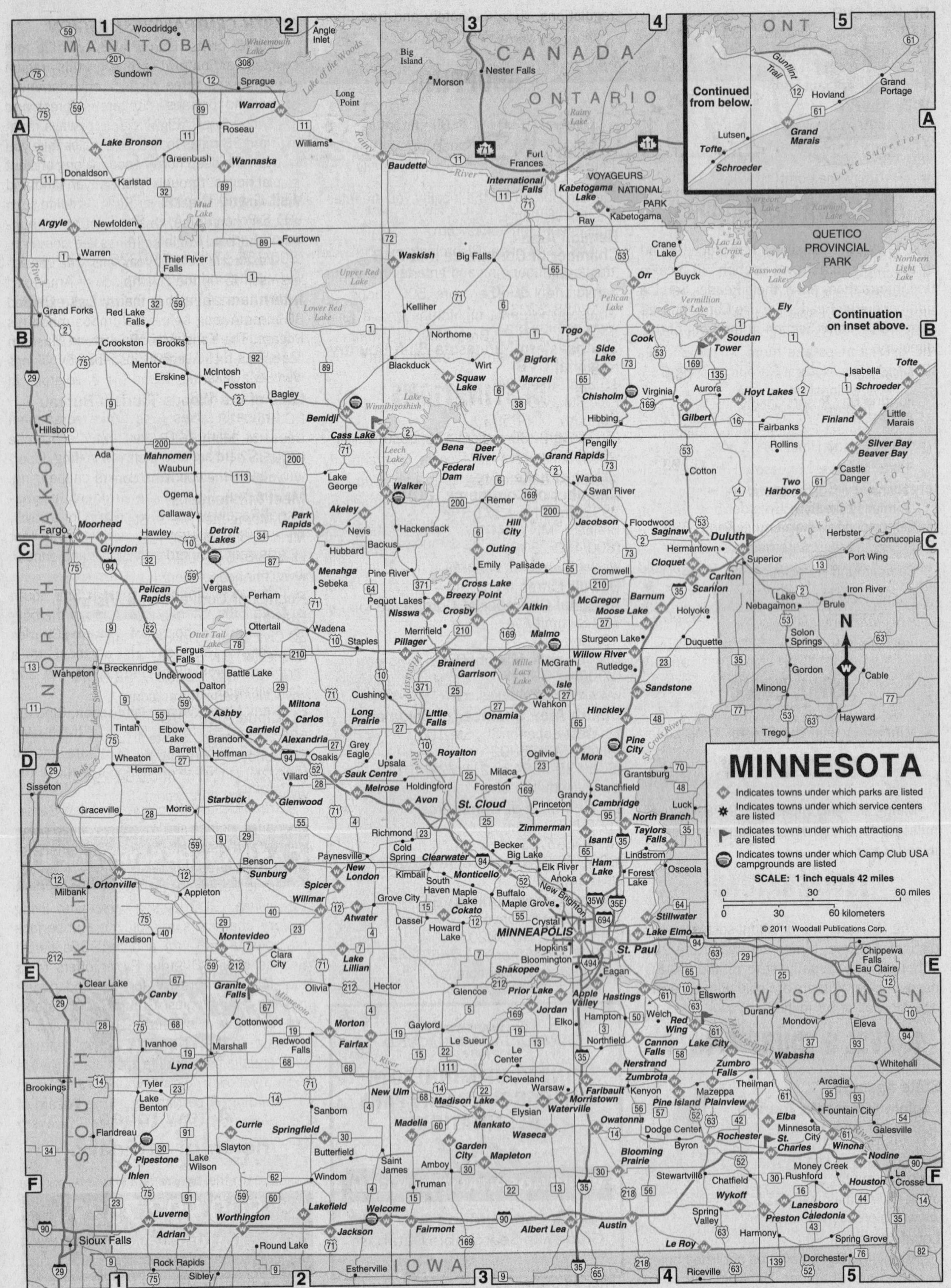
MINNESOTA
Indicates towns under which parks are listed
Indicates towns under which service centers are listed
Indicates towns under which attractions are listed
Indicates towns under which Camp Club USA campgrounds are listed
SCALE: 1 inch equals 42 miles
0 30 60 miles
0 30 60 kilometers
© 2011 Woodall Publications Corp.
MANITOBA
CANADA
ONTARIO
ONT
NORTH DAKOTA
SOUTH DAKOTA
IOWA
WISCONSIN
Continued from below.
Continuation on inset above.
VOYAGEURS NATIONAL PARK
QUETICO PROVINCIAL PARK
Lake Superior
Lake of the Woods
Red River
Rainy River
Mississippi River
Minnesota River
St. Croix River
Leech Lake
Mille Lacs Lake
Upper Red Lake
Lower Red Lake
Otter Tail Lake
Lake Winnibigoshish
Gunflint Trail
Grand Portage
Hovland
Grand Marais
Lutsen
Tofte
Schroeder
Woodridge
Sundown
Sprague
Angle Inlet
Big Island
Morson
Nester Falls
Long Point
Warroad
Roseau
Williams
Baudette
International Falls
Fort Frances
Kabetogama Lake
Kabetogama
Ray
Lake Bronson
Greenbush
Wannaska
Donaldson
Karlstad
Argyle
Newfolden
Fourtown
Warren
Thief River Falls
Waskish
Big Falls
Crane Lake
Orr
Buyck
Ely
Grand Forks
Red Lake Falls
Kelliher
Northome
Togo
Cook
Soudan
Tower
Crookston
Brooks
Mentor
Erskine
McIntosh
Fosston
Bagley
Blackduck
Wirt
Bigfork
Side Lake
Squaw Lake
Marcell
Chisholm
Virginia
Aurora
Hoyt Lakes
Isabella
Bemidji
Cass Lake
Hibbing
Gilbert
Fairbanks
Finland
Little Marais
Hillsboro
Ada
Mahnomen
Waubun
Bena
Deer River
Grand Rapids
Pengilly
Rollins
Silver Bay
Beaver Bay
Lake George
Federal Dam
Warba
Cotton
Castle Danger
Two Harbors
Ogema
Walker
Swan River
Remer
Callaway
Akeley
Park Rapids
Hill City
Jacobson
Floodwood
Saginaw
Duluth
Fargo
Moorhead
Hawley
Detroit Lakes
Glyndon
Nevis
Hackensack
Hubbard
Backus
Outing
Hermantown
Superior
Herbster
Cornucopia
Port Wing
Menahga
Sebeka
Pine River
Emily
Palisade
Cromwell
Cloquet
Carlton
Scanlon
Pelican Rapids
Vergas
Perham
Cross Lake
Pequot Lakes
Breezy Point
Nisswa
Crosby
Aitkin
McGregor
Barnum
Moose Lake
Holyoke
Lake Nebagamon
Brule
Iron River
Ottertail
Wadena
Staples
Merrifield
Pillager
Malmo
Sturgeon Lake
Duquette
Solon Springs
Fergus Falls
Wahpeton
Breckenridge
Underwood
Battle Lake
Brainerd
Garrison
McGrath
Willow River
Rutledge
Gordon
Cable
Dalton
Ashby
Miltona
Carlos
Cushing
Long Prairie
Little Falls
Onamia
Isle
Wahkon
Sandstone
Minong
Tintah
Elbow Lake
Garfield
Alexandria
Grey Eagle
Hinckley
Hayward
Trego
Brandon
Barrett
Hoffman
Wheaton
Herman
Osakis
Upsala
Royalton
Ogilvie
Pine City
Mora
Sisseton
Villard
Sauk Centre
Melrose
Holdingford
Milaca
Foreston
Grantsburg
Graceville
Morris
Starbuck
Glenwood
Avon
St. Cloud
Grandy
Stanchfield
Princeton
Cambridge
North Branch
Luck
Richmond
Zimmerman
Isanti
Taylors Falls
Becker
Big Lake
Paynesville
Cold Spring
Clearwater
Benson
Sunburg
New London
Kimball
South Haven
Monticello
Elk River
Anoka
Ham Lake
Forest Lake
Lindstrom
Osceola
Milbank
Ortonville
Appleton
Spicer
Willmar
Maple Lake
Buffalo
Grove City
Atwater
Cokato
Dassel
Howard Lake
Maple Grove
Crystal
MINNEAPOLIS
St. Paul
New Brighton
Stillwater
Lake Elmo
Madison
Montevideo
Clara City
Lake Lillian
Hopkins
Bloomington
Eagan
Shakopee
Chippewa Falls
Eau Claire
Clear Lake
Canby
Granite Falls
Olivia
Hector
Glencoe
Prior Lake
Apple Valley
Hastings
Ellsworth
Jordan
Elko
Hampton
Welch
Red Wing
Durand
Mondovi
Eleva
Cottonwood
Morton
Gaylord
Le Sueur
Le Center
Northfield
Cannon Falls
Lake City
Wabasha
Ivanhoe
Marshall
Redwood Falls
Fairfax
Lynd
Nerstrand
Zumbrota
Zumbro Falls
Theilman
Whitehall
Brookings
Tyler
Lake Benton
New Ulm
Madison Lake
Cleveland
Warsaw
Faribault
Morristown
Kenyon
Mazeppa
Pine Island
Plainview
Arcadia
Fountain City
Sanborn
Elysian
Waterville
Currie
Springfield
Madelia
Mankato
Waseca
Owatonna
Dodge Center
Rochester
Elba
Minnesota City
St. Charles
Winona
Galesville
Flandreau
Pipestone
Lake Wilson
Slayton
Butterfield
Garden City
Mapleton
Blooming Prairie
Byron
Nodine
Ihlen
Saint James
Amboy
Truman
Windom
Stewartville
Chatfield
Money Creek
Rushford
Houston
La Crosse
Luverne
Adrian
Worthington
Lakefield
Welcome
Jackson
Fairmont
Albert Lea
Austin
Wykoff
Spring Valley
Lanesboro
Preston
Caledonia
Harmony
Spring Grove
Sioux Falls
Round Lake
Le Roy
Rock Rapids
Sibley
Estherville
Riceville
Dorchester

St. Paul CVB
175 W. Kellogg Blvd. Ste. 502
St. Paul, MN 55102
(800/627-6101)
www.visitsaintpaul.com

Winona CVB
160 Johnson St
Winona, MN 55987
(800/657-4972)
www.visitwinona.com

RECREATIONAL INFO

Canoeing: Minnesota Canoe Assn., www.canoe-kayak.org

Fishing: For a copy of the Minnesota Fishing guide, call Explore Minnesota Tourism (888/868-7476) For information on regulations, lake maps and more, see Minnesota Department of Natural Resources (888/646-6367) www.dnr.state.mn.us

Golf: To find a golf course near your destination, contact Explore Minnesota Tourism (888/868-7476)

Historic Sites: Minnesota Historical Society (888/727-8386) www.mnhs.org

Winter Recreation: To order brochures on skiing and snowmobiling, call (888/868-7476) or www.exploreminnesota.com. Also available are reports on snow depths and trail conditions, info on dog sledding excursions, snowmobile rentals, ice fishing reports and ice fish house rentals. For snowmobiling regulations, permits, safety and trail information, see www.dnr.state.mn.us

SHOPPING

General Store of Minnetonka, Minnetonka. Find Minnesota gifts and housewares at this locally owned family business. Experience turn of the century personalized service. On Hwy. 7. www.generalstoreofminnetonka.com

Mall of America, Bloomington. Experience the largest shopping and entertainment center in the US. There are 500 shops, an amusement park, nightclubs and a giant aquarium. 60 E. Broadway, Bloomington, MN 55425 www.mallofamerica.com

DESTINATIONS

Though Minnesota is approximately 1,000 miles from either coast, it's practically a seaboard state, thanks to Lake Superior. Millions of years ago, glaciers flattened all but its southeast corner, and gouged out more than 15,000 lakes. Ninety-five percent of the population lives within ten minutes of a body of water, and the very name, "Minnesota", is a Sioux word meaning, "land of sky-tinted water".

NORTH-CENTRAL/WEST REGION

Noted for its fishing lakes, wildlife and spectacular natural scenery, this region encompasses three distinct environments: plains and prairies, coniferous forest and hardwood forest. Eight scenic byways ranging from 28 miles to over 500 miles take you through the deep north woods, along ancient glacial ridges, through Paul Bunyan land and following the Great River Road. Wildlife such as bear, porcupine, deer and otter is abundant and bald eagle sightings are common.

Alexandria Lakes Area. This area considers itself to be the "birthplace of America." Many here claim that the Vikings explored Minnesota long before Columbus made his voyage. The **Kensington Runestone Museum** features a rock allegedly inscribed by Vikings in 1362. A farmer found the large stone in his field in 1898.

Brainerd Lakes Area. This recreational area has nearly 500 lakes within a 50-mile radius. There are also plenty of golfing opportunities—as scenic as they are challenging. Racing fans flock to the **Brainerd International Raceway** and if you're out for a stroll, try the **Paul Bunyan Recreational Trail** that begins near Brainerd and Baxter and ends in Bemidji.

Charles A. Lindbergh Historic Site, south of Little Falls, offers guided tours of the boyhood summer home of aviator Charles Lindbergh. The home is adjacent to a museum chronicling Lindbergh's life and achievements.

Frank Lloyd Wright Gas Station, Cloquet. Built in 1958, the station is a three-level steel and cement block structure with a glass-walled observation lounge above the main office.

Grand Casino Hinckley, Hinckley. Games of chance include slot machines, video poker games and blackjack tables. Live entertainment is featured daily.

Grand Rapids. At the **Forest History Center**, visit a 1900 logging camp with living history characters role-playing lumberjack life, plus a museum and a 1930s Forest Service cabin. **Blandin Paper** offers tours that focus on forestry, logging and papermaking technologies. Grand Rapids is also the birthplace of Judy Garland and a museum in the old Central School features memorabilia from her life and career. There's even a yellow brick sidewalk leading up to the building. A carriage from the Wizard of Oz is featured at the **Children's Discovery Museum**.

Mille Lacs Indian Museum, Mille Lacs Lake. Learn the culture of a Native American tribe at one of the finest museums in the country. Dedicated to telling the story of the Mille Lacs Band of Ojibwe, past and present, the site features displays and exhibits such as the "Season's" exhibit, Pow Wow display

and a crafts room that houses a demonstration area. Also on-site is a trading post that was restored to its 1930s appearance.

St. Cloud. This is the commercial hub of central Minnesota offering a variety of activities in and around the city. **Munsinger and Clemens Gardens** lie on the banks of the Mississippi and feature beautiful gardens with blooms from May through September. The **Stearns History Museum** has a children's gallery, a miniature circus, a 1919 Pan automobile and a replica granite quarry. Nearby is **Quarry Park** with swimming, scuba diving and fishing.

NORTHEASTERN REGION

Bordered by Lake Superior on the east, this is the region of 1000 Grand Lakes although there are actually over 1600 lakes providing some of the best fishing in the U.S. Northern pike, lake trout, walleye, smallmouth bass and panfish are among the fish that cruise these waters. On land you can see moose, bear, wolves, bald eagles and countless other birds and small mammals. This was the land of the Ojibwe Indians, where explorers, trappers, miners and lumbermen came to make their fortune. Much of this land is still pristine with unspoiled wilderness areas.

Duluth is the world's largest freshwater port—hundreds of foreign vessels visit the harbor each year. At **Canal Park**, the aerial lift bridge rises to let massive seafaring vessels enter the harbor. It's easy to spot ships carrying the flags of countries halfway around the world. The **Maritime Visitor Center** has exhibits on Great Lakes shipping, including tragic shipwrecks. The **Great Lakes Floating Museum** offers tours of a retired ore carrier, the William A. Irvin and a retired Coast Guard cutter, the Sundew. Another waterfront attraction in Duluth is the **Lakewalk**, a boardwalk for strolling or jogging, plus a bike path and trail for carriage rides. The Lakewalk extends eastward from Canal Park to the **Rose Gardens** with more than 3,000 rose bushes. **Bayfront Festival Park** has outdoor concerts and a creative playground. The **Great Lakes Aquarium** focuses on the fish, wildlife and history of Lake Superior and its shoreline. Journey back in time at **Glensheen**, a 7.6-acre site containing the 1905 Jacobean Revival mansion of Chester

BUSINESSES OFFERING

	Things to See & Do	RV Sales	RV Service
CASS LAKE			
Canal House Restaurant & Bar	▶		
DULUTH			
Willard Munger Inn	▶		
GRANITE FALLS			
Prairie's Edge Casino Resort	▶		
RED WING			
Treasure Island Resort & Casino	▶		
ST. CHARLES			
Lazy D Trail Rides	▶		
TOWER			
Fortune Bay Resort Casino	▶		

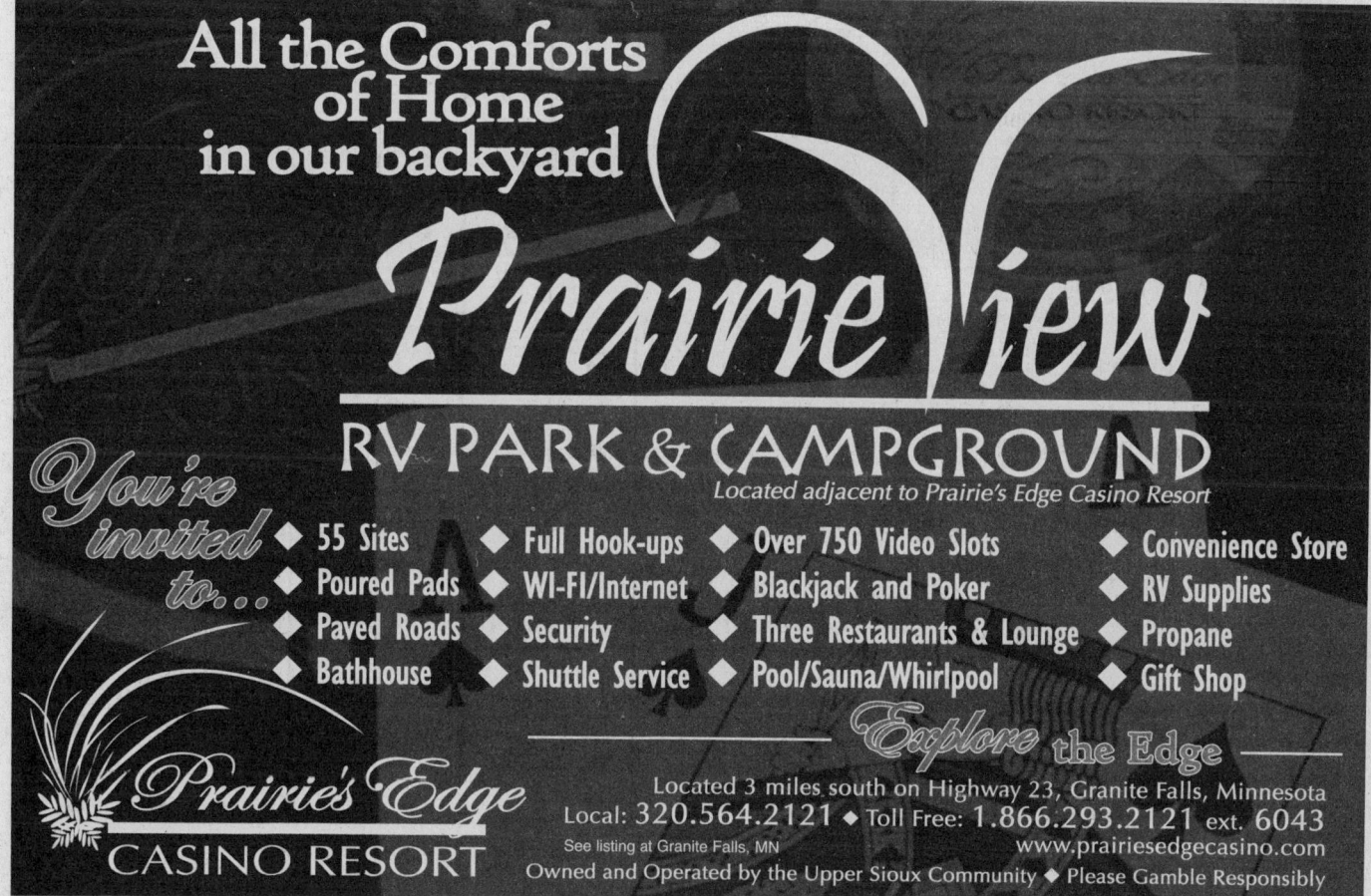

QUICK REFERENCE CHART FOR WOODALL'S FEATURED PARKS

	Green Friendly	RV Lots for Sale	Park Models-Onsite Ownership	Park Membership for Sale	Big Rigs Welcome	Internet Friendly	Pets Welcome
APPLE VALLEY							
Lebanon Hills Campground (Dakota County Park)					▲	●	■
AUSTIN							
Beaver Trails Jellystone Park Camp-Resort	🍂				▲	●	■
CANNON FALLS							
Lake Byllesby Campground (Dakota County Park)					▲		■
CASS LAKE							
Stony Point Resort Trailer Park & Campground	🍂				▲	●	■
CLEARWATER							
A-J Acres Campground	🍂					●	■
DULUTH							
Indian Point Campground					▲	●	■
Lakehead Boat Basin, Inc					▲	●	■
GRANITE FALLS							
Prairie View RV Park & Campground					▲	●	■
HINCKLEY							
Grand Casino Hinckley RV Resort					▲	●	■
LAKE CITY							
Lake Pepin Campgrounds & Trailer Court	🍂				▲		■
MINNEAPOLIS							
KOA-Minneapolis Southwest					▲	●	■
Lowry Grove	🍂				▲		■
Minneapolis NW KOA Campground	🍂				▲	●	■
MONTICELLO							
River Terrace Park					▲		■
PIPESTONE							
Pipestone RV Campground	🍂				▲	●	■
RED WING							
Treasure Island RV Park	🍂				▲	●	■
ROCHESTER							
Autumn Woods RV Park	🍂				▲	●	■
KOA-Rochester/Marion	🍂					●	■
ST. CHARLES							
Lazy D Campground & Trail Rides	🍂					●	■
TOWER							
Fortune Bay Resort, Casino & RV Park					▲	●	■
WABASHA							
Pioneer Campsite Resort	🍂				▲	●	■
WASECA							
Kiesler's Campground & R.V. Resort	🍂				▲	●	■

Green Friendly 🍂; RV Lots for Sale ✖; Park Models/Onsite Onwership ✱; Park Memberships for Sale ✔; Big Rigs Welcome ▲; Internet Friendly ●; Internet Friendly-WiFi ●; Pets Welcome ■

A. Congdon. The 39-room mansion features exotic woods, rich textiles and beautiful art glass. The **Duluth Omnimax Theatre**, with its 72-foot domed screen, is also near the waterfront. Other attractions include: **Fitger's-on-the-Lake**, a shopping complex in an old brewery, **Spirit Mountain Recreation Area, Duluth Zoo** and the **North Shore Scenic Railroad**. Duluth marks the beginning of the scenic North Shore Drive along Lake Superior on Highway 61 to the Canadian border. Traversing approximately 150 miles, the route is a nationally designated All-American Road.

International Wolf Center. Explore the habits of these fascinating animals through extensive exhibits, video programs and lectures. Special activities include winter and summer aerial flights over prime wolf territory and wolf howl evenings. On-site is a 1.5-acre enclosure housing a pack of four wolves raised by center staff.

Grand Marais. This village on Lake Superior is noted for its community of artists and features numerous art galleries, artists' workshops, a folk art school and community theater and the **Grand Marais Playhouse**.

Grand Portage National Monument features a reconstructed North West Company fur trading post from the late 1700s. Explore the Heritage Center with stories of the Anishinabe or Ojibwe people of Grand Portage and the North West Company of the North American fur trade. Follow pathways into a distant time. Take in the sights and smells of a bustling depot, reconstructed over its original footprint. Listen for the echo of the drum over Grand Portage Bay.

Ironworld Discovery Center, Chisholm. The story of the miner's heritage is well told at this entertainment complex. **Festival Park** features a rolling brook, ponds, the Avenue of the Nations, strolling minstrels and artisans and a variety of ethnic foods. A trolley delivers passengers to an early 1900s railroad roadhouse where they catch a ride on a 1915 steam train, which takes them to view two open pit mines.

TWIN CITIES AREA

The exciting and vibrant Minneapolis-St. Paul area is the entertainment and cultural center of the state. Contemporary skylines, historic architecture and greenways of parks, lakes and the Mississippi and Minnesota rivers converge in this cosmopolitan area.

Bloomington. See over 4,500 living sea creatures and touch real sharks at the **Underwater Adventures Aquarium**, the world's largest underground aquarium; located at **Mall of America**. Also at Mall of America, visit **Camp Snoopy** for family fun.

Chanhassen. Landscape Arboretum, an extensive 900-acre nature-lover's "playground" houses the **Seisu Tei** (Garden of Pure Water), the **National Display Garden for the Hosta Society**, the **Francis de Voss Home Demonstration Gardens**, five specialty herb gardens, six miles of hiking trails, paved roads to tour the grounds by car and countless flowers, trees and shrubs in their natural environment.

Minneapolis. The heart of the downtown area is **Nicollet Mall**, a 12-block pedestrian/transit mall lined with shops. Most of the downtown is linked by indoor walkways called skyways. A the end of the mall, a pedestrian greenway leads to **Loring Park**, the **Minneapolis Sculpture Garden** and the newly expanded **Walker Art Center** featuring contemporary visual and performing arts. The **Mill City Museum** explains the impact of flour milling, rising eight stories inside the limestone ruins of the Washburn A. Mill. A rooftop observation deck offers sweeping views of the Mississippi River. The **Minneapolis Institute of Arts,** with a new wing of galleries, has collections representing diverse cultures from around the world. Other Minneapolis museums include the **Museum of Russian Art** and the **Weisman Art Museum**, in a striking riverfront building on the University of Minnesota campus. Other attractions include the **IDS Center**, a 57-story monolith; **Guthrie Theatre**, which has moved to a new riverfront home; the **Min-**

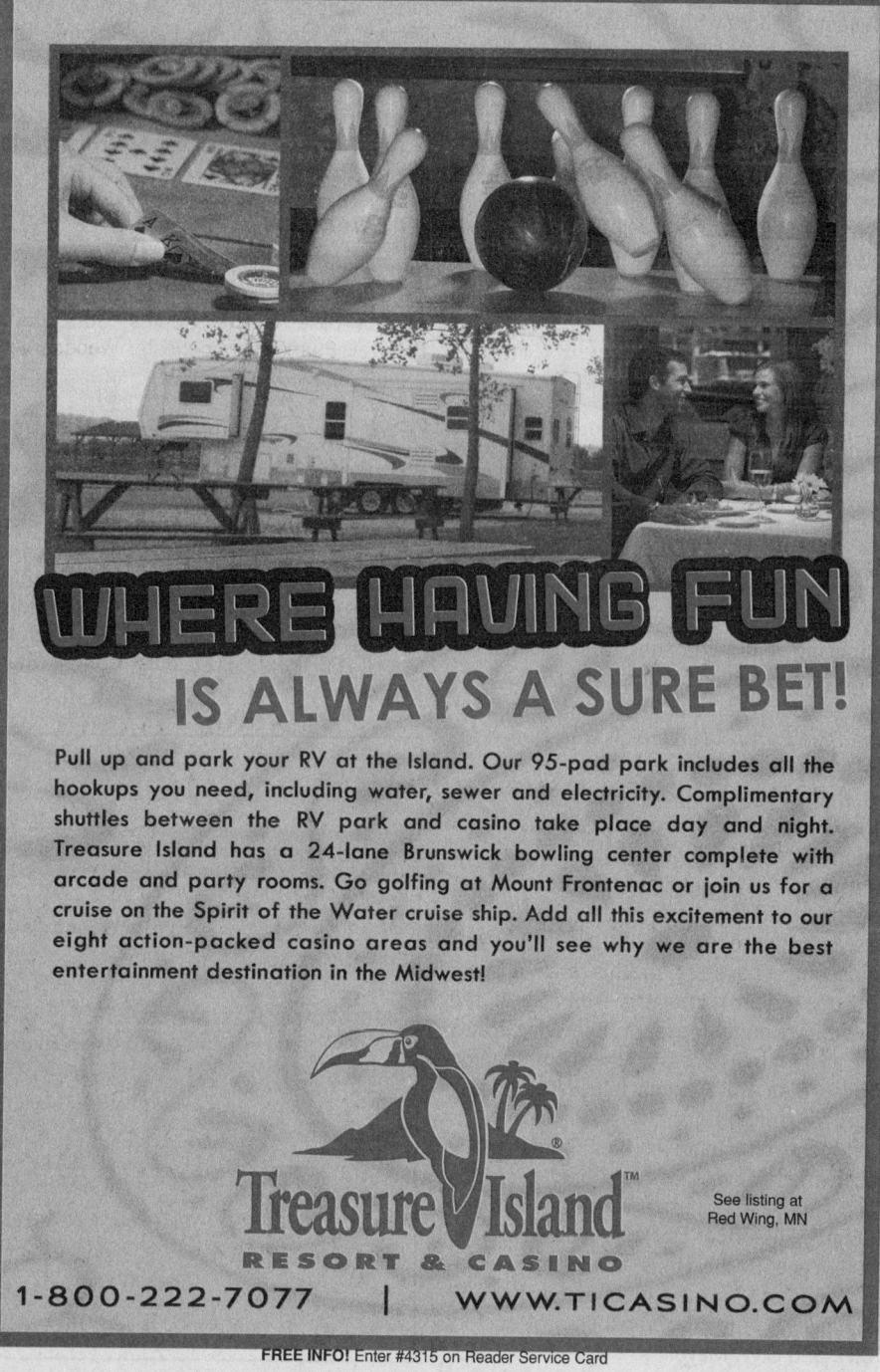

nesota Orchestra and Orchestra Hall; and scenic paths and drives around city lakes.

Plymouth. At **Hennepin Parks,** a series of nature centers provide year-round nature programs, wildlife observation, wildflowers and maple sugaring.

St. Paul. This capital city has an old-world charm with renovated 19th-century buildings and grand edifices around Rice Park and Mears Park. The **Science Museum of Minnesota** lets visitors experience audio-visual voyages through space and time. The popular museum features hands-on, fun science exhibits and a domed Omnitheater. Como Town Amusement Park, located at **Como Zoo & Conservatory,** features new interactive rides, games and a theater. Other highlights include the **Minnesota Children's' Museum**, filled with fun learning experiences; **Fort Snelling,** a living museum depicting 1800s fort life complete with costumed guides; the historic **Landmark Center**, with museums, art galleries and a full schedule of entertainment; the **Ordway Center for the Performing Arts** features the St. Paul Chamber Orchestra, as well as national and international artists and entertainment. An architectural masterpiece, the **Minnesota History Center** features unique hands-on exhibits; climb into a grain elevator replica or a 24-ton boxcar.

SOUTHERN REGION

This is the region of peaceful plains and prairies where pioneers came to farm the land. Buffalo, sod houses and ethnic festivals speak of the rich heritage of this area.

Blue Earth claims to be the "birthplace of the ice cream sandwich." But its most imposing feature is the 55-foot tall Jolly Green Giant, which attracts over 10,000 visitors a year. The community was named for the Blue Earth River, which was named for its blue-green clay riverbed

Red Wing. Historic buildings, antique shops and cobbled streets await you in this home of the **Red Wing Shoe Store and Museum**. At **Hobgoblin Music**, watch crafts people build folk harps, dulcimers, banjos and bodhrans or visit the antique instrument museum. The story of this area and its Dakota Indian heritage is well told at the **Goodhue County Museum.** Red Wing is also the eastern trail access for the scenic Cannon Valley Bike Trail, which follows a winding river to Cannon Falls.

Rochester. Tours of the internationally acclaimed **Mayo Clinic** are held each day and include an informative movie. **Olmsted County Historical Society**, located on the outskirts of Rochester, is an information center and also owns and operates tours of **Mayowood**, the 55-room home of doctors C.H. and C.W. Mayo.

ANNUAL EVENTS

JANUARY

St. Paul Winter Carnival, St. Paul; Annual Warmer By the Lake, Duluth; Polar Days Festival, Bemidji; Urban Fxpedition, St. Paul; Back to Hack, Hackensack; Frozen River Film Festival, Winona; Sled Dog Marathon, Duluth; Polar Bear Plunge; St. James Winter Carnival, St. James.

FEBRUARY

Grumpy Old Men Festival, Wabasha; Celebration of the Lakes, Center City; Annual Logging Days, Bemidiji; Buffalo Lake Winterfest, Buffalo Lake; Ole & Lena Days, Granite Falls; Laskiainen Finnish Sliding Festival, Aurora; Waseca Sleigh & Cutter Festival, Waseca; Winter Fete, Bloomington; Carlton Winterfest, Carlton; Rochester Winterfest, Rochester; Winterfest, St. Peter; Ely Winter Festival, Ely; Duluth Boat, Sports & Travel Show, Duluth; Frost Festival, Olivia; Winter Tracks, Grand Marais.

MARCH

International Festival of Owls, Houston; Deer & Turkey Expo, Owatonna; 2nd to Last Chance Spiel, Grand Rapids; State Polka Festival, Plymouth; Rochester Woodcarvers Annual Show, Rochester.

APRIL

Sweetwater Shakedown Spring Festival, Lutsen; Alpaca Expo, Owatonna; World Festival, Rochester; Mountain Meltdown Music Festival, Lusten; Ibsen Festival, Lanesboro; Red Bridge Film Festival, Park Rapids; Annual Pioneer Power Swap Meet, Le Sueur; Minnesota Horse Expo, St. Paul; St. Paul Art Crawl, St. Paul; 100 Mile Garage Sale, Wabasha.

MAY

100 Mile Garage Sale, Winona; Annual Fishing Opener BBQ, Grand Rapids; Minnesota Dance Festival, St. Paul; Scottish Fair & Highland Games, Farmington; Olmsted County Gold Rush, Rochester; Shepherds Harvest Festival, Lake Elmo; Minnesota in May BBQ, Austin; Art Festival & Farmers Market, Montrose; Art-A-Whirl, Minneapolis; Festival of Birds, Detroit Lakes; Annual Spring Bluegrass Festival, Houston; Dylan Days, Virginia; Grand Marais Jazz Fest, Lutsen.

JUNE

Boreal Birding & Northern Landscapes Festival, Grand Marais; Buffalo Days, Luverne; Great Camden Campout, Lynd; Tower Days Community Celebration, Spring Lake Park; Rhubarb Festival, Lanesboro; Scandinavian Festival, Roseau; Buffalo Days, Buffalo; Father Hennepin Festival, Champlin; Grand Cities Art fest, Grand Forks; Olde World Renaissance Faire, Twig; Riverfest, Windom; Windsurfing Regatta & Music Festival, Worthington; Mountain Lake Pow Wow Festival, Mountain Lake; Bluegrass Festival, Grand Rapids; Covered Bridge Festival, Zumbrota; Fairbault Heritage Celebration, Fairbault; Fulda Wood Duck Festival, Fulda; Midsummer Days, North Branch; Art in the Air, Red Wng; Henderson Sauerkraut Days, Henderso; Kaposia Days, St. Paul; Heartland Days, Lewiston; Rochesterfest, Rochester; Scandinavian Festival, Moorhead; St. James Rail Road Days, St. James.

JULY

Freedomfest, Austin; PBR Challenger Tour Bull Ride, Park Rapids; Polka Fest Days, Bird Island; Taste of Minnesota, St. Paul; St. Louis River Rendezvous, Cloquet; Sweetheart Days, Hackensack; Sidewalk Days, Duluth; Corn & Clover Carnival, Hinckley; Fourth of July Festival, Elysian; Pan-O-Prog, Lakeville.

Where to Find CCUSA Parks

List City	Park Name	Map Coordinates
BEMIDJI		
	Hamilton's Fox Lake Campground	B-2
CHISHOLM		
	Iron Trail RV Park & Campground	B-4
DETROIT LAKES		
	Country Campground	C-2
MALMO		
	Pete's Retreat Family Campground & RV Park	C-3
PINE CITY		
	Pokegama Lake RV Park & Golf Course	D-4
PIPESTONE		
	Pipestone RV Campground	F-1
WALKER		
	Trails RV Park	C-3
WELCOME		
	Checkers Welcome Campground	F-2

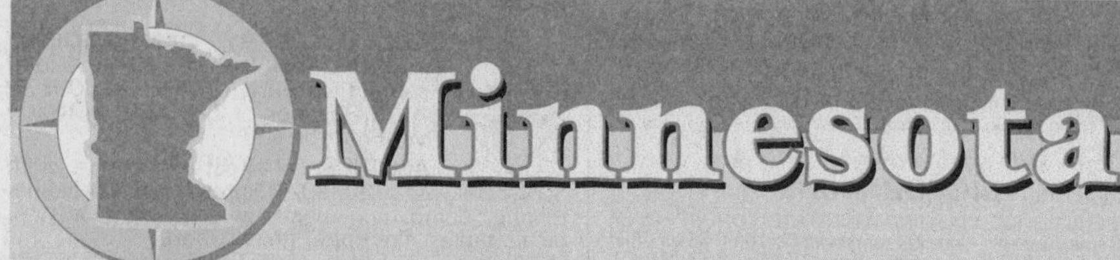

All privately owned campgrounds personally inspected by WOODALL'S Representatives

Dave and Kate Reikofski

ADRIAN—F-1

(W) ADRIAN CAMPGROUND (Municipal Park)—(Nobles) *From jct I-90 & Hwy 91: Go 1 block S on Hwy 91, then 2 blocks W on Franklin St.* FACILITIES: 100 sites, 46 full hkups, 64 W&E, 30 pull-thrus, tenting, dump, laundry. RECREATION: swim pool, playground. Partial handicap access. Open May 1 - Oct 15. Phone: (507)483-2820.

AITKIN—C-3

(S) Hickory Lake Campground—(Aitkin) *From S jct Hwy 210 & US 169: Go 7 mi S on US 169. Enter on L.* ◆◆◆FACILITIES: 56 sites, typical site width 30 ft, 56 full hkups, (20/30/50 amps), 5 pull-thrus, family camping, tenting, dump, laundry, ltd groc. ◆◆◆◆RECREATION: swim pool, lake swim, boating, canoeing, ramp, dock, lake fishing, playground. Pets welcome, breed restrict. Open May 1 - Sept 30. Rate in 2010 $42-59 for 4 persons. Phone: (218)927-6001.

AKELEY—C-2

(W) AKELEY CITY CAMPGROUND—(Hubbard) *From jct Hwy 64 & Hwy 34: Go 4 blocks W on Hwy 34. Enter on R.* FACILITIES: 24 sites, (30 amps), 24 no hkups, 26 pull-thrus, tenting, dump. RECREATION: lake swim, boating, canoeing, ramp, dock, lake fishing. Open May 15 - Sept 15. Phone: (218) 652-2172.

ALBERT LEA—F-3

(E) Albert Lea/Austin KOA Kampground—(Freeborn) *From jct I-35 & I-90: Go 8 mi E on I-90 (exit 166), then 1/2 mi NE on CR 46. Enter on R.* ◆◆◆FACILITIES: 82 sites, typical site width 45 ft, 20 full hkups, 62 W&E, (20/30/50 amps), 43 pull-thrus, family camping, tenting, dump, laundry, ltd groc. ◆◆◆RECREATION: swim pool, play equipment. Pets welcome, breed restrict. Open Apr 15 - Oct 15. Big rigs welcome. Rate in 2010 $32-44 for 2 persons. Phone: (507)373-5170. KOA discount.

(N) Crystal Springs RV Resort (TOO NEW TO RATE)—(Steele) *From jct of I-35 (exit 26) & SR 30: Go 100 yds E on SR 30, then 1/2 mi S on Frontage Rd. Enter on L.* FACILITIES: 20 sites, typical site width 40 ft, accepts full hkup units only, 20 full hkups, 2 pull-thrus. RECREATION: canoeing, pond fishing. Pets welcome, breed restrict. No tents. Open May 1 - Oct 31. Big rigs welcome. Rate in 2010 $25-27. Phone: (507) 684-2406.

(SE) MYRE-BIG ISLAND STATE PARK—(Freeborn) *From jct I-35 & CR 46: Go 1/2 mi E on CR 46, then S on CR 38 to the end.* FACILITIES: 93 sites, 32 E, 61 no hkups, tenting, dump. RECREATION: canoeing, lake fishing. Open all yr. Phone: (507) 379-3403.

ALEXANDRIA—D-2

(S) Alexandria Shooting Park & RV Campground—(Douglas) *From jct I-94 (exit 103) & Hwy 29: Go 1 mi S on Hwy 29, then 1 mi E on CR 87. Enter on L.* ◆◆◆FACILITIES: 146 sites, typical site width 25 ft, 146 W&E, (30/50 amps), 146 pull-thrus, family camping, tenting, dump, laundry, ltd groc. ◆◆◆RECREATION: playground. Pets welcome. Open May 1 - Oct 30. Big rigs welcome. Rate in 2010 $18 per vehicle. Phone: (320)763-5315.

(S) Lakes Area Motel & RV Park—(Douglas) *From jct I-94 (exit 103) & Hwy 29: Go 1 mi N on Hwy 29, then 1/4 mi W on Hwy 27. Enter on L.* ◆◆◆FACILITIES: 40 sites, typical site width 25 ft, accepts full hkup units only, 40 full hkups, (20/30/50 amps), family camping, laundry. ◆◆RECREATION: playground. Pets welcome. No tents. Open May 1 - Oct 30. Big rigs welcome. Rate in 2010 $27.50 for 4 persons. Phone: (800)733-1793.

Minnesota State Nicknames: "The Gopher State", "The North Star State"

APPLE VALLEY—E-4

(SE) LEBANON HILLS CAMPGROUND (Dakota County Park)—(Dakota) *From jct I-494 & I-35 E: Go 5 mi S on I-35 E (exit 93), then 3/4 mi E on Cliff Rd, then 1-1/4 mi S on Johnny Cake Ridge Rd. Enter on L.*

FACILITIES: 93 sites, 58 full hkups, 24 E, (20/30/50 amps), 11 no hkups, 3 pull-thrus, WiFi Internet central location, tenting, dump, non-guest dump $, laundry, ltd groc, RV supplies, ice, picnic tables, fire rings, grills, wood.

RECREATION: canoeing, kayaking, 4 canoe/4 kayak rentals, lake fishing, play equipment, hiking trails. Rec open to public.

Pets welcome. Partial handicap access. Open Early May - Oct 17. Big rigs welcome. MC/VISA/Debit. Member MRA.

Phone: (651)688-1376
Address: 12100 Johnny Cake Ridge Rd, Apple Valley, MN 55124
Lat/Lon: 44.77343/-93.18707
Web: www.co.dakota.mn.us/parks/index.htm

SEE AD TRAVEL SECTION PAGE 411

ARGYLE—A-1

(NE) OLD MILL STATE PARK—(Mill) *From town: Go 12 mi E on CR 4, then 1 mi N on CR 4.* FACILITIES: 26 sites, 10 E, (30 amps), 16 no hkups, tenting. RECREATION: canoeing, river fishing, playground. Partial handicap access. Open all yr. Phone: (218)437-8174.

ASHBY—D-2

(S) Prairie Cove Campground & RV Park—(Grant) *From jct I-94 (exit 77) & Hwy 78: Go 1 block N on Hwy 78. Enter on R.* ◆◆◆◆FACILITIES: 22 sites, typical site width 20 ft, 6 full hkups, 16 W&E, (20/30/50 amps), 12 pull-thrus, family camping, tenting, dump, ltd groc. ◆◆RECREATION: playground. Pets welcome ($). Open Apr 15 - Oct 15. Facilities fully operational May 1 - Oct 1. Rate in 2010 $30 for 2 persons. Phone: (218)747-2931.

ATWATER—E-2

(N) KANDIYOHI COUNTY PARK NUMBER 3—(Kandiyohi) *From jct US-12 & CR-2: Go 3 mi W on US-12, then 4 mi N on CR-4.* FACILITIES: 84 sites, 84 E, dump, ltd groc. RECREATION: lake swim, boating, ramp, dock, lake fishing, playground. Open May - Oct. Phone: (320)974-8520.

We all know that one of the best parts about camping is the food! Woodall's Campsite Cookbook is a classic cookbook containing such fun campsite and RV recipes as Roadside Spuds, The Fastest Sauce in the West, and Hairy Squares (which taste a lot better than they sound!) To order your copy go to www.woodalls.com/shop.

AUSTIN—F-4

(E) BEAVER TRAILS JELLYSTONE PARK CAMP-RESORT—(Mower) *From jct US 218 (South at Austin) & I-90: Go 7-1/2 mi E on I-90 (exit 187), then 25 yards S on CR 20. Enter on R.*

◆◆◆◆◆FACILITIES: 320 sites, typical site width 30 ft, 225 full hkups, 75 W&E, (20/30/50 amps), 50 amps ($), 20 no hkups, some extd stay sites, 200 pull-thrus, WiFi Instant Internet at site, WiFi Internet central location, family camping, tenting, RV's/park model rentals, cabins, RV storage, dump, non-guest dump $, portable dump, laundry, full svc store, RV supplies, LP gas by weight/by meter, ice, picnic tables, patios, fire rings, wood, controlled access.

◆◆◆◆◆RECREATION: rec hall, rec room/area, pavilion, coin games, swim pool, wading pool, 3 pedal boat rentals, pond/stream fishing, mini-golf, ($), golf nearby, bsktball, 17 bike rentals, playground, activities, (wkends), horseshoes, sports field, hiking trails, v-ball. Rec open to public.

Pets welcome. Partial handicap access. Open Apr 15 - Oct 1. Big rigs welcome. Clubs welcome. Green Friendly. Rate in 2010 $38-55 for 2 persons. MC/VISA/DISC/Debit. ATM. Member ARVC. FCRV discount. FMCA discount.

Phone: (800)245-6281
Address: 21943 630th Ave, Austin, MN 55912
Lat/Lon: 43.67256/-92.79469
Email: camping@beavertrails.com
Web: www.beavertrailsjellystone.com

SEE AD THIS PAGE

AVON—D-3

(S) El Rancho Manana—(Stearns) *From jct I-94 (exit 153) & CR 9: Go 9 mi S on CR 9, then 1/2 mi E on Manana Rd, then 2 mi N on Ranch Rd. (gravel road). Enter at end.* ◆◆◆FACILITIES: 120 sites, typical site width 45 ft, 90 full hkups, 30 W&E, (20/30/50 amps), 50 amps ($), 30 pull-thrus, family camping, tenting, dump, laundry, groceries. ◆◆◆◆RECREATION: lake swim, boating, canoeing, ramp, dock, lake fishing, playground. Pets welcome. Open May 4 - Oct 5. Rate in 2010 $25-50 per family. Member MRA. Phone: (320) 597-2740.

BARNUM—C-4

(NE) Bent Trout Lake Campground—(Carlton) *From jct I-35 (exit 220) & CR 6: Go 1/4 mi E on CR 6, then 5-3/4 mi N Bent Trout Lake Rd. (CR 140). Enter on R.* ◆◆◆FACILITIES: 80 sites, typical site width 25 ft, 35 ft max RV length, 80 W&E, (20/30 amps), 5 pull-thrus, family camping, tenting, dump, ltd groc. ◆◆◆◆RECREATION: lake swim, boating, electric motors only, canoeing, ramp, dock, lake fishing, playground. Pets welcome. Open May 15 - Oct 1. Rate in 2010 $30 for 4 persons. Phone: (218)389-6322.

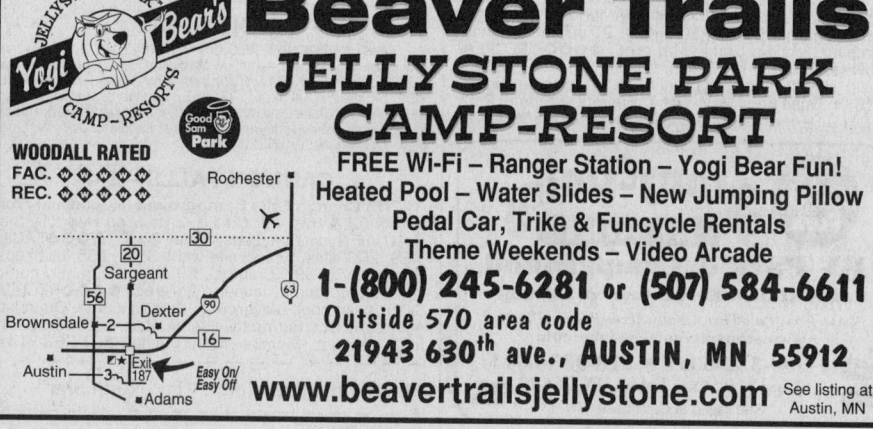

BAUDETTE—A-3

(N) Lake-of-the-Woods Campground—(Lake of the Woods) *From jct Hwy 11 & Hwy 172: Go 9 mi N on Hwy 172, then 1/2 mi E on CR 32. Enter on R.* ◇◇◇FACILITIES: 88 sites, typical site width 40 ft, 79 full hkups, 9 W&E, (20/30/50 amps), 50 amps ($), 56 pull-thrus, family camping, tenting, dump, laundry, groceries. ◇◇◇RECREATION: swim pool, lake/river fishing, playground. Pets welcome. Open May 1 - Oct 1. Big rigs welcome. Green Friendly. Rate in 2010 $25-32 for 2 persons. Phone: (218)634-1694.

ZIPPEL BAY STATE PARK—(Lake of the Woods) *From jct Hwy 11 & Hwy 172: Go 12 mi N on Hwy 172, then 6 mi W on CR 8, then 1 mi N on CR 34.* FACILITIES: 57 sites, 30 ft max RV length, 57 no hkups, tenting, dump. RECREATION: lake swim, boating, canoeing, ramp, lake/river fishing, playground. Partial handicap access. Open all yr. Facilities fully operational Mid May - Late Sept. Phone: (218)783-6252.

BEAVER BAY—C-5

SPLIT ROCK LIGHTHOUSE STATE PARK—(Lake) *From town: Go 5 mi S on Hwy 61.* FACILITIES: 24 sites, 24 no hkups, tenting. RECREATION: lake/river fishing. Partial handicap access. Open all yr. Phone: (218)226-6377.

BEMIDJI—B-2

(N) Hamilton's Fox Lake Campground—(Beltrami) *From jct US 2 & US 71: Go 10 mi N on US 71, then 4 mi W on CR 22. Enter on L.* ◇◇◇◇FACILITIES: 70 sites, typical site width 30 ft, 70 full hkups, (20/30/50 amps), 12 pull-thrus, cable TV, ($), WiFi Instant Internet at site, WiFi Internet central location, family camping, tenting, RV storage, dump, laundry, ltd groc, RV supplies, LP gas by weight, marine gas, ice, picnic tables, patios, fire rings, wood. ◇◇◇◇RECREATION: lake swim, boating, canoeing, ramp, dock, lake fishing, bsktball, 7 bike rentals, playground, hiking trails, v-ball. Pets welcome. Partial handicap access. Open May 4 - Sep 13. Big rigs welcome. Rate in 2010 $35 per family. MC/VISA/DISC/Debit. Member MRA. CCUSA 50% Discount. CCUSA reservations Recommended, CCUSA max stay 4 days. Discount not available Jul 1- Jul 9. Credit card required to confirm reservation. Must cancel 7 days before arrival. Cash only accepted for discounted rate. Discounts may not be combined. Max 4 discounted nights in 30 days. Check in 3 PM. Check out 2 PM.

Phone: (218)586-2231
Address: 2556 Island View Dr NE, Bemidji, MN 56601-7143
Lat/Lon: 47.61481/-94.84109
Email: jgducharme1@gmail.com
Web: www.camponfoxlake.com

(W) KOA-Bemidji Kampground—(Beltrami) *From jct US 71 & US 2: Go 2-1/2 mi W on US 2. Enter on R.* ◇◇◇◇FACILITIES: 68 sites, typical site width 20 ft, 32 full hkups, 27 W&E, 9 E, (20/30/50 amps), 50 amps ($), 36 pull-thrus, family camping, tenting, dump, laundry, groceries. ◇◇◇◇RECREATION: swim pool, playground. Pets welcome, breed restrict. Open Apr 1 - Nov 1. Big rigs welcome. Rate in 2010 $35-49 for 2 persons. Member MRA. Phone: (800)562-1742. KOA discount.

(NE) LAKE BEMIDJI STATE PARK—(Beltrami) *From south city limits: Go 2 mi N on US 197, then 4 mi N on CR 21, then 2 mi E on CR 20.* FACILITIES: 98 sites, 43 E, (30 amps), 55 no hkups, 4 pull-thrus, tenting, dump. RECREATION: lake swim, boating, ramp, dock, lake fishing. Partial handicap access. Open all yr. Facilities fully operational May - Sep. Phone: (218)755-3843.

(S) Royal Oaks RV Park—(Beltrami) *(E bnd)From N jct SR 197/ US 71/ US 2 (stay in Rt lane): Go 5-1/3 mi S on US 2, then 600 ft N on SR 197.(W Bnd) From S jct US 71/ US 2/ SR 197: Go 600 ft N on SR 197. Enter on R.* ◇◇◇◇FACILITIES: 63 sites, typical site width 30 ft, 63 full hkups, (20/30/50 amps), 50 amps ($), 7 pull-thrus, tenting, laundry. ◇◇RECREATION: play equipment. Pets welcome. Partial handicap access. Open May 1 - Oct 5. Big rigs welcome. Green Friendly. Rate in 2010 $26 for 2 persons. Member MRA. Phone: (218)751-8357.

(N) Summer Haven RV Resort—(Beltrami) *From jct US 2 & US 71: Go 10-1/4 mi N on US 71, then 6 mi N on CR 23. Enter on R.* ◇◇◇◇FACILITIES: 121 sites, 121 full hkups, (20/30/50 amps), 21 pull-thrus, family camping, tenting, laundry, ltd groc. ◇◇◇◇◇RECREATION: swim pool, lake swim, boating, canoeing, ramp, dock, lake fishing, playground. Pets welcome, breed restrict. Open Early May - Oct 1. Big rigs welcome. Rate in 2010 $44-49 for 4 persons. Phone: (218)586-2842.

BENA—C-3

(NE) CHIPPEWA NATIONAL FOREST (Tamarack Point Campground)—(Cass) *1-1/2 mi E on US-2, then 5-2/3 mi NE on CR-9, then 3-1/2 mi NW on FR-2163.* FACILITIES: 31 sites, 22 ft max RV length, 31 no hkups, tenting. RECREATION: lake swim, boating, ramp, dock, lake fishing. Open May 5 - Jul 7. Phone: (218)246-2123.

BIGFORK—B-3

(SE) GEORGE WASHINGTON STATE FOREST (Owen Lake Campground)—(Itasca) *From town: Go 10 mi SE on CR-7, then 7 mi E on CR-340, then follow signs 3-1/2 mi N.* FACILITIES: 20 sites, 20 ft max RV length, 20 no hkups, tenting. RECREATION: lake swim, boating, ramp, lake fishing. Partial handicap access. Open May 1 - Oct 30. Phone: (218)743-3362.

(SE) SCENIC STATE PARK—(Itasca) *From town: Go 7 mi E on CR-7.* FACILITIES: 95 sites, 20 E, 75 no hkups, 20 pull-thrus, tenting, dump. RECREATION: lake swim, boating, canoeing, ramp, dock, lake fishing. Partial handicap access. Open all yr. Phone: (218)743-3362.

BLOOMING PRAIRIE—F-4

(SE) Brookside Campground—(Mower) *From jct Hwy 30 & US 218: Go 4 mi S on US 218, then 1 mi E on CR 1. Enter on L.* ◇◇◇FACILITIES: 90 sites, typical site width 30 ft, 50 full hkups, 40 W&E, (20/30/50 amps), 12 pull-thrus, family camping, tenting, dump, ltd groc. ◇◇◇◇RECREATION: swim pool, river fishing, playground. Pets welcome, breed restrict. Open May 1 - Sep 30. Big rigs welcome. Green Friendly. Rate in 2010 $35-45 for 2 persons. Phone: (507)583-2979.

BRAINERD—D-3

(S) CROW WING STATE PARK—(Cass) *From town: Go 8 mi SW on Hwy-371, then 1 mi W on CR-27.* FACILITIES: 59 sites, typical site width 12 ft, 12 E, 47 no hkups, tenting, dump. RECREATION: river swim, boating, canoeing, ramp, river fishing, playground. Partial handicap access. Open all yr. Phone: (218)825-3075.

(S) Don & Mayva's Crow Wing Lake Campground—(Crow Wing) *From jct Hwys 18, 371 & 210: Go 10 mi S on Hwy 371. Enter on L.* ◇◇◇◇FACILITIES: 100 sites, typical site width 30 ft, 80 full hkups, 10 W&E, 10 E, (20/30/50 amps), 17 pull-thrus, family camping, tenting, dump, laundry, groceries. ◇◇◇◇◇RECREATION: swim pool, boating, canoeing, ramp, dock, lake fishing, playground. Pets welcome. Open May 1 - Oct 1. Big rigs welcome. Rate in 2010 $40-57 for 2 persons. Member ARVC, MRA. Phone: (218)829-6468.

(N) GULL LAKE RECREATION AREA (COE)—(Cass) *From town: Go 8 mi N on US-371, then 3 mi W on Crow Wing CR-125.* FACILITIES: 39 sites, typical site width 25 ft, 39 E, (30 amps), tenting, dump. RECREATION: lake swim, boating, ramp, dock, lake/river fishing, playground. Partial handicap access. Open all yr. Phone: (218)829-3334.

BREEZY POINT—C-3

(N) Highview Campground & RV Park—(Crow Wing) *From jct of SR 371 & CR 11: Go 8-1/2 mi E on CR 11, then 1/2 mi N on CR 39, then 200 yds N on Highview St. Enter on L.* ◇◇◇FACILITIES: 147 sites, typical site width 30 ft, 147 full hkups, (20/30/50 amps), 3 pull-thrus, family camping, tenting, dump, laundry. ◇◇◇◇RECREATION: lake swim, boating, canoeing, ramp, dock, lake fishing, playground. Pets welcome. Open May 1 - Oct 1. Rate in 2010 $34-38 for 2 persons. Member ARVC, MRA. Phone: (218)543-4526.

CALEDONIA—F-5

(W) BEAVER CREEK VALLEY STATE PARK—(Houston) *From town: Go 1/2 mi N on Hwy-76, then 4 mi W on CR-1.* FACILITIES: 42 sites, 16 E, 26 no hkups, tenting, dump. RECREATION: stream fishing, playground. Partial handicap access. Open all yr. Phone: (507)724-2107.

CAMBRIDGE—D-4

(E) FAIRGROUNDS CAMPGROUND (Isanti Co. Agricultural Society)—(Isanti) *From jct Hwy 65 & Hwy 95: Go 1/2 mi E on Hwy 95. Enter on L.* FACILITIES: 48 sites, 48 W&E, tenting, dump. RECREATION: lake/river fishing. Partial handicap access. Open May 1 - Oct 1. Phone: (763)689-2555.

CANBY—E-1

(SW) STONEHILL REGIONAL PARK (Lac Qui Parle Yellow Bank Watershed)—(Yellow Medicine) *From jct US 75 & Hwy 68: Go 3 blocks W on Hwy 68, then 1 mi S and 1 mi W.* FACILITIES: 54 sites, 6 full hkups, 48 W&E, 4 pull-thrus, tenting, dump. RECREATION: lake swim, boating, canoeing, ramp, dock, lake/stream fishing, playground. Partial handicap access. Open May - Oct. Phone: (507)223-7586.

CANNON FALLS—E-4

(E) Cannon Falls Campground—(Goodhue) *From jct US 52 & Hwy 19: Go 2-1/2 mi E on Hwy 19, then 2/10 mi S on Oak Lane. Enter on R.* ◇◇◇◇FACILITIES: 200 sites, typical site width 35 ft, 135 full hkups, 65 W&E, (20/30/50 amps), 50 amps ($), family camping, tenting, dump, laundry, ltd groc. ◇◇◇◇RECREATION: swim pool, playground. Pets welcome. Open late Apr - early Oct. Big rigs welcome. Rate in 2010 $32-42 for 4 persons. Member MRA. Phone: (507)263-3145.

Minnesota State Motto: "The North Star"

CANNON FALLS—Continued

(SE) LAKE BYLLESBY CAMPGROUND (Dakota County Park)—(Dakota) *From jct US 52 & CR 86: Go 30 ft. W on CR 86, then 2 1/2 mi S on Harry Ave. Enter on L.*

FACILITIES: 57 sites, typical site width 30 ft, 35 W&E, (20/30/50 amps), 22 no hkups, tenting, dump, non-guest dump $, ltd groc, ice, picnic tables, fire rings, grills, wood.

RECREATION: pavilion, lake swim, boating, canoeing, kayaking, ramp, dock, lake fishing, golf nearby, playground, sports field, hiking trails. Rec open to public.

Pets welcome. Partial handicap access. Open Early May - Mid Oct. Big rigs welcome. Clubs welcome. MC/VISA. Member MRA.

Text 82174 to (440)725-8687 to see our Visual Tour.

Phone: (507)263-4447
Address: 7650 Echo Point Rd, Cannon Falls, MN 55009
Lat/Lon: 44.51449/-92.94648
Web: www.co.dakota.mn.us/parks/index.htm

SEE AD TRAVEL SECTION PAGE 411

CARLOS—D-2

(W) LAKE CARLOS STATE PARK—(Douglas) *From town: Go 1 mi W on CR 13, then 1 mi N on Hwy 29, then 1-1/2 mi W on Hwy 38.* FACILITIES: 123 sites, 81 E, 42 no hkups, tenting, dump. RECREATION: lake swim, boating, ramp, lake fishing. Partial handicap access. Open all yr. Facilities fully operational Mid May - Mid Sept. Phone: (320)852-7200.

CARLTON—C-4

(E) JAY COOKE STATE PARK—(Carlton) *From town: Go 3 mi E on Hwy-210.* FACILITIES: 80 sites, 21 E, 59 no hkups, 1 pull-thrus, tenting, dump. RECREATION: river fishing, playground. Partial handicap access. Open all yr. Phone: (218)384-4610.

CASS LAKE—B-2

(E) CANAL HOUSE RESTAURANT & BAR—*From jct Hwy 371 & US 2; Go 2 mi E on US 2.* Waterside dining specializing in Bar-B-Q Ribs & broasted chicken. Full soup & salad bar, burgers & sandwiches with Northwoods Gift Shop. Open May 1 - Sep 15. MC/VISA/DISC/AMEX/Debit.

Phone: (218)335-2136
Address: 5510 US 2 NW, Cass Lake, MN 56633
Lat/Lon: 47.37860/-94.57475
Web: www.stonyptresortcasslake.com

SEE AD BEMIDJI THIS PAGE

(E) CHIPPEWA NATIONAL FOREST (Chippewa Campground)—(Cass) *From town: Go 4-1/4 mi E on US 2, then 3/4 mi N on FR 2171.* FACILITIES: 46 sites, 46 E, tenting, dump, ltd groc. RECREATION: lake swim, boating, ramp. Partial handicap access. Open May 7 - Oct 26. Phone: (218)335-8600.

(E) CHIPPEWA NATIONAL FOREST (Norway Beach Campground)—(Cass) *From town: Go 4 mi E on US-2, then 1/4 mi N on FR-2171, then 1/3 mi N on FR-2007.* FACILITIES: 54 sites, 54 no hkups, 1 pull-thrus, tenting, dump, ltd groc. RECREATION: lake swim, boating, ramp, lake fishing. Partial handicap access. Open May 26 - Sep 8. Phone: (218)335-8560.

(E) CHIPPEWA NATIONAL FOREST (Wanaki Campground)—(Cass) *4-1/4 mi E on US-2, then 2 mi NE on FR-2171.* FACILITIES: 46 sites, 46 no hkups, 1 pull-thrus, tenting, dump. RECREATION: lake swim, boating, ramp, lake fishing. Partial handicap access. Open May 13 - Sep 9. Phone: (218)335-8600.

(NE) CHIPPEWA NATIONAL FOREST (Winnie Dam Campground)—(CASS) *6 mi E on US-2, then 2-1/3 mi N on CR-10, then 7 mi NE on FR-2171, then 3-1/2 mi SE on FR-2168.* FACILITIES: 35 sites, (30 amps), 35 no hkups, tenting, dump. RECREATION: boating, ramp, lake fishing. Open May 13 - Oct 25. Phone: (218)326-6128.

(N) Marclay Point Resort Campground/RV Park—(Cass) *From jct Hwy 371 & US 2: Go 500 ft E on US 2, then 3/4 mi N on CR 60(changes to CR 148), then 1 mi N on CR 148(turns E), then 1/4 mi N on Anglers Beach Rd, then 1/4 mi E on Marclay Point Rd (gravel). Enter on R.* ◇◇◇FACILITIES: 91 sites, typical site width 25 ft, 30 ft max RV length, accepts self-contained units only, 91 full hkups, (20/30 amps), 4 pull-thrus, family camping. ◇◇◇◇RECREATION: lake swim, boating, ramp, dock, lake fishing, play equipment. Pets welcome. Partial handicap access. No tents. Open May 1 - Sep 20. Rate in 2010 $41 for 4 persons. Phone: (218)335-6589.

CASS LAKE—Continued on next page

Minnesota's waters flow outward in three directions: north to Hudson Bay in Canada, east to the Atlantic Ocean, and south to the Gulf of Mexico.

CASS LAKE—Continued

(E) STONY POINT RESORT TRAILER PARK & CAMPGROUND—(Cass) *From jct Hwy 371 & US 2: Go 2 mi E on US 2. Enter on L.*

◊◊◊◊FACILITIES: 165 sites, typical site width 35 ft, 135 full hkups, 30 W&E, (20/30/50 amps), many extd stay sites, 29 pull-thrus, WiFi Instant Internet at site ($), family camping, tenting, cabins, RV storage, dump, non-guest dump $, laundry, ltd groc, RV supplies, LP gas by weight/by meter, marine gas, ice, picnic tables, patios, fire rings, grills, wood.

◊◊◊◊◊RECREATION: rec hall, rec room/area, pavilion, coin games, lake swim, boating, canoeing, kayaking, ramp, dock, 3 pontoon/2 canoe/8 kayak/6 pedal boat/7 motorboat rentals, lake/pond fishing, fishing supplies, fishing guides, golf nearby, bsktball, playground, activities, horseshoes, sports field, v-ball. Rec open to public.

Pets welcome. Open May 1 - Oct 15. Big rigs welcome. Clubs welcome. Green Friendly. Rate in 2010 $30.75-35.50 for 2 persons. MC/VISA/DISC/AMEX/Debit. Member MRA.

Phone: (800)332-6311
Address: 5510 US Hwy 2 NW, Cass Lake, MN 56633
Lat/Lon: 47.37864/-94.57495
Email: stonypoint@arvig.net
Web: www.stonyptresortcasslake.com

SEE AD BEMIDJI PAGE 418

CHISHOLM—B-4

(C) Iron Trail RV Park & Campground—(St. Louis) *From jct US 169 & Hwy 73: Go 1/2 mi N on Hwy 73. (Hwy 73 & 6th Ave SW, on Frontage Road). Enter on L.* ◊◊◊FACILITIES: 42 sites, typical site width 25 ft, 27 full hkups, 15 W&E, (20/30/50 amps), 8 pull-thrus, cable TV, ($), family camping, tenting, dump, non-guest dump $, laundry, RV supplies, ice, picnic tables, wood. ◊RECREATION: bsktball. Pets welcome. Open May 1 - Oct 1. Rate in 2010 $19.24-23.51 for 2 persons. CCUSA 50% Discount. CCUSA reservations Recommended, CCUSA max stay 1 days, Cash only for CCUSA disc., CCUSA disc. not avail holidays. No discount during local area special events. Call for details.

Phone: (800)711-7789
Address: 115 SW 6th Ave, Chisholm, MN 55719
Lat/Lon: 47.48848/-92.88891
Web: www.irontrailcampground.com

CLEARWATER—D-3

(SE) A-J ACRES CAMPGROUND—(Stearns) *From jct I-94 (exit 178) & Hwy 24: Go 50 yards S on Hwy 24, then 1 mi SW on CR 145, then 1/2 mi W on 195th St E. Enter at end.*

◊◊◊FACILITIES: 196 sites, typical site width 30 ft, 150 full hkups, 46 W&E, (20/30/50 amps), many extd stay sites, 15 pull-thrus, WiFi Internet central location, family camping, tenting, RV storage, dump, non-guest dump $, laundry, ltd groc, RV supplies, ice, picnic tables, fire rings, wood, controlled access.

◊◊◊◊◊RECREATION: rec hall, lake swim, boating, 5 hp limit, canoeing, ramp, dock, 5 rowboat/3 canoe rentals, lake fishing, fishing supplies, golf nearby, playground, activities, (wkends), horseshoes, hiking trails, v-ball.

Pets welcome. Open May 1 - Sep 30. Big rigs welcome. Clubs welcome. Green Friendly. Rate in 2010 $38 per family. MC/VISA/DISC/Debit. Member ARVC, MRA.

CLEARWATER—Continued
A-J ACRES CAMPGROUND—Continued

Phone: (320)558-2847
Address: 1300 195th St E., Clearwater, MN 55320
Lat/Lon: 45.40557/-94.08927
Email: ajacres@frontiernet.net
Web: www.ajacrescampground.com

SEE AD ST. CLOUD PAGE 426

(E) St. Cloud/Clearwater RV Park—(Stearns) *From jct I-94 (exit 178) & Hwy 24: Go 1/2 mi N on Hwy 24, then 1 mi W on CR 75, then 1/4 mi SW on CR 143. Enter on R.* ◊◊◊◊FACILITIES: 120 sites, typical site width 40 ft, 58 full hkups, 46 W&E, 8 E, (20/30/50 amps), 50 amps ($), 8 no hkups, 65 pull-thrus, family camping, tenting, dump, laundry, ltd groc. ◊◊◊◊RECREATION: swim pool, playground. Pets welcome, breed restrict. Open May 1 - Oct 8. Big rigs welcome. Rate in 2010 $34-48 for 4 persons. Member MRA. Phone: (320)558-2876.

CLOQUET—C-4

(S) Cloquet/Duluth KOA—(Carlton) *From jct I-35 (exit 239) & Hwy 45: Go 2 mi S on Hwy 45, then 1 mi W on CR-3. Enter on R.* ◊◊◊◊FACILITIES: 50 sites, typical site width 40 ft, 10 full hkups, 40 W&E, (20/30/50 amps), 50 amps ($), 26 pull-thrus, family camping, tenting, dump, laundry, ltd groc. ◊◊◊RECREATION: swim pool, playground. Pets welcome, breed restrict. Age restrict may apply. Open May 1 - Oct 15. Big rigs welcome. Green Friendly. Rate in 2010 $34-45 for 2 persons. Member MRA. Phone: (218)879-5726. KOA discount.

COKATO—E-3

(N) Cokato Lake RV Resort—(Wright) *From jct Hwy 15 & US 12: Go 7 mi E on US 12, then 3 mi N on CR 4. Enter on L.* ◊◊◊◊FACILITIES: 220 sites, typical site width 25 ft, 220 full hkups, (20/30 amps), 7 pull-thrus, tenting, dump, laundry, groceries. ◊◊◊◊◊RECREATION: swim pool, boating, canoeing, dock, lake fishing, playground. Pets welcome. Open May 1 - Oct 1. Rate in 2010 $39-42 for 2 persons. Phone: (320)286-5779.

COOK—B-4

(N) KABETOGAMA STATE FOREST (Wakemup Bay Campground)—(St. Louis) *From town: Go 2-1/2 mi N on CR 24, then 3 mi E on CR 78, then 1 mi N.* FACILITIES: 23 sites, 23 no hkups, tenting. RECREATION: lake swim, boating, canoeing, ramp, lake fishing. Partial handicap access. Open May 10 - Sep 15. Phone: (218)753-2245.

CROSBY—C-3

(NW) CROW WING STATE FOREST (Greer Lake Campground)—(Crow Wing) *From town: Go 12 mi N on Hwy-6, then 3 mi W on CR-36, then 3-1/2 mi SW on CR-14. Follow signs.* FACILITIES: 29 sites, 20 ft max RV length, 29 no hkups, tenting. RECREATION: lake swim, boating, ramp, dock, lake fishing. Open May 1 - Oct 1. Phone: (218)546-5926.

CROSS LAKE—C-3

RONALD LOUIS CLOUTIER REC AREA (COE-Crosslake)—(Crow Wing) *In town at jct CR 3 & CR 66.* FACILITIES: 119 sites, 69 E, (30 amps), 50 no hkups, tenting, dump, laundry. RECREATION: lake/river swim, boating, canoeing, ramp, dock, lake/river fishing, playground. Partial handicap access. Open all yr. Phone: (218)692-2025.

CURRIE—F-2

(NW) LAKE SHETEK STATE PARK—(Murray) *From town: Go 1-1/2 mi N on CR 38, then 1-1/2 mi W on CR 37.* FACILITIES: 97 sites, 66 E, 31 no hkups, 1 pull-thrus, tenting, dump. RECREATION: lake swim, boating, canoeing, ramp, dock, lake fishing, playground. Partial handicap access. Open all yr. Phone: (507) 763-3256.

(N) Schreier's on Shetek—(Murray) *From jct Hwy 30 & CR 38: Go 2 mi N on CR 38, then W 500 ft on CR 37, then 1 mi N on 200 Ave (gravel road), then 1/2 mi W on 181st St, then 1/4 mi N on Resort Rd. Enter at end.* ◊◊◊◊FACILITIES: 120 sites, typical site width 35 ft, 111 full hkups, 6 E, (20/30/50 amps), 3 no hkups, family camping, tenting, dump, laundry, ltd groc.

CURRIE—Continued
Schreier's on Shetek—Continued

◊◊◊◊◊RECREATION: lake swim, boating, canoeing, ramp, dock, lake fishing, playground. Pets welcome. Open May 1 - Oct 15. Green Friendly. Rate in 2010 $26-30 per family. Member MACO. Phone: (507)763-3817.

DEER RIVER—C-3

(S) SCHOOLCRAFT STATE PARK—(Cass) *From jct US 2 & Hwy 6: Go 8 mi S on Hwy 6, then 1/2 mi W on CR 28, then 2 mi W on CR 65, then 1 mi N on CR 74.* FACILITIES: 28 sites, 35 ft max RV length, 28 no hkups, tenting. RECREATION: boating, canoeing, ramp, dock, river fishing. Open all yr. Phone: (218)247-7215.

DETROIT LAKES—C-2

(S) Country Campground—(Becker) *From jct US 10, Hwy 34 & US 59: Go 4-1/2 mi S on US 59,then 50 yrds NE on CR 22, then 1 mi E on 130th St, then 3/4 mi N on 260th Ave. Enter on R.* ◊◊◊◊FACILITIES: 30 sites, typical site width 40 ft, 30 full hkups, (20/30/50 amps), 16 pull-thrus, WiFi Instant Internet at site, WiFi Internet central location, family camping, tenting, dump, non-guest dump $, laundry, ltd groc, RV supplies, LP gas by weight, ice, picnic tables, fire rings, grills, wood. ◊◊◊◊◊RECREATION: rec hall, pavilion, dock, lake fishing, mini-golf, bsktball, playground, horseshoes, hiking trails, v-ball. Pets welcome. Open May 1 - Oct 1. Big rigs welcome. Green Friendly. Rate in 2010 $30 per family. MC/VISA/Debit. CCUSA 50% Discount. CCUSA reservations Accepted, CCUSA max stay Unlimited, CCUSA disc. not avail S, CCUSA disc. not avail F,Sa, CCUSA disc. not avail holidays. Not available month of Jul & first week of Aug.

Phone: (800)898-7901
Address: 2123 260th Ave., Detroit Lakes, MN 56501
Lat/Lon: 46.76970/-95.85699
Email: ccdlmn@lakesnet.net
Web: www.countrycampground.org

(W) Forest Hills Golf & RV Resort—(Becker) *From jct Hwy 34, US 59, & US 10: Go 3 mi W on US 10. Enter on L.* ◊◊◊◊FACILITIES: 180 sites, typical site width 25 ft, 180 full hkups, (30/50 amps), 10 pull-thrus, family camping, laundry. ◊◊◊◊RECREATION: swim pool, playground. Pets welcome, breed restrict. No tents. Open May 1 - Oct 1. Big rigs welcome. Rate in 2010 $30-35 per vehicle. Phone: (800)482-3441.

(W) Long Lake Campsite & RV Resort—(Becker) *From jct Hwy 34, US 59 & US 10: Go 2-1/2 mi W on US 10, then 1/2 mi S on W Long Lake Rd. Enter on L.* ◊◊◊FACILITIES: 105 sites, typical site width 25 ft, 29 full hkups, 76 W&E, (30 amps), 19 pull-thrus, family camping, dump, ltd groc. ◊◊◊◊RECREATION: lake swim, boating, canoeing, ramp, dock, lake fishing, play equipment. Pets welcome, breed restrict. No tents. Open May 1 - Sep 23. Rate in 2010 $26 for 4 persons. Member MRA. Phone: (218)847-8920.

DULUTH—C-4

See listings at Barnum, Cloquet, Saginaw, Scanlon & Two Harbors.

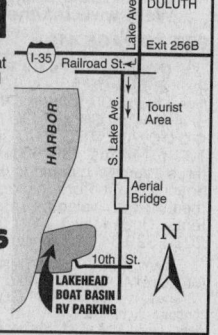

DULUTH—Continued on next page

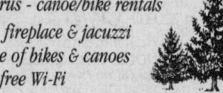

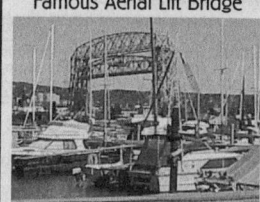

DULUTH—Continued

(SW) Buffalo Valley Camping—(St. Louis) *From jct I-35 (exit 245) & Hwy 61, then 100 yds E on Hwy 61, then 100 yds N on CR 3, then 1/4 mi E on Guss Rd. Enter at end.* ◊◊◊FACILITIES: 63 sites, 12 full hkups, 33 W&E, 18 E, (20/30/50 amps), 8 pull-thrus, tenting, dump. Pets welcome. Partial handicap access. Open all yr. Facilities fully operational May 10 - Oct 1. Big rigs welcome. Rate in 2010 $30-35 per vehicle. Phone: (218)628-7019.

(SW) Fond du Lac Campground & Boat Landing—(St.Louis) *From jct US 53 & I-35 (exit 255): Go 11 mi S on I-35 (exit 246), then 3-3/4 mi S on Hwy 13, then 4-1/4 mi W on Hwy 23/Commonwealth Ave. Enter on L.* ◊◊FACILITIES: 49 sites, typical site width 25 ft, 30 ft max RV length, 4 full hkups, 21 W&E, (20/30 amps), 24 no hkups, 10 pull-thrus, family camping, tenting, dump. ◊◊RECREATION: boating, canoeing, ramp, dock, river fishing. Pets welcome, breed restrict, quantity restrict. Partial handicap access. Open May 8 - Oct 1. Rate in 2010 $28-30 per family.

Phone: (218)749-5388
Address: Junction Hwy 23 & Hwy 210, Duluth, MN 55808
Lat/Lon: 46.66078/-92.28030
Email: vinebritt@aol.com
Web: www.fondulaccampground.com

(SW) INDIAN POINT CAMPGROUND—(St. Louis) *N'bound: From I-35 (exit 251A): Go 1/2 mi E on Cody St, then 1/4 mi S on 59th Ave W, then 1-1/4 mi S on Grand, then 1/4 mi E on 75th Ave W. S'bound: From I-35 (exit 251B): Go 1-1/4 mi S on Grand, then 1/4 mi E on 75th Ave W. Enter at end.*

WELCOME

◊◊◊FACILITIES: 51 sites, typical site width 35 ft, 7 full hkups, 21 W&E, 23 E, (20/30/50 amps), 9 pull-thrus, WiFi Instant Internet at site, family camping, tenting, shower$, dump, non-guest dump $, laundry, RV supplies, ice, picnic tables, fire rings, wood.

◊◊◊RECREATION: pavilion, canoeing, kayaking, 4 canoe/6 pedal boat rentals, river fishing, golf nearby, bike rental 25 bike rentals, playground, sports field, hiking trails.

Pets welcome. Partial handicap access. Open all yr. Facilities fully operational May 1 - Oct 15. Big rigs welcome. Clubs welcome. Rate in 2010 $25-32 per vehicle. MC/VISA/DISC/AMEX/Debit. Member MRA.

Phone: (800)982-2453
Address: 7000 Pulaski St, Duluth, MN 55807
Lat/Lon: 46.72226/-92.18590
Email: munger@mungerinn.com
Web: www.indianpointcampground.com

SEE AD PAGE 419

(E) LAKEHEAD BOAT BASIN, INC (RV SPACES)—(St. Louis) *From jct US 53 & I-35 (exit 255): Go 1 mi N on I-35 (exit 256B), then 1 block SE on Lake Ave (get in rt ln), then 1 block SW on Railroad St, (get in lft ln) then 3/4 mi SE on (over Aerial Bridge), then 1 block W on 10th St. Enter at end.*

WELCOME

FACILITIES: 30 sites, typical site width 24 ft, 12 full hkups, 18 W&E, (15/30/50 amps), some extd stay sites, WiFi Instant Internet at site, laundry, RV supplies, marine gas, ice, wood.

RECREATION: boating, canoeing, kayaking, dock, lake fishing, fishing guides.

Pets welcome. No tents. Open May 15 - Sep 15. Big rigs welcome. Rate in 2010 $29-34 per vehicle. MC/VISA/DISC/AMEX/Debit.

Phone: (218)722-1757
Address: 1000 Minnesota Ave, Duluth, MN 55802
Lat/Lon: 46.77436/-92.09153
Email: lbb@lakeheadboatbasin.com
Web: www.lakeheadboatbasin.com

SEE AD PAGE 419

(NW) Ogston's RV Park—(St. Louis) *From jct I-35 (exit 255) & US 53: Go 13 mi W on US 53/Miller Trunk Hwy, then 500 ft N on CR 859/Caribou Lake Rd, then 3/4 mi W on CR 982/Old Miller Trunk Hwy. Enter on R.* ◊◊◊◊FACILITIES: 100 sites, typical site width 40 ft, 100 full hkups, (30/50 amps), 50 amps ($), 41 pull-thrus, family camping, laundry. ◊◊◊RECREATION: boating, no motors, canoeing, pond fishing, play equipment. Pets welcome. Partial handicap access. No tents. Open May 1 - Oct 1. Big rigs welcome. Rate in 2010 $29-34 per family. Phone: (218)729-9528.

(W) SPIRIT MOUNTAIN CAMPGROUND (City Park)—(St. Louis) *At I-35 (exit 249) & Spirit Mountain Place.* FACILITIES: 73 sites, typical site width 20 ft, 39 W&E, 34 E, 13 pull-thrus, tenting, dump. RECREATION: playground. Partial handicap access. Open May - Oct. Phone: (218)628-2891.

DULUTH—Continued

(SW) WILLARD MUNGER INN—*N'bnd: From I-35 (exit 251A): Go 1/2 mi E on Cody St, then 1/4 mi S on 59th Ave W, then 1-1/4 mi S on Grand to 75th Ave W (enter on L). S'bnd: From I-35 (exit 251B): Go 1-1/4 on S on Grand to 75th Ave W (enter on L).* The Historic Willard Munger Inn offers unique Suites - some w/wood burning fireplaces, jacuzzis, or walk-out decks. Free use of bicycles, canoes & kayaks. Free Zoo tickets, Continental Brkfast & high speed wi-fi in all rooms. The Munger Trail starts here. Open all yr. MC/VISA/DISC/AMEX/Debit.

WELCOME

Phone: (800)982-2453
Address: 7408 Grand Ave, Duluth, MN 55807
Web: www.mungerinn.com

SEE AD PAGE 419

ELBA—F-5

WHITEWATER STATE PARK—(Winona) *From town: Go 2 mi S on Hwy 74.* FACILITIES: 106 sites, 47 E, (50 amps), 59 no hkups, 5 pull-thrus, tenting, dump. RECREATION: river fishing, playground. Partial handicap access. Open all yr. Phone: (507) 932-3007.

ELY—B-5

(NE) Canoe Country Campground & Cabins—(Lake) *From jct Hwy 1 & Hwy 169: Go 17 mi E on Hwy 169, then 1-1/2 mi W on Moose Lake Rd/ CR 183. Enter on L.* ◊◊◊FACILITIES: 19 sites, typical site width 30 ft, 35 ft max RV length, 10 full hkups, 2 W&E, (20/30 amps), 7 no hkups, family camping, tenting, laundry, ltd groc. ◊◊◊RECREATION: lake swim, boating, canoeing, dock, lake fishing. Pets welcome. Open May 15 - Oct 1. Rate in 2010 $27-29 for 2 persons. Member MACO. Phone: (800)752-2306.

(S) SUPERIOR NATIONAL FOREST (Birch Lake Campground)—(Lake) *9 mi SE on Hwy 1, then 4-1/2 mi S on Little Lake Road.* FACILITIES: 29 sites, typical site width 14 ft, 29 no hkups, tenting. RECREATION: boating, ramp, lake fishing. Open May - Sep. Phone: (218)365-4966.

(N) SUPERIOR NATIONAL FOREST (Fenske Lake Campground)—(Lake) *From Ely: Go 1 mi E on State Hwy 169 (toward Winton), then left 2 mi on CR 88, then right 8 mi on Echo Trail to campground. Enter on R.* FACILITIES: 15 sites, 15 no hkups, tenting. RECREATION: lake swim, canoeing, ramp, lake fishing. Open May 15 - Sep 30. Phone: (218)365-4966.

(S) SUPERIOR NATIONAL FOREST (South Kawishiwi River Campground)—(Lake) *From town: Go 12 mi S on Hwy-1.* FACILITIES: 31 sites, typical site width 12 ft, 31 no hkups, tenting. RECREATION: river swim, boating, canoeing, ramp, river fishing. Open May - Sep. Phone: (218)365-4966.

(E) SUPERIOR NF (Fall Lake Campground)—(Lake) *From jct Hwy 1 & Hwy 169: Go 5 mi E on Hwy 169, then 2 mi N on Country Rd 182 (Fall Lake Rd). Enter on L.* FACILITIES: 29 sites, 29 no hkups, 5 pull-thrus, tenting, ltd groc. RECREATION: saltwater swim, boating, canoeing, ramp, lake fishing. Partial handicap access. Open May 1 - Oct 1. Phone: (218)365-5638.

FAIRFAX—E-2

(S) FORT RIDGELY STATE PARK—(Nicollet) *From jct Hwys-19 & 4: Go 7 mi S on 4.* FACILITIES: 39 sites, 15 E, (30/50 amps), 24 no hkups, 1 pull-thrus, tenting, dump. RECREATION: stream fishing, playground. Partial handicap access. Open all yr. Phone: (507)426-7840.

FAIRMONT—F-3

(W) Flying Goose Campground—(Martin) *From jct I-90 (exit 107) & CR 53: Go 1 mi S on CR 53, then 1 mi W on 115th St/CR 26. Enter on L.* ◊◊◊◊FACILITIES: 110 sites, typical site width 35 ft, 40 full hkups, 70 W&E, (20/30/50 amps), 50 amps ($), 30 pull-thrus, family camping, tenting, dump, laundry, ltd groc. ◊◊◊◊RECREATION: lake swim, boating, canoeing, ramp, dock, playground. Pets welcome. Open May 1 - Oct 31. Big rigs welcome. Rate in 2010 $32-40 per family. Member MRA. Phone: (507)235-3458.

FARIBAULT—F-4

(S) Camp Faribo—(Rice) *From jct I-35 (exit 56) & Hwy 60: Go 1/4 mi E on Hwy 60, then 1-1/2 mi S on Western Ave. Enter on L.* ◊◊◊◊FACILITIES: 71 sites, typical site width 30 ft, 71 full hkups, (20/30/50 amps), 50 amps ($), 25 pull-thrus, family camping, tenting, dump, laundry, ltd groc. ◊◊◊◊RECREATION: swim pool, playground. Pets welcome. Open Apr 1 - Oct 15. Big rigs welcome. Rate in 2010 $31-35 for 4 persons. Member MRA. Phone: (507)332-8453.

FEDERAL DAM—C-3

(W) LEECH LAKE RECREATION AREA (COE Leech Lake Reservoir)—(Cass) *From jct US 2 & CR 8: Go 7 mi S on CR 8.* FACILITIES: 79 sites, 75 E, (50 amps), 4 no hkups, 3 pull-thrus, tenting, dump, laundry, ltd groc. RECREATION: lake/river swim, boating, canoeing, ramp, dock, lake/river fishing, playground. Partial handicap access. Open May - Oct. Phone: (218)654-3145.

FINLAND—B-5

(E) FINLAND STATE FOREST (Eckbeck Campground)—(Lake) *From town: Go 3 mi S on Hwy 1.* FACILITIES: 30 sites, 21 ft max RV length, 30 no hkups, tenting. RECREATION: river fishing. Partial handicap access. Open May - Sep. Phone: (218) 226-6365.

FINLAND—Continued

(E) FINLAND STATE FOREST (Finland Campground)—(Lake) *From town: Go 1/2 mi E on CR 6.* FACILITIES: 39 sites, 21 ft max RV length, 18 E, 21 no hkups, tenting. RECREATION: river fishing. Partial handicap access. Open May - Sep 30. Phone: (218)226-6365.

(NE) GEORGE CROSBY MANITOU STATE PARK—(Lake) *From town: Go 8 mi NE on Lake CR 7.* FACILITIES: 21 sites, 21 no hkups, tenting. RECREATION: lake swim, boating, no motors, canoeing, lake/river fishing. Open all yr. Phone: (218)226-6365.

GARDEN CITY—F-3

(E) SHADY OAKS CAMPGROUND—(Blue Earth) *S'Bnd US 169 & 173rd St: Go 1/2 mi E on 173rd St (street changes names to Washington St and then to Fairground St). Enter at end.* FACILITIES: 70 sites, typical site width 30 ft, 20 W&E, 50 E, (30/50 amps), tenting, dump, ltd groc. RECREATION: river fishing, playground. Open May 1 - Oct 31. Member MRA. Phone: (507)546-3986.

GARFIELD—D-2

(S) Oak Park Kampground—(Douglas) *From jct I-94 (exit 97) & Hwy 114/CR 40: Go 1-1/2 mi N on CR 40, then 1-1/4 mi W on CR 8. Enter on R.* ◊◊◊◊FACILITIES: 43 sites, typical site width 40 ft, 15 full hkups, 28 W&E, (20/30/50 amps), 30 pull-thrus, family camping, tenting, dump, laundry. ◊◊◊RECREATION: swim pool, playground. Pets welcome. Partial handicap access. Open May 1 - Oct 1. Big rigs welcome. Rate in 2010 $25-30 for 2 persons. Member MRA. Phone: (320)834-2345.

GARRISON—D-3

(N) Camp Holiday Resort & Campground—(Crow Wing) *From jct US 169 & Hwy 18: Go 3-1/2 mi N on Hwy 18, then 1/4 mi E on CR 10, then 2 mi E on Round Lake Rd. Enter on L.* ◊◊◊FACILITIES: 40 sites, typical site width 25 ft, 24 full hkups, 16 W&E, (20/30/50 amps), 3 pull-thrus, family camping, tenting, dump, laundry, ltd groc. ◊◊◊◊RECREATION: lake swim, boating, canoeing, ramp, dock, lake fishing, playground. Pets welcome. Open May 1 - Sep 30. Rate in 2010 $24-45 for 2 persons. Phone: (800)450-2495.

GILBERT—B-4

SHERWOOD FOREST CAMPGROUND (City Park)—(St. Louis) *From jct Hwy 37 (Broadway) & Wisconsin Ave: Go 2 blocks S on Wisconsin Ave. Enter on R.* FACILITIES: 57 sites, 20 full hkups, 19 W&E, 4 E, 14 no hkups, tenting, dump. RECREATION: lake swim, boating, canoeing, ramp, dock, lake fishing, playground. Partial handicap access. Open May 1 - Oct 31. Phone: (800)403-1803.

GLENWOOD—D-2

(S) BARSNESS PARK-CHALET CAMPGROUND (Municipal Park)—(Pope) *1/2 mi S on Hwy-104.* FACILITIES: 50 sites, 5 full hkups, 45 E, (50 amps), tenting. RECREATION: lake swim, boating, playground. Open May 1 - Sep 30. Phone: (320) 634-5433.

GLYNDON—C-1

(E) BUFFALO RIVER STATE PARK—(Clay) *From town: Go 4 mi E on US-10.* FACILITIES: 44 sites, 35 E, (20/30/50 amps), 9 no hkups, tenting, dump. RECREATION: river fishing. Partial handicap access. Open all yr. Phone: (218)498-2124.

GRAND MARAIS—A-5

(SW) CASCADE RIVER STATE PARK—(Cook) *From town: Go 10 mi W on Hwy 61 to milepost 101.* FACILITIES: 40 sites, 35 ft max RV length, 40 no hkups, 3 pull-thrus, tenting, dump. RECREATION: lake/river/stream fishing. Open all yr. Phone: (218) 387-3053.

(S) GRAND MARAIS RECREATION AREA (Municipal Park)—(Cook) *In town, off US 61 & Eighth Ave.* FACILITIES: 300 sites, typical site width 28 ft, 152 full hkups, 104 W&E, (20/30/50 amps), 44 no hkups, 30 pull-thrus, family camping, tenting, dump. RECREATION: swim pool, boating, canoeing, ramp, dock, lake fishing, playground. Pets welcome. Partial handicap access. Open May 1 - Oct 15. Big rigs welcome. Member ARVC, MRA. Phone: (800)998-0959.

(N) Gunflint Pines Resort & Campground—(Cook) *From jct US 61 & CR 12 (Gunflint Trail): Go 43-1/4 mi NW on CR 12, then 1 mi N on CR 50. Enter on L.* ◊◊◊FACILITIES: 14 sites, typical site width 35 ft, 38 ft max RV length, 14 W&E, (20/30/50 amps), family camping, tenting, dump, laundry, groceries. ◊◊◊◊◊RECREATION: lake swim, boating, canoeing, ramp, dock, lake fishing, playground. Pets welcome. Open all yr. Facilities fully operational May 1 - Oct 4. Rate in 2010 $34-40 for 2 persons. Member ARVC, MRA. Phone: (800)533-5814.

(NE) JUDGE C R MAGNEY STATE PARK—(Cook) *From town: Go 14 mi NE on Hwy 61.* FACILITIES: 27 sites, 27 no hkups, tenting. RECREATION: lake/river/stream fishing. Partial handicap access. Open all yr. Facilities fully operational May - Sep. Phone: (218)387-3039.

(NW) SUPERIOR NATIONAL FOREST (East Bearskin Lake Campground)—(Cook) *From jct US 61 & CR 12 (Gunflint Trail): Go 25-1/2 mi NW on CR 12, then 1-1/2 mi NE on FR 146.* FACILITIES: 33 sites, typical site width 13 ft, 33 no hkups, tenting, ltd groc. RECREATION: lake swim, boating, canoeing, ramp, lake fishing. Open May 1 - Nov 1. Phone: (218)388-4410.

GRAND MARAIS—Continued on next page

(NW) SUPERIOR NATIONAL FOREST (Trails End Campground)—(Cook) *From jct US 61 & CR 12 (Gunflint Trail): Go 58 mi NW on CR 12.* FACILITIES: 33 sites, 33 no hkups, tenting, ltd groc. RECREATION: lake swim, boating, canoeing, ramp, lake fishing. Open May - Oct. Phone: (218)387-1750.

(N) SUPERIOR NATIONAL FOREST (Two Island Lake Campground)—(Cook) *3-3/4 mi N on CR-12 (Gunflint Trail), then 1 mi W on CR-6, then 4-3/4 mi NW on CR-8, then 4-1/3 mi NW on CR-27.* FACILITIES: 37 sites, 32 ft max RV length, 37 no hkups, tenting. RECREATION: boating, ramp, lake fishing. Open May - Sep. Phone: (218)387-1750.

GRAND RAPIDS—C-3

(N) Prairie Lake Campground—(Itasca) *From W jct US 169 & US 2: Go 3 blocks W on US 2, then 6-1/2 mi N on Hwy 38/NW 3rd Ave, then 1/2 mi E on CR 49. Enter on R.* ◊◊◊FACILITIES: 55 sites, typical site width 30 ft, 26 full hkups, 29 W&E, (20/30/50 amps), 4 pull-thrus, family camping, tenting, dump. ◊◊◊RECREATION: lake swim, boating, canoeing, ramp, dock, lake fishing, playground. Pets welcome. Open May 1 - Sep 30. Rate in 2010 $24.95-29.95 for 2 persons. Member MACO. Phone: (218)326-8486.

(S) Sugar Bay Campground/Resort—(Itasca) *From west jct US 2 & US 169: Go 7-1/2 mi S on US 169, then 6 mi W CR 17, then 1/2 mi E on Moose Point Rd (CR 239). Enter on L.* ◊◊◊FACILITIES: 23 sites, typical site width 40 ft, 10 full hkups, 13 W&E, (20/30 amps), 4 pull-thrus, tenting, dump. ◊◊◊RECREATION: lake swim, boating, canoeing, ramp, dock, lake fishing. Pets welcome. Open May 1 - Oct 1. Rate in 2010 $25.50-31.50 for 2 persons. Member MRA. Phone: (218)326-8493.

GRANITE FALLS—E-2

(S) PRAIRIE VIEW RV PARK & CAMPGROUND—(Yellow Medicine) *From jct of Hwy 212 & Hwy 23: Go 3 mi S on Hwy 23, then 1/2 mi E on Hwy 274, then 1 mi E on Prairie's Edge Ln. Enter on L.*

WELCOME

COMFORTS OF HOME IN OUR BACKYARD!
Southwest Minnesota's largest and Newest RV Park. Featuring long pull-thrus, paved patios, storm shelter, 24/7 security, Free Wi-Fi, Laundry and Surveillance. Big Rigs Welcome!

◊◊◊◊◊FACILITIES: 55 sites, 26 full hkups, (30/50 amps), 29 no hkups, 26 pull-thrus, WiFi Instant Internet at site, WiFi Internet central location, family camping, tenting, laundry, groceries, RV supplies, LP gas by weight/by meter, ice, picnic tables, patios, fire rings, wood.

◊◊◊◊◊RECREATION: pavilion, coin games, swim pool, wading pool, hot tub, golf nearby, bsktball, playground, shuffleboard court shuffleboard court, horseshoes, sports field.

Pets welcome. Partial handicap access. Open May 4 - Oct 21. Big rigs welcome. Clubs welcome. Rate in 2010 $16-24 per vehicle. MC/VISA/DISC/AMEX/Debit.

Phone: (866)293-2121
Address: 5616 Prairie's Edge Ln, Granite Falls, MN 56241
Lat/Lon: 44.76399/-95.52939
Email: rvpark@prairieviewrvpark.com
Web: www.prairieviewrvpark.com

SEE AD TRAVEL SECTION PAGE 413

(S) PRAIRIE'S EDGE CASINO RESORT—*From jct of Hwy 212 & Hwy 23: Go 2.4 mi W on Hwy 23, then 0.4 mi S on Hwy 274, then 0.8 mi E on Prairie's Edge Ln. Enter at end.* New casino with hotel and convention facility. Separate non-smoking casino building. New expansions for casino & hotel to be completed Spring 2011. Open all yr. MC/VISA/DISC/AMEX/Debit. ATM.

WELCOME

Phone: (866)293-2121
Address: 5616 Prairie's Edge Ln, Granite Falls, MN 56241
Lat/Lon: 44.76305/-95.52720
Web: www.prairiesedgecasino.com

SEE AD TRAVEL SECTION PAGE 413

UPPER SIOUX AGENCY STATE PARK—(Yellow Medicine) *From jct Hwy 23 & Hwy 67 south of town: Go 8 mi E on Hwy 67.* FACILITIES: 34 sites, 14 E, (30/50 amps), 20 no hkups, 20 pull-thrus, tenting. RECREATION: boating, canoeing, ramp, river fishing, play equipment. Partial handicap access. Open all yr. Phone: (320)564-4777.

HAM LAKE—E-4

(N) Ham Lake Campground—(Anoka) *From jct Hwy 65 & Constance Blvd: Go 1 mi E on Constance Blvd (CR 60). Enter on R.* ◊◊◊◊FACILITIES: 143 sites, 55 full hkups, 75 W&E, (20/30/50 amps), 13 no hkups, 6 pull-thrus, family camping, tenting, dump, laundry, ltd groc. ◊◊◊◊RECREATION: lake swim, canoeing, lake/pond fishing, playground. Pets welcome ($). Partial handicap access. Age restrict may apply. Open May 1 - Nov 1. Rate in 2010 $30 per family. Member ARVC, MRA. Phone: (763)434-5337.

HASTINGS—E-4

(N) AFTON STATE PARK—(Dakota) *From jct US 61 & Hwy 95: Go 5 mi N on Hwy 95, then 3 mi E on CR 20.* FACILITIES: 24 sites, 24 no hkups, tenting. RECREATION: river swim, boating, canoeing, river fishing. Partial handicap access. Open all yr. Phone: (651)436-5391.

ST. CROIX BLUFFS REGIONAL PARK (Washington County Park)—(Washington) *From Hwy 95 & CR 76: Go 3 mi E on CR 76, then 1 mi S on CR 21. Enter on L.* FACILITIES: 62 sites, 21 W&E, 41 E, (50 amps), 26 pull-thrus, tenting, dump. RECREATION: river swim, boating, canoeing, ramp, river fishing, playground. No pets. Open all yr. Facilities fully operational May 28 - Oct 11. Phone: (651)430-8240.

HILL CITY—C-3

(S) Quadna Mountain Campground & RV Park—(Aitken) *From jct Hwy 200 & US 169: Go 1 mi S on US 169, then 1 mi E on CR 82 (Register at Lodge). Enter at end.* ◊◊◊FACILITIES: 49 sites, typical site width 30 ft, 31 full hkups, 18 W&E, (20/30/50 amps), 1 pull-thrus, tenting, dump. RECREATION: swim pool, lake swim, boating, canoeing, lake fishing. Pets welcome. Open May 1 - Oct 15. Rate in 2010 $18-20 for 2 persons. Phone: (800)422-6649.

HINCKLEY—D-4

(E) GRAND CASINO HINCKLEY RV RESORT—(Pine) *From jct I-35 & Hwy 48: Go 1 mi E on Hwy 48. Enter on R.*

WELCOME

◊◊◊◊◊FACILITIES: 271 sites, typical site width 35 ft, 271 full hkups, (30/50 amps), cable TV, ($), WiFi Instant Internet at site, family camping, cabins, RV storage, laundry, groceries, RV supplies, ice, picnic tables, patios, fire rings, grills, wood, controlled access.

◊◊◊◊◊RECREATION: rec room/area, pavilion, equipped pavilion, coin games, swim pool, hot tub, golf nearby, bsktball, playground, shuffleboard court 2 shuffleboard courts, activities, horseshoes, sports field, v-ball.

Pets welcome. Partial handicap access. No tents. Open all yr. Facilities fully operational Apr - Nov. Limited sites - Winter. Big rigs welcome. Clubs welcome. Rate in 2010 $23-28 MC/VISA/DISC/AMEX/Debit. Member MRA. FMCA discount.

Phone: (800)995-4726
Address: 1326 Fire Monument Rd., Hinckley, MN 55037
Lat/Lon: 46.01101/-92.91087
Email: hinsmk@grcasinos.com
Web: www.grandcasinosmn.com

SEE AD TRAVEL SECTION PAGE 412

(E) St. Croix Haven Campground—(Pine) *From jct I-35 & Hwy 48: Go 23-1/2 mi E on Hwy 48, then 1 mi N on CR 173 (Just before the river). Enter on R.* ◊◊◊FACILITIES: 166 sites, typical site width 50 ft, 70 full hkups, 92 W&E, 4 E, (20/30/50 amps), 2 pull-thrus, family camping, tenting, dump, laundry, groceries. ◊◊◊◊RECREATION: swim pool, river swim, canoeing, river fishing, playground. Pets welcome ($). Open May 1 - Oct 20. Big rigs welcome. Rate in 2010 $36-46 for 2 persons. Member MRA. Phone: (800)280-0166.

(SE) ST. CROIX STATE PARK—(Pine) *From jct I-35 (Hinckley exit) & Hwy 48: Go 15 mi E on Hwy 48, then 5 mi S on CR 22.* FACILITIES: 211 sites, 42 E, (20 amps), 169 no hkups, tenting, dump, laundry, ltd groc. RECREATION: river swim, canoeing, river/stream fishing, playground. Partial handicap access. Open all yr. Phone: (320)384-6591.

HOUSTON—F-5

(NW) Money Creek Haven, Inc.—(Houston) *From jct I-90 & Hwy 76: Go 8 mi S on Hwy 76, then 1/4 mi W on Hwy 26. Enter on R.* ◊◊◊FACILITIES: 205 sites, typical site width 50 ft, 14 full hkups, 178 W&E, (20/30/50 amps), 13 no hkups, 13 pull-thrus, family camping, tenting, dump, laundry, ltd groc. ◊◊◊RECREATION: swim pool, pond fishing, play equipment. Pets welcome. Open Apr 10 - Nov 30. Big rigs welcome. Green Friendly. Rate in 2010 $33-37 per family. Member MRA. Phone: (507)896-3544.

HOYT LAKES—B-4

(W) FISHERMAN'S POINT CAMPGROUND (City Park)—(St. Louis) *From jct Hwy 135 & CR 110: Go 5 mi N on CR 110 to Campground Rd. Enter on R.* FACILITIES: 70 sites, 64 E, 6 no hkups, 11 pull-thrus, tenting. RECREATION: boating, ramp, lake fishing, playground. Partial handicap access. Open May 1 - Sep 15. Phone: (218)225-3337.

IHLEN—F-1

SPLIT ROCK CREEK STATE PARK—(Pipestone) *From jct Hwy 23 & CR 2: Go 1/4 mi E on CR 2, then 1/2 mi S on CR 20.* FACILITIES: 28 sites, 19 E, 9 no hkups, tenting, dump. RECREATION: lake swim, boating, 9 hp limit, canoeing, ramp, dock, lake fishing, playground. Partial handicap access. Open May - Sep. Phone: (507)348-7908.

INTERNATIONAL FALLS—A-3

(S) Arnold's Campground & RV Park—(Koochiching) *From jct US 71/Hwy 11 & US 53: Go 1-1/4 mi S on US 53. Enter on L.* ◊◊◊FACILITIES: 19 sites,

10 full hkups, 9 E, (20/30/50 amps), 12 pull-thrus, family camping, tenting, dump. ◊RECREATION: play equipment. Pets welcome. Open May 1 - Oct 31. Rate in 2010 $15-20 per vehicle. Member MRA. Phone: (218)285-9100.

ISANTI—D-4

(SW) Country Camping RV Park—(Isanti) *From north town limits: Go 2-1/4 mi W on CR 5, then 1/2 mi S on Palm St NW/CR 8 /CR 10, then 1 mi S on Strike Blvd NW/CR 68, then 500 ft E on 277th Ave NW, then 1/2 mi S on Palm St NW. Enter at end.* ◊◊◊◊FACILITIES: 95 sites, typical site width 25 ft, 37 full hkups, 44 W&E, (20/30/50 amps), 14 no hkups, 6 pull-thrus, family camping, tenting, dump, laundry, ltd groc. ◊◊◊◊RECREATION: swim pool, river swim, canoeing, river fishing, playground. Pets welcome. Open May 1 - Oct 1. Big rigs welcome. Rate in 2010 $33-38 per family. Member MRA. Phone: (763)444-9626.

ISLE—D-3

(SW) FATHER HENNEPIN STATE PARK—(Cook) *From town: Go 1/4 mi W on Hwy 27.* FACILITIES: 103 sites, 41 E, (20/30 amps), 62 no hkups, tenting, dump. RECREATION: lake swim, boating, canoeing, ramp, dock, lake fishing, playground. Partial handicap access. Open all yr. Phone: (320)676-8763.

(SE) South Isle Family Campground—(Kanabec) *From jct of Hwy 27 & Hwy 47: Go 2 mi S on Hwy 47. Enter on L.* ◊◊◊FACILITIES: 130 sites, typical site width 40 ft, 43 full hkups, 87 W&E, (20/30/50 amps), 50 amps ($), family camping, tenting, dump, ltd groc. ◊◊◊◊RECREATION: swim pool, pond fishing, playground. Pets welcome. Open May 1 - Oct 1. Green Friendly. Rate in 2010 $27-46 for 2 persons. Member ARVC, MRA. Phone: (320)676-8538.

JACKSON—F-2

(N) Jackson-KOA—(Jackson) *From jct I-90 (exit 73) & US 71: Go 1/4 mi N on US 71, then 500 feet W on access road. Enter on L.* ◊◊◊◊FACILITIES: 76 sites, typical site width 35 ft, 34 full hkups, 27 W&E, 5 E, (20/30/50 amps), 50 amps ($), 10 no hkups, 51 pull-thrus, family camping, tenting, dump, laundry, groceries. ◊◊◊◊RECREATION: swim pool, playground. Pets welcome. Partial handicap access. Open Apr 15 - Oct 15. Big rigs welcome. Green Friendly. Rate in 2010 $26-39 for 2 persons. Member MRA. Phone: (800)KOA-5670. KOA discount.

JACOBSON—C-4

SAVANNA STATE FOREST (Hay Lake Campground)—(Aitkin) *From town: Go 2-1/2 mi S on Hwy 65,then 3 mi E, then 1 mi S.* FACILITIES: 20 sites, 20 ft max RV length, 20 no hkups, tenting. RECREATION: lake swim, boating, canoeing, ramp, lake fishing. Open all yr. Phone: (218)426-3271.

JORDAN—E-3

MINNESOTA VALLEY STATE PARK—(Hennepin) *From jct Hwy 282 & US 169: follow state park signs.* FACILITIES: 25 sites, 25 no hkups, tenting. RECREATION: river fishing. Open all yr. Phone: (952)492-6400.

KABETOGAMA LAKE—A-4

(NW) KABETOGAMA STATE FOREST (Woodenfrog Campground)—(St. Louis) *From jct US 53 & CR 122: Go 2-1/2 mi N on CR 122, then 3-1/3 mi W on CR 122, then 3/4 mi N on Waltz Rd.* FACILITIES: 61 sites, 61 no hkups, tenting, groceries. RECREATION: lake swim, boating, canoeing, ramp, dock, lake fishing. Partial handicap access. Open May 1 - Nov 30. Phone: (218)365-7229.

LAKE BRONSON—A-1

(E) LAKE BRONSON STATE PARK—(Kittson) *From town: Go 2 mi E on CR 28.* FACILITIES: 157 sites, 35 E, (20/30 amps), 122 no hkups, tenting, dump. RECREATION: lake swim, boating, canoeing, ramp, dock, lake/river fishing, playground. Partial handicap access. Open all yr. Phone: (218)754-2200.

LAKE CITY—E-4

(NW) FRONTENAC STATE PARK—(Wabasha) *From jct US 63 & US 61: Go 7 mi NW on US 63/61 (Frontenac), then 1 mi E on CR 2.* FACILITIES: 58 sites, 19 E, (30 amps), 39 no hkups, tenting, dump. RECREATION: lake/river/stream fishing. Partial handicap access. Open all yr. Facilities fully operational May 1 - Oct 22. Phone: (651)345-3401.

LAKE CITY—Continued on next page

LAKE CITY—Continued

(N) LAKE PEPIN CAMPGROUNDS & TRAILER COURT—(Goodhue) *From south jct US 63 & US 61: Go 1-1/4 mi NW on US 61/63. Enter on L.*

WELCOME

◆◆◆FACILITIES: 58 sites, typical site width 30 ft, 18 full hkups, 18 W&E, 10 E, (20/30/50 amps), 12 no hkups, some extd stay sites, 5 pull-thrus, family camping, tenting, RV storage, dump, RV supplies, ice, picnic tables, fire rings, wood.

◆RECREATION: golf nearby, bsktball, playground, sports field.

Pets welcome. Open Apr 15 - Oct 15. No outside firewood allowed. Big rigs welcome. Green Friendly. Rate in 2010 $17-28 for 2 persons. Member MRA.

Phone: (651)345-2909
Address: 1818 N High, Lake City, MN 55041
Lat/Lon: 44.46272/-92.28643

SEE AD PAGE 421

LAKE ELMO—E-4

(SW) LAKE ELMO PARK RESERVE (Washington County Park)—(Washington) *From jct I-694 & I-94: Go 3 mi E on I-94, then 1 mi N on CR 19. Enter at end.* FACILITIES: 80 sites, 80 E, (20/30 amps), 6 pull-thrus, tenting, dump. RECREATION: boating, canoeing, ramp, dock, lake fishing, playground. Partial handicap access. Open May - Oct. Phone: (651)430-8370.

LAKE LILLIAN—E-2

(W) KANDIYOHI COUNTY PARK NUMBER 1—(Kandiyohi) *From jct Hwy-7 & CR-8: Go 5 mi W on Hwy-7, then 3 mi N on CR-81.* FACILITIES: 94 sites, 94 E, 25 pull-thrus, tenting, dump, laundry, groceries. RECREATION: lake swim, boating, canoeing, ramp, dock, lake fishing, playground. Partial handicap access. Open May - Oct. Phone: (320)995-6599.

(N) KANDIYOHI COUNTY PARK NUMBER 2—(Kandiyohi) *From jct Hwy-7 & CR-8: Go 4 mi N on CR-8, then 1-3/4 mi NW on CR-132.* FACILITIES: 105 sites, 75 E, 30 no hkups, tenting, dump, ltd groc. RECREATION: lake swim, boating, canoeing, ramp, dock, lake fishing, playground. Partial handicap access. Open May 3 - Oct 30. Phone: (320)644-4707.

LAKEFIELD—F-2

(NE) KILEN WOODS STATE PARK—(Jackson) *From jct I-90 & Hwy 86: Go 6 mi N on Hwy 86, then 5 mi E on CR 24.* FACILITIES: 33 sites, 11 E, 22 no hkups, 3 pull-thrus, tenting, dump. RECREATION: boating, canoeing, river fishing. Partial handicap access. Open all yr. Phone: (507)662-6258.

LANESBORO—F-5

(NE) Eagle Cliff Campground & Lodging—(Fillmore) *From jct US 52 & Hwy 16: Go 9 mi E on Hwy 16. Enter on L.* ◆◆◆◆FACILITIES: 214 sites, typical site width 45 ft, 109 full hkups, 53 W&E, 6 E, (20/30/50 amps), 46 no hkups, 18 pull-thrus, family camping, tenting, dump, laundry, ltd groc. ◆◆◆◆◆RECREATION: river swim, canoeing, river fishing, playground. Pets welcome. Partial handicap access. Open Apr 1 - Dec 1. Big rigs welcome. Green Friendly. Rate in 2010 $24-29 for 2 persons. Member MRA. Phone: (507)467-2598.

(N) Highway 250 Campground—(Fillmore) *From jct SR 16 & SR 250 : Go 1 mi NE thru Lanesboro on Hwy 250. Enter on R.* ◆◆FACILITIES: 98 sites, 65 full hkups, 33 W&E, (20/30/50 amps), 20 pull-thrus, family camping, tenting, dump. ◆◆◆RECREATION: river swim, canoeing, river fishing. Pets welcome. Open Apr 1 - Nov 1. Rate in 2010 $25 for 2 persons. Phone: (507)467-3395.

LE ROY—F-4

(N) LAKE LOUISE STATE PARK—(Mower) *From town: Go 1-1/2 mi N on CR 14.* FACILITIES: 20 sites, 11 E, 9 no hkups, tenting, dump. RECREATION: lake swim, boating, electric motors only, canoeing, lake/river fishing. Partial handicap access. Open all yr. Phone: (507)324-5249.

LITTLE FALLS—D-3

(SW) CHARLES A LINDBERGH STATE PARK—(Harrison) *From jct Hwy 27 & CR 52 (Lindbergh Drive S): Go 1-1/2 mi SW on CR 52.* FACILITIES: 38 sites, 15 E, 23 no hkups, tenting, dump. RECREATION: boating, canoeing, ramp, river fishing, playground. Partial handicap access. Open all yr. Phone: (320)616-2525.

LONG PRAIRIE—D-2

(N) Camp RnL RV Park/Campground—(Todd) *From N jct SR-27 & US-71: Go 3/4 mi N on US 71. Enter on L.* ◆◆◆FACILITIES: 24 sites, typical site width 40 ft, 18 full hkups, 4 W&E, 2 E, (20/30/50 amps), 8 pull-thrus, family camping, tenting, dump. Pets welcome. Partial handicap access. Open Apr 10 - Oct 10. Rate in 2010 $22 for 2 persons. Member MRA. Phone: (800)226-7765.

LUVERNE—F-1

(NE) BLUE MOUNDS STATE PARK—(Rock) *From town: Go 4 mi N on US 75, then 1 mi E on CR 20.* FACILITIES: 73 sites, 40 E, 33 no hkups, tenting, dump. RECREATION: lake/river swim, boating, no motors, canoeing, lake fishing, playground. Partial handicap access. Open all yr. Phone: (507)283-1307.

LYND—E-1

(SW) CAMDEN STATE PARK—(Lyon) *From town: Go 2 mi SW on Hwy 23.* FACILITIES: 80 sites, 29 E, (30 amps), 51 no hkups, 7 pull-thrus, tenting, dump. RECREATION: boating, electric motors only, canoeing, ramp, lake/river fishing, playground. Partial handicap access. Open all yr. Phone: (507)865-4530.

MADELIA—F-3

WATONA PARK (City Park)—(Watonwan) *In town at jct Hwys-60 & 15.* FACILITIES: 32 sites, 14 full hkups, 10 W&E, 8 E, tenting, dump. RECREATION: swim pool, canoeing, ramp, river fishing, playground. Open Apr 15 - Oct 15. Phone: (507)642-3245.

MADISON LAKE—F-3

(N) BRAY PARK (Blue Earth County Park)—(Blue Earth) *From jct US-14 & Hwy-60: Go 4 mi N on Hwy-60, then 1-1/2 mi E on Hwy-60, then 2 mi S on CR-48.* FACILITIES: 43 sites, typical site width 8 ft, 43 W&E, tenting, dump. RECREATION: lake swim, boating, ramp, dock, lake fishing, playground. Partial handicap access. Open May 1 - Oct 31. Phone: (507)243-3885.

MAHNOMEN—C-1

(S) Shooting Star RV Park and Casino—(Mahnomen) *From jct Hwy 200 & US 59: Go 1 mi S on US 59. Enter on R.* ◆◆◆◆FACILITIES: 47 sites, typical site width 30 ft, 47 full hkups, (20/30/50 amps), 28 pull-thrus, dump, laundry. ◆◆◆RECREATION: swim pool, play equipment. Pets welcome. Open May 15 - Oct 15. Big rigs welcome. Rate in 2010 $18-20 per vehicle. Member MRA. Phone: (800)453-STAR.

MALMO—C-3

(N) Pete's Retreat Family Campground & RV Park—(Aitkin) *From jct Hwy 18 & Hwy 47: Go 9 mi N on Hwy 47. Enter on L.* ◆◆◆◆◆FACILITIES: 99 sites, 99 full hkups, (20/30/50 amps), 20 pull-thrus, cable TV, WiFi Instant Internet at site, family camping, tenting, RV storage, ltd groc, RV supplies, ice, picnic tables, fire rings, wood. ◆◆◆◆◆RECREATION: pavilion, swim pool, wading pool, hot tub, pond fishing, bsktball, playground, activities, horseshoes, v-ball. Pets welcome. Partial handicap access. Open May 1 - Oct 1. Big rigs welcome. Rate in 2010 $44-52 for 4 persons. MC/VISA/DISC/Debit. Member MRA. CCUSA 50% Discount. CCUSA reservations Required, CCUSA max stay Unlimited, CCUSA disc. not avail F,Sa, CCUSA disc. not avail holidays.

CAMPCLUB USA

Phone: (866)578-7275
Address: 22337 State Hwy 47, Aitkin, MN 56431
Lat/Lon: 46.33822/-93.51612
Email: joan@petesretreat.com
Web: www.petesretreat.com

MANKATO—F-3

(W) MINNEOPA STATE PARK—(Blue Earth) *From jct US 169/Hwy 60 & Hwy 68W: Go 1 mi W on Hwy 68W, follow signs.* FACILITIES: 61 sites, 6 E, 55 no hkups, tenting. RECREATION: boating, canoeing, river/stream fishing. Partial handicap access. Open all yr. Phone: (507)389-5464.

MAPLETON—F-3

(S) DALY PARK (Blue Earth County Park)—(Blue Earth) *From town: Go 3 mi S on CR-7, then 2 mi W on CR-191.* FACILITIES: 86 sites, 67 W&E, 19 no hkups, tenting, dump. RECREATION: lake swim, boating, ramp, dock, lake fishing, playground. Open May 1 - Oct 31. Phone: (507)524-3000.

Minnesota State Gem: Lake Superior Agate

MARCELL—B-3

(NE) CHIPPEWA NATIONAL FOREST (Clubhouse Lake Campground)—(Itasca) *From town: Go 1/2 mi N on Hwy-38, then 5 mi E on CR-45, then 1-1/4 mi N on FR-2181, then 1-1/4 mi E on FR-3758.* FACILITIES: 47 sites, 47 no hkups, tenting. RECREATION: lake swim, boating, ramp, lake fishing. Partial handicap access. Open May 5 - Oct 13. Phone: (218)246-2123.

(SE) CHIPPEWA NATIONAL FOREST (North Star Campground)—(Itasca) *From town: Go 3-1/2 mi SE on Hwy 38.* FACILITIES: 38 sites, 38 no hkups, tenting, dump. RECREATION: lake swim, boating, ramp. Partial handicap access. Open May 5 - Oct 13. Phone: (218)832-3161.

MCGREGOR—C-4

(N) SANDY LAKE RECREATION AREA (COE Sandy Lake Reservoir)—(Aitkin) *From town: Go 12 mi N on Hwy 65.* FACILITIES: 43 sites, 36 ft max RV length, 43 E, 5 pull-thrus, tenting, dump, laundry. RECREATION: lake/river swim, boating, canoeing, ramp, dock, lake/river fishing, playground. Partial handicap access. Open May - Sep. Phone: (218)426-3482.

(NE) SAVANNA PORTAGE STATE PARK—(Aitkin) *From town: Go 7 mi N on Hwy 65, then 10 mi NE on CR 14.* FACILITIES: 61 sites, 18 E, 43 no hkups, 4 pull-thrus, tenting, dump. RECREATION: lake swim, boating, electric motors only, canoeing, ramp, dock, lake/river fishing, playground. Partial handicap access. Open all yr. Facilities fully operational May 15 - Sep 15. Phone: (218)426-3271.

MELROSE—D-2

(NE) BIRCH LAKE STATE FOREST (Birch Lake Campground)—(Stearns) *From jct I-94/US 52 & CR 13: Go 5-1/2 mi N on CR 13, then 1-1/2 mi E on CR 17, then 3-1/2 mi N on township road.* FACILITIES: 29 sites, 20 ft max RV length, 29 no hkups, tenting. RECREATION: lake swim, boating, ramp, dock, lake fishing, playground. Partial handicap access. Open May 1 - Oct 15. Phone: (320)616-2525.

MENAHGA—C-2

(E) HUNTERSVILLE STATE FOREST (Huntersville Landing)—(Wadena) *From jct CR 17 & CR 23: Go 1 mi N on CR 23, then 3 mi E on CR 18, then 1 mi S, then 2 mi E.* FACILITIES: 24 sites, 20 ft max RV length, 24 no hkups, tenting. RECREATION: river swim, boating, canoeing, river fishing. Partial handicap access. Open May 15 - Sep 15. Phone: (218)472-2100.

MILTONA—D-2

(NE) Lazy Days Campground—(Douglas) *From S jct County 14 & SR 29: Go 2 mi N on SR 29, then 4 mi E on County Rd 36. Enter on L.* ◆◆◆FACILITIES: 99 sites, typical site width 55 ft, 99 full hkups, (30/50 amps), 10 pull-thrus, family camping, tenting, ltd groc. ◆◆◆◆RECREATION: swim pool, playground. Pets welcome ($), quantity restrict. Partial handicap access. Open May 1 - Oct 1. Big rigs welcome. Rate in 2010 $32 for 4 persons. Member MRA.

Phone: (218)943-3000
Address: 10247 County Road 36 NE, Miltona, MN 56354
Lat/Lon: 46.07820/-95.23643
Web: www.lazydaysmiltona.com

MINNEAPOLIS—E-4

ST. PAUL/MINNEAPOLIS AREA MAP

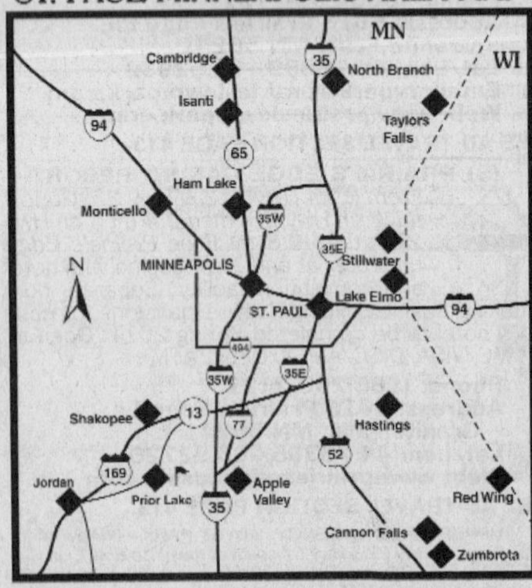

Symbols on map indicate towns within a 50 mi radius of St. Paul where campgrounds (diamonds), attractions (flags), & RV service centers & camping supply outlets (gears) are listed. Check listings for more information.

Tell Them Woodall's Sent You!

MINNEAPOLIS—Continued on next page

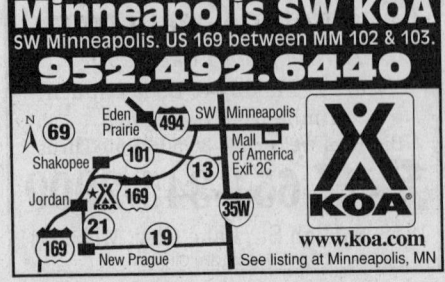

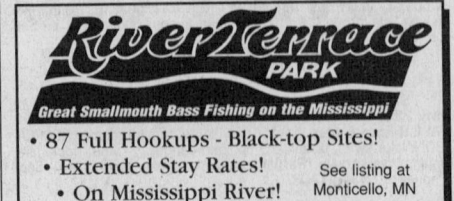

MINNEAPOLIS—Continued

(SW) KOA-MINNEAPOLIS SOUTHWEST—(Scott) *From jct I-494 & US 169: Go 18 mi S on US 169, then 500 ft E on E 166th St. Enter at end.*

WELCOME

◊◊◊◊FACILITIES: 118 sites, typical site width 35 ft, 35 full hkups, 66 W&E, (20/30/50 amps ($), 17 no hkups, 50 pull-thrus, WiFi Instant Internet at site, family camping, tenting, cabins, dump, non-guest dump $, laundry, groceries, RV supplies, LP gas by weight/by meter, ice, picnic tables, patios, fire rings, wood.

◊◊◊◊RECREATION: rec hall, rec room/area, swim pool, mini-golf, ($), golf nearby, bsktball, 6 bike rentals, playground, activities, (wkends), horseshoes, sports field, v-ball.

Pets welcome, breed restrict. Open May 1 - Oct 15. Big rigs welcome. Escort to site. Clubs welcome. Rate in 2010 $32-42 for 2 persons. MC/VISA/Debit. Member MRA. KOA discount.

Phone: (952)492-6440
Address: 3315 W 166th St, Jordan, MN 55352
Lat/Lon: 44.70940/-93.59103
Email: minneapolisswkoa@hotmail.com
Web: www.koa.com

SEE AD PAGE 422

(N) LOWRY GROVE—(Hennepin) *From jct I-694 & I-35W: Go 5 mi S on I-35W (exit 22), then 1 mi N on St. Anthony Pkwy, then 1/2 mi W on Kenzie Terrace. Enter on R.*

WELCOME

◊◊◊FACILITIES: 64 sites, typical site width 25 ft, 64 full hkups, (30/50 amps), some extd stay sites, 3 pull-thrus, phone Internet central location, family camping, RV storage, laundry, picnic tables, patios.

RECREATION: golf nearby.

Pets welcome. No tents. Open all yr. Seasonals must be in by Oct 31 & spend entire winter. No overnight sites after Oct 31. Big rigs welcome. Clubs welcome. Green Friendly. Rate in 2010 $45 per vehicle. MC/VISA/Debit. Member MRA.

Phone: (612)781-3148
Address: 2501 Lowry Ave NE, St. Anthony Village, MN 55418
Lat/Lon: 45.01384/-93.22499
Email: adeline@pljrealty.com
Web: www.pljrealty.com

SEE AD THIS PAGE

(NW) MINNEAPOLIS NW KOA CAMPGROUND—(Hennepin) *From I-94 (exit 213): Go 300 yds S on Maple Grove Pkwy, then 1-1/2 mi W on CR 30, then 3/4 mi N on CR 101. Enter on R.*

WELCOME

◊◊◊◊FACILITIES: 170 sites, typical site width 35 ft, 40 full hkups, 110 W&E, (20/30/50 amps), 50 amps ($), 20 no hkups, some extd stay sites, 50 pull-thrus, WiFi Instant Internet at site, WiFi Internet central location, family camping, tenting, cabins, dump, non-guest dump $, portable dump, laundry, groceries, RV supplies, LP gas by weight/by meter, ice, picnic tables, fire rings, grills, wood.

MINNEAPOLIS—Continued
MINNEAPOLIS NW KOA CAMPGROUND—Continued

◊◊◊◊RECREATION: rec hall, rec room/area, coin games, swim pool, mini-golf, ($), golf nearby, bsktball, playground, shuffleboard court 2 shuffleboard courts, horseshoes, sports field.

Pets welcome, breed restrict. Open Apr 1 - Oct 15. Big rigs welcome. Clubs welcome. Green Friendly. Rate in 2010 $31-40 for 2 persons. MC/VISA/Debit. Member MRA. KOA discount.

Phone: (763)420-2255
Address: 10410 Brockton Ln N, Maple Grove, MN 55311
Lat/Lon: 45.14442/-93.52189
Email: mplsnwkoa@aol.com
Web: www.mplsnwkoa.com

SEE AD THIS PAGE

(S) Town & Country Campground & RV Park—(Scott) *From jct I-35 W (exit 3B) & CR 13: Go 4-1/2 mi W on CR 13, then follow CR 13 S, then 1/2 mi W on 126th St, then 50 ft S on Boone Ave. Enter on L.* ◊◊◊◊FACILITIES: 85 sites, typical site width 30 ft, 50 full hkups, 34 W&E, (20/30/50 amps), 50 amps ($), 1 no hkups, 18 pull-thrus, family camping, tenting, dump, laundry, ltd groc. ◊◊◊RECREATION: swim pool, stream fishing, playground. Pets welcome ($), breed restrict. Partial handicap access. Age restrict may apply. Open all yr. Facilities fully operational Apr 15 - Oct 15. Big rigs welcome. Rate in 2010 $36-38 for 2 persons. Member ARVC, MRA. Phone: (952)445-1756.

MONTEVIDEO—E-2

(NW) LAC QUI PARLE STATE PARK—(Chippewa) *From town: Go 12 mi NW on US 59, then 4 mi W on CR 13 and CR 33.* FACILITIES: 67 sites, 9 full hkups, 37 E, 21 no hkups, tenting, dump. RECREATION: lake/river swim, boating, canoeing, ramp, dock, lake/river fishing. Partial handicap access. Open all yr. Facilities fully operational May 13 - Oct 23. Phone: (320)752-4736.

MONTICELLO—E-3

(W) RIVER TERRACE PARK—(Wright) *From jct I-94 (exit 193) & Hwy 25: Go 1/2 mi NE on Hwy 25, then 1 mi W on Broadway (Hwy 75), then 1/2 mi N on Ottercreek Rd. Turns to River Street West. Enter on R.*

WELCOME

◊◊◊◊FACILITIES: 87 sites, typical site width 35 ft, 87 full hkups, (20/30/50 amps), many extd stay sites, 15 pull-thrus, family camping, tenting, RV storage, dump, non-guest dump $, laundry, ice, picnic tables, fire rings, wood.

◊◊◊RECREATION: rec hall, coin games, boating, canoeing, ramp, river fishing, golf nearby, bsktball, playground, horseshoes, v-ball.

Pets welcome. Open Apr 1 - Oct 30. Facilities fully operational Memorial Day - Labor Day. Big rigs welcome. Clubs welcome. Rate in 2010 $29-33 for 6 persons.

MONTICELLO—Continued
RIVER TERRACE PARK—Continued

Phone: (763)295-2264
Address: 1335 River St W, Monticello, MN 55362
Lat/Lon: 45.31568/-93.81699

SEE AD MINNEAPOLIS PAGE 422

MOORHEAD—C-1

(E) KOA-Fargo-Moorhead—(Clay) *From jct US 75 & I-94 (exit 1): Go 1-1/2 mi E on I-94 (exit 2), then 1 mi E on north side frontage road (gravel). Enter on L.* ◊◊◊◊FACILITIES: 75 sites, typical site width 20 ft, 16 full hkups, 59 W&E, (20/30/50 amps), 27 pull-thrus, family camping, tenting, dump, laundry, groceries. ◊◊◊RECREATION: swim pool, playground. Pets welcome, breed restrict. Open May 1 - Oct 15. Big rigs welcome. Rate in 2010 $32.47-39.59 for 6 persons. Member MRA. Phone: (800)KOA-0271. KOA discount.

MOOSE LAKE—C-4

(W) MOOSE LAKE CITY PARK—(Carlton) *From jct I-35 & Hwy 73N: Go 1 mi N on Hwy 73N, then 3 blocks E on 2nd St, then 2 blocks N on Birch St, then E on 4th St.* FACILITIES: 87 sites, 22 full hkups, 65 W&E, (30/50 amps), 6 pull-thrus, tenting, dump. RECREATION: lake swim, boating, canoeing, ramp, dock, lake fishing, playground. Partial handicap access. Open May - Sep. Phone: (218)485-4761.

MOOSE LAKE STATE PARK—(Pine) *From jct I-35 & CR 137: Go 1/4 mi E on CR 137.* FACILITIES: 33 sites, 20 E, (30 amps), 13 no hkups, tenting. RECREATION: lake swim, boating, ramp, lake/river fishing, playground. Partial handicap access. Open all yr. Facilities fully operational May 15 - Sep 30. Phone: (218)485-5420.

MORA—D-4

(N) Captain Dan's Crow's Nest Resort—(Kanabec) *From jct Hwy 23 & Hwy 65: Go 8 mi N on Hwy 65. Enter on L.* ◊◊◊FACILITIES: 57 sites, typical site width 25 ft, 35 full hkups, 22 W&E, (20/30 amps), 5 pull-thrus, family camping, tenting, dump, laundry, groceries. ◊◊◊RECREATION: lake swim, boating, canoeing, dock, lake fishing, play equipment. Pets welcome. Open May 1 - Oct 1. Rate in 2010 $38.48 for 4 persons. Phone: (320)679-1977.

MORRISTOWN—F-3

(W) Camp Maiden Rock West—(Rice) *Jct I-35 & Hwy 60: Go 8 1/2 mi W on Hwy 60, then 1/4 mi N on cty Rd 99. Enter on R.* ◊◊◊FACILITIES: 66 sites, typical site width 35 ft, 25 full hkups, 25 W&E, (20/30/50 amps), 16 no hkups, 2 pull-thrus, tenting, dump. ◊◊◊RECREATION: swim pool, canoeing, river/pond fishing. Pets welcome. Open May 15 - Oct 1. Rate in 2010 $32-38 for 4 persons. Phone: (507)685-2240.

Although often called the "Land of 10,000 Lakes", Minnesota actually has over 12,000 lakes.

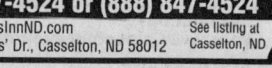

MORTON—E-2

Jackpot Junction RV Park—(Redwood) *From jct US 71/Hwy 19 & CR 2: Go 1 mi S on CR 2. Enter on R.* ◊◊◊◊FACILITIES: 70 sites, 70 full hkups, (20/30/50 amps), 24 pull-thrus, dump, groceries. Pets welcome. Partial handicap access. No tents. Open Mid Apr - Mid Oct. Big rigs welcome. Rate in 2010 $16-40 for 2 persons. Member MRA. Phone: (800)946-0077.

NERSTRAND—E-4

(W) NERSTRAND BIG WOODS STATE PARK—(Rice) *From town: Go 2 mi W.* FACILITIES: 51 sites, 27 W&E, 24 no hkups, 1 pull-thrus, tenting, dump. RECREATION: playground. Partial handicap access. Open all yr. Phone: (507)333-8848.

NEW LONDON—E-2

(W) KANDIYOHI COUNTY PARK NUMBER 7—(Kandiyohi) *From jct US 71 & CR 40: Go 4 mi W on CR 40, then 2 mi N on CR 5.* FACILITIES: 56 sites, 56 W&E, (50 amps), tenting, dump, laundry, ltd groc. RECREATION: lake swim, boating, canoeing, ramp, dock, lake fishing, playground. Partial handicap access. Open May - Oct. Phone: (320)354-4453.

NEW ULM—F-3

(SW) FLANDRAU STATE PARK—(Brown) *From jct Hwy 15 & Hwy 68 in town: Go 2/3 mi SW on 10th St, then S on Summit Ave.* FACILITIES: 92 sites, 34 E, (30 amps), 58 no hkups, 1 pull-thrus, tenting, dump. RECREATION: swim pool, river fishing, playground. Partial handicap access. Open all yr. Facilities fully operational May 1 - mid Oct. Phone: (507)233-9800.

NISSWA—C-3

(W) Fritz's Resort, Campground & Golf Course—(CrowWing) *From jct CR 77/33 & SR 371 (N town limit): Go 3 mi N on SR 371. Enter on L.* ◊◊◊◊FACILITIES: 92 sites, typical site width 25 ft, 92 full hkups, (20/30/50 amps), 50 amps ($), 15 pull-thrus, family camping, dump, laundry, ltd groc. ◊◊◊◊RECREATION: lake swim, boating, canoeing, dock, lake fishing, playground. No pets. No tents. Open May 1 - Oct 1. Rate in 2010 $39 for 4 persons. Phone: (218)568-8988.

NODINE—F-5

(N) GREAT RIVER BLUFFS STATE PARK—(Winona) *From jct I-90 (exit 266) & CR 12: Go N to end of CR 12, then 1 mi E on CR 3 (Scenic Apple Blossom Dr), then right 1 mi on gravel access road.* FACILITIES: 31 sites, 31 no hkups, tenting. RECREATION: playground. Partial handicap access. Open May 26 - Sep 3. Phone: (507)643-6849.

NORTH BRANCH—D-4

(W) Kozy Oaks Kamp—(Isanti) *From jct I-35 (exit 147) & Hwy 95: Go 1 mi W on Hwy 95, then 2-1/4 mi W on CR 13, then 2-1/2 mi S on CR 18, then 1/2 mi E on 277th Ave NE. Enter on R.* ◊◊FACILITIES: 100 sites, typical site width 25 ft, 86 W&E, (20/30 amps), 14 no hkups, 10 pull-thrus, family camping, tenting, dump, ltd groc. ◊◊◊RECREATION: swim pool, canoeing, dock, play equipment. Pets welcome. Open Apr 15 - Oct 15. Rate in 2010 $20.50-23 per family. Phone: (651)674-8471.

WILD RIVER STATE PARK—(Chicago) *From jct I-35 (North Branch exit) & Hwy 95: Go 12 mi E on Hwy 95, then 3 mi N on CR 12.* FACILITIES: 96 sites, 17 E, 79 no hkups, 2 pull-thrus, tenting, dump. RECREATION: boating, canoeing, ramp, river/stream fishing. Partial handicap access. Open all yr. Phone: (651)583-2125.

ONAMIA—D-3

(NW) MILLE LACS KATHIO STATE PARK—(Mille Lacs) *From town: Go 8 mi NW on US 169, then 3/4 mi S on CR 26.* FACILITIES: 70 sites, 22 E, (20/30 amps), 48 no hkups, 3 pull-thrus, tenting, dump. RECREATION: river swim, boating, canoeing, ramp, dock, lake/river fishing, playground. Partial handicap access. Open all yr. Facilities fully operational May - Mid Oct. Phone: (320)532-3523.

ORR—B-4

(S) Pine Acres Resort & Campground—(St. Louis) *From jct US 53 & CR 23: Go 1-1/2 mi S on US 53, then 1/2 mi W on CR 23, then 3/4 mi N on Hitchcock Rd. (CR 515) 3/4 mi strait ahead on gravel road. Enter on R.* ◊◊◊FACILITIES: 70 sites, typical site width 20 ft, 34 ft max RV length, 20 full hkups, 50 W&E, (20/30 amps), family camping, tenting, dump, ltd groc. ◊◊◊◊RECREATION: lake swim, boating, canoeing, ramp, dock, lake fishing, playground. Pets welcome, breed restrict. Open May 10 - Sep 15. Rate in 2010 $26-33 per family. Phone: (800)777-7231.

SUPERIOR NATIONAL FOREST (Echo Lake Campground)—(St. Louis) *From town: Go 15 mi NE on CR-23, then 4 mi N on CR-24, then 1 mi SE on CR-116 (Echo Trail), then 3/4 mi N on FR-841.* FACILITIES: 24 sites, 24 no hkups, tenting. RECREATION: lake swim, boating, ramp, dock, lake fishing, playground. Open May 15 - Oct 5. Phone: (218)666-5251.

ORTONVILLE—E-1

(NW) BIG STONE LAKE STATE PARK—(Big Stone) *From jct Hwy-7 & US-12: Go 8 mi NW on Hwy-7.* FACILITIES: 37 sites, 10 E, 27 no hkups, tenting, dump. RECREATION: lake swim, boating, ramp, lake fishing, playground. Partial handicap access. Open Apr 1 - Dec 31. Phone: (320)839-3663.

(N) Lakeshore RV Park, Inc—(Big Stone) *From jct US 12 & Hwy 7: Go 3 mi N on Hwy 7. Enter on L.* ◊◊◊◊FACILITIES: 94 sites, typical site width 20 ft, 94 full hkups, (20/30/50 amps), 30 pull-thrus, tenting, laundry, ltd groc. ◊◊◊◊◊RECREATION: swim pool, boating, ramp, dock, lake fishing, playground. Pets welcome. Open Apr 15 - Oct 1. Big rigs welcome. Rate in 2010 $32.95 for 4 persons. Member ARVC, MRA. Phone: (800)936-7386.

OUTING—C-3

(N) LAND O'LAKES STATE FOREST (Clint Converse Memorial Campground)—(Cass) *From town: Go 2 mi N on Hwy-6, then 1-1/2 mi W on CR-48.* FACILITIES: 31 sites, 26 ft max RV length, 31 no hkups, tenting. RECREATION: lake swim, boating, ramp, dock, lake fishing. Pets welcome. Partial handicap access. Open May - Nov. Phone: (218)546-5926.

OWATONNA—F-4

(E) RICE LAKE STATE PARK—(Steele) *From I-35 (exit 42A-Owatonna): Go E & S on Hoffman Dr to third stoplight, then 8 mi E on Rose St (becomes CR 19 at city limits).* FACILITIES: 42 sites, 16 E, 26 no hkups, tenting. RECREATION: lake swim, boating, canoeing, ramp, dock, lake fishing, playground. Partial handicap access. Open all yr. Phone: (507)455-5871.

(S) Riverview Campground—(Steele) *From jct I-35 (exit 40) & US-14E/US-218: Go 1-1/2 mi E on US-14E/US-218, then 1/2 mi S on CR-45, then 1-1/2 mi W on CR-18. Enter on R.* ◊◊◊◊FACILITIES: 145 sites, typical site width 30 ft, 83 full hkups, 51 W&E, (30/50 amps), 11 no hkups, 12 pull-thrus, family camping, tenting, dump, laundry, groceries. ◊◊◊◊RECREATION: swim pool, river fishing, playground. Pets welcome. Open May 1 - Oct 1. Big rigs welcome. Rate in 2010 $35-45 for 2 persons. Member MRA. Phone: (507)451-8050.

PARK RAPIDS—C-2

(N) Breeze Camping & RV Resort—(Hubbard) *From jct Hwy-34 & US-71: Go 9 mi N on US-71, then 1/2 block E on CR-89. Enter on R.* ◊◊◊◊FACILITIES: 123 sites, typical site width 35 ft, 35 ft max RV length, 88 full hkups, 35 W&E, (20/30/50 amps), family camping, tenting, dump, laundry, ltd groc. ◊◊◊◊RECREATION: swim pool, boating, canoeing, ramp, dock, lake fishing, playground. Pets welcome. Open May 1 - Oct 1. Rate in 2010 $30-34 for 2 persons. Member MRA. Phone: (218)732-5888.

(N) ITASCA STATE PARK—(Hubbard) *From jct Hwy 34 & US 71: Go 21 mi N on US 71 to south entrance.* FACILITIES: 223 sites, 100 E, 123 no hkups, tenting, dump. RECREATION: lake swim, boating, canoeing, ramp, lake/river/stream fishing, playground. Partial handicap access. Open all yr. Phone: (218)266-2100.

PAUL BUNYAN STATE FOREST (Mantrap Lake Campground)—(Hubbard) *From town: Go 12 mi NE on CR-4, then 1-1/2 mi E on CR-24, then 3/4 mi N on CR-104.* FACILITIES: 38 sites, 26 ft max RV length, 38 no hkups, tenting. RECREATION: lake swim, boating, ramp, dock, lake fishing, playground. Partial handicap access. Open May - Oct. Phone: (218)266-2100.

(N) Vagabond Village Campground—(Hubbard) *From jct Hwy 34 & US 71: Go 7 mi N on US 71, then 6 mi E on CR 40, then 1/2 mi S on Green Pines Rd. Enter on R.* ◊◊◊◊FACILITIES: 125 sites, typical site width 50 ft, 98 full hkups, 27 W&E, (20/30/50 amps), 10 pull-thrus, family camping, tenting, dump, laundry, ltd groc. ◊◊◊◊◊RECREATION: swim pool, lake swim, boating, canoeing, ramp, dock, lake fishing, playground. Pets welcome. Open May 15 - Oct 1. Big rigs welcome. Rate in 2010 $38-41 for 2 persons. Member ARVC, MRA. Phone: (218)732-5234.

PELICAN RAPIDS—C-1

(E) MAPLEWOOD STATE PARK—(Otter Tail) *From jct US 59 & Hwy 108: Go 7 mi E on Hwy 108.* FACILITIES: 71 sites, 35 ft max RV length, 32 E, (50 amps), 39 no hkups, tenting, dump. RECREATION: lake swim, boating, canoeing, ramp, lake fishing. Partial handicap access. Open all yr. Phone: (218)863-8383.

SHERIN MEMORIAL CAMPGROUND (City Park)—(Otter Tail) *In town on Hwy-108.* FACILITIES: 30 sites, 35 ft max RV length, 10 E, (15/20/30/50 amps), 20 no hkups, tenting, dump, laundry, ltd groc. RECREATION: swim pool, lake fishing, playground. Open May 15 - Sep 15. Phone: (218)863-6571.

PILLAGER—D-3

(N) PILLSBURY STATE FOREST (Rock Lake Campground)—(Cass) *From jct Hwy 210 & CR 1: Go 6 mi N on CR 1, then follow signs W along the lake.* FACILITIES: 48 sites, 20 ft max RV length, 48 no hkups, tenting. RECREATION: lake swim, boating, canoeing, ramp, dock, lake fishing. Partial handicap access. Open May - Oct. Phone: (218)825-3075.

PINE CITY—D-4

(E) CHENGWATANA STATE FOREST (Snake River Campground)—(Pine) *From town: Go 9 mi E on CRs 8 & 118, then 1/2 mi N.* FACILITIES: 26 sites, 20 ft max RV length, 26 no hkups, tenting. RECREATION: canoeing, river fishing. Open May 10 - Nov 1. Phone: (651)583-2125.

(W) Pokegama Lake RV Park & Golf Course—(Pine) *From jct I-35 (Exit 171) & CR 11: Go 4 mi W on CR 11, then 1 blk S on Island Resort Rd. Enter on R.* ◊◊◊FACILITIES: 179 sites, typical site width 20 ft, 153 full hkups, 26 W&E, (20/30/50 amps), 26 pull-thrus, WiFi Internet central location, family camping, shower$, dump, non-guest dump $, ltd groc, ice, picnic tables, fire rings, wood. ◊◊◊RECREATION: pavilion, swim pool, boating, ramp, dock, lake fishing, putting green, bsktball, play equipment, activities horseshoes. Pets welcome. No tents. Open May 1 - Oct 1. Big rigs welcome. Rate in 2010 $28-32 for 2 persons. MC/VISA/DISC/Debit. CCUSA 50% Discount. CCUSA reservations Required, CCUSA max stay 5 days, CCUSA disc. not avail F,Sa, CCUSA disc. not avail holidays.

Phone: (800)248-6552
Address: 19193 Island Resort Rd, Pine City, MN 55063
Lat/Lon: 45.87162/-93.04688
Email: pokegamarvpark@yahoo.com
Web: www.woischkes.com

PINE ISLAND—F-4

(SE) Hidden Meadows RV Park—(Olmsted) *From jct US 52 & CR 31: Go 1 mi SW on CR 31, then 1 mi E on 120th St, then 3/4 mi N on CR 90. Enter on L.* ◊◊◊◊FACILITIES: 109 sites, typical site width 45 ft, 46 full hkups, 63 W&E, (20/30/50 amps), 50 amps ($), 40 pull-thrus, family camping, tenting, dump, laundry, ltd groc. ◊◊◊◊RECREATION: river swim, river fishing, playground. Pets welcome. Open Apr 8 - Nov 1. Green Friendly. Rate in 2010 $28-30 for 2 persons. Phone: (507)356-8594.

PIPESTONE—F-1

(C) PIPESTONE RV CAMPGROUND—(Pipestone) *From jct Hwy 23 & Hwy 30: Go 1/4 mi W on Hwy 30, then 1-1/4 mi N on Hiawatha Ave. Enter on R.* ◊◊◊FACILITIES: 62 sites, typical site width 30 ft, 38 full hkups, 24 W&E, (30/50 amps), some extd stay sites, 24 pull-thrus, cable TV, WiFi/cable Instant Internet at site, family camping, tenting, RV storage, dump, laundry, ltd groc, RV supplies, ice, picnic tables, fire rings, grills, wood.

◊◊◊RECREATION: rec hall, rec room/area, coin games, swim pool, golf nearby, bsktball, playground, activities, (wkends), horseshoes, sports field, v-ball.

Pets welcome. Open May 1 - Sep 30. Big rigs welcome. Clubs welcome. Green Friendly. Rate in 2010 $27-32 for 2 persons. MC/VISA/DISC/Debit. Member MRA. CCUSA 50% Discount. CCUSA reservations Required, CCUSA max stay 4 days, Cash only for CCUSA disc., CCUSA disc. not avail holidays. Discount not valid Thu, Fri & Sat between Memorial Day & Labor Day weekends. Not available for groups.

Phone: (507)825-2455
Address: 919 N. Hiawatha Ave., Pipestone, MN 56164
Lat/Lon: 44.00876/-96.31583
Email: pipestonervcampground@gmail.com
Web: www.pipestonervcampground.com

SEE AD THIS PAGE

PLAINVIEW—F-4

(S) CARLEY STATE PARK—(Wabana) *From town: Go 4 mi S on CR 10.* FACILITIES: 20 sites, 30 ft max RV length, 20 no hkups, tenting. RECREATION: river fishing, playground. Partial handicap access. Open all yr. Phone: (507)932-3007.

PRESTON—F-5

(W) Maple Springs Campground—(Fillmore) *From jct US 52 & Hwy 16: Go 8 mi W on Hwy 16, then 4 mi S on CR 5, then 1-1/2 mi E on CR 118. Enter on L.* ◊◊◊FACILITIES: 69 sites, typical site width 30 ft, 43 W&E, (20/30/50 amps), 34 no hkups, family camp-

Maple Springs Campground—Continued on next page

PRESTON—Continued
Maple Springs Campground—Continued

ing, tenting, ltd groc. ◆◆RECREATION: river swim, river fishing. Pets welcome, breed restrict. Open Apr 15 - Nov 1. Big rigs welcome. Green Friendly. Rate in 2010 $27 for 6 persons. Member MRA. Phone: (507)352-2056.

(NE) Old Barn Resort—(Fillmore) *From jct US 52 & CR 17 at west edge of Preston: Go 4 mi E on CR 17, then 1 mi S on Heron Rd. Enter on L.* ◆◆FACILITIES: 170 sites, typical site width 30 ft, 63 full hkups, 70 W&E, (20/30/50 amps), 37 no hkups, 10 pull-thrus, family camping, tenting, dump, laundry, ltd groc. ◆◆◆RECREATION: swim pool, river swim, canoeing, river fishing, playground. Pets welcome. Open Apr 1 - Nov 15. Big rigs welcome. Rate in 2010 $36 for 2 persons. Member MRA. Phone: (800)552-2512.

(N) Valley View Campground, Inc—(Fillmore) *From jct Hwy 52 & Hwy 16 (N of Preston): Go 1 mi N on Hwy 52. Enter on R.* ◆◆◆FACILITIES: 49 sites, typical site width 50 ft, 12 full hkups, 37 W&E, (20/30/50 amps), 5 pull-thrus, family camping, tenting, dump, ltd groc. ◆◆◆RECREATION: stream fishing, play equipment. Pets welcome. Partial handicap access. Open Apr 15 - Oct 15. Big rigs welcome. Rate in 2010 $30 for 2 persons. Phone: (507)765-2227.

PRIOR LAKE—E-3

(SW) Dakotah Meadows RV Park & Campground—(Scott) *From jct I-35 E & CR 42: Go 11 mi W on CR 42, then 2 mi S on CR 83, then 1/4 mi W on 154th St, then 2 blks N on Mystic Lake Rd. Enter on R.* ◆◆◆◆FACILITIES: 122 sites, 122 full hkups, (30/50 amps), 93 pull-thrus, family camping, dump, laundry, groceries. ◆◆◆◆◆RECREATION: playground. Pets welcome. Partial handicap access. No tents. Open all yr. Facilities fully operational Mar 1 - Oct 31. Big rigs welcome. Rate in 2010 $30.99 per vehicle. Member MRA. Phone: (952)445-8800. FMCA discount.

RED WING—E-4

(S) Haycreek Valley Campground—(Goodhue) *From jct US 61 & US 63/SR 58: Go 6-1/2 mi S on SR 58. Enter on R.* ◆◆◆FACILITIES: 175 sites, typical site width 40 ft, 15 full hkups, 150 W&E, 2 E, (20/30/50 amps), 50 amps ($), 8 no hkups, 40 pull-thrus, family camping, tenting, dump, laundry, ltd groc. ◆◆◆◆RECREATION: swim pool, stream fishing, playground. Pets welcome. Partial handicap access. Open all yr. Big rigs welcome. Rate in 2010 $33-35 Member MRA. Phone: (651)388-3998.

(NW) TREASURE ISLAND RESORT & CASINO—*From jct SR 19 & US 61: Go 2-1/4 NW on US 61, then 2-3/4 mi N on CR 18, then 1-1/4 mi E on Sturgeon Lake Rd. Enter on L.* Tropical-themed resort and casino featuring over 1500 slots, table games, video poker and more. Resort complex includes 250-room hotel, show lounge, restaurant, RV park & campground and marina on the Mississippi River. Open all yr. MC/VISA/DISC/AMEX.

Phone: (800)222-7077
Address: 5734 Sturgeon Lake Road, Welch, MN 55089
Lat/Lon: 44.62981/-92.65394
SEE AD TRAVEL SECTION PAGE 415

(NW) TREASURE ISLAND RV PARK—(Goodhue) *From jct SR 19 & US 61: Go 2 1/4 mi NW on US 61, then 2 3/4 mi N on CR 18, then 1 1/4 mi E on Sturgeon Lake Rd. Enter on L.*

TREASURE ISLAND RESORT & CASINO
Good times are in the cards! Visit one of our action-packed gaming areas, bowl at family-friendly Island Xtreme Bowl or relax in our luxury hotel today! With excitement for everyone, it's worth the drive to The Island.

◆◆◆◆FACILITIES: 95 sites, typical site width 20 ft, 95 full hkups, (30/50 amps), 50 amps ($), some extd stay sites, 88 pull-thrus, WiFi Instant Internet at site, WiFi Internet central location, tenting, dump, non-guest dump $, laundry, marine gas, ice, picnic tables.

RED WING—Continued
TREASURE ISLAND RV PARK—Continued

◆◆◆◆RECREATION: rec room/area, pavilion, coin games, swim pool, hot tub, boating, canoeing, kayaking, ramp, dock, river fishing, golf nearby. Rec open to public.

Pets welcome. Open Apr 1 - Oct 31. Big rigs welcome. Clubs welcome. Green Friendly. Rate in 2010 $23-30 per vehicle. MC/VISA/DISC/AMEX/Debit. Member MRA.

Phone: (651)267-3060
Address: 5630 Sturgeon Lake Rd, Welch, MN 55089
Lat/Lon: 44.62963/-92.64637
Web: www.treasureislandcasino.com
SEE AD TRAVEL SECTION PAGE 415

ROCHESTER—F-4

(S) AUTUMN WOODS RV PARK—(Olmsted) *From jct I-90 (exit 209) & US 63: Go 2.5 mi N on US 63, then 50 feet W on Hwy 16, then 0.5 mi N on 11th Ave SW. Enter on R.*

◆◆◆◆FACILITIES: 93 sites, typical site width 34 ft, accepts self-contained units only, 93 full hkups, (20/30/50 amps), 32 pull-thrus, cable TV, WiFi Instant Internet at site, family camping, RV storage, laundry, picnic tables, patios, fire rings.

◆RECREATION: rec hall, golf nearby, horseshoes, sports field.

Pets welcome. Partial handicap access. No tents. Open Feb 15 - Nov 30. Call for reservations. Big rigs welcome. Clubs welcome. Green Friendly. Rate in 2010 $32-40 per family. MC/VISA/DISC/Debit.

Phone: (507)990-2983
Address: 1067 Autumn Woods Circle SW, Rochester, MN 55902
Lat/Lon: 43.92703/-92.47827
Email: autumnwoods01@dybb.com
Web: www.autumnwoodsrvpark.com
SEE AD THIS PAGE

(SE) KOA-ROCHESTER/MARION—(Olmsted) *From jct I-90 (exit 218) & US 52: Go 1/4 mi S on US 52 (Marion), then 500 feet E on 54th St SE, then 100 feet N on 65th Ave SE. Enter on R.*

◆◆◆◆FACILITIES: 72 sites, typical site width 30 ft, 56 full hkups, 16 W&E, (20/30/50 amps), 15 pull-thrus, WiFi Instant Internet at site, family camping, tenting, cabins, laundry, groceries, RV supplies, LP gas by weight/by meter, ice, picnic tables, patios, fire rings, grills, wood.

◆◆◆RECREATION: swim pool, golf nearby, bsktball, playground, activities, (wkends), horseshoes, sports field, v-ball.

Pets welcome, breed restrict. Open Mar 15 - Oct 31. Limited services only before May 1 & after Oct 15. Clubs welcome. Green Friendly. Rate in 2010 $29-40 for 2 persons. MC/VISA/Debit. ATM. Member MRA. KOA discount.

Phone: (507)288-0785
Address: 5232 65th Ave SE, Rochester, MN 55904
Lat/Lon: 43.94350/-92.34852
Email: kamp@rochesterkoa.com
Web: www.rochesterKOA.com
SEE AD THIS PAGE

(N) Silver Lake Motorcoach Resort—(Olmsted) *From jct Hwy-14 & US-63: Go 2 mi N on US 63, then 1 blk W on 14th St. Enter on L.* ◆◆◆FACILITIES: 58 sites, typical site width 25 ft, 40 ft max RV length, 58 full hkups, (20/30/50 amps), family camping, laundry. Pets welcome. Partial handicap access. No tents. Open Apr 1 - Nov 1. Rate in 2010 $34 for 2 persons. Phone: (888)284-6412.

(N) Tilly's American Traveler's RV Resort—(Olmsted) *From jct US N 14 & US 52: Go 2-1/2 mi N on US 52, then 1/2 mi W on 100th St NW, then 1/2 mi N on 3rd Ave SW, then 1/4 mi E on 12th St W, then 1/4*

ROCHESTER—Continued
Tilly's American Traveler's RV Resort—Continued

mi N on Shady Lake Ln. Enter on L. ◆◆◆◆FACILITIES: 33 sites, 33 full hkups, (30/50 amps), 17 pull-thrus, family camping, laundry. Pets welcome. Partial handicap access. No tents. Open Apr 15 - Nov 15. Big rigs welcome. Rate in 2010 $30 per vehicle.

Phone: (507)367-2400
Address: 1155 Lake Shady Avenue South, Oronoco, MN 55960
Lat/Lon: 44.15399/-92.53429
Email: tillysrvpark@pitel.net
Web: www.tillysrvresort.com

ROYALTON—D-3

(S) Two Rivers Campground & Tubing—(Benton) *From jct US 10 & Halfway Crossing (CR 40): Go 100 feet SW on Halfway Crossing (CR 40), then 1 mi S on CR 73 (45th Ave NW), then 1/2 mi W on 145th St NW. Enter at end.* ◆◆◆◆FACILITIES: 185 sites, typical site width 55 ft, 106 full hkups, 79 W&E, (20/30/50 amps), 40 pull-thrus, family camping, tenting, dump, laundry, ltd groc. ◆◆◆◆◆RECREATION: swim pool, river swim, boating, canoeing, river fishing, playground. Pets welcome. Open May 1 - Oct 1. Big rigs welcome. Green Friendly. Rate in 2010 $38-49 per family. Member MRA. Phone: (320)584-5125.

SAGINAW—C-4

(SE) Saginaw Campground—(St. Louis) *From jct US 2 & SR 194: Go 500 feet S on US 2. Enter on R.* ◆◆◆FACILITIES: 36 sites, typical site width 35 ft, 27 full hkups, 9 W&E, (20/30/50 amps), 50 amps ($), 18 pull-thrus, family camping, tenting, dump, laundry. Pets welcome. Partial handicap access. Open May 1 - Oct 1. Big rigs welcome. Rate in 2010 $23-27 per vehicle. Phone: (218)729-4908.

ST. CHARLES—F-5

(N) LAZY D CAMPGROUND & TRAIL RIDES—(Winona) *From jct I-90 (exit 233) & Hwy 74: Go 9-1/2 mi N on Hwy 74, then 150 yards W on CR 39. Enter on R.*

◆◆◆◆FACILITIES: 122 sites, typical site width 40 ft, 112 W&E, (20/30/50 amps), 50 amps ($), 10 no hkups, some extd stay sites, 2 pull-thrus, WiFi Internet central location, family camping, tenting, cabins, shower$, dump, non-guest dump $, laundry, ltd groc, RV supplies, ice, picnic tables, fire rings, wood.

◆◆◆◆◆RECREATION: rec hall, rec room/area, pavilion, coin games, swim pool, river swim, canoeing, 6 canoe/13 pedal boat rentals, float trips, river/stream fishing, fishing supplies, golf nearby, bsktball, playground, activities, (wkends), horseshoes, sports field, v-ball, local tours. Rec open to public.

Pets welcome. Open Apr 15 - Nov 30. Clubs welcome. Green Friendly. Rate in 2010 $27-44 for 2 persons. MC/VISA/DISC/Debit. Member MRA.

Phone: (507)932-3098
Address: 18748 Cty Rd 39, Altura, MN 55910
Lat/Lon: 44.07284/-92.03874
Email: lazydcamp@aol.com
Web: www.lazydcampground.com
SEE AD THIS PAGE

(N) LAZY D TRAIL RIDES—*From jct I-90 (exit 233) & Hwy 74: Go 9 mi N on Hwy 74, then 150 yds W on CR 39. Enter on R.* Horseback trail rides in the scenic Whitewater Valley of Southern Minnesota. Open Apr 15 - Nov 30. MC/VISA/DISC/Debit.

LAZY D TRAIL RIDES—Continued on next page

ST. CHARLES—Continued
LAZY D TRAIL RIDES—Continued

Phone: (507)932-3098
Address: 18748 Cty Rd 39, Altura, MN 55910
Lat/Lon: 44.07284/-92.03874
Email: lazydcamp@aol.com
Web: www.lazydcampground.com

SEE AD PAGE 425

ST. CLOUD—D-3

See listings at Avon, Clearwater, Little Falls, Monticello & Royalton.

(E) St. Cloud Campground & RV Park—(Benton) *From jct US 10 & Hwy 23: Go 1/4 mi E on Hwy 23, then 1 block S on 14th Ave SE, then 1 mi E on CR 8. Enter on L.* ◆◆◆◆FACILITIES: 102 sites, typical site width 30 ft, 77 full hkups, 18 W&E, (20/30/50 amps), 50 amps ($), 7 no hkups, 48 pull-thrus, family camping, tenting, dump, laundry, ltd groc. ◆◆◆◆RECREATION: swim pool, playground. Pets welcome. Age restrict may apply. Open Apr 20 - Oct 15. Big rigs welcome. Green Friendly. Rate in 2010 $30-33 for 2 persons. Member ARVC, MRA. Phone: (320)251-4463. FMCA discount.

Reserve Online at Woodalls.com

ST. PAUL—E-4

ST. PAUL/MINNEAPOLIS AREA MAP

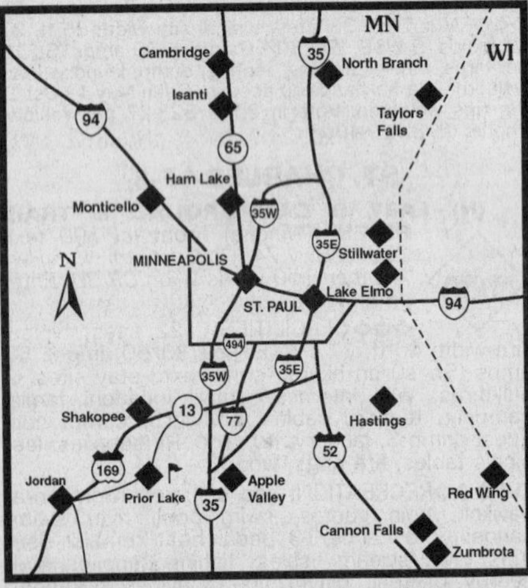

Symbols on map indicate towns within a 50 mi radius of St. Paul where campgrounds (diamonds), attractions (flags), & RV service centers & camping supply outlets (gears) are listed. Check listings for more information.

Tell Them Woodall's Sent You!

(E) ST. PAUL EAST RV PARK—(Washington) *From jct I-694/494/94: Go 3 mi E on I-94 (exit 253), then 100 yds S on CR 15/Manning Ave S, then 1 mi W on Hudson Rd, then 1/4 mi S on CR 72/Settlers Ridge Pkwy. Enter on R.* ◆◆◆◆◆FACILITIES: 84 sites, typical site width 30 ft, 35 full hkups, 39 W&E, (20/30/50 amps), 50 amps ($), 10 no hkups, 45 pull-thrus, WiFi Internet central location, family camping, tenting, cabins, dump, non-guest dump $, laundry, LP gas by weight/by meter, ice, picnic tables, fire rings, wood, controlled access. ◆◆◆RECREATION: swim pool, golf nearby, playground, horseshoes, sports field, v-ball.

Pets welcome, breed restrict. Partial handicap access. Open Apr 20 - Oct 1. Big rigs welcome. Clubs welcome. Rate in 2010 $31-41 for 2 persons. MC/VISA/Debit.

Phone: (651)436-6436
Address: 568 Settlers Ridge Pkwy, Woodbury, MN 55129
Lat/Lon: 44.94085/-92.88339
Email: stpauleastrvpark@aol.com
Web: stpauleastrvpark.com

SEE AD MINNEAPOLIS PAGE 423

SANDSTONE—D-4

(E) BANNING STATE PARK—(Pine) *From jct I-35 (exit 195) & Hwy 23: Go 1/2 mi E on Hwy 23.* FACILITIES: 33 sites, 11 E, (30 amps), 22 no hkups, tenting, dump. RECREATION: boating, no motors, canoeing, ramp, river fishing, playground. Partial handicap access. Open all yr. Phone: (320)245-2668.

SAUK CENTRE—D-2

(N) SINCLAIR LEWIS CAMPGROUND (City Park)—(Stearns) *From jct I-94 & US-71: Go 1 mi N on US-71, then 1/4 mi W on 1st St S.* FACILITIES: 70 sites, 35 ft max RV length, 40 full hkups, 30 W&E, tenting, dump. RECREATION: ramp, dock, playground. Open May 1 - Oct 15. Phone: (320)333-9546.

SCANLON—C-4

(E) Knife Island Campground—(Carlton) *From jct I-35 (exit 239) and Hwy 45 : Go 1/4 mi N on Hwy 45, then 1/4 mi E on Hwy 61. (End of bridge). Enter on R.* ◆◆FACILITIES: 30 sites, typical site width 25 ft, 30 W&E, (20/30/50 amps), 7 pull-thrus, family camping, tenting, dump, ltd groc. ◆◆RECREATION: boating, canoeing, river fishing. Pets welcome, breed restrict. Open May 1 - Oct 1. Rate in 2010 $20-28 for 2 persons. Phone: (218)879-6063.

SCHROEDER—B-5

(E) Lamb's Campground—(Cook) *In town on US 61. Enter on R.* ◆◆FACILITIES: 40 sites, typical site width 20 ft, 9 full hkups, 28 W&E, 3 E, (20/30/50 amps), family camping, tenting. ◆◆◆◆RECREATION: lake swim, canoeing, lake/river fishing, playground. Pets welcome ($). Open May 1 - Oct 21. Rate in 2010 $23-33 per vehicle. Member MRA. Phone: (218)663-7292.

(NE) TEMPERANCE RIVER STATE PARK—(Cook) *From town: Go 1 mi N on Hwy-61.* FACILITIES: 55 sites, 18 E, 37 no hkups, 2 pull-thrus, tenting. RECREATION: boating, canoeing, lake/river fishing. Partial handicap access. Open all yr. Facilities fully operational Mid May - Sept. Phone: (218)663-7476.

SHAKOPEE—E-3

(S) Shakopee Valley RV Park—(Scott) *From jct US 169 & CR 101: Go 5 1/2 mi W on CR 101, then 1 blk N on Marschall. Enter on R.* ◆◆◆FACILITIES: 160 sites, typical site width 25 ft, 80 full hkups, 20 W&E, (20/30/50 amps), 50 amps ($), 60 no hkups, 40 pull-thrus, family camping, tenting, dump, laundry, ltd groc. ◆◆RECREATION: swim pool, river fishing, playground. Pets welcome. Open all yr. Facilities fully operational Apr 15 - Sep 15. Big rigs welcome. Rate in 2010 $30-38 per vehicle. Member ARVC, MACO. Phone: (952) 445-7313.

SIDE LAKE—B-4

MCCARTHY BEACH STATE PARK—(Itasca) *From jct CR 5 & CR 915 (McCarthy Beach Rd): Go 1 mi W on CR 915.* FACILITIES: 86 sites, 18 E, (30 amps), 68 no hkups, tenting, dump. RECREATION: lake swim, boating, canoeing, ramp, lake fishing. Partial handicap access. Open May - Oct. Phone: (218)254-7979.

SILVER BAY—C-5

TETTEGOUCHE STATE PARK—(Lake) *From town: Go 4-1/2 mi NE on Hwy 61.* FACILITIES: 28 sites, 28 no hkups, tenting. RECREATION: boating, no motors, canoeing, lake/river fishing. Partial handicap access. Open all yr. Facilities fully operational Apr 20 - Mid Oct. Phone: (218)226-6365.

SOUDAN—B-4

(N) MCKINLEY PARK CAMPGROUND (Breitung Twp Park)—(St. Louis) *From jct Hwy 169 & Main St: Go 1/4 mi N on Main St, then 1-1/2 mi NW on McKinley Park Rd. Enter on R.* FACILITIES: 90 sites, typical site width 30 ft, 81 W&E, (50 amps), 9 no hkups, 12 pull-thrus, tenting, dump, laundry, ltd groc. RECREATION: lake swim, boating, canoeing, ramp, dock, lake fishing, playground. Partial handicap access. Open May 1 - Sep 30. Member MRA. Phone: (218)753-5921.

SPICER—E-2

KANDIYOHI COUNTY PARK NUMBER 5—(Kandiyohi) *From jct US 23 & CR 10: Go 2 mi E on CR 10, then 4 mi NE on Indian Beach Rd around Green Lake.* FACILITIES: 54 sites, 45 E, 9 no hkups, tenting, dump, ltd groc. RECREATION: lake swim, boating, ramp, dock, lake fishing, playground. Open Apr - Oct. Phone: (320)796-5564.

SPRINGFIELD—F-2

(C) ROTHENBURG CAMPGROUND—(Brown) *From jct Hwy 258 & US 14: Go 3-3/4 mi W on US 14, then 1/2 mi S on Cass Ave. Enter on R.* FACILITIES: 38 sites, typical site width 35 ft, 38 W&E, (30/50 amps), family camping, dump. RECREATION: swim pool, playground. Pets welcome. No tents. Open Apr 30 - Oct 15. Phone: (507)723-3517.

SQUAW LAKE—B-3

(SW) CHIPPEWA NATIONAL FOREST (Deer Lake Campground)—(Itasca) *From jct Hwy-46 & CR-33: Go 3 mi SW on CR-33, then 1 mi S on FR-3153.* FACILITIES: 48 sites, 35 ft max RV length, 48 no hkups, tenting. RECREATION: lake swim, boating, ramp, lake fishing. Partial handicap access. Open May 5 - Oct 13. Phone: (218)246-2123.

(SE) CHIPPEWA NATIONAL FOREST (O-ne-gum-e Campground)—(Itasca) *From town: Go 7 mi SE on Hwy-46, then 1/10 mi E on FR-2507.* FACILITIES: 48 sites, 43 E, 5 no hkups, tenting, ltd groc. RECREATION: lake swim, boating, ramp, lake fishing. Partial handicap access. Open May 5 - Oct 13. Phone: (218)246-2123.

STARBUCK—D-2

(S) GLACIAL LAKES STATE PARK—(Pope) *From town: Go 3 mi S on Hwy-29, then 2 mi S on CR-41.* FACILITIES: 39 sites, 14 E, 25 no hkups, 1 pull-thrus, tenting, dump. RECREATION: lake swim, boating, electric motors only, canoeing, ramp, dock, lake fishing, playground. Partial handicap access. Open all yr. Phone: (320)239-2860.

STILLWATER—E-4

WILLIAM O'BRIEN STATE PARK—(Washington) *From town: Go 16 mi N on Hwy-95.* FACILITIES: 124 sites, 61 E, (30 amps), 63 no hkups, tenting, dump. RECREATION: lake swim, boating, electric motors only, canoeing, ramp, river fishing, playground. Partial handicap access. Open all yr. Facilities fully operational May - Mid Oct. Phone: (763)433-0500.

SUNBURG—E-2

MONSON LAKE STATE PARK—(Swift) *From town: Go 1-1/2 mi W on Hwy 9, then 2-1/2 mi S on CR 95.* FACILITIES: 20 sites, 20 no hkups, tenting. RECREATION: boating, canoeing, ramp, dock, lake fishing. Open all yr. Phone: (320)366-3797.

TAYLORS FALLS—D-4

(N) Camp Waub-O-Jeeg—(Chisago) *From jct US 8 & Hwy 95: Go 1/2 mi N on Hwy 95, then 2 mi N on CR 16 (Steep uphill to campsites). Enter on L.* ◆◆FACILITIES: 76 sites, typical site width 20 ft, 32 ft max RV length, 26 W&E, (20/30 amps), 50 no hkups, 1 pull-thrus, family camping, tenting, dump, ltd groc. ◆RECREATION: play equipment. Pets welcome. Open Apr 15 - Oct 15. Rate in 2010 $30-36 for 4 persons. Phone: (651)465-3500.

(S) INTERSTATE STATE PARK—(Chicago) *From town: Go 1-1/2 mi S on US 8.* FACILITIES: 37 sites, 22 E, (20/30 amps), 15 no hkups, tenting, dump. RECREATION: boating, canoeing, ramp, river fishing, playground. Partial handicap access. Open all yr. Facilities fully operational May 1 - Sept 30. Phone: (612)465-5711.

(SW) Wildwood Campground—(Chisago) *From jct Hwy 95 & US 8: Go 3 mi W on US 8. Enter on R.* ◆◆◆FACILITIES: 113 sites, typical site width 35 ft, 63 full hkups, 50 W&E, (20/30/50 amps), 18 pull-thrus, family camping, tenting, dump, ltd groc. ◆◆◆◆RECREATION: swim pool, canoeing, playground. Pets welcome ($). Open May 1 - Oct 1. Big rigs welcome. Rate in 2010 $40-46 per family. Member MRA. Phone: (800) 447-4958.

TOFTE—B-5

(N) SUPERIOR NATIONAL FOREST (Crescent Lake Campground)—(Cook) *From town: Go 1/2 mi NE on US-61, then 17 mi N on CR-2 (Sawbill Trail), then 7 mi NE on FR-165.* FACILITIES: 33 sites, typical site width 13 ft, 33 no hkups, tenting. RECREATION: boating, ramp, lake fishing. Partial handicap access. Open May 10 - Oct 11. Phone: (218)663-7280.

(N) SUPERIOR NATIONAL FOREST (Sawbill Lake Campground)—(Cook) *From town: Go 1/2 mi NE on US-61, then 24 mi N on CR-2 (Sawbill Trail).* FACILITIES: 52 sites, typical site width 20 ft, 52 no hkups, tenting, laundry, groceries. RECREATION: boating, ramp, lake fishing. Partial handicap access. Open May 10 - Oct 1. Phone: (218)663-7150.

TOGO—B-4

(S) GEORGE WASHINGTON STATE FOREST (Bear Lake Campground)—(Itasca) *From town: Go 12 mi S on Hwy-65, then 2 mi W on CR-52 (Venning Rd), then 2 mi S on access road.* FACILITIES: 27 sites, 20 ft max RV length, 27 no hkups, tenting. RECREATION: lake swim, boating, ramp, lake fishing. Partial handicap access. Open May 10 - Sep 10. Phone: (218)254-7979.

(W) GEORGE WASHINGTON STATE FOREST (Thistledew Lake Campground)—(St. Louis) *From town: Go 4-1/2 mi W on Hwy 1, then 2 mi S on access road.* FACILITIES: 21 sites, 20 ft max RV length, 21 no hkups, tenting. RECREATION: lake swim, boating, canoeing, ramp, dock, lake fishing. Partial handicap access. Open May 15 - Sep 15. Phone: (218)254-7979.

TOWER—B-4

(E) BEAR HEAD LAKE STATE PARK—(St. Louis) *From town: Go 9 mi E on Hwy 169, then 7 mi S on CR 128 (Bear Head State Park Rd).* FACILITIES: 73 sites, 26 E, 47 no hkups, tenting, dump. RECREATION: lake swim, boating, canoeing, dock, lake/stream fishing. Partial handicap access. Open all yr. Phone: (218)365-7229.

TOWER—Continued on next page

TOWER—Continued

(NW) FORTUNE BAY RESORT CASINO —*From jct Hwy 1/Hwy 169 & Hwy 135: Go 4 mi W on Hwy 1/Hwy 169, then 1-3/4 mi N on CR 77, then 2 mi E on CR 104. Enter on L.* Lakeside resort complex featuring 24-hour casino with 174 room resort entertainment, dining room, deli, marina and RV sites. Heritage Museum, 18-hole championship golf course - Lake Vermilion. Open all yr. MC/VISA/DISC/AMEX/Debit. ATM.

Phone: (800)992-PLAY
Address: 1430 Bois Forte Rd, Tower, MN 55790
Lat/Lon: 47.82079/-92.34026
Web: www.fortunebay.com

SEE AD TRAVEL SECTION PAGE 409

(NW) FORTUNE BAY RESORT, CASINO & RV PARK—(St. Louis) *From jct Hwy 1/Hwy 169 & Hwy 135: Go 4 mi W on Hwy 1/Hwy 169, then 1-3/4 mi N on CR 77, then 2 mi E on CR 104. Enter on L.*

◊◊◊◊FACILITIES: 36 sites, typical site width 35 ft, 16 W&E, (20/30/50 amps), 20 no hkups, 16 pull-thrus, WiFi Internet central location, tenting, dump, non-guest dump $, laundry, marine gas, ice, picnic tables, wood.

◊◊◊◊RECREATION: swim pool, wading pool, hot tub, boating, canoeing, ramp, dock, 3 pontoon/3 canoe/2 pedal boat/5 motorboat rentals, lake fishing, fishing supplies, fishing guides, golf nearby.

Pets welcome. Open all yr. Big rigs welcome. Clubs welcome. Rate in 2010 $25-30 per vehicle. MC/VISA/DISC/AMEX/Debit. ATM.

Phone: (800)992-7529
Address: 1430 Bois Forte Rd, Tower, MN 55790
Lat/Lon: 47.81968/-92.34055
Web: www.fortunebay.com

SEE AD TRAVEL SECTION PAGE 409

(N) HOODOO POINT CAMPGROUND (City Park)—(St. Louis) *From jct Cedar St & N 3rd St: Go 1-1/2 mi on N 3rd St.* FACILITIES: 85 sites, 30 full hkups, 26 W&E, (50 amps), 29 no hkups, 13 pull-thrus, tenting, dump, laundry, ltd groc. RECREATION: lake swim, boating, ramp, dock, lake fishing, playground. Partial handicap access. Open May 1 - Sep 30. Facilities fully operational May 1 - Sep 30. Phone: (218)753-6868.

TWIN CITIES—D-3

See area maps under Minneapolis & St. Paul for locations of campgrounds & service centers within a 50 mi radius of the Twin Cities.

TWO HARBORS—C-5

(N) BURLINGTON BAY CAMPGROUND (City Park)—(Lake) *In town off US-61 on Park Rd. Enter on L.* FACILITIES: 102 sites, typical site width 25 ft, 36 full hkups, 66 W&E, (30 amps), dump. RECREATION: boating, ramp, dock, lake fishing. Open May 7 - Oct 10. Member ARVC, MRA. Phone: (218)834-2021.

(N) CLOQUET VALLEY STATE FOREST (Indian Lake Campground)—(Lake) *From town: Go 13 mi N on CR 2, then 12 mi W on CR 14, then 1 mi N.* FACILITIES: 25 sites, 26 ft max RV length, 25 no hkups, tenting. RECREATION: lake swim, boating, canoeing, ramp, lake fishing. Partial handicap access. Open May 1 - Oct 31. Phone: (218)226-6377.

(NE) GOOSEBERRY FALLS STATE PARK—(Lake) *From town: Go 13 mi NE on Hwy 61.* FACILITIES: 70 sites, 70 no hkups, 3 pull-thrus, tenting, dump. RECREATION: lake/river fishing. Partial handicap access. Open all yr. Phone: (218)834-3855.

(S) Knife River Campground—(Lake) *From jct US 61 & Scenic Hwy Drive 61: Go 7 mi S on Scenic Hwy Drive 61. Enter on L.* ◊◊◊FACILITIES: 29 sites, typical site width 30 ft, 4 full hkups, 20 W&E, (20/30/50 amps), 5 no hkups, 12 pull-thrus, tenting, dump. ◊◊RECREATION: river fishing, playground. Pets welcome. Open Apr 15 - Oct 15. Big rigs welcome. Rate in 2010 $26-31 for 2 persons. Member MRA. Phone: (218)834-5044.

(S) Penmarallter Campsite—(Lake) *From jct US 61 & Scenic CR 61: Go 2-1/2 mi S on Scenic CR 61. Enter on R.* ◊◊FACILITIES: 24 sites, typical site width 50 ft, 5 full hkups, 19 W&E, (30/50 amps), 24 pull-thrus, family camping, tenting, dump. Pets welcome. Open May 1 - Oct 1. Big rigs welcome. Rate in 2010 $26-32 for 2 persons. Phone: (218)834-4603.

WABASHA—E-5

(S) PIONEER CAMPSITE RESORT—(Wabasha) *From jct Hwy 60 & US 61: Go 4 mi S on US 61, then 3/4 mi N on CR 30 E, then 2-1/2 mi E on CR 24, then 1/4 mi E on Prairie Lane, then 1/2 mi S on Pioneer Dr. Enter on R.*

◊◊FACILITIES: 240 sites, typical site width 35 ft, 205 full hkups, 35 W&E, (20/30/50 amps), mostly extd stay sites, 60 pull-thrus, WiFi Instant Internet at site, family camping, tenting, RV stor-

WABASHA—Continued
PIONEER CAMPSITE RESORT—Continued

age, shower$, dump, non-guest dump, $, ltd groc, RV supplies, ice, picnic tables, fire rings, wood.

◊◊◊◊◊RECREATION: rec hall, rec room/area, equipped pavilion, coin games, swim pool, boating, canoeing, kayaking, ramp, rowboat/4 canoe/2 kayak rentals, river fishing, fishing supplies, mini-golf, ($), golf nearby, bsktball, playground, horseshoes, sports field, hiking trails, v-ball.

Pets welcome. Open Apr 15 - Oct 15. Big rigs welcome. Clubs welcome. Green Friendly. Rate in 2010 $28-30 per family. Member MRA.

Phone: (651)565-2242
Address: 64739 140th Ave, Wabasha, MN 55981
Lat/Lon: 44.31952/-91.94611
Web: www.pioneercampsite.com

SEE AD THIS PAGE

(S) Wabasha Motel & RV—(Wabasha) *From jct US 61 & Hwy 60: Go 3/4 mi N on Hwy 60, then 3/4 mi E on Hiawatha Dr E (Hwy 30). Enter on R.* ◊◊◊◊FACILITIES: 16 sites, 14 full hkups, 2 W&E, (30/50 amps), 50 amps ($), 1 pull-thrus, family camping, tenting. Pets welcome. Open Mid Apr - Mid Oct. Big rigs welcome. Rate in 2010 $32.50 per vehicle. Member ARVC, MRA. Phone: (866)565-9932.

WALKER—C-3

(NE) CHIPPEWA NATIONAL FOREST (Stony Point Campground)—(Cass) *From town: Go 4 mi SE on US-371, then 1-3/4 mi E on Hwy-200, then 4-1/3 mi N on CR-13, then 4-3/4 mi NE on FR-3792.* FACILITIES: 44 sites, 44 E, 13 pull-thrus, tenting, dump. RECREATION: lake swim, boating, ramp, dock, lake fishing. Partial handicap access. Open May 13 - Oct 4. Phone: (218)547-1044.

(C) Pine Creek RV Park—(Cass) *From jct Hwy 34 & Hwy 371: Go 100 ft N on Hwy 371. Enter on L.* ◊◊◊◊FACILITIES: 13 sites, typical site width 20 ft, accepts full hkup units only, 13 full hkups, (30/50 amps), 13 pull-thrus, family camping. ◊◊RECREATION: swim pool. Pets welcome. No tents. Open Early May - Late Oct. Big rigs welcome. Rate in 2010 $39 per vehicle. Phone: (218)547-2200.

(N) Trails RV Park—(Cass) *From jct Hwy 34 & Hwy 371: Go 4 mi N on Hwy 371. Enter on R.* ◊◊◊◊FACILITIES: 84 sites, typical site width 45 ft, 84 full hkups, (20/30/50 amps), 12 pull-thrus, cable TV, WiFi Instant Internet at site, WiFi Internet central location, family camping, tenting, laundry, ltd groc, ice, picnic tables, fire rings, wood. ◊◊◊RECREATION: swim pool, bsktball, playground, activities, horseshoes, hiking trails. Pets welcome ($). Open May 1 - Oct 15. Big rigs welcome. Green Friendly. Rate in 2010 $35-39 for 4 persons. MC/VISA/DISC/Debit. CCUSA 50% Discount. CCUSA reservations Recommended, CCUSA max stay Unlimited, CCUSA disc. not avail F,Sa, CCUSA disc. not avail holidays.

Phone: (877)280-0322
Address: 9424 State 371 NW, Walker, MN 56484
Lat/Lon: 47.14387/-94.63338
Web: www.trailsrvpark.com

WANNASKA—A-2

(E) HAYES LAKE STATE PARK—(Roseau) *From jct Hwy 89 & CR 4: Go 9 mi E on CR 4.* FACILITIES: 35 sites, 18 E, 17 no hkups, tenting, dump. RECREATION: lake swim, boating, electric motors only, canoeing, ramp, lake/river fishing, playground. Partial handicap access. Open all yr. Phone: (218)425-7504.

Name origin: From Dakota Sioux word "Minisota", meaning "cloudy water" or "sky-tinted water" of the Minnesota River.

WARROAD—A-2

(E) WARROAD MUNICIPAL PARK—(Roseau) *From Hwy 11 in town: Go 1 mi E on Lake St NE.* FACILITIES: 182 sites, 32 ft max RV length, 80 full hkups, 32 W&E, 60 E, (50 amps), 10 no hkups, 27 pull-thrus, tenting, dump, laundry. RECREATION: 2 swim pools, boating, canoeing, ramp, dock, lake/river fishing, playground. Pets welcome. Partial handicap access. Open May - Oct. Phone: (218)386-1454.

WASECA—F-3

(E) KIESLER'S CAMPGROUND & R.V. RESORT—(Waseca) *From jct I-35 & US 14 (exit 42): Go 12 mi W on US 14. Enter on L.*

◊◊◊◊◊FACILITIES: 308 sites, typical site width 40 ft, 229 full hkups, 79 W&E, (20/30/50 amps), 50 amps ($), many extd stay sites, 2 pull-thrus, cable TV, WiFi Instant Internet at site, family camping, tenting, dump, non-guest dump $, laundry, ltd groc, RV supplies, LP gas by weight/by meter, ice, picnic tables, fire rings, wood, controlled access.

◊◊◊◊◊RECREATION: rec hall, rec room/area, coin games, swim pool, wading pool, boating, ramp, dock, rowboat/7 motorboat rentals, lake fishing, fishing supplies, mini-golf, ($), golf nearby, bsktball, playground, shuffleboard court 2 shuffleboard courts, activities, horseshoes, sports field, v-ball.

Pets welcome. Open Apr 14 - Sep 25. Big rigs welcome. Clubs welcome. Green Friendly. Rate in 2010 $38-61 for 2 persons. MC/VISA/DISC/Debit. Member ARVC, MRA.

Phone: (507)835-3179
Address: 14360 Hwy 14 E, Waseca, MN 56093
Lat/Lon: 44.07966/-93.47948
Email: camp@kieslers.com
Web: www.kieslers.com

SEE AD THIS PAGE

WASKISH—B-3

(NE) RED LAKE STATE FOREST (Waskish Campground)—(Beltrami) *From jct CR-40 & Hwy-72: Go 100 yards S on Hwy-72.* FACILITIES: 30 sites, 30 no hkups, tenting. RECREATION: boating, ramp, dock, river fishing. Partial handicap access. Open May - Oct. Phone: (218)647-8592.

WATERVILLE—F-3

(NE) Kamp Dels—(Le Sueur) *From S jct Hwy-60 & Hwy-13: Go 1 mi N on Hwy-13, then 1/2 mi E on CR-131. Enter on L.* ◊◊◊◊FACILITIES: 400 sites, typical site width 40 ft, 305 full hkups, 87 W&E, (20/30/50 amps), 8 no hkups, 9 pull-thrus, family camping, tenting, dump, laundry, groceries. ◊◊◊◊◊RECREATION: 2 swim pools, boating, canoeing, ramp, dock, lake fishing, playground. Pets welcome. Open Apr 20 - Oct 20. Facilities fully operational May 30 - Sep 1. Rate in 2010 $43.50-60 for 2 persons. Member MRA. Phone: (507)362-8616.

(E) SAKATAH LAKE STATE PARK—(Le Sueur) *From jct Hwys-13 & 60: Go 2 mi E on Hwy-60.* FACILITIES: 62 sites, 14 E, 48 no hkups, tenting, dump. RECREATION: lake swim, boating, canoeing, dock, lake/river fishing, playground. Partial handicap access. Open all yr. Facilities fully operational Mid May - Oct 24. Phone: (507)362-4438.

WELCOME—F-2

(N) Checkers Welcome Campground—(Martin) *From jct I-90 & Hwy 263 (exit 93): Go 1/2 mi S on Hwy 263. Enter on R.* ◊◊◊FACILITIES: 43 sites, typical site width 25 ft, 43 full hkups, (20/30/50 amps), 50 amps ($), 14 pull-thrus, WiFi Instant Internet at site, family camping, tenting, laundry, ltd groc, RV supplies, LP gas by weight/by meter, ice, picnic tables, fire rings, wood.

Checkers Welcome Campground—Continued on next page

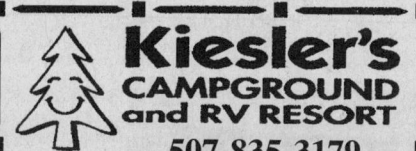

WELCOME—Continued
Checkers Welcome Campground—Continued

◆◆RECREATION: pavilion, bsktball, play equipment, activities horseshoes, v-ball. Pets welcome. Open Apr 1 - Nov 15. Rate in 2010 $24-25 for 2 persons. Member MRA. CCUSA 50% Discount. CCUSA reservations Accepted, CCUSA max stay 3 days, Cash only for CCUSA disc.

Phone: (507)728-8811
Address: 601 N Guide St, Welcome, MN 56181
Lat/Lon: 43.67582/-94.61520
Email: welcomecampground@frontiernet.net
Web: www.checkerswelcomecampground.com

WILLMAR—E-2

SIBLEY STATE PARK—(Kandiyohi) *From jct US-71 & 12: Go 15 mi N on US-71 (New London).* FACILITIES: 132 sites, 53 E, 79 no hkups, 9 pull-thrus, tenting, dump. RECREATION: lake swim, boating, ramp, lake/stream fishing. Partial handicap access. Open all yr. Phone: (320)354-2055.

WILLOW RIVER—D-4

(E) GENERAL C.C. ANDREWS STATE FOREST (Willow River Campground)—(Pine) *E on North St to Int-35 service road.* FACILITIES: 39 sites, 22 ft max RV length, 39 no hkups, tenting. RECREATION: boating, ramp, river fishing. Partial handicap access. Open May 1 - Oct 30. Phone: (320)245-2668.

WINONA—F-5

(SE) PLA-Mor Campground—(Winona) *From jct Hwy 43 & US 61/14: Go 6 mi S on US 61/14. Enter on R.* ◆◆◆FACILITIES: 150 sites, typical site width 30 ft, 30 full hkups, 120 W&E, (20/30/50 amps), 22 pull-

WINONA—Continued
PLA-Mor Campground—Continued

thrus, family camping, tenting, dump, laundry, groceries. ◆◆◆RECREATION: swim pool, boating, canoeing, ramp, dock, river fishing, playground. Pets welcome. Open Apr 15 - Oct 15. Rate in 2010 $35-40 for 2 persons. Phone: (507)454-2851.

(N) PRAIRIE ISLAND CAMPGROUND (City Park)—(Winona) *From jct US 61/US 14 & Hwy 44: Go 1 mi N on Huff St, then 1 mi W on Riverview Dr, then 1 mi N/NW on Prairie Island Rd. Enter on R.* FACILITIES: 201 sites, typical site width 45 ft, 111 W&E, (20/30/50 amps), 50 amps ($), 90 no hkups, 20 pull-thrus, tenting, dump, ltd groc. RECREATION: river swim, boating, canoeing, ramp, dock, river fishing, playground. Pets welcome. Open Apr - Nov. Phone: (507)452-4501.

WORTHINGTON—F-2

(NW) OLSON PARK CAMPGROUND (Municipal Park)—(Nobles) *From jct I-90 & Hwy 266: Go S on Hwy 266, then 1 mi W on CR 35, then 2 mi S on CR 10. Enter on L.* FACILITIES: 68 sites, 32 ft max RV length, 63 E, (20/30/50 amps), 5 no hkups, 30 pull-thrus, tenting, dump, laundry. RECREATION: lake swim, lake fishing, playground. Open Apr 1 - Oct 31. Phone: (507)329-0760.

WYKOFF—F-4

(SE) FORESTVILLE-MYSTERY CAVE STATE PARK—(Fillmore) *From town: Go 5 mi S on CR-5, then 2 mi E on CR-12.* FACILITIES: 73 sites, typical site width 12 ft, 23 E, (30 amps), 50 no hkups, tenting, dump. RECREATION: stream fishing. Partial handicap access. Open all yr. Phone: (507)352-5111.

Minnesota State Flower: Lady's Slipper

ZIMMERMAN—D-3

(W) SAND DUNES STATE FOREST (Ann Lake Campground)—(Sherburne) *From jct US-169 & CR-4: Go 6 mi W on CR-4, then follow signs 1-1/2 mi S.* FACILITIES: 36 sites, 20 ft max RV length, 36 no hkups, tenting. RECREATION: lake swim, lake fishing. Partial handicap access. Open Apr - Nov. Phone: (763)878-2325.

ZUMBRO FALLS—F-4

(W) Bluff Valley Campground—(Wabasha) *From jct US 63 & Hwy 60: Go 1-1/2 mi W on Hwy 60, then 1-1/2 mi S on Bluff Valley Rd (hilly gravel road). Enter on L.* ◆◆◆FACILITIES: 275 sites, typical site width 40 ft, 275 W&E, (20/30/50 amps), 50 amps ($), 60 pull-thrus, family camping, tenting, dump, groceries. ◆◆◆◆◆RECREATION: swim pool, river swim, river fishing, playground. Pets welcome. Partial handicap access. Open Apr 15 - Sep 25. Big rigs welcome. Rate in 2010 $42-49 for 2 persons. Phone: (800)226-7282.

ZUMBROTA—F-4

(NW) Shades of Sherwood Campground—(Goodhue) *From jct Hwy 60W & US 52: Go 2-1/2 mi N on US 52, then 2 mi W on Sherwood Trail (gravel road). Enter on L.* ◆◆◆◆FACILITIES: 355 sites, typical site width 35 ft, 103 full hkups, 246 W&E, (30/50 amps), 6 no hkups, 5 pull-thrus, family camping, tenting, dump, laundry, groceries. ◆◆◆◆◆RECREATION: swim pool, river fishing, playground. Pets welcome. Open Apr 25 - Oct 5. Big rigs welcome. Green Friendly. Rate in 2010 $29-49 for 2 persons. Phone: (507)732-5100.

READER SERVICE INFO

The following business has placed an ad in the Mississippi Travel Section. To receive free information, enter their Reader Service number on the Reader Service Card opposite page 48/Discover Section in the front of this directory:

Advertiser	RS #
Mississippi State Parks	754

TIME ZONE

Mississippi is in the Central Time Zone.

TOPOGRAPHY

The greater part of the state is a rolling-to-hilly portion of the coastal plain, rising from the Gulf Coast to the north and west. From sea level on the Gulf Coast, elevation reaches 806 feet in northern Mississippi, though most of the state ranges from about 100 to 500 feet above sea level.

TEMPERATURE

While the state has a change of seasons, the moderate climate is mild all year. Average low in January is 50° and summer highs are in the 90s.

TRAVEL & TOURISM INFO

State Agency:

Mississippi Development Authority
P.O. Box 849
Jackson, MS 39205
(866/SEE-MISS)
www.visitmississippi.org

Regional Agencies:

Mississippi Gulf Coast CVB
P.O. Box 6128
Gulfport, MS 39506-6128
(888/467-4853 or 228/896-6699)
www.gulfcoast.org

Tenn-Tom Tourism Association
P.O. Drawer 671
Columbus, MS 39703
(662/328-8936) www.tenntom.org

Mississippi Delta Tourism Association
P.O. Box 68
Greenville, MS 38701
(877/DELTA-MS)
www.visitthedelta.com

Local Agencies:

For information on an area not listed here, contact the Chamber of Commerce or Tourism Bureau for the locality you are interested in visiting.

Mississippi's West Coast-Hancock County Tourism Development Bureau
P. O. Box 3002
Bay St. Louis, MS 39521
(228/463-9222 or 800/466-9048)
www.mswestcoast.org

Columbus-Lowndes Convention and Visitors Bureau
P.O. Box 789
Columbus, MS 39703-0789
(662/329-1191 or 800/327-2686)
www.columbus-ms.org

Greenville/Washington County Convention and Visitors Bureau
216 S. Walnut St.
Greenville, MS 38701
(662/334-2711 or 800/467-3582)
www.visitgreenville.org

Hattiesburg Convention and Visitors Bureau
Five Convention Center Plaza
Hattiesburg, MS 39401
(601/296-7475 or 866/442-8843)
www.visithattie.com

Jackson Convention and Visitors Bureau
111 East Capitol St., Ste. 102
P.O. Box 1450
Jackson, MS 39215-1450
(601/960-1891 or 800/354-7695)
www.visitjackson.com

McComb Community Relations & Tourism Bureau
P.O. Box 667
McComb, MS 39649
(601/684-8664)
www.DiscoverMccomb.com

Natchez Convention and Visitors Bureau
640 South Canal St. #C
Natchez, MS 39120
(601/446-6345 or 800/647-6724)
www.visitnatchez.org

Ocean Springs Chamber of Commerce
1000 Washington Avenue
Ocean Springs, MS 39564
(228/875-4424)
www.oceanspringschamber.com

Jackson County Chamber of Commerce
P.O. Drawer 480
Pascagoula, MS 39568-0480
(228/762-3391)
www.jcchamber.com

Greater Picayune Area Chamber of Commerce
P.O. Box 448
Picayune, MS 39466
(601/798-3122)
www.picayunechamber.org

Tupelo Convention and Visitors Bureau
P.O. Drawer 47
Tupelo, MS 38802-0047
(662/841-6521 or 800/533-0611)
www.tupelo.net

Yazoo County Convention and Visitors Bureau
P.O. Box 186
Yazoo City, MS 39194

BUSINESSES OFFERING

	Things to See & Do	RV Sales	RV Service
GREENWOOD			
Florewood State Park	⚑		
SOUTHAVEN			
Southaven RV Supercenter		🚌	✱
TUNICA			
Harrah's Casino Tunica	⚑		
TUPELO			
Camper City		🚌	✱
WOODVILLE			
Clark Creek Nature Park	⚑		

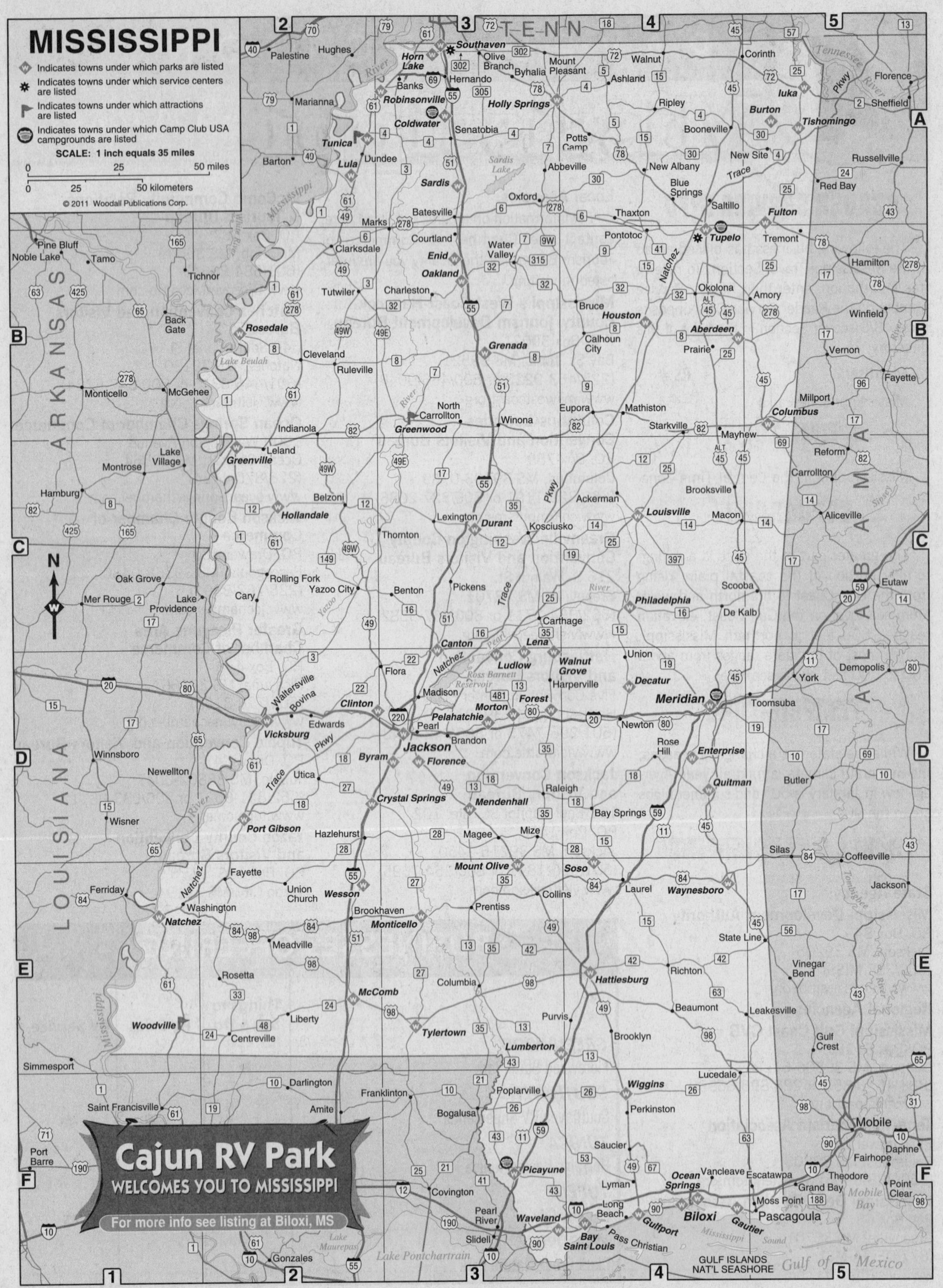

MISSISSIPPI
Indicates towns under which parks are listed
Indicates towns under which service centers are listed
Indicates towns under which attractions are listed
Indicates towns under which Camp Club USA campgrounds are listed
SCALE: 1 inch equals 35 miles
0 25 50 miles
0 25 50 kilometers
© 2011 Woodall Publications Corp.
TENN
ARKANSAS
LOUISIANA
ALABAMA
Southaven
Horn Lake
Hernando
Olive Branch
Byhalia
Mount Pleasant
Walnut
Corinth
Iuka
Florence
Sheffield
Tishomingo
Burton
Booneville
Holly Springs
Robinsonville
Coldwater
Tunica
Senatobia
Lula
Dundee
Sardis
Batesville
Oxford
Abbeville
New Albany
Ripley
Ashland
Potts Camp
Blue Springs
Saltillo
New Site
Russellville
Red Bay
Fulton
Tupelo
Tremont
Pontotoc
Thaxton
Marks
Clarksdale
Courtland
Water Valley
Enid
Oakland
Tutwiler
Charleston
Bruce
Houston
Okolona
Amory
Hamilton
Winfield
Aberdeen
Prairie
Calhoun City
Grenada
Rosedale
Cleveland
Ruleville
Vernon
Fayette
Millport
Columbus
North Carrollton
Greenwood
Winona
Eupora
Mathiston
Starkville
Mayhew
Indianola
Leland
Greenville
Lake Village
Montrose
Hamburg
Belzoni
Hollandale
Lexington
Durant
Kosciusko
Ackerman
Louisville
Brooksville
Macon
Reform
Carrollton
Aliceville
Thornton
Rolling Fork
Yazoo City
Benton
Pickens
Cary
Oak Grove
Mer Rouge
Lake Providence
Philadelphia
Scooba
De Kalb
Eutaw
Carthage
Canton
Lena
Walnut Grove
Ludlow
Union
Decatur
Flora
Madison
Harperville
Forest
Morton
Pelahatchie
Meridian
Toomsuba
Demopolis
York
Clinton
Waltersville
Bovina
Vicksburg
Edwards
Jackson
Pearl
Brandon
Newton
Byram
Florence
Rose Hill
Enterprise
Quitman
Butler
Winnsboro
Newellton
Utica
Crystal Springs
Mendenhall
Raleigh
Bay Springs
Wisner
Port Gibson
Hazlehurst
Magee
Mize
Silas
Coffeeville
Mount Olive
Soso
Laurel
Waynesboro
Jackson
Ferriday
Fayette
Union Church
Wesson
Collins
Washington
Natchez
Brookhaven
Monticello
Prentiss
Meadville
State Line
Rosetta
Columbia
Hattiesburg
Richton
Vinegar Bend
McComb
Liberty
Beaumont
Leakesville
Woodville
Centreville
Tylertown
Purvis
Brooklyn
Gulf Crest
Lumberton
Simmesport
Darlington
Franklinton
Poplarville
Wiggins
Lucedale
Saint Francisville
Amite
Bogalusa
Perkinston
Mobile
Saucier
Port Barre
Picayune
Daphne
Fairhope
Ocean Springs
Vancleave
Escatawpa
Theodore
Lyman
Covington
Grand Bay
Point Clear
Long Beach
Gulfport
Biloxi
Gautier
Moss Point
Pascagoula
Pearl River
Waveland
Slidell
Bay Saint Louis
Pass Christian
Gonzales
Lake Pontchartrain
Lake Maurepas
GULF ISLANDS NAT'L SEASHORE
Gulf of Mexico
Mississippi Sound
Mobile Bay
Ross Barnett Reservoir
Sardis Lake
Lake Beulah
Natchez Trace Pkwy
Cajun RV Park
WELCOMES YOU TO MISSISSIPPI
For more info see listing at Biloxi, MS

(662/746-1815 or 800/381-0662)
www.yazoo.org

RECREATIONAL INFO

Canoeing/Kayaking: Mississippi Outdoor Club, c/o Charles West, 5535 Marblehead Drive, Jackson, MS 39211 www.mscanoeclub.org

Fishing/Boating & Hunting: Mississippi Dept. of Wildlife, Fisheries & Parks, 1505 Eastover Drive, Jackson, MS 39211-6374 (601/432-2400)
www.mdwfp.com

Golf: Mississippi Golf Information, P.O. Box 849, Jackson, MS 39205 (601/359-3297) www.visitmississippi.org/golf

Outdoor Recreation & Outfitters: Mississippi Outdoor Inquiry, P. O. Box 849, Jackson, MS 39205 (601/866-733-6477) www.visitmississippi.org/outdoor%5Frec/

SHOPPING

Biking: Mississippi Department of Transportation (for local cycling clubs, online maps, bike trails). www.gomdot.com/home/travel/bicycling/bicycling.aspx

Factory Stores Outlet Mall of MS, Batesville. This factory-direct outlet offers furnishings for the home, books, entertainment items, apparel and a food court. 325 Lakewood Dr., Batesville, MS. www.discoverourtown.com/MS/Batesville/shopping-398.html

Gulfport Factory Stores, Gulfport. Famous-name merchandise is featured at over 70 exciting shops. A food court and playground is also on-site.10000 Factory Store Blvd., Gulfport, MS. (662/563-5491) (888/260-7609)
www.primeoutlets.com/cntrdefault.asp?cntnd=1025.

The Mississippi Gift Company, 300 Howard Street, Greenwood. Mississippi made marinades and spices, collegiate items, books and cookbooks and Mississippi gourmet food baskets.

Vicksburg Factory Outlet, Vicksburg. Shop at 24 nationally known stores, located across I-20 from the Vicksburg National Military Park. Off E. Clay St., overlooking I-20 at 4000 S. Frontage Rd., Vicksburg, MS. www.vicksburgfactoryoutlet.com/

DESTINATIONS

Mississippi's culture and heritage can be seen in the state's museums, historical homes, Civil War sites and landmarks, and in the unfolding of the Civil Rights Movement and contributions to literature, fine arts and crafts. This is the heart of the Deep South.

Antebellum mansions, historic homes and plantations are often open to the public through scheduled tours. Check with the local chamber of commerce in the city you are visiting for times and availability. The Mississippi Blues Trail is an unforgettable journey that allows visitors to follow the paths of blues musicians born in Mississippi. Walk where they walked, dance where they danced and experience the blues where they were born.

The Natchez Trace Parkway is renowned for its unspoiled, natural beauty. The Trace stretches diagonally across Mississippi from Natchez to Nashville, Tennessee and is lined with markers that point out important sites and fascinating history. First used by Native Americans thousands of years ago, it was later a major trade route during frontier days. Starting from Natchez, you travel through Port Gibson, Jackson, Ridgeland, Kosciusko and Tupelo. Sites along the way include magnificent antebellum homes, spectacular views of the Mississippi River, Cypress Swamp and Tishomingo State Park.

Tennessee-Tombigee Waterway. Located in the northeast corner of Mississippi, the Tenn-Tom boasts 234 miles of adventure. Thousands of acres of water and natural woodlands invite outdoor enthusiasts. Pleasure boaters and skiers delight in the easy current, while avid anglers partake in big money fishing tournaments. Nature trails, secluded campsites and abundant wildlife can be found along the Tenn-Tom's shores.

THE HILLS REGION

Most of the more than 500 Civil War battles waged on Mississippi soil were fought in this area, which brings thousands of history buffs to Corinth to walk the carefully preserved battlefields, and tour the gracious antebellum mansions of nearby Holly Springs. This region also includes **Tupelo**, birthplace of "The King", Elvis Presley. Thousands come from all over the world to see the home where he grew up.

Corinth. Be sure to have a slugburger while visiting this city. During the Depression years, diner cooks sought to stretch ground beef to get more burgers per pound. Originally these hamburgers were made using potato flour as an extender. Today, the beef mixture contains soybean grits. The slugburger is made into small patties, which are fried in canola oil. They are traditionally served topped with mustard, dill pickles, and onions on a small 5-inch hamburger bun. According to town legend, though not a fact, the term "slugburger" comes from the slang term for a nickel. Stop by the Corinth Chamber of Commerce and pick up a brochure and tape describing the Corinth Driving Tour, providing hours of Civil War history.

Corinth National Cemetery/Memphis National Cemetery. This section of the Corinth Civil War Battlefield is the final resting place for 6,000 soldiers. Sadly, most of the tombstones read "Unknown Soldier."

Civil War Earthworks. Corinth has the largest number of intact Civil War earthworks in the nation. They were constructed by both the Confederate and Union armies stationed at Corinth and were used in the defense of the city.

Holly Springs. Known as the Antebellum Capital of the Mid-South, this town has over 100 antebellum structures still standing and more than 64 houses, churches and buildings that pre-date the Civil War. **Walter Place** is the town's crown jewel antebellum home with a variety of architectural styles. The center section is Greek Revival, flanked by massive Medieval Gothic towers. Other attractions in Holly Springs include:

At the **Marshall County Historical Museum,** you can view artifacts that were used by the people of this county. On display are relics of wars from the War of 1812 to the Korean conflict, farm tools, quilts, as well as special Civil War rooms.

Montrose. Visit this Greek Revival brick mansion that was built in 1858 to serve as the Holly Springs Garden Club's headquarters. Today, the lushly landscaped grounds are designated as a state arboretum.

Oxford. The historic downtown square has been the center of life in this university town for over 150 years. The rich history of Oxford Square is honored with the recent

CAMPCLUB USA

Where to Find CCUSA Parks

List City	Park Name	Map Coordinates
COLDWATER		
	Memphis South campground & RV Park	A-3
MERIDIAN		
	Benchmark Coach and RV Park	D-4
PICAYUNE		
	Sun Roamers RV Resort	F-3
TUPELO		
	Natchez Trace RV Park	B-4

QUICK REFERENCE CHART FOR WOODALL'S FEATURED PARKS

	Green Friendly	RV Lots for Sale	Park Models-Onsite Ownership	Park Membership for Sale	Big Rigs Welcome	Internet Friendly	Pets Welcome
BAY ST. LOUIS							
Bay Hide Away RV & Camping Resort	🍃				▲	●	■
BILOXI							
Cajun RV Park	🍃				▲	●	■
Mazalea Travel Park					▲		■
Oaklawn RV Park					▲	●	■
Parker's Landing RV Park					▲	●	■
Southern Comfort Camping Resort					▲	●	■
BYRAM							
Swinging Bridge RV Park					▲	●	■
COLDWATER							
Memphis South campground & RV Park					▲	●	■
COLUMBUS							
Lake Lowndes SP							■
CRYSTAL SPRINGS							
Shiloh Estates RV Park							■
DURANT							
Holmes County SP							■
FLORENCE							
Wendy Oaks RV Resort					▲		■
GAUTIER							
Indian Point RV Resort					▲	●	■
Santa Maria RV Park					▲	●	■
Shepard SP							■
GRENADA							
Hugh White SP							■
GULFPORT							
Baywood RV Park and Campground, Inc.					▲		■
Country Side RV Park					▲		■
HATTIESBURG							
Okatoma Resort & RV Park					▲		■
Paul B Johnson SP							■
HOLLANDALE							
Leroy Percy SP							■
HOLLY SPRINGS							
Wall Doxey SP							■
IUKA							
JP Coleman SP							■
JACKSON							
LeFleur's Bluff SP & Golf Course							■

Green Friendly 🍃; RV Lots for Sale ✖; Park Models/Onsite Onwership ✱; Park Memberships for Sale ✔; Big Rigs Welcome ▲; Internet Friendly ●; Internet Friendly-WiFi ●; Pets Welcome ■

QUICK REFERENCE CHART FOR WOODALL'S FEATURED PARKS

	Green Friendly	RV Lots for Sale	Park Models-Onsite Ownership	Park Membership for Sale	Big Rigs Welcome	Internet Friendly	Pets Welcome
LOUISVILLE							
Legion SP							■
MCCOMB							
Percy Quin SP & Quail Hollow Golf Course							■
MERIDIAN							
Benchmark Coach and RV Park					▲	●	■
Nanabe Creek Campground					▲	●	■
MORTON							
Roosevelt SP							■
NATCHEZ							
Natchez SP							■
OAKLAND							
George Payne Cossar SP							■
PICAYUNE							
Sun Roamers RV Resort					▲	●	■
QUITMAN							
Clarkco SP							■
ROSEDALE							
Great River Road SP							■
SARDIS							
John Kyle SP & Mallard Point Golf Course							■
SOUTHAVEN							
EZ Daze RV Park					▲	●	■
TISHOMINGO							
Tishomingo SP							■
TUNICA							
Harrah's Casino RV Resort					▲	●	■
TUPELO							
Campgrounds at Barnes Crossing					▲	●	■
Natchez Trace RV Park					▲	●	■
Tombigbee SP							■
Trace SP							■
TYLERTOWN							
Hidden Springs Resort				✔	▲		■
VICKSBURG							
Magnolia RV Park Resort					▲	●	■
River Town Campground					▲	●	■
WAVELAND							
Buccaneer SP							■
WESSON							
Lake Lincoln SP							■

Green Friendly 🍃; RV Lots for Sale ✖; Park Models/Onsite Onwership ✱; Park Memberships for Sale ✔; Big Rigs Welcome ▲; Internet Friendly ●; Internet Friendly-WiFi ●; Pets Welcome ■

release of the Tourism Council's Audio Walking Tour, a 45-minute tape filled with historical facts and personal reminiscences about the city's downtown area. Rowan Oak, the antebellum home of Nobel Prize winner William Faulkner, features the outline of his novel, A Fable, written on the study wall.

University of Mississippi, Oxford. "Ole Miss" housed soldiers wounded from the Civil War battles of Shiloh and Corinth. Today the university provides visitors with a scenic and interesting walking tour. Don't miss the **Center for the Study of Southern Culture**—a unique research center which focuses on Southern music, history, lifestyles and folklore. University of Mississippi Blues Archives boasts an extensive blues collection including the personal collection of blues great B.B. King.

Tupelo. Popular attractions in Tupelo include **Tupelo National Battlefield Site**, the two-room home in which Elvis Presley was born and lived as a small child and the **Natchez Trace Parkway Visitors Center** with an audio-visual program on the history of the Trace. The recently opened **Tupelo Automobile Museum** is a first of its kind in Mississippi and offers visitors a unique experience in touring its more than 100 restored automobiles. This 120,000 square foot museum features state-of-the-art automobile displays with interactive speakers detailing the history of each car. Open-viewing restoration bays, hundreds of antique automotive signs, a replica of an old garage and a gift shop are also included. The **Tupelo Buffalo Park** is a thriving park and zoo. Visitors can ride through the park in open-air trolleys and see herds of buffalo or their family of giraffes. The park also features a rare white buffalo, camels, zebra, ostriches and more. It also includes a petting zoo and a re-created Chickasaw Indian village.

THE PINES REGION

This region is filled with rolling hills, Native American homelands, and historic towns. A portion of the Tennessee-Tombigbee Waterway system offers numerous lakes, rivers and reservoirs, locks and dams that are teeming with bass, catfish and panfish.

Aberdeen. Make an appointment to tour some of Mississippi's finest antebellum and Victorian homes. You'll enjoy the beautiful **Holiday Haven** (1850), **The Magnolias** (1850) and **Victoria** (1879), just to name a few.

Antebellum homes await your arrival in lovely **Columbus. Amzi Love**, **Lee Home Museum, Rosewood Manor, Temple Heights** and **Tennessee Williams Home** are all open to tourists year-round. **Waverly Plantation Mansion**, circa 1852, is a four-story mansion with fluted columns and wrought-iron balcony railings topped with a magnificent octagonal cupola, completely renovated to its former glory over the last 45 years by the Snow family. Also in Columbus are riverboats, offering sightseeing and romantic dinner cruises on the **Tennessee-Tombigee Waterway**. **Friendship Cemetery** is the final resting place for 2,194 Confederate soldiers who fell at the Battle of Shiloh. Set among the towering oaks and magnolias are marble cherubs and angels, making it popular with photographers and filmmakers.

Meridian. Dunn's Falls, a 65-ft. waterfall was once a power source for the neighboring Carroll Richardson grist mill, which is open for tours. Also on-site are a natural wildlife refuge and gristmill pond.

Turkey Creek Water Park, located 15 miles southwest of Decatur, is part of the **Pat Harrison Waterway District**—a series of water parks offering a variety of recreation. Turkey Creek features excellent bass fishing, boating, water-skiing, camping, biking, an old-fashioned swimming hole and beach, boat rentals, a playground and a nature trail.

THE DELTA

This region has long been known as the birthplace of the blues. Visitors can still visit some of the old juke joints that helped put blues on the map, or visit some of the surrounding cities that are known for hosting lively festival celebrating the areas rich music heritage.

Belzoni. Make an appointment to tour **Mama's Dream World**—the home of **Ethel Wright Mohamed** (the "Grandma Moses of Stitchery") featuring over 100 stitchery "memory pictures." Then view beauty of another sort at **Wister Gardens** with its 14 acres of scenic gardens and domestic and exotic birds.

Birthplace of the Kermit the Frog Exhibit. Commemorates the Delta boyhood of Jim Henson, creator of the Sesame Street characters and his delightful Muppets. Kermit the Frog is displayed along with other Henson memorabilia.

Chatham. Take a step back in time on the **Lake Washington Scenic Tour**. Visit **Roy's Country Store** for a cold soda and a snack of hoop cheese and crackers.

Clarksdale. Learn about Mississippi and blues history in this town. Highlights include **Cat Head Delta Blues & Folk Art, Delta Blues Museum** and **Muddy Waters Cabin Site & Marker.**

Cleveland. Built in 1915, **Cleveland Depot Library** is one of the oldest surviving buildings in Cleveland. This historic depot contains local railroad history and literacy exhibits. The **Roy Lee Wiley Planetarium** location provides educational and entertaining programs related to astronomy.

Greenville. At **Winterville Mounds** view 17 earthen structures believed to be constructed by ancient ancestors of the known Mississippi tribes—Choctaw, Chickasaw and Natchez. Stroll through the museum to view artifacts discovered in the area. Other highlights include **Greenville Air Force Base Museum, Greenville History Museum** and **The Great Wall of Mississippi,** a levee system longer and taller than the Great Wall of China, constructed by the U.S. Army Corps of Engineers.

Greenwood. Cotton is certainly king in this Mississippi Delta town. The Delta's rich and varied history is presented at the **Cottonlandia Museum**. The museum has a large collection of Mississippi artwork, an extensive archaeology collection and a room dedicated to the agricultural history of the region. A life-size, walk-through diorama of a Mississippi swamp (complete with sound effects), coupled with a hands-on natural science room are always favorites of younger visitors. The Leflore County Military History exhibit displays uniforms, veteran lists, victory posters and artifacts from the wars and the homefront.

Fort Pemberton. Located on a narrow strip of land between the Yazoo and Tallahatchie rivers, the fort was named for the Confederate commander-in-chief in Mississippi. The Union gunboat Star of the West was positioned here to prevent the advancement in the Yazoo Pass expedition.

Indianola. Newly opened in 2008, the **B.B. King Museum and Delta Interpretive Center** honors the blues icon and his delta heritage. Exhibits will explore the Delta, Beale Street, WDIA radio station and B.B.'s career. Plans also include an experiential hands-on Blues Studio where visitors can create their own music.

Leland. Leland is the birthplace of the Frog. This town commemorates the Delta boyhood of Jim Hensen, creator of Sesame Street. The original Muppets are displayed in addition to Henson's Christmas card designs, videos of Hensen's early television appearances as well as other various memorabilia. Stop in at the famous **Highway 61 Blues Museum**, and get to know the famous Bluesmen who originated from the area. This area also contains several historic plantations and antebellum homes. The Belmont Plantation was one of the few homes in the Mississippi Delta to escape the torch of Union soldiers during the Civil War.

Tunica. While this town is known as the South's Casino Capital, Tunica also offers championship golf courses, antique shopping in a charming historic district and the **Tunica Museum** with exhibits on the town and Delta area. The **Tunica RiverPark** has a museum showcasing unique items and natural aquatic exhibits. The Tunica Queen offers paddlewheel cruises three times daily.

Yazoo City. The historic downtown and residential districts contain 20 of the most beautiful Victorian and antebellum homes in Mississippi. Among them are Estes House, a modified Queen Anne with wraparound porch; the castle-like Parker House; and the Wilson-Gilruth House, the largest surviving home from the pre-Civil War period in Yazoo City. The nearby **Triangle Cultural Center**, a former school building built in 1904, houses several museums, a theatre and historical displays. **Oakes African-American Cultural Center** is a restored home showcasing the skills, craftsmanship and unyielding determination of one African-American family. Careful restoration has preserved the uniqueness of the construction and the building is now listed on the State and National Register of Historic Places. Native American Mounds west of Yazoo City date to 1000 A.D.

THE CAPITAL/RIVER REGION

Visitors to this region will be given a glimpse of Old South grandeur, and Civil War reenactments. This region of the state features at least one historic bed and breakfast, Civil War battle sight or monument in every ten-mile stretch. This area is also home to Natchez, who boasts one of the largest collections of Antebellum mansions in the nation.

Clinton. The **Clinton Community Nature Center** is comprised of thirty-three acres of woodlands near Olde Towne Clinton. It includes 2.5 miles of all weather walking trails, an array of native trees and flowers and a museum/education building.

Fayette. The **Springfield Plantation** (circa 1786-91) is the site of Andrew Jackson's wedding to Rachel Robars in 1791. This was one of the first houses in America to feature a full colonnade across the front facade and the first of its kind built in the Mississippi valley. Also noteworthy is its beautiful 18th century hand-carved interior woodwork.

Flora. Don't miss the **Mississippi Petrified Forest**. This natural landmark is the only petrified forest in the eastern U.S. It depicts 36 million years of geological history preserved in huge stone logs. It also features colorful Badlands, a nature trail, a campground, a museum and a lapidary shop.

Jackson. This "City with Soul" has some of the best blues music in the world. You can take a self-guided tour along the **Mississippi Blues Trail** or engage your own private blues tour. Shop for that rare, hard-to-find CD at Bebop Records and enjoy authentic Southern cuisine at one of the 300 restaurants. The **Mississippi Sports Hall of Fame and Museum** is located here as is the **Eudora Welty House, Jackson Zoological Park** and the **Mississippi Museum of Art**. Other highlights of the city include:

Farish Street Historical District. On the National Register of Historic Places, this neighborhood is currently under extensive renovation to become a Mecca of jazz and blues bars, museums, shopping and more.

Mississippi Museum of Natural Science features living displays showcasing the state's natural heritage. Includes over 200 species of fish in giant aquariums and "The Swamp", a 1,700- sq. ft. greenhouse and 20,000-gallon aquarium.

Vicksburg. Visit the **Vicksburg National Military Park/U.S.S. Cairo Museum**. At the visitor center, view "In Memory of Men," an 18-minute film about the Confederate army. The 1,800-acre park features monuments built for both Confederate and Union forces. There is a large variety of antebellum homes as well. View scale models of several waterways, including Niagara Falls, at **Waterways Experiment Station**. This facility is the principal research, testing and development center for the Army Corps. of Engineers.

Woodville. The childhood home of Jefferson Davis, **Rosemont Plantation**, features original furnishings, a family cemetery and a windowsill carved with the names of the Davis children. Also visit the Wilkinson County Museum, which is housed in the original building of the old West Feliciana Railroad Co. since 1838.

THE COASTAL REGION

The coastal region is home to beaches, marshes, bayous and thick timber, and provides access to kayaking, swimming, fishing, and many other outdoor activities. This area is well known for its outstanding fresh and saltwater fishing in a variety of beautiful rivers and streams that feed into the coastal marshes and estuaries. This area is also home to Hattiesburg and Laurel, who both showcase beautiful Victorian mansions originally built by lumber barons.

Although the Mississippi coast was devastated by Hurricane Katrina, there is much that was untouched or has been reconstructed. Tourists are encouraged to visit and see the improved Gulf Coast; however, you are encouraged to research your coastal destination before leaving home. The following bureaus can give you up-to-date information on the area you are visiting: Mississippi Division of Tourism (866/733-6477); Hancock County Tourism Development Bureau (800/466-9048); Jackson County Chamber (228/762-3391); Mississippi Gulf Coast CVB (888/467-4853); Ocean Springs Chamber of Commerce (228/875-4424).

Bay St. Louis. For a sample of the infamous Mississippi Bayou, spend some time touring the marshes, the bayous, the Jordan River and the bay. Visit several historic sites near a charming bayside shopping district. The **Historic Downtown Walking Tour** begins at the **Kate Lobrano House**. Take a guided tour of NASA's space shuttle main engine-testing complex at the **John C. Stennis Space Center**. Also on-site are a museum and a theater that features filmed and live presentations of space and related subjects. The Visitors Center exhibits include moon rocks, rockets and space suits. The Apollo 4 command module is also on display.

Biloxi/Gulfport Area is a popular vacation spot offering 26 miles of sandy beaches, golfing, deep sea fishing, boating, swimming, gambling cruises, nightclubs, historic sites and a scenic coast drive. The area is also known for its fine seafood restaurants.

Beauvoir Jefferson Davis Shrine, Biloxi. The historic last home of Jefferson Davis now contains a Confederate museum and a cemetery, where 700 Confederate soldiers are buried. The **Tomb of the Unknown Soldier of the Confederate States of America** was dedicated here. Although badly damaged by Katrina, the home survived and has undergone an intensive historic restoration. It is open 7 days a week, from 9 am to 4 pm, all year long.

Biloxi Lighthouse has shined its beacon out across the Gulf for 157 years. Its light can be seen for 13 miles. Although its brick exterior suffered some hurricane damage, it survived and was photographed after the storm, standing on the ravaged beach with an American flag flying from its top. It is currently closed for tours.

Ship Island Excursions. This is the Biloxi point of departure for daily cruises to Ship Island, which is part of Gulf Islands National Seashore. **Fort Massachusetts**, used by Union General Benjamin "Beast" Butler during the Civil War as a P.O.W camp, is also located here. In addition to being a beautiful beach and the place where the Mississippi Sound meets the Gulf of Mexico, this was also the launch site for Union forces in the battle for New Orleans.

Hattiesburg. Called the "Hub" for its central location, this city is known for its genuine Southern hospitality. Cultural highlights include **USM's Museum of Art, Armed Forces Museum at Camp Shelby,** and the **Lucile Parker Art Gallery**. For recreation visit **Longleaf Trace**, 39 miles of historic railway converted to a beautiful nature trail.

Laurel. The **Lauren Rogers Museum of Art** in Laurel's historic district houses one of the most impressive collections of art in the South including works by Winslow Homer, John Singer Sargent, Mary Cassat, Grandma Moses and many more. Other Laurel attractions include **Landrum's Country Homestead and Village,** a re-creation of a late 1800's settlement with over 50 buildings and displays; **Veterans Memorial Museum** commemorating our military history and **Laurel's Historic District** which encompasses over 360 buildings.

ABERDEEN—B-4

(N) BLUE BLUFF CAMPGROUND (COE-Tennessee/Tombigbee Waterway)—(Monroe) *from jct US 45 (Commerce St) & Meridian St (center of downtown): Go 1 mi N on Meridian St, then 1/2 mi E & N on paved roads.* FACILITIES: 92 sites, 92 W&E, (30 amps), tenting, dump, laundry. RECREATION: lake swim, boating, canoeing, ramp, dock, lake/river fishing, playground. Pets welcome. Partial handicap access. Open all yr. Phone: (662)369-2832.

(E) MORGAN'S LANDING PARK—(Monroe) *From jct MS 8 & MS 25 & US 45: Go 1-1/2 mi E on US 45 then 1/2 mi S on Darracot Access Rd, then 1 mi E on Sharpley Bottom Rd. Enter at end.*

WELCOME

FACILITIES: 14 sites, 1 full hkups, 13 W&E, (30/50 amps), tenting, dump.

RECREATION: pavilion, boating, ramp.

Open all yr. Rate in 2010 $10 per vehicle.

Phone: (662)369-7815
Address: 10186 Sharpley Bottom Rd, Aberdeen, MS 39730

SEE AD THIS PAGE

The Natchez Trace Parkway, named an All-American Road by the federal government, extends from Natchez to just south of Nashville, Tennessee. The Trace began as an Indian trail more than 8,000 years ago.

BAY ST. LOUIS—F-4

(W) BAY HIDE AWAY RV & CAMPING RESORT—(Hancock) *From jct I-10 W (exit 13) & Hwy 43/603: Go 6 mi S on Hwy 43/603, then 4.8 mi W on US 90, then 1/2 mi S on Lakeshore Rd. Enter on L.*

WELCOME

FRIENDLIEST CAMPING ON THE COAST!!!
Close to EVERYTHING on the Gulf Coast & New Orleans, Casinos-Beach-Golf-Shops-Fishing-Food! Enjoy true Southern Hospitality in our country setting! Pull Thru - POOL - 9-hole DISC GOLF! A perfect Summer Getaway & Winter Retreat!

◊◊◊◊FACILITIES: 46 sites, typical site width 30 ft, 46 full hkups, (20/30/50 amps), some extd stay sites, 41 pull-thrus, WiFi Instant Internet at site, phone Internet central location, laundry, RV supplies, ice, picnic tables, patios, fire rings, wood.

◊◊◊◊RECREATION: rec hall, equipped pavilion, swim pool, pond fishing, golf nearby, playground, activities, (wkends), horseshoes, sports field, hiking trails, v-ball.

Pets welcome. Partial handicap access. No tents. Open all yr. Big rigs welcome. Escort to site. Clubs welcome. Green Friendly. Rate in 2010 $30-40 for 2 persons. MC/VISA. Member ARVC.

Phone: (228)466-0959
Address: 8374 Lakeshore Rd, Bay St Louis, MS 39520
Lat/Lon: 30.29193/-89.45654
Email: bhacamping@aol.com
Web: www.bayhideaway.com

SEE AD THIS PAGE

CAJUN RV PARK—*From jct Hwy 43/603 & I-10 (exit 13): Go 33 mi E on I-10 (exit 46), then 4 mi S on I-110, then 3 mi W on US 90. Enter on R.*

WELCOME

SEE PRIMARY LISTING AT BILOXI AND AD MAP PAGE 430

(N) Hollywood Casino RV Park—(Hancock) *From jct I-10 (exit 13) & Hwys 43/603: Go 6 mi S on Hwys 43/603, then 2 mi E on US 90 to jct Main St & Blue Meadow Rd, then 1/2 mi N on Blue Meadow Rd, then 1 mi E on Hollywood Blvd. (follow signs). Enter at end.* ◊◊◊◊FACILITIES: 101 sites, typical site width 45 ft, 101 full hkups, (30/50 amps), 6 pull-thrus, laundry. ◊◊◊◊RECREATION: swim pool, boating, ramp, saltwater fishing. Pets welcome. Partial handicap access. No tents. Open all yr. Big rigs welcome. Rate in 2010 $32 per vehicle. Phone: (866)7LUCKY-1.

MCLEOD WATER PARK—*From town: Go 10 mi N on Hwy 603, then turn W on Texas Flatt Rd.* FACILITIES: 70 sites, 70 W&E, tenting, dump, laundry, ltd groc. RECREATION: lake swim, boating, canoeing, ramp, dock, river fishing, playground. Partial handicap access. Open all yr. Phone: (228)467-1894.

Mississippi State Song: "Way Down South In Mississippi"

BILOXI—F-4

(C) CAJUN RV PARK—(Harrison) *From jct I-10 & I-110: Go 4 mi S on I-110, then 3 mi W on US 90. Enter on R.*

WELCOME

EXPLORE. PLAY. RELAX. IN BILOXI
Come enjoy our spacious sites, friendly staff and beautiful park. Across from the beach. Complimentary casino shuttles, Cable TV, Internet kiosk high-speed WIFI access. 1-877-225-8699 www.cajunrvpark.com

◊◊◊◊◊FACILITIES: 130 sites, typical site width 26 ft, 130 full hkups, (20/30/50 amps), many extd stay sites (winter), 68 pull-thrus, cable TV, WiFi Instant Internet at site, RV storage, dump, non-guest dump $, laundry, RV supplies, LP gas by weight/by meter, ice, picnic tables.

◊◊◊◊RECREATION: rec room/area, pavilion, swim pool, golf nearby, playground, activities, horseshoes, sports field.

Pets welcome, breed restrict. No tents. Open all yr. Big rigs welcome. Clubs welcome. Green Friendly. Rate in 2010 $39.98 for 2 persons. MC/VISA/DISC/AMEX/Debit. Member ARVC. FMCA discount.

Text 81292 to (440)725-8687 to see our Visual Tour.

Phone: (877)225-8699
Address: 1860 Beach Blvd, Biloxi, MS 39531
Lat/Lon: 30.39378/-88.94928
Email: cajunrvpark@gmail.com
Web: www.cajunrvpark.com

Reserve Online at Woodalls.com

SEE AD NEXT PAGE AND AD MAP PAGE 430

(C) Majestic Oaks RV Resort—(Harrison) *From jct I-110 & Hwy 90 (Beach Rd): Go 2-3/4 mi W on Hwy 90, then 1 mi N on Rodenberg Ave, then 1/8 mi W on Pass Rd. Enter on R.* ◊◊◊◊◊FACILITIES: 95 sites, 95 full hkups, (30/50 amps), 11 pull-thrus, laundry.

Majestic Oaks RV Resort—Continued on next page

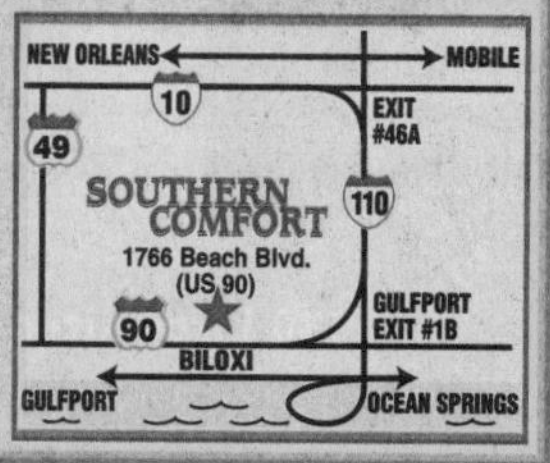

BILOXI—Continued
Majestic Oaks RV Resort—Continued

◆◆RECREATION: swim pool. Pets welcome, breed restrict, quantity restrict. Partial handicap access. No tents. Open all yr. Big rigs welcome. Rate in 2010 $38.50-44 for 2 persons. Phone: (228)436-4200. FMCA discount.

(N) MAZALEA TRAVEL PARK—(Harrison) *From jct I-110 & I-10 (exit 46): Go 4 mi W on I-10 (exit 41), then 300 yards S on Hwy 67. Enter on R.*

WELCOME

◆◆◆◆◆FACILITIES: 151 sites, typical site width 25 ft, 151 full hkups, (20/30/50 amps), many extd stay sites, 45 pull-thrus, cable TV, RV's/park model rentals, cabins, RV storage, dump, non-guest dump $, laundry, groceries, RV supplies, LP gas by weight/by meter, ice, picnic tables, patios.

◆◆RECREATION: rec hall, rec room/area.

Pets welcome, breed restrict. No tents. Open all yr. Big rigs welcome. Escort to site. Clubs welcome. Rate in 2010 $28-30 for 2 persons. MC/VISA/Debit. Member ARVC. FMCA discount.

Phone: (800)877-8575
Address: 8220 W Oaklawn Rd, Biloxi, MS 39532
Lat/Lon: 30.45738/-88.97282
Email: wmsentr@aol.com
Web: www.southernrvparks.com

SEE AD PAGE 440

BILOXI—Continued

(N) OAKLAWN RV PARK—(Harrison) *From jct I-110 & I-10 (exit 46): Go 4 mi W on I-10 (exit 41), then 1/2 mi S on Hwy 67. Enter on R.*

WELCOME

◆◆◆◆FACILITIES: 49 sites, typical site width 25 ft, accepts full hkup units only, 49 full hkups, (30/50 amps), 24 pull-thrus, WiFi Instant Internet at site, laundry, ice, picnic tables.

RECREATION: golf nearby.

Pets welcome, breed restrict. No tents. Open all yr. Big rigs welcome. Escort to site. Rate in 2010 $30 for 2 persons.

Phone: (228)392-1233
Address: 8400 W Oaklawn Rd #37, Biloxi, MS 39532
Lat/Lon: 30.45724/-88.97775
Email: oaklawnrv@gmail.com
Web: oaklawnrvpark.net

SEE AD PAGE 437

In 1902, while on a hunting expedition in Sharkey County, President Theodore (Teddy) Roosevelt refused to shoot a captured baby bear. This act resulted in the creation of the world-famous "teddy bear".

BILOXI—Continued

(N) PARKER'S LANDING RV PARK—(Harrison) *From jct I-110 & I-10 (exit 46): Go 4 mi W on I-10 (exit 41), then 500 ft S on Hwy 67, then 1/4 mi E on Oaklawn Rd. Enter on R.*

WELCOME

◆◆◆◆◆FACILITIES: 130 sites, 130 full hkups, (20/30/50 amps), some extd stay sites, 20 pull-thrus, cable TV, WiFi Instant Internet at site ($), phone on site Internet (needs activ), tenting, cabins, RV storage, laundry, ltd groc, RV supplies, LP gas by weight/by meter, ice, picnic tables, patios.

◆◆◆◆RECREATION: rec hall, rec room/area, swim pool, boating, ramp, dock, river fishing, fishing guides, golf nearby, local tours.

Pets welcome. Partial handicap access. Open all yr. Big rigs welcome. Escort to site. Clubs welcome. Rate in 2010 $30-32 for 2 persons. MC/VISA/AMEX. Member ARVC.

Phone: (228)392-7717
Address: 7577 East Oaklawn Rd, Biloxi, MS 39532
Lat/Lon: 30.45813/-88.96790
Email: parkerslan@aol.com
Web: parkerslandingpark.com

SEE AD NEXT PAGE

BILOXI—Continued on next page

BILOXI—Continued

(C) SOUTHERN COMFORT CAMPING RESORT—(Harrison) *From jct I-10 (exit 46A) & I-110: Go 2 mi S on I-110 (exit 1B), then 2-3/4 mi W on US 90. Enter on R.*

CLOSEST RV PARK TO CASINOS & BEACH
Mississippi's Gulf Coast is renewing itself. Join us & relax, have fun, play on the beach or casino's. Enjoy deep-sea fishing, restaurants & shopping. 1-1/2 hrs to New Orleans - 1 hr to Mobile. Large sites - Cable TV. WiFi at sites.

◆◆◆◆FACILITIES: 129 sites, typical site width 30 ft, 86 full hkups, 43 W&E, (20/30/50 amps), some extd stay sites, 57 pull-thrus, cable TV, WiFi Instant Internet at site, phone Internet central location, tenting, RV storage, dump, laundry, RV supplies, LP gas by weight/by meter, ice, picnic tables, patios.

◆◆◆RECREATION: rec hall, rec room/area, coin games, swim pool, wading pool, golf nearby, local tours.

Pets welcome, breed restrict. Partial handicap access. Open all yr. Big rigs welcome. Escort to site. Clubs welcome. Rate in 2010 $25-32 for 2 persons. MC/VISA.

Phone: (877)302-1700
Address: 1766 Beach Blvd, Biloxi, MS 39531
Lat/Lon: 30.39426/-88.94124

SEE AD PAGE 437

BURTON—A-5

PINEY GROVE CAMPGROUND (COE-Tennessee/Tombigbee Waterway)—(Prentiss) *From jct Hwy 365 & Hwy 30: Go 2 mi W on Hwy 30, then 3 mi S on CR 3501, then follow sign.* FACILITIES: 144 sites, 144 W&E, tenting, dump, laundry. RECREATION: lake swim, boating, ramp, lake fishing, playground. Partial handicap access. Open Mar 1 - Nov 13. Phone: (662)728-1134.

BYRAM—D-3

(C) SWINGING BRIDGE RV PARK—(Hinds) *From I-55 (exit 85-Byram exit): Go 1 block E, then 1/4 mi N on Frontage Rd. Enter on R.*

◆◆◆◆FACILITIES: 131 sites, typical site width 30 ft, 131 full hkups, (20/30/50 amps), mostly extd stay sites, cable TV, cable on-site Internet (needs activ), RV storage, laundry, RV supplies, LP gas by weight/by meter, ice, patios.

◆◆◆RECREATION: pavilion, swim pool, pond fishing, golf nearby, bsktball, sports field.

Pets welcome, breed restrict. Partial handicap access. No tents. Open all yr. Big rigs welcome. Rate in 2010 $30 for 2 persons. MC/VISA/DISC/AMEX/Debit.

Phone: (601)502-1101
Address: 100 Holiday Rambler Ln, Jackson, MS 39272
Lat/Lon: 32.18513/-90.25309
Email: info@rvresort.net
Web: www.rvresort.net

SEE AD JACKSON PAGE 444

CANTON—D-3

(W) Movietown RV Resort—(Madison) *From jct I 55 (exit 119) & Hwy 22: Go 1/4 mi W on Hwy 22, then 1/4 mi N on Virlilia Rd. Enter on R.* ◆◆◆◆FACILITIES: 114 sites, 114 full hkups, (20/30/50 amps), 75 pull-thrus, tenting, laundry. ◆RECREATION: playground. Pets welcome. Partial handicap access. Open all yr. Big rigs welcome. Rate in 2010 $25 per vehicle. Phone: (601)859-7990.

CLINTON—D-2

(SE) Springridge RV Park—(Hinds) *From I-20 (exit 36): Go 2 blocks S on Springridge Rd. Enter on L.* ◆◆◆◆FACILITIES: 42 sites, typical site width 25 ft, 42 full hkups, (30/50 amps), 30 pull-thrus, tenting, laundry. ◆◆◆RECREATION: swim pool, playground. Pets welcome. Open all yr. Big rigs welcome. Rate in 2010 $26-29 for 2 persons. Phone: (601)924-0947.

COLDWATER—A-3

DUB PATTON CAMPGROUND (COE-Arkabutla Lake) —(Tate) *From town: Go 10 mi W on Arkabutla Rd. Follow signs N to the dam.* FACILITIES: 66 sites, 66 W&E, (20/30 amps), tenting, dump. RECREATION: lake swim, boating, ramp, lake fishing. Partial handicap access. Open all yr. Phone: (662)562-6261.

HERNANDO POINT (COE - Arkabutla Lake)—(Tate) *From town: Go 4 mi N on US-51, then 5 mi W on Wheeler Rd.* FACILITIES: 83 sites, 83 W&E, tenting, dump. RECREATION: lake swim, boating, ramp, lake fishing, playground. Open all yr. Phone: (662)562-6261.

COLDWATER—Continued

(C) MEMPHIS SOUTH CAMPGROUND & RV PARK—(Tate) *From I-55 (exit 271) & Hwy 306: Go 200 ft W on Hwy 306. Enter on L.*

◆◆◆◆FACILITIES: 82 sites, typical site width 50 ft, 82 full hkups, (20/30/50 amps), some extd stay sites, 82 pull-thrus, WiFi Instant Internet at site, tenting, RV storage, laundry, picnic tables, wood.

◆◆RECREATION: equipped pavilion, swim pool, pond fishing, golf nearby, bsktball, play equipment.

Pets welcome, size restrict. Partial handicap access. Open all yr. Pool open Apr - Mid Oct. Big rigs welcome. Clubs welcome. Rate in 2010 $32 for 2 persons. MC/VISA/Debit. CCUSA 50% Discount. CCUSA reservations Recommended, CCUSA max stay 2, Cash only for CCUSA disc.

Phone: (662)622-0056
Address: 256 Campground Dr, Coldwater, MS 38618
Lat/Lon: 34.69884/-89.96716
Email: memphissouthrv@aol.com
Web: www.memphissouthrv.com

SEE AD MEMPHIS, TN PAGE 732

SOUTH ABUTMENT CAMPGROUND (COE-Arkabutla Lake)—(Tate) *From town: Go 10 mi W on Arkabutla Rd. Follow signs N to the dam.* FACILITIES: 80 sites, 80 W&E, tenting, dump. RECREATION: lake swim, boating, ramp, lake fishing, playground. Partial handicap access. Open all yr. Phone: (662)562-6261.

COLUMBUS—B-5

DEWAYNE HAYES CAMPGROUND (COE-Tennessee/Tombigbee Waterway)—(Lowndes) *From jct US 45 & Hwy 50W/Hwy 373N: Go 1-1/2 mi NW on Hwy 373, then 1/2 mi left on Barton Ferry Rd.* FACILITIES: 110 sites, 100 W&E, (30/50 amps), 10 no hkups, tenting, dump, laundry. RECREATION: lake swim, boating, ramp, lake fishing, playground. Pets welcome. Partial handicap access. Open all yr. Phone: (662)434-6939.

(SE) LAKE LOWNDES SP—(Lowndes) *From town: Go 4 mi SE on Hwy-69, then 4 mi SE follow signs.*

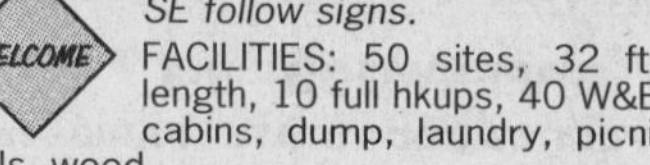

FACILITIES: 50 sites, 32 ft max RV length, 10 full hkups, 40 W&E, tenting, cabins, dump, laundry, picnic tables, grills, wood.

RECREATION: rec hall, rec room/area, equipped pavilion, coin games, lake swim, boating, ramp, dock, 6 rowboat/6 pedal boat rentals, lake fishing, bsktball, 8 bike rentals, playground, activities, (wkends), tennis, sports field, hiking trails, v-ball. Rec open to public.

Pets welcome. Open all yr. MC/VISA.

Phone: (662)328-2110
Address: 3319 Lake Lowndes Rd, Columbus, MS 39702
Lat/Lon: 33.43490/-88.30065
Email: lowndesl@ayrix.net
Web: campingconnection.com

SEE AD TRAVEL SECTION PAGE 431 AND AD LA TRAVEL SECTION PAGE 278

(NW) TOWN CREEK CAMPGROUND (COE-Tennessee/Tombigbee Waterway)—(Clay) *From jct US 45 & Hwy 50: Go W on Hwy 50 to west side of Tenn-Tom Bridge, then follow signs N on county roads.* FACILITIES: 110 sites, 100 W&E, (30 amps), 10 no hkups, tenting, dump, laundry. RECREATION: lake swim, boating, ramp, dock, lake/river fishing, playground. Pets welcome. Partial handicap access. Open all yr. Phone: (662)494-4885.

DECATUR—D-4

(W) TURKEY CREEK WATER PARK (Pat Harrison Waterway District)—(Newton) *From jct I-20 (exit 109) & Hwy 15: Go 7 mi N on Hwy 15 to Decatur, then 4-1/2 mi W on park road. Follow signs.* FACILITIES: 22 sites, typical site width 23 ft, 38 ft max RV length, 22 W&E, tenting, dump, laundry. RECREATION: lake swim, boating, canoeing, ramp, dock, lake fishing, playground. Open all yr. Phone: (601)635-3314.

DURANT—C-3

(S) HOLMES COUNTY SP—(Attala) *From jct I-55 (exit 156) & Hwy 12: Go 5 mi S on I-55 (exit 150), then 1 mi E on park access road.*

FACILITIES: 28 sites, 28 W&E, 2 pull-thrus, tenting, cabins, dump, laundry, ice, picnic tables.

RECREATION: rec hall, pavilion, coin games, lake swim, boating, ramp, dock, 6 rowboat/6 pedal boat rentals, lake fishing, playground, sports field, hiking trails, v-ball. Rec open to public.

Pets welcome. Open all yr. MC/VISA.

Mississippi State Fish: Largemouth or Black Bass

DURANT—Continued
HOLMES COUNTY SP—Continued

Phone: (662)653-3351
Address: Old Holmes Park Rd, Durant, MS 39063
Lat/Lon: 33.02635/-89.91692
Web: campingconnection.com

SEE AD TRAVEL SECTION PAGE 431 AND AD LA TRAVEL SECTION PAGE 278

ENID—B-3

CHICKASAW HILL CAMPGROUND (COE-Enid Lake) —(Yalobusha) *From jct I-55 (exit 233) & Enid Dam Rd (CR 36): Go 1 mi E on Enid Dam Rd, then 3 mi N on Chapel Hill Rd, then 7 mi E on Pope-Water Valley Rd, then 1-1/2 mi S on Chickasaw Rd.* FACILITIES: 51 sites, typical site width 12 ft, 51 W&E, (50 amps), tenting, dump. RECREATION: lake swim, boating, ramp, lake fishing, playground. Partial handicap access. Open all yr. Phone: (662)563-4571.

(NE) PERSIMMON HILL-SOUTH ABUTMENT (COE-Enid Lake)—(Yalobusha) *From jct I-55 (exit 233) & Enid Dam Rd (CR 36): Go 1 mi E on Enid Dam Rd (CR 36), then 2 mi S across top of the dam, then follow signs.* FACILITIES: 72 sites, typical site width 12 ft, 72 W&E, (30 amps), tenting, dump. RECREATION: lake swim, boating, ramp, lake fishing, playground. Partial handicap access. Open all yr. Facilities fully operational Mar 1 - Oct 31. Phone: (662)563-4571.

WALLACE CREEK (COE-Enid Lake)—(Yalobusha) *From jct I-55 (exit 233) & CR 36: Go 2-1/2 mi E on CR 36 & follow signs.* FACILITIES: 99 sites, typical site width 12 ft, 99 W&E, (30 amps), 8 pull-thrus, tenting, dump. RECREATION: lake swim, boating, ramp, lake fishing, playground. Pets welcome. Partial handicap access. Open all yr. Phone: (662)563-4571.

WATER VALLEY LANDING CAMPGROUND (COE-Enid Lake)—(Yalobusha) *From jct I-55 (exit 227) & Hwy 32: Go 1-1/4 mi E on Hwy 32, then 2 mi N on CR 553. Enter on R.* FACILITIES: 29 sites, 29 W&E, (30 amps), tenting, dump. RECREATION: lake swim, boating, ramp, lake fishing, playground. Pets welcome. Partial handicap access. Open Mar 1 - Oct 31. Phone: (662)563-4571.

ENTERPRISE—D-4

DUNN'S FALLS WATER PARK (Pat Harrison Waterway District)—(Clarke) *From jct I-20 & I-59: Go 6 mi S on I-59 (exit 142), then 4 mi W & S on paved road (cross back over I-59, follow signs).* FACILITIES: 15 sites, typical site width 20 ft, 15 no hkups. RECREATION: lake swim, canoeing, lake/river fishing. Open all yr. Phone: (601)655-8550.

FLORENCE—D-3

(S) WENDY OAKS RV RESORT—(Rankin) *From jct I-20 (exit 47) & Hwy 49: Go 13 mi S on Hwy 49 to Florence (traffic light), then 5 mi S on US Hwy 49, then go under railroad trestle, then make a U turn and go 1/2 mi N on Us Hwy 49. Enter on R.*

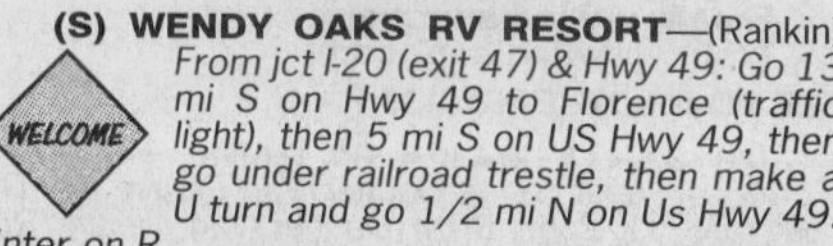

◆◆◆◆FACILITIES: 32 sites, 32 full hkups, (20/30/50 amps), some extd stay sites, 18 pull-thrus, tenting, laundry, picnic tables, fire rings, wood.

◆◆RECREATION: boating, electric motors only, canoeing, ramp, pedal boat rentals, lake fishing, fishing supplies, bsktball, horseshoes.

Pets welcome, breed restrict. Partial handicap access. Open all yr. Big rigs welcome. Rate in 2010 $27-32 for 2 persons.

Phone: (601)845-CAMP
Address: 4160 Hwy 49 S, Florence, MS 39073
Lat/Lon: 32.10961/-90.05539
Email: wendyoaksrvresort@windstream.net

SEE AD THIS PAGE

FOREST—D-3

(SE) BIENVILLE NATIONAL FOREST (Marathon Campground)—(Smith) *From town: Go 11 mi SE on Hwy-501, then 3-1/2 mi SE on FR-506, then 1/3 mi S on FR 520.* FACILITIES: 34 sites, 22 ft max RV length, 34 W&E, (30/50 amps), tenting, dump. RECREATION: lake swim, boating, 10 hp limit, ramp, dock, lake fishing. Open all yr. Phone: (601)469-3811.

Huge catches of seafood are taken from the gulf yearly.

FULTON—A-5

WHITTEN PARK—(Itawamba) *From jct US 78 & Hwy 25: Go N on Hwy 25, then W on Main St to the waterway, then 2 mi N on access roads.* FACILITIES: 61 sites, 61 W&E, (30 amps), tenting, dump, laundry. RECREATION: lake swim, boating, ramp, dock, lake/river fishing, playground. Partial handicap access. Open all yr. Phone: (662)862-7070.

GAUTIER—F-4

(NW) INDIAN POINT RV RESORT—(Jackson) *From I-10 (exit 61) & Gautier/VanCleave Rd: Go 3/4 mi S on Gautier/VanCleave Rd, then E on Indian Point Rd to gate. Enter at end.*

RELAX OR PLAY IN OUR 5W RESORT!
Located between Mobile & New Orleans - just minutes from Biloxi. Enjoy our 5W Resort on Sioux Bayou. Take a boat ride on the bayou. Swimming, Fishing, Activities & Restaurant on site. Near casinos, golf courses, shopping.

◊◊◊◊◊FACILITIES: 200 sites, typical site width 40 ft, 200 full hkups, (20/30/50 amps), many extd stay sites, 13 pull-thrus, cable TV, WiFi Instant Internet at site, WiFi Internet central location, RV's/park model rentals, cabins, RV storage, dump, non-guest dump $, laundry, RV supplies, LP gas by weight/by meter, ice, picnic tables, patios, wood.

◊◊◊◊◊RECREATION: rec hall, rec room/area, equipped pavilion, 2 swim pools, boating, canoeing, ramp, dock, river fishing, fishing guides, minigolf, golf nearby, bsktball, playground, shuffleboard court 2 shuffleboard courts, activities (wkends), horseshoes, sports field, hiking trails.

Pets welcome, breed restrict. Partial handicap access. No tents. Open all yr. Big rigs welcome. Clubs welcome. Rate in 2010 $25-30 for 2 persons. MC/VISA/DISC/AMEX/Debit. Member ARVC.

Text 100600 to (440)725-8687 to see our Visual Tour.

Phone: (228)497-1011
Address: 1600 Indian Point Parkway, Gautier, MS 39553
Lat/Lon: 30.41235/-88.62956
Email: ip@indianpt.com
Web: www.indianpt.com

SEE AD BILOXI PAGE 439

(N) SANTA MARIA RV PARK—*From I-10 (exit 61) & Gautier/Van Cleave Rd: Go 1/2 mi S on Gautier/Van Cleave Rd, then 1-1/2 mi E on Martin Bluff Rd.*

ENJOY TRANQUILITY AT SANTA MARIA
Located at 5800 Martin Bluff Rd in Gautier. You can swim, fish or just grill out and relax. Close to golfing, shopping and casinos. We offer laundry services, workout room, propane onsite, WiFi, spacious lots and more.

◊◊◊FACILITIES: 142 sites, 142 full hkups, (30/50 amps), some extd stay sites, WiFi Instant Internet at site, family camping, RV's/park model rentals, laundry, LP gas by weight/by meter, ice.

◊◊◊◊RECREATION: swim pool, lake/river fishing, golf nearby, bsktball, playground, horseshoes, sports field, v-ball.

Pets welcome. Partial handicap access. No tents. Open all yr. Big rigs welcome. Clubs welcome. Rate in 2010 $28 for 2 persons. MC/VISA/DISC/AMEX/Debit.

Text 108020 to (440)725-8687 to see our Visual Tour.

GAUTIER—Continued
SANTA MARIA RV PARK—Continued

Phone: (228)522-3009
Address: 5800 Martin Bluff Rd, Gautier, MS 39553
Lat/Lon: 30.42820/-88.63155
Web: santamariarvpark.com

SEE AD BILOXI PAGE 440

(S) SHEPARD SP—(Jackson) *From I-10 (exit 61): Go S on Van Cleave Rd, then E on US 90 to first stoplight, then 1-1/2 mi S to Graveline Rd.*

FACILITIES: 28 sites, 28 W&E, tenting, cabins, dump, picnic tables, grills, controlled access.

RECREATION: pavilion, boating, ramp, dock, 6 rowboat/6 canoe rentals, saltwater fishing, playground, sports field, hiking trails. Rec open to public.

Pets welcome. Open all yr.

Phone: (228)497-2244
Address: 1034 Gravelinde Rd, Gautier, MS 39553
Lat/Lon: 30.37395/-88.62709
Web: campingconnection.com

SEE AD TRAVEL SECTION PAGE 431 AND AD LA TRAVEL SECTION PAGE 278

GREENVILLE—C-2

PECAN GROVE RV PARK—*From jct Hwy 1 & US 82: Go 19 mi W on US 82 (over the Mississippi River). Enter on L.*

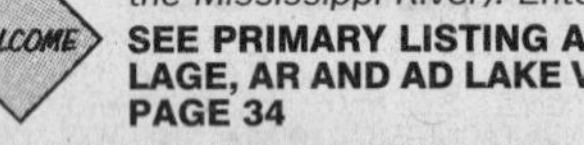

SEE PRIMARY LISTING AT LAKE VILLAGE, AR AND AD LAKE VILLAGE, AR PAGE 34

(W) WARFIELD POINT PARK (Washington County Park)—(Washington) *From jct Hwy 1 & US 82: Go 5-1/2 mi W on US 82, then at Warfield Point Park sign go 3 mi N.* FACILITIES: 75 sites, typical site width 35 ft, 52 full hkups, (20/30 amps), 23 no hkups, tenting, dump. RECREATION: boating, canoeing, ramp, river fishing, playground. Partial handicap access. Open all yr. Phone: (662)335-7275.

GREENWOOD—B-3

(W) FLOREWOOD STATE PARK—*From Greenwood: Go 2 mi W on US 82.* State Park - Day use only. For picnics with picnic pavilions. Open all yr. Day use only.

Phone: (662)455-3904
Address: 1999 County Road 145, Greenwood, MS 38930
Web: www.mdwfp.com

SEE AD TRAVEL SECTION PAGE 431 AND AD LA TRAVEL SECTION PAGE 278

GRENADA—B-3

(N) Frog Hollow Campground/RV Park—(Grenada) *From north jct I-55 (exit 211) & Hwy 7: Go 500 feet E on Hwy 7. Enter on R.* ◊◊◊FACILITIES: 49 sites, typical site width 25 ft, 49 full hkups, (20/30/50 amps), 24 pull-thrus, tenting, laundry. Pets welcome, breed restrict. Open all yr. Big rigs welcome. Rate in 2010 $24-26 for 2 persons. Member ARVC. Phone: (662)226-9042.

(NE) HUGH WHITE SP—(Grenada) *From jct I-55 (exit 206) & Hwy 8: Go 5 mi E on Hwy 8, then 2-1/2 mi N on Hwy 333. Follow signs.*

FACILITIES: 173 sites, 34 ft max RV length, 173 W&E, tenting, cabins, dump, laundry, ltd groc, ice.

RECREATION: rec hall, pavilion, swim pool, lake swim, boating, ramp, dock, 6 rowboat rentals, lake fishing, fishing supplies, bike rental bike rental, playground, tennis, hiking trails. Rec open to public.

Pets welcome. Open all yr.

Phone: (662)226-4934
Address: 3170 Hugh White State Park Rd, Grenada, MS 38902
Lat/Lon: 33.81210/-89.77334
Web: campingconnection.com

SEE AD TRAVEL SECTION PAGE 431 AND AD LA TRAVEL SECTION PAGE 278

Natchez was settled by the French in 1716 and is the oldest permanent settlement on the Mississippi River. It once had 500 millionaires, more than any other city except New York City.

GULFPORT—F-4

(W) BAYWOOD RV PARK AND CAMPGROUND, INC.—(Harrison) *From jct I-10 (exit 38) & Lorraine/Cowen Rd: Go 3 mi S on Lorraine/Cowen Rd. Enter on L.*

◊◊◊◊FACILITIES: 118 sites, typical site width 25 ft, 118 full hkups, (15/30/50 amps), some extd stay sites, 8 pull-thrus, cable TV, RV's/park model rentals, RV storage, dump, laundry, groceries, RV supplies, LP gas by weight/by meter, ice, picnic tables, patios.

◊◊RECREATION: rec hall, swim pool, golf nearby, playground.

Pets welcome, breed restrict. No tents. Open all yr. Big rigs welcome. Escort to site. Clubs welcome. Rate in 2010 $28-30 for 2 persons. MC/VISA/Debit. Member ARVC. FMCA discount.

Phone: (888)747-4840
Address: 1100 Cowan Road, Gulfport, MS 39507
Lat/Lon: 30.40116/-89.02648
Email: wmsentr@aol.com
Web: www.southernrvparks.com

SEE AD NEXT PAGE

(N) COUNTRY SIDE RV PARK—(Harrison) *From jct I-10 (exit 34B) & US 49: Go 10 mi N on US 49. Enter on R.*

◊◊◊◊FACILITIES: 32 sites, typical site width 29 ft, 32 full hkups, (20/30/50 amps), some extd stay sites (winter), 2 pull-thrus, cable TV, tenting, laundry, RV supplies, LP gas by weight/by meter, ice, picnic tables.

◊◊◊RECREATION: rec room/area, pavilion, swim pool, pond fishing, golf nearby, activities, local tours.

Pets welcome. Partial handicap access. Open all yr. Big rigs welcome. Escort to site. Clubs welcome. Rate in 2010 $27 for 2 persons.

Phone: (228)539-0807
Address: 20278 US Highway 49, Saucier, MS 39574
Lat/Lon: 30.57507/-89.12514
Email: csrv@bellsouth.net
Web: www.countrysidervpark.com

SEE AD THIS PAGE

HARRISON COUNTY FAIRGROUNDS—(Harrison) *From jct I-10 (exit 28) & County Farm Rd: Go 7-1/2 mi N on County Farm Rd. Enter on L.* FACILITIES: 130 sites, 130 W&E. RECREATION: Open all yr. Phone: (228)832-8620.

HATTIESBURG—E-4

Cypress Hill RV Park—(Forrest) *From S edge of town: Go 8-3/4 mi S on Hwy 49. Enter on R.* ◊◊◊◊FACILITIES: 30 sites, 30 full hkups, (30/50 amps), 5 pull-thrus, laundry. ◊◊RECREATION: swim pool, pond fishing. Pets welcome. No tents. Open all yr. Big rigs welcome. Rate in 2010 $23-26 for 2 persons. Phone: (601)545-3090.

MILITARY PARK (Lake Walker Family Campground-Camp Shelby)—(Forrest) *From jct I-59 & US 98: Go 1 mi E on US 98, then S on US 49 to South Gate. Check in at Bldg 1480. On base.* FACILITIES: 36 sites, 32 full hkups, (30/50 amps), 4 no hkups, tenting, dump, laundry. RECREATION: swim pool, boating, electric motors only, ramp, lake fishing. Pets welcome. Open all yr. Facilities fully operational Apr - Sep. Phone: (601)558-2397.

(NW) OKATOMA RESORT & RV PARK—(Covington) *From jct I-59 (exit 67B) & US 49N: Go 8 mi N on Hwy 49, then 1 mi E on Lux Rd, then 1 mi N on Okatoma River Rd.*

◊◊◊FACILITIES: 55 sites, 54 full hkups, 1 W&E, (30/50 amps), some extd stay sites, 11 pull-thrus, tenting, dump.

◊◊◊◊RECREATION: rec hall, equipped pavilion, swim pool, river swim, lake/river fishing, golf nearby, bsktball, playground, horseshoes, sports field, hiking trails, v-ball.

Pets welcome, breed restrict. Open all yr. Big rigs welcome. Escort to site. Clubs welcome. Rate in 2010 $22 for 2 persons. MC/VISA/DISC/AMEX/Debit.

Phone: (601)520-6631
Address: 221 Okatoma River Rd, Hattiesburg, MS 39401
Lat/Lon: 31.45683/-89.42044
Email: Fabaker2001@okatomaresort.com
Web: www.okatomaresort.com

SEE AD NEXT PAGE

HATTIESBURG—Continued on next page

Natchez now has more than 500 buildings that are on the National Register of Historic Places.

HATTIESBURG—Continued

(S) PAUL B JOHNSON SP—(Forrest) *From town: Go 14 mi S on Hwy 49.*

FACILITIES: 108 sites, 36 ft max RV length, 23 full hkups, 85 W&E, 22 pull-thrus, tenting, cabins, dump, laundry, ice, picnic tables, grills, wood, controlled access.

RECREATION: rec hall, pavilion, coin games, lake swim, boating, canoeing, ramp, dock, 6 rowboat/6 canoe/6 pedal boat rentals, lake fishing, playground, sports field, hiking trails. Rec open to public.

Pets welcome. Open all yr. MC/VISA.

Phone: (601)582-7721
Address: 319 Gieger Lake Rd, Hattiesburg, MS 39401
Lat/Lon: 31.13448/-89.24326
Web: campingconnection.com

SEE AD TRAVEL SECTION PAGE 431 AND AD LA TRAVEL SECTION PAGE 278

HOLLANDALE—C-2

(W) LEROY PERCY SP—(Washington) *From jct US 61 & Hwy 12: Go 6 mi W on Hwy 12.*

FACILITIES: 16 sites, typical site width 35 ft, 34 ft max RV length, 15 W&E, 1 no hkups, tenting, cabins, dump, laundry, ltd groc, ice, picnic tables, patios, fire rings, grills, wood, controlled access.

RECREATION: pavilion, equipped pavilion, swim pool, boating, 10 hp limit, ramp, dock, 10 rowboat/5 pedal boat rentals, lake fishing, playground, sports field, hiking trails, v-ball. Rec open to public.

Pets welcome. Open all yr. MC/VISA.

Phone: (662)827-5436
Address: 1400 Highway 12 E A, Hollandale, MS 38748
Lat/Lon: 33.16089/-90.93615
Web: campingconnection.com

SEE AD TRAVEL SECTION PAGE 431 AND AD LA TRAVEL SECTION PAGE 278

HOLLY SPRINGS—A-3

HOLLY SPRINGS NATIONAL FOREST (Chewalla Lake Campground)—(Marshall) *From town: Go 5 mi NE on Hwy 4, then 1 mi S on CR 634, then 1 mi E on FR 611.* FACILITIES: 36 sites, 22 ft max RV length, 9 W&E, 27 no hkups, tenting, dump. RECREATION: lake swim, boating, ramp, lake fishing, playground. Partial handicap access. Open all yr. Phone: (662)236-6550.

(S) WALL DOXEY SP—(Benton) *From jct US 78 & Hwy 7: Go 6 mi S on Hwy 7.*

FACILITIES: 64 sites, 64 W&E, tenting, cabins, RV storage, dump, laundry, ice, picnic tables, patios, fire rings, grills, wood.

RECREATION: rec hall, pavilion, lake swim, boating, electric motors only, canoeing, ramp, dock, 6 rowboat/6 canoe/6 pedal boat rentals, lake fishing, mini-golf, bsktball, playground, sports field, hiking trails, v-ball. Rec open to public.

Pets welcome. Open all yr. MC/VISA.

Phone: (662)252-4231
Address: 3946 Hwy 7, South, Holly Springs, MS 38635
Lat/Lon: 34.66302/-89.46409
Web: campingconnection.com

SEE AD TRAVEL SECTION PAGE 431 AND AD LA TRAVEL SECTION PAGE 278

HORN LAKE—A-3

(S) Memphis Jellystone Camp Resort—(DeSoto) *From jct I-55 & Church Rd (exit 287): Go 1 mi W on Church Rd, then 3/4 mi N on US 51, then 500 ft E on Audubon Point Dr. Enter at end.* ◆◆◆◆◆FACILITIES: 116 sites, 116 full hkups, (20/30/50 amps), 60 pull-

HORN LAKE—Continued
Memphis Jellystone Camp Resort—Continued

thrus, tenting, laundry. ◆◆◆◆RECREATION: swim pool, playground. Pets welcome, quantity restrict. Partial handicap access. Open all yr. Big rigs welcome. Rate in 2010 $45-55 for 2 persons. Member ARVC. Phone: (662)280-8282.

HOUSTON—B-4

TOMBIGBEE NATIONAL FOREST (Davis Lake Campground)—(Chickasaw) *From town: Go 10 mi NE on Hwy-15, then 3 mi E on CR 903.* FACILITIES: 25 sites, 22 ft max RV length, 25 W&E, (20 amps), tenting, dump. RECREATION: lake swim, boating, ramp, dock, lake fishing. Pets welcome. Open May 1 - Sep 15. Phone: (662)285-3264.

Woodall's Tip... 100% Money Back Guarantee... If for any reason you're not satisfied with this Directory, please return it to us by December 31, 2011 along with your sales receipt, and we'll reimburse you for the amount you paid for the Directory.

IUKA—A-5

(NE) JP COLEMAN SP—(Tishomingo) *From jct US 17 & Hwy 25: Go 5 mi N on Hwy 25, then 8 mi NE on paved road. Follow signs.*

FACILITIES: 74 sites, 32 ft max RV length, 74 W&E, tenting, cabins, dump, laundry, ice, picnic tables, grills.

RECREATION: pavilion, swim pool, lake swim, boating, ramp, dock, 6 rowboat rentals, lake fishing, mini-golf, playground, sports field. Rec open to public.

Pets welcome. Open all yr. MC/VISA.

Phone: (662)423-6515
Address: 612 CR 321, Luka, MS 38852
Lat/Lon: 34.93085/-88.16707
Web: campingconnection.com

SEE AD TRAVEL SECTION PAGE 431 AND AD LA TRAVEL SECTION PAGE 278

Jimmy Buffet, singer and songwriter, is from Mississippi.

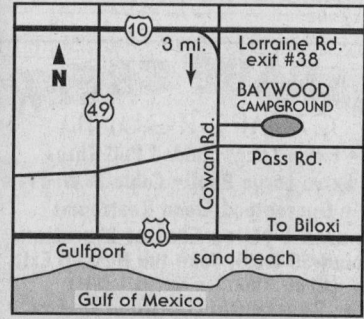

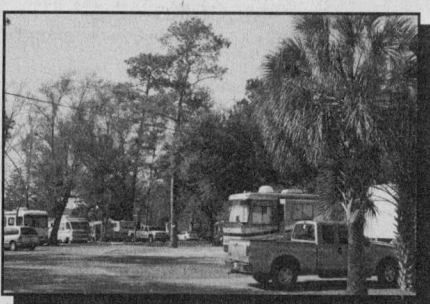

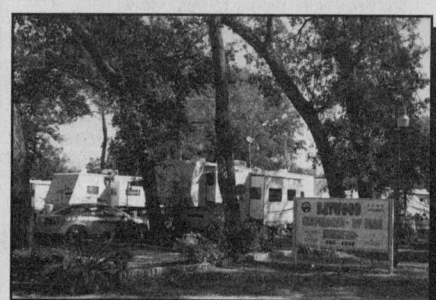

JACKSON—D-3

(NE) GOSHEN SPRINGS CAMPGROUND (Pearl River Valley Water Supply District)—(Rankin) *From Natchez Trace Pkwy & Hwy-43: Go 3 mi E on Hwy-43. Enter on L.* FACILITIES: 169 sites, typical site width 25 ft, 169 full hkups, (20/30/50 amps), dump, laundry. RECREATION: swim pool, lake/river swim, boating, canoeing, ramp, dock, lake/river fishing, playground. Pets welcome. Partial handicap access. No tents. Open all yr. Big rigs welcome. Phone: (601)829-2751.

(N) LEFLEUR'S BLUFF SP & GOLF COURSE—(Hinds) *From jct I-55 (exit 98B-Carthage/Lakeland) & Hwy 25N: Go 1 mi E on Hwy 25N to camping entrance.*

WELCOME

FACILITIES: 30 sites, 30 W&E, tenting, dump, ltd groc, picnic tables, grills, wood, controlled access.

RECREATION: pavilion, swim pool, boating, electric motors only, canoeing, ramp, 8 rowboat/6 canoe/8 pedal boat rentals, lake fishing, putting green, playground, tennis, sports field, hiking trails. Rec open to public.

Pets welcome. Open all yr.

Phone: (601)987-3923
Address: 2140 Riverside Dr., Jackson, MS 39202
Lat/Lon: 32.33268/-90.15032
Web: campingconnection.com

SEE AD TRAVEL SECTION PAGE 431 AND AD LA TRAVEL SECTION PAGE 278

MISSISSIPPI STATE PARKS—(Hinds) *From I-55 (exit 98A) & Woodrow Wilson Ave: Go 3/4 mi W on Woodrow Wilson, then 1/2 mi N on State St.*

WELCOME

Offer 22 campgrounds w/dev campsites, tenting, group camping & cabins-rustic to deluxe.

Address: 1505 Eastover Dr, Jackson, MS 39211
Lat/Lon: 32.31818/-90.17207
Email: tjack2013@mowfp.state.ms.us
Web: www.mdwfp.com

SEE AD TRAVEL SECTION PAGE 431 AND AD LA TRAVEL SECTION PAGE 278

(NE) TIMBERLAKE CAMPGROUND (Pearl River Valley Water Supply District)—(Rankin) *From jct I-55 & Lakeland Dr: Go 7 mi E on Lakeland Dr, then 4 mi N on Old Fannin Rd. Enter on L.* FACILITIES: 272 sites, typical site width 25 ft, 272 full hkups, (15/30/50 amps), tenting, dump, laundry. RECREATION: swim pool, lake swim, boating, ramp, dock, lake fishing, playground. Pets welcome. Partial handicap access. Open all yr. Big rigs welcome. Phone: (601)992-9100.

LENA—D-3

(W) LEAKE COUNTY WATER PARK (Pearl River Valley Water Supply District)—(Leake) *From jct Natchez Trace Parkway & Hwy 43: Go 7 mi E on Hwy 43, then 10 mi N on Hwy 25, then 3 mi NW on Utah Rd, then 3 mi W on Park Rd (follow signs). Enter at end.* FACILITIES: 42 sites, typical site width 25 ft, 42 full hkups, (15/30/50 amps), tenting, dump, laundry. RECREATION: swim pool, river swim, boating, canoeing, ramp, dock, river fishing, playground. Pets welcome. Partial handicap access. Open all yr. Big rigs welcome. Phone: (601)654-9359.

(W) LOW HEAD DAM (Pearl River Valley Water Supply District)—(Leake) *From jct Natchez Trace Parkway & Hwy 43: Go 7 mi E on Hwy 43, then 10 mi N on Hwy 25, then 3 mi NW on Utah Rd, then 5 mi W on Lowhead Dam Rd. Enter at end.* FACILITIES: 13 sites, 13 W&E, (15/30/50 amps), tenting. RECREATION: swim pool, river swim, boating, canoeing, ramp, river fishing. Pets welcome. Partial handicap access. Open all yr. Big rigs welcome. Phone: (601)654-9359.

Greenwood is the home of Cotton Row, which is the second largest cotton exchange in the nation and is on the National Register of Historic Places.

LOUISVILLE—C-4

(N) LEGION SP—(Winston) *From Hwy 14E (Main St) in town: Go 2 mi N on N Columbus Ave (Bypass Hwy 25). Enter on L.*

WELCOME

FACILITIES: 15 sites, 15 no hkups, tenting, cabins, picnic tables, grills, wood, controlled access.

RECREATION: pavilion, boating, electric motors only, 6 rowboat/pedal boat rentals, lake fishing, bsktball, hiking trails. Rec open to public.

Pets welcome. Open all yr. For tent camping only. No RVs.

Phone: (662)773-8323
Address: 635 Legion State Park Rd, Louisville, MS 39339
Lat/Lon: 33.14608/-89.04113
Web: campingconnection.com

SEE AD TRAVEL SECTION PAGE 431 AND AD LA TRAVEL SECTION PAGE 278

LUDLOW—D-3

(W) COAL BLUFF PARK (Pearl River Valley Water Supply District)—(Scott) *From jct Natchez Trace Parkway & Hwy 43: Go 7 mi E on Hwy 43, then 9 mi N on Hwy 25, then 3 mi W on Riverbend Rd, then 4 mi N on Coal Bluff Rd. Enter at end.* FACILITIES: 50 sites, typical site width 25 ft, 39 full hkups, 11 E, (15/30/50 amps), 3 pull-thrus, tenting, dump, laundry. RECREATION: swim pool, river swim, boating, canoeing, ramp, river/pond fishing, playground. Pets welcome. Partial handicap access. Open all yr. Big rigs welcome. Phone: (601)654-7726.

LULA—A-2

(W) Isle of Capri RV Park (RV SPACES)—(Coahoma) *From jct US 61 & US 49: Go 10 mi W on US 49. Enter on R.* FACILITIES: 28 sites, accepts full hkup units only, 28 full hkups, 28 pull-thrus, dump, laundry. Pets welcome. No tents. Open all yr. Rate in 2010 $14.95. Phone: (800)789-5825.

LUMBERTON—E-3

LITTLE BLACK CREEK WATER PARK (Pat Harrison Waterway District)—(Lamar) *From jct I-59 (exit 41) & Hwy 13: Go 3 mi W on Hwy 13, then 1/3 mi N on US 11, then 7 mi NW on Mynich Rd. Follow signs.* FACILITIES: 106 sites, typical site width 23 ft, 82 full hkups, 24 W&E, (30/50 amps), tenting, dump, laundry, ltd groc. RECREATION: lake swim, boating, canoeing, ramp, dock, lake fishing, playground. Open all yr. Phone: (601) 794-2957.

MCCOMB—E-2

(E) BOGUE CHITTO WATER PARK CAMPGROUND (Pearl River Basin Dev. Dist.)—(Pike) *From jct I-55 & Hwy 98 east (exit 15A): Go 12 mi E on Hwy 98, then at Brown Bogue Chitto Water Park sign, go 1 mi S on Dogwood Trail. Enter at end.* FACILITIES: 91 sites, typical site width 28 ft, 7 full hkups, 74 W&E, (20/30/50 amps), 10 no hkups, tenting, dump. RECREATION: river swim, boating, canoeing, ramp, river fishing, playground. Pets welcome. Partial handicap access. Open all yr. Big rigs welcome. Phone: (601)684-9568.

(W) PERCY QUIN SP & QUAIL HOLLOW GOLF COURSE—(Pike) *From jct I-55 (exit 13) & Fernwood Rd: Go 3/4 mi W on Fernwood Rd, then 1/4 mi N on Hwy 48.*

WELCOME

FACILITIES: 100 sites, 32 ft max RV length, 100 W&E, tenting, cabins, dump, laundry, ltd groc, ice, picnic tables, wood.

RECREATION: rec hall, pavilion, swim pool, lake swim, boating, canoeing, ramp, dock, 6 rowboat/6 canoe/6 pedal boat rentals, lake fishing, mini-golf, bsktball, playground, tennis, sports field, hiking trails. Rec open to public.

Pets welcome. Open all yr. MC/VISA.

Phone: (601)684-3938
Address: 1156 Camp Beaver Dr, McComb, MS 39648
Lat/Lon: 31.18863/-90.51064
Web: campingconnection.com

SEE AD TRAVEL SECTION PAGE 431 AND AD LA TRAVEL SECTION PAGE 278

Mississippi State Motto: "By Valor and Arms"

MENDENHALL—D-3

D'LO WATER PARK (Pearl River Basin Dev. Dist.)—(Simpson) *From town: Go 2 mi W on Old US 49 (D'Lo).* FACILITIES: 12 sites, 12 full hkups, (30/50 amps), dump. RECREATION: river swim, boating, canoeing, ramp, dock, river fishing, playground. Open all yr. Phone: (601)847-4310.

MERIDIAN—D-4

(E) BENCHMARK COACH AND RV PARK—(Lauderdale) *From jct I-20/59 (exit 157B) & Hwy 45: Go 2 mi N on US 45 N to Marion Russell exit, then 1 mi W on Marion Russell, then 1 mi N on Dale Dr.*

WELCOME

◇◇◇◇FACILITIES: 35 sites, typical site width 30 ft, 35 full hkups, (20/30/50 amps), some extd stay sites, 27 pull-thrus, cable TV, WiFi Instant Internet at site, laundry, LP gas by weight/by meter, ice, picnic tables.

CAMPCLUB USA

Pets welcome, breed restrict. No tents. Open all yr. Big rigs welcome. Clubs welcome. Rate in 2010 $25-30 for 2 persons. MC/VISA/Debit. Member ARVC. FMCA discount. CCUSA 50% Discount. CCUSA reservations Required, CCUSA max stay Unlimited, Cash only for CCUSA disc. Cash only. Subject to availability. Must specify CCUSA prior to making reservations or checking site availability. No electric heaters.

Phone: (601)483-7999
Address: 6420 Dale Dr, Meridian, MS 39342
Lat/Lon: 32.42747/-88.64545
Email: bigrigs@benchmarkrv.net
Web: www.benchmarkrv.net

SEE AD THIS PAGE

(E) NANABE CREEK CAMPGROUND—(Lauderdale) *From jct US 45 & I-20/59 (exit 157): Go 3-1/2 mi E on I-20/59 (exit 160), then 1 mi N on Russell Rd. Enter on R.*

WELCOME

◇◇◇◇FACILITIES: 75 sites, typical site width 28 ft, 55 full hkups, 10 W&E, (20/30/50 amps), 50 amps ($), 10 no hkups, some extd stay sites, 30 pull-thrus, WiFi Instant Internet at site, phone Internet central location, tenting, RV storage, laundry, RV supplies, LP gas by weight/by meter, ice, picnic tables, fire rings, wood.

◇◇◇RECREATION: rec room/area, pavilion, swim pool, pond fishing, golf nearby, play equipment, sports field, v-ball. Rec open to public.

Pets welcome. Open all yr. Big rigs welcome. Escort to site. Clubs welcome. Rate in 2010 $25-28 for 2 persons. FCRV discount. FMCA discount.

Phone: (601)485-4711
Address: 1933 Russell-Mt. Gilead Rd., Meridian, MS 39301
Lat/Lon: 32.40286/-88.59116
Email: maryjo@nanabervpark.com
Web: nanabervpark.com

SEE AD THIS PAGE

OKATIBBEE WATER PARK (Pat Harrison Waterway District)—(Lauderdale) *From jct I-20/59 (exit 150) & Hwy 19: Go 5 mi N on Hwy 19, then 8 mi N on Pine Spring Rd. Follow signs.* FACILITIES: 105 sites, typical site width 25 ft, 75 full hkups, 30 W&E, (50 amps), 6 pull-thrus, tenting, dump, laundry. RECREATION: swim pool, lake swim, boating, canoeing, ramp, dock, lake fishing, playground. Open all yr. Phone: (601)737-2370.

TWILTLEY BRANCH CAMPING AREA (COE-Okatibbee Lake)—(Lauderdale) *From town: Go 10 mi NW on Hwy 19, then 2 mi E on CR 17.* FACILITIES: 61 sites, 50 W&E, (30 amps), 11 no hkups, 3 pull-thrus, tenting, dump, laundry. RECREATION: lake swim, boating, canoeing, ramp, lake fishing, playground. Partial handicap access. Open all yr. Phone: (601)626-8068.

MONTICELLO—E-3

ATWOOD WATER PARK (Pearl River Basin Dev. Dist.)—(Lawrence) *From town: Go 1 mi E on Hwy-84.* FACILITIES: 44 sites, 44 W&E, tenting, dump. RECREATION: boating, ramp, river fishing, playground. Partial handicap access. Open Mar - Oct. Phone: (601)587-2711.

MORTON—D-3

(N) ROOSEVELT SP—(Scott) *From jct I-20 (exit 77) & Hwy 13: Go 1/2 mi N on Hwy 13.*

WELCOME

FACILITIES: 109 sites, 28 full hkups, 81 W&E, 1 pull-thrus, tenting, cabins, dump, laundry, picnic tables, patios.

RECREATION: rec hall, rec room/area, pavilion, swim pool, lake swim, boating, canoeing, ramp, dock, 6 rowboat/6 canoe/6 pedal boat rentals, lake fishing, mini-golf, playground, tennis, sports field, hiking trails, v-ball. Rec open to public.

Pets welcome. Open all yr. MC/VISA.

Phone: (601)732-6316
Address: 2149 Hwy 13 S, Morton, MS 39117
Lat/Lon: 32.31930/-89.66770
Web: campingconnection.com

SEE AD TRAVEL SECTION PAGE 431 AND AD LA TRAVEL SECTION PAGE 278

MOUNT OLIVE—E-3

DRY CREEK WATER PARK (Pat Harrison Waterway District)—(Covington) *From jct US 49 & park road: Go 4-1/2 mi W on park road. Follow signs.* FACILITIES: 36 sites, typical site width 23 ft, 38 ft max RV length, 8 full hkups, 28 W&E, tenting, dump. RECREATION: lake swim, boating, canoeing, ramp, lake fishing, playground. Open all yr. Phone: (601)797-4619.

NATCHEZ—E-1

(NE) NATCHEZ SP—(Adams) *From north jct US 84/98 & US 61: Go 5-1/4 mi NE on US 61, then 3/4 mi E on park road.*

WELCOME

FACILITIES: 50 sites, 32 ft max RV length, 6 full hkups, 44 W&E, tenting, cabins, dump, picnic tables, grills.

RECREATION: pavilion, boating, ramp, dock, 6 rowboat/6 pedal boat rentals, lake fishing, playground, hiking trails. Rec open to public.

Pets welcome. Open all yr.

Phone: (601)442-2658
Address: 230-B Wickcliff Rd, Natchez, MS 39120
Lat/Lon: 31.59687/-91.21585
Email: natchez@tacinfo.com
Web: campingconnection.com

SEE AD TRAVEL SECTION PAGE 431 AND AD LA TRAVEL SECTION PAGE 278

RIVER VIEW RV PARK—*From Natchez(jct US Hwy 61 & US Hwy 65/84): Go 3 1/2 mi W on US Hwy 65/84, (to West End of Mississippi River Bridge) then 1 mi S on SR 131, then 1 block E on Black Top Rd. Enter at end.*

WELCOME

SEE PRIMARY LISTING AT VIDALIA, LA AND AD THIS PAGE

OAKLAND—B-3

(NE) GEORGE PAYNE COSSAR SP—(Tallahatchie) *From jct I-55 (exit 227) & Hwy 32: Go 2-1/2 mi E on Hwy 32, then 1-3/4 mi N on park access road.*

WELCOME

FACILITIES: 84 sites, 32 ft max RV length, 84 W&E, tenting, cabins, dump, laundry, ice, picnic tables, patios, fire rings, grills, wood, controlled access.

RECREATION: rec hall, pavilion, swim pool, boating, ramp, 6 rowboat rentals, lake fishing, mini-golf, bike rental 8 bike rentals, playground, sports field, hiking trails, v-ball. Rec open to public.

Pets welcome. Open all yr. Church services Memorial Day to Labor Day. MC/VISA.

Phone: (662)623-7356
Address: 165 County Rd 170, Oakland, MS 38948
Lat/Lon: 34.13049/-89.88125
Web: campingconnection.com

SEE AD TRAVEL SECTION PAGE 431 AND AD LA TRAVEL SECTION PAGE 278

OCEAN SPRINGS—F-4

GULF ISLANDS NATIONAL SEASHORE (Davis Bayou Area)—*From town: Go 2 mi E on US 90, then 1 mi S on Park Rd.* FACILITIES: 51 sites, 45 ft max RV length, 51 W&E, (30 amps), tenting, dump. RECREATION: boating, ramp, dock, saltwater fishing, playground. Partial handicap access. Open all yr. Phone: (228)875-3962.

PASCAGOULA—F-5

See listings at Gautier

PELAHATCHIE—D-3

(N) Yogi On The Lake—(Rankin) *From I-20 (exit 68) & Hwy 43, then 2 mi N on Hwy 43, then 1/2 mi W on Lake Rd to Campgrounds Rd.* ◆◆◆◆◆FACILITIES: 150 sites, 150 full hkups, (20/30/50 amps), family camping, tenting, laundry, ltd groc. ◆◆◆◆◆RECREATION: swim pool, lake swim, boating, ramp, lake fishing, playground. Pets welcome, breed restrict. Partial handicap access. Open all yr. Big rigs welcome. Rate in 2010 $26-46 for 2 persons. Member ARVC. Phone: (601)854-6859.

PHILADELPHIA—C-4

(W) Frog Level RV Park—(Neshoba) *From jct Hwy 15 & Hwy 16W: Go 500 feet W on Hwy 16W. Enter on R.* ◆◆◆FACILITIES: 52 sites, typical site width 30 ft, 52 full hkups, (20/30/50 amps), 52 pull-thrus, laundry, full svc store. Pets welcome, breed restrict. Partial handicap access. No tents. Open all yr. Big rigs welcome. Rate in 2010 $20 for 4 persons. Phone: (601) 650-0044.

PICAYUNE—F-3

(NE) Clearwater RV Park—(Pearl River) *From jct I-59 & Hwy 43 (exit 4): Go 1 mi E on Hwy 43, then 7-1/2 mi N on Ceasar Rd. Enter on L.* ◆◆◆◆FACILITIES: 64 sites, 64 full hkups, (20/30/50 amps), 3 pull-thrus, laundry, ltd groc. ◆◆◆RECREATION: pond fishing, playground. Pets welcome. Partial handicap access. No tents. Open all yr. Big rigs welcome. Rate in 2010 $25-26 for 2 persons. Phone: (601)749-8142.

(E) SUN ROAMERS RV RESORT—(Pearl River) *From jct I-59 & Hwy 43 (exit 4): Go 3/4 mi E on Hwy 43 then 1/2 mi S on Stafford Rd. Enter on R.*

WELCOME

◆◆◆◆FACILITIES: 154 sites, typical site width 50 ft, 154 full hkups, (30/50 amps), some extd stay sites, WiFi Instant Internet at site, cabins, RV storage, dump, non-guest dump $, laundry, LP gas by weight/by meter, ice, picnic tables.

◆◆◆◆RECREATION: rec hall, rec room/area, equipped pavilion, swim pool, lake fishing, mini-golf, ($), golf nearby, play equipment, horseshoes, sports field, hiking trails, v-ball.

Pets welcome, breed restrict, size restrict. No tents. Open all yr. Big rigs welcome. Escort to site. Clubs welcome. Rate in 2010 $26-38 for 2 persons. MC/VISA/Debit. FMCA discount. CCUSA 50% Discount. CCUSA reservations Accepted, CCUSA max stay 14 days. Discount available on selected sites. $5 electrical surcharge May thru Sept.

Phone: (601)798-5818
Address: 41 Mississippi Pines Blvd, Picayune, MS 39466
Lat/Lon: 30.51012/-89.64970
Email: rvreserve@sunroamers.com
Web: www.sunroamers.com

Reserve Online at Woodalls.com

SEE AD THIS PAGE

PORT GIBSON—D-2

(NW) GRAND GULF MILITARY PARK CAMPGROUND (State)—(Claiborne) *From jct US 61 & Hwy 462: Go 7 mi W on paved road (follow signs). Enter on R.* FACILITIES: 42 sites, typical site width 35 ft, 42 full hkups, (30 amps), 2 pull-thrus, tenting, dump, laundry. RECREATION: Partial handicap access. Open all yr. Phone: (601)437-5911.

PORT GIBSON—Continued

(NE) NATCHEZ TRACE PARKWAY (Rocky Springs Campground)—(Claiborne) *From jct Hwy 18 & Natchez Trace Pkwy: Go 13 mi N on Natchez Trace Pkwy. Enter on L.* FACILITIES: 22 sites, 35 ft max RV length, 22 no hkups, tenting. RECREATION: Pets welcome. Open all yr. Phone: (662)680-4025.

QUITMAN—D-4

(NW) ARCHUSA CREEK WATER PARK (Pat Harrison Waterway District)—(Clarke) *From jct I-59 (exit 126) & Hwy 18: Go 9 mi E on Hwy 18, then 3 mi N on US 45/Hwy 18, then 1-1/4 mi E on Hwy 18, then 1 mi E on Hwy 511. Follow signs.* FACILITIES: 69 sites, typical site width 25 ft, 38 ft max RV length, 56 full hkups, 13 W&E, (30/50 amps), tenting, dump, laundry. RECREATION: lake swim, boating, canoeing, ramp, dock, lake fishing, playground. Open all yr. Phone: (601)776-6956.

(N) CLARKCO SP—(Clarke) *From town: Go 5 mi N on US-45.*

FACILITIES: 43 sites, 32 ft max RV length, 43 W&E, 2 pull-thrus, cabins, dump, laundry, groceries, picnic tables, wood.

RECREATION: rec hall, pavilion, lake swim, boating, canoeing, ramp, dock, 6 rowboat/6 canoe/6 pedal boat rentals, lake fishing, playground, tennis, sports field, hiking trails. Rec open to public.

Pets welcome. Open all yr. MC/VISA.

Phone: (601)776-6651
Address: 386 Clarkco Rd, Quitman, MS 39355
Lat/Lon: 32.10241/-88.70075
Web: www.mdwfp.com/parkview/parks

SEE AD TRAVEL SECTION PAGE 431 AND AD LA TRAVEL SECTION PAGE 278

ROBINSONVILLE—A-3

(E) BUCK ISLAND MHC (RV SPACES) —(TUNICA) *From jct Hwy 61 & CR-304: Go 1-1/2 mi E on CR 304, then 2 mi S on Kirby Rd.*

WELCOME

FACILITIES: 44 sites, accepts full hkup units only, 44 full hkups, (30/50 amps), some extd stay sites.

Pets welcome, breed restrict, size restrict. No tents. Open all yr. No restrooms. Big rigs welcome. Rate in 2010 $22 for 2 persons.

Phone: (662)363-0121
Address: 2466 Kirby Rd, Robinsonville, MS 38664
Lat/Lon: 34.79245/-90.27278
Email: buckisland@wildblue.net

SEE AD TUNICA NEXT PAGE AND AD MEMPHIS, TN PAGE 734 AND AD MILLINGTON, TN PAGE 736

ROSEDALE—B-2

(W) GREAT RIVER ROAD SP—(Bolivar) *From jct Hwys 1/8: Go 1 mi W on park access road.*

WELCOME

FACILITIES: 61 sites, 61 W&E, tenting, dump, laundry, ice, picnic tables, patios, grills, wood, controlled access.

RECREATION: rec hall, rec room/area, pavilion, lake/river swim, boating, no motors, canoeing, ramp, 6 rowboat/6 canoe/6 pedal boat rentals, lake/river fishing, bsktball, 8 bike rentals, playground, sports field, hiking trails. Rec open to public.

Pets welcome. Open all yr. MC/VISA.

Phone: (662)759-6762
Address: Highway 1 S, Rosedale, MS 28769
Lat/Lon: 33.84551/-91.04611
Web: www.wildernet.com

SEE AD TRAVEL SECTION PAGE 431 AND AD LA TRAVEL SECTION PAGE 278

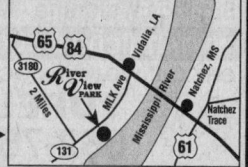

SARDIS—A-3

(E) JOHN KYLE SP & MALLARD POINT GOLF COURSE—(Panola) *From jct I-55 (exit 252) & Hwy 315: Go 7 mi SE on Hwy 315.*

FACILITIES: 200 sites, 200 W&E, tenting, cabins, dump, laundry, ice, picnic tables, grills, wood.

RECREATION: rec hall, pavilion, swim pool, lake swim, boating, ramp, rowboat rentals, lake fishing, bike rental 8 bike rentals, playground, tennis, sports field, hiking trails. Rec open to public.

Pets welcome. Open all yr. MC/VISA.

Phone: (662)487-1345
Address: 4235 State Park Rd, Sardis, MS 38666
Lat/Lon: 34.41072/-89.80556
Web: mdwfp.com

SEE AD TRAVEL SECTION PAGE 431 AND AD LA TRAVEL SECTION PAGE 278

SOSO—E-4

(W) BIG CREEK WATER PARK (Pat Harrison Waterway District)—(Jones) *From jct I-59 & US 84: Go 12 mi W on US 84, then 1 mi S on park road. Follow signs.* FACILITIES: 49 sites, 38 ft max RV length, 40 full hkups, 9 W&E, 6 pull-thrus, tenting, dump, laundry. RECREATION: lake swim, boating, canoeing, ramp, dock, lake fishing, playground. Open all yr. Phone: (601) 763-8555.

SOUTHAVEN—A-3

(S) EZ DAZE RV PARK—(Desoto) *From jct I-55 (exit 287) & Church Rd: Go 1/8 mi W on Church Rd, then 3/4 mi N on Pepper Chase Dr, then 1 block W on WE Ross Parkway. Enter on R.*

BRAND NEW RV PARK DESIGNED JUST FOR YOU!

Location, Location - It's central to Memphis attractions and Tunica Casinos. Relax on our veranda, chill out in our gazebo - enclosed hot tub or let our massage therapist relax those tired muscles. It's a first-class RV Park.

◆◆◆◆◆FACILITIES: 87 sites, 87 full hkups, (20/30/50 amps), some extd stay sites, 5 pull-thrus, cable TV, WiFi Instant Internet at site, phone Internet central location, laundry, RV supplies, LP gas by weight/by meter, ice, picnic tables, patios.

◆◆RECREATION: pavilion, swim pool, hot tub.

Pets welcome, breed restrict. Partial handicap access. No tents. Open all yr. Big rigs welcome. Clubs welcome. Rate in 2010 $30-33 for 2 persons. MC/VISA/DISC/AMEX/Debit.

Text 116514 to (440)725-8687 to see our Visual Tour.

Phone: (662)342-7720
Address: 536 W E Ross Parkway, Southaven, MS 38671
Lat/Lon: 34.94188/-89.99888
Email: ezdazervpark@yahoo.com
Web: ezdazervpark.info

SEE AD MEMPHIS, TN PAGE 734

(N) Southaven RV Park—(DeSoto) *From I-55 (exit 291/Stateline Rd): Go 2 blocks E. Enter on L.* ◆◆◆◆FACILITIES: 44 sites, typical site width 29 ft, 44 full hkups, (20/30/50 amps), 14 pull-thrus, laundry. Pets welcome. Partial handicap access. No tents. Open all yr. Big rigs welcome. Rate in 2010 $28 per vehicle. Phone: (662)393-8585.

(S) SOUTHAVEN RV SUPERCENTER—*From I-55 (exit 287) & Church Rd: Go 1/8 mi W on Church Rd, then 1/2 mi N on Pepper Chase. Enter on L.* SALES: travel trailers, park models, 5th wheels, Class A motorhomes, Class C motorhomes, fold-down camping trailers, pre-owned unit sales. SERVICES: full-time mech, RV appliance repair, body work/collision repair, sells parts/accessories, installs hitches. Open all yr. MC/VISA/DISC.

Phone: (662)393-9948
Address: 5485 Pepper Chase, Southaven, MS 38671
Lat/Lon: 34.93990/-89.99608
Email: mhixson@southavenrv.com
Web: www.southavenrv.com

SEE AD MEMPHIS, TN PAGE 736

TISHOMINGO—A-5

(SE) TISHOMINGO SP—(Tishomingo) *From town: Go 1 mi S on Hwy 25, then 2 mi E on park road.*

FACILITIES: 62 sites, 32 ft max RV length, 62 W&E, tenting, cabins, dump, laundry, picnic tables, wood.

RECREATION: pavilion, swim pool, boating, 10 hp limit, canoeing, ramp, dock, 6 rowboat/6 canoe/6 pedal boat rentals, float trips, lake/river fishing, mini-golf, bsktball, 8 bike rentals, playground, sports field, hiking trails, v-ball. Rec open to public.

Pets welcome. Open all yr. MC/VISA.

Phone: (662)438-6914
Address: 105 County Road 90, Tishomingo, MS 38773
Lat/Lon: 34.61172/-88.20121
Web: campingconnection.com

SEE AD TRAVEL SECTION PAGE 431 AND AD LA TRAVEL SECTION PAGE 278

TUNICA—A-2

(C) HARRAH'S CASINO RV RESORT—(Tunica) *From jct US 61 & Grand Casino Pkwy: Go 2-1/2 mi W on Grand Casino Pkwy. Enter at end.*

◆◆◆◆◆FACILITIES: 200 sites, 200 full hkups, (20/30/50 amps), 79 pull-thrus, cable TV, WiFi Instant Internet at site ($), WiFi Internet central location, laundry, ltd groc, RV supplies, LP gas by weight/by meter, ice, picnic tables, patios, controlled access.

◆◆◆◆◆RECREATION: rec room/area, pavilion, coin games, swim pool, putting green, bsktball, playground, shuffleboard court shuffleboard court, tennis, sports field, v-ball.

Pets welcome. Partial handicap access. No tents. Open all yr. Big rigs welcome. Clubs welcome. Rate in 2010 $16-20 per family. MC/VISA/DISC/AMEX.

Phone: (800)WIN 4-WIN
Address: 111 Resort Village Rd, Robinsonville, MS 38664
Lat/Lon: 34.84652/-90.29109
Web: www.harrahs.com

SEE AD DISCOVER SECTION PAGE 41

HARRAH'S CASINO TUNICA—*From jct US 61 & Grand Casino Pkwy: Go 2-1/2 mi W on Grand Casino Pkwy. Enter at end.* The largest casino between Las Vegas and Atlantic City and the closest casino to Memphis with seven restaurants. Open all yr. MC/VISA/DISC/AMEX. ATM.

Phone: (800)WIN-4-WIN
Address: 13615 Old US Highway 61 N, Robinsonville, MS 38664
Lat/Lon: 34.85562/-90.29390
Web: www.harrastunica.com

SEE AD DISCOVER SECTION PAGE 41

(C) Hollywood Casino RV Resort—(Tunica) *From jct US 61 & Hwy 304: Go 5-1/2 mi W on Hwy 304. Enter at end.* ◆◆◆◆◆FACILITIES: 122 sites, typical site width 30 ft, accepts full hkup units only, 122 full hkups, (50 amps), 14 pull-thrus, dump, laundry. ◆◆◆◆RECREATION: swim pool. Pets welcome. Partial handicap access. No tents. Open all yr. Big rigs welcome. Rate in 2010 $18 per vehicle. Phone: (800)871-0711.

(C) Sam's Town RV Park—(Hilsborough) *From jct 61 & Hwy 304 (Robinsonville exit): Go 5-1/2 mi W on Hwy 304 (Crossover Mississippi River Levee) Follow Signs. Enter on L.* ◆◆◆◆◆FACILITIES: 100 sites, typical site width 32 ft, 100 full hkups, (30/50 amps), 15 pull-thrus, laundry, ltd groc. ◆◆◆◆RECREATION: swim pool. Pets welcome, quantity restrict. Partial handicap access. No tents. Open all yr. Big rigs welcome. Rate in 2010 $15.99 per vehicle. Phone: (800) 456-0711.

TUPELO—B-4

(SW) CAMPER CITY—*From jct US 78 & Natchez Trace Pkwy: Go SW on Natchez Trace Pkwy (Cliff Gookin Exit), then 1/4 mi W on Cliff Gookin Rd. Enter on L.* SALES: pre-owned unit sales. SERVICES: full-time mech, RV appliance repair, body work/collision repair, sells parts/accessories, installs hitches. Open all yr.

Phone: (662)844-2371
Address: 4895 Cliff Gookin Blvd, Tupelo, MS 38801
Lat/Lon: 34.24000/-88.77020

SEE AD NEXT PAGE

(N) CAMPGROUNDS AT BARNES CROSSING—(Lee) *From jct Natchez Trace Pkwy & US 78: Go 1-1/4 mi E on US 78, then 1-1/4 mi N on US 45, then 1/2 mi W on Barnes Crossing Rd, then 1/2 mi N on Old 45/145 to County Rd 1698. Enter on R.*

◆◆◆◆FACILITIES: 54 sites, 54 full hkups, (30/50 amps), some extd stay sites, 25 pull-thrus, cable TV, WiFi Instant Internet at site, phone Internet central location, dump, non-guest dump $, laundry, RV supplies, ice, picnic tables.

◆RECREATION: golf nearby, hiking trails.

Pets welcome. No tents. Open all yr. Big rigs welcome. Escort to site. Clubs welcome. Rate in 2010 $32 for 2 persons.

Phone: (662)844-6063
Address: 125 Road 1698, Tupelo, MS 38804
Lat/Lon: 34.32293/-88.70624
Email: cgbarnescrossing@comcast.net
Web: www.cgbarnescrossing.com

SEE AD NEXT PAGE

ELVIS PRESLEY LAKE & CAMPGROUND (County Park)—(Lee) *From jct US 45 & US 78: Go 1 mi E on US 78 (Veterans Blvd Exit), then 1 block N on Veterans Blvd, then 1 3/4 mi E on CR 1460, then 1/2 mi NE on CR 995. Enter on R.* FACILITIES: 66 sites, typical site width 30 ft, 16 W&E, 50 no hkups, 1 pull-thrus, tenting, dump. RECREATION: boating, ramp, dock, lake fishing. Open all yr. Phone: (662)841-1304.

(SW) NATCHEZ TRACE RV PARK—(Lee) *From jct Hwy 78 & Natchez Trace Pkwy: Go 12 mi S on Natchez Trace Pkwy, exit between milepost 251 & 252, then 250 yards E on Pontocola Rd. Enter on R.*

◆◆◆◆FACILITIES: 32 sites, typical site width 30 ft, 21 full hkups, 11 W&E, (30/50 amps), some extd stay sites, 20 pull-thrus, phone Internet cen-

NATCHEZ TRACE RV PARK—Continued on next page

TUPELO—Continued
NATCHEZ TRACE RV PARK—Continued

tral location, tenting, dump, laundry, ltd groc, RV supplies, LP gas by weight/by meter, ice, picnic tables, wood.

◆◆◆RECREATION: rec room/area, pavilion, swim pool, pond fishing, fishing supplies, horseshoes, v-ball.

Pets welcome. Open all yr. Big rigs welcome. Clubs welcome. Rate in 2010 $23-25 per vehicle. FMCA discount. CCUSA 50% Discount. CCUSA reservations Not Accepted, CCUSA max stay 3 days, Cash only for CCUSA disc., Check only for CCUSA disc., CCUSA disc. not avail holidays. Not valid Mar thru May or Sep thru Nov. Pets must be on leash.

Phone: (662)767-8609
Address: 189 County Rd 506, Shannon, MS 38868
Lat/Lon: 34.14606/-88.81811
Email: wez@dixieconnect.com
Web: www.natcheztracervpark.com

SEE AD PAGE 446

(SE) TOMBIGBEE SP—(Lee) *From town: Go 3 mi SE on Hwy 6, then 3 mi E on state park road.*

WELCOME

FACILITIES: 20 sites, 20 W&E, tenting, cabins, dump, laundry, ice, picnic tables, fire rings, grills, wood.

RECREATION: rec hall, rec room/area, pavilion, lake swim, boating, canoeing, ramp, dock, 8 rowboat/6 canoe/6 pedal boat rentals, lake fishing, playground, tennis, sports field, hiking trails, v-ball. Rec open to public.

Pets welcome. Open all yr. MC/VISA.

John Grisham, novelist, is from Mississippi.

TUPELO—Continued
TOMBIGBEE SP—Continued

Phone: (662)842-7669
Address: 264 Cabin Dr, Tupelo, MS 38804
Lat/Lon: 34.22990/-88.62011
Email: tombigb@bellsouth.net
Web: campingconnection.com

SEE AD TRAVEL SECTION PAGE 431 AND AD LA TRAVEL SECTION PAGE 278

(W) TRACE SP—(Lee) *From Natchez Trace Parkway: Go 6 mi W on Hwy 6, then 2-1/2 mi N on CR 65.*

WELCOME

FACILITIES: 52 sites, 32 ft max RV length, 52 W&E, 3 pull-thrus, tenting, cabins, RV storage, dump, laundry, picnic tables, grills, wood.

RECREATION: pavilion, lake swim, boating, ramp, dock, 6 pedal boat rentals, lake fishing, bike rental 8 bike rentals, playground, sports field, hiking trails. Rec open to public.

Pets welcome. Open all yr.

Phone: (662)489-2958
Address: 2139 Faulkner Rd, Belden, MS 38826
Lat/Lon: 34.26034/-88.88669
Email: tracesp@avrix.net
Web: campingconnection.com

SEE AD TRAVEL SECTION PAGE 431 AND AD LA TRAVEL SECTION PAGE 278

The Mississippi River is the longest river in North America and is the nation's chief waterway. Its nicknames include "Old Man River" and "Ole Miss".

TYLERTOWN—E-3

HIDDEN SPRINGS RESORT—(Wathall) *From jct SH 27 & US Hwy 98: Go 4-1/2 mi W on US Hwy 98, then 3 mi S on Mesa Walker Bridge Rd. Enter on R.*

WELCOME

◆◆◆FACILITIES: 60 sites, 19 full hkups, 41 W&E, (30/50 amps), 6 pull-thrus, tenting, cabins, dump, laundry, picnic tables, fire rings.

◆◆◆◆RECREATION: equipped pavilion, 2 swim pools, river swim, boating, electric motors only, canoeing, ramp, river fishing, golf nearby, bsktball, playground, tennis, sports field, hiking trails.

Pets welcome. Open all yr. Big rigs welcome. Rate in 2010 $19-22 for 4 persons.

Phone: (601)876-4151
Address: 16 Clyde Rhodue Rd, Tylertown, MS 39667
Lat/Lon: 31.13710/-90.24758
Email: sheilalynnmcdaniel@yahoo.com
Web: resortmanagementinc.com

SEE AD THIS PAGE AND AD PALM SPRINGS, CA PAGE 154 AND AD SPRINGFIELD, OH PAGE 632

VICKSBURG—D-2

(C) Ameristar RV Park—(Warren) *From jct I-20 (exit 1A) & Washington St: Go 1/2 mi N on Washington St. Enter on R.* ◆◆◆◆◆FACILITIES: 67 sites, typical site width 30 ft, accepts full hkup units only, 67 full hkups, (30/50 amps), 67 pull-thrus, laundry. ◆◆RECREATION: swim pool, play equipment. Pets welcome. No tents. Open all yr. Big rigs welcome. Rate in 2010 $25-30 per family. Phone: (800)700-7770.

VICKSBURG—Continued on next page

William Faulkner, novelist, was from Mississippi.

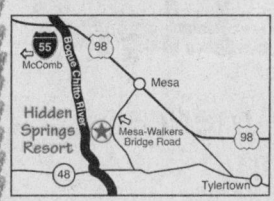

(S) MAGNOLIA RV PARK RESORT—(Warren) *From jct I-20 (exit 1B) & US 61: Go 1 mi S on US 61, then 1/4 mi W on Miller St. Enter on R.*

WELCOME

◆◆◆◆FACILITIES: 66 sites, 66 full hkups, (20/30/50 amps), 66 pull-thrus, cable TV, ($), WiFi Instant Internet at site, RV storage, laundry, ltd groc, RV supplies, LP gas by weight/by meter, ice, picnic tables.

◆◆◆RECREATION: rec hall, rec room/area, swim pool, golf nearby, bsktball, playground, sports field, local tours.

Pets welcome, breed restrict, quantity restrict. Partial handicap access. No tents. Open all yr. Big rigs welcome. Clubs welcome. Rate in 2010 $24-27 for 4 persons. MC/VISA/DISC/Debit. FMCA discount.

Phone: (601)631-0388
Address: 211 Miller St, Vicksburg, MS 39180
Lat/Lon: 32.29963/-90.89556
Email: guestservices@magnoliarvparkresort.com
Web: www.magnoliarvparkresort.com

SEE AD THIS PAGE

(S) River Town Campground—(Warren) *From I-20 (exit 1B) & US Hwy 61 S: Go 6 mi S on Hwy 61 S. Enter on L.* ◆◆◆◆FACILITIES: 148 sites, typical site width 45 ft, 148 full hkups, (20/30/50 amps), 60 pull-thrus, dump, laundry. ◆◆◆RECREATION: swim pool, playground. Pets welcome. Partial handicap access. Open all yr. Big rigs welcome. Rate in 2010 $22-26 per vehicle. Phone: (866)442-2267.

WALNUT GROVE—D-3

(E) GOLDEN MEMORIAL STATE PARK—(Leake) *From jct SH 35 & CR 492: Go 5 mi E on CR 492.*

WELCOME

FACILITIES: 8 sites, 8 W&E, (20/30/50 amps).

Open all yr. Day use all year.

WALNUT GROVE—Continued
GOLDEN MEMORIAL STATE PARK—Continued

Address: 2104 Hwy 492 E, Walnut Grove, MS 39189
Web: www.mdwfp.com

SEE AD TRAVEL SECTION PAGE 431 AND AD LA TRAVEL SECTION PAGE 278

WAVELAND—F-3

(W) BUCCANEER SP—(Hancock) *From jct Hwys 43/603 & US 90: Go 1-3/4 mi S on Nicholson Ave, then 3-1/2 mi W on Beach Blvd.*

WELCOME

FACILITIES: 149 sites, 90 full hkups, 59 W&E, tenting, dump, laundry, picnic tables, patios, controlled access.

RECREATION: rec room/area, pavilion, swim pool, wading pool, saltwater swim, boating, saltwater fishing, bsktball, playground, tennis, sports field, hiking trails. Rec open to public.

Pets welcome. Open all yr. MC/VISA.

Phone: (228)467-3822
Address: 1150 South Beach Blvd, Waveland, MS 39576
Lat/Lon: 30.26286/-89.40504
Web: campingconnection.com

SEE AD TRAVEL SECTION PAGE 431 AND AD LA TRAVEL SECTION PAGE 278

WAYNESBORO—E-4

(W) MAYNOR CREEK WATER PARK (Pat Harrison Waterway District)—(Wayne) *From town: Go 2 mi W on US 84, then 3 mi S on Reservoir Rd. Follow signs.* FACILITIES: 69 sites, typical site width 23 ft, 35 full hkups, 34 W&E, tenting, dump, laundry. RECREATION: lake swim, boating, canoeing, ramp, dock, lake fishing, playground. Open all yr. Phone: (601)735-4365.

WESSON—E-2

(E) LAKE LINCOLN SP—(Lincoln) *From town Go 6 mi E on Timberlane Rd.*

FACILITIES: 61 sites, 61 W&E, 61 pull-thrus, tenting, dump, laundry, picnic tables, fire rings, grills, controlled access.

RECREATION: pavilion, lake swim, boating, canoeing, ramp, dock, 6 canoe/6 motorboat rentals, lake fishing, playground, sports field, hiking trails. Rec open to public.

Pets welcome. Open all yr. MC/VISA.

Phone: (601)643-9044
Address: 2573 Sunset Dr, Wesson, MS 39191
Lat/Lon: 31.67429/-90.34115
Web: campingconnection.com

SEE AD TRAVEL SECTION PAGE 431 AND AD LA TRAVEL SECTION PAGE 278

WIGGINS—F-4

(NE) FLINT CREEK WATER PARK (Pat Harrison Waterway District)—(Stone) *From jct US 49 (Wiggins exit) & Hwy 29: Go 4 mi NE on Hwy 29. Follow signs.* FACILITIES: 156 sites, typical site width 22 ft, 77 full hkups, 79 W&E, (20/30/50 amps), 15 pull-thrus, tenting, dump, laundry, ltd groc. RECREATION: lake swim, boating, canoeing, ramp, dock, lake fishing, playground. Open all yr. Phone: (601)928-3051.

WOODVILLE—E-1

(W) CLARK CREEK NATURE PARK—*From jct SH 61 & CR-24: Go 13 mi W on CR-34.* Daylight to dark park. Comprising more than 700 acres, it is highlighted by some 50 waterfalls, ranging in size 10 to more than 30 ft in height. Hiking, bird-watching, photography and botanizing are available on the established trails. Open all yr. Day use only.

WELCOME

Phone: (601)888-6040
Address: 366 Ft. Adams Pond Rd, Woodville, MS 39669
Web: www.mdwfp.com

SEE AD TRAVEL SECTION PAGE 431 AND AD LA TRAVEL SECTION PAGE 278

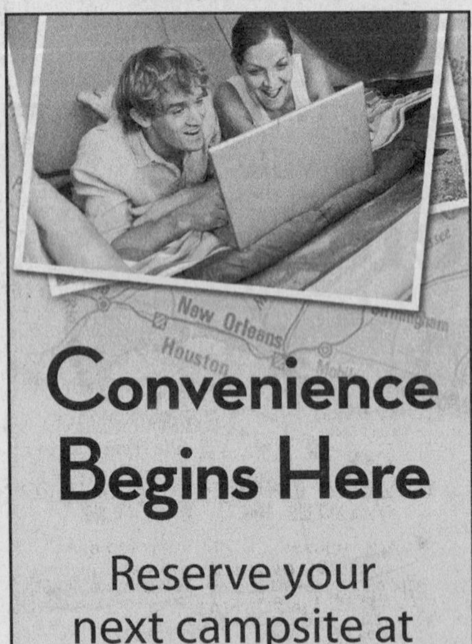

READER SERVICE INFO

The following businesses have placed an ad in the Missouri Travel Section. To receive free information, enter their Reader Service number on the Reader Service Card opposite page 48/ Discover Section in the front of this directory:

Advertiser	RS#
Boomland RV Park & Campground	4271
Branson Lakes Area Chamber of Commerce & CVB	3766
Division of State Parks Missouri	3028
Lady Luck RV Park & Nature Trail	3465
Missouri Association of RV Parks	3147
Missouri Division of Tourism	3338

TIME ZONE

Missouri is in the Central Time Zone.

TEMPERATURE

Average daily temperatures in winter range from 25° to 35°. In summer, Missouri is generally humid with temps varying from 78° to 80°.

TOPOGRAPHY

Missouri has 4 major types of terrain: glacial, in the northern part of the state along the Mississippi River; fertile prairie in the central and northwest portions; hills, forests, rivers and lakes in the Ozarks; and alluvial plains in the extreme southeastern portion.

TRAVEL & TOURISM INFO

State Agency:
Missouri Div. of Tourism
P.O. Box 1055
Jefferson City, MO 65102
(573/751-4133)
www.VisitMo.com
To order a free copy of the "Missouri Travel Guide" call (800/519-4800).

Local Agencies:

For information on local areas, contact the Chamber of Commerce or Tourism Bureau for the locality you are interested in visiting. Contact the state agency for addresses.

Hannibal Convention & Visitors Bureau
505 North Third St.
Hannibal, MO 63401
(800/1-TOMANDHUCK or 573/221-2477)
www.visithannibal.com

Jefferson City Convention & Visitors Bureau
P.O. Box 2227
100 E. High Street
Jefferson City, MO 65101
(573/632-2820)
www.visitjeffersoncity.com

Kansas City Convention & Visitor Association
1100 Main St., Ste. 2200
Kansas City, MO 64105-2195
(816/221-5242)
www.visitkc.com

Lake of the Ozarks Convention & Visitor Bureau
P.O. Box 1498
Osage Beach, MO 65065
(573/348-1599 or 800/386-5253)
www.funlake.com

St. Louis Convention & Visitors Commission
701 Convention Plaza, Suite 300
St. Louis, MO 63101
(314/421-1023 or 800/325-7962)
www.explorestlouis.com

Welcome Centers:

Missouri has six welcome centers located throughout the state to assist you while traveling. Welcome centers are an excellent resource if you need maps, directions and brochures about regional attractions, events and accommodations or friendly advice about the best places to visit.

Eagleville, 11687 I-35 South (exit 112). P.O. Box 123, Eagleville, MO 64442 (660/867-5566)

Hannibal, Hwy. 61 P.O. Box 575, Hannibal, MO 63401 (573/248-2420)

Joplin, I-44, Mile Marker 2 Rest Area, P.O. Box 2275, Joplin, MO 64803 (417/629-3030)

Kansas City, 4010 Blue Ridge Cut-Off, Kansas City, MO 64133 (816/889-3330)

New Madrid, Marston Rest Area, P.O. Box 246, New Madrid, MO 63869 (573/643-2654)

Rock Port, Hwy. Rest Area I-29, P.O. Box 69, Rock Port, MO 64482 (660/744-6300)

St. Louis, I-270 at Riverview Drive, P.O. Box 38182, St. Louis, MO 63138 (314/869-7100)

RECREATIONAL INFO

Canoeing Information: Missouri Canoe & Floaters Assn., 28425 Spring Rd., Richland, MO 65556. www.missouricanoe.org

Cave Exploration: National Caves Association (270/749-2228). www.cavern.com

Fishing & Hunting: Missouri Dept. of Conservation, P.O. Box 180, Jefferson City, MO 65109 (573/751-4115). www.mdc.mo.gov/fish

SHOPPING

Bluestem Missouri Crafts, Columbia. A gallery representing over 250 of the state's finest craft artists. 13 S. 9th St., Columbia.

Engler Block, Branson. Demonstrating Arts and Crafts Mall, which includes 30 upscale shops, plus demonstrating crafts-

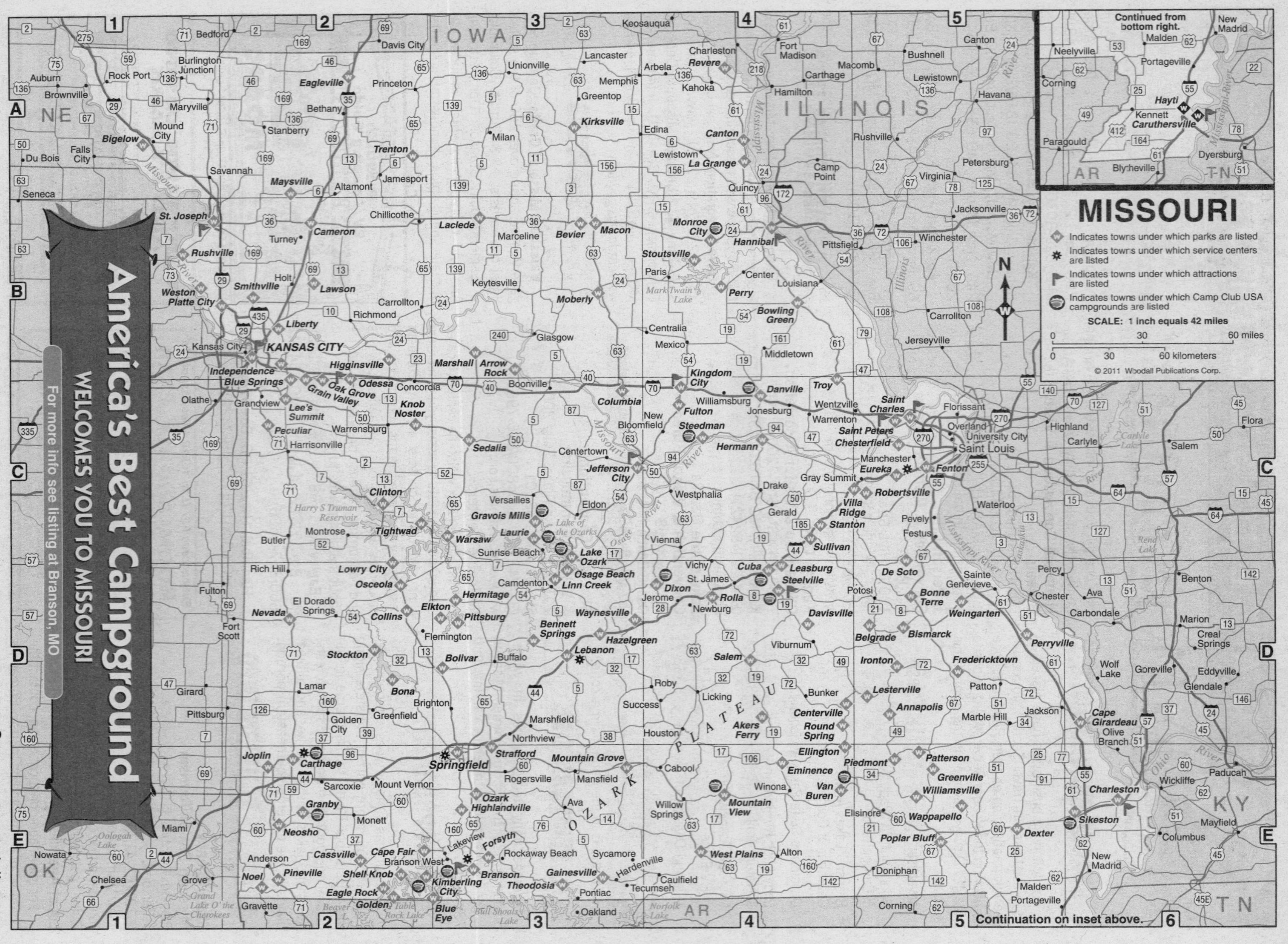
MISSOURI
Indicates towns under which parks are listed
Indicates towns under which service centers are listed
Indicates towns under which attractions are listed
Indicates towns under which Camp Club USA campgrounds are listed
SCALE: 1 inch equals 42 miles
0 30 60 miles
0 30 60 kilometers
© 2011 Woodall Publications Corp.
Continued from bottom right.
Continuation on inset above.
IOWA
ILLINOIS
KY
TN
AR
OK
NE
OZARK
PLATEAU
KANSAS CITY
Saint Louis
Springfield
Jefferson City
America's Best Campground
WELCOMES YOU TO MISSOURI
For more info see listing at Branson, MO

people at work. There are musicians and two food facilities. 1335 W. Rt 76.

Riverport Market, Glasgow. Located in a 19th century bank on the banks of the Missouri River, the market showcases the work of Missouri artists and craftsmen.

St. Charles Historic District, St. Charles. Missouri's largest district on the National Register of Historic Places. Eighty-eight restored buildings dating to the 1790s. More than 125 craft and specialty shops. Main Street, St. Charles.

Sikeston Factory Outlet Stores, Sikeston. Visit the only outlet shopping center between St. Louis and Memphis. Wide variety of stores including a VF outlet. Something for everyone. 100 Outlet Dr., Sikeston.

UNIQUE FEATURES

Missouri is known as the Gateway to the West for it's location at the confluence of the Mississippi and Missouri rivers, that were once major routes for pioneers traveling west. Divided into several distinct regions, Missouri welcomes visitors from far and wide to enjoy a variety of cultural sights, events, and outdoor activities.

Missouri is also known as the Cave State. More than 5,500 caves tunnel underneath it. From towering columns to intricately woven draperies of rock, the caves will captivate explorers of all ages. Guided tours vary from daily to seasonal and can be affected by rainfall so it is wise to call ahead for availability. Listed below are some of the more famous and accessible caves.

Bluff Dwellers Caverns & Browning Museum is located two miles South of Noel on Hwy. 59. This is one of the more scenic caves due to the varied types of cave growth. A tour takes forty-five minutes to an hour. A Museum of Rocks, Mineral, Fossils, Arrowheads and Antiques is included on the tour.

Bridal Cave can be found two miles north of Camdenton on Hwy 5. Local folklore tells of a legendary Indian wedding ceremony held in the cave in the early 1800s. Today, the cave can be reserved for a romantic wedding chapel. Ongoing exploration recently uncovered beautiful chambers including the crystal clear waters of Mystery Lake. Guided tours last approximately one hour. Bridal Cave features giant columns, delicate soda straws, massive draperies and more onyx formations than any other known cave or cavern.

Cameron Cave: On Cave Hollow Rd in Hannibal. Discovered in 1925, Cameron Cave has hosted guided lantern tours that are more geographical in nature since 1978. Unique and intricate formations are found in its 260 passages, which total six miles in length if they were to be put end to end.

Cathedral Cave: In Onandanga Cave State Park. Flowstone, several slump pits, a natural bridge and a nearly eighty-foot ceiling, stromatolites (fossilized algae beds), wind-bent stalactites and great amounts of cave coral are outstanding features. Come for the weekend lantern tours.

Crystal Cave is located on Hwy H, 5 mi. N of Springfield and features guided tours daily. Its unique features include the Upside Down Well, an unusual solution cavity; Rainbow Falls, a flowstone formation; the Cathedral, a complex of stalactites, stalagmites, columns, draperies, flowstone cones, popcorn, grapes and coral; and the Castle, a truly massive dripstone column, about three times as thick as it is high.

Fantastic Caverns: 4872 North Farm Road 125, Springfield. Tours every 20-30 min. America's only ride-through cave, the tour follows the path of an ancient underground river. The Cave is toured in jeep-drawn trams so you can enjoy the beauty of a natural cave without the long walks or steep climbs.

Fishers Cave: Meramec State Park, Fisher. Naturalist-led tours, offered on a seasonal basis, take you from low, narrow streamside passages to the huge rooms filled with calcite deposits. Inside these rooms and passages are well-preserved bear claw marks, cave wildlife and a vast array of calcite deposits ranging from intricate hellectites to massive columns 30 feet tall.

Jacob's Cave: Off Hwy. 5 on State Rd. TT. Famous for its depth illusion, reflective pools, ceiling sponge-work, prehistoric bones (mastodon, bear and peccary) and the world's largest geode. The tour covers a mile-long track. Evidence of six ice ages and three earthquakes can be seen. The temperature remains a constant 53° inside the cave. Jacob's Cave is handicap accessible.

Mark Twain Cave: 1 mile South of Hannibal on Highway 79. The oldest show cave in Missouri, the cave has also served as a place of hiding for Indians, trappers of animals for trade, the infamous Jesse James

and slaves searching for freedom via the Underground Railroad.

Meramec Caverns: On 44 West, Exit 230 Stanton. Guided tours of caverns chronicle over 400 million years of history. Learn how Mother Nature built an ancient limestone "Wine Table" and an entire 7-story mansion... all underground. On tour you will see both the rarest and largest cave formations in the world. All cavern facilities are accessible to the disabled.

Onondaga Cave: 7556 Hwy. H, Leasburg. Deposits of tall stalagmites, dripping stalactites, active flowstones and many other colorful deposits.

Ozark Caverns: Lake of the Ozarks State Park. Angel Showers, an unusual cave phenomenon, is a featured part of the Ozark Caverns tour. The never-ending shower of water seems to come out of the solid ceiling of rock. Tours are 1-1/2 hrs. Children's tour runs from 30-45 min.

Round Spring Caverns: The National Park Service conducts lantern tours for the public. These somewhat strenuous "underground hikes" are limited to the first 15 people. Wear sturdy shoes and bring a jacket or sweater.

Talking Rocks Cavern: S of jct. Hwy 76 and Hwy 13 in Branson West. The 50 min. tours showcase thousands of naturally beautiful living crystal cave formations of many different kinds with colors and textures growing closely together.

Tower Rock is a majestic landmark in the Mississippi River in Perry County. The less-than-one-acre limestone rock towers more than 90 feet above the Mississippi River bed. Water is turbulent as it passes around the rock and returns to the main channel, especially when the river is high. Sightseers can walk on flat rocks near river level, or climb a bluff near Tower Rock, for better views. Tower Rock is accessible by foot only during extremely low water. Adjacent Missouri land features a 32-acre natural forest, including a 10-mile hiking trail.

DESTINATIONS

CENTRAL REGION

Central Missouri is characterized by true Midwestern hospitality and a wide variety of attractions. Home to Columbia, this part of the state features many cultural and historic sites that appeal to a wide variety of travelers. Lake Ozark is a prominent feature of this region, and is a natural attraction for watersports and beach activities.

Appleton City Historical District, Appleton City. See an 1870 railroad depot caboose, railroad park, the original W.H. Library and a museum.

Barrels of Fun, Lebanon. Tour the largest wooden-barrel factory in the world. Independent Stave Company produces more than 50 percent of barrels worldwide. Tours highlight the care and skill involved in producing these barrels, which are used to age fine bourbons and wines. Viewing windows and TV screens offer a "live eye" look at the production process.

Berlin Wall "Breakthrough" Sculpture, Fulton. A 32-foot sculpture created by Edwina Sandys, granddaughter of Sir Winston Churchill, commemorating the fall of the Berlin Wall. The "Breakthrough" Sculpture, formed from sections of the actual wall, stands near the Churchill Memorial on the campus of Westminster College, where Sir Winston made his famous "iron curtain" speech.

Big Surf Waterpark, Linn Creek. Enjoy 27 acres of water play areas, Zambezi falls, wave pool, space bowl, flumes, rapids, activity pool and tropical splash island for babies and toddlers.

Bridal Cave/Thunder Mountain Park, Camdenton. Experience one of America's most scenic cave tours.

Carl's Gun Shop Museum, El Dorado Springs. View 1,000 guns in glass cases; ammunition used by the Warren Commission for ballistic testing in the J.F.K. assassination; Smiley Burnett's Colt 45; an arrowhead collection; WWI U.S. Cavalry blacksmith forge; 48-star US flag flown for the first time Dec. 25th, 1918 over U.S. naval air station in Ireland; and many mounted animals and other items of interest.

Carnahan Memorial Gardens, Jefferson City. Located next to the Governor's Mansion, the gardens were constructed in the late 1930s. The site is filled with flowers, pools and walkways.

Columbia. The **YouZeum** is a fascinating interactive learning environment designed to give visitors a better understanding of the workings of the human body and the healthful choices they can make. It is opened daily except on Sundays. **Columbia** was once roamed by Osage and Missouri Indians. The Lewis and Clark Expedition passed within a few miles of the area on the Missouri River 1803. In 1806, Daniel Boone and his sons established a salt lick in the area about 40 miles northwest of Columbia. The Booneslick Trail traveled from Kentucky to St. Charles, Missouri and on through this region.

Devil's Icebox Cave, located 7 miles south of Columbia. Devil's Icebox Cave, a natural rock bridge and numerous sinkholes in **Rock Bridge Memorial State Park,** are part of a limestone-cave system dating back thousands of years.

House of Butterflies, Osage Beach. View butterflies in their natural setting.

Lake of the Ozarks, mid-Missouri. One of the largest man-made lakes in the world with more than 1,150 miles of shoreline and virtually every form of water recreation imaginable, including fishing for white and black bass, striper, catfish and crappie.

Lakes Truman, Stockton & Pomme de Terre are the 3 major lakes in the Osage Lakes region. These recreational paradises offer 1,369 miles of undeveloped shoreline and 16 full-service marinas.

Lebanon-Laclede County Route 66 Museum, Lebanon. Museum, gift shop and café located in library building. Memorabilia of historic Route 66 maps and books; vignettes of a motel room, a diner and a gas station, along with other must-see collectibles.

Memoryville U.S.A., Rolla. One of the largest antique and classic automobile restoration galleries in the area. Currently displaying a 1938 Nash Lafayette owned by news commentator Paul Harvey and his wife Angel.

Missouri Governor's Mansion, Jefferson City. The mansion was constructed in 1871 as the official residence of Missouri's first family. Guided tours of the authentically restored first floor are offered. Reservations are required at least 24 hours in advance.

Missouri State Capitol and Missouri State Museum, Jefferson City. The east and west wings of the first floor of the Capitol house the Missouri State Museum. Tours, given hourly, include two large galleries, which provide a sample of the state's natural resources and rich history.

Museums at Fort Leonard Wood. An unusual complex of military museums. A World War II camp replica with barracks, chapel and mess hall. Army Engineer Museum with maps and tools dating to the Revolutionary War. Exhibits at the Military Police Museum cover the times from U.S. frontier army-post life to the Iraq wars.

Onyx Mountain Caverns National Historic Site, Newburg. Caverns feature artifacts from the Woodland Indians, an underground river and twin dripstone formations.

Ozark Caverns, Linn Creek. Choose from three tours to explore these remarkable caverns.

Orion Science Center, Camdenton, offers interactive science and natural history exhibits. Indoor and outdoor hands-on science activities.

Pleasant Green Plantation House, Pilot Grove. Built in 1820 by the pioneer Walk family, with additions in 1835 and the 1850s of brush-fired brick, reflecting 7 generations.

Powell Gardens, Kingsville. Features unique architecture, a 12-acre lake, a perennial garden, a rock and waterfall garden, terrace gardens and a wildflower meadow.

BUSINESSES OFFERING

	Things to See & Do	RV Sales	RV Service
BRANSON			
Branson Lakes Area Chamber of Commerce & Convention & Visitors Bureau	⚑		
Sam's Trailer Service		🚌	✱
Whistle Stop Cafe	⚑		
CARTHAGE			
Coachlight RV Sales		🚌	✱
CARUTHERSVILLE			
Lady Luck Casino Caruthersville	⚑		
The Lone Wolf	⚑		
CHARLESTON			
Boomland	⚑		
EUREKA			
Byerly RV Center		🚌	✱
HANNIBAL			
Mark Twain Cave	⚑		
JEFFERSON CITY			
Division of State Parks Missouri	⚑		
Missouri Division of Tourism	⚑		
KANSAS CITY			
Oceans of Fun	⚑		
Worlds of Fun	⚑		
KINGDOM CITY			
Hanson Hills Campground Kitchen	⚑		
LEBANON			
Happy Trails RV Center		🚌	✱
ODESSA			
One Good Taste Country Store	⚑		
SPRINGFIELD			
Reliable RV Center		🚌	✱
Thomas & Sons RV Supply		🚌	✱
ST. CHARLES			
Sundermeier Banquet & Conference Center	⚑		
Sundermeier Beef Eaters Restaurant	⚑		
ST. JOSEPH			
Glore Psychiatric Museum	⚑		
National Military Heritage Museum	⚑		
Patee House Museum & Jesse James Home	⚑		
Pony Express National Museum	⚑		
Robidoux Row Museum	⚑		
St. Joseph Visitors Bureau	⚑		
Terrible's St. Jo Frontier Casino	⚑		
The Black Archives of St. Joseph	⚑		
The St. Joseph Museum	⚑		
Wyeth-Tootle Museum	⚑		
ST. PETERS			
St. Peters Rec-Plex	⚑		
STEELVILLE			
Bass' River Resort Canoe Rental	⚑		
Huzzah Valley Resort Canoe Rental	⚑		

QUICK REFERENCE CHART FOR WOODALL'S FEATURED PARKS

	Green Friendly	RV Lots for Sale	Park Models-Onsite Ownership	Park Membership for Sale	Big Rigs Welcome	Internet Friendly	Pets Welcome
BOWLING GREEN							
Cozy C RV Campground					▲	●	■
BRANSON							
Acorn Acres RV Park & Campground	🍃				▲	●	■
America's Best Campground					▲	●	■
Branson Shenanigans RV Park					▲	●	■
Branson View Estates					▲		■
Branson's Ozark Country Campground	🍃				▲	●	■
Compton Ridge Campground	🍃				▲	●	■
Cooper Creek Campground	🍃				▲	●	■
Oak Grove RV Resort					▲	●	■
CANTON							
City of Canton Mississippi River Park					▲		■
CARTHAGE							
Big Red Barn RV Park					▲	●	■
Coachlight Campground					▲	●	■
CARUTHERSVILLE							
Lady Luck RV Park and Nature Trail					▲	●	■
CHARLESTON							
Boomland RV Park & Campground					▲		■
COLUMBIA							
Cottonwoods RV Park	🍃				▲	●	■
DANVILLE							
Lazy Day Campground					▲	●	■
EUREKA							
KOA St. Louis West/Historic Rt 66					▲	●	■
HANNIBAL							
Injun Joe Campground					▲	●	■
Mark Twain Cave and Campground					▲	●	■
HAYTI							
Hayti-Portageville KOA					▲	●	■
INDEPENDENCE							
Stadium RV Park					▲	●	■
JEFFERSON CITY							
Osage Campground & More							■
KANSAS CITY							
Worlds of Fun Village					▲	●	■
KINGDOM CITY							
Hanson Hills Campground						●	■
LEBANON							
Happy Trails RV Park					▲	●	■
OAK GROVE							
Kansas City East KOA					▲	●	■

Green Friendly 🍃; RV Lots for Sale ✖; Park Models/Onsite Onwership ✱; Park Memberships for Sale ✔; Big Rigs Welcome ▲; Internet Friendly ●; Internet Friendly-WiFi ●; Pets Welcome ■

Sculpture Garden, William Woods University, Fulton. A massive sculpture garden created by California sculptor Will Nettleship.

NORTHEAST REGION

The Northeast Region is home to Hannibal, Mark Twain's boyhood home, and home to Molly Brown, perhaps the most recognizable survivor of the Titanic. This area also features a variety of outdoor activities including hiking trails, and great fishing spots. Long Branch Lake is a favorite haven for water sports enthusiasts.

Anheuser-Busch Budweiser Brewery Tour, St. Louis. Experience a century-old brewing tradition on a complimentary Budweiser brewery tour. See how beer is brewed. Visit the historic brew house, Budweiser Clydesdales and gift shop.

Artisans at Work, Clarksville. Watch potters, cabinet makers and blacksmiths at work. See a Windsor chair maker, a metal and glass artist, a glassblower and a painter doing their things.

Battle of Athens State Historic Site, Athens. Union troops defeated pro-South Missouri State Guard in 1861 on this site, the northernmost location of a Civil War battle fought west of Mississippi River.

Chatillon DeMenil Mansion and Museum, St. Louis. Historic house and museum that showcases the founding of St. Louis, westward expansion and 1904 World's Fair. Home of Henri Chatillon, guide and hunter for the American Fur Company.

City Museum, St. Louis. Art, science, history and fun weave together in this one-of-a-kind downtown attraction. Built of recycled materials, the museum includes World Aquarium at City Museum.

First Missouri State Capitol, St. Charles. Now a state historic site, the buildings housed the Missouri government from 1821 to 1826.

Fort Belle Fontaine Historic Site, St. Louis. Visit the site of the first American fort west of the Mississippi River, site of Lewis and Clark's first stop and the final stop of their journey of discovery. Located on the banks of the Missouri River, it served as a trading post for local American Indian tribes.

Gateway Arch, St. Louis. This 630-ft arch is the nation's tallest man-made national monument and symbolizes the city's role as the "Gateway to the West."

Grant's Farm (the ancestral home of the Busch family) in St. Louis features a 160-acre game preserve, Grant's Cabin, coach and carriage collections, a Bier Garten and the world famous Budweiser Clydesdale horses.

Hannibal. The home Samuel Clemens lived in is now a museum of Twain memorabilia. At the **1894 and More Museum** you'll see guns, local artifacts from the area, old photographs, deeds, hand tools, beautiful organs, kerosene lamps and vintage postcards. The **Mark Twain Cave** is the cave made famous by Mark Twain, where Tom Sawyer and Becky Thatcher were lost in the cave where Injun Joe hid his treasure.

QUICK REFERENCE CHART FOR WOODALL'S FEATURED PARKS

	Green Friendly	RV Lots for Sale	Park Models-Onsite Ownership	Park Membership for Sale	Big Rigs Welcome	Internet Friendly	Pets Welcome
ODESSA							
Country Gardens RV Park					▲	●	■
OSAGE BEACH							
Osage Beach RV Park					▲	●	■
PECULIAR							
Peculiar Park Place RV Park					▲	●	■
PERRYVILLE							
Perryville Campground					▲	●	■
SIKESTON							
Town & Country RV Resort					▲	●	■
ST. CHARLES							
Sundermeier RV Park & Conference Center	🍃				▲	●	■
ST. JOSEPH							
Beacon RV Park					▲	●	■
ST. PETERS							
370 Lakeside Park RV & Campground					▲	●	■
STEELVILLE							
Bass' River Resort					▲	●	■
Huzzah Valley Resort					▲	●	■
STRAFFORD							
Paradise In The Woods RV Park & Campground					▲		■
RV Park Strafford					▲		■
WARSAW							
DeerRest CampPark							■

Green Friendly 🍃; RV Lots for Sale ✖; Park Models/Onsite Onwership ✱; Park Memberships for Sale ✔; Big Rigs Welcome ▲; Internet Friendly ●; Internet Friendly-WiFi ●; Pets Welcome ■

Historic Daniel Boone Home, Defiance. Take an exciting, educational and historical trip back to the days of Daniel Boone. Visit the Boone Home and Boonesfield Village. The Daniel Boone home overlooks the Boonesfield Village, which is comprised of over a dozen 19th century buildings including the Old Peace Chapel, grist mill, schoolhouse, and carpenter's shop. Each building has been moved to the site from within 50 miles of the local area. The buildings offer visitors a glimpse into life as a frontiersman and the chance to witness the hard work and dedication these men and women possessed.

Mastodon State Historic Site, Imperial. The excavation of American mastodon remains and Indian artifacts make this one of North America's most important sites for the study of ice-age men and animals.

Meramec Caverns, Stanton. Guided tours of a seven story natural wonder that was a Jesse James hideout.

Missouri History Museum, St. Louis. The museum offers exciting exhibitions and interactive galleries as well as special exhibits throughout the year. Permanent exhibits include Seeking St. Louis, 1904 World's Fair, and Lindbergh.

Petroglyphs, Kirksville. American Indian rock carvings, over 1,500 years old, at Thousand Hills State Park.

Shaw Arboretum of the Missouri Botanical Garden, Gray Summit. Featured are 2,400 acres of a rich diversity of plants and animals in restored and constructed natural habitats: a restored 19th-century home, housing "People on the Land."

Six Flags St. Louis, southwest of St. Louis. Ride breathtaking roller coasters like "Batman" and "Thunder River." The little ones are sure to enjoy Looney Tunes Town.

St. Charles. The Saint Charles Historic District, Missouri's largest district on the National Register of Historic Places, surrounds the site of Missouri's first capitol building. There are eighty-eight restored buildings dating to the 1790s. The gas lit, brick streets offer more than 125 specialty and craft shops, plus numerous restaurants. At the Lewis & Clark Center, you'll experience 3-D exhibits, walk-through exhibits and hands-on activities dealing with the amazing discoveries of their journey.

Discovery Expedition of St. Charles is building and operating three replica boats used by Lewis and Clark. The 55-foot keelboat construction and two completed 40-foot pirogues can be viewed in the riverside pavilion.

Saint Louis Art Museum contains more than 30,000 works. Its collections include works from virtually every culture and time period. Designed by architect Cass Gilbert as the Palace of Fine Arts for the 1904 World's Fair, the Museum is the only permanent building remaining from that fair.

St. Louis Zoo. The 90 beautiful acres of the Zoo are home to 11,400 exotic animals, many of them rare and endangered. Animals live in natural habitats. The Penguin and Puffin Coast offers a spectacular underwater view of these oceanic birds. Underwater viewing of hippos is available. Asian elephants, a children's zoo, the insectarium, a carousel and the cypress swamp are among the newer attractions. Free admission.

St. Louis Children's Aquarium, Brentwood. This is a fun, interactive and educational public aquarium for children of all ages. See the humpback whale exhibit, pet a shark, pick up turtles and explore a cave.

Wabash, Frisco & Pacific Steam Railway, Wildwood. Ride a steam-powered miniature railway from Glencoe on a scenic two-mile trip along Meramec River.

Where to Find CCUSA Parks

List City	Park Name	Map Coordinates
BRANSON		
	Branson Stagecoach RV Park	E-3
	Branson View Campground (Not visited)	E-3
	Branson's Ozark Country Campground	E-3
	Pea Patch RV Park	E-3
CARTHAGE		
	Big Red Barn RV Park	E-2
CUBA		
	Meramec Valley RV Camp Resort	D-4
DANVILLE		
	Kan-Do Kampground & RV Park	C-4
DIXON		
	Boiling Spring Campground	D-4
GRANBY		
	Hwy 60 RV Park	E-2
GRAVOIS MILLS		
	Hava Space RV Park	C-3
KIMBERLING CITY		
	Water's Edge on Table Rock Lake	E-2
LAKE OZARK		
	Cross Creek RV Park	C-3
LAURIE		
	Laurie RV Park	C-3
MONROE CITY		
	Mark Twain Landing Resort	B-4
MOUNTAIN VIEW		
	Ozarks Mountain Springs RV Park	E-4
SIKESTON		
	Town & Country RV Resort	E-6
STEEDMAN		
	Wildwood	C-4
STEELVILLE		
	Bass' River Resort	D-4
VAN BUREN		
	Yogi Bear's Jellystone Park At Van Buren	E-4

SOUTHEAST REGION

This region is a canoeing and kayaking paradise. Deep springs, sparkling rivers, wilderness areas and historic towns make it a major recreation destination. Travelers will also find Ste. Genevieve, established by the French in the 1730's, which contains the greatest concentration of original French colonial buildings in North America. This area is also home to Cape Girardeau, an early 19th century trading post, and Mississippi River port. Trail of Tears State Park marks the spot where Cherokee Indians crossed the Mississippi on their forced march to Oklahoma in the 1830's.

Alley Spring Mill. This historic gristmill sits along the Jack's Fork River near Eminence.

Bonne Terre Mine Tours, Bonne Terre. Tour a cavernous room supported by giant rock pillars where miners dug for lead ore. Or take a boat tour of the "Billion Gallon Lake," the largest subterranean lake in the world, once dived and filmed by Jacques Cousteau. The mine, consisting of five levels, covers an underground area larger than the town of Bonne Terre. It is has been named a National Geographic Top 10 Adventure.

Mississippi River Observation Deck, New Madrid. Enjoy the scenic views of the grand Mississippi. The observation deck extends over the Mississippi River.

Missouri Mines State Historic Site, Park Hills. This milling complex was used in the days when Missouri's "Lead Belt" produced nearly 80 percent of the nation's mined lead.

Sainte Genevieve Winery, Ste. Genevieve, is housed in a circa 1900 mansion.

SOUTHWEST REGION

The Southwest Region is home to Branson, which welcomes thousands of travelers every year with its live music, variety theaters, comedians, acrobats, and other entertainers. This region is also home to The Titanic Museum, which offers stories and artifacts from passengers of the doomed ocean liner. Another big attraction is the Ozarks, where fishing and boating opportunities are endless.

Branson. Attractions include **Silver Dollar City,** a re-created 1880s mining town. **Marvel Cave** is America's third largest cavern. Take a trip down memory lane at the **Roy Rogers-Dale Evans Museum and Happy Trails Theater.** See Trigger, the Smartest Horse in the Movies, Bullet the Wonder Dog, Dale's horse Buttermilk, Trigger Jr., Nellybelle and many of Roy and Dale's personal items on display. **Lake Taneycomo** flows through the heart of historic downtown Branson and offers easy access to water activities and some of the finest year-round trout fishing available.

Carthage. This historic city was the site of the first full-scale land battle of the Civil War. Visit the **Powers Museum** or take a drive along historic Route 66. Tour the beautiful **Jasper County Courthouse** or stroll the historical downtown square. Carthage has one of the state's largest historic districts on the National Register of Historic Places. Whatever you choose to do, you're sure to discover what makes Carthage one of the most unique cities in Missouri. See the beautiful murals of artist Sam Butcher at the **Precious Moments Chapel**.

Discovery Center of Springfield, Springfield. An interactive science center, newly expanded with a "green" building and science-oriented ChromoZone gallery. The energy-works exhibit demonstrates different forms of energy. The Exploratory Lab presents hands-on experiments in science, earth science and energy. Wonderland is a toddler and preschool area.

Fantastic Caverns, Springfield. America's only ride-through cave, the tour follows the path of an ancient underground river. Enjoy the beauty of a natural cave without the long walks or steep climbs.

George Washington Carver National Monument, located off Hwy. 59, south of Carthage. This teacher, lecturer, scientist, artist, researcher and humanitarian is honored for his legendary achievements.

Laura Ingalls Wilder Historic Home, Mansfield. The author of the Little House on the Prairie books lived in this home from 1894 until her death in 1957.

Osage Village State Historic Site, Walker. Visit the location of Big Osage Indian village between 1700 and 1777. On National Historic Register, the site was home of the Osage when they were first encountered by the Europeans.

NORTHWEST REGION

This region was once the jumping-off point for pioneers forging west to settle the country. Home to St. Joseph, known historically as the start of the Pony Express, and the famed location of the assassination of Jesse James in 1882, which draws visitors every year wishing to experience a Wild West revival.

Airline History Museum, Kansas City. Dedicated to propeller-driven commercial aircraft, the museum contains a collection that will bring you the true flavor of an age gone by including a rare Martin 404 and a unique 24-passenger Douglas DC-3.

American Jazz Museum, Kansas City. The sights and sounds of a uniquely American art form come alive at the American Jazz Museum. The museum includes interactive exhibits and educational programs. Also, enjoy the Blue Room, a working jazz club and the Gem Theater.

Arabia Steamboat Museum, Kansas City. In 1856, the steamboat Arabia sank near Kansas City with 200 tons of cargo bound for towns to the west. In 1988 the Arabia excavation began and resulted in the astonishing discovery of pre-Civil War artifacts that are now on display.

Chariton County Historical Society, Salisbury. See county memorabilia, pioneer artifacts, hand-made tools and much more.

Fort Osage, Sibley. This reconstructed 1808 fur-trade fort above the Missouri River offers a living-history program and tours.

Green City Railroad Depot, Green City. Listed on the National Register of Historic Places, this railroad depot contains an 1883 caboose, railroad items, jacks, telegraph equipment and a baggage cart.

Hercules Glades Wilderness. Panoramic views of the Ozark Plateau, as well as the St. Francis and Boston mountains to the south.

Jesse James Bank Museum, Liberty. Visit the site of the first successful daylight bank robbery, which was eventually credited to Frank, Jesse and the "James Gang."

Kansas City. After massive reconstruction, stunning architectural showpieces are evident in this city, including the new **Nelson-Atkins Museum of Art** and the nine-block **Power and Light District**. Situated on 202 acres of rolling hills in Swope Park, the **Kansas City Zoo** is home to almost 900 animals from six continents. The newly opened KidZone allows kids and adults to experience small exotic animals up close and personal. Visitors to the expanded **National World War I Museum** will find themselves on a glass floor suspended over a field of poppies one minute, then immersed in the sights and sounds of the trenches the next. Formerly the Liberty Memorial Museum, the landmark is the nation's only public museum dedicated exclusively to the history of World War I.

St. Joseph features attractions such as the Pony Express National Memorial and the St. Joseph Museum. St. Joseph's Doll Museum displays over 600 dolls from 1840.

Jesse James Home. This was the house where outlaw Jesse James was killed in 1882.

Pony Express Museum. See the historic stable where Pony Express began in 1860.

State Theater, Mound City. Visit a restored 1939 movie theater.

ANNUAL EVENTS

JANUARY

Annual Ice Carving Event, Branson; Eagle Days, Clarksville/St. Louis; Orchid Show, St. Louis (through March).

FEBRUARY

Chocolate Wine Trail, Hermann; Soulard Mardi Gras, St. Louis; Winter Bluegrass Festival, Hannibal.

MARCH

Wurstfest, Hermann; Annual IMAX FilmFest, Branson.

APRIL

River Arts Festival, Excelsior Springs; Affton Chamber Buddy Bass Fishing Tournament, Camdenton; Coalition of Historic Trekkers, Sibley; Mississippi Valley Scenic Tour, Cape Girardeau; Mid-Missouri Storytelling Festival, Jefferson City; Civil War Reenactment-Summer of 1863, St. Joseph.

MAY

Faust Fine Art & Folk Festival, St. Louis; Bluegrass & BBQ Festival, Branson; Perryville Mayfest, Perryville; Annual Art Fair & Winefest, Washington; Annual Rib America Festival, St. Louis; Lewis and Clark Rendezvous, St. Charles.

All privately owned campgrounds personally inspected by WOODALL'S Representatives

Lee and Mary Franck

AKERS FERRY—D-4

(E) Jason Place Campground—(Shannon) *From jct Hwy 32 & Hwy 19: Go 20 mi S on Hwy 19, then 4 mi W on Hwy KK. Enter on R.* ◆◆FACILITIES: 180 sites, typical site width 25 ft, 20 W&E, 50 E, (30 amps), 110 no hkups, tenting, dump, laundry, ltd groc. ◆◆◆RECREATION: swim pool, boating, canoeing, play equipment. Pets welcome. Open all yr. Rate in 2010 $23-28.50 for 2 persons. Member ARVC. Phone: (800)333-5628. FMCA discount.

ANNAPOLIS—D-5

(N) Big Creek RV Park—(Iron) *From jct K & Hwy 49N: Go 4.8 mi N on Hwy 49N,. Enter on R.* ◆◆◆FACILITIES: 40 sites, typical site width 35 ft, 40 full hkups, (30/50 amps), 10 pull-thrus, laundry, ltd groc. ◆◆◆RECREATION: river/stream fishing, play equipment. Pets welcome, quantity restrict. Partial handicap access. No tents. Open all yr. Big rigs welcome. Green Friendly. Rate in 2010 $28 for 2 persons. Member ARVC, MOARC.

Phone: (573)598-1064
Address: 47247 Hwy 49, Annapolis, MO 63620
Lat/Lon: 37.42567/-90.69673
Email: bigcreekrvpark@hughes.net
Web: www.bigcreekrvpark.com

HIGHWAY K PARK (COE Clearwater Lake)—(St. Francois) *From jct Hwy-49 & CR-K: Go 4 mi SW on CR-K.* FACILITIES: 82 sites, typical site width 17 ft, 21 W&E, 35 E, (20/30 amps), 26 no hkups, tenting, dump. RECREATION: river swim, boating, canoeing, river fishing, playground. Partial handicap access. Open all yr. Phone: (573)223-7777.

ARROW ROCK—B-3

(N) ARROW ROCK STATE HISTORIC SITE—(Saline) *From jct I-70 & Hwy 41: Go 13 mi N on Hwy 41. Enter on R.*

WELCOME

FACILITIES: 47 sites, typical site width 25 ft, 1 full hkups, 34 W&E, (30/50 amps), 12 no hkups, tenting, dump, picnic tables, fire rings, grills, wood, controlled access.

RECREATION: pavilion, lake/pond fishing, playground, hiking trails. Rec open to public.

Partial handicap access. Open all yr. Facilities fully operational Apr 1 - Oct 31. Max stay 15 days. MC/VISA/DISC/AMEX.

Phone: (660)837-3330
Address: 4th & van Buren Streets, Arrow Rock, MO 65320
Lat/Lon: 39.063361/-92.946389
Web: www.mostateparks.com

SEE AD TRAVEL SECTION PAGE 451

BELGRADE—D-5

MARK TWAIN NATIONAL FOREST (Council Bluff Lake Campground)—(Iron) *From town: Go 5 mi W on Hwy C, then 7 mi S on Hwy DD.* FACILITIES: 54 sites, 54 no hkups, tenting. RECREATION: lake swim, boating, 10 hp limit, lake fishing. Partial handicap access. Open Apr 15 - Nov 15. Phone: (573)766-5646.

BENNETT SPRINGS—D-3

(NW) BENNETT SPRING STATE PARK—(Dallas/Laclede) *From jct Hwy 5 & Hwy 64: Go 12 mi W on Hwy 64.*

WELCOME

FACILITIES: 193 sites, 48 full hkups, 130 E, (30 amps), 15 no hkups, 48 pull-thrus, tenting, cabins, dump, laundry, ltd groc, ice, picnic tables, fire rings, grills, wood.

RECREATION: pavilion, swim pool, canoeing, canoe rentals, river fishing, hiking trails.

BENNETT SPRINGS—Continued
BENNETT SPRING STATE PARK—Continued

Open all yr. Facilities fully operational Apr 1 - Oct 31. MC/VISA/DISC/AMEX.

Phone: (417)532-4338
Address: 26250 State Highway 64A, Lebanon, MO 65536
Lat/Lon: 37.897778/-92.729167
Web: www.mostateparks.com

SEE AD TRAVEL SECTION PAGE 451

BEVIER—B-3

(N) Shoemaker RV Park—(Macon) *From jct US 63 & US 36: Go 5 mi W on US 36 to Bevier exit, then 1/4 mi E on south frontage road. Enter on R.* ◆◆◆FACILITIES: 101 sites, typical site width 25 ft, 81 full hkups, 20 W&E, (20/30/50 amps), 50 amps ($), 54 pull-thrus, tenting, dump, laundry. ◆◆RECREATION: pond fishing. Pets welcome. Open all yr. Big rigs welcome. Rate in 2010 $20 for 2 persons. Member ARVC, MOARC. Phone: (660)773-5313.

BIGELOW—A-1

(SW) BIG LAKE STATE PARK—(Holt) *From jct US 29 & Hwy 118: Go 13 mi W on Hwy 118, then go 3 mi S on Hwy 111. Enter on R.*

WELCOME

FACILITIES: 75 sites, typical site width 20 ft, 57 E, (20/30 amps), 18 no hkups, 20 pull-thrus, tenting, cabins, dump, laundry, ltd groc, picnic tables, fire rings, grills, wood.

RECREATION: pavilion, swim pool, boating, canoeing, ramp, dock, lake fishing, playground, horseshoes.

Open all yr. Facilities fully operational May - Sep. Max stay 15 days. No pool in off season. MC/VISA/DISC/AMEX.

Phone: (660)442-3770
Address: 204 Lake Shore Drive, Craig, MO 64437
Lat/Lon: 40.093889/-95.353583
Web: www.mostateparks.com

SEE AD TRAVEL SECTION PAGE 451

BISMARCK—D-5

(S) SAINT JOE STATE PARK—(St. Francois) *From jct Hwy-32 & CR-B: Go 1 mi SW on CR-B (Elvins). Enter on R.*

WELCOME

FACILITIES: 96 sites, 30 ft max RV length, 53 E, (30 amps), 43 no hkups, 15 pull-thrus, tenting, dump, laundry, picnic tables, fire rings, grills, wood, controlled access.

RECREATION: pavilion, lake swim, boating, ramp, lake fishing, hiking trails.

Partial handicap access. Open all yr. Facilities fully operational Apr 1 - Oct 31. MC/VISA/DISC/AMEX.

Phone: (573)431-1069
Address: 2800 Pimville Rd, Park Hills, MO 63601
Web: www.mostateparks.com

SEE AD TRAVEL SECTION PAGE 451

BLUE EYE—E-3

BAXTER PARK (COE Table Rock Lake)—(Taney) *From jct Hwy-86 & Hwy-13: Go 2-1/2 mi N on Hwy-13, then 4-3/4 mi W on CR-H.* FACILITIES: 54 sites, typical site width 20 ft, 25 W&E, (30 amps), 29 no hkups, tenting, dump, ltd groc. RECREATION: lake swim, boating, ramp, dock, lake fishing, playground. Open Apr 1 - Sep 30. Phone: (417)779-5370.

COW CREEK PARK (COE Table Rock Lake)—(Stone) *From town: Go 2 mi S on Hwy-86, then 2 mi N on access road.* FACILITIES: 23 sites, 23 no hkups, tenting, dump. RECREATION: lake swim, boating, ramp, lake fishing. Open May 1 - Sep 5. Phone: (417)779-5377.

MILL CREEK PARK (COE Table Rock Lake)—(Taney) *From jct Hwy-86 & Hwy-13: Go 5-3/4 mi N on Hwy-13.* FACILITIES: 68 sites, typical site width 20 ft, 23 W&E, 36 E, (30 amps), 9 no hkups, tenting, dump. RECREATION: lake swim, boating, ramp, lake fishing, playground. Open May 1 - Sep 30. Phone: (417)779-5378.

(E) OLD HIGHWAY 86 PARK (COE Table Rock Lake)—(Taney) *From town: Go 6 mi N & E on Hwy-86, then 1-1/2 mi NE on access road.* FACILITIES: 71 sites, 23 W&E, 40 E, (30 amps), 8 no hkups, tenting, dump. RECREATION: lake swim, boating, ramp, lake fishing, playground. Pets welcome. Partial handicap access. Open May 1 - Sep 30. Phone: (417)779-5376.

BLUE SPRINGS—C-2

BLUE SPRINGS LAKE CAMPGROUND (Jackson County Park)—(Jackson) *From jct I-70 & I-470: Go 2 mi S on I-470 to exit 14, then 2/10 mi E on Bowlin Rd to park entrance, then N to campground entrance.* FACILITIES: 59 sites, 22 full hkups, 17 W&E, 20 E, (20/30/50 amps), 10 pull-thrus, tenting, dump, laundry. RECREATION: lake swim, boating, canoeing, ramp, dock, lake/pond fishing, playground. Open May 16 - Sep 30. Phone: (816)795-8200.

BOLIVAR—D-3

(S) SPEEDWAY RV PARK (NOT VISITED)—(Polk) *From jct Hwy 13 & Bus Hwy 83: Go 1/2 mi S on Outer Rd (Scenic Ave). Enter on L.*

WELCOME

FACILITIES: 31 sites, typical site width 40 ft, 31 full hkups, (30/50 amps), 18 pull-thrus, cable TV, WiFi Instant Internet at site, family camping, RV storage, laundry, RV supplies, LP gas by weight/by meter, ice, picnic tables, wood.

RECREATION: pavilion, golf nearby, activities, sports field.

Pets welcome, quantity restrict. Partial handicap access. No tents. Open all yr. Big rigs welcome. Escort to site. Rate in 2010 $26-33 for 2 persons. MC/VISA/DISC/AMEX/Debit.

Phone: (417)326-2219
Address: 5100 Scenic Ave, Bolivar, MO 65613
Email: cowboy@windstream.net
Web: www.speedwayrv.net

SEE AD THIS PAGE

BONA—D-2

CEDAR RIDGE AREA (COE Stockton Lake)—(Dade) *From jct Hwy 215 & Hwy 245: Go 1 mi N on Hwy 245 & CR RA.* FACILITIES: 54 sites, typical site width 12 ft, 21 E, (20/30 amps), 33 no hkups, tenting, dump. RECREATION: lake swim, boating, ramp, dock, lake fishing. Partial handicap access. Open all yr. Phone: (417)995-2045.

BONNE TERRE—D-5

(N) SAINT FRANCOIS STATE PARK—(St. Francois) *From jct Hwy 47 & US 67: Go 4 mi N on US 67. Enter on R.*

WELCOME

FACILITIES: 110 sites, 63 E, (30 amps), 47 no hkups, 28 pull-thrus, tenting, dump, laundry, picnic tables, fire rings, grills, wood, controlled access.

RECREATION: pavilion, river swim, boating, no motors, canoeing, float trips, river/stream fishing, hiking trails.

Open all yr. Facilities fully operational Apr 1 - Oct 31. MC/VISA/DISC/AMEX.

Phone: (573)358-2173
Address: 8920 US Hwy 67 N, Bonne Terre, MO 63628
Web: www.mostateparks.com

SEE AD TRAVEL SECTION PAGE 451

The second most powerful earthquake to strike the United States, with a magnitude of 8.0 on the Richter scale, occurred in 1811, centered in New Madrid, Missouri. The quake shook more than one million square miles, and was felt as far as 1,000 miles away.

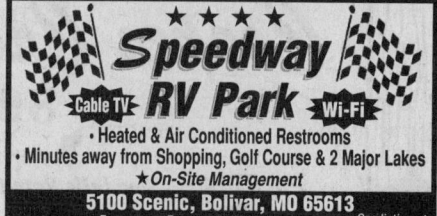

BOWLING GREEN—B-4

(NE) COZY C RV CAMPGROUND—(Pike) *From jct US 61 & US 54: Go 2-1/2 mi E on US 54. Enter on R.*

WELCOME

◆◆◆◆FACILITIES: 45 sites, typical site width 25 ft, 45 full hkups, (20/30/50 amps), some extd stay sites, 15 pull-thrus, cable TV, ($), WiFi Instant Internet at site ($), family camping, tenting, RV storage, laundry, ltd groc, RV supplies, LP gas by weight/by meter, ice, picnic tables, patios.

◆◆RECREATION: rec hall, pavilion, mini-golf, ($), golf nearby.

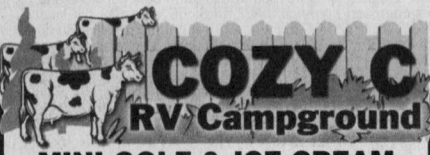

BOWLING GREEN—Continued
COZY C RV CAMPGROUND—Continued

Pets welcome, breed restrict. Open all yr. Must be registered before dark. Big rigs welcome. Clubs welcome. Rate in 2010 $25.50 for 2 persons. MC/VISA/DISC/Debit. Member ARVC, MOARC.

Phone: (573)324-3055
Address: 16733 US Highway 54, Bowling Green, MO 63334
Lat/Lon: 39.37276/-91.16423
Email: cozycamp@wildblue.net
Web: www.cozyccampground.com

SEE AD THIS PAGE

BRANSON—E-3

(W) ACORN ACRES RV PARK & CAMPGROUND—(Stone) *From jct US 65 & US 465 (Ozark Mtn Highroad): Go 8 mi W on US 465 (Ozark Mtn Highroad), then 2-1/2 mi W on Hwy 76. Enter on L.*

WELCOME

◆◆◆◆◆FACILITIES: 79 sites, typical site width 40 ft, 79 full hkups, (30/50 amps), many extd stay sites, 15 pull-thrus, cable TV, WiFi Instant Internet at site, phone Internet central location, family camping, tenting, cabins, RV storage, dump, laundry, ltd groc, RV supplies, LP gas by weight/by meter, ice, picnic tables, patios, fire rings, grills, wood.

◆◆◆◆◆RECREATION: rec room/area, equipped pavilion, coin games, swim pool, golf nearby, bsktball, playground, activities, horseshoes, sports field, v-ball, local tours.

Pets welcome, quantity restrict. Partial handicap access. Open all yr. Big rigs welcome. Clubs welcome. Green Friendly. Rate in 2010 $24-52 for 2 persons. MC/VISA/DISC/Debit. Member ARVC, MOARC.

Phone: (417)338-2500
Address: 159 Acorn Acres Lane, Branson West, MO 65737
Lat/Lon: 36.68936/-93.34351
Email: camp@bestbransonrvpark.com
Web: www.bestbransonrvpark.com

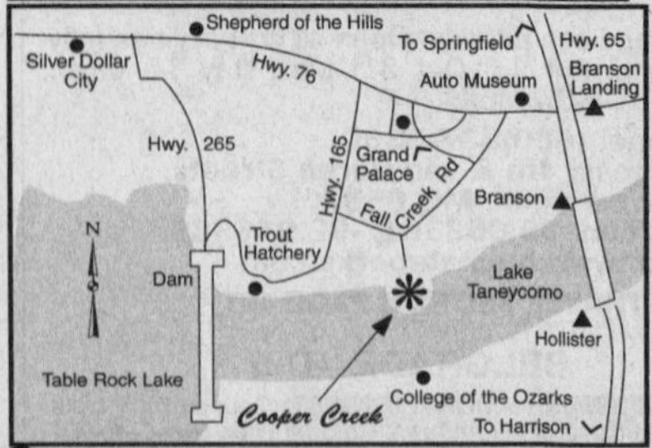

SEE AD THIS PAGE

America's Best Campground
2003-2010
Winner
8-Year Welcome Mat Winner
Most RV-Friendly Good Sam Park in the nation as voted by the Good Sam Club Membership
Good Sam Park
Come See Why!!
BRANSON, MO
800-671-4399
FREE
WiFi
See listing at Branson, MO
City Close, Country Quiet
To Springfield
0.3 mi.
248
Buena Vista Rd.
1.3 mi.
Tri Lakes Center
Shepherd of the Hills Expwy.
1.7 mi.
KMART SC
Outlet Mall
Gretna Rd.
Epps Rd.
65
Roark Valley Rd.
Forsythe Rd.
Business 65
Lake Taneycomo
Old Downtown Branson & Waterfront
76
165
Dots Indicate Branson Music Shows & Attractions
Green Mtn. Drive
Wildwood Drive
Fall Creek Rd.
To Arkansas
N
TL RATED
9.5/9.5★/9
Woodall's Rated
Fac: WWWWW
Rec: WWWWW
15% OFF!
For Good Sam and Veterans when paying with cash or check
499 Buena Vista Rd.
Branson, MO 65616
www.abc-branson.com
fun4uabc@aol.com
417-336-4399
Win Tickets to these Fabulous Shows with advance reservation. Call for Details.
WE SELL BRANSON SHOW TICKETS!
George Dyer
Righteous Brothers' Bill Medley
Legends in Concert
The Texas Tenors
Red, Hot... & Blue!
Barbara Fairchild
Smoke on the Mountain
Yakov's Moscow Circus Dinner Experience
The Duttons
IMAX
Clay Cooper's Country Music Express
Titanic World's Largest Museum Attraction
The World Famous Platters
Buck Trent Morning Show
The Hughes Brothers Celebrity Theatre
Grand Jubilee
Tribute to Marty Robbins
Strait Country!
Neal McCoy
Jeerk
Comedy Jamboree
The Thomas Brothers
Sunday Gospel Jubilee
The Yakov Smirnoff Show
John Denver
Hamner Barber Variety Show
Ripley's Believe It or Not!
Island Fire
Rankin Brothers
Cassandre
Swingin Doors Classic Country
Hank Williams Revisited
Hollywood Wax Museum
Haygoods
Tony Roi's Elvis Experience
Buckets N Boards
Doug Gabriel

Find a Campground Woodall's Does Not List? Tell Us About It At www.woodalls.com!

OAK GROVE RV PARK

CABLE TV

FREE WIFI

- Branson Show Tickets on Site
- 3/4 mile S of Titanic
- Clean Restrooms

417-334-4781

www.oakgrovervpark.com

email: reservations@oakgrovervpark.com

780 State Hwy 165, Branson, MO 65616

See listing at Branson, MO

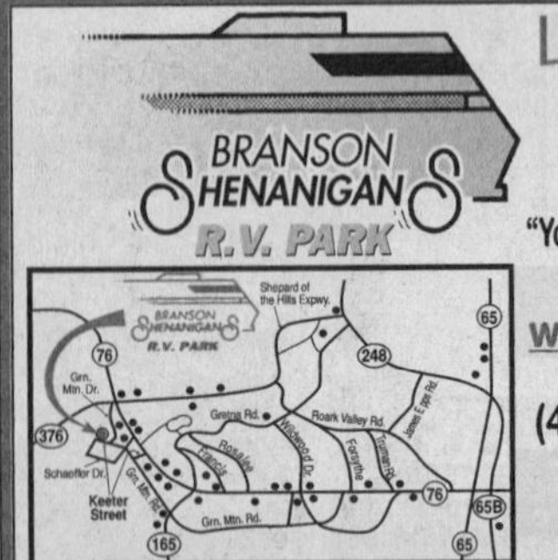

Save $10.00*

and see why guests say this about

BRANSON SHENANIGANS RV PARK...

"We've been in every state but two, this is the nicest park we've been to!"

"You really ARE close to everything, but it's so quiet with the woods all around!"

Full hookup, free Wi-Fi and Cable TV

www.bransonRVparks.com • bsrvpark@aol.com

3675 Keeter St., Branson, MO 65616

(417) 334-1920 for info • (800) 338-7275 for reservations

*Mention this ad and receive $10 off a 3 night stay

Not valid with any other discount

See listing at Branson, MO

Branson's
Ozark Country Campground
Branson, Missouri
IN THE CENTER OF IT ALL!

Free Wi-Fi

Clubs Welcome

• Cable • Big Rigs • Pool

(800) 968-1300

www.bransoncampground.com

Email – occ@bransoncampground.com

679 Quebec Dr., Branson, MO

See listing at Branson, MO

COMPTON RIDGE CAMPGROUND

Where Campers Come First

Cabins – Lodge/Motel Rooms – Cafe – WI-FI

Groups Welcome • Large Meeting Room

Free Shuttle to Silver Dollar City

New Restrooms • Fun Bike Rental

Store – Discounted Show Tickets

Doggie Park • Outdoor Family Movies

5040 State Hwy 265
Branson, MO 65616

417-338-2911

New Owners

Woodalls Rated:
Fac: WWWWW
Rec: WWWWW
See listing at Branson, MO

800-233-8648 *(Resv. Only)*

www.comptonridge.com

Email: info@comptonridge.com

BRANSON—Continued

(N) AMERICA'S BEST CAMPGROUND—(Taney) *From jct US 65 & Hwy 248 (Shepherd of the Hills Expwy): Go 1-3/4 mi W on Hwy 248 (Shepherd of the Hills Expwy), then keep right to Hwy 248 (1/2 mi N of Tri-Lake Center), then 1-1/4 mi N on Hwy 248, then 300 yards W on Buena Vista Rd. Enter on L.*

"EXPERIENCE THE DIFFERENCE" AT ABC!
America's Best Campground's convenient location is City Close and Country Quiet. ENJOY FREE WIFI; even in your RV! Rallies welcome! Come see why the Good Sam Club members keep voting us their favorite park year after year.

◆◆◆◆◆FACILITIES: 161 sites, typical site width 30 ft, 159 full hkups, 2 W&E, (30/50 amps), 136 pull-thrus, cable TV, phone/WiFi Instant Internet at site, phone Internet central location, family camping, tenting, cabins, RV storage, dump, non-guest dump $, laundry, groceries, RV supplies, LP gas by meter, ice, picnic tables, patios, grills.

◆◆◆◆◆RECREATION: rec hall, rec room/area, coin games, swim pool, hot tub, golf nearby, bsktball, playground, activities, horseshoes, v-ball, local tours.

Pets welcome. Partial handicap access. Open all yr. Facilities fully operational Mid Mar - Mid Dec. Planned activities in season only. Rental units open Mid Mar - Mid Dec. Big rigs welcome. Escort to site. Clubs welcome. Rate in 2010 $35 for 2 persons. MC/VISA/DISC. Member ARVC, MOARC.

Text 83390 to (440)725-8687 to see our Visual Tour.

Phone: (800)671-4399
Address: 499 Buena Vista Rd, Branson, MO 65616
Lat/Lon: 36.68326/-93.26055
Email: fun4uabc@aol.com
Web: www.abc-branson.com

SEE AD PAGE 461 AND AD MAP PAGE 450

(W) Branson KOA—(Taney) *From jct US 65 & Hwy 76: Go 3-1/4 mi W on Hwy 76, then 1/2 mi S on Hwy 165, then 200 yards W on Animal Safari Rd. Enter on L.* ◆◆◆◆◆FACILITIES: 146 sites, typical site width 23 ft, 140 full hkups, 6 W&E, (20/30/50 amps), 115 pull-thrus, family camping, tenting, dump, laundry, groceries. ◆◆◆◆◆RECREATION: swim pool, playground. Pets welcome, breed restrict. Partial handicap access. Open all yr. Big rigs welcome. Green Friendly. Rate in 2010 $30-47 for 2 persons. Member ARVC, MOARC. Phone: (800)467-7611. KOA discount.

(N) BRANSON LAKES AREA CHAMBER OF COMMERCE & CONVENTION & VISITORS BUREAU—*From jct Hwy 76 & US 65: Go 1 mi N on US 65, then 100 feet W on Hwy 248. Enter on L.* Open all yr.

Phone: (417)334-4136
Address: 269 Hwy 248, Branson, MO 65615
Lat/Lon: 36.39554/-93.13499
Email: info@bransoncvb.com
Web: www.explorebranson.com

SEE AD PAGE 462 AND AD KANSAS CITY PAGE 470 AND AD ST. LOUIS PAGE 478 AND AD TRAVEL SECTION PAGE 453

(W) BRANSON SHENANIGANS RV PARK—(Taney) *From jct US 65 & Hwy 76: Go 2 mi W on Hwy 76, then 2 mi S on Green Mtn Drive, then straight on W Keeter. Enter on R.*

WALK TO BRANSON SHOWS!
All the amenities & the best location in town! A park like setting minutes from all the fun & excitement Branson offers. Quick access to shows, outlet shopping & dining. Golf, fishing & boating just a 7 minute drive. Let us spoil you.

◆◆◆◆FACILITIES: 40 sites, typical site width 26 ft, 40 full hkups, (30/50 amps), 33 pull-thrus, cable TV, WiFi Instant Internet at site, WiFi Internet central location, family camping, laundry, ice, picnic tables.

◆RECREATION: rec room/area, golf nearby.

Pets welcome. Partial handicap access. No tents. Open all yr. Big rigs welcome. Clubs welcome. Rate in 2010 $29.81-37.50 for 2 persons. MC/VISA/Debit. Member ARVC, MOARC.

Phone: (800)338-7275
Address: 3675 Keeter St, Branson, MO 65616
Lat/Lon: 36.64568/-93.29182
Email: bsrvpark@aol.com
Web: www.bransonrvparks.com

SEE AD PAGE 462

BRANSON—Continued
Branson Stagecoach RV Park—Continued

(SW) Branson Stagecoach RV Park—(Taney) *From jct Hwy 76 & US 65: Go 3 mi S on US 65, then 5 mi W on Hwy 165. Enter on R.* ◆◆◆◆FACILITIES: 47 sites, typical site width 32 ft, 47 full hkups, (20/30/50 amps), 27 pull-thrus, cable TV, WiFi Instant Internet at site, phone Internet central location, laundry, LP gas by weight/by meter, ice, picnic tables, fire rings, grills, wood. ◆◆RECREATION: rec hall, swim pool, hot tub, playground. Pets welcome. Partial handicap access. No tents. Open Mar 1 - Dec 15. Big rigs welcome. Rate in 2010 $40 for 2 persons. MC/VISA/DISC/Debit. Member ARVC, MOARC. FMCA discount. CCUSA 50% Discount. CCUSA reservations Recommended, CCUSA max stay Unlimited.

Phone: (800)446-7110
Address: 5751 State Hwy 165, Branson, MO 65616
Lat/Lon: 36.70344/-93.14224
Email: contact@bransonstagecoachrv.com
Web: www.bransonstagecoachrv.com

Branson View Campground (Not visited)—(Taney) FACILITIES: RECREATION: No tents. Open all yr. Rate in 2010 $44 for 2 persons. CCUSA 50% Discount. CCUSA reservations Required, CCUSA max stay 5 days.

Phone: (800)992-9055
Address: 2362 Hwy 265, Branson, MO 65616
Lat/Lon: 36.63224/-93.30410
Web: www.thebransonviewcampground.com

(N) BRANSON VIEW ESTATES (RV SPACES)—(Taney) *From jct Hwy 76 & US 65: Go 5 mi N on US 65, then 2 mi SE on MO 7. Enter on L.*

FACILITIES: 10 sites, typical site width 25 ft, 10 full hkups, (20/50 amps), tenting.

Pets welcome. Open all yr. Big rigs welcome. Rate in 2010 $20 per vehicle.

Phone: (417)561-2255
Address: 2543 State Hwy 7, Branson, MO 65616

SEE AD PAGE 460

(SW) BRANSON'S OZARK COUNTRY CAMPGROUND—(Taney) *From jct US 65 & Hwy 248 (that becomes Gretna Rd at 2nd light): Go 1-3/4 mi S on Hwy 248, then 3-1/4 mi S on Gretna Rd & cross over Hwy 76 & it becomes Hwy 165, then go 2-1/2 mi S on Hwy 165 to Quebec Dr, then go 1/2 mi W on Quebec Dr. Enter on L.*

◆◆◆◆FACILITIES: 72 sites, typical site width 35 ft, 72 full hkups, (20/30/50 amps), some extd stay sites, 10 pull-thrus, cable TV, WiFi Instant Internet at site, phone Internet central location, laundry, RV supplies, LP gas by weight/by meter, ice, picnic tables, fire rings, grills, wood.

◆◆◆RECREATION: rec hall, rec room/area, equipped pavilion, swim pool, golf nearby, play equipment, hiking trails.

Pets welcome. Partial handicap access. No tents. Open all yr. Big rigs welcome. Clubs welcome. Green Friendly. Rate in 2010 $24-36 for 2 persons. MC/VISA/DISC/AMEX/Debit. Member ARVC, MOARC. FMCA discount. CCUSA 50% Discount. CCUSA reservations Accepted, CCUSA max stay Unlimited, Cash only for CCUSA disc. Discount not available Jan thru Mar. Standard discounted rate applies at that time.

Phone: (800)968-1300
Address: 679 Quebec Dr., Branson, MO 65616
Lat/Lon: 36.63052/-93.21652
Email: occ@bransoncampground.com
Web: www.bransoncampground.com

SEE AD PAGE 462

(W) COMPTON RIDGE CAMPGROUND—(Stone) *From jct US 65 & US 465 (Ozark Mt High Rd): Go 7 mi S on US 465, then 1/4 mi W on US 76, then 1/2 mi S on Hwy 265. Enter on L.*

◆◆◆◆◆FACILITIES: 219 sites, typical site width 30 ft, 178 full hkups, 41 W&E, (20/30/50 amps), 53 pull-thrus, cable TV, WiFi Instant Internet at site, family camping, tenting, cabins, RV storage, laundry, groceries, RV supplies, LP gas by weight/by meter, ice, picnic tables, patios, fire rings, grills, wood.

◆◆◆◆◆RECREATION: rec hall, rec room/area, equipped pavilion, coin games, 3 swim pools, wading pool, golf nearby, bsktball, 7 bike rentals, playground, activities, tennis, hiking trails, v-ball, local tours.

BRANSON—Continued
COMPOTON RIDGE CAMPGROUND—Continued

Pets welcome. Partial handicap access. Open Mar 15 - Dec 15. Big rigs welcome. Escort to site. Clubs welcome. Green Friendly. Rate in 2010 $27.50-42 for 2 persons. MC/VISA/DISC/AMEX/Debit. ATM. Member ARVC, MOARC.

Phone: (417)338-2911
Address: 5040 State Hwy 265, Branson, MO 65616
Lat/Lon: 36.66679/-93.33022
Email: info@comptonridge.com
Web: www.comptonridge.com

SEE AD PAGE 462

(S) COOPER CREEK CAMPGROUND—(Taney) *From jct US 65 & Hwy 76: Go 1 mi W on Hwy 76, then 2 mi S on Fall Creek Rd. Enter on L.*

◆◆◆◆FACILITIES: 75 sites, typical site width 31 ft, 75 full hkups, (20/30/50 amps), 26 pull-thrus, cable TV, WiFi Internet central location, family camping, cabins, dump, laundry, ltd groc, RV supplies, marine gas, ice, picnic tables, fire rings, wood.

◆◆◆◆RECREATION: rec room/area, equipped pavilion, coin games, 2 swim pools, boating, ramp, dock, pontoon/4 motorboat rentals, lake fishing, fishing supplies, fishing guides, golf nearby, bsktball, playground, horseshoes.

Pets welcome, breed restrict. Partial handicap access. No tents. Open Mar 10 - Dec 1. Big rigs welcome. Clubs welcome. Green Friendly. Rate in 2010 $28-37 for 2 persons. MC/VISA/DISC/Debit. FMCA discount.

Phone: (800)261-8398
Address: 471 Cooper Creek Rd., Branson, MO 65616
Lat/Lon: 36.61847/-93.24842
Email: coopercreek@suddenlink.net
Web: www.coopercreekcampground.com

SEE AD PAGE 460

(SW) OAK GROVE RV RESORT—(Taney) *From jct US 65 & Hwy 248: Go 6 mi W on Hwy 248, (Hwy 248 turns into Gretna Rd) proceed straight ahead on Gretna Rd and cross US 76. Enter on L.*

◆◆◆◆FACILITIES: 130 sites, 130 full hkups, (30/50 amps), 7 pull-thrus, cable TV, WiFi Instant Internet at site, WiFi Internet central location, family camping, tenting, RV storage, laundry, LP gas by weight/by meter, ice, picnic tables, fire rings, grills, wood.

◆RECREATION: equipped pavilion, golf nearby, playground, activities, (wkends).

Pets welcome, size restrict, quantity restrict. Open all yr. Big rigs welcome. Escort to site. Clubs welcome. Rate in 2010 $30-34 for 2 persons. MC/VISA/DISC/Debit. Member ARVC, MOARC.

OAK GROVE RV RESORT—Continued on next page

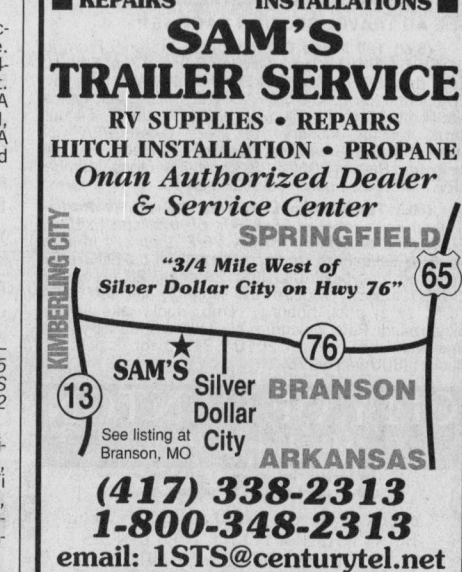

BRANSON—Continued
OAK GROVE RV RESORT—Continued

Phone: (888)334-4781
Address: 780 State Hwy 165, Branson, MO 65616
Lat/Lon: 36.62764/-93.28048
Email: reservations@oakgrovervpark.com
Web: www.oakgrovervpark.com

SEE AD PAGE 462

(C) Pea Patch RV Park—(Taney) *From jct US 65 & Hwy 248: Go 6 mi W on Hwy 248 (Hwy 248 turns into Gretna Rd): Go straight on Gretna Rd to US 76, then 1/2 blk W on US 76, then 500 ft on Harvey Ln (behind Ruby Tuesday). Enter on L.* ◆◆◆FACILITIES: 31 sites, 31 full hkups, (20/30/50 amps), cable TV, WiFi Instant Internet at site, family camping, tenting, laundry, RV supplies, picnic tables. ◆◆RECREATION: swim pool, play equipment. Pets welcome. Partial handicap access. Open Mar 1 - Dec 1. Rate in 2010 $29.95-39.95 for 2 persons. MC/VISA/DISC/AMEX/Debit. CCUSA 50% Discount. CCUSA max stay Unlimited. Reservations not accepted Memorial Day thru Labor Day weekends. $3 pull thru surcharge. Limited cable.

CAMPCLUB USA

Phone: (417)335-3958
Address: 3330 W Harvey Ln, Branson, MO 65616
Lat/Lon: 36.63689/-93.28362
Email: peapatch@suddenlinkmail.com
Web: www.peapatchrvpark.com

Reserve Online at Woodalls.com

(W) SAM'S TRAILER SERVICE—*From jct US 65 & US 465 (Ozark Mtn High Rd): Go 7 mi S on US 465, then 1-1/2 mi W on Hwy 76. Enter on L.* SALES: pre-owned unit sales. SERVICES: full-time mech, RV appliance repair, body work/collision repair, LP gas by weight/by meter, sells parts/accessories, installs hitches. Open all yr. MC/VISA/DISC/AMEX/Debit.

WELCOME

Phone: (800)348-2313
Address: 8810 State Hwy 76, Reeds Spring, MO 65737
Lat/Lon: 36.68089/-93.34051
Email: 1sts@centurytel.net

SEE AD PAGE 463

(W) TABLE ROCK STATE PARK—(Taney) *From jct Hwy-76 & Hwy-165: Go 5 mi W on Hwy-165. Enter on L.*

WELCOME

FACILITIES: 161 sites, 30 ft max RV length, 29 full hkups, 89 E, (30/50 amps), 43 no hkups, tenting, dump, laundry, ltd groc, picnic tables, fire rings, grills, wood.

RECREATION: pavilion, lake swim, boating, canoeing, ramp, dock, canoe rentals, lake fishing, hiking trails.

Partial handicap access. Facilities fully operational Apr 1 - Oct 31. MC/VISA/DISC/AMEX.

Phone: (417)334-4707
Address: 5272 State Highway 165, Branson, MO 65616
Web: www.mostateparks.com

SEE AD TRAVEL SECTION PAGE 451

(SW) Tall Pines Campground—(Stone) *From jct US 65 & US 465 (Ozark Mtn High Rd): Go 7 mi S on US 465, then 1/4 mi W on US 76, then 100 yds S on Hwy 265. Enter on L.* ◆◆◆◆FACILITIES: 71 sites, typical site width 35 ft, 71 full hkups, (30/50 amps), 14 pull-thrus, tenting, laundry, ltd groc. ◆◆RECREATION: swim pool. Pets welcome. Open Mar 1 - Dec 1. Big rigs welcome. Rate in 2010 $28-32 for 2 persons. Member ARVC, MOARC. Phone: (417)338-2445.

(NE) Taneycomo Lakefront Resort/RV Park—(Taney) *From jct Hwy 65 & Bus 65 (Hollister Exit): Go 1-3/4 mi E on Bus 65 to Hwy 76 E, then 1/4 mi E on 76 E to Lakeshore Dr, then 2 mi N on Lakeshore Dr. Enter on L.* ◆◆◆FACILITIES: 28 sites, 28 full hkups, (30/50 amps), 9 pull-thrus, laundry. ◆◆◆RECREATION: swim pool, boating, ramp, dock, lake fishing, playground. Pets welcome. No tents. Open all yr. Big rigs welcome. Rate in 2010 $21.95 for 2 persons. Phone: (800)949-9975.

BRANSON—Continued

(SW) The Wilderness at Silver Dollar City—(Stone) *From jct US 65 & US 465 (Ozark Mountain High Rd): Go 7 mi S on US 465, then 1/4 mi W on US 76, then 1/2 mi S on Hwy 265. Enter on R.* ◆◆◆◆FACILITIES: 175 sites, typical site width 30 ft, 112 full hkups, 23 W&E, (30/50 amps), 50 amps ($), 40 no hkups, 22 pull-thrus, family camping, tenting, dump, laundry, full svc store. ◆◆◆RECREATION: swim pool, playground. Pets welcome. Partial handicap access. Open Mar 1 - Dec 31. Big rigs welcome. Rate in 2010 $26-35 for 2 persons. Member ARVC, MOARC. Phone: (800)477-5164.

(W) Treasure Lake RV Resort—(Taney) *From jct Hwy 248 & 65N: Go 2 mi W on Hwy 248, then 3-1/4 mi SW on Shepherd of the Hills Expwy to entrance. Enter on R.* ◆◆◆◆◆FACILITIES: 550 sites, typical site width 25 ft, 550 full hkups, (30/50 amps), 81 pull-thrus, family camping, tenting, dump, laundry, ltd groc. ◆◆◆◆◆RECREATION: 2 swim pools, pond fishing, playground. Pets welcome. Partial handicap access. Open all yr. Big rigs welcome. Phone: (417)334-1040.

(E) Turkey Creek RV Village—(Taney) *(N'Bnd/S'Bnd) From jct Hwy 76 & Hwy 65: Go 1 mi S on Hwy 65 to Hollister Business 65, then 2 mi on Business 65 on the left. Do not go US 65 Bus or SR 76 through Old Branson with an RV. Enter on L.* ◆◆◆◆FACILITIES: 67 sites, typical site width 32 ft, 67 full hkups, (30/50 amps), 50 amps ($), 11 pull-thrus, tenting, dump, laundry. ◆◆RECREATION: boating, ramp, lake fishing. Pets welcome. Partial handicap access. Open all yr. Big rigs welcome. Rate in 2010 $20.50-21.50 for 2 persons. Phone: (417)335-8004.

(W) WHISTLE STOP CAFE—*From jct US 65 & US 465 (Ozark Mtn High Rd): Go 7 mi S on US 465, then 1/4 mi W on US 76, then 1/2 mi S on Hwy 265. Enter on L.* Home style economical. Family meals open breakfast & dinner every day. Delivery available and catering for groups. Check out our fresh baked pizza shop and weekly specials! Open May 15 - Oct 31. MC/VISA/DISC.

WELCOME

Phone: (417)338-8345
Address: 5040 State Hwy 265, Branson, MO 65616
Lat/Lon: 36.66679/-93.33022
Web: www.comptonridge.com

SEE AD PAGE 462

CAMERON—B-2

(S) WALLACE STATE PARK—(Clinton) *From jct US-69 & 36: Go 6 mi S on Hwy-69, then 2 mi E on Hwy-121. Enter on R.*

WELCOME

FACILITIES: 77 sites, typical site width 20 ft, 42 E, (30/50 amps), 35 no hkups, tenting, dump, laundry, picnic tables, fire rings, wood.

RECREATION: pavilion, lake swim, boating, electric motors only, canoeing, lake fishing, playground, horseshoes, hiking trails.

Partial handicap access. Open all yr. No reservations. Max stay 15 days. MC/VISA/DISC/AMEX.

Phone: (816)632-3745
Address: 10621 NE Hwy 121, Cameron, MO 64429
Lat/Lon: 39.658083/-94.214361
Email: moparks@mail.dnr.state.mo.us
Web: www.mostateparks.com

SEE AD TRAVEL SECTION PAGE 451

Situated within a day's drive of 50% of the U.S. population, Branson and the Tri-Lakes area serves up to 65,000 visitors daily. Branson has been a "rubber tire" destination with the vast majority of tourists arriving by vehicles, RVs and tour buses. Branson has also become one of America's top motor coach vacation destinations with an estimated 4,000 buses arriving each year.

CANTON—A-4

(C) CITY OF CANTON MISSISSIPPI RIVER PARK—(Lewis) *From jct US 61 & SR-P: Go 1-1/4 mi E on SR-P, then 1/2 mi N on 4th St, then 1/4 mi E on Henderson. Enter at end.*

WELCOME

FACILITIES: 23 sites, typical site width 25 ft, 14 full hkups, 9 W&E, (20/30/50 amps), mostly extd stay sites, tenting, dump, picnic tables, fire rings, grills.

RECREATION: boating, ramp, river fishing, golf nearby, playground.

Pets welcome. Open all yr. No restrooms. Big rigs welcome. Clubs welcome.

Phone: (573)288-4413
Address: 106 N 5th St, Canton, MO 63435
Lat/Lon: 40.13605/-91.51559

SEE AD THIS PAGE

CAPE FAIR—E-2

(S) CAPE FAIR DOCK & PARK (COE Table Rock Lake)—(Taney) *From town: Go 1 mi W on Lake Rd 76-82.* FACILITIES: 82 sites, typical site width 20 ft, 36 W&E, 33 E, (30 amps), 13 no hkups, tenting, dump, ltd groc. RECREATION: lake swim, boating, ramp, dock, lake fishing, playground. Partial handicap access. Open Apr 1 - Oct 31. Phone: (417)538-2220.

CAPE GIRARDEAU—D-6

(SW) Cape Camping & RV Park—(Cape Girardeau) *From jct I-55 & Hwy 61 (exit 99): Go 1-1/2 mi E on Hwy 61. Enter on L.* ◆◆◆◆FACILITIES: 102 sites, typical site width 25 ft, 90 full hkups, (20/30/50 amps), 12 no hkups, 90 pull-thrus, family camping, tenting, laundry. ◆◆◆◆RECREATION: swim pool, pond fishing, playground. Pets welcome. Partial handicap access. Open all yr. Big rigs welcome. Rate in 2010 $30 for 2 persons. Phone: (573)332-8888.

(N) TRAIL OF TEARS STATE PARK—(Cape Girardeau) *From town: Go 10 mi N on Hwy 177. Enter on R.*

WELCOME

FACILITIES: 52 sites, 7 full hkups, 10 E, (30 amps), 35 no hkups, tenting, dump, laundry, picnic tables, fire rings, grills, wood, controlled access.

RECREATION: pavilion, lake swim, boating, ramp, lake/river fishing, hiking trails.

Partial handicap access. Open all yr. Facilities fully operational Apr 1 - Oct 31. MC/VISA/DISC/AMEX.

Phone: (573)290-5268
Address: 429 Moccasin Springs, Jackson, MO 63755
Web: www.mostateparks.com

SEE AD TRAVEL SECTION PAGE 451

CARTHAGE—E-2

(S) Ballards Campground—(Jasper) *From jct I-44 (exit 18A) & Hwy 59: Go 1/4 mi S on Hwy 59. Enter on L.* ◆◆FACILITIES: 30 sites, typical site width 20 ft, 8 full hkups, 12 W&E, 10 E, (20/30/50 amps), 24 pull-thrus, tenting, dump, laundry. RECREATION: pond fishing. Pets welcome. Open all yr. Rate in 2010 $15-21 for 2 persons. Phone: (417)359-0359.

(SE) BIG RED BARN RV PARK—(Jasper) *N'bnd: jct I-44 & US 71 (exit 18-B): Go 3-1/2 mi N on US 71 to Garrison. Go 1 mi S on Grand Ave/Outer Rd, then 1/3 mi E on Elm. S'bnd: jct US 71 & HH/Fir: Go 3/4 mi E on HH/Fir, then 1/3 mi S on Garrison/571, then 1/2 mi on Grand, then 1/2 mi on Elm. Enter on L.*

WELCOME

◆◆◆◆◆FACILITIES: 65 sites, typical site width 30 ft, 57 full hkups, 8 W&E, (20/30/50 amps), some extd stay sites, 55 pull-thrus, cable TV, WiFi Instant Internet at site, phone Internet central location, family camping, tenting, RV's/park model rentals, RV storage, dump, non-guest dump $, laundry, LP gas by weight/by meter, ice, picnic tables, patios.

◆◆◆RECREATION: rec hall, rec room/area, golf nearby, bsktball, playground, horseshoes, sports field, v-ball.

CAMPCLUB USA

Pets welcome. Partial handicap access. Open all yr. Big rigs welcome. Escort to site. Clubs welcome. Rate in 2010 $35-45 for 2 persons. MC/VISA/DISC/Debit. Member ARVC, MOARC. FMCA discount. CCUSA 50% Discount. CCUSA reservations Recommended, CCUSA max stay 2 days. Subject to availability. Discount applies to regular sites-premium sites addl. Cannot be used with other discounts. Discounts not available during special events or with rally/group rates. Call for details.

BIG RED BARN RV PARK—Continued on next page

CARTHAGE—Continued
BIG RED BARN RV PARK—Continued

Phone: (417)358-2432
Address: 5089 County Lane 138, Carthage, MO 64836
Lat/Lon: 37.12579/-94.30441
Email: reserve@bigredbarnrvpark.com
Web: www.bigredbarnrvpark.com

SEE AD PAGE 464

WELCOME **(S) COACHLIGHT CAMPGROUND**—(Jasper) *From jct I-44 (exit 18B) & US 71: Go 3/4 mi N on US 71 to Cedar Rd exit, then W 300 ft. Enter on R.*

◆◆◆◆◆FACILITIES: 80 sites, typical site width 15 ft, accepts full hkup units only, 80 full hkups, (20/30/50 amps), some extd stay sites, 57 pull-thrus, cable TV, WiFi Instant Internet at site, phone Internet central location, family camping, RV storage, dump, non-guest dump $, laundry, RV supplies, LP gas by weight/by meter, ice, patios.

◆◆RECREATION: rec hall, rec room/area.

Pets welcome, breed restrict. No tents. Open all yr. No restrooms. Big rigs welcome. Escort to site. Clubs welcome. Rate in 2010 $25 per vehicle. MC/VISA/Debit. Member ARVC, MOARC.

Phone: (417)358-3666
Address: 5305 S Garrison Rd, Carthage, MO 64836
Lat/Lon: 37.09502/-94.31413
Email: campground@coachlightrv.com
Web: www.coachlightrv.com

SEE AD THIS PAGE

WELCOME **(S) COACHLIGHT RV SALES**—*From jct I-44 (exit 18B) & US 71: Go 3/4 mi N on US 71 to Cedar Rd exit, then W 300 ft. Enter on R.* SALES: travel trailers, 5th wheels, Class A motorhomes, Class C motorhomes, fold-down camping trailers, pre-owned unit sales. SERVICES: full-time mech, RV appliance repair, body work/collision repair, LP gas by weight/by meter, dump station, sells parts/accessories, installs hitches. Open all yr. MC/VISA/Debit.

Phone: (800)799-7444
Address: 5327 S Garrison Rd, Carthage, MO 64836
Lat/Lon: 37.09395/-94.31304
Email: sales@coachlightrv.com
Web: www.coachlightrv.com

SEE AD THIS PAGE

CARUTHERSVILLE—A-6

WELCOME **(S) LADY LUCK CASINO CARUTHERSVILLE**—*From jct I-55 & Hwy 84 (exit 19): Go 5 mi E on Hwy 84. Enter at end.* Full service riverboat casino with amphitheater. Expo Center, Restaurant & Sidelines entertainment lounge. Ample parking. Open all yr. MC/VISA/DISC/AMEX/Debit. ATM.

Phone: (888)ladyluck
Address: 777 East Third St, Caruthersville, MO 63830
Lat/Lon: 36.18982/-89.65012
Email: ladyluckcaruthersville@ islecorp.com
Web: www.ladyluckcaruthersville.com

SEE AD TRAVEL SECTION PAGE 449

WELCOME **(S) LADY LUCK RV PARK AND NATURE TRAIL**—(Pemiscot) *From jct I-55 & Hwy 84 (exit 19): Go 5 mi E on Hwy 84. Enter at end.*

◆◆◆◆◆FACILITIES: 27 sites, 27 full hkups, (20/30/50 amps), 18 pull-thrus, cable TV, WiFi Instant Internet at site, dump, laundry, ice, grills.

◆◆◆RECREATION: rec room/area, equipped pavilion, golf nearby.

Pets welcome, quantity restrict. Partial handicap access. No tents. Open all yr. Big rigs welcome. Clubs welcome. Rate in 2010 $20 for 2 persons. MC/VISA/DISC/AMEX/Debit. ATM.

Phone: (573)333-6000
Address: 777 East Third St, Caruthersville, MO 63830
Lat/Lon: 36.19068/-89.65111
Email: ladyluckcaruthersville@ islecorp.com
Web: ladyluckcaruthersville.com

SEE AD TRAVEL SECTION PAGE 449

Ages ago, the Ozarks were a region of volcanic peaks.

CARUTHERSVILLE—Continued

WELCOME **(S) THE LONE WOLF**—*From jct I-55 & Hwy 84 (exit 19): Go 5 mi E on Hwy 84. Enter at end.* From Karaoke contests, to ladies nights, DJ dance parties & non-stop sports action, Lone Wolf always the place to be. Open all yr.

Phone: (888)ladyluck
Address: 777 E Third St, Caruthersville, MO 63830
Lat/Lon: 36.18982/-89.65012
Email: ladyluckcaruthersville@ islecorp.com
Web: www.ladyluckcaruthersville.com

SEE AD TRAVEL SECTION PAGE 449

CASSVILLE—E-2

(E) BIG M BOAT DOCK & PARK (COE - Table Rock Lake)—(Barry) *From town: Go 9 mi E on Hwy-76, then 7 mi S on CR-M (Mano).* FACILITIES: 60 sites, typical site width 20 ft, 14 full hkups, 4 E, (30 amps), 42 no hkups, tenting, dump, ltd groc. RECREATION: lake swim, boating, ramp, dock, lake fishing, playground. Partial handicap access. Open Apr 1 - Sep 30. Phone: (417)271-3190.

(S) Oak Hill Court & RV Park—(Barry) *From jct Bus 37 & Hwy 112: Go 4-1/2 mi S on Hwy 112. Enter on L.* ◆◆◆FACILITIES: 23 sites, 15 full hkups, 8 W&E, (30/50 amps), 15 pull-thrus, dump, laundry. ◆◆◆RECREATION: swim pool, playground. Pets welcome. Partial handicap access. No tents. Open Mar 1 - Oct 31. Rate in 2010 $20 for 2 persons. Phone: (800)291-9442.

WELCOME **(S) ROARING RIVER STATE PARK**—(Barry) *From jct Hwy 248 & Hwy 112: Go 12 mi S on Hwy 112. Enter on R.*

FACILITIES: 185 sites, 137 E, (30 amps), 48 no hkups, 15 pull-thrus, tenting, cabins, dump, laundry, ltd groc, ice, picnic tables, fire rings, grills, wood.

RECREATION: pavilion, swim pool, river fishing, hiking trails.

Partial handicap access. Open all yr. Facilities fully operational Feb 25 - Oct 31. MC/VISA/DISC/AMEX.

Phone: (417)847-2539
Address: 12716 Farm Road 2239, Cassville, MO 65625
Web: www.mostateparks.com

SEE AD TRAVEL SECTION PAGE 451

CENTERVILLE—D-4

MARK TWAIN NATIONAL FOREST (Sutton Bluff Campground)—(Reynolds) *From town: Go 3 mi NE on Hwy-21, then 7 mi NW on FR-2233, then 3 mi S on FR-2236.* FACILITIES: 34 sites, 34 no hkups, tenting. RECREATION: river swim, boating, canoeing, river fishing. Open Apr 1 - Dec 1. Phone: (573)648-9293.

The east end of the Pony Express was in St. Joseph, Missouri.

CHARLESTON—E-6

WELCOME **(S) BOOMLAND**—*From jct I-57 & Hwy 105 (exit 10): Go 300 ft S on Hwy 105 to bottom of ramp, then 500 ft E on Beasley Rd. Enter on R.* 70,000 Sq ft of gifts, fireworks, souvenirs. Gas/Diesel, restaurant & snack bar. Open all yr. MC/VISA/DISC/Debit.

Phone: (573)683-6108
Address: 100 Beasley Park Rd, Charleston, MO 63834
Lat/Lon: 36.90346/-89.35369
Email: boomland01@yahoo.com
Web: www.boomland.com

SEE AD TRAVEL SECTION PAGE 449

WELCOME **(S) BOOMLAND RV PARK & CAMPGROUND**—(Mississippi) *From jct I-57 (exit 10) & Hwy 105: Go 300 feet S on Hwy 105 to bottom of ramp, then E on Beasley Rd. Enter on R.*

◆◆◆FACILITIES: 36 sites, typical site width 25 ft, 36 full hkups, (20/30/50 amps), 34 pull-thrus, tenting, ice.

Pets welcome. Open all yr. Big rigs welcome. Clubs welcome. Rate in 2010 $12 for 2 persons.

Phone: (573)683-6108
Address: 100 Beasley Park Rd, Charleston, MO 63834
Lat/Lon: 36.90339/-89.34988
Email: boomland01@yahoo.com
Web: www.boomland.com

SEE AD TRAVEL SECTION PAGE 449

CHESTERFIELD—C-5

WELCOME **(N) BABLER STATE PARK**—*From jct I-44/US 50 & Hwy 109 (exit 264): Go 10 mi N on Hwy 109.*

FACILITIES: 73 sites, 43 E, (30/50 amps), 30 no hkups, tenting, dump, picnic tables, fire rings, grills, wood, controlled access.

RECREATION: pavilion, swim pool, tennis, sports field, hiking trails.

Partial handicap access. Open all yr. Facilities fully operational Apr 1 - Oct 31. MC/VISA/DISC/AMEX.

Phone: (636)458-3813
Address: 800 Guy Park Dr, Wildwood, MO 63005
Web: www.mostateparks.com

SEE AD TRAVEL SECTION PAGE 451

CLINTON—C-2

(S) Cozy Corner RV Park—(Henry) *From jct Hwy 7 & Hwy 13 & 52: Go 4-1/2 mi S on Hwy 13 to CR 450 SE (Sparrow Foot exit), then 1 mi E on blacktop. Enter on R.* ◆◆◆FACILITIES: 108 sites, typical site width 30 ft, 108 full hkups, (20/30/50 amps), 50 amps ($), 43

Cozy Corner RV Park—Continued on next page

CLINTON—Continued
Cozy Corner RV Park—Continued

pull-thrus, tenting, laundry, groceries. ◇◇◇RECREATION: swim pool, boating, lake/pond fishing, play equipment. Pets welcome. Open all yr. Big rigs welcome. Rate in 2010 $27 for 2 persons. Member ARVC, MOARC. Phone: (660)885-8824. FMCA discount.

(SE) SPARROWFOOT (COE - Harry S. Truman Reservoir)—(Henry) *From town: Go 5 mi S on Hwy 13, then 1 mi E on paved access road.* FACILITIES: 48 sites, typical site width 20 ft, 48 E, (30 amps), tenting, dump, laundry. RECREATION: lake swim, boating, ramp, lake fishing, playground. Partial handicap access. Open all yr. Phone: (660)438-7317.

COLLINS—D-2

(W) Arrowhead Point RV Park & Campground —(St. Clair) *From jct Hwy 13 & US 54: Go 10 mi W on US 54. Enter on R.* ◇◇◇FACILITIES: 42 sites, typical site width 35 ft, 42 full hkups, (30/50 amps), 50 amps ($), 42 pull-thrus, tenting, dump, laundry. ◇◇◇RECREATION: pond fishing, play equipment. Pets welcome. Partial handicap access. Open all yr. Big rigs welcome. Rate in 2010 $18-23 for 2 persons. Phone: (888)881-5720. FMCA discount.

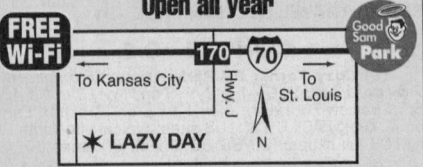

COLUMBIA—C-3

(N) COTTONWOODS RV PARK—(Boone) *From jct I-70 (exit 128A) & US 63: Go 3 mi N on US 63, then 1/4 mi NE on Oakland Gravel Rd. (paved road). Enter on R.*

A NICE PLACE FOR A NICE PEOPLE!
Lovely, landscaped park with many amenities. Just off I 70 we are conveniently located to Historic Downtown, Univ of MO, Stephens & Columbia Colleges. Best Pro, fine dining, golf, museums. 30 min to Jefferson City Capital.

◇◇◇◇◇FACILITIES: 117 sites, typical site width 30 ft, 97 full hkups, (20/30/50 amps), 50 amps ($), 20 no hkups, some extd stay sites, 74 pull-thrus, WiFi Instant Internet at site, family camping, tenting, dump, non-guest dump $, laundry, groceries, RV supplies, LP gas by weight/by meter, ice, picnic tables, patios, fire rings, wood.

◇◇◇◇RECREATION: rec hall, rec room/area, equipped pavilion, swim pool, golf nearby, bsktball, playground, activities, (wkends), horseshoes, sports field.

Pets welcome. Partial handicap access. Open all yr. Big rigs welcome. Clubs welcome. Green Friendly. Rate in 2010 $30 for 2 persons. MC/VISA/DISC/Debit. Member ARVC, MOARC.

Phone: (888)303-3313
Address: 5170 Oakland Gravel Rd, Columbia, MO 65202
Lat/Lon: 39.00740/-92.30189
Email: cottonwoodsrv@aol.com
Web: www.cottonwoodsrv.com

SEE AD THIS PAGE

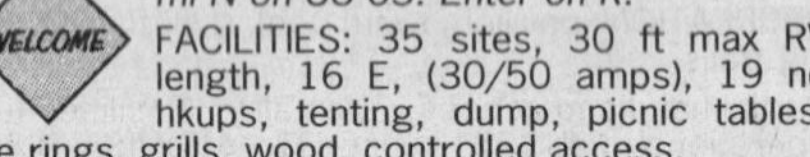

(N) FINGER LAKES STATE PARK—(Boone) *From jct I-70 & US 63: Go 10 mi N on US 63. Enter on R.*
FACILITIES: 35 sites, 30 ft max RV length, 16 E, (30/50 amps), 19 no hkups, tenting, dump, picnic tables, fire rings, grills, wood, controlled access.

RECREATION: lake swim, boating, ramp, lake fishing.

Partial handicap access. Open all yr. Facilities fully operational Apr 1 - Oct 31. MC/VISA/DISC/AMEX.

Phone: (573)443-5315
Address: 1505 E Peabody Rd, Columbia, MO 65202
Web: www.mostateparks.com

SEE AD TRAVEL SECTION PAGE 451

CUBA—D-4

(W) Ladybug RV Park & Campground—(Crawford) *From jct I-44 (exit 203) & Hwy 7: Go 1/4 mi N on Hwy 7. Enter on R.* ◇◇◇FACILITIES: 32 sites, typical site width 35 ft, 32 full hkups, (20/30/50 amps), 23 pull-thrus, family camping, tenting, dump, laundry, ltd groc. ◇◇◇RECREATION: swim pool, pond fishing, play equipment. Pets welcome, breed restrict. Partial handicap access. Open all yr. Facilities fully operational Mar - Nov. Rate in 2010 $17-25 for 2 persons. Member ARVC, MOARC.

Phone: (573)885-3622
Address: 355 Hwy F, Cuba, MO 65453
Email: mslh19@gmail.com
Web: www.ladybugrvpark.com

(NE) Meramec Valley RV Camp Resort—(Crawford) *From jct I-44 & Rt UU (exit 210): Go 1 mi N on Hwy UU. Enter on L.* ◇◇◇FACILITIES: 470 sites, typical site width 25 ft, 111 full hkups, 359 W&E, (30 amps), 60 no hkups, 125 pull-thrus, WiFi Internet central location, family camping, tenting, RV storage, dump, laundry, ltd

CUBA—Continued
Meramec Valley RV Camp Resort—Continued

groc, RV supplies, LP gas by weight/by meter, ice, picnic tables, fire rings, wood. ◇◇◇◇RECREATION: rec hall, equipped pavilion, 2 swim pools, wading pool, boating, electric motors only, dock, float trips, lake fishing, fishing supplies, mini-golf, bsktball, playground, shuffleboard court shuffleboard court, activities, tennis, horseshoes, hiking trails, v-ball. Pets welcome. Partial handicap access. Open all yr. Rate in 2010 $27-29 per vehicle. MC/VISA/Debit. CCUSA 50% Discount. CCUSA reservations Recommended, CCUSA max stay 2 days, CCUSA disc. not avail holidays. Not valid May 22-25, Jul 2-6, Sep 3-8, Oct 9-11.

Phone: (573)885-2541
Address: 1360 Hwy UU, Cuba, MO 65453
Lat/Lon: 38.11060/-91.35928
Email: meramec@centurytel.net
Web: www.meramecvalleycampresort.com

DANVILLE—C-4

(NW) GRAHAM CAVE STATE PARK—(Montgomery) *From jct I-70 & US 161: Go 1 mi W on I-70, then go 1 mi NW on CR-TT. Enter on L.*
FACILITIES: 52 sites, typical site width 12 ft, 35 ft max RV length, 18 E, (20/30 amps), 34 no hkups, tenting, dump, picnic tables, fire rings, wood.

RECREATION: pavilion, boating, ramp, river fishing, playground, hiking trails.

Pets welcome. Partial handicap access. Open Apr 1 - Oct 31. Max stay 15 days. MC/VISA/DISC/AMEX.

Phone: (573)564-3476
Address: 217 Hwy TT, Montgomery City, MO 63361
Lat/Lon: 38.909222/-91.572778
Web: www.mostateparks.com

SEE AD TRAVEL SECTION PAGE 451

(W) Kan-Do Kampground & RV Park—(Montgomery) *From jct I-70 & Hwy 19: Go 5 mi W on I-70 to exit 170, then N to Hwy TT, then 1 mi W on Hwy TT (on dead end road). Enter on R.* ◇◇◇◇FACILITIES: 69 sites, typical site width 25 ft, 45 full hkups, 24 W&E, (15/30/50 amps), 21 pull-thrus, WiFi Instant Internet at site, family camping, tenting, RV storage, dump, non-guest dump $, laundry, ltd groc, RV supplies, LP gas by weight/by meter, ice, picnic tables, fire rings, grills, wood. ◇◇◇RECREATION: equipped pavilion, swim pool, pond fishing, fishing supplies, playground, activities, horseshoes, v-ball. Pets welcome. Open all yr. Big rigs welcome. Rate in 2010 $25-30 for 2 persons. MC/VISA/DISC/Debit. CCUSA 50% Discount. CCUSA reservations Required, CCUSA max stay 3 days, CCUSA disc. not avail S, CCUSA disc. not avail F,Sa, CCUSA disc. not avail holidays. Not available Jun-Sep.

Phone: (573)564-7993
Address: 99 Highway TT, Montgomery City, MO 63361
Lat/Lon: 38.90592/-91.55679
Web: www.kandocampground.com

DANVILLE—Continued on next page

Woodall's Tip... If you're ever lost in the forest, you can tell your direction from the trees. The bark will be thicker on the north side of trees.

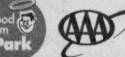

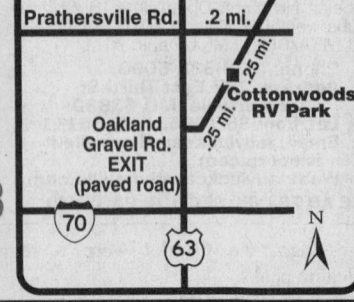

DANVILLE—Continued

(W) LAZY DAY CAMPGROUND—(Montgomery) *From jct I-70 (exit 170) & Hwy J: Go 1-1/4 mi S on Hwy J. Enter on L.*

HIGHEST RATED CAMPGROUND IN AREA
A quiet, lovely country park conveniently located for great day trips to Historic St. Charles, Mark Twain's Hannibal or Jefferson City, Hermann-Wine Country. We offer large, level pull-thrus, swimming pool, WiFi & 30/50 amps.

◆◆◆◆◆FACILITIES: 61 sites, typical site width 30 ft, 52 full hkups, 9 W&E, (30/50 amps), 60 pull-thrus, WiFi Instant Internet at site, family camping, tenting, RV storage, dump, non-guest dump $, laundry, ltd groc, RV supplies, LP gas by weight/by meter, ice, picnic tables, fire rings, wood.

◆◆◆RECREATION: rec hall, rec room/area, swim pool, lake/pond fishing, fishing supplies, golf nearby, bsktball, shuffleboard court shuffleboard court, activities (wkends), horseshoes. Rec open to public.

Pets welcome. Partial handicap access. Open all yr. Big rigs welcome. Escort to site. Clubs welcome. Rate in 2010 $30-32 for 2 persons. MC/VISA/DISC/Debit. Member ARVC, MOARC. FMCA discount.

Phone: (573)564-2949
Address: 214 Highway J, Montgomery City, MO 63361
Lat/Lon: 38.89637/-91.56046
Email: lazydaycamping@aol.com
Web: www.lazydaycampground.net

SEE AD PAGE 466 AND AD TRAVEL SECTION PAGE 451

DAVISVILLE—D-4

(E) MARK TWAIN NATIONAL FOREST (Red Bluff Campground)—(Crawford) *From town: Go 1 mi E on Hwy-V, then 1 mi N on FR-2011.* FACILITIES: 43 sites, typical site width 15 ft, 43 no hkups, tenting. RECREATION: river swim, river fishing. Open Apr 15 - Oct 15. Phone: (573)743-6042.

DE SOTO—D-5

(N) WASHINGTON STATE PARK—(Washington) *From jct Hwy 47 & Hwy 21: Go 6 mi N on Hwy 21. Enter on L.*

FACILITIES: 50 sites, 24 E, (30 amps), 26 no hkups, tenting, cabins, dump, laundry, ltd groc, ice, picnic tables, fire rings, grills, wood.

RECREATION: pavilion, swim pool, canoeing, canoe rentals, river fishing, hiking trails.

Open all yr. Facilities fully operational Apr 1 - Oct 31. MC/VISA/DISC/AMEX.

Phone: (636)586-2995
Address: 13041 State Hwy. 104, DeSoto, MO 63020
Web: www.mostateparks.com

SEE AD TRAVEL SECTION PAGE 451

DEXTER—E-5

(W) Wildwood RV Park—(Stoddard) *From Intersection of Hwy 60 & Hwy AD: Go 1/4 mi E on North Outer Rd, then turn left into driveway at American Outdoor Store. Office in Audibel Hearing Aid Center. Enter on L.* ◆◆FACILITIES: 22 sites, accepts full hkup units only, 22 full hkups, (20/30/50 amps), 22 pull-thrus. Pets welcome. No tents. Open all yr. Big rigs welcome. Rate in 2010 $25 per family. Phone: (573)624-5421.

DIXON—D-4

(S) Boiling Spring Campground—(Pulaski) *From jct I-44 & Hwy 28, (Exit 163): Go 6 mi N on Hwy 28, then 3.5 miles E on Hwy PP or from jct I-70 & Hwy 63 (exit 128A): Go 15 mi S on Hwy 63, then 25 mi SW on Hwy 58, then 3-1/2 mi E on Hwy PP. Enter at end.* ◆◆FACILITIES: 55 sites, typical site width 20 ft, 38 ft max RV length, 35 full hkups, 12 W&E, 2 E, (30/50 amps), 6 no hkups, 3 pull-thrus, WiFi Instant Internet at site, family camping, tenting, RV storage, dump, non-guest dump $, laundry, ltd groc, RV supplies, ice, picnic tables, fire rings, grills, wood. ◆◆◆RECREATION: pavilion, river swim, canoeing, ramp, float trips, river fishing, fishing supplies, fishing guides, activities, horseshoes, hiking trails, v-ball. Pets welcome. Open all yr. Facilities fully operational Apr 15 - Nov 15. Green Friendly. Rate in 2010 $22-26 for 4 persons. MC/VISA/DISC/Debit. Member ARVC, MOARC. CCUSA 50% Discount. CCUSA reservations Recommended, CCUSA max stay 30 days, CCUSA disc. not avail S, CCUSA disc. not avail F,Sa, CCUSA disc. not avail holidays. No vicious pets. Normal camping Apr 15 thru Nov 15, weather permitting. Addl surcharges: $2 electric heaters, $3 riverview sites.

DIXON—Continued
Boiling Spring Campground—Continued

Phone: (573)759-7294
Address: 18700 Cliff Rd, Dixon, MO 65459
Lat/Lon: 37.88849/-92.04170
Email: larryh@yhti.net
Web: www.bscfloattrips.com

EAGLE ROCK—E-2

(E) EAGLE ROCK BOAT DOCK & PARK (COE Table Rock Lake)—(Barry) *From town: Go 2-1/2 mi W on Hwy-86.* FACILITIES: 63 sites, typical site width 20 ft, 34 ft max RV length, 1 full hkups, (30 amps), 62 no hkups, tenting, dump, ltd groc. RECREATION: lake swim, boating, ramp, dock, lake fishing, playground. Pets welcome. Partial handicap access. Open Apr 1 - Sep 30. Phone: (417)271-3215.

(S) PARADISE COVE CAMPING RESORT—(Barry) *From jct Hwy 86 & Hwy P: Go 1 mi S on Hwy P to Missouri/Arkansas State Line, then 2-1/2 mi W on Lake Rd P3 (Stateline Rd). Enter on R.*

◆◆◆FACILITIES: 67 sites, typical site width 25 ft, 35 ft max RV length, 5 full hkups, 12 E, (20/30 amps), 50 no hkups, WiFi Internet central location, family camping, tenting, cabins, RV storage, laundry, ice, picnic tables, patios, fire rings, grills, wood.

◆◆◆RECREATION: pavilion, lake swim, boating, canoeing, 4 pedal boat rentals, lake fishing, playground, horseshoes. Rec open to public.

Pets welcome, breed restrict, size restrict. Partial handicap access. Open all yr. Clubs welcome. Rate in 2010 $19-23 for 2 persons.

Phone: (417)271-4888
Address: 18828 FR 2300, Eagle Rock, MO 65641
Lat/Lon: 36.528917/-93.728722
Email: paradisecove2@centurytel.net
Web: www.passport-america.com/campgrounds

SEE AD THIS PAGE

EAGLEVILLE—A-2

(S) Eagle Ridge RV Park—(Harrison) *S'Bnd from jct I-35 (exit 106) & CR N: Go 1/4 mi W on CR N, then 1 mi S on US 69 (Ent R): N'bnd from jct I-35 (exit 99) & CR A: Go 1/4 mi W on CR A, then 5 mi N on US 69 (Ent L). Enter on R.* ◆◆◆FACILITIES: 47 sites, typical site width 30 ft, 19 full hkups, 8 W&E, (20/30/50 amps), 20 no hkups, 17 pull-thrus, family camping, tenting, dump, laundry, ltd groc. ◆◆◆◆RECREATION: swim pool, pond fishing, playground. Pets welcome. Partial handicap access. Open Mar 1 - Nov 30. Big rigs welcome. Rate in 2010 $26.50 for 2 persons.

Phone: (660)867-5518
Address: 22708 W 182 St, Eagleville, MO 64442
Lat/Lon: 40.44834/-93.99274
Email: eagleridgervparkmo@gmail.com
Web: www.eagleridgervpark.webs.com

ELKTON—D-3

LIGHTFOOT PUBLIC USE AREA (COE Pomme de Terre Lake)—(Hickory) *From jct Hwy 83 & CR RB: Go 3 mi E on CR RB.* FACILITIES: 40 sites, typical site width 20 ft, 29 W&E, (30/50 amps), 11 no hkups, 1 pull-thrus, tenting, dump. RECREATION: lake swim, boating, ramp, dock, lake fishing, playground. Partial handicap access. Open all yr. Phone: (417)282-6890.

ELLINGTON—E-4

(SE) WEBB CREEK PARK (COE - Clearwater Lake)—(Wayne) *From jct Hwy-21 & CR-H: Go 10 mi SE on CR-H.* FACILITIES: 35 sites, typical site width 15 ft, 25 E, (30 amps), 10 no hkups, tenting, dump. RECREATION: lake swim, boating, ramp, dock, lake fishing, playground. Partial handicap access. Open all yr. Phone: (573)223-7777.

EMINENCE—E-4

(N) Jacks Fork Canoe Rental & Campground—(Shannon) *From jct Hwy 19 & Hwy 106: Go 1/4 mi E on Hwy 106. Enter on L.* ◆◆FACILITIES: 132 sites, typical site width 30 ft, 14 full hkups, 26 W&E, 22 E, (30 amps), 70 no hkups, 4 pull-thrus, tenting, dump, ltd groc. ◆◆◆RECREATION: river swim, boating, canoeing, river fishing, play equipment. Pets welcome. Open May 15 - Oct 15. Facilities fully operational Memorial Day - Labor Day. Rate in 2010 $24-30 for 2 persons. Phone: (800)333-5628. FMCA discount.

(W) OZARK NATIONAL SCENIC RIVERWAYS (Alley Spring)—(Carter) *From town: Go 6 mi W on Hwy-106.* FACILITIES: 162 sites, typical site width 15 ft, 162 no hkups, tenting, dump, ltd groc. RECREATION: river swim, boating, ramp, river fishing, playground. Partial handicap access. Open all yr. Phone: (573) 323-4236.

EUREKA—C-5

(N) BYERLY RV CENTER—*From jct I-44 (exit 264) & Hwy 109: Go 1/10 mi N on Hwy 109, then 3/10 mi E on 5th St. Enter on L.* SALES: travel trailers, park models, truck campers, 5th wheels, Class A motorhomes, Class C motorhomes, Class B motorhomes, fold-down camping trailers, pre-owned unit sales. SERVICES: full-time mech, RV appliance repair, body work/collision repair, LP gas by weight/by meter, RV rentals, sells parts/accessories, installs hitches. Open all yr. MC/VISA/DISC/Debit.

EUREKA—Continued
BYERLY RV CENTER—Continued

Phone: (636)938-2000
Address: 295 E 5th St, Eureka, MO 63025
Lat/Lon: 38.50657/-90.61781
Email: sales@byerlyrv.com
Web: www.byerlyrv.com

SEE AD ST. LOUIS PAGE 478

(W) KOA ST. LOUIS WEST/HISTORIC RT 66—(St. Louis) *From jct I-44 (exit 261) & Six Flags Rd, then W'bnd 3/4 mi SW on Six Flags Rd to Bus Loop 44 (Hist Rt 66). E'bnd: 3/4 mi on bus Loop 44 (Hist Rt 66). Enter on R.*

KOA-SIX FLAGS-SIMPLY THE BEST!
Fun park on Historic Rt 66. Great RV sites. Kamping Kabins & Tent Sites. Base Camp for St Louis Attractions, Restaurants, shopping & antique mall. A/C restrooms. Free WiFi! 1 day to Branson.

◆◆◆◆◆FACILITIES: 140 sites, typical site width 25 ft, 45 full hkups, 42 W&E, (30/50 amps), 53 no hkups, 77 pull-thrus, WiFi Instant Internet at site, phone Internet central location, family camping, tenting, cabins, dump, non-guest dump $, laundry, ltd groc, RV supplies, LP gas by weight/by meter, ice, picnic tables, fire rings, grills, wood.

◆◆◆RECREATION: rec hall, rec room/area, pavilion, coin games, swim pool, golf nearby, playground, horseshoes, sports field.

Pets welcome, breed restrict. Open Mar 1 - Nov 1. Big rigs welcome. Escort to site. Clubs welcome. Rate in 2010 $28.25-49.75 for 2 persons. MC/VISA/DISC/Debit. Member ARVC, MOARC. KOA discount.

Phone: (636)257-3018
Address: 18475 Historic Rt 66/Bus Loop 44, Eureka, MO 63025
Lat/Lon: 38.50108/-90.68931
Email: stlwkoa@fidnet.com
Web: www.stlwkoa.com

SEE AD ST. LOUIS PAGE 478

(W) Yogi Bear's Jellystone Park Resort at Six Flags—(St. Louis) *From jct I-270 & I-44: Go 15 mi W on I-44 to Six Flags/Allenton exit (exit 261), then 1/2 mi W on Fox Creek Rd (N service road). Enter on R.* ◆◆◆FACILITIES: 87 sites, typical site width 25 ft, 35 full hkups, 25 W&E, (30/50 amps), 27 no hkups, 17 pull-thrus, family camping, tenting, dump, laundry, groceries. ◆◆◆◆◆RECREATION: swim pool, playground. Pets welcome. Partial handicap access. Open Apr 1 - Oct 1. Rate in 2010 $34.95-54.95 for 2 persons. Member ARVC, MOARC. Phone: (800)861-3020.

FENTON—C-5

(S) Belleville Mobile Home and RV Estates (RV SPACES)—(Jefferson) *From jct I-270 & I-44: Go 2-1/2 mi S on I-270 (exit 3), then 2-1/2 mi S on Hwy 30, then 2-3/4 mi S on Hwy 141 to Fiedler Ln, then 1 block E to Old 141, then 1 Block S to Cool Valley Rd, then 1 block E on Clearwater Rd. Enter on R.* FACILITIES: 37 sites, typical site width 30 ft, accepts self-contained units only, 37 full hkups, (30/50 amps). Pets welcome. No tents. Open all yr. Big rigs welcome. Rate in 2010 $35 for 2 persons. Phone: (636)343-9182.

FORSYTH—E-3

(SE) BEAVER CREEK CAMPGROUND (COE Bull Shoals Lake)—(Taney) *From jct US-160 & CR-O: Go 4 mi S on CR-O.* FACILITIES: 37 sites, typical site width 20 ft, 30 ft max RV length, 37 E, (30/50 amps), tenting, dump. RECREATION: boating, ramp, dock, lake fishing, playground. Partial handicap access. Open all yr. Phone: (417)546-3708.

FORSYTH—Continued on next page

Saint Genevieve, Missouri's oldest community, was founded as early as 1735.

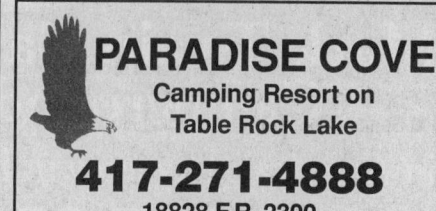

FORSYTH—Continued

(S) RIVER RUN PARK (COE Bull Shoals Lake)—(Taney) *From town: Go 1-1/2 mi SE.* FACILITIES: 32 sites, typical site width 15 ft, 30 ft max RV length, 32 E, (30 amps), tenting, dump. RECREATION: boating, ramp, lake fishing, playground. Partial handicap access. Open all yr. Phone: (870)546-3646.

(S) SHADOW ROCK PARK & CAMPGROUND (City Park)—(Taney) *From jct US 160 & Hwy 76: Go 50 feet E on US 160. Enter on L.* FACILITIES: 110 sites, 99 W&E, (20/30/50 amps), 11 no hkups, tenting, dump. RECREATION: ramp, lake/stream fishing, playground. Pets welcome. Partial handicap access. Open Mar - Oct. Big rigs welcome. Phone: (417)546-2876.

FREDERICKTOWN—D-5

(W) MARK TWAIN NATIONAL FOREST (Silver Mines Campground)—(Madison) *From town: Go 6-1/2 mi W on Hwy 72, then 3 mi SW on Hwy D.* FACILITIES: 72 sites, typical site width 15 ft, 11 E, 61 no hkups, tenting. RECREATION: canoeing. Pets welcome. Partial handicap access. Open Apr 15 - Oct 31. Phone: (573)783-3769.

FULTON—C-4

(W) Red Maples Community (RV SPACES)—(Callaway) *From jct US 5 & I-70: Go 9 mi W on US 54 to Hwy H, then 50 ft E to NN, then 300 yds S on NN. Enter on L.* FACILITIES: 24 sites, accepts full hkup units only, 24 full hkups, (30/50 amps). Pets welcome. No tents. Open all yr. Big rigs welcome. Rate in 2010 $20 for 2 persons. Phone: (573)642-4282.

GAINESVILLE—E-3

PONTIAC PARK (COE Bull Shoals Lake)—(Ozark) *From jct US-160 & Hwy-5: Go 5 mi S on Hwy-5, then 7-1/4 mi W on CR-W (Pontiac).* FACILITIES: 37 sites, 35 ft max RV length, 37 E, (20/30 amps), 12 pull-thrus, tenting, dump, ltd groc. RECREATION: lake swim, boating, ramp, dock, lake fishing, playground. Partial handicap access. Open all yr. Phone: (417)679-2222.

GOLDEN—E-2

(NW) VINEY CREEK PARK (COE Table Rock Lake)—(Stone) *From jct Hwy-86 & CR-J: Go 4 mi NW on CR-J.* FACILITIES: 46 sites, typical site width 20 ft, 24 W&E, (30 amps), 22 no hkups, tenting, dump. RECREATION: lake swim, boating, ramp, lake fishing, playground. Pets welcome. Partial handicap access. Open May 1 - Sept 14. Phone: (417)271-3860.

GRAIN VALLEY—C-2

(N) TRAILSIDE RV PARK—(Jackson) *From jct Hwy 88 & I-70 (exit 24): Go 200 ft S on CR AA, then 300 yds W on US 40, then 500 ft N, then 1/4 mi W on R.D. Mize Rd. Enter on R.*

◆◆◆◆FACILITIES: 85 sites, typical site width 25 ft, 46 full hkups, 39 W&E, (30/50 amps), some extd stay sites, 75 pull-thrus, WiFi Instant Internet at site, phone Internet central location, tenting, RV storage, dump, non-guest dump $, portable dump, laundry, ltd groc, RV supplies, LP gas by weight/by meter, ice, picnic tables, grills.

◆◆RECREATION: swim pool, golf nearby, bsktball, playground.

Pets welcome, breed restrict. Partial handicap access. Open all yr. Big rigs welcome. Clubs welcome. Rate in 2010 $29.93 for 2 persons. MC/VISA/DISC/AMEX/Debit. Member ARVC, MOARC. FMCA discount.

Phone: (816)229-2267
Address: 1000 R D Mize Rd, Grain Valley, MO 64029
Lat/Lon: 39.02164/-94.21093
Email: info@trvpark.com
Web: www.trvpark.com

SEE AD KANSAS CITY PAGE 470

GRANBY—E-2

(NW) Hwy 60 RV Park—(Newton) *From jct Hwy 59 & US 60: Go 11-1/2 mi E on US 60. Enter on R.* ◆◆◆FACILITIES: 21 sites, typical site width 25 ft, 21 full hkups, (30/50 amps), 22 pull-thrus, phone on-site Internet (needs activ), tenting, RV storage, dump, non-guest dump $, laundry, ltd groc, ice, picnic tables. REC-

GRANBY—Continued
Hwy 60 RV Park—Continued

REATION: Pets welcome, breed restrict. Partial handicap access. Open all yr. Big rigs welcome. Rate in 2010 $36 per vehicle. CCUSA 50% Discount. CCUSA reservations Accepted, CCUSA max stay Unlimited, CCUSA disc. not avail F,Sa, CCUSA disc. not avail holidays.

Phone: (417)476-2116
Address: 29135 US Hwy 60, Stark City, MO 64866
Lat/Lon: 36.91809/-94.11565

GRAVOIS MILLS—C-3

(S) Hava Space RV Park—(Morgan) *From jct Hwy 5 & Hwy P: Go 100 ft W on Montana Rd. Enter on L.* ◆◆◆FACILITIES: 28 sites, 28 full hkups, (30/50 amps), 20 pull-thrus, cable TV, WiFi Instant Internet at site, RV storage, dump, laundry, picnic tables, fire rings. ◆◆RECREATION: swim pool, playground, horseshoes, hiking trails. Pets welcome. No tents. Open all yr. Big rigs welcome. Rate in 2010 $25-28 for 2 persons. MC/VISA/DISC/AMEX. CCUSA 50% Discount. CCUSA reservations Required, CCUSA max stay 1 day, CCUSA disc. not avail S,Th, CCUSA disc. not avail F,Sa, CCUSA disc. not avail holidays. Discount available Sep-Apr. 55 Plus Park-children may stay short term.

Phone: (573)372-3466
Address: 13242 Montana Rd, Gravois Mills, MO 65037
Lat/Lon: 38.26476/-92.82777
Email: havaspace@hughes.net
Web: www.havaspacervpark.com

GREENVILLE—E-5

(S) GREENVILLE (COE - Wappapello Lake)—(Wayne) *From jct Hwy D & US 67: Go 1 mi S on US 67.* FACILITIES: 111 sites, 106 E, (30 amps), 5 no hkups, 2 pull-thrus, tenting, dump. RECREATION: boating, canoeing, ramp, dock, lake/river fishing, playground. Partial handicap access. Open Apr 1 - Mid Nov. Phone: (573)224-3884.

HANNIBAL—B-4

(S) INJUN JOE CAMPGROUND—(Ralls) *From jct US 36/US 72 & US 61: Go 6-1/2 mi S on US 61. Enter on R.*

◆◆◆FACILITIES: 160 sites, typical site width 25 ft, 110 full hkups, 20 W&E, (30/50 amps), 30 no hkups, some extd stay sites, 15 pull-thrus, WiFi Internet central location, tenting, RV storage, dump, non-guest dump $, laundry, ltd groc, LP bottle exch, ice, picnic tables, patios, wood.

◆◆◆◆RECREATION: rec room/area, equipped pavilion, coin games, swim pool, lake fishing, mini-golf, ($), golf nearby, bsktball, playground. Rec open to public.

Pets welcome. Partial handicap access. Open all yr. Facilities fully operational May 15 - Nov 1. Big rigs welcome. Clubs welcome. Rate in 2010 $26.50-29 for 2 persons. Member ARVC, MOARC.

Phone: (573)985-3581
Address: 14113 Clemens Dr, New London, MO 63459
Lat/Lon: 39.62747/-91.41409
Email: injunjoe@uid.onemain.com
Web: www.hanmo.com/clemenslanding/campground.html

SEE AD THIS PAGE

(S) MARK TWAIN CAVE—*From jct US 61 & US 72: Go 1/2 mi W on US 72 (exit 157), then 2 mi S on Hwy 79. Enter on R.* Natural cave, registered natural landmark. Souvenir shop and rock shop. Fudge shop, wine shop and hand-carved candle shop also available. Open all yr. MC/VISA/DISC.

HANNIBAL—Continued
MARK TWAIN CAVE—Continued

Phone: (573)221-1656
Address: Hwy 79 S. Cave Hollow Rd, Hannibal, MO 63401
Lat/Lon: 39.68846/-91.33192
Web: www.MARKTWAINCAVE.com

SEE AD THIS PAGE

(S) MARK TWAIN CAVE AND CAMPGROUND—(Marion) *From jct US 61 & US 72: Go 1/2 mi E on US 72 (exit 157), then 2 mi S on Hwy 79. Enter on R.*

◆◆◆◆FACILITIES: 95 sites, typical site width 25 ft, 60 full hkups, 9 W&E, 10 E, (20/30/50 amps), 16 no hkups, 22 pull-thrus, WiFi Instant Internet at site, phone Internet central location, family camping, tenting, dump, non-guest dump $, laundry, ltd groc, RV supplies, ice, picnic tables, fire rings, grills, wood.

◆◆RECREATION: equipped pavilion, golf nearby, playground, hiking trails, local tours.

Pets welcome, breed restrict. Open Apr 1 - Oct 31. Big rigs welcome. Clubs welcome. Rate in 2010 $25-32 for 4 persons. MC/VISA/DISC/Debit. Member ARVC, MOARC.

Phone: (573)221-1656
Address: 300 Cave Hollow Rd, Hannibal, MO 63401
Lat/Lon: 39.69119/-91.33208
Email: cavecity@marktwaincave.com
Web: www.marktwaincave.com

SEE AD THIS PAGE

HAYTI—A-6

(E) HAYTI-PORTAGEVILLE KOA—(Pemiscot) *S'bnd: From jct I-55 (exit 27) & Wardell: Go 3 mi S on Outer Rd (L). N'bnd: From jct I-55 (exit 19) & Hwy 84: Go 500 ft. E on Hwy 84, then 6 mi N on Outer Road (R). Enter on R.*

◆◆◆FACILITIES: 45 sites, typical site width 25 ft, 26 full hkups, 11 W&E, 2 E, (20/30/50 amps), 6 no hkups, some extd stay sites, 30 pull-thrus, WiFi Instant Internet at site, family camping, tenting, cabins, dump, non-guest dump $, laundry, RV supplies, ice, picnic tables, patios, grills, wood.

◆◆◆RECREATION: rec hall, rec room/area, swim pool, dock, bsktball, playground, v-ball.

Pets welcome. Partial handicap access. Age restrict may apply. Open Mar 15 - Nov 15. Big rigs welcome. Clubs welcome. Rate in 2010 $27-37 for 2 persons. MC/VISA/DISC/Debit.

Phone: (573)359-1580
Address: 2824 MO State East Outer Road, Portageville, MO 63873
Email: rdeflavis@live.com
Web: www.koa.com

SEE AD THIS PAGE AND AD FL TRAVEL SECTION PAGE 74

Bill Bradley, basketball player, is from Missouri.

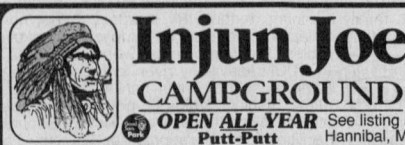

HAZELGREEN—D-3

(E) Gasconade Hills Resort—(Pulaski) *From jct I-44 (exit 145) & SR 133: Go 100 ft S on SR 133, then 150 yds E on NB Hwy, then 1-1/2 mi S on Spring Rd (gravel). Enter on R.* ◆◆◆FACILITIES: 49 sites, typical site width 30 ft, 19 full hkups, 10 W&E, (20/30/50 amps), 20 no hkups, 10 pull-thrus, family camping, tenting, dump, laundry, ltd groc. ◆◆◆◆RECREATION: swim pool, canoeing, ramp, river fishing, playground. Pets welcome, breed restrict. Open Apr 1 - Nov 1. Rate in 2010 $26 for 2 persons. Phone: (800)869-6861.

HERMANN—C-4

(SW) HERMANN RV & TRAILER PARK (City Park)—(Gasconade) *From jct Hwy 19 & Hwy 100 (S): Go 1/2 mi N on Hwy 100, then W 1 block to Gasconade St. Enter on L.* FACILITIES: 50 sites, 18 full hkups, 24 W&E, 8 E, (20/30/50 amps), 5 pull-thrus, tenting, dump. RECREATION: swim pool, lake fishing. Pets welcome. Partial handicap access. Open Apr 1 - Nov 1. Big rigs welcome. Phone: (573)486-5400.

HERMITAGE—D-3

(S) DAMSITE CAMP AREA (COE Pomme de Terre Lake)—(Hickory) *From town: Go 3 mi S on Hwy 254.* FACILITIES: 128 sites, typical site width 20 ft, 39 W&E, 24 E, (30/50 amps), 65 no hkups, 16 pull-thrus, tenting, dump, laundry. RECREATION: boating, dock, lake fishing, playground. Partial handicap access. Open all yr. Phone: (417)745-2244.

(S) NEMO PARK (COE Pomme de Terre Lake)—(Hickory) *From town: Go 7 mi S on Hwys-254/64.* FACILITIES: 120 sites, typical site width 20 ft, 11 W&E, 48 E, (30 amps), 61 no hkups, 5 pull-thrus, tenting, dump, laundry. RECREATION: lake swim, boating, ramp, dock, lake fishing, playground. Partial handicap access. Open all yr. Phone: (417)993-5529.

(SW) OUTLET AREA (COE Pomme de Terre Lake)—(Hickory) *From town: Go 4-1/2 mi S & W on Hwy 254.* FACILITIES: 28 sites, typical site width 20 ft, 14 W&E, (30 amps), 14 no hkups, tenting. RECREATION: boating, canoeing, ramp, river fishing, playground. Partial handicap access. Open all yr. Phone: (417)745-2290.

WHEATLAND PARK (COE Pomme de Terre Lake)—(Hickory) *From town: Go 8 mi S & W on Hwy 254, then 1 mi S on CR 205.* FACILITIES: 83 sites, typical site width 20 ft, 41 W&E, 26 E, (30 amps), 16 no hkups, 2 pull-thrus, tenting, dump. RECREATION: lake swim, boating, ramp, dock, lake fishing, playground. Partial handicap access. Open all yr. Phone: (417)282-5267.

HIGGINSVILLE—B-2

(S) The Great Escape RV & Camp Resort—(Lafayette) *From jct I-70 & Hwy 13 (exit 49): Go 100 ft S on Hwy 13, then 1/4 mi W on Old Hwy 40. Enter on L.* ◆◆◆◆FACILITIES: 51 sites, typical site width 25 ft, 51 full hkups, (20/30/50 amps), 30 pull-thrus, tenting, laundry. ◆◆◆◆RECREATION: swim pool, pond fishing, playground. Pets welcome. Partial handicap access. Open all yr. Big rigs welcome. Rate in 2010 $26-28 for 4 persons. Phone: (800)690-2267.

HIGHLANDVILLE—E-3

(S) Hwy 160 RV Park—(Christian) *From jct US 160 and County Road EE: Go 2 mi S on Hwy 160. Enter on L.* ◆◆◆FACILITIES: 18 sites, accepts self-contained units only, 18 full hkups, (30/50 amps). Pets welcome. No tents. Open all yr. Big rigs welcome. Rate in 2010 $15 for 2 persons.

Phone: (417)443-5000
Address: 8180 Hwy 160 South, Highlandville, MO 65669
Lat/Lon: 36.89968/-93.28692
Email: hwy160rvpark@gmail.com
Web: www.cookiesantiqueworld.com

INDEPENDENCE—B-2

(C) Campus RV Park—(Jackson) *From I-70 (exit 14): Go 3-1/2 mi N on Lee's Summit Rd, then 1-1/2 mi W on Truman Rd, then 5 blks S on Osage St, then 1-1/2 blks W on Pacific Ave. From I-435 (exit 60): Go 3-3/4 mi E on Truman Rd, then 5 blks S on Osage St, then 1-1/2 blks W on Pacific Ave. Enter on R.* ◆◆◆FACILITIES: 46 sites, typical site width 26 ft, 30 full hkups, 16 W&E, (30/50 amps), dump, laundry. Pets welcome, quantity restrict. Partial handicap access. No tents. Open all yr. Big rigs welcome. Rate in 2010 $29.50 for 2 persons. Phone: (888)254-3750. FMCA discount.

(E) STADIUM RV PARK (RV SPACES)—(Jackson) *W'bnd from jct I-70 (exit 11): Go 3/4 mi W on US 40. E'bnd from I-70 (exit 9): Go 1/4 mi N on Blue Ridge Cutoff, then 1/4 mi E on Hwy 40. Entrance on right.*

FACILITIES: 22 sites, 22 full hkups, (20/30/50 amps), some extd stay sites, WiFi Instant Internet at site, laundry, patios.

RECREATION: golf nearby.

Pets welcome. No tents. Open all yr. Big rigs welcome. Escort to site. Rate in 2010 $25 for 2 persons. Member ARVC, MOARC.

Phone: (816)353-0242
Address: 10021 US Hwy 40 E, Independence, MO 64055
Lat/Lon: 39.05457/-94.46037
Web: www.gocampingamerica.com/stadium

SEE AD KANSAS CITY NEXT PAGE

IRONTON—D-5

MARK TWAIN NATIONAL FOREST (Marble Creek Campground)—(Madison) *From jct Hwy-72 & Hwy-21: Go 1 mi S on Hwy-21, then 12 mi SE on Hwy-E.* FACILITIES: 25 sites, typical site width 15 ft, 25 no hkups, tenting. RECREATION: Partial handicap access. Open Apr 15 - Oct 31. Phone: (573)438-5427.

(SW) TAUM SAUK STATE PARK—(Madison) *From jct Hwy 21 and Hwy CC: Go 4 mi W on Hwy CC. Enter on R.*

FACILITIES: 12 sites, 12 no hkups, tenting, non-flush toilets only, picnic tables.

RECREATION: hiking trails.

Open all yr. Facilities fully operational Apr 1 - Oct 31. No showers, no reservations. MC/VISA/DISC.

Phone: (573)546-2450
Address: HCR 1, Middlebrook, MO 63656
Web: www.mostateparks.com

SEE AD TRAVEL SECTION PAGE 451

JEFFERSON CITY—C-3

(C) DIVISION OF STATE PARKS MISSOURI—Tourism Bureau for the Division of State Parks of Missouri. Open all yr.

Phone: (573)751-8463
Address: 1659 E Elm St, Jefferson, MO 65707
Lat/Lon: 38.33360/-92.09163
Web: www.mostateparks.com

SEE AD TRAVEL SECTION PAGE 451

(C) MISSOURI DIVISION OF TOURISM—*From jct US 50 & US 54/63: Go 1/2 mi W on US 50.* From Fall vacations, golf getaways to everthing in between, MO has something for everyone. Tour one of our award winning wineries. Experience our exciting festivals and events or take in the beautiful Fall foilage w/a scenic drive through our countryside.

Phone: (314)751-3246
Address: 301 W. High St. Truman Bldg Rm 290, Jefferson City, MO 65101
Lat/Lon: 38.34621/-92.10615
Email: tourism@ded.mo.gov
Web: visitmo.com

SEE AD TRAVEL SECTION PAGE 452

(E) OSAGE CAMPGROUND & MORE—(Cole) *From jct US 54 & Hwy 50/63 (Jefferson City): Go 10 mi E on Hwy 50/63 to Marina Rd, then 1/2 mi E on Marina Rd. Enter on L.*

◆◆FACILITIES: 78 sites, typical site width 30 ft, 14 full hkups, 24 W&E, (30/50 amps), 40 no hkups, some extd stay sites, 26 pull-thrus, phone Internet central location, family camping, tenting, RV storage, dump, non-guest dump $, laundry, ltd groc, RV supplies, marine gas, ice, picnic tables, fire rings, grills, wood.

◆◆◆RECREATION: rec room/area, equipped pavilion, coin games, boating, pond fishing, fishing supplies, golf nearby, bsktball, play equipment, horseshoes, sports field.

Pets welcome. Open all yr. Clubs welcome. Rate in 2010 $20.50 for 2 persons. MC/VISA/DISC/AMEX/Debit.

Phone: (573)395-4066
Address: 10407 Marina Rd, Jefferson City, MO 65101
Lat/Lon: 38.49469/-92.01313
Email: uscats1@aol.com

SEE AD NEXT PAGE

JOPLIN—E-2

(SW) KOA-Joplin—(Newton) *At jct I-44 & Hwy 43 (Seneca exit 4): Go 1/8 mi S on Hwy 43, turn E at traffic light to Outer Road. Enter on R.* ◆◆◆◆FACILITIES: 75 sites, typical site width 40 ft, 59 full hkups, 12 W&E, (30/50 amps), 4 no hkups, 54 pull-thrus, family camping, tenting, dump, laundry, ltd groc. ◆◆◆RECREATION: swim pool, pond fishing, playground. Pets welcome, breed restrict. Partial handicap access. Open all yr. Big rigs welcome. Rate in 2010 $32-63 for 2 persons. Phone: (417)623-2246. KOA discount.

Woodall's Tip... Looking for a place to stay for an extended period of time? Check out our Extended Stay Guide (the yellow pages in the middle of this Directory).

KANSAS CITY—B-2

See listings at Blue Springs, Grain Valley, Higginsville, Holt, Independence, Lee's Summit, Liberty, Oak Grove, Peculiar, Platte City, St. Joseph, Smithville, in MO, and in KS: Gardner, Lawrence, Louisburg

METROPOLITAN KANSAS CITY AREA MAP

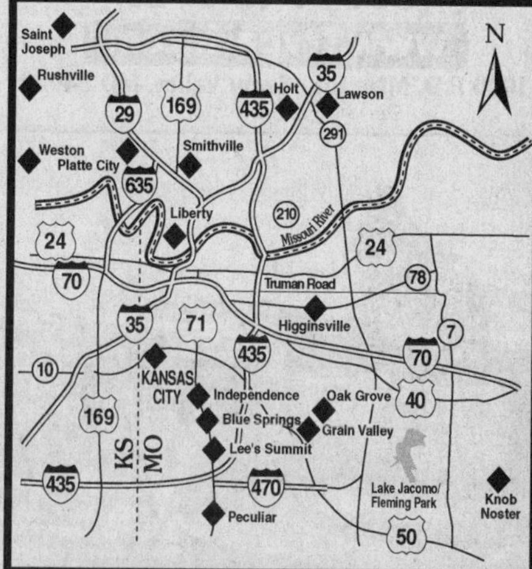

Symbols on map indicate towns within a 60 mi radius of Kansas City where campgrounds (diamonds), attractions (flags), & RV service centers & camping supply outlets (gears) are listed. Check listings for more information.

Tell Them Woodall's Sent You!

LONGVIEW LAKE CAMPGROUND (Jackson County Park)—(Jackson) *From jct I-470 & Hwy 50: Go 2 mi W on I-470 (exit 5), then 2 mi S on View High Dr. Enter on R.* FACILITIES: 113 sites, 17 full hkups, 59 E, (20/30/50 amps), 37 no hkups, 10 pull-thrus, tenting, dump, laundry. RECREATION: lake swim, boating, canoeing, ramp, dock, lake/pond fishing, playground. Pets welcome. Open Apr 17 - Sep 30. Phone: (816)795-8200.

(NE) OCEANS OF FUN—*From jct I-35 & I-435: Go 2 mi S on I-435 to exit 54, then 1/2 mi E on Parvin Rd to Oceans of Fun. Enter on L.* Worlds of Fun & Oceans of Fun-the Midwest's premier family entertainment destination-features 235 acres of rides and attractions for guests of all ages, lazy river, water slides & more. Open May 28 - Sep 18. MC/VISA/DISC/AMEX.

Phone: (816)454-4545
Address: 4545 Worlds of Fun Ave, Kansas City, MO 64161
Lat/Lon: 39.16853/-94.48463
Web: www.worldsoffun.com

SEE AD THIS PAGE

The tallest man in US documented medical history was Robert Pershing Wadlow from St. Louis. He was 8 feet, 11.1 inches tall.

Staying close to home next year? Pre-order the 2012 Directory in a smaller regional version. It contains all the great information Woodall's North American Directory contains, but in a handy to-go version, specific to the states or provinces you need.

KANSAS CITY—Continued

(NE) WORLDS OF FUN—*From East loop of I-435 (exit 54): Go 1/2 mi E on Parrim Rd. enter RV Park through Oceans of Fun parking lot. Enter on R.* Worlds of Fun & Oceans of Fun-The Midwest's premier family entertainment destination-features 235 acres of rides & attractions including roller coasters for guests of all ages. Meet the "Peanuts" character in Camp Snoopy. Open Apr 15 - Oct 30. MC/VISA/DISC/AMEX.

Phone: (816)454-4545
Address: 4545 Worlds of Fun Ave, Kansas City, MO 64161
Lat/Lon: 39.10100/-94.29076
Web: www.worldsoffun.com

SEE AD PAGE 470

(NE) WORLDS OF FUN VILLAGE—(Clay) *From East Loop of I-435 (exit 54): Go 1/2 mi E on Parvin Rd. Enter RV Park through Oceans of Fun parking lot. Enter on L.*

◆◆◆◆◆FACILITIES: 82 sites, 82 full hkups, (20/30/50 amps), 35 pull-thrus, cable TV, WiFi Instant Internet at site, phone Internet central location, family camping, cabins, laundry, groceries, RV supplies, ice, picnic tables, patios, grills.

◆◆◆◆◆RECREATION: rec room/area, coin games, swim pool, hot tub, activities, local tours.

Pets welcome. Partial handicap access. No tents. Open Mar 15 - Nov 15. Big rigs welcome. Clubs welcome. Rate in 2010 $37.95-39.95 for 6 persons. MC/VISA/DISC/AMEX. Member ARVC, MOARC.

Phone: (816)454-4545
Address: 4545 Worlds of Fun Ave, Kansas City, MO 64161
Lat/Lon: 39.16906/-94.48763
Email: wof@worldsoffun.com
Web: www.worldsoffun.com

SEE AD PAGE 470

KIMBERLING CITY—E-2

(NW) AUNTS CREEK PARK (COE Table Rock Lake) (Stone) *From town: Go 2 mi N on Hwy-13, then 3 mi W on Hwy-00 to Lake Rd 00-9.* FACILITIES: 55 sites, typical site width 20 ft, 34 ft max RV length, 52 E, (30 amps), 3 no hkups, tenting, dump, ltd groc. RECREATION: lake swim, boating, ramp, lake fishing, playground. Partial handicap access. Open May 1 - Oct 30. Phone: (417)739-2792.

(S) Water's Edge on Table Rock Lake—(Stone) *From jct Hwy 76/265 & Hwy 13: Go 6 mi S on Hwy 13 to Kimberling Blvd, then 1/4 mi N on Marina Way. Enter on R.* ◆◆◆FACILITIES: 123 sites, typical site width 40 ft, 41 full hkups, 11 W&E, 41 E, (30/50 amps), 30 no hkups, 9 pull-thrus, WiFi Instant Internet at site, family camping, tenting, RV storage, dump, non-guest dump $, RV supplies, marine gas, ice, picnic tables, fire rings, grills, wood. ◆◆◆RECREATION: pavilion, lake swim, boating, ramp, lake fishing, bsktball, playground, tennis, hiking trails. Pets welcome. Open all yr. Big rigs welcome. Rate in 2010 $21-29 for 2 persons. MC/VISA/Debit. Member ARVC, MOARC. CCUSA 50% Discount. CCUSA reservations Accepted, CCUSA max stay 14 days, CCUSA disc. not avail S,Th, CCUSA disc. not avail F,Sa, CCUSA disc. not avail holidays. Discount valid Mon-Wed from Apr thru Sep & valid all days from Oct thru Mar. No other discounts apply.

Phone: (800)439-3500
Address: 72 Marina Way, Kimberling City, MO 65686
Email: info@watersedgetr.com
Web: www.watersedgetr.com

Woodall's Tip... If you think Woodall's Ratings mean Good, Better, Best...think again. See the "How to Use" section in the front of this Directory for an explanation of our Rating System.

KINGDOM CITY—C-4

(W) HANSON HILLS CAMPGROUND—(Callaway) *From jct US 54 & I-70: Go 2 mi W on I-70 (exit 144), then 1 mi W on Outer Road, then 7 mi S on Hwy HH, then 1-1/4 mi N on CR 221. Enter on L.*

◆◆◆FACILITIES: 80 sites, typical site width 25 ft, 48 full hkups, 6 W&E, 6 E, (30/50 amps), 50 amps ($), 20 no hkups, 28 pull-thrus, WiFi Internet central location, family camping, tenting, tent rentals, RV's/park model rentals, dump, non-guest dump $, laundry, ltd groc, RV supplies, ice, picnic tables, fire rings, wood.

◆◆◆RECREATION: rec hall, pavilion, swim pool, hot tub, pond fishing, fishing supplies, golf nearby, bsktball, playground, shuffleboard court shuffleboard court, activities (wkends), horseshoes, sports field, hiking trails, v-ball. Rec open to public.

Pets welcome. Partial handicap access. Open all yr. Big rigs welcome. Escort to site. Clubs welcome. Rate in 2010 $23-28 for 2 persons. MC/VISA/DISC/Debit.

KINGDOM CITY—Continued
HANSON HILLS CAMPGROUND—Continued

Phone: (877)642-6060
Address: 3643 CR 221, Kingdom City, MO 65262
Lat/Lon: 38.92972/-92.01126
Email: hanson.hills@gmail.com
Web: www.hansonhillscampground.com

SEE AD THIS PAGE

(W) HANSON HILLS CAMPGROUND KITCHEN—*From jct US 54 & I-70: Go 2 mi W on I-70 (exit 144). Enter on R.* Fresh baked pizza with your choice of toppings. Grilled short orders with daily specials Mon - Fri. Open all yr. MC/VISA/DISC/AMEX.

HANSON HILLS CAMPGROUND KITCHEN—Continued on next page

James C. Penney, founder of J.C. Penney's, was from Missouri.

KINGDOM CITY—Continued
HANSON HILLS CAMPGROUND KITCHEN—Continued

Phone: (573)642-8600
Address: 3643 CR 221, Kingdom City, MO 65262
Lat/Lon: 38.92972/-92.01126

SEE AD PAGE 471

KIRKSVILLE—A-3

(SW) THOUSAND HILLS STATE PARK—(Adair) *From jct US-63 & Hwy-6: Go 4 mi W on Hwy-6, then 2 mi S on Hwy-157.*

WELCOME

FACILITIES: 57 sites, typical site width 20 ft, 42 E, (30 amps), 15 no hkups, 11 pull-thrus, tenting, cabins, dump, ltd groc, marine gas, ice, picnic tables, fire rings, wood.

RECREATION: rec room/area, pavilion, lake swim, boating, 90 hp limit, canoeing, ramp, dock, canoe rentals, lake fishing, playground, activities, hiking trails.

Partial handicap access. Open all yr. No reservations. Max stay 14 days. MC/VISA/DISC/AMEX.

Phone: (660)665-6995
Address: 20431 St Hwy 157, Kirksville, MO 63501
Lat/Lon: 40.189972/-92.648194
Web: www.mostateparks.com

SEE AD TRAVEL SECTION PAGE 451

KNOB NOSTER—C-2

(S) KNOB NOSTER STATE PARK—(Johnson) *From jct US 50 & Hwy 23: Go 2 mi S on Hwy 23. Enter on R.*

WELCOME

FACILITIES: 76 sites, 30 ft max RV length, 37 E, (30 amps), 39 no hkups, tenting, dump, laundry, ltd groc, picnic tables, fire rings, grills, wood.

RECREATION: pavilion, lake fishing, sports field, hiking trails.

Partial handicap access. Open all yr. Facilities fully operational Apr 1 - Oct 31. MC/VISA/DISC/AMEX.

Phone: (660)563-2463
Address: 873 SE 10th, Knob Noster, MO 65336
Web: www.mostateparks.com

SEE AD TRAVEL SECTION PAGE 451

LA GRANGE—A-4

(S) WAKONDA STATE PARK—(Lewis) *From jct CR C & US 61: Go 3 mi S on US 61. Enter on L.*

WELCOME

FACILITIES: 81 sites, 4 full hkups, 65 E, (30/50 amps), 12 no hkups, 21 pull-thrus, tenting, cabins, dump, laundry, ice, picnic tables, fire rings, grills, wood, controlled access.

RECREATION: pavilion, lake swim, boating, 10 hp limit, canoeing, ramp, canoe rentals, lake fishing, hiking trails.

Partial handicap access. Open all yr. Facilities fully operational Apr 15 - Oct 31. MC/VISA/DISC/AMEX.

Phone: (573)655-2280
Address: 32836 State Park Rd, La Grange, MO 63448
Email: moparks@dnr.mo.gov
Web: www.mostateparks.com

SEE AD TRAVEL SECTION PAGE 451

Prepare gourmet meals in your RV kitchen! Woodall's Cooking on the Road with Celebrity Chefs includes dozens of tips and sidebars that make recipes easier to use while traveling. Go to www.woodalls.com/shop and check it out.

LACLEDE—B-3

(W) PERSHING STATE PARK—(Linn) *From jct Hwy 5 & US 36: Go 2 mi W on US 36, then 1-1/2 mi S on Hwy 130. Enter on R.*

WELCOME

FACILITIES: 38 sites, typical site width 12 ft, 26 E, (20/30 amps), 12 no hkups, 4 pull-thrus, tenting, dump, laundry, picnic tables, fire rings, wood.

RECREATION: rec room/area, pavilion, lake swim, lake fishing, playground, horseshoes, hiking trails.

Partial handicap access. Open all yr. Max stay 15 days. MC/VISA/DISC/AMEX.

Phone: (660)963-2299
Address: 29277 Hwy 130, Laclede, MO 64651
Lat/Lon: 39.758556/-93.212944
Web: www.mostateparks.com

SEE AD TRAVEL SECTION PAGE 451

LAKE OF THE OZARKS—C-3

See listings at Bennett Springs, Camdenton, Eldon, Gravois Mills, Lake Ozark, Laurie, Linn Creek, Osage Beach, Versailles, Vienna

LAKE OF THE OZARKS AREA MAP

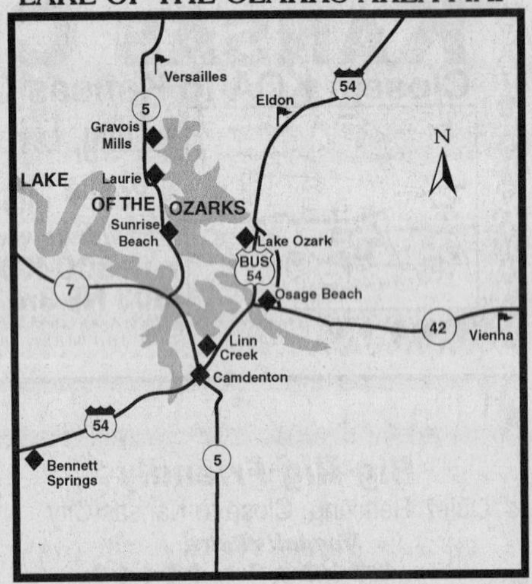

Symbols on map indicate towns within a 15 mi radius of Lake of the Ozarks where campgrounds (diamonds), attractions (flags), & RV service centers & camping supply outlets (gears) are listed. Check listings for more information.

Tell Them Woodall's Sent You!

LAKE OZARK—C-3

(N) Cross Creek RV Park—(Miller) *From jct US 54 & Hwy W: Go 2-1/2 mi NW (of Bagnell Dam) on Hwy W, then 1 mi N on Gilliam Rd, (gravel road). Enter at end.* ◇◇◇FACILITIES: 62 sites, typical site width 25 ft, 38 ft max RV length, 50 full hkups, (30/50 amps), 12 no hkups, 7 pull-thrus, WiFi Instant Internet at site, phone Internet central location, family camping, tenting, laundry, groceries, RV supplies, ice, picnic tables, fire rings, wood. ◇◇◇◇RECREATION: rec hall, equipped pavilion, swim pool, boating, canoeing, kayaking, dock, lake fishing, fishing supplies, mini-golf, bsktball, play equipment, 2 shuffleboard courts, activities horseshoes, hiking trails, v-ball. Pets welcome, breed restrict. Partial handicap access. Open Apr 1 - Nov 1. Green Friendly. Rate in 2010 $25-30 for 2 persons. MC/VISA/DISC. Member ARVC, MOARC. FMCA discount. CCUSA 50% Discount. CCUSA max stay Unlimited, CCUSA disc. not avail F,Sa, CCUSA disc. not avail holidays. Discount not available for lakefront sites or for any holiday weekends.

CAMPCLUB USA

Phone: (888)250-3885
Address: 41 Old Trail Rd, Lake Ozark, MO 65049
Lat/Lon: 38.24422/-92.65887
Email: camp@crosscreekrvpark.com
Web: www.crosscreekrvpark.com

(N) Majestic Oaks Park—(Miller) *From jct of Hwy 54 & CR W: Go 4-1/4 mi NW on CR W. Enter on R.* ◇◇◇FACILITIES: 84 sites, typical site width 30 ft, 62 full hkups, 9 W&E, 1 E, (30/50 amps), 50 amps ($), 12 no hkups, 10 pull-thrus, family camping, tenting, laundry, ltd groc. ◇◇◇◇RECREATION: swim pool, playground. Pets welcome. Open all yr. Facilities fully operational Apr 1 - Nov 30. Big rigs welcome. Rate in 2010 $25-31 for 4 persons. Member ARVC, MOARC. Phone: (573)365-1890. FMCA discount.

The capital of Missouri is Jefferson City.

LAKE OZARK—Continued
Majestic Oaks Park—Continued

(E) Riverview RV Park—(Miller) *From west jct Business 54 & US 54: Go 1 mi E on US 54 to immediately before Osage River Bridge. Entrance on right. From north jct Business US 54 & US 54: Go 2-1/3 mi W on US 54 to immediately after Osage River Bridge. Enter on L.* ◇◇◇◇FACILITIES: 79 sites, typical site width 25 ft, 72 full hkups, (20/30/50 amps), 7 no hkups, 7 pull-thrus, family camping, tenting, dump, laundry, groceries. ◇◇◇◇RECREATION: swim pool, boating, canoeing, ramp, dock, river/pond fishing, playground. Pets welcome. Partial handicap access. Open all yr. Facilities fully operational Mar 1 - Nov 15. Big rigs welcome. Rate in 2010 $26-28 for 2 persons. Phone: (573)365-1122.

LAURIE—C-3

(NE) Laurie RV Park—(Morgan) *From jct Hwy 5 & Hwy O: Go 1 mi E on Hwy O. Enter on R.* ◇◇◇FACILITIES: 18 sites, typical site width 24 ft, 18 full hkups, (30/50 amps), 18 pull-thrus, WiFi Internet central location, RV storage, laundry, ice, picnic tables, fire rings, wood. ◇RECREATION: pond fishing. Pets welcome. No tents. Open all yr. Facilities fully operational Apr 1 - Nov 1. Big rigs welcome. Rate in 2010 $20-22 per vehicle. MC/VISA. Member ARVC, MOARC. CCUSA 50% Discount. CCUSA reservations Recommended, CCUSA max stay Unlimited.

CAMPCLUB USA

Phone: (573)374-8469
Address: 515 Highway O, Laurie, MO 65037
Lat/Lon: 38.20352/-92.82552
Email: laurievpark@charterinternet.com
Web: www.laurievpark.com

LAWSON—B-2

(NW) WATKINS WOOLEN MILL STATE PARK—(Clay) *From jct US 69 & Hwy 92: Go 1 mi W on Hwy 92 to CR RA, then go 4 mi N. Enter at end.*

WELCOME

FACILITIES: 98 sites, 75 E, (30/50 amps), 23 no hkups, tenting, dump, laundry, picnic tables, fire rings, grills, wood, controlled access.

RECREATION: pavilion, lake swim, boating, canoeing, ramp, lake fishing, hiking trails.

Open all yr. Facilities fully operational Apr 1 - Oct 31. MC/VISA/DISC/AMEX.

Phone: (816)580-3387
Address: 26600 Park Rd N, Lawson, MO 64062
Web: www.mostateparks.com

SEE AD TRAVEL SECTION PAGE 451

LEASBURG—D-4

(SE) ONONDAGA CAVE STATE PARK—(Crawford) *From jct I-44 & Hwy-H (Leasburg Exit): Go 7 mi SE on Hwy-H. Enter on R.*

WELCOME

FACILITIES: 66 sites, typical site width 20 ft, 47 W&E, (50 amps), 19 no hkups, 2 pull-thrus, tenting, dump, laundry, ltd groc, ice, picnic tables, fire rings, grills, wood.

RECREATION: pavilion, river swim, boating, ramp, river fishing, playground, activities, hiking trails.

Partial handicap access. Open all yr. No reservations. Max stay 15 days. MC/VISA/DISC/AMEX.

Phone: (573)245-6576
Address: 7556 Hwy H, Leasburg, MO 65535
Lat/Lon: 38.062806/-91.228278
Web: www.mostateparks.com

SEE AD TRAVEL SECTION PAGE 451

(S) Ozark Outdoors/Riverfront Resort—(Crawford) *From jct I-44 (exit 214) & Hwy H: Go 7-1/2 mi S on Hwy H across Meramec River. Enter on L.* ◇◇◇FACILITIES: 410 sites, typical site width 40 ft, 60 full hkups, 50 W&E, (30/50 amps), 300 no hkups, 20 pull-thrus, tenting, dump, laundry, ltd groc. ◇◇◇RECREATION: swim pool, canoeing, river fishing, playground. Pets welcome. Partial handicap access. Open all yr. Big rigs welcome. Rate in 2010 $21 for 2 persons. Member ARVC, MOARC. Phone: (800) 888-0023.

Woodall's Tip... Rate information is based on the campground's published rate last year. These rates aren't guaranteed, and you should always call ahead for the most updated rate information.

LEBANON—D-3

✽ **(W) HAPPY TRAILS RV CENTER**—*From jct I-44 (exit 123): Go 500 ft E on South Outer Rd. Enter on R.* SALES: travel trailers, park models, 5th wheels, fold-down camping trailers, pre-owned unit sales. SERVICES: full-time mech, RV appliance repair, body work/collision repair, LP gas by meter, RV rentals, sells parts/accessories, installs hitches. Open all yr. MC/VISA/DISC/AMEX/ Debit.

Phone: (417)533-7530
Address: 18256 Campground Rd, Phillipsburg, MO 65722
Lat/Lon: 37.60079/-92.71117
Email: office@happytrailsrvcenter.com
Web: www.happytrailsrvcenter.com

SEE AD SPRINGFIELD PAGE 480

(W) HAPPY TRAILS RV PARK—(Laclede) *From Hwy-5 & I-44: Go 6 mi W on I-44 (exit 123), then 500 ft E on South outer road. Enter on R.*

◆◆◆FACILITIES: 49 sites, typical site width 30 ft, 19 full hkups, 16 W&E, 6 E, (20/30/50 amps), 8 no hkups, some extd stay sites, 35 pull-thrus, WiFi Instant Internet at site, family camping, tenting, cabins, dump, non-guest dump $, laundry, ltd groc, RV supplies, LP gas by meter, ice, picnic tables, fire rings, grills, wood.

◆◆◆RECREATION: rec hall, swim pool, pond fishing, golf nearby, playground, horseshoes, sports field, v-ball.

Pets welcome. Open all yr. Big rigs welcome. Clubs welcome. Rate in 2010 $24-30 for 2 persons. MC/VISA/DISC/Debit.

Phone: (417)532-3422
Address: 18376 Campground Rd, Phillipsburg, MO 65722-1823
Lat/Lon: 37.60154/-92.71102
Web: www.happytrailrvpark.com

Reserve Online at Woodalls.com

SEE AD SPRINGFIELD PAGE 480

LEE'S SUMMIT—C-2

JACOMO CAMPGROUND AT FLEMING PARK (Jackson County Park)—*W'bound from I-470 (exit 10A): Go 1-3/4 mi E on Colbern Rd to park entrance, then 1/2 mi N to campground entrance. E'bound from I-470 (exit 9) & Douglas St: Go 1/4 mi N, then 2-1/2 mi E on Colbern Rd to park entrance, then 1/2 mi N to campground entrance. Enter on L.* FACILITIES: 60 sites, 19 full hkups, 21 E, (20/30/50 amps), 20 no hkups, 10 pull-thrus, tenting, dump, laundry. RECREATION: lake swim, boating, 25 hp limit, canoeing, ramp, dock, lake fishing, play equipment. Partial handicap access. Open all yr. Facilities fully operational Apr 1 - Oct 31. Phone: (816)795-8200.

LESTERVILLE—D-5

(N) JOHNSON'S SHUT-INS STATE PARK—(Reynolds) *From jct Hwy 40 & Hwy 72: Go 1/2 mi E on Hwy 40, then go 8 mi N on Hwy N. Enter on R.*

FACILITIES: 49 sites, 23 E, (30 amps), 26 no hkups, 6 pull-thrus, tenting, dump, laundry, ltd groc, picnic tables, fire rings, grills, wood, controlled access.

RECREATION: pavilion, river fishing, hiking trails.

No pets. Partial handicap access. Open all yr. Facilities fully operational Apr 1 - Oct 31. MC/VISA/ DISC/AMEX.

Phone: (573)546-2450
Address: 148 Taum Sauk Trl, Middlebrook, MO 63656
Web: www.mostateparks.com

SEE AD TRAVEL SECTION PAGE 451

LIBERTY—B-2

(NE) Miller's Kampark—(Clay) *From jct I-35 (exit 17) & Hwy 291: Go 1 mi S on Hwy 291, then 1 block S on Stewart Rd. Enter on L.* ◆◆FACILITIES: 51 sites, typical site width 20 ft, 41 full hkups, 10 W&E, (30/50 amps), 13 pull-thrus, dump, laundry. ◆RECREATION: swim pool. Pets welcome. No tents. Open all yr. Rate in 2010 $25.71-31.08 for 2 persons. Member ARVC, MOARC. Phone: (816)781-7724.

LINN CREEK—D-3

MILITARY PARK (Lake of the Ozarks Rec Area-Fort Leonard Wood)—(Camden) *Off base. From jct I-44 & Hwy 7N: Go 9-3/10 mi N on Hwy 7N, then 20 mi N on Hwy A, then 5 mi on Hwy A33.* FACILITIES: 38 sites, 17 W&E, (20/30 amps), 21 no hkups, tenting, dump, laundry, ltd groc. RECREATION: lake swim, boating, canoeing, ramp, dock, lake fishing. Open Mar - Oct. Phone: (573)346-5640.

(NW) Ozark Trails RV Park—(Camden) *E'bnd From jct Hwy 5 & US 54: Go 4 mi E on US 54. W'bnd from jct Hwy & US 54: Go 1 mi W on Hwy 54. Enter on L.* ◆◆◆◆FACILITIES: 86 sites, typical site width 30 ft, 64 full hkups, 2 W&E, (20/30/50 amps), 20 no hkups,

LINN CREEK—Continued
Ozark Trails RV Park—Continued

23 pull-thrus, family camping, tenting, dump, laundry. ◆◆◆RECREATION: swim pool, playground. Pets welcome. Open all yr. Big rigs welcome. Rate in 2010 $24-27.50 for 2 persons. Member ARVC, MOARC. Phone: (573)346-5490.

LOWRY CITY—D-2

(E) TALLEY BEND (COE - Harry S. Truman Reservoir) —(St. Clair) *From town: Go 5 mi E on CR C to CR HH.* FACILITIES: 76 sites, typical site width 20 ft, 76 E, (30 amps), tenting, dump, laundry. RECREATION: lake swim, boating, ramp, lake fishing, playground. Partial handicap access. Open all yr. Phone: (417) 644-2446.

MACON—B-3

(W) LONG BRANCH STATE PARK—(Macon) *From jct US-63 & US-36: Go 2 mi W on US-36.*

FACILITIES: 73 sites, typical site width 18 ft, 64 E, (30/50 amps), 9 no hkups, 1 pull-thrus, tenting, dump, ltd groc, marine gas, ice, picnic tables, fire rings, grills, wood.

RECREATION: pavilion, lake swim, boating, ramp, dock, lake fishing, hiking trails, v-ball.

Partial handicap access. Open all yr. No reservations. Max stay 15 days. MC/VISA/DISC/AMEX.

Phone: (660)773-5229
Address: 28615 Visitor Center Rd, Macon, MO 63552
Lat/Lon: 39.775556/-92.532556
Web: www.mostateparks.com

SEE AD TRAVEL SECTION PAGE 451

MARK TWAIN LAKE AREA—B-4

See listings at Bowling Green, Canton, Hannibal & Monroe City.

MARSHALL—B-3

(S) Lazy Day Camping—(Saline) *From jct I-70 (exit 78B) & US 65: Go 1/4 mi N on US 65, then 3/4 mi E on North Outer Rd. Enter on L.* ◆◆FACILITIES: 55 sites, typical site width 15 ft, 20 full hkups, 15 W&E, (30/50 amps), 20 no hkups, 20 pull-thrus, tenting, dump, laundry, ltd groc. ◆◆RECREATION: swim pool, pond fishing, playground. Pets welcome. Partial handicap access. Open all yr. Rate in 2010 $18-22 for 2 persons. Phone: (660)879-4411.

(N) VAN METER STATE PARK—(Saline) *From jct Hwy 41 & Hwy 122: Go 4 mi W on Hwy 122.*

FACILITIES: 21 sites, typical site width 20 ft, 12 E, (30 amps), 9 no hkups, tenting, picnic tables, fire rings, grills, wood.

RECREATION: pavilion, lake swim, lake fishing, hiking trails.

Partial handicap access. Open all yr. Open Apr 1 - Oct 31. Max stay 15 days. No reservations. MC/ VISA/DISC.

Phone: (660)886-7537
Address: Rt 1, Miami, MO 65344
Lat/Lon: 39.264417/-93.267111
Email: moparks@mail.dnr.state.mo.us
Web: mostateparks.com

SEE AD TRAVEL SECTION PAGE 451

MAYSVILLE—A-2

(S) Pony Express RV Park & Campground—(DeKalb) *From jct I-35 & US 36: Go 8 mi W on US 36, then 6 mi N on Hwy 33. Enter on L.* ◆◆◆FACILITIES: 60 sites, typical site width 30 ft, 60 full hkups, (30/50 amps), 12 pull-thrus, family camping, tenting, dump, laundry, ltd groc. ◆◆◆RECREATION: pond fishing, playground. Pets welcome. Open Apr 1 - Oct 31. Big rigs welcome. Rate in 2010 $27 for 2 persons. Phone: (816)449-2039.

MOBERLY—B-3

ROTHWELL PARK CAMPGROUND (City Park)—(Randolph) *From jct US 63 & US 24: Go 3 mi W on US 24, then 1/4 mi S on Rothwell Park Rd. Enter on R.* FACILITIES: 36 sites, 36 W&E, 18 pull-thrus, tenting, dump. RECREATION: swim pool, boating, 10 hp limit, lake fishing, playground. Pets welcome. Open all yr. Phone: (660)263-6757.

MONROE CITY—B-4

(S) INDIAN CREEK (COE - Mark Twain Lake)—(Ralls) *From jct US 24 & Hwy HH: Go 2 mi S on Hwy HH, then 3 mi E on access road.* FACILITIES: 220 sites, typical site width 20 ft, 30 full hkups, 190 E, (20/30 amps), tenting, dump. RECREATION: lake swim, boating, ramp, dock, lake fishing, playground. Partial handicap access. Open Mar 30 - Nov 20. Phone: (573)735-4097.

(S) Mark Twain Landing Resort—(Ralls) *From jct US 36 & US 61: Go 14 mi W on 36 to J Road, then 7-1/2 mi S on J Road. Enter on R.* ◆◆◆◆◆FACILITIES: 233 sites, typical site width 35 ft, 233 full hkups, (30/50 amps), cable TV, WiFi Instant Internet at site,

MONROE CITY—Continued
Mark Twain Landing Resort—Continued

WiFi Internet central location, family camping, tenting, RV storage, laundry, groceries, RV supplies, LP gas by weight/by meter, ice, picnic tables, patios, fire rings, grills, wood. ◆◆◆◆◆RECREATION: rec hall, pavilion, equipped pavilion, swim pool, wading pool, boating, lake/pond fishing, fishing supplies, mini-golf, ($), bsktball, playground, activities, horseshoes, v-ball. Pets welcome, breed restrict. Open all yr. Facilities fully operational Apr 1 - Oct 31. Big rigs welcome. Rate in 2010 $27-39 for 4 persons. MC/VISA/Debit. ATM. Member ARVC, MOARC. FMCA discount. CCUSA 50% Discount. CCUSA reservations Not Accepted, CCUSA max stay 7 days, CCUSA disc. not avail F,Sa. Limited amenities Nov 1-Apr 1. Discount not available holiday weekends or Jun 28-Jul 10. Limited availability holiday weeks. Special Events weekends, please call.

Phone: (573)735-9422
Address: 42819 Landing Ln, Monroe City, MO 63456
Lat/Lon: 39.56260/-91.65999
Email: info@marktwainlanding.com
Web: www.marktwainlanding.com

MOUNTAIN GROVE—E-3

(W) Missouri Park & Campground—(Wright) *From jct Hwy 95 & US 60: Go 2 mi W on US 60, to Business US 60 exit, then 1 mi W on North Outer Rd (follow signs). Enter on R.* ◆◆◆FACILITIES: 90 sites, typical site width 30 ft, 60 full hkups, 10 W&E, (20/30/50 amps), 20 no hkups, 35 pull-thrus, tenting, dump, laundry. ◆◆RECREATION: swim pool, pond fishing. Pets welcome. Partial handicap access. Open all yr. Big rigs welcome. Rate in 2010 $26 for 2 persons. Phone: (417)926-4104.

MOUNTAIN VIEW—E-4

(W) Ozarks Mountain Springs RV Park—(Howell) *From jct Hwy 60 & Hwy 63 (at Willow Springs): Go 4 mi E on Hwy 60 (8 mi W of Mountain View). Enter on L.* ◆◆◆◆FACILITIES: 48 sites, typical site width 25 ft, 48 full hkups, (30/50 amps), 37 pull-thrus, WiFi Instant Internet at site, phone Internet central location, family camping, tenting, laundry, full svc store, RV supplies, ice, picnic tables, patios, fire rings, wood. ◆◆RECREATION: rec hall, activities, horseshoes, v-ball. Pets welcome, breed restrict. Partial handicap access. Open all yr. Big rigs welcome. Rate in 2010 $24.50-32 for 2 persons. MC/VISA. Member ARVC, MOARC. CCUSA 50% Discount. CCUSA reservations Accepted, CCUSA max stay 2 days, Cash only for CCUSA disc., CCUSA disc. not avail holidays.

Phone: (417)469-3351
Address: 5400 CR 3200 #19, Mountain View, MO 65548
Lat/Lon: 36.59162/-91.52831
Email: lisatate@gmail.com
Web: ozarksrvpark.com

NEOSHO—E-2

(NW) Stage Stop Campground—(Newton) *From jct US 71 & Hwy 86: Go 1/4 mi E on Hwy 86 to Hammer Rd, then go 1 mi N on Hammer Rd. Enter on R.* ◆◆◆FACILITIES: 16 sites, typical site width 25 ft, 16 full hkups, (30/50 amps), 5 pull-thrus, tenting. Pets welcome. Open all yr. Big rigs welcome. Rate in 2010 $20 for 2 persons. Phone: (417)456-1010.

NEVADA—D-2

(N) Osage Prairie RV Park—(Vernon) *From jct US 54 & US 71: Go 1 mi N on US 71 to Highland Ave exit, then 1/2 mi S on West Outer Road. Enter on R.* ◆◆◆◆FACILITIES: 45 sites, typical site width 20 ft, 35 full hkups, (20/30/50 amps), 10 no hkups, 18 pull-thrus, family camping, tenting, dump, laundry, ltd groc. ◆◆◆RECREATION: swim pool. Pets welcome. Open all yr. Big rigs welcome. Rate in 2010 $27 for 2 persons. Member ARVC, MOARC. Phone: (417)667-2267. FMCA discount.

NOEL—E-2

(N) River Ranch RV Park & Campground—(McDonald) *From jct Hwy-90 & Hwy-59: Go 100 yards N on Hwy-59. Enter on L.* ◆◆◆FACILITIES: 124 sites, typical site width 25 ft, 19 full hkups, 24 E, (20/30/50 amps), 81 no hkups, family camping, tenting, dump, ltd groc. ◆◆◆RECREATION: river swim, boating, canoeing, ramp, river fishing, playground. Pets welcome, breed restrict, size restrict. Partial handicap access. Open May 15 - Sep. Big rigs welcome. Rate in 2010 $30 for 2 persons. Member ARVC, MOARC. Phone: (800)951-6121.

Woodall's Tip... Is a new Woodall's Directory needed every year? You bet! Each year the Woodall's North American Directory averages over 350,000 changes from the previous year.

OAK GROVE—C-2

(N) KANSAS CITY EAST KOA—(Jackson) *From jct I-70 & CR H (exit 28): Go 1 blk N on Hwy H, 2 blks E on 3rd St. Enter on R.*

WELCOME

CLOSEST KOA TO KANSAS CITY
You'll feel like you are getting away from it all when you pull into this KOA, where half the 20 acre campground is wooded, yet close to all the city sights. You'll be greeted with a smile and a big welcome.

◆◆◆◆FACILITIES: 85 sites, typical site width 30 ft, 56 full hkups, 15 W&E, (30/50 amps), 14 no hkups, 42 pull-thrus, WiFi Instant Internet at site, family camping, tenting, cabins, RV storage, dump, non-guest dump $, laundry, ltd groc, RV supplies, LP gas by weight/by meter, ice, picnic tables, fire rings, wood.

◆◆◆◆RECREATION: rec hall, rec room/area, coin games, swim pool, mini-golf, golf nearby, bsktball, playground, sports field, v-ball.

Pets welcome, breed restrict. Partial handicap access. Open all yr. Big rigs welcome. Escort to site. Clubs welcome. Rate in 2010 $27-32 for 2 persons. MC/VISA/DISC/Debit. KOA discount.

Phone: (816)690-6660
Address: 303 NE 3rd St, Oak Grove, MO 64075
Lat/Lon: 39.01763/-94.12623
Email: KCEASTKOA@AOL.COM
Web: www.koa.com

SEE AD KANSAS CITY PAGE 471

(S) LAKE PARADISE RESORT (CAMP RESORT)—(Jackson) *From jct I-470 & I-70: Go 13 mi E on I-70 to Hwy F (exit 28), then 7 mi S to Cline Rd, then 1-1/2 mi E on Cline Rd. Enter at end.*

WELCOME

"WHERE MEMORIES ARE MADE"
Only 10 minutes from I-70 (exit 28) close to Kansas City. Enjoy 260 acres of lakes, trees and fun! Huge swimming pool, putt-putt golf, restaurant, 5 lakes, fishing and much, much more. Come for the day or stay for a month!

FACILITIES: 515 sites, typical site width 30 ft, 350 full hkups, 125 W&E, 40 E, (30/50 amps), some extd stay sites, 25 pull-thrus, WiFi Internet central location, family camping, tenting, cabins, RV storage, dump, laundry, ltd groc, LP gas by weight/by meter, ice, picnic tables, patios, fire rings, grills, wood, controlled access.

RECREATION: rec hall, rec room/area, pavilion, swim pool, wading pool, boating, canoeing, ramp, 5 rowboat rentals, lake fishing, fishing supplies, mini-golf, golf nearby, bsktball, playground, shuffleboard court 2 shuffleboard courts, activities (wkends), horseshoes, sports field, hiking trails, v-ball. Rec open to public.

Pets welcome, breed restrict. Partial handicap access. Open all yr. Facilities fully operational Apr 1 - Oct 31. Big rigs welcome. Escort to site. Clubs welcome. Rate in 2010 $32 for 4 persons. MC/VISA/DISC/Debit. Member ARVC, MOARC.

Phone: (816)690-4113
Address: 985 NW 1901 Rd, Lone Jack, MO 64070
Lat/Lon: 38.91552/-94.10120
Web: www.lakeparadiseresort.com

SEE AD KANSAS CITY PAGE 471

ODESSA—C-2

(W) COUNTRY GARDENS RV PARK—(Lafayette) *From jct I-70 & Rt 131, exit 37 (Odessa Mall): Go N on Rt 131 for 100 ft, then 1/2 mi W on Outer Rd. Enter on R.*

WELCOME

I-70 ACCESS, BUT FEELS LIKE COUNTRY
Paved sites, nestled between green lawns, make it best stop near Kansas City. 25 min from historic Independence & Lexington. Country Store onsite: over 100 varieties cheese, Amish style jarred goods, spices, candy, snacks.

◆◆◆◆FACILITIES: 30 sites, 30 full hkups, (30/50 amps), some extd stay sites, 7 pull-thrus, WiFi Internet central location, tenting, RV storage, dump, non-guest dump $, laundry, ltd groc, LP gas by weight, picnic tables.

◆RECREATION: horseshoes.

Pets welcome. Open all yr. Big rigs welcome. Rate in 2010 $27-30 for 2 persons. MC/VISA/Debit.

Text 108009 to (440)725-8687 to see our Visual Tour.

ODESSA—Continued
COUNTRY GARDENS RV PARK—Continued

Phone: (816)633-8720
Address: 7089 Outer Rd, Odessa, MO 64076
Lat/Lon: 39.00928/-93.97768
Email: info@countrygardensrv.com
Web: www.countrygardensrv.com

SEE AD KANSAS CITY PAGE 470

(W) ONE GOOD TASTE COUNTRY STORE —*From I-70 & Rt 131, exit 37 (Odessa Mall): Go 100 feet N on Rt 131, then 1/2 mi W on Outer Rd. Enter on R.* Unique country store featuring Osceola cheese & many others (samples), gourmet coffees, Amish style bulk foods & spices, Amish furniture & gifts. Open all yr. MC/VISA/Debit.

WELCOME

Phone: (816)633-8720
Address: 7089 Outer Rd, Odessa, MO 64076
Lat/Lon: 39.00928/-93.97768
Email: info@countrygardensrv.com
Web: www.onegoodtaste.com

SEE AD KANSAS CITY PAGE 470

OSAGE BEACH—D-3

(S) LAKE OF THE OZARKS STATE PARK —(Camden) *From jct Hwy-42 & Hwy-134: Go 5 mi S on Hwy-134. Enter on R.*

WELCOME

FACILITIES: 189 sites, 30 ft max RV length, 88 E, (30/50 amps), 101 no hkups, 21 pull-thrus, tenting, cabins, dump, laundry, ltd groc, ice, picnic tables, fire rings, grills, wood.

RECREATION: pavilion, lake swim, boating, ramp, dock, lake fishing, hiking trails.

Partial handicap access. Open all yr. Facilities fully operational Apr 1 - Oct 31. MC/VISA/DISC/AMEX.

Phone: (573)348-2694
Address: Junction Hwy 42 & 134, Kaiser, MO 65047
Web: www.mostateparks.com

SEE AD TRAVEL SECTION PAGE 451

(N) OSAGE BEACH RV PARK—(Miller) *From jct US 54 & Hwy 42: Go 1/3 mi E on Hwy 42. Enter on R.*

WELCOME

◆◆◆◆FACILITIES: 75 sites, typical site width 34 ft, 75 full hkups, (20/30/50 amps), some extd stay sites, 33 pull-thrus, cable TV, WiFi Instant Internet at site, WiFi Internet central location, family camping, cabins, dump, non-guest dump $, laundry, RV supplies, LP gas by weight/by meter, ice, picnic tables, patios, fire rings.

◆◆◆RECREATION: rec hall, equipped pavilion, swim pool, wading pool, golf nearby, bsktball, playground, shuffleboard court 2 shuffleboard courts, horseshoes.

Pets welcome, breed restrict. Partial handicap access. No tents. Open Mar 24 - Nov 6. Big rigs welcome. Clubs welcome. Rate in 2010 $27.95-29.95 for 4 persons. MC/VISA/DISC/Debit. FMCA discount.

Phone: (573)348-3445
Address: 3949 Campground Lane, Osage Beach, MO 65065
Lat/Lon: 38.15248/-92.60151
Email: info@osagebeachrvpark.net
Web: www.osagebeachrvpark.net

Reserve Online at Woodalls.com

SEE AD LAKE OF THE OZARKS PAGE 472

OSCEOLA—D-2

(W) OSCEOLA RV PARK—(St. Clair) *From jct SR-13 & Business 13 (Truman Rd): Go 1/2 mi W on Business 13/Truman Rd, then 300 ft N on Parkview Dr. Enter on L.* FACILITIES: 52 sites, 38 full hkups, 14 W&E, (30/50 amps), 33 pull-thrus, tenting, dump, laundry. RECREATION: boating, dock, lake fishing, playground. Pets welcome. Open all yr. Facilities fully operational Mar 15 - Nov 26. Big rigs welcome. Phone: (417)646-8675.

OZARK—E-3

(E) Ozark RV Park—(Christian) *From jct US 65 & Hwy 14: Go 400 ft W on Hwy 14. Enter on L.* ◆◆◆FACILITIES: 44 sites, accepts full hkup units only, 44 full hkups, (30/50 amps), 44 pull-thrus, dump. Pets welcome. No tents. Open all yr. Big rigs welcome. Rate in 2010 $20 per vehicle. Phone: (417)581-3203.

(E) Stage Stop RV Park—(Christian) *From jct US 65 & exit CC & J: Go 1/2 mi E on Rte J, then 1/4 mi S on 17th St. Enter on R.* ◆◆◆FACILITIES: 34 sites, typical site width 25 ft, accepts self-contained units only, 34 full hkups, (30/50 amps), 34 pull-thrus. Pets welcome. No tents. Open all yr. Big rigs welcome. Rate in 2010 $20 per vehicle.

OZARK—Continued
Stage Stop RV Park—Continued

Phone: (417)581-6482
Address: 5251 N 17th Street, Ozark, MO 65721
Lat/Lon: 37.06858/-93.22491
Email: stagestoprv@aol.com
Web: www.STAGESTOPRV.com

PATTERSON—E-5

(N) SAM A BAKER STATE PARK—(Wayne) *From jct Hwy-34 & Hwy-143: Go 3 mi N on Hwy-143. Enter on R.*

WELCOME

FACILITIES: 198 sites, 30 ft max RV length, 132 E, (30/50 amps), 66 no hkups, tenting, cabins, dump, laundry, ltd groc, ice, picnic tables, fire rings, grills, wood, controlled access.

RECREATION: pavilion, river swim, boating, no motors, canoeing, ramp, canoe rentals, river/stream fishing, hiking trails.

Partial handicap access. Open all yr. Facilities fully operational Apr 1 - Oct 31. MC/VISA/DISC/AMEX.

Phone: (573)856-4411
Address: Hwy 143, Patterson, MO 63956
Web: www.mostateparks.com

SEE AD TRAVEL SECTION PAGE 451

PECULIAR—C-2

(E) PECULIAR PARK PLACE RV PARK—(Cass) *From jct Hwy 58 & US 71: Go 6 mi S on US 71, (Peculiar exit), then 300 ft E on CR J, then 1-1/2 mi S on E Outer Rd. Enter on L.*

WELCOME

◆◆◆◆◆FACILITIES: 60 sites, typical site width 35 ft, 46 full hkups, 14 W&E, (20/30/50 amps), some extd stay sites, 30 pull-thrus, WiFi Instant Internet at site, phone Internet central location, RV storage, dump, non-guest dump $, laundry, RV supplies, LP gas by weight/by meter, ice, picnic tables, patios.

◆◆RECREATION: rec room/area, equipped pavilion, golf nearby, shuffleboard court shuffleboard court, horseshoes, hiking trails.

Pets welcome, breed restrict, quantity restrict. Partial handicap access. No tents. Open all yr. Big rigs welcome. Escort to site. Clubs welcome. Rate in 2010 $27-29 for 2 persons. Member ARVC, MOARC. FMCA discount.

Phone: (816)779-6300
Address: 22901 SE Outer Rd, Peculiar, MO 64078
Lat/Lon: 38.70607/-94.43832
Email: ppprvpark@aol.com
Web: www.peculiarparkplacervpark.com

SEE AD KANSAS CITY PAGE 470

PERRY—B-4

FRANK RUSSELL REC. AREA (COE - Mark Twain Lake) —(Rails) *From jct Hwy 154 & Hwy J: Go 11 mi N on Hwy J.* FACILITIES: 65 sites, typical site width 20 ft, 65 E, (20/30 amps), tenting, dump. RECREATION: boating, canoeing, lake fishing, playground. Open Mar 30 - Sep 24. Phone: (573)735-4097.

(N) RAY BEHRENS RECREATION AREA (COE - Mark Twain Lake)—(Ralls) *From jct Hwy 154 & Hwy J: Go 8 mi N on Hwy J.* FACILITIES: 165 sites, typical site width 20 ft, 165 E, (50 amps), tenting, dump. RECREATION: boating, ramp, dock, lake fishing, playground. Partial handicap access. Open Mar 16 - Nov 21. Phone: (573)735-4097.

PERRYVILLE—D-5

(W) PERRYVILLE CAMPGROUND—(Perry) *From jct I-55 (exit 129) & Hwy 51: Go 1 mi N on access road on west side of interstate. Enter on L.*

WELCOME

◆◆◆◆FACILITIES: 108 sites, typical site width 25 ft, 98 full hkups, 10 W&E, (20/30/50 amps), 85 pull-thrus, WiFi Instant Internet at site, family camping, tenting, RV's/park model rentals, cabins, RV storage, dump, non-guest dump $, laundry, groceries, RV supplies, LP gas by weight/by meter, ice, picnic tables, fire rings, grills, wood.

◆◆◆RECREATION: equipped pavilion, pond fishing, fishing supplies, golf nearby, bsktball, playground, activities, (wkends), horseshoes, sports field, hiking trails, v-ball. Rec open to public.

Pets welcome. Open all yr. Big rigs welcome. Escort to site. Clubs welcome. Rate in 2010 $30-38 for 2 persons. MC/VISA/DISC/Debit.

PERRYVILLE CAMPGROUND—Continued on next page

Woodall's Tip... Each state/province begins with travel information and a map, both of which are updated annually.

PERRYVILLE—Continued
PERRYVILLE CAMPGROUND—Continued

Phone: (573)547-8303
Address: 300 Lake Dr, Perryville, MO 63775
Lat/Lon: 37.72565/-89.90427
Email: perryvillecampground@charterinternet.com
Web: www.perryvillecampground.com

SEE AD THIS PAGE

PIEDMONT—E-5

(NW) BLUFF VIEW PARK (COE Clearwater Lake)—(Reynolds) *From town: Go 2-1/2 mi N on Hwy-49, then 7 mi W on CR-AA.* FACILITIES: 61 sites, typical site width 15 ft, 20 W&E, (30/50 amps), 41 no hkups, tenting, dump. RECREATION: boating, ramp, dock, lake fishing, playground. Partial handicap access. Open all yr. Facilities fully operational May 13 - Sep 13. Phone: (573)223-7777.

(SW) PIEDMONT PARK (COE Clearwater Lake)—(Reynolds) *From town: Go 1 mi S on Hwy-34, then 5-1/2 mi SW & NW on CR-HH.* FACILITIES: 97 sites, typical site width 15 ft, 76 E, (30 amps), 21 no hkups, 3 pull-thrus, tenting, dump. RECREATION: lake swim, boating, ramp, dock, lake fishing, playground. Partial handicap access. Open all yr. Phone: (573)223-7777.

(SW) RIVER ROAD PARK (COE Clearwater Lake)—(Wayne) *From town: Go 1 mi S on Hwy-34, then 4 mi SW & NW on CR-HH.* FACILITIES: 97 sites, typical site width 15 ft, 97 E, (20/30 amps), 3 pull-thrus, tenting, dump. RECREATION: lake swim, boating, canoeing, ramp, lake/river fishing, playground. Partial handicap access. Open all yr. Phone: (573)223-7777.

PINEVILLE—E-2

(W) Big Elk Camp & Canoe Rental—(McDonald) *At jct of Bus 71 & CR H. (Pineville/H exit). Enter on L.* ◆◆◆FACILITIES: 93 sites, typical site width 20 ft, 73 full hkups, 15 W&E, 5 E, (20/30/50 amps), 21 pull-thrus, family camping, tenting, dump. ◆◆◆◆RECREATION: river/boating, canoeing, river fishing. Pets welcome, breed restrict. Open all yr. Big rigs welcome. Rate in 2010 $25 for 2 persons. Member ARVC, MOARC.

Phone: (417)223-4635
Address: 402 Bus Hwy 71, Pineville, MO 64856
Lat/Lon: 36.58759/-94.38613
Email: paddle_us@yahoo.com
Web: www.bigelkcampcanoe.com

PITTSBURG—D-3

(S) PITTSBURG PARK (COE Pomme de Terre Lake)—(Hickory) *From jct Hwy 64 & CR RA: Go 2-1/2 mi E on CR RA.* FACILITIES: 65 sites, typical site width 20 ft, 65 no hkups, tenting, dump, laundry. RECREATION: lake swim, boating, ramp, dock, lake fishing. Open all yr. Phone: (417)852-4291.

(SW) POMME DE TERRE STATE PARK—(Hickory) *From jct US 54 & Hwy 254: Go 5 mi S on Hwy 254 to Hwy 64, then go 8 mi S to 64B, then go 4 mi W on 64B. Enter at end.*

WELCOME

FACILITIES: 184 sites, 20 full hkups, 123 E, (30/50 amps), 41 no hkups, 10 pull-thrus, tenting, dump, laundry, ice, picnic tables, fire rings, grills, wood.

RECREATION: pavilion, lake swim, boating, ramp, dock, lake fishing, hiking trails.

Open all yr. Facilities fully operational Apr 1 - Oct 31. MC/VISA/DISC/AMEX.

Phone: (417)852-4291
Address: HC 77 Hwy 64B, Pittsburg, MO 65724
Web: www.mostateparks.com

SEE AD TRAVEL SECTION PAGE 451

PLATTE CITY—B-2

(E) Basswood Country Resort—(Platte) *From jct I-29 & Hwy 92 (exit 18): Go 3-3/4 mi E on Hwy 92, then 1-3/4 mi N on Winan Rd, then 2 blocks W on Interurban Rd. Enter on L.* ◆◆◆◆◆FACILITIES: 159 sites, typical site width 30 ft, 159 full hkups, (20/30/50 amps), 44 pull-thrus, family camping, tenting, laundry, full svc store. ◆◆◆◆◆RECREATION: swim pool, lake fishing, playground. Pets welcome. Partial handicap access. Open all yr. Big rigs welcome. Green Friendly. Rate in 2010 $34 for 2 persons. Member ARVC, MOARC. Phone: (816)858-5556. FCRV discount. FMCA discount.

POPLAR BLUFF—E-5

(N) Camelot RV Campground—(Butler) *W'bnd on US 60: Take Springfield/St. Louis exit, go 1-1/2 mi NW on 60/67 to park entrance road (enter on right). E'bnd from jct US 60 & Poplar Bluff exit: Go 3 mi on Poplar Bluff (enter on left). Enter on L.* ◆◆◆◆FACILITIES: 76 sites, typical site width 30 ft, 76 full hkups, (20/30/50 amps), 34 pull-thrus, laundry. Pets welcome. No tents. Open all yr. Big rigs welcome. Rate in 2010 $27-33 for 2 persons. Member ARVC, MOARC. Phone: (573)785-1016. FMCA discount.

Missouri State Tree: Flowering Dogwood

REVERE—A-4

BATTLE OF ATHENS STATE HISTORIC SITE—(Clark) *From jct Hwy 81 & CR CC: Go E on CR CC.* FACILITIES: 29 sites, 15 E, (30 amps), 14 no hkups, tenting, dump. RECREATION: boating, ramp, lake fishing. Partial handicap access. Open Mar 1 - Nov 30. Phone: (660)877-3871.

ROBERTSVILLE—C-5

(E) ROBERTSVILLE STATE PARK—(Franklin) *From jct I-44 & Hwy O: Go 5 mi E on Hwy O. Enter on L.*

WELCOME

FACILITIES: 26 sites, typical site width 20 ft, 14 E, (30 amps), 12 no hkups, tenting, dump, portable dump, laundry, picnic tables, fire rings, grills, wood, controlled access.

RECREATION: pavilion, boating, canoeing, ramp, river fishing, playground, hiking trails.

Partial handicap access. Open all yr. No reservations. Max stay 15 days. MC/VISA/DISC/AMEX.

Phone: (636)257-3788
Address: 900 State Park Dr, Robertsville, MO 63072
Lat/Lon: 38.418139/-90.817444
Email: moparks@mail.dnr.state.mo.us
Web: www.mostateparks.com

SEE AD TRAVEL SECTION PAGE 451

ROLLA—D-4

MARK TWAIN NATIONAL FOREST (Lane Spring Campground)—(Phelps) *From jct Hwy-72 & US-63: Go 12 mi S on US-63, then 1 mi W on FR-1892.* FACILITIES: 18 sites, 18 no hkups, 2 pull-thrus, tenting. RECREATION: stream fishing, playground. Partial handicap access. Open all yr. Phone: (573)364-4621.

(S) Three Springs RV Park & Campground—(Phelps) *From jct I-44 & US 63 (exit 186): Go 18 mi S on US 63 to CR 6050, then go 1/4 mi E on CR 6050. Enter on R.* ◆◆◆FACILITIES: 33 sites, 30 full hkups, 3 W&E, (20/30/50 amps), 26 pull-thrus, family camping, tenting, laundry. ◆◆◆RECREATION: swim pool, play equipment. Pets welcome. Open all yr. Big rigs welcome. Rate in 2010 $20 for 2 persons. Member ARVC. Phone: (573)201-1579.

ROUND SPRING—D-4

OZARK NATIONAL SCENIC RIVERWAYS (Pulltite)—(Carter) *From town: Go 4 mi N on Hwy-19, then 4 mi W on CR-EE.* FACILITIES: 55 sites, typical site width 15 ft, 55 no hkups, tenting, ltd groc. RECREATION: river swim, boating, ramp, river fishing. Partial handicap access. Open all yr. Phone: (573)323-4236.

OZARK NATIONAL SCENIC RIVERWAYS (Round Spring Campground)—(Carter) *In town on Hwy-19.* FACILITIES: 60 sites, typical site width 15 ft, 60 no hkups, tenting, dump, laundry, ltd groc. RECREATION: river swim, boating, ramp, river fishing, playground. Partial handicap access. Open all yr. Phone: (573)323-4236.

RUSHVILLE—B-1

(SW) LEWIS & CLARK STATE PARK—(Buchanan) *From jct US-59 & Hwy-45: Go 1 mi S on Hwy-45, then 1 mi W on Hwy-138. Enter on R.*

WELCOME

FACILITIES: 70 sites, typical site width 25 ft, 63 E, (50 amps), 7 no hkups, 15 pull-thrus, tenting, dump, laundry, picnic tables, fire rings, grills, wood.

RECREATION: pavilion, lake swim, boating, ramp, lake fishing, playground.

Partial handicap access. Open all yr. No reservations. Max stay 15 days. MC/VISA/DISC/AMEX.

Phone: (816)579-5564
Address: 801 Lake Crest Blvd, Rushville, MO 64484
Lat/Lon: 39.542278/-95.043611
Web: www.mostateparks.com

SEE AD TRAVEL SECTION PAGE 451

Burt Bacharach, songwriter, is from Missouri.

ST. CHARLES—C-5

(N) SUNDERMEIER BANQUET & CONFERENCE CENTER—*From jct Hwy 370 & N 3rd St/Hwy 94 (exit 7): Go 3/10 mi W on Hwy 94, then 2 blocks E on Transit St. Enter at end.* Banquet facilities and outside patios for up to 300 with unlimited food service. Event Room with seating up to 80. Clubhouse for up to 40. Rallies, reunions, conventions, caravans, etc. welcome. Open all yr.

WELCOME

Phone: (636)940-7712
Address: 111 Transit St, St. Charles, MO 63301
Lat/Lon: 38.79764/-90.47368

SEE AD ST. LOUIS PAGE 477

(N) SUNDERMEIER BEEF EATERS RESTAURANT—*From jct Hwy 370 & N 3rd St/Hwy 94 (exit 7): Go 3/10 mi W on Hwy 94, then 2 blocks E on Transit St. Enter at end.* Comfortable casual atmosphere. Steaks & Prime Rib grilled to perfection, our speciality. Delicious Entress-Chops, Chicken, Fresh Seafood & Pasta, prepared by our own chef. Cocktails available. Open Mon - Fri 11am-9:30pm, Sat & Sun, 4pm-9:30pm. Open all yr. MC/VISA/DISC/AMEX/Debit.

WELCOME

Phone: (636)916-5874
Address: 111 Transit St, St. Charles, MO 63301
Lat/Lon: 38.79764/-90.47368

SEE AD ST. LOUIS PAGE 477

(N) SUNDERMEIER RV PARK & CONFERENCE CENTER—(St. Charles) *From jct Hwy 370 & N 3rd St/Hwy 94 (exit 7): Go 3/10 mi W on Hwy 94, then 2 blocks E on Transit St. Enter at end.*

WELCOME

HISTORIC ST. CHARLES & ST. LOUIS

Our Best Parks In America with it's 5W rating offers deluxe amenities, gourmet restaurant, & more. History comes alive in St. Charles's 19th Century district-dining, antique/craft shopping, casinos. www.sundermeierrvpark.com.

◆◆◆◆◆FACILITIES: 106 sites, typical site width 28 ft, 106 full hkups, (20/30/50 amps), some extd stay sites, 39 pull-thrus, cable TV, phone/WiFi Instant Internet at site, cabins, RV storage, laundry, ltd groc, RV supplies, LP gas by weight/by meter, ice, picnic tables, patios.

◆◆◆RECREATION: rec hall, rec room/area, equipped pavilion, golf nearby, hiking trails, local tours.

Pets welcome, breed restrict. No tents. Open all yr. Full handicap access. Big rigs welcome. Clubs welcome. Green Friendly. Rate in 2010 $50-55 for 2 persons. MC/VISA/DISC/Debit. Member ARVC, MOARC. FMCA discount.

Text 107995 to (440)725-8687 to see our Visual Tour.

Phone: (800)929-0832
Address: 111 Transit St, St. Charles, MO 63301-0949
Lat/Lon: 38.79770/-90.47375
Email: reservations@sundermeierrvpark.com
Web: www.sundermeierrvpark.com

SEE AD ST. LOUIS PAGE 477 AND AD TRAVEL SECTION PAGE 451

Find a park or campground Woodall's does not list? Tell us about it! Use Reader Comment Forms located after the Alphabetical Quick Reference pages.

ST. JOSEPH—B-1

(SE) **BEACON RV PARK**—(Buchanan) *From jct I-29 (exit 46B) and US 36W: Go 1/4 mi W on US 36 (exit Belt Hwy), then 3/4 mi N on Belt Hwy. Enter on L.*

WELCOME

◆◆◆◆FACILITIES: 59 sites, typical site width 25 ft, 59 full hkups, (20/30/50 amps), 50 amps ($), some extd stay sites, 17 pull-thrus, cable TV, ($), WiFi Instant Internet at site ($), family camping, tenting, RV storage, laundry, RV supplies, LP gas by weight/by meter, ice, picnic tables, patios.

◆◆RECREATION: rec hall, rec room/area, golf nearby, horseshoes.

Pets welcome. Partial handicap access. Open all yr. Big rigs welcome. Escort to site. Clubs welcome. Rate in 2010 $25.53-33.01 for 2 persons. MC/VISA/DISC/AMEX/Debit. Member ARVC, MOARC. FMCA discount.

Phone: (816)279-5417
Address: 822 S Belt Hwy, St. Joseph, MO 64505
Lat/Lon: 39.75878/-94.80387
Email: beaconrvparks@aol.com
Web: www.beaconrvpark.com

SEE AD THIS PAGE

(C) **GLORE PSYCHIATRIC MUSEUM**—*From jct US 36 & US 29: Go 2 mi N on Frederick Blvd, then go 1 mi W on Frederick Blvd. Enter on R.* Nationally recognized as "one of the 50 most unusual museums in the country," uses full sized replicas, illustrates how mental illness has been portrayed and treated for the past 7500 years. Open all yr. Closed Sunday, Holidays.

WELCOME

Phone: (816)364-1209
Address: 3406 Frederick, St. Joseph, MO 64506
Lat/Lon: 39.77713/-94.81573
Web: www.stjosephmuseum.org

SEE AD THIS PAGE

Woodall's Tip... If a park's management welcomes camping clubs, we'll indicate that in the listing.

ST. JOSEPH—Continued

(C) **NATIONAL MILITARY HERITAGE MUSEUM**—*From jct US 29 & US 36: Go 2 mi W on US 36 to 10th St, then go 3 blocks N to Messanie. Enter on L.* A tribute to all branches of the Armed Forces and their contributions to the United States from 1800 to present. Open all yr. 9-5 Mon-Fri. 9-12 Sat.

WELCOME

Phone: (816)233-4321
Address: 701 Messanie, St. Joseph, MO 64501
Lat/Lon: 39.76393/-94.85275
Web: www. nationalmilitaryheritagemuseum.org

SEE AD THIS PAGE

(C) **PATEE HOUSE MUSEUM & JESSE JAMES HOME**—*From jct US 29 & US 36: Go 2 mi W on US 36 to 10th St, then 1/2 mi N on 10th St to Penn, then 1/4 mi E on Penn. Enter on R.* This Nat'l Landmark was a pioneer hotel and head-quarters for the Pony Express in 1860. Visit the streets of "Old St Joe." New carousel. See Jesse James house. Open all yr.

WELCOME

Phone: (816)232-8206
Address: 1202 Penn St, St. JOseph, MO 64503
Lat/Lon: 39.75684/-94.84555
Web: www.stjoseph.net/ponyexpress/ museums

SEE AD THIS PAGE

(W) **PONY EXPRESS NATIONAL MUSEUM**—*From jct US 29 & US 36: Go 2 mi W on US 36, then 1/2 mi N on 10th St to Penn St, then 1/2 mi W on Penn St. Enter on L.* The State-of-the-art exhibits illustrate the need, creation, operation and termination of the Pony Express. Open all yr.

WELCOME

Phone: (816)279-5059
Address: 914 Penn, St. Joseph, MO 64503
Lat/Lon: 39.75676/-94.85022
Web: www.ponyexpress.org

SEE AD THIS PAGE

ST. JOSEPH—Continued

(NE) **ROBIDOUX ROW MUSEUM**—*From jct I-229 & US 36: Go 1 mi N on I-229 to St. Joseph Ave, then 3 blocks N to 3rd St, then E 100 feet on 3rd St. Enter on R.* Built in 1843 by Joseph Robidoux, the founder of St. Joseph, to help meet the needs for temporary housing during the pioneer period. Open all yr. Closed January, Monday, Holidays.

WELCOME

Phone: (816)232-5861
Address: Third and Poulin, St. Joseph, MO 64501
Lat/Lon: 39.77650/-94.85542
Web: www.robidouxrow.com

SEE AD THIS PAGE

(C) **ST. JOSEPH VISITORS BUREAU**—*From jct US 36 & I-229: Go 1/2 mi E on I-229 to Felix St (exit 6A), then 1/4 mi to 4th St, then 1 block S on 4th St. Enter on L.* Information on St. Joseph & all area attractions. Ample parking. Restrooms. Open all yr.

WELCOME

Phone: (800)785-0360
Address: 109 S 4th St, St. Joseph, MO 64501
Lat/Lon: 39.75849/-94.85493
Web: www.STJOMO.com

SEE AD THIS PAGE

(W) **TERRIBLE'S ST. JO FRONTIER CASINO**—*From jct I-229 & US 36: Go 2 mi N on I-229 to Highland Ave, then 1/4 mi W on Highland to river. Enter on L.* Riverboat casino with an 1800's atmosphere of fun and action, slot machines & table games, steakhouse, buffet & lounge, and banquet & entertainment center. Open all yr. MC/VISA/DISC. ATM.

WELCOME

Phone: (800)888-2946
Address: 777 Winners Circle, St. Joseph, MO 64505
Lat/Lon: 39.46936/-94.52501
Web: www.stjocasino.com

SEE AD THIS PAGE

(C) **THE BLACK ARCHIVES OF ST. JOSEPH**—*From jct I-29 & Frederick Ave: Go W 1.1 mi. Enter on L.* Features exhibits & displays on the St. Joseph American Experience. Includes Integration, Education, Music and Underground Railroad. Open all year. Closed Holidays. Open all yr.

WELCOME

Phone: (816)232-8471
Address: 3406 Frederick, St. Joseph, MO 64501

SEE AD THIS PAGE

(C) **THE ST. JOSEPH MUSEUM**—*From jct I-29 & Frederick Ave: Go W 1.1 mi. Enter on L.* Dedicated to the history of St. Joseph from prehistoric times to today. Extensive Native American Collection. Ruth Warrick Memorial. Open all year. Closed Holidays. Open all yr.

WELCOME

Phone: (816)232-8471
Address: 3406 Frederick Ave, St. Joseph, MO 64508

SEE AD THIS PAGE

(N) **WYETH-TOOTLE MUSEUM**—*From jct US 36 & US 29: Go 2 mi W on US 36 to 10th St, then 1 mi N on 10th Street to Charles, then go 1 block E on Charles. Enter on R.* The St. Joseph Museum is housed in a 19th century museum. Featured exhibits include an internationally famous Native American collection, St. Joseph history and natural history. Open all yr. Closed Thanksgiving, Dec 24,25,31 & Jan 1.

WELCOME

Phone: (816)232-8471
Address: 1100 Charles, St Joseph, MO 64502-0128
Lat/Lon: 39.76584/-94.84579
Web: www.stjosephmuseum.org

SEE AD THIS PAGE

ST. LOUIS—C-5

See listings at, Bowling Green, Danville, Eureka, Hannibal, Monroe City, Perryville, St. Charles, Stanton, Sullivan, MO and Ava, Cahokia, Carlinville, Carlyle, Chester, Grafton, Granite City, Litchfield, Mulberry Grove, Nashville, New Douglas, Pocahontas, IL

ST. LOUIS—Continued on next page

ST. LOUIS AREA MAP

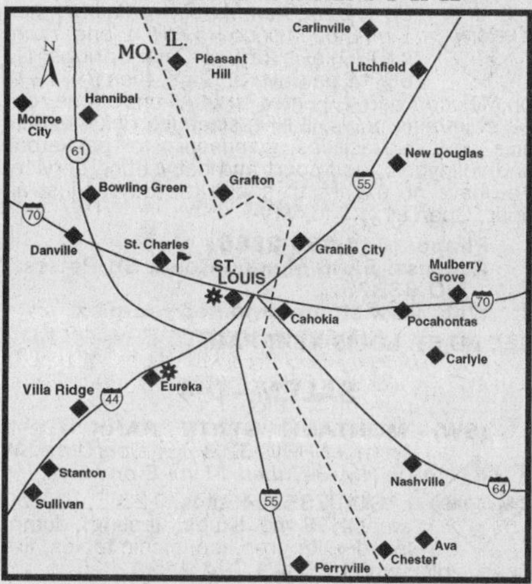

Symbols on map indicate towns within a 60 mi radius of St. Louis where campgrounds (diamonds), attractions (flags), & RV service centers & camping supply outlets (gears) are listed. Check listings for more information.

Tell Them Woodall's Sent You!

ST. LOUIS—Continued on next page

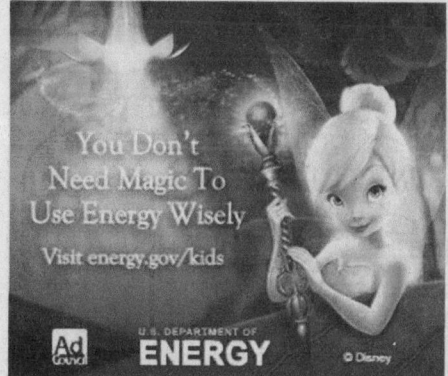

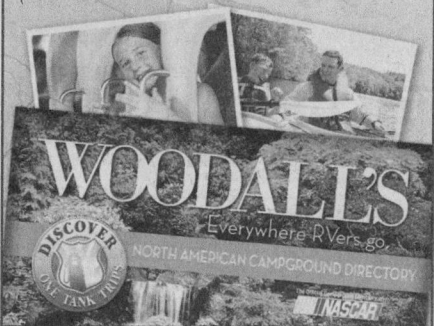

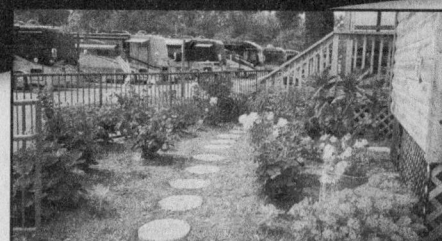

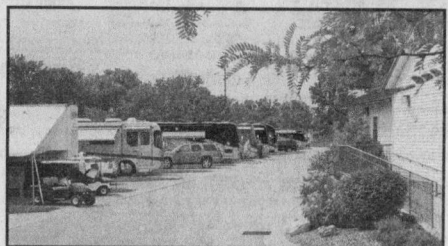

SUNDERMEIER RV PARK & CONFERENCE CENTER—*From jct I-270 (exit 22) & Hwy 370: Go 5-1/2 mi W on Hwy 370 to N 3rd St/Hwy 94 (exit 7), then 3/10 mi W on Hwy 94, then 2 blocks E on Transit St. Enter at end.*

SEE PRIMARY LISTING AT ST. CHARLES AND AD PAGE 477

ST. PETERS—C-5

(N) 370 LAKESIDE PARK RV & CAMPGROUND (UNDER CONSTRUCTION) —(St. Charles) *From jct I-70 (exit 224) & Hwy 370: Go 1 mi N on Hwy 370 (exit 2), then 1 blk N on Truman Rd/Lakeside Park Dr. Enter at end.*

FACILITIES: 100 sites, typical site width 30 ft, 50 full hkups, (20/30/50 amps), 50 no hkups, 20

pull-thrus, WiFi Instant Internet at site, family camping, tenting, laundry, ltd groc, ice, picnic tables, patios, fire rings, grills, wood.

RECREATION: boating, electric motors only, ramp, lake fishing, fishing supplies, golf nearby, bike rental 9 bike rentals, sports field, hiking trails.

Pets welcome. Partial handicap access. Open all yr. Big rigs welcome. Rate in 2010 $35-45 for 7 persons. MC/VISA.

Phone: (636)387-5253
Address: 1000 Lakeside Park Dr, St. Peters, MO 63376
Web: www.stpetersmo.net/rvpark

SEE AD ST. LOUIS NEXT PAGE

T.S. Eliot, poet, was from Missouri.

(W) ST. PETERS REC-PLEX—*W'bnd: From jct I-70 (exit 222) & Mid Rivers Mall Dr: Go 1/2 mi S on Mid River Mall Dr, then 1 mi E on Mexico Rd - (R). E'bnd: From jct I-70 (exit 225) & Cave Springs: Go 600' S on Cave Springs, then 3/4 mi W on Mexico Road (L). Enter on L.* All under one roof - 2 swimming pools, 3 NHL sized ice rinks, expansive work out facilities, gymnasuim for basketball and volleyball, food court and babysitting service. You have no excuse to spend the day or just an hour. Open all yr. MC/VISA.

Phone: (636)939-2386
Address: 5200 Mexico Road, St. Peters, MO 63376
Web: www.stpetersmo.net/rec-plex

SEE AD ST. LOUIS NEXT PAGE

SALEM—D-4

(SW) MONTAUK STATE PARK—(Dent) *From jct Hwys-32 & 19: Go 10 mi SW on Hwy-32, then 11 mi S on Hwy-119.*

FACILITIES: 154 sites, 123 E, (30/50 amps), 31 no hkups, tenting, dump, laundry, ltd groc, ice, picnic tables, fire rings, grills, wood.

RECREATION: pavilion, river/stream fishing, hiking trails.

Partial handicap access. Open all yr. Facilities fully operational Apr 1 - Oct 31. MC/VISA/DISC/AMEX.

Phone: (573)548-2201
Address: 345 County Road 6670, Salem, MO 65560
Lat/Lon: 37.450667/-91.687250
Web: www.mostateparks.com

SEE AD TRAVEL SECTION PAGE 451

SALEM—Continued on next page

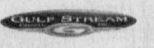

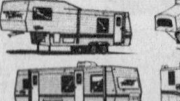

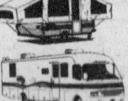

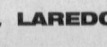

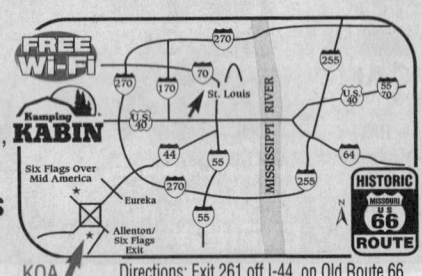

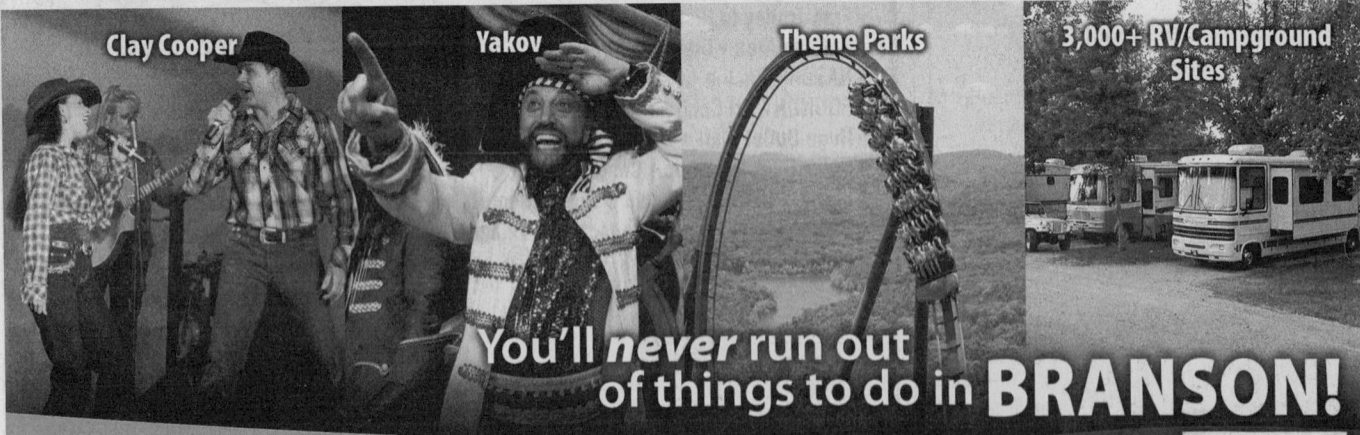

SALEM—Continued

OZARK NATIONAL SCENIC RIVERWAYS (Akers)—(Dent) *From jct Hwy-32 & Hwy-19: Go 19 mi S on Hwy-19, then 6 mi W on CR-KK.* FACILITIES: 66 sites, 66 no hkups, tenting, ltd groc. RECREATION: river swim, boating, river fishing. Open all yr. Phone: (573)323-4236.

SEDALIA—C-3

(S) Countryside Adult & Senior RV Park—(Pettis) *From jct Hwy 50 & US 65: Go 2-3/4 mi S on US 65. Enter on R.* ◊◊◊FACILITIES: 28 sites, typical site width 25 ft, accepts self-contained units only, 28 full hkups, (30/50 amps), 7 pull-thrus, dump, laundry. Pets welcome. Partial handicap access. No tents. Age restrict may apply. Open Apr 1 - Oct 15. Big rigs welcome. Rate in 2010 $23-25 for 2 persons. Member ARVC, MOARC. Phone: (660)827-6513. FMCA discount.

(W) MISSOURI STATE FAIR RV PARK—(Pettis) *From jct Hwy 50 & Hwy 65: Go 1/2 m S on Hwy 65 to 16th St, then 500 ft W on 16th St. Enter at end.* FACILITIES: 2500 sites, 1000 full hkups, 1500 W&E, (20/30/50 amps), 200 pull-thrus, tenting, dump. RECREATION: Pets welcome. Open all yr. Big rigs welcome. Phone: (660)530-5600.

SHELL KNOB—E-2

(E) CAMPBELL POINT BOAT DOCK & PARK (COE Table Rock Lake)—(Stone) *From jct Hwy-39 & CR-YY: Go 6 mi SE on CR-YY.* FACILITIES: 76 sites, typical site width 20 ft, 38 E, (30 amps), 38 no hkups, tenting, dump, ltd groc. RECREATION: lake swim, boating, ramp, dock, lake fishing, playground. Open Apr 1 - Oct 31. Phone: (417)858-3903.

(S) MARK TWAIN NATIONAL FOREST (Big Bay Campground)—(Stone) *From town: Go 1 mi SE on Hwy-39, then 3 mi SE on Hwy-YY.* FACILITIES: 38 sites, typical site width 12 ft, 38 no hkups, tenting. RECREATION: lake swim, boating, ramp, lake fishing. Partial handicap access. Open all yr. Phone: (417)847-2144.

VIOLA BOAT DOCK & PARK (COE Table Rock Lake)—(Barry) *From town: Go 6 mi S on Hwy-39, then 1 mi W on Lake Rd-39-48.* FACILITIES: 57 sites, typical site width 20 ft, 6 W&E, 21 E, (20/30 amps), 30 no hkups, tenting, dump. RECREATION: lake swim, boating, ramp, dock, lake fishing, playground. Pets welcome. Partial handicap access. Open Apr 1 - Sep 30. Phone: (417)858-3904.

Betty Grable, actress, was from Missouri.

SIKESTON—E-6

(W) HINTON PARK—(Scott) *From jct I-55 (Bertrand exit 67) & US 62: Go 2 blocks E on US 62. Enter on R.*

WELCOME

◊◊◊FACILITIES: 58 sites, typical site width 30 ft, 58 full hkups, (30/50 amps), 44 pull-thrus, cable TV, phone/WiFi Instant Internet at site, phone Internet central location, tenting, dump, non-guest dump $, laundry, RV supplies, LP gas by weight/by meter, ice, picnic tables.

Pets welcome. Partial handicap access. Open all yr. Big rigs welcome. Escort to site. Clubs welcome. Rate in 2010 $29 for 2 persons. MC/VISA/DISC/Debit. Member ARVC, MOARC. FMCA discount.

Phone: (800)327-1457
Address: 2863 E Malone Ave, Sikeston, MO 63801
Lat/Lon: 36.89426/-89.52740
Email: reservations@hintonrvpark.com
Web: www.hintonrvpark.com

SEE AD THIS PAGE

(W) TOWN & COUNTRY RV RESORT—(Scott) *From jct I-55 (exit 67 Bertrand) & US 62: Go 1-1/2 mi E on US 62. Enter on R.*

WELCOME

◊◊◊◊FACILITIES: 80 sites, typical site width 30 ft, 50 full hkups, 10 W&E, (30/50 amps), 20 no hkups, some extd stay sites, 60 pull-thrus, cable TV, WiFi Instant Internet at site, tenting, RV storage, laundry, LP gas by weight/by meter, ice, picnic tables, patios.

CAMPCLUB USA

Pets welcome. Partial handicap access. Open all yr. Big rigs welcome. Clubs welcome. Member ARVC, MOARC. FMCA discount. CCUSA 50% Discount. CCUSA reservations Required, CCUSA max stay Unlimited, Cash only for CCUSA disc., Check only for CCUSA disc.

Phone: (800)771-1339
Address: Hwy 62 East, Sikeston, MO 63801
Lat/Lon: 36.89981/-89.50806
Web: www.passport-america.com/campgrounds/CampgroundDetails.asp?CampgroundID=I054

SEE AD THIS PAGE

SMITHVILLE—B-2

(NE) CAMP BRANCH CAMPGROUND & MARINA (Clay County Park)—(Clay) *From jct I-29 & US 169N: Go N on US 169, then 6 mi E on Hwy 92, then 3 mi N on CR E, follow signs. Enter on R.* FACILITIES: 362 sites, 36 E, (30 amps), 326 no hkups, 35 pull-thrus, tenting, dump, laundry. RECREATION: lake swim, boating, canoeing, ramp, dock, lake/river/pond fishing. Pets welcome. Partial handicap access. Open all yr. Facilities fully operational Apr 15 - Oct 15. Phone: (816)407-3400.

CROWS CREEK (Clay County Park)—(St. Clair) *From jct I-35 & Hwy 92: Go 4-1/2 mi W on Hwy 92, then 3-1/2 mi N on CR E. Enter on L.* FACILITIES: 415 sites, 82 W&E, 111 E, 222 no hkups, 40 pull-thrus, tenting, dump, laundry. RECREATION: lake swim, boating, canoeing, ramp, dock, lake/river fishing, playground. Pets welcome. Partial handicap access. Open all yr. Facilities fully operational Mar 15 - Oct 15. Phone: (816)532-0803.

(NE) SMITH'S FORK CAMPGROUND—(Clay) *From jct I-435 & US 169 (exit 41B): Go N 1/2 mi on US 169 to CR-DD, then E 1-3/4 mi to Dam Rd, then E 100 ft. Enter on L.* FACILITIES: 82 sites, 82 full hkups, (30/50 amps), 20 pull-thrus, laundry. RECREATION: lake swim, boating, ramp, dock, lake fishing. Pets welcome. No tents. Open Apr 15 - Oct 15. Phone: (816)532-1028.

SPRINGFIELD—E-3

✲ **(S) RELIABLE RV CENTER**—*From jct US 65 & Chestnut Expwy: Go 200 feet W on Chestnut Expwy, then 1/4 mi S on Ingram Mill Ave. Enter on L.* SALES: travel trailers, 5th wheels, Class A motorhomes, Class C motorhomes, pre-owned unit sales. SERVICES: full-time mech, engine/chassis repair, RV appliance repair, body work/collision repair, RV towing, LP gas by

WELCOME

RELIABLE RV CENTER—Continued on next page

SPRINGFIELD—Continued
RELIABLE RV CENTER—Continued

weight/by meter, dump station, sells parts/accessories, installs hitches. Open all yr. MC/VISA/DISC/AMEX/Debit.

Phone: (866)898-2762
Address: 438 S Ingram Mill Ave, Springfield, MO 65802
Lat/Lon: 37.20359/-93.22732
Email: sales@reliablerv.com
Web: www.reliablerv.com

SEE AD THIS PAGE

(W) Springfield/Route 66 KOA—(Greene) *From jct I-44 (exit 70) & CR MM: Go 1 block S on MM, then 1 mi E on Farm Rd 140. Enter on L.* ◊◊◊◊FACILITIES: 77 sites, typical site width 32 ft, 44 full hkups, 33 W&E, (20/30/50 amps), 63 pull-thrus, family camping, tenting, dump, laundry, full svc store. ◊◊◊◊RECREATION: swim pool, playground. Pets welcome. Partial handicap access. Open all yr. Big rigs welcome. Rate in 2010 $34-45 for 2 persons. Phone: (800)562-1228. KOA discount.

(NE) THOMAS & SONS RV SUPPLY—*From jct I-44 (exit 80A) & Glenstone: Go 1 mi S on Glenstone. (Business 44). Enter on L.* SALES: pre-owned unit sales. SERVICES: full-time mech, RV appliance repair, body work/collision repair, RV storage, sells parts/accessories, installs hitches. Open all yr. MC/VISA/DISC/Debit.

Phone: (417)865-6125
Address: 1930 N Glenstone, Springfield, MO 65803
Lat/Lon: 37.23316/-93.26092
Email: thomassls@aol.com
Web: www.thomassonsrv.com

SEE AD PAGE 479

STANTON—C-4

(S) Stanton/Meramec KOA—(Franklin) *From jct I-44 & CR-W (Stanton exit 230): Go 1 block S on CR-W. Enter on R.* ◊◊◊◊FACILITIES: 51 sites, typical site width 25 ft, 16 full hkups, 14 W&E, (30/50 amps), 21 no hkups, 30 pull-thrus, tenting, dump, laundry, groceries. ◊◊◊◊RECREATION: swim pool, canoeing, pond fishing, playground. Pets welcome, breed restrict, quantity restrict. Partial handicap access. Open Mar 1 - Dec 1. Big rigs welcome. Rate in 2010 $33-50 for 2 persons. Member ARVC, MOARC. Phone: (573)927-5215. KOA discount.

STEEDMAN—C-4

(N) Wildwood—(Callaway) *From jct I-70 & US 54: Go 3-1/2 mi S on US 54 to US 54 Bus, then 2 mi S on Bus US 54 to Hwy O, then 12 mi E on Hwy O. Enter on L.* ◊◊◊FACILITIES: 19 sites, 39 ft max RV length, 19 full hkups, (30/50 amps), 6 pull-thrus, phone Internet central location, tenting, dump, laundry, groceries, ice, picnic tables, wood. ◊◊◊◊◊RECREATION: rec hall, pavilion, equipped pavilion, swim pool, wading pool, boating, 10 hp limit, ramp, dock, lake fishing, fishing supplies, bsktball, playground, shuffleboard court shuffleboard court, activities tennis, horseshoes, v-ball. Pets welcome. Partial handicap access. Open all yr. Rate in 2010 $10 for 2 persons. MC/VISA/DISC. CCUSA 50% Discount. CCUSA reservations Recommended, CCUSA max stay Unlimited.

Phone: (573)676-5317
Address: 7233 Wildwood Estates Dr, Steedman, MO 65077
Lat/Lon: 38.79320/-91.77589
Email: wloa@ktis.net
Web: www.wildwoodassociation.com

Whether you're dreaming about buying a new RV or are actively shopping, 2011 RV Buyer's Guide is your best source. It contains all the information you need to make an intelligent buying decision. Over 450 vehicles are profiled with complete information about construction features, dimensions, popular options, and more, making comparing models easy. To order your copy go to www.woodalls.com/shop.

STEELVILLE—D-4

(E) BASS' RIVER RESORT—(Crawford) *From jct Hwy 19 & Hwy 8: Go 10-1/4 mi E on Hwy 8, then 1-1/2 mi NE on asphalt entrance road. Enter on L.* ◊◊◊◊FACILITIES: 290 sites, typical site width 25 ft, 40 full hkups, 60 W&E, (30/50 amps), 190 no hkups, 20 pull-thrus, WiFi Internet central location, family camping, tenting, cabins, dump, laundry, ltd groc, ice, picnic tables, fire rings, grills, wood.

◊◊◊◊◊RECREATION: rec room/area, equipped pavilion, coin games, swim pool, river swim, canoeing, kayaking, 350 canoe/80 kayak rentals, float trips, river fishing, fishing supplies, bsktball, playground, activities, (wkends), sports field, hiking trails, v-ball.

Pets welcome. Partial handicap access. Open all yr. Facilities fully operational Mar - Nov. Big rigs welcome. Clubs welcome. Rate in 2010 $27.50-35 for 2 persons. MC/VISA/DISC/AMEX/Debit. ATM. Member ARVC, MOARC. CCUSA 50% Discount. CCUSA reservations Recommended, CCUSA max stay 2 days, CCUSA disc. not avail holidays. Discount available Oct 1-Apr 30.

Phone: (800)392-3700
Address: 204 Butts Rd, Steelville, MO 65565
Lat/Lon: 37.99222/-91.17544
Email: fdicbass@misn.com
Web: www.bassresort.com

SEE AD THIS PAGE

(E) BASS' RIVER RESORT CANOE RENTAL—*From jct Hwy 19 & Hwy 8: Go 10-1/4 mi E on Hwy 8, then 1-1/2 mi NE on asphalt entrance road. Enter on L.* Float trips from 2 hours to 2 days on the beautiful Courtois, Meramec or Huzzah Rivers. Your choice of canoes, rafts, kayaks or tubes. Open all yr. MC/VISA/DISC.

Phone: (800)392-3700
Address: 204 Butts Rd, Steelville, MO 65565
Lat/Lon: 37.99222/-91.179544
Email: fdicbass@misn.com
Web: www.basscanoeresort.com

SEE AD THIS PAGE

STEELVILLE—Continued on next page

Woodall's Tip... If you are camping in bear country, be sure to cook at least 300 feet downwind of your sleeping area. Use baking soda to rid your clothes and hands of cooking odors.

STEELVILLE—Continued

(E) HUZZAH VALLEY RESORT—(Crawford) *From jct Hwy-19 & Hwy-8: Go 9-1/2 mi E on Hwy-8. Enter on R.*

◇◇◇◇FACILITIES: 348 sites, typical site width 30 ft, 43 full hkups, 55 W&E, (20/30/50 amps), 250 no hkups, 12 pull-thrus, WiFi Instant Internet at site, family camping, tenting, cabins, RV storage, showerS, dump, laundry, ltd groc, RV supplies, ice, picnic tables, fire rings, grills, wood.

◇◇◇◇RECREATION: equipped pavilion, river swim, canoeing, kayaking, 2 rowboat/433 canoe/100 kayak rentals, float trips, river fishing, fishing supplies, playground, sports field, hiking trails, v-ball.

Pets welcome. Partial handicap access. Open all yr. Facilities fully operational Mar 1 - Nov 1. Big rigs welcome. Clubs welcome. MC/VISA/DISC/AMEX/ Debit. ATM. Member ARVC, MOARC.

Phone: (800)367-4516
Address: 970 E State Highway 8, Steelville, MO 65565
Lat/Lon: 37.97312/-91.20120
Email: vacation@huzzahvalley.com
Web: www.huzzahvalley.com

SEE AD PAGE 480

(E) HUZZAH VALLEY RESORT CANOE RENTAL—*From jct Hwy 19 & Hwy 8: Go 9-1/2 mi E on Hwy 8. Enter on R.* Canoe, raft or kayak trips on the scenic Huzzah and Courtois Rivers. Trips from 2 hours to 2 days. Open Mar 1 - Nov 1. MC/VISA.

Phone: (800)367-4516
Address: 970 E State Highway 8, Steelville, MO 65565
Lat/Lon: 37.97312/-91.20120
Email: vacation@huzzahvalley.com
Web: www.huzzahvalley.com

SEE AD PAGE 480

STOCKTON—D-2

(E) CRABTREE COVE (COE Stockton Lake)—(Cedar) *From town: Go 3-1/2 mi SE on Hwy-32, then 1/2 mi SW. 1 mi S of the dam.* FACILITIES: 58 sites, typical site width 20 ft, 31 E, (30 amps), 27 no hkups, 2 pull-thrus, tenting, dump. RECREATION: boating, ramp, dock, lake fishing. Partial handicap access. Open all yr. Phone: (417)276-6799.

(S) HAWKER POINT (COE - Stockton Lake)—(Cedar) *From town: Go 6 mi S on Hwy 39, then 5.2 mi E on CR H.* FACILITIES: 62 sites, typical site width 15 ft, 30 E, (20/30 amps), 32 no hkups, tenting, dump. RECREATION: lake swim, boating, ramp, dock, lake fishing. Open all yr. Phone: (417)276-7266.

(SE) MASTERS AREA (COE Stockton Lake)—(Cedar) *From town: Go 10 mi SE on Hwy-32, then 3-1/2 mi S on CR-RA.* FACILITIES: 66 sites, typical site width 15 ft, 66 no hkups, tenting, dump. RECREATION: lake swim, boating, ramp, dock, lake fishing. Partial handicap access. Open all yr. Phone: (417)276-3113.

MUTTON CREEK (COE Stockton Lake)—(Dade) *From town: Go 12 mi S on Hwy-39, then 5 mi E on CR-Y (Arcola).* FACILITIES: 12 sites, 12 E, (20/30 amps), tenting, dump. RECREATION: lake swim, boating, ramp, dock, lake fishing. Open all yr. Facilities fully operational Apr - Sep. Phone: (417)995-3355.

(S) ORLEANS TRAIL MARINA & PUBLIC USE AREA (COE Stockton Lk)—(Cedar) *From jct Hwy-39 & CR-RB: Go 3/4 mi E on CR-RB.* FACILITIES: 118 sites, typical site width 15 ft, 12 E, 106 no hkups, tenting, dump, groceries. RECREATION: lake swim, boating, ramp, dock, lake fishing. Partial handicap access. Open all yr. Phone: (417)276-6948.

(S) RUARK BLUFF (COE Stockton Lake)—(Dade) *From town: Go 12 mi S on Hwy-39, then 4 mi E on CR-Y, then 1 mi S on CR-H(Arcola).* FACILITIES: 165 sites, typical site width 15 ft, 68 E, (30 amps), 97 no hkups, tenting, dump. RECREATION: lake swim, boating, ramp, dock, lake fishing, playground. Partial handicap access. Open all yr. Phone: (417)637-5279.

(SE) STOCKTON STATE PARK—(Cedar) *From Hwy 32 & Hwy 39: Go 6 mi S on Hwy 39, then go 6 mi SE on Hwy 215. Enter on L.*

FACILITIES: 74 sites, 60 E, (30/50 amps), 14 no hkups, tenting, dump, laundry, ltd groc, picnic tables, fire rings, grills, wood.

RECREATION: pavilion, lake swim, boating, canoeing, ramp, dock, canoe rentals, lake fishing, hiking trails.

Partial handicap access. Open all yr. Facilities fully operational Apr 1 - Oct 31. MC/VISA/DISC/AMEX.

Phone: (417)276-4259
Address: 19100 S Hwy 215, Dadeville, MO 65635
Web: www.mostateparks.com

SEE AD TRAVEL SECTION PAGE 451

Vincent Price, actor, was from Missouri.

STOUTSVILLE—B-4

(S) MARK TWAIN STATE PARK—(Monroe) *From jct US-24 & Hwy-107: Go 6 mi S on Hwy-107. Enter on L.*

FACILITIES: 97 sites, 75 E, (30/50 amps), 22 no hkups, tenting, dump, laundry, picnic tables, fire rings, grills, wood.

RECREATION: pavilion, lake swim, boating, ramp, lake fishing, hiking trails.

Open all yr. Facilities fully operational Apr 1 - Oct 31. MC/VISA/DISC/AMEX.

Phone: (573)565-3440
Address: 20057 State Park Office Rd., Stoutsville, MO 65283
Web: www.mostateparks.com

SEE AD TRAVEL SECTION PAGE 451

STRAFFORD—E-3

(E) PARADISE IN THE WOODS RV PARK & CAMPGROUND—(Webster) *From jct I-44 (exit 96) & Evergreen: Go 2-1/4 mi W on N Service Rd, then 1 block N on Grier Branch Rd. Enter on R.*

A PRIVATE PARADISE FOR CAMPERS
Getting away from it all is why we take vacations. This is a quiet & peaceful park. Just 10 min from Springfield, 30 min from Branson. Visit the fast paced adventures, then come, relax in the solitude of PARADISE IN THE WOODS RV PARK.

◇◇◇FACILITIES: 43 sites, typical site width 25 ft, 43 full hkups, (20/30/50 amps), 43 pull-thrus, phone Internet central location, family camping, tenting, dump, non-guest dump $, laundry, ltd groc, LP gas by weight/by meter, ice, picnic tables, patios, wood.

◇◇◇RECREATION: rec room/area, swim pool, pond fishing, golf nearby, playground, horseshoes.

Pets welcome. Partial handicap access. Open all yr. Big rigs welcome. Escort to site. Clubs welcome. Rate in 2010 $20-25 for 2 persons. MC/ VISA/DISC/AMEX/Debit. Member ARVC, MOARC.

Phone: (417)859-2175
Address: 2481 Grier Branch Rd, Strafford, MO 65757
Lat/Lon: 37.28730/-93.04163
Email: paradiserv55@yahoo.com

SEE AD SPRINGFIELD PAGE 480

(E) RV PARK STRAFFORD—(Greene) *From jct I-44 (exit 88) & Hwy 125: Go 1 block S on Hwy 125, then 200 feet E on Hwy OO. Enter on L.*

◇◇◇FACILITIES: 50 sites, typical site width 15 ft, 50 full hkups, (30/50 amps), some extd stay sites, 24 pull-thrus, RV storage, dump, non-guest dump $, laundry, LP gas by weight/by meter, picnic tables.

Pets welcome. No tents. Open all yr. Big rigs welcome. Clubs welcome. Rate in 2010 $20 for 2 persons. MC/VISA/Debit.

Phone: (417)736-3382
Address: 313 E. Old Rte 66, Straford, MO 65757
Lat/Lon: 37.26918/-93.11214

SEE AD SPRINGFIELD PAGE 480

SULLIVAN—C-4

(S) MERAMEC STATE PARK—(Franklin) *From jct I-44 & Hwy 185: Go 3 mi S on Hwy 185. Enter on R.*

FACILITIES: 209 sites, 18 full hkups, 14 W&E, 125 E, (20/30/50 amps), 52 no hkups, 13 pull-thrus, tenting, cabins, dump, laundry, ltd groc, ice, picnic tables, wood, controlled access.

RECREATION: pavilion, river swim, boating, canoeing, ramp, canoe rentals, river fishing, hiking trails.

Partial handicap access. Open all yr. Facilities fully operational Apr 1 - Oct 31. MC/VISA/DISC/AMEX.

Phone: (573)468-6072
Address: 115 Meramec Park Dr, Sullivan, MO 63080
Web: www.mostateparks.com

SEE AD TRAVEL SECTION PAGE 451

THEODOSIA—E-3

BUCK CREEK PARK (COE - Bull Shoals Lake)—(Taney) *From jct US 160 & Hwy 125: Go 9-1/2 mi S on Hwy 125 (Protem).* FACILITIES: 38 sites, typical site width 15 ft, 36 ft max RV length, 36 E, (30 amps), 2 no hkups, tenting, dump, ltd groc. RECREATION: lake swim, boating, ramp, dock, lake fishing, playground. Partial handicap access. Open all yr. Phone: (870)785-4313.

THEODOSIA—Continued

(E) THEODOSIA PARK (COE Bull Shoals Lake)—(Ozark) *In town S of US-160.* FACILITIES: 108 sites, 106 E, (30/50 amps), 2 no hkups, tenting, dump, ltd groc. RECREATION: lake swim, boating, ramp, dock, lake fishing, playground. Partial handicap access. Open all yr. Phone: (417)273-4626.

TIGHTWAD—C-2

BUCKSAW POINT (COE - Harry S. Truman Reservoir) —(Henry) *From jct Hwy-7 & CR-U: Go 4 mi S on CR-U.* FACILITIES: 308 sites, typical site width 20 ft, 115 E, (50 amps), 193 no hkups, 38 pull-thrus, tenting, dump, laundry. RECREATION: lake swim, boating, ramp, dock, lake fishing, playground. Partial handicap access. Open all yr. Facilities fully operational Apr 15 - Oct 15. Phone: (660)438-7317.

WINDSOR CROSSING (COE - Harry S Truman Reservoir)—(Henry) *From jct Hwy-7 & CR-PP: Go 5 mi N on CR-PP.* FACILITIES: 47 sites, typical site width 20 ft, 47 no hkups, 7 pull-thrus, tenting. RECREATION: lake swim, boating, ramp, dock, lake/river fishing. Partial handicap access. Open all yr. Facilities fully operational May - Oct 15. Phone: (660)438-7317.

TRENTON—A-2

(NW) CROWDER STATE PARK—(Grundy) *From jct US 65 & Hwy 5: Go 5 mi W on Hwy 5, then go 1 mi N on Hwy 146. Enter on R.*

FACILITIES: 41 sites, typical site width 15 ft, 31 E, (30 amps), 10 no hkups, 8 pull-thrus, tenting, dump, laundry, picnic tables, fire rings, wood.

RECREATION: pavilion, lake swim, boating, canoeing, ramp, lake/stream fishing, playground, sports field, hiking trails.

Partial handicap access. Open Mar 1 - Nov 30. No reservations. Max stay 15 days. MC/VISA/DISC/ AMEX.

Phone: (660)359-6473
Address: 76 Hwy 128, Trenton, MO 64683
Lat/Lon: 40.094472/-93.662194
Web: www.mostateparks.com

SEE AD TRAVEL SECTION PAGE 451

TROY—C-4

(NE) CUIVRE RIVER STATE PARK—(Lincoln) *From jct US 61 & Hwy 47: Go 3 mi E on Hwy 47, then go 1 mi N on Hwy 147. Enter on R.*

FACILITIES: 106 sites, 31 full hkups, 23 E, (30 amps), 52 no hkups, tenting, dump, laundry, picnic tables, fire rings, grills, wood.

RECREATION: pavilion, lake swim, boating, electric motors only, ramp, lake/stream fishing, hiking trails.

Partial handicap access. Open all yr. Facilities fully operational Apr 1 - Oct 31. MC/VISA/DISC/AMEX.

Phone: (636)528-7247
Address: 678 State Route 147, Troy, MO 63379
Web: www.mostateparks.com

SEE AD TRAVEL SECTION PAGE 451

VAN BUREN—E-4

(SE) Big Spring RV Camp—(Carter) *From jct US 60 & Hwy 103: Go 1/4 mi S on Hwy 103, then 1/2 mi E on E. Chicopee Rd. Enter on L.* ◇◇◇FACILITIES: 50 sites, typical site width 40 ft, 50 full hkups, (20/30/50 amps), family camping, tenting, dump, laundry, ltd groc. ◇◇◇◇RECREATION: river swim, ramp, river fishing. Pets welcome, breed restrict. Partial handicap access. Open all yr. Facilities fully operational May 26 - Labor Day. Big rigs welcome. Rate in 2010 $26.70 for 2 persons. Phone: (800)354-6295.

Reserve Online at Woodalls.com

(S) OZARK NATIONAL SCENIC RIVERWAYS (Big Spring)—(Carter) *From town: Go 4 mi S on Hwy-103.* FACILITIES: 123 sites, typical site width 15 ft, 123 no hkups, tenting. RECREATION: river swim, boating, ramp, river fishing, playground. Partial handicap access. Open all yr. Phone: (573)323-4236.

(N) Yogi Bear's Jellystone Park At Van Buren —(Carter) *From jct US 60 & County Road M: Go 2-1/2 mi N on County Road M, then 3/4 mi E on paved entrance road. Enter on R.* ◇◇◇◇FACILITIES: 106 sites, 10 full hkups, 69 W&E, (20/30/50 amps), 27 no hkups, 5 pull-thrus, cable TV, WiFi Instant Internet at site, phone Internet central location, family camping, tenting, dump, portable dump, laundry, groceries, RV supplies, ice, picnic tables, fire rings, grills, wood. ◇◇◇◇◇RECREATION: rec hall, swim pool, river swim, canoeing, kayaking, ramp, float trips, river fishing, fishing supplies, mini-golf, ($), playground, activities, v-ball. Pets welcome. Partial handicap access. Open all yr. Facilities fully operational Mar 15 - Oct 15. Big rigs welcome. Rate in 2010 $38-47 for 2 persons. MC/ VISA/DISC/AMEX/Debit. Member ARVC, MOARC.

CAMPCLUB USA

Yogi Bear's Jellystone Park At Van Buren—Continued on next page

VAN BUREN—Continued
Yogi Bear's Jellystone Park At Van Buren—Continued

CCUSA 50% Discount. CCUSA reservations Recommended, CCUSA max stay 7 days. No holidays or weekends Memorial Day thru Labor Day weekends.

Phone: (888)763-5628
Address: Cty Rd M 127, Van Buren, MO 63965
Lat/Lon: 37.01667/-91.03334
Email: contactjellystone@yahoo.com
Web: www.currentriverjellystone.com

VILLA RIDGE—C-5

(W) Pin Oak Creek RV Park—(Franklin) *W'bnd: From jct I-44 (exit 247) & Hwy 50 W: Go 1/4 mi W on Hwy 50, then 1 mi E on Hwy AT (R). E'bnd: From jct I-44 (exit 247) & Hwy 50/AT: Go 1/4 mi W (left at bottom of exit, then 1/2 mi E on Hwy AT (R). Enter on R.* ◊◊◊◊FACILITIES: 179 sites, typical site width 25 ft, 150 full hkups, 9 W&E, (20/30/50 amps), 20 no hkups, 75 pull-thrus, family camping, tenting, laundry, groceries. ◊◊◊◊◊RECREATION: swim pool, lake fishing, playground. Pets welcome. Partial handicap access. Open all yr. Big rigs welcome. Rate in 2010 $35.62-45.23 for 4 persons. Member ARVC, MOARC. Phone: (888)474-6625.

WAPPAPELLO—E-5

(N) PEOPLES CREEK CAMPGROUND (COE Wappapello Lake)—(Wayne) *From North end of dam: Go 1/2 mi N on Hwy-D.* FACILITIES: 57 sites, 57 E, (50 amps), 2 pull-thrus, tenting. RECREATION: lake swim, boating, ramp, dock, lake fishing. Partial handicap access. Open all yr. Phone: (573)222-8234.

(S) REDMAN CREEK CAMPGROUNDS (COE Wappapello Lake)—(Butler) *From S end of dam: Go 1/2 mi S on Hwy T.* FACILITIES: 116 sites, typical site width 15 ft, 30 full hkups, 80 E, (20 amps), 6 no hkups, tenting, dump. RECREATION: lake swim, boating, ramp, dock, lake fishing, playground. Partial handicap access. Open Apr 1 - Oct 31. Phone: (573)222-8233.

WARSAW—C-3

(W) BERRY BEND (COE - Harry S. Truman Reservoir)—(Benton) *From town: Go 4 mi W on Hwy 7, then 3 mi W on CR Z, then 2 mi S on paved access road.* FACILITIES: 113 sites, typical site width 20 ft, 113 E, (30 amps), 4 pull-thrus, tenting, dump, laundry. RECREATION: lake swim, boating, ramp, dock, lake/river fishing, playground. Partial handicap access. Open all yr. Facilities fully operational Apr 15 - Oct 15. Phone: (660)438-3872.

(S) DEERREST CAMPPARK—(Benton) *From jct US 65 & Hwy 7 (N of town): Go 3/4 mi S on US 65 to Warsaw exit (E Main), then 1/4 mi W to Hackberry Dr. Enter on R.*

◊◊◊FACILITIES: 34 sites, typical site width 25 ft, 14 full hkups, 14 W&E, (20/30 amps), 6 no hkups, some extd stay sites, 7 pull-thrus, tenting, RV storage, dump, non-guest dump $, picnic tables, fire rings.

◊RECREATION: equipped pavilion, lake fishing.

Pets welcome. Partial handicap access. Open Mar 15 - Oct 30. Rate in 2010 $15-20 for 2 persons. Member ARVC, MOARC.

Woodall's Tip... Looking for a particular campground? Use our Alphabetical Quick Reference in the middle & near the end of this Directory.

WARSAW—Continued
DEERREST CAMPPARK—Continued

Phone: (660)438-6005
Address: 807 Gasoline Alley, Warsaw, MO 65355
Lat/Lon: 38.23866/-93.36886
Email: deerrest@iland.net
Web: www.gocampingamerica.com/deerrest

SEE AD THIS PAGE

(NW) HARRY S. TRUMAN STATE PARK—(Benton) *From jct I-65 & US 7: Go 5 mi W on US 7, then go 3 mi N on CR UU. Enter on L.*

FACILITIES: 198 sites, 98 E, (30/50 amps), 100 no hkups, tenting, dump, laundry, ltd groc, picnic tables, fire rings, grills, wood, controlled access.

RECREATION: pavilion, lake swim, boating, ramp, dock, lake fishing, hiking trails.

Partial handicap access. Open all yr. Facilities fully operational Apr 1 - Oct 31. MC/VISA/DISC/AMEX.

Phone: (660)438-7711
Address: 28761 State Park Rd, Warsaw, MO 65355
Web: www.mostateparks.com

SEE AD TRAVEL SECTION PAGE 451

(W) LONGSHOAL (COE - Harry S Truman Reservoir)—(Benton) *From jct US-65 & Hwy-7: Go 10 mi W on Hwy-7.* FACILITIES: 123 sites, typical site width 20 ft, 96 E, (30 amps), 27 no hkups, tenting, dump, laundry. RECREATION: lake swim, boating, ramp, dock, lake fishing, playground. Partial handicap access. Open all yr. Phone: (660)438-7317.

(S) OSAGE BLUFF (COE - Harry S Truman Reservoir)—(Benton) *From jct US 65 & Hwy 83: Go 4 mi S on Hwy 83.* FACILITIES: 68 sites, typical site width 20 ft, 42 E, (20/30 amps), 26 no hkups, tenting, dump, laundry. RECREATION: boating, ramp, dock, lake/river fishing, playground. Partial handicap access. Open all yr. Phone: (660)438-3873.

(N) THIBAUT POINT (COE - Harry S. Truman Reservoir)—(Benton) *From town: Go 5 mi N on US 65, then 3 mi W on CR T, then 1 mi S on gravel road.* FACILITIES: 51 sites, typical site width 20 ft, 26 E, (30 amps), 25 no hkups, tenting, dump, laundry. RECREATION: lake swim, boating, ramp, lake fishing. Partial handicap access. Open all yr. Phone: (660)438-2767.

WAYNESVILLE—D-3

ROUBIDOUX SPRINGS CAMPGROUND (City Park)—(Pulaski) *From jct I-44 (exit 156) & Hwy H & Business I-44: Go 1-3/4 mi NE on Business I-44. Enter on L.* FACILITIES: 36 sites, 36 full hkups, (30/50 amps), 18 pull-thrus, tenting, dump. RECREATION: river swim, river fishing. Pets welcome. Open all yr. Facilities fully operational Mar 1 - Nov 15. Big rigs welcome. Phone: (573)774-6171.

WEINGARTEN—D-5

(S) HAWN STATE PARK—(Ste. Genevieve) *From jct Hwy 32 & Hwy 144: Go 4 mi S on Hwy 144. Enter at end.*

FACILITIES: 50 sites, 26 E, (30 amps), 24 no hkups, tenting, dump, laundry, picnic tables, fire rings, grills, wood, controlled access.

RECREATION: pavilion, hiking trails.

Partial handicap access. Open all yr. Facilities fully operational Apr 1 - Oct 31. MC/VISA/DISC/AMEX.

WEINGARTEN—Continued
HAWN STATE PARK—Continued

Phone: (573)883-3603
Address: 12096 Park Drive, Ste Genevieve, MO 63670
Web: www.mostateparks.com

SEE AD TRAVEL SECTION PAGE 451

WEST PLAINS—E-4

(N) Road Runner RV Park—(Howell) *From jct US 63 & Hwy 14: Go 1 mi N on US 63. Enter on L.* ◊◊◊FACILITIES: 63 sites, 63 full hkups, (20/30/50 amps), 56 pull-thrus, tenting, laundry. ◊◊RECREATION: swim pool, playground. Pets welcome. Open all yr. Big rigs welcome. Rate in 2010 $25 for 2 persons. Phone: (417)255-0213.

WESTON—B-1

(S) WESTON BEND STATE PARK—(Platte) *From jct Hwy 273 & Hwy 45: Go 1 mi S on Hwy 45.*

FACILITIES: 36 sites, typical site width 20 ft, 32 E, (50 amps), 4 no hkups, tenting, dump, laundry, picnic tables, fire rings, grills, wood.

RECREATION: pavilion, river fishing, playground, activities, hiking trails.

Partial handicap access. Open all yr. Max stay 15 days. MC/VISA/DISC/AMEX.

Phone: (816)640-5443
Address: 16600 Hwy 45 N, Weston, MO 64098
Lat/Lon: 39.387083/-94.864806
Email: moparks@mail.dnr.state.mo.us
Web: www.mostateparks.com

SEE AD TRAVEL SECTION PAGE 451

WILLIAMSVILLE—E-5

(E) LAKE WAPPAPELLO STATE PARK—(Wayne) *From jct US-67 & Hwy-172: Go 9 mi E on Hwy-172. Enter at end.*

FACILITIES: 78 sites, 71 E, (30/50 amps), 7 no hkups, 10 pull-thrus, tenting, cabins, dump, laundry, ltd groc, ice, picnic tables, fire rings, grills, wood.

RECREATION: pavilion, lake swim, boating, ramp, lake fishing, hiking trails.

Partial handicap access. Open all yr. Facilities fully operational Apr 1 - Oct 31. MC/VISA/DISC/AMEX.

Phone: (573)297-3232
Address: HC 2 Hwy 172, Williamsville, MO 63967
Web: www.mostateparks.com

SEE AD TRAVEL SECTION PAGE 451

(W) MARK TWAIN NATIONAL FOREST (Markham Springs Campground)—(Wayne) *From town: Go 3 mi W on Hwy-49, then 1/2 mi N on FR-2997.* FACILITIES: 40 sites, typical site width 15 ft, 11 E, 29 no hkups, tenting, dump. RECREATION: boating, canoeing, ramp, river fishing. Partial handicap access. Open May 1 - Sept 30. Phone: (573)785-1475.

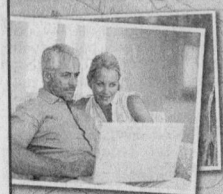

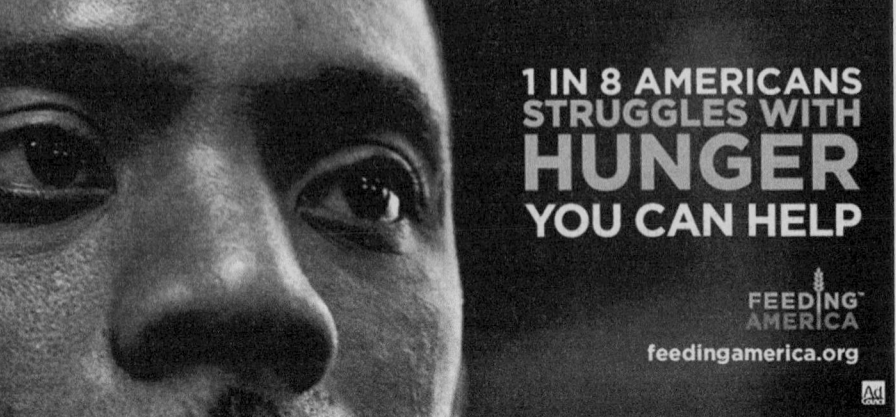

TRAVEL SECTION

New Hampshire

READER SERVICE INFO

The following businesses have placed an ad in the New Hampshire Travel Section. To receive free information, enter their Reader Service number on the Reader Service Card opposite page 48/Discover Section in the front of this directory:

Advertiser	RS#
Great Bay Camping/Shell	4309
Tamworth Camping Area	4331
White Mountain Attractions	730

TIME ZONE

New Hampshire is in the Eastern Time Zone.

TOPOGRAPHY

There are 1,300 lakes and ponds, 40,000 miles of streams and 18 miles of seacoast within New Hampshire. 84 percent of the land is forested and 182 mountains are over 3,000 ft. high.

TEMPERATURE

The average temperature in January is 21°, while July has 70° days. The average monthly precipitation is 3.2."

TRAVEL & TOURISM INFO

State Agency:

State of New Hampshire Dept of Tourism
172 Pembroke Rd.
Box 1856
Concord, NH 03302
(603/271-2665
www.visitnh.gov

Regional Agencies:

Androscoggin Valley Chamber of Commerce
961 Main St.
Berlin, NH 03570
(800/992-7480 or 603/752-6060)
www.androscogginvalleychamber.com

Hanover Area Chamber of Commerce
P.O. Box 5105
Hanover, NH
(603/643-3115).
www.hanoverchamber.org

Lakes Region Association
P.O. Box 430
260 Rt 104
New Hampton, NH 03256
(800/60-LAKES or 603/744-8664)
www.lakesregion.org

North Country Chamber of Commerce
Rt. 3 Rest Area
Colebrook, NH 03576
(603/237-8939 or 800/698-8939)
www.northcountrychamber.org

Northern Gateway Regional Chamber of Commerce
P.O. Box 537
Lancaster, NH 03584
(877/788-2530 or 603/788-2530)
www.northerngatewaychamber.org

White Mountains Attractions
P.O. Box 10
North Woodstock, NH 03262
(800/FIND MTS or 603/745-8720).
www.visitwhitemountains.com

Local Agencies:

For local information, contact the Chamber of Commerce or Tourism Bureau for the locality you are interested in visiting.

RECREATIONAL INFO

Alpine/Cross Country Ski Conditions: Ski New Hampshire, P.O. Box 528, North Woodstock, NH 03262 (800/88-SKI-NH) www.skinh.com

New Hampshire Fish & Game Dept., 11 Hazen Dr., Concord, NH 03301 (603/271-3511) www.wildlife.state.nh.us

New Hampshire State Parks, 172 Pembroke Rd, Box 1856, Concord, NH 03302 (603/271-3556). www.nhstateparks.org

New Hampshire Snowmobile Assn., 614 Laconia Rd., Unit 4, Tilton, NH 03276 (603/273-0220) www.nhsa.com/

New Hampshire State Forest, P.O. Box 1856, Concord, NH 03302-1856 (603/271-2214) www.nhdfl.org

SHOPPING

Shopping in New Hampshire is tax-free! For information on antiques and collectibles,

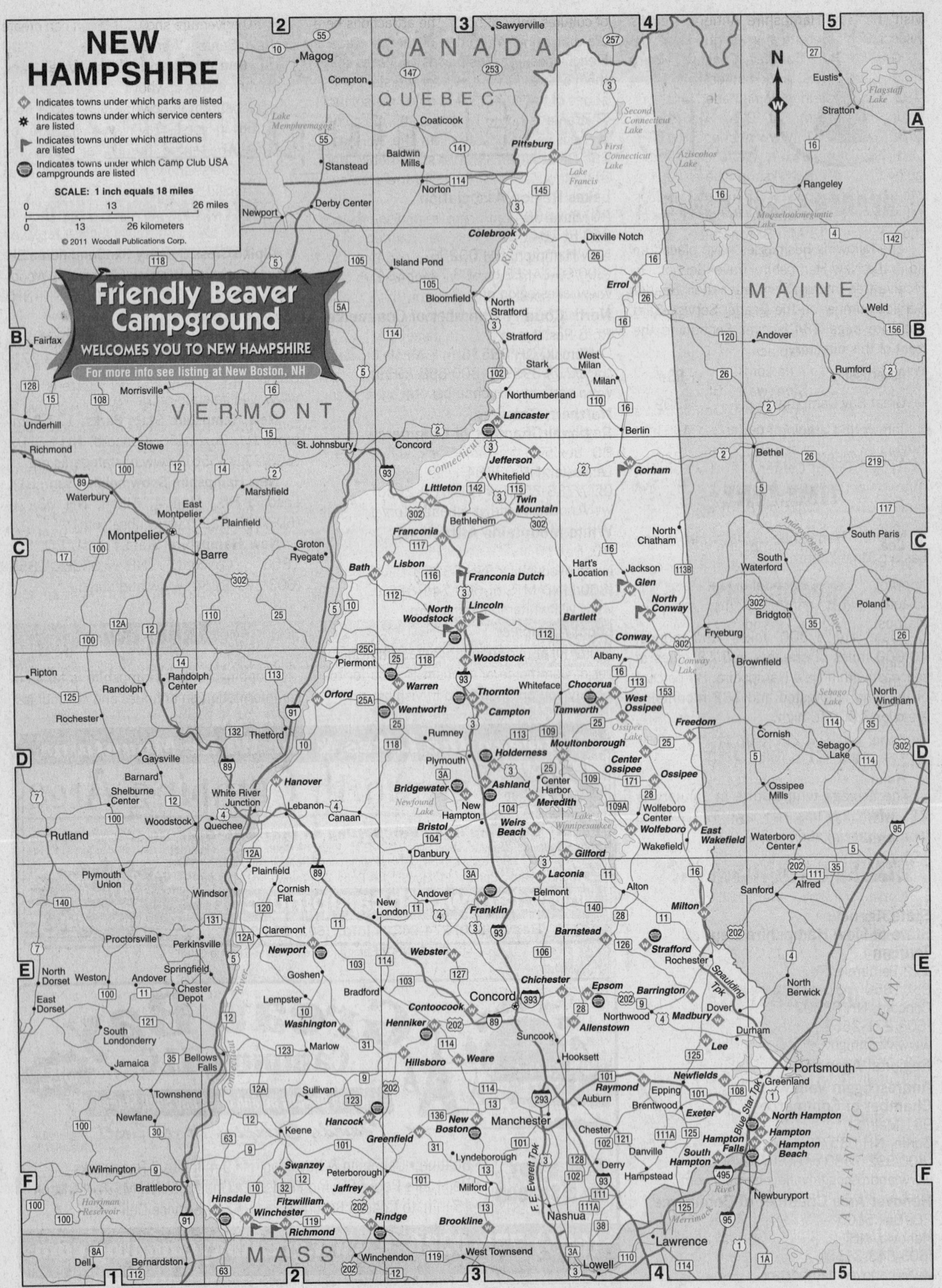
NEW HAMPSHIRE
Indicates towns under which parks are listed
Indicates towns under which service centers are listed
Indicates towns under which attractions are listed
Indicates towns under which Camp Club USA campgrounds are listed
SCALE: 1 inch equals 18 miles
0 13 26 miles
0 13 26 kilometers
© 2011 Woodall Publications Corp.
Friendly Beaver Campground
WELCOMES YOU TO NEW HAMPSHIRE
For more info see listing at New Boston, NH
CANADA
QUEBEC
VERMONT
MAINE
MASS
ATLANTIC OCEAN
N
Sawyerville
Magog
Compton
Coaticook
Lake Memphremagog
Baldwin Mills
Stanstead
Norton
Derby Center
Newport
Pittsburg
Second Connecticut Lake
First Connecticut Lake
Lake Francis
Aziscohos Lake
Eustis
Flagstaff Lake
Stratton
Rangeley
Mooselookmeguntic Lake
Colebrook
Dixville Notch
Island Pond
Errol
Bloomfield
North Stratford
Stratford
Weld
Andover
Fairfax
Morrisville
Stark
West Milan
Milan
Rumford
Northumberland
Lancaster
Berlin
Underhill
Richmond
Stowe
St. Johnsbury
Concord
Jefferson
Gorham
Bethel
Whitefield
Littleton
Twin Mountain
Waterbury
Marshfield
East Montpelier
Plainfield
Bethlehem
Montpelier
Barre
Franconia
North Chatham
South Paris
Groton
Ryegate
Bath
Lisbon
Franconia Dutch
Hart's Location
Jackson
Glen
South Waterford
North Conway
Bartlett
North Woodstock
Lincoln
Poland
Bridgton
Fryeburg
Conway
Woodstock
Albany
Conway Lake
Brownfield
Piermont
Ripton
Randolph
Randolph Center
Warren
Thornton
Whiteface
Chocorua
West Ossipee
Orford
Wentworth
Campton
Tamworth
Sebago Lake
North Windham
Rochester
Rumney
Freedom
Thetford
Moultonborough
Ossipee Lake
Cornish
Sebago Lake
Gaysville
Plymouth
Holderness
Center Ossipee
Ossipee
Barnard
Hanover
Center Harbor
Shelburne Center
White River Junction
Bridgewater
Ashland
Ossipee Mills
Newfound Lake
Meredith
Lebanon
Canaan
New Hampton
Wolfeboro Center
Woodstock
Quechee
Rutland
Bristol
Weirs Beach
Lake Winnipesaukee
Wolfeboro
East Wakefield
Waterboro Center
Wakefield
Danbury
Gilford
Plainfield
Laconia
Plymouth Union
Cornish Flat
Alton
Alfred
Sanford
Windsor
Andover
Belmont
New London
Franklin
Milton
Claremont
Proctorsville
Perkinsville
Barnstead
Newport
Webster
Strafford
Rochester
Spaulding Tpk
Springfield
North Dorset
Weston
Andover
Chester Depot
Goshen
Chichester
Epsom
Barrington
North Berwick
East Dorset
Lempster
Bradford
Concord
Dover
Contoocook
Northwood
Madbury
Washington
Henniker
Allenstown
Durham
South Londonderry
Marlow
Suncook
Jamaica
Bellows Falls
Hillsboro
Weare
Lee
Hooksett
Portsmouth
Newfields
Greenland
Townshend
Sullivan
Raymond
Epping
Auburn
Brentwood
North Hampton
Newfane
Keene
Hancock
New Boston
Manchester
Exeter
Greenfield
Chester
Hampton
Hampton Falls
Hampton Beach
Lyndeborough
Blue Star Tpk
Danville
South Hampton
Swanzey
Peterborough
Derry
Hampstead
Wilmington
Brattleboro
Jaffrey
Milford
F.E. Everett Tpk
Newburyport
Harriman Reservoir
Hinsdale
Fitzwilliam
Winchester
Richmond
Rindge
Brookline
Nashua
Merrimack River
Lawrence
Winchendon
West Townsend
Lowell
Dell
Bernardston
Connecticut River
Androscoggin River

visit the New Hampshire Antique Dealers Association's website at www.nhada.org.

Granite State Candies, Concord. Handmade chocolates and confections since 1927. Now featuring homemade, super premium ice cream. At 9-17 Warren St. (888/225-2591) www.nhchocolates.com

Hampshire Pewter, Wolfeboro. Take a guided tour of the workshop where they create the beautiful pewter gifts, serving pieces, tableware, jewelry and more before visiting the gift shop. 43 Mill St (one block off Rte 109). (603/569-4944). www.hampshirepewter.com

Keepsake Quilting, Center Harbor. America's largest quilt shop sells quilting supplies and handmade quilts. (603/253-4026), Senter's Marketplace, Rt 25B www.keepsakequilting.com

Salmon Falls Stoneware, Dover. Handmade stoneware dinnerware, lamps, crocks and more in a variety of patterns. Oak Street Engine House, Dover. (603/749-1467)

Tanger Outlet Center, 120 Laconia Rd, Tilton. Over 50 designer and brand name outlet stores. (603/286-7880) www.tangeroutlet.com/tilton

League of New Hampshire Craftsmen. The League was established in 1932 as a nonprofit craft educational organization dedicated to preserving and inspiring New Hampshire's fine handcraft tradition. www.nhcrafts.org

Eight retail galleries are located throughout the state at the following locations:

Center Sandwich, 32 Main St., (603/284-6831)

Concord, 36 North Main St. (603/228-8171)

Hanover, 13 Lebanon St., (603/643-5050)

Littleton, 81 Main St., (603/444-1099)

Meredith, 279 Daniel Webster Hwy., (603/279-7920)

Nashua, 98 Main Street. 603-595-8233

North Conway, Main St./Route 16, (603/356-2441)

Wolfeboro, 15 North Main St., (603/569-3309)

DESTINATIONS

New Hampshire is a state filled with natural beauty, cultural events, and New England living. From the White Mountains to the north, through the Lakes Region to the state's strip of Atlantic seacoast, New Hampshire is a vacationland of rugged outdoor adventure, and urban charm.

GREAT NORTH WOODS REGION

With 97 percent of the Great North Woods forested, it has been described as a little piece of Alaska or Labrador. Because of its close proximity to Canada, there is a mix of cultures and outlooks. The attractions here are all natural and much of the populace is French-speaking. The woods and lakes shape the life here, so camp under the stars or fish at one of the streams and enjoy the solitude. This area is home to one of the most comprehensive trail systems in the Northeast. The Great North Woods' snowmobile trails bring thousands of riders to the area each winter.

Moose are common here and some weigh up to 1,000 lbs. Use caution when approaching them, even in a car. If you see one, slow down and be prepared to stop. Resume speed only after you have passed them. Moose and wildlife tours are available from Northern Forest Heritage Park.

Christies' Maple Farm & Maple Museum, Lancaster. Learn how maple syrup is made in an authentic sugarhouse. Gift shop, picnic area with spectacular views.

Dixville Notch State Park, Dixville. Enjoy the day hiking to **Table Rock**, waterfalls and a scenic gorge. Two picnic areas are available.

The Old Meeting House, Groveton. See historical items from the area on display in this 1799 Meeting House.

Santa's Village, Jefferson. Includes 16 action-packed rides, live performances and a new 3D adventure show. Children can create crafts in Santa's Workshop.

Six Gun City & Fort Splash Water Park, Jefferson. Watch cowboys, bank robbers and sheriffs perform in cowboy skits and a frontier show. Horse-drawn vehicles are on display. The entire family will enjoy the miniature horse show. Amusement park rides and waterslides will complete the fun.

Stark's Covered Bridge, Stark. Built in 1862, it is over 134' long. Almost replaced in the 1950s, the passionate public outcry led the state to restore the historic span.

WHITE MOUNTAINS REGION

The 800,000-acre **White Mountain National Forest** touches or is part of every town in this region. The fall foliage is spectacular. From mid-September through mid to late October, scenic drives are a favorite pastime for residents and tourists. Bear Notch Road joins the Kancamagus Highway west of Conway and ends at Route 302 in the center of Barlett. Several scenic overlooks provide stunning views, particularly to the west and Crawford Notch.

This is also a major winter sport area with six major downhill ski areas within an hour

drive and miles of cross-country ski trails and snowmobile trails.

Conway Scenic Railroad, North Conway Village. Experience nostalgic train rides of varying durations through the scenic New Hampshire countryside. The "Valley Train" offers first class seating on the restored Pullman Parlor-Observation Car "Gertrude Emma" on its excursions to Conway and Bartlett, while the "Notch Train" carries passengers through spectacular Crawford Notch and past the finest natural scenery in the East.

The Frost Place, Franconia. Poet Robert Frost's farmhouse and farm, with a museum and nature trail.

Flume Gorge at Franconia Notch State Park offers a spectacular walk through a natural chasm, over covered bridges and past waterfalls, scenic pools and mountain views.

Story Land is located adjacent to Heritage-New Hampshire. You'll find an adventure around every corner, where family fun has been a tradition for over 45 years. Hop aboard the **Huff Puff & Whistle Railroad** for a ride through this beautifully landscaped 35-acre park. Visit Africa, Holland, the Alps, a south-of-the-border town, Antarctica and even outer space. Then become part of the show at the **Tales of Wonder Theater**. Meet Timothy Tree, the talking tree house and "leaf" your name on one of his branches.

Littleton Grist Mill, Littleton. Restored Grist Mill complex and basic mill workings complete with wooden gears, four-foot millstones and a waterheel. Still produces flours and mixes available in the gift shop.

Lost River Gorge and Boulder Caves, North Woodstock. Lost River Gorge was created when glaciers ground their way across North America, shaping the land. Today, you can follow Lost River as it appears and disappears through the narrow, steep-walled gorge, the tumbled granite, crevasses, caverns and falls. You'll learn about the natural history, ecology and plant life of the area.

Mount Washington Observatory, North Conway. Located on the summit of Mt. Washington, this new observatory features a research facility, exhibits, displays and science activities for the whole family.

Mount Washington Cog Railway, Bretton Woods. Built in 1869, this National Historic Engineering Landmark takes you on a three-hour round trip up Mount Washington in replica era coaches. On a clear day, the view spans four states, Canada and the Atlantic Ocean.

Mt. Washington Auto Road, Gorham offers two-hour guided trips to the summit of Mt. Washington.

Museum of American Weather, Haverhill. See major weather events including the 1888 blizzard, the 1927 Vermont flood, the 1938 hurricane and the Worcester tornado graphically illustrated.

Nestlenook Farm Victorian Recreation Park, Jackson. Experience the magic of a Winter Wonderland—travel by a horse drawn Austrian sleigh on a path through the woods and along the Ellis River, enjoying the timeless beauty of a Victorian Estate. Ice skate on Emerald Lake and try snowshoeing on Nestlenook's trail system. Enjoy a full day of festivities stuffed with the magic of Christmas morning. Visit with Santa, feed his reindeer and get your good luck ring from the Village Smithy. Santa has rides including the cool "Yule Log Flume" and "Rudy's Rapid Transit" coaster. Three magic shows are also offered.

New England Ski Museum, Franconia. See this fascinating collection and exhibits of historic ski memorabilia, plus vintage videos, books and posters in the museum shop.

Polar Caves Park, Plymouth. Hike the amazing series of caves and passages formed by great blocks of granite loosened by melting glaciers. Includes main lodge, Rock Garden of the Giants and Maple Sugar Museum.

Wildcat Mountain Gondola, Pinkham Notch. Breathtaking scenery and amazing views of Mt. Washington. Experience New England's most exciting new thrill ride, the ZipRider, at this scenic ski area.

Waterfalls, White Mountain. **White Mountain Waterfalls** are refreshing and powerful waters are displayed in Mother Nature's finest formations. These spectacular sights are awe inspiring to all who visit. Contact the **White Mountains Attractions Visitor Center** in North Woodstock for detailed locations.

BUSINESSES OFFERING

	Things to See & Do	RV Sales	RV Service
FRANCONIA NOTCH			
The Flume/Franconia Notch State Park	⚑		
GLEN			
Story Land	⚑		
GORHAM			
Mt. Washington Auto Road	⚑		
JEFFERSON			
Santa's Village	⚑		
LINCOLN			
Loon Mountain	⚑		
The Whale's Tale Water Park	⚑		
NORTH CONWAY			
Conway Scenic Railroad	⚑		
NORTH WOODSTOCK			
Clark's Trading Post	⚑		
Lost River Gorge & Boulder Caves	⚑		
White Mountain Attractions Visitors Center	⚑		
RICHMOND			
Museum of Family Camping	⚑		
WINCHESTER			
Forest Lake Pitch and Putt	⚑		

DARTMOUTH/LAKE SUNAPEE REGION

This historic area was shaped by two major communities. The Shakers practiced equality and pacifism and built more than 200 buildings including the **Great Stone Dwelling**, the largest Shaker dwelling ever built. The Cornish Colony was a group of artists, writers, musicians and others involved in the arts that summered in the area.

Charlestown Historic District features over 60 historic structures along beautiful Main Street. Rural activities include miles of snowmobile trails through two state forests.

Enfield Shaker Museum includes gardens, exhibits and artifacts relating to the Shaker way of life.

Fort at No. 4 Living History Museum, Charlestown. Experience what life was like in the northern-most outpost of the frontier between New England and New France. See 18th-century skills such as open hearth cooking and candlemaking demonstrated.

Hood Museum of Art, Darthmouth College, Hanover. One of the oldest and largest college museums in the country houses an outstanding collection of works of art and artifacts.

Mt. Kearsarge Indian Museum, Education and Cultural Center, Warner. Over 1,000 artifacts showcase the Native American culture and way of life. See Native dwelling reproductions, Medicine Woods and Anna's Garden.

LAKES REGION

There are 273 lakes and ponds in this region, dominated by 72-square-mile Lake Winnipesaukee, and the Squam Lakes, offer water sports all year. From the extremes of sunbathing in the summer, to ice fishing in the winter.

Castle in the Clouds, Moultonborough. This 5,000-acre estate nestles high in the Ossipee Mountains with spectacular views of Lake Winnipesaukee and the surrounding area.

Daniel Webster Birthplace, Franklin. One of the U.S.'s most distinguished statesmen and orators was born in this two-room frame house in 1782. It has been restored with period furnishings.

Lake Winnipesaukee, New Hampshire's largest lake, is surrounded by three mountain ranges, has 183 miles of shoreline and over 250 islands. Cruises on the M/S Mount Washington are available from Weirs Beach, Wolfeboro, Alton Bay, Center Harbor and Meredith.

Loon Center and Markus Wildlife Sanctuary, Moultonborough. Learn about loons and the ecology of New Hampshire at this year-round facility.

Museum of Childhood of Wakefield. This museum of memories is for all ages. Displayed are a children's sled exhibit, 3,500 dolls, teddy bears, trains, dollhouses, musicals and 1890-period rooms.

New Hampshire Boat Museum, Wolfeboro Falls. Boating displays, artifacts and mementos that recall a way of life that is still evident today.

New Hampshire Farm Museum, Milton. Visit this 19th-century agricultural museum,

QUICK REFERENCE CHART FOR WOODALL'S FEATURED PARKS

	Green Friendly	RV Lots for Sale	Park Models-Onsite Ownership	Park Membership for Sale	Big Rigs Welcome	Internet Friendly	Pets Welcome
ASHLAND							
Ames Brook Campground					▲	●	■
BARRINGTON							
Ayers Lake Farm Campground						●	■
BRIDGEWATER							
Newfound RV Park					▲	●	■
CAMPTON							
Branch Brook Campground						●	■
CHOCORUA							
Chocorua Camping Village KOA					▲	●	■
EPSOM							
Circle 9 Ranch					▲	●	■
FRANCONIA							
Fransted Family Campground						●	■
GILFORD							
Gunstock Mountain Resort						●	■
GLEN							
Green Meadow Camping Area						●	■
GORHAM							
Timberland Campground						●	■
HAMPTON FALLS							
Wakeda Campground						●	■
HENNIKER							
Keyser Pond Campground						●	■
Mile Away Campground						●	■
LACONIA							
Silver Lake Park Campground						●	
LEE							
Ferndale Acres Campground						●	■
Wadleigh Falls Campground						●	■
LITTLETON							
Crazy Horse Campground & RV Park					▲	●	■
MEREDITH							
Clearwater Campground					▲	●	■
Harbor Hill Camping Area						●	■
Meredith Woods 4 Season Camping Area					▲	●	■
Twin Tamarack Family Camping and RV Resort						●	■

Green Friendly ; RV Lots for Sale ✖; Park Models/Onsite Onwership ✱; Park Memberships for Sale ✔; Big Rigs Welcome ▲; Internet Friendly ●; Internet Friendly-WiFi ●; Pets Welcome ■

house and barn tour, rural artifacts, blacksmith, cobbler shops, gardens and emerging 1890's family farm with animals.

Squam Lakes Natural Science Center, Holderness. Spend a day at the 200-acre nature center. Observe live native New Hampshire wildlife—bears, deer, otters, fox, owls, bald eagles and more in woodland enclosures. Enjoy the nature trails and hands-on exhibits.

MONADNOCK REGION

Monadnock is an Abenaki term meaning "highest land around." On a clear day you can see all six New England states from the summit of Mount Monadnock. Step back in time when visiting this region full of 200-year-old inns and 18th and 19th century historic homes.

Horatio Colony Museum, Keene. The 1806 home of Horatio Colony contains worldwide collections of art, furniture, books, silver and other cultural treasures.

Monadnock State Park, Jaffrey. Mt. Monadnock is one of the most frequently climbed mountains in the world, offering 40 miles of trails—many leading to its 3,165 ft. summit.

Shieling State Forest, Peterborough. Explore over two miles of self-guided foot trails and visit the **Forestry Learning Center**, featuring an exhibit area that includes a small woodlot management demonstration.

Stonewall Farm, Keene. Working farm and nonprofit educational center has Belgian horses, Holstein cows, hayrides, sleigh rides, farm products and gift shop.

MERRIMACK VALLEY REGION

For almost 200 years, the Merrimack Valley has been the seat of New Hampshire's government. You'll find many historical places to visit, family attractions and plenty of outdoor recreation.

America's Stonehenge, North Salem. See one of the largest and possibly the oldest megalithic (stone-constructed) sites in North America. Artifacts found at the excavation site suggest a Native American or migrant

QUICK REFERENCE CHART FOR WOODALL'S FEATURED PARKS

	Green Friendly	RV Lots for Sale	Park Models-Onsite Ownership	Park Membership for Sale	Big Rigs Welcome	Internet Friendly	Pets Welcome
MILTON							
Mi-Te-Jo Campground					▲	●	■
MOULTONBOROUGH							
Long Island Bridge Campground						●	■
NEW BOSTON							
Friendly Beaver Campground					▲	●	■
NEWFIELDS							
Great Bay Camping/Shell					▲	●	■
NEWPORT							
Crow's Nest Campground						●	■
NORTH CONWAY							
Saco River Camping Area						●	■
NORTH HAMPTON							
Shel-Al Campground						●	■
RICHMOND							
Shir-Roy Camping Area						●	■
SWANZEY							
Swanzey Lake Camping Area						●	■
TAMWORTH							
Tamworth Camping Area						●	■
WEARE							
Cold Springs Camp Resort					▲	●	■
WEIRS BEACH							
Pine Hollow Park						●	■
WINCHESTER							
Forest Lake Campground, Inc							■
WOLFEBORO							
Wolfeboro Campground							■

Green Friendly ; RV Lots for Sale ✖; Park Models/Onsite Onwership ✱; Park Memberships for Sale ✔; Big Rigs Welcome ▲; Internet Friendly ●; Internet Friendly-WiFi ●; Pets Welcome ■

European population constructed this mystery to determine specific solar and lunar events of the year.

Canobie Lake Park, Salem. Antique carousel, authentic 24-Gauge Steam Train, high-tech thrill rides, games, shows, arcades, swimming pool, flower gardens and tree-lined promenades.

Canterbury Shaker Village, Canterbury. Outdoor museum featuring historic buildings, tours, crafts, organic food and flower gardens, trails, festivals, family activities, farm stand. Museum Store and The Shaker Table Restaurant.

Capitol Center for the Arts, Concord. Presents the finest in nationally touring Broadway musicals, popular entertainers, family performances, dance, comedy, drama and classical music.

Charmingfare Farm, Candia. This 180-acre farm is home to over 200 animals, consisting of 30 different species, the largest collection of agricultural animals and North America wildlife in New Hampshire. You will encounter wolves, cougars, wolverines, lynx, American black bears, fishers, reindeer, river otters and more.

Christa McAuliffe Planetarium, Concord. Take an exciting flight through the Universe. You'll see spectacular stellar wonders that fill the state-of-the-art domed theater. Space travelers of all ages can blast off for hour-long cosmic adventures.

SEACOAST REGION

Along an 18-mile coastline, much of which is public land, are long sandy beaches, picturesque villages and working ports. Bike down scenic roads, golf, hike, fish or take an ocean cruise to offshore islands.

Hampton Beach has world-class attractions, events, festivals, nightly entertainment and an outstanding fireworks schedule. It is an active place for swimming, para-sailing, jet skiing (there's a separate beach for surf boards) or strolling the historic boardwalk. Sunbathers will find Hampton's miles of clean white beach unsurpassed. Deep-sea fishing or whale watching is available and there is also a nearby golf course.

Portsmouth. Explore Portsmouth, a 375 year-old city, by walking the **Portsmouth Harbour Trail**. The Map and Guide (available for sale throughout the city) leads you down the city's narrow streets, past the waterfront, historic sites and gardens. Other attractions include **Albacore Park** where you can tour the world's fastest submarine; **Governor John Langdon House**, the home of John Langdon, merchant, signer of the Constitution and three-term governor of New Hampshire, who built this imposing house in 1784.

Water Country in Portsmouth is New England's largest waterpark. Among its activities are the Tahiti Treehouse with two waterslides, squirting guns and a huge dumping bucket; the Geronimo, Polaroid Shoot and the Screamer, a wave pool, Adventure River, Whirlpool and Racing Rapids.

Strawberry Banke Museum, Portsmouth. Tour one of America's oldest settlements, dating back four centuries. Costumed interpreters demonstrate their skills.

Water Country, Portsmouth. Enjoy an all-day adventure at New England's largest waterpark. From high-energy thrill rides to wave pools and Kiddie Kove, there's something to please everyone in your family.

The **Children's Museum in Dover** includes a space shuttle cockpit, submarine, lobster boat, Music Matrix and Pattern Palace among other hands-on exhibits.

ANNUAL EVENTS

JANUARY

Winter Wine Festival, New Castle (through February); State Snow Sculpture Competition, Jackson; New England Dog Sled Race, Tamworth.

FEBRUARY

Farm & Forest Exposition, Manchester; Meredith Rotary Fishing Derby, Meredith; Annual Winter Carnival, Newport; Wolfeboro Winter Carnival, Wolfeboro.

Where to Find CCUSA Parks

List City	Park Name	Map Coordinates
ASHLAND		
	Ames Brook Campground	D-3
BRIDGEWATER		
	Newfound RV Park	D-3
EPSOM		
	Blake's Brook Family Campground	E-4
	Circle 9 Ranch	E-4
FRANKLIN		
	Thousand Acres Family Campground	E-3
HAMPTON		
	Tidewater Campground	F-5
HAMPTON FALLS		
	Wakeda Campground	F-5
HANCOCK		
	Seven Maples Campground	F-2
HENNIKER		
	Keyser Pond Campground	E-3
	Mile Away Campground	E-3
HINSDALE		
	Hinsdale Campground	F-2
HOLDERNESS		
	Bethel Woods Campground	D-3
LANCASTER		
	Mountain Lake Campground & RV Park	B-3
NEW BOSTON		
	Friendly Beaver Campground	F-3
NEWPORT		
	Crow's Nest Campground	E-2
NORTH WOODSTOCK		
	Lost River Valley Campground	C-3
RINDGE		
	Woodmore Family Campground & RV Park	F-2
STRAFFORD		
	Crown Point Campground	E-4
TAMWORTH		
	Tamworth Camping Area	D-4
THORNTON		
	Goose Hollow Camp & RV Park	D-3
WARREN		
	Scenic View Campground	D-3
WENTWORTH		
	Pine Haven Campground	D-3

New Hampshire

ALLENSTOWN—E-4

BEAR BROOK SP—(Merrimack) *From jct US 3 & Hwy 28: Go 3 mi NE on Hwy 28, then follow signs.* FACILITIES: 101 sites, 101 no hkups, tenting, dump, laundry, ltd groc. RECREATION: boating, no motors, canoeing, pond/stream fishing, playground. Pets welcome. Partial handicap access. Open early May - mid Oct. Phone: (603)485-9869.

ASHLAND—D-3

(SE) AMES BROOK CAMPGROUND—(Grafton) *From jct I-93 (exit 24) & US 3: Go 3/4 mi S on US 3, then 1/4 mi S on Hwy 132, then 1/2 mi S on Winona Rd. Enter on R.*

◆◆◆◆FACILITIES: 79 sites, typical site width 50 ft, 76 full hkups, 3 W&E, (20/30/50 amps), some extd stay sites (summer), 7 pull-thrus, cable TV, WiFi Instant Internet at site ($), cable Internet central location, family camping, tenting, dump, non-guest dump $, portable dump, laundry, ltd groc, RV supplies, LP gas by weight/by meter, ice, picnic tables, fire rings, wood.

◆◆◆◆RECREATION: rec hall, rec room/area, coin games, swim pool, stream fishing, fishing supplies, golf nearby, bsktball, playground, activities, (wkends), horseshoes, sports field, v-ball.

Pets welcome, quantity restrict. Open May 15 - Oct 22. Big rigs welcome. Escort to site. Clubs welcome. Rate in 2010 $34-39 for 2 persons. MC/VISA. Member NE-HA-CA. CCUSA 50% Discount. CCUSA reservations Accepted, CCUSA max stay 5 days, Cash only for CCUSA disc., CCUSA disc. not avail F,Sa, CCUSA disc. not avail holidays. Not available Motorcycle week. Call for details.

Phone: (603)968-7998
Address: 104 Winona Rd, Ashland, NH 03217
Lat/Lon: 43.68796/-71.62323
Email: info@amesbrook.com
Web: www.amesbrook.com

SEE AD THIS PAGE AND AD TRAVEL SECTION PAGE 485

(S) Yogi Bear's Jellystone Park Camp Resort—(Belknap) *From jct I-93 (exit 23): Go 1/2 mi E on Hwy 104, then 4 mi N on Hwy 132N. Enter on L.* ◆◆◆FACILITIES: 207 sites, typical site width 25 ft, 77 full hkups, 130 W&E, (20/30/50 amps), family camping, tenting, dump, laundry, groceries. ◆◆◆◆RECREATION: swim pool, river swim, canoeing, river fishing, playground. Pets welcome, breed restrict, quantity restrict. Partial handicap access. Open 3rd wknd May - Mid-Oct. Rate in 2010 $39-69 per family. Member ARVC, NE-HA-CA. Phone: (603)968-9000.

BARNSTEAD—E-4

(N) Sun River Campground—(Belknap) *From jct Hwy 107 & Hwy 28: Go 4-1/4 mi N on Hwy 28. Enter on R.* ◆◆◆FACILITIES: 85 sites, typical site width 40 ft, 38 ft max RV length, 25 full hkups, 53 W&E, (30/50 amps), 7 no hkups, family camping, tenting, dump. ◆◆◆RECREATION: river swim, river fishing, playground. Pets welcome. Partial handicap access. Open mid May - Mid Oct. Rate in 2010 $30 per family. Member NE-HA-CA. Phone: (603)269-3333.

BARRINGTON—E-4

(NW) AYERS LAKE FARM CAMPGROUND—(Strafford) *From jct Hwy 16 (Spaulding Tpk) (exit 13) & US 202: Go 5 mi SW on US 202. Enter on R.*

◆◆◆FACILITIES: 52 sites, 46 full hkups, 5 W&E, (20/30/50 amps), 1 no hkups, many extd stay sites (summer), 3 pull-thrus, cable TV, ($), WiFi Internet central location, family camping, tenting, cabins, dump, laundry, ice, picnic tables, fire rings, wood, controlled access.

◆◆◆◆RECREATION: lake swim, boating, canoeing, kayaking, 2 rowboat/4 canoe/6 kayak rentals, lake fishing, golf nearby, bsktball, play equipment, horseshoes.

Pets welcome, breed restrict, size restrict, quantity restrict. Open May 20 - Late Sep. Rate in 2010 $39-48 per family. Member ARVC, NE-HA-CA.

Phone: (866)335-1110
Address: 557 Rte 202, Barrington, NH 03825
Lat/Lon: 43.24852/-71.04981
Web: www.ucampnh.com/ayerslake

SEE AD THIS PAGE

(S) Barrington Shores Campground—(Strafford) *From jct Hwy 4 & Hwy 125: Go 3 mi N on Hwy 125, then 1 mi W on Beauty Hill Rd, then 1 mi S on Hall Rd. Enter on R.* ◆◆◆◆FACILITIES: 136 sites, typical site width 35 ft, 113 full hkups, 23 W&E, (20/30/50 amps), family camping, tenting, dump, laundry, ltd groc. ◆◆◆◆RECREATION: lake swim, boating, canoeing, ramp, dock, lake fishing, playground. Pets welcome. Partial handicap access. Open Mid May - Mid Sep. Big rigs welcome. Rate in 2010 $34-55 per family. Member ARVC, NE-HA-CA. Phone: (603)664-9333.

BARTLETT—C-4

CRAWFORD NOTCH SP (Dry River Campground)—(Carroll) *From town: Go 12 mi NW on US 302.* FACILITIES: 36 sites, 36 no hkups, tenting, laundry. RECREATION: river fishing. Partial handicap access. Open end May - mid Dec. Phone: (603) 374-2272.

(S) WHITE MOUNTAIN NATIONAL FOREST (Jigger Johnson Campground)—(Carroll) *From jct US 302 & FR 26: Go 9 mi S on FR 26, then 1/4 mi W on Hwy 112.* FACILITIES: 74 sites, 30 ft max RV length, 74 no hkups, tenting. RECREATION: river fishing. Open late May - mid Oct. Phone: (603)447-5448.

BATH—C-2

(W) Twin River RV Park & Cottages—(Grafton) *From jct US 302 & Hwy 112: Go 100 yards SE on Hwy 112. Enter on R.* ◆◆◆FACILITIES: 103 sites, typical site width 32 ft, 50 full hkups, 45 W&E, (20/30/50 amps), 50 amps ($), 8 no hkups, family camping, tenting, dump, laundry, ltd groc. ◆◆◆RECREATION: swim pool, river fishing, play equipment. Pets welcome, breed restrict, quantity restrict. Partial handicap access. Open May 15 - Oct 15. Rate in 2010 $31-36 per family. Member ARVC, NE-HA-CA. Phone: (603)747-3640. FMCA discount.

BRIDGEWATER—D-3

(N) NEWFOUND RV PARK—(Grafton) *From jct I-93 & Hwy 104: Go 6 mi W on Hwy 104, then 4-1/2 mi N on Hwy 3A. Enter on R.*

◆◆◆◆FACILITIES: 45 sites, 45 full hkups, (20/30/50 amps), some extd stay sites (summer), 39 pull-thrus, cable TV, WiFi Instant Internet at site, WiFi Internet central location, family camping, tenting, laundry, ltd groc, RV supplies, LP gas by weight/by meter, ice, picnic tables, fire rings, wood.

◆◆RECREATION: rec hall, stream fishing, golf nearby, horseshoes, v-ball.

Pets welcome, breed restrict. Partial handicap access. Open Mid May - Mid Oct. Big rigs welcome. Clubs welcome. Rate in 2010 $40-48 for 2 persons. MC/VISA/DISC. Member NE-HA-CA. FMCA discount. CCUSA 50% Discount. CCUSA reservations Recommended, CCUSA max stay 3 days, CCUSA disc. not avail S,M, CCUSA disc. not avail F,Sa, CCUSA disc. not avail holidays. Not available during special events. Call for details.

Phone: (603)744-3344
Address: 792 Mayhew Tpk (Rte 3A), Bridgewater, NH 03222
Lat/Lon: 43.65478/-71.73658
Email: newfoundrv@aol.com
Web: www.newfoundrvpark.com

SEE AD MEREDITH PAGE 497 AND AD TRAVEL SECTION PAGE 485

BRISTOL—D-3

(E) Davidson's Countryside Campground—(Grafton) *From I-93 (exit 23) & Hwy-104: Go 1-1/2 mi W on Hwy-104, then 1/2 mi N on River Rd. Enter on R.* ◆◆◆FACILITIES: 132 sites, typical site width 55 ft, 84 full hkups, 24 W&E, (20/30/50 amps), 50 amps ($), 24 no hkups, 18 pull-thrus, family camping, tenting, dump. ◆◆◆RECREATION: river swim, canoeing, river fishing, playground. Pets welcome. Open Memorial Day - Columbus Day. Rate in 2010 $32-34 per family. Member NE-HA-CA. Phone: (603)744-2403.

BROOKLINE—F-3

(NW) Field and Stream RV Park—(Hillsborough) *From jct US 3 (exit 6) & Hwy 130: Go 12 mi W on Hwy 130, then 1 mi S on Hwy 13, then 1 mi W on Mason Rd, then 1/4 mi N on Dupaw Gould Rd. Enter on R.* ◆◆◆◆FACILITIES: 54 sites, typical site width 35 ft, 54 full hkups, (30/50 amps), 5 pull-thrus, dump, laundry. ◆RECREATION: canoeing, pond/stream fishing, play equipment. Pets welcome, breed restrict. No tents. Open all yr. Facilities fully operational Apr 1 - Nov 1. Big rigs welcome. Rate in 2010 $37 for 2 persons. Member NE-HA-CA. Phone: (603)673-4677.

CAMPTON—D-3

(W) BRANCH BROOK CAMPGROUND—(Grafton) *From jct I-93 (exit 28) & Hwy-49: Go 1 mi W on Hwy-49. Enter on R.*

◆◆◆FACILITIES: 199 sites, typical site width 40 ft, 70 full hkups, 87 W&E, 29 E, (20/30/50 amps), 13 no hkups, some extd stay sites (summer), cable TV, WiFi Internet central location, family camping, tenting, RV's/park model rentals, dump, ltd groc, RV supplies, LP gas by weight/by meter, ice, picnic tables, fire rings, wood, controlled access.

BRANCH BROOK CAMPGROUND—Continued on next page

CAMPTON—Continued
BRANCH BROOK CAMPGROUND—Continued

◇◇◇◇RECREATION: rec hall, rec room/area, coin games, swim pool, river swim, canoeing, kayaking, 6 canoe/6 kayak rentals, float trips, river/pond fishing, fishing supplies, golf nearby, playground, shuffleboard court shuffleboard court, activities, sports field, v-ball.

Pets welcome. Partial handicap access. Open all yr. Facilities fully operational May 1 - Nov 1. Electric only Nov 1 thru May 1. Clubs welcome. Rate in 2010 $41-45 per family. MC/VISA/DISC.

Phone: (603)726-7001
Address: 101 Branch Brook Rd, Campton, NH 03223
Lat/Lon: 43.84855/-71.66236
Email: branchbrook@myfairpoint.net
Web: www.campnh.com

SEE AD PAGE 491

(E) WHITE MOUNTAIN NATIONAL FOREST (Campton Campground)—(Grafton) *From I-93 (exit 28): Go 2 mi E on Hwy-49.* FACILITIES: 58 sites, 30 ft max RV length, 58 no hkups, tenting, ltd groc. RECREATION: river swim, boating, canoeing, river fishing. Open Apr 14 - Oct 13. Phone: (603)536-1310.

WHITE MOUNTAIN NATIONAL FOREST (Waterville Campground)—(Grafton) *From town: Go 1/4 mi N on Hwy-175, then 9 mi E on Hwy-49, then 1/4 mi N on FR-30.* FACILITIES: 20 sites, 22 ft max RV length, 20 no hkups. RECREATION: canoeing. Partial handicap access. Open Apr 30 - Oct 13. Phone: (603)536-1310.

CENTER OSSIPEE—D-4

(SW) Terrace Pines—(Carroll) *From jct Hwy 16 & Center Ossipee Business District Rd: Go 500 feet W & 500 feet S, then 1/2 mi W on Main St to Center Ossipee Village, then 1-1/2 mi W on Moultinville Rd, then 1-3/4 mi SW on Valley Rd, then 1/2 mi W on Bents Rd. Enter at end.* ◇◇◇FACILITIES: 185 sites, typical site width 45 ft, 30 ft max RV length, 184 full hkups, 1 W&E, (20/30/50 amps), family camping, tenting, dump, laundry, ltd groc. ◇◇◇◇◇RECREATION: lake swim, boating, canoeing, ramp, dock, lake fishing, playground. Pets welcome. Partial handicap access. Open Mid May - Columbus Day. Rate in 2010 $37-42 per family. Member NE-HA-CA. Phone: (603)539-6210.

CHICHESTER—E-3

(E) Hillcrest Campground—(Merrimack) *From jct I-93 (exit 15E) & I-393: Go 4 mi E on I-393, then 2 mi E on US 4. Enter on L.* ◇◇◇FACILITIES: 149 sites, typical site width 30 ft, 90 full hkups, 43 W&E, (30/50 amps), 16 no hkups, 5 pull-thrus, family camping, tenting, dump, laundry, ltd groc. ◇◇◇◇RECREATION: swim pool, boating, no motors, canoeing, pond fishing, playground. Pets welcome, quantity restrict. Partial handicap access. Open mid Apr - mid Oct. Big rigs welcome. Rate in 2010 $29-37 per family. Member NE-HA-CA. Phone: (603)798-5124.

CHOCORUA—D-4

(S) CHOCORUA CAMPING VILLAGE KOA—(Carroll) *From north jct Hwy 25 & Hwy 16: Go 3 mi N on Hwy 16. Enter on R.*

WELCOME

A QUIET LAKESIDE FAMILY CAMPGROUND!
A very special KOA for your Family in the Foothills of the White Mountains, Central to area attractions, with miles of Trails, Boating, Fishing and other Fun Family-Oriented Activities. National Park of the Year 06/07/08/09.

◇◇◇◇◇FACILITIES: 132 sites, typical site width 50 ft, 106 full hkups, 22 W&E, (20/30/50 amps), 4 no hkups, some extd stay sites (summer), 18 pull-thrus, cable TV, WiFi Instant Internet at site ($), family camping, tenting, RV's/park model rentals, cabins, RV storage, dump, non-guest dump $, portable dump, laundry, ltd groc, RV supplies, LP gas by weight/by meter, ice, picnic tables, fire rings, grills, wood, controlled access.

CHOCORUA—Continued
CHOCORUA CAMPING VILLAGE KOA—Continued

◇◇◇◇◇RECREATION: rec hall, rec room/area, coin games, swim pool, lake swim, boating, electric motors only, canoeing, kayaking, dock, 3 rowboat/3 canoe/5 kayak/2 pedal boat rentals, lake/river fishing, fishing supplies, golf nearby, bsktball, playground, activities, horseshoes, hiking trails, v-ball.

Pets welcome, breed restrict, quantity restrict. Partial handicap access. Open May 1 - Mid Oct. Limited off season camping available. Big rigs welcome. Escort to site. Clubs welcome. Rate in 2010 $32-63 per family. MC/VISA/DISC. Member ARVC, NE-HA-CA. KOA discount. FMCA discount.

Phone: (888)237-8642
Address: 893 White Mtn Hwy (Rte 16), Chocorua, NH 03817
Lat/Lon: 43.85581/-71.20593
Email: info@chocoruacamping.com
Web: www.chocoruacamping.com

SEE AD THIS PAGE

COLEBROOK—B-3

COLEMAN SP—(Coos) *From jct US 3 & Hwy 26: Go 6-3/4 mi E on Hwy 26, then 5-1/2 mi N on Diamond Pond Rd.* FACILITIES: 25 sites, 30 ft max RV length, 25 no hkups, tenting, dump, laundry. RECREATION: boating, 10 hp limit, canoeing, ramp, lake fishing, playground. Open Mid Jun - Mid Oct. Phone: (603)237-5382.

(E) Mohawk Valley Camping Area—(Coos) *From jct US 3 & Hwy 26: Go 4-1/2 mi E on Hwy 26, then 1/4 mi S on Bungy Rd. Enter on L.* ◇◇FACILITIES: 100 sites, typical site width 20 ft, 2 full hkups, 28 W&E, 8 E, (20/30 amps), 62 no hkups, 30 pull-thrus, tenting, dump. ◇◇RECREATION: river swim, river fishing, play equipment. Pets welcome. Open Memorial Day - Mid Oct. Rate in 2010 $22-25 for 2 persons. Phone: (603) 237-5756.

(E) Notch View Country Inn & RV Resort—(Coos) *From jct US 3 & Hwy 26: Go 3 mi E on Hwy 26, then 3/4 mi NE on East Colebrook Rd, then 1/4 mi N on Lyman Forbes Rd. Enter on R.* ◇◇◇FACILITIES: 41 sites, typical site width 35 ft, 41 full hkups, (30/50 amps), 3 pull-thrus, dump, laundry. ◇◇RECREATION: swim pool, pond fishing, play equipment. Pets welcome. Partial handicap access. No tents. Open May 15 - Oct 15. Rate in 2010 $35-45 for 2 persons. Phone: (603)237-4237.

CONCORD—E-3

See listings at Chichester, Contocook ,Epsom, Henniker & Weare.

CONTOOCOOK—E-3

(SE) Sandy Beach RV Resort—(Merrimack) *From jct I-89 (exit 6) & Hwy 127: Go 1 mi N on Hwy 127, then 2-1/2 mi W on Pine st, then 1/2 mi S on Clement Hill Rd. Enter on R.* ◇◇◇FACILITIES: 182 sites, typical site width 40 ft, 182 full hkups, 105 E, (20/30/50 amps), family camping, tenting, laundry. ◇◇◇◇RECREATION: lake swim, boating, electric motors only, canoeing, ramp, dock, lake fishing, playground. Pets welcome. Partial handicap access. Open Early May - Mid Oct. Big rigs welcome. Rate in 2010 $29-39 per family. Member ARVC, NE-HA-CA. Phone: (603)746-3591.

Reserve Online at Woodalls.com

CONWAY—C-4

(SE) Cove Camping Area on Conway Lake—(Carroll) *From north jct Hwy 16 & Hwy 113: Go 1 mi E on Hwy 113, then 1-3/4 mi S on Stark Rd, then 1 mi E on Cove Rd. Enter at end.* ◇◇◇FACILITIES: 95 sites, typical site width 30 ft, 30 ft max RV length, 48 W&E, (20/30 amps), 47 no hkups, family camping, tenting, dump, laundry, ltd groc. ◇◇◇◇RECREATION: lake swim, boating, canoeing, ramp, dock, lake fishing, playground. No pets. Open Memorial Day - Columbus Day. Rate in 2010 $26-51 per family. Member NE-HA-CA. Phone: (603)447-6734.

CONWAY—Continued

SACO RIVER CAMPING AREA—*From center of town: Go 4 mi N on Hwy 16. Enter on L.*

SEE PRIMARY LISTING AT NORTH CONWAY AND AD NORTH CONWAY PAGE 502

(W) WHITE MOUNTAIN NATIONAL FOREST (Blackberry Crossing Campground)—(Carroll) *From jct Hwy 16 & Hwy 112: Go 6-1/2 mi W on Hwy 112 (Kancamagus Scenic Hwy).* FACILITIES: 26 sites, 30 ft max RV length, 26 no hkups, tenting. RECREATION: river swim, river fishing. Partial handicap access. Open all yr. Phone: (603)447-5448.

(W) WHITE MOUNTAIN NATIONAL FOREST (Covered Bridge Campground)—(Carroll) *From jct Hwy-16 & Hwy-112: Go 6-1/2 mi W on Hwy-112, then 1/3 mi SE on FR-60.* FACILITIES: 49 sites, 30 ft max RV length, 49 no hkups, tenting. RECREATION: Open May 6 - Oct 8. Phone: (603)447-5448.

(W) WHITE MOUNTAIN NATIONAL FOREST (Passaconaway Campground)—(Carroll) *From jct Hwy-16 & Hwy-112: Go 14-1/3 mi W on Hwy-112.* FACILITIES: 33 sites, 30 ft max RV length, 33 no hkups, tenting. RECREATION: river fishing. Open mid May - late Oct. Phone: (603)447-5448.

(S) WHITE MOUNTAIN NATIONAL FOREST (White Ledge Campground)—(Carroll) *From jct Hwy-16 & Hwy-112: Go 5 mi SW on Hwy-16.* FACILITIES: 28 sites, 22 ft max RV length, 28 no hkups, tenting. RECREATION: Open mid May - mid Oct. Phone: (603)447-5448.

DOVER—E-4

See listings at Barrington, Lee & Madbury

EAST WAKEFIELD—D-4

(N) Lake Ivanhoe Campground—(Carroll) *From jct Hwy 109 & Hwy 16: Go 1-3/4 mi N on Hwy 16, then 1/2 mi E on Wakefield Rd, then 2-1/2 mi N on Hwy 153, then 1-1/4 mi E on Acton Ridge Rd. Enter on L.* ◇◇◇FACILITIES: 75 sites, typical site width 40 ft, 60 full hkups, 9 W&E, 3 E, (20/30 amps), 3 no hkups, 4 pull-thrus, family camping, tenting, dump, laundry. ◇◇◇RECREATION: lake swim, boating, canoeing, lake fishing, play equipment. Pets welcome, breed restrict, quantity restrict. Open May 1 - Mid Oct. Rate in 2010 $39-44 per family. Member NE-HA-CA. Phone: (603) 522-8824.

EPSOM—E-4

(E) Blake's Brook Family Campground—(Merrimack) *From jct Hwy 28 & US 4/202/Hwy 9 (Epsom Traffic Circle): Go 1-1/2 mi E on US 4/202/Hwy 9, then 1-1/2 mi SE on Center Hill Rd, then 1/4 mi W on Mountain Rd. Enter on R.* ◇◇◇FACILITIES: 48 sites, 36 ft max RV length, 34 full hkups, 13 W&E, (20/30 amps), 1 no hkups, heater not allowed, family camping, tenting, shower$, dump, RV supplies, ice, picnic tables, fire rings, wood. ◇◇RECREATION: rec hall, swim pool, bsktball, play equipment, horseshoes. Pets welcome, breed restrict, quantity restrict. Open May 1 - Oct 15. Rate in 2010 $34 per family. Member NE-HA-CA. CCUSA 50% Discount. CCUSA reservations Recommended, CCUSA max stay 7 days, Cash only for CCUSA disc., Check only for CCUSA disc., CCUSA disc. not avail holidays. Not available Nascar weekends. Cabins not discounted.

CAMPCLUB USA

Phone: (603)736-4793
Address: 76 Mountain Rd, Epsom, NH 03234
Lat/Lon: 43.20739/-71.31003
Email: blakes@tds.net
Web: www.BLAKESBROOK.com

EPSOM—Continued on next page

New Hampshire's state motto is "Live Free or Die". The motto comes from a statement written by the Revolutionary General John Stark, hero of the Battle of Bennington.

See listing at Chocorua, NH

See listing at Epsom, NH

EPSOM—Continued

(S) CIRCLE 9 RANCH—(Merrimack) *From jct US 4/202/Hwy 9 & Hwy 28 (Epsom Traffic Circle): Go 1/4 mi S on Hwy 28, then 1/4 mi W on Windymere Dr. Enter on R.*

◆◆◆FACILITIES: 116 sites, typical site width 25 ft, 80 full hkups, 26 W&E, (20/30/50 amps), 10 no hkups, some extd stay sites (summer), 17 pull-thrus, cable TV, WiFi Instant Internet at site, WiFi Internet central location, family camping, tenting, RV storage, dump, non-guest dump $, laundry, ltd groc, RV supplies, ice, picnic tables, fire rings, wood, controlled access.

◆◆◆RECREATION: rec room/area, coin games, swim pool, pond/stream fishing, golf nearby, bsktball, playground, activities, (wkends), horseshoes.

Pets welcome. Partial handicap access. Open all yr. Facilities fully operational May 1 - Oct 15. Rates higer during holidays & special events. Big rigs welcome. Clubs welcome. Rate in 2010 $18-85 per family. MC/VISA/DISC. Member ARVC, NE-HA-CA. CCUSA 50% Discount. CCUSA reservations Accepted, CCUSA max stay 5 days, CCUSA disc. not avail F,Sa, CCUSA disc. not avail holidays. Hot Showers metered. Cable tv premium sites-summer only.

Phone: (603)736-9656
Address: 39 Windymere Dr, Epsom, NH 03234
Lat/Lon: 43.22205/-71.36808
Email: info@circle9ranch.com
Web: www.circle9campground.com

Reserve Online at Woodalls.com

SEE AD PAGE 492

(N) Epsom Valley Campground—(Merrimack) *From jct US 4/202 & Hwy 28: Go 1/4 mi N on Hwy 28. Enter on R.* ◆◆◆FACILITIES: 65 sites, typical site width 25 ft, 42 full hkups, 22 W&E, (30 amps), 1 no hkups, 6 pull-thrus, family camping, tenting, dump, laundry. ◆◆◆RECREATION: river swim, canoeing, river fishing, play equipment. Pets welcome, breed restrict, quantity restrict. Open May 15 - Mid October. Rate in 2010 $28-35 per family. Member NE-HA-CA. Phone: (603)736-9758.

(N) Lazy River Family Campground—(Merrimack) *From jct Hwys 4/202 & Hwy 28: Go 2 mi N on Hwy 28, then 1/2 mi E on Depot Rd. Enter on R.* ◆◆FACILITIES: 109 sites, typical site width 35 ft, 35 ft max RV length, 59 full hkups, 50 W&E, (20/30/50 amps), family camping, tenting, dump, laundry. ◆◆◆RECREATION: swim pool, river swim, canoeing, river fishing, playground. Pets welcome. Open May 15 - Oct 15. Rate in 2010 $26-30 per family. Phone: (603) 798-5900.

ERROL—B-4

MOLLIDGEWOCK SP—(Coos) *From jct Hwy 26 & Hwy 16: Go 2-3/4 mi S on Hwy 16. Enter on L.* FACILITIES: 37 sites, 37 no hkups, tenting. RECREATION: river swim, boating, canoeing, ramp, river fishing. Pets welcome. Partial handicap access. Open Mar 1 - Feb 9. Phone: (603)482-3373.

UMBAGOG LAKE CAMPGROUND SP—(Coos) *From jct Hwy 16 & Hwy 26: Go 7-3/4 mi E on Hwy 26. Enter on L.* FACILITIES: 69 sites, 35 W&E, 34 no hkups, tenting, dump, ltd groc. RECREATION: lake swim, boating, canoeing, ramp, dock, lake fishing, play equipment. Pets welcome. Open Jun 11 - Oct 11. Phone: (603)482-7795.

EXETER—F-4

(S) Exeter Elms Family Campground—(Rockingham) *From jct Hwy 111 & Hwy 108: go 1-1/2 mi S on Hwy 108. Enter on L.* ◆◆FACILITIES: 201 sites, typical site width 30 ft, 79 full hkups, 61 W&E, (15/30/50 amps), 61 no hkups, family camping, tenting, dump, laundry, ltd groc. ◆◆◆RECREATION: swim pool, canoeing, river fishing, playground. Pets welcome ($). Partial handicap access. Open mid-May - Mid Oct. Rate in 2010 $39-50 per family. Member NE-HA-CA. Phone: (603)778-7631.

Reserve Online at Woodalls.com

(S) The Green Gate Camping Area—(Rockingham) *From jct Hwy-111 & Hwy-108: Go 1-1/2 mi S on Hwy-108. Enter on R.* ◆◆◆FACILITIES: 109 sites, typical site width 25 ft, 35 ft max RV length, 85 full hkups, 24 W&E, (20/30/50 amps), 50 amps ($), 3 pull-thrus, family camping, tenting, laundry. ◆◆◆RECREATION: swim pool, river fishing, playground. Pets welcome, breed restrict, quantity restrict. Partial handicap access. Open May 15 - Sep 15. Rate in 2010 $33-36.50 per family. Member NE-HA-CA. Phone: (603)772-2100.

FITZWILLIAM—F-2

(S) Laurel Lake Campground—(Cheshire) *From jct Hwy 12 & Hwy 119: Go 1-1/2 mi W on Hwy 119, then 1-1/2 mi S on East Lake Rd. Enter on R.* ◆◆FACILITIES: 65 sites, typical site width 40 ft, 32 ft max RV length, 11 full hkups, 54 W&E, (20 amps),

FITZWILLIAM—Continued
Laurel Lake Campground—Continued

family camping, tenting, dump, ltd groc. ◆◆◆RECREATION: lake swim, boating, canoeing, dock, lake fishing, play equipment. Pets welcome. Open Mid May - Mid Oct. Rate in 2010 $27 per family. Member NE-HA-CA. Phone: (603)585-3304.

FRANCONIA—C-3

FRANCONIA NOTCH SP (Echo Lake RV Park)—(Grafton) *From Franconia: Go 5 mi S on I-93/Franconia Notch Pkwy to exit 3.* FACILITIES: 7 sites, typical site width 20 ft, accepts full hkup units only, 7 full hkups, (50 amps), dump. RECREATION: lake swim, boating, 20 hp limit, canoeing, ramp, dock, lake fishing. No pets. No tents. Open all yr. Facilities fully operational mid May - late Oct. Phone: (603)823-8800.

FRANCONIA NOTCH SP (Lafayette Place Campground) —(Grafton) *No N'bound access. N'bound on I-93: turn around at Tramway exit 2, then go back 2-1/2 mi S on I-93. S'bound: At I-93 (Lafayette Place/Campground exit). Enter on R.* FACILITIES: 97 sites, 97 no hkups, tenting. RECREATION: stream fishing. No pets. Partial handicap access. Open mid May - mid Oct. Phone: (603)823-9513.

(S) FRANSTED FAMILY CAMPGROUND —(Grafton) *From jct I-93 (exit 38): Go 50 feet W, then 1 mi S on Hwy 18. Enter on R.*

◆◆◆◆FACILITIES: 100 sites, typical site width 30 ft, 41 full hkups, 20 W&E, (30/50 amps), 39 no hkups, some extd stay sites (summer), 7 pull-thrus, cable TV, WiFi Instant Internet at site, WiFi Internet central location, family camping, tenting, RV's/park model rentals, dump, portable dump, laundry, ltd groc, RV supplies, LP gas by weight/by meter, ice, picnic tables, fire rings, wood.

◆◆◆◆RECREATION: equipped pavilion, river swim, stream fishing, fishing supplies, mini-golf, ($), golf nearby, bsktball, playground, activities, (wkends), horseshoes, sports field, hiking trails, v-ball.

Pets welcome, breed restrict, quantity restrict. Open May 1 - Nov 1. Accepts SCU only between Oct 15 - Nov 1. Escort to site. Clubs welcome. Rate in 2010 $42-45 per family. MC/VISA. Member ARVC, NE-HA-CA.

Phone: (603)823-5675
Address: 974 Profile Rd, Rte 18, Franconia, NH 03580
Lat/Lon: 44.21689/-71.73026
Email: fransted@aol.com
Web: www.franstedcampground.com

SEE AD THIS PAGE AND AD TRAVEL SECTION PAGE 485

FRANCONIA NOTCH—C-3

THE FLUME/FRANCONIA NOTCH STATE PARK—*From jct I-93 (exit 34A) & US 3: Go S along US 3. Enter on L.* This stunning natural wonder will leave you spellbound as you stroll the path from the Visitors Center to the Flume & back. Walk among towering moss-covered granite walls, past cascading waterfalls, historic covered bridges, glacial boulders & much more! Open mid May - Mid Oct. Weather permitting in early & late season. MC/VISA.

Phone: (603)745-8391
Address: Rt 3, Franconia Notch, NH 03580
Lat/Lon: 44.0989/-71.6706
Email: nhparks@dred.state.nh.us
Web: www.nhstateparks.org

SEE AD TRAVEL SECTION PAGE 486

FRANKLIN—E-3

(S) Thousand Acres Family Campground—(Merrimack) *S'bound from jct I-93 (exit 20) & US 3: Go 8-1/2 mi S on US 3. N'bound from I-93 (exit 17) & US 3: Go 10 mi N on US 3. Enter on R.* ◆◆◆FACILITIES: 150 sites, typical site width 40 ft, 94 full hkups, 30 W&E, (20/30/50 amps), 26 no hkups, cable TV, ($), WiFi Internet central location, family camping, tenting, shower$, dump, non-guest dump $, RV supplies, ice, picnic tables, fire rings, wood. ◆◆◆RECREATION: rec hall, pavilion, swim pool, canoeing, pond fishing, fishing supplies, bsktball, playground, activities, horseshoes, v-ball. Pets welcome. Partial handicap access. Open Mid May - Oct 1. Big rigs welcome. Rate in 2010 $28-35 for 2 persons. MC/VISA/DISC. Member ARVC, NE-HA-CA. CCUSA 50% Discount. CCUSA reservations Accepted, CCUSA max stay 2 days, CCUSA disc. not avail S, CCUSA disc. not avail F,Sa, CCUSA disc. not avail holidays. Not available during special events. Call for schedule.

Phone: (603)934-4440
Address: 1079 S Main St, (Rte 3), Franklin, NH 03235
Lat/Lon: 43.39260/-71.64475
Email: camp1k@metrocast.net
Web: www.THOUSANDACRESCAMP.com

FREEDOM—D-4

(NW) DANFORTH BAY CAMPING & RV RESORT—(Carroll) *From jct Hwy 16 & Hwy 41: Go 1/2 mi N on Hwy 41, then 4-3/4 mi E on Ossipee Lake Rd, then 1 mi NE on Shawtown Rd. Enter on R.*

PREMIER LAKESIDE CAMPING & RVING
Located between the Lakes Region and White Mountains of NH, family-owned Danforth Bay Camping & RV Resort offers large private sites and sandy beaches. Amenities include heated pools, WiFi, rec. programs and theme weekends.

◆◆◆◆◆FACILITIES: 300 sites, typical site width 30 ft, 254 full hkups, 46 W&E, (30/50 amps), some extd stay sites (summer), 24 pull-thrus, cable TV, WiFi Instant Internet at site, WiFi Internet central location, family camping, tenting, RV's/park model rentals, cabins, RV storage, shower$, dump, non-guest dump $, laundry, groceries, RV supplies, LP gas by weight/by meter, LP bottle exch, ice, picnic tables, fire rings, grills, wood, controlled access.

◆◆◆◆◆RECREATION: rec hall, rec room/area, equipped pavilion, coin games, 2 swim pools, wading pool, lake swim, boating, canoeing, kayaking, ramp, dock, 2 rowboat/8 canoe/15 kayak/3 pedal boat/2 motorboat rentals, lake/river fishing, fishing supplies, golf nearby, bsktball, playground, activities, tennis, horseshoes, sports field, hiking trails, v-ball.

Pets welcome, quantity restrict. Partial handicap access. Open all yr. Facilities fully operational Memorial Day - Columbus Day. Big rigs welcome. Clubs welcome. Rate in 2010 $34-71 per family. MC/VISA/DISC. ATM. Member NE-HA-CA.

Phone: (603)539-2069
Address: 196 Shawtown Rd, Freedom, NH 03836
Lat/Lon: 43.83204/-71.11036
Email: reservations@danforthbay.com
Web: www.danforthbay.com

SEE AD NORTH CONWAY PAGE 502

(NW) THE BLUFFS ADULT RV RESORT—(Carroll) *From jct Hwy 16 & Hwy 41: Go 1/2 mi N on Hwy 41, then 4-3/4 mi E on Ossipee Lake Rd, then 1-1/4 m NE on Shawtown Rd. Enter on R.*

NEW ENGLAND'S NEW ADULT-ONLY RV RESORT!
Located between the Lakes Region and White Mountains of NH, The Bluffs RV Resort offers large extended-stay rental RV sites for active adults age 50+. Amenities include a clubhouse, heated pools, tennis, court games and more.

◆◆◆◆◆FACILITIES: 240 sites, typical site width 50 ft, 240 full hkups, (20/30/50 amps), many extd stay sites (summer), cable TV, WiFi Instant Internet at site, WiFi Internet central location, shower$, laundry, groceries, RV supplies, LP gas by weight/by meter, LP bottle exch, ice, picnic tables, fire rings, grills, wood, controlled access.

◆◆◆◆◆RECREATION: rec hall, rec room/area, coin games, 5 swim pools, lake swim, boating, canoeing, kayaking, ramp, dock, 2 rowboat/8 canoe/15 kayak/3 pedal boat/2 motorboat rentals, lake/river fishing, fishing supplies, golf nearby, bsktball, playground, activities, tennis, horseshoes, sports field, hiking trails, v-ball.

Pets welcome, quantity restrict. Partial handicap access. No tents. Age restrict may apply. Open Mid-April - Mid-November. Facilities fully operational May 1 - October 31. Min 1 week stay. Big rigs welcome. Escort to site. Rate in 2010 $44 for 2 persons. MC/VISA/DISC. ATM. Member NE-HA-CA.

THE BLUFFS ADULT RV RESORT—Continued on next page

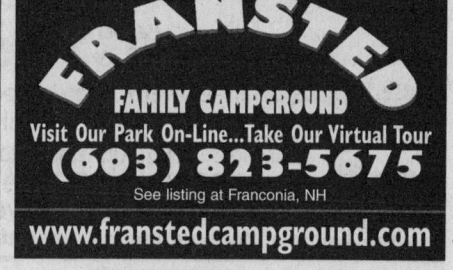

FREEDOM—Continued
THE BLUFFS ADULT RV RESORT—Continued

Phone: (603)539-2069
Address: 196 Shawtown Rd., Freedom, NH 03836
Lat/Lon: 43.83204/-71.11036
Email: seasonal@danforthbay.com
Web: www.nhrvresort.com

SEE AD NORTH CONWAY PAGE 502

GILFORD—D-4

ELLACOYA SP—(Belknap) *From north jct Hwy 3 & Hwy 11: Go 5 mi S on Hwy 11.* FACILITIES: 38 sites, typical site width 30 ft, 38 full hkups, (50 amps), 8 pull-thrus, laundry, ltd groc. RECREATION: lake swim, boating, canoeing, ramp, lake fishing. No pets. Partial handicap access. No tents. Open May 28 - Oct 10. Phone: (603)293-7821.

(E) GUNSTOCK MOUNTAIN RESORT—(Belknap) *From North edge of town: Go 1 mi N on Hwy-11B, then 3-1/2 mi E on Hwy-11A. Enter on R.*

FACILITIES: 311 sites, typical site width 25 ft, 73 full hkups, 71 W&E, (20/30/50 amps), 167 no hkups, some extd stay sites (summer), 14 pull-thrus, WiFi Internet central location, family camping, tenting, cabins, dump, non-guest dump $, laundry, ltd groc, RV supplies, LP gas by weight, ice, picnic tables, fire rings, wood, controlled access.

RECREATION: rec hall, rec room/area, pavilion, coin games, swim pool, lake swim, no motors, canoeing, kayaking, canoe/9 kayak/6 pedal boat rentals, pond fishing, fishing supplies, mini-golf, ($), golf nearby, bsktball, 50 bike rentals, playground, activities, horseshoes, sports field, hiking trails, v-ball. Rec open to public.

Pets welcome. Partial handicap access. Open Memorial Day - Columbus Day. Must be 18 to register. Winter camping mid Dec-mid Mar. Seasonal winter camping available. Clubs welcome. MC/VISA/DISC/AMEX. ATM. Member NE-HA-CA.

Phone: (800)GUNSTOCK
Address: 719 Cherry Valley Rd, Gilford, NH 03249
Lat/Lon: 43.55041/-71.35900
Email: camping@gunstock.com
Web: www.gunstock.com

SEE AD THIS PAGE

GLEN—C-4

(W) Glen Ellis Family Campground—(Carroll) *From north jct Hwy-16 & US-302: Go 1/4 mi W on US-302. Enter on L.* ◊◊◊FACILITIES: 215 sites, typical site width 45 ft, 84 full hkups, 77 W&E, (30/50 amps), 54 no hkups, 17 pull-thrus, family camping, tenting, dump, laundry, ltd groc. ◊◊◊◊◊RECREATION: swim pool, river swim, canoeing, river fishing, playground. No pets. Partial handicap access. Open Memorial Day - Columbus Day. Rate in 2010 $35-50 per family. Member NE-HA-CA. Phone: (603)383-4567.

New Hampshire State Gem: Smokey Quartz

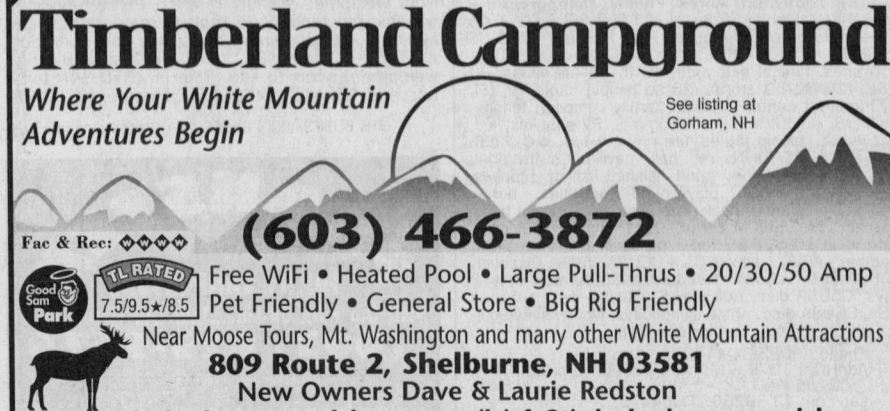

(N) GREEN MEADOW CAMPING AREA—(Carroll) *From north jct Hwy 302 & Hwy 16: Go 1/4mi N on Hwy 16. Enter on R.*

◊◊◊FACILITIES: 92 sites, typical site width 25 ft, 36 full hkups, 35 W&E, (20/30/50 amps), 50 amps ($), 21 no hkups, some extd stay sites (summer), heater not allowed, cable TV, WiFi Internet central location, family camping, tenting, shower$, dump, laundry, RV supplies, ice, picnic tables, fire rings, grills, wood.

◊◊◊RECREATION: swim pool, golf nearby, bsktball, playground, horseshoes, sports field, v-ball.

Pets welcome. Partial handicap access. Open Memorial Day - Columbus Day. Clubs welcome. Rate in 2010 $28-36 per family. MC/VISA. Member NE-HA-CA.

Phone: (603)383-6801
Address: Green Meadow Ln (Rte 16), Glen, NH 03838
Lat/Lon: 44.11356/-71.18196
Web: www.greenmeadowcampingarea.com

SEE AD THIS PAGE

(NE) STORY LAND—*From jct US 302 & Hwy 16: Go 1/2 mi N on Hwy 16. Enter on R.* 21 wonderfully themed rides in a story-book setting, as well as visits with story-book characters, live shows. A favorite of Parents, Grandparents & Children. Open late May - mid Oct. Weekends only late May-mid Jun & early Sep -mid Oct. MC/VISA.

Phone: (603)383-4186
Address: Rt 16, Glen, NH 03838
Lat/Lon: 44.11672/-71.18436
Email: fun@storylandnh.com
Web: www.storylandnh.com

SEE AD TRAVEL SECTION PAGE 486

GORHAM—C-4

MOOSE BROOK SP—(Coos) *From west jct Hwy 16 & US 2: Go 1-1/4 mi W on US 2, then 1/2 mi N on Jimtown Rd. Enter on R.* FACILITIES: 59 sites, 59 no hkups, tenting, ltd groc. RECREATION: stream fishing, play equipment. Partial handicap access. Open mid May - mid Oct. Phone: (603)466-3860.

(S) MT. WASHINGTON AUTO ROAD—*From east jct US 2 & Hwy 16: Go 8 mi S on Hwy 16. Enter on R.* Scenic eight-mile tollroad leading to the summit of Mt. Washington, New England's highest peak. Audio tour on CD available. Also 1.5 hour guided van tours. Souvenirs, cafe & indoor climbing walls at base of road. Open mid May - late Oct. Early & late season: as weather permits. MC/VISA/DISC/AMEX.

Phone: (603)466-3988
Address: Rt 16, Pinkham Notch, Gorham, NH 03581
Lat/Lon: 44.28922/-71.22703
Email: info@mtwashingtonautoroad.com
Web: www.mtwashingtonautoroad.com

SEE AD TRAVEL SECTION PAGE 486

Stay with a Campground in Woodall's

GORHAM—Continued

(E) TIMBERLAND CAMPGROUND—(Coos) *From east jct Hwy-16 & US-2: Go 5 mi E on US-2. Alternate: From NH/ME State Line: Go 4-1/2 mi W on US 2. Enter on R. Enter on L.*

◊◊◊◊FACILITIES: 113 sites, typical site width 30 ft, 41 full hkups, 37 W&E, (20/30/50 amps), 50 amps ($), 35 no hkups, 20 pull-thrus, cable TV, WiFi Internet central location, family camping, tenting, shower$, dump, laundry, ltd groc, RV supplies, ice, picnic tables, fire rings, grills, wood, controlled access.

◊◊◊◊RECREATION: rec hall, rec room/area, coin games, swim pool, golf nearby, bsktball, playground, horseshoes, v-ball.

Pets welcome, breed restrict. Open May 10 - Mid Oct. Clubs welcome. Rate in 2010 $26-32 for 2 persons. MC/VISA/DISC. Member NE-HA-CA.

Phone: (603)466-3872
Address: 809 Rte. 2, Shelburne, NH 03581
Lat/Lon: 44.40836/-71.08868
Email: info@timberlandcampgroundnh.com
Web: www.timberlandcampgroundnh.com

SEE AD THIS PAGE

(E) White Birches Camping Park—(Coos) *From east jct Hwy 16 & US 2: Go 1 1/2 mi E on US 2. Enter on R.* ◊◊◊FACILITIES: 110 sites, 47 full hkups, 16 W&E, (20/30 amps), 47 no hkups, family camping, tenting, dump, laundry. ◊◊◊RECREATION: swim pool, canoeing. Pets welcome. Open May 1 - end of Oct. Rate in 2010 $25-27 per family. Member NE-HA-CA. Phone: (603)466-2022.

(S) WHITE MOUNTAIN NATIONAL FOREST (Dolly Copp Campground)—(Coos) *From jct US-2 & Hwy-16: Go 6 mi SW on Hwy-16.* FACILITIES: 121 sites, 32 ft max RV length, 121 no hkups, tenting. RECREATION: river swim, river fishing. Open mid May - mid Oct. Phone: (603)466-2713.

GREENFIELD—F-3

(W) GREENFIELD SP—(Hillsborough) *From jct Hwy-31 & Hwy-136: Go 1 mi W on Hwy-136. Enter on R.* FACILITIES: 257 sites, 257 no hkups, tenting, dump, ltd groc. RECREATION: lake swim, boating, canoeing, ramp, lake/river/pond/stream fishing, playground. Pets welcome. Partial handicap access. Open mid May - Columbus Day. Phone: (603)547-3497.

HAMPTON—F-5

See listings at Hampton Beach, Hampton Falls, North Hampton, Newfields, Salisbury, MA & Salisbury Beach MA

HAMPTON—Continued on next page

New Hampshire State Nickname: Granite State

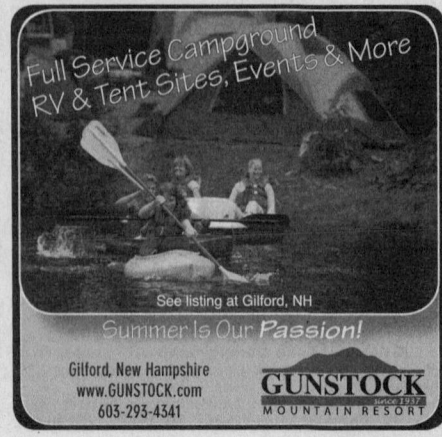

HAMPTON—Continued

(S) **TIDEWATER CAMPGROUND**—(Rockingham) *From jct Hwy 101 & US 1: Go 160 yards S on US 1. Enter on R.*

◆◆◆◆FACILITIES: 225 sites, typical site width 30 ft, 185 full hkups, (20/30/50 amps), 50 amps ($), 40 no hkups, many extd stay sites (summer), 4 pull-thrus, heater not allowed, WiFi Instant Internet at site, family camping, tenting, shower$, ltd groc, RV supplies, ice, picnic tables, fire rings, wood, controlled access.

◆◆◆RECREATION: rec hall, coin games, swim pool, golf nearby, bsktball, playground, horseshoes, sports field.

No pets. Partial handicap access. Open May 15 - Oct 15. Big rigs welcome. Rate in 2010 $41 per family. MC/VISA/DISC. Member ARVC, NE-HA-CA. CCUSA 50% Discount. CCUSA reservations Required, CCUSA max stay 1 day, CCUSA disc. not avail F,Sa, CCUSA disc. not avail holidays. Not available Jun 15 thru Labor Day, special events. No Dogs.

Phone: (603)926-5474
Address: 160 Lafayette Rd, Hampton, NH 03842
Lat/Lon: 42.93074/-70.84512
Web: www.ucampnh.com/tidewater

SEE AD THIS PAGE AND AD TRAVEL SECTION PAGE 485

HAMPTON BEACH—F-5

See listings at Hampton, Hampton Falls, Newfields, North Hampton, NH and Salisbury & Salisbury Beach, MA

HAMPTON BEACH SP—(Rockingham) *From jct I-95 (exit 2) & Hwy 51: Go 3 mi S on Hwy 51, then 1 mi S on Hwy 1A. Enter on L.* FACILITIES: 28 sites, typical site width 35 ft, accepts full hkup units only, 28 full hkups, (30/50 amps), 13 pull-thrus, dump, ltd groc. RECREATION: saltwater swim, boating, ramp, dock, saltwater fishing, playground, play equipment. No tents. Open all yr. Phone: (603)926-8990.

HAMPTON FALLS—F-5

(W) **WAKEDA CAMPGROUND**—(Rockingham) *From jct US 1 & Hwy 88: Go 4 mi W on Hwy 88. Enter on L.*

CAMP IN THE PINES NEAR HAMPTON BEACH
Enjoy Camping Cabins, 70' 50 amp Pull Thrus, Tent & 2 or 3 way Sites, Trading Post, Game Room, Mini Golf, Playground, Laundry, Ice Cream Stand, Clean Modern Facilities and Very Friendly Staff! 14 mi to Portsmouth, 44 mi to Boston.

◆◆◆◆FACILITIES: 408 sites, typical site width 35 ft, 232 full hkups, 111 W&E, (30/50 amps), 65 no hkups, some extd stay sites (summer), 5 pull-thrus, cable Internet central location, family camping, tenting, RV's/park model rentals, RV storage, shower$, dump, non-guest dump $, laundry, ltd groc, RV supplies, ice, picnic tables, fire rings, grills, wood.

HAMPTON FALLS—Continued
WAKEDA CAMPGROUND—Continued

◆◆◆◆RECREATION: rec hall, rec room/area, pavilion, coin games, mini-golf, ($), golf nearby, bsktball, playground, horseshoes, sports field, v-ball.

Pets welcome, breed restrict, quantity restrict. Partial handicap access. Open May 15 - Oct 1. Trading Post,Gameroom,Mini Golf,Ice Cream Socials & Pancake Breakfasts Jun 30-Labor Day. Escort to site. Clubs welcome. Rate in 2010 $37-46 per family. MC/VISA. Member NE-HA-CA. CCUSA 50% Discount. CCUSA reservations Recommended, CCUSA max stay 2 days, CCUSA disc. not avail F,Sa, CCUSA disc. not avail holidays. Not available Jul & Aug.

Phone: (603)772-5274
Address: 294 Exeter Rd (Rt 88), Hampton Falls, NH 03844
Lat/Lon: 42.95617/-70.90452
Web: www.wakedacampground.com

SEE AD THIS PAGE

HANCOCK—F-2

(N) **Seven Maples Campground**—(Hillsborough) *From jct Hwy 123 & Hwy 137: Go 1/2 mi N on Hwy 137, then 1/8 mi N on Longview Rd. Enter on L.* ◆◆◆FACILITIES: 125 sites, typical site width 25 ft, 50 full hkups, 54 W&E, (20/30/50 amps), 50 amps ($), 21 no hkups, WiFi Instant Internet at site, WiFi Internet central location, family camping, tenting, dump, non-guest dump $, ltd groc, RV supplies, LP gas by weight/by meter, ice, picnic tables, fire rings, wood. ◆◆◆◆RECREATION: rec hall, swim pool, canoeing, kayaking, pond fishing, fishing supplies, bsktball, playground, shuffleboard court shuffleboard court, horseshoes. Pets welcome, quantity restrict. Open Early May - Mid Oct. Facilities fully operational Mother's Day -

HANCOCK—Continued
Seven Maples Campground—Continued

Columbus Day. Rate in 2010 $30-33 per family. MC/VISA. Member ARVC, NE-HA-CA. FCRV discount. FMCA discount. CCUSA 50% Discount. CCUSA reservations Accepted, CCUSA max stay 4 days, Cash only for CCUSA disc., CCUSA disc. not avail F,Sa, CCUSA disc. not avail holidays. Not available July 4th week. Max stay per month: 4 nights, Mon-Thu. Coin operated showers. $15 dump surcharge if not staying in park.

Phone: (603)525-3321
Address: 24 Longview Rd, Hancock, NH 03449
Lat/Lon: 42.98466/-71.97874
Email: info@sevenmaples.com
Web: www.sevenmaples.com

HANOVER—D-2

STORRS POND RECREATION AREA—(Grafton) *From jct I-89 & I-91 in VT: Go 5 mi N on I-91 (exit 13-Hanover, NH-Dartmouth College), then turn E and cross the Connecticut River into Hanover, NH (street becomes Wheelock St), 1 mi E on Wheelock St, 1 mi N on Hwy 10, then 1 mi E on Reservoir. Enter on L.* FACILITIES: 31 sites, typical site width 45 ft, 35 ft max RV length, 19 W&E, (15/30 amps), 12 no hkups, 2 pull-thrus, tenting, dump. RECREATION: swim pool, canoeing, pond fishing, play equipment. Partial handicap access. Open Mid May - Mid Oct. Facilities fully operational Jul 1 - Aug 31. Phone: (603)643-2134.

New Hampshire State Tree: White Birch

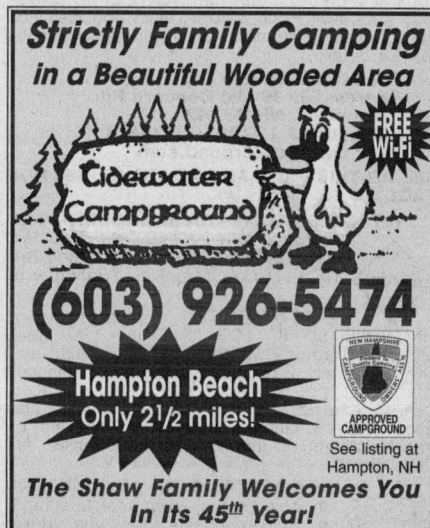

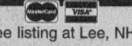

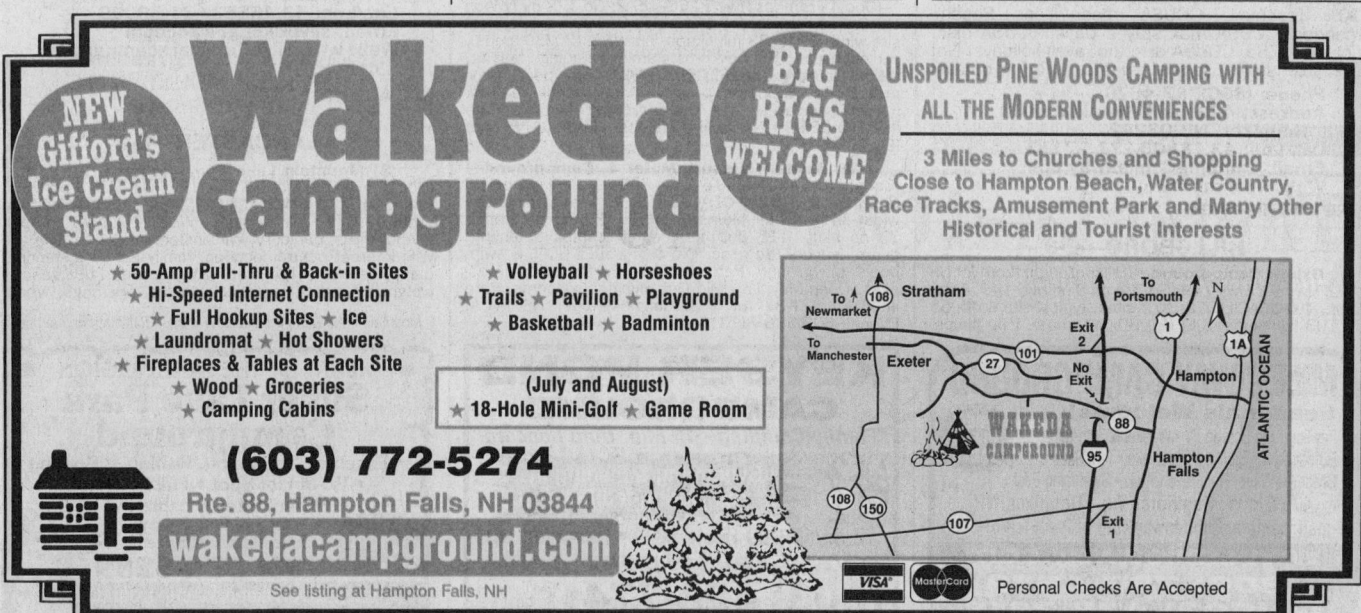

HENNIKER—E-3

(E) KEYSER POND CAMPGROUND—(Merrimack) *From N'bnd jct I-89 (exit 5) & Hwy 202: Go 3-1/2 mi W on Hwy 202, then 300 yds S on Old Concord Rd. From SB I-89 (exit 6) to Hwy 127, then 3-1/4 mi S on Hwy 127, then (cross US 202) 300 yds S on Old Concord Rd. Enter on R.*

◊◊◊FACILITIES: 118 sites, typical site width 50 ft, 66 full hkups, 43 W&E, (20/30 amps), 9 no hkups, some extd stay sites (summer), WiFi Internet central location, family camping, tenting, RV's/park model rentals, shower$, dump, non-guest dump $, laundry, ltd groc, RV supplies, LP gas by weight/by meter, ice, picnic tables, fire rings, wood, controlled access.

◊◊◊◊RECREATION: rec hall, coin games, boating, electric motors only, canoeing, kayaking, 3 rowboat/5 canoe/3 kayak/2 pedal boat rentals, pond fishing, fishing supplies, mini-golf, ($), golf nearby, bsktball, playground, shuffleboard court 3 shuffleboard courts, activities (wkends), horseshoes, v-ball.

Pets welcome. Open mid May - mid Oct. Rate in 2010 $32-40 per family. MC/VISA/DISC. Member NE-HA-CA. CCUSA 50% Discount. CCUSA reservations Accepted, CCUSA max stay 2 days, CCUSA disc. not avail F,Sa, CCUSA disc. not avail holidays. Not available month of July or special events. Call for details.

Phone: (603)428-7741
Address: 1739 Old Concord Rd, Henniker, NH 03242
Lat/Lon: 43.17786/-71.75881
Web: www.keyserpond.com

SEE AD THIS PAGE AND AD TRAVEL SECTION PAGE 485

(E) MILE AWAY CAMPGROUND—(Merrimack) *From jct I-89 (exit 5) & Hwy 202: Go 5 mi W on Hwy 202, then 1 mi NE on Old West Hopkinton Rd. Enter on L.*

◊◊◊◊FACILITIES: 159 sites, typical site width 50 ft, 129 full hkups, 30 W&E, (20/30/50 amps), 50 amps ($), many extd stay sites (summer), 2 pull-thrus, cable TV, WiFi Instant Internet at site, cable Internet central location, family camping, tenting, shower$, dump, non-guest dump $, laundry, ltd groc, RV supplies, LP gas by weight/by meter, ice, picnic tables, fire rings, wood.

◊◊◊◊RECREATION: rec hall, pavilion, coin games, swim pool, boating, 6 hp limit, canoeing, kayaking, dock, rowboat/3 canoe/4 pedal boat rentals, pond fishing, fishing supplies, mini-golf, golf nearby, bsktball, playground, shuffleboard court 2 shuffleboard courts, activities (wkends), horseshoes, v-ball.

Pets welcome. Partial handicap access. Open all yr. Facilities fully operational May - Oct. Escort to site. Clubs welcome. Rate in 2010 $35 per family. MC/VISA/DISC. Member ARVC, NE-HA-CA. CCUSA 50% Discount. CCUSA reservations Recommended, CCUSA max stay 2 days, CCUSA disc. not avail F,Sa, CCUSA disc. not avail holidays. Not available during special events. Call for details.

Phone: (800)787-4679
Address: 479 Old W Hopkinton Rd, Henniker, NH 03242
Lat/Lon: 43.18803/-71.77113
Email: camping@mileaway.com
Web: www.mileaway.com

SEE AD THIS PAGE

HILLSBORO—E-3

Oxbow Campground—(Hillsborough) *From jct US 202/Hwy 9 & Hwy 149: Go 3/4 mi S on Hwy 149. Enter on L.* ◊◊◊FACILITIES: 112 sites, typical site width 55 ft, 103 full hkups, 8 E, (20/30/50 amps), 1 no hkups,

HILLSBORO—Continued
Oxbow Campground—Continued

4 pull-thrus, family camping, tenting, laundry. ◊◊◊◊RECREATION: lake swim, no motors, pond fishing, playground. Pets welcome, breed restrict. Partial handicap access. Open May 1 - Oct 15. Big rigs welcome. Rate in 2010 $34 per family. Member NE-HA-CA. Phone: (603)464-5952.

HINSDALE—F-2

(W) Hinsdale Campground—(Cheshire) *From I-91 in VT, take exit 1 E on Rt 5: Go 1 mi, cross over Green Bridge. Follow Rte 119 4.8 mi E to Hinsdale Campground. Enter on L.* ◊◊◊◊FACILITIES: 113 sites, typical site width 30 ft, 88 full hkups, 16 W&E, (20/30/50 amps), 9 no hkups, cable TV, ($), WiFi Internet central location, family camping, tenting, RV storage, dump, non-guest dump $, laundry, RV supplies, LP gas by weight/by meter, ice, picnic tables, fire rings, grills, wood. ◊◊◊◊RECREATION: rec hall, equipped pavilion, swim pool, wading pool, playground, activities, horseshoes, hiking trails. Pets welcome, breed restrict, quantity restrict. Partial handicap access. Open Apr 1 - Oct 31. Big rigs welcome. Rate in 2010 $39-42.50 for 4 persons. MC/VISA. Member NE-HA-CA. FMCA discount. CCUSA 50% Discount. CCUSA reservations Recommended, CCUSA max stay 3 days, CCUSA disc. not avail Th, CCUSA disc. not avail F,Sa, CCUSA disc. not avail holidays.

Phone: (603)336-8906
Address: 29 Pine St, Hinsdale, NH 03451
Lat/Lon: 42.79793/-72.51322
Email: hinsdale@campingnow.com
Web: www.campingnow.com

HOLDERNESS—D-3

(SE) Bethel Woods Campground—(Grafton) *From jct I-93 (exit 24) & US 3: Go 7-1/2 mi on US 3 South. Enter on R.* ◊◊◊FACILITIES: 107 sites, typical site width 50 ft, 75 full hkups, 11 W&E, (20/30 amps), 21 no hkups, WiFi Instant Internet at site, WiFi Internet central location, family camping, tenting, dump, laundry, ltd groc, RV supplies, LP gas by weight, ice, picnic tables, fire rings, wood. ◊◊◊RECREATION: rec hall, swim pool, bsktball, playground, horseshoes. Pets welcome, breed restrict. Open Mid May - Columbus Day. Rate in 2010 $35-38 per family. MC/VISA. Member ARVC, NE-HA-CA. CCUSA 50% Discount. CCUSA reservations Recommended, CCUSA max stay 4 days, Cash only for CCUSA disc., CCUSA disc. not avail F,Sa. Not valid during special events, call for details.

Phone: (603)279-6266
Address: 245 Rte 3, Holderness, NH 03245
Lat/Lon: 43.71858/-71.53820
Email: camp@bethelwoods.com
Web: www.bethelwoods.com

JAFFREY—F-2

MONADNOCK SP—(Cheshire) *From jct US 202 & Hwy 124: Go 2-1/4 mi W on Hwy 124, then 1-1/2 mi N on Dublin Rd, then follow signs. Enter at end.* FACILITIES: 28 sites, 28 no hkups, tenting, ltd groc. RECREATION: No pets. Partial handicap access. Open all yr. Facilities fully operational Apr 1 - Veteran's Day. Phone: (603)532-8862.

JEFFERSON—C-3

(E) Fort Jefferson Campground at Six Gun City—(Coos) *From jct Hwy 115 & US 2: Go 1/2 mi NW on US 2. Enter on L.* ◊◊◊FACILITIES: 100 sites, typical site width 20 ft, 33 full hkups, 28 W&E, (20/30 amps), 39 no hkups, 83 pull-thrus, family camping, tenting, dump, laundry. ◊◊RECREATION: swim pool, playground. Pets welcome, breed restrict, quantity restrict. Partial handicap access. Open Mid May - Mid Oct. Rate in 2010 $25-29 per family. Member NE-HA-CA. Phone: (603)586-4510.

(W) Lantern Resort Motel & Campground—(Coos) *From jct Hwy 116 & US 2: Go 1/2 mi NW on US 2. Enter on R.* ◊◊◊◊FACILITIES: 91 sites, typical site width 35 ft, 46 full hkups, 30 W&E, (20/30/50 amps), 15 no hkups, 15 pull-thrus, family camping, tenting, dump, laundry, ltd groc. ◊◊◊◊RECREATION: 2 swim pools, playground. Pets welcome. Partial handicap access. Open May 15 - Mid Oct. Big rigs welcome. Rate in 2010 $27-37 for 2 persons. Member NE-HA-CA. Phone: (603)586-7151.

JEFFERSON—Continued

SANTA'S VILLAGE—*From jct Hwy 116 & US 2: Go 3/4 mi NW on US 2. Enter on L.* Visit Santa's summer home & enjoy all his special rides new Ho Ho H20 Water Feature, Reindeer Carousel, Sleigh Ride, Log Flume & more. Rides for all ages. Take in special shows. See Santa's elves & reindeer. Open late May - mid Oct. Weekends thru mid Jun & after early Sep & wknds during Chrismas Season. MC/VISA.

Phone: (603)586-4445
Address: 528 Presidential Hwy (Rte 2), Jefferson, NH 03583
Lat/Lon: 44.43419/-71.51083
Email: santa@santasvillage.com
Web: www.santasvillage.com

SEE AD TRAVEL SECTION PAGE 486

KEENE—F-2

See listings at Fitzwilliam, Hinsdale, Richmond & Winchester

LACONIA—E-3

(N) Hack-Ma-Tack Family Campground—(Belknap) *From jct Hwy 104 & US 3: Go 2-1/2 mi S on US 3. Enter on L.* ◊◊◊FACILITIES: 100 sites, typical site width 30 ft, 74 full hkups, 17 W&E, (20/30/50 amps), 9 no hkups, family camping, tenting, dump, laundry, ltd groc. ◊◊◊RECREATION: swim pool, playground. Pets welcome ($), breed restrict, size restrict, quantity restrict. Open May 10 - Columbus Day. Big rigs welcome. Rate in 2010 $30-35 for 2 persons. Phone: (603)366-5977.

(S) SILVER LAKE PARK CAMPGROUND—(Belknap) *From N'bound jct I-93 (exit 20) & US 3: Cross US 3 to Hwy 140, then Go 2-3/4 mi E on Hwy 140, then 2 mi N on Jamestown Rd. From S'bnd jct I-93 (exit 20) & US 3: Go 1/4 mi E on US 3, then 2-3/4 mi E on Hwy 140, then 2 mi N on Jamestown Rd. Enter on L.*

◊◊◊◊FACILITIES: 72 sites, typical site width 25 ft, 35 ft max RV length, 71 full hkups, 1 W&E, (20/30 amps), mostly extd stay sites (summer), 73 pull-thrus, cable TV, WiFi Internet central location, family camping, tenting, cabins, dump, non-guest dump $, laundry, ltd groc, RV supplies, ice, picnic tables, fire rings, grills, wood, controlled access.

◊◊◊◊RECREATION: equipped pavilion, lake swim, boating, canoeing, kayaking, ramp, 2 canoe/4 kayak/2 pedal boat rentals, lake fishing, golf nearby, bsktball, playground, activities, (wkends), horseshoes, sports field, v-ball.

No pets. Partial handicap access. Open Early May - Columbus Day Wknd. Weather Permitting. Rate in 2010 $30-40 for 2 persons. MC/VISA/DISC. Member ARVC, NE-HA-CA.

Phone: (603)524-6289
Address: 389 Jamestown Rd, Belmont, NH 03220
Lat/Lon: 43.46553/-71.53099
Email: silverlkcpgr@aol.com
Web: www.silverlakeparkcampground.com

SEE AD THIS PAGE

LANCASTER—B-3

(S) Mountain Lake Campground & RV Park—(Coos) *From east jct US 2 & US 3: Go 4 mi S on US 3. Enter on R.* ◊◊◊◊FACILITIES: 94 sites, typical site width 30 ft, 50 full hkups, 44 W&E, (20/30/50 amps), 10 pull-thrus, cable TV, WiFi Instant Internet at site ($), WiFi Internet central location, family camping, tenting, dump, laundry, ltd groc, RV supplies, LP gas by weight/by meter, ice, picnic tables, fire rings, wood.

Mountain Lake Campground & RV Park—Continued on next page

LANCASTER—Continued
Mountain Lake Campground & RV Park—Continued

◇◇◇◇◇RECREATION: rec hall, swim pool, lake swim, boating, canoeing, kayaking, ramp, lake fishing, fishing supplies, playground, shuffleboard court shuffleboard court, activities, horseshoes, hiking trails. Pets welcome ($), breed restrict, quantity restrict. Open May 1 - Oct 31. Facilities fully operational Mid May - Mid Oct. Big rigs welcome. Rate in 2010 $42-52.50 per family. MC/VISA. Member NE-HA-CA. CCUSA 50% Discount. CCUSA reservations Accepted, CCUSA max stay 7 days. Discount not available Memorial Day weekend, Jun 21 thru Labor Day weekends. 2 day minimum stay. Rates subject to change-call to confirm.

Phone: (603)788-4509
Address: 485 Prospect St, Lancaster, NH 03584
Lat/Lon: 44.42950/-71.58954
Email: mtnlake@ne.rr.com
Web: www.mtnlakecampground.com

(E) Roger's Campground—(Coos) *From east jct US 3 & US 2: Go 1-1/2 mi E on US 2. Enter on R.* ◇◇◇◇FACILITIES: 456 sites, typical site width 30 ft, 302 full hkups, 91 W&E, 17 E, (30/50 amps), 50 amps ($), 46 no hkups, 302 pull-thrus, family camping, tenting, dump, laundry, ltd groc. ◇◇◇◇◇RECREATION: 2 swim pools, playground. Pets welcome. Partial handicap access. Open Late Apr. - Mid Oct. Rate in 2010 $27-46 for 2 persons. Member ARVC, NE-HA-CA. Phone: (603)788-4885.

LEE—E-4

FERNDALE ACRES CAMPGROUND—(Strafford) *From jct US 4 & Hwy 155: Go 2-1/2 mi S on Hwy 155, then 1-1/2 mi E on Wednesday Hill Rd, then 1 mi S on entry road. Enter at end.*

◇◇◇FACILITIES: 145 sites, typical site width 25 ft, 36 ft max RV length, 110 full hkups, 35 W&E, (20/30 amps), some extd stay sites (summer), 5 pull-thrus, heater not allowed, cable TV, WiFi Internet central location, family camping, tenting, shower$, dump, laundry, ltd groc, RV supplies, ice, picnic tables, fire rings, wood.

◇◇◇◇RECREATION: rec hall, rec room/area, coin games, swim pool, river swim, canoeing, kayaking, river fishing, golf nearby, bsktball, playground, shuffleboard court shuffleboard court, activities (wkends), horseshoes, sports field, v-ball.

Pets welcome, breed restrict, quantity restrict. Partial handicap access. Open Mid May - Mid Sep. Clubs welcome. Rate in 2010 $34 for 2 persons. MC/VISA/AMEX. Member ARVC, NE-HA-CA.

Phone: (603)659-5082
Address: 130 Wednesday Hill Rd, Lee, NH 03861
Lat/Lon: 43.12279/-70.98355
Email: fac132@aol.com
Web: www.ferndaleacres.com

SEE AD THIS PAGE

(S) WADLEIGH FALLS CAMPGROUND—(Strafford) *From jct Hwy 125 & Hwy 152: Go 2 mi E on Hwy 152, then 1/4 mi S on Campground Rd. Enter on R.*

◇◇◇FACILITIES: 115 sites, 79 full hkups, 34 W&E, (20/30/50 amps), 2 no hkups, many extd stay sites (summer), 19 pull-thrus, heater not allowed, WiFi Internet central location, family camping, tenting, shower$, dump, non-guest dump $, portable dump, laundry, RV supplies, ice, picnic tables, fire rings, wood.

◇◇◇◇RECREATION: rec hall, rec room/area, coin games, swim pool, canoeing, kayaking, 3

LEE—Continued
WADLEIGH FALLS CAMPGROUND—Continued

canoe rentals, river fishing, mini-golf, ($), golf nearby, bsktball, playground, activities, (wkends), horseshoes, sports field, v-ball.

Pets welcome. Partial handicap access. Open Mid May - Mid Oct. Clubs welcome. Rate in 2010 $27-34 per family. MC/VISA. Member ARVC, NE-HA-CA.

Phone: (603)659-1751
Address: 16 Campground Rd, Lee, NH 03861
Lat/Lon: 43.08922/-71.00941
Email: wadleighfalls@comcast.net
Web: www.wadleighfalls.com

SEE AD HAMPTON PAGE 495

LINCOLN—C-3

(N) Country Bumpkins Campground & Cabins—(Grafton) *From jct I-93 (exit 33) & US 3: Go 1/2 mi S on US 3. Enter on L.* ◇◇◇◇FACILITIES: 45 sites, typical site width 25 ft, 6 full hkups, 13 W&E, (20/30 amps), 26 no hkups, family camping, tenting, dump, laundry, ltd groc. ◇◇RECREATION: river swim, river fishing, play equipment. Pets welcome, breed restrict. Open Mid May - Mid Oct. Rate in 2010 $25-29 per family. Member NE-HA-CA. Phone: (603)745-8837.

LOON MOUNTAIN—*From jct I-93 (exit 32) & Kancamagus Hwy: Go 3 mi E on Kancamagus Hwy. Enter on R.* The state's longest aerial ride - 7,000 feet to the summit. Cafeteria, observation tower, glacial caves & boardwalk, Artisans Village & playground. At Loon's base - two climbing walls & zipline, festivals & concerts, Mountain Biking. Open all yr. Closed mid Apr - mid Jun & mid Oct - mid Nov. MC/VISA/DISC/AMEX.

Phone: (603)745-8111
Address: 60 Loon Mountain Rd, Lincoln, NH 03251
Email: info@loonmtn.com
Web: www.loonmtn.com

SEE AD TRAVEL SECTION PAGE 486

THE WHALE'S TALE WATER PARK—*From I-93, take exit 33 N Lincoln to Route 3 N. Continue N on Rte 3 1/2 mi. Enter on L.* Full size waterpark with wave pool, waterslides & lazy river. New Banzai Pipeline and Shipwreck Island Adventure. Open Mid June - Early Sept. Open 10am-6pm.

Phone: (603)745-8810
Address: 481 DW Hwy, Lincoln, NH 03251
Email: info@whalestalewaterpark.net
Web: www.whalestalewaterpark.net

SEE AD TRAVEL SECTION PAGE 486

(E) WHITE MOUNTAIN NATIONAL FOREST (Big Rock Campground)—(Grafton) *From jct US-3 & FH-112: Go 8 mi E on FH-112 (Kancamagus Hwy).* FACILITIES: 28 sites, 30 ft max RV length, 28 no hkups, tenting. RECREATION: lake fishing. Open all yr. Phone: (603)536-1310.

(E) WHITE MOUNTAIN NATIONAL FOREST (Hancock Campground)—(Grafton) *From jct US 3 & Hwy 112: Go 4 mi E on Hwy 112 (Kancamagus Scenic Hwy).* FACILITIES: 56 sites, 30 ft max RV length, 56 no hkups, tenting. RECREATION: river swim. Open all yr. Phone: (603)536-1310.

LISBON—C-3

(SW) Littleton/Lisbon KOA—(Grafton) *From jct I-93 (exit 42) & US 302: Go 5-1/2 mi W on US 302. Enter on L.* ◇◇◇◇FACILITIES: 60 sites, typical site width 34 ft, 19 full hkups, 22 W&E, (20/30/50 amps), 19 no hkups, 14 pull-thrus, family camping, tenting, dump, laundry, ltd groc. ◇◇◇◇RECREATION: swim pool, river swim, river fishing, playground. Pets welcome. Open May 1 - Oct 17. Big rigs welcome. Rate in 2010 $36-49 for 2 persons. Member NE-HA-CA. Phone: (800)562-5836. KOA discount.

LITTLETON—C-3

(NW) CRAZY HORSE CAMPGROUND & RV PARK—(Grafton) *From I-93 (exit 43) and CR 18 (Dalton Rd): Go 1/10 mi S on CR 18, then 1 mi W on CR 135 (St Johnsbury Rd), then 1-1/2 mi NW on Hilltop Rd. Enter on R.*

◇◇◇◇FACILITIES: 179 sites, typical site width 35 ft, 135 full hkups, 36 W&E, (30/50 amps), 8 no hkups, many extd stay sites (summer), 16 pull-thrus, cable TV, WiFi Instant Internet at site, WiFi Internet central location, family camping, tenting, RV's/park model rentals, RV storage, shower$, dump, laundry, ltd groc, RV supplies, LP gas by weight/by meter, ice, picnic tables, fire rings, wood.

◇◇◇◇RECREATION: rec hall, pavilion, coin games, swim pool, canoeing, kayaking, 6 canoe/3 kayak rentals, lake/pond fishing, fishing supplies, golf nearby, bsktball, playground, activities, (wkends), horseshoes, sports field, hiking trails, v-ball.

Pets welcome. Partial handicap access. Open all yr. Limited facilities Oct 15 - Dec 1 & Apr 1 - May 15. Big rigs welcome. Escort to site. Clubs welcome. Rate in 2010 $33-39 per family. MC/VISA/DISC. Member NE-HA-CA.

Phone: (603)444-2204
Address: 788 Hilltop Rd, Littleton, NH 03561
Lat/Lon: 44.32194/-71.84924
Email: mail@crazyhorsenh.com
Web: www.crazyhorsenh.com

SEE AD THIS PAGE AND AD TRAVEL SECTION PAGE 485

MADBURY—E-4

(W) Old Stage Campground—(Strafford) *From jct Hwy 125 & Hwy 9: Go 3 mi E on Hwy 9, then 1 mi S on Old Stage Rd. Enter on R.* ◇◇◇FACILITIES: 158 sites, typical site width 35 ft, 151 full hkups, 7 W&E, (30 amps), 4 pull-thrus, family camping, tenting, dump, laundry, ltd groc. ◇◇◇◇RECREATION: swim pool, river/pond fishing, playground. Pets welcome, breed restrict. Open Early May - Columbus Day. Rate in 2010 $38 per family. Member ARVC, NE-HA-CA. Phone: (603) 742-4050.

MEREDITH—D-3

(W) CLEARWATER CAMPGROUND—(Belknap) *From jct I-93 (exit 23) & Hwy-104: Go 3 mi E on Hwy-104. Enter on R.*

◇◇◇◇FACILITIES: 141 sites, typical site width 35 ft, 69 full hkups, 32 W&E, (20/30/50 amps), many extd stay sites (summer), 4 pull-thrus, cable TV, WiFi Instant Internet at site ($), family camping, tenting, cabins, dump, portable dump, laundry, groceries, RV supplies, ice, picnic tables, fire rings, wood, controlled access.

CLEARWATER CAMPGROUND—Continued on next page

MEREDITH—Continued
CLEARWATER CAMPGROUND—Continued

◊◊◊◊◊RECREATION: rec hall, rec room/area, coin games, lake swim, boating, canoeing, kayaking, ramp, dock, rowboat/2 canoe/3 kayak/3 pedal boat rentals, lake fishing, fishing supplies, golf nearby, bsktball, playground, activities, horseshoes, sports field, v-ball.

Pets welcome. Open mid May - Columbus Day. Big rigs welcome. Rate in 2010 $25-46 per family. MC/VISA/DISC/AMEX. Member NE-HA-CA.

Text 107996 to (440)725-8687 to see our Visual Tour.

Phone: (603)279-7761
Address: 556 Rte 104, Meredith, NH 03253
Lat/Lon: 43.61924/-71.58601
Email: info@clearwatercampground.com
Web: www.clearwatercampground.com

SEE AD THIS PAGE AND AD TRAVEL SECTION PAGE 485

(E) HARBOR HILL CAMPING AREA—(Belknap) *From jct US 3 & Hwy 25: Go 1-1/2 mi E on Hwy 25. Enter on R.*

WELCOME

◊◊◊◊FACILITIES: 140 sites, typical site width 25 ft, 96 full hkups, 30 W&E, (20/30/50 amps), 14 no hkups, many extd stay sites (summer), 4 pull-thrus, heater not allowed, cable TV ($), WiFi Internet central location, family camping, tenting, RV's/park model rentals, cabins, shower$, dump, laundry, ltd groc, RV supplies, LP gas by weight/by meter, ice, picnic tables, fire rings, wood, controlled access.

◊◊◊◊RECREATION: rec room/area, coin games, swim pool, golf nearby, bsktball, playground, shuffleboard court shuffleboard court, horseshoes.

MEREDITH—Continued
HARBOR HILL CAMPING AREA—Continued

Pets welcome, breed restrict, quantity restrict. Open Memorial Day - Columbus Day. Escort to site. Rate in 2010 $36 per family. MC/VISA/Debit. Member ARVC, NE-HA-CA.

Phone: (603)279-6910
Address: 189 NH Rt 25, Meredith, NH 03253-6411
Lat/Lon: 43.67507/-71.48099
Email: hhcamp@hhcamp.com
Web: www.HHCAMP.com

SEE AD THIS PAGE

(W) MEREDITH WOODS 4 SEASON CAMPING AREA—(Belknap) *From jct I-93 (exit 23) & Hwy 104: Go 3 mi E on Hwy 104. Enter on L.*

WELCOME

◊◊◊◊FACILITIES: 99 sites, typical site width 40 ft, 99 full hkups, (20/30/50 amps), mostly extd stay sites, cable TV, WiFi Instant Internet at site ($), family camping, tenting, cabins, laundry, ltd groc, RV supplies, ice, picnic tables, fire rings, wood, controlled access.

◊◊◊◊◊RECREATION: rec hall, rec room/area, coin games, swim pool, lake swim, hot tub, boating, canoeing, kayaking, ramp, dock, rowboat/2 canoe/3 kayak/3 pedal boat rentals, lake fishing, fishing supplies, golf nearby, bsktball, playground, activities, horseshoes, sports field, hiking trails, v-ball.

Pets welcome. Partial handicap access. Open all yr. Big rigs welcome. Rate in 2010 $32-46 per family. MC/VISA/DISC/AMEX. Member ARVC, NE-HA-CA.

Phone: (603)279-5449
Address: 551 Rte 104, Meredith, NH 03253
Lat/Lon: 43.61990/-71.58573
Email: info@meredithwoods.com
Web: www.MEREDITHWOODS.com

SEE AD THIS PAGE AND AD TRAVEL SECTION PAGE 485

The granite profile "Old Man of the Mountain" is one of the most famous natural landmarks in the state. The Old Man's head measures 40 feet from chin to forehead and is made up of five ledges. Nature carved this profile thousands of years ago. The natural sculpture is 1,200 feet above Echo Lake.

MEREDITH—Continued

(W) TWIN TAMARACK FAMILY CAMPING AND RV RESORT—(Belknap) *From jct I-93 (exit 23) & Hwy-104: Go 2-1/2 mi E on Hwy-104. Enter on L.*

WELCOME

◊◊◊◊FACILITIES: 243 sites, typical site width 40 ft, 147 full hkups, 96 W&E, (30/50 amps), 50 amps ($), some extd stay sites (summer), 7 pull-thrus, WiFi Internet central location, family camping, tenting, RV's/park model rentals, cabins, dump, non-guest dump $, portable dump, laundry, ltd groc, RV supplies, ice, picnic tables, fire rings, wood, controlled access.

◊◊◊◊RECREATION: rec room/area, pavilion, coin games, swim pool, lake swim, hot tub, boating, canoeing, kayaking, ramp, dock, 2 rowboat/4 canoe/3 kayak/2 pedal boat rentals, lake fishing, fishing supplies, golf nearby, bsktball, playground, activities, (wkends), horseshoes, sports field, v-ball.

Pets welcome, breed restrict, quantity restrict. Partial handicap access. Open Late May - Columbus Day. Motorcycles ok during Bike Week. Escort to site. Clubs welcome. Rate in 2010 $34-39 per family. MC/VISA/DISC. Member NE-HA-CA.

Phone: (603)279-4387 Address: Twin Tamarack Rd.
Lat/Lon: 43.62075/-71.59192
Email: twintamarack@metrocast.net
Web: www.twintamarackcampground.com

SEE AD THIS PAGE AND AD TRAVEL SECTION PAGE 485

Whether you're dreaming about buying a new RV or are actively shopping, 2011 RV Buyer's Guide is your best source. It contains all the information you need to make an intelligent buying decision. Over 450 vehicles are profiled with complete information about construction features, dimensions, popular options, and more, making comparing models easy. To order your copy go to www.woodalls.com/shop.

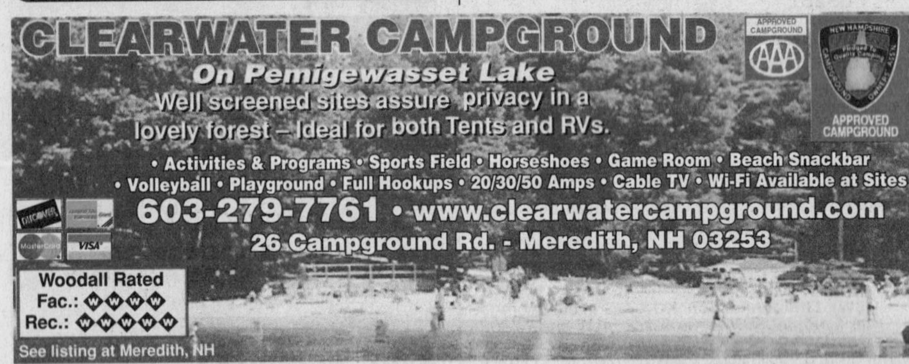

MILTON—E-4

(NE) MI-TE-JO CAMPGROUND—(Strafford) *From Hwy 16/Spaulding Tpk (exit 17): Go 3/4 mi E on Hwy 75, then 3-1/4 mi N on Hwy 125, then 1 mi E on Townhouse Rd. Enter on L.*

COME RELAX AND ENJOY YOUR FAMILY!! Less than 1 hour from the White Mountains, Ocean Beaches, and tax free Outlet Shopping. We offer Large Full-Hookup Sites, Cabins, Boating & Fishing, Lake Swimming, Playgrounds, Basketball, Rec Halls, Tennis, Wi-Fi & more!

◊◊◊◊FACILITIES: 198 sites, typical site width 50 ft, 198 full hkups, (20/30/50 amps), many extd stay sites (summer), 15 pull-thrus, cable TV, WiFi Instant Internet at site, WiFi Internet central location, family camping, tenting, cabins, dump, non-guest dump $, laundry, ltd groc, RV supplies, LP gas by weight/by meter, ice, picnic tables, fire rings, wood, controlled access.

◊◊◊◊◊RECREATION: rec hall, rec room/area, pavilion, coin games, lake swim, boating, canoeing, kayaking, ramp, dock, 4 canoe/8 kayak/3 pedal boat rentals, lake fishing, fishing supplies, golf nearby, bsktball, playground, shuffleboard court shuffleboard court, tennis, horseshoes, sports field, v-ball.

Pets welcome. Partial handicap access. Open May 15 - Columbus Day. Big rigs welcome. Escort to site. Clubs welcome. Rate in 2010 $41-46 per family. MC/VISA. Member ARVC, NE-HA-CA.

Phone: (603)652-9022
Address: 111 Mi-Te-Jo Rd, Milton, NH 03851
Lat/Lon: 43.43628/-70.96818
Email: info@mi-te-jo.com
Web: www.mi-te-jo.com

SEE AD THIS PAGE

MOULTONBOROUGH—D-4

LONG ISLAND BRIDGE CAMPGROUND —(Carroll) *From jct Hwy 109 & Hwy 25: Go 4 mi SW on Hwy 25, then 6-1/2 mi S on Moultonborough Neck Rd. Enter on L.*

◊◊◊◊FACILITIES: 114 sites, typical site width 25 ft, 36 ft max RV length, 76 full hkups, 25 W&E, (20/30 amps), 13 no hkups, many extd stay sites (summer), 4 pull-thrus, cable TV, WiFi Internet central location, family camping, tenting, RV's/park model rentals, cabins, shower$, dump, laundry, RV supplies, ice, picnic tables, fire rings, grills, wood, controlled access.

◊◊◊RECREATION: lake swim, boating, canoeing, kayaking, ramp, dock, 2 canoe/kayak rentals, lake fishing, fishing supplies, golf nearby, bsktball, playground, sports field, v-ball.

Pets welcome, breed restrict, quantity restrict. Partial handicap access. Open Mid May - Mid Oct. Escort to site. Rate in 2010 $25-37 per family. Member NE-HA-CA.

Phone: (603)253-6053
Address: 29 Long Island Rd, Moultonborough, NH 03254
Lat/Lon: 43.66676/-71.34696
Email: libcg1@juno.com
Web: www.longislandbridgecampground.com

SEE AD THIS PAGE

Check out our web site www.woodalls.com

NEW BOSTON—F-3

(W) FRIENDLY BEAVER CAMPGROUND —(Hillsborough) *From jct Hwy 77 & Hwy 136 & Hwy 13: Go 100 feet S on Hwy 13, then 2 mi W on Old Coach Rd. Enter on R.*

NEW ENGLAND'S #1 FUN DESTINATION! THE Super Vacation Spot in Southern New Hampshire, Friendly Beaver has LOTS of Activities for All Ages! From our Indoor and 3 Outdoor Pools to Theme Weekends and Activities for Children Young and Old, there'll be NO BOREDOM!!

◊◊◊◊◊FACILITIES: 278 sites, typical site width 40 ft, 213 full hkups, 62 W&E, (20/30/50 amps), 3 no hkups, many extd stay sites, heater not allowed, WiFi Instant Internet at site ($), WiFi Internet central location ($), family camping, tenting, dump, portable dump, laundry, groceries, RV supplies, ice, picnic tables, fire rings, grills, wood.

◊◊◊◊◊RECREATION: rec hall, rec room/area, pavilion, coin games, 4 swim pools, wading pool, golf nearby, bsktball, playground, activities, horseshoes, sports field, hiking trails, v-ball.

Pets welcome. Partial handicap access. Open all yr. Entire facility fully operational during Winter months. Big rigs welcome. Escort to site. Clubs welcome. Rate in 2010 $36-42 per family. MC/VISA. ATM. Member ARVC, NE-HA-CA. CCUSA 50% Discount. CCUSA reservations Required, CCUSA max stay 2 days, CCUSA disc. not avail F,Sa, CCUSA disc. not avail holidays. Not available month of July. Addl surcharges: $4 sewer, $5 WiFi.

Text 86103 to (440)725-8687 to see our Visual Tour.

Phone: (603)487-5570
Address: 88 Cochran Hill Rd, New Boston, NH 03070
Lat/Lon: 42.96871/-71.72274
Email: reservations@friendlybeaver.com
Web: www.friendlybeaver.com

SEE AD PAGES 500-501 AND AD MAP PAGE 484

John Irving, author, is from New Hampshire.

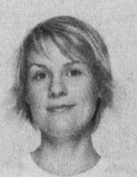

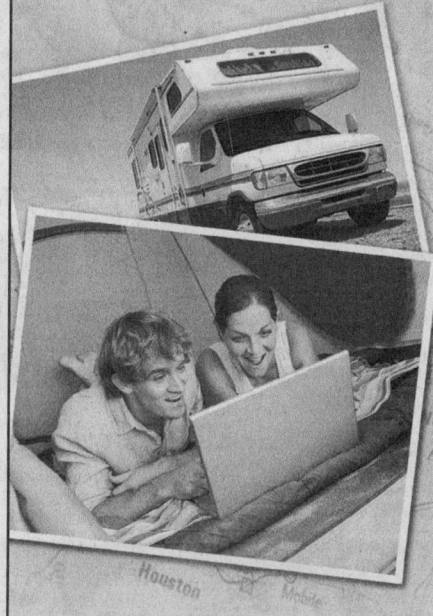

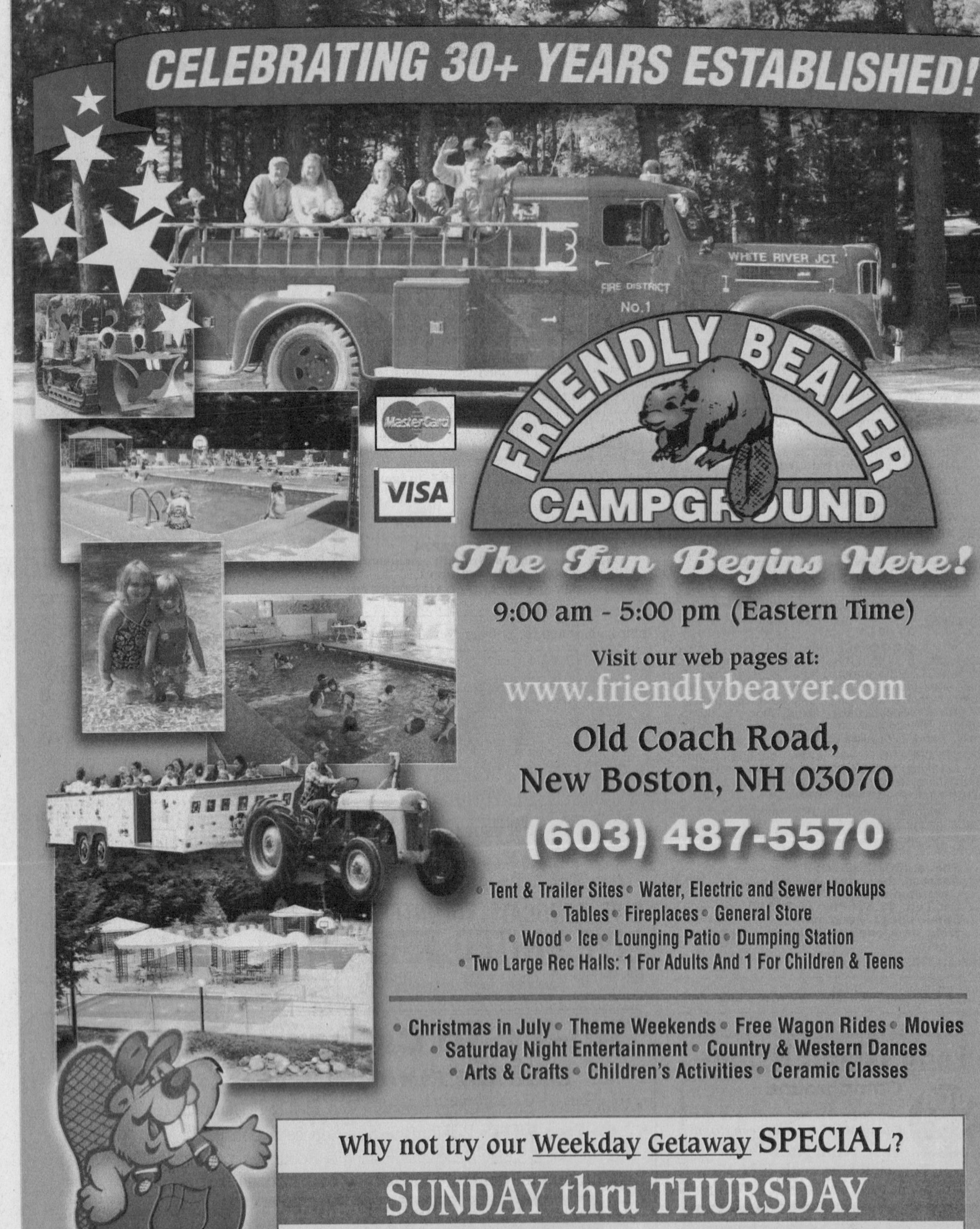
CELEBRATING 30+ YEARS ESTABLISHED!
WHITE RIVER JCT.
FIRE DISTRICT
No.1
MasterCard
VISA
FRIENDLY BEAVER
CAMPGROUND
The Fun Begins Here!
9:00 am - 5:00 pm (Eastern Time)
Visit our web pages at:
www.friendlybeaver.com
Old Coach Road,
New Boston, NH 03070
(603) 487-5570
• Tent & Trailer Sites • Water, Electric and Sewer Hookups
• Tables • Fireplaces • General Store
• Wood • Ice • Lounging Patio • Dumping Station
• Two Large Rec Halls: 1 For Adults And 1 For Children & Teens
• Christmas in July • Theme Weekends • Free Wagon Rides • Movies
• Saturday Night Entertainment • Country & Western Dances
• Arts & Crafts • Children's Activities • Ceramic Classes
Why not try our Weekday Getaway SPECIAL?
SUNDAY thru THURSDAY
Camp TWO Nights and Receive a THIRD Night FREE!
Must request discount at time of making your reservation

NEWFIELDS—F-4

(N) **GREAT BAY CAMPING/SHELL**—(Rockingham) *From I-95 (exit 2) & Hwy 101 W: Go 3-1/2 mi W on Hwy 101 W, then 4 mi N on Hwy 108 (turn in at Shell gas station). Enter on R.*

WOODED CAMPSITES, SALTWATER FISHING
Come enjoy our Quiet Country Setting! Direct boat access to saltwater! Camp in our natural atmosphere under oaks and pines or relax at the pool. Weekend activities for ALL ages. FAMILY CAMPING AT ITS BEST!!!

◆◆◆FACILITIES: 85 sites, typical site width 45 ft, 60 full hkups, 6 W&E, (20/30/50 amps), 19 no hkups, some extd stay sites (summer), WiFi Instant Internet at site, WiFi Internet central location, family camping, tenting, laundry, groceries, RV supplies, LP gas by weight/by meter, ice, picnic tables, fire rings, grills, wood.

◆◆◆RECREATION: rec hall, swim pool, boating, canoeing, kayaking, ramp, dock, canoe/4 kayak rentals, saltwater fishing, golf nearby, bsktball, activities, (wkends), horseshoes, v-ball.

Pets welcome, breed restrict, quantity restrict. Open May 15 - Oct 1. Big rigs welcome. Rate in 2010 $40 per family. MC/VISA. ATM. Member NE-HA-CA.

Phone: (603)778-0226
Address: 58 Rte 108, Newfields, NH 03856
Lat/Lon: 43.04629/-70.93085
Email: info@greatbaycamping.com
Web: www.greatbaycamping.com

SEE AD TRAVEL SECTION PAGE 485 AND AD TRAVEL SECTION PAGE 483

NEWPORT—E-2

(W) **CROW'S NEST CAMPGROUND**—(Sullivan) *From jct Hwy-11 & Hwy-10: Go 2 mi S on Hwy-10. Enter on R.*

◆◆◆◆FACILITIES: 115 sites, typical site width 30 ft, 42 full hkups, 61 W&E, (20/30/50 amps), 12 no hkups, some extd stay sites (summer), 4 pull-thrus, WiFi Instant Internet at site, WiFi Internet central location, family camping, tenting, tent rentals, RV's/park model rentals, cabins, shower$, dump, non-guest dump $, laundry, ltd groc, RV supplies, LP gas by weight/by meter, ice, picnic tables, fire rings, wood.

◆◆◆◆RECREATION: rec hall, rec room/area, coin games, swim pool, wading pool, river swim, river fishing, fishing supplies, mini-golf, ($), golf nearby, playground, activities, (wkends), horseshoes, sports field, v-ball.

Pets welcome, breed restrict, quantity restrict. Partial handicap access. Open Mid May - Mid Oct. Open Dec 1-Apr 1, water not available at all sites. Escort to site. Clubs welcome. Rate in 2010 $32-40 per family. MC/VISA/DISC. Member ARVC, NE-HA-CA. CCUSA 50% Discount. CCUSA reservations Required, CCUSA max stay 2 days, CCUSA disc. not avail F,Sa, CCUSA disc. not avail holidays. Open May 15-Oct 15 and again Dec 1-Apr 1.

Phone: (603)863-6170
Address: 529 S. Main St, Newport, NH 03773
Lat/Lon: 43.33403/-72.16835
Email: camping@crowsnestcampground.com
Web: www.crowsnestcampground.com

SEE AD SUNAPEE PAGE 504

(S) **Northstar Campground**—(Sullivan) *From jct Hwy 11 & Hwy 10: Go 3-1/2 mi S on Hwy 10, then 1/4 mi W on Coon Brook Rd. Enter on R.* ◆◆FACILITIES: 68 sites, typical site width 50 ft, 35 ft max RV length,

NEWPORT—Continued
Northstar Campground—Continued

25 full hkups, 25 W&E, (20/30 amps), 18 no hkups, family camping, tenting, dump. ◆◆RECREATION: lake swim, river fishing, playground. Pets welcome. Partial handicap access. Open May 15 - Oct 15. Rate in 2010 $30-32 for 2 persons. Member NE-HA-CA. Phone: (603) 863-4001.

NORTH CONWAY—C-4

(S) **Beach Camping Area**—(Carroll) *From south jct Hwy 302 & Hwy 16: Go 1 mi S on Hwy 16. Enter on R.* ◆◆◆FACILITIES: 120 sites, typical site width 35 ft, 113 full hkups, 1 W&E, (20/30 amps), 6 no hkups, 13 pull-thrus, family camping, tenting, dump, laundry, ltd groc. ◆◆◆◆RECREATION: river swim, canoeing, river fishing, playground. Pets welcome ($), breed restrict, quantity restrict. Open mid May - mid Oct. Rate in 2010 $28-39 per family. Member ARVC, NE-HA-CA. Phone: (603)447-2723. FMCA discount.

CONWAY SCENIC RAILROAD—*From south jct US 302 & Hwy 16: Go 2-1/2 mi N on US 302/Hwy 16, then 100 yards W on Norcross St. Enter at end.* Scenic 11-mile, 21-mile & 60-mile round-trip train rides through the Mt. Washington Valley countryside and surrounding White Mountains with live commentary on the history and folklore of the area. Open Mid Apr - Dec. Call for times. MC/VISA.

Phone: (603)356-5251
Address: 38 Norcross Circle, North Conway, NH 03860
Email: info@conwayscenic.com
Web: www.conwayscenic.com

SEE AD TRAVEL SECTION PAGE 486

(S) **SACO RIVER CAMPING AREA**—(Carroll) *From south jct US 302 & Hwy 16: Go 1/4 mi N on Hwy 16/US 302. Enter on L.*

◆◆◆◆FACILITIES: 144 sites, typical site width 40 ft, 95 full hkups, 44 W&E, (20/30/50 amps), 5 no hkups, 29 pull-thrus, cable TV, WiFi Instant Internet at site, family camping, tenting, RV's/park model rentals, shower$, dump, laundry, ltd groc, RV supplies, LP gas by weight/by meter, ice, picnic tables, fire rings, grills, wood, controlled access.

◆◆◆◆RECREATION: rec hall, pavilion, coin games, swim pool, river swim, canoeing, kayaking, 20 canoe/20 kayak rentals, river fishing, fishing supplies, golf nearby, bsktball, 25 bike rentals, playground, activities, horseshoes, sports field, hiking trails, v-ball.

Pets welcome ($), breed restrict, quantity restrict. Open Mid May - Mid Oct. Clubs welcome. Rate in 2010 $35-45 per family. MC/VISA/DISC/AMEX. Member ARVC, NE-HA-CA.

Phone: (603)356-3360
Address: 1550 White Mountain Hwy (Rte 16), North Conway, NH 03860
Lat/Lon: 44.02129/-71.11668
Email: reservations@sacorivercampingarea.com
Web: www.sacorivercampingarea.com

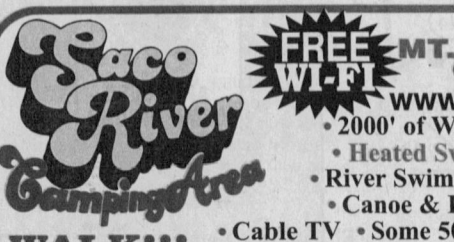

SEE AD THIS PAGE

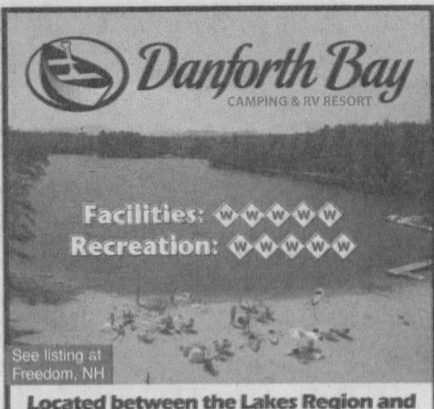

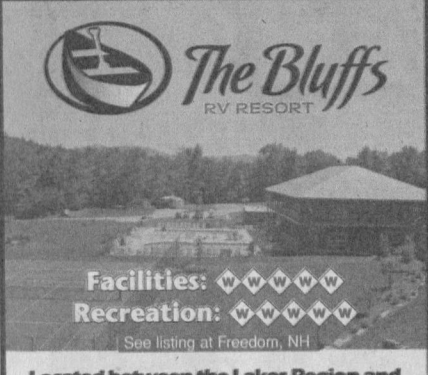

NORTH HAMPTON—F-5

(N) SHEL-AL CAMPGROUND—(Rockingham) *From jct Hwy 111 & US 1: Go 1/2 mi N on US 1. Enter on R.*

WELCOME ◆◆◆FACILITIES: 183 sites, typical site width 20 ft, 32 ft max RV length, 94 full hkups, 32 W&E, 30 E, (20/30/50 amps), 50 amps ($), 27 no hkups, some extd stay sites (summer), heater not allowed, WiFi Internet central location, family camping, tenting, RV's/park model rentals, shower$, RV supplies, ice, picnic tables, fire rings, grills, wood.

◆◆◆RECREATION: rec hall, coin games, golf nearby, bsktball, playground, shuffleboard court shuffleboard court, horseshoes, v-ball.

Pets welcome, quantity restrict. Open May 15 - Oct 1. Facilities fully operational May 15 - Sep 15. Escort to site. Rate in 2010 $32-42 per family. Member NE-HA-CA.

Phone: (603)964-5730
Address: 115 Lafayette Rd (Rt 1), North Hampton, NH 03862
Lat/Lon: 42.98245/-70.83132
Email: camp@shel-al.com
Web: www.shel-al.com

SEE AD HAMPTON PAGE 494

NORTH WOODSTOCK—C-3

(N) CLARK'S TRADING POST—*From jct I-93 (exit 32) & Hwy 112: Go 3/4 mi W on Hwy 112, then 1-1/2 mi N on US 3. Enter on R.* WELCOME Performances by trained bears; 2.5 mi train ride on standard gauge steam locomotive; visit 1884 replica of Hook & Ladder Fire House with authentic horsedrawn fire equipment;Americana Bumper Boats, Ice Cream Parlor, Peppermint Saloon & antique style photos. Open mid May - mid Oct. Weekends only mid May - mid Jun & Labor Day - mid Oct. MC/VISA.

Phone: (603)745-8913
Address: 110 US Rte 3, Lincoln, NH 03251
Lat/Lon: 44.04344/-71.68865
Email: info@clarkstradingpost.com
Web: www.clarkstradingpost.com

SEE AD TRAVEL SECTION PAGE 486

(W) LOST RIVER GORGE & BOULDER CAVES—*From jct I-93 (exit 32) & Hwy 112: Go 6 mi W on Hwy 112. Enter on R.* WELCOME Natural gorge with scenic views of rock formations & waterfalls. Self-guided tours along boardwalks and thru boulder caves, geologic display, nature garden, gift shop & snack bar. Open mid May - mid Oct. Weather permitting. MC/VISA.

Phone: (603)745-8031
Address: 1712 Lost River Rd, North Woodstock, NH 03262
Lat/Lon: 44.03720/-71.78514
Email: info@lostrivergorge.com
Web: www.lostrivergorge.com

SEE AD TRAVEL SECTION PAGE 486

(W) Lost River Valley Campground—(Grafton) *From jct I-93 (exit 32) & Hwy 112: Go 3-1/2 mi W on Hwy 112. Enter on L.* ◆◆◆FACILITIES: 132 sites, typical site width 40 ft, 32 ft max RV length, 8 full hkups, 53 W&E, (20/30/50 amps), 71 no hkups, 8 pull-thrus, WiFi Internet central location, family camping, tenting, shower$, dump, laundry, groceries, RV supplies, LP gas by weight/by meter, ice, picnic tables, fire rings, grills, wood. CAMPCLUB USA ◆◆◆◆RECREATION: kayaking, stream fishing, fishing supplies, bsktball, playground, tennis, horseshoes, v-ball. Pets welcome, breed restrict, quantity restrict. Partial handicap access. Open May 15 - Columbus Day. Rate in 2010 $30-36 for 2 persons. MC/VISA/DISC. ATM. Member ARVC, NE-HA-CA. CCUSA 50% Discount. CCUSA reservations Recommended, CCUSA max stay Unlimited, CCUSA disc. not avail F,Sa, CCUSA disc. not avail holidays. May stay unlimited length of time depending on availability but full price must be paid on Fri & Sat. Discount available May 15-Jun 20 and again after Labor Day to Columbus Day.

Phone: (800)370-5678
Address: 951 Lost River Rd, North Woodstock, NH 03262
Lat/Lon: 44.01923/-71.74326
Email: jim@lostriver.com
Web: www.lostriver.com

(W) Maple Haven Camping, Cottages, & Lodge—(Grafton) *From jct I-93 (exit 32) & Hwy 112: Go 1 mi W on Hwy 112. Enter on L.* ◆◆FACILITIES: 42 sites, 22 W&E, (20/30 amps), 20 no hkups, 1 pull-thru, family camping, tenting, dump. ◆◆◆RECREATION: river/pond fishing, playground. Pets welcome. Open Memorial Day - End of Sep. Rate in 2010 $30-40 per family. Phone: (603)745-3350.

NORTH WOODSTOCK—Continued

WHITE MOUNTAIN ATTRACTIONS VISITORS CENTER—*From jct I-93 (exit 32) & Hwy 112 (Kancamagus Hwy): Go 200 yds E on Hwy 112. Enter on R.* WELCOME Located at exit 32 off I-93. Free information & directions to White Mountain area family attractions, historic sites, scenic drives, camping, lodging, tax-free shopping, dining, maps, brochures and more. Open all yr.

Phone: (800)346-3687
Address: 200 Kancamagus Hwy, North Woodstock, NH 03262
Lat/Lon: 44.03574/-71.67703
Email: info@visitwhitemountains.com
Web: www.visitwhitemountains.com

SEE AD TRAVEL SECTION PAGE 486

(S) WHITE MOUNTAIN NATIONAL FOREST (Russell Pond Campground)—(Grafton) *From jct US-3 & Hwy-175: Go 2-3/4 mi S on Hwy-175, then 2 mi E on FR-30, then 3 mi N on FR-90.* FACILITIES: 86 sites, 22 ft max RV length, 86 no hkups, tenting. RECREATION: boating, no motors, ramp, dock, lake fishing. Partial handicap access. Open May 15 - Oct 15. Phone: (603)536-1310.

WHITE MOUNTAIN NATIONAL FOREST (Wildwood Campground)—(Grafton) *From jct Hwy-112 & US-3: Go 8-2/3 mi W on Hwy-112.* FACILITIES: 26 sites, 22 ft max RV length, 26 no hkups, tenting. RECREATION: Partial handicap access. Open mid May - Dec. Phone: (603)536-1310.

ORFORD—D-2

(S) The Pastures—(Grafton) *From I-91 (exit 15) Vermont: Go 100 yards E to US 5, then 3/4 mi N on US 5 to Hwy 25A, cross bridge on Hwy 25A, then 1 block S on Hwy 10. Enter on R.* ◆◆◆FACILITIES: 61 sites, typical site width 50 ft, 35 ft max RV length, 24 full hkups, 37 W&E, (20/30/50 amps), 2 pull-thrus, family camping, tenting, dump. ◆◆◆RECREATION: swim pool, boating, canoeing, dock, river fishing, playground. Pets welcome, quantity restrict. Open mid May - Mid Oct. Rate in 2010 $26 per family. Member ARVC, NE-HA-CA. Phone: (603)353-4579.

OSSIPEE—D-4

(S) Beaver Hollow Campground—(Carroll) *From jct Hwy 28 & Hwy 16: Go 1-1/2 mi S on Hwy 16. Enter on L.* ◆◆FACILITIES: 160 sites, typical site width 25 ft, 140 full hkups, (20/30/50 amps), 20 no hkups, 100 pull-thrus, family camping, tenting, laundry. ◆◆◆RECREATION: swim pool, playground. Pets welcome, breed restrict, quantity restrict. Partial handicap access. Open Mid May - Mid Oct. Rate in 2010 $35 per family. Member NE-HA-CA. Phone: (603)539-4800.

PITTSBURG—A-3

CONNECTICUT LAKES SF (Deer Mountain Campground)—(Coos) *From town: Go 20 mi N on Hwy 3.* FACILITIES: 25 sites, 25 no hkups. RECREATION: lake swim, canoeing, lake fishing. Partial handicap access. Open End May - mid Oct. Phone: (603)538-6965.

LAKE FRANCIS SP—(Coos) *From town: Go 7 mi N on US-3.* FACILITIES: 43 sites, 43 no hkups, tenting, dump, ltd groc. RECREATION: boating, canoeing, ramp, lake fishing, playground. Open mid May - mid Dec. Facilities fully operational mid May - mid Oct. Phone: (603)538-6965.

RAYMOND—F-4

PAWTUCKAWAY SP—(Rockingham) *From jct Hwy 101 (exit 5) & Hwy 156: Go 2 mi N on Hwy 156, then 2 mi NW on Mountain Rd.* FACILITIES: 195 sites, 195 no hkups, tenting, ltd groc. RECREATION: lake swim, boating, canoeing, ramp, dock, lake fishing, playground. No pets. Partial handicap access. Open May 15 - mid Oct. Phone: (603)895-3031.

(SE) Pine Acres RV Resort, LLC (Morgan RV Resorts)—(Rockingham) *From Hwy 101 (exit 5): Go 3/4 mi S on Hwy 107. Enter on L.* ◆◆◆◆FACILITIES: 403 sites, typical site width 30 ft, 292 full hkups, 91 W&E, (20/30/50 amps), 20 no hkups, family camping, tenting, dump, laundry, full svc store. ◆◆◆◆◆RECREATION: river swim, boating, 7.5 hp limit, canoeing, ramp, dock, river fishing, playground. Pets welcome. Partial handicap access. Open Mid Apr - Mid Oct. Big rigs welcome. Rate in 2010 $39-56 per family. Member ARVC, NE-HA-CA. Phone: (603)895-2519.

RICHMOND—F-2

(N) MUSEUM OF FAMILY CAMPING—*From jct Hwy 119 & Hwy 32: Go 1 mi S on Hwy 32. Enter on L.* WELCOME A series of exhibits showing evolution of camping, camping vehicles, and camping memorabilia. Open Memorial Day - Columbus Day.

Phone: (603)239-4768
Address: 136 Athol Rd (Rte 32), Richmond, NH 03470
Lat/Lon: 42.74408/-72.27086
Web: www.museumoffamilycamping.com

SEE AD THIS PAGE

(S) SHIR-ROY CAMPING AREA—(Cheshire) *From jct Hwys 119 & 32: Go 1 mi S on Hwy 32. Enter on L.*

WELCOME ◆◆◆FACILITIES: 122 sites, typical site width 30 ft, 120 full hkups, 1 W&E, 1 E, (20/30/50 amps), some extd stay sites (summer), 18 pull-thrus, WiFi Internet central location, family camping, tenting, cabins, dump, non-guest dump $, laundry, ltd groc, RV supplies, ice, picnic tables, fire rings, grills, wood.

◆◆◆◆RECREATION: rec hall, rec room/area, coin games, lake swim, boating, canoeing, kayaking, ramp, 3 rowboat/5 canoe/5 kayak/3 pedal

SHIR-ROY CAMPING AREA—Continued on next page

RICHMOND—Continued
SHIR-ROY CAMPING AREA—Continued

boat rentals, lake fishing, fishing supplies, golf nearby, bsktball, playground, activities, (wkends), horseshoes, sports field, v-ball.

Pets welcome, quantity restrict. Partial handicap access. Open Memorial Day weekend - Columbus Day. Open some wkends only, after Columbus Day in Oct, by reservation. Clubs welcome. Rate in 2010 $28-39 per family. Member ARVC, NE-HA-CA.

Phone: (603)239-4768
Address: 136 Athol Rd (Rte 32), Richmond, NH 03470
Lat/Lon: 42.74408/-72.27086
Web: www.ucampnh.com/shir-roy

SEE AD PAGE 503

RINDGE—F-2

(E) Woodmore Family Campground & RV Park—(Cheshire) *From west jct Hwy 119 & US 202: Go 1 mi N on US 202, then 1/4 mi E on S. Woodbound Rd, then 1/2 mi N on Woodbound Rd. Enter on L.* ◊◊◊FACILITIES: 135 sites, typical site width 50 ft, 87 full hkups, 46 W&E, (30/50 amps), 2 no hkups, heater not allowed, cable TV, phone Internet central location, family camping, tenting, RV storage, shower$, dump, non-guest dump $, laundry, groceries, RV supplies, LP gas by weight, ice, picnic tables, fire rings, grills, wood. ◊◊◊◊RECREATION: rec hall, pavilion, swim pool, boating, canoeing, kayaking, dock, lake fishing, fishing supplies, bsktball, playground, activities, horseshoes, v-ball. Pets welcome. Partial handicap access. Open Early May - Late Oct. Big rigs welcome. Rate in 2010 $32-40 per family. MC/VISA. Member ARVC, NE-HA-CA. FMCA discount. CCUSA 50% Discount. CCUSA reservations Recommended, CCUSA max stay 1 day, Cash only for CCUSA disc., CCUSA disc. not avail F,Sa, CCUSA disc. not avail holidays. Not available Jul, Aug or holiday weeks. Electric heater not allowed.

Phone: (603)899-3362
Address: 21 Woodmore Dr, Rindge, NH 03461
Lat/Lon: 42.77806/-72.02508
Email: info@woodmorecampground.com
Web: www.woodmorecampground.com

SOUTH HAMPTON—F-4

Tuxbury Pond Resort—(Rockingham) ◊◊◊FACILITIES: 315 sites, 297 full hkups, 8 W&E, (50 amps), 10 no hkups, 18 pull-thrus, family camping, tenting, laundry, ltd groc. ◊◊◊◊RECREATION: swim pool, boating, 10 hp limit, canoeing, lake fishing, playground. Pets welcome. Partial handicap access. Open May 1 - Mid Oct. Rate in 2010 $40-48 per family. Phone: (800)585-7660.

Reserve Online at Woodalls.com

STRAFFORD—E-4

(E) Crown Point Campground—(Strafford) *From jct Spaulding Tpk (Hwy 16-exit 14) & Ten Rod Rd: Go 1/2 mi SE on Hwy 11 (Main St), then 1/2 mi SW on Twombley St, then 4 mi W on Hwy 202A, then 1/4 mi N on First Crown Point Rd. Enter on L.* ◊◊◊◊FACILITIES: 135 sites, typical site width 45 ft, 132 full hkups, 3 W&E, (20/30/50 amps), cable TV, WiFi Internet central location, family camping, tenting, dump, non-guest dump $, laundry, ltd groc, RV supplies, LP gas by weight/by meter, ice, picnic tables, fire rings, wood. ◊◊◊◊RECREATION: rec hall, pavilion, swim pool, lake swim, canoeing, kayaking, pond fishing, fishing supplies, bsktball, playground, activities, horseshoes. Pets welcome, breed restrict, quantity restrict. Open Early May - Columbus Day. Big rigs welcome. Green Friendly. Rate in 2010 $25-41 for 2 persons. MC/VISA/DISC. Member ARVC, NE-HA-CA. CCUSA 50% Discount.

STRAFFORD—Continued
Crown Point Campground—Continued

Phone: (603)332-0405
Address: 79 First Crown Point Rd, STRAFFORD, NH 03884
Lat/Lon: 43.28681/-71.06731
Email: camp@crownpointcampground.com
Web: www.crownpointcampground.com

SUNAPEE—E-2

See listing at Newport

SWANZEY—F-2

(E) SWANZEY LAKE CAMPING AREA—(Cheshire) *From jct Hwy 12 & Hwy 32: Go 5 mi S on Hwy 32, then 2 mi SW on Swanzey Lake Rd, then 1/2 mi N on East Shore Rd. Enter on L.*

◊◊◊FACILITIES: 100 sites, 34 ft max RV length, 86 full hkups, 11 W&E, (20/30 amps), 3 no hkups, many extd stay sites (summer), cable TV, ($), WiFi Internet central location, family camping, tenting, cabins, shower$, dump, non-guest dump $, laundry, ltd groc, RV supplies, LP gas by weight/by meter, ice, picnic tables, fire rings, wood.

◊◊◊RECREATION: rec hall, lake swim, boating, canoeing, kayaking, dock, 4 rowboat/3 canoe/4 kayak/2 pedal boat rentals, lake fishing, fishing supplies, golf nearby, play equipment, horseshoes.

Pets welcome. Partial handicap access. Open Apr 15 - Nov 1. Rate in 2010 $32-34 per family. MC/VISA/DISC/AMEX. Member NE-HA-CA.

Phone: (603)352-9880
Address: 88 E Shore Rd, Swanzey, NH 03446
Lat/Lon: 42.84243/-72.29961
Email: info@swanzeylake.com
Web: www.SWANZEYLAKE.com

SEE AD THIS PAGE

TAMWORTH—D-4

(SW) Riverbend RV Resort—(Carroll) *From jct Hwy 16 & Hwy 25: Go 7 mi W on Hwy 25, then 100 ft N on Hwy 113 (Bearcamp Hwy). Enter on L.* ◊◊◊FACILITIES: 27 sites, typical site width 30 ft, 27 full hkups, (30/50 amps), 8 pull-thrus, family camping, tenting, dump, laundry. ◊◊◊RECREATION: swim pool, river swim, canoeing, river fishing, playground. Pets welcome, breed restrict, quantity restrict. Partial handicap access. Open Mid May - End Oct. Big rigs welcome. Rate in 2010 $30 per family. Member ARVC, NE-HA-CA. Phone: (603)323-9133.

(SE) TAMWORTH CAMPING AREA—(Carroll) *From jct Hwy 16 & Hwy 25W: Go 3/4 mi N on Hwy 16, then 3 mi W on Depot Rd. Enter on L.*

◊◊◊FACILITIES: 100 sites, typical site width 50 ft, 49 full hkups, 40 W&E, (20/30/50 amps), 11 no hkups, some extd stay sites (summer), 1 pull-thrus, WiFi Internet central location, family camping, tenting, RV's/park model rentals, RV storage, shower$, dump, non-guest dump $, portable dump, laundry, RV supplies, LP gas by weight, ice, picnic tables, fire rings, grills, wood, controlled access.

◊◊◊◊RECREATION: rec hall, rec room/area, pavilion, coin games, river swim, river fishing, fishing supplies, mini-golf, ($), golf nearby, bsktball, playground, shuffleboard court 2 shuffleboard courts, activities (wkends), horseshoes, sports field, v-ball.

TAMWORTH—Continued
TAMWORTH CAMPING AREA—Continued

Pets welcome. Open May 15 - Dec 1. Facilities fully operational May 15 - Columbus Day. Clubs welcome. Rate in 2010 $30-43 per family. MC/VISA/DISC. Member ARVC, NE-HA-CA. CCUSA 50% Discount.

Phone: (800)274-8031
Address: 194 Depot Rd, Tamworth, NH 03886
Lat/Lon: 43.84705/-71.25749
Email: info@tamworthcamping.com
Web: www.tamworthcamping.com

SEE AD TRAVEL SECTION PAGE 483

THORNTON—D-3

(E) Goose Hollow Camp & RV Park—(Crafton) *From jct I-93 (exit 28) & Hwy 49: Go 3-3/4 mi E on Hwy 49, then 100 yards N on Burbank Hill Rd. Enter on R.* ◊◊◊FACILITIES: 175 sites, typical site width 40 ft, 128 full hkups, 47 W&E, (20/30/50 amps), 50 amps ($), 3 pull-thrus, WiFi Internet central location, family camping, tenting, RV storage, dump, non-guest dump $, portable dump, laundry, ltd groc, RV supplies, ice, picnic tables, fire rings, wood. ◊◊◊◊RECREATION: rec hall, swim pool, river swim, river fishing, fishing supplies, bsktball, 20 bike rentals, playground, shuffleboard court 2 shuffleboard courts, horseshoes, v-ball. Pets welcome, quantity restrict. Partial handicap access. Open all yr. Rate in 2010 $34-37 per family. MC/VISA. Member NE-HA-CA. CCUSA 50% Discount.

Phone: (603)726-2000
Address: 35 Burbank Hill Rd, Thornton, NH 03285
Lat/Lon: 43.88224/-71.59750
Email: info@nhcampgounds.com
Web: www.nhcampgrounds.com

TWIN MOUNTAIN—C-3

(S) Ammonoosuc Campground—(Coos) *From jct US 302 & US 3: Go 1/4 mi S on US 3. Enter on L.* ◊◊◊FACILITIES: 112 sites, typical site width 30 ft, 36 ft max RV length, 75 full hkups, 13 W&E, (20/30 amps), 24 no hkups, family camping, tenting, dump, laundry. ◊◊RECREATION: swim pool, playground. Pets welcome, quantity restrict. Open May 15 - Oct 15. Rate in 2010 $28 per family. Member NE-HA-CA. Phone: (603) 846-5527.

(W) Beech Hill Campground—(Coos) *From jct US-3 & US-302: Go 2 mi W on US-302. Enter on R.* ◊◊◊FACILITIES: 142 sites, typical site width 50 ft, 56 full hkups, 42 W&E, (20/30 amps), 44 no hkups, family camping, tenting, dump, laundry, ltd groc. ◊◊◊RECREATION: swim pool, river swim, river fishing. Pets welcome. Partial handicap access. Open Mid May - Mid Oct. Rate in 2010 $36-41 per family. Member ARVC, NE-HA-CA. Phone: (603)846-5521.

(E) Living Water Campground—(Coos) *From jct US 3 & US 302: Go 1/4 mi E on US 302. Enter on R.* ◊◊◊FACILITIES: 70 sites, typical site width 35 ft, 6 full hkups, 31 W&E, (20/30 amps), 33 no hkups, family camping, tenting, dump, ltd groc. ◊◊◊RECREATION: swim pool, river swim, river fishing, playground. No pets. Open all yr. Facilities fully operational Early May - Late Oct. Rate in 2010 $35-39 for 2 persons. Member NE-HA-CA. Phone: (603)846-5513.

(W) Tarry-Ho Campground & Cottages—(Coos) *From jct US-3 & US-302: Go 3/4 mi W on US-302. Enter on L.* ◊◊◊FACILITIES: 55 sites, typical site width 33 ft, 34 full hkups, 15 W&E, (20/30/50 amps), 50 amps ($), 6 no hkups, family camping, tenting, dump. ◊◊◊RECREATION: swim pool, river swim, canoeing, river fishing, playground. Pets welcome, breed restrict, size restrict. Open all yr. Rate in 2010 $44-88 per family. Member NE-HA-CA. Phone: (603) 846-5577.

(N) Twin Mountain KOA—(Coos) *From jct US 302 & US 3: Go 2 mi N on US 3, then 3/4 mi NE on Hwy 115. Enter on R.* ◊◊◊FACILITIES: 78 sites, typical site width 25 ft, 41 full hkups, 20 W&E, 6 E, (20/30/50 amps), 50 amps ($), 11 no hkups, 21 pull-thrus, family camping, tenting, dump, laundry, ltd groc. ◊◊◊RECREATION: swim pool, playground. Pets welcome, breed restrict. Partial handicap access. Open mid May - mid Oct. Big rigs welcome. Rate in 2010 $33.98-52.23 for 2 persons. Member NE-HA-CA. Phone: (800)562-9117. KOA discount.

(E) WHITE MOUNTAIN NATIONAL FOREST (Sugarloaf I Campground)—(Coos) *From jct US 3 & US 302: Go 2-1/3 mi E on US 302, then at Zealand Recreation Area follow signs 1/2 mi S on FR 16.* FACILITIES: 29 sites, 22 ft max RV length, 29 no hkups, tenting. RECREATION: Partial handicap access. Open mid May - mid Oct. Phone: (603)869-2626.

(E) WHITE MOUNTAIN NATIONAL FOREST (Sugarloaf II Campground)—(Coos) *From jct US 3 & US 302: Go 2-1/4 mi E on US 302, then at Zealand Recreation Area follow signs 1/2 mi S on FR 16.* FACILITIES: 21 sites, 22 ft max RV length, 21 no hkups, tenting. RECREATION: Partial handicap access. Open mid May - mid Oct. Phone: (603)869-2626.

WARREN—D-3

(NE) Moose Hillock Campground—(Grafton) *From jct I-93 (exit 26) & Hwy 25W: Go 20 mi W on Hwy 25, then 1 mi N on Hwy 118. Enter on R.* ◇◇◇FACILITIES: 298 sites, typical site width 40 ft, 230 full hkups, 50 W&E, (20/30/50 amps), 18 no hkups, family camping, tenting, dump, laundry, ltd groc. ◇◇◇◇RECREATION: swim pool, pond/stream fishing, playground. Pets welcome. Partial handicap access. Open May 14 - Oct 10. Rate in 2010 $44-63 per family. Member NE-HA-CA. Phone: (603)764-5294.

(S) Scenic View Campground—(Grafton) *From jct I-93 (exit 26) & Hwy 25: Go 18 mi W on Hwy 25. Enter on L.* ◇◇◇◇FACILITIES: 96 sites, typical site width 36 ft, 57 full hkups, 29 W&E, (20/30/50 amps), 10 no hkups, 14 pull-thrus, cable TV, ($), WiFi Instant Internet at site, family camping, tenting, shower$, dump, non-guest dump $, laundry, ltd groc, RV supplies, LP gas by weight/by meter, ice, picnic tables, fire rings, wood. ◇◇◇◇RECREATION: rec hall, pavilion, swim pool, bsktball, playground, activities, horseshoes. Pets welcome. Partial handicap access. Open Mothers Day - Columbus Day. Big rigs welcome. Rate in 2010 $36-47 per family. MC/VISA. Member NE-HA-CA. CCUSA 50% Discount. CCUSA reservations Recommended, CCUSA max stay 4 days, CCUSA disc. not avail holidays. Not available Fri & Sat in Jul & Aug-is available Sun. thru Thu. Discount available every night in May, Jun, Sep & Oct.

Phone: (603)764-9380
Address: 18 Gingerbread Ln, Warren, NH 03279
Lat/Lon: 43.90617/-71.89005
Email: info@scenicviewnh.com
Web: www.scenicviewnh.com

WASHINGTON—E-2

PILLSBURY SP—(Sullivan) *From town: Go 4 mi N on Hwy 31. Enter on R.* FACILITIES: 40 sites, 40 no hkups, tenting. RECREATION: boating, electric motors only, canoeing, ramp, pond/stream fishing, playground. Partial handicap access. Open Jun 11 - Oct 11. Phone: (603)863-2860.

WEARE—E-3

(S) Autumn Hills Campground—(Hillsborough) *From jct Hwy 149 & Hwy 114: Go 2-1/2 mi SE on Hwy 114. Enter on R.* ◇◇◇FACILITIES: 113 sites, typical site width 25 ft, 92 full hkups, 11 W&E, (20/30 amps), 10 no hkups, family camping, tenting, dump, laundry, ltd groc. ◇◇◇◇RECREATION: swim pool, lake swim, canoeing, lake fishing, playground. Pets welcome, breed restrict. Open May 1 - Oct 15. Rate in 2010 $36-39 per family. Member NE-HA-CA. Phone: (603) 529-2425.

(S) COLD SPRINGS CAMP RESORT—(Hillsborough) *From jct Hwy 149 & Hwy 114: Go 1 mi SE on Hwy 114, then 1/4 mi E on Barnard Hill Rd. Enter on R.*

*****THE MOST FUN CAMPGROUND IN NH*****

First Class Fun & First Class Amenities is what you'll find here! Close to NH Motor Speedway, Golf, Fishing & Shopping, we have a Campsite or Cabin rentals to suit you! Come play in our Pools & enjoy our Many Activities.

◇◇◇◇◇FACILITIES: 400 sites, typical site width 25 ft, 392 full hkups, 8 W&E, (20/30/50 amps), many extd stay sites (summer), 16 pull-thrus, heat-

WEARE—Continued
COLD SPRINGS CAMP RESORT—Continued

er not allowed, cable TV, WiFi Instant Internet at site, WiFi Internet central location, family camping, tenting, cabins, shower$, dump, laundry, groceries, RV supplies, ice, picnic tables, fire rings, wood, controlled access.

◇◇◇◇◇RECREATION: rec hall, rec room/area, pavilion, equipped pavilion, coin games, 4 swim pools, wading pool, hot tub, golf nearby, bsktball, playground, shuffleboard court 2 shuffleboard courts, activities, horseshoes, sports field, v-ball.

Pets welcome ($), breed restrict. Partial handicap access. Open May 1 - Columbus Day. Big rigs welcome. Escort to site. Clubs welcome. Rate in 2010 $50-54 for 2 persons. MC/VISA/DISC. Member ARVC, NE-HA-CA.

Phone: (603)529-2528
Address: 62 Barnard Hill Rd, Weare, NH 03281
Lat/Lon: 43.05466/-71.68983
Email: info@coldspringscampresort.com
Web: www.COLDSPRINGSCAMPRESORT.com

SEE AD THIS PAGE

WEBSTER—E-3

(S) COZY POND CAMPING RESORT (NOT VISITED)—(Merrimack) *From jct I-89 (exit 7) & Hwy 103: Go 3/4 mi E on Hwy 103, then 3 mi N on Hwy 127. Enter on L.*

FACILITIES: typical site width 50 ft, 82 full hkups, 30 W&E, (20/30 amps), 17 no hkups, 6 pull-thrus, family camping, tenting, dump, non-guest dump $, laundry, ice, picnic tables, fire rings, wood.

RECREATION: pavilion, canoeing, kayaking, river/pond fishing, bsktball, playground, shuffleboard court shuffleboard court, horseshoes, v-ball.

Pets welcome ($). Open Mother's Day - Columbus Day. Clubs welcome. Rate in 2010 $40-45 per family. MC/VISA. Member ARVC, NE-HA-CA.

Phone: (603)428-7701
Address: 541 Battle Street (Rt. 127), Webster, NH 03303
Email: info@cozypond.com
Web: www.cozypond.com

SEE AD THIS PAGE

WEIRS BEACH—D-3

(W) Paugus Bay Campground—(Belknap) *From jct Hwy 104 & US 3: Go 4 mi S on US 3, then 2/10 mi W on Hilliard Rd. Enter on L.* ◇◇◇FACILITIES: 173 sites, typical site width 25 ft, 36 ft max RV length, 146 full hkups, 27 W&E, (20/30 amps), 3 pull-thrus, family camping, tenting, dump, laundry, ltd groc. ◇◇◇RECREATION: lake swim, boating, canoeing, ramp, lake fishing, playground. Pets welcome, size restrict. Open May 15 - Oct 15. Rate in 2010 $39-43 per family. Member NE-HA-CA. Phone: (603)366-4757.

WEIRS BEACH—Continued

(N) PINE HOLLOW PARK—(Belknap) *From jct Hwy 104 & US 3: Go 2-3/4 mi S on US 3. Enter on R.*

◇◇◇FACILITIES: 80 sites, typical site width 35 ft, 40 full hkups, (30 amps), 40 no hkups, some extd stay sites (summer), cable TV, ($), WiFi Instant Internet at site, WiFi Internet central location, family camping, tenting, dump, laundry, ice, picnic tables, fire rings, wood, controlled access.

◇◇RECREATION: rec hall, swim pool.

Pets welcome, breed restrict. Open Memorial Day - Columbus Day. Escort to site. Rate in 2010 $38 per family. MC/VISA/AMEX.

Phone: (603)366-2222
Address: 656 Endicott N, Weirs Beach, NH 03247
Lat/Lon: 43.61581/-71.48027
Email: camp@pinehollowcampground.com
Web: www.pinehollowcampground.com

SEE AD THIS PAGE

WENTWORTH—D-3

(S) Pine Haven Campground—(Grafton) *From jct I-93 (exit 26) & Hwy-25: Go 12 mi W on Hwy-25. Enter on L.* ◇◇◇FACILITIES: 117 sites, typical site width 35 ft, 77 full hkups, 22 W&E, (30/50 amps), 18 no hkups, 7 pull-thrus, heater not allowed, cable TV, WiFi Instant Internet at site, WiFi Internet central location, family camping, tenting, shower$, dump, laundry, ltd groc, RV supplies, LP gas by weight, ice, picnic tables, fire rings, grills, wood. ◇◇◇◇RECREATION: rec hall, pavilion, swim pool, river swim, river fishing, bsktball, playground, shuffleboard court shuffleboard court, activities, horseshoes. Pets welcome, breed restrict, quantity restrict. Open May 15 - Oct 15. Rate in 2010 $35-41 per family. MC/VISA/DISC/AMEX. Member NE-HA-CA. CCUSA 50% Discount. CCUSA reservations Recommended, CCUSA max stay 3 days, CCUSA disc. not avail F,Sa, CCUSA disc. not avail holidays. Not available last week of Jun thru Labor Day. Electric heater not allowed.

Phone: (603)786-2900
Address: 29 Pine Haven Campground Rd (Rte 25), Wentworth, NH 03282
Lat/Lon: 43.82722/-71.89462
Email: info@pinehavencampground.com
Web: www.pinehavencampground.com

WEST OSSIPEE—D-4

WHITE LAKE SP—(Carroll) *From jct Hwy 16 & Hwy 25: Go 1-1/2 mi N on Hwy 16.* FACILITIES: 200 sites, 200 no hkups, tenting, dump, ltd groc. RECREATION: lake swim, boating, electric motors only, canoeing, lake fishing, playground. No pets. Partial handicap access. Open May 28 - Oct 4. Phone: (603)323-7350.

WINCHESTER—F-2

(N) FOREST LAKE CAMPGROUND, INC —(Cheshire) *From jct I-91 (exit 28A, Northfield, Mass. exit) & Hwy 10: Go 15 mi N on Hwy 10. Enter on R.*

WELCOME

◆◆◆FACILITIES: 175 sites, typical site width 35 ft, 35 ft max RV length, 156 full hkups, 9 W&E, (20/30 amps), 10 no hkups, mostly extd stay sites (summer), 5 pull-thrus, heater not allowed, cable TV, family camping, tenting, dump, portable dump, LP gas by weight/by meter, ice, picnic tables, fire rings, grills, wood, controlled access.

◆◆◆◆RECREATION: rec hall, lake swim, boating, canoeing, kayaking, ramp, rowboat/canoe/pedal boat rentals, lake fishing, putting green, golf nearby, bsktball, playground, shuffleboard court 3 shuffleboard courts, activities (wkends), tennis, horseshoes, sports field, hiking trails, v-ball.

Pets welcome. Open May 1 - Oct 1. Rate in 2010 $27-30 per family. Member NE-HA-CA.

Phone: (603)239-4267
Address: 331 Keene Rd, Winchester, NH 03470
Lat/Lon: 42.79431/-72.37267
Email: forestlake1@flcg.comcastbiz.net
Web: www.ucampnh.com/forestlake

SEE AD THIS PAGE

FOREST LAKE CAMPGROUND
Lakeside Camping in a Wooded Setting
• FHU Pull-Thrus • Boat Launch
• Swimming Beach • Activities • Driving Range
• Near Speedways, Mtns, Covered Bridges
(603) 239-4267 See listing at Winchester, NH
www.ucampnh.com/forestlake

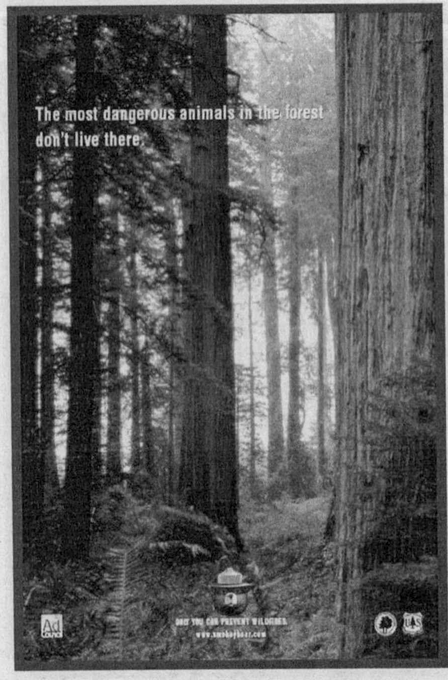

WINCHESTER—Continued

(N) FOREST LAKE PITCH AND PUTT— *From jct I-91, exit 28A, (Northfield MA exit): Go 15 mi N on Hwy 10. Enter on R.* Nine-hole Pitch and Putt with full driving range. On-site exercise facility with Hoggan Sprint equipment. Open Thursdays - Sundays during season. Open May 1 - Oct 1.

WELCOME

Phone: (603)239-4585
Address: 297 Keene Rd, Winchester, NH 03470
Lat/Lon: 42.79431/-72.37267
Email: forestlake1@flcg.comcastbiz.net
Web: www.ucampnh.com/forestlake

SEE AD THIS PAGE

WOLFEBORO—D-4

(E) WOLFEBORO CAMPGROUND—(Carroll) *From south jct Hwy 109 & Hwy 28: Go 4-1/2 mi N on Hwy 28, then 1/4 mi E on Haines Hill Rd. Enter on R.*

WELCOME

◆◆◆FACILITIES: 50 sites, typical site width 35 ft, 32 ft max RV length, 30 full hkups, 10 W&E, (20/30 amps), 10 no hkups, some extd stay sites (summer), family camping, tenting, shower$, dump, portable dump, ltd groc, LP gas by weight/by meter, ice, picnic tables, fire rings, grills, wood.

WOLFEBORO—Continued
WOLFEBORO CAMPGROUND—Continued

RECREATION: sports field.

Pets welcome. Open May 15 - Oct 15. Rate in 2010 $30 per family. MC/VISA. Member NE-HA-CA.

Phone: (603)569-9881
Address: 61 Haines Hill Rd, Wolfeboro, NH 03894
Lat/Lon: 43.63385/-71.15381
Web: www.wolfeborocampground.com

SEE AD THIS PAGE

WOODSTOCK—D-3

(S) Woodstock KOA—(Grafton) *From I-93 (exit 31): Go 2 mi S on Hwy-175. Enter on R.* ◆◆◆FACILITIES: 135 sites, typical site width 50 ft, 28 full hkups, 64 W&E, (20/30 amps), 43 no hkups, 43 pull-thrus, tenting, dump, laundry, ltd groc. ◆◆◆◆RECREATION: swim pool, river/pond fishing, playground. Pets welcome. Open May 1 - Oct 31. Rate in 2010 $35.29-44.99 for 2 persons. Member NE-HA-CA. Phone: (603) 745-8008. KOA discount.

The Irish-born American sculptor Augustus Saint-Gaudens lived and worked in Cornish from 1885 until his death at age 59 in 1907.

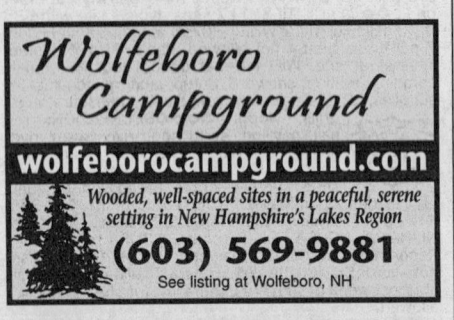

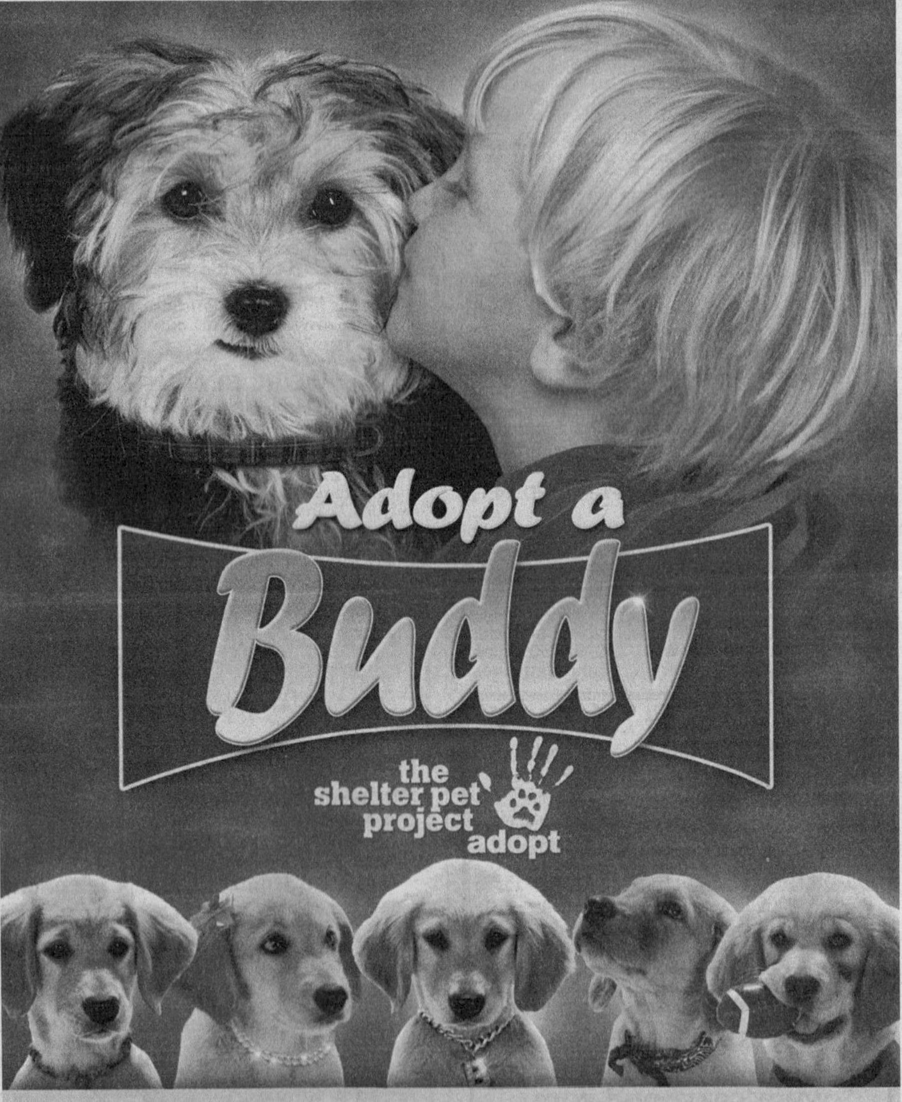

Adopt a Buddy
the shelter pet project
adopt
Visit a local shelter and bring home your new Buddy!
TheShelterPetProject.org
© Disney

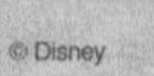

TRAVEL SECTION

New Jersey

READER SERVICE INFO

The following businesses have placed an ad in the New Jersey Travel Section. To receive free information, enter their Reader Service number on the Reader Service card opposite page 48/Discover Section in the front of this directory:

Advertiser	RS#
New Jersey Campground Assoc	574
Ocean View Resort Campground	958
Seashore Campsites	4021

TIME ZONE

New Jersey is in the Eastern Time Zone.

TOPOGRAPHY

The state of New Jersey is 166 miles long and ranges in width from 32 to 60 miles. Total area is 8,204 square miles. Much of that area is farmland and forests and 699 square miles consist of lakes and other inland waters. From the southeastern coastal plain, the terrain rises in elevations through the Appalachian Highland, the Appalachian Valley and the Kittatinny Mountains. The highest point of elevation is 1,803 feet at High Point in Sussex County.

TEMPERATURE

New Jersey lies in a temperate zone where winters are fairly moderate and summers are warm. In the mountain-lakes region of the north, temperatures are several degrees cooler and the rainfall and snowfall are heavier than in central and southern New Jersey. Average monthly temperatures range from 22° to 36° in January and 81° to 87° in July. Snowfall ranges from an average of 13 inches in Cape May County to around 50 inches in the northwestern hills.

TRAVEL & TOURISM INFO

State Agency:

New Jersey Dept of Tourism
P.O. Box 460
Trenton, NJ 08625
(800/VISIT NJ or 609/777-0885)
www.visitnj.org

Regional Agencies:

Atlantic City Convention & Visitors Authority
2314 Pacific Ave.
Atlantic City, NJ 08401
(888/228-4748)
www.atlanticcitynj.com

South Jersey Tourism Corp.
One Port Ctr, Ste 102
2 Riverside Dr.
Camden, NJ 08103
(856/757-9400)
www.visitsouthjersey.com

Meadowlands Liberty CVB
1 Harmon Plaza
Secaucus, NJ 07094
(877/MLCVB-US)
www.meadowlandslibertcvb.com

Monmouth County Department of Economic Development & Tourism
31 East Main St.
Freehold, NJ 07728
(732/431-7476 or 800/523-2587)
www.visitmonmouth.com

Ocean County Public Affairs and Tourism
101 Hooper Ave., Room 109
P.O. Box 2191
Toms River, NJ 08754
(732/929-2000)
www.oceancountytourism.com

Skylands Tourism Council
P.O. Box 464
Belvidere, NJ
(800/4SKYLAND)
www.skylandstourism.org

Southern Shore Tourism Council
(609/463-6415 or 800/227-2297)
www.njsouthernshore.com

Local Agencies:

For local information, contact the Chamber of Commerce or Tourism Bureau for the locality you interested in visiting.

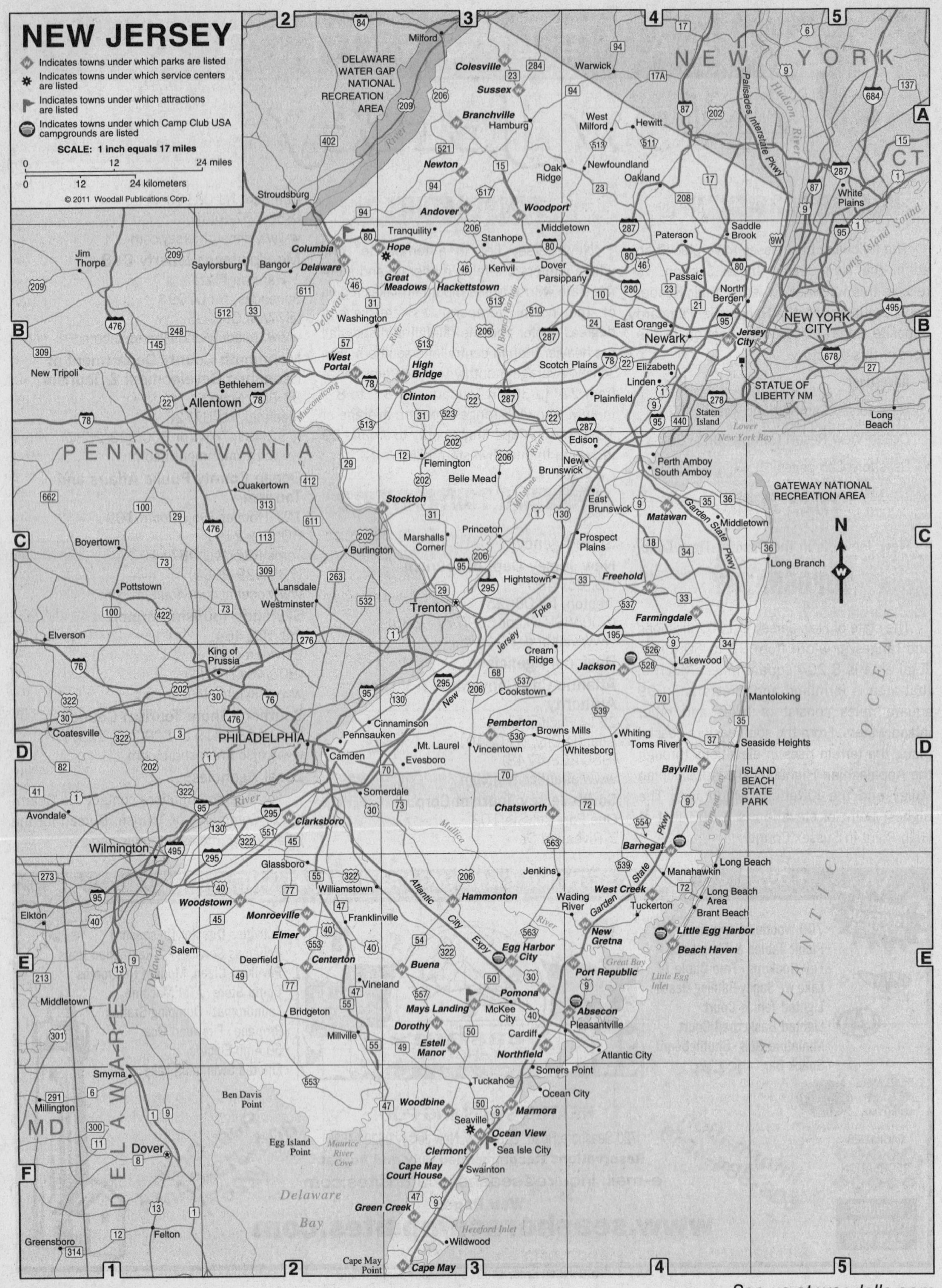

NEW JERSEY
Indicates towns under which parks are listed
Indicates towns under which service centers are listed
Indicates towns under which attractions are listed
Indicates towns under which Camp Club USA campgrounds are listed
SCALE: 1 inch equals 17 miles
0 12 24 miles
0 12 24 kilometers
© 2011 Woodall Publications Corp.
DELAWARE WATER GAP NATIONAL RECREATION AREA
NEW YORK
CT
PENNSYLVANIA
MD
DELAWARE
ATLANTIC OCEAN
GATEWAY NATIONAL RECREATION AREA
STATUE OF LIBERTY NM
ISLAND BEACH STATE PARK
NEW YORK CITY
PHILADELPHIA
Milford
Colesville
Sussex
Branchville
Hamburg
Warwick
West Milford
Hewitt
Newton
Oak Ridge
Newfoundland
Oakland
Andover
Woodport
Middletown
Stroudsburg
Tranquility
Stanhope
Paterson
Saddle Brook
White Plains
Columbia
Hope
Delaware
Great Meadows
Hackettstown
Kenvil
Dover
Parsippany
Passaic
North Bergen
Jim Thorpe
Saylorsburg
Bangor
Washington
East Orange
Newark
Jersey City
West Portal
High Bridge
Clinton
Scotch Plains
Elizabeth
Linden
Plainfield
New Tripoli
Bethlehem
Allentown
Staten Island
Long Beach
Lower New York Bay
Edison
Flemington
New Brunswick
Perth Amboy
South Amboy
Belle Mead
Quakertown
Stockton
East Brunswick
Matawan
Middletown
Princeton
Prospect Plains
Boyertown
Marshalls Corner
Burlington
Long Branch
Pottstown
Lansdale
Westminster
Hightstown
Freehold
Trenton
Farmingdale
Elverson
King of Prussia
Cream Ridge
Jackson
Lakewood
Cookstown
Mantoloking
Coatesville
Cinnaminson
Pennsauken
Pemberton
Browns Mills
Whiting
Toms River
Seaside Heights
Camden
Mt. Laurel
Evesboro
Vincentown
Whitesbog
Bayville
Somerdale
Avondale
Chatsworth
Clarksboro
Wilmington
Barnegat
Glassboro
Jenkins
Long Beach
Manahawkin
Williamstown
Hammonton
West Creek
Wading River
Long Beach Area
Tuckerton
Brant Beach
Elkton
Woodstown
Monroeville
Franklinville
Elmer
Little Egg Harbor
New Gretna
Beach Haven
Salem
Deerfield
Centerton
Egg Harbor City
Buena
Great Bay
Little Egg Inlet
Port Republic
Vineland
Pomona
Middletown
Bridgeton
Mays Landing
McKee City
Absecon
Dorothy
Cardiff
Pleasantville
Millville
Estell Manor
Northfield
Atlantic City
Smyrna
Somers Point
Ben Davis Point
Tuckahoe
Ocean City
Millington
Woodbine
Marmora
Seaville
Ocean View
Egg Island Point
Maurice River Cove
Clermont
Sea Isle City
Dover
Swainton
Cape May Court House
Delaware Bay
Green Creek
Hereford Inlet
Felton
Greensboro
Wildwood
Cape May Point
Cape May
Palisades Interstate Pkwy
Hudson River
Long Island Sound
Garden State Pkwy
New Jersey Tpke
Atlantic City Expy
Delaware River
Musconetcong
N Branch Raritan
Millstone River
Raritan River
Mullica
Barnegat Bay

RECREATIONAL INFO

Charter Boats: For a New Jersey Party and Charter Boat Directory, contact the New Jersey Div. of Fish & Wildlife, P.O. Box 400, Trenton, NJ 08625 (609/292-2965). www.nj.gov/dep/

Fishing & Hunting: New Jersey Div. of Fish and Wildlife, P.O. Box 400, Trenton, NJ 08625 (609/292-2965). www.nj.gov/dep/

Golf: New Jersey State Golf Association 1700 Galloping Hill Rd, Kenilworth, NJ 07033 (908/241-GOLF). www.njsga.org

Lighthouses: New Jersey Lighthouse Society, P.O. Box 332, Navesink, NJ 07752. www.njlhs.org

New Jersey Turnpike — EXIT 2

TIMBERLANE CAMPGROUND— *From Exit 2: Go 4 mi E on US 322, then 7 mi N on I-295 (Exit 18), then 3/4 mi SE on Timberlane Rd. Enter on R.*

See listing at Clarksboro, NJ

I-295 — EXIT 18-/18AB

TIMBERLANE CAMPGROUND— *From N'bnd Exit 18: Go 3/4 mi SE on Timberlane Rd, Enter on R. From S'bnd Exit 18AB: Go 1 mi S on Hwy 667 (Cohawkin Rd), then 1/4 mi SW on Friendship Rd, then 1/4 mi NW on Timberlane Rd. Enter on L.*

See listing at Clarksboro, NJ

Wineries: Garden State Wine Growers Association, P.O. Box 2631, Hamilton Square, NJ 08690. www.newjerseywines.com

SHOPPING

New Jersey offers great shopping at the following factory outlet malls:

Atlantic City Outlets - The Walk, N. Michigan Ave. (609/343-0081)

Circle Factory Outlet Center, 1407 West Atlantic Ave., Manasquan (732/223-2300)

Jackson Premium Outlets, Exit 16 off I-195 (732/833-0503) www.premiumoutlets.com/jackson

Jersey Gardens, Exit 13A off the NJ Tpk, Elizabeth (908/354-5900) www.jerseygardens.com

Liberty Village Premium Outlets, 1 Church St, Flemington (908/782-8550) www.premiumoutlets.com/libertyvillage

Olde Lafayette Village. 75 Rt. 15, Lafayette (973/383-8323) www.lafayettevillageshops.com

Outlets at the Cove, 45 Meadowlands Pky., Secaucus (201/348-4780) www.hartzmountain.com

The Marketplace, 439 Rt. 34, Old Bridge (732/583-8700)

Turntable Junction, Church St., Central Ave. & Fulper Rd. Flemington (908/782-1919)

Where to Find CCUSA Parks

List City	Park Name	Map Coordinates
ABSECON		
	Shady Pines Carefree RV Resort	E-4
BARNEGAT		
	Long Beach Carefree RV Resort	D-4
EGG HARBOR CITY		
	Turtle Run Campground	E-3
JACKSON		
	Timberland Lake Campground	D-4
LITTLE EGG HARBOR		
	Baker's Acres Campground	E-4

FREE INFO! Enter #958 on Reader Service Card

DESTINATIONS

SKYLANDS REGION

Located less than 40 miles from Manhattan, the Skylands region includes mountains, lakes and swamps, and can truly claim that George Washington slept here! This region also contains two National Parks at its edges, and the rustic nature of this region is perfectly complemented by many towns and villages that offer numerous cultural and entertainment opportunities.

Alexandria Field Airport, Pittstown has a daily air show and is the home of many antique and experimental aircraft.

Colonial Park Gardens, East Millstone. Stroll along all-America rose selections, flowering perennials, annuals, shrubs and trees. Also on-site is a fragrance and sensory garden for the visually impaired.

Cooper Gristmill, Chester. Corn, wheat, rye and buckwheat are ground here by millstones into meal or flour. A six-ton outside waterwheel provides the power to this restored 1826 mill located on the Black River.

Delaware Water Gap National Recreation Area, Columbia. Visit this 70,000-acre recreation center. Canoe trips are available.

Duke Farms, Hillsborough. This attraction contains 11 traditional gardens of many countries. Particularly outstanding are the Chinese, Japanese, tropical, French, Italian and desert gardens. In nearby Somerville is the Wallace House, Washington's headquarters during the Middlebrook encampment of 1778-79.

Great Swamp National Wildlife Refuge, Basking Ridge. This 7,000-acre refuge is the nesting ground for a large number of birds. A half-mile boardwalk, two observation blinds and ten miles of marked trails provide great opportunities for viewing.

Hunterdon Historical Museum, Clinton. Telling the story of the county's rural heritage since 1963, there are more than 40,000 changing exhibits, special events and objects.

Kittatinny Valley State Park, Andover. The park includes Lake Aeroflex and Gardner's Pond, Paulinskill Valley Trail and Sussex Branch Trail. Fishing, biking, hiking, boating, picnicking, horseback riding and cross-country skiing are offered throughout the area.

Lakota Wolf Preserve, Columbia. View Tundra, Timber and Arctic wolves in a natural surrounding. Catch photo opportunities of a lifetime. Bobcats and foxes also reside in the preserve.

Land of Make Believe, Hope. This family amusement and water park offers 30 acres of rides, shows, attractions and games.

Morristown. This quaint town is filled with centuries of historical treasures well worth exploring. Public sites include the **Morris**

County Courthouse, The First Baptist Church founded in 1771 and the **Independent Hose Company**, Morristown's first fire department. Many beautiful private homes and mansions built in the 19th century are open to the public.

U.S.G.A. Golf House & Museum, Far Hills. View this renowned collection of golf memorabilia, fine art and decorative arts. There is a 13,000-volume library, as well as high-tech displays in the **Research & Test Center**.

Wild West City, Netcong. Continuous live action shows bring the old west to life in a setting inspired by Dodge City in the 1880's and includes living history demonstrations, a petting zoo, panning for gold, a train, a stagecoach and pony rides.

GATEWAY REGION

Known as the "Gateway to Freedom," for the thousands of immigrants that passed through Ellis Island, this area is also renowned for many first—from the first organized baseball game, to the first brewery, steam locomotive, diner and much more.

East Jersey Olde Towne, Piscataway. More than 30 houses and shops comprise a reconstruction of a colonial village depicting the life of early colonists.

Edison National Historic Site, West Orange. View the inventor's laboratory and workshops where he developed the motion picture camera and the phonograph. You'll also be able to see Edison's early movies as well as take a tour of Glenmont—his 23-room estate.

Fairy Tale Forest, Oak Ridge. Children's Storyland Park with over 20 displays of classic fairytales.

Fort Lee Historic Park offers views of the Hudson River and New York skyline. Visitor's Center with Revolutionary War information.

The Hermitage, a national historic landmark that is a 14-room Gothic Revival home built in 1847. Exhibitions, lectures, special events and craft shows.

Lady Cruises, Jersey City. At the **Lady Liberty Landing Marina Liberty State Park**, take a cruise viewing the Manhattan Skyline and Statue of Liberty on an authentic 85' paddlewheel riverboat.

Liberty Science Center, Liberty State Park. This hands-on science museum fea-

BUSINESSES OFFERING

	Things to See & Do	RV Sales	RV Service
COLUMBIA			
Buck Stop Gift Shop	⚑		
Lakota Wolf Preserve at Camp Taylor	⚑		
HOPE			
George's RV Repair			✱
MAYS LANDING			
Winding River Canoeing & Kayaking	⚑		
OCEAN VIEW			
Ocean View Trailer Sales		🚌	✱
Shore Gate Golf Club	⚑		

QUICK REFERENCE CHART FOR WOODALL'S FEATURED PARKS

	Green Friendly	RV Lots for Sale	Park Models-Onsite Ownership	Park Membership for Sale	Big Rigs Welcome	Internet Friendly	Pets Welcome
ABSECON							
Shady Pines Carefree RV Resort			✱		▲	●	■
BARNEGAT							
Brookville Campground							■
Long Beach Carefree RV Resort			✱			●	■
BEACH HAVEN							
Long Beach Island Trailer Park							■
BRANCHVILLE							
Harmony Ridge Campground						●	■
CAPE MAY							
Seashore Campsites	🍃				▲	●	■
The Depot Travel Park					▲	●	■
CAPE MAY COURT HOUSE							
Big Timber Lake Camping Resort					▲	●	■
CHATSWORTH							
Wading Pines Camping Resort					▲		■
CLARKSBORO							
Timberlane Campground					▲	●	■
CLERMONT							
Avalon Campground						●	■
COLUMBIA							
Camp Taylor Campground						●	■
DOROTHY							
Country Oaks Campground					▲	●	■
EGG HARBOR CITY							
Turtle Run Campground						●	■
FREEHOLD							
Pine Cone Resort					▲	●	■
HACKETTSTOWN							
Goodland Country Club & Spa	🍃					●	■
HOPE							
Triplebrook Camping Resort	🍃				▲	●	■
JACKSON							
Tip Tam Camping Resort					▲	●	■
JERSEY CITY							
Liberty Harbor RV Park					▲		■
LITTLE EGG HARBOR							
Baker's Acres Campground						●	■
MAYS LANDING							
Winding River Campground						⚫	■
MONROEVILLE							
Old Cedar Campground						●	■
OCEAN VIEW							
Ocean View Resort Campground	🍃				▲	●	■
POMONA							
Pomona RV Park					▲	●	■
WEST PORTAL							
Jugtown Mountain Campsites					▲	●	■
WOODSTOWN							
Four Seasons Campground					▲	●	■

Green Friendly 🍃; RV Lots for Sale ✖; Park Models/Onsite Onwership ✱; Park Memberships for Sale ✔; Big Rigs Welcome ▲;
Internet Friendly ⚫; Internet Friendly-WiFi ●; Pets Welcome ■

tures the world's largest OMNIMAX Theater, laser light show, living salt marsh, touch tunnel and illusion labyrinth.

Liberty State Park/Statue of Liberty/Ellis Island. Take a ferry from Liberty State Park to America's symbols of freedom—the Statue of Liberty and Ellis Island.

Meadowlands Environment Center. Exhibits, programs on birds and meadowlands ecology and walking trails are found here.

Spirit of New Jersey. Cruise around New York Harbor during any season. It features outdoor strolling areas, spectacular views of the city and a lunch or dinner program.

Turtle Back Zoo, West Orange. View wild and domestic animals on 16-acres with a train ride and petting zoo.

SHORE REGION

This area is known for its 127 miles of white sand beaches, picturesque seaside towns and historic lighthouses.

Barnegat Light Museum & Historical Society, Barnegat. Formerly a one-room schoolhouse, the building is now a museum that features maritime exhibits, an original lighthouse lens and more.

Deep Cut Gardens, Middletown. Visit this 53-acre park that contains a variety of year-round gardens and a horticultural center. Also on-site are home gardening experts, a reference library and a display greenhouse.

Fort Hancock Gateway National Recreation Area. Sandy Hook Unit, Highlands. Fort Hancock, located at the tip of a six-mile peninsula, has the oldest operating lighthouse, as well as the only surviving colonial lighthouse, in the United States.

Guggenheim Memorial Library, West Long Branch. Once the summer residence of the mining magnate, the library was patterned after the Petit Trianon at Versailles.

Island Beach State Park, Seaside Park. **Aeolium Nature Center** and **Emily deCap Herbarium** is housed in one of the last relatively undisturbed barrier beaches found in New Jersey. Explore more than 1,900 acres of sand dunes, saltwater marshes and freshwater bogs.

National Guard Militia Museum of New Jersey, Sea Girt. This museum includes displays of artifacts and memorabilia of the militia and National Guard of New Jersey, which portray the many contributions of the citizen soldier to both the state and nation.

Naval Air Engineering Station at Lakehurst, Lakehurst. This is the site of the 1937 Hindenburg crash. There are free tours.

Navesink Light Station at Twin Lights Historic Site, Highlands. About 256-feet above the water, the two-beacon lighthouse overlooks Sandy Hook and the Atlantic Ocean. Artifacts of marine history are displayed in the museum at the state park.

Point Pleasant Beach. You'll find games, amusements, entertainment, miniature golf and restaurants along the boardwalk. At **Jenkinson's Aquarium** you can see exotic fish, mammals, birds, a petting tank, seals, alligators and penguins. Nature programs are offered throughout the summer.

Six Flags Great Adventure & Wild Safari, Jackson. The state's largest theme park features 25 new rides and attractions. The Kingda Ka—the tallest, fastest roller coaster on earth, takes riders 45 stories high for an unforgettable journey.

Village Inn, Englishtown. This historic tavern/inn was frequented by Revolutionary War militia and served as a stage stop, courtroom and church.

GREATER ATLANTIC CITY REGION

This is an area that never sleeps, full of beautiful beaches, 24-hour gaming, the world's first boardwalk and the Miss America contest. There is so much more to this area! Outdoor enthusiasts will find endless opportunities from biking, to canoeing and kayaking, or whale and dolphin watching.

Absecon Lighthouse, Atlantic City. Built in 1857, the lighthouse was designed by George Meade, famous Civil War general. It's the tallest lighthouse in New Jersey and the third tallest in the US.

Atlantic City, the gaming and entertainment center of the east. It is renowned for its hotels and casinos, floor shows and gourmet restaurants, sandy beaches and saltwater taffy. Also known for its six-and-a-half-mile-long oceanfront boardwalk, offering rolling chairs, shops, bicycling, games, refreshments and two amusement piers. Don't miss attractions such as the **Atlantic City Historical Museum, Ripley's Believe It or Not** or the **Ocean Life Center** and the **Absecon Lighthouse** while in the city. In neighboring communities, catch these attractions:

SOUTHERN SHORE REGION

The Southern Shore Region is the place for a great romantic getaway full of beautiful seaside resorts, nature preserves and championship golf and fishing. It's no wonder this area is called a "resort for all seasons", with its many indoor and outdoor activities! This area is also home to great cultural places, like the incredible Woodruff Museum of Indian Artifacts, that houses more than 20,000 artifacts created by the Leni Lenape Indians.

Bridgeton Historic District, Bridgeton. New Jersey's largest historic district is comprised of 2,200 homes and buildings from the Colonial, Federalist and Victorian periods. Brick walkways, lanterns and benches lining the scenic **Riverfront Promenade** and **Fountain Plaza** give the town its charming aura.

The Jersey Cape. This popular resort area includes attractions such as **Wetlands Institute** (a research and education center emphasizing salt marshes and coastal ecology), **Stone Harbor Bird Sanctuary, Cape May Court House, Cold Spring Village** (authentic re-creation of a 19th-century town and site for special events), **Leaming's Run Botanical Gardens** in Swainton and the **Ocean City Historical Museum. Mid-Atlantic Center for the Arts** provides year-round tours of Victorian Cape May's National Landmark District. Experience the mansions through gaslight tours during the summer, April's Tulip Garden Trolley Tour, the June Music Festival and other event tours.

Cape May County Park & Zoo. Visit nearly 250 animals here and enjoy the scenic views of Cape May County's parks.

Ocean City offers lots of family entertainment including amusement park rides, go-karts, miniature golf, a three-mile boardwalk, the **Ocean City Arts Center,** the **Discovery Sea Shell Museum** and the **Ocean City Historical Museum.**

Ocean Discovery Center, Wildwood Crest. A whale and dolphin watch is included in this environmental cruise and presentation, open April through late October.

DELAWARE RIVER REGION

This is a historical region that includes the site of Washington's famous crossing of the Delaware and other Revolutionary War sites. The Powhatan Renape Nation resides here. These peoples are descended from an ancient confederation that at one point comprised more than 30 tribes. Travelers will also find living historical farms, more than a million acres of pine trees, and numerous buildings associated with the French and Revolutionary Wars.

Air Victory Museum, Medford. This 24,000 square foot military aviation museum contains aircraft and engine collections, along with replicas of the Wright Brothers and Spirit of St. Louis aircraft.

Batsto Historic Village, Hammonton. A principal source of ammunition for the Revolution, this iron mine continued to produce iron through the 19th century. Traditional crafts are still practiced today.

Berlin is home to the **South Jersey Museum** of American History, displaying political history, pre-Columbian exhibits and the restored 1894 Berlin Post Office. The **Berlin Railroad Station** was built in 1853. It is the oldest remaining railroad in the state and is listed in both State and National Historic Registries.

Garden State Discovery Museum, Cherry Hill. This hands-on museum offers interactive children's exhibits.

Glassboro. The **Heritage Glass Museum** displays glassware, glassblowing tools and memorabilia from the 18th century.

Glassboro Wildlife Management Area contains 2,337 acres of woodlands and fields. Excellent rabbit, quail, grouse and squirrel hunting is available.

Indian King Tavern Museum, Haddonfield. Built in 1750, this early American public house and tavern was a Revolutionary War meeting place for New Jersey's General Assembly. The Great Seal of the State was adopted here. Guided tours are available.

Pine Barrens. Experience the primeval majesty of nature in the one million acres of legendary Pine Barrens, the largest tract of space on the Mid-Atlantic coast and home to more than 1,000 species of plants and animals.

Princeton. Visit this world-renowned center of cultural and educational activity. You'll enjoy **Princeton University's Art Museum, McCarter Theatre** and library. Also featured are **Bainbridge House**, Einstein's residence; **Clarke House on the Princeton Battlefield, Morven,** home of the New Jersey Historical Society; and **Drumthwacket**, the governor's mansion.

Camden. The **New Jersey State Aquarium** is home to the 760,000 gallon Open Ocean tank with more than 1,400 fish. Over 4,000 aquatic animals can be found here. Daily seal and dive shows and interactive exhibits are offered. **Children's Garden** offers a horticultural playground to delight children of all ages. **USS New Jersey,** the most decorated battleship in US Navy History, is permanently berthed on the Camden Waterfront as a floating museum.

Trenton. The capital of New Jersey prides itself on having the second oldest State House in continuous use in the United States. Attractions include the old colonial barracks (used by the British and Hessian troops) and the William Trent House with its Queen Anne architecture, period furniture and exhibits.

Washington Crossing State Park, Titusville. Site of Washington's 1776 Christmas crossing of the Delaware. Attractions include the McKonkey Ferry House, an arboretum, an open-air theater, hiking trails, fishing in the Delaware and Raritan Canal, bird watching and group camping.

ANNUAL EVENTS

JANUARY

First Day at the Beach, Ocean City; Model RR Open House, Richland; Fire & Ice, Mount Holly.

MARCH

St. Patrick's Day Parade, Ringwood.

APRIL

Dover Fleamarket & Street Fair, Dover.

MAY

Flemington Spring Crafts Festival, Lambertville; Harbor Safari, Cape May; Cape May's Spring Festival, Cape May; Rakkasah Spring Caravan, Somerset; Annual Spring Festival, Hackettstown; Multicultural Arts Festival, Elizabeth; Seaport Irish Festival, Tuckerton; Spring Beach Jam, Wildwood; Mayfest, Smithville; Strawberry Fair, Oceanport; International Kite Festival, Wildwood; Blues and Wine Festival, Peapack/Gladstone.

JUNE

New Jersey International Film Festival, New Brunswick; NJ Quilt Convention, Edison; Mummers Brigade Weekend, North Wildwood; Family Fun Day, Madison; North Plainfield Lions Club Chili Cook Off Competition, North Plainfield; North Plainfield Street Fair, North Plainfield; Locke Ave Fun Day, Woolwich; Skimmer Weekend Seaside Craft Market, Sea Isle City; Summer Flea Market, Farmingdale; MeadowFest, Secaucus; Fishawack Festival, Chatham; Annual Family Carnival, Hamilton Square; Pathmark Multicultural Arts Festival, Woodbridge; Harbor Fest, Cape May; State Fair Meadowlands, East Rutherford; Annual North Wildwood Original Italian American Festival, North Wildwood; Red Bank Jazz & Blues Festival, Red Bank; Celtic Festival, Cape May; Annual Nanticoke Lenni-Lanape Indian Pow Wow, Woodstown; Seafood Festival, Belmar; Ghost Walking Tours, Beach Haven (through September); Miss New Jersey Pageant, Ocean City; Big, Fat Greek Festival, Flemington; Family Carnival, Hamilton Square.

JULY

Carnival Extravaganza, Roselle Park; Oceanfest 2011, Long Branch; Whale of a Day Family Festival, Townbank; Sussex County Native American Heritage Celebration, Augusta; New Jersey State Barbeque Championship/Anglesea Blues Festival, North Wildwood; Showhouse at the Shore, Margate; Seafood Festival, Vineland; Firefly Festival, Princeton; Merchants in Venice Seafood Festival, Ocean City; New Jersey State Ice Cream Festival, Toms River; Mid Summer Festival at the Gazebo, Wildwood Crest; Multicultural Festival, Dover; Warren County Farmers Fair & Balloon Festival, Phillipsburg; Annual Clam Festival, Highlands; Independence Week Tubing, Frenchtown; Freedom Festival, Wildwood Crest; Cumberland County Fair, Millville; Farm Days, Cape May; Passiac County Fair, West Paterson; Puerto Rican Festival, Vineland; Monmouth County Fair, East Freehold; Burlington County Fair, Lumberton; Gloucester Co. 4-H Fair & New Jersey Peach Festival, Mullica Hill; Festival of Ballooning, Whitehouse Station.

AUGUST

New Jersey State Fair, Augusta; Railroad Days, Cape May; Peaches N Cream Festival, Bridgeton; Ocean Township Italian Festival, Ocean Township; Miss Crustacean Hermit Crab Beauty Pageant, Ocean City; Annual Anderson House Seafood Festival, Flemington; Jersey Fresh Wine & Food Festival, Pennington; Annual Clam Bake, Waretown; Weird Week, Ocean City; Carnival, Lindenwold; International Food and Cultural Festival, Vineland; Wildwood Block Party & Festival, Wildwood; Scandinavian Fest, Budd Lake; Middlesex County Fair, East Brunswick; Maritime Heritage Festival, Tuckerton; Festival of the Sea, Long Beach Township; Salem County Fair, Woodstown; Clamfest, Highlands; Italian Festival, Oakhurst; Colts Neck Country Fair, Colts Neck.

SEPTEMBER

Italian American Fest, West Windsor; St. Demetrios Green Festival, Union; Union County MusicFest, Cranford; New Jersey Film Festival, New Brunswick; Victorian Days, Belvidere; Railroaders Weekend, Farmingdale; Fido's Festival USA, Woodstown; Street Faire, Avalon; Edison Fall Family Spectacular Music Festival, Edison; Fall Family Festival Seaside Craft Market, Sea Isle City; Irish Fall Festival, North Wildwood/Sea Isle City; Renaissance Faire, Lakewood; Sunset Lake Seafarers Celebration, Wildwood Crest; Ocean City Air Festival, Ocean City; Annual Bloomfield Harvestfest Street Fair, Bloomfield; Pumpkin Palooza, Cherry Hill; Mercer County Italian American Festival, West Windsors.

OCTOBER

Sugarloaf Crafts Festival, Somerset; Festival of Fine Craft, Millville; Chowderfest Merchants Mart, Beach Haven; Wildwoods Seafood and Blues Festival, Wildwood; Oktoberfest, Smithville; Harvest Fest, Califon; 1770s Festival, Basking Ridge; Annual Hackensack Street Fair, Hackensack; Indian Summer Weekend, Ocean City; Seafood Fest, Avalon; Irish Festival, Smithville; Apple Festival, Medford; Ghost Walk, Mays Landing; Annual Pumpkin Festival, Cape May; Fall Craft Festival, Haddonfield; Italian Street Festival, Seaside Heights; Fall Festival/Civil War Re-enactment, Mullica Hill.

NOVEMBER

Celebrate Frogs, Point Pleasant Beach; Quiet Festival, Ocean City; Dickens Days, Clinton; Holly Days, Morristown; Red Bank Annual Window Walk, Red Bank; Quiet Festival, Ocean City.

DECEMBER

Holiday Candlelight Tour, Clifton; Festival of Trees, Basking Ridge; Walk of Lights, Bridgeton; Snowflake Parade, Millburn; Carolfest, Ocean City; Victorian Holiday Festival:Houses and Inns on Tour, Ocean Grove; Christkindlmarkt, Tuckerton.

All privately owned campgrounds personally inspected by WOODALL'S Representatives

Dave and Jaynie Carlson

ABSECON—E-4

(W) SHADY PINES CAREFREE RV RESORT—(Atlantic) *From jct US 9 & US 30: Go 1-1/2 mi W on US 30, then 1-1/2 mi N on Sixth Ave. Enter on L.*

◊◊◊◊FACILITIES: 140 sites, typical site width 30 ft, 140 full hkups, (20/30/50 amps), many extd stay sites, WiFi Internet central location, family camping, RV's/park model rentals, dump, non-guest dump $, laundry, LP gas by weight/by meter, ice, picnic tables, fire rings, wood.

◊◊RECREATION: pavilion, swim pool, golf nearby, play equipment, shuffleboard court, horseshoes.

Pets welcome. No tents. Open Mar 1 - Nov 1. Big rigs welcome. Clubs welcome. Rate in 2010 $39 for 4 persons. MC/VISA/Debit. Member ARVC, NJCOA. FCRV discount. FMCA discount. CCUSA 50% Discount. CCUSA reservations Recommended, CCUSA max stay 5 days, CCUSA disc. not avail S, CCUSA disc. not avail F,Sa, CCUSA disc. not avail holidays. Not available Jun 13-Sep 1.

Phone: (609)652-1516
Address: 443 S 6th Ave, Galloway, NJ 08205
Lat/Lon: 39.45668/-74.50405
Web: www.carefreeresorts.com/newjerseyrvparks/shady_pines_rv_resort

SEE AD NEXT PAGE

ANDOVER—A-3

(S) Panther Lake Camping Resort—(Sussex) *From jct I-80 (exit 25) & US 206: Go 4-1/2 mi N on US 206. Enter on R.* ◊◊◊◊FACILITIES: 435 sites, typical

ANDOVER—Continued
Panther Lake Camping Resort—Continued

site width 40 ft, 300 full hkups, 135 W&E, (15/20/30 amps), family camping, tenting, dump, laundry, ltd groc. ◊◊◊◊RECREATION: swim pool, lake swim, boating, no motors, canoeing, ramp, lake/pond fishing, playground. Pets welcome. Partial handicap access. Open Apr 1 - Nov 1. Rate in 2010 $41-46 for 2 persons. Member ARVC, NJCOA. Phone: (973)347-4440.

ATLANTIC CITY—E-4

See listings at Absecon, Chatsworth, Egg Harbor City, Marmora, Mays Landing, New Gretna, Ocean City, Pomona, Port Republic & Wading River

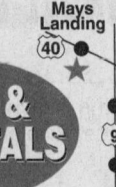

JUGTOWN MOUNTAIN CAMPSITES
E-Z ON & OFF I-78 (Exit 11)
Swimming Pool • Rental RV'S • Pets Welcome
LP Gas & RV Dump Available • RV Parts & Accessories
West Portal, New Jersey
(908) 735-5995
www.jugtownmountaincampsites.com
See listing at West Portal, NJ

EXPLORE NEW JERSEY WITH ENCORE RV RESORTS

CHESTNUT LAKE
631 CHESTNUT NECK ROAD
PORT REPUBLIC (*Atlantic City*)

LAKE AND SHORE
515 CORSON TAVERN ROAD
OCEAN VIEW (*Sea Isle City*)

SEA PINES
U.S. ROUTE 9, BOX 1535
SWAINTON (*Avalon/Cape May*)

SEASONAL SITES AVAILABLE

www.RVontheGo.com

Call to make your reservations today!
888.481.6348
See listing at Port Republic, NJ

Equity *LifeStyle* Properties

NEW JERSEY COAST

WINDING RIVER CAMPGROUND

Woodall's Rated Fac: ◊◊◊◊ Rec: ◊◊◊◊ TRAILER LIFE RATED 6/8★/8

WE'VE GOT IT ALL . . . LARGE SHADED SITES, A HEATED POOL, TUBING, CANOEING, KAYAKING AND CAMPING ON THE GREAT EGG HARBOR RIVER!

AND . . . • Fishing • Rec Hall with Fireplace • Game Room • Activities • Laundry • Shaded Sites

Canoe & Kayak Rentals

A Nature Lover's Dream . . . Unique in all the World
Experience the scenic quiet of planned trips on the beautiful Great Egg Harbor River

CABIN & RV RENTALS

Mays Landing (40) — Atlantic City (25 Min.) — Ocean City (25 Min.) — (9) — Wildwood (50 Min.) — Cape May Ferry (60 Min.) — N

NATIONAL ARVC

For Reservations, Information, Or A Free Brochure:
(609) 625-3191 - www.windingrivercamping.com
E-Mail: windingrivercampgroundnj@msn.com
6752 Weymouth Road, Mays Landing, NJ 08330 See listing at Mays Landing, NJ

AVALON—F-3

See primary listing at Clermont

BARNEGAT—D-4

(W) BROOKVILLE CAMPGROUND—(Ocean) *From Garden State Parkway South (exit 69) & Hwy 532: Go 4 mi W on Hwy 532, then 1-1/2 mi SW on Brookville Rd, then 1/2 mi E on Jones Rd. Enter on R.*

◆◆◆FACILITIES: 100 sites, typical site width 35 ft, 72 full hkups, (20/30 amps), 28 no hkups, some extd stay sites, family camping, tenting, RV's/park model rentals, RV storage, dump, non-guest dump $, ice, picnic tables, wood.

◆◆◆RECREATION: pavilion, swim pool, lake fishing, golf nearby, bsktball, playground, horseshoes, sports field, hiking trails, v-ball.

Pets welcome. Open May 1 - Oct 1. Rate in 2010 $35 for 2 persons. Member ARVC, NJCOA.

Phone: (609)698-3134
Address: 224 Jones Rd, Barnegat, NJ 08005
Lat/Lon: 39.77865/-74.30074

SEE AD THIS PAGE

LONG BEACH CAREFREE RV RESORT—(Ocean County) *From jct Garden State Pkwy (exit 63) & Hwy 72: Go 4 mi W on Hwy 72. Enter on R.*

WELCOME TO CAREFREE RV RESORTS
The best way to see the Jersey Shore and beautiful Long Beach Island! This casual, family-oriented resort is full of fun things to do such as mini-golf, bicycling and swimming. You can do it all, or nothing at all!

LONG BEACH CAREFREE RV RESORT—Continued on next page

Frank Sinatra, singer, was from New Jersey.

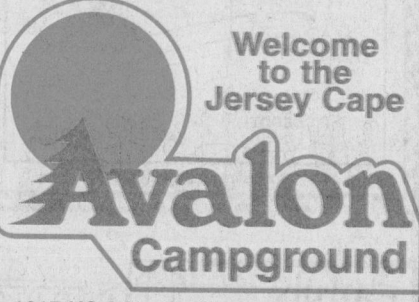

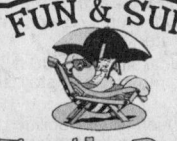

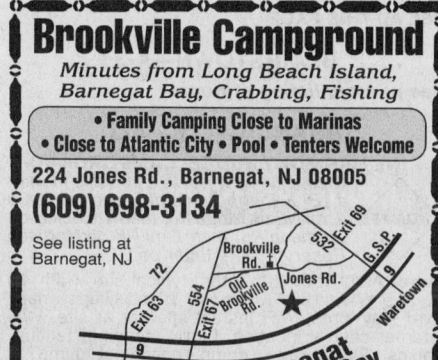

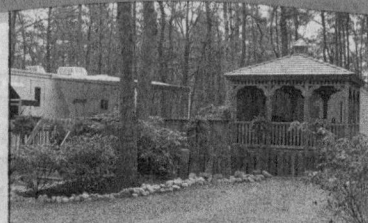

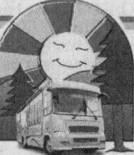

BARNEGAT—Continued
LONG BEACH CAREFREE RV RESORT—Continued

◆◆◆FACILITIES: 226 sites, 226 W&E, (30/50 amps), many extd stay sites, cable TV, WiFi Instant Internet at site ($), family camping, tenting, cabins, RV storage, dump, non-guest dump $, portable dump, laundry, ltd groc, RV supplies, LP bottle exch, ice, picnic tables, fire rings, grills, wood, controlled access.

◆◆◆◆RECREATION: rec hall, rec room/area, equipped pavilion, coin games, swim pool, mini-golf, ($), golf nearby, bsktball, 12 bike rentals, playground, shuffleboard court shuffleboard court, activities (wkends), horseshoes, hiking trails.

Pets welcome. Open Apr 1 - Oct 31. Escort to site. Rate in 2010 $29-57 for 2 persons. MC/VISA. Member ARVC, NJCOA. CCUSA 50% Discount. CCUSA reservations Recommended, CCUSA max stay 5 days, CCUSA disc. not avail F,Sa, CCUSA disc. not avail holidays. Not available Jun 13-Sep 1.

Phone: (609)698-5684
Address: 30 Rt 72, Barnegat, NJ 08005
Lat/Lon: 39.75901/-74.31654
Email: longbeachrv@comcast.net
Web: www.carefreervresorts.com/newjerseyrvparks/long_beach_rv_resort/

SEE AD ATLANTIC CITY PAGE 515

BAYVILLE—D-4

(S) Cedar Creek Campground—(Ocean) *From jct Hwy 530 & US 9: Go 6 1/2 mi S on US 9. Enter on R.* ◆◆◆FACILITIES: 220 sites, typical site width 35 ft, 100 full hkups, 85 W&E, (20/30/50 amps), 35 no hkups, 20 pull-thrus, family camping, tenting, dump, laundry, full svc store. ◆◆◆◆RECREATION: swim pool, boating, canoeing, playground. Pets welcome. Partial handicap access. Open all yr. Rate in 2010 $48.50-54.50 for 2 persons. Member ARVC, NJCOA. Phone: (732)269-1413.

New Jersey State Motto: "Liberty and Prosperity"

BEACH HAVEN—E-4

(S) LONG BEACH ISLAND TRAILER PARK (RV SPACES)—(Ocean) *From jct Garden State Pkwy (exit 63) & Hwy 72: Go 6-3/4 mi SE on Hwy 72, then 9 mi S on Long Beach Blvd, then 1/2 block W on Harding Ave. Enter on R.*

WELCOME

FACILITIES: 146 sites, typical site width 30 ft, 146 full hkups, (30/50 amps), mostly extd stay sites, cable TV, picnic tables.

Pets welcome. No tents. Open all yr. Facilities fully operational Apr 1 - Nov 1. Very limited overnight sites avail. Reservations strongly suggested. Big rigs welcome. Rate in 2010 $50-75 for 2 persons. Member NJCOA.

Phone: (609)492-9151
Address: 19 Harding Ave, Beach Haven, NJ 08008
Lat/Lon: 39.53384/-74.26202

SEE AD THIS PAGE

BLAIRSTOWN—A-3

See primary listing at Hope

BRANCHVILLE—A-3

(N) HARMONY RIDGE CAMPGROUND—(Sussex) *From jct US 206 (Mile Marker 118) & Ridge Rd (N of Branchville): Go 1 mi NE on Ridge Rd, then 1 block N on Mattison Rd, then 1 mi NE on Mattison Reservoir Ave. Enter on L.*

WELCOME

◆◆◆FACILITIES: 225 sites, typical site width 40 ft, 215 W&E, (20/30 amps), 10 no hkups, many extd stay sites, WiFi Instant Internet at site, WiFi Internet central location, family camping, tenting, cabins, RV storage, dump, non-guest dump $, portable dump, laundry, ltd groc, RV supplies, LP gas by weight/by meter, ice, picnic tables, fire rings, wood.

◆◆◆◆RECREATION: rec room/area, coin games, swim pool, boating, no motors, ramp, 6 pedal boat rentals, lake fishing, fishing supplies, golf nearby, bsktball, playground, shuffleboard court 2 shuffleboard courts, horseshoes, sports field, hiking trails, v-ball.

BRANCHVILLE—Continued
HARMONY RIDGE CAMPGROUND—Continued

Pets welcome. Open all yr. Clubs welcome. Rate in 2010 $15 for 1 persons. MC/VISA/AMEX/Debit. Member ARVC, NJCOA.

Phone: (973)948-4941
Address: 23 Risdon Dr, Branchville, NJ 07826
Lat/Lon: 41.18978/-74.73652
Email: harmony@nac.net
Web: www.harmonyridge.com

SEE AD THIS PAGE

(N) Kymer's Camping Resort—(Sussex) *From jct US 206 & CR-519: Go 4-3/4 mi N on CR-519, then 1 mi W on Kymer Rd. Enter on R.* ◆◆◆FACILITIES: 250 sites, typical site width 35 ft, 40 ft max RV length, 111 full hkups, 139 W&E, (20/30 amps), family camping, tenting, dump, laundry, ltd groc. ◆◆◆◆RECREATION: swim pool, pond fishing, playground. Pets welcome. Open Apr 1 - Oct 31. Rate in 2010 $40-45 for 2 persons. Member ARVC, NJCOA. Phone: (973)875-3167.

STOKES STATE FOREST—(Sussex) *From jct CR-519 & US-206: Go 3 mi NW on US-206.* FACILITIES: 51 sites, 51 no hkups, tenting. RECREATION: lake swim, boating, no motors, canoeing, lake fishing, playground. No pets. Open all yr. Phone: (973)948-3820.

BUENA—E-3

(E) Buena Vista Camping Resort (Morgan RV Resorts)—(Atlantic) *From jct Hwy 54 & Hwy 40: Go 500 feet E on Hwy 40. Enter on L.* ◆◆◆◆FACILITIES: 648 sites, typical site width 30 ft, 310 full hkups, 338 W&E, (20/30/50 amps), 2 pull-thrus, family camping, tenting, dump, laundry, groceries. ◆◆◆◆◆RECREATION: swim pool, lake swim, pond fishing, playground. Pets welcome. Partial handicap access. Open all yr. Big rigs welcome. Rate in 2010 $20-55 per family. Member ARVC, NJCOA. Phone: (856)697-5555.

CAPE MAY—F-3

(N) Beachcomber Camping Resort—(Cape May) *From jct Hwy 47 & US 9: Go 1-1/4 mi S on US 9, then 1 block W on Sally Marshall Crossing, then 1 block N on Seashore Rd. Enter on L.* ◆◆◆◆◆FACILITIES: 725 sites, typical site width 35 ft, 700 full hkups, 25 W&E, (30/50 amps), family camping, tenting, dump, laundry, groceries. ◆◆◆◆◆RECREATION: 3 swim pools, lake swim, boating, no motors, canoeing, lake fishing, playground. Pets welcome. Open Mid-April - Oct 31. Big rigs welcome. Rate in 2010 $30-69 for 2 persons. Member ARVC, NJCOA. Phone: (609)886-6035.

CAPE MAY—Continued on next page

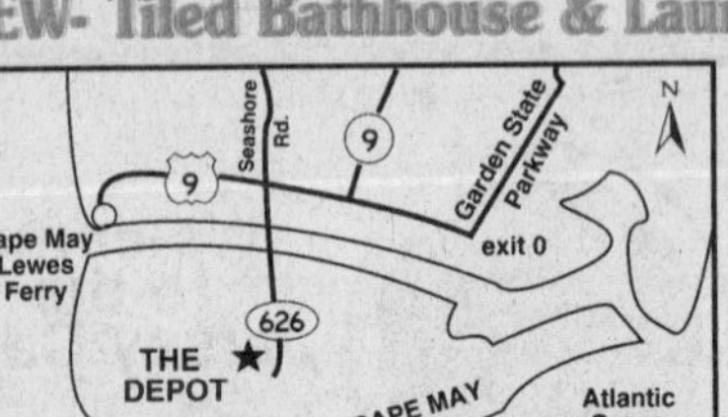

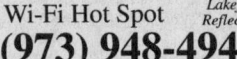

CAPE MAY—Continued

(N) Holly Shores Campground—(Cape May) *From jct Hwy-47 & US-9: Go 1-1/4 mi S on US-9. Enter on L.* ◆◆◆◆◆FACILITIES: 300 sites, typical site width 40 ft, 270 full hkups, 30 W&E, (20/30/50 amps), family camping, tenting, dump, laundry, groceries. ◆◆◆◆RECREATION: swim pool, playground. Pets welcome. Partial handicap access. Open Mid Apr - Late Oct. Big rigs welcome. Rate in 2010 $32-65 for 2 persons. Member ARVC, NJCOA. Phone: (609)886-1234.

(N) Lake Laurie Campground (Morgan RV Resorts)—(Cape May) *From jct Hwy 47 & US 9: Go 2-1/2 mi S on US 9. Enter on L.* ◆◆◆FACILITIES: 750 sites, typical site width 30 ft, 300 full hkups, 390 W&E, (20/30/50 amps), 60 no hkups, 3 pull-thrus, family camping, tenting, dump, laundry, groceries. ◆◆◆◆RECREATION: swim pool, lake swim, boating, no motors, canoeing, lake fishing, playground. Pets welcome. Partial handicap access. Open Apr 1 - Oct 1. Facilities fully operational Mid Jun - Mid Sep. Rate in 2010 $38.99-44.99 for 2 persons. Member ARVC, NJCOA. Phone: (609)884-3567.

(N) SEASHORE CAMPSITES—(Cape May) *From jct Hwy 47 & US 9: Go 2-3/4 mi S on US 9, then 500 ft W over tracks on Bennetts Crossing, then 500 ft N on Hwy 626. (Seashore Rd). Enter on L.*

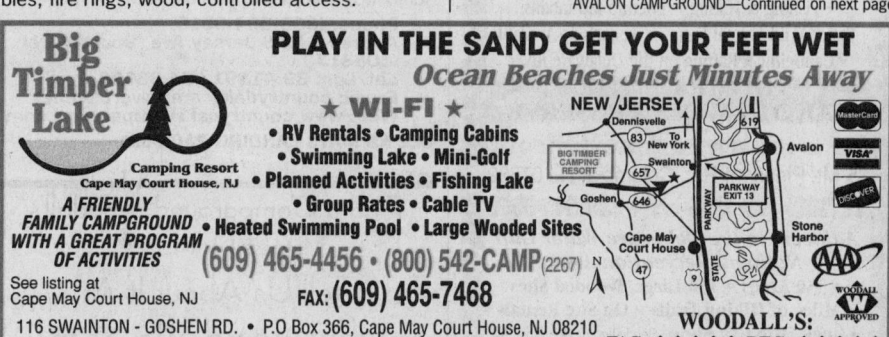

WE'RE JUST 5 MINUTES FROM THE BEACH
Enjoy the beach and Victorian Cape May. Swim, fish, surf or sunbathe to your heart's content. Enjoy daily activities or just relax around a campfire. Close to area attractions. A vacation spot surrounded by natural beauty!

◆◆◆◆◆FACILITIES: 700 sites, typical site width 40 ft, 514 full hkups, 130 W&E, (20/30/50 amps), 56 no hkups, many extd stay sites, 22 pull-thrus, cable TV, WiFi Instant Internet at site ($), WiFi Internet central location, family camping, tenting, shower$, dump, non-guest dump $, portable dump, laundry, groceries, RV supplies, LP gas by weight/by meter, ice, picnic tables, patios, wood.

◆◆◆◆◆RECREATION: rec hall, rec room/area, equipped pavilion, coin games, swim pool, wading pool, lake swim, mini-golf, ($), golf nearby, bsktball, playground, shuffleboard court 2 shuffleboard courts, activities, tennis, horseshoes, v-ball, local tours.

Pets welcome. Open Apr 15 - Oct 31. 3 day min. Jul & Aug with reservations. Big rigs welcome. Clubs welcome. Green Friendly. Rate in 2010 $25-62 for 2 persons. MC/VISA/DISC/AMEX/Debit. ATM. Member ARVC, NJCOA. FMCA discount.

Phone: (609)884-4010
Address: 720 Seashore Rd, Cape May, NJ 08204
Lat/Lon: 38.97620/-74.90380
Email: inquire@seashorecampsites.com
Web: www.seashorecampsites.com

SEE AD TRAVEL SECTION PAGE 507

(N) THE DEPOT TRAVEL PARK—(Cape May) *From jct Garden State Pkwy (exit 0) & Hwy 109: Go 1 mi W on Hwy 109/US 9, then 1 mi S on CR 626 (Seashore Rd). From jct Cape May - Lewes Ferry & US 9: Go 2 mi E on US 9, then 1-3/4 mi S on CR 626 (Seashore Rd). Enter on R.*

◆◆◆◆FACILITIES: 135 sites, typical site width 40 ft, 100 full hkups, 35 W&E, (20/30/50 amps), some extd stay sites, heater not allowed, cable TV, WiFi Internet central location, family camping, tenting, RV's/park model rentals, dump, non-guest dump $, laundry, LP gas by weight/by meter, ice, picnic tables.

◆◆RECREATION: pavilion, golf nearby, playground, horseshoes, sports field.

Pets welcome. Partial handicap access. Open May 1 - Columbus Day. Big rigs welcome. Clubs welcome. Rate in 2010 $42.50-45 for 4 persons. Member ARVC, NJCOA.

Phone: (609)884-2533
Address: 800 Broadway, West Cape May, NJ 08204
Lat/Lon: 38.94386/-74.92944
Web: www.thedepottravelpark.com

SEE AD PAGE 516

CAPE MAY COURT HOUSE—F-3

(S) Adventure Bound Camping Resorts - Cape May—(Cape May) *From jct Garden State Pkwy (exit 9) & Shellbay Ave: Go 1 mi W on Shellbay Ave. Enter on R.* ◆◆FACILITIES: 400 sites, 125 full hkups, 109 W&E, (20/30 amps), 166 no hkups, 29 pull-thrus, family camping, tenting, dump, laundry, groceries. ◆◆RECREATION: swim pool, playground. Pets welcome. Partial handicap access. Open Mid Apr - Mid Oct.

CAPE MAY COURT HOUSE—Continued
Adventure Bound Camping Resorts - Cape May—Continued

Rate in 2010 $20-58 for 2 persons. Member ARVC, NJCOA. Phone: (800)752-4882.

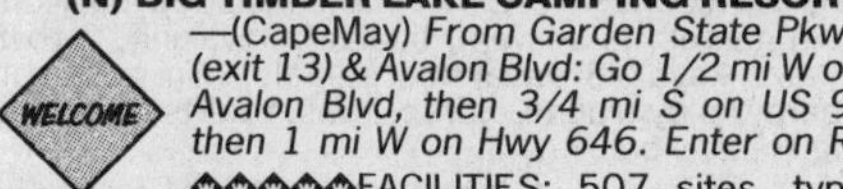

(N) BIG TIMBER LAKE CAMPING RESORT—(CapeMay) *From Garden State Pkwy (exit 13) & Avalon Blvd: Go 1/2 mi W on Avalon Blvd, then 3/4 mi S on US 9, then 1 mi W on Hwy 646. Enter on R.*

◆◆◆◆◆FACILITIES: 507 sites, typical site width 35 ft, 438 full hkups, 69 W&E, (20/30/50 amps), many extd stay sites, cable TV, WiFi Instant Internet at site ($), family camping, tenting, RV's/park model rentals, cabins, shower$, dump, non-guest dump $, laundry, ltd groc, RV supplies, LP gas by weight/by meter, ice, picnic tables, fire rings, wood.

◆◆◆◆◆RECREATION: rec hall, rec room/area, equipped pavilion, coin games, swim pool, wading pool, lake swim, canoeing, kayaking, 8 kayak rentals, pond fishing, fishing supplies, mini-golf, ($), golf nearby, bsktball, playground, shuffleboard court 2 shuffleboard courts, activities, horseshoes, sports field, v-ball.

Pets welcome. Partial handicap access. Open Apr 29 - Oct 15. 3 day min. weekends Jul-Aug, 4 day min. Jul 4 weekend by reservation. Big rigs welcome. Clubs welcome. Rate in 2010 $50-72 for 2 persons. MC/VISA/DISC/Debit. ATM. Member ARVC, NJCOA.

Phone: (609)465-4456
Address: 116 Swainton-Goshen Rd, Cape May Court House, NJ 08210-0366
Lat/Lon: 39.12362/-74.80700
Email: camp@bigtimberlake.com
Web: www.bigtimberlake.com/wdl

Reserve Online at Woodalls.com

SEE AD THIS PAGE

(N) King Nummy Trail Campground—(Cape May) *From jct Garden State Parkway (exit 6) & Hwy 147: Go 1 block W on Hwy 147 (turns into Hwy 618), then 3 mi W on Hwy 618, then 1 block SE on Hwy 47. Enter on R.* ◆◆◆FACILITIES: 300 sites, typical site width 40 ft, 118 full hkups, 182 W&E, (20/30/50 amps), family camping, tenting, dump, laundry, groceries. ◆◆◆◆RECREATION: 2 swim pools, playground. Pets welcome. Partial handicap access. Open Apr 24 - Oct 1. Rate in 2010 $40-44 for 2 persons. Member ARVC, NJCOA. Phone: (609)465-4242.

(S) Shellbay Campground—(Cape May) *From Garden State Parkway (exit 9): Go 1 mi W on Shellbay Ave. Enter on L.* ◆◆◆FACILITIES: 300 sites, typical site width 40 ft, 280 full hkups, 20 W&E, (20/30/50 amps), family camping, tenting, dump, laundry, ltd groc. ◆◆◆◆◆RECREATION: swim pool, playground. Pets welcome. Partial handicap access. Open May 15 - Oct 1. Rate in 2010 $43 for 4 persons. Member ARVC, NJCOA. Phone: (609)465-4770.

CENTERTON—E-2

PARVIN STATE PARK—(Salem) *From jct CR 553 & CR 540: Go 2 mi E on CR 540.* FACILITIES: 56 sites, 24 ft max RV length, 56 no hkups, tenting, dump, laundry. RECREATION: lake swim, boating, electric motors only, canoeing, ramp, dock, lake fishing, playground. No pets. Partial handicap access. Open Apr 1 - Oct 31. Phone: (856)358-8616.

CHATSWORTH—D-3

(S) WADING PINES CAMPING RESORT—(Burlington) *From jct Garden State Pkwy (exit 63) & Hwy 72: Go 17 mi W on Hwy 72, then 13 mi S on Hwy 563, then 3/4 mi W on Godfrey Bridge Rd. Enter on L.*

◆◆◆◆FACILITIES: 300 sites, 130 full hkups, 170 W&E, (20/30/50 amps), many extd stay sites (summer), 20 pull-thrus, cable TV, family camping, tenting, cabins, dump, laundry, groceries, RV supplies, LP gas by weight/by meter, ice, picnic tables, fire rings, wood, controlled access.

CHATSWORTH—Continued
WADING PINES CAMPING RESORT—Continued

◆◆◆◆◆RECREATION: rec hall, rec room/area, coin games, swim pool, canoeing, kayaking, 35 canoe/7 kayak rentals, float trips, river/pond fishing, fishing supplies, bsktball, playground, shuffleboard court 2 shuffleboard courts, activities (wkends), tennis, horseshoes, hiking trails, v-ball.

Pets welcome. Open Mar 1 - Nov 15. Big rigs welcome. Clubs welcome. Rate in 2010 $40-50 for 2 persons. MC/VISA/DISC/Debit. Member ARVC, NJCOA.

Phone: (609)726-1313
Address: 85 Godfrey Bridge Rd, Chatsworth, NJ 08019
Lat/Lon: 39.68710/-74.53962
Email: wadingpinescr@aol.com
Web: www.wadingpines.com

SEE AD ATLANTIC CITY PAGE 515

CLARKSBORO—D-2

(S) TIMBERLANE CAMPGROUND—(Gloucester) *N'bnd from jct I-295 & Timberlane Rd (exit 18): Go 3/4 mi SE on Timberlane Rd. Ent on rt. S'bnd from I-295 (exit 18AB):Go 1 mi S on Hwy 667 (Cohawkin Rd), then 1/4 mi SW on Friendship Rd, then 1/4 mi NW on Timberlane Rd.*

◆◆◆◆FACILITIES: 96 sites, typical site width 30 ft, 82 full hkups, (20/30/50 amps), 14 no hkups, some extd stay sites, 51 pull-thrus, cable TV, WiFi Internet central location, family camping, tenting, cabins, RV storage, dump, non-guest dump $, laundry, RV supplies, LP gas by weight/by meter, ice, picnic tables, fire rings, wood.

◆◆◆◆RECREATION: rec room/area, pavilion, coin games, swim pool, wading pool, pond fishing, fishing supplies, golf nearby, bsktball, playground, shuffleboard court shuffleboard court, horseshoes, sports field, v-ball.

Pets welcome. Partial handicap access. Open all yr. Big rigs welcome. Rate in 2010 $42-45 for 2 persons. MC/VISA/Debit. Member ARVC, NJCOA.

Phone: (856)423-6677
Address: 117 Timberlane Road, Clarksboro, NJ 08210
Lat/Lon: 39.80458/-75.23582
Email: info@timberlanecampground.com
Web: www.timberlanecampground.com

SEE AD PHILADELPHIA, PA PAGE 673 AND AD TRAVEL SECTION PAGE 509

CLERMONT—F-3

(S) AVALON CAMPGROUND—(Cape May) *From Garden State Parkway & Hwy 601 (exit 13): Go 1/2 mi W on Hwy 601, then 1-1/2 mi N on US 9. Enter on L.*

◆◆◆FACILITIES: 360 sites, 200 full hkups, 120 W&E, (20/30/50 amps), 40 no hkups, many extd stay sites, cable TV, WiFi Instant Internet at site, WiFi Internet central location, family camping, tenting, RV's/park model rentals, cabins, RV storage, dump, non-guest dump $, laundry, ltd groc, RV supplies, LP gas by weight, ice, picnic tables, fire rings, wood, controlled access.

◆◆◆◆◆RECREATION: rec hall, rec room/area, pavilion, equipped pavilion, coin games, 2 swim pools, mini-golf, ($), golf nearby, bsktball, playground, shuffleboard court 2 shuffleboard courts, activities, horseshoes, sports field, v-ball.

Pets welcome. Open Mid Apr - Mid Oct. 3 Day Min Holiday Wknds by reservation. 4 Day Min Jul & Aug

AVALON CAMPGROUND—Continued on next page

CLERMONT—Continued
AVALON CAMPGROUND—Continued

by reservation. Clubs welcome. Rate in 2010 $44-56 for 4 persons. MC/VISA/DISC. Member ARVC, NJCOA.

Phone: (609)624-0075
Address: 1917 Rte 9 North, Clermont, NJ 08210
Lat/Lon: 39.14667/-74.76478
Email: avaloncmpg@aol.com
Web: www.avaloncampground.com

SEE AD AVALON PAGE 515

CLINTON—B-3

ROUND VALLEY STATE RECREATION AREA—(Hunterdon) *From jct Hwy 31 & US 22: Go 8 mi E on US 22, then 1-1/2 mi S on Lebanon Stanton Rd to office, then hike or boat (3-6 mi) to campsites.* FACILITIES: 85 sites, 85 no hkups, tenting. RECREATION: lake swim, boating, 10 hp limit, canoeing, ramp, lake fishing, playground. No pets. Open Apr 1 - Oct 31. Phone: (908) 236-6355.

COLESVILLE—A-3

HIGH POINT STATE PARK—(Sussex) *From town: Go 3 mi N on Hwy-23.* FACILITIES: 50 sites, 50 no hkups, tenting. RECREATION: lake swim, boating, electric motors only, ramp, lake fishing, playground. No pets. Partial handicap access. Open Apr 1 - Oct 31. Phone: (973)875-4800.

COLUMBIA—B-2

(NE) BUCK STOP GIFT SHOP—*From jct I-80 & Hwy 94 (exit 4C): Go 3-1/2 mi N on Hwy 94, then 1/2 mi W on Benton Rd, then 1/4 mi N on Frog Pond Rd, then 1-1/2 mi N on Wishing Well Rd, then 1/2 mi S on Mt. Pleasant Rd. (Do not take Mt. Pleasant Rd directly from Hwy 94 due to incline). Enter on R.* Variety of unique gifts for all occasions. Online orders from website. Wolf Figurines, Earrings, Necklaces & Pendants, Bracelets, Journals & Plush items. Gifts from nature, Fine Crafts & Jewelry. Open all yr. MC/VISA/DISC/AMEX/Debit.

Phone: (908)496-4333
Address: 85 Mt Pleasant Rd, Columbia, NJ 07832
Lat/Lon: 40.97126/-75.07252
Web: www.buckstopgiftship.com

SEE AD THIS PAGE

(NE) CAMP TAYLOR CAMPGROUND—(Warren) *From jct I-80 & Hwy 94 (exit 4C): Go 3-1/2 mi N on Hwy 94, then 1/2 mi W on Benton Rd, then 1/4 mi N on Frog Pond Rd, then 1-1/2 mi N on Wishing Well Rd, then 1/2 mi S on Mt Pleasant Rd (Caution: do not take Mt Pleasant Rd directly from Hwy 94 d/t incline). Enter on R.*

◆◆◆FACILITIES: 150 sites, typical site width 40 ft, 102 W&E, (20/30/50 amps), 48 no hkups, some extd stay sites, WiFi Instant Internet at site, family camping, tenting, RV's/park model rentals,

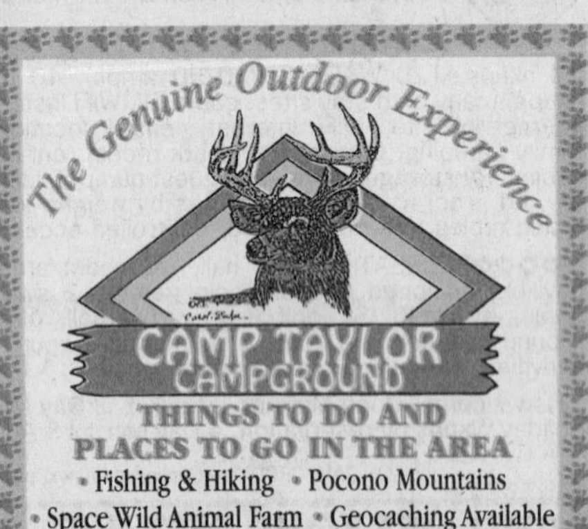

COLUMBIA—Continued
CAMP TAYLOR CAMPGROUND—Continued

cabins, shower$, dump, portable dump, LP gas by weight, ice, picnic tables, fire rings, wood.

◆◆◆◆RECREATION: rec hall, equipped pavilion, coin games, lake swim, boating, kayaking, 2 rowboat/2 kayak/3 pedal boat rentals, mini-golf, golf nearby, playground, horseshoes, sports field, hiking trails, v-ball.

Pets welcome, quantity restrict. Partial handicap access. Open Mid Apr - Nov 1. Lakota Wolf Preserve open year round. Clubs welcome. Rate in 2010 $33 for 2 persons. MC/VISA/DISC/AMEX/Debit. Member ARVC, NJCOA.

Phone: (908)496-4333
Address: 85 Mt. Pleasant Rd, Columbia, NJ 07832
Lat/Lon: 40.97126/-75.07252
Web: www.camptaylor.com

SEE AD THIS PAGE

(NE) LAKOTA WOLF PRESERVE AT CAMP TAYLOR—*From jct I-80 & Hwy 94 (exit 4): Go 3-1/2 mi N on Hwy 94, then 1/2 mi W on Benton Rd, then 2/10 mi N on Frog Pond Rd, then 1-1/2 mi N on Wishing Well Rd, then 1/2 mi S on Mt Pleasant Rd. Caution: do not take Mt Pleasant Rd directly from Hwy 94 d/t incline. Enter on R.* Wolf Watch program features informal talks, question & answer sessions daily at 10:30 a.m. & 4 p.m. Photography sessions also available by reservation only. (10:30 a.m. & 3:00 p.m. fall & Winter) Closed Mondays. Weekdays by appointment only. Open all yr.

Phone: (877)SEE-WOLF
Address: 85 Mt Pleasant Rd, Columbia, NJ 07832
Lat/Lon: 40.97126/-75.07252
Web: www.lakotawolf.com

SEE AD THIS PAGE

DELAWARE—B-2

(S) Delaware River Family Campground—(Warren) *From jct I-80, Hwy 94 & US 46: Go 3-1/2 mi E on US 46. Enter on R.* ◆◆◆FACILITIES: 171 sites, typical site width 25 ft, 171 W&E, (20/30 amps), family camping, tenting, dump, laundry, ltd groc. ◆◆◆◆RECREATION: swim pool, boating, canoeing, ramp, river fishing, playground. Pets welcome. Partial handicap access. Open Apr 1 - Oct 31. Rate in 2010 $41 for 2 persons. Member ARVC, NJCOA. Phone: (908)475-4517.

DOROTHY—E-3

(N) COUNTRY OAKS CAMPGROUND—(Atlantic) *From jct Hwy 50 & Hwy 557: Go 8 mi SE on Hwy 557 (Tuckahoe Rd), then 50 feet E on 14th St (across RR tracks), then 1/2 mi N on S Jersey Ave. Enter on R.*

◆◆◆FACILITIES: 140 sites, typical site width 40 ft, 127 full hkups, 13 W&E, (20/30/50 amps), many extd stay sites, 5 pull-thrus, cable TV, WiFi Instant Internet at site, WiFi Internet central location, family camping, tenting, cabins, dump, non-guest dump $, laundry, ltd groc, RV supplies, LP gas by weight/by meter, ice, picnic tables, fire rings, wood, controlled access.

◆◆◆◆RECREATION: rec hall, pavilion, coin games, swim pool, wading pool, golf nearby, bsktball, playground, shuffleboard court shuffleboard court, activities, horseshoes, sports field, v-ball.

Pets welcome. Partial handicap access. Open April 15 - Oct 15. Big rigs welcome. Escort to site. Clubs welcome. Rate in 2010 $40-50 for 4 persons. MC/VISA/Debit. Member ARVC, NJCOA.

Phone: (800)694-0315
Address: 13 S Jersey Ave, Dorothy, NJ 08317
Lat/Lon: 39.41591/-74.83636
Email: countryoakscamp@verizon.net
Web: www.countryoakscampground.com

SEE AD MAYS LANDING PAGE 520

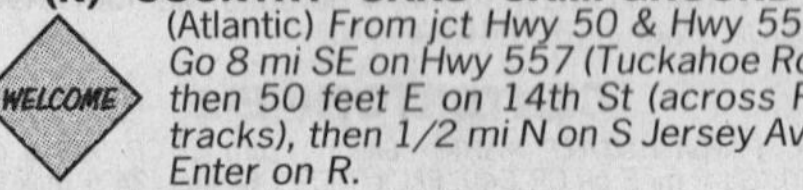

EGG HARBOR CITY—E-3

(S) Best Holiday Trav-L-Park/Holly Acres—(Atlantic) *From jct Hwy 50 & US 30: Go 2 mi SE on US 30, then 1-1/2 mi NE on Frankfurt Ave. Enter on R.* ◆◆◆◆FACILITIES: 175 sites, typical site width 35 ft, 125 full hkups, 50 W&E, (30/50 amps), 50 amps ($), 20 pull-thrus, family camping, tenting, dump, laundry, ltd groc. ◆◆◆◆RECREATION: swim pool, pond fishing, playground. Pets welcome. Partial handicap access. Open Apr 15 - Oct 31. Big rigs welcome. Rate in 2010 $38-43 for 2 persons. Member ARVC, NJCOA. Phone: (609)965-2287.

(C) TURTLE RUN CAMPGROUND—(Burlington) *From jct. Garden State Pkwy & US 9 (exit 50). Go 1 mi N on US 9, then 3-1/2 mi NW on CR 542, then 1/4 mi W on Turtle Creek Rd.*

◆◆◆FACILITIES: 109 sites, typical site width 35 ft, 53 full hkups, 36 W&E, (30/50 amps), 20 no hkups, some extd stay sites, 2 pull-thrus, WiFi Instant Internet at site, family camping, tenting, cabins, RV storage, dump, non-guest dump $, portable dump, laundry, groceries, RV supplies, LP gas by weight/by meter, ice, picnic tables, fire rings, grills, wood, controlled access.

◆◆◆◆RECREATION: rec hall, rec room/area, pavilion, coin games, swim pool, spray ground, boating, canoeing, kayaking, river fishing, fishing supplies, mini-golf, ($), golf nearby, bsktball, 8 bike rentals, playground, activities, (wkends), horseshoes, sports field, hiking trails, v-ball.

Pets welcome. Partial handicap access. Open April 1 - Oct 31. Clubs welcome. Rate in 2010 $32-42 for 4 persons. MC/VISA/DISC/AMEX/Debit. Member ARVC, NJCOA. CCUSA 50% Discount. CCUSA reservations Required, CCUSA max stay 14 days, CCUSA disc. not avail S, CCUSA disc. not avail F,Sa, CCUSA disc. not avail holidays.

Phone: (609)965-5343
Address: 3 Cedar Ln, Egg Harbor City, NJ 08215
Lat/Lon: 39.61294/-74.50158
Web: www.turtleruncampground.com

SEE AD ATLANTIC CITY PAGE 515

ELMER—E-2

(W) Yogi Bear Jellystone Park at Tall Pines Resort—(Salem) *From jct Hwy 40 & Hwy 77 & Hwy 635: Go 6-1/4 mi SW on CR 635 (Daretown Rd), then 1/4 mi E on Beal Rd. Enter on R.* ◆◆◆FACILITIES: 262 sites, typical site width 25 ft, 195 full hkups, 55 W&E, (20/30/50 amps), 12 no hkups, family camping, tenting, dump, laundry, groceries. ◆◆◆◆RECREATION: swim pool, pond/stream fishing, playground. Pets welcome, breed restrict, quantity restrict. Partial handicap access. Open Apr 1 - Nov 30. Rate in 2010 $32-69 per family. Member ARVC, NJCOA. Phone: (800)252-2890.

ESTELL MANOR—E-3

(N) Pleasant Valley Family Campground—(Weymouth) *From south jct Hwy 40 & Hwy 50: Go 1-1/4 mi S on Hwy 50. Enter on R.* ◆◆◆◆FACILITIES: 250 sites, 250 full hkups, (20/30/50 amps), family camping, laundry. ◆◆◆◆RECREATION: swim pool, playground. Pets welcome, breed restrict. No tents. Open Apr 15 - Oct 15. Big rigs welcome. Rate in 2010 $45 for 4 persons. Member ARVC, NJCOA. Phone: (609) 625-1238.

FARMINGDALE—C-4

(S) ALLAIRE STATE PARK—(Monmouth) *From jct I-195 & CR 547: Go 1/4 mi N on CR 547, then 1-1/4 mi E on CR 524.* FACILITIES: 45 sites, 45 no hkups, 12 pull-thrus, dump. RECREATION: canoeing, playground. No pets. Partial handicap access. Open all yr. Phone: (732)938-2371.

FREEHOLD—C-4

(W) PINE CONE RESORT—(Monmouth) *From jct Hwy 195 (exit 28) & Hwy 9: Go 1-1/2 mi N on Hwy 9, then 1-1/2 mi W on West Farms Rd. Enter on L.*

◆◆◆◆FACILITIES: 125 sites, typical site width 40 ft, 35 full hkups, 90 W&E, (20/30/50 amps), some extd stay sites, 15 pull-thrus, cable TV, WiFi Instant Internet at site, family camping, tenting, cabins, RV storage, dump, non-guest dump $, portable dump, laundry, ltd groc, RV supplies, ice, picnic tables, fire rings, wood.

◆◆◆◆RECREATION: rec room/area, coin games, swim pool, golf nearby, bsktball, playground, activities, (wkends), tennis, horseshoes, sports field, v-ball.

Pets welcome. Partial handicap access. Open all yr. 3 day min holidays by reservation. Big rigs welcome. Clubs welcome. Rate in 2010 $43-55 for 2 persons. MC/VISA/DISC/AMEX/Debit. Member ARVC, NJCOA.

PINE CONE RESORT—Continued on next page

FREEHOLD—Continued
PINE CONE RESORT—Continued

Phone: (732)462-2230
Address: 340 Georgia Rd, Freehold, NJ 07728
Lat/Lon: 40.17442/-74.27213
Email: pineconeresort@aol.com
Web: www.pineconenj.com

SEE AD THIS PAGE

(SW) TURKEY SWAMP (Monmouth County Park)—(Monmouth) *From jct US-9 & CR-524: Go 1-1/4 mi W on CR-524, then 1-3/4 mi SW on Georgia Rd.* FACILITIES: 64 sites, 30 ft max RV length, 64 W&E, (20/30 amps), 64 pull-thrus, tenting, dump, laundry. RECREATION: boating, electric motors only, canoeing, dock, lake fishing, playground. Pets welcome. Partial handicap access. Open Mar 15 - Nov 30. Phone: (732)462-7286.

GREAT MEADOWS—B-3

JENNY JUMP STATE FOREST—(Warren) *From jct US 46 & Hwy 611: Go 5 mi NW on Hwy 611 to Far View Rd.* FACILITIES: 22 sites, 25 ft max RV length, 22 no hkups, tenting. RECREATION: boating, electric motors only, canoeing, ramp, lake fishing, playground. No pets. Partial handicap access. Open Apr 1 - Oct 31. Phone: (908)459-4366.

GREEN CREEK—F-3

(N) Acorn Campground—(Cape May) *From jct Garden State Parkway (exit 4A) & Hwy 47: Go 3-1/2 mi NW on Hwy 47. Enter on L.* ◆FACILITIES: 330 sites, typical site width 40 ft, 270 full hkups, 60 W&E, (20/30/50 amps), 5 pull-thrus, family camping, tenting, dump, laundry, ltd groc. ◆◆◆RECREATION: 2 swim pools, pond fishing, playground. Pets welcome. Open Memorial Day - Labor Day. Rate in 2010 $46-52 per family. Member ARVC, NJCOA. Phone: (609)886-7119.

HACKETTSTOWN—B-3

(S) GOODLAND COUNTRY CLUB & SPA (NUDIST RESORT)—(Morris) *In Hackettstown: Call for directions.*

WELCOME

FACILITIES: 60 sites, 25 full hkups, 5 W&E, (15/20/30/50 amps), 30 no hkups, WiFi Internet central location, tenting, cabins, dump, laundry, picnic tables, fire rings, wood.

RECREATION: rec hall, pavilion, swim pool, hot tub, golf nearby, bsktball, shuffleboard court 2 shuffleboard courts, activities (wkends), horseshoes, hiking trails, v-ball.

Pets welcome. Open May 1 - Sep 30. Call for reservations. Off season RV sites Avail. Construction workers welcome. Green Friendly. Rate in 2010 $25-60 for 2 persons. MC/VISA/AMEX. Member ARVC, NJCOA.

Phone: (908)850-1300
Address: Hackettstown, NJ 07840
Email: info@goodlandcc.com
Web: www.goodlandcc.com

SEE AD THIS PAGE

STEPHENS STATE PARK—(Warren) *From town: Go 2 mi N on Willow Grove Rd.* FACILITIES: 40 sites, 16 ft max RV length, 40 no hkups, tenting. RECREATION: boating, river fishing, playground. No pets. Partial handicap access. Open Apr 1 - Oct 31. Phone: (908)852-3790.

HAMMONTON—E-3

WHARTON STATE FOREST (Atsion Rec. Area)—(Burlington) *From jct US 30 & US 206: Go 7 mi N on US 206.* FACILITIES: 50 sites, 26 ft max RV length, 50 no hkups, tenting, dump. RECREATION: lake swim, boating, electric motors only, canoeing, ramp, dock, lake/river fishing, playground. No pets. Partial handicap access. Open Apr 1 - Dec 15. Phone: (609)268-0444.

WHARTON STATE FOREST (Godfrey Bridge Camp)—(Burlington) *From jct US 30 & CR 542: Go 15 mi NE on CR 542 & CR 563.* FACILITIES: 49 sites, 21 ft max RV length, 49 no hkups, tenting. RECREATION: boating, electric motors only, canoeing, pond/stream fishing. No pets. Open all yr. Phone: (609)561-0024.

HIGH BRIDGE—B-3

(N) VOORHEES STATE PARK—(Hunterdon) *From jct Hwy-31 & I-78: Go 5 mi N on Hwy-31 & Hwy-513.* FACILITIES: 47 sites, 47 no hkups, tenting, dump. RECREATION: pond fishing, playground. No pets. Partial handicap access. Open Apr 1 - Oct 31. Phone: (908)638-6969.

HOPE—B-3

✱ **(S) GEORGE'S RV REPAIR**—*From jct I-80 (exit 12) & CR 521: Go 1 mi S on CR 521, then 3 mi W on CR 609, then 1 mi N on Nightingale Rd, then 1/2 mi E on Honeyrun Rd (at Triplebrook Camping Resort). Enter on L.* SERVICES: full-time mech, RV appliance repair, LP gas by weight/by meter, sells parts/accessories. Open all yr. MC/VISA/DISC/AMEX.

WELCOME

Phone: (800)340-1312
Address: 58 Honeyrun Rd, Blairstown, NJ 07825
Web: www.triplebrook.com

SEE AD BLAIRSTOWN PAGE 516

New Jersey State Tree: Red Oak

HOPE—Continued

(S) TRIPLEBROOK CAMPING RESORT—(Warren) *From jct I-80 (exit 12) & CR 521: Go 1 mi S on CR 521, then 3 mi W on CR 609, then 1 mi N on Nightingale Rd, then 1/2 mi E on Honey Run Rd. Enter on L.*

WELCOME

◆◆◆◆FACILITIES: 217 sites, typical site width 40 ft, 110 full hkups, 101 W&E, (20/30/50 amps), 6 no hkups, some extd stay sites, 6 pull-thrus, WiFi Instant Internet at site, WiFi Internet central location, family camping, tenting, cabins, RV storage, dump, non-guest dump $, portable dump, laundry, ltd groc, RV supplies, LP gas by weight/by meter, ice, picnic tables, wood.

◆◆◆◆RECREATION: rec room/area, equipped pavilion, coin games, 2 swim pools, hot tub, boating, canoeing, kayaking, 6 rowboat/4 pedal boat rentals, pond fishing, fishing supplies, mini-golf, ($), golf nearby, bsktball, playground, shuffleboard court shuffleboard court, activities, tennis, horseshoes, sports field, hiking trails, v-ball.

Pets welcome. Open all yr. 3 day min. stay holiday wkends with reservations. Dec 1-Mar 31 by reservation only. Big rigs welcome. Clubs welcome. Green Friendly. Rate in 2010 $39-45 for 2 persons. MC/VISA/DISC/AMEX. Member ARVC, NJCOA.

Phone: (908)459-4079
Address: 58 Honey Run Rd, Blairstown, NJ 07825
Lat/Lon: 40.91177/-75.01913
Email: info@triplebrook.com
Web: www.triplebrook.com

SEE AD BLAIRSTOWN PAGE 516

JACKSON—D-4

(E) Butterfly Camping Resort—(Ocean) *From jct I-195 (exit 21) & Hwy 527: Go 5-1/4 mi S on Hwy 527, then 1/2 mi N on Butterfly Rd. Enter on L.* ◆◆◆FACILITIES: 135 sites, typical site width 40 ft, 80 full hkups, 55 W&E, (30/50 amps), 8 pull-thrus, family camping, tenting, dump, laundry, groceries. ◆◆◆◆RECREATION: swim pool, boating, canoeing, ramp, lake fishing, playground. Pets welcome. Partial handicap access. Open Apr 1 - Oct 31. Rate in 2010 $50-55 per family. Member ARVC, NJCOA. Phone: (732)928-2107.

(W) Indian Rock Resort—(Ocean) *From jct I-195 (exit 16B) & Hwy 537: Go 1 mi SE on Hwy 537, then 4-1/2 mi S on Hwy 571, then 1-1/2 mi W on Hwy 528. Enter on R.* ◆◆◆FACILITIES: 210 sites, typical site width 40 ft, 90 full hkups, 120 W&E, (20/30 amps), 1

Indian Rock Resort—Continued on next page

JACKSON—Continued
Indian Rock Resort—Continued

pull-thrus, family camping, tenting, dump, laundry, groceries. ◆◆◆◆RECREATION: swim pool, pond fishing, playground. Pets welcome. Partial handicap access. Open all yr. Rate in 2010 $45 for 2 persons. Member ARVC, NJCOA. Phone: (732)928-0034.

(W) TIMBERLAND LAKE CAMPGROUND—(Ocean) *From jct I-195 & Hwy 537 (exit 16): Go 3-1/4 mi SW on Hwy 537, then 1/4 mi S on Hawkins Rd, then 1/2 mi SE on Reed Rd. Enter on R.*

CLOSEST CAMPGROUND TO SIX FLAGS!
Just a short drive from New York City, Philadelphia & Atlantic City. Enjoy our Olympic size pool, fishing & beach. New 50A Big Rig sites & WiFi! Relax by a campfire or enjoy our planned group activities.

◆◆◆FACILITIES: 200 sites, typical site width 40 ft, 30 full hkups, 170 W&E, (20/30/50 amps), some extd stay sites, 60 pull-thrus, cable TV, WiFi Internet central location, family camping, tenting, cabins, dump, non-guest dump $, portable dump, groceries, RV supplies, LP gas by weight/by meter, ice, picnic tables, fire rings, wood, controlled access.

◆◆◆RECREATION: pavilion, coin games, swim pool, canoeing, 8 row-boat/3 canoe/8 pedal boat rentals, lake fishing, fishing supplies, mini-golf, ($), golf nearby, bsktball, playground, activities, horseshoes, hiking trails, v-ball.

Pets welcome. Open Mar 1 - Dec 1. 3 day min on holiday wknds. Big rigs welcome. Clubs welcome. Rate in 2010 $44-51 for 2 persons. MC/VISA/DISC/AMEX/Debit. Member ARVC, NJCOA. FCRV discount. CCUSA 50% Discount. CCUSA reservations Recommended, CCUSA max stay 5 days, CCUSA disc. not avail F,Sa, CCUSA disc. not avail holidays.

Phone: (732)928-0500
Address: 1335 Reed Rd, Cream Ridge, NJ 08514
Lat/Lon: 40.12258/-74.46688
Email: timberlandlakecampground@yahoo.com
Web: www.timberlandlakecampground.com

SEE AD PAGE 519

(E) TIP TAM CAMPING RESORT—(Ocean) *From jct I-195 (exit 21) & Hwy 527: Go 1/4 mi S on Hwy 527, then 5-3/4 mi E on Hwy 526, then 1-3/4 mi S on Brewers Bridge Rd. Enter on L.*

◆◆◆◆FACILITIES: 200 sites, typical site width 35 ft, 168 full hkups, 32 W&E, (20/30/50 amps), some extd stay sites, cable TV, WiFi Instant Internet at site, family camping, tenting, RV's/park model rentals, cabins, shower$, dump, laundry, ltd groc, RV supplies, LP gas by weight/by meter, ice, picnic tables, fire rings, wood, controlled access.

◆◆◆◆RECREATION: rec hall, rec room/area, pavilion, equipped pavilion, coin games, 2 swim pools, wading pool, mini-golf, ($), golf nearby, bsktball, 2 bike rentals, playground, shuffleboard court shuffleboard court, activities, horseshoes, sports field, v-ball.

Pets welcome. Open Apr 15 - Sep 30. Big rigs welcome. Clubs welcome. Rate in 2010 $46-49 for 4 persons. MC/VISA/DISC. Member ARVC, NJCOA. FCRV discount.

In Cape May, New Jersey, more than 600 turn-of-the-century buildings stand as tribute to Victorian-era architecture.

JACKSON—Continued
TIP TAM CAMPING RESORT—Continued

Phone: (732)363-4036
Address: 301 Brewers Bridge Rd, Jackson, NJ 08527
Lat/Lon: 40.10013/-74.27028
Email: tiptam@aol.com
Web: www.tiptam.com

SEE AD THIS PAGE

JERSEY CITY—B-4

(C) LIBERTY HARBOR RV PARK—(Hudson) *From jct I-78, NJ Turnpike (exit 14C) and Jersey City/Columbus Dr exit (last exit before Holland Tunnel), keep right at end of ramp: Go 7 blocks E on Christopher Columbus Dr, then 6 blocks S on Marin Blvd to end. Enter at end.*

◆◆◆FACILITIES: 50 sites, typical site width 25 ft, 50 W&E, (30/50 amps), 2 pull-thrus, phone Internet central location, family camping, tenting, dump, laundry, marine gas, ice, picnic tables.

◆◆RECREATION: boating, dock, saltwater fishing, golf nearby, local tours.

Pets welcome. Partial handicap access. Open all yr. Big rigs welcome. Clubs welcome. Rate in 2010 $60 per family. MC/VISA/DISC/AMEX. Member ARVC, NJCOA. FMCA discount.

Text 108017 to (440)725-8687 to see our Visual Tour.

Phone: (201)386-7500
Address: 11 Marin Blvd, Jersey City, NJ 07302
Lat/Lon: 40.70775/-74.03957
Email: carmen.aponte@libertyharbor.com
Web: www.libertyharborrv.com

SEE AD NEW YORK CITY, NY PAGE 555 AND AD DISCOVER SECTION PAGE 24

LITTLE EGG HARBOR—E-4

(N) BAKER'S ACRES CAMPGROUND—(Ocean) *From jct Garden State Pkwy (exit 58) & Hwy 539: Go 1/4 mi SE on Hwy 539, then 1-3/4 mi E on Thomas Ave, then 1/4 mi SE on Railroad Dr. Enter on R.*

◆◆◆FACILITIES: 250 sites, typical site width 40 ft, 35 ft max RV length, 50 full hkups, 170 W&E, (20/30 amps), 30 no hkups, many extd stay sites (summer), 6 pull-thrus, cable TV, WiFi Instant Internet at site, WiFi Internet central location, family camping, tenting, cabins, RV storage, shower$, dump, portable dump, laundry, groceries, RV supplies, LP gas by weight, ice, picnic tables, fire rings, wood.

◆◆◆RECREATION: equipped pavilion, coin games, swim pool, wading pool, golf nearby, playground, activities, (wkends), horseshoes, hiking trails, v-ball.

Pets welcome. Partial handicap access. Open May 1 - Nov 1. Clubs welcome. Rate in 2010 $42-46 for 4 persons. MC/VISA/DISC/AMEX/Debit. Member ARVC, NJCOA. CCUSA 50% Discount. CCUSA reservations Recommended, CCUSA max stay 3 days, CCUSA disc. not avail F,Sa, CCUSA disc. not avail holidays. Not available Memorial Day thru Labor Day weekend.

Phone: (800)648-2227
Address: 230 Willets Ave, Little Egg Harbor, NJ 08087
Lat/Lon: 39.63479/-74.31405
Email: mrsacres@bakersacres.com
Web: www.BakersAcres.com/Woodalls

SEE AD TUCKERTON PAGE 522

LONG BEACH ISLAND—E-4

BROOKVILLE CAMPGROUND—*From jct US 9 & Hwy 72: Go 5-1/4 mi NW on Hwy 72, then 3/4 mi E on Hwy 554, then 3/4 mi N on Brookville Rd, then 1/2 mi E on Jones Rd. Enter on R.*

SEE PRIMARY LISING AT BARNEGAT AND AD BARNEGAT PAGE 515

MARMORA—F-3

(S) Whippoorwill Campground—(Cape May) *From jct Garden State Parkway (exit 25) & Hwy 623: Go 1 block W on Hwy 623, then 1-1/2 mi S on US 9. Enter on R.* ◆◆◆◆FACILITIES: 288 sites, typical site width 45 ft, 226 full hkups, 58 W&E, (20/30/50 amps), 4 no hkups, family camping, tenting, dump, laundry, ltd groc. ◆◆◆◆RECREATION: swim pool, playground. Pets welcome. Partial handicap access. Open Apr 1 - Oct 31. Rate in 2010 $53.50 for 2 persons. Member ARVC, NJCOA. Phone: (800)424-8275.

MATAWAN—C-4

(NE) CHEESEQUAKE STATE PARK—(Middlesex) *From Garden State Pkwy (exit 120): Bear right, then turn right at second traffic light.* FACILITIES: 53 sites, 53 no hkups, tenting, dump. RECREATION: lake swim, boating, electric motors only, canoeing, lake fishing, playground. No pets. Open Apr 1 - Oct 31. Facilities fully operational Memorial Day - Labor Day. Phone: (732) 566-2161.

MAYS LANDING—E-3

(W) Nascar at May's Landing RV Resort (Morgan RV Resorts)—(Atlantic) *From jct Hwy 50 & Hwy 40: Go 1/2 mi S on Hwy 50, then 4 mi W on Hwy 669, then 1/4 mi N on Beach Rd, then 500 feet E on 12th Ave. Enter on R.* ◆◆◆FACILITIES: 164 sites, typical site width 35 ft, 142 full hkups, 22 W&E, (20/30/50 amps), family camping, tenting, dump, laundry, groceries. ◆◆◆RECREATION: swim pool, pond fishing, playground. Pets welcome. Partial handicap access. Open Apr 1 - Oct 31. Rate in 2010 $41.99-54.99 for 4 persons. Member ARVC, NJCOA. Phone: (609)476-2811.

(N) WINDING RIVER CAMPGROUND—(Atlantic) *From jct Hwy 50 & Hwy 40 & Hwy 616: Go 1/4 mi N on Hwy 616, then 4 mi NE on Hwy 559. Enter on R.*

◆◆◆◆FACILITIES: 133 sites, 105 full hkups, 28 W&E, (20/30 amps), many extd stay sites, phone Internet central location, family camping, tenting, RV's/park model rentals, cabins, RV storage, shower$, dump, non-guest dump $, laundry, ltd groc, LP gas by weight, ice, picnic tables, fire rings, wood.

◆◆◆◆RECREATION: rec room/area, equipped pavilion, coin games, swim pool, boating, 20 hp limit, canoeing, kayaking, ramp, 34 canoe/40 kayak rentals, float trips, river/pond fishing, fishing supplies, golf nearby, bsktball, playground, activities, (wkends), horseshoes, v-ball.

WINDING RIVER CAMPGROUND—Continued on next page

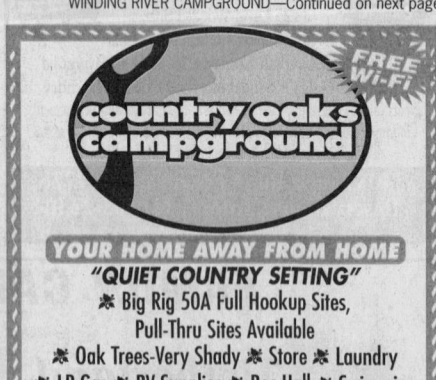

MAYS LANDING—Continued
WINDING RIVER CAMPGROUND—Continued

Pets welcome. Open May 1 - Oct 15. 3 day min. stay Holiday Weekends with Reservations. Rate in 2010 $39-44 for 2 persons. MC/VISA/DISC/Debit. ATM. Member ARVC, NJCOA.

Text 107912 to (440)725-8687 to see our Visual Tour.

Phone: (609)625-3191
Address: 6752 Weymouth Rd, Mays Landing, NJ 08330
Lat/Lon: 39.48858/-74.76993
Email: windingrivercampgroundnj@msn.com
Web: www.windingrivercamping.com

SEE AD ATLANTIC CITY PAGE 514

(N) WINDING RIVER CANOEING & KAYAKING—*From jct Hwy 50 & Hwy 40 & Hwy 616: Go 1/4 mi N on Hwy 616, then 4 mi NE on Hwy 559.* Scenic Great Egg Harbor River, canoeing, kayaking & tubing trips. Open May 1 - Oct 15. MC/VISA/DISC/Debit.

Phone: (609)625-3191
Address: 6752 Weymouth Rd, Mays Landing, NJ 08330
Lat/Lon: 39.48858/-74.76993
Email: windingrivercampgroundnj@msn.com
Web: www.windingrivercamping.com

SEE AD ATLANTIC CITY PAGE 514

MONROEVILLE—E-2

(S) OLD CEDAR CAMPGROUND—(Gloucester) *From jct Hwy 77 & Hwy 604: Go 2-1/4 mi SE on Hwy 604, then 1/2 mi N on Hwy 609, then 3/4 mi E on Foote Ln. Enter on L.*

◆◆◆FACILITIES: 200 sites, typical site width 40 ft, 160 full hkups, 35 W&E, (15/20/30/50 amps), 5 no hkups, some extd stay sites, 25 pull-thrus, WiFi Internet central location, family camping, tenting, cabins, dump, non-guest dump $, laundry, ltd groc, RV supplies, LP gas by weight/by meter, ice, picnic tables, fire rings, wood, controlled access.

◆◆◆RECREATION: rec room/area, pavilion, coin games, lake swim, mini-golf, ($), golf nearby, bsktball, playground, shuffleboard court 3 shuffleboard courts, activities (wkends), tennis, horseshoes, sports field, hiking trails, v-ball. Rec open to public.

Pets welcome. Partial handicap access. Open Apr 1 - Nov 1. Clubs welcome. Rate in 2010 $32 for 2 persons. MC/VISA/DISC/AMEX/Debit. Member ARVC, NJCOA.

Phone: (856)358-4881
Address: 274 Richwood Rd, Monroeville, NJ 08343
Lat/Lon: 39.63805/-75.15940
Email: reservations@oldcedarcampground.com
Web: www.oldcedarcampground.com

SEE AD THIS PAGE

(S) Oldman's Creek Campground—(Gloucester) *From jct US 322 & Hwy 45: Go 3/4 mi S on Hwy 45, then 4 mi S on Hwy 77, then 1/2 mi E on Hwy 538, then 1/2 mi S on Hwy 641, then 3/4 mi S on Laux Rd. Enter on L.* ◆◆◆FACILITIES: 143 sites, typical site width 32 ft, 135 full hkups, 8 W&E, (20/30/50 amps), 2 pull-thrus, family camping, tenting, dump, laundry. ◆◆◆◆RECREATION: swim pool, lake swim, boating, no motors, canoeing, lake fishing, playground. Pets welcome, breed restrict. Open all yr. Rate in 2010 $37.50 for 4 persons. Member ARVC, NJCOA. Phone: (856)478-4502.

NEW GRETNA—E-4

(N) BASS RIVER STATE FOREST—(Burlington) *From jct US-9 & State Parkway: Go 1-1/2 mi W on US-9 into town, then 3 mi NE on Stage Rd.* FACILITIES: 176 sites, 176 no hkups, dump, laundry. RECREATION: lake/river swim, boating, electric motors only, canoeing, playground. No pets. Partial handicap access. Open all yr. Phone: (609)296-1114.

(N) Timberline Lake Camping Resort—(Burlington) *From jct US 9 & Hwy 679: Go 3-3/4 mi NW on Hwy 679. Enter on L.* ◆◆◆FACILITIES: 158 sites, typical site width 45 ft, 68 full hkups, 80 W&E, (20/30/50 amps), 10 no hkups, 10 pull-thrus, family camping, tenting, dump, laundry, ltd groc. ◆◆◆RECREATION: swim

New Jersey State Nickname: Garden State

NEW GRETNA—Continued
Timberline Lake Camping Resort—Continued

pool, lake swim, boating, no motors, canoeing, lake fishing, playground. Pets welcome. Open May 1 - mid Oct. Big rigs welcome. Rate in 2010 $37-45 for 4 persons. Member ARVC, NJCOA. Phone: (609)296-7900.

NEWTON—A-3

SWARTSWOOD STATE PARK—(Sussex) *From town: Go 7 mi NW on Newton Swartswood Rd.* FACILITIES: 65 sites, 65 no hkups, tenting, dump, laundry. RECREATION: lake swim, boating, electric motors only, canoeing, ramp, dock, lake fishing, playground. No pets. Partial handicap access. Open Apr 1 - Oct 31. Phone: (973)383-5230.

NORTHFIELD—E-3

BIRCH GROVE PARK (City Park)—(Atlantic) *From jct US-322 & US-9: Go 2 mi S on US-9, then 1/4 mi W on Hwy 662 (Mill Rd), then 1/8 mi N on Burton Rd.* FACILITIES: 50 sites, 17 full hkups, 20 W&E, 13 no hkups, tenting, dump, laundry. RECREATION: pond fishing, playground. Open Apr - Oct 14. Phone: (609)641-3778.

OCEAN VIEW—F-3

(W) Frontier Campground—(Cape May) *From jct US 9 & Hwy 50: Go 2-1/2 mi N on Hwy 50. Enter on R.* ◆◆◆FACILITIES: 196 sites, typical site width 35 ft, 130 full hkups, 57 W&E, (20/30/50 amps), 9 no hkups, family camping, tenting, laundry, ltd groc. ◆◆RECREATION: playground. No pets. Partial handicap access. Open Mid Apr - Mid Oct. Rate in 2010 $31-45 for 4 persons. Member ARVC, NJCOA. Phone: (609)390-3649.

LAKE AND SHORE—*Take Garden State Pkwy S to Sea Isle City (Exit 17), then left at stop sign, then W 1/2 mi to Rt 9, then R onto Rt 9. Go N on Rt 9 (1/2 mi) to Rt 550, then left on Rt 550 & follow to Corson Tavern Rd, then right on Corson Tavern Rd & travel 1/4 mi to camp. Enter on L.*

FACILITIES: 218 sites, 218 full hkups, family camping, tenting, RV's/park model rentals, groceries.

LAKE AND SHORE—Continued on next page

OCEAN VIEW—Continued
LAKE AND SHORE—Continued

RECREATION: coin games, swim pool, lake swim, boating, lake fishing, mini-golf, bsktball, playground, shuffleboard court shuffleboard court, horseshoes, v-ball.

Pets welcome. Open all yr.

Phone: (877)730-5935
Address: 545 Corsen Tavern Rd, Ocean View, NJ 08230
Email: tripexpert@1000trails.com
Web: oneparkmembership.com

SEE AD ABSECON PAGE 514

(S) OCEAN VIEW RESORT CAMPGROUND—(Cape May) *From jct Garden State Pkwy South (exit 17) & Hwy 625 (Sea Isle Blvd): Go 1/4 mi W on Hwy 625, then 1/4 mi N on US 9. Enter on L.*

JERSEY SHORE CAMPING AT IT'S BEST!
New Jersey's largest privately owned campground! Close to beaches, golf, shopping, restaurants & an abundance of activities. Enjoy historic Cape May, Wildwood & Atlantic City. Jersey shore memories are waiting to be made!

◇◇◇◇FACILITIES: 1175 sites, 1175 full hkups, (20/30/50 amps), some extd stay sites (summer), 40 pull-thrus, heater not allowed, cable TV, WiFi Instant Internet at site, WiFi Internet central location, family camping, tenting, RV's/park model rentals, cabins, RV storage, shower$, laundry, full svc store, RV supplies, LP gas by weight/by meter, ice, picnic tables, fire rings, wood, controlled access.

◇◇◇◇◇RECREATION: rec hall, rec room/area, equipped pavilion, coin games, swim pool, wading pool, lake swim, boating, 6 pedal boat rentals, pond fishing, fishing supplies, mini-golf, ($), golf nearby, bsktball, playground, shuffleboard court 2 shuffleboard courts, activities, tennis, sports field, v-ball, local tours.

Pets welcome. Partial handicap access. Open Mid Apr - Sep 30. Weekends only early season. Big rigs welcome. Green Friendly. Rate in 2010 $39-79 for 4 persons. MC/VISA/DISC/Debit. ATM. Member ARVC, NJCOA.

Phone: (609)624-1675
Address: 2555 Shore Rd (US9), Ocean View, NJ 08230
Lat/Lon: 39.17467/-74.72440
Email: camp@ovresort.com
Web: www.ovresort.com

SEE AD PAGE 521 AND AD TRAVEL SECTION PAGE 509

(S) OCEAN VIEW TRAILER SALES—*Garden State Pkwy South (exit 17) & Hwy 625 (Sea Isle Blvd): Go 1/4 mi W on Hwy 625, then 1/4 mi N on US 9. Enter on L.* SALES: travel trailers, park models, pre-owned unit sales. SERVICES: full-time mech, RV appliance repair, LP gas by weight/by meter, RV storage, sells parts/accessories, installs hitches. Open all yr. MC/VISA/DISC.

Phone: (609)624-0370
Address: 2555 US Rte 9, Ocean View, NJ 08230
Lat/Lon: 39.17467/-74.72440
Email: ovts@comcast.net
Web: www.oceanviewtrailersales.com

SEE AD PAGE 521

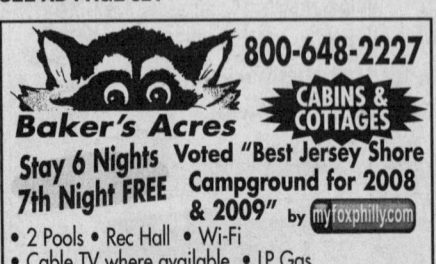

OCEAN VIEW—Continued

(S) Sea Grove Camping Resort—(Cape May) *From jct Garden State Pkwy South (exit 17) & Hwy 625 (Sea Isle Blvd): Go 1/4 mi W on Hwy 625, then 1 mi N on US 9. Enter on L.* ◇◇◇FACILITIES: 190 sites, 135 full hkups, 35 W&E, (20/30/50 amps), 20 no hkups, family camping, tenting, dump, laundry, ltd groc. ◇◇◇RECREATION: swim pool, playground. Pets welcome. Partial handicap access. Open Apr 1 - Nov 1. Rate in 2010 $30-50 for 4 persons. Member ARVC, NJCOA. Phone: (609)624-3529.

(S) SHORE GATE GOLF CLUB—*From jct Garden State Pkwy South (exit 17) & Hwy 625 (Sea Isle Blvd): Go 1/4 mi W on Hwy 625, then 1/4 mi W on School House Ln.* 18-hole Championship Golf Course located adjacent to Ocean View Resort Campground. Pro Shop & Snack Bar. Practice facilities. PGA professionals available. Open all yr. MC/VISA.

Phone: (609)624-TEES
Address: 35 School House Ln, Ocean View, NJ 08230
Lat/Lon: 39.17862/-74.73697
Web: www.shoregategolfclub.com

SEE AD PAGE 521

(S) Tamerlane Campground—(Cape May) *From jct Garden State Pkwy (exit 17) & Hwy 625 (Sea Isle Blvd): Go 1/4 mi N on Hwy 625, then 1 mi S on US 9. Enter on R.* ◇◇◇FACILITIES: 250 sites, typical site width 35 ft, 30 ft max RV length, 250 full hkups, (20/30/50 amps), family camping, tenting, dump, laundry, ltd groc. ◇◇◇RECREATION: swim pool, playground. Pets welcome. Partial handicap access. Open Apr 1 - Oct 1. Rate in 2010 $45 for 4 persons. Member ARVC, NJCOA. Phone: (609)624-0767.

PEMBERTON—D-3

BYRNE STATE FOREST—(Burlington) *From jct US-206 & Hwy-70: Go 10 mi E on Hwy-70.* FACILITIES: 79 sites, 79 no hkups, tenting, dump, laundry. RECREATION: lake fishing, playground. No pets. Partial handicap access. Open Apr 1 - Oct 31. Phone: (609)726-1191.

POMONA—E-3

(N) Evergreen Woods Lakefront Resort—(Atlantic) *From jct US 30 & Hwy 575: Go 4 mi N on Hwy 575, then 100 yards E on Hwy Alt 561S (Moss Mill Rd). Enter on R.* ◇◇◇FACILITIES: 225 sites, 175 full hkups, 50 W&E, (20/30 amps), 30 pull-thrus, family camping, tenting, dump, laundry, ltd groc. ◇◇◇RECREATION: swim pool, boating, no motors, canoeing, dock, lake fishing, playground. Pets welcome. Partial handicap access. Open Mar 31 - Oct 31. Rate in 2010 $40 for 2 persons. Member ARVC, NJCOA. Phone: (609)652-1577.

(S) POMONA RV PARK—(Atlantic) *From jct US 30 & Hwy 575: Go 1/2 mi S on Hwy 575. Enter on L.*

◇◇◇◇FACILITIES: 125 sites, typical site width 25 ft, 125 full hkups, (20/30/50 amps), some extd stay sites, 7 pull-thrus, cable TV, WiFi Instant Internet at site, WiFi Internet central location, family camping, tenting, RV's/park model rentals, laundry, ltd groc, RV supplies, LP gas by weight, ice, picnic tables, patios, fire rings, wood.

◇◇◇RECREATION: rec room/area, coin games, swim pool, hot tub, golf nearby, playground, activities, (wkends), horseshoes, sports field, v-ball.

Pets welcome. Open Apr 1 - Nov 1. Limited winter camping. Big rigs welcome. Clubs welcome. Rate in 2010 $45-50 for 2 persons. MC/VISA/DISC/Debit. Member ARVC, NJCOA.

Phone: (609)965-2123
Address: 536 South Pomona Rd, Galloway, NJ 08240
Lat/Lon: 39.47158/-74.58347
Email: info@pomonarvpark.com
Web: www.pomonarvpark.com

SEE AD ATLANTIC CITY PAGE 515

PORT REPUBLIC—E-4

(N) Atlantic City Blueberry Hill RV Park (Morgan RV Resorts)—(Atlantic) *From jct Garden State Parkway (South) exit 48 & US 9: Go 1/4 mi S on US 9, then 1-1/2 mi S on CR 575, then 1 mi S on CR 650, then 1/4 mi W on CR 624. Enter on L.* ◇◇◇FACILITIES: 173 sites, typical site width 40 ft, 47 full hkups, 124 W&E, (20/30/50 amps), 50 amps ($), 2 no hkups, 50 pull-thrus, family camping, tenting, dump, laundry, ltd groc. ◇◇◇◇RECREATION: swim pool, playground. Pets welcome. Partial handicap access. Open Feb 1 - Dec 15. Rate in 2010 $29.99-43.99 for 4 persons. Member ARVC, NJCOA. Phone: (609)652-1644.

Atlantic City has the longest boardwalk in the world.

PORT REPUBLIC—Continued

(N) CHESTNUT LAKE CAMPGROUND—(Atlantic) *From jct Garden State Parkway (Exit 48). Go 1/4 mi E then 1/4 mi W on Hwy 575. Enter on R.*

◇◇◇FACILITIES: 185 sites, typical site width 30 ft, 40 ft max RV length, 65 full hkups, 120 W&E, (30 amps), some extd stay sites, 120 pull-thrus, WiFi Internet central location, family camping, tenting, RV storage, dump, non-guest dump $, portable dump, laundry, RV supplies, LP gas by weight, ice, picnic tables, grills, controlled access.

◇◇◇RECREATION: rec hall, swim pool, bsktball, playground, shuffleboard court 3 shuffleboard courts, horseshoes, sports field.

Pets welcome. Partial handicap access. Open May 1 - Oct 15. Clubs welcome. Rate in 2010 $48 for 2 persons. MC/VISA/DISC/AMEX. Member ARVC, NJCOA.

Phone: (609)652-1005
Address: 631 Chestnut Neck Road, Port Republic, NJ 08241
Lat/Lon: 39.54028/74.46892
Web: www.1000trails.com

SEE AD ABSECON PAGE 514

STOCKTON—C-3

DELAWARE AND RARITAN CANAL STATE PARK (Bull's Island Section)—(Hunterdon) *From town: Go 3 mi NW on Hwy 29.* FACILITIES: 69 sites, 69 no hkups, tenting, dump. RECREATION: boating, electric motors only, canoeing, ramp, river/stream fishing, playground. No pets. Open Apr 1 - Oct 31. Phone: (609)397-2949.

SUSSEX—A-3

(N) Pleasant Acres Farm Campground—(Sussex) *From jct Hwy-284 & Hwy-23: Go 4-3/4 mi N on Hwy-23, then 1 mi E on Dewitt Rd. Enter on R.* ◇◇◇◇FACILITIES: 300 sites, typical site width 35 ft, 300 full hkups, (20/30/50 amps), 6 pull-thrus, family camping, dump, laundry, groceries. ◇◇◇◇RECREATION: swim pool, pond/stream fishing, playground. Pets welcome. Partial handicap access. No tents. Open all yr. Big rigs welcome. Rate in 2010 $52 for 2 persons. Member ARVC, NJCOA. Phone: (800)722-4166.

SWAINTON—F-3

(S) OUTDOOR WORLD-SEA PINES CAMPGROUND (CAMP RESORT)—(Cape May) *From jct Garden State Pkwy (exit 13) & Hwy 601: Go 1/2 mi W on Hwy 601, then 1/2 mi S on US 9. Enter on R.*

FACILITIES: 485 sites, 236 full hkups, 249 W&E, (30/50 amps), some extd stay sites, family camping, tenting, RV's/park model rentals, RV storage, dump, laundry, ltd groc, RV supplies, LP gas by weight/by meter, ice, picnic tables, patios, fire rings, grills, wood.

RECREATION: rec hall, rec room/area, pavilion, equipped pavilion, coin games, swim pool, wading pool, canoeing, kayaking, 4 kayak rentals, lake fishing, mini-golf, golf nearby, bsktball, playground, shuffleboard court shuffleboard court, activities, sports field, v-ball.

Pets welcome. Partial handicap access. Open Mid-May - Mid-Oct. Clubs welcome. MC/VISA/DISC/AMEX. Member ARVC, NJCOA.

Phone: (609)465-4517
Address: 1535 Rt 9N, Swainton, NJ 08210
Lat/Lon: 39.12190/-74.78520
Web: www.1000trails.com

SEE AD ABSECON PAGE 514

TUCKERTON—E-4

See primary listing at Little Egg Harbor

WEST CREEK—E-4

(S) Sea Pirate Campground—(Ocean) *From jct Hwy-72 & US-9: Go 5 mi S on US-9. Enter on L.* ◇◇◇◇FACILITIES: 184 sites, typical site width 50 ft, 84 full hkups, 95 W&E, (20/30/50 amps), 5 no hkups, 15 pull-thrus, family camping, tenting, dump, laundry, groceries. ◇◇◇◇RECREATION: swim pool, boating, canoeing, saltwater/pond fishing, playground. Pets welcome. Partial handicap access. Open May 1 - Nov 1. Big rigs welcome. Rate in 2010 $52-62 per family. Member ARVC, NJCOA. Phone: (609)296-7400.

On Christmas Eve, 1776, General George Washington crossed the Delaware River into New Jersey, surprising the British Troops at Trenton.

WEST PORTAL—B-2

(C) JUGTOWN MOUNTAIN CAMPSITES —(Hunterdon) *Westbound: From jct I-78 (exit 11) & Hwy 173: Go 1-1/2 mi W on Hwy 173. Eastbound: From jct I-78 (exit 7) & Hwy 173: Go 3 mi E on Hwy 173.*

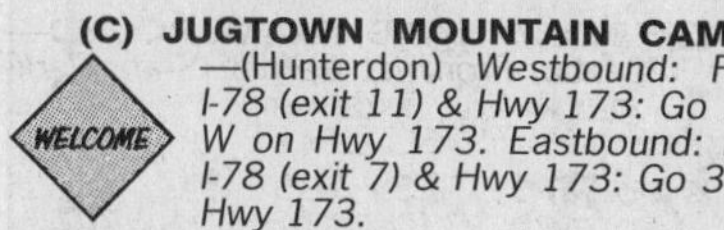

◆◆◆FACILITIES: 150 sites, typical site width 30 ft, 75 W&E, (15/30/50 amps), 50 amps ($), 75 no hkups, some extd stay sites, 25 pull-thrus, WiFi Internet central location, family camping, tenting, RV's/park model rentals, RV storage, dump, non-guest dump $, portable dump, RV supplies, LP gas by weight/by meter, ice, picnic tables, fire rings, wood.

◆◆RECREATION: swim pool, golf nearby, play equipment, sports field, hiking trails, v-ball.

Pets welcome. Open all yr. Big rigs welcome. Clubs welcome. Rate in 2010 $31 for 2 persons. MC/VISA/DISC/AMEX/Debit. ATM. Member ARVC, NJCOA.

Phone: (908)735-5995
Address: 1074 Hwy 173, Asbury, NJ 08802
Lat/Lon: 40.65235/-75.01855
Web: www.jugtownmountaincampsites.com

SEE AD ANDOVER PAGE 514

WOODBINE—F-3

(N) BELLEPLAIN STATE FOREST—(Cape May) *N'bound from jct Hwy 557 & CR 550: Go 2-1/2 mi W on CR 550.* FACILITIES: 169 sites, 169 no hkups, tenting, dump, laundry. RECREATION: lake swim, boating, electric motors only, canoeing, ramp, dock, lake fishing, playground. No pets. Partial handicap access. Open all yr. Phone: (609)861-2404.

WOODPORT—A-3

MAHLON DICKERSON RESERVATION (Morris County Park)—(Morris) *From jct I-80 (exit 34) & Hwy 15: Go 5 mi N on Hwy 15, then 4 mi E on Weldon Rd.* FACILITIES: 30 sites, 35 ft max RV length, 18 W&E, 12 no hkups, tenting, dump. RECREATION: canoeing, pond fishing. Partial handicap access. Open all yr. Facilities fully operational May 1 - Nov 1. Phone: (973)663-0200.

WOODSTOWN—E-2

(W) FOUR SEASONS CAMPGROUND—(Salem) *From jct Hwy 45 & US 40: Go 3-3/4 mi E on US 40, then 1-1/2 mi S on CR 581, then 300 feet W on Woodstown Rd-Daretown Rd. Enter on R.*

WELCOME

◆◆◆FACILITIES: 487 sites, typical site width 25 ft, 395 full hkups, 92 W&E, (20/30/50 amps), mostly extd stay sites, 30 pull-thrus, cable TV, WiFi Internet central location ($), family camping, tenting, cabins, dump, non-guest dump $, laundry, groceries, RV supplies, LP gas by weight, ice, picnic tables, fire rings, wood.

◆◆◆◆RECREATION: rec hall, rec room/area, pavilion, coin games, lake swim, boating, no motors, canoeing, kayaking, rowboat/canoe/2 pedal boat rentals, lake/pond fishing, fishing supplies, golf nearby, bsktball, playground, activities, (wkends), horseshoes, v-ball.

Pets welcome. Partial handicap access. Open all yr. Facilities fully operational Feb 1 - Dec 31. 3 Day Min. Holiday Weekends by Reservation. Big rigs welcome. Escort to site. Rate in 2010 $31-36 per family. MC/VISA/DISC/AMEX/Debit. ATM. Member ARVC, NJCOA.

Phone: (856)769-3635
Address: 158 Woodstown-Daretown Rd, Pilesgrove, NJ 08098
Lat/Lon: 39.60983/-75.27177
Email: info@fourseasonscamping.com
Web: www.fourseasonscamping.com

SEE AD THIS PAGE

Asbury Park—Home of Jersey Shore Rock n' RollMWhere legendary Bruce Springsteen first tuned his guitar in the late 60's.

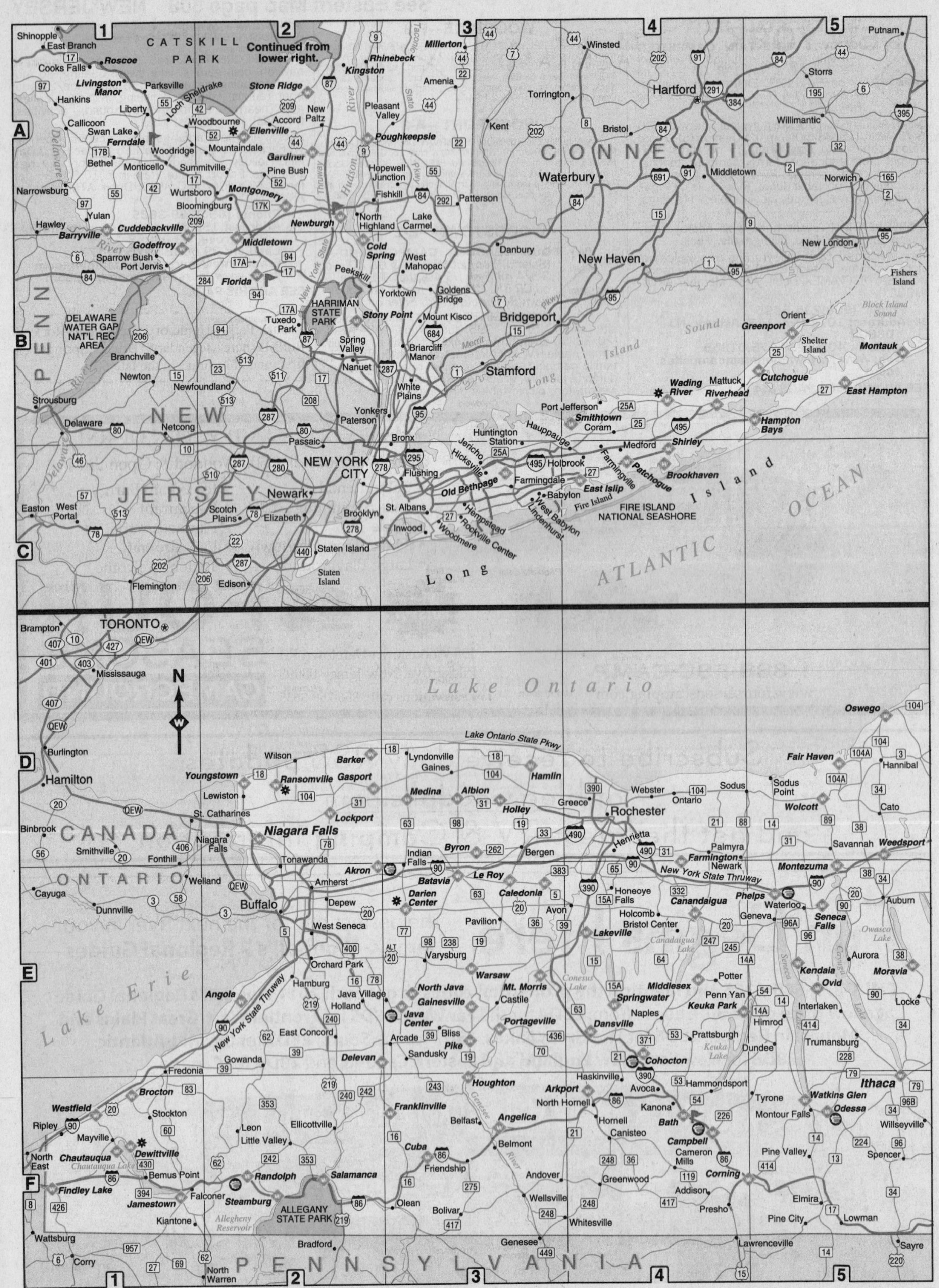

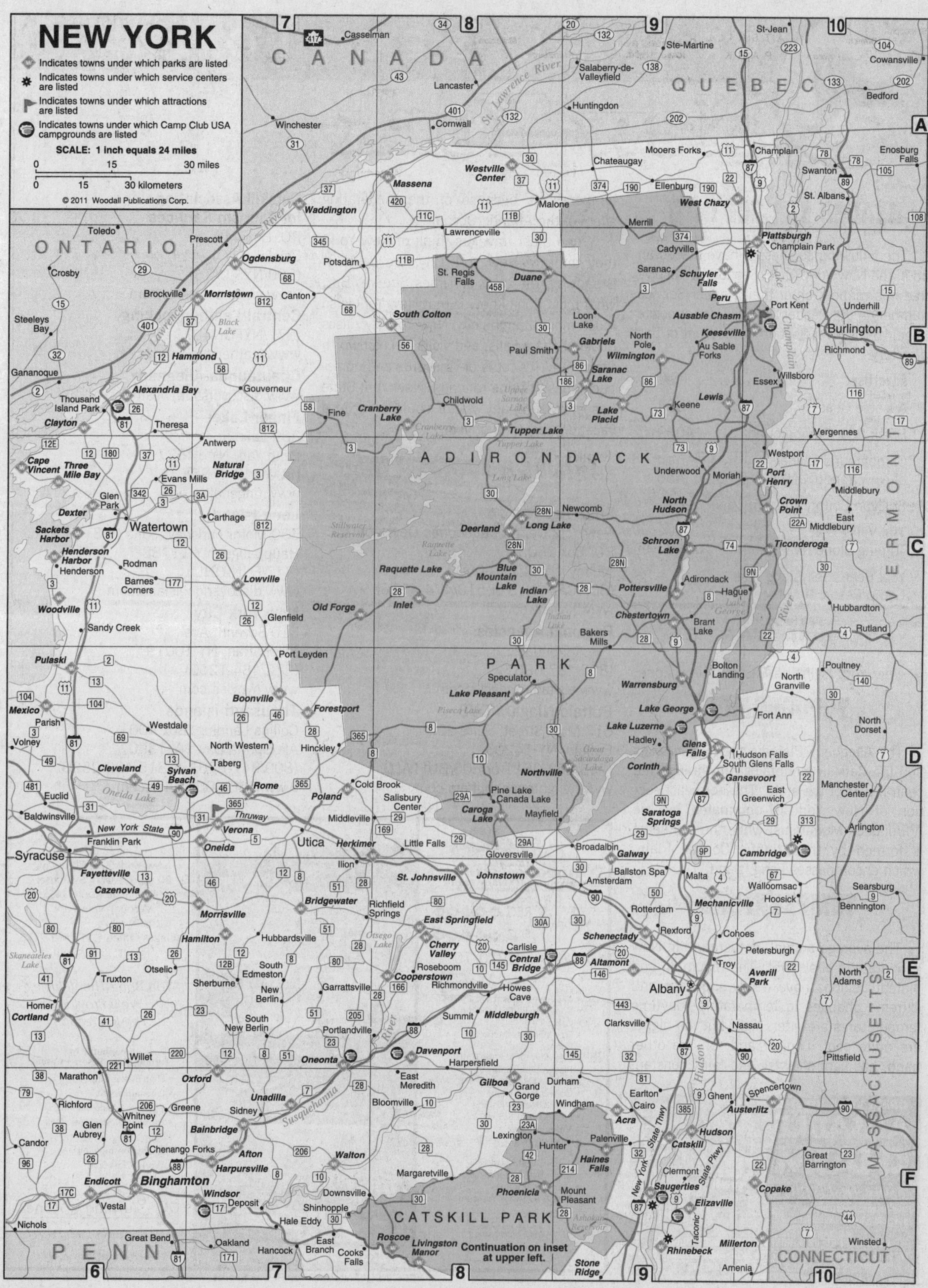

NEW YORK
Indicates towns under which parks are listed
Indicates towns under which service centers are listed
Indicates towns under which attractions are listed
Indicates towns under which Camp Club USA campgrounds are listed
SCALE: 1 inch equals 24 miles
0 15 30 miles
0 15 30 kilometers
© 2011 Woodall Publications Corp.
CANADA
QUEBEC
ONTARIO
ADIRONDACK PARK
CATSKILL PARK
VERMONT
MASSACHUSETTS
CONNECTICUT
PENN
Continuation on inset at upper left.
St. Lawrence River
Casselman
Lancaster
Cornwall
Winchester
Ste-Martine
Salaberry-de-Valleyfield
Huntingdon
St-Jean
Cowansville
Bedford
Champlain
Mooers Forks
Chateaugay
Westville Center
Massena
Waddington
Malone
Ellenburg
West Chazy
Enosburg Falls
Swanton
St. Albans
Toledo
Prescott
Ogdensburg
Lawrenceville
Potsdam
Merrill
Plattsburgh
Champlain Park
Cadyville
Saranac
Schuyler Falls
Peru
Crosby
Brockville
Morristown
Canton
St. Regis Falls
Duane
Loon Lake
Ausable Chasm
Keeseville
Port Kent
Underhill
Burlington
Steeleys Bay
Black Lake
South Colton
North Pole
Au Sable Forks
Richmond
Gananoque
Hammond
Paul Smith
Gabriels
Wilmington
Saranac Lake
Willsboro
Essex
Thousand Island Park
Alexandria Bay
Gouverneur
Fine
Cranberry Lake
Childwold
Upper Saranac Lake
Lake Placid
Keene
Lewis
Clayton
Theresa
Antwerp
Tupper Lake
Vergennes
Cape Vincent
Three Mile Bay
Natural Bridge
Evans Mills
Long Lake
Underwood
Moriah
Westport
Port Henry
Middlebury
Glen Park
Dexter
Sackets Harbor
Watertown
Carthage
Stillwater Reservoir
Newcomb
Deerland
North Hudson
Crown Point
East Middlebury
Henderson Harbor
Henderson
Rodman
Raquette Lake
Blue Mountain Lake
Schroon Lake
Ticonderoga
Barnes Corners
Lowville
Indian Lake
Pottersville
Adirondack
Hague
Lake George
Hubbardton
Woodville
Old Forge
Inlet
Chestertown
Brant Lake
Glenfield
Sandy Creek
Bakers Mills
Rutland
Port Leyden
Speculator
Bolton Landing
Poultney
Pulaski
Warrensburg
North Granville
Boonville
Lake Pleasant
Piseco Lake
Forestport
Fort Ann
Mexico
Parish
Westdale
Lake Luzerne
Hadley
North Dorset
Volney
North Western
Hinckley
Glens Falls
Hudson Falls
South Glens Falls
Taberg
Cleveland
Sylvan Beach
Oneida Lake
Rome
Cold Brook
Northville
Great Sacandaga Lake
Corinth
Gansevoort
Euclid
Poland
Salisbury Center
Pine Lake
Canada Lake
Caroga Lake
Mayfield
Saratoga Springs
East Greenwich
Manchester Center
Baldwinsville
Thruway
New York State
Verona
Middleville
Arlington
Franklin Park
Syracuse
Oneida
Utica
Herkimer
Little Falls
Gloversville
Broadalbin
Galway
Cambridge
Ilion
St. Johnsville
Johnstown
Ballston Spa
Malta
Fayetteville
Cazenovia
Amsterdam
Walloomsac
Searsburg
Hoosick
Bennington
Morrisville
Bridgewater
Richfield Springs
Mechanicville
Rotterdam
East Springfield
Hamilton
Hubbardsville
Otsego Lake
Cherry Valley
Carlisle
Schenectady
Rexford
Cohoes
Skaneateles Lake
Central Bridge
Altamont
Petersburgh
Troy
South Edmeston
Roseboom
Cooperstown
Richmondville
Averill Park
North Adams
Otselic
Truxton
Sherburne
New Berlin
Garrattsville
Howes Cave
Albany
Homer
Cortland
South New Berlin
Summit
Middleburgh
Clarksville
Nassau
Portlandville
Willet
Davenport
Oneonta
Harpersfield
Pittsfield
Marathon
Oxford
East Meredith
Gilboa
Grand Gorge
Durham
Earlton
Ghent
Spencertown
Richford
Unadilla
Susquehanna
Sidney
Bloomville
Windham
Cairo
Austerlitz
Whitney Point
Greene
Glen Aubrey
Bainbridge
Lexington
Hunter
Palenville
Acra
Hudson
Candor
Chenango Forks
Afton
Walton
Haines Falls
Catskill
Great Barrington
Harpursville
Margaretville
Clermont
Endicott
Binghamton
Windsor
Deposit
Downsville
Phoenicia
Mount Pleasant
Saugerties
Copake
Vestal
Shinhopple
Hale Eddy
Ashokan Reservoir
Elizaville
Nichols
Great Bend
Oakland
Hancock
East Branch
Cooks Falls
Roscoe
Livingston Manor
Stone Ridge
Rhinebeck
Millerton
Winsted
Amenia
New York State Thwy
Taconic State Pkwy
Hudson River
Lake Champlain
Champlain

READER SERVICE INFO

The following businesses have placed an ad in the New York Travel Section. To receive free information, enter their Reader Service number on the Reader Service Card opposite page 48/Discover Section in the front of this directory:

Advertiser	RS#
Ausable Chasm	4364
Black Bear Campground	4029
Campground Owners of New York (CONY)	456
Sullivan County Tourism	689
The Villages at Turning Stone RV Park	3574
Yogi Bear's Jellystone Park Camp Resort at Mexico	659

TIME ZONE

New York is in the Eastern Time Zone.

TOPOGRAPHY

The Allegheny Plateau, the Finger Lakes and the Catskill Mountains run through the central part of the state. The northeast section of New York is dominated by the Adirondack Mountains, while the southeast is formed by the Atlantic Coastal Plain, which encompasses Long Island.

TEMPERATURE

The average annual temperature in New York state is about 45°. The mountain and plateau regions have heavy snowfalls and extreme changes in temperature; daytime temperatures are often high, but the nights are quite cool. Long Island, on the other hand, has light snowfall and fairly constant temperatures because of the moderating effect of the Atlantic Ocean.

When most travelers think of New York, they think of New York City, the lights of Broadway, the buzz of Times Square. But, what most don't know is that New York is so much more than the city. New York is cruises under Niagara Falls, and visits to Letchworth State Park. It's tours of vineyards and horseback rides at dude ranches. New York State has everything any visitor could want in a vacation, any time of year.

TRAVEL & TOURISM INFO

State Agency:
New York Dept. of Economic Development
P.O. Box 2603
Albany, NY 12220-0603
(800/CALL-NYS or 518/474-4116)
www.iloveny.com

Regional Agencies:
The Adirondacks
(800/487-6867)
www.visitadirondacks.com

Buffalo Niagara CVB
617 Main Street, Suite 200
Buffalo, NY 14203
(716/852-0511 or 800/BUFFALO
www.wrightnowinbuffalo.com

Catskill Association for Tourism Services
P.O. Box 449
Catskill, NY 12414
(800/NYS-CATS)
www.visitthecatskills.com

Central-Leatherstocking
(877/NYFUN4U)
www.leatherstockingny.com

Chautauqua-Allegheny
www.discoversouthwestny.com

Finger Lakes
309 Lake St
Penn Yan, NY 14527
(800/548-4386)
www.fingerlakes.org

Long Island
330 Motor Parkway, Suite 203
Hauppauge, NY 11788
(877/FUN-ONLI)
www.discoverlongisland.com

New York City
810 Seventh Ave
Manhattan, NY 10019
(212/484-1200)
www.nycvisit.com

Thousand Islands
Collins Landing, Box 400
Alexandria Bay, NY 13607
(800/847-5263 or 315/482-2520)
www.visit1000islands.com

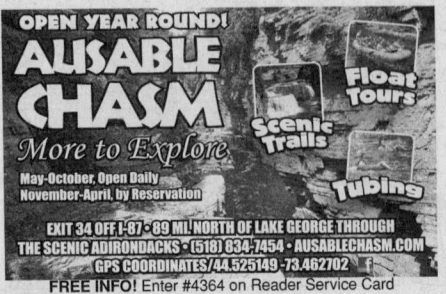

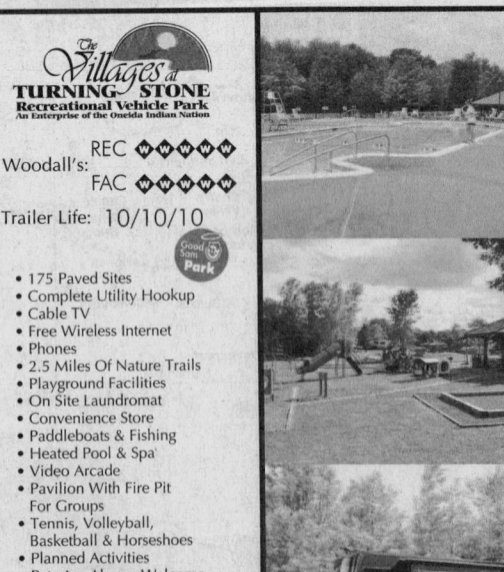

Local Agencies:

Albany Co. CVB
25 Quackenbush Sq
Clinton Ave @ Broadway
Albany, NY 12207
(800/258-3582 or 518/434-1217)
www.albany.org

Columbia Co. Tourism
401 State St
Hudson, NY 12534
(800/724-1846 or 518/828-3375)
www.BestCountryRoads.com

Dutchess Co. Tourism
3 Neptune Rd, Suite Q-17
Poughkeepsie, NY 12601
(800/445-3131 or 845/463-4000)
www.dutchesstourism.com

Franklin Co. Tourism
10 Elm St, Ste 2
Malone, NY 12953
(800/709-4895 or 518/483-9470
www.adirondacklakes.com

Lake Placid/Essex Co. Visitors Bureau
49 Parkside Drive, Suite 2
Lake Placid, NY 12946
(518/523-2445)
www.lakeplacid.com

Madison County Tourism
Morrisville, NY 13408
(800/684-7320 or 315/684-7320)
www.madisontourism.com

Montgomery County Chamber of Commerce
12 South Bridge St.
Fonda, NY 12068
(800/743-7337 or 518/853-1800)
www.montgomerycountyny.com

Niagara County Tourism
345 Third Street, Ste. 605
Niagara Falls, NY 14303
(877/FALLS-US or 716/282-8992)
www.niagara-usa.com

Oneida County CVB
I-90 Exit 31
Utica, NY 13503
(800/426-3132 or 315/724-7221)
www.oneidacountycvb.com

Greater Rochester Visitors Assn.
45 East Ave, Ste. 400
Rochester, NY 14604
(800/677-7282 or 585/279-8300)
www.visitrochester.com

Saratoga County Chamber of Commerce
28 Clinton St.
Saratoga Springs, NY 12866
(518/584-3255)
www.saratoga.org

St. Lawrence County Chamber of Commerce
101 Main St
Canton, NY 13617
(877/228-7810)
www.northcountryguide.com

Ulster County Tourism
10 Westbrook Ln
Kingston, NY 12401
(800/342-5826 or 845/340-3566)
www.ulstertourism.info

RECREATIONAL INFO

Amusement Parks: Splish Splash Water Park, Riverhead, Long Island; Playland Park, Rye; Great Escape and Splashwater Kingdom, Lake George; Water Slide World, Lake George; Broome County's Carousels, Binghamton; Martin's Fantasy Island, Grand Island; Six Flags, Darien Lake; Seabreeze Park, Rochester; Midway Park, Maple Springs; Zoom Flume Water Park, East Durham; Roseland Waterpark, Canandaigua.

Boating: For a free New York State Boater's Guide and/or Launch Site Book, contact Marine & Recreational Vehicles, State Parks, Empire State Plaza, Albany, NY 12238 (518/474-0456) www.nysparks.com

Canoeing: For navigational information about canoeing in the Adirondacks, Dept. of Environmental Conservation, Preserve Protection & Management, 625 Broadway, Albany, NY 12233. (518/ 402-8540)

Fishing & Hunting: Hunting, trapping and fishing licenses may be obtained at all town clerk offices, many village and county clerk offices and at most sporting goods and retail stores throughout the state. For fishing information contact: NYSDEC, Resources Bureau of Fisheries, 625 Broadway, Albany, NY 12233-4753.

Hiking, Biking, Horseback Riding Trails: More than 17,000 miles of multi-use trail networks criss-cross the state. For a free copy of **Empire State Trails**, a comprehensive guide to NYS trails, contact NYS Office of Parks, Recreation and Historic Preservation, Empire State Plaza, Agency Building 1, Albany, NY 12238 www.nysparks.com. For **Trail Finder Maps**, a guide to 90 trails for walking, biking, in-line skating and cross-country skiing, contact Parks and Trails New York, 29 Elk St., Albany, NY 12207 www.ptny.org

Off-Road Vehicles: NYS Off-Highway Recreational Vehicle Association, Inc., P.O. Box 2, Macedon, NY 14502. www.nysorva.org

Outfitters/guides: NYS Outdoor Guides Association, 1936 Saranac Ave., Ste. 2-150, Lake Placid, NY 12946. www.nysoga.com

Wineries: Wine Trails, New York Wine & Grape Foundation, 800 South Main Street, Suite 200, Canandaigua, NY 14424. www.newyorkwines.org

SHOPPING

Hickory Dickory Dock, Nyack. Over 300 clocks on display: wall, grandfather, mantle, brass miniatures & German cuckoos. Also music boxes, puzzles, wood toys and unique gifts.

Where It All Began Bat Company, Cooperstown. Bats made to order. Worlds largest wooden baseball bat on display at retail store (87 Main). Company factory open for tours during the summer. www.wiab.com.

NBC Experience Store, New York City. Tour features NBC's operations, including the opportunity to visit some of our famous studios, such as those that broadcast Saturday Night Live and the Today Show. High-tech, interactive store contains hundreds of items from all your favorite NBC shows. nbcexperiencestore.com

UNIQUE FEATURES

NEW YORK STATE'S CANAL SYSTEM

The 524-mile canal system links the Great Lakes with the Hudson River and the inland waterways of the East Coast, connecting hundreds of miles of lakes and rivers across New York. The 4 canals that make up the system are the **Erie, Cayuga-Seneca, Oswego** and **Champlain**. The Canalway Trail runs parallel to the canal system and currently encompasses 220 miles. For more information on biking, hiking, boating, fishing or exploring the Canal System call (800/4CANAL4) or see their website at: www.canals.state.ny.us.

DESTINATIONS

THE ADIRONDACKS REGION

Visitors to the Adirondacks have a plethora of outdoor adventures just waiting to be had. Kayaking, canoeing, whitewater rafting, horseback riding, hiking, and in winter, add to the list; skiing, snowshoeing, and snowmobiling! The forests are filled with hundreds of pristine lakes and ponds, endless miles of rivers and streams, and the famous Adirondack Mountains. The Adirondacks are where people and nature meet!

Adirondacks Interpretive Centers, Newcomb and Paul Smiths. Open daily, these informative centers provide visitors with interpretive trails, exhibit halls, theater and classroom presentations, demonstrations and festival programs.

Adirondack Museum, Blue Mountain. One of America's finest outdoor museums is renowned for the breadth of its collections that include historic artifacts, photographs, archival materials and fine art documenting the Adirondack region's past. Twenty-two exhibit spaces and galleries tell the stories of the men and women who have lived, worked and played in the largest wilderness area east of the Mississippi River.

Ausable Chasm. Take a walking tour and boat ride through one-and-a-half-mile long natural scenic wonder. When Major John Howe first discovered the chasm, he made a perilous descent suspended on ropes. Today visitors proceed along stone galleries by way of stairs and steel bridges at various levels or by boat.

Bluff Point, Plattsburgh. See small static displays interpreting the Lighthouse and the surrounding area, the Fresnel lens, the Iron Tower, the Architecture, the Lighthouse Keeper's family life, geology and ecology of the island and the history of the island. Visitors needing transportation to the island should contact the Champlain Valley Transportation Museum. The museum provides transportation to Valcour Island and Crab Island aboard the replica Sail Ferry "Weatherwax".

Crown Point State Historic Site, Crown Point. See the ruins of **Fort St. Frederic,** "His Majesty's Fort of Crown Point," surrounding lands and original 18th-century structures. The modern visitor center features exhibits interpreting the French, British and American chapters of Crown Point's history.

Fort Ticonderoga, Ticonderoga. This "Gibraltar of the North" played a key role in the wars for Empire and Freedom in the New World. Today, the fort houses a great

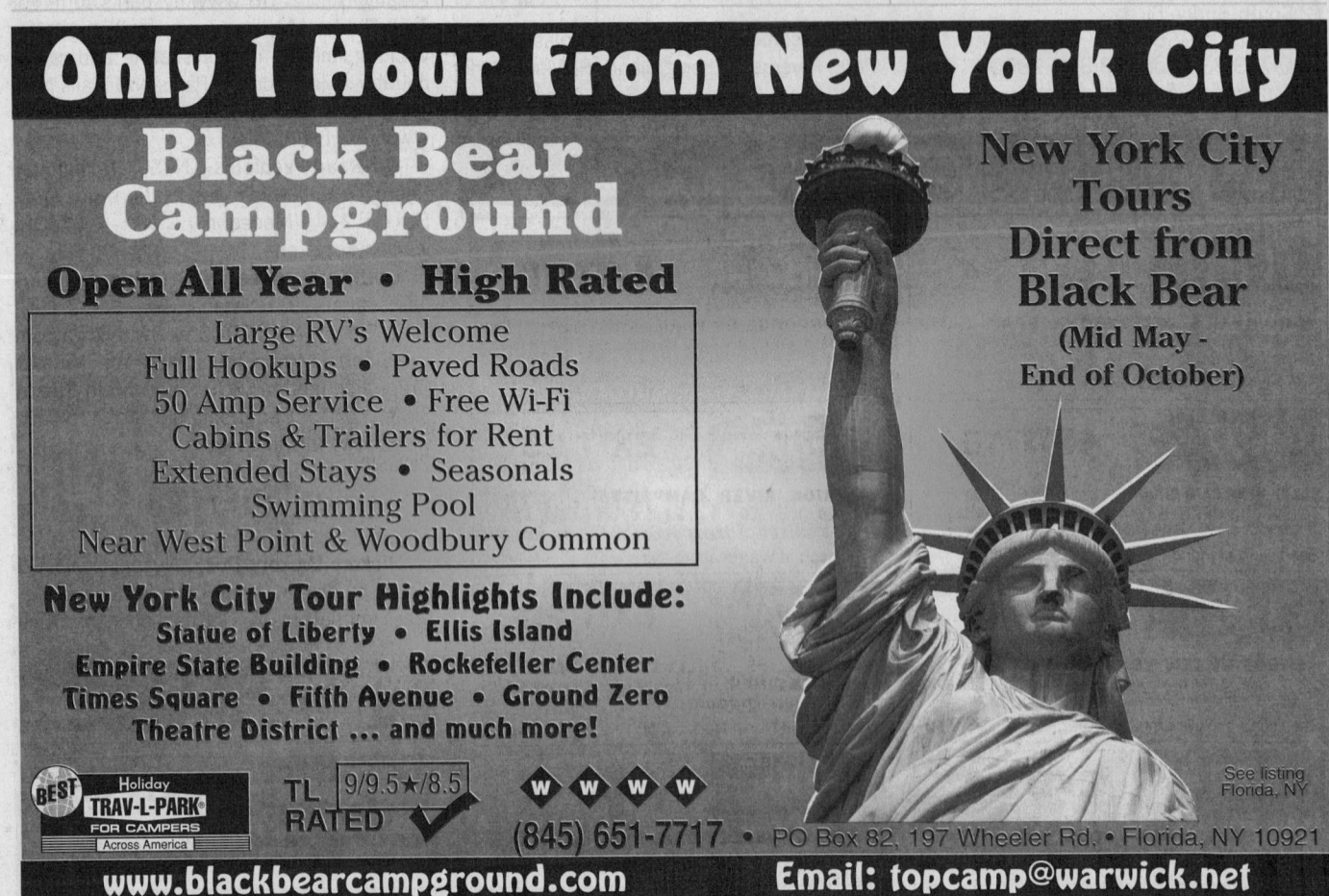

BUSINESSES OFFERING

	Things to See & Do	RV Sales	RV Service
AUSABLE CHASM			
Ausable Chasm	⚑		
BATH			
Finger Lakes Wellness Center & Health Spa	⚑		
CAMBRIDGE			
Doug's RV Repairs			✲
DARIEN CENTER			
Skyline RV Sales & Service		🚌	✲
DEWITTVILLE			
Chautauqua Lake RV & Park Model Sales		🚌	
ELLENVILLE			
Skyway RV Sales		🚌	✲
FERNDALE			
Sullivan County Visitors Association	⚑		
FLORIDA			
New York City Tours-Black Bear Campground	⚑		
NEWBURGH			
New York City Tours - KOA-Newburgh/New York City North	⚑		
PLATTSBURGH			
Bull's RV Center		🚌	✲
RANSOMVILLE			
Niagara Woodland Service Center			✲
RHINEBECK			
Interlake Trailer Sales		🚌	✲
SAUGERTIES			
Rip Van Winkle RV Sales			✲
VERONA			
Turning Stone Resort & Casino	⚑		
WADING RIVER			
W.E.S. Trailer Sales Inc.		🚌	✲

museum collection of 18th-century artifacts and collection of cannons.

High Falls Gorge, Wilmington. The gorge offers a spectacular view of falls and rock formations from modern steel walks.

Lake George. This resort area offers an array of campgrounds and RV parks, dinner theatres, arcades, water parks, fine restaurants, steamboat cruises and the **Factory Outlets of Lake George** on the "Million Dollar Half-Mile."

Lake Placid. Enjoy nature trails, boat trips, boat regattas and a winter sports museum. Tour the **Lake Placid Olympic Facilities,** home of the 1932 and 1980 Winter Olympic Games. The Lake Placid Winter Museum and Hall of Fame showcases the USA hockey team's "Miracle on Ice" and other highlights. Tour the Olympic Jumping Complex, bobsled and luge run, then take a ride on the Whiteface Mountain chairlift and skyride.

Olympic Sports Complex. This is the only bobsled run in the U.S. Take a trolley car ride up Mt. Van Hoevenberg to get a close look at the mile-long Olympic track. Be sure to see the Olympic luge run and displays of bobsledding and luge equipment. Try the runs in winter.

CAPITAL-SARATOGA REGION

This region's Dutch heritage and neighborly feel go back hundreds of years, and this can be seen in the architecture and learned from its history.

Albany. The state capital boasts 300 years of history, making it one of the oldest cities in the U.S. It's Capitol, fashioned after Paris' city hall, was the most expensive building of its time. Daily tours include the building's beautiful "Million Dollar Staircase." Other Albany attractions include:

Governor Nelson A. Rockefeller Empire State Plaza. Free tours are offered of this government complex, encompassing a convention center, performing arts center, the NYS Museum, world's largest contemporary art collection, reflecting pools and more. **St. Peter's Church**, **Old Episcopal Church** dating back to 1712 and **Schuyler Mansion State Historic Site,** 1761 home of the Revolutionary War general and his family.

Central Park Rose Garden, Schenectady. Over 4,500 roses (200 varieties) in bloom from June until frost. The Central Park Rose Garden is located at the Wright Avenue entrance to Schenectady's Central Park.

Fulton County Court House in Johnstown was built in 1772. The oldest colonial courthouse in NYS still used today.

Saratoga Springs. This resort city has over 60 restaurants, offering everything from French cuisine to Bavarian delicacies. Sidewalk cafés, factory outlets, amusement parks, world-class thoroughbred racing, year-round harness racing and spas featuring mineral baths from natural springs have made Saratoga Springs a "top destination." Visit the **Petrified Sea Gardens** and view fossils over 500 million years old.

Watervliet Arsenal Museum, Watervliet. Exhibits depict the story of the Arsenal's service to the U.S. armed forces. Cannon development is traced from the earliest times to the present day.

HUDSON VALLEY REGION

For more than three centuries, this region has been a destination for visitors from all over the world. This historic region offers mansion tours, museums, performing arts centers, and numerous historic sites. The Hudson River cuts a great, sinuous path through its valley. The vistas created in the spring and summer are of deep green and river sky. In the fall the colors burst; in the winter they fade to white.

Alice and Hamilton Fish Library, Garrison. This three million dollar library emphasizes the Revolutionary War period by displaying original documents signed by Washington, Jefferson, Hamilton and others.

Caramoor Center of Music & the Arts, Katonah. This Mediterranean-style villa and home of the Rosens on 117 wooded acres houses nine centuries of imported collectibles. Summer outdoor music performances are held here.

Chuang Yen Monastery, Carmel. Hall of 10,000 Buddhas circling Buddha Vairocana. Largest Buddha in Western Hemisphere.

Dia, Beacon. Houses Dia Art Foundation's renowned collection, comprised of art from the 1960's to the present. 300,000 sq ft facility located on the Hudson River. Artists' work on view includes Joseph Beuys, Donald Judd, On Kawara, Agnes Martin, Richard Serra and Andy Warhol.

FASNY Museum of Firefighting, Hudson. The premiere collection of American firefighting objects in the world, featuring over 90 pieces of apparatus on display.

Franklin D. Roosevelt National Historic Site, Hyde Park. The 32nd President's home maintains its 1945 appearance and is the burial site of both Franklin and Eleanor.

Hammond Museum & Oriental Stroll Gardens, North Salem. Visit the **Museum of the Humanities and Gardens** on a three-and-a-half-acre site. Fifteen of these gardens provide the tranquility of the Stroll Garden, which began in Japan to refresh the spirit.

Kykuit, Sleepy Hollow. Take a tour of this three-generation home of the Rockefellers. You'll enjoy the panoramic views of the Hudson River, along with the beautiful house and garden.

Museum Village in Orange County, Monroe. This rural 19th-century village features 30 working exhibits including a blacksmith shop, a log cabin and a 1-room schoolhouse. Live farm animals fill the barn and the general store offers the same items found in a typical 1800s store. Sheep shearing, wool

QUICK REFERENCE CHART FOR WOODALL'S FEATURED PARKS

	Green Friendly	RV Lots for Sale	Park Models-Onsite Ownership	Park Membership for Sale	Big Rigs Welcome	Internet Friendly	Pets Welcome
AFTON							
Kellystone Park Campsite					▲	●	■
ALEXANDRIA BAY							
1000 Islands Campground					▲	●	■
AUSTERLITZ							
Woodland Hills Campground						●	■
AVERILL PARK							
Alps Family Campground	🍃					●	■
BATH							
Hickory Hill Camping Resort	🍃				▲	●	■
CAMBRIDGE							
Lake Lauderdale Campground	🍃					●	■
CAMPBELL							
Camp Bell Campground	🍃					●	■
CHAUTAUQUA							
Camp Chautauqua Camping Resort	🍃				▲	●	■
COOPERSTOWN							
Cooperstown Shadow Brook Campground						●	■
Hartwick Highlands Campground					▲	●	■
COPAKE							
KOA Copake					▲	●	■
CORNING							
Ferenbaugh Campground						●	■
DARIEN CENTER							
Skyline Resort Campground						●	■
DEWITTVILLE							
Chautauqua Heights Camping Resort					▲	●	■
ELLENVILLE							
Skyway Camping Resort						●	■
Yogi Bear's Jellystone Park at Birchwood Acres					▲	●	■
FLORIDA							
Black Bear Campground					▲	●	■
GAINESVILLE							
Woodstream Campsite						●	■
GARDINER							
Yogi Bear's Jellystone Park Camp-Resort at Lazy River					▲	●	■
GILBOA							
Country Roads Campground						●	■
Nickerson Park Campground						●	■
GREENPORT							
Eastern Long Island Kampground						●	■
HENDERSON HARBOR							
Association Island RV Resort & Marina					▲	●	■
HERKIMER							
KOA-Herkimer Diamond Resort					▲	●	■
HOLLEY							
Red Rock Ponds RV Resort					▲	●	■
HOUGHTON							
Camping at Mariposa Ponds						●	■
LAKE GEORGE							
Adirondack Adventure Resorts-Schroon River							■
Adirondack Camping Village					▲	●	■
King Phillip's Campground & Resort	🍃					●	■
Lake George RV Park	🍃				▲	●	■
Ledgeview RV Park					▲	●	

Green Friendly 🍃; **RV Lots for Sale** ✖; **Park Models/Onsite Onwership** ✱; **Park Memberships for Sale** ✔; **Big Rigs Welcome** ▲;
Internet Friendly ●; **Internet Friendly-WiFi** ●; **Pets Welcome** ■

QUICK REFERENCE CHART FOR WOODALL'S FEATURED PARKS

	Green Friendly	RV Lots for Sale	Park Models-Onsite Ownership	Park Membership for Sale	Big Rigs Welcome	Internet Friendly	Pets Welcome
LOCKPORT							
Niagara County Camping Resort						WiFi	■
MASSENA							
Massena International Kampground						●	■
MEXICO							
Yogi Bear's Jellystone Park Camp Resort at Mexico						WiFi	■
NATURAL BRIDGE							
Adirondack 1000 Islands Campground					▲	WiFi	■
NEWBURGH							
KOA-Newburgh/New York City North					▲	WiFi	■
NIAGARA FALLS							
AA Royal Campground & Motel					▲	WiFi	■
KOA-Niagara Falls North					▲	WiFi	■
Niagara's Lazy Lakes Camping Resort					▲	WiFi	■
NORTH HUDSON							
Yogi Bear's Jellystone Park at Paradise Pines					▲	WiFi	■
ONEONTA							
Susquehanna Trail Campground						WiFi	■
PHELPS							
Cheerful Valley Campground						●	■
Junius Ponds Cabins & Campgrounds					▲	WiFi	■
POLAND							
Adirondack Gateway Campground & Lodge					▲	●	■
PORTAGEVILLE							
Four Winds Campground					▲	●	■
RANDOLPH							
Pope Haven Campground	Leaf					WiFi	■
RANSOMVILLE							
Niagara Woodland Campground & RV Service Center	Leaf					WiFi	■
RHINEBECK							
Interlake RV Park & Sales					▲	WiFi	■
SAUGERTIES							
Blue Mountain Campground	Leaf					WiFi	■
KOA-Saugerties/Woodstock	Leaf				▲	WiFi	■
Rip Van Winkle Campgrounds					▲	WiFi	■
SCHENECTADY							
Arrowhead Marina & RV Park					▲	●	■
SENECA FALLS							
Oak Orchard Marina & Campground							■
SPRINGWATER							
Holiday Hill Campground						WiFi	■
VERONA							
The Villages at Turning Stone RV Park					▲	WiFi	■
WARRENSBURG							
Schroon River Campsites						WiFi	■
WATKINS GLEN							
Clute Memorial Park & Campground	Leaf				▲	WiFi	■
WESTFIELD							
Brookside Beach Campground					▲	WiFi	■
WESTVILLE CENTER							
Babbling Brook RV Park	Leaf					WiFi	■
WILMINGTON							
North Pole Camping Resort	Leaf				▲	WiFi	■

Green Friendly (leaf); RV Lots for Sale ✖; Park Models/Onsite Onwership ✱; Park Memberships for Sale ✔; Big Rigs Welcome ▲; Internet Friendly ●; Internet Friendly-WiFi (gray ●); Pets Welcome ■

spinning and open hearth cooking are demonstrated.

Newburgh. One-hour tours of historic homes and points of interest are offered.

Rhinebeck. Site of the oldest hotel in the U.S., (circa 1700), Old Rhinebeck Aerodrome has a world-famous display of vintage WWI and earlier aircraft.

Shaker Museum, Old Chatham. The finest collection of Shaker-made artifacts in the world depicts over 200 years of Shaker history and culture. Walking trails and an herb garden are also on the premises.

Tarrytown. Sleepy Hollow country was made famous by Washington Irving. Highlights include **Sunnyside**, the author's delightful home (built in 1835) on the banks of the Hudson. **Union Church of Pocantico Hills** boasts stained glass windows by modern masters Henri Matisse and Marc Chagall.

United States Military Academy, West Point. Visit the Military Museum, chapels, Trophy Point, Fort Putman and take a driving tour to the cemetery.

NEW YORK CITY REGION

No visit would be complete without a stop in one of the world's busiest cities. Here are some things you won't want to miss:

Get a panoramic view of New York at the **Empire State Building**. Stop at the **New York Stock Exchange** to see where the real action takes place. Don't miss the **South Street Seaport,** where you can visit over 120 stores, pubs, restaurants and food vendors in this restored 19th-century seaport district. Over 40 percent of America's population can trace their ancestry through **Ellis Island,** part of the **Statue of Liberty National Monument. Ellis Island** is now a museum and American Family Immigration History Center containing manifests of 25 million immigrants, passengers and crew members who entered New York Harbor between 1892 and 1924. If you plan on entering the **Statue of Liberty** you will need a "monument access" pass, free with the purchase of a ferry ticket. Only a limited number are available so you may want to order in advance to avoid disappointment.

Central Park is a green oasis in the middle of New York City. Entirely man-made, the park encompasses 843 acres including woodlands, lawns and 150 acres of water. Within the park are sculptures, bridges, arches, playgrounds and miles of pedestrian and bridle paths. Over 275 species of migratory birds have been sighted in Central Park, a major stopping point on the Atlantic flyway.

For a taste of New York, visit one of the many museums or performing arts buildings. The **Metropolitan Museum of Art**, the **Guggenheim Museum**, the **Children's Museum of Manhattan**, the **Museum of Modern Art** and the **Bronx Museum of the Arts** are just a few of the museums to see. New York is a world famous performing arts center. You won't want to miss the talent at **Broadway, Carnegie Hall, Lincoln Center for the Performing Arts, Radio City Music Hall, Madison Square Garden** and **Rockefeller Center**. And just for fun, take a ride to **Coney Island**, home of the **Astroland Amusement Park**. For the animal lover in you, stop by the **Bronx Zoo** and the **Central Park Zoo.**

THE CATSKILLS REGION

Buddhist Centers are located throughout the wooded hills and valleys of the Catskills, among them Zen Mountain Monastery, Mount Tremper; The Karma Triyana Dharmachakra, Woodstock; The International Dai Bosatsu Zendo, Livingston Manor.

Delaware & Ulster Rail Ride, Arkville. Relive the golden age of railroading along the **Catskill Scenic Trail**, a network of country roads and trails suitable for hiking, biking and driving. Enjoy magnificent mountain scenery and pastoral landscapes from the vintage coach or open-air car.

Eagle Institute, Barryville. Watch eagles in their natural habitat.

Hanford Mills Museum, East Meredith. More than 10 authentic 19th-century machines have been made operational. Listed in both the New York and National Registers of Historic Places, the museum is also engaged in the business of custom woodworking. If you are having trouble matching wood in an older house you are

CAMPCLUB USA

Where to Find CCUSA Parks

List City	Park Name	Map Coordinates
AKRON	Sleepy Hollow Lake Campground	E-2
ALEXANDRIA BAY	1000 Islands Campground	B-6
AUSABLE CHASM	Ausable River Campsite	B-10
CAMBRIDGE	Lake Lauderdale Campground	D-10
CAMPBELL	Camp Bell Campground	F-4
CENTRAL BRIDGE	Hide-A-Way Campsites	E-8
COHOCTON	Tumble Hill Campground	E-4
DAVENPORT	Beaver Spring Lake Campground	E-8
ELIZAVILLE	Brook N Wood Family Campground	F-9
JAVA CENTER	Beaver Meadow Family Campground	E-3
LAKE GEORGE	King Phillip's Campground & Resort	D-9
LAKE LUZERNE	Mt. Kenyon Family Campground	D-9
ODESSA	Cool-Lea Camp	F-5
ONEONTA	Susquehanna Trail Campground	E-7
PHELPS	Cheerful Valley Campground	E-5
RANDOLPH	Pope Haven Campground	F-2
SAUGERTIES	Blue Mountain Campground	F-9
SYLVAN BEACH	Treasure Isle RV Park	D-6
WINDSOR	Forest Lake Campground	F-7

restoring, Hanford Mills can probably solve your problem.

Hunter Mountain, Hunter, is host to major ethnic music festivals during the summer and fall. Enjoy fantastic views of the Northeast from the longest, highest chairlift in the Catskills.

Kittatinny Canoes, Barryville. Experience exciting Delaware River canoeing and whitewater rafting, whether you're a beginner or have lots of experience.

Livingston Manor. Self-guided tours at the **Catskill State Fish Hatchery** or visit the **Catskill Fly Fishing Center and Museum** dedicated to fly-fishing and protecting its environment.

CENTRAL-LEATHERSTOCKING REGION

In this region, visitors will step back in time and tour a 19th century village, be pampered at a historic spa in Sharon Springs, visit a Native American museum, explore underground caverns, or relax by a sparkling waterfall. The unspoiled beauty and nostalgic charm of this region is just waiting to be explored!

Binghamton. Highlights include the **Anderson Center for the Performing Arts, Roberson Center for the Arts & Sciences, Kopernik Observatory** and **Ross Park Zoo.**

Cherry Valley Museum, Cherry Valley. This 250-year-old village was the scene of one of the most memorable battles of the American Revolution and the site of the Cherry Valley Massacre, where British troops and a Mohawk legion attacked the settlement.

Fenimore House. View an extensive collection of American folk art, distinguished by strong design and vigorous colors.

Herkimer Diamond Mine & Museum, Herkimer. A cluster of diamonds was found at the Herkimer Diamond Mines on September 11, 2001 at approximately 9:30 am. It is most unusual in size, quantity, quality and structure. The cluster is configured in the shape of a cross. It is on display at the Museum at The Herkimer Diamond Mine.

Kopernik Observatory and Space Education Center, Vestal. Three observatories; astronomy, physics, earth science and computer labs; teaching darkroom. Public astronomy programs.

Through Their Eyes: Images of the Iroquois, Howes Cave. An exhibit of art works, many from recent acquisitions to the permanent collection, in the Hanks Gallery of Contemporary Iroquois Art.

FINGER LAKES REGION

Canandaigua Lake. New in 2006 is the **Finger Lakes Wine & Culinary Center,** situated at the north end of Canandaigua Lake. Guest chefs, hands-on cooking classes and a wine tasting room.

Auburn. Ward O'Hara Agricultural Museum. 15,000 square foot museum has over 3,000 artifacts depicting the rural and agricultural heritage of Cayuga County.

Corning. Gateway to the southern Finger Lakes region, this town is home to the **Corning Museum of Glass,** a unique complex depicting the art, history, science and industry of glass, complete with a tour of the museum, **Technology Gallery, Hall of Science and Industry** and **Steuben Glass Factory**. Also in Corning is the **Rockwell Museum**, housing the largest collection of Western American art, Native American artifacts and Steuben glass. The **Rockwell Gallery** contains the world's largest collection of Carder Steuben Glass.

Center at High Falls. Be sure to visit the hands-on exhibits, a simulated open raceway of running water, the Pont de Rennes pedestrian bridge, an archaeological site and seasonal laser, light and sound shows in the Gorge at High Falls.

George Eastman House includes the **International Museum of Photography,** which is dedicated to the art and science of photography spanning 130 years. Also onsite is the Kodak founder's renovated mansion and gardens.

Rome. Visit a reconstructed 19th century settlement on the site where the first shovelful of earth was turned for the construction of the original Erie Canal. Guests can ride a mule drawn packet boat and a narrow gauge steam train.

Syracuse. Visit the **Salt Museum** (a reconstructed 1856 salt factory); the **Milton J. Rubenstein Museum of Science & Technology;** the **Onondaga Historical Assn. Museum; Erie Canal Museum**; and the **Everson Museum of Art**. Syracuse is also home to the **Burnet Park Zoo**, with over 1,000 animals.

Watkins Glen. Be sure to stop at Seneca Market on the historic and picturesque lakefront. Over 30 shops, cafes and pushcarts set in a 19th-century aura.

International Race Track. This world-class auto racing circuit is tops in the nation.

Wineries. Fine wines, comparable in taste and quality to any in the world, are produced in the Finger Lakes region. Wineries such as Taylor Gold Seal are located in Bluff Point, Branchport, Conesus, Dundee, Hammondsport, Hector, Lodi, Naples, Burdett, Fairport, Himrod, Interlaken, Romulus and Valois.

CHAUTAUQUA-ALLEGHENY REGION

This region is just as rich in culture and history as the rest of New York! Vast open land lakes and lush forests are just waiting to be explored, as well as wineries, and Amish culture.

Bemus Point. The 181-year—old **Bemus Point-Stow Ferry** is a cable-drawn, wooden ferry that carries passengers, cars, vans and cows back and forth to each community located in the middle of Chautauqua Lake. Visit the Casino where you can still hear the "big band" sound.

Jamestown. The birthplace of Lucille Ball hosts **Lucyfest**, a Lucille Ball Festival of Comedy, each May. The Lucy-Desi Museum celebrates this revered comedienne's life. At the **Audubon Nature Center,** 1600 Riverside Road, the interpretive building houses a large collection of exhibits, a children's hands-on discovery room, an arboretum and special programs.

Mayville is homeport for the **Chautauqua Bell**, a paddlewheel steamship with one-and-a-half-hour-cruises on Chautauqua Lake. Also, be sure to take a **Webb's Goatmilk Fudge & Candy Factory tour**. The town is also the seat of Chautauqua County government and the home of **Chautauqua Institution**, a nationally known center for the arts, education, religion and recreation.

Panama Rocks, Panama. Visit the world's most extensive outcrop of glacially cut ocean quartz—a conglomerate of cliffs, crevices, cavernous dens and caves. The **Trail's End Gallery** has limited editions and originals, hand-carved Native American pottery, secondary market prints, wildlife art and custom framing.

GREATER NIAGARA REGION

Of course, planning a trip to this region has to include a trip the breathtaking Niagara Falls! Visitors can also look to this area for world-class symphony, a historic zoo, top collections of modern art, major league sports, awesome food, and some incredible scenery and parks. Travelers to this region will soon learn why every visitor falls in love with the Greater Niagara Falls Region!

Buffalo. The state's second largest city has such outstanding attractions as the **Albright-Knox Art Gallery**, containing one of the foremost art collections in the world dating back to 3,000 B.C.; **Allentown**, one of the largest historic preservation sites in the U.S.; **Broadway Market**, an Old World market where farmers sell fresh, field-grown products; **Buffalo & Erie County Naval & Servicemen's Park**, the only inland naval park in the nation and **Buffalo Museum of Science**, displaying such unique exhibits as dinosaurs, mummies and Chinese jades.

Niagara Falls. Visit the natural wonder of Niagara's thundering waters. Other points of interest include: **Aquarium of Niagara Falls,** with hourly dolphin and sea lion performances; **Niagara's Wax Museum of History** with life-size figures; **Rainbow Centre**, a one-stop fashion, shopping, dining and entertainment experience.

Woodall's Camping Life magazine is the perfect family camping companion to any of Woodall's Directories and Guides. With 7 monthly issues per year, containing camping stories, destination articles, buyer's guides and more, Camping Life is a valuable resource for any family camper. Visit www.campinglife.com for more info.

We all know that one of the best parts about camping is the food! Woodall's Campsite Cookbook is a classic cookbook containing such fun campsite and RV recipes as Roadside Spuds, The Fastest Sauce in the West, and Hairy Squares (which taste a lot better than they sound!) To order your copy go to www.woodalls.com/shop.

All privately owned campgrounds personally inspected by WOODALL'S Representatives

Greg and Maureen Baron

ACCORD—A-2

(W) RONDOUT VALLEY RESORT (CAMP RESORT)—(Ulster) *From jct Hwy 44/55 & Hwy 209: Go 3 mi NE on Hwy 209, then 1/2 mi N on Mettacohonts Rd. Enter on L.*

WELCOME

FACILITIES: 387 sites, typical site width 35 ft, 170 full hkups, 197 W&E, (30/50 amps), 20 no hkups, some extd stay sites (summer), 2 pull-thrus, cable TV, ($), WiFi Internet central location, family camping, tenting, RV's/park model rentals, cabins, RV storage, dump, portable dump, laundry, ltd groc, RV supplies, LP gas by weight/by meter, ice, picnic tables, fire rings, grills, wood, controlled access.

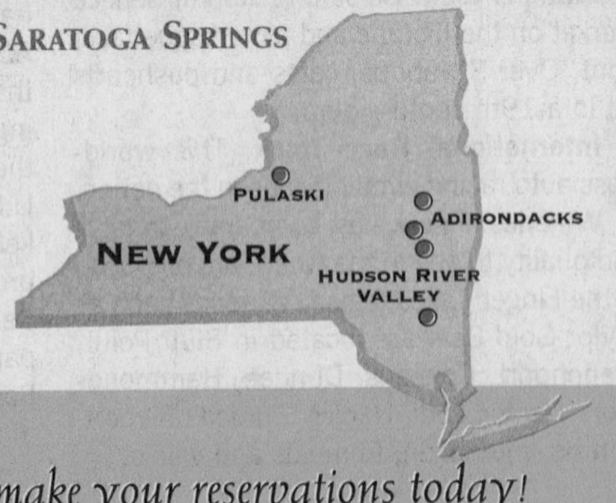

RECREATION: rec hall, rec room/area, pavilion, coin games, swim pool, pond/stream fishing, fishing supplies, mini-golf, ($), golf nearby, bsktball, 10 bike rentals, playground, shuffleboard court 2 shuffleboard courts, activities (wkends), horseshoes, sports field, hiking trails, v-ball.

Pets welcome. Partial handicap access. Open all yr. Clubs® welcome. Rate in 2010 $45-50 for 4 persons. MC/VISA/DISC/AMEX/Debit. Member ARVC, CONY.

Phone: (845)626-5521
Address: 105 Mettacohonts Rd, Accord, NY 12404
Lat/Lon: 41.79518/-74.24793
Email: rvrsor@aol.com
Web: www.rondoutvalley.com

SEE AD ACRA THIS PAGE

ACRA—F-9

(S) Whip-O-Will Campsite—(Greene) *From jct Hwy-145 & Hwy-23: Go 2-1/4 mi W on Hwy-23, then 2 mi S on CR-31. Enter on L.* ◊◊◊FACILITIES: 236 sites, typical site width 28 ft, 32 ft max RV length, 95 full hkups, 110 W&E, (20/30/50 amps), 31 no hkups, family camping, tenting, dump, laundry, ltd groc. ◊◊◊RECREATION: swim pool, boating, no motors, dock, lake fishing, playground. Pets welcome. Open Apr 15 - Oct 15. Rate in 2010 $25-28 per family. Member ARVC, CONY. Phone: (518)622-3277.

AFTON—F-7

(S) KELLYSTONE PARK CAMPSITE—(Broome) *From jct I-88 (Afton exit 7) & Hwy 41: Go 5 mi S on Hwy 41, then 1/4 mi E on Hawkins Rd. Enter on L.*

WELCOME

◊◊◊FACILITIES: 170 sites, typical site width 20 ft, 150 full hkups, 20 W&E, (20/30/50 amps), mostly extd stay sites (summer), 20 pull-thrus, phone Internet central location, family camping, tenting, RV storage, shower$, dump, non-guest dump $, portable dump, laundry, ltd groc, RV supplies, ice, picnic tables, fire rings, wood.

◊◊◊◊RECREATION: rec hall, pavilion, coin games, swim pool, pond fishing, fishing supplies, golf nearby, bsktball, playground, activities, (wkends), tennis, horseshoes, sports field, hiking trails, v-ball.

Pets welcome. Partial handicap access. Open Apr 15 - Oct 1. Facilities fully operational May 1 - Oct 1. Big rigs welcome. Clubs welcome. Rate in 2010 $28-32 per family. MC. Member ARVC, CONY.

KELLYSTONE PARK CAMPSITE—Continued on next page

AFTON—Continued
KELLYSTONE PARK CAMPSITE—Continued

Phone: (607)639-1090
Address: 51 Hawkins Rd, Nineveh, NY 13813
Lat/Lon: 42.16439/-75.52798
Email: kellystone_park@yahoo.com
Web: www.kellystonepark.net

SEE AD BINGHAMTON NEXT PAGE

AKRON—E-2

(S) Sleepy Hollow Lake Campground—(Erie) *From jct I-90 (exit 48A) & Hwy 77: Go 1/2 mi S on Hwy 77, then 4 mi W on Hwy 5, then 4 mi S on Crittenden Rd, then 1/4 mi E on Siehl Rd. Enter on L.* ◇◇◇FACILITIES: 200 sites, typical site width 25 ft, 200 W&E, (30/50 amps), 5 pull-thrus, heater not allowed, WiFi Instant Internet at site, phone Internet central location, family camping, tenting, dump, non-guest dump $, portable dump, groceries, RV supplies, LP gas by weight/by meter, ice, picnic tables, wood. ◇◇◇RECREATION: rec hall, pavilion, lake swim, boating, no motors, canoeing, kayaking, lake fishing, fishing supplies, mini-golf, ($), bsktball, 4 bike rentals, playground, activities, tennis, horseshoes, hiking trails, v-ball. Pets welcome. Open Apr 27 - Oct 31. Big rigs welcome. Rate in 2010 $31-34 per family. MC/VISA/DISC. Member ARVC, CONY. FMCA discount. CCUSA 50% Discount. CCUSA reservations Accepted, CCUSA max stay 7 days, CCUSA disc. not avail holidays. Addl. surcharges: electric heater: $2, extra vehicle over 2: $1.

Phone: (716)542-4336
Address: 13800 Siehl Rd, Akron, NY 14001
Lat/Lon: 42.95469/-78.47174
Email: sleepyhollowlake@yahoo.com
Web: www.sleepyhollowlakeresort.com

ALBANY—E-9

See listings at Averill Park & Schenectady

(S) CHERRYSTONE FAMILY CAMPING RESORT—*From Albany Go: 450 mi S on I-87/I-95/US 13, then at US 13 & Hwy 680 (Town Fields Dr), then 1-1/2 mi W on Hwy 680 (Town Fields Dr). Enter at end.*

◇◇◇◇◇FACILITIES: 725 sites, typical site width 28 ft, 403 full hkups, 303 W&E, (20/30/50 amps), 19 no hkups, 110 pull-thrus, WiFi Instant Internet at site, WiFi Internet central location, family camping, tenting, RV's/park model rentals, cabins, RV storage, dump, portable dump, laundry, full svc store, RV supplies, LP gas by weight/by meter, ice, picnic tables, wood, controlled access.

◇◇◇◇◇RECREATION: rec hall, equipped pavilion, coin games, 4 swim pools, spray ground, saltwater swim, boating, canoeing, kayaking, ramp, dock, 9 kayak/15 pedal boat/40 motorboat rentals, saltwater fishing, fishing supplies, fishing guides, mini-golf ($), golf nearby, bsktball, 60 bike rentals, playground, shuffleboard court 2 shuffleboard courts, activities, tennis, horseshoes, sports field, v-ball.

Pets welcome, breed restrict, quantity restrict. Partial handicap access. Open all yr. Big rigs welcome. Clubs welcome. Rate in 2010 $17-68 for 2 persons. MC/VISA/AMEX/Debit. ATM. Member ARVC, VCA.

Phone: (757)331-3063
Address: 1511 Townfield Dr, Cheriton, VA 23316
Lat/Lon: 37.28590/-76.01084
Email: mail@cherrystoneva.com
Web: cherrystoneva.com

SEE PRIMARY LISTING AT CHERITON AND AD CHERITON, VA PAGE 771

ALBION—D-3

(E) Hickory Ridge Golf & RV Resort—(Orleans) *From jct Hwy 98 & Hwy 31: Go 5-1/2 mi E on Hwy 31, then veer right onto Paddleford Rd, then 1/4 mi S, then 400 feet W on Lynch Rd. Enter on L.* ◇◇◇◇FACILITIES: 54 sites, typical site width 40 ft, 51 full hkups, 3 W&E, (20/30/50 amps), 31 pull-thrus, family camping, dump, laundry, ltd groc. ◇◇◇RECREATION: canoeing, lake fishing, playground. Pets welcome, quantity restrict. Partial handicap access. No tents. Open May 1 - Oct 31. Big rigs welcome. Rate in 2010 $35-40 per family. Member ARVC, CONY. Phone: (585)638-0220. FMCA discount.

(N) LAKESIDE BEACH STATE PARK—(Orleans) *From town: Go 10 mi N on Hwy-98, then 2 mi W on Lake Ontario Pkwy.* FACILITIES: 274 sites, 274 E, (20 amps), tenting, dump, laundry, groceries. RECREATION: boating, canoeing, lake fishing, playground. Partial handicap access. Open Apr 23 - Nov 8. Phone: (585)682-4888.

New York State Nickname: Empire State

ALEXANDRIA BAY—B-6

(S) 1000 ISLANDS CAMPGROUND—(Jefferson) *From jct I-81 (exit 50 S) & NYS Route 12: Go 1-3/4 mi S on NYS Route 12. Enter on R.*

◇◇◇FACILITIES: 88 sites, typical site width 30 ft, 41 full hkups, 37 W&E, (20/30/50 amps), 50 amps ($), some extd stay sites, 17 pull-thrus, WiFi Internet central location, family camping, tenting, RV's/park model rentals, RV storage, dump, ice, picnic tables, fire rings, wood.

◇◇RECREATION: golf nearby, bsktball, playground, horseshoes.

Pets welcome, quantity restrict. Partial handicap access. Open mid May - Columbus Day. Big rigs welcome. Clubs welcome. Rate in 2010 $30-33 for 5 persons. MC/VISA. CCUSA 50% Discount. CCUSA reservations Recommended, CCUSA max stay 7 days, CCUSA disc. not avail holidays. Discount not available Jun 24 through Sep 6. Electric surcharge refers to 20 amp. Honeywagon surcharge $3.

Phone: (315)686-2600
Address: 42099 Rt 12, Alexandria Bay, NY 13607
Lat/Lon: 44.27688/-75.99723
Email: 1000islandscampground@earthlink.net
Web: www.1000islandscampground.com

SEE AD THIS PAGE

GRASS POINT STATE PARK—(Niagara) *From business center: Go 5 mi S on Hwy-12.* FACILITIES: 78 sites, 21 E, (20 amps), 57 no hkups, tenting, dump. RECREATION: boating, canoeing, ramp, dock, river fishing, playground. Partial handicap access. Open Mid May - Columbus Day. Phone: (315)686-4472.

(S) KEEWAYDIN STATE PARK—(Jefferson) *From business center: Go 1/2 mi S on Hwy 12.* FACILITIES: 41 sites, 41 no hkups, tenting. RECREATION: swim pool, boating, canoeing, ramp, dock, river fishing, playground. Partial handicap access. Open all yr. Facilities fully operational Mid May - Labor Day. Phone: (315)482-3331.

(N) KRING POINT STATE PARK—(Jefferson) *From town: Go 6 mi NE on Hwy 12.* FACILITIES: 92 sites, 21 E, (20/30 amps), 71 no hkups, 20 pull-thrus, tenting, dump, ltd groc. RECREATION: river swim, boating, canoeing, ramp, dock, river fishing, playground. Pets welcome. Partial handicap access. Open all yr. Facilities fully operational Last Fri in Apr - Columbus Day. Phone: (315)482-2444.

WELLESLEY ISLAND STATE PARK—(Jefferson) *From business center: Go 6 mi S on Hwy 12, then cross 1000 Island Bridge (Toll).* FACILITIES: 429 sites, 57 full hkups, 74 E, 298 no hkups, tenting, dump, groceries. RECREATION: boating, canoeing, ramp, dock, river fishing, playground. Pets welcome. Partial handicap access. Open all yr. Facilities fully operational Late Apr - Mid Oct. Phone: (315)482-2722.

ALTAMONT—E-9

THOMPSON'S LAKE STATE PARK—(Jefferson) *From business center: Go 4 mi S on 156, then 1 mi SE on Hwy-157.* FACILITIES: 140 sites, 30 ft max RV length, 140 no hkups, tenting, dump. RECREATION: lake swim, boating, no motors, canoeing, ramp, lake fishing, playground. Partial handicap access. Open all yr. Facilities fully operational May 12 - Oct 8. Phone: (518)872-1674.

ANGELICA—F-3

(N) Evergreen Trails Campground—(Allegany) *From jct I-86/Hwy 17 (exit 30) & Hwy 19: Go 2 mi N on Hwy 19, then 3 mi E on Hwy 16, then 4-1/2 mi N on Hwy 15. Enter on L.* ◇◇◇FACILITIES: 74 sites, 32 ft max RV length, 2 full hkups, 67 W&E, (20/30/50 amps), 5 no hkups, family camping, tenting, dump, laundry, ltd groc. ◇◇◇RECREATION: lake swim, pond fishing, playground. Pets welcome. Open Apr 25 - Nov 30. Rate in 2010 $26-30 for 4 persons. Phone: (585)466-7993.

ANGOLA—E-2

EVANGOLA STATE PARK—(Erie) *From business center: Go 4 mi W on Hwy-5 (Silver Creek exit for NY thruway).* FACILITIES: 77 sites, typical site width 25 ft, 77 E, (30/50 amps), tenting, dump, laundry, groceries. RECREATION: lake swim, lake fishing, playground. Partial handicap access. Open Apr 21 - Oct 23. Phone: (716)549-1802.

New York State Tree: Sugar Maple

ARKPORT—F-4

(N) Sun Valley Campsites—(Allegany) *From jct I-86/Hwy 17 (exit 34) & Hwy 36: Go 7 mi N on Hwy 36, then 1 mi W on Hwy 70, then 1/4 mi N on Poags Hole Rd. Enter at end.* ◇◇◇FACILITIES: 281 sites, 214 full hkups, 57 W&E, (20/30 amps), 10 no hkups, 4 pull-thrus, family camping, tenting, dump, laundry, ltd groc. ◇◇◇◇RECREATION: swim pool, pond/stream fishing, playground. Pets welcome. Partial handicap access. Open May 1 - Mid Oct. Rate in 2010 $29-37 per family. Phone: (607)545-8388.

AUSABLE CHASM—B-10

(E) AUSABLE CHASM—*From jct Hwy 373 & US 9: Go 800 feet S on US 9. Enter on R.* Walking & boat tour of Ausable Chasm with picnic grounds & amusement park. The oldest and largest natural attraction in the Adirondacks. Open Mid May - Late Oct. MC/VISA/AMEX.

Phone: (518)834-7454
Address: 2144 Rte 9, Keeseville, NY 12944
Lat/Lon: 44.52522/-73.46256
Web: www.ausablechasm.com

SEE AD TRAVEL SECTION PAGE 526

(E) Ausable Chasm Campground—(Essex) *From jct I-87 (exit 34) & Hwy 9N: Go 1-1/2 mi E on Hwy 9N, then 1 mi N on Hwy 9, then 800 ft E on Hwy 373. Enter on L.* ◇◇FACILITIES: 147 sites, typical site width 25 ft, 35 full hkups, 55 W&E, (20/30/50 amps), 57 no hkups, 70 pull-thrus, family camping, tenting, dump, laundry, ltd groc. ◇◇◇RECREATION: swim pool, playground. Pets welcome. Partial handicap access. Open Memorial Day - mid Oct. Big rigs welcome. Rate in 2010 $27-29 for 2 persons. Member ARVC, CONY. Phone: (518)834-9990.

(W) Ausable River Campsite—(Clinton) *From jct I-87 (exit 34) & Hwy 9N: Go 1/4 mi W on Hwy 9N, then 3/4 mi S on entry road. Enter on L.* ◇◇◇FACILITIES: 112 sites, 99 full hkups, (20/30/50 amps), 13 no hkups, 18 pull-thrus, WiFi Instant Internet at site ($), family camping, tenting, RV storage, laundry, ltd groc, RV supplies, ice, picnic tables, fire rings, wood. ◇◇◇RECREATION: pavilion, swim pool, canoeing, kayaking, river fishing, bsktball, playground, activities, horseshoes, v-ball. Pets welcome, breed restrict. Partial handicap access. Open May 15 - Oct 15. Rate in 2010 $28-35 for 4 persons. MC/VISA/AMEX. Member ARVC, CONY. CCUSA 50% Discount. CCUSA reservations Accepted, CCUSA max stay 2 days, CCUSA disc. not avail holidays. Riverfront sites not discounted. Reservations by phone only. Credit card surcharge $1. WiFi surcharge $3.

Phone: (518)834-9379
Address: 367 Rt 9N, Keesville, NY 12944
Lat/Lon: 44.49438/-73.50561
Email: ausablerivcamp@aol.com
Web: www.ausablerivercampsite.com

AUSTERLITZ—F-10

(NW) WOODLAND HILLS CAMPGROUND—(Columbia) *From jct I-90 (exit B-3) & Hwy-22: Go 2 mi S on Hwy-22, then 1/2 mi W onMiddle Rd, then 3/4 mi N on Fog Hill Rd. Enter on L.*

◇◇◇FACILITIES: 202 sites, typical site width 40 ft, 149 full hkups, 41 W&E, (20/30 amps), 12 no hkups, many extd stay sites (summer), heater not allowed, WiFi Internet central location, family camping, tenting, RV's/park model rentals, RV storage, shower$, dump, non-guest dump $, portable dump, laundry, ltd groc, RV supplies, LP gas by weight/by meter, ice, picnic tables, fire rings, wood.

◇◇◇◇RECREATION: rec hall, rec room/area, coin games, lake swim, boating, no motors, 2 pedal boat rentals, pond fishing, fishing supplies, golf nearby, bsktball, playground, activities, (wkends), horseshoes, sports field, v-ball. Rec open to public.

WOODLAND HILLS CAMPGROUND—Continued on next page

AUSTERLITZ—Continued
WOODLAND HILLS CAMPGROUND—Continued

Pets welcome. Open May 15 - Columbus Day. Clubs welcome. Rate in 2010 $31-35 per family. MC/VISA/DISC. Member ARVC, CONY.

Phone: (518)392-3557
Address: 386 Fog Hill Rd, Austerlitz, NY 12017
Lat/Lon: 42.34537/-73.44170
Email: woodlandhills@whcg.net
Web: www.whcg.net

SEE AD THIS PAGE

AVERILL PARK—E-10

(E) ALPS FAMILY CAMPGROUND—(Rensselaer) *From jct Hwy 66 & Hwy 43: Go 3 mi SE on Hwy 66/Hwy 43, then 1-1/2 mi SE on Hwy 43. Enter on L.*

WELCOME

◆◆◆FACILITIES: 89 sites, typical site width 40 ft, 53 full hkups, 36 W&E, (20/30 amps), many extd stay sites (summer), 3 pull-thrus, heater not allowed, WiFi Instant Internet at site, WiFi Internet central location, family camping, tenting, cabins, dump, non-guest dump $, laundry, groceries, RV supplies, LP gas by weight/by meter, ice, picnic tables, fire rings, wood.

◆◆◆RECREATION: rec hall, rec room/area, coin games, swim pool, pond/stream fishing, fishing supplies, golf nearby, bsktball, playground, activities, (wkends), horseshoes, sports field, hiking trails, v-ball.

Pets welcome. Open all yr. Facilities fully operational May 1 - Oct 15. Clubs welcome. Green Friendly. Rate in 2010 $30-32 per family. MC/VISA/Debit. Member ARVC, CONY.

Phone: (518)674-5565
Address: 1928 NY 43, Averill Park, NY 12018
Lat/Lon: 42.59004/-73.49555
Email: alpscamp@capital.net
Web: www.alpscg.com

SEE AD ALBANY PAGE 537

BAINBRIDGE—F-7

(E) OQUAGA CREEK STATE PARK—(Broome) *From I-88 (exit 8) & Hwy 206: Go E on Hwy 206, then S on CR 20. Enter on L.* FACILITIES: 94 sites, typical site width 40 ft, 94 no hkups, 20 pull-thrus, tenting, dump, ltd groc. RECREATION: lake swim, boating, no motors, canoeing, ramp, lake fishing, playground. Partial handicap access. Open June 4 - Sep 5. Phone: (607)467-4160.

(S) Riverside RV Camping—(Chenango) *From jct I-88 (exit 8) & Hwy 206: Go 1/4 mi W on Hwy 206, then 100 yds S on Hwy 39. Enter on R.* ◆◆◆FACILITIES: 12 sites, 3 full hkups, 9 W&E, (20/30 amps). Pets welcome. No tents. Phone: (607)967-2102.

(NE) Tall Pines Riverfront Campground, Canoeing & Country Store—(Chenango) *From jct I-88 (exit 9) & Hwy 8: Go 3-3/4 mi N on Hwy 8, then 1/8 mi E on CR 35. Enter on L.* ◆◆◆◆FACILITIES: 98 sites, typical site width 25 ft, 44 full hkups, 47 W&E, (20/30/50 amps), 7 no hkups, 10 pull-thrus, family camping, tenting, dump, groceries. ◆◆◆◆RECREATION: swim pool, boating, canoeing, dock, river fishing, playground. Pets welcome. Open Apr - Oct. Rate in 2010 $25-39 for 2 persons. Member ARVC, CONY. Phone: (607)563-8271.

BARKER—D-2

(N) GOLDEN HILL STATE PARK—(Hamilton) *From business center: Go 6 mi NE on Lower Lake Rd.* FACILITIES: 54 sites, 54 E, (30 amps), tenting, dump. RECREATION: boating, canoeing, ramp, lake fishing, playground. Partial handicap access. Open all yr. Facilities fully operational Mid Apr - Mid Oct. Phone: (716)795-3885.

BARRYVILLE—A-1

(W) Kittatinny Campgrounds—(Sullivan) *From jct Hwy-55 & Hwy-97: Go 2 mi NW on Hwy-97. Enter on R.* ◆◆FACILITIES: 352 sites, typical site width 25 ft, 100 W&E, (20 amps), 252 no hkups, tenting, dump, laundry, groceries. ◆◆◆RECREATION: swim pool, boating, canoeing, river/stream fishing, playground. Pets welcome, quantity restrict. Open Apr 15 - Oct 31. Rate in 2010 $34 for 2 persons. Member ARVC, CONY. Phone: (845)557-8611.

BATAVIA—E-3

(S) LEI-TI Campground—(Genesee) *From jct Hwy-5 and Hwy-63: Go 2-1/2 mi SE on Hwy-63, then 1/2 mi S on Shepherd Rd, then 3/4 mi W on Putnam Rd, then 2 mi S on Francis Rd. Enter on L.* ◆◆◆◆FACILITIES: 228 sites, typical site width 30 ft, 212 W&E, (20/30/50 amps), 16 no hkups, 7 pull-thrus, family camping, dump, laundry, ltd groc. ◆◆◆◆RECREATION: swim pool, lake swim, boating, no motors, lake fishing, playground. Pets welcome, breed restrict, quantity restrict. Partial handicap access. No tents. Open all yr. Facilities fully operational May 1 - Oct 25. Rate in 2010 $35-40 per family. Member ARVC, CONY. Phone: (800)HI-LEITI.

BATH—F-4

(S) Babcock Hollow Campground—(Steuben) *From jct Hwy 17 (exit 39) & Hwy 415/Hwy 11: Go 2 mi S on Hwy 11. Enter on L.* ◆◆◆FACILITIES: 100 sites, typical site width 20 ft, 62 full hkups, 38 W&E, (20/30 amps), family camping, tenting, dump, laundry. ◆◆◆RECREATION: swim pool, boating, electric motors only, canoeing, pond fishing, playground. Pets welcome. Open May 1 - Oct 31. Rate in 2010 $24.50-26 per family. Phone: (607)776-7185.

(SW) Campers Haven—(Steuben) *From Hwy 17 (exit 38) & Hwy 415: Go 1-1/2 mi N on Hwy 415, then 2-1/2 mi SW on Knight Settlement Rd. (Hwy 15). Enter on L.* ◆◆◆FACILITIES: 136 sites, typical site width 20 ft, 48 full hkups, 73 W&E, (30/50 amps), 15 no hkups, 10 pull-thrus, family camping, tenting, dump, laundry, ltd groc. ◆◆◆RECREATION: swim pool, boating, no motors, pond fishing, playground. Pets welcome. Partial handicap access. Open mid Apr - Oct. Rate in 2010 $27-34 for 4 persons. Phone: (607)776-0328.

(N) FINGER LAKES WELLNESS CENTER & HEALTH SPA—*From jct I-86/Hwy 17 (exit 38) & Hwy 54: Go 1 mi E & N following Hwy 54, then 2 mi N on Haverling St. Enter on L. Located at Hickory Hill Camping Resort.* Massage Therapy, Facials, Nail Care, Signature Grape Seed Bodywork Sessions, and Manual Therapy for Medical concerns. MC/VISA/DISC/Debit. ATM.

WELCOME

Phone: (607)776-3737
Address: 7531 County Rte 13, Bath, NY 14810
Lat/Lon: 42.36449/-77.30983
Email: email@fingerlakeswellness.com
Web: www.fingerlakeswellness.com

SEE AD CORNING PAGE 542

(N) HICKORY HILL CAMPING RESORT—(Steuben) *From jct I-86/Hwy 17 (exit 38) & Hwy 54: Go 1 mi E & N following Hwy 54, then 2 mi N on Haverling St. Enter on L.*

WELCOME

◆◆◆◆◆FACILITIES: 199 sites, typical site width 30 ft, 176 full hkups, 17 W&E, (20/30/50 amps), 3 no hkups, some extd stay sites (summer), 40 pull-thrus, cable TV, WiFi Instant Internet at site, phone Internet central location, family camping, tenting, cabins, dump, non-guest dump $, laundry, groceries, RV supplies, LP gas by weight/by meter, ice, picnic tables, fire rings, wood.

◆◆◆◆◆RECREATION: rec hall, rec room/area, pavilion, coin games, 2 swim pools, pond fishing, fishing supplies, mini-golf, golf nearby, bsktball, 6 bike rentals, playground, shuffleboard court shuffleboard court, activities, horseshoes, sports field, hiking trails, v-ball.

Pets welcome. Partial handicap access. Open May 1 - Oct 31. Big rigs welcome. Clubs welcome.

BATH—Continued
HICKORY HILL CAMPING RESORT—Continued

Green Friendly. Rate in 2010 $42-62 per family. MC/VISA/DISC/Debit. ATM. Member ARVC, CONY. FMCA discount.

Phone: (800)760-0947
Address: 7531 County Route 13, Bath, NY 14810
Lat/Lon: 42.36449/-77.30983
Email: camp@hickoryhillcampresort.com
Web: www.hickoryhillcampresort.com

SEE AD CORNING PAGE 542

BINGHAMTON—F-6

(E) CHENANGO VALLEY STATE PARK—(Broome) *E'bound from I-88 (exit 3): Go 5 mi N on Hwy 369, then W on Hwy 8. S'bound from I-81 (exit 8): Go 12 mi E on Hwy 79, cross Chenango River, then right 4 mi on Pigeon Hill Rd.* FACILITIES: 216 sites, typical site width 15 ft, 35 ft max RV length, 51 E, (15/30 amps), 165 no hkups, tenting, dump. RECREATION: lake swim, boating, no motors, canoeing, lake fishing, playground. Partial handicap access. Open all yr. Phone: (607)648-5251.

BLUE MOUNTAIN LAKE—C-8

LAKE DURANT (Adirondack SF)—(Hamilton) *From jct Hwy 30 & Hwy 28: Go 3 mi E on Hwy 28.* FACILITIES: 61 sites, 30 ft max RV length, 61 no hkups, tenting, dump. RECREATION: lake swim, boating, canoeing, ramp, lake fishing. Partial handicap access. Open May 16 - Oct 13 (Columbus Day). Phone: (518)352-7797.

BOONVILLE—D-7

PIXLEY FALLS STATE PARK—(Oneida) *From town: Go 6 mi S on Hwy 46. Enter on R.* FACILITIES: 22 sites, 30 ft max RV length, 22 no hkups, tenting, dump. RECREATION: stream fishing. Open all yr. Phone: (315)942-4713.

BRIDGEWATER—E-7

(N) Lake Chalet Campground & Motel—(Oneida) *From jct US 20 & Hwy 8: Go 1 mi N on Hwy 8. Enter on L.* ◆◆FACILITIES: 50 sites, typical site width 30 ft, 22 W&E, (20/30/50 amps), 50 amps ($), 28 no hkups, family camping, tenting, dump, laundry, ltd groc. ◆◆◆RECREATION: lake swim, boating, no motors, canoeing, dock, lake/river fishing, playground. Pets welcome. Open May 1 - Oct 15. Rate in 2010 $24-29 for 2 persons. Member ARVC, CONY. Phone: (315)822-6074.

BROCTON—F-1

(N) LAKE ERIE STATE PARK—(Chautauqua) *From New York Thruway (Exit 59-Dunkirk): Go S on Hwy-5.* FACILITIES: 97 sites, 33 E, (20 amps), 64 no hkups, tenting, dump. RECREATION: lake swim, boating, canoeing, lake fishing, playground. Partial handicap access. Open Apr 28 - Oct 28. Phone: (716)792-9214.

BROOKHAVEN—C-4

SOUTHHAVEN COUNTY PARK—(Suffolk) *From Long Island Expwy (I-495, exit 68S): Go S on William Floyd Pkwy to 4th traffic light, then W on Victory Ave, then 1/2 mi N on River Rd.* FACILITIES: 150 sites, 150 no hkups, tenting, dump. RECREATION: lake/stream fishing, playground. Open Thur-Sat Apr 1 - Sep 12. Facilities fully operational May 13 - Sep 12. Phone: (631)854-1414.

BUFFALO—E-2

See listings at Akron, Darien Center, Gainesville & North Java

BYRON—D-3

(E) Southwoods RV Resort—(Genesee) *From jct I-90 (exit 47) & Hwy 19: Go 3-1/2 mi N on Hwy 19, then 4-1/2 mi W on Hwy 262. Enter on L.* ◆◆◆◆FACILITIES: 215 sites, typical site width 45 ft, 150 full hkups, 65 W&E, (20/30/50 amps), 74 pull-thrus, family camping, tenting, dump, laundry, ltd groc. ◆◆◆RECREATION: swim pool, playground. Pets welcome. Partial handicap access. Open May 1 - Oct 31. Big rigs welcome. Rate in 2010 $28-36 per family. Member ARVC, CONY. Phone: (585)548-9002.

Presidents Martin Van Buren, Millard Fillmore, Theodore Roosevelt & Franklin D. Roosevelt were all born in New York.

CALEDONIA—E-3

(W) Genesee Country Campground—(Livingston) *From jct Hwy 36 N (center of town) & Hwy 5: Go 3 mi W on Hwy 5, then 1/2 mi NE on Flint Hill Rd. Enter on L.* ◇◇◇◇FACILITIES: 155 sites, typical site width 30 ft, 125 W&E, (20/30/50 amps), 30 no hkups, 30 pull-thrus, family camping, tenting, dump, laundry, ltd groc. ◇◇◇RECREATION: playground. Pets welcome. Partial handicap access. Open May 1 - Oct 31. Big rigs welcome. Rate in 2010 $25-28 per family. Member ARVC, CONY. Phone: (585)538-4200.

CAMBRIDGE—D-10

(N) DOUG'S RV REPAIRS—*From jct Hwy 372 & Hwy 22: Go 4-1/2 mi N on Hwy 22, then 3/4 mi E on CR 61 (Shushan Rd). Enter on R.* SERVICES: full-time mech, RV appliance repair, LP gas by weight/by meter, dump station, RV storage, sells parts/accessories, installs hitches. On site repairs. Open May 1 - Oct 15. MC/VISA.

Phone: (518)677-8855
Address: 744 County Road 61, Cambridge, NY 12816
Lat/Lon: 43.09518/-73.36726
Email: joanllc@yahoo.com
Web: www.lakelauderdalecampground.com

SEE AD THIS PAGE

(N) LAKE LAUDERDALE CAMPGROUND—(Washington) *From jct Hwy 372 & Hwy 22: Go 4-1/2 mi N on Hwy 22, then 3/4 mi E on Hwy 61 (Shushan Rd). Enter on R.*

◇◇◇FACILITIES: 75 sites, typical site width 40 ft, 44 ft max RV length, 17 full hkups, 43 W&E, (20/30/50 amps), 15 no hkups, many extd stay sites (summer), 11 pull-thrus, cable TV, WiFi Instant Internet at site, WiFi Internet central location, family camping, tenting, RV's/park model rentals, cabins, RV storage, dump, non-guest dump $, portable dump, laundry, ltd groc, RV supplies, LP gas by weight/by meter, ice, picnic tables, fire rings, wood.

◇◇◇RECREATION: equipped pavilion, golf nearby, playground, activities, (wkends), horseshoes, sports field, hiking trails, v-ball.

Pets welcome. Open May 1 - Oct 15. Clubs welcome. Green Friendly. Rate in 2010 $29-32 per family. MC/VISA. Member ARVC, CONY. FMCA discount. CCUSA 50% Discount. CCUSA reservations Recommended, CCUSA max stay 4 days, Cash only for CCUSA disc., CCUSA disc. not avail S, CCUSA disc. not avail F,Sa, CCUSA disc. not avail holidays.

Phone: (518)677-8855
Address: 744 County Rd 61, Cambridge, NY 12816
Lat/Lon: 43.09518/-73.36726
Email: joanllc@yahoo.com
Web: www.lakelauderdalecampground.com

SEE AD THIS PAGE

CAMPBELL—F-4

(NW) CAMP BELL CAMPGROUND—(Steuben) *From jct I-86 (exit 41) & Hwy 333: Go 1/2 mi E on Hwy 333, then 3/4 mi N on Hwy 415. Enter on L.*

◇◇◇FACILITIES: 96 sites, typical site width 40 ft, 96 W&E, (20/30 amps), some extd stay sites (summer), 20 pull-thrus, cable TV, WiFi Instant Internet at site, family camping, tenting, RV's/park model rentals, cabins, dump, non-guest dump $, portable dump, laundry, ltd groc, RV supplies, LP gas by weight/by meter, ice, picnic tables, fire rings, wood.

Eighteen languages were spoken in N.Y. in 1644.

CAMPBELL—Continued
CAMP BELL CAMPGROUND—Continued

◇◇◇◇RECREATION: rec hall, pavilion, coin games, swim pool, mini-golf, ($), golf nearby, bsktball, playground, activities, (wkends), horseshoes, sports field, hiking trails, v-ball.

Pets welcome. Partial handicap access. Open May 1 - Oct 15. Clubs welcome. Green Friendly. Rate in 2010 $28-35 per family. MC/VISA/DISC. Member ARVC, CONY. FCRV discount. FMCA discount. CCUSA 50% Discount.

Phone: (607)527-3301
Address: 8700 SR 415, Campbell, NY 14821
Lat/Lon: 42.23577/-77.18465
Email: campbellcampground@yahoo.com
Web: www.campbellcampground.com

SEE AD CORNING PAGE 541

CANANDAIGUA—E-4

(W) Bristol Woodlands Campground—(Ontario) *From jct Hwy 20/5 & Hwy 64: Go 7 mi S on Hwy 64, then 1-1/2 mi W on CR 32, then 1 mi S on South Hill Rd. (Weight limit 10 tons). Enter on L.* ◇◇◇FACILITIES: 84 sites, typical site width 60 ft, 59 full hkups, 2 W&E, (20/30 amps), 23 no hkups, family camping, tenting, dump. ◇◇◇RECREATION: swim pool, pond fishing, playground. Pets welcome, breed restrict. Open May 1 - Oct 20. Rate in 2010 $38 per family. Member ARVC, CONY. Phone: (585)229-2290.

CAPE VINCENT—C-6

BURNHAM POINT STATE PARK—(Jefferson) *From business center: Go 3 mi E on Hwy-12E.* FACILITIES: 52 sites, 22 E, (20 amps), 30 no hkups, tenting, dump. RECREATION: boating, canoeing, ramp, dock, river fishing, playground. Partial handicap access. Open mid May - Labor Day. Phone: (315)654-2522.

CAROGA LAKE—D-8

(S) CAROGA LAKE CAMPGROUND (Adirondack SF)—(Fulton) *From jct Hwy-10 & Hwy-29A: Go 1 mi S on Hwy-29A (Campground on E Caroga Lake).* FACILITIES: 161 sites, 161 no hkups, tenting, dump. RECREATION: lake swim, boating, canoeing, ramp, lake fishing. Partial handicap access. Open Mid May - Labor Day. Phone: (518)835-4241.

CATSKILL—F-9

(W) Indian Ridge Campground—(Greene) *From jct NY Thruway I-87 (exit 21) & Hwy 23 B: Go 1/4 mi W on Hwy 23 B, then 1/2 mi N on Forest Hills Ave (3-way interseciton). Campground straight ahead. Enter at end.* ◇◇◇FACILITIES: 70 sites, 59 W&E, (20/30/50 amps), 11 no hkups, family camping, tenting, dump, laundry, ltd groc. ◇◇◇RECREATION: swim pool, playground. Pets welcome. Open May 15 - Oct 15. Rate in 2010 $35-50 per family. Member ARVC, CONY. Phone: (518)943-4513.

New York was named in honor of the Duke of York.

CAZENOVIA—E-6

(N) CHITTENANGO FALLS STATE PARK—(Madison) *From jct US 20 & Hwy 13: Go 4 mi N on Hwy 13.* FACILITIES: 24 sites, typical site width 15 ft, 20 ft max RV length, 24 no hkups, 22 pull-thrus, tenting. RECREATION: stream fishing, playground. Partial handicap access. Open May 5 - Oct 8. Phone: (315)655-9620.

CENTRAL BRIDGE—E-8

(NW) Hide-A-Way Campsites—(Schoharie) *From jct I-88 (Central Bridge exit 23) & Hwy 7/30A: Go 1-1/4 mi W on Hwy 7/30A, then 3/4 mi W & N on Hwy 30A, then 1/8 mi N on State Rd, then 1-1/4 mi W on Grovenors Corners Rd, then 1/2 mi N on CR 10, then 1/4 mi E on Woodman Rd. Enter on L.* ◇◇◇FACILITIES: 50 sites, typical site width 30 ft, 41 W&E, (20/30/50 amps), 9 no hkups, 2 pull-thrus, WiFi Internet central location, family camping, tenting, RV storage, dump, non-guest dump $, portable dump, laundry, LP gas by weight/by meter, ice, picnic tables, fire rings, wood.

◇◇◇RECREATION: swim pool, pond fishing, bsktball, playground, activities, horseshoes, hiking trails, v-ball. Pets welcome. Open May 11 - Columbus Day. Rate in 2010 $28-30 for 2 persons. MC/VISA. Member ARVC, CONY. FCRV discount. FMCA discount. CCUSA 50% Discount. CCUSA reservations Recommended, CCUSA max stay 3 days, CCUSA disc. not avail Th, CCUSA disc. not avail F,Sa, CCUSA disc. not avail holidays. No check-in after 9 pm.

Phone: (518)868-9975
Address: 107 Janice Ln, Central Bridge, NY 12035
Lat/Lon: 42.72778/-74.36372
Email: hideawaycampsites@hotmail.com
Web: www.hide-a-waycampsites.com

(W) Locust Park—(Schoharie) *From jct I-88 (Central Bridge exit) & Hwy 7/Hwy 30A: Go 1 mi W on Hwy 7. Enter on L.* ◇◇◇FACILITIES: 32 sites, typical site width 30 ft, 30 full hkups, (20/30 amps), 2 no hkups, 14 pull-thrus, family camping, tenting, dump. Pets welcome, breed restrict. Open May 1 - Nov 1. Rate in 2010 $25 for 4 persons. Phone: (518)868-9927.

CHAUTAUQUA—F-1

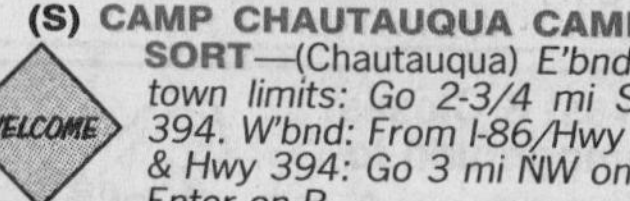

(S) CAMP CHAUTAUQUA CAMPING RESORT—(Chautauqua) *E'bnd: From SE town limits: Go 2-3/4 mi SE on Hwy 394. W'bnd: From I-86/Hwy 17 (exit 8) & Hwy 394: Go 3 mi NW on Hwy 394. Enter on R.*

EXPERIENCE CAMPING AT IT'S FINEST

...On the shores of Chautauqua Lake. Camp Chautauqua, a family resort with all amenities in the heart of western New York's natural playground. 2000 ft of lakeside w/docks. Near Chautauqua Institution. Open all year. 5/5 rating.

◇◇◇◇◇FACILITIES: 250 sites, typical site width 40 ft, 125 full hkups, 100 W&E, (20/30/50 amps), 25 no hkups, many extd stay sites (summer), 114 pull-thrus, cable TV, WiFi Instant Internet at site, WiFi Internet central location, family camping, tent-

CAMP CHAUTAUQUA CAMPING RESORT—Continued on next page

CHAUTAUQUA—Continued
CAMP CHAUTAUQUA CAMPING RESORT—Continued

ing, dump, non-guest dump $, portable dump, laundry, full svc store, RV supplies, LP gas by weight/by meter, ice, picnic tables, patios, fire rings, grills, wood, controlled access.

◊◊◊◊◊RECREATION: rec hall, rec room/area, equipped pavilion, coin games, swim pool, wading pool, lake swim, boating, canoeing, kayaking, ramp, dock, lake/pond fishing, golf nearby, bsktball, playground, activities, (wkends), tennis, sports field, v-ball.

Pets welcome, quantity restrict. Partial handicap access. Open all yr. Facilities fully operational Apr 15 - Oct 15. Big rigs welcome. Clubs welcome. Green Friendly. Rate in 2010 $38-60 per family. MC/VISA/DISC/Debit. ATM. Member ARVC, CONY.

Text 107997 to (440)725-8687 to see our Visual Tour.

Phone: (716)789-3435
Address: 3900 W Lake Rd, Stow, NY 14785
Lat/Lon: 42.16918/-79.43985
Email: camp@campchautauqua.com
Web: www.campchautauqua.com

SEE AD THIS PAGE

CHERRY VALLEY—E-8

(S) Belvedere Lake Campground—(Otsego) *From jct Hwy 54 & Hwy 166: Go 4 mi S on Hwy 166, then 1/2 mi SE on Hwy 165, then 1/8 mi E on Hwy 57, then 3/4 mi N on Gage Rd. Enter on R.* ◊◊◊FACILITIES: 175 sites, typical site width 30 ft, 135 full hkups, 40 W&E, (20/30 amps), family camping, tenting, dump, laundry, ltd groc. ◊◊◊◊RECREATION: lake swim, boating, electric motors only, canoeing, dock, lake fishing, playground. Pets welcome. Partial handicap access. Open May 1 - Columbus Day. Rate in 2010 $35-40 for 2 persons. Member ARVC, CONY. Phone: (607)264-8182.

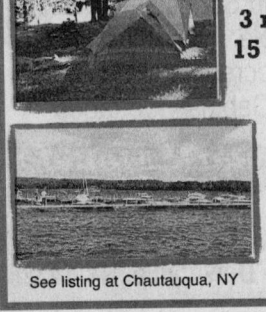

CHESTERTOWN—C-9

(E) Rancho Pines—(Warren) *From jct I-87 (exit 25) & Hwy 8: Go 50 yards E on Hwy 8, then 1 mi S on Schroon River Rd. Enter on L.* ◊◊◊FACILITIES: 68 sites, typical site width 28 ft, 35 ft max RV length, 58 full hkups, (20/30 amps), 10 no hkups, family camping, tenting, laundry. ◊◊◊RECREATION: swim pool, boating, canoeing, river fishing, playground. Pets welcome. Partial handicap access. Open May 15 - Oct 15. Rate in 2010 $27-32 for 2 persons. Member ARVC, CONY. Phone: (518)494-3645.

CLAYTON—B-6

(SW) CEDAR POINT STATE PARK—(Jefferson) *From business center: Go 6 mi W on Hwy-12E.* FACILITIES: 179 sites, 26 full hkups, 57 E, 96 no hkups, tenting, dump. RECREATION: boating, canoeing, ramp, river fishing, playground. Open Early May - Columbus Day. Phone: (315)654-2522.

(SW) Merry Knoll 1000 Islands Campground—(Jefferson) *From jct Hwy-12 & Hwy-12 E: Go 2-1/2 mi SW on Hwy-12E. Enter on R.* ◊◊◊FACILITIES: 87 sites, typical site width 30 ft, 77 full hkups, 10 W&E, (20/30/50 amps), 50 amps ($), 12 pull-thrus, family camping, tenting, dump, laundry, ltd groc. ◊◊◊◊RECREATION: swim pool, boating, canoeing, dock, river fishing, playground. Pets welcome. Open Mid May - Oct 15. Big rigs welcome. Rate in 2010 $35-37 for 2 persons. Member ARVC, CONY. Phone: (315)686-3055.

CLEVELAND—D-6

(E) Lazy K RV Ranch—(Oneida) *From jct I-81 (exit 32) & Hwy 49: Go 16 mi E on Hwy 49, then 1-1/2 mi N on Hall Rd, then 1/8 mi E on Stonebarn Rd. Enter on L.* ◊◊◊FACILITIES: 99 sites, typical site width 33 ft, 47 full hkups, 28 W&E, (20/30/50 amps), 24 no hkups, 56 pull-thrus, family camping, tenting, dump, laundry, ltd groc. ◊◊◊RECREATION: swim pool, boating, no motors, canoeing, dock, pond fishing, playground. Pets welcome, quantity restrict. Open Apr 25 - Mid Oct. Rate in 2010 $29-50 per family. Member ARVC, CONY. Phone: (888)381-6415.

COHOCTON—E-4

(N) Tumble Hill Campground—(Steuben) *From I-390 (exit 2): Go 2/10 mi E to Hwy 415, then 1/2 mi S on Hwy 415, then 1/2 mi N on Hwy 371, then 1/2 mi W on Atlanta Back Rd. Enter on L.* ◊◊◊FACILITIES: 38 sites, typical site width 40 ft, 34 full hkups, (20/30/50 amps), 4 no hkups, 5 pull-thrus, cable TV, phone Internet central location, family camping, tenting, laundry, LP gas by weight/by meter, ice, picnic tables, fire rings, wood. ◊◊◊RECREATION: rec hall, playground, activities, horseshoes, hiking trails, v-ball. Pets welcome. Open May 1 - Oct 31. Big rigs welcome. Rate in 2010 $27 for 2 persons. Member ARVC, CONY. CCUSA 50% Discount. CCUSA reservations Recommended, CCUSA max stay 4 days, Cash only for CCUSA disc., CCUSA disc. not avail Th, CCUSA disc. not avail F,Sa, CCUSA disc. not avail holidays.

Phone: (585)384-5248
Address: 10551 Atlanta Back Rd, Cohocton, NY 14826
Lat/Lon: 42.51289/-77.48797
Email: tumblehill@aol.com
Web: www.tumblehill.com

COLD SPRING—B-2

CLARENCE FAHNESTOCK MEMORIAL STATE PARK—(Putnam) *From jct Hwy-9 & Hwy-301: Go 8 mi E on Hwy-301.* FACILITIES: 80 sites, 80 no hkups, tenting, ltd groc. RECREATION: lake swim, boating, no motors, canoeing, ramp, lake fishing, playground. No pets. Open Mid May - Late Oct. Phone: (845) 225-7207.

COOPERSTOWN—E-8

(S) Cooperstown Beaver Valley Cabins & Campsites—(Otsego) *From jct Hwy 80 & Hwy 28 in town: Go 4 mi S on Hwy 28, then 2-1/4 mi W on Seminary Rd. Enter on L.* ◊◊◊FACILITIES: 90 sites, typical site width 30 ft, 10 full hkups, 60 W&E, (20/30 amps), 20 no hkups, 17 pull-thrus, family camping, tenting, dump, laundry, ltd groc. ◊◊◊◊RECREATION: swim pool, boating, no motors, dock, pond fishing, playground. Pets welcome. Open May 15 - Oct 11. Rate in 2010 $25-39 per family. Member ARVC, CONY. Phone: (800)726-7314. FCRV discount. FMCA discount.

(SW) Cooperstown Famous Family Tent & Trailer Campground—(Otsego) *From Hwy 28 (in Cooperstown): Go 2-1/2 mi S on Hwy 28, then 4 mi W on CR 11, then 1/2 mi NE on Petkewec Rd. Enter on R.* ◊◊FACILITIES: 100 sites, typical site width 50 ft, 12 full hkups, 73 W&E, (30/50 amps), 50 amps ($), 15 no hkups, 8 pull-thrus, family camping, tenting, dump, laundry, ltd groc. ◊◊◊RECREATION: swim pool, pond fishing, playground. Pets welcome. Open May 15 - Oct 15. Rate in 2010 $26-32 for 2 persons. Member ARVC, CONY. Phone: (607)293-7766.

(N) Cooperstown Ringwood Farms Campground—(Otsego) *From jct Hwy 28 & Hwy 80: Go 9 mi N on Hwy 80. Enter on L.* ◊◊FACILITIES: 104 sites, typical site width 30 ft, 74 full hkups, (20/30 amps), 30 no hkups, family camping, tenting, dump, laundry, ltd

Cooperstown Ringwood Farms Campground—Continued on next page

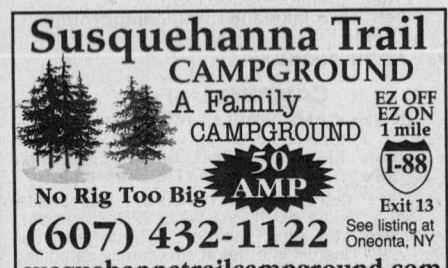

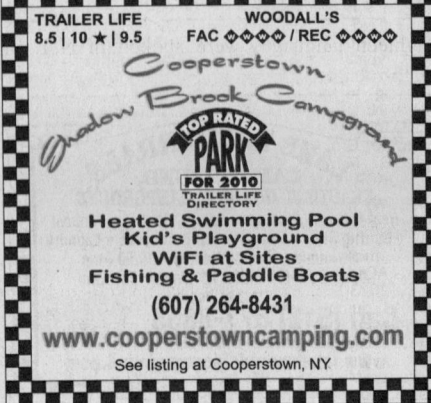

COOPERSTOWN—Continued
Cooperstown Ringwood Farms Campground—Continued

groc. ◊◊◊RECREATION: swim pool, pond fishing. Pets welcome. Partial handicap access. Open all yr. Facilities fully operational Apr 15 - Oct 15. Rate in 2010 $39 for 2 persons. Member ARVC, CONY. Phone: (800) 231-9114.

(N) COOPERSTOWN SHADOW BROOK CAMPGROUND—(Otsego) *From center of town at jct Main St & Hwy 80E: Go 10-3/4 mi N on Hwy 80E, then 4 mi E on Hwy 20, then 1 mi S on CR 31 (Or 1 mi S of US Hwy 20 at E Springfield). Enter on R.*

COOPERSTOWN'S HIGHEST RATED CAMPGROUND!
Only 9 mi from the center of Cooperstown. Heated pool, wireless internet, playground, video game room, rec center with billiards & ping pong, fishing pond with paddle boats, cabin & house rentals, and spacious RV & tent sites.

◊◊◊◊FACILITIES: 100 sites, typical site width 30 ft, 16 full hkups, 73 W&E, (30 amps), 11 no hkups, some extd stay sites (summer), 20 pull-thrus, WiFi Instant Internet at site ($), WiFi Internet central location ($), family camping, tenting, cabins, dump, portable dump, laundry, ltd groc, RV supplies, LP gas by weight/by meter, ice, picnic tables, fire rings, wood.

◊◊◊◊RECREATION: rec hall, rec room/area, pavilion, coin games, swim pool, boating, no motors, canoeing, 3 pedal boat rentals, pond fishing, fishing supplies, golf nearby, bsktball, playground, activities, horseshoes, sports field, v-ball.

Pets welcome, breed restrict. Partial handicap access. Open May 20 - Oct 10. Escort to site. Clubs welcome. Rate in 2010 $28-50 for 2 persons. MC/VISA/DISC/Debit. Member ARVC, CONY.

Phone: (607)264-8431
Address: 2149 County Hwy 31, Cooperstown, NY 13326
Lat/Lon: 42.81639/-74.82485
Email: reservations@cooperstowncamping.com
Web: www.cooperstowncamping.com

SEE AD PAGE 540

(S) HARTWICK HIGHLANDS CAMPGROUND—(Otsego) *From jct Hwy 80 & Hwy 28 in town: Go 4 mi S on Hwy 28, then 1-1/2 mi W on Seminary Rd. Enter at end.*

◊◊◊◊FACILITIES: 69 sites, typical site width 45 ft, 54 full hkups, 5 W&E, (20/30/50 amps), 10 no hkups, 16 pull-thrus, WiFi Instant Internet at site, WiFi Internet central location, family camping, tenting, cabins, dump, laundry, ltd groc, RV supplies, LP gas by weight/by meter, ice, picnic tables, fire rings, wood, controlled access.

◊◊◊◊RECREATION: rec room/area, equipped pavilion, coin games, swim pool, golf nearby, playground, horseshoes, sports field, hiking trails.

Pets welcome. Partial handicap access. Open May 15 - Oct 15. Big rigs welcome. Clubs welcome. Rate in 2010 $31-43 per family. MC/VISA/DISC. Member ARVC, CONY.

Phone: (607)547-1996
Address: 131 Burke Hill Rd, Milford, NY 13807
Lat/Lon: 42.65806/-74.98430
Email: camping@hartwickhighlandscg.com
Web: www.hartwickhighlandscg.com

SEE AD PAGE 540

(N) KOA-Cooperstown—(Herkimer) *From jct Hwy-28 & Hwy-80: Go 11 mi NE on Hwy-80, then 1/2 mi W on US-20, then 3/4 mi N on McShane Rd, then 1/4 mi W on Edick Rd. Enter on R.* ◊◊◊FACILITIES: 101 sites, typical site width 30 ft, 27 full hkups, 51 W&E, (20/30/50 amps), 23 no hkups, 58 pull-thrus, family camping, tenting, dump, laundry, ltd groc. ◊◊◊RECREATION: swim pool, playground. Pets welcome. Partial handicap access. Open Apr 15 - Oct 31. Big rigs welcome. Green Friendly. Rate in 2010 $39-51 for 2 persons. Member ARVC, CONY. Phone: (800)562-3402. KOA discount.

(SW) Meadow-Vale Campsites—(Otsego) *From jct Hwy 80 & Hwy 28 (Chestnut St): Go 2-1/2 mi S on Hwy 28, then 7-1/2 mi W on CR 11, then 4 mi SW on CR 14, then 1/4 mi S on Gilbert Lake Rd. Enter on R.* ◊◊◊FACILITIES: 110 sites, typical site width 35 ft, 96 W&E, (20/30/50 amps), 14 no hkups, family camping, tenting, dump, laundry, groceries. ◊◊◊◊RECREATION: swim pool, boating, no motors, canoeing, dock, pond fishing, playground. Pets welcome. Open May 14 - Oct 11. Big rigs welcome. Rate in 2010 $33-38 for 4 persons. Member ARVC, CONY. Phone: (607)293-8802.

COOPERSTOWN—Continued

(W) Yogi Bear's Jellystone Park at Crystal Lake—(Otsego) *From jct Hwy 28 & Hwy 80: Go 10-3/4 mi W on Hwy 80, then 5-3/4 mi S on CR 16, then 3/4 mi N on Hwy 51, then 1 mi W on CR 17, then 100' N on East Turtle Lake Rd. Enter on L.* ◊◊◊FACILITIES: 250 sites, typical site width 25 ft, 32 full hkups, 212 W&E, (20/30/50 amps), 50 amps ($), 6 no hkups, 5 pull-thrus, family camping, tenting, dump, laundry, groceries. ◊◊◊◊◊RECREATION: swim pool, boating, no motors, canoeing, dock, lake fishing, playground. Pets welcome, breed restrict. Partial handicap access. Open Mid May - Mid Sep. Big rigs welcome. Rate in 2010 $55 per family. Member ARVC, CONY. Phone: (607)965-8265.

COPAKE—F-10

(N) Camp Waubeeka Family Campground (Morgan RV Resorts)—(Columbia) *From jct Hwy 23 & Hwy 22: Go 4 mi S on Hwy 22, then 2 mi S on Farm Rd. Enter on R.* ◊◊◊FACILITIES: 426 sites, typical site width 34 ft, 370 full hkups, 5 W&E, (20/30/50 amps), 51 no hkups, 11 pull-thrus, family camping, tenting, ltd groc. ◊◊◊◊RECREATION: lake swim, boating, electric motors only, canoeing, lake/river fishing, playground. Pets welcome, breed restrict. Open May 1 - Oct 15. Big rigs welcome. Rate in 2010 $35-45 per family. Member ARVC, CONY. Phone: (518)329-4681.

(SW) KOA COPAKE—(Columbia) *From jct I-87 & Hwy 23: Go 15 mi E on Hwy 23, then 5 mi S on Hwy 22, then 2 mi SW on Hwy 7A. Enter on R.*

SCENIC TACONIC MTNS BORDERS MASS, CT, NY
Copake KOA is on a historic 110-acre property in Columbia County. The area is rich in history and fun! Antiquing, Bash Bish Falls, Museums, Catamount Adventure Park, Apple picking, Tanglewood, Lime Rock, Wineries and more!

◊◊◊◊FACILITIES: 250 sites, typical site width 50 ft, 240 full hkups, (20/30/50 amps), 10 no hkups, some extd stay sites, 20 pull-thrus, heater not allowed, cable TV, WiFi Instant Internet at site ($), family camping, tenting, cabins, laundry, ltd groc, RV supplies, LP gas by weight/by meter, ice, picnic tables, fire rings, wood, controlled access.

◊◊◊◊RECREATION: rec room/area, pavilion, coin games, swim pool, golf nearby, bsktball, 5 bike rentals, playground, activities, (wkends), tennis, horseshoes, sports field, hiking trails, v-ball.

Pets welcome, breed restrict, quantity restrict. Partial handicap access. Open May 15 - Oct 15. Self contained units only after Columbus Weekend. Big rigs welcome. Escort to site. Clubs welcome. Rate in 2010 $45-62 per family. MC/VISA/Debit. Member ARVC, CONY.

Phone: (518)329-2811
Address: 2236 County Rte 7, Copake, Ny 12516
Lat/Lon: 42.09360/-73.58148
Email: copake@hotmail.com
Web: www.copakekoa.com

SEE AD CANAAN, CT PAGE 47

CORINTH—D-9

(SE) ALPINE LAKE RV RESORT, LLC (CAMP RESORT)—(Saratoga) *From south village limits: Go 1-1/4 mi S on Hwy 9N, then 1-1/4 mi E on Heath Rd. Enter on L.*

FACILITIES: 530 sites, typical site width 60 ft, 500 full hkups, (30/50 amps), 30 no hkups, some extd stay sites (summer), 300 pull-thrus, cable TV, ($), WiFi Instant Internet at site ($), cable Internet central location, family camping, tenting, RV's/park model rentals, cabins, RV storage, shower$, laundry, groceries, RV supplies, LP gas by weight/by meter, ice, picnic tables, patios, fire rings, wood, controlled access.

RECREATION: rec hall, rec room/area, pavilion, coin games, 2 swim pools, lake swim, boating, electric motors only, canoeing, kayaking, 10 rowboat/5 canoe/5 kayak/5 pedal boat rentals, lake fishing, fishing supplies, golf nearby, bsktball, 18 bike rentals, playground, shuffleboard court 2 shuffleboard courts, activities, tennis, horseshoes, sports field, hiking trails, v-ball, local tours.

Pets welcome. Partial handicap access. Open May 1 - Oct 15. Big rigs welcome. Escort to site. Clubs welcome. Rate in 2010 $45-52 for 2 persons. MC/VISA/DISC/AMEX. ATM. Member ARVC, CONY.

New York was the 11th state admitted to the Union.

CORINTH—Continued
ALPINE LAKE RV RESORT, LLC—Continued

Phone: (518)654-6260
Address: 78 Heath Rd, Corinth, NY 12822
Lat/Lon: 43.21056/-73.84116
Email: alpine_lake@mhchomes.com
Web: www.alpinelakervresort.com

Reserve Online at Woodalls.com

SEE AD ACRA PAGE 536 AND AD LAKE GEORGE PAGE 549

(N) River Road Campground—(Saratoga) *From jct Hwy 10 & Hwy 9N: Go 3-1/2 mi N on Hwy 9N. Enter on R.* ◊◊FACILITIES: 75 sites, typical site width 30 ft, 30 ft max RV length, 39 full hkups, 24 W&E, (20/30/50 amps), 12 no hkups, 6 pull-thrus, family camping, tenting, dump, ltd groc. ◊◊◊RECREATION: swim pool, river swim, boating, canoeing, ramp, dock, river/stream fishing, playground. Pets welcome. Open Memorial Day - Columbus Day. Rate in 2010 $37-39 for 2 persons. Member ARVC, CONY. Phone: (518)654-6630. FMCA discount.

CORNING—F-4

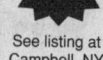

(N) FERENBAUGH CAMPGROUND—(Steuben) *From jct I-86/Hwy 17 (exit 46) & Hwy 414: Go 5 mi N on Hwy 414. Enter on R.*

CENTRAL TO CORNING & WATKINS GLEN!
274 acres of open, wooded & creekside camping. Private shaded & open campsites in a beautiful forest hillside & scenic valley setting. A 40 ft wide trout stream flows through the center of the campground. Big Rigs Welcome!

◊◊◊◊FACILITIES: 149 sites, typical site width 50 ft, 33 full hkups, 97 W&E, (20/30/50 amps), 19 no hkups, 40 pull-thrus, cable TV, ($), WiFi Instant Internet at site, WiFi Internet central location, family camping, tenting, cabins, dump, non-guest dump $, portable dump, laundry, ltd groc, RV supplies, LP gas by weight/by meter, ice, picnic tables, fire rings, wood.

◊◊◊◊RECREATION: rec room/area, pavilion, coin games, swim pool, pond/stream fishing, fishing supplies, mini-golf, golf nearby, bsktball, playground, activities, (wkends), horseshoes, sports field, hiking trails, v-ball.

Pets welcome. Partial handicap access. Open Apr 15 - Nov 1. Facilities fully operational May 1 - Nov 1. Clubs welcome. Rate in 2010 $29-54 per family. MC/VISA/DISC/AMEX/Debit. Member ARVC, CONY. FMCA discount.

Phone: (607)962-6193
Address: 4248 SR 414, Corning, NY 14830
Lat/Lon: 42.20532/-76.99229
Email: ferenbaugh@ferenbaugh.com
Web: www.ferenbaugh.com

SEE AD NEXT PAGE

CORTLAND—E-6

(E) Cortland's Country Music Park & Campground—(Cortland) *From jct I-81 (exit 11) & Hwy 13: Go 1-1/4 mi NE on Hwy 13. Enter on R.* ◆◆◆FACILITIES: 105 sites, 83 W&E, (30 amps), 22 no hkups, family camping, tenting, dump. ◆◆◆RECREATION: pond fishing, playground. Pets welcome. Open all yr. Rate in 2010 $22 per family. Phone: (607)753-0377.

(NE) Yellow Lantern Kampground—(Cortland) *From jct I-81 (exit 11) & Hwy 13: Go 1 mi NE on Hwy 13. Enter on R.* ◆◆FACILITIES: 205 sites, 70 full hkups, 135 W&E, (20/30/50 amps), family camping, tenting, dump, laundry, ltd groc. ◆◆RECREATION: swim pool, river fishing, playground. Pets welcome. Open Mar 15 - Nov 15. Rate in 2010 $23.50-30 for 4 persons. Phone: (607)756-2959.

CRANBERRY LAKE—B-8

CRANBERRY LAKE CAMPGROUND (Adirondack SF) —(St. Lawrence) *From town: Go 1-1/2 mi off Hwy 3.* FACILITIES: 172 sites, 172 no hkups, tenting, dump. RECREATION: lake swim, boating, canoeing, lake fishing. Partial handicap access. Open Mid May - Late Oct. Phone: (315)848-2315.

CROWN POINT—C-10

(N) CROWN POINT RESERVATION CAMPGROUND (Adirondack SF)—(Essex) *From town: Go 8 mi N on Hwy 9N.* FACILITIES: 70 sites, typical site width 40 ft, 70 no hkups, tenting, dump. RECREATION: boating, canoeing, ramp, dock, lake fishing, playground. Partial handicap access. Open May 2 - Oct 13 (Columbus Day). Phone: (518)597-3603.

CUBA—F-3

(N) Maple Lane Campground & RV Park—(Allegany) *From jct Hwy 17/I-86 (exit 28) & Hwy 305: Go 300 yards N on Hwy 305, then 300 yards W & N on Maple Ln. Enter on L.* ◆◆◆FACILITIES: 46 sites, 20 full hkups, 26 W&E, (30/50 amps), 24 pull-thrus, family camping, tenting, dump, laundry. Pets welcome. Partial handicap access. Open Apr 1 - Oct. Facilities fully operational Apr 15 - Oct. Big rigs welcome. Rate in 2010 $24-26 per vehicle. Member ARVC, CONY. Phone: (585)968-1677.

CUDDEBACKVILLE—B-1

(W) Oakland Valley Campground—(Orange) *From jct Hwy 17 & Hwy 209: Go 9 mi S on Hwy 209, then 1-3/4 mi W on Hwy 7. Enter on L.* ◆◆◆FACILITIES: 110 sites, typical site width 50 ft, 25 full hkups, 35 W&E, (20/30 amps), 50 no hkups, family camping,

CUDDEBACKVILLE—Continued
Oakland Valley Campground—Continued

tenting, dump, laundry, ltd groc. ◆◆◆RECREATION: swim pool, river swim, river fishing, playground. Pets welcome, breed restrict, quantity restrict. Partial handicap access. Open May 1 - Oct 15. Rate in 2010 $38-43 per family. Member ARVC, CONY. Phone: (845)754-8732.

CUTCHOGUE—B-5

(C) Cliff and Ed's Trailer Park—(Suffolk) *From jct I-495 (exit 73) & Hwy 25: Go 15-1/4 mi E on Hwy 25, then 1 block N on Depot Lane, then 1 block W on Schoolhouse Rd. Enter on R.* ◆◆◆◆FACILITIES: 24 sites, typical site width 36 ft, accepts full hkup units only, 24 full hkups, (20/30/50 amps), family camping. Pets welcome, breed restrict. Partial handicap access. No tents. Open Apr 1 - Nov 1. Big rigs welcome. Rate in 2010 $45-55 per vehicle. Member ARVC, CONY. Phone: (631)298-4091.

DANSVILLE—E-4

(W) Skybrook Campground—(Livingston) *From jct I-390 (exit 4) & Hwy 36: Go 1-1/2 mi N on Hwy 36, then 1/2 mi W on Hwy 436, then 1 mi S on Ossian Hill Rd, then 2-3/4 mi SE on McCurdy Rd. Enter on L.* ◆◆FACILITIES: 470 sites, typical site width 40 ft, 20 full hkups, 350 W&E, (30/50 amps), 100 no hkups, family camping, tenting, dump, laundry, ltd groc. ◆◆◆RECREATION: swim pool, pond fishing, playground. Pets welcome. Open May 1 - Oct 1. Rate in 2010 $26-30 for 2 persons. Phone: (585)335-6880.

(S) STONY BROOK STATE PARK—(Livingston) *From business center: Go 3 mi S on Hwy-36.* FACILITIES: 125 sites, 125 no hkups, tenting, dump. RECREATION: swim pool, stream fishing, playground. Pets welcome. Partial handicap access. Open all yr. Facilities fully operational May 1 - Mid Oct. Phone: (585)335-8111.

(S) Sugar Creek Glen Campground—(Livingston) *From jct I-390 (exit 4) & Hwy 36: Go 500 feet S on Hwy 36, then 5 mi SW on Poags Hole Rd. Enter at end.* ◆◆◆FACILITIES: 139 sites, typical site width 35 ft, 35 ft max RV length, 100 W&E, 2 E, (20/30 amps), 37 no hkups, family camping, tenting, dump, ltd groc. ◆◆◆RECREATION: river swim, stream fishing, playground. Pets welcome. Open May 1 - Oct 15. Rate in 2010 $30-35 for 2 persons. Member ARVC, CONY. Phone: (585)335-6294.

DARIEN CENTER—E-3

(W) DARIEN LAKES STATE PARK—(Genessee) *From jct I-90/NYS Thruway (exit 48A) & Hwy 77: Go 6 mi S on Hwy 77, then 2-1/2 mi W on US 20, then 1/4 mi N on Harlow Rd. Enter on R.* FACILITIES: 158 sites, typical site width 25 ft, 45 E, (20/30 amps), 113 no hkups, 15 pull-thrus, tenting, dump. RECREATION: lake swim, lake fishing, playground. Partial handicap access. Open May 3 - Early Sep. Phone: (585)547-9242.

(E) SKYLINE RESORT CAMPGROUND—(Genesee) *From jct Hwy 77 & US 20: Go 4 mi E on US 20, then 1 mi S on Townline Rd. Enter on L.*

WELCOME

◆◆◆FACILITIES: 300 sites, typical site width 30 ft, 40 full hkups, 260 W&E, (30/50 amps), mostly extd stay sites (summer), WiFi Internet central location, family camping, tenting, RV storage, shower$, dump, portable dump, ltd groc, RV supplies, LP gas by weight, ice, picnic tables, wood, controlled access.

◆◆◆◆RECREATION: rec hall, rec room/area, pavilion, coin games, 2 swim pools, spray ground, lake fishing, fishing supplies, mini-golf, ($), golf nearby, bsktball, playground, shuffleboard court 2 shuffleboard courts, activities (wkends), tennis, horseshoes, v-ball.

SKYLINE RESORT CAMPGROUND—Continued on next page

DARIEN CENTER—Continued
SKYLINE RESORT CAMPGROUND—Continued

Pets welcome, quantity restrict. Partial handicap access. Open May 2 - Columbus Day. Clubs welcome. Rate in 2010 $30-40 for 2 persons. MC/VISA/DISC. Member ARVC, CONY.

Phone: (585)591-2021
Address: 10933 Townline Rd, Darien Center, NY 14040
Lat/Lon: 42.88494/-78.30744
Email: adele@skylinervresort.com
Web: www.skylinervresort.com

SEE AD NIAGARA FALLS PAGE 558

(E) SKYLINE RV SALES & SERVICE—*From jct Hwy 77 & US 20: Go 4 mi E on US 20, then 1 mi S on Townline Rd. Enter on L.* SALES: travel trailers, park models, 5th wheels, fold-down camping trailers, pre-owned unit sales. SERVICES: full-time mech, RV appliance repair, body work/collision repair, LP gas by weight, dump station, RV storage, sells parts/accessories, installs hitches. Open all yr. MC/VISA/DISC.

Phone: (585)591-2021
Address: 10933 Townline Rd., Darien Center, NY 14040
Lat/Lon: 42.88494/-78.30744
Web: www.skylinervresort.com

SEE AD NIAGARA FALLS PAGE 558

DAVENPORT—E-8

(E) Beaver Spring Lake Campground—(Delaware) *From jct I-88 & Hwy 23: Go 10 mi E on Hwy 23, then 1/4 mi N on Beaver Spring Rd. Enter at end.* ◇◇◇FACILITIES: 120 sites, typical site width 30 ft, 70 full hkups, 30 W&E, (20/30 amps), 20 no hkups, 12 pull-thrus, WiFi Internet central location, family camping, tenting, RV storage, dump, laundry, ltd groc, RV supplies, LP gas by weight/by meter, ice, picnic tables, fire rings, wood. ◇◇◇RECREATION: pavilion, swim pool, boating, electric motors only, canoeing, lake/stream fishing, fishing supplies, bsktball, playground, activities, horseshoes, hiking trails, v-ball. Pets welcome. Open Apr 15 - Oct 31. Rate in 2010 $34-40 per family. MC/VISA/DISC/Debit. ATM. Member ARVC, CONY. CCUSA 50% Discount. CCUSA reservations Recommended, CCUSA max stay 14 days, Cash only for CCUSA disc., CCUSA disc. not avail holidays. Discount not available special event weekends-call for details. Check in: between 2PM & 9 PM; Check out: by 2 PM. Addl surcharges:Electric heater-$3, sewer (if available)-$5, visitors-$5 day/$7 overnight.

Phone: (607)278-5293
Address: 263 Beaver Spring Rd, Davenport, NY 13750
Lat/Lon: 42.47839/-74.83275
Email: bslcg@stny.rr.com
Web: www.beaverspringlake.com

DEERLAND—C-8

FORKED LAKE CAMPGROUND (Adirondack SF)—(Hamilton) *From business center: Go 3 mi W off Hwy-30 (access by foot or boat only).* FACILITIES: 77 sites, 77 no hkups, tenting, groceries. RECREATION: boating, canoeing, ramp, lake fishing. Partial handicap access. Open May 16 - Sep 1. Facilities fully operational Mid May - Labor Day. Phone: (518)624-6646.

DELEVAN—E-2

(S) Arrowhead Camping Area—(Cattaraugus) *From jct Hwy 39 & Hwy 16: Go 7 mi S on Hwy 16. Enter on R.* ◇◇◇FACILITIES: 200 sites, typical site width 50 ft, 190 W&E, (20/30/50 amps), 10 no hkups, 10 pull-thrus, family camping, tenting, dump, laundry, ltd groc. ◇◇◇RECREATION: lake swim, boating, no motors, pond/stream fishing, playground. Pets welcome. Partial handicap access. Open Memorial Day wknd - Columbus Day wknd. Rate in 2010 $25 per family. Member ARVC, CONY. Phone: (716)492-3715.

DEWITTVILLE—F-1

(S) CHAUTAUQUA HEIGHTS CAMPING RESORT—(Chautauqua) *From jct I-86 (exit 10) & Hwy 430: Go 6-1/2 mi W on Hwy 430, then 1/2 mi E on Thumb Rd. Enter on L.*

◇◇◇◇FACILITIES: 180 sites, typical site width 35 ft, 151 full hkups, 28 W&E, (20/30/50 amps), 1 no hkups, mostly extd stay sites (summer), 61 pull-thrus, cable TV, WiFi Instant Internet at site, family camping, tenting, cabins, RV storage, dump, laundry, ltd groc, RV supplies, LP gas by weight, ice, picnic tables, fire rings, wood, controlled access.

◇◇◇◇RECREATION: rec hall, rec room/area, pavilion, coin games, swim pool, mini-golf, golf nearby, bsktball, playground, activities, horseshoes, sports field, hiking trails, v-ball.

Pets welcome. Partial handicap access. Open May 1 - Oct 15. Pets require rabies certification. Big

DEWITTVILLE—Continued
CHAUTAUQUA HEIGHTS CAMPING RESORT—Continued

rigs welcome. Escort to site. Clubs welcome. Rate in 2010 $25-45 per family. MC/VISA/DISC/Debit. Member ARVC, CONY.

Phone: (716)386-3804
Address: 5652 Thumb Rd., Dewittville, NY 14728
Lat/Lon: 42.22827/-79.42972
Email: contact@chautauquahgts.com
Web: www.chautauquahgts.com

SEE AD CHAUTAUQUA PAGE 539

(S) CHAUTAUQUA LAKE RV & PARK MODEL SALES—*From jct I-86 (exit 10) & Hwy 430: Go 6-1/2 mi W on Hwy 430, then 1/2 mi E on Thumb Rd. Enter on L.* SALES: park models, pre-owned unit sales. SERVICES: Open May 1 - Oct 15. MC/VISA/DISC/Debit.

Phone: (716)386-3804
Address: 5652 Thumb Rd, Dewittville, NY 14728
Lat/Lon: 42.22827/-79.42972
Email: contact@chautauquahgts.com
Web: www.chautauquahgts.com

SEE AD CHAUTAUQUA PAGE 539

DEXTER—C-6

(C) Black River Bay Campground—(Jefferson) *From jct I-81 (exit 46) & Hwy 12F (Coffeen Rd): Go 5-1/2 mi W on Hwy 12F (Coffeen Rd), then 1/8 mi W on Foster Park Rd. Enter on R.* ◇◇◇FACILITIES: 150 sites, typical site width 40 ft, 82 full hkups, 25 W&E, (20/30 amps), 43 no hkups, 11 pull-thrus, family camping, tenting, dump, laundry, ltd groc. ◇◇◇RECREATION: boating, canoeing, ramp, dock, river fishing, playground. Pets welcome. Partial handicap access. Open May 1 - Oct 15. Rate in 2010 $29-31 for 2 persons. Member ARVC, CONY. Phone: (315)639-3735.

DUANE—B-8

(C) Deer River Campsite—(Franklin) *From jct Hwy 30, Hwy 99 & Hwy 14: Go 1-1/2 mi W on Hwy 14 (Red Tavern Rd). Enter on L.* ◇◇◇◇FACILITIES: 79 sites, typical site width 35 ft, 19 full hkups, 54 W&E, (30 amps), 6 no hkups, 3 pull-thrus, family camping, dump, laundry, groceries. ◇◇◇◇◇RECREATION: lake swim, boating, 9.5 hp limit, canoeing, dock, lake fishing, playground. Pets welcome, breed restrict, quantity restrict. Partial handicap access. No tents. Open May 15 - Oct 1. Rate in 2010 $26-30 for 2 persons. Member ARVC, CONY. Phone: (518)483-0060.

MEACHAM LAKE CAMPGROUND (Adirondack SF)—(Franklin) *From jct Hwy 99 & Hwy 30: Go 10 mi S on Hwy 30.* FACILITIES: 224 sites, 224 no hkups, tenting, dump. RECREATION: lake swim, boating, canoeing, ramp, lake fishing, playground. Partial handicap access. Open Mid May - Columbus Day. Phone: (518)483-5116.

EAST HAMPTON—B-5

CEDAR POINT (Suffolk County Park)—(Suffolk) *From town: Go E on Hwy 27 (Montauk Hwy), then N on Stephens Hands Path to Old Northwest Rd, then follow signs to Alewive Brook Rd.* FACILITIES: 190 sites, 190 no hkups, tenting, dump, full svc store. RECREATION: boating, saltwater fishing, playground. Open Thurs-Sat Apr 1 - Oct 12. Facilities fully operational May 13 - Sep 12. Phone: (631)852-7620.

EAST ISLIP—C-4

HECKSCHER STATE PARK—(Suffolk) *From jct Hwy-27A & Southern State Pkwy (exit 45): Go 1-1/2 mi S on Southern State Pkwy.* FACILITIES: 69 sites, 69 no hkups, tenting, dump. RECREATION: swim pool, saltwater swim, boating, canoeing, ramp, saltwater fishing, playground. Partial handicap access. Open all yr. Facilities fully operational May 26 - Sep 3. Phone: (631)581-2100.

EAST SPRINGFIELD—E-8

GLIMMERGLASS STATE PARK—(Otsego) *From jct US 20 & CR 31: Go 5 mi S on CR 31. Enter on R.* FACILITIES: 37 sites, typical site width 20 ft, 37 no hkups, tenting, dump. RECREATION: lake swim, canoeing, ramp, lake/stream fishing, playground. Partial handicap access. Open May 14 - Oct 10. Phone: (607)547-8662.

ELIZAVILLE—F-9

(N) Brook N Wood Family Campground—(Columbia) *From jct Hwy 199 & US 9: Go 9 mi N on US 9, then 2 mi E on Hwy 8. Enter on R.* ◇◇◇FACILITIES: 174 sites, typical site width 40 ft, 124 full hkups, 30 W&E, (20/30/50 amps), 20 no hkups, cable TV, WiFi Instant Internet at site, family camping, tenting, dump, non-guest dump $, laundry, ltd groc, RV supplies, LP gas by weight/by meter, ice, picnic tables, fire rings, wood. ◇◇◇RECREATION: rec hall, swim pool, stream fishing, fishing supplies, mini-golf, ($), bsktball, playground, activities, horseshoes, hiking trails, v-ball. Pets welcome, breed restrict. Open Apr 1 - Mid Nov. Big rigs welcome. Rate in 2010 $43-52 per family. MC/VISA/DISC. Member ARVC, CONY. CCUSA 50% Discount.

ELIZAVILLE—Continued
Brook N Wood Family Campground—Continued

Phone: (888)588-8622
Address: 1947 County Route 8, Elizaville, NY 12523
Lat/Lon: 42.09112/-73.78832
Email: camp@brooknwood.com
Web: www.brooknwood.com

ELLENVILLE—A-2

(W) SKYWAY CAMPING RESORT—(Ulster) *From jct US 209 & Hwy 52: Go 5 mi W on Hwy 52, then 1 mi S on Skyway RV Rd (immediate right fork). Enter on L.*

◇◇◇◇◇FACILITIES: 180 sites, typical site width 30 ft, 160 full hkups, 20 W&E, (30/50 amps), some extd stay sites (summer), cable TV, WiFi Instant Internet at site, WiFi Internet central location, family camping, tenting, RV's/park model rentals, RV storage, laundry, ltd groc, RV supplies, LP gas by weight/by meter, ice, picnic tables, fire rings, wood.

◇◇◇◇◇RECREATION: rec hall, rec room/area, coin games, swim pool, hot tub, boating, no motors, 2 kayak/4 pedal boat rentals, lake fishing, fishing supplies, golf nearby, bsktball, playground, shuffleboard court, shuffleboard court, activities (wkends), tennis, horseshoes, sports field.

Pets welcome, breed restrict. Partial handicap access. Open May 1 - Columbus Day. Clubs welcome. MC/VISA/DISC/AMEX. Member ARVC, CONY.

Phone: (845)647-5747
Address: 99 Mountaindale Rd, Greenfield Park, NY 12435
Lat/Lon: 41.72893/-74.50894
Email: skywaymail@skywaycamping.com
Web: www.skywaycamping.com

SEE AD TRAVEL SECTION PAGE 530

(W) SKYWAY RV SALES—*From jct US 209 & Hwy 52: Go 5 mi W on Hwy 52. Enter on L.* SALES: travel trailers, park models, 5th wheels, pre-owned unit sales. SERVICES: LP gas by weight/by meter, sells parts/accessories. Open Apr - Oct. MC/VISA.

Phone: (800)832-3132
Address: Mountaindale Rd, Greenfield Park, NY 12435
Lat/Lon: 41.72741/-74.49004

SEE AD TRAVEL SECTION PAGE 530

(W) YOGI BEAR'S JELLYSTONE PARK AT BIRCHWOOD ACRES—(Ulster) *From jct US-209 & Hwy-52: Go 8 mi W on Hwy-52, then 1 mi S on Martinfeld Rd. Enter on L.*

FAMILIES LOVE JELLYSTONE PARK!
Families with kids enjoy our heated spray pool, activities, cabins, deluxe lodges and sites with free Wi-Fi, cable TV, and nearby hiking and performing arts center, what are you waiting for? Call us for your camping fun!

◇◇◇◇◇FACILITIES: 218 sites, typical site width 40 ft, 131 full hkups, 77 W&E, (20/30/50 amps), 50 amps ($), 10 no hkups, some extd stay sites (summer), heater not allowed, cable TV, WiFi Instant Internet at site, WiFi Internet central location, family camping, tenting, RV's/park model rentals, cabins, RV storage, dump, laundry, groceries, RV supplies, LP gas by weight/by meter, ice, picnic tables, fire rings, wood.

◇◇◇◇◇RECREATION: rec hall, rec room/area, coin games, swim pool, spray ground, hot tub, boating, electric motors only, canoeing, kayaking, 2 rowboat/kayak/6 pedal boat rentals, lake fishing, fishing supplies, golf nearby, bsktball, playground, shuffleboard court 3 shuffleboard courts, activities, tennis, horseshoes, sports field, v-ball.

Pets welcome, breed restrict, quantity restrict. Partial handicap access. Open May 1 - Columbus Day. Pools and snack bar Memorial Day to Labor Day. Big rigs welcome. Clubs welcome. Rate in 2010 $60-62 for 2 persons. MC/VISA/AMEX/Debit. Member ARVC, CONY.

Phone: (800)552-4724
Address: 85 Martinfeld Rd, Woodridge, NY 12789
Lat/Lon: 44.74088/-74.54456
Email: reservations@nyjellystone.com
Web: www.nyjellystone.com

SEE AD TRAVEL SECTION PAGE 530

ENDICOTT—F-6

(NW) Pine Valley RV Park and Campground—(Broome) *From jct Hwy 17 (exit 66) & Rt 17C: Go 3-1/2 mi E on Rt 17C to Glendale Dr (2nd light), then 1-3/4 mi N on Glendale (becomes Leona), then 1/2 mi W on Day Hollow Rd, then 2-1/2 mi N on Boswell Hill Rd. Enter on R.* ◊◊◊FACILITIES: 118 sites, typical site width 45 ft, 53 full hkups, 50 W&E, (20/30/50 amps), 50 amps ($), 15 no hkups, family camping, tenting, dump, laundry, ltd groc. ◊◊◊RECREATION: lake swim, boating, electric motors only, canoeing, lake fishing, playground. Pets welcome. Partial handicap access. Open May 1 - Oct 15. Big rigs welcome. Rate in 2010 $27-35 for 2 persons. Member ARVC, CONY. Phone: (607)785-6868.

FAIR HAVEN—D-5

(N) FAIR HAVEN BEACH STATE PARK—(Cayuga) *From Hwy 104A in town: Go 2 mi N on State Park Rd.* FACILITIES: 184 sites, 46 E, (15 amps), 138 no hkups, tenting, dump, ltd groc. RECREATION: lake swim, boating, canoeing, ramp, dock, lake fishing, playground. Partial handicap access. Open all yr. Facilities fully operational Apr 1 - End of Oct. Phone: (315)947-5205.

FARMINGTON—E-4

(S) KOA-Canandaigua/Rochester—(Ontario) *From jct Hwy 28 & Farmington Townline Rd: Go 1-3/4 mi W on Farmington Townline Rd. Enter on R.* ◊◊◊◊FACILITIES: 117 sites, typical site width 22 ft, 42 full hkups, 52 W&E, 6 E, (20/30/50 amps), 50 amps ($), 17 no hkups, family camping, tenting, dump, laundry, ltd groc. ◊◊◊◊RECREATION: swim pool, pond fishing, playground. Pets welcome, breed restrict. Open Apr 1 - Oct 31. Big rigs welcome. Rate in 2010 $33-44 for 2 persons. Member ARVC, CONY. Phone: (585)398-3582. KOA discount.

FAYETTEVILLE—E-6

(E) GREEN LAKES STATE PARK—(Onondaga) *From I-481 (exit 5): Go 1 mi E, then 1 mi S on Fremont Rd, then 3-1/2 mi E on Hwy 290. Enter on R.* FACILITIES: 137 sites, typical site width 12 ft, 42 E, (20/30 amps), 95 no hkups, tenting, dump. RECREATION: lake swim, boating, canoeing, lake fishing, playground. Partial handicap access. Open all yr. Facilities fully operational May 19 - Oct 8. Phone: (315)637-6111.

FERNDALE—A-1

(C) SULLIVAN COUNTY VISITORS ASSOCIATION—*From jct Hwy 17 (exit 101) & Hwy 175 (Sullivan Ave): Go 1/4 mi N on Hwy 175 (Sullivan Ave). Enter on L.* Tourist information center for the Sullivan County Catskills and the magnificant Delaware River. Long known as a quiet & scenic resort area, it is also an action-packed playground for adults and children, including the Monticello Gaming & Raceway. Open all yr.

Phone: (845)747-4449
Address: 100 Sullivan Ave, Ferndale, NY 12734
Lat/Lon: 41.78008/-74.73018
Email: info@scva.net
Web: www.scva.net

SEE AD TRAVEL SECTION PAGE 530

FINDLEY LAKE—F-1

(S) Paradise Bay Park—(Chautauqua) *From jct I-86/17 & Hwy 426 (exit 4): Go 1 mi S on Hwy 426, then 1-3/4 mi S on Shadyside Rd. Enter on L.* ◊◊◊FACILITIES: 100 sites, typical site width 25 ft, 100 W&E, (20/30/50 amps), 3 pull-thrus, family camping, tenting, dump, ltd groc. ◊◊◊RECREATION: lake swim, boating, canoeing, ramp, dock, lake fishing, playground. Pets welcome. Open May 1 - Oct 1. Big rigs welcome. Rate in 2010 $28 per family. Member ARVC, CONY. Phone: (716)769-7582.

Woodall's Tip... 100% Money Back Guarantee... If for any reason you're not satisfied with this Directory, please return it to us by December 31, 2011 along with your sales receipt, and we'll reimburse you for the amount you paid for the Directory.

FLORIDA—B-2

(W) BLACK BEAR CAMPGROUND—(Orange) *From jct Hwy 17 (exit 124) & Hwy 17A: Go 5-1/2 mi SW on Hwy 17A, turn right at light (Bridge St), then 1-1/2 mi W on CR 41. Enter on L.*

◊◊◊◊FACILITIES: 160 sites, typical site width 30 ft, 154 full hkups, 6 W&E, (20/30/50 amps), some extd stay sites, 10 pull-thrus, cable TV, WiFi Instant Internet at site, family camping, RV's/park model rentals, cabins, dump, portable dump, laundry, ltd groc, RV supplies, ice, picnic tables, fire rings, grills, wood.

◊◊◊◊RECREATION: equipped pavilion, coin games, swim pool, mini-golf, golf nearby, bsktball, playground, activities, (wkends), horseshoes, sports field, v-ball, local tours.

Pets welcome, breed restrict. Partial handicap access. No tents. Open all yr. Big rigs welcome. Clubs welcome. Rate in 2010 $42-50 for 2 persons. MC/VISA/Debit. Member ARVC, CONY.

Phone: (845)651-7717
Address: 197 Wheeler Rd, Florida, NY 10921
Lat/Lon: 41.32225/-74.37359
Email: topcamp@warwick.net
Web: www.blackbearcampground.com

SEE AD NEW YORK CITY PAGE 556 AND AD TRAVEL SECTION PAGE 528 AND AD TRAVEL SECTION PAGE 527

(W) NEW YORK CITY TOURS-BLACK BEAR CAMPGROUND—*From jct Hwy 17 (exit 124) & Hwy 17A: Go 5-1/2 mi SW on Hwy 17, right at light (Bridge St), then 1-1/2 mi W on CR 41. Enter on L.* Guided bus or van tours of New York City-individuals or groups. Reservation recommended. Direct tours to New York City from our Campground! Open Mid May - Mid Oct. MC/VISA/DISC.

Phone: (845)651-7717
Address: 197 Wheeler Rd, Florida, NY 10921
Lat/Lon: 41.32225/-74.37359
Email: topcamp@warwick.net
Web: www.blackbearcampground.com

SEE AD NEW YORK CITY PAGE 556

FORESTPORT—D-7

(S) Kayuta Lake Campground—(Oneida) *From jct Hwy 12 & Hwy 28: Go 1-1/2 mi N on Hwy 28, then 2 mi SE on Woodhull Rd, then 2 mi S on Bardwell Mills Rd. Enter on L.* ◊◊◊FACILITIES: 164 sites, 78 full hkups, 70 W&E, (20/30/50 amps), 50 amps ($), 16 no hkups, 10 pull-thrus, family camping, tenting, dump, laundry, ltd groc. ◊◊◊◊RECREATION: lake swim, boating, canoeing, ramp, dock, lake/stream fishing, playground. Pets welcome. Partial handicap access. Open May 1 - Oct 1. Rate in 2010 $28-34 per family. Phone: (315)831-5077.

FRANKLINVILLE—F-3

(W) Triple R Camping Resort & Trailer Sales—(Cattaraugus) *From south jct Hwy 98 & Hwy 16: Go 1 mi N on Hwy 16/98, then 1-/1/2 mi W on Elm St, then 1/3 mi SW on Bryant Hill Rd. Enter on L.* ◊◊◊◊FACILITIES: 215 sites, typical site width 45 ft, 215 full hkups, (30/50 amps), 24 pull-thrus, family camping, tenting, dump, laundry, groceries. ◊◊◊◊RECREATION: swim pool, pond fishing, playground. Pets welcome. Partial handicap access. Open Apr 15 - Oct 15. Big rigs welcome. Rate in 2010 $33-38 per family. Member ARVC, CONY. Phone: (716)676-3856.

GABRIELS—B-9

BUCK POND (Adirondack SF)—(Franklin) *From jct Hwy 86 & CR 30: Go 6 mi N on CR 30.* FACILITIES: 116 sites, typical site width 18 ft, 30 ft max RV length, 116 no hkups, tenting, dump. RECREATION: boating, canoeing, ramp, pond fishing. Pets welcome. Partial handicap access. Open May 16 - Sep 1. Phone: (518)891-3449.

GAINESVILLE—E-3

(S) WOODSTREAM CAMPSITE—(Wyoming) *From jct Hwy-78 & Hwy-19: Go 1-1/2 mi S on Hwy-19, then 1/2 mi E on School Rd. Enter on R.*

◊◊◊FACILITIES: 250 sites, typical site width 30 ft, 16 full hkups, 214 W&E, (20/30/50 amps), 20 no hkups, many extd stay sites (summer), 10 pull-thrus, WiFi Internet central location, family camping, tenting, RV's/park model rentals, cabins, RV storage, shower$, dump, portable dump, laundry, ltd groc, RV supplies, LP gas by weight/by meter, ice, picnic tables, fire rings, wood.

◊◊◊◊RECREATION: rec hall, rec room/area, pavilion, coin games, lake swim, stream fishing,

fishing supplies, mini-golf, ($), golf nearby, bsktball, playground, activities, (wkends), horseshoes, sports field, v-ball.

Pets welcome. Partial handicap access. Open May 1 - Oct 15. Clubs welcome. Rate in 2010 $28-36 for 4 persons. MC/VISA/DISC. Member ARVC, CONY.

Phone: (877)CAMPNOW
Address: 5440 School Rd, Gainesville, NY 14066
Lat/Lon: 42.63019/-78.12271
Web: www.woodstreamcampsite.com

SEE AD THIS PAGE

GALWAY—D-9

(E) McConchies Heritage Acres—(Saratoga) *From jct Hwy 147 & Hwy 67: Go 1-1/2 mi E on Hwy 67, then 1 mi N on Division St. Enter on L.* ◊◊FACILITIES: 190 sites, typical site width 50 ft, 170 W&E, (15/20/30 amps), 20 no hkups, family camping, tenting, dump, laundry, ltd groc. ◊◊◊RECREATION: swim pool, pond fishing, playground. Pets welcome. Open May 1 - Oct 1. Rate in 2010 $28-30 for 2 persons. Member ARVC, CONY. Phone: (518)882-6605.

(NW) Pop's Lake Campground—(Saratoga) *From jct Hwy 147 & Hwy 29: Go 2 mi W on Hwy 29, then 1-3/4 mi N on Fishhouse Rd, then 3/4 mi NE on Centerline Rd. Enter on L.* ◊◊◊FACILITIES: 82 sites, typical site width 20 ft, 35 ft max RV length, 40 full hkups, 24 W&E, (20/30 amps), 18 no hkups, 3 pull-thrus, family camping, tenting, dump, ltd groc. ◊◊◊RECREATION: lake swim, lake fishing, playground. Pets welcome. Open May 15 - Sep 30. Rate in 2010 $26.50-28.50 per family. Phone: (518)883-8678.

GANSEVOORT—D-9

(NW) Adirondack Gateway RV Resort (Morgan RV Resorts)—(Saratoga) *From jct I-87 (exit 17N) & US 9: Go 1/2 mi NE on US 9, then 1/4 mi S on Fawn Rd, then 1/4 mi SE on Fortsville Rd. Enter on R.* ◊◊◊FACILITIES: 327 sites, typical site width 30 ft, 155 full hkups, 172 W&E, (20/30/50 amps), 62 pull-thrus, family camping, tenting, dump, laundry, ltd groc. ◊◊◊◊◊RECREATION: 2 swim pools, pond/stream fishing, playground. Pets welcome, breed restrict, quantity restrict. Open May 1 - Oct 15. Rate in 2010 $35-39 for 2 persons. Phone: (518)792-0485.

(SW) Coldbrook RV Resort (Morgan RV Resorts)—(Saratoga) *From jct I-87 (exit 16) & Ballard Rd: Go 300 feet E on Ballard Rd, then 1 mi N on Gurnsprings Rd. Enter on R.* ◊◊◊◊FACILITIES: 279 sites, 268 full hkups, (20/30/50 amps), 11 no hkups, 7 pull-thrus, family camping, tenting, dump, laundry, ltd groc. ◊◊◊◊RECREATION: swim pool, pond/stream fishing, playground. Pets welcome, breed restrict, quantity restrict. Open May 1 - Oct 7. Big rigs welcome. Rate in 2010 $38-41 for 4 persons. Member ARVC, CONY. Phone: (518)584-8038.

(S) Saratoga RV Park—(Saratoga) *From jct I-87 (exit 15 Northway) & Hwy 50: Go 8 mi NE on Hwy 50. Enter on L.* ◊◊◊FACILITIES: 152 sites, 152 full hkups, (20/30/50 amps), 21 pull-thrus, family camping, dump, laundry, ltd groc. ◊◊◊RECREATION: swim pool, playground. Pets welcome. No tents. Open May 1 - Oct 31. Big rigs welcome. Rate in 2010 $32-39 for 4 persons. Phone: (518)798-1913.

GARDINER—A-2

(W) YOGI BEAR'S JELLYSTONE PARK CAMP-RESORT AT LAZY RIVER—(Ulster) *From jct Hwy-208 & Hwy-44/55: Go 2-1/2 mi W on Hwy-44/55, then 2/10 mi S on Albany Post Rd, then 1/2 mi E on Bevier Rd. Enter at end.*

◊◊◊◊◊FACILITIES: 168 sites, typical site width 45 ft, 90 full hkups, 68 W&E, (20/30/50 amps), 10 no hkups, some extd stay sites (summer), 30 pull-thrus, cable TV, WiFi Instant Internet at site, WiFi Internet central location, family camping, tenting, cabins, RV storage, dump, non-guest dump $, portable dump, laundry, groceries, RV supplies, LP gas by weight/by meter, ice, picnic tables, fire rings, wood, controlled access.

◊◊◊◊◊RECREATION: rec hall, rec room/area, pavilion, coin games, 2 swim pools, river swim, boating, no motors, canoeing, kayaking, 18 kayak rentals, river fishing, fishing supplies, mini-golf, ($), golf nearby, bsktball, 25 bike rentals, playground, shuffleboard court 2 shuffleboard courts, activities, horseshoes, sports field.

Pets welcome, quantity restrict. Partial handicap access. Open May 1 - Columbus Day. Big rigs welcome. Clubs welcome. Rate in 2010 $42-65 for 4 persons. MC/VISA/DISC/Debit. ATM. Member ARVC, CONY.

YOGI BEAR'S JELLYSTONE PARK CAMP-RESORT AT LAZY RIVER—Continued on next page

GARDINER—Continued
YOGI BEAR'S JELLYSTONE PARK CAMP-RESORT AT LAZY RIVER—Continued

Phone: (845)255-5193
Address: 50 Bevier Rd, Gardiner, NY 12525
Lat/Lon: 41.68324/-74.16555
Web: www.lazyriverny.com

SEE AD THIS PAGE

GASPORT—D-2

(N) Niagara Hartland RV Resort—(Niagara) *From jct Hwy 104 & Hartland Rd: Go 3-3/4 mi N on Hartland Rd. Enter on R.* ◇◇◇FACILITIES: 100 sites, typical site width 25 ft, 75 full hkups, 15 W&E, (30/50 amps), 50 amps ($), 10 no hkups, 17 pull-thrus, family camping,

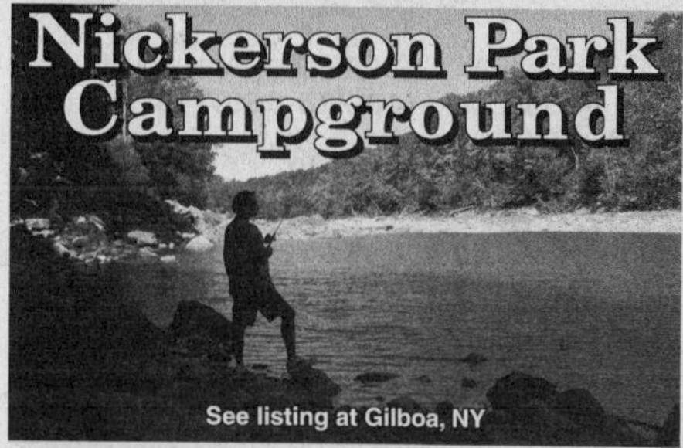

See listing at Gilboa, NY

GASPORT—Continued
Niagara Hartland RV Resort—Continued

tenting, dump, laundry, ltd groc. ◇◇◇RECREATION: lake swim, canoeing, lake/pond fishing, playground. Pets welcome, breed restrict. Partial handicap access. Open May 15 - Oct 15. Rate in 2010 $24-29 for 2 persons. Phone: (716)795-3812. FMCA discount.

GENEVA—E-5

See listing at Phelps

Mae West, actress, was from NY.

GILBOA—F-8

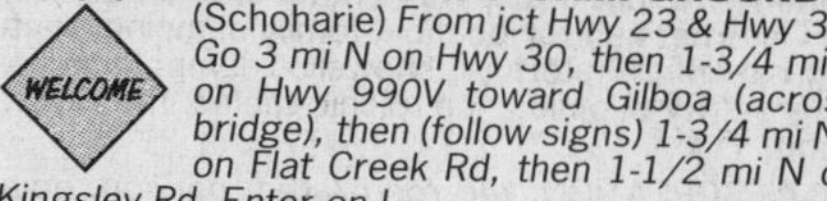

(N) COUNTRY ROADS CAMPGROUND—(Schoharie) *From jct Hwy 23 & Hwy 30: Go 3 mi N on Hwy 30, then 1-3/4 mi E on Hwy 990V toward Gilboa (across bridge), then (follow signs) 1-3/4 mi NE on Flat Creek Rd, then 1-1/2 mi N on Kingsley Rd. Enter on L.*

◇◇◇◇FACILITIES: 118 sites, typical site width 35 ft, 62 full hkups, 35 W&E, (20/30/50 amps), 50 amps ($), 21 no hkups, some extd stay sites

COUNTRY ROADS CAMPGROUND—Continued on next page

See listing at Gardiner, NY

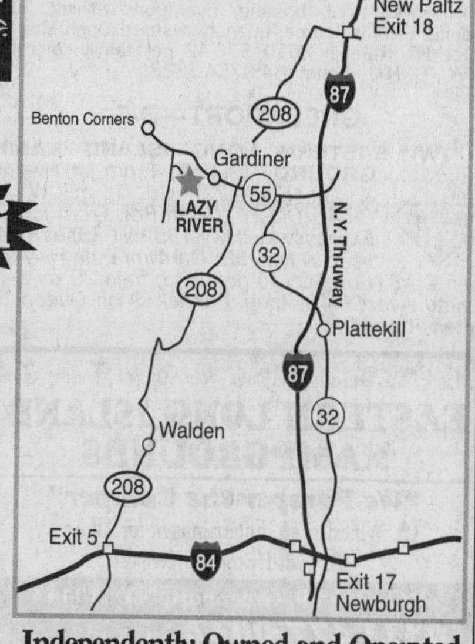

GILBOA—Continued
COUNTRY ROADS CAMPGROUND—Continued

(summer), 2 pull-thrus, WiFi Instant Internet at site, WiFi Internet central location, family camping, tenting, cabins, RV storage, shower$, dump, laundry, ltd groc, RV supplies, ice, picnic tables, fire rings, wood.

◊◊◊RECREATION: rec room/area, pavilion, coin games, swim pool, hot tub, golf nearby, playground, activities, (wkends), horseshoes, sports field, hiking trails, v-ball.

Pets welcome. Open May 15 - Columbus Day. Clubs welcome. Rate in 2010 $34-38 for 2 persons. MC/VISA/DISC/Debit. Member ARVC, CONY. FMCA discount.

Phone: (518)827-6397
Address: 144 Peaceful Rd, Gilboa, NY 12076
Lat/Lon: 42.43424/-74.42305
Email: camp@countryroadscampground.com
Web: www.countryroadscampground.com

SEE AD PAGE 545

(NW) NICKERSON PARK CAMPGROUND—(Schoharie) *From jct Hwy 23 & Hwy 30: Go 5-1/2 mi N on Hwy 30, then 1 mi E on Stryker Rd (CR 13). Enter on L.*

WELCOME

◊◊◊FACILITIES: 377 sites, typical site width 50 ft, 264 full hkups, 18 W&E, (20/30/50 amps), 95 no hkups, many extd stay sites (summer), WiFi Internet central location, family camping, tenting, dump, non-guest dump $, portable dump, laundry, ltd groc, RV supplies, LP gas by weight, ice, picnic tables, fire rings, wood.

◊◊◊RECREATION: rec hall, equipped pavilion, coin games, swim pool, river swim, river fishing, golf nearby, bsktball, playground, activities, (wkends), horseshoes, sports field, v-ball.

Pets welcome. Open May 1 - Columbus Day. Clubs welcome. Rate in 2010 $31-38 per family. MC/VISA. Member ARVC, CONY.

Phone: (607)588-7327
Address: 378 Stryker Rd, Gilboa, NY 12076
Lat/Lon: 42.41364/-74.46341
Email: info@nickersonparkcampground.com
Web: www.nickersonparkcampground.com

SEE AD PAGE 545

GLENS FALLS—D-9

MOREAU LAKE STATE PARK—(Saratoga) *From business center: Go 5 mi S on US-9.* FACILITIES: 147 sites, 147 no hkups, tenting, dump. RECREATION: lake swim, boating, no motors, canoeing, ramp, dock, lake fishing, playground. Partial handicap access. Open all yr. Facilities fully operational Mid May - Mid Oct. Phone: (518)793-0511.

GODEFFROY—B-1

(E) American Family Campground, Inc—(Orange) *From jct US 6 & US 209: Go 6 mi NE on US 209, then 1/2 mi E on Guymard Turnpike. Enter on R.* ◊◊◊FACILITIES: 200 sites, 55 full hkups, 50 W&E, (20/30 amps), 95 no hkups, 5 pull-thrus, family camping, tenting, dump, laundry, ltd groc. ◊◊◊◊RECREATION: swim pool, boating, river/pond fishing, playground. Pets welcome, quantity restrict. Open May 15 - Oct 15. Rate in 2010 $36-42 per family. Member ARVC, CONY. Phone: (845)754-8388.

GREENPORT—B-5

(W) EASTERN LONG ISLAND KAMPGROUND—(Suffolk) *From jct Hwy-25 & CR-48/Old-27: Go 1 mi W on CR-48/Old-27 (North Rd). From jct L.I. Expressway (Hwy-495 exit 73) at Riverhead & Hwy-58: Go 4 mi E on Hwy-58, then 2 mi N on 105 to deadend, then 20 mi E on Sound Ave/CR-48, then 1 block S on Queen St. Enter at end.*

WELCOME

GREENPORT—Continued
EASTERN LONG ISLAND KAMPGROUND—Continued

◊◊◊◊FACILITIES: 186 sites, typical site width 30 ft, 38 ft max RV length, 101 full hkups, 52 W&E, (20/30 amps), 33 no hkups, some extd stay sites (summer), heater not allowed, WiFi Instant Internet at site, family camping, tenting, RV's/park model rentals, RV storage, dump, non-guest dump $, portable dump, laundry, ltd groc, RV supplies, ice, picnic tables, fire rings, wood.

◊◊◊RECREATION: rec hall, swim pool, golf nearby, bsktball, playground, shuffleboard court shuffleboard court, activities (wkends), horseshoes, sports field, v-ball.

Pets welcome, breed restrict. Partial handicap access. Open May 1 - Nov 1. Escort to site. Clubs welcome. Rate in 2010 $50-60 per family. MC/VISA/DISC/AMEX. Member ARVC, CONY.

Phone: (631)477-0022
Address: 690 Queen St, Greenport Long Island, NY 11944
Lat/Lon: 41.10482/-72.38073
Email: mydon1@aol.com
Web: www.easternlikampground.com

SEE AD THIS PAGE

HAINES FALLS—F-9

(NE) NORTH/SOUTH LAKE CAMPGROUND (Catskills SF)—(Greene) *From town: Go 3 mi NE on CR 18.* FACILITIES: 219 sites, 219 no hkups, tenting, dump. RECREATION: lake swim, boating, no motors, canoeing, ramp, lake fishing. Partial handicap access. Open May 5 - Oct 21. Phone: (518)589-5058.

HAMILTON—E-7

(W) Lebanon Reservoir Campground—(Madison) *From jct Hwy 12B & Hwy 75: Go 2-1/2 mi SW on Hwy 75, then 1 mi NW on Hwy 66, then 2 mi SW on Reservoir Rd. Enter on R.* ◊◊◊FACILITIES: 135 sites, 95 full hkups, 30 W&E, (30 amps), 10 no hkups, 45 pull-thrus, family camping, tenting, dump, ltd groc. ◊◊◊RECREATION: lake swim, boating, canoeing, dock, lake fishing, playground. Pets welcome. Partial handicap access. Open May 15 - Oct 10. Rate in 2010 $28-35 per family. Member ARVC, CONY. Phone: (315) 824-2278.

HAMLIN—D-3

HAMLIN BEACH STATE PARK—(Monroe) *From business center: Go 4 mi N on Hwy 19, then 2 mi W on Lake Ontario Pkwy. Enter on R.* FACILITIES: 264 sites, 264 E, tenting, dump, laundry, groceries. RECREATION: lake swim, lake fishing, playground. Pets welcome. Partial handicap access. Open Mid May - Early Oct. Phone: (585)964-2121.

HAMMOND—B-6

(NE) McLear's Cottage Colony & Campground—(St. Lawrence) *From jct Hwy 37 & Hwy 6 (Lake St): Go 3-1/2 mi NE on Lake St (Hwy 6). Enter on R.* ◊◊◊FACILITIES: 35 sites, typical site width 22 ft, 32 ft max RV length, 21 full hkups, 14 W&E, (20/30 amps), family camping, tenting, dump, ltd groc. ◊◊◊RECREATION: lake swim, boating, dock, lake fishing, playground. Pets welcome ($), quantity restrict. Partial handicap access. Open May 1 - Oct 15. Rate in 2010 $29-50 for 2 persons. Member ARVC, CONY. Phone: (315)375-6508.

HAMPTON BAYS—B-5

SEARS BELLOWS (Suffolk County Park)—(Suffolk) *From Sunrise Hwy (Hwy 27, exit 65N): Go N on Bellows Pond Rd.* FACILITIES: 70 sites, 70 no hkups, tenting, dump. RECREATION: lake swim, pond fishing, playground. Open Thurs-Sat Apr 1 - Sep 12. Facilities fully operational May 13 - Sep 12. Phone: (631)852-8290.

HARPURSVILLE—F-7

(NW) Belden Hill Campground—(Broome) *From jct I-88 (exit 5) & Martin Hill Rd: Go 1/2 mi N on Martin Hill Rd, then 1/4 mi E on Hwy 7. Enter on L.* ◊◊◊FACILITIES: 140 sites, typical site width 25 ft, 123 full hkups, 7 W&E, (30/50 amps), 10 no hkups, 23 pull-thrus, family camping, tenting, dump, laundry. ◊◊◊RECREATION: lake swim, pond fishing, playground. Pets welcome, quantity restrict. Open Apr 1 - Oct. Rate in 2010 $29-30 for 2 persons. Phone: (607) 693-1645.

HENDERSON HARBOR—C-6

(W) ASSOCIATION ISLAND RV RESORT & MARINA—(Jefferson) *From I-81 (exit 41) & Hwy 178: Go 12 mi W on Hwy 178, then 2 mi N on Snowshoe Rd, cross bridge to 2nd Island. Enter at end.*

WELCOME

YOUR ONE-OF-A-KIND ISLAND GET-AWAY!
Watch world class sunsets from our unique island resort located a mile into Lake Ontario, accessed by bridge. Enjoy activities on-site or in the local Thousand Islands Region. Our non-membership resort welcomes all RV'ers.

HENDERSON HARBOR—Continued
ASSOCIATION ISLAND RV RESORT & MARINA—Continued

◊◊◊◊◊FACILITIES: 305 sites, typical site width 40 ft, 305 full hkups, (20/30/50 amps), 29 pull-thrus, cable TV, WiFi Instant Internet at site ($), WiFi Internet central location ($), family camping, cabins, dump, laundry, ltd groc, RV supplies, ice, picnic tables, fire rings, wood, controlled access.

◊◊◊◊◊RECREATION: rec hall, rec room/area, coin games, swim pool, lake swim, boating, canoeing, kayaking, ramp, dock, 4 kayak rentals, lake fishing, fishing supplies, fishing guides, golf nearby, bsktball, playground, shuffleboard court shuffleboard court, activities (wkends), tennis, sports field, hiking trails.

Pets welcome, breed restrict, quantity restrict. Partial handicap access. No tents. Open May 15 - Columbus Day. Big rigs welcome. Clubs welcome. Rate in 2010 $35-70 for 2 persons. MC/VISA. ATM. Member ARVC, CONY. FMCA discount.

Text 85386 to (440)725-8687 to see our Visual Tour.

Phone: (800)393-4189
Address: 15530 Snowshoe Rd, Henderson, NY 13650
Lat/Lon: 43.88696/-76.23008
Email: info@airesort.com
Web: www.associationislandresort.com

SEE AD NEXT PAGE

(NE) The Willows on the Lake RV Park & Resort—(Jefferson) *From jct I-81 (exit 41) & Hwy 178: Go 9 mi W on Hwy 178, then 5 mi NE on Hwy 3. Enter on L.* ◊◊◊FACILITIES: 100 sites, 71 full hkups, 9 W&E, (30/50 amps), 20 no hkups, family camping, tenting, dump, laundry, ltd groc. ◊◊◊RECREATION: lake swim, boating, canoeing, dock, lake fishing, play equipment. Pets welcome. Open Apr 15 - Oct 15. Rate in 2010 $28-40 per family. Member ARVC, CONY. Phone: (315)938-5977.

HERKIMER—D-7

(N) GEMS ALONG THE MOHAWK—*From I-90 (exit 30): Go straight 100 yds. Enter at end.* Legends & Heritage of Central N.Y.-68 retail stores under one roof, waterfront dining, boat tours, historic displays & interpretive center. Official Mohawk Valley Visitor's Center. Open all yr.

WELCOME

Phone: (315)717-0077
Address: 5661 St Rt 5, Herkimer, NY 13350
Lat/Lon: 43.01698/-74.99435
Email: diamonds@ntcnet.com
Web: www.gemsalongmohawk.com

SEE AD NEXT PAGE

(N) HERKIMER CRYSTAL CHANDELIER RESTAURANT—*From NE jct Hwy-5 & Hwy-28: Go 7 mi N on Hwy-28. Enter on L.* Casual dining restaurant with chicken, veal, steaks and house specialty ribs. Open May - Oct. Serving dinners Thurs-Sun. MC/VISA/DISC/AMEX.

WELCOME

Phone: (315)891-3366
Address: 4601 St Rt 28 N, Herkimer, NY 13350
Lat/Lon: 43.12773/-74.97672
Email: diamonds@ntcnet.com
Web: www.herkimerdiamond.com

SEE AD NEXT PAGE

(N) HERKIMER DIAMOND MINES—*From NE jct Hwy-5 & Hwy-28: Go 7 mi N on Hwy-28. Enter on L.* Rock shop, gift shop, geological museum, prospecting for Herkimer diamonds, fossiling, childrens reading room. Open Apr 1 - Dec 1. Hours: 9-5, 7 days a week. MC/VISA/DISC.

WELCOME

Phone: (315)891-7355
Address: 4601 St Rt 28 N, Herkimer, NY 13350
Lat/Lon: 43.12856/-74.97606
Email: diamonds@ntcnet.com
Web: www.herkimerdiamond.com

SEE AD NEXT PAGE

(N) KOA-HERKIMER DIAMOND RESORT—(Herkimer) *From northeast jct Hwy 5 & Hwy 28: Go 7 mi N on Hwy 28. Enter on R.*

WELCOME

◊◊◊◊FACILITIES: 117 sites, typical site width 25 ft, 50 full hkups, 45 W&E, (30/50 amps), 50 amps ($), 22 no hkups, some extd stay sites, 31 pull-thrus, cable TV, WiFi Instant Internet at site, phone Internet central location, family camping, tenting, cabins, RV storage, dump, non-guest dump $, laundry, ltd groc, RV

KOA-HERKIMER DIAMOND MINES—Continued on next page

HERKIMER—Continued
KOA-HERKIMER DIAMOND RESORT—Continued

supplies, LP gas by weight/by meter, ice, picnic tables, fire rings, grills, wood.

◇◇◇◇◇RECREATION: rec room/area, equipped pavilion, coin games, swim pool, river swim, canoeing, river fishing, fishing supplies, golf nearby, bsktball, playground, activities, horseshoes, sports field, v-ball.

Pets welcome. Open Apr 15 - Nov 1. Big rigs welcome. Clubs welcome. Rate in 2010 $30-60 for 2 persons. MC/VISA/DISC/AMEX/Debit. KOA discount.

Phone: (800)562-0897
Address: 4621 St Rt 28 N, Herkimer, NY 13350
Lat/Lon: 43.12946/-74.97462
Email: diamonds@ntcnet.com
Web: www.herkimerdiamond.com

SEE AD THIS PAGE

HOLLEY—D-3

(NW) RED ROCK PONDS RV RESORT—(Orleans) *From jct Hwy 98 & Hwy 104: Go 5 mi E on Hwy 104, then 2-1/4 mi S on Fancher Rd, then 1 mi E on Canal Rd. Enter on L.*

WELCOME

◇◇◇◇FACILITIES: 110 sites, typical site width 35 ft, 110 full hkups, (20/30/50 amps), many extd stay sites, 13 pull-thrus, cable TV, WiFi Internet central location, family camping, cabins, dump, non-guest dump $, laundry, ltd groc, RV supplies, LP gas by meter, picnic tables, fire rings, wood.

◇◇◇◇RECREATION: rec room/area, pavilion, coin games, lake swim, 2 rowboat/2 kayak/2 pedal boat rentals, pond fishing, bsktball, playground, activities, (wkends), horseshoes, hiking trails, v-ball.

Pets welcome, breed restrict, quantity restrict. Partial handicap access. No tents. Open May 1 - Oct 31. Big rigs welcome. Rate in 2010 $38 per family. MC/VISA/DISC/AMEX/Debit.

HOLLEY—Continued
RED ROCK PONDS RV RESORT—Continued

Phone: (585)638-2445
Address: 16097 Canal Road, Holley, NY 14470
Lat/Lon: 43.25412/-78.07685
Email: contactus@redrockponds.com
Web: www.redrockponds.com

SEE AD NEXT PAGE

HOUGHTON—F-3

(W) CAMPING AT MARIPOSA PONDS—(Allegany) *From jct Hwy 243 & Hwy 19: Go 3 mi N on Hwy 19, then 1/4 mi W on Hougton College Rd (CR 35), then 1-1/2 mi W on Centerville Rd. Enter on R.*

◆◆◆◆FACILITIES: 82 sites, typical site width 25 ft, 36 ft max RV length, 80 full hkups, 2 W&E, (20/30/50 amps), some extd stay sites (summer), 5 pull-thrus, WiFi Internet central location, family camping, tenting, RV's/park model rentals, cabins, dump, non-guest dump $, portable dump, ltd groc, RV supplies, LP gas by weight, ice, picnic tables, fire rings, wood.

◆◆◆◆◆RECREATION: rec hall, pavilion, swim pool, pond fishing, golf nearby, bsktball, playground, activities, horseshoes, sports field, hiking trails, v-ball.

Pets welcome, quantity restrict. Partial handicap access. Open May 1 - Oct 15. Clubs welcome. Rate in 2010 $27-30 for 4 persons. MC/VISA/DISC. Member ARVC, CONY.

Phone: (585)567-4211
Address: 7632 Centerville Rd, Houghton, NY 14744
Lat/Lon: 42.44026/-78.16905
Email: mariposaponds@frontiernet.net
Web: www.mariposaponds.com

SEE AD THIS PAGE

HUDSON—F-9

LAKE TAGHKANIC STATE PARK—(Columbia) *From business center: Go 11 mi S on Hwy-82.* FACILITIES: 171 sites, 171 no hkups, tenting, dump, groceries. RECREATION: lake swim, boating, no motors, canoeing, ramp, lake fishing, playground. No pets. Partial handicap access. Open all yr. Facilities fully operational Early May - Oct 30. Phone: (518)851-3633.

INDIAN LAKE—C-8

(S) LEWEY LAKE PUBLIC CAMPGROUND (Adirondack SF)—(Hamilton) *From business center: Go 12 mi S on Hwy-30.* FACILITIES: 181 sites, 181 no hkups, tenting, dump. RECREATION: lake swim, boating, canoeing, ramp, lake fishing. Open May 16 - Oct 13. Phone: (518)648-5266.

INLET—C-8

(E) LIMEKILN LAKE (Adirondack SF)—(Hamilton) *From business center: Go 1 mi E on Hwy-28, then 2 mi S.* FACILITIES: 271 sites, 271 no hkups, tenting, dump. RECREATION: lake swim, boating, canoeing, ramp, lake fishing. Partial handicap access. Open May 16 - Sep 1. Phone: (315)357-4401.

ITHACA—F-5

(SW) BUTTERMILK FALLS STATE PARK—(Tompkins) *From business center: Go 2 mi S on Hwy-13.* FACILITIES: 60 sites, typical site width 20 ft, 35 ft max RV length, 60 no hkups, 5 pull-thrus, tenting, dump. RECREATION: lake/stream fishing, playground. Partial handicap access. Open all yr. Facilities fully operational Mid May - Mid Oct. Phone: (607)273-5761.

The "New York Post", established in 1803 by Alexander Hamilton, is the oldest running newspaper in the United States.

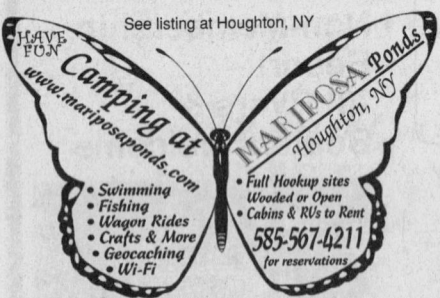

ITHACA—Continued

(W) PINECREEK CAMPGROUND—(Tompkins) *From jct Hwy 13 & Hwy 79: Go 7 mi S on Hwy 79, then 3-1/2 mi S on CR 327 (Hulsey Valley), then 1/4 mi S on Hines Rd, then 500 ft W on Rockwell Rd. Enter on R.*

◆◆◆FACILITIES: 162 sites, typical site width 40 ft, 57 full hkups, 56 W&E, (20/30/50 amps), 49 no hkups, some extd stay sites (summer), 5 pull-thrus, family camping, tenting, RV's/park model rentals, cabins, RV storage, dump, non-guest dump $, ltd groc, ice, picnic tables, fire rings, wood.

◆◆◆RECREATION: rec room/area, pavilion, coin games, swim pool, pond/stream fishing, golf nearby, bsktball, playground, horseshoes, sports field, v-ball.

Pets welcome, breed restrict. Open May 1 - Oct 15. Big rigs welcome. Rate in 2010 $32-45 for 4 persons. MC/VISA. Member ARVC, CONY.

Phone: (607)273-1974
Address: 28 Rockwell Rd, Newfield, NY 14867
Lat/Lon: 42.40734/-76.61138
Email: info@pinecreekcampground.com
Web: www.pinecreekcampground.com

SEE AD THIS PAGE

(S) ROBERT H TREMAN STATE PARK—(Tompkins) *From business center: Go 5 mi S on Hwy-13, then E on 327.* FACILITIES: 72 sites, 11 E, (15 amps), 61 no hkups, tenting, dump. RECREATION: lake swim, stream fishing, playground. Pets welcome. Partial handicap access. Open all yr. Facilities fully operational Mid May - Nov 30. Phone: (607)273-3440.

(N) Spruce Row Campground—(Tompkins) *From north jct Hwy 13 & Hwy 96: Go 7 mi NW on Hwy 96, then 1/2 mi N on Jacksonville Rd, then 1-1/4 mi E on Kraft Rd. Enter on R.* ◆◆◆FACILITIES: 213 sites, typical site width 40 ft, 38 ft max RV length, 99 full hkups, 99 W&E, (20/30 amps), 15 no hkups, 30 pull-thrus, family camping, tenting, dump, ltd groc. ◆◆◆◆RECREATION: swim pool, pond fishing, playground. Pets welcome, quantity restrict. Partial handicap access. Open May 1 - Columbus Day. Rate in 2010 $33-36 per family. Member ARVC, CONY. Phone: (607)387-9225.

TAUGHANNOCK FALLS STATE PARK—(Tompkins) *From business center: Go 8 mi N on Hwy-89.* FACILITIES: 76 sites, 16 E, 60 no hkups, tenting, dump. RECREATION: lake swim, boating, canoeing, ramp, dock, lake fishing, playground. Partial handicap access. Open all yr. Facilities fully operational Apr 24 - Mid Oct. Phone: (607)387-6739.

JAMESTOWN—F-1

(S) Hidden Valley Camping Area—(Chautauqua) *From jct I-86 & SR-60 (exit 12): Go 5.9 mi S on SR-60, then 3.1 mi S on SR-62, then 0.6 mi W on Riverside Rd, then 500 ft S on Kiantone Rd. Enter on R.* ◆◆◆FACILITIES: 225 sites, typical site width 40 ft, 225 W&E, (20/30/50 amps), 30 pull-thrus, family camping, tenting, dump, laundry, ltd groc. ◆◆◆◆RECREATION: swim pool, pond fishing, playground. Pets welcome. Open Apr 15 - Oct 15. Rate in 2010 $28 for 2 persons. Member ARVC, CONY. Phone: (716)569-5433. FMCA discount.

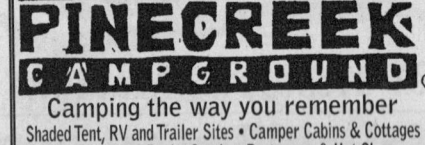

JAVA CENTER—E-3

(N) Beaver Meadow Family Campground—(Wyoming) *From jct Hwy 78/98/77: Go 3/4 mi N on Hwy 77, then 500 ft E on Beaver Meadow Rd. Enter on L.* ◆◆◆FACILITIES: 290 sites, typical site width 30 ft, 150 W&E, (20/30/50 amps), 50 amps ($), 140 no hkups, family camping, tenting, dump, non-guest dump $, portable dump, laundry, ltd groc, RV supplies, LP gas by weight/by meter, ice, picnic tables, wood. ◆◆◆RECREATION: swim pool, lake swim, pond fishing, fishing supplies, playground, activities, horseshoes, hiking trails, v-ball. Pets welcome. Open May 1 - Columbus Day. Rate in 2010 $20-30 per family. MC/VISA. Member ARVC, CONY. CCUSA 50% Discount.

Phone: (585)457-3101
Address: 1455 Beaver Meadow Rd, Java Center, NY 14082
Lat/Lon: 42.66123/-78.38541
Email: beavermeadowcampground@yahoo.com
Web: www.beavermeadowcampground.com

Reserve Online at Woodalls.com

JOHNSTOWN—E-8

(W) Royal Mountain Campsite—(Fulton) *From jct I-90 (exit 29) & Hwy 10: Go 13 mi N on Hwy 10. Enter on L.* ◆◆◆FACILITIES: 69 sites, typical site width 30 ft, 65 W&E, (15/20/30/50 amps), 4 no hkups, 6 pull-thrus, tenting, dump, laundry. ◆◆RECREATION: pond fishing. Pets welcome. Open Apr 1 - Nov 1. Rate in 2010 $27 for 2 persons. Phone: (518)762-1946.

KEESEVILLE—B-10

POKE-O-MOONSHINE CAMPGROUND (Adirondack SF)—(Essex) *From town: Go 6 mi S on Hwy 9.* FACILITIES: 25 sites, 30 ft max RV length, 25 no hkups, tenting. RECREATION: playground. Partial handicap access. Open Mid May - Labor Day. Phone: (518)834-9045.

KENDAIA—E-5

SAMPSON STATE PARK—(Seneca) *In town off Hwy 96A.* FACILITIES: 362 sites, typical site width 15 ft, 35 ft max RV length, 301 E, (30 amps), 61 no hkups, tenting, dump, ltd groc. RECREATION: lake swim, boating, canoeing, ramp, dock, lake fishing, playground. Pets welcome. Partial handicap access. Open all yr. Facilities fully operational Late Apr - Mid Nov. Phone: (315)585-6392.

KEUKA PARK—E-4

KEUKA LAKE STATE PARK—(Yates) *From west town limits: Go 1 mi SW on Hwy-54A.* FACILITIES: 150 sites, 53 E, (30 amps), 97 no hkups, tenting, dump, ltd groc. RECREATION: lake swim, boating, 45 hp limit, canoeing, ramp, lake fishing, playground. Open all yr. Facilities fully operational May 4 - Oct 21. Phone: (315)536-3666.

KINGSTON—F-9

See listings at Saugerties

LAKE CHAMPLAIN—B-10

See listings at Ausable Chasm & Plattsburgh, NY & Grand Isle, North Hero & South Hero, VT

LAKE GEORGE—D-9

LAKE GEORGE—Continued on next page

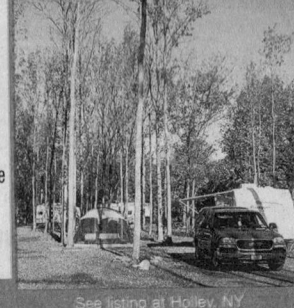

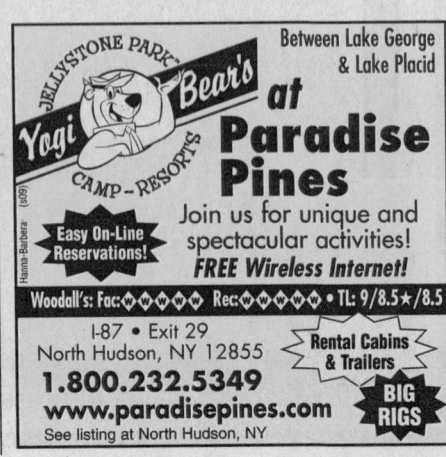

Just off Exit 20 of Interstate 87, near the area's most popular attractions, restaurants and shops.

Rated one of the finest resorts in the Adirondacks, Lake George RV Park offers the heart and soul of camping plus every amenity you can imagine.

HERE'S SOME OF OUR INCLUDED AMENITIES!

- **25 On-site RV Rentals available**
- 390 perfectly designed campsites
- WI-FI Internet Service at all sites ($)
- 30 and 50 amps, water, sewer & cable TV at all sites
- Paved roads throughout Park
- 2 hot water Laundromats
- Fully stocked general store
- 2 video arcades with 10 pool tables
- "Camper Café" and ice cream parlor*
- Adirondack style adult lounge
- 4 playgrounds
- Indoor heated pool
- 2 outdoor heated pools*
- 2 kiddie pools*
- 2 indoor movie theaters*
- Professional live entertainment (Summer)
- Free trolley shuttle to over 100 outlet stores/restaurants*
- Municipal trolley service to Lake George Village ($)
- 7 all-weather tennis courts
- Paved bike trails
- 8 free paddle boats on private pond*
- Adult fitness center
- Extensive sports courts
- Stocked bass fishing pond
- French Mountain hiking trail

*Available summer season and most weekends

FAC: ⓌⓌⓌⓌⓌ
REC: ⓌⓌⓌⓌⓌ

Rated First Choice for RV Camping and Wilderness Lodging.

518-792-3775 • WWW.LAKEGEORGERVPARK.COM • 74 STATE ROUTE 149, LAKE GEORGE, NY 12845-3501 TL RATED: 9.5/10★/9.5

LAKE GEORGE—Continued

(N) ADIRONDACK ADVENTURE RESORTS-SCHROON RIVER—(Warren) *From jct I-87 (exit 23) & Diamond Point Rd: Go 1/4 mi E on Diamond Point Rd, then 4-1/2 mi N on E Schroon River Rd. Enter on L.*

WELCOME

◆◆◆FACILITIES: 153 sites, typical site width 25 ft, 96 full hkups, 57 W&E, (30 amps), 70 pull-thrus, family camping, tenting, RV's/park model rentals, cabins, RV storage, dump, non-guest dump $, laundry, ltd groc, RV supplies, LP gas by weight/by meter, ice, picnic tables, fire rings, grills, wood.

◆◆◆RECREATION: rec hall, swim pool, boating, canoeing, 2 rowboat/6 canoe rentals, river fishing, bsktball, playground, shuffleboard court shuffleboard court, activities (wkends), horseshoes.

Pets welcome, breed restrict. Partial handicap access. Open May 15 - Columbus Day. Clubs welcome. Rate in 2010 $35-39 for 2 persons. MC/VISA. Member ARVC, CONY.

Phone: (800)340-CAMP
Address: 969 E Schroon River Rd, Diamond Point, NY 12824
Lat/Lon: 43.55058/-73.73833
Email: camping@charterinternet.com
Web: www.adirondackadventureresorts.com

SEE AD NEXT PAGE

(N) ADIRONDACK CAMPING VILLAGE—(Warren) *From jct I-87 (exit 20) & US9: Go 4 -3/4 mi N on I-87 (exit 22) & Hwy 9N/US 9, then 1-1/2 mi N on US 9. Enter on R.*

WELCOME

◆◆◆◆FACILITIES: 175 sites, typical site width 35 ft, 74 full hkups, 90 W&E, (20/30/50 amps), 11 no hkups, some extd stay sites (sum-

ADIRONDACK CAMPING VILLAGE—Continued on next page

mer), 13 pull-thrus, cable TV, WiFi Internet central location, family camping, tenting, shower$, dump, laundry, ltd groc, RV supplies, ice, picnic tables, fire rings, wood, controlled access.

◇◇◇◇RECREATION: rec room/area, pavilion, coin games, swim pool, wading pool, fishing supplies, golf nearby, bsktball, playground, shuffleboard court 2 shuffleboard courts, activities, horseshoes, sports field, hiking trails, v-ball.

Pets welcome. Open Mid May - Mid Sept. Big rigs welcome. Clubs welcome. Rate in 2010 $30-54 for 2 persons. MC/VISA/DISC/AMEX/Debit. Member ARVC, CONY.

Text 107940 to (440)725-8687 to see our Visual Tour.

Phone: (518)668-5226
Address: 43 Finkle Farm Rd, Lake George, NY 12845
Lat/Lon: 43.45261/-73.73376
Email: info@adirondackcampingvillage.com
Web: www.adirondackcampingvillage.com

SEE AD PAGE 551

(N) HEARTHSTONE POINT CAMPGROUND (Adirondack SF)—(Warren) *From business center: Go 2 mi N on Hwy-9N.* FACILITIES: 251 sites, 251 no hkups, 5 pull-thrus, tenting, dump. RECREATION: boating, canoeing, lake fishing, playground. Partial handicap access. Open May 16 - Sep 7. Phone: (518)668-5193.

(S) KING PHILLIP'S CAMPGROUND & RESORT—(Warren) *From jct I-87 & Rt 9N (exit 21): Go 1/4 mi N on Rt 9N, then 3/4 mi S on Rt 9, then 100 yards E on Bloody Pond Rd. Enter on R.*

WELCOME

CONVENIENTLY LOCATED TO ATTRACTIONS
We are a CLEAN & QUIET family campground surrounded by activities sure to please the whole family. We are the closest to Lake George Village and Beaches and are on the Trolley and Bike routes to area attractions.

◇◇◇◇FACILITIES: 215 sites, typical site width 40 ft, 196 full hkups, 16 W&E, (20/30 amps), 3 no hkups, many extd stay sites (summer), 15 pull-thrus, cable TV, WiFi Instant Internet at site, family camping, tenting, dump, laundry, groceries, RV supplies, LP gas by weight/by meter, ice, picnic tables, fire rings, wood, controlled access.

◇◇◇RECREATION: rec room/area, pavilion, coin games, swim pool, golf nearby, bsktball, playground, activities, (wkends), horseshoes, sports field, hiking trails, v-ball.

Pets welcome. Open May 1 - Nov 1. Escort to site. Clubs welcome. Green Friendly. Rate in 2010 $29-45 for 2 persons. MC/VISA/Debit. Member ARVC, CONY. CCUSA 50% Discount. CCUSA reservations Required, CCUSA max stay Unlimited, CCUSA disc. not avail F,Sa, CCUSA disc. not avail holidays. Discount available May 1-June 24 & Sep 12-Nov 1, excluding special events.

Phone: (518)668-5763
Address: 14 Bloody Pond Rd, Lake George, NY 12845
Lat/Lon: 43.39534/-73.70214
Email: info@kingphillipscampground.com
Web: www.kingphillipscampground.com

SEE AD PAGE 551

(S) LAKE GEORGE BATTLEGROUND CAMPGROUND (Adirondack SF)—(Warren) *From town: Go 1/4 mi S on US-9.* FACILITIES: 68 sites, 68 no hkups, tenting, dump. RECREATION: boating, lake fishing. Partial handicap access. Open May 2 - Oct 13. Phone: (518)668-3348.

(S) Lake George Campsites (Morgan RV Resorts)—(Warren) *S'bound from jct I-87 (exit 20) & US 9: Go 1 mi S on US 9. Entrance on right. N'bound from jct I-87 (exit 19) & US 9: Go 1 mi N on US 9. Enter on L.* ◇◇◇FACILITIES: 245 sites, typical site width 25 ft, 57 full hkups, 160 W&E, (20/30 amps), 28 no hkups, 45 pull-thrus, family camping, tenting, dump, laundry, ltd groc. ◇◇◇RECREATION: swim pool, playground. Pets welcome, breed restrict. Partial handicap access. Open all yr. Facilities fully operational Apr 15 - Oct 15. Rate in 2010 $33-49 for 2 persons. Member ARVC, CONY. Phone: (518)798-6218.

(N) LAKE GEORGE ESCAPE RESORT—(Warren) *From jct I-87 (Exit 23) & Diamond Point Rd: Go 1/4 mi E on Diamond Point Rd, then 3/4 mi N on East Schroon River Rd. Enter on L.*

WELCOME

◇◇◇◇◇FACILITIES: 519 sites, typical site width 40 ft, 278 full hkups, 151 W&E, (20/30/50 amps), 90 no hkups, 97 pull-thrus, cable TV, WiFi Instant Internet at site, cable Internet central location, family camping, tenting, RV's/park model rentals, cabins, RV storage, dump, laundry, groceries, RV supplies, LP gas by weight/by meter, ice, picnic tables, patios, fire rings, wood, controlled access.

◇◇◇◇◇RECREATION: rec hall, equipped pavilion, coin games, 2 swim pools, river swim, boating, 10 hp limit, canoeing, kayaking, dock, 16 rowboat/25 canoe/10 kayak/20 motorboat rentals, river/pond fishing, fishing supplies, mini-golf, ($), golf nearby, bsktball, 10 bike rentals, playground, shuffleboard court 2 shuffleboard courts, activities, tennis, horseshoes, sports field, hiking trails, v-ball, local tours. Rec open to public.

Pets welcome, quantity restrict. Partial handicap access. Open May 1 - Nov 15. Big rigs welcome. Clubs welcome. Green Friendly. Rate in 2010 $24-65 for 2 persons. MC/VISA/DISC/AMEX. ATM. Member ARVC, CONY.

Phone: (800)327-3188
Address: 175 E Schroon River Rd, Lake George, NY 12845
Lat/Lon: 43.50105/-73.74795
Email: info@lakegeorgeescape.com
Web: www.lakegeorgeescape.com

Reserve Online at Woodalls.com

SEE AD PAGE 549 AND AD ACRA PAGE 536

(S) LAKE GEORGE RV PARK—(Warren) *From jct I-87 (Exit 20-Northway) & Hwy-149/US-9: Go 3/4 mi N on Hwy-149/US-9, then 1/2 mi E on Hwy-149. Enter on R.*

GET READY FOR THE TIME OF YOUR LIFE!
Lake George RV Park embodies the heart and soul of the camping experience plus so much more. Rated one of the finest resorts in the Adirondacks. With every amenity you can imagine. Located near the best family attractions.

◇◇◇◇◇FACILITIES: 390 sites, typical site width 40 ft, 390 full hkups, (30/50 amps), 250 pull-thrus, cable TV, WiFi Instant Internet at site ($), phone Internet central location, family camping, RV's/park model rentals, RV storage, dump, laundry, groceries, RV supplies, LP gas by weight/by meter, ice, picnic tables, patios, fire rings, grills, wood, controlled access.

◇◇◇◇◇RECREATION: rec hall, rec room/area, pavilion, coin games, 3 swim pools, wading pool, 9 pedal boat rentals, pond/stream fishing, fishing supplies, golf nearby, bsktball, playground, shuffleboard court 4 shuffleboard courts, activities, tennis, horseshoes, sports field, hiking trails, v-ball, local tours.

Pets welcome. Partial handicap access. No tents. Open First Fri in May - Columbus Day. Big rigs welcome. Clubs welcome. Green Friendly. Rate in 2010 $50-72 for 2 persons. MC/VISA/DISC/AMEX/Debit. ATM. Member ARVC.

Text 86100 to (440)725-8687 to see our Visual Tour.

Phone: (518)792-3775
Address: 74 State Route 149, Lake George, NY 12845-3501
Lat/Lon: 43.37076/-73.69112
Email: info@lakegeorgervpark.com
Web: www.lakegeorgervpark.com

SEE AD PAGE 550 AND AD TRAVEL SECTION PAGE 527

(SE) LEDGEVIEW RV PARK—(Warren) *From jct I-87 (exit 20-Northway) & Hwy 149/US 9: Go 3/4 mi N on Hwy 149/US 9, then 1-1/2 mi E on Hwy 149. Enter on L.*

WELCOME

LEDGEVIEW - COZY, QUALITY CAMPING
Our clean and impeccably maintained facilities are conveniently located near all of the favorite Lake George attractions - yet just far enough away to guarantee your peace and privacy. 30 & 50 Amp service. No pets.

LEDGEVIEW RV PARK—Continued on next page

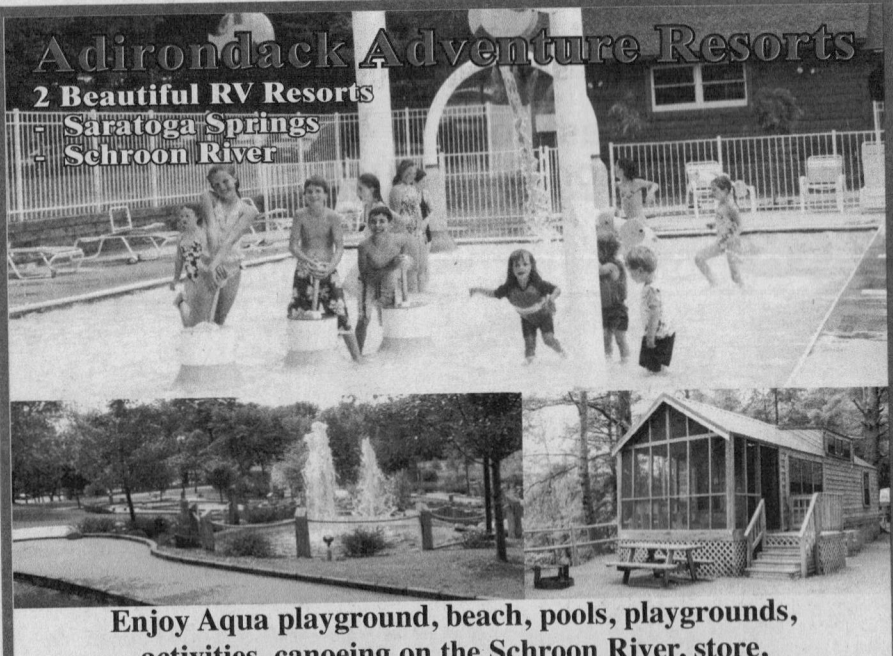

LAKE GEORGE—Continued
LEDGEVIEW RV PARK—Continued

◇◇◇◇◇FACILITIES: 130 sites, typical site width 50 ft, 130 full hkups, (30/50 amps), 50 amps ($), some extd stay sites (summer), 17 pull-thrus, cable TV, WiFi Internet central location, family camping, RV storage, laundry, ltd groc, RV supplies, ice, picnic tables, fire rings, wood, controlled access.

◇◇◇◇RECREATION: rec hall, pavilion, coin games, swim pool, golf nearby, bsktball, 10 bike rentals, playground, shuffleboard court 2 shuffleboard courts, horseshoes, v-ball.

No pets. Partial handicap access. No tents. Open May 1 - Columbus Day. No pets. Big rigs welcome. Clubs welcome. Rate in 2010 $39-45 for 2 persons. MC/VISA/Debit. Member ARVC, CONY.

Phone: (518)798-6621
Address: 321 State Route 149, Lake George, NY 12845
Lat/Lon: 43.37554/-73.66998
Email: info1@ledgeview.com
Web: www.ledgeview.com

SEE AD PAGE 551

(NW) River View Campground—(Warren) *From jct I-87 (exit 23) & Hwy 35: Go 1/4 mi W on Hwy 35, then 1/4 mi N on Hwy 9. Enter on R.* ◇◇◇FACILITIES: 135 sites, 70 full hkups, 55 W&E, (20/30 amps), 10 no hkups, family camping, tenting, dump, ltd groc. ◇◇◇RECREATION: swim pool, river swim, river fishing, playground. Pets welcome, breed restrict. Open May 15 - Oct 15. Rate in 2010 $37-47. Phone: (518) 623-9444.

(S) Whippoorwill Campground—(Warren) *From jct I-87 (Northway exit 21) & Hwy-9N/US-9: Go 1-1/4 mi S on US-9. Enter on L.* ◇◇FACILITIES: 46 sites, typical site width 40 ft, 4 full hkups, 33 W&E, 9 E, (20/30/50 amps), 12 pull-thrus, family camping, tenting, dump, laundry. ◇◇RECREATION: swim pool, playground. Pets welcome. Open Memorial Day - Labor Day. Big rigs welcome. Rate in 2010 $33-37 for 2 persons. Phone: (518)668-5565.

LAKE LUZERNE—D-9

(N) Half Mile Ranch Camping Resort—(Warren) *From jct I-87 (exit 21) & Hwy 9N: Go 8-1/4 mi SW on Hwy 9N. Enter on R.* ◇◇FACILITIES: 98 sites, typical site width 25 ft, 30 full hkups, 38 W&E, (20/30/50 amps), 30 no hkups, tenting, dump. ◇◇◇RECREATION: swim pool, lake fishing, playground. Pets welcome. Open all yr. Big rigs welcome. Rate in 2010 $34-39 per family. Phone: (518)696-3113.

(N) Mt. Kenyon Family Campground—(Warren) *From jct I-87 (Northway exit 21) & Hwy-9N: Go 3-3/4 mi S on Hwy-9N. Enter on R.* ◇◇◇FACILITIES: 110 sites, typical site width 25 ft, 28 full hkups, 57 W&E, 7 E, (15/20 amps), 18 no hkups, a/c not allowed, WiFi Internet central location, family camping, tenting, dump, laundry, ltd groc, ice, picnic tables, fire rings, wood. ◇◇◇RECREATION: swim pool, stream fishing, playground, shuffleboard court shuffleboard court, horseshoes, hiking trails. Pets welcome. Open May 15 - Sep 30. Rate in 2010 $28-30 for 4 persons. MC/VISA/DISC. CCUSA 50% Discount. CCUSA reservations Recommended, CCUSA max stay 2 days, Cash only for CCUSA disc., CCUSA disc. not avail S,M,Th, CCUSA disc. not avail F,Sa, CCUSA disc. not avail holidays. A/C not allowed.

Phone: (518)696-2905
Address: 1571 Lake Ave, Lake Luzerne, NY 12846
Lat/Lon: 43.37963/-73.77773
Web: www.mtkenyon.com

LAKE PLACID—B-9

NORTH POLE CAMPING RESORT—*From Lake Placid Village: Go 12-3/4 mi NE on Hwy 86. Enter on R.*
SEE PRIMARY LISTING AT WILMINGTON AND AD THIS PAGE

(S) Whispering Pines Campground—(Essex) *From jct Hwy 86 & Hwy 73: Go 6 mi E on Hwy 73 (Caution poor visibility). Enter on L.* ◇◇FACILITIES: 80 sites, typical site width 35 ft, 9 full hkups, 42 W&E, 2 E, (15/20/30 amps), 27 no hkups, 35 pull-thrus, family camping, tenting, dump, groceries. ◇◇RECREATION: playground. Pets welcome. Open May 15 - Oct 15. Rate in 2010 $25-32 for 2 persons. Phone: (518)523-9322.

LAKE PLEASANT—D-8

LITTLE SAND POINT (Adirondack SF)—(Hamilton) *From business center: Go 7 mi SW on Hwy 8, then 3 mi N on Old Piseco Rd.* FACILITIES: 78 sites, 78 no hkups, tenting, dump. RECREATION: boating, canoeing, ramp, lake fishing. Partial handicap access. Open May 16 - Sep 1. Phone: (518)548-7585.

LAKEVILLE—E-4

(S) Conesus Lake Campground—(Livingston) *From jct I-390 (exit 8) & US 20A: Go 2-1/2 mi E on US 20A, then 5-3/4 mi S on E Lake Rd. Enter on L.* ◇◇◇FACILITIES: 115 sites, typical site width 35 ft, 35 ft max RV length, 75 full hkups, 35 W&E, (20/30/50 amps), 5 no hkups, family camping, tenting, dump, laundry, groceries. ◇◇◇◇RECREATION: swim pool, lake swim, boating, canoeing, dock, lake fishing, playground. Pets welcome, quantity restrict. Partial handicap access. Open May 15 - Oct 15. Rate in 2010 $32-37 per family. Member ARVC, CONY. Phone: (585) 346-2267.

LE ROY—E-3

(N) FROST RIDGE CAMPGROUND—(Genesee) *From jct I-90 (exit 47) & Hwy 19: Go 1/2 mi S on Hwy 19, then 1/2 mi E on North Rd., then 1/2 mi S on Conlon Rd. Enter on L.*

◇◇◇FACILITIES: 120 sites, typical site width 50 ft, 50 full hkups, 55 W&E, (20/30/50 amps), 15 no hkups, many extd stay sites (summer), 15 pull-thrus, WiFi Instant Internet at site, WiFi Internet central location, family camping, tenting, RV's/park model rentals, cabins, RV storage, dump, non-guest dump $, portable dump, laundry, ltd groc, RV supplies, LP gas by weight/by meter, ice, picnic tables, fire rings, wood.

◇◇◇◇RECREATION: rec hall, pavilion, coin games, swim pool, mini-golf, ($), golf nearby, bsktball, 5 bike rentals, playground, activities, (wkends), horseshoes, sports field, hiking trails.

Pets welcome, breed restrict, quantity restrict. Partial handicap access. Open all yr. Facilities fully operational May 1 - Oct 31. Big rigs welcome. Escort to site. Clubs welcome. Rate in 2010 $28-32 per family. MC/VISA/DISC/Debit. Member ARVC, CONY.

LE ROY—Continued
FROST RIDGE CAMPGROUND—Continued

Phone: (585)768-4883
Address: 8101 Conlon Rd, Leroy, NY 14482
Lat/Lon: 43.02060/-77.95474
Email: info@frostridge.com
Web: frostridge.com

SEE AD ROCHESTER PAGE 562

(N) Timberline Lake Park—(Genesee) *From jct I-90 (exit 47), Hwy 19 & I-490: Go 1/10 mi N on I-490 (exit 1), then 1/10 mi SW on Hwy 19, then 1 mi E on Vallance Rd. Westbound I-490 (exit 1): Go 1/10 mi NE on county road, then 1 mi E on Vallance Rd. Enter on R.* ◇◇◇FACILITIES: 130 sites, typical site width 35 ft, 94 full hkups, 36 W&E, (20/30/50 amps), 10 pull-thrus, family camping, tenting, dump, laundry, ltd groc. ◇◇◇RECREATION: swim pool, pond fishing, playground. Pets welcome. Open May 1 - Oct 15. Big rigs welcome. Rate in 2010 $26-28 per family. Member ARVC, CONY. Phone: (585)768-6635. FMCA discount.

LEWIS—B-9

(N) Magic Pines Family Campground—(Essex) *From jct I-87 (exit 32 Lewis) & Hwy 12: Go 1-1/2 mi W on Hwy 12, then 3 mi N on US 9. Enter on R.* ◇◇FACILITIES: 95 sites, typical site width 50 ft, 42 full hkups, 32 W&E, (20/30/50 amps), 50 amps ($), 21 no hkups, 5 pull-thrus, family camping, tenting, dump, laundry. ◇◇◇RECREATION: swim pool, playground. Pets welcome. Open May 15 - Oct 15. Rate in 2010 $24-28 for 2 persons. Phone: (518)873-2288.

LIVINGSTON MANOR—F-8

BEAVERKILL CAMPGROUND (Catskills SF)—(Sullivan) *From business center: Go 7 mi NE on CR 151.* FACILITIES: 52 sites, 30 ft max RV length, 52 no hkups, 45 pull-thrus, tenting, dump. RECREATION: river fishing. Partial handicap access. Open Mid May - Labor Day. Phone: (845)439-4281.

LIVINGSTON MANOR—Continued on next page

LIVINGSTON MANOR—Continued

(NW) LITTLE POND CAMPGROUND (Catskill SF)—(Delaware) *From Hwy 17 in town: Go 14 mi NE on county roads 151, 152 & 154, then 1/10 mi NE on Big Pond Rd, then NW on Little Pond Rd.* FACILITIES: 75 sites, 75 no hkups, tenting, dump. RECREATION: lake swim, boating, no motors, canoeing, ramp, lake fishing, playground. Partial handicap access. Open May 19 - Oct 8. Phone: (845)439-5480.

(NE) MONGAUP POND (Catskills SF)—(Sullivan) *From business center: Go 6 mi E on CR 81 & CR 82 to DeBruce, then 3 mi N on Mongaup Rd.* FACILITIES: 163 sites, 163 no hkups, tenting, dump. RECREATION: lake swim, boating, no motors, canoeing, ramp, pond fishing. Partial handicap access. Open May 19 - Oct 8. Phone: (845)439-4233.

LOCKPORT—D-2

(NE) NIAGARA COUNTY CAMPING RESORT—(Niagara) *From jct Hwy 31 & Hwy 78: Go 4 mi N on Hwy 78, then 1/4 mi N on Hwy 78/104, then 2-1/2 mi E on Wheeler Rd. Enter on L.*

WELCOME

◊◊◊FACILITIES: 240 sites, 180 W&E, (20/30/50 amps), 60 no hkups, many extd stay sites (summer), 47 pull-thrus, cable TV, WiFi Instant Internet at site, family camping, tenting, cabins, dump, portable dump, ltd groc, RV supplies, ice, picnic tables, fire rings, wood, controlled access.

◊◊◊RECREATION: pavilion, lake swim, lake fishing, fishing supplies, mini-golf, golf nearby, bsktball, playground, activities, (wkends), horseshoes, sports field.

Pets welcome. Open May 15 - Oct 15. Clubs welcome. Rate in 2010 $29-31 per family. MC/VISA/DISC/Debit. Member ARVC, CONY.

Phone: (716)434-3991
Address: 7369 Wheeler Rd, Lockport, NY 14094
Lat/Lon: 43.22915/-78.63009
Email: camp@niagaracamping.com
Web: www.niagaracamping.com

SEE AD NIAGARA FALLS PAGE 558

LONG ISLAND—B-3

W.E.S. TRAILER SALES INC.—*From I-495 (Long Island Expy) (exit 68) & Hwy 46: Go 4 mi N on Hwy 46, then 3 mi E on Hwy 25. Enter on L.*

WELCOME

SEE PRIMARY LISTING AT WADING RIVER AND AD WADING RIVER PAGE 564

LONG LAKE—C-8

(NW) LAKE EATON CAMPGROUND (Adirondack SF)—(Hamilton) *From business center: Go 2 mi NW on Hwy-30.* FACILITIES: 135 sites, 30 ft max RV length, 135 no hkups, tenting, dump. RECREATION: lake swim, boating, canoeing, ramp, lake fishing. Partial handicap access. Open May 2 - Oct 13. Phone: (518)624-2641.

LAKE HARRIS CAMPGROUND (Adirondack SF)—(Essex) *From business center: Go 14 mi E on Hwy-28N to Newcomb then 3 mi N.* FACILITIES: 90 sites, 90 no hkups, tenting, dump. RECREATION: boating, canoeing, ramp, lake fishing. Partial handicap access. Open Mid May - Early Sep. Phone: (518)582-2503.

LOWVILLE—C-7

(S) WHETSTONE GULF STATE PARK—(Lewis) *From business center: Go 8 mi S on Hwy 26 S.* FACILITIES: 62 sites, 62 no hkups, tenting, dump. RECREATION: lake swim, canoeing, lake fishing, playground. Pets welcome. Partial handicap access. Open May 18 - Sep 17. Phone: (315)376-6630.

MALONE—A-8

See listings at Duane & Westville Center

MASSENA—A-8

(E) MASSENA INTERNATIONAL KAMPGROUND—(St. Lawrence) *From jct Hwy 56 & Hwy 37: Go 6 mi E on Hwy 37, then 200' N on O'Neil Rd, then 1/4 mi E on Trippany Rd, then 1/4 mi N on Hwy 42A. Enter on R.*

WELCOME

◊◊◊◊FACILITIES: 142 sites, typical site width 35 ft, 99 full hkups, 40 W&E, (20/30/50 amps), 50 amps ($), 3 no hkups, some extd stay sites

MASSENA—Continued
MASSENA INTERNATIONAL KAMPGROUND—Continued

(summer), 1 pull-thrus, cable TV, cable Internet central location, family camping, tenting, cabins, RV storage, dump, non-guest dump $, laundry, ltd groc, RV supplies, LP gas by weight/by meter, ice, picnic tables, fire rings, grills, wood.

◊◊◊RECREATION: rec hall, swim pool, wading pool, river fishing, golf nearby, bsktball, playground, activities, (wkends), horseshoes, sports field, v-ball.

Pets welcome. Open May 1 - Oct 15. Big rigs welcome. Clubs welcome. Rate in 2010 $30-35 for 2 persons. MC/VISA/AMEX/Debit. Member ARVC, CONY.

Phone: (315)769-9483
Address: 84 CR 42 A, Massena, NY 13662
Lat/Lon: 44.95790/-74.82966
Email: massenakamp@earthlink.net
Web: www.massenainternationalkampground.com

SEE AD THIS PAGE

(E) ROBERT MOSES STATE PARK—(St. Lawrence) *From town: Go 5 mi NE on Hwy 131, then 3 mi N.* FACILITIES: 197 sites, 104 E, (15/30 amps), 93 no hkups, tenting, dump. RECREATION: river swim, boating, canoeing, ramp, river fishing, playground. Partial handicap access. Open May 26 - Oct 8. Phone: (315)769-8663.

MECHANICVILLE—E-9

(E) Adventure Bound Camping Resort at Deer Run—(Rensselaer) *From jct I-87 (Northway exit 9) & Hwy 146: Go 5 mi NE on Hwy 146, then 2-1/4 mi N on Hwy 4/Hwy32, then 1-1/4 mi E on Hwy 67, then 1-1/2 mi N on Deer Run Dr. Enter at end.* ◊◊◊FACILITIES: 394 sites, typical site width 30 ft, 370 full hkups, 24 W&E, (30 amps), 230 pull-thrus, family camping, tenting, dump, laundry, ltd groc. ◊◊◊◊◊RECREATION: 3 swim pools, playground. Pets welcome. Partial handicap access. Open May 1 - Oct 15. Rate in 2010 $25-48 per family. Member ARVC, CONY. Phone: (866)333-7462.

MEDINA—D-3

(NW) KOA-Medina/Wildwook Lake—(Orleans) *From jct Hwy 31 & Hwy 63: Go 4 mi N on Hwy 63, then 4 mi W on Hwy 104, then 2 mi N on Hwy 269. Enter on R.* ◊◊◊FACILITIES: 310 sites, typical site width 20 ft, 84 full hkups, 220 W&E, (30/50 amps), 6 no hkups, family camping, tenting, dump, laundry. ◊◊◊◊RECREATION: swim pool, lake swim, boating, dock, lake fishing, playground. Pets welcome. Open May 1 - Columbus Day. Rate in 2010 $33.50-48.50 per family. Member ARVC, CONY. Phone: (585)735-3310.

MEXICO—D-6

(N) YOGI BEAR'S JELLYSTONE PARK CAMP RESORT AT MEXICO—(Oswego) *From west jct Hwy 3 & Hwy 104 & CR 16 (Academy St): Go 2-3/4 mi N on CR 16. Enter on L.*

WELCOME

◊◊◊◊FACILITIES: 110 sites, typical site width 50 ft, 15 full hkups, 87 W&E, (20/30/50 amps), 8 no hkups, some extd stay sites (summer), 15 pull-thrus, WiFi Instant Internet at site, WiFi Internet central location, family camping, tenting, RV's/park model rentals, cabins, RV storage, dump, portable dump, laundry, groceries, RV supplies, LP gas by weight/by meter, ice, picnic tables, fire rings, wood, controlled access.

◊◊◊◊◊RECREATION: rec room/area, pavilion, coin games, swim pool, river fishing, fishing supplies, mini-golf, ($), golf nearby, bsktball, 4 bike rentals, playground, activities, horseshoes, sports field, v-ball.

Pets welcome, breed restrict, quantity restrict. Partial handicap access. Open Apr 15 - Oct 25. Escort to site. Clubs welcome. Rate in 2010 $29-55 for 2 persons. MC/VISA/DISC/Debit. Member ARVC, CONY.

Phone: (800)248-7096
Address: 601 CR 16, Mexico, NY 13114
Lat/Lon: 43.49752/-76.24983
Email: office@jellystonecny.com
Web: www.jellystonecny.com

SEE AD TRAVEL SECTION PAGE 527 AND AD TRAVEL SECTION PAGE 529

MIDDLEBURGH—E-8

(S) MAX V. SHAUL STATE PARK—(Schoharie) *From business Center: Go 5 mi S on Hwy-30.* FACILITIES: 30 sites, 30 no hkups, tenting. RECREATION: playground. Open Mid May - Columbus Day. Phone: (518)827-4711.

MIDDLESEX—E-4

(E) Flint Creek Campgrounds—(Yates) *From jct Hwy 247 & Hwy 364: Go 1/2 mi SE on Hwy 364, then 1-1/2 mi W on Phelps Rd. Enter on L.* ◊◊FACILITIES: 125 sites, typical site width 50 ft, 91 full hkups, 14

MIDDLESEX—Continued
Flint Creek Campgrounds—Continued

W&E, (20/30 amps), 20 no hkups, family camping, tenting, dump, laundry, ltd groc. ◊◊◊RECREATION: swim pool, pond/stream fishing, playground. Pets welcome, breed restrict. Open May 1 - Oct 31. Rate in 2010 $25-27 for 4 persons. Phone: (585)554-3567.

MIDDLETOWN—B-2

(NW) Korn's Campgrounds—(Orange) *From jct Rt 17 (exit 118) & Rt 17M: Go 1-1/4 mi NW on 17M, then 3 mi SW on Prosperous Valley Rd, then 200 yards W on Brola Rd, then 250 yards W on Meyer Rd. Enter on R.* ◊◊◊FACILITIES: 91 sites, typical site width 25 ft, 36 ft max RV length, 45 full hkups, 45 W&E, (20/30 amps), 1 no hkups, family camping, tenting, laundry, ltd groc. ◊◊◊RECREATION: swim pool, stream fishing, playground. Pets welcome ($), breed restrict, quantity restrict. Open May 1 - Oct 15. Rate in 2010 $35-42 for 2 persons. Member ARVC, CONY. Phone: (845)386-3433.

MILLERTON—F-10

TACONIC SP (Copake Falls Area)—(Columbia) *From business center: Go 13 mi NE on Hwy-22 & Hwy-344.* FACILITIES: 106 sites, 22 ft max RV length, 106 no hkups, tenting, dump. RECREATION: river swim, boating, canoeing, river fishing, playground. Pets welcome. Partial handicap access. Open all yr. Facilities fully operational May 6 - Dec 3. Phone: (518)329-3993.

TACONIC SP (Rudd Pond)—(Columbia) *From business center: Go 2 mi N on Hwy-22.* FACILITIES: 41 sites, 30 ft max RV length, 41 no hkups, tenting. RECREATION: lake swim, boating, no motors, canoeing, ramp, playground. Pets welcome. Open all yr. Facilities fully operational May 6 - Sep 4. Phone: (518)789-3059.

MONTAUK—B-5

(W) HITHER HILLS STATE PARK—(Suffolk) *From town: Go 8 mi W on Hwy 27A (Old Montauk Hwy).* FACILITIES: 168 sites, 168 no hkups, tenting, dump, laundry, ltd groc. RECREATION: saltwater swim, saltwater fishing, playground. No pets. Open June 11 - Sept 12. Phone: (631)668-2554.

MONTEZUMA—E-5

(S) Hejamada Campground and RV Park—(Cayuga) *From jct Hwy 20/5 & Hwy 90: Go 3 mi N on Hwy 90, then 200 yds S on Fuller Rd., then 1 mi SE on McDonald. Enter on R.* ◊◊◊FACILITIES: 188 sites, typical site width 40 ft, 20 full hkups, 168 W&E, (20/30/50 amps), 50 amps ($), family camping, tenting, dump, laundry, ltd groc. ◊◊◊RECREATION: swim pool, pond fishing, playground. Pets welcome. Partial handicap access. Open May1 - Oct 15. Rate in 2010 $25-30 for 2 persons. Member ARVC, CONY. Phone: (315)776-5887. FMCA discount.

MONTGOMERY—A-2

(W) WINDING HILLS PARK (Orange County Park)—(Orange) *From jct I-84 (exit 5) & Hwy-208: Go 1 mi N on Hwy-208, then 4 mi W on Hwy-17K, then 1/4 mi NW on Old Route 17K. Enter on R.* FACILITIES: 51 sites, 29 ft max RV length, 10 E, 41 no hkups, 4 pull-thrus, tenting, dump. RECREATION: boating, no motors, ramp, dock, pond fishing, playground. Open 1st Fri in May - 4th Sun in Oct. Phone: (845)457-4918.

MORAVIA—E-5

(S) FILLMORE GLEN STATE PARK—(Cayuga) *From business center: Go 1 mi S on Hwy-38.* FACILITIES: 60 sites, typical site width 20 ft, 14 E, (20/30/50 amps), 46 no hkups, tenting, dump. RECREATION: swim pool, playground. Pets welcome. Partial handicap access. Open May 7 - Oct 10. Phone: (315)497-0130.

MORRISTOWN—B-7

(W) JACQUES CARTIER STATE PARK—(St. Lawrence) *From jct Hwy 37 & Hwy 12: Go 3 mi W on Hwy 12S.* FACILITIES: 89 sites, 24 E, (15 amps), 65 no hkups, tenting, dump, ltd groc. RECREATION: river swim, boating, canoeing, ramp, dock, river fishing, playground. Partial handicap access. Open May 19 - Columbus Wknd. Phone: (315)375-6371.

MORRISVILLE—E-7

(N) Cedar Valley Campsite—(Madison) *From center of town at jct US 20 & Cedar St: Go 3 mi N on Cedar St, then 1/4 mi E on Fearon Rd (CR 47), then 1/2 mi N on South Butler Rd. Enter on L.* ◊◊◊FACILITIES: 68 sites, 46 full hkups, 19 W&E, (30/50 amps), 3 no hkups, 3 pull-thrus, family camping, tenting, dump. ◊◊RECREATION: stream fishing, playground. Pets welcome. Open May 15 - Oct 15. Rate in 2010 $20-27 for 2 persons. Phone: (315)684-3033.

MT. MORRIS—E-3

LETCHWORTH STATE PARK—(Wyoming) *From jct I-390 (exit 7) & Hwy 408S: Go 2 mi SW on Hwy 408, then 2 mi N on Hwy 36, then 6 mi S on main park road. Enter on L.* FACILITIES: 270 sites, 270 E, (20 amps), tenting, dump, laundry, ltd groc. RECREATION: swim pool, canoeing, river/pond/stream fishing, playground. Partial handicap access. Open all yr. Facilities fully operational May 7 - Oct 23. Phone: (585)493-3600.

Dairying is New York's most important farming activity with over 18,000 cattle and/or calves farms.

NATURAL BRIDGE—C-7

(E) ADIRONDACK 1000 ISLANDS CAMPGROUND—(Lewis) *From jct I-81 (exit 48) & Hwy 342: Go 7 mi E on Hwy 342, then 7 mi E on Hwy 3, then 5 mi E on Hwy 3A, then 6 mi E on Hwy 3. Enter on L.*

◆◆◆FACILITIES: 74 sites, 30 full hkups, 31 W&E, (20/30/50 amps), 50 amps ($), 13 no hkups, 37 pull-thrus, WiFi Internet central location, family camping, tenting, RV's/park model rentals, cabins, RV storage, dump, non-guest dump $, laundry, ltd groc, RV supplies, ice, picnic tables, fire rings, grills, wood.

◆◆◆RECREATION: rec room/area, equipped pavilion, swim pool, golf nearby, bsktball, playground, activities, (wkends), horseshoes, sports field, hiking trails, v-ball.

Pets welcome. Partial handicap access. Open May 15 - Oct 11. Big rigs welcome. Clubs welcome. Rate in 2010 $32-35 for 4 persons. Member ARVC, CONY.

Phone: (315)644-4098
Address: 6081 State Route 3, Natural Bridge, NY 13665
Lat/Lon: 44.07421/-75.47371
Email: aticampground@yahoo.com
Web: www.adirondack1000islandscampground.com

SEE AD UTICA PAGE 564 AND AD WATERTOWN PAGE 565

NEW YORK CITY—C-2

BLACK BEAR CAMPGROUND—*About 1-hr NW on I-87 to exit 16 (US 17W), then 13 mi W on US 17 to exit 124, then 5-1/2 mi SW on Hwy 17A, then right at light (Bridge St), then 1-1/2 mi W on CR-41. Enter on L.*

SEE PRIMARY LISTING AT FLORIDA AND AD NEXT PAGE

NEW YORK CITY—Continued on next page

Lucille Ball, comedienne, was from New York.

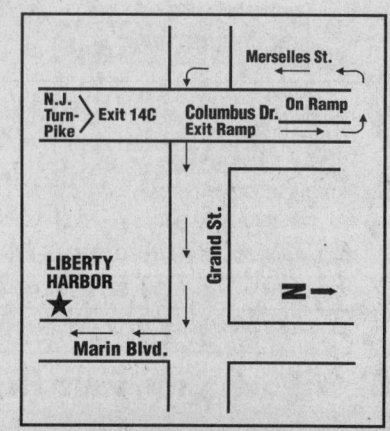

NEW YORK CITY—Continued

LIBERTY HARBOR RV PARK—*From jct Hwy 9A & I-78 (entrance to Holland Tunnel W): Go 3-3/4 mi W on I-78, then 3/4 mi E on Grand St., then 1/4 mi S on Marin Blvd. (Caution: Vehicles with LP gas tanks not allowed in tunnel.). Enter at end.*

SEE PRIMARY LISTING AT JERSEY CITY, NJ AND AD PAGE 555

NEWBURGH—A-2

(N) KOA-NEWBURGH/NEW YORK CITY NORTH—(Ulster) *From jct I-84 (exit 7N) & I-87 (exit 17): Go 4 mi N on Hwy-300, then 5 mi N on Hwy-32, then 1/2 mi NE on Freetown Hwy. Enter on L.*

◆◆◆◆◆FACILITIES: 145 sites, typical site width 32 ft, 93 full hkups, 44 W&E, (20/30/50 amps), 8 no hkups, some extd stay sites, 20 pull-thrus, cable TV, WiFi Instant Internet at site, phone Internet central location, family camping, tenting, cabins, RV storage, dump, non-guest dump $, laundry, groceries, RV supplies, LP gas by weight/by meter, ice, picnic tables, fire rings, wood.

◆◆◆◆◆RECREATION: rec hall, rec room/area, coin games, 2 swim pools, pond fishing, mini-golf, ($), golf nearby, bsktball, 15 bike rentals, playground, shuffleboard court 2 shuffleboard courts, activities, horseshoes, sports field, hiking trails, v-ball, local tours.

Pets welcome, breed restrict, quantity restrict. Open Apr 1 - Oct 31. Big rigs welcome. Clubs welcome. Rate in 2010 $50-65 for 2 persons. MC/VISA/DISC. Member ARVC, CONY. KOA discount.

Phone: (845)564-2836
Address: 119 Freetown Hwy, Plattekill, NY 12568
Lat/Lon: 41.63715/-74.09599
Email: nnycnkoa@aol.com
Web: www.newburghkoa.com

SEE AD NEW YORK CITY PAGE 556 AND AD TRAVEL SECTION PAGE 527

Kareem Abdul-Jabbar, basketball player, is from New York.

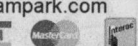

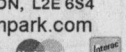

KIDS STAY FREE 2 per site

Campark Resorts

Holiday TRAV-L-PARK FOR CAMPERS Across America

Only Minutes from the Falls & Casino!

- Shuttle to Falls & Casino • Open All Year
- Cabins • Activities • Groceries
- RV Supplies • Laundry • Heated Pool
- Hot Tub • Imagimaze Playground
- Volleyball and Basketball Courts

....And Much More!

1-877-CAMPARK

9387 Lundy's Lane Niagara Falls, ON, L2E 6S4
info@campark.com www.campark.com

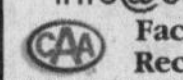
Fac: ◆◆◆◆◆
Rec: ◆◆◆◆◆
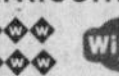

NEWBURGH—Continued

MILITARY CAMPGROUND (Round Pond Recreation Area-West Point USMA)—(Orange) *Off I-87 & US 9W. On base.* FACILITIES: 28 sites, 28 W&E, (30/50 amps), tenting, dump. RECREATION: lake swim, boating, electric motors only, dock, lake fishing, playground. Open Apr 15 - Nov 15. Facilities fully operational Apr 15 - Oct 15. Phone: (845)938-2503.

(N) NEW YORK CITY TOURS - KOA-NEWBURGH/NEW YORK CITY NORTH—*From I-84 (exit 7N) & I-87 (exit 17): Go 4 mi N on Hwy 300, then 5 mi N on Hwy 32, then 1/2 mi NE on Freetown Hwy. Enter on L.* Guided bus or van tours of New York City. Individual & groups. Reservations recommended. Open mid May - mid Oct. MC/VISA/DISC.

Phone: (845)564-2836
Address: 119 Freetown Hwy, Plattekill, NY 12568
Lat/Lon: 41.63715/-74.09599
Email: nnycnkoa@aol.com
Web: www.newburghkoa.com

SEE AD NEW YORK CITY PAGE 556

NIAGARA FALLS—D-2

(E) AA ROYAL CAMPGROUND & MOTEL—(Niagara) *From jct I-290 (exit 3) & US 62 (Niagara Falls Blvd): Go 6 mi N on US 62. Enter on R.*

NICEST CAMPGROUND IN AREA

Avoid the congestion! Most convenient RV park! Large paved sites while you visit the FALLS, Casinos, Forts & Canada. *WiFi*, Grayline, Bedore & Niagara Majestic Tours pick up here! Restaurants, Univ close too! Open all year!

◆◆◆◆FACILITIES: 33 sites, typical site width 30 ft, 30 full hkups, (30/50 amps), 3 no hkups, 6 pull-thrus, WiFi Instant Internet at site, WiFi Internet central location, family camping, tenting, laundry, ice, picnic tables, patios, fire rings, wood.

AA ROYAL CAMPGROUND & MOTEL—Continued on next page

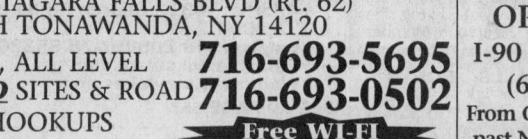

...located directly on Lake Erie
between Erie, PA & Niagara Falls
(1 hr. to falls)

FREE WI-FI

BROOKSIDE BEACH CAMPGROUND

- Full Hookups with 30 & 50 Amp Service
- Private Beach * Beautiful Sunsets
- Nearby Wineries, Restaurants, Antique Shops, Golf Courses & Boat Launch

Groups Welcome * Quality Municipal Water

brooksidebeach.com

PO Box 130, Westfield, NY 14787
(716) 326-9945 or (716) 326-3096
(2.5 miles from I-90, exit 60, west on Route 5)

See listing at Westfield, NY

Good Sam Park

Gateway to NIAGARA FALLS - Only 9 Miles

AA ROYAL CAMPGROUND & MOTEL

3333 NIAGARA FALLS BLVD (Rt. 62)
NORTH TONAWANDA, NY 14120

LARGE, ALL LEVEL **716-693-5695**
PAVED SITES & ROAD **716-693-0502**
FULL HOOKUPS
PULL-THRU SITES
TENT SITES
FIRE RINGS, ICE, WOOD

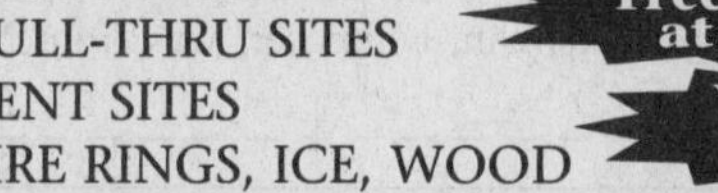

BIG RIGS WELCOME • DAILY, WEEKLY & MONTHLY RATES • **EZ COME EZ GO**

visit us at: www.royalmotelandcampground.com

OPEN ALL YEAR
I-90 to 290(w) to exit 3 (62N) 5.7 mi on R
From Canada: take US 62S 3 mi past Niagara Falls Airport on L

GUIDED TOURS DIRECTLY FROM CAMPGROUND

☆ CLOSE TO UNIVERSITY, RV SERVICES, GROCERIES & MALL

See listing at Niagara Falls, NY

4312 Church Road • Cambria, NY 14094 • 1 (800) 874-2957

Your home away from home...

15 Minutes to Niagara Falls, Seneca Niagara Casino, Historic Lewiston, Fort Niagara, Great Restaurants, Golfing & Wineries!

Open May 1 - November 1
24 Hour Security
Big Rig Friendly
Motorhomes / 5th Wheels
Travel Trailers
265 Sites

- **2 Spring-Fed Lakes**
- **2 Heated Pools With Lifeguards**
- **4000 Sq. Ft. Activity Lodge w/Deck**
- **4 "10 Star" Restrooms w/Showers**
- **2 Laundry Facilities**
- **3 Dump Stations**
- **Country Store • Playground**

See listing at Niagara Falls, NY

LAZYLAKES.COM

NO DRIVE-UPS • RESERVATIONS REQUIRED

NIAGARA FALLS—Continued
AA ROYAL CAMPGROUND & MOTEL—Continued

◆RECREATION: local tours.

Pets welcome. Partial handicap access. Open all yr. Big rigs welcome. Clubs welcome. Rate in 2010 $39-59 for 2 persons. MC/VISA/DISC/Debit. Member ARVC, CONY.

Phone: (716)693-5695
Address: 3333 Niagara Falls Blvd, N Tonawanda, NY 14120
Lat/Lon: 43.07516/-78.86167
Email: mike@royalmotelandcampground.com
Web: www.royalmotelandcampground.com

SEE AD PAGE 557

BRANCHES OF NIAGARA CAMPGROUND & RESORT (TOO NEW TO RATE) —(Erie) *From jct I-90 (exit 19) & Whitehaven Rd: Go 3/4 mi on Whitehaven Rd. Enter on R.*

FACILITIES: 68 sites, 30 full hkups, 38 W&E, (20/30/50 amps), WiFi Instant Internet at site, WiFi Internet central location, family camping, tenting, cabins, dump, laundry.

RECREATION: swim pool, lake swim, boating, 3 canoe/3 pedal boat rentals, lake fishing, bike rental, playground, shuffleboard court shuffleboard court, activities (wkends), horseshoes, v-ball.

Pets welcome. Open Memorial Day Wknd - Oct 31. Rate in 2010 $48-88 for 4 persons. MC/VISA/AMEX.

Phone: (877)321-CAMP
Address: 2659 Whitehaven Road, Grand Island, NY 14072
Lat/Lon: 43.021303/-78.990474
Email: info@branchesofniagara.com
Web: branchesofniagara.com

SEE AD THIS PAGE

(S) Cinderella Campsite & Motel—(Erie) *From jct I-190 (exit 20B & Hwy 324): Go 1-1/2 mi E on Hwy 324 (Grand Island Blvd). Enter on L.* ◆◆◆FACILITIES: 60 sites, typical site width 18 ft, 30 full hkups, 30 E, (20/30/50 amps), family camping, tenting, dump, laundry. Pets welcome. Open Apr - Oct. Rate in 2010 $40 for 2 persons. Phone: (716)773-4095.

(S) KOA-Niagara Falls—(Erie) *From jct I-190 (exit 20B) & Hwy 324: Go 2 mi E on Hwy 324 (Grand Island Blvd), then 3/4 mi N on Hwy 324 (Grand Island Blvd). Enter on R.* ◆◆◆◆FACILITIES: 293 sites, typical site width 20 ft, 211 full hkups, 76 W&E, (20/30/50 amps), 6 no hkups, 153 pull-thrus, family camping, tenting, dump, laundry, groceries. ◆◆◆◆RECREATION: 2 swim pools, pond fishing, playground. Pets welcome. Partial handicap access. Open Apr 1 - Oct 31. Big rigs welcome. Rate in 2010 $50-80 for 2 persons. Member ARVC, CONY. Phone: (716)773-7583. KOA discount.

(N) KOA-NIAGARA FALLS NORTH—(Niagara) *From north jct I-190 (exit 25B) & Robert Moses Pkwy: Go 3 mi N on Robert Moses Pkwy, then 1-3/4 mi E on Pletcher Rd. Enter on R.*

◆◆◆◆FACILITIES: 90 sites, typical site width 24 ft, 18 full hkups, 54 W&E, (20/30/50 amps), 50 amps ($), 18 no hkups, 40 pull-thrus, WiFi Instant Internet at site, WiFi Internet central location, family camping, tenting, RV's/park model rentals, cabins, dump, non-guest dump $, laundry, groceries, RV supplies, LP gas by weight/by meter, ice, picnic tables, fire rings, wood.

◆◆◆RECREATION: rec room/area, swim pool, golf nearby, bsktball, 6 bike rentals, playground, activities, (wkends), horseshoes, v-ball, local tours.

NIAGARA COUNTY
CAMPING RESORT
Lowest Rates in Niagara Falls Area
• Free Wi-Fi • Free Cable TV • Free Miniature Golf
• Lake Front Cabins & Cottages • Planned Activities
• Groups Welcome • 3 Miles to Erie Canal • 30/50 Amps
• 2 Lakes • Petting Zoo • Swimming • Fishing • Pets Welcome
www.niagaracamping.com
Good Sam Park
TL RATED 6.5/8★/8
716-434-3991
See listing at Lockport, NY

NIAGARA FALLS—Continued
KOA-NIAGARA FALLS NORTH—Continued

Pets welcome, breed restrict. Partial handicap access. Open Apr 15 - Columbus Day. Big rigs welcome. Escort to site. Clubs welcome. Rate in 2010 $47-62 for 2 persons. MC/VISA/DISC/Debit. Member ARVC, CONY. KOA discount.

Phone: (716)754-8013
Address: 1250 Pletcher Rd, Youngstown, NY 14174
Lat/Lon: 43.20887/-78.99004
Email: franp@msn.com
Web: www.niagarafallsnorthkoa.com

SEE AD THIS PAGE

(E) Niagara Falls Campground—(Niagara) *N'bound: From jct I-290 (exit 3) & US 62: Go 9 mi N on US 62. Entrance on right. S'bound: From jct I-190 (exit 22) & US 62: Go 4-1/2 mi S on US 62. Entrance on left.* ◆◆◆FACILITIES: 73 sites, typical site width 15 ft, 49 full hkups, 6 W&E, 5 E, (20/30/50 amps), 13 no hkups, 32 pull-thrus, family camping, tenting, dump, laundry. ◆◆RECREATION: swim pool, playground. Pets welcome. Open Mar 15 - Nov 15. Big rigs welcome. Rate in 2010 $49-59 for 2 persons. Member ARVC, CONY. Phone: (716)731-3434.

(NE) NIAGARA'S LAZY LAKES CAMPING RESORT—(Niagara) *From jct Hwy 429 & Hwy 104: Go 1 mi E on Hwy 104, then 1/4 mi N on Church Rd. Enter on L.*

"YOUR HOME AWAY FROM HOME..."
Lazy Lakes Resort is called the best kept secret in Western New York. 15 minutes from Niagara Falls, 9 miles East of Historic Lewiston in the Town of Cambria. Nearby Restaurants, Casinos, Amusement Parks, Shopping & more.

◆◆◆◆FACILITIES: 265 sites, typical site width 35 ft, 51 full hkups, 214 W&E, (30/50 amps), WiFi Instant Internet at site, WiFi Internet central location, family camping, cabins, dump, portable dump, laundry, ltd groc, RV supplies, ice, picnic tables, fire rings, wood.

◆◆◆◆RECREATION: rec hall, pavilion, coin games, 2 swim pools, lake swim, boating, canoeing, 2 rowboat/2 canoe/8 pedal boat rentals, lake fishing, fishing supplies, golf nearby, bsktball, playground, shuffleboard court 2 shuffleboard courts, activities (wkends), horseshoes, sports field, v-ball.

Pets welcome, quantity restrict. Partial handicap access. No tents. Open May 1 - Nov 1. Reservations required. No drive-ups. Big rigs welcome. Rate in 2010 $55 per family. ATM.

Phone: (800)874-2957
Address: 4312 Church Rd, Lockport, NY 14094
Lat/Lon: 43.20585/-78.85326
Email: lazylks@aol.com
Web: www.lazylakes.com

SEE AD PAGE 557

George Gershwin, composer, was from New York.

NIAGARA FALLS—Continued

YOGI BEAR'S JELLYSTONE PARK CAMP-RESORT—*From Rainbow Bridge: Go 3.2 km/2 mi W on Hwy 420, then 3.2 km/2 mi S on QEW, then 183 meters/200 yards E on McLeod Rd., then 2.4 km/1-1/2 mi S on Oakwood Dr.*

SEE PRIMARY LISTING AT NIAGARA FALLS, ON AND AD NIAGARA FALLS, ON PAGE 880

NORTH HUDSON—C-9

(W) YOGI BEAR'S JELLYSTONE PARK AT PARADISE PINES—(Essex) *From jct I-87 (exit 29-North Hudson) & Blue Ridge Rd: Go 750 feet E on Blue Ridge Rd. Enter on L.*

◆◆◆◆◆FACILITIES: 173 sites, typical site width 30 ft, 125 full hkups, 45 W&E, (20/30/50 amps), 3 no hkups, some extd stay sites (summer), 40 pull-thrus, cable TV, WiFi Instant Internet at site, WiFi Internet central location, family camping, tenting, RV's/park model rentals, cabins, RV storage, dump, non-guest dump $, portable dump, laundry, groceries, RV supplies, LP gas by weight/by meter, ice, picnic tables, fire rings, grills, wood, controlled access.

◆◆◆◆◆RECREATION: rec hall, rec room/area, equipped pavilion, coin games, 2 swim pools, wading pool, river swim, canoeing, kayaking, 6 kayak rentals, river fishing, mini-golf, ($), golf nearby, bsktball, 20 bike rentals, playground, shuffleboard court shuffleboard court, activities, horseshoes, sports field, v-ball.

Pets welcome, breed restrict. Partial handicap access. Open May 1 - Mid Oct. Big rigs welcome. Escort to site. Clubs welcome. Rate in 2010 $42-61 per family. MC/VISA/Debit. Member ARVC, CONY.

Phone: (518)532-7493
Address: 4035 Blue Ridge Rd, North Hudson, NY 12855
Lat/Lon: 43.95192/-73.73096
Email: office@paradisepines.com
Web: www.paradisepines.com

SEE AD LAKE GEORGE PAGE 548 AND AD TRAVEL SECTION PAGE 527

NORTH JAVA—E-3

(SE) Yogi Bear's Jellystone Park of Western New York—(Wyoming) *From jct Hwy 98 & Hwy 78 (at Five Corners): Go 1-1/2 mi E on Pee Dee Rd, then 3/4 mi S Youngers Rd. Enter on R.* ◆◆◆◆FACILITIES: 245 sites, typical site width 40 ft, 106 full hkups, 109 W&E, (20/30/50 amps), 50 amps ($), 30 no hkups, 45 pull-thrus, family camping, tenting, dump, laundry, groceries. ◆◆◆◆◆RECREATION: swim pool, lake swim, boating, no motors, lake/pond fishing, playground. Pets welcome. Partial handicap access. Open May 2 - Columbus Day. Big rigs welcome. Rate in 2010 $30-84 per family. Member ARVC, CONY. Phone: (585)457-9644.

Adirondack Park is larger than Yellowstone, Yosemite, Grand Canyon, Glacier, and Olympic Parks combined.

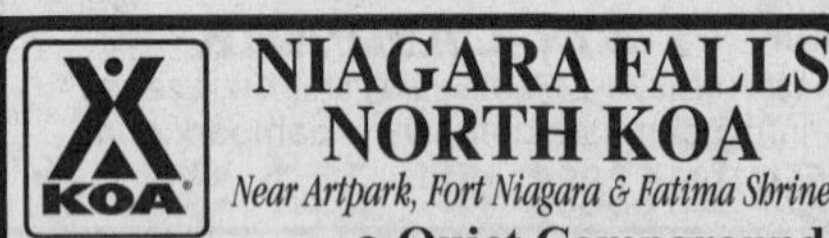

NORTHVILLE—D-9

NORTHAMPTON BEACH CAMPGROUND (Adirondack SF)—(Fulton) *From business center: Go 1-1/2 mi S on Hwy 30, then SE.* FACILITIES: 224 sites, 224 no hkups, tenting, dump. RECREATION: lake swim, boating, canoeing, ramp, lake fishing, playground. Partial handicap access. Open May 2 - Oct 13. Phone: (518)863-6000.

(S) SACANDAGA CAMPGROUND (Adirondack SF)—(Hamilton) *From town: Go 8 mi N on Hwy-30.* FACILITIES: 144 sites, 144 no hkups, tenting, dump. RECREATION: Pets welcome. Partial handicap access. Open May 16 - Oct 12. Phone: (518)924-4121.

ODESSA—F-5

(E) Cool-Lea Camp—(Schuyler) *From jct Hwy 14 & Hwy 224: Go 3-1/2 mi E on Hwy 224, then 2-1/2 mi N on Hwy 228. Enter on R.* ◇◇◇FACILITIES: 90 sites, typical site width 30 ft, 8 full hkups, 72 W&E, (20/30 amps), 10 no hkups, heater not allowed, family camping, tenting, RV storage, shower$, dump, portable dump, ice, picnic tables, fire rings, wood. ◇◇◇RECREATION: equipped pavilion, lake swim, boating, canoeing, ramp, dock, lake fishing, bsktball, playground, activities, horseshoes, hiking trails. Pets welcome. Partial handicap access. Open May 15 - Oct 15. Rate in 2010 $25-40 per family. MC/VISA/AMEX/Debit. CCUSA 50% Discount. CCUSA reservations Required, CCUSA max stay 5 days, Cash only for CCUSA disc., CCUSA disc. not avail F,Sa, CCUSA disc. not avail holidays. Pet surcharge for more than 1-$6/day.

Phone: (607)594-3500
Address: 2540 Rt 228, Odessa, NY 14869
Lat/Lon: 42.36217/-76.74901
Email: coollea2@aol.com
Web: www.coolleacamp.com

OGDENSBURG—B-7

(NE) LISBON BEACH AND CAMPGROUND—(St. Lawrence) *From jct Hwy 812 & Hwy 37: Go 5 mi E on Hwy 37. Enter on L.* FACILITIES: 70 sites, typical site width 35 ft, 10 full hkups, 46 W&E, 4 E, (20/30/50 amps), 10 no hkups, family camping, tenting, dump. RECREATION: river swim, boating, canoeing, ramp, river fishing, playground. Pets welcome. Open May 1 - Oct 15. Phone: (315)393-5374.

OLD BETHPAGE—C-3

BATTLE ROW CAMPGROUND (Nassau County Park)—(Nassau) *From jct I-495 (exit 48) & Round Swamp Rd: Go 1-3/4 mi SE on Round Swamp Rd, then 1 block E on Bethpage-Sweethollow Rd, then 1 block S on Claremont Rd. Enter on R.* FACILITIES: 64 sites, 31 W&E, (20/30 amps), 33 no hkups, tenting, dump. RECREATION: playground. Pets welcome. Partial handicap access. Open Apr 1 - Last Sun in Nov. Phone: (516)572-8690.

OLD FORGE—C-7

NICK'S LAKE CAMPGROUND (Adirondack SF)—(Herkimer) *From business center: Go 2 mi SE on Hwy-28.* FACILITIES: 112 sites, 112 no hkups, tenting, dump. RECREATION: lake swim, boating, no motors, canoeing, lake fishing, playground. Partial handicap access. Open May 2 - Oct 13. Phone: (315)369-3314.

(S) Singing Waters Campground—(Herkimer) *From jct Gilbert St (center of town) & Hwy 28: Go 5-3/4 mi S on Hwy-28. Enter on L.* ◇◇FACILITIES: 145 sites, typical site width 25 ft, 60 full hkups, 72 W&E, (15/20/30 amps), 13 no hkups, family camping, tenting, dump. ◇◇◇RECREATION: river swim, boating, canoeing, river fishing, play equipment. Pets welcome. Open all yr. Facilities fully operational May 15 - Nov 15. Rate in 2010 $40-45 for 2 persons. Phone: (315)369-6618.

ONEIDA—D-7

VERONA BEACH STATE PARK—(Oneida) *From jct I-90 & Hwy-13: Go 7 mi NW on Hwy-13.* FACILITIES: 45 sites, 45 no hkups, tenting, dump, ltd groc. RECREATION: lake swim, canoeing, lake fishing, playground. Pets welcome. Partial handicap access. Open all yr. Facilities fully operational May 1 - Oct 9. Phone: (315)762-4463.

ONEONTA—E-7

(N) GILBERT LAKE STATE PARK—(Otsego) *From business center: Go 12 mi N on Hwy 205, then 1 mi W/NW on CR 11, then 2 mi SW on Braun Rd/Townline Rd.* FACILITIES: 219 sites, typical site width 15 ft, 219 E, (20 amps), tenting, dump. RECREATION: lake swim, boating, canoeing, lake fishing, playground. Partial handicap access. Open all yr. Open May 14 - Oct 11. Phone: (607)432-2114.

(W) SUSQUEHANNA TRAIL CAMPGROUND—(Otsego) *From jct I-88 (exit 13) & Hwy 205: Go 1/2 mi N on Hwy 205, then 1/2 mi W on Hwy 7. Enter on R.*

◇◇◇FACILITIES: 68 sites, typical site width 30 ft, 45 full hkups, 8 W&E, (20/30/50 amps), 50 amps ($), 15 no hkups, some extd stay sites (summer), 10 pull-thrus, cable TV, ($), WiFi Internet central location, family camping, tenting, RV's/park model rentals, RV storage, dump, ltd groc, RV supplies, ice, picnic tables, fire rings, wood, controlled access.

Michael Jordan, basketball player, is from New York.

ONEONTA—Continued
SUSQUEHANNA TRAIL CAMPGROUND—Continued

◇◇◇RECREATION: pavilion, swim pool, stream fishing, golf nearby, bsktball, playground, activities, (wkends), horseshoes, sports field, v-ball.

Pets welcome. Partial handicap access. Open Apr 1 - Nov 15. Escort to site. Clubs welcome. Rate in 2010 $35-42 for 2 persons. MC/VISA/DISC. Member ARVC, CONY. FCRV discount. FMCA discount. CCUSA 50% Discount. CCUSA reservations Recommended, CCUSA max stay 14 days, CCUSA disc. not avail holidays. Discount not available weekends Memorial Day weekend thru Labor Day. Discount applies to back-in sites only. No discount on tent sites.

Phone: (607)432-1122
Address: 4292 State Highway 7, Oneonta, NY 13820
Lat/Lon: 42.43751/-75.11724
Email: info@susquehannatrailcampground.com
Web: www.susquehannatrailcampground.com

Reserve Online at Woodalls.com

SEE AD COOPERSTOWN PAGE 540

OSWEGO—D-5

(W) Sunset RV Park—(Oswego) *From jct Hwy 48 & Hwy 104: Go 2-1/4 mi W on Hwy 104, then 3/4 mi NW on Fred Haynes Blvd, then 100 feet N on CR 89. Enter on R.* ◇◇FACILITIES: 26 sites, typical site width 25 ft, 22 full hkups, (30/50 amps), 4 no hkups, family camping, tenting, dump. ◇◇◇RECREATION: swim pool, boating, canoeing, lake fishing, playground. Pets welcome. Open May 1 - Oct 15. Big rigs welcome. Rate in 2010 $25-34 for 2 persons. Phone: (315)343-2166.

OVID—E-5

(E) Sned-Acres Family Campground—(Seneca) *From jct Hwy 96 & Hwy 138: Go 1-1/2 mi E on Hwy 138, then 1 mi N on Hwy 89, then 500 ft W on S Cayuga Lake Rd. Enter on L.* ◇◇◇FACILITIES: 85 sites, typical site width 30 ft, 34 full hkups, 41 W&E, (20/30 amps), 10 no hkups, 6 pull-thrus, family camping, tenting, dump, laundry, ltd groc. ◇◇◇RECREATION: swim pool, pond fishing, playground. Pets welcome. Open Mid Apr - Nov 1. Rate in 2010 $27-31 per family. Member ARVC, CONY. Phone: (607)869-9787.

OXFORD—F-7

(W) BOWMAN LAKE STATE PARK—(Chenango) *From jct Hwy 12 & Hwy 220: Go 6 mi NW on Hwy 220.* FACILITIES: 199 sites, typical site width 20 ft, 35 ft max RV length, 199 no hkups, 4 pull-thrus, tenting, dump, ltd groc. RECREATION: lake swim, boating, canoeing, ramp, lake fishing, playground. Open all yr. Phone: (607)334-2718.

PATCHOGUE—C-4

FIRE ISLAND NAT'L SEASHORE (Watch Hill Campground)—(Suffolk) *Access by private boat or passenger ferry only (Fire Island).* FACILITIES: 26 sites, 26 no hkups, tenting, ltd groc. RECREATION: saltwater swim, boating, canoeing, dock, saltwater fishing. Partial handicap access. Open May 8 - Oct 25. Phone: (631)597-6633.

PERU—B-9

(S) AUSABLE POINT CAMPGROUND (Adirondack SF)—(Clinton) *From jct I-87 & Hwy 442: Go 3 mi E on Hwy 422, then 1/2 mi S on US 9.* FACILITIES: 123 sites, (20/30 amps), 123 no hkups, tenting, dump. RECREATION: lake swim, boating, canoeing, ramp, lake fishing, playground. Partial handicap access. Open May 16 - Oct 13. Phone: (518)561-7080.

(E) Iroquois RV Park & Campground—(Clinton) *From jct I-87 (exit 35) & Hwy-442: Go 1-1/2 mi E on Hwy-442. Enter on L.* ◇◇◇FACILITIES: 170 sites, typical site width 25 ft, 170 full hkups, (20/30/50 amps), 40 pull-thrus, family camping, tenting, dump, laundry, ltd groc. ◇◇◇RECREATION: swim pool, pond fishing, playground. Pets welcome. Open May 1 - Oct 1. Rate in 2010 $32 for 3 persons. Member ARVC, CONY. Phone: (518)643-9057.

PHELPS—E-5

(E) CHEERFUL VALLEY CAMPGROUND—(Ontario) *From jct I-90 (exit 42) & Hwy-14: Go 1/2 mi N on Hwy-14. (Lyons Rd). Enter on L.*

IN THE HEART OF THE FINGER LAKES
Unbelievably beautiful lush river valley. Winding, willow-lined river filled with hungry fish await your arrival. Enjoy all that the Finger Lakes has to offer: wineries, parks, and quaint towns nestled between the lakes.

◇◇◇◇FACILITIES: 130 sites, typical site width 45 ft, 37 full hkups, 88 W&E, (20/30/50 amps), 5 no hkups, some extd stay sites (summer), 10 pull-thrus, phone Internet central location, family camping, tenting, cabins, dump, non-guest dump $, portable dump, laundry, ltd groc, RV supplies, LP gas by weight/by meter, ice, picnic tables, fire rings, wood.

PHELPS—Continued
CHEERFUL VALLEY CAMPGROUND—Continued

◇◇◇◇RECREATION: rec room/area, equipped pavilion, coin games, swim pool, canoeing, kayaking, river fishing, fishing supplies, golf nearby, bsktball, playground, shuffleboard court 2 shuffleboard courts, activities (wkends), horseshoes, sports field, v-ball.

Pets welcome, quantity restrict. Open Apr 15 - Oct 15. Pool open Memorial Day-Labor Day. Clubs welcome. Rate in 2010 $30-48 for 2 persons. MC/VISA/Debit. Member ARVC, CONY. CCUSA 50% Discount. CCUSA reservations Accepted, CCUSA max stay 1 day, Cash only for CCUSA disc., CCUSA disc. not avail F,Sa, CCUSA disc. not avail holidays. Discount available Apr 15-Memorial Day & Labor Day-Oct 15. Cash only for discount. No on-line or credit card reservations.

Phone: (315)781-1222
Address: 1412 Rte 14 (Lyons Rd), Phelps, NY 14532
Lat/Lon: 42.96401/-76.97802
Email: cheerfulvalley@rochester.rr.com
Web: www.cheerfulvalleycampground.com

SEE AD ROCHESTER PAGE 561 AND AD TRAVEL SECTION PAGE 527

(E) JUNIUS PONDS CABINS & CAMPGROUNDS—(Seneca) *From jct I-90 (exit 42-Geneva) & Hwy 318: Go 3/4 mi E on Hwy 318, then 1/4 mi N on W Townline Rd. Enter at end.*

◇◇◇◇FACILITIES: 230 sites, typical site width 50 ft, 205 full hkups, 20 W&E, (20/30/50 amps), 50 amps ($), 5 no hkups, many extd stay sites (summer), 30 pull-thrus, WiFi Instant Internet at site ($), WiFi Internet central location, family camping, tenting, RV's/park model rentals, cabins, RV storage, dump, non-guest dump $, laundry, ltd groc, RV supplies, LP gas by weight/by meter, ice, picnic tables, fire rings, wood.

◇◇◇◇RECREATION: rec hall, rec room/area, pavilion, coin games, swim pool, pond fishing, fishing supplies, golf nearby, bsktball, playground, activities, horseshoes, sports field, hiking trails, v-ball.

Pets welcome. Partial handicap access. Open Apr 15 - Oct 15. Big rigs welcome. Clubs welcome. Rate in 2010 $29-32 per family. MC/VISA/AMEX/Debit. Member ARVC, CONY.

Phone: (315)781-5120
Address: 1475 W Townline Rd, Phelps, NY 14532
Lat/Lon: 42.95490/-76.96107
Email: hcdadson@yahoo.com
Web: www.juniuspondscabinsandcampground.com

SEE AD ROCHESTER PAGE 561

PHOENICIA—F-8

KENNETH L. WILSON CAMPGROUND (Catskills SF)—(Ulster) *From jct Hwy-28 & Hwy-212: Go 1/2 mi E on Hwy-212, then 4 mi SE on CR-40.* FACILITIES: 76 sites, 76 no hkups, tenting, dump. RECREATION: boating, no motors, canoeing, ramp, playground. Partial handicap access. Open May 12 - Oct 8. Phone: (845)679-7020.

(SW) WOODLAND VALLEY CAMPGROUND (Catskill SF)—(Ulster) *From town: Go 6 mi SW off Hwy-28.* FACILITIES: 72 sites, 72 no hkups, tenting, dump. RECREATION: river fishing. Partial handicap access. Open Mid May - Columbus Day. Phone: (845)688-7647.

PIKE—E-3

(W) Rolling Acres Golf Course & Campground—(Wyoming) *From jct Hwy 39 & Hwy 19: Go 1 mi S on Hwy 19, then 4 mi S on DeWitt Rd. (Hwy 36). Enter on L.* ◇◇◇FACILITIES: 80 sites, typical site width 20 ft, 80 W&E, (20/30 amps), family camping, tenting, dump. ◇◇RECREATION: playground. Pets welcome. Open May 1 - Oct 15. Rate in 2010 $27 for 4 persons. Member ARVC, CONY. Phone: (585)567-8557.

PLATTSBURGH—B-10

(W) BULL'S RV CENTER—*From jct I-87 (exit 38 N) & Hwy-374: Go 11 mi W on Hwy-374. Enter on L.* SALES: travel trailers, 5th wheels, fold-down camping trailers, pre-owned unit sales. SERVICES: full-time mech, RV appliance repair, LP gas by meter, dump station, RV rentals, RV storage, sells parts/accessories, installs hitches. Sells truck caps, bed liners. Open all yr. MC/VISA.

BULL'S RV CENTER—Continued on next page

PLATTSBURGH—Continued
BULL'S RV CENTER—Continued

Phone: (518)492-7007
Address: 699 RT-374, Cadyville, NY 12918
Lat/Lon: 44.71518/-73.68369
Email: sales@bullsrv.com
Web: www.bullsrv.com

SEE AD THIS PAGE

(NE) CUMBERLAND BAY STATE PARK—(Clinton) *From jct US 9 & Hwy 314: Go 1 mi E on Hwy 314.* FACILITIES: 152 sites, typical site width 15 ft, 13 E, (20/30 amps), 139 no hkups, tenting, dump. RECREATION: lake swim, boating, canoeing, playground. Pets welcome. Partial handicap access. Open all yr. Open Early May - Columbus Day. Phone: (518)563-5240.

(N) Plattsburgh RV Park—(Clinton) *From jct I-87 (exit 39) & Hwy 314: Go 500 feet E on Hwy 314, then 1/4 mi N on US 9. Enter on R.* ◊◊◊FACILITIES: 162 sites, typical site width 30 ft, 88 full hkups, 70 W&E, (20/30/50 amps), 4 no hkups, family camping, tenting, dump, laundry. ◊◊◊RECREATION: swim pool, pond fishing, playground. Pets welcome. Partial handicap access. Open May 1 - Oct 15. Rate in 2010 $32-37 for 2 persons. Member ARVC, CONY. Phone: (518)563-3915.

(N) Shady Oaks RV Park—(Clinton) *From jct I-87 (exit 39) & Hwy 314/Moffitt Rd: Go 1/4 mi NW on Moffitt Rd. Enter on R.* ◊◊FACILITIES: 103 sites, 103 full hkups, (20/30/50 amps), 8 pull-thrus, family camping, tenting, laundry. ◊◊RECREATION: swim pool, playground. Pets welcome, quantity restrict. Partial handicap access. Open May 1 - Oct 15. Rate in 2010 $30 for 4 persons. Member ARVC, CONY. Phone: (518) 562-0561.

POLAND—D-7

(N) ADIRONDACK GATEWAY CAMPGROUND & LODGE—(Oneida) *From jct Hwy 28 N & Hwy 8: Go 5 mi N on Hwy 8, then 1/2 mi E on Hall Rd, then 1/4 mi N on Burt Rd. Enter on R.*

◊◊◊FACILITIES: 72 sites, typical site width 40 ft, 37 full hkups, 14 W&E, (20/30/50 amps), 50 amps ($), 21 no hkups, 7 pull-thrus, phone Internet central location, family camping, tenting, cabins, RV storage, dump, laundry, ice, picnic tables, fire rings, wood.

◊◊◊RECREATION: rec hall, rec room/area, swim pool, pond fishing, golf nearby, playground, activities, (wkends), horseshoes, sports field, v-ball.

Pets welcome. Open May 15 - Oct 15. Big rigs welcome. Clubs welcome. Rate in 2010 $28-30 for 6 persons.

Phone: (315)826-5335
Address: 244 Burt Rd, Coldbrook, NY 13324
Lat/Lon: 43.26593/-74.98170
Email: AGCcoldbrook@yahoo.com
Web: www.adirondackgatewaycampground.net

SEE AD UTICA PAGE 564 AND AD WATERTOWN PAGE 565

(N) West Canada Creek Campsites—(Oneida) *From jct I-90 (exit 31) & Hwy 8 North: Go 11 mi N on Hwy 8. Enter on L.* ◊◊◊◊FACILITIES: 81 sites, typical site width 35 ft, 50 full hkups, 18 W&E, (20/30/50 amps), 13 no hkups, 10 pull-thrus, family camping, tenting, dump, laundry, ltd groc. ◊◊◊◊RECREATION: swim pool, river swim, boating, canoeing, river fishing, playground. Pets welcome. Partial handicap access. Open Apr 15 - Oct 15. Rate in 2010 $23-53 per family. Member ARVC, CONY. Phone: (888)461-2267.

PORT HENRY—C-10

(S) BULWAGGA BAY CAMPGROUND & RV PARK—(Essex) *From center of town: Go 1/4 mi S on Hwy 9N/22, then 500 feet E on Bulwagga Rd (follow signs). Enter on L.* FACILITIES: 175 sites, typical site width 40 ft, 168 W&E, (20/30 amps), 7 no hkups, 50 pull-thrus, family camping, tenting, dump. RECREATION: lake swim, boating, canoeing, ramp, dock, lake fishing, playground. Pets welcome. Partial handicap access. Open May - Oct. Phone: (518)546-7500.

(NE) PORT HENRY CHAMP BEACH CAMPGROUND & RV PARK—(Essex) *From center of town (Hwy 9N/22): Go 100 yards E on Dock St, then 1/4 mi N on Hwy 9N/22, then 1/8 mi E on Beach Rd (curve to the right). Enter on R.* FACILITIES: 120 sites, typical site width 40 ft, 120 W&E, (20/30 amps), 25 pull-thrus, family camping, tenting, dump. RECREATION: lake swim, boating, canoeing, lake fishing, playground. Pets welcome. Partial handicap access. Open May - Oct. Phone: (518)546-7123.

PORT HENRY—Continued
PORT HENRY CHAMP BEACH CAMPGROUND & RV PARK—Continued

PORTAGEVILLE—E-3

(SW) FOUR WINDS CAMPGROUND—(Wyoming) *From south jct Hwy 436 & Hwy 19A: Go 1/4 mi N on Hwy 19A to state park entrance, then 1-3/4 mi W on Griffith Rd, then 1-1/4 mi S on Tenefly Rd. Enter on R.*

◊◊◊FACILITIES: 154 sites, 94 full hkups, 28 W&E, (20/30/50 amps), 32 no hkups, some extd stay sites (summer), 10 pull-thrus, phone Internet central location, family camping, tenting, dump, non-guest dump $, laundry, ltd groc, RV supplies, LP gas by weight/by meter, ice, picnic tables, fire rings, wood.

◊◊◊◊RECREATION: rec room/area, pavilion, coin games, lake swim, stream fishing, fishing supplies, golf nearby, bsktball, playground, shuffleboard court shuffleboard court, activities (wkends), horseshoes, sports field, hiking trails, v-ball.

Pets welcome. Partial handicap access. Open May 2 - Oct 6. Big rigs welcome. Clubs welcome. Rate in 2010 $35-37 per family. MC/VISA/DISC/Debit. Member ARVC, CONY. FCRV discount. FMCA discount.

Phone: (585)493-2794
Address: 7350 Tenefly Rd, Portageville, NY 14536
Lat/Lon: 42.54917/-78.08910
Email: 4winds@wycol.com
Web: www.fourwindscampground.com

SEE AD THIS PAGE

POTTERSVILLE—C-9

(N) EAGLE POINT CAMPGROUND (Adirondack SF)—(Warren) *From town: Go 2 mi N on US 9.* FACILITIES: 72 sites, typical site width 15 ft, 35 ft max RV length, 72 no hkups, tenting, dump. RECREATION: lake swim, boating, canoeing, ramp, lake fishing, playground. Partial handicap access. Open May 16 - Sep 1. Phone: (518)494-2220.

(E) Ideal Campground—(Warren) *N'bound: From jct I-87 jct (Northway exit 26) & Valley Farm Rd: Go 1/4 mi S on Valley Farm Rd. S'bound: From jct I-87 (Northway exit 26) & Hwy 9: Go 1-1/4 mi S on Hwy 9, then 1/2 mi E & S on Valley Farm Rd. Enter on L.* ◊◊◊FACILITIES: 68 sites, typical site width 30 ft, 30 full hkups, 25 W&E, (20/30 amps), 13 no hkups, 56 pull-thrus, family camping, tenting, dump. ◊◊◊RECREATION: river swim, boating, canoeing, dock, river fishing, playground. Pets welcome. Open May 15 - Oct 15. Rate in 2010 $23 for 2 persons. Member ARVC, CONY. Phone: (518)494-2096.

POUGHKEEPSIE—A-2

MILLS-NORRIE STATE PARK—(Dutchess) *From town: Go 9 mi N on US-9.* FACILITIES: 45 sites, 45 no hkups, 15 pull-thrus, tenting, dump. RECREATION: boating, canoeing, ramp, dock, river fishing, playground. Partial handicap access. Open May 12 - Oct 29. Phone: (845)889-4646.

PULASKI—D-6

(W) BRENNAN BEACH RV RESORT—(Oswego) *From jct Hwy 13 & Hwy 3: Go 1 mi N on Hwy 3, then follow signs 1/2 mi W on entry road. Enter on L.*

◊◊◊◊FACILITIES: 198 sites, typical site width 40 ft, 198 full hkups, (30/50 amps), many extd stay sites, 150 pull-thrus, cable TV, WiFi Internet central location, family camping, tenting, RV's/park model rentals, shower$, laundry, ltd groc, RV supplies, LP gas by weight/by meter, ice, picnic tables, patios, fire rings, wood, controlled access.

◊◊◊◊RECREATION: rec hall, rec room/area, coin games, 2 swim pools, wading pool, lake swim, boating, canoeing, lake/stream fishing, fishing supplies, golf nearby, bsktball, playground, shuffleboard court 4 shuffleboard courts, activities, tennis, horseshoes, sports field, hiking trails, v-ball.

PULASKI—Continued
BRENNAN BEACH RV RESORT—Continued

Pets welcome. Partial handicap access. Open May 1 - Oct 15. Big rigs welcome. Clubs welcome. Green Friendly. Rate in 2010 $41-57 for 2 persons. MC/VISA/DISC/Debit. Member ARVC, CONY.

Phone: (888)891-5979
Address: 80 Brennan Beach, Pulaski, NY 13142
Lat/Lon: 43.57963/-76.18093
Email: brennanbeach@mhchomes.com
Web: www.brennanbeachrvresort.com

Reserve Online at Woodalls.com

SEE AD ACRA PAGE 536

(W) SELKIRK SHORES STATE PARK—(Oswego) *From jct I-81 & Hwy 13: Go 3 mi W on Hwy 13, then 1-1/2 mi S on Hwy 3. Enter on R.* FACILITIES: 148 sites, 84 E, (20 amps), 64 no hkups, tenting, dump, ltd groc. RECREATION: lake swim, boating, canoeing, ramp, lake/river fishing, playground. Partial handicap access. Open all yr. Facilities fully operational Apr 1 - Nov 25. Phone: (315)298-5737.

(S) Streamside RV Park & Golf Course—(OSWEGO) *From jct I-81 (exit 35) & Hwy 28: Go 1/4 mi E on Hwy 28 (Tinker Tavern Rd). Enter on L.* ◊◊◊FACILITIES: 60 sites, accepts self-contained units only, 60 full hkups, (20/30/50 amps), family camping, dump, laundry. Pets welcome. No tents. Rate in 2010 $25 for 2 persons. Phone: (315)298-6887.

RANDOLPH—F-2

(N) POPE HAVEN CAMPGROUND—(Cattaraugus) *From jct Hwy 17/I-86 (exit 16) & Hwy 394: Go 1-1/2 mi NE on Hwy 394, then 3-1/2 mi N on Hwy 241, then 1/4 mi N on Pope Rd. Enter on L.*

◊◊◊FACILITIES: 152 sites, typical site width 45 ft, 5 full hkups, 146 W&E, (20/30/50 amps), 1 no hkups, some extd stay sites (summer), 10 pull-thrus, WiFi Instant Internet at site ($), WiFi Internet central location, family camping, tenting, RV's/park model rentals, cabins, shower$, dump, portable dump, laundry, ltd groc, RV supplies, LP gas by weight/by meter, ice, picnic tables, fire rings, wood.

◊◊◊RECREATION: rec room/area, pavilion, coin games, swim pool, pond fishing, fishing supplies, golf nearby, bsktball, playground, activities, (wkends), horseshoes, sports field, hiking trails, v-ball.

Pets welcome. Partial handicap access. Open May 1 - Columbus Day. Escort to site. Clubs welcome. Green Friendly. Rate in 2010 $26-36 per family. MC/VISA/Debit. Member ARVC, CONY. CCUSA 50% Discount. CCUSA reservations Recommended, CCUSA max stay 2 days, Cash only for CCUSA disc., Check only for CCUSA disc., CCUSA disc. not avail F,Sa, CCUSA disc. not avail holidays. $2 surcharge/person for swimming.

Phone: (716)358-4900
Address: 11948 Pope Rd, Randolph, NY 14772
Lat/Lon: 42.20749/-78.99736
Email: rangermike@popehaven.com
Web: www.popehaven.com

SEE AD SALAMANCA PAGE 562

RANSOMVILLE—D-2

(E) NIAGARA WOODLAND CAMPGROUND & RV SERVICE CENTER—(Niagara) *From jct Hwy 104 & Hwy 425: Go 1-3/4 mi N on Hwy 425, then 1-1/2 mi W on New Rd. Enter on R.*

◊◊◊FACILITIES: 168 sites, 119 full hkups, 44 W&E, 4 E, (15/30/50 amps), 1 no hkups, mostly extd stay sites, WiFi Instant Internet at site, family camping, tenting, RV storage, dump, non-guest dump $, laundry, ltd groc, RV supplies, LP gas by weight/by meter, ice, picnic tables, fire rings, wood, controlled access.

◊◊◊RECREATION: rec room/area, equipped pavilion, coin games, swim pool, wading pool, mini-golf, ($), golf nearby, bsktball, playground, activities, (wkends), horseshoes, sports field, local tours.

Pets welcome, breed restrict. Open 2nd Fri of May - Weekend after Columbus Day. Clubs welcome. Green Friendly. Rate in 2010 $32-35 for 4 persons. MC/VISA. Member ARVC, CONY.

NIAGARA WOODLAND CAMPGROUND & RV SERVICE CENTER—Continued on next page

RANSOMVILLE—Continued
NIAGARA WOODLAND CAMPGROUND & RV SERVICE CENTER—Continued

Phone: (716)791-3101
Address: 3435 New Rd, Ransomville, NY 14131
Lat/Lon: 43.24236/-78.85867
Email: niagarawoodlandcampground@roadrunners.com
Web: www.niagarawoodland.com

SEE AD NIAGARA FALLS PAGE 558

(E) NIAGARA WOODLAND SERVICE CENTER—*From jct State Hwy 104 & Hwy 425: Go 1-3/4 mi N on Hwy 425, then 1-1/2 mi W on New Rd. Enter on R.* SERVICES: full-time mech, RV appliance repair, body work/collision repair, mobile RV svc, RV storage, sells parts/accessories, installs hitches. Open all yr. MC/VISA. FMCA discount.

Phone: (716)791-3101
Address: 3435 New Rd., Ransomville, NY 14131
Lat/Lon: 43.24236/-78.85867
Email: niagarawoodlandcampground@roadrunners.com
Web: www.niagarawoodland.com

SEE AD NIAGARA FALLS PAGE 558

RAQUETTE LAKE—C-8

BROWN TRACT POND CAMPGROUND (Adirondack SF)—(Hamilton) *From business center: Go 2 mi NW on Town Rd.* FACILITIES: 90 sites, 30 ft max RV length, 90 no hkups, tenting, dump. RECREATION: boating, no motors, canoeing, ramp, pond fishing. Partial handicap access. Open Mid May - Labor Day. Phone: (315)354-4412.

EIGHTH LAKE (Adirondack SF)—(Hamilton) *From town: Go 5 mi W on Hwy-28.* FACILITIES: 116 sites, 116 no hkups, tenting, dump. RECREATION: lake swim, boating, canoeing, ramp, lake fishing. Partial handicap access. Open May 21 - Oct 10. Phone: (315)354-4120.

(N) GOLDEN BEACH (Adirondack SF)—(Hamilton) *From town: Go 3 mi N on Hwy-28.* FACILITIES: 195 sites, 30 ft max RV length, 195 no hkups, tenting, dump. RECREATION: lake swim, boating, canoeing, ramp, lake fishing. Partial handicap access. Open May 16 - Sep 1. Phone: (315)354-4230.

RHINEBECK—F-9

(E) INTERLAKE RV PARK & SALES—(Dutchess) *From jct US 9 & Hwy 9G in Rhinebeck: Go 3-1/2 mi S on Hwy 9G, then 3-1/2 mi E on Slate Quarry Rd (Hwy 19), then 1/2 mi S on Lake Drive. Enter on L.*

◆◆◆◆FACILITIES: 159 sites, typical site width 30 ft, 41 full hkups, 112 W&E, (20/30/50 amps), 6 no hkups, many extd stay sites (summer), cable TV, WiFi Instant Internet at site, WiFi Internet central location, family camping, tenting, RV's/park model rentals, shower$, dump, non-guest dump $, portable dump, laundry, ltd groc, RV supplies, ice, picnic tables, fire rings, wood, controlled access.

◆◆◆◆RECREATION: rec hall, coin games, swim pool, wading pool, boating, no motors, canoeing, kayaking, 6 rowboat rentals, lake/pond fishing, fishing supplies, golf nearby, bsktball, playground, activities, (wkends), horseshoes, v-ball.

Pets welcome. Open Apr 15 - Oct 15. Big rigs welcome. Clubs welcome. Rate in 2010 $44-53 for 2 persons. MC/VISA/DISC/Debit. Member ARVC, CONY.

Phone: (845)266-5387
Address: 428 Lake Dr, Rhinebeck, NY 12572-3213
Lat/Lon: 41.90401/-73.81339
Email: interlakervpark@aol.com
Web: www.interlakervpark.com

SEE AD THIS PAGE

(E) INTERLAKE TRAILER SALES—*From jct US 9 & Hwy 9G in Rhinebeck: Go 3-1/2 mi S on HWy 9G, then 3-1/2 mi E on Slate Quarry Hill Rd (CR 19), then 1/2 mi S on Lake Dr. Enter on L.* SALES: travel trailers, park models, 5th wheels, pre-owned unit sales. SERVICES: full-time mech, RV appliance repair. Open all yr. MC/VISA/DISC.

Phone: (845)266-5387
Address: 428 Lake Dr, Rhinebeck, NY 12572-3213
Lat/Lon: 41.90401/-73.81337

SEE AD THIS PAGE

RIVERHEAD—B-4

INDIAN ISLAND PARK (Suffolk County Park)—(Suffolk) *From jct Hwy 24 & CR 105: Go E on CR 105 past golf course.* FACILITIES: 150 sites, 150 no hkups, tenting, dump. RECREATION: saltwater fishing, playground. Open all yr. Phone: (631) 854-4949.

ROCHESTER—D-4

See listings at Leroy & Phelps

ROCHESTER—Continued on next page

The first capital of the United States was New York City. In 1789 George Washington took his oath as president on the balcony at Federal Hall.

Can you trust the Woodall's ratings? 25 evaluation teams have scoured North American campgrounds to provide you with accurate, up to date information & ratings. Find a rating you don't agree with? Send a letter or email our way, and we'll give it extra attention for 2012.

ROCHESTER—Continued

CHEERFUL VALLEY CAMPGROUND—*From Rochester: Take I-90 (Thruway) east to exit 42, then 1/2 mi N on Hwy 14. Enter on L.*

WELCOME

SEE PRIMARY LISTING AT PHELPS AND AD PAGE 561

ROME—D-7

(N) DELTA LAKE STATE PARK—(Oneida) *From town: Go 6 mi N on Hwy-46.* FACILITIES: 101 sites, typical site width 15 ft, 30 ft max RV length, 101 no hkups, tenting, dump, laundry, ltd groc. RECREATION: lake swim, boating, canoeing, ramp, lake fishing, playground. Partial handicap access. Open all yr. Phone: (315)337-4670.

ROSCOE—F-8

(NW) Russell Brook Campsite—(Delaware) *WESTBOUND: From Hwy 17 (Quickway) take exit 93 Cooks Falls: Go 500 feet W on Old Hwy-17, then 3/4 mi N on Russell Brook Rd. EASTBOUND: From Hwy-17 (Quickway) take exit 92: Go 1-1/2 mi SE on Old Hwy-17, then 3/4 mi N on Russell Brook Rd. Enter on L.* ◇◇◇FACILITIES: 140 sites, typical site width 40 ft, 140 W&E, (20/30 amps), 5 pull-thrus, family camping, tenting, dump, laundry, ltd groc. ◇◇◇◇RECREATION: swim pool, river swim, pond/stream fishing, playground. Pets welcome ($), quantity restrict. Open May 1 - Oct 31. Green Friendly. Rate in 2010 $35 for 2 persons. Phone: (607)498-5416.

SACKETS HARBOR—C-6

(SE) Bedford Creek Marina & Campground—(Jefferson) *From jct I-81 & Hwy 3 (exit 45): Go 9 mi S on Hwy 3. Enter on R.* ◇◇FACILITIES: 202 sites, typical site width 22 ft, 146 full hkups, 32 W&E, (20/30 amps), 24 no hkups, 3 pull-thrus, family camping, tenting, dump, laundry, ltd groc. ◇◇◇RECREATION: lake swim, boating, canoeing, ramp, dock, lake fishing, play equipment. Pets welcome, quantity restrict. Open Apr 15 - Oct 15. Rate in 2010 $26-30 for 2 persons. Member ARVC, CONY. Phone: (315)646-2486.

Norman Rockwell, painter and illustrator, was from New York.

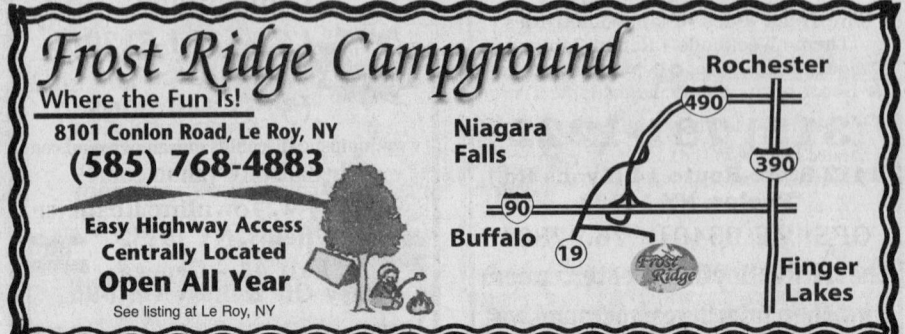

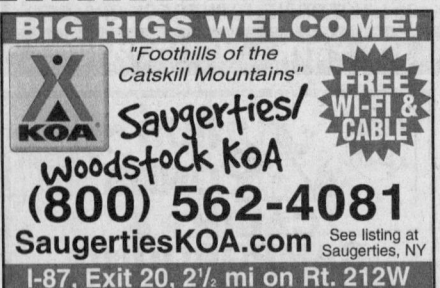

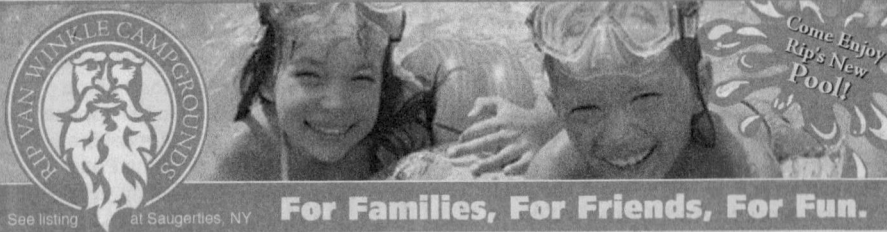

SACKETS HARBOR—Continued

WESCOTT BEACH STATE PARK—(Jefferson) *From town: Go 3 mi S on Hwy 3.* FACILITIES: 154 sites, 83 E, (20/30 amps), 71 no hkups, tenting, dump. RECREATION: lake swim, boating, canoeing, ramp, dock, lake fishing, playground. Pets welcome. Partial handicap access. Open Early May - Columbus Day. Phone: (315)646-2239.

ST. JOHNSVILLE—E-8

(N) Crystal Grove Diamond Mine & Campground—(Fulton) *From jct Hwy 29 & Hwy 114: Go 1/4 mi S on Hwy 114. Enter on L.* ◇◇◇FACILITIES: 32 sites, typical site width 40 ft, 22 W&E, (15/30 amps), 10 no hkups, 6 pull-thrus, family camping, tenting, dump. ◇◇RECREATION: stream fishing, playground. Pets welcome. Open Apr 15 - Oct 15. Rate in 2010 $32 per family. Member ARVC, CONY. Phone: (800)579-3426.

ST. JOHNSVILLE CAMPSITE & MARINA (City Park)—(Montgomery) *From I-90 (Canajoharie exit): Cross Mohawk River and go 10 mi W on Hwy 5, then 1/4 mi S on Bridge St to Marina Dr.* FACILITIES: 21 sites, 15 full hkups, 6 E, 6 pull-thrus, tenting, dump. RECREATION: river swim, boating, canoeing, ramp, dock, river fishing. Open May 15 - Oct 15. Phone: (518)568-7406.

SALAMANCA—F-2

ALLEGANY STATE PARK (Quaker Area)—(Cattarougus) *From Hwy-17 (Exit 18): Go S on Hwy-280, then E on Park Rd 3.* FACILITIES: 189 sites, 91 E, 98 no hkups, tenting, dump, laundry, ltd groc. RECREATION: lake swim, boating, 5 hp limit, electric motors only, canoeing, ramp, lake/stream fishing, playground. Pets welcome. Partial handicap access. Open all yr. Phone: (716)354-9121.

ALLEGANY STATE PARK (Red House Area)—(Cattarougus) *From Hwy 17 (exit 19): Go E on Allegany State Park Rd 2, then S on Allegany State Park Rd 1.* FACILITIES: 130 sites, 66 E, 64 no hkups, 3 pull-thrus, tenting, dump, laundry, ltd groc. RECREATION: lake swim, boating, no motors, canoeing, ramp, lake/stream fishing, playground. Partial handicap access. Open all yr. Phone: (716)354-9121.

SARANAC LAKE—B-9

MEADOWBROOK CAMPGROUND (Adirondack SF)—(Essex) *From town: Go 4 mi E on Hwy-86.* FACILITIES: 62 sites, 30 ft max RV length, 62 no hkups, tenting, dump. RECREATION: playground. Partial handicap access. Open May 16 - Sep 1. Phone: (518)891-4351.

SARATOGA SPRINGS—D-9

(N) ADIRONDACK ADVENTURE RESORTS-SARATOGA SPRINGS—(Saratoga) *From jct I-87 (exit 16) & Hwy 33: Go 2 mi W on Ballard Rd (RT 33), then 1-3/4 mi S on RT 9, then 3 mi W on Gailor Rd, then 1 mi NW on Brigham Rd. Enter on L.*

WELCOME

◇◇◇◇FACILITIES: 78 sites, 68 W&E, (30 amps), 10 no hkups, 10 pull-thrus, cable TV, ($), WiFi Internet central location, family camping, tenting, cabins, RV storage, dump, non-guest dump $, portable dump, laundry, ltd groc, RV supplies, LP gas by weight/by meter, ice, picnic tables, fire rings, wood.

SARATOGA SPRINGS—Continued
ADIRONDACK ADVENTURE RESORTS-SARATOGA SPRINGS—Continued

◇◇◇◇RECREATION: rec room/area, swim pool, spray ground, lake swim, boating, dock, lake fishing, mini-golf, ($), golf nearby, playground, sports field, hiking trails.

Pets welcome. Partial handicap access. Open May 15 - Columbus Day. Clubs welcome. Rate in 2010 $45 for 2 persons. MC/VISA/DISC/AMEX. Member ARVC, CONY.

Phone: (800)340-CAMP
Address: 265 Brigham Rd, Greenfield Center, NY 12833
Lat/Lon: 43.14658/-73.81882
Email: camping@charterinternet.com
Web: www.adirondackadventureresorts.com

SEE AD LAKE GEORGE PAGE 552

(NW) Whispering Pines Campsites—(Saratoga) *From jct I-87 (Exit 15) & Hwy 50: Go 2 mi SW on Hwy 50, then 3 mi W & NW on Van Dam/Church/State Hwy 9 N, then 3-1/4 mi W on Middle Grove Rd (Hwy 21), then 2 mi N on Sand Hill Rd. Enter on L.* ◇◇◇FACILITIES: 112 sites, 46 full hkups, 29 W&E, (20/30/50 amps), 37 no hkups, 8 pull-thrus, family camping, tenting, dump, laundry, ltd groc. ◇◇◇RECREATION: swim pool, pond/stream fishing, playground. Pets welcome. Open May 1 - Oct 31. Rate in 2010 $35-41 for 2 persons. Member ARVC, CONY. Phone: (518)893-0416.

SAUGERTIES—F-9

(NW) BLUE MOUNTAIN CAMPGROUND—(Ulster) *From jct I-87 (exit 20) & Hwy 212: Go 1/8 mi W on Hwy 212, then 4-1/2 mi N on Hwy 32. Enter on L.*

WELCOME

◇◇◇FACILITIES: 60 sites, 20 full hkups, 20 W&E, (20/30/50 amps), 20 no hkups, some extd stay sites, WiFi Instant Internet at site, WiFi Internet central location, family camping, tenting, dump, laundry, ltd groc, ice, picnic tables, fire rings, wood.

◇◇◇RECREATION: coin games, swim pool, golf nearby, bsktball, playground, activities, (wkends), sports field, v-ball.

Pets welcome. Open Mid Apr - Mid Oct. Green Friendly. Rate in 2010 $45 for 2 persons. MC/VISA/DISC/AMEX. Member ARVC, CONY. CCUSA 50% Discount. CCUSA reservations Recommended, CCUSA max stay 14 days, CCUSA disc. not avail F,Sa, CCUSA disc. not avail holidays.

BLUE MOUNTAIN CAMPGROUND—Continued on next page

Find a park or campground Woodall's doesn't list? Tell us!

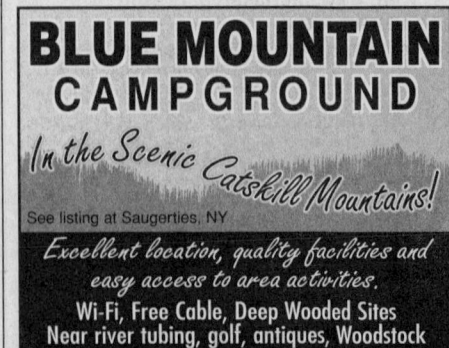

SAUGERTIES—Continued
BLUE MOUNTAIN CAMPGROUND—Continued

Phone: (845)246-7564
Address: 3783 Rte 32, Saugerties, NY 12477
Lat/Lon: 42.14174/-74.00209
Email: bluemtncampground@yahoo.com
Web: www.bluemountaincampground.com

SEE AD PAGE 562

(W) KOA-SAUGERTIES/WOODSTOCK—(Ulster) *From jct I-87 (exit 20) & Hwy 212: Go 2-1/2 mi W on Hwy 212. Enter on R.*

◇◇◇◇FACILITIES: 81 sites, typical site width 30 ft, 29 full hkups, 29 W&E, (20/30/50 amps), 23 no hkups, 21 pull-thrus, cable TV, WiFi Instant Internet at site, family camping, tenting, cabins, RV storage, dump, non-guest dump $, laundry, groceries, RV supplies, LP gas by weight/by meter, ice, picnic tables, fire rings, wood.

◇◇◇◇RECREATION: rec hall, rec room/area, coin games, swim pool, pond fishing, fishing supplies, mini-golf, golf nearby, bike rental 10 bike rentals, playground, activities, (wkends), horseshoes, hiking trails.

Pets welcome, breed restrict. Partial handicap access. Open Mid March - Oct 31. Pool open Memorial Day to Labor Day. Big rigs welcome. Escort to site. Clubs welcome. Green Friendly. Rate in 2010 $35-60 for 2 persons. MC/VISA/DISC/AMEX/Debit. Member ARVC, CONY. KOA discount.

Phone: (800)562-4081
Address: 882 Rt 212, Saugerties, NY 12477
Lat/Lon: 42.08344/-74.01568
Email: saugertieskoa@hotmail.com
Web: www.saugertieskoa.com

SEE AD PAGE 562 AND AD TRAVEL SECTION PAGE 527

(W) RIP VAN WINKLE CAMPGROUNDS—(Ulster) *S'bound from I-87 (exit 20-Saugerties) & Hwy 32: Go 1/8 mi S on Hwy 32, 2 mi W on Hwy 212, then 1/2 mi N at Centerville Fork on CR 35. N'bound from jct I-87 (exit 20-Saugerties) & Hwy 212: Go 2 mi W on Hwy 212, then 1/2 mi N at Centerville Fork on CR 35. Enter on L.*

◇◇◇◇FACILITIES: 170 sites, typical site width 60 ft, 114 full hkups, 6 W&E, (20/30/50 amps), 50 no hkups, some extd stay sites (summer), 37 pull-thrus, cable TV, WiFi Instant Internet at site ($), WiFi Internet central location, family camping, tenting, RV storage, shower$, dump, laundry, ltd groc, RV supplies, LP gas by weight/by meter, ice, picnic tables, fire rings, wood, controlled access.

◇◇◇◇RECREATION: rec hall, coin games, swim pool, river swim, 2 pedal boat rentals, river/pond fishing, fishing supplies, golf nearby, playground, activities, (wkends), sports field, hiking trails, v-ball.

Pets welcome. Partial handicap access. Open May 1 - Oct 15. Big rigs welcome. Clubs welcome. Rate in 2010 $45-50 per family. MC/VISA/DISC/Debit. ATM. Member ARVC, CONY. FMCA discount.

Phone: (800)724-1239
Address: 149 Blue Mountain Rd, Saugerties, NY 12477
Lat/Lon: 42.09237/-74.01753
Email: camping@ripvanwinklecampgrounds.com
Web: www.ripvanwinklecampgrounds.com

SEE AD PAGE 562

Woodall's Tip... If a campground's management escorts your RV right to your site, we let you know in the listing.

SAUGERTIES—Continued

✲ **(W) RIP VAN WINKLE RV SALES**—*From jct I-87 (exit 20 Saugerties) & Hwy 212: Go 2 mi W on Hwy 212, then 1/2 mi N on Centerville Fork on Hwy 35. Enter on L.* SALES: travel trailers, park models, 5th wheels, SERVICES: LP gas by weight/by meter. Open May 1 - Oct 15. MC/VISA/DISC/Debit. ATM.

Phone: (800)724-1239
Address: 149 Blue Mountain Rd, Saugerties, NY 12477
Email: camping@ripvanwinklecampgrounds.com
Web: www.ripvanwinklecampgrounds.com

SEE AD PAGE 562

SCHENECTADY—E-9

(W) ARROWHEAD MARINA & RV PARK—(Schenectady) *From jct I-90 (exit 26) & Hwy 5: Go 1 mi NW on Hwy 5, then 1 block W on Hwy 5, then 1/4 mi W on Van Buren Lane, cross over railroad tracks, then 1/4 mi NW on Pump House Rd. Enter on L.*

◇◇◇◇FACILITIES: 65 sites, typical site width 30 ft, 34 full hkups, 26 W&E, 3 E, (20/30/50 amps), 2 no hkups, some extd stay sites (summer), 10 pull-thrus, cable TV, phone Internet central location, family camping, tenting, dump, non-guest dump $, portable dump, laundry, RV supplies, marine gas, ice, picnic tables, patios, fire rings, grills, wood.

◇◇RECREATION: boating, canoeing, ramp, dock, river fishing, fishing supplies, golf nearby, activities, (wkends), horseshoes. Rec open to public.

Pets welcome. Open May 15 - Oct 15. Big rigs welcome. Clubs welcome. Rate in 2010 $29-32 per family. Member ARVC, CONY.

Phone: (518)382-8966
Address: 2 Van Buren Lane, Glenville, NY 12302
Lat/Lon: 42.85232/-74.01215
Email: arrowheadmrvp@gmail.com
Web: www.arrowheadmrvp.com

SEE AD THIS PAGE

SCHROON LAKE—C-9

(N) SHARP BRIDGE CAMPGROUND (Adirondack SF)—(Essex) *From town: Go 15 mi N on Hwy-9.* FACILITIES: 40 sites, 40 no hkups, tenting, dump. RECREATION: river fishing, playground. Partial handicap access. Open May 16 - Sep 1. Phone: (518)532-7538.

SCHUYLER FALLS—B-9

(W) MACOMB RESERVATION STATE PARK—(Clinton) *From the center of the village at jct Hwy 22B & Norrisville Rd: Go 2 mi W on Norrisville Rd.* FACILITIES: 173 sites, 173 no hkups, tenting, dump. RECREATION: lake swim, boating, canoeing, river fishing, playground. Partial handicap access. Open May 12 - Sep 3. Phone: (518)643-9952.

SENECA FALLS—E-5

(E) CAYUGA LAKE STATE PARK—(Seneca) *From town: Go 3 mi E on Bayard St, then S on Hwy 89.* FACILITIES: 250 sites, (30 amps), 250 no hkups, tenting, dump. RECREATION: lake swim, boating, canoeing, ramp, dock, lake fishing, playground. Partial handicap access. Open Apr 24 - Oct 28. Phone: (315)568-5163.

Woodall's Tip... Time Zone, temperature & topography information is located in the Travel Section in front of each state/province.

SENECA FALLS—Continued

(N) OAK ORCHARD MARINA & CAMPGROUND—(Seneca) *From jct Hwy 5/US 20 & Hwy 89: Go 4 mi N on Hwy 89. Enter on L.*

◇◇◇FACILITIES: 79 sites, typical site width 40 ft, 7 full hkups, 62 W&E, (20/30/50 amps), 10 no hkups, some extd stay sites (summer), family camping, tenting, cabins, RV storage, dump, laundry, ltd groc, RV supplies, LP gas by meter, ice, picnic tables, fire rings, wood.

◇◇◇RECREATION: rec room/area, pavilion, coin games, swim pool, boating, kayaking, ramp, dock, 3 rowboat/2 canoe/pedal boat rentals, river fishing, fishing supplies, golf nearby, playground, activities, (wkends), hiking trails.

Pets welcome, breed restrict. Open May 1 - Oct 15. Rate in 2010 $27-29 for 4 persons. MC/VISA/DISC/AMEX.

Phone: (315)365-3000
Address: 508 Rt 89, Savannah, NY 13146
Lat/Lon: 43.00090/-76.76443
Email: oakorchardcampground@yahoo.com
Web: www.oakorchard.com

SEE AD THIS PAGE

SHIRLEY—C-4

SMITH POINT PARK (Suffolk County Park)—(Suffolk) *From Long Island Expwy (I-495, exit 68): Go S on William Floyd Pkwy to the end on Fire Island.* FACILITIES: 220 sites, 220 no hkups, tenting, dump. RECREATION: saltwater swim, saltwater fishing, playground. Open all yr. Facilities fully operational Apr - Oct. Phone: (631)852-1313.

SMITHTOWN—B-4

(W) BLYDENBURGH PARK (Suffolk County Park)—(Suffolk) *From Long Island Expwy (I-495, exit 57): Go 4 mi N.* FACILITIES: 50 sites, 50 no hkups, tenting, dump. RECREATION: boating, electric motors only, dock, pond fishing, playground. Partial handicap access. Open all yr. Phone: (631)854-3712.

SOUTH COLTON—B-8

HIGLEY FLOW STATE PARK—(St. Lawrence) *From town: Go 1-1/2 mi W off Hwy-56 on Coldbrook.* FACILITIES: 135 sites, 43 E, (20 amps), 92 no hkups, tenting, dump. RECREATION: lake swim, boating, canoeing, ramp, river fishing, playground. Partial handicap access. Open Memorial Day - Labor Day. Phone: (315) 262-2880.

SPRINGWATER—E-4

(SE) HOLIDAY HILL CAMPGROUND—(Livingston) *From jct I-390 (exit 3) & Hwy 15: Go 4 mi N on Hwy 15, then 1/2 mi E on Walker Rd, then 3 mi NW on Strutt St, then 1/2 mi S on Marvin Hill Rd. Enter on L.*

◇◇◇FACILITIES: 168 sites, typical site width 35 ft, 22 full hkups, 146 W&E, (20/30 amps), many extd stay sites (summer), cable TV, WiFi Instant Internet at site, WiFi Internet central location, family camping, tenting, RV's/park model rentals, cabins, dump, non-guest dump $, portable dump, laundry, groceries, RV supplies, LP gas by weight, ice, picnic tables, fire rings, wood.

◇◇◇◇RECREATION: rec hall, rec room/area, pavilion, coin games, swim pool, pond fishing, fishing supplies, mini-golf, ($), golf nearby, bsktball, playground, activities, (wkends), horseshoes, sports field, hiking trails, v-ball.

HOLIDAY HILL CAMPGROUND—Continued on next page

SPRINGWATER—Continued
HOLIDAY HILL CAMPGROUND—Continued

Pets welcome. Partial handicap access. Open May 1 - Columbus Day. Clubs welcome. Rate in 2010 $37-41 for 4 persons. MC/VISA/DISC/Debit. Member ARVC, CONY.

Phone: (585)669-2600
Address: 7818 Marvin Hill Rd, Springwater, NY 14560
Lat/Lon: 42.62860/-77.56767
Email: hilltoprec@gmail.com
Web: www.holidayhillcampground.com

SEE AD PAGE 563

STEAMBURG—F-2

(S) ONOVILLE MARINA AND CAMPGROUND—(Cattaraugus) *From I-86 (exit 17): Go 9-1/4 mi S on West Perimeter Rd. Enter on L.* FACILITIES: 65 sites, 40 W&E, 17 E, (20/30 amps), 8 no hkups, family camping, tenting, dump, laundry, ltd groc. RECREATION: lake swim, boating, canoeing, ramp, dock, lake fishing. Pets welcome. Partial handicap access. Open May - Sep. Phone: (716)354-2615.

STONE RIDGE—A-2

(NW) So-Hi Campground—(Ulster) *From jct US 209 & CR 2: Go 4 mi NW on CR 2, then 1/4 mi N on Woodland Rd. Enter on R.* ◇◇FACILITIES: 130 sites, 100 full hkups, (20/30 amps), 30 no hkups, family camping, tenting, laundry, ltd groc. ◇◇◇RECREATION: swim pool, pond fishing, playground. Pets welcome, breed restrict. Open May 15 - Oct 14. Rate in 2010 $34-40 for 2 persons. Member ARVC, CONY. Phone: (845)687-7377.

STONY POINT—B-2

HARRIMAN SP (Beaver Pond Campground)—(Rockland) *5 mi W of town on Gate Hill Rd.* FACILITIES: 200 sites, 200 no hkups, tenting, dump. RECREATION: lake swim, boating, no motors, ramp, lake fishing. Open mid Apr - Last Wknd of Oct. Phone: (845)786-2701.

SYLVAN BEACH—D-6

(E) Mayfair Campground—(Oneida) *From jct Hwy 49 & Hwy 13: Go 2-1/4 mi S on Hwy 13, then 4 mi NE on Vienna Rd/Haskins Rd. Enter on R.* ◇◇◇FACILITIES: 76 sites, 76 full hkups, (20/30/50 amps), family camping, dump, laundry, ltd groc. ◇◇RECREATION: river swim, boating, ramp, river fishing, playground. Pets welcome. Partial handicap access. No tents. Open May 1 - Oct 15. Big rigs welcome. Rate in 2010 $31-35 per family. Member ARVC, CONY. Phone: (315)245-3870.

(E) Ta-Ga-Soke Campgrounds—(Oneida) *From jct I-90 (exit 34) & Hwy 13 N: Go 9 mi N on Hwy 13, then 2-1/2 mi NE on Vienna Rd, then 100 feet E on Higginsville Rd. Enter on L.* ◇◇◇FACILITIES: 212 sites, typical site width 30 ft, 75 full hkups, 120 W&E, (15/30/50 amps), 17 no hkups, 45 pull-thrus, family camping, tenting, dump, laundry, ltd groc. ◇◇◇◇RECREATION: river swim, boating, canoeing, ramp, dock, river fishing, playground. Pets welcome. Partial handicap access. Open May 1 - mid Oct. Rate in 2010 $28-32 per family. Member ARVC, CONY. Phone: (800)831-1744.

(C) The Landing Campground—(Oneida) *From jct Hwy 49 & Hwy 13: Go 2-1/4 mi S on Hwy 13, then 2-1/4 mi NE on Vienna Rd, then 100 feet E on Kellogg Rd. Enter on R.* ◇◇FACILITIES: 74 sites, typical site width 30 ft, 74 full hkups, (15/20/30 amps), 4 pull-thrus, family camping, tenting, dump, laundry, ltd groc. ◇◇◇RECREATION: river swim, boating, canoeing, ramp, dock, river fishing, playground. Pets welcome. Open Apr 1 - Nov 1. Rate in 2010 $30-35 for 2 persons. Member ARVC, CONY. Phone: (315)245-9951.

(W) Treasure Isle RV Park—(Oneida) *From jct Hwy 49 & Hwy 13: Go 2-1/4 mi S on Hwy 13, then 3-1/2 mi NE on Vienna Rd/Haskins Rd. Enter on R.* ◇◇FACILITIES: 70 sites, typical site width 45 ft, 66 W&E, (20/30/50 amps), 50 amps ($), 4 no hkups, 12 pull-thrus, WiFi Internet central location, family camping, tenting, RV storage, dump, portable dump, laundry, ltd groc, RV supplies, ice, picnic tables, fire rings, wood.

SYLVAN BEACH—Continued
Treasure Isle RV Park—Continued

CAMPCLUB USA

◇◇◇RECREATION: pavilion, river swim, boating, canoeing, kayaking, dock, river/pond fishing, fishing supplies, bsktball, playground, activities, horseshoes, hiking trails, v-ball. Pets welcome, quantity restrict. Partial handicap access. Open Mid Apr - Mid Oct. Big rigs welcome. Green Friendly. Rate in 2010 $31-37 per family. MC/VISA. Member ARVC, CONY. CCUSA 50% Discount. CCUSA reservations Required, CCUSA max stay Unlimited, Cash only for CCUSA disc., CCUSA disc. not avail holidays. Fee for dumping on way in. Fee for RV & vehicle washing. Cash only for discount. Call ahead for availability.

Phone: (315)245-5228
Address: 3132 Haskins Rd, Blossvale, NY 13308
Lat/Lon: 43.23173/-75.67744
Email: leannesilber@gmail.com
Web: www.treasureislervpark.com

SYRACUSE—D-6

WELCOME

YOGI BEAR'S JELLYSTONE PARK CAMP RESORT AT MEXICO—*From jct I-90 (exit) & I-81: Go 28 mi N on I-81 (exit 34), then 5 mi W on Hwy 104, then 3 mi N on CR 16. Enter on L.*

SEE PRIMARY LISTING AT MEXICO AND AD TRAVEL SECTION PAGE 529

THREE MILE BAY—C-6

(S) LONG POINT STATE PARK (Thousand Islands Region)—(Jefferson) *From town: Go 2 mi W on Hwy 12E, then 9 mi S on access road.* FACILITIES: 80 sites, 39 E, (15 amps), 41 no hkups, tenting, dump. RECREATION: boating, canoeing, ramp, dock, lake fishing, playground. Partial handicap access. Open May 19 - Sep 15. Phone: (315)649-5258.

TICONDEROGA—C-10

PARADOX LAKE CAMPGROUND (Adirondack SF)—(Essex) *From town: Go 8 mi W on Hwy-74.* FACILITIES: 58 sites, typical site width 50 ft, 58 no hkups, 9 pull-thrus, tenting, dump. RECREATION: lake swim, boating, canoeing, ramp, lake fishing, playground. Partial handicap access. Open May 16 - Oct 13. Phone: (518)532-7451.

PUTNAM POND CAMPSITE (Adirondack SF)—(Essex) *From town: Go 6 mi SW on Hwy-74 & FR.* FACILITIES: 72 sites, 72 no hkups, tenting, dump. RECREATION: lake swim, boating, canoeing, ramp, pond fishing, playground. Partial handicap access. Open May 16 - Sep 1. Phone: (518)585-7280.

ROGERS ROCK CAMPGROUND (Adirondack SF)—(Warren) *From town: Go 7 mi SW on Hwy-9N.* FACILITIES: 321 sites, 321 no hkups, tenting, dump. RECREATION: lake swim, boating, canoeing, ramp, lake fishing, playground. Partial handicap access. Open May 2 - Oct 13. Phone: (518)585-6746.

TUPPER LAKE—B-8

(E) FISH CREEK PONDS CAMPGROUND (Adirondack SF)—(Franklin) *From town: Go 12 mi E on Hwy-30.* FACILITIES: 324 sites, typical site width 12 ft, 324 no hkups, tenting, dump. RECREATION: lake swim, boating, canoeing, ramp, playground. Partial handicap access. Open Apr 11 - Oct 26. Phone: (518)891-4560.

(N) ROLLINS POND CAMPGROUND (Adirondack SF)—(Franklin) *From town: Go 12 mi NE on Hwy-30.* FACILITIES: 268 sites, 268 no hkups, tenting, dump. RECREATION: boating, 25 hp limit, canoeing, ramp. Pets welcome. Partial handicap access. Open May 16 - Sep 1. Phone: (518)891-3239.

UNADILLA—F-7

(E) KOA-UNADILLA/Delaware Valley—(Delaware) *From jct I-88 (exit 11) & Hwy 357: Go 1/4 mi W on Hwy 357, then 2 mi NE on Covered Bridge Rd, then 1 mi S on CR 44, then 1/4 mi W on Union Church Rd. Enter on L.* ◇◇◇FACILITIES: 88 sites, typical site width 20 ft, 79 W&E, (20/30/50 amps), 50 amps ($), 9 no hkups, 21 pull-thrus, family camping, tenting, dump, laundry, ltd groc. ◇◇◇RECREATION: swim pool, pond/stream fishing, playground. Pets welcome. Open May 1 - Oct 15. Rate in 2010 $40 for 2 persons. Member ARVC, CONY. Phone: (800)562-7658. KOA discount.

UTICA—D-7

See listing at Poland

VERONA—D-7

WELCOME

(SW) THE VILLAGES AT TURNING STONE RV PARK—(Oneida) *From jct I-90 (NY Thruway) (exit 33) & Hwy 365: Go 1-1/2 mi W on Hwy 365. Enter on R.*

ADVENTURE ABOUNDS IN VERONA, NY
Enjoy nature's playground at this top-rated New York park. Hike and bike acres of terrain, swim, and enjoy themed weekends the whole season through. Entire world-class resort experience is just a 5 min. shuttle ride away!

◇◇◇◇◇FACILITIES: 175 sites, typical site width 40 ft, 175 full hkups, (20/30/50 amps), some extd stay sites (summer), 50 pull-thrus, cable TV, WiFi Instant Internet at site, cable Internet central location, family camping, dump, non-guest dump $, laundry, ltd groc, RV supplies, LP gas by weight/by meter, ice, picnic tables, patios, fire rings, grills, wood.

◇◇◇◇◇RECREATION: rec hall, rec room/area, equipped pavilion, coin games, swim pool, wading pool, hot tub, 5 pedal boat rentals, pond fishing, fishing supplies, golf nearby, bsktball, playground, activities, (wkends), tennis, horseshoes, hiking trails, v-ball, local tours.

Pets welcome. Partial handicap access. No tents. Open Mid Apr - Oct. Big rigs welcome. Clubs welcome. Rate in 2010 $40-55 for 4 persons. MC/VISA/DISC/AMEX/Debit. Member ARVC, CONY. FMCA discount.

Text 81698 to (440)725-8687 to see our Visual Tour.

Phone: (315)361-7275
Address: 5065 SR 365, Verona, NY 13478
Lat/Lon: 43.10577/-75.60483
Email: info@turningstone.com
Web: www.turningstone.com/lodging/rvpark/

SEE AD TRAVEL SECTION PAGE 526

WELCOME

(SW) TURNING STONE RESORT & CASINO—*From jct I-90 (NY Thruway-exit 33) & Hwy 365: Go 1 mi S on Hwy 365. Enter on L.* Around the clock casino action with exciting table games, six restaurants, gift and smoke shop. The casino is an enterprise of the Oneida Indian Nation, a Sovereign Indian Nation. Open all yr. MC/VISA/DISC/AMEX/Debit. ATM.

Phone: (800)771-7711
Address: Hwy 365, Verona, NY 13478
Lat/Lon: 43.11712/-75.59498
Email: info@turningstone.com
Web: www.turningstone.com

SEE AD TRAVEL SECTION PAGE 526

WADDINGTON—A-7

(E) COLES CREEK STATE PARK—(St. Lawrence) *From town: Go 5 mi N on Hwy-37.* FACILITIES: 235 sites, typical site width 20 ft, 154 E, (15/30 amps), 81 no hkups, tenting, dump, ltd groc. RECREATION: boating, canoeing, ramp, dock, river fishing, playground. Partial handicap access. Open Mid May - After Columbus Day. Phone: (315)388-5636.

WADING RIVER—B-4

WELCOME

(S) W.E.S. TRAILER SALES INC.—*From jct Hwy 46 & Hwy 25: Go 3 mi E on Hwy 25. Enter on L.* SALES: travel trailers, 5th wheels, Class A motorhomes, Class C motorhomes, fold-down camping trailers, pre-owned unit sales. SERVICES: full-time mech, RV appliance repair, body work/collision repair, LP gas by weight/by meter, dump station, RV storage, sells parts/accessories, installs hitches. Expert Welding Services. Open all yr. MC/VISA/DISC.

W.E.S. TRAILER SALES INC.—Continued on next page

WADING RIVER—Continued
W.E.S. TRAILER SALES INC.—Continued

Phone: (631)727-5852
Address: 6166 Rte 25 & Wading River Manor Rd, Wading River, Long Island, NY 11792
Lat/Lon: 40.91454/-72.83467
Email: westrailers@yahoo.com
Web: www.westrailersales.com

SEE AD PAGE 564 AND AD TRAVEL SECTION PAGE 527

(NE) WILDWOOD STATE PARK—(Suffolk) *From jct I-495 (Long Island Expwy) (Exit 68) & Hwy 46: Go 7 mi N on Hwy 46, then 4 mi E on Hwy 25A (follow signs).* FACILITIES: 314 sites, 80 full hkups, 234 no hkups, tenting, dump, ltd groc. RECREATION: saltwater swim, saltwater fishing, playground. No pets. Partial handicap access. Open May 21 - Oct 10. Phone: (631)929-4314.

WALTON—F-7

(SE) BEAR SPRING MOUNTAIN (Catskill SF)—(Delaware) *From town: Go 5 mi SE on Hwy 206.* FACILITIES: 41 sites, typical site width 12 ft, 30 ft max RV length, 41 no hkups, tenting, dump. RECREATION: lake swim, boating, no motors, canoeing, ramp, pond fishing. Partial handicap access. Open Late April - Early Dec. Phone: (607)865-6989.

WARRENSBURG—D-9

(N) LAKE GEORGE/SCHROON VALLEY RESORT—(Warren) *From I-87 (exit 24/Bolton Landing): Go 50 yds E, then 3/4 mi S on Schroon River Rd. Enter on L.*

◇◇◇◇FACILITIES: 150 sites, typical site width 35 ft, 80 full hkups, 70 W&E, (20/30/50 amps), some extd stay sites (summer), 26 pull-thrus, WiFi Instant Internet at site, phone Internet central location, family camping, tenting, RV's/park model rentals, cabins, dump, portable dump, laundry, ltd groc, RV supplies, LP gas by weight/by meter, ice, picnic tables, fire rings, wood, controlled access.

◇◇◇◇RECREATION: rec room/area, coin games, 2 swim pools, canoeing, kayaking, float trips, river fishing, fishing supplies, golf nearby, bsktball, 7 bike rentals, playground, activities, (wkends), horseshoes, sports field, v-ball.

Pets welcome, breed restrict. Open Mothers Day - Columbus Day. Big rigs welcome. Clubs welcome. Rate in 2010 $22-43 for 2 persons. MC/VISA/Debit. ATM. Member ARVC, CONY.

Phone: (800)958-2267
Address: 1730 Schroon River Rd, Warrensburg, NY 12885
Lat/Lon: 43.59258/-73.73215
Email: info2@lakegeorgecamping.com
Web: www.lakegeorgecamping.com

SEE AD ACRA PAGE 536 AND AD LAKE GEORGE PAGE 549

(NE) SCHROON RIVER CAMPSITES—(Warren) *From jct I-87 (exit 23-Warrensburg) & Diamond Point Rd: Go 200 feet W on Diamond Point Rd, then 1/2 mi N on US 9, then 3 mi N on Horicon Ave/Schroon River Rd. Enter on R.*

◇◇◇FACILITIES: 300 sites, typical site width 30 ft, 250 full hkups, 50 W&E, (15/20/30/50 amps), many extd stay sites (summer), heater not allowed, cable TV, WiFi Internet central location, family camping, tenting, cabins, dump, non-guest dump $, laundry, groceries, RV supplies, LP gas by weight, ice, picnic tables, fire rings, wood.

◇◇◇◇RECREATION: rec room/area, coin games, swim pool, river swim, boating, canoeing, kayaking, 2 rowboat/7 canoe/2 kayak rentals, float trips, river fishing, fishing supplies, golf nearby, bsktball, playground, activities, (wkends), horseshoes, sports field, v-ball.

Pets welcome. Open May 13 - Oct 2. Clubs welcome. Rate in 2010 $27-45 for 2 persons. MC/VISA/Debit. Member ARVC, CONY.

Phone: (518)623-2171
Address: 686 Schroon River Rd, Warrensburg, NY 12885
Lat/Lon: 43.53123/-73.75544
Email: info@schroonrivercampsites.com
Web: www.schroonriver.com

SEE AD LAKE GEORGE PAGE 553 AND AD TRAVEL SECTION PAGE 527

(E) Warrensburg Travel Park—(Warren) *From jct I-87 (exit 23-Warrensburg) & Diamond Point Rd: Go 1,000 feet W on Diamond Point Rd, then 1/2 mi N on US 9, then 3/4 mi NE on Horicon Rd. Enter on R.* ◇◇FACILITIES: 140 sites, typical site width 28 ft, 68 full hkups, 68 W&E, (20 amps), 4 no hkups, 77 pull-thrus, family camping, tenting, dump, laundry, ltd groc.

Woodall's — Trusted for Over 75 Years.

WARRENSBURG—Continued
Warrensburg Travel Park—Continued

◇◇◇◇RECREATION: swim pool, river swim, boating, 5 hp limit, canoeing, river fishing, playground. Pets welcome. Open May 1 - Columbus Day. Rate in 2010 $27-34 for 2 persons. Member ARVC, CONY. Phone: (518) 623-9833.

WARSAW—E-3

(W) KOA- Warsaw/Dream Lake—(Wyoming) *From jct Hwy 19 & Hwy 20A: Go 1-1/2 mi W on Hwy 20A, then 1-1/2 mi N on Blackhouse Rd, then 1-1/4 mi W on Buffalo Rd. Enter on R.* ◇◇◇FACILITIES: 98 sites, typical site width 25 ft, 7 full hkups, 91 W&E, (20/30 amps), 15 pull-thrus, family camping, tenting, dump, laundry. ◇◇◇RECREATION: lake swim, boating, electric motors only, ramp, lake fishing, playground. Pets welcome. Open Apr 25 - Columbus Day. Rate in 2010 $36-54 for 4 persons. Member ARVC, CONY. Phone: (585)786-5172. KOA discount.

WATERTOWN—C-6

See listing at Dexter.

WATKINS GLEN—F-5

(C) CLUTE MEMORIAL PARK & CAMPGROUND—(Schuyler) *From North jct of Hwy 14 & Hwy 414: Go 5 blks N on Hwy 414. Enter on R.*

FACILITIES: 138 sites, typical site width 30 ft, 130 full hkups, (20/30/50 amps), 8 no hkups, some extd stay sites (summer), 16 pull-thrus, cable TV, WiFi Instant Internet at site, family camping, tenting, dump, non-guest dump $, LP bottle exch, ice, picnic tables, fire rings, wood.

RECREATION: rec hall, pavilion, lake swim, boating, canoeing, kayaking, ramp, lake fishing, golf nearby, bsktball, playground, tennis, horseshoes, sports field, hiking trails, v-ball.

Pets welcome. Partial handicap access. Open Second wknd in May - Columbus day. Big rigs welcome. Escort to site. Clubs welcome. Green Friendly. MC/VISA/Debit.

Phone: (607)535-4438
Address: 155 S Clute Park Dr, Watkins Glen, NY 14891
Lat/Lon: 42.38419/-76.86003
Email: vofwgparks@stny.rr.com
Web: www.watkinsglen.us

SEE AD THIS PAGE

FERENBAUGH CAMPGROUND—*From Watkins Glen: Go 14 mi SW on Hwy 414. Enter on L.*

SEE PRIMARY LISTING AT CORNING AND AD CORNING PAGE 542

(W) KOA-Watkins Glen/Corning Resort—(Schuyler) *From South jct Hwy-14 & Hwy-414: Go 4-1/2 mi S on Hwy-414. Enter on L.* ◇◇◇◇FACILITIES: 145 sites, typical site width 35 ft, 104 full hkups, 32 W&E, (20/30/50 amps), 9 no hkups, 42 pull-thrus, family camping, tenting, dump, laundry, groceries. ◇◇◇◇◇RECREATION: swim pool, pond/stream fishing, playground. Pets welcome, breed restrict. Partial handicap access. Open Apr 18 - Nov 1. Big rigs welcome. Rate in 2010 $40-80 for 2 persons. Member ARVC, CONY. Phone: (800)562-7430. KOA discount.

(N) Paradise Park Campground—(Schuyler) *From North jct Hwy-414 & Hwy-14: Go 3-1/2 mi N on Hwy-14, then 1-1/2 mi NW on Hwy-14A, then 1 mi W on Church Rd, then 1/4 mi N on Cross Rd. Enter on R.* ◇◇FACILITIES: 198 sites, typical site width 35 ft, 198 W&E, (30 amps), 25 pull-thrus, family camping, tenting, dump, laundry, ltd groc. ◇◇◇RECREATION: swim pool, pond fishing, playground. Pets welcome. Partial handicap access. Open May 1 - Oct 15. Rate in 2010 $23.95-26.95 for 4 persons. Member ARVC, CONY. Phone: (607)535-6600.

(S) WATKINS GLEN STATE PARK—(Schuyler) *At jct Hwy-14 & Hwy-414.* FACILITIES: 305 sites, 20 ft max RV length, 54 E, (30/50 amps), 251 no hkups, tenting, dump, ltd groc. RECREATION: swim pool, canoeing, playground. Open May 5 - Oct 21. Phone: (607)535-4511.

WEEDSPORT—D-5

(N) Riverforest Park—(Cayuga) *From jct I-90 (exit 40) & Hwy-34: Go 1/4 mi N on Hwy-34, then 3/4 mi NW on Stickle Rd. Enter at end.* ◇◇FACILITIES: 250 sites, typical site width 22 ft, 250 W&E, (20/30 amps), family camping, tenting, dump, laundry, ltd groc. ◇◇◇RECREATION: swim pool, boating, ramp, dock, river/pond fishing, playground. Pets welcome. Open Apr 21 - Oct 10. Rate in 2010 $33-38 for 2 persons. Phone: (315) 834-9458.

WEST CHAZY—A-9

(SW) Twin Ells Campsites—(Clinton) *From jct I-87 (exit 37) & Hwy 3: Go 1-1/2 mi W on Hwy 3, then 8 mi NW on Hwy 190, then 1 mi E on La Plante Rd. Enter on R.* ◇◇◇FACILITIES: 240 sites, 240 full hkups, (20/30/50 amps), 14 pull-thrus, family camping, tenting, dump, laundry, ltd groc. ◇◇◇RECREATION: swim pool, playground. Pets welcome. Partial handicap access. Open May - Oct. Big rigs welcome. Rate in 2010 $24 per family. Phone: (518)493-6151.

WESTFIELD—F-1

(SW) BROOKSIDE BEACH CAMPGROUND—(Chautauqua) *From jct I-90 (exit 60) & Hwy 394: Go 1/4 mi N on Hwy 394, then 2-1/4 mi W on Hwy 5. Enter on R.*

CAMPGROUND DIRECTLY ON LAKE ERIE
Enjoy the many "moods" of Lake Erie and beautiful sunsets right from your campsite. Brookside's private beach is "exclusive" for our patrons. With nearby attractions and only 1 hour to Niagara Falls, we are ideally located.

◇◇◇FACILITIES: 70 sites, typical site width 30 ft, 55 full hkups, 15 E, (30/50 amps), many extd stay sites, 10 pull-thrus, WiFi Instant Internet at site, family camping, tenting, RV storage, dump, portable dump, laundry, picnic tables, fire rings, wood.

◇◇◇RECREATION: pavilion, lake swim, lake fishing, golf nearby, play equipment, shuffleboard court, horseshoes, sports field, hiking trails.

Pets welcome. Open May 1 - Oct 15. Big rigs welcome. Escort to site. Clubs welcome. Rate in 2010 $32 for 4 persons. Member ARVC, CONY.

Phone: (716)326-3096
Address: 8862 W Lake Rd (Rt 5), Westfield, NY 14787
Lat/Lon: 42.31691/-79.63781
Email: brooksidebeach@hotmail.com
Web: brooksidebeach.com

SEE AD NIAGARA FALLS PAGE 557

(NE) KOA-Westfield-Lake Erie—(Chautauqua) *From jct I-90 (exit 60) & Hwy-394: Go 1/4 mi N on Hwy-394, then 1 mi NE on Hwy-5. Enter on R.* ◇◇◇◇FACILITIES: 117 sites, typical site width 35 ft, 51 full hkups, 47 W&E, (20/30/50 amps), 50 amps ($), 19 no hkups, 80 pull-thrus, family camping, tenting, dump, laundry, groceries. ◇◇◇RECREATION: swim pool, pond fishing, playground. Pets welcome. Partial handicap access. Open Apr 15 - Oct 15. Big rigs welcome. Rate in 2010 $28-45 for 2 persons. Member ARVC, CONY. Phone: (716)326-3573. KOA discount.

Sam Wilson, a meatpacker from Troy who's caricature Uncle Sam came to personify the United States, is buried at Troy's Oakwood Cemetery. During the War of 1812, he stamped "U.S. Beef" on his products which soldiers interpreted the U.S. abbreviation as meaning Uncle Sam.

WESTVILLE CENTER—A-8

(N) BABBLING BROOK RV PARK—(Franklin) *From jct Hwy 122 & Hwy 37: Go 1 mi NW on Hwy 37, then 400' W on Hwy 4. Enter on R.*

WELCOME

◇◇◇FACILITIES: 57 sites, typical site width 35 ft, 57 full hkups, (30/50 amps), 50 amps ($), 30 pull-thrus, WiFi Instant Internet at site, family camping, tenting, cabins, shower$, dump, non-guest dump $, laundry, ice, picnic tables, fire rings, wood, controlled access.

◇◇◇RECREATION: rec room/area, pavilion, stream fishing, golf nearby, playground, activities, (wkends), horseshoes, sports field.

Pets welcome, quantity restrict. Partial handicap access. Open May 11 - Sep 30. Clubs welcome. Green Friendly. Rate in 2010 $26-29 for 2 persons. MC/VISA.

Phone: (518)358-4245
Address: 1623 CR 4, Westville Center, NY 12926
Lat/Lon: 44.95414/-74.41355
Email: Snyders_2001@yahoo.com
Web: www.babblingbrookrvparkny.com

SEE AD THIS PAGE

WILMINGTON—B-9

(S) KOA-Lake Placid Whiteface Mountain—(Essex) *From jct Hwy 431 & Hwy 86: Go 2 mi SW on Hwy 86, then 1/4 mi E on Fox Farm Rd. Enter on L.* ◇◇◇◇FACILITIES: 187 sites, typical site width 50 ft, 48 full hkups, 49 W&E, 13 E, (20/30/50 amps), 50 amps ($), 77 no hkups, 82 pull-thrus, family camping, tenting, dump, laundry, groceries. ◇◇◇◇◇RECREATION: swim pool, river fishing, playground. Pets welcome, breed restrict, quantity restrict. Partial handicap access. Open Apr 29 - Oct 21. Rate in 2010 $30-40 for 2 persons. Member ARVC, CONY. Phone: (518)946-7878. KOA discount.

(S) NORTH POLE CAMPING RESORT—(Essex) *From jct Hwy 87 (exit 30) & Hwy 73: Go 16 mi NW on Hwy 73, then 10 mi N on Hwy 9N, then 5 mi W on Hwy 86, then 1/4 mi W on Hwy 86 (at Hwy 431 jct). Enter on L.*

WELCOME

◇◇◇◇FACILITIES: 169 sites, typical site width 30 ft, 67 full hkups, 48 W&E, (30/50 amps), 54 no hkups, 50 pull-thrus, cable TV, cable on-site Internet (needs activ), WiFi Internet central location, family camping, tenting, RV's/park model rentals, cabins, RV storage, dump, laundry, groceries, RV supplies, LP gas by weight/by meter, ice, picnic tables, fire rings, wood.

◇◇◇◇◇RECREATION: rec hall, rec room/area, coin games, 2 swim pools, boating, 10 hp limit, canoeing, kayaking, 3 rowboat/6 canoe/5 kayak/pedal boat rentals, lake/river fishing, fishing

WILMINGTON—Continued
NORTH POLE CAMPING RESORT—Continued

supplies, mini-golf, ($), golf nearby, bsktball, 5 bike rentals, playground, activities, (wkends), horseshoes, hiking trails, v-ball. Rec open to public.

Pets welcome, breed restrict, quantity restrict. Partial handicap access. Open all yr. Facilities fully operational May 1 - Nov 1. Big rigs welcome. Escort to site. Clubs welcome. Green Friendly. Rate in 2010 $37-40 per family. MC/VISA/DISC/Debit. Member ARVC, CONY. FMCA discount.

Phone: (800)245-0228
Address: 5644 Rt 86, Wilmington, NY 12997
Lat/Lon: 44.38766/-73.82475
Email: info@northpoleresorts.com
Web: www.northpoleresorts.com

SEE AD LAKE PLACID PAGE 553

(S) WILMINGTON NOTCH CAMPGROUND (Adirondack SF)—(Essex) *From town: Go 4 mi W on Hwy-86.* FACILITIES: 54 sites, 30 ft max RV length, 54 no hkups, tenting, dump. RECREATION: river fishing. Pets welcome. Open May 5 - Oct 8. Phone: (518)946-7172.

WINDSOR—F-7

(NE) Forest Lake Campground—(Broome) *From jct Hwy 17 & Old Hwy 17 (exit 80): Go 3-3/4 mi E on Old Hwy 17 (Ostander Rd). Enter on R.* ◇◇FACILITIES: 97 sites, typical site width 30 ft, 75 full hkups, 7 W&E, (20/30 amps), 15 no hkups, 7 pull-thrus, family camping, tenting, dump, laundry, ltd groc, ice, picnic tables, fire rings, wood. ◇◇◇RECREATION: pavilion, lake swim, boating, dock, lake fishing, playground, activities, horseshoes, hiking trails, v-ball. Pets welcome, breed restrict. Open May 15 - Oct 15. Rate in 2010 $26.95-38.95 per family. MC/VISA/DISC/AMEX. CCUSA 50% Discount. CCUSA reservations Required, CCUSA max stay 7 days, CCUSA disc. not avail holidays. No snakes, pitbulls, rottweilers or dobermans. Pet owners, please bring pet papers & tags with you.

CAMPCLUB USA

Phone: (607)655-1444
Address: 574 Ostrander Rd, Windsor, NY 13865
Lat/Lon: 42.09404/-75.59933
Email: forestlakecampground@yahoo.com
Web: www.forestlakeny.net

(S) LAKESIDE CAMPGROUND—(Broome) *From jct Hwy 17 (exit 79) & Hwy 79: Go 4 mi S on Hwy 79, then 3-1/2 mi W on Edson Rd (CR 16), then 1 mi SW on Hargrave Rd. Enter on L.*

WELCOME

◇◇◇◇FACILITIES: 100 sites, 74 full hkups, 26 W&E, (20/30/50 amps), some extd stay sites (summer), 9 pull-thrus, WiFi Instant Internet at site, family camping, tenting, RV's/park model rentals, cabins, shower$, dump, laundry, ltd groc, RV supplies, LP gas by weight/by meter, ice, picnic tables, fire rings, wood, controlled access.

◇◇◇◇RECREATION: rec room/area, equipped pavilion, coin games, lake swim, boating, electric motors only, canoeing, 3 rowboat/3 canoe/5 ped-

WINDSOR—Continued
LAKESIDE CAMPGROUND—Continued

al boat rentals, lake fishing, fishing supplies, golf nearby, bsktball, playground, activities, (wkends), tennis, horseshoes, sports field.

Pets welcome. Open May 15 - Oct 15. Big rigs welcome. Clubs welcome. Rate in 2010 $32.95-35.95 for 2 persons. MC/VISA/DISC/AMEX. Member ARVC, CONY.

Phone: (607)655-2694
Address: 336 Hargrave Rd, Windsor, NY 13865
Lat/Lon: 42.01919/-75.68358
Email: theresa@ilovecamping.com
Web: www.ilovecamping.com

SEE AD BINGHAMTON PAGE 538

(S) Pine Crest Campground—(Broome) *From jct Hwy 17 & Hwy 79: Go 1/4 mi E on Chapel St, then 6 mi S on Hwy 79. Enter on L.* ◇◇◇FACILITIES: 104 sites, 86 full hkups, 18 W&E, (20/30 amps), 7 pull-thrus, family camping, dump, laundry. ◇◇◇RECREATION: swim pool, boating, canoeing, dock, river/pond fishing, playground. Pets welcome. No tents. Open May 15 - Oct 1. Rate in 2010 $32-41 per family. Member ARVC, CONY. Phone: (607)655-1515.

WOLCOTT—D-5

(E) Cherry Grove Campground—(Wayne) *From jct Hwy 414 & Hwy 104: Go 6 mi E on Hwy 104, then 300 feet NW on Ridge Rd. Enter on R.* ◇◇◇FACILITIES: 110 sites, typical site width 30 ft, 105 full hkups, (20/30/50 amps), 5 no hkups, 32 pull-thrus, family camping, tenting, dump, laundry. ◇◇◇RECREATION: swim pool, playground. Pets welcome, breed restrict, quantity restrict. Open Apr 15 - Oct 15. Big rigs welcome. Rate in 2010 $27-32 per family. Member ARVC, CONY. Phone: (315)594-8320.

(NW) Lake Bluff Campground—(Wayne) *From jct Hwy 104 & Hwy 414: Go 3-1/2 mi N on Hwy 414 (Lake Bluff Rd), then 1/4 mi N on Garner Rd. Enter on R.* ◇◇◇FACILITIES: 150 sites, typical site width 40 ft, 94 full hkups, 56 W&E, (20/30/50 amps), family camping, tenting, dump, ltd groc. ◇◇◇RECREATION: swim pool, pond fishing, playground. Pets welcome. Open Apr 15 - Oct 31. Rate in 2010 $29-32 for 2 persons. Member ARVC, CONY. Phone: (888)588-4517.

WOODVILLE—C-6

(W) SOUTHWICK BEACH STATE PARK—(Jefferson) *From town: Go 3 mi W on Hwy 3.* FACILITIES: 100 sites, 69 E, (15 amps), 31 no hkups, tenting, dump, groceries. RECREATION: lake swim, canoeing, ramp, lake fishing, playground. Partial handicap access. Open Early May - Columbus Day Wknd. Phone: (315) 846-5338.

YOUNGSTOWN—D-2

FORT NIAGARA SP (Four Mile Campsite)—(Niagara) *From town: Go 4 mi E on Hwy-18.* FACILITIES: 266 sites, 102 E, (30/50 amps), 164 no hkups, tenting, dump. RECREATION: swim pool, ramp, lake/stream fishing, playground. Pets welcome. Partial handicap access. Open all yr. Open Mid Apr - Late Oct. Phone: (716)745-7273.

READER SERVICE INFO

The following businesses have placed an ad in the North Carolina Travel Section. To receive free information, enter their Reader Service number on the Reader Service Card opposite page 48/Discover Section in the front of this directory:

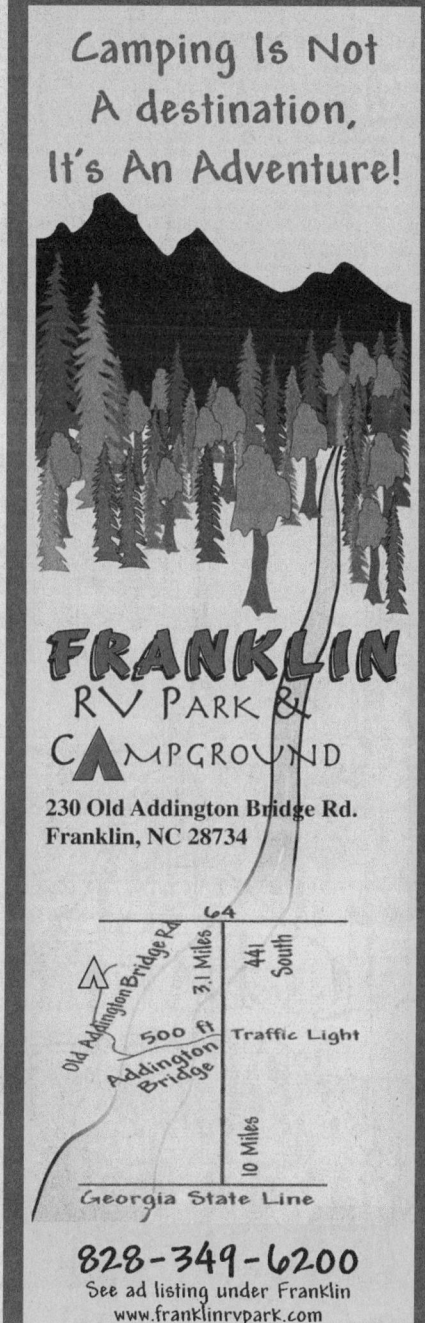

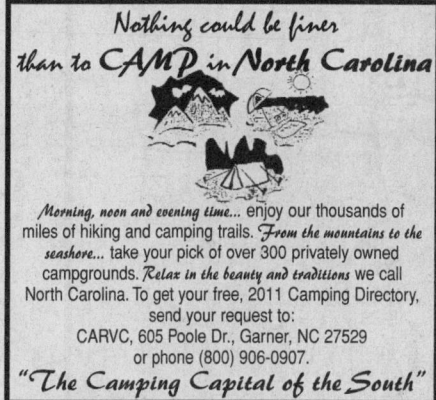

Advertiser	RS#
Carolina RV Parks & Campground Assoc	3591
Daly RV	3527
Franklin RV Park & Campground	3617
Outer Banks Visitors Bureau	3398
The Refuge	3707

TIME ZONE

North Carolina is located in the Eastern Time Zone.

TOPOGRAPHY

The state is divided into three distinct topographical regions: the Coastal Plain, the Heartland and the Mountains.

TEMPERATURE

North Carolina's average January temperatures range from 27° to 48.7°; July temperatures range from 59.2° to 80.2°.

TRAVEL & TOURISM INFO

State Agency:
North Carolina Dept of Tourism
301 North Wilmington St.
Raleigh, NC 27601—2825
(800/VISIT-NC or 919/733-4171)
www.visitnc.com

Local Agencies:
Asheville Convention & Visitors Bureau
P.O. Box 1010
Asheville, NC 28802-1010
(828/258-6102 or 800/257-1300)
www.exploreasheville.com

Blowing Rock Tourism Development Authority
P.O. Box 2445
Blowing Rock, NC 28605
(877/750-4636 or 828/295-4636)
www.visitblowingrock.com

Boone Convention & Visitors Bureau
208 Howard Street
Boone, NC 28607-4037
(828/262-3516 or 800/852-9506)
www.visitboonenc.com

NC Brunswick Islands
P.O. Box 1186
Shallotte, NC 28459
(800/795-7263 or 910/755-5517)
www.ncbrunswick.com

Burlington/Alamance County Convention & Visitors Bureau
610 S. Lexington Avenue
Burlington, NC 27215
(800/637-3804 or 336/570-1444)
www.burlington-area-nc.org

Cabarrus County Convention & Visitors Bureau
3003 Dale Earnhardt Blvd., Suite 200
Kannapolis, NC 28083
(800/848-3740 or 704/782-4340)
www.cabarruscvb.com

Wilmington/Cape Fear Coast Convention & Visitors Bureau
24 North Third Street
Wilmington, NC 28401

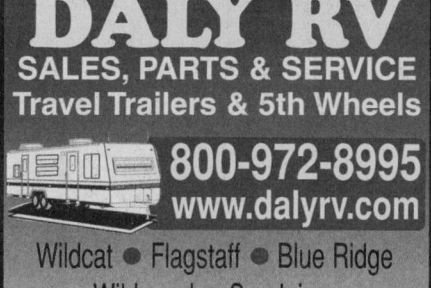

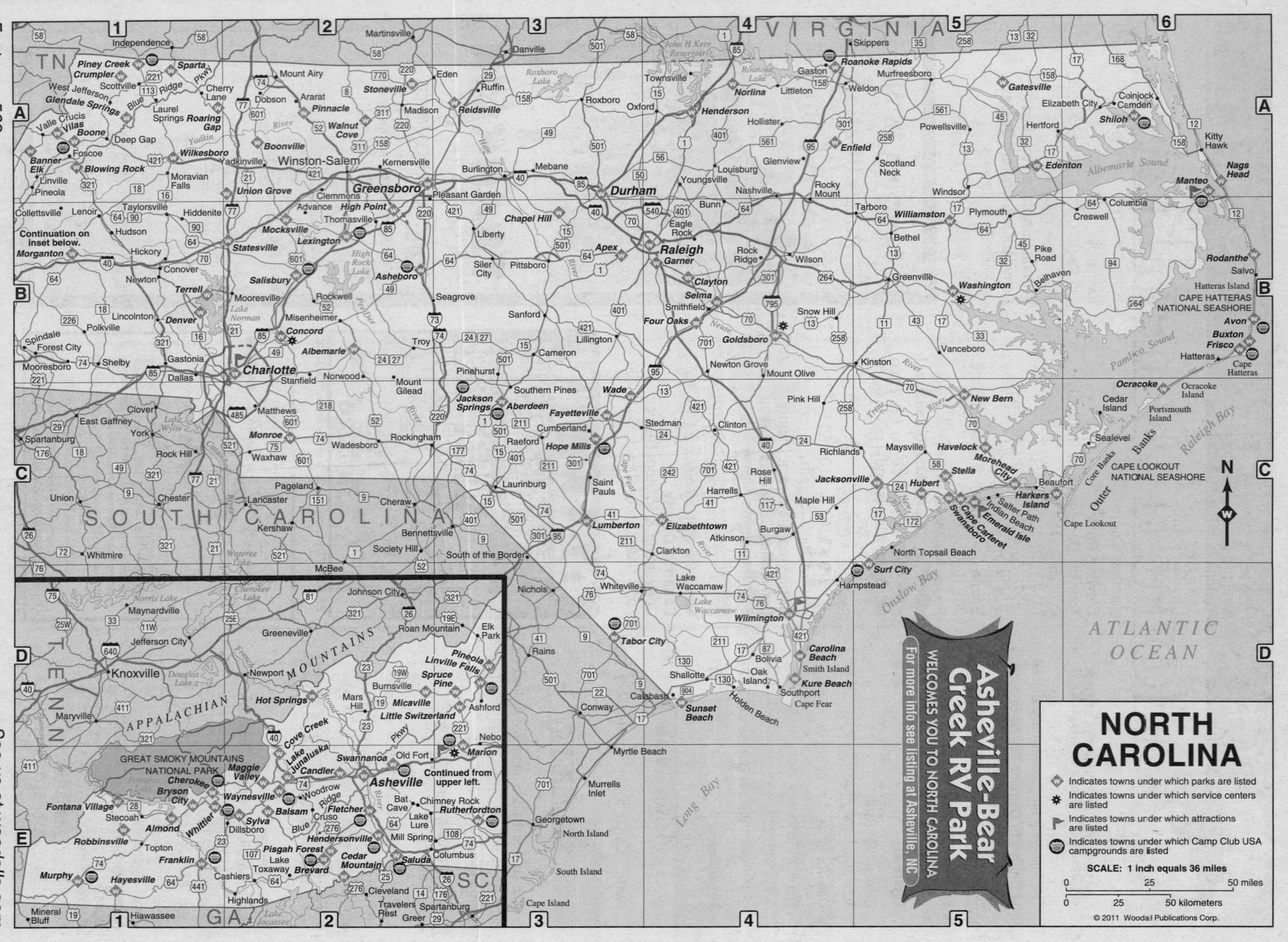

NORTH CAROLINA
Indicates towns under which parks are listed
Indicates towns under which service centers are listed
Indicates towns under which attractions are listed
Indicates towns under which Camp Club USA campgrounds are listed
SCALE: 1 inch equals 36 miles
0 25 50 miles
0 25 50 kilometers
© 2011 Woodall Publications Corp.
Asheville-Bear Creek RV Park
WELCOMES YOU TO NORTH CAROLINA
For more info see listing at Asheville, NC
ATLANTIC OCEAN
VIRGINIA
SOUTH CAROLINA
TENN
Continuation on inset below.
Continued from upper left.
GREAT SMOKY MOUNTAINS NATIONAL PARK
APPALACHIAN MOUNTAINS
CAPE HATTERAS NATIONAL SEASHORE
CAPE LOOKOUT NATIONAL SEASHORE

(866/266-9690 or 910/341-4030)
www.gocapefearcoast.com

Chapel Hill/Orange County Visitors Bureau
501 West Franklin Street
Chapel Hill, NC 27516
(919/968-2060)
www.chocvb.org

**Visit Charlotte
The Convention and Visitors Bureau**
500 South College Street, Suite 300
Charlotte, NC 28202
(800/722-1994 or 704/334-2282)
www.visitcharlotte.com

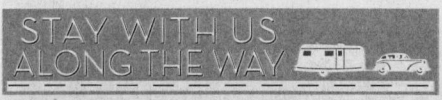

Cleveland County Economic Development/Travel & Tourism
P.O. Box 879
Shelby, NC 28151
(704/487-8521)
www.clevelandchamber.org

Columbus County Tourism Bureau
104 East Walter Street
P.O. Box 1352
Whiteville, NC 28472
(800/845-8419 or 910/640-2818)
www.discovercolumbus.org

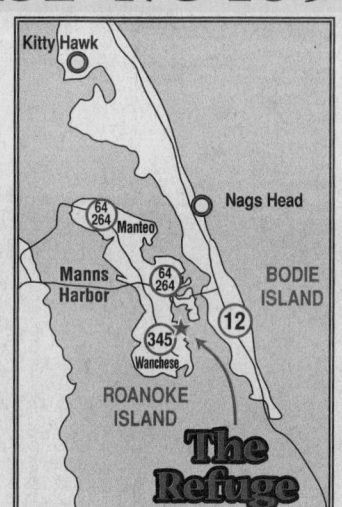

Durham Convention & Visitors Bureau
101 East Morgan Street
Durham, NC 27701
(800/446-8604 or 919/687-0288)
www.durham-nc.com

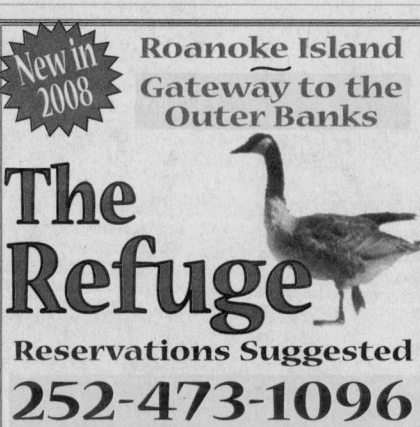

Fayetteville Area Convention & Visitors Bureau
245 Person Street
Fayetteville, NC 28301
(800/255-8217 or 910/483-5311)
www.visitfayettevillenc.com

Gaston County Department of Tourism
620 North Main Street
Belmont, NC 28012
(800/849-9994 or 704/825-4044
www.gastontourism.com

Greensboro Area Convention & Visitors Bureau
317 South Greene Street
Greensboro, NC 27401-2615
(800/344-2282 or 336/274-2282)
www.visitgreensboro.com

Greenville-Pitt County Convention & Visitors Bureau
303 SW Greenville Blvd.
Greenville, NC 27834
(800/537-5564 or 252/329-4200)
www.visitgreenvillenc.com

Hickory Metro Convention and Visitors Bureau
1960-A Thirteenth Avenue Drive S.E.
Hickory, NC 28602
(800/509-2444 or 828/322-1335)
www.hickorymetro.com

Johnston County Visitors Bureau
1115 Industrial Park Drive
Smithfield, NC 27577
(800/441-7829 or 919/989-8687)
www.johnstoncountync.org

Lake Norman Convention and Visitors Bureau
19900 West Catawaba Avenue
Cornelius, NC 28031
(704/987-3300)
www.lakenorman.org

Lexington Tourism Authority
16 East Center Street
P.O. Box 2103
Lexington, NC 27292
(336/236-4218 or 866/604-2389)
www.visitlexingtonnc.com

Martin County Travel & Tourism Authority
P.O. Box 382
Williamston, NC 27892
(800/776-8566 or 252/792-6605)
www.visitmartincounty.com

Monroe Tourism & Visitors Bureau
100 West Jefferson Street
Monroe, NC 28112
(704/225-1085)
www.visitmonroenc.org

Mooresville Convention & Visitors Bureau
265 North Main Street
Mooresville, NC 28115
(704/799-2400 or 800/661-1234)
www.racecityusa.org

New Bern/Craven County Convention & Visitors Bureau
203 South Front Street
New Bern, NC 28563

(800/437-5767 or 252/637-9400)
www.visitnewbern.com

Pinehurst, Southern Pines & Aberdeen Area CVB
10677 US Highway 15-501
Southern Pines, NC 28388
(800/346-5362 or 910/692-3330)
www.homeofgolf.com

Greater Raleigh Convention & Visitors Bureau
421 Fayetteville Street Mall, Suite 1505
P.O. Box 1879 (27602)
Raleigh, NC 27601-2946
(800/849-8499 or 919/834-5900)
www.visitraleigh.com

Randolph County Tourism Development Authority
222 Sunset Ave, Suite 107
Asheboro, NC 27203
(800/626-2672 or 336/626-0364)
www.visitrandolphcounty.com

Rockingham County Partnership for Economic and Tourism Development
P.O. Box 205
Wentworth, NC 27375
(336/342-8138)
www.ncnorthstar.com

Rowan County Convention & Visitors Bureau
204 East Innes Street, Suite 120
Salisbury, NC 28144
(800/332-2343 or 704/638-3100)
www.visitsalisburync.com

Rutherford County Tourism Development Authority
1990 US Highway 221 South
Forest City, NC 28043
(800/849-5998 or 828/245-1492)
www.rutherfordtourism.com

Stanly County Convention & Visitors Bureau
116 East North Street
P.O. Box 1456
Albemarle, NC 28002
(704/986-2583 or 800/650-1476)
www.stanlycvb.org

Statesville Convention & Visitors Bureau
111 Depot Lane
P.O. Box 1109
Statesville, NC 28687
(704/878-3480 or 877/531-1819)
www.visitstatesville.org

Washington Tourism Development Authority
138 South Market Street
P.O. Box 1765
Washington, NC 27889
(800/999-3857 or 252/948-9415)
www.originalwashington.com

Wilson Visitors Bureau
124 East Nash Street
Wilson, NC 27894
(800/497-7398 or 252/243-8440)
www.wilson-nc.com

Winston-Salem Convention & Visitors Bureau
200 Brookstown Avenue
Winston-Salem, NC 27101
(866/728-4200 or 336/728-4200)
www.visitwinstonsalem.com

RECREATIONAL INFO

Fishing & Hunting: NC Wildlife Resources Commission, 512 N. Salisbury, Raleigh, NC 27699 (919/733-3391) www.ncwildlife.org

Golf: For a free copy of the Official North Carolina Golf Guide, call 800/VISIT-NC or visit www.visitnc.com.

NC Beach Buggy Association, Box 940, Manteo, NC 27954. (252/473-4880) www.ncbba.org

Skiing: NC Ski Areas Association, P.O. Box 106, Blowing Rock, NC 28605 (828/295-7828) www.goskinc.com

Wineries: NC Wine & Grape Council, 4324 MSC, Raleigh, NC 27699-1615 (919/715-9463) www.visitncwine.com

BUSINESSES OFFERING

	Things to See & Do	RV Sales	RV Service
CHARLOTTE			
Carowinds	▶		
CONCORD			
Tom Johnson Camping Center		🚌	✱
EMERALD ISLE			
Emerald Isle Wine Market	▶		
GOLDSBORO			
Daly RV		🚌	✱
MANTEO			
Outer Banks Visitors Bureau	▶		
MARION			
Buck Creek Driving Range	▶		
Tom Johnson Camping Center		🚌	✱
WASHINGTON			
Crisp RV Center		🚌	✱
WILMINGTON			
Battleship North Carolina	▶		

SHOPPING

Appalachian Craft Center, Asheville. Authentic mountain handicrafts, pottery, face jugs, quilts, mountain-made toys, rugs and more. 10 N. Spruce St. www.appalachian-craftcenter.com

Carolina Premium Outlets, Smithfield. Shop at over 80 factory-direct designer and brand name outlets offering savings of 25%-65%. Off I-95, Exit 95, Smithfield, NC. www.premiumoutlets.com/carolina

Ninth Street Shopping District, Durham. Locally owned specialty shops in 25,000 square foot mall in the eclectic shopping district near Duke University East Campus at Main St. and Club Blvd. www.ninthst.com.

North Carolina Remembered, Raleigh. The most complete NC products store in the state. A vast array of items, pottery, foods, suncatchers, flags, toys, pens, pencils, local sports items, etc. They will custom make gift baskets while you wait. 4325 Glenwood Ave. www.ncremembered.citysearch.com

Wilcox Emporium Warehouse, Boone. Over 180 vendors in the historic downtown area selling unique antiques, art and collectibles. 161 Howard St., Boone, NC

DESTINATIONS

North Carolina is one of the largest and most beautifully diverse states in the nation. Stretching from the Smoky Mountains to the Atlantic, it is one of the most popular destinations for travelers seeking a relaxing coastal getaway, skiing, hiking, biking, and fishing.

THE MOUNTAINS

The Mountains region of the state is home to one of the largest protected areas east of the Mississippi River, the Great Smokey Mountains National Park. Visitors from all over come to these mountains to view nature, hike, fish, camp, and get away from the normal day-to-day grind.

Appalachian Trail. Over 2,150 miles of the wilderness route from Maine to Georgia follow high ridges in the **Pisgah National Park**, which is home to **Sliding Rock**, a natural water slide, **Nantahala National Forest**

QUICK REFERENCE CHART FOR WOODALL'S FEATURED PARKS

	Green Friendly	RV Lots for Sale	Park Models-Onsite Ownership	Park Membership for Sale	Big Rigs Welcome	Internet Friendly	Pets Welcome
ABERDEEN							
Pine Lake RV Resort						●	■
ASHEBORO							
Deep River Campground & RV Park					▲	●	■
Holly Bluff Family Campground					▲	●	■
Trails End Family Camping					▲	●	■
ASHEVILLE							
Asheville-Bear Creek RV Park					▲	●	■
Campfire Lodgings					▲	●	■
BALSAM							
Moonshine Creek Campground						●	■
BANNER ELK							
Grandfather Campground					▲	●	■
BOONE							
Flintlock Campground						●	■
KOA-Boone					▲	●	■
BRYSON CITY							
Country Girl's RV Park					▲	●	■
Ela Campground						●	■
BUXTON							
Cape Woods Campground					▲	●	■
CEDAR MOUNTAIN							
Black Forest Family Camping Resort					▲	●	■
CHAPEL HILL							
Spring Hill Park					▲	●	■
CHARLOTTE							
Carowinds Camp Wilderness Resort					▲	●	■
Elmore Mobile Home & RV Park					▲		■
CHEROKEE							
Great Smokey Mountain RV Camping Resort							■
CLAYTON							
Cooper's Mobile Home Park & RV's					▲	●	■
CONCORD							
Charlotte Motor Speedway Camping					▲		■
EMERALD ISLE							
Holiday Trav-L-Park Resort For Campers					▲	●	■
FAYETTEVILLE							
Lazy Acres Campground					▲	●	■
FLETCHER							
Rutledge Lake RV Park					▲	●	■
FOUR OAKS							
Four Oaks RV Resort					▲	●	■
FRANKLIN							
Country Woods RV Park						●	■
Franklin RV Park & Campground					▲	●	■
FRISCO							
Frisco Woods Campground					▲	●	■
GLENDALE SPRINGS							
Raccoon Holler Campground						●	■
GREENSBORO							
Greensboro Campground					▲	●	■

Green Friendly 🍃; RV Lots for Sale ✖; Park Models/Onsite Onwership ✱; Park Memberships for Sale ✔; Big Rigs Welcome ▲;
Internet Friendly ●; Internet Friendly-WiFi ●; Pets Welcome ■

QUICK REFERENCE CHART FOR WOODALL'S FEATURED PARKS

	Green Friendly	RV Lots for Sale	Park Models-Onsite Ownership	Park Membership for Sale	Big Rigs Welcome	Internet Friendly	Pets Welcome
HARKERS ISLAND							
Cape Pointe RV Park					▲	●	■
HENDERSONVILLE							
Jaymar Travel Park					▲	●	■
Lakewood RV Resort			✱		▲	●	■
HIGH POINT							
Oak Hollow Family Campground					▲	●	■
HUBERT							
Hawkins Creek Campground					▲		■
JACKSONVILLE							
Cabin Creek Campground					▲	●	■
LEXINGTON							
Cross Winds Family Campground					▲	●	■
LINVILLE FALLS							
Linville Falls Trailer Lodge & Campground							■
LUMBERTON							
Sleepy Bear's RV Park	🍃				▲	●	■
MANTEO							
The Refuge					▲	●	■
MARION							
Buck Creek RV Park Campground					▲	●	■
Mountain Stream RV Park					▲	●	■
The Campground at Tom Johnson Camping Center					▲	●	■
MOREHEAD CITY							
Whispering Pines RV Park					▲	●	■
ROANOKE RAPIDS							
The RV Resort at Carolina Crossroads					▲	●	■
RODANTHE							
Camp Hatteras	🍃				▲	●	■
Ocean Waves Campground					▲	●	■
SALUDA							
Orchard Lake Campground & RV Park					▲	●	■
SELMA							
RVacation Campground					▲	●	■
SWANNANOA							
Asheville East-KOA					▲	●	■
Mama Gertie's Hideaway Campground					▲	●	■
SYLVA							
Ft. Tatham RV Park (Carefree RV Resort)			✱			●	■
TABOR CITY							
Yogi Bear's Jellystone Park at Daddy Joe's					▲	●	■
VILAS							
Vanderpool Campground					▲	●	■
WADE							
Fayetteville KOA					▲	●	■
WHITTIER							
Tuckaseegee R.V. Resort		✖			▲	●	■
WILLIAMSTON							
Green Acres Family Campground						●	■

Green Friendly 🍃; RV Lots for Sale ✖; Park Models/Onsite Onwership ✱; Park Memberships for Sale ✔; Big Rigs Welcome ▲; Internet Friendly ●; Internet Friendly-WiFi ●; Pets Welcome ■

and the **Great Smoky Mountain National Park.**

Asheville. The newly opened **Blue Ridge Parkway Destination Center** highlights the diversity, traditions and recreational aspects of the Blue Ridge Parkway. Or explore the 250 rooms of the **Biltmore House**, home of the Vanderbilts and the largest home in America. For amazing panoramic views visit **Chimney Rock Park.**

Belmont Abbey, Belmont. Once the only abbey cathedral in the nation, its beautiful painted-glass windows won a gold prize in 1893.

Blowing Rock. Enjoy a leisurely scenic walk overlooking John's River Gorge. The **Appalachian Heritage Museum** features costumed interpreters demonstrating skills of the period. **Mystery Hill** offers a fascinating way to explore science and optical illusion.

Blue Ridge Parkway. Over 250 miles of this scenic road skim the crest of the mountains between the North Carolina-Virginia line and the entrance to the **Great Smoky Mountains National Park** near Cherokee. The new Blue Ridge Parkway Destination Center houses exhibits featuring things to see and do in the region.

Boone. Step back into the 1800s in this historical town. At **Hickory Ridge Homestead**, a costumed interpreter will explain how early settlers lived and survived in the mountains of North Carolina. *Honor in the West* is an outdoor drama depicting the story of Daniel Boone and the Colonial Settlers in their struggle to free themselves from British tyranny.

Bottomless Pools is located in the hickory Nut Gorge of western North Carolina. The pools opened in 1916. Three pools each have their own waterfall and unique, lovely natural setting.

Brevard/Cashiers Area. Known as the "Land of Waterfalls," the Brevard area contains many beautiful waterfalls, including **Connestee Falls, Looking Glass Falls, Toxaway Falls, High Falls, Rainbow Falls and Whitewater Falls. Brevard Station** is a museum portraying pictures, artifacts and documents from the past, including the discovery of the Bigleaf Magnolia in the area in 1795.

Cherokee/Qualla Boundary, located east of Bryson City at the Great Smoky Mountain National Park entrance, is now considered the **Cherokee Native American Reservation** by the descendants of the first mountain dwellers. See what life was like in an 18th-century Cherokee village. Visitors can follow the development of the Cherokee nation and learn about their language and important historical figures in tribal history at the **Museum of the Cherokee Indian**. Other attractions to visit include **Qualla Arts & Crafts Mutual; Unto These Hills,** an outdoor drama that

Where to Find CCUSA Parks

List City	Park Name	Map Coordinates
ABERDEEN		
	Long Leaf Pine Oasis	C-3
ASHEBORO		
	Deep River Campground & RV Park	B-2
AVON		
	Sands of Time Campground	B-6
BOONE		
	Honey Bear Campground	A-1
BREVARD		
	Adventure Village & Lodgings	E-2
CHEROKEE		
	Fort Wilderness Campground and RV Resort	E-1
FLETCHER		
	Rutledge Lake RV Park	E-2
FRANKLIN		
	Country Woods RV Park	E-1
	River Vista Mountain Village	E-1
FRISCO		
	Frisco Woods Campground	B-6
HENDERSONVILLE		
	Jaymar Travel Park	E-2
HOPE MILLS		
	Lake Waldo's Beach Campground	C-3
LEXINGTON		
	Cross Winds Family Campground	B-2
LINVILLE FALLS		
	Linville Falls Trailer Lodge & Campground	D-3
MANTEO		
	The Refuge	A-6
MARION		
	The Campground at Tom Johnson Camping Center	E-3
MURPHY		
	Crawford's Campground & Cabin Rentals	E-1
	Rivers Edge Mountain RV Resort	E-1
PINEY CREEK		
	RiverCamp USA RV Park & Campground	A-1
ROANOKE RAPIDS		
	The RV Resort at Carolina Crossroads	A-4
RUTHERFORDTON		
	Four Paws Kingdom	E-3
SALISBURY		
	Bass Lake	B-2
SALUDA		
	Orchard Lake Campground & RV Park	E-2
SHILOH		
	North River Campground & RV Park	A-6
SURF CITY		
	Lanier's Campground	D-5
SWANNANOA		
	Mama Gertie's Hideaway Campground	E-2
SYLVA		
	Ft. Tatham RV Park (Carefree RV Resort)	E-2
TABOR CITY		
	Carrollwoods RV Park at Grapefull Sisters Vineyard	D-3
WAYNESVILLE		
	Pride RV Resort	E-2
	Trails End RV Park	E-2

illustrates the struggle of the Cherokee nation against the U.S.; **Aarrak's Cherokee Casino,** the size of 3 football fields; **Tribal Bingo**, with nightly games and **Santa's Land** amusement park.

Daniel Stow Botanical Garden is one of the finest perennial gardens in the Southeast with extensive landscaping, a glass-domed pavilion and more on 110 acres. The newly opened Orchid Conservatory is devoted to tropical plants.

Grandfather Mountain (5,964 feet) is located in the Linville area and features a mile-high swinging bridge. The highest peaks can be reached only by trail in an undeveloped 5,000-acre area.

Great Smoky Mountains National Park. Located half in North Carolina and half in Tennessee, the park contains 514,093 acres and offers camping, fishing, hiking, picnicking, sightseeing, an observation tower and guided nature tours.

Green River Plantation, Rutherford. This 1804 mansion has 42 rooms on 366 acres of land bordered by lagoons. It is on the National Register of Historic Places.

Historic Hendersonville & Flat Rock Area, nestled in the beautiful Blue Ridge Mountains. Boasting antique stores, specialty shops and restaurants, this town has a history of tradition with a hometown charm. Visit the **Western North Carolina Air Museum,** the first of its kind in the "first in flight" state and **Jump Off Rock**, a scenic overlook which supplies a panoramic view of rolling pastures and Blue Ridge and Pisgah mountains. This rock also holds a Native American legend. The **Carl Sandburg Home** contains a collection of 10,000 books, notes and papers.

Labyrinth Center, Fairview dates back to prehistoric time and has been an integral part of many cultures including Celtic, Native American and Mayan.

Lake Lure has been named by National Geographic as one of the ten most spectacular man-made lakes in the world. Besides cruises and tours, boats of all kind are available for rent.

Linville Gorge Wilderness Area features one of eastern America's most scenic and rugged gorges. Stop by the district ranger's office (in Marion) for the permit required to enter the area. **Linville Caverns** is NC's only show cave– a natural limestone cavern with an underground stream.

Maggie Valley. Maggie Mountaineer Crafts has memorabilia and handcrafted items from local artisans. The newly reopened **Ghost Town in the Sky**, one of North Carolina's oldest family theme parks, features staged gunfights, special performances, historical and heritage exhibits.

Magic Mountain Gem Mine lets you mine for your own gems. Equipment is provided.

Oconaluflee Indian Village, Cherokee. An authentic replica of an 18th century Cherokee community. Artisans demonstrate their arts and crafts. Replica of a 7-sided Council House and Cherokee homes.

Schiele Museum of Natural History. Largest collection of land mammal species in the southeast; includes a planetarium with changing exhibits.

Sparta. Scheduled to open the summer of 2008 is the **Sparta Teapot Museum**, a multi-million dollar international collection of tea-themed treasures. The collection of more than 10,000 objects represents many cultures and includes priceless antique teapots from the 1700s, as well as contemporary ones.

Spruce Pine. Nearby is the **North Carolina Museum of Minerals**; the **Pemland School of Crafts**, the oldest and largest school for high quality mixed media arts and crafts; and the **Crossmore School**, home to the Weaving Room, where demonstrations of this traditional mountain craft are available.

THE HEARTLAND

The Heartland region of the state is filled with cosmopolitan centers and plenty of historic sites worth exploring. A great vacation destination that offers countless entertainment, dining and cultural venues.

Chapel Hill. This community is home to **Ackland Art Museum; Morehead Planetarium**, which offers daily public programs; and **North Carolina Botanical Garden**, a 307-acre woodland with a large collection of native plants and herbs.

Charlotte. Attractions in the Charlotte area include:

Paramount's Carowinds. Enjoy this theme park located on the border of North and South Carolina. Featured are over 30 rides, a wave pool, rock concerts and historic attractions.

Discovery Place & OMNI-MAX Theater is North Carolina's largest privately owned museum of science and technology and offers a variety of exhibits and hands-on activities.

Mint Museum of Art. One of the leading museums in the Southeast, the Mint is not only the first branch of the U.S. Mint, but North Carolina's first art museum as well. Holdings include American and European paintings; African, Spanish and pre-Columbian art; furniture and decorative arts; regional crafts; historic costumes and an internationally acclaimed collection of pottery and porcelain.

Nature Museum. The museum features nature exhibits that encourage you to touch them, a nature trail, live animals, a planetarium and a puppet theater.

The U.S. National Whitewater Center (USNWC). This new outdoor recreation and environmental education center features the world's only multi-channel re-circulating whitewater river. With something for outdoor enthusiasts of all abilities, the facility offers mountain-biking and running trails, a climbing center, challenge course and the customized whitewater river for rafting and canoeing/kayaking.

Clemmons Educational State Forest, Clayton. Kids will enjoy the "talking" trees and rocks, telling tales about the forest.

Gold Hill is a preserved mining town once known as "the richest mining property east of the Mississippi."

Greensboro. Start your tour of this interesting town with a stroll through the Downtown Greensboro Historic District. On the North Carolina A&T University campus is the **African Heritage Museum,** which houses one of the finest collections of African artifacts in the nation. The **Natural Science Center** is a multi-dimensional experience. It contains a botanical garden, petting zoo, nature museum and trails, a marine gallery, planetarium and newly opened Animal Discovery Zoological Park. This 500-acre addition features tigers, wallabies, meerkats and others.

Lake Norman. North Carolina's "inland sea" offers 32,500 acres of water for swimming, boating and sailing.

National Railroad Museum, Hamlet. Located in the old depot, the museum's collection of railroad equipment includes rolling stock, maps and photographs.

North Carolina Museum of Life & Science, Durham. View extensive prehistoric exhibits, an outstanding aerospace exhibit, the zoo, a wildlife sanctuary and a mile-long, narrow gauge railroad for visitors to enjoy.

North Carolina Zoological Park, Asheboro. The park is the largest walk-through natural habitat zoo in the U.S., encompassing more than 550 acres, with both African and North American-style acreage. The new expansion called Watani Grasslands Reserve, features elephants and rhinoceros.

Old Salem, Winston-Salem. Stroll through this restored town of Moravian ancestry and visit the **Museum of Early Southern Decorative Arts**, the **Herbst House**, where visitors may view candlemaking and saddlemaking, or the **Timothy Vogler Gun Shop,** a rifle-smithing facility.

Piedmont Carolina Railroad Museum, Belmont. Located at the old Piedmont and Northern Railroad Depot, this museum houses a large collection of railroad equipment and rolling stock.

Pinehurst. Golfers thrill to this charming village with over 35 courses within a 15-mile radius of the Pinehurst-Southern Pines area. Stop by the **PGA World of Golf Hall of Fame** to view clubs, golf artifacts and portraits of golf legends inducted into the hall of fame.

Raeford. Paraclete XP, one of the world's largest bodyflight centers is also one of the biggest vertical wind tunnels on the planet.

Raleigh. Learn about the state's history and culture at North Carolina's capital and enjoy the arts and natural beauty of the city.

Exploris is the world's first global learning center and features hands-on exhibits for all ages.

North Carolina Museum of Art is home to the finest collection of Old Master paintings in the Southeast.

North Carolina State Museum of Natural Sciences offers hands-on programs every day. See the state's natural treasures, ranging from salamanders to a 2-toed sloth.

Reed Gold Mine State Historic Site, Georgeville. Visit the site of the first documented discovery of gold in the country. Found in 1799, mining of the gold took place from 1803 to 1912.

Sciworks, Winston Salem. Travel the Solar System, come face-to-face with river otters in our Environmental Park and enjoy interactive hands-on exhibits.

Scotland Neck. Sylvan Heights Waterfowl Center, a breeding center with the world's largest collection of waterfowl including many rare and endangered species, opened a new flamingo exhibit in January 2008.

THE COAST

The Coastal region is as enchanting as the western mountains, even if the scenery is completely different. Here travelers can enjoy quiet beaches and view marine birds and other aquatic animals, including sea turtles at one of many wildlife sanctuaries. The region attracts surfers, hang-gliders, and wildlife watchers.

Bald Head Island. Accessible only by ferry or boat, this picturesque island has many points of interest including **Old Baldy Lighthouse** (1817), **Smith Island Museum of History** and the **Fort Holmes Site**.

Brunswick Islands. This colonial seaport, location of the Stamp Act Rebellion, was burned by British troops in 1776. Current attractions include the **Ingram Planetarium** featuring a domed theater and exhibits, the **Museum of Coastal Carolina**, a natural history museum with live reptile and turtle information programs and the **USS North Carolina Battleship Memorial.**

Calabash. Enjoy delicious Calabash cooking (lightly fried seafood) at this Intracoastal Waterway village.

Oak Island Beaches, Caswell, Long and Yaupon. These southern coastal vacation spots offer year-round fishing, boating, golfing and swimming, as well as a chance to see the **Oak Island Lighthouse.**

Cape Fear Coast is a world of history, sports, island beaches and incredible natural beauty—with four distinct yet mild seasons.

Highlights of the Cape Fear Coast include the newly renovated **Aquarium at Fort Fisher**, the historic **Wilmington** and the **Brunswick Islands**. Miles of beaches line the southeastern coast and offer excellent year-round recreational activities, including fishing, golf, boating and swimming.

The Battleship North Carolina. Take a tour to experience the inspiring "Through Their Eyes" exhibits. You'll see one of the few Kingfisher float planes still in existence.

Wilmington. The historic port of Wilmington affords visitors the unique opportunity to enjoy an exciting area rich in shopping, dining, culture and the arts, while being only minutes away from white sandy beaches. It has one of the largest districts listed in the National Register of Historic Places. In 2008, the National Trust for Historic Preservation named Wilmington as one of a "Dozen Distinctive Destinations".

Cape Hatteras National Seashore was the first national seashore. It runs 75 miles along NC 12. The seashore is famous for windsailing, surf and deep-sea fishing, as well as nature study and historic sites. **Pea Island National Wildlife Refuge** comprises 5,915 acres and has observation stands for wildlife viewing. The **Cape Hatteras Lighthouse** was built in 1870. At 208 ft. tall, it is the tallest lighthouse in the country. Visitors can climb the 268-step staircase for a spectacular view.

Cape Lookout National Seashore, Harkers Island. This 56-mile-long section of the Outer Banks consists of three undeveloped barrier islands that offer many natural and historical features.

Croatan National Forest. This coastal national forest covers over 155,000 acres and offers camping, picnicking, boating, canoeing, swimming, birdwatching and fishing.

Core Sound Waterfowl Museum, Harkers Island. Visit the exhibit gallery and artifacts and educational facilities.

Crystal Coast. Known as the "Southern Outer Banks," this area is recognized for its magnificent beaches and numerous water sports, such as swimming, fishing and surfing.

Dismal Swamp. Access to the swamp is finally possible with the newly opened state park with an 80-foot swing bridge across the historic Dismal Swamp Canal, the oldest continually operating man-made canal in the U.S.

Duplin Wine Cellars, Rose Hill. North Carolina's largest and oldest operating winery offers tours and tastings.

Elizabeth City Historic District. Grab a brochure at the local Chamber of Commerce and take a self-guided tour of the downtown area, highlighting 32 National Register historic sites and structures.

Fort Fisher State Historic Site and Civil War Museum. Before its fall in January, 1865, Fort Fisher, the South's largest earthen fort, protected blockade runners en route to Wilmington. The Second Battle was the largest land-sea battle of the Civil War. Wayside exhibits mark the tour trail. Guided tours. 1610 Fort Fisher Blvd. South, Kure Beach. Hours: Mon.-Sat. 9am-5pm, Sun. 1-5pm (Apr.-Sept.), Tues.-Sat. 10am-4pm, (Oct.-Mar.) Free, donations welcomed. www.fortfisher.nchistoricsites.org 910/458-5538

Greenville Museum of Art, Greenville. The museum houses an impressive collection of 20th-century American art and the largest display of Jugtown Pottery in the eastern part of the state.

Historic Bath. Incorporated in 1705, Bath is the state's oldest town and was the first meeting place of the Colonial Assembly of the Province. Several important 18th- and 19th-century structures have been restored and contain period furnishings, all of which are open for public viewing. These include **Palmer Marse House, St. Thomas Church, William House, Van Der Veer House, Bonner House** and **Swindell's Store.**

History Place, Morehead City. View artifacts of Native Americans, costumes and furnishings of the 18th and 19th centuries, Civil War artifacts and visiting exhibits.

Museum of the Albemarle, Elizabeth City. Learn about the regional history of the 10-county area of northeastern North Carolina. Exhibits recount the area's government, education, religion and economy, as well as its geology and history.

North Carolina Aquarium at Fort Fisher. Sharks, stingrays, seahorses, alligators & more, including: octopus, lionfish, sea turtles, and exotic fish. Programs include divers, feedings, touch-pool talks, sleepovers, canoeing, and camps. Food, gardens, gift shop. U. S. 421, 15-min. from Wilmington or ferry from Southport. Hours: Open 9am-5pm. Admission charged. www.ncaquariums.com 866/301-3476

North Carolina Maritime Museum, Beaufort. The exhibits explore maritime history and coastal natural history.

Outer Banks. Comprised of several barrier islands stretched along the coast, the Outer Banks offers historic sites, quaint villages, a variety of recreational activities, and miles of scenery.

Cape Hatteras Lighthouse, Buxton. View the tallest brick lighthouse in North America.

Cape Hatteras National Seashore encompasses over 30,000 acres of land on Bodie, Hatteras and Ocracoke Islands. Enjoy camping, surf and sport fishing, swimming and the picturesque village of Ocracoke.

Cape Lookout National Seashore. Accessible only by boat, the seashore extends over 50 miles up to Ocracoke Inlet.

Roanoke Island is the site of the first English attempt to colonize the New World. **The Waterside Theatre,** home of America's oldest outdoor drama *The Lost Colony*, is found here. This drama tells the history of Sir Walter Raleigh's Roanoke Voyages.

Wright Brothers National Memorial, near Kitty Hawk and Kill Devil Hills. Site of the Wright Brothers' historic 1903 flight, the memorial is now home to a monument, markers, a museum, a reconstructed hangar and an airport.

ANNUAL EVENTS

JANUARY

Pooh Day, Greensboro; Boat Show, Raleigh; Ultimate Wine Glass Competition & Toast, Ocean Isle Beach; Ft. Fisher Anniversary Event, Kure Beach.

FEBRUARY

Camper & RV Show, Concord; Art Exhibit, Marion; Carolina Chocolate Festival, Morehead City; Valentine Faire, Elizabeth City; Carolina Garden Expo, Charlotte; Annual Civil War Living History, Elizabeth City; Carolina Power & Sailboat Show, Raleigh; Folk Art Festival at Fearrington, Pittsboro; Native American Powwow, Durham; Native American Art Show, Raleigh.

MARCH

Fly a Kite Day, Tryon; Biltmore Estate's Festival of Flowers, Asheville; Annual Coastal Home and Garden Show, Morehead City; Rumba on the Lumber Festival, Lumberton; American Music Jubilee, Selma; Great Outdoor Expo, Morganton; Seafood Festival Fun Fest, Morehead City; Spring Craft Fair, Raleigh; NC Jazz Festival, Wilmington; Civil War Living History Re-enactment, Wilmington.

APRIL

French Broad River Festival, Hot Springs; Festival of Flowers, Asheville; NC Azalea Festival, Wilmington; NC Pickle Festival, Mount Olive; Annual National Juried Art Exhibition, Rocky Mount; Blue Ridge Wine Festival, Blowing Rock; Annual International Whistlers Convention, Louisburg; Annual Redbud Festival, Saxapahaw; Spring Wine Festival, Wagram; Antique Show and Sale, Greenville.

MAY

Daniel Boone Family Festival, Mocksville; Ole Time Fiddlers' & Bluegrass Festival, Union Grove; Olde Tyme Music Festival, Hendersonville; Springfest, Saluda; NC Seafood Festival Golf Extravaganza, Morehead City; Spring Festival, Murphy; Annual North Carolina Forest Festival, Plymouth; Annual May Fest & Auto Show, Rutherfordton; Ramp Festival, Waynesville; Ribfest, Eden; Butterfly Festival, Hudson; Annual Celtic Festival and Highland Game, Winston-Salem; Wilmington Greek Festival, Wilmington; Bimbe Cultural Arts Festival, Durham; Salisbury Cultural Arts Festival, Salisbury; Music Festival, Beaufort; Dale Earnhardt Mayfest, Newton; Paddlefest, Denton; Lil John's Mountain Music Festival, Snow Camp; Fiddler's Grove Festival, Union Grove.

JUNE

American Dance Festival, Durham; Big Rock Blue Marlin Fishing Tournament, Atlantic Beach; National Hollerin' Contest, Spivey's Corner; Eastern Music Festival, Greensboro; Annual Bluegrass Festival, Aberdeen; Festival of the Vino, Chapel Hill; Tar River Festival, Louisburg; Big Lick Bluegrass Festival, Oakboro; Annual Blue Ridge Barbecue Festival, Tryon; Annual Piedmont Pottery Festival, Eden; Bluff Mountain Festival, Marshall; Arts by the Sea Festival, Swansboro; Taste of Scotland, Franklin; Beach Music Festival, Carolina Beach; Ocrafolk Music & Story Festival, Ocracoke; Anniversary Celebration, Bethania; Under the Oaks Arts Festival, Corolla.

JULY

Festival for the Eno, Durham; Blackberry Festival, Lenoir; Hatteras Kite Festival, Hatteras; Jazz Festival, Morehead City; Doc Watson Music Fest, Sugar Grove; Art in the Park, Blowing Rock; Peach Festival, Candor; Cherokee Rodeo, Cherokee; Parade of Lawnmowers/Watermelon Festival, Cooleemee; Wright Kite Festival, Kill Devil Hills; Croaker Festival, Oriental; Battleship Blast July 4th Celebration, Wilmington; Cape Fear Blues Festival, Wilmington; North Carolina 4th of July Festival, Southport; Red White and Bluegrass Festival, Morganton; Waldensian Festival, Valdese.

AUGUST

Art on Main, Hendersonville; Mountain Dance and Folk Festival, Asheville; Art & Craft Fair, Asheville; Sourwood Festival, Black Mountain; Mount Mitchell Craft Fair, Burnsville; Shrimp by the Bay, Edenton; Cape Lookout Lighthouse Open House, Harkers Island; Festival of Crafts, Hickory; Watermelon Festival, Murfreesboro; Blackberry Festival, Mars Hill; Annual Jack Tales Festival, Blowing Rock; Waldensian Festival, Valdese.

SEPTEMBER

Pow Wow, Spruce Pine; NC Mountain State Fair, Asheville; Mule Days, Benson; Tomato Festival, Bryson City; Bull Durham Blues Festival, Durham; Apple Festival, Hendersonville; Bar-B-Q Blow Out, Maggie Valley; Grape Day/Gourd Festival, Raleigh; Purple Feet Festival, Ocean Isle Beach; Winston-Salem Crafts Guild Fall Craft Show, Winston Salem; Flatwoods Festival, Bennett; Historic Morganton Festival, Morganton; Greek Festival, Greensboro; Apple Festival, Winston-Salem; Mountain Heritage Festival, Sparta; Southern Coastal Bluegrass Festival, Kure Beach; Wagram's Annual Pig Pickin' Festival, Wagram; Blues, Brews & BBQ, Charlotte.

OCTOBER

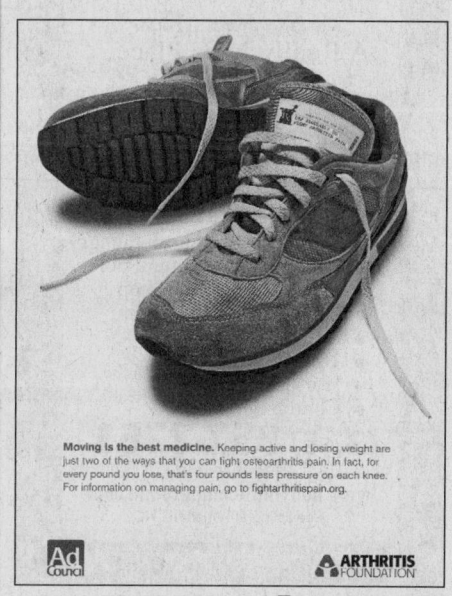

Peanut Festival, Enfield; Heritage Day Festival, Black Creek; North Carolina State Fair, Raleigh; International Sardine Festival, Aberdeen; Oktoberfest at Sugar Mountain, Banner Elk; Carolina Kite Fest, Atlantic Beach; Maple Leaf Festival, Bryson City; Great Grapes! Wine & Music Festival, Charlotte; Festifall, Chapel Hill; Dam Jam, Fontana Dam; North Carolina Seafood Festival, Morehead City; Oyster Festival, Ocean Isle Beach; Annual Cornshucking Frolic, Pinnacle; Hillbilly Heritage Festival, Spruce Pine; Riverfest, Wilmington; Mountain Music Homecoming Jamboree, Maggie Valley.

NOVEMBER

Christmas at Biltmore Estate, Asheville; Weaverville Art Safari, Weaverville; Kites with Lights, Nags Head; Colossal Collard Day, Raleigh; Pecan Day, Raleigh; Wings Over Water, Kill Devil Hills; Pottery Festival, Seagrove; Storytelling Festival, Tryon; Holiday Season in Old Salem, Winston-Salem; NC Holiday Flotilla, Wrightsville Beach.

DECEMBER

Sugarfest, Banner Elk; Creekside Christmas, Archdale; A Carolina Mountain Christmas, Arden; Twilight Tour, Brevard; Winterfest, Burnsville; Island of Lights Festival of Homes, Carolina Beach; Window Wonderland, Franklin; Christmas Boat Parade, Lake Lure; Old Wilmington By Candlelight, Wilmington; Christmas by the Sea Festival, Southport.

North Carolina

ABERDEEN—C-3

(S) Long Leaf Pine Oasis—(Scotland) *From jct of Hwy 211 & US 15/501: Go 14-1/2 mi S on US 15/501, then 2 mi W on Palmer Rd. Enter on L.* ◆◆FACILITIES: 26 sites, typical site width 20 ft, accepts self-contained units only, 14 full hkups, 12 E, (30/50 amps), 14 pull-thrus, WiFi Instant Internet at site, family camping, dump, picnic tables, fire rings. RECREATION: Pets welcome. No tents. Open all yr. Big rigs welcome. Rate in 2010 $38 per vehicle. Member ARVC, CARVC. CCUSA 50% Discount. CCUSA reservations Recommended, CCUSA max stay 3 days, Cash only for CCUSA disc., Check only for CCUSA disc., CCUSA disc. not avail F,Sa, CCUSA disc. not avail holidays. Not available during Pinehurst Deercroft golfing events or special events @ St Andrews College-call for details. Reservations may be made by phone. Tent camping available-call for rates.

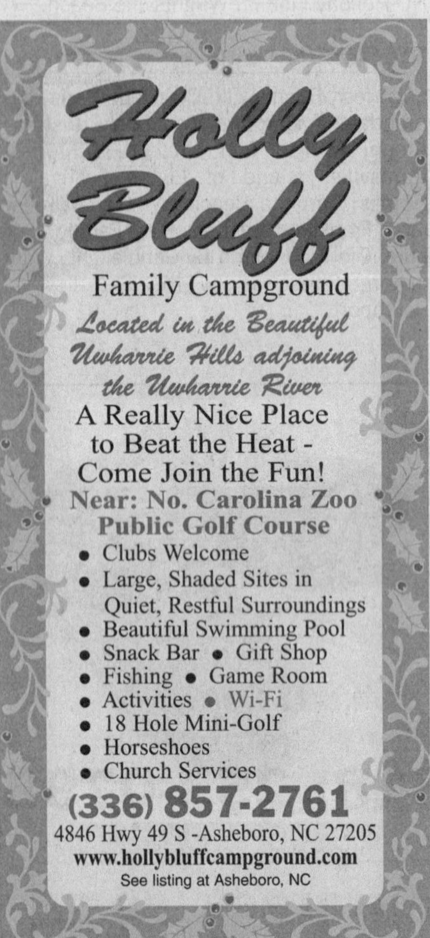

Holly Bluff
Family Campground
Located in the Beautiful Uwharrie Hills adjoining the Uwharrie River
A Really Nice Place to Beat the Heat - Come Join the Fun!
Near: No. Carolina Zoo
Public Golf Course
• Clubs Welcome
• Large, Shaded Sites in Quiet, Restful Surroundings
• Beautiful Swimming Pool
• Snack Bar • Gift Shop
• Fishing • Game Room
• Activities • Wi-Fi
• 18 Hole Mini-Golf
• Horseshoes
• Church Services
(336) 857-2761
4846 Hwy 49 S -Asheboro, NC 27205
www.hollybluffcampground.com
See listing at Asheboro, NC

ABERDEEN—Continued
Long Leaf Pine Oasis—Continued

Phone: (910)266-8372
Address: 15340 Palmer Rd, Marston, NC 28363
Lat/Lon: 34.90446/-79.46770
Email: longleafpineoasis@yahoo.com
Web: longleafpineoasis.com

Reserve Online at Woodalls.com

(SE) PINE LAKE RV RESORT—(Scotland) *From jct of Hwy 211 & US 15/US 501: Go 9-1/2 mi S on US 15/501, then 2 mi E on Hill Creek Rd. Enter on R.*

WELCOME

◆◆FACILITIES: 90 sites, typical site width 28 ft, 85 full hkups, 5 W&E, (30/50 amps), some extd stay sites, 80 pull-thrus, WiFi Instant Internet at site, WiFi Internet central location, family camping, RV's/park model rentals, cabins, RV storage, dump, non-guest dump $, laundry, RV supplies, LP gas by weight/by meter, ice, picnic tables, fire rings, wood, controlled access.

◆◆◆RECREATION: rec room/area, pavilion, swim pool, boating, no motors, canoeing, kayaking, pond fishing, playground, horseshoes, hiking trails.

Pets welcome. No tents. Open all yr. Clubs welcome. Rate in 2010 $34-38 per family. MC/VISA. FCRV discount. FMCA discount.

Phone: (800)746-3505
Address: 32482 Hill Creek Rd, Wagram, NC 28396
Lat/Lon: 34.98497/-79.41535
Email: pinelakeresort@earthlink.net
Web: pinelakervresortcamp.com

SEE AD THIS PAGE

ALBEMARLE—B-2

(NE) MORROW MOUNTAIN STATE PARK—(Stanly) *From town: Go 5 mi E on Hwy 24/27/73/740.* FACILITIES: 106 sites, 26 ft max RV length, 22 E, (30/50 amps), 84 no hkups, 1 pull-thrus, tenting, dump. RECREATION: swim pool, boating, canoeing, ramp, lake fishing. Pets welcome. Partial handicap access. Open all yr. Phone: (704)982-4402.

ALMOND—E-1

(W) NANTAHALA NATIONAL FOREST (Tsali Recreational Area)—(Swain) *From town: Go 2 mi W on Hwy 28, then 1-1/2 mi N on FR 361.* FACILITIES: 41 sites, 22 ft max RV length, 41 no hkups, tenting. RECREATION: boating, ramp, lake fishing. Partial handicap access. Open Apr 15 - Oct 31. Phone: (828)479-6431.

(NW) Tumbling Waters Campground—(Graham) *From west jct US 19/74 & Hwy 28: Go 5-1/4 mi NW on Hwy 28, then 1-3/4 mi W on Panther Creek Rd. Enter at end.* ◆◆◆FACILITIES: 32 sites, typical site width 20 ft, 32 full hkups, (30 amps), 5 pull-thrus, family camping, tenting, laundry. ◆RECREATION: river swim, pond/stream fishing. Pets welcome. Open Mar 1 - Dec 1. Rate in 2010 $23-26 for 2 persons. Phone: (828) 479-3814.

APEX—B-3

JORDAN LAKE STATE REC. AREA (Crosswinds Campground)—(Chatham) *From jct US 1 & US 64: Go 11 mi W on US 64.* FACILITIES: 129 sites, 129 W&E, tenting, dump. RECREATION: boating, ramp, lake fishing, playground. Partial handicap access. Open all yr. Facilities fully operational Mar 21 - Nov 15. Phone: (919)362-0586.

JORDAN LAKE STATE REC. AREA (Parkers Creek)—(Chatham) *From jct Hwy 1 & US 64: Go W on US 64.* FACILITIES: 250 sites, 150 W&E, (20 amps), 100 no hkups, tenting, dump. RECREATION: lake swim, boating, canoeing, ramp, lake fishing, playground. No pets. Partial handicap access. Open all yr. Phone: (919)362-0586.

JORDAN LAKE STATE REC. AREA (Poplar Point)—(Chatham) *From town: Go 10 mi W on US 64 to Wilsonville, then 2 mi S on Hwy 1008.* FACILITIES: 579 sites, 363 W&E, (30/50 amps), 216 no hkups, tenting, dump. RECREATION: lake swim, boating, canoeing, ramp, dock, lake fishing, playground. No pets. Partial handicap access. Open Mar 15 - Nov 30. Phone: (919) 362-0586.

JORDAN LAKE STATE REC. AREA (Vista Point)—(Chatham) *From town: Go 12 mi W on US 64 to Griffins Crossroads, then 3 mi S on Pea Ridge Rd.* FACILITIES: 50 sites, 50 W&E, dump. RECREATION: lake swim, boating, canoeing, ramp, dock, lake fishing. No pets. No tents. Open Mar 15 - Nov 30. Phone: (919)362-0586.

ASHEBORO—B-2

(NE) DEEP RIVER CAMPGROUND & RV PARK—(Randolph) *From jct I-73/I-74/US 220 & US 64/Hwy 40: Go 7 mi E on US 64/Hwy 49, then 1-1/2 mi N on Loflin Pond Rd, then 1/4 mi E on McDowell Country Trail. Enter on L.*

WELCOME

◆◆◆FACILITIES: 61 sites, typical site width 45 ft, 45 full hkups, 16 W&E, (30/50 amps), many extd stay sites, 38 pull-thrus, cable TV, WiFi Instant Internet at site, family camping, tenting, cabins,

DEEP RIVER CAMPGROUND & RV PARK—Continued on next page

ASHEBORO—Continued
DEEP RIVER CAMPGROUND & RV PARK—Continued

dump, non-guest dump $, laundry, LP gas by weight/by meter, ice, picnic tables, fire rings, wood.

◆◆◆RECREATION: rec room/area, pavilion, coin games, 2 swim pools, canoeing, kayaking, canoe/2 kayak rentals, lake/river fishing, bsktball, play equipment, horseshoes, v-ball. Rec open to public.

Pets welcome, breed restrict. Open all yr. Big rigs welcome. Clubs welcome. Rate in 2010 $24-30 for 4 persons. MC/VISA. Member ARVC, CARVC. CCUSA 50% Discount. CCUSA reservations Recommended, CCUSA max stay 5 days, CCUSA disc. not avail F,Sa, CCUSA disc. not avail holidays.

Phone: (336)629-4069
Address: 814 McDowell Country Trail, Asheboro, NC 27203
Lat/Lon: 35.74597/-79.73067
Email: drcampground@earthlink.net
Web: www.deeprivercampground.com

SEE AD PAGE 578

(SW) HOLLY BLUFF FAMILY CAMPGROUND—(Randolph) *From jct I-73/I-74/US 220 & US 64/Hwy 49: Go 1/2 mi W on US 64/Hwy 49, then 7 mi S on Hwy 49. Enter on R.*

COME JOIN THE FUN!
We take pride in our family campground. Enjoy our mini-golf course. We keep everything up-to-date & ship-shape. There's lots to do (swim in our pool, fish at the river) and we're in a great location near the zoo.

◆◆◆FACILITIES: 98 sites, typical site width 25 ft, 93 full hkups, (20/30/50 amps), 5 no hkups, some extd stay sites, 10 pull-thrus, WiFi Instant Internet at site, family camping, tenting, RV storage, dump, non-guest dump $, ice, picnic tables, fire rings.

◆◆◆RECREATION: rec hall, equipped pavilion, coin games, swim pool, river fishing, fishing supplies, mini-golf, ($), golf nearby, bsktball, playground, activities, (wkends), horseshoes, hiking trails, v-ball.

ASHEBORO—Continued
HOLLY BLUFF FAMILY CAMPGROUND—Continued

Pets welcome. Open all yr. Self-contained units only in winter. Big rigs welcome. Clubs welcome. Rate in 2010 $28-32 for 4 persons.

Phone: (336)857-2761
Address: 4846 NC Hwy 49 South, Asheboro, NC 27205
Lat/Lon: 35.64432/-79.95623
Web: www.hollybluffcampground.com

SEE AD PAGE 578

(SE) TRAILS END FAMILY CAMPING—(Randolph) *From SR 64 & Zoo Pkwy: Go 2 mi S on Zoo Pkwy, then SE 3 mi on Old Cox Rd. Enter on R.*

◆◆◆FACILITIES: 100 sites, typical site width 18 ft, 43 full hkups, 11 W&E, (30/50 amps), 46 no hkups, some extd stay sites (summer), WiFi Instant Internet at site, WiFi Internet central location, family camping, tenting, dump, laundry, ice, picnic tables, fire rings, wood, controlled access.

◆◆◆RECREATION: equipped pavilion, coin games, swim pool, lake/stream fishing, activities, (wkends), horseshoes, hiking trails. Rec open to public.

Pets welcome. Open Apr 1 - Nov 1. Big rigs welcome. Rate in 2010 $20-25 for 2 persons. MC/VISA/DISC/AMEX. Member ARVC, CARVC.

Phone: (336)629-5353
Address: 2846 Old Cox Rd., Asheboro, NC 27205
Lat/Lon: 35.63319/-79.77102
Web: trailsendcampground.net

SEE AD THIS PAGE

ASHEVILLE—E-2

ASHEVILLE EAST-KOA—*From Asheville: Go E on I-40 to exit 59, then 1/2 mi N on Patton Cove Rd, then 1-1/2 mi E on US 70. Enter on L.*

SEE PRIMARY LISTING AT SWANNANOA AND AD PAGE 581

Tell them Woodall's sent you!

ASHEVILLE—Continued

(SW) ASHEVILLE-BEAR CREEK RV PARK—(Buncombe) *From jct I-40 (exit 47) & Hwy 191: Westbound: Go across Hwy 191, then 1/2 mi W on S Bear Creek Rd. Eastbound: Go 1/2 mi N on Hwy 191, then 1/2 mi W on S Bear Creek Rd. Enter on L.*

◆◆◆◆FACILITIES: 90 sites, typical site width 30 ft, 90 full hkups, (30/50 amps), 32 pull-thrus, cable TV, WiFi Instant Internet at site, WiFi Internet central location, cabins, laundry, RV supplies, LP gas by weight/by meter, ice, picnic tables, patios.

◆◆◆RECREATION: rec hall, rec room/area, swim pool, golf nearby, bsktball, play equipment, v-ball.

Pets welcome. Partial handicap access. No tents. Open all yr. Big rigs welcome. Clubs welcome. Rate in 2010 $38-45 for 2 persons. MC/VISA/Debit. Member ARVC, CARVC. FMCA discount.

ASHEVILLE-BEAR CREEK RV PARK—Continued on next page

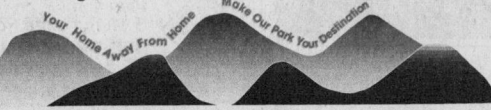

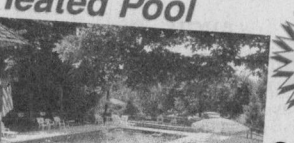

ASHEVILLE—Continued
ASHEVILLE-BEAR CREEK RV PARK—Continued

Phone: (828)253-0798
Address: 81 S Bear Creek Rd, Asheville, NC 28806
Email: hbbercreek@bellsouth.net
Web: www.ashevillebearcreek.com

SEE AD PAGE 579 AND AD MAP PAGE 568

BLUE RIDGE NATIONAL PARKWAY (Mt. Pisgah)—(Haywood) *From town: Go 24 mi W on Blue Ridge Pkwy at Milepost 409.* FACILITIES: 119 sites, 30 ft max RV length, 119 no hkups, tenting, dump, ltd groc. RECREATION: Pets welcome. Partial handicap access. Open May 14 - Oct 31. Phone: (828)298-0398.

(N) CAMPFIRE LODGINGS—(Buncombe) *From jct I-40/ I-26 and I-240: Go 4 mi NE on I-240 (exit 4A), then 5-3/4 mi N on US 19/23 (exit 21), then E on New Stock Rd, then 3/4 mi S on US 19 Bus (Weaverville Hwy), then 1/4 mi W on Old Marshall Hwy. Enter on L.*

WELCOME

◊◊◊◊FACILITIES: 29 sites, typical site width 40 ft, 22 full hkups, (20/30/50 amps), 7 no hkups, 0 pull-thrus, cable TV, WiFi Instant Internet at site, family camping, tenting, cabins, laundry, RV supplies, LP gas by weight/by meter, picnic tables, patios, fire rings, wood.

◊◊RECREATION: pond fishing, horseshoes, hiking trails.

Pets welcome. Partial handicap access. Open all yr. Big rigs welcome. Rate in 2010 $40-55 for 2 persons. MC/VISA/AMEX. Member ARVC, CARVC.

Phone: (800)933-8012
Address: 116 Old Marshall Hwy, Asheville, NC 28804
Lat/Lon: 35.65999/-82.59255
Email: info@campfirelodgings.com
Web: www.campfirelodgings.com

SEE AD NEXT PAGE

(S) PISGAH NATIONAL FOREST (Lake Powhatan Rec. Area)—(Haywood) *From town: Go 4 mi S on Hwy-191, then 3-1/2 mi W on FR-806.* FACILITIES: 98 sites, 35 ft max RV length, 9 full hkups, 1 W&E, 1 E, 87 no hkups, 7 pull-thrus, dump. RECREATION: lake swim, lake fishing. Open Apr 1 - Oct 31. Phone: (828) 670-5627.

(S) PISGAH NATIONAL FOREST (North Mills River Rec. Area)—(Haywood) *From town: Go 13-1/2 mi S on Hwy-19, then 5 mi W on FR-478.* FACILITIES: 30 sites, 22 ft max RV length, 30 no hkups, tenting, dump. RECREATION: river fishing. Open all yr. Facilities fully operational Apr 1 - Oct 31. Phone: (828)890-3284.

RUTLEDGE LAKE RV PARK—*From jct I-40 & I-26: Go 9 mi S on I-26 to exit 40, then 1 mi E on Hwy 280, then 3/4 mi S on Rutledge Rd. Enter on L.*

SEE PRIMARY LISTING AT FLETCHER AND AD THIS PAGE

(E) Taps RV Park (RV SPACES)—(Buncombe) *From jct I-240 & I-40/I-26: Go 9 mi E on I-40 (exit 55), then 1/4 mi W on US 70 (Tunnel Rd). Enter on L.* FACILITIES: 46 sites, typical site width 25 ft, 32 full hkups, 14 W&E, (20/30/50 amps), 23 pull-thrus, dump. RECREATION: river fishing. Pets welcome. No tents. Open all yr. Big rigs welcome. Phone: (800)831-4385.

AVON—B-6

(C) Sands of Time Campground—(Dare) *From jct of Hwy 12 & Harbor Rd: Go 1/4 mi W on Harbor Rd, then 300 feet N on N End Rd. Enter on R.* ◊◊◊FACILITIES: 62 sites, typical site width 30 ft, 57 full hkups, (30/50 amps), 50 amps ($), 5 no hkups, cable TV, WiFi Instant Internet at site ($), tenting, dump, laundry, picnic

Sands of Time Campground—Continued on next page

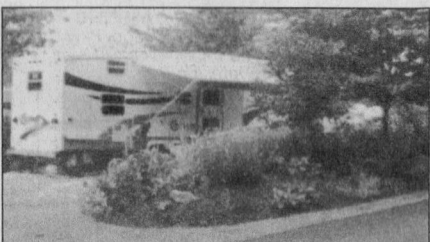

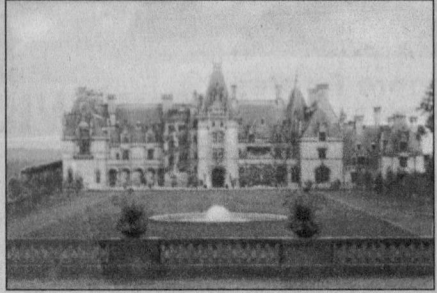

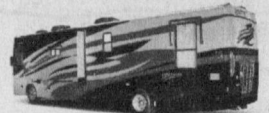

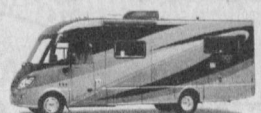

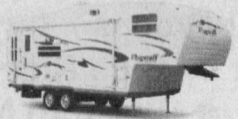

AVON—Continued
Sands of Time Campground—Continued

tables. RECREATION: Pets welcome ($), breed restrict. Open all yr. Big rigs welcome. Rate in 2010 $34-44 for 2 persons. CCUSA 50% Discount.

Phone: (252)995-5596
Address: 40523 North End Road, Avon, NC 27915
Lat/Lon: 35.35499/-75.50745
Email: sandsoftime1@aol.com
Web: www.sandsoftimecampground.com

BALSAM—E-2

(SW) **MOONSHINE CREEK CAMPGROUND**—(Jackson) *From jct Blue Ridge Pkwy (exit MP 443.1) & US 23/US 74: Go 1/2 mi S & W on US 23/74, then 2 mi SW on Candlestick Lane/CR-1471 which becomes Dark Ridge Rd. Enter on L.*

◆◆◆FACILITIES: 100 sites, typical site width 25 ft, 55 full hkups, 45 W&E, (20/30/50 amps), some extd stay sites, cable TV, ($), WiFi Internet central location, tenting, cabins, dump, laundry, groceries, RV supplies, LP gas by weight/by meter, ice, picnic tables, patios, fire rings, grills, wood.

◆◆RECREATION: equipped pavilion, pond/stream fishing, fishing supplies, play equipment, horseshoes, hiking trails.

Pets welcome, breed restrict. Open Apr 1 - Nov 1. Clubs welcome. Rate in 2010 $30-37 for 2 persons. MC/VISA. Member ARVC, CARVC.

Phone: (828)586-6666
Address: 27 Moonshine CR Trail, Balsam, NC 28707
Lat/Lon: 35.41464/-83.09978
Email: moonshinecreek@hotmail.com
Web: www.moonshinecreekcampground.com

SEE AD CHEROKEE PAGE 586

BANNER ELK—A-1

(S) **GRANDFATHER CAMPGROUND**—(Watauga) *From jct US 321 & Hwy 105: Go 10 mi S on Hwy 105. Enter on L.*

◆◆◆FACILITIES: 128 sites, typical site width 40 ft, 60 full hkups, 12 W&E, 7 E, (20/30/50 amps), 49 no hkups, 19 pull-thrus, cable TV, WiFi Instant Internet at site, WiFi Internet central location, family camping, tenting, cabins, RV storage, dump, non-guest dump $, laundry, ltd groc, RV supplies, ice, picnic tables, fire rings, grills, wood.

◆◆RECREATION: rec room/area, pavilion, stream fishing, golf nearby, activities, (wkends), horseshoes, hiking trails.

Pets welcome. Partial handicap access. Open all yr. Big rigs welcome. Clubs welcome. Rate in 2010 $26-33 for 2 persons. MC/VISA/DISC. Member ARVC, CARVC.

Phone: (800)788-2582
Address: 125 Riverside Dr, Banner Elk, NC 28604
Lat/Lon: 36.14440/-81.79725
Email: grandfatherrv@charter.net
Web: www.grandfatherrv.com

SEE AD BOONE NEXT PAGE

BLOWING ROCK—A-1

(S) BLUE RIDGE NATIONAL PARKWAY (Julian Price Memorial Campground)—*From town: Go 1 mi N on US-221 & 321, then 5 mi SW on Blue Ridge Pkwy to MP-297.* FACILITIES: 68 sites, 30 ft max RV length, 68 no hkups, tenting, dump. RECREATION: boating, canoeing, ramp, dock, lake fishing. Pets welcome. Partial handicap access. Open Mid May - End of Oct. Phone: (828)963-5911.

BOONE—A-1

(SW) **FLINTLOCK CAMPGROUND**—(Watauga) *From jct US 321 & Hwy 105: Go 3 mi SW on Hwy 105. Enter on R.*

◆◆◆FACILITIES: 92 sites, typical site width 24 ft, 61 full hkups, 31 W&E, (15/20/30/50 amps), some extd stay sites, 6 pull-thrus, cable TV, WiFi Internet central location, tenting, cabins, RV storage, dump, laundry, ice, picnic tables, patios, wood.

◆◆RECREATION: rec room/area, pavilion, bsktball, play equipment, horseshoes, v-ball.

Pets welcome. Partial handicap access. Open Apr 1 - Early Nov. Clubs welcome. Rate in 2010 $25-33 for 2 persons. MC/VISA.

FLINTLOCK CAMPGROUND—Continued on next page

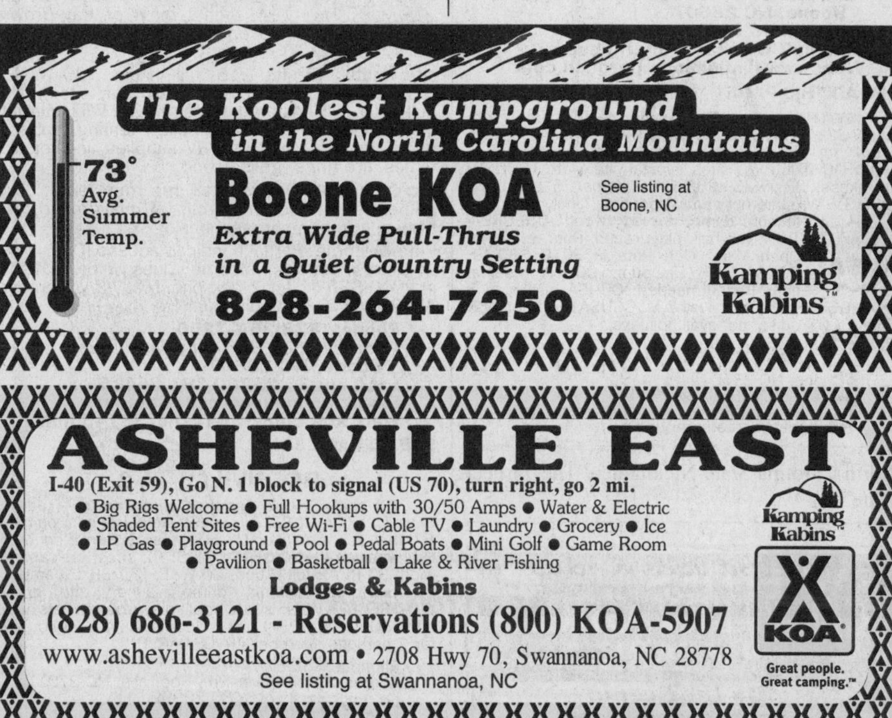

BOONE—Continued
FLINTLOCK CAMPGROUND—Continued

Phone: (888)850-9997
Address: 171 Flintlock Campground Dr, Boone, NC 28607
Lat/Lon: 36.20473/-81.72855
Email: FCG@charterinternet.com
Web: www.flintlockcampground.com

SEE AD THIS PAGE

(SW) Honey Bear Campground—(Watauga) *From jct US 321 & Hwy 105: Go 1-1/2 mi S on Hwy 105, then 1-1/4 mi E on Poplar Grove Rd. Enter on L.* ◆◆◆FACILITIES: 73 sites, typical site width 18 ft, 40 full hkups, 33 W&E, (20/30/50 amps), 6 pull-thrus, cable TV, WiFi Internet central location, family camping, tenting, dump, laundry, wood. ◆RECREATION: rec hall, playground. Pets welcome. Open Mar - Oct. Rate in 2010 $30-39. CCUSA 50% Discount. CCUSA reservations Recommended, CCUSA max stay 3 days, CCUSA disc. not avail S,M, CCUSA disc. not avail F,Sa, CCUSA disc. not avail holidays.

Phone: (828)963-4586
Address: 229 Honey Bear Campground Rd, Boone, NC 28607
Lat/Lon: 36.19668/-81.71119
Email: vacation@honeybearcampground.com
Web: honeybearcampground.com

North Carolina State Nickname: "The Tarheel State"

BOONE—Continued

KOA-BOONE—(Watauga) *From jct US 421/Hwy 194 & US 321/221: Go 1 mi NE on US 221/194, then 3 mi NW on Hwy 194, then 1 mi W on Ray Brown Rd. Enter on R.*

◆◆◆FACILITIES: 135 sites, typical site width 45 ft, 115 full hkups, 20 W&E, (15/20/30/50 amps), some extd stay sites, 100 pull-thrus, WiFi Instant Internet at site, WiFi Internet central location, family camping, tenting, cabins, dump, laundry, ltd groc, RV supplies, ice, picnic tables, fire rings, grills, wood.

◆◆◆RECREATION: rec hall, rec room/area, coin games, swim pool, mini-golf, ($), playground, activities, (wkends), horseshoes.

Pets welcome. Partial handicap access. Open May 1 - Oct 31. Big rigs welcome. Clubs welcome. Rate in 2010 $35-41 for 2 persons. MC/VISA. Member ARVC, CARVC. KOA discount.

Phone: (828)264-7250
Address: 123 Harmony Mtn Lane, Boone, NC 28607
Lat/Lon: 36.25780/-81.66476
Email: boonekoa@bellsouth.net
Web: koa.com/where/nc/33145.htm

SEE AD PAGE 581

BOONVILLE—A-2

(N) Holly Ridge Family Campground—(Yadkin) *From jct I-77 (exit 82) & Hwy 67: Go 6-1/2 mi E on Hwy 67, then 1-1/4 mi N on US 601, then 1/2 mi E on River Rd. Enter on L.* ◆◆◆FACILITIES: 62 sites, typical site width 30 ft, 42 full hkups, 20 W&E, (20/30/50 amps), 17 pull-thrus, tenting, dump, laundry, ltd groc. ◆◆◆RECREATION: swim pool, playground. Pets welcome. Open all yr. Big rigs welcome. Rate in 2010 $37 for 2 persons. Member ARVC, CARVC.

Phone: (336)367-7756
Address: 5140 River Rd., Boonville, NC 27011
Lat/Lon: 36.25718/-80.70999
Email: hollyridge@yadtel.net
Web: www.hollyridgecampground.tripod.com

BREVARD—E-2

(W) Adventure Village & Lodgings—(Transylvania) *From jct US 276 & US 64: Go 5-1/2 mi W on US 64, then 150 yds N on Adventure Ridge/Israel Rd. Enter on L.* ◆◆FACILITIES: 50 sites, typical site width 25 ft, 30 full hkups, (20/30/50 amps), 20 no hkups, WiFi Internet central location, family camping, tenting, ltd groc, RV supplies, picnic tables, fire rings, grills.

Save time! Plan ahead with WOODALL'S!

BREVARD—Continued
Adventure Village & Lodgings—Continued

◆◆◆RECREATION: wading pool, fishing supplies, bsktball, playground, horseshoes, v-ball. Pets welcome. Partial handicap access. Open all yr. Big rigs welcome. Rate in 2010 $30 for 4 persons. MC/VISA/Debit. CCUSA 50% Discount. CCUSA reservations Recommended, CCUSA max stay Unlimited, CCUSA disc. not avail holidays. $5 surcharge fishing pond.

Phone: (828)862-5411
Address: 129 Israel Rd, Brevard, NC 28712
Lat/Lon: 35.16534/-82.81526
Email: adventurevillage@citcom.net
Web: www.theadventurevillage.com

BLACK FOREST FAMILY CAMPING RESORT—*From jct US 64 & US 276: Go 12-1/2 mi S on US 276, then 1/4 mi E on Summer Rd.*

SEE PRIMARY LISTING AT CEDAR MOUNTAIN AND AD THIS PAGE

(N) PISGAH NATIONAL FOREST (Davidson River Campground)—(Transylvania) *From jct US-64 & US-276: Go 1-1/2 mi N on US-276.* FACILITIES: 160 sites, 12 full hkups, 3 E, (30 amps), 145 no hkups, 13 pull-thrus, tenting, dump. RECREATION: river fishing, play equipment. Partial handicap access. Open all yr. Phone: (828)862-5960.

BRYSON CITY—E-1

(E) COUNTRY GIRL'S RV PARK—(Swain) *From US 74 (exit 69): Go 1-1/4 mi N on Hyatt Creek Rd (SR 1190). Enter on L.*

◆◆FACILITIES: 75 sites, typical site width 25 ft, 75 full hkups, (30/50 amps), some extd stay sites, WiFi Internet central location, family camping, tenting, laundry, ice, picnic tables, fire rings, wood.

◆RECREATION: river fishing.

Pets welcome, breed restrict, size restrict. Open all yr. Big rigs welcome. Rate in 2010 $25 for 2 persons.

Phone: (828)488-8807
Address: 1367 Hyatt Creek Rd, Bryson City, NC 28713
Lat/Lon: 35.45133/-83.39867
Web: countrygirlsrvpark.com

SEE AD THIS PAGE

(NE) Deep Creek Tube Center & Campground—(Swain) *From US 74 (exit 67): Go 3/4 mi NW on Veterans Blvd, then 2 blocks E on US 19, then 1/4 mi*

Deep Creek Tube Center & Campground—Continued on next page

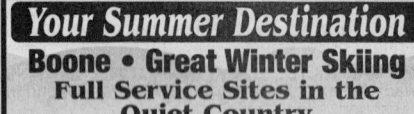

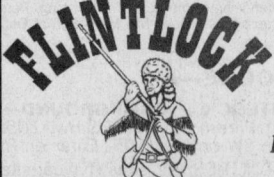

BRYSON CITY—Continued
Deep Creek Tube Center & Campground—Continued

N on Everett St, then 2 blocks E on Depot St, then 1-1/4 mi NE on Deep Creek Rd. Enter on R. ◊◊◊FACILITIES: 46 sites, typical site width 25 ft, 30 full hkups, 3 W&E, (20/30/50 amps), 50 amps ($), 13 no hkups, 3 pull-thrus, tenting, laundry, ltd groc. ◊◊RECREATION: river fishing, play equipment. Pets welcome. Partial handicap access. Open Apr 1 - Oct 31. Big rigs welcome. Rate in 2010 $25-37 for 4 persons. Member ARVC, CARVC. Phone: (828)488-6055.

(E) ELA CAMPGROUND—(Swain) *From US 74 (exit 69): Go 2 mi N on Hyatt Creek Rd (SR 1190), then 1/2 mi E on US 19. Enter on R.*

WELCOME

◊◊FACILITIES: 163 sites, typical site width 22 ft, 35 ft max RV length, 152 full hkups, 11 W&E, (30/50 amps), many extd stay sites, 14 pull-thrus, cable TV, WiFi Instant Internet at site, WiFi Internet central location, family camping, tenting, RV's/park model rentals, cabins, RV storage, dump, laundry, groceries, RV supplies, LP gas by weight/by meter, ice, picnic tables, fire rings, wood.

◊◊◊RECREATION: rec hall, equipped pavilion, swim pool, river fishing, fishing supplies, bsktball, playground, activities, (wkends), horseshoes, v-ball.

Pets welcome. Open all yr. Escort to site. Clubs welcome. Rate in 2010 $35 for 4 persons. MC/VISA/DISC/AMEX. Member ARVC, CARVC.

Phone: (828)488-2410
Address: 5100 Ela Rd, Bryson City, NC 28713
Lat/Lon: 35.44902/-83.38562
Email: info@elacampground.com
Web: elacampground.com

SEE AD CHEROKEE PAGE 586

(N) GREAT SMOKY MOUNTAINS NATIONAL PARK (Deep Creek Campground)—(Swain) *From town: Follow brown & white signs 3 mi N.* FACILITIES: 92 sites, 26 ft max RV length, 92 no hkups, tenting, dump. RECREATION: Open Apr 1 - Oct 31. Phone: (865)436-1200.

BUXTON—B-6

(S) CAPE HATTERAS NATIONAL SEASHORE (Cape Point Campground)—(Dare) *From Hwy-12 in town: Go 3-1/2 mi SE on park road.* FACILITIES: 202 sites, 202 no hkups, 10 pull-thrus, tenting, dump, groceries. RECREATION: saltwater swim, saltwater fishing. Partial handicap access. Open May 27 - Sep 5. Phone: (252)473-2111.

(SW) CAPE WOODS CAMPGROUND—(Dare) *From north jct Hwy 12 & Hwy 1232 S (Buxton Back Rd): Go 1/2 mi S on Hwy 1232 (Buxton Back Rd). Enter on L.*

WELCOME

◊◊◊FACILITIES: 115 sites, typical site width 30 ft, 98 full hkups, 6 W&E, (30/50 amps), 11 no hkups, many extd stay sites, 10 pull-thrus, cable TV, WiFi Internet central location, family camping, tenting, cabins, dump, laundry, ice, picnic tables, patios, fire rings, grills, wood, controlled access.

◊◊◊RECREATION: rec room/area, pavilion, coin games, swim pool, pond fishing, playground.

Pets welcome. Partial handicap access. Open Mar 1 - Late Dec. Big rigs welcome. Rate in 2010 $30-52 per family. MC/VISA.

Phone: (252)995-5850
Address: 47649 Buxton Back Rd, Buxton, NC 27920
Lat/Lon: 35.26505/-75.54056
Web: www.capewoods.com

SEE AD THIS PAGE

CANDLER—E-2

(W) Asheville West KOA—(Buncombe) *From jct I-40 (exit 37) & US Hwys 19/23/74: Go 200 yards S on connecting road, then 1/2 mi W on 19/23/74, then 200 yards N on Wiggins Rd. Enter on R.* ◊◊◊FACILITIES: 68 sites, typical site width 24 ft, 44 full hkups, 24 W&E, (20/30/50 amps), 23 pull-thrus, family camping, tenting, dump, laundry, ltd groc. ◊◊RECREATION: swim pool, pond fishing, play equipment. Pets welcome, breed restrict. Partial handicap access. Open all yr. Big rigs welcome. Rate in 2010 $32-40 for 2 persons. Phone: (828)665-7015. KOA discount.

CAPE CARTERET—C-5

(E) Goose Creek Resort Family Campground—(Carteret) *From jct Hwy 58 & Hwy 24: Go 4 mi NE on Hwy 24, then 3/4 mi S on Red Barn Rd. Enter on R.* ◊◊◊◊FACILITIES: 771 sites, typical site width 32 ft, 747 full hkups, 15 W&E, (20/30/50 amps), 9 no hkups, 12 pull-thrus, tenting, dump, laundry, groceries. ◊◊◊◊RECREATION: swim pool, saltwater swim,

CAPE CARTERET—Continued
Goose Creek Resort Family Campground—Continued

boating, canoeing, ramp, dock, saltwater fishing, playground. Pets welcome. Partial handicap access. Open all yr. Big rigs welcome. Rate in 2010 $45-55 per vehicle. Member ARVC, CARVC. Phone: (252)393-2628.

Reserve Online at Woodalls.com

CAPE HATTERAS—B-6

See listings at Avon, Buxton, Frisco and Rodanthe

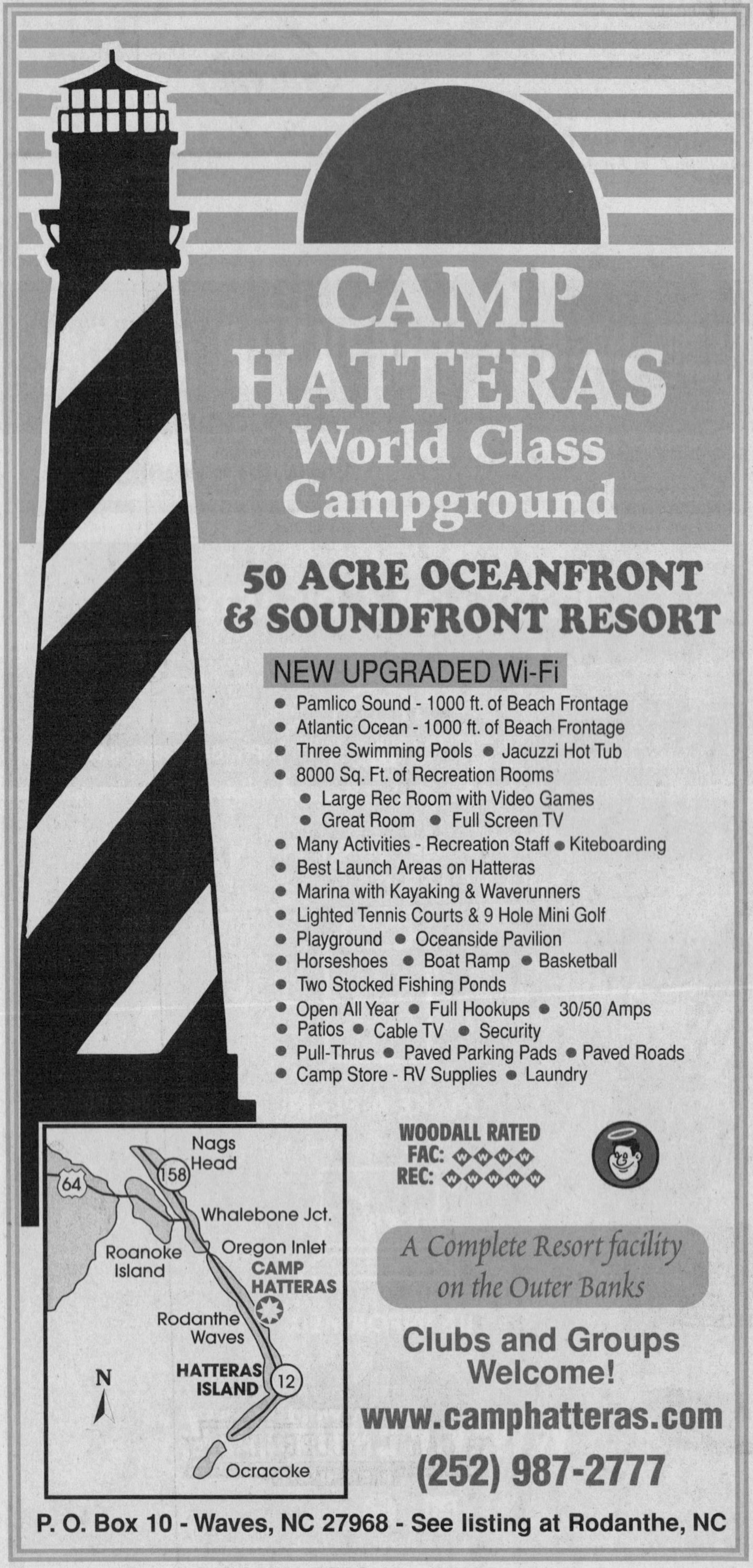

CAROLINA BEACH—D-4

(N) CAROLINA BEACH STATE PARK—(New hanover) *From town: Go 1 mi N on US-421, then 1/2 mi W on Dow Rd.* FACILITIES: 83 sites, 83 no hkups, tenting, dump. RECREATION: boating, ramp, dock, river fishing. Partial handicap access. Open all yr. Phone: (910)458-8206.

CEDAR MOUNTAIN—E-2

(E) BLACK FOREST FAMILY CAMPING RESORT—(Transylvania) *From Cascade Ln & US 276: Go 1-1/2 mi S on 276, then 1/4 mi E on Summer Rd. Enter on R.*

◇◇◇◇FACILITIES: 108 sites, typical site width 35 ft, 52 full hkups, 56 W&E, (20/30/50 amps), 50 amps ($), WiFi Internet central location, family camping, tenting, RV's/park model rentals, cabins, dump, non-guest dump $, laundry, groceries, RV supplies, ice, picnic tables, fire rings, grills, wood, controlled access.

◇◇◇◇RECREATION: rec hall, rec room/area, coin games, swim pool, golf nearby, playground, activities, (wkends), horseshoes, sports field, hiking trails, v-ball.

Pets welcome. Partial handicap access. Open all yr. Limited facilities in winter-call for availability. Big rigs welcome. Escort to site. Rate in 2010 $32-38 for 2 persons. MC/VISA. Member ARVC, CARVC.

Phone: (828)884-2267
Address: 100 Summer Rd, Cedar Mountain, NC 28718
Lat/Lon: 35.13379/-82.63525
Web: www.blackforestcampground.com

SEE AD BREVARD PAGE 582

CHAPEL HILL—B-3

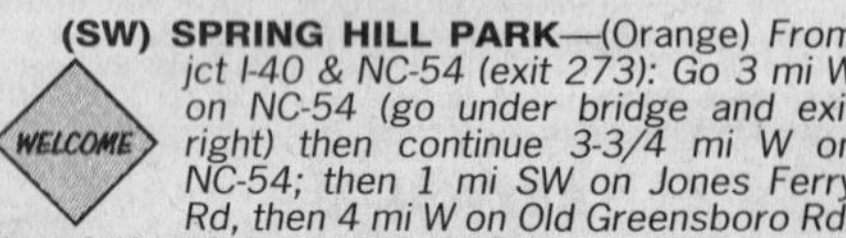

(SW) SPRING HILL PARK—(Orange) *From jct I-40 & NC-54 (exit 273): Go 3 mi W on NC-54 (go under bridge and exit right) then continue 3-3/4 mi W on NC-54; then 1 mi SW on Jones Ferry Rd, then 4 mi W on Old Greensboro Rd, then 1/4 mi N on Spring Hill Rd.*

◇◇◇FACILITIES: 50 sites, typical site width 35 ft, accepts full hkup units only, 50 full hkups, (30/50 amps), some extd stay sites, 7 pull-thrus, cable TV, WiFi Instant Internet at site, family camping, RV storage, LP gas by meter.

RECREATION: golf nearby, play equipment, sports field.

Pets welcome. No tents. Open all yr. Reservations recommended. Big rigs welcome. Rate in 2010 $30 per family. MC/VISA.

Phone: (800)824-8807
Address: 3500 Old Greensboro Rd, Chapel Hill, NC 27516
Lat/Lon: 35.89678/-79.16984
Web: springhillpark.com

SEE AD THIS PAGE

CHARLOTTE—B-2

(SW) CAROWINDS—*From jct I-85 & I-77: Go 13-1/2 mi S on I-77 (SC exit 90), then 3/4 mi W on Carowinds Blvd. Enter on R.* 100-acre family theme park. with the widest selection of rides, shows and attractions in the Carolinas. Open Late Mar - Mid Oct. Open weekends only Spring & Fall. MC/VISA/DISC/AMEX. ATM.

CAROWINDS—Continued on next page

CHARLOTTE—Continued
CAROWINDS—Continued

Phone: (800)888-4FUN
Address: 14523 Carowinds Blvd, Charlotte, NC 28241
Lat/Lon: 35.10158/-80.93516
Web: carowinds.com

SEE AD THIS PAGE

The Biltmore Estate in Asheville is America's largest home, and includes a 255-room chateau, an award-winning winery and extensive gardens.

CHARLOTTE—Continued

(SW) CAROWINDS CAMP WILDERNESS RESORT—(Mecklenburg) *From jct I-85 & I-77: Go 13-1/2 mi S on I-77 (SC exit 90), then 1 mi W on Carowinds Blvd, then 1/4 mi N on Catawba Trace. Enter on L.*

◊◊◊◊FACILITIES: 197 sites, typical site width 30 ft, 141 full hkups, 56 W&E, (20/30/50 amps), 39 pull-thrus, WiFi Instant Internet at site, WiFi Internet central location, family camping, tenting, cabins, dump, laundry, ltd groc, RV supplies, ice, grills.

CAROWINDS CAMP WILDERNESS RESORT—Continued on next page

I-85 Exit #41 Only RV Park in the City of Charlotte
Elmore RV Park
704-597-1323
Reservations Required
Bus to NASCAR Museum & Epi Center
Mention Woodall's, Save $$
See listing at Charlotte, NC

CAMPGROUNDS

CAMP WITH US RACE DAY OR ANY DAY.

Camping Amenities
- ★ 430 sites
- ★ Full hookups
- ★ 20/30/50 Electric
- ★ Clean modern showers
- ★ Picnic tables at sites
- ★ Groups welcome
- ★ Private pavilion
- ★ Laundry facility
- ★ Pets welcome
- ★ Paved roads with gravel pads

Visa,MasterCard and Discover accepted

Racing Attractions and Entertainment
- ★ Speedway tours
- ★ NASCAR Hall of Fame
- ★ NASCAR SpeedPark
- ★ NASCAR, NHRA, and other races
- ★ Numerous restaurants and other attractions!

Other Entertainment
- ★ Concord Mills Shopping Mall
- ★ Rocky River Golf Course
- ★ Intimidators Baseball
- ★ Wineries
- ★ Carowinds Amusement Park
- ★ Reed Gold Mine

See listing at Concord, NC

(704)455-4445

6600 Bruton Smith Blvd, Concord NC 28027
Exit 49 off I-85

www.charlottemotorspeedway.com/camping
camping1@charlottemotorspeedway.com

GPS: 35.358895, -80.690449

Camping with a twist!

Stay at Camp Wilderness and wake up to a day full of twisty-twirly fun at Carowinds amusement park! Sleep under the stars at our tent/pop-up sites, stay at the luxury Great Wilderness Lodge, or park your RV at one of our deluxe sites, and enjoy a private pool, mini-golf, games, and more! Come take on Intimidator, the tallest, fastest, longest coaster in the Southeast. Plus, our 20-acre waterpark, Boomerang Bay™, is included in the price of admission too. And in summer 2011, we're introducing the Snoopy Starlight Spectacular, a dazzling new nighttime light and sound experience. We're also extending our hours during the summer! So make it a camping trip to remember at Carowinds Camp Wilderness Resort.

Charlotte, NC | 704.588.2600
Book online now at carowinds.com

See listing at Charlotte, NC

CHARLOTTE—Continued
CAROWINDS CAMP WILDERNESS RESORT—Continued

◆◆◆◆RECREATION: rec room/area, swim pool, mini-golf, playground, shuffleboard court shuffleboard court, v-ball.

Pets welcome. Open all yr. Big rigs welcome. Rate in 2010 $40-70 for 2 persons. MC/VISA/DISC/AMEX/Debit. ATM.

Phone: (800)888-4386
Address: 205 Wilderness Trace, Charlotte, NC 28273
Lat/Lon: 35.10260/-80.94627
Web: www.carowinds.com/campground

SEE AD PAGE 585

(S) CHARLOTTE MOTOR SPEEDWAY CAMPING—(Charlotte) *From jct US 21 & I-85: Go 6-1/4 mi N on I-85, then 1/4 mi E on NC 24, then 1/2 mi W on Harris Blvd, then 4-3/4 mi N on Tryon St. Enter on R.*

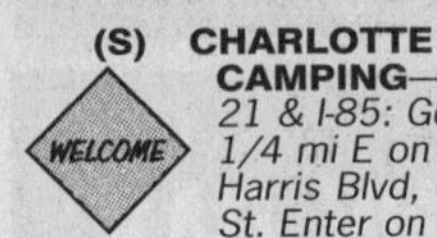

◆◆◆◆FACILITIES: 430 sites, typical site width 20 ft, 430 full hkups, (20/30/50 amps), 8 pull-thrus, phone Internet central location, family camping, tenting, dump, non-guest dump $, laundry, ice, picnic tables, wood.

RECREATION: equipped pavilion, play equipment.

Pets welcome, size restrict. Open all yr. Big rigs welcome. Clubs welcome. Rate in 2010 $25-30 per vehicle. MC/VISA/DISC/Debit. Member ARVC, CARVC.

Phone: (704)455-4445
Address: 5555 Concord Pkwy S, Concord, NC 28027
Lat/Lon: 35.35859/-80.69081
Email: camping1@charlottemotorspeedway.com
Web: www.charlottemotorspeedway.com/tickets/camping

SEE PRIMARY LISTING AT CONCORD AND AD PAGE 585

CHARLOTTE—Continued

ELMORE MOBILE HOME & RV PARK (RV SPACES)—(Mecklinburg) *From jct I-77 & I-85: Go E 2 mi on I-85 to exit 41, then 5-1/2 mi on Sugar Creek Rd, then E 1/2 mi on Tryon St (US 29). Enter on R.*

FACILITIES: 50 sites, accepts full hkup units only, 50 full hkups, (30/50 amps), many extd stay sites.

Pets welcome. No tents. Open all yr. 2 night min stay. Big rigs welcome. Rate in 2010 $25 for 2 persons. MC/VISA.

Phone: (704)597-1323
Address: 4824 N Tryon St, Charlotte, NC 28213
Lat/Lon: 35.25742/-80.78529
Email: rvpark@carolina.rr.com
Web: www.elmorervpark.com

SEE AD PAGE 585

(SW) MCDOWELL NATURE PRESERVE CAMPGROUND—(Mecklenburg) *From jct I-85 & I-77: Go 13-1/2 mi S on I-77 (exit 90), then 2 mi W on Carowinds Blvd, then 4 mi S on York Rd (Hwy 49). Enter on R.* FACILITIES: 66 sites, 56 W&E, (30/50 amps), 10 no hkups, 13 pull-thrus, tenting, dump. RECREATION: Pets welcome. Open all yr. Phone: (704)583-1284.

CHEROKEE—E-1

(S) Fort Wilderness Campground and RV Resort—(Jackson) *From west jct US 19 and US 441: Go 3 1/2 mi S on US 441, then 1/4 mi W on Shoal Creek Rd., then NE on County Road. Enter on R.* ◆◆◆FACILITIES: 130 sites, typical site width 25 ft, 42 ft max RV length, 110 full hkups, 10 W&E, (15/30/50 amps), 10 no hkups, 15 pull-thrus, cable TV, ($), WiFi Instant Internet at site, phone Internet central location, family camping, tenting, dump, non-guest dump $, laundry, ltd groc, RV supplies, ice, picnic tables, patios, fire rings, wood. ◆◆◆RECREATION: pavilion, swim pool, bsktball, play equipment, v-ball. Pets welcome, breed restrict. Open all yr. Facilities fully operational May 1 - Oct 31. Rate in 2010 $31-39 per family. MC/VISA. Member ARVC. CCUSA 50% Discount. CCUSA reservations

CHEROKEE—Continued
Fort Wilderness Campground and RV Resort—Continued

Accepted, Cash only for CCUSA disc., CCUSA disc. not avail S, CCUSA disc. not avail F,Sa. Discount not available Memorial Day, 4th of July or Labor Day. Not valid month of Jul & Oct.

Phone: (828)497-9331
Address: 284 Fort Wilderness Rd, Whittier, NC 28789
Lat/Lon: 35.44201/-83.33178
Email: fortwild@gmail.com
Web: www.fortwilderness.net

Reserve Online at Woodalls.com

(S) GREAT SMOKEY MOUNTAIN RV CAMPING RESORT—(Jackson) *From West jct US 19 & US 441: Go 1-1/2 mi S on US 441. Enter on L.*

CHEROKEE CASINO - BLUE RIDGE PRKWY
Quiet camping resort catering to adults - just 3/4 mi from Harrah's Casino. We've got everything you need here, and lots to do nearby. Enjoy great weather Spring, Summer & Fall.

◆◆◆FACILITIES: 251 sites, typical site width 20 ft, 251 full hkups, (20/30 amps), mostly extd stay sites, 100 pull-thrus, cable TV, family camping, laundry, ltd groc, LP gas by weight/by meter, ice, picnic tables, patios, fire rings, wood.

◆◆RECREATION: rec room/area, coin games, swim pool, river fishing, fishing supplies, bsktball, playground, shuffleboard court 2 shuffleboard courts.

GREAT SMOKEY MOUNTAIN RV CAMPING RESORT—Continued on next page

Pets welcome, size restrict. No tents. Open May 1 - Oct 31. Clubs welcome. Rate in 2010 $30 for 2 persons. Member ARVC, CARVC.

Phone: (828)497-2470
Address: 17 Old Soco Rd, Whittier, NC 28789
Lat/Lon: 35.45993/-83.31349

SEE AD PAGE 586

GREAT SMOKY MOUNTAINS NATIONAL PARK (Balsam Mountain Campground)—(Swain) *From town: Go 4 mi N on US 441, 12 mi E on Blue Ridge Pkwy to MP 458, then 8 mi N on Balsam Mtn. Rd.* FACILITIES: 46 sites, 30 ft max RV length, 46 no hkups, tenting. RECREATION: Open May 8 - Oct 12. Phone: (423)436-1200.

(N) GREAT SMOKY MOUNTAINS NATIONAL PARK (Smokemont Campground)—(Swain) *From town: Go 6 mi N on US-441.* FACILITIES: 142 sites, 27 ft max RV length, 142 no hkups, tenting, dump. RECREATION: Open all yr. Facilities fully operational mid May - Oct 31. Phone: (865)436-1200.

(E) Happy Holiday RV Village—(Jackson) *From west jct US Business 441 & US 19: Go 3 mi NE on US 19 N. Enter on L.* ◇◇◇FACILITIES: 389 sites, typical site width 45 ft, 300 full hkups, 66 W&E, (20/30/50 amps), 23 no hkups, 159 pull-thrus, family camping, tenting, dump, laundry, groceries. ◇◇◇RECREATION: swim pool, lake/stream fishing, playground. Pets welcome, breed restrict. Partial handicap access. Open Apr - Oct. Big rigs welcome. Rate in 2010 $34-42 for 2 persons. Member ARVC, CARVC. Phone: (877)782-2765. FMCA discount.

(NE) KOA-Cherokee Great Smokies—(Swain) *From jct US 441 & US 19/441: Go 2 mi N on US 441, then 4 1/4 mi N on Big Cove Rd. Enter on R.* ◇◇◇◇FACILITIES: 400 sites, typical site width 40 ft, 257 full hkups, 123 W&E, (30/50 amps), 20 no hkups, 133 pull-thrus, tenting, dump, laundry, full svc store. ◇◇◇◇◇RECREATION: 2 swim pools, river swim, river/pond fishing, playground. Pets welcome. Partial handicap access. Open all yr. Big rigs welcome. Member ARVC, CARVC. Phone: (828)497-9711. KOA discount.

(S) Timberlake Campground—(Swain) *From jct US 441 & US 74: Go 1-1/2 mi W on US 74 (exit 72), then 1/4 mi N on Whittier Rd, then 1/4 mi W on Main St, then 1/2 mi S on Whittier Depot St, then 200 yards W on Old Bryson City Rd, then 3-1/4 mi S on Conleys Creek Rd. Enter on R.* ◇◇FACILITIES: 44 sites, typical site width 50 ft, 35 ft max RV length, 42 W&E, (20/30 amps), 2 no hkups, family camping, tenting, dump, laundry. ◇◇RECREATION: lake/pond fishing. Pets welcome. Open May 1 - Nov 1. Rate in 2010 $25-27 for 2 persons.

Phone: (828)497-7320
Address: 3270 Conleys Creek Rd, Whittier, NC 28789
Lat/Lon: 35.39418/-83.35292
Email: bettyfb@dnet.net
Web: campingnc.com/timberlake

(NE) Yogi in the Smokies—(Swain) *From west jct US 441 & US 19/441: Go 1/2 mi W on US 19/441, then 2 mi N on US 441, then 100 yards E on Acquoni Rd, then 7 mi N on Big Cove Rd, then E on Galamore Bridge Rd. Continue 1/2 mi S on Sherrill Cove Rd. Enter at end.* ◇◇◇FACILITIES: 149 sites, typical site width 25 ft, 89 full hkups, 53 W&E, (15/20/30/50 amps), 7 no hkups, 20 pull-thrus, family camping, tenting, dump, laundry, groceries. ◇◇◇◇RECREATION: swim pool, river swim, river fishing, play equipment. Pets welcome, breed restrict. Partial handicap access. Open all yr. Facilities fully operational 2nd week in Mar - 2nd week in Nov. Big rigs welcome. Rate in 2010 $39-64 for 2 persons. Member ARVC, CARVC. Phone: (828)497-9151.

CLAYTON—B-4

(W) COOPER'S MOBILE HOME PARK & RV'S (RV SPACES)—(Johnston) *From jct I-40 (exit 306) & US 70: Go 4 mi E on US 70. Enter on L.*

WELCOME

FACILITIES: 40 sites, accepts full hkup units only, 40 full hkups, (20/30/50 amps), mostly extd stay sites, cable TV, WiFi Instant Internet at site, RV storage.

Pets welcome. No tents. Open all yr. No restrooms. Big rigs welcome. Rate in 2010 $35 per family.

Phone: (919)868-4896
Address: 13528 Hwy 70 W, Clayton, NC 27520
Lat/Lon: 35.67110/-78.50863
Web: www.campinraleigh.com

SEE AD RALEIGH PAGE 598 AND AD TRAVEL SECTION PAGE 569

Morehead City is home to the North Carolina Seafood Festival, held the first weekend in October every year.

CONCORD—B-2

(S) CHARLOTTE MOTOR SPEEDWAY CAMPING—(Cabarrus) *From jct I-85 (exit 49) & Concord Mills/Burton Smith Blvds: Go 1-1/4 mi E on Burton Smith Blvd. Enter on L.*

NOT JUST FOR RACING WEEK

Great location, great sites and great people make us the first choice in the Charlotte area. Right across from the speedway with special events all year long. Close to area attractions, shopping and great restaurants.

◇◇◇◇FACILITIES: 430 sites, typical site width 20 ft, 430 full hkups, (20/30/50 amps), 8 pull-thrus, phone Internet central location, tenting, dump, non-guest dump $, laundry, ice, picnic tables, wood.

RECREATION: equipped pavilion, play equipment.

Pets welcome, size restrict. Open all yr. Big rigs welcome. Clubs welcome. Rate in 2010 $25-30 per vehicle. MC/VISA/DISC/Debit. Member ARVC, CARVC.

Phone: (704)455-4445
Address: 5555 Concord Pkwy S, Concord, NC 28027
Lat/Lon: 35.35859/-80.69081
Email: camping1@charlottemotorspeedway.com
Web: www.charlottemotorspeedway.com/tickets/camping/

SEE AD CHARLOTTE PAGE 585 AND AD DISCOVER SECTION PAGE 42

(S) TOM JOHNSON CAMPING CENTER —*From jct I-85 (exit 49) & Concord Mills/Bruton Smith Blvds: Go 1-1/4 mi E on Bruton Smith Blvd. Enter on L.* SALES: travel trailers, park models, 5th wheels, Class A motorhomes, Class C motorhomes, fold-down camping trailers, pre-owned unit sales. SERVICES: full-time mech, engine/chassis repair, RV appliance repair, body work/collision repair, LP gas by weight/by meter, dump station, sells parts/accessories, installs hitches. Open all yr. MC/VISA.

WELCOME

Phone: (888)450-1440
Address: 6700 Bruton Smith Blvd, Concord, NC 28027
Lat/Lon: 35.35991/-80.69275
Email: concordsales@tomjohnsoncamping.com
Web: www.tomjohnsoncamping.com

SEE AD ASHEVILLE PAGE 580

COVE CREEK—E-2

(SW) GREAT SMOKY MOUNTAINS NATIONAL PARK (Cataloochee Campground)—(Hawood) *From jct I-40 & US 276: Go 1/2 mi SW on US 276, then NW on Cove Creek Rd.* FACILITIES: 27 sites, 31 ft max RV length, 27 no hkups, tenting. RECREATION: river fishing. Open Mar 13 - Oct 31. Phone: (423) 436-1200.

CRUMPLER—A-1

(NE) Twin Rivers Family Campground—(Ashe) *From center of town: Go 1 mi S on US16, then 2 mi NE on Chestnut Hill Rd (SR-1567), then 2-1/2 mi NE on Geo McMillan Rd (SR-1565), then 1 mi NW on Garvey Bridge. Enter on R.* ◇◇FACILITIES: 60 sites, 8 full hkups, 14 W&E, (20/30 amps), 38 no hkups, tenting, dump. ◇◇RECREATION: boating, no motors, canoeing, river fishing. Pets welcome. Open Late Apr - Late Oct. Rate in 2010 $18-20 for 2 persons. Phone: (336)982-3456.

DENVER—B-1

(N) Cross Country Campground—(Catawba) *From jct Hwy 16 & Hwy 150: Go 2-1/2 mi E on Hwy 150. Enter on L.* ◇◇◇FACILITIES: 407 sites, typical site width 25 ft, 347 full hkups, 60 W&E, (15/20/30/50 amps), 87 pull-thrus, tenting, dump, laundry, ltd groc. ◇◇◇◇RECREATION: swim pool, pond fishing, playground. Pets welcome, breed restrict, size restrict. Partial handicap access. Open all yr. Big rigs welcome. Rate in 2010 $30 for 4 persons. Phone: (704)483-5897.

DURHAM—A-3

(SW) Birchwood RV Park (RV SPACES) —(Orange) *From jct I-40 & Hwy 86 (exit 266): Go 1-1/2 mi N on Hwy 86, then 4-1/2 mi E on Mt. Sinai Rd, then 1/4 mi S on Wilkins Dr. Enter on L.* FACILITIES: 60 sites, typical site width 20 ft, accepts self-contained units only, 50 full hkups, 10 W&E, (30/50 amps), dump, laundry. RECREATION: play equipment. Pets welcome. No tents. Open all yr. Big rigs welcome. Rate in 2010 $29-34 for 2 persons.

Two U.S. Presidents were born in North Carolina: James K. Polk, Andrew Johnson

Phone: (919)493-1557
Address: 5901 Wilkins Dr, Lot #1, Durham, NC 27705
Lat/Lon: 35.98817/-79.00073
Email: birchwoodrvpark@yahoo.com
Web: www.birchwoodrv.com

EDENTON—A-5

(N) Rocky Hock Campground—(Chowan) *From jct of US 17 and Hwy 32: Go 5 mi N on Hwy 32, then 1-1/4 mi W on Rocky Hock Creek Rd, then 1/4 mi S on Rocky Hock Rd, then 1-3/4 mi W on Harris Landing Rd, then 3/4 mi N on Tynch Town Rd. Enter on L.* ◇◇◇FACILITIES: 32 sites, typical site width 35 ft, 32 full hkups, (30/50 amps), tenting, laundry. ◇◇RECREATION: boating, canoeing, pond fishing. Pets welcome. Open all yr. Big rigs welcome. Rate in 2010 $29-31 for 2 persons.

Phone: (252)221-4695
Address: 1008 David's Red Barn Ln, Edenton, NC 27932
Lat/Lon: 36.15568/-76.70922
Email: rhcampground@net-change.com
Web: www.rockyhockcampground.com

ELIZABETHTOWN—C-4

(N) JONES LAKE STATE PARK—(Bladen) *From town: Go 4 mi N on Hwy 242.* FACILITIES: 20 sites, 30 ft max RV length, 1 W&E, 19 no hkups, tenting. RECREATION: lake swim, canoeing, dock, lake fishing. Open all yr. Phone: (910)588-4550.

EMERALD ISLE—C-5

EMERALD ISLE WINE MARKET—*From jct Hwy 24 & Hwy 58: Go 2 mi SE on Hwy 58, then W on Coast Guard Rd. Enter on L.* Extensive selection of wines from North Carolina and around the world, as well as gifts and accesories for wine lovers. Open all yr. MC/VISA.

WELCOME

Phone: (252)354-8466
Address: 9102 Coast Guard Rd, Emerald Isle, NC 28594
Lat/Lon: 34.66007/-77.05972

SEE AD NEXT PAGE

EMERALD ISLE—Continued on next page

Home of the tallest lighthouse in the U.S.A.

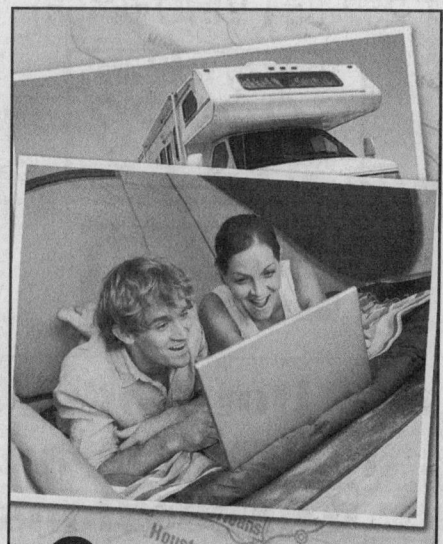

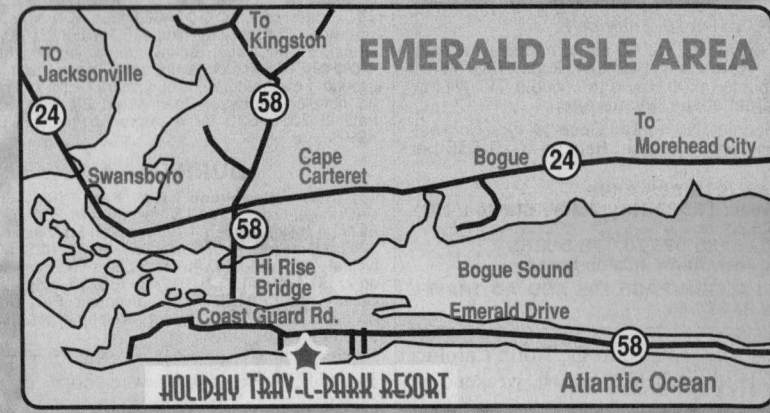

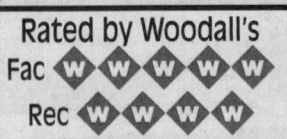

EMERALD ISLE—Continued

(C) **HOLIDAY TRAV-L-PARK RESORT FOR CAMPERS**—(Carteret) *From jct Hwy 24 & Hwy 58: Go 2 mi SE on Hwy 58, then W on Coast Guard Rd. Enter on L.*

5W RESORT ON THE BEACH
RV and tent campers love our beautiful 5W resort. All campsites are grassy and you can walk directly to the beach. Lots to do for all ages. Unique meeting facility; catering available for groups.

◇◇◇◇◇FACILITIES: 334 sites, typical site width 35 ft, 278 full hkups, 21 W&E, (20/30/50 amps), 50 amps ($), 35 no hkups, some extd stay sites, 150 pull-thrus, cable TV, ($), WiFi Instant Internet at site ($), family camping, tenting, RV storage, dump, non-guest dump $, laundry, groceries, RV supplies, LP gas by weight/by meter, ice, picnic tables, controlled access.

◇◇◇◇RECREATION: rec hall, pavilion, coin games, swim pool, wading pool, saltwater swim, saltwater fishing, bike rental 10 bike rentals, playground, activities, hiking trails.

Pets welcome ($), breed restrict. Partial handicap access. Open Mar 1 - Dec 1. Big rigs welcome. Clubs welcome. Rate in 2010 $50-101 for 2 persons. MC/VISA. ATM. Member ARVC, CARVC.

Text 82613 to (440)725-8687 to see our Visual Tour.

Phone: (252)354-2250
Address: 9102 Coast Guard Rd, Emerald Isle, NC 28594
Lat/Lon: 34.66007/-77.05972
Email: htpresort@mynetrocks.com
Web: htpresort.com

SEE AD PAGE 588 AND AD DISCOVER SECTION PAGE 44

ENFIELD—A-4

(E) **KOA-Enfield-Rocky Mt.**—(Halifax) *From jct I-95 (exit 154) & Hwy 481: Go 3/4 mi W on Hwy 481. Enter on R.* ◇◇◇FACILITIES: 80 sites, typical site width 30 ft, 33 full hkups, 47 W&E, (15/20/30/50 amps), 50 amps ($), 67 pull-thrus, family camping, tenting, dump, laundry, groceries. ◇◇RECREATION: swim pool, playground. Pets welcome. Open all yr. Big rigs welcome. Rate in 2010 $32-40 for 2 persons. Phone: (252)445-5925. KOA discount.

FAYETTEVILLE—C-3

FAYETTEVILLE KOA—*From jct I-95 & Bus Rd I-95: Go 5-1/2 mi N on I-95 to exit 61, then 1/2 mi E on Wade Stedman Rd. Enter on L.*

SEE PRIMARY LISTING AT WADE. AND AD THIS PAGE

(SE) **LAZY ACRES CAMPGROUND**—(Cumberland) *From I-95 (exit 44): Go 1 mi N on Claude Lee Rd, then 1/4 mi E on Lazy Acres St. Enter at end.*

◇◇◇FACILITIES: 50 sites, typical site width 30 ft, 46 full hkups, 4 W&E, (30/50 amps), some extd stay sites, 45 pull-thrus, cable TV, WiFi Instant Internet at site, family camping, RV storage, dump, non-guest dump $, laundry, LP gas by weight/by meter, ice, picnic tables, patios, fire rings, wood.

◇◇RECREATION: pavilion, swim pool, pond fishing, play equipment.

Pets welcome. No tents. Open all yr. Big rigs welcome. Escort to site. Rate in 2010 $30-32 for 2 persons. MC/VISA/DISC. Member ARVC, CARVC.

Phone: (910)425-9218
Address: 821 Lazy Acres St., Fayetteville, NC 28306
Lat/Lon: 34.97447/-78.88721
Email: bob@lazyacrescampground.net
Web: www.lazyacrescampground.net

SEE AD THIS PAGE AND AD TRAVEL SECTION PAGE 569

MILITARY PARK (Fort Bragg Travel Camp)—(Cumberland) *Off Hwy 24. On base. Adjacent to Smith Lake Rec. Area.* FACILITIES: 31 sites, 22 full hkups, 9 W&E, (30/50 amps), tenting, dump, laundry. RECREATION: lake swim, boating, ramp, lake fishing. Open all yr. Phone: (910)396-5979.

FLETCHER—E-2

(N) **RUTLEDGE LAKE RV PARK**—(Henderson) *From I-26 (exit 40) & Hwy 280: Go 1 mi E on Hwy 280, then 3/4 mi S on Rutledge Rd. Enter on L.*

IN THE HEART OF THE BLUE RIDGE
Close to Asheville's Biltmore Estate, Chimney Rock, Hendersonville and the scenic Blue Ridge Parkway. Make us your base camp for exploring. Enjoy the fun right here at our beautiful heated pool or fish our pond.

◇◇◇◇◇FACILITIES: 78 sites, typical site width 40 ft, 77 full hkups, 1 W&E, (20/30/50 amps), some extd stay sites, 6 pull-thrus, cable TV, WiFi Instant Internet at site, family camping, tenting, RV's/park model rentals, cabins, RV storage, laundry, RV supplies, LP gas by weight/by meter, ice, picnic tables, patios, fire rings, wood, controlled access.

◇◇◇RECREATION: rec hall, pavilion, swim pool, boating, no motors, canoeing, kayaking, 3 canoe/2 kayak/5 pedal boat rentals, pond fishing, golf nearby, bsktball, playground, activities, (wkends), horseshoes, hiking trails, v-ball.

Pets welcome, breed restrict. Partial handicap access. Open all yr. Big rigs welcome. Escort to site. Clubs welcome. Rate in 2010 $43-55 for 2 persons. MC/VISA. Member ARVC, CARVC. FMCA discount. CCUSA 50% Discount. CCUSA reservations Not Accepted, CCUSA max stay See rest., Cash only for CCUSA disc., CCUSA disc. not avail S, CCUSA disc. not avail F,Sa, CCUSA disc. not avail holidays. Discount does not apply to pull-thrus,

FLETCHER—Continued
RUTLEDGE LAKE RV PARK—Continued

lake front sites or special events. Max stay 3 days (Sun -Wed)in May-July dependent on availability. Max stay 4 days (Sun-Thu) Aug-May. All dogs must be on leash.

Text 88523 to (440)725-8687 to see our Visual Tour.

Phone: (828)654-7873
Address: 170 Rutledge Rd, Fletcher, NC 28732
Lat/Lon: 35.44054/-82.52361
Email: rutledgelakepark@bellsouth.net
Web: www.rutledgelake.com

SEE AD ASHEVILLE PAGE 580 AND AD TRAVEL SECTION PAGE 569

FONTANA VILLAGE—E-1

(S) NANTAHALA NATIONAL FOREST (Cable Cove Campground)—(Graham) *From town: Go 4-1/2 mi NE on Hwy-28, then 1-1/2 mi NE on FR-3618.* FACILITIES: 26 sites, 26 no hkups, tenting. RECREATION: boating, ramp, lake fishing. Open Apr 15 - Oct 31. Phone: (828)479-6431.

FOUR OAKS—B-4

(S) **FOUR OAKS RV RESORT** (RV SPACES)—(Johnston) *From jct US 70 & I-95: Go 5 mi S on I-95 to exit 90, then 1/4 mi S on US 301. Enter on R.*

FACILITIES: 20 sites, typical site width 25 ft, accepts full hkup units only, 20 full hkups, (20/30/50 amps), 4 pull-thrus, cable TV, WiFi Instant Internet at site, ice, picnic tables.

RECREATION: pavilion, golf nearby, bsktball, horseshoes, v-ball.

Pets welcome. No tents. Open all yr. Big rigs welcome. Escort to site. Rate in 2010 $19-30 for 2 persons. MC/VISA/DISC/AMEX. Member ARVC, CARVC.

Phone: (919)963-3596
Address: 4606 US Hwy 301 S, Four Oaks, NC 27524
Lat/Lon: 35.38971/-78.51929
Email: info@fouroaksrvresort.com
Web: www.fouroaksrvresort.com

SEE AD SMITHFIELD PAGE 599 AND AD TRAVEL SECTION PAGE 569

(S) **Smithfield KOA**—(Johnston) *From jct US 70 & I-95: Go 5 mi S on I-95 to exit 90, then 1/4 mi S on US 701. Enter on L.* ◇◇◇FACILITIES: 111 sites, typical site width 25 ft, 107 full hkups, (30/50 amps), 4 no hkups, 77 pull-thrus, tenting, dump, laundry, groceries. ◇◇◇RECREATION: swim pool, playground. Pets welcome. Partial handicap access. Open all yr. Big rigs welcome. Rate in 2010 $37-40 for 2 persons. Member ARVC, CARVC. Phone: (800)562-5897. KOA discount.

FRANKLIN—E-1

(S) **Cardinal Ridge Farm RV & B** (TOO NEW TO RATE)—(Macon) *From west jct US 64 & US 44/23: Go 5-1/4 mi S on US 23/441, then 1/2 mi E on Riverside Rd, then 1 mi S on Hickory Knoll Rd. Enter on L.* FACILITIES: 3 sites, typical site width 30 ft, accepts full hkup units only, 3 full hkups, (30/50 amps), family camping. Pets welcome. No tents. Open all yr. Big rigs welcome. Rate in 2010 $40-55 for 2 persons.

Phone: (828)524-8090
Address: 1722 Hickory Knoll Rd, Franklin, NC 28734
Email: kathleen@cardinalridgefarmrvandb.com
Web: cardinalridgefarmrvandb.com

FRANKLIN—Continued on next page

North Carolina's mountains are the highest east of the Mississippi.

Pepsi was invented and first served in New Bern in 1898.

Camping Is Not A Destination, It's An Adventure!

Best Rally Pavilion
Own Your Own Lot

FRANKLIN—Continued

(W) Cartoogechaye Creek Campground—(Macon) *From west jct US 441 & US 64: Go 6-1/4 mi W on US 64. Enter on L.* ◆◆FACILITIES: 60 sites, typical site width 25 ft, 40 full hkups, 20 W&E, (30/50 amps), 50 amps ($), tenting, dump, laundry. ◆RECREATION: stream fishing, play equipment. Pets welcome. Open all yr. Facilities fully operational Apr 1 - Oct 31. Rate in 2010 $25-35 for 2 persons. FMCA discount.

Phone: (828)524-8553
Address: 91 No Name Rd, Franklin, NC 28734
Lat/Lon: 35.13729/-83.49108
Email: vhatch0818@aol.com
Web: www.franklin-chamber.com/cartoogechaye

(S) COUNTRY WOODS RV PARK—(Macon) *From west jct US 64 & US 441/23: Go 2-1/4 mi S on US 441/23. Enter on R.*

WELCOME

A HUB TO EVERYTHING

Escape the heat on a level shaded site. Close to gem mines, waterfalls, a farmers market and performing arts center. Free Wi-Fi, movie night Fridays & Picking on the Square Saturdays.

◆◆◆FACILITIES: 72 sites, typical site width 35 ft, 72 full hkups, (30/50 amps), mostly extd stay sites (summer), 3 pull-thrus, cable TV, WiFi Instant Internet at site, WiFi Internet central location, laundry, picnic tables, patios, fire rings, wood.

◆◆RECREATION: rec room/area, equipped pavilion, hiking trails.

CAMPCLUB USA

Pets welcome. No tents. Open Apr 1 - Oct 31. Escort to site. Rate in 2010 $30-35 for 2 persons. MC/VISA/DISC. CCUSA 50% Discount. CCUSA reservations Recommended, CCUSA max stay 2 days, Cash only for CCUSA disc., Check only for CCUSA disc. Discount not available Memorial Day or Labor Day weekends. Not available in Jul & Oct.

Phone: (828)524-4339
Address: 60 Country Woods Dr., Franklin, NC 28734
Lat/Lon: 35.13517/-83.39919
Email: cwoodsrv@dnet.net
Web: www.countrywoodsrvpark.com

SEE AD PAGE 589

(S) FRANKLIN RV PARK & CAMPGROUND—(Macon) *From jct US 64 & US 441 Bus: Go 3.1 mi S on US 441/23, then 300 feet SW on Addington Bridge Rd, then NW on Old Addington Bridge Rd. Enter on L.*

WELCOME

◆◆◆◆FACILITIES: 27 sites, typical site width 20 ft, 23 full hkups, 4 W&E, (20/30/50 amps), 3 pull-thrus, cable TV, WiFi Instant Internet at site, tenting, picnic tables, fire rings.

◆RECREATION: equipped pavilion.

Pets welcome, breed restrict, quantity restrict. Open Apr 1 - Dec 1. Big rigs welcome. Rate in 2010 $32-40 for 2 persons.

Phone: (828)349-6200
Address: 230 Old Addington Rd, Franklin, NC 28734
Lat/Lon: 35.12329/-83.39529
Email: info@franklinrvpark.com
Web: www.franklinrvpark.com

SEE AD THIS PAGE AND AD TRAVEL SECTION PAGE 567

(S) NANTAHALA NATIONAL FOREST (Standing Indian Campground)—(Macoh) *From town: Go 10 mi SW on US 64, then 2 mi E on Wallace Gap Rd (Old US 64), then 2 mi S on FR 67.* FACILITIES: 81 sites, 22 ft max RV length, 81 no hkups, 4 pull-thrus, tenting. RECREATION: river swim, river fishing. Facilities fully operational Apr 1 - Dec 1. Phone: (828)524-6441.

(W) Pines RV Park—(Macon) *From west jct US 441 bypass & US 64: Go 4-3/4 mi W on US 64. Enter on L.* ◆◆◆FACILITIES: 66 sites, typical site width 21 ft, 55 full hkups, 11 W&E, (30/50 amps), 50 amps ($), tenting, dump, laundry. ◆RECREATION: playground. Pets welcome. Open all yr. Rate in 2010 $24-29 for 2 persons. Member ARVC, CARVC.

Phone: (828)524-4490
Address: 4724 Murphy Rd, Franklin, NC 28734
Lat/Lon: 35.14865/-83.46769
Email: pinesrvparknc@aol.com
Web: www.gocampin.net/pinesrvpark

FRANKLIN—Continued on next page

In 1903, the Wright Brothers made the first successful powered flight by man at Kill Devil Hill near Kitty Hawk. The Wright Memorial at Kitty Hawk now commemorates their achievement.

FRANKLIN—Continued

(S) RIVER VISTA MOUNTAIN VILLAGE—(Macon) *From jct of US 64 & US 441/23: Go 13 mi S on US 441/23,then 1 mi E on Hwy 246. Enter on R.*

◆◆◆◆◆FACILITIES: 144 sites, typical site width 35 ft, 144 full hkups, (20/30/50 amps), some extd stay sites, 27 pull-thrus, cable TV, WiFi Instant Internet at site, WiFi Internet central location, family camping, cabins, laundry, ltd groc, LP gas by weight/by meter, ice, picnic tables, grills.

◆◆◆RECREATION: rec hall, pavilion, 2 swim pools, hot tub, pond fishing, golf nearby, bsktball, play equipment, activities, horseshoes.

Pets welcome. Partial handicap access. No tents. Open all yr. Big rigs welcome. Escort to site. Clubs welcome. Rate in 2010 $24-49 per vehicle. MC/VISA/DISC/AMEX/Debit. Member CARVC. FMCA discount. CCUSA 50% Discount.

Phone: (888)850-7275
Address: 20 River Vista Dr, Dillard, GA 30537
Lat/Lon: 34.98600/-83.36850
Email: relax@rvountainvillage.com
Web: www.rvmountainvillage.com

SEE PRIMARY LISTING AT DILLARD AND AD PAGE 590 AND AD DILLARD, GA PAGE 199

(N) The Great Outdoors RV Resort—(Macon) *From west jct US 64 & US 441/23: Go 6-1/2 mi N on US 441/23, then 100 yards W on Echo Valley Rd. Enter on R.* ◆◆◆◆◆FACILITIES: 66 sites, typical site width 35 ft, accepts self-contained units only, 66 full hkups, (30/50 amps), laundry, ltd groc. ◆◆RECREATION: swim pool. Pets welcome, breed restrict. Partial handicap access. No tents. Open all yr. Facilities fully operational Apr 1 - Dec 1. Big rigs welcome. Rate in 2010 $36-41 for 2 persons. Member ARVC, CARVC. Phone: (828)349-0412.

FRISCO—B-6

CAPE HATTERAS NATIONAL SEASHORE (Frisco Campground)—(Dare) *From center of town on Hwy 12: Go 2 mi E following signs.* FACILITIES: 127 sites, (20/30 amps), 127 no hkups, tenting. RECREATION: saltwater swim, saltwater fishing. Open Mar 1 - Dec 15. Phone: (252)473-2111.

(N) FRISCO WOODS CAMPGROUND—(Dare) *Located in center of town on Hwy 12. Entrance on West side of Hwy.*

PAMLICO SOUND WATERFRONT CAMPING
New full hook-up sites & great ameneties in a natural setting. Relax at our large pool overlooking the Bay or get active with Kayaking, windsurfing or kite surfing. Your outdoor recreation destination on Hatteras Island.

◆◆◆FACILITIES: 236 sites, typical site width 25 ft, 80 full hkups, 106 W&E, (15/20/30/50 amps), 50 amps ($), 50 no hkups, cable TV, WiFi Instant Internet at site, WiFi Internet central location, family camping, tenting, cabins, dump, non-guest dump $, laundry, full svc store, RV supplies, LP gas by weight/by meter, ice, picnic tables.

◆◆◆RECREATION: rec room/area, swim pool, saltwater swim, boating, canoeing, kayaking, 20 kayak rentals, saltwater fishing, play equipment, horseshoes, hiking trails, v-ball. Rec open to public.

Pets welcome. Open Mar 1 - Dec 15. Big rigs welcome. Clubs welcome. Rate in 2010 $38-62 for 4 persons. MC/VISA/DISC/AMEX. Member ARVC, CARVC. CCUSA 50% Discount. CCUSA reservations Recommended, CCUSA max stay 2 days, Cash only for CCUSA disc., CCUSA disc. not avail F,Sa, CCUSA disc. not avail holidays. Not available Memorial Day thru Labor Day.

Text 83398 to (440)725-8687 to see our Visual Tour.

Phone: (252)995-5208
Address: 53124 Hwy 12 S, Frisco, NC 27936
Lat/Lon: 35.23948/-75.61991
Web: outer-banks.com/friscowoods

SEE AD THIS PAGE

North Carolina was the 12th state admitted to the Union.

GARNER—B-4

(E) 70 East Mobile Acres & RV Park (RV SPACES)—(Wake) *From jct I-40 (exit 306) & US 70: Go 1 mi E on US 70. Enter on L.* FACILITIES: 65 sites, typical site width 40 ft, accepts full hkup units only, 65 full hkups, (20/30/50 amps), 25 pull-thrus. Pets welcome. No tents. Open all yr. Big rigs welcome. Rate in 2010 $30-35 per vehicle. Phone: (919)772-6568.

GATESVILLE—A-5

MERCHANTS MILLPOND STATE PARK—(Gates) *From town: Go 6 mi NE on Hwy 1403.* FACILITIES: 20 sites, 20 no hkups, tenting. RECREATION: canoeing, pond fishing. Partial handicap access. Open all yr. Facilities fully operational Mar 15 - Nov 30. Phone: (252)357-1191.

The first English colony in America was located on Roanoke Island, founded by Walter Raleigh. The colonists mysteriously vanished with no trace except for the word "Croatoan" scrawled on a nearby tree.

GLENDALE SPRINGS—A-1

(N) RACCOON HOLLER CAMPGROUND—(Ashe) *From jct Blue Ridge Pkwy (milepost 257-3/4) & Raccoon Holler Rd: Go 1/4 mi W on Raccoon Holler Rd. Enter on R.*

◆◆◆◆FACILITIES: 213 sites, typical site width 25 ft, 165 full hkups, 48 W&E, (20/30/50 amps), many extd stay sites, 12 pull-thrus, cable TV, ($), WiFi Internet central location, family camping, tenting, RV's/park model rentals, RV storage, dump, laundry, ltd groc, RV supplies, LP gas by weight/by meter, ice, picnic tables, fire rings, wood.

◆◆◆RECREATION: rec hall, coin games, lake fishing, fishing supplies, bsktball, playground, shuffleboard court shuffleboard court, activities (wkends), sports field, v-ball.

Pets welcome, breed restrict, quantity restrict. Partial handicap access. Open Apr 25 - Oct 31. Clubs welcome. Rate in 2010 $28-32 per family. Member ARVC.

RACCOON HOLLER CAMPGROUND—Continued on next page

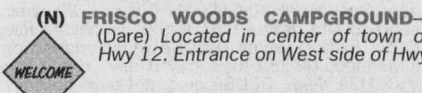

GLENDALE SPRINGS—Continued
RACCOON HOLLER CAMPGROUND—Continued

Phone: (336)982-2706
Address: 493 Raccoon Holler Rd, Glendale Spgs, NC 28629
Lat/Lon: 36.33661/-81.37467
Email: janmill@skybest.com
Web: www.raccoonholler.com

SEE AD THIS PAGE

GOLDSBORO—B-4

CLIFFS OF THE NEUSE STATE PARK—(Wayne) *From town: Go 14 mi SE on Hwy-111, then 1 mi E.* FACILITIES: 35 sites, 35 ft max RV length, 35 no hkups, tenting, dump. RECREATION: lake swim, boating, river fishing. Open Mar 15 - Nov 30. Phone: (919)778-6234.

✽ **(W) DALY RV**—*From jct Hwy 581 & US 70: Go 1 mi W on US 70. Enter on L.*

WELCOME

SALES: travel trailers, 5th wheels, pre-owned unit sales. SERVICES: full-time mech, RV appliance repair, body work/collision repair, LP gas by weight/by meter, sells parts/accessories, installs hitches. Open all yr. MC/VISA/DISC.

Phone: (919)734-4616
Address: 3369 Hwy 70 W, Goldsboro, NC 27530
Lat/Lon: 35.43785/-78.08336
Email: info@dalyrv.com
Web: www.dalyrv.com

SEE AD TRAVEL SECTION PAGE 567

GREENSBORO—A-2

(E) GREENSBORO CAMPGROUND—(Guilford) *From jct I-40 & Bus 85: Go 4-1/4 mi NE on Bus I-40/Bus 40 (exit 224), then 1/4 mi SE on E Lee St, then 1 mi W on Sharpe Rd, then 1/4 mi N on Trox St. Enter on L.*

WELCOME

STAY A NIGHT-OR A LITTLE LONGER

EZ on/off I-40, but far enough that you'll want to stay awhile. The perfect home base while you enjoy everything the Piedmont is known for - shopping, museums, NASCAR, golf. Or just relax at our sparkling clean pool.

◆◆◆FACILITIES: 76 sites, accepts full hkup units only, 76 full hkups, (20/30/50 amps), many extd stay sites, 70 pull-thrus, WiFi Instant Internet at site, WiFi Internet central location, family camping, cabins, RV storage, dump, non-guest dump $, laundry, ltd groc, RV supplies, LP gas by weight/by meter, ice, picnic tables, fire rings, wood, controlled access.

◆◆RECREATION: rec room/area, pavilion, swim pool, golf nearby, playground, horseshoes.

Pets welcome, breed restrict. Partial handicap access. No tents. Open all yr. Big rigs welcome. Rate in 2010 $30-35 for 4 persons. MC/VISA/DISC. Member ARVC, CARVC.

Phone: (336)274-4143
Address: 2300 Montreal Ave, Greensboro, NC 27406
Lat/Lon: 36.04701/-79.74672
Email: greensborocampgr@bellsouth.net
Web: www.GreensboroCampground.com

SEE AD THIS PAGE

HARKERS ISLAND—C-5

CAPE POINTE RV PARK (TOO NEW TO RATE)—(Carteret) *From jct Hwy 70 in Otway & Harkers Island Rd: Go 9 mi on Harkers Island Rd. Enter on R.*

WELCOME

FACILITIES: 102 sites, typical site width 35 ft, accepts full hkup units only, 102 full hkups, (30/50 amps), 50 amps ($), cable TV, WiFi Instant Internet at site, family camping, picnic tables, fire rings, grills, controlled access.

RECREATION: boating, kayaking, 2 kayak rentals, saltwater fishing, bike rental 10 bike rentals, playground, horseshoes, v-ball.

Pets welcome, breed restrict. No tents. Open all yr. No cash payments. Big rigs welcome. Rate in 2010 $40-80 for 4 persons. MC/VISA/DISC.

Phone: (252)515-2302
Address: 1200 Island Rd, Harkers Island, NC 28531
Email: ashley@capepointervpark.com
Web: capepointervpark.com

SEE AD OUTER BANKS PAGE 598

HAVELOCK—C-5

MILITARY PARK (Cherry Point MCAS Travel Camp)—(Craven) *On Fontana Rd, on base.* FACILITIES: 20 sites, 20 full hkups, tenting, dump, laundry, ltd groc. RECREATION: swim pool, boating, ramp. Open all yr. Phone: (252)466-2197.

Howard Cosell, sports journalist, was from North Carolina.

HAYESVILLE—E-1

(E) NANTAHALA NATIONAL FOREST (Jackrabbit Mountain Campground)—(Clay) *From town: Go 6 mi E on US-64, then 2-1/2 mi S on Hwy-175, then 1-1/2 mi W on CR-1155.* FACILITIES: 100 sites, 22 ft max RV length, 100 no hkups, 5 pull-thrus, tenting, dump. RECREATION: lake swim, boating, ramp, lake fishing. Open May 1 - Sept 30. Phone: (828)837-5152.

HENDERSON—A-4

(N) KERR STATE REC. AREA (Bullocksville)—(Vance) *From town: Go 6 mi N on US-1, then 5 mi NW on Hwy-1369, then 1366.* FACILITIES: 60 sites, 30 ft max RV length, 29 W&E, 31 no hkups, tenting, dump. RECREATION: lake swim, boating, ramp, dock, lake fishing, playground. Open Apr - Sep. Phone: (252)438-7791.

(N) KERR STATE REC. AREA (Henderson Point)—(Vance) *From town: Go 20 mi N on Hwy-39, then CR-1356, then 1359.* FACILITIES: 79 sites, 45 E, (30 amps), 34 no hkups, tenting, dump. RECREATION: boating, ramp, playground. Open Mar - Sep. Phone: (252)438-7791.

(N) KERR STATE REC. AREA (Hibernia)—(Vance) *Go 15 mi N on Hwy 39, then right on to 1347.* FACILITIES: 150 sites, 50 E, 100 no hkups, tenting, dump. RECREATION: boating, ramp, playground. Open all yr. Phone: (252)438-7791.

(N) KERR STATE REC. AREA (Nutbush Bridge)—(Vance) *From town: Go 6 mi N on Hwy-39, then 1308.* FACILITIES: 103 sites, 60 W&E, 43 no hkups, tenting, dump. RECREATION: boating, ramp, playground. Open Apr 1 - Nov 1. Facilities fully operational Spring - Fall. Phone: (252)438-7791.

(N) KERR STATE REC. AREA (Satterwhite Points)—(Vance) *From town: Take exit 217 off I-85, go 7 mi N on Hwy 1319.* FACILITIES: 119 sites, 60 E, (30 amps), 59 no hkups, tenting, dump. RECREATION: boating, playground. Open all yr. Phone: (252)438-7791.

HENDERSONVILLE—E-2

(NE) JAYMAR TRAVEL PARK—(Henderson) *From jct of I-26 (exit 49A) & US 64: Go 2 1/2 mi E on US 64. Enter on L.*

WELCOME

◆◆◆FACILITIES: 200 sites, typical site width 20 ft, accepts full hkup units only, 200 full hkups, (30/50 amps), mostly extd stay sites, 12 pull-thrus, cable TV, ($), WiFi Instant Internet at site, WiFi Internet central location, laundry, picnic tables.

CAMPCLUB USA

◆◆RECREATION: rec hall, rec room/area, golf nearby, shuffleboard court shuffleboard court, activities, horseshoes.

Pets welcome, quantity restrict. No tents. Open April 20 - Nov 1. Big rigs welcome. Escort to site. Rate in 2010 $28-33 per vehicle. CCUSA 50% Discount. CCUSA reservations Recommended, CCUSA max stay 2 days, Cash only for CCUSA disc., CCUSA disc. not avail holidays.

JAYMAR TRAVEL PARK—Continued on next page

HENDERSONVILLE—Continued
JAYMAR TRAVEL PARK—Continued

Phone: (828)685-3771
Address: 140 Jaymar Park Dr, Hendersonville, NC 28792
Lat/Lon: 35.35451/-82.41271
Email: jaymarnc@yahoo.com
Web: www.web.mac.com/jaymarnc

SEE AD PAGE 592

(SE) LAKEWOOD RV RESORT—(Henderson) *From jct US 64 & I-26: Go 3-1/2 mi SE on I-26 to exit 53, then 1/4 mi E on Upward Rd, then 1/4 mi N on Ballenger Rd. Enter on R.*

A PREMIER RESORT CATERING TO ADULTS
Make us your Blue Ridge Mountain home. We are close to area attractions but with our quality amenities you may not want to venture far from your large shaded site and concrete patio.

◆◆◆◆FACILITIES: 100 sites, typical site width 24 ft, 100 full hkups, (30/50 amps), 24 pull-thrus, cable TV, WiFi Instant Internet at site, phone Internet central location, RV storage, laundry, ice, picnic tables, patios.

◆◆◆RECREATION: rec hall, swim pool, pond fishing, golf nearby, shuffleboard court 2 shuffleboard courts, activities, horseshoes.

Pets welcome, breed restrict, quantity restrict. Partial handicap access. No tents. Open all yr. Big rigs welcome. Rate in 2010 $39 for 4 persons. MC/VISA/DISC/AMEX. Member ARVC, CARVC. FMCA discount.

Phone: (888)819-4200
Address: 15 Timmie Lane, Flat Rock, NC 28731
Lat/Lon: 35.30141/-82.40198
Email: info@lakewoodrvresort.com
Web: www.lakewoodrvresort.com

SEE AD THIS PAGE

RUTLEDGE LAKE RV PARK—*From jct US 64 & I-26: Go 9 mi N on I-26 to exit 40, then 1 mi E on Hwy 280, then 3/4 mi S on Rutledge Rd. Enter on L.*

SEE PRIMARY LISTING AT FLETCHER AND AD ASHEVILLE PAGE 580

(SE) Twin Ponds RV Park—(Henderson) *From jct I-26 & Upward Rd (exit 53): Go 1/2 mi E on Upward Rd, then 4/10 mi N on S Orchard Rd. Enter on L.* ◆◆FACILITIES: 150 sites, typical site width 30 ft, 150 full hkups, (30/50 amps), 7 pull-thrus, laundry. ◆◆RECREATION: swim pool, pond fishing. Pets welcome, breed restrict. Partial handicap access. No tents. Open all yr. Big rigs welcome. Member ARVC, CARVC. Phone: (828)693-4018.

HIGH POINT—B-2

(N) OAK HOLLOW FAMILY CAMPGROUND—(Davidson) *From Bus I-85 & 311 By-Pass N: Go 4 1/2 mi N to exit 66, then go 5 1/8 mi on Johnson St, then E 1/2 mi on Oakview Rd, then left on Centennial for 600 yds. Enter on L.*

◆◆◆◆FACILITIES: 121 sites, typical site width 30 ft, 108 full hkups, 13 E, (20/30/50 amps), cable TV, WiFi Instant Internet at site, WiFi Internet central location, family camping, tenting, laundry, RV supplies, ice, picnic tables, grills, controlled access.

◆◆◆RECREATION: pavilion, swim pool, boating, ramp, dock, lake fishing, golf nearby, playground, tennis. Rec open to public.

Pets welcome. Open all yr. All sites first come, first served. Call for site availability during Apr & Oct. Big rigs welcome. Clubs welcome. Rate in 2010 $30 for 6 persons. MC/VISA/DISC/AMEX/Debit.

Phone: (336)883-3492
Address: 3415 N Centennial St, High Point, NC 27265
Lat/Lon: 36.00960/-80.00591
Web: www.oakhollowcampground.com

SEE AD THIS PAGE

HOPE MILLS—C-3

(SE) Fayetteville Spring Valley Park—(Cumberland) *From jct I-95 (exit 41) & Hwy 59: Go 3/4 mi NW on Hwy 59, crossing I-95 Business Loop US 301, then 1 mi N on west service road. Enter on L.* ◆◆◆FACILITIES: 21 sites, typical site width 30 ft, 14 full hkups, 7 W&E, (30/50 amps), 50 amps ($), 22 pull-thrus, dump. Pets welcome. No tents. Open all yr. Big rigs welcome. Rate in 2010 $37-42 for 2 persons. Phone: (910)425-1505.

(W) Lake Waldo's Beach Campground (TOO NEW TO RATE)—(Cumberland) *From jct I-95 (exit 41) & Hwy 59: Go 3 mi N on Hwy 59 (Main St), then 2 mi W on Rockfish Rd, then 1-1/4 mi W on Camden Rd, then*

HOPE MILLS—Continued
Lake Waldo's Beach Campground—Continued

1-1/2 mi SW on Waldo's Beach Rd. FACILITIES: 23 sites, 23 full hkups, (30/50 amps), tenting, ice. RECREATION: swim pool, lake/pond fishing. Pets welcome. Open all yr. Big rigs welcome. Rate in 2010 $28-36 for 2 persons. CCUSA 50% Discount.

Phone: (910)818-2618
Address: 6742 Waldo's Beach Rd, Fayetteville, NC 28306
Lat/Lon: 34.95811/-79.02193
Web: lakewaldosbeachcampground.com

HOT SPRINGS—D-2

(C) Hot Springs Campground & Suites—(Madison) *From jct Hwy 209 & US 25/US 70: Go 1/4 mi E on US 25/US 70. Enter on R.* ◆◆FACILITIES: 104 sites, typical site width 40 ft, 34 full hkups, 9 W&E, (20/30/50 amps), 61 no hkups, 2 pull-thrus, tenting, dump, full svc store. ◆◆RECREATION: canoeing, river fishing, play equipment. Pets welcome. Partial handicap access. Open all yr. Rate in 2010 $30-40 for 4 persons. Phone: (828)622-7267.

(S) PISGAH NATIONAL FOREST (Rocky Bluff Campground)—(Madison) *From town: Go 3 mi S on Hwy-209.* FACILITIES: 30 sites, 30 ft max RV length, 30 no hkups, tenting. RECREATION: Open May 1 - Oct 31. Phone: (828)622-3202.

HUBERT—C-5

(NW) HAWKINS CREEK CAMPGROUND—(Onslow) *From center of town: Go 1-3/4 mi NW on Hwy 24, then 1/4 mi S on Hwy 172, then 1/4 mi E on Starling Rd. Enter at end.*

◆◆◆FACILITIES: 65 sites, typical site width 30 ft, 58 full hkups, 5 W&E, 2 E, (20/30/50 amps), 8 pull-thrus, cable TV, family camping, tenting, dump, non-guest dump $, laundry, picnic tables.

◆RECREATION: pavilion, canoeing, kayaking, pond fishing, hiking trails.

Pets welcome. Open all yr. Big rigs welcome. Rate in 2010 $25 for 2 persons.

Phone: (910)353-0144
Address: 252 Reid Acres Ln, Hubert, NC 28539
Lat/Lon: 34.70933/-77.22890
Email: reid@hawkinscreekcampground.com
Web: www.hawkinscreekcampground.com

SEE AD JACKSONVILLE NEXT PAGE

Woodall's Tip... Looking for a particular campground? Use our Alphabetical Quick Reference in the middle & near the end of this Directory.

Oak Hollow
FAMILY CAMPGROUND
OPEN YEAR ROUND
Great Value
$30
Full Hookups
Cable & Wi-Fi Included
Paved Sites - Shaded or Open
336-883-3492
800 acres lake • Marina
Pete Dye Golf Course
Tennis • Swimming Pool
Lots More
oakhollowcampground.com
See listing at High Point, NC

JACKSONVILLE—C-5

(SW) CABIN CREEK CAMPGROUND—(Onslow) *From west jct Hwy 24 & US 17: Go 4 3/4 mi S on US 17. Enter on R.*

◆◆◆FACILITIES: 100 sites, typical site width 30 ft, 93 full hkups, (30/50 amps), 7 no hkups, 30 pull-thrus, cable TV, WiFi Instant Internet at site, WiFi Internet central location, family camping, tenting, RV's/park model rentals, cabins, RV storage, laundry, RV supplies, LP gas by weight/by meter, ice, picnic tables.

◆RECREATION: rec hall, rec room/area, pavilion, mini-golf, ($), golf nearby, play equipment, hiking trails.

Pets welcome, quantity restrict. Open all yr. Big rigs welcome. Escort to site. Rate in 2010 $32-39 per family. MC/VISA/AMEX/Debit. Member ARVC, CARVC.

CABIN CREEK CAMPGROUND—Continued on next page

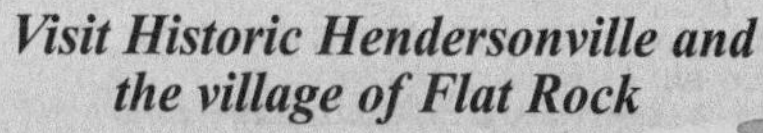

JACKSONVILLE—Continued
CABIN CREEK CAMPGROUND—Continued

Phone: (910)346-4808
Address: 3200 Wilmington Hwy, Jacksonville, NC 28540
Lat/Lon: 34.69154/-77.47894
Email: cabincreekcampground@yahoo.com
Web: www.cabincreekcampground.com

SEE AD THIS PAGE

MILITARY PARK (New River Rec. Area)—(Onslow) *From jct Hwy 24 & US 17: Go 5 mi S on US 17 to Main Gate. On base.* FACILITIES: 10 sites, 10 no hkups, tenting. RECREATION: saltwater swim, boating, canoeing, ramp, dock, saltwater fishing, playground. Open all yr. Phone: (910)449-6578.

MILITARY PARK (Onslow Beach Recreation Area-Camp Lejeune MCB)—(Onslow) *Off jct US 17 & Hwy 24. On base.* FACILITIES: 44 sites, typical site width 15 ft, 44 full hkups, (50 amps), tenting, dump, laundry, ltd groc. RECREATION: saltwater swim, saltwater fishing, play equipment. Open all yr. Phone: (910) 450-7502.

KURE BEACH—D-4

MILITARY PARK (Fort Fisher Air Force Rec. Area)—(New Hanover) *Off base, about 100 mi S of Seymour Johnson AFB (Goldsboro). Located 20 mi S of Wilmington on US 421 at Kure Beach.* FACILITIES: 36 sites, 16 full hkups, 20 no hkups, tenting, dump, laundry, ltd groc. RECREATION: swim pool, saltwater swim, boating, canoeing, ramp, saltwater/river fishing, playground. Open all yr. Phone: (910)458-6546.

LAKE JUNALUSKA—E-2

(S) Camp Adventure Family Campground—(Haywood) *From jct I-40 (exit 27) & US 19/US 23: Go 3 mi SW on US 19. Enter on L.* ◆◆◆FACILITIES: 54 sites, typical site width 25 ft, 44 full hkups, 10 W&E, (30/50 amps), 12 pull-thrus, tenting, dump. ◆RECREATION: playground. Pets welcome. Partial handicap access. Open Apr 1 - Oct 31. Big rigs welcome. Rate in 2010 $27-32 for 4 persons. Phone: (828)452-5887.

The first American born to English parents was born in North Carolina (Virginia Dare).

LEXINGTON—B-2

(S) CROSS WINDS FAMILY CAMPGROUND—(Davidson) *From I-85 S (exit 85) & Clark Rd: Go 500 ft NW on Clark Rd, then 1 mi SW on Old Salisbury Rd, then cross Hwy 150 and continue 1/4 mi, then 300 ft on Sowers Rd. Enter on R.*

CELEBRATING OUR THIRD YEAR

Great big sites on paved roads plus full amenities await you. Expore Central North Carolina from our convenient location. We're close to Childress Winery, the NC Transportation Museum, Threshers Reunion, NASCAR and NC Zoo.

◆◆◆◆FACILITIES: 55 sites, typical site width 70 ft, 55 full hkups, (30/50 amps), some extd stay sites, 21 pull-thrus, cable TV, WiFi Instant Internet at site, WiFi Internet central location, family camping, tenting, laundry, LP gas by weight/by meter, ice, picnic tables, fire rings, wood.

◆◆RECREATION: pavilion, swim pool, golf nearby, playground, horseshoes, hiking trails.

CAMPCLUB USA

Pets welcome. Open all yr. Big rigs welcome. Clubs welcome. Rate in 2010 $34 for 4 persons. MC/VISA. Member ARVC, CARVC. CCUSA 50% Discount. CCUSA reservations Not Accepted, CCUSA max stay 3 days, Cash only for CCUSA disc. Discount not available Fri, Sat or holidays May 1-Oct 31. Cash payment required. Not available for groups or clubs or with any other discount. Call ahead for availability-no advance reservations. Discount based on 90% or less capacity.

Richard Gatling, inventor, was from North Carolina.

LEXINGTON—Continued
CROSS WINDS FAMILY CAMPGROUND—Continued

Phone: (336)853-4567
Address: 160 Campground Ln, Linwood, NC 27299
Lat/Lon: 35.73098/-80.38250
Email: camping@crosswindsfamilycampground.com
Web: www.crosswindsfamilycampground.com

SEE AD THIS PAGE AND AD TRAVEL SECTION PAGE 569

(S) High Rock Lake Marina & Campground—(Davidson) *From jct I-85 (exit 91) & Hwy 8: Go 7 mi S on Hwy 8, then 1-3/4 mi E on Wafford Rd. Enter on L.* ◆◆◆FACILITIES: 81 sites, typical site width 20 ft, 81 full hkups, (20/30/50 amps), 30 pull-thrus, dump, laundry, ltd groc. ◆◆◆RECREATION: swim pool, boating, canoeing, ramp, dock, lake fishing, playground. Pets welcome, breed restrict. No tents. Open all yr. Rate in 2010 $38 for 4 persons. Member ARVC. Phone: (800) 382-3239. FMCA discount.

LINVILLE FALLS—D-3

BLUE RIDGE NATIONAL PARKWAY (Linville Falls Campground)—(haywood) *At milepost 316 on Blue Ridge Pkwy.* FACILITIES: 70 sites, 30 ft max RV length, 70 no hkups, tenting, dump. RECREATION: lake/river fishing. Open Apr 1 - Oct 23. Phone: (828)298-0398.

WELCOME

(NW) LINVILLE FALLS TRAILER LODGE & CAMPGROUND—(Avery) *From jct Blue Ridge Pkwy (between mileposts 317 & 318) & US 221: Go 500 feet S on US 221, then 3/4 mi W on Gurney Franklin Rd. Enter on L.*

◆◆◆FACILITIES: 48 sites, typical site width 20 ft, 40 ft max RV length, 35 full hkups, (15/20/30 amps), 13 no hkups, some extd stay sites, phone Internet central location, family camping, tenting, cabins, laundry, ltd groc, ice, picnic tables, fire rings, wood.

LINVILLE FALLS TRAILER LODGE & CAMPGROUND—Continued on next page

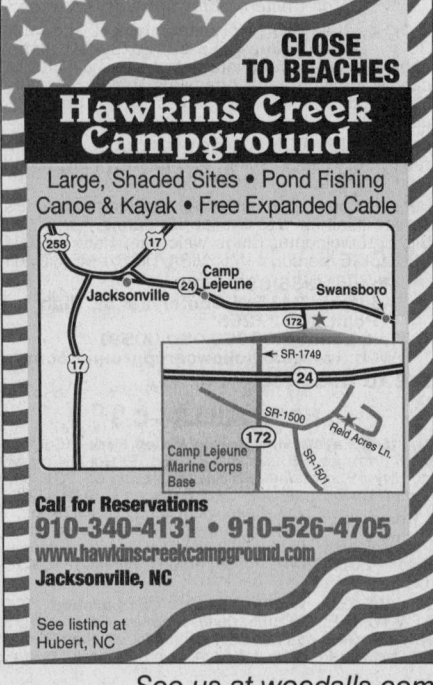

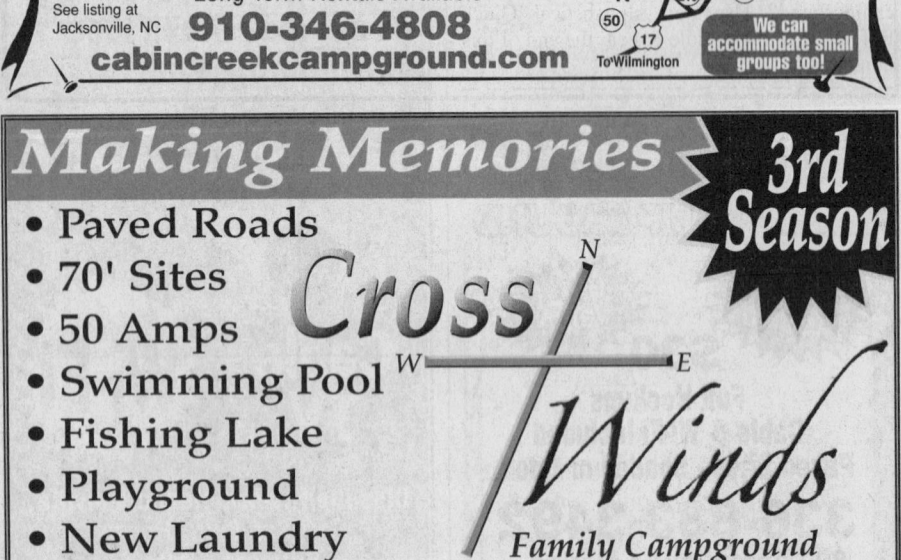

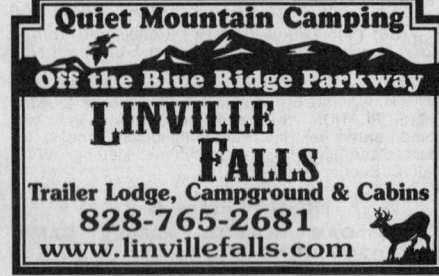

LINVILLE FALLS—Continued
LINVILLE FALLS TRAILER LODGE & CAMPGROUND—Continued

◇◇RECREATION: equipped pavilion, bsktball, play equipment, horseshoes, v-ball.

Pets welcome. Open May 1 - Oct 31. Rate in 2010 $32-35 for 2 persons. Member ARVC, CARVC. CCUSA 50% Discount. CCUSA reservations Recommended, CCUSA max stay 2 days, Cash only for CCUSA disc., CCUSA disc. not avail Th, CCUSA disc. not avail F,Sa, CCUSA disc. not avail holidays. Not available Highland Games & other special events. Call for details. Electric heater surcharge $2.

Phone: (828)765-2681
Address: 717 Gurney Franklin Rd, Linville Falls, NC 28647
Lat/Lon: 35.95638/-81.95303
Email: campwood05@aol.com
Web: www.linvillefalls.com

SEE AD PAGE 594

LITTLE SWITZERLAND—D-3

BLUE RIDGE NATIONAL PARKWAY (Crabtree Meadows Campground)—(Haywood) *From town: Go 5 mi NE on Hwy-226A, then 3 mi S on Blue Ridge Pkwy to MP-339.* FACILITIES: 22 sites, 30 ft max RV length, 22 no hkups, tenting, dump. RECREATION: Open May 14 - Oct 31. Phone: (828)298-0398.

LUMBERTON—C-3

(SW) SLEEPY BEAR'S RV PARK—(Robeson) *From jct I-95 (exit 17) & NC 72: Go 1/8 mi W on NC 72, then 2-1/2 mi S on Kenric Dr. Enter on R.*

OUR FAMILY WELCOMES YOUR FAMILY
We are proud to offer a restful retreat just off I-95. There's a lot to do here in the park and nearby - but feel free just to chill on your paved pull-thru site or beside our colorful pool. Just make yourself at home!

◇◇◇◇FACILITIES: 106 sites, typical site width 27 ft, 82 full hkups, 24 W&E, (20/30/50 amps), 91 pull-thrus, WiFi Instant Internet at site, phone Internet central location, family camping, tenting, RV's/park model rentals, cabins, RV storage, dump, non-guest dump $, laundry, ltd groc, RV supplies, LP gas by weight/by meter, ice, picnic tables, fire rings, grills, wood.

◇◇◇◇RECREATION: rec hall, rec room/area, pavilion, coin games, swim pool, river fishing, mini-golf, golf nearby, bsktball, playground, shuffleboard court shuffleboard court, horseshoes. Rec open to public.

Pets welcome. Partial handicap access. Open all yr. Big rigs welcome. Clubs welcome. Green Friendly. Rate in 2010 $32 for 2 persons. MC/VISA. Member ARVC, CARVC. FMCA discount.

Text 107993 to (440)725-8687 to see our Visual Tour.

Phone: (910)739-4372
Address: 465 Kenric Rd, Lumberton, NC 28360
Lat/Lon: 34.60523/-79.09883
Email: sleepybear@bellsouth.net
Web: www.sleepybearsrvpark.com

SEE AD THIS PAGE AND AD TRAVEL SECTION PAGE 569

MAGGIE VALLEY—E-2

(E) NASCAR RV Resorts at Stonebridge—(Haywood) *From west jct US 276 and US 19: Go 2 mi SW on US 19. Enter on R.* ◇◇◇FACILITIES: 380 sites, typical site width 25 ft, 380 full hkups, (20/30/50 amps), 160 pull-thrus, family camping, tenting, laundry. ◇◇◇RECREATION: swim pool, river swim, stream fishing, playground. Pets welcome, breed restrict. Partial handicap access. Open Apr - Oct. Big rigs welcome. Rate in 2010 $25-45 for 4 persons. Phone: (877)313-0899.

MANTEO—A-6

(W) OUTER BANKS VISITORS BUREAU—*From jct US 158 & US 64: Go 5 1-1/4 mi W on US 64/264. Enter on L.* Provides information about North Carolina's barrier islands: beaches, windsurfing, kite flying, surf & deep sea fishing, historical sites, outdoor dramas, NC Aquarium & Roanoak Island Festival Park. Open all yr.

Phone: (877)629-4386
Address: One Visitors Center Cir, Manteo, NC 27954
Lat/Lon: 35.88697/-75.66673
Web: outerbanks.org

SEE AD TRAVEL SECTION PAGE 570 AND AD DISCOVER SECTION PAGE 1

MANTEO—Continued

(S) THE REFUGE—(Dare) *From jct US 264/US 64 and Hwy 345: Go 2-3/4 mi S on Hwy 345. Enter on L.*

OUTER BANKS ONE OF A KIND CAMPING
Spacious campsites in an environmentally sound conditon on Roanoke Island, near the active fishing village of Wanchese. Venture into the marsh on elevated walkways, fish in our stocked ponds or relax at the pristine pool.

◇◇◇◇FACILITIES: 59 sites, typical site width 30 ft, 59 full hkups, (30/50 amps), many extd stay sites, cable TV, WiFi Instant Internet at site, family camping, laundry, picnic tables.

◇◇RECREATION: pavilion, swim pool, canoeing, kayaking, pond fishing, golf nearby, horseshoes.

Pets welcome. Partial handicap access. No tents. Open all yr. Big rigs welcome. Clubs welcome. Rate in 2010 $40-60 for 4 persons. MC/VISA/Debit. CCUSA 50% Discount. CCUSA reservations Required, CCUSA max stay 2 days, Cash only for CCUSA disc., CCUSA disc. not avail F,Sa, CCUSA disc. not avail holidays. Discount available Oct 1-May. No refunds/rainchecks only valid for 12 mos from dates of reservation cancellation.

Text 84842 to (440)725-8687 to see our Visual Tour.

Stay with a Campground in Woodall's

MANTEO—Continued
THE REFUGE—Continued

Phone: (252)473-1096
Address: 2881 NC-345, Wanchese, NC 27981
Lat/Lon: 35.85273/-75.64351
Web: www.therefuge-roanokeisland.com

SEE AD TRAVEL SECTION PAGE 569

MARION—E-3

(W) BUCK CREEK DRIVING RANGE—*From jct I-40 (exit 86) & Hwy 226: Go 6 mi N on Hwy 226/US 221 bypass, then 1-3/4 mi W on US 70, then 1-3/4 mi N on Hwy 80, then 100 ft NE on Tom's Creeek Rd. Enter on L.* Large, level driving range. Open Mar 1 - Nov 30.

Phone: (828)724-4888
Address: 2576 Toms Creek Rd, Marion, NC 28752
Lat/Lon: 35.71764/-82.07250

SEE AD NEXT PAGE

(W) BUCK CREEK RV PARK CAMPGROUND—(McDowell) *From jct I-40 (exit 86) & Hwy 226: Go 6 mi N on Hwy 226/US 221 bypass, then 1-3/4 mi W on US 70, then 1-3/4 mi N on Hwy 80, then 100 ft NE on Tom's Creek Rd. Enter on L.*

◇◇◇◇FACILITIES: 74 sites, typical site width 30 ft, 74 full hkups, (20/30/50 amps), many extd stay sites (summer), 5 pull-thrus, cable TV, WiFi Instant

BUCK CREEK RV PARK CAMPGROUND—Continued on next page

MARION—Continued
BUCK CREEK RV PARK CAMPGROUND—Continued

Internet at site, cable Internet central location, family camping, RV storage, laundry, ice, picnic tables, fire rings, grills, wood.

◇◇RECREATION: equipped pavilion, river swim, river fishing, golf nearby, bsktball, horseshoes, sports field.

Pets welcome. No tents. Open Apr 1 - Nov 1. Off season by reservation only. Big rigs welcome. Clubs welcome. Rate in 2010 $33-44 for 2 persons.

Phone: (828)724-4888
Address: 2576 Tom's Creek Rd, Marion, NC 28752
Lat/Lon: 35.71764/-82.07250
Web: www.buckcreekcampground.com

SEE AD THIS PAGE

LAKE JAMES STATE PARK—(McDowell) *From town: Go 5 mi NE on Hwy 126.* FACILITIES: 20 sites, 20 no hkups, tenting. RECREATION: lake swim, boating, canoeing, ramp, lake fishing. Partial handicap access. Open Mar 1 - Nov 30. Phone: (828)652-5047.

(W) MOUNTAIN STREAM RV PARK—(McDowell) *From jct I-40W (exit 86) & Hwy 226: Go 6 mi N on Hwy 226/US 221 bypass, then 1-3/4 mi W on US 70, then 7 mi N on Hwy 80. From jct I-40E (exit 72) & US 70: Go 9 mi E on US 70, then 7 mi N on Hwy 80. Enter on R.*

PRETTIEST PARK THIS SIDE OF HEAVEN
God gave us a beautiful creek side setting. We added the level, big rig sites with gravel pads and manicured lawns. Come enjoy nature at its best (and Sat. night Gospel music) just 5 mi off the scenic Blue Ridge Parkway.

◇◇◇FACILITIES: 35 sites, typical site width 30 ft, 35 full hkups, (20/30/50 amps), 50 amps ($), cable TV, WiFi Instant Internet at site, WiFi Internet central location, family camping, ltd groc, RV supplies, ice, picnic tables, fire rings, grills, wood.

◇◇RECREATION: rec room/area, pavilion, stream fishing, fishing supplies, bsktball, activities, (wkends), horseshoes.

Pets welcome. Partial handicap access. No tents. Open all yr. Facilities fully operational Apr 1 - Nov 30. Big rigs welcome. Clubs welcome. Rate in 2010 $35-50 per family. MC/VISA/DISC/Debit. Member ARVC, CARVC. FMCA discount.

Phone: (877)724-9013
Address: 6954 Buck Creek Rd, Marion, NC 28752
Lat/Lon: 35.73980/-82.13283
Email: camp@mountainstreamrvpark.com
Web: www.mountainstreamrvpark.com

SEE AD PAGE 595

WELCOME **(W) THE CAMPGROUND AT TOM JOHNSON CAMPING CENTER**—(McDowell) *From jct I-40 W (exit 86) & Hwy 226: Go 6 mi N on Hwy 226/US 221 Bypass, then 1-1/2 mi W on US 70, then 1/4 mi S on Resistoflex Rd. From jct I-40E (exit 72) & US 70: Go 9-1/2 mi E on US 70, then 1/4 mi S on Resistoflex Rd. Enter on L.*

◇◇◇FACILITIES: 66 sites, 66 full hkups, (50 amps), WiFi Internet central location, laundry, LP gas by weight/by meter, patios, controlled access.

Woodall's Directory is split, East/West. You can buy a Directory with all of North America, or you can buy only the Eastern or Western editions. Browse our bookstore at www.woodalls.com/shop for more details.

MARION—Continued
THE CAMPGROUND AT TOM JOHNSON CAMPING CENTER—Continued

◇RECREATION: rec room/area.

Pets welcome. Partial handicap access. No tents. Open all yr. Big rigs welcome. Clubs welcome. Rate in 2010 $24-30 per vehicle. MC/VISA/DISC/AMEX. CCUSA 50% Discount. CCUSA reservations Required, CCUSA max stay 1 day, Cash only for CCUSA disc., CCUSA disc. not avail holidays. Not available rallies or special events. Call for details.

Phone: (800)225-7802
Address: Resistoflex Rd, Marion, NC 28752
Lat/Lon: 35.68755/-82.06187
Email: camping@tomjohnsoncamping.com
Web: tomjohnsoncamping.com

SEE AD ASHEVILLE PAGE 580

✱ WELCOME **(W) TOM JOHNSON CAMPING CENTER**—*From jct I-40 (exit 86) & Hwy 226: Go 3/4 mi N on Hwy 226, then 5 mi N on Hwy 226/US 221, then 1-1/2 mi W on US 70. Enter on L.* SALES: travel trailers, park models, 5th wheels, Class A motorhomes, Class C motorhomes, fold-down camping trailers, pre-owned unit sales. SERVICES: full-time mech, engine/chassis repair, RV appliance repair, LP gas by weight/by meter, dump station, RV rentals, sells parts/accessories, installs hitches. Open all yr. MC/VISA/DISC/AMEX.

Phone: (800)225-7802
Address: 1885 US 70W, Marion, NC 28752
Lat/Lon: 36.69097/-82.05927
Email: marionsales@tomjohnsoncamping.com
Web: www.tomjohnsoncamping.com

SEE AD ASHEVILLE PAGE 580

(SE) Yogi Bear's Jellystone Park Camp Resort—(McDowell) *From jct I-40 (exit 86) & Hwy 226: Go 300 yds on Hwy 226, then 1 mi E on Fairview Rd, then 1-1/4 mi SE on Deacon Dr. Enter on R.* ◇◇◇FACILITIES: 81 sites, typical site width 30 ft, 68 full hkups, 13 W&E, (30/50 amps), 10 pull-thrus, family camping, tenting, dump, laundry, ltd groc. ◇◇◇◇RECREATION: swim pool, boating, electric motors only, canoeing, lake fishing, playground. Pets welcome. Partial handicap access. Open Late Mar - Nov 15. Big rigs welcome. Rate in 2010 $40-60 per family. Phone: (828)652-7208.

MICAVILLE—D-2

PISGAH NANTAHALA NATIONAL FOREST (Carolina Hemlock Park)—(Yancey) *From town: Go 8-3/4 mi S on Hwy-80.* FACILITIES: 33 sites, 22 ft max RV length, 33 no hkups, 4 pull-thrus, tenting, ltd groc. RECREATION: river swim, river fishing. Open Apr 15 - Oct 31. Phone: (828)837-5152.

PISGAH NATIONAL FOREST (Black Mountain Campground)—(Yancey) *From town: Go 12 mi S on Hwy-80, then 3 mi on FR-472.* FACILITIES: 46 sites, 22 ft max RV length, 46 no hkups, 2 pull-thrus, tenting. RECREATION: river fishing. Open Apr 14 - Oct 31. Phone: (828)682-6146.

MOCKSVILLE—B-2

(NW) Lake Myers RV Resort—(Davie) *From jct I-40 (exit 168) & US 64: Go 2-1/2 mi NW on US 64. Enter on R.* ◇◇◇FACILITIES: 425 sites, typical site width 25 ft, 40 ft max RV length, 400 full hkups, 25 W&E, (20/30/50 amps), 50 amps ($), 17 pull-thrus, tenting, dump, laundry, ltd groc. ◇◇RECREATION: 2 swim pools, canoeing, lake/pond fishing, playground. Pets welcome. Partial handicap access. Open all yr. Facilities fully operational Memorial Day - Labor Day. Rate in 2010 $35-56 for 4 persons. Member ARVC, CARVC. Phone: (336)492-7736.

Billy Graham, evangelist, is from North Carolina.

MONROE—C-2

CANE CREEK PARK (Union County Park)—(Union) *From town: Go 11 mi S on Hwy 200, then 3 mi SE on Potters Rd, then 2 mi SW on Cane Creek Rd. Enter on R.* FACILITIES: 108 sites, typical site width 25 ft, 49 full hkups, 59 W&E, (50 amps), tenting, dump, ltd groc. RECREATION: lake swim, boating, canoeing, ramp, lake fishing, playground. Partial handicap access. Open all yr. Phone: (704)843-3919.

MOREHEAD CITY—C-5

WELCOME **(W) WHISPERING PINES RV PARK**—(Carteret) *From jct US 70 & Hwy 24: Go 8 mi W on Hwy 24. Enter on L.*

◇◇◇FACILITIES: 184 sites, typical site width 30 ft, 184 full hkups, (30/50 amps), mostly extd stay sites, 12 pull-thrus, cable TV, WiFi Instant Internet at site, family camping, RV storage, laundry, RV supplies, ice, picnic tables, wood.

◇◇RECREATION: rec room/area, swim pool, boating, ramp, dock, pond fishing, golf nearby, bsktball, playground.

Pets welcome, quantity restrict. Partial handicap access. No tents. Open all yr. Big rigs welcome. Rate in 2010 $44-55 for 4 persons. MC/VISA. Member ARVC, CARVC.

Phone: (252)726-4902
Address: 25 Whispering Pines, Newport, NC 28570
Lat/Lon: 34.72614/-76.92894
Email: info@wprvpark.com
Web: wprvpark.com

SEE AD NEXT PAGE

MORGANTON—B-1

(NW) Steele Creek Park—(Burke) *From jct I-40 (exit 105) & Hwy 18: Go 2-1/2 mi NW on Hwy 18, then 13-1/2 mi N on Hwy 181. Enter on L.* ◇◇◇FACILITIES: 334 sites, typical site width 30 ft, 249 full hkups, 60 W&E, (20/30/50 amps), 25 no hkups, 9 pull-thrus, family camping, tenting, dump, laundry, ltd groc. ◇◇◇◇RECREATION: swim pool, river/pond/stream fishing, playground. Pets welcome, breed restrict, size restrict. Open all yr. Facilities fully operational Apr 1 - Oct 31. Rate in 2010 $25-35 for 2 persons. Member ARVC, CARVC.

Phone: (828)433-5660
Address: 7081 NC Highway 181, Morganton, NC 28655
Lat/Lon: 35.87285/-81.79265
Web: www.steelecreekpark.com

MURPHY—E-1

(NW) Crawford's Campground & Cabin Rentals—(Cherokee) *From jct US 64 & US 19/74/129: Go 3-1/4 mi W on Tennessee St. which becomes Joe Brown Hwy, then 8 mi N on Hanging Dog Rd, then bear left and go 3-1/2 mi W on Beaver Dam Rd. Enter on R.* ◇◇◇FACILITIES: 46 sites, typical site width 25 ft, 24 full hkups, 12 W&E, (30/50 amps), 10 no hkups, WiFi Internet central location, family camping, tenting, RV storage, dump, laundry, groceries, RV supplies, LP gas by weight, ice, picnic tables, fire rings, wood. ◇◇RECREATION: pavilion, stream fishing, playground, horseshoes, hiking trails. Pets welcome. Open all yr. Big rigs welcome. Rate in 2010 $25-35 for 2 persons. MC/VISA/DISC/Debit. CCUSA 50% Discount. CCUSA reservations Recommended, CCUSA max stay 2 days. 20% off additional days.

Phone: (828)837-9077
Address: 87 Horton Rd, Murphy, NC 28906
Lat/Lon: 35.20285/-84.08846
Email: crawfords_campground@yahoo.com
Web: www.crawfordsattellico.com

(N) NANTAHALA NATIONAL FOREST (Hanging Dog Campground)—(Cherokee) *From town: Go 5 mi NW on Hwy-1326.* FACILITIES: 52 sites, 52 no hkups, 1 pull-thrus, tenting. RECREATION: boating, ramp, lake fishing. Open Apr 1 - Oct 31. Phone: (828)837-5152.

(NE) Peace Valley KOA at Murphy—(Cherokee) *From east jct US 64 and US 19/74/129: Go 4 mi NE on US 19/74/129. Enter on R.* ◇◇◇FACILITIES: 66 sites, typical site width 30 ft, 47 full hkups, 9 W&E, (30/50 amps), 10 no hkups, 20 pull-thrus, tenting, dump, laundry. ◇◇◇RECREATION: swim pool, canoeing, river fishing. Pets welcome. Open all yr. Big rigs welcome. Rate in 2010 $30-40 for 2 persons. Member ARVC, CARVC. Phone: (828)837-6223.

(W) Rivers Edge Mountain RV Resort—(Cherokee) *From jct US/19/129/74 & US 64: Go 6-1/2 mi W on US 64/74. Enter on R.* ◇◇◇◇FACILITIES: 49 sites, typical site width 55 ft, 49 full hkups, (30/50 amps), 38 pull-thrus, cable TV, WiFi Instant Internet at site, laundry, LP gas by weight/by meter, picnic tables, patios, fire

Rivers Edge Mountain RV Resort—Continued on next page

Ava Gardner, actress, was from North Carolina.

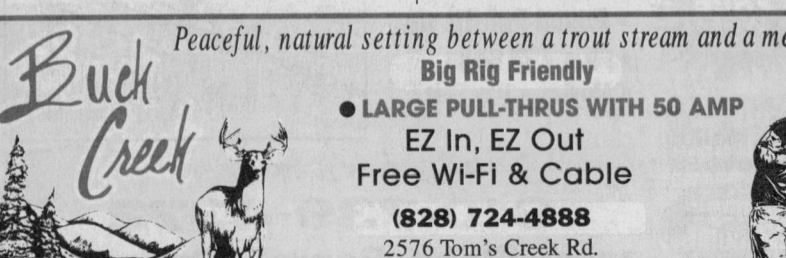

MURPHY—Continued
Rivers Edge Mountain RV Resort—Continued

CAMPCLUB USA rings, wood. ◆RECREATION: pavilion, river fishing. Pets welcome. No tents. Open all yr. Big rigs welcome. Rate in 2010 $35-55 for 2 persons. MC/VISA/DISC/Debit. CCUSA 50% Discount. CCUSA reservations Recommended, CCUSA max stay 1 day, Cash only for CCUSA disc., CCUSA disc. not avail holidays.

Phone: (828)361-4517
Address: 1750 Hilltop Rd, Murphy, NC 28906
Lat/Lon: 35.02934/-84.11558
Web: www.riversedgemountainrvresort.com

NAGS HEAD—A-6

(S) CAPE HATTERAS NATIONAL SEASHORE (Oregon Inlet Campground)—(Dare) *From jct US-64/264 & Hwy-12: Go 8 mi S on Hwy-12.* FACILITIES: 120 sites, 120 no hkups, tenting, dump. RECREATION: saltwater swim, saltwater fishing. Open Apr 3 - Oct 12. Phone: (252)473-2111.

NEW BERN—C-5

(NW) New Bern KOA—(Craven) *From jct US 70 & US 17: Go 8-1/2 mi E on US 17/NC 55 toward Bayboro/Washington. Enter on L.* ◆◆◆◆FACILITIES: 79 sites, typical site width 30 ft, 60 full hkups, 16 W&E, (30/50 amps), 3 no hkups, 31 pull-thrus, tenting, dump, laundry, groceries. ◆◆◆RECREATION: swim pool, boating, canoeing, ramp, dock, river/pond fishing, playground. Pets welcome, breed restrict. Open all yr. Big rigs welcome. Rate in 2010 $35-85 for 2 persons. Member ARVC. Phone: (252)638-2556. KOA discount.

NORLINA—A-4

KERR STATE REC. AREA (County Line Park)—(Vance) *From town: Take exit 223 off I-85: Go W on Manson Rd 2.5 mi to Drewry, turn right on Drewry-Valine Rd. Go 2.5 mi Turn left on Buchanan Store Rd. Go 1 mi, then right on County line rd 1.5 mi to the park.* FACILITIES: 84 sites, 41 W&E, 43 no hkups, tenting, dump. RECREATION: lake swim, boating, ramp, lake fishing, playground. Open Apr - Mid Sept. Phone: (252)438-7791.

KERR STATE REC. AREA (Kimball Point Park)—(Vance) *From town: take exit 223 of I-85: Go W on Manson Rd 2.5 mi to Drewry. Go N on Drewry-Virgina Line Rd 5 mi. Turn let on Kimball Pt Rd. for 1.5 mi.* FACILITIES: 91 sites, 23 E, (30 amps), 68 no hkups, tenting, dump. RECREATION: lake swim, boating, ramp, lake fishing, playground. Open Apr 1 - Nov 1. Phone: (252) 438-7791.

OCRACOKE—C-6

(C) Beachcomber Campground (RV SPACES) —(Hyde) *From Cedar Island-Ocracoke Ferry Landing: Go 1 mi N on Hwy 12. Enter on R.* FACILITIES: 29 sites, typical site width 15 ft, 29 W&E, (20/30/50 amps), tenting, dump, full svc store. Pets welcome. Open all yr. Rate in 2010 $35-48 for 2 persons. Phone: (252)928-4031.

(E) CAPE HATTERAS NATIONAL SEASHORE (Ocracoke Campground)—(Hyde) *From town: Go 4 mi E on Hwy-12.* FACILITIES: 136 sites, 136 no hkups, tenting, dump, groceries. RECREATION: saltwater swim, boating, ramp, dock, lake fishing. Partial handicap access. Open Apr 3 - Oct 26. Phone: (800)365-CAMP.

Sugar Ray Leonard, boxer, is from North Carolina.

OUTER BANKS—B-6

OUTER BANKS AREA MAP

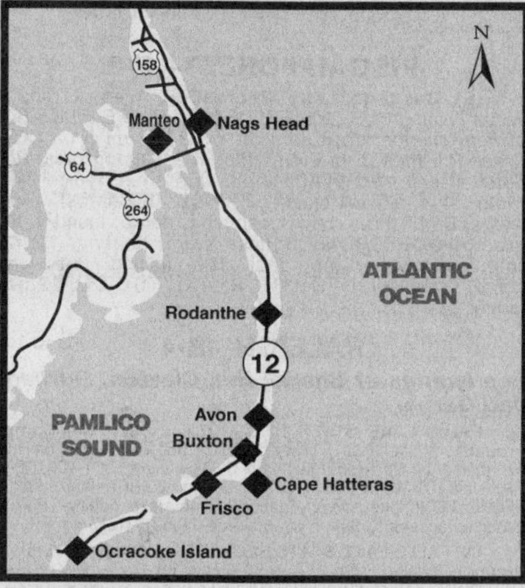

Symbols on map indicate towns within the Outer Banks where campgrounds (diamonds), attractions (flags), & RV service centers & camping supply outlets (gears) are listed. Check listings for more information.

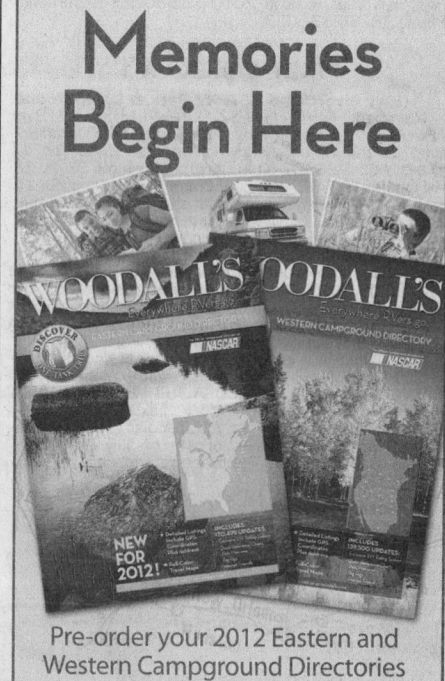

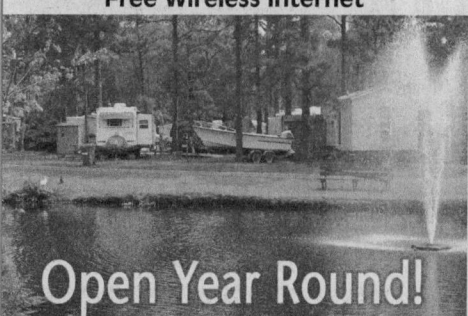

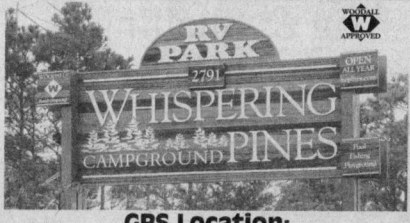

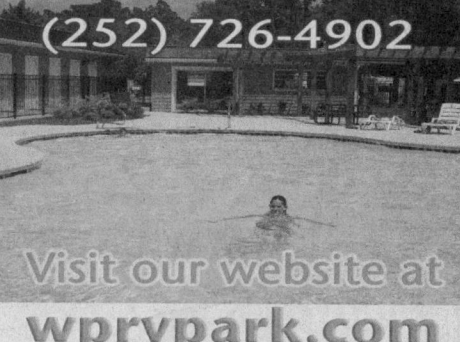

Tell Them Woodall's Sent You!

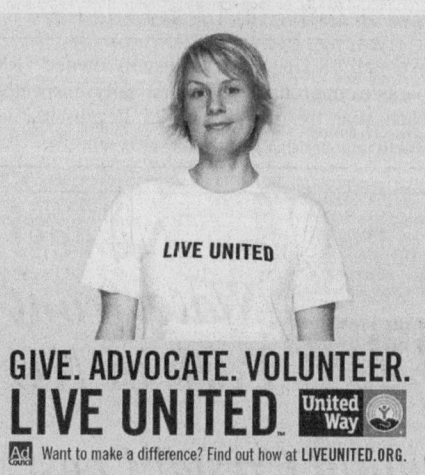

PINEHURST—B-3

PINE LAKE RV RESORT—*From jct Hwy 2 & US 15/501 (Pinehurst Traffic Cir): Go 4 mi S on US 15/501, then 2 mi S on US 15/US 2, then 9-1/2 mi S on US 15/501, then 2 mi E on Hill Creek Rd.*

SEE PRIMARY LISTING IN ABERDEEN, NC AND AD ABERDEEN PAGE 578

PINEOLA—D-3

(S) Down By The River Campground—(Avery) *From jct US 221 & Hwy 181: Go S 1/4 mi on Hwy 181. Enter on R.* ◆◆◆FACILITIES: 124 sites, 124 full hkups, (30/50 amps), 30 pull-thrus, family camping, tenting, dump, laundry. ◆◆RECREATION: river fishing. Pets welcome, quantity restrict. Open May 1 - Oct 31. Big rigs welcome. Rate in 2010 $30-50 for 2 persons. Phone: (828)733-5057.

PINEY CREEK—A-1

(SW) RiverCamp USA RV Park & Campground—(Alleghany) *From jct US 221 & Hwy 113: Go 4-1/2 mi N on Hwy 113, then 1/2 mi W on South Fork Church Rd, then 2 mi W on Kings Creek Rd. Enter on L.* ◆◆◆FACILITIES: 61 sites, typical site width 35 ft, 38 full hkups, 13 W&E, (20/30/50 amps), 50 amps ($), 10 no hkups, WiFi Instant Internet at site ($), phone Internet central location, family camping, tenting, RV storage, dump, non-guest dump $, laundry, ltd groc, RV supplies, ice, picnic tables, patios, fire rings, grills, wood.

◆◆RECREATION: pavilion, boating, no motors, canoeing, kayaking, float trips, river fishing, fishing supplies, fishing guides, play equipment, horseshoes, v-ball. Pets welcome, breed restrict. Partial handicap access. Open Apr 15 - Nov 1. Big rigs welcome. Rate in 2010 $26 for 2 persons. MC/VISA. Member ARVC, CARVC. FMCA discount. CCUSA 50% Discount. CCUSA reservations Required, CCUSA max stay 5 days, CCUSA disc. not avail F,Sa, CCUSA disc. not avail holidays. Not available week of 4th of July or special events. Call for details. Pet breed restrictions. WiFi surcharge $2.

Phone: (336)359-2267
Address: 2221 Kings Creek Rd, Piney Creek, NC 28663
Lat/Lon: 36.52704/-81.33603
Email: info@RIVERCAMPUSA.COM
Web: WWW.RIVERCAMPUSA.COM

PINNACLE—A-2

(N) PILOT MOUNTAIN STATE PARK—(Surry) *From town: Go 3 mi W on US 52.* FACILITIES: 49 sites, 49 no hkups, tenting. RECREATION: boating, canoeing, river fishing. Open Mar 15 - Nov 30. Phone: (336)325-2355.

PISGAH FOREST—E-2

(E) Cascade Lake Recreation Area—(Transylvania) *From jct US 276 & US 64: Go 3 mi E on US 64, at convenience store go right for 2-1/2 mi S on Crab Creek Rd, then 2 mi E on Little River Campground Rd. Enter at end.* ◆◆◆FACILITIES: 165 sites, typical site width 24 ft, 85 full hkups, 73 W&E, (50 amps), 7 no hkups, 8 pull-thrus, family camping, dump, laundry, ltd groc. ◆◆◆RECREATION: lake swim, boating, 12 hp limit, canoeing, ramp, dock, lake fishing. Pets welcome. Open Apr 1 - Oct 31. Rate in 2010 $15-42 per family.

RALEIGH—B-4

See listings at Chapel Hill, Clayton, Durham and Garner

FALLS LAKE STATE REC. AREA (Holly Point Campground)—(Wake) *From jct Hwy 50 & Hwy 98: Go 1/2 mi E on Hwy 98, then N on Ghoston Rd, then N on New Light Rd.* FACILITIES: 186 sites, 89 W&E, (20/30 amps), 97 no hkups, tenting, dump. RECREATION: lake swim, boating, ramp, lake fishing. Partial handicap access. Open all yr. Phone: (919)676-1027.

(N) FALLS LAKE STATE REC. AREA (Rollingview Campground)—(Wake) *From jct Hwy 50 & Hwy 98: Go 8 mi W on Hwy 98, then N on Baptist Rd.* FACILITIES: 117 sites, 82 W&E, (20/30 amps), 35 no hkups, tenting. RECREATION: lake swim, boating, ramp, lake fishing. Open all yr. Phone: (919)676-1027.

(W) WILLIAM B UMSTEAD STATE PARK—(Wake) *From town: Go 6 mi NW on US 70.* FACILITIES: 28 sites, 20 ft max RV length, 28 no hkups, tenting. RECREATION: boating, lake fishing. Open Mar 15 - Dec 15. Phone: (919)571-4170.

REIDSVILLE—A-3

LAKE REIDSVILLE RECREATION PARK (City Park)—(Rockingham) *From town: Go 5 mi S on US 29, then 1 mi E on Waterworks Rd. Enter on L.* FACILITIES: 46 sites, typical site width 12 ft, 46 W&E, (50 amps), 10 pull-thrus, tenting, dump, ltd groc. RECREATION: boating, canoeing, ramp, dock, lake fishing, playground. Open Apr 1 - Nov 1. Phone: (336)349-4738.

Woodall's Tip... All privately-owned RV parks/campgrounds are personally inspected each year by one of our 25 Representative Teams.

ROANOKE RAPIDS—A-4

(S) THE RV RESORT AT CAROLINA CROSSROADS—(Halifax) *From jct I-95 (exit 171) & Hwy 125: Go 1/10 mi S on Hwy 125 to first stoplight, then E on Carolina Crossroads Blvd. Stay right at traffic circle and continue 1/2 mi E on Wallace Fork Rd (NC 1698). Enter on R.*

◆◆◆◆FACILITIES: 89 sites, typical site width 35 ft, 89 full hkups, (50 amps), 68 pull-thrus, cable TV, ($), WiFi Instant Internet at site, cable Internet central location, family camping, tenting, laundry, RV supplies, LP gas by weight/by meter, ice, picnic tables, patios, fire rings, wood.

◆◆RECREATION: rec hall, pavilion, swim pool, hot tub, mini-golf, golf nearby, play equipment, horseshoes.

Pets welcome. Partial handicap access. Open all yr. Big rigs welcome. Clubs welcome. Rate in 2010 $25-37.50 for 2 persons. MC/VISA. Member ARVC, CARVC. CCUSA 50% Discount.

Phone: (252)538-9776
Address: 415 Wallace Fork Rd, Roanoke Rapids, NC 27870
Lat/Lon: 36.40572/-77.63100
Email: rvresort@embarqmail.com
Web: www.rvresortatcc.com

SEE AD THIS PAGE

ROARING GAP—A-1

STONE MOUNTAIN STATE PARK—(Wilkes) *From jct US 21 & Hwy 1002: Go 7 mi SW on Hwy 1002 to John P. Frank Pkwy.* FACILITIES: 47 sites, 47 no hkups, tenting, laundry. RECREATION: river fishing. Open all yr. Facilities fully operational Mar 15 - Dec 15. Phone: (336)957-8185.

ROBBINSVILLE—E-1

NANTAHALA NATIONAL FOREST (Cheoah Point Rec. Area)—(Graham) *From town: Go 8 mi NW on US-129.* FACILITIES: 23 sites, 22 ft max RV length, 23 no hkups, 1 pull-thrus, tenting. RECREATION: boating, ramp, lake fishing. Open Apr 15 - Oct 31. Phone: (828)479-6431.

RODANTHE—B-6

(N) CAMP HATTERAS—(Dare) *From the business center: Go 1 mi S on Hwy 12. Enter on L.*

◆◆◆◆FACILITIES: 403 sites, typical site width 40 ft, 403 full hkups, (30/50 amps), 9 pull-thrus, cable TV, ($), WiFi Instant Internet at site, family camping, tenting, laundry, ltd groc, RV supplies, ice, picnic tables, patios, controlled access.

◆◆◆◆◆RECREATION: rec hall, rec room/area, pavilion, coin games, 2 swim pools, wading pool, saltwater swim, hot tub, boating, canoeing, kayaking, ramp, 10 kayak rentals, saltwater/pond fishing, fishing supplies, mini-golf, ($), bsktball, 10 bike rentals, playground, shuffleboard court 4 shuffleboard courts, activities, tennis, v-ball.

Pets welcome. Partial handicap access. Open all yr. Big rigs welcome. Clubs welcome. Green Friendly. Rate in 2010 $43-94 for 2 persons. MC/VISA/DISC/AMEX. Member ARVC, CARVC. FMCA discount.

Text 107916 to (440)725-8687 to see our Visual Tour.

Phone: (252)987-2777
Address: 24798 Hwy 12, Rodanthe, NC 27968
Lat/Lon: 35.57820/-75.46660
Email: camping@camphatteras.com
Web: www.camphatteras.com

SEE AD CAPE HATTERAS PAGE 584 AND AD DISCOVER SECTION PAGE 44

(S) Cape Hatteras KOA—(Dare) *From the business center: Go 1-1/4 mi S on Hwy 12. Enter on L.* ◆◆◆FACILITIES: 345 sites, typical site width 25 ft, 161 full hkups, 154 W&E, (20/30/50 amps), 30 no hkups, 109 pull-thrus, family camping, tenting, dump, laundry, groceries. ◆◆◆◆◆RECREATION: swim pool, saltwater swim, canoeing, saltwater fishing, playground. Pets welcome. Partial handicap access. Open all yr. Big rigs welcome. Rate in 2010 $43-94 for 6 persons. Phone: (252)987-2307. KOA discount.

(S) OCEAN WAVES CAMPGROUND—(Dare) *From business center: Go 1-1/2 mi S on Hwy 12. Enter on L.*

◆◆◆◆FACILITIES: 68 sites, typical site width 30 ft, 64 full hkups, (20/30/50 amps), 4 no hkups, cable TV, ($), WiFi Instant Internet at site, WiFi Internet central location, tenting, laundry, ltd groc, ice, picnic tables.

◆◆RECREATION: rec room/area, coin games, swim pool, saltwater swim, saltwater fishing, fishing supplies, play equipment.

Pets welcome. Partial handicap access. Open Mar 15 - Nov 15. Big rigs welcome. Rate in 2010 $38 per family. MC/VISA/DISC. Member ARVC, CARVC.

Phone: (252)987-2556
Address: 25313 Hwy 12, Waves, NC 27982
Lat/Lon: 35.57162/-75.46710
Web: www.oceanwavescampground.com

SEE AD THIS PAGE

RUTHERFORDTON—E-3

(W) Four Paws Kingdom—(Rutherford) *From jct US 64/74A and Coopers Gap Rd: Go 3-1/4 mi W on Coopers Gap Rd to Lazy Creek Dr. Enter on R.* ◆◆◆FACILITIES: 47 sites, 41 full hkups, 6 W&E, (20/30/50 amps), 50 amps ($), cable TV, WiFi Instant Internet at site, WiFi Internet central location, laundry, ltd groc, RV supplies, ice, picnic tables, fire rings,

Check out our web site www.woodalls.com

RUTHERFORDTON—Continued
Four Paws Kingdom—Continued

wood. ◆◆RECREATION: equipped pavilion, pond fishing, horseshoes, hiking trails. Pets welcome, breed restrict. Partial handicap access. No tents. Age restrict may apply. Open Apr 7 - Nov 27. Big rigs welcome. Rate in 2010 $35-44 for 2 persons. MC/VISA/DISC. Member ARVC, CARVC. CCUSA 50% Discount. CCUSA reservations Not Accepted, CCUSA max stay 4 days, Cash only for CCUSA disc., CCUSA disc. not avail S, CCUSA disc. not avail F,Sa, CCUSA disc. not avail holidays. Call ahead for availability. Park closed Aug 1-17. Adults only campground.

Phone: (828)287-7324
Address: 335 Lazy Creek Dr, Rutherfordton, NC 28139
Lat/Lon: 35.37451/-82.02878
Email: camping@4pawskingdom.com
Web: www.4pawskingdom.com

SALISBURY—B-2

(N) Bass Lake—(Rowan) *From jct I-40 (exit 170) & Hwy 601: Go 13 1/2 mi S on Hwy 601. Enter on L.* ◆◆◆FACILITIES: 68 sites, 38 full hkups, 30 W&E, (30/50 amps), 50 amps ($), WiFi Instant Internet at site ($), family camping, dump, laundry. ◆◆◆RECREATION: rec hall, pavilion, swim pool, pond fishing, mini-golf, bsktball, playground, activities, horseshoes. No tents. Open May - Oct 15. Rate in 2010 $30 per vehicle. CCUSA 50% Discount.

Phone: (704)642-0035
Address: 185 Jim Neely Dr., Salisbury, NC 28144
Lat/Lon: 35.75945/-80.51086
Email: basslake@whrus.com
Web: westernhorizontoday.com

(E) DAN NICHOLAS PARK (Rowan County Park)—(Rowan) *From jct US 52 & I-85: Go 1-3/4 mi N on I-85 (exit 79), then 1-1/4 mi SE on Choate Rd, then 1/2 mi SE on McCaules Rd, then 5 mi E on Bringle Ferry Rd. Enter on L.* FACILITIES: 70 sites, 67 E, (30/50 amps), 3 no hkups, 13 pull-thrus, tenting, dump, ltd groc. RECREATION: lake fishing, playground. Open all yr. Phone: (704)216-7808.

SALUDA—E-2

(SW) ORCHARD LAKE CAMPGROUND & RV PARK—(Polk) *From I-26 (exit 59): Go 1-1/4 mi SW on Ozone Rd, then 1/2 mi SW on US 176, then 3 mi SE on Mountain Page Rd, then 1-1/2 mi E on left fork (Mine Mtn Rd), then 1/2 mi SE on Orchard Lake Rd. Enter on L.*

◆◆◆FACILITIES: 127 sites, typical site width 25 ft, 104 full hkups, 23 W&E, (20/30/50 amps), some extd stay sites, 10 pull-thrus, WiFi Instant Internet at site, phone Internet central location, family camping, tenting, cabins, RV storage, dump, laundry, ltd groc, RV supplies, ice, picnic tables, patios, fire rings, wood.

◆◆◆◆RECREATION: rec hall, pavilion, lake swim, boating, electric motors only, canoeing, kayaking, dock, 4 rowboat/8 canoe/3 pedal boat rentals, lake/pond fishing, fishing supplies, bsktball, playground, shuffleboard court shuffleboard court, activities (wkends), horseshoes, sports field, hiking trails, v-ball. Rec open to public.

Pets welcome. Open Apr 1 - Oct 31. Big rigs welcome. Clubs welcome. Rate in 2010 $40 per family. MC/VISA/DISC. Member ARVC, CALARVC. CCUSA 50% Discount. CCUSA reservations Recommended, CCUSA max stay 1 day, Cash only for CCUSA disc.

Visit a Dealer/Service Location in Woodall's.

SALUDA—Continued
ORCHARD LAKE CAMPGROUND & RV PARK—Continued

Phone: (828)749-3901
Address: 460 Orchard Lake Rd, Saluda, NC 28773
Lat/Lon: 35.20133/-82.35670
Email: mgr@orchardlakecampground.com
Web: www.orchardlakecampground.com

SEE AD HENDERSONVILLE PAGE 592

SELMA—B-4

(NE) RVACATION CAMPGROUND—(Johnston) *From jct I-95 & Pine Level - Selma Rd (exit 98): Go 100 ft E on Pine Level - Selma Rd (CR 1927), then 1/2 mi N on campground Rd. Enter on R.*

◆◆◆◆FACILITIES: 50 sites, typical site width 50 ft, 45 full hkups, 5 W&E, (30/50 amps), 45 pull-thrus, WiFi Instant Internet at site, RV storage, dump, non-guest dump $, laundry, ltd groc, RV supplies, LP gas by weight/by meter, ice, picnic tables.

◆RECREATION: lake fishing, fishing supplies, golf nearby, playground.

Pets welcome. No tents. Open all yr. Big rigs welcome. Escort to site. Rate in 2010 $25-37 for 2 persons. MC/VISA. Member ARVC, CARVC.

Phone: (919)965-5923
Address: 428 Campground Rd, Selma, NC 27576-8947
Lat/Lon: 35.53166/-78.26287
Email: camping@rvacation.us
Web: rvacation.us

SEE AD THIS PAGE

SHILOH—A-6

(E) North River Campground & RV Park—(Camden) *From jct US 158 & Indian Town Rd: Go 6 mi S on Indian Town Rd, then 1-1/2 mi E on Garrington Island Rd. Enter at end.* ◆◆◆◆FACILITIES: 83 sites, typical site width 35 ft, 73 full hkups, 10 W&E, (30/50 amps), 4 pull-thrus, cable TV, WiFi Instant Internet at site ($), WiFi Internet central location, tenting, RV storage, dump, non-guest dump $, laundry, ltd groc, LP gas by weight/by meter, ice, picnic tables, grills, wood. ◆◆◆RECREATION: rec hall, equipped pavilion, lake swim, lake fishing, mini-golf, ($), play equipment, activities horseshoes, v-ball. Pets welcome. Partial handicap access. Open all yr. Big rigs welcome. Rate in 2010 $35 for 2 persons. MC/VISA/DISC/AMEX. CCUSA 50% Discount. CCUSA reservations Recommended, CCUSA max stay 3 days, Cash only for CCUSA disc., CCUSA disc. not avail F,Sa, CCUSA disc. not avail holidays.

Phone: (252)336-4414
Address: 256 Garrington Island Rd, Shawboro, NC 27973
Lat/Lon: 36.30448/-76.02154
Web: northrivercampground.com

SMITHFIELD—B-4

RVACATION CAMPGROUND—*From jct US 70 Bus/I-95: Go 3 mi N on I-95 to exit 98, then 25 yds E on CR 1927 (Pine Level-Selma Rd), then 1/2 mi N on Campground Rd.*

SEE PRIMARY LISTING AT SELMA AND AD THIS PAGE

Woodall's Tip... For bridge, tunnel & ferry regulations, check out the Rules of the Road section in front of this Directory.

SPARTA—A-1

E NATIONAL PARKWAY (Doughton Park -(Alleghany) *From town: Go 7 mi S on US 21, n Blue Ride Pkwy to milepost 239.* FACILITIES: 24 ax RV length, 24 no hkups, tenting, dump. RECREA- May 14 - Oct 31. Phone: (336)372-8568.

SPRUCE PINE—D-3

SE) Bear Den Campground—(McDowell) *From JS 19 E & Hwy 226: Go 4-1/2 mi E on Hwy 226, en 6 mi N on Blue Ridge Pkwy to milepost 324.8. nter on R.* ◇◇◇FACILITIES: 142 sites, typical site width 20 ft, 29 full hkups, 113 W&E, (20/30/50 amps), 11 pull-thrus, family camping, tenting, dump, laundry, ltd groc. ◇◇◇◇RECREATION: lake swim, canoeing, pond fishing, playground. Pets welcome ($). Open Mar 1 - Nov 30. Rate in 2010 $40-45 for 2 persons. Member ARVC, CARVC. Phone: (828)765-2888.

STATESVILLE—B-2

LAKE NORMAN STATE PARK—(Iredell) *From town: Go 10 mi S on Hwy 1569.* FACILITIES: 33 sites, 33 no hkups, tenting, dump. RECREATION: lake swim, boating, canoeing, ramp, lake fishing. Open Mar 15 - Nov 30. Phone: (704)528-6350.

(NE) Statesville East I-40/Winston Salem KOA—(Davie) *From jct I-77 & I-40: Go 9 mi E on I-40 to exit 162, then 1/4 mi S on US 64, then 1/4 mi E on Campground Road. Enter on L.* ◇◇◇FACILITIES: 83 sites, typical site width 25 ft, 47 full hkups, 25 W&E, (20/30/50 amps), 11 no hkups, 39 pull-thrus, family camping, tenting, dump, laundry, groceries. ◇◇◇◇RECREATION: swim pool, lake fishing, playground. Pets welcome, breed restrict. Open all yr. Big rigs welcome. Rate in 2010 $36-48 for 2 persons. Member ARVC, CARVC. Phone: (800)562-8651. KOA discount.

(S) Statesville/I-77 KOA—(Iredell) *From jct I-40 & I-77: Go 6 mi S on I-77 (exit 45), then 1/2 mi N on E frontage road. Enter on L.* ◇◇◇FACILITIES: 88 sites, typical site width 34 ft, 37 full hkups, 51 W&E, (20/30/50 amps), 50 amps ($), 49 pull-thrus, tenting, dump, laundry, groceries. ◇◇RECREATION: swim pool, playground. Pets welcome, breed restrict. Partial handicap access. Open all yr. Big rigs welcome. Rate in 2010 $33-41 for 2 persons. Phone: (704)873-5560. KOA discount.

STELLA—C-5

(S) White Oak Shores Camping & RV Resort—(Carteret) *From jct Hwy 24 & Hwy 58: Go 8-1/2 mi N on Hwy 58, then 1 mi S on Morristown Rd, then 3/4 mi W on Wetherington Rd. Enter on L.* ◇◇◇◇FACILITIES: 250 sites, typical site width 30 ft, 250 full hkups, (20/30/50 amps), 35 pull-thrus, family camping, tenting, laundry, groceries. ◇◇◇◇RECREATION: swim pool, boating, canoeing, ramp, dock, river fishing, playground. Pets welcome, breed restrict. Open all yr. Big rigs welcome. Rate in 2010 $42-60 for 2 persons. Phone: (252)393-3244.

STONEVILLE—A-2

(SW) Dan River Campground—(Rockingham) *From jct US 220 & Hwy 135: Go 1 blk W on Hwy 135, then 1/2 mi S on Dan Valley Rd, then 2 mi E on River Rd, then 1 mi SE on Webster Rd. Enter on R.* ◇◇FACILITIES: 42 sites, typical site width 35 ft, 20 full hkups, 18 W&E, (20/30/50 amps), 4 no hkups, 2 pull-thrus, family camping, tenting, dump. ◇◇RECREATION: swim pool, canoeing, river fishing, play equipment. Pets welcome, breed restrict. Open all yr. Rate in 2010 $23-25 for 2 persons. Member ARVC, CARVC. Phone: (336)427-8530.

SUNSET BEACH—D-4

(W) KOA Shallotte/Brunswick Beaches—(Brunswick) *From jct US 17 & Hwy 904: Go 1/4 mi SE on Hwy 904. Enter on R.* ◇◇◇FACILITIES: 93 sites, typical site width 30 ft, 70 full hkups, 23 W&E, (20/30/50 amps), 80 pull-thrus, tenting, dump, laundry, ltd groc. ◇◇RECREATION: swim pool, pond fishing, playground. Pets welcome. Partial handicap access. Open all yr. Big rigs welcome. Rate in 2010 $35-54 for 2 persons. Phone: (888)562-4240. KOA discount.

SURF CITY—D-5

(C) Lanier's Campground—(Pender) *From jct US 17 & Hwy 210: Go 2-3/4 mi E on Hwy 210, continue 1 mi SE on Hwy 210, then 1/2 mi S on Little Kinston Rd., then 1/2 mi W on Spot Lane. Enter at end.* ◇◇◇FACILITIES: 443 sites, typical site width 25 ft, 40 ft max RV length, 214 full hkups, 229 W&E, (30/50 amps), 2 pull-thrus, WiFi Internet central location, tenting, dump, non-guest dump $, ltd groc, RV supplies, ice, picnic tables, fire rings, wood. ◇◇◇RECREATION: pavilion, swim pool, boating, canoeing, kayaking, ramp, dock, saltwater fishing, playground, activities, horseshoes. Pets welcome, breed restrict. Partial handicap access. Open all yr. Rate in 2010 $28-38 for 5 persons. MC/VISA/AMEX. Member ARVC, CARVC. CCUSA 50% Discount. CCUSA reservations Recommended, CCUSA max stay 2 days, CCUSA disc. not avail holidays. Discount availabe Nov thru Feb.

SURF CITY—Continued
Lanier's Campground—Continued

Phone: (910)328-9431
Address: 1161 Spot Ln, Surf City, NC 28445
Lat/Lon: 34.43192/-77.56940
Email: CampLanier@aol.com
Web: www.lanierscampground.com

SWANNANOA—E-2

(E) ASHEVILLE EAST-KOA—(Buncombe) *From I-40 (exit 59) & Patton Cove Rd: Go 1/2 mi N on Patton Cove Rd, then 1-1/2 mi E on US 70. Enter on L.*

◇◇◇FACILITIES: 227 sites, typical site width 22 ft, 85 full hkups, 136 W&E, 4 E, (20/30/50 amps), 2 no hkups, 15 pull-thrus, cable TV, ($), WiFi Instant Internet at site, phone Internet central location, family camping, tenting, RV's/park model rentals, cabins, RV storage, dump, non-guest dump $, laundry, groceries, RV supplies, LP gas by weight/by meter, ice, picnic tables, fire rings, wood.

◇◇◇◇RECREATION: rec room/area, pavilion, coin games, swim pool, river swim, boating, electric motors only, 3 rowboat/3 pedal boat rentals, lake/river fishing, fishing supplies, mini-golf, ($), golf nearby, bsktball, 14 bike rentals, playground, activities, (wkends), horseshoes, hiking trails.

Pets welcome, breed restrict. Open all yr. Big rigs welcome. Escort to site. Clubs welcome. Rate in 2010 $32-46 for 2 persons. MC/VISA/DISC. KOA discount.

Phone: (828)686-3121
Address: 2708 US Hwy 70 East, Swannanoa, NC 28778
Lat/Lon: 35.60056/-82.37867
Email: akoaeast@bellsouth.net
Web: www.ashevilleeastkoa.com

SEE AD ASHEVILLE PAGE 581 AND AD TRAVEL SECTION PAGE 569

(S) MAMA GERTIE'S HIDEAWAY CAMPGROUND—(Buncombe) *From jct I-40 (exit 59) & Patton Cove Rd: Go 1/2 mi S on Patton Cove Rd. Enter on L.*

◇◇◇◇◇FACILITIES: 33 sites, typical site width 30 ft, 19 full hkups, 14 W&E, (20/30/50 amps), 13 pull-thrus, cable TV, WiFi Instant Internet at site, phone Internet central location, family camping, tenting, cabins, dump, laundry, ltd groc, RV supplies, LP gas by weight/by meter, ice, picnic tables, patios, fire rings, wood, controlled access.

◇◇◇RECREATION: rec hall, rec room/area, equipped pavilion, coin games, golf nearby, horseshoes, hiking trails.

Pets welcome. Partial handicap access. Open all yr. Big rigs welcome. Escort to site. Rate in 2010 $30-46 for 2 persons. MC/VISA/DISC. Member ARVC, CARVC. FMCA discount. CCUSA 50% Discount. CCUSA reservations Required, CCUSA max stay 2 days, Cash only for CCUSA disc., CCUSA disc. not avail holidays. Discount not available May thru Oct.

Phone: (828)686-4258
Address: 15 Uphill Rd, Swannanoa, NC 28778
Lat/Lon: 35.58697/-82.40562
Email: info@mamagerties.com
Web: www.mamagerties.com

SEE AD ASHEVILLE PAGE 581

(W) Miles Motors RV Campground (RV SPACES)—(Buncombe) *From jct I-40 (exit 59) & Patton Cove Rd: Go 1/4 mi N on Patton Cove Rd, then W on Reece Dr. Enter at end.* FACILITIES: 60 sites, typical site width 24 ft, 60 full hkups, (30/50 amps), 8 pull-thrus, dump. Pets welcome. No tents. Open all yr. Big rigs welcome. Rate in 2010 $25 for 2 persons. Phone: (800)982-5315.

SWANSBORO—C-5

(S) CROATAN NATIONAL FOREST (Cedar Point Campground)—(carterette) *From town: Go 3-1/4 mi SE on Hwy-24, then 3/4 mi NE on Hwy-58, then 1/2 mi NW on Hwy-1114, then 3/4 mi SW on FR-153A.* FACILITIES: 40 sites, 22 ft max RV length, 40 E, 1 pull-thrus, tenting. RECREATION: boating, no motors, canoeing, ramp, river fishing. Partial handicap access. Open all yr. Phone: (252)638-5628.

Can you trust the Woodall's ratings? 25 evaluation teams have scoured North American campgrounds to provide you with accurate, up to date information & ratings. Find a rating you don't agree with? Send a letter or email our way, and we'll give it extra attention for 2012.

SYLVA—E-2

(SW) FT. TATHAM RV PARK (Carefree RV Resort)—(Jackson) *From jct US 23 & US 441: Go 6-1/2 mi S on US 441. Enter on L.*

◇◇◇FACILITIES: 90 sites, 86 full hkups, 4 W&E, (30/50 amps), mostly extd stay sites, WiFi Instant Internet at site, family camping, tenting, cabins, RV storage, dump, laundry, ice, picnic tables.

◇◇◇RECREATION: rec hall, equipped pavilion, swim pool, pond/stream fishing, bsktball, playground, shuffleboard court 2 shuffleboard courts, activities, horseshoes, v-ball.

Pets welcome, breed restrict. Open Apr 1 - Nov 1. Escort to site. Clubs welcome. Rate in 2010 $22-26 for 2 persons. MC/VISA. CCUSA 50% Discount. CCUSA reservations Required, CCUSA max stay 4 days, CCUSA disc. not avail F,Sa.

Phone: (828)586-6662
Address: 175 Tathams Creek Rd, Sylva, NC 28779
Lat/Lon: 35.29312/-83.26945
Email: fttathumrv@verizon.net
Web: www.carefreervresorts.com

SEE AD FRANKLIN PAGE 590

TABOR CITY—D-3

(E) Carrollwoods RV Park at Grapefull Sisters Vineyard (TOO NEW TO RATE)—(Columbus) *From jct US 701 Byp & Hwy 904: Go 10 mi E on Hwy 904, then 1 mi SE on Guide Rd, then 100 yds N on Ramsey Rd. Enter on R.* FACILITIES: 22 sites, typical site width 40 ft, 22 full hkups, (20/30/50 amps), 30 pull-thrus, WiFi Internet central location, family camping, tenting, laundry, picnic tables, grills, wood. RECREATION: pond fishing, playground, horseshoes. Pets welcome. Partial handicap access. Open all yr. Big rigs welcome. Rate in 2010 $30-55 per family. MC/VISA. Member ARVC, CARVC. CCUSA 50% Discount. CCUSA reservations Required, CCUSA max stay 3 days.

Phone: (910)653-5538
Address: 4903 Ramsey Ford Rd, Tabor City, NC 28463
Lat/Lon: 34.05873/-78.71135
Email: info@grapefullsistersvineyard.com
Web: www.carrollwoods.com

(SE) YOGI BEAR'S JELLYSTONE PARK AT DADDY JOE'S—(Columbus) *From jct Hwy 410 & US 701: Go 1/2 mi S on US 701, then 1/2 mi E on Richard Wright Rd. Enter on R.*

◇◇◇◇FACILITIES: 102 sites, typical site width 45 ft, 102 full hkups, (20/30/50 amps), some extd stay sites, 76 pull-thrus, WiFi Instant Internet at site, family camping, tenting, cabins, RV storage, dump, non-guest dump $, laundry, groceries, RV supplies, LP gas by weight/by meter, ice, picnic tables, patios, fire rings, grills, wood.

◇◇◇◇◇RECREATION: rec hall, pavilion, coin games, 2 swim pools, spray ground, boating, electric motors only, canoeing, kayaking, lake fishing, fishing supplies, bsktball, playground, shuffleboard court shuffleboard court, activities (wkends), horseshoes, sports field, hiking trails, v-ball.

Pets welcome. Partial handicap access. Open all yr. Big rigs welcome. Clubs welcome. Rate in 2010 $28-62 per family. MC/VISA/AMEX. Member ARVC, CARVC.

Phone: (910)653-2155
Address: 626 Richard Wright Rd, Tabor City, NC 28463
Lat/Lon: 34.15351/-78.85005
Email: yogi@taborcityjellystone.com
Web: www.taborcityjellystone.com

SEE AD MYRTLE BEACH, SC PAGE 706

TERRELL—B-1

(N) Wildlife Woods Campground—(Catawba) *From jct I-77 & Hwy 150 (exit 36): Go 10-1/2 mi W on Hwy 150. Enter on L.* ◇◇◇FACILITIES: 300 sites, typical site width 30 ft, 280 full hkups, 20 W&E, (20/30/50 amps), 80 pull-thrus, tenting. ◇◇◇RECREATION: swim pool, lake swim, boating, canoeing, ramp, dock, lake fishing. Pets welcome, breed restrict. Open all yr. Rate in 2010 $30-35 for 4 persons. Member ARVC, CARVC. Phone: (704)483-5611.

UNION GROVE—A-2

(E) Van Hoy Farms Family Campground—(Iredell) *From jct I-77 (exit 65) & Hwy-901: Go 200 yds E on Hwy 901, then 1/4 mi S on Jericho Rd. Enter on L.* ◇◇◇FACILITIES: 60 sites, typical site width 30 ft, 50

Van Hoy Farms Family Campground—Continued on next page

UNION GROVE—Continued
Van Hoy Farms Family Campground—Continued

full hkups, 10 W&E, (15/30/50 amps), 21 pull-thrus, family camping, tenting, dump, laundry. ◆◆RECREATION: swim pool. Pets welcome. Open all yr. Big rigs welcome. Rate in 2010 $30-35 for 2 persons. Member ARVC, CARVC. Phone: (704)539-5493.

VILAS—A-1

(E) VANDERPOOL CAMPGROUND—(Watauga) *From jct NC 321 & Hwy 421N: Go 1 mi NE on Hwy 421, then 100 yds S on Vanderpool Rd, then 50 ft S on Charlie Thompson Rd. Enter on R.*

◆◆◆FACILITIES: 42 sites, typical site width 27 ft, 37 full hkups, 5 W&E, (20/30/50 amps), mostly extd stay sites (summer), 10 pull-thrus, cable TV, WiFi Instant Internet at site, WiFi Internet central location, tenting, RV storage, dump, non-guest dump $, laundry, RV supplies, ice, picnic tables, patios, fire rings, wood.

RECREATION: pavilion.

Pets welcome. Open all yr. Big rigs welcome. Escort to site. Clubs welcome. Rate in 2010 $28 for 2 persons. MC/VISA/DISC.

Phone: (828)297-3486
Address: 180 Vanderpool Rd, Vilas, NC 28692
Lat/Lon: 36.26365/-81.75894
Email: gsnipas@vanderpoolcampground.com
Web: www.vanderpoolcampground.com

SEE AD BOONE PAGE 582

WADE—C-3

(E) FAYETTEVILLE KOA—(Cumberland) *From jct I-95 (exit 61) & Wade Stedman Rd: Go 1/2 mi E on Wade Stedman Rd. Enter on L.*

◆◆◆◆FACILITIES: 73 sites, typical site width 45 ft, 60 full hkups, 13 W&E, (30/50 amps), 60 pull-thrus, cable TV, WiFi Instant Internet at site, cable Internet central location, family camping, tenting, cabins, RV storage, dump, laundry, groceries, RV supplies, LP gas by weight/by meter, ice, picnic tables, grills, wood.

◆◆◆RECREATION: rec hall, swim pool, pond fishing, bsktball, playground, horseshoes, hiking trails, v-ball.

Pets welcome. Partial handicap access. Open all yr. Big rigs welcome. Escort to site. Clubs welcome. Rate in 2010 $33-57 for 2 persons. MC/VISA/DISC. Member ARVC, CARVC. KOA discount.

Phone: (910)484-5500
Address: 6250 Wade-Stedman Rd., Wade, NC 28395-0067
Lat/Lon: 35.15810/-78.70453
Email: fayettevillekoa@hotmail.com
Web: www.koa.com/where/nc/33123.htm

SEE AD FAYETTEVILLE PAGE 589 AND AD TRAVEL SECTION PAGE 569

WALNUT COVE—A-2

HANGING ROCK STATE PARK—(Stokes) *From town: Go 11 mi NW on Hwy-89, then 12 mi SW on Hwy-1001.* FACILITIES: 73 sites, 73 no hkups, tenting. RECREATION: lake swim, lake fishing. Partial handicap access. Open all yr. Phone: (336)593-8480.

WASHINGTON—B-5

✱ **(S) CRISP RV CENTER**—*From jct US-264 & US-17: Go 2 mi S on US-17. Enter on R.* SALES: travel trailers, park models, 5th wheels, toy hauler, Class C motorhomes, fold-down camping trailers, pre-owned unit sales. SERVICES: full-time mech, RV appliance repair, body work/collision repair, LP gas by weight/by meter, dump station, RV rentals, sells parts/accessories, installs hitches. Open all yr. MC/VISA/DISC/AMEX.

Phone: (252)946-0311
Address: 2042 Hwy 17 South, Chocowinity, NC 27817
Lat/Lon: 35.52656/-77.07929
Email: mailbox@crisprv.com
Web: www.crisprv.com

SEE AD THIS PAGE

(NW) Tranter's Creek Resort & Campground—(Pitt) *From jct US 17 & US 264: Go 1-1/2 mi W on US 264, then 1-1/2 mi S on Clarks Neck Rd. Enter on R.* ◆◆◆◆FACILITIES: 196 sites, typical site width 40 ft, 196 full hkups, (20/30/50 amps), 12 pull-thrus, tenting, laundry, ltd groc. ◆◆◆◆RECREATION: swim pool, boating, canoeing, ramp, dock, river fishing, playground. Pets welcome. Partial handicap access. Open all yr. Big rigs welcome. Rate in 2010 $31-43 for 2 persons. Member ARVC, CARVC.

WASHINGTON—Continued
Tranter's Creek Resort & Campground—Continued

Phone: (252)948-0850
Address: 6573 Clark's Neck Rd, Washington, NC 27889
Lat/Lon: 35.56549/-77.10278
Email: camp@tranterscreekresort.com
Web: www.tranterscreekresort.com

(S) Twin Lakes Camping Resort and Yacht Basin—(Beaufort) *From jct US 264 & US 17: Go 1-1/2 mi S on US 17, then 1-1/2 mi SE on Whichards Beach Rd. Enter on R.* ◆◆◆FACILITIES: 483 sites, typical site width 34 ft, 40 ft max RV length, 409 full hkups, 74 W&E, (30/50 amps), 55 pull-thrus, tenting, dump, laundry, ltd groc. ◆◆◆◆RECREATION: swim pool, boating, canoeing, ramp, dock, lake/river/pond fishing, playground. Pets welcome. Open all yr. Rate in 2010 $32-45 for 2 persons. Member ARVC, CARVC. Phone: (252)946-5700.

Reserve Online at Woodalls.com

WAYNESVILLE—E-2

(NW) Creekwood Farm RV Park—(Haywood) *From jct I-40 (exit 20) & US 276: Go 1 mi S on US 276. Enter on L.* ◆◆◆◆FACILITIES: 125 sites, typical site width 25 ft, 125 full hkups, (30/50 amps), 15 pull-thrus, tenting, laundry. ◆◆RECREATION: stream fishing. Pets welcome. Open all yr. Big rigs welcome. Rate in 2010 $35-45 for 2 persons. Phone: (828)926-7977.

(NW) Pride RV Resort—(Haywood) *From jct I-40 (exit 20) & US 276: Go 1-1/4 mi S on US 276. Enter on L.* ◆◆◆◆FACILITIES: 148 sites, 140 full hkups, 8 W&E, (20/30/50 amps), cable TV, WiFi Instant Internet at site, WiFi Internet central location, family camping, tenting, RV storage, dump, non-guest dump $, laundry, LP gas by weight/by meter, ice, picnic tables, wood. ◆◆◆◆RECREATION: rec hall, equipped pavilion, swim pool, pond/stream fishing, mini-golf, bsktball, playground, activities, horseshoes, v-ball. Pets welcome, breed restrict, size restrict, quantity restrict. Partial handicap access. Open Apr - Nov 15. Big rigs welcome. Rate in 2010 $38-48 for 2 persons. MC/VISA/DISC/AMEX. CCUSA 50% Discount. CCUSA reservations Recommended, CCUSA max stay 2 days, Cash only for CCUSA disc., CCUSA disc. not avail holidays. Not available Jun thru Oct. Nonaggressive pet breeds under 30 lbs welcome.

Phone: (800)926-8191
Address: 4394 Jonathan Creek Rd, Waynesville, NC 28785
Lat/Lon: 35.58344/-83.01240
Email: info@pridervresort.com
Web: pridervresort.com

Trails End RV Park—*From I-40 (exit 20) to 276: Go 3.1 mi, R on Hemphill, L on Shelton Cove Rd. Enter on L.* FACILITIES: 28 sites, 28 full hkups, (20/30/50 amps), cable TV, cable/WiFi Internet central location, dump, laundry, picnic tables, fire rings, grills. RECREATION: pavilion, river fishing, bsktball, horseshoes, v-ball. Pets welcome. No tents. Open all yr. Rate in 2010 $31-42 per vehicle. CCUSA 50% Discount. CCUSA reservations Accepted, Cash only for CCUSA disc., CCUSA disc. not avail S,Th, CCUSA disc. not avail F,Sa. Discount not available Memorial Day, or Labor Day. Not valid month of Jul, Aug & Oct.

Phone: (828)421-5295
Address: 219 Shelton Cove, Waynesville, NC 28785
Lat/Lon: 35.5569/-83.0407
Email: trailsend@cbvnol.com
Web: www.pngusa.net/trailsend/

(NW) Winngray Family Campground—(Haywood) *From jct I-40 (exit 20) & US 276: Go 3 mi S on US 276. Enter on R.* ◆◆◆FACILITIES: 150 sites, typical site width 25 ft, 122 full hkups, 18 W&E, (20/30/50

Visit Woodall's blog at blog.woodalls.com

WAYNESVILLE—Continued
Winngray Family Campground—Continued

amps), 10 no hkups, 35 pull-thrus, tenting, dump, laundry. ◆RECREATION: river swim, stream fishing. Pets welcome, size restrict. Open all yr. Rate in 2010 $33-36 for 2 persons. Member ARVC, CARVC. Phone: (828) 926-3170.

WHITTIER—E-1

TUCKASEEGEE R.V. RESORT (UNDER CONSTRUCTION)—(Jackson) *From jct US 74 & US 441: Go 2 mi SE on US 441/US 74. Enter on R.*

FACILITIES: 63 sites, typical site width 25 ft, 53 full hkups, (30/50 amps), 10 no hkups, 0 pull-thrus, WiFi Instant Internet at site, family camping, tenting, dump, picnic tables, patios.

Pets welcome. Open all yr. Big rigs welcome.

Phone: (828)497-3578
Address: 78 Wilmont Rd, Whittier, NC 28789
Lat/Lon: 35.40348/-83.31342
Web: tuckaseegeervresort.com

SEE AD CHEROKEE PAGE 586

WILKESBORO—A-1

(W) BANDIT'S ROOST PARK (COE-W. Kerr Scott Reservoir)—(Wilkes) *From jct US-421 & Hwy-268: Go 5 mi W on Hwy-268, then 1/2 mi on RPR-1141.* FACILITIES: 100 sites, 30 ft max RV length, 83 W&E, (30 amps), 17 no hkups, 10 pull-thrus, tenting, dump, laundry. RECREATION: lake swim, boating, ramp, dock, lake/river fishing, playground. Partial handicap access. Open Apr 1 - Oct 31. Phone: (336)921-3190.

(W) WARRIOR CREEK PARK (COE-W. Kerr Scott Reservoir)—(Wilkes) *From jct US-421 & Hwy-268: Go 7-1/2 mi W on Hwy-268.* FACILITIES: 54 sites, 30 ft max RV length, 34 W&E, (30 amps), 20 no hkups, 4 pull-thrus, tenting, dump. RECREATION: lake swim, boating, lake fishing, playground. Partial handicap access. Open Apr 15 - Oct 15. Phone: (336)921-2177.

WILLIAMSTON—B-5

(S) GREEN ACRES FAMILY CAMPGROUND—(Martin) *From jct US 64/US 13 (exit 514) and US 17: Go 3 mi S on US 17, then 1 mi W on Rodgers School Rd. Enter on R.*

◆◆FACILITIES: 175 sites, typical site width 20 ft, 40 ft max RV length, 89 full hkups, 75 W&E, (20/30/50 amps), 50 amps ($), 11 no hkups, some extd stay sites, 155 pull-thrus, WiFi Instant Internet at site, WiFi Internet central location, family camping, tenting, cabins, RV storage, dump, non-guest dump $, laundry, ltd groc, RV supplies, LP gas by weight/by meter, ice, picnic tables, fire rings, wood.

◆◆◆◆RECREATION: rec hall, rec room/area, equipped pavilion, coin games, 2 swim pools, no motors, canoeing, kayaking, 3 canoe/2 kayak/5 pedal boat rentals, pond fishing, fishing supplies, mini-golf, ($), bsktball, playground, shuffleboard court shuffleboard court, activities (wkends), tennis, horseshoes, sports field, v-ball.

Pets welcome. Open all yr. Clubs welcome. Rate in 2010 $25-31 for 2 persons. MC/VISA/DISC/AMEX. Member ARVC, CARVC.

Phone: (252)792-3939
Address: 1679 Green Acres Rd, Williamston, NC 27892
Lat/Lon: 35.78113/-77.08739
Email: bgreene@embarqmail.com
Web: greenacresnc.com

SEE AD THIS PAGE

WILMINGTON—D-4

(W) **BATTLESHIP NORTH CAROLINA**—*On the west side of the Wilmington Bridge from jct US 17, US 74, US 76 & US 421: Go 1/2 mi N on US 421 North. Enter on R.* A WW II battleship museum and memorial. Visitors may take a self-guided tour. Located on the Cape Fear River across from historic downtown Wilmington. Parking for busses and RVs. No overnight camping. A National Historic Landmark. Open all yr. 7 days a wk; 8am-8pm Memorial Day weekend to Labor Day & 8am-5pm Labor Day to Memorial Day. MC/VISA.

Text 107884 to (440)725-8687 to see our Visual Tour.

Phone: (910)251-5797
Address: Eagle Island, Wilmington, NC 28402
Lat/Lon: 34.23543/-77.95336
Email: leads@battleshipnc.com
Web: www.battleshipnc.com

SEE AD DISCOVER SECTION PAGE 43

Wilmington-KOA—(New Hanover) *From jct I-40 (exit 416) & Hwy 17: Go 4-3/4 mi N on Hwy 17, then 2-1/2 mi S on Bus 17 S. Enter on R.* ◇◇◇◇FACILITIES: 81 sites, typical site width 30 ft, 47 full hkups, 22 W&E, (30/50 amps), 12 no hkups, 46 pull-thrus, tenting, dump, laundry, ltd groc. ◇◇◇RECREATION: swim pool, playground. Pets welcome, breed restrict. Open all yr. Big rigs welcome. Rate in 2010 $30-85 per vehicle. Member ARVC, CARVC. Phone: (888)562-5699. KOA discount.

The Biltmore Estate in Asheville is America's largest home, and includes a 255-room chateau, an award-winning winery and extensive gardens.

Woodall's Tip... If you're ever lost in the forest, you can tell your direction from the trees. The bark will be thicker on the north side of trees.

TRAVEL SECTION

Ohio

READER SERVICE INFO

The following businesses have placed an ad in the Ohio Travel Section. To receive free information, enter their Reader Service number on the Reader Service Card opposite page 48/Discover Section in the front of this directory:

Advertiser	RS#
Cedar Point Camper Village/Lighthouse Point	2807
Ohio Campground Owners Assoc.	411
Ohio Department of Natural Resources	4277
RV Wholesalers	3779

TIME ZONE

Ohio is in the Eastern Time Zone.

TOPOGRAPHY

The northern portion of Ohio, which is part of the Great Lakes Basin, is flat. The southern and eastern portions of the state bordering the Ohio River are hilly. There are 50,000 lakes, ponds and reservoirs in the state, as well as over seven million acres of forests.

TEMPERATURE

Spring temperatures in Ohio range from 37° – 70°F in the northeast and 41° – 72°F in the southwest. Summer is warm and sunny, with most areas seeing 90°F temperatures for at least a few days. Fall is the sunniest season, resulting in some of most beautiful fall foliage to be found; temperatures range from 42° – 71°F. Winters can be cold at times ranging from 17° – 43°F, with plenty of snow in northern Ohio near Lake Erie for travelers looking for outdoor winter fun.

TRAVEL & TOURISM INFO

State Agency:

Ohio Tourism Division
77 S. High St., 29th Floor
Columbus, OH 43215
(800/BUCKEYE)
www.DiscoverOhio.com

Regional Agencies:

Ashland Area CVB
211 Claremont Ave.
Ashland, OH 44805
(877/581-2345, Ext. 1003)
www.visitashlandohio.com

Belmont County TC
Ohio Valley Mall
Unit 485
67800 Mall Ring Road
St. Clairsville, OH 43950
(800/356-5082)
www.belmontcountytourism.org

Cincinnati USA Regional Tourism Network
50 E. Rivercenter Blvd., Ste. 810
Covington, KY 41011
(859/581-2260)
www.cincinnatiusa.com

Delaware County CVB
44 E. Winter St.
Delaware, OH 43015
(888/335-6446)
www.visitdelohio.com

Dublin CVB
9 S. High St.
Dublin, OH 43017

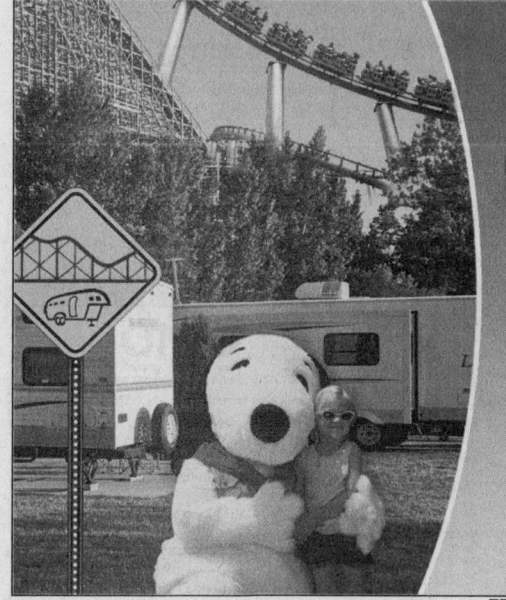

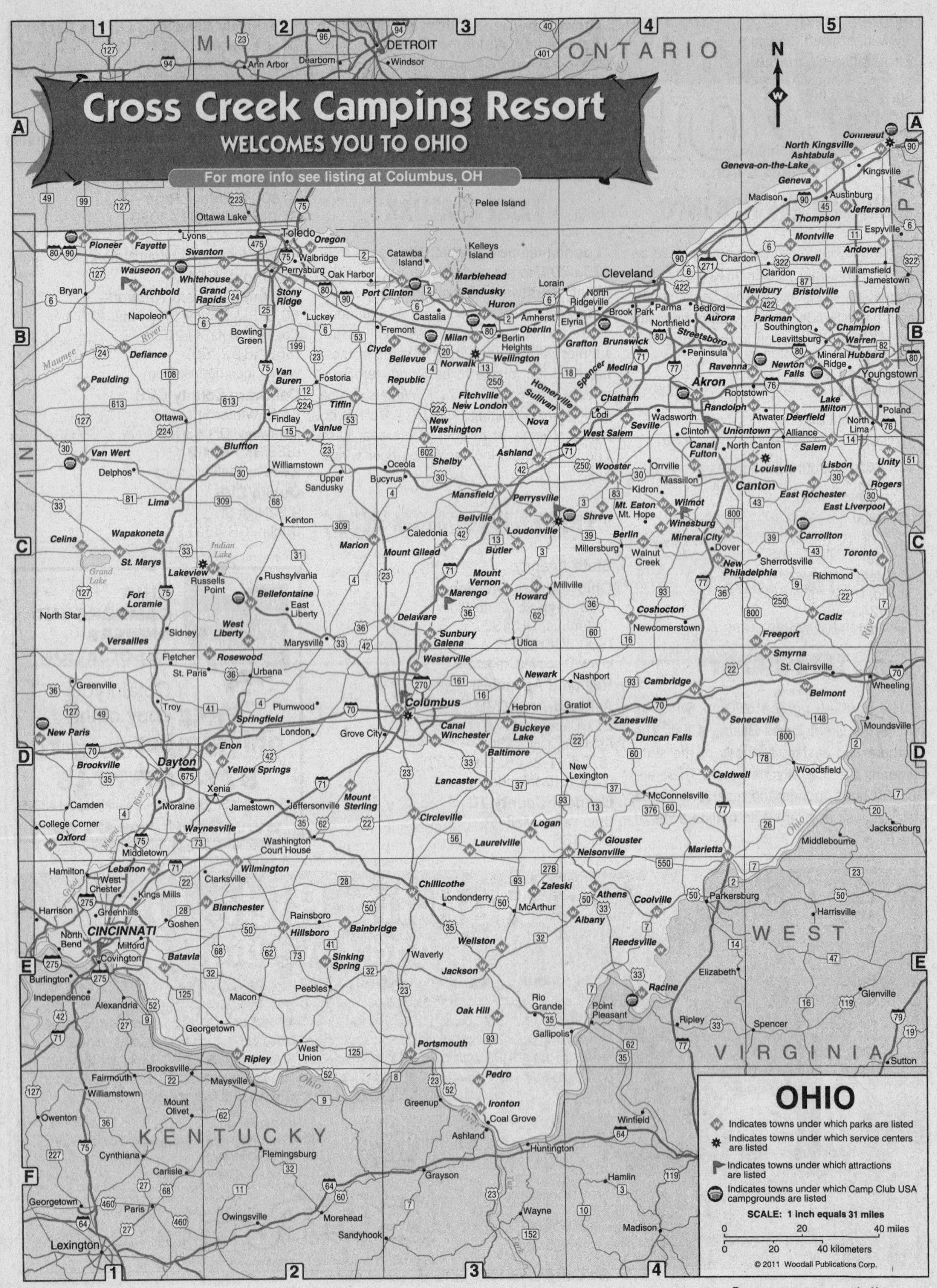

Cross Creek Camping Resort
WELCOMES YOU TO OHIO
For more info see listing at Columbus, OH
ONTARIO
DETROIT
Windsor
Ann Arbor
Dearborn
Toledo
Cleveland
Akron
Canton
Youngstown
Columbus
Dayton
CINCINNATI
Pelee Island
WEST
VIRGINIA
KENTUCKY
OHIO
Indicates towns under which parks are listed
Indicates towns under which service centers are listed
Indicates towns under which attractions are listed
Indicates towns under which Camp Club USA campgrounds are listed
SCALE: 1 inch equals 31 miles
0 20 40 miles
0 20 40 kilometers
© 2011 Woodall Publications Corp.

(800/245-8387)
www.irishisanattitude.com

Experience Columbus
277 W. Nationwide Blvd.
Suite 125
Columbus, OH 43215
(866/397-2657)
www.experiencecolumbus.com

Fairfield Co. Visitors & Convention Bureau
124 W. Main St.
Lancaster, OH 43130
(800/626-1296)
www.visitfairfieldcounty.org

Fremont/Sandusky Co. CVB
712 North Street, Suite 102
Fremont, OH 43420
(800/255-8070)
www.lakeeriesfavoriteneighbor.com

Gahanna CVB
181 Granville ST, Ste. 200
Gahanna, OH 43230
(614/418-9122)
www.visitgahanna.org

Greater Springfield CVB
20 S. Limestone St., Suite 100
Springfield, OH 45502
(800/803-1553)
www.visitspringfieldohio.com

Greater Toledo CVB
401 Jefferson Ave.
Toledo, OH 43604
(800/243-4667)
www.dotoledo.org/gtcvb/

Grove City Area Visitors & Convention Bureau and Welcome Center
3378 Park St.
Grove City, OH 43123
(800/539-0405 or 614/539-8747)
www.visitgrovecityoh.com

Licking County CVB and Welcome Center
455 Hebron Road (State Route 79)
Heath, OH 43056
(800/589-8224)
www.lccvb.com

Loudonville/Mohican CVB
131 W. Main St.
Loudonville, OH 44842
(877/266-4422)
www.loudonville-mohican.com

Mansfield/Richland County CVB
124 N. Main St.
Mansfield, OH 44902
(800/642-8282)
www.mansfieldtourism.com

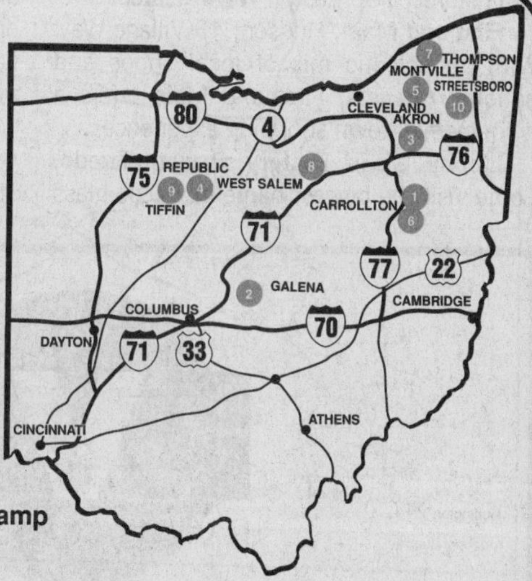

Marion Area Convention & Visitors Bureau and Welcome Center
1713 Marion-Mt. Gilead Rd., Suite 110
Marion, OH 43302
(800/371-6688)
www.visitmarionohio.com

Pickaway County Visitors Bureau
325 W. Main St.
Circleville, OH 43113
(888/770-PICK)
www.pickaway.com

Positively Cleveland Visitors Center
The Highbee Bldg
100 Public Sq, Ste. 100
Cleveland, OH 44113
(800/321-1004)
www.positivelycleveland.com

Reynoldsburg Visitors and Community Activities Bureau
7374 E. Main St.
Reynoldsburg, OH 43068
(614/866-4888)
www.visitreynoldsburg.com

Sandusky/Erie County VCB
4424 Milan Road, Suite A
Sandusky, OH 44870
(800/255-3743)
www.shoresandislands.com

Union Co. CVB & Welcome Center
227 E. 5th St.
Marysville, OH 43040
(937/642-6279)
www.unioncountycvb.com

Westerville CVB & Visitor Information Center
20 W. Main St.
Westerville, OH 43081
(800/824-8461)
www.visitwesterville.org

CVB of Worthington
P.O. Box 225
579 High Street
Worthington, OH 43085
(800/871-3070)
www.visitworthingtonohio.com

Local Agencies:

For information on local areas, contact the Chamber of Commerce or Tourism Bureau for the locality you are interested in.

RECREATIONAL INFO

Fishing & Hunting: Ohio Dept. of Natural Resources, Wildlife Division, 2045 Morse Road Building G, Columbus, OH 43229 (614/265-6300 or 800/945-3543). www.ohiodnr.com/wildlife

Winery Tours & Tastings: For brochures and maps, contact the Ohio Wine Producers Assn., 33 Tegam Way, Geneva, OH 44041 (800/227-6972 or 440/466-4417). www.ohiowines.org

SHOPPING

Aurora Premium Outlets, Aurora. Early American-styled village with 70 upscale outlet stores with savings of 25% to 65%. On Route 43.

Chapel Hill Mall, Akron. Shop at more than 80 department and specialty stores, then take a ride on the full-size carousel. 2000 Brittain Rd., Akron, OH 44310

The Holmes County Flea Market, 4568 State Route 39, Millersburg, OH, 44654 330/893-0900

Easton Town Center, Columbus. Indoor and outdoor entertainment, restaurants and retail stores. 160 Easton Town Center.

First and Main, Hudson, 43 Village Way. With an eclectic mix of local shops and national retailers, First and Main offers a unique small-town shopping experience.

Libbey Glass Factory Outlet, Toledo. Come visit the biggest name in Toledo glass and get big savings on thousands of pieces of glassware at their factory outlet. 205 S. Erie St., Toledo, OH (419/727-2374 or 888/794-8469). www.libbey.com.

Prime Outlets, Jeffersonville I & II. You'll find great bargains at more than 160 manufacturer outlet stores. Located off I-71 at Exits 65 & 69.

Lodi Station Outlets, Burbank. Northeast Ohio's largest outlet center featuring over 90 of the nation's top name brand manufacturer's outlet stores. I-71 & Route 83, Exit 204.

DESTINATIONS

They say that Ohio is just too much fun for one day, so why not make a vacation of it? Travelers can visit world-class museums, and wineries, blow their minds on record setting roller coasters, or expand it at some of the best hands-on science museums in the country. From prehistoric and Native American history, to the Underground Railroad - just take a look around and discover just how much fun Ohio can be!

NORTHWEST

Much of this region was the Great Black Swamp until the mud-19th century, when the swamp was drained, but travelers can still see the remaining portions in Pearson Metropark. Toledo has a history in shipping, and visitors can relive a piece of that history on the S.S. Willis B. Boyer, a former Great Lakes freightliner that has been transformed into a museum.

AuGlaize Village, Defiance. The village consists of seventeen restored and reconstructed buildings, typical of rural northwestern Ohio in the early 19th century. See craft demonstrations, cider and cane mills, a broom factory, and blacksmith shop.

Miami & Erie Canal Restoration. Take a trip back to the mid 1800s and see a working mule-drawn canal boat, canal lock and historic water-powered saw and grain mill.

Sauder Village. Experience life on a farm at the turn of the last century on this working farm in Ohio's fertile northwest. Your visit will include hands-on learning activities.

West Liberty. Visit the beautiful countryside that is home to two Piatt castles. In the 1820s, the U.S. Government had taken possession of the Shawnee territory called Mac-A-Creek. Shortly thereafter, the Piatt family moved to the area. Their two children built their homes there—Abram Sanders Piatt built **Mac-A-Chee Castle** atop a hill that offers a breathtaking view of the surrounding landscape. His brother, Donn Piatt, built **Mac-O-Chee Castle,** nestled on a hillside. Ohio Caverns, a 35-acre park, is home to colored walls and milk-white stalactites and stalagmites. A level, concrete path weaves through rooms filled with beautiful formations.

Zane Shawnee Caverns, Bellefontaine. Tour guides lead visitors through caverns famous for their sparkling cave "pearls." Descend 132 ft. below the ground and experience pure air while viewing nature's greatest treasures.

NORTH CENTRAL

African Safari Wildlife Park, Port Clinton. Visitors can get a close-up view of freely roaming wild animals through a self-guided driving tour. Camel and pony rides and educational programs are also available.

Cedar Point, Sandusky. This amazing amusement park has more than 70 rides, including more roller coasters than any other place on earth, four theaters, a water park, a beach, a marina, a campground and more.

Edison Birthplace, Milan. The house where Thomas Edison was born is now a museum, offering guided tours of seven furnished rooms containing mementos from the inventor's career.

Grand Rapids. A steady pace of renovation and restoration has caused this quaint river town to blossom. During spring's high-water season, visitors seek higher ground and watch the mighty Maumee rage over the rapids that give the town its name.

Inland Seas Maritime Museum, Vermilion. The collection includes ship models, marine relics, paintings and photographs relating to the history of the Great Lakes.

Lagoon Deer Park, Sandusky. Walk with and hand-feed more than 200 exotic animals. Each summer dozens of baby animals are born. Fish in one of the on-site lakes stocked with bullheads, channel cat, bass, crappies and trout.

Mad River & NKP Railroad Society Museum, Bellevue. Rail fans delight in a railroad yard loaded with engines, passenger cars, freight cars and cabooses. Also on-site are a station house and a museum filled with railroad memorabilia. While in Bellevue, take a trip back in time at **Historic Lyme Village**, a restored collection of buildings spanning 1830-1930. Take a guided tour through the Victorian Wright Mansion, one room school, log church, Seymour house, blacksmith shop, woodworking shop and more.

Marblehead Lighthouse State Park is the oldest continuously operating lighthouse on the Great Lakes. Open for tours.

Toledo. There's lots of family entertainment in Toledo, including the following attractions:

Toledo Glass Pavilion. Opened in 2006, the postmodern Glass Pavilion is the new home of the Toledo Museum of Art's world-renowned glass collection, featuring more than 5,000 works of art.

Maumee Bay State Park, located southeast of Toledo, provides acres of swimming, boating, fishing and hiking.

Toledo Botanical Garden. Stroll through picturesque gardens and meadows alive with dazzling colors and fragrances.

Toledo Zoo. One of the nation's best family-friendly zoos. See the Kingdom of the Apes, the Hippoquarium, the renovated Aviary and the Primate Forest.

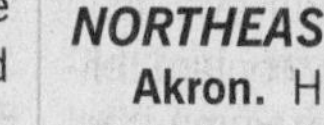

NORTHEAST

Akron. Highlights include a passenger steam train ride at Cuyahoga Valley National Park, a 19th-century re-created **Hale Farm & Village**, interactive exhibits at the **Inventure Place**, the **National Inventors Hall of Fame, Blossom Music Center**, **Akron Zoo** and the **Stan Hywet Hall and Gardens.** Take a Chocolate Factory tour in nearby North Canton. The **Akron Art Museum** has just tripled its space with a new addition featuring paintings, sculpture and photography exhibits.

Ashtabula County, in Ohio's highest-yielding wine region, has dozens of boutique vintners who offer cellar tours. The county also is home to the state's largest concentration of covered bridges.

Aurora. Located southeast of Cleveland, Aurora has a variety of antique shops and Ohio's oldest and largest flea market.

Cleveland. Situated on Lake Erie, the city's attractions include the **Cleveland Museum of Art; Great Lakes Science Center, Playhouse Square; Crawford Auto-Aviation Museum,** displaying nearly 200 various types of vehicles; **Metroparks Zoo** features a unique two-acre rainforest; the **Museum of Natural History,** where you'll learn all about the world around you—past and present; the hands-on **Health Museum**; and the glass-domed **Arcade**, America's first indoor shopping center. At the **Rock and Roll Hall of Fame and Museum** you can learn about the development of rock 'n' roll.

Wildwater Kingdom. Enjoy the thrilling coasters and water park in Aurora.

Kirtland. Holden Arboretum is one of the largest and one of the most diverse arboretums in the United States. About 20 miles of interpretive trails wind through woods and natural areas on the 3,100 acres of land.

Shaker Historical Museum, Shaker Heights. This religious sect that once had four settlements in Ohio is portrayed through extensive collections of furniture, clothing, tools and rare books.

Steamship William G. Mather Museum. Visit northeast Ohio's only floating maritime museum housed in a 618-foot restored Great Lakes freighter.

Terminal Tower. This 57-story building is the tallest building in Ohio and is the distinctive architectural symbol of Cleveland. In 1990 **The Avenue** opened. It is a three-level marble, brass and glass complex of entertainment, dining and retail establishments.

University Circle, located four miles east of downtown Cleveland, features the country's largest concentration of cultural arts and educational institutions within one square mile.

EAST CENTRAL

Amish Country locations are south of Cleveland in Holmes, Wayne, Tuscarawas,

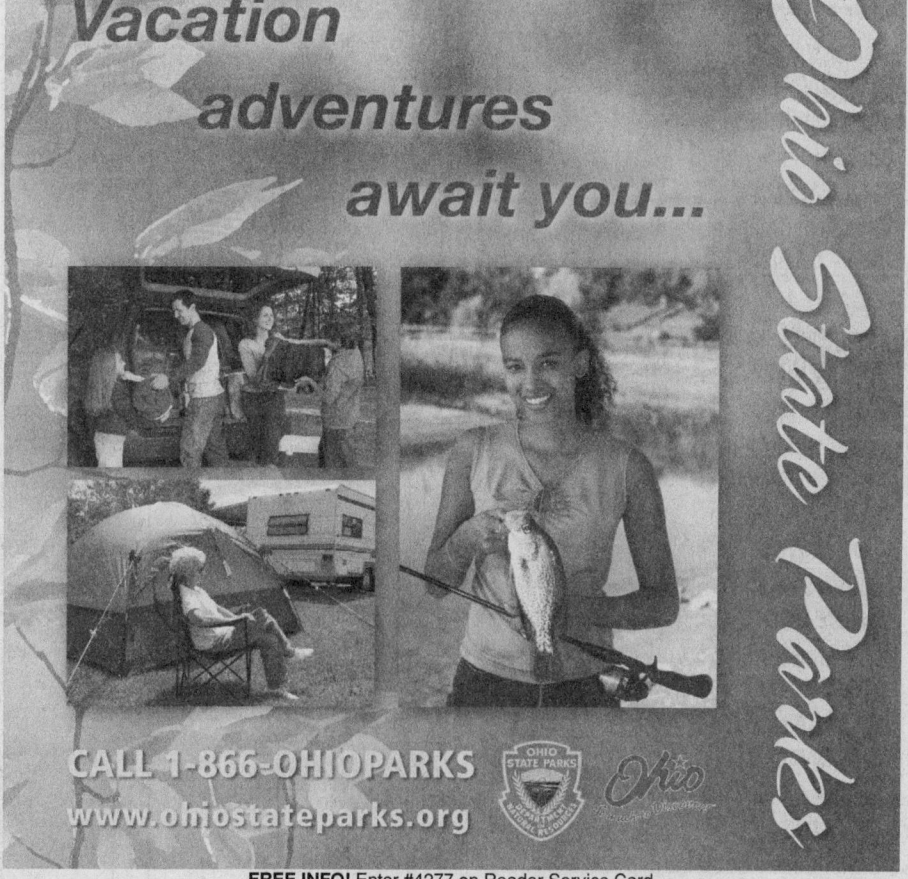

Coshocton, Stark, Geauga and Madison counties. Please respect the privacy and religion of the Amish people by refraining from taking pictures.

Berlin. Tour historical homes and explore quaint side streets. Try free samples of over 50 Amish cheeses and purchase smoked Amish meats and homemade delights. **Wendell August Forge** (creators of unique hand-crafted metal giftware) offers museum and production tours, a gift shop and a mini-theater. View the world's largest Amish buggy. At the **Amish Farm & Home**, you can tour the Miller residence and the Dawdy Hause, view a slide presentation and take a buggy ride. The **Behalt-Mennonite Information Center** offers books on Amish and Mennonite culture. View the mural depicting Amish, Mennonite and Hutterite history. **Kauffman's Country Baker of Bunker Hill Village** uses an old-fashioned stone hearth oven. Breakfast is served seven days a week. Visit **Schrock's Amish Farm & Home.** Take a buggy ride and a guided tour of an Amish home, where you can witness their customs and lifestyles. **'Tis the Season** is a year-round Christmas shop that displays over 100 decorated trees and hundreds of ornaments and lights.

Canal Fulton, just northwest of Canton. Journey back 200 years to taste the foods of the time, see the master craftsmen demonstrate their skills and enjoy the entertainment of pioneer America at the Yankee Peddler Festival that takes place for three weekends in September.

Canton. Located in the middle of Stark County, Canton is home to the **Pro Football Hall of Fame.** This four-building complex offers a theater showing football films; a research library; twin enshrinement halls; and special exhibition areas that include tapes, television monitors and slide machines. At **The First Ladies National Historic Site,** you can witness the accomplishments of our presidents' wives. If you're into historic automobiles, check out the **Canton Classic Car Museum** with its displays of vintage cars. Travel 10 miles south of Canton and you'll discover **Zoar Village.** Spend an afternoon browsing through a reconstructed wagon shop, blacksmith shop, tin shop, gardens, greenhouse, **Bimeler Museum** and restored bakery.

McKinley Museum features the world's largest collection of William McKinley memorabilia. Also on-site is **Discover World**—an interactive children's science center with toys, dolls and a model HO train layout; a life-size historical town; a planetarium; and the **McKinley National Memorial.**

Coshocton. Monticello II Canal Boat. Travel the Ohio and Erie Canals in a replica of the boats used in the 1800s.

Roscoe Village. This restored canal town on the former Ohio and Erie Canal offers horse-drawn trolley and canal boat rides, shopping at quaint shops, dining and self-guided tours.

Kidron. Tucked away on a country road north of US 250 and south of US 30 in Wayne County, Kidron's country charm beckons. Find just what you're looking for at Lehman's. This huge general store has served the Amish community for two generations. In stock are cast-iron cookware, unusual hand tools, non-electric lighting and Ohio's largest selection of wood stoves. You'll also find a **Lehman's** in the town of Kidron, located just north of Berlin. Lehmans at Mt. Hope is a leading Amish supplier of crocks, kegs, kitchen supplies and oil lamps.

Museum of Ceramics, East Liverpool. This elegant, marble-floored building contains ceramic collections, dioramas of turn-of-the-century pottery and a nine-projector slide show on the pottery industry. Antique malls and pottery outlet shops are also in town. Nearby, **Beaver Creek State Park** offers a pioneer village and a nationally designated wild and scenic river.

Trumpet in the Land Outdoor Drama, New Philadelphia. Enjoy theater under the stars! Humor, drama, music and dance portray the story of a missionary and Native Americans caught in the conflict of the American Revolution.

Warther's, Dover. World's master carver Ernest Warther presents an amazing display of hand-carved (walnut, ebony, ivory and pearl) wonders. The display includes the history of steam locomotives and trains.

Sugarcreek. A part of Ohio's Amish Country, this village of 4,000 residents welcomes over 100,000 people the first weekend in October for the Ohio Swiss Festival. While there, visit **Swiss Village Quilts & Crafts,** where quilts of high quality are made, along with wall hangings, pillows and wood items. There are many unique items, including toys for children 1 to 100.

Walnut Creek. Come with a hearty appetite to **Der Dutchman Restaurant.** Their family style dinners are sure to fill even the hungriest guest. After you've eaten, browse through three floors of elegant gifts at **Carlisle House Gifts,** located in a beautiful Victorian house.

BUSINESSES OFFERING

	Things to See & Do	RV Sales	RV Service
ARCHBOLD			
Sauder Village	⚑		
CINCINNATI			
Hamilton County Park District	⚑		
Hickey's Barber Shop	⚑		
COLUMBUS			
Ohio Department of Natural Resources (Div. of Parks & Rec.)		⚑	
Post's Traveland		🚌	⚙
CONNEAUT			
Evergreen Lake RV Sales		🚌	⚙
LAKEVIEW			
RV Wholesalers		🚌	⚙
LOUDONVILLE			
Mohican Adventures Canoe & Fun Center	⚑		
Mohican RV Center		🚌	⚙
LOUISVILLE			
Cutty's Sunset RV Service			⚙
MARENGO			
Ole Farmstead Inn	⚑		
NORWALK			
Hy-Tek Truck & Auto Center, LTD			⚙
UNIONTOWN			
Clearwater Park	⚑		
WILMOT			
Baylor Beach Water Park	⚑		

QUICK REFERENCE CHART FOR WOODALL'S FEATURED PARKS

	Green Friendly	RV Lots for Sale	Park Models-Onsite Ownership	Park Membership for Sale	Big Rigs Welcome	Internet Friendly	Pets Welcome
AKRON							
Cherokee Park Campground						●	■
Countryside Campground						●	■
ARCHBOLD							
Sauder Village Campground					▲	●	■
ASHLAND							
Hickory Lakes Campground						●	■
BELLEFONTAINE							
Back Forty Ltd						●	■
BELLEVUE							
Lazy J RV Resort	🍃					●	■
BERLIN							
Scenic Hills RV Park					▲	●	■
BROOKVILLE							
KOA-Dayton Tall Timbers Resort					▲	●	■
BRUNSWICK							
Willow Lake Park Inc.						●	■
BUCKEYE LAKE							
Buckeye Lake/Columbus East KOA Kamping Resort					▲	●	■
CAMBRIDGE							
Spring Valley Campground					▲	●	■
CANAL FULTON							
Clay's Park Resort						●	■
CANTON							
KOA-Bear Creek Resort Ranch					▲	●	■
CARROLLTON							
ABC Country Camping & Cabins							■
Cozy Ridge Campground							■
CELINA							
Kozy Kamp Ground							■
CHILLICOTHE							
Sun Valley Campground	🍃				▲		■
CINCINNATI							
Hidden Valley Mobile Home Park					▲		■
Indian Springs Campground					▲	●	■
Winton Woods Campground (Hamilton County Park)					▲	●	■
CLYDE							
Leafy Oaks Campground						●	■
COLUMBUS							
Alton RV Park					▲	●	■
Cross Creek Camping Resort					▲	●	■
CONNEAUT							
Evergreen Lake Park						●	■

Green Friendly 🍃; RV Lots for Sale ✖; Park Models/Onsite Onwership ✱; Park Memberships for Sale ✔; Big Rigs Welcome ▲; Internet Friendly ●; Internet Friendly-WiFi ●; Pets Welcome ■

QUICK REFERENCE CHART FOR WOODALL'S FEATURED PARKS

	Green Friendly	RV Lots for Sale	Park Models-Onsite Ownership	Park Membership for Sale	Big Rigs Welcome	Internet Friendly	Pets Welcome
DEERFIELD							
Philabaun's Hidden Cove Resort						●	■
ENON							
Enon Beach Campground					▲	●	■
GALENA							
Berkshire Lake Campgrounds					▲	●	■
GRAFTON							
American Wilderness Campground					▲	●	■
HOMERVILLE							
Wild Wood Lakes Campground						●	■
HURON							
Huron River Valley Campground & Marina							■
JEFFERSON							
Millbrook Outdoor Resort (Formerly Wagon Trail Resort)						●	■
LOGAN							
Hocking Hills KOA	🍃				▲	●	■
LOUDONVILLE							
Camp Toodik Family Campground Cabins & Canoeing						●	■
Mohican Adventures Camp and Cabins					▲	●	■
Mohican Reservation Campgrounds and Canoeing						●	■
LOUISVILLE							
Cutty's Sunset Camping Resort						●	■
MARBLEHEAD							
Surf Motel & RV Campground						●	■
MARENGO							
Cardinal Center Campground					▲	●	■
MARION							
Hickory Grove Lake Campground						⬤	■
MONTVILLE							
Country Lakes Family Campground							■
MOUNT GILEAD							
Dogwood Valley Camping Resort						●	■
MOUNT VERNON							
Rustic Knolls Campground					▲	●	■
MT. EATON							
Evergreen Park RV Resort	🍃				▲	●	■
NEW PARIS							
Natural Springs Resort					▲	●	■
NEW PHILADELPHIA							
Wood's Tall Timber Lake Resort					▲		■
NEWARK							
Lazy River at Granville	🍃				▲	●	■
PORT CLINTON							
Cedarlane RV Park	🍃					●	■

Green Friendly 🍃; RV Lots for Sale ✖; Park Models/Onsite Onwership ✱; Park Memberships for Sale ✔; Big Rigs Welcome ▲; Internet Friendly ⬤; Internet Friendly-WiFi ●; Pets Welcome ■

QUICK REFERENCE CHART FOR WOODALL'S FEATURED PARKS

	Green Friendly	RV Lots for Sale	Park Models-Onsite Ownership	Park Membership for Sale	Big Rigs Welcome	Internet Friendly	Pets Welcome
PORTSMOUTH							
Wolford's Landing Campground						●	■
RAVENNA							
Country Acres Campground					▲	●	■
REPUBLIC							
Clinton Lake Camping							■
SANDUSKY							
Cedar Point Camper Village/Lighthouse Point					▲		■
Sandusky Bayshore KOA					▲	●	■
SEVILLE							
Maple Lakes Recreational Park					▲	●	■
SHELBY							
Shelby/Mansfield KOA (Wagon Wheel Campground)					▲	●	■
SPRINGFIELD							
Tomorrow's Stars RV Resort				✔			■
STREETSBORO							
Streetsboro/Cleveland SE KOA (Mar-Lynn lake Park)					▲	●	■
Woodside Lake Park					▲	●	■
THOMPSON							
Heritage Hills Family Campground						●	■
TIFFIN							
Walnut Grove Campground							■
TORONTO							
Austin Lake Park and Campground	🍃				▲	●	■
UNIONTOWN							
Clearwater Park Camping Resort					▲	●	■
VAN BUREN							
Findlay/Van Buren KOA	🍃				▲	●	■
VANLUE							
Heritage Springs Campground							■
WAPAKONETA							
Wapakoneta/Lima South - KOA	🍃				▲	●	■
WEST SALEM							
Town & Country Camp Resort					▲	●	■
WILMINGTON							
Beechwood Acres Camping Resort					▲	●	■
WILMOT							
Baylor Beach Park					▲	●	■
WINESBURG							
Amish Country Campsites						●	■
ZANESVILLE							
Wolfies Campground					▲	●	■

Green Friendly 🍃; RV Lots for Sale ✖; Park Models/Onsite Onwership ✱; Park Memberships for Sale ✔; Big Rigs Welcome ▲; Internet Friendly ●; Internet Friendly-WiFi ●; Pets Welcome ■

Wilmot. If you're looking for handmade furniture to grace your home, look no further than the **Amish Door**. Also on-site is a restaurant specializing in Amish kitchen cooking. Shop for antiques at six nearby gift shops.

CENTRAL

Columbus. Ohio's state capital features the **Ohio Historical Center, Ohio Village, Expositions Center, German Village, Center of Science & Industry, Wyandot Lake Adventure Park, COSI (Center for Science and Industry)** and the **Park of Roses** containing over 36,000 roses. Other Columbus highlights include the **Wexner Center for the Arts** and the **Franklin Park Conservatory**. The **Columbus Zoo & Aquarium** has just opened Asia Quest, an outdoor, ancient Asia city complete with sights and sounds of a Himalayan village. Includes interactive exhibits and, of course, the animals of Asia – sun bears, pheasants, red pandas and a Siberian tiger.

The **Columbus Museum of Art** features Eye Spy: Adventures in Art—an interactive exhibition for kids and their families.

Motorcycle Hall of Fame Museum. Explore the Hall of Fame Gallery, showcasing motorcycles from 1924 to the present.

Anheuser-Busch Brewery Tour. Enjoy a complimentary tour of the brewery and uncover the special ingredients that go into the family of fine beers. Learn about the natural brewing process that has been used for more than a century. Also featured is a gift shop filled with unique merchandise.

Ohio Village is a re-created 19th-century community with costumed "townspeople" who explain period customs and demonstrate craftsmanship common over a century ago. Summer weekends often include musical entertainment and 19th-century-style baseball games.

Ohio Railway Museum. View a 30-piece collection of equipment, including electric inter-urban and street railway cars.

Olentangy Indian Caverns. Experience Native American lore and the awesome beauties of this natural wonderland. The temperature in the caverns is a constant 54 degrees and 30-minute tours are available April through October. Also on-site are a snack bar, picnic grounds, playground, mini-golf and campground with a swimming pool.

Granville. This quiet New England-style village is well known for the hospitality of its local inns and the architecture of its buildings.

Grove City. Just minutes from downtown Columbus, the Grove City area has a lot to offer. **Beulah Park Jockey Club**, Ohio's original "home" of Thoroughbred racing, offers an afternoon of fun at the races; The **Gardens at Gantz Farm** are not only among the region's most educational community gardens, but also one of the most beautiful. **Grove City Town Center** offers the charm of an early era from its gas streetlights to its distinctive shops, offering everything from gourmet coffee to custom jewelry. Fall and summer are highlighted by Grove City's Community Festivals and Markets, held every Saturday morning from mid-July to mid-September.

Leatherlips Monument, Dublin. This stone marker commemorates the site of the Wyandot Native American chief's execution in 1810. Nearby are the **Olentangy Indian Caverns.**

Mansfield. Legendary John "Johnny Appleseed" Chapman planted hundreds of apple trees in the land surrounding Mansfield.

Marion. Located north of Columbus, Marion is home to the **Harding Home & Museum** as well as the **Harding Memorial,** a Grecian-style monument made from white Georgian marble. The structure stands on 10 acres of beautifully landscaped grounds and marks the burial place of President Warren Harding and his wife.

Moundbuilders Earthworks houses the nation's first museum devoted exclusively to prehistoric Native American art.

The **National Heisey Glass Museum**. This museum was established in 1957 by those who collected Heisey glassworks, so that the beautiful artwork might be seen by a wider audience. Eight rooms hold thousands of pieces—from whimsical animal shapes to colorful pattern glass.

Sherman House State Memorial, Lancaster. Visit the birthplace of Civil War General William T. Sherman and brother Senator John Sherman, author of the Sherman Anti-Trust Act.

Where to Find CCUSA Parks

List City	Park Name	Map Coordinates
AKRON		
	Countryside Campground	B-4
BELLEFONTAINE		
	Ohio State Eagles Family Recreation Park	C-2
BELLEVUE		
	Lazy J RV Resort	B-3
CARROLLTON		
	Cozy Ridge Campground	C-5
CLEVELAND		
	American Wilderness Campground	B-4
CONNEAUT		
	Windy Hill Golf Course & Campground	A-5
GRAFTON		
	American Wilderness Campground	B-4
HURON		
	Huron River Valley Campground & Marina	B-3
LOUDONVILLE		
	Mohican Reservation Campgrounds and Canoeing	C-3
	Wally World Camping Resort	C-3
NEW PARIS		
	Arrowhead Campground	D-1
	Natural Springs Resort	D-1
NEWTON FALLS		
	Ridge Ranch Campground	B-5
PIONEER		
	Loveberry's Funny Farm Campground	B-1
PORT CLINTON		
	Tall Timbers Campground	B-3
RACINE		
	Kountry Resort	E-4
RAVENNA		
	Country Acres Campground	B-5
VAN WERT		
	Timberwoods Camping Resort	C-1
WAUSEON		
	Sunny's Campground	B-1

AKRON—B-4

See listings at Randolph, Ravenna & Seville

(E) CHEROKEE PARK CAMPGROUND—(Portage) *From jct I-76 (exit 33) & Hwy 43: Go 2 mi S on Hwy 43. Enter on L.*

WELCOME

◊◊◊FACILITIES: 115 sites, typical site width 35 ft, 115 W&E, (20/30/50 amps), 50 amps ($), mostly extd stay sites (summer), 8 pull-thrus, heater not allowed, WiFi Internet central location, family camping, tenting, RV storage, dump, non-guest dump $, laundry, LP gas by weight/by meter, ice, picnic tables, fire rings, wood.

◊◊◊◊RECREATION: rec hall, rec room/area, pavilion, lake swim, 2 pedal boat rentals, lake fishing, golf nearby, bsktball, 6 bike rentals, playground, shuffleboard court 2 shuffleboard courts, activities (wkends), horseshoes, sports field, v-ball.

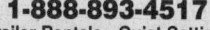

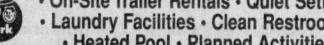

Pets welcome. Partial handicap access. Open Apr 20 - Oct 20. Escort to site. Rate in 2010 $25-26 for 4 persons. MC/VISA/DISC/Debit. Member ARVC, OCOA.

Phone: (330)673-1964
Address: 3064 SR 43, Mogadore, OH 44260
Lat/Lon: 41.07267/-81.34692
Email: cherokeepark@cherokeeparkcampground.com
Web: www.cherokeeparkcampground.com

SEE AD TRAVEL SECTION PAGE 605

(E) COUNTRYSIDE CAMPGROUND—(Portage) *From jct I-76 (exit 33) & Hwy 43: Go 2 mi S on Hwy 43. Enter on R.*

WELCOME

◊◊◊FACILITIES: 96 sites, typical site width 25 ft, 86 full hkups, (20/30 amps), 10 no hkups, many extd stay sites (summer), 8 pull-thrus, WiFi Instant Internet at site, phone Internet central location, family camping, tenting, RV's/park model rentals, RV storage, dump, non-guest dump $, laundry, ltd groc, RV supplies, LP gas by weight/by meter, LP bottle exch, ice, picnic tables, fire rings, wood, controlled access.

◊◊◊RECREATION: rec hall, rec room/area, coin games, swim pool, lake fishing, fishing supplies, golf nearby, bsktball, playground, activities, (wkends), sports field, hiking trails.

Pets welcome, breed restrict. Open May 1 - Oct 15. Escort to site. Rate in 2010 $30-33 for 2 persons. MC/VISA/DISC/AMEX/Debit. Member ARVC, OCOA. CCUSA 50% Discount. CCUSA reservations Recommended, CCUSA max stay 2 days, CCUSA disc. not avail F,Sa, CCUSA disc. not avail holidays. Fully operational May 1- Oct 15.

Phone: (888)893-4517
Address: 2687 State Route 43, Mogadore, OH 44260
Lat/Lon: 41.06202/-81.34744
Email: gtbrain@aol.com
Web: www.countrysidecampgrounds.com

SEE AD THIS PAGE

AKRON—Continued on next page

John Glenn was the first American to orbit the earth on February 20, 1962. In October of 1998, at age 77, he returned to the space program and traveled back into space and became the oldest man to venture into outer space.

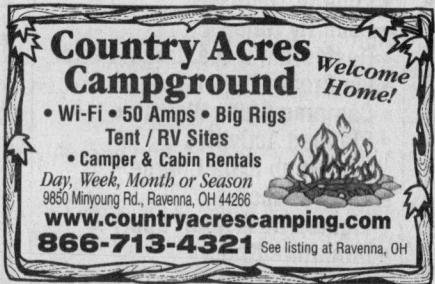

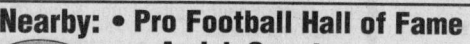

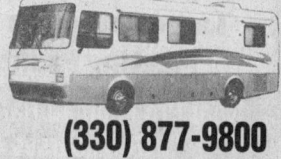

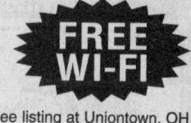

AKRON—Continued

PORTAGE LAKES STATE PARK—(Summit) *From jct Hwy 619(Waterloo Rd) & S Main St in town: Go 2 mi S on Main St, then 2 mi E on Caston to Christman.* FACILITIES: 74 sites, 35 ft max RV length, 74 no hkups, tenting, dump. RECREATION: lake swim, boating, 400 hp limit, canoeing, ramp, lake fishing. Pets welcome. Open all yr. Facilities fully operational Apr - Oct. Phone: (330)644-2220.

ALBANY—E-4

(E) LAKE SNOWDEN EDUCATIONAL AND RECREATION PARK—(Athens) *From jct US 50/32 & CR 681: Go 1 mi N on US 50/32. Enter on L.* FACILITIES: 135 sites, 117 E, (20/30 amps), 18 no hkups, 13 pull-thrus, tenting, dump, laundry, ltd groc. RECREATION: lake swim, boating, canoeing, ramp, dock, lake fishing. No pets. Partial handicap access. Open Apr 1 - Dec 15. Facilities fully operational Apr 1 - Oct 31. Member ARVC, OCOA. Phone: (740)698-6373.

ANDOVER—B-5

(SE) Bay Shore Resort—(Ashtabula) *From jct US 6 / Hwy 7 & Hwy 85: Go 1-1/2 mi E on Hwy-85, then 4-1/4 miS on Pymatuning Lake Rd. Enter on L.* ◇◇◇◇FACILITIES: 390 sites, typical site width 40 ft, 375 full hkups, 15 W&E, (30 amps), 17 pull-thrus, family camping, tenting, dump, laundry. ◇◇◇◇◇RECREATION: swim pool, boating, 20 hp limit, canoeing, ramp, dock, lake fishing, playground. Pets welcome, breed restrict, size restrict. Partial handicap access. Open Apr 15 - Oct 15. Rate in 2010 $38-46 for 2 persons. Member ARVC, OCOA. Phone: (440)293-7202.

(SE) PYMATUNING STATE PARK—(Ashtabula) *From town: Go 6 mi SE on Lake Rd.* FACILITIES: 370 sites, 35 ft max RV length, 18 full hkups, 331 E, (20/30 amps), 21 no hkups, tenting, dump, laundry, ltd groc. RECREATION: lake swim, boating, 10 hp limit, canoeing, ramp, dock, lake fishing, playground. Open all yr. Facilities fully operational Apr - Oct. Phone: (440)293-6030.

(S) Wildwood Acres Family Campground—(Ashtabula) *From jct Hwy 85 & US 6/Hwy 7: Go 2 mi S on Hwy-7, then 1/4 mi E on Marvin Rd. Enter on L.* ◇◇◇FACILITIES: 302 sites, typical site width 38 ft, 38 ft max RV length, 278 W&E, (20/30 amps), 24 no hkups, family camping, tenting, dump, groceries. ◇◇◇◇RECREATION: 2 swim pools, pond fishing, playground. Pets welcome. Open mid Apr - mid Oct. Rate in 2010 $25 for 4 persons. Phone: (440)293-6838.

ARCHBOLD—B-1

(N) SAUDER VILLAGE—*From jct I-80/90 (exit 25) & SR 66/US 20A: Go 4 mi S on US 20A/SR 66, then 1/4 mi E on SR 2. Enter on R.* 1800's-Era Farm & Craft village with staff in period costumes and skilled craftsmen at work. Restaurant, bakery, gift center, 98-room inn & conference center. Allow 4 hours for visit. Two-day passes available. Open mid Apr - end of Oct. Restaurant, Bakery, gift center & inn open all year,. MC/VISA/Debit.

Phone: (800)590-9755
Address: 22611 State Highway 2, Archbold, OH 43502
Lat/Lon: 41.54328/-84.30155
Email: info@saudervillage.org
Web: www.SAUDERVILLAGE.com

SEE AD THIS PAGE

(N) SAUDER VILLAGE CAMPGROUND—(Fulton) *From I80/90 (exit 25) & US 20A/SR 66: Go 4 mi S on US 20A/SR 66, then 1/4 mi E on SR 2. Enter on R.*
◇◇◇FACILITIES: 37 sites, 3 full hkups, 23 W&E, 11 E, (20/30/50 amps), 11 pull-thrus, WiFi Instant Internet at site, family camping, tenting, dump, laundry, ice, picnic tables, fire rings, wood.
◇◇◇RECREATION: pavilion, swim pool, lake fishing, golf nearby, playground, shuffleboard court 2 shuffleboard courts, sports field, hiking trails, local tours.
Pets welcome. Partial handicap access. Open Late Apr - End of Oct. Big rigs welcome. Clubs welcome. Rate in 2010 $29-36 per vehicle. MC/VISA/DISC/AMEX/Debit. ATM.

ARCHBOLD—Continued
SAUDER VILLAGE CAMPGROUND—Continued

Phone: (800)590-9755
Address: 22611 St Rt 2, Archbold, OH 43502
Lat/Lon: 41.54328/-84.30155
Email: sauderheritageinn@saudervillage.org
Web: www.SAUDERVILLAGE.org

SEE AD THIS PAGE

ASHLAND—C-3

(E) HICKORY LAKES CAMPGROUND—(Ashland) *From jct I-71 (exit 186) & US 250: Go 6 mi E on US 250, then 1 mi N on Twp Rd 63, then 1/2 mi E on Twp Rd 1300. Enter on R.*
◇◇◇FACILITIES: 220 sites, typical site width 40 ft, 220 W&E, (20/30/50 amps), 50 amps ($), many extd stay sites (summer), 14 pull-thrus, WiFi Internet central location, family camping, tenting, cabins, dump, non-guest dump $, portable dump, laundry, groceries, RV supplies, LP gas by weight/by meter, ice, picnic tables, fire rings, wood, controlled access.
◇◇◇RECREATION: rec hall, rec room/area, coin games, lake swim, 2 pedal boat rentals, lake fishing, golf nearby, bsktball, playground, activities, (wkends), horseshoes, sports field, hiking trails, v-ball.
Pets welcome. Partial handicap access. Open Apr 15 - Sep 30. Escort to site. Clubs welcome. Rate in 2010 $28 for 2 persons. MC/VISA. Member ARVC, OCOA.

Phone: (419)869-7587
Address: 23 Twp Rd 1300 (Meyers Rd), West Salem, OH 44287
Lat/Lon: 40.87139/-82.12967
Email: hickorylake@bright.net
Web: www.hickorylakescampground.com

SEE AD THIS PAGE

ASHTABULA—A-5

(NW) Buccaneer Campsites—(Ashtabula) *From jct I-90 (exit 223) & Hwy 45: Go 1 mi S on Hwy 45, then 3 mi E on Hwy 307. Enter on R.* ◇◇◇FACILITIES: 170 sites, typical site width 45 ft, 112 W&E, 45 E, (20/30/50 amps), 50 amps ($), 13 no hkups, 10 pull-thrus, tenting, dump, ltd groc. ◇◇◇RECREATION: lake swim, boating, canoeing, dock, lake/river fishing, playground. Pets welcome. Partial handicap access. Open May 1 - Oct 31. Rate in 2010 $25 for 2 persons. Member ARVC, OCOA. Phone: (440)576-2881. FCRV discount.

(S) Hide-A-Way Lakes Campground—(Ashtabula) *From jct I-90 & Hwy 45: Go 2 mi N on Hwy 45, then 3 mi E on Hwy 84. Enter on R.* ◇◇◇FACILITIES: 300 sites, typical site width 40 ft, 75 full hkups, 155 W&E, (15/20/30/50 amps), 70 no hkups, 4 pull-thrus, family camping, tenting, dump, laundry, ltd groc. ◇◇◇RECREATION: swim pool, pond fishing, playground. Pets welcome. Open Apr 15 - Oct 15. Rate in 2010 $30-35 for 2 persons. Member ARVC, OCOA. Phone: (440)992-4431.

ATHENS—E-4

STROUDS RUN STATE PARK—(Athens) *From jct US 33 (Columbus Rd exit) & N Lancaster Rd: Go E on N Lancaster Rd, which becomes Columbia Ave then Strouds Run Rd (CR 20).* FACILITIES: 76 sites, 76 no hkups, tenting, dump. RECREATION: lake swim, boating, 10 hp limit, ramp, lake fishing, playground. Pets welcome. Open all yr. Facilities fully operational Apr - Oct. Phone: (740)592-2302.

AURORA—B-4

See listings at Ravenna & Streetsboro

(E) Yogi Bear's Jellystone Park (Morgan RV Resorts)—(Portage) *From jct Hwy 43 & Hwy 82: Go 4-1/4 mi E on Hwy 82. Enter on R.* ◇◇◇◇◇FACILITIES: 418 sites, typical site width 30 ft, 154 full hkups, 149 W&E, (30/50 amps), 50 amps ($), 115 no hkups, 41 pull-thrus, family camping, tenting, dump, laundry, grocer-

Yogi Bear's Jellystone Park (Morgan RV Resorts)—Continued on next page

AURORA—Continued
Yogi Bear's Jellystone Park (Morgan RV Resorts)—Continued

ies. ◆◆◆◆◆RECREATION: swim pool, lake swim, boating, electric motors only, canoeing, ramp, dock, lake fishing, playground. Pets welcome. Partial handicap access. Open May 1 - Oct 15. Facilities fully operational mid Jun - Labor Day. Rate in 2010 $47-55 for 2 persons. Member ARVC, OCOA. Phone: (800)344-9644.

BAINBRIDGE—E-2

(N) PAINT CREEK STATE PARK—(Highland) *From jct Hwy 41 & US 50: Go 6 mi W on US 50. Enter on L.* FACILITIES: 197 sites, 197 E, (30/50 amps), tenting, dump, laundry, ltd groc. RECREATION: lake swim, boating, canoeing, ramp, dock, lake fishing, play equipment. Pets welcome. Open all yr. Facilities fully operational Apr - Oct. Phone: (937)365-1401.

(SE) PIKE LAKE STATE PARK—(Highland) *From jct Hwy 41 & US 50: Go 1 mi E on US 50, then 6 mi S on CR 28 (Potts Hill Rd) & CR 4 (Pike Lake Rd). Enter at end.* FACILITIES: 101 sites, 35 ft max RV length, 101 E, (30/50 amps), tenting, dump, ltd groc. RECREATION: lake swim, boating, 4.5 hp limit, electric motors only, canoeing, lake fishing, playground. Pets welcome. Open all yr. Facilities fully operational Apr - Oct. Phone: (740)493-2212.

BALTIMORE—D-3

(NW) Rippling Stream Campground—(Fairfield) *From jct I-70 (exit 112A) & SR 256: Go 4-1/2 mi S on SR 256, then 5-1/2 mi E on SR 256. Enter on L.* ◆◆FACILITIES: 132 sites, typical site width 25 ft, 132 W&E, (20/30 amps), tenting, dump. ◆◆◆RECREATION: swim pool, playground. Pets welcome, breed restrict. Open Apr 1 - Oct 31. Rate in 2010 $25 for 4 persons. Member ARVC, OCOA. Phone: (740)862-6065.

BATAVIA—E-1

(E) EAST FORK STATE PARK—(Clermont) *From jct I-275 & Hwy 32: Go 10 mi E on Hwy 32, then 1/4 mi S on Half Acre Rd, then 500 feet E on access road.* FACILITIES: 396 sites, 39 ft max RV length, 7 full hkups, 389 E, (30/50 amps), tenting, dump. RECREATION: lake swim, boating, ramp, lake fishing, playground. Pets welcome. Open all yr. Facilities fully operational Apr - Oct. Phone: (513)734-4323.

BELLEFONTAINE—C-2

(N) BACK FORTY LTD—(Logan) *From jct US 33 & US 68: Go 7 mi N on US 68, then 1 mi E on CR 111. Enter on L.*

◆◆◆FACILITIES: 82 sites, typical site width 40 ft, 82 W&E, (20/30 amps), mostly extd stay sites (summer), 20 pull-thrus, heater not allowed, WiFi Internet central location, family camping, cabins, dump, non-guest dump $, portable dump, ltd groc, ice, picnic tables, fire rings, wood, controlled access.

◆◆◆◆RECREATION: rec room/area, pavilion, coin games, lake swim, lake fishing, golf nearby, playground, activities, (wkends), horseshoes, hiking trails, v-ball.

Pets welcome, breed restrict. No tents. Open 1st weekend of May - Last weekend of Oct. Clubs welcome. Rate in 2010 $30-32 per family. MC/VISA/DISC.

Phone: (937)468-7492
Address: 959 CR 111 E, Rushsylvania, OH 43347
Lat/Lon: 40.47704/-83.69083
Email: backfortycampground@embarqmail.com
Web: www.backfortycampground.com

SEE AD THIS PAGE

(N) Ohio State Eagles Family Recreation Park—(Logan) *From jct US 33 & US 68: Go 4 mi N on US 68. Enter on R.* ◆◆◆FACILITIES: 205 sites, typical site width 35 ft, 40 ft max RV length, 133 full hkups, 32 W&E, (30/50 amps), 40 no hkups, family camping, tenting, shower$, dump, non-guest dump $, portable dump, laundry, ltd groc, RV supplies, LP gas by weight/by meter, ice, picnic tables, fire rings, wood. ◆◆◆◆RECREATION: pavilion, equipped pavilion, lake swim, boating, lake fishing, fishing supplies, bsktball, playground, activities, horseshoes, v-ball. Pets welcome, breed restrict. Partial handicap access. Open Apr 1 - Oct 31. Rate in 2010 $21 for 4 persons.

BELLEFONTAINE—Continued
Ohio State Eagles Family Recreation Park—Continued

CCUSA 50% Discount. CCUSA reservations Recommended, CCUSA max stay 4 days, Cash only for CCUSA disc., Check only for CCUSA disc., CCUSA disc. not avail S,Th, CCUSA disc. not avail F,Sa, CCUSA disc. not avail holidays. Not available months of Jun or Jul.

Phone: (937)593-1565
Address: 5118 US 68N, Bellefontaine, OH 43311
Lat/Lon: 40.43261/-83.73721
Email: eaglesrecpark@loganrec.net
Web: www.eaglesrecpark.com

BELLEVUE—B-3

(E) LAZY J RV RESORT—(Huron) *From jct Ohio Tpk I-80/90 (exit 110) & Hwy 4: Go 7 mi S on Hwy 4, then 1-1/2 mi E on US 20. Enter on L.*

◆◆◆FACILITIES: 109 sites, typical site width 30 ft, 109 W&E, (20/30/50 amps), 50 amps ($), some extd stay sites (summer), 64 pull-thrus, WiFi Instant Internet at site, family camping, tenting, cabins, RV storage, dump, non-guest dump $, portable dump, laundry, ltd groc, RV supplies, LP gas by weight/by meter, ice, picnic tables, fire rings, grills, wood.

◆◆◆◆RECREATION: rec hall, rec room/area, pavilion, coin games, swim pool, 3 pedal boat rentals, lake/pond fishing, fishing supplies, mini-golf, ($), golf nearby, bsktball, playground, activities, (wkends), horseshoes, sports field, v-ball. Rec open to public.

Pets welcome. Partial handicap access. Open May 1 - Oct 31. Escort to site. Clubs welcome. Green Friendly. Rate in 2010 $30-41 for 2 persons. MC/VISA/DISC/Debit. Member ARVC, OCOA. FMCA discount. CCUSA 50% Discount. CCUSA reservations Recommended, CCUSA max stay 2 days, CCUSA disc. not avail F,Sa. Not available Jun, Jul, Aug or any holiday weekends.

BELLEVUE—Continued
LAZY J RV RESORT—Continued

Phone: (800)305-9644
Address: 4888 US Hwy 20 E, Bellevue, OH 44811
Lat/Lon: 41.26129/-82.76750
Email: info@lazy-j.com
Web: www.lazy-j.com

SEE AD SANDUSKY PAGE 631

BELLVILLE—C-3

(SW) Lake Timberlin Camp Resort—(Richland) *From jct I-71 (exit 165) & Hwy 97: Go 1-1/2 mi SE on Hwy 97, then 3 mi W on Mock Rd, then 4 mi S on Hwy 546, then 1/4 mi SW on Black Rd. Enter on R.* ◆◆◆FACILITIES: 253 sites, typical site width 50 ft, 136 full hkups, 17 W&E, (15/20/30/50 amps), 50 amps ($), 100 no hkups, 3 pull-thrus, family camping, tenting, dump, laundry, groceries. ◆◆◆◆RECREATION: swim pool, lake swim, boating, canoeing, ramp, dock, lake fishing, playground. Pets welcome, breed restrict. Partial handicap access. Open Apr 15 - Oct 30. Rate in 2010 $33-40 per family. Member ARVC, OCOA. Phone: (419)886-2267.

BELMONT—D-5

(S) BARKCAMP STATE PARK—(Belmont) *From jct Hwy-147 & Hwy-149: Go 2 mi NE off Hwy-149.* FACILITIES: 123 sites, 35 ft max RV length, 123 E, (50 amps), tenting, dump, ltd groc. RECREATION: lake swim, boating, electric motors only, ramp, dock, lake fishing, playground. Pets welcome. Partial handicap access. Open all yr. Facilities fully operational Apr - Oct. Phone: (740)484-4064.

BERLIN—C-4

See listings at Mt. Eaton, Shreve, Wilmot & Winesburg.

BERLIN—Continued on next page

Marblehead is the oldest operating lighthouse on the Great Lakes.

BERLIN—Continued

(S) SCENIC HILLS RV PARK—(Holmes) *From jct I-77 (exit 83) & SR-39: Go 18 mi W on SR-39, then 1/4 mi S on TR 367 (blinking light) 1 mi E of Berlin. Enter on R.*

WELCOME

◇◇◇◇FACILITIES: 112 sites, typical site width 36 ft, accepts full hkup units only, 112 full hkups, (30/50 amps), 40 pull-thrus, WiFi Instant Internet at site, family camping, RV storage, dump, non-guest dump $, laundry, RV supplies, picnic tables, fire rings, wood.

RECREATION: sports field.

Pets welcome, breed restrict. No tents. Open Apr 1 - Nov 1. No restrooms. Big rigs welcome. Clubs welcome. Rate in 2010 $27-35 for 2 persons. Member ARVC, OCOA.

Phone: (330)893-3607
Address: 4483 Township Hwy 367, Millersburg, OH 44654
Lat/Lon: 40.54947/-81.78249
Email: shrvp@wifi7.com
Web: www.scenichillsrvpark.com

SEE AD PAGE 615

BLANCHESTER—E-2

STONELICK STATE PARK—(Clinton) *From jct Hwy-28 & Hwy-133: Go 6 mi SW on Hwy-133 (Edonton), then 1-1/2 mi S on Hwy-727.* FACILITIES: 114 sites, 35 ft max RV length, 108 E, (50 amps), 6 no hkups, tenting, dump, laundry, ltd groc. RECREATION: lake swim, boating, electric motors only, ramp, lake fishing, playground. Pets welcome. Open all yr. Facilities fully operational Apr - Oct. Phone: (513)734-4323.

BLUFFTON—C-2

(NE) Twin Lakes Park—(Hancock) *From jct I-75 (exit 145) & SR 235: Go 200 yards S on SR 235, then 1/2 mi E on Twp Rd 34. Enter on L.* ◇◇◇FACILITIES: 85 sites, typical site width 30 ft, 14 full hkups, 71 W&E, (20/30/50 amps), 50 amps ($), 4 pull-thrus, family camping, tenting, dump, laundry, full svc store. ◇◇◇◇RECREATION: lake swim, boating, electric motors only, lake fishing, playground. Pets welcome. Partial handicap access. Open all yr. Facilities fully operational May 1 - Nov 1. Big rigs welcome. Rate in 2010 $34.50-49.50 for 2 persons. Member ARVC, OCOA. Phone: (888)436-3610.

Reserve Online at Woodalls.com

BRISTOLVILLE—B-5

(S) Paradise Lakes Family Campground—(Trumbull) *From jct Hwy-88 & Hwy-45: Go 1-1/2 mi S on Hwy-45, then 1/4 mi E on Housel-Craft Rd. Enter on L.* ◇◇FACILITIES: 163 sites, typical site width 40 ft, 123 full hkups, 40 W&E, (30 amps), 50 pull-thrus, tenting, dump, laundry, ltd groc. ◇◇◇RECREATION: lake swim, boating, electric motors only, canoeing, lake fishing, playground. Pets welcome. Open May 1 - Oct 15. Rate in 2010 $28 per family. Phone: (330)889-3031.

BROOKVILLE—D-1

(NE) KOA-DAYTON TALL TIMBERS RESORT—(Montgomery) *From jct I-70 (exit 24) & SR 49: Go 1/2 mi N on SR 49, then 1/2 mi W on Pleasant Plains Rd, then 1/4 mi S on Wellbaum Rd. Enter on L.*

WELCOME

◇◇◇◇FACILITIES: 228 sites, typical site width 30 ft, 110 full hkups, 77 W&E, 31 E, (20/30/50 amps), 50 amps ($), 10 no hkups, 77 pull-thrus, WiFi Instant Internet at site, family camping, tenting, cabins, dump, non-guest dump $, laundry, full svc store, RV supplies, LP gas by meter, ice, picnic tables, patios, fire rings, grills, wood.

◇◇◇◇◇RECREATION: pavilion, equipped pavilion, swim pool, 3 pedal boat rentals, lake/stream fishing, fishing supplies, mini-golf, ($), golf nearby, bsktball, 52 bike rentals, playground, activities, horseshoes, sports field, hiking trails, v-ball.

Pets welcome, breed restrict. Partial handicap access. Open Apr 1 - Nov 1. Big rigs welcome. Escort to site. Clubs welcome. Rate in 2010 $41.41-56 for 2 persons. MC/VISA/DISC/Debit. Member ARVC, OCOA. KOA discount.

BROOKVILLE—Continued
KOA-DAYTON TALL TIMBERS RESORT—Continued

Text 107945 to (440)725-8687 to see our Visual Tour.

Phone: (937)833-3888
Address: 7796 Wellbaum Rd, Brookville, OH 45309
Lat/Lon: 39.85795/-84.38782
Email: camp@daytonkoa.com
Web: www.daytonkoa.com

SEE AD DAYTON PAGE 623 AND AD TRAVEL SECTION PAGE 606

BRUNSWICK—B-4

(S) WILLOW LAKE PARK INC.—(Medina) *From jct I-71 (exit 226) & Hwy 303: Go 3 mi W on Hwy 303, then 2 mi S on Sub-Station. Enter on R.*

WELCOME

◇◇◇FACILITIES: 247 sites, 247 W&E, (20/30/50 amps), 50 amps ($), mostly extd stay sites (summer), 20 pull-thrus, heater not allowed, WiFi Instant Internet at site, phone Internet central location, family camping, tenting, RV storage, shower$, dump, non-guest dump $, portable dump, ltd groc, RV supplies, ice, picnic tables, fire rings, grills, wood.

◇◇◇◇RECREATION: rec hall, pavilion, coin games, lake swim, lake fishing, fishing supplies, mini-golf, ($), golf nearby, bsktball, playground, activities, (wkends), horseshoes, sports field, v-ball. Rec open to public.

Pets welcome, breed restrict. Open May 1 - Oct 24. Park closes the last Sunday in Oct. Clubs welcome. Rate in 2010 $28-35 per family. Member ARVC, OCOA.

Phone: (330)225-6580
Address: 2400 Sub Station Rd, Medina, OH 44256
Lat/Lon: 41.20929/-81.86060
Email: ajkwlp@aol.com
Web: www.willowlakepark.net

SEE AD THIS PAGE

BUCKEYE LAKE—D-3

(SW) BUCKEYE LAKE/COLUMBUS EAST KOA KAMPING RESORT—(Licking) *From jct I-70 (exit 129A) & SR 79: Go 1-1/2 mi S on SR 79. Enter on R.*

WELCOME

◇◇◇◇◇FACILITIES: 258 sites, typical site width 35 ft, 113 full hkups, 73 W&E, 22 E, (20/30/50 amps), 50 no hkups, 134 pull-thrus, cable TV, WiFi Instant Internet at site, phone Internet central location, family camping, tenting, cabins, dump, non-guest dump $, laundry, full svc store, RV supplies, LP gas by weight/by meter, ice, picnic tables, patios, fire rings, grills, wood.

◇◇◇◇◇RECREATION: rec hall, rec room/area, pavilion, equipped pavilion, coin games, swim pool, mini-golf, ($), golf nearby, bsktball, 20 bike rentals, playground, shuffleboard court 2 shuffleboard courts, activities (wkends), horseshoes, sports field.

Pets welcome, breed restrict. Partial handicap access. Open Apr 1 - Oct 31. Big rigs welcome. Escort to site. Clubs welcome. Rate in 2010 $39.71-90.25 for 2 persons. MC/VISA/DISC/AMEX/Debit. Member ARVC, OCOA. KOA discount.

Clark Gable, actor, was from Ohio.

BUCKEYE LAKE—Continued
BUCKEYE LAKE/COLUMBUS EAST KOA KAMPING RESORT—Continued

Phone: (740)928-0706
Address: 4460 Walnut Rd., Buckeye Lake, OH 43008
Lat/Lon: 39.92921/-82.49530
Email: buckeyelakekoa@midohio.twcbc.com
Web: www.koa.com

SEE AD COLUMBUS PAGE 622

BUTLER—C-3

(SE) KOA-Butler/Mohican—(Richland) *From jct Hwy-95 & Hwy-97: Go 3-1/2 mi E on Hwy-97, then 2 mi S on Bunkerhill Rd. Enter on R.* ◇◇◇◇FACILITIES: 86 sites, typical site width 35 ft, 33 full hkups, 31 W&E, (20/30/50 amps), 22 no hkups, 18 pull-thrus, family camping, tenting, dump, laundry, groceries. ◇◇◇◇RECREATION: swim pool, lake fishing, playground. Pets welcome, breed restrict. Open May 1 - Oct 31. Big rigs welcome. Rate in 2010 $20-33 for 2 persons. Member ARVC, OCOA. Phone: (419)883-3314. KOA discount.

(NW) River Trail Crossing RV Park—(Richland) *From jct Hwy 95 & Hwy 97: Go 2 mi W on Hwy 97. Enter on R.* ◇◇◇FACILITIES: 42 sites, typical site width 50 ft, 29 full hkups, 9 W&E, (30/50 amps), 4 no hkups, 3 pull-thrus, family camping, tenting, dump, laundry, ltd groc. ◇◇RECREATION: river fishing, playground. Pets welcome, breed restrict, quantity restrict. Partial handicap access. Open May 1 - Oct 15. Big rigs welcome. Rate in 2010 $29-31 per family. Member ARVC, OCOA. Phone: (419)883-3888.

CADIZ—C-5

TAPPAN LAKE PARK (Muskingum Watershed Conservancy Dist)—(Harrison) *From town: Go 7-1/2 mi W on US 250, then 3 mi S on CR 55.* FACILITIES: 600 sites, 32 full hkups, 76 W&E, 492 E, (30 amps), 12 pull-thrus, tenting, dump, laundry, ltd groc. RECREATION: lake swim, boating, 299 hp limit, canoeing, ramp, dock, lake fishing, playground. Partial handicap access. Open all yr. Phone: (740)922-3649.

CALDWELL—D-4

WOLF RUN STATE PARK—(Noble) *From jct Hwy-78 & I-77: Go 5 mi N on I-77, then exit 5, follow signs.* FACILITIES: 137 sites, 35 ft max RV length, 72 E, (50 amps), 65 no hkups, tenting, dump, laundry, ltd groc. RECREATION: lake swim, boating, 10 hp limit, ramp, lake fishing, playground. Pets welcome. Open all yr. Facilities fully operational Apr - Oct. Phone: (740)732-5035.

CAMBRIDGE—D-4

(NE) Hillview Acres Campground—(Guernsey) *From jct I-77 (exit 47) & US 22: Go 4 mi E on US 22, then 1/4 mi S on Wolf's Den Rd. Enter on R.* ◇◇FACILITIES: 200 sites, typical site width 33 ft, 200 W&E, (20/30 amps), 7 pull-thrus, family camping, tenting, dump, groceries. ◇◇RECREATION: pond fishing, playground. Pets welcome, breed restrict. Partial handicap access. Open Apr 15 - Oct 31. Rate in 2010 $24 for 4 persons. Member ARVC, OCOA. Phone: (740)439-3348.

(E) SALT FORK STATE PARK—(Guernsey) *From jct I-70 & I-77: Go 3-1/2 mi N on I-77, then 6 mi E on Hwy-22. Enter on L.* FACILITIES: 212 sites, 35 ft max RV length, 20 full hkups, 192 E, (30/50 amps), tenting, dump, laundry, ltd groc. RECREATION: lake swim, boating, ramp, dock, lake fishing, playground. Pets welcome. Partial handicap access. Open all yr. Facilities fully operational Apr - Oct. Phone: (740)439-3521.

CAMBRIDGE—Continued on next page

Alan Freed, a Cleveland disc jockey, was the first to coin the phrase "Rock-N-Roll" during a 1951 broadcast.

CAMBRIDGE—Continued

(S) SPRING VALLEY CAMPGROUND—(Guernsey) *From jct I-77 & I-70: Go 1 mi W on I-70 (exit 178) then 50 yards S on SR 209, then 1 mi W on Dozer Rd. Enter on L.*

◊◊◊◊FACILITIES: 199 sites, typical site width 35 ft, 154 full hkups, 45 W&E, (20/30/50 amps), some extd stay sites (summer), 39 pull-thrus, cable TV, ($), WiFi Instant Internet at site, family camping, tenting, cabins, dump, non-guest dump $, laundry, groceries, RV supplies, LP gas by weight/by meter, ice, picnic tables, fire rings, wood.

◊◊◊◊RECREATION: pavilion, equipped pavilion, swim pool, lake swim, lake fishing, golf nearby, bsktball, playground, activities, (wkends), horseshoes, sports field, hiking trails, v-ball. Rec open to public.

Pets welcome, breed restrict. Partial handicap access. Open all yr. Facilities fully operational Apr 1 - Oct 31. Swimming Pool open Memorial Day through Labor Day. Big rigs welcome. Clubs welcome. Rate in 2010 $29-35 for 4 persons. MC/VISA/Debit.

Phone: (740)439-9291
Address: 8000 Dozer Rd, Cambridge, OH 43725
Lat/Lon: 40.00260/-81.59224
Email: mail@campspringvalley.com
Web: www.campspringvalley.com

SEE AD THIS PAGE

CANAL FULTON—C-4

(S) CLAY'S PARK RESORT—(Stark) *From jct Hwy 21 & Hwy 93: Go 2 mi S on Hwy 93, then 1/2 mi E on Patterson Rd. Enter on L.*

◊◊◊◊FACILITIES: 650 sites, typical site width 45 ft, 367 full hkups, 188 W&E, (20/30/50 amps), 95 no hkups, many extd stay sites (summer), 30 pull-thrus, WiFi Internet central location, family camping, tenting, cabins, RV storage, dump, non-guest dump $, portable dump, laundry, ltd groc, RV supplies, ice, picnic tables, patios, fire rings, wood, controlled access.

◊◊◊◊◊RECREATION: rec hall, rec room/area, pavilion, coin games, swim pool, lake swim, hot tub, boating, no motors, canoeing, kayaking, dock, 6 rowboat/6 canoe/4 kayak/10 pedal boat rentals, lake fishing, mini-golf, golf nearby, bsktball, bike rental, playground, shuffleboard court 2 shuffleboard courts, activities (wkends), tennis, horseshoes, sports field, hiking trails, v-ball. Rec open to public.

Pets welcome, breed restrict, quantity restrict. Partial handicap access. Open May 1 - Nov 1. Big rigs welcome. Clubs welcome. Rate in 2010 $32.95-41.95 for 2 persons. MC/VISA/DISC/Debit. Member ARVC, OCOA.

Phone: (800)860-4386
Address: 13190 Patterson Rd NW, North Lawrence, OH 44666
Lat/Lon: 40.85819/-81.59420
Email: info@clayspark.com
Web: www.clayspark.com

SEE AD AKRON PAGE 613

CANAL WINCHESTER—D-3

(SE) Jackson Lake Park—(Fairfield) *From East jct I-70 & I-270: Go 3-1/2 mi SW on I-270, then 5 mi E on US 33, then 2-1/2 mi S on Gender Rd (Hwy 674), then 2 mi SE on Lithopolis Rd, then 1/2 mi SW on Cedar Hill Rd. Enter on R.* ◊FACILITIES: 200 sites, typical site width 40 ft, 28 ft max RV length, 80 full hkups, 80 W&E, 40 E, (20/30/50 amps), family camping, tenting, dump. ◊◊RECREATION: swim pool, lake fishing. Pets welcome, breed restrict. Open all yr. Facilities fully operational May 1 - Sep 30. Rate in 2010 $35 for 2 persons. Phone: (614)837-2656.

CANTON—C-4

See listings at Canal Fulton, Louisville & Uniontown

CLEARWATER PARK CAMPING RESORT—*From I-77 (exit 107): Go 11 mi N on I-77 (exit 118) & Hwy 241, then 1/2 m N on Hwy 241, then 4-1/2 mi E on SR 619 (Edison St).*

SEE PRIMARY LISTING AT UNIONTOWN AND AD AKRON PAGE 613

(S) KOA-BEAR CREEK RESORT RANCH—(Stark) *From jct Hwy 30 & I-77: Go 4-1/2 mi S on I-77 (exit 99), then 1/2 mi W on Fohl Rd, then 2-1/2 mi S on Sherman Church Rd, then 1/2 mi E on Haut Rd, then 100 yards SE on Downing St. Enter on R.*

◊◊◊◊FACILITIES: 92 sites, typical site width 35 ft, 60 full hkups, 24 W&E, (20/30/50 amps), 8 no hkups, 50 pull-thrus, WiFi Instant Internet at site, family camping, tenting, cabins, dump, non-guest dump $, laundry, groceries, RV supplies, LP gas by weight/by meter, ice, picnic tables, fire rings, grills, wood.

◊◊◊◊◊RECREATION: rec hall, rec room/area, pavilion, coin games, swim pool, 4 pedal boat rentals, lake fishing, fishing supplies, mini-golf, ($), golf nearby, bsktball, playground, activities, (wkends), horseshoes, sports field, hiking trails, v-ball. Rec open to public.

Pets welcome, breed restrict, quantity restrict. Partial handicap access. Open all yr. Big rigs welcome. Escort to site. Clubs welcome. Rate in 2010 $32-51 for 2 persons. MC/VISA/DISC/AMEX. Member ARVC, OCOA. KOA discount.

Phone: (330)484-3901
Address: 3232 Downing St S.W., East Sparta, OH 44626
Lat/Lon: 40.68559/-81.41280
Email: koabearcreek@gmail.com
Web: www.bearcreek.us

SEE AD THIS PAGE

CARROLLTON—C-5

(SE) A1 Twin Valley Campground—(Carroll) *From jct Hwy 39 & Hwy 43: Go 3 mi S on Hwy 43, then 3 mi E on CR 27 (Bay Rd). Enter on R.* ◊◊FACILITIES: 135 sites, 68 full hkups, 47 W&E, (30/50 amps), 20 no hkups, 30 pull-thrus, tenting, dump, laundry, ltd groc. ◊◊◊RECREATION: swim pool, pond fishing, playground. Pets welcome, breed restrict. Open all yr. Facilities fully operational May 1 - Oct 15. Rate in 2010 $23-28 for 2 persons. Member ARVC, OCOA. Phone: (330)739-2811.

(W) ABC COUNTRY CAMPING & CABINS—(Carroll) *From jct Hwy 39 & Hwy 43: Go 4 mi N on Hwy 43, then 3-1/2 mi W on Hwy 171, then 1-3/4 mi S on Avalon Rd (CR 20), then 1/4 mi W on Fresno Rd. Enter on R.*

◊◊◊FACILITIES: 135 sites, 135 W&E, (15/20/30/50 amps), many extd stay sites (summer), 30 pull-thrus, family camping, tenting, cabins, RV storage, dump, portable dump, ltd groc, ice, picnic tables, fire rings, wood.

◊◊◊◊RECREATION: rec room/area, pavilion, coin games, swim pool, pond fishing, bsktball, playground, shuffleboard court shuffleboard court, activities (wkends), horseshoes, sports field, v-ball.

Pets welcome ($). Open May 1 - Oct 15. Clubs welcome. Rate in 2010 $21 per family.

Phone: (330)735-3220
Address: 4105 Fresno Rd NW, Carrollton, OH 44615
Lat/Lon: 40.59949/-81.17570
Email: abccampingandcabins@yahoo.com
Web: www.abccampingandcabins.com

SEE AD TRAVEL SECTION PAGE 605

(W) COZY RIDGE CAMPGROUND—(Carroll) *From jct Hwy 39 & Hwy 43: Go 4 mi N on Hwy 43, then 3-1/2 mi W on Hwy 171, then 1-3/4 mi S on Avalon Rd (CR 20), then 1/2 mi W on Fresno Rd. Enter at end.*

◊◊◊FACILITIES: 150 sites, typical site width 35 ft, 150 full hkups, (20/30/50 amps), some extd stay sites (summer), 50 pull-thrus, tenting, dump, portable dump, ice, picnic tables, fire rings, wood.

◊◊◊RECREATION: rec room/area, pavilion, coin games, swim pool, pond fishing, bsktball, playground, horseshoes, sports field, hiking trails, v-ball.

Pets welcome. Partial handicap access. Open Apr 15 - Oct 15. Clubs welcome. Rate in 2010 $20-25 for 2 persons. Member ARVC, OCOA. FMCA discount. CCUSA 50% Discount. CCUSA reservations Recommended, CCUSA max stay 3 days, Cash only for CCUSA disc., Check only for CCUSA disc., CCUSA disc. not avail F,Sa, CCUSA disc. not avail holidays.

Phone: (330)735-2553
Address: 4145 Fresno Rd NW, Carrollton, OH 44615
Lat/Lon: 40.59951/-81.17780
Email: cozyridge@eohio.net

SEE AD TRAVEL SECTION PAGE 605

PETERSBURG MARINA (Muskingum Conservancy District)—(Carroll) *From town: Go 4 mi S on Hwy-332, then W on CR-22.* FACILITIES: 88 sites, 35 ft max RV length, 14 full hkups, 74 E, tenting, dump, ltd groc. RECREATION: boating, 10 hp limit, canoeing, ramp, dock, lake fishing, playground. Open Apr 16 - Oct 31. Phone: (330)627-4270.

CELINA—C-1

(S) KOZY KAMP GROUND—(Mercer) *From jct US 33 & US 127: Go 10 mi S on US 127, then 1 mi SE on 703W, then 1/4 mi E on Its It Rd. Enter on R.*

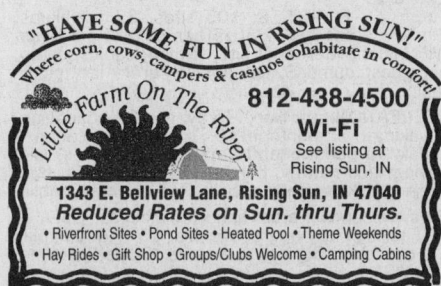

◆◆◆FACILITIES: 600 sites, 10 full hkups, 580 W&E, (15/20/30 amps), 10 no hkups, many extd stay sites (summer), family camping, tenting, dump, non-guest dump $, portable dump, ltd groc, RV supplies, LP gas by weight, ice, picnic tables, wood.

◆◆◆◆RECREATION: rec hall, pavilion, coin games, swim pool, boating, canoeing, kayaking, ramp, dock, lake/pond fishing, fishing supplies, mini-golf, ($), golf nearby, bsktball, playground, sports field, v-ball.

Pets welcome, breed restrict. Open all yr. Facilities fully operational Apr 1 - Oct 15. Clubs welcome. Rate in 2010 $25-30 for 2 persons. MC/VISA/DISC. Member ARVC, OCOA.

Phone: (419)268-2275
Address: 5134 Its It Rd, Celina, OH 45822
Lat/Lon: 40.49848/-84.56011
Email: kozykamp@bright.net
Web: www.kozykampground.com

SEE AD THIS PAGE

CHAMPION—B-5

(N) Willow Lake Park—(Trumbull) *From jct I-80 (Ohio Tpk, exit 209) & Hwy 5: Go 8 mi E on Hwy 5, then 4-1/2 mi N on Hwy 45/Mahoning Ave (through Champion). Enter on L.* ◆◆◆FACILITIES: 187 sites, typical site width 35 ft, 187 W&E, (15/20/30 amps), 150 pull-thrus, family camping, tenting, dump, laundry, ltd groc. ◆◆◆RECREATION: swim pool, playground. Pets welcome. Open May 1 - Sep 30. Rate in 2010 $28 for 2 persons. Phone: (330)847-8614.

CHATHAM—B-4

(S) Honey-Do Campground—(Medina) *From jct Hwy-162 & Hwy-83: Go 1 mi S on Hwy-83. Enter on R.* ◆◆FACILITIES: 210 sites, typical site width 50 ft, 210 W&E, (20/30 amps), 8 pull-thrus, tenting, dump, ltd groc. ◆◆◆◆RECREATION: lake swim, lake fishing, playground. Pets welcome. Open May 1 - Oct 15. Rate in 2010 $25 for 2 persons. Member ARVC, OCOA. Phone: (330)667-2295.

Orville Wright, inventor, was from Ohio.

CHILLICOTHE—E-3

(N) GREAT SEAL STATE PARK—(Ross) *From jct US 23 & Hwy 159: Go 3 mi E on Delano Rd, then S on Marietta. Enter on L.* FACILITIES: 15 sites, typical site width 10 ft, 35 ft max RV length, 15 no hkups, tenting, dump. RECREATION: playground. Pets welcome. Open all yr. Facilities fully operational Apr - Oct. Phone: (740)887-4818.

(S) SCIOTO TRAIL STATE PARK—(Ross) *From jct Hwy 104 & US 23: Go 7 mi NE on US 23 & Hwy 372. Enter on R.* FACILITIES: 73 sites, typical site width 10 ft, 40 E, (30/50 amps), 33 no hkups, 15 pull-thrus, tenting, dump, ltd groc. RECREATION: lake swim, boating, electric motors only, canoeing, ramp, lake fishing, playground. Pets welcome. Open all yr. Facilities fully operational Apr - Oct. Phone: (740)663-2125.

(NW) SUN VALLEY CAMPGROUND—(Ross) *From jct SR-104 & US 35: Go 4 mi NW on US 35, then 2 mi W on CR 550. Enter on R.*

◆◆◆◆FACILITIES: 60 sites, typical site width 40 ft, 20 full hkups, 25 W&E, (20/30/50 amps), 50 amps ($), 15 no hkups, some extd stay sites (summer), 3 pull-thrus, phone Internet central location, family camping, tenting, dump, non-guest dump $, picnic tables, patios, fire rings, wood.

◆◆◆RECREATION: rec hall, pavilion, pond fishing, golf nearby, bsktball, playground, horseshoes, sports field, v-ball.

Pets welcome, breed restrict. Open all yr. Facilities fully operational Apr 15 - Oct 15. Big rigs welcome. Clubs welcome. Green Friendly. Rate in 2010 $25.50-35.50 for 2 persons. Member ARVC, OCOA.

Phone: (740)775-3490
Address: 10105 CR 550, Chillicothe, OH 45601
Lat/Lon: 39.38218/-83.08557
Email: btcope@roadrunners.com
Web: www.sunvalleycampground.freeservers.com

SEE AD THIS PAGE

The Warner Bros. started out in Youngstown, Ohio. Sam was a carnival barker, Jack a delivery man, Albert sold soap, and Harry sold meat.

CINCINNATI—E-1

CINCINNATI AREA MAP

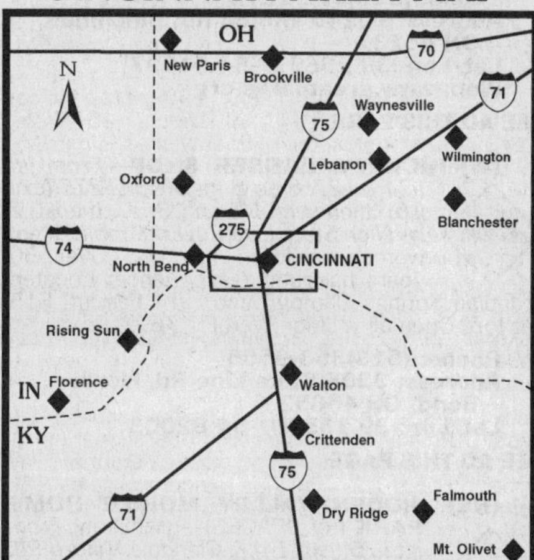

Symbols on map indicate towns within a 40 mi radius of Cincinnati where campgrounds (diamonds), attractions (flags), & RV service centers & camping supply outlets (gears) are listed. Check listings for more information.

Tell Them Woodall's Sent You!

(C) HAMILTON COUNTY PARK DISTRICT—Call for reservations: (513)851-CAMP to visit Miami Whitewater Forest (West), Winton Woods (North), Steamboat Bend (East). Open all yr.

HAMILTON COUNTY PARK DISTRICT—Continued on next page

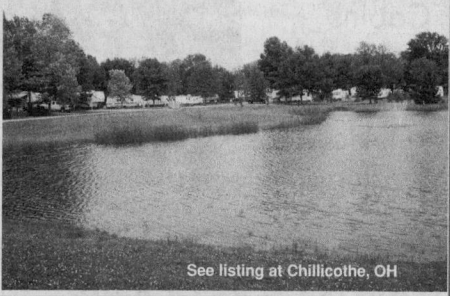

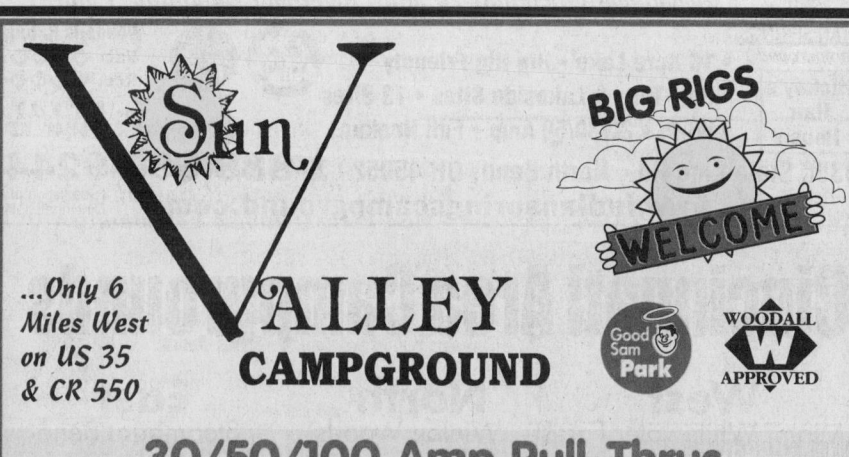

CINCINNATI—Continued
HAMILTON COUNTY PARK DISTRICT—Continued

Phone: (513)521-7275
Address: 10245 Winton Rd, Cincinnati, OH 45231
Lat/Lon: 39.25697/-84.51997
Web: www.greatparks.org

SEE AD THIS PAGE

(W) HICKEY'S BARBER SHOP—*From jct I-74 & I-275: Go 8 mi SW on I-275 (exit 16), then 3 mi NE on US 50, then 1/2 mi N on State Line Rd. Enter on R.* Men, women, children haircuts. Over 60 years haircutting experience. Located at Indian Springs Campground. $14 haircut, $15 flat top. Open all yr. Mon,Wed,Fri 9-6.

Phone: (513)353-9555
Address: 3306 State Line Rd, North Bend, OH 45052
Lat/Lon: 39.15570/-84.82003

SEE AD THIS PAGE

(NE) HIDDEN VALLEY MOBILE HOME PARK (RV SPACES)—(Hamilton) *From jct I-75 (exit 14) & Glendale Milford Rd: Go 1 mi E on Glendale Milford Rd, then 1 mi S on Reading Rd. Enter on R.*

FACILITIES: 50 sites, typical site width 20 ft, accepts self-contained units only, 50 full hkups, (30/50 amps), 2 pull-thrus, patios.

Pets welcome, size restrict, quantity restrict. No tents. Open all yr. Big rigs welcome. Rate in 2010 $40 for 2 persons. VISA/DISC/AMEX/Debit.

Phone: (513)733-5330
Address: 9797 Reading Rd, Cincinnati, OH 45215
Lat/Lon: 39.23940/-84.43040
Email: ksh@hiddenvalley-rv.com
Web: www.hiddenvalley-rv.com

SEE AD PAGE 619

CINCINNATI—Continued

(W) INDIAN SPRINGS CAMPGROUND—(Hamilton) *From jct I-74 & I-275: Go 8 mi SW on I-275 (exit 16), then 3 mi NE on US 50, then 1/2 mi N on State Line Rd. Enter on R.*

◇◇◇◇FACILITIES: 73 sites, typical site width 31 ft, 73 full hkups, (20/30/50 amps), some extd stay sites (summer), 13 pull-thrus, WiFi Instant Internet at site, family camping, dump, laundry, RV supplies, LP gas by weight/by meter, ice, picnic tables, fire rings, wood.

◇◇◇◇RECREATION: rec hall, rec room/area, coin games, boating, electric motors only, canoeing, kayaking, ramp, dock, 2 rowboat/4 pedal boat rentals, lake fishing, playground, horseshoes.

Pets welcome, breed restrict. No tents. Open all yr. Call for reservations Dec, Jan, Feb. Big rigs welcome. Clubs welcome. Rate in 2010 $38 for 2 persons. MC/VISA/Debit. Member ARVC, OCOA. FMCA discount.

Phone: (888)550-9244
Address: 3306 State Line Rd, North Bend, OH 45052
Lat/Lon: 39.15570/-84.82003
Email: info@indianspringscampground.com
Web: www.indianspringscampground.com

SEE AD THIS PAGE

Can you trust the Woodall's ratings? 25 evaluation teams have scoured North American campgrounds to provide you with accurate, up to date information & ratings. Find a rating you don't agree with? Send a letter or email our way, and we'll give it extra attention for 2012.

CINCINNATI—Continued

(W) MIAMI WHITEWATER FOREST CAMPGROUND (Hamilton County Park)—(Hamilton) *From I-74 (exit 3): Go 1 mi N on Dry Fork Rd, then 1/4 mi E on West Rd. Enter on L.*

FACILITIES: 46 sites, typical site width 42 ft, 46 E, (30 amps), tenting, dump, ice, picnic tables, fire rings, wood.

RECREATION: spray ground, 4 hp limit, 2 pontoon/50 rowboat/25 pedal boat/3 motorboat rentals, lake fishing, golf nearby, bike rental 50 bike rentals, playground, sports field, hiking trails, v-ball. Rec open to public.

Partial handicap access. Open all yr. Facilities fully operational Apr 15 - Nov 1. Max 14 day stay. Clubs welcome. MC/VISA.

Phone: (513)367-9632
Address: 9001 Mt Hope Rd, Harrison, OH 45030
Email: camping@greatprks.org
Web: www.hamiltoncountyparks.org

SEE AD THIS PAGE

(S) STEAMBOAT BEND (Hamilton County Park)—(Hamilton) *From jct I-275E & US 52: go 6 mi E on US 52, then S on Nine Mile Rd, then 3/4 mi W on Steamboat Dr. Enter on L.*

FACILITIES: 55 sites, typical site width 35 ft, accepts self-contained units only, 55 W&E, (30 amps), mostly extd stay sites (summer), phone/cable on-site Internet (needs activ), dump, portable dump, picnic tables, fire rings.

RECREATION: pavilion, river fishing.

No tents. Open Apr 1 - Oct 31. No restrooms. Must have advanced weekly or montly reservations. MC/VISA.

Phone: (513)851-2267
Address: 8401 Steamboat Dr, Cincinnati, OH 45255
Lat/Lon: 39.03011/-84.32922
Email: camping@greatparks.org
Web: www.greatparks.org

SEE AD THIS PAGE

(C) WINTON WOODS CAMPGROUND (Hamilton County Park)—(Hamilton) *From I-275 (exit 39): Go 3-1/2 mi S on Winton Rd. Enter on L.*

FACILITIES: 105 sites, 37 full hkups, 68 E, (20/30/50 amps), 12 pull-thrus, WiFi Instant Internet at site, tenting, cabins, dump, non-guest dump $, laundry, ltd groc, ice, picnic tables, fire rings, wood.

RECREATION: pavilion, spray ground, canoeing, kayaking, 3 pontoon/40 rowboat/6 canoe/4 kayak/25 pedal boat/10 motorboat rentals, lake fishing, golf nearby, bsktball, 4 bike rentals, playground, hiking trails, v-ball. Rec open to public.

Pets welcome. Partial handicap access. Open all yr. Facilities fully operational Mar 15 - Nov 11. Max 14 day stay. Big rigs welcome. Clubs welcome. MC/VISA.

Phone: (513)851-2267
Address: 10245 Winton Rd, Cincinnati, OH 45231
Lat/Lon: 39.25697/-84.51997
Email: camping@greatparks.org
Web: www.greatparks.org

SEE AD THIS PAGE

CIRCLEVILLE—D-3

(E) A.W. MARION STATE PARK—(Pickaway) *From jct US-23 & US-22: Go 6 mi E on US-22, then 1-1/2 mi N on East Ringgold Southern Rd, then W on Warner Huffer Rd.* FACILITIES: 58 sites, 35 ft max RV length, 30 E, (50 amps), 28 no hkups, tenting, dump. RECREATION: boating, electric motors only, ramp, dock, lake fishing, playground. Pets welcome. Open Apr 1 - Oct 30. Phone: (740)869-3124.

CLEVELAND—B-4

See listings at Aurora, Brunswick, Grafton, Streetsboro & Thompson

(SW) AMERICAN WILDERNESS CAMPGROUND—(Lorain) *From jct I-71S & I-480W: Take I-480W to Rt 10W. First exit on Rt 10W is SR 83. Go 8-1/2 mi S on SR 83. Enter on L.*

◆◆◆FACILITIES: 160 sites, typical site width 30 ft, 135 W&E, (20/30/50 amps), 25 no hkups, many extd stay sites (summer), 23 pull-thrus, heater not allowed, WiFi Instant Internet at site, phone Internet central location, family camping, tenting, cabins, RV storage, dump, non-guest dump $, portable dump, laundry, groceries, RV supplies, ice, picnic tables, fire rings, grills, wood, controlled access.

◆◆◆◆RECREATION: rec hall, rec room/area, pavilion, coin games, lake swim, canoeing, 2 rowboat/canoe/3 pedal boat rentals, lake fishing, bsktball, playground, activities (wkends), horseshoes, sports field, hiking trails, v-ball.

Pets welcome, breed restrict. Partial handicap access. Open May 1 - Oct 15. Big rigs welcome. Clubs welcome. Rate in 2010 $32-35 per family. MC/VISA/DISC/AMEX/Debit. Member ARVC, OCOA. CCUSA 50% Discount.

Phone: (440)926-3700
Address: 17273 Avon Belden Rd (St Rt 83), Grafton, OH 44044
Lat/Lon: 41.23336/-82.02296
Email: staff@americanwildernesscampground.com
Web: www.americanwildernesscampground.com

SEE LISTING IN GRAFTON AND AD THIS PAGE

HERITAGE HILLS FAMILY CAMPGROUND—*From jct I-490 & I-90: Go 42 mi E on I-90 (exit 212, Madison/Thompson), then 2 mi S on Hwy 528, then 2 mi E on Ledge Rd. Enter on L.*

SEE PRIMARY LISTING AT THOMPSON, OH AND AD TRAVEL SECTION PAGE 605

CLEVELAND—Continued

STREETSBORO/CLEVELAND SE KOA (Mar-Lynn Lake Park)—*From jct I-490 & I-90: Go 24 mi SE on I-480, then 1 mi SE on Hwy 14, then 2 mi W on Hwy 303. Enter on R.*

SEE PRIMARY LISTING AT STREETSBORO AND AD AKRON PAGE 613

CLYDE—B-3

(SW) LEAFY OAKS CAMPGROUND—(Seneca) *From jct US 20 & SR 101 (at Clyde): Go 8 mi S on SR 101. Enter on L.*

◆◆◆FACILITIES: 235 sites, typical site width 40 ft, 90 full hkups, 120 W&E, (20/30/50 amps), 25 no hkups, many extd stay sites (summer), WiFi Internet central location, family camping, tenting, cabins, RV storage, dump, non-guest dump $, portable dump, laundry, full svc store, RV supplies, LP gas by weight/by meter, ice, picnic tables, fire rings, grills, wood, controlled access.

◆◆◆RECREATION: rec room/area, pavilion, coin games, lake swim, lake fishing, fishing supplies, golf nearby, bsktball, playground, shuffleboard court shuffleboard court, activities (wkends), horseshoes, sports field, hiking trails, v-ball.

Pets welcome, quantity restrict. Partial handicap access. Open Apr 15 - Mid Oct. Big rigs welcome.

CLYDE—Continued
LEAFY OAKS CAMPGROUND—Continued

Escort to site. Clubs welcome. Rate in 2010 $25-32 for 5 persons. MC/VISA/DISC/Debit. Member ARVC, OCOA.

Phone: (419)639-2887
Address: 6955 N State Rte 1, Clyde, OH 43410
Lat/Lon: 41.13697/-83.01503
Email: leafyoakscamp@aol.com
Web: www.leafyoaks.com

SEE AD THIS PAGE

COLUMBUS—D-3

See listings at Baltimore, Buckeye Lake, Delaware, Galena, Lancaster, Mount Sterling, Sunbury & Westerville.

(W) ALTON RV PARK—(Franklin) *From Columbus Outerbelt jct I-270 & West Broad St (US 40) exit 7 or 7B west side of Columbus: Go 3 mi W on West Broad St. (US 40). Enter on R.*

◆◆◆FACILITIES: 35 sites, typical site width 30 ft, 35 full hkups, (20/30/50 amps), some extd stay sites, 23 pull-thrus, WiFi Instant Internet at site, tenting, dump, non-guest dump $, picnic tables, wood.

Pets welcome, breed restrict. Partial handicap access. Open all yr. Facilities fully operational Apr 15 - Nov 15. Bathhouses closed mid Nov - mid Apr.

ALTON RV PARK—Continued on next page

COLUMBUS—Continued
ALTON RV PARK—Continued

Big rigs welcome. Escort to site. Clubs welcome. Rate in 2010 $30-35 for 2 persons. MC/VISA/DISC/Debit. Member ARVC, OCOA.

Phone: (614)878-9127
Address: 6552 W Broad St, Galloway, OH 43119
Lat/Lon: 39.95037/-83.17601
Email: altonrvpark@sbcglobal.net
Web: www.altonrvpark.com

SEE AD THIS PAGE

(N) CROSS CREEK CAMPING RESORT —(Delaware) *From jct I-71 (exit 131) & SR 36/37: Go 3 mi W on SR 36/37, then 3 mi S on Lackey (Old State Rd.). Enter on R.*

OHIO'S NUMBER ONE PREMIER RV RESORT
Located 20 minutes N of Columbus & only 8 minutes off I-71 exit #131. 03 & 04 ARVC National Midsize Park of the year. Many full hookup 50 amp sites! Near all major attractions. Adjacent to Alum Creek State Park & Marina.

◇◇◇◇◇FACILITIES: 200 sites, typical site width 35 ft, 139 full hkups, 61 W&E, (20/30/50 amps), some extd stay sites (summer), 41 pull-thrus, WiFi Instant Internet at site, family camping, tenting, RV's/park model rentals, cabins, RV storage, dump, non-guest dump $, laundry, ltd groc, RV supplies, LP gas by weight/by meter, ice, picnic tables, patios, fire rings, grills, wood, controlled access.

◇◇◇◇◇RECREATION: rec hall, rec room/area, pavilion, coin games, swim pool, lake swim, boating, canoeing, kayaking, 9 pontoon/2 canoe/2 kayak/4 pedal boat/3 motorboat rentals, lake fishing, fishing supplies, golf nearby, bsktball, bike rental, playground, shuffleboard court 2 shuffleboard courts, activities (wkends), tennis, horseshoes, sports field, hiking trails, v-ball.

Pets welcome. Partial handicap access. Open all yr. Big rigs welcome. Escort to site. Clubs welcome. Rate in 2010 $31-43 for 2 persons. MC/VISA/DISC/Debit. Member ARVC, OCOA.

Text 84300 to (440)725-8687 to see our Visual Tour.

Phone: (740)549-2267
Address: 3190 S Old State Rd, Delaware, OH 43015
Lat/Lon: 40.23203/-82.98526
Email: crosscreek@alumcreek.com
Web: www.ALUMCREEK.com

SEE AD PAGE 621 AND AD TRAVEL SECTION PAGE 606 AND AD MAP PAGE 604

COLUMBUS—Continued

(C) OHIO DEPARTMENT OF NATURAL RESOURCES (Div. of Parks & Rec.) —Call for reservations: (866)644-6727 to visit any of the Ohio State Parks. Open all yr.

Phone: (614)265-6508
Address: 2045 Morse Rd, C-3, Columbus, OH 43229
Lat/Lon: 40.05815/-82.96494
Web: www.ohiostateparks.org

SEE AD TRAVEL SECTION PAGE 607

(NE) POST'S TRAVELAND—*From east jct I-70 & I-270: Go 14 mi N on I-270 (exit 29), then 3 mi S on SR 3 (Westerville Rd). Enter on L.* SALES: travel trailers, truck campers, 5th wheels, toy hauler, fold-down camping trailers, pre-owned unit sales. SERVICES: full-time mech, RV appliance repair, body work/collision repair, LP gas by weight/by meter, RV rentals, RV storage, sells parts/accessories, installs hitches. Open all yr. MC/VISA/DISC/AMEX/Debit.

Phone: (614)471-0550
Address: 4330 Westerville Rd, Columbus, OH 43231
Lat/Lon: 40.05965/-82.93621
Web: www.postrv.com

SEE AD THIS PAGE

WOLFIES CAMPGROUND—*From E jct I-270 & I-40: Go 46 mi E on I-70 (exit 155) & OH 146 W. (E'b I-70 go left, at bottom of ramp on Elbron), then 1/4 mi W on OH 146, then right on OH 666, then 3/4 mi N & left on Lewis (OH 166), then first right past Riverside Park is Buckeye Dr. Enter at end.*

SEE PRIMARY LISTING AT ZANESVILLE, OH AND AD THIS PAGE

CONNEAUT—A-5

(S) EVERGREEN LAKE PARK—(Ashtabula) *From jct I-90 (exit 241) & Hwy 7: Go 1/2 mi N on Hwy 7, then 1 block W on Gateway Ave, then 1/2 mi S on Center Rd. Enter on R.*

◇◇◇FACILITIES: 304 sites, typical site width 50 ft, 66 full hkups, 210 W&E, (20/30/50 amps), 50 amps ($), 28 no hkups, many extd stay sites (summer), 24 pull-thrus, WiFi Instant Internet at site ($), tenting, cabins, RV storage, dump, non-guest dump $, portable dump, ltd groc, RV supplies, LP gas by weight/by meter, ice, picnic tables, patios, fire rings, wood.

◇◇◇◇RECREATION: rec room/area, pavilion, coin games, lake swim, boating, no motors,

CONNEAUT—Continued
EVERGREEN LAKE PARK—Continued

canoeing, lake fishing, fishing supplies, mini-golf, golf nearby, bsktball, playground, shuffleboard court 2 shuffleboard courts, activities (wkends), horseshoes, sports field, v-ball.

Pets welcome, breed restrict. Open May 1 - Oct 15. Clubs welcome. Rate in 2010 $28-33 for 2 persons. MC/VISA/DISC/Debit. ATM. Member ARVC, OCOA. FMCA discount.

Phone: (440)599-8802
Address: 703 Center Road, Conneaut, OH 44030
Lat/Lon: 41.91722/-80.57184
Email: camper@suite224.net
Web: www.evergreenlake.com

SEE AD ERIE, PA PAGE 656

(S) EVERGREEN LAKE RV SALES—*From jct I-90 (exit 241) & Hwy 7: Go 1/2 mi N on Hwy 7, then 1 block W on Gateway Ave, then 1/2 mi S on Center Rd. Enter on R.* SALES: travel trailers, park models, 5th wheels, toy hauler, pre-owned unit sales. SERVICES: full-time mech, RV appliance repair, LP gas by weight/by meter, dump station, RV storage, sells parts/accessories, installs hitches. Open May 1 - Oct 15. MC/VISA/DISC.

Phone: (440)599-8802
Address: 703 Center Rd, Conneaut, OH 44030
Lat/Lon: 41.91722/-80.57184
Web: www.evergreenlake.com

SEE AD ERIE, PA PAGE 656

Windy Hill Golf Course & Campground—(Ashtabula) *From jct I-90 (exit 241) & Hwy 7: Go 3 mi S on Hwy 7, then 1/2 mi E on Weaver Rd. Enter on L.* FACILITIES: 80 sites, 50 W&E, (20/30 amps), 30 no hkups, 10 pull-thrus, tenting, RV storage, dump, portable dump, ice, picnic tables, fire rings, wood. RECREATION: pavilion, pond fishing, bsktball, play equipment, shuffleboard court, activities, horseshoes. Pets welcome. Open May 1 - Oct 31. Rate in 2010 $40 per vehicle. CCUSA 50% Discount. CCUSA reservations Required, CCUSA max stay 4 days. Discount not available holiday weekends.

Windy Hill Golf Course & Campground—Continued on next page

CONNEAUT—Continued
Windy Hill Golf Course & Campground—Continued

Phone: (440)594-5251
Address: 6231 Weaver Rd, Conneaut, OH 44030
Lat/Lon: 41.87033/-80.56145
Email: windy@suite224.net
Web: www.windyhillgolf.com

COOLVILLE—E-4

(W) Carthage Gap Campground—(Athens) *From jct SR 7 & US 50: Go 3-1/2 mi W on US 50, then 1/2 mi N on CR 56. Enter on R.* ◆◆◆◆FACILITIES: 135 sites, typical site width 40 ft, 135 full hkups, (20/30/50 amps), 50 amps ($), 21 pull-thrus, family camping, tenting, dump, laundry. ◆◆◆RECREATION: lake swim, lake fishing, playground. Pets welcome, breed restrict. Partial handicap access. Open Apr 15 - Oct 31. Big rigs welcome. Rate in 2010 $28-30 per family. Member ARVC, OCOA. Phone: (740)667-3072.

CORTLAND—B-5

(W) MOSQUITO LAKE STATE PARK—(Trumbull) *From jct Hwy 11 & Hwy 305: Go 4-1/2 mi W on Hwy 305, then 1/2 mi N on Hougland-Blackstub Rd. Enter on R.* FACILITIES: 234 sites, 35 ft max RV length, 218 E, (50 amps), 16 no hkups, tenting, laundry, ltd groc. RECREATION: lake swim, boating, ramp, dock, lake fishing, playground. Open all yr. Facilities fully operational Apr - Oct. Phone: (330)637-2856.

COSHOCTON—C-4

(N) LAKE PARK RECREATION AREA (County Park)—(Coshocton) *From jct Hwy-16 & US-36: Go 1/4 mi E on US-36, then 1/4 mi N on Hwy-83. Enter on L.* FACILITIES: 69 sites, typical site width 35 ft, 69 E, (30 amps), 10 pull-thrus, tenting, dump. RECREATION: swim pool, boating, electric motors only, canoeing, lake/river fishing, playground. Partial handicap access. Open Apr 1 - Nov 1. Phone: (740)622-7528.

DAYTON—D-1

See listings at Brookville, Enon, New Paris, Springfield

MILITARY PARK (Wright-Patterson AFB FAMCAMP)—(Montgomery) *From I-70 (exit 41): Go S of Fairborn on Hwy 444. On base.* FACILITIES: 54 sites, 54 W&E, (20/30/50 amps), tenting, dump. RECREATION: lake fishing, playground. Pets welcome. Open all yr. Big rigs welcome. Phone: (937)257-2579.

DEERFIELD—B-5

MILL CREEK RECREATION AREA (COE - Berlin Reservoir)—(Mahoning) *From jct Hwy-14 & US-224: Go 5 mi SE on US-224 & Bedell Rd.* FACILITIES: 348 sites, 35 ft max RV length, 47 E, (30 amps), 301 no hkups, tenting, dump. RECREATION: lake swim, boating, ramp, lake fishing, playground. Partial handicap access. Open May 21 - Sep 10. Phone: (330)547-8180.

(SE) PHILABAUN'S HIDDEN COVE RESORT—(Portage) *From jct Hwy 14 & Hwy 224: Go 1 mi E on Hwy 224, then 1/4 mi S on Edgewater Blvd. Enter at end.*

WELCOME

◆◆◆FACILITIES: 210 sites, typical site width 33 ft, 170 W&E, (20/30/50 amps), 40 no hkups, many extd stay sites (summer), 4 pull-thrus, heater not allowed, WiFi Internet central location, tenting, cabins, RV storage, shower$, dump, non-guest dump $, portable dump, ltd groc, RV supplies, LP bottle exch, ice, picnic tables, fire rings, wood.

◆◆◆RECREATION: rec hall, coin games, lake swim, boating, canoeing, kayaking, ramp, 2 pontoon/4 canoe rentals, lake fishing, golf nearby, bsktball, playground, activities, (wkends), horseshoes, sports field, hiking trails, v-ball. Rec open to public.

Pets welcome, breed restrict. Open Last wk in Apr - Second Weekend of Oct. Clubs welcome. Rate in 2010 $40 per family. MC/VISA/DISC/AMEX/Debit. Member ARVC, OCOA.

Phone: (330)584-3695
Address: 1115 Edgewater Blvd, Deerfield, OH 44411
Lat/Lon: 41.01968/-81.03370
Email: bphilabaun@yahoo.com
Web: www.philabaunshiddencoveresort.com

SEE AD THIS PAGE

DEFIANCE—B-1

INDEPENDENCE DAM STATE PARK—(Defiance) *From jct Hwy-15 & Hwy-424: Go 5 mi E on Hwy-424.* FACILITIES: 40 sites, 30 ft max RV length, 40 no hkups, tenting, dump. RECREATION: boating, canoeing, ramp, river fishing, playground. Open all yr. Facilities fully operational Apr - Oct. Phone: (419)237-1503.

DELAWARE—C-3

(SE) ALUM CREEK STATE PARK—(Delaware) *From jct I-71 & Hwy-36/37: Go 1 mi W on Hwy 36/37.* FACILITIES: 290 sites, 35 ft max RV length, 3 full hkups, 287 E, (50 amps), tenting, dump, ltd groc. RECREATION: lake swim, boating, canoeing, ramp, dock, lake fishing, playground. Open all yr. Facilities fully operational Apr - Oct. Phone: (740)548-4631.

(N) DELAWARE STATE PARK—(Delaware) *From jct US-36 & US-23: Go 6 mi N on US-23.* FACILITIES: 211 sites, 35 ft max RV length, 211 E, (20 amps), tenting, dump, laundry, ltd groc. RECREATION: lake swim, boating, ramp, dock, lake fishing, playground. Pets welcome. Partial handicap access. Open Apr - Dec. Phone: (740)363-4561.

DUNCAN FALLS—D-4

BLUE ROCK STATE PARK—(Muskingum) *From jct Hwy-555 & Hwy-60: Go 5 mi SE on Hwy-60, then 6 mi SE on CR-45.* FACILITIES: 97 sites, 97 no hkups, tenting, dump, ltd groc. RECREATION: lake swim, boating, electric motors only, canoeing, ramp, lake fishing, playground. Pets welcome. Open all yr. Facilities fully operational Apr - Oct. Phone: (740)453-4377.

EAST LIVERPOOL—C-5

BEAVER CREEK STATE PARK—(Columbiana) *From jct Hwy-267 & Hwy-7: Go N on Hwy-7, then E on Bell School Rd.* FACILITIES: 48 sites, 35 ft max RV length, 48 no hkups, tenting, dump. RECREATION: canoeing, river/stream fishing, playground. Pets welcome. Open all yr. Facilities fully operational Apr - Oct. Phone: (330)385-3091.

EAST ROCHESTER—C-5

(NE) Paradise Lake Park—(Columbiana) *From jct Hwy 183 & Hwy 172: Go 5 mi E on Hwy 172, then 3/4 mi N on Rochester Rd. Enter on R.* ◆FACILITIES: 500 sites, typical site width 35 ft, 500 W&E, (20/30 amps), 100 pull-thrus, family camping, tenting, dump, laundry,

Annie Oakley, markswoman, was from Ohio.

EAST ROCHESTER—Continued
Paradise Lake Park—Continued

groceries. ◆◆◆◆RECREATION: lake swim, boating, electric motors only, canoeing, ramp, lake fishing, playground. Pets welcome. Partial handicap access. Open Apr 15 - Oct 15. Member ARVC, OCOA. Phone: (330) 525-7726.

ENON—D-2

(N) ENON BEACH CAMPGROUND—(Clark) *W'bnd from I-70W (exit 48): Go 175 yds N on Enon Rd. E'bnd from jct I-70W & OH 4N (exit 47): Go 1-1/4 mi N on OH 4N, then exit 175 yds S toward Enon, then 175 yds S on Enon Rd.*

WELCOME

◆◆FACILITIES: 150 sites, typical site width 30 ft, 44 full hkups, 86 W&E, (20/30/50 amps), 20 no hkups, some extd stay sites (summer), 32 pull-thrus, WiFi Instant Internet at site, WiFi Internet central location, family camping, tenting, cabins, RV storage, dump, non-guest dump $, laundry, ltd groc, RV supplies, LP bottle exch, ice, picnic tables, fire rings, grills, wood.

◆◆◆RECREATION: rec room/area, pavilion, coin games, lake swim, boating, electric motors only, canoeing, kayaking, dock, rowboat/6 canoe/5 pedal boat rentals, lake fishing, golf nearby, playground, activities, (wkends), horseshoes, hiking trails.

Pets welcome, breed restrict. Partial handicap access. Open all yr. Facilities fully operational Apr 15 - Oct 15. Big rigs welcome. Clubs welcome. Rate in 2010 $27-35 for 4 persons. Member ARVC, OCOA.

ENON BEACH CAMPGROUND—Continued on next page

John James Audubon practiced taxidermy in Cincinnati.

ENON—Continued
ENON BEACH CAMPGROUND—Continued

Phone: (937)882-6431
Address: 2401 Enon Rd, Springfield, OH 45502
Lat/Lon: 39.88993/-83.93581
Web: www.enonbeach.com

SEE AD PAGE 623 AND AD TRAVEL SECTION PAGE 606

FAYETTE—B-1

(SW) HARRISON LAKE STATE PARK—(Fulton) *From I-80/90-Ohio Tpk (exit 2): Go 4 mi N on Hwy 15, then 10 mi E on US 20, then 2 mi S on CR 27.* FACILITIES: 199 sites, 35 ft max RV length, 174 E, (50 amps), 25 no hkups, tenting, dump, laundry. RECREATION: lake swim, boating, electric motors only, canoeing, ramp, lake fishing, playground. Pets welcome. Open all yr. Facilities fully operational Apr 1 - Nov 1. Phone: (419)237-2593.

FITCHVILLE—B-3

(N) Indian Trail Campground—(Huron) *From jct I-80 (Ohio Turnpike exit 7) & US 250: Go 18 mi S on US 250. Enter on L.* ◊◊◊◊FACILITIES: 226 sites, typical site width 35 ft, 109 full hkups, 67 W&E, (30/50 amps), 50 amps ($), 50 no hkups, 1 pull-thrus, family camping, tenting, dump, laundry, groceries. ◊◊◊◊RECREATION: swim pool, boating, electric motors only, canoeing, dock, lake fishing, playground. Pets welcome, breed restrict. Partial handicap access. Open Apr 27 - Oct 7. Rate in 2010 $28-33 for 2 persons. Member ARVC, OCOA. Phone: (419)929-1135.

FORT LORAMIE—C-1

LAKE LORAMIE STATE PARK—(Shelby) *From jct Hwy 66 & Hwy 362: Go 3 mi E on Hwy 362.* FACILITIES: 161 sites, 35 ft max RV length, 160 E, (30 amps), 1 no hkups, 2 pull-thrus, tenting, dump, laundry, ltd groc. RECREATION: lake swim, boating, canoeing, ramp, dock, lake fishing, play equipment. Open all yr. Facilities fully operational Apr - Oct. Phone: (937)295-2011.

FREEPORT—C-5

CLENDENING MARINA (Muskingum Watershed Conservancy Dist)—(Harrison) *From jct Hwy 800 & Hwy 799: Go 2 mi E on Hwy 799.* FACILITIES: 80 sites, 35 ft max RV length, 50 E, (30 amps), 30 no hkups, tenting, dump. RECREATION: boating, 10 hp limit, canoeing, ramp, dock, lake fishing, playground. Partial handicap access. Open Apr 1 - Oct 31. Phone: (740)658-3691.

GALENA—C-3

(NW) BERKSHIRE LAKE CAMPGROUNDS—(Delaware) *From jct I-71 (exit 131) & SR 36/37: Go 3/4 mi E on SR 36/37, then 3 mi S on S Galena Rd (at 5 way cont on S Galena Rd), then 1/2 mi SW on Alexander. Enter on R.*

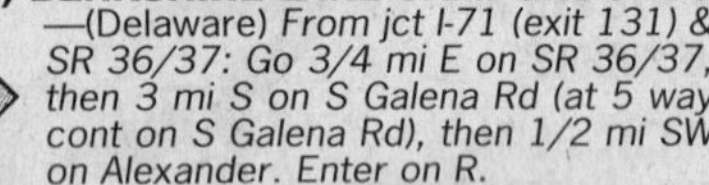

◊◊◊◊FACILITIES: 285 sites, accepts full hkup units only, 285 full hkups, (20/30/50 amps), mostly extd stay sites (summer), 15 pull-thrus, WiFi Instant Internet at site, WiFi Internet central location, family camping, RV storage, shower$, laundry, ltd groc, RV supplies, LP bottle exch, ice, picnic tables, fire rings, wood, controlled access.

◊◊◊◊RECREATION: rec room/area, pavilion, coin games, swim pool, lake fishing, mini-golf, ($), golf nearby, bsktball, playground, horseshoes, sports field, v-ball.

Pets welcome. No tents. Open all yr. Facilities fully operational Memorial Day - Labor Day. Big rigs welcome. Clubs welcome. Rate in 2010 $35 for 2 persons. MC/VISA/Debit. ATM.

Phone: (740)965-2321
Address: 1848 Alexander Rd, Galena, OH 43021
Lat/Lon: 40.23174/-82.89388
Email: berkshirelake@embarqmail.com
Web: www.berkshirelakecampground.com

SEE AD TRAVEL SECTION PAGE 605

The first ambulance service was established in Cincinnati in 1865.

GENEVA—A-5

GENEVA STATE PARK—(Ashtabula) *From jct US-20 & Hwy-534: Go 4 mi N on Hwy-534.* FACILITIES: 100 sites, 4 full hkups, 89 E, (30 amps), 7 no hkups, tenting, dump, laundry, ltd groc. RECREATION: lake swim, boating, ramp, dock, lake fishing, playground. Pets welcome. Open Apr - Nov. Phone: (440)466-8400.

(SE) Kenisee's Grand River Camp & Canoe—(Ashtabula) *From jct I-90 (exit 218) & Hwy 534: Go 1/4 mi S on Hwy 534, then 1 mi E on Hwy 307. Enter on R.* ◊◊◊◊FACILITIES: 300 sites, typical site width 40 ft, 12 full hkups, 288 W&E, (20/30/50 amps), 12 pull-thrus, family camping, tenting, dump, groceries. ◊◊◊◊RECREATION: lake swim, lake/river fishing, playground. Pets welcome. Partial handicap access. Open May 1 - Oct 15. Rate in 2010 $30 for 2 persons. Member ARVC, OCOA. Phone: (440)466-2320.

GENEVA-ON-THE-LAKE—A-5

(E) Indian Creek Camping Resort (Morgan RV Resorts)—(Ashtabula) *From jct I-90 (exit 223) & Hwy 45: Go 6 mi N on Hwy 45, then 4 mi W on Hwy 531. Enter on L.* ◊◊◊◊◊FACILITIES: 632 sites, typical site width 45 ft, 329 full hkups, 150 W&E, (20/30/50 amps), 153 no hkups, 110 pull-thrus, family camping, tenting, dump, laundry, full svc store. ◊◊◊◊◊RECREATION: 2 swim pools, lake/pond fishing, playground. Pets welcome, breed restrict, quantity restrict. Partial handicap access. Open all yr. Facilities fully operational May 1 - Oct 15. Big rigs welcome. Rate in 2010 $29.99-56.99 for 2 persons. Member ARVC, OCOA. Phone: (440)466-8191.

GLOUSTER—D-4

(N) BURR OAK STATE PARK—(Morgan) *From jct Hwy-13 & Hwy-78: Go 4 mi N on Hwy-13, then 2-1/2 mi E on CR-107.* FACILITIES: 94 sites, 30 ft max RV length, 94 no hkups, tenting, dump, laundry. RECREATION: swim pool, lake swim, boating, 10 hp limit, ramp, dock, lake fishing, playground. Pets welcome, quantity restrict. Open all yr. Facilities fully operational Apr - Oct. Phone: (740)767-3683.

GRAFTON—B-4

(SE) AMERICAN WILDERNESS CAMPGROUND—(Lorain) *From jct Hwy 303 & Hwy 83: Go 1/4 mi S on Hwy 83. Enter on L.*

◊◊◊FACILITIES: 160 sites, typical site width 30 ft, 135 W&E, (20/30/50 amps), 25 no hkups, many extd stay sites (summer), 23 pull-thrus, heater not allowed, WiFi Instant Internet at site, phone Internet central location, family camping, tenting, cabins, RV storage, dump, non-guest dump $, portable dump, laundry, groceries, RV supplies, ice, picnic tables, fire rings, grills, wood, controlled access.

◊◊◊◊RECREATION: rec hall, rec room/area, pavilion, coin games, lake swim, canoeing, 2 rowboat/2 canoe/3 pedal boat rentals, lake fishing, bsktball, playground, activities, (wkends), horseshoes, sports field, hiking trails, v-ball.

Pets welcome, breed restrict. Partial handicap access. Open May 1 - Oct 15. Big rigs welcome. Clubs welcome. Rate in 2010 $32-35 per family. MC/VISA/DISC/AMEX/Debit. Member ARVC, OCOA. CCUSA 50% Discount. CCUSA max stay Unlimited, CCUSA disc. not avail S,Th, CCUSA disc. not avail F,Sa, CCUSA disc. not avail holidays. First night is discounted. If member stays 2nd night at full price, 3rd night will be discounted also.

Phone: (440)926-3700
Address: 17273 Avon Belden Rd (St Rt 83), Grafton, OH 44044
Lat/Lon: 41.23336/-82.02296
Email: staff@americanwildernesscampground.com
Web: www.americanwildernesscampground.com

SEE AD CLEVELAND PAGE 621

GRAND RAPIDS—B-2

MARY JANE THURSTON STATE PARK—(Wood) *From jct US 24 & Hwy 578: Go S on Hwy 578, then SW on Hwy 65.* FACILITIES: 35 sites, 35 ft max RV length, 35 no hkups, tenting, dump. RECREATION: boating, ramp, dock, river fishing, playground. Pets welcome. Open all yr. Facilities fully operational Apr - Oct. Phone: (419)832-7662.

HILLSBORO—E-2

(SE) ROCKY FORK STATE PARK—(Highland) *From town: Go 4 mi SE on Hwy-124, then E on North Shore Dr.* FACILITIES: 171 sites, 35 ft max RV length, 44 full hkups, 96 E, (50 amps), 31 no hkups, tenting, dump, laundry, ltd groc. RECREATION: lake swim, boating, ramp, dock, lake fishing, playground. Pets welcome. Open all yr. Facilities fully operational Apr - Oct. Phone: (937)393-4284.

Woodall's — Trusted for Over 75 Years.

HOMERVILLE—B-4

(SE) WILD WOOD LAKES CAMPGROUND—(Medina) *From jct US 224 & Hwy 301: Go 3/4 mi S on Hwy 301, then 1 mi E on Crawford Rd. Enter on R.*

◊◊◊◊FACILITIES: 240 sites, typical site width 35 ft, 231 full hkups, (20/30/50 amps), 9 no hkups, mostly extd stay sites (summer), 35 pull-thrus, WiFi Internet central location, family camping, tenting, cabins, RV storage, laundry, groceries, RV supplies, LP gas by weight/by meter, ice, picnic tables, fire rings, wood, controlled access.

◊◊◊◊RECREATION: rec hall, rec room/area, pavilion, coin games, lake swim, lake fishing, golf nearby, bsktball, playground, activities, (wkends), horseshoes, sports field, hiking trails, v-ball.

Pets welcome, breed restrict, quantity restrict. Partial handicap access. Open Apr 16 - Oct 17. Big rigs welcome. Escort to site. Clubs welcome. Rate in 2010 $36 for 2 persons. MC/VISA. Member ARVC, OCOA.

Phone: (330)625-2817
Address: 11450 Crawford Rd, Homerville, OH 44235
Lat/Lon: 41.01680/-82.10326
Email: wildwoodlakes@verizon.net
Web: www.wildwoodlakes.com

SEE AD MEDINA PAGE 627

HOWARD—C-3

(E) Kokosing Valley Camp & Canoe—(Knox) *From jct Hwy 62 & US 36: Go 1/4 mi W on US 36. Enter on L.* ◊◊FACILITIES: 170 sites, typical site width 50 ft, 145 W&E, (20/30 amps), 25 no hkups, family camping, tenting, dump, laundry, ltd groc. ◊◊◊RECREATION: swim pool, canoeing, river fishing, playground. Pets welcome, breed restrict. Open May 1 - Oct 15. Rate in 2010 $23-27 per family. Phone: (740)599-7056.

HUBBARD—B-5

(N) Chestnut Ridge Park & Campground—(Trumbull) *From jct I-80 (exit 234) & Hwy 7: Go 1 mi N on Hwy 7, then 1 mi W on Chestnut Ridge Rd. Enter on L.* ◊◊FACILITIES: 319 sites, typical site width 35 ft, 39 full hkups, 80 W&E, (20/30 amps), 200 no hkups, 8 pull-thrus, tenting, dump, laundry. ◊◊◊◊RECREATION: lake swim, lake/pond fishing, playground. Pets welcome. Partial handicap access. Open May 1 - Oct 1. Rate in 2010 $25-30 per family. Member ARVC, OCOA. Phone: (330)534-2352.

(N) Hubbard's Haven Family Campground—(Trumbull) *From jct I-80 (eastbound exit 234B) & (westbound exit 234) & Hwy 7: Go 1-1/2 mi N on Hwy 7 (Brookfield Rd). Enter on L.* ◊FACILITIES: 77 sites, 54 full hkups, 6 W&E, (20/30/50 amps), 17 no hkups, 10 pull-thrus, family camping, tenting, dump, laundry, ltd groc. ◊◊◊RECREATION: swim pool, playground. Pets welcome. Open all yr. Facilities fully operational May 1 - Nov 1. Rate in 2010 $21-29 for 4 persons. Phone: (330)448-4858.

HURON—B-3

(S) HURON RIVER VALLEY CAMPGROUND & MARINA—(Erie) *From jct SR 13 & SR 2: Go 2-1/4 mi E on SR 2, then 3/4 mi S on Berlin Rd, then 1-1/2 mi W on Knight Rd, then 500 ft S on River Rd. Enter on R.*

◊◊◊FACILITIES: 200 sites, typical site width 30 ft, 147 W&E, (30 amps), 53 no hkups, many extd stay sites (summer), 5 pull-thrus, family camping, tenting, RV storage, dump, non-guest dump $, portable dump, laundry, ltd groc, RV supplies, ice, picnic tables, fire rings, wood, controlled access.

◊◊◊RECREATION: river swim, boating, canoeing, ramp, dock, river fishing, fishing supplies, golf nearby, bsktball, playground, activities, (wkends), horseshoes, hiking trails, v-ball. Rec open to public.

Pets welcome, breed restrict, quantity restrict. Partial handicap access. Open May 1 - Oct 10. Escort to site. Rate in 2010 $29.95-30.95 per family. MC/VISA/DISC/Debit. Member ARVC, OCOA. CCUSA 50% Discount. CCUSA reservations Recommended, CCUSA max stay 3 days, CCUSA disc. not avail holidays. No aggressive dog breeds. Boat ramp fee $5.

Phone: (419)433-4118
Address: 9019 River Rd, Huron, OH 44839
Lat/Lon: 41.35675/-82.54961
Email: letscamp@huronrivervalley.com
Web: www.huronrivervalley.com

SEE AD THIS PAGE

IRONTON—F-3

WAYNE NATIONAL FOREST (Lake Vesuvius Campground)—(Lawrence) *From town: Go 6 mi N on Hwy 93, then 1 mi E on CR 29.* FACILITIES: 81 sites, 16 E, 65 no hkups, tenting, dump, ltd groc. RECREATION: lake swim, ramp, lake fishing, playground. Partial handicap access. Facilities fully operational Apr 15 - Oct 31. Phone: (740)534-6500.

JACKSON—E-3

(NE) Lazy Dog Camp Resort—(Jackson) *From jct US 35 & Hwy 124/32: Go 5 mi E on Hwy 124/32, then 400 ft N on McGiffins Ln. Enter on R.* ◊◊◊FACILITIES: 83 sites, typical site width 25 ft, 83 full hkups, (30/50 amps), 25 pull-thrus, tenting, dump, laundry. ◊◊◊RECREATION: swim pool, lake fishing, playground. Pets welcome ($). Partial handicap access. Open all yr. Big rigs welcome. Rate in 2010 $24.99-29.99 per family. Member ARVC, OCOA. Phone: (800) 282-2167.

JEFFERSON—A-5

(S) MILLBROOK OUTDOOR RESORT (Formerly Wagon Trail Resort) (CAMP RESORT)—(Ashtabula) *From jct Rt 6 & Rt 46: Go 2-1/2 mi N on Rt 46. Enter on L.*

WELCOME

FACILITIES: 200 sites, 37 ft max RV length, 200 W&E, (20/30 amps), 10 pull-thrus, WiFi Internet central location, tenting, cabins, dump, laundry, picnic tables.

RECREATION: rec hall, pavilion, swim pool, lake swim, boating, canoeing, dock, 4 rowboat/canoe/pedal boat rentals, lake fishing, mini-golf, bsktball, playground, shuffleboard court shuffleboard court, activities (wkends), horseshoes, sports field, v-ball.

Pets welcome, breed restrict. Open all yr. Facilities fully operational Apr 15 - Oct 31. Closed Tuesday/Camping dates open Apr 15 - Oct 31. MC/VISA/DISC/AMEX.

Text 108013 to (440)725-8687 to see our Visual Tour.

Phone: (440)294-3991
Address: 4051 State Route 46S, Jefferson, OH 44047
Lat/Lon: 41.63966/-80.78072
Email: wagontrailsresort@hotmail.com
Web: www.gomilbrook.com

SEE AD THIS PAGE

LAKE MILTON—B-5

(NE) Green Acres Lake Park Resort—(Mahoning) *From jct I-76 (exit 54) & Hwy 534: Go 1/4 mi N on Hwy 534, then 1/4 mi E on Creed Rd. Enter on R.* ◊◊◊FACILITIES: 169 sites, typical site width 35 ft, 89 full hkups, 80 W&E, (15/20/30/50 amps), 50 amps ($), 8 pull-thrus, tenting, dump, ltd groc. ◊◊◊RECREATION: lake swim, boating, lake fishing, playground. Pets welcome, breed restrict. Partial handicap access. Open May 1 - Oct 1. Rate in 2010 $20-35 for 2 persons. Member ARVC, OCOA. Phone: (330)538-2194.

LAKEVIEW—C-2

(N) INDIAN LAKE STATE PARK—(Logan) *From jct US 33 & Hwy 235: Go 3 mi N on Hwy 235. Enter on R.* FACILITIES: 459 sites, 39 ft max RV length, 19 full hkups, 440 E, (30/50 amps), dump, laundry, ltd groc. RECREATION: lake swim, boating, canoeing, ramp, dock, lake fishing, playground. Pets welcome. No tents. Open all yr. Facilities fully operational Apr - Oct. Phone: (937)843-2717.

✽ **(N) RV WHOLESALERS**—*From jct US 33 & SR 235: Go 1 blk S on SR 235 to 1st stoplight, then 1/2 mi N (right turn) on North Main St. Enter on R.* SALES: travel trailers, park models, 5th wheels, toy hauler, SERVICES: full-time mech, RV appliance repair, body work/collision repair, LP gas by weight, LP bottle exch, sells parts/accessories, installs hitches. Open all yr. MC/VISA/DISC/AMEX/Debit.

WELCOME

50% of the United States population lives within a 500 mile radius of Columbus.

LAKEVIEW—Continued
RV WHOLESALERS—Continued

Phone: (937)843-9000
Address: 530 North Main St, Lakeview, OH 43331
Lat/Lon: 40.49301/-83.92921
Email: sales@rvwholesalers.com
Web: www.rvwholesalers.com

SEE AD TRAVEL SECTION PAGE 606

LANCASTER—D-3

(SE) Lakeview RV Park—(Fairfield) *From jct US 22 & US Bus 33: Go 2-3/4 mi S on US 33 (Memorial Dr), then 1/2 mi NE on Wilson Lane Rd, then 1/4 mi SE on Sugar Grove Rd SE. Enter on R.* ◊◊◊FACILITIES: 70 sites, typical site width 35 ft, 25 full hkups, 45 W&E, (30/50 amps), 50 amps ($), 16 pull-thrus, family camping, tenting, dump, laundry. ◊◊◊RECREATION: lake swim, boating, electric motors only, canoeing, ramp, dock, lake fishing, play equipment. Pets welcome, breed restrict. Partial handicap access. Open all yr. Facilities fully operational Apr 15 - Oct 15. Big rigs welcome. Rate in 2010 $29-35 for 2 persons. Member ARVC, OCOA. Phone: (740)653-4519.

(W) Lancaster RV Camp Ground—(Fairfield) *From jct US 22 & Bus US 33 (Memorial Dr): Go 3/4 mi N on US 33, then 1-1/2 mi W on Fair Ave. Enter on R.* ◊◊◊FACILITIES: 24 sites, typical site width 35 ft, 24 W&E, (20/30/50 amps), dump, laundry. ◊◊◊RECREATION: swim pool, playground. Pets welcome. No tents. Open Apr 1 - Oct 31. Big rigs welcome. Rate in 2010 $20 for 2 persons. Phone: (740)653-2261.

LAURELVILLE—D-3

(S) TAR HOLLOW STATE PARK—(Hocking) *From town: Go 7 mi S on Hwy-327.* FACILITIES: 99 sites, 35 ft max RV length, 71 E, (50 amps), 28 no hkups, tenting, dump, laundry, ltd groc. RECREATION: lake swim, boating, 4 hp limit, electric motors only, canoeing, ramp, lake fishing, playground. Pets welcome. Open all yr. Facilities fully operational Apr - Oct. Phone: (740)887-4818.

LEBANON—E-1

(NW) Cedarbrook Campground—(Warren) *From jct I-71 (exit 28) & SR 48: Go 4 mi N on SR 48, then 1-1/2 mi N on Hwy 123. Enter on R.* ◊◊◊FACILITIES: 134 sites, typical site width 50 ft, 84 full hkups, 31 W&E, (20/30/50 amps), 19 no hkups, 26 pull-thrus, tenting, dump, laundry, ltd groc. ◊◊◊RECREATION: swim pool, playground. Pets welcome, breed restrict. Open all yr. Big rigs welcome. Rate in 2010 $28-42 for 2 persons. Member ARVC, OCOA. Phone: (513)932-7717.

LIMA—C-1

(SE) Sun Valley Family Campground—(Allen) *From jct US 33 & Hwy 196: Go 8 mi N on Hwy 196, then 3 mi E on Amherst Rd, then 2 mi N on Hay Rd, then 1 blk W on Faulkner Rd. Enter on R.* ◊◊◊FACILITIES: 242 sites, typical site width 30 ft, 242 full hkups, (20/30/50 amps), 5 pull-thrus, family camping, tenting, laundry, ltd groc. ◊◊◊◊RECREATION: lake swim,

LIMA—Continued
Sun Valley Family Campground—Continued

boating, electric motors only, dock, lake/pond fishing, playground. Pets welcome, breed restrict, size restrict. Partial handicap access. Open Apr 1 - Oct 31. Big rigs welcome. Rate in 2010 $27 for 2 persons. Member ARVC, OCOA. Phone: (419)648-2235.

(SW) Winona Lake Campground—(Allen) *From jct US 33 & I-75: Go 9 mi N on I-75 (exit 120), then 4-1/2 mi W on Breese Rd. Enter on L.* ◊◊◊FACILITIES: 45 sites, 30 full hkups, 15 W&E, (30/50 amps), family camping, tenting, dump. ◊◊◊RECREATION: lake swim, pond fishing, play equipment. Pets welcome. Open May 1 - Oct 15. Rate in 2010 $25-30 for 2 persons. Member ARVC, OCOA. Phone: (419)999-6571.

LISBON—C-5

GUILFORD LAKE STATE PARK—(Columbiana) *Southbound: From jct US-45 & US-30: Go 2 mi N on US-30, then 5 mi NW on Hwy-172.* FACILITIES: 41 sites, 35 ft max RV length, 41 E, (50 amps), tenting, dump, ltd groc. RECREATION: lake swim, boating, 10 hp limit, ramp, dock, lake fishing, playground. Open all yr. Facilities fully operational Apr - Oct. Phone: (330)222-1712.

(SE) Lock 30 Woodlands RV Resort—(Columbiana) *From jct Hwy 11 & Hwy 154: Go 1-1/2 mi E on Hwy 154, then 3-1/2 mi E on CR 419. Enter on R.* ◊◊◊FACILITIES: 98 sites, typical site width 35 ft, 75 full hkups, 8 W&E, (20/30/50 amps), 15 no hkups, 5 pull-thrus, family camping, tenting, dump, laundry, full svc store. ◊◊◊◊RECREATION: swim pool, canoeing, lake/river fishing, playground. Pets welcome. Open all yr. Big rigs welcome. Rate in 2010 $25-41 for 2 persons. Member ARVC, OCOA. Phone: (330)424-9197.

LODI—B-4

See listings at Chatham, Homerville & Seville

LOGAN—D-3

(SW) HOCKING HILLS KOA—(Hocking) *From jct US 33 & SR-664: Go 6-3/4 mi SW on SR 664. Enter on L.*

WELCOME

◊◊◊◊FACILITIES: 92 sites, typical site width 50 ft, 24 full hkups, 38 W&E, 11 E, (20/30/50 amps), 19 no hkups, 45 pull-thrus, WiFi Instant Internet at site, family camping, tenting, RV's/park model rentals, cabins, dump, non-guest dump $, portable dump, laundry, ltd groc, RV supplies, LP gas by weight/by meter, ice, picnic tables, fire rings, wood.

◊◊◊◊◊RECREATION: rec hall, rec room/area, pavilion, coin games, swim pool, bsktball, playground, activities, (wkends), horseshoes, sports field, hiking trails, v-ball. Rec open to public.

Pets welcome, breed restrict. Partial handicap access. Open Apr 1 - Oct 31. Big rigs welcome. Clubs welcome. Green Friendly. Rate in 2010 $31-66 for 2 persons. MC/VISA/DISC/Debit. Member ARVC, OCOA. KOA discount.

HOCKING HILLS KOA—Continued on next page

LOGAN—Continued
HOCKING HILLS KOA—Continued

Phone: (740)385-4295
Address: 29150 Pattor Rd, Logan, OH 43138
Lat/Lon: 39.46884/-82.49049
Email: camp@hockinghillskoa.com
Web: www.hockinghillskoa.com

SEE AD PAGE 625

(S) HOCKING HILLS STATE PARK (Old Man's Cave)—(Hocking) *From jct US 33 & Hwy-664: Go 12 mi SW on Hwy-664 & Hwy-374.* FACILITIES: 169 sites, 156 E, (20/30/50 amps), 13 no hkups, tenting, dump, laundry, ltd groc. RECREATION: swim pool, lake fishing, playground. Pets welcome. Open all yr. Facilities fully operational Apr - Oct. Phone: (740)385-6841.

LOUDONVILLE—C-3

(E) CAMP TOODIK FAMILY CAMPGROUND CABINS & CANOEING—(Holmes) *From jct Hwy 3 & Hwy 60: Go 2-1/2 mi SE on Hwy 60, then 3/4 mi N on Twp Rd 462. Enter on R.*

WELCOME

◊◊◊FACILITIES: 188 sites, typical site width 45 ft, 46 full hkups, 126 W&E, (20/30/50 amps), 16 no hkups, some extd stay sites (summer), 2 pull-thrus, WiFi Internet central location, family camping, tenting, cabins, RV storage, dump, laundry, groceries, RV supplies, LP gas by weight/by meter, ice, picnic tables, fire rings, wood, controlled access.

◊◊◊◊RECREATION: rec room/area, pavilion, coin games, swim pool, boating, canoeing, kayaking, 69 canoe/34 kayak rentals, float trips, river/pond fishing, mini-golf, golf nearby, bsktball, playground, shuffleboard court 2 shuffleboard courts, activities (wkends), horseshoes, sports field, hiking trails, v-ball.

Pets welcome, breed restrict. Partial handicap access. Open Apr - Oct 31. Clubs welcome. Rate in 2010 $37-44 for 2 persons. MC/VISA/DISC/Debit. Member ARVC, OCOA.

Phone: (877)886-7866
Address: 7700 TR 462, Loudonville, OH 44842
Lat/Lon: 40.63275/-82.18723
Email: mrtoodik@hughes.net
Web: www.camptoodik.com

SEE AD THIS PAGE

(NE) **Lake Wapusun Campground**—(Wayne) *From jct Hwy 60 & Hwy 3: Go 8 mi NE on Hwy 3, then 1-1/2 mi N on Snoddy Rd (Twp Rd 31), then 1/4 mi E on Molter Rd. Enter on L.* ◊◊FACILITIES: 400 sites, typical site width 35 ft, 351 W&E, (20/30 amps), 49 no hkups, 24 pull-thrus, family camping, tenting, dump, laundry, groceries. ◊◊◊RECREATION: lake swim, boating, electric motors only, lake fishing, playground. Pets welcome. Open mid Apr - mid Oct. Rate in 2010 $19-25 for 2 persons. Member ARVC, OCOA. Phone: (330)496-2355.

(SW) MOHICAN ADVENTURES CAMP AND CABINS—(Ashland) *From jct Hwy 60 & Hwy 3: Go 1-1/2 mi S on Hwy 3. Enter on R.*

WELCOME

◊◊◊◊FACILITIES: 434 sites, typical site width 35 ft, 189 full hkups, (20/30/50 amps), 245 no hkups, 100 pull-thrus, WiFi Instant Internet at site ($), family camping, tenting, RV's/park model rentals, cabins, dump, non-guest dump $, ltd groc, RV supplies, ice, picnic tables, fire rings, grills, wood, controlled access.

◊◊◊◊◊RECREATION: rec room/area, pavilion, swim pool, hot tub, boating, canoeing, kayaking, 500 canoe/200 kayak/6 pedal boat rentals, float trips, lake/pond fishing, fishing supplies, mini-golf, ($), golf nearby, bsktball, playground, activities, (wkends), horseshoes, sports field, hiking trails, v-ball. Rec open to public.

Pets welcome. Partial handicap access. Open Apr 2 - Dec 5. Facilities fully operational May 1 - Oct 31. Big rigs welcome. Clubs welcome. MC/VISA/DISC/Debit. Member ARVC, OCOA.

LOUDONVILLE—Continued
MOHICAN ADVENTURES CAMP AND CABINS—Continued

Phone: (888)909-7400
Address: 3058 SR 3, Loudonville, OH 44842
Lat/Lon: 40.61715/-82.25321
Email: campgrounds@mohicanadventures.com
Web: www.mohicanadventures.com

SEE AD THIS PAGE

(SW) MOHICAN ADVENTURES CANOE & FUN CENTER—*From jct Hwy 60 & Hwy 3: Go 1-1/2 mi S on Hwy 3. Enter on L.* Canoes & kayaks on the Mohican river from 2 hours up to 2 days. Group rates, packages, 4 picnic shelters with grills. Adventure golf, adventure go-karts. Open Apr 1 - Oct 31. MC/VISA/DISC.

WELCOME

Phone: (800)MO-CANOE
Address: 3045 State Hwy 3 South, Loudonville, OH 44842
Lat/Lon: 40.61713/-82.25264
Email: mocanoe@neo.rr.com
Web: www.mohicanadventures.com

SEE AD THIS PAGE

(S) MOHICAN RESERVATION CAMPGROUNDS AND CANOEING—(Knox) *From jct Hwy 60 & Hwy 3: Go 1/2 mi S on Hwy 3, then 7 mi S on Wally Rd (CR 3175). Enter on L.*

WELCOME

◊◊◊FACILITIES: 238 sites, typical site width 35 ft, 209 W&E, (20/30/50 amps), 29 no hkups, some extd stay sites (summer), WiFi Instant Internet at site, family camping, tenting, tent rentals, cabins, RV storage, shower$, dump, non-guest dump $, portable dump, laundry, ltd groc, RV supplies, LP bottle exch, ice, picnic tables, fire rings, grills, wood, controlled access.

CAMPCLUB USA

◊◊◊RECREATION: rec room/area, pavilion, coin games, river swim, boating, canoeing, kayaking, 500 canoe/100 kayak rentals, float trips, river fishing, bsktball, playground, activities, (wkends), horseshoes, sports field, v-ball.

Pets welcome, quantity restrict. Partial handicap access. Open Apr 1 - Nov 1. Clubs welcome. Rate in 2010 $25-30 for 2 persons. MC/VISA/DISC/AMEX/Debit. Member ARVC, OCOA. CCUSA 50% Discount. CCUSA reservations Recommended, CCUSA max stay Unlimited. Not valid holiday and special event weekends. Call for details. Special group rates & packages.

Phone: (800)766-CAMP
Address: 23720 Wally Rd (CR 3175), Loudonville, OH 44842
Lat/Lon: 40.57012/-82.18866
Email: info@mohicanreservation.com
Web: www.mohicanreservation.com

SEE AD THIS PAGE

(SW) **Mohican RV Center**—*From jct Hwy 60 & Hwy 3: Go 1-1/4 mi S on Hwy 3, then 100 yds NE on S Mt. Vernon Ave. Enter on L.* SALES: travel trailers, park models, pre-owned unit sales. SERVICES: RV appliance repair, LP gas by meter, sells parts/accessories. Open all yr.

Phone: (866)290-4994
Address: 3036 CR 3A, Loudonville, OH 44842
Lat/Lon: 40.62029/-82.25022
Email: mohicanrv@verizon.net
Web: www.mohicanrv.com

(S) MOHICAN STATE PARK—(Ashland) *From jct Hwy-97 & Hwy-3: Go 1 mi N on Hwy-3.* FACILITIES: 186 sites, 39 ft max RV length, 33 full hkups, 118 E, (50 amps), 35 no hkups, 33 pull-thrus, tenting, dump, laundry, ltd groc. RECREATION: swim pool, boating, canoeing, river fishing, playground. Pets welcome. Open all yr. Facilities fully operational Apr - Oct. Phone: (419)994-5125.

(S) **Mohican Wilderness**—(Knox) *From jct Hwy 60 & Hwy 3: Go 3/4 mi S on Hwy 3, then 8 mi SE on Wally Rd (CR-3175). Enter on L.* ◊◊FACILITIES: 239 sites, typical site width 80 ft, 177 W&E, (30 amps), 62 no hkups, 10 pull-thrus, family camping, tenting, dump,

LOUDONVILLE—Continued
Mohican Wilderness—Continued

laundry, groceries. ◊◊◊RECREATION: river swim, boating, canoeing, river fishing, playground. Pets welcome. Open May 1 - Oct 31. Rate in 2010 $34-42 for 2 persons. Member ARVC, OCOA. Phone: (740)599-6741.

(S) **River Run Family Campground & Canoe Livery**—(Ashland) *From jct Hwy-60 & Hwy-3. Go 3/4 mi S on Hwy-3, then 1-1/4 mi SE on Wally Rd. Enter on R.* ◊◊◊FACILITIES: 250 sites, typical site width 33 ft, 164 W&E, 86 E, (20/30 amps), 12 pull-thrus, tenting, dump, ltd groc. ◊◊◊◊RECREATION: swim pool, river swim, boating, canoeing, river fishing, playground. Pets welcome, breed restrict. Open May 1 - Oct 16. Rate in 2010 $32-34 for 2 persons. Member ARVC, OCOA. Phone: (419)994-5257.

(S) **Smith's Pleasant Valley Campground & Cabins**—(Holmes) *From jct Hwy 60 & Hwy 3: Go 3/4 mi S on Hwy 3, then 4 mi SE on Wally Rd (CR 3175). Enter on L.* ◊◊◊FACILITIES: 170 sites, typical site width 40 ft, 170 W&E, (20/30/50 amps), 6 pull-thrus, family camping, tenting, dump, ltd groc. ◊◊◊◊RECREATION: swim pool, river swim, boating, canoeing, river fishing, playground. Pets welcome. Open Apr 15 - Oct 31. Big rigs welcome. Rate in 2010 $30-35 for 2 persons. Member ARVC, OCOA. Phone: (800)3SMITHS.

(S) **Wally World Camping Resort**—(Holmes) *From jct Hwy 60 & Hwy 3: Go 3/4 mi S on Hwy 3, then 4-3/4 mi SE on Wally Rd (CR 3175). Enter on L.* ◊◊◊FACILITIES: 332 sites, 1 full hkups, 331 W&E, (20/30 amps), 60 pull-thrus, tenting, RV storage, dump, laundry, ice, picnic tables, fire rings, wood.

CAMPCLUB USA

◊◊◊◊RECREATION: rec hall, swim pool, river fishing, mini-golf, bsktball, playground, activities, horseshoes, v-ball. Pets welcome, breed restrict. Open all yr. Facilities fully operational May 1 - Nov 1. Rate in 2010 $34 per vehicle. MC/VISA/DISC/Debit. CCUSA 50% Discount. CCUSA reservations Accepted, CCUSA max stay 5 days. May 27,28,29,30; Jul 1, 2,3,4,; Sep 2,3,4,5. No pit bulls, rottweilers or Doberman pinschers.

Phone: (419)994-4828
Address: 16121 CR 23, Loudonville, OH 44842
Lat/Lon: 40.59193/-82.19057
Email: services@wallyworldresort.com
Web: www.wallyworldresort.com

LOUISVILLE—C-5

(N) CUTTY'S SUNSET CAMPING RESORT—(Stark) *From jct US 62 & Hwy 44: Go 7 mi N on Hwy 44, then 1/4 mi E on Hwy 619. Enter on R.*

WELCOME

◊◊◊◊FACILITIES: 480 sites, typical site width 35 ft, 430 full hkups, 50 W&E, (30/50 amps), 50 amps ($), mostly extd stay sites (summer), 15 pull-thrus, WiFi Instant Internet at site ($), WiFi Internet central location, family camping, tenting, dump, non-guest dump $, laundry, full svc store, RV supplies, LP gas by weight/by meter, ice, picnic tables, fire rings, wood, controlled access.

◊◊◊◊◊RECREATION: rec hall, rec room/area, pavilion, coin games, swim pool, spray ground, mini-golf, ($), golf nearby, bsktball, playground, shuffleboard court 4 shuffleboard courts, activities, tennis, horseshoes, sports field, v-ball.

Pets welcome, breed restrict. Partial handicap access. Open May 1 - Oct 15. Big rigs welcome. Clubs welcome. Rate in 2010 $29-36 for 2 persons. MC/VISA/DISC/Debit. Member ARVC, OCOA.

Text 107966 to (440)725-8687 to see our Visual Tour.

Phone: (330)935-2431
Address: 8050 Edison St NE, Louisville, OH 44641
Lat/Lon: 40.95147/-81.24645
Email: info@cuttyssunset.com
Web: www.cuttyssunset.com

SEE AD AKRON PAGE 614

LOUISVILLE—Continued on next page

LOUISVILLE—Continued

✲ **(N) CUTTY'S SUNSET RV SERVICE**— *From jct US 62 & Hwy 44: Go 7 mi N on Hwy 44, then 1/4 mi E on Hwy 619. Enter on R.* SERVICES: full-time mech, RV appliance repair, LP gas by weight/by meter, dump station, sells parts/accessories, installs hitches. Open all yr. MC/VISA.

WELCOME

Phone: (330)935-2733
Address: 8050 Edison St NE, Louisville, OH 44641
Lat/Lon: 40.95147/-81.24645
Email: info@cuttyssunset.com
Web: www.cuttyssunset.com

SEE AD AKRON PAGE 614

MANSFIELD—C-3

See listings at Ashland, Bellville, Butler, Loudonville, Perrysville, Shelby & Mount Vernon.

(E) CHARLES MILL LAKE PARK (Muskingum Watershed Conservancy Dist)—(Ashland) *From jct I-71 & US 30: Go 2 mi E on US 30, then 1/4 mi S on Hwy 603 to Hwy 430.* FACILITIES: 500 sites, 257 E, 243 no hkups, 50 pull-thrus, tenting, dump. RECREATION: lake swim, boating, 10 hp limit, ramp, dock, lake fishing, playground. Open all yr. Facilities fully operational Memorial Day - Labor Day. Phone: (419)368-6885.

MALABAR FARM STATE PARK—(Richland) *From jct Hwy 603 & Pleasant Valley Rd: Go 1 mi W on Pleasant Valley Rd.* FACILITIES: 15 sites, 15 no hkups, tenting. RECREATION: pond fishing, playground. Open all yr. Facilities fully operational Apr - Oct. Phone: (419)892-2784.

MARBLEHEAD—B-3

(W) Kamp Kozy—(Ottawa) *From US 2 & Hwy 163: Go 1 mi E on Hwy 163, then 2 mi S on Church Rd, then 3/4 mi SW on Bayshore, then 1/2 mi S on Meter 222 Rd. Enter on R.* ◆◆◆FACILITIES: 187 sites, 175 W&E, (30/50 amps), 12 no hkups, tenting, dump, ltd groc. ◆◆◆RECREATION: lake swim, boating, ramp, dock, lake fishing, playground. Pets welcome, breed restrict. Open May 1 - Oct 31. Rate in 2010 $32 for 2 persons. Phone: (419)732-2421.

Ohio is the home state of two of the U.S.'s most famous astronauts: John H. Glenn (first American to orbit the Earth) and Neil Armstrong (first man to walk on the moon).

MARBLEHEAD—Continued

(C) SURF MOTEL & RV CAMPGROUND —(Ottawa) *From jct of St Rt 269 & St Rt 163: Go 5 mi E on St Rt 163. Enter on R.*

WELCOME

◆◆◆FACILITIES: 89 sites, 60 full hkups, 14 W&E, (20/30/50 amps), 15 no hkups, many extd stay sites, 10 pull-thrus, WiFi Instant Internet at site, WiFi Internet central location, tenting, laundry, ltd groc, ice, picnic tables, grills.

◆◆RECREATION: pavilion, swim pool, pond fishing, fishing supplies, playground, horseshoes, v-ball.

Pets welcome. Partial handicap access. Open Apr 1 - Nov 1. Rate in 2010 $25-40 for 4 persons. MC/VISA/DISC/AMEX/Debit. Member ARVC, OCOA.

Phone: (419)798-4823
Address: 230 E Main St, Marblehead, OH 43440
Lat/Lon: 41.54073/-82.71866
Email: service@surfmotelohio.com
Web: www.surfmotelohio.com

SEE AD THIS PAGE

MARENGO—C-3

(SW) CARDINAL CENTER CAMPGROUND —(Morrow) *From jct I-71 (exit 140) & SR 61: Go 1/2 mi N on SR 61. Enter on L.*

WELCOME

◆◆◆◆◆FACILITIES: 384 sites, 200 full hkups, 184 W&E, (20/30/50 amps), 53 pull-thrus, WiFi Instant Internet at site, family camping, tenting, cabins, dump, non-guest dump $, laundry, ltd groc, RV supplies, LP gas by weight/by meter, ice, picnic tables, fire rings, wood.

◆◆◆◆RECREATION: rec hall, rec room/area, pavilion, swim pool, pond fishing, golf nearby, bsktball, playground, activities, (wkends), horseshoes, sports field, v-ball.

Pets welcome. Partial handicap access. Open all yr. Big rigs welcome. Escort to site. Clubs welcome. Rate in 2010 $26-39 per family. MC/VISA/DISC/AMEX/Debit.

Phone: (419)253-0800
Address: 616 State Route 61, Marengo, OH 43334
Lat/Lon: 40.37882/-82.82928
Email: cardinalcentercamp@yahoo.com
Web: www.cardinalcentercamp.com

SEE AD COLUMBUS PAGE 622

⚑ **(SW) OLE FARMSTEAD INN**—*From jct I-71 (exit 140) & SR-61: Go 1/4 mi N on SR-61. Enter on L.* Fine food in a friendly hometown atmosphere. Open all yr.

WELCOME

MARENGO—Continued
OLE FARMSTEAD INN—Continued

Address: State Rte 61, Marengo, OH 43334
Lat/Lon: 40.37601/-82.82964

SEE AD COLUMBUS PAGE 622

MARIETTA—D-4

WASHINGTON COUNTY FAIR PARK—(Washington) *From jct I-77 & Hwy 821: Go 2-1/2 mi S on Hwy 821, then 6 blocks S on Hwy 60 to Washington County Fairgrounds. Enter on L.* FACILITIES: 180 sites, typical site width 30 ft, 140 full hkups, 40 W&E, (20/30 amps), 12 pull-thrus, tenting, dump, laundry. RECREATION: swim pool, boating, canoeing, river fishing, playground. Pets welcome. Partial handicap access. Open all yr. Facilities fully operational May 1 - Oct 1. Phone: (740)373-1347.

MARION—C-2

(W) HICKORY GROVE LAKE CAMPGROUND—(Marion) *From jct US 23 & SR-309: Go 7-1/2 mi W on SR-309, then 1/4 mi S on SR-203, then 1 mi W on Decliff-Big Island Rd, then 1/2 mi S on Hoch Rd. Enter on R.*

WELCOME

◆◆◆FACILITIES: 196 sites, typical site width 35 ft, 100 full hkups, 70 W&E, (20/30/50 amps), 50 amps ($), 26 no hkups, many extd stay sites (summer), 8 pull-thrus, phone Internet central location, family camping, tenting, RV's/park model rentals, RV storage, dump, non-guest dump $, groceries, RV supplies, ice, picnic tables, fire rings, wood.

◆◆◆◆RECREATION: rec hall, pavilion, coin games, lake swim, boating, electric motors only, canoeing, 3 rowboat/3 pedal boat rentals, lake fishing, fishing supplies, mini-golf, ($), bsktball, playground, activities, (wkends), horseshoes, sports field, v-ball. Rec open to public.

Pets welcome, breed restrict. Partial handicap access. Open all yr. Facilities fully operational Apr 15 - Oct 15. Electricity only in winter months. Escort to site. Clubs welcome. Rate in 2010 $27-30 for 2 persons. Member ARVC, OCOA.

Phone: (740)382-8584
Address: 805 Hoch Rd., Marion, OH 43302
Lat/Lon: 40.60057/-83.23679
Email: hickorygrovelk@live.com

SEE AD THIS PAGE

(E) River Bend Family Campground—(Marion) *From jct US 23 & SR 95: Go 4 mi E on SR 95, then 1 mi S on Whetstone River Rd. Enter on L.* ◆◆◆FACILITIES: 240 sites, typical site width 35 ft, 180 full hkups, 60 W&E, (20/30/50 amps), family camping, tenting, dump. ◆◆◆◆RECREATION: swim pool, boating, canoeing, dock, pond fishing, playground. Pets welcome, breed restrict. Open Apr 15 - Oct 15. Rate in 2010 $25-30 per family. Phone: (740)389-5371.

MEDINA—B-4

(SW) Pier-Lon Park—(Medina) *Fom jct Hwy 83 & Hwy 162: Go 1 mi E on Hwy 162, then 1/2 mi N on CR 31 (Vandemark Rd). Enter on L.* ◆◆◆FACILITIES: 350

Pier-Lon Park—Continued on next page

sites, typical site width 40 ft, 220 full hkups, 110 W&E, (20/30/50 amps), 20 no hkups, 50 pull-thrus, family camping, tenting, dump, laundry, groceries. ◊◊◊◊RECREATION: lake swim, lake fishing, playground. Pets welcome, breed restrict. Open Apr 15 - 3rd weekend in Oct. Big rigs welcome. Rate in 2010 $27.50-36 per family. Member ARVC, OCOA. Phone: (330)667-2311.

MILAN—B-3

(NW) Milan Travel Park—(Erie) *From jct I-90/80 & US 250: Go 1/4 mi N on US 250. Enter on R.* ◊◊◊◊FACILITIES: 141 sites, typical site width 30 ft, 49 full hkups, 42 W&E, (20/30/50 amps), 50 amps ($), 50 no hkups, 52 pull-thrus, family camping, tenting, dump, laundry, ltd groc. ◊◊◊RECREATION: swim pool, playground. Pets welcome, breed restrict. Partial handicap access. Open May 1 - Nov 1. Facilities fully operational May 1 - Oct 15. Big rigs welcome. Rate in 2010 $34-36 for 2 persons. Phone: (800)433-4627.

MINERAL CITY—C-4

(E) ATWOOD LAKE PARK (Muskingum Watershed Conservancy Dist)—(Tuscarwas) *From jct I-77 & Hwy-212: Go 12-1/2 mi SE on Hwy-212, then N on CR-93.* FACILITIES: 537 sites, 62 full hkups, 475 E, (30 amps), tenting, dump, laundry, groceries. RECREATION: lake swim, boating, 25 hp limit, canoeing, ramp, dock, lake fishing, playground. No pets. Partial handicap access. Open all yr. Facilities fully operational Memorial Day - Labor Day. Phone: (330)343-6780.

MONTVILLE—B-5

(E) COUNTRY LAKES FAMILY CAMPGROUND—(Geauga) *From jct I-90 (exit 212) & Hwy 528: Go 10 mi S on Hwy 528, then 1 mi E on Hwy 6. Enter on R.*

WELCOME

◊◊◊FACILITIES: 235 sites, typical site width 35 ft, 175 W&E, (20/30 amps), 60 no hkups, many extd stay sites (summer), 2 pull-thrus, family camping, tenting, cabins, RV storage, dump, portable dump, laundry, ltd groc, RV supplies, ice, picnic tables, fire rings, wood, controlled access.

◊◊◊◊RECREATION: rec hall, rec room/area, pavilion, coin games, swim pool, lake swim, lake fishing, fishing supplies, bsktball, playground, activities, (wkends), horseshoes, sports field, v-ball.

Pets welcome, breed restrict. Open Last wknd of Apr - First wknd of Oct. Escort to site. Clubs welcome. Rate in 2010 $29 for 2 persons. MC/VISA. Member ARVC, OCOA.

Phone: (440)968-3400
Address: 17147 G.A.R. Hwy, Montville, OH 44064
Lat/Lon: 41.60692/-81.02954
Email: harrietk@SBCglobal.net
Web: www.countrylakescampground.com

SEE AD TRAVEL SECTION PAGE 605

MOUNT GILEAD—C-3

(N) DOGWOOD VALLEY CAMPING RESORT—(Morrow) *From jct SR 95 & US 42/SR 61: Go 2 mi N on SR 61, then 1/2 mi E on Twp Rd 99. Enter on L.*

WELCOME

◊◊◊◊FACILITIES: 202 sites, typical site width 35 ft, 50 full hkups, 137 W&E, (15/20/30/50 amps), 15 no hkups, some extd stay sites (summer), 27 pull-thrus, cable TV, WiFi Internet central location, family camping, tenting, RV's/park model rentals, dump, non-guest dump $, portable dump, groceries, RV supplies, ice, picnic tables, fire rings, grills, wood.

◊◊◊◊RECREATION: rec room/area, pavilion, equipped pavilion, 2 swim pools, lake swim, boating, canoeing, kayaking, dock, 2 rowboat/2 canoe/4 kayak/9 pedal boat rentals, lake fishing, fishing supplies, bsktball, playground, activities, (wkends), horseshoes, hiking trails, v-ball. Rec open to public.

Pets welcome, breed restrict, quantity restrict. Partial handicap access. Open May 1 - Oct 15. Big rigs welcome. Escort to site. Clubs welcome. Rate in 2010 $36-65 per family. MC/VISA/DISC/Debit. Member ARVC, OCOA.

Phone: (419)946-5230
Address: 4185 Twp Rd 99, Mt. Gilead, OH 43338
Lat/Lon: 40.57901/-82.81530
Email: dogwoodvalley@gmail.com
Web: www.dogwoodvalleycamping.com

SEE AD THIS PAGE

(E) Hidden Lakes Community Assoc.—(Morrow) *From jct I-71 (exit 151) & US 95: Go 4-1/4 mi W on US 95, then 1 mi E on CR 109, then 1/2 mi N on TR 108. Enter on L.* ◊◊FACILITIES: 40 sites, accepts self-contained units only, 40 W&E, (30 amps), 4 pull-thrus, dump, laundry, ltd groc. ◊◊◊RECREATION: swim pool, lake fishing, playground. Pets welcome, breed restrict. Partial handicap access. No tents. Open May 1 - Oct 31. Phone: (419)946-7050.

(W) MT. GILEAD STATE PARK—(Morrow) *From jct US-42 & Hwy-95: Go 1 mi E on Hwy-95.* FACILITIES: 59 sites, 39 ft max RV length, 59 E, (50 amps), tenting, dump, ltd groc. RECREATION: boating, electric motors only, canoeing, ramp, lake fishing, playground. Open all yr. Facilities fully operational Apr - Oct. Phone: (740)369-2761.

MOUNT STERLING—D-2

(S) DEER CREEK STATE PARK—(Pickaway) *From jct Hwy-56 & Hwy-207: Go 5 mi S on Hwy-207, then E on Yankeetown Rd.* FACILITIES: 227 sites, 39 ft max RV length, 227 E, (30 amps), tenting, dump, laundry, ltd groc. RECREATION: lake swim, boating, ramp, dock, lake fishing, playground. Pets welcome. Open all yr. Facilities fully operational Apr - Oct. Phone: (740)869-3124.

MOUNT VERNON—C-3

(SW) RUSTIC KNOLLS CAMPGROUND—(Knox) *From jct Hwy 13 & Hwy 36/3: Go 2-1/2 mi S on 36/3, then 2-1/2 mi W on Pleasant Valley Rd, then 1/4 mi S on Twp Rd 363 (Keys Rd). Enter on L.*

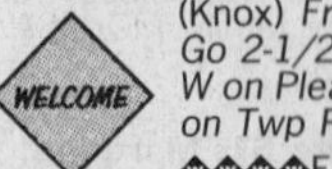

◊◊◊◊FACILITIES: 150 sites, typical site width 30 ft, 119 full hkups, 21 W&E, (20/30/50 amps), 10 no hkups, many extd stay sites (summer), 3 pull-thrus, WiFi Instant Internet at site, WiFi Internet central location, family camping, tenting, cabins, RV storage, dump, non-guest dump $, laundry, ltd groc, LP bottle exch, ice, picnic tables, fire rings, wood, controlled access.

◊◊◊◊RECREATION: rec hall, rec room/area, equipped pavilion, coin games, lake swim, lake fishing, golf nearby, bsktball, playground, activities, (wkends), horseshoes, sports field, v-ball. Rec open to public.

Pets welcome, breed restrict, quantity restrict. Partial handicap access. Open Apr 15 - Oct 15. Big rigs welcome. Clubs welcome. Rate in 2010 $26-30 for 4 persons. MC/VISA/Debit. Member ARVC, OCOA.

Phone: (740)397-9318
Address: 8664 Keys Rd, Mt. Vernon, OH 43050
Lat/Lon: 40.36761/-82.55931
Email: rusticknolls@embarqmail.com
Web: www.rusticknollscampground.com

SEE AD THIS PAGE

MT. EATON—C-4

(E) EVERGREEN PARK RV RESORT—(Wayne) *From jct Hwy 62 & US 250: Go 4 mi W on US 250. Enter on L.*

WELCOME

RIGHT IN THE HEART OF AMISH COUNTRY
Our Luxurious RV Resort features beautifully Landscaped paved full hookup 50 amp sites. Many pull thrus & a large indoor pool & commercial Laundromat on site. Only minutes to great Amish restaurants, attractions & stores.

◊◊◊◊◊FACILITIES: 87 sites, typical site width 30 ft, 87 full hkups, (20/30/50 amps), 52 pull-thrus, cable TV, WiFi Instant Internet at site, tenting, cabins, dump, non-guest dump $, laundry, ltd groc, RV supplies, LP gas by weight/by meter, ice, picnic tables, fire rings, wood.

◊◊◊◊◊RECREATION: rec room/area, pavilion, equipped pavilion, coin games, swim pool, hot tub, golf nearby, bsktball, 10 bike rentals, playground, shuffleboard court 2 shuffleboard courts, activities (wkends), horseshoes, sports field, hiking trails, v-ball, local tours.

Pets welcome. Partial handicap access. Open all yr. Big rigs welcome. Clubs welcome. Green Friendly. Rate in 2010 $45 for 2 persons. MC/VISA/DISC/AMEX/Debit. ATM. Member ARVC, OCOA.

Text 83406 to (440)725-8687 to see our Visual Tour.

Phone: (888)359-6429
Address: 16359 US 250, Mt Eaton, OH 44659
Lat/Lon: 40.69129/-81.69429
Email: evergreenpark@wifi7.com
Web: www.evergreenparkrvresort.com

SEE AD BERLIN PAGE 616

NELSONVILLE—D-4

(SW) Happy Hills Campground & Cabins—(Hocking) *From jct US 33 & SR 278: Go 8 mi S on SR 278. Enter on R.* ◊◊◊FACILITIES: 63 sites, typical site width 35 ft, 17 full hkups, 31 W&E, 5 E, (15/20/30 amps), 10 no hkups, 10 pull-thrus, tenting, dump, laundry, ltd groc. ◊◊◊◊RECREATION: swim pool, lake swim, dock, lake fishing, playground. Pets welcome, breed restrict. Facilities fully operational Mid Apr - Oct 31. Rate in 2010 $36-53 for 4 persons. Member ARVC, OCOA. Phone: (740)385-6720.

NEW LONDON—B-3

(S) NEW LONDON VILLAGE RESERVOIR PARK—(Huron) *From jct Hwy-162 & Hwy-60: Go 1 mi S on Hwy-60, then 3/4 mi W on Town Line Rd, then 1/4 mi N on Euclid Rd.* FACILITIES: 114 sites, 57 full hkups, 42 E, (30/50 amps), 15 no hkups, 4 pull-thrus, tenting, dump, ltd groc. RECREATION: lake swim, boating, 5 hp limit, electric motors only, canoeing, ramp, lake fishing, playground. Pets welcome. Partial handicap access. Open Apr 15 - Oct 15. Phone: (419)929-8609.

NEW PARIS—D-1

(S) Archway Campground—(Darke) *From jct I-70 (exit 156B in Indiana) & US 40: Go 1/2 mi E on US 40, then S on Old National Rd. Enter on R.* ◊◊FACILITIES: 30 sites, 30 W&E, (30/50 amps), tenting. ◊◊RECREATION: play equipment. Pets welcome. Open Apr 1 - Oct 31. Big rigs welcome. Rate in 2010 $25 for 2 persons. Phone: (937)273-2022.

(NE) Arrowhead Campground—(Darke) *From jct I-70 (exit 156B in Indiana) & US 40: Go 1 mi E on US 40, then 2 mi N on SR 320, then 7-1/4 mi N on SR 121, then 1 mi N on Thomas Rd. Enter on L.* ◊◊◊◊FACILITIES: 131 sites, typical site width 28 ft, 120 full hkups, 6 E, (20/30/50 amps), 50 amps ($), 5 no hkups, 7 pull-thrus, family camping, tenting, dump, non-guest dump $, laundry, groceries, RV supplies, LP gas by meter, ice, picnic tables, patios, fire rings, grills, wood.

CAMPCLUB USA

◊◊◊◊RECREATION: pavilion, swim pool, boating, pond fishing, fishing supplies, bsktball, playground, activities, horseshoes, v-ball. Pets welcome, breed restrict. Open Apr 15 - Oct 31. Big rigs welcome. Rate in 2010 $25-39 for 4 persons. MC/VISA/Debit. Member ARVC, OCOA. CCUSA 50% Discount. CCUSA reservations Accepted, CCUSA max stay Unlimited, CCUSA disc. not avail F,Sa, CCUSA disc. not avail holidays.

Phone: (937)996-6203
Address: 1361 Thomas Rd, New Paris, OH 45347
Lat/Lon: 39.95302/-84.74638
Email: patmcc@arrowhead-campground.com
Web: www.arrowhead-campground.com

NEW PARIS—Continued on next page

Cleveland became the world's first city to be lighted electrically in 1879.

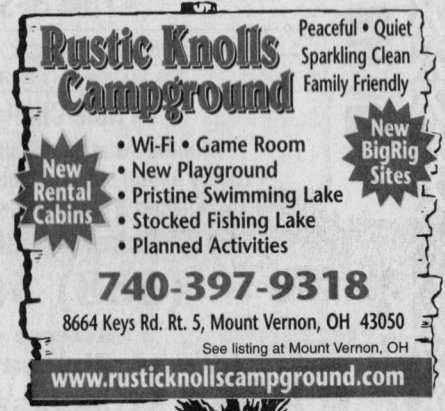

NEW PARIS—Continued

(S) NATURAL SPRINGS RESORT—(Preble) *From jct I-70 (exit 156 B in Indiana) & US 40: Go 1 mi E on US 40, then 1 mi N on SR 320. Enter on L.*

◆◆◆◆FACILITIES: 240 sites, typical site width 35 ft, 200 full hkups, 30 W&E, (20/30/50 amps), 10 no hkups, some extd stay sites (summer), 18 pull-thrus, WiFi Instant Internet at site, tenting, RV's/park model rentals, cabins, RV storage, dump, non-guest dump $, laundry, groceries, RV supplies, LP gas by weight, ice, picnic tables, patios, fire rings, grills, wood, controlled access.

◆◆◆◆◆RECREATION: rec hall, rec room/area, pavilion, swim pool, lake swim, boating, electric motors only, canoeing, kayaking, ramp, dock, 2 pedal boat rentals, lake/pond fishing, fishing supplies, mini-golf, ($), golf nearby, bsktball, playground, shuffleboard court 3 shuffleboard courts, activities (wkends), horseshoes, sports field, hiking trails, v-ball. Rec open to public.

Pets welcome ($), breed restrict, quantity restrict. Partial handicap access. Open all yr. Facilities fully operational Mid Apr - Nov 1. Big rigs welcome. Escort to site. Clubs welcome. Rate in 2010 $27-44 per family. MC/VISA/DISC/Debit. Member ARVC, OCOA. CCUSA 50% Discount. CCUSA reservations Recommended, CCUSA max stay 3 days, CCUSA disc. not avail F,Sa, CCUSA disc. not avail holidays.

Phone: (937)437-5771
Address: 500 S. Washington St, New Paris, OH 45347
Lat/Lon: 39.85253/-84.79295
Email: webmaster@naturalspringsresort.com
Web: www.naturalspringsresort.com

SEE AD RICHMOND, IN PAGE 242

NEW PHILADELPHIA—C-4

(E) WOOD'S TALL TIMBER LAKE RESORT—(Tuscarawas) *From jct I-77 (exit 81) & SR 39: Go 7 mi E on SR 39, then 1/2 mi NE on Tall Timber Rd NE (County Road 88). Enter on R.*

ONE OF OHIO'S FINEST RV RESORTS
Enjoy our 7 Acre Lake, Swim, Fish & Paddleboats. Rental Cottages, Clubhouse, Bait Shop, Concession Stand. Deluxe Paved RV sites, w/30/50 amp. Minutes off I-77 Exit #81. Near Restaurants & the World's Largest Amish Country.

◆◆◆◆◆FACILITIES: 155 sites, 104 full hkups, 15 E, (30/50 amps), 50 amps ($), 36 no hkups, some extd stay sites, 40 pull-thrus, family camping, tenting, cabins, RV storage, dump, laundry, ltd groc, LP bottle exch, ice, picnic tables, patios, fire rings, wood.

◆◆◆◆◆RECREATION: rec hall, rec room/area, pavilion, equipped pavilion, coin games, lake swim, 12 pedal boat rentals, lake fishing, fishing supplies, mini-golf, ($), golf nearby, bsktball, playground, activities, (wkends), hiking trails, v-ball, local tours.

Pets welcome, breed restrict. Partial handicap access. Open Apr 1 - Nov 1. Facilities fully operational Memorial Wknd - Labor Day Wknd. Big rigs welcome. Escort to site. Clubs welcome. Rate in 2010 $31-35 per family. MC/VISA/DISC/Debit. Member ARVC, OCOA.

Text 107964 to (440)725-8687 to see our Visual Tour.

Phone: (330)602-4000
Address: 1921 Tall Timber Road NE, New Philadelphia, OH 44663
Lat/Lon: 40.50386/-81.37300
Email: info@woodstalltimberlake.com
Web: www.woodstalltimberlake.com

SEE AD THIS PAGE AND AD TRAVEL SECTION PAGE 606

NEW WASHINGTON—B-3

(E) Auburn Lake Park—(Crawford) *From jct Hwy-602 & Hwy-103: Go 3-1/2 mi E on Hwy-103. Enter on R.* ◆◆FACILITIES: 111 sites, typical site width 40 ft, 83 full hkups, 28 W&E, (20/30 amps), family camping, tenting, dump, ltd groc. ◆◆◆RECREATION: lake swim, boating, lake fishing, playground. Pets welcome. Open Apr 15 - Oct 15. Rate in 2010 $30 for 2 persons. Member ARVC, OCOA. Phone: (419)492-2110.

NEWARK—D-3

(NE) Hidden Hill Campground—(Licking) *From jct SR 13 & SR 16: Go 3 mi E on SR 16, then 1 block N on Dayton Rd, then 2-1/2 mi NE on Swans Rd, then 1-1/2 mi E on Loper Rd (Twp 361). Enter on R.* ◆◆FACILITIES: 62 sites, typical site width 35 ft, 30 ft max RV length, 62 W&E, (20/30 amps), 13 pull-thrus, tenting, dump. RECREATION: playground. Pets welcome. Open Apr 15 - Oct 15. Phone: (740)763-2750.

(NW) LAZY RIVER AT GRANVILLE—(Licking) *From jct I-70 (exit 126) & SR 37: Go 8 mi N on SR 37, then 4-1/2 mi N on SR 661, then 1-1/4 mi E on Dry Creek Rd NE (CR 10). Enter on R.*

◆◆◆◆◆FACILITIES: 195 sites, typical site width 38 ft, 124 full hkups, 56 W&E, (20/30/50 amps), 15 no hkups, some extd stay sites (summer), 40 pull-thrus, WiFi Instant Internet at site, family camping, tenting, cabins, RV storage, dump, laundry, groceries, RV supplies, LP gas by weight/by meter, ice, picnic tables, patios, fire rings, wood.

◆◆◆◆◆RECREATION: rec hall, rec room/area, pavilion, coin games, swim pool, spray ground, stream fishing, mini-golf, ($), golf nearby, bsktball, 8 bike rentals, playground, shuffleboard court shuffleboard court, activities, horseshoes, sports field, hiking trails, v-ball.

Pets welcome. Partial handicap access. Open all yr. Big rigs welcome. Escort to site. Clubs welcome. Green Friendly. Rate in 2010 $28-43 for 2 persons. MC/VISA/DISC/Debit. Member ARVC, OCOA.

Phone: (740)366-4385
Address: 2340 Dry Creek Rd. NE, Granville, OH 43023
Lat/Lon: 40.12364/-82.49444
Email: camp@lazyriveratgranville.com
Web: www.lazyriveratgranville.com

SEE AD COLUMBUS PAGE 622

NEWBURY—B-5

(E) PUNDERSON STATE PARK—(Geauga) *From jct Hwy-44 & Hwy-87: Go 2 mi W on Hwy-87.* FACILITIES: 201 sites, 35 ft max RV length, 5 full hkups, 184 E, (20/30/50 amps), 12 no hkups, tenting, dump, laundry, ltd groc. RECREATION: 2 swim pools, boating, electric motors only, ramp, dock, lake fishing, playground. Pets welcome. Open all yr. Facilities fully operational Apr - Oct. Phone: (440)564-2279.

NEWTON FALLS—B-5

(N) Ridge Ranch Campground—(Trumbull) *From jct I-80 (Tpk exit 209) & Hwy 5: Go 1 mi W on Hwy 5, then 2-1/2 mi N on Hwy 534, then 1/4 mi W on Hwy 82/Hwy 303, then 1/2 mi W on Hwy 303. Enter on L.* ◆◆FACILITIES: 207 sites, typical site width 35 ft, 101 full hkups, 72 W&E, 20 E, (20/30/50 amps), 14 no hkups, 30 pull-thrus, WiFi Instant Internet at site, WiFi Internet central location, tenting, dump, non-guest dump $, portable dump, laundry, ltd groc, RV supplies, LP gas by weight/by meter, ice, picnic tables, fire rings, wood. ◆◆◆◆RECREATION: pavilion, lake swim, boating, lake fishing, fishing supplies, mini-golf, ($), bsktball, playground, activities, horseshoes, v-ball. Pets welcome. Open May 1 - Oct 15. Rate in 2010 $23-27 per family. MC/VISA. Member ARVC, OCOA. CCUSA 50% Discount. CCUSA reservations Required, CCUSA max stay 5 days, Cash only for CCUSA disc., CCUSA disc. not avail F,Sa, CCUSA disc. not avail holidays. 2 day minimum stay, 5 day maximum.

Phone: (330)898-8080
Address: 5219 SR 303 NW, Newton Falls, OH 44444
Lat/Lon: 41.23581/-80.98566
Web: www.ridgeranchcampground.com

NORTH KINGSVILLE—A-5

(N) VILLAGE GREEN CAMPGROUND (City Park)—(Ashtabula) *From jct I-90 (N Kingsville, exit 235) & Hwy 193: Go 3 mi N on Hwy 193, then 1/4 mi E on Village Green Dr. Enter on L.* FACILITIES: 72 sites, 60 W&E, (20/30 amps), 12 no hkups, 6 pull-thrus, tenting, dump, laundry, ltd groc. RECREATION: lake fishing, playground. Partial handicap access. Open Apr 15 - Oct 15. Phone: (440)224-0310.

NORWALK—B-3

(E) Hy-Tek Truck & Auto Center, LTD—*From jct US 250 & Hwy 61: Go 3/4 mi N on Hwy 61, then 1/2 mi E on Cleveland Rd. Enter on R.* SERVICES: full-time mech, engine/chassis repair, bus. hrs emerg rd svc, RV towing. Open all yr. MC/VISA/DISC/AMEX.

Phone: (877)729-3987
Address: 240 Cleveland Rd, Norwalk, OH 44857
Lat/Lon: 41.24744/-82.58810
Email: hytek@accnorwalk.com
Web: www.hytekauto.com

NOVA—B-3

(NW) Country Stage Campground—(Ashland) *From jct US 18 & Hwy 511: Go 8 mi S on Hwy 511, then 1-1/2 mi W on CR 40. Enter at end.* ◆◆◆FACILITIES: 129 sites, typical site width 50 ft, 24 full hkups, 105 W&E, (30 amps), 7 pull-thrus, family camping, tenting, dump, laundry, ltd groc. ◆◆◆RECREATION: swim pool, lake fishing, playground. Pets welcome. Open May 1 - Oct 18. Rate in 2010 $27 for 30 persons. Member ARVC, OCOA. Phone: (419)652-2267.

OAK HILL—E-3

JACKSON LAKE STATE PARK—(Jackson) *From jct Hwy-93 & Hwy-279: Go 2 mi W on Hwy-279.* FACILITIES: 34 sites, 35 ft max RV length, 34 E, (50 amps), tenting, dump, ltd groc. RECREATION: lake swim, boating, 10 hp limit, ramp, lake fishing, playground. Pets welcome. Open Apr 1 - Oct 30. Phone: (740) 682-6197.

OBERLIN—B-3

(SW) Schaun Acres Campground—(Lorain) *From jct Hwy 511 & Hwy 303: Go 1/2 mi W on Hwy 303. Enter on R.* ◆◆FACILITIES: 130 sites, typical site width 35 ft, 35 full hkups, 75 W&E, (30 amps), 20 no hkups, family camping, tenting, dump, laundry, groceries. ◆◆◆◆RECREATION: swim pool, pond fishing, playground. Pets welcome. Open May 1 - Oct 1. Rate in 2010 $28-33 for 4 persons. Member ARVC, OCOA. Phone: (440)775-7122.

OREGON—B-2

(E) MAUMEE BAY STATE PARK—(Lucas) *From jct I-280 & Hwy 2: Go 6 mi E on Hwy 2, then 2-1/2 mi N on N Curtice Rd. Enter at end.* FACILITIES: 252 sites, 252 E, (30 amps), tenting, dump, laundry, ltd groc. RECREATION: lake swim, boating, electric motors only, canoeing, lake/pond fishing, play equipment. Pets welcome. Open all yr. Facilities fully operational Apr - Oct. Phone: (419)836-7758.

ORWELL—B-5

(N) Pine Lakes Campground—(Ashtabula) *From jct US 322 & Hwy 45: Go 1 mi N on Hwy 45, then 1/2 mi E on Hague Rd. Enter on L.* ◆◆FACILITIES: 240 sites, typical site width 40 ft, 240 W&E, (20/30/50 amps), 40 pull-thrus, family camping, tenting, dump. ◆◆◆RECREATION: lake swim, boating, electric motors only, lake fishing, playground. Pets welcome. Open May 1 - Oct 15. Rate in 2010 $21-27 for 4 persons. Member ARVC, OCOA. Phone: (440)437-6218.

OXFORD—D-1

HUESTON WOODS STATE PARK—(Butler) *From jct US-27 & Hwy-732: Go 6 mi N on Hwy-732. Enter on L.* FACILITIES: 488 sites, typical site width 30 ft, 35 ft max RV length, 252 E, (30 amps), 236 no hkups, 66 pull-thrus, tenting, dump, laundry, ltd groc. RECREATION: lake swim, boating, 10 hp limit, canoeing, ramp, dock, lake fishing, playground. Pets welcome. Open all yr. Facilities fully operational Apr - Oct. Phone: (513)523-6347.

PARKMAN—B-5

(SE) Kool Lakes Family Campground—(Portage) *From jct Hwy 88 & US-422: Go 2 mi E on US 422, then 1/2 mi S on Hwy 282. Enter on L.* ◆◆◆FACILITIES: 203 sites, typical site width 45 ft, 169 full hkups, 34 W&E, (20/30/50 amps), 5 pull-thrus, tenting, dump, laundry, ltd groc. ◆◆◆◆RECREATION: lake swim, boating, electric motors only, canoeing, dock, lake fishing, playground. Pets welcome. Partial handicap access. Open May 1 - Oct 15. Big rigs welcome. Rate in 2010 $25-30 for 2 persons. Member ARVC, OCOA. Phone: (440)548-8436.

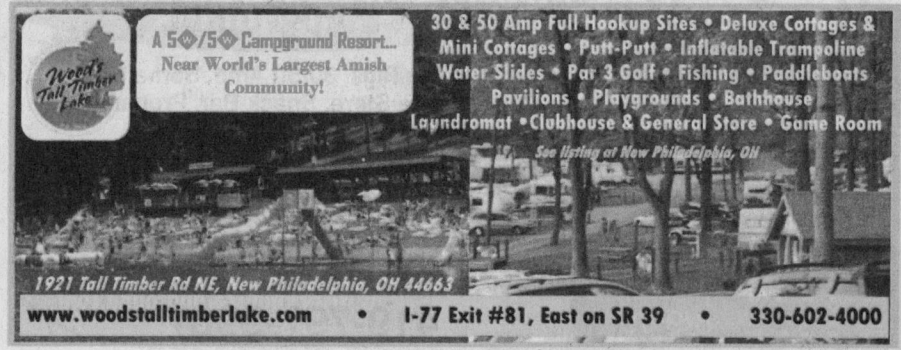

PAULDING—B-1

(SE) Woodbridge Campground—(Paulding) *From jct Hwy 24/127 & Hwy 127/111: Go 9 mi S on Hwy 127, then 4 mi E on SR 613, then 1/2 mi N on Road 137. Enter on R.* ◆◆◆FACILITIES: 143 sites, typical site width 45 ft, 143 W&E, (15/20/30/50 amps), 4 pull-thrus, family camping, tenting, dump, groceries. ◆◆◆RECREATION: swim pool, boating, lake fishing, playground. Pets welcome ($). Partial handicap access. Open all yr. Facilities fully operational Apr 26 - Oct 20. Rate in 2010 $25-30 per family. Phone: (419) 399-2267.

PEDRO—F-3

(SE) WAYNE NATIONAL FOREST (Iron Ridge Campground)—(Lawrence) *From town: Go 1-3/4 mi S Hwy 93, then 1-1/2 mi E on CR 29.* FACILITIES: 41 sites, 22 ft max RV length, 17 E, (15 amps), 24 no hkups, tenting. RECREATION: lake swim, boating, electric motors only, canoeing, ramp, dock, lake fishing. Pets welcome. Partial handicap access. Open Apr 3 - Oct 31. Phone: (614)532-3223.

PERRYSVILLE—C-3

(W) PLEASANT HILL LAKE PARK (Muskingum Watershed Conservancy Dist)—(Ashland) *From jct Hwy 39 & Hwy 95: Go 2-1/2 mi SW on Hwy 95.* FACILITIES: 380 sites, 62 full hkups, 80 W&E, 238 E, (15/30 amps), 20 pull-thrus, tenting, dump, ltd groc. RECREATION: lake swim, boating, canoeing, ramp, dock, lake fishing, playground. Pets welcome. Partial handicap access. Open all yr. Facilities fully operational Memorial Day - Labor Day. Phone: (419)938-7884.

PIONEER—B-1

(SW) Lazy River Resort Campground—(Williams) *From jct I-80 Ohio Turnpike (exit 13) and Alt US 20/SR 15: Go 2 mi N on Alt US 20/SR 15, then 1 mi W on Alt US 20, then 200 yards W on US 20. Enter on L.* ◆◆FACILITIES: 500 sites, typical site width 30 ft, 260 full hkups, 200 W&E, (15/30 amps), 40 no hkups, 340 pull-thrus, tenting, dump, laundry, groceries. ◆◆◆RECREATION: swim pool, lake swim, river/pond fishing, playground. Pets welcome. Partial handicap access. Open all yr. Facilities fully operational Apr 15 - Oct 15. Rate in 2010 $28 per family. Phone: (419)485-4411.

(NW) Loveberry's Funny Farm Campground—(Williams) *From jct I-80 Ohio Turnpike (exit 13) & Alt US 20/SR 15: Go 5 mi N on SR 15, then 2 mi W on First St (CR-R), then 1-1/2 mi N on CR 12. Enter on R.* ◆◆◆FACILITIES: 300 sites, typical site width 35 ft, 32 full hkups, 188 W&E, (20/30/50 amps), 50 amps ($), 80 no hkups, 20 pull-thrus, WiFi Instant Internet at site, WiFi Internet central location, family camping, tenting, RV storage, dump, non-guest dump $, portable dump, laundry, groceries, RV supplies, LP gas by weight/by meter, ice, picnic tables, fire rings, wood. ◆◆◆RECREATION: pavilion, swim pool, pond fishing, bsktball, playground, activities, horseshoes, v-ball. Pets welcome, breed restrict. Open 3rd week of Apr - 2nd weekend in Oct. Rate in 2010 $28-30 for 2 persons. MC/VISA/Debit. CCUSA 50% Discount. CCUSA max stay 2 days, CCUSA disc. not avail F,Sa, CCUSA disc. not avail holidays.

CAMPCLUB USA

Phone: (419)737-2467
Address: 19452 CR 12, Pioneer, OH 43554
Lat/Lon: 41.70114/-84.59209
Email: dougloveberry@verizon.net
Web: www.loveberrysfunnyfarm.com

Early general stores in Ohio measured cloth by brass tacks set at intervals in a counter. According to local stories, this is where the phrase "Get down to brass tacks" originated.

PORT CLINTON—B-3

(NE) CEDARLANE RV PARK—(Ottawa) *From jct SR 2 (exit 124) & N SR 53: Go 4 mi N on SR 53. Enter on L.*

WELCOME

◆◆◆◆FACILITIES: 291 sites, typical site width 33 ft, 5 full hkups, 265 W&E, 7 E, (20/30/50 amps), 14 no hkups, many extd stay sites (summer), 32 pull-thrus, WiFi Instant Internet at site, WiFi Internet central location, family camping, tenting, RV's/park model rentals, cabins, RV storage, dump, non-guest dump $, portable dump, laundry, groceries, RV supplies, LP gas by weight/by meter, ice, picnic tables, patios, fire rings, wood, controlled access.

◆◆◆◆RECREATION: rec room/area, coin games, 2 swim pools, wading pool, spray ground, golf nearby, bsktball, playground, shuffleboard court 2 shuffleboard courts, horseshoes, sports field, v-ball.

Pets welcome, breed restrict. Partial handicap access. Open May 1 - Oct 15. Big rigs welcome. Escort to site. Clubs welcome. Green Friendly. Rate in 2010 $32-43 for 2 persons. MC/VISA/Debit. Member ARVC, OCOA.

Phone: (419)797-9907
Address: 2926 NE Catawba Rd (Hwy 53), Port Clinton, OH 43452
Lat/Lon: 41.56445/-82.83261
Email: reservations@yahoo.com
Web: www.cedarlanervpark.com

SEE AD THIS PAGE

(W) Chet's Place—(Ottawa) *From jct SR 53 & US 2: Go 3 mi W on US 2, then 4 mi W on SR 163W. Enter on L.* ◆◆◆FACILITIES: 75 sites, typical site width 30 ft, 35 ft max RV length, 75 W&E, (30/50 amps), family camping, tenting, dump, ltd groc. ◆◆RECREATION: boating, ramp, dock, lake/river fishing, play equipment. Pets welcome. Open May 1 - Oct 31. Rate in 2010 $22 for 2 persons. Member ARVC, OCOA. Phone: (419)898-1104.

EAST HARBOR STATE PARK—(Ottawa) *From jct Hwy 2 & Hwy 269: Go 4 mi N on Hwy 269. Enter on R.* FACILITIES: 572 sites, 23 full hkups, 353 E, (50 amps), 196 no hkups, 150 pull-thrus, tenting, dump, laundry, ltd groc. RECREATION: lake swim, boating, ramp, dock, lake fishing, playground. Open all yr. Facilities fully operational Apr - Oct. Phone: (419)734-5857.

KELLEYS ISLAND STATE PARK (Lake Erie Islands SP)—(Ottawa) *From town: Go E on Hwy 163 to Marblehead Peninsula. Then take ferry (cars/trailers/boats) from Newman Boat Lines or Kelley Island Ferry Boat Line - 20 min. ride to Kelleys Island. Park is approx. 2 mi from ferry docks.* FACILITIES: 125 sites, 35 ft max RV length, 82 E, (50 amps), 43 no hkups, tenting, dump. RECREATION: lake swim, boating, ramp, lake fishing, playground. Pets welcome. Partial handicap access. Open all yr. Facilities fully operational Apr - Oct. Phone: (419)746-2546.

MIDDLE BASS ISLAND STATE PARK—(Ottawa) *From jct US 2 & SR-53: Go 5 mi N on SR-53, then Ferry N to South Bass Island, then Ferry N to Middle Bass Island. Enter on R.* FACILITIES: 21 sites, 21 no hkups, tenting. RECREATION: lake swim, boating, dock, lake fishing, playground. Pets welcome. Open all yr. Phone: (419)797-4530.

(NE) St. Hazards Village (Not Visited)—(Ottawa) *From jct US 2 & SR 53: Go 7 mi N on SR 53, then by Miller's ferry to Middle Bass Island. Advance reservations necessary on ferry. Enter on R.* FACILITIES: 60 sites, 20 full hkups, (20/30/50 amps), 40 no hkups, tenting, laundry. RECREATION: swim pool, pond fishing. No pets. Open May 1 - Oct 31. Big rigs welcome. Rate in 2010 $19-29.50 for 2 persons. Member ARVC, OCOA. Phone: (800)837-5211.

(NE) Shade Acres Campground & Cottages—(Ottawa) *From jct US 2 & SR 53: Go 1-1/2 mi N on SR 53 (just over Causeway), then 1-3/4 mi W on Catawba Rd. Enter on L.* ◆◆FACILITIES: 50 sites, 35 ft max RV

PORT CLINTON—Continued
Shade Acres Campground & Cottages—Continued

length, 50 W&E, (30 amps), family camping, tenting, dump. RECREATION: play equipment. Pets welcome. Open Apr 15 - Oct 15. Rate in 2010 $28 for 4 persons. Phone: (419)797-4681.

Reserve Online at Woodalls.com

SOUTH BASS ISLAND STATE PARK (Lake Erie Islands SP)—(Ottawa) *From jct Hwy 163 & Hwy 53: Go N on Hwy 53 to tip of Catawba Island Peninsula to Miller Boat Line. Then 20-min ferry (cars/trailers/boats) ride to South Bass Island. Park is 1 mi from ferry dock.* FACILITIES: 131 sites, 35 ft max RV length, 11 full hkups, (50 amps), 120 no hkups, tenting, dump, ltd groc. RECREATION: lake swim, boating, ramp, dock, lake fishing, playground. Open all yr. Facilities fully operational Apr - Oct. Phone: (419)797-4530.

(E) Tall Timbers Campground—(Ottawa) *From jct US 2 & SR 53: Go 1-1/4 mi N on SR 53, then 1-1/2 mi W on SR 163, then 1/4 mi S on Christy Chapel Rd. Enter on R.* ◆◆◆FACILITIES: 409 sites, typical site width 30 ft, 409 W&E, (30/50 amps), 5 pull-thrus, WiFi Instant Internet at site, WiFi Internet central location, family camping, tenting, dump, non-guest dump $, portable dump, laundry, groceries, RV supplies, LP gas by weight/by meter, ice, picnic tables, patios, fire rings, wood. ◆◆◆◆RECREATION: pavilion, lake swim, pond fishing, bsktball, playground, activities, horseshoes, v-ball. Pets welcome, breed restrict. Partial handicap access. Open May 1 - Oct 31. Rate in 2010 $32-35 for 2 persons. MC/VISA/Debit. CCUSA 50% Discount. CCUSA reservations Accepted, CCUSA max stay 2 days, CCUSA disc. not avail F,Sa, CCUSA disc. not avail holidays. No vicious dog breeds.

CAMPCLUB USA

Phone: (419)732-3938
Address: 340 Christy Chapel Rd., Port Clinton, OH 43452
Lat/Lon: 41.51354/-82.88595
Email: talltimbers@cros.net
Web: www.camplakeerie.com

PORTSMOUTH—E-3

(SW) Lazy Village Campground & RV Park—(Scioto) *From jct US 23 & US 52: Go 6 mi W on US 52. Enter on L.* ◆◆◆FACILITIES: 104 sites, typical site width 30 ft, 44 full hkups, 35 W&E, (20/30/50 amps), 25 no hkups, 5 pull-thrus, tenting, dump, laundry, groceries. ◆◆◆RECREATION: swim pool, stream fishing, playground. Pets welcome, breed restrict. Open all yr. Facilities fully operational Apr 1 - Oct 31. Big rigs welcome. Rate in 2010 $35 for 2 persons. Member ARVC, OCOA. Phone: (740)858-2409.

SHAWNEE STATE PARK—(Scioto) *From jct US-23 & US-52: Go 10 mi SW on US-52, then W on Hwy-125.* FACILITIES: 107 sites, 35 ft max RV length, 99 E, (20/30 amps), 8 no hkups, tenting, dump, laundry, ltd groc. RECREATION: lake swim, boating, electric motors only, canoeing, ramp, dock, lake fishing, playground. Pets welcome. Open all yr. Facilities fully operational Apr - Oct. Phone: (740)858-6652.

(E) WOLFORD'S LANDING CAMPGROUND—(Scioto) *From jct US 23 & US 52: Go 7 mi E on US 52, then 100 ft S on Webster St, then 1/4 mi E on East Front St. Enter on R.*

WELCOME

◆◆◆◆FACILITIES: 83 sites, typical site width 25 ft, 50 full hkups, 33 W&E, (30/50 amps), 50 amps ($), many extd stay sites (summer), 2 pull-thrus, WiFi Instant Internet at site, tenting, dump, ice, picnic tables, patios, fire rings, wood.

◆◆◆RECREATION: pavilion, river swim, river fishing, bike rental 10 bike rentals, playground, shuffleboard court shuffleboard court, activities (wkends), horseshoes.

Pets welcome. Open all yr. Facilities fully operational Apr 1 - Nov 1. Rate in 2010 $25-30 for 2 persons.

Phone: (740)776-9956
Address: 6888 E. Front St., Portsmouth, OH 45662
Lat/Lon: 38.74791/-82.87369

SEE AD THIS PAGE

John Lambert of Ohio City made America's first automobile in 1891.

RACINE—E-4

(N) Kountry Resort—(Meigs) *From jct Hwy 7 & US 33: Go 3 mi E on US 33, then 1 block SW on Cr 34, then 1/2 mi NW on Lazy T Rd. Enter on L.* ◆◆◆FACILITIES: 268 sites, 210 full hkups, 40 W&E, (20/30/50 amps), 18 no hkups, 10 pull-thrus, phone Internet central location, family camping, tenting, RV storage, dump, non-guest dump $, laundry, ltd groc, RV supplies, LP gas by meter, ice, picnic tables, fire rings, wood. ◆◆◆RECREATION: pavilion, swim pool, boating, no motors, canoeing, lake/pond fishing, bsktball, playground, horseshoes, hiking trails, v-ball. Pets welcome, breed restrict. Partial handicap access. Open all yr. Rate in 2010 $30 per family. MC/VISA/DISC. CCUSA 50% Discount. CCUSA reservations Required, CCUSA max stay 14 days, CCUSA disc. not avail holidays. Pets must have up to date shot record. No water on sites from Nov.-Apr.

Phone: (740)992-6488
Address: 44705 Resort Rd, Racine, OH 45771
Lat/Lon: 39.04585/-81.96154
Web: ww.krccamping.com

RANDOLPH—B-5

(N) Friendship Acres Park, Inc.—(Portage) *From jct I-76 & Hwy 44: Go 3-1/2 mi S on Hwy 44. Enter on L.* ◆◆◆FACILITIES: 250 sites, typical site width 30 ft, 250 W&E, (20/30 amps), 10 pull-thrus, family camping, tenting, dump, laundry, groceries. ◆◆◆RECREATION: swim pool, lake swim, pond fishing. Pets welcome. Open May 1 - Oct 15. Rate in 2010 $24-28 for 4 persons. Member ARVC, OCOA. Phone: (330)325-9527.

RAVENNA—B-5

(E) COUNTRY ACRES CAMPGROUND—(Portage) *From jct I-80 (exit 209) & Hwy 5: Go 5 mi W on Hwy 5, then 100 yards S on Hwy 225, then 1 mi E on Minyoung Rd. Enter on R.*

◆◆◆◆FACILITIES: 191 sites, typical site width 30 ft, 36 full hkups, 115 W&E, (20/30/50 amps), 50 amps ($), 40 no hkups, many extd stay sites (summer), 12 pull-thrus, WiFi Instant Internet at site, tenting, RV's/park model rentals, cabins, RV storage, dump, non-guest dump $, portable dump, laundry, ltd groc, RV supplies, LP gas by weight, ice, picnic tables, fire rings, grills, wood, controlled access.

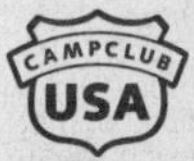

◆◆◆◆RECREATION: rec room/area, pavilion, coin games, swim pool, wading pool, rowboat/3 pedal boat rentals, lake fishing, fishing supplies, golf nearby, bsktball, playground, activities, (wkends), horseshoes, sports field, hiking trails, v-ball. Rec open to public.

Pets welcome. Partial handicap access. Open all yr. Facilities fully operational Apr 22 - Oct 16. Winter by reservation only. Big rigs welcome. Escort to site. Clubs welcome. Rate in 2010 $28.90-39.90 for 2 persons. MC/VISA/DISC/Debit. Member ARVC, OCOA. FCRV discount. FMCA discount. CCUSA 50% Discount. CCUSA reservations Recommended, CCUSA max stay Unlimited, Cash only for CCUSA disc., CCUSA disc. not avail F,Sa, CCUSA disc. not avail holidays. 2 night minimum stay, not valid w/ other offers/discounts. Cash only. Winter camping by appt. only.

Phone: (866)713-4321
Address: 9850 Minyoung Rd, Ravenna, OH 44266
Lat/Lon: 41.17820/-81.03400
Email: countryacres1@aol.com
Web: www.countryacrescamping.com

SEE AD AKRON PAGE 613

(E) WEST BRANCH STATE PARK—(Portage) *From jct Hwy 14 & Hwy 5: Go 5 mi E on Hwy 5, then S on Rouchspring Rd.* FACILITIES: 199 sites, 35 ft max RV length, 29 full hkups, 156 E, (30/50 amps), 14 no hkups, tenting, dump, laundry, ltd groc. RECREATION: lake swim, boating, ramp, dock, lake fishing, playground. Pets welcome. Open all yr. Facilities fully operational Apr - Oct. Phone: (330)296-3239.

Book your reservation online at woodalls.com

REEDSVILLE—E-4

(S) FORKED RUN STATE PARK—(Meigs) *From jct Hwy-681 & Hwy-124: Go 3 mi S on Hwy-124.* FACILITIES: 145 sites, 30 ft max RV length, 81 E, (50 amps), 64 no hkups, tenting, dump, laundry, ltd groc. RECREATION: lake swim, boating, 10 hp limit, ramp, dock, lake fishing, playground. Pets welcome. Partial handicap access. Open all yr. Facilities fully operational Apr - Oct. Phone: (740)378-6206.

REPUBLIC—B-3

(NW) CLINTON LAKE CAMPING—(Seneca) *From jct US 224 & SR 67: Go 1/4 mi E on SR 67, then 5 mi N on CR 43, then 1-1/10 mi W on Twp Rd 122. Enter on L.*

◆◆◆FACILITIES: 200 sites, typical site width 30 ft, 160 W&E, (30 amps), 40 no hkups, many extd stay sites (summer), 10 pull-thrus, family camping, tenting, dump, portable dump, groceries, RV supplies, ice, picnic tables, fire rings, wood.

◆◆◆◆RECREATION: rec room/area, pavilion, coin games, lake swim, boating, electric motors only, dock, lake fishing, fishing supplies, bsktball, playground, activities, (wkends), horseshoes, sports field, v-ball.

Pets welcome. Partial handicap access. Open May 1 - Oct 15. Clubs welcome. Rate in 2010 $23-26 per family. MC/VISA/DISC. Member ARVC, OCOA.

Phone: (419)585-3331
Address: 4990 E Twp Rd-122, Republic, OH 44867
Lat/Lon: 41.13869/-83.07422
Email: clinton_lake20@yahoo.com

SEE AD TRAVEL SECTION PAGE 605

RIPLEY—E-2

EAGLE CREEK MARINA (COE)—(Brown) *From jct US-52 & US-62/68: Go 1-1/2 mi E on US-52/62/68.* FACILITIES: 75 sites, 60 W&E, 15 E, (30 amps), 8 pull-thrus, tenting, dump, ltd groc. RECREATION: boating, ramp, dock, river fishing, playground. Open Apr 1 - Oct 31. Phone: (937)392-4989.

ROGERS—C-5

(N) Terrace Lakes—(Columbiana) *From jct Hwy 14 & Hwy 7: Go 5 mi S on Hwy 7. Enter on R.* ◆◆FACILITIES: 200 sites, typical site width 35 ft, 140 full hkups, 60 W&E, (20/30 amps), 14 pull-thrus, tenting, dump, laundry, ltd groc. ◆◆◆RECREATION: lake swim, boating, lake fishing, playground. Pets welcome, breed restrict. Partial handicap access. Open last wk Apr - mid Oct. Rate in 2010 $25-30 for 4 persons. Member ARVC, OCOA. Phone: (330)227-9606.

ROSEWOOD—D-2

KISER LAKE STATE PARK—(Champaign) *From jct US-36 & Hwy-235: Go 5 mi N on Hwy-235.* FACILITIES: 118 sites, 39 ft max RV length, 10 E, 108 no hkups, tenting, dump, ltd groc. RECREATION: lake swim, boating, no motors, ramp, dock, lake fishing, playground. Pets welcome. Open all yr. Facilities fully operational Apr - Oct. Phone: (937)362-3822.

ST. MARYS—C-1

(NE) Easy Campground—(Auglaize) *From jct I-75 & US 33: Go 9 mi W on US 33, then 100 yds N on CR 71. Enter on R.* ◆◆◆FACILITIES: 50 sites, 42 full hkups, 8 W&E, (20/30/50 amps), 13 pull-thrus, family camping, tenting, dump, ltd groc. ◆◆RECREATION: pond fishing, play equipment. Pets welcome. Open Apr 1 - Nov 1. Big rigs welcome. Rate in 2010 $30 per family. Phone: (419)394-3836.

GRAND LAKE ST. MARY'S STATE PARK—(Auglaize) *From jct Hwy-29 & Hwy-364: Go 1 mi S on Hwy-364, then E on Hwy-703. Enter on R.* FACILITIES: 204 sites, 35 ft max RV length, 166 E, (50 amps), 38 no hkups, 50 pull-thrus, tenting, dump, laundry, ltd groc. RECREATION: lake swim, boating, canoeing, ramp, dock, lake fishing, playground. Pets welcome. Partial handicap access. Open all yr. Facilities fully operational Apr - Oct. Phone: (419)394-2774.

SALEM—C-5

(N) Chaparral Family Campground—(Mahoning) *From jct Hwy 224 & Hwy 45: Go 4-1/2 mi S on Hwy 45, then 1/2 mi E on Middletown Rd. Enter on L.*

SALEM—Continued
Chaparral Family Campground—Continued

◆◆◆FACILITIES: 215 sites, typical site width 35 ft, 135 full hkups, 55 W&E, (20/30 amps), 25 no hkups, 13 pull-thrus, family camping, tenting, dump, ltd groc. ◆◆◆◆RECREATION: lake swim, boating, electric motors only, canoeing, lake fishing, playground. Pets welcome. Partial handicap access. Open Apr 15 - Nov 15. Rate in 2010 $24-25.50 for 4 persons. Member ARVC, OCOA. Phone: (330)337-9381.

(SW) Timashamie Family Campground—(Columbiana) *From jct Hwy 224 & Hwy 45: Go 7-1/2 mi S on Hwy 45, then 5-1/2 mi SW on CR 400 (Georgetown Rd). Enter on L.* ◆◆◆FACILITIES: 175 sites, typical site width 35 ft, 175 full hkups, (20/30/50 amps), 40 pull-thrus, family camping, tenting, laundry. ◆◆◆◆RECREATION: swim pool, boating, electric motors only, lake fishing, playground. Pets welcome. Open Apr 1 - Oct 31. Rate in 2010 $31 per family. Phone: (330)525-7054. FCRV discount.

SANDUSKY—B-3

(NE) CEDAR POINT CAMPER VILLAGE/ LIGHTHOUSE POINT—(Sandusky) *From jct Hwy 2 & US 250: Go 5 mi NW on US 250, then 1 mi E on US 6, then 4 mi N on Causeway Dr. Enter at end.*

◆◆◆◆FACILITIES: 209 sites, typical site width 35 ft, 97 full hkups, 112 E, (20/30/50 amps), 58 pull-thrus, family camping, cabins, dump, laundry, groceries, RV supplies, ice, picnic tables, patios, grills, controlled access.

◆◆◆◆RECREATION: rec room/area, coin games, swim pool, wading pool, hot tub, boating, shuffleboard court 4 shuffleboard courts.

Pets welcome. Partial handicap access. No tents. Open Early May - Labor Day. Weekends only during Sep & mid Oct. Big rigs welcome. Clubs welcome. Rate in 2010 $65-90 per family. MC/VISA/DISC/AMEX/Debit. ATM. Member ARVC, OCOA.

Text 107975 to (440)725-8687 to see our Visual Tour.

Phone: (419)627-2106
Address: 1 Cedar Point Dr, Sandusky, OH 44870
Lat/Lon: 41.48865/-82.69066
Web: www.cedarpoint.com

SEE AD TRAVEL SECTION PAGE 603

(W) Crystal Rock Campground—(Erie) *From jct SR 2 & US 6: Go 3 mi W on US 6, then 1/2 mi W on Wahl Rd, then 1/4 mi N on Crystal Rock Rd. Enter on R.* ◆◆◆◆FACILITIES: 184 sites, 14 full hkups, 40 W&E, 72 E, (20/30/50 amps), 58 no hkups, 10 pull-thrus, family camping, tenting, dump, laundry, ltd groc. ◆◆◆RECREATION: playground. Pets welcome, breed restrict. Open Apr 1 - Nov 15. Big rigs welcome. Rate in 2010 $32-37 for 2 persons. Phone: (800)321-7177.

(E) SANDUSKY BAYSHORE KOA—(Erie) *From jct US 250 & US 6: Go 1-3/4 mi E on US 6. Enter on L.*

CLOSEST CAMPGROUND TO CEDAR POINT!
RV's campers & tents welcome, or rent a 1-3 BR park model. Pull-thru and shaded sites; in ground pool and much more. For details and to make your plans and reservations, visit our website at koasandusky.com.

◆◆◆◆◆FACILITIES: 572 sites, typical site width 40 ft, 168 full hkups, 106 W&E, 56 E, (20/30/50 amps), 242 no hkups, some extd stay sites (summer), 49 pull-thrus, cable TV, WiFi Instant Internet at site, WiFi Internet central location, family camping, tenting, RV's/park model rentals, dump, non-

SANDUSKY BAYSHORE KOA—Continued on next page

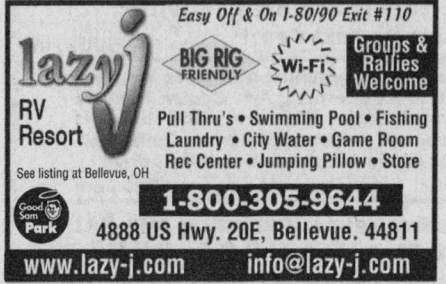

guest dump $, laundry, groceries, RV supplies, ice, picnic tables, fire rings, wood, controlled access.

◊◊◊◊◊RECREATION: rec room/area, pavilion, coin games, swim pool, lake/pond fishing, golf nearby, bsktball, playground, shuffleboard court 2 shuffleboard courts, activities, horseshoes, v-ball, local tours.

Pets welcome. Partial handicap access. Open May 1 - Oct 31. Big rigs welcome. Escort to site. Clubs welcome. Rate in 2010 $34.50-66.50 for 2 persons. MC/VISA/DISC/AMEX/Debit. ATM. Member ARVC, OCOA. KOA discount.

Text 89810 to (440)725-8687 to see our Visual Tour.

Phone: (800)562-2486
Address: 2311 Cleveland Rd, Sandusky, OH 44870
Lat/Lon: 41.43732/-82.66540
Email: reservations@koasandusky.com
Web: www.koasandusky.com

Reserve Online at Woodalls.com

SEE AD PAGE 631

SENECAVILLE—D-4

(S) SENECA LAKE PARK (Muskingum Watershed Conservancy Dist)—(Guernsey) *From jct Hwy 313 & Hwy 574: Go 3 mi S on Hwy 574.* FACILITIES: 513 sites, 156 full hkups, 357 E, (30/50 amps), 22 pull-thrus, family camping, tenting, dump, laundry. RECREATION: lake swim, boating, 299 hp limit, canoeing, ramp, dock, lake fishing, playground. Open Apr 31 - Oct 1. Phone: (740)685-6013.

SENECA MARINA POINT (Muskingum Watershed Conservancy Dist)—(Guernsey) *From jct I-77 & Hwy 313: Go 5 mi E on Hwy 313.* FACILITIES: 513 sites, 156 full hkups, 357 E, (30/50 amps), 22 pull-thrus, tenting, dump, laundry. RECREATION: boating, 180 hp limit, ramp, dock, lake fishing, playground. Partial handicap access. Open Apr 1 - Oct 31. Phone: (740)685-6013.

SEVILLE—B-4

(NE) **MAPLE LAKES RECREATIONAL PARK**—(Medina) *From jct I-76 & Hwy-3: Go 1 mi NE on Hwy 3, then 1 mi E on CR-118 (Blake Rd). Enter on L.*

◊◊◊◊FACILITIES: 225 sites, typical site width 35 ft, 40 full hkups, 185 W&E, (20/30/50 amps), mostly extd stay sites (summer), 20 pull-thrus, WiFi Instant Internet at site, WiFi Internet central location, family camping, tenting, RV's/park model rentals, dump, non-guest dump $, portable dump, laundry, ltd groc, LP gas by weight, ice, picnic tables, fire rings, grills, wood, controlled access.

◊◊◊◊RECREATION: rec room/area, pavilion, coin games, swim pool, wading pool, lake fishing, golf nearby, bsktball, playground, activities, (wkends), horseshoes, sports field, v-ball. Rec open to public.

Pets welcome, breed restrict. Partial handicap access. Open Apr 15 - Oct 1. Big rigs welcome. Clubs welcome. Rate in 2010 $35-39 for 2 persons. MC/VISA/DISC/AMEX. Member ARVC, OCOA.

Phone: (330)336-2251
Address: 4275 Blake Rd, Seville, OH 44273-0086
Lat/Lon: 41.04721/-81.84319
Email: maplelk@gte.net
Web: www.maplelakes.com

SEE AD THIS PAGE

SHELBY—C-3

(NW) **SHELBY/MANSFIELD KOA (Wagon Wheel Campground)**—(Crawford) *From jct Hwy 61 & Hwy 39: Go 4 mi W on Hwy 39, then 4-1/2 mi N on Baker Rd. Enter on R.*

◊◊◊◊◊FACILITIES: 198 sites, typical site width 35 ft, 144 full hkups, 54 W&E, (20/30/50 amps), some extd stay sites (summer), 49 pull-thrus, cable TV, WiFi Instant Internet at site, WiFi Internet central location, family camping, tenting, cabins, RV storage, dump, non-guest dump $, laundry, groceries, RV supplies, LP gas by weight/by meter, ice, picnic tables, patios, fire rings, grills, wood, controlled access.

◊◊◊◊◊RECREATION: rec hall, rec room/area, pavilion, equipped pavilion, coin games, swim pool, wading pool, hot tub, 9 pedal boat rentals, lake fishing, fishing supplies, mini-golf, ($), golf nearby, bsktball, 19 bike rentals, playground, shuffleboard court 2 shuffleboard courts, activities, tennis, horseshoes, sports field, hiking trails, v-ball. Rec open to public.

Pets welcome, breed restrict. Partial handicap access. Open May 1 - Oct 15. Big rigs welcome. Escort to site. Clubs welcome. Rate in 2010 $31-75 for 2 persons. MC/VISA/DISC/AMEX/Debit. ATM. Member ARVC, OCOA. KOA discount.

The Rome Beauty Apple was named not after the city in Italy, but Rome, Ohio. It was in that township that the first tree was planted.

Phone: (419)347-1392
Address: 6787 Baker 47, Shelby, OH 44875
Lat/Lon: 40.94870/-82.74317
Email: camp@shelbymansfieldkoa.com
Web: www.shelbymansfieldkoa.com

SEE AD MANSFIELD PAGE 627

SHREVE—C-4

(SW) **Whispering Hills Family Campground**—(Holmes) *From jct Hwy 226 & Hwy 514: Go 2 mi S on Hwy 514. Enter on R.* ◊◊◊◊FACILITIES: 250 sites, 105 full hkups, 133 W&E, (20/30/50 amps), 12 no hkups, 35 pull-thrus, family camping, tenting, dump, laundry, ltd groc. ◊◊◊◊RECREATION: swim pool, boating, electric motors only, dock, lake fishing, playground. Pets welcome, breed restrict. Partial handicap access. Open Apr 23 - Oct 24. Big rigs welcome. Rate in 2010 $32-47 for 2 persons. Member ARVC, OCOA. Phone: (800)992-2435.

SINKING SPRING—E-2

(NE) **Long's Retreat Family Resort**—(Pike) *From jct Hwy 41 & SR 124: Go 5-1/4 mi E on SR 124, then 100 ft NW on Bell Hollow Rd. Enter on R.* ◊◊◊◊FACILITIES: 598 sites, typical site width 40 ft, 142 full hkups, 131 W&E, 225 E, (15/20/30/50 amps), 100 no hkups, 75 pull-thrus, family camping, tenting, dump, laundry, groceries. ◊◊◊◊◊RECREATION: lake swim, boating, electric motors only, canoeing, lake fishing, playground. Pets welcome. Partial handicap access. Open Apr 1 - Oct 31. Big rigs welcome. Rate in 2010 $25-32 per family. Member ARVC, OCOA. Phone: (937)588-3725.

SMYRNA—D-5

PIEDMONT MARINA (Muskingum Watershed Conservancy Dist)—(Belmont) *From jct Hwy-800 & CR-893: Go E on CR-893.* FACILITIES: 90 sites, 35 ft max RV length, 26 full hkups, 64 W&E, (30 amps), tenting, dump, ltd groc. RECREATION: boating, 10 hp limit, canoeing, ramp, dock, lake fishing, playground. Partial handicap access. Open Apr 1 - Oct 31. Phone: (740)658-3735.

SPENCER—B-4

(NE) **Sunset Lake Campground**—(Medina) *From jct Hwy-301 & Hwy-162: Go 2-1/2 mi E on Hwy-162, then 1-1/2 mi N on CR-58 (Root Rd). Enter on L.* ◊◊FACILITIES: 205 sites, typical site width 35 ft, 127 full hkups, 63 W&E, (20/30/50 amps), 50 amps ($), 15 no hkups, 5 pull-thrus, family camping, tenting, dump, laundry, ltd groc. ◊◊◊RECREATION: lake swim, boating, electric motors only, canoeing, lake fishing, playground. Pets welcome. Open May 1 - 2nd wknd in Oct. Big rigs welcome. Rate in 2010 $27 for 4 persons. Member ARVC, OCOA. Phone: (330)667-2686.

SPRINGFIELD—D-2

(E) **BEAVER VALLEY RESORT** (CAMP RESORT)—(Clark) *From jct I-70 (exit 62) & US 40: Go 1/4 mi E on US 40. Enter on R.*

FACILITIES: 345 sites, typical site width 35 ft, 275 full hkups, 70 W&E, (20/30/50 amps), some extd stay sites, 10 pull-thrus, cabins, RV storage, dump, non-guest dump $, laundry, ice, picnic tables, patios, fire rings, wood.

RECREATION: rec hall, rec room/area, pavilion, coin games, 1 swim pools, river/pond fishing, mini-golf, golf nearby, bsktball, playground, shuf-

BEAVER VALLEY RESORT—Continued on next page

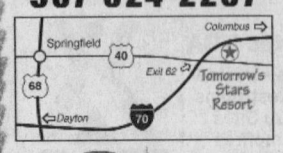

SPRINGFIELD—Continued
BEAVER VALLEY RESORT—Continued

fleboard court 2 shuffleboard courts, activities (wkends), horseshoes, v-ball. Rec open to public.

Pets welcome. Partial handicap access. No tents. Open all yr. Facilities fully operational Apr 15 - Oct 15. Big rigs welcome. Escort to site. Clubs welcome. Rate in 2010 $30 per family. MC/VISA/DISC/Debit.

Phone: (937)324-3263
Address: 6725 E National Rd, S. Charleston, OH 45368
Lat/Lon: 39.92448/-83.67888
Web: www.beavervalley.com

SEE AD THIS PAGE

(E) BUCK CREEK STATE PARK—(Clark) *From I-70 (exit 62): Go 2-1/2 mi W, then 1-1/2 mi N on Bird Rd (Harmony).* FACILITIES: 111 sites, 35 ft max RV length, 89 E, (30 amps), 22 no hkups, tenting, dump, laundry, ltd groc. RECREATION: lake swim, boating, ramp, dock, lake fishing, playground. Pets welcome. Open all yr. Facilities fully operational Apr 1 - Oct 30. Phone: (937)322-5284.

(E) TOMORROW'S STARS RV RESORT—(Clark) *From I-70 & US 40 (exit 62) : Go 1/4 mi E on US 40. Enter on L.* ◆◆◆FACILITIES: 210 sites, typical site width 40 ft, 210 full hkups, (30/50 amps), 50 amps ($), some extd stay sites, 15 pull-thrus, heater not allowed, tenting, RV storage, laundry, ice, picnic tables, patios, fire rings, wood.

◆◆◆◆RECREATION: rec hall, rec room/area, pavilion, swim pool, pond fishing, mini-golf, golf nearby, bsktball, play equipment, shuffleboard court, activities (wkends), horseshoes, sports field, hiking trails, v-ball. Rec open to public.

Pets welcome. Partial handicap access. Open all yr. Facilities fully operational Apr 15 - Oct 15. Big rigs welcome. Clubs welcome. Rate in 2010 $30-32 per vehicle. MC/VISA/DISC/AMEX/Debit.

Phone: (937)324-2267
Address: 6716 E National Rd, South Charleston, OH 45368
Lat/Lon: 39.92508/-83.67897
Web: www.letsgocamping.com

SEE AD PAGE 632 AND AD PALM SPRINGS, CA PAGE 154 AND AD TYLERTOWN, MS PAGE 447

STEUBENVILLE—C-5

See listing at Toronto

STONY RIDGE—B-2

(E) Toledo East/Stony Ridge KOA—(Wood) *From jct I-80/90 (exit 71) & SR 420: Go 1/2 mi S on SR 420, then 1-1/2 mi W on SR 163, then 1/4 mi S on Luckey Rd. Enter on R.* ◆◆◆◆FACILITIES: 59 sites, typical site width 30 ft, 27 full hkups, 23 W&E, (20/30/50 amps), 50 amps ($), 9 no hkups, 26 pull-thrus, tenting, dump, laundry, full svc store. ◆◆◆◆RECREATION: swim pool, playground. Pets welcome. Partial handicap access. Open Mar 15 - Oct 31. Big rigs welcome. Rate in 2010 $38-49 for 2 persons. Member ARVC, OCOA. Phone: (419)837-6848. KOA discount.

Staying close to home next year? Pre-order the 2012 Directory in a smaller regional version. It contains all the great information Woodall's North American Directory contains, but in a handy to-go version, specific to the states or provinces you need.

STREETSBORO—B-4

(W) STREETSBORO/CLEVELAND SE KOA (Mar-Lynn lake Park)—(Summit) *From jct Ohio Turnpike (I-80) & Hwy 14: Go 1 mi SE on Hwy 14, then 2 mi W on Hwy 303. Enter on R.*

◆◆◆◆FACILITIES: 250 sites, typical site width 42 ft, 225 full hkups, 25 W&E, (20/30/50 amps), many extd stay sites (summer), 15 pull-thrus, WiFi Instant Internet at site, WiFi Internet central location, family camping, tenting, cabins, RV storage, dump, non-guest dump $, laundry, groceries, RV supplies, LP gas by weight/by meter, ice, picnic tables, fire rings, wood, controlled access.

◆◆◆◆RECREATION: rec room/area, pavilion, coin games, lake swim, lake fishing, golf nearby, bsktball, 9 bike rentals, playground, activities, (wkends), horseshoes, sports field, v-ball. Rec open to public.

Pets welcome, breed restrict. Open May 1 - Oct 15. Big rigs welcome. Escort to site. Clubs welcome. Rate in 2010 $28-52 for 2 persons. MC/VISA/DISC/Debit. Member ARVC, OCOA. KOA discount.

Phone: (800)562-0804
Address: 187 SR 303, Streetsboro, OH 44241
Lat/Lon: 41.23991/-81.38750
Email: marcamp303@aol.com
Web: www.streetsborokoa.com

SEE AD AKRON PAGE 613

(NE) WOODSIDE LAKE PARK—(Portage) *From jct Ohio Turnpike (I-80) & Hwy 14: Go 1-1/2 mi SE on Hwy 14, then 1-1/2 mi N on Hwy 43, then 2-1/4 mi E on Frost Rd, then 200 yds S on Elliman. Enter on R.*

◆◆◆FACILITIES: 250 sites, typical site width 35 ft, 210 W&E, (20/30/50 amps), 50 amps ($), 40 no hkups, many extd stay sites (summer), 14 pull-thrus, WiFi Instant Internet at site, phone Internet central location, family camping, tenting, cabins, dump, non-guest dump $, portable dump, laundry, ltd groc, RV supplies, LP gas by weight/by meter, ice, picnic tables, fire rings, wood.

◆◆◆◆RECREATION: rec hall, rec room/area, pavilion, coin games, lake swim, boating, 3 pedal boat rentals, lake/stream fishing, fishing supplies, golf nearby, bsktball, playground, activities, (wkends), horseshoes, sports field, hiking trails, v-ball. Rec open to public.

Pets welcome. Open Apr 15 - Oct 15. Big rigs welcome. Escort to site. Clubs welcome. Rate in 2010 $32-34 for 2 persons. MC/VISA/DISC/Debit. Member ARVC, OCOA.

Phone: (866)241-0492
Address: 2486 Frost Rd., Streetsboro, OH 44241
Lat/Lon: 41.25908/-81.30312
Email: woodside@woodsidelake.com
Web: www.woodsidelake.com

SEE AD TRAVEL SECTION PAGE 605

SULLIVAN—B-4

(N) Rustic Lakes Campgrounds Inc.—(Lorain) *From jct Hwy 224 & Hwy 58: Go 2-1/2 mi N on Hwy 58, then 1 mi E on New London/Eastern Rd. Enter on R.* ◆◆FACILITIES: 290 sites, typical site width 45 ft, 37 full hkups, 253 W&E, (20/30/50 amps), family camping, tenting, dump, laundry, ltd groc. ◆◆◆RECREATION: swim pool, lake fishing, playground. Pets welcome, breed restrict. Open May 1 - Oct 15. Rate in 2010 $28-31 for 2 persons. Member ARVC, OCOA. Phone: (440)647-3804.

Say you saw it in Woodall's!

SUNBURY—C-3

(NE) Autumn Lakes Family Campground—(Delaware) *From jct US 36 & SR 61: Go 4 mi N on SR 61, then 3-1/2 mi NE on SR 656, then 200 feet S on Porter Central Rd. Enter on L.* ◆◆◆FACILITIES: 98 sites, 92 W&E, (20/30/50 amps), 6 no hkups, 16 pull-thrus, family camping, tenting, dump, ltd groc. ◆◆◆◆RECREATION: swim pool, boating, no motors, canoeing, pond fishing, playground. Pets welcome, breed restrict. Open Apr 15 - Nov 1. Big rigs welcome. Rate in 2010 $30-42 per family. Member ARVC, OCOA. Phone: (740)625-6600.

SWANTON—B-2

(SE) Big Sandy Toledo/Maumee Campground—(Lucas) *From Ohio Turnpike (I-80/90, exit 52) & SR 2: Go 2 mi W on SR 2, then 2 mi S on SR 295. Enter on L.* ◆◆◆FACILITIES: 180 sites, typical site width 40 ft, 10 full hkups, 150 W&E, (20/30/50 amps), 50 amps ($), 20 no hkups, 16 pull-thrus, family camping, tenting, dump, laundry, groceries. ◆◆◆◆RECREATION: lake swim, boating, electric motors only, canoeing, lake fishing, playground. Pets welcome. Open Apr 22 - Oct 1. Big rigs welcome. Rate in 2010 $25-30 for 2 persons. Phone: (419)826-8784.

THOMPSON—A-5

(E) HERITAGE HILLS FAMILY CAMPGROUND—(Geauga) *From jct I-90 (Madison/Thompson exit 212) & Hwy 528: Go 2 mi S on Hwy 528, then 2 mi E on Ledge Rd. Enter on L.*

◆◆◆FACILITIES: 120 sites, typical site width 60 ft, 49 full hkups, 71 W&E, (20/30/50 amps), many extd stay sites (summer), 11 pull-thrus, heater not allowed, WiFi Instant Internet at site, WiFi Internet central location, family camping, tenting, dump, portable dump, ltd groc, RV supplies, ice, picnic tables, fire rings, grills, wood, controlled access.

◆◆◆◆RECREATION: rec room/area, pavilion, coin games, lake swim, lake fishing, fishing supplies, golf nearby, bsktball, playground, activities, (wkends), horseshoes, sports field, hiking trails, v-ball. Rec open to public.

Pets welcome, quantity restrict. Partial handicap access. Open May 1 - Oct 1. Escort to site. Clubs welcome. Rate in 2010 $26-29 for 2 persons. MC/VISA/DISC/Debit. Member ARVC, OCOA.

Phone: (440)298-1311
Address: 6445 Ledge Rd, Thompson, OH 44086
Lat/Lon: 41.41836/-81.02267
Email: hhcafamilycampground@juno.com
Web: heritagehillscamp.com

SEE AD TRAVEL SECTION PAGE 605

TIFFIN—B-2

(S) WALNUT GROVE CAMPGROUND—(Seneca) *From jct US 224 & SR 53: Go 7 mi S on SR 53, then 1 mi E on CR 6, then 1-1/2 mi S on TWP Rd 131. Enter on L.*

◆◆◆FACILITIES: 235 sites, typical site width 35 ft, 149 full hkups, 56 W&E, 30 E, (15/20/30/50 amps), many extd stay sites (summer), 39 pull-thrus, family camping, tenting, cabins, dump, laundry, groceries, RV supplies, LP gas by weight, ice, picnic tables, fire rings, wood.

◆◆◆◆RECREATION: rec hall, rec room/area, pavilion, coin games, swim pool, wading pool, boating, canoeing, ramp, 5 canoe/3 pedal boat rentals, river/pond fishing, fishing supplies, golf nearby, bsktball, playground, activities, (wkends), horseshoes, sports field, hiking trails.

WALNUT GROVE CAMPGROUND—Continued on next page

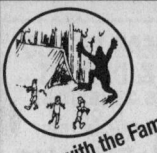

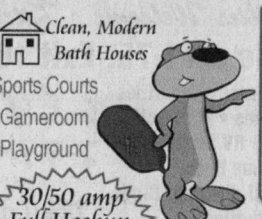

TIFFIN—Continued
WALNUT GROVE CAMPGROUND—Continued

Pets welcome. Open May 1 - Oct 31. Big rigs welcome. Clubs welcome. Rate in 2010 $21-33 for 2 persons. MC/VISA/DISC/Debit. ATM. Member ARVC, OCOA.

Phone: (419)448-0914
Address: 7325 S Twp Rd 131, Tiffin, OH 44883
Lat/Lon: 41.01723/-83.20396
Email: walnutgrove@bright.net
Web: www.walnutgrovecampground.com

SEE AD TRAVEL SECTION PAGE 605

TOLEDO—B-2

See listings at Swanton, OH & Monroe & Petersburg, MI

TORONTO—C-5

(W) AUSTIN LAKE PARK AND CAMPGROUND—(Jefferson) *From jct Hwy 7 & Hwy 22: Go 5 mi W on Hwy 22, then 5 mi NW on Hwy 43, then 4 mi N on Hwy 152, then 1-1/2 mi W on Twp Hwy 285A. Enter at end.*

◆◆◆◆FACILITIES: 250 sites, typical site width 45 ft, 220 W&E, (20/30/50 amps), 30 no hkups, many extd stay sites (summer), 3 pull-thrus, WiFi Instant Internet at site, WiFi Internet central location, family camping, tenting, RV storage, shower$, dump, portable dump, laundry, ltd groc, LP gas by weight/by meter, ice, picnic tables, fire rings, grills, wood, controlled access.

◆◆◆◆◆RECREATION: rec hall, rec room/area, pavilion, coin games, lake swim, boating, 25 hp limit, canoeing, kayaking, ramp, dock, 2 rowboat/10 canoe/12 kayak/8 pedal boat rentals, lake/pond/stream fishing, fishing supplies, bsktball, 12 bike rentals, playground, activities, (wkends), horseshoes, sports field, hiking trails, v-ball. Rec open to public.

Pets welcome, breed restrict, quantity restrict. Partial handicap access. Open all yr. Facilities fully operational May 1 - Oct 31. Limited Service Nov 1 thru Apr 30. Big rigs welcome. Clubs welcome. Green Friendly. Rate in 2010 $30-37 for 4 persons. MC/VISA/Debit. Member ARVC, OCOA.

Ohio gave America its first hot dog in 1900. Harry M. Stevens created the popular dining dog.

TORONTO—Continued
AUSTIN LAKE PARK AND CAMPGROUND—Continued

Phone: (888)249-5685
Address: 1002 Twp Highway 285A, Toronto, OH 43964
Lat/Lon: 40.48385/-80.73605
Email: austinlakepark@hughes.net
Web: www.austinlakepark.com

SEE AD STEUBENVILLE PAGE 633

UNIONTOWN—B-4

(E) CLEARWATER PARK—*From jct I-77 (Exit 118) & Hwy 241: Go 1/2 mi N on Hwy 241, then 4-1/2 mi E on SR 619 (Edison St). Enter on R.* Swimming, 145' water slide, adventure mini-golf, campground adjacent to water park, snack bar, & gem panning. Open May 1 - Oct 15. MC/VISA.

Phone: (330)877-9800
Address: 12712 Hoover Ave NW, Uniontown, OH 44685
Lat/Lon: 40.97594/-81.37811
Email: clearwaterpark@hotmail.com
Web: www.clearwaterpark.net

SEE AD AKRON PAGE 613

(E) CLEARWATER PARK CAMPING RESORT—(Stark) *From jct I-77 (exit 118) & Hwy 241: Go 1/2 mi N on Hwy 241, then 4-1/2 mi E on SR 619 (Edison St). Enter on R.*

◆◆◆◆FACILITIES: 175 sites, typical site width 30 ft, 150 full hkups, 25 W&E, (30/50 amps), many extd stay sites (summer), 20 pull-thrus, WiFi Instant Internet at site, WiFi Internet central location, family camping, tenting, RV's/park model rentals, RV storage, dump, non-guest dump $, ltd groc, RV supplies, LP gas by weight/by meter, LP bottle exch, ice, picnic tables, fire rings, wood.

◆◆◆◆RECREATION: rec room/area, pavilion, equipped pavilion, swim pool, mini-golf, ($), playground, sports field, v-ball. Rec open to public.

Pets welcome, breed restrict. Open May 1 - Oct 15. Big rigs welcome. Clubs welcome. Rate in 2010 $29-39 for 2 persons. MC/VISA/Debit. Member ARVC, OCOA.

Charles Kettering of Loundonville invented the automobile self-starter in 1911.

UNIONTOWN—Continued
CLEARWATER PARK CAMPING RESORT—Continued

Phone: (330)877-9800
Address: 12712 Hoover Ave NW, Uniontown, OH 44685
Lat/Lon: 40.97594/-81.37811
Email: clearwaterpark@hotmail.com
Web: www.clearwaterpark.net

SEE AD AKRON PAGE 613

UNITY—C-5

(NW) Flying Finn Campground—(Columbiana) *From jct Hwy 7 & Hwy 14: Go 5 mi E on Hwy 14, then 2 mi NW on Hwy 165, then 1/2 mi W on Brushville Rd. Enter on R.* ◆◆FACILITIES: 167 sites, typical site width 35 ft, 167 W&E, (30 amps), 25 pull-thrus, dump. ◆◆◆RECREATION: swim pool, boating, electric motors only, ramp, lake fishing, playground. Pets welcome. No tents. Open May 1 - Oct 1. Phone: (330)457-2167.

VAN BUREN—B-2

(E) FINDLAY/VAN BUREN KOA—(Hancock) *From jct I-75 (exit 164) & SR 613: Go 3/4 mi E on SR 613, then 1/4 mi SE on Twp 218. Enter on R.*

◆◆◆FACILITIES: 380 sites, typical site width 32 ft, 244 full hkups, 136 W&E, (20/30/50 amps), 50 amps ($), many extd stay sites (summer), 22 pull-thrus, WiFi Instant Internet at site, WiFi Internet central location, family camping, tenting, cabins, RV storage, dump, non-guest dump $, portable dump, laundry, groceries, RV supplies, LP gas by weight/by meter, ice, picnic tables, fire rings, wood, controlled access.

◆◆◆◆◆RECREATION: rec hall, rec room/area, pavilion, coin games, swim pool, boating, no motors, canoeing, kayaking, 6 canoe/2 kayak rentals, pond fishing, fishing supplies, mini-golf, ($), golf nearby, bsktball, playground, shuffleboard court 4 shuffleboard courts, activities, horseshoes, sports field, v-ball. Rec open to public.

Pets welcome, breed restrict, quantity restrict. Partial handicap access. Open all yr. Facilities fully operational mid Apr - mid Oct. 22 sites with Winter water off season. Big rigs welcome. Clubs welcome. Green Friendly. Rate in 2010 $29.95-43.95 per family. MC/VISA/Debit. Member ARVC, OCOA. KOA discount.

Phone: (419)299-3897
Address: 12611 Twp Rd 218, Van Buren, OH 45889
Lat/Lon: 41.13814/-83.63783
Email: campfire7@verizon.net
Web: www.koa.com

SEE AD THIS PAGE

(E) VAN BUREN STATE PARK—(Hancock) *From jct I-75 & Hwy-613: Go 1 mi E on Hwy-613.* FACILITIES: 75 sites, 35 ft max RV length, 75 no hkups, tenting, dump. RECREATION: boating, electric motors only, canoeing, ramp, lake fishing, playground. Pets welcome. Open all yr. Facilities fully operational Apr - Oct. Phone: (419)832-7662.

VAN WERT—C-1

(E) Huggy Bear Campground—(Van Wert) *From jct US 30 & US 127: Go 1-1/2 mi S on US 127, then 5 mi E on Lincoln Hwy, then 1/2 mi S on Ringwald Rd. Enter on L.* ◆◆◆◆FACILITIES: 400 sites, typical site width 30 ft, 350 full hkups, 50 W&E, (20/30/50 amps), 50 amps ($), 95 pull-thrus, family camping, tenting, dump, laundry, groceries. ◆◆◆◆RECREATION: swim pool, boating, no motors, pond fishing, playground. Pets welcome. Partial handicap access. Open all yr. Facilities fully operational Apr 15 - Oct 15. Big rigs welcome. Rate in 2010 $30-35 per family. Phone: (419)968-2211.

(SW) Timberwoods Camping Resort—(Van Wert) *From jct US 127 & US 30: Go 2-1/4 mi W on US 30, then 2-3/4 mi W on US 224, then 1/2 mi S on Liberty Union Rd. Enter on R.* ◆◆◆FACILITIES: 158 sites, typical site width 25 ft, 84 full hkups, 59 W&E, (20/30/50 amps), 15 no hkups, 4 pull-thrus, WiFi In-

Timberwoods Camping Resort—Continued on next page

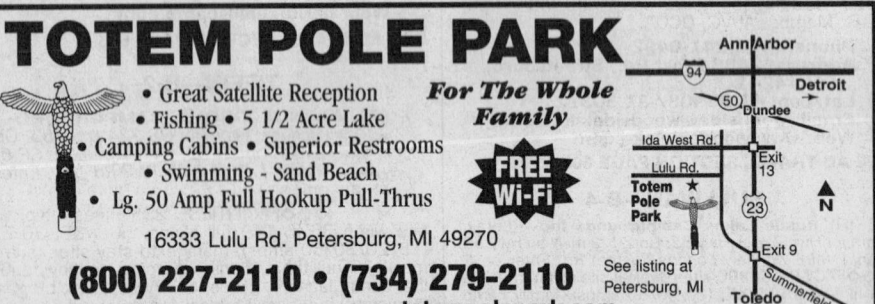

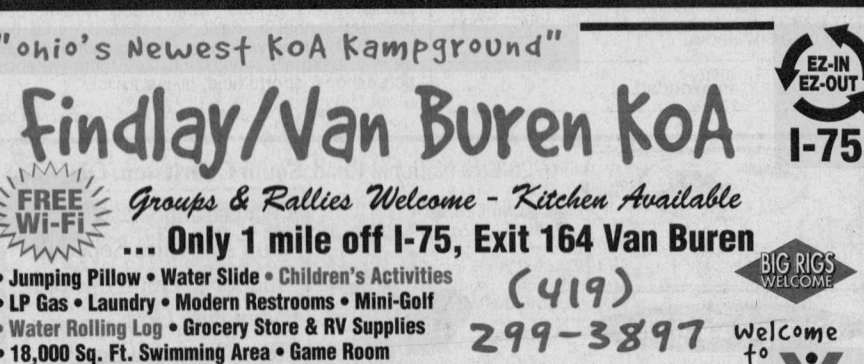

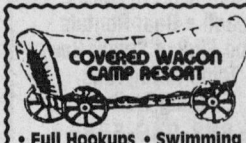

VAN WERT—Continued
Timberwoods Camping Resort—Continued

stant Internet at site ($), family camping, tenting, dump, non-guest dump $, laundry, groceries, RV supplies, LP gas by weight, ice, picnic tables, fire rings, grills, wood. ◊◊◊◊RECREATION: pavilion, swim pool, pond fishing, mini-golf, ($), bsktball, playground, activities, horseshoes, v-ball. Pets welcome. Open Apr 15 - Nov 1. Rate in 2010 $28-32 per family. MC/VISA. CCUSA 50% Discount. CCUSA reservations Required, CCUSA max stay 1 day, CCUSA disc. not avail S,M,Th, CCUSA disc. not avail F,Sa, CCUSA disc. not avail holidays. Discount available Apr, Sep and Oct only.

Phone: (419)238-1124
Address: 10856A Liberty Union Rd, Van Wert, OH 45891
Lat/Lon: 40.84629/-84.62946
Email: wagnerjerri@yahoo.com
Web: www.timberwoodscampgrounds.com

VANLUE—B-2

(E) HERITAGE SPRINGS CAMPGROUND—(Hancock) *From jct SR 15 & SR 330: Go 1/2 mi N on SR 330, then 2 blocks E on Main St, then 100 yards S on East St, then 1/2 mi E on Amanda (TWP 171/199). Enter on L.*

◊◊◊FACILITIES: 166 sites, typical site width 33 ft, 144 full hkups, 22 W&E, (20/30 amps), many extd stay sites (summer), 8 pull-thrus, family camping, RV storage, dump, non-guest dump $, laundry, groceries, RV supplies, LP gas by weight, ice, picnic tables, fire rings, wood, controlled access.

◊◊◊◊RECREATION: rec room/area, coin games, lake swim, lake fishing, fishing supplies, golf nearby, bsktball, playground, shuffleboard court 2 shuffleboard courts, activities (wkends), tennis, horseshoes, sports field, v-ball.

Pets welcome, breed restrict. No tents. Open Apr 30 - Oct 31. Clubs welcome. Rate in 2010 $25-27 per family. MC/VISA/Debit. Member ARVC, OCOA.

Phone: (419)387-7738
Address: 13891 Twp Rd 199, Vanlue, OH 45890
Lat/Lon: 40.96423/-83.46703
Email: mickeymopar24@aol.com
Web: www.heritagespringscampground.com

SEE AD THIS PAGE

VERSAILLES—C-1

(N) Cottonwood Lakes—(Darke) *From jct Main St & Center St (in town): Go 6-1/2 mi N on Center St/Reed Rd (Center St becomes Reed Rd), then 1/2 mi W on Althoff Rd. Enter on L.* ◊◊◊FACILITIES: 120 sites, typical site width 25 ft, 80 full hkups, 38 W&E, (20/30/50 amps), 2 no hkups, family camping, tenting, dump. ◊◊◊RECREATION: lake swim, boating, no motors, lake fishing, playground. Pets welcome. Open Apr 15 - Oct 15. Big rigs welcome. Rate in 2010 $25 per vehicle. Phone: (419)582-2610.

WAPAKONETA—C-1

(E) WAPAKONETA/LIMA SOUTH - KOA—(Auglaize) *From jct I-75 N'bnd exit 110 & S'bnd exit 111: Go 1/2 block east to first intersection, then 3/4 mi N on Cemetery Rd. Enter on L.*

◊◊◊◊◊FACILITIES: 66 sites, typical site width 27 ft, 51 full hkups, 15 W&E, (20/30/50 amps), some extd stay sites (summer), 49 pull-thrus, WiFi Instant Internet at site, family camping, tenting, cabins, RV storage, dump, non-guest dump $, laundry, groceries, RV supplies, LP gas by weight/by meter, LP bottle exch, ice, picnic tables, patios, fire rings, grills, wood.

◊◊◊◊RECREATION: rec hall, rec room/area, equipped pavilion, coin games, swim pool, mini-golf, ($), golf nearby, bsktball, playground, shuffleboard court shuffleboard court, activities (wkends), horseshoes, sports field, v-ball.

Pets welcome, breed restrict. Partial handicap access. Open Mar 1 - Nov 30. Big rigs welcome. Escort to site. Clubs welcome. Green Friendly. Rate in 2010 $35-50 for 2 persons. MC/VISA/Debit. Member ARVC, OCOA. KOA discount.

Phone: (419)738-6016
Address: 14719 Cemetery Rd, Wapakoneta, OH 45895
Lat/Lon: 40.56606/-84.16477
Email: wapakonetaoh@mykoa.com
Web: www.wapakonetakoa.com

SEE AD LIMA PAGE 625

WARREN—B-5

See listings at Bristolville, Champion, Deerfield, Hubbard, Lake Milton, Newton Falls & Parkman

WARREN—Continued

(NW) Valley Lake Park—(Trumbull) *From jct Hwy-534 & Hwy-305: Go 3/4 mi E on Hwy-305. Enter on R.* ◊◊FACILITIES: 99 sites, typical site width 45 ft, 78 W&E, (20/30 amps), 21 no hkups, 3 pull-thrus, tenting, dump, laundry. ◊◊◊RECREATION: lake swim, boating, canoeing, lake fishing, playground. Pets welcome. Open May 1 - Sep 30. Rate in 2010 $18 per family. Phone: (330)898-1819.

WAUSEON—B-1

(NE) Sunny's Campground—(Fulton) *From jct I-80 (Ohio Turnpike exit 34) & SR 108: Go 3-1/2 mi N on SR 108, then 2 mi E on CR M, then 1/2 mi N on CR 13. Enter on L.* ◊◊◊FACILITIES: 801 sites, typical site width 50 ft, 8 full hkups, 793 W&E, (30/50 amps), 32 pull-thrus, WiFi Instant Internet at site, WiFi Internet central location, family camping, tenting, dump, non-guest dump $, portable dump, ltd groc, RV supplies, LP gas by weight/by meter, ice, picnic tables, fire rings, wood. ◊◊◊◊RECREATION: rec hall, pavilion, lake swim, boating, electric motors only, canoeing, lake fishing, fishing supplies, mini-golf, ($), bsktball, playground, shuffleboard court 2 shuffleboard courts, activities horseshoes, v-ball. Pets welcome. Partial handicap access. Open Apr 23 - Oct 3. Big rigs welcome. Rate in 2010 $23-30 for 2 persons. MC/VISA/Debit. CCUSA 50% Discount. CCUSA reservations Accepted, CCUSA max stay 3 days, CCUSA disc. not avail S,Th, CCUSA disc. not avail F,Sa, CCUSA disc. not avail holidays. Sewer surcharge $2.

Phone: (419)337-3101
Address: 12399 CR #13, Wauseon, OH 43567
Lat/Lon: 41.64616/-84.11292
Web: www.sunnyscampground.com

WAYNESVILLE—D-1

(E) CAESAR CREEK STATE PARK—(Warren) *From jct I-71 & Hwy-73: Go 1 mi E on Hwy-73, then 5 mi N on Hwy-380, then W on Center Rd (Harveysburg).* FACILITIES: 283 sites, 283 E, (20/30 amps), tenting, dump, ltd groc. RECREATION: lake swim, boating, ramp, dock, lake fishing, playground. Pets welcome. Open all yr. Facilities fully operational Apr - Oct. Phone: (513)897-3055.

WELLINGTON—B-3

(SW) Clare-Mar Lakes Campground—(Lorain) *From jct Hwy-162 & Hwy-58: Go 2-1/4 mi S on Hwy-58, then 1-3/4 mi W on New London/Eastern Rd. Enter on L.* ◊◊◊FACILITIES: 500 sites, typical site width 35 ft, 440 W&E, (20/30/50 amps), 60 no hkups, 10 pull-thrus, family camping, tenting, dump. ◊◊◊◊RECREATION: lake swim, boating, electric motors only, canoeing, lake fishing, playground. Pets welcome, breed restrict. Open May 1 - Oct 15. Member ARVC, OCOA. Phone: (440)647-3318.

(S) FINDLEY STATE PARK—(Lorain) *From jct Hwy-18 & Hwy-58: Go 3 mi S on Hwy-58.* FACILITIES: 270 sites, 39 ft max RV length, 90 E, (50 amps), 180 no hkups, tenting, dump, laundry, ltd groc. RECREATION: lake swim, boating, electric motors only, canoeing, ramp, lake fishing, playground. Pets welcome, quantity restrict. Open all yr. Facilities fully operational Apr - Oct. Phone: (440)647-5749.

WELLSTON—E-3

LAKE ALMA STATE PARK—(Jackson) *From jct Hwy 160 & Hwy 349: Go 1 mi S on Hwy 349. Enter on L.* FACILITIES: 81 sites, typical site width 15 ft, 72 E, (30/50 amps), 9 no hkups, tenting, dump, ltd groc. RECREATION: lake swim, boating, electric motors only, canoeing, ramp, dock, lake/river fishing, playground. Pets welcome. Open all yr. Facilities fully operational Apr - Oct. Phone: (740)384-4474.

WEST LIBERTY—C-2

(NW) Oak Crest Campground—(Logan) *From jct Hwy-245 & US-68: Go 2-1/2 mi N on US-68, then 2 mi W on Twp Rd 30, then 1 mi N on Twp Rd 187. Enter on L.* ◊◊◊FACILITIES: 136 sites, typical site width 32 ft, 34 full hkups, 102 W&E, (15/20/30 amps), 50 pull-thrus, family camping, tenting, dump, ltd groc. ◊◊◊RECREATION: swim pool, boating, dock, lake fishing, playground. Pets welcome, breed restrict, quantity restrict. Open all yr. Facilities fully operational Apr 15 - Oct 31. Rate in 2010 $30-35 for 4 persons. Phone: (937)593-7211.

WEST SALEM—B-4

(SE) TOWN & COUNTRY CAMP RESORT—(Wayne) *From jct I-71 (exit 198) & Hwy 539: Go 1 mi N on Hwy 539, then 1 mi E on Shilling Rd. Enter at end.*

◊◊◊◊FACILITIES: 200 sites, typical site width 50 ft, 196 full hkups, 4 W&E, (20/30/50 amps), mostly extd stay sites (summer), 7 pull-thrus, WiFi Instant Internet at site, WiFi Internet central location, family camping, tenting, RV storage, laundry, ltd groc, RV supplies, LP gas by weight/by meter, ice, picnic tables, fire rings, wood, controlled access.

◊◊◊◊RECREATION: rec hall, pavilion, equipped pavilion, coin games, swim pool, pond fishing, fishing supplies, bsktball, playground, activities, (wkends), horseshoes, sports field, hiking trails, v-ball.

WEST SALEM—Continued
TOWN & COUNTRY CAMP RESORT—Continued

Pets welcome. Open Apr 1 - Oct 31. Big rigs welcome. Clubs welcome. Rate in 2010 $30 per family. MC/VISA/DISC/Debit. Member ARVC, OCOA.

Phone: (419)853-4550
Address: 7555 Shilling Rd, West Salem, OH 44287
Lat/Lon: 40.96150/-82.07288
Email: tccampground@verizon.net
Web: www.tccamp.com

SEE AD TRAVEL SECTION PAGE 605

WESTERVILLE—D-3

(NE) Tree Haven Campground—(Delaware) *From jct I-270 (exit 30) & SR 161: Go 4-1/2 mi E on SR 161 Bypass, then 1-1/4 mi N on New Albany Rd, then 1 block N on SR 605, then 3-7/10 mi N on Schleppi Rd/Miller Paul Rd. Enter on R.* ◊◊FACILITIES: 130 sites, 130 W&E, (20/30/50 amps), 50 amps ($), 20 pull-thrus, family camping, tenting, dump, ltd groc. ◊◊◊RECREATION: swim pool, playground. Pets welcome ($), breed restrict. Open May 1 - Nov 1. Rate in 2010 $33-38 for 2 persons. Member ARVC, OCOA. Phone: (740)965-3469.

WHITEHOUSE—B-2

(NW) Twin Acres Campground—(Lucas) *From Ohio Tpk I-80/90 (exit 52) & SR 2: Go 2 mi SW on SR 2, then 4 mi S on SR 295, then 1/4 mi N on SR 64. Enter on L.* ◊◊◊FACILITIES: 200 sites, typical site width 30 ft, 100 full hkups, 100 W&E, (20/30/50 amps), 50 amps ($), family camping, tenting, dump, ltd groc. ◊◊◊RECREATION: lake swim, pond fishing, playground. Pets welcome, breed restrict. Open May 1 - Oct 15. Rate in 2010 $22-25 per family. Phone: (419) 877-2684.

WILMINGTON—E-2

(SW) BEECHWOOD ACRES CAMPING RESORT—(Clinton) *From US 22 & US 68: Go 6-1/4 mi S on US 68, then 2 mi W on SR 350, then 3/4 mi N on Yankee Rd. Enter on R.*

◊◊◊◊FACILITIES: 95 sites, typical site width 35 ft, 95 W&E, (20/30/50 amps), some extd stay sites (summer), 17 pull-thrus, heater not allowed, WiFi Instant Internet at site, family camping, tenting, cabins, shower$, dump, non-guest dump $, portable dump, laundry, ltd groc, RV supplies, LP gas by weight/by meter, ice, picnic tables, fire rings, grills, wood.

◊◊◊◊◊RECREATION: rec room/area, pavilion, coin games, swim pool, lake fishing, fishing supplies, golf nearby, bsktball, 12 bike rentals, playground, activities, (wkends), hiking trails, v-ball.

Pets welcome, breed restrict. Partial handicap access. Open Apr 15 - Oct 31. Big rigs welcome. Clubs welcome. Rate in 2010 $35-40 per family. MC/VISA/DISC/Debit. Member ARVC, OCOA.

Phone: (937)289-2202
Address: 855 Yankee Rd, Wilmington, OH 45177
Lat/Lon: 39.37961/-83.89778
Email: beechwoodacres@hotmail.com
Web: www.beechwoodacres.com

SEE AD NEXT PAGE

WILMINGTON—Continued on next page

WILMINGTON—Continued

(SW) COWAN LAKE STATE PARK—(Clinton) *From jct Hwy-3/22 & US-68: Go 3 mi S on US-68, then 2 mi W on Dalton Rd.* FACILITIES: 254 sites, 35 ft max RV length, 237 E, (50 amps), 17 no hkups, tenting, dump, laundry, ltd groc. RECREATION: lake swim, boating, 10 hp limit, canoeing, ramp, dock, lake fishing, playground. Pets welcome. Partial handicap access. Open all yr. Facilities fully operational Apr - Oct. Phone: (937)383-3751.

WILMOT—C-4

(NE) BAYLOR BEACH PARK—(Stark) *From jct US 250 & US 62: Go 2 mi E on US 62 (at jct US 62 & Hwy 93). Enter on L.*

WELCOME

◆◆◆◆FACILITIES: 60 sites, typical site width 30 ft, 10 full hkups, 50 W&E, (30/50 amps), 32 pull-thrus, WiFi Instant Internet at site, tenting, RV storage, dump, non-guest dump $, portable dump, ice, picnic tables, fire rings, grills, wood, controlled access.

◆◆◆◆RECREATION: pavilion, equipped pavilion, swim pool, spray ground, lake swim, boating, kayaking, 6 kayak/8 pedal boat rentals, mini-golf, ($), golf nearby, bsktball, playground, horseshoes, sports field, v-ball. Rec open to public.

Pets welcome, breed restrict. Partial handicap access. Open May 1 - Oct 15. Waterpark open Memorial Day thru Labor Day. Big rigs welcome. Clubs welcome. Rate in 2010 $25-30 for 2 persons. MC/VISA/DISC/Debit. Member ARVC, OCOA.

Phone: (330)767-3031
Address: 8725 Manchester Ave SW, Navarre, OH 44662
Lat/Lon: 40.68686/-81.59955
Web: www.baylorbeachpark.com

SEE AD BERLIN PAGE 617

(NE) BAYLOR BEACH WATER PARK—*From jct US 250 & US 62: Go 2 mi E on US 62 (at jct US 62 & Hwy 93). Enter on L.* 2 acre swimming lake, sand bottom, grassy beaches. 90" Tube of Terror & 4 kid slides, diving boards, log rolls picnicking, grills, concessions, mini golf, funyaks, aquabikes, volleyball, & more. Shelters available for rental. Season membership available. Open Memorial Day - Labor Day. MC/VISA/DISC.

WELCOME

Phone: (330)767-3031
Address: 8725 Manchester Ave. SW, Navarre, OH 44662
Lat/Lon: 40.68686/-81.59955
Web: www.baylorbeachpark.com

SEE AD BERLIN PAGE 617

WINESBURG—C-4

(N) AMISH COUNTRY CAMPSITES—(Holmes) *From jct US 250 & US 62: Go 4 mi W on US 62. Enter on L.*

WELCOME

◆◆◆◆FACILITIES: 60 sites, typical site width 25 ft, 60 W&E, (20/30 amps), 15 pull-thrus, WiFi Instant Internet at site, tenting, dump, non-guest dump $, ice, picnic tables, fire rings, wood.

◆RECREATION: pavilion, playground.

Pets welcome. Partial handicap access. Open all yr. Clubs welcome. Rate in 2010 $25 for 2 persons. MC/VISA/DISC/Debit. Member ARVC, OCOA.

Phone: (330)359-5226
Address: 1930 SR 62 E, Winesburg, OH 44690
Lat/Lon: 40.62381/-81.69099
Web: www.amishcountrycampsites.com

SEE AD BERLIN PAGE 615

WOOSTER—C-4

See listings at Ashland & Shreve

(N) Meadow Lake Park—(Wayne) *From jct US 30 & Hwy 83/3 :Go 8 mi N on Hwy 3, then 2 mi W on Fulton Rd, then 100 yds S on Canaan Center Rd, then 1 bl W on CR 27. Enter on L.* ◆◆FACILITIES: 165 sites, typical site width 35 ft, 165 W&E, (20/30/50 amps), 50 amps ($), 145 pull-thrus, family camping, tenting, dump. ◆◆◆RECREATION: lake swim, lake fishing. Pets welcome. Open May 1 - Oct 31. Big rigs welcome. Rate in 2010 $25-30 for 4 persons. Phone: (330)435-6652.

YELLOW SPRINGS—D-2

JOHN BRYAN STATE PARK—(Greene) *From jct US-68 & Hwy-343: Go 2-1/2 mi E on Hwy-343 & Hwy-370.* FACILITIES: 98 sites, 39 ft max RV length, 10 E, (50 amps), 88 no hkups, tenting, dump, ltd groc. RECREATION: canoeing, ramp, river fishing, playground. Pets welcome. Open all yr. Facilities fully operational Apr - Oct. Phone: (937)767-1274.

YOUNGSTOWN—B-5

See listings at Hubbard

ZALESKI—E-3

(SW) LAKE HOPE STATE PARK—(Vinton) *From jct Hwy-677 & Hwy-278: Go 5 mi N on Hwy-278.* FACILITIES: 187 sites, 46 E, (50 amps), 141 no hkups, tenting, dump, laundry, ltd groc. RECREATION: lake swim, boating, electric motors only, canoeing, ramp, lake fishing, playground. Pets welcome. Partial handicap access. Open all yr. Facilities fully operational Apr - Oct. Phone: (740)596-4938.

ZANESVILLE—D-4

DILLON STATE PARK—(Muskingum) *From jct Hwy-60 & Hwy-146: Go 9 mi NW on Hwy-146. Enter on L.* FACILITIES: 195 sites, 183 E, (50 amps), 12 no hkups, tenting, dump, laundry, ltd groc. RECREATION: lake swim, boating, ramp, dock, lake fishing, playground. Pets welcome. Partial handicap access. Open all yr. Facilities fully operational Apr - Oct. Phone: (740)452-1083.

(S) MUSKINGUM RIVER PARKWAY STATE PARK—(Muskingum) *From jct I-70 & Hwy 60: Go 6 mi N on Hwy 60, then NE on CR 49.* FACILITIES: 20 sites, 35 ft max RV length, 20 no hkups, tenting. RECREATION: boating, canoeing, ramp, river fishing. Pets welcome. Open all yr. Facilities fully operational Apr - Oct. Phone: (740)674-4794.

(E) National Road Campground—(Muskingum) *From jct I-70 (exit 157) & Hwy 93: Go 100 yards S on Hwy 93, then 50 feet W on US 40/Hwy 93 (quick left in front of Marathon gas station), then 3/4 mi S on S Pleasant Grove Rd. Enter on R.* ◆◆◆FACILITIES: 85 sites, typical site width 35 ft, 35 ft max RV length, 38 full hkups, 47 W&E, (20/30 amps), 32 pull-thrus, tenting, dump, laundry, groceries. ◆◆RECREATION: canoeing, pond fishing, play equipment. Pets welcome. Open Apr 1 - Nov 1. Rate in 2010 $26-28 for 2 persons. Member ARVC, OCOA. Phone: (740)452-5025.

(E) WOLFIES CAMPGROUND—(Muskingum) *From jct I-70 (exit 155) & OH 146 W (E'bnd I-70 go left at bottom of ramp onto Elberon): Go 1/4 mi W on OH 146, then right onto OH 666 3/4, then left onto Lewis (OH 666) 3/4 mi, then first right past "Riverside Park" is Buckeye Dr, to campground. Enter at end.*

WELCOME

◆◆◆◆FACILITIES: 54 sites, typical site width 30 ft, 46 full hkups, 8 W&E, (20/30/50 amps), 50 amps ($), 23 pull-thrus, WiFi Instant Internet at site, family camping, tenting, RV's/park model rentals, cabins, RV storage, dump, non-guest dump $, laundry, ltd groc, RV supplies, ice, picnic tables, fire rings, wood.

◆◆◆RECREATION: rec room/area, equipped pavilion, coin games, swim pool, golf nearby, bsktball, playground, activities, (wkends), horseshoes. Rec open to public.

Pets welcome. Partial handicap access. Open all yr. Limited facilities Nov to Apr. Big rigs welcome. Escort to site. Clubs welcome. Rate in 2010 $26-30 for 2 persons. MC/VISA/AMEX/Debit. Member ARVC, OCOA.

Phone: (740)454-0925
Address: 101 Buckeye Dr, Zanesville, OH 43701
Lat/Lon: 39.96226/-81.98749
Email: wolfieskamping1@yahoo.com
Web: www.wolfiescampground.com

SEE AD COLUMBUS PAGE 622

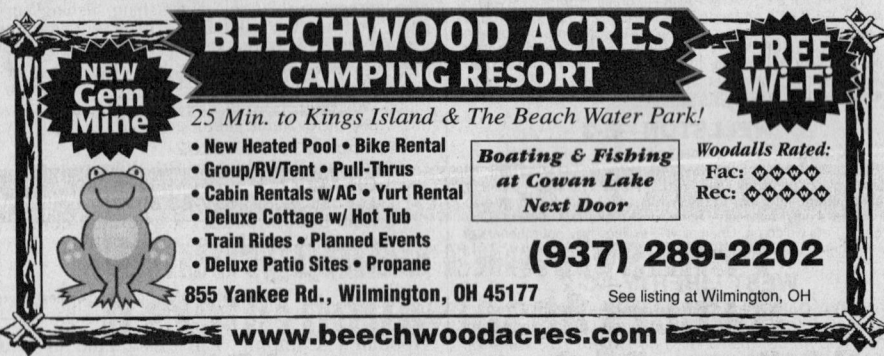

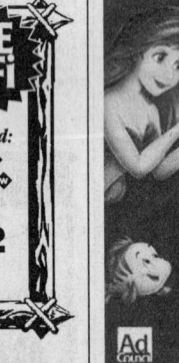

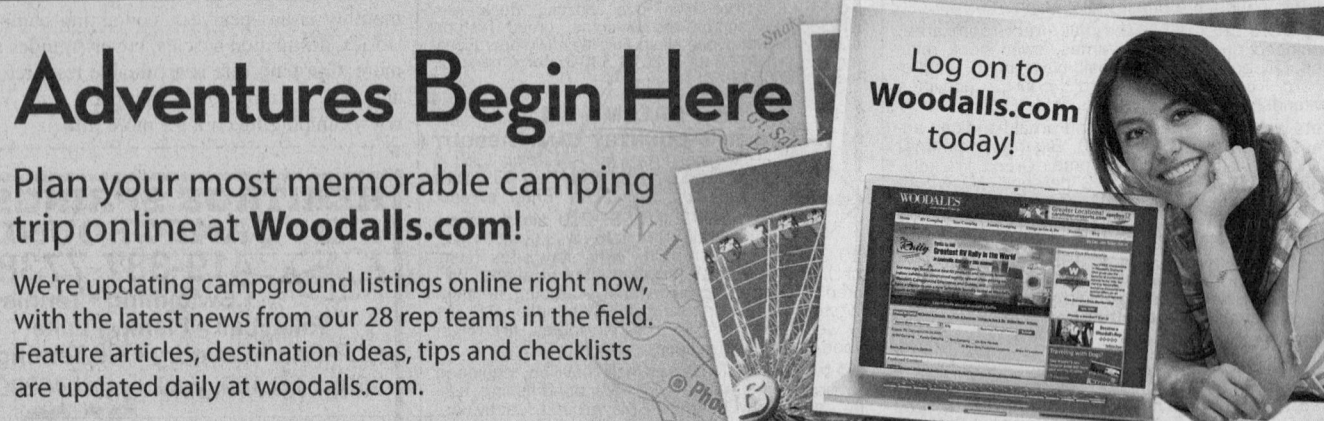

TRAVEL SECTION

Pennsylvania

READER SERVICE INFO

The following business has placed an ad in the Pennsylvania Travel Section. To receive free information, enter their Reader Service number on the Reader Service Card opposite page 48/Discover Section in the front of this directory:

Advertiser	RS#
Bear Run Campground	3568
Boyer RV Center	3739
Dale Smith's Camper Sales	3743
Mellott Brothers RV	3704
Pennsylvania Campground Owners' Association	515
The Foote Rest Campground	3584

TIME ZONE

Pennsylvania is in the Eastern Time Zone.

TOPOGRAPHY

In the northern and western parts of Pennsylvania, the Allegheny Plateau rises to 2,000 ft. in the north and to 1,200 ft. south of Pittsburgh. The eastern portion of the state is made up of the great Appalachian Valley and Mountains, lowlands and plateaus that slope to the Delaware River.

TEMPERATURE

Annual temperatures range from 14° to 35° in January and between 60° and 85° in July.

Pennsylvania was once inhabited by Delaware and Susquehannock Native Americans prior to 1609. This state was among the thirteen colonies that opposed England during the Revolutionary War, and the Declaration of Independence was signed in Philadelphia. This state was also the sight of The Battle of Gettysburg during the Civil war. Emigrants from Sweden, Netherlands and England were some of the first to settle in this area, and their rich cultural history can still be seen in many areas of the state today.

TRAVEL & TOURISM INFO

State Agency:
Pennsylvania Tourism Office
Commonwealth Keystone Bldg, 4th Flr.
400 North St.
Harrisburg, PA 17120
(800/847-4872)
www.visitpa.com

Regional Agencies:
Allegheny Mountains CVB
One Convention Ctr. Dr.
Altoona, PA 16602
(800/842-5866 or 814/943-4183)
www.alleghenymountains.com

Armstrong County Tourist Bureau
125 Market Street
Kittanning, PA 16201
(724/543-4003 or 888/265-9954)
www.armstrongcounty.com

Bedford County Visitors Bureau
131 S. Juliana St.
Bedford, PA 15522
(800/765-3331)
www.bedfordcounty.net

Brandywine Conference and Visitors Bureau
One Beaver Valley Road
Chadds Ford, PA 19317
(610/565-3679 or 800/343-3983)
www.brandywinecountry.org

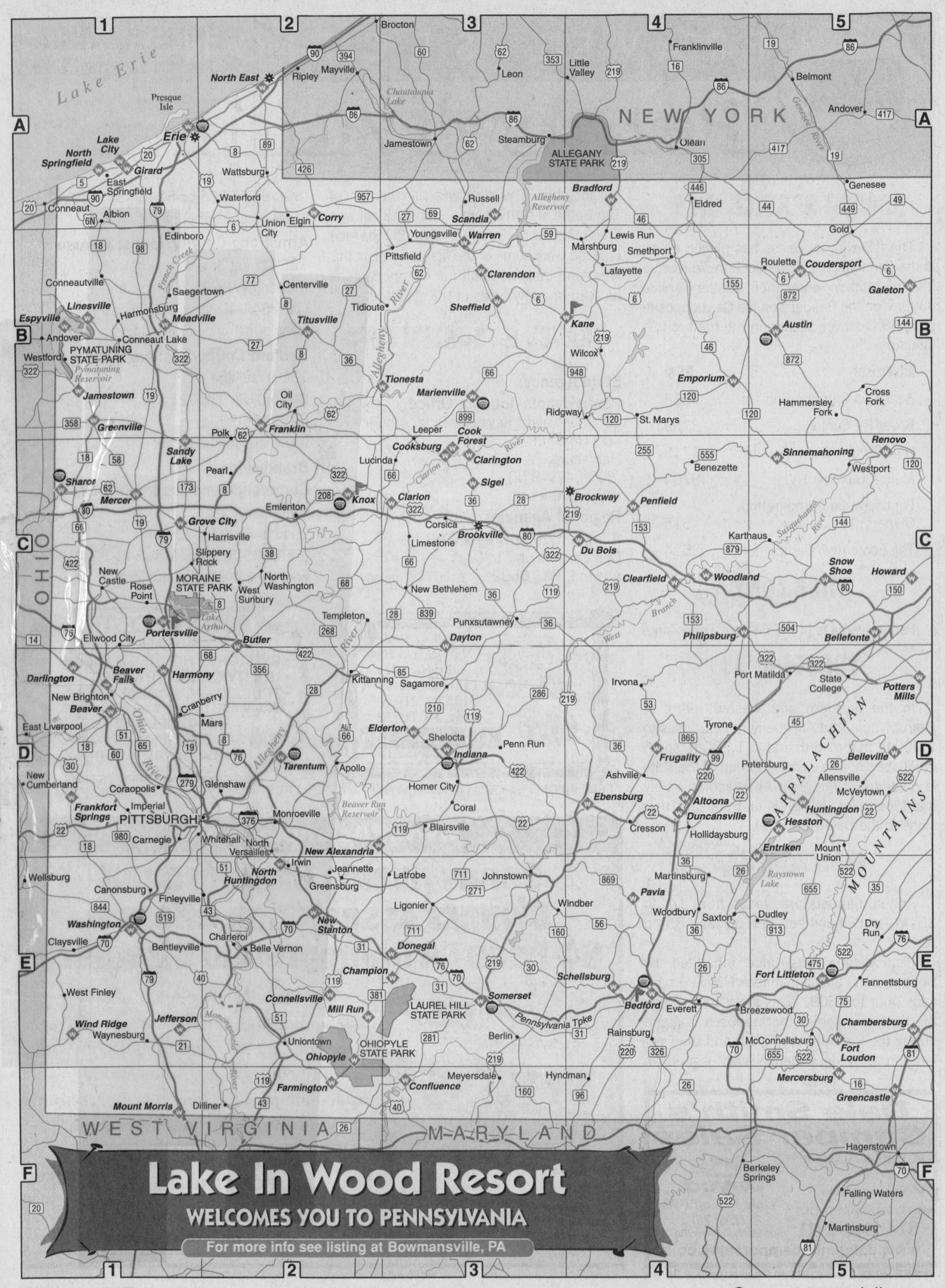
Lake Erie
NEW YORK
OHIO
WEST VIRGINIA
MARYLAND
APPALACHIAN MOUNTAINS
Brocton
Franklinville
Ripley
Mayville
Chautauqua Lake
Leon
Little Valley
Belmont
Andover
North East
Presque Isle
Erie
Jamestown
Steamburg
ALLEGANY STATE PARK
Olean
Lake City
North Springfield
Girard
East Springfield
Wattsburg
Bradford
Genesee
Conneaut
Albion
Waterford
Russell
Allegheny Reservoir
Eldred
Union City
Elgin
Corry
Scandia
Lewis Run
Gold
Edinboro
Youngsville
Warren
Marshburg
Smethport
Pittsfield
Roulette
Coudersport
Lafayette
Clarendon
Conneautville
French Creek
Saegertown
Centerville
Galeton
Linesville
Harmonsburg
Tidioute
Sheffield
Kane
Espyville
Meadville
Titusville
Austin
Andover
Conneaut Lake
Wilcox
Westford
PYMATUNING STATE PARK
Pymatuning Reservoir
Tionesta
Emporium
Cross Fork
Jamestown
Oil City
Marienville
Hammersley Fork
Ridgway
St. Marys
Greenville
Polk
Franklin
Leeper
Cook Forest
Renovo
Sandy Lake
Cooksburg
Sinnemahoning
Lucinda
Clarington
Benezette
Westport
Pearl
Sharon
Sigel
Mercer
Knox
Clarion
Brockway
Penfield
Emlenton
Corsica
Brookville
Grove City
Harrisville
Limestone
Karthaus
Du Bois
Slippery Rock
Snow Shoe
Howard
New Castle
North Washington
Clearfield
Woodland
Rose Point
MORAINE STATE PARK
West Sunbury
New Bethlehem
Lake Arthur
Templeton
Punxsutawney
Portersville
Ellwood City
Butler
Dayton
Philipsburg
Bellefonte
Darlington
Beaver Falls
Harmony
Kittanning
Sagamore
Port Matilda
State College
Potters Mills
Irvona
New Brighton
Beaver
Cranberry
Mars
Tyrone
East Liverpool
Elderton
Shelocta
Penn Run
Frugality
Belleville
Tarentum
Apollo
Indiana
Petersburg
Allensville
New Cumberland
Coraopolis
Glenshaw
Ashville
McVeytown
Homer City
Altoona
Frankfort Springs
Imperial
Coral
Ebensburg
Duncansville
Huntingdon
PITTSBURGH
Monroeville
Beaver Run Reservoir
Hollidaysburg
Hesston
Carnegie
Whitehall
North Versailles
Blairsville
Cresson
Entriken
Mount Union
New Alexandria
Irwin
Wellsburg
Jeannette
North Huntingdon
Latrobe
Johnstown
Martinsburg
Raystown Lake
Canonsburg
Greensburg
Pavia
Finleyville
Ligonier
Windber
Woodbury
Saxton
Dudley
Washington
New Stanton
Dry Run
Claysville
Charleroi
Bentleyville
Belle Vernon
Donegal
Champion
Schellsburg
Fort Littleton
West Finley
Connellsville
LAUREL HILL STATE PARK
Somerset
Fannettsburg
Mill Run
Bedford
Everett
Breezewood
Jefferson
Wind Ridge
Waynesburg
Pennsylvania Tpke
Berlin
Rainsburg
Chambersburg
Uniontown
OHIOPYLE STATE PARK
Ohiopyle
McConnellsburg
Fort Loudon
Meyersdale
Hyndman
Farmington
Confluence
Mercersburg
Greencastle
Mount Morris
Dilliner
Hagerstown
Berkeley Springs
Falling Waters
Martinsburg
Lake In Wood Resort
WELCOMES YOU TO PENNSYLVANIA
For more info see listing at Bowmansville, PA

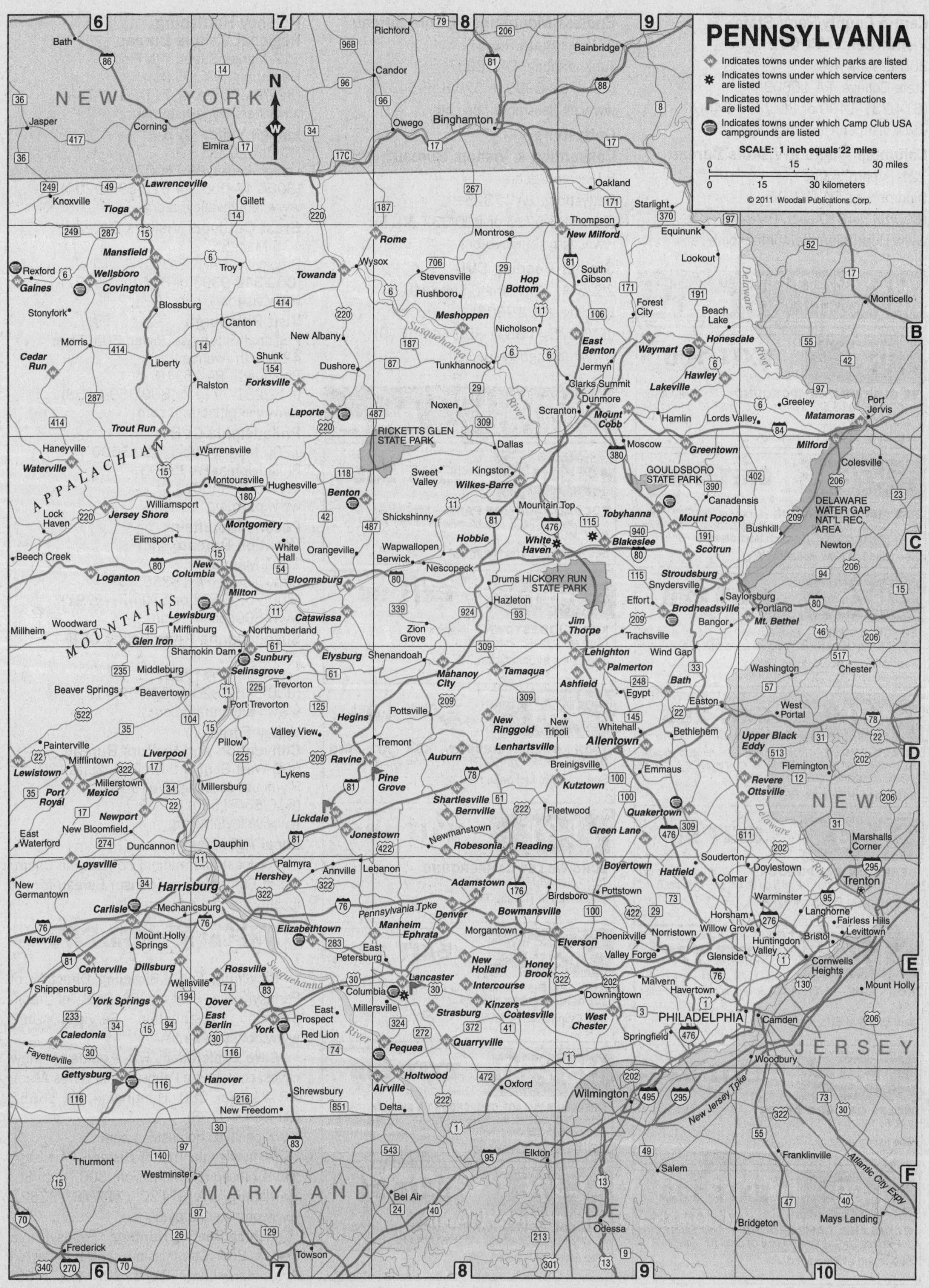
PENNSYLVANIA
Indicates towns under which parks are listed
Indicates towns under which service centers are listed
Indicates towns under which attractions are listed
Indicates towns under which Camp Club USA campgrounds are listed
SCALE: 1 inch equals 22 miles
0 15 30 miles
0 15 30 kilometers
© 2011 Woodall Publications Corp.
NEW YORK
N
W
Bath
Jasper
Corning
Elmira
Richford
Candor
Owego
Binghamton
Bainbridge
Oakland
Starlight
Thompson
New Milford
Equinunk
Lookout
Monticello
Lawrenceville
Knoxville
Tioga
Gillett
Mansfield
Rexford
Gaines
Wellsboro
Covington
Stonyfork
Blossburg
Troy
Canton
Towanda
Wysox
Rome
Montrose
Stevensville
Rushboro
Hop Bottom
South Gibson
Forest City
Beach Lake
Meshoppen
Nicholson
East Benton
Waymart
Honesdale
Morris
Cedar Run
Liberty
Ralston
Shunk
New Albany
Dushore
Forksville
Tunkhannock
Jermyn
Hawley
Lakeville
Clarks Summit
Dunmore
Scranton
Mount Cobb
Hamlin
Lords Valley
Greeley
Port Jervis
Matamoras
Laporte
Noxen
Trout Run
RICKETTS GLEN STATE PARK
Dallas
Moscow
Greentown
Milford
Haneyville
Warrensville
Waterville
APPALACHIAN
Montoursville
Hughesville
Sweet Valley
Kingston
Wilkes-Barre
GOULDSBORO STATE PARK
Colesville
Williamsport
Benton
Canadensis
Lock Haven
Jersey Shore
Mountain Top
Tobyhanna
Mount Pocono
DELAWARE WATER GAP NAT'L REC. AREA
Montgomery
Shickshinny
Bushkill
Elimsport
White Hall
Orangeville
Wapwallopen
Hobbie
White Haven
Blakeslee
Scotrun
Newton
Beech Creek
Berwick
Nescopeck
Loganton
New Columbia
Bloomsburg
Drums
HICKORY RUN STATE PARK
Stroudsburg
Snydersville
Milton
Hazleton
Effort
Saylorsburg
Portland
Brodheadsville
Bangor
Mt. Bethel
MOUNTAINS
Lewisburg
Catawissa
Zion Grove
Jim Thorpe
Trachsville
Millheim
Woodward
Mifflinburg
Northumberland
Glen Iron
Shamokin Dam
Sunbury
Elysburg
Shenandoah
Lehighton
Wind Gap
Washington
Chester
Middleburg
Selinsgrove
Mahanoy City
Tamaqua
Palmerton
Beaver Springs
Beavertown
Trevorton
Ashfield
Bath
Egypt
Easton
West Portal
Port Trevorton
Pottsville
Hegins
New Ringgold
New Tripoli
Whitehall
Bethlehem
Allentown
Painterville
Pillow
Valley View
Tremont
Lenhartsville
Upper Black Eddy
Mifflintown
Liverpool
Lewistown
Ravine
Auburn
Breinigsville
Emmaus
Flemington
Millerstown
Lykens
Pine Grove
Kutztown
Revere
Port Royal
Mexico
Millersburg
Ottsville
Shartlesville
Bernville
Fleetwood
NEW
Newport
New Bloomfield
Lickdale
Quakertown
Newmanstown
Green Lane
East Waterford
Duncannon
Dauphin
Jonestown
Robesonia
Reading
Marshalls Corner
Loysville
Palmyra
Annville
Lebanon
Boyertown
Souderton
Doylestown
Hershey
Hatfield
Colmar
Trenton
New Germantown
Harrisburg
Adamstown
Birdsboro
Pottstown
Warminster
Carlisle
Mechanicsburg
Pennsylvania Tpke
Denver
Bowmansville
Horsham
Langhorne
Fairless Hills
Levittown
Elizabethtown
Manheim
Ephrata
Morgantown
Phoenixville
Norristown
Willow Grove
Bristol
Newville
Mount Holly Springs
Huntingdon Valley
East Petersburg
Elverson
Valley Forge
Glenside
Cornwells Heights
Centerville
Dillsburg
New Holland
Honey Brook
Lancaster
Wellsville
Rossville
Malvern
Havertown
Mount Holly
Shippensburg
Columbia
Intercourse
Downingtown
York Springs
Dover
Millersville
Kinzers
Coatesville
West Chester
PHILADELPHIA
Camden
East Berlin
East Prospect
Strasburg
Springfield
Caledonia
York
Red Lion
Quarryville
Fayetteville
Pequea
JERSEY
Woodbury
Gettysburg
Holtwood
Oxford
Hanover
Shrewsbury
Airville
Wilmington
New Freedom
Delta
New Jersey Tpke
Franklinville
Thurmont
Elkton
Westminster
Salem
MARYLAND
Bel Air
DE
Atlantic City Expy
Mays Landing
Bridgeton
Odessa
Frederick
Towson
Susquehanna River
Delaware River
6
7
8
9
10
B
C
D
E
F

Centre County/Penn State Visitor Center/CPCVB
800 E. Park Ave.
State College, PA 16803
(814/231-1400 or 800/358-5466)
www.visitpennstate.org

Columbia Montour Visitors Bureau
121 Papermill Rd.
Bloomsburg, PA 17815
(800/847-4810 or 570/784-8279)
www.iTourColumbiaMontour.com

Endless Mountains Visitors Bureau
4 Werks Plaza Rte 6
Tunkhannock, PA 18657
(800/769-8999 or 570/836-5431)
www.endlessmountains.org

Gettysburg Convention & Visitors Bureau
8 Lincoln Square
Gettysburg, PA 17325
(866/486-5735 or 800/337-5015))
www.gettysburgcvb.org

Greater Reading CVB
2525 N. 12th Street, Suite 101
Reading, PA 19605
(610/375-4085 or 800/443-6610)
www.readingberkspa.com

Hershey Harrisburg Regional Visitors Bureau
112 Market Street, 4th Floor
Harrisburg, PA 17101
(877/PA-PULSE or 717/231-7788)
www.hersheyharrisburg.org

Lehigh Valley CVB
PO Box 20785
Lehigh Valley, PA 18002
(800/747-0561 or 610/882-9200)
www.lehighvalleypa.org

Great Outdoors Visitors Bureau
175 Main St.
Brookville, PA 15825
(800/348-9393 or 814/849-5197)
www.visitpago.com

Visit Pittsburgh
Regional Enterprise Tower, 30th Floor
425 Sixth Avenue
Pittsburgh, PA 15219
(412/281-7711 or 800/359-0758)
www.visitpittsburgh.com

Philadelphia CVB
1700 Market Street, Ste. 3000
Philadelphia, PA 19103
(215/636-3300)
www.pcvb.org

Pocono Mountains Vacation Bureau, Inc.
1004 Main St.
Stroudsburg, PA 18360
(800/762-6667 or 570/421-5791)
www.800poconos.com

Susquehanna River Valley CVB
81 Hafer Rd.
Lewisburg, PA 17837
(800/525-7320 or 570/524-7234)
www.visitcentralpa.org.

Valley Forge Convention and Visitors Bureau
600 West Germantown Pike, Suite 130,
Plymouth Meeting, PA 19462
(610/834-1550)
www.valleyforge.org

Local Agencies:

For local information, contact the Chamber of Commerce or Tourism Bureau for the locality you are interested in.

RECREATIONAL INFO

Bicycling: For a Bicycling Directory of Pennsylvania, contact: PA Dept. of Transportation, Distribution Services Unit, www.dot.state.pa.us

Cave Exploration: For a guide to show caves, contact the Pennsylvania Caves Assn., RR #1, Box 280, Huntington, PA 16652 (814/643-0268). www.pacaves.homestead.com

Pennsylvania Trail of History: PA Historical & Museum Commission, 300 North St., Harrisburg, PA 17120 (717/787-3362). www.phmc.state.pa.us/

Fishing/Boating/Hunting: Pennsylvania Fish & Boat Commission, 1601 Elmerton Ave, Harrisburg, PA 17106 (717/705-

7800).
www.fish.state.pa.us/

Golf: For information: (814/849-5197). www.playandstayinpa.com

Hiking: Department of Conservation and Natural Resources, Rachel Carson State Office Building, PO Box 8767, 400 Market Street, Harrisburg, PA 17105-8767. (888/PA-PARKS) www.dcnr.state.pa.us/

RVing: PA Recreation Vehicle & Camping Association, 4000 Trindle Rd., Camp Hill, PA 17011 (888/303-2887 or 717/303-0295). www.prvca.org

Skiing: Pennsylvania Ski Areas Association, P.O. Box 27, White Haven, PA 18661 (570/443-0963). www.skipa.com

SHOPPING

Statewide website:
www.shoppinginpa.com

There is no sales tax on clothing in Pennsylvania. It has become a major shopping destination, with areas known as:

Antiques Capital USA, Adamstown. This town in the heart of Pennsylvania Dutch Country is a premier antiques destination accessible from exit 286 off the Pennsylvania Turnpike. Antique shops and villages include: Stoudtburg Antiques Mall, Clock Tower Antiques, Country French Collection, European Pine Antiques, Heritage Antiques, Antique Complex of Fleetwood I and II and more.

For more information and a free map write: Dept. PVG, Antiques Capital USA, PO Box 814, Adamstown, PA 19501. www.antiquescapital.com

VF Outlet, Reading. On Wyomissing Blvd. Outlet stores offer name brands from stores such as Vanity Fair, Lee, Wrangler, Nautica, JanSport and Lily of France. www.vffo.com

Volant Shops, Volant. Offers 30 quaint shops, historic mill and winery in the Amish countryside. On Route 208. www.volantshops.com.

Wendell August Forge, Grove City. Skilled craftsmen create unique metal giftware. 620 Madison Ave. (724/458-8360). www.wendellaugust.com

DESTINATIONS

PENNSYLVANIA GREAT LAKES

This region contains more than 32,000 acres of inland lakes as well as hundreds of miles of rivers. The soil is fertile here, making it an important farming area. During the spring and summer, the peach, apple and cherry orchards are in full bloom.

Amusement Parks. This region has several family oriented theme parks to choose from including: **Waldameer Park and Water World,** an amusement and water park complex set amid beautifully landscaped grounds; **Conneaut Lake Park,** which includes an amusement park, Kiddieland, beach and boardwalk, live entertainment and golf; and **Splash Lagoon**, an indoor water park rising up four stories.

DeBence Antique Music World, Franklin. Home of the happiest music on earth. Nickelodeons, carousel organs, music boxes, pianos and organs.

Erie Art Museum at Discovery Square. Exhibitions encompass folk art, contemporary craft, multi-disciplinary installations, community-based work and public art as well as traditional media. Their collection of over 5,000 objects includes American ceramics, Tibetan paintings, Indian bronzes and a variety of other categories.

Erie Maritime Museum. Along the shores of historic Lake Erie sits the re-creation of the U.S. Brig Niagara, Commodore Perry's flagship during the Battle of Lake Erie in the War of 1812.

Erie Zoo & Botanical Gardens. Fifteen-acre park, carousel rides, petting zoo.

ExpERIEnce Children's Museum, Erie. More than 55 hands-on exhibits.

Flight 93 National Memorial. A temporary memorial honoring the victims of the 9/11 attack is in place overlooking the crash site while the permanent memorial is under construction.

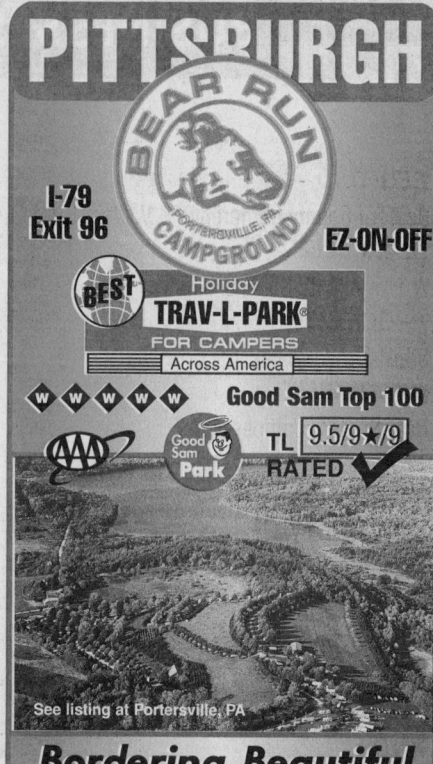

Lake Erie Arboretum at Frontier, Erie. Tree museum with more than 250 varieties of trees.

Splash Lagoon Indoor Water Park, Erie. Year-round indoor water slides, pools and hot tubs.

Tyred Wheels Museum, Pleasantville. Antique cars, car and plane memorabilia and 5,000 models.

Venango Museum of Art, Science and Industry, Oil City. Home of the Black Gold/ Black Magic exhibit.

Presque Isle State Park. The vast beaches and magnificent sunsets of this haven on the shores of Lake Erie have garnered national acclaim.

Pymatuning Lake Area. These 17,000 acres of lake, 8,000 acres of land and 70 miles of shoreline are located along the state lines of Ohio and Pennsylvania. At the southern-most point is Pymatuning Deer Park, featuring over 250 animals and birds from around the world.

PENNSYLVANIA WILDS

In addition to the Allegheny National Forest itself, this region boasts more acres of state game land than anywhere else in the Commonwealth. Black bear, whitetail deer, turkey, grouse, pheasant and more make their homes here. Trout, muskie and walleye fishing are popular in this region—the record muskie was caught at Kinzua Dam in Warren County.

Eldred World War II Museum, Eldred. Spectacular exhibits, award-winning introductory video, large research library.

Gobbler's Knob & Groundhog Zoo, Punxsutawney. Punxsutany Phil's annual Groundhog Day prediction takes place here at Gobbler's Knob.

Pennsylvania Lumber Museum, Galeton. An outdoor museum depicting the lumber industry.

Pine Creek Gorge, Wellsboro. Almost 50 miles long and over 1,000 feet deep, it is known as the Grand Canyon of Pennsylvania. It offers spectacular views, abundant wildlife and beautiful foliage. Stop in the quaint town of Wellsboro where you'll see gas-lit streets and Victorian mansions that date back to the early 1800s.

Oil Creek & Titusville Railroad, Oil City. Take this leisurely 2-1/2-hour, 27-mile train ride through oil boom country. Enjoy the fun of train travel and re-live early history.

Zippo/Case Visitors Center, Bradford. Exhibits of Zippo lighters and Case cutlery.

NORTHEASTERN MOUNTAINS

This region provides scenic vistas and plateaus in its Pocono and Endless Mountain ranges. The Appalachian Trail, America's first scenic trail, enters the state at the Delaware Water Gap.

Dorflinger Glass Museum / Dorflinger-Suydam Wildlife Sanctuary, White Mills. Located on a 600-acre wildlife sanctuary, the museum features magnificent glass works produced during the 19th century. Over 900 pieces of cut, engraved, etched, gilded and enameled crystal.

Bushkill Falls, Bushkill. Referred to as the "Niagara of Pennsylvania," these 8 waterfalls are famous for their scenic beauty and nature trails.

Endless Mountains. Bradford, Sullivan, Susquehanna and Wyoming counties are home to a chain of mountains boasting great fishing, hunting and hiking.

Houdini Museum Tour and Magic Show, Scranton. World's only building devoted to Houdini. Great guided tour, world's rarest films of Houdini and a live stage magic show with famous magicians and live animals.

Kittatinny Canoes, Dingmans Ferry, Milford and Matamoras. Canoeing, kayaking and white water rafting are offered for all skill levels on the Delaware River.

Lackawanna Coal Mine Tour, Scranton. Journey 300 feet underground to explore a once active coal mine with a retired miner.

Pocono Indian Museum, Bushkill. The museum traces the history of the Delaware Indians. View ancient artifacts, weapons and tools used throughout the centuries.

BUSINESSES OFFERING

	Things to See & Do	RV Sales	RV Service
BEDFORD			
Bedford County Conference & Visitors Bureau	⚑		
BLAKESLEE			
W T Family RV Sales & Service		🚌	✱
BROCKWAY			
Starr's Trailer Sales		🚌	✱
BROOKVILLE			
Dale Smith's Camper Sales		🚌	✱
ERIE			
Boyer RV Center		🚌	✱
GETTYSBURG			
Adventure Golf at Granite Hill	⚑		
Gettysburg Bluegrass Festival	⚑		
National Riding Stables	⚑		
KANE			
Allegheny National Forest Vacation Bureau	⚑		
KNOX			
Barnwell Cafe'	⚑		
LANCASTER			
Mellott Brothers Trailer Sales		🚌	✱
Pennsylvania Dutch Convention & Visitors Bureau	⚑		
LICKDALE			
Lickdale Campground & Canoe Rentals	⚑		
Twin Grove Restaurant	⚑		
NORTH EAST			
Ray Wakley's RV Center		🚌	✱
PINE GROVE			
Twin Grove Amusement Park	⚑		
PORTERSVILLE			
Bear Run Campground Canoe Rental	⚑		
STRASBURG			
The National Toy Train Museum	⚑		
WHITE HAVEN			
Lehigh Gorge RV Center		🚌	✱

QUICK REFERENCE CHART FOR WOODALL'S FEATURED PARKS

	Green Friendly	RV Lots for Sale	Park Models-Onsite Ownership	Park Membership for Sale	Big Rigs Welcome	Internet Friendly	Pets Welcome
ADAMSTOWN							
Dutch Cousin Campground					▲	●	■
ALLENTOWN							
KOA-Allentown-Lehigh Valley Kampground					▲	●	■
BATH							
Evergreen Lake Campground						●	■
BEDFORD							
Choice Camping Court					▲		■
Friendship Village Campground & RV Park					▲	●	■
Heritage Cove Resort					▲	●	■
BELLEFONTE							
KOA-Bellefonte/State College					▲	●	■
BENTON							
Whispering Pines Camping Estates					▲	●	■
BLAKESLEE							
W T Family Camping						●	■
BLOOMSBURG							
Indian Head Recreational Campgrounds						●	■
BOWMANSVILLE							
Lake In Wood Resort	🍃		*		▲	●	■
BOYERTOWN							
Lazy-K Campground					▲	●	■
BRODHEADSVILLE							
Silver Valley Campsites						●	■
CARLISLE							
Dogwood Acres Campground						●	■
Mountain Creek Campground						●	■
Western Village RV Park, Inc.						●	■
COATESVILLE							
Hidden Acres Camping Grounds						●	■
COOK FOREST							
Deer Meadow Campground						●	■
DENVER							
Shady Grove Campground					▲	●	■
DOVER							
Cedar Lake Campground					▲	●	■
DU BOIS							
Clearview Campground							■
ERIE							
Hill's Family Campground					▲	●	■
KOA-Erie					▲	●	■
Lampe Marina Campground					▲		■
Sparrow Pond Family Campground					▲	●	■
FORT LITTLETON							
Ye Olde Mill Campground					▲	●	■
GAINES							
Kenshire Campground							■
GETTYSBURG							
Artillery Ridge Camping Resort					▲	●	■
Gettysburg Campground					▲	●	■
Granite Hill Camping Resort						●	■

Green Friendly 🍃; RV Lots for Sale ✖; Park Models/Onsite Onwership *; Park Memberships for Sale ✔; Big Rigs Welcome ▲; Internet Friendly ●; Internet Friendly-WiFi ●; Pets Welcome ■

QUICK REFERENCE CHART FOR WOODALL'S FEATURED PARKS

	Green Friendly	RV Lots for Sale	Park Models-Onsite Ownership	Park Membership for Sale	Big Rigs Welcome	Internet Friendly	Pets Welcome
GROVE CITY							
Kozy Rest Kampground	🍃					●	■
HATFIELD							
Village Scene Park					▲	●	■
HERSHEY							
Hershey Highmeadow Campground					▲	●	■
HOLTWOOD							
Tucquan Park Family Campground					▲	●	■
HOP BOTTOM							
Shore Forest Campground					▲	●	■
INTERCOURSE							
Beacon Hill Camping						●	■
JIM THORPE							
Jim Thorpe Camping Resort					▲	●	■
JONESTOWN							
KOA-Jonestown						●	■
KANE							
The Foote Rest Campground						●	■
KNOX							
Wolfs Camping Resort					▲	●	■
LAKE CITY							
Camp Eriez Campground							■
LANCASTER							
Country Acres Campground					▲	●	■
Flory's Cottages & Camping					▲	●	■
Mill Bridge Village & Campresort					▲	●	■
Old Mill Stream Campground					▲	●	■
LAPORTE							
Pioneer Campground						●	■
LENHARTSVILLE							
Blue Rocks Family Campground						●	■
LEWISTOWN							
WaterSide Campground & RV Park					▲	●	■
LICKDALE							
Lickdale Campground					▲	●	■
Twin Grove Resort KOA at Pine Grove					▲	●	■
LOYSVILLE							
Paradise Stream Family Campground						●	■
MANHEIM							
Pinch Pond Family Campground & RV Park						●	■
MEADVILLE							
Brookdale Family Campground						●	■
MOUNT BETHEL							
Driftstone on the Delaware					▲	●	■
MT. COBB							
Clayton Park Recreation Area	🍃					●	■
NEW HOLLAND							
Country Haven Campground					▲	●	■
Red Run Campground						●	■
NEW STANTON							
Fox Den Acres Campground					▲	●	■

Green Friendly 🍃; RV Lots for Sale ✖; Park Models/Onsite Onwership ✱; Park Memberships for Sale ✔; Big Rigs Welcome ▲; Internet Friendly ●; Internet Friendly-WiFi ●; Pets Welcome ■

QUICK REFERENCE CHART FOR WOODALL'S FEATURED PARKS

	Green Friendly	RV Lots for Sale	Park Models-Onsite Ownership	Park Membership for Sale	Big Rigs Welcome	Internet Friendly	Pets Welcome
NORTH HUNTINGDON							
Dusty Rhodes Mobile Home Village							■
PEQUEA							
Pequea Creek Campground (PPL)						●	■
PORTERSVILLE							
Bear Run Campground						●	■
Rose Point Cabins & Camping	🍃					●	■
QUAKERTOWN							
Homestead Campground					▲	●	■
Quakerwoods Campground						●	■
QUARRYVILLE							
Yogi Bear's Jellystone Park Camp-Resort-Lancaster South/Quarryville					▲	●	■
RAVINE							
Echo Valley Campground					▲	●	■
REVERE							
Colonial Woods Family Camping Resort						●	■
SELINSGROVE							
Penn Avon Campground					▲	●	■
SHARON							
Shenango Valley RV Park					▲	●	■
STRASBURG							
White Oak Campground						●	■
STROUDSBURG							
Delaware Water Gap/Pocono Mt. KOA					▲	●	■
Mountain Vista Campground					▲	●	■
Otter Lake Camp Resort						●	■
Pocono Vacation Park						●	■
TAMAQUA							
Rosemount Camping Resort							■
TITUSVILLE							
Oil Creek Family Campground						●	■
TROUT RUN							
Sheshequin Campground					▲	●	■
WAYMART							
Keen Lake Camping & Cottage Resort						●	■
Valleyview Farm & Campground					▲		■
WELLSBORO							
Canyon Country Campground						●	■
Stony Fork Creek Campground					▲	●	■
WHITE HAVEN							
Lehigh Gorge Campground	🍃					●	■
WOODLAND							
Woodland Campground					▲	●	■

Green Friendly 🍃; RV Lots for Sale ✖; Park Models/Onsite Onwership ✱; Park Memberships for Sale ✔; Big Rigs Welcome ▲; Internet Friendly ●; Internet Friendly-WiFi ●; Pets Welcome ■

Where to Find CCUSA Parks

List City	Park Name	Map Coordinates
AUSTIN		
	Austin Campground	B-5
BEDFORD		
	Shawnee Sleepy Hollow Campground	E-4
BENTON		
	Whispering Pines Camping Estates	C-7
BRODHEADSVILLE		
	Silver Valley Campsites	C-9
CARLISLE		
	Western Village RV Park, Inc.	E-6
ELIZABETHTOWN		
	Hershey Conewago Campground	E-7
ERIE		
	West Haven at Lake Erie RV Park and Family Campground	A-1
FORT LITTLETON		
	Ye Olde Mill Campground	E-5
GAINES		
	Kenshire Campground	B-6
GETTYSBURG		
	Artillery Ridge Camping Resort	F-6
	Gettysburg Campground	F-6
HESSTON		
	Pleasant Hills Resort	D-5
HONESDALE		
	Countryside Family Campground	B-9
	Ponderosa Pines Campground	B-9
INDIANA		
	Wheel-In Campground	D-3
KNOX		
	Wolfs Camping Resort	C-2
LANCASTER		
	Mill Bridge Village & Campresort	E-8
LAPORTE		
	Pioneer Campground	B-7
LEWISBURG		
	Little Mexico Campground	C-7
MARIENVILLE		
	Forest Ridge Campground (Not Visited)	B-3
PEQUEA		
	Pequea Creek Campground (PPL)	E-8
PORTERSVILLE		
	Bear Run Campground	C-1
QUAKERTOWN		
	Quakerwoods Campground	D-9
SHARON		
	Shenango Valley RV Park	C-1
SOMERSET		
	Hickory Hollow Campground	E-3
SUNBURY		
	Fantasy Island Campground	D-7
TARENTUM		
	Mountain Top Campground	D-2
TOBYHANNA		
	Hemlock Campground & Cottages	C-9
WASHINGTON		
	Pine Cove Beach & RV Park	E-1
	Whispering Pines Family Campground	E-1
WELLSBORO		
	Canyon Country Campground	B-6
YORK		
	Ben Franklin RV Park	E-7

Pocono Museum Unlimited, Lehighton. For kids and model train buffs, this museum has it all – over 2,000 feet of track, a highway with moving vehicles, an amusement park and a zoo.

Pocono International Raceway, Long Pond. Each season, Pocono hosts two NASCAR Nextel Cup races, an SCCA National, and a number of SCCA Regionals.

PHILADELPHIA COUNTRYSIDE

This region is a mixture of the city of Brotherly Love and the surrounding countryside. It is particularly significant historically, because more Revolutionary War battles were fought within a 50-mile radius of Philadelphia than in all of the New England states combined.

Air Museums. This region is a Mecca for the aircraft enthusiast. The **Allied Air Force Museum** in Allentown displays several full-scale airplanes and helicopters. In Reading, the **Mid-Atlantic Air Museum** collection ranges from military trainers, transports and bombers to helicopters, experimental planes and classic airliners. **Wings of Freedom Air and Space Museum** in Willow Grove offers a large collection of aircraft and archives full of documents and artifacts.

Brandywine Battlefield Park. The Battle of Brandywine in 1777 was the largest single day land battle of the American Revolution. Tours include an introductory video, exhibits, discussion of battle tactics and historic house tour.

Longwood Gardens, Kennett Square. The 350 acres of outdoor gardens and fountain displays and 3-1/2 acres of indoor conservatories make this one of the most elegant gardens in the country.

Philadelphia. This historic city welcomes visitors with fine restaurants, extensive gardens and arboretums, professional theater companies and orchestras. **Independence National Historical Park** is the most historic square mile in the most historic city in America. Locally referred to as **Independence Mall**, it covers several blocks of Old City Philadelphia. All of the park buildings and sites are associated with colonial Philadelphia and the American Revolution. Major attractions include the **Liberty Bell, Independence Hall**, where the Declaration of Independence was adopted; the **Second Bank of the U.S., Franklin Court** and **City Tavern**. Spanning approximately 45 acres, the park has about 20 buildings open to the public.

The Crayola Factory, Easton. Watch Crayola® crayons and markers being made, learn about the colorful Crayola history and experience interactive exhibits, projects and activities.

Fairmount Park. At 8,000 acres, this is the world's largest landscaped city park. It also houses the oldest zoo in America.

Choose your method of transportation (trolley, bus, car, bicycle, or foot), then explore the park and listen to concerts along the banks of the Schuylkill River.

Neshaminy Valley Music Theatre, Bucks County. This community theater has provided Broadway-style musical productions for over 40 years. Proceeds from these productions fund annual scholarship grants to fine arts or performing-arts students.

Neon Museum of Philadelphia. Enjoy the magic of the 1950's again through animated, pictorial neon signs.

The Philadelphia Zoo. America's first zoo houses over 1,500 exotic animals and the country's first white lions. Experience Talking Storybooks and explore the zoo's 42 acres year-round.

Sesame Place. Visit the street of your child's dreams... Sesame Street! March in the AmaZing Alphabet Parade or play in Twiddlebug Land, where everything is larger than life. Enjoy any of the other outdoor interactive rides and attractions along with regular appearances from Elmo, Big Bird and many other Sesame Street friends. Then try the "Sky Splash" water ride.

Valley Forge. Visit scenic Valley Forge, known to every American. It was here that George Washington's Army retreated during the winter of 1777, just beyond reach of British troops in Philadelphia. The area's great past is apparent everywhere, from colonial mansions to national historical parks. Also, explore Valley Forge's contemporary attractions, including lush gardens, renowned art collections and delightful restaurants.

PENNSYLVANIA DUTCH COUNTRY

The Amish and Mennonite farmers who have cultivated the farmland here live in this region among its rolling hills and golden fields. It is truly farm country, an area of rich soil and neatly tended crops and homes. It is also a history buff's paradise, with an abundance of historic sites whose events shook an entire nation.

Gettysburg. Attractions within the Gettysburg area include **Gettysburg National Military Park**. See the vast site of the famous Civil War battle and Lincoln's Gettysburg Address.

Gettysburg Steam Railroad. This old-time steam train transports riders through the Gettysburg countryside. Civil War re-enactments are featured at scheduled times.

Lincoln Room Museum. View the room where President Lincoln wrote the Gettysburg Address.

Hershey. The chocolate capital of America features **Hersheypark**, an 87-acre family theme park offering over 50 rides and attractions; **Hershey Gardens**, 23 acres of beautifully tended gardens; **Zoo America North American Wildlife Park**, an 11-acre walk-through zoo featuring plants and animals from 5 regions of North America; and **Hershey's Chocolate World Visitors Center Park**, where visitors can experience a chocolate-making tour ride and taste a free sample!

Lancaster. Popular attractions in this part of the Pennsylvania Dutch Country are the **Amish Homestead**, **Dutch Wonderland** amusement park and the **National Wax Museum.**

Mill Bridge Village, Strasburg. This reconstructed early American village will show you traditions of colonial Pennsylvania with shops, craftsmen and an operating mill.

Millersburg Ferry, Liverpool. Take a ride on this historic ferry between Liverpool and Millersburg that has been in operation since 1825.

CENTRAL MOUNTAINS & VALLEYS

This region is crisscrossed with rivers, creeks and streams. Traditional river towns are abundant along the Susquehanna, called the "Currier and Ives" of rivers by many artists. A prime area for outdoor activities, the rolling hills and small peaks of this region mark the beginning of the Allegheny Mountains. Lake Raystown is favored by nature lovers and boaters. Indiana County is home to quaint Amish settlements nestled among acres of farmland and timber. Mining and manufacturing towns, many dating back to the Industrial Revolution, fill the narrow winding valleys below the highlands. There is also a charming network of covered bridges built to cross the river's many tributaries.

Knoebels Amusement-Resort, Elysburg. Visit Pennsylvania's largest free admission amusement park with free parking and over 50 rides. It was voted best amusement park for families and best amusement park food.

Fallingwater, Mill Run. This fantastic home was built by Frank Lloyd Wright. It integrates cantilevered construction with a rushing mountain waterfall and is one of the most architecturally significant buildings in America.

Fort Ligonier, Ligonier. This full-scale, onsite reconstructed fort features a museum with elegant period rooms from the 1700s.

Ohiopyle Area. The wild Youghiogheny River winds 14 miles and drops 60 ft. in 1 mile to create the spectacular Ohiopyle Falls. Guides for white water excursions are available from several rafting companies in the Ohiopyle area.

Old Bedford Village, Bedford, is a reconstructed pioneer town where visitors can watch craftsmen in action.

PITTSBURGH & COUNTRYSIDE

One of the pleasures of touring this region is the proximity of city to country. The historic small towns and Amish farmlands are just a short drive from the city of Pittsburgh.

Armstrong Rails to Trails, Kittanning. 52-mile rail trail running the east bank of the Allegheny River.

Dane Castle Museum, Strongstown. A recreation of a 12th-century medieval castle. Tour of the Great Hall with weapons, armor and art.

Meadowcroft Museum of Rural Life, Avella. Features exhibit on site of longest continuous human habitation in North America. Also see the living history village with 19th century log homes, schoolhouse, blacksmith shop and covered bridge.

Carnegie Institute Museum of Art and Museum of Natural History. Changing exhibitions, tours, holiday programs and more.

Nationality Rooms. Tour 26 rooms depicting the heritages of Pittsburgh's ethnic communities in the Cathedral of Learning.

ANNUAL EVENTS

JANUARY

Pennsylvania Farm Show, Harrisburg; Lights on the Lake, Altoona; Winterfest, Clarendon.

FEBRUARY

Winter Festival, Punxsutawney; Annual Clarks Summit Festival of Ice, Clarks Summit; Ridgway Chainsaw Carvers Rendezvous, Ridgway.

MARCH

Berks Jazz Festival, Reading; Pennsylvania Maple Festival, Meyersdale.

APRIL

Spring Flowering Tree and Bulb Display, Hershey; Greater Lehigh Valley Auto Show, Bethlehem; Pear Blossom Festival, Milford; Flower Show, Kingston; Native American Cultural Festival, Horsham.

MAY

Blair County Arts Festival, Altoona; Antiques & Collectibles, Carlisle; Scots-Irish Festival, Elizabethtown; Spring Fling, Danville; Spring Festival, Washington Crossing; Apple Blossom Festival, Arendtsville; Peddler's Village Strawberry Festival, Lahaska; Corn Festival, Allentown; Chestnut Hill Garden Festival, Philadelphia; Fort Pitt Royal American Regiment's Parade of the Soldier, Pittsburgh; Herb and Garden Faire, Lancaster; All Truck Show, Boyertown; Spring Craft Fair, Leesport; Rhubarb Festival, Intercourse; Craft and Activity Day, Horsham; Wilhelm Winery Festival, Hadley; Jimmy Stewart Festival Week, Indiana; Edinboro Arts & Music Festival, Edinboro; Philadelphia International Children's Theatre Festival, Philadelphia; Annual Spring Festival, Farmington.

All privately owned campgrounds personally inspected by

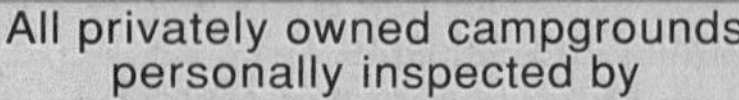

Representatives

Johnny and Nancy Johnson

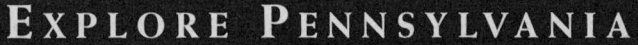

ADAMSTOWN—E-8

(W) DUTCH COUSIN CAMPGROUND—(Lancaster) *From jct I-76 (exit 286) & SR 272: Go 1/4 mi N on SR 272, then 1 mi W on Hill Rd. Enter on L.*

WELCOME

IN THE DUTCH TRADITION
Camping is a wonderful way to spend time with your family and Dutch Cousin Campground lets you camp the way you want! From "primitive" to "full hookup" & rental cabin camping. Simple, clean accomodations are a strong Dutch tradition.

◊◊◊FACILITIES: 95 sites, typical site width 25 ft, 62 full hkups, 28 W&E, (20/30/50 amps), 5 no hkups, some extd stay sites, 3 pull-thrus, cable TV, WiFi Instant Internet at site, family camping, tenting, cabins, dump, portable dump, laundry, ltd groc, LP gas by weight/by meter, ice, picnic tables, fire rings, wood.

◊RECREATION: rec room/area, golf nearby, playground.

Pets welcome. Partial handicap access. Open all yr. Limited water to sites in Winter. Big rigs welcome. Rate in 2010 $36-38 per family. MC/VISA/DISC/Debit. Member ARVC, PCOA.

Phone: (717)336-6911
Address: 446 Hill Rd, Denver, PA 17517
Lat/Lon: 40.23775/-76.10135
Email: bubblygroff@aol.com
Web: www.dutchcousin.com

SEE AD LANCASTER PAGES 664-666 AND AD TRAVEL SECTION PAGE 640

(E) Sill's Family Campground—(Lancaster) *From jct Pa Tpk (exit 286/21) & SR 272: Go 3-1/2 mi N on SR 272, then 1/4 mi E on Bowmansville Rd. Enter on L.* ◊◊◊FACILITIES: 132 sites, typical site width 30 ft, 126 full hkups, (15/20/30/50 amps), 6 no hkups, 1 pull-thrus, family camping, tenting, dump, laundry, ltd groc. ◊◊◊RECREATION: swim pool, playground. Pets welcome, breed restrict, quantity restrict. Partial handicap access. Open all yr. Big rigs welcome. Rate in 2010 $39.50-42 for 2 persons. Member ARVC, PCOA. Phone: (717)484-4806.

AIRVILLE—F-8

(NE) Otter Creek Campground (PPL)—(York) *From jct SR 74 & Hwy 425: Go 4 mi N on Hwy 425. Enter on L.* ◊◊◊FACILITIES: 86 sites, typical site width 30 ft, 86 W&E, (20/30/50 amps), 8 pull-thrus, family camping, tenting, dump, laundry, ltd groc. ◊◊◊RECREATION: river swim, boating, canoeing, ramp, dock, river/stream fishing, playground. Pets welcome. Partial handicap access. Open all yr. Facilities fully operational Apr 15 - Oct 31. Big rigs welcome. Rate in 2010 $30 per family. Member ARVC, PCOA. Phone: (717)862-3628.

ALLENTOWN—D-9

(NW) KOA-ALLENTOWN-LEHIGH VALLEY KAMPGROUND—(Lehigh) *From jct PA Tpk (exit 56) & US 22: Go 3 mi W on US 22/78 (exit 49B), then 6-1/2 mi N on SR-100, then 1/2 mi W on Narris Rd. Enter on R.*

WELCOME

◊◊◊◊◊FACILITIES: 99 sites, typical site width 28 ft, 38 full hkups, 61 W&E, (20/30/50 amps), some extd stay sites (summer), 27 pull-thrus, ca-

KOA-ALLENTOWN-LEHIGH VALLEY KAMPGROUND—Continued on next page

ALLENTOWN—Continued
KOA-ALLENTOWN-LEHIGH VALLEY KAMPGROUND—Continued

ble TV, WiFi Instant Internet at site, WiFi Internet central location, family camping, tenting, cabins, dump, non-guest dump $, laundry, groceries, RV supplies, LP gas by weight/by meter, ice, picnic tables, fire rings, wood.

◆◆◆◆◆RECREATION: rec hall, rec room/area, pavilion, coin games, swim pool, wading pool, stream fishing, fishing supplies, mini-golf, ($), golf nearby, bsktball, 4 bike rentals, playground, activities, (wkends), horseshoes, sports field, hiking trails, v-ball.

Pets welcome, breed restrict. Partial handicap access. Open Apr 1 - Nov 1. Big rigs welcome. Escort to site. Clubs welcome. Rate in 2010 $38-48.50 for 2 persons. MC/VISA/DISC/Debit. KOA discount.

Phone: (610)298-2160
Address: 6750 KOA Drive, New Tripoli, PA 18066
Lat/Lon: 40.65924/-75.69243
Email: alvkoa@ptd.net
Web: www.allentownkoa.com

SEE AD THIS PAGE

ALTOONA—D-4

(S) Wright's Orchard Station Campground—(Blair) *From jct I-99/US 220 (Plank Rd exit 31) & Business US 220: Go 1 mi S on Business US 220. Enter on R.* ◆◆FACILITIES: 42 sites, typical site width 30 ft, 17 full hkups, 20 W&E, (20/30/50 amps), 50 amps ($), 5 no hkups, 9 pull-thrus, family camping, tenting, dump, laundry, ltd groc. Pets welcome. Partial handicap access. Open May 1 - Oct 31. Big rigs welcome. Rate in 2010 $27-33 for 2 persons. Member ARVC, PCOA. Phone: (814)695-2628.

ASHFIELD—D-9

(SW) Blue Ridge Campground—(Carbon) *From jct PA Tpk (exit 74) & US 209: Go 1-1/2 mi S on US 209, then 3 mi SE on SR-248, then 6-1/2 mi W on SR-895. Enter on L.* ◆◆FACILITIES: 114 sites, typical site width 29 ft, 35 ft max RV length, 100 full hkups, 14 W&E, (20/30 amps), family camping, tenting, laundry, ltd groc. ◆◆◆RECREATION: swim pool, stream fishing, playground. Pets welcome, quantity restrict. Partial handicap access. Open Apr 8 - Oct 31. Rate in 2010 $40 per family. Member ARVC, PCOA. Phone: (570) 386-2911.

AUBURN—D-8

(NE) Christmas Pines Campground—(Schuylkill) *From north jct SR-61 & SR-895: Go 2 mi W on SR-895, then 1/2 mi N on Hickory Rd, then 3/4 mi N on Red Church Rd (last 1/2 mi steep grade). Enter on L.* ◆◆◆FACILITIES: 130 sites, typical site width 27 ft, 127 W&E, (30/50 amps), 3 no hkups, family camping, tenting, dump, laundry, groceries. ◆◆◆RECREATION: swim pool, pond fishing, playground. Pets welcome. Partial handicap access. Open Mid Apr - Late Oct. Big rigs welcome. Rate in 2010 $25-32 for 4 persons. Member ARVC, PCOA. Phone: (570)366-8866.

AUSTIN—B-5

(S) Austin Campground—(Potter) *From jct of SR-872 & SR-607: Go 6-1/2 mi S on SR-872, then 1 mi NE on Nelson Run Rd. Enter on R.* ◆◆◆FACILITIES: 128 sites, typical site width 45 ft, 39 W&E, 89 E,

AUSTIN—Continued
Austin Campground—Continued

(20/30/50 amps), 6 pull-thrus, WiFi Instant Internet at site, WiFi Internet central location, family camping, tenting, RV storage, dump, non-guest dump $, portable dump, ltd groc, RV supplies, ice, picnic tables, fire rings, wood. ◆◆◆RECREATION: pavilion, stream fishing, fishing supplies, bsktball, playground, activities, horseshoes, hiking trails, v-ball. Pets welcome. Open all yr. Facilities fully operational Apr - Nov. Big rigs welcome. Rate in 2010 $20-25 per family. MC/VISA/DISC/AMEX/Debit. Member ARVC, PCOA. CCUSA 50% Discount. CCUSA reservations Recommended, CCUSA max stay Unlimited.

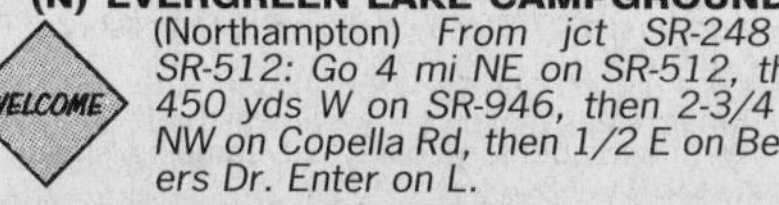

Phone: (800)878-0889
Lat/Lon: 41.56882/-78.02135
Email: campnjohnny@gmail.com
Web: www.austincampground.com

BATH—D-9

(N) EVERGREEN LAKE CAMPGROUND—(Northampton) *From jct SR-248 & SR-512: Go 4 mi NE on SR-512, then 450 yds W on SR-946, then 2-3/4 mi NW on Copella Rd, then 1/2 E on Benders Dr. Enter on L.*

◆◆◆◆FACILITIES: 300 sites, typical site width 28 ft, 100 full hkups, 200 W&E, (20/30 amps), many extd stay sites (summer), 10 pull-thrus, heater not allowed, cable TV ($), WiFi Internet central location, family camping, tenting, dump, non-guest dump $, portable dump, laundry, ltd groc, RV supplies, LP gas by weight/by meter, ice, picnic tables, fire rings, wood.

◆◆◆◆RECREATION: rec hall, rec room/area, pavilion, coin games, lake swim, 5 rowboat/3 pedal boat rentals, lake fishing, fishing supplies, mini-golf, ($), golf nearby, bsktball, playground, activities, (wkends), horseshoes, sports field, hiking trails.

Pets welcome, breed restrict. Open Apr 15 - Oct 15. Clubs welcome. Rate in 2010 $29-36 per family. Member ARVC, PCOA.

Phone: (610)837-6401
Address: 2375 Benders Dr, Bath, PA 18014
Lat/Lon: 40.81262/-75.40170
Web: www.evergreenlake.net

SEE AD THIS PAGE

BEAVER—D-1

(W) Orchard Grove Campsites—(Beaver) *From jct SR-68 & SR-60: Go 2 mi N on SR-60 (Brighton exit), then 4-1/2 mi W on Tuscarawas Rd. Enter on R.* ◆◆FACILITIES: 40 sites, typical site width 25 ft, accepts full hkup units only, 40 full hkups, (20/30/50 amps), 20 pull-thrus, laundry. Pets welcome. No tents. Open May 1 - Oct 15. Big rigs welcome. Rate in 2010 $25 for 2 persons. Phone: (724)495-7828.

BEAVER FALLS—D-1

Harts Content Campground—(Beaver) *From jct US 19 & SR 588: Go 6 mi W on SR 588, then 1/4 mi S on Glendale Rd. (Weight limit 7 1/2 tons.). Enter on L.* ◆◆FACILITIES: 125 sites, typical site width 30 ft, 40 ft max RV length, 125 full hkups, (20/30/50 amps), 4 pull-thrus, family camping, tenting, dump, laundry. ◆◆RECREATION: swim pool, playground. Pets welcome, quantity restrict. Partial handicap access. Open Apr 15 - Oct 15. Rate in 2010 $25 for 4 persons. Member ARVC, PCOA. Phone: (724)846-0005.

Pennsylvania State Motto: "Virtue, Liberty & Independence"

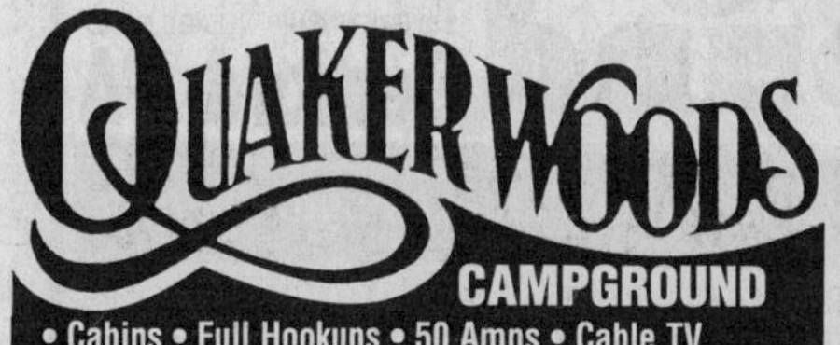

BEDFORD—E-4

(S) BEDFORD COUNTY CONFERENCE & VISITORS BUREAU—*From jct PA Tpk & I-99/US 220 (exit 146): Go 3 mi S on US 220, then 1-3/4 mi E on Bus US 30, then 1/8 mi S on Juliana St. Enter on L.* Tourism and resort information bureau for Bedford County. Mon-Fri 9am-5pm, Sat 10am-2pm. Open all yr. MC/VISA/DISC/Debit.

Phone: (800)765-3331
Address: 131-S Juliana St, Bedford, PA 15522
Lat/Lon: 40.01820/-78.50370
Email: bccvb@bedford.net
Web: www.bedfordcounty.net

SEE AD NEXT PAGE

(W) CHOICE CAMPING COURT—(Bedford) *From jct US 220 & US 30: Go 5 mi W on US 30, then 2-1/2 mi SW on SR-31, then 400 yds NW on Watson Rd. Enter on L.*

◆◆◆FACILITIES: 240 sites, typical site width 26 ft, 175 full hkups, 65 W&E, (20/30/50 amps), many extd stay sites (summer), 20 pull-thrus, cable TV, ($), family camping, tenting, RV's/park model rentals, dump, non-guest dump $, laundry, ice, picnic tables, fire rings, wood.

◆◆◆RECREATION: rec hall, rec room/area, pavilion, coin games, stream fishing, golf nearby, bsktball, playground, activities, (wkends), horseshoes, sports field, v-ball.

Pets welcome. Partial handicap access. Open Apr 15 - Oct 1. Big rigs welcome. Clubs welcome. Rate in 2010 $20-24 for 4 persons.

Phone: (814)623-5586
Address: 209 Choice Campground Rd, Manns Choice, PA 15550
Lat/Lon: 40.01533/-78.58972

SEE AD NEXT PAGE

(NW) FRIENDSHIP VILLAGE CAMPGROUND & RV PARK—(Bedford) *From jct PA Tpk & Bus US 220 (exit 146): Go 300 yds N on Bus US 220, then 1-1/2 mi S on US 220, then 1-1/2 mi NW on US 30, then 1/2 mi NE on Friendship Village Rd. Enter at end.*

◆◆◆◆◆FACILITIES: 252 sites, typical site width 40 ft, 210 full hkups, 27 W&E, (20/30/50 amps), 50 amps ($), 15 no hkups, some extd stay sites (summer), 54 pull-thrus, cable TV, WiFi Instant Internet at site, WiFi Internet central location, family camping, tenting, cabins, RV storage, dump, non-guest dump $, laundry, ltd groc, RV supplies, LP gas by weight/by meter, ice, picnic tables, fire rings, wood.

◆◆◆◆◆RECREATION: rec hall, rec room/area, pavilion, coin games, 2 swim pools, 2 rowboat/2 pedal boat rentals, lake/river/pond/stream fishing, fishing supplies, mini-golf, ($), golf nearby, bsktball, playground, shuffleboard court 2 shuffleboard courts, activities, horseshoes, sports field, hiking trails, v-ball.

Pets welcome, quantity restrict. Partial handicap access. Open all yr. Facilities fully operational Apr 15 - Oct 15. Big rigs welcome. Escort to site. Clubs welcome. Rate in 2010 $27-40 for 4 persons. MC/VISA/DISC/Debit. Member ARVC, PCOA.

FRIENDSHIP VILLAGE CAMPGROUND & RV PARK—Continued on next page

BEDFORD—Continued
FRIENDSHIP VILLAGE CAMPGROUND & RV PARK—Continued

Phone: (800)992-3528
Address: 348 Friendship Village Rd, Bedford, PA 15522
Lat/Lon: 40.04469/-78.51921
Email: friendshipvillage@comcast.net
Web: www.friendshipvillagecampground.com

SEE AD THIS PAGE AND AD TRAVEL SECTION PAGE 640

(NE) HERITAGE COVE RESORT—(Bedford) *From jct SR-26 & SR-913: Go 3 mi E on SR-913 (Follow directional signs), then 1 mi N on Weaver Falls Rd, (cross bridge), then 1 mi W on River Rd. Enter at end.*

◆◆◆◆FACILITIES: 195 sites, typical site width 50 ft, 195 full hkups, (20/30/50 amps), some extd stay sites (summer), 20 pull-thrus, WiFi Internet central location, family camping, tenting, cabins, RV storage, laundry, ltd groc, RV supplies, ice, picnic tables, fire rings, wood.

◆◆◆◆RECREATION: rec room/area, pavilion, swim pool, boating, canoeing, kayaking, ramp, dock, pontoon/10 canoe/16 kayak/2 pedal boat rentals, lake fishing, fishing supplies, golf nearby, playground, shuffleboard court shuffleboard court, horseshoes, sports field, v-ball.

Pets welcome. Partial handicap access. Open Apr - Oct. Big rigs welcome. Escort to site. Clubs welcome. Rate in 2010 $42-50 for 4 persons. MC/VISA/DISC/Debit. Member ARVC, PCOA. FMCA discount.

Phone: (814)635-3386
Address: 1172 River Rd, Saxton, PA 16678
Lat/Lon: 40.23489/-78.24039
Email: heritagecove@heritagecoveresort.com
Web: www.heritagecoveresort.com

SEE AD PAGE 649

Merritt Pond Campground (TOO NEW TO RATE) —(Bedford) *From jct US 30 & PA 220: Go 6-3/4 mi S on PA 220, then 1/2 mi SE on Browns Rd, then right on Teaberry Rd, then left 1/4 mi on Shobers Run Ln, then 1/2 mi on Flyng Dutchman Rd. Enter on L.* FACILITIES:

BEDFORD—Continued
Merritt Pond Campground—Continued

20 sites, typical site width 35 ft, 20 full hkups, (30/50 amps), 20 pull-thrus, family camping, dump. Pets welcome, quantity restrict. Open all yr. Big rigs welcome. Rate in 2010 $27-30 per family. Phone: (814)623-1509.

(NW) Shawnee Sleepy Hollow Campground—(Bedford) *From jct US 220 & US 30: Go 7 mi W on US 30. Enter on R.* ◆◆FACILITIES: 88 sites, typical site width 26 ft, 68 W&E, (20/30/50 amps), 50 amps ($), 20 no hkups, 4 pull-thrus, family camping, tenting, RV storage, dump, non-guest dump $, portable dump, laundry, RV supplies, ice, picnic tables, fire rings, wood.

◆◆RECREATION: pavilion, swim pool, bsktball, playground, shuffleboard court 2 shuffleboard courts, horseshoes, hiking trails, v-ball. Pets welcome ($), size restrict. Open Apr 15 - Oct 31. Rate in 2010 $27-29 for 4 persons. MC/VISA. FMCA discount. CCUSA 50% Discount.

Phone: (814)733-4380
Address: 147 Sleepy Hollow Rd, Schellsburg, PA 15559
Lat/Lon: 40.05042/-78.60621
Email: sleepyhollow147@comcast.net
Web: www.bedfordcounty.net/camping/sleepy

BELLEFONTE—C-5

(NE) KOA-BELLEFONTE/STATE COLLEGE—(Centre) *From jct I-80 & SR-26 (exit 161): Go 2 mi N on SR-26. Enter on L.*

◆◆◆◆◆FACILITIES: 163 sites, typical site width 26 ft, 65 full hkups, 62 W&E, (20/30/50 amps), 36 no hkups, 28 pull-thrus, cable TV, WiFi Instant Internet at site, WiFi Internet central location, family camping, tenting, cabins, RV storage, dump, laundry, full svc store, RV supplies, LP gas by weight/by meter, ice, picnic tables, patios, fire rings, wood.

◆◆◆◆◆RECREATION: rec hall, rec room/area, pavilion, equipped pavilion, coin games, swim pool, wading pool, pond fishing, fishing supplies, golf nearby, bsktball, 6 bike rentals, playground, activities, horseshoes, sports field, hiking trails, v-ball.

Pets welcome. Partial handicap access. Open Apr 1 - Mid Nov. Big rigs welcome. Escort to site. Clubs welcome. Rate in 2010 $30-59 for 2 persons. MC/VISA/DISC/AMEX/Debit. Member ARVC, PCOA. KOA discount.

Phone: (800)562-8127
Address: 2481 Jacksonville Rd, Bellefonte, PA 16823
Lat/Lon: 40.96177/-77.68616
Email: bellkoa@verizon.net
Web: www.bellefontekoa.com

SEE AD STATE COLLEGE PAGE 677

BELLEVILLE—D-5

GREENWOOD FURNACE STATE PARK—(Huntingdon) *From business center: Go 5 mi W on Hwy 305. Enter on L.* FACILITIES: 51 sites, typical site width 26 ft, 44 E, (30/50 amps), 50 amps ($), 7 no hkups, tenting, dump, ltd groc. RECREATION: lake swim, lake fishing, playground. Pets welcome, quantity restrict. Partial handicap access. Open Apr 10 - Oct 31. Phone: (814)667-1800.

BENTON—C-7

RICKETTS GLEN STATE PARK—(Luzerne/Sullivan) *From business center: Go 12 mi NE on Hwy 487 (Caution: steep road). Heavy RV units should use Hwy 487S from Dushore.* FACILITIES: 120 sites, 35 ft max RV length, 120 no hkups, tenting, dump. RECREATION: lake swim, boating, electric motors only, ramp, dock, lake fishing. No pets. Partial handicap access. Open all yr. Phone: (570)477-5675.

(E) WHISPERING PINES CAMPING ESTATES—(Columbia) *From jct SR-487 & SR-239: Go 4 mi SE on SR-239, then 1 mi S on North Bendertown Rd. Enter on R.*

◆◆◆FACILITIES: 64 sites, typical site width 35 ft, 54 full hkups, (20/30/50 amps), 10 no hkups, some extd stay sites (summer), 5 pull-thrus, WiFi Instant Internet at site, WiFi Internet central location, family camping, tenting, RV's/park model rentals, cabins, RV storage, dump, laundry, groceries, RV supplies, ice, picnic tables, fire rings, wood.

◆◆RECREATION: pavilion, coin games, boating, no motors, rowboat/pedal boat rentals, pond fishing, bsktball, play equipment, activities (wkends), horseshoes, sports field, hiking trails, v-ball.

Pets welcome, breed restrict. Partial handicap access. Open all yr. Big rigs welcome. Escort to site. Clubs welcome. Rate in 2010 $20-40 per family. MC/VISA/DISC/Debit. Member ARVC, PCOA. CCUSA 50% Discount.

Phone: (570)925-6810
Address: 1557 N Bendertown Rd., Stillwater, PA 17878
Lat/Lon: 41.17929/-76.31863
Email: info@wpce.com
Web: www.wpce.com

SEE AD THIS PAGE

BLAKESLEE—C-9

(N) Pocono Raceway Campground—(Monroe) *From jct of I-80 & SR-115 (exit 284): Go 3-1/4 mi S on SR-115, then 1/4 mi E on Long Pond Rd, (Register at Race Track Office), then 1 mi E on Long Pond Rd, then 1/4 mi S on Clearview Rd. Enter on R.* ◆◆FACILITIES: 100 sites, typical site width 25 ft, 37 full hkups, 26 W&E, (20/30/50 amps), 37 no hkups, family camping, tenting, dump. ◆◆RECREATION: swim pool, stream fishing. Pets welcome. Open Late Apr - Oct 31. Big rigs welcome. Rate in 2010 $24-108 for 2 persons. Member ARVC, PCOA. Phone: (570)646-2300.

(S) W T FAMILY CAMPING—(Monroe) *From jct I-80 & SR 115 (exit 284): Go 5-1/2 mi S on SR 115. Enter on R.*

◆◆◆FACILITIES: 110 sites, typical site width 28 ft, 42 full hkups, 40 W&E, (20/30 amps), 28 no hkups, some extd stay sites (summer), 7 pull-thrus, WiFi Internet central location, family camping, tenting, RV's/park model rentals, RV storage, dump, portable dump, ltd groc, RV supplies, LP gas by weight/by meter, ice, picnic tables, fire rings, wood, controlled access.

W T FAMILY CAMPING—Continued on next page

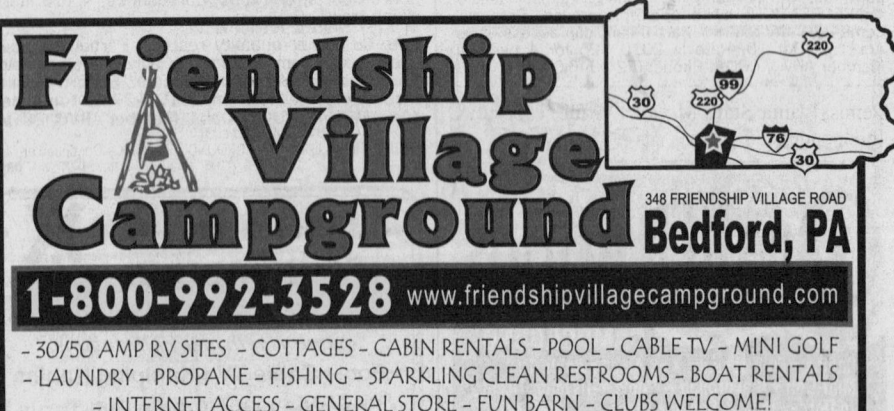

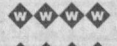

BLAKESLEE—Continued
W T FAMILY CAMPING—Continued

◆◆◆◆RECREATION: rec hall, rec room/area, pavilion, coin games, swim pool, wading pool, mini-golf, ($), golf nearby, bsktball, playground, activities, (wkends), horseshoes, sports field, hiking trails, v-ball.

Pets welcome. Partial handicap access. Open Apr 1 - Oct 31. Clubs welcome. Rate in 2010 $33-41 per family. MC/VISA/DISC/Debit. ATM. Member ARVC, PCOA.

Phone: (570)646-9255
Address: Rt 115 HC 1 Box 1486, Blakeslee, PA 18610
Lat/Lon: 41.02831/-75.49746
Email: wtcamp@epix.net
Web: www.wtfamily.com

SEE AD THIS PAGE

✱ **(S) W T FAMILY RV SALES & SERVICE**—*From jct I-80 & SR-115 (exit 284): Go 5-1/2 mi S on SR-115. Enter on R.* SALES: travel trailers, truck campers, 5th wheels, fold-down camping trailers, pre-owned unit sales. SERVICES: full-time mech, RV appliance repair, body work/collision repair, bus. hrs emerg rd svc, RV towing, LP gas by weight/by meter, RV storage, sells parts/accessories, installs hitches. 2000 Sq Ft Pop-up Showroom. Open all yr. MC/VISA/DISC.

WELCOME

Phone: (570)646-4040
Address: Rt 115 HC 1 Box 1486, Blakeslee, PA 18610
Lat/Lon: 41.02831/-75.49746
Email: wtrvfam@epix.net
Web: www.wtfamily.com

SEE AD THIS PAGE

BLOOMSBURG—C-7

Deihl's Camping Resort, Inc—(Columbia) *From jct I-80 & SR 487 (exit 236): Go 3-1/2 mi N on SR 487 to Charmund Rd, 1/2 mi N to Mt. Pleasant Rd, 1/4 mi W to Deihl's Rd, then 1/2 mi N. Enter on R.* ◆◆◆FACILITIES: 160 sites, typical site width 30 ft, 40 ft max RV length, 150 full hkups, (20/30 amps), 10 no hkups, 18 pull-thrus, family camping, tenting, dump, groceries. ◆◆◆RECREATION: swim pool, playground. Pets welcome. Partial handicap access. Open Apr 15 - Oct 15. Rate in 2010 $30 for 4 persons. Phone: (570) 683-5212.

(S) INDIAN HEAD RECREATIONAL CAMPGROUNDS—(Columbia) *From jct I-80 & SR 42 (exit 232): Go 3 mi S on SR 42, then 1/2 mi E on Train St. Enter on L.*

WELCOME

◆◆◆FACILITIES: 229 sites, typical site width 28 ft, 24 full hkups, 163 W&E, (20/30/50 amps), 42 no hkups, some extd stay sites (summer), 62 pull-thrus, WiFi Instant Internet at site ($), family camping, tenting, RV storage, dump, non-guest dump $, portable dump, groceries, RV supplies, ice, picnic tables, fire rings, wood.

◆◆◆RECREATION: rec room/area, pavilion, boating, canoeing, kayaking, ramp, river/stream fishing, fishing supplies, golf nearby, bsktball, playground, sports field, hiking trails.

Pets welcome. Partial handicap access. Open May 1 - End of Oct. Big rigs welcome. Clubs welcome. Rate in 2010 $32-38 for 2 persons. MC/VISA. Member ARVC, PCOA. FCRV discount. FMCA discount.

Phone: (570)784-6150
Address: 340 Reading St, Bloomsburg, PA 17815
Lat/Lon: 40.97818/-76.47072
Email: tal@sunlink.net
Web: www.indianheadcampground.com

SEE AD THIS PAGE

Pennsylvania State Tree: Hemlock

BOWMANSVILLE—E-8

(E) LAKE IN WOOD RESORT—(Lancaster) *From SR-625 & E Maple Grove Rd: Go 3/4 mi E on Maple Grove Rd, then 1/2 mi S on Oaklyn Dr, then 1-1/2 mi E on Yellow Hill Rd. Enter on R.*

WELCOME

◆◆◆◆◆FACILITIES: 400 sites, typical site width 32 ft, 389 full hkups, 10 W&E, (20/30/50 amps), 1 no hkups, many extd stay sites (summer), 36 pull-thrus, cable TV, phone/WiFi Instant Internet at site, family camping, tenting, RV's/park model rentals, cabins, RV storage, dump, laundry, full svc store, RV supplies, ice, picnic tables, fire rings, wood, controlled access.

◆◆◆◆◆RECREATION: rec hall, rec room/area, pavilion, equipped pavilion, coin games, 3 swim pools, wading pool, spray ground, lake swim, hot tub, boating, no motors, canoeing, kayaking, 4 rowboat/5 pedal boat rentals, lake fishing, fishing supplies, mini-golf, ($), golf nearby, bsktball, 12 bike rentals, play equipment, 4 shuffleboard courts, activities, horseshoes, sports field, hiking trails, v-ball.

Pets welcome, quantity restrict. Partial handicap access. Open Apr 1 - Nov 1. Big rigs welcome. Escort to site. Clubs welcome. Green Friendly. Rate in 2010 $30-61 for 2 persons. MC/VISA/DISC/Debit. ATM. Member ARVC, PCOA.

Text 107933 to (440)725-8687 to see our Visual Tour.

Phone: (717)445-5525
Address: 576 Yellow Hill Rd, Narvon, PA 17555
Lat/Lon: 40.19423/-75.97147
Email: lakeinwoodcamp@juno.com
Web: www.lakeinwoodcampground.com

SEE AD LANCASTER PAGES 664-666 AND AD MAP PAGE 638 AND AD DISCOVER SECTION PAGE 25

(E) Oak Creek Campground—(Lancaster) *From jct SR 625 & East Maple Grove Rd: Go 1-1/2 mi E on East Maple Grove Rd. Enter on R.* ◆◆◆◆FACILITIES: 280 sites, typical site width 40 ft, 232 full hkups, 48 W&E, (30/50 amps), 12 pull-thrus, family camping, dump, laundry, ltd groc. ◆◆◆◆RECREATION: swim pool, pond/stream fishing, playground. Pets welcome, breed restrict, size restrict, quantity restrict. Partial handicap access. No tents. Open all yr. Facilities fully operational Apr 1 - Nov 1. Big rigs welcome. Rate in 2010 $40-45 for 4 persons. Member ARVC, PCOA. Phone: (800)446-8365.

(NE) SUN VALLEY CAMPGROUND—(Lancaster) *From SR 625 & E Maple Grove Rd: Go 2 mi E on E. Maple Grove Rd. Enter on L.*

WELCOME

◆◆◆◆FACILITIES: 265 sites, typical site width 32 ft, 219 full hkups, 36 W&E, (20/30/50 amps), 10 no hkups, many extd stay sites, 9 pull-thrus, cable TV, WiFi Instant Internet at site, phone Internet central location, family camping, tenting, cabins, RV storage, dump, non-guest dump $, laundry, ltd groc, RV supplies, LP gas by weight/by meter, ice, picnic tables, fire rings, wood, controlled access.

BOWMANSVILLE—Continued
SUN VALLEY CAMPGROUND—Continued

◆◆◆RECREATION: rec hall, rec room/area, equipped pavilion, coin games, swim pool, pond fishing, fishing supplies, golf nearby, bsktball, playground, activities, horseshoes, v-ball.

Pets welcome. Partial handicap access. Open all yr. Facilities fully operational Apr 1 - Nov 1. Limited sites avail in winter. Big rigs welcome. Clubs welcome. Rate in 2010 $40-46 per family. MC/VISA/Debit. Member ARVC, PCOA.

Phone: (717)445-6262
Address: 451 E Maple Grove Rd, Bowmansville, PA 17507
Lat/Lon: 40.20537/-75.98883
Email: sun_valley@equitylifestyle.com
Web: www.sunvalleycamping.com

SEE AD ADAMSTOWN PAGE 648

BOYERTOWN—E-9

(N) LAZY-K CAMPGROUND—(Berks) *From jct SR 73 & SR 100: Go 2-1/2 mi N on SR 100, then 200 yds E on Township Line Rd. Enter on R.*

WELCOME

◆◆◆◆FACILITIES: 84 sites, typical site width 25 ft, 84 full hkups, (20/30/50 amps), 50 amps ($), cable TV, WiFi Instant Internet at site, WiFi Internet central location, family camping, tenting, RV's/park model rentals, RV storage, dump, laundry, RV supplies, ice, picnic tables, fire rings, wood.

RECREATION: golf nearby, playground.

Pets welcome. Open all yr. Call for water availability in Winter. Big rigs welcome. Escort to site. Clubs welcome. Rate in 2010 $39-42 for 2 persons. MC/VISA. Member ARVC, PCOA.

Phone: (610)367-8576
Address: 61 Washington Rd, Bechtelsville, PA 19505
Lat/Lon: 40.35884/-75.62530
Email: camp@lazycamping.com
Web: www.lazykcamping.com

SEE AD THIS PAGE

BRADFORD—A-4

(W) ALLEGHENY NATIONAL FOREST (Tracy Ridge Campground)—(McKean) *From business center: Go 16 mi W on Hwy 346, then 3 mi SE on Hwy 321.* FACILITIES: 120 sites, 120 no hkups, tenting, dump. RECREATION: Open Mid Apr - Mid Dec. Phone: (814)368-4158.

(W) ALLEGHENY NATIONAL FOREST (Willow Bay Campground)—(McKean) *From business center: Go 15 mi W on Hwy 346.* FACILITIES: 102 sites, 33 E, (30 amps), 69 no hkups, tenting, dump. RECREATION: lake swim, boating, canoeing, ramp, dock, lake/stream fishing, playground. Partial handicap access. Open Mid Apr - Mid Dec. Phone: (814)362-4613.

Woodhaven Acres—(Mckean) *From jct US 219/PA 59: Go 6.7 mi NW on PA 59. Enter on L.* ◆◆◆FACILITIES: 25 sites, typical site width 25 ft, 25 full hkups, (30 amps), 6 pull-thrus, family camping, tenting, dump, laundry, ltd groc. RECREATION: playground. Pets welcome. Open all yr. Rate in 2010 $30 for 4 persons. Phone: (814)368-6806.

BROCKWAY—C-4

✱ **(E) Starr's Trailer Sales**—*From jct SR-28 & US 219: Go 2 mi N on US 219. Enter on L.* SALES: travel trailers, truck campers, 5th wheels, fold-down camping trailers, pre-owned unit sales. SERVICES: full-time mech, RV appliance repair, LP gas by weight/by meter, sells parts/accessories, installs hitches. Open all yr. MC/VISA/DISC/AMEX/Debit.

Starr's Trailer Sales—Continued on next page

BROCKWAY—Continued
Starr's Trailer Sales—Continued

Phone: (814)265-0632
Address: 3673 Rt 219, Brockway, PA 15824
Lat/Lon: 41.24734/-78.74844
Email: greg@starrstrailersales.com
Web: www.starrstrailersales.com

BRODHEADSVILLE—C-9

(S) Chestnut Lake Campground—(Monroe) *From jct SR-115 & US-209: Go 1-1/4 mi NE on US-209, then 1/4 mi S on Frable Rd, then 1/4 mi W on Frantz Rd. Enter on R.* ◇◇◇FACILITIES: 153 sites, typical site width 30 ft, 88 full hkups, 25 W&E, (20/30/50 amps), 50 amps ($), 40 no hkups, family camping, tenting, dump, laundry, ltd groc. ◇◇◇RECREATION: lake swim, boating, no motors, canoeing, lake fishing, playground. Pets welcome, breed restrict, size restrict, quantity restrict. Partial handicap access. Open all yr. Facilities fully operational May 1 - Nov 1. Big rigs welcome. Rate in 2010 $30-32 for 2 persons. Member ARVC, PCOA. Phone: (570)992-6179.

Tell them Woodall's sent you!

BRODHEADSVILLE—Continued

(N) SILVER VALLEY CAMPSITES—(Monroe) *From jct US 209 & SR 115: Go 1 mi NE on US 209, then 3/4 mi N on Silver Valley Rd, then 1/4 mi NE on Deer Ln, then 1/8 mi W on Kennel Rd. Enter on R.*

◇◇◇◇FACILITIES: 138 sites, typical site width 30 ft, 119 full hkups, 1 W&E, (20/30/50 amps), 18 no hkups, some extd stay sites (summer), 9 pull-thrus, cable TV, WiFi Instant Internet at site, WiFi Internet central location, family camping, tenting, RV's/park model rentals, cabins, dump, non-guest dump $, laundry, groceries, RV supplies, LP gas by weight/by meter, ice, picnic tables, fire rings, wood.

◇◇◇◇RECREATION: rec hall, rec room/area, coin games, 2 swim pools, pond fishing, fishing supplies, golf nearby, playground, activities, horseshoes, v-ball.

Pets welcome, breed restrict, size restrict, quantity restrict. Partial handicap access. Open all yr. Facilities fully operational May 1 - 2nd week of Oct.

BRODHEADSVILLE—Continued
SILVER VALLEY CAMPSITES—Continued

Big rigs welcome. Escort to site. Clubs welcome. Rate in 2010 $42.50-44.50 per family. MC/VISA/DISC/Debit. Member ARVC, PCOA. CCUSA 50% Discount. CCUSA reservations Required, CCUSA max stay Unlimited, Cash only for CCUSA disc., CCUSA disc. not avail F,Sa. CCUSA disc. not avail holidays. Discount not available Mother's Day, Father's Day, during race events in Jun & Jul, holiday weekends & entire week of July 4th.

Phone: (570)992-4824
Address: RR 4 Box 4214, Saylorsburg, PA 18353
Lat/Lon: 40.95310/-75.37718
Email: svc1@ptd.net
Web: www.silvervalleycamp.com

SEE AD STROUDSBURG PAGE 678

BROOKVILLE—C-3

(N) DALE SMITH'S CAMPER SALES—*From jct I-80 (exit 78) & SR-36: Go 1-3/4 mi N on SR-36. Enter on R.* SALES: travel trailers, 5th wheels, toy hauler, Class C motorhomes, pre-owned unit sales. SERVICES: full-time mech, engine/chassis repair, RV appliance repair, body work/collision repair, bus. hrs emerg rd svc, mobile RV svc, LP gas by weight/by meter, sells parts/accessories, installs hitches. Open all yr. MC/VISA/DISC/Debit.

Phone: (814)849-2911
Address: 1648 Rt 36 North, Brookville, PA 15825
Lat/Lon: 41.19553/-79.10691
Email: dscamper@windstream.net
Web: www.dalesmithcampersales.com

SEE AD TRAVEL SECTION PAGE 637

BUTLER—C-2

(W) Buttercup Woodlands Campground—(Butler) *From jct I-79 (exit 83) & SR-528: Go 1-1/2 mi E on SR-528, then 8 mi E on SR-68. Enter on L.* ◇◇◇FACILITIES: 330 sites, typical site width 25 ft, 40 ft max RV length, 300 full hkups, (30/50 amps), 30 no hkups, 6 pull-thrus, family camping, tenting, laundry, groceries. ◇◇RECREATION: swim pool, playground. Pets welcome. Partial handicap access. Open Mid Apr - Mid Oct. Rate in 2010 $30 for 4 persons. Member ARVC, PCOA. Phone: (724)789-9340.

CALEDONIA—E-6

CALEDONIA STATE PARK—(Franklin) *From jct US-30 & Hwy-233: Go 1/4 mi N on Hwy-233.* FACILITIES: 175 sites, 35 E, (30/50 amps), 50 amps ($), 140 no hkups, 10 pull-thrus, tenting, dump. RECREATION: swim pool, stream fishing, playground. No pets. Partial handicap access. Open Apr 11 - Dec 15. Phone: (717)352-2161.

CARLISLE—E-6

(S) Deer Run Campgrounds—(Cumberland) *From jct of I-81 & SR 34 (exit 47): Go 8 mi S on SR 34, then 1-1/2 mi S on SR-94, then 1/2 mi E on Sheet Iron Roof Rd. Enter on L.* ◇◇◇FACILITIES: 173 sites, typical site width 30 ft, 127 full hkups, 6 W&E, 11 E, (30/50 amps), 29 no hkups, 25 pull-thrus, family camping, tenting, dump, laundry, ltd groc. ◇◇◇◇RECREATION: swim pool, pond fishing, playground. Pets welcome. Open all yr. Facilities fully operational Apr 1 - Oct 31. Big rigs welcome. Rate in 2010 $33-35 per family. Member ARVC, PCOA. Phone: (800)955-0208.

CARLISLE—Continued on next page

Can you trust the Woodall's ratings? 25 evaluation teams have scoured North American campgrounds to provide you with accurate, up to date information & ratings. Find a rating you don't agree with? Send a letter or email our way, and we'll give it extra attention for 2012.

CARLISLE—Continued

(N) DOGWOOD ACRES CAMPGROUND —(Cumberland) *From jct SR 641 & SR 233: Go 5 mi N on SR 233, then 2-1/2 mi E on SR 944. Enter on L.*

WELCOME

◆◆◆◆FACILITIES: 100 sites, typical site width 30 ft, 80 full hkups, 8 W&E, (20/30/50 amps), 50 amps ($), 12 no hkups, many extd stay sites (summer), 6 pull-thrus, WiFi Instant Internet at site ($), family camping, tenting, RV's/park model rentals, cabins, RV storage, dump, non-guest dump $, portable dump, ltd groc, RV supplies, LP gas by weight/by meter, ice, picnic tables, fire rings, wood, controlled access.

◆◆◆◆◆RECREATION: rec room/area, equipped pavilion, coin games, swim pool, no motors, dock, rowboat/2 pedal boat rentals, pond fishing, fishing supplies, golf nearby, bsktball, 5 bike rentals, playground, shuffleboard court shuffleboard court, activities (wkends), horseshoes, sports field, hiking trails, v-ball.

Pets welcome, breed restrict, quantity restrict. Partial handicap access. Open Apr 1 - Oct 31. Big rigs welcome. Escort to site. Clubs welcome. Rate in 2010 $39-45 per family. MC/VISA/Debit. Member ARVC, PCOA.

Phone: (717)776-5203
Address: 4500 Enola Rd, Newville, PA 17241
Lat/Lon: 40.23429/-77.39976
Email: info@dogwoodcamping.com
Web: www.dogwoodcamping.com

SEE AD PAGE 652

(S) MOUNTAIN CREEK CAMPGROUND —(Cumberland) *From I-81 & SR 34 (exit 47A): Go 7 mi S on SR 34, then 1/2 mi W on Green Mt. Rd, then 1 mi W on Pine Grove Rd. Enter on R.*

WELCOME

FAMILY CAMPING AT ITS BEST!
Join us and enjoy hayrides, tubing, fishing and all those other outdoor activities which make family camping a wonderful experience. Or if that much fun sounds tiring, just build a fire, relax and enjoy the great PA outdoors.

◆◆◆◆FACILITIES: 213 sites, typical site width 40 ft, 27 full hkups, 172 W&E, (20/30/50 amps), 50 amps ($), 14 no hkups, some extd stay sites, 10 pull-thrus, WiFi Instant Internet at site, WiFi Internet central location, family camping, tenting, RV's/park model rentals, cabins, RV storage, dump, non-guest dump $, portable dump, laundry, groceries, RV supplies, LP gas by weight/by meter, ice, picnic tables, fire rings, wood, controlled access.

◆◆◆◆◆RECREATION: rec hall, pavilion, coin games, swim pool, wading pool, hot tub, pond/stream fishing, fishing supplies, mini-golf, ($), golf nearby, bsktball, playground, shuffleboard court shuffleboard court, activities (wkends), horseshoes, sports field, hiking trails, v-ball.

Pets welcome, breed restrict, quantity restrict. Partial handicap access. Open all yr. Facilities fully operational Apr 1 - Oct 31. By reservation only Nov 1 through Apr 1. (Limited water in Winter). Big rigs welcome. Clubs welcome. Rate in 2010 $27-40.50 per family. MC/VISA/DISC/AMEX/Debit. Member ARVC, PCOA.

Phone: (717)486-7681
Address: 349 Pine Grove Rd, Gardners, PA 17324
Lat/Lon: 40.06361/-77.22624
Email: mtncreekcg@embarqmail.com
Web: www.mtncreekcg.com

SEE AD GETTYSBURG PAGE 657

(SW) WESTERN VILLAGE RV PARK, INC. —(Cumberland) *From I-81 (exit 45): Go 1-1/2 mi SW on Walnut Bottom Rd, then 400 yds SW on Greenview Dr. Enter at end.*

WELCOME

◆◆◆◆FACILITIES: 250 sites, typical site width 27 ft, 145 full hkups, 105 W&E, (20/30/50 amps), some extd stay sites, 22 pull-thrus, WiFi Instant Internet at site, WiFi Internet central location, family camping, tenting, cabins, RV storage, dump, non-guest dump $, laundry, groceries, RV supplies, LP gas by weight/by meter, ice, picnic tables, fire rings, wood.

CAMPCLUB USA

◆◆◆◆RECREATION: rec hall, rec room/area, pavilion, coin games, swim pool, mini-golf, ($), golf nearby, bsktball, playground, shuffleboard court 2 shuffleboard courts, activities (wkends), horseshoes, sports field, hiking trails, v-ball.

CARLISLE—Continued
WESTERN VILLAGE RV PARK, INC.—Continued

Pets welcome. Partial handicap access. Open all yr. Big rigs welcome. Clubs welcome. Rate in 2010 $32-40 for 4 persons. MC/VISA/Debit. Member ARVC, PCOA. CCUSA 50% Discount. CCUSA reservations Recommended, CCUSA max stay 2 days, Cash only for CCUSA disc., CCUSA disc. not avail F,Sa, CCUSA disc. not avail holidays. Not available during local car show dates. Available Nov 15-Feb 27 7 days/wk, Mar 1-May 31 & Sep 15-Nov 15 back-in sites only. Discount not available on cabins or 50 amp.

Phone: (717)243-1179
Address: 200 Greenview Dr, Carlisle, PA 17015
Lat/Lon: 40.17103/-77.22634
Email: camp@westernvillagervpark.com
Web: www.westernvillagervpark.com

SEE AD PAGE 652

CATAWISSA—C-7

(SW) J and D Campground—(Columbia) *From north jct SR 42 & SR 487: Go 5 mi S on SR 487. Enter on R.* ◆◆◆◆FACILITIES: 255 sites, typical site width 31 ft, 255 full hkups, (20/30/50 amps), 50 amps ($), 10 pull-thrus, family camping, dump, ltd groc. ◆◆RECREATION: swim pool, pond fishing, playground. Pets welcome. Partial handicap access. No tents. Open May 1 - Mid Oct. Big rigs welcome. Rate in 2010 $40 per family. Phone: (570)356-7700.

(S) Knoebels Lake Glory Campground—(Columbia) *From jct US 11 & SR 42: Go 3-3/4 mi S on SR 42, then 2-3/4 mi S on SR 487, then 1 mi E on Ashton Hollow Rd, then 1/4 mi E on Hemlock Dr, then 200 yards N on Eisenhower Rd. Enter on L.* ◆◆◆FACILITIES: 175 sites, typical site width 30 ft, 72 full hkups, 86 W&E, (20/30/50 amps), 17 no hkups, family camping, tenting, dump, laundry, groceries. ◆◆◆RECREATION: lake fishing, playground. Pets welcome. Partial handicap access. Open Apr 15 - Oct 31. Big rigs welcome. Rate in 2010 $38-40 per vehicle. Member ARVC, PCOA. Phone: (570)356-7392.

CEDAR RUN—B-6

(E) Pettecote Junction Campground—(Lycoming) *From jct Rte 44 & Rte 414 (Waterville): Go 19 mi NE on Rte 414, then 1/4 mi N on Beuahland Rd, then 150 yds on Beach Rd. Enter at end.* ◆◆◆FACILITIES: 144 sites, typical site width 30 ft, 42 ft max RV length, 119 W&E, (30/50 amps), 25 no hkups, family camping, tenting, dump, ltd groc. ◆◆◆RECREATION: boating, canoeing, stream fishing, playground. Pets welcome. Partial handicap access. Open Apr 1 - Oct 31. Rate in 2010 $32 per family. Member ARVC, PCOA. Phone: (570)353-7183.

CENTERVILLE—E-6

PINE GROVE FURNACE STATE PARK—(Cumberland) *From jct I-81 (exit 37) & Hwy 233: Go 8 mi S on Hwy 233.* FACILITIES: 70 sites, 27 E, (30/50 amps), 50 amps ($), 43 no hkups, 4 pull-thrus, tenting, dump, ltd groc. RECREATION: lake swim, boating, electric motors only, canoeing, ramp, dock, lake/stream fishing. Pets welcome ($). Partial handicap access. Open all yr. Phone: (717)486-7174.

CHAMBERSBURG—E-5

(W) Twin Bridge Meadow Family Campground —(Franklin) *From jct I-81 (exit 16/6) & US 30: Go 6 mi W on US 30, then 1-1/4 mi N on Twin Bridge Rd. Enter on L.* ◆FACILITIES: 150 sites, typical site width 30 ft, 30 full hkups, 120 W&E, (30 amps), 28 pull-thrus, family camping, tenting, dump, ltd groc. ◆RECREATION: stream fishing, playground. Pets welcome. Open Apr 15 - Oct 15. Rate in 2010 $20-23 per family. Member ARVC, PCOA. Phone: (717)369-2216.

CHAMPION—E-3

(S) Mountain Pines RV Resort (Morgan Rv Resorts)—(Westmoreland) *From jct PA Turnpike & SR-31 (exit 91): Go 2 mi E on SR-31, then 2 mi S on SR-711. Enter on L.* ◆◆◆FACILITIES: 745 sites, typical site width 30 ft, 707 full hkups, 28 W&E, (20/30 amps), 10 no hkups, family camping, tenting, dump, laundry, ltd groc. ◆◆◆RECREATION: 2 swim pools, stream fishing, playground. Pets welcome. Partial handicap access. Open Mid Apr - Mid Oct. Rate in 2010 $27-42 for 2 persons. Member ARVC, PCOA. Phone: (724)455-3300.

CLARENDON—B-3

(SW) CHAPMAN STATE PARK—(Warren) *From US 6 in town: Go 5 mi SW on Chapman Dam Rd/Railroad St.* FACILITIES: 82 sites, 39 E, (30/50 amps), 50 amps ($), 43 no hkups, tenting, dump, ltd groc. RECREATION: lake swim, boating, electric motors only, canoeing, ramp, dock, lake/stream fishing, playground. No pets. Partial handicap access. Open Apr 15 - Dec 15. Phone: (814)723-0250.

CLARINGTON—C-3

(SW) White's Haven Campground & Cabins—(Jefferson) *From jct of SR 899 & SR 36: Go 2 mi W on SR 36, then 1-3/4 mi S on Cathers Run Rd. Enter on L.* ◆◆◆FACILITIES: 152 sites, typical site width 35 ft, 65

CLARINGTON—Continued
White's Haven Campground & Cabins—Continued

full hkups, 70 W&E, (20/30 amps), 17 no hkups, 2 pull-thrus, family camping, tenting, dump, laundry, ltd groc. ◆◆RECREATION: pond fishing, playground. Pets welcome. Partial handicap access. Open all yr. Rate in 2010 $28 for 4 persons. Member ARVC, PCOA. Phone: (814)752-2205.

CLARION—C-3

(W) Rustic Acres Campgrounds—(Clarion) *From jct I-80 & SR-66 (exit 60): Go 3 mi N on SR-66, then 1/2 mi W on Pine Terrace Rd. Enter on L.* ◆FACILITIES: 103 sites, typical site width 30 ft, 91 full hkups, (20/30 amps), 12 no hkups, 21 pull-thrus, family camping, tenting, dump, laundry. RECREATION: playground. Pets welcome. Partial handicap access. Open Mid Apr - Mid Oct. Rate in 2010 $26 for 2 persons. Member ARVC, PCOA. Phone: (814)226-9850.

CLEARFIELD—C-4

S B ELLIOTT STATE PARK—(Clearfield) *From town: Go 7 mi N on Hwy 153.* FACILITIES: 25 sites, 25 no hkups, tenting, dump. RECREATION: stream fishing, playground. No pets. Partial handicap access. Open mid Apr - Early Oct. Phone: (814)765-0630.

COATESVILLE—E-8

(NW) Birchview Farm Campground—(Chester) *From jct US 30 & SR-82: Go 1/8 mi N on SR-82, then 3 mi W on SR 340, then 1 mi N on N Bonsall School Rd, then 1-1/2 mi E on Martins Corner Rd. Enter on L.* ◆◆FACILITIES: 200 sites, typical site width 28 ft, 181 full hkups, 19 W&E, (20/30/50 amps), family camping, tenting, dump, laundry, full svc store. ◆◆◆RECREATION: swim pool, pond fishing, playground. Pets welcome. Partial handicap access. Open Mid April - Mid Oct. Rate in 2010 $34-39 per family. Member ARVC, PCOA. Phone: (610)384-0500.

(NW) HIDDEN ACRES CAMPING GROUNDS—(Chester) *From jct US-30 & SR-82: Go 1/8 mi N on SR-82, then 5 mi W on SR-340, then 1/2 mi N on Cambridge Rd, then 1/4 mi E on Baldwin Rd. Enter on L.*

◆◆◆FACILITIES: 255 sites, typical site width 25 ft, 40 ft max RV length, 65 full hkups, 180 W&E, (20/30/50 amps), 10 no hkups, some extd stay sites (summer), heater not allowed, WiFi Internet central location, family camping, tenting, dump, laundry, groceries, RV supplies, ice, picnic tables, fire rings, wood.

◆◆◆RECREATION: rec hall, rec room/area, pavilion, coin games, swim pool, pond fishing, golf nearby, bsktball, playground, sports field, v-ball.

Pets welcome. Partial handicap access. Open Mid Apr - Late Oct. Facilities fully operational Memorial Day - Labor Day. Clubs welcome. Rate in 2010 $27-45 per family. Member ARVC, PCOA.

Phone: (610)857-3990
Address: 103 Hidden Acres Rd, Coatesville, PA 19320
Lat/Lon: 40.02905/-75.90292
Email: camp@hiddenacrespa.com
Web: www.hiddenacrespa.com

SEE AD PHILADELPHIA PAGE 673

CONFLUENCE—F-3

OUTFLOW RECREATION AREA (COE-Youghioheny Lake)—(Fayette) *From business center: Go 1 mi S on Hwy 281.* FACILITIES: 60 sites, 4 full hkups, 26 W&E, (50 amps), 30 no hkups, tenting, dump. RECREATION: dock, playground. Open May 19 - Sep 10. Phone: (814)395-3242.

(S) TUB RUN RECREATION AREA (COE-Youghiogheny Lake)—(Fayette) *From business centers: Go 8 mi S on Hwy 281.* FACILITIES: 101 sites, 30 E, (30/50 amps), 71 no hkups, tenting, dump. RECREATION: lake swim, boating, ramp, lake fishing, playground. Open May 19 - Sep 4. Phone: (814)395-3242.

CONNELLSVILLE—E-2

Rivers Edge Camping and Cabins—(Fayette) *From jct SR 195 & SR 201: Go 1-1/2 mi N on US 201, then 1/1/2 mi E on Adelaide Rd.* ◆◆◆FACILITIES: 120 sites, typical site width 22 ft, 120 full hkups, (30/50 amps), 4 pull-thrus, family camping, tenting, dump, laundry, ltd groc. ◆◆◆RECREATION: swim pool, river swim, canoeing, river fishing, playground. Pets welcome. Partial handicap access. Open all yr. Facilities fully operational Apr 15 - Oct 15. Big rigs welcome. Rate in 2010 $32-53 for 2 persons. Member ARVC. Phone: (724)628-4880.

COOK FOREST—C-3

(N) DEER MEADOW CAMPGROUND—(Clarion) *From jct SR-36 & SR-66: Go 5 mi N on SR-66, then 3 mi S on SR-1015 (Forest Rd). Enter on R.*

◆◆◆◆FACILITIES: 375 sites, typical site width 40 ft, 265 full hkups, 110 W&E, (20/30 amps), many extd stay sites (summer), 12 pull-thrus, heater not allowed, cable TV, WiFi Internet central location, family camping, RV storage, dump, non-guest dump $, laundry, groceries, RV supplies, LP gas by weight/by meter, ice, picnic tables, fire rings, wood, controlled access.

◆◆◆◆RECREATION: rec room/area, pavilion, coin games, swim pool, mini-golf, ($), golf nearby, bsktball, playground, activities, (wkends), horseshoes, sports field, hiking trails, v-ball.

Pets welcome, breed restrict. Partial handicap access. No tents. Open Memorial Day - Labor Day. Clubs welcome. Rate in 2010 $30-40 for 2 persons. MC/VISA/DISC/Debit. Member ARVC, PCOA.

Phone: (800)294-9561
Address: 2761 Forest Rd., Cook Forest, PA 16217
Lat/Lon: 41.36761/-79.21826
Email: teabetz@gmail.com
Web: www.deermeadow.com

SEE AD THIS PAGE

(N) Kalyumet Camping & Cabins—(Clarion) *From jct I-80 & (exit 62), then 2 mi N on SR-68, then 9-1/2 mi NE on 5th Ave/Miola Rd. Enter on R.* ◆◆◆◆FACILITIES: 164 sites, typical site width 30 ft, 110 full hkups, 30 W&E, (20/30 amps), 24 no hkups, 19 pull-thrus, family camping, tenting, dump, laundry, ltd groc. ◆◆◆◆RECREATION: swim pool, pond fishing, playground. Pets welcome. Partial handicap access. Open May 1 - Oct 31. Rate in 2010 $30-45 for 4 persons. Member ARVC, PCOA. Phone: (814)744-9622.

COOKSBURG—C-3

(N) RIDE CAMPGROUND-COOK STATE FOREST—(Clarion) *Clarion River Bridge at Cooksburg: Go NW 1 mi on Hwy 36 N. Enter on R.* FACILITIES: 226 sites, typical site width 40 ft, 60 E, (50 amps), 50 amps ($), 166 no hkups, 4 pull-thrus, tenting, dump, laundry. RECREATION: swim pool, no motors, canoeing, river/stream fishing, play equipment. Partial handicap access. Open all yr. Facilities fully operational late May - early Oct. Phone: (814)744-8407.

CORRY—A-2

(N) Harecreek Campground—(Erie) *From jct US 6 & SR-426: Go 1/2 mi E on US 6, then 400 yds on Sciota St. Enter on R.* ◆◆◆FACILITIES: 100 sites, typical site width 50 ft, 80 full hkups, (20/30/50 amps), 20 no hkups, 10 pull-thrus, family camping, tenting, dump, laundry, ltd groc. ◆◆◆RECREATION: swim pool, stream fishing, play equipment. Pets welcome. Open all yr. Facilities fully operational May 1 - Sept 30. Big rigs welcome. Rate in 2010 $29-33 for 4 persons. Member ARVC, PCOA. Phone: (814)664-9684.

COUDERSPORT—B-5

(E) Allegheny River Campground—(Potter) *From US 6 & Main St (East jct): Go 5 mi W on US 6. Enter on L.* ◆◆FACILITIES: 95 sites, typical site width 40 ft, 16 full hkups, 79 W&E, (15/20/30/50 amps), 10 pull-thrus, family camping, tenting, dump, laundry, ltd groc. ◆◆RECREATION: river swim, canoeing, river fishing, playground. Pets welcome. Open Mid Apr - Mid Dec. Green Friendly. Rate in 2010 $22-34 per family. Member ARVC, PCOA. Phone: (814)544-8844.

CHERRY SPRINGS STATE PARK—(Potter) *From business center: Go 12 mi S on Hwy-44.* FACILITIES: 30 sites, 30 no hkups, tenting, dump. RECREATION: No pets. Partial handicap access. Open Apr 10 - Dec 13. Phone: (814)435-5010.

(E) Potter County Family Campground—(Potter) *From jct US 6 & SR 49 (Coudersport): Go 8 mi E on US 6. Enter on L.* ◆◆◆◆FACILITIES: 90 sites, typical site width 40 ft, 31 full hkups, 55 W&E, (20/30/50 amps), 4 no hkups, family camping, tenting, dump, ltd groc. ◆◆RECREATION: playground. Pets welcome. Partial handicap access. Open all yr. Big rigs welcome. Rate in 2010 $22-25 for 2 persons. Phone: (814)274-5010.

COVINGTON—B-6

(SE) Tanglewood Camping—(Tioga) *From jct US 6 & US 15: Go 2-1/4 mi S on US 15, then 1/2 mi N on US 15 Bus, then 3-1/2 mi SE on Canoe Camp CK (creek) Rd, then 1-1/4 mi E on Old State Road then 1-1/2 mi S on Tangelwood Rd (last 1/2 mi Steep grade). (10 ton limit roads). Enter at end.* ◆◆◆FACILITIES: 107 sites, typical site width 30 ft, 40 ft max RV length, 85 W&E, (20/30/50 amps), 50 amps ($), 22 no hkups, 10 pull-thrus, family camping, tenting, dump, laundry, ltd groc. ◆◆◆RECREATION: lake swim, boating, no motors, canoeing, dock, lake fishing, playground. Pets welcome, size restrict, quantity restrict. Open May 1 - Oct 31. Rate in 2010 $36-38 for 4 persons. Member ARVC, PCOA. Phone: (570)549-8299.

Reserve Online at Woodalls.com

DARLINGTON—D-1

(S) Crawford's Camping Park—(Beaver) *From jct SR-51 & SR-168: Go 1 mi S on SR-168, then 3/4 mi W on Hodgson Rd. Enter on L.* ◆◆◆FACILITIES: 109 sites, typical site width 28 ft, 34 full hkups, 63 W&E, (20/30/50 amps), 12 no hkups, 20 pull-thrus, family camping, tenting, dump. ◆◆◆RECREATION: swim pool, pond fishing, playground. Pets welcome. Open Apr 15 - Oct 15. Big rigs welcome. Rate in 2010 $25-27 for 2 persons. Phone: (724)846-5964.

DAYTON—C-3

(N) Milton Loop Campground—(Armstrong) *From jct SR-85 & SR-839: Go 9 mi N on SR-839. Enter on L.* ◆◆◆FACILITIES: 62 sites, typical site width 80 ft, 32 W&E, 12 E, (20/30/50 amps), 18 no hkups, family camping, tenting, dump, ltd groc. ◆◆◆RECREATION: boating, 9.9 hp limit, canoeing, ramp, lake/stream fishing, playground. Pets welcome, breed restrict. Partial handicap access. Open Apr 1 - Nov 1. Big rigs welcome. Rate in 2010 $25 for 4 persons. Member ARVC, PCOA. Phone: (814)257-0131.

DENVER—E-8

(E) Hickory Run Family Camping Resort—(Lancaster) *From jct PA Tpk & SR 272 (exit 286): Go 1-3/4 mi S on SR 272, then 2 mi W on Church/Main St, then 2 mi E on Leisy Rd / Greenville Rd. Enter on L.* ◆◆◆FACILITIES: 211 sites, typical site width 32 ft, 87 full hkups, 122 W&E, 2 E, (20/30/50 amps), 24 pull-thrus, family camping, tenting, dump, laundry, groceries. ◆◆◆RECREATION: swim pool, lake swim, boating, no motors, canoeing, dock, lake fishing, playground. Pets welcome. Partial handicap access. Open Apr 1 - Nov 1. Big rigs welcome. Rate in 2010 $40-43 for 2 persons. Member ARVC, PCOA. Phone: (717)336-5564.

(W) SHADY GROVE CAMPGROUND—(Lancaster) *From jct Pa Tpk (exit 286) & Hwy 272: Go 1-1/4 mi N on Hwy 272, then 1/2 mi NW on Hwy 897, then 1/8 mi S on Poplar Dr. Enter on R.*

IN THE HEART OF ANTIQUE COUNTRY
Shady Grove offers a newly renovated family camping experience. Convenient to Antique Shopping, Lancaster/Pennsylvania Dutch Country, Hershey Park and Reading. We welcome clubs and reunions or just come by yourself.

◆◆◆FACILITIES: 118 sites, typical site width 30 ft, 112 full hkups, (20/30/50 amps), 6 no hkups, some extd stay sites, 3 pull-thrus, cable TV, WiFi Instant Internet at site, family camping, tenting, cabins, RV storage, laundry, ltd groc, RV supplies, LP gas by weight/by meter, ice, picnic tables, fire rings, wood.

◆◆◆◆RECREATION: rec room/area, pavilion, coin games, swim pool, lake swim, boating, electric motors only, canoeing, kayaking, dock, 2 rowboat/4 pedal boat rentals, lake fishing, fishing supplies, golf nearby, bsktball, playground, activities, (wkends), horseshoes, sports field, v-ball.

Pets welcome. Partial handicap access. Open all yr. Facilities fully operational Apr 1 - End of Oct. Big rigs welcome. Clubs welcome. Rate in 2010 $42 for 4 persons. MC/VISA/DISC/Debit. Member ARVC, PCOA.

DENVER—Continued
SHADY GROVE CAMPGROUND—Continued

Phone: (717)484-4225
Address: 65 Poplar Dr, Denver, PA 17517
Lat/Lon: 40.23870/-76.08550
Email: shadygrovecampground@yahoo.com
Web: www.shadygrovecampground.com

SEE AD LANCASTER PAGES 664-666 AND AD TRAVEL SECTION PAGE 640

DILLSBURG—E-6

(S) Walmar Manor Campground—(York) *From SR 74 & US 15: Go 3-3/4 mi S on US 15, then 3/4 mi S on Franklin Church Rd. Enter on R.* ◆◆◆FACILITIES: 63 sites, 33 full hkups, 30 W&E, (50 amps), family camping, tenting, dump, laundry. ◆◆RECREATION: swim pool, play equipment. Pets welcome. Partial handicap access. Open all yr. Big rigs welcome. Rate in 2010 $31-33 for 2 persons. Member ARVC, PCOA. Phone: (717)432-4523.

DONEGAL—E-3

(W) Donegal Campground—(Westmoreland) *From jct PA Tpk & SR-31 (exit 91): Go 1/2 mi W on SR-31. Enter on L.* ◆◆FACILITIES: 47 sites, typical site width 26 ft, 36 full hkups, 4 W&E, (30/50 amps), 50 amps ($), 7 no hkups, 38 pull-thrus, family camping, tenting. RECREATION: swim pool, play equipment. Pets welcome. Open Mar 15 - Dec 15. Big rigs welcome. Rate in 2010 $26-28 for 2 persons. Phone: (724)593-7717.

KOOSER STATE PARK—(Somerset) *From jct I-70/76 & Hwy 31: Go 9 mi SE on Hwy 31. Enter on R.* FACILITIES: 47 sites, typical site width 25 ft, 30 ft max RV length, 14 E, (30 amps), 33 no hkups, 10 pull-thrus, tenting, dump. RECREATION: lake swim, lake/stream fishing, playground. No pets. Partial handicap access. Open Apr 9 - Oct 17. Phone: (814)445-8673.

(SE) Laurel Highlands Campland—(Westmoreland) *From jct PA Tpk & SR-31 (exit 91): Go 3/4 mi E on SR-31. Enter on R.* ◆◆◆◆FACILITIES: 248 sites, typical site width 26 ft, 248 full hkups, (30/50 amps), 30 pull-thrus, family camping, dump, laundry, ltd groc. ◆◆◆◆RECREATION: 2 swim pools, pond fishing, playground. Pets welcome. Partial handicap access. No tents. Open all yr. Big rigs welcome. Rate in 2010 $38 for 4 persons. Member ARVC, PCOA.

Phone: (724)593-6325
Address: 1001 Clubhouse Dr, Donegal, PA 15628
Lat/Lon: 40.10343/-79.36990
Email: 1hc1001@live.com
Web: www.LHcampland.com

DOVER—E-7

CEDAR LAKE CAMPGROUND—(York) *From jct SR 194 & SR 234: Go 4 mi E on SR 234, then 2 mi N on Big Mount Rd, then 1 mi E on Pine Hill Rd. Enter on L.*

◆◆◆FACILITIES: 160 sites, typical site width 28 ft, 125 full hkups, 4 W&E, (30/50 amps), 31 no hkups, many extd stay sites, WiFi Instant Internet at site, family camping, tenting, RV's/park model rentals, RV storage, dump, non-guest dump $, laundry, ltd groc, RV supplies, LP gas by weight/by meter, ice, picnic tables, fire rings, wood.

◆◆◆RECREATION: rec room/area, pavilion, coin games, swim pool, lake swim, boating, electric motors only, canoeing, kayaking, ramp, dock, lake fishing, fishing supplies, golf nearby, bsktball, playground, activities, (wkends), horseshoes, v-ball.

Pets welcome. Partial handicap access. Open all yr. Big rigs welcome. Escort to site. Clubs welcome. Rate in 2010 $47 for 37 persons. MC/VISA/DISC/Debit.

Phone: (717)292-2918
Address: 5051 Pine Hill Road, Dover, PA 17315
Lat/Lon: 40.04313/-98.51928
Email: cedarlakecamp@aol.com
Web: www.cedarlakefamilycampground.com

SEE AD THIS PAGE

GETTYSBURG FARM - OUTDOOR WORLD (CAMP RESORT)—
FACILITIES: 265 sites.

Phone: (800)579-4987
Address: 6200 Big Mount Rd, Dover, PA 17315
Web: www.oneparkmembership.com

SEE AD ADAMSTOWN PAGE 648

DU BOIS—C-4

(N) Cayman Landing at Treasure Lake—(Clearfield) *From jct I-80 (exit 101) & SR-255: Go 3/4 mi N on SR-255, (entrance to Treasure Lake), then 5-1/4 mi on Bay Rd. Enter at end.* ◆◆◆◆FACILITIES: 379 sites, typical site width 30 ft, 15 full hkups, 364 W&E, (20/30 amps), 50 pull-thrus, family camping, tenting, dump, laundry, ltd groc. ◆◆◆◆RECREATION: 2 swim pools, boating, canoeing, ramp, dock, lake fishing, playground. Pets welcome. Partial handicap access. Open all yr. Facilities fully operational Apr 1 - mid Dec. Rate in 2010 $26.50-50.70 per vehicle. Phone: (814) 913-1437.

(NE) CLEARVIEW CAMPGROUND—(Clearfield) *From jct I-80 (exit 101) & SR-255: Go 1-1/4 mi N on SR-255, then 1/2 mi N on Hungry Hollow Rd, then 1/2 mi NE on Salada Rd. Enter on L.*

◆◆◆FACILITIES: 74 sites, typical site width 26 ft, 68 full hkups, 6 W&E, (20/30 amps), many extd stay sites (summer), 3 pull-thrus, family camping, tenting, RV's/park model rentals, dump, non-guest dump $, laundry, ice, picnic tables, fire rings, wood.

◆◆RECREATION: pavilion, golf nearby, bsktball, play equipment, horseshoes, sports field, v-ball.

Pets welcome. Open May 1 - Oct 31. Clubs welcome. Rate in 2010 $25 for 2 persons.

Phone: (814)371-9947
Address: 69 Giles Rd, Du Bois, PA 15801
Lat/Lon: 41.15062/-78.68062

SEE AD THIS PAGE

DUNCANSVILLE—D-4

(N) 764 Campground (RV SPACES)—(Blair) *From jct I-99/US 22 (exit 28): Go 1/4 mi N on SR 764, then 250 yards, then 1/2 mi W on Carson Valley Rd, then 450 yards E on Spencer Creek. Enter on R.* FACILITIES: 41 sites, typical site width 40 ft, 41 full hkups, (20/30/50 amps), 8 pull-thrus, family camping, tenting, dump, laundry. Pets welcome. Open all yr. Big rigs welcome. Rate in 2010 $30 per vehicle. Phone: (814) 695-0932.

EAST BENTON—B-9

LACKAWANNA STATE PARK—(Lackawanna) *From I-81 (exit 199): Go 3 mi W on Hwy 524, then N on Hwy 407. Enter on L.* FACILITIES: 92 sites, 61 E, (50 amps), 31 no hkups, tenting, dump. RECREATION: swim pool, boating, electric motors only, ramp, dock, lake fishing, playground. No pets. Partial handicap access. Open Apr 10 - Oct 18. Phone: (570)945-3239.

EAST BERLIN—E-7

(N) Conewago Isle Campground—(York) *From jct SR 194 & SR 234: Go 4 mi E on SR 234, then 3 mi N on Big Mount Rd. Enter on L.* ◆FACILITIES: 75 sites, typical site width 28 ft, 30 full hkups, 45 W&E, (20/30 amps), 9 pull-thrus, tenting, dump. ◆RECREATION: river swim, canoeing, dock, stream fishing, play equipment. Pets welcome. Open all yr. Facilities fully operational Apr 2 - Oct 31. Rate in 2010 $30 per family. Member ARVC, PCOA. Phone: (717)292-1461.

EAST STROUDSBURG—C-9

TIMOTHY LAKE NORTH - OUTDOOR WORLD (CAMP RESORT)—(Monroe) *Timothy Lake Rd RR6 Box 6627., East Stroudsburg, PA 18301.*

Phone: (800)579-4987
Address: Timothy Lake Rd, RR6 Box 6627, East Stroudsburg, PA 18301
Web: www.oneparkmembership.com

SEE AD ADAMSTOWN PAGE 648

TIMOTHY LAKE SOUTH - OUTDOOR WORLD (CAMP RESORT)—(Monroe) *Timothy Lake Rd, RR6 Box 6647, East Stroudsburg, PA 18301.*

Phone: (800)579-4987
Address: Timothy Lake Rd, RR6 Box 6647, East Stroudsburg 18301
Web: www.oneparkmembership.com

SEE AD ADAMSTOWN PAGE 648

EBENSBURG—D-4

(SW) Woodland Park Inc—(Cambria) *From west jct US 219 & US 22: Go 1-1/4 mi W on US 22, then 1/4 mi S on Campground Rd. Enter on L.* ◆◆FACILITIES: 200 sites, typical site width 26 ft, 185 full hkups, 15 W&E, (20/30/50 amps), 8 pull-thrus, family camping, tenting, dump, laundry, groceries. ◆◆RECREATION: pond fishing, playground. Pets welcome. Open Apr 15 - Oct 15. Rate in 2010 $18-24 per family. Phone: (814) 472-9857.

ELDERTON—D-3

Silver Canoe Campground—(Armstrong) *From jct of US 422 & ST 210: Go 9 mi N on 210. Enter on L.* ◆◆◆FACILITIES: 71 sites, typical site width 40 ft, 50 full hkups, 5 W&E, (30/50 amps), 16 no hkups, 5 pull-thrus, family camping, tenting, dump, ltd groc. ◆◆◆RECREATION: canoeing, dock, lake fishing, playground. Pets welcome, quantity restrict. Open all yr. Facilities fully operational Apr 1 - Oct 30. Big rigs welcome. Rate in 2010 $18-27 for 2 persons. Member ARVC, PCOA. Phone: (724)783-6000.

ELIZABETHTOWN—E-7

(SW) Elizabethtown/Hershey KOA—(Lancaster) *From jct SR 283 & SR 743 (Hershey/Elizabethtown exit): Go 1-1/2 mi S on SR 743, then 1/2 mi SW on SR 241 (High St), (High St. Bridge height 13' 3"), then 2-1/2 mi NW on Turnpike Rd. Enter on L.* ◆◆◆◆FACILITIES: 134 sites, typical site width 27 ft, 92 full hkups, 32 W&E, (20/30/50 amps), 10 no hkups, 17 pull-thrus, family camping, tenting, dump, laundry, full svc store. ◆◆◆◆RECREATION: swim pool, pond fishing, playground. Pets welcome, breed restrict. Partial handicap access. Open Apr 10 - Early Nov. Big rigs welcome. Rate in 2010 $47.75-66.49 per family. Member ARVC, PCOA. Phone: (717)367-7718. KOA discount.

(N) HERSHEY CONEWAGO CAMPGROUND—(Dauphin) *From jct of SR-283 & SR-743: Go 1-1/2 mi N on SR-743. Enter on R.*

HERSHEY/LANCASTER/PA DUTCH COUNTRY

6 mi South of Hershey & 30 minutes to PA Dutch Country, we offer long & wide shaded campsites for tents to motor homes. Family reunions & clubs welcome. Also, stay in our 20-room motel. Many attractions within 30 minutes.

◆◆◆FACILITIES: 160 sites, typical site width 30 ft, 58 full hkups, 82 W&E, (20/30 amps), 20 no hkups, some extd stay sites (summer), 18 pull-thrus, WiFi Instant Internet at site, phone on-site Internet (needs activ), WiFi Internet central location, family camping, tenting, cabins, RV storage, dump, non-guest dump $, laundry, ltd groc, RV supplies, LP gas by weight/by meter, ice, picnic tables, fire rings, grills, wood.

◆◆◆RECREATION: rec room/area, pavilion, coin games, swim pool, pond fishing, mini-golf, ($), golf nearby, bsktball, playground, activities, (wkends), tennis, horseshoes, sports field, v-ball.

Pets welcome. Open Early Apr - Early Nov. Clubs welcome. Rate in 2010 $33-50 per family. MC/VISA/DISC/AMEX/Debit. Member ARVC, PCOA. CCUSA 50% Discount. CCUSA reservations Recommended, CCUSA max stay 1 day, Cash only for CCUSA disc., CCUSA disc. not avail S,Th, CCUSA disc. not avail F,Sa, CCUSA disc. not avail holidays. Not available Jun thru Aug & special events. Call for details.

Phone: (717)367-1179
Address: 1590 Hershey Rd, Elizabethtown, PA 17022
Lat/Lon: 40.19806/-76.60895
Email: camp@hersheyconewago.com
Web: www.hersheyconewago.com

SEE AD HERSHEY PAGE 661

ELVERSON—E-9

(NE) FRENCH CREEK STATE PARK—(Berks) *From jct Hwy 23 & Hwy 345: Go N on Hwy 345. Enter on R.* FACILITIES: 201 sites, typical site width 15 ft, 60 E, (30/50 amps), 50 amps ($), 141 no hkups, tenting, dump. RECREATION: swim pool, boating, electric motors only, canoeing, ramp, lake fishing. Pets welcome. Partial handicap access. Open all yr. Facilities fully operational mid Apr - mid Dec. Phone: (610)582-9680.

ELYSBURG—D-7

(E) Knoebels Grove Campground—(Columbia) *From jct SR-487 & SR-54: Go 2 mi N on SR-487, then 1/2 mi E on paved road. Enter on R.* ◆◆◆FACILITIES:

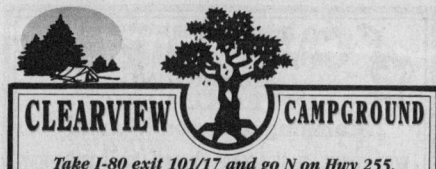

ELYSBURG—Continued
Knoebels Grove Campground—Continued

500 sites, typical site width 30 ft, 500 E, (15/20/50 amps), 50 amps ($), 25 pull-thrus, family camping, tenting, dump, laundry, groceries. ◆◆◆◆RECREATION: 2 swim pools, stream fishing, playground. Pets welcome. Partial handicap access. Open Apr 15 - Oct 15. Rate in 2010 $38-40 per vehicle. Member ARVC, PCOA. Phone: (570)672-9555.

EMPORIUM—B-4

(N) SIZERVILLE STATE PARK—(Cameron/Potter) *From town: Go 6 mi N on Hwy 155. Enter on R.* FACILITIES: 23 sites, 18 E, (20/50 amps), 5 no hkups, tenting, dump. RECREATION: swim pool, stream fishing, playground. No pets. Partial handicap access. Open mid Apr - mid Dec. Phone: (814)486-5605.

ENTRIKEN—D-5

(SE) Hemlock Hideaway Campground—(Huntingdon) *From jct SR-26 & SR-994: Go 6 mi E on SR-994. Enter on R.* ◆◆◆FACILITIES: 111 sites, typical site width 30 ft, 28 ft max RV length, 54 full hkups, 54 W&E, (20/30/50 amps), 3 no hkups, family camping, tenting, dump, laundry, ltd groc. ◆◆◆RECREATION: swim pool, pond fishing, playground. Pets welcome. Partial handicap access. Open all yr. Facilities fully operational Apr 1 - Dec 1. Rate in 2010 $30 for 4 persons. Phone: (814)658-3663.

(SE) Lake Raystown Resort and Lodge—(Huntingdon) *From jct SR-26 & SR-994: Go 4 mi E on SR-994. Enter on R.* ◆◆◆◆FACILITIES: 221 sites, typical site width 32 ft, 221 W&E, (20/30/50 amps), 50 amps ($), 14 pull-thrus, family camping, tenting, dump, laundry, groceries. ◆◆◆◆◆RECREATION: swim pool, lake swim, boating, canoeing, ramp, dock, lake fishing, playground. Pets welcome. Partial handicap access. Open Mid April - Oct 31. Rate in 2010 $32-59 for 6 persons. Member ARVC, PCOA. Phone: (814)658-3500.

TROUGH CREEK STATE PARK—(Huntingdon) *From jct Hwy 26 & Hwy 994: Go 3 mi S on Hwy 994, then 2 mi E at Park Sign to entrance.* FACILITIES: 29 sites, 26 ft max RV length, 29 E, (20/30 amps), tenting, dump. RECREATION: lake/stream fishing. No pets. Partial handicap access. Open mid Apr - mid Dec. Phone: (814)658-3847.

EPHRATA—E-8

(NW) Starlite Camping Resort—(Lancaster) *From jct SR 272 & US 322: Go 4 mi W on US 322, then 1 mi N on Clay Rd, then 1/2 mi E on Hopeland Rd, then 1/2 mi N on Kleinfeltersville Rd, then 1/4 mi E on Forest Hill Rd, then 1/2 mi N on Furnance Hill Rd. Enter on L.* ◆◆◆FACILITIES: 220 sites, typical site width 28 ft, 38 ft max RV length, 143 full hkups, 77 W&E, (20/30/50 amps), 50 amps ($), family camping, tenting, dump, laundry, groceries. ◆◆◆◆RECREATION: swim pool, playground. Pets welcome. Open May 1 - Nov 1. Rate in 2010 $38-40 for 2 persons. Member ARVC, PCOA. Phone: (800)521-3599.

ERIE—A-1

See listings at Corry, Lake City, North East & North Springfield,Waterford

ERIE—Continued on next page

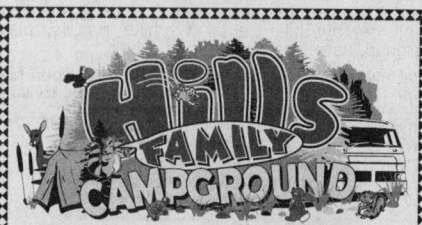

ERIE—Continued

✽ **(E) BOYER RV CENTER**—*From jct I-90 (exit 24) & US 19: Go 1 mi S on US 19. Enter on L.* SALES: travel trailers, park models, truck campers, 5th wheels, toy hauler, fold-down camping trailers, pre-owned unit sales. SERVICES: full-time mech, RV appliance repair, body work/collision repair, LP gas by weight, sells parts/accessories, installs hitches. Open all yr. MC/VISA/DISC/Debit.

Phone: (814)868-7561
Address: 8495 Peach St (US 19), Erie, PA 16509
Lat/Lon: 42.03911/-80.06820
Email: webmail@boyerrv.com
Web: www.boyerrv.com

SEE AD TRAVEL SECTION PAGE 637

(SW) HILL'S FAMILY CAMPGROUND—(Erie) *From jct I-90 (exit 18) & SR 832: Go 500 feet N on SR 832. Enter on L.*

◆◆◆◆FACILITIES: 174 sites, typical site width 30 ft, 121 full hkups, 13 W&E, (20/30/50 amps), 40 no hkups, some extd stay sites (summer), 60 pull-thrus, cable TV, WiFi Internet central location, family camping, tenting, RV's/park model rentals, cabins, RV storage, laundry, groceries, RV supplies, ice, picnic tables, fire rings, wood.

◆◆RECREATION: rec room/area, pavilion, coin games, golf nearby, play equipment.

Pets welcome, breed restrict. Partial handicap access. Open Apr 1 - Oct 31. Big rigs welcome. Clubs welcome. Rate in 2010 $30-36 for 2 persons. MC/VISA/DISC. Member ARVC, PCOA. FCRV discount.

Phone: (814)833-3272
Address: 6300 Sterrettania Rd, Fairview, PA 16415
Lat/Lon: 42.02161/-80.18595
Email: hillscampground@gmail.com
Web: www.hillsfamilycampground.com

SEE AD PAGE 655

(SW) KOA-ERIE—(Erie) *From jct I-79 (exit 174): Go 1 mi W on West Rd. Enter on L.*

◆◆◆◆◆FACILITIES: 113 sites, typical site width 28 ft, 46 full hkups, 37 W&E, (15/20/30/50 amps), 50 amps ($), 30 no hkups, some extd stay sites (summer), 26 pull-thrus, cable TV, WiFi Instant Internet at site, WiFi Internet central location, family camping, tenting, RV's/park model rentals, cabins, dump, non-guest dump $, portable dump, laundry, full svc store, RV supplies, LP gas by weight/by meter, ice, picnic tables, patios, fire rings, grills, wood.

◆◆◆◆RECREATION: rec room/area, pavilion, coin games, swim pool, wading pool, boating, 2 pedal boat rentals, lake fishing, fishing supplies, golf nearby, bike rental 13 bike rentals, playground, activities, horseshoes, v-ball.

Pets welcome. Partial handicap access. Open Mid Apr - Mid Oct. Big rigs welcome. Escort to site.

ERIE—Continued
KOA-ERIE—Continued

Clubs welcome. Rate in 2010 $36-66 for 2 persons. MC/VISA/DISC/AMEX. Member ARVC, PCOA. KOA discount.

Text 107951 to (440)725-8687 to see our Visual Tour.

Phone: (800)562-7610
Address: 6645 West Rd, McKean, PA 16426
Lat/Lon: 42.00305/-80.19270
Email: camp@eriekoa.com
Web: www.eriekoa.com

SEE AD THIS PAGE AND AD TRAVEL SECTION PAGE 640

(N) LAMPE MARINA CAMPGROUND—(Erie) *At North end on I-79, continue 5 mi E on Bayfront Parkway, then 1-3/4 mi N on East Ave, then turn N onto Port Access Rd. Enter at end.*

FACILITIES: 42 sites, typical site width 50 ft, 42 W&E, (20/30/50 amps), family camping, tenting, dump, non-guest dump $, laundry, ice, picnic tables, patios, fire rings, grills, wood.

RECREATION: boating, ramp, dock, lake fishing, golf nearby, hiking trails.

Pets welcome. Partial handicap access. Open May 1 - Oct 31. Big rigs welcome. Clubs welcome. MC/VISA/DISC.

Phone: (814)455-7557
Address: Foot of Port Access Rd, Erie, PA 16507
Lat/Lon: 42.15004/-80.07940
Web: www.porterie.org

SEE AD THIS PAGE

(W) Sara's Campground—(Erie) *From jct I-79 & SR 5 (exit 183B): Go 1-1/4 mi W on SR 5, then 3/4 mi N on SR 832. Enter on L.* ◆◆◆FACILITIES: 400 sites, typical site width 25 ft, 30 ft max RV length, 300 full hkups, 50 W&E, (20/30/50 amps), 50 no hkups, family camping, tenting, dump, laundry, ltd groc. ◆◆◆RECREATION: lake swim, lake fishing, playground. Pets welcome. Open Apr 1 - Oct 31. Rate in 2010 $28-32 per family. Member ARVC, PCOA. Phone: (814)833-4560.

(S) SPARROW POND FAMILY CAMPGROUND—(Erie) *From jct of I-90 (exit 24) & US 19: Go 6 mi S on US 19. Enter on L.*

◆◆◆◆FACILITIES: 133 sites, typical site width 45 ft, 117 full hkups, 5 W&E, (20/30/50 amps), 11 no hkups, some extd stay sites (summer), 18 pull-thrus, WiFi Internet central location, family camping, tenting, cabins, dump, non-guest dump $, portable dump, laundry, ltd groc, RV supplies, LP gas by weight/by meter, ice, picnic tables, fire rings, grills, wood, controlled access.

◆◆◆◆◆RECREATION: rec hall, rec room/area, pavilion, coin games, swim pool, wading pool, pond fishing, fishing supplies, golf nearby, bsktball, playground, activities, (wkends), horseshoes, sports field, hiking trails, v-ball.

Pets welcome. Partial handicap access. Open Mid Apr - Oct 30. Big rigs welcome. Clubs welcome. Rate in 2010 $32-45 for 4 persons. MC/VISA/DISC/Debit. Member ARVC, PCOA.

ERIE—Continued
SPARROW POND FAMILY CAMPGROUND—Continued

Phone: (814)796-6777
Address: 11103 Rt 19 N, Waterford, PA 16441
Lat/Lon: 41.97930/-80.01373
Email: sparrowpondcamp@aol.com
Web: www.sparrowpond.com

SEE AD THIS PAGE

West Haven at Lake Erie RV Park and Family Campground—(Erie) *From jct of I-90 (exit 18) and SR 832: Go 1/2 mi S on SR 832. Enter on L.* ◆◆◆FACILITIES: 167 sites, typical site width 40 ft, 144 full hkups, 21 W&E, (30/50 amps), 2 no hkups, 5 pull-thrus, WiFi Instant Internet at site, WiFi Internet central location, family camping, tenting, RV storage, shower$, dump, non-guest dump $, ice, picnic tables, fire rings, wood. ◆◆◆RECREATION: pavilion, equipped pavilion, swim pool, kayaking, pond fishing, playground, horseshoes, hiking trails. Pets welcome. Partial handicap access. Open May 1 - Late Oct. Big rigs welcome. Rate in 2010 $30-39 for 4 persons. Member ARVC, PCOA. CCUSA 50% Discount. CCUSA reservations Recommended, CCUSA max stay 1 day, Cash only for CCUSA disc., CCUSA disc. not avail S,M,Th, CCUSA disc. not avail F,Sa, CCUSA disc. not avail holidays.

Phone: (814)838-1082
Address: 6601 Sterrettania Rd, Fairview, PA 16415
Email: reservations@westhavenrvpark.com
Web: www.westhavenrvpark.com

ESPYVILLE—B-1

PYMATUNING STATE PARK (Tuttle Camp)—(Crawford) *Jct State Hwy 285 & N. Lake Rd: Go 2 mi N on N Lake Rd. Entrance at end of N. Lake RD. Enter at end.* FACILITIES: 657 sites, typical site width 25 ft, 30 ft max RV length, 165 E, (30 amps), 492 no hkups, tenting, dump, laundry, groceries. RECREATION: lake swim, boating, 10 hp limit, canoeing, ramp, dock, lake fishing, play equipment. No pets. Partial handicap access. Open 2nd wkd Apr - Mid Oct. Phone: (724)932-3141.

FARMINGTON—F-2

(N) Benner's Meadow Run Camping & Cabins—(Fayette) *From jct SR-381 & US 40: Go 1 mi W on US 40, then 2 mi N on Nelson Rd. Enter on L.* ◆◆◆FACILITIES: 160 sites, typical site width 28 ft, 100 full hkups, 8 W&E, (30/50 amps), 50 amps ($), 52 no hkups, 3 pull-thrus, family camping, tenting, laundry, groceries. ◆◆◆◆RECREATION: swim pool, pond fishing, playground. Pets welcome, breed restrict. Partial handicap access. Open Mid Apr - Mid Oct. Big rigs welcome. Rate in 2010 $37-47 for 4 persons. Member ARVC, PCOA. Phone: (724)329-4097.

FORKSVILLE—B-7

(S) WORLDS END STATE PARK—(Sullivan) *From town: Go 2 mi S on Hwy-154. Enter on R.* FACILITIES: 70 sites, typical site width 15 ft, 32 E, (30/50 amps), 50 amps ($), 38 no hkups, 1 pull-thrus, tenting, dump. RECREATION: river swim, canoeing, stream fishing. No pets. Partial handicap access. Open all yr. Phone: (570)924-3287.

FORT LITTLETON—E-5

(E) YE OLDE MILL CAMPGROUND—(Fulton) *From jct Pa Tpk (exit 180/13) & US 522: Go 4-1/2 mi NE on US 522, then 1/2 mi E on SR-1010 (Grist Mill Rd). Enter on R.*

◆◆◆FACILITIES: 32 sites, typical site width 25 ft, 32 W&E, (20/30/50 amps), some extd stay sites (summer), 12 pull-thrus, cable TV, WiFi Instant Internet at site, tenting, RV's/park model rentals, RV storage, dump, non-guest dump $, portable dump, laundry, groceries, RV supplies, LP gas by weight/by meter, ice, picnic tables, fire rings, wood.

YE OLDE MILL CAMPGROUND—Continued on next page

Drake Well Museum in Titusville is on the site where Edwin L. Drake drilled the world's first oil well in 1859 and launched the modern petroleum industry.

FORT LITTLETON—Continued
YE OLDE MILL CAMPGROUND—Continued

◆◆RECREATION: pavilion, stream fishing, fishing supplies, golf nearby, bsktball, playground, activities, (wkends), horseshoes, sports field, hiking trails, v-ball.

Pets welcome. Open all yr. Facilities fully operational Apr 1 - Early Dec. No water to sites in winter. Big rigs welcome. Clubs welcome. Rate in 2010 $25-34 per family. MC/VISA/DISC/Debit. Member ARVC, PCOA. CCUSA 50% Discount. CCUSA reservations Recommended, CCUSA max stay 2 days, CCUSA disc. not avail F,Sa, CCUSA disc. not avail holidays. Not available during special events. Call for details.

Phone: (717)987-3244
Address: 582 Grist Mill Rd, Burnt Cabins, PA 17215
Lat/Lon: 40.07763/-77.88799
Email: info@historicmillandcamping.com
Web: www.historicmillandcamping.com

SEE AD THIS PAGE AND AD TRAVEL SECTION PAGE 640

FORT LOUDON—E-5

(NW) COWANS GAP STATE PARK—(Fulton) *From jct US 30 & Hwy 75: Go 4 mi N on Hwy 75, then W on Richmond Furnace Rd.* FACILITIES: 224 sites, 64 E, (30/50 amps), 160 no hkups, tenting, dump, ltd groc. RECREATION: lake swim, boating, electric motors only, canoeing, ramp, dock, lake/stream fishing. No pets. Partial handicap access. Open Apr 9 - Dec 12. Phone: (717)485-3948.

FRANKFORT SPRINGS—D-1

(N) RACCOON CREEK STATE PARK—(Beaver) *Franfort Springs: Go 1 mi N on Rte 18, then 1 mi E on Main Park Rd. Enter on L.* FACILITIES: 172 sites, 65 E, (50 amps), 50 amps ($), 107 no hkups, tenting, dump. RECREATION: lake swim, boating, electric motors only, canoeing, ramp, dock, lake/stream fishing, playground. Pets welcome. Partial handicap access. Open all yr. Facilities fully operational Mid Apr - Mid Oct. Phone: (724)899-2200.

FRANKLIN—B-2

(NE) TWO MILE RUN COUNTY PARK—(Venango) *From jct of SR 8 & US 322: Go 1/2 mi W on US 322, then 6 mi N on SR 417, then 1/2 mi E on Cherrytree Rd, then 3/4 mi S on Beach Rd. Enter on L.* FACILITIES: 70 sites, 12 full hkups, 28 E, (20/30 amps), 30 no hkups, tenting, dump, ltd groc. RECREATION: lake swim, boating, electric motors only, canoeing, ramp, dock, lake fishing, playground. Pets welcome. Open all yr. Facilities fully operational May 22 - Nov 1. Phone: (814)676-6116.

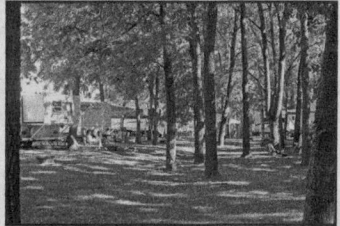

FRUGALITY—D-4

PRINCE GALLITZIN STATE PARK—(Cambria) *From jct Hwy 53 & Hwy 253: Go 1-3/4 mi S on Hwy 53, then 3 mi W on Marina Rd.* FACILITIES: 401 sites, 85 E, (30/50 amps), 316 no hkups, tenting, dump, laundry, ltd groc. RECREATION: lake swim, boating, 20 hp limit, ramp, dock, lake fishing, playground. No pets. Partial handicap access. Open mid Apr - mid Dec. Phone: (814)674-1000.

GAINES—B-6

(W) KENSHIRE CAMPGROUND—(Tioga) *From jct SR-349 & US 6: Go 1/2 mi W on US 6. Enter on L.*

◆◆◆FACILITIES: 145 sites, typical site width 32 ft, 10 full hkups, 131 W&E, (20/30/50 amps), 50 amps ($), 4 no hkups, some extd stay sites, 4 pull-thrus, cable TV, family camping, tenting, RV's/park model rentals, cabins, RV storage, shower$, dump, non-guest dump $, portable dump, laundry, ltd groc, RV supplies, ice, picnic tables, fire rings, wood.

◆◆◆RECREATION: rec room/area, pavilion, river swim, canoeing, kayaking, float trips, river fishing, fishing supplies, golf nearby, bsktball, 7 bike rentals, playground, activities, (wkends), horseshoes, sports field, v-ball.

Pets welcome. Partial handicap access. Open all yr. Escort to site. Clubs welcome. Rate in 2010 $30-40 per family. MC/VISA/DISC/AMEX/Debit. Member ARVC, PCOA. CCUSA 50% Discount. CCUSA reservations Accepted, CCUSA max stay 4 days, Cash only for CCUSA disc., Check only for CCUSA disc., CCUSA disc. not avail F,Sa, CCUSA disc. not avail holidays.

Phone: (814)435-6764
Address: 112 John Deere Ln, Gaines, PA 16921
Lat/Lon: 41.75098/-77.56680
Email: kenshirecamp@verizon.net
Web: www.pavisnet.com/kenshirekampsite

SEE AD THIS PAGE

Erie is the home port of one of the last remaining early, 19th-century warships, the U.S. Brig Niagara.

GALETON—B-5

(NW) LYMAN RUN STATE PARK—(Potter) *From business center: Go 7 mi W on West Branch Rd. Enter on R.* FACILITIES: 35 sites, 29 E, (30/50 amps), 6 no hkups, 5 pull-thrus, tenting, dump. RECREATION: lake swim, boating, electric motors only, ramp, dock, lake/stream fishing, playground. No pets. Partial handicap access. Open Apr 1 - Dec 13. Phone: (814)435-5010.

(S) OLE BULL STATE PARK—(Potter) *From jct Hwy-144 & US-6: Go 20 mi S on Hwy-144, follow signs.* FACILITIES: 43 sites, 36 ft max RV length, 43 E, (30/50 amps), tenting, dump. RECREATION: river swim, stream fishing, playground. No pets. Partial handicap access. Open all yr. Facilities fully operational Memorial Day - Labor Day. Phone: (814)435-5000.

GETTYSBURG—F-6

See listings at Carlisle, Chambersburg, East Berlin, Gettysburg, York and York Springs.

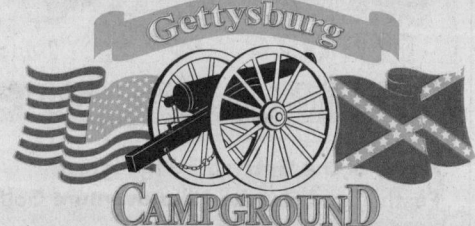

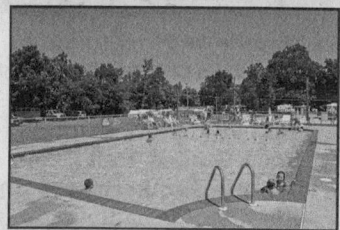

GETTYSBURG—Continued

(W) ADVENTURE GOLF AT GRANITE HILL—*From jct US 30 & Bus US 15: Go 1 block S on Bus US 15, then 6 mi W on SR 116. Enter on L.* Sculpted from a stone mountain, Adventure Golf is a state of the art miniature golfing experience. 18-holes w/practice green; full service snack bar, picnic area, kayaks & paddle boats. Buses welcome. Open Apr - Oct. MC/VISA. ATM.

Phone: (717)642-8749
Address: 3340 Fairfield Rd, Gettysburg, PA 17325
Lat/Lon: 39.80674/-77.33382
Email: camp@granitehillcampingresort.com
Web: www.granitehillcampingresort.com

SEE AD THIS PAGE

(S) ARTILLERY RIDGE CAMPING RESORT—(Adams) *From jct US 30 & Business US 15: Go 3 mi S on Business US 15, then 1-1/4 mi SE on Hwy 134. Enter on L.*

◆◆◆◆FACILITIES: 188 sites, typical site width 27 ft, 124 full hkups, 24 W&E, (30/50 amps), 40 no hkups, some extd stay sites (summer), 57 pull-thrus, WiFi Instant Internet at site, WiFi Internet central location, family camping, tenting, RV's/park model rentals, cabins, dump, non-guest dump $, portable dump, laundry, groceries, RV supplies, ice, picnic tables, fire rings, wood.

◆◆◆◆RECREATION: rec hall, rec room/area, coin games, swim pool, pedal boat rentals, pond fishing, fishing supplies, golf nearby, bsktball, playground, activities, (wkends), horseshoes, v-ball, local tours.

Pets welcome. Partial handicap access. Open Apr 1 - Nov 30. Big rigs welcome. Clubs welcome. Rate in 2010 $44-48 per family. MC/VISA/DISC/AMEX/Debit. Member ARVC, PCOA. CCUSA 50% Discount. CCUSA reservations Recommended, CCUSA max stay 5 days, CCUSA disc. not avail F,Sa, CCUSA disc. not avail holidays. Dump station surcharge is for non-guest dumping.

Text 107936 to (440)725-8687 to see our Visual Tour.

GETTYSBURG—Continued
ARTILLERY RIDGE CAMPING RESORT—Continued

Phone: (717)334-1288
Address: 610 Taneytown Rd, Gettysburg, PA 17325
Lat/Lon: 39.80213/-77.22932
Email: artilleryridge@comcast.net
Web: www.artilleryridge.com

SEE AD THIS PAGE

(E) Drummer Boy Camping Resort—(Adams) *From jct US 30 & Bus US 15: Go 1/4 mi E on US 30, then 1 mi E on SR 116, then 1/8 mi N on Rocky Grove Rd. Enter on L.* ◆◆◆◆◆FACILITIES: 409 sites, typical site width 32 ft, 330 full hkups, 48 W&E, (20/30/50 amps), 31 no hkups, 111 pull-thrus, family camping, tenting, dump, laundry, full svc store. ◆◆◆◆◆RECREATION: 2 swim pools, pond fishing, playground. Pets welcome, breed restrict, quantity restrict. Partial handicap access. Open End of Mar - Early Nov. Big rigs welcome. Rate in 2010 $36-61 per family. Member ARVC, PCOA. Phone: (800)293-2808.

(W) GETTYSBURG BLUEGRASS FESTIVAL—*From jct of US 30 & Bus US 15: Go 1 block S on Bus US 15, then 6 mi W on SR 116. Enter on L.* A Bluegrass tradition since 1979! Presenting the greatest lineup of the world's top bluegrass artists in a beautiful outdoor setting. Just minutes from Historic Gettysburg at Granite Hill Camping Resort. May 13-16, 2010 and Aug 19-22, 2010. MC/VISA. ATM.

Phone: (717)642-8749
Address: 3340 Fairfield Rd, Gettysburg, PA 17325
Lat/Lon: 39.80674/-77.33382
Email: camp@granitehillcampingresort.com
Web: www.gettysburgbluegrass.com

SEE AD THIS PAGE

(W) GETTYSBURG CAMPGROUND—(Adams) *From jct Business US 15 & SR-116: Go 3 mi W on SR-116. Enter on L.*

LOCATED IN HISTORIC GETTYSBURG, PA
Gettysburg Campground is a full-facility, family campground along beautiful Marsh Creek. Convenient to Gettysburg Battlefields, Lancaster, Hershey, Baltimore, and Washington, DC.

◆◆◆◆◆FACILITIES: 260 sites, typical site width 30 ft, 124 full hkups, 116 W&E, (20/30/50 amps), 50 amps ($), 20 no hkups, 48 pull-thrus, cable TV, WiFi Instant Internet at site, WiFi Internet central location, family camping, tenting, cabins, dump, non-guest dump $, portable dump, laundry, groceries, RV supplies, LP gas by weight/by meter, ice, picnic tables, patios, fire rings, wood.

GETTYSBURG—Continued
GETTYSBURG CAMPGROUND—Continued

◆◆◆◆◆RECREATION: rec hall, rec room/area, pavilion, coin games, swim pool, canoeing, stream fishing, fishing supplies, mini-golf, ($), golf nearby, bike rental bike rental, playground, shuffleboard court shuffleboard court, activities, horseshoes, sports field, v-ball, local tours.

Pets welcome. Partial handicap access. Open Apr - Nov. Big rigs welcome. Escort to site. Clubs welcome. Rate in 2010 $35-50 per family. MC/VISA/DISC/Debit. Member ARVC, PCOA. CCUSA 50% Discount. CCUSA reservations Recommended, CCUSA max stay 3 days, Cash only for CCUSA disc., CCUSA disc. not avail F,Sa, CCUSA disc. not avail holidays. Rate is for basic W/E back-in or pull thru site. Discount not available month of Jul. Limited facility camping in winter months.

Text 89807 to (440)725-8687 to see our Visual Tour.

Phone: (888)879-2241
Address: 2030 Fairfield Rd, Gettysburg, PA 17325
Lat/Lon: 39.81820/-77.28534
Email: camp@gettysburgcampground.com
Web: www.gettysburgcampground.com

SEE AD PAGE 657

(W) GRANITE HILL CAMPING RESORT—(Adams) *From jct US 30 & Bus US 15: Go 1 block S on Bus US 15, then 6 mi W on SR 116. Enter on L.*

◆◆◆◆FACILITIES: 320 sites, typical site width 27 ft, 131 full hkups, 139 W&E, (20/30/50 amps), 50 no hkups, 109 pull-thrus, cable TV, WiFi Internet central location, family camping, tenting, cabins, RV storage, dump, non-guest dump $, laundry, groceries, RV supplies, LP gas by weight/by meter, ice, picnic tables, fire rings, wood, controlled access.

◆◆◆◆◆RECREATION: rec hall, rec room/area, pavilion, coin games, swim pool, kayaking, 6 kayak/6 pedal boat rentals, pond fishing, fishing supplies, mini-golf, ($), golf nearby, bsktball, play equipment, 2 shuffleboard courts, activities, tennis, horseshoes, sports field, hiking trails, v-ball, local tours. Rec open to public.

Pets welcome. Partial handicap access. Open Apr 1 - Nov 30. Call for availability in winter. Escort to site. Clubs welcome. Rate in 2010 $35-53 for 2 persons. MC/VISA. ATM. Member ARVC, PCOA.

Text 108011 to (440)725-8687 to see our Visual Tour.

GRANITE HILL CAMPING RESORT—Continued on next page

Pennsylvania is also known as "The Keystone State".

CAMPING RESORT
AND NATIONAL RIDING STABLES
Closest Campground to Visitor Center
"Experience the battlefields at Gettysburg like a Civil War Cavalry Soldier ...from the back of a horse."
Re-live history through Daily Guided Trail Rides with our Gentle Horses on the historic battlefields.
Our Horse or Yours!
Gettysburg's only Horse Friendly Resort, with facilities for over 90 guest horses.
(717) 334-1288
610 Taneytown Rd.
Gettysburg, PA 17325
See listing at Gettysburg, PA

AAA Approved

Gettysburg Bluegrass Festival – May 12-15 and August 18-21, 2011

Home of the Gettysburg Bluegrass Festival and Granite Hill Adventure Golf!

Whether you come to re ax, to de ve into Civi War history or to enjoy t e great outdoors, you wi discover an unforgettab e vacation experience at Granite Hi Camping Resort, Bed & Breakfast and Adventure Go f.

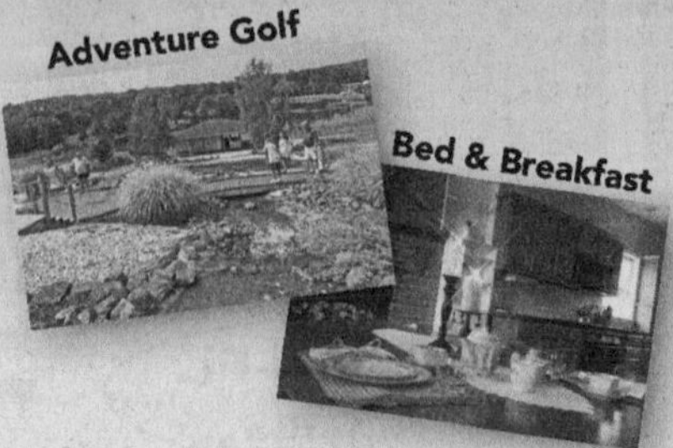

3340 Fairfield Road | Gettysburg, PA 17325
www.granitehillcampingresort.com | camp@granitehillcampingresort.com
800-642-TENT
See listing at Gettysburg, PA

Family Owned & Operated Since 1972!

Phone: (800)642-TENT (8368)
Address: 3340 Fairfield Rd, Gettysburg, PA 17325
Lat/Lon: 39.80674/-77.33382
Email: camp@granitehillcampingresort.com
Web: www.granitehillcampingresort.com

SEE AD PAGE 658

(W) KOA-Gettysburg—(Adams) *From jct US-30 & Business US-15: Go 3 mi W on US-30, then 2-1/2 mi S on Knoxlyn Rd, then 1/2 mi W on Knox Rd. Enter on L.* ◊◊◊◊◊FACILITIES: 90 sites, typical site width 26 ft, 56 full hkups, 18 W&E, (20/30/50 amps), 50 amps ($), 16 no hkups, 12 pull-thrus, family camping, tenting, dump, laundry, groceries. ◊◊◊◊◊RECREATION: swim pool, playground. Pets welcome. Partial handicap access. Open Apr 1 - Oct 31. Rate in 2010 $25-67 per family. Member ARVC, PCOA. Phone: (800)KOA-1869. KOA discount.

(S) NATIONAL RIDING STABLES—*From jct US 30 & Business US 15: Go 3 mi S on Business US 15, then 1-1/4 mi SE on Hwy 134. Enter on L.* Guided horse tours of the Battlefied. Horse camping and stable facilities available. Open Apr 1 - Nov 1. MC/VISA/DISC/AMEX/Debit.

Phone: (717)334-1288
Address: 610 Taneytown Rd, Gettysburg, PA 17325
Lat/Lon: 39.80213/-77.22932
Email: artilleryridge@comcast.net
Web: www.artilleryridge.com

SEE AD PAGE 658

(S) Round Top Campground—(Adams) *From jct US 30 & Bus US 15: Go 1-1/2 mi S on Bus US 15, then 2-3/4 mi SE on SR-134, then 1/2 mi W on Knight Rd. Enter on L.* ◊◊◊FACILITIES: 292 sites, typical site width 30 ft, 218 full hkups, 64 W&E, (30/50 amps), 50 amps ($), 10 no hkups, 12 pull-thrus, family camping, tenting, dump, laundry, groceries. ◊◊◊RECREATION: swim pool, playground. Pets welcome. Partial handicap access. Open all yr. Big rigs welcome. Rate in 2010 $35-60 per family. Member ARVC, PCOA. Phone: (717) 334-9565.

GIRARD—A-1

Folly's End Campground—(Erie) *From jct I-90 & SR 98 (exit 60): Go 2 mi S on Sr 98. Enter on R.* ◊◊FACILITIES: 100 sites, typical site width 40 ft, 2 full hkups, 81 W&E, (30/50 amps), 17 no hkups, 2 pull-thrus, family camping, tenting, dump. ◊◊RECREATION: river swim, river fishing, playground. Pets welcome. Open all yr. Big rigs welcome. Rate in 2010 $22-24 per family. Member ARVC, PCOA. Phone: (814) 474-5730.

GLEN IRON—C-6

(W) Sunsational Family Campground—(Union) *From jct SR 45 & SR 235: Go 3 mi S on SR 235, then 3 mi W on Creek Rd. Enter at end.* ◊◊FACILITIES: 114 sites, typical site width 25 ft, 40 ft max RV length, 105 W&E, (20/30/50 amps), 9 no hkups, 20 pull-thrus, family camping, tenting, dump, laundry, ltd groc. ◊◊RECREATION: canoeing, stream fishing, playground. Pets welcome, quantity restrict. Open 2nd wk of Apr - 2nd wk of Oct. Rate in 2010 $25-30 for 4 persons. Member ARVC, PCOA. Phone: (570)922-2267.

GREEN LANE—D-9

(NE) Boulder Woods Campground—(Bucks) *From jct SR 309 & SR 313: Go 2 mi S on SR 309, then 1/5 mi W on Tollgate Rd, then 3.1 mi on Trumbauersville Rd, the S 0.7 mi on Nursery Rd, then 0.2 mi E on Upper Ridge Rd, then 0.7 mi S on Camp Sky Mount Rd. Enter on R.* ◊◊FACILITIES: 208 sites, typical site width 30 ft, 188 W&E, (30/50 amps), 20 no hkups, 7 pull-thrus, family camping, tenting, dump, laundry, groceries. ◊◊RECREATION: 2 swim pools, lake swim, lake fishing, playground. Pets welcome. Partial handicap access. Open Apr 1 - Oct 31. Big rigs welcome. Rate in 2010 $35 per family. Member ARVC, PCOA. Phone: (215)257-7178.

GREENCASTLE—F-5

(S) Keystone RV Campground (RV SPACES) —(Franklin) *At jct I-81 (exit 1) & MD/PA State Line. Enter on R.* FACILITIES: 27 sites, typical site width 25 ft, accepts self-contained units only, 27 W&E, (20/30/50 amps), 6 pull-thrus, family camping, dump. Pets welcome. No tents. Open all yr. Big rigs welcome. Rate in 2010 $30 for 2 persons. Phone: (800)232-3279.

GREENTOWN—C-9

(NE) Ironwood Point Recreation Area (PPL)—(Pike) *From jct I-84 & Hwy 507 (exit 20): Go 2-1/4 mi N on Hwy 507, then 1/2 mi W on Burns Hill Rd. Enter at end.* ◊◊◊FACILITIES: 62 sites, typical site width 30 ft, 40 ft max RV length, 60 W&E, (20/30 amps), 2 no hkups, family camping, tenting, dump, laundry, ltd groc.

◊◊◊RECREATION: lake swim, boating, canoeing, ramp, dock, lake fishing, playground. No pets. Partial handicap access. Open End of Apr - Mid Oct. Rate in 2010 $22-30 per family. Member ARVC, PCOA. Phone: (570)857-0880.

(N) Ledgedale Recreation Area (PPL)—(Pike) *From jct I-84 & SR-507 (exit 20): Go 1/2 mi N on SR-507, then 2 mi W on Ledgedale Rd. Enter on R.* ◊◊◊FACILITIES: 70 sites, typical site width 30 ft, 34 ft max RV length, 70 W&E, (20/30 amps), 4 pull-thrus, family camping, tenting, dump, laundry, ltd groc. ◊◊◊RECREATION: lake swim, boating, canoeing, ramp, dock, lake fishing, playground. No pets. Partial handicap access. Open End of Apr - Mid Oct. Rate in 2010 $26-30 per family. Member ARVC, PCOA. Phone: (570)689-2181.

PROMISED LAND STATE PARK—(Pike) *From jct I-84 (exit 26) & Hwy 309: Go 5 mi S on Hwy 390.* FACILITIES: 513 sites, typical site width 30 ft, 35 ft max RV length, 155 E, (30/50 amps), 50 amps ($), 358 no hkups, tenting, dump. RECREATION: lake swim, boating, electric motors only, canoeing, ramp, dock, lake fishing, play equipment. Partial handicap access. Open all yr. Phone: (570)676-3428.

GREENVILLE—B-1

(E) Farma Family Campground—(Mercer) *From jct I-79 (exit 130) & SR-358: Go 7 mi W on SR-358, then 1 mi S on Hughey Rd. Enter on L.* ◊◊◊FACILITIES: 250 sites, typical site width 40 ft, 250 full hkups, (30/50 amps), 6 pull-thrus, family camping, tenting, dump, laundry, ltd groc. ◊◊◊◊RECREATION: swim pool, pond/stream fishing, playground. Pets welcome. Partial handicap access. Open May 1 - Oct 1. Big rigs welcome. Rate in 2010 $30-45 for 4 persons. Member ARVC, PCOA. Phone: (724)253-4535.

GROVE CITY—C-1

(E) KOZY REST KAMPGROUND—(Butler) *From jct I-79 & SR-208 (exit 113): Go 4 mi E on SR-208, then 4 mi E on SR-58, then 2 mi N on Campground Rd. Enter on L.*

◊◊◊◊◊FACILITIES: 173 sites, typical site width 27 ft, 141 full hkups, 28 W&E, (20/30/50 amps), 50 amps ($), 4 no hkups, many extd stay sites (summer), 23 pull-thrus, WiFi Instant Internet at site, WiFi Internet central location, family camping, tenting, cabins, RV storage, dump, non-guest dump $, laundry, groceries, RV supplies, LP gas by weight/by meter, ice, picnic tables, fire rings, wood, controlled access.

◊◊◊◊◊RECREATION: rec hall, rec room/area, pavilion, coin games, swim pool, mini-golf, ($), golf nearby, bsktball, 8 bike rentals, playground, shuffleboard court shuffleboard court, activities (wkends), horseshoes, sports field, hiking trails, v-ball.

Pets welcome. Partial handicap access. Open Apr 15 - Oct 31. Big rigs welcome. Escort to site. Clubs welcome. Green Friendly. Rate in 2010 $31-48 for 4 persons. MC/VISA/Debit. ATM. Member ARVC, PCOA.

Phone: (724)735-2417
Address: 449 Campground Rd, Harrisville, PA 16038
Lat/Lon: 41.14776/-79.96629
Email: kozyrest@kozyrestkampground.com
Web: www.kozyrestkampground.com

SEE AD THIS PAGE

HANOVER—F-7

(SE) CODORUS STATE PARK—(York) *From jct Hwy 116 & Hwy 216: Go 2 mi E on Hwy 216 to park entrance, then 1/2 mi S on Dubb's Church Rd. Enter on R.* FACILITIES: 198 sites, typical site width 10 ft, 93 E, (30/50 amps), 50 amps ($), 105 no hkups, tenting, dump. RECREATION: swim pool, lake swim, boating, 20 hp limit, canoeing, ramp, dock, lake fishing. Pets welcome. Partial handicap access. Open Apr 15 - Oct 21. Phone: (717)637-2816.

HARMONY—C-3

(NW) Indian Brave Campground—(Butler) *From jct I-79 & SR-68: Go 1 mi W on SR-68, then 3/4 mi N on US 19. Enter on R.* ◊◊◊FACILITIES: 221 sites, typical site width 35 ft, 171 full hkups, (30/50 amps), 50 no hkups, 25 pull-thrus, family camping, tenting, dump, laundry, ltd groc. ◊◊◊RECREATION: 1 swim pools, stream fishing, playground. Pets welcome, breed restrict. Partial handicap access. Open all yr. Open April 15 - October 15. Big rigs welcome. Rate in 2010 $35-38 for 4 persons. Member ARVC, PCOA. Phone: (724)452-9204.

HARRISBURG—E-7

See listings at Carlisle, Dillsburg, East Berlin, Elizabethtown, Hershey, Jonestown, Lickdale, Manheim, York and York Springs.

(SE) Harrisburg East Campground—(Dauphin) *From jct I-283 (exit 2): Go 1 mi S on Eisenhower Blvd. Enter on L.* ◊◊◊FACILITIES: 75 sites, typical site width 40 ft, 40 ft max RV length, 45 full hkups, 16 W&E, (20/30/50 amps), 14 no hkups, 53 pull-thrus, family camping, tenting, dump, laundry. ◊◊◊RECREATION: swim pool, play equipment. Pets welcome. Partial handicap access. Open all yr. Rate in 2010 $29-40 for 4 persons. Member ARVC, PCOA. Phone: (717)939-4331.

WATERSIDE CAMPGROUND & RV PARK—*From jct of Maday St/US 22: Go 55 mi to Loop Rd, then W 1 mi on Loop Rd to Locust Rd, then S 1/2 mi. Enter at end.*

SEE PRIMARY LISTING AT LEWISTOWN AND AD LEWISTOWN PAGE 669

HATFIELD—E-9

(NW) Oak Grove Park & Sales (RV SPACES) —(Montgomery) *From jct SR 463 & Vine St: Go 1 mi N on SR 463 (Cowpath Rd). Enter on R.* FACILITIES: 70 sites, 70 full hkups, (30/50 amps), 2 pull-thrus, family camping, dump, laundry. RECREATION: playground. Pets welcome. No tents. Open all yr. Big rigs welcome. Rate in 2010 $35 for 2 persons. Phone: (215)723-2007.

(W) VILLAGE SCENE PARK—(Montgomery) *From jct SR 463 & Vine St: Go 3/4 mi SW on S Vine St, then 300 yards N on Koffel Rd. Enter on R.*

◊◊◊◊FACILITIES: 30 sites, typical site width 25 ft, accepts full hkup units only, 30 full hkups, (30/50 amps), WiFi Instant Internet at site, WiFi Internet central location, family camping, dump, non-guest dump $, laundry, picnic tables.

RECREATION: playground.

Pets welcome, quantity restrict. Partial handicap access. No tents. Open Apr 1 - Nov 30. Call for winter availability. Big rigs welcome. Escort to site. Rate in 2010 $30 per vehicle.

Phone: (215)362-6030
Address: 2151 Koffel Rd, Hatfield, PA 19440
Lat/Lon: 40.27025/-75.30551
Email: sallebachvs@verizon.net

SEE AD PHILADELPHIA PAGE 673 AND AD TRAVEL SECTION PAGE 640

HAWLEY—B-9

(S) Wilsonville Recreation Area (PPL)—(Pike) *From jct SR-590 & US 6: Go 2 mi E on US 6. Enter on R.* ◊◊◊FACILITIES: 161 sites, typical site width 25 ft, 161 W&E, (20/30 amps), family camping, tenting, dump, laundry, groceries. ◊◊RECREATION: lake swim, boating, canoeing, ramp, dock, lake fishing, playground. No pets. Partial handicap access. Open End of Apr - 3rd weekend in Oct. Rate in 2010 $26-30 per family. Member ARVC, PCOA. Phone: (570)226-4382.

HEGINS—D-7

(E) Camp-A-While Inc—(Schuylkill) *From jct of I-81 & SR 25 (exit 112): Go 1/2 mi W on SR 25. Enter on L.* ◊◊◊◊FACILITIES: 123 sites, typical site width 30 ft, 95 full hkups, (20/30 amps), 28 no hkups, 4 pull-thrus, family camping, tenting, laundry, groceries. ◊◊◊◊RECREATION: swim pool, pond fishing, playground. Pets welcome. Partial handicap access. Open Mid Apr - Late Oct. Rate in 2010 $28-32 per family. Member ARVC, PCOA. Phone: (570)682-8696.

HERSHEY—E-7

See listings at Dillsburg, East Berlin, Elizabethtown, Harrisburg, Jonestown, Lickdale, Liverpool, Manheim, Ravine, Pine Grove, York & York Springs.

HERSHEY—Continued on next page

HERSHEY—Continued

(W) HERSHEY HIGHMEADOW CAMPGROUND—(Dauphin) *From jct US 422 & SR-743: Go 2-1/4 mi SW on US 422, then 1/2 mi N on Hershey Park Dr (SR-39). Enter on L.*

◆◆◆◆FACILITIES: 300 sites, typical site width 24 ft, 105 full hkups, 133 W&E, (20/30/50 amps), 62 no hkups, 87 pull-thrus, cable TV, WiFi Instant Internet at site, WiFi Internet central location, family camping, tenting, RV's/park model rentals, cabins, RV storage, dump, non-guest dump $, laundry, full svc store, RV supplies, LP gas by weight/by meter, ice, picnic tables, fire rings, grills, wood.

◆◆◆◆◆RECREATION: rec room/area, pavilion, coin games, 2 swim pools, wading pool, stream fishing, golf nearby, bsktball, playground, shuffleboard court 2 shuffleboard courts, activities, horseshoes, sports field, v-ball, local tours.

Pets welcome. Partial handicap access. Open all yr. Facilities fully operational Mid Apr - Oct 31. 2 Night Min, no water to sites in Winter. Big rigs welcome. Clubs welcome. Rate in 2010 $41-53 per family. MC/VISA/DISC/AMEX/Debit. ATM. Member ARVC, PCOA.

Phone: (717)534-8999
Address: 1200 Matlack Rd., Hummelstown, PA 17036
Lat/Lon: 40.27301/-76.69006
Email: mpanassow@hersheypa.com
Web: www.hersheypa.com

SEE AD PAGE 660

TWIN GROVE RESORT KOA AT PINE GROVE—*From jct I-81 & SR 443 (exit 100): Go 5 mi W on SR 443. Enter on R.*

SEE PRIMARY LISTING AT LICKDALE AND AD THIS PAGE AND AD TRAVEL SECTION PAGE 640

HESSTON—D-5

(E) Pleasant Hills Resort—(Huntingdon) *From jct Hwy 26 & (SR-3011) Seven Points Rd: Go 2-1/4 mi E on (SR-3011) Seven Points Rd, then 1 mi NE on Pleasant Hills Dr. Enter at end.* ◆◆◆FACILITIES: 156 sites, typical site width 28 ft, 35 ft max RV length, 156 full hkups, (20/30/50 amps), 28 pull-thrus, WiFi Internet central location, family camping, tenting, RV storage, laundry, ltd groc, ice, picnic tables, fire rings, wood. ◆◆RECREATION: pavilion, swim pool, mini-golf, bsktball, playground, activities, horseshoes, v-ball. Pets welcome, breed restrict. Open Mid Apr - Mid Oct. Rate in 2010 $36 for 2 persons. MC/VISA. Member ARVC, PCOA. CCUSA 50% Discount. CCUSA reservations Required, CCUSA max stay Unlimited. Discount available May (except Memorial weekend), Jun, Sep after Labor Day.

Phone: (814)658-3986
Address: 86 Pleasant Hills Dr., Hesston, PA 16647
Lat/Lon: 40.41357/-78.08822
Email: phrcamp@hotmail.com
Web: www.pleasanthills.net

HOBBIE—C-8

(S) Moyer's Grove Campground—(Luzerne) *From jct I-80 (exit 256) & SR 93: Go 3-3/4 mi N on SR 93, then 3/4 mi NE on SR 239, then 1-1/2 mi NE on Hobbie Rd, then 1-3/4 mi NE on Ridge Rd. Note: Entrance to camping area has covered bridge. 13' Clearance. Enter on R.* ◆◆FACILITIES: 147 sites, typical site width 28 ft, 40 ft max RV length, 70 full hkups, 70 W&E, (20/30/50 amps), 7 no hkups, 4 pull-thrus, family

HOBBIE—Continued
Moyer's Grove Campground—Continued

camping, tenting, dump, laundry, groceries. ◆◆◆RECREATION: swim pool, canoeing, pond/stream fishing, playground. Pets welcome. Partial handicap access. Open all yr. Rate in 2010 $30-37 per family. Phone: (800)722-1912.

HOLTWOOD—F-8

(NE) Muddy Run Recreation Park (Exelon Energy)—(Lancaster) *From jct SR 272 & SR 372: Go 3-1/2 mi W on SR 372, then 1/4 mi S on Bethesda Church Rd. Enter on L.* ◆◆◆FACILITIES: 189 sites, typical site width 28 ft, 148 W&E, (20/30 amps), 41 no hkups, 1 pull-thrus, family camping, tenting, dump, laundry, ltd groc. ◆◆◆RECREATION: lake swim, boating, electric motors only, canoeing, ramp, dock, lake fishing, playground. Pets welcome. Partial handicap access. Open End of Mar - End of Oct. Rate in 2010 $25 for 6 persons. Phone: (717)284-5850.

(N) TUCQUAN PARK FAMILY CAMPGROUND—(Lancaster) *From jct SR 272 & SR 372: Go 5 mi W on SR 372, then 2 mi N on River Rd. (Call for Big Rig directions). Enter on R.*

◆◆◆FACILITIES: 198 sites, typical site width 31 ft, 128 full hkups, 10 W&E, (20/30/50 amps), 60 no hkups, some extd stay sites (summer), 20 pull-thrus, WiFi Instant Internet at site, WiFi Internet central location, family camping, tenting, cabins, RV storage, dump, non-guest dump $, laundry, ltd groc, RV supplies, LP gas by weight/by meter, ice, picnic tables, fire rings, wood.

◆◆◆RECREATION: rec hall, rec room/area, pavilion, coin games, swim pool, boating, 2 row-boat/pedal boat rentals, pond fishing, fishing supplies, golf nearby, bsktball, playground, shuffleboard court shuffleboard court, activities (wkends), horseshoes, sports field, hiking trails, v-ball.

Pets welcome. Partial handicap access. Open all yr. Facilities fully operational Apr 1 - Oct 30. Snack Bar open weekends. Big rigs welcome. Escort to site. Clubs welcome. Rate in 2010 $40 per family. MC/VISA/DISC/Debit. Member ARVC, PCOA.

Phone: (717)284-2156
Address: 917 River Rd, Holtwood, PA 17532
Lat/Lon: 39.85890/-76.33077
Email: tucquanpark@aol.com
Web: www.camptucquanpark.com

SEE AD LANCASTER PAGES 664-666

HONESDALE—B-9

(SW) Cherry Ridge Campsites & Lodging—(Wayne) *From jct US 6 & SR-191: Go 3-1/2 mi S on SR-191, then 2-1/2 W mi on Owego Tpk, then 1 mi S*

HONESDALE—Continued
Cherry Ridge Campsites & Lodging—Continued

on Melody Rd, then 1/2 mi S on Camp Rd. Enter on R. ◆◆FACILITIES: 101 sites, typical site width 26 ft, 94 full hkups, 4 W&E, (15/20/30/50 amps), 3 no hkups, 2 pull-thrus, family camping, tenting, laundry, ltd groc. ◆◆RECREATION: lake swim, boating, electric motors only, canoeing, dock, lake fishing, playground. Pets welcome, breed restrict. Open May 1 - Oct 30. Big rigs welcome. Rate in 2010 $32-37 per family. Member ARVC, PCOA. Phone: (570)488-6654.

(N) Countryside Family Campground—(Wayne) *From north jct US 6 & SR-191: Go 1/2 mi N on SR-191, then 6-1/4 mi N on SR-670. Enter on L.* ◆◆◆FACILITIES: 138 sites, typical site width 30 ft, 19 full hkups, 101 W&E, (20/30/50 amps), 18 no hkups, 6 pull-thrus, WiFi Instant Internet at site, WiFi Internet central location, family camping, tenting, RV storage, dump, portable dump, laundry, groceries, RV supplies, LP gas by weight/by meter, ice, picnic tables, fire rings, wood. ◆◆◆◆RECREATION: pavilion, equipped pavilion, swim pool, pond fishing, mini-golf, ($), bsktball, playground, activities, horseshoes, v-ball. Pets welcome, breed restrict. Partial handicap access. Open Mar 1 - Dec 23. Big rigs welcome. Rate in 2010 $35-40 per family. MC/VISA/DISC/Debit. Member ARVC, PCOA. CCUSA 50% Discount. CCUSA reservations Recommended, CCUSA max stay 2 days, Cash only for CCUSA disc., Check only for CCUSA disc., CCUSA disc. not avail F,Sa. Not available during Wayne County Fair. Fully operational Apr-Dec.

Phone: (570)253-0424
Address: 50 Countryside Ln, Honesdale, PA 18431
Lat/Lon: 41.66010/-75.31578
Email: countrysidecamping@verizon.net
Web: www.countrysidefamilycampground.com

(NW) Ponderosa Pines Campground—(Wayne) *From North jct US 6 & SR-191: Go 1-1/2 mi W on US 6, then 4-3/4 mi N on Beech Grove Rd, then 1 mi N on Alden Rd. Enter on R.* ◆◆◆FACILITIES: 107 sites, typical site width 30 ft, 11 full hkups, 86 W&E, (20/30/50 amps), 10 no hkups, 3 pull-thrus, heater not allowed, WiFi Instant Internet at site, WiFi Internet central location, family camping, tenting, RV storage, dump, non-guest dump $, portable dump, laundry, ltd groc, RV supplies, LP gas by weight, ice, picnic tables, fire rings,

Ponderosa Pines Campground—Continued on next page

Edgar Allan Poe lived in Philadelphia from 1837 to 1844.

HONESDALE—Continued
Ponderosa Pines Campground—Continued

wood. ◆◆◆RECREATION: rec hall, pavilion, swim pool, lake swim, boating, electric motors only, canoeing, kayaking, lake fishing, fishing supplies, mini-golf, ($), bsktball, playground, activities, horseshoes, hiking trails, v-ball. Pets welcome, breed restrict, quantity restrict. Open Apr 23 - Oct 31. Rate in 2010 $35-45 per family. MC/VISA/DISC/Debit. Member ARVC, PCOA. CCUSA 50% Discount. CCUSA reservations Recommended, CCUSA max stay 3 days, CCUSA disc. not avail holidays. Not available special event weekends-call for details. Not available on seasonal sites. Addl surcharges: Portable dump: $10, Sewer: $5, Wifi: $2.

Phone: (570)253-2080
Address: 31 Ponderosa Dr, Honesdale, PA 18431
Lat/Lon: 41.65569/-75.33583
Email: ponderosapines@verizon.net
Web: www.ponderosapinescampground.com

HONEY BROOK—E-8

(SE) Two Log Campground—(Chester) *From jct US 322 & SR 10: Go 2-3/4 mi S on SR 10, then 1-3/4 mi E on Beaver Dam Rd. Enter on R.* ◆◆FACILITIES: 95 sites, typical site width 28 ft, 40 ft max RV length, 80 W&E, (15/30/50 amps), 15 no hkups, 2 pull-thrus, family camping, tenting, dump, ltd groc. ◆◆RECREATION: lake swim, boating, electric motors only, canoeing, dock, lake fishing, play equipment. Pets welcome. Open Apr 15 - Oct 15. Phone: (610)273-3068.

HOP BOTTOM—B-8

(NE) SHORE FOREST CAMPGROUND—(Susquehanna) *From jct US 6 & US 11: Go 12.6 mi N on US 11, then 0.5 mi E on Forest St. Enter on L.*

WELCOME

◆◆◆FACILITIES: 170 sites, typical site width 28 ft, 40 ft max RV length, 150 full hkups, 20 W&E, (20/30/50 amps), many extd stay sites (summer), 7 pull-thrus, cable TV, ($), WiFi Internet central location, family camping, tenting, cabins, dump, laundry, ltd groc, RV supplies, LP gas by weight/by meter, ice, picnic tables, fire rings, wood.

◆◆◆RECREATION: rec hall, rec room/area, coin games, swim pool, hot tub, boating, no motors, canoeing, kayaking, 3 rowboat/2 canoe/2 kayak/2 pedal boat rentals, lake fishing, fishing supplies, golf nearby, bsktball, playground, activities, (wkends), horseshoes, v-ball.

Pets welcome. Open Mid Apr - Early Nov. Big rigs welcome. Escort to site. Clubs welcome. Rate in 2010 $28-43 per family. MC/VISA/DISC/Debit. Member ARVC, PCOA.

Phone: (570)289-4666
Address: 121 The Driveway, Hop Bottom, PA 18824
Lat/Lon: 41.70981/-75.75681
Email: shoreforest@gmail.com
Web: www.shoreforestcampground.com

SEE AD SCRANTON PAGE 676

HOWARD—C-5

BALD EAGLE STATE PARK (Russel P. Letterman Campground)—(Centre) *From jct I-80 (exit 158) & Hwy 150: Go 9 mi N on Hwy 150. Enter on R.* FACILITIES: 97 sites, 82 E, (30/50 amps), 50 amps ($), 15 no hkups, tenting, dump. RECREATION: lake swim, boating, canoeing, ramp, dock, lake fishing, playground. No pets. Partial handicap access. Open 2nd Fri in Apr - Mid Dec. Phone: (814)625-2775.

Pennsylvania is the home of the world's largest cocoa & chocolate factory.

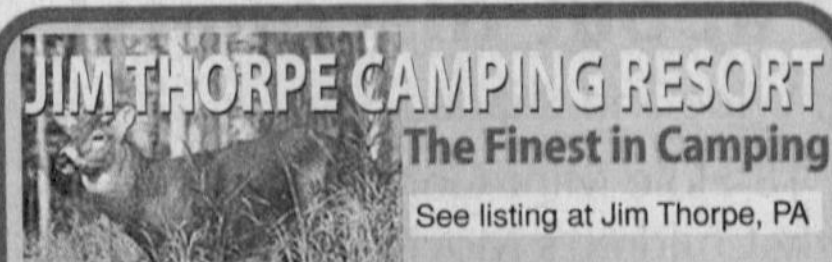

HOWARD—Continued

PRIMITIVE CAMPGROUND AT BALD EAGLE STATE PARK—(Centre) *I-80 (exit 158) & Hwy 150: Go 8 mi N on Rt 150 to Rt 26 S and turn right, go another 1.5 mi and left at the sign (Primitive Campground). Enter on L.* FACILITIES: 35 sites, 35 ft max RV length, 35 no hkups, 3 pull-thrus, tenting, dump. RECREATION: boating, canoeing, lake fishing. No pets. Partial handicap access. Open Apr 15 - Dec 15. Phone: (814)625-2775.

HUNTINGDON—D-5

(SW) HUNTINGDON FAIRGROUNDS CAMPGROUND—(Huntingdon) *From jct US 22 & SR-3035: Go 1 mi SW on SR-3035. Enter on L.* FACILITIES: 63 sites, typical site width 25 ft, 63 full hkups, (20/30/50 amps), tenting, dump. RECREATION: stream fishing. Pets welcome. Open Apr - Mid Oct. Phone: (814) 643-2274.

INDIANA—D-3

(NE) Wheel-In Campground—(Armstrong) *From jct US 422 & US 119: Go 12 mi W on US 422, then 1/2 mi NE on Dutch Run Rd, then 1/4 mi N on Plum Creek Rd. Enter on L.* ◆◆◆FACILITIES: 100 sites, typical site width 45 ft, 8 full hkups, 92 W&E, (20/30 amps), 10 pull-thrus, WiFi Internet central location, family camping, tenting, RV storage, dump, non-guest dump $, portable dump, RV supplies, ice, picnic tables, fire rings, wood.

CAMPCLUB USA

◆◆◆RECREATION: rec hall, pavilion, boating, no motors, canoeing, stream fishing, bsktball, playground, shuffleboard court 2 shuffleboard courts, activities horseshoes, v-ball. Pets welcome. Open Mid Apr - Mid Oct. Rate in 2010 $27-29 for 4 persons. MC/VISA. Member ARVC, PCOA. CCUSA 50% Discount. CCUSA reservations Recommended, CCUSA max stay 4 days, Cash only for CCUSA disc., Check only for CCUSA disc. Apr 20-Memorial Day Weekend-no restrictions; Memorial Day Weekend thru Labor Day Weekend no Fri, Sat or Sun; after Labor Day till closing-no restrictions. Discount not available opening day of trout season weekend.

Phone: (724)354-3693
Address: 113 Wheelin Campground, Shelocta, PA 15774
Lat/Lon: 40.69272/-79.32730
Email: wheelin@windstream.net
Web: www.wheel-incampground.com

(SE) Yellow Creek Campground—(Indiana) *From jct of US 119 & US 422: Go 9-3/4 mi E on US 422. Enter on L.* ◆◆FACILITIES: 130 sites, typical site width 30 ft, 105 W&E, (20/30/50 amps), 25 no hkups, 1 pull-thrus, family camping, tenting, dump, ltd groc. ◆◆RECREATION: stream fishing, playground. Pets welcome. Open Apr 15 - Oct 15. Rate in 2010 $22.50 for 2 persons. Phone: (724)465-4169.

INTERCOURSE—E-8

(N) BEACON HILL CAMPING—(Lancaster) *From jct SR 340 & SR 772: Go 1/2 mi NW on SR 772, then 1/8 mi E on Beacon Hill Rd. Enter on L.*

WELCOME

◆◆◆◆FACILITIES: 42 sites, typical site width 25 ft, 42 full hkups, (20/30/50 amps), 50 amps ($), 12 pull-thrus, WiFi Instant Internet at site, tenting, cabins, dump, laundry, RV supplies, LP gas by weight/by meter, ice, picnic tables, fire rings, wood.

◆RECREATION: pavilion, golf nearby.

Pets welcome. Partial handicap access. Age restrict may apply. Open Apr 1 - Nov 1. Rate in 2010 $33-34 for 2 persons. MC/VISA/DISC/Debit. Member ARVC, PCOA.

Phone: (717)768-8775
Address: 128 Beacon Hill Dr, Intercourse, PA 17534
Lat/Lon: 40.04712/-76.11480
Email: beaconhillcamping@frontiernet.net
Web: www.beaconhillcamping.com

SEE AD LANCASTER PAGES 664-666

JAMESTOWN—B-1

(NW) PYMATUNING STATE PARK (Jamestown Camp)—(Crawford) *From business center: Go 5 mi W on US 322.* FACILITIES: 331 sites, typical site width 25 ft, 30 ft max RV length, 165 E, (30/50 amps), 166 no hkups, tenting, dump, laundry, groceries. RECREATION: lake swim, boating, 10 hp limit, canoeing, ramp, dock, lake fishing, playground. No pets. Partial handicap access. Open 2nd wkd Apr - 3 wkd Oct. Phone: (724) 932-3141.

JEFFERSON—E-1

(NE) Firehouse RV Campground—(Greene) *From jct I-79 (exit 19) & SR-19: Go 300 yds S on SR-19, then 4 mi E on SR-221, then 4 mi E on SR-188. Enter on L.* ◆◆◆FACILITIES: 48 sites, typical site width 30 ft, 48 full hkups, (30/50 amps), 20 pull-thrus, tenting, laundry. Pets welcome. Open all yr. Big rigs welcome. Rate in 2010 $30 for 2 persons. Phone: (724)883-1955.

Hershey is considered the Chocolate Capital of the United States.

JERSEY SHORE—C-6

RAVENSBURG STATE PARK—(Clinton) *From town: Go 12 mi S on Hwy 44 & Hwy 880. Enter on L.* FACILITIES: 21 sites, 21 no hkups, tenting. RECREATION: stream fishing, playground. No pets. Open Mid Apr - Late Oct. Phone: (570)966-1455.

Susquehanna Campground (TOO NEW TO RATE)—(Lycoming) *From jct of PA 44 & US 220: Go 2 mi E on US 220, then 1 mi N on Susquehanna Dr. Enter on R.* FACILITIES: 160 sites, typical site width 50 ft, 30 full hkups, 130 W&E, (20/30 amps), 15 pull-thrus, family camping, tenting, dump. RECREATION: river swim, canoeing, ramp, river fishing, playground. Pets welcome, breed restrict. Open Apr 15 - Oct 15. Rate in 2010 $22-30 per family. Member ARVC, PCOA. Phone: (570)398-0462.

JIM THORPE—C-9

(W) JIM THORPE CAMPING RESORT—(Carbon) *From jct US 209 & SR-903: Go 1/4 mi N on US 209, then 2-1/4 mi W on Broadway. Enter on L.*

WELCOME

◆◆FACILITIES: 200 sites, typical site width 28 ft, 40 ft max RV length, 150 full hkups, 20 W&E, (20/30/50 amps), 30 no hkups, some extd stay sites (summer), 75 pull-thrus, cable TV, WiFi Internet central location, family camping, tenting, cabins, RV storage, dump, non-guest dump $, laundry, groceries, RV supplies, LP gas by weight/by meter, ice, picnic tables, fire rings, wood.

◆◆◆RECREATION: rec hall, rec room/area, pavilion, coin games, swim pool, wading pool, stream fishing, fishing supplies, golf nearby, bsktball, playground, shuffleboard court shuffleboard court, activities (wkends), horseshoes, hiking trails, v-ball.

Pets welcome. Partial handicap access. Open Apr 1 - Oct 31. Escort to site. Clubs welcome. Rate in 2010 $33-40 for 2 persons. MC/VISA. Member ARVC, PCOA.

Phone: (570)325-2644
Address: 129 Lentz Trail, Jim Thorpe, PA 18229
Lat/Lon: 40.85422/-75.77601
Email: camper1@ptd.net
Web: www.jimthorpecamping.com

SEE AD THIS PAGE

JONESTOWN—D-7

(NE) KOA-JONESTOWN—(Lebanon) *From jct SR 72 & US 22: Go 2 mi E on US 22, then 1/2 mi S on Old Rt 22. Enter on R.*

WELCOME

◆◆◆◆FACILITIES: 129 sites, typical site width 25 ft, 67 full hkups, 36 W&E, 8 E, (20/30/50 amps), 50 amps ($), 18 no hkups, some extd stay sites, 50 pull-thrus, WiFi Instant Internet at site, WiFi Internet central location, family camping, tenting, cabins, RV storage, dump, non-guest dump $, laundry, groceries, RV supplies, LP gas by meter, ice, picnic tables, fire rings, wood.

◆◆◆◆RECREATION: rec room/area, pavilion, coin games, swim pool, wading pool, mini-golf, ($), golf nearby, bsktball, playground, activities, (wkends), horseshoes, v-ball. Rec open to public.

Pets welcome. Partial handicap access. Open all yr. Limited sites in Winter. Big rigs welcome. Escort to site. Clubs welcome. Rate in 2010 $36-53 per family. MC/VISA/DISC/AMEX/Debit. Member ARVC, PCOA. KOA discount.

Phone: (717)865-2526
Address: 145 Old Rt 22, Jonestown, PA 17038
Lat/Lon: 40.42197/-76.46594
Email: jonestownkoa145@comcast.net
Web: www.koa.com/where/pa/38105

SEE AD HERSHEY PAGE 661 AND AD TRAVEL SECTION PAGE 640

KANE—B-4

(NW) ALLEGHENY NATIONAL FOREST (Kiasutha Campground)—(McKean) *From business center: Go 8 mi NW on Hwy-321, then 2 mi NW on FR-262.* FACILITIES: 90 sites, 90 no hkups, 47 pull-thrus, tenting, dump. RECREATION: lake swim, boating, ramp, dock, lake fishing, playground. Open May 22 - Sep 7. Phone: (814)945-6511.

(NW) ALLEGHENY NATIONAL FOREST (Red Bridge Campground)—(McKean) *From business center: Go 9 mi NW on Hwy-321.* FACILITIES: 67 sites, 12 full hkups, 13 E, 42 no hkups, tenting, dump. RECREATION: lake swim, lake fishing, playground. Partial handicap access. Open Apr - Mid Dec. Phone: (814)945-6511.

(SE) ALLEGHENY NATIONAL FOREST (Twin Lakes Campground)—(Elk) *From town: Go 8 mi S on Hwy 321, then 1-1/2 mi W on FR 191. Railroad underpass on entrance road has a 10-ft clearance.* FACILITIES: 51 sites, 28 ft max RV length, 23 E, (30 amps), 28 no hkups, tenting, dump. RECREATION: lake swim, lake/stream fishing, playground. Partial handicap access. Open Apr 10 - Dec 8. Phone: (814)362-4613.

KANE—Continued on next page

KANE—Continued

(N) ALLEGHENY NATIONAL FOREST VACATION BUREAU—*From jct US 219 & US 6: Go 1/4 mi N on US 219. Enter on L.* Distributes information and brochures pertaining to Allegheny National Forest Region. Open all yr.

Phone: (800)473-9370
Address: 3183 Rt 219, Kane, PA 16735
Lat/Lon: 41.71446/-78.69494
Web: www.visitanf.com

SEE AD TRAVEL SECTION PAGE 637

(NE) THE FOOTE REST CAMPGROUND—(McKean) *From jct US 219 & US 6: Go 1/4 mi N on US 219. Enter on L.* ◊◊◊◊FACILITIES: 162 sites, typical site width 28 ft, 25 full hkups, 117 W&E, (20/30 amps), 20 no hkups, many extd stay sites (summer), 135 pull-thrus, cable TV, ($), WiFi Instant Internet at site, family camping, tenting, cabins, RV storage, dump, non-guest dump $, portable dump, laundry, groceries, RV supplies, LP gas by weight/by meter, ice, picnic tables, fire rings, wood.

◊◊◊◊RECREATION: rec room/area, pavilion, coin games, swim pool, mini-golf, ($), golf nearby, bsktball, playground, shuffleboard court 2 shuffleboard courts, activities (wkends), horseshoes, sports field, hiking trails, v-ball.

Pets welcome. Partial handicap access. Open all yr. Facilities fully operational Apr - Oct. Limited water to sites in Winter. Escort to site. Clubs welcome. Rate in 2010 $30-32 for 2 persons. MC/VISA/DISC/Debit. Member ARVC, PCOA.

Phone: (814)778-5336
Address: 3183 Rt 219, Kane, PA 16735
Lat/Lon: 41.7142/-78.6947
Email: forms@footerestcampground.com
Web: www.footerestcampground.com

SEE AD TRAVEL SECTION PAGE 637

KINZERS—E-8

(E) Roamers' Retreat Campground—(Lancaster) *From jct SR 30 & Kinzer Rd: Go 3/4 mi E on SR 30. Enter on L.* ◊◊FACILITIES: 108 sites, typical site width 30 ft, 108 full hkups, (30/50 amps), 50 amps ($), 41 pull-thrus, family camping, tenting, dump, laundry, ltd groc. RECREATION: playground. Pets welcome. Open all yr. Big rigs welcome. Rate in 2010 $40-57 per family. Member ARVC, PCOA. Phone: (800)525-5605.

Reserve Online at Woodalls.com

(SE) The Loose Caboose Campground—(Lancaster) *From jct SR-30. Enter on R.* ◊◊◊FACILITIES: 67 sites, typical site width 30 ft, 54 full hkups, 3 W&E, (20/30/50 amps), 10 no hkups, 5 pull-thrus, family camping, tenting, dump. RECREATION: playground. Pets welcome. Open all yr. Facilities fully operational Early Apr - Late Oct. Big rigs welcome. Rate in 2010 $30-38 per family. Member ARVC, PCOA. Phone: (717) 442-8429.

KNOX—C-2

(S) BARNWELL CAFE'—*From jct I-80 (exit 53) & SR-338: Go 1/8 mi N on SR-338. Enter on R.* Full service restaurant serving breakfast, lunch & dinner. Open Apr 1 - Mid Dec. MC/VISA/DISC/Debit. ATM.

Phone: (814)797-1109
Address: 308 Timberwolf Run, Knox, PA 16232
Lat/Lon: 41.18814/-79.54226

SEE AD THIS PAGE

(S) WOLFS CAMPING RESORT—(Clarion) *From jct I-80 (exit 53) & SR-338: Go 1/8 mi N on SR-338. Enter on R.* ◊◊◊FACILITIES: 500 sites, typical site width 30 ft, 455 full hkups, 35 W&E, (20/30/50 amps), 15 no hkups, mostly extd stay sites (summer), 92 pull-thrus, cable TV, ($), WiFi Internet central location, family camping, tenting, RV's/park model rentals, cabins, RV storage, dump, non-guest dump $, laundry, groceries, RV supplies, LP gas by weight/by meter, ice, picnic tables, fire rings, wood, controlled access.

◊◊◊◊RECREATION: rec hall, rec room/area, pavilion, coin games, swim pool, wading pool, spray ground, lake swim, hot tub, canoeing, kayaking, lake fishing, fishing supplies, mini-golf, ($), putting green, golf nearby, bsktball, playground, shuffleboard court 6 shuffleboard courts, activities, horseshoes, sports field, v-ball. Rec open to public.

Pets welcome. Partial handicap access. Open Apr 15 - Oct 31. Big rigs welcome. Clubs welcome.

KNOX—Continued
WOLFS CAMPING RESORT—Continued

Rate in 2010 $32-45 for 2 persons. MC/VISA/DISC/Debit. ATM. Member ARVC, PCOA. FCRV discount. FMCA discount. CCUSA 50% Discount. CCUSA max stay 1 day, Cash only for CCUSA disc., CCUSA disc. not avail F,Sa, CCUSA disc. not avail holidays. $3.50 sewer surcharge.

Phone: (814)797-1103
Address: 308 Timberwolf Run, Knox, PA 16232
Lat/Lon: 41.18816/-79.54225
Email: info@wolfscampingresort.com
Web: www.wolfscampingresort.com

SEE AD THIS PAGE AND AD TRAVEL SECTION PAGE 640

KUTZTOWN—D-9

(N) Pine Hill RV Park—(Berks) *From jct I-78/US 22 (exit 40) & SR 737: Go 1/8 mi N on SR 737, then 1-1/2 mi E on Old US 22. Enter on R.* ◊◊◊◊FACILITIES: 123 sites, typical site width 30 ft, accepts full hkup units only, 123 full hkups, (20/30/50 amps), 90 pull-thrus, family camping, laundry, groceries. ◊◊◊RECREATION: play equipment. Pets welcome. Partial handicap access. No tents. Open Apr 1 - Nov 1. Big rigs welcome. Rate in 2010 $38-42 per family. Member ARVC, PCOA. Phone: (800)217-6776.

LAKE CITY—A-1

(W) CAMP ERIEZ CAMPGROUND—(Erie) *From jct I-90 (exit 16) & SR-98: Go 3-1/2 mi N on SR-98, then 2.7 mi W on SR-5. Enter on R.*

◊◊◊◊FACILITIES: 177 sites, typical site width 35 ft, 162 full hkups, 15 W&E, (20/30/50 amps), mostly extd stay sites (summer), 15 pull-thrus, heater not allowed, family camping, RV storage, dump, picnic tables, fire rings, wood, controlled access.

◊◊◊◊RECREATION: rec hall, rec room/area, coin games, swim pool, lake swim, boating, lake fishing, golf nearby, bsktball, playground, activities, (wkends), sports field, v-ball.

Pets welcome. Partial handicap access. No tents. Open Mid Apr - Mid Oct. Escort to site. Clubs welcome. Rate in 2010 $25-28 for 4 persons.

Phone: (814)774-8381
Address: 9356 W Lake Rd, Lake City, PA 16423
Lat/Lon: 42.03309/-80.32125
Email: bart4262@yahoo.com

SEE AD ERIE PAGE 656

LAKEVILLE—B-9

(N) Secluded Acres Campground—(Wayne) *From jct SR-196 & SR-590: Go 7-1/2 mi NE on SR-590, then 1-3/4 mi NW on Avoy Rd. Enter on R.* ◊◊◊FACILITIES: 264 sites, typical site width 50 ft, 184 full hkups, 31 W&E, (30/50 amps), 49 no hkups, 8 pull-thrus, family camping, tenting, dump, laundry, groceries. ◊◊◊RECREATION: lake swim, boating, electric motors only, canoeing, ramp, lake fishing, playground. Pets welcome. Partial handicap access. Open Mid Apr - Mid Oct. Big rigs welcome. Rate in 2010 $35 per family. Member ARVC, PCOA. Phone: (570)226-9959.

LANCASTER—E-8

LANCASTER AREA MAP

Newmanstown
Adamstown
Bowmansville
Denver
Manheim
Ephrata
New Holland
Honey Brook
Elizabethtown
LANCASTER
Intercourse
Kinzers
Coatesville
Willow Street
Strasburg
Quarryville
Pequea
Airville
Holtwood
PA Tpk.
76
222
283
30
SR 222/272

Symbols on map indicate towns within a 30 mi radius of Lancaster where campgrounds (diamonds), attractions (flags), & RV service centers & camping supply outlets (gears) are listed. Check listings for more information.

CIRCLE M - OUTDOOR WORLD (CAMP RESORT)—(Lancaster) *2111 Millersville Rd, Lancaster, PA 17603.*
FACILITIES: 380 sites.
RECREATION: rec hall, swim pool.

Phone: (800)579-4987
Address: 2111 Millersville Rd, Lancaster, PA 17603
Web: www.oneparkmembership.com

SEE AD ADAMSTOWN PAGE 648

LANCASTER—Continued on next page

Lancaster County℠

The Heart of Pennsylvania Dutch Country®

www.PaDutchCountry.com 1-800-PA DUTCH

"Where the Amish are our neighbors."

Hosts:
Claudette,
Lou & Shelly

(717) 687-6670

99 N. Ronks Rd • PO Box 308
Ronks, PA 17572
Between US 30 & Rte. 340

Level Shaded
*Campsites
E,W,S
Cable TV
Wi-Fi

Pet Free
Smoke Free
*Cottages
*Guest Rooms

*Camp Store
*Pavilion
*Laundry
*Bathhouses

IN THE HEART OF LANCASTER COUNTY

Overlooking 5 miles of Amish Farmland

COUNTRY HAVEN CAMPGROUND

Full Hookups on Spacious Terraced Sites, Pull Throughs or Wooded Sites Available. Free Cable TV & Wi-Fi. Leash Free Dog Park.

Big Rigs Welcome

(717) 354-7926

Bob and Bonnie Patterson
354 Springville Rd.,
New Holland, PA 17557
www.countryhaven.com

See listing at New Holland
No Planned Activities

You've Got a Friend In Lancaster County

A COMPLETE CAMPING RESORT

EXCLUSIVE AMENITIES

- Free Local telephone calls
- Wireless Internet Access
- Dedicated pet play/exercise area
- Warm hospitality
- Complimentary coffee and tea
- Exclusive RVing & Camping
- Vacation and VIP Treatment

Camping Experience

Woodall Ratings:

Facilities 

Recreation 

400 Wooded & Open Sites * 30 & 50 Amp 5-Pt Hookups (W/S/E/CTV/Ph) * Dust Free Roads 6 Acre Lake * Rustic to Deluxe Cabin Rentals * Security Gate & Patrol * Full Service Store & Gift Shop * Outdoor & Indoor Pool Complex with Spa * Planned Group Activities * Fishing * Boating Mini Golf * World Fitness Trail * Hiking Trails * Fun Cycles * Golf Cart Rentals * Entertainment Hall with Pipe Organ * Close to Golf Courses and Pennsylvania Dutch Tourist Attractions

576 Yellow Hill Rd., Narvon, PA 17555
(Near Bowmansville)
(717) 445-5525
WWW.LAKEINWOODCAMPGROUND.COM
Online Reservations with E-Mail Confirmation

Lake in Wood is ours by deed,
God's by Creation.

See listing at Bowmansville

LANCASTER—Continued

(SE) COUNTRY ACRES CAMPGROUND—(Lancaster) *From jct SR 896 & US 30: Go 2-1/2 mi E on US 30. Enter on L.*

♦♦♦♦FACILITIES: 84 sites, typical site width 32 ft, 60 full hkups, 18 W&E, (20/30/50 amps), 6 no hkups, 22 pull-thrus, cable TV, WiFi Instant Internet at site, phone Internet central location, family camping, tenting, cabins, dump, non-guest dump $, laundry, ltd groc, RV supplies, ice, picnic tables, fire rings, wood, controlled access.

♦♦♦♦RECREATION: rec room/area, pavilion, coin games, swim pool, wading pool, golf nearby, bsktball, playground, shuffleboard court 2 shuffleboard courts, horseshoes, sports field, v-ball, local tours.

Pets welcome. Partial handicap access. Open Mar 17 - Nov 26. Big rigs welcome. Clubs welcome. Rate in 2010 $35-50 for 2 persons. MC/VISA/DISC/Debit. Member ARVC, PCOA.

Phone: (866)675-4745
Address: 20 Leven Rd, Gordonville, PA 17529
Lat/Lon: 40.01393/-76.14441
Email: countryacres@bird-in-hand.com
Web: www.countryacrescampground.com

SEE AD PAGES 664-666

COUNTRY HAVEN CAMPGROUND—*From Lancaster NE on US 222: Go 1 mi to US 322, then 7 mi S on SR 897, then 5-1/2 mi S on SR 897.*

LANCASTER AND AD PAGES 664-666

(E) FLORY'S COTTAGES & CAMPING—(Lancaster) *From East jct SR 462 & US-30: Go 3-1/2 mi E on US 30, then 1/2 mi N on Ronks Rd. Enter on R.*

♦♦♦♦FACILITIES: 71 sites, typical site width 26 ft, 71 full hkups, (20/30/50 amps), 50 amps ($), cable TV, ($), WiFi Instant Internet at site ($), family camping, tenting, RV's/park model rentals, cabins, dump, laundry, ltd groc, RV supplies, ice, picnic tables.

LANCASTER—Continued
FLORY'S COTTAGES & CAMPING—Continued

♦♦♦RECREATION: rec hall, rec room/area, pavilion, coin games, golf nearby, bsktball, playground, activities, (wkends).

Pets welcome. Open all yr. Limited water to sites in Winter. Big rigs welcome. Clubs welcome. Rate in 2010 $30-50 for 2 persons. MC/VISA/Debit. Member ARVC, PCOA.

Phone: (717)687-6670
Address: 99 North Ronks Rd, Ronks, PA 17572
Lat/Lon: 40.02486/-76.16804
Email: info@floryscamping.com
Web: www.floryscamping.com

SEE AD PAGES 664-666

✽ **(S) MELLOTT BROTHERS TRAILER SALES**—*From jct SR 462 and US 222 South (Lancaster): Go 4-1/2 mi S on US 222/SR 272 South to W Penn Grant Rd, then E 400 yds on W Penn Grant Rd to Willow Street Pike, then 5 mi N on Willow Street Pike. Enter on L.* SALES: travel trailers, truck campers, 5th wheels, toy hauler, Class A motorhomes, Class C motorhomes, Class B motorhomes, fold-down camping trailers, pre-owned unit sales. SERVICES: full-time mech, RV appliance repair, body work/collision repair, LP gas by weight/by meter, dump station, sells parts/accessories, installs hitches. Open all yr. MC/VISA/DISC/Debit.

Phone: (800)826-3556
Address: 2718 Willow Street Pike, Rte 272 North, Willow Street, PA 17584
Lat/Lon: 39.98001/-76.27722
Email: sales@mellottbrothers.com
Web: www.mellottbrothers.com

SEE AD TRAVEL SECTION PAGE 641

(SE) MILL BRIDGE VILLAGE—*From east jct Hwy 462 & US 30: Go 3-1/2 mi E on US 30, then 1/2 mi S on Ronks Rd. Enter on L.* Oldest continuous operating Historic Village in PA Amish Country: 1738 Grist Mill. Village Store & Farm Museum. Listed on the National Registry of Historic Places. Also longest Double-Span covered

LANCASTER—Continued
MILL BRIDGE VILLAGE—Continued

bridge in Lancaster Cnty. Open Mar 27 - Oct 26. MC/VISA.

Phone: (717)687-8181
Address: 101 S Ronks Rd, Ronks, PA 17572
Email: info@millbridge.com
Web: www.millbridge.com

SEE AD PAGES 664-666

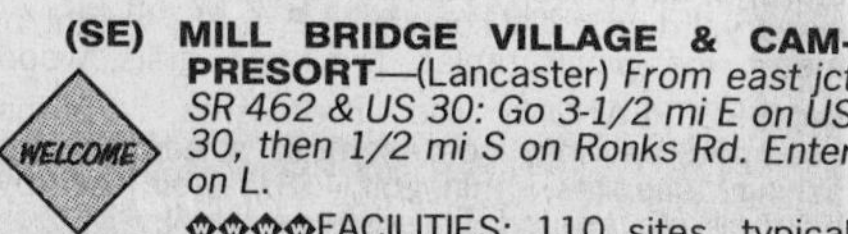

(SE) MILL BRIDGE VILLAGE & CAMPRESORT—(Lancaster) *From east jct SR 462 & US 30: Go 3-1/2 mi E on US 30, then 1/2 mi S on Ronks Rd. Enter on L.*

♦♦♦♦FACILITIES: 110 sites, typical site width 26 ft, 70 full hkups, 40 W&E, (20/30/50 amps), 50 amps ($), 23 pull-thrus, cable TV, WiFi Instant Internet at site, family camping, tenting, cabins, dump, non-guest dump $, laundry, ltd groc, RV supplies, ice, picnic tables, fire rings, wood.

♦♦♦♦RECREATION: rec hall, rec room/area, pavilion, coin games, swim pool, canoeing, 2 canoe rentals, stream fishing, fishing supplies, golf nearby, bsktball, playground, activities, (wkends), horseshoes, local tours.

Pets welcome, breed restrict. Open all yr. Big rigs welcome. Clubs welcome. Rate in 2010 $37-56 per family. MC/VISA/DISC/Debit. ATM. Member ARVC, PCOA. CCUSA 50% Discount. CCUSA reservations Required, CCUSA max stay 2 days, CCUSA disc. not avail S,Th, CCUSA disc. not avail F,Sa, CCUSA disc. not avail holidays. 2 night minimum. Discount available Mar 15-May 20 & Sep 7-Nov 30.

Phone: (800)645-2744
Address: 101 S Ronks Rd, Ronks, PA 17572
Lat/Lon: 40.00905/-76.16188
Email: info@millbridge.com
Web: www.millbridge.com

SEE AD PAGES 664-666

LANCASTER—Continued on next page

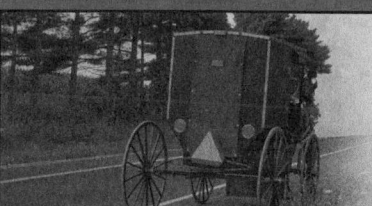

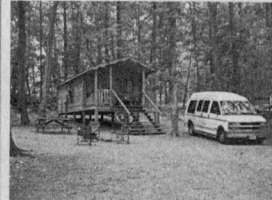

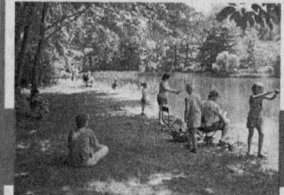

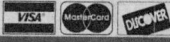

LANCASTER—Continued

(E) OLD MILL STREAM CAMPGROUND—(Lancaster) *From east jct SR 462 & US 30: Go 1 mi E on US 30. Enter on L.*

◊◊◊◊FACILITIES: 163 sites, typical site width 30 ft, 144 full hkups, 11 W&E, (20/30/50 amps), 8 no hkups, 8 pull-thrus, cable TV, WiFi Instant Internet at site, phone Internet central location, family camping, tenting, RV storage, dump, non-guest dump $, portable dump, laundry, ltd groc, RV supplies, LP gas by weight/by meter, ice, picnic tables, fire rings, grills, wood.

◊◊◊RECREATION: rec room/area, pavilion, equipped pavilion, coin games, stream fishing, fishing supplies, mini-golf, ($), golf nearby, bsktball, playground, horseshoes, v-ball.

Pets welcome. Partial handicap access. Open all yr. Limited water in Winter. Big rigs welcome. Clubs welcome. Rate in 2010 $37-44 for 4 persons. MC/VISA/DISC/Debit. ATM. Member ARVC, PCOA.

Phone: (717)299-2314
Address: 2249 Lincoln Hwy E, Lancaster, PA 17602
Lat/Lon: 40.02863/-76.21491
Email: info@oldmillstreamcampground.com
Web: www.oldmillstreamcampground.com

SEE AD PAGES 664-666

(E) PENNSYLVANIA DUTCH CONVENTION & VISITORS BUREAU—*From jct SR 23 & US 30: Go 1-1/2 mi E on US 30, then 1/8 mi N on Greenfield Rd. Enter on R.* The heart of Pennsylvania Dutch Country. You'll find informative brochures and maps, coupons, tickets, self-guided audio tours, and seasonal farmland tours. Open all yr. Daily 8 a.m.-6 p.m. MC/VISA/DISC.

Phone: (800)PADUTCH
Address: 501 Greenfield Rd, Lancaster, PA 17601
Lat/Lon: 40.05063/-76.25547
Email: info@padutchcountry.com
Web: www.padutchcountry.com

SEE AD PAGES 664-666

SHADY GROVE CAMPGROUND—*From jct PA Tpk (exit 286) & Hwy 272: Go 1-1/4 mi N on Hwy 272, then 1/2 mi NW on Hwy 897, then 1/8 mi S on Poplar Rd.*

SEE PRIMARY LISTING AT DENVER AND AD PAGES 664-666

TUCQUAN PARK FAMILY CAMPGROUND—*From Lancaster: Go S on US 222 to SR 272, then S on SR 272 to SR 372, then 5 mi W on SR 372, then 2 mi N on River Rd. Enter on R.*

SEE PRIMARY LISTING AT HOLTWOOD AND AD PAGES 664-666

YOGI BEAR'S JELLYSTONE PARK CAMP-RESORT-LANCASTER SOUTH/QUARRYVILLE—*From Lancaster: Go 12 mi S on US 222/SR 272, then 3-1/4 mi E on SR 372/Buck Rd, then 2-3/4 mi S on US 222, then 1-1/2 mi SE on Blackburn Rd. Enter on L.*

SEE PRIMARY LISTING AT QUARRYVILLE AND AD PAGES 664-666

Each year on Christmas Day the "Crossing of the Delaware" is reenacted at Washington Crossing.

LAPORTE—B-7

(S) PIONEER CAMPGROUND—(Sullivan) *From SR 154 & US 220: Go 2-1/2 mi S on US 220, then 1/2 mi W on Pioneer Trail. Enter at end.*

◊◊◊◊◊FACILITIES: 100 sites, typical site width 35 ft, 42 ft max RV length, 71 W&E, (20/30/50 amps), 29 no hkups, some extd stay sites (summer), cable TV, WiFi Instant Internet at site, WiFi Internet central location, family camping, tenting, cabins, RV storage, dump, non-guest dump $, portable dump, laundry, groceries, RV supplies, LP gas by weight/by meter, ice, picnic tables, fire rings, wood.

◊◊◊◊RECREATION: rec room/area, pavilion, coin games, swim pool, saltwater swim, bsktball, playground, activities, (wkends), horseshoes, sports field, hiking trails, v-ball.

Pets welcome. Partial handicap access. Open Early Apr - Early Dec. Escort to site. Clubs welcome. Rate in 2010 $30-42 per family. MC/VISA/DISC/Debit. Member ARVC, PCOA. CCUSA 50% Discount. CCUSA reservations Recommended, CCUSA max stay 1 day, Cash only for CCUSA disc., CCUSA disc. not avail S,M,Th, CCUSA disc. not avail F,Sa, CCUSA disc. not avail holidays. $10 extra tent on site surcharge.

Phone: (570)946-9971
Address: 307 Pioneer Trail, Muncy Valley, PA 17758
Lat/Lon: 41.39885/-76.50008
Email: info@pioneercampground.com
Web: www.pioneercampground.com

SEE AD THIS PAGE

LAWRENCEVILLE—A-6

TOMPKINS REC AREA (COE - Cowanesque Lake)—(Tioga) *From jct Hwy 49 & US 15: Go 1/4 mi N on US 15, then 3 mi W on Bliss Rd. Enter on L.* FACILITIES: 86 sites, 59 W&E, 27 no hkups, tenting, dump, ltd groc. RECREATION: lake swim, boating, ramp, dock, lake/river/pond fishing, playground. Open Memorial Day - Labor Day. Phone: (570)835-5281.

LEBANON—E-7

HERSHEY-THOUSAND TRAILS (CAMP RESORT)—(Lebanon) *493 S Mt. Pleasant Rd, Lebanon, PA 17042.*

FACILITIES: tenting.

Open all yr. Rate in 2010 $32 for 2 persons.

Phone: (800)405-6188
Address: 493 South Mt. Pleasant Rd, Lebanon, PA 17042
Email: tripexpert@1000trails.com

SEE AD ADAMSTOWN PAGE 648

LEHIGHTON—D-9

(S) Stoneybrook Estates—(Carbon) *From jct I-309 & PA 895: Go 6 mi E on PA 895, then 1/2 mi S on Lauchner Rd to end, then E on Germans Rd. to Stoneybrook Campground. Enter on L.* ◊◊◊◊FACILITIES: 58 sites, typical site width 50 ft, 58 full hkups, (20/30/50 amps), family camping, dump, laundry, ltd groc. ◊◊RECREATION: swim pool. Pets welcome, quantity restrict. Partial handicap access. No tents. Open all yr. Big rigs welcome. Rate in 2010 $40 for 4 persons. Member ARVC, PCOA. Phone: (570)386-4088.

LENHARTSVILLE—D-8

(NW) BLUE ROCKS FAMILY CAMPGROUND—(Berks) *From jct I-78/US 22 (exit 35) & SR 143: Go 3/4 mi N on SR 143, then 100 yards W on Mountain Rd, then 1/2 mi W on Blue Rocks Rd, then 300 yds N on Sousley Rd. Enter on L.*

◊◊◊FACILITIES: 200 sites, typical site width 26 ft, 40 ft max RV length, 45 full hkups, 60 W&E,

LENHARTSVILLE—Continued
BLUE ROCKS FAMILY CAMPGROUND—Continued

(15/20/30 amps), 95 no hkups, many extd stay sites (summer), 4 pull-thrus, WiFi Internet central location, family camping, tenting, RV's/park model rentals, cabins, dump, portable dump, laundry, groceries, RV supplies, LP gas by weight/by meter, ice, picnic tables, fire rings, wood, controlled access.

◊◊◊◊RECREATION: rec hall, rec room/area, pavilion, coin games, swim pool, wading pool, pond fishing, fishing supplies, golf nearby, bsktball, playground, activities, (wkends), horseshoes, hiking trails, v-ball. Rec open to public.

Pets welcome. Partial handicap access. Open Apr 1 - Nov 1. Winter camping by reservation only. Clubs welcome. Rate in 2010 $40-46 per family. MC/VISA/DISC/Debit. Member ARVC, PCOA.

Phone: (866)GR8-KAMPN
Address: 341 Sousley Rd, Lenhartsville, PA 19534
Lat/Lon: 40.59007/-75.90881
Email: camp@bluerockscampground.com
Web: www.bluerockscampground.com

SEE AD THIS PAGE

(NE) ROBIN HILL CAMPING RESORT—(Berks) *E'Bnd from jct I-78/US 22 (exit 35) & SR 143: Go 1/2 mi S on SR 143, then 1-1/2 mi E on Old US 22, then 150 yds N on Donat Rd, then 300 yds N on Little Round Top Rd, then 1/2 mi N on Robin Hill Rd. Enter on R.*

◊◊◊◊FACILITIES: 274 sites, typical site width 40 ft, 250 full hkups, 18 W&E, (20/30/50 amps), 6 no hkups, many extd stay sites (summer), 1 pull-thrus, cable TV, WiFi Instant Internet at site, WiFi Internet central location, family camping, tenting, cabins, dump, non-guest dump $, portable dump, laundry, full svc store, RV supplies, LP gas by weight/by meter, ice, picnic tables, fire rings, wood.

◊◊◊◊RECREATION: rec hall, rec room/area, pavilion, coin games, swim pool, wading pool, lake swim, boating, no motors, canoeing, kayaking, dock, 4 pedal boat rentals, lake fishing, fishing supplies, golf nearby, bsktball, playground, activities, (wkends), horseshoes, sports field, v-ball.

Pets welcome. Partial handicap access. Open Apr 1 - Oct 31. Big rigs welcome. Clubs welcome. Rate in 2010 $46-56 per family. MC/VISA/Debit. Member ARVC, PCOA.

Phone: (800)732-5267
Address: 149 Robin Hill Rd, Lenhartsville, PA 19534
Lat/Lon: 40.58958/-75.85612
Email: robinhill@equitylifestyle.com
Web: www.robinhillrvresort.com

SEE AD ADAMSTOWN PAGE 648

LEWISBURG—C-7

(W) Hidden Valley Camping Resort—(Union) *From jct US 15 & SR 192: Go W 9 mi on SR 192. Enter on L.* ◊◊◊FACILITIES: 486 sites, typical site width 26 ft, 280 full hkups, 191 W&E, (20/30/50 amps), 17 no hkups, family camping, tenting, dump, laundry, groceries. ◊◊◊◊RECREATION: swim pool, lake swim, lake fishing, playground. Pets welcome, breed restrict. Partial handicap access. Open Mid Apr - Oct 31. Big rigs welcome. Rate in 2010 $36-41 for 4 persons. Member ARVC, PCOA. Phone: (570)966-1330. FMCA discount.

LEWISBURG—Continued on next page

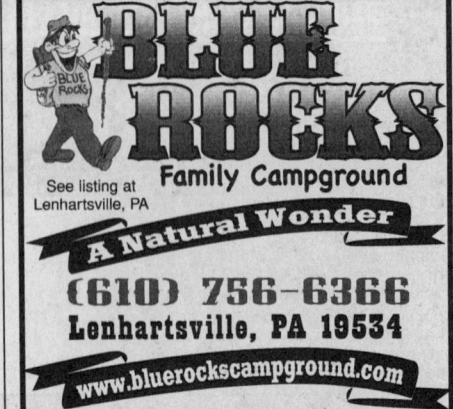

LEWISBURG—Continued

(SW) Little Mexico Campground—(Snyder) *From jct US 15 & SR-45: Go 4 mi S on US 15, then 6 mi W on SR-304, then 1 mi S on Little Mexico Rd. Enter on L.* ◆◆◆FACILITIES: 265 sites, typical site width 30 ft, 40 ft max RV length, 35 full hkups, 226 W&E, (20/30/50 amps), 4 no hkups, 20 pull-thrus, cable TV, WiFi Instant Internet at site, family camping, tenting, RV storage, dump, non-guest dump $, portable dump, laundry, groceries, RV supplies, LP gas by weight/by meter, ice, picnic tables, fire rings, wood. ◆◆◆RECREATION: pavilion, equipped pavilion, swim pool, canoeing, kayaking, pond/stream fishing, fishing supplies, mini-golf, ($), bsktball, playground, activities, horseshoes, v-ball. Pets welcome, quantity restrict. Partial handicap access. Open 3rd wknd Apr - 3rd wknd Oct. Rate in 2010 $31-33 for 4 persons. MC/VISA/DISC/Debit. Member ARVC, PCOA. CCUSA 50% Discount. CCUSA reservations Accepted, CCUSA max stay Unlimited, CCUSA disc. not avail F,Sa, CCUSA disc. not avail holidays. Not available 2nd weekend of Oct. $4 pet surcharge if 3 or more.

Phone: (570)374-9742
Address: 1640 Little Mexico Rd, Winfield, PA 17889
Lat/Lon: 40.87395/-76.94145
Email: camping@littlemexico.net
Web: www.littlemexico.net

R. B. WINTER STATE PARK—(Union) *From jct US 15 & Hwy 192: Go 18 mi W on Hwy 192.* FACILITIES: 59 sites, 21 E, (50 amps), 38 no hkups, 1 pull-thrus, tenting, dump. RECREATION: lake swim, stream fishing, playground. No pets. Partial handicap access. Open Apr 10 - Dec 15. Phone: (570)966-1455.

(S) River Edge RV Camp & Marina—(Union) *From jct US 15 & SR 45: Go 4-1/2 mi S on US 15, then 100 yds SE on 7 Kitchens Rd, then 100 ft NE on Reitz Rd, then 1/4 mi E on Riveredge Lane. Enter at end.* ◆◆FACILITIES: 140 sites, typical site width 27 ft, 3 full hkups, 123 W&E, 7 E, (20/30/50 amps), 7 no hkups, 8 pull-thrus, family camping, tenting, dump, laundry, ltd groc. ◆◆RECREATION: river swim, boating, canoeing, ramp, dock, river fishing, playground. Pets welcome, breed restrict. Partial handicap access. Open Apr 1 - Oct 31. Big rigs welcome. Rate in 2010 $32-35 per family. Member ARVC, PCOA. Phone: (570)524-0453.

LEWISTOWN—D-6

(S) WATERSIDE CAMPGROUND & RV PARK—(Mifflin) *From jct US 22 & SR-322: Go 4 mi W on US 22, (take Bus-22 exit), then 1 mi SE on Industrial Park Rd, then 1 mi S on Locust Rd. Enter at end.*

◆◆◆FACILITIES: 240 sites, typical site width 34 ft, 230 full hkups, (20/30/50 amps), 10 no hkups, some extd stay sites, cable TV, WiFi Instant Internet at site, WiFi Internet central location, family camping, tenting, cabins, RV storage, shower$, dump, non-guest dump $, laundry, ltd groc, RV supplies, LP gas by weight/by meter, ice, picnic tables, fire rings, wood, controlled access.

◆◆◆◆RECREATION: rec hall, rec room/area, coin games, swim pool, river swim, boating, canoeing, kayaking, ramp, river fishing, fishing supplies, golf nearby, bsktball, playground, activities, horseshoes, sports field, hiking trails, v-ball.

Pets welcome. Partial handicap access. Open all yr. Big rigs welcome. Escort to site. Clubs welcome. Rate in 2010 $35 per family. MC/VISA/DISC/Debit. ATM. Member ARVC, PCOA.

Text 107994 to (440)725-8687 to see our Visual Tour.

Phone: (717)248-3974
Address: 475 Locust Road, Lewistown, PA 17044
Lat/Lon: 40.55918/-77.59924
Email: info@watersidecampground.com
Web: www.watersidecampground.com

SEE AD THIS PAGE

LICKDALE—D-7

(E) LICKDALE CAMPGROUND—(Lebanon) *From jct I-81 & SR 72 (exit 90): Go 999 ft E on Lickdale Rd. Enter on L.*

◆◆◆◆FACILITIES: 90 sites, typical site width 30 ft, 85 full hkups, 2 W&E, (30/50 amps), 3 no hkups, some extd stay sites (summer), 39 pull-thrus, cable TV, WiFi Instant Internet at site, family camping, tenting, cabins, RV storage, dump, non-guest dump $, laundry, full svc store, RV supplies, LP gas by weight/by meter, ice, picnic tables, patios, fire rings, wood.

◆◆◆RECREATION: rec hall, rec room/area, coin games, river swim, boating, no motors, canoeing, kayaking, 10 canoe/4 kayak rentals, float trips, stream fishing, fishing supplies, golf nearby, bsktball, 10 bike rentals, playground, shuffleboard court shuffleboard court, activities (wkends), horseshoes, hiking trails, v-ball, local tours.

LICKDALE—Continued
LICKDALE CAMPGROUND—Continued

Pets welcome. Partial handicap access. Open all yr. Big rigs welcome. Escort to site. Clubs welcome. Rate in 2010 $32.50-40 per family. MC/VISA/DISC/Debit. ATM. Member ARVC, PCOA.

Phone: (877)865-6411
Address: 11 Lickdale Rd, Jonestown, PA 17038
Lat/Lon: 40.45180/-76.51134
Email: camp@lickdalecampground.com
Web: www.lickdalecampground.com

SEE AD THIS PAGE

(E) LICKDALE CAMPGROUND & CANOE RENTALS—*From jct I-81 & SR 72: Go 999 ft E on Lickdale Rd. Enter on L.* General Store open 5am to 9pm Mon-Fri and Sat & Sun 6am to 9pm. Canoe, kayak and tube rentals with livery service 7 days a week. Open May 1 - Oct 31. MC/VISA/DISC/Debit. ATM.

Phone: (877)865-6411
Address: 11 Lickdale Rd, Jonestown, PA 17038
Lat/Lon: 40.45180/-76.51134
Email: camp@lickdalecampground.com
Web: www.lickdalecampground.com

SEE AD THIS PAGE

(N) TWIN GROVE RESORT KOA AT PINE GROVE—(Lebanon) *From jct I-81 & SR-443 (exit 100): Go 5 mi W on SR-443. Enter on R.*

◆◆◆◆◆FACILITIES: 183 sites, typical site width 38 ft, 170 full hkups, 4 E, (30/50 amps), 9 no hkups, some extd stay sites (summer), 65 pull-thrus, cable TV, WiFi Instant Internet at site, WiFi Internet central location, family camping, tenting, cabins, dump, non-guest dump $, laundry, full svc store, RV supplies, LP gas by weight/by meter, LP bottle exch, ice, picnic tables, fire rings, wood, controlled access.

◆◆◆◆◆RECREATION: rec hall, rec room/area, pavilion, equipped pavilion, coin games, swim pool, stream fishing, mini-golf, ($), golf nearby, bsktball, playground, shuffleboard court shuffleboard court, activities, horseshoes, sports field, v-ball. Rec open to public.

Pets welcome, breed restrict, quantity restrict. Partial handicap access. Open all yr. Big rigs welcome. Escort to site. Clubs welcome. Rate in 2010 $30-63 per family. MC/VISA/DISC/Debit. ATM. Member ARVC, PCOA. KOA discount.

Phone: (800)562-5471
Address: 1445 Suedburg Rd, Pine Grove, PA 17963
Lat/Lon: 40.51417/-76.51250
Email: info@twingrove.com
Web: www.twingrove.com

SEE AD HERSHEY PAGE 661 AND AD TRAVEL SECTION PAGE 640

(W) TWIN GROVE RESTAURANT—*From jct of I-81 & SR 443 (exit 100): Go 5 mi W on SR 443. Enter on R.* Casual dining of PA Dutch cooking. Homemade cakes and pies. Serving breakfast, lunch and dinner. Open Apr - Oct. MC/VISA/DISC.

Phone: (800)562-5471
Address: 1445 Suedburg Rd, Pine Grove, PA 17963
Lat/Lon: 40.51417/-76.51250
Email: info@twingrovepark.com
Web: www.twingrove.com

SEE AD HERSHEY PAGE 661

LINESVILLE—B-1

(NW) Mallards Landing Family Campground—(Crawford) *From jct US 6 & Linesville Rd: Go 3-3/4 mi W on US 6, then 1/2 mi S on Footsville Rd. Enter on L.* ◆◆◆FACILITIES: 98 sites, typical site width 40 ft, 54 full hkups, 32 W&E, 2 E, (20/30/50 amps), 10 no hkups, 20 pull-thrus, family camping, tenting, dump, ltd

LINESVILLE—Continued
Mallards Landing Family Campground—Continued

groc. ◆◆◆RECREATION: swim pool, pond fishing, playground. Pets welcome. Partial handicap access. Open Apr 15 - Oct 15. Big rigs welcome. Rate in 2010 $24-26 for 2 persons. Member ARVC, PCOA. Phone: (814)683-5870.

(NE) Pineview Camplands, LLC—(Crawford) *From jct US 6 & Linesville-Hartstown Rd: Go 1 mi E on US 6, then 1-3/4 mi E on Harmonsburg Rd, then 3/4 mi N on Shermansville Rd. Enter on L.* ◆◆◆FACILITIES: 117 sites, typical site width 30 ft, 94 full hkups, 23 W&E, (20/30/50 amps), family camping, tenting, dump, ltd groc. ◆◆RECREATION: pond fishing, play equipment. Pets welcome, breed restrict, quantity restrict. Open Apr 15 - Oct 15. Big rigs welcome. Rate in 2010 $20-30 per family. Member ARVC, PCOA. Phone: (814)683-5561.

PYMATUNING STATE PARK (Linesville Camp)—(Crawford) *From town: Go 2 mi W on W Erie St. Enter at end.* FACILITIES: 115 sites, 30 ft max RV length, 68 E, (30/50 amps), 47 no hkups, tenting, dump, laundry. RECREATION: lake swim, boating, 10 hp limit, canoeing, ramp, lake fishing, playground. No pets. Partial handicap access. Open Mid Apr - Mid Dec. Phone: (724) 932-3141.

LIVERPOOL—D-6

(S) Ferryboat Campsites—(Perry) *From jct Hwy 17 & US 11/15: Go 2 mi S on US 11/15. Use highway turn around to go N 1 mi to entrance. Enter on R.* ◆◆◆FACILITIES: 305 sites, typical site width 28 ft, 40 ft max RV length, 287 full hkups, 3 W&E, (20/30 amps), 15 no hkups, 20 pull-thrus, family camping, tenting, dump, laundry, groceries. ◆◆◆RECREATION: river swim, boating, ramp, dock, river/pond fishing, playground. Pets welcome. Partial handicap access. Open Apr 15 - Oct 31. Rate in 2010 $30-43 for 4 persons. Member ARVC, PCOA. Phone: (800)759-8707.

LOGANTON—C-6

(NE) Holiday Pines Campground—(Clinton) *From jct I-80 (exit 185) & SR-477: Go 1/4 mi N on SR-477, then 2 mi E on Rockey Rd. Enter on R.* ◆◆FACILITIES: 84 sites, typical site width 28 ft, 20 full hkups, 48 W&E, (20/30 amps), 16 no hkups, 38 pull-thrus, family camping, tenting, dump, laundry, groceries. ◆◆◆RECREATION: swim pool, playground. Pets welcome. Partial handicap access. Open Apr 1 - Dec 15. Rate in 2010 $35-39 for 4 persons. Member ARVC, PCOA. Phone: (570)725-2267.

Woodall's Tip... To be considered a "Big Rig Friendly" park, the campground must meet the following requirements: minimum of 50 amps, adequate road width, overhead access clearance, site clearance to accommodate the tallest and widest rigs built. Often not every site can accommodate a big rig, so we recommend that you call ahead for availability.

LOYSVILLE—E-6

(W) PARADISE STREAM FAMILY CAMPGROUND—(Perry) *From east jct SR 850 & SR 274: Go 5 mi W on SR 274, then 1/4 mi S on SR 3008 (Couchtown Rd). Enter on R.*

◆◆◆◆FACILITIES: 145 sites, typical site width 40 ft, 128 full hkups, 17 W&E, (20/30/50 amps), 50 amps ($), many extd stay sites (summer), 19 pull-thrus, heater not allowed, WiFi Internet central location, family camping, tenting, cabins, RV storage, dump, non-guest dump $, laundry, ltd groc, RV supplies, LP gas by weight/by meter, ice, picnic tables, fire rings, wood, controlled access.

◆◆◆◆◆RECREATION: rec hall, rec room/area, pavilion, equipped pavilion, coin games, swim pool, boating, no motors, canoeing, kayaking, 2 canoe/2 pedal boat rentals, lake/stream fishing, fishing supplies, mini-golf, ($), golf nearby, bsktball, playground, shuffleboard court shuffleboard court, activities (wkends), horseshoes, sports field, hiking trails, v-ball.

Pets welcome, quantity restrict. Partial handicap access. Open Mid April - End of Oct. Big rigs welcome. Clubs welcome. Rate in 2010 $38-41 per family. MC/VISA/DISC/Debit. Member ARVC, PCOA.

Phone: (717)789-2117
Address: 693 Paradise Stream Rd, Loysville, PA 17047
Lat/Lon: 40.34584/-77.42769
Email: camparadise@embarqmail.com
Web: www.campparadisestream.com

SEE AD THIS PAGE

MAHANOY CITY—D-8

LOCUST LAKE STATE PARK—(Schuylkill) *From I-81N & PA 54W (exit 131B): Go 1-1/4 mi Left on to PA -1008, then 1 mi left onto PA 1006, then 1-1/2 mi straight onto PA 1011, then 1 mi right on Township Rd 489.* FACILITIES: 282 sites, typical site width 15 ft, 80 E, 202 no hkups, tenting, dump, ltd groc. RECREATION: lake swim, boating, electric motors only, canoeing, ramp, dock, lake fishing, playground. Pets welcome. Partial handicap access. Open mid Apr - mid Oct. Phone: (570)467-2404.

MANHEIM—E-8

(NW) Gretna Oaks Camping—(Lancaster) *From jct Pa Tpk (exit 266/20) & SR 72: Go 1 mi S on SR 72, then 1/2 mi W on Cider Press Rd, then 3/4 mi N on Pinch Rd, then 1/2 mi W on Camp Rd. Enter on L.* ◆◆FACILITIES: 38 sites, typical site width 27 ft, 39 ft max RV length, 28 full hkups, 3 W&E, (20/30/50 amps), 7 no hkups, family camping, tenting, dump, laundry, ltd groc. Pets welcome. Open Apr 15 - Oct 31. Rate in 2010 $32-35 for 4 persons. Phone: (717)665-7120. FMCA discount.

PA DUTCH COUNTY - OUTDOOR WORLD (CAMP RESORT)—(Lancaster) *185 Lehman Rd. Manheim, PA 17545.*

Phone: (800)579-4987
Address: 185 Lehman Rd, Manheim, PA 17545
Email: www.oneparkmembership.com

SEE AD ADAMSTOWN PAGE 648

(NW) PINCH POND FAMILY CAMPGROUND & RV PARK—(Lancaster) *From jct PA Tpk (exit 266/20) & SR 72: Go 1 mi S on SR 72, then 1/2 mi W on Cider Press Rd, then 1 mi N on Pinch Rd. Enter on R.*

◆◆◆◆◆FACILITIES: 190 sites, typical site width 35 ft, 168 full hkups, 17 W&E, (20/30/50 amps), 5 no hkups, some extd stay sites, 42 pull-thrus, cable TV, WiFi Instant Internet at site ($), WiFi Internet central location, family camping, tenting, cabins, RV storage, dump, non-guest dump $, laundry,

MANHEIM—Continued
PINCH POND FAMILY CAMPGROUND & RV PARK—Continued

groceries, RV supplies, LP gas by weight/by meter, ice, picnic tables, fire rings, wood, controlled access.

◆◆◆◆◆RECREATION: rec hall, rec room/area, equipped pavilion, coin games, swim pool, pond/stream fishing, fishing supplies, golf nearby, bsktball, playground, activities, (wkends), horseshoes, sports field.

Pets welcome. Partial handicap access. Open all yr. Limited service in winter months. Big rigs welcome. Escort to site. Clubs welcome. Rate in 2010 $38-45 per family. MC/VISA/DISC. Member ARVC, PCOA. FMCA discount.

Phone: (800)659-7640
Address: 3075 Pinch Rd, Manheim, PA 17545
Lat/Lon: 40.22942/-76.45225
Email: jmspond@aol.com
Web: www.pinchpond.com

SEE AD LANCASTER PAGES 664-666 AND AD LANCASTER PAGE 667

MANSFIELD—B-6

(NE) Bucktail Camping Resort—(Tioga) *From jct US 15 & US 6: Go 400 yds E on US 6, then 1-1/4 mi N on Lambs Creek Rd (10 ton limit), then 1 mi SW on Mann Creek Rd (Entrance has a steep grade). Enter on L.* ◆◆◆FACILITIES: 175 sites, typical site width 25 ft, 151 full hkups, 24 W&E, (20/30/50 amps), 10 pull-thrus, family camping, tenting, dump, laundry, ltd groc. ◆◆◆RECREATION: swim pool, pond fishing, playground. Pets welcome. Partial handicap access. Open Apr 15 - Oct 31. Big rigs welcome. Rate in 2010 $19-59.75 per family. Member ARVC, PCOA. Phone: (570) 662-2923.

MARIENVILLE—B-3

(N) ALLEGHENY NATIONAL FOREST (Beaver Meadows Campground)—(Forest) *From business center: Go 4 mi N on FR-128 follow signs.* FACILITIES: 38 sites, 38 no hkups, tenting. RECREATION: boating, no motors, canoeing, ramp, lake fishing, playground. Partial handicap access. Open all yr. Facilities fully operational Apr 1 - Dec 14. Phone: (814)927-6628.

ALLEGHENY NATIONAL FOREST (Loleta Campground)—(Elk) *From town: Go 6 mi S on Hwy 27027.* FACILITIES: 38 sites, 20 E, 18 no hkups, tenting. RECREATION: lake swim, canoeing, lake/stream fishing. Partial handicap access. Open Mid Apr - Mid Dec. - Apr 1. Phone: (814)927-6628.

(S) Forest Ridge Campground (Not Visited)—(Forest) *From jct SR-899 & SR-66: Go 1 mi N on SR-66, then 2-1/4 mi S on S. Forest St/Loleta Rd. Enter on R.* FACILITIES: 63 sites, typical site width 30 ft, 45 full hkups, 12 W&E, (20/30 amps), 6 no hkups, 3 pull-thrus, WiFi Instant Internet at site, family camping, tenting, ltd groc, LP gas by weight, ice, picnic tables, fire rings, wood. RECREATION: pavilion, bsktball, playground, horseshoes, hiking trails, v-ball. Pets welcome, breed restrict, quantity restrict. Open May 1 - mid Dec. Rate in 2010 $23-30 for 2 persons. MC/VISA. Member ARVC, PCOA. CCUSA 50% Discount. CCUSA reservations Recommended, CCUSA max stay 1 day, Cash only for CCUSA disc., CCUSA disc. not avail F,Sa, CCUSA disc. not avail holidays.

Phone: (814)927-8340
Address: HC 3 Box 214, Marienville, PA 16239
Lat/Lon: 41.43873/-79.11800
Email: forestridgecabins@verizon.net
Web: www.forestridgecabins.com

MARSHALLS CREEK—C-9

OTTER LAKE CAMP RESORT—*From Marshalls Creek (jct US 209 & Hwy 402): Go 300 feet NW on SR 402, then 7-1/2 mi N on Marshalls Creek Rd. Enter on L.*

SEE PRIMARY LISTING AT STROUDSBURG AND AD STROUDSBURG PAGE 680

MATAMORAS—B-10

(S) Tri-State RV Park—(Pike) *From jct I-84 (exit 53 w/bound) & US 209: Go 1/4 mi S on US 209/US 6, then 3/4 mi E on Reuben Bell Dr. Enter at end.* ◆◆FACILITIES: 53 sites, typical site width 26 ft, 30 full hkups, 23 W&E, (15/20/30/50 amps), 15 pull-thrus, family camping, tenting, dump, laundry. ◆RECREATION: boating, 10 hp limit, canoeing, ramp, river fishing. Pets welcome. Partial handicap access. Open all yr. Big rigs welcome. Rate in 2010 $33-35 for 4 persons. Phone: (800)562-2663.

MEADVILLE—B-1

(E) BROOKDALE FAMILY CAMPGROUND—(Crawford) *I-79 (exit 147A) SR 6 & SR 19 to Park Ave exit. Go straight up Park Ave to North St. Follow SR 77 until it turns left. Follow SR 27 E 5 mi (straight). Enter on L.*

◆◆◆◆FACILITIES: 162 sites, typical site width 25 ft, 124 full hkups, 23 W&E, (30/50 amps), 50 amps ($), 15 no hkups, some extd stay sites (summer), 33 pull-thrus, WiFi Instant Internet at site, WiFi Internet central location, family camping, tenting, cabins, RV storage, dump, non-guest dump $, laundry, groceries, RV supplies, LP gas by weight/by meter, ice, picnic tables, fire rings, wood, controlled access.

◆◆◆◆◆RECREATION: rec hall, rec room/area, pavilion, coin games, swim pool, 6 pedal boat rentals, lake/pond fishing, fishing supplies, mini-golf, ($), golf nearby, bsktball, 2 bike rentals, playground, activities, (wkends), horseshoes, sports field, hiking trails, v-ball.

Pets welcome. Partial handicap access. Open Apr 29 - Oct 17. Escort to site. Clubs welcome. Rate in 2010 $31-44 per family. MC/VISA/DISC/Debit. ATM. Member ARVC, PCOA.

Phone: (814)789-3251
Address: 25164 State Hwy 27, Meadville, PA 16335
Lat/Lon: 41.62231/-80.03849
Email: camp@brookdalecampground.com
Web: www.brookdalecampground.com

SEE AD THIS PAGE

MERCER—C-1

(SE) KOA-Mercer/Grove City—(Mercer) *From jct I-80 & I-79: Go 3 mi S on I-79 to exit 113, then 3 mi N on SR-258. Enter on R.* ◆◆◆FACILITIES: 158 sites, typical site width 26 ft, 143 full hkups, 15 W&E, (20/30/50 amps), 33 pull-thrus, family camping, tenting, laundry, groceries. ◆◆◆RECREATION: swim pool, lake fishing, playground. Pets welcome. Partial handicap access. Open Apr 1 - Oct 31. Big rigs welcome. Rate in 2010 $40-65 for 4 persons. Member ARVC, PCOA. Phone: (724)748-3160. KOA discount.

(NW) RV Village Camping Resort—(Mercer) *I-80 (exit 15) & US 19: Go 3 mi N on US 19,then 2 blks W on SR 62, then 3 mi NW on SR-258, then 1/2 mi S on Skyline Dr. Enter on R.* ◆◆◆FACILITIES: 296 sites, 190 full hkups, 106 W&E, (20/30/50 amps), 10 pull-thrus, family camping, tenting, dump, laundry, ltd groc. ◆◆◆RECREATION: swim pool, pond fishing, playground. Pets welcome. Open Apr 1 - Oct 31. Big rigs welcome. Rate in 2010 $28 per family. Member ARVC, PCOA. Phone: (724)662-4560.

MERCERSBURG—F-5

Saunderosa Park Inc—(Franklin) *From jct St 16 & St 456: Go 2 mi S on ST 456. Enter on R.* ◆◆◆FACILITIES: 310 sites, typical site width 50 ft, 250 full hkups, 60 W&E, (30/50 amps), 10 pull-thrus, family camping, tenting, dump, laundry, ltd groc. ◆◆◆RECREATION: swim pool, lake swim, lake fishing, playground. Open May 1 - Nov 1. Big rigs welcome. Rate in 2010 $28-30. Phone: (717)328-2216.

Penn Township, officially referred to as the Township of Penn, was named after the founder of Pennsylvania, William Penn.

MESHOPPEN—B-8

(N) Day's End Campground—(Susquehanna) *From jct SR-267 & US 6: Go 8-3/4 mi N on SR-267, then 2 mi E on SR 3004, then 1/2 mi N on Chase Rd. Enter on R.* ◆◆◆FACILITIES: 55 sites, typical site width 30 ft, 45 W&E, (15/20/30 amps), 10 no hkups, tenting, dump, ltd groc. ◆◆◆RECREATION: pond fishing. Pets welcome, size restrict. Age restrict may apply. Open May 1 - Mid Oct. Rate in 2010 $24-26 for 2 persons. Phone: (570)965-2144.

(SE) Slumber Valley Campground—(Wyoming) *From jct SR-267 & US 6: Go 1 mi E on US 6, then 1 mi N on SR 4008. Enter on L.* ◆◆FACILITIES: 67 sites, typical site width 50 ft, 4 full hkups, 43 W&E, (20/30 amps), 20 no hkups, 10 pull-thrus, family camping, tenting, dump, laundry, ltd groc. ◆◆◆◆RECREATION: swim pool, pond/stream fishing, playground. Pets welcome. Partial handicap access. Open Mid Apr - Mid Oct. Rate in 2010 $30-32 per family. Member ARVC, PCOA. Phone: (570)833-5208.

MEXICO—D-6

(SW) Buttonwood Campground—(Juniata) *From jct US 22/322 & SR 75: Go 1/2 mi S on SR 75, then 1 mi SE on Old US 322, then 1/4 mi S on Front St, then 1/4 mi SW on River Rd. Enter on R.* ◆◆◆◆FACILITIES: 270 sites, typical site width 30 ft, 248 full hkups, 16 W&E, (15/20/30/50 amps), 6 no hkups, 26 pull-thrus, family camping, tenting, dump, laundry, ltd groc. ◆◆◆◆◆RECREATION: swim pool, river swim, boating, ramp, river fishing, playground. Pets welcome. Partial handicap access. Open Apr 1 - Oct 31. Big rigs welcome. Rate in 2010 $36-42.50 per family. Member ARVC, PCOA. Phone: (717)436-8334.

MILFORD—C-10

(NE) River Beach Campsites on the Delaware-Kittatinny Canoes—(Pike) *From jct I-84 (exit 53) & US 209: Go 3 mi S on US 209. Enter on L.* ◆◆◆FACILITIES: 165 sites, typical site width 26 ft, 54 W&E, (20/30 amps), 111 no hkups, 11 pull-thrus, family camping, tenting, dump, laundry, ltd groc. ◆◆◆◆RECREATION: river swim, boating, canoeing, ramp, river fishing. Pets welcome, quantity restrict. Partial handicap access. Open Apr 1 - Oct 31. Rate in 2010 $32 for 4 persons. Member ARVC, PCOA. Phone: (800)FLOAT-KC.

MILL RUN—E-2

(S) Yogi Bear's Jellystone Park Camp-Resort-Mill Run—(Fayette) *From south town limits: Go 1/8 mi S on SR-381. Enter on R.* ◆◆◆◆◆FACILITIES: 201 sites, typical site width 30 ft, 160 full hkups, 10 W&E, (20/30/50 amps), 31 no hkups, 40 pull-thrus, family camping, tenting, dump, laundry, groceries. ◆◆◆◆◆RECREATION: 2 swim pools, pond fishing, playground. Pets welcome ($), breed restrict. Partial handicap access. Open all yr. Facilities fully operational Apr 15 - Oct 31. Big rigs welcome. Rate in 2010 $53-63 per family. Member ARVC, PCOA. Phone: (800)439-9644.

MILTON—C-7

(S) Yogi At Shangri-La On the Creek—(Northumberland) *From I-80 (exit 212A/31A) & SR 147: Go 8 mi S on SR 147, then 1/4 mi NW on SR 405, then 3/4 mi E on Hidden Paradise Rd. Enter at end.* ◆◆◆◆FACILITIES: 162 sites, typical site width 30 ft, 45 full hkups, 102 W&E, (20/30/50 amps), 15 no hkups, 32 pull-thrus, family camping, tenting, dump, laundry, groceries. ◆◆◆◆◆RECREATION: swim pool, canoeing, pond/stream fishing, playground. Pets welcome, quantity restrict. Partial handicap access. Open all yr. Facilities fully operational Mid Apr - Nov 1. Rate in 2010 $34-46 per family. Member ARVC, PCOA. Phone: (570)524-4561. FMCA discount.

MONTGOMERY—C-7

(S) Riverside Campground—(Lycoming) *From jct US 15 & SR 54: Go 3 mi E on SR 54, then 1/4 mi E on S Main St. Enter at end.* ◆◆FACILITIES: 141 sites, typical site width 30 ft, 91 full hkups, 30 W&E, (20/30/50 amps), 20 no hkups, 8 pull-thrus, family camping, tenting, dump, laundry. ◆◆RECREATION: swim pool, river swim, boating, canoeing, dock, river fishing. Pets welcome. Partial handicap access. Open all yr. Big rigs welcome. Rate in 2010 $36-40 for 2 persons. Member ARVC, PCOA. Phone: (570)547-6289.

MOUNT BETHEL—C-10

(SE) DRIFTSTONE ON THE DELAWARE—(Northampton) *From jct SR-611 & Portland-Columbia Bridge/River Rd: Go 3-3/4 mi S on River Rd. Enter on L.*

WELCOME

◆◆◆◆FACILITIES: 190 sites, typical site width 50 ft, 40 ft max RV length, 184 W&E, (20/30/50 amps), 6 no hkups, some extd stay sites (summer), 7 pull-thrus, cable TV, WiFi Instant Internet at site, WiFi Internet central location, family camping, tenting, dump, portable dump, laundry, groceries, RV supplies, LP gas by weight/by meter, ice, picnic tables, fire rings, wood, controlled access.

MOUNT BETHEL—Continued
DRIFTSTONE ON THE DELAWARE—Continued

◆◆◆◆◆RECREATION: rec hall, rec room/area, coin games, swim pool, wading pool, river swim, boating, 50 hp limit, canoeing, kayaking, ramp, dock, 18 canoe/34 kayak rentals, float trips, river fishing, fishing supplies, golf nearby, bsktball, playground, activities, horseshoes, sports field, v-ball.

Pets welcome, quantity restrict. Partial handicap access. Open Mid May - Mid Sep. Rate in 2010 $33-52 for 2 persons. MC/VISA/Debit. Member ARVC, PCOA.

Phone: (570)897-6859
Address: 2731 River Rd, Mt Bethel, PA 18343
Lat/Lon: 40.87374/-75.05746
Email: office@driftstone.com
Web: www.driftstone.com

SEE AD THIS PAGE

MOUNT MORRIS—F-1

(N) Mt. Morris Travel Trailer Park—(Greene) *From I-79 (exit 1): Go 1/2 mi W on Locust Ave, then 1 mi N on US 19. Enter on L.* ◆◆◆FACILITIES: 30 sites, typical site width 37 ft, 17 full hkups, 13 W&E, (15/20/30 amps), 8 pull-thrus, family camping, tenting, dump, laundry. Pets welcome, breed restrict. Open all yr. Facilities fully operational Apr 1 - Nov 1. Rate in 2010 $33 for 2 persons. Phone: (724)324-2432.

MOUNT POCONO—C-9

(N) Mount Pocono Campground—(Monroe) *From jct SR-611, PA 940 & SR-196: Go 3/4 mi N on SR-196, then 1/2 mi E (Right turn) on Edgewood Rd. Enter at end.* ◆◆◆◆FACILITIES: 191 sites, typical site width 40 ft, 123 full hkups, 25 W&E, 6 E, (20/30/50 amps), 37 no hkups, 23 pull-thrus, family camping, tenting, laundry, groceries. ◆◆◆◆RECREATION: swim pool, playground. Pets welcome. Partial handicap access. Age restrict may apply. Open May 1 - Oct 31. Big rigs welcome. Rate in 2010 $40-50 for 2 persons. Member ARVC, PCOA. Phone: (570)839-8950.

MT. COBB—B-9

(NE) CLAYTON PARK RECREATION AREA—(Wayne) *From jct I-84 (exit 8) & Rt 247: Go 250 yds N on Rt 247, then 1/2 mi E on Rt 348 (Mt Cobb Rd), then 4-1/2 mi N on Cortez Rd, then 1/2 mi SE on Maplewood Rd, then 1/4 mi E on Swoyer Rd. Enter on R.*

◆◆◆FACILITIES: 96 sites, typical site width 35 ft, 29 full hkups, 58 W&E, (30/50 amps), 9 no hkups, many extd stay sites (summer), 5 pull-thrus, WiFi Instant Internet at site, WiFi Internet central location, family camping, tenting, RV's/park model rentals, RV storage, shower$, dump, non-guest dump $, laundry, ltd groc, RV supplies, LP bottle exch, ice, picnic tables, fire rings, wood.

◆◆RECREATION: rec room/area, pavilion, lake swim, boating, canoeing, kayaking, ramp, dock, 7 rowboat/2 canoe rentals, lake fishing, fishing supplies, golf nearby, bsktball, playground, activities, (wkends), horseshoes, hiking trails.

Pets welcome, breed restrict. Open May 1 - Oct 15. Big rigs welcome. Escort to site. Green Friendly. Rate in 2010 $30-44 per family. MC/VISA/Debit. Member ARVC, PCOA.

Phone: (570)698-6080
Address: 26 Eagle Eye Dr, Lake Ariel, PA 18436
Lat/Lon: 41.45540/-75.45149
Email: camp@claytonpark.net
Web: www.claytonpark.net

SEE AD POCONO MOUNTAINS PAGE 675

NEW ALEXANDRIA—D-2

KEYSTONE STATE PARK—(Westmoreland) *From jct US 22 & Hwy 981: Go 1/4 mi S on Hwy 981, then follow signs 2-1/2 mi E.* FACILITIES: 100 sites, 25 E, (30/50 amps), 75 no hkups, 28 pull-thrus, tenting, dump, ltd groc. RECREATION: lake swim, boating, electric motors only, canoeing, ramp, dock, lake fishing. Pets welcome. Partial handicap access. Open all yr. Facilities fully operational Early Apr - Mid Oct. Phone: (724)668-2939.

NEW COLUMBIA—C-7

(W) Williamsport South/Nittany Mountain KOA—(Union) *From jct I-80 (exit 210 South) & US 15: Go 1/4 mi S on US 15, then 4-1/4 mi W on New Columbia Rd, then 1/4 mi N on Miller's Bottom Rd. Enter on R.* ◆◆◆FACILITIES: 347 sites, typical site width 35 ft, 37 full hkups, 303 W&E, (20/30/50 amps), 50 amps ($), 7 no hkups, 25 pull-thrus, family camping, tenting, dump, laundry, groceries. ◆◆◆◆RECREATION: swim pool, pond fishing, playground. Pets welcome, quantity restrict. Partial handicap access. Open Apr 1 - Nov 1. Big rigs welcome. Rate in 2010 $34-52 for 2 persons. Member ARVC, PCOA. Phone: (570)568-5541. KOA discount.

NEW HOLLAND—E-8

(SE) COUNTRY HAVEN CAMPGROUND—(Lancaster) *From jct SR 23 & SR 897: Go 5-1/2 mi S on SR 897. Enter on R.*

WELCOME

◆◆◆◆FACILITIES: 58 sites, typical site width 26 ft, 58 full hkups, (20/30/50 amps), 8 pull-thrus, cable TV, WiFi Instant Internet at site, WiFi Internet central location, family camping, tenting, RV storage, dump, laundry, RV supplies, LP gas by weight/by meter, ice, picnic tables, fire rings, wood, controlled access.

◆◆◆RECREATION: play equipment.

Pets welcome. Partial handicap access. Open Apr 1 - Nov 1. Big rigs welcome. Escort to site. Clubs welcome. Rate in 2010 $41-55 per family. MC/VISA. Member ARVC, PCOA.

Phone: (717)354-7926
Address: 354 Springville Rd, New Holland, PA 17557
Lat/Lon: 40.05778/-76.02002
Web: www.countryhaven.com

SEE AD LANCASTER PAGES 664-666

(N) RED RUN CAMPGROUND—(Lancaster) *From jct SR 23 & US 322: Go 3 mi W on US 322, then 3 mi N on Grist Mill Rd, then 1/8 mi E on Martin Church Rd. Enter on L.*

WELCOME

◆◆◆◆FACILITIES: 125 sites, typical site width 26 ft, 40 ft max RV length, 125 W&E, (20/30/50 amps), some extd stay sites (summer), 21 pull-thrus, WiFi Internet central location, family camping, tenting, cabins, RV storage, dump, non-guest dump $, portable dump, laundry, ltd groc, RV supplies, LP gas by meter, ice, picnic tables, fire rings, wood.

◆◆◆◆RECREATION: rec hall, rec room/area, coin games, swim pool, boating, no motors, canoeing, kayaking, canoe/3 pedal boat rentals, pond/stream fishing, fishing supplies, golf nearby, bsktball, 5 bike rentals, playground, activities, (wkends), horseshoes, sports field, v-ball.

RED RUN CAMPGROUND—Continued on next page

NEW HOLLAND—*Continued*
RED RUN CAMPGROUND—*Continued*

Pets welcome. Open Apr 1 - Oct 31. Clubs welcome. Rate in 2010 $35-39 per family. MC/VISA/DISC/Debit. Member ARVC, PCOA.

Phone: (717)445-4526
Address: 877 Martin Church Rd, New Holland, PA 17557
Lat/Lon: 40.17543/-76.07969
Email: redruncampground@frontiernet.net
Web: www.REDRUNCAMPGROUND.com

SEE AD LANCASTER PAGES 664-666 AND AD TRAVEL SECTION PAGE 640

(SE) SPRING GULCH RESORT CAMPGROUND—(Lancaster) *From jct SR 23 & SR 897: Go 4 mi S on SR 897, then 50 yards E on Lynch Rd. Enter on L.*

◊◊◊◊FACILITIES: 420 sites, typical site width 32 ft, 290 full hkups, 110 W&E, (20/30/50 amps), 20 no hkups, some extd stay sites (summer), 40 pull-thrus, cable TV, WiFi Instant Internet at site ($), phone Internet central location, family camping, tenting, RV's/park model rentals, cabins, RV storage, dump, laundry, groceries, RV supplies, LP gas by weight/by meter, ice, picnic tables, fire rings, wood, controlled access.

◊◊◊◊RECREATION: rec hall, rec room/area, pavilion, coin games, 2 swim pools, lake swim, hot tub, lake fishing, fishing supplies, mini-golf, ($), golf nearby, bsktball, playground, shuffleboard court 2 shuffleboard courts, activities, tennis, horseshoes, sports field, hiking trails, v-ball.

Pets welcome, breed restrict. Partial handicap access. Open Late Mar - Early Nov. Big rigs welcome. Clubs welcome. Rate in 2010 $40-68 for 2 persons. MC/VISA/DISC/AMEX/Debit. ATM. Member ARVC, PCOA.

Phone: (717)354-3100
Address: 475 Lynch Rd, New Holland, PA 17557
Lat/Lon: 40.06539/-76.01719
Email: spring_gulch@equitylifestyle.com
Web: www.rvonthego.com

Reserve Online at Woodalls.com

SEE AD ADAMSTOWN PAGE 648

NEW MILFORD—B-9

(W) Montrose Campsites—(Susquehanna) *From I-81 (eixt 223) & Rt 492: Go 1/2 mi W on Rt 492, then 1 mi W on Rt 11, then 5-3/4 mi on Rt 706, then 1/4 mi NW on Rt 1026, then 1/4 mi N on Rt 1039, then 1 mi N on T776, then 1/4 mi N on Pratt Rd. Enter on L.* ◊◊FACILITIES: 60 sites, typical site width 40 ft, 50 full hkups, (20/30/50 amps), 10 no hkups, family camping, tenting, dump, laundry. ◊◊◊RECREATION: swim pool, playground. Pets welcome. Open Apr 15 - Oct 15. Big rigs welcome. Rate in 2010 $30 per family. Member ARVC, PCOA. Phone: (570)278-9999.

The Camp at East Lake (TOO NEW TO RATE)—*From jct of I-81 (exit 223) and PA 492: Go E .6 mi, then N on PA 1012 for 3.1 mi, then straight when PA 1012 ends. PA1012 turns into East Lake Road. Enter on L.* FACILITIES: 65 sites, typical site width 40 ft, 63 full hkups, 2 W&E, (30/50 amps), 12 pull-thrus, family camping, tenting, dump, laundry, groceries. RECREATION: lake swim, boating, lake fishing, playground. Pets welcome. Open May 1 - Dec 1. Big rigs welcome. Rate in 2010 $30-40 per family. Member ARVC, PCOA. Phone: (570)465-2267.

NEW RINGGOLD—D-8

(NE) Laurel Lake Campsites—(Schuylkill) *From jct SR 895 & SR 443: Go 1/2 mi W on SR 895. Enter on L.* ◊◊FACILITIES: 69 sites, typical site width 27 ft, 65 W&E, (15/20/30/50 amps), 4 no hkups, 4 pull-thrus, family camping, tenting, dump. ◊RECREATION: pond/stream fishing, play equipment. Pets welcome. Open Memorial Day - Labor Day. Rate in 2010 $25 per family. Member ARVC, PCOA. Phone: (570)386-5301.

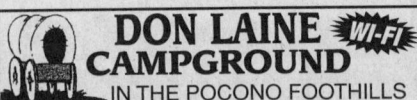

NEW STANTON—E-2

(NE) FOX DEN ACRES CAMPGROUND—(Westmoreland) *From I-70 (E'bnd: exit 57, W'bnd: exit 57B): Go 2 mi N on North Center Ave. Enter on L.*

◊◊◊FACILITIES: 350 sites, typical site width 28 ft, 260 full hkups, 20 W&E, 20 E, (20/30/50 amps), 50 no hkups, some extd stay sites (summer), 105 pull-thrus, heater not allowed, cable TV, WiFi Instant Internet at site, WiFi Internet central location, family camping, tenting, shower$, dump, non-guest dump $, full svc store, RV supplies, LP gas by weight/by meter, ice, picnic tables, fire rings, wood.

◊◊◊RECREATION: rec room/area, pavilion, coin games, swim pool, wading pool, lake swim, lake fishing, golf nearby, bsktball, playground, activities, (wkends), horseshoes, sports field, v-ball.

Pets welcome. Partial handicap access. Open May 1 - Oct 31. Big rigs welcome. Escort to site. Clubs welcome. Rate in 2010 $32 for 2 persons. MC/VISA/Debit.

Phone: (724)925-7054
Address: 390 Wilson Fox Rd, New Stanton, PA 15672
Lat/Lon: 40.23880/-79.59478
Email: steve@foxdenacres.com
Web: www.foxdenacres.com

SEE AD PITTSBURGH PAGE 674

(W) KOA-Madison/Pittsburgh—(Westmoreland) *From jct I-70 (exit 54) & Madison Rd: Go 3/4 mi N on Madison Rd. Enter on R.* ◊◊◊◊FACILITIES: 92 sites, typical site width 26 ft, 78 full hkups, 14 W&E, (20/30/50 amps), 101 pull-thrus, family camping, tenting, dump, laundry, groceries. ◊◊◊◊RECREATION: swim pool, canoeing, lake fishing, playground. Pets welcome. Partial handicap access. Open Apr 1 - Nov 1. Big rigs welcome. Rate in 2010 $36-52 for 2 persons. Member ARVC, PCOA. Phone: (800)562-4034. KOA discount.

NEWPORT—D-6

(SW) LITTLE BUFFALO FAMILY CAMPING—(Perry) *From jct US 22 & SR 34: Go 3 mi S on SR 34, then 3 mi W on Little Buffalo Rd, then 1/2 m N on Blackhill Rd. Enter on L.* FACILITIES: 40 sites, typical site width 40 ft, 12 full hkups, 19 W&E, (15/20/30 amps), 9 no hkups, 5 pull-thrus, tenting, dump. RECREATION: swim pool, boating, pond fishing, playground. Pets welcome. Partial handicap access. Open all yr. Facilities fully operational Apr - Mid Oct. Phone: (717)567-7370.

NEWVILLE—E-6

(N) COLONEL DENNING STATE PARK—(Cumberland) *From business center: Go 9 mi N on Hwy-233.* FACILITIES: 52 sites, 30 ft max RV length, 18 E, (30/50 amps), 34 no hkups, tenting, dump. RECREATION: lake swim, lake fishing, playground. No pets. Partial handicap access. Open Apr 17 - Dec 12. Phone: (717)776-5272.

NORTH EAST—A-2

Creekside Campground—(Erie) *From jct PA 430 and PA 89: Go 1 mi S on PA 89. Enter on R.* ◊FACILITIES: 100 sites, typical site width 40 ft, 34 ft max RV length, 60 W&E, (20 amps), 40 no hkups, family camping, tenting, dump, laundry, ltd groc. RECREATION: river swim, river fishing, playground. Pets welcome. Open May 1 - Sep 31. Rate in 2010 $30 per family. Phone: (814)725-5523. FMCA discount.

(SE) Family Affair Campground—(Erie) *From jct I-90 (exit 41) & SR- 89: Go 3/4 mi S on SR-89, then 2 mi E on Cole Rd, then 1 mi S on SR-426. Enter on R.* ◊◊FACILITIES: 299 sites, typical site width 31 ft, 100 full hkups, 149 W&E, (15/20/30/50 amps), 50 no hkups, 25 pull-thrus, family camping, tenting, dump, groceries. ◊◊◊RECREATION: 2 swim pools, boating, no motors, lake fishing, playground. Pets welcome, breed restrict. Partial handicap access. Open Apr 25 - Oct 15. Big rigs welcome. Rate in 2010 $25-30 per family. Member ARVC, PCOA. Phone: (814)725-8112.

✲ **(W) Ray Wakley's RV Center**—*From jct of SR 89 & US 20: Go 1-3/4 mi W on US 20. Enter on L.* SALES: travel trailers, 5th wheels, toy hauler, Class A motorhomes, Class C motorhomes, fold-down camping trailers, pre-owned unit sales. SERVICES: full-time mech, RV appliance repair, body work/collision repair, LP gas by weight/by meter, LP bottle exch, RV rentals, sells parts/accessories, installs hitches. Open all yr. MC/VISA/DISC/Debit.

Phone: (814)725-9608
Address: 10261 W Main Rd, North East, PA 16428
Lat/Lon: 42.20498/-79.86311
Email: brandall@wakleyrv.com
Web: www.wakleyrv.com

Woodall's Tip... Rate information is based on the campground's published rate last year. These rates aren't guaranteed, and you should always call ahead for the most updated rate information.

NORTH HUNTINGDON—E-2

(S) DUSTY RHODES MOBILE HOME VILLAGE (RV SPACES)—(Westmoreland) *From Intersection of Sr 48 & US 30, take US 30 .5 mi S. Enter on R.*

FACILITIES: 4 sites, 40 ft max RV length, accepts full hkup units only, 4 full hkups, (50 amps), family camping.

RECREATION: golf nearby.

Pets welcome. No tents. Open all yr. Rate in 2010 $30 for 4 persons.

Phone: (412)849-5341
Address: 14940 Rte 30, North Huntingdon, PA 15642
Lat/Lon: 40.36377/-79.77173

SEE AD PITTSBURGH PAGE 674

NORTH SPRINGFIELD—A-1

(W) Virginia's Beach Campground—(Erie) *From jct of I-90 & SR 215 (exit 6): Go 3-3/4 mi N on SR 215, then 1-1/2 N on Holliday Rd. Enter on R.* ◊◊FACILITIES: 141 sites, typical site width 30 ft, 126 full hkups, 10 W&E, (20/30/50 amps), 5 no hkups, 13 pull-thrus, family camping, tenting, dump, ltd groc. ◊◊RECREATION: lake swim, boating, ramp, lake/pond fishing, playground. Pets welcome, quantity restrict. Open mid May - mid Oct. Rate in 2010 $35-42 per family. Member ARVC, PCOA. Phone: (814)922-3261.

OHIOPYLE—E-2

(S) OHIOPYLE STATE PARK—(Fayette) *From business center: Go 1/4 mi S on Hwy-381 follow signs.* FACILITIES: 226 sites, typical site width 15 ft, 34 E, (20/30/50 amps), 50 amps ($), 192 no hkups, 6 pull-thrus, tenting, dump. RECREATION: canoeing, river/stream fishing, playground. No pets. Partial handicap access. Open Mar 1 - mid Dec. Phone: (724)329-8591.

OTTSVILLE—D-10

(NE) Beaver Valley Family Campground—(Bucks) *Call for directions (low weight limit bridges). Enter on L.* ◊◊FACILITIES: 85 sites, typical site width 30 ft, 35 ft max RV length, 85 W&E, (30 amps), 2 pull-thrus, family camping, tenting, dump, laundry, ltd groc. ◊◊◊RECREATION: swim pool, playground. Pets welcome, breed restrict, quantity restrict. Open Apr 2 - Oct 31. Rate in 2010 $33 for 2 persons. Member ARVC, PCOA. Phone: (610)847-5643.

PA GRAND CANYON

See listings at Covington, Gaines, Mansfield, Morris, Tioga & Wellsboro.

PALMERTON—D-9

(S) DON LAINE CAMPGROUND—(Carbon) *From south town limits: Go 1 mi SE on Church Dr, then 3/4 mi E on 57 Dr. Enter on R.*

◊◊◊FACILITIES: 166 sites, typical site width 27 ft, 100 full hkups, 66 W&E, (20/30/50 amps), many extd stay sites (summer), 37 pull-thrus, cable TV, ($), WiFi Instant Internet at site ($), WiFi Internet central location, family camping, tenting, RV storage, dump, non-guest dump $, laundry, full svc store, RV supplies, LP gas by weight/by meter, ice, picnic tables, fire rings, wood, controlled access.

◊◊◊RECREATION: rec hall, rec room/area, pavilion, coin games, swim pool, golf nearby, bsktball, playground, activities, (wkends), horseshoes, sports field, hiking trails, v-ball.

Pets welcome. Partial handicap access. Open End of April - End of Oct. Big rigs welcome. Clubs welcome. Rate in 2010 $27-33.50 per family. MC/VISA/DISC/Debit. Member ARVC, PCOA.

Phone: (610)381-3381
Address: 790 57 Drive, Palmerton, PA 18071
Lat/Lon: 40.86720/-75.51419
Email: dlaine@ptd.net
Web: www.donlaine.com

SEE AD THIS PAGE

PAVIA—E-4

(N) BLUE KNOB STATE PARK—(Bedford) *From small village follow signs 2 mi N.* FACILITIES: 45 sites, 25 E, (30/50 amps), 20 no hkups, tenting, dump. RECREATION: swim pool, stream fishing, playground. Open Apr 10 - Oct 18. Phone: (814) 276-3576.

PENFIELD—C-4

(N) PARKER DAM STATE PARK—(Clearfield) *From business center: Go 2 mi S on Hwy-153, then 2-1/2 mi E on park entrance road.* FACILITIES: 110 sites, 80 E, (30/50 amps), 30 no hkups, tenting, dump. RECREATION: lake swim, boating, ramp, dock, playground. Partial handicap access. Open mid Apr - late Dec. Phone: (814)765-0630.

PEQUEA—E-8

(N) PEQUEA CREEK CAMPGROUND (PPL)—(Lancaster) *From jct SR 324 & River Rd: Go 3/4 mi SW on SR 324 (Pequea Blvd), then S on (Fox Hollow Road bridge 11' 6" Hgt 5 ton limit). Or call for alternate route. Enter on L.*

◆◆◆FACILITIES: 107 sites, typical site width 27 ft, 105 W&E, (30 amps), 2 no hkups, many extd stay sites (summer), 19 pull-thrus, cable TV, ($), WiFi Internet central location, family camping, tenting, RV storage, shower$, dump, non-guest dump $, portable dump, laundry, ltd groc, RV supplies, LP gas by weight, ice, picnic tables, fire rings, wood.

◆◆◆RECREATION: equipped pavilion, coin games, boating, no motors, canoeing, kayaking, ramp, stream fishing, fishing supplies, golf nearby, bsktball, playground, activities, (wkends), horseshoes, sports field, hiking trails, v-ball.

Pets welcome. Partial handicap access. Open Apr 1 - Oct 31. Facilities fully operational Mid Apr - Mid Oct. Bridge has 5 ton, 11' 6" height limit. Clubs welcome. Rate in 2010 $32 per family. MC/VISA/DISC/AMEX/Debit. Member ARVC, PCOA. CCUSA 50% Discount. CCUSA reservations Recommended, CCUSA max stay 1 day, Cash only for CCUSA disc., CCUSA disc. not avail S, CCUSA disc. not avail F,Sa. Discount available Apr 1-weekend before Memorial Day & after Labor Day-Oct 31. Bridge has 5 ton, 11'6" limit.

Phone: (717)284-4587
Address: 86 Fox Hollow Rd, Pequea, PA 17565
Lat/Lon: 39.89848/-76.34248
Email: pequeacamp@comcast.net
Web: www.pequeacreekcampground.com

SEE AD LANCASTER PAGES 664-666 AND AD LANCASTER PAGE 667

Benjamin Franklin founded the Philadelphia Zoo, the first public zoo in the United States.

PHILADELPHIA—E-10

PHILADELPHIA AREA MAP

N
Upper Black Eddy · Revere · Stockton · Quakertown · Boyertown · Ottsville · Hatfield · Pemberton · Honey Brook · Coatesville · W. Chester · PHILADELPHIA · Chatsworth · Clarksboro · Glassboro · Williamstown · Woodstown · New Castle · Hammonton · Elmer · Buena · PA · DE · NJ · N.J.TPK. · 9 · 611 · 95 · 195 · 422 · 76 · 276 · 30 · 202 · 206 · 295 · 55 · 322 · 40 · 54

Symbols on map indicate towns within a 30 mi radius of Philadelphia where campgrounds (diamonds), attractions (flags), & RV service centers & camping supply outlets (gears) are listed. Check listings for more information.

Tell Them Woodall's Sent You!

PHILADELPHIA—Continued on next page

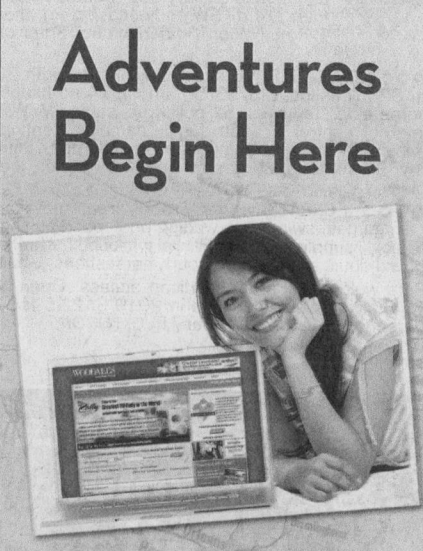

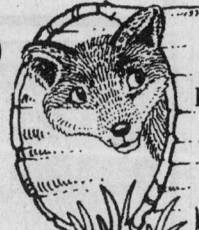

Pennsylvania State Animal: White-tailed Deer

PHILADELPHIA—Continued

(E) TIMBERLANE CAMPGROUND—*From I-95 & I-76 E: Go 4-1/4 mi SE on I-76E, then 8-1/2 mi SW on I-295, (exit 18AB), then 1 mi S on Hwy 667 (Cohawkin Rd), then 1/4 mi SW on Friendship Rd, then 1/4 mi NW on Timberlane Rd. Enter on L.*

♦♦♦♦FACILITIES: 96 sites, typical site width 30 ft, 82 full hkups, (20/30/50 amps), 14 no hkups, some extd stay sites, 51 pull-thrus, cable TV, WiFi Internet central location, family camping, tenting, cabins, RV storage, dump, non-guest dump $, laundry, RV supplies, LP gas by weight/by meter, ice, picnic tables, fire rings, wood.

♦♦♦♦RECREATION: rec room/area, pavilion, coin games, swim pool, wading pool, pond fishing, fishing supplies, bsktball, playground, shuffleboard court shuffleboard court, horseshoes, v-ball.

Pets welcome. Partial handicap access. Open all yr. Big rigs welcome. Rate in 2010 $42-45 for 2 persons. MC/VISA. Member ARVC, NJCOA.

See listing at Revere, PA

PHILADELPHIA—Continued
TIMBERLANE CAMPGROUND—Continued

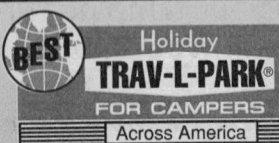

Phone: (856)423-6677
Address: 117 Timberlane Rd, Clarksboro, NJ 08020
Email: info@timberlanecampground.com
Web: www.timberlanecampground.com

SEE PRIMARY LISTING AT CLARKSBORO, NJ AND AD PAGE 673

PHILIPSBURG—C-4

BLACK MOSHANNON STATE PARK—(Centre) *From business center: Go 9 mi E on Hwy 504, then 1/4 mi after park entrance, go 1/2 mi N on Cassanova-Munson Rd. Enter on R.* FACILITIES: 80 sites, 30 ft max RV length, 55 E, (20/30/50 amps), 50 amps ($), 25 no hkups, 3 pull-thrus, tenting, dump, ltd groc. RECREATION: lake swim, boating, electric motors only, ramp, dock, lake/stream fishing, playground. No pets. Partial handicap access. Open mid Apr - late Dec. Phone: (814)342-5960.

PINE GROVE—D-8

(N) TWIN GROVE AMUSEMENT PARK—*From jct I-81 & SR 443 (exit 100): Go 5 mi W on SR 443. Enter on R.* Family oriented amusement park adjacent to Pine Grove KOA. Open Memorial Day - Labor Day. MC/VISA/DISC.

WELCOME

Phone: (800)562-5471
Address: 1445 Suedburg Rd, Pine Grove, PA 17963
Lat/Lon: 40.51417/-76.51250
Email: info@twingrove.com
Web: www.twingrove.com

SEE AD HERSHEY PAGE 661

Woodall's Tip... Looking for a place to stay for an extended period of time? Check out our Extended Stay Guide (the yellow pages in the middle of this Directory).

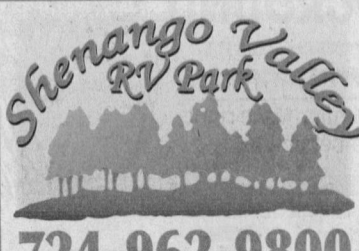

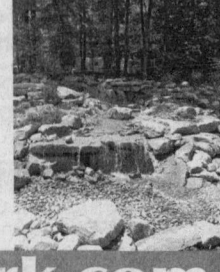

PITTSBURGH—D-2

PITTSBURGH AREA MAP

Symbols on map indicate towns within a 30 mi radius of Pittsburgh where campgrounds (diamonds), attractions (flags), & RV service centers & camping supply outlets (gears) are listed. Check listings for more information.

Tell Them Woodall's Sent You!

PITTSBURGH—Continued on next page

The word Pennsylvania is misspelled in the inscription on the Liberty Bell.

PITTSBURGH—Continued

FOX DEN ACRES CAMPGROUND—*From jct I-376 & I-279: Go 14 mi E on I-376, then 18 mi E on I-76, then 1/4 mi W on I-70 (exit 57B-New Stanton), then 2 mi N on North Center Ave. Enter on L.*

SEE LISTING IN NEW STANTON AND AD PAGE 674

POCONO MOUNTAINS—C-9

See listings at Stroudsburg Matamoras, Marshalls Creek, Mount Pocono, Tobyhanna, Blakeslee, Broadheadsville, Trachsville, White Haven

DELAWARE WATER GAP/POCONO MT. KOA—*From jct I-80 (exit 309) & US 209: Go 6-1/2 mi N on US 209, then 1 mi E on Hollow Rd. Enter on L.*

SEE PRIMARY LISTING AT STROUDSBURG AND AD STROUDSBURG PAGE 678

OTTER LAKE CAMP RESORT—*From Pocono Mountains (jct I-80 exit 309 & US 209): Go 4 mi N on US 209, then 300 feet NW on SR 402, then 7-1/2 mi N on Marshalls Creek Rd. Enter on L.*

SEE PRIMARY LISTING AT STROUDSBURG AND AD STROUDSBURG PAGE 680

POCONO VACATION PARK—*From jct US 209 & I-80 (exit 309): Go W on I-80 to exit 305, then 2 mi S on Business US 209, then 1/2 mi W on Shafer's School House Rd. Enter on L.*

SEE PRIMARY LISTING AT STROUDSBURG AND AD STROUDSBURG PAGE 678

PORT ROYAL—D-6

(SW) Shoops Country Campground—(Juniata) *From jct SR-75 & SR-333: Go 6 mi SW on SR-75, then 1/2 mi SW on Mill Lane Rd, then 1/4 mi NE on Mountain Rd. Enter on R.* ◊◊FACILITIES: 115 sites, typical site width 30 ft, 115 full hkups, (30 amps), 1 pull-thrus, family camping, tenting, dump. ◊◊RECREATION: playground. Pets welcome. Partial handicap access. Open Apr 1 - End of Nov. Rate in 2010 $25-28 per family. Phone: (717)527-4885.

PORTERSVILLE—C-1

(E) BEAR RUN CAMPGROUND—(Butler) *From jct I-79 (exit 96) & Hwy 488: Go 50 yards E on Hwy 488, then 1/2 mi N on Badger Hill Rd. Enter on R.*

◊◊◊◊◊FACILITIES: 300 sites, typical site width 30 ft, 188 full hkups, 48 W&E, (20/30/50 amps), 64 no hkups, many extd stay sites (summer), 26 pull-thrus, WiFi Instant Internet at site, WiFi Internet central location, family camping, tenting, RV's/park model rentals, cabins, shower$, dump, laundry, full svc store, RV supplies, LP gas by weight/by meter, ice, picnic tables, fire rings, wood, controlled access.

◊◊◊◊◊RECREATION: rec room/area, pavilion, equipped pavilion, coin games, swim pool, lake swim, boating, canoeing, kayaking, ramp, dock, 6 canoe/4 kayak rentals, lake/pond fishing, fishing supplies, golf nearby, bsktball, playground, activities, (wkends), horseshoes, sports field, hiking trails, v-ball.

Pets welcome, breed restrict, quantity restrict. Partial handicap access. Open Apr 15 - Oct 30. Escort to site. Clubs welcome. Rate in 2010 $40-60 for 4 persons. MC/VISA/DISC/Debit. ATM. Member ARVC, PCOA. FCRV discount. FMCA discount. CCUSA 50% Discount. CCUSA reservations Recommended, CCUSA max stay See rest., CCUSA disc. not avail S, CCUSA disc. not avail F,Sa, CCUSA disc. not avail holidays. Discount not available in July. Max stay 1 day-pull-thrus, 2 days-full hookups & tent sites, 3 days-water & electric.

Text 107974 to (440)725-8687 to see our Visual Tour.

Phone: (888)737-2605
Address: 184 Badger Hill Rd, Portersville, PA 16051
Lat/Lon: 40.92997/-80.12627
Email: brcinc@earthlink.net
Web: www.bearruncampground.com

SEE AD TRAVEL SECTION PAGE 640 AND AD TRAVEL SECTION PAGE 641

PORTERSVILLE—Continued

(E) BEAR RUN CAMPGROUND CANOE RENTAL—*From jct I-79 & SR-488 (exit 96): Go 50 yds E on SR-488, then 1/2 mi N on Badger Hill Rd. Enter on R.* Explore 44 mi shoreline of beautiful Lake Arthur within Moraine State Park. Open Apr 15 - Oct 31. MC/VISA/DISC/Debit.

Phone: (888)737-2605
Address: 184 Badger Hill Rd, Portersville, PA 16051
Lat/Lon: 40.92997/-80.12627
Email: brcinc@earthlink.net
Web: www.bearruncampground.com

SEE AD TRAVEL SECTION PAGE 641

(W) ROSE POINT CABINS & CAMPING—(Lawrence) *From jct I-79 (exit 99) & US 422: Go 3 mi W on US 422, then 1/4 mi N on Old Rt. 422. Enter on L.*

◊◊◊◊FACILITIES: 137 sites, typical site width 30 ft, 121 full hkups, 10 W&E, (20/30/50 amps), 6 no hkups, many extd stay sites, 7 pull-thrus, WiFi Instant Internet at site, family camping, tenting, cabins, RV storage, dump, non-guest dump $, laundry, groceries, RV supplies, LP gas by weight/by meter, ice, picnic tables, fire rings, wood, controlled access.

◊◊◊◊RECREATION: rec hall, rec room/area, pavilion, equipped pavilion, coin games, swim pool, stream fishing, fishing supplies, golf nearby, bsktball, playground, activities, horseshoes, sports field, hiking trails, v-ball.

Pets welcome, breed restrict. Partial handicap access. Open all yr. Facilities fully operational Apr 1 - Nov 1. Limited sites in Winter. Big rigs welcome. Escort to site. Clubs welcome. Green Friendly. Rate in 2010 $40 for 2 persons. MC/VISA/DISC/Debit. Member ARVC, PCOA.

Phone: (724)924-2415
Address: 8775 Old U.S. 422, New Castle, PA 16101
Lat/Lon: 40.97180/-80.18398
Email: info@rosepointpark.com
Web: www.rosepointpark.com

SEE AD PITTSBURGH PAGE 674

POTTERS MILLS—D-5

POE PADDY STATE PARK—(Centre) *Drive 1.5 mi S on Rt 322 to unpaved Sand Mtn Rd, follow marked state roads to P, about 10 mi. Just go 3.5 mi past PV on paved/unpaved roads.* FACILITIES: 41 sites, 41 no hkups, tenting. RECREATION: stream fishing, playground. Partial handicap access. Open mid Apr - mid Dec. Phone: (814)349-2460.

POE VALLEY STATE PARK—(Centre) *Drive 1.5 mi S on rt 322 to unpaved Sand Mountain Rd. Follow marked state roads to PV, about 10 mi.* FACILITIES: 67 sites, 30 ft max RV length, 67 E, tenting, dump. RECREATION: lake swim, boating, electric motors only, ramp, lake fishing, playground. No pets. Partial handicap access. Open mid Apr - mid Dec. Phone: (814)349-2460.

(S) Seven Mountains Campground—(Centre) *From jct SR-144 & US 322: Go 2-1/2 mi E on US 322. Enter on R.* ◊◊◊FACILITIES: 70 sites, typical site width 22 ft, 28 full hkups, 42 W&E, (20/30/50 amps), 7 pull-thrus, family camping, tenting, dump, laundry. RECREATION: playground. Pets welcome. Partial handicap access. Open Apr 1 - Dec 10. Facilities fully operational Apr 1 - Nov 1. Rate in 2010 $40 for 4 persons. Member ARVC, PCOA. Phone: (888)468-2556.

QUAKERTOWN—D-9

(NE) HOMESTEAD CAMPGROUND—(Bucks) *From SR 309 & SR 313: Go 2 mi S on SR 309, then 1-1/2 mi W on Tollgate Dr, then 400 yds S on E Broad St, then 1-1/2 mi S on Allentown Rd. Enter on R.*

◊◊◊FACILITIES: 125 sites, typical site width 30 ft, 40 full hkups, 70 W&E, (30/50 amps), 15 no hkups, 10 pull-thrus, cable TV, WiFi Instant Internet at site, WiFi Internet central location, family camping, tenting, dump, non-guest dump $, laundry, ltd groc, RV supplies, LP gas by weight/by meter, ice, picnic tables, fire rings, wood.

QUAKERTOWN—Continued
HOMESTEAD CAMPGROUND—Continued

◊◊◊RECREATION: rec hall, rec room/area, pavilion, coin games, swim pool, pond fishing, golf nearby, bsktball, playground, horseshoes, v-ball.

Pets welcome. Partial handicap access. Open all yr. Big rigs welcome. Escort to site. Clubs welcome. Rate in 2010 $25 for 4 persons. MC/VISA/Debit. Member ARVC, PCOA.

Phone: (215)257-3445
Address: 1150 Allentown Rd, Green Lane, PA 18054
Lat/Lon: 40.38971/-75.37479
Email: homesteadcampground@comcast.net
Web: www.homesteadcampground.com

SEE AD THIS PAGE

(E) Little Red Barn Campgrounds, LLC—(Bucks) *From jct SR 313 & SR-309: Go 4 mi E on SR 313, then 2-1/4 mi N on SR 563, then 3/4 mi W on Old Bethlehem Rd. Enter on L.* ◊◊◊FACILITIES: 150 sites, typical site width 27 ft, 40 ft max RV length, 100 W&E, (20/30/50 amps), 50 no hkups, 5 pull-thrus, family camping, tenting, dump, laundry, groceries. ◊◊◊RECREATION: swim pool, playground. Pets welcome. Age restrict may apply. Open Apr 1 - Nov 1. Rate in 2010 $35 for 4 persons. Member ARVC, PCOA. Phone: (866)434-1711.

(NW) QUAKERWOODS CAMPGROUND—(Bucks) *From jct SR 309 & SR 313/SR 663: Go 1/4 mi SW on SR 663, then 4 mi N on Old Bethlehem Pk, then 1/2 mi W on Rosedale Rd. Enter on L.*

◊◊◊FACILITIES: 213 sites, typical site width 28 ft, 110 full hkups, 83 W&E, (20/30/50 amps), 50 amps ($), 20 no hkups, some extd stay sites (summer), 4 pull-thrus, cable TV, WiFi Instant Internet at site ($), family camping, tenting, RV's/park model rentals, cabins, RV storage, dump, non-guest dump $, laundry, groceries, RV supplies, LP gas by weight/by meter, ice, picnic tables, fire rings, wood.

◊◊◊RECREATION: rec hall, rec room/area, pavilion, coin games, swim pool, wading pool, pond fishing, fishing supplies, mini-golf, ($), golf nearby, bsktball, playground, shuffleboard court 2 shuffleboard courts, activities (wkends), horseshoes, sports field, hiking trails, v-ball.

Pets welcome. Age restrict may apply. Open Apr 1 - Oct 31. Big rigs welcome. Clubs welcome. Rate in 2010 $35-44 for 2 persons. MC/VISA/DISC/Debit. Member ARVC, PCOA. CCUSA 50% Discount. CCUSA reservations Accepted, CCUSA max stay 2 days, CCUSA disc. not avail F,Sa, CCUSA disc. not avail holidays. Only RV sites discounted.

Phone: (800)235-2350
Address: 2225 Rosedale Rd., Quakertown, PA 18951
Lat/Lon: 40.46861/-75.40067
Email: quakerwoods@verizon.net
Web: www.quakerwoods.com

SEE AD ALLENTOWN PAGE 649

(NW) Tohickon Family Campground—(Bucks) *From jct SR-309 & SR-313: Go 3-1/4 mi E on SR-313, then 1-1/4 mi E on Steiner Mill Rd, then 1-1/4 mi N on Richlandtown Rd, then 500 yds N on Covered Bridge Dr. (12'4" high, one lane covered bridge). Enter on R.* ◊◊FACILITIES: 190 sites, typical site width 30 ft, 104 full hkups, 71 W&E, (20/30/50 amps), 15 no hkups, family camping, tenting, dump, laundry, groceries. ◊◊RECREATION: swim pool, boating, no motors, canoeing, stream fishing, playground. Pets welcome. Open all yr. Facilities fully operational Apr 1 - Oct 31. Big rigs welcome. Rate in 2010 $42 per family. Member ARVC, PCOA. Phone: (215)536-7951.

The Rockville Bridge in Harrisburg is the longest stone arch bridge in the world.

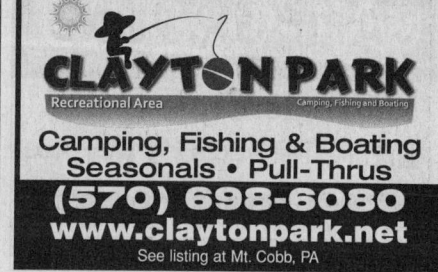

QUARRYVILLE—E-8

(S) YOGI BEAR'S JELLYSTONE PARK CAMP-RESORT-LANCASTER SOUTH/QUARRYVILLE—(Lancaster) *From east jct SR 372 & US 222: Go 2-1/2 mi S on US 222, then 1-1/2 mi E on Blackburn Rd. Enter on L.*

◊◊◊FACILITIES: 160 sites, typical site width 32 ft, 119 full hkups, 41 W&E, (20/30/50 amps), 15 pull-thrus, cable TV, WiFi Internet central location, family camping, tenting, cabins, RV storage, dump, laundry, full svc store, LP gas by weight, ice, picnic tables, patios, fire rings, grills, wood.

◊◊◊◊RECREATION: rec room/area, pavilion, coin games, swim pool, wading pool, spray ground, lake fishing, fishing supplies, golf nearby, bsktball, playground, shuffleboard court 3 shuffleboard courts, activities, horseshoes, sports field, hiking trails, v-ball.

Pets welcome, breed restrict, quantity restrict. Partial handicap access. Open Apr 20 - Nov 1. Big rigs welcome. Escort to site. Clubs welcome. Rate in 2010 $42-120 per family. MC/VISA/DISC/Debit. ATM. Member ARVC, PCOA.

Phone: (717)786-3458
Address: 340 Blackburn Rd, Quarryville, PA 17566
Lat/Lon: 39.85353/-76.12685
Email: yogilanc@aol.com
Web: www.jellystonepa.com

SEE AD LANCASTER PAGES 664-666

RAVINE—D-7

(NE) ECHO VALLEY CAMPGROUND—(Schuylkill) *From jct I-81 (exit 104) turn right on Molly's Town Road, follow signs to campground. Enter on R.*

◊◊◊FACILITIES: 121 sites, typical site width 25 ft, 107 full hkups, 4 W&E, (15/20/30/50 amps), 50 amps ($), 10 no hkups, some extd stay sites, 13 pull-thrus, cable TV, ($), WiFi Instant Internet at site ($), family camping, tenting, RV's/park model rentals, cabins, RV storage, dump, non-guest dump $, laundry, ltd groc, RV supplies, LP bottle exch, ice, picnic tables, fire rings, wood.

◊◊◊RECREATION: rec hall, rec room/area, pavilion, coin games, swim pool, stream fishing, golf nearby, bsktball, playground, activities, (wkends), horseshoes, hiking trails, v-ball.

Pets welcome. Partial handicap access. Open all yr. Big rigs welcome. Clubs welcome. Rate in 2010 $30-40 for 4 persons. MC/VISA/DISC/Debit. Member ARVC, PCOA.

Phone: (570)695-3659
Address: 52 Camp Rd, Tremont, PA 17981
Lat/Lon: 40.59890/-76.39110
Email: echovalley@comcast.net
Web: www.echovalleycamp.com

SEE AD THIS PAGE AND AD TRAVEL SECTION PAGE 640

READING—D-8

See listings at Adamstown, Auburn, Bernville, Bowmansville, Boyertown, Denver, Kutztown, Lenhartsville & Shartlesville

(N) Bluefalls Grove Waterpark & Campground (RV SPACES)—(Berks) *From jct of SR 61 & SR 73: Go 1/2 mi S on SR 61, then 1 mi E on Wileys Ln. Enter on L.* FACILITIES: 38 sites, typical site width 30 ft, 38 W&E, (20/30/50 amps), 8 pull-thrus, tenting, dump.

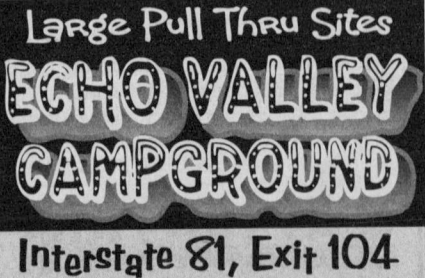

READING—Continued
Bluefalls Grove Waterpark & Campground—Continued

RECREATION: swim pool, boating, no motors, canoeing, ramp, dock, stream fishing, playground. Pets welcome. Partial handicap access. Open all yr. Rate in 2010 $32 per family. Member ARVC, PCOA. Phone: (610)926-4017.

LAKE IN WOOD RESORT—*Take US 222 S to SR 625 S to Bowmansville, then 3/4 mi E on Maple Grove, then 1/2 mi S on Oaklyn Dr, then 1-1/2 mi E on Yellow Hill Rd. Enter on R.*

SEE PRIMARY LISTING AT BOWMANSVILLE AND AD DISCOVER SECTION PAGE 25

RENOVO—C-5

HYNER RUN STATE PARK—(Clinton) *From Renova go 6 mi E on Hwy 120. At Hyner intersection turn left, go 3 mi N of Hyner.* FACILITIES: 30 sites, 30 no hkups, tenting, dump. RECREATION: swim pool, stream fishing, playground. No pets. Partial handicap access. Open Apr 10 - Dec 15. Phone: (570)923-6000.

(NW) KETTLE CREEK STATE PARK—(Clinton) *From business center: Go 6 mi W on Hwy 120 to Westport, then 7 mi N on SR 4001, follow signs.* FACILITIES: 68 sites, 36 ft max RV length, 48 E, (20/50 amps), 20 no hkups, tenting, dump. RECREATION: lake swim, boating, electric motors only, ramp, dock, lake/stream fishing, playground. No pets. Open Apr 2 - Dec 5. Phone: (570)923-6004.

REVERE—D-10

(N) COLONIAL WOODS FAMILY CAMPING RESORT—(Bucks) *From south jct SR 412 & SR 611: Go 1-1/2 mi N on SR 611, then 1-1/2 mi E on Marienstein Rd, then 1/2 mi N on Lonely Cottage Dr. (15 Ton Bridge). Enter on R.*

◊◊◊◊FACILITIES: 235 sites, typical site width 30 ft, 235 W&E, (20/30 amps), many extd stay sites (summer), 10 pull-thrus, cable TV, WiFi Instant Internet at site ($), WiFi Internet central location, family camping, tenting, RV's/park model rentals, cabins, RV storage, dump, portable dump, laundry, groceries, RV supplies, LP gas by weight/by meter, ice, picnic tables, fire rings, wood, controlled access.

◊◊◊◊◊RECREATION: rec hall, rec room/area, pavilion, equipped pavilion, coin games, swim pool, wading pool, spray ground, hot tub, boating, no motors, canoeing, kayaking, pond fishing, fishing supplies, mini-golf, ($), golf nearby, bsktball, playground, shuffleboard court 2 shuffleboard courts, activities, tennis, horseshoes, sports field, v-ball.

Pets welcome. Partial handicap access. Open Mid Apr - Early Nov. Clubs welcome. Rate in 2010 $38-45 per family. MC/VISA/DISC/Debit. Member ARVC, PCOA.

Phone: (800)887-CAMP
Address: 545 Lonely Cottage Dr, Upper Black Eddy, PA 18972
Lat/Lon: 40.53398/-75.15418
Email: camping@colonialwoods.com
Web: www.colonialwoods.com

SEE AD PHILADELPHIA PAGE 674

ROBESONIA—D-8

(SW) Adventure Bound Camping Resort at Eagles Peak—(Lebanon) *From jct US 422 & SR 419: Go 3 mi S on SR 419, then 2 mi E on S. Fort Zellers Rd, then 350 yds E on Eagles Peak Rd. Enter on R.* ◊◊◊FACILITIES: 347 sites, typical site width 30 ft, 316 full hkups, 31 W&E, (30/50 amps), 5 pull-thrus, family camping, tenting, dump, laundry, ltd groc. ◊◊◊◊◊RECREATION: 2 swim pools, boating, pond fishing, playground. Pets welcome. Partial handicap access. Open Apr 1 - Nov 1. Big rigs welcome. Rate in 2010 $32-57 for 4 persons. Member ARVC, PCOA. Phone: (800)336-0889.

ROME—B-8

(N) Pine Cradle Lake Family Campground—(Bradford) *From jct SR-187 & SR-467: Go 2-3/4 mi NE on SR-187, then 3 mi N on SR-1055, then 250 yds W on Parks Rd, then 1 mi S on Shoemaker Rd. Enter on*

ROME—Continued
Pine Cradle Lake Family Campground—Continued

L. ◊◊◊FACILITIES: 185 sites, typical site width 45 ft, 181 full hkups, 2 W&E, (20/30/50 amps), 2 no hkups, 11 pull-thrus, family camping, tenting, dump, laundry, ltd groc. ◊◊◊◊RECREATION: swim pool, boating, electric motors only, canoeing, dock, lake fishing, playground. Pets welcome, quantity restrict. Partial handicap access. Open May 1 - Oct 15. Big rigs welcome. Rate in 2010 $28-42 for 4 persons. Member ARVC, PCOA. Phone: (570)247-2424.

ROSSVILLE—E-7

GIFFORD PINCHOT STATE PARK—(York) *From jct Hwy 177 & Hwy 74: Go 1 mi S on Hwy 74, then E on camping area road.* FACILITIES: 339 sites, 75 E, (30/50 amps), 264 no hkups, tenting, dump. RECREATION: lake swim, boating, electric motors only, canoeing, ramp, dock, lake fishing, playground. No pets. Partial handicap access. Open Apr 10 - Oct 31. Phone: (717)432-5011.

SANDY LAKE—C-1

(N) Goddard Park Vacationland Campground—(Mercer) *From jct I-79 & SR-358 (exit 130): Go 1/8 mi W on SR-358, then 1 mi NW on Sheakleyville Rd, then 3-1/2 mi E on Lake Wilhelm Rd, then 1/4 mi N on Georgetown Rd. Enter on R.* ◊◊◊◊FACILITIES: 602 sites, typical site width 26 ft, 513 full hkups, 49 W&E, (30 amps), 40 no hkups, 175 pull-thrus, family camping, tenting, dump, laundry, groceries. ◊◊◊◊◊RECREATION: 2 swim pools, playground. Pets welcome. Partial handicap access. Open Apr 15 - Oct 15. Rate in 2010 $31.50-36.75 for 2 persons. Member ARVC, PCOA. Phone: (724)253-4645.

SCANDIA—A-3

(NE) Red Oak Campground—(Warren) *From jct Cole Hill Rd & Scandia-Onoville Rd, (north town limits): Go 6 mi N on Scandia-Onoville Rd. Enter on R.* ◊◊FACILITIES: 225 sites, typical site width 35 ft, 145 full hkups, 60 W&E, (20/30 amps), 20 no hkups, family camping, tenting, dump, laundry, groceries. ◊◊RECREATION: swim pool, playground. Pets welcome. Partial handicap access. Open all yr. Facilities fully operational May - Oct 15. Rate in 2010 $31-36 per family. Member ARVC, PCOA. Phone: (814)757-8507.

SCHELLSBURG—E-4

(S) SHAWNEE STATE PARK—(Bedford) *From business center: 2 mi S on Hwy-96.* FACILITIES: 293 sites, 98 E, (30/50 amps), 195 no hkups, 19 pull-thrus, tenting, dump, ltd groc. RECREATION: lake swim, boating, electric motors only, ramp, dock, lake fishing, playground. Partial handicap access. Open mid Apr - mid Dec. Phone: (814)733-4218.

SCOTRUN—C-9

(S) Four Seasons Campgrounds—(Monroe) *From jct SR-715 & SR-611: Go 1 mi N on SR-611, then 1/4 mi SW (left) on Scotrun Ave, then 3/4 mi W on Babbling Brook Rd. Enter on R.* ◊◊◊◊FACILITIES: 130 sites, typical site width 30 ft, 40 ft max RV length, 116 full hkups, 14 W&E, (20/30/50 amps), 50 amps ($), 19 pull-thrus, family camping, tenting, dump, laundry, groceries. ◊◊◊◊RECREATION: swim pool, playground. Pets welcome. Partial handicap access. Open mid Apr - Columbus Wknd. Rate in 2010 $43-51 for 2 persons. Member ARVC, PCOA. Phone: (570)629-2504.

SCOTRUN - OUTDOOR WORLD (CAMP RESORT)—(Monroe) *PO Box 428, Route 611, Scotrun, PA 18355.*

Phone: (800)579-4987
Address: Scotrun, PA 18355
Web: www.oneparkmembership.com

SEE AD ADAMSTOWN PAGE 648

SCRANTON—B-9

See listings at Clarks Summit, Hop Bottom, Meshoppen, South Gibson, Tunkhannock, Waymart, Rome, Lakeville, & Greentown.

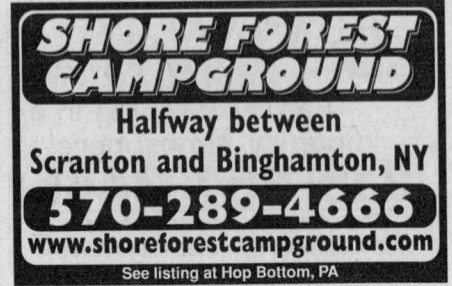

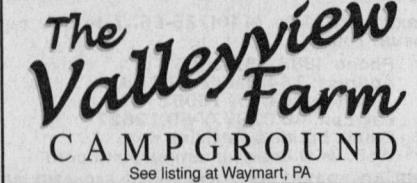

SELINSGROVE—D-7

(N) PENN AVON CAMPGROUND—(Snyder) *From jct US 11/15 & US 522: Go 1 mi SW on US 522, then 1-1/2 N on SR 204. Enter on R.*

◆◆◆FACILITIES: 49 sites, typical site width 30 ft, 43 full hkups, (20/30/50 amps), 6 no hkups, some extd stay sites, 3 pull-thrus, cable TV, WiFi Instant Internet at site, WiFi Internet central location, family camping, tenting, dump, non-guest dump $, ice, picnic tables, fire rings, wood.

◆◆RECREATION: pavilion, stream fishing, golf nearby, bsktball, play equipment, horseshoes.

Pets welcome. Partial handicap access. Open Apr 1 - Oct 31. Big rigs welcome. Escort to site. Clubs welcome. Rate in 2010 $36 per family. MC/VISA/DISC. Member ARVC, PCOA.

Phone: (570)374-9468
Address: 22 Penn Avon Trail, Rte 204, Selinsgrove, PA 17870
Lat/Lon: 40.83215/-76.87241
Email: pennavon@ptd.net
Web: www.pennavon.com

SEE AD THIS PAGE

SHARON—C-1

SHENANGO PUBLIC USE AREA (COE-Shenango Lake) —(Mercer) *From jct I-80 & Hwy 18: Go 6-1/2 mi N on Hwy 18. Enter on L.* FACILITIES: 330 sites, typical site width 12 ft, 85 E, 245 no hkups, tenting, dump, laundry. RECREATION: lake swim, boating, canoeing, ramp, lake fishing, playground. Partial handicap access. Open Memorial Day - Labor Day. Phone: (724)646-1124.

(NE) SHENANGO VALLEY RV PARK—(Mercer) *From jct of I-80 & SR18 (exit 4B): Go 11 mi N on SR 18 then 1/2 mi E on Reynolds Industrial Park Rd, then 1 mi SE on Crestview Dr, then left at Y intersetion onto East Crestview Dr. Enter on L.*

◆◆◆◆◆FACILITIES: 198 sites, typical site width 40 ft, 189 full hkups, 9 W&E, (20/30/50 amps), mostly extd stay sites (summer), 5 pull-thrus, cable TV, WiFi Instant Internet at site, WiFi Internet central location, family camping, tenting, shower$, dump, laundry, ltd groc, RV supplies, LP gas by weight/by meter, LP bottle exch, ice, picnic tables, fire rings, wood, controlled access.

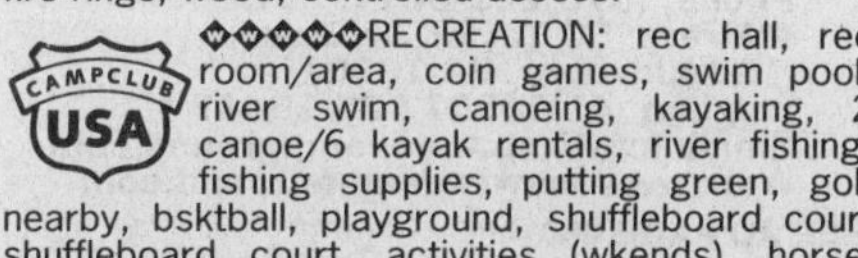

◆◆◆◆◆RECREATION: rec hall, rec room/area, coin games, swim pool, river swim, canoeing, kayaking, 2 canoe/6 kayak rentals, river fishing, fishing supplies, putting green, golf nearby, bsktball, playground, shuffleboard court shuffleboard court, activities (wkends), horseshoes, sports field, hiking trails, v-ball.

Pets welcome, breed restrict, quantity restrict. Partial handicap access. Open May 1 - Oct 15. Big rigs welcome. Escort to site. Clubs welcome. Rate in 2010 $38-45 for 2 persons. MC/VISA/DISC/AMEX/Debit. Member ARVC, PCOA. CCUSA 50% Discount. CCUSA reservations Recommended, CCUSA max stay 1 day, CCUSA disc. not avail S, CCUSA disc. not avail F,Sa, CCUSA disc. not avail holidays.

Text 107943 to (440)725-8687 to see our Visual Tour.

Phone: (724)962-9800
Address: 559 E Crestview Dr, Transfer, PA 16154
Lat/Lon: 41.33323/-80.37746
Email: info@shenangovalleyrvpark.com
Web: www.shenangovalleyrvpark.com

SEE AD PITTSBURGH PAGE 674

SHARTLESVILLE—D-8

(NW) APPALACHIAN CAMPSITES—(Berks) *From jct I-78/US 22 (exit 23) & Mountain Road: Go 1/8 mi W on Motel Dr. Enter at end.*

◆◆◆◆FACILITIES: 328 sites, typical site width 30 ft, 228 full hkups, 100 W&E, (20/30/50 amps), many extd stay sites, 26 pull-thrus, cable TV, WiFi Instant Internet at site, WiFi Internet central location, family camping, tenting, RV's/park model rentals, cabins, RV storage, dump, non-guest dump $, portable dump, laundry, ltd groc, RV supplies, LP gas by weight/by meter, ice, picnic tables, fire rings, wood, controlled access.

◆◆◆◆RECREATION: rec hall, rec room/area, pavilion, coin games, swim pool, wading pool, lake swim, pond fishing, fishing supplies, mini-golf, ($), golf nearby, bsktball, playground, activities, (wkends), horseshoes, sports field, hiking trails, v-ball.

SHARTLESVILLE—Continued
APPALACHIAN CAMPSITES—Continued

Pets welcome. Partial handicap access. Open Apr 1 - Nov 1. Big rigs welcome. Clubs welcome. Rate in 2010 $34-50 for 4 persons. MC/VISA/DISC/AMEX/Debit. Member ARVC, PCOA.

Phone: (800)424-5746
Address: 60 Motel Drive, Shartlesville, PA 19554
Lat/Lon: 40.51435/-76.11828
Email: appalachianrv@equitylifestyle.com
Web: www.appalachianrvresort.com

SEE AD ADAMSTOWN PAGE 648

(NE) Mountain Springs Camping Resort—(Berks) *From jct I-78/US 22 (exit 23) & Shartlesville Rd: Go 1 mi N on Mountain Rd. Enter on L.* ◆◆◆◆FACILITIES: 292 sites, typical site width 30 ft, 113 full hkups, 168 W&E, (20/30/50 amps), 11 no hkups, 13 pull-thrus, family camping, tenting, dump, laundry, ltd groc. ◆◆◆◆RECREATION: swim pool, lake swim, pond/stream fishing, playground. Pets welcome. Partial handicap access. Open Apr 1 - Oct 31. Big rigs welcome. Rate in 2010 $35-41 per family. Member ARVC, PCOA. Phone: (610)488-6859.

(NW) Pennsylvania Dutch Campsite—(Berks) *From jct I-78/US 22 (exit 23) & Shartlesville Rd: Go 1/8 mi S on Shartlesville Rd, then 1 mi W on Old US 22, then 1/4 mi N on North Northkill Rd, then 3/4 mi W on Campsite Rd. Enter on L.* ◆◆FACILITIES: 233 sites, typical site width 27 ft, 225 full hkups, 8 W&E, (30/50 amps), 25 pull-thrus, family camping, tenting, dump, ltd groc. ◆◆RECREATION: swim pool, playground. Pets welcome. Open 2nd Wkd in April - 4th Wkd in October. Big rigs welcome. Rate in 2010 $39-42 per family. Member ARVC, PCOA. Phone: (610)488-6268.

SHEFFIELD—B-3

(E) Whispering Winds Campground—(Warren) *From jct SR 666 & US 6: Go 3/4 mi E on US 6, then 1/4 mi N on Tollgate Rd. Enter on R.* ◆◆◆FACILITIES: 35 sites, typical site width 30 ft, 21 full hkups, 14 W&E, (20/30 amps), family camping, tenting, dump, laundry, ltd groc. ◆◆◆RECREATION: swim pool, stream fishing, playground. Pets welcome. Open all yr. Facilities fully operational Apr 1 - Nov 1. Rate in 2010 $24-28 per family. Member ARVC, PCOA. Phone: (814)968-4377.

Reserve Online at Woodalls.com

SIGEL—C-3

(N) Campers Paradise Campground & Cabins—(Jefferson) *From jct SR 36 & SR 949: Go 3 mi N on SR 949. Enter on R.* ◆◆◆◆FACILITIES: 118 sites, typical site width 26 ft, 58 full hkups, 38 W&E, (20/30 amps), 22 no hkups, 5 pull-thrus, family camping, tenting, dump, groceries. ◆◆◆◆RECREATION: swim pool, stream fishing, playground. Pets welcome, quantity restrict. Open all yr. Facilities fully operational mid Apr - mid Oct. Rate in 2010 $30-39 for 4 persons. Member ARVC, PCOA. Phone: (814)752-2393.

(NW) CLEAR CREEK STATE PARK—(Jefferson) *Take Rt 36 N 10 mi to Rt 949 at Sigel. Turn Right on Rt 949 N, take Rt 949 four mi to Clear Creek State Park on the left.* FACILITIES: 53 sites, typical site width 20 ft, 30 E, (30/50 amps), 50 amps ($), 23 no hkups, 5 pull-thrus, tenting, dump. RECREATION: lake/river swim, no motors, canoeing, ramp, pond/stream fishing, playground. No pets. Partial handicap access. Open Apr 10 - Dec 18. Phone: (814)752-2368.

SINNEMAHONING—C-5

(N) SINNEMAHONING STATE PARK—(Cameron) *From jct Hwy 120 & Hwy 872: Go 8 mi N on Hwy 872. Enter on R.* FACILITIES: 35 sites, 22 E, (30/50 amps), 50 amps ($), 13 no hkups, tenting, dump. RECREATION: boating, electric motors only, canoeing, ramp, lake/pond/stream fishing, playground. Pets welcome. Partial handicap access. Open all yr. Phone: (814) 647-8401.

SNOW SHOE—C-5

(W) SNOW SHOE PARK (City Park)—(Centre) *From jct I-80 (exit 147) & SR-144: Go 1/2 mi N on SR-144.* FACILITIES: 84 sites, typical site width 22 ft, 84 full hkups, (20/30/50 amps), tenting, dump. RECREATION: swim pool, playground. Pets welcome. Partial handicap access. Open Apr 15 - Oct 15. Phone: (814)387-6299.

SOMERSET—E-3

(SW) Hickory Hollow Campground—(Somerset) *From jct PA Tpk & SR 601 (exit 110): Go 1/2 mi S on SR 601, then 6-1/2 mi S on SR 281. Enter on R.* ◆◆◆◆FACILITIES: 107 sites, typical site width 40 ft, 86 full hkups, 14 W&E, (20/30/50 amps), 7 no hkups, 29 pull-thrus, cable TV, WiFi Internet central location, family camping, tenting, RV storage, dump, non-guest dump $, laundry, ltd groc, RV supplies, LP gas by weight/by meter, ice, picnic tables, fire rings, wood. ◆◆◆◆RECREATION: pavilion, swim pool, lake fishing, fishing supplies, bsktball, playground, activities, horseshoes, hiking trails, v-ball. Pets welcome. Partial handicap access. Open Apr 15 - Oct 31. Big rigs welcome. Rate in 2010 $28-30 for 4 persons. MC/VISA/DISC/Debit. Member ARVC, PCOA. CCUSA 50% Discount. CCUSA reservations Recommended, CCUSA max stay Unlimited, Cash only for CCUSA disc., CCUSA disc. not avail F,Sa, CCUSA disc. not avail holidays. Max 6 persons/site.

Phone: (814)926-4636
Address: 176 Big Hickory Rd, Rockwood, PA 15557
Lat/Lon: 39.96024/-79.18190
Email: info@hickoryhollowcampground.com
Web: www.hickoryhollowcampground.com

(SW) LAUREL HILL STATE PARK—(Somerset) *From jct I-70/76 (exit 110) & Hwy 31: Go 10 mi W on Hwy 31, then follow signs 2 mi S. Enter on R.* FACILITIES: 264 sites, 30 ft max RV length, 149 E, (30/50 amps), 50 amps ($), 115 no hkups, tenting, dump. RECREATION: lake swim, boating, electric motors only, canoeing, ramp, lake/stream fishing, playground. No pets. Partial handicap access. Open Apr 3 - Oct 18. Phone: (814)445-7725.

(W) Pioneer Park Campground—(Somerset) *From jct PA Tpk & SR-601 (exit 110): Go 1/2 mi S on SR 601, then 7 mi W on SR 31, then 1/4 mi S on Trent Rd. From jct PA 711 & SR 31 (exit 91): Go 12 mi E on SR 31, then 1/4 mi S on Trent Rd. Enter on R.* ◆◆◆◆FACILITIES: 340 sites, typical site width 31 ft, 245 full hkups, 20 W&E, (20/30/50 amps), 75 no hkups, 120 pull-thrus, family camping, tenting, dump, laundry, groceries. ◆◆◆◆◆RECREATION: swim pool, lake fishing, playground. Pets welcome. Partial handicap access. Open Early Apr - End of Oct. Big rigs welcome. Rate in 2010 $32-37 for 2 persons. Member ARVC, PCOA. Phone: (814)445-6348.

(SW) Scottyland Camping Resort—(Somerset) *From jct PA Tpk & SR-601 (exit 110): Go 1/2 mi S on SR-601, then 10 mi S on SR-281, then 1 mi W on SR-653. Enter on R.* ◆◆◆FACILITIES: 714 sites, typical site width 32 ft, 540 full hkups, 50 W&E, (20/30/50 amps), 124 no hkups, 36 pull-thrus, tenting, dump, laundry, ltd groc. ◆◆◆◆RECREATION: swim pool, river swim, lake/river/pond/stream fishing, playground. Pets welcome. Partial handicap access. Open all yr. Facilities fully operational Apr 15 - Oct 15. Big rigs welcome. Rate in 2010 $26-28 for 2 persons. Member ARVC, PCOA. Phone: (800)242-2267. FMCA discount.

(N) Woodland Campsites—(Somerset) *From jct PA Tpk & SR-601 (exit 110): Go 1-3/4 mi N on SR-601, then 1/2 mi E on Gilmour Rd. Enter on R.* ◆FACILITIES: 110 sites, typical site width 23 ft, 60 full hkups, 40 W&E, (15/20/30 amps), 10 no hkups, 3 pull-thrus, family camping, tenting, dump, laundry. ◆RECREATION: swim pool, lake fishing, play equipment. Pets welcome, breed restrict, quantity restrict. Open Apr 1 - Nov 1. Rate in 2010 $27-30 for 2 persons. Member ARVC, PCOA. Phone: (814)445-8860.

STATE COLLEGE—D-5

See listings at Bellefonte, Lewistowon, Potters Mills.

STATE COLLEGE—Continued on next page

Pennsylvania was the 2nd state admitted to the Union.

STATE COLLEGE—Continued

WATERSIDE CAMPGROUND & RV PARK *—From jct of PA 26, US 322E: Go 28 mi on US 322 E, then 4-1/2 mi S on US 22 Bus, then W on Industrial Park Rd 1 mi, then S on Locust Rd 1/2 mi.*

WELCOME

SEE PRIMARY LISTING AT LEWISTOWN AND AD LEWISTOWN PAGE 669

STRASBURG—E-8

(E) THE NATIONAL TOY TRAIN MUSEUM *—From jct of SR 896 & SR 741: Go 1 mi E on SR 741, then 1/2 mi N on Paradise Ln. Enter on R.* Marvel at over one hundred years of toy train history with the museum's interactive operating layouts in five different gauges, colorful displays and all day presentations of toy train videos. Gift Shop. Open May 1 - Oct 31. Weekends only, Apr, Nov & Dec. MC/VISA.

WELCOME

Phone: (717)687-8976
Address: 300 Paradise Lane, Strasburg, PA 17579
Lat/Lon: 39.98718/-76.15228
Email: info@nttmuseum.org
Web: www.nttmuseum.org

SEE AD LANCASTER PAGES 664-666 AND AD LANCASTER PAGE 667

(SE) WHITE OAK CAMPGROUND—(Lancaster) *From west jct SR 741 & SR 896/Decatur St: Go 3-3/4 mi S on Decatur St/May Post Office Rd, then 400 yds E on White Oak Rd. Enter on L.*

WELCOME

◆◆◆◆FACILITIES: 210 sites, typical site width 30 ft, 150 full hkups, 45 W&E, (20/30 amps), 15 no hkups, some extd stay sites, 20 pull-thrus, WiFi Internet central location, family camping, tenting, dump, groceries, RV supplies, ice, picnic tables, fire rings, wood.

◆◆RECREATION: rec hall, rec room/area, coin games, golf nearby, playground, sports field.

Pets welcome. Partial handicap access. Open all yr. Limited facilities in winter. Clubs welcome. Rate in 2010 $30-33 per family. MC/VISA/DISC/Debit. Member ARVC, PCOA.

Phone: (717)687-6207
Address: 3156 White Oak Rd, Quarryville, PA 17566
Lat/Lon: 39.94408/-76.13859
Email: info@whiteoakcampground.com
Web: www.whiteoakcampground.com

SEE AD LANCASTER PAGES 664-666 AND AD LANCASTER PAGE 667

John Updike & Louisa May Alcott, authors, were from Pennsylvania.

STROUDSBURG—C-9

STROUDSBURG AREA MAP

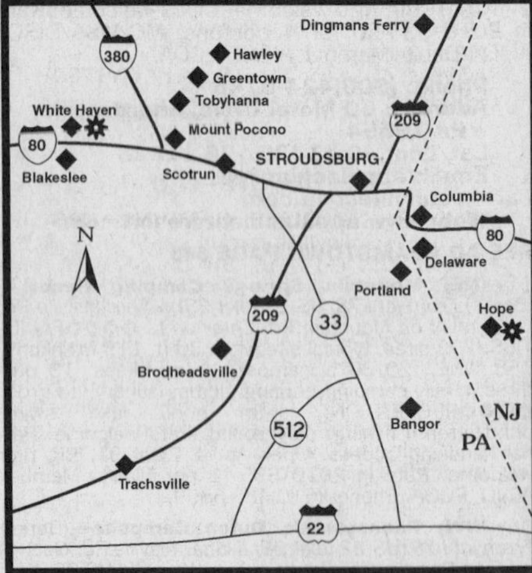

Symbols on map indicate towns within a 30 mi radius of Stroudsburg where campgrounds (diamonds), attractions (flags), & RV service centers & camping supply outlets (gears) are listed. Check listings for more information.

Tell Them Woodall's Sent You!

(NE) DELAWARE WATER GAP/POCONO MT. KOA—(Monroe) *From jct I-80 (exit 309) & US 209: Go 6 mi N on US 209, then 1 mi E on Hollow Rd. Enter on L.*

WELCOME

◆◆◆◆FACILITIES: 194 sites, typical site width 30 ft, 176 W&E, (20/30/50 amps), 18 no hkups, some extd stay sites, 51 pull-thrus, cable TV, WiFi Instant Internet at site, family camping, tenting, RV's/park model rentals, cabins, RV storage, dump, portable dump, laundry, groceries, RV supplies, LP gas by weight/by meter, ice, picnic tables, fire rings, wood.

◆◆◆◆RECREATION: rec hall, rec room/area, pavilion, coin games, swim pool, mini-golf, ($), golf nearby, bsktball, 16 bike rentals, playground, activities, (wkends), horseshoes, sports field, v-ball.

Pets welcome, breed restrict. Open all yr. Facilities fully operational Apr 1 - Oct 31. Big rigs welcome. Clubs welcome. Rate in 2010 $39.49-60.49 for 2 persons. MC/VISA/DISC/Debit. Member ARVC, PCOA. KOA discount.

STROUDSBURG—Continued
DELAWARE WATER GAP/POCONO MT. KOA—Continued

Phone: (570)223-8000
Address: 233 Hollow Rd, East Stroudsburg, PA 18302
Lat/Lon: 41.04927/-75.07970
Email: information@poconokoa.com
Web: www.poconokoa.com

SEE AD THIS PAGE

(NE) Foxwood Family Campground—(Monroe) *From jct I-80 (exit 309) & US 209: Go 1-1/2 mi N on US 209, then 1/4 mi E on Buttermilk Falls Rd, then 1 mi N on Mt Nebo Rd. Enter on L.* ◆FACILITIES: 350 sites, typical site width 27 ft, 164 full hkups, 186 W&E, (20/30/50 amps), 12 pull-thrus, family camping, tenting, dump, laundry, ltd groc. ◆◆RECREATION: swim pool, pond fishing, playground. Pets welcome, breed restrict, quantity restrict. Partial handicap access. Open Mid Apr - End of Oct. Big rigs welcome. Rate in 2010 $38 per family. Member ARVC, PCOA. Phone: (570)421-1424.

(N) MOUNTAIN VISTA CAMPGROUND—(Monroe) *From jct I-80 (exit 309) & US 209: Go 350 yds N on US 209, then 2 mi NW on SR-447, then 3 mi N on Business US 209, then 1 mi W on Craig's Meadow Rd, then 500 feet SW on Taylor Dr. Enter on R.*

WELCOME

◆◆◆◆◆FACILITIES: 195 sites, typical site width 40 ft, 175 full hkups, 20 W&E, (20/30/50 amps), many extd stay sites, 21 pull-thrus, heater not allowed, cable TV, WiFi Instant Internet at site, WiFi Internet central location, family camping, tenting, cabins, dump, portable dump, laundry, full svc store, RV supplies, LP bottle exch, ice, picnic tables, fire rings, wood.

◆◆◆◆◆RECREATION: rec room/area, equipped pavilion, coin games, swim pool, pond fishing, fishing supplies, golf nearby, bsktball, playground, shuffleboard court shuffleboard court, activities, tennis, horseshoes, sports field, hiking trails, v-ball.

Pets welcome. Partial handicap access. Open Mid Apr - Nov 1. Big rigs welcome. Escort to site. Clubs welcome. Rate in 2010 $35-53 for 2 persons. ATM. Member ARVC, PCOA.

Text 107930 to (440)725-8687 to see our Visual Tour.

Phone: (570)223-0111
Address: 50 Taylor Dr, East Stroudsburg, PA 18301
Lat/Lon: 41.04567/-75.15447
Email: info@mtnvistacampground.com
Web: www.mtnvistacampground.com

SEE AD PAGE 680

(N) OTTER LAKE CAMP RESORT—(Monroe) *From jct I-80 & US 209 (exit 309): Go 4 mi N on US 209, then 300 feet NW on SR 402, then 7-1/2 mi N on Marshalls Creek Rd. Enter on L.*

WELCOME

BEAUTIFUL PRIVATE LAKE

Family camping at only 5W-5W Camp Resort in Pocconos. 300 wooded acres. 60-acre private lake. No fishing license required. From tent sites to Wi-Fi, something for everyone. Seasonal Planned Activities. Softball, Archery, Ceramics.

◆◆◆◆◆FACILITIES: 300 sites, typical site width 33 ft, 35 ft max RV length, 250 full hkups, 50 W&E, (20/30 amps), many extd stay sites, 25 pull-thrus, cable TV, WiFi Instant Internet at site, WiFi Internet central location, family camping, tenting, dump, non-guest dump $, laundry, full svc store, RV supplies, LP gas by weight/by meter, ice, picnic tables, fire rings, wood, controlled access.

◆◆◆◆◆RECREATION: rec hall, rec room/area, pavilion, coin games, 2 swim pools, wading pool, lake swim, hot tub, boating, electric motors only, canoeing, kayaking, ramp, dock, 8 rowboat/8

OTTER LAKE CAMP RESORT—Continued on next page

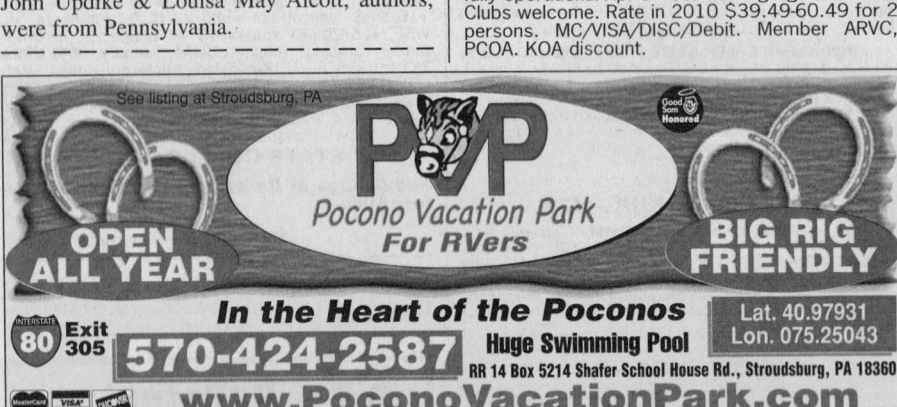

STROUDSBURG—Continued
OTTER LAKE CAMP RESORT—Continued

canoe/4 kayak/6 pedal boat rentals, lake fishing, fishing supplies, golf nearby, bsktball, playground, shuffleboard court 2 shuffleboard courts, activities, tennis, horseshoes, sports field, hiking trails, v-ball.

Pets welcome. Partial handicap access. Open all yr. Facilities fully operational Apr 1 - Nov 1. 5 night min. Jul & Aug. No water to winter sites. Clubs welcome. Rate in 2010 $37-67 for 2 persons. MC/VISA/Debit. ATM. Member ARVC, PCOA.

Text 107929 to (440)725-8687 to see our Visual Tour.

Phone: (800)345-1369
Address: 4805 Marshalls Creek Rd, East Stroudsburg, PA 18302
Lat/Lon: 41.14123/-75.15143
Email: otterlake@otterlake.com
Web: www.otterlake.com

SEE AD NEXT PAGE

(E) POCONO VACATION PARK—(Monroe) *From jct I-80 (exit 305) & Business US 209: Go 2 mi S on Business US 209, then 1/2 mi W on Shafer School House Rd. Enter on L.*

WELCOME

◊◊◊◊FACILITIES: 325 sites, typical site width 30 ft, 315 full hkups, 10 W&E, (20/30/50 amps), many extd stay sites (summer), 300 pull-thrus, cable TV, WiFi Instant Internet at site, family camping, RV storage, dump, non-guest dump $, laundry, ltd groc, LP gas by weight/by meter, ice, picnic tables, fire rings, wood.

◊◊◊◊RECREATION: rec hall, rec room/area, pavilion, coin games, swim pool, wading pool, mini-golf, putting green, golf nearby, bsktball, playground, shuffleboard court shuffleboard court, activities (wkends), horseshoes, sports field, v-ball.

Pets welcome. Partial handicap access. No tents. Open all yr. Facilities fully operational Apr 1 - Oct 31. Big rigs welcome. Escort to site. Clubs welcome. Rate in 2010 $28-33 for 2 persons. MC/VISA/DISC/Debit. Member ARVC, PCOA.

Text 107928 to (440)725-8687 to see our Visual Tour.

Phone: (570)424-2587
Address: RR 14 Box 5214 Shafers School House Rd, Stroudsburg, PA 18360
Lat/Lon: 40.97931/-75.25043
Email: info@poconovacationpark.com
Web: www.poconovacationpark.com

SEE AD PAGE 678 AND AD TRAVEL SECTION PAGE 640

SUNBURY—D-7

(N) Fantasy Island Campground—(Northumberland) *From jct US-11 & SR-147: Go 1/4 mi S on SR-147, then 100 yards E on Park Dr. Enter on L.* ◊◊◊◊FACILITIES: 99 sites, typical site width 30 ft, 40 ft max RV length, 99 full hkups, (20/30 amps), cable TV, WiFi Instant Internet at site, WiFi Internet central location, family camping, tenting, shower$, dump, non-guest dump $, laundry, ltd groc, RV supplies, LP gas by weight/by meter, ice, picnic tables, patios, fire rings, wood. ◊◊◊◊RECREATION: rec hall, equipped pavilion, swim pool, river swim, boating, canoeing, kayaking, ramp, dock, river fishing, fishing supplies, mini-golf, ($), bsktball, play equipment, shuffleboard court, activities horseshoes, v-ball. Pets welcome, breed restrict, quantity restrict. Partial handicap access. Open Apr 15 - Oct 15. Rate in 2010 $38-42 for 4 persons. MC/VISA/Debit. CCUSA 50% Discount.

CAMPCLUB USA

SUNBURY—Continued
Fantasy Island Campground—Continued

CCUSA reservations Not Accepted, CCUSA max stay 2 days, Cash only for CCUSA disc., CCUSA disc. not avail F,Sa, CCUSA disc. not avail holidays.

Phone: (866)882-1307
Address: 401 Park Drive, Sunbury, PA 17801
Lat/Lon: 40.88708/-76.78703
Email: fantasyislandcampground@yahoo.com
Web: www.fantasyislandcampground.com

TAMAQUA—D-8

(SW) ROSEMOUNT CAMPING RESORT —(Schuylkill) *From jct SR-309 & US 209: Go 4 mi SW on US 209, then 2-1/2 mi S on Catawissa, then 1-1/4 mi W on Valley Rd. Enter on R.*

WELCOME

◊◊◊◊FACILITIES: 200 sites, typical site width 30 ft, 36 ft max RV length, 145 full hkups, 55 W&E, (20/30 amps), many extd stay sites (summer), cable TV, ($), family camping, tenting, cabins, dump, non-guest dump $, portable dump, laundry, full svc store, RV supplies, ice, picnic tables, fire rings, wood.

◊◊◊◊RECREATION: rec hall, rec room/area, pavilion, coin games, swim pool, wading pool, boating, no motors, 2 pedal boat rentals, lake fishing, fishing supplies, golf nearby, bsktball, playground, shuffleboard court shuffleboard court, activities, horseshoes, sports field, hiking trails, v-ball.

Pets welcome. Open Apr 15 - Oct 15. Escort to site. Clubs welcome. Rate in 2010 $32-34 per family. MC/VISA/DISC/Debit. Member ARVC, PCOA.

Phone: (570)668-2580
Address: 285 Valley Rd, Tamaqua, PA 18252
Lat/Lon: 40.72103/-76.04640
Web: www.rosemountcampingresort.com

SEE AD THIS PAGE

TARENTUM—D-2

(NW) Mountain Top Campground—(Allegheny) *From jct SR-28 & Millerstown SR-908 (exit 16): Go 4-3/4 mi W on SR-908, then 1/4 mi N on Thompson Rd, then 1/4 E on Sun Mine Rd. Enter on L.* ◊◊◊FACILITIES: 215 sites, 15 full hkups, 200 W&E, (20/30/50 amps), 50 amps ($), 200 pull-thrus, family camping, dump, non-guest dump $, portable dump, picnic tables, fire rings, wood. RECREATION: pavilion, hiking trails. Pets welcome, breed restrict. No tents. Open all yr. Big rigs welcome. Rate in 2010 $50 per vehicle. MC/VISA/DISC/AMEX. CCUSA 50% Discount. CCUSA reservations Accepted, CCUSA max stay Unlimited. No animals known to be vicious. $50/night (standard rate):water & 30 amp electric sites. Monthly rate $500-no discount.

CAMPCLUB USA

Phone: (724)224-1511
Address: 873 Sun Mine Rd, Tarentum, PA 15084
Lat/Lon: 40.65822/-79.80213
Email: camp@mountaintopcampground.com
Web: www.mountaintopcampground.com

TIOGA—A-6

IVES RUN RECREATION AREA (COE-Hammond Lake) —(Tioga) *From jct US 15 & Hwy 287: Go 2 mi S to Tioga, turn W on continue 4 mi S on Hwy 287. Enter on L.* FACILITIES: 160 sites, 45 full hkups, 86 W&E, 29 no hkups, tenting, dump, ltd groc. RECREATION: lake swim, boating, ramp, dock, lake/stream fishing, playground. Partial handicap access. Open Apr 20 - Dec 1. Phone: (570)835-5281.

(NW) Tioga Heritage Campground (REBUILDING) —(Tioga) *From jct SR-287 & US 15: Go 3-1/2 mi S on SR-287, then 2-1/4 mi W on Elkhorn, then 3/4 mi N on Howe Hill Rd, then 1/2 mi E on Petticrew Rd (Scenic View Dr).* FACILITIES: 85 sites, typical site width 35 ft, 50 full hkups, (30 amps), 35 no hkups, family camping, tenting, dump, laundry, ltd groc. RECREATION: canoeing, pond fishing, playground. Pets welcome, quantity restrict. Open End of April - Oct 31. Rate in 2010 $30-35 for 4 persons. Member ARVC, PCOA. Phone: (570) 835-5700.

TIONESTA—B-3

(S) OUTFLOW CAMPING AREA (COE-Tionesta Lake) —(Forest) *From town: Go 1 mi S on Hwy 36 (follow signs). Enter on L.* FACILITIES: 40 sites, 20 ft max RV length, 40 no hkups, tenting, dump. RECREATION: lake swim, boating, canoeing, ramp, dock, lake/stream fishing, play equipment. Open all yr. Facilities fully operational 3rd week in May - Oct. Phone: (814) 755-3512.

(S) TIONESTA RECREATION AREA (COE - Tionesta Lake)—(Forest) *From business center: Go 1 mi S on Hwy-36 follow signs. Enter on L.* FACILITIES: 125 sites, 20 ft max RV length, 61 E, (30 amps), 64 no hkups, tenting, dump, ltd groc. RECREATION: lake/river swim, boating, canoeing, ramp, lake/river/stream fishing, play equipment. Pets welcome. Open May 19 - Oct 12. Phone: (814)755-3512.

TITUSVILLE—B-2

(S) OIL CREEK FAMILY CAMPGROUND —(Venango) *From jct SR-8 & SR-27: Go 4 mi S on SR-8, then 3/4 mi E on Turkey Farm Rd, then 1/2 mi S on Shreve Rd. Enter on L.*

WELCOME

◊◊◊FACILITIES: 97 sites, typical site width 27 ft, 64 full hkups, 26 W&E, (20/30/50 amps), 50 amps ($), 7 no hkups, some extd stay sites (summer), 47 pull-thrus, phone Internet central location, family camping, tenting, RV's/park model rentals, cabins, RV storage, dump, non-guest dump $, portable dump, ltd groc, RV supplies, ice, picnic tables, fire rings, wood.

◊◊◊◊RECREATION: rec room/area, pavilion, coin games, swim pool, pond fishing, fishing supplies, golf nearby, bsktball, 16 bike rentals, playground, activities, (wkends), horseshoes, sports field, hiking trails, v-ball.

Pets welcome. Partial handicap access. Open mid Apr - Nov 1. Clubs welcome. Rate in 2010 $25-27 for 2 persons. MC/VISA/DISC/Debit. Member ARVC, PCOA.

Phone: (814)827-1023
Address: 340 Shreve Rd, Titusville, PA 16354
Lat/Lon: 41.55750/-79.67662
Email: dturner@csonline.net
Web: www.oilcreekcampground.com

SEE AD THIS PAGE

TOBYHANNA—C-9

(SE) Hemlock Campground & Cottages—(Monroe) *From jct I-380 (exit 8) & SR 611: Go 1-3/4 mi S on SR 611, then 1-1/4 mi SE on Hemlock Dr. Enter on L.* ◊◊◊◊FACILITIES: 82 sites, typical site width 27 ft, 63 full hkups, 11 W&E, (30 amps), 8 no hkups, 2 pull-thrus, cable TV, WiFi Instant Internet at site, WiFi Internet central location, family camping, tenting, RV storage, dump, non-guest dump $, portable dump, laundry, ltd groc, RV supplies, LP gas by weight, ice, picnic tables, fire rings, wood. ◊◊◊◊RECREATION: rec hall, pavilion, equipped pavilion, swim pool, bsktball, playground, activities, horseshoes. Pets welcome, breed restrict, quantity restrict. Open May 1 - Oct 31. Rate in 2010 $31-43 per family. MC/VISA/DISC/Debit. Member ARVC, PCOA. FMCA discount. CCUSA 50% Discount. CCUSA reservations Accepted, CCUSA max stay 5 days, Cash only for CCUSA disc., CCUSA disc. not avail F,Sa, CCUSA disc. not avail holidays. No animals known to be vicious. $50/night (standard rate):water & 30 amp electric sites. Monthly rate $500-no discount.

CAMPCLUB USA

Phone: (570)894-4388
Address: 362 Hemlock Dr., Tobyhanna, PA 18466
Lat/Lon: 41.15241/-75.37654
Email: camp@hemlockcampground.com
Web: www.hemlockcampground.com

(N) TOBYHANNA STATE PARK—(Monroe) *From jct I-380 (exit 8) & Hwy 423: Go 3 mi N on Hwy 423. Enter on L.* FACILITIES: 140 sites, 140 no hkups, tenting, dump. RECREATION: lake swim, boating, electric motors only, canoeing, ramp, dock, lake/stream fishing, playground. No pets. Partial handicap access. Open mid Apr - mid Dec. Phone: (570)894-8336.

TOWANDA—B-7

(E) Riverside Acres Campground—(Bradford) *From jct US 6 & SR-187: Go 3/4 mi S on SR-187, then 1-1/2 mi E on Echo Beach Rd. Enter on L.* ◊◊FACILITIES: 41 sites, typical site width 30 ft, 40 ft max RV length, 12 full hkups, 24 W&E, (20/30 amps), 5 no hkups, family camping, tenting, dump, laundry. ◊◊RECREATION: boating, canoeing, ramp, river fishing, play equipment. Pets welcome. Open all yr. Rate in 2010 $28-35 per family. Member ARVC, PCOA. Phone: (570)265-3235.

Woodall's Tip... 100% Money Back Guarantee... If for any reason you're not satisfied with this Directory, please return it to us by December 31, 2011 along with your sales receipt, and we'll reimburse you for the amount you paid for the Directory.

OUR CAMPGROUND FEATURES:
- Large Wooded Sites
- Water and Sewer Hookups
- 50/30/20 Amp Electric
- Big Rig Friendly
- Free Cable TV & WiFi
- Laundry
- Swimming Pool
- Tennis Court
- Stocked Fishing Pond
- Sand Volleyball Court
- Outdoor-Fit Exercise Multigym
- Game Room
- Table Tennis
- Shuffleboard
- Bocce Court
- Horseshoe Pits
- Playground

NEARBY ALL POCONO ATTRACTIONS

DISCOUNT TICKETS AVAILABLE

MOUNTAIN VISTA CAMPGROUND

Pocono Mountains

Escape, Relax, Enjoy

50 Taylor Drive
East Stroudsburg, PA 18301
570-223-0111
www.mtnvistacampground.com

WOODALL'S 5 FACILITIES 5 RECREATION

WOODALL'S RATED 5W 5W

WOODALL'S 5 FACILITIES 5 RECREATION

OTTER LAKE

300 Wooded Acres • 60 Acre Lake • 300 Campsites
Full Hookups • Cable TV • WiFi • 2 Laundries • Store • LP Gas
Fishing (no fishing license required) • Boat Rentals
Year Round Indoor Pool Complex Featuring A Sauna & 2 Whirlpools
Large Outdoor Pool & Kiddie Pool • 4 Tennis Courts
2 Racquetball Courts • Basketball • Sports Field
Seasonal Planned Activities Including:
DJ's • Archery • Ceramics • Free Truck Rides • Bingo

PO Box 850 • Marshalls Creek, PA 18301 • 570-223-0123 • www.otterlake.com

TROUT RUN—B-6

(NE) SHESHEQUIN CAMPGROUND—(Lycoming) *From jct Rte 15 & Rte 14: Go 9 mi N on Rte 14, then 200 yds E on Pleasant Stream Rd. Enter on L.*

WELCOME

◆◆◆FACILITIES: 90 sites, typical site width 30 ft, 90 W&E, (20/30/50 amps), WiFi Internet central location, family camping, tenting, dump, portable dump, ice, picnic tables, fire rings, wood.

◆◆◆RECREATION: pavilion, river swim, canoeing, kayaking, float trips, stream fishing, bsktball, playground, horseshoes, sports field, v-ball.

Pets welcome, breed restrict. Open Mid Apr - Mid Oct. Big rigs welcome. Clubs welcome. Rate in 2010 $25-28 per family. MC/VISA/DISC/Debit. Member ARVC, PCOA.

Phone: (570)995-9230
Address: 389 Marsh Hill Rd, Trout Run, PA 17771
Lat/Lon: 41.47665/-76.97689
Email: sheshequincampground@yahoo.com
Web: www.sheshequincampground.com

SEE AD THIS PAGE

UPPER BLACK EDDY—D-10

(SW) Ringing Rocks Family Campground—(Bucks) *From jct SR 32 & Bridgeton Hill Rd: Go 2-1/2 mi W on Bridgeton Hill Rd (6 ton weight limit on bridge), then 1/4 mi N on Woodland Dr. Enter on R.* ◆◆◆FACILITIES: 114 sites, typical site width 30 ft, 30 ft max RV length, 5 full hkups, 105 W&E, (20/30/50 amps), 4 no hkups, family camping, tenting, dump, laundry, ltd groc. ◆◆◆RECREATION: swim pool, playground. Pets welcome, breed restrict, quantity restrict. Open Apr 1 - Oct 31. Rate in 2010 $35 per family. Phone: (610)982-5552.

WARREN—B-3

(W) ALLEGHENY NATIONAL FOREST (Buckaloons Campground)—(Warren) *From business center: Go 6 mi W on US-6.* FACILITIES: 57 sites, 43 E, (30/50 amps), 14 no hkups, tenting, dump. RECREATION: river swim, boating, canoeing, ramp, river fishing, playground. Pets welcome. Partial handicap access. Open May 7 - Oct 11. Phone: (814)563-9631.

(E) ALLEGHENY NATIONAL FOREST (Dewdrop Campground)—(Warren) *From town: Go 11 mi E on Hwy 59, then 4 mi S on FR 262 (Longhouse Scenic Dr).* FACILITIES: 74 sites, 22 ft max RV length, 74 no hkups, tenting, dump. RECREATION: lake swim, boating, ramp, lake/stream fishing. Open May 22 - Sep 7. Phone: (814)945-6511.

(S) ALLEGHENY NATIONAL FOREST (Hearts Content Campground)—(Warren) *From business center: Go 12 mi SW on Hwy-337, then 4 mi S on FR-18.* FACILITIES: 26 sites, 26 no hkups, tenting, dump. RECREATION: playground. Partial handicap access. Open all yr. Phone: (814)968-3232.

WASHINGTON—E-1

(E) KOA-Washington—(Washington) *From east jct I-70 & I-79: Go 3/4 mi S on I-79 (exit 33), then 1/2 mi W on US 40, then 1 mi N on Vance Station Rd. Enter on L.* ◆◆◆FACILITIES: 78 sites, typical site width 27 ft, 60 full hkups, 5 W&E, 2 E, (20/30/50 amps), 50 amps ($), 11 no hkups, 33 pull-thrus, family camping, tenting, dump, laundry, full svc store. ◆◆◆RECREATION: swim pool, pond fishing, playground. Pets welcome. Partial handicap access. Open Mar 1 - Dec 1. Big rigs welcome. Rate in 2010 $32-40 for 2 persons. Phone: (724)225-7590. KOA discount.

WASHINGTON—Continued

(E) Pine Cove Beach & RV Park—(Washington) *From jct I-70 & SR 481 (exit 35): Go 1/4 mi N on SR 481. Enter on L.* ◆◆◆◆FACILITIES: 38 sites, typical site width 38 ft, 38 full hkups, (30/50 amps), heater not allowed, cable TV, WiFi Internet central location, family camping, RV storage, laundry, ice, picnic tables, fire rings, grills, wood. ◆◆◆◆RECREATION: pavilion, swim pool, wading pool, hot tub, pond fishing, bsktball, playground, activities, horseshoes, v-ball. Pets welcome. Partial handicap access. No tents. Open Apr 1 - Oct 31. Big rigs welcome. Rate in 2010 $35-50 for 4 persons. MC/VISA/DISC/Debit. Member ARVC, PCOA. CCUSA 50% Discount. CCUSA reservations Accepted, CCUSA max stay 1 day, CCUSA disc. not avail S, CCUSA disc. not avail F,Sa, CCUSA disc. not avail holidays.

CAMPCLUB USA

Phone: (724)239-2900
Address: 1495 Route 481, Charleroi, PA 15022
Lat/Lon: 40.12830/-79.95638
Web: www.pinecovebeachclub.com

(N) Whispering Pines Family Campground—(Washington) *From jct I-70 & Hwy 18 (exit 17): Go 4-1/2 mi N on Hwy 18. Enter on L.* ◆◆FACILITIES: 44 sites, typical site width 26 ft, 13 full hkups, 12 W&E, 4 E, (15/20/30/50 amps), 15 no hkups, 3 pull-thrus, family camping, tenting, RV storage, dump, non-guest dump $, LP gas by weight/by meter, ice, picnic tables, fire rings, wood. ◆◆◆RECREATION: swim pool, mini-golf, bsktball, playground, activities, horseshoes, hiking trails, v-ball. Pets welcome. Open Apr 15 - Oct 31. Rate in 2010 $22-26 for 2 persons. MC/VISA/Debit. FCRV discount. FMCA discount. CCUSA 50% Discount. CCUSA reservations Recommended, CCUSA max stay 2 days, CCUSA disc. not avail F,Sa, CCUSA disc. not avail holidays. Discount available Sun thru Thu Memorial Day-Labor Day weekend.

CAMPCLUB USA

Phone: (724)222-9830
Address: 1969 Henderson Ave, Washington, PA 15301
Lat/Lon: 40.23643/-80.29788

WATERVILLE—C-6

(N) Happy Acres Resort—(Lycoming) *From jct SR-44 & SR-4001: Go 3-1/4 mi N on SR-4001. Enter on L.* ◆◆◆FACILITIES: 161 sites, typical site width 30 ft, 71 full hkups, 41 W&E, (20/30/50 amps), 49 no hkups, 5 pull-thrus, family camping, tenting, dump, laundry, groceries. ◆◆◆RECREATION: swim pool, playground. Pets welcome, breed restrict. Open all yr. Big rigs welcome. Rate in 2010 $30-40 for 4 persons. Member ARVC, PCOA. Phone: (570)753-8000.

(N) LITTLE PINE STATE PARK—(Lycoming) *From jct Hwy 44 & LR 4001: Go 4 mi N on LR 4001.* FACILITIES: 99 sites, 30 ft max RV length, 66 E, (50 amps), 33 no hkups, tenting, dump. RECREATION: lake swim, boating, electric motors only, canoeing, ramp, dock, lake/stream fishing, playground. No pets. Partial handicap access. Open Early Apr - Mid Dec. Phone: (570)753-6000.

WAYMART—B-9

(W) KEEN LAKE CAMPING & COTTAGE RESORT—(Wayne) *From jct US-6 & SR-296: Go 1-1/2 mi E on US-6. Enter on R.*

WELCOME

◆◆◆◆FACILITIES: 338 sites, typical site width 25 ft, 40 ft max RV length, 216 full hkups, 81 W&E, (20/30/50 amps), 50 amps ($), 41 no hkups, some extd stay sites (summer), 5 pull-thrus, cable TV, ($), WiFi Instant Internet at site, WiFi Internet central location, family camping, tenting, RV's/park model rentals, cabins, RV storage, shower$, dump, laundry, full svc store, RV supplies, ice, picnic tables, fire rings, wood.

◆◆◆◆◆RECREATION: rec hall, rec room/area, pavilion, equipped pavilion, coin games, swim pool, lake swim, boating, electric motors only, canoeing, kayaking, ramp, dock, 16 rowboat/6 canoe/7 kayak/5 pedal boat rentals, lake/stream fishing, fishing supplies, golf nearby, bsktball, playground, shuffleboard court 2 shuffleboard courts, activities, horseshoes, sports field, hiking trails, v-ball.

WAYMART—Continued
KEEN LAKE CAMPING & COTTAGE RESORT—Continued

Pets welcome, quantity restrict. Partial handicap access. Open May 1 - Columbus Day. Clubs welcome. Rate in 2010 $42-55 for 2 persons. MC/VISA/DISC/Debit. ATM. Member ARVC, PCOA.

Text 107931 to (440)725-8687 to see our Visual Tour.

Phone: (570)488-6161
Address: 155 Keen Lake Rd, Waymart, PA 18472
Lat/Lon: 41.59283/-75.37656
Email: camping@keenlake.com
Web: www.keenlake.com

SEE AD THIS PAGE

(N) VALLEYVIEW FARM & CAMPGROUND—(Wayne) *From jct US 6 & SR-296 (Belmont Tpk): Go 7-1/4 mi N on SR-296 (Belmont Tpk), then follow signs for 1/2 mi on paved road. Enter on L.*

WELCOME

◆◆FACILITIES: 94 sites, typical site width 50 ft, 71 full hkups, 4 W&E, (20/30/50 amps), 19 no hkups, some extd stay sites (summer), family camping, tenting, RV's/park model rentals, cabins, RV storage, dump, non-guest dump $, laundry, ltd groc, RV supplies, LP gas by weight/by meter, ice, picnic tables, fire rings, wood.

◆◆RECREATION: rec hall, swim pool, pond fishing, mini-golf, ($), golf nearby, bsktball, playground, hiking trails.

Pets welcome. Partial handicap access. Open May 15 - Oct 15. Big rigs welcome. Clubs welcome. Rate in 2010 $28 for 4 persons. MC/VISA. Member ARVC, PCOA.

Phone: (570)448-2268
Address: 1576 Belmont Tpk, Waymart, PA 18472
Lat/Lon: 41.68909/-75.41228
Email: rvcamp@nep.net
Web: www.valleyviewfarmcampground.com

SEE AD SCRANTON PAGE 676

WELLSBORO—B-6

(SW) CANYON COUNTRY CAMPGROUND—(Tioga) *From jct US 6 and SR-660: Go 9 mi W on SR-660, then 1/4 mi SW on Wilson Road. Enter on R.*

WELCOME

◆◆◆◆FACILITIES: 68 sites, typical site width 60 ft, 30 full hkups, 17 W&E, 7 E, (20/30 amps), 14 no hkups, 17 pull-thrus, WiFi Internet central location, family camping, tenting, cabins, dump, laundry, ltd groc, RV supplies, LP gas by weight/by meter, ice, picnic tables, fire rings, wood.

CANYON COUNTRY CAMPGROUND—Continued on next page

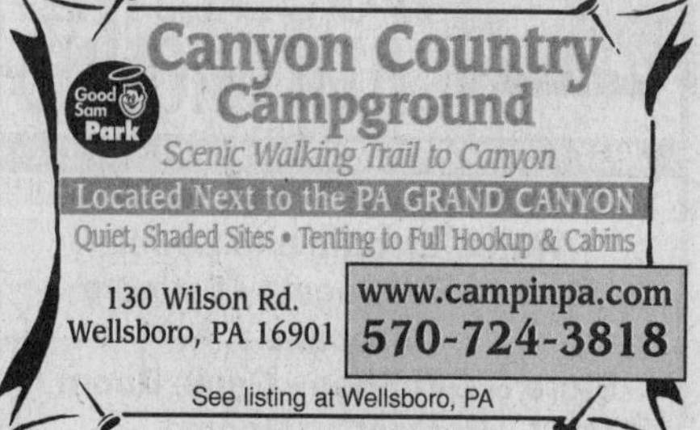

WELLSBORO—Continued
CANYON COUNTRY CAMPGROUND—Continued

◆◆◆RECREATION: rec room/area, pavilion, coin games, golf nearby, bsktball, playground, horseshoes, sports field, hiking trails, v-ball.

Pets welcome, quantity restrict. Open Apr 15 - Oct 31. Escort to site. Clubs welcome. Rate in 2010 $29-33 per family. MC/VISA/DISC/Debit. Member ARVC, PCOA. CCUSA 50% Discount. CCUSA reservations Not Accepted, CCUSA max stay 2 days, Cash only for CCUSA disc., CCUSA disc. not avail F,Sa, CCUSA disc. not avail holidays. Discount available Apr 15-May 15, after Labor Day-Sep 30 & Oct 15-Oct 31. Max 2 pets. May call ahead same day for availability. Discount not available on cabins.

Phone: (570)724-3818
Address: 130 Wilson Rd, Wellsboro, PA 16901
Lat/Lon: 41.69320/-77.43840
Email: info@campinpa.com
Web: www.campinpa.com

SEE AD PAGE 681

COLTON POINT STATE PARK—(Tioga) *From business center: Go 11 mi W on US 6, then 6 mi S on Colton Point Rd.* FACILITIES: 25 sites, 20 ft max RV length, 25 no hkups, tenting, dump. RECREATION: stream fishing, playground. No pets. Partial handicap access. Open Apr 9 - Oct 17. Phone: (570)724-3061.

(NW) HILLS CREEK STATE PARK—(Tioga) *From junction of 660 and Rt 6, go 4 mi E on US 6, then N on access rd.* FACILITIES: 85 sites, 26 E, (30/50 amps), 59 no hkups, tenting, dump. RECREATION: lake swim, boating, electric motors only, ramp, lake fishing, playground. Partial handicap access. Open mid Apr - late Oct. Phone: (570)724-4246.

(W) LEONARD HARRISON STATE PARK—(Tioga) *From business center: Go 10 mi SW on Hwy-660.* FACILITIES: 30 sites, 35 ft max RV length, 9 E, (50 amps), 21 no hkups, tenting, dump. RECREATION: ramp, dock, lake fishing, playground. No pets. Partial handicap access. Open Apr 10 - Oct 18. Phone: (570)724-3061.

(SW) STONY FORK CREEK CAMPGROUND—(Tioga) *From jct US 6 & SR-660: Go 3/4 mi W on SR-660, then 7 mi S on Kelsey St/SR 3007, then 1-1/4 mi S on Stony Fork Creek Rd. Enter on R.*

WELCOME

◆◆◆◆FACILITIES: 213 sites, typical site width 35 ft, 98 full hkups, 52 W&E, 2 E, (20/30/50 amps), 61 no hkups, some extd stay sites (summer), WiFi Instant Internet at site, family camping, tenting, RV's/park model rentals, cabins, RV storage, dump, non-guest dump $, portable dump, laundry, groceries, RV supplies, ice, picnic tables, fire rings, wood.

◆◆◆◆RECREATION: rec room/area, pavilion, coin games, swim pool, boating, no motors, canoeing, kayaking, rowboat/3 pedal boat rentals, pond/stream fishing, fishing supplies, golf nearby, bsktball, playground, activities, (wkends), horseshoes, sports field, hiking trails, v-ball.

Pets welcome. Partial handicap access. Open all yr. Facilities fully operational Memorial Day wknd - end of Oct. Limited sites with water in winter. Big rigs welcome. Clubs welcome. Rate in 2010 $30-35 for 4 persons. MC/VISA/Debit. Member ARVC, PCOA.

Phone: (570)724-3096
Address: 658 Stony Fork Creek Rd., Wellsboro, PA 16901
Lat/Lon: 41.63953/-77.37078
Email: simba61@epix.net
Web: www.stonyforkcamp.com

SEE AD PAGE 681

(S) Twin Streams Campground—(Tioga) *From north jct SR-287 & SR-414: Go 1/4 mi N on SR-287. Enter on L.* ◆◆◆FACILITIES: 150 sites, typical site width 27 ft, 100 full hkups, 20 W&E, (20/30/50 amps), 50 amps ($), 30 no hkups, 7 pull-thrus, family camping, tenting, dump, laundry, groceries. ◆◆◆RECREATION: stream fishing, playground. Pets welcome. Partial handicap access. Open Apr 15 - Early Dec. Big rigs welcome. Rate in 2010 $28-33 for 4 persons. Member ARVC, PCOA. Phone: (570)353-7251.

WEST CHESTER—E-9

(SW) KOA-Philadelphia/West Chester—(Chester) *From jct US 202 & US 1: Go 9 mi SW on US 1, then 3 mi NW on SR 82, then 3 mi E on SR 162. Enter on L.* ◆◆◆◆FACILITIES: 94 sites, typical site width 28 ft, 39 full hkups, 27 W&E, 3 E, (20/30/50 amps), 50 amps ($), 25 no hkups, 15 pull-thrus, family camping, tenting, dump, laundry, groceries. ◆◆◆◆RECREATION: swim pool, boating, no motors, canoeing, river fishing, playground. Pets welcome. Partial handicap access. Open Apr 1 - Oct 31. Big rigs welcome. Rate in 2010 $45-68 per family. Member ARVC, PCOA. Phone: (610)486-0447. KOA discount.

WHITE HAVEN—C-8

(E) HICKORY RUN STATE PARK—(Carbon) *From jct I-80 (exit 274) & Hwy 534: Go 6 mi E on Hwy 534. Enter on R.* FACILITIES: 381 sites, typical site width 10 ft, 64 E, (30/50 amps), 317 no hkups, tenting, dump, ltd groc. RECREATION: lake swim, lake/stream fishing, play equipment. No pets. Partial handicap access. Open Apr 9 - Dec 19. Phone: (570)443-0400.

(E) LEHIGH GORGE CAMPGROUND—(Carbon) *From jct I-80 (exit 274) & West SR-534: Go 1/4 mi, then 1/4 mi W on SR-940. Enter on R.*

WELCOME

◆◆◆◆FACILITIES: 240 sites, typical site width 26 ft, 200 full hkups, (30 amps), 40 no hkups, many extd stay sites (summer), 20 pull-thrus, cable TV, WiFi Instant Internet at site, family camping, tenting, laundry, groceries, RV supplies, LP gas by weight/by meter, ice, picnic tables, fire rings, wood, controlled access.

◆◆◆◆RECREATION: rec room/area, equipped pavilion, coin games, swim pool, lake swim, lake fishing, fishing supplies, golf nearby, bsktball, playground, activities, (wkends), horseshoes, hiking trails, v-ball.

Pets welcome, quantity restrict. Partial handicap access. Open Mid Mar - Mid Dec. Call for availability in Winter. Clubs welcome. Green Friendly. Rate in 2010 $37 per family. MC/VISA/DISC/Debit.

Phone: (570)443-9191
Address: 4585 State St Rt 940, White Haven, PA 18661
Lat/Lon: 41.06585/-75.75272
Email: liz@lehighgorgecampground.com
Web: www.lehighgorgecampground.com

SEE AD BLAKESLEE PAGE 651

✽ **(E) LEHIGH GORGE RV CENTER**—*From jct I-80 (exit 274) & West SR-534: Go 1/4 mi, then 1/4 mi W on SR-940. Enter on R.* SALES: travel trailers, truck campers, 5th wheels, toy hauler, pre-owned unit sales. SERVICES: full-time mech, RV appliance repair, body work/collision repair, LP gas by weight/by meter, sells parts/accessories, installs hitches. Open all yr. MC/VISA/DISC.

WELCOME

Phone: (570)443-9876
Address: 4585 State St Rt 940, White Haven, PA 18661
Email: jay@lehighgorgerv.com
Web: www.lehighgorgerv.com

SEE AD BLAKESLEE PAGE 651

WILKES-BARRE—C-8

FRANCES SLOCUM STATE PARK—(Luzerne) *From jct I-81 (exit 170B) & Hwy 309: Go 7 mi N on Hwy 309, then 4 mi E on Carverton Rd, then 1 mi N on Eighth St, then 1 mi W on Mt. Olivet Rd.* FACILITIES: 100 sites, 35 ft max RV length, 54 E, 46 no hkups, tenting, dump. RECREATION: swim pool, boating, electric motors only, ramp, lake fishing, playground. No pets. Partial handicap access. Open Apr 9 - Oct 17. Phone: (570)696-3525.

WIND RIDGE—E-1

(SW) RYERSON STATION STATE PARK (McNay Ridge Campground)—(Greene) *From business center: Go 2 mi SW on Hwy 21, follow signs, then 2 mi S on Hwy 3022 (Bristoria Rd), then 1/2 mi E on McNay Ridge Rd. Enter on L.* FACILITIES: 48 sites, 16 E, (30/50 amps), 32 no hkups, 20 pull-thrus, tenting, dump. RECREATION: swim pool, boating, electric motors only, ramp, dock, lake/stream fishing, playground. No pets. Open all yr. Phone: (724)428-4254.

WOODLAND—C-4

(N) WOODLAND CAMPGROUND—(Clearfield) *From jct I-80 (exit 123) & SR-970: Go 3/4 mi N on SR-970, then 1/4 mi E on Egypt Rd. Enter on R.*

WELCOME

◆◆◆◆FACILITIES: 80 sites, typical site width 26 ft, 67 full hkups, 2 W&E, (20/30/50 amps), 11 no hkups, some extd stay sites (summer), 36 pull-thrus, cable TV, WiFi Instant Internet at site, family camping, tenting, RV's/park model rentals, cabins, RV storage, dump, non-guest dump $, portable dump, laundry, groceries, RV supplies, LP gas by weight/by meter, ice, picnic tables, fire rings, wood.

◆◆◆RECREATION: rec room/area, pavilion, coin games, lake swim, hot tub, boating, electric motors only, canoeing, kayaking, dock, rowboat/2 kayak/2 pedal boat rentals, pond fishing, fishing supplies, golf nearby, bsktball, playground, activities, (wkends), horseshoes, hiking trails, v-ball.

Pets welcome, breed restrict. Partial handicap access. Open all yr. Facilities fully operational Apr 1 - Dec 21. Big rigs welcome. Escort to site. Clubs welcome. Rate in 2010 $36 per family. MC/VISA/DISC/Debit. Member ARVC, PCOA. FMCA discount.

Phone: (814)857-5388
Address: 314 Egypt Rd, Woodland, PA 16881
Lat/Lon: 41.03027/-78.33544
Email: woodlandcampground@yahoo.com
Web: www.woodlandpa.com

SEE AD THIS PAGE AND AD TRAVEL SECTION PAGE 640

YORK—E-7

(SW) Ben Franklin RV Park—(York) *From I-83 & US-30: Go 6 mi W on US-30, then 100 yards S on SR-616 (Trinity Rd), then 1/4 mi E on Woodberry Rd. Enter on L.* ◆◆FACILITIES: 29 sites, typical site width 30 ft, accepts self-contained units only, 29 full hkups, (20/30/50 amps), 1 pull-thrus, WiFi Instant Internet at site, family camping. RECREATION: Pets welcome. No tents. Open all yr. Big rigs welcome. Rate in 2010 $30 for 4 persons. MC/VISA/DISC. CCUSA 50% Discount. CCUSA reservations Recommended, CCUSA max stay 1 day, CCUSA disc. not avail F,Sa. No restrooms. Accepts self-contained units only.

CAMPCLUB USA

Phone: (717)792-9612
Address: 1350 Woodberry Rd, York, PA 17408
Lat/Lon: 39.93427/-76.80071
Email: ben@benfranklinrvpark.com
Web: www.benfranklinrvpark.com

(S) Indian Rock Campground—(York) *From jct I-83 (exit 14) & SR 182: Go 2-1/2 mi W on SR 182/Indian Rock Dam Rd, then 100 yards S on Croll School Rd. Enter on R.* ◆◆FACILITIES: 46 sites, typical site width 27 ft, 34 ft max RV length, 30 full hkups, 6 W&E, (20/30 amps), 10 no hkups, 3 pull-thrus, family camping, tenting, dump, ltd groc. Pets welcome. Partial handicap access. Open all yr. Facilities fully operational Apr 1 - Nov 1. Rate in 2010 $26 for 2 persons. Member ARVC, PCOA. Phone: (717)741-1764.

YORK SPRINGS—E-6

(SE) Hershey's Fur Center Camping Area (Not Visited)—(Adams) *From jct US 15 & Hwy 94: Go 1/4 mi S on Hwy 94. Enter on R.* FACILITIES: 25 sites, typical site width 27 ft, 22 ft max RV length, 6 full hkups, 15 W&E, (20/30 amps), 4 no hkups, 2 pull-thrus, family camping, tenting, dump. RECREATION: lake swim, lake/stream fishing, playground. Pets welcome, size restrict. Open May 1 - Oct 30. Rate in 2010 $25-30 for 4 persons. Phone: (717)528-4412.

TIME ZONE

Rhode Island is in the Eastern Time Zone.

TOPOGRAPHY

Rhode Island, the smallest state in the US, has a total area of 1,214 sq. miles, a length of 48 miles and a width of 37 miles at the longest points. In addition, the state has 400 miles of coastline. Other physical features include 5 major bays and several saltwater rivers. High, rocky cliffs dominate the Atlantic southeast coastline.

TEMPERATURE

The warming influence of Narragansett Bay makes the climate of Rhode Island milder, and with fewer high and low extremes, than that of the other New England states. Average annual precipitation is about 40 inches in the north part of the state and about 50 inches along the coast. January temperatures average about 30°. In July, temperatures average about 72°.

TRAVEL & TOURISM INFO

State Agency:
Rhode Island Tourism Division
315 Iron Horse Way, Suite 101
Providence, RI 02908 (800/556-2484)
www.VisitRhodeIsland.com

South County Rhode Island
4808 Tower Hill Rd
Wakefield, RI 02879
(800/548-4662 or 401/789-4422)
www.southcountryri.com

RECREATIONAL INFO

Fishing: Rhode Island Dept. of Environmental Management, Div. of Fish & Wildlife, 4808 Tower Hill Rd., Wakefield, RI 02879 (401/789-3094 or 401/222-3575).

SHOPPING

Bowen's Wharf, Newport. Twenty-five shops and art galleries with hand-blown glass, locally crafted scrimshaw, jewelry, men and women's fashions, toys, candles, bags, imports from Ireland and Bali, Italian leather.

Only in Rhode Island, Newport. Unique products created in Rhode Island include photography, jewelry, gourmet food, candles, pottery, books, music and artwork. Located at The Shops at Long Wharf.

DESTINATIONS

This state is packed with 400 miles of coastline and 20 percent of the country's historic landmarks. Newport is the sailing capital of the world, and home to the famed Gilded Age mansions.

Blackstone Valley. The valley, with the mighty Blackstone River, offers an abundance of scenic vistas, historic homes, factory outlets and special events.

Block Island is a popular resort area with many recreational opportunities and historical sites. Popular attractions include Mohegan Bluffs, which rise abruptly about 200 ft. above the sea and stretch for several miles along the southeastern shore. Southeast Lighthouse has the most powerful beacon on the eastern coast of the United States.

Bristol. Popular attractions include **Blithewold Mansion & Gardens**, a 45-room mansion and 33 acres of landscaped grounds bordering Bristol Harbor; the **Bristol Art Museum; Coggeshall Farm Museum**, an 18th-century working farm restoration featuring a colonial orchard, herb garden, farm animals and craft demonstrations; **Colt State Park**, featuring playing fields, picnic areas, saltwater fishing and a scenic drive around the shoreline of the former Colt family estate on the east side of Narragansett Bay.

Narragansett Bay. Visit lighthouses and charming harbor towns along the bay. Or enjoy a variety of water sports in the pro-

Where to Find CCUSA Parks

List City	Park Name	Map Coordinates
HOPE VALLEY		
	Whispering Pines Campground	D-2

QUICK REFERENCE CHART FOR WOODALL'S FEATURED PARKS

	Green Friendly	RV Lots for Sale	Park Models-Onsite Ownership	Park Membership for Sale	Big Rigs Welcome	Internet Friendly	Pets Welcome
FOSTER							
Ginny-B Family Campground							■
HARMONY							
Holiday Acres Camping Resort						●	■
HOPE VALLEY							
Whispering Pines Campground					▲	●	■

Green Friendly ; RV Lots for Sale ✖; Park Models/Onsite Onwership ✱; Park Memberships for Sale ✔; Big Rigs Welcome ▲; Internet Friendly ●; Internet Friendly-WiFi ●; Pets Welcome ■

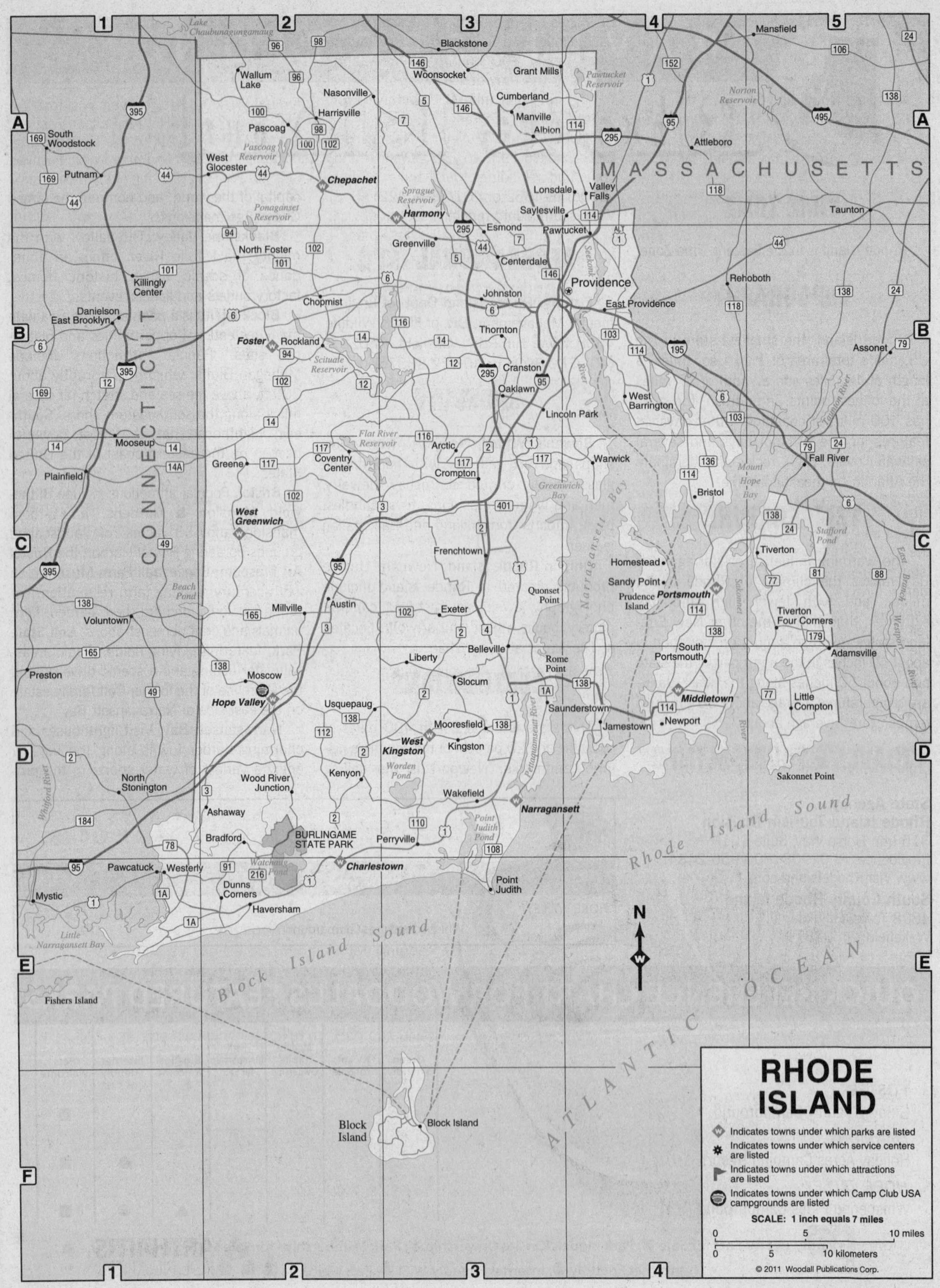
RHODE ISLAND
MASSACHUSETTS
CONNECTICUT
Indicates towns under which parks are listed
Indicates towns under which service centers are listed
Indicates towns under which attractions are listed
Indicates towns under which Camp Club USA campgrounds are listed
SCALE: 1 inch equals 7 miles
0 5 10 miles
0 5 10 kilometers
Providence
Block Island Sound
Rhode Island Sound
ATLANTIC OCEAN
Narragansett Bay
Block Island
Fishers Island
Woonsocket
Pawtucket
Cranston
Warwick
Newport
Westerly
Narragansett
Charlestown
Portsmouth
Middletown
Chepachet
Harmony
Foster
West Greenwich
Hope Valley
West Kingston
BURLINGAME STATE PARK

tected harbors and inlets. Parasailing, scuba diving, fishing, sailing, whale watching and kayaking are all available in the bay's marinas.

Newport. Stroll along the beautiful Cliff Walk (3 miles) and view the rocky coast on one side and several estates on the other. **Newport Mansions** are fabled for their extravagant opulence. Six are owned and operated by the Preservation Society of Newport County.

Additional Newport attractions include: **Touro Synagogue**, the oldest in America; **Trinity Church**, an Episcopal church of colonial times; **Friends Meeting House**, the oldest Quaker meeting house in America; and **Old Stone Mill**. **Fort Adams State Park** offers picnicking, swimming, boating and fishing.

The **Newport Jazz Festival** features outstanding music every August by legendary performers as well as rising stars.

Providence. The capital is known as the site of **Brown University**, as well as for countless other educational and historic attractions. Among them are the **First Baptist Meeting House**, built in 1774-75 and the **Old State House**, where the Rhode Island General Assembly renounced allegiance to King George III in May 1776. The Capitol building itself has one of only four self-supporting domes in the world. It houses the original Rhode Island Charter and the historic portrait of George Washington painted by Gilbert Stuart. The **Roger Williams Park & Zoo** affords a relaxing retreat on 430 acres of woodlands, waterways and winding drives. **Providence Children's Museum** makes science fun with its "hands-on" approach. In the summer and fall, a must see is **Waterfire Providence**, when nearly 100 bonfires illuminate the waters of the Providence River and thread through one half mile of downtown Providence's WaterPlace Park.

South County Museum, Narragansett. Established in 1933 to inspire wonder and a better understanding of rural and agricultural village life in coastal Rhode Island. Six exhibit buildings highlight blacksmith, carpentry, printing and textile trades and a Living History Farm.

ANNUAL EVENTS

FEBRUARY

Spring Flower & Garden Show, Providence; Newport Winter Festival, Newport.

MARCH

Irish Heritage Month, Newport; Maple Sugar Thanksgiving, Exeter; Celtic Festival, West Kingston.

APRIL

Annual Pawcatuck River Duck Race, Westerly.

MAY

Gaspee Days Arts & Crafts Festival, Pawtuxet Village; Rhode Island Lighthouse Cruise & Newport Harbor Tours, North Kingstown; Virtu Art Festival, Westerly; Kenyon's Grist Mill Open House, South Kingston.

JUNE

Main Street Stroll, East Greenwich; Scottish Highland Festival, Richmond; Strawberry Festival, Wickford; Annual Narragansett Art Fetstival, Narragansett.

JULY

Annual Wickford Art Festival, Wickford Village; South County Hot Air Balloon Festival, Kingston; Annual Art of the Ocean State, Wickford; Kingston Chamber Music Festival, Kingston; Annual Blessing of the Fleet Weekend, Narragansett; Annual Folk Art Quilt Show, Narragansett; Crabman Sprint Triathlon, Matunuck Beach.

AUGUST

JVC Jazz Festival, Newport; Annual Meeting Green Corn Festival, Charlestown; RI International Film Festival, West Kingston; Annual Wine Tasting by the Sea, West Kingston; Annual Washington County Fair, Richmond.

SEPTEMBER

International Boat Show, Newport; Annual Rhythm and Roots Festival, Charlestown; Annual Hopkinton Colonial Crafts Festival, Ashaway; Summer's End Festival, Narragansett; Wickford Harbour Fest, North Kingston; Swamp Yankee Days Festival, Ashaway.

OCTOBER

Stuart Fall Festival, Saunderstown; Pumpkin Fest, Narragansett.

NOVEMBER

Holiday Pottery & Art Sale, Kingston.

DECEMBER

Wickford Festival of Lights, Wickford Village; Annual Artcraft Show & Sale, West Kingston.

Rhode Island

All privately owned campgrounds personally inspected by
WOODALL'S
Representatives
Greg and Maureen Baron

CHARLESTOWN—E-2

(W) BURLINGAME STATE PARK—(Washington) *From Jct Hwy 2, Hwy 212 & Hwy 1: Go 3.6 S on Hwy 1, then 2/10 mi W on Camping Area exit ramp, then 1/10 mi N on Klondike Rd. Enter on R.* FACILITIES: 700 sites, typical site width 40 ft, 700 no hkups, 36 pull-thrus, tenting, dump, full svc store. RECREATION: lake swim, boating, canoeing, ramp, lake fishing, playground. No pets. Partial handicap access. Open Apr 15 - Oct 31. Phone: (401)322-7994.

CHARLESTOWN—Continued

(S) CHARLESTOWN BREACHWAY (State Camping Area)—(Washington) *From town: Go S on Charlestown Beach Rd.* FACILITIES: 75 sites, 75 no hkups. RECREATION: saltwater swim, boating, ramp, saltwater fishing. No pets. Partial handicap access. No tents. Open Apr 15 - Oct 31. Phone: (401)364-7000.

CHEPACHET—A-2

(W) Bowdish Lake Camping Area—(Providence) *From jct Hwy 102 & US 44: Go 6-1/2 mi W on US 44. Enter on R.* ◇◇FACILITIES: 400 sites, typical site width 40 ft, 400 W&E, (15/20/30/50 amps), 50 amps ($), 6 pull-thrus, family camping, tenting, dump, ltd groc. ◇◇◇◇RECREATION: lake swim, boating, 10 hp limit, canoeing, ramp, lake fishing, playground. Pets welcome ($), breed restrict. Open May 14 - Columbus Day. Rate in 2010 $30-100 per family. Member ARVC, RICOA. Phone: (401)568-8890.

GEORGE WASHINGTON MANAGEMENT AREA (SP) —(Providence) *From jct US-44 & Hwy-102: Go 6 mi W on US-44.* FACILITIES: 45 sites, 45 no hkups, tenting. RECREATION: lake swim, boating, ramp, lake fishing, playground. No pets. Partial handicap access. Open Apr 11 - Oct 15. Phone: (401)568-2013.

Rhode Island State Flower: Violet

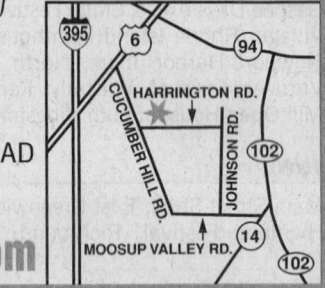

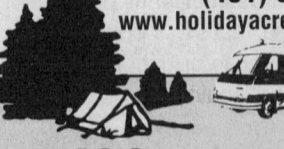

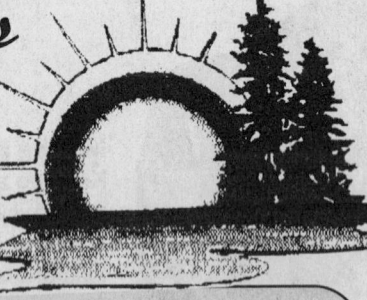

FOSTER—B-2

(SW) GINNY-B FAMILY CAMPGROUND —(Providence) *From jct Hwy-94 & US-6: Go 3-1/4 mi W on US-6, then 3-1/2 mi S on Cucumber Hill Rd, then 1/2 mi E on Harrington Rd. Enter on L.*

◇◇◇FACILITIES: 200 sites, typical site width 35 ft, 50 full hkups, 150 W&E, (20/30/50 amps), many extd stay sites (summer), 35 pull-thrus, family camping, tenting, dump, portable dump, laundry, ltd groc, ice, picnic tables, fire rings, wood.

◇◇◇RECREATION: rec room/area, pavilion, lake swim, pond/stream fishing, fishing supplies, golf nearby, bsktball, playground, activities, (wkends), horseshoes, sports field, v-ball.

Pets welcome. Partial handicap access. Open May 1 - Sep 30. Clubs welcome. Rate in 2010 $31-32 for 2 persons. Member ARVC, RICOA.

Phone: (401)397-9477
Address: 7 Harrington Rd, Foster, RI 02825
Lat/Lon: 41.75383/-71.75455
Email: gnnyb@aol.com
Web: www.ginny-bcampground.com

SEE AD THIS PAGE

HARMONY—A-3

(W) HOLIDAY ACRES CAMPING RESORT —(Providence) *From jct I-295 & Hwy 44: Go 2-1/2 mi W on Hwy 44, then 1-1/2 mi S on Hwy 116 (Smith Ave), then 2-3/4 mi W on Snake Hill Rd. Enter on R.*

◇◇◇FACILITIES: 233 sites, typical site width 50 ft, 165 full hkups, 68 W&E, (20/30/50 amps), 50 amps ($), many extd stay sites (summer), 7 pull-thrus, cable Internet central location, family camping, tenting, dump, portable dump, laundry, ltd groc, RV supplies, LP gas by weight/by meter, ice, picnic tables, fire rings, wood.

◇◇◇◇RECREATION: rec hall, rec room/area, pavilion, coin games, lake swim, boating, electric motors only, canoeing, kayaking, ramp, 5 rowboat/7 canoe/2 kayak/8 pedal boat rentals, lake fishing, fishing supplies, mini-golf, ($), bsktball, playground, shuffleboard court 2 shuffleboard courts, activities (wkends), horseshoes, sports field, hiking trails, v-ball.

Pets welcome. Open all yr. Facilities fully operational Apr 15 - Oct 30. Clubs welcome. Rate in 2010 $40-55 per family. MC/VISA. Member ARVC.

Phone: (401)934-0780
Address: 591 Snake Hill Rd., N Scituate, RI 02857
Lat/Lon: 41.87909/-71.62210
Email: lyon421@aol.com
Web: www.holidayacrescampground.com

SEE AD THIS PAGE

HOPE VALLEY—D-2

(NW) WHISPERING PINES CAMPGROUND—(Washington) *From jct I-95 (exit 3B) & Hwy 138: Go 3 mi W on Hwy 138, then 1/2 mi N on Saw Mill Rd. Enter on L.*

◇◇◇FACILITIES: 212 sites, typical site width 25 ft, 126 full hkups, 76 W&E, (20/30/50 amps), 10 no hkups, many extd stay sites (summer), 20 pull-thrus, WiFi Internet central location, family camping, tenting, cabins, dump, portable dump, laundry, ltd groc, RV supplies, LP gas by meter, ice, picnic tables, fire rings, grills, wood, controlled access.

◇◇◇◇RECREATION: rec hall, pavilion, coin games, swim pool, canoeing, 5 rowboat/3 canoe/5 pedal boat rentals, pond/stream fishing, fishing supplies, mini-golf, ($), bsktball, 20 bike rentals, playground, activities, (wkends), horseshoes, sports field, v-ball.

Pets welcome, breed restrict. Open Mid Apr - Columbus Day. Facilities fully operational Memorial

WHISPERING PINES CAMPGROUND—Continued on next page

HOPE VALLEY—Continued
WHISPERING PINES CAMPGROUND—Continued

Day - Labor Day. 3 day minimum on holiday weekends. Big rigs welcome. Escort to site. Clubs welcome. Rate in 2010 $31-52 per family. MC/VISA/AMEX. Member ARVC, RICOA. CCUSA 50% Discount. CCUSA reservations Recommended, CCUSA max stay Unlimited, CCUSA disc. not avail holidays. Discount available Apr 10-May 20 and Sep 10-Oct 15.

Phone: (401)539-7011
Address: 41 Saw Mill Rd, Hope Valley, RI 02832
Lat/Lon: 41.52847/-71.73658
Email: wpinesri@aol.com
Web: www.whisperingpinescamping.com

SEE AD THIS PAGE

MIDDLETOWN—D-4

(S) Meadowlark RV & Mobile Home Park (RV SPACES)—(Newport) *From jct Hwy 138 & Hwy 138A: Go 1-1/2 mi S on Hwy 138A, then 1/4 mi E on Prospect Ave. Enter on R.* FACILITIES: 40 sites, typical site width 22 ft, accepts self-contained units only, 40 full hkups, (30 amps), family camping, dump. Pets welcome. No tents. Open Apr 15 - Oct 30. Rate in 2010 $30-45 for 2 persons. Phone: (401)846-9455.

NARRAGANSETT—D-3

(S) FISHERMEN'S MEMORIAL STATE PARK—(Washington) *From town: Go S on Hwy-108 (Point Judith Rd), then E.* FACILITIES: 182 sites, 40 full hkups, 107 W&E, 35 no hkups, tenting, dump. RECREATION: playground. No pets. Partial handicap access. Open all yr. Facilities fully operational Apr 15 - Oct 31. Phone: (401)789-8374.

PORTSMOUTH—C-4

(SW) MELVILLE PONDS CAMPGROUND (City Park)—(Newport) *N'bound: from jct Hwy 138 & Hwy 114: Go 4-3/4 mi N on Hwy 114, then 1/2 mi W on Stringham Rd, then 1/2 mi N on Sullivan Rd. S'bound: from jct Hwy 24 & Hwy 114: Go 1-1/2 mi S on Hwy 114, then 1/2 mi W on Stringham, then N on Sullivan.* FACILITIES: 133 sites, 35 full hkups, 35 W&E, 63 no hkups, tenting, dump. RECREATION: boating, electric motors only, canoeing, pond fishing, playground. Pets welcome. Partial handicap access. Open Apr 1 - Oct 31. Phone: (401)682-2424.

PROVIDENCE—B-4

See listings at Foster, Harmony, Hope Valley & West Greenwich.

WEST GREENWICH—C-2

(SW) Oak Embers Campground—(Kent) *From jct Hwy 3 & Hwy 165: Go 5-1/4 mi W on Hwy 165, then 1-1/2 mi N on Escoheag Hill Rd. Enter on L.* ◇◇◇FACILITIES: 92 sites, typical site width 30 ft, 40 full hkups, 40 W&E, (20/30/50 amps), 12 no hkups, 17

WEST GREENWICH—Continued
Oak Embers Campground—Continued

pull-thrus, family camping, tenting, dump, laundry, ltd groc. ◇◇◇RECREATION: swim pool, play equipment. Pets welcome. Open May 1 - Nov 30. Rate in 2010 $35-40 per family. Member ARVC, RICOA. Phone: (401) 397-4042.

WEST KINGSTON—D-3

(N) Wawaloam Campground—(Washington) *From jct I-95 (exit 5A) & Hwy 102: Go 2 mi S on Hwy 102, then 1/2 mi SW on Town Hall Rd, then 2 mi S on Gardiner Rd. Enter on R.* ◇◇◇FACILITIES: 300 sites, typical site width 50 ft, 140 full hkups, 160 W&E, (20/30/50 amps), 50 amps ($), family camping, tenting, dump, laundry, groceries. ◇◇◇◇RECREATION: swim pool, pond fishing, playground. Pets welcome. Open all yr. Facilities fully operational May 1 - Oct 31. Rate in 2010 $40-45 per family. Member ARVC, RICOA. Phone: (401)294-3039.

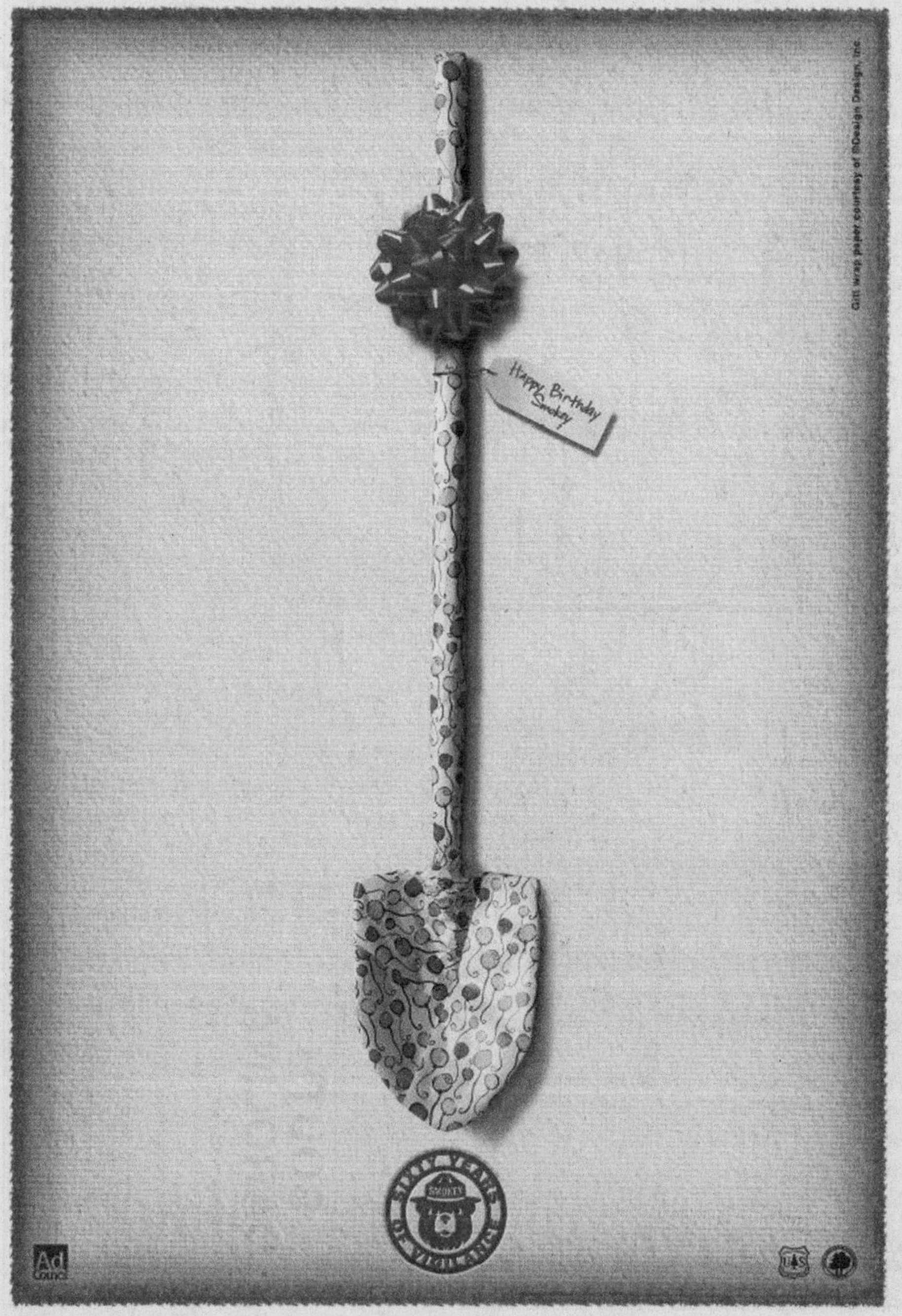

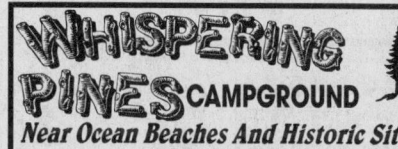

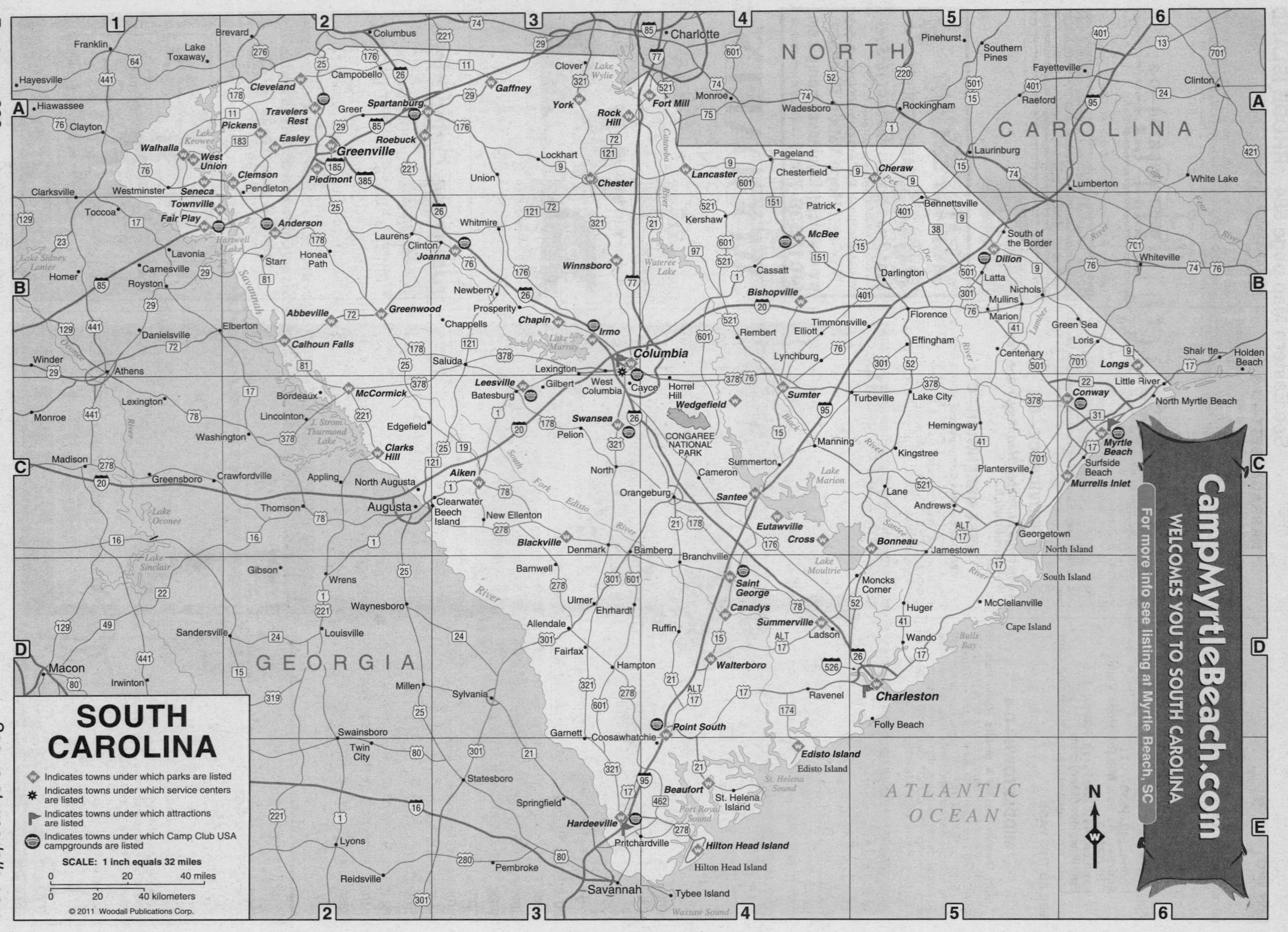

CampMyrtleBeach.com
WELCOMES YOU TO SOUTH CAROLINA
For more info see listing at Myrtle Beach, SC
SOUTH CAROLINA
Indicates towns under which parks are listed
Indicates towns under which service centers are listed
Indicates towns under which attractions are listed
Indicates towns under which Camp Club USA campgrounds are listed
SCALE: 1 inch equals 32 miles
0 20 40 miles
0 20 40 kilometers
© 2011 Woodall Publications Corp.
NORTH CAROLINA
GEORGIA
ATLANTIC OCEAN
Charlotte
Columbia
Charleston
Myrtle Beach
North Myrtle Beach
Murrells Inlet
Surfside Beach
Conway
Longs
Little River
Florence
Dillon
Cheraw
McBee
Bishopville
Sumter
Lancaster
Fort Mill
Rock Hill
Chester
Winnsboro
York
Gaffney
Spartanburg
Greenville
Roebuck
Piedmont
Anderson
Easley
Travelers Rest
Cleveland
Pickens
Clemson
West Union
Walhalla
Seneca
Townville
Fair Play
Greenwood
Abbeville
Calhoun Falls
McCormick
Clarks Hill
Joanna
Irmo
Chapin
Leesville
Aiken
Swansea
Wedgefield
Santee
Eutawville
Cross
Bonneau
Saint George
Canadys
Summerville
Walterboro
Blackville
Point South
Beaufort
Hilton Head Island
Hardeeville
Edisto Island
Augusta
Savannah
CONGAREE NATIONAL PARK

TRAVEL SECTION

South Carolina

READER SERVICE INFO

The following businesses have placed an ad in the South Carolina Travel Section. To receive free information, enter their Reader Service number on the Reader Service Card opposite page 48/Discover Section in the front of this directory:

Advertiser	RS#
Carolina Campground Assoc	3592
Magnolia RV Park & Campground	3667
Myrtle Beach Campground Association	4278

TIME ZONE

South Carolina is located in the Eastern Time Zone.

TEMPERATURE

South Carolina's climate is generally mild and humid. The average temperature varies substantially across the state. During the winter months, the average temperature ranges from the mid-30s in the mountains to approximately 50° F near the southern coast. Summer average temperatures range from the low 70s to mid 80s. Rainfall varies across the state with the heaviest rain occurring in the northwest and the least rain falling in the central part of the state. Hurricane season annually runs from June through early November.

TRAVEL & TOURISM INFO

State Agency:

South Carolina Dept. of Parks & Tourism
1205 Pendleton St.
Columbia, SC 29201
(866/224-9339 or 803/734-1700)
www.discoversouthcarolina.com

Regional Agencies:

Discover Upcountry Carolina Assn.
P.O. Box 3116
Greenville, SC 29602
(800/849-4766 or 864/233-2690)
www.TheUpcountry.com

Capital City/Lake Murray Country Tourism Region & Visitor Center
2184 N. Lake Dr.
Columbia, SC 29210
(866/725-3935 or 803/781-5940)
http://lakemurraycountry.com/

Lowcountry & Resort Islands Tourism Commission
P.O. Box 615
Yemassee, SC 29945
(800/528-6870 or 843/717-3090)
www.southcarolinalowcountry.com

Olde English District Tourism Commission
116 Gadsden Street
Chester, SC 29706
(800/968-5909 or 803/385-6800)
www.sctravel.net

Pee Dee Tourism Commission
P.O. Box 3093
Florence, SC 29502
(800/325-9005 or 843/669-0950)
www.peedeetourism.com

I-20 EXIT 58

BARNYARD RV PARK— *From Exit 58: Go 2 mi NE on Hwy 1. Enter on L.*
See listing at Columbia, SC

I-26 EXIT 60

MAGNOLIA RV PARK & CAMPGROUND— *From Exit 60: Go 1/10 mi W on Hwy 66, then 1/2 mi S on Fairview Church Rd. Enter on L.*
See listing at Joanna, SC

I-26 EXIT 111-A

BARNYARD RV PARK— *From Exit 111A: Go 3 mi SW on US 1. Enter on R.*
See listing at Columbia, SC

I-85 EXIT 39

IVY ACRES RV PARK— *From Exit 39: Go 1-1/4 mi E on River Rd. Enter on L.*
See listing at Piedmont, SC

I-85 EXIT 44

SPRINGWOOD RV PARK— *From Exit 44: Go 2-3/4 mi S on White Horse Rd, then 1/2 mi S on Donaldson Rd. Enter on R.*
See listing at Greenville, SC

I-95 EXIT 193

BASS LAKE RV CAMPGROUND— *From jct I-95 (Exit 193) & Hwy 9/Hwy 57: Go 50 ft W on Hwy 9/Hwy 57, then 1/4 mi N on Frontage Rd. Enter at end.*
See listing at Dillon, SC

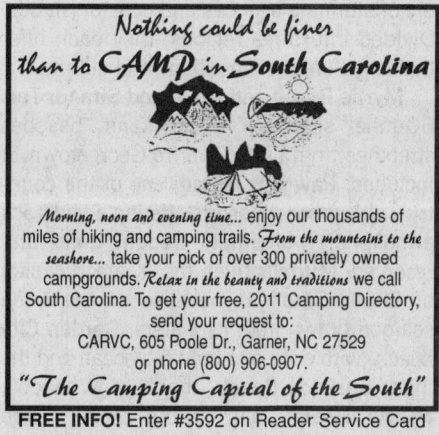

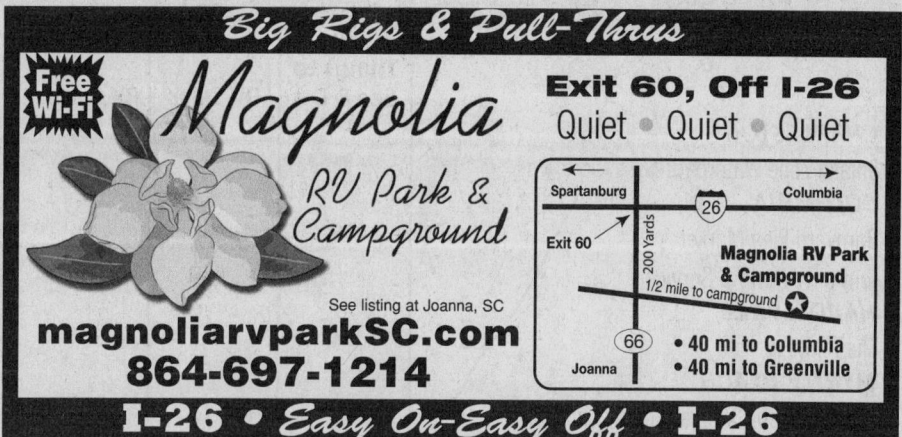

Pendleton District Historical Recreational & Tourism Commission
125 East Queen St.
Pendleton, SC 29670
(800/862-1795 or 864/646-3782)
www.pendleton-district.org

Santee Cooper Counties Promotion Commission and Visitor Center
9302 Old #6 Hwy
PO drawer 40
Santee, SC 29142
(800/227-8510 or 803/854-2131)
www.santeecoopercountry.org

Thoroughbred Country
P.O. Box 850
Aiken, SC 29802
(888/834-1654 or 803/649-7981)
www.tbredcountry.org

Local Agencies:
Charleston Area CVB
423 King St.
Charleston, SC 29403
(843/853-8000)
www.charlestoncvb.com

Clarendon Co. Chamber of Commerce
19 N. Brooks St.
Manning, SC 29102
(803/435-4405 or 800/731-5253)
www.clarendoncounty.com

Columbia Metropolitan CVB
1101 Lincoln St.
Columbia, SC 29201
(800/264-4884 or 803/545-0000)
www.columbiacvb.com

Edisto Chamber of Commerce
P.O. Box 206
Edisto Island, SC 29438
(843/869-3867 or 888/333-2781)
www.edistochamber.com

Hilton Head Island-Bluffton Chamber of Commerce & Visitor and Convention Center
1 Chamber Dr.
Hilton Head, SC 29938
(800/523-3373 or 843/785-3673)
www.hiltonheadisland.org

Kershaw County Chamber of Commerce Visitor Center
607 S. Broad St.
Camden, SC 29020
(800/968-4037 or 803/432-2525)
www.camden-sc.org

Lancaster County Chamber of Commerce
604 N. Main St.
Lancaster, SC 29721
(803/283-4105)
www.lancasterchambersc.org

Myrtle Beach Area Chamber of Commerce & Visitor Center
1200 N. Oak St.
Myrtle Beach, SC 29577
(843/626-7444 or 800/356-3016)
www.myrtlebeachinfo.com

North Myrtle Beach Area Chamber of Commerce & CVB
270 Hwy 17 N.
North Myrtle Beach, SC 29582
(877/332-2662 or 843/281-2662)
www.northmyrtlebeachchamber.com

Sumter Convention & Visitors Bureau
21 N. Main St.
Sumter, SC 29150
(803/436-2500)
www.sumter-sc.com

RECREATIONAL INFO

Arts & Culture: SC Arts Commission, 1800 Gervais St., Columbia, SC 29201 (803/734-8696). www.state.sc.us/arts

Fishing & Hunting: South Carolina Dept. of Natural Resources, Rembert C. Dennis Bldg., 1000 Assembly St., Columbia, SC 29201 (803/734-3833). www.dnr.state.sc.us

History: SC Dept. of Archives & History, 8301 Parklane Rd., Columbia, SC 29223 (803/896-6100). www.state.sc.gov

SHOPPING

Barefoot Landing, North Myrtle Beach. Reminiscent of an old fishing village, over 100 shops and waterfront restaurants surround a 27-acre lake. On Hwy 17 S.

Broadway at the Beach, Myrtle Beach. A 350-acre shopping and dining complex features over 100 specialty shops. 1325 Celebrity Circle.

Catawba Cultural Center, Rock Hill. Features the distinctive Catawba pottery. 1536 Tom Stevens Rd.

The Old City Market, Charleston. Built in 1841, it features several small shops, restaurants and a flea market, offering everything from produce to antiques. Located on Market St., between Meeting and E Bay St.

South Carolina Artisans Center, Walterboro. Declared, "The Official Folk Art and Craft Center for South Carolina" by the South Carolina Legislature. Representing the work of over 200 of the state's finest artists... blown and formed glass, sweetgrass baskets, furniture, carvings, pottery, jewelry, quilts, tatting, whimsical folk art, metalwork and much more. The center also offers a yearlong series of craft demonstrations on site. Located at 344 Wichman Street in Walterboro, SC. (843/549-0011)

State Farmers Market, Columbia. One of the largest produce markets in the Southeast receives truckloads of fresh fruits and vegetables daily in addition to perennial and annual flowers and plants. 1001 Bluff Rd.

UNIQUE FEATURES

The beautiful terrain, and interesting historical sites fuel tourism to North Carolina. This state is home to the Great Smoky Mountains National Park, and the Blue Ridge Parkway in the west, and the Outer Banks in the east. The coast is dotted with lighthouses, the oldest being the Cape Hatteras Lighthouse.

BEACHES

The South Carolina coastline offers a variety of stunning beaches and coastal islands. Divided into three regions, they each offer their own unique attractions and culture.

Myrtle Beach and the Grand Strand: This 60-mile span of white sand beaches stretches from Little River to Georgetown. It includes: **Pawley's Island**, one of the country's oldest beach resorts offering a laid back atmosphere; **Litchfield Beach**, quiet and reserved; **Murrells Inlet**, the "seafood capital of South Carolina" because of the fresh seafood drawn from its waters; **Garden City** beach, with access to both the ocean and the inlet; **Surfside Beach**, the "family beach"; **Myrtle Beach**, one of the most visited

BUSINESSES OFFERING

	Things to See & Do	RV Sales	RV Service
CHARLESTON			
Splash Zone Waterpark	⚑		
COLUMBIA			
Barnyard Flea Market	⚑		
Tony's RV Parts & Service		🚌	✱
HARDEEVILLE			
The Pink Pig	⚑		
MYRTLE BEACH			
Myrtle Beach Campground Association	⚑		

beaches on the East Coast; and **North Myrtle Beach**, known for its family beach atmosphere, fishing piers and wonderfully wide beaches. **Little River** offers a slightly slower pace of life than the rest of the Grand Strand, lying just below the North Carolina border along what is now the Intracoastal Waterway.

Historic Charleston & Resort Beaches: Idyllic beach resorts at Kiawah Island, Seabrook, Wild Dunes and Edisto Island offer miles of unspoiled beaches and marshlands. Other beach areas include **Bulls Island**, part of the 60,000-acre **Cape Romain National Wildlife Refuge; Folly Beach**, complete with lighthouse and fishing pier; **Isle of Palms** a semi-tropical retreat; **Kiawah Island**, with 10 miles of undisturbed Atlantic beach; **Seabrook Island**, where you can wander miles of private beach or tour the island on horseback.

DESTINATIONS

DISCOVER UPCOUNTRY REGION

This area in the far northwest section of the state is the most economically and geographically diverse area with foothills and the rugged mountains of the Blue Ridge.

Bob Jones University Museum & Gallery, Greenville, contains 30 galleries of art, tapestries, furniture, sculpture and architectural motifs from 5 centuries.

Chattooga National Wild & Scenic River. Forming 40 miles of the South Carolina/Georgia border, this famous whitewater paddling spot was featured in the movie *Deliverance*.

Greenville County Museum of Art, Greenville, contains works of art with a southern accent. See Andrew Wyeth pieces along with contemporary collections from artists such as Georgia O'Keefe and Andy Warhol.

Hollywild Animal Park in Inman is home to over 500 animals, many of which roam freely inside large natural enclosures or on man-made islands. The Outback Safari takes visitors through 80 acres of free-roaming animals.

The Peachoid is the best-known, most photographed water tank in the U.S., painted to match the kind of peaches grown in Cherokee County. Along I-85 near Gaffney.

Pendleton Village Green is one of the largest historic districts in the nation featuring shops, restaurants and 19th century restored buildings.

SC Botanical Garden, Clemson features a unique collection of 12 nature-based sculptures. Also includes "niche gardens," a 70-acre arboretum, the **Bob Campbell Geology Museum** and the ca.1716 French Huguenot Hanover House.

Whitewater Falls is the highest series of falls in eastern North America with the Lower Falls having a 200-foot drop. Six different waterfalls along the NC/SC border comprise the chain. Off SC 130 at Duke Power's Bad Creek Hydroelectric Station.

OLDE ENGLISH DISTRICT

This area is alive with period homes, historic sites, and a rich Civil and Revolutionary War history. No matter the final destination, this is a must experience for any traveler in search of picturesque areas, and some Olde English charm.

Andrew Jackson State Park, located north of Lancaster. On-site are a museum, one-room school, fishing, nature trail and year-round interpretive programs.

Carolina Sandhills National Wildlife Refuge, McBee. See a diverse species of flora and fauna from observation towers, biking trails or by car in this 45,000-acre national wildlife refuge.

Cheraw Historic District & Town Green. Laid out in 1768, more than 50 antebellum buildings and numerous Victorian and classical revival homes line the streets. The **Cheraw Museum and History Company** is part museum, part antique shop.

Museum of York County. Visit more than 200 animal exhibits from seven continents. This museum also houses Native American artifacts that mirror the heritage of the first Carolinians. A planetarium, three art galleries and a nature trail are also on-site.

Paramount's Carowinds, Fort Mill. Theme park with more than 50 rides; a water park and high-speed roller coaster highlight the park.

Rose Hill Plantation State Historic Site, Union. Home of SC's "Secession Governor," William H. Gist, the site offers a look at antebellum SC with a restored mansion, period furnishing and beautiful grounds.

PEE DEE COUNTRY

An area steeped in romance and history, the Pee Dee area was originally home to the Pee Dee Indians who thrived here. Avid sportsmen are drawn to the fields and streams here, where wildlife is plentiful. The Great Pee Dee is just one of the rivers that meander through the area providing a scenic backdrop for many different outdoor adventures.

Florence. This bustling city began with the railroad in the 1880s. Located just west of the Pee Dee River, you'll find:

Dooley Planetarium at Francis Marion University. Visitors experience the day and night sky through a Spitz-512 Star Projector capable of producing 2,354 stars, several prominent galaxies and star clusters onto a 33-foot dome suspended from the ceiling by 14 chains. The instruments display the sky as seen from anywhere on earth for any time, for any day, for any year.

Pee Dee State Farmer's Market. Fresh fruits and veggies, flowers, hanging baskets and homemade goods are displayed Monday through Saturday.

Florence Museum of Art, Science & History. Changing art exhibits, regional history, Asian, African, ancient Mediterranean and southwest Pueblo cultures are featured.

Fryar's Topiary Garden, Bishopville. Three acres of meticulously sculpted plants include graceful arches, spirals, geometrics and fantasies.

SC Cotton Museum, Bishopville. Explore the state's cotton culture through interactive exhibits, stories, original tools and interpretive center.

OLD 96 DISTRICT

Old 96 is an area of living history, friendly towns, retirement communities, open country, deep woodlands and wide water. Area attractions include:

Burt-Stark Mansion, Abbeville. Built in the 1830s, this Greek Revival house was the site of the first reading of the secession papers, giving birth to the Confederacy. Contains family antiques.

Sumter National Forest. Explore over 118,000 acres of woodland wonderland filled with wildlife and recreation areas. Enjoy hiking, camping, picnicking and fishing.

Greenwood. This scenic small city is nestled at the foot of the rolling hills of the Upstate. Our mild climate offers year-round golfing with ideal weather conditions. Take a stroll along **Greenwood's Heritage Trail** while visiting. One can enjoy this 2-1/2 mile paved path for biking, walking or skating. Beautiful Lake Greenwood encompasses more than 11,400 acres of sparkling water. Along the 200-mile shoreline, find commercial and public boat landings, bait and tackle shops, fishing piers and a variety of restaurants for continuous adventure and entertainment.

CAPITAL CITY & LAKE MURRAY COUNTRY

This region boasts southern hospitality, state museums, historical southern homes, and challenging golf courses. Lake Murray is a popular destination in this area, and a haven for all types of water related sports.

Columbia. The capital city offers a multitude of activities and places of interest.

Columbia Museum of Art features collections of European and American fine and decorative art including masterpieces from the Italian Renaissance.

South Carolina State House. Bronze stars signify where General Sherman's army fired on the 145-year-old facility.

South Carolina State Museum. Visit four floors representing various fields of interest such as art, natural history, technology and science. There are hands-on exhibits about pioneering South Carolina inventors.

QUICK REFERENCE CHART FOR WOODALL'S FEATURED PARKS

	Green Friendly	RV Lots for Sale	Park Models-Onsite Ownership	Park Membership for Sale	Big Rigs Welcome	Internet Friendly	Pets Welcome
AIKEN							
Aiken RV Park					▲	◍	■
CHARLESTON							
Campground at James Island County Park					▲	◍	■
Lake Aire RV Park and Campground					▲	◍	■
Mt. Pleasant/Charleston KOA					▲	◍	■
Oak Plantation Campground					▲	◍	■
CLEVELAND							
Solitude Pointe					▲	◍	■
COLUMBIA							
Barnyard RV Park					▲	◍	■
CONWAY							
Big Cypress Lake RV Park & Fishing Retreat					▲	●	■
CROSS							
Cross/Santee Cooper Lakes Campground						◍	■
DILLON							
Bass Lake RV Campground					▲	◍	■
EUTAWVILLE							
Rocks Pond Campground & Marina					▲	◍	■
FORT MILL							
Crown International Campground					▲	◍	■
GREENVILLE							
Rainbow RV Park						◍	■
Springwood RV Park					▲	◍	■
HARDEEVILLE							
Hardeeville RV-Thomas' Parks and Sites					▲	◍	■
HILTON HEAD ISLAND							
Hilton Head Harbor RV Resort & Marina		✖			▲	◍	■
Hilton Head Island Motorcoach Resort		✖			▲	◍	■
JOANNA							
Magnolia RV Park & Campground					▲	◍	■
LEESVILLE							
Cedar Pond Campground							■
LONGS							
WillowTree Resort					▲	◍	■
MYRTLE BEACH							
Apache Family Campground					▲	◍	■
Briarcliffe RV Resort, Inc				✔	▲	◍	■
KOA-Myrtle Beach					▲	◍	■
Lakewood Camping Resort	🍃		✱		▲	◍	■
Myrtle Beach Travel Park					▲	◍	■

Green Friendly 🍃; RV Lots for Sale ✖; Park Models/Onsite Onwership ✱; Park Memberships for Sale ✔; Big Rigs Welcome ▲;
Internet Friendly ●; Internet Friendly-WiFi ◍; Pets Welcome ■

Lake Murray, just west of Columbia. A 50,000-acre impoundment, located just west of the metro-Columbia area, it has 520 miles of scenic shoreline, a host of marinas and campgrounds, excellent fishing and abundant water recreation.

Riverbanks Zoo and Botanical Garden, Riverbanks. This 170-acre park features 2,000 animals, a microcosmic rainforest, a desert, an undersea kingdom, a southern farm, an aquarium/reptile complex and a botanical garden. The Ndoki Forest is River-bank's new home for elephants, meerkats and gorillas. Also included are historic ruins, plant collections and 70 acres of woodland gardens.

THOROUGHBRED COUNTRY

This is horse and rider heaven. Famed as a winter resort for some of America's wealthiest who enjoyed the unpaved roads, equestrian stoplights, beautiful gardens, and a restored 19th century inn, all that recalls the area's golden era.

Aiken. Aiken is unique in that the city is home to over 150 different species of trees that make up its **Citywide Arboretum**, which is spread over 176 parkways covering 15 miles in length. **Hitchcock Woods**, the largest urban forest in the U.S., offers peace and beauty in the midst of an urban area. To explore the city, take a 2-hour trolley tour that will take you past its many historic homes, churches, Civil War sites and more. **DuPont Planetarium**, located at the campus of USC-Aiken, the 45-seat theater has a 30-foot diameter tilted dome with a projector system that displays more than 9,000 stars. **Aiken County Historical Museum**. The museum is housed in a 1931 winter colony mansion with three floors of exhibits telling the history of Aiken County from past to present. Admission is free.

Other Aiken attractions include:

Hopelands Gardens is a 14-acre estate opened in 1969 as a public garden. Paths shaded by 100-year-old oaks, deodar cedars and magnolias curve through the gardens. Within the gardens is the **Thoroughbred Racing Hall of Fame & Museum**. Horses trained in Aiken who have gone on to become National Champions are enshrined in the Hall of Fame. Visitors may view trophies and photographs from the careers of some of America's best-known equestrian riders, polo players and steeplechase riders. Adjacent to the property is **The Wetlands** featuring a floating boardwalk and a tranquil marshland setting.

Agricultural Heritage Museum, Blackville. The museum consists of an Agricultural Heritage Museum, a Discovery Center and a Hands-On Learning Center, providing a unique opportunity for the public to revisit the past and observe modern agricultural research as it is being conducted.

DuPont Planetarium. The 45-seat planetarium is equipped with state-of-the-art special effects systems and is augmented by sundials and telescopes. Various shows are available throughout the year.

Healing Springs. Indians believed in the springs' natural healing powers and brought wounded Revolutionary War soldiers here to drink. Locals still believe in the springs' powers and drink its water. In 1944, the acre of land the springs are on was legally deeded to GOD by LP "Luke" Boylston. Open during daylight hours.

SANTEE COOPER COUNTRY

This area is one of the state's most celebrated sports and recreational sites. More than 171,000 acres of water fill the basin, which teems with bass, crappie and catfish.

QUICK REFERENCE CHART FOR WOODALL'S FEATURED PARKS

	Green Friendly	RV Lots for Sale	Park Models-Onsite Ownership	Park Membership for Sale	Big Rigs Welcome	Internet Friendly	Pets Welcome
MYRTLE BEACH(Continued)							
Ocean Lakes Family Campground	🍂				▲	●	■
Pirateland Family Camping Resort	🍂				▲	●	■
PIEDMONT							
Ivy Acres RV Park					▲	●	■
ROEBUCK							
Pine Ridge Campground					▲	●	■
SANTEE							
Santee Lakes Campground						●	■
SENECA							
Crooked Creek RV Park					▲	●	■
ST. GEORGE							
Jolly Acres RV Park & Storage					▲	●	■
SWANSEA							
Yogi Bear's Jellystone Park @ River Bottom Farms					▲	●	■
TRAVELERS REST							
Valley Park Resort						●	■
WALTERBORO							
New Green Acres R.V. Park					▲	●	■

Green Friendly 🍂; RV Lots for Sale ✖; Park Models/Onsite Onwership ✱; Park Memberships for Sale ✔; Big Rigs Welcome ▲; Internet Friendly ●; Internet Friendly-WiFi ●; Pets Welcome ■

Cypress Gardens, Moncks Corner. You can tour this 175-acre swamp garden on foot or in the famous beateaus (flat-bottomed boats). Features include a butterfly house, freshwater aquarium and reptile center.

Edisto Memorial Gardens & Horne Wetlands Park, Orangeburg. The north fork of the Edisto River winds through colorful and graceful gardens. Within the gardens, the Wetlands Park features an extensive boardwalk for viewing wetland wildlife. Adjacent to the gardens is the **Orangeburg Arts Center** with a gallery on the second floor.

Sumter. Swan Lake Iris Gardens surrounds the black waters of Swan Lake, where all eight known species of the world's swans swim.

MYRTLE BEACH AREA/ THE GRAND STRAND

For decades, this area has been a Mecca for vacationers looking for a great escape. Stretching more than 60 miles along the Atlantic Coast, this string of beach resorts includes popular destinations like Myrtle Beach, Atlantic Beach, Surfside, and Pawleys Island. Each year, this area welcomes millions in search of swimming, sunning, boating and shelling.

The Grand Strand is a 60-mile stretch of white sandy beaches along the Atlantic Coast. Popular beaches include **Myrtle Beach**, **Huntington Beach State Park**, **Surfside Beach**, **Garden City**, **Litchfield Beach** and **Cherry Grove Beach**. Golfers thrill to over 100 championship courses, while anglers cast their lines into abundant fishing waters.

Georgetown. This first settlement in North America failed in 1526, but is now a thriving community with several marinas on the Intracoastal Waterway and the **Harborwalk**, an array of restaurants and shops. Sixteen blocks of the downtown area are listed on the National Historic Register.

Myrtle Beach. This is a camper's paradise for golf, beaches, shows, fishing and plantations. Attractions in Myrtle Beach include **NASCAR Speedpark**—a racing-theme park with seven race tracks, miniature golf and a 12,000-sq. ft. SpeedDome that features interactive arcade games and other racing memorabilia. See some of the most feared and fascinating members of the reptile world at **Alligator Adventure.** Visit **Ripley's Aquarium**, where you'll see an extensive aquatic collection in a unique way. Travel the aquarium's *Dangerous Reef* tunnel on a moving glide path surrounded on all sides by sharks up to 10 feet long. The Ripley complex also includes **Ripley's Believe It or Not! Museum** of the weird, incredible, rare and unbelievable in 12 galleries; **Ripley's Haunted Adventure** with high-tech animations and special effects; **Ripley's 4-D Moving Theater**, a movie that you actually ride featuring a digital 6-channel surround-sound system and giant 70mm films. The **Myrtle Beach Pavilion Amusement Park** is an 11-acre playground with a category 5 Hurricane roller coaster, an antique Herschel-Spillman Merry-Go-Round, 4-D Adventure Theater and a giant 1900 German Pipe Organ. See over 100 species of animals at the 500-acre **Waccatee Zoological Farm**, which includes a wildlife sanctuary and breeding ground for several species of migratory birds and alligators.

LOWCOUNTRY & RESORT BEACHES REGION

This area is home to Hilton Head Island, known for its recreation facilities and over two dozen championship golf courses, one of which hosts the nationally televised golf tournament annually. Travelers will find this area hauntingly beautiful, with miles of white beaches, endless marshes, and trees laden with Spanish moss.

Barrier Sea Islands is a string of barrier sea islands south of Charleston where modern resorts have been carved out of semi-tropical thickets. Golf, play tennis, beachcomb, boat, swim and camp in this peaceful environment. Major islands include **Seabrook**, **Kiawah**, **Edisto**, **Daufuskie**, **Hunting**, **Fripp** and **Hilton Head**.

Hilton Head Island. The **Coastal Discovery Museum** combines hands-on exhibits in coastal history and nature at its main location, with 15 different tours and cruises at various locations.

Lowcountry Visitors Center & Museum, Yemassee, features a re-created plantation parlor and displays from the region's 10 museums and the SC Artisans Center.

Parris Island Museum, Parris Island, focuses on the history of the island with exhibits that cover archaeology, Native Americans and 16th-century French and Spanish settlements.

Where to Find CCUSA Parks

List City	Park Name	Map Coordinates
ANDERSON		
	Lake Hartwell Camping & Cabins	B-2
COLUMBIA		
	Barnyard RV Park	B-3
CONWAY		
	Big Cypress Lake RV Park & Fishing Retreat	C-6
DILLON		
	Bass Lake RV Campground	B-5
FAIR PLAY		
	Lake Hartwell RV Park	B-1
HARDEEVILLE		
	Hardeeville RV-Thomas' Parks and Sites	E-3
IRMO		
	Woodsmoke Family Campground	B-3
JOANNA		
	Magnolia RV Park & Campground	B-3
LEESVILLE		
	Cedar Pond Campground	C-3
MCBEE		
	The Farm Campground	B-4
MYRTLE BEACH		
	Briarcliffe RV Resort, Inc	C-6
	Carrollwoods RV Park at Grapefull Sisters Vineyard	C-6
	Pirateland Family Camping Resort	C-6
POINT SOUTH		
	The Oaks at Point South RV Resort	D-4
SPARTANBURG		
	Cunningham RV Park	A-2
ST. GEORGE		
	Jolly Acres RV Park & Storage	D-4
	St. George RV Park	D-4
SWANSEA		
	Yogi Bear's Jellystone Park @ River Bottom Farms	C-3
TRAVELERS REST		
	Valley Park Resort	A-2

South Carolina

ABBEVILLE—B-2

(S) SUMTER NATIONAL FOREST (Parson's Mountain Lake Campground)—(Abbeville) *From town: Go 2 mi S on Hwy 28, then 1-1/2 mi E on FR SI-257.* FACILITIES: 23 sites, 22 ft max RV length, 23 no hkups, tenting, dump. RECREATION: lake swim, boating, no motors, ramp, lake fishing. Open Apr 1 - Dec 15. Phone: (803)637-5247.

AIKEN—C-3

(NE) AIKEN RV PARK—(Aiken) *From jct I-20 (exit 22) & US 1: Go 1 mi S on US 1. Enter on L.*

WELCOME

◇◇◇FACILITIES: 47 sites, typical site width 15 ft, 47 full hkups, (30/50 amps), mostly extd stay sites, 9 pull-thrus, cable TV, WiFi Instant Internet at site, laundry, picnic tables, patios, grills.

RECREATION: pavilion, horseshoes.

Pets welcome. No tents. Open all yr. Big rigs welcome. Escort to site. Rate in 2010 $25 for 2 persons. Member CALARVC.

Phone: (803)648-4056
Address: 2424 Columbia Hwy N, Aiken, SC 29801
Lat/Lon: 33.59883/-81.68771
Email: staywithus@aikenrvpark.com
Web: www.aikenrvpark.com

SEE AD AUGUSTA, GA PAGE 194

(E) AIKEN STATE NATURAL AREA—(Aiken) *From jct Hwy 19 & US 78: Go 16 mi E on US 78, then 7 mi N on CR 53. Enter on R.* FACILITIES: 25 sites, 35 ft max RV length, 25 W&E, (30 amps), 2 pull-thrus, family camping, tenting, dump. RECREATION: boating, canoeing, lake/river/pond fishing. Pets welcome. Open all yr. Phone: (803)649-2857.

(NE) Pine Acres Campground (RV SPACES)—(Aiken) *From jct I-20 (exit 22) & US 1: Go 4-3/4 mi S on US 1. Enter on L.* FACILITIES: 40 sites, typical site width 30 ft, 40 full hkups, (30/50 amps), 22 pull-thrus, dump, laundry. Pets welcome. No tents. Open all yr. Big rigs welcome. Rate in 2010 $30 for 2 persons. Phone: (803)648-5715.

ANDERSON—B-2

(NW) Anderson/Lake Hartwell KOA—(Anderson) *From jct I-85 (Exit 11) & Hwy 24: Go 3 mi E on I-85 (exit 14), then 1 mi SE on Hwy 187. Enter on L.* ◇◇◇FACILITIES: 86 sites, typical site width 35 ft, 49 full hkups, 33 W&E, (20/30/50 amps), 50 amps ($), 4 no hkups, 65 pull-thrus, tenting, dump, laundry, ltd groc. ◇◇RECREATION: swim pool, playground. Pets welcome. Partial handicap access. Open all yr. Member ARVC, CARVC. Phone: (864)287-3161. KOA discount.

(NW) Lake Hartwell Camping & Cabins—(Anderson) *From jct I-85 (exit 11) & Hwy 24: Go 2-1/2 mi W on Hwy 24, then 1/2 mi N on O'Neal Ferry Rd, then 1/2 mi E on Ponderosa Rd. Enter at end.* ◇◇◇FACILITIES: 120 sites, typical site width 35 ft, 80 full hkups, 40 W&E, (20/30/50 amps), 45 pull-thrus, WiFi Instant Internet at site, WiFi Internet central location, family camping, tenting, RV storage, dump, non-guest dump $, laundry, ltd groc, RV supplies, LP gas by weight/by meter, ice, picnic tables, fire rings, grills, wood. ◇◇◇RECREATION: rec hall, pavilion, swim pool, wading pool, boating, canoeing, kayaking, ramp, dock, lake fishing, mini-golf, bsktball, playground, tennis, horseshoes, hiking trails, v-ball. Pets welcome. Open all yr. Rate in 2010 $25-33 for 4 persons. MC/VISA/DISC/AMEX. FMCA discount. CCUSA 50% Discount. CCUSA reservations Accepted, CCUSA max stay Unlimited. Discount not available Memorial Day thru Labor Day weekends.

CAMPCLUB USA

ANDERSON—Continued
Lake Hartwell Camping & Cabins—Continued

Phone: (888)427-8935
Address: 400 Ponderosa Pt Rd, Townville, SC 29689
Lat/Lon: 34.56366/-82.85731
Email: info@camplakehartwell.com
Web: camplakehartwell.com

(W) Tiger Cove Campground—(Anderson) *From jct I-85 (exit 11) & Hwy 24: Go 2-3/4 mi E on Hwy 24, continue straight for 1-1/2 mi SE on Hwy 187, then 1/2 mi S on Old Asbury Rd, then 1/4 mi W on Hwy 34, (Whitehall Rd). Enter on L.* ◇◇FACILITIES: 42 sites, 40 ft max RV length, 20 full hkups, 22 W&E, (30 amps), family camping, tenting, dump. ◇◇RECREATION: lake swim, canoeing, dock, lake fishing. Pets welcome. Open all yr. Rate in 2010 $24-35 for 4 persons. Member ARVC, CARVC. Phone: (864)225-5993.

BEAUFORT—E-4

(E) Tuck In The Wood Campground—(Beaufort) *From jct Hwy 170 & US 21: Go 12 mi SE on US 21, then 2-1/4 mi W on Martin L King/Lands End Rd. Enter on L.* ◇◇◇FACILITIES: 71 sites, typical site width 30 ft, 71 full hkups, (20/30/50 amps), 50 amps ($), 11 pull-thrus, tenting, dump, laundry. ◇◇RECREATION: pond fishing, playground. Pets welcome, breed restrict. Partial handicap access. Open all yr. Phone: (843)838-2267.

BISHOPVILLE—B-4

(SE) LEE STATE NATURAL AREA—(Lee) *From jct I-20 & Hwy-341: Go 3 mi E on I-20, then 1-1/2 mi N on S-22.* FACILITIES: 25 sites, typical site width 30 ft, 36 ft max RV length, 25 W&E, (20/30 amps), 11 pull-thrus, family camping, tenting. RECREATION: river fishing. Pets welcome. Partial handicap access. Open all yr. Phone: (803)428-5307.

BLACKVILLE—C-3

(SW) BARNWELL STATE PARK—(Barnwell) *From jct US 78 & Hwy 3: Go 2 mi S on Hwy 3.* FACILITIES: 33 sites, 36 ft max RV length, 8 full hkups, 25 W&E, (20/30/50 amps), family camping, tenting, dump. RECREATION: lake fishing, playground. Pets welcome. Open all yr. Phone: (803)284-2212.

BONNEAU—C-5

MILITARY PARK (Short Stay Rec Area-Charleston Naval Sta.)—(Berkeley) *Off base, 35 mi N of Charleston Naval Base. Located W of Bonneau, off US 52, on Lake Moultrie.* FACILITIES: 127 sites, 111 W&E, (30 amps), 16 no hkups, tenting, dump, groceries. RECREATION: lake swim, boating, lake fishing, playground. Open all yr. Phone: (800)447-2178.

CALHOUN FALLS—B-2

(N) CALHOUN FALLS STATE RECREATION AREA—(Abbeville) *From town: Go 1/2 mi N on Hwy 81. Enter on L.* FACILITIES: 100 sites, 40 ft max RV length, 86 W&E, (20/30 amps), 14 no hkups, 31 pull-thrus, family camping, tenting, dump, laundry, ltd groc. RECREATION: lake swim, boating, ramp, dock, lake fishing, playground. Pets welcome. Open all yr. Phone: (864)447-8267.

Woodall's Tip... Get FREE Information—Use the Reader Service card.

CANADYS—D-4

(N) Shuman's RV Trailer Park (RV SPACES)—(Colleton) *From I-95 (exit 68) & Hwy 61: Go 2-3/4 mi E on Hwy 61, then 1/4 mi N on Hwy 15. Enter on R.* FACILITIES: 20 sites, typical site width 20 ft, accepts full hkup units only, 20 full hkups, (20/30/50 amps), 50 amps ($), 11 pull-thrus, dump. Pets welcome. No tents. Open all yr. Rate in 2010 $17 per vehicle. Phone: (888) 533-8731.

CHAPIN—B-3

(SW) DREHER ISLAND STATE RECREATION AREA—(Newberry) *From jct I-26 (exit 91) & Hwy 48: Go W on Hwy 48, then 1/8 mi S on US 76, then 4 mi S on CR 29, then 3 mi S on Hwy 231 (Dreher Isl Rd).* FACILITIES: 112 sites, typical site width 30 ft, 45 ft max RV length, 97 W&E, (20/30 amps), 15 no hkups, 7 pull-thrus, family camping, tenting, dump, ltd groc. RECREATION: boating, ramp, lake fishing, playground. Pets welcome. Open all yr. Phone: (803)364-4152.

CHARLESTON—D-5

(SW) CAMPGROUND AT JAMES ISLAND COUNTY PARK—(Charleston) *From jct I-26 (exit 221) & US 17: Go 2 mi S on US 17, then 1 mi S on Hwy 171, then 1-1/2 mi W on Hwy 700, then 1-3/4 mi S on Riverland Dr. Enter on R.*

EXPLORE CHARLESTON & THE LOWCOUNTRY

Discover the history, charm, fine dining, antiques, plantations, antebellum homes, parks and sandy beaches. All can be found just minutes from your private retreat within our 643-acre Park's beautiful campground.

◇◇◇◇FACILITIES: 124 sites, typical site width 25 ft, 118 full hkups, 6 W&E, (20/30/50 amps), 11 pull-thrus, WiFi Instant Internet at site, family camping, tenting, cabins, dump, non-guest dump $, laundry, groceries, RV supplies, LP gas by weight/by meter, ice, picnic tables, fire rings, grills, wood, controlled access.

◇◇◇◇RECREATION: rec room/area, pavilion, spray ground, boating, canoeing, kayaking, dock, 8 kayak/16 pedal boat rentals, lake/stream fishing, golf nearby, bike rental 75 bike rentals, playground, sports field, hiking trails. Rec open to public.

Pets welcome. Partial handicap access. Open all yr. Big rigs welcome. Clubs welcome. Rate in 2010 $41-43 for 6 persons. MC/VISA/DISC/AMEX.

Text 87744 to (440)725-8687 to see our Visual Tour.

Phone: (843)795-7275
Address: 871 Riverland Dr, Charleston, SC 29412
Lat/Lon: 32.73592/-79.98266
Email: campground@ccprc.com
Web: www.ccprc.com

SEE AD PAGE 698 AND AD DISCOVER SECTION PAGE 46

CHARLESTON—Continued on next page

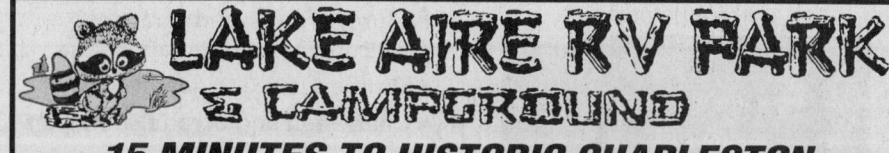

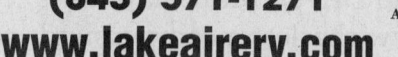

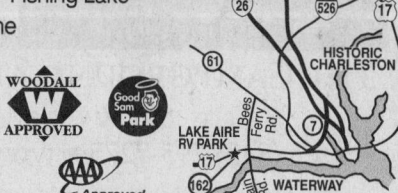

DISCOVER HISTORIC *Charleston*

Play in Charleston
& explore the...

HISTORY · CHARM · FINE DINING · ANTIQUES · PLANTATIONS
ANTEBELLUM HOMES · SANDY BEACHES · GOLF COURSES

Other campground
highlights...
Splash Zone Waterpark
open every summer.

The annual
Holiday Festival of Lights
within the park.

Stay with us...

The Campground at James Island County Park

A full service campground located within a beautiful, wooded 640-acre park locatd 10 minutes from downtown Charleston.

Features

- 125 wooded RVsites
- 50 amp sites
- Pull thrus, full hookups
- 24 hour security
- Group Meeting Facilities
- Campground Store
- Clubs, groups, and caravans welcome with reservations
- Shuttle service to downtown
- Charleston and ocean fishing pier
- Reservations accepted one week in advance
- Wi-Fi Internet Service

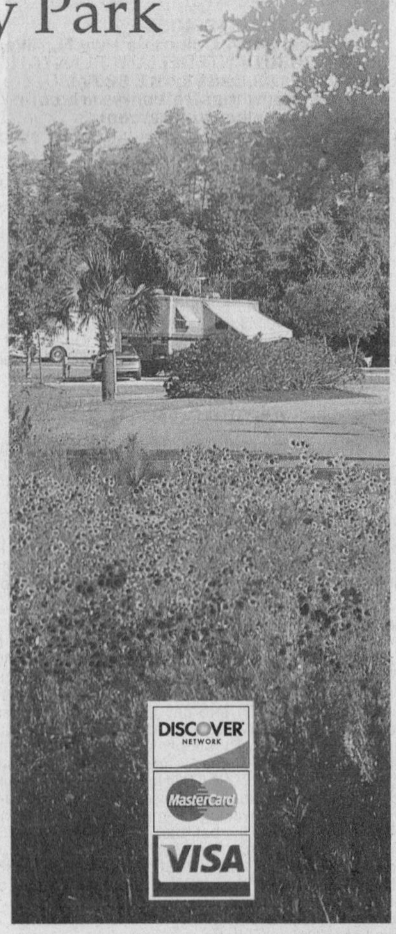

THE CAMPGROUND AT JAMES ISLAND COUNTY PARK
871 Riverland Drive, South Carolina
(843) 795-7275 • www.charlestoncampgrounds.com

CHARLESTON—Continued

(NW) KOA-Charleston—(Charleston) *From jct I-26 (exit 205A) & US 78: Go 1 mi W on US 78. Enter on R.* ◊◊◊FACILITIES: 150 sites, typical site width 35 ft, 105 full hkups, 45 W&E, (20/30/50 amps), 65 pull-thrus, family camping, tenting, dump, laundry, groceries. ◊◊RECREATION: swim pool, playground. Pets welcome. Partial handicap access. Open all yr. Big rigs welcome. Rate in 2010 $27-30 for 2 persons. Member ARVC, CARVC. Phone: (800)KOA-5812. KOA discount.

(W) LAKE AIRE RV PARK AND CAMPGROUND—(Charleston) *From jct I-526 & US 17: Go 7-1/2 mi S on US 17, then 1000 feet S on Hwy 162. Enter on L.*

WELCOME

◊◊◊FACILITIES: 113 sites, 66 full hkups, 21 W&E, (20/30/50 amps), 26 no hkups, some extd stay sites, 75 pull-thrus, WiFi Instant Internet at site, WiFi Internet central location, family camping, tenting, dump, laundry, ltd groc, RV supplies, LP gas by weight/by meter, ice, picnic tables, fire rings, wood.

◊◊◊RECREATION: pavilion, swim pool, boating, electric motors only, canoeing, pedal boat rentals, lake fishing, bsktball, playground, horseshoes, sports field, hiking trails.

Pets welcome. Partial handicap access. Open all yr. Big rigs welcome. Clubs welcome. Rate in 2010 $28-33 for 2 persons. MC/VISA/DISC. FMCA discount.

Phone: (843)571-1271
Address: 4375 State Highway 162, Hollywood, SC 29449
Lat/Lon: 32.77797/-80.15007
Email: lakeairerv@juno.com
Web: www.lakeairerv.com

SEE AD PAGE 697

MILITARY PARK (Shady Oaks Family Campground-Charleston AFB)—(Charleston) *From I-26 (exit 211-Aviation Ave): Go 1/2 mi W on Aviation Ave, then N on Arthur Rd around the runways, thru the gate to Outdoor Rec. Center. On base.* FACILITIES: 30 sites, 30 W&E, tenting, dump, laundry. RECREATION: swim pool, lake/saltwater swim, boating, canoeing, saltwater/lake/river fishing, play equipment. Partial handicap access. Open all yr. Phone: (803)566-5270.

(NE) MT. PLEASANT/CHARLESTON KOA—(Charleston) *From jct I-26 (exit 212C) & I-526: Go 12 mi E on I-526, then 5 mi N on US 17. Enter on R.*

WELCOME

STAY ON AN ANTEBELLUM PLANTATION
Enjoy a beautiful, quiet location on a 30-acre lake with lots of fun things to do. Fish, boat, bike or hike. Walk next door to Blackbeard's Cove Family Fun Park. Close to Charleston for dining, shopping and tours.

◊◊◊◊FACILITIES: 114 sites, typical site width 35 ft, 70 full hkups, 40 W&E, (20/30/50 amps), 4 no hkups, some extd stay sites, 62 pull-thrus, cable TV, WiFi Instant Internet at site, phone Internet central location, family camping, tenting, cabins, dump, non-guest dump $, laundry, groceries, RV supplies, LP gas by weight/by meter, ice, picnic tables, fire rings, grills, wood.

◊◊◊RECREATION: rec hall, swim pool, boating, no motors, canoeing, kayaking, 4 canoe/3 kayak/2 pedal boat rentals, lake fishing, fishing supplies, bsktball, 8 bike rentals, playground, sports field, hiking trails, v-ball.

MT. PLEASANT/CHARLESTON KOA—Continued on next page

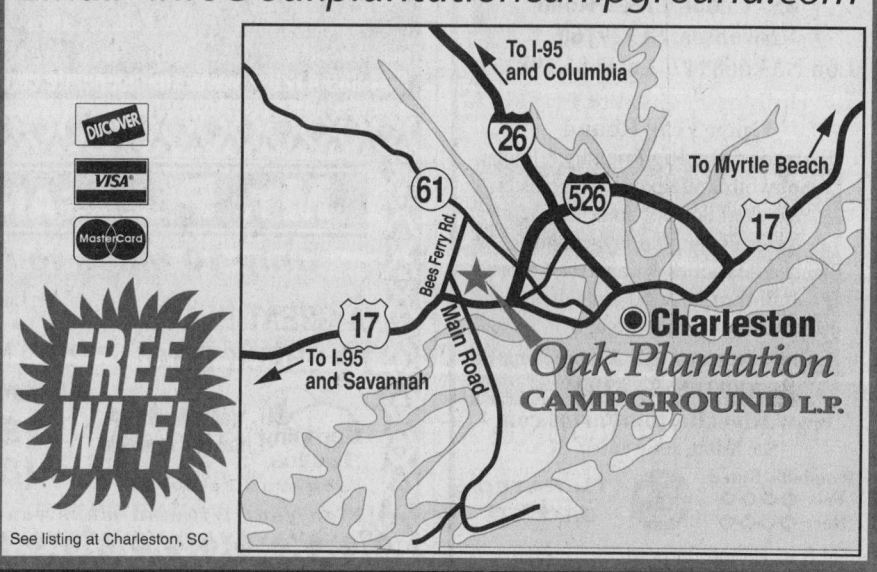

CHARLESTON—Continued
MT. PLEASANT/CHARLESTON KOA—Continued

Pets welcome. Partial handicap access. Open all yr. Big rigs welcome. Clubs welcome. Rate in 2010 $40-59 for 2 persons. MC/VISA/DISC/AMEX. Member ARVC, CARVC. KOA discount.

Phone: (800)KOA-5796
Address: 3157 US Hwy 17 N, Mt. Pleasant, SC 29466
Lat/Lon: 32.86828/-79.78140
Email: StayKOA@aol.com
Web: www.koamountpleasantSC.com

SEE AD THIS PAGE

(W) OAK PLANTATION CAMPGROUND—(Charleston) *From west jct I-526 & US 17 South: Go 4 mi SW on US 17. Enter on R.*

WELCOME

15 MINUTES FROM HISTORIC CHARLESTON
Guests appreciate the friendly staff and picturesque facility as well as our convenient location to the many attractions in the Charleston area. For sightseeing or just relaxing, let us host your next camping experience.

◆◆◆◆◆FACILITIES: 298 sites, typical site width 28 ft, 144 full hkups, 80 W&E, (20/30/50 amps), 74 no hkups, 87 pull-thrus, WiFi Instant Internet at site, WiFi Internet central location, family camping, RV storage, dump, non-guest dump $, laundry, ltd groc, RV supplies, LP gas by meter, ice, picnic tables, wood.

◆◆◆RECREATION: pavilion, swim pool, lake fishing, playground, horseshoes, sports field.

Pets welcome. No tents. Open all yr. Big rigs welcome. Clubs welcome. Rate in 2010 $26-35 for 2 persons. MC/VISA/DISC.

Text 107889 to (440)725-8687 to see our Visual Tour.

Campbell's Covered Bridge built in 1909, is the only remaining covered bridge in South Carolina. It is located off Hwy 14 near Gowensville.

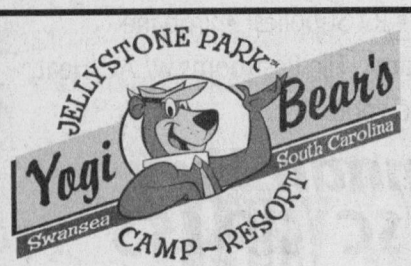

CHARLESTON—Continued
OAK PLANTATION CAMPGROUND—Continued

Phone: (866)658-2500
Address: 3540 Savannah Hwy, Charleston, SC 29455
Lat/Lon: 32.80307/-80.10732
Email: info@oakplantationcampground.com
Web: www.oakplantationcampground.com

SEE AD PAGE 699

(SW) SPLASH ZONE WATERPARK—*From jct I-26 (exit 221) & US 17: Go 2 mi S on US 17, then 1 mi S on Hwy 171, then 1 1/2 mi W on Hwy 700, then 1 3/4 mi S on Riverland Dr. Enter on R.* Fun for the entire family featuring tube and open slides, 500 foot lazy river, Caribbean play structure with slides, wheels and sprays plus a recreational pool. Open May - Labor Day. Call for hours & days of operation.

WELCOME

Phone: (843)795-4386
Address: 871 Riverland Dr, Charleston, SC 29412
Lat/Lon: 32.73592/-79.98266
Web: www.ccprc.com

SEE AD PAGE 698

CHERAW—A-5

(S) CHERAW STATE RECREATION AREA—(Chesterfield) *From town: Go 4 mi S on US 52. Enter on R.* FACILITIES: 17 sites, 40 ft max RV length, 17 W&E, (20/30 amps), 2 pull-thrus, family camping, tenting, dump. RECREATION: lake swim, boating, 10 hp limit, canoeing, lake fishing, playground. Pets welcome. Open all yr. Phone: (843)537-9656.

CHESTER—A-3

(SW) CHESTER STATE PARK—(Chester) *From jct Hwy 9 & Hwy 72: Go 3 mi SW on Hwy 72.* FACILITIES: 25 sites, 33 ft max RV length, 25 W&E, (20/30 amps), 5 pull-thrus, family camping, tenting, dump. RECREATION: lake fishing, playground. Pets welcome. Partial handicap access. Open all yr. Phone: (803)385-2680.

(W) SUMTER NF (Woods Ferry Campground)—(Chester) *From jct Hwy 72 & Hwy 25: Go 2 mi N on Hwy 25, then 3-1/2 mi N on Hwy 49, then 3-1/2 mi NW on Hwy 574.* FACILITIES: 29 sites, 22 ft max RV length, 29 no hkups. RECREATION: boating, ramp. Open May 1 - Sept 30. Phone: (864)427-9858.

CLARKS HILL—C-2

MODOC CAMPGROUND (COE-J. Strom Thurmond Lake)—(McCormick) *Northbound, from jct Hwy-28 & US-221: Go 3-1/2 mi N on US-221 (Modoc), then 1-1/2 mi SW on paved road.* FACILITIES: 49 sites, 35 W&E, (30 amps), 14 no hkups, 20 pull-thrus, tenting, dump, laundry. RECREATION: lake swim, boating, ramp, lake fishing, playground. Open all yr. Phone: (864)333-2272.

Visit our website www.woodalls.com

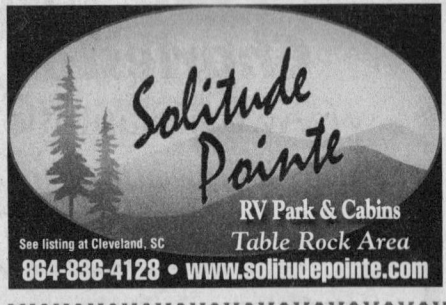

CLEMSON—A-2

(SW) TWIN LAKES CAMPGROUND (COE-Hartwell Lake)—(Pickens) *From jct US 123 & US 76: Go 2 mi SE on US 76, then 5 mi SW on CR 56.* FACILITIES: 102 sites, 102 W&E, (50 amps), 25 pull-thrus, tenting, dump. RECREATION: lake swim, boating, ramp, lake fishing, playground. Open Mar 1 - Nov 30. Phone: (888)893-0678.

CLEVELAND—A-2

(NW) SOLITUDE POINTE—(Greenville) *From jct Hwy 11 & US 276: Go 5 mi NW on Hwy 11/US 276 then stay on US 276 for 1 mi, then turn sharply left onto Hwy 8, then go 1/4 mi, then turn right on Table Rock Rd. Enter on R.*

WELCOME

◆◆◆◆FACILITIES: 14 sites, typical site width 40 ft, 13 full hkups, 1 W&E, (30/50 amps), WiFi Instant Internet at site, WiFi Internet central location, family camping, tenting, cabins, laundry, ice, picnic tables, fire rings, grills, wood.

◆◆RECREATION: rec hall, pavilion, canoeing, 2 canoe rentals, river fishing, bsktball, play equipment, horseshoes, hiking trails.

Pets welcome, breed restrict. Open all yr. Big rigs welcome. Escort to site. Rate in 2010 $28-35 per vehicle. Member ARVC, CARVC.

Phone: (864) 836-4128
Address: 102 Table Rock Rd, Cleveland, SC 29635
Lat/Lon: 35.06581/-82.62410
Email: info@solitudepointe.com
Web: solitudepointe.com

SEE AD THIS PAGE

COLUMBIA—B-3

(W) BARNYARD FLEA MARKET—*From jct I-26 (exit 111A) & US 1: Go 3 mi SW on US 1. Enter on R. Or from jct I-20 (exit 58) & US 1: Go 2 mi NE on US 1. Enter on L.* One of the premier flea markets in South Carolina, with over 550 spaces stocked wtih a wide variety of items, new and old. Open Fri, Sat & Sun. Open all yr.

WELCOME

Phone: (803)957-6570
Address: 4414 Augusta Rd, Lexington, SC 29073
Lat/Lon: 33.97429/-81.15731

SEE AD NEXT PAGE

COLUMBIA—Continued on next page

Stretching 60 miles from Little River to Georgetown, South Carolina's Grand Strand is one of the most popular tourist destinations in the United States.

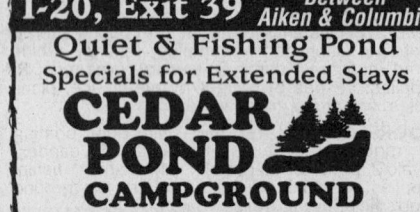

COLUMBIA—Continued

(W) **BARNYARD RV PARK**—(Lexington) *From jct I-26 (exit 111A) & US 1: Go 3 mi SW on US 1. Enter on R. Or from jct I-20 (exit 58) & US 1: Go 2 mi NE on US 1. Enter on L.*

TALK ABOUT CONVENIENCE!
Located off Hwy 1, just minutes from I-20, I-26 and many area attractions. Come stay with us, kick back, relax and we will make you feel right at home. On weekends, experience Southern hospitality at our huge flea market.

◆◆◆◆FACILITIES: 129 sites, typical site width 40 ft, 129 full hkups, (30/50 amps), some extd stay sites, 82 pull-thrus, cable TV, WiFi Instant Internet at site ($), phone on-site Internet (needs activ), phone Internet central location, RV storage, dump, non-guest dump $, laundry, RV supplies, ice, picnic tables, patios.

RECREATION: pavilion, horseshoes.

Pets welcome. Partial handicap access. No tents. Open all yr. Big rigs welcome. Clubs welcome. Rate in 2010 $28-31 for 2 persons. MC/VISA/DISC. CCUSA 50% Discount. CCUSA reservations Accepted, CCUSA max stay 1 day, CCUSA disc. not avail S,Th, CCUSA disc. not avail F,Sa. Not available during special events. Call for details. No tents.

Text 107886 to (440)725-8687 to see our Visual Tour.

Phone: (803)957-1238
Address: 201 Oak Dr, Lexington, SC 29073
Lat/Lon: 33.97660/-81.15818
Email: barnyardrvpark@sc.rr.com
Web: www.barnyardrvpark.com

SEE AD THIS PAGE AND AD TRAVEL SECTION PAGE 689

MILITARY PARK (Weston Lake Rec. Area-Ft. Jackson) —(Lexington) *From I-20 (exit 80): Go S on Clemson Rd to end, then E on Percival, then S on Wildcat, then 2-1/2 mi E on Hwy 262 (Leesburg Rd). On base.* FACILITIES: 30 sites, 13 full hkups, 5 W&E, 12 no hkups, tenting, dump. RECREATION: lake swim, boating, canoeing, ramp, dock, lake fishing. Open all yr. Phone: (803) 751-5253.

(NE) SESQUICENTENNIAL STATE PARK—(Richland) *From jct I-20 & US 1: Go 3 mi NE on US 1. Enter on R.* FACILITIES: 84 sites, typical site width 30 ft, 35 ft max RV length, 84 W&E, (30 amps), 14 pull-thrus, family camping, tenting, dump. RECREATION: lake swim, lake fishing, playground. Pets welcome. Partial handicap access. Open all yr. Phone: (803)788-2706.

Tony's RV Parts & Service—*From I-20 (exit 55) & Hwy 6: Go 3-3/4 mi S on Hwy 6, then 5 mi W on Platt Spring Rd (SC-34). Enter on R.* SALES: pre-owned unit sales. SERVICES: full-time mech, engine/chassis repair, RV appliance repair, body work/collision repair, mobile RV svc, LP gas by weight/by meter, dump station, RV storage, sells parts/accessories, installs hitches. Renovations, Paint, Body & Warranty Work. Open all yr. MC/VISA/DISC/AMEX. FMCA discount.

Phone: (803)894-3071
Address: 130 Pond Branch Road, Lexington, SC 29073
Lat/Lon: 33.86660/-81.28810
Email: darlene@tonysrv.com
Web: www.tonysrv.com

CONWAY—C-6

(NW) **BIG CYPRESS LAKE RV PARK & FISHING RETREAT**—(Horry) *From jct US 501 & Hwy 378: Go 1-1/2 mi SW on US 701, then 5-3/4 mi W on Janette St./Cates Bay Hwy. Then 1/2 mi S on Brown's Way Shortcut Rd. Enter on L.*

◆◆◆FACILITIES: 45 sites, typical site width 25 ft, 30 full hkups, (20/30/50 amps), 50 amps ($), 15 no hkups, some extd stay sites, 10 pull-thrus, heater not allowed, phone Internet central location, family camping, tenting, RV storage, picnic tables, patios, fire rings, wood.

◆RECREATION: pavilion, boating, electric motors only, ramp, dock, lake fishing, hiking trails.

Pets welcome. Open all yr. Big rigs welcome. Clubs welcome. Rate in 2010 $35-55 for 2 persons. MC/VISA. Member ARVC, CARVC. CCUSA 50% Discount. CCUSA reservations Required, CCUSA max stay Unlimited, Cash only for CCUSA disc., CCUSA disc. not avail F,Sa, CCUSA disc. not avail holidays. Minimum stay 2 nights. Discount available Sep thru Mar. Must identify as CCUSA upon making reservation & present card upon arrival. Limited # of sites. Electric heater not allowed. $5 surcharge for RV greater than 32'.

CONWAY—Continued
BIG CYPRESS LAKE RV PARK & FISHING RETREAT—Continued

Phone: (843)902-3418
Address: 6531 Brown's Way Shortcut Rd., Conway, SC 29527
Lat/Lon: 33.78962/-79.16589
Email: rvpark@sccoast.net
Web: www.bigcypresslake.com

SEE AD MYRTLE BEACH PAGE 706

CROSS—C-4

(N) **CROSS/SANTEE COOPER LAKES KOA** (TOO NEW TO RATE)—(Burkley) *From jct I-95 (exit 90) & US 176: Go 2-1/2 mi E on Hwy 176, then at 5 way stop go toward Eutawville for 19-1/2 mi NE on SR 45 which becomes SR 6, continue 1 mi on Hwy 6/Ranger Dr. Enter on L.*

FACILITIES: 62 sites, 42 ft max RV length, 62 full hkups, (20/30/50 amps), 10 pull-thrus, WiFi Internet central location, family camping, tenting, laundry, ice, picnic tables, wood, controlled access.

RECREATION: lake swim, canoeing, kayaking, ramp, dock, lake fishing, hiking trails.

Pets welcome, breed restrict, quantity restrict. Open all yr. Escort to site. Rate in 2010 $33 for 2 persons. MC/VISA/DISC. KOA discount.

Phone: (843)753-2818
Address: 2060 Ranger Dr, Cross, SC 29436
Email: saraj47@yahoo.com
Web: www.koa.com

SEE AD NEXT PAGE

Woodall's Tip... To be considered a "Big Rig Friendly" park, the campground must meet the following requirements: minimum of 50 amps, adequate road width, overhead access clearance, site clearance to accommodate the tallest and widest rigs built. Often not every site can accommodate a big rig, so we recommend that you call ahead for availability.

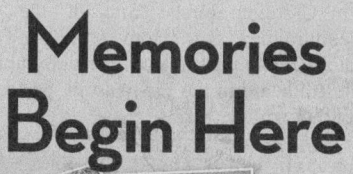

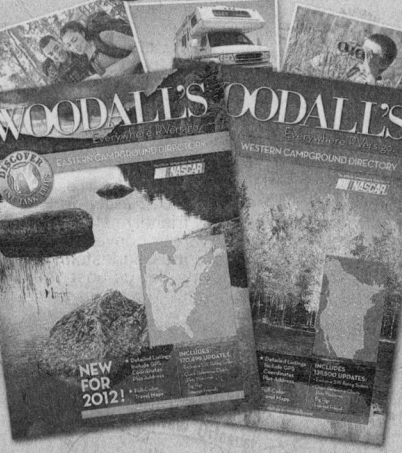

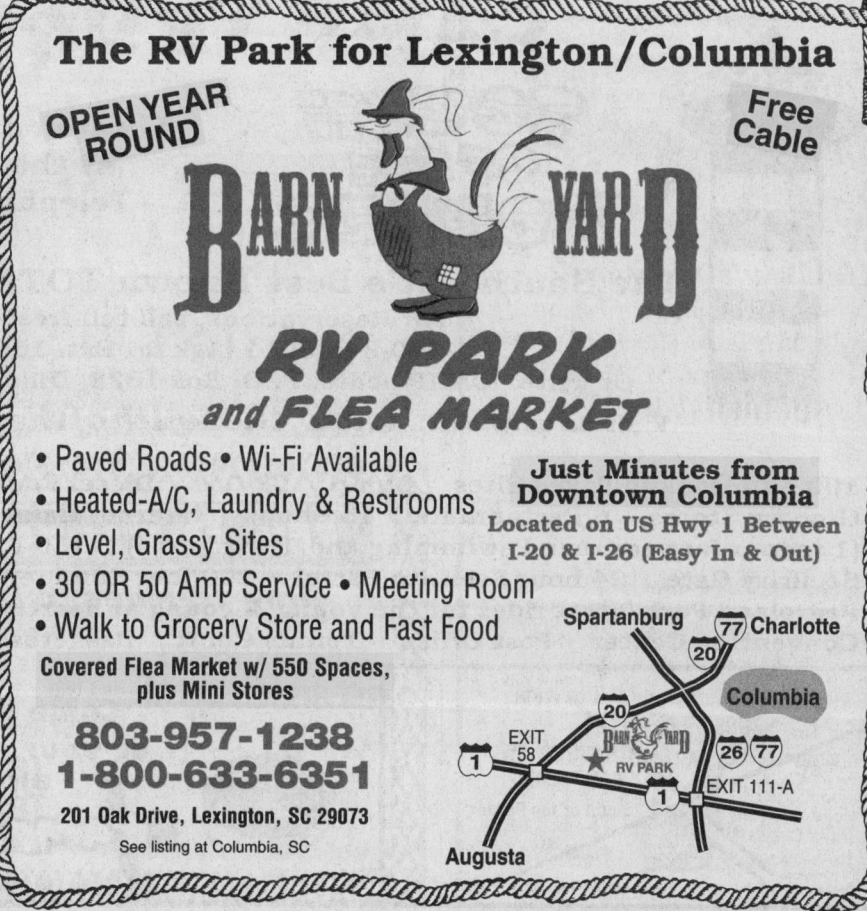

South Carolina Firsts: Site of the First Museum in the U.S.A., Home of the First Real Theater, First Opera and First Symphony Orchestra heard in the U.S.A. were performed in South Carolina.

Can you trust the Woodall's ratings? 25 evaluation teams have scoured North American campgrounds to provide you with accurate, up to date information & ratings. Find a rating you don't agree with? Send a letter or email our way, and we'll give it extra attention for 2012.

DILLON—B-5

(NW) BASS LAKE RV CAMPGROUND—(Dillon) *From jct I-95 (exit 193) & Hwy 9/ Hwy 57: Go 50 ft W on Hwy 9/Hwy 57, then 1/4 mi N on Frontage Road. Enter at end.*

◆◆◆FACILITIES: 48 sites, typical site width 30 ft, 43 full hkups, 5 W&E, (20/30/50 amps), 34 pull-thrus, WiFi Instant Internet at site, family camping, tenting, RV storage, dump, laundry, ltd groc, RV supplies, LP gas by weight/by meter, ice, picnic tables.

◆◆RECREATION: rec room/area, pavilion, lake fishing, play equipment.

Pets welcome. Open all yr. Big rigs welcome. Clubs welcome. Rate in 2010 $20-30 for 2 persons. MC/VISA/DISC/AMEX. CCUSA 50% Discount. CCUSA reservations Required, CCUSA max stay 5 days. Discount not available special events. Call for details.

Phone: (843)774-9100
Address: 1149 Bass Lake Place, Dillon, SC 29536
Lat/Lon: 34.44674/-79.36641
Email: basslakerv@att.net
Web: www.basslakecampground.net

SEE AD NEXT PAGE AND AD TRAVEL SECTION PAGE 689

(C) CAMP PEDRO—(Dillon) *From jct I-95 (exit 1) & US-301: Go 1/10 mi S on US-301. Enter on L.*

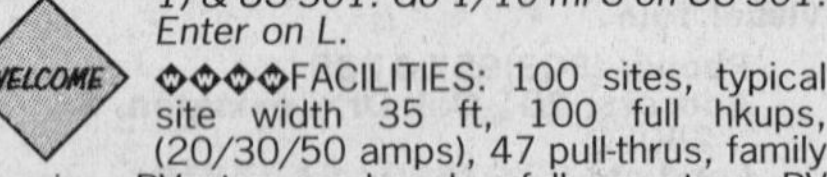

◆◆◆◆FACILITIES: 100 sites, typical site width 35 ft, 100 full hkups, (20/30/50 amps), 47 pull-thrus, family camping, RV storage, laundry, full svc store, RV supplies, LP gas by weight/by meter, ice, picnic tables, grills, controlled access.

◆◆◆RECREATION: rec room/area, coin games, 2 swim pools, mini-golf, ($), bsktball, playground, tennis. Rec open to public.

Pets welcome. Partial handicap access. No tents. Open all yr. Big rigs welcome. Clubs welcome. Rate in 2010 $22-25 per vehicle. MC/VISA/DISC/AMEX. ATM. Member ARVC, CARVC.

CAMP PEDRO—Continued on next page

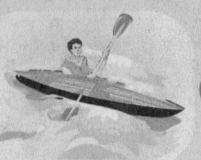

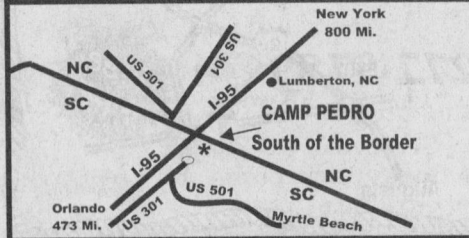

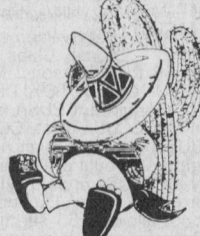

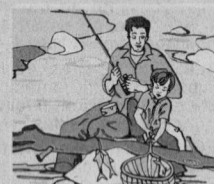

DILLON—Continued
CAMP PEDRO—Continued

Phone: (800)845-6011
Address: US Highway 301/501, South of the Border, SC 29547
Lat/Lon: 34.49978/-79.30677
Web: www.thesouthoftheborder.com

SEE AD PAGE 702

(S) LITTLE PEE DEE STATE PARK—(Dillon) *From jct US 301 & Hwy 9: Go 9 mi SE on Hwy 9, then 2 mi SW on CR 22 (State Park Rd).* FACILITIES: 50 sites, typical site width 22 ft, 32 W&E, (20/30 amps), 18 no hkups, 4 pull-thrus, family camping, tenting, dump. RECREATION: boating, lake fishing, playground. Pets welcome. Partial handicap access. Open all yr. Phone: (843)774-8872.

SOUTH OF THE BORDER—*From jct I-95 & US-301: Go 1/10 mi S on US-301. Enter on L.* Tourist complex with variety of six restaurants, shops, arcades and hotel/motel convention center. Also features children's amusement park, mini-golf, observation tower & post office. Open all yr. MC/VISA/DISC/AMEX. ATM.

Phone: (843)774-2411
Address: US Highway 301/501, South of the Border, SC 29547
Lat/Lon: 34.49978/-79.30677
Web: www.thesouthoftheborder.com

SEE AD PAGE 702

EASLEY—A-2

(N) April Valley RV Park—(Pickens) *From jct Hwy 123 & Hwy 135: Go 6-1/2 mi N on Hwy 135, then 2-1/4 mi W on Jameson Rd. Enter on R.* ◇◇FACILITIES: 27 sites, accepts full hkup units only, 27 full hkups, (20/30/50 amps). ◇RECREATION: lake/pond fishing. Pets welcome. No tents. Open all yr. Big rigs welcome. Rate in 2010 $25 per vehicle. Phone: (864)855-1200.

EDISTO ISLAND—E-4

(S) EDISTO BEACH STATE PARK—(Charleston) *From jct US 17 & Hwy 174: Go 28 mi S on Hwy 174.* FACILITIES: 116 sites, typical site width 20 ft, 111 W&E, (30/50 amps), 5 no hkups, 3 pull-thrus, family camping, tenting, dump. RECREATION: saltwater swim, boating, canoeing, ramp, saltwater fishing, playground. Pets welcome. Open all yr. Phone: (843)869-2756.

EUTAWVILLE—C-4

(E) ROCKS POND CAMPGROUND & MARINA—(Orangeburg) *From jct Hwy 45 & Hwy 6: Go 5-3/4 mi E on Hwy 6 (Old Number Six Hwy), then 1-1/4 mi N on Rock Pond Road, then 1/2 mi E on Campground Rd. Enter at end.*

◇◇◇FACILITIES: 500 sites, typical site width 50 ft, 500 full hkups, (20/30/50 amps), some extd stay sites, 290 pull-thrus, WiFi Instant Internet at site ($), WiFi Internet central location, family camping, tenting, RV's/park model rentals, RV storage, laundry, full svc store, RV supplies, LP gas by meter, marine gas, ice, picnic tables, fire rings, wood, controlled access.

EUTAWVILLE—Continued
ROCKS POND CAMPGROUND & MARINA—Continued

◇◇◇◇RECREATION: rec hall, rec room/area, equipped pavilion, coin games, lake swim, boating, canoeing, kayaking, ramp, dock, 3 pontoon/7 rowboat rentals, lake/pond fishing, fishing supplies, fishing guides, mini-golf ($), bsktball, playground, activities, (wkends), sports field. Rec open to public.

Pets welcome, breed restrict. Partial handicap access. Open all yr. Big rigs welcome. Clubs welcome. Rate in 2010 $27-37 for 4 persons. MC/VISA. Member ARVC, CARVC.

Phone: (803)492-7711
Address: 108 Campground Rd, Eutawville, SC 29048
Lat/Lon: 33.40361/-80.23503
Email: feedback@rockspondcampground.com
Web: www.rockspondcampground.com

SEE AD SANTEE PAGE 709

FAIR PLAY—B-1

Lake Hartwell RV Park—(Oconee) *From jct I-85 (exit 1) & Hwy 11: Go 4 mi N on Hwy 11. Enter on R.* ◇◇◇FACILITIES: 14 sites, typical site width 28 ft, accepts full hkup units only, 14 full hkups, (30/50 amps), WiFi Instant Internet at site, RV storage. RECREATION: No tents. Open all yr. Big rigs welcome. Rate in 2010 $30-34 for 2 persons. MC/VISA. CCUSA 50% Discount. CCUSA reservations Recommended, CCUSA max stay 2 days, Cash only for CCUSA disc., CCUSA disc. not avail S, CCUSA disc. not avail F,Sa, CCUSA disc. not avail holidays.

Phone: (866)972-0378
Address: 14503 Hwy 11, Westminster, SC 29693
Lat/Lon: 34.55177/-83.04933

(W) LAKE HARTWELL STATE RECREATION AREA—(Oconee) *At jct I-85 & Hwy 11.* FACILITIES: 128 sites, typical site width 25 ft, 40 ft max RV length, 115 W&E, (20/30 amps), 13 no hkups, 8 pull-thrus, family camping, tenting, dump, laundry, ltd groc. RECREATION: boating, ramp, lake fishing, playground. Pets welcome. Open all yr. Phone: (864)972-3352.

FORT MILL—A-4

(N) Charlotte/Fort Mill KOA—(York) *From jct I-77 (exit 88) & Gold Hill Rd: Go 1/2 mi W on Gold Hill Rd. Enter on R.* ◇◇◇◇FACILITIES: 236 sites, typical site width 35 ft, 164 full hkups, 47 W&E, 25 E, (20/30/50 amps), 63 pull-thrus, family camping, tenting, dump, laundry, full svc store. ◇◇◇RECREATION: swim pool, playground. Pets welcome. Partial handicap access. Open all yr. Big rigs welcome. Rate in 2010 $35-65 for 2 persons. Phone: (888)562-4430. KOA discount.

FORT MILL—Continued

(NE) CROWN INTERNATIONAL CAMPGROUND—(York) *From jct I-77 & Carowinds Blvd (exit 90): Go 1 mi S on Hwy 21 to Regent Park Marble Entrance sign, then 2-1/4 mi E on Regent Pkwy. Enter on R.*

◇◇FACILITIES: 127 sites, 108 full hkups, 19 W&E, (30/50 amps), some extd stay sites, 91 pull-thrus, cable TV, WiFi Instant Internet at site, family camping, dump, laundry, picnic tables.

RECREATION: lake fishing.

Pets welcome. No tents. Open all yr. Big rigs welcome. Rate in 2010 $35 per family. MC/VISA/DISC.

Phone: (803)547-3500
Address: 8332 Regent Pkwy, Fort Mill, SC 29715
Lat/Lon: 35.06011/-80.90462
Email: Jeremy@coulstoninc.com

SEE AD CHARLOTTE, NC PAGE 586

GAFFNEY—A-3

(W) Spartanburg NE/Gaffney KOA—(Cherokee) *From jct I-85 (exit 87) & Road 39: Go 50 yds S on Rd-39, then 1 mi E on Overbrook Dr exit(east frontage rd), then 200 yds S on Sarratt School Rd. Enter on R.* ◇◇◇FACILITIES: 108 sites, typical site width 26 ft, 91 full hkups, 17 W&E, (20/30/50 amps), 28 pull-thrus, family camping, tenting, dump, laundry, ltd groc. ◇◇◇RECREATION: swim pool, pond fishing, playground. Pets welcome. Partial handicap access. Open all yr. Big rigs welcome. Rate in 2010 $30-38 for 4 persons. Phone: (864)489-2022. KOA discount.

GREENVILLE—A-2

IVY ACRES RV PARK—*From jct I-85 (exit 39) & SR 143 (River Rd): Go 1-1/4 mi E on River Rd. Enter on L.*

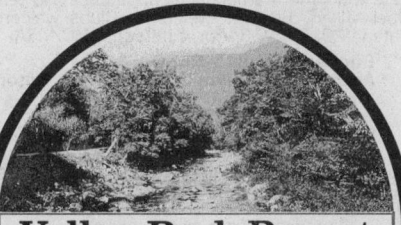

SEE PRIMARY LISTING AT PIEDMONT AND AD NEXT PAGE

(N) PARIS MOUNTAIN STATE PARK—(Greenville) *From jct US 276 & Hwy 253: Go 6 mi NE on Hwy 253, then NW on park road.* FACILITIES: 52 sites, typical site width 35 ft, 40 ft max RV length, 39 W&E, (20/30 amps), 13 no hkups, 3 pull-thrus, family camping, tenting, dump. RECREATION: lake swim, lake fishing, playground. Pets welcome. Partial handicap access. Open all yr. Phone: (864)244-5565.

GREENVILLE—Continued on next page

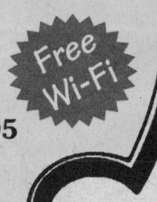

GREENVILLE—Continued

(NE) RAINBOW RV PARK—(Greenville) *N'bound from jct I-85 (exit 42) & US 29: Go 11-6/10 mi NE on US 29, then 200 feet NW on Rutherford Rd. S'bound from jct I-85 (exit 66) & US 29: Go 15 mi W on US 29, then 200 feet NW on Rutherford Rd. Enter on R.*

◇◇FACILITIES: 50 sites, typical site width 25 ft, 40 ft max RV length, accepts full hkup units only, 50 full hkups, (30/50 amps), mostly extd stay sites, 10 pull-thrus, WiFi Internet central location, RV storage, patios.

Pets welcome, size restrict. No tents. Open all yr. No restrooms. Rate in 2010 $27-30 for 2 persons.

Phone: (864)244-1271
Address: 3553 Rutherford Rd., Taylors, SC 29687
Lat/Lon: 34.91659/-82.32059
Web: www.rainbowrvpark.com

SEE AD THIS PAGE

(SE) Scuffletown USA Campground—(Greenville) *From jct I-85 (exit 51) & Hwy 146 (Woodruff Rd): Go 4-3/4 mi E on Hwy 146, then 1-1/2 mi S on Scuffletown Rd to campground. Enter on L.* ◇◇FACILITIES: 68 sites, typical site width 35 ft, 35 full hkups, 15 W&E, 8 E, (20/30/50 amps), 50 amps ($), 10 no hkups, 4 pull-thrus, tenting, dump, laundry. RECREATION: lake fishing, play equipment. Pets welcome. Open all yr. Big rigs welcome. Rate in 2010 $27-32 for 2 persons. Phone: (864)967-2276.

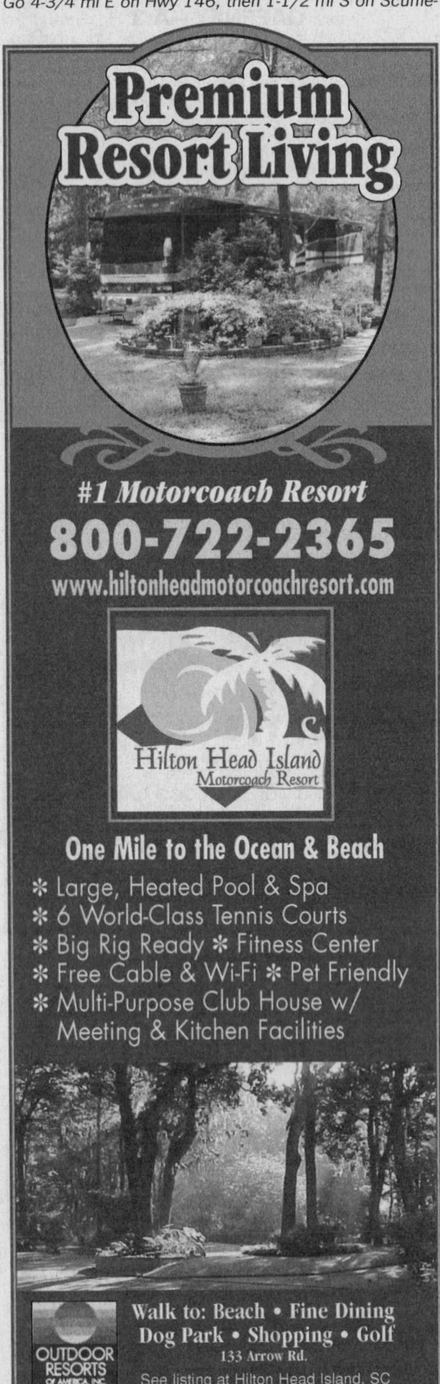

Premium Resort Living
#1 Motorcoach Resort
800-722-2365
www.hiltonheadmotorcoachresort.com
Hilton Head Island Motorcoach Resort
One Mile to the Ocean & Beach
* Large, Heated Pool & Spa
* 6 World-Class Tennis Courts
* Big Rig Ready * Fitness Center
* Free Cable & Wi-Fi * Pet Friendly
* Multi-Purpose Club House w/ Meeting & Kitchen Facilities
Walk to: Beach • Fine Dining
Dog Park • Shopping • Golf
133 Arrow Rd.
OUTDOOR RESORTS OF AMERICA, INC.
See listing at Hilton Head Island, SC

(S) SPRINGWOOD RV PARK—(Greenville) *From I-85 (exit 44) & US 25/White Horse Rd: go 2-3/4 mi S on White Horse Rd, then 1/2 mi S on Donaldson Rd. Enter on R.*

◇◇◇FACILITIES: 65 sites, typical site width 30 ft, 65 full hkups, (30/50 amps), many extd stay sites, 5 pull-thrus, WiFi Instant Internet at site, WiFi Internet central location, patios.

Pets welcome. No tents. Open all yr. Big rigs welcome. Rate in 2010 $25-30 for 2 persons. MC/VISA.

Text 107950 to (440)725-8687 to see our Visual Tour.

Phone: (864)277-9789
Address: 810 Donaldson Rd, Greenville, SC 29605
Lat/Lon: 34.76017/-82.38466
Email: wyattpark@aol.com
Web: www.springwoodrvpark.com

SEE AD PAGE 703 AND AD TRAVEL SECTION PAGE 689

GREENWOOD—B-2

(E) LAKE GREENWOOD STATE RECREATION AREA —(Greenwood) *From jct US 178-25 & Hwy 34: Go 14 mi E on Hwy 34, then 3 mi N on Hwy 702.* FACILITIES: 125 sites, typical site width 25 ft, 125 W&E, (20/30 amps), 0 no hkups, 32 pull-thrus, family camping, tenting, dump, ltd groc. RECREATION: boating, ramp, lake fishing. Pets welcome. Open all yr. Phone: (864)543-3535.

(E) Moon Landing RV Park & Marina—(Laurens) *From jct of hwy 72 & Hwy 39: Go 2 mi SE on Hwy 39, then 4 mi SW on Watts Bridge Rd. Enter on L.* ◇◇◇FACILITIES: 70 sites, typical site width 30 ft, 40 ft max RV length, 56 full hkups, 14 W&E, (30/50 amps), 15 pull-thrus, family camping, dump, laundry, ltd groc. ◇◇◇RECREATION: lake swim, boating, ramp, dock, lake fishing. Pets welcome. Partial handicap access. No tents. Open all yr. Rate in 2010 $20-35 per family. Member ARVC, CARVC. Phone: (864)998-4292.

HARDEEVILLE—E-3

(SE) HARDEEVILLE RV-THOMAS' PARKS AND SITES—(Jasper) *From I-95 (exit 5) & jct US 17: Go N 1 mi on US 17, then E 5 mi on Hwy 46, then 1/4 mi W on Hwy 170 and continue straight on Hwy 170-A for 3 mi. Enter on L.*

◇◇◇FACILITIES: 100 sites, typical site width 35 ft, accepts full hkup units only, 100 full hkups, (30/50 amps), 50 amps ($), some extd stay sites, 30 pull-thrus, cable TV, WiFi Instant Internet at site, laundry, ice, picnic tables, fire rings, wood.

HARDEEVILLE—Continued
HARDEEVILLE RV-THOMAS' PARKS AND SITES—Continued

RECREATION: hiking trails.

Pets welcome. No tents. Open all yr. No restrooms. Big rigs welcome. Rate in 2010 $34 for 2 persons. Member ARVC, CARVC. CCUSA 50% Discount. CCUSA reservations Required, CCUSA max stay Unlimited. Discount not available Mar or Apr: not available to club organizations or rallies. No restrooms/showers.

Phone: (843)784-6210
Address: 2942 S Okatie Hwy, Hardeeville, SC 29927
Lat/Lon: 32.18878/-81.02996
Web: www.hardeevillerv.com

SEE AD SAVANNAH, GA PAGE 206

(SE) THE PINK PIG—*From jct I-95 (exit 5) & jct US 17: Go 1 mi N on US 17, then 5 mi E on Hwy 46, then 1/4 mi W on Hwy 170 and continue straight on Hwy 170-A for 2-1/2 mi. Enter on L.* The Pink Pig is a family owned and operated restaurant featuring a slow roasting bbq method. All sauces and other recipes were created by the founder. The restaurant has been featured on The Food Channel. Open all yr.

Phone: (843)784-3635
Address: 3508 South Okatie Hwy, Hardeeville, SC 29927
Lat/Lon: 32.19432/-81.02953
Web: www.the-pink-pig.com

SEE AD SAVANNAH, GA PAGE 206

HILTON HEAD ISLAND—E-4

(W) HILTON HEAD HARBOR RV RESORT & MARINA—(Beaufort) *From jct I-95 (exit 8) & US 278: Go 19 mi E on US 278 1/2 mi past bridge, then 1/4 mi N on Jenkins Rd. Enter on L.*

STAY ON THE INTRACOASTAL WATERWAY
Beautiful Waterside Resort with landscaped sites and concrete pads. Enjoy fine dining at the Sunset Grille. Charter a boat at our marina. Beautiful beaches and premier golf are minutes away. Ask about lot sales.

◇◇◇◇FACILITIES: 200 sites, typical site width 40 ft, accepts full hkup units only, 200 full hkups, (20/30/50 amps), cable TV, phone/WiFi Instant Internet at site, WiFi Internet central location, laundry, ltd groc, marine gas, ice, picnic tables, patios, grills.

◇◇◇RECREATION: rec room/area, 2 swim pools, hot tub, boating, canoeing, kayaking, ramp, dock, pontoon/2 kayak/motorboat rentals, saltwater/river fishing, fishing guides, golf nearby, playground, tennis.

Pets welcome. Partial handicap access. No tents. Open all yr. Big rigs welcome. Clubs welcome. Rate in 2010 $49-64 for 4 persons. MC/VISA.

Phone: (800)845-9560
Address: 43-A Jenkins Island Rd, Hilton Head Island, SC 29926
Lat/Lon: 32.22314/-80.77074
Email: info@hiltonheadharbor.com
Web: hiltonheadharbor.com

SEE AD NEXT PAGE AND AD DISCOVER SECTION PAGE 46

HILTON HEAD ISLAND—Continued on next page

South Carolina State Motto: "Dum Spiro Spero" (While I breathe, I hope)

HILTON HEAD ISLAND—Continued

(C) **HILTON HEAD ISLAND MOTOR-COACH RESORT**—(Beaufort) *From jct I-95 (exit 8) & US 278: Go 22 mi E on US 278, then 5-1/2 mi E on Cross Island Pkwy, then 1/4 mi N on Target Rd, then E on Arrow Rd. Enter on L.*

LUXURY RESORT ONLY 1 MILE TO OCEAN

ORA Motorcoach Only Resort with 401 beautiful sites on Hilton Head Island - 45 minutes off I-95. Gated access with large swimming pool, 6 tennis courts & fitness center. Bicycle or walk to beach, golf dining and shopping.

◆◆◆◆◆FACILITIES: 401 sites, typical site width 40 ft, accepts full hkup units only, 401 full hkups, (30/50 amps), 6 pull-thrus, cable TV, WiFi Instant Internet at site, laundry, ice, picnic tables, patios, controlled access.

◆◆◆◆RECREATION: rec hall, rec room/area, swim pool, hot tub, pond fishing, golf nearby, bsktball, play equipment, 2 shuffleboard courts, activities, tennis.

Pets welcome. Partial handicap access. No tents. Open all yr. Motor Coaches Only. Big rigs welcome. Escort to site. Clubs welcome. Rate in 2010 $55-75 for 4 persons. MC/VISA/AMEX. Member ARVC, CARVC. FMCA discount.

Text 107882 to (440)725-8687 to see our Visual Tour.

Phone: (800)722-2365
Address: 133 Arrow Rd, Hilton Head Island, SC 29928
Lat/Lon: 32.15940/-80.76140
Email: outdoorresort@hargray.com
Web: www.hiltonheadmotorcoachresort.com

SEE AD PAGE 704

RIVER'S END CAMPGROUND & RV PARK—*From jct I-95 (exit 8) & US 278: Go 3 mi S on I-95, then 15 mi S on US 17, then 1 mi on Hwy 25 (W. Oglethorpe/W Broad), then 1 mi E on Bay St, then 15 mi E on President St (becomes Island Expwy then US 80 to Tybe Island), then 2 blks N on Polk St.*

SEE PRIMARY LISTING AT TYBEE ISLAND, GA AND AD SAVANNAH, GA PAGE 206

IRMO—B-3

(SE) **Woodsmoke Family Campground**—(Newberry) *From jct I-26 (exit 97) & US 176: Go 1 mi W on US 176. Enter on R.* ◆◆◆FACILITIES: 34 sites, 32 full hkups, 2 W&E, (30/50 amps), 10 pull-thrus, WiFi Instant Internet at site ($), family camping, tenting, dump, non-guest dump $, laundry, LP gas by weight, ice, picnic tables, wood. ◆◆RECREATION: pond fishing, bsktball, playground, horseshoes, v-ball. Pets welcome, breed restrict. Partial handicap access. Open all yr. Big rigs welcome. Rate in 2010 $23-28 for 2 persons. CCUSA 50% Discount. CCUSA reservations Recommended, CCUSA max stay 1 day, Cash only for CCUSA disc., CCUSA disc. not avail S, CCUSA disc. not avail F,Sa, CCUSA disc. not avail holidays.

Phone: (803)781-3451
Address: 11302 Broad River Rd, Irmo, SC 29063
Lat/Lon: 34.15723/-81.25179
Web: woodsmoke.webs.com

JOANNA—B-3

(E) **MAGNOLIA RV PARK & CAMP-GROUND**—(Laurens) *From jct I-26 (exit 60) & Hwy 66: Go 1/10 mi W on Hwy 66, then 1/2 mi S on Fairview Church Rd. Enter on L.*

◆◆◆FACILITIES: 45 sites, typical site width 30 ft, 25 full hkups, 20 W&E, (20/30/50 amps), some extd stay sites, 29 pull-thrus, WiFi Instant Internet at site, phone Internet central location, family camping, tenting, cabins, RV storage, dump, non-guest dump $, laundry, RV supplies, LP gas by weight/by meter, ice, picnic tables, fire rings, wood.

◆◆RECREATION: rec room/area, pavilion, swim pool, play equipment. Rec open to public.

Pets welcome, quantity restrict. Open all yr. Big rigs welcome. Escort to site. Rate in 2010 $26-32 for 4 persons. MC/VISA/DISC. Member ARVC, CARVC. CCUSA 50% Discount. CCUSA reservations Recommended, CCUSA max stay Unlimited, CCUSA disc. not avail F,Sa, CCUSA disc. not avail holidays. Discount not available on weekly or monthly rates. $3 sewer surcharge.

JOANNA—Continued
MAGNOLIA RV PARK & CAMPGROUND—Continued

Phone: (864)697-1214
Address: 567 Fairview Church Rd, Kinards, SC 29355
Lat/Lon: 34.43233/-81.75619
Email: info@magnoliarvparksc.com
Web: www.magnoliarvparksc.com

Reserve Online at Woodalls.com

SEE AD TRAVEL SECTION PAGE 689

LAKE HARTWELL—B-2

See lisings at Anderson, Clemson, Fair Play, Senea & Townville

LAKE KEOWEE—A-1

See listings at Clemson, Fairplay, Seneca, Townville

LANCASTER—A-4

(N) ANDREW JACKSON STATE PARK—(Lancaster) *Northbound, from jct Hwy 9 & US 521: Go 9 mi N on US 521. Enter on R.* FACILITIES: 25 sites, typical site width 30 ft, 36 ft max RV length, 25 W&E, 5 pull-thrus, family camping, tenting, dump. RECREATION: lake fishing, playground. Pets welcome. Partial handicap access. Open all yr. Phone: (803)285-3344.

LEESVILLE—C-3

(SE) **CEDAR POND CAMPGROUND**—(Lexington) *From jct I-20 (exit 39) & US 178: Go 1-1/2 mi E on US 178. Enter on R.*

◆◆◆FACILITIES: 32 sites, typical site width 30 ft, 40 ft max RV length, 26 full hkups, 6 W&E, (20/30/50 amps), some extd stay sites, 6 pull-thrus, tenting, dump, non-guest dump $, laundry, LP gas by weight/by meter, picnic tables.

◆◆RECREATION: pavilion, boating, electric motors only, dock, pond fishing, play equipment, horseshoes, v-ball.

Pets welcome. Open all yr. Rate in 2010 $20 for 4 persons. MC/VISA/DISC. CCUSA 50% Discount.

Phone: (803)657-5993
Address: 4721 Fairview Rd, Batesburg - Leesville, SC 29070
Lat/Lon: 33.79917/-81.43043
Email: cedarpondcamp@aol.com

SEE AD COLUMBIA PAGE 700

LONGS—B-6

(SE) **WILLOWTREE RESORT**—(Horry) *From jct SC-9 and SC 905: Go 1-3/4 mi NE on SC 905, then 1-1/2 mi N on Old Buck Creek Rd. Enter on R.*

NEWEST & BEST IN MYRTLE BEACH AREA

A true RV resort, planned and developed to meet the needs of today's discerning RVers. Large paved sites. Superior customer service. Picture-perfect setting. 21st century amenities.

◆◆◆◆◆FACILITIES: 106 sites, typical site width 45 ft, 106 full hkups, (20/30/50 amps), some extd stay sites, 98 pull-thrus, WiFi Instant Internet at site, WiFi Internet central location, family camping, cabins, RV storage, dump, non-guest dump $, laundry, ltd groc, RV supplies, LP gas by meter, ice, picnic tables, patios, fire rings, grills, wood, controlled access.

◆◆◆◆◆RECREATION: rec hall, rec room/area, coin games, swim pool, wading pool, lake swim, hot tub, boating, electric motors only, canoeing, canoe/6 pedal boat/5 motorboat rentals, lake fishing, fishing supplies, golf nearby, bsktball, 12 bike rentals, playground, activities, horseshoes, hiking trails, v-ball.

LONGS—Continued
WILLOWTREE RESORT—Continued

Pets welcome. Partial handicap access. No tents. Open all yr. Big rigs welcome. Escort to site. Clubs welcome. Rate in 2010 $30-88 per family. MC/VISA/DISC. Member ARVC, CARVC.

Text 83409 to (440)725-8687 to see our Visual Tour.

Phone: (866)207-2267
Address: 520 Southern Sights Drive, Longs, SC 29568
Lat/Lon: 33.97505/-78.71937
Email: reservations@willowtreervr.com
Web: www.willowtreervr.com

SEE AD MYRTLE BEACH PAGE 707 AND AD TRAVEL SECTION PAGE 691 AND AD DISCOVER SECTION PAGE 45

MCBEE—B-4

(E) **The Farm Campground**—(Chesterfield) *From jct US 1 & Hwy 151: Go 6 mi E on Hwy 151, then 1/10 mi on Tabernackle Church Rd, then 1/2 mi N on Hillcrest Ln. Enter on R.* ◆◆◆FACILITIES: 20 sites, typical site width 25 ft, 40 ft max RV length, 20 full hkups, (30/50 amps), 6 pull-thrus, WiFi Instant Internet at site, family camping, tenting, laundry, picnic tables, fire rings, wood. RECREATION: horseshoes, hiking trails. Pets welcome. Open all yr. Rate in 2010 $20-60 per family. CCUSA 50% Discount. CCUSA reservations Recommended, CCUSA max stay Unlimited, Cash only for CCUSA disc. Discount not available race week or special events. Call for details.

Phone: (843)339-1338
Address: 604 Hillcrest Ln, Mcbee, SC 29101
Lat/Lon: 34.43345/-80.18144
Email: info@thefarmcampground.net
Web: thefarmcampground.net

MCCORMICK—C-2

(W) BAKER CREEK STATE PARK—(McCormick) *From jct Hwy 28 & US 378: Go 3-1/2 mi SW on US 378, then 1 mi N on park road. Enter on L.* FACILITIES: 100 sites, 50 W&E, (20/30 amps), 50 no hkups, 8 pull-thrus, family camping, tenting, dump. RECREATION: boating, ramp, lake fishing, playground. Pets welcome. Partial handicap access. Open all yr. Phone: (864)443-2457.

(SE) HAMILTON BRANCH STATE RECREATION AREA—(McCormick) *From town: Go 12 mi SE on US-221.* FACILITIES: 140 sites, typical site width 32 ft, 40 ft max RV length, 140 W&E, (20/30 amps), 10 pull-thrus, family camping, tenting, dump. RECREATION: boating, ramp, dock, lake fishing, playground. Pets welcome. Open all yr. Phone: (864)333-2223.

(W) HAWE CREEK CAMPGROUND (COE-J. Strom Thurmond Lake)—(McCormick) *From jct US-221 & US-378: Go 2-1/2 mi SW on US-378, then 4 mi S on paved road.* FACILITIES: 28 sites, 10 W&E, (30/50 amps), 18 no hkups, 7 pull-thrus, tenting, dump. RECREATION: lake swim, boating, ramp, lake fishing. Partial handicap access. Open Mar - Dec. Phone: (864)443-5441.

(W) HICKORY KNOB STATE RESORT PARK—(McCormick) *From town: Go 6 mi SW on US 378, then 2 mi N on Hwy 7, then 2 mi W on park road.* FACILITIES: 44 sites, typical site width 20 ft, 30 ft max RV length, 44 W&E, 8 pull-thrus, family camping, tenting, dump. RECREATION: boating, ramp, dock, lake fishing, playground. Pets welcome. Open all yr. Phone: (800)491-1764.

MT. CARMEL CAMPGROUND (COE-J. Strom Thurmond Lake)—(McCormick) *From jct Hwy-28 & US-378: Go 15 mi NW on Hwy-28 & Hwy-81.* FACILITIES: 43 sites, 21 W&E, (30 amps), 22 no hkups, 10 pull-thrus, tenting, dump. RECREATION: lake swim, boating, ramp, lake fishing, playground. Open all yr. Phone: (864)391-2711.

The Edisto River Canoe & Kayak Trail covers 66 miles of the river for which it's named. The Edisto is reputed to be the world's longest free-flowing "blackwater" stream.

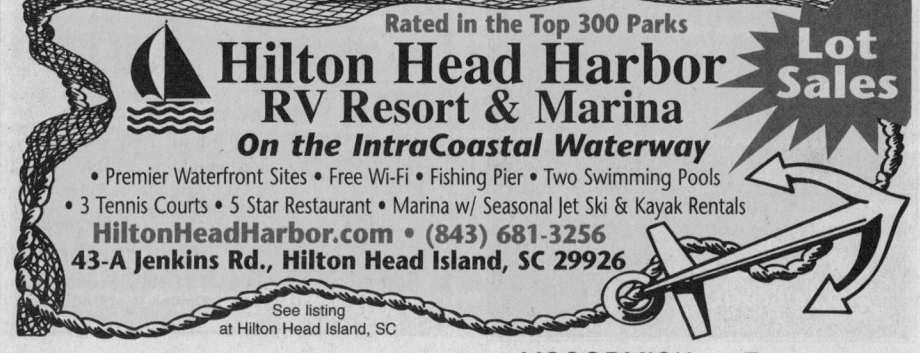

MURRELLS INLET—C-6

(SW) HUNTINGTON BEACH STATE PARK—(Georgetown) *Westbound, from jct Hwy-544 & US-17: Go 3 mi S on US-17.* FACILITIES: 137 sites, typical site width 40 ft, 24 full hkups, 107 W&E, (20/30 amps), 6 no hkups, 2 pull-thrus, family camping, tenting, dump. RECREATION: saltwater swim, saltwater fishing. Pets welcome. Open all yr. Phone: (843)237-4440.

MYRTLE BEACH—C-6

WELCOME

(N) APACHE FAMILY CAMPGROUND—(Horry) *From jct US 501 & US 17: Go 9-3/4 mi N on US 17, then 1/2 mi E on Chestnut Rd, then 1/4 mi S on Kings Rd. Enter on L.*

LONGEST PIER ON EASTERN SEABOARD
From your campsite or rental enjoy great fishing, dancing or casual oceanfront dining at Croakers on our 1220' Pier. With planned activities, a large arcade or nightly entertainment. Relax at a great family value.

◆◆◆◆FACILITIES: 937 sites, typical site width 32 ft, 931 full hkups, 6 W&E, (30/50 amps), some extd stay sites, 18 pull-thrus, cable TV, WiFi Instant Internet at site ($), phone Internet central location, family camping, tenting, RV's/park model rentals, RV storage, dump, laundry, full svc store, RV supplies, LP gas by weight/by meter, ice, picnic tables, controlled access.

◆◆◆◆RECREATION: rec room/area, equipped pavilion, coin games, swim pool, wading pool, saltwater swim, saltwater fishing, fishing supplies, golf nearby, bsktball, playground, activities, v-ball. Rec open to public.

Pets welcome, breed restrict, quantity restrict. Partial handicap access. Open all yr. Big rigs welcome. Clubs welcome. Rate in 2010 $27-58 for 4 persons. MC/VISA. Member ARVC, CARVC.

Text 107871 to (440)725-8687 to see our Visual Tour.

Phone: (800)553-1749
Address: 9700 Kings Rd, Myrtle Beach, SC 29572
Lat/Lon: 33.76909/-78.78801
Web: www.apachefamilycampground.com

SEE AD THIS PAGE

WELCOME

BATTLESHIP NORTH CAROLINA—*From jct US 501 & US 17: Go 4-1/2 mi N on US 17 then 15 mi N on Hwy 31, then 1-3/4 mi N on Hwy 9/US 17, then 50 mi N on US 17, then 1/2 mi N on US 421. Enter on R.*

SEE PRIMARY LISTING AT WILMINGTON, SC AND AD DISCOVER SECTION PAGE 43

WELCOME

(N) BRIARCLIFFE RV RESORT, INC—(Horry) *From jct US 501 & US 17: Go 11 mi N on US 17. Enter on L.*

◆◆◆◆FACILITIES: 174 sites, typical site width 35 ft, 174 full hkups, (30/50 amps), some extd stay sites, cable TV, WiFi Instant Internet at site, WiFi Internet central location, RV's/park model rentals, laundry, ice, picnic tables, patios, controlled access.

CAMPCLUB USA

◆◆◆RECREATION: rec hall, swim pool, mini-golf, golf nearby, bsktball, play equipment, 2 shuffleboard courts, activities, horseshoes.

Pets welcome. Partial handicap access. No tents. Age restrict may apply. Open all yr. Big rigs welcome. Clubs welcome. Rate in 2010 $33-47 for 8 persons. MC/VISA/DISC. CCUSA 50% Discount. CCUSA reservations Required, CCUSA max stay Unlimited, CCUSA disc. not avail F,Sa, CCUSA disc. not avail holidays. Phone sites available for additional charge.

Text 107870 to (440)725-8687 to see our Visual Tour.

Phone: (843)272-2730
Address: 10495 N Kings Hwy, Myrtle Beach, SC 29572
Lat/Lon: 33.79548/-078.75097
Email: briarcliffervresort@sc.rr.com
Web: www.briarcliffervresort.com

SEE AD THIS PAGE

MYRTLE BEACH—Continued on next page

"Carolina Shag" is the state dance of South Carolina.

HOLIDAY TRAV-L-PARK RESORT FOR CAMPERS—*From jct US 501 & US 17 in Myrtle Beach, SC: Go 103 mi N on US 17, then 22 mi SE on Hwy 24, then 2 mi SE on Hwy 58, then W on Coast Guard Rd. Enter on L.*

SEE PRIMARY LISTING AT EMERALD ISLE, NC AND AD EMERALD ISLE, NC PAGE 588

(C) KOA-MYRTLE BEACH—(Horry) *From jct US 17 & US 501: Go 2-1/2 mi E on US 501, then 1 mi S on US 17 Bus, W on 5th Ave S. Enter on L.*

◇◇◇◇FACILITIES: 543 sites, typical site width 40 ft, 392 full hkups, 102 W&E, (20/30/50 amps), 49 no hkups, some extd stay sites, 47 pull-thrus, cable TV, phone/WiFi Instant Internet at site ($), phone Internet central location, family camping, tenting, RV's/park model rentals, cabins, RV storage, dump, non-guest dump $, laundry, full svc store, RV supplies, LP gas by weight/by meter, ice, picnic tables, fire rings, grills, wood, controlled access.

◇◇◇◇RECREATION: rec room/area, coin games, swim pool, wading pool, spray ground, pond fishing, bsktball, bike rental, playground, activities, v-ball, local tours.

Pets welcome. Partial handicap access. Open all yr. Big rigs welcome. Escort to site. Clubs welcome. MC/VISA/DISC. ATM. Member ARVC, CARVC. KOA discount.

Phone: (800)255-7614
Address: 613 5th Ave S, Myrtle Beach, SC 29577
Lat/Lon: 33.68413/-78.89667
Web: www.koa.com

SEE AD PAGE 707 AND AD TRAVEL SECTION PAGE 691 AND AD DISCOVER SECTION PAGE 45

(S) LAKEWOOD CAMPING RESORT—(Horry) *From jct US 501 & 544: Go E 14 mi on Hwy 544, then N 1/2 mi on US 17 Bus. Enter on R.*

FUN FOR THE WHOLE FAMILY

You choose - oceanfront or shaded camping. Then enjoy great new water attractions, fishing, miniature golf, pool parties, canoe and kayak rentals, planned activities for the kids & teens, bonfires and more.

◇◇◇◇◇FACILITIES: 1900 sites, typical site width 34 ft, 1874 full hkups, 26 W&E, (20/30/50 amps), some extd stay sites, 45 pull-thrus, cable TV, WiFi Instant Internet at site, WiFi Internet central location, family camping, tenting, RV's/park model rentals, cabins, RV storage, dump, laundry, full svc store, RV supplies, LP gas by weight/by meter, ice, picnic tables, wood, controlled access.

◇◇◇◇◇RECREATION: rec hall, rec room/area, equipped pavilion, coin games, 2 swim pools, wading pool, saltwater swim, hot tub, canoeing, kayaking, 9 canoe/10 kayak/20 pedal boat rentals, saltwater/lake/pond fishing, fishing supplies, mini-golf, ($), golf nearby, bsktball, 40 bike rentals, playground, shuffleboard court 3 shuffleboard courts, activities, horseshoes, v-ball, local tours.

Pets welcome, breed restrict. Partial handicap access. Open all yr. Big rigs welcome. Clubs welcome. Green Friendly. Rate in 2010 $26-65 for 5 persons. MC/VISA/DISC. ATM. Member ARVC, CARVC.

Text 82628 to (440)725-8687 to see our Visual Tour.

Phone: (843)238-5161
Address: 5901 S Kings Hwy, Myrtle Beach, SC 29575-4997
Lat/Lon: 33.63420/-78.95652
Email: info@lakewoodcampground.com
Web: www.lakewoodcampground.com

SEE AD PAGE 707 AND AD TRAVEL SECTION PAGE 691 AND AD DISCOVER SECTION PAGE 45

(W) MYRTLE BEACH CAMPGROUND ASSOCIATION—Association of six Myrtle Beach Campgrounds which promotes tourism in the area.

Text 108018 to (440)725-8687 to see our Visual Tour.

Read interesting travel facts in the front of every state/province.

Phone: (800)356-3016x26001
Address: 3023 Church St, Myrtle Beach, SC 29577
Lat/Lon: 33.72413/-78.87719
Email: ashepherd@brandonadvertising.com
Web: www.campmyrtlebeach.com

SEE AD PAGE 707 AND AD TRAVEL SECTION PAGE 691 AND AD MAP PAGE 688 AND AD DISCOVER SECTION PAGE 45

(SW) MYRTLE BEACH STATE PARK—(Horry) *From jct US-501 & US-17: Go 3 mi S on US-17, then 1 mi on park road.* FACILITIES: 347 sites, typical site width 30 ft, 40 ft max RV length, 302 W&E, (20/30 amps), 45 no hkups, 3 pull-thrus, family camping, tenting, dump, laundry, ltd groc. RECREATION: swim pool, saltwater swim, dock, saltwater fishing, playground. Pets welcome. Open all yr. Phone: (843)238-5325.

(NE) MYRTLE BEACH TRAVEL PARK—(Horry) *From jct US-501 & US-17: Go 9-3/4 mi N on US-17, then 1/2 mi E on Chestnut Rd, then 1/4 mi N on Kings Rd. Enter on R.*

125 ACRES OF OCEANFRONT CAMPING

Enjoy a wide variety of campsites, oceanfront lakeside, or wooded. We have beachcombing, swimming, fishing or just relaxing on the beach. Our restrooms are beautifully refurbished. www.myrtlebeachtravelpark.com

◇◇◇◇◇FACILITIES: 1100 sites, typical site width 35 ft, 1080 full hkups, 20 W&E, (20/30/50 amps), some extd stay sites, 500 pull-thrus, cable TV, WiFi Instant Internet at site ($), phone Internet central location, family camping, tenting, RV's/park model rentals, RV storage, dump, non-guest dump, laundry, full svc store, RV supplies, LP gas by weight, ice, picnic tables, controlled access.

◇◇◇◇◇RECREATION: rec room/area, pavilion, coin games, 3 swim pools, wading pool, saltwater swim, hot tub, dock, saltwater/pond fishing, golf nearby, bsktball, playground, activities, hiking trails, v-ball, local tours.

Pets welcome. Partial handicap access. Open all yr. Big rigs welcome. Clubs welcome. Rate in 2010 $32-62 for 4 persons. MC/VISA/DISC/AMEX. Member ARVC, CARVC.

Text 107875 to (440)725-8687 to see our Visual Tour.

Phone: (800)255-3568
Address: 10108 Kings Rd, Myrtle Beach, SC 29572
Lat/Lon: 33.77757/-78.77362
Email: timbryant@scrr.com
Web: www.myrtlebeachtravelpark.com

SEE AD PAGE 707 AND AD TRAVEL SECTION PAGE 691 AND AD DISCOVER SECTION PAGE 45

(S) OCEAN LAKES FAMILY CAMPGROUND—(Horry) *From jct US-501 & SC Hwy 544: Go 14 mi E on SC Hwy 544. Enter at end.*

GUEST RATED "A" AGAIN

Oceanfront & shaded sites. Big Rig friendly. Reserve by site number up to 18 mo in advance. All pull-thru sites. Large rally facility-no add'l fee. Concrete pads 45'x18' avail. All inclusive rates.

◇◇◇◇◇FACILITIES: 3447 sites, typical site width 40 ft, 3447 full hkups, (20/30/50 amps), many extd stay sites, 893 pull-thrus, cable TV, phone/WiFi Instant Internet at site ($), WiFi Internet central location, family camping, tenting, cabins, RV storage, laundry, full svc store, RV supplies, LP gas by weight/by meter, ice, picnic tables, controlled access.

◇◇◇◇◇RECREATION: rec hall, rec room/area, equipped pavilion, coin games, 3 swim pools, wading pool, saltwater swim, saltwater/lake fishing, fishing supplies, mini-golf, ($), golf nearby, bsktball, 15 bike rentals, playground, shuffleboard court 3 shuffleboard courts, activities, horseshoes, v-ball, local tours.

Pets welcome, breed restrict. Partial handicap access. Open all yr. Big rigs welcome. Clubs welcome. Green Friendly. Rate in 2010 $27-67 per family. MC/VISA/DISC. ATM. Member ARVC, CARVC.

Text 81835 to (440)725-8687 to see our Visual Tour.

South Carolina was the 8th state admitted to the Union

Phone: (800)876-4306
Address: 6001 S. Kings Highway, Myrtle Beach, SC 29575
Lat/Lon: 33.62897/-78.96236
Email: camping@oceanlakes.com
Web: www.oceanlakes.com

SEE AD PAGE 707 AND AD TRAVEL SECTION PAGE 691 AND AD DISCOVER SECTION PAGE 45

(S) PIRATELAND FAMILY CAMPING RESORT—(Horry) *From jct US 17 & US 544: Go 2 mi E on US 544, then 1 mi N on US 17 Bus. Enter on R.*

OCEANFRONT, PLUS 510' LAZY RIVER

Looking for the absolute best in oceanfront camping? Look no further. We have redefined the standards of family outdoor fun to bring you an unbeatable camping experience. Check out our specials at www.pirateland.com

◇◇◇◇◇FACILITIES: 1493 sites, typical site width 40 ft, 1493 full hkups, (30/50 amps), some extd stay sites, 39 pull-thrus, cable TV, WiFi Instant Internet at site ($), WiFi Internet central location, family camping, tenting, RV's/park model rentals, RV storage, laundry, full svc store, RV supplies, LP gas by weight/by meter, ice, picnic tables, controlled access.

◇◇◇◇◇RECREATION: rec hall, rec room/area, equipped pavilion, coin games, 3 swim pools, wading pool, saltwater swim, 4 canoe/15 pedal boat rentals, saltwater/lake/pond fishing, fishing supplies, mini-golf, ($), golf nearby, bsktball, playground, activities, local tours.

Pets welcome, breed restrict. Partial handicap access. Open all yr. Facilities fully operational Easter Wknd, then memorial Day - Labor Day. Big rigs welcome. Clubs welcome. Green Friendly. Rate in 2010 $27-73 for 4 persons. MC/VISA. ATM. Member ARVC, CARVC. CCUSA 50% Discount. CCUSA reservations Recommended, CCUSA max stay 2 days. Discount available only after Labor Day and before Friday of Memorial Day weekend. Discount not available Easter & Thanksgiving weekends. Maximum stay 2 nights at CCUSA rate within a 7 day time frame.

Text 87742 to (440)725-8687 to see our Visual Tour.

Phone: (800)443-2267
Address: 5401 S Kings Hwy, Myrtle Beach, SC 29575
Lat/Lon: 33.64191/-78.94713
Email: pirateland@pirateland.com
Web: www.pirateland.com

SEE AD PAGE 707 AND AD TRAVEL SECTION PAGE 691 AND AD DISCOVER SECTION PAGE 45

(SE) WILLOWTREE RESORT—(Horry) *From jct US 17 & US 501: Go W on US 501, then N on Hwy 31 to end, then 5-1/2 mi W on Hwy 9, then 1-3/4 mi NE on Hwy 905, then 1-1/2 mi N on Old Buck Creek Rd. Enter on R.*

◇◇◇◇◇FACILITIES: 106 sites, typical site width 45 ft, 106 full hkups, (20/30/50 amps), some extd stay sites, 98 pull-thrus, WiFi Instant Internet at site, WiFi Internet central location, family camping, cabins, RV storage, dump, non-guest dump $, laundry, ltd groc, RV supplies, LP gas by meter, ice, picnic tables, patios, fire rings, grills, wood, controlled access.

◇◇◇◇◇RECREATION: rec hall, rec room/area, swim pool, wading pool, lake swim, hot tub, canoeing, canoe/6 pedal boat/5 motorboat rentals, lake fishing, fishing supplies, golf nearby, bsktball, 12 bike rentals, playground, activities, horseshoes, hiking trails, v-ball.

Pets welcome. Partial handicap access. No tents. Open all yr. Big rigs welcome. Escort to site. Clubs welcome. Rate in 2010 $30-88 per family. MC/VISA/DISC. Member ARVC, CARVC.

Phone: (866)207-2267
Address: 520 Southern Sights Dr, Longs, SC 29568
Lat/Lon: 33.97505/-78.71937
Email: reservations@willowtreervr.com
Web: www.willowtreervr.com

SEE PRIMARY LISTING AT LONGS AND AD PAGE 707

Site of more Revolutionary War battles than any other state.

PICKENS—A-2

(NW) KEOWEE-TOXAWAY STATE NATURAL AREA—(Pickens) *From jct US 178 & Hwy 11: Go 9 mi W on Hwy 11.* FACILITIES: 24 sites, typical site width 20 ft, 40 ft max RV length, 10 W&E, (20/30 amps), 14 no hkups, 2 pull-thrus, family camping, tenting, dump. RECREATION: boating, lake fishing. Pets welcome. Open all yr. Phone: (864)868-2605.

TABLE ROCK STATE PARK—(Pickens) *From jct Hwy 183 & US 178: Go 9 mi N on US 178, then 4 mi E on Hwy 11, then 1 mi N on park road.* FACILITIES: 100 sites, typical site width 30 ft, 40 ft max RV length, 94 W&E, (20/30 amps), 6 no hkups, 27 pull-thrus, family camping, tenting, dump, laundry, ltd groc. RECREATION: lake swim, boating, canoeing, ramp, lake fishing. Pets welcome. Open all yr. Phone: (864)878-9813.

PIEDMONT—A-2

(NW) IVY ACRES RV PARK—(Greenville) *From jct I-85 (exit 39) & SR 143 (River Rd): Go 1-1/4 mi E on River Rd. Enter on L.*

WELCOME

◆◆◆FACILITIES: 40 sites, typical site width 35 ft, accepts full hkup units only, 40 full hkups, (20/30/50 amps), many extd stay sites, 11 pull-thrus, WiFi Instant Internet at site, WiFi Internet central location, RV storage, dump, non-guest dump $, picnic tables, fire rings, wood.

◆RECREATION: pavilion, river/pond fishing, golf nearby, horseshoes, hiking trails.

Pets welcome, breed restrict, quantity restrict. No tents. Age restrict may apply. Open all yr. Big rigs welcome. Escort to site. Rate in 2010 $30 per vehicle. MC/DISC/Debit.

Phone: (864)220-9680
Address: 201 Ivy Acres Dr, Piedmont, SC 29673
Lat/Lon: 34.74177/-82.47283
Email: chill627@juno.com
Web: www.ivyacresrvpark.com

SEE AD GREENVILLE PAGE 704 AND AD TRAVEL SECTION PAGE 689

POINT SOUTH—D-4

(S) KOA-Point South—(Jasper) *From jct I-95 (exit 33) & US 17: Go 200 yards E on US 17, then S (first right) on Yemassee Rd, then 1/2 mi W on Campground Rd. Enter at end.* ◆◆◆FACILITIES: 58 sites, typical site width 20 ft, 29 full hkups, 29 W&E, (20/30/50 amps), 50 amps ($), 32 pull-thrus, tenting, dump, laundry, groceries. ◆◆◆RECREATION: swim pool, lake fishing, playground. Pets welcome. Open all yr. Big rigs welcome. Rate in 2010 $35-48 for 2 persons. Member ARVC, CARVC. Phone: (843)726-5733. KOA discount. FMCA discount.

(S) The Oaks at Point South RV Resort—(Jasper) *From jct I-95 (exit 33) & US 17: Go 1/4 mi E on US 17, then S on Yemassee Rd, then 1/2 mi E on Campground Rd. Enter on R.* ◆◆◆FACILITIES: 93 sites, typical site width 25 ft, 88 full hkups, (20/30/50 amps), 5 no hkups, 88 pull-thrus, cable TV, WiFi Instant Internet at site ($), phone Internet central location, tenting, RV storage, laundry, ice, picnic tables. ◆◆RECREATION: pavilion, swim pool, lake fishing, mini-golf, playground, hiking trails. Pets welcome. Open all yr. Big rigs welcome. Rate in 2010 $30-45 for 2 persons. MC/VISA/DISC. CCUSA 50% Discount. CCUSA reservations Recommended, CCUSA max stay 2 days. Call for holiday restrictions.

CAMPCLUB USA

Phone: (843)726-5728
Address: 1292 Campground Rd, Yemassee, SC 29945
Lat/Lon: 32.62773/-80.87058

ROCK HILL—A-3

(N) EBENEZER PARK—(York) *From jct I-77 & SR 161 (exit 82): Go 3/4 mi W on SR 161 to Mt. Gallant Rd., then 4 mi NE to Boatshore Rd., then 1/2 mi E to park. Enter on L.* FACILITIES: 69 sites, 69 full hkups, 3 pull-thrus, tenting, dump. RECREATION: lake swim, boating, canoeing, ramp, dock, lake fishing, playground. Partial handicap access. Open all yr. Phone: (803)366-6620.

"Carolina Shag" is the state dance of South Carolina.

ROEBUCK—A-2

(SE) PINE RIDGE CAMPGROUND—(Spartanburg) *From jct I-26 (exit 28) & US 221: Go 500 yds NE on US 221, then 1 mi E on Stillhouse Rd, then 1 1/2 mi N on Otts Shoals Rd, then 1000 feet E on Pine Ridge Campground Rd. Enter at end.*

WELCOME

◆◆◆FACILITIES: 50 sites, typical site width 25 ft, 50 full hkups, (30/50 amps), many extd stay sites, 12 pull-thrus, WiFi Instant Internet at site, family camping, RV's/park model rentals, cabins, RV storage, dump, laundry, RV supplies, LP gas by meter, ice, picnic tables, patios, fire rings, grills, wood.

◆◆◆RECREATION: rec room/area, pavilion, swim pool, pond fishing, play equipment, horseshoes.

Pets welcome. No tents. Open all yr. Big rigs welcome. Escort to site. Clubs welcome. Rate in 2010 $25-30 for 3 persons. MC/VISA.

Phone: (866)576-0302
Address: 199 Pineridge Campground Rd., ROEBUCK, SC 29376
Lat/Lon: 34.84940/-81.94350
Email: camp@pineridgecampground.com
Web: pineridgecampground.com

SEE AD THIS PAGE

ST. GEORGE—D-4

(E) JOLLY ACRES RV PARK & STORAGE—(Dorchester) *From jct I-95 (exit 77) & Hwy 78: Go 5-1/2 mi E on Hwy 78, then 1/2 mi N on Horne Taylor Rd. Enter on L.*

WELCOME

◆◆◆◆FACILITIES: 31 sites, typical site width 30 ft, 19 full hkups, 12 W&E, (20/30/50 amps), 50 amps ($), some extd stay sites, 12 pull-thrus, WiFi Instant Internet at site ($), WiFi Internet central location, RV's/park model rentals, RV storage, dump, laundry, ltd groc, RV supplies, LP gas by weight/by meter, ice, picnic tables, fire rings, grills, wood.

◆◆RECREATION: pond fishing, play equipment, activities (wkends), hiking trails.

CAMPCLUB USA

Pets welcome. No tents. Open all yr. Big rigs welcome. Clubs welcome. Rate in 2010 $30 for 2 persons. MC/VISA. Member CARVC. CCUSA 50% Discount. CCUSA reservations Accepted, CCUSA max stay Unlimited, CCUSA disc. not avail F,Sa. No tenting. Check-In 2 PM. Sunday hours 2-6 PM.

Phone: (843)563-8303
Address: 289 Horne Taylor Rd, St. George, SC 29477
Lat/Lon: 33.17957/-80.51365
Email: jollyacres@hughes.net
Web: www.syrrrun.com

SEE AD THIS PAGE

(W) St. George RV Park—(Dorchester) *From jct I-95 (exit 77) & Hwy 78: Go 1/4 mi E on Hwy 78, then 1/4 mi W on Frontage Rd. Enter at end.* ◆◆◆FACILITIES: 20 sites, 40 ft max RV length, 20 full hkups, (20/30/50 amps), 0 pull-thrus, WiFi Instant Internet at site, WiFi Internet central location, laundry, ice. ◆RECREATION: swim pool. Pets welcome. No tents. Open all yr. Rate in 2010 $25 per vehicle. CCUSA 50% Discount. CCUSA reservations Recommended, CCUSA max stay 7 days, Cash only for CCUSA disc.

CAMPCLUB USA

Phone: (843)563-4180
Address: 139 Motel Drive, St. George, SC 29477
Lat/Lon: 33.19482/-80.60438
Email: sccomfortinn@aol.com

SANTEE—C-4

(NE) SANTEE LAKES CAMPGROUND—(Clarendon) *From jct Hwy 6 & I-95 (exit 98): Go 4 mi N on I-95 to exit 102, then 200 yards E on Rd 400, then 1/4 mi S on Dingle Pond Rd. Enter on R.*

WELCOME

◆◆FACILITIES: 185 sites, typical site width 35 ft, 70 full hkups, 115 W&E, (30 amps), some extd stay sites, 185 pull-thrus, WiFi Instant Internet at site, WiFi Internet central location, family camping, tenting, dump, non-guest dump $, laundry, ltd groc, RV supplies, ice, picnic tables.

◆◆◆RECREATION: rec room/area, coin games, swim pool, wading pool, lake swim, boating, canoeing, kayaking, ramp, dock, lake fishing, mini-golf, bsktball, playground, v-ball.

Pets welcome. Open all yr. Clubs welcome. Rate in 2010 $28-33 for 3 persons. MC/VISA/Debit.

Phone: (803)478-2262
Address: 1268 Gordon Rd, Summerton, SC 29148
Lat/Lon: 33.51726/-80.42909
Web: www.santeelakes-campground.com

SEE AD THIS PAGE

SANTEE STATE PARK—(Orangeburg) *From I-95 (exit 98) & Hwy 6: Go 3-1/2 mi NW on Hwy 6, then N on access road.* FACILITIES: 158 sites, 40 ft max RV length, 158 W&E, (30 amps), 17 pull-thrus, family camping, tenting, dump, laundry, ltd groc. RECREATION: lake swim, boating, ramp, dock, lake fishing, playground. Pets welcome. Open all yr. Phone: (803)854-2408.

SENECA—A-1

(NW) CROOKED CREEK RV PARK—(Oconee) *From jct I-85 & US 76 W/SC 28 (exit 19B): Go 11 mi W on US 76 W/SC 28, then 9 mi W on US 76/US 123/SC 28, then 1-1/4 mi NW on SC 28, then 3-1/4 mi NE on SC 188 (Keowee School Rd), then 1-3/4 mi N on Ebenezer Rd to Arvee Ln. Enter on R.*

WELCOME

◆◆◆◆FACILITIES: 110 sites, typical site width 35 ft, 97 full hkups, 13 W&E, (20/30/50 amps), 97 pull-thrus, cable TV, phone/WiFi Instant Internet at site, WiFi Internet central location, family camping, tenting, RV storage, laundry, ltd groc, RV supplies, LP gas by weight/by meter, marine gas, ice, picnic tables, wood.

◆◆◆◆RECREATION: rec room/area, pavilion, coin games, swim pool, wading pool, lake swim, boating, canoeing, kayaking, ramp, dock, pontoon/2 kayak/pedal boat rentals, lake fishing, fishing supplies, golf nearby, bsktball, playground, horseshoes, v-ball.

Pets welcome, breed restrict. Partial handicap access. Open all yr. Big rigs welcome. Clubs welcome. Rate in 2010 $30-40 for 4 persons. MC/VISA/DISC/AMEX. ATM. FMCA discount.

CROOKED CREEK RV PARK—Continued on next page

SENECA—Continued
CROOKED CREEK RV PARK—Continued

Phone: (864)882-5040
Address: 777 Arvee Lane, West Union, SC 29696
Lat/Lon: 34.76172/-82.97798
Email: ccrvp@trivergent.net
Web: www.crookedcreekrvpark.com

SEE AD THIS PAGE

SPARTANBURG—A-2

(SE) CROFT STATE NATURAL AREA—(Spartanburg) *From town: Go 3 mi SE on Hwy 56, then E on Daisy Ridge Rd.* FACILITIES: 50 sites, typical site width 30 ft, 40 ft max RV length, 50 W&E, (20/30/50 amps), 6 pull-thrus, family camping, tenting, dump. RECREATION: swim pool, boating, electric motors only, lake fishing, playground. Pets welcome. Open all yr. Phone: (864) 585-1283.

(NW) Cunningham RV Park—(Spartanburg) *From jct I-85 (exit 70) & I-26: Go 2-1/2 mi W on I-26 to exit 17, then 1/4 mi W on New Cut Rd, then 1 mi S on Campground Rd. Enter on R.* ◆◆FACILITIES: 95 sites, typical site width 40 ft, 57 full hkups, 38 W&E, (20/30/50 amps), 69 pull-thrus, WiFi Internet central location, family camping, tenting, RV storage, dump, non-guest dump $, laundry, LP gas by weight/by meter, ice, picnic tables, wood. ◆◆RECREATION: swim pool, playground. Pets welcome. Partial handicap access. Open all yr. Big rigs welcome. Rate in 2010 $28-34 for 2 persons. MC/VISA/DISC. Member ARVC, CARVC. CCUSA 50% Discount. CCUSA reservations Not Accepted, CCUSA max stay 1 day, CCUSA disc. not avail S, CCUSA disc. not avail F,Sa, CCUSA disc. not avail holidays. Not available Jun, Jul, Aug, Oct.

Phone: (864)576-1973
Address: 600 Campground Rd, Spartanburg, SC 29303
Lat/Lon: 34.98551/-82.04047
Email: info@cunninghamrvpark.com
Web: www.cunninghamrvpark.com

SUMMERVILLE—D-4

(SW) GIVHANS FERRY STATE PARK—(Dorchester) *From jct US-78 & US-17A: Go 7 mi SW on US-17A, then 8 mi NW on Hwy-61.* FACILITIES: 25 sites, typical site width 25 ft, 40 ft max RV length, 25 W&E, (20/30 amps), family camping, tenting, dump. RECREATION: boating, canoeing, river fishing. Pets welcome. Open all yr. Phone: (843)873-0692.

SUMTER—C-4

MILITARY PARK (Wateree Recreation Area and FAMCAMP-Shaw AFB)—(Sumter) *Off base. From jct US 521 & Hwy 97: Go 10 mi NW on Hwy 97.* FACILITIES: 13 sites, 13 W&E, tenting, dump, ltd groc. RECREATION: lake swim, boating, ramp, dock, lake fishing, playground. Open all yr. Phone: (803)432-7976.

SWANSEA—C-3

(SW) YOGI BEAR'S JELLYSTONE PARK @ RIVER BOTTOM FARMS—(Lexington) *From jct US 321 & S.C. 3: Go W 6-1/2 mi on S.C. 3, then NW 1/2 mi on US 178, then W 1/2 mi on Cedar Creek Rd. Enter on L.*

◆◆◆◆FACILITIES: 70 sites, typical site width 40 ft, 52 full hkups, 14 W&E, 4 E, (30/50 amps), some extd stay sites, 25 pull-thrus, WiFi Instant Internet at site, WiFi Internet central location, family camping, tenting, cabins, RV storage, laundry, RV supplies, LP gas by weight/by meter, ice, picnic tables, fire rings, grills, wood.

◆◆◆◆RECREATION: rec hall, pavilion, coin games, swim pool, river/pond fishing, fishing supplies, play equipment, activities (wkends), horseshoes, sports field, hiking trails, v-ball.

Pets welcome. Partial handicap access. Open all yr. Big rigs welcome. Clubs welcome. Rate in 2010 $30-32 per family. MC/VISA. Member ARVC, CARVC. CCUSA 50% Discount. CCUSA max stay

SWANSEA—Continued
YOGI BEAR'S JELLYSTONE PARK @ RIVER BOTTOM FARMS—Continued

Unlimited, CCUSA disc. not avail S, CCUSA disc. not avail F,Sa, CCUSA disc. not avail holidays. Not available May 1-Oct 31.

Phone: (803)568-4182
Address: 357 Cedar Creek Rd, Swansea, SC 29160
Lat/Lon: 33.68947/-81.19251
Email: rbfrvresort@pbtcomm.net
Web: www.columbiajellystone.com

SEE AD COLUMBIA PAGE 700

TOWNVILLE—B-1

(N) CONEROSS CAMPGROUND (COE-Hartwell Lake)—(Oconee) *From town: Go 2 mi W on Hwy 24, then 1 mi N on CR 184, then 1 mi E on county road.* FACILITIES: 106 sites, 94 W&E, (30/50 amps), 12 no hkups, 36 pull-thrus, tenting, dump. RECREATION: lake swim, boating, ramp, dock, lake fishing, playground. Open May 1 - Sep 29. Phone: (888)893-0678.

(N) OCONEE POINT CAMPGROUND (COE - Hartwell Lake)—(Oconee) *From town: Go 2 mi W on Hwy 24, then 4 mi N on CR 184, then 3 mi E on CR 21.* FACILITIES: 70 sites, 70 W&E, (50 amps), tenting, dump. RECREATION: lake swim, boating, ramp, lake fishing, playground. Partial handicap access. Open May 1 - Sep 9. Phone: (888)893-0678.

TRAVELERS REST—A-2

(N) VALLEY PARK RESORT—(Greenville) *From jct US 276 & US 25: Go 8 1/2 mi N on US 25. Enter on R.*

◆◆◆FACILITIES: 42 sites, typical site width 30 ft, 44 ft max RV length, 42 full hkups, (30/50 amps), many extd stay sites, cable TV, WiFi Instant Internet at site, WiFi Internet central location, family camping, tenting, cabins, RV storage, dump, laundry, LP gas by weight, picnic tables, patios.

◆◆RECREATION: pavilion, swim pool, hiking trails.

Pets welcome, quantity restrict. Open all yr. Rate in 2010 $36-38 per vehicle. MC/VISA/DISC/Debit. Member CARVC. CCUSA 50% Discount. CCUSA reservations Recommended, CCUSA max stay Unlimited, Cash only for CCUSA disc., Check only for CCUSA disc., CCUSA disc. not avail F,Sa, CCUSA disc. not avail holidays. No discount on cabins or pull thru sites. Anyone over 12 yrs considered adult for surcharge purposes. Pull-thru surcharge $5.

Text 81262 to (440)725-8687 to see our Visual Tour.

Phone: (864)834-8150
Address: 2400 North Hwy 25, Travelers Rest, SC 29690
Lat/Lon: 35.06147/-82.42828
Web: www.valleyparkresort.com

SEE AD GREENVILLE PAGE 703

WALHALLA—A-1

(NE) DEVILS FORK STATE PARK—(Oconee) *From jct Hwy 183 & Hwy 11: Go 13 mi NE on Hwy 11, then 3 mi N on Hwy 25.* FACILITIES: 84 sites, typical site width 22 ft, 36 ft max RV length, 59 W&E, (20/30 amps), 25 no hkups, 5 pull-thrus, family camping, tenting, dump, laundry, ltd groc. RECREATION: boating, ramp, lake fishing, playground. Pets welcome. Open all yr. Phone: (864)944-2639.

(N) OCONEE STATE PARK—(Oconee) *From jct Hwy-11 & Hwy-28: Go 10 mi NW on Hwy-28, then 2 mi N on Hwy-107.* FACILITIES: 155 sites, typical site width 25 ft, 35 ft max RV length, 140 W&E, (20/30 amps), 15 no hkups, 46 pull-thrus, family camping, tenting, dump, laundry, ltd groc. RECREATION: lake swim, canoeing, lake fishing, playground. Pets welcome. Partial handicap access. Open all yr. Phone: (864)638-5353.

(NW) SUMTER NF (Cherry Hill Campground)—(Oconee) *From jct Hwy-11 & Hwy-28: Go 9 mi NW on Hwy-28, then 7-1/3 mi N on Hwy-107. Enter on R.* FACILITIES: 28 sites, 22 ft max RV length, 28 no hkups, dump, ltd groc. RECREATION: Open May 1 - Sept 30. Phone: (864)638-9568.

WALTERBORO—D-4

(SW) NEW GREEN ACRES R.V. PARK—(Colleton) *From jct I-95 (exit 53) & Hwy 63: Go W on Hwy 63, then take first right on Campground Rd. Enter on R.*

◆◆◆FACILITIES: 106 sites, typical site width 50 ft, 70 full hkups, 31 W&E, (30/50 amps), 50 amps ($), 5 no hkups, some extd stay sites, 101 pull-thrus, cable TV, ($), WiFi Instant Internet at site, phone Internet central location, tenting, RV storage, dump, non-guest dump $, laundry, RV supplies, LP gas by weight/by meter, ice, picnic tables, patios, fire rings.

◆◆RECREATION: rec hall, swim pool, playground.

Pets welcome. Open all yr. Big rigs welcome. Clubs welcome. Rate in 2010 $24-28 for 2 persons. MC/VISA. Member ARVC, CARVC.

Phone: (800)474-3450
Address: 396 Campground Rd., Walterboro, SC 29488
Lat/Lon: 32.89974/-80.70706
Email: greenacres53@lowcountry.com
Web: newgreenacres.com

SEE AD THIS PAGE

WEDGEFIELD—C-4

(S) POINSETT STATE PARK—(Sumter) *From jct Hwy 763 & Hwy 261: Go 6 mi S on Hwy 261, then 3 mi W on CR 34 & park road.* FACILITIES: 50 sites, typical site width 20 ft, 40 ft max RV length, 24 W&E, (20/30 amps), 26 no hkups, family camping, tenting, dump. RECREATION: lake fishing, playground. Pets welcome. Open all yr. Phone: (803)494-8177.

WEST UNION—A-1

Keowee Falls Rv Park (Not Visited)—*From jct I-85 & US 76 W/SC 28/US 123 S/US 76 W, then 1/2 mi on State Rd 37/214, then 3-1/2 mi on Blue Ridge Blvd, then 1/4 on W Union Rd, then 3/4 mi on Jefferson Rd.* FACILITIES: 100 sites, accepts self-contained units only, 100 full hkups, (30 amps). RECREATION: lake swim, boating, ramp, dock, lake/pond fishing, playground. Pets welcome, breed restrict. No tents. Open all yr. Rate in 2010 $30-35 per vehicle.

WINNSBORO—B-3

(E) LAKE WATEREE STATE RECREATION AREA—(Fairfield) *From jct I-77 (exit 41) & Hwy 41: Go 3 mi E on Hwy 41, then 3 mi N on US 21, then 5-1/2 mi E on Secondary Rd 101 (River Rd). Enter on L.* FACILITIES: 72 sites, typical site width 20 ft, 40 ft max RV length, 72 W&E, (20/30 amps), 5 pull-thrus, family camping, tenting, dump, ltd groc. RECREATION: boating, ramp, dock, lake fishing, playground. Pets welcome. Open all yr. Phone: (803)482-6401.

YORK—A-3

(E) KINGS MOUNTAIN STATE PARK—(York) *From jct Hwy 5 & US 321: Go 4 mi N on US 321, then 9 mi NW on Hwy 161, then 2 mi W on park road.* FACILITIES: 125 sites, typical site width 30 ft, 40 ft max RV length, 115 W&E, (20/30 amps), 10 no hkups, 30 pull-thrus, family camping, tenting, dump, laundry. RECREATION: lake swim, canoeing, lake fishing, playground. Pets welcome. Open all yr. Phone: (803)222-3209.

Woodall's Tip... To be considered a "Big Rig Friendly" park, the campground must meet the following requirements: minimum of 50 amps, adequate road width, overhead access clearance, site clearance to accommodate the tallest and widest rigs built. Often not every site can accommodate a big rig, so we recommend that you call ahead for availability.

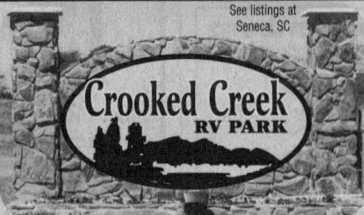

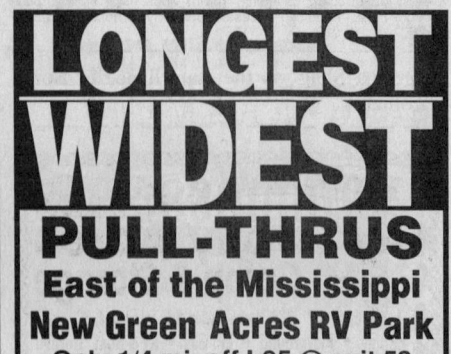

READER SERVICE INFO

The following businesses have placed an ad in the Tennessee Travel Section. To receive free information, enter their Reader Service number on the Reader Service Card opposite page 48/Discover Section in the front of this directory:

Advertiser	RS#
Tennessee ARVC	4340
Tennessee State Parks Dept	3342

TIME ZONE

The eastern portion of Tennessee is on Eastern Standard Time. Middle and Western Tennessee are on Central Standard Time.

TEMPERATURE

Located in the Temperate Zone, Tennessee has a generally mild climate year-round, yet still has four distinct seasons. During the winter, the average high temperature is 49.4° and the average low is 30.4°. In the summer, the average high temperature is 89° and the average low is 67°. The average annual rainfall is 49.7".

TRAVEL & TOURISM INFO

State Agency:
Tennessee Department of Tourist Development
312 Eighth Ave. N., 25th Floor
William Snodgrass Building
Nashville, TN 37243
(615/741-2159)
www.tnvacation.com

Regional Agencies:

Memphis CVB
47 Union Ave.
Memphis, TN 38103
(901/543-5300)
www.memphistravel.com

Nashville CVB
One Nashville Place
150 Fourth Ave N., Ste. G-250
Nashville, TN 37219
(800/657-6910)
www.musiccityusa.com

Middle Tennessee Tourism Council
501 Union St., 6th Flr.
Nashville, TN 37219
(615/862-8828)
www.middletennesseetourism.com

Northeast Tennessee Tourism Assn.
P.O. Box 415
Jonesborough, TN 37659
(800/468-6882 or 423/913-5550)
www.netta.com

Northwest Tennessee Tourism Council
P.O. Box 807
Big Sandy, TN 38221
(866/698-6386 or 731/593-0171)
www.kentuckylaketourism.com

Southeast Tennessee Tourism Association
P.O. Box 4757
Chattanooga, TN 37405
(423/424-4267)
www.southeasttennessee.com

Tourism Association of Southwest Tennessee
P.O. Box 10543
Jackson, TN 38308
(800/462-8366 or 731/616-7474)
www.tast.tn.org

RECREATIONAL INFO

Fishing/Hunting/Boating: Tennessee Wildlife Resources Agency (615/781-6500) www.state.tn.us/twra.

SHOPPING

Ada's, the Unusual Country Store, Bethel Springs. More than 75 Amish, Mennonite and Allergy-Free cookbooks. Also cheeses, teas and herbal remedies. On Hwy 45 N.

Belz Factory Outlet Center, Pigeon Forge. Buy direct from the manufacturer and save up to 75%. 2655 Teaster Ln., Pigeon Forge, TN.

Brooks Collection, Collierville. A unique gift and garden shop located in Collierville's Historic Town Square. 110 E. Mulberry St.

Holloway's Quilts, Cosby. Specializing in handcrafted, American-made quilts. Special orders accepted.

Market Street Antique Mall, Paris. Browse through one of the largest antique malls in the country. 414 N. Market St. (Hwy 641), Paris; TN.

Opry Mills, Nashville. One of Tennessee's great retail, dining and entertainment destination with 200 interactive retailers offering value shopping, theme dining and entertainment. Adjacent to Grand Ole Opry at 433 Opry Mills Dr. www.oprymills.com.

Phillips General Store Antiques, Bell Buckle. Over 100-year-old dry goods store with original fixtures, vignettes of antique

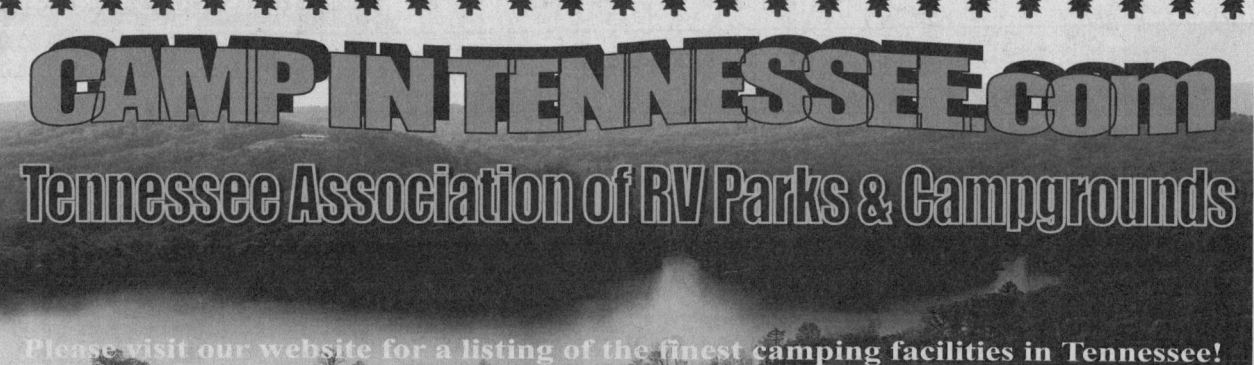

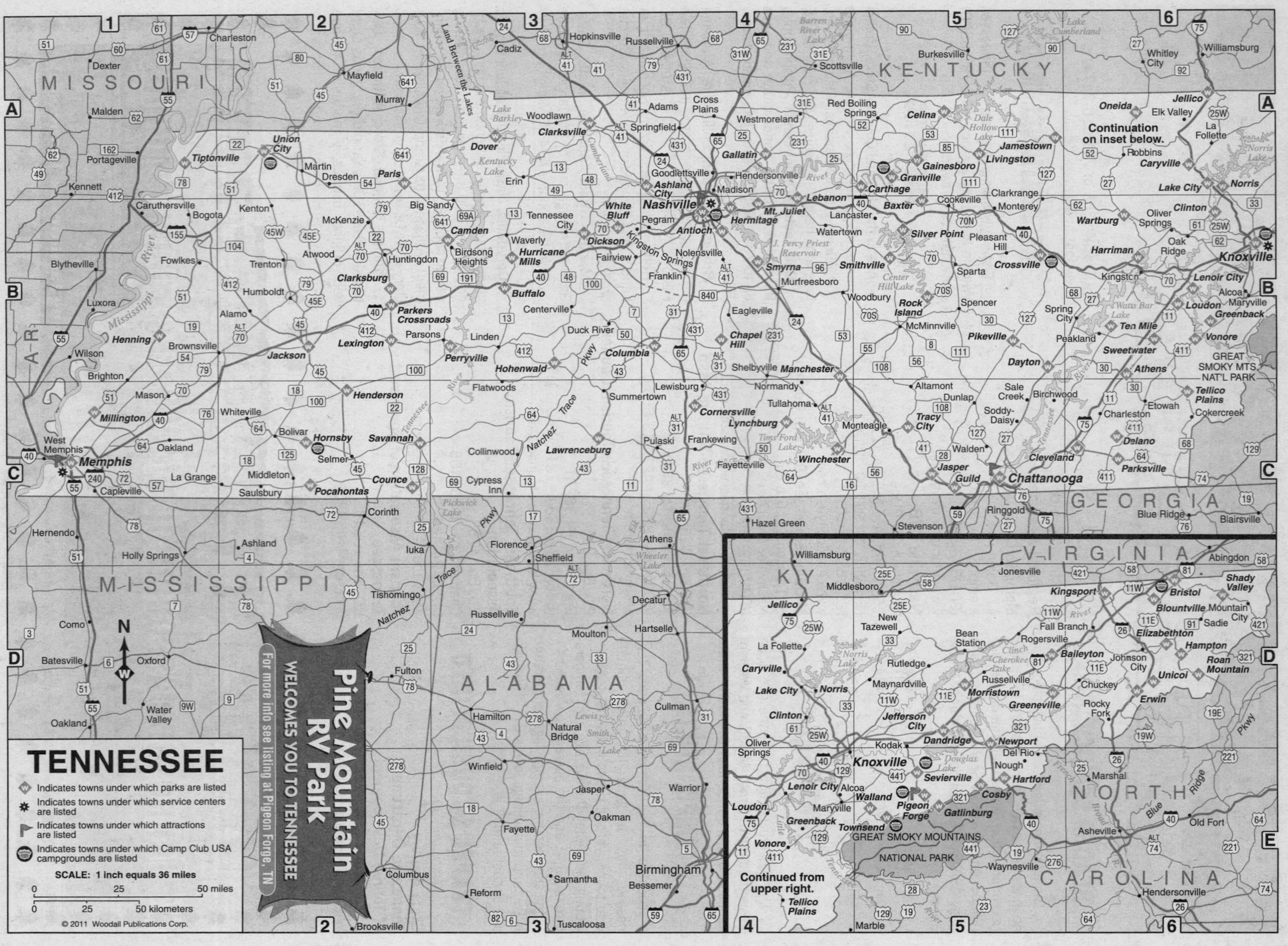
TENNESSEE
Indicates towns under which parks are listed
Indicates towns under which service centers are listed
Indicates towns under which attractions are listed
Indicates towns under which Camp Club USA campgrounds are listed
SCALE: 1 inch equals 36 miles
50 miles
50 kilometers
© 2011 Woodall Publications Corp.
Pine Mountain RV Park
WELCOMES YOU TO TENNESSEE
For more info see listing at Pigeon Forge, TN
Continuation on inset below.
Continued from upper right.
KENTUCKY
MISSOURI
ARKANSAS
MISSISSIPPI
ALABAMA
GEORGIA
VIRGINIA
NORTH CAROLINA
GREAT SMOKY MOUNTAINS NATIONAL PARK

treasures, primitives, architectural fragments and textiles. 4 Railroad Square.

Rivergate Mall, Goodlettsville. More than 150 stores. Easy access off I-85 at exit 96.

DESTINATIONS

Located in the southeast region of the nation, Tennessee shares a border with eight states, and has long been a melting pot of musical styles. From the mountains came Appalachian folk songs and bluegrass, while Memphis is known world-wide as the home of the blues, which gave birth to rock 'n' roll. Thousands flock every year to Memphis to see Graceland, the home of "The King". More than half the sate is forested, and great tracts set aside as state and national parks, wilderness areas, and game preserves.

EAST REGION

An area of natural beauty, this region has the **Great Smoky Mountains National Park,** the largest wilderness area east of the Mississippi. Theme parks, shopping and sightseeing in resort towns make this an area of family fun.

American Museum of Science and Industry, Oak Ridge. Learn about and experiment with energy forms and discover their uses through demonstrations, audiovisuals, machines and other devices.

Athens. McMinn County Living Heritage Museum has 30 permanent exhibit areas over three floors that trace the history of McMinn County from the Cherokee through the 1940's. Special events and classes throughout the year, including an annual quilt show. At the **Mayfield Dairy Visitor Center,** you can tour the dairy plant to see how milk is bottled and ice cream is made.

Benton. Just off Hwy 411 sits **Fort Marr,** built in the early 19th century to safeguard Andrew Jackson's shipping trains. It was also used as protection for the Cherokee Indians, who were fighting the Creek Indians at the time. Ironically, it later became a stockade that was used to detain Cherokee Indians prior to their forced removal on the Trail of Tears. The blockhouse remains.

Bays Mountain Park & Planetarium, Kingsport. This 3,300-acre nature preserve has an excellent nature center, barge rides on a 44-acre lake, a museum, a planetarium, hiking trails, a saltwater tidal pool, marine aquariums, wildlife habitats and a variety of exhibits.

Briarwood Ranch Safari Park, Bybee. View hundreds of animals and more than 35 exotic species during the four-mile safari at this great park. The tour winds through beautiful hills and pastureland. You can feed the animals right from your car.

Bristol Caverns, Bristol. Caverns feature geologic formations and a paved walkway.

Butler Museum, Butler. View a replica of the train depot on "Old Butler" - the town that wouldn't drown. It houses artifacts and memorabilia of the only incorporated town "drowned" by the TVA.

Chattanooga. Many of Chattanooga's attractions reflect its early railroad history. **Chattanooga Choo Choo** is an immense complex of restaurants, shops, lounges and gardens. Enjoy trolley car rides, tennis courts and an ice skating rink. View one of the largest model railroad displays in the world. **Audubon Acres** has miles of hiking trails that enable naturalists to view a variety of birds and wildflowers. Other attractions include:

Creative Discovery Museum where you can pilot a riverboat, dig for dinosaur bones, make sculptures and build robots.

Lake Winnepesaukah Amusement Park. Over 30 rides and attractions including roller coasters, paddleboats, mini-golf and games.

Tennessee Aquarium. Learn the details of freshwater ecosystems; journey through two living forests and a 60-ft. canyon where over 7,000 animals fly, swim and crawl about their natural habitats. Enjoy the film at the IMAX® 3D Theater.

Houston Museum of Decorative Arts houses 18th-, 19th- and early 20th-century decorative art objects.

Hunter Museum of American Art is the most complete collection of American art in the Southeast.

National Medal of Honor Museum of Military History preserves the memory of those who served in America's military conflicts from the Revolutionary War through today.

Coker Creek. Try your hand at gold panning. Take a horseback ride or drive to Buck Bald to watch the sunset. Browse through the nearby **Coker Creek Crafts Gallery.**

Copperhill. As you explore the downtown of this copper mining town, look for the stone steps that were built in the early days of the 20th century to allow miners to park their motorcars at the bottom of the hill and walk home.

Cherokee National Forest consists of 600,000 acres of mountains, forests and meadows. Hiking, fishing, white water rafting, canoeing, skiing, hunting and camping keep visitors busy year-round.

Ducktown. Listed on the National Register of Historic Places, the **Ducktown Basin Museum** offers seasonal tours of the Burra Burra Mine Shops and Change House to complement permanent exhibits that depict the mining heritage of the Copper Basin. Near Ducktown and Copperhill is the **Ocoee Whitewater Center**. Built for the 1996 Olympic Whitewater Races, this visitor center includes the Olympic race channel, a native plant garden, paved walkways on both sides of the river, pools of water for wading or feeding fish and the historic Old Copper Road, open for hiking and biking.

Etowah. The 18-room **Louisville & Nashville Depot and Railroad Museum** resides in a restored Victorian Depot and features a museum "Growing Up With the L&N: Life and Times in a Railroad Town." In downtown Etowah, you'll find the historic **Gem Theater** with special events throughout the year.

Farragut Folklife Museum, Farragut. See a remarkable collection of East Tennessee artifacts including an extensive collection from Admiral David Farragut.

Gatlinburg. No longer a small mountain village, Gatlinburg has developed into a major resort area with over 400 shops and a large concentration of working craftspeople. At **Ober Gatlinburg Ski Resort & Amusement Park** you can enjoy indoor ice skating, alpine slide, a Black Bear Habitat, water raft rides, winter sports and a scenic aerial tramway.

Christus Gardens of Gatlinburg. Experience the Greatest Story Ever Told in a series of breathtaking dioramas, peopled with over 100 life-size wax figures in realistic settings. It's one of the Best Hours in the Smokies! Also featured at Christus Gardens is **The Promise**—a 900 square foot original mural featuring over 30 characters from the Old Testament, as well as **The Place of Parables**—a series of life-size paintings depicting the beloved stories told by Jesus. **Biblical Era Coins** features America's finest collection of Ancient coins from the Holy Land and Imperial Rome. **The Carraca Face of Christ** is a 6-ton marble sculpture of the head of Christ, so skillfully crafted not only the eyes but also

QUICK REFERENCE CHART FOR WOODALL'S FEATURED PARKS

	Green Friendly	RV Lots for Sale	Park Models-Onsite Ownership	Park Membership for Sale	Big Rigs Welcome	Internet Friendly	Pets Welcome
BAILEYTON							
Baileyton RV Park	🍃				▲	○	■
BRISTOL							
Lakeview RV Park	🍃				▲	○	■
CHATTANOOGA							
Best Holiday Trav-L-Park					▲	○	■
Chattanooga's Raccoon Mtn. Caverns & Campground	🍃				▲	○	■
CLARKSVILLE							
Clarksville RV Park & Campground	🍃				▲	○	■
CLEVELAND							
KOA-Chattanooga North/Cleveland					▲	○	■
CLINTON							
Fox Inn Campground/Norris					▲	○	■
COLUMBIA							
Campers RV Park					▲	○	■
CROSSVILLE							
Bean Pot Campground	🍃				▲	○	■
Deer Run RV Resort					▲	○	■
DAYTON							
Blue Water Marina/Campground						○	■
ELIZABETHTON							
Stoney Creek RV Park							■
GATLINBURG							
Great Smoky Jellystone Park Camp Resort						○	■
Twin Creek RV Resort	🍃				▲	○	■
HARRIMAN							
Caney Creek RV Resort & Marina	🍃				▲	○	■
JACKSON							
Jackson RV Park					▲	○	■
KINGSPORT							
KOA-Bristol/Kingsport					▲	○	■
KNOXVILLE							
Southlake RV Park						●	■
LAKE CITY							
Mountain Lake Marina & Campground					▲	○	■
LEBANON							
Countryside RV Resort					▲	○	■

Green Friendly 🍃; RV Lots for Sale ✖; Park Models/Onsite Onwership ✱; Park Memberships for Sale ✔; Big Rigs Welcome ▲; Internet Friendly ●; Internet Friendly-WiFi ○; Pets Welcome ■

QUICK REFERENCE CHART FOR WOODALL'S FEATURED PARKS

	Green Friendly	RV Lots for Sale	Park Models-Onsite Ownership	Park Membership for Sale	Big Rigs Welcome	Internet Friendly	Pets Welcome
LENOIR CITY							
Soaring Eagle Campground & RV Park					▲	●	■
LOUDON							
Express RV Park						●	■
MANCHESTER							
KOA-Manchester	🍂				▲	●	■
MEMPHIS							
Agricenter RV Park						●	■
Memphis/Graceland RV Park & Campground					▲	●	■
Redwood Estates							■
MILLINGTON							
Shady Oaks Community							■
NASHVILLE							
Nashville Country RV Park	🍂				▲	●	■
Stonegate RV Park					▲	●	■
Two Rivers Campground					▲	●	■
NEWPORT							
KOA-Newport I-40/Smoky Mtns					▲	●	■
PARKERS CROSSROADS							
Parker's Crossroads RV Park & Campground						●	■
PIGEON FORGE							
Cove Mountain Resorts RV Park					▲	●	■
Eagle's Nest Campground					▲	●	■
Foothills RV Park & Cabins						●	■
King's Holly Haven RV Park					▲	●	■
Pine Mountain RV Park					▲	●	■
River Plantation RV Park					▲	●	■
Riverbend Campground					▲	●	■
Riveredge RV Park	🍂				▲	●	■
Twin Mountain RV Park and Campground					▲	●	■
SEVIERVILLE							
Ripplin' Waters Campground					▲	●	■
Riverside RV Park & Resort					▲	●	■
SMYRNA							
Nashville I-24 Campground					▲	●	■
SWEETWATER							
KOA-Sweetwater Valley					▲	●	■
TOWNSEND							
Big Meadow Family Campground	🍂				▲	●	■

Green Friendly 🍂; RV Lots for Sale ✖; Park Models/Onsite Onwership ✱; Park Memberships for Sale ✔; Big Rigs Welcome ▲;
Internet Friendly ●; Internet Friendly-WiFi ●; Pets Welcome ■

the entire face seems to follow your movements.

Guinness World of Records Museum, Gatlinburg. Hundreds of exhibits and 10 shows with memorabilia of famous record-holders.

Great Smoky Mountains Heritage Center. The Mission of the Great Smoky Mountain Heritage Center is to preserve, protect and promote the unique history and rich culture of the residents and Native Americans who inhabited the East Tennessee mountain communities. The Center will be a 15,000 square foot structure on three acres, including two classrooms, a museum, a store, an auditorium, a Native American gallery, an Early History gallery, a Temporary gallery, a Collection storage and a Fabrication shop. A 500-seat amphitheater has also been added to the Heritage Center.

Great Smoky Mountains National Park, Gatlinburg. Located partly in North Carolina and partly in Tennessee, this 500,000-acre park has beautiful mountain scenery, over 800 miles of hiking trails, mile-high peaks and countless opportunities for fishing, biking, horseback riding and camping. Wildflowers abound in late April and early May and autumn's pageantry of color usually peaks during mid-October.

Hiwassee & Ocoee Scenic Rivers, Delano. Spend a leisurely afternoon canoeing, fishing, hiking and photographing nature along the Hiwassee River.

John Muir Trail. This 18.8-mile trail, which follows the Hiwassee River, begins at Childers Creek near Reliance and ends near Hwy 68 at Farner. The first three-mile section has been designed for senior citizens. Named for naturalist John Muir, the trail allows you to experience some of the most diverse and unique terrain in the Cherokee National Forest.

Knoxville. Enjoy the following areas, in and around Knoxville:

Ijams Nature Center offers 80 acres of trails, winding through wooded areas and wildflower meadows, past sinkholes, ponds and bluffs.

Knoxville Zoological Park features more than 1,000 animals, rides for adults and children, a playground, miniature golf and picnic facilities.

TVA Lakes. Located within 30 miles of Knoxville are six Tennessee Valley Authority lakes: **Norris, Douglas, Cherokee, Fort Loudon, Melton Hill and Watts Bar**. Most of the campgrounds around these lakes are open year-round; some have houseboats for rent and all offer year-round fishing.

Museum of Appalachia, Norris. Known as the most authentic and complete replica of pioneer Appalachian life in the world, this 65-acre museum has more than 250,000 pioneer relics, more than 30 log structures and the Appalachia Hall of Fame.

CAMP CLUB USA

Where to Find CCUSA Parks

List City	Park Name	Map Coordinates
BRISTOL		
	Lakeview RV Park	D-6
CROSSVILLE		
	Bean Pot Campground	B-5
	Deer Run RV Resort	B-5
GRANVILLE		
	Maple Grove Campground	A-5
HORNSBY		
	Big Buck Camping Resort	C-2
KNOXVILLE		
	Volunteer Park	B-6
NASHVILLE		
	Nashville Country RV Park	B-4
PIGEON FORGE		
	Creekside RV Park	E-5
	Eagle's Nest Campground	E-5
	Smoker Holler RV Resort	E-5
	Waldens Creek Campground	E-5
SEVIERVILLE		
	Ripplin' Waters Campground	E-5
TOWNSEND		
	Misty River Cabins & RV Resort, LLC	E-5
UNION CITY		
	AAA RV Park	A-2

Paramount Center for the Arts, Bristol, is a historic 1931 landmark theater restored to its original art deco style.

Niota. Built in 1853, the **Niota Depot** is the oldest standing railroad depot in Tennessee. Now used as offices for the town, the depot is open for tours during business hours.

Ocoee Scenic Byway. US Highway 64. The first National Forest Scenic Byway in the United States is located in the Cherokee National Forest and consists of 26 miles of highway that winds alongside the Ocoee River in Polk County and up to the Chilhowee Campground on Forest Service Road 77. The highway passes through scenic areas dominated by rock bluffs, mountain peaks and historic sites such as the Ocoee Flume Line and Powerhouses, Confederate Camp and Old Copper Road. The panoramic views from the Chilhowee Overlooks and Boyd Gap are favorites of photographers.

Pigeon Forge. This family-fun town, located north of Gatlinburg, has numerous music shows, entertainment parks and more than 200 discount stores. Homespun fun can be found at **Dollywood**, a theme park, which brings to life the fun and folklore of the Smoky Mountains. Flyaway, one of only three such facilities in the world, lets visitors experience the thrill of flying inside a wind tunnel.

Sweetwater. The **Tennessee Meji Gakuin Culture Enrichment Center** bridges the gap between Japanese and American cultures. Exhibits, classes and enrichment programs. Special events include the annual Japanese Quilt Show. Other highlights include: **Sweetwater Heritage Museum** featuring memorabilia and photographs that help visitors step back in time; **Lost Sea**, the world's largest underground lake. Designated a Registered National Landmark, the earliest known visitor to the cave was a saber-toothed tiger, whose fossilized remains are now in the Museum of Natural History. A guided walk to the bottom of the cavern is rewarded with a trip in a glass bottom boat.

Tellico Plains. Pause in this small mountain town and look for Babcock Street, where houses built by Babcock Lumber Company stand. At the end of the street, you'll see the old **Stokely Cannery**, where German prisoners of war worked in the cannery fields during WWII.

Vonore. Fort Loudon State Historic Area commemorates the first planned British fort in the land of the Overhill Cherokee. The reconstructed fort was originally built in 1756. Re-enactments and other celebrations add to museum exhibits on site. Picnicking and swimming. Other highlights include the **Sequoyah Birthplace Museum** located on the banks of Tellico Lake on tribal land. The museum examines the history of the Cherokee people and honors Sequoyah, creator of the Cherokee written language. Cherokee crafts and historical information are for sale in the gift shop.

MIDDLE REGION

Besides Nashville, the country music capital of the world, the middle region has picturesque communities, beautiful scenery, restored antebellum mansions and more.

101st Airborne Division's Don F. Pratt Memorial Museum at Clarksville tells the story of Fort Campbell and the 101st Airborne Division featuring a large collection of weapons, aircraft and vehicles.

Beachaven Vineyards & Winery, Clarksville, provides a look into historic wine making procedures. Free tours and tastings are available.

Beechcraft Heritage Museum, Tullahoma. **The Staggerwing Museum** commemorates Walter Beech's Model 17 "Staggerwing" as a milestone of 1930's aviation development. Various Beech aircraft are on display including: Travel Airs, Beech 18, and Bonanza. The museum currently houses 17 airplanes.

Bell Witch Cave, Adams. This cave is associated with a famous spirit of the early 1800s and is considered to be one of the most haunted areas in America.

Big South Fork National River and Recreation Area, Jamestown. This area includes over 105,000 acres of the **Cumberland Plateau**. In addition to scenic beauty, the area offers camping, hiking, horseback riding, mountain biking, swimming, fishing, hunting, canoeing and whitewater paddling.

Bowen Campbell Plantation House, Goodlettsville. The area's earliest residence and region's oldest brick structure is furnished in 1790s style.

Carnton Plantation, Franklin. This antebellum plantation served as a field hospital during the Civil War Battle of Franklin. The largest private Confederate cemetery is adjacent to the grounds.

Clay County Courthouse, Celina. The stately redbrick structure, built in 1872, is one of the oldest working courthouses in Tennessee.

Cumberland Caverns, McMinnville. Tennessee's largest show cave displays some of the largest underground rooms and spectacular formations in eastern America, featuring waterfalls, gleaming pools and even a 3/4-ton chandelier.

Cumberland River Walk, Clarksville. Meandering riverfront walk is the center of this 200-year-old city's River District.

Ethridge is an Amish community with more than 200 families of farmers and craftspeople. Shops and galleries offer homemade food items, quilts, custom woodwork, baskets and furniture.

Fort Defiance, Clarksville. Well preserved Civil War fortification of earthen ramparts overlooks the Cumberland and Red rivers and the town of Clarksville.

Homeplace - 1850, A Living History Museum, Dover. Life in the mid 19th century is recreated with authentic houses and barns, interpreters in period clothing and demonstrations of daily chores.

Land Between the Lakes National Recreation Area, Dover, is made up of over 170,000 acres. Attractions include a living history farm, nature center, planetarium, wildlife viewing area and campgrounds.

Historic Mansker's Station Frontier Life Center, Goodlettsville. Fort reconstruction is considered to be one of the nation's most historically accurate. Tour with video and period dress interpreters.

Nashville. Welcome to "Music City USA," home of the famous **Grand Ole Opry,** dozens of recording studios, music shows and music-related attractions. The District in downtown Nashville has been renovated with imagination and flair; turn-of-the-century buildings house restaurants, trendy shops, contemporary art galleries and Nashville nightspots. Visit the **Country Music Hall of Fame & Museum,** which offers displays of country music's greatest stars and live music daily. Interactive features will allow you to create a custom CD of songs. Other attractions include the **Adventure Science Center** where you can discover the wonders of science through interactive displays and exhibits; **Cheekwood Botanical Garden & Museum of Art, Belle Meade Plantation, Frist Center for the Visual Arts**, and **Buchanan Log House**.

Stones River National Battlefield, Murfreesboro. These 509 acres commemorate the Civil War **Battle of Stones River**, where 23,000 casualties occurred in a 2-day period. On-site are a national cemetery, a visitors' center and a museum.

Thomas Drugs, Cross Plains. Old-fashioned 1915 drugstore with operating soda fountain.

WEST REGION

Western Tennessee is a region of barbecues, blues and the mighty Mississippi. Natural wonders include the Reelfoot Lake, Kentucky Lake, and the Tennessee River Freshwater Pearl Farm. Civil War grounds offer a glimpse into Tennessee's history.

American Museum of Science & Energy, Oak Ridge. Center for exploration dedicated to the WWII Manhattan Project history. Live demonstrations, interactive exhibits and presentations.

Collierville Train Museum, Collierville. Working with the Smithsonian, the Norfolk Southern Railroad and the Southern Railway Historical Society, the museum brings back to life The Tennessean. The museum features a 2-8-2 Frisco Steam Locomotive, a Southern Caboose and a former Business Car from the Seaboard Railroad.

Cotton Museum of the South, Bells, features a 1915 cotton gin located in a rural antique village with dining, shops, country church, arboretum, log buildings and one-room schoolhouse.

Dixie Gun Works Old Car Museum, Union City. View 36 antique autos, over 2,000 antique auto accessories, farm and steam engines and whistles.

Jackson. Visit the historic home of America's railroad legend at the **Casey Jones Home & Railroad Museum** with a 130-ton engine on display. Then head on over to the **International Rock-A-Billy Hall of Fame and Museum** featuring this country music sound with a blend of the blues.

Memphis. Hop aboard a **Main Street Trolley** for an entertaining tour of downtown. No trip to Memphis is complete without a walk through the **Beale Street Historic District,** known as the "birthplace of the blues." See Elvis Presley's home, **Graceland**, his auto collection and the Lisa Marie jet. The **National Civil Rights Museum** brings to life the sights, sounds and tensions of the Civil Rights Movement. See Ya Ya and Le Le, two giant pandas, at the **Memphis Zoo** along with more than 3,500 other animals. Then head to **Mud Island River Park** with its museum, riverwalk and recreation such as canoeing, kayaking and bicycling.

A. Schwab Dry Goods Store located on Beale St. was started in 1876 and is still owned and operated by three generations of the family. Incredible array of merchandise.

Art Museum of the University of Memphis contains changing exhibits of contemporary art throughout the year. Permanent collections include Egyptian Antiquities and the Neil Nokes West African Art Collection.

Peabody Hotel is home to the famous Peabody Ducks who have made their twice-daily marches through the lobby since the 1930s.

Stax Museum of American Soul Music which presents the legacy of Stax Records whose recording artists included such legends as Otis Redding, Isaac Hayes, Booker T and more.

Shiloh was the site of one of the Civil War's bloodiest battles. Union and Confederate casualties reached a combined total of 23,746. **Shiloh National Military Park** commemorates this battle with 150 monuments, 217 cannons and 450 historic markers throughout its 4,000 acres. The Shiloh Civil War Relics & Museum features bullets, cannons, books, buckles and many more authentic Civil War artifacts.

Smokey Says

Only You Can Prevent Wildfires

SMOKEY

- Never play with matches or lighters.
- Inspect your campsite before leaving.
- Build campfires away from low-hanging tree branches and all vegetation.
- Never use fireworks on public lands.
- Never use stoves, lanterns, or heaters inside a tent or near combustibles.
- Don't leave a fire unattended.
- Use existing fire rings or build fire rings for camp fires.

Our day in the forest

Paste your photos here.

YMI
YOUNG MINDS INSPIRED

ANTIOCH—B-4

ANDERSON ROAD CAMPGROUND (Corps of Engineers)—(Davison) *From I-40, exit 219, and Stewarts Ferry Pike.: Go S on Stewarts Ferry Pike, becomes Bell Rd., then 5 mi E on Smith Springs Rd., then 1 mi N on Anderson Rd. Enter on L.* FACILITIES: 37 sites, 37 no hkups, tenting, dump, laundry. RECREATION: lake swim, boating, ramp, lake fishing, playground. Partial handicap access. Open May 15 - Sep 2. Phone: (615)361-1980.

ASHLAND CITY—A-4

LOCK A CAMPGROUND (COE - Cheatham Lake)—(Cheatham) *From jct Ashland City: Go W 8 mi on US 12 to Cheap Hill, then W 4 mi on Cheatham Dam Rd. Enter on R.* FACILITIES: 45 sites, 45 W&E, (50 amps), tenting, dump, laundry. RECREATION: lake swim, boating, canoeing, ramp, lake fishing, playground. Pets welcome. Partial handicap access. Open Apr 1 - Sep 8. Phone: (615)792-3715.

ATHENS—B-6

(W) Athens I-75 Campground—(McMinn) *From jct I-75 (exit 49) & Hwy 30: Go 1/2 mi E on Hwy 30. Enter on R.* ◇◇FACILITIES: 60 sites, typical site width 25 ft, 44 full hkups, 6 W&E, (20/30/50 amps), 50 amps ($), 10 no hkups, 24 pull-thrus, tenting, dump, laundry. ◇◇RECREATION: swim pool, stream fishing, play equipment. Pets welcome. Open all yr. Rate in 2010 $17-18 for 2 persons. Phone: (423)745-9199.

(N) Over-Niter RV Park—(McMinn) *From jct I-75 (exit 52) & Hwy 305: Go 3/4 mi E on US 305. Enter on L.* ◇◇◇FACILITIES: 16 sites, typical site width 30 ft, 16 full hkups, (20/30/50 amps), 11 pull-thrus, tenting, laundry. Pets welcome. Open all yr. Big rigs welcome. Rate in 2010 $22-25 for 2 persons. Phone: (423)507-0069.

BAILEYTON—D-5

(E) BAILEYTON RV PARK—(Greene) *From jct I-81 (exit 36) & Van Hill Rd: Go 3/4 mi N on Van Hill Rd, then 1 mi E on Horton Hwy. Enter on L.*

WELCOME

◇◇◇◇FACILITIES: 60 sites, typical site width 30 ft, 55 full hkups, 5 W&E, (20/30/50 amps), some extd stay sites, 30 pull-thrus, cable TV, WiFi Instant Internet at site, phone on-site Internet (needs activ), phone Internet central location, tenting, cabins, RV storage, dump, non-guest dump $, laundry, RV supplies, LP gas by weight/by meter, ice, picnic tables, grills, wood.

◇◇RECREATION: equipped pavilion, pond fishing, fishing supplies, golf nearby, horseshoes, hiking trails, v-ball.

Pets welcome. Open all yr. Big rigs welcome. Escort to site. Clubs welcome. Green Friendly. Rate

BAILEYTON—Continued
BAILEYTON RV PARK—Continued

in 2010 $32-34 for 2 persons. MC/VISA/DISC/Debit. Member ARVC, TNARVC. FMCA discount.

Phone: (423)234-4992
Address: 7485 Horton Hwy, Baileyton, TN 37745
Lat/Lon: 36.33932/-82.82324
Email: baileytonrvpark@gmail.com
Web: www.baileytonrvpark.com

SEE AD GREENEVILLE PAGE 728 AND AD TRAVEL SECTION PAGE 713

BAXTER—B-5

(W) Twin Lakes Catfish Farm & Campground—(Putnam) *From jct I-40 & Hwy 56 (exit 280): Go 2-3/4 mi N on Hwy 56. Enter on L.* ◇◇◇FACILITIES: 32 sites, typical site width 30 ft, 28 full hkups, (20/30/50 amps), 4 no hkups, 9 pull-thrus, family camping, tenting. ◇◇◇RECREATION: lake fishing. Pets welcome. Partial handicap access. Open all yr. Big rigs welcome. Rate in 2010 $27 for 2 persons. Phone: (931)858-2333.

BLOUNTVILLE—D-6

(E) Rocky Top Campground & RV Park—(Sullivan) *From jct I-81 (exit 63 Tri-City Airport) & Browder Rd: Go 1/2 mi N on Browder Rd, then 3/4 mi SW on Pearl Lane. Enter on R.* ◇◇◇◇◇FACILITIES: 35 sites, typical site width 25 ft, 35 full hkups, (20/30/50 amps), 8 pull-thrus, family camping, tenting, dump, laundry, groceries. ◇◇◇RECREATION: playground. Pets welcome. Open all yr. Big rigs welcome. Rate in 2010 $33-37 for 2 persons. Member ARVC, TNARVC. FMCA discount.

Phone: (800)452-6456
Address: 496 Pearl Lane, Blountville, TN 37617
Lat/Lon: 36.51121/-82.44001
Email: camping@rockytopcampground.com
Web: www.rockytopcampground.com

BRISTOL—D-6

See listing at Bristol, VA & Blountville, Johnson City & Kingsport, TN

CHEROKEE NATIONAL FOREST (Little Oak Campground)—(Sullivan) *From town: Go 14 mi E on US-421, then 7 mi SW on FR-87.* FACILITIES: 70 sites, 70 no hkups, tenting, dump. RECREATION: lake swim, boating, canoeing, ramp, lake fishing. Open Mid Apr - Dec 1. Phone: (423)735-1500.

(S) LAKEVIEW RV PARK—(Sullivan) *From jct I-81 (exit 69) & SR 394: Go 5-1/4 mi E on SR-394, then 3 mi S on US Hwy 11E. Enter on R.*

WELCOME

◇◇◇◇FACILITIES: 151 sites, typical site width 30 ft, 151 full hkups, (20/30/50 amps), 2 pull-thrus, cable TV, WiFi Instant Internet at site, WiFi Internet central location, family camping, tenting, RV's/park model rentals, RV storage, laundry, ltd groc, RV supplies, LP gas by weight/by meter, ice, picnic tables.

CAMPCLUB USA

◇◇◇◇RECREATION: rec room/area, equipped pavilion, swim pool, boating, canoeing, kayaking, dock, 2 pontoon/2 rowboat/2 kayak rentals, lake fishing, fishing supplies, golf nearby, playground, activities, horseshoes, sports field, v-ball.

Pets welcome. Partial handicap access. Open all yr. Big rigs welcome. Escort to site. Clubs welcome. Green Friendly. Rate in 2010 $28-39 for 4

BRISTOL—Continued
LAKEVIEW RV PARK—Continued

persons. MC/VISA/DISC/Debit. Member ARVC, TNARVC. FMCA discount. CCUSA reservations Accepted, CCUSA 50% Discount. CCUSA max stay 6 days. Discount not available 7 days before & after Bristol Motor Speedway Event.

Phone: (866)800-0777
Address: 4550 US Hwy 11 E Lot 1, Bluff City, TN 37618
Lat/Lon: 36.46499/-82.28550
Email: camping@lakeviewrvpark.com
Web: www.lakeviewrvpark.com

Reserve Online at Woodalls.com

SEE AD THIS PAGE

BUFFALO—B-3

(E) KOA-Buffalo—(Humphreys) *From jct I-40 (exit 143) & Hwy 13: Go 200 yards N on Hwy 13, then 1/4 mi E. Follow signs. Enter on R.* ◇◇◇◇FACILITIES: 62 sites, typical site width 22 ft, 23 full hkups, 19 W&E, 10 E, (20/30/50 amps), 50 amps ($), 28 pull-thrus, family camping, tenting, dump, laundry, full svc store. ◇◇◇RECREATION: swim pool, playground. Pets welcome, breed restrict. Open all yr. Big rigs welcome. Rate in 2010 $27-40 for 2 persons. Phone: (931)296-1306. KOA discount.

CAMDEN—B-3

(S) Birdsong Resort, Marina & Lakeside Campground—(Benton) *From jct I-40 (exit 133) & Hwy 191N: Go 9 mi N on Hwy 191, then 1 blk W on Marina Rd. Enter on R.* ◇◇◇FACILITIES: 84 sites, typical site width 24 ft, 64 full hkups, (20/30/50 amps), 20 no hkups, 10 pull-thrus, family camping, tenting, dump, ltd groc. ◇◇◇RECREATION: swim pool, lake swim, boating, canoeing, ramp, dock, lake fishing, playground. Pets welcome. Partial handicap access. Open all yr. Big rigs welcome. Rate in 2010 $32.50-38 for 2 persons. Phone: (731)584-7880.

(E) NATHAN BEDFORD FORREST STATE PARK—(Benton) *From town: Go 10 mi NE on Hwy 191 (Eva). Enter at end.*

WELCOME

FACILITIES: 51 sites, 38 W&E, (20/30/50 amps), 13 no hkups, tenting, cabins, dump, picnic tables, grills, wood.

RECREATION: lake swim, boating, ramp, lake fishing, playground, activities, sports field, hiking trails, v-ball. Rec open to public.

Partial handicap access. Open Apr 1 - Nov 15. No reservations.

Phone: (800)715-7305
Address: 1825 Pilot Knob Rd., Eva, TN 38333
Lat/Lon: 36.085917/-87.981111
Web: www.state.tn.us

SEE AD TRAVEL SECTION PAGE 714

CARTHAGE—A-5

(N) DEFEATED CREEK PARK (Corps of Engineers)—(Smith) *From Carthage: Go 4 mi W on SR 25, then N on US 80, then E on SR 85, 7 mi from Carthage.* FACILITIES: 155 sites, 63 full hkups, 92 W&E, (20/30 amps), 32 pull-thrus, tenting, dump, laundry. RECREATION: swim pool, lake swim, boating, ramp, dock, lake fishing, playground. Partial handicap access. Open Mar 17 - Nov 11. Phone: (615)774-3141.

Tennessee State Motto: "Agriculture and Commerce"

CARYVILLE—A-6

(NE) COVE LAKE STATE PARK—(Campbell) *From jct I-75 & US 25W: Go 1/2 mi NE on US 25W. Enter on L.*

FACILITIES: 105 sites, 101 W&E, (30 amps), 4 no hkups, 2 pull-thrus, tenting, dump, ice, picnic tables, grills.

RECREATION: equipped pavilion, swim pool, boating, electric motors only, dock, 8 rowboat/10 pedal boat rentals, lake fishing, playground, shuffleboard court shuffleboard court, activities, tennis, horseshoes, sports field, hiking trails, v-ball.

Pets welcome. Partial handicap access. Open all yr. Facilities fully operational Apr 1 - Oct 31. No reservations.

Phone: (423)566-9701
Address: 110 Cove Lake Lane, Caryville, TN 37714
Lat/Lon: 36.30898/-84.21108
Web: www.state.tn.us

SEE AD TRAVEL SECTION PAGE 714

CELINA—A-5

(E) DALE HOLLOW DAM CAMPGROUND (COE-Dale Hollow Lake)—(Clay) *From town: Go 3 mi E on Hwy-53.* FACILITIES: 79 sites, 78 W&E, (50 amps), 1 no hkups, 13 pull-thrus, tenting, dump, laundry. RECREATION: boating, canoeing, ramp, dock, river fishing, playground. Partial handicap access. Open Apr 1 - Oct 31. Phone: (931)243-3136.

CHAPEL HILL—B-4

(S) HENRY HORTON STATE PARK—(Marshall) *From town: Go 3 mi S on US 31A. Enter on R.*

WELCOME

FACILITIES: 63 sites, 54 W&E, (30 amps), 9 no hkups, tenting, cabins, dump, picnic tables, grills.

RECREATION: pavilion, swim pool, boating, canoeing, ramp, river fishing, putting green, bsktball, playground, activities, tennis, sports field, hiking trails, v-ball.

Pets welcome. Open all yr. Facilities fully operational Apr 1 - Oct 31.

Phone: (800)250-8612
Address: 4209 Nashville Hwy, Chapel Hill, TN 37034
Lat/Lon: 35.59103/-86.70245
Web: www.state.tn.us

SEE AD TRAVEL SECTION PAGE 714

CHATTANOOGA—C-5

CHATTANOOGA AREA MAP

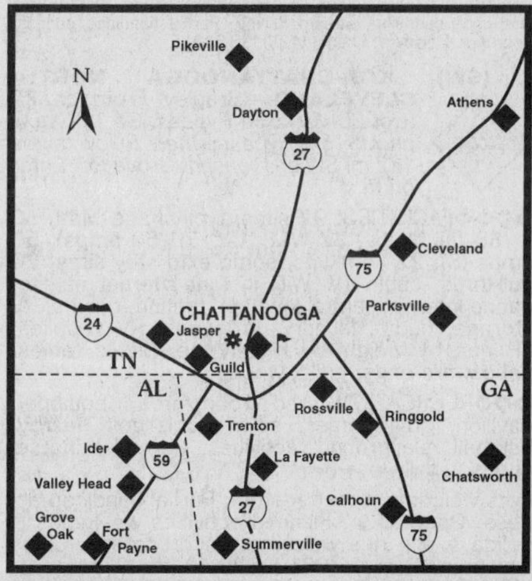

Symbols on map indicate towns within a 45 mi radius of Chattanooga where campgrounds (diamonds), attractions (flags), & RV service centers & camping supply outlets (gears) are listed. Check listings for more information.

Tell Them Woodall's Sent You!

CHATTANOOGA—Continued on next page

Reputed "Turtle Capital of the World", Reelfoot Lake also features thousands of sliders, stinkpots, mud and map turtles.

Tennessee ties with Missouri as the most neighborly state in the union. It is bordered by eight states.

Sequoyah, a Tsalagi leader, created an alphabet for the Tsalagi or Cherokee people.

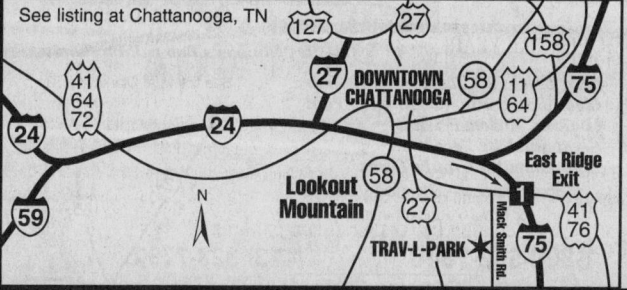

(S) BEST HOLIDAY TRAV-L-PARK—(Hamilton) *From jct I-24 & I-75: Go 1/2 mi S on I-75 (S bound exit 1, N bound exit 1B), then 1/4 mi W on US 41N, then 1/2 mi S on Mack Smith Rd. Enter on R.*

CHATTANOOGA KEEPS GETTING BETTER!

And so do we! Make our 5W park your home while you re-live Civil War history, visit the world's largest freshwater aquarium or ride the Incline Railroad. We offer well-groomed, shaded sites with every amenity-just 1/2 mi off I-75.

◆◆◆◆◆FACILITIES: 171 sites, typical site width 30 ft, 131 full hkups, 22 W&E, (20/30/50 amps), 18 no hkups, some extd stay sites, 130 pull-thrus, cable TV, WiFi Instant Internet at site, phone on-site Internet (needs activ), cable Internet central location, family camping, tenting, cabins, RV storage, dump, non-guest dump $, laundry, ltd groc, RV supplies, LP gas by weight/by meter, ice, picnic tables, patios, fire rings, wood.

◆◆◆◆RECREATION: rec hall, rec room/area, pavilion, swim pool, golf nearby, bsktball, playground, shuffleboard court 2 shuffleboard courts, horseshoes, sports field, v-ball.

Pets welcome, breed restrict. Partial handicap access. Open all yr. Big rigs welcome. Clubs welcome. Rate in 2010 $35-37 for 2 persons. MC/VISA/Debit. Member ARVC, TNARVC. FCRV discount. FMCA discount.

Text 107909 to (440)725-8687 to see our Visual Tour.

Phone: (800)693-2877
Address: 1709 Mack Smith Rd, Chattanooga, TN 37412
Lat/Lon: 34.97932/-85.21240
Email: campmail@chattacamp.com
Web: www.chattacamp.com

SEE AD PAGE 721 AND AD TRAVEL SECTION PAGE 713

(W) CHATTANOOGA'S RACCOON MTN. CAVERNS & CAMPGROUND—(Hamilton) *From jct I-24 (exit 174) & US 41/64: Go 1-1/4 mi N on US 41/64, then 1/2 mi SW on West Hill Rd. Enter on L.*

◆◆◆◆FACILITIES: 136 sites, typical site width 22 ft, 61 full hkups, 44 W&E, (30/50 amps), 31 no hkups, 61 pull-thrus, cable TV, WiFi Instant Internet at site, phone Internet central location, tenting, cabins, RV storage, dump, non-guest dump $, laundry, groceries, RV supplies, LP gas by weight/by meter, ice, picnic tables, patios, fire rings, grills, wood.

◆◆◆◆RECREATION: rec hall, equipped pavilion, coin games, swim pool, golf nearby, bsktball, playground, horseshoes, sports field, hiking trails, local tours.

Pets welcome, breed restrict. Open all yr. Facilities fully operational May - Oct 31. Pool seasonal. Big rigs welcome. Clubs welcome. Green Friendly. Rate in 2010 $30-33 for 4 persons. MC/VISA/DISC/Debit. Member ARVC, TNARVC. FMCA discount.

The city of Murfreesboro lies in the exact geographical center of the state.

CHATTANOOGA—Continued
CHATTANOOGA'S RACCOON MTN. CAVERNS & CAMPGROUND—Continued

Phone: (423)821-9403
Address: 319 West Hills Rd, Chattanooga, TN 37419
Lat/Lon: 35.02174/-85.40733
Email: raccoonl@racoonmountain.com
Web: www.raccoonmountain.com

SEE AD THIS PAGE

(W) CHATTANOOGA'S RACCOON MTN. CRYSTAL CAVERNS—*From jct I-24 (exit 174) & US 41/64: Go 1-1/4 mi N on US 41/64, then 1/2 mi SW on West Hill Rd. Enter on L.* Caverns tours, gift shop. Wild Cave tours available by reservation. Batting cage. Go carts available. Gem panning. Open all yr. MC/VISA/DISC.

Phone: (423)821-9403
Address: 319 West Hills Rd, Chattanooga, TN 37419
Lat/Lon: 35.02174/-85.40733

SEE AD THIS PAGE

(N) CHESTER FROST PARK (Hamilton County Park) —(Hamilton) *From jct Hwy-153 & Hixson Pike: Go 10 mi N on Hixon Pike, then 1 mi N on Gold Point Circle.* FACILITIES: 200 sites, 180 W&E, (30/50 amps), 20 no hkups, 35 pull-thrus, tenting, dump, laundry. RECREATION: lake swim, boating, ramp, dock, lake fishing, playground. Pets welcome. Partial handicap access. Open all yr. Facilities fully operational Apr - Nov. Phone: (423)842-0177.

HARRISON BAY STATE PARK—(Hamilton) *From town: Go 11 mi NE on Hwy 58. Enter on L.*

FACILITIES: 163 sites, 135 W&E, (30 amps), 28 no hkups, tenting, dump, ltd groc, marine gas, ice, picnic tables, grills.

RECREATION: rec hall, pavilion, swim pool, boating, canoeing, ramp, dock, lake fishing, bsktball, playground, shuffleboard court shuffleboard court, activities, tennis, horseshoes, sports field, hiking trails, v-ball.

Pets welcome. Partial handicap access. Open all yr. No reservations. MC/VISA/DISC/AMEX.

Phone: (423)344-7966
Address: 8411 Harrison Bay Rd, Harrison, TN 37341
Lat/Lon: 35.17181/-85.12436
Web: www.state.tn.us

SEE AD TRAVEL SECTION PAGE 714

(S) Shipp's RV Campground—(Hamilton) *From jct I-75 (exit 1) & US-41: Go 1/2 mi SE on US-41. Enter on R.* ◆◆◆FACILITIES: 60 sites, typical site width 20 ft, 60 full hkups, (20/30/50 amps), 50 amps ($), 50 pull-thrus, dump. ◆◆RECREATION: swim pool, boating, no motors, lake fishing, playground. Pets welcome. Partial handicap access. No tents. Open all yr. Phone: (423)892-0144.

CLARKSBURG—B-2

NATCHEZ TRACE STATE PARK—(Henderson) *From jct Hwy 114 & I-40 (exit 116): Follow signs.*

FACILITIES: 209 sites, 77 full hkups, 87 W&E, (30/50 amps), 45 no hkups, 9 pull-thrus, tenting, cabins, dump, laundry, ltd groc, picnic tables, fire rings, grills.

RECREATION: lake swim, boating, no motors, ramp, lake fishing, playground, hiking trails. Rec open to public.

CLARKSBURG—Continued
NATCHEZ TRACE STATE PARK—Continued

Pets welcome. Partial handicap access. Open all yr. Facilities fully operational Apr 1 - Oct 31. No reservations.

Phone: (800)250-8616
Address: 24845 Natchez Trace Park, Wildersville, TN 38388
Web: www.state.tn.us

SEE AD TRAVEL SECTION PAGE 714

CLARKSVILLE—A-3

(NE) CLARKSVILLE RV PARK & CAMPGROUND—(Montgomery) *From jct I-24 (exit 1) & Hwy 48: Go 1/4 mi N on Hwy 48, then 1/4 mi W on Tylertown Rd. Enter on L.*

BIG RIG SITES!! 50 AMPS!! WIFI!!

We can handle your big rig with our long level pull thru 30/50 amp sites. We have high speed Internet access and we're close to restaurants & shopping. Stay with us once and you'll keep coming back. We also Welcome rallies.

◆◆◆◆FACILITIES: 75 sites, typical site width 25 ft, 55 full hkups, 12 W&E, (20/30/50 amps), 8 no hkups, some extd stay sites, 51 pull-thrus, WiFi Instant Internet at site, phone Internet central location, family camping, tenting, cabins, dump, non-guest dump $, laundry, ltd groc, RV supplies, LP gas by weight/by meter, ice, picnic tables, wood.

◆◆◆RECREATION: rec hall, swim pool, golf nearby, playground, horseshoes, sports field, v-ball.

Pets welcome. Open all yr. Swimming Pool open Memorial Day thru Labor Day. Big rigs welcome. Clubs welcome. Green Friendly. Rate in 2010 $32-35 for 2 persons. MC/VISA/DISC/Debit. Member ARVC, TNARVC.

Phone: (888)287-8638
Address: 1270 Tylertown Rd, Clarksville, TN 37040
Lat/Lon: 36.63480/-87.32233
Email: info@clarksvillervpark.com
Web: www.clarksvillervpark.com

SEE AD THIS PAGE AND AD TRAVEL SECTION PAGE 713

CLEVELAND—C-6

(E) CHEROKEE NATIONAL FOREST (Chilhowee Campgrounds)—(Polk) *From town: Go 17-3/10 mi E on US-64, then 7-4/10 mi NW on FR-77.* FACILITIES: 82 sites, 25 E, 57 no hkups, 1 pull-thrus, tenting, dump. RECREATION: boating, electric motors only, canoeing, stream fishing. Partial handicap access. Open Apr 1 - Nov 9. Phone: (423)338-5201.

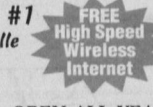

(SW) KOA-CHATTANOOGA NORTH/ CLEVELAND—(Bradley) *From jct I-75 (exit 20) & US 64 Bypass: Go 1/2 mi W on US 64 Bypass, then follow signs 1/2 mi SW on Pleasant Grove Rd. Enter on R.*

◆◆◆◆FACILITIES: 97 sites, typical site width 30 ft, 38 full hkups, 37 W&E, (20/30/50 amps), 50 amps ($), 22 no hkups, some extd stay sites, 20 pull-thrus, cable TV, WiFi Instant Internet at site, phone Internet central location, tenting, cabins, RV storage, dump, laundry, groceries, RV supplies, LP gas by weight/by meter, ice, picnic tables, patios, fire rings, grills, wood.

◆◆◆RECREATION: rec room/area, equipped pavilion, coin games, swim pool, golf nearby, bsktball, playground, activities, (wkends), horseshoes, v-ball.

Pets welcome, breed restrict. Partial handicap access. Open all yr. Planned activities weekends & holidays. Big rigs welcome. Escort to site. Clubs welcome. Rate in 2010 $29-40 for 2 persons. MC/VISA/DISC/Debit. KOA discount.

KOA-CHATTANOOGA NORTH/ CLEVELAND—Continued on next page

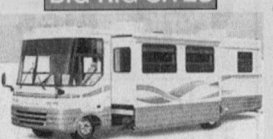

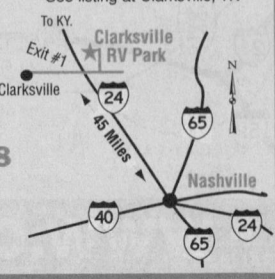

CLEVELAND—Continued
KOA-CHATTANOOGA NORTH/ CLEVELAND—Continued

Phone: (423)472-8928
Address: 648 Pleasant Grove Rd SW, McDonald, TN 37353
Lat/Lon: 35.15059/-84.96041
Email: koacleveland@charter.net
Web: koa.com

SEE AD CHATTANOOGA PAGE 721

CLINTON—B-6

(E) FOX INN CAMPGROUND/NORRIS—(Anderson) *From jct I-75 (exit 122) & Hwy 61: Go 500 ft E on Hwy 61. Enter on L.*

◆◆◆◆FACILITIES: 93 sites, typical site width 25 ft, 57 full hkups, 36 W&E, (20/30/50 amps), some extd stay sites, 70 pull-thrus, cable TV, WiFi Instant Internet at site, phone Internet central location, family camping, tenting, cabins, dump, non-guest dump $, laundry, ltd groc, RV supplies, LP gas by weight/by meter, ice, picnic tables, fire rings, wood.

◆◆◆◆RECREATION: rec room/area, equipped pavilion, coin games, swim pool, wading pool, golf nearby, bsktball, play equipment, horseshoes, sports field, v-ball.

Pets welcome. Open all yr. Big rigs welcome. Escort to site. Clubs welcome. Rate in 2010 $28-32 for 2 persons. MC/VISA/Debit. Member ARVC, TNARVC. FMCA discount.

Phone: (865)494-9386
Address: 2423 N Charles G Seivers Blvd, Clinton, TN 37716
Lat/Lon: 36.16933/-84.07906
Email: foxinncamp@comcast.net
Web: www.foxinncampground.com

SEE AD KNOXVILLE PAGE 730

COLUMBIA—B-4

(E) CAMPERS RV PARK (NOT VISITED)—(Maury) *From jct I-65 (exit 46) & Hwy 99: Go 1 mi E on Hwy 99. Enter on R.*

FACILITIES: 128 sites, 83 full hkups, 28 W&E, (30/50 amps), 17 no hkups, 34 pull-thrus, WiFi Internet central location, family camping, tenting, cabins, dump, non-guest dump $, laundry, LP gas by weight/by meter, ice, picnic tables, fire rings, wood.

RECREATION: pavilion, swim pool, play equipment, activities (wkends).

Pets welcome. Open all yr. Big rigs welcome. Clubs welcome. Rate in 2010 $25-30 per vehicle. MC/VISA/DISC/AMEX.

Phone: (931)381-4112
Address: 1792 Bear Creek Pike, Columbia, TN 38401
Lat/Lon: 35.64150/-86.87784
Email: campersrvpark@yahoo.com
Web: www.campersrvtn.com

SEE AD THIS PAGE

Aretha Franklin, singer, is from Tennessee.

CORNERSVILLE—C-4

(W) Texas "T" Campground—(Marshall) *From jct I-65 (exit 27) & Hwy 129: Go 1/8 mi E on Hwy 129. Enter on R.* ◆◆◆FACILITIES: 40 sites, typical site width 30 ft, 40 full hkups, 4 W&E, (30/50 amps), 40 pull-thrus, tenting, dump, laundry. ◆◆RECREATION: play equipment. Pets welcome, breed restrict. Open all yr. Big rigs welcome. Rate in 2010 $23.25-30.81 per family. Phone: (931)293-2500.

COSBY—E-5

(S) GREAT SMOKY MOUNTAINS NATIONAL PARK (Cosby Campground)—(Sevier) *From town: Go 2 mi S on Hwy 32.* FACILITIES: 175 sites, 25 ft max RV length, 175 no hkups, tenting, dump. RECREATION: stream fishing. Pets welcome. Partial handicap access. Open Late May - Oct 31. Phone: (423)487-5418.

COUNCE—C-2

(N) PICKWICK DAM (TVA-Pickwick Lake)—(Hardin) *From jct Hwy-57 & Hwy-128: Go 1-1/2 mi N on Hwy-128 across dam, then W below dam.* FACILITIES: 95 sites, 66 W&E, (30/50 amps), 29 no hkups, 20 pull-thrus, tenting, dump. RECREATION: swim pool, lake swim, boating, ramp, river fishing, play equipment. Pets welcome. Partial handicap access. Open all yr. Phone: (731) 925-4346.

CROSSVILLE—B-5

(NE) BEAN POT CAMPGROUND—(Cumberland) *From jct I-40 (exit 322) & Peavine Rd: Go 1-1/2 mi N on Peavine Rd, then 1 blk on Bean Pot Campground. Enter on R.*

◆◆◆◆FACILITIES: 64 sites, typical site width 28 ft, 36 full hkups, 28 W&E, (20/30/50 amps), 50 pull-thrus, cable TV, WiFi Instant Internet at site, phone Internet central location, tenting, cabins, RV storage, dump, non-guest dump $, laundry, groceries, RV supplies, LP gas by weight/by meter, ice, picnic tables, fire rings, grills, wood.

◆◆◆◆RECREATION: rec hall, coin games, swim pool, wading pool, golf nearby, bsktball, playground, activities, (wkends), horseshoes, hiking trails, v-ball.

Pets welcome, breed restrict. Partial handicap access. Open all yr. Big rigs welcome. Escort to site. Clubs welcome. Green Friendly. Rate in 2010 $24-27 for 2 persons. MC/VISA/DISC/AMEX/Debit. Member ARVC, TNARVC. FMCA discount. CCUSA 50% Discount. CCUSA reservations Required, CCUSA max stay 1 day, CCUSA disc. not avail F,Sa, CCUSA disc. not avail holidays. Not available Jun, Jul, Aug, Oct.

Phone: (877)848-7958
Address: 23 Bean Pot Campground Loop, Crossville, TN 38571
Lat/Lon: 35.97832/-84.96323
Email: beanpotcampground@yahoo.com
Web: www.beanpotcampground.com

SEE AD THIS PAGE AND AD TRAVEL SECTION PAGE 713

(E) Crossville KOA Campground—(Cumberland) *(W'bnd) From jct I-40 (exit 329) & Hwy 70: Go 1 block N to Hwy 70, then 4 mi W on Hwy 70. (E'bnd) From jct I-40 (exit 332) & Hwy 101/Peavine Rd: Go 1 mi S on Hwy 101, then 4 mi E on Hwy 70. Enter at end.* ◆◆◆FACILITIES: 48 sites, typical site width 35 ft, 17 full hkups, 21 W&E, (20/30/50 amps), 10 no hkups, 22 pull-thrus, family camping, tenting, laundry, groceries. ◆◆◆RECREATION: pond fishing, playground. Pets welcome. Partial handicap access. Open all yr. Big rigs welcome. Rate in 2010 $35-42 for 2 persons. Phone: (931)707-5349.

The Tulip Poplar was chosen as the state tree because it was used extensively by the Tennessee pioneers to construct their houses, barns and other buildings.

CROSSVILLE—Continued

(S) CUMBERLAND MOUNTAIN STATE PARK—(Cumberland) *From I-40 (exit 317): Go 8-1/2 mi S on US 127. Enter on R.*

FACILITIES: 153 sites, 14 full hkups, 139 W&E, (20/30 amps), tenting, cabins, dump, ltd groc, ice, picnic tables, grills.

RECREATION: rec hall, swim pool, wading pool, boating, no motors, canoeing, dock, 10 rowboat/8 canoe/24 pedal boat rentals, lake fishing, bsktball, playground, activities, tennis, sports field, hiking trails, v-ball. Rec open to public.

Pets welcome. Partial handicap access. Open all yr. Facilities fully operational Apr 1 - Sep 31. No reservations. No boat dock in winter. MC/VISA/DISC/AMEX.

Phone: (800)250-8618
Address: 24 Office Dr., Crossville, TN 38555
Lat/Lon: 35.90046/-84.99712
Web: www.state.tn.us

SEE AD TRAVEL SECTION PAGE 714

(NE) DEER RUN RV RESORT—(Cumberland) *From jct I-40 (exit 322) & Peavine Rd: Go 2 mi N on Peavine Rd, then 3-1/2 mi W on Firetower Rd. Enter on L.*

◆◆◆◆FACILITIES: 100 sites, typical site width 30 ft, 100 full hkups, (20/30/50 amps), many extd stay sites, 11 pull-thrus, WiFi Instant Internet at site, WiFi Internet central location, family camping, tenting, RV's/park model rentals, cabins, RV storage, laundry, groceries, RV supplies, LP gas by weight/by meter, ice, picnic tables, fire rings, grills, wood, controlled access.

◆◆◆◆RECREATION: rec room/area, equipped pavilion, swim pool, lake swim, electric motors only, canoeing, kayaking, ramp, dock, lake fishing, fishing supplies, golf nearby, bsktball, playground, shuffleboard court shuffleboard court, activities (wkends), tennis, horseshoes, sports field, v-ball.

Pets welcome, quantity restrict. Partial handicap access. Open all yr. Big rigs welcome. Escort to site. Clubs welcome. Rate in 2010 $29 per family. MC/VISA/Debit. Member ARVC, TNARVC. FMCA discount. CCUSA 50% Discount. CCUSA reservations Recommended, CCUSA max stay 6 days, CCUSA disc. not avail F,Sa, CCUSA disc. not avail holidays. No other discounts in combination.

Phone: (931)484-3333
Address: 3609 Peavine Firetower rd, Crossville, TN 38571
Lat/Lon: 36.02120/-84.92945
Email: info@deerrunrvresort.com
Web: deerrunrvresort.com

SEE AD THIS PAGE

(NE) Spring Lake RV Resort—(Cumberland) *From jct I-40 (exit 322) & Hwy 101 (Peavine Rd): Go 3-1/2 mi N on Peavine Rd, then turn 1/4 mi E on Fairview Dr. Enter on L.* ◆◆◆◆FACILITIES: 64 sites, typical site width 50 ft, 45 ft max RV length, 61 full hkups, 3 W&E, (30/50 amps), 5 pull-thrus, laundry. ◆◆RECREATION: lake fishing. Pets welcome, breed restrict. No tents. Open all yr. Big rigs welcome. Rate in 2010 $27-30 for 2 persons. Member ARVC, TNARVC. Phone: (877)707-1414. FMCA discount.

DANDRIDGE—D-5

(E) Lake Cove Resort—(Jefferson) *From jct I-40 (exit 424) & Hwy 113: Go 1-1/4 mi W on Hwy 113/ Oak Grove Rd. Enter on L.* ◆◆◆FACILITIES: 38 sites, 36 ft

Lake Cove Resort—Continued on next page

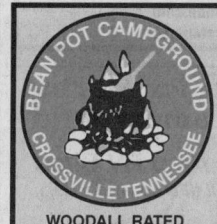

DANDRIDGE—Continued
Lake Cove Resort—Continued

max RV length, 30 full hkups, 8 W&E, (30 amps), 6 pull-thrus, tenting. ◆◆◆RECREATION: swim pool, boating, ramp, dock, lake fishing, playground. Pets welcome. Open Apr 15 - Nov 1. Rate in 2010 $33-38 for 4 persons.

DAYTON—B-5

(E) BLUE WATER MARINA/ CAMPGROUND (REBUILDING) —(Rhea) *From jct US 27 Bypass & Hwy 30: Go 1/2 mi E on Hwy 30 to Double "S" Rd, then 1-3/4 mi S on Double "S" Rd. Enter at end.*

FACILITIES: 34 sites, typical site width 40 ft, 34 full hkups, (20/30/50 amps), cable TV, WiFi Instant Internet at site, tenting, dump, ltd groc, RV supplies, marine gas, ice, picnic tables.

RECREATION: rec room/area, pavilion, coin games, boating, ramp, dock, lake fishing, fishing supplies, golf nearby.

Pets welcome. Open all yr. Rate in 2010 $25.50-27.50 for 4 persons. MC/VISA/Debit.

Phone: (423)775-3265
Address: 220 Bluewater Campground Rd., Dayton, TN 37321
Lat/Lon: 35.48066/-84.97768

SEE AD THIS PAGE

DELANO—C-6

HIAWASSEE STATE SCENIC RIVER & OCOEE RIVER (Gee Creek Campground)—(Polk) *From north jct Hwy 30 & US 411: Go 6 mi S on US 411 to Hwy 163, then 1 mi SE on Spring Creek Rd. Enter on L.*

FACILITIES: 47 sites, 47 no hkups, 47 pull-thrus, tenting, picnic tables, fire rings, grills, controlled access.

RECREATION: river swim, boating, canoeing, ramp, river fishing, horseshoes, hiking trails, v-ball.

Pets welcome. Partial handicap access. Open all yr. Facilities fully operational Apr 1 - Oct 31. No reservations.

Phone: (423)263-0050
Address: 404 Spring Creek Rd, Delano, TN 37325
Web: www.state.tn.us

SEE AD TRAVEL SECTION PAGE 714

DICKSON—B-3

(S) Dickson RV Park—(Dickson) *At jct I-40 (exit 172) & Hwy 46: Go 1 blk N on Hwy 46, then 1 blk W on W Christie Rd. Enter at end.* ◆◆FACILITIES: 60 sites, typical site width 30 ft, 38 ft max RV length, 51 full hkups, 5 W&E, 4 E, (20/30/50 amps), 50 amps ($), 60 pull-thrus, tenting, laundry, groceries. ◆◆RECREATION: swim pool, playground. Pets welcome. Open all yr. Facilities fully operational Memorial Day - Labor Day. Rate in 2010 $28-30 for 2 persons. Phone: (615)446-9925.

DOVER—A-3

BUMPUS MILLS RECREATIONAL AREA (COE-Lk Barkley)—(Stewart) *From town: Go 13 mi NW on Hwy-120.* FACILITIES: 33 sites, 15 W&E, (20/30 amps), 18 no hkups, tenting, dump, laundry, ltd groc. RECREATION: lake swim, boating, ramp, dock, lake fishing, playground. Partial handicap access. Open Early Apr - Mid Oct. Phone: (931)232-8831.

(N) GATLIN POINT (LBL) National Recreation Area (Lake Access Site Only)—(Stewart) *From jct US 79 & The Trace: Go 4 mi N on The Trace, then follow signs 3 mi E.* FACILITIES: 25 sites, 25 no hkups, tenting. RECREATION: boating, ramp, lake fishing. Open all yr. Phone: (270)924-2000.

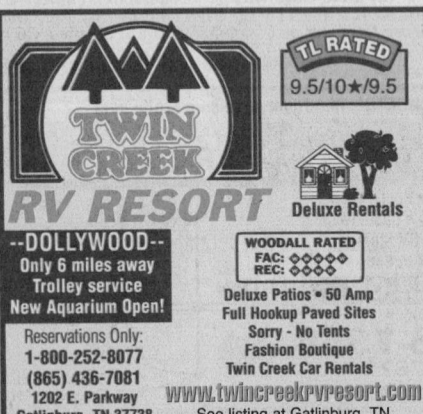

DOVER—Continued

(W) PINEY (LBL) National Recreation Area—(Stewart) *From town: Go 9-1/2 mi W on US 79, then 3 mi on CR 230 (Fort Henry Rd). Follow signs. Enter at end.* FACILITIES: 384 sites, 44 full hkups, 281 E, (30/50 amps), 59 no hkups, 6 pull-thrus, tenting, dump, laundry, groceries. RECREATION: lake swim, boating, ramp, dock, lake/pond fishing, playground. Pets welcome. Open Mar 1 - Nov 30. Phone: (931)232-5331.

ELIZABETHTON—D-6

STONEY CREEK RV PARK—(Sullivan) *From jct I-26 (exit 24) & Hwy 321/67: Go 8 mi E on Hwy 321/67 to jct US 19E/321 & Hwy 91, then 3 mi N on Hwy 91, then 175 yds E on Blue Springs Rd, then 1-1/4 mi N on Willow Springs Rd (Stay left at Y), then 100 ft W on Price Rd. Enter on L.*

◆◆◆FACILITIES: 13 sites, typical site width 25 ft, accepts full hkup units only, 13 full hkups, (30/50 amps), 50 amps ($), 4 pull-thrus, dump, non-guest dump $, picnic tables, fire rings, grills, wood.

RECREATION: horseshoes.

Pets welcome. No tents. Open all yr. No restrooms. Rate in 2010 $17-20 for 2 persons.

Phone: (423)474-3505
Address: 108 Price Rd., Elizabethton, TN 37643
Lat/Lon: 36.37754/-82.13777

SEE AD THIS PAGE

ERWIN—D-6

CHEROKEE NATIONAL FOREST (Rock Creek Campgrounds)—(Unicoi) *From town: Go 1 mi N on US-23, then 3 mi E on FR-30.* FACILITIES: 34 sites, 13 E, (20/30 amps), 21 no hkups, tenting, dump. RECREATION: stream fishing. Partial handicap access. Open May 1 - Oct 1. Phone: (423)638-4109.

GAINESBORO—A-5

SALT LICK CREEK CAMPGROUND (Corps of Engineers)—(Jackson) *From Carthage, TN: Go 4 mi W on SR 25, then N on US 80, then E on SR 85 to Gladdice, follow signs, then right on Smith Bend Rd.* FACILITIES: 150 sites, 31 full hkups, 119 W&E, (30/50 amps), tenting, dump, laundry. RECREATION: lake swim, boating, ramp, lake fishing, playground. Partial handicap access. Open Apr 22 - Oct 14. Phone: (931)678-4718.

GALLATIN—A-4

(E) BLEDSOE CREEK STATE CAMPING PARK—(Sumner) *From town: Go 6 mi E on Hwy 25, then 1-1/2 mi S on Zeigler Fort Rd. Enter on L.*

FACILITIES: 71 sites, 71 W&E, (30 amps), 8 pull-thrus, tenting, dump, laundry, picnic tables, fire rings, controlled access.

RECREATION: boating, ramp, lake fishing, playground, hiking trails.

Pets welcome. Partial handicap access. Open all yr. Day use only. Limited water avail in winter months.

Phone: (615)452-3706
Address: 400 Zeigler Fort Rd., Gallatin, TN 37066
Lat/Lon: 36.37846/-86.36096
Web: www.state.tn.us

SEE AD TRAVEL SECTION PAGE 714

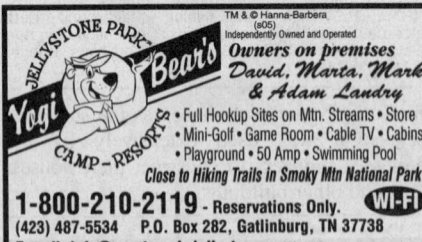

GATLINBURG—E-5

(E) Adventure Bound Camping Resort Gatlinburg (formerly Crazy Horse Camping & RV Resort)—(Sevier) *From jct US-441 & US 321 N: Go 12 mi E on US 321 N. Enter on L.* ◆◆◆FACILITIES: 207 sites, typical site width 30 ft, 75 full hkups, 132 W&E, (20/30/50 amps), 29 pull-thrus, family camping, tenting, dump, laundry, ltd groc. ◆◆◆◆RECREATION: swim pool, pond fishing, playground. Pets welcome. Partial handicap access. Open Apr 1 - Nov 30. Rate in 2010 $28-49 for 2 persons. Member ARVC, TNARVC. Phone: (865)436-4434.

(E) Arrow Creek Campground—(Sevier) *From jct I-40 (exit #440) & Hwy 32/321: Go 14-1/2 mi S on Hwy 321. Enter on L.* ◆◆◆FACILITIES: 52 sites, typical site width 30 ft, 35 ft max RV length, 37 full hkups, 12 W&E, (30/50 amps), 3 no hkups, 3 pull-thrus, family camping, tenting, dump, laundry, ltd groc. ◆◆RECREATION: swim pool, play equipment. Pets welcome. Open Apr 1 - Nov 1. Rate in 2010 $27.50-29.50 for 2 persons. Member ARVC, TNARVC. Phone: (865)430-7433.

(E) Camping in the Smokies—(Sevier) *From jct US 441 & Hwy 321: Go 3 mi E on Hwy 321. Enter on R.* ◆◆◆FACILITIES: 53 sites, typical site width 35 ft, 41 full hkups, 11 W&E, (20/30/50 amps), 2 pull-thrus, family camping, tenting, laundry. ◆RECREATION: swim pool. Pets welcome, breed restrict. Open Mar 15 - Nov 1. Rate in 2010 $31.95-52.95 for 2 persons. Member ARVC, TNARVC. Phone: (865)430-3594.

(E) GREAT SMOKY JELLYSTONE PARK CAMP RESORT—(Cocke) *E'bnd from jct I-40 (exit 435) & Hwy 321: G0 15 mi S on Hwy 321. W'bnd from jct I-40 (exit 440) & Hwy 73: Go 15 mi S on Hwy 321. Enter on L.*

◆◆◆◆◆FACILITIES: 89 sites, typical site width 35 ft, 44 full hkups, 30 W&E, (20/30/50 amps), 15 no hkups, 4 pull-thrus, cable TV, WiFi Instant Internet at site, phone Internet central location, family camping, tenting, cabins, dump, non-guest dump $, laundry, full svc store, RV supplies, LP gas by weight/by meter, ice, picnic tables, fire rings, wood.

◆◆◆◆◆RECREATION: rec hall, equipped pavilion, coin games, swim pool, wading pool, stream fishing, fishing supplies, mini-golf, ($), golf nearby, bsktball, playground, activities, horseshoes, hiking trails.

Pets welcome, breed restrict. Partial handicap access. Open Mar 15 - Nov 30. Escort to site. Clubs welcome. Rate in 2010 $25-49 for 2 persons. MC/VISA/DISC/Debit. Member ARVC, TNARVC.

Phone: (423)487-5534
Address: 4946 Hooper Hwy, Gatlinburg, TN 37738
Lat/Lon: 35.77171/-83.26789
Email: gatlyogi@comcast.net
Web: www.greatsmokyjellystone.com

SEE AD THIS PAGE

Greenbrier Island Campground—(Sevier) *From jct US-441 & Hwy-321: Go 6-1/4 mi E on Hwy-321, then 250 yards N on Pittman-Center Rd. Enter on L.* ◆◆◆FACILITIES: 116 sites, typical site width 40 ft, 48 full hkups, 34 W&E, (20/30 amps), 34 no hkups, 10 pull-thrus, family camping, tenting, dump, laundry. ◆◆◆RECREATION: river swim, river fishing, play equipment. Pets welcome, quantity restrict. Open Apr 1 - Oct 31. Rate in 2010 $26-30 for 2 persons. Phone: (865)436-4243.

(E) Smoky Bear Campground—(Sevier) *From jct I-40 (exit 435 or 440) & Hwy 321: Go 12 or 17 mi S on US 321. Enter on R.* ◆◆◆◆FACILITIES: 49 sites, typical site width 30 ft, 49 full hkups, (20/30/50 amps), 9 pull-thrus, family camping, tenting, laundry. ◆◆◆RECREATION: swim pool, playground. Pets welcome. Partial handicap access. Open Mar - Dec. Big rigs welcome. Green Friendly. Rate in 2010 $32-44 for 4 persons. Member ARVC, TNARVC. Phone: (800)850-8372.

Reserve Online at Woodalls.com

GATLINBURG—Continued on next page

Dolly Parton, singer, is from Tennessee.

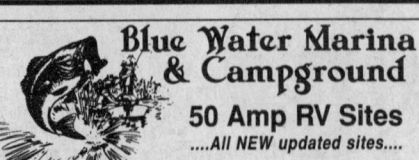

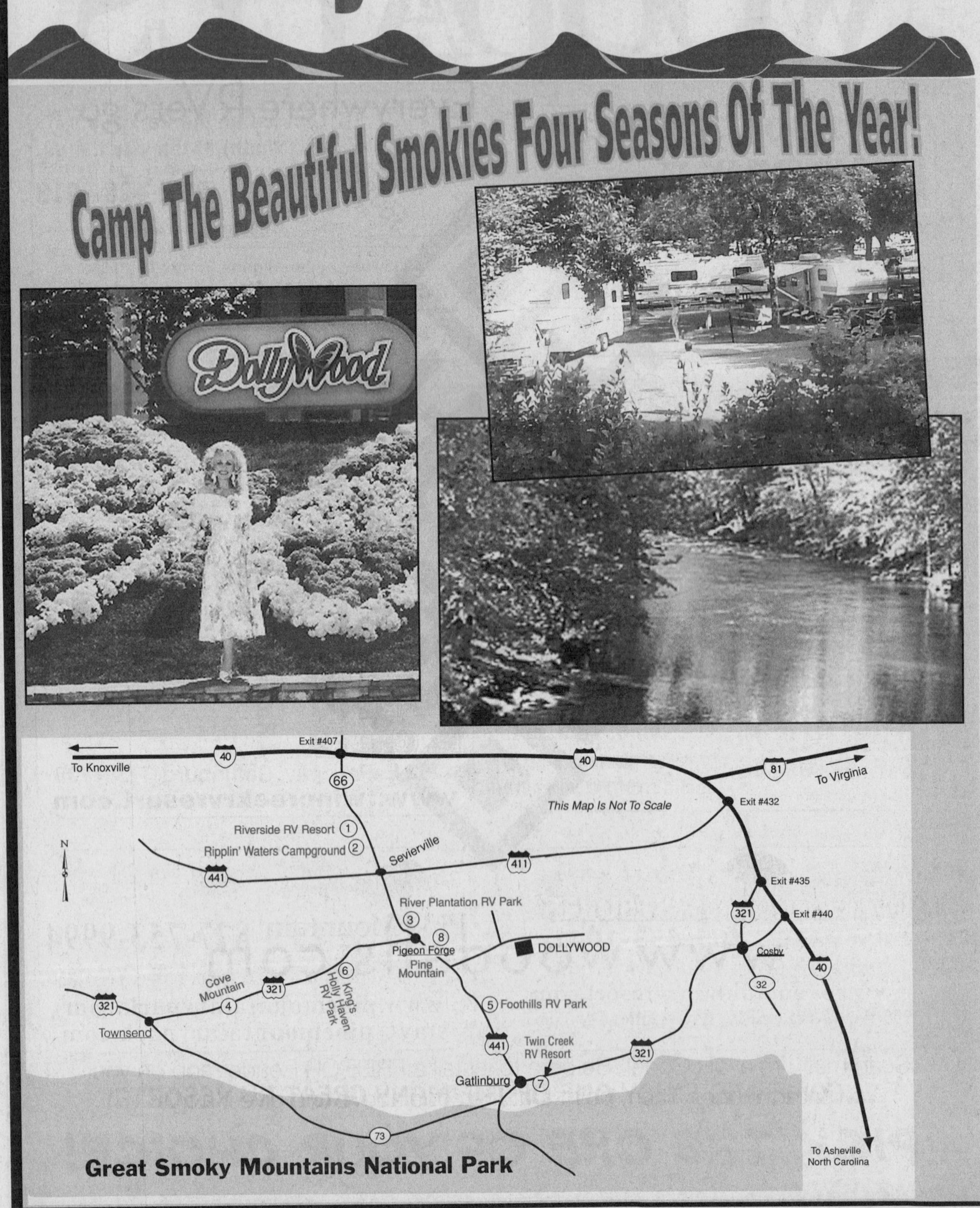
Smoky Mountains
Camp The Beautiful Smokies Four Seasons Of The Year!
Dollywood
To Knoxville
Exit #407
40
66
81
To Virginia
This Map Is Not To Scale
Exit #432
Riverside RV Resort 1
Ripplin' Waters Campground 2
Sevierville
441
411
Exit #435
River Plantation RV Park
3
321
Exit #440
8
Pigeon Forge
DOLLYWOOD
Cosby
Pine Mountain
6
King's Holly Haven RV Park
Cove Mountain
4
32
321
5 Foothills RV Park
Townsend
Twin Creek RV Resort
Gatlinburg
7
73
To Asheville North Carolina
Great Smoky Mountains National Park

Gatlinburg - Pigeon Forge - Sevierville

Tennessee's Camping Capital

1-800-341-7534 ①
(Reservation Only)

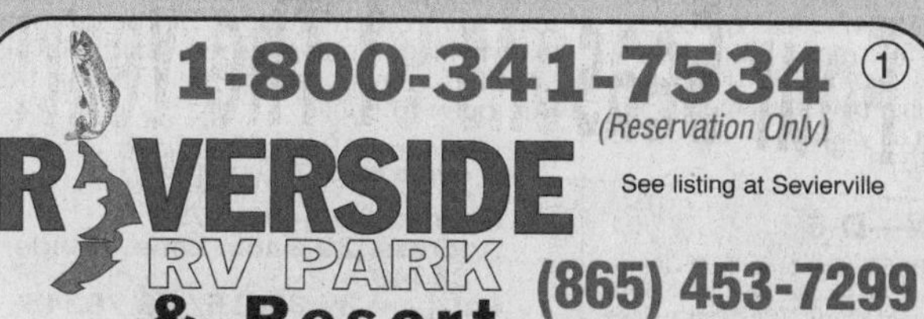

See listing at Sevierville

(865) 453-7299

4280 Boyds Creek Hwy., Sevierville, TN 37876
www.riversidecamp.com

Located on the Parkway ⑤
(South) at the City Limits
www.foothillsrvparkandcabins.com

(865) 428-3818
Trolley Stop
See listing at Pigeon Forge
4235 Huskey St., Pigeon Forge, TN 37863
camp@foothillsrvpark.info

See listing at Sevierville ②

1930 Winfield Dunn Pkwy.
Sevierville, TN 37876

Campground & Cabins

Toll Free Reservations Only
1-888-Ripplin
(747-7546)

or call
(865) 453-4169
www.ripplinwatersrv.com

⑥
For Reservations Only
Toll FREE: 1-888-204-0247
www.hollyhavenrvpark.com
(865) 453-5352
See listing at Pigeon Forge
647 Wears Valley Rd.
Pigeon Forge, TN 37863

③
For Reservations Only:
1-800-758-5267
1004 Parkway
Sevierville, TN 37862
www.riverplantationrv.com
email: riverrv@aol.com
See listing at Pigeon Forge

⑦
Reservations Only:
1-800-252-8077
(865) 436-7081
Trolley Stop
See listing at Gatlinburg
1202 E. Parkway, Gatlinburg, TN 37738
www.twincreekrvresort.com

④
COVE MOUNTAIN RESORTS
RV PARK 865-453-1041
2 miles to Great Smoky Mtn Park
www.covemountainrvresort.com
3958 Wears Valley Rd., Sevierville, TN 37862
See listing at Pigeon Forge

⑧
Pine Mountain
RV Park by the Creek
Trolley Stop
See listing at Pigeon Forge
877-753-9994
411 Pine Mountain Road, Pigeon Forge, TN 37863
www.pinemountainrvpark.com
stay@pinemountainrvpark.com

....COME AND ENJOY ONE OF THE MANY GREAT RV RESORTS!

PICK THE ONE OF YOUR CHOICE!

GATLINBURG—Continued

(E) TWIN CREEK RV RESORT—(Sevier) *From jct US 441 & US 321: Go 2 1/4 mi E on US 321 N. Enter on R.*

WELCOME

◊◊◊◊◊FACILITIES: 83 sites, typical site width 30 ft, 83 full hkups, (20/30/50 amps), 15 pull-thrus, cable TV, WiFi Instant Internet at site, phone Internet central location, family camping, cabins, laundry, groceries, RV supplies, ice, picnic tables, patios, fire rings, grills, wood.

◊◊◊◊RECREATION: rec room/area, coin games, swim pool, wading pool, hot tub, stream fishing, fishing supplies, golf nearby, playground, activities, (wkends), hiking trails, local tours.

Pets welcome, breed restrict, quantity restrict. Partial handicap access. No tents. Open Mid Mar - Dec 5. Big rigs welcome. Escort to site. Clubs welcome. Green Friendly. MC/VISA/Debit. Member ARVC, TNARVC. FMCA discount.

Phone: (800)252-8077
Address: 1202 E. Parkway, Gatlinburg, TN 37738
Lat/Lon: 35.72591/-83.48277
Web: www.twincreekrvresort.com

SEE AD PAGES 726-727 AND AD PAGE 724 AND AD PIGEON FORGE PAGE 740

GRANVILLE—A-5

(S) Maple Grove Campground—(Jackson) *From jct I-40 (exit 268) & Rte 96: Go 4 mi N on Rte 96, then 4 mi W on Hwy 70N, then 5 mi N on Rte 53. Enter on L.* ◊◊◊FACILITIES: 38 sites, typical site width 25 ft, 38 full hkups, (20/30/50 amps), 50 amps ($), 22 pull-thrus, family camping, tenting, dump, non-guest dump $, ltd groc, RV supplies, picnic tables. ◊◊RECREATION: pavilion, swim pool, wading pool, lake fishing, bsktball, play equipment, hiking trails, v-ball. Pets welcome. Open all yr. Rate in 2010 $18.50-22.50 for 4 persons. FCRV discount. CCUSA 50% Discount. CCUSA reservations Not Accepted, CCUSA max stay Unlimited, Cash only for CCUSA disc., Check only for CCUSA disc., CCUSA disc. not avail holidays.

CAMPCLUB USA

Phone: (931)653-4486
Address: 6878 Granville Hwy, Granville, TN 38564
Lat/Lon: 36.26778/-85.79836
Email: info@maplegrovecampground.com
Web: www.maplegrovecampground.com

GREAT SMOKY MOUNTAINS NATIONAL PARK—E-5

See listings at Gatlinburg, Pigeon Forge, Sevierville, Townsend, Walland & Newport

GREENBACK—B-6

LOTTERDALE COVE—(Loudon) *From jct Hwy 95 & US 411: Go 3-1/4 mi SW on US 411, then follow signs 4-1/4 mi N. Enter on L.* FACILITIES: 90 sites, (30/50 amps), 90 no hkups, 8 pull-thrus, tenting, dump. RECREATION: lake swim, boating, canoeing, ramp, lake fishing, playground. Pets welcome. Partial handicap access. Open Apr - Oct. Phone: (423)856-3832.

GREENEVILLE—D-5

See listing at Baileyton

DAVY CROCKETT BIRTHPLACE HISTORICAL SP—(Greene) *From jct US 11E & Limestone Rd.: Go 3 mi S & follow signs. Enter on R.*

WELCOME

FACILITIES: 88 sites, 35 full hkups, 36 W&E, (30 amps), 17 no hkups, tenting, dump, ice, picnic tables, grills, controlled access.

RECREATION: swim pool, wading pool, boating, ramp, river fishing, bsktball, playground, hiking trails.

Pets welcome. Partial handicap access. Open all yr. Facilities fully operational Apr 1 - Oct 31.

GREENEVILLE—Continued
DAVY CROCKETT BIRTHPLACE HISTORICAL SP—Continued

Phone: (423)257-2167
Address: 1245 Davy Crockett Park Rd., Limestone, TN 37681
Lat/Lon: 36.20978/-82.65894
Web: www.state.tn.us

SEE AD TRAVEL SECTION PAGE 714

KINSER PARK (City Park)—(Greene) *From jct US 321 & Hwy 70: Go 5 mi S on Hwy 70, then 5 mi E on Allens Bridge Rd.* FACILITIES: 157 sites, 149 full hkups, 8 W&E, (30/50 amps), tenting, groceries. RECREATION: swim pool, boating, ramp, lake/river fishing, playground. Pets welcome. Open Apr 1 - Oct 31. Phone: (423)639-5912.

GUILD—C-5

(W) Camp on the Lake Campground—(Marion) *From jct I-24 (exit 161) & Hwy 156: Go 1/8 mi S on Hwy 156. Enter on R.* ◊◊FACILITIES: 42 sites, typical site width 35 ft, 19 W&E, (20/30/50 amps), 23 no hkups, 3 pull-thrus, tenting, dump. ◊◊RECREATION: lake swim, boating, ramp, lake fishing, play equipment. Pets welcome, breed restrict. Open all yr. Rate in 2010 $25 per family. Phone: (423)942-4078.

HAMPTON—D-6

CHEROKEE NATIONAL FOREST (Cardens Bluff Campground)—(Carter) *From town: Go 4 mi NE on US-321.* FACILITIES: 42 sites, 42 no hkups, tenting. RECREATION: boating, lake fishing. Partial handicap access. Open Apr 30 - Oct 12. Phone: (423)735-1500.

HARRIMAN—B-6

(W) CANEY CREEK RV RESORT & MARINA—(Roane) *From jct I-40 (exit 350) & Hwy 29: Go 1/2 mi S on Hwy 29, then 3 mi W on Hwy 70. Enter on L.*

WELCOME

CANEY CREEK RV RESORT & MARINA
Brand new resort on beautiful Watts Bar Lake. 178 sites, many on lake, inc. pull-thru's & face-to-face. Pool, playground, pavilion, marina, cable, WiFi, full hook-ups year round, 30/50 amp. Big Rig friendly. (865)882-4042

◊◊◊◊FACILITIES: 178 sites, 178 full hkups, (20/30/50 amps), some extd stay sites, 6 pull-thrus, cable TV, ($), WiFi Instant Internet at site, laundry, ltd groc, RV supplies, LP gas by weight/by meter, LP bottle exch, ice, picnic tables, patios, fire rings, grills, wood.

◊◊◊◊RECREATION: pavilion, swim pool, wading pool, lake swim, boating, ramp, dock, 2 pontoon/2 canoe/2 pedal boat/2 motorboat rentals, lake fishing, fishing supplies, fishing guides, golf nearby, bsktball, 8 bike rentals, playground, shuffleboard court shuffleboard court, activities (wkends), horseshoes, sports field, hiking trails, v-ball.

Pets welcome, breed restrict, quantity restrict. Partial handicap access. No tents. Open all yr. Big rigs welcome. Clubs welcome. Green Friendly. Rate in 2010 $49-65 for 4 persons. MC/VISA/DISC/AMEX/Debit. Member ARVC, TNARVC.

Phone: (865)882-4042
Address: 3615 Roane State Hwy, Harriman, TN 37748
Lat/Lon: 35.86715/-84.59574
Email: reservations@caneycreekrvresort.com
Web: www.caneycreekrvresort.com

SEE AD THIS PAGE AND AD TRAVEL SECTION PAGE 713

HARTFORD—E-5

(SW) Shauan's RV Park—(Cocke) *From jct I-40 (exit 447) & Hartford Rd: Go 1/4 mi S on Hartford Rd, then 100 yds W on Trail Hollow Rd. Enter on R.*

HARTFORD—Continued
Shauan's RV Park—Continued

◊◊◊◊FACILITIES: 14 sites, typical site width 25 ft, 14 full hkups, (30/50 amps), family camping, tenting. ◊◊RECREATION: boating, ramp, river fishing. Pets welcome. Open all yr. Rate in 2010 $25-35 for 2 persons. Phone: (423)487-4400.

HENDERSON—C-2

(W) CHICKASAW STATE PARK—(Hardeman/Chester) *From jct Hwy 45 & Hwy 100 in Henderson: Go 8 mi W on Hwy 100. Enter on L.*

WELCOME

FACILITIES: 113 sites, 84 W&E, (30 amps), 29 no hkups, tenting, cabins, dump, picnic tables, grills.

RECREATION: pavilion, lake swim, boating, no motors, ramp, 15 rowboat/30 pedal boat rentals, lake fishing, putting green, bsktball, playground, activities, tennis, sports field, hiking trails, v-ball. Rec open to public.

Pets welcome. Partial handicap access. Open all yr. MC/VISA/DISC/AMEX/Debit.

Phone: (800)458-1752
Address: 20 Cabin Lane, Henderson, TN 38340
Lat/Lon: 35.39016/-88.78245
Web: www.state.tn.us

SEE AD TRAVEL SECTION PAGE 714

HENNING—B-1

FORT PILLOW STATE HISTORIC AREA—(Lauderdale) *From jct US 51 & Hwy 87: Go 17 mi W on 87, then 1 mi N on Hwy 207. Enter at end.*

WELCOME

FACILITIES: 32 sites, 32 no hkups, tenting, picnic tables, grills.

RECREATION: lake/river fishing, playground, activities, hiking trails.

Pets welcome. Partial handicap access. Open all yr. For tent camping only.

Phone: (731)738-5581
Address: 3122 Park Rd., Henning, TN 38041
Web: www.state.tn.us

SEE AD TRAVEL SECTION PAGE 714

HERMITAGE—B-4

(E) SEVEN POINTS CAMPGROUND (Corps of Engineers)—(Davison) *From jct I-40, exit 221B, and Old Hickory Blvd.: Go 1 mi S on Old Hickory Blvd., then 1 mi E on Bell Rd., then 1 mi S on New Hope Rd., then E on Stewart Ferry Rd. follow signs. Enter on R.* FACILITIES: 60 sites, 60 W&E, (30/50 amps), tenting, dump, laundry. RECREATION: lake swim, boating, canoeing, ramp, lake fishing. Partial handicap access. Open Apr 1 - Oct 29. Phone: (615)889-5198.

HOHENWALD—B-3

NATCHEZ TRACE CAMPGROUND (CAMP RESORT)—(Lewis) *1363 Napier Rd., Hohenwald, TN 38462.*

WELCOME

RECREATION: rec hall, swim pool.

Phone: (800)579-4987
Address: 1363 Napier Rd, Hohenwald, TN 38462
Web: www.oneparkmembership.com

SEE AD NASHVILLE PAGE 738

HOHENWALD—Continued on next page

HOHENWALD—Continued

(E) NATCHEZ TRACE PARKWAY (Meriwether Lewis Campground)—(Lewis) *From town: Go 7 mi E on Hwy-20.* FACILITIES: 32 sites, 32 no hkups, tenting. RECREATION: Pets welcome. Open all yr. Phone: (800)305-7417.

HORNSBY—C-2

(E) Big Buck Camping Resort—(Hardeman) *From jct Hwy 18 & US 64: Go 12 mi E on US 64, then 1/4 mi N on Sparks Rd. Enter on R.* ◊◊◊FACILITIES: 125 sites, 125 W&E, (30/50 amps), WiFi Internet central location, family camping, tenting, dump, non-guest dump $, laundry, ice, picnic tables, patios, fire rings, grills, wood. ◊◊◊◊RECREATION: rec hall, pavilion, equipped pavilion, swim pool, boating, dock, lake fishing, bsktball, playground, activities, horseshoes, v-ball. Pets welcome. Partial handicap access. Open all yr. Rate in 2010 $25 per vehicle. MC/VISA/DISC/AMEX/Debit. CCUSA 50% Discount. CCUSA reservations Recommended, CCUSA max stay 7 days, CCUSA disc. not avail holidays. Burning restrictions Aug thru May.

Phone: (731)658-2246
Address: 205 Sparks Rd, Hornsby, TN 38044
Lat/Lon: 35.22068/-88.79452
Email: bigbuck@aeneas.net
Web: www.bigbuckresort.com

HURRICANE MILLS—B-3

Loretta Lynn's Ranch—(Humphreys) *From jct I-40 (exit 143) & Hwy-13: Go 8 mi N on Hwy-13. Enter on L.* ◊◊◊◊FACILITIES: 465 sites, typical site width 35 ft, 102 full hkups, 213 W&E, (20/30/50 amps), 150 no hkups, 70 pull-thrus, family camping, tenting, dump, laundry, groceries. ◊◊◊◊◊RECREATION: swim pool, river swim, boating, canoeing, pond/stream fishing, playground. Pets welcome. Open Apr 1 - Oct 31. Facilities fully operational Memorial Day - Labor Day. Big rigs welcome. Member ARVC. Phone: (931)296-7700.

JACKSON—B-2

(S) JACKSON RV PARK (RV SPACES) —(Madison) *From jct I-40 (exit 79) & Hwy 412: Go 1/4 mi S on Hwy 412. Enter on L.*

FACILITIES: 36 sites, accepts self-contained units only, 36 full hkups, (15/30/50 amps), some extd stay sites, 15 pull-thrus, WiFi Instant Internet at site, laundry.

RECREATION: bsktball.

Pets welcome. No tents. Open all yr. Big rigs welcome. Rate in 2010 $20 per family.

Phone: (731)668-1147
Address: 2223 Hollywood Dr, Jackson, TN 38305
Lat/Lon: 35.65456/-88.87158
Web: www.jacksonrvpark.com

SEE AD THIS PAGE

(N) Joy-O RV Park—(Madison) *From jct I-40 (exit 68) & Hwy 138: Go 1/4 mi S on Hwy 138 (Providence Rd). Enter on L.* ◊◊◊FACILITIES: 30 sites, 20 full hkups, 10 W&E, (30/50 amps), 50 amps ($), 20 pull-thrus, tenting, dump, laundry. ◊RECREATION: swim pool. Pets welcome. Open all yr. Rate in 2010 $20.95-44.60 for 2 persons. Member ARVC, TNARVC. Phone: (731)424-3725.

(W) Parkway Village (RV SPACES)—(Madison) *From jct Hwy 20 & I-40: Go 8 mi E on I-40 (exit 87), then 3-1/2 mi SW on Hwy 70 W. Enter on R.* FACILITIES: 23 sites, typical site width 25 ft, accepts full hkup units only, 23 full hkups, (30/50 amps), laundry. RECREATION: swim pool, play equipment. Pets welcome, size restrict. No tents. Open all yr. Big rigs welcome. Rate in 2010 $20 per vehicle. Phone: (731)423-3331.

(W) Whispering Pines RV Park (RV SPACES) —(Madison) *From jct I-40 (exit 76) & Hwy 223: Go 3 mi S on Hwy 223, then 1/4 mi W on US 70, then 1/4 mi N on McKenzie Rd.* FACILITIES: 30 sites, accepts full hkup units only, 30 full hkups, (30/50 amps), 50 amps ($), 9 pull-thrus, laundry. Pets welcome. No tents. Open all yr. Big rigs welcome. Rate in 2010 $23 for 2 persons. Phone: (731)422-3682.

JAMESTOWN—A-5

(N) Maple Hill RV Park—(Fentress) *From jct I-40 (exit 317) & US 127: Go 36 mi N on US 127. Enter on R.* ◊◊◊FACILITIES: 22 sites, typical site width 25 ft, 19 full hkups, 3 W&E, (20/30/50 amps), 9 pull-thrus, tenting, dump, laundry. Pets welcome. Partial handicap access. Open all yr. Big rigs welcome. Rate in 2010 $20-25 for 2 persons. Phone: (931)879-3025.

The Great Smoky Mountains National Park is the most visited national park in the United States. The park was named for the smoke-like bluish haze that often envelops these fabled mountains.

JAMESTOWN—Continued

(NW) PICKETT STATE PARK—(Pickett) *From Jamestown: Go 15 mi NE on Hwy 154. Enter on L.*

FACILITIES: 54 sites, 25 ft max RV length, 32 W&E, (20/30 amps), 22 no hkups, tenting, cabins, dump, laundry, ice, picnic tables, grills, wood, controlled access.

RECREATION: rec hall, lake swim, boating, no motors, canoeing, 5 rowboat/3 canoe rentals, lake fishing, bsktball, playground, tennis, hiking trails, v-ball. Rec open to public.

Pets welcome. Partial handicap access. Open all yr. Facilities fully operational Apr 1 - Oct 31. No reservations. MC/VISA/DISC/AMEX.

Phone: (877)260-0010
Address: 4605 Pickett Park Hwy, Jamestown, TN 38556
Lat/Lon: 36.55070/-84.79613
Web: www.state.tn.us

SEE AD TRAVEL SECTION PAGE 714

JASPER—C-5

SHELLMOUND-NICKAJACK DAM RESERVATION (TVA-Nickajack Lake)—(Marion) *From I-24 (exit 158): Go 2-1/4 mi S on paved TVA road to Nickajack Dam Reservation, then E at entrance to Shellmound Recreation Area.* FACILITIES: 50 sites, 50 W&E, (30/50 amps), tenting, dump. RECREATION: lake swim, boating, canoeing, ramp, dock, lake/river fishing, playground. Pets welcome. Partial handicap access. Open Late Apr - Nov 1. Phone: (423)942-9857.

JEFFERSON CITY—D-5

(N) GREENLEE OF MAY SPRINGS—(Grainger) *From jct US 11-E & Hwy 92: Go 5 mi N on Hwy 92, then 4-1/2 mi NE on Hwy 375 (Lake Shore Dr), then follow signs 1/2 mi S.* FACILITIES: 170 sites, 100 full hkups, 35 W&E, (30/50 amps), 35 no hkups, tenting, dump, laundry, ltd groc. RECREATION: lake swim, boating, ramp, dock, lake fishing. Partial handicap access. Open all yr. Phone: (866)828-4802.

(N) TVA/CHEROKEE DAM - CHEROKEE LAKE—(Grainger) *From town: Go 1-1/2 mi W on US-11-E, then follow signs 4-1/2 mi N to Cherokee Dam Reservation.* FACILITIES: 42 sites, 42 W&E, (30 amps), 10 pull-thrus, tenting, dump. RECREATION: lake swim, boating, ramp, lake/river fishing, play equipment. Open Mar 18 - Nov 7. Phone: (423)585-2120.

JELLICO—A-6

INDIAN MOUNTAIN STATE PARK—(Campbell) *From jct I-75 (exit #160 & US 25 NW: Follow signs 3 mi N to park. Enter on R.*

FACILITIES: 49 sites, 49 W&E, (20/30 amps), tenting, dump, picnic tables, grills.

RECREATION: swim pool, boating, no motors, 10 pedal boat rentals, lake fishing, playground, hiking trails.

Pets welcome. Open all yr. Facilities fully operational Apr 1 - Oct 31.

Phone: (423)784-7958
Address: 143 State Park Circle, Jellico, TN 37762
Web: www.state.tn.us

SEE AD TRAVEL SECTION PAGE 714

JOHNSON CITY—D-6

See listings at Bristol, Elizabethton, Kingsport & Unicoi

KINGSPORT—D-6

(E) KOA-BRISTOL/KINGSPORT—(Sullivan) *From I-81 (exit 63 Tri-City Airport) & TN 357: Go 1/2 mi N on TN 357 (Browder Rd), then 3/4 mi SW on Pearl Lane, then 1/4 mi S on Rocky Branch Rd. Enter on R.*

◊◊◊◊FACILITIES: 72 sites, typical site width 35 ft, 72 full hkups, (20/30/50 amps), 50 amps ($), many extd stay sites, 12 pull-thrus, cable TV, WiFi Instant Internet at site, phone Internet central location, tenting, cabins, RV storage, dump, non-guest

KINGSPORT—Continued
KOA-BRISTOL/KINGSPORT—Continued

dump $, laundry, groceries, RV supplies, LP gas by weight/by meter, ice, picnic tables, patios, fire rings, grills, wood.

◊◊◊◊◊RECREATION: rec room/area, equipped pavilion, coin games, swim pool, golf nearby, bsktball, playground, activities, horseshoes, sports field, hiking trails, v-ball.

Pets welcome. Partial handicap access. Open all yr. Big rigs welcome. Escort to site. Clubs welcome. Rate in 2010 $37-64 for 2 persons. MC/VISA/DISC/AMEX/Debit. KOA discount.

Phone: (800)562-7640
Address: 425 Rocky Branch Rd, Blountville, TN 37617
Lat/Lon: 36.50809/-82.44312
Email: bristolkptkoa@charter.net
Web: www.bristolkptkoa.com

SEE AD BRISTOL PAGE 720 AND AD TRAVEL SECTION PAGE 713

(E) WARRIOR'S PATH STATE PARK—(Sullivan) *From I-81 & Hwy 36: Go 1 mi NW on Hwy 36, then 1 mi N on access roads. Enter at end.*

FACILITIES: 134 sites, 94 W&E, (30/50 amps), 40 no hkups, tenting, dump, marine gas, ice, picnic tables, grills.

RECREATION: swim pool, boating, canoeing, ramp, dock, 2 canoe/2 kayak/10 pedal boat rentals, lake fishing, putting green, bsktball, playground, activities, tennis, horseshoes, hiking trails, v-ball.

Pets welcome. Partial handicap access. Open all yr.

Phone: (423)239-8531
Address: 490 Hemlock Rd, Kingsport, TN 37763
Lat/Lon: 36.49767/-82.48375
Web: www.state.tn.us

SEE AD TRAVEL SECTION PAGE 714

Whether you're dreaming about buying a new RV or are actively shopping, 2011 RV Buyer's Guide is your best source. It contains all the information you need to make an intelligent buying decision. Over 450 vehicles are profiled with complete information about construction features, dimensions, popular options, and more, making comparing models easy. To order your copy go to www.woodalls.com/shop.

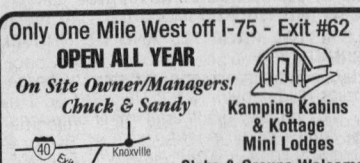

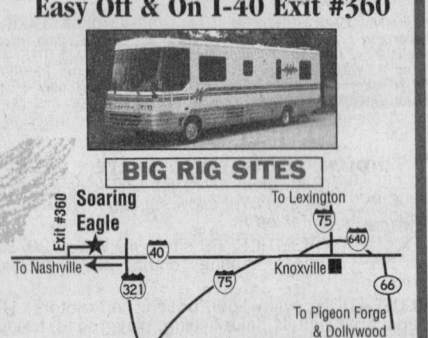

Whether you're dreaming about buying a new RV or are actively shopping, 2011 RV Buyer's Guide is your best source. It contains all the information you need to make an intelligent buying decision. Over 450 vehicles are profiled with complete information about construction features, dimensions, popular options, and more, making comparing models easy. To order your copy go to www.woodalls.com/shop.

KNOXVILLE—B-6

NASHVILLE AREA MAP

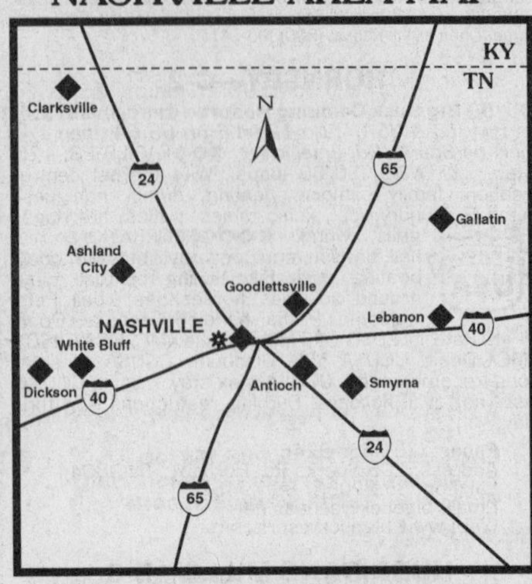

Symbols on map indicate towns within a 40 mi radius of Nashville where campgrounds (diamonds), attractions (flags), & RV service centers & camping supply outlets (gears) are listed. Check listings for more information.

Tell Them Woodall's Sent You!

(N) Escapees Raccoon Valley RV Park—(Knox) *From jct I-640 & I-75: Go 9 mi N on I-75/Raccoon Valley Rd, (exit 117), then 3/4 mi W on Raccoon Valley Road. Enter on L.* ◆◆◆FACILITIES: 64 sites, typical site width 30 ft, 64 full hkups, (20/30/50 amps), 50 amps ($), 38 pull-thrus, dump, laundry. ◆◆RECREATION: swim pool. Pets welcome. No tents. Open all yr. Big rigs welcome. Rate in 2010 $21.50-22.50 for 2 persons. Phone: (865)947-9776.

KNOXVILLE—Continued on next page

The second largest earthquake in American history, the New Madrid Earthquake, occurred in the winter of 1811-12 in northwestern Tennessee. Reelfoot Lake located in Obion and Lake Counties was formed during this earthquake.

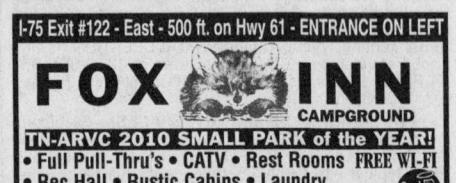

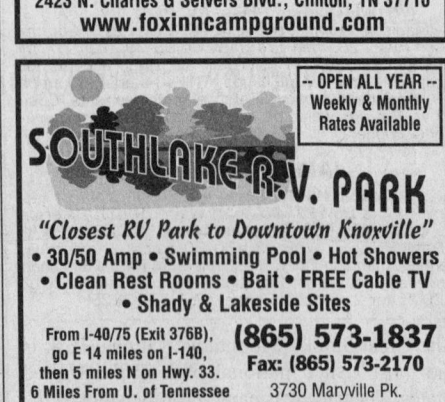

KNOXVILLE—Continued

(S) SOUTHLAKE RV PARK—(Knox) *From jct I-40/75 (exit 376) and I-140: Go 14 mi SE on I-140/162, then 5 mi N on Hwy 33. Enter on L.*

◊◊◊FACILITIES: 123 sites, typical site width 35 ft, 98 full hkups, 25 W&E, (30/50 amps), 50 amps ($), some extd stay sites, 4 pull-thrus, cable TV, phone Internet central location, family camping, tenting, RV storage, dump, non-guest dump $, laundry, ltd groc, RV supplies, ice, picnic tables, grills, wood.

◊◊◊RECREATION: rec room/area, swim pool, boating, dock, lake fishing, fishing supplies, golf nearby, playground, horseshoes.

Pets welcome. Open all yr. Clubs welcome. Rate in 2010 $25-35 for 2 persons. MC/VISA/DISC/AMEX/Debit.

Phone: (865)573-1837
Address: 3730 Maryville Pike, Knoxville, TN 37920
Lat/Lon: 35.87236/-83.94340
Email: southlakervpark@yahoo.com
Web: www.southlakervpark.com

SEE AD PAGE 730

✽ **(E) TENNESSEE RV CAMPING WORLD** *—From jct I-640E & I-40: Go 5 mi E on I-40 (exit 398), then 1 blk N on Strawberry Plains. Enter on L.* SALES: travel trailers, 5th wheels, Class A motorhomes, Class C motorhomes, preowned unit sales. SERVICES: full-time mech, engine/chassis repair, RV appliance repair, body work/collision repair, bus. hrs emerg rd svc, LP gas by weight/by meter, sells parts/accessories, installs hitches. Open all yr. MC/VISA/DISC/AMEX.

Phone: (800)678-2233
Address: 835 Huckleberry Springs Rd, Knoxville, TN 37924
Lat/Lon: 36.00537/-83.76933
Email: sales@tennesseerv.com
Web: www.tennesseerv.com

SEE AD PAGE 730

(N) Volunteer Park—(Knox) *From jct I-640 & I-75: Go 9 mi N on I-75/Raccoon Valley Rd (exit 17), then 1/4 mi W on Raccoon Valley Rd. Enter on L.* ◊◊◊◊FACILITIES: 144 sites, typical site width 35 ft, 100 full hkups, 44 W&E, (30/50 amps), 30 pull-thrus, cable TV, ($), WiFi Instant Internet at site, phone Internet central location, tenting, dump, non-guest dump $, laundry, groceries, RV supplies, LP gas by weight/by meter, ice, picnic tables, fire rings, wood. ◊◊◊◊RECREATION: rec hall, swim pool, wading pool, bsktball, playground, activities, horseshoes, hiking trails, v-ball. Pets welcome. Open all yr. Big rigs welcome. Rate in 2010 $35 for 4 persons. MC/VISA/DISC/Debit. FMCA discount. CCUSA 50% Discount. CCUSA reservations Accepted, CCUSA max stay Unlimited. Discount not valid 2nd week in Oct. Limit 2 pets /site. Drive-ups welcome. No discount on tenting sites.

Phone: (865)938-6600
Address: 9514 Diggs Gap Rd, Heiskell, TN 37754-2172
Lat/Lon: 36.10284/-84.02594
Email: volunteerpark@aol.com
Web: www.volpark.com

Bristol is known as the "Birthplace of Country Music".

LAKE CITY—A-6

(N) MOUNTAIN LAKE MARINA & CAMPGROUND (TOO NEW TO RATE)—(Anderson) *From jct I-75 (exit 128) & US 441: Go 1-1/4 mi SE on US 441, then 2 mi NE on Oak Grove Rd, then 3/4 mi E on Lindsey Mill Circle/Campground Rd. Follow signs. Enter at end.*

FACILITIES: 196 sites, 180 full hkups, 16 W&E, (20/30/50 amps), 50 amps ($), some extd stay sites, 24 pull-thrus, cable TV, ($), WiFi Instant Internet at site, phone Internet central location, tenting, cabins, RV storage, dump, laundry, ltd groc, RV supplies, LP bottle exch, ice, picnic tables, patios, fire rings, wood.

RECREATION: rec hall, rec room/area, coin games, swim pool, boating, canoeing, ramp, dock, 2 pontoon/motorboat rentals, lake fishing, fishing supplies, fishing guides, golf nearby, shuffleboard court 2 shuffleboard courts, activities (wkends), horseshoes, v-ball.

Pets welcome. Partial handicap access. Open all yr. Big rigs welcome. Clubs welcome. Rate in 2010 $30.95-42 for 2 persons. MC/VISA/DISC/Debit. Member ARVC, TNARVC.

Phone: (877)686-2267
Address: 136 Campground Rd, Lake City, TN 37769
Lat/Lon: 36.25901/-84.15082
Email: mountainlakemarina@comcast.net
Web: www.mountainlakemarina.com

SEE AD THIS PAGE AND AD TRAVEL SECTION PAGE 713

• LAWRENCEBURG—C-3

(W) DAVID CROCKETT STATE PARK—(Lawrence) *From town: Go 1/2 mi W on US 64. Enter on R.*

FACILITIES: 112 sites, 107 W&E, (30 amps), 5 no hkups, tenting, dump, ice, picnic tables, grills, controlled access.

RECREATION: pavilion, swim pool, boating, no motors, dock, 7 pedal boat rentals, lake fishing, bsktball, playground, tennis, v-ball. Rec open to public.

Pets welcome. Partial handicap access. Open all yr. Facilities fully operational Apr 1 - Oct 31. Swimming pool and boat rentals from Memorial Day to middle August. MC/VISA/DISC/AMEX.

Phone: (931)762-9408
Address: 1400 W Gaines, Lawrenceburg, TN 38464
Lat/Lon: 35.24499/-87.35172
Web: www.state.tn.us

SEE AD TRAVEL SECTION PAGE 714

LEBANON—B-4

(S) CEDARS OF LEBANON STATE PARK *—(Wilson) From I-40 (exit 238) & US 231: Go 6 mi S on US 231. Enter on L.*

FACILITIES: 117 sites, 38 ft max RV length, 117 W&E, (20/30/50 amps), 45 pull-thrus, tenting, cabins, dump, laundry, ltd groc, ice, picnic tables, fire rings, grills.

RECREATION: rec hall, coin games, swim pool, playground, activities, tennis, horseshoes, sports field, hiking trails, v-ball. Rec open to public.

Pets welcome. Partial handicap access. Open all yr. Facilities fully operational Apr 1 - Oct 31. Camp store closed in winter. MC/VISA/DISC/AMEX.

LEBANON—Continued
CEDARS OF LEBANON STATE PARK—Continued

Phone: (800)713-5180
Address: 328 Cedar Forest Rd., Lebanon, TN 37090
Lat/Lon: 36.09207/-86.33110
Web: www.state.tn.us

SEE AD TRAVEL SECTION PAGE 714

(W) COUNTRYSIDE RV RESORT—(Wilson) *From jct I-40 (exit 232) & Hwy 109: Go 1 block S on TN 109, then 2 mi E on Safari Camp Rd. Enter on R.*

◊◊◊◊FACILITIES: 120 sites, typical site width 35 ft, 68 full hkups, 52 W&E, (20/30/50 amps), 50 amps ($), some extd stay sites (summer), 40 pull-thrus, WiFi Instant Internet at site, phone Internet central location, tenting, dump, laundry, full svc store, RV supplies, LP gas by weight/by meter, ice, picnic tables, fire rings, wood.

◊◊◊RECREATION: equipped pavilion, swim pool, golf nearby, bsktball, playground, tennis, horseshoes, sports field, v-ball.

Pets welcome. Open all yr. Big rigs welcome. Clubs welcome. Rate in 2010 $28.60-30.60 for 2 persons. MC/VISA/Debit. Member ARVC, TNARVC.

Phone: (615)449-5527
Address: 2100 Safari Camp Rd, Lebanon, TN 37090
Lat/Lon: 36.18356/-86.36947
Email: countryside@countrysideresort.com
Web: www.countrysideresort.com

SEE AD NASHVILLE PAGE 738

(SE) Shady Acres Campground—(Wilson) *From jct I-40 (Exit 238) & US-231: Go 2 mi S on US-231. Enter on L.* ◊◊◊FACILITIES: 140 sites, typical site width 30 ft, 135 full hkups, 5 E, (30/50 amps), 50 amps ($), 115 pull-thrus, dump, laundry, ltd groc. ◊◊RECREATION: swim pool, playground. Pets welcome. No tents. Open all yr. Big rigs welcome. Rate in 2010 $20 for 2 persons. Phone: (615)449-5400.

LENOIR CITY—B-6

(N) MELTON HILL DAM (TVA-Melton Hill Reservoir)—(Anderson) *From jct I-40 (exit 364) & Hwy 95: Go 1/2 mi N on Hwy 95, then follow signs E to Melton Hill Dam Reservation.* FACILITIES: 57 sites, 8 full hkups, 33 W&E, 16 no hkups, tenting, dump. RECREATION: lake swim, boating, ramp, lake/river fishing. Partial handicap access. Open all yr. Facilities fully operational May 8 - Sep 8. Phone: (865)986-8329.

(W) SOARING EAGLE CAMPGROUND & RV PARK—(Roane) *From jct I-40 (exit 360) & Buttermilk Rd: Go 100 feet N on Buttermilk Rd. Enter on R.*

◊◊◊FACILITIES: 125 sites, typical site width 28 ft, 76 full hkups, 39 W&E, (20/30/50 amps), 50 amps ($), 10 no hkups, some extd stay sites, 44 pull-thrus, WiFi Instant Internet at site, WiFi Internet central location, family camping, tenting, RV storage, dump, non-guest dump $, laundry, ltd groc, RV supplies, LP gas by weight/by meter, ice, picnic tables, patios, grills, wood.

◊◊◊RECREATION: equipped pavilion, swim pool, boating, canoeing, ramp, dock, lake fishing, golf nearby, bsktball, play equipment, horseshoes, v-ball.

Pets welcome, breed restrict. Partial handicap access. Open all yr. Big rigs welcome. Clubs wel-

SOARING EAGLE CAMPGROUND & RV PARK—Continued on next page

LENOIR CITY—Continued
SOARING EAGLE CAMPGROUND & RV PARK—Continued

come. Rate in 2010 $27-30 for 2 persons. MC/VISA/DISC/Debit. Member ARVC, TNARVC. FMCA discount.

Phone: (865)376-9017
Address: 3152 Buttermilk Rd W, Lenoir City, TN 37771
Lat/Lon: 35.87223/-84.37724
Web: www.soaringeaglecampgroundrvpark.com

SEE AD KNOXVILLE PAGE 730 AND AD TRAVEL SECTION PAGE 713

LEXINGTON—B-2

(N) Beech Lake Family Camping Resort—(Henderson) *From jct I-40 (exit 108) & Hwy 22: Go 6-1/2 mi S on Hwy 22, then 1-1/2 mi W on Crazy Doe Rd. Enter on L.* ◇◇◇FACILITIES: 104 sites, typical site width 30 ft, 100 W&E, (30 amps), 4 no hkups, 7 pull-thrus, family camping, tenting, dump, laundry, ltd groc. ◇◇◇◇RECREATION: lake swim, boating, canoeing, ramp, dock, lake fishing, playground. Pets welcome. Partial handicap access. Age restrict may apply. Open all yr. Facilities fully operational Apr 1 - Nov 30. Rate in 2010 $22-27 for 4 persons. Phone: (731)968-9542.

LIVINGSTON—A-5

LILLYDALE CAMPGROUND (COE-Dale Hollow Lake)—(Clay) *From town: Go 5 mi NE on Hwy 111/294, then 14 mi N on Hwy 294, then 1 mi N on access road.* FACILITIES: 114 sites, 99 W&E, (20/30/50 amps), 15 no hkups, 3 pull-thrus, tenting, dump, laundry. RECREATION: lake swim, boating, ramp, lake fishing, playground. Partial handicap access. Open Apr 15 - Oct 15. Phone: (931)823-4155.

OBEY RIVER CAMPGROUND (COE-Dale Hollow Lake)—(Clay) *From town: Go 16 mi NE on Hwy-42 to the Obey River Bridge.* FACILITIES: 132 sites, 80 W&E, (30/50 amps), 52 no hkups, 13 pull-thrus, tenting, dump, laundry. RECREATION: lake swim, boating, ramp, lake fishing, playground. Partial handicap access. Open Apr 16 - Oct 18. Phone: (931)864-6388.

The Ocoee River in southeastern Tennessee is rated among the top white water recreational rivers in the nation and was the site for the Olympic white water canoe/kayak competition in the 1996 Olympics.

LIVINGSTON—Continued

(NW) STANDING STONE STATE PARK—(Overton) *From town: Go 12 mi NW on Hwy 52, then 2 mi S on Hwy 136. Enter on L.*

FACILITIES: 36 sites, 36 W&E, (20/30/50 amps), tenting, cabins, dump, laundry, ice, picnic tables, grills.

RECREATION: rec hall, equipped pavilion, swim pool, wading pool, boating, electric motors only, 10 rowboat rentals, lake/stream fishing, bsktball, playground, activities, tennis, sports field, hiking trails, v-ball. Rec open to public.

Pets welcome. Partial handicap access. Open all yr. MC/VISA/DISC/AMEX.

Phone: (800)73-5157
Address: 1674 Standing Stone Park Rd., Hilham, TN 38568
Lat/Lon: 36.47101/-85.41536
Web: state.tn.us

SEE AD TRAVEL SECTION PAGE 714

WILLOW GROVE (COE-Dale Hollow Lake)—(Clay) *From town: Go 5 mi NE on Hwy 111/294, then 16 mi N on Hwy 294. Enter at end.* FACILITIES: 83 sites, 62 W&E, (30/50 amps), 21 no hkups, tenting, dump, laundry. RECREATION: lake swim, boating, ramp, lake fishing, playground. Partial handicap access. Open May 15 - Sep 6. Phone: (931)823-4285.

LOUDON—B-6

(E) EXPRESS RV PARK (RV SPACES)—(Loudon) *From jct I-75 (exit 72) & Hwy 72: Go 1/4 mi W on Hwy 72. Enter on R.*

FACILITIES: 15 sites, 15 W&E, (30/50 amps), 16 pull-thrus, WiFi Instant Internet at site, tenting, dump, non-guest dump $, laundry.

RECREATION: swim pool.

Pets welcome. Open all yr. Rate in 2010 $20-25 for 2 persons. MC/VISA/DISC/AMEX/Debit.

Phone: (865)458-5855
Address: 15100 Hwy 72, Loudon, TN 37774
Lat/Lon: 35.73436/-84.39820

SEE AD THIS PAGE AND AD TRAVEL SECTION PAGE 713

LYNCHBURG—C-4

(S) Lynchburg Wilderness RV Park—(Moore) *From Lynchburg's only traffic light on Hwy 55 (Majors Blvd): Go 2 blocks west on Majors Blvd, then 1/2 mi S on Elm St which turns into Main St. Enter on L.* ◇◇FACILITIES: 48 sites, 48 full hkups, (20/30/50 amps), 10 pull-thrus, tenting, laundry. ◇◇RECREATION: stream fishing. Pets welcome. Partial handicap access. Open all yr. Rate in 2010 $20-35 per vehicle. Member ARVC, TNARVC. Phone: (931)580-2680. FMCA discount.

MANCHESTER—B-4

(S) KOA-MANCHESTER—(Coffee) *From jct I-24 (exit 114) & US 41: Go 100 yards on US 41, then 1/2 mi N on Kampground Rd (Frontage Rd). Enter on R.*

◇◇◇◇◇FACILITIES: 54 sites, typical site width 33 ft, 40 full hkups, 10 E, (20/30/50 amps), 4 no hkups, 42 pull-thrus, cable TV, WiFi Instant Internet at site, family camping, tenting, cabins, dump, non-guest dump $, laundry, full svc store, RV supplies, LP gas by weight/by meter, ice, picnic tables, patios, fire rings, grills, wood.

◇◇◇◇◇RECREATION: rec room/area, pavilion, swim pool, spray ground, hot tub, pond/stream fishing, fishing supplies, putting green, golf nearby, bsktball, 2 bike rentals, playground, activities, (wkends), horseshoes, sports field, hiking trails, v-ball, local tours.

Pets welcome. Partial handicap access. Open all yr. Big rigs welcome. Escort to site. Clubs welcome. Green Friendly. Rate in 2010 $32-65 for 2 persons. MC/VISA/DISC/AMEX/Debit. Member ARVC. KOA discount.

Phone: (800)562-7785
Address: 586 Campground Rd, Manchester, TN 37355
Lat/Lon: 35.46310/-86.05401
Email: manchesterkoa@earthlink.net
Web: www.koa.com

SEE AD THIS PAGE

MILITARY PARK (FAMCAMP-Arnold AFB)—(Franklin) *From I-24 (exit 117): Go W on Wattendorf Hwy past Gate 2, then S on Pump Station Rd, then 1-1/2 mi W on Northshore Dr. On base. Enter on R.* FACILITIES: 83 sites, typical site width 14 ft, 25 ft max RV length, 26 W&E, (30/50 amps), 57 no hkups, 2 pull-thrus, tenting, dump, laundry, ltd groc. RECREATION: lake swim, boating, canoeing, ramp, dock, lake fishing, playground. Open all yr. Phone: (931)454-4520.

(W) OLD STONE FORT STATE ARCHAEOLOGICAL AREA—(Coffee) *From jct Hwy 53 & US 41: Go 1/2 mi W on US 41. Enter on L.*

FACILITIES: 51 sites, 51 W&E, tenting, dump, picnic tables, grills, controlled access.

RECREATION: boating, electric motors only, canoeing, lake/river fishing, playground, activities, hiking trails.

Pets welcome. Partial handicap access. Open all yr. No reservations. MC/VISA/DISC/AMEX.

Phone: (931)723-5073
Address: 732 Stone Fort Dr., Manchester, TN 37355
Lat/Lon: 35.49192/-86.10664
Web: www.state.tn.us

SEE AD TRAVEL SECTION PAGE 714

MEMPHIS—C-1

See listings at Millington, TN; West Memphis, AR; Southhaven, Tunica & Coldwater & Robinsonville, MS

MEMPHIS—Continued on next page

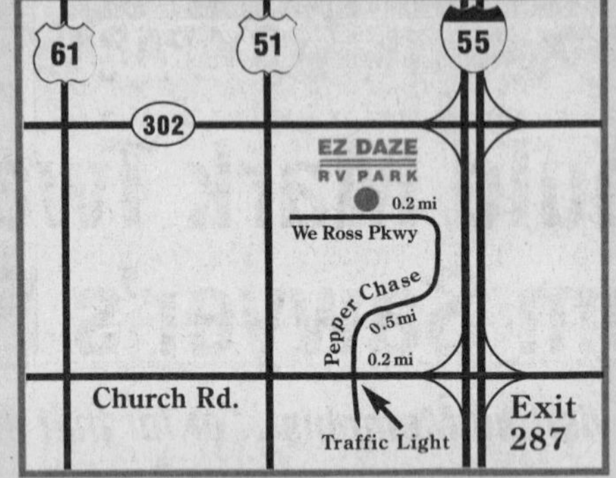

MEMPHIS—Continued

(S) AGRICENTER RV PARK—(Shelby) *From jct I-40 & Germantown Rd (W'bound exit 16A/E'bound exit 16): Go 4 mi S on Germantown Pkwy, then 2/10 mi W on Timber Creek Rd. Enter on R.*

WELCOME

FACILITIES: 400 sites, typical site width 40 ft, 146 full hkups, 254 W&E, (30/50 amps), some extd stay sites, 400 pull-thrus, WiFi Instant Internet at site, WiFi Internet central location, dump, portable dump, laundry, ltd groc, ice.

RECREATION: pond fishing, golf nearby, activities, (wkends), sports field, hiking trails.

Pets welcome. No tents. Open all yr. Clubs welcome. MC/VISA/DISC/AMEX/Debit.

Phone: (901)355-1977
Address: 7777 Walnut Grove Rd, Memphis, TN 38120
Lat/Lon: 35.12727/-89.79866
Email: mhoggard@agricenter.org
Web: www.agricenter.org

SEE AD PAGE 732

MEMPHIS—Continued on next page

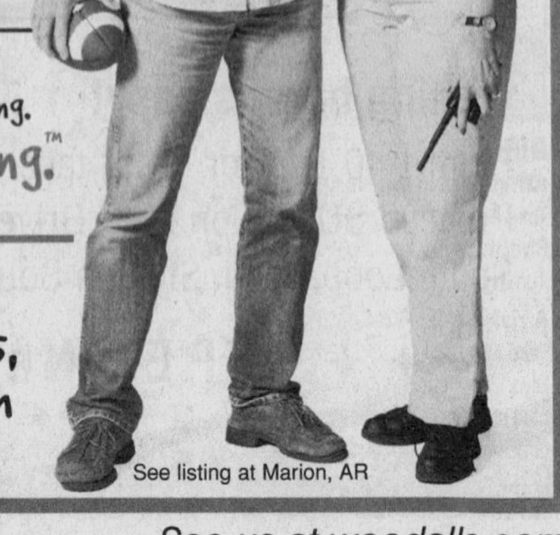

MEMPHIS—Continued

✲ **Davis Motorhome/D & N Camper Sales**—*From jct I-240 & I-55: Go 1/2 mi S on I-55 (exit 5B) & US 51, then 1 block E on Brooks Rd.* SALES: travel trailers, 5th wheels, Class A motorhomes, Class C motorhomes, pre-owned unit sales. SERVICES: full-time mech, RV appliance repair, body work/collision repair, sells parts/accessories. Open all yr. MC/VISA/DISC/AMEX.

Phone: (800)772-3414
Address: 1145 East Brooks Rd, Memphis, TN 38116
Lat/Lon: 35.06138/-90.02590
Email: jody@dandncampersales.com
Web: dandncampersales.com

(S) Elvis Presley Blvd RV Park—(Shelby) *From jct I-240 & I-55: Go 1/2 mi S on I-55 (exit 5B) & US 51 (Elvis Presley Blvd), then 1-1/2 mi S on US 51 (Elvis Presley Blvd). Enter on R.* ◇◇FACILITIES: 60 sites, typical site width 20 ft, 60 full hkups, (20/30/50 amps), 50 amps ($), 2 pull-thrus, tenting, dump, laundry. Pets welcome. Open all yr. Rate in 2010 $32-36 for 2 persons. Phone: (901)332-3633.

⚑ **(S) GRACELAND**—*From jct I-240 & I-55: Go 1/2 mi S on I-55 (exit 5B) & US 51 (Elvis Presley Blvd), then 1-1/4 mi S on US 51 (Elvis Presley Blvd). Enter on R.* Elvis Presley's Graceland, where the King of Rock 'n Roll called Home. Tour Elvis' home, see videos, photos, stage costumes & an amazing display of gold & platinum awards. Tour Elvis' automobile museum & board The Lisa Marie, Elvis' custom jet. Open all yr. MC/VISA/DISC/AMEX.

MEMPHIS—Continued
GRACELAND—Continued

Phone: (800)238-2000
Address: 3717 Elvis Presley Blvd, Memphis, TN 38116
Lat/Lon: 35.04626/-90.02508

SEE AD THIS PAGE

(E) Memphis East Campground—(Shelby) *From jct I-40 (exit 20) & Canada Rd: Go 3/4 mi S on Canada Rd, then 1/4 mi E on Monroe St. Enter on L.* ◇◇◇FACILITIES: 82 sites, typical site width 22 ft, 64 full hkups, 10 W&E, 8 E, (20/30/50 amps), 50 amps ($), 38 pull-thrus, tenting, dump, laundry, groceries. ◇◇RECREATION: swim pool, pond fishing, playground. Pets welcome. Partial handicap access. Open all yr. Rate in 2010 $24.50-27 for 2 persons. Phone: (901) 388-3053.

MEMPHIS KOA—*From jct Mississippi River Bridge & I-40: Follow I-40/I-55 to I-55 N Cut off, then 7 mi N on I-55 to exit 14, then follow camping logo signs to entrance on west service road. Enter on R.*

SEE PRIMARY LISTING AT MARION, AR AND AD PAGE 734

Memphis, Tennessee is the site of Sun Studios... Elvis Presley's first recording studio.

MEMPHIS—Continued

(S) MEMPHIS/GRACELAND RV PARK & CAMPGROUND—(Shelby) *From jct I-240 & I-55: Go 1/2 mi S on I-55 (exit 51B) & US 51 (Elvis Presley Blvd), then 1 mi S on US 51 (Elvis Presley Blvd). Enter on R.*

◇◇◇◇FACILITIES: 106 sites, typical site width 22 ft, 71 full hkups, 16 W&E, (20/30/50 amps), 19 no hkups, some extd stay sites, 31 pull-thrus, WiFi Instant Internet at site, phone Internet central location, tenting, cabins, dump, laundry, ltd groc, RV supplies, LP gas by weight/by meter, ice, picnic tables.

◇◇◇RECREATION: equipped pavilion, swim pool, golf nearby, bsktball, playground, horseshoes, sports field, v-ball, local tours.

Pets welcome. Partial handicap access. Open all yr. Big rigs welcome. Clubs welcome. Rate in 2010 $34-39 for 2 persons. MC/VISA/DISC/AMEX/Debit.

MEMPHIS/GRACELAND RV PARK & CAMPGROUND—Continued on next page

The Tulip Poplar was chosen as the state tree because it was used extensively by the Tennessee pioneers to construct their houses, barns and other buildings.

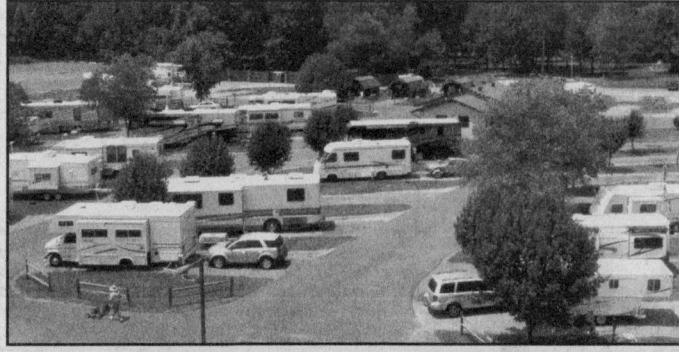

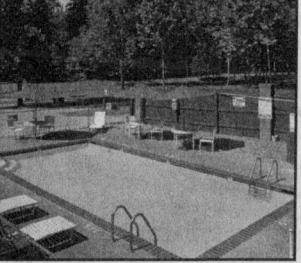

MEMPHIS—Continued
MEMPHIS/GRACELAND RV PARK & CAMPGROUND—Continued

Phone: (901)396-7125
Address: 3691 Elvis Presley Blvd, Memphis, TN 38116
Lat/Lon: 35.04905/-90.02690
Web: www.memphisgracelandrvpark.com

SEE AD PAGE 735 AND AD TRAVEL SECTION PAGE 713

(N) **REDWOOD ESTATES** (RV SPACES) —(Shelby) *From jct I-40 (exit 2A) & I-240: Go 3 mi N on US 51/North Thomas St. Enter on R.*

WELCOME

FACILITIES: 22 sites, accepts full hkup units only, 22 full hkups, (30/50 amps), phone on-site Internet (needs activ), laundry.

RECREATION: bsktball.

Pets welcome, breed restrict. No tents. Open all yr.

Phone: (901)358-0485
Address: 4144 North Thomas St, Memphis, TN 38127
Lat/Lon: 35.23859/-90.01136
Web: www.redwoodestatesmhc.com

SEE AD PAGE 734 AND AD MILLINGTON THIS PAGE AND AD TUNICA, MS PAGE 446

(SW) **T.O. FULLER STATE PARK**—(Shelby) *From I-55 & US 61: Go 2 mi S on US 61, then 6 mi W on Mitchell Rd, then S on Plant Rd, then 1/2 mi E on Boxtown Rd. Enter on L.*

WELCOME

FACILITIES: 45 sites, 45 W&E, (30/50 amps), 19 pull-thrus, tenting, dump, laundry, picnic tables, fire rings, grills.

RECREATION: equipped pavilion, swim pool, putting green, bsktball, playground, tennis, hiking trails.

Pets welcome. Partial handicap access. Open all yr. No reservations. MC/VISA/DISC/AMEX.

Phone: (901)543-7581
Address: 1500 Mitchell Rd., Memphis, TN 38109
Lat/Lon: 35.05959/-90.11403
Web: www.state.tn.us

SEE AD TRAVEL SECTION PAGE 714

Staying close to home next year? Pre-order the 2012 Directory in a smaller regional version. It contains all the great information Woodall's North American Directory contains, but in a handy to-go version, specific to the states or provinces you need.

MILLINGTON—C-1

(W) **MEEMAN-SHELBY FOREST STATE PARK**—(Shelby) *From I-240 (exit 2A): Go 3 mi N on US 51, then 8 mi N on Watkins N, then 1 mi W on Locke-Cuba, then 1 mi N on Bluff Rd.*

WELCOME

FACILITIES: 49 sites, 40 ft max RV length, 49 W&E, (20/30/50 amps), tenting, cabins, dump, picnic tables, fire rings, grills.

RECREATION: rec hall, pavilion, swim pool, wading pool, boating, electric motors only, ramp, dock, 25 rowboat rentals, lake fishing, playground, sports field, hiking trails.

Pets welcome. Partial handicap access. Open all yr. MC/VISA/DISC/AMEX.

Phone: (800)471-5293
Address: 910 Riddick Rd, Millington, TN 38053
Lat/Lon: 35.34374/-90.03257
Web: www.state.tn.us

SEE AD TRAVEL SECTION PAGE 714

(E) **SHADY OAKS COMMUNITY** (RV SPACES)—(Shelby) *From jct US 51 & Navy Rd: Go 1 mi E on Navy Rd, then 1/2 block S on Raleigh Millington Rd. Enter on L.*

WELCOME

FACILITIES: 35 sites, typical site width 30 ft, accepts full hkup units only, 35 full hkups, (20/30 amps), heater not allowed, phone on-site Internet (needs activ), laundry, patios.

RECREATION: golf nearby, play equipment.

Pets welcome, breed restrict. No tents. Open all yr. No restrooms.

Phone: (901)872-3168
Address: 7860 Raleigh Millington Rd, Millington, TN 38053
Lat/Lon: 35.34046/-89.89381
Email: shadyoaks@bigriver.net
Web: www.shadyoaksmhc.com

SEE AD THIS PAGE AND AD MEMPHIS PAGE 734 AND AD TUNICA, MS PAGE 446

MORRISTOWN—D-5

(E) **Heron Point Marina & Campground**—(Hamblen) *From jct Hwy 25E & Hwy 11E: Go 1-1/2 mi NE on Hwy 11E, then 2-1/4 mi N on Mahle Dr - Cedar Creek Rd (2nd Stop light), then 1-1/2 mi E on Brights Pike (3 way stop), then 3/4 mi W on Fall Creek Dock Rd. Enter at end.* ◊◊◊FACILITIES: 60 sites, typical site width 25 ft, 32 ft max RV length, 30 full hkups, 15 W&E, (20/30/50 amps), 15 no hkups, 13 pull-thrus, tenting, ltd groc. ◊◊◊RECREATION: lake swim, boating, canoeing, ramp, dock, lake fishing, playground. Pets welcome. Open May 1 - Oct 31. Rate in 2010 $28-35 for 4 persons. Phone: (423)581-4701.

Dolly Parton, singer, is from Tennessee.

MORRISTOWN—Continued

(W) **PANTHER CREEK STATE PARK**—(Hamblen) *From jct US 11E & Hwy 342: Go 2 mi W on Hwy 342. Enter on R.*

WELCOME

FACILITIES: 51 sites, 40 ft max RV length, 51 W&E, (20/30 amps), tenting, dump, laundry, picnic tables, patios, fire rings, grills, controlled access.

RECREATION: pavilion, swim pool, wading pool, boating, ramp, lake fishing, bsktball, playground, tennis, sports field, hiking trails, v-ball. Rec open to public.

Pets welcome. Partial handicap access. Open all yr.

Phone: (423)587-7046
Address: 2010 Panther Creek Rd., Morristown, TN 37814
Lat/Lon: 36.20670/-83.40650
Web: www.state.tn.us

SEE AD TRAVEL SECTION PAGE 714

MT. JULIET—B-4

CEDAR CREEK CAMPGROUND (COE-Old Hickory Lake)—(Wilson) *From jct Hwy 171 & US 70W: Go 1 mi W on US 70, then 2 mi N on Nonaville Rd, then 1 mi E on Saundersville Rd. Enter on L.* FACILITIES: 59 sites, typical site width 14 ft, 59 W&E, (30/50 amps), 4 pull-thrus, tenting, dump, laundry, ltd groc. RECREATION: lake swim, boating, ramp, dock, lake fishing, playground. Partial handicap access. Open Apr 1 - Oct 28. Phone: (615)754-4947.

NASHVILLE—B-4

KNOXVILLE AREA MAP

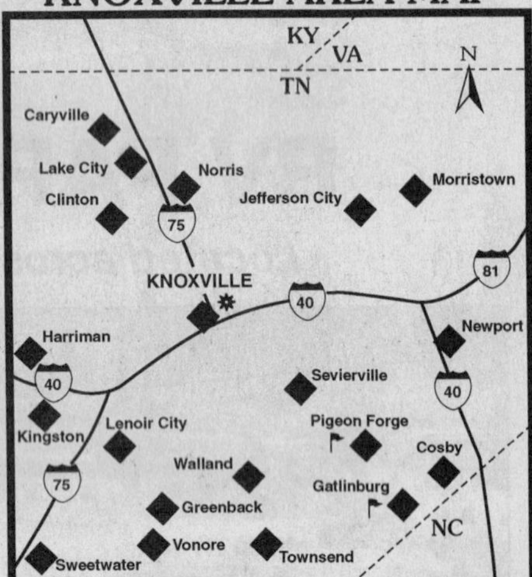

Symbols on map indicate towns within a 50 mi radius of Knoxville where campgrounds (diamonds), attractions (flags), & RV service centers & camping supply outlets (gears) are listed. Check listings for more information.

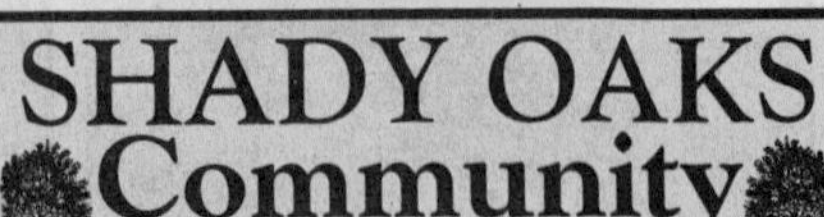

NASHVILLE—Continued on next page

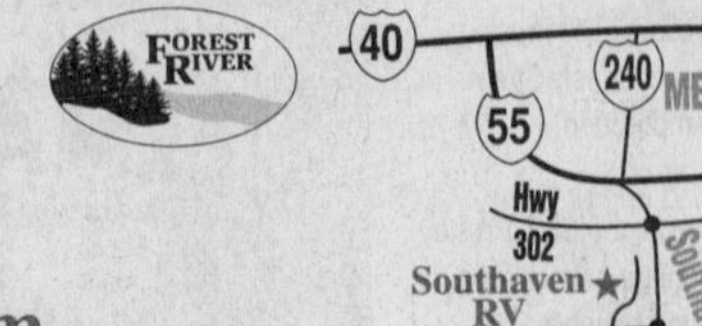

NASHVILLE—Continued

✲ **(NE) Cullum & Maxey Camping Center**—*From I-40 E (exit 215-Briley Pkwy): Go 5-1/2 mi N on Briley Pkwy, then 1/4 mi W on McGavock Pike, then 1 mi N on Music Valley Dr. Enter on L.* SALES: travel trailers, 5th wheels, Class A motorhomes, Class C motorhomes, pre-owned unit sales. SERVICES: full-time mech, engine/chassis repair, RV appliance repair, body work/collision repair, LP gas by weight/by meter, dump station, sells parts/accessories, installs hitches. Open all yr. MC/VISA.

Phone: (615)889-1600
Address: 2614 Music Valley Dr, Nashville, TN 37214
Lat/Lon: 36.23302/-86.70243

WELCOME

NASHVILLE COUNTRY RV PARK—(Sumner) *From I-24 West & I-65 North: Go 10 mi N on I-65, (exit 98) US31 W, then 1-3/4 mi N on US 31 W. Enter on L.*

◆◆◆◆FACILITIES: 95 sites, typical site width 30 ft, 83 full hkups, 12 W&E, (20/30/50 amps), 50 amps ($), some extd stay sites, 57 pull-thrus, cable TV, WiFi Instant Internet at site, phone Internet central location, family camping, tenting, RV's/park model rentals, cabins, RV storage, dump, non-guest dump $, laundry, ltd groc, RV supplies, LP gas by weight/by meter, LP bottle exch, ice, picnic tables, patios, grills, wood.

NASHVILLE COUNTRY RV PARK—Continued on next page

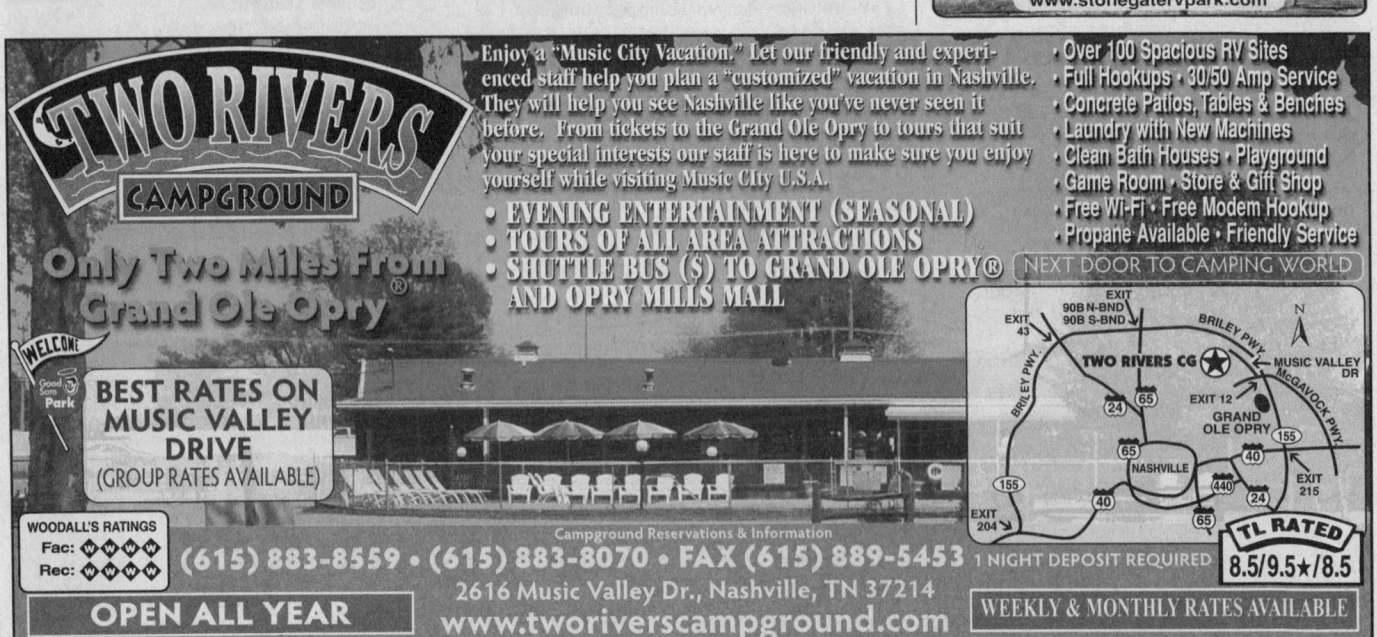

Wilma Rudolph, athlete, was from Tennessee.

NASHVILLE—Continued
NASHVILLE COUNTRY RV PARK—Continued

◊◊◊◊◊RECREATION: rec room/area, equipped pavilion, swim pool, stream fishing, golf nearby, playground, shuffleboard court 3 shuffleboard courts, activities, horseshoes, hiking trails, local tours.

Pets welcome. Open all yr. Pet playground. Big rigs welcome. Clubs welcome. Green Friendly. Rate in 2010 $34.50-39.50 for 2 persons. MC/VISA/Debit. Member ARVC, TN ARVC. FCRV discount. FMCA discount. CCUSA 50% Discount. CCUSA reservations Recommended, CCUSA max stay Unlimited, CCUSA disc. not avail Th, CCUSA disc. not avail F,Sa. Not available special events-call for details. 10% discount Thu thru Sat. $5 surcharge for big rig or premium sites. Cash only 3 days or less.

Phone: (615)859-0348
Address: 1200 Louisville Hwy, Goodlettsville, TN 37072
Lat/Lon: 36.37355/-86.70929
Email: camp@nashvillecountryrvpark.com
Web: www.nashvillecountryrvpark.com

SEE AD PAGE 738

(NE) Nashville KOA—(Davidson) *From jct I-40 (exit 215) & Briley Pkwy: Go 5-1/2 mi N on Briley Pkwy (exit 12). S'Bnd: From I-65N (Opryland exit 90B) & Briley Pkwy: Go 4-1/2 mi S on Briley Pkwy (exit 12), then 1/4 mi W on McGavock Pike, then 2 mi N on Music Valley Dr. Enter on L.* ◊◊◊◊FACILITIES: 389 sites, typical site width 30 ft, 271 full hkups, 62 W&E, (20/30/50 amps), 50 amps ($), 56 no hkups, 112 pull-thrus, family camping, tenting, dump, laundry, full svc store. ◊◊◊◊◊RECREATION: swim pool, playground. Pets welcome. Partial handicap access. Open all yr. Big rigs welcome. Member ARVC, TN ARVC. Phone: (800)KOA-7789. KOA discount.

(E) NASHVILLE SHORES RV CAMPGROUND (NOT VISITED)—(Davidson) *W'bnd from jct I-40 (exit 221B) & Old Hickory. E'bnd I-40 (exit 221B) & Old Hickory: Go 1/2 mi S on Old Hickory. Enter on L.*

FACILITIES: 125 sites, typical site width 24 ft, 30 ft max RV length, 100 full hkups, 25 E, (50 amps), WiFi Instant Internet at site, family camping, tenting, cabins, laundry, ltd groc, RV supplies, ice, picnic tables, fire rings, wood, controlled access.

RECREATION: rec hall, equipped pavilion, lake swim, ramp, 20 pontoon rentals, lake fishing, fishing supplies, playground, activities, horseshoes, hiking trails, v-ball. Rec open to public.

Pets welcome, breed restrict. Open Apr 1 - Nov 1. Clubs welcome. Rate in 2010 $30-50 per vehicle. MC/VISA/DISC/AMEX/Debit.

Text 107990 to (440)725-8687 to see our Visual Tour.

Phone: (615)889-7050
Address: 4001 Bell Rd, Hermitage, TN 37076
Lat/Lon: 36.16393/-86.60088
Email: info@nashvilleshores.com
Web: www.nashvilleshores.com

SEE AD PAGE 737

(E) NASHVILLE SHORES WATER PARK—*W'bnd from jct I-40 (exit 221B) & Old Hickory: Go 1/2 mi S on Old Hickory. Enter on L.* Located on Percy Priest Lake. Brave the wavepool or float in Breaker Bay. Enjoy our 8 water slides or cool off with "Giant Bucket of Fun" or chill by the 3 pools, volleyball or enjoy a cruise. There is all-day, all-you-can-play water fun for everyone. Open Mid May - Mid Sep. MC/VISA/DISC/AMEX/Debit.

Phone: (615)889-7050
Address: 4001 Bell Road, Hermitage, TN 37076
Lat/Lon: 36.16393/-86.60088
Email: info@nashvilleshores.com

SEE AD PAGE 737

(NE) Nashville's Jellystone Park—(Davidson) *Westbound: From I-40E (exit 215-Briley Pkwy): Go 5-1/2 mi N on Briley Pkwy. Southbound: From I-65 N & Briley Pkwy (Opryland exit): Go 4-1/2 mi S on Briley Pkwy. Both From Briley Pkwy: Go 1/4 mi W on McGavock Pike, then 1 mi N on Music Valley Dr. Enter on L.* ◊◊◊◊FACILITIES: 263 sites, typical site width 35 ft, 171 full hkups, 62 W&E, (20/30/50 amps), 50 amps ($), 30 no hkups, 238 pull-thrus, family camping, tenting, dump, laundry, full svc store. ◊◊◊◊◊RECREATION: swim pool, playground. Pets welcome, breed restrict. Partial handicap access. Open all yr. Big rigs welcome. Green Friendly. Rate in 2010 $43-56 for 2 persons. Member ARVC, TN ARVC. Phone: (800)547-4480. FMCA discount.

NASHVILLE—Continued

STONEGATE RV PARK (NOT VISITED)—(Wilson) *From jct I-40 & Exit 226B: Go 1/4 N Exit 226B. Enter on R.*

FACILITIES: 50 sites, typical site width 40 ft, accepts full hkup units only, 50 full hkups, (30/50 amps), some extd stay sites, cable TV, WiFi Internet central location, RV storage.

RECREATION: rec room/area, swim pool, golf nearby, playground.

Pets welcome, breed restrict, size restrict, quantity restrict. No tents. Open all yr. No restrooms. Big rigs welcome. Escort to site. Rate in 2010 $35 for 4 persons. MC/VISA/Debit.

Phone: (877)590-8646
Address: 699 Stonegate Dr, Mt Juliet, TN 37122
Lat/Lon: 36.17554/-86.51219
Email: stonegatervpark@tds.net
Web: www.stonegatervpark.com

SEE AD PAGE 738

TENNESSEE STATE PARKS DEPARTMENT OF ENVIRONMENT AND CONSERVATION—

Phone: (615)532-4580
Address: 401 Church St-L & C Tower Flr, Nashville, TN 37243
Web: www.tnstateparks.com

SEE AD TRAVEL SECTION PAGE 714

(NE) TWO RIVERS CAMPGROUND—(Davidson) *W'bnd: From I-40E (exit 215-Briley Pkwy): Go 5-1/2 mi N on Briley Pkwy (exit 12) S'bnd: From I-65N & Briley Pkwy (Opryland exit) 90 B: Go 4-1/2 mi S on Briley Pkwy. Both From Briley Pkwy: Go 1/4 mi W on McGavock Pike, then 1 mi N on Music Valley Dr. Enter on L.*

◊◊◊◊FACILITIES: 104 sites, typical site width 30 ft, 72 full hkups, 32 W&E, (30/50 amps), 50 amps ($), 11 pull-thrus, WiFi Instant Internet at site, phone Internet central location, family camping, dump, laundry, full svc store, RV supplies, LP gas by weight/by meter, ice, picnic tables, patios.

◊◊◊◊RECREATION: rec room/area, coin games, swim pool, golf nearby, bsktball, playground, activities, local tours.

Pets welcome. Partial handicap access. No tents. Open all yr. Big rigs welcome. Clubs welcome. Rate in 2010 $36-46 for 2 persons. MC/VISA/DISC/Debit. Member ARVC, TNARVC. FMCA discount.

Text 107901 to (440)725-8687 to see our Visual Tour.

Phone: (615)883-8559
Address: 2616 Music Valley Dr, Nashville, TN 37214
Lat/Lon: 36.23443/-86.70377
Email: tworiverscamp@bellsouth.net
Web: www.tworiverscampground.com

SEE AD PAGE 738 AND AD TRAVEL SECTION PAGE 713

US ARMY CORPS OF ENGINEERS/VOLUNTEER CLEARING HOUSE—Beautiful lakes, parks & visitor centers! the US Army offers nationwide volunteer opportunities to help in campgrounds & visitor centers, maintain park facilities, trails, wildlife habitat & more. Free campsite often provided.

Phone: (800)865-8337
Address: 801 Broadway, A-626, Nashville, TN 37202
Email: Volunteer.Clearinghouse@lrn02.usace.army.mil
Web: www.corpslakes.us/volunteer

SEE AD DISCOVER SECTION PAGE 47

NEWPORT—D-5

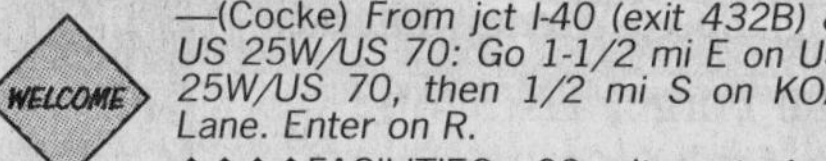

(W) KOA-NEWPORT I-40/SMOKY MTNS—(Cocke) *From jct I-40 (exit 432B) & US 25W/US 70: Go 1-1/2 mi E on US 25W/US 70, then 1/2 mi S on KOA Lane. Enter on R.*

◊◊◊◊FACILITIES: 99 sites, typical site width 35 ft, 47 full hkups, 52 W&E, (20/30/50 amps), 50 amps ($), 45 pull-thrus, cable TV, ($), WiFi Internet at site, family camping, tenting, RV's/park model rentals, cabins, RV storage, dump, non-guest dump $, laundry, groceries, RV supplies, LP gas by meter, ice, picnic tables, wood.

NEWPORT—Continued
KOA-NEWPORT I-40/SMOKY MTNS—Continued

◊◊◊RECREATION: equipped pavilion, swim pool, golf nearby, bsktball, playground, horseshoes, v-ball. Rec open to public.

Pets welcome. Open all yr. Big rigs welcome. Escort to site. Clubs welcome. Rate in 2010 $32-37 for 2 persons. MC/VISA/Debit. KOA discount.

Phone: (800)562-9016
Address: 240 KOA Lane, Newport, TN 37821
Lat/Lon: 35.97027/-83.22626
Email: k644@bellsouth.net
Web: www.koa.com

SEE AD THIS PAGE

NORRIS—A-6

BIG RIDGE STATE PARK—(Union) *From jct I-75 (exit 122) & Hwy 61: Go 12 mi E on Hwy 61. Enter on L.*

FACILITIES: 50 sites, 50 W&E, (30/50 amps), 3 pull-thrus, tenting, cabins, dump, laundry, picnic tables, fire rings, grills.

RECREATION: lake swim, boating, canoeing, ramp, 6 rowboat/5 canoe/5 pedal boat rentals, lake fishing, bsktball, playground, activities, tennis, sports field, hiking trails, v-ball.

Pets welcome. Partial handicap access. Open all yr. Facilities fully operational Apr 1 - Oct 31. No reservations. Bathhouses closed winter months. MC/VISA/DISC/AMEX.

Phone: (800)471-5305
Address: 1015 Big Ridge Park Rd, Maynardville, TN 37807
Lat/Lon: 36.24250/-83.93055
Web: www.state.tn.us

SEE AD TRAVEL SECTION PAGE 714

(E) LOYSTON POINT (TVA - Norris Reservoir)—(Anderson) *From jct US-441 & Hwy-61: Go 2 mi E on Hwy-61, then 3 3/4 mi N on ParkRd, then 1/2 mi E on Boy Scout Rd, then follow signs 2-1/2 mi NE/S/E onLoyston Point Rd.* FACILITIES: 64 sites, 39 E, 25 no hkups, 8 pull-thrus, tenting, dump. RECREATION: lake swim, boating, ramp, lake fishing. Open Mid Apr - Mid Oct. Phone: (865)494-9369.

NORRIS DAM STATE PARK—(Campbell) *From jct I-75 (exit 128): Go 2-1/2 mi S on US 441. Enter on R.*

FACILITIES: 85 sites, 35 ft max RV length, 75 W&E, (20/30 amps), 10 no hkups, tenting, cabins, dump, laundry, marine gas, picnic tables, grills.

RECREATION: pavilion, boating, ramp, dock, motorboat rentals, lake fishing, playground, activities, tennis, hiking trails, v-ball. Rec open to public.

Pets welcome. Partial handicap access. Open all yr. Facilities fully operational Apr 1 - Oct 31. some activities available in season only.

Phone: (800)543-9335
Address: 125 Village Green Cir, Lake City, TN 37769
Web: www.state.tn.us

SEE AD TRAVEL SECTION PAGE 714

ONEIDA—A-6

BIG SOUTH FORK NAT'L. RIVER & REC. AREA (Bandy Creek Campground)—(Scott) *From jct US 27 & Hwy 297: Go 15 mi W on Hwy 297. Enter on R.* FACILITIES: 178 sites, 100 W&E, 78 no hkups, tenting, dump. RECREATION: swim pool, boating, no motors, canoeing, river fishing, play equipment. Partial handicap access. Open all yr. Facilities fully operational Apr 1 - Oct 31. Phone: (423)569-9778.

PARIS—A-2

(E) Buchanan Resort—(Henry) *From jct US 641 & US 79: Go 12 mi NE on US 79, then 1-1/2 mi SE on Antioch Rd, then 3/4 mi NE on Buchanan Resort Rd. Enter on L.* ◊◊FACILITIES: 50 sites, typical site width

Buchanan Resort—Continued on next page

PARIS—Continued
Buchanan Resort—Continued

35 ft, 38 ft max RV length, 50 W&E, (20/30/50 amps), 4 pull-thrus, tenting, dump. ◆◆◆RECREATION: swim pool, lake swim, boating, ramp, dock, lake/river fishing, playground. Pets welcome. Open Mar 15 - Nov 1. Rate in 2010 $22 for 4 persons. Phone: (731)642-2828.

Eagles Nest Campground—(Henry) *From jct Hwy 641 & Hwy 79: Go 13 mi E on Hwy 79, then 3/4 mi S on Eagle Nest Rd. Enter on R.* ◆◆◆◆FACILITIES: 33 sites, typical site width 35 ft, 33 full hkups, (20/30/50 amps), family camping, laundry. Pets welcome. No tents. Open all yr. Rate in 2010 $30 for 2 persons. Phone: (731)363-2692.

(E) KOA-Paris Landing—(Henry) *From jct US 641 & US 79: Go 12 mi NE on US 79, then 1/4 mi SE on E Antioch Rd. Enter on L.* ◆◆◆FACILITIES: 41 sites, typical site width 25 ft, 19 full hkups, 19 W&E, 3 E, (20/30/50 amps), 39 pull-thrus, family camping, tenting, dump, laundry, groceries. ◆◆◆RECREATION: swim pool, playground. Pets welcome. Open Apr 1 - Oct 30. Big rigs welcome. Rate in 2010 $26-29 for 2 persons. Phone: (800)562-2815. KOA discount.

(E) Little Eagle RV Park—(Henry) *From jct Hwy 641 & Hwy 79: Go 13-1/2 mi E on Hwy 79. Enter on R.* ◆◆◆◆FACILITIES: 48 sites, typical site width 35 ft, 34 full hkups, 14 W&E, (20/30/50 amps), 3 pull-thrus, tenting, laundry. ◆◆RECREATION: boating, ramp, dock, lake fishing, play equipment. Pets welcome. Partial handicap access. Open all yr. Big rigs welcome. Rate in 2010 $29 for 4 persons. Phone: (731)642-4669.

(NE) PARIS LANDING STATE PARK—(Henry) *From town: Go 16 mi NE on US 79. Enter on R.*

WELCOME

FACILITIES: 63 sites, 45 W&E, (20/30 amps), 18 no hkups, 4 pull-thrus, tenting, cabins, dump, laundry, marine gas, ice, picnic tables, grills, wood.

RECREATION: swim pool, lake/river swim, boating, canoeing, ramp, dock, lake/river fishing, fishing supplies, bsktball, playground, tennis, horseshoes, hiking trails, v-ball. Rec open to public.

Pets welcome. Partial handicap access. Open all yr. Facilities fully operational Apr 1 - Oct 31. No reservatons.

PARIS—Continued
PARIS LANDING STATE PARK—Continued

Phone: (800)250-8614
Address: 16055 Hwy 79 N, Buchanon, TN 38222
Lat/Lon: 36.43904/-88.08261
Web: www.state.tn.us

SEE AD TRAVEL SECTION PAGE 714

PARKERS CROSSROADS—B-2

(S) PARKER'S CROSSROADS RV PARK & CAMPGROUND—(Henderson) *From jct I-40 (exit 108) & Hwy 22: Go 1-1/4 mi N on Hwy 22. Enter on R.*

WELCOME

◆◆◆FACILITIES: 36 sites, 24 full hkups, 12 W&E, (30/50 amps), 30 pull-thrus, cable TV, WiFi Instant Internet at site, cable on-site Internet (needs activ), phone Internet central location, tenting, cabins, RV storage, dump, non-guest dump $, laundry, groceries, RV supplies, LP gas by weight/by meter, ice, picnic tables, wood.

◆◆◆RECREATION: rec room/area, swim pool, pond fishing, golf nearby, play equipment, horseshoes, sports field.

Pets welcome. Partial handicap access. Open all yr. Escort to site. Clubs welcome. Rate in 2010 $24.50-28.50 for 2 persons. MC/VISA/DISC/Debit.

Phone: (731)968-9939
Address: 22580 Highway 22 N, Yuma, TN 38390
Lat/Lon: 35.80934/-88.38904
Email: steve@franklintenn.com
Web: www.parkerscrossroadsrvpark.com

SEE AD JACKSON PAGE 729

PARKSVILLE—C-6

CHEROKEE NATIONAL FOREST (Parksville Lake Campground)—(Polk) *From jct US-64 & Hwy-30: Go 1/2 mi NE on Hwy-30.* FACILITIES: 16 sites, 16 E, (20/30 amps), 2 pull-thrus, tenting, dump. RECREATION: boating, ramp, lake fishing. Partial handicap access. Open Late Mar - Mid Nov. Phone: (423) 338-5201.

PERRYVILLE—B-3

BEECH BEND (Decatur County Pk)—*From jct US 412/Hwy 20 & Hwy 100: Go 1-1/2 mi S on Hwy 100.* FACILITIES: 74 sites, 56 W&E, (20 amps), 18 no hkups, tenting, dump, ltd groc. RECREATION: boating, canoeing, ramp, river fishing, playground. Pets welcome. Open all yr. Phone: (731)847-4252.

MOUSETAIL LANDING STATE PARK—(Perry) *From jct I-40 (exit 126) & Hwy 69: Go 14 mi S on Hwy 69, then 6 mi E on Hwy 412, then 2-1/2 mi S on Hwy 438. Enter on R.*

WELCOME

FACILITIES: 46 sites, typical site width 37 ft, 25 W&E, (20/50 amps), 21 no hkups, tenting, dump, laundry, ice, picnic tables, fire rings, grills.

RECREATION: equipped pavilion, river swim, boating, canoeing, ramp, river/stream fishing, bsktball, playground, sports field, v-ball. Rec open to public.

Partial handicap access. Open all yr. Facilities fully operational Apr 1 - Oct 31.

Phone: (731)847-0841
Address: Rt 3 Box 2808, Linden, TN 37096
Lat/Lon: 35.65606/-88.00652
Web: www.state.tn.us

SEE AD TRAVEL SECTION PAGE 714

PIGEON FORGE—E-5

(W) Clabough's Campground & RV Resort—(Sevier) *From north city limits at jct US 441 & Wears Valley Rd: Go 1/4 mi W on Wears Valley Rd. Enter on L.* ◆◆◆◆FACILITIES: 320 sites, typical site width 30 ft, 320 full hkups, (30/50 amps), 50 amps ($), 90 pull-thrus, tenting, laundry, full svc store. ◆◆◆◆RECREATION: 2 swim pools, stream fishing, playground. Pets welcome, quantity restrict. Open all yr. Big rigs welcome. Rate in 2010 $25-37 for 4 persons. Member ARVC, TNARVC. Phone: (800)965-8524.

PIGEON FORGE—Continued on next page

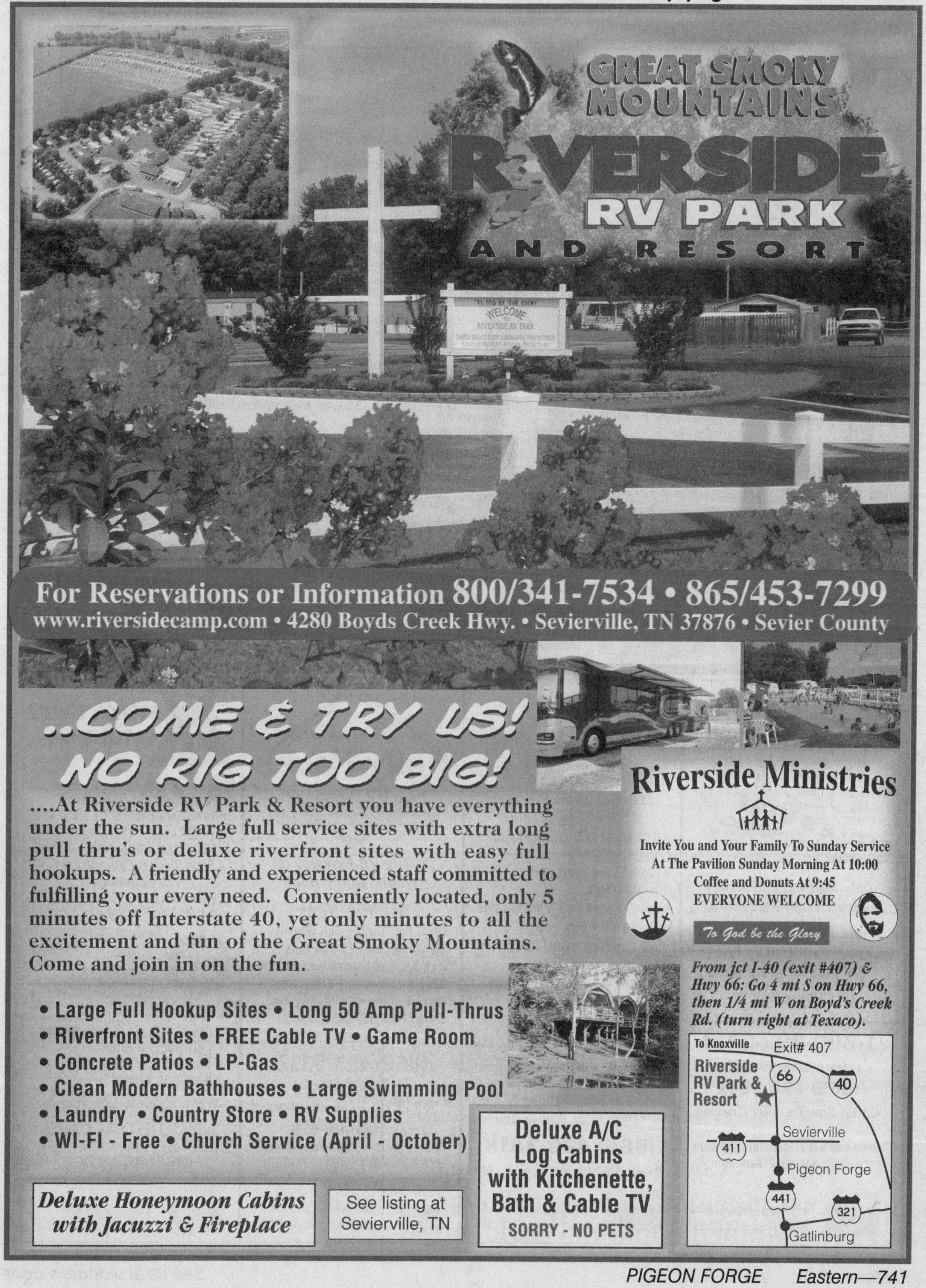

GREAT SMOKY MOUNTAINS

RIVERSIDE RV PARK AND RESORT

For Reservations or Information 800/341-7534 • 865/453-7299

www.riversidecamp.com • 4280 Boyds Creek Hwy. • Sevierville, TN 37876 • Sevier County

..COME & TRY US! NO RIG TOO BIG!

....At Riverside RV Park & Resort you have everything under the sun. Large full service sites with extra long pull thru's or deluxe riverfront sites with easy full hookups. A friendly and experienced staff committed to fulfilling your every need. Conveniently located, only 5 minutes off Interstate 40, yet only minutes to all the excitement and fun of the Great Smoky Mountains. Come and join in on the fun.

- Large Full Hookup Sites • Long 50 Amp Pull-Thrus
- Riverfront Sites • FREE Cable TV • Game Room
- Concrete Patios • LP-Gas
- Clean Modern Bathhouses • Large Swimming Pool
- Laundry • Country Store • RV Supplies
- WI-FI - Free • Church Service (April - October)

Riverside Ministries

Invite You and Your Family To Sunday Service At The Pavilion Sunday Morning At 10:00

Coffee and Donuts At 9:45

EVERYONE WELCOME

To God be the Glory

From jct I-40 (exit #407) & Hwy 66: Go 4 mi S on Hwy 66, then 1/4 mi W on Boyd's Creek Rd. (turn right at Texaco).

Deluxe Honeymoon Cabins with Jacuzzi & Fireplace

See listing at Sevierville, TN

Deluxe A/C Log Cabins with Kitchenette, Bath & Cable TV

SORRY - NO PETS

Where rest meets recreation.

Nothing beats camping in Pigeon Forge at the foothills of the Great Smoky Mountains. From traditional tent camping to deluxe RV camping, there is a spot for everyone. The fun and excitement of the Parkway is right around the corner. Pigeon Forge is the place where you can do everything or just sit back and take it all in. Either way, you're smiling.

MyPigeonForge.com

THE CENTER OF FUN IN THE SMOKIES
ACTION ★ PACKED
PIGEON FORGE
TENNESSEE

---

10 Minutes To Dollywood & Outlet Malls

Only 1-1/2 Mi. off Parkway On Wears Valley Rd. (Hwy 321)

Cable TV • Laundry • Pool
Level Full Hookup Sites
Bathhouse • Tent Sites
Camping Cabins

Toll Free Reservations Only
1-800-892-2714
For Information Call
(865) 428-5841

Chain Saw Tree Art Carving

www.eaglesnestcampground.com
e-mail: encamp2@aol.com

Trolley Stop

1111 Wears Valley Rd.
Pigeon Forge, TN 37863

Located on the Parkway at the South City Limits

- 5 Minutes to Dollywood and Outlet Malls
- Walk to the River and Restaurants
- Level Paved Full Hookup Sites
- Cable TV • Firewood
- RV Supplies • Concrete Patios
- Laundry • Ice
- Cabins with Bath Facilities
- Sleeping Cabins
- New Enlarged Pool
- Deluxe AC/Heated Bathhouse
- 30/50 Amp Service
- Free Wi-Fi

For Reservations & Information Please Call
(865) 428-3818
www.foothillsrvparkandcabins.com

Trolley Stop

4235 Huskey St.
Pigeon Forge, TN 37863

1 Mile Off Parkway on Wears Valley Road

Big Rig Sites

Level Pull Thrus • Full Hookups
Creekside Sites • 30/50 Amp
2 Lg A/C Bathhouses & Laundries
Open Air Pavilion • Playground
Creek Fishing • Swimming Pool
E-mail Station • Cable TV

(865) 453-5352
For Reservations Only
Toll FREE: 1-888-204-0247
Fax: (865) 453-5551
e-mail: hollyhavenrvpark@aol.com
www.hollyhavenrvpark.com

Trolley Stop

647 Wears Valley Rd.
Pigeon Forge, TN 37863

KOA
PIGEON FORGE GATLINBURG

In Town-Turn East Off US Hwy. 441 At Traffic Light #8 Dollywood Lane Through Next Traffic Light - on Left

The Closest Campground To Dollywood
Special Dollywood Tickets Available Plus Dollywood's Splash Country

Deluxe Sites
- *50 Amp*
- *Patio*
- *Patio Furniture*
- *Chimineas*
- *Landscaped & Much More*

- Super Clean Bathhouses
- Store • Pool • Game Room
- Full Hookup Sites
- Campsites on the River
- Kamping Kabins

www.pigeonforgekoa.com
1-800-KOA-7703
(Reservations Only)
(865) 453-7903
Information

Trolley Stop

P.O. Box 310
3122 Veterans Blvd.
Pigeon Forge, TN 37868

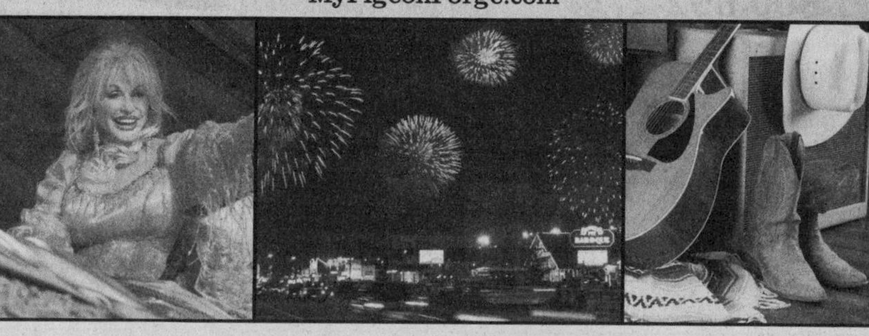

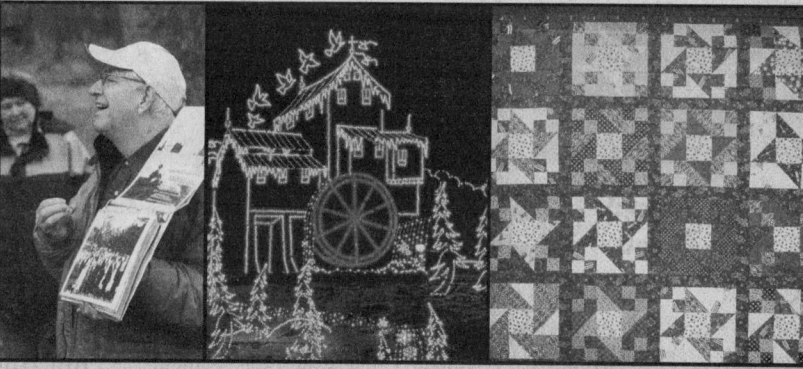

Tina Turner, singer, is from Tennessee.

Stay on top of the latest RV Camping news, tips and more by signing up for RSS or email feeds at blog.woodalls.com

PIGEON FORGE—Continued

(S) COVE MOUNTAIN RESORTS RV PARK —(Sevier) *From north city limits at jct US 441 & Wear's Valley Rd (US 321) stop light #3: Go 9.7 mi W on Wears Valley Rd. Enter on R.*

◆◆◆◆FACILITIES: 55 sites, typical site width 50 ft, accepts full hkup units only, 55 full hkups, (20/30/50 amps), some extd stay sites, 4 pull-thrus, cable TV, WiFi Instant Internet at site, family camping, picnic tables.

◆◆RECREATION: equipped pavilion, swim pool, pond fishing.

Pets welcome. No tents. Open all yr. No restrooms. Big rigs welcome. Escort to site. Clubs welcome. Rate in 2010 $30.50-37 for 2 persons. MC/VISA/DISC.

Phone: (865)453-1041
Address: 3958 Wears Valley Rd, Sevierville, TN 37862
Lat/Lon: 35.70985/-83.66528
Web: www.covemountainrvresort.com

SEE AD GATLINBURG PAGES 726-727

(W) Creekside RV Park—(Sevier) *From north city limits at US 441 & US 321 (traffic light #3): Go 1/2 mi W on Wear's Valley Rd/US 321, then 1/4 mi NW on Henderson Springs Rd. Enter on R.* ◆◆◆◆FACILITIES: 110 sites, typical site width 30 ft, 110 full hkups, (30/50 amps), 50 amps ($), 5 pull-thrus, cable TV, WiFi Instant Internet at site, laundry, RV supplies, ice, picnic tables, patios, wood. ◆◆RECREATION: pavilion, swim pool, stream fishing, activities. Pets welcome. Partial handicap access. No tents. Open Mar 1 - Jan 5. Big rigs welcome. Rate in 2010 $33-37 for 2 persons. MC/VISA/DISC/Debit. CCUSA 50% Discount. CCUSA reservations Recommended, Cash only for CCUSA disc., Check only for CCUSA disc., CCUSA disc. not avail F,Sa, CCUSA disc. not avail holidays. Not available Oct & Special Events-call for details. Max stay based on availability. $2 surcharge creekside site.

Phone: (800)498-4801
Address: 2475 Henderson Springs Rd, Pigeon Forge, TN 37863
Lat/Lon: 35.80178/-83.58885
Email: creeksidervpark@creeksidervpark.com
Web: www.creeksidervpark.com

(W) EAGLE'S NEST CAMPGROUND—(Sevier) *From north city limits at jct US 441 & Wears Valley Rd: Go 1-1/2 mi W on Wears Valley Rd/Hwy 321. Enter on L.*

◆◆◆FACILITIES: 244 sites, typical site width 35 ft, 135 full hkups, 50 W&E, (20/30/50 amps), 50 amps ($), 59 no hkups, some extd stay sites, 24 pull-thrus, cable TV, WiFi Instant Internet at site, phone Internet central location, family camping, tenting, cabins, dump, laundry, RV supplies, ice, picnic tables, fire rings, wood.

◆◆RECREATION: rec room/area, coin games, swim pool, stream fishing, golf nearby, play equipment, horseshoes, sports field.

Pets welcome. Partial handicap access. Open all yr. Big rigs welcome. Clubs welcome. Rate in 2010 $29-32.50 for 2 persons. MC/VISA/DISC/Debit. FMCA discount. CCUSA 50% Discount. CCUSA reservations Accepted, CCUSA max stay Unlimited. Not valid month of Oct or holiday weeks. Credit/debit cards accepted with stay of 4 days or longer-cash only on 1-3 day stays. $5 service charge for cancellations prior to 48 hrs before scheduled arrival/no show or cancellation less than 48 hr prior chrgd 1 night.

Phone: (800)892-2714
Address: 1111 Wears Valley Rd, Pigeon Forge, TN 37863
Lat/Lon: 35.79277/-83.60205
Email: encamp2@aol.com
Web: www.eaglesnestcampground.com

SEE AD PAGES 742-743

(S) FOOTHILLS RV PARK & CABINS—(Sevier) *At south city limits at jct US 441 & Huskey St & Parkway. Enter on L.*

◆◆◆◆FACILITIES: 39 sites, typical site width 22 ft, 34 ft max RV length, 37 full hkups, 2 W&E, (20/30/50 amps), 50 amps ($), cable TV, WiFi Instant Internet at site, family camping, cabins, laundry, RV supplies, ice, picnic tables, patios, fire rings, wood.

◆RECREATION: swim pool, golf nearby, local tours.

FOOTHILLS RV PARK & CABINS—Continued on next page

PIGEON FORGE—Continued
FOOTHILLS RV PARK & CABINS—Continued

Pets welcome. Partial handicap access. No tents. Open Apr 1 - Nov 1. Rate in 2010 $32 for 2 persons. MC/VISA/Debit.

Phone: (865)428-3818
Address: 4235 Huskey St, Pigeon Forge, TN 37863
Lat/Lon: 35.77353/-83.53661
Email: camp@foothillsrvpark.info
Web: www.foothillsrvparkandcabins.com

SEE AD PAGES 742-743 AND AD GATLINBURG PAGES 726-727

(W) KING'S HOLLY HAVEN RV PARK—(Sevier) *From north city limits at jct US 441 & Wear's Valley Rd (US 321) stop light #3: Go 1 mi W on Wear's Valley Rd (US 321). Enter on L.*

NEAR IT ALL-BUT AWAY FROM THE NOISE.
Our quiet family RV Park features creekside sites & long 50 amp pull thrus's, large pool, 2 laundries, pavilion & friendly folks await you. Near Outlet Malls & all attractions. Great Family Rates. Trolley stops at our entrance.

◊◊◊◊FACILITIES: 161 sites, typical site width 30 ft, 161 full hkups, (20/30/50 amps), 50 amps ($), some extd stay sites, 12 pull-thrus, cable TV, WiFi Instant Internet at site, laundry, ltd groc, RV supplies, ice, picnic tables, patios, fire rings, grills, wood.

◊◊RECREATION: equipped pavilion, swim pool, stream fishing, golf nearby, playground, activities, local tours.

Pets welcome. Partial handicap access. No tents. Open all yr. Big rigs welcome. Clubs welcome. Rate in 2010 $22-32 for 2 persons. MC/VISA/Debit. Member ARVC, TNARVC.

Phone: (865)453-5352
Address: 647 Wear's Valley Rd, Pigeon Forge, TN 37863
Lat/Lon: 35.79586/-83.59106
Email: hollyhavenrvpark@aol.com
Web: hollyhavenrvpark.com

SEE AD PAGES 742-743 AND AD GATLINBURG PAGES 726-727

(E) KOA-Pigeon Forge/Gatlinburg—(Sevier) *From center of town at jct US 441 & Dollywood Lane #8: Go 1/4 mi E on Dollywood Lane, then 1,000 feet N on Veterans Blvd. Enter on L.* ◊◊◊◊◊FACILITIES: 181 sites, typical site width 40 ft, 118 full hkups, 56 W&E, (30/50 amps), 50 amps ($), 7 no hkups, 80 pull-thrus, family camping, tenting, dump, laundry, groceries. ◊◊◊◊◊RECREATION: swim pool, river fishing, playground. Pets welcome, quantity restrict. Partial handicap access. Open Apr 1 - Nov 30. Big rigs welcome. Rate in 2010 $32-80 for 2 persons. Phone: (865)453-7903. KOA discount.

(N) PIGEON FORGE DEPARTMENT OF TOURISM—*From North City Limits: Go 3/4 mi S on US 441. Enter on R.* Tourism Department of Pigeon Forge. Call toll free 1-800-251-9100 (nationwide & Canada) for information. Brochures and information available. Open all yr.

Phone: (800)251-9100
Address: 2450 Parkway, Pigeon Forge, TN 37868
Lat/Lon: 35.81012/-83.57903
Email: inquire@mypigeonforge.com
Web: www.mypigeonforge.com

SEE AD PAGES 742-743

(W) PINE MOUNTAIN RV PARK—(Sevier) *From jct US 321 & US 441: Go S on US 441 to traffic light #6, then, 1/4 mi W on Pine Mountain Rd. Enter on L.*

◊◊◊◊◊FACILITIES: 61 sites, typical site width 25 ft, 61 full hkups, (30/50 amps), 50 amps ($), 25 pull-thrus, cable TV, WiFi Instant Internet at site, family camping, RV's/park model rentals, laundry, ltd groc, ice, picnic tables, patios, fire rings, wood.

◊◊RECREATION: rec room/area, 2 swim pools, hot tub, golf nearby, local tours.

Pets welcome, breed restrict, size restrict, quantity restrict. No tents. Open all yr. Big rigs welcome. Clubs welcome. Rate in 2010 $35-53 for 2 persons. MC/VISA/DISC/AMEX/Debit. Member ARVC, TNARVC. FMCA discount.

Text 81417 to (440)725-8687 to see our Visual Tour.

Read interesting travel facts in the front of every state/province.

PIGEON FORGE—Continued
PINE MOUNTAIN RV PARK—Continued

Phone: (865)453-9994
Address: 411 Pine Mountain Rd, Pigeon Forge, TN 37863
Lat/Lon: 35.78918/-83.56722
Email: stay@pinemountainrvpark.com
Web: www.pinemountainrvpark.com

SEE AD PAGES 742-743 AND AD PAGE 740 AND AD GATLINBURG PAGES 726-727 AND AD MAP PAGE 712

(N) RIVER PLANTATION RV PARK—(Sevier) *From jct Hwy 66 & US 441: Go 1 mi S on US 441. Enter on L.*

◊◊◊◊◊FACILITIES: 297 sites, typical site width 30 ft, 297 full hkups, (20/30/50 amps), 50 amps ($), some extd stay sites (summer), 58 pull-thrus, cable TV, WiFi Instant Internet at site, phone Internet central location, family camping, cabins, RV storage, laundry, groceries, RV supplies, LP gas by weight/by meter, ice, picnic tables, patios, fire rings, wood.

◊◊◊◊◊RECREATION: rec hall, rec room/area, equipped pavilion, coin games, 2 swim pools, wading pool, river swim, hot tub, river fishing, golf nearby, bsktball, playground, activities, horseshoes, v-ball, local tours.

Pets welcome. No tents. Open all yr. Big rigs welcome. Clubs welcome. Rate in 2010 $22.50-49.50 for 2 persons. MC/VISA/DISC/Debit. ATM. Member ARVC, TNARVC.

Text 107986 to (440)725-8687 to see our Visual Tour.

Phone: (865)429-5267
Address: 1004 Pkwy, Sevierville, TN 37862
Lat/Lon: 35.85144/-83.56968
Email: riverplantation@gmail.com
Web: www.riverplantationrv.com

SEE AD PAGE 744 AND AD GATLINBURG PAGES 726-727

(E) RIVERBEND CAMPGROUND—(Sevier) *From North city limits: Go 1/2 mi S on US 441, then 1/2 mi W on Henderson Chapel Rd. Enter on L.*

◊◊◊◊FACILITIES: 131 sites, typical site width 40 ft, 126 full hkups, 5 W&E, (30/50 amps), some extd stay sites, 35 pull-thrus, heater not allowed, cable TV, WiFi Instant Internet at site, phone Internet central location, tenting, laundry, ice, picnic tables, patios.

◊◊RECREATION: equipped pavilion, river swim, river fishing, golf nearby.

Pets welcome. Open Mar 15 - Dec 1. Church services during season only. Big rigs welcome. Clubs welcome. Rate in 2010 $32 for 2 persons.

Phone: (865)453-1224
Address: 2479 Riverbend Loop Lot 1, Pigeon Forge, TN 37863
Lat/Lon: 35.80950/-83.58792
Email: riverbend@earthlink.net
Web: www.riverbendcampground.com

SEE AD PAGES 742-743

(S) RIVEREDGE RV PARK—(Sevier) *South city limits at jct US 441 & Cates Ln (left exit before stop light #10): Go 1 blk E on Cates Ln. Enter on R.*

◊◊◊◊◊FACILITIES: 177 sites, typical site width 30 ft, 177 full hkups, (20/30/50 amps), 50 amps ($), cable TV, WiFi Instant Internet at site, phone Internet central location, family camping, cabins, laundry, ltd groc, RV supplies, ice, picnic tables, patios, fire rings, wood.

◊◊◊◊RECREATION: rec room/area, coin games, swim pool, wading pool, hot tub, stream fishing, golf nearby, playground, local tours.

Pets welcome. Partial handicap access. No tents. Open all yr. Big rigs welcome. Clubs welcome. Green Friendly. Rate in 2010 $39 for 2 persons. MC/VISA/Debit.

Text 107900 to (440)725-8687 to see our Visual Tour.

Phone: (800)477-1205
Address: 4220 Huskey St., Pigeon Forge, TN 37863
Lat/Lon: 35.77364/-83.53696
Email: info@stayriveredge.com
Web: www.stayriveredge.com

SEE AD PAGES 742-743 AND AD PAGE 740

(S) Shady Oaks Campground Pigeon Forge/Gatlinburg—(Sevier) *From south city limits at jct US 441 & Conner Hgts Rd: Go 1/4 mi W on Conner Hgts Rd. Enter on R.* ◊◊FACILITIES: 150 sites, typical

PIGEON FORGE—Continued
Shady Oaks Campground Pigeon Forge/Gatlinburg—Continued

site width 30 ft, 75 full hkups, 45 W&E, (15/20/30/50 amps), 30 no hkups, 4 pull-thrus, family camping, tenting, dump, laundry. ◊◊◊RECREATION: swim pool, pond fishing, playground. Pets welcome. Open all yr. Phone: (865)453-3276.

(E) Smoker Holler RV Resort—(Sevier) *From jct US 441 & Hwy 321: Go 11 mi W on Hwy 321. Enter on L.* ◊◊◊FACILITIES: 33 sites, typical site width 38 ft, 33 full hkups, (20/30/50 amps), 9 pull-thrus, cable TV, WiFi Instant Internet at site, phone Internet central location, ice, picnic tables, fire rings, wood. ◊RECREATION: equipped pavilion, horseshoes, v-ball. Pets welcome. No tents. Open all yr. Big rigs welcome. Rate in 2010 $25-32 for 2 persons. MC/VISA/DISC/Debit. Member ARVC, TNARVC. FMCA discount. CCUSA 50% Discount. CCUSA reservations Recommended, CCUSA max stay 7 days, CCUSA disc. not avail holidays. Not available month of Oct.

Phone: (866)453-8777
Address: 4119 Wears Valley Rd, Sevierville, TN 37862
Lat/Lon: 35.70471/-83.67128
Email: smokerholler@aol.com
Web: www.smokerholler.us

(S) TWIN MOUNTAIN RV PARK AND CAMPGROUND—(Sevier) *From jct US 321 & US 441: Go S on US 441 through traffic light #8, then 1/2 mi S, then E on Golf Dr at Duff's Rest, then 1/4 mi E on Golf Dr. Enter on R.*

◊◊◊◊FACILITIES: 122 sites, typical site width 35 ft, 117 full hkups, (30/50 amps), 5 no hkups, cable TV, WiFi Instant Internet at site, phone Internet central location, family camping, tenting, laundry, RV supplies, ice, picnic tables, fire rings, wood.

◊◊◊◊RECREATION: rec room/area, coin games, swim pool, float trips, river fishing, golf nearby, bsktball, playground, activities, tennis, horseshoes, local tours.

Pets welcome. Open all yr. Big rigs welcome. Clubs welcome. Rate in 2010 $29-39 for 2 persons. MC/VISA/Debit.

Phone: (800)848-9097
Address: 304 Day Springs Rd, Pigeon Forge, TN 37863
Lat/Lon: 35.77847/-83.54193
Email: creek@usit.net
Web: www.twinmountainrvpark.com

SEE AD PAGES 742-743 AND AD PAGE 744

(E) Waldens Creek Campground—(Sevier) *From north city limits at jct US 441 & Wear's Valley Rd (US 321): Go 1/2 mi W on Wear's Valley Rd (US 321), then 1/4 mi NW on Henderson Springs Rd. Enter on R.* ◊◊◊FACILITIES: 45 sites, typical site width 30 ft, 35 full hkups, 10 E, (20/30/50 amps), 50 amps ($), cable TV, WiFi Instant Internet at site, WiFi Internet central location, tenting, laundry, ice, picnic tables, patios, fire rings, wood. ◊RECREATION: pavilion, river swim, stream fishing, bsktball, activities. Pets welcome. Open all yr. Big rigs welcome. Rate in 2010 $25-35 for 2 persons. MC/VISA/Debit. CCUSA 50% Discount. CCUSA reservations Recommended, CCUSA max stay 5 days, CCUSA disc. not avail holidays. Not available month of Oct and Special Events-call for details. Stay may be extended depending on availability & at manager discretion.

Phone: (865)908-2727
Address: 2485 Henderson Springs Rd, Pigeon Forge, TN 37863
Lat/Lon: 35.80077/-83.58824
Email: info@waldenscreekcampground.com
Web: www.waldenscreekcampground.com

PIKEVILLE—B-5

(NW) FALL CREEK FALLS STATE PARK—(Van Buren) *From jct US 127 & Hwy 30: Go 14 mi W on Hwy 30, then 2 mi SW on Hwy 284, then at park entrance continue 7-1/2 mi to campground. Enter on L.*

FACILITIES: 237 sites, 228 W&E, (20/50 amps), 9 no hkups, tenting, cabins, dump, laundry, ltd groc, ice, picnic tables, fire rings, grills.

RECREATION: rec hall, pavilion, swim pool, wading pool, boating, electric motors only, canoeing, 37 rowboat/11 canoe/18 pedal boat/37 motorboat rentals, lake fishing, putting green, bsktball, playground, activities, tennis, sports field, hiking trails, v-ball. Rec open to public.

Pets welcome. Partial handicap access. Open all yr. Facilities fully operational Apr 1 - Oct 31. MC/VISA/DISC.

FALL CREEK FALLS STATE PARK—Continued on next page

PIKEVILLE—Continued
FALL CREEK FALLS STATE PARK—Continued

Phone: (800)250-8611
Address: Rt 3 2009 Village Camp Rd, Pikeville, TN 37367
Lat/Lon: 35.65545/-85.35471
Web: www.state.tn.us

SEE AD TRAVEL SECTION PAGE 714

(W) Mountain Glen RV Park—(Bledsoe) *From jct State Hwy 111 & Hwy 284: Go 1 mi E on Hwy 284, then 1 mi S on Old Hwy 111, then 6-1/4 mi E on Brockdell Rd. Enter on R.* ◆◆◆FACILITIES: 42 sites, 42 full hkups, (50 amps), 42 pull-thrus, tenting, dump, laundry, ltd groc. ◆◆RECREATION: pond fishing. Pets welcome, breed restrict. Partial handicap access. Open Apr 1 - Oct 31. Big rigs welcome. Rate in 2010 $28 for 2 persons. Member ARVC, TNARVC. Phone: (877)716-4493.

POCAHONTAS—C-2

BIG HILL POND STATE PARK—(McNairy) *From town: Go 5 mi E on Hwy 57. Enter on R.*

WELCOME

FACILITIES: 28 sites, 28 no hkups, tenting, picnic tables, grills, controlled access.

RECREATION: boating, electric motors only, canoeing, ramp, lake fishing, bsktball, playground, hiking trails.

Pets welcome. Partial handicap access. Open all yr.

Phone: (731)645-7967
Address: 984 John Howell Rd, Pocahontas, TN 38061
Web: www.state.tn.us

SEE AD TRAVEL SECTION PAGE 714

Can you trust the Woodall's ratings? 25 evaluation teams have scoured North American campgrounds to provide you with accurate, up to date information & ratings. Find a rating you don't agree with? Send a letter or email our way, and we'll give it extra attention for 2012.

ROAN MOUNTAIN—D-6

(S) ROAN MOUNTAIN STATE RESORT PARK—(Carter) *From jct US 9E & Hwy 143: Go 5 mi S on Hwy 143. Enter at end.*

WELCOME

FACILITIES: 107 sites, 87 W&E, (30 amps), 20 no hkups, tenting, cabins, dump, laundry, ice, picnic tables, fire rings, grills, wood, controlled access.

RECREATION: rec room/area, equipped pavilion, coin games, swim pool, river swim, river/stream fishing, bsktball, playground, shuffleboard court shuffleboard court, tennis, horseshoes, sports field, hiking trails, v-ball.

Pets welcome. Partial handicap access. Open all yr. Facilities fully operational Apr 1 - Oct 31. No reservations. MC/VISA/DISC/AMEX.

Phone: (800)250-8620
Address: 1015 Hwy 143, Roan Mountain, TN 37687
Lat/Lon: 36.15958/-82.09990
Web: www.state.tn.us

SEE AD TRAVEL SECTION PAGE 714

ROCK ISLAND—B-5

(W) ROCK ISLAND STATE PARK—(Warren) *From jct US 705 & Hwy 136: Go on Hwy 136 to Hwy 287, then W on Hwy 287 (follow signs). Enter on R.*

WELCOME

FACILITIES: 60 sites, typical site width 46 ft, 50 W&E, (20/30 amps), 10 no hkups, tenting, cabins, dump, laundry, ltd groc, ice, picnic tables, grills, controlled access.

RECREATION: pavilion, lake swim, boating, canoeing, ramp, lake/river fishing, bsktball, playground, tennis, sports field, hiking trails, v-ball. Rec open to public.

Pets welcome. Partial handicap access. Open all yr. Facilities fully operational Apr 1 - Oct 31. MC/VISA/DISC/AMEX.

Phone: (800)713-6065
Address: 82 Beach Rd., Rock Island, TN 38581
Lat/Lon: 35.80993/-85.64207
Web: www.state.tn.us

SEE AD TRAVEL SECTION PAGE 714

SAVANNAH—C-2

PICKWICK LANDING STATE RESORT PARK—(Hardin) *From town: Go 10 mi S on Hwy 128 to jct Hwy 28 & Hwy 57. Enter on L.*

WELCOME

FACILITIES: 48 sites, 48 W&E, (20/30/50 amps), 2 pull-thrus, tenting, cabins, dump, laundry, marine gas, picnic tables, grills.

RECREATION: pavilion, lake swim, boating, ramp, dock, 10 motorboat rentals, lake fishing, putting green, bsktball, playground, tennis, sports field, hiking trails, v-ball. Rec open to public.

Pets welcome. Partial handicap access. Open all yr. Facilities fully operational Apr 1 - Oct 30.

Phone: (800)250-8615
Address: 855 Hardin Dock Rd, Pickwick Dam, TN 38365
Lat/Lon: 35.051944/-88.237139
Web: www.state.tn.us

SEE AD TRAVEL SECTION PAGE 714

SEVIERVILLE—E-5

(N) DOUGLAS DAM TAILWATER (TVA - Douglas Reservoir)—(Jefferson) *From jct US 411 & Hwy 66: Go 7 mi N on Hwy 66, then 3-1/2 mi E on Hwy 139, then 1/2 mi S on Hwy 338, follow signs.* FACILITIES: 60 sites, 60 W&E, (30 amps), 25 pull-thrus, tenting, dump, ltd groc. RECREATION: lake swim, boating, ramp, river fishing, play equipment. Partial handicap access. Open Apr - Oct. Phone: (423)585-2120.

(N) DOUGLAS HEADWATER (TVA - Douglas Reservoir)—(Jefferson) *From jct US 411 & Hwy 66: Go 7 mi N on Hwy 66, then 3-1/2 mi E on Hwy 139, then 2-1/2 mi S on Hwy 338, then follow signs 1 mi N.* FACILITIES: 65 sites, 61 W&E, 4 no hkups, tenting, dump. RECREATION: lake swim, boating, ramp, lake fishing. Partial handicap access. Open Mid Apr - Late Oct. Phone: (423)585-2120.

SEVIERVILLE—Continued on next page

Prepare gourmet meals in your RV kitchen! Woodall's Cooking on the Road with Celebrity Chefs includes dozens of tips and sidebars that make recipes easier to use while traveling. Go to www.woodalls.com/shop and check it out.

SEVIERVILLE—Continued

(N) RIPPLIN' WATERS CAMPGROUND—(Sevier) *From jct I-40 (exit 407) & Hwy 66: Go 5 mi S on Hwy 66. Enter on R.*

CHECK OUT OUR LOW LOW RATES!

Our quiet family campground features riverside sites & long 50 amp pull thrus! Our large pool, pavilion & country store await you. Near all the attractions with great facilities & great family rates.

◊◊◊◊FACILITIES: 155 sites, typical site width 25 ft, 155 full hkups, (20/30/50 amps), 50 amps ($), 5 pull-thrus, cable TV, WiFi Instant Internet at site, family camping, cabins, laundry, groceries, RV supplies, LP gas by weight/by meter, LP bottle exch, ice, picnic tables, patios, wood.

◊◊◊RECREATION: rec room/area, equipped pavilion, swim pool, river fishing, golf nearby, bsktball, playground.

Pets welcome, breed restrict. Partial handicap access. No tents. Open all yr. Big rigs welcome. Escort to site. Clubs welcome. Rate in 2010 $28-33 for 2 persons. MC/VISA/DISC/Debit. ATM. Member ARVC, TNARVC. CCUSA 50% Discount.

Phone: (888)747-7546
Address: 1930 Winfield Dunn Pkwy, Sevierville, TN 37876
Lat/Lon: 35.92078/-83.58123
Email: ripplinwatersrv@ripplinwatersrv.com
Web: www.ripplinwatersrv.com

SEE AD PAGE 746 AND AD GATLINBURG PAGES 726-727 AND AD TRAVEL SECTION PAGE 713

(N) RIVERSIDE RV PARK & RESORT—(Sevier) *From jct I-40 (exit 407) & Hwy 66: Go 4 mi S on Hwy 66, then 1/4 mi W on Boyds Creek Rd (turn right at Marathon). Enter on R.*

◊◊◊◊◊FACILITIES: 316 sites, typical site width 30 ft, 296 full hkups, 20 W&E, (30/50 amps), 50 amps ($), some extd stay sites (summer), 101 pull-thrus, cable TV, WiFi Instant Internet at site, family camping, RV's/park model rentals, cabins, RV storage, laundry, groceries, RV supplies, LP gas by weight/by meter, ice, picnic tables, patios, fire rings, grills, wood.

◊◊◊◊RECREATION: rec room/area, equipped pavilion, coin games, swim pool, boating, ramp, river fishing, fishing supplies, golf nearby, bsktball, playground, activities.

Pets welcome. No tents. Open all yr. Big rigs welcome. Clubs welcome. Rate in 2010 $30-32 for 2 persons. MC/VISA/Debit.

Text 101120 to (440)725-8687 to see our Visual Tour.

Phone: (800)341-7534
Address: 4280 Boyds Creek Hwy, Sevierville, TN 37876
Lat/Lon: 35.92848/-83.58674
Email: KVOLUNTEER@aol.com
Web: www.riversidecamp.com

SEE AD GATLINBURG PAGES 726-727 AND AD PIGEON FORGE PAGE 741 AND AD TRAVEL SECTION PAGE 713

(N) Two Rivers Landing Resort—(Sevier) *From jct I-40 (exit 407) & Hwy 66: Go 3 mi S on Hwy 66, then 1/4 mi W on Knife Works Ln, then 1/4 mi N on Business Center Circle. Enter on R.* ◊◊◊◊◊FACILITIES: 55 sites, typical site width 32 ft, 55 full hkups, (30/50 amps), family camping, laundry. ◊◊◊RECREATION: swim pool, river fishing, playground. Pets welcome. Partial handicap access. No tents. Open all yr. Big rigs welcome. Rate in 2010 $45-65 for 6 persons. Phone: (866)727-5781.

SHADY VALLEY—D-6

CHEROKEE NATIONAL FOREST (Jacobs Creek Campgrounds)—(Sullivan) *From town: Go 9 mi NW on US-421, then 2 mi N on CR-32, then 7/10 mi W on FR-337.* FACILITIES: 27 sites, 27 no hkups, dump. RECREATION: lake swim, boating, lake fishing. Partial handicap access. Open May 1 - Oct 1. Phone: (423) 735-1500.

SILVER POINT—B-5

FLOATING MILL (COE-Center Hill Reservoir)—(DeKalb) *From I-40 (exit 273): Go 5 mi S on Hwy-56 to Hurricane Dock Rd., then 1 mi W on Hurricane Dock Rd to campground.* FACILITIES: 118 sites, 30 ft max RV length, 2 full hkups, 88 W&E, (20/30/50 amps), 28 no hkups, tenting, dump, laundry, ltd groc. RECREATION: lake swim, boating, canoeing, ramp, lake fishing, playground. Partial handicap access. Open Apr 16 - Sep 15. Phone: (931)858-4845.

SILVER POINT—Continued

LONG BRANCH (COE - Center Hill Reservoir)—(DeKalb) *From I-40 (exit 268): Go 5 mi S on Bob Steber Rd, then 2 mi W on Hwy-141.* FACILITIES: 60 sites, 3 full hkups, 57 W&E, (20/30/50 amps), tenting, dump, laundry. RECREATION: lake swim, boating, canoeing, ramp, lake fishing, playground. Open Apr 15 - Oct 31. Phone: (615)548-8002.

SMITHVILLE—B-5

EDGAR EVINS STATE RUSTIC PARK—(DeKalb) *From jct US 70 & Hwy 56: Go 16 mi N on Hwy 56, then 6 mi N on Hwy 141. Enter on L.*

FACILITIES: 69 sites, 45 ft max RV length, 60 W&E, (20/30/50 amps), 9 no hkups, tenting, cabins, dump, laundry, marine gas, ice, picnic tables, fire rings, grills.

RECREATION: swim pool, lake swim, boating, canoeing, ramp, dock, lake fishing, bsktball, playground, activities, hiking trails, v-ball. Rec open to public.

Pets welcome. Partial handicap access. Open all yr. No reservations.

Phone: (800)250-8619
Address: 1630 Edgar Evins Pk Rd, Silver Point, TN 38582
Lat/Lon: 36.08747/-85.81391
Web: www.state.tn.us

SEE AD TRAVEL SECTION PAGE 714

(E) RAGLAND BOTTOM (COE - Center Hill Reservoir)—(DeKalb) *From jct Hwy-56 & Hwy-70: Go 8 mi E on Hwy-70, then 1 mi N on county road.* FACILITIES: 57 sites, 41 W&E, (30/50 amps), 16 no hkups, 15 pull-thrus, tenting, dump, laundry. RECREATION: lake swim, boating, canoeing, ramp, lake fishing, playground. Partial handicap access. Open May 1 - Sep 15. Phone: (931)761-3616.

SMYRNA—B-4

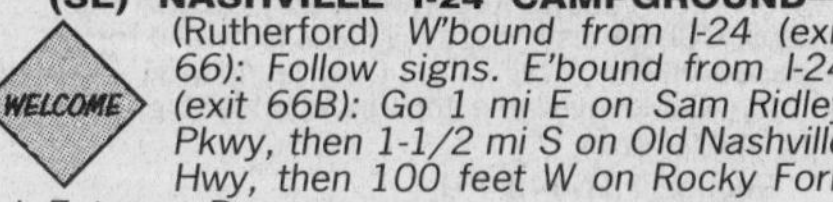

(SE) NASHVILLE I-24 CAMPGROUND—(Rutherford) *W'bound from I-24 (exit 66): Follow signs. E'bound from I-24 (exit 66B): Go 1 mi E on Sam Ridley Pkwy, then 1-1/2 mi S on Old Nashville Hwy, then 100 feet W on Rocky Fork Rd. Enter on R.*

◊◊◊FACILITIES: 148 sites, typical site width 25 ft, 110 full hkups, 38 W&E, (20/30/50 amps), 50 amps ($), some extd stay sites (summer), 75 pull-thrus, WiFi Instant Internet at site, phone Internet central location, family camping, tenting, cabins, RV storage, dump, non-guest dump $, laundry, groceries, RV supplies, LP gas by weight/by meter, LP bottle exch, ice, picnic tables.

◊◊RECREATION: rec room/area, coin games, swim pool, golf nearby, bsktball, playground, v-ball.

Pets welcome, breed restrict. Open all yr. Big rigs welcome. Escort to site. Clubs welcome. Rate in 2010 $25-29 for 2 persons. MC/VISA/Debit. Member ARVC.

Phone: (615)459-5818
Address: 1130 Rocky Fork Rd, Smyrna, TN 37167
Lat/Lon: 35.96630/-86.52996
Web: www.nashvillet24kampground.com

SEE AD NASHVILLE PAGE 738

SWEETWATER—B-6

(W) KOA-SWEETWATER VALLEY—(Loudon) *From jct I-75 (exit 62) & Oakland Rd: Go 3/4 mi W on Oakland Rd, then 1/4 mi S on Murrays Chapel Rd. Enter on L.*

◊◊◊◊FACILITIES: 62 sites, typical site width 30 ft, 56 full hkups, 6 W&E, (20/30/50 amps), some extd stay sites, 62 pull-thrus, cable TV, WiFi Instant Internet at site, phone Internet central location, tenting, cabins, RV storage, dump, non-guest dump $, laundry, groceries, RV supplies, LP gas by weight/by meter, LP bottle exch, ice, picnic tables, patios, fire rings, grills, wood.

◊◊◊◊◊RECREATION: rec hall, rec room/area, pavilion, equipped pavilion, coin games, swim pool, pond fishing, fishing supplies, golf nearby, bsktball, playground, activities, horseshoes, sports field, hiking trails, v-ball.

Pets welcome, breed restrict. Partial handicap access. Open all yr. Planned group activities on holidays & special weekends. Big rigs welcome. Escort to site. Clubs welcome. Rate in 2010 $28.50-56.50 for 2 persons. MC/VISA/DISC/AMEX/Debit. KOA discount.

SWEETWATER—Continued
KOA-SWEETWATER VALLEY—Continued

Phone: (800)562-9224
Address: 269 Murrays Chapel Rd, Sweetwater, TN 37874
Lat/Lon: 35.62284/-84.50571
Email: sweetwaterkoa@hotmail.com
Web: www.sweetwaterkoa.com

SEE AD KNOXVILLE PAGE 730

TELLICO PLAINS—C-6

(NE) CHEROKEE NATIONAL FOREST (Indian Boundary A & Overflow Areas)—(Monroe) *From jct Hwy 68 & Hwy 165: Go 15 mi NE on Hwy 165, then 1-1/2 mi NE on FR 35.* FACILITIES: 88 sites, 22 ft max RV length, 88 E, (20 amps), 1 pull-thrus, tenting, dump, ltd groc. RECREATION: lake swim, boating, electric motors only, canoeing, ramp, lake fishing. Partial handicap access. Open all yr.

(E) KOA Tellico Plains—(Monroe) *From jct I-75 (exit 60) & Hwy 68: Go 25 mi S on Hwy 68, then 1 mi E on Hwy 165, then 1/2 mi N on Hwy 360 (in NW corner of Hwy 165 & Hwy 360). Enter on L.* ◊◊◊◊FACILITIES: 108 sites, 70 full hkups, 38 W&E, (30/50 amps), 56 pull-thrus, tenting, dump, laundry, groceries. ◊◊◊◊RECREATION: swim pool, river fishing, playground. Pets welcome. Partial handicap access. Open Mar 12 - Nov 13. Big rigs welcome. Rate in 2010 $35-47 for 2 persons. Member ARVC, TNARVC. Phone: (423)253-2447. KOA discount.

TEN MILE—B-6

(SW) FOOSHEE PASS—(Meigs) *From jct Hwy 68 & Hwy 304: Go 1-3/4 mi N on Hwy 304, then 1-3/4 mi W following signs. Enter on R.* FACILITIES: 55 sites, 52 W&E, (30 amps), 3 no hkups, tenting, dump. RECREATION: lake swim, boating, ramp, lake fishing, playground. Partial handicap access. - Sep. Phone: (423) 334-4842.

(S) HORNSBY HOLLOW (Watts Bar Lake)—(Meigs) *From jct Hwy 68 & Hwy 58: Go 3-1/2 mi N on Hwy 58, then follow signs 2-1/2 mi W, then 1/2 mi N on Hwy 304. Enter on L.* FACILITIES: 99 sites, 99 W&E, (30/50 amps), tenting, dump, laundry, ltd groc. RECREATION: lake swim, boating, canoeing, ramp, dock, lake fishing, playground. Pets welcome. Partial handicap access. Open Apr - Oct. Phone: (423)334-1709.

TIPTONVILLE—A-1

(E) REELFOOT LAKE STATE PARK—(Lake) *From town: Go 5 mi E on Hwy 21. Enter on R.*

FACILITIES: 100 sites, 100 W&E, (30 amps), 4 pull-thrus, tenting, cabins, dump, laundry, ice, picnic tables, grills, controlled access.

RECREATION: pavilion, swim pool, boating, 10 hp limit, canoeing, ramp, dock, lake fishing, playground, tennis, hiking trails.

Pets welcome. Partial handicap access. Open all yr. Facilities fully operational Apr 1 - Oct 31. No reservations.

Phone: (800)250-8617
Address: 3120 State Rte 213, Tiptonville, TN 38079
Lat/Lon: 36.35212/-89.40221
Web: state.tn.us

SEE AD TRAVEL SECTION PAGE 714

TOWNSEND—E-5

(N) BIG MEADOW FAMILY CAMPGROUND—(Blount) *From jct Scenic Hwy 73 & US 321: Go 350 yds NE on US 321, then 100 yds W on Cedar Creek Rd (end of bridge). Enter on L.*

◊◊◊◊◊FACILITIES: 77 sites, typical site width 35 ft, 77 full hkups, (30/50 amps), 58 pull-thrus, cable TV, WiFi Instant Internet at site, WiFi Internet central location, family camping, RV storage, laundry, RV supplies, LP gas by weight/by meter, ice, picnic tables, patios, controlled access.

◊◊◊◊RECREATION: rec room/area, equipped pavilion, coin games, river swim, float trips, river fishing, golf nearby, bsktball, playground, activities, horseshoes, v-ball.

Pets welcome. No tents. Open all yr. Planned activities & church services during season only. Big rigs welcome. Escort to site. Clubs welcome. Green Friendly. Rate in 2010 $40-50 for 4 persons. MC/VISA/Debit. Member ARVC, TNARVC.

Phone: (888)497-0625
Address: 8215 Cedar Creek Rd, Townsend, TN 37882
Lat/Lon: 35.68202/-83.73393
Email: bigmeadow@msn.com
Web: www.bigmeadowcampground.com

SEE AD NEXT PAGE

TOWNSEND—Continued on next page

TOWNSEND—Continued

GREAT SMOKY MOUNTAINS NATIONAL PARK (Cades Cove Campground)—(Blount) *From jct US 321 & Scenic Hwy 73: Go 9 mi S on Scenic Hwy 73 to Laurel Creek Rd.* FACILITIES: 159 sites, 35 ft max RV length, 159 no hkups, tenting, dump, groceries. RECREATION: Pets welcome. Partial handicap access. Open all yr. Facilities fully operational May 15 - Oct 31. Phone: (865)436-1200.

Lazy Daze Campground—(Blount) *From jct Hwy 321 & Scenic Hwy 73: Go 1/2 mi E on Scenic Hwy 73. Enter on L.* ◇◇◇FACILITIES: 68 sites, typical site width 25 ft, 68 full hkups, (30/50 amps), 0 pull-thrus, family camping, tenting, laundry, groceries. ◇◇◇◇RECREATION: swim pool, river swim, river fishing, playground. Pets welcome. Open all yr. Rate in 2010 $38-44 for 2 persons. Member ARVC, TNARVC. Phone: (865)448-6061.

(W) Misty River Cabins & RV Resort, LLC—(Blount) *From jct US 321 & Hwy 73: Go 8 mi W on Hwy 321, then N on E Millers Cove (gas station on corner), then 1/2 mi W on Old Walland Hwy (quick left off bridge). Enter on L.* ◇◇◇FACILITIES: 72 sites, typical site width 35 ft, 72 full hkups, (30/50 amps), 59 pull-thrus, cable TV, WiFi Instant Internet at site, family camping, RV storage, laundry, ltd groc, RV supplies, LP gas by weight/by meter, ice, picnic tables, patios, fire rings, wood. ◇◇◇◇RECREATION: swim pool, river swim, hot tub, canoeing, kayaking, river fishing, fishing supplies, playground, horseshoes, v-ball. Pets welcome. Partial handicap access. No tents. Open all yr. Big rigs welcome. Green Friendly. Rate in 2010 $25-45 per vehicle. MC/VISA. Member ARVC, TNARVC. CCUSA 50% Discount. CCUSA reservations Recommended, CCUSA max stay 4 days, Cash only for CCUSA disc., CCUSA disc. not avail F,Sa, CCUSA disc. not avail holidays. Discount not available for special events, rallies or groups. Credit cards accepted only for reservation deposit.

Phone: (865)981-4300
Address: 5050 Old Walland Hwy, Walland, TN 37886
Lat/Lon: 35.73716/-83.82165
Email: info@mistyriverrv.com
Web: www.mistyriverrv.com

(E) Mountaineer Campground—(Blount) *From jct Hwy-321 & Scenic Hwy-73: Go 3/4 mi E on Scenic Hwy-73. Enter on L.* ◇◇◇FACILITIES: 50 sites, typical site width 25 ft, 39 full hkups, 11 W&E, (30/50 amps), 50 amps ($), family camping, tenting, dump, laundry, ltd groc. ◇◇◇RECREATION: swim pool, river swim, river fishing, playground. Pets welcome. Open Mar 1 - Nov 15. Rate in 2010 $27-41 for 2 persons. Member ARVC, TNARVC. Phone: (865)448-6421.

(S) Townsend Great Smokies KOA—(Blount) *From jct Hwy-321 & Scenic Hwy-73: Go 1 mi E on Scenic Hwy-73. Enter on L.* ◇◇◇◇FACILITIES: 126 sites, typical site width 25 ft, 62 full hkups, 39 W&E, (20/30/50 amps), 25 no hkups, 23 pull-thrus, family camping, tenting, dump, laundry, full svc store. ◇◇◇◇◇RECREATION: swim pool, river swim, canoeing, stream fishing, playground. Pets welcome, breed restrict. Partial handicap access. Open all yr. Big rigs welcome. Rate in 2010 $25-75 for 2 persons. Member ARVC, TN ARVC. Phone: (865)448-2241. KOA discount.

TOWNSEND—Continued

(S) Tremont Outdoor Resort—(Blount) *From jct Hwy-321 & Scenic Hwy-73: Go 1-1/4 mi E on Scenic Hwy-73. Enter on L.* ◇◇◇◇FACILITIES: 121 sites, typical site width 35 ft, 90 full hkups, 23 W&E, (20/30/50 amps), 8 no hkups, 3 pull-thrus, family camping, tenting, dump, laundry, groceries. ◇◇◇◇RECREATION: swim pool, river swim, river fishing, playground. Pets welcome. Partial handicap access. Open all yr. Big rigs welcome. Rate in 2010 $26-65 for 2 persons. Member ARVC, TNARVC. Phone: (800)448-6373.

TRACY CITY—C-5

FOSTER FALLS (TVA)—(Marion) *From town: Go 5 mi E on Hwy 150/US 41.* FACILITIES: 26 sites, 26 no hkups, tenting. RECREATION: Partial handicap access. Open Late Apr - Mid Oct. Phone: (423)942-5759.

UNICOI—D-6

(W) Woodsmoke Campground—(Unicoi) *From jct I-26 (exit 32) & TN 173: Go 175 yds W on TN 173. Enter on R.* ◇◇◇FACILITIES: 33 sites, 29 full hkups, (30/50 amps), 4 no hkups, tenting. Pets welcome. Partial handicap access. Open Mar 15 - Dec 1. Rate in 2010 $26 for 2 persons. Phone: (423)743-2116.

UNION CITY—A-2

(S) AAA RV Park—(Obin) *From jct US Hwy 45W & Hwy 51: Go 2 mi SE on Hwy 51, then 1/2 mi S on Phebus Lane. Enter on R.* ◇◇◇FACILITIES: 22 sites, typical site width 28 ft, 22 full hkups, (30/50 amps), 22 pull-thrus, cable TV, ($), WiFi Instant Internet at site, family camping, tenting, dump, non-guest dump $, laundry, RV supplies, picnic tables, fire rings. RECREATION: play equipment. Pets welcome. Partial handicap access. Open all yr. Big rigs welcome. Rate in 2010 $30 for 4 persons. MC/VISA. Member ARVC, TNARVC. FMCA discount. CCUSA 50% Discount. CCUSA reservations Recommended, CCUSA max stay 2 days, CCUSA disc. not avail F,Sa. Not valid for groups & based on site availability. Coin laundry-$1.75 wash, $1 dry. Cable available thru independent provider for long term stays.

Phone: (731)446-4514
Address: 2029 Phebus Ln, Union City, TN 38261
Email: billshirley@bellsouth.net
Web: www.aaarvpark.com

VONORE—B-6

NOTCHY CREEK—(Monroe) *From jct US 411 & CR 400: Go 3 mi S on CR 400, then 1-3/4 mi E (follow signs). Enter on L.* FACILITIES: 51 sites, 51 E, (50 amps), tenting, dump. RECREATION: lake swim, boating, ramp, dock, lake fishing. Open Apr - Oct. Phone: (423)884-6280.

TOQUA BEACH CAMPGROUND—(Monroe) *From jct US 411 & Hwy 360: Go 3 mi E on Hwy 360. Enter on L.* FACILITIES: 24 sites, 20 E, (30/50 amps), 4 no hkups, tenting, dump. RECREATION: lake swim, boating, ramp, dock, lake fishing. Open Apr - Oct. Phone: (423)884-2344.

WALLAND—E-5

GREAT SMOKY MOUNTAINS NATIONAL PARK (Look Rock Campground)—(Blount) *From town: Go 11 mi SW on Foothills Pkwy.* FACILITIES: 68 sites, 35 ft max RV length, 68 no hkups, tenting. RECREATION: Open Memorial Day - Labor Day. Phone: (423)436-1200.

WARTBURG—B-6

FROZEN HEAD STATE PARK—(Morgan) *From Hwy 27 in Harriman: Go N on Hwy 27, then 2 mi E on Hwy 62, then 4 mi N on Flat Fork Rd to park entrance.*

FACILITIES: 20 sites, 20 no hkups, tenting, picnic tables, fire rings, grills.

RECREATION: bsktball, playground, horseshoes, sports field, hiking trails, v-ball.

Pets welcome. Partial handicap access. Open all yr.

Phone: (423)346-3318
Address: 964 Flat Fork Road, Wartburg, TN 37887

SEE AD TRAVEL SECTION PAGE 714

WHITE BLUFF—B-3

MONTGOMERY BELL STATE PARK—(Dickson) *From town: Go 4 mi W on US 70. Enter on R.*

FACILITIES: 116 sites, 40 full hkups, 40 W&E, (30/50 amps), 36 no hkups, 2 pull-thrus, tenting, cabins, dump, picnic tables, fire rings, grills.

RECREATION: pavilion, lake swim, boating, electric motors only, ramp, canoe rentals, lake fishing, putting green, playground, shuffleboard court shuffleboard court, sports field, hiking trails, v-ball, local tours. Rec open to public.

Pets welcome. Partial handicap access. Open all yr. Facilities fully operational Apr 1 - Oct 31. MC/VISA/DISC/AMEX.

Phone: (615)797-9052
Address: 1020 Jackson Hill Rd, Burns, TN 37029
Lat/Lon: 36.10068/-87.28519
Web: state.tn.us

SEE AD TRAVEL SECTION PAGE 714

WINCHESTER—C-4

(NW) TIMS FORD STATE RUSTIC PARK—(Franklin) *From town: Go 5 mi W on Hwy 50, then 5 mi N on Mansford Rd. Enter on L.*

FACILITIES: 140 sites, 35 ft max RV length, 30 full hkups, 90 W&E, (30 amps), 20 no hkups, tenting, cabins, shower$, dump, laundry, ice, picnic tables, fire rings, grills.

RECREATION: rec hall, equipped pavilion, swim pool, wading pool, lake swim, boating, canoeing, ramp, dock, lake/river fishing, putting green, playground, activities, hiking trails, v-ball. Rec open to public.

Pets welcome. Partial handicap access. Open all yr. Facilities fully operational Apr 1 - Oct 31. No reservations. MC/VISA/DISC/AMEX.

Phone: (800)471-5295
Address: 570 Tims Ford Rd., Winchester, TN 37398
Lat/Lon: 35.22052/-86.25542
Web: www.state.tn.us

SEE AD TRAVEL SECTION PAGE 714

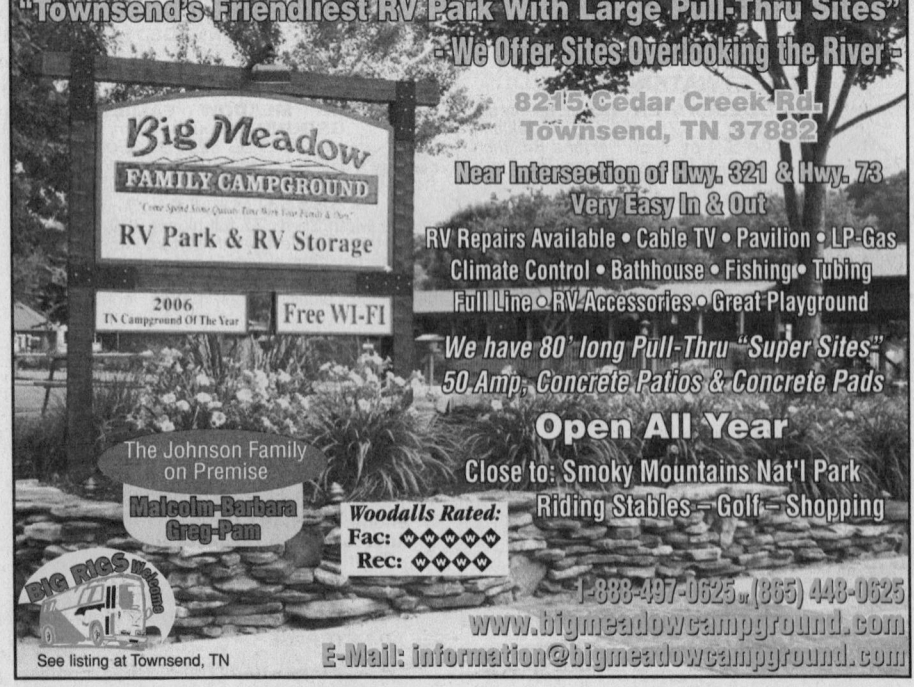

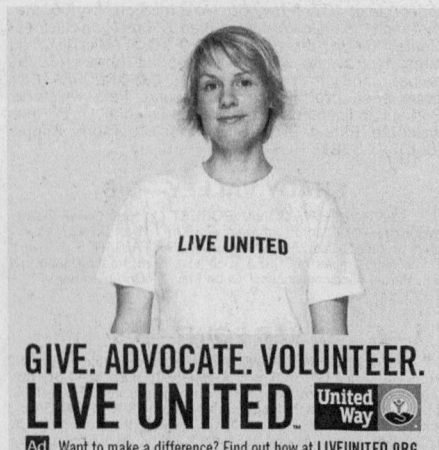

READER SERVICE INFO

The following businesses have placed an ad in the Vermont Travel Section. To receive free information, enter the Reader Service number on the Reader Service Card opposite page 48/Discover Section in the front of this directory:

Advertiser	RS#
Greenwood Lodge & Campsites	4302
Lone Pine Campsites	4342
Quechee Pine Valley KOA	2293
Vermont Campground Owners Association	3148

TIME ZONE

Vermont is in the Eastern Time Zone.

TOPOGRAPHY

Vermont enjoys four distinct seasons and, thanks to its diverse geography, distinctive regional weather. Within Vermont's 9,609 square mile area are mountains, lakes, islands, thousands of miles of fishable waterways and trails for hiking, biking or winter sports.

TEMPERATURE

Vermont enjoys a full 4-season climate. The temperature and precipitation varies among the different regions of the state. The average temperatures range from the low 30s in winter to the low 80s in summer.

TRAVEL & TOURISM INFO

State Agency:
Vermont Department of Tourism
National Life Bldg., 6th Floor, Drawer 20
Montpelier, VT 05620-0501
(802/828-3676 or 800/VERMONT)
www.vermontvacation.com.

The Vermont Campground Guide may be requested via 1/800-VERMONT or viewed online at www.campvermont.com.

Local Agencies:

Addison County Chamber of Commerce
2 Court St.
Middlebury, VT 05753
(802/388-7951 or 800/733-8376)
www.addisoncounty.com

Barton Area Chamber of Commerce
P.O. Box 403
Barton, VT 05822
(802/525-1137)
www.centerofthekingdom.com

Bennington Area Chamber of Commerce
Veterans Memorial Drive
Bennington, VT 05201
(800/229-0252 or 802/447-3311)
www.bennington.com

Brandon Chamber of Commerce
P.O. Box 267
Brandon, VT 05733
(802/247-6401)
www.brandon.org

Brattleboro Area Chamber of Commerce
180 Main St.
Brattleboro, VT 05301
(802/254-4565)
www.brattleborochamber.com

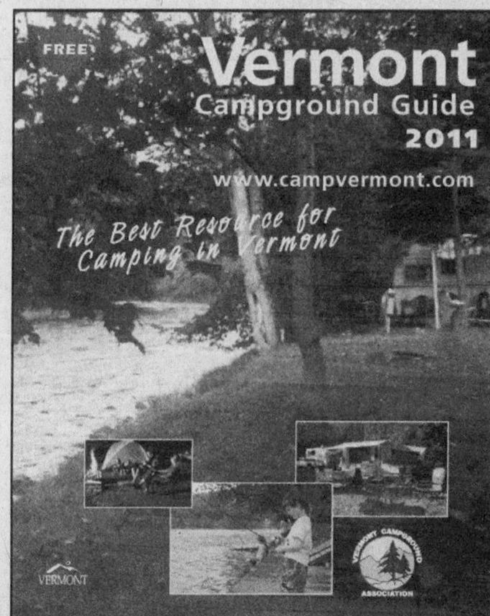

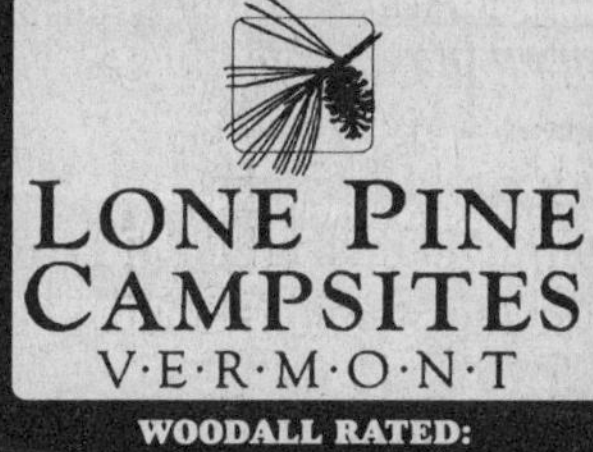

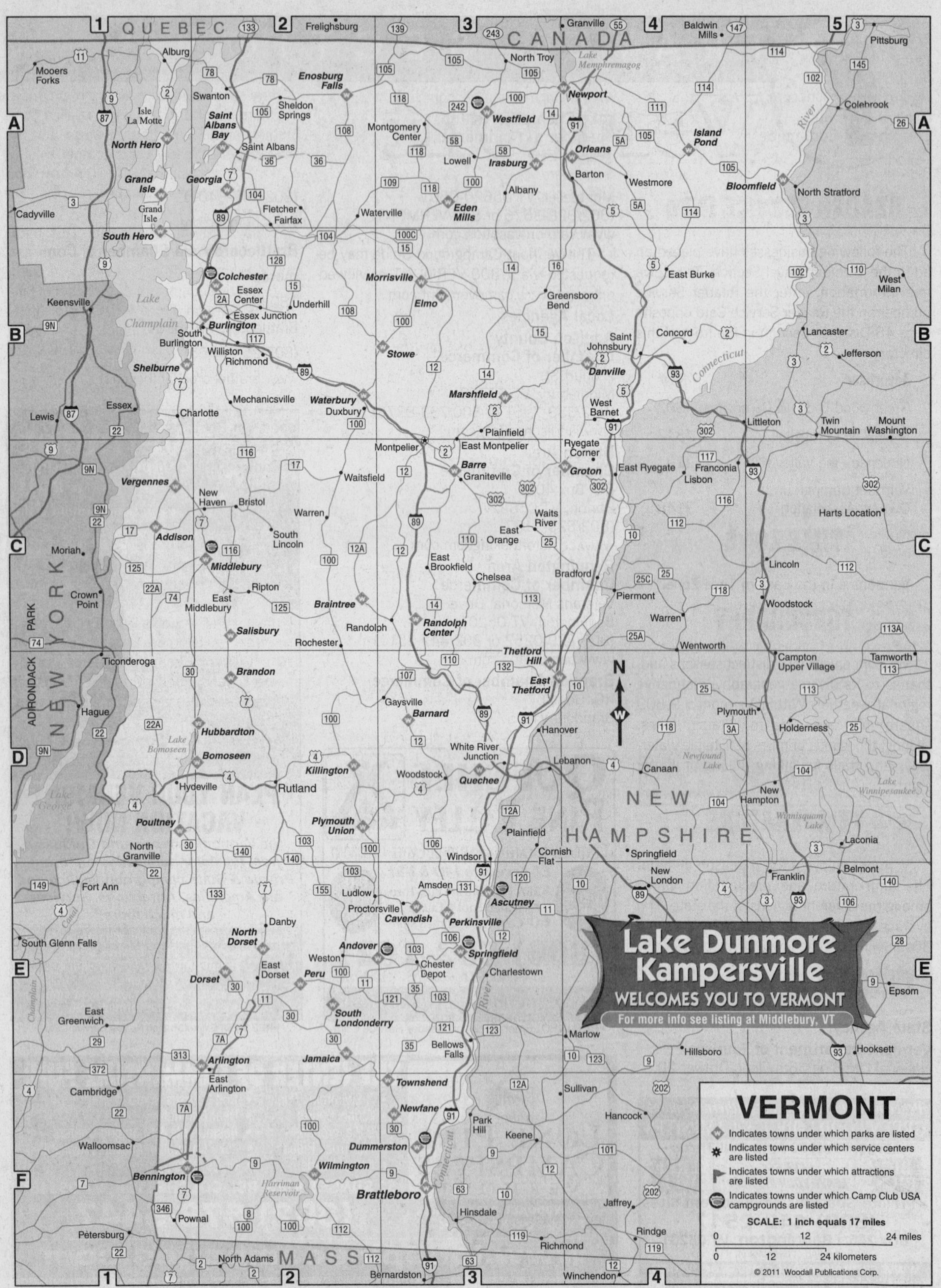

QUEBEC
CANADA
NEW YORK
ADIRONDACK PARK
NEW HAMPSHIRE
MASS
Lake Memphremagog
Lake Champlain
Lake Bomoseen
Lake George
Newfound Lake
Lake Winnipesaukee
Winnisquam Lake
Harriman Reservoir
Connecticut River
Mooers Forks
Alburg
Swanton
Isle La Motte
North Hero
Saint Albans Bay
Saint Albans
Sheldon Springs
Enosburg Falls
Frelighsburg
North Troy
Newport
Westfield
Montgomery Center
Lowell
Irasburg
Orleans
Barton
Westmore
Island Pond
Bloomfield
North Stratford
Colebrook
Pittsburg
Baldwin Mills
Granville
Grand Isle
Georgia
Fletcher
Fairfax
Cadyville
South Hero
Waterville
Eden Mills
Albany
East Burke
West Milan
Colchester
Essex Center
Essex Junction
Underhill
Morrisville
Elmo
Greensboro Bend
Keensville
Burlington
South Burlington
Williston
Richmond
Stowe
Saint Johnsbury
Concord
Lancaster
Jefferson
Danville
Shelburne
Mechanicsville
Waterbury
Duxbury
Marshfield
West Barnet
Littleton
Twin Mountain
Mount Washington
Essex
Lewis
Charlotte
Plainfield
Montpelier
East Montpelier
Ryegate Corner
Groton
East Ryegate
Franconia
Lisbon
Barre
Graniteville
Waitsfield
Vergennes
New Haven
Bristol
Warren
Waits River
East Orange
Harts Location
Addison
South Lincoln
Moriah
Middlebury
East Brookfield
Chelsea
Bradford
Lincoln
Crown Point
East Middlebury
Ripton
Piermont
Woodstock
Braintree
Randolph
Randolph Center
Salisbury
Rochester
Warren
Wentworth
Ticonderoga
Brandon
Thetford Hill
East Thetford
Campton Upper Village
Tamworth
Gaysville
Barnard
Plymouth
Holderness
Hague
Hanover
Hubbardton
White River Junction
Bomoseen
Killington
Lebanon
Canaan
Hydeville
Rutland
Woodstock
Quechee
New Hampton
Poultney
Plymouth Union
Plainfield
Laconia
North Granville
Windsor
Cornish Flat
Springfield
Fort Ann
Ludlow
Amsden
Ascutney
New London
Franklin
Belmont
Proctorsville
Cavendish
Perkinsville
Danby
North Dorset
Andover
Springfield
South Glenn Falls
Weston
Chester Depot
Charlestown
East Dorset
Dorset
Peru
Epsom
East Greenwich
South Londonderry
Marlow
Hooksett
Jamaica
Bellows Falls
Hillsboro
Arlington
East Arlington
Cambridge
Townshend
Sullivan
Newfane
Park Hill
Hancock
Keene
Walloomsac
Dummerston
Wilmington
Bennington
Brattleboro
Jaffrey
Pownal
Hinsdale
Petersburg
Rindge
Richmond
North Adams
Bernardston
Winchendon
N
W
Lake Dunmore Kampersville
WELCOMES YOU TO VERMONT
For more info see listing at Middlebury, VT
VERMONT
Indicates towns under which parks are listed
Indicates towns under which service centers are listed
Indicates towns under which attractions are listed
Indicates towns under which Camp Club USA campgrounds are listed
SCALE: 1 inch equals 17 miles
0 12 24 miles
0 12 24 kilometers
© 2011 Woodall Publications Corp.

Burke Area Chamber of Commerce
P.O. Box 347
East Burke, VT 05832
(802/626-4124)
www.burkevermont.com

Central Vermont Chamber of Commerce
P.O. Box 336
Barre, VT 05641
(802/229-5711)
www.central-vt.com

Dorset Chamber of Commerce
P.O. Box 121, Dorset, VT 05251
(802/867-2450)
www.dorsetvt.com

Franklin County Regional Chamber of Commerce
2 North Main St., Ste 101
St. Albans, VT 05478
(802/524-2444)
www.stalbanschamber.com

Hardwick Area Chamber of Commerce
P.O. Box 111
Hardwick, VT 05843
(802/472-5906)
www.hardwickvtarea.com

Hartford Area Chamber of Commerce
211 N. Main St., Suite #4
White River Junction., VT 05001
(802/295-7900 or 800/295-5451)
www.hartfordvtchamber.com

Jay Peak Area Association
P.O. Box 177
Troy, VT 05868
(802/326-3232)
www.jaypeakvermont.org

Killington Chamber of Commerce
P.O. Box 114
Killington, VT 05751
(802/773-4181)
www.killingtonchamber.com

Lake Champlain Islands Chamber of Commerce
P.O. Box 213
North Hero, VT 05474-0213
(802/372-8400; 800/262-5226)
www.champlainislands.com

Lake Champlain Regional Chamber of Commerce
60 Main Street, Suite 100
Burlington, VT 05401-8418
(802/863-3489)
www.vermont.org

Vermont Chamber of Commerce
P.O. Box 37
Montpelier, VT 05601
(802/223-3443)
www.vtchamber.com

Vermont's North Country Chamber of Commerce
246 Causeway
Newport, VT 05855
(802-334-7782)
www.vtnorthcountry.org

Windsor-Mt Ascutney Regional Chamber of Commerce
P.O. Box 41
Windsor, VT 05089
(802/674-5910)
www.windsorvt.com/

RECREATIONAL INFO

Biking: Vermont Outdoor Guide Association, P.O. Box 10, North Ferrisburg, VT 05473 (800/425-8747 or 802/425-6211). www.voga.org

Bike Vermont, 52 Pleasant St., Woodstock, VT 05091 (802/457-3553). www.bikevt.com

Fishing and Hunting: Vermont Fish & Wildlife Dept. 10 South, 103 South Main St., Waterbury, VT (802/241-3700). www.vtfishandwildlife.com

Golf: Play Northeast Golf, 5197 Main St, Ste. 8, Waitsfield, VT 05673 (800/639-1941 or 802/496-7575). www.PlayNortheastGolf.com

Hiking: Vermont Outdoor Guide Association, P.O. Box 10, N Ferrisburg, VT 05473 (800/425-8747). www.voga.org

Skiing, Downhill & Cross-Country/Snowboarding: Vermont Ski Areas Association, 26 State St, Montpelier, VT 05602 (802/223-2439).
www.skivermont.com

Snowmobiling: Vermont Association of Snow Travelers, 26 Vast Lane, Berlin, VT 05641 (802/229-0005) www.vtvast.org

Waterfalls: www.northeastwaterfalls.com

SHOPPING

The Vermont landscape is dotted with country stores carrying a variety of products, but more important, bringing a relaxed community spirit and timelessness to the shopping experience. For a complete list of country stores, visit the **Vermont Association of Independent Country Stores** at www.vaics.org

Willey's Store, Greensboro. This traditional country store has wood floors and carries everything from hardware and clothing to hunting equipment and custom meats.

Falls General Store & Deli, Northfield Falls. An amazing array of products including groceries, dry goods, furniture, souvenirs, artwork and Vermont products. Play checkers in the summer, sit by the woodstove in the winter or watch the suspended G-scale train year round. On Rt. 12, corner of Cox Brook Rd.

Newfane Country Store, Newfane. Specializing in handmade quilts and Newfane pottery hand painted by a local artist, the store also carries a wide assortment of Vermont fare including fudge, maple syrup, jams, jellies and more. On Rt. 30, Main St.

Vermont Country Store, Weston. Established in 1946, this was the first restored rural store in the nation. They carry hard-to-find items and products that you remember from years ago and have been looking forever since. Clothing, household items, candy, apothecary and products ranging from Green Goddess salad dressing to Dippity Do Styling Gel. Route 100

Vermont Teddy Bear Company, Shelburne. Tours reveal how teddy bears are hand crafted. Browse for gifts in the Bear Shop or create your own teddy. At 6655 Shelburne Rd.

UNIQUE FEATURES

Vermont is known for its great skiing. Recent renovations and upgrades to their ski resorts have resulted in expanded terrain and increased snowmaking coverage. Popular ski resorts include:

Bolton Valley Resort, Bromley Mountain, Burke Mountain Ski Area, Jay Peak Resort, Killington Resort, Mad River Glen, Magic Mountain, Middlebury College Snow Bowl, Mount Snow Resort, Okemo Mountain Resort, Pico Mountain, Smugglers' Notch Resort, Stowe Mountain Resort, Stratton Mountain Resort and Sugarbush Resort.

DESTINATIONS

STATEWIDE

Vermont has a total of 114 covered bridges, more than 50 state parks, dozens of great private campgrounds, lots of hands-on and history-based museums and an abundance of high quality artisans and specialty food producers.

NORTHERN VERMONT

Vermont's Islands and Farms Region is home to **St. Anne's Shrine**, beautiful island parks and rolling farmland. Fishing, wildlife watching, water sports and biking are great draws. Nearly three-dozen covered bridges are in northern Vermont. **Missisquoi National Wildlife Refuge** in Swanton has over 6,600 acres of forest, marsh and wetlands.

The Northeast Kingdom is known for its mountains, lakes, wilderness and wildlife as well as its delightful small villages, fairs and foliage festivals and mountain resorts. And with some of the most abundant snowfalls in the northeast, this area is a Nordic skier's paradise.

Kingdom Trails, noted among the "Top Ten" best mountain biking trails in the world by the International Mountain Biking Association, winds its way through forests, meadows, fields and mountains.

Birds of Vermont Museum, Huntington. See loons and 464 other life-size woodcarvings of Vermont birds. The museum also features extinct and endangered birds. See live birds at feeders or walk the 100 acres on hiking trails.

ECHO at the Leahy Center for Lake Champlain, Burlington, is a world-class lake aquarium and science center. Over 60 species of live fish, amphibians and reptiles. 100 interactive exhibits. 2.6-acre site highlights **Lake Champlain Navy Memorial** & heroic "Lone Sailor" statue. Live animal feedings and demonstrations daily.

Ethan Allen Homestead Museum, Burlington. The Homestead offers hands-on history, spectacular scenery and riverside picnic areas and walks.

Fairbanks Museum & Planetarium, St. Johnsbury. Victorian masterpiece with largest display of mounted birds and mammals in northern New England. Also features antique tools and toys, dolls and dinosaurs, artifacts from Vermont and around the world. Vermont's only public planetarium and weather gallery.

Vermont Ski Museum, Stowe. Located in an historic 1818 Old Town Hall, the museum collects, preserves and celebrates Vermont's rich skiing history. Permanent and changing exhibits include handcrafted eight-foot skis to lost ski areas to the story of the 10th Mountain Division.

CENTRAL VERMONT

The **Lake Champlain Basin** extends along the western side of Vermont through the greater Burlington, Middlebury/ Vergennes and Rutland areas. Water sports, cruises, underwater archaeological preserves, waterfront dining, a downtown pedestrian shopping mall, **Frog Hollow State Crafts Center**, great performing arts events and year-round venues, farm attractions includ-

QUICK REFERENCE CHART FOR WOODALL'S FEATURED PARKS

	Green Friendly	RV Lots for Sale	Park Models-Onsite Ownership	Park Membership for Sale	Big Rigs Welcome	Internet Friendly	Pets Welcome
BARRE							
Limehurst Lake Campground					▲	●	■
BENNINGTON							
Greenwood Lodge and Campsites					▲	●	■
Pine Hollow Campground					▲	●	■
BRANDON							
Smoke Rise Campground							■
BURLINGTON							
North Beach Campground					▲	●	■
COLCHESTER							
Lone Pine Campsites					▲	●	■
DANVILLE							
Sugar Ridge RV Village & Campground					▲	●	■
DORSET							
Dorset RV Park					▲	●	■
IRASBURG							
Tree Corners Family Campground					▲	●	■
MIDDLEBURY							
Lake Dunmore Kampersville					▲	●	■
QUECHEE							
Quechee Pine Valley KOA					▲	●	■
SHELBURNE							
Shelburne Camping Area					▲	●	■
SOUTH HERO							
Apple Island Resort					▲	●	■
STOWE							
Gold Brook Campground (at Nichols Lodge).						●	■

Green Friendly 🍃**; RV Lots for Sale ✖; Park Models/Onsite Onwership ✱; Park Memberships for Sale ✔; Big Rigs Welcome ▲; Internet Friendly ●; Internet Friendly-WiFi ●; Pets Welcome ■**

ing the **UVM Morgan Horse Farm** and myriad restaurants and museums are a few of the area's great experiences. At the **Lake Champlain Maritime Museum** you can explore the history of Lake Champlain through hands-on exhibits featuring shipwrecks, antique boats and a working conservation lab.

The Henry Sheldon Museum of Vermont History is the oldest chartered community history museum in the United States, welcoming visitors and researchers since 1882. It offers lively tours, exhibits and programs to enrich our understanding of Vermont's past. Visitors can now enter through the original door on the front porch of the Museum's 1829 brick house on Park Street. The Museum Shop has also moved to the front of the building, where it can more easily be a part of the commercial mix of downtown Middlebury.

Historic Shelburne Village includes **Shelburne Museum,** displaying a large selection of Americana and **Shelburne Farms** as well as the **Shelburne Craft School** that offers two-day weekend workshops in different art mediums including wood, clay, fine arts, metal and stained glass. While in Shelburne, visit the **Vermont Wildflower Farm** featuring six acres of wildflower gardens.

The **Barre-Montpelier** section of central Vermont is well known for **The Vermont State House**, **Rock of Ages Granite** and many beautiful examples of stonecutting expertise exhibited in local monuments and statues. The Vermont Historical Society has moved to a historic Barre building. **Cabot Creamery**, **Ben and Jerry's, Cold Hollow, Bragg Farm** and others showcase Vermont's agricultural products. Learn the art of sugaring from Vermont's oldest maple family at **Morse Farm Maple Sugarworks**. Includes a **Sugar House**, **Woodshed Theatre** and famous wood carved dioramas.

Montshire Museum of Science, Norwich. Outdoor science park and learning center with live animals, aquariums, exhibits on space, nature and technology with many hands-on exhibits.

SOUTHERN VERMONT

Outdoor enthusiasts will find southern Vermont, half of it within the **Green Mountain National Forest**, has some of the best terrain in the East for hiking, biking, water and winter sports. **D&K Butterfly Farm**, Jamaica, **Robert Frost Museum**, Shaftsbury and the **Vermont Covered Bridge Museum**, Bennington are great attractions. The area is rich in Vermont arts and culture venues of all types, including the **Southern Vermont Arts Center, Simon Pearce and Bellows Falls Village**. **Bennington Museum** houses a collection of Grandma Moses paintings among other regional art. View a corn maze and dancing leaves at the **Apple Barn** and strolling of the heifers through downtown **Brattleboro.**

The Precision Valley, from Springfield to Ludlow, was known as the center of the machine tool industry during much of the 19th and 20th centuries; many inventions crucial to industrialization came from this area.

Manchester is home to the **American Museum of Fly Fishing**, the largest public collection of angling art and artifacts. For family fun, visit the **Bromley Mountain Thrill Zone** and ride the Alpine Slide, Vermont's longest waterslide ride. Also features roller coasters, climbing wall, mini golf and kiddie fun park.

Wilmington. Try milking goats or take a scenic hayride to bear caves at **Adams Farm,** a sixth generation working farm with sheep herding demonstrations, livestock barn, Vermont made products.

ANNUAL EVENTS

JANUARY

Hildene Holidays, Manchester; Annual Stowe Winter Carnival, Stowe; Yankee Sportsman's Classic Hunting Fishing & Outdoor Show, Essex Junction; Brookfield Ice Harvest, Brookfield.

FEBRUARY

Lake Hortonia Ice Fishing Derby, Hortonia; Vermont Boat Show, Essex Junction; Brattleboro Winter Carnival, Middlebury; Magic Hat Mardi Gras, Burlington; Jay Peak Mardi Gras, Jay; Vermont Recreation Vehicle & Camping Show, Essex Junction.

MARCH

Maple Festival, Lunenberg; Burlington Home Show, Burlington; US Open Snowboarding Championships, Stratton; Vermont Maple Open House, Statewide; Reggaefest, West Dover; Annual Spring Loaded, Killington.

APRIL

Spring Summit Celebration, Stowe; Annual Vermont Maple Festival, St. Albans; Everything Equine & Horses, Essex Junction.

MAY

Vermont Chocolate Show, Essex; Jamaica Fiber Festival, Jamaica; Blackfly Festival, Adamant; Annual Flavors of the Valley, White River Junction; Annual Essex Craft & Fine Art Show, Essex; Vermont Business Expo, Burlington.

JUNE

Strolling of the Heifers Parade & Festival, Brattleboro; Vermont Dairy Festival, Sheldon; Discover Jazz Festival, Burlington; Annual Manchester Antique & Classic Car Show, Manchester; Quechee Hot Air Balloon Festival, Quechee; Vermont Quilt Festival, Essex Junction and Colchester; Killington Music Festival, Killington; Annual Vermont Food Festival, Burlington; Stowe Garden Festival, Stowe.

JULY

Kaleidoscope Festival, Stowe; Stoweflake Hot Air Balloon Festival, Stowe; Basin Bluegrass Festival, Brandon; Washington County Fair & Field Days, East Montpelier; SolarFest, Tinmouth; Windsor County Agricultural Fair, Springfield; Vermont Mozart Festival, Burlington; Marlboro Music Festival, Marlboro; Middlebury Festival on the Green, Middlebury; Connecticut Valley Fair, Bradford; Cobras in the Mountains, Stowe; Annual Cracker Barrel Festival, Newbury.

CAMPCLUB USA

Where to Find CCUSA Parks

List City	Park Name	Map Coordinates
ANDOVER		
	Horseshoe Acres Campground	E-2
ASCUTNEY		
	Getaway Mountain Campground	E-3
	Running Bear Camping Area	E-3
BENNINGTON		
	Pine Hollow Campground	F-1
COLCHESTER		
	Lone Pine Campsites	B-2
DUMMERSTON		
	Hidden Acres Campground	F-3
MIDDLEBURY		
	Lake Dunmore Kampersville	C-2
SPRINGFIELD		
	Tree Farm Campground	E-3
WESTFIELD		
	Barrewood Campground	A-3

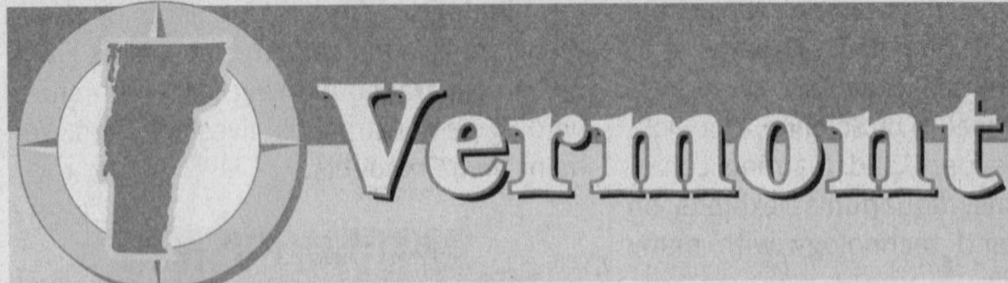

All privately owned campgrounds personally inspected by WOODALL'S Representatives

John and Carla Skolburg

ADDISON—C-1

(W) DAR SP—(Addison) *From jct Hwy-22A & Hwy-17: Go 7 mi SW on Hwy-17.* FACILITIES: 70 sites, 70 no hkups, tenting, dump. RECREATION: lake swim, boating, lake fishing, playground. Pets welcome. Open mid May - early Sep. Phone: (802) 759-2354.

ANDOVER—E-2

Horseshoe Acres Campground—*From jct Hwy 103 & Hwy 11: 4 mi W on Hwy 11, 3-1/2 mi N on Andover/Weston Rd. Enter on R.* FACILITIES: 173 sites, 38 ft max RV length, 36 full hkups, 137 W&E, (20/30 amps), 12 pull-thrus, cable TV, tenting, RV storage, dump, portable dump, laundry, groceries, RV supplies, ice, picnic tables, fire rings, wood. RECREATION: rec hall, pavilion, swim pool, lake fishing, mini-golf, bsktball, playground, shuffleboard court shuffleboard court, horseshoes, v-ball. Pets welcome. Open May 15 - Nov 1. Rate in 2010 $30-35 per vehicle. CCUSA 50% Discount. CCUSA reservations Required, CCUSA max stay 4 days, CCUSA disc. not avail F,Sa, CCUSA disc. not avail holidays. Campground closed Nov 1-May 15. $10 surcharge for portable dump, $2.50 for mini-golf round.

Phone: (802)875-2960
Address: 1978 Weston-Andover Rd, Andover, VT 05143
Lat/Lon: 43.2842/-72.7146
Email: horseshoe@vermontel.net
Web: www.horseshoeacrescampground.com

ARLINGTON—E-2

(N) Camping on The Battenkill—(Bennington) *From north jct US 7A & Hwy 313: Go 3/4 mi N on US 7A. Enter on L.* ◇◇◇FACILITIES: 100 sites, typical site width 25 ft, 46 full hkups, 54 W&E, (20/30/50 amps), 50 amps ($), 13 pull-thrus, family camping, tenting, dump. ◇◇RECREATION: river swim, canoeing, river fishing, playground. Pets welcome, quantity restrict. Partial handicap access. Open mid Apr - mid Oct. Big rigs welcome. Rate in 2010 $30-32 for 2 persons. Member ARVC, VCA. Phone: (802)375-6663.

ASCUTNEY—E-3

ASCUTNEY SP—(Windsor) *From I-91 (exit 8): Go 2 mi N on US 5, then 1 mi NW on Hwy 44a road to mountain top.* FACILITIES: 39 sites, 39 no hkups, tenting, dump. RECREATION: playground. Pets welcome. Open May 20 - Oct 15. Phone: (802)674-2060.

ASCUTNEY—Continued

(S) Getaway Mountain Campground—(Windsor) *From jct I-91 (exit 8) & Hwy 131: Go 1/2 mi E on Hwy 131, then 1-1/2 mi S on US 5. Enter on R.* ◇◇◇FACILITIES: 99 sites, typical site width 30 ft, 87 full hkups, 6 W&E, (20/30/50 amps), 6 no hkups, 10 pull-thrus, heater not allowed, family camping, tenting, shower$, dump, non-guest dump $, laundry, ltd groc, LP gas by weight/by meter, ice, picnic tables, fire rings, grills, wood. ◇◇◇RECREATION: swim pool, hot tub, bsktball, playground, horseshoes, v-ball. Pets welcome. Partial handicap access. Open May 1 - End Oct. Rate in 2010 $27-30 for 3 persons. Member VCA. CCUSA 50% Discount. CCUSA reservations Recommended, CCUSA max stay 1 day, Cash only for CCUSA disc., CCUSA disc. not avail F,Sa, CCUSA disc. not avail holidays. Discount not available on seasonal sites. Electric heater not allowed.

Phone: (802)674-2812
Address: 3628 Rte 5S, Ascutney, VT 05030
Lat/Lon: 43.38693/-72.41201

(N) Running Bear Camping Area—(Windsor) *From jct I-91 (exit 8) & Hwy 131: Go 1/2 mi E on Hwy 131, then 1 mi N on US 5. Enter on L.* ◇◇◇FACILITIES: 97 sites, typical site width 25 ft, 46 full hkups, 41 W&E, (20/30/50 amps), 10 no hkups, WiFi Instant Internet at site, family camping, tenting, RV storage, dump, non-guest dump $, portable dump, laundry, ltd groc, RV supplies, LP gas by weight/by meter, ice, picnic tables, fire rings, wood. ◇◇◇◇RECREATION: rec hall, swim pool, bsktball, playground, activities, horseshoes, v-ball. Pets welcome, breed restrict. Open all yr. Facilities fully operational May 1 - Oct 15. Rate in 2010 $32-37 per family. MC/VISA. Member ARVC, VCA. CCUSA 50% Discount. CCUSA reservations Recommended, CCUSA max stay 5 days, Cash only for CCUSA disc., CCUSA disc. not avail F,Sa, CCUSA disc. not avail holidays.

Phone: (802)674-6417
Address: 6248 Rt 5, Ascutney, VT 05030
Lat/Lon: 43.42216/-72.40304
Email: girards@runningbearvt.com
Web: www.runningbearvermont.com

Reserve Online at Woodalls.com

(S) WILGUS SP—(Windsor) *From jct I-91 (exit 8) & US 5: Go 1-1/2 mi S on US 5.* FACILITIES: 17 sites, 17 no hkups, tenting, dump. RECREATION: lake swim, boating, canoeing, river fishing, playground. Pets welcome. Open May 26 - Oct 9. Phone: (802)674-5422.

BARNARD—D-3

(N) SILVER LAKE SP—(Windsor) *From town: Go 1/4 mi N on Town Rd.* FACILITIES: 40 sites, 40 no hkups, tenting, dump. RECREATION: lake swim, boating, no motors, lake fishing, playground. Pets welcome. Open Memorial Day - Labor Day. Phone: (802)234-9451.

BARRE—C-3

(W) Lazy Lions Campground—(Washington) *From I-89 (exit 6): Go 4 mi E on Hwy 63 to Hwy 14, then 1 mi straight ahead from stop light. Enter on L.* ◇◇◇FACILITIES: 42 sites, typical site width 30 ft, 23 full hkups, 4 W&E, 4 E, (20/30 amps), 11 no hkups, 4 pull-thrus, family camping, tenting, dump, laundry. ◇◇RECREATION: swim pool. Pets welcome. Partial handicap access. Open Early May - End of Oct. Rate in 2010 $35 per family. Member VCA. Phone: (802)479-2823.

BARRE—Continued
Lazy Lions Campground—Continued

(S) LIMEHURST LAKE CAMPGROUND—(Orange) *From jct I-89 (exit 6) & Hwy 63: Go 4 mi E on Hwy 63, then 6 mi S on Hwy 14. Enter on R.*

◇◇◇◇FACILITIES: 73 sites, typical site width 35 ft, 30 full hkups, 27 W&E, 2 E, (30/50 amps), 14 no hkups, some extd stay sites (summer), 8 pull-thrus, cable TV, WiFi Instant Internet at site, WiFi Internet central location, family camping, tenting, RV's/park model rentals, cabins, RV storage, shower$, dump, portable dump, laundry, ltd groc, RV supplies, LP gas by weight/by meter, ice, picnic tables, fire rings, grills, wood, controlled access.

◇◇◇◇◇RECREATION: rec room/area, equipped pavilion, coin games, lake swim, canoeing, kayaking, 3 rowboat/4 canoe/2 kayak/5 pedal boat rentals, lake fishing, fishing supplies, golf nearby, bsktball, playground, shuffleboard court 2 shuffleboard courts, activities (wkends), horseshoes, sports field, hiking trails, v-ball. Rec open to public.

Pets welcome, breed restrict. Partial handicap access. Open Apr 15 - Oct 25. Facilities fully operational May 1 - Oct 15. Big rigs welcome. Escort to site. Clubs welcome. Rate in 2010 $24-39 per family. MC/VISA. Member ARVC, VCA. FCRV discount. FMCA discount.

Phone: (802)433-6662
Address: 4104 VT Rte 14, Williamstown, VT 05679
Lat/Lon: 44.09846/-72.54774
Email: limehurstlake@myfairpoint.net
Web: www.limehurstlake.com

SEE AD THIS PAGE AND AD TRAVEL SECTION PAGE 751

BENNINGTON—F-1

(E) GREENWOOD LODGE AND CAMPSITES—(Bennington) *From jct US 7 & Hwy 9: Go 8 mi E on Hwy 9. Enter on R.*

◇◇◇◇FACILITIES: 40 sites, typical site width 35 ft, 20 W&E, (20/30/50 amps), 20 no hkups, 8 pull-thrus, WiFi Instant Internet at site, WiFi Internet central location, family camping, tenting, RV storage, dump, non-guest dump $, portable dump, picnic tables, fire rings, grills, wood.

◇◇◇RECREATION: rec hall, rec room/area, boating, canoeing, 2 rowboat/3 canoe rentals, bsktball, horseshoes, sports field, hiking trails, v-ball.

GREENWOOD LODGE AND CAMPSITES—Continued on next page

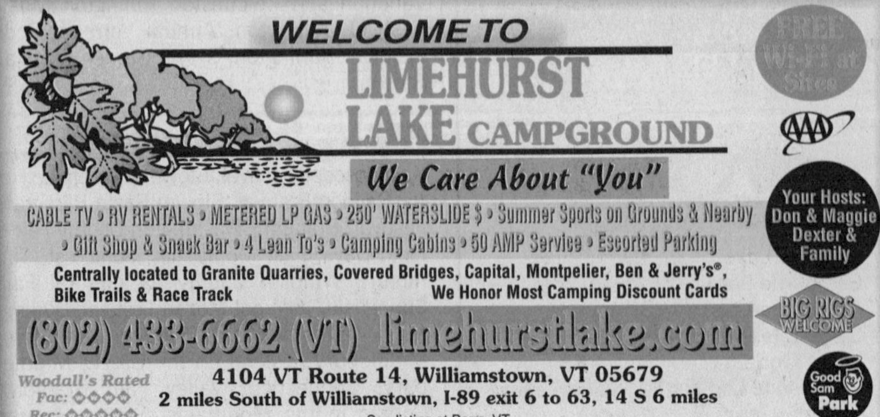

BENNINGTON—Continued
GREENWOOD LODGE AND CAMPSITES—Continued

Pets welcome, breed restrict. Partial handicap access. Open May 20 - Oct 26. Big rigs welcome. Escort to site. Clubs welcome. Rate in 2010 $31-33 for 2 persons. Member ARVC, VCA.

Phone: (802)442-2547
Address: 311 Greenwood Dr, Woodford, VT 05201
Lat/Lon: 42.87585/-73.08099
Email: campgreenwood@aol.com
Web: www.campvermont.com/greenwood

SEE AD TRAVEL SECTION PAGE 749

(S) PINE HOLLOW CAMPGROUND—(Bennington) *From jct US 7 & SR 9: Go 6-1/4 mi S on US 7, then 1-1/2 mi E on Barbers Pond Rd, then 3/4 mi S on Old Military Rd, then 1/4 mi W on Pine Hollow Rd. Enter at end.*

◇◇◇◇FACILITIES: 60 sites, typical site width 25 ft, 24 full hkups, 34 W&E, (20/30/50 amps), 2 no hkups, cable TV, ($), WiFi Instant Internet at site, family camping, tenting, dump, portable dump, ice, picnic tables, fire rings, wood.

◇◇◇RECREATION: lake swim, electric motors only, canoeing, canoe/2 pedal boat rentals, pond fishing, fishing supplies, play equipment, shuffleboard court, horseshoes, v-ball.

Pets welcome, breed restrict. Open Mid May - Mid Oct. Big rigs welcome. Escort to site. Clubs welcome. Rate in 2010 $30-37 for 4 persons. Member ARVC, VCA. CCUSA 50% Discount. CCUSA reservations Recommended, CCUSA max stay 1 day, Cash only for CCUSA disc., CCUSA disc. not avail F,Sa, CCUSA disc. not avail holidays. $2 electric heater surcharge.

Phone: (802)823-5569
Address: 342 Pine Hollow Rd, Pownal, VT 05261
Lat/Lon: 42.78642/-73.19909
Web: www.pinehollowcamping.com

SEE AD THIS PAGE

WOODFORD SP—(Bennington) *From town: Go 10 mi E on Hwy-9.* FACILITIES: 103 sites, 103 no hkups, tenting, dump. RECREATION: lake swim, boating, no motors, lake fishing, playground. Pets welcome. Open May 26 - Oct 9. Phone: (802)447-7169.

BLOOMFIELD—A-5

MAIDSTONE SP—(Essex) *From town: Go 5 mi S on Hwy-102, then 5 mi SW on State Forest highway.* FACILITIES: 82 sites, 82 no hkups, tenting, dump. RECREATION: lake swim, boating, ramp, lake fishing, playground. Pets welcome. Open May 26 - Sep 5. Phone: (802)676-3930.

BOMOSEEN—D-2

BOMOSEEN SP—(Rutland) *From jct US 4 (exit 4) & Hwy 30: Go 1 mi S on Hwy 30, then 2 mi W on US 4, then 4 mi N on West Shore Rd.* FACILITIES: 66 sites, 19 ft max RV length, 66 no hkups, tenting, dump. RECREATION: lake swim, boating, ramp, dock, lake fishing, playground. Pets welcome. Open Memorial Day - Labor Day. Phone: (802)265-4242.

(N) LAKE BOMOSEEN CAMPGROUND—(Rutland) *From jct US-4 & Hwy-30 (Exit 4): Go 5 mi N on Hwy-30. Enter on L.*

◇◇◇◇FACILITIES: 148 sites, typical site width 50 ft, 60 full hkups, 43 W&E, (30/50 amps), 45 no hkups, some extd stay sites (summer), 11 pull-thrus, cable TV, WiFi Instant Internet at site ($), WiFi Internet central location ($), family camping, tenting, RV's/park model rentals, cabins, RV storage, shower$,

BOMOSEEN—Continued
LAKE BOMOSEEN CAMPGROUND—Continued

dump, non-guest dump $, laundry, full svc store, RV supplies, LP gas by weight/by meter, ice, picnic tables, fire rings, wood, controlled access.

◇◇◇◇◇RECREATION: rec hall, rec room/area, pavilion, coin games, swim pool, wading pool, hot tub, boating, canoeing, kayaking, ramp, dock, 2 pontoon/2 rowboat/4 canoe/4 kayak/8 motorboat rentals, lake/stream fishing, fishing supplies, mini-golf, ($), golf nearby, bsktball, 14 bike rentals, playground, shuffleboard court shuffleboard court, activities (wkends), horseshoes, sports field, hiking trails, v-ball.

Pets welcome ($), breed restrict. Partial handicap access. Open May 1 - Oct 1. Big rigs welcome. Escort to site. Clubs welcome. Rate in 2010 $28-43 per family. MC/VISA/DISC/AMEX. Member ARVC, VCA.

Phone: (802)273-2061
Address: 18 Campground Dr, Bomoseen, VT 05732
Lat/Lon: 43.68348/-73.18905
Email: camplbc@aol.com
Web: www.lakebomoseen.com

SEE AD RUTLAND PAGE 758

BRAINTREE—C-2

(S) Abel Mountain Campground—(Orange) *From jct I-89 (exit 4) & Hwy-66: Go 2-1/2 mi W on Hwy-66, then 2 mi N on Hwy-12A. Enter on L.* ◇◇◇FACILITIES: 101 sites, typical site width 25 ft, 87 full hkups, 14 W&E, (20/30/50 amps), 28 pull-thrus, family camping, tenting, dump. ◇◇◇RECREATION: swim pool, playground. Pets welcome. Partial handicap access. Open May 15 - Oct 15. Big rigs welcome. Rate in 2010 $30-35 for 4 persons. Member VCA. Phone: (802)728-5548.

BRANDON—D-2

(N) Country Village Campground—(Addison) *From jct US-7 & Hwy-73: Go 3 mi N on US-7. Enter on L.* ◇◇◇FACILITIES: 41 sites, typical site width 30 ft, 36 W&E, (20/30 amps), 5 no hkups, 3 pull-thrus, family camping, tenting, dump, ltd groc. ◇◇◇RECREATION: swim pool, playground. Pets welcome. Partial handicap access. Open mid May - Columbus Day. Rate in 2010 $32 per family. Member VCA. Phone: (802)247-3333.

(N) SMOKE RISE CAMPGROUND—(Rutland) *From jct Hwy 73 & US 7: Go 2 mi N on US 7. Enter on R.*

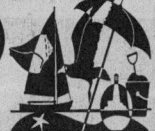

◇◇FACILITIES: 52 sites, typical site width 25 ft, 23 full hkups, 29 W&E, (30 amps), 23 pull-thrus, heater not allowed, family camping, tenting, shower$, dump, non-guest dump $, laundry, LP gas by weight/by meter, ice, picnic tables, fire rings, wood, controlled access.

◇◇◇RECREATION: pavilion, swim pool, golf nearby, bsktball, play equipment, 2 shuffleboard courts, horseshoes, sports field, v-ball. Rec open to public.

Pets welcome. Open May 15 - Oct 15. Rate in 2010 $23-28 per family.

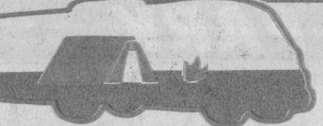

BRANDON—Continued
SMOKE RISE CAMPGROUND—Continued

Phone: (802)247-6984
Address: 2145 Grove St, Brandon, VT 05733
Lat/Lon: 43.82916/-73.10461

SEE AD THIS PAGE

BRATTLEBORO—F-3

(S) FORT DUMMER SP—(Windham) *From jct I-91 (exit 1) & US-5: Go 1/10 mi N on US-5, then 1/2 mi E on Fairground Rd, then 1 mi S on Main St & Old Guilford Rd.* FACILITIES: 60 sites, 60 no hkups, tenting, dump. RECREATION: playground. Pets welcome. Open May 26 - Sep 6. Phone: (802)254-2610.

BURLINGTON—B-2

See listings at Colchester & South Hero, Shelburne

(N) NORTH BEACH CAMPGROUND—(Chittenden) *From jct I-89 (exit 14W) & US 2: Go 1-3/4 mi W on Main St, then 1/2 mi N on Battery St, then 100 yds W on Sherman St, then 1-1/4 mi N on North Ave. Enter on L.*

FACILITIES: 137 sites, typical site width 28 ft, 27 full hkups, 39 W&E, (30/50 amps), 71 no hkups, WiFi Instant Internet at site, family camping, tenting, shower$, dump, laundry, ice, picnic tables, fire rings, wood, controlled access.

RECREATION: pavilion, lake swim, boating, canoeing, kayaking, 20 canoe/20 kayak rentals, lake fishing, golf nearby, playground, horseshoes, hiking trails, v-ball.

Pets welcome. Partial handicap access. Open May 1 - Oct 15. Big rigs welcome. Escort to site. Clubs welcome. MC/VISA/DISC/AMEX. Member VCA.

Phone: (802)862-0942
Address: 60 Institute Rd, Burlington, VT 05401
Lat/Lon: 44.49463/-73.23618
Email: clinnell@ci.burlington.vt.us
Web: www.enjoyburlington.com

SEE AD THIS PAGE

CAVENDISH—E-3

(E) Caton Place Campground—(Windsor) *From jct Hwy 103 & Hwy 131: Go 4-1/2 mi E on Hwy 131, then 1-1/2 mi NE on Tarbell Hill Rd, then 1/4 mi W on East Rd. Enter on R.* ◇◇FACILITIES: 85 sites, typical site width 33 ft, 38 full hkups, 40 W&E, 7 E, (15/20/30 amps), 14 pull-thrus, family camping, tenting, dump, laundry. ◇◇RECREATION: swim pool, playground. Pets welcome, quantity restrict. Open May 1 - Oct 15. Rate in 2010 $17-25 for 4 persons. Member VCA. Phone: (802)226-7767.

Ben & Jerry's Ice Cream company gives their ice cream waste to the local Vermont farmers who use it to feed their hogs. The hogs seem to like all of the flavors except Mint Oreo.

COLCHESTER—B-2

(N) LONE PINE CAMPSITES—(Chittenden) *N'bound from jct I-89 (exit 16) & US 2/7: Go 3-1/4 mi N on US 2/7, then 1 mi left on Bay Rd (blinking light). Enter on R.*

◊◊◊◊FACILITIES: 266 sites, typical site width 30 ft, 210 full hkups, 56 W&E, (30/50 amps), some extd stay sites (summer), 2 pull-thrus, cable TV, WiFi Instant Internet at site ($), WiFi Internet central location ($), family camping, tenting, RV storage, shower$, dump, non-guest dump $, portable dump, laundry, groceries, RV supplies, LP gas by weight/by meter, ice, picnic tables, fire rings, grills, wood.

◊◊◊◊RECREATION: rec hall, rec room/area, coin games, 2 swim pools, mini-golf, ($), golf nearby, bsktball, playground, shuffleboard court shuffleboard court, activities (wkends), tennis, horseshoes, sports field, v-ball.

Pets welcome, breed restrict, quantity restrict. Partial handicap access. Open May 1 - Oct 15. 3 day minimum stay holiday weekends, by reservation. Big rigs welcome. Escort to site. Clubs welcome. Rate in 2010 $32-45 per family. MC/VISA. Member ARVC, VCA. CCUSA 50% Discount. CCUSA reservations Accepted, CCUSA max stay 5 days, Cash only for CCUSA disc., CCUSA disc. not avail holidays. Discount not available July & Aug.

Text 86096 to (440)725-8687 to see our Visual Tour.

Phone: (802)878-5447
Address: 52 Sunset View Rd, Colchester, VT 05446
Lat/Lon: 44.55479/-73.18539
Email: suzanne@lonepinecampsites.com
Web: www.lonepinecampsites.com

SEE AD TRAVEL SECTION PAGE 751 AND AD TRAVEL SECTION PAGE 749

(NW) Malletts Bay Campgrounds—(Chittenden) *From jct I-89 (exit 16) & US 2/7: Go 2 mi N on US 2/7, then 3 mi W on Hwy 127 S (Blakely Rd.). Enter on L.* ◊◊FACILITIES: 150 sites, typical site width 25 ft, 84 full hkups, 26 W&E, (20/30/50 amps), 40 no hkups, family camping, tenting, dump, laundry, ltd groc. ◊◊RECREATION: swim pool, playground. Pets welcome, breed restrict. Open May 1 - Oct 15. Rate in 2010 $38-39 per family. Member VCA. Phone: (802) 863-6980.

DANVILLE—B-4

(E) SUGAR RIDGE RV VILLAGE & CAMPGROUND—(Caledonia) *From jct I-91 (exit 21) & US 2: Go 4-1/2 mi W on US 2. Enter on L.*

◊◊◊◊◊FACILITIES: 150 sites, typical site width 50 ft, 133 full hkups, 7 W&E, (30/50 amps), 10 no hkups, some extd stay sites (summer), 5 pull-thrus, cable TV, WiFi Instant Internet at site, phone Internet central location, family camping, tenting, RV's/park model rentals, dump, non-guest dump $, laundry, groceries, RV supplies, LP gas by weight/by meter, ice, picnic tables, fire rings, grills, wood, controlled access.

◊◊◊◊◊RECREATION: rec hall, coin games, 2 swim pools, pond fishing, fishing supplies, mini-golf, ($), golf nearby, bsktball, playground, shuffleboard court shuffleboard court, activities, tennis, horseshoes, sports field, hiking trails, v-ball.

Pets welcome. Partial handicap access. Open Mothers Day Weekend - Week after Columbus Day. Big rigs welcome. Clubs welcome. Rate in 2010 $39.50-41.50 for 4 persons. MC/VISA/DISC. Member VCA.

Admiral George Dewey was from Vermont.

DANVILLE—Continued
SUGAR RIDGE RV VILLAGE & CAMPGROUND—Continued

Phone: (802)684-2550
Address: 24 Old Stagecoach Rd, Danville, VT 05828
Lat/Lon: 44.42231/-72.11511
Email: sugarridge@kingcon.com
Web: www.sugarridgervpark.com

SEE AD ST. JOHNSBURY PAGE 758

DORSET—E-2

(S) DORSET RV PARK—(Bennington) *From jct US 7A & Hwy 30 (in Manchester): Go 4 mi N on Hwy 30. Enter on L.*

◊◊◊◊FACILITIES: 40 sites, typical site width 25 ft, 20 full hkups, 7 W&E, (30/50 amps), 50 amps ($), 13 no hkups, some extd stay sites (summer), 6 pull-thrus, cable TV, WiFi Instant Internet at site, WiFi Internet central location, family camping, tenting, RV storage, dump, non-guest dump $, portable dump, laundry, ltd groc, RV supplies, LP bottle exch, ice, picnic tables, fire rings, grills, wood.

◊◊◊RECREATION: rec hall, coin games, golf nearby, bsktball, playground, shuffleboard court 2 shuffleboard courts, activities (wkends), horseshoes, sports field, v-ball.

Pets welcome. Partial handicap access. Open Beginning of May - End of October. Big rigs welcome. Escort to site. Clubs welcome. Rate in 2010 $25-40 per family. MC/VISA. Member VCA.

Phone: (802)867-5754
Address: 1567 State Rt 30, Dorset, VT 05251
Lat/Lon: 43.23282/-73.08062
Email: hasgas@aol.com
Web: www.dorsetrvpark.com

SEE AD THIS PAGE

DUMMERSTON—F-3

(N) Brattleboro North-KOA—(Windham) *From jct I-91 (exit 3), Hwy 9 & US 5: Take Round About and Go 3-1/2 mi N on US 5. Enter on R.* ◊◊◊◊FACILITIES: 41 sites, typical site width 50 ft, 12 full hkups, 29 W&E, (20/30/50 amps), 34 pull-thrus, family camping, tenting, dump, laundry, ltd groc. ◊◊◊RECREATION: swim pool, playground. Pets welcome. Open Mid Apr - Early Nov. Big rigs welcome. Rate in 2010 $34-48 for 2 persons. Member VCA. Phone: (800)562-5909. KOA discount.

(N) Hidden Acres Campground—(Windham) ◊◊◊FACILITIES: 40 sites, 9 full hkups, 31 W&E, (30 amps), 25 pull-thrus, WiFi Instant Internet at site, WiFi Internet central location, family camping, tenting, shower$, dump, non-guest dump $, portable dump, laundry, ltd groc, RV supplies, LP gas by weight/by meter, ice, picnic tables, fire rings, wood. ◊◊◊◊RECREATION: rec hall, swim pool, mini-golf, ($), bsktball, playground, shuffleboard court 2 shuffleboard courts, activities horseshoes, hiking trails, v-ball. Pets welcome. Partial handicap access. Open Apr 15 - Oct 15. Rate in 2010 $36-40 per family. MC/VISA. Member VCA. CCUSA 50% Discount. CCUSA reservations Required, CCUSA max stay 5 days, CCUSA disc. not avail F,Sa, CCUSA disc. not avail holidays. Pool open Memorial Day weekend thru Labor Day.

Phone: (802)254-2098
Address: 792 US Rt. 5, Dummerston, VT 05301
Lat/Lon: 42.91598/-72.53645
Email: hacrvt@sover.net
Web: hiddenacresvt.net

EAST THETFORD—D-3

(W) Rest N' Nest Campground—(Orange) *From jct I-91 (exit 14) & Hwy-113: Go 200 feet E on Hwy-113, then 1/8 mi N on Latham Rd. Enter on R.* ◊◊◊FACILITIES: 90 sites, typical site width 50 ft, 59 full hkups, 19

EAST THETFORD—Continued
Rest N' Nest Campground—Continued

W&E, (20/30/50 amps), 12 no hkups, 6 pull-thrus, family camping, tenting, dump, laundry, ltd groc. ◊◊◊RECREATION: swim pool, playground. Pets welcome. Open Apr 30 - Oct 15. Rate in 2010 $32-39 per family. Member VCA. Phone: (802)785-2997.

EDEN MILLS—A-3

(NE) Lakeview Camping Area—(Lamoille) *From jct Hwy-118 & Hwy-100: Go 2 mi N on Hwy-100. Enter on L.* ◊◊FACILITIES: 75 sites, typical site width 30 ft, 38 ft max RV length, 72 W&E, 3 E, (20/30 amps), 6 pull-thrus, family camping, tenting, dump, laundry, ltd groc. ◊◊RECREATION: lake swim, boating, canoeing, lake fishing, play equipment. Pets welcome. Partial handicap access. Open May 15 - Oct 15. Rate in 2010 $25 for 2 persons. Member VCA. Phone: (802)635-2255.

ELMO—B-3

ELMORE SP—(Lamoille) *From town: Go 5 mi S on Hwy-12 (Lake Elmore).* FACILITIES: 60 sites, 60 no hkups, tenting, dump. RECREATION: lake swim, boating, ramp, lake fishing, playground. Pets welcome. Open May 26 - Oct 15. Phone: (802)888-2982.

ENOSBURG FALLS—A-2

(W) LAKE CARMI SP—(Franklin) *From town: Go 3 mi W on Hwy-105, then 3 mi N on Hwy-236.* FACILITIES: 177 sites, 177 no hkups, tenting, dump. RECREATION: lake swim, boating, ramp, lake fishing, playground. Pets welcome. Open May 20 - Sep 5. Phone: (802)933-8383.

GEORGIA—A-2

(S) Homestead Campground—(Franklin) *From jct I-89 (exit 18) & Hwy-7: Go 1/4 mi S on Hwy-7. Enter on L.* ◊◊◊FACILITIES: 150 sites, typical site width 30 ft, 150 W&E, (20/30/50 amps), 59 pull-thrus, family camping, tenting, dump, laundry. ◊◊◊RECREATION: 2 swim pools, playground. Pets welcome, quantity restrict. Partial handicap access. Open May 1 - Oct 5. Rate in 2010 $33 per family. Member ARVC, VCA. Phone: (802)524-2356.

GRAND ISLE—A-1

GRAND ISLE SP—(Grand Isle) *From town: Go 1 mi S on US-2.* FACILITIES: 157 sites, 157 no hkups, tenting, dump. RECREATION: lake swim, boating, ramp, lake fishing, playground. Pets welcome. Open May 20 - Oct 10. Phone: (802)372-4300.

GROTON—C-4

NEW DISCOVERY CAMPGROUND (Groton SF)—(Caledonia) *From town: Go 2 mi W on US-302, then 9-1/2 mi N on Hwy-232.* FACILITIES: 61 sites, 61 no hkups, tenting, dump. RECREATION: lake fishing, playground. Pets welcome. Open May 26 - Sep 5. Phone: (802)426-3042.

RICKER CAMPGROUND (Groton SF)—(Caledonia) *From town: Go 2 mi W on US-302, then 2-1/2 mi N on Hwy-232.* FACILITIES: 58 sites, 58 no hkups, tenting, dump. RECREATION: boating, ramp, pond fishing. Pets welcome. Open Mid May - Early Sep. Phone: (802)584-3821.

(N) STILLWATER CAMPGROUND (Groton SF)—(Caledonia) *From town: Go 2 mi W on US 302, then 6 mi N on Hwy 232, then 1/2 mi E on Boulder Beach Rd.* FACILITIES: 62 sites, 62 no hkups, tenting, dump. RECREATION: lake swim, boating, ramp, playground. Pets welcome. Open May 20 - Oct 15. Phone: (802) 584-3822.

HUBBARDTON—D-2

HALF MOON POND SP—(Rutland) *From town: Go 2 mi N on Hwy 30, then 2 mi N on Town Rd, then 1-1/2 mi S on Town Rd.* FACILITIES: 63 sites, 63 no hkups, tenting, dump. RECREATION: boating, no motors, canoeing, ramp, pond fishing, playground. Pets welcome. Open May 26 - Oct 9. Phone: (802)273-2848.

IRASBURG—A-3

(N) TREE CORNERS FAMILY CAMPGROUND—(Orleans) *From jct I-91 (exit 26) & RT 58: Go 3-3/4 mi W on Hwy 58, then 1-1/4 mi N on Hwy 14/58, then 50 yards W on Hwy 58. Enter on L.*

◊◊◊◊FACILITIES: 131 sites, typical site width 50 ft, 57 full hkups, 73 W&E, (30/50 amps), 1 no hkups, some extd stay sites (summer), 10 pull-

TREE CORNERS FAMILY CAMPGROUND—Continued on next page

IRASBURG—Continued
TREE CORNERS FAMILY CAMPGROUND—Continued

thrus, cable TV, WiFi Instant Internet at site ($), family camping, tenting, cabins, shower$, dump, non-guest dump $, laundry, ltd groc, RV supplies, LP gas by weight/by meter, ice, picnic tables, fire rings, wood, controlled access.

◆◆◆◆RECREATION: rec hall, rec room/area, coin games, 2 swim pools, golf nearby, bsktball, playground, shuffleboard court shuffleboard court, activities (wkends), horseshoes.

Pets welcome, breed restrict. Partial handicap access. Open Mid May - Mid Oct. Big rigs welcome. Clubs welcome. Rate in 2010 $29-33 per family. MC/VISA. Member VCA.

Phone: (802)754-6042
Address: 95 Rte 58 W, Irasburg, VT 05845
Lat/Lon: 44.81532/-72.29611
Email: info@treecorners.com
Web: www.treecorners.com

SEE AD PAGE 756 AND AD TRAVEL SECTION PAGE 751

ISLAND POND—A-4

(E) BRIGHTON SP—(Essex) *From town: Go 2 mi E on Hwy-105, then 3/4 mi S on local road.* FACILITIES: 84 sites, 84 no hkups, tenting, dump. RECREATION: lake swim, boating, no motors, lake/pond fishing, playground. Pets welcome. Open Memorial Day - Columbus Day. Phone: (802)723-4360.

(E) Lakeside Campground—(Essex) *From jct Hwy 114 & Hwy 105 (center of town): Go 1-1/2 mi E on Hwy 105. Enter on R.* ◆◆◆FACILITIES: 200 sites, 193 full hkups, (30 amps), 7 no hkups, family camping, tenting, dump, laundry, ltd groc. ◆◆◆RECREATION: lake swim, boating, canoeing, dock, lake fishing, playground. Pets welcome. Open May 15 - Week after Labor Day. Rate in 2010 $35-38 per family. Member VCA. Phone: (802)723-6649.

JAMAICA—E-2

(N) JAMAICA SP—(Windham) *From Hwy 30 in town: Go 1/2 mi N on town road.* FACILITIES: 59 sites, 59 no hkups, tenting, dump. RECREATION: river swim, river fishing, playground. Pets welcome. Open May 8 - Oct 15. Phone: (802)874-4600.

KILLINGTON—D-2

GIFFORD WOODS SP—(Rutland) *From jct US-4 & Hwy-100: Go 1/2 mi N on Hwy-100.* FACILITIES: 42 sites, 42 no hkups, tenting, dump. RECREATION: pond fishing, playground. Pets welcome. Open May 21 - Oc 19. Phone: (802)775-5354.

LAKE CHAMPLAIN—B-2

See listings at Burlington, Colchester, Middlebury & South Hero

MARSHFIELD—B-3

(E) Groton Forest Road Campground—(Washington) *From jct US 2 & Hwy 232: go 2-1/2 mi S on Hwy 232. Enter on R.* ◆◆FACILITIES: 40 sites, 32 W&E, 2 E, (15/30 amps), 6 no hkups, 9 pull-thrus, family camping, tenting, dump, laundry. ◆◆RECREATION: swim pool, play equipment. Pets welcome, breed restrict. Open May 15 - Oct 10. Rate in 2010 $28.50 per family. Phone: (802)426-4122.

Woodall's Tip... If you are camping in bear country, be sure to cook at least 300 feet downwind of your sleeping area. Use baking soda to rid your clothes and hands of cooking odors.

MIDDLEBURY—C-2

(S) LAKE DUNMORE KAMPERSVILLE—(Addison) *From jct Hwy 125 & Hwy 30, & US 7: Go 6 mi S on US 7, then 1-1/2 mi S on Hwy 53. Enter on L.*

******VERMONT CAMPING AT ITS BEST******
OPEN ALL YEAR, in the Champlain Valley & the Foot of the Green Mountains on Sparkling Lake Dunmore, enjoy our pools, beach, fishing, boating (w/rental), sports fields, rec hall, arcade, playground-See WWW.KAMPERSVILLE.COM for much more

◆◆◆◆FACILITIES: 210 sites, typical site width 35 ft, 119 full hkups, 81 W&E, (30/50 amps), 10 no hkups, some extd stay sites (summer), 2 pull-thrus, cable TV, WiFi Instant Internet at site ($), phone Internet central location, family camping, tenting, RV's/park model rentals, cabins, RV storage, dump, non-guest dump $, portable dump, laundry, full svc store, RV supplies, LP gas by weight/by meter, marine gas, ice, picnic tables, fire rings, grills, wood.

◆◆◆◆◆RECREATION: rec hall, rec room/area, equipped pavilion, coin games, 2 swim pools, wading pool, spray ground, lake swim, hot tub, boating, canoeing, kayaking, ramp, dock, 3 rowboat/4 canoe/6 kayak/5 pedal boat/6 motorboat rentals, lake fishing, fishing supplies, mini-golf, ($), bsktball, playground, shuffleboard court 4 shuffleboard courts, activities, horseshoes, sports field, hiking trails, v-ball.

Pets welcome. Partial handicap access. Open all yr. Facilities fully operational May 1 - Oct 15. Big rigs welcome. Escort to site. Clubs welcome. Rate in 2010 $39-43 per family. MC/VISA/DISC/AMEX. ATM. Member VCA. CCUSA 50% Discount. CCUSA reservations Accepted, CCUSA max stay Unlimited, CCUSA disc. not avail holidays. Discount available May, Jun, last 2 weeks of Aug, Sep & Oct. In season rates $28-46/Out of season-$20-35. Call or visit website for details.

Phone: (802)352-4501
Address: 1457 Lake Dunmore Rd, Salisbury, VT 05769
Lat/Lon: 43.92134/-73.08418
Email: info@kampersville.com
Web: www.kampersville.com

SEE AD THIS PAGE AND AD MAP PAGE 750

(N) Rivers Bend Campground—(Addison) *From jct Hwy 125 & US 7 (in North Middlebury): Go 3 mi N on US 7, then 3/4 mi W on Dog Team Rd. Enter on L.* ◆◆FACILITIES: 67 sites, typical site width 50 ft, 67 W&E, (20/30/50 amps), 10 pull-thrus, tenting, dump, laundry. ◆◆◆RECREATION: swim pool, river swim, canoeing, river fishing, play equipment. Pets welcome. Open May 1 - Mid Oct. Rate in 2010 $33-35 per family. Member ARVC, VCA. Phone: (802)388-9092.

MONTPELIER—B-3

See listings at Barre, Morrisville, Randolph Center & Stowe

MORRISVILLE—B-3

(E) Mountain View Campground—(Lamoille) *From south jct Hwy 100 & Hwy 15: Go 3 mi E on Hwy 15. Enter on R.* ◆◆◆◆FACILITIES: 68 sites, typical site width 25 ft, 24 full hkups, 29 W&E, 6 E, (30 amps), 9 no hkups, family camping, tenting, dump, laundry, ltd groc. ◆◆◆◆RECREATION: 2 swim pools, canoeing, river fishing, playground. Pets welcome ($), breed restrict. Partial handicap access. Open May 1 - Mid Oct. Rate in 2010 $35-40 per family. Member VCA. Phone: (802)888-2178.

NEWFANE—F-3

(E) Kenolie Village Campground—(Windham) *From village of Newfane on Hwy 30: Go 2 mi N on Hwy 30, then 1 mi E on Radway Rd., then S on Gravel Rd (before bridge). Enter on R.* ◆◆◆FACILITIES: 200 sites, typical site width 30 ft, 190 W&E, (30/50 amps), 10 no hkups, 7 pull-thrus, family camping, tenting, dump, laundry, ltd groc. ◆◆◆RECREATION: river swim, canoeing, river fishing, playground. Pets welcome. Partial handicap access. Open Apr 1 - Late Nov. Rate in 2010 $21.75-23.75 for 2 persons. Phone: (802)365-7671.

NEWPORT—A-4

PROUTY BEACH CAMPGROUND (City Park)—(Orleans) *From jct I-91 (exit 27) & Hwy 191: Go 2 mi toward Newport, 1st traffic light continue straight, R at 2nd set of lights on to Union St. Enter on R.* FACILITIES: 56 sites, 40 ft max RV length, 52 full hkups, (30/50 amps), 4 no hkups, tenting, dump, laundry. RECREATION: lake swim, boating, canoeing, lake/river fishing, playground. Pets welcome. Partial handicap access. Open May 9 - Oct 12. Phone: (802)334-7951.

NORTH DORSET—E-2

EMERALD LAKE SP—(Bennington) *In town on US-7.* FACILITIES: 104 sites, 104 no hkups, tenting, dump. RECREATION: lake swim, boating, no motors, ramp, lake fishing, playground. Pets welcome. Open May 29 - Oct 9. Phone: (802)362-1655.

NORTH HERO—A-1

(N) NORTH HERO SP—(Grand Isle) *From town: Go 6 mi SW on US 2, then 3 mi NE on town road.* FACILITIES: 20 sites, 20 no hkups, tenting. RECREATION: lake swim, boating, ramp, lake fishing, playground. Pets welcome. Open May 26 - Sep 5. Phone: (802)372-8727.

ORLEANS—A-4

(E) Will-O-Wood Campground—(Orleans) *From jct I-91 (exit 26) & Hwy 58: Go 6-1/4 mi E on Hwy 58, then 1/2 mi S on Hwy 5A. Enter on R.* ◆◆◆FACILITIES: 117 sites, typical site width 30 ft, 57 full hkups, 54 W&E, (20/30 amps), 6 no hkups, 8 pull-thrus, tenting, dump, laundry, ltd groc. ◆◆◆RECREATION: swim pool, playground. Pets welcome. Open May 1 - Oct 15. Rate in 2010 $25-28 per family. Member VCA. Phone: (802)525-3575.

PERKINSVILLE—E-3

(N) Crown Point Camping Area—(Weathersfield) *From jct I-91 (exit 7) & Hwy 106: Go 10 mi N on Hwy 106, then 1 mi E on Stoughton Pond Rd. Enter on L.* ◆◆◆FACILITIES: 146 sites, typical site width 35 ft, 74 full hkups, 52 W&E, (20/30/50 amps), 20 no hkups, 11 pull-thrus, tenting, dump, laundry. ◆◆◆RECREATION: boating, canoeing, ramp, lake fishing, playground. Pets welcome, breed restrict. Open May 1 - Oct 30. Rate in 2010 $25-30 per family. Member VCA. Phone: (802)263-5555.

PERU—E-2

(NE) GREEN MOUNTAIN NF (Hapgood Pond Campground)—(Bennington) *From town: Go 1-3/4 mi NE on Hapgood Pond Rd (FR 3).* FACILITIES: 28 sites, 32 ft max RV length, 28 no hkups, tenting. RECREATION: boating, electric motors only, canoeing, pond/stream fishing, playground. Open May 26 - Oc 15. Phone: (802)888-1349.

Vermont State Nickname: Green Mountain State

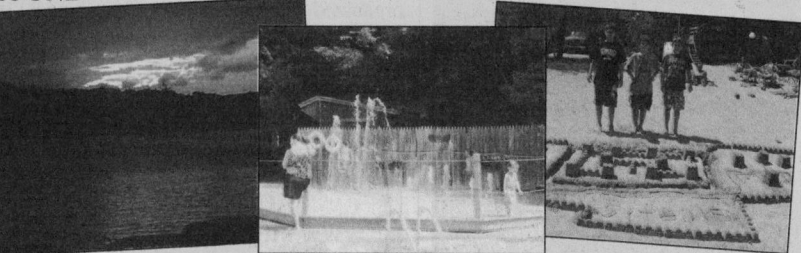

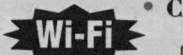

PLYMOUTH UNION—D-2

COOLIDGE SP—(Windsor) *From jct Hwy 100 & Hwy 100A: Go 3 mi N on Hwy 100A.* FACILITIES: 62 sites, 62 no hkups, tenting, dump. RECREATION: playground. Pets welcome. Open mid May - mid Oct. Phone: (802)672-3612.

POULTNEY—D-1

(S) LAKE ST. CATHERINE SP—(Rutland) *From town: Go 3 mi S on Hwy-30.* FACILITIES: 61 sites, 61 no hkups, tenting, dump, ltd groc. RECREATION: lake swim, boating, ramp, dock, lake fishing, playground. Pets welcome. Open May 26 - Oc 15. Phone: (802)287-9158.

QUECHEE—D-3

QUECHEE GORGE SP—(Windsor) *From jct I-89 (exit 1) & US 4: Go 3 mi W on US 4.* FACILITIES: 54 sites, 54 no hkups, tenting, dump. RECREATION: river fishing, playground. Pets welcome. Open May 26 - Oct 19. Phone: (802)295-2990.

(NE) **QUECHEE PINE VALLEY KOA**—(Windsor) *From jct I-89 (exit 1) & US 4: Go 1/2 mi W on US 4. Enter on L.*

WELCOME

◆◆◆◆FACILITIES: 90 sites, typical site width 30 ft, 49 full hkups, 41 W&E, (20/30/50 amps), 19 pull-thrus, cable TV, WiFi Instant Internet at site, WiFi Internet central location, family camping, tenting, RV's/park model rentals, cabins, dump, laundry, ltd groc, RV supplies, LP gas by weight/by meter, ice, picnic tables, fire rings, wood.

◆◆◆RECREATION: rec hall, rec room/area, swim pool, canoeing, 2 canoe/pedal boat rentals, pond fishing, fishing supplies, golf nearby, bike rental 5 bike rentals, playground.

Pets welcome, breed restrict. Partial handicap access. Open May 1 - Late Oct. Open thru Late Oct, weather permitting. Pool open Memorial Day. Big rigs welcome. Escort to site. Clubs welcome. Rate in 2010 $36-47 for 2 persons. MC/VISA/DISC. Member ARVC, VCA. KOA discount.

Phone: (802)296-6711
Address: 3700 Woodstock Rd, White River Junction, VT 05001
Lat/Lon: 43.65887/-72.38717
Email: info@pinevalleyrv.com
Web: www.quecheepinevalley.com

SEE AD TRAVEL SECTION PAGE 749 AND AD TRAVEL SECTION PAGE 751

RANDOLPH CENTER—C-3

(N) **Lake Champagne Campground**—(Orange) *From jct I-89 (exit 4) & Hwy 66: Go 1 mi E on Hwy 66, then 200 yds E (right) on Furnace Rd. Enter on L.* ◆◆◆◆FACILITIES: 123 sites, typical site width 40 ft, 66 full hkups, 43 W&E, (30/50 amps), 14 no hkups, 41 pull-thrus, family camping, tenting, dump, laundry. ◆◆◆◆RECREATION: lake swim, playground. Pets welcome. Partial handicap access. Open Mid May - Mid Oct. Big rigs welcome. Rate in 2010 $30-36 per family. Member VCA. Phone: (802)728-5293.

RUTLAND—D-2

See listings at Bomoseen & Brandon

ST. ALBANS BAY—A-2

BURTON ISLAND SP—(Franklin) *From town: Go 2-1/2 mi SW on town road, Lake Rd & Point Rd to Kill Kare Area. Then take passenger ferry or private boat to Burton Island.* FACILITIES: 43 sites, 43 no hkups, tenting, dump. RECREATION: lake swim, boating, ramp, lake fishing, playground. Pets welcome. Open mid May - Early Sep. Phone: (802)524-6353.

ST. JOHNSBURY—B-4

See primary listing at Franconia & Littleton

SALISBURY—C-2

BRANBURY SP—(Addison) *From jct US-7 & Hwy-53: Go 2 mi S on Hwy-53.* FACILITIES: 22 sites, 22 no hkups, tenting, dump. RECREATION: lake swim, boating, lake fishing, playground. Pets welcome. Open May 26 - Oct 15. Phone: (802)247-5925.

SHELBURNE—B-1

(N) **SHELBURNE CAMPING AREA**—(Chittenden) *From jct I-89 (exit 13) & I-189: Go 3/4 mi W on I-189, then 3-1/2 mi S on US 7. Enter on L.*

WELCOME

◆◆◆FACILITIES: 78 sites, typical site width 40 ft, 28 full hkups, 40 W&E, (20/30/50 amps), 10 no hkups, some extd stay sites (summer), 7 pull-thrus, cable TV, WiFi Instant Internet at site, WiFi Internet central location, family camping, tenting, RV's/park model rentals, RV storage, dump, non-guest dump $, portable dump, laundry, ltd groc, RV supplies, LP gas by weight/by meter, ice, picnic tables, fire rings, grills, wood.

SHELBURNE—Continued
SHELBURNE CAMPING AREA—Continued

◆◆◆RECREATION: rec room/area, 2 swim pools, golf nearby, bsktball, playground, horseshoes, sports field, v-ball.

Pets welcome. Partial handicap access. Open all yr. Facilities fully operational Apr 1 - Nov 1. Limited facilities in winter. Big rigs welcome. Clubs welcome. Rate in 2010 $26-42 for 2 persons. MC/VISA/DISC. Member ARVC, VCA.

Phone: (802)985-2540
Address: 4385 Shelburne Rd, Shelburne, VT 05482
Lat/Lon: 44.39264/-73.21971
Email: shelbcamp@aol.com
Web: www.shelburnecamping.com

SEE AD BURLINGTON PAGE 755

SOUTH HERO—B-1

(SE) **APPLE ISLAND RESORT**—(Grand Isle) *From I-89 (exit 17) & US-2: Go 6 mi NW on US-2. Enter on L.*

WELCOME

◆◆◆◆FACILITIES: 250 sites, typical site width 40 ft, 216 full hkups, 34 W&E, (30/50 amps), many extd stay sites (summer), 20 pull-thrus, WiFi Instant Internet at site, WiFi Internet central location, family camping, tenting, RV's/park model rentals, cabins, RV storage, dump, laundry, groceries, RV supplies, marine gas, ice, picnic tables, fire rings, wood.

◆◆◆◆◆RECREATION: rec hall, rec room/area, swim pool, hot tub, boating, canoeing, kayaking, ramp, dock, 2 pontoon/3 rowboat/2 canoe/4 kayak rentals, lake fishing, fishing supplies, golf nearby, playground, activities, sports field, hiking trails.

Pets welcome, breed restrict, quantity restrict. Partial handicap access. Open May 1 - Oct 20. Big rigs welcome. Escort to site. Clubs welcome. Rate in 2010 $40-49 per family. MC/VISA/DISC. Member ARVC, VCA. FMCA discount.

Phone: (802)372-3800
Address: 71 US Rte. 2, South Hero, VT 05486
Lat/Lon: 44.63546/-73.26700
Email: info@appleislandresort.com
Web: www.appleislandresort.com

SEE AD ADDISON PAGE 754

SOUTH LONDONDERRY—E-2

WINHALL BROOK CAMPING AREA (COE-Ball Mountain Lake)—(Windham) *From town: Go 2-1/2 mi S on Hwy 100, then E on Windhall Station Rd. Enter on L.* FACILITIES: 111 sites, 6 W&E, 105 no hkups, tenting, dump. RECREATION: river swim, river/stream fishing, playground. Partial handicap access. Open Apr 21 - Oct 9. Phone: (802)874-4881.

SPRINGFIELD—E-3

(E) **Tree Farm Campground**—(Windsor) *From I-91, exit 7 & Hwy 11: Go 3 mi W on Hwy 11, then 1/2 mi N on Bridge St, then 1/2 mi E on Hwy 143. Enter on R.* ◆◆◆FACILITIES: 118 sites, typical site width 35 ft, 80 full hkups, 29 W&E, (20/30 amps), 9 no hkups, 16 pull-thrus, cable TV, family camping, tenting, RV storage, dump, RV supplies, LP gas by weight, ice, picnic tables, fire rings, wood. ◆◆RECREATION: bsktball, play equipment, horseshoes, hiking trails, v-ball. Pets welcome. Open May 1 - Oct 31. Rate in 2010 $30 per family. Member VCA. CCUSA 50% Discount.

CAMPCLUB USA

Phone: (802)885-2889
Address: 53 Skitchewaug Trail, Springfield, VT 05156
Lat/Lon: 43.29198/-72.46254
Email: campvermont@treefarmcampground.com
Web: www.treefarmcampground.com

Woodall's Tip... The North American Edition is split into Eastern and Western sections; each organized alphabetically starting with Alabama in the East and Alaska in the West.

STOWE—B-3

(S) GOLD BROOK CAMPGROUND (at Nichols Lodge).—(Lamoille) *From jct I-89 (exit 10) & Hwy 100: Go 7-1/2 mi N on Hwy 100. Enter on L.*

◇◇◇FACILITIES: 79 sites, typical site width 35 ft, 26 full hkups, 24 W&E, (20/30/50 amps), 29 no hkups, cable TV, WiFi Internet central location ($), family camping, tenting, RV storage, dump, non-guest dump $, laundry, ice, picnic tables, fire rings, grills, wood.

◇◇◇RECREATION: rec room/area, swim pool, river swim, canoeing, kayaking, river fishing, golf nearby, bsktball, playground, shuffleboard court shuffleboard court, horseshoes, sports field, v-ball.

Pets welcome. Open all yr. From Dec 1 thru Apr: Open by reservation only. Clubs welcome. Rate in 2010 $28-40 per family. MC/VISA/DISC. Member ARVC, VCA.

Phone: (802)253-7683
Address: 1900 Waterbury Rd, Stowe, VT 05672
Lat/Lon: 44.44277/-72.70470
Email: mnic997808@aol.com
Web: www.staywired.com/goldbrook

SEE AD THIS PAGE

(NW) SMUGGLERS NOTCH CAMPGROUND (Mount Mansfield SF)—(Lamoille) *From jct Hwy-100 & Hwy-108: Go 10 mi NW on Hwy-108.* FACILITIES: 34 sites, 34 no hkups, tenting, dump. RECREATION: playground. Pets welcome. Open Mid May - Oct 18. Phone: (802)253-4014.

THETFORD HILL—D-3

THETFORD HILL SP—(Orange) *From jct I-91 (exit 14) & Hwy 113A: Go 1 mi W on Hwy 113A, then 1 mi S on Academy Rd. Enter on R.* FACILITIES: 16 sites, typical site width 30 ft, 36 ft max RV length, 16 no hkups, tenting, dump. RECREATION: play equipment. Pets welcome. Open May 26 - Sep 5. Phone: (802)885-8855.

TOWNSHEND—F-3

(S) Bald Mountain Campground—(Windham) *From jct I-91 (exit 3) & US 5: Go 3 mi S on US 5, then 15-1/2 mi NW on State Forest TH 4. Enter on R.* ◇◇◇FACILITIES: 200 sites, typical site width 25 ft, 190 W&E, (15/20/30 amps), 10 no hkups, 62 pull-thrus, family camping, tenting, dump, laundry. ◇◇◇RECREATION: river swim, canoeing, river fishing, playground. Pets welcome. Open Early May - Columbus Day. Rate in 2010 $27-31 per family. Member VCA. Phone: (802)365-7510.

TOWNSHEND SF—(Windham) *From jct Hwy 30 & Town Rd: Go 3 mi N on Town Rd.* FACILITIES: 34 sites, 16 ft max RV length, 34 no hkups, tenting. RECREATION: boating. Pets welcome. Open May 26 - Sep 5. Phone: (802)365-7500.

VERGENNES—C-1

(W) BUTTON BAY SP—(Addison) *From town: Go 1/2 mi S on Hwy-22A, then 6-1/2 mi NW on local roads.* FACILITIES: 73 sites, 73 no hkups, tenting, dump. RECREATION: swim pool, lake swim, boating, ramp, dock, lake fishing, playground. Pets welcome. Open May 26 - Sep 6. Phone: (802)475-2377.

WATERBURY—B-2

(W) LITTLE RIVER SP—(Washington) *From jct Hwy-100 & US-2: Go 1-1/2 mi W on US-2, then 3-1/2 mi N on Little River Rd.* FACILITIES: 101 sites, 101 no hkups, tenting, dump. RECREATION: lake swim, ramp, lake/stream fishing, playground. Pets welcome. Open May 26 - Oct 9. Phone: (802)244-7103.

WESTFIELD—A-3

(S) Barrewood Campground—(Orleans) *From jct Hwy 87 (North Hill Rd) & Hwy 100: Go 1-1/2 mi S on Hwy 100. Enter on R.* ◇◇◇FACILITIES: 38 sites, typical site width 30 ft, 6 full hkups, 32 W&E, (20/30 amps), 6 pull-thrus, family camping, tenting, dump, non-guest dump $, laundry, ice, picnic tables, fire rings, wood. ◇◇◇RECREATION: pavilion, swim pool, stream fishing, bsktball, playground, shuffleboard court shuffleboard court, horseshoes, hiking trails, v-ball. Pets welcome, quantity restrict. Partial handicap access. Open May 1 - Oct 31. Rate in 2010 $24-26 per family. Member VCA. CCUSA 50% Discount. CCUSA reservations Recommended, CCUSA max stay Unlimited, Cash only for CCUSA disc., CCUSA disc. not avail F,Sa, CCUSA disc. not avail holidays.

Phone: (802)744-6340
Address: 2998 VT RTE 100, Westfield, VT 05874
Lat/Lon: 44.86153/-72.43452
Email: barrewood@earthlink.net

WILMINGTON—F-2

(E) MOLLY STARK SP—(Windham) *From jct Hwy-100 & Hwy-9: Go 3 mi E on Hwy-9.* FACILITIES: 34 sites, 30 ft max RV length, 34 no hkups, tenting, dump. RECREATION: playground. Pets welcome. Open mid May - mid Oct. Phone: (802)464-5460.

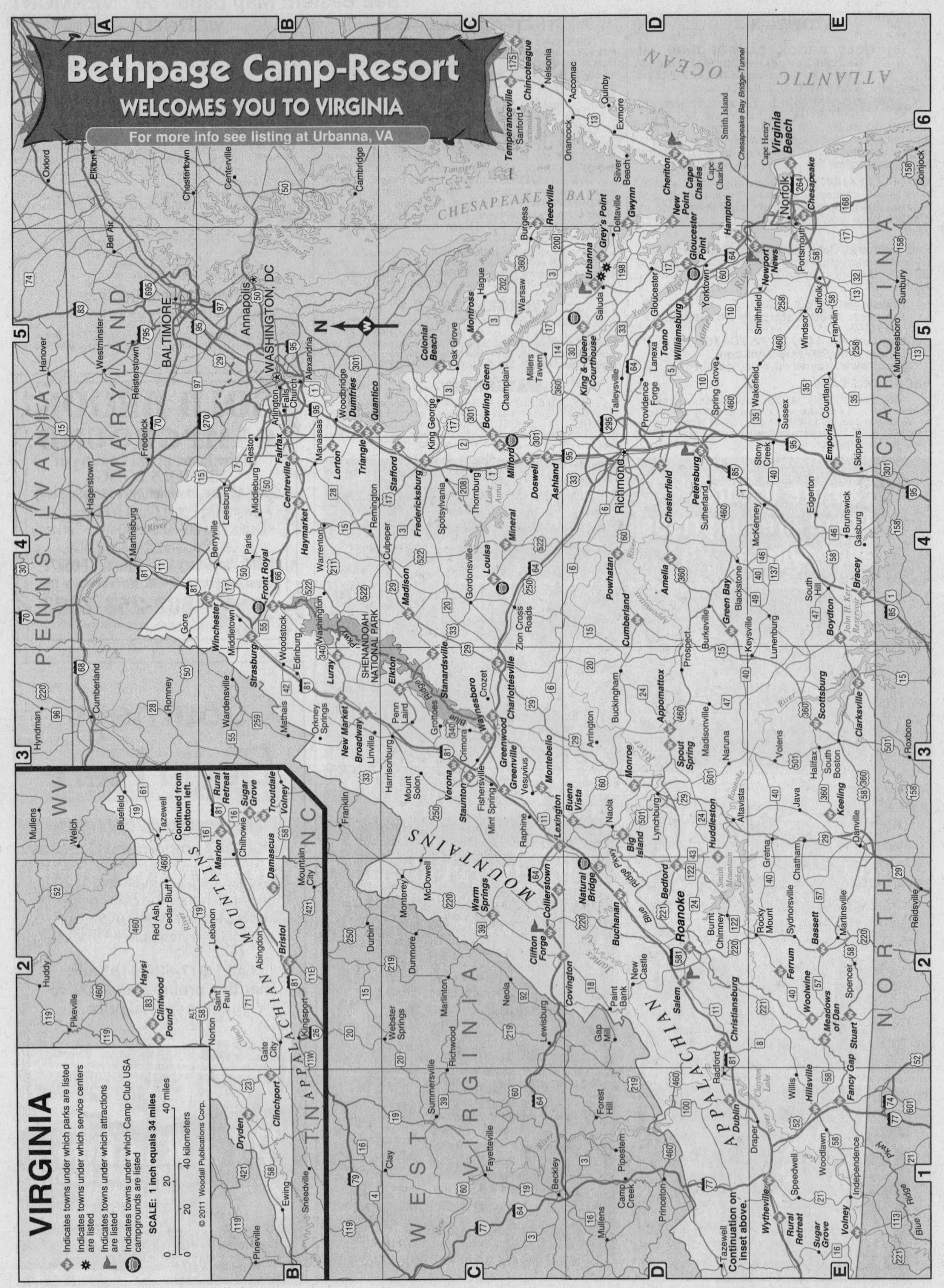
Bethpage Camp-Resort
WELCOMES YOU TO VIRGINIA
For more info see listing at Urbanna, VA
VIRGINIA
Indicates towns under which parks are listed
Indicates towns under which service centers are listed
Indicates towns under which attractions are listed
Indicates towns under which Camp Club USA campgrounds are listed
SCALE: 1 inch equals 34 miles
0 20 40 miles
0 20 40 kilometers
© 2011 Woodall Publications Corp.
Continued from bottom left.
Continuation on inset above.
PENNSYLVANIA
MARYLAND
WEST VIRGINIA
NORTH CAROLINA
APPALACHIAN MOUNTAINS
SHENANDOAH NATIONAL PARK
CHESAPEAKE BAY
ATLANTIC OCEAN
WASHINGTON, DC
BALTIMORE
Richmond
Roanoke
Norfolk
Virginia Beach

READER SERVICE INFO

The following businesses have placed an ad in the Virginia Travel Section. To receive free information, enter the Reader Service number on the Reader Service Card opposite page 48/Discover Section in the front of this directory:

Advertiser	RS#
Bethpage Camp Resort	568
Cherrystone Family Camping Resort	538
KOA Williamsburg	4319
Virginia Campground Assoc	3757

TIME ZONE

Virginia is in the Eastern Time Zone.

TOPOGRAPHY

Virginia is made up of three natural topographic regions: the Tidewater or Coastal Plains, the Piedmont Plateau of middle Virginia and the Western Mountain region.

TEMPERATURE

Virginia experiences four distinct seasons, with winters mild on the coast and snow in the higher elevations. Summers are mild throughout the state. Normal January daily high temperatures range from 33° in the southwestern mountains to 48° along the southeastern coast. Normal July daily high temperatures range from 87° in the southwest to 88° along the eastern coast.

TRAVEL & TOURISM INFO

State Agency:
Virginia Tourism Corporation
901 E. Byrd St.
Richmond, VA 23219
(800/847-4882)
www.virginia.org

Regional Agencies:
Heart of Appalachia Tourism Authority
16620 East Riverside Dr., P.O. Box 926
Lebanon, VA 24266
(276/762-0011)
www.heartofappalachia.com

Eastern Shore Tourism Commission
24391 Lankford Hwy.
P.O. Box 72
Tasley, VA 23441
(757/787-8268)
www.esvatourism.org

River Country Tourism Council
125 Bowden St., P.O. Box 286
Saluda, VA 23149
(800/527-6360 or 804/758-4917)
www.visitrivercountry.org

Local Agencies:
Abingdon Convention & Visitors Bureau
335 Cummmings St.,
Abingdon, VA 24210
(276/676-2282 or 800/435-3440)
www.abingdon.com

Alexandria Convention & Visitors Association
421 King St.,
Alexandria, VA 22314
(703/838-4200 or 800/388-9119)
www.visitalexandriava.com

Arlington County Visitors Center
1301 S. Joyce St.
Arlington, VA 22202
(800/296-7996 or 703/416-0784)
www.stayarlington.com

Bedford Area Welcome Center
816 Burks Hill Road
Bedford, VA 24523
(540/587-5681 or 540/587-5983)
www.visitbedford.com

Bristol Convention & Visitors Bureau
20 Volunteer Pkwy.
P.O. Box 519
Bristol, VA 24203
(423/989-4850)
www.bristolchamber.org

Charlottesville Albemarle County Convention & Visitors Bureau
610 East Main Street
Charlottesville, VA 22902
(877/386-1103 or 434/293-6789)
www.pursuecharlottesville.com

Chesapeake Conventions & Tourism
3815 Bainbridge Blvd.
Chesapeake, VA 23324
(888/889-5551)
www.visitchesapeake.com

Chincoteague Chamber of Commerce
6733 Maddox Blvd.,
Chincoteague, VA 23336
(757/336-6161)
www.chincoteaguechamber.com

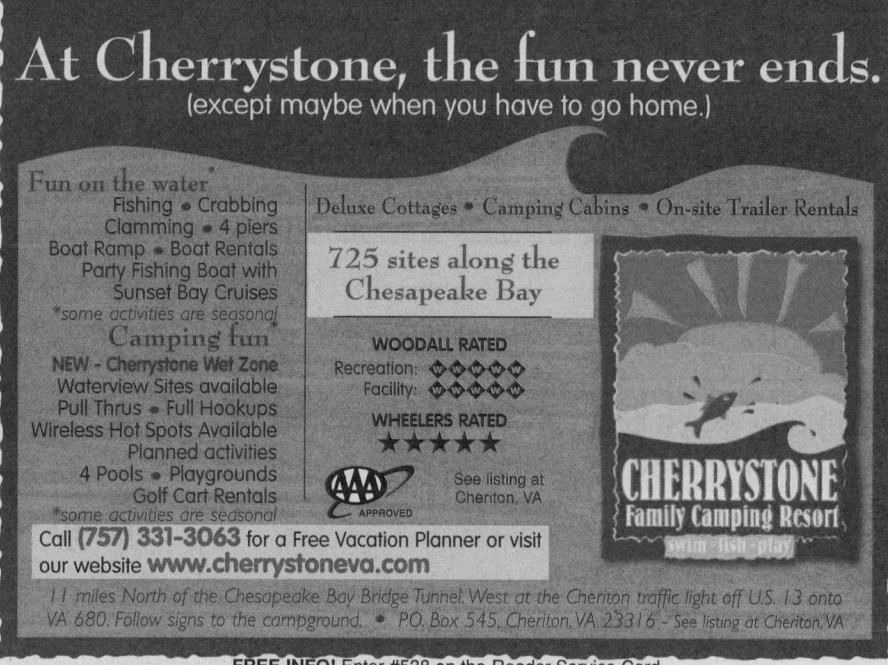

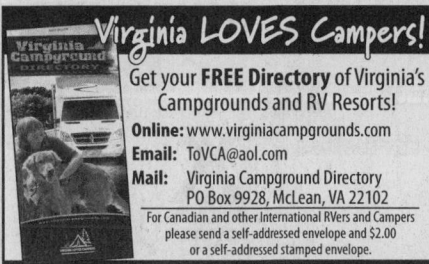

Danville Welcome Center
645 River Park Drive
Danville, VA 24540
(434/793-4636)
www.visitdanville.com

Fairfax County Visitors Center
10209 Main Street
Lorton, VA 22079
(800/732-4732)
www.fxva.com

Fredericksburg Visitor Center
706 Caroline Street
Fredericksburg, VA 22401
(800/678-4748)
www.visitfred.com

Front Royal Warren County Visitor Center
414 E. Main Street
Front Royal, VA 22630
(540/635-5788)
www.ci.front-royal.va.us

Harrisonburg Tourism and Visitor Services
212 South Main St.
Harrisonburg, VA 22801
(540/432-8935)
www.harrisonburgtourism.com

Lexington Rockbridge Area Visitor Center
106 E. Washington Street
Lexington, VA 24450
(877/453-9822)
www.lexingtonvirginia.com

Loudoun County Visitors Center
222 Catoctin Circle SE, Ste. 100
Leesburg, VA 20175
(800/752-6118 or 703/771-2617)
www.visitloudoun.org

Lynchburg Regional Convention & Visitors Bureau
216 Twelfth St. at Church
Lynchburg, VA 24504
(800/732-5821)
www.discoverlynchburg.org

Newport News Tourism Development Office
700 Town Center Dr., Suite 320
Fountain Plaza Two
Newport News, VA 23606
(888/493-7386 or 757/926-1400)
www.newport-news.org

Norfolk Convention & Visitors Bureau
232 E. Main St.
Norfolk, VA 23510
(757/664-6620 or 800/368-3097)
www.norfolkcvb.com

Petersburg Visitors Center
425 Cockade Alley
Petersburg, VA 23803
(804/733-2400 or 800/368-3595)
www.petersburg-va.org

Portsmouth Convention & Visitor's Bureau
505 Crawford St.
Portsmouth, VA 23704
(757/393-5327 or800/767-8782)
www.portsva.com

Prince William County Convention & Visitors Bureau
8609 Sudley Road, Suite 105
Manassas, VA 20110
(800/432-1792 or 703/396-7130)
www.visitpwc.com

Richmond Metropolitan Convention and Visitors Bureau
401 N. 3rd Street
Richmond, VA 23219
(804/783-7450)
www.visit.richmondva.com

Roanoke Valley Visitor Information Center
101 Shenandoah Ave. NE
Roanoke, VA 24016
(800/635-5535)
www.visitroanokeva.com

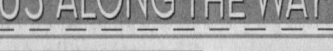

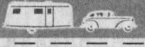

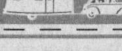

Shenandoah Valley Travel Association
P.O. Box 1040
New Market, VA 22844
(800/847-4878)
www.visitshenandoah.org

Smith Mountain Lake Visitor Center
16430 Booker T. Washington Hwy.,
Bridgewater Plaza Suite 2
Moneta, VA 24121
(540/721-1203 or 800/676-8203)
www.visitsmithmountainlake.com

Staunton Convention & Visitors Bureau
116 W. Beverly St.
Staunton, VA 24401
(540/332-3865 or 800/342-7982)
www.staunton.com

Virginia Beach Visitor Information Center
2100 Parks Avenue
Virginia Beach, VA 23451
(800/822-3224)
www.vbfun.com

Greater Williamsburg Chamber & Tourism Alliance
421 N. Boundary St.
Williamsburg, VA 23185
(757/229-6511 or 800/368-6511)
www.williamsburgcc.com

Winchester-Frederick County CVB
1400 S. Pleasant Valley Road
Winchester, VA 22601
(877/871-1326)
www.visitwinchesterva.com

Wytheville Convention & Visitors Bureau
975 Tazewell Street
Wytheville, VA 24382
(877/347-8307)
www.visitwytheville.com

RECREATIONAL INFO

Birding: For copy of VA Birding & Wildlife Trail Guide, call 804/367-8747.

Horseback Riding: For a trip to Virginia's Horse Country, call 877-TROT2VA. www.virginiahousecouncil.org

Freshwater Fishing: Virginia Department of Game and Inland Fisheries, 4010 West Broad Street, Richmond, VA 23230 (804/367-1000). www.dgif.virginia.gov

Saltwater Fishing: Virginia Marine Resources Commission, 2600 Washington Avenue, 3rd Floor, Newport News, VA 23607 (757/247-2200)www.mrc.virginia.gov

Golf: Virginia Golf Association, (800/932-2259) www.virginia.org/golf

SHOPPING

Made in Virginia, Fredericksburg. Products made by the people of Tidewater, Shenandoah Valley, Blue Ridge Mountains, Piedmont and Chesapeake Bay areas of Virginia. Unique collection of gifts, souvenirs, crafts, wines and foodstuffs.

Potomac Mills, Exit 156 off I-95. (703/496-9355). www.potomacmills.com. Over 225 stores offering savings of 30%-70% off retail.

Tysons Corner Center, 1961 Chain Bridge Rd., McLean. www.ShopTysons.com. Largest shopping mall in VA (10th largest in US), with 5 anchors and more than 250 stores and restaurants.

Prime Outlets at Williamsburg, 5715-62A Richmond Rd., Williamsburg. Over 90 brand-name stores with savings of 25%-65% off retail.

UNIQUE FEATURES

This statewide effort identifies Civil War sites and installs interpretive signs with maps, illustrations and text. Regional driving tours that connect significant sites are identified in maps and brochures available at many visitor centers and museums. For infor-

BUSINESSES OFFERING

	Things to See & Do	RV Sales	RV Service
CHERITON			
Miss Jennifer Charter Fishing	▶		
CLIFTON FORGE			
The Buckhorne Country Store	▶		
GREYS POINT			
RV Adventures		🚌	
NEWPORT NEWS			
Newport News Golf Club at Deer Run	▶		
Newport News Visitors Center	▶		
PETERSBURG			
Bear's Den Restaurant	▶		
SALEM			
Dixie Caverns	▶		
URBANNA			
Bethpage Mini-Golf & Ice Creamery	▶		
RV Adventures		🚌	

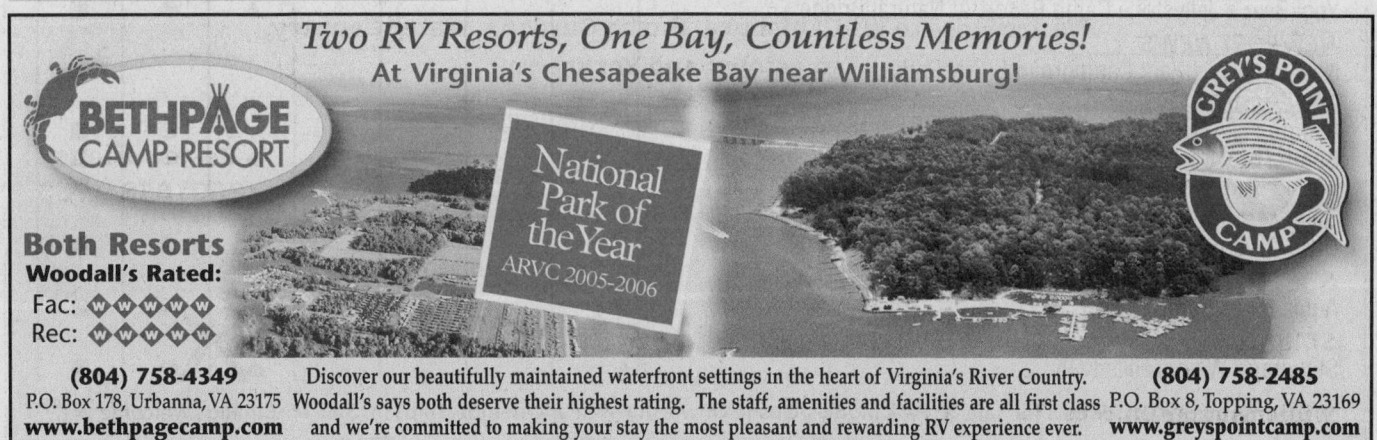

QUICK REFERENCE CHART FOR WOODALL'S FEATURED PARKS

	Green Friendly	RV Lots for Sale	Park Models-Onsite Ownership	Park Membership for Sale	Big Rigs Welcome	Internet Friendly	Pets Welcome
ASHLAND							
Americamps KOA Richmond-North					▲	●	■
BROADWAY							
Harrisonburg / Shenandoah Valley KOA					▲	●	■
CHARLOTTESVILLE							
KOA-Charlottesville					▲	●	■
CHERITON							
Cherrystone Family Camping Resort					▲	●	■
CHESAPEAKE							
Chesapeake Campground							■
CLIFTON FORGE							
The Buckhorne Country Store & Campground						●	■
COLONIAL BEACH							
Monroe Bay Campground							■
DUMFRIES							
Travel Trailer Village at Prince William Forest Park	🍃					●	■
EMPORIA							
Yogi Bear's Jellystone Park Camp Resort Emporia					▲	●	■
FAIRFAX							
Burke Lake Park (Fairfax County Park Authority)							■
FREDERICKSBURG							
KOA-Fredericksburg/Washington DC						●	■
FRONT ROYAL							
Front Royal RV Campground						●	■
GLOUCESTER POINT							
Gloucester Point Family Campground						●	■
GREY'S POINT							
Grey's Point Camp			*		▲	●	■
HAYMARKET							
Greenville Farm Family Campground							■
KING & QUEEN COURTHOUSE							
Rainbow Acres Campground					▲	●	■
LURAY							
Luray RV Resort -The Country Waye					▲	●	■
MADISON							
Madison/Shenandoah Hills KOA	🍃				▲	●	■
MEADOWS OF DAN							
Meadows of Dan Campground					▲	●	■
MILFORD							
R & D Family Campground					▲	●	■
NATURAL BRIDGE							
Yogi Bear's Jellystone Camp Resort At Natural Bridge					▲	●	■
NEWPORT NEWS							
Newport News Park Campground (City Park)							■
PETERSBURG							
Picture Lake Campground						●	■
South Forty Camp Resort					▲	●	■
Spring Gardens Mobile Home Park							■
SALEM							
Dixie Caverns Campground					▲	●	■
STAFFORD							
Aquia Pines Camp Resort					▲	●	■
STAUNTON							
Staunton / Walnut Hills KOA					▲	●	■

Green Friendly 🍃; RV Lots for Sale ✖; Park Models/Onsite Onwership ✱; Park Memberships for Sale ✔; Big Rigs Welcome ▲;
Internet Friendly ●; Internet Friendly-WiFi ●; Pets Welcome ■

mation call 888/CIVIL WAR or visit www.civilwartraveler.com/virginia.

DESTINATION

Virginia is known as the gateway to the South, and one of the most historic and scenic states. With more than 250 Civil War sites to discover across the state, the Blue Ridge and Allegheny Mountains, Virginia offers something for history seekers, and adventure seekers alike. The Chesapeake Bay is a complex ecosystem with a long history of pirates and shipwrecks, but today it has thriving oyster farms, and is a popular spot for fishing, swimming, boating and sailing. There's always something to discover in Virginia.

NORTHERN VIRGINIA REGION

This region is next door to the nation's capital, yet has its own distinctive character that is reminiscent of colonial times, with rambling plantations, equestrian farms and cobblestoned streets.

Alexandria. Located south of the nation's capital, this historic seaport is lined with cobblestone streets. Several taverns have become museums and many structures harbor a fascinating history. Cruises down the Potomac River are as informative as they are relaxing. **The Lyceum** offers exhibits and public programs. This history museum features maps, photos, silver, Civil War artifacts and more.

Arlington. **Arlington National Cemetery's Arlington House** was constructed on top of a hill by Martha Washington's grandson. His daughter, Maryann Randolph Custis, married Robert E. Lee and they spent much of their life there. During the Civil War, the area was converted into a national cemetery, site of the graves of noted Americans such as Presidents Taft and Kennedy, General John J. Pershing and Supreme Court Justice Oliver Wendell Holmes. A narrated tour makes several stops, allowing you to leisurely view the Kennedys' resting place, visit **Arlington House** and watch the **Changing of the Guard** at the **Tomb of the Unknown Soldier**. The **Old Guard Museum** is a museum of the oldest active U.S. Army infantry unit.

The Pentagon. Tour the world's largest office building and home to the **U.S. Department of Defense**.

Fredericksburg. Located 50 miles south of Washington, DC, this historic town contains four Civil War battlefields, a multitude of antique shops and a national historic district. Before you begin your tour, stop by the Fredericksburg Visitor Center. Fredericksburg and **Spotsylvania National Military Park** are the sites of four devastating Civil War battles that claimed more than 100,000 lives.

Civil War Life Museum features extensive displays of original equipment, weapons and personal effects.

Ferry Farm. George Washington's boyhood home where he supposedly uttered the famous words, "I cannot tell a lie," after cutting down the cherry tree.

Stonewall Jackson Shrine marks where the Civil War general died.

The Manassas Museum. Visit an array of exhibits as you journey back in time, including railway, Civil War, Victorian items and custom videos.

Manassas National Battlefield Park. Located 26 miles southwest of Washington, DC, the park commemorates two major Civil War battles in which 28,626 men lost their lives.

Mount Vernon. George Washington's beloved home overlooks the Potomac River. The 30 acres include a dozen buildings, all open to the public. Explore the mansion, greenhouse, slave quarters, gardens, pioneer farmer site and gristmill.

National Air and Space Museum, Dulles Airport. This addition to the Smithsonian museum houses 80 aircraft as well as space shuttles and has an observation tower where visitors can take in the air traffic at Dulles.

SOUTHERN VIRGINIA REGION

Southern Virginia was once the heart of the states tobacco growing region, and where the rhythms of life rose and fell with fortunes made here. This area is rich in Revolutionary and Civil War history, an easy lure for any history buff. For those looking for something a little fast pace, the region is also home to six speedways and raceways!

Visit Clarksville for easy access to Virginia's **Buggs Island Lake**, Virginia's largest with 50,000 acres of fresh water and 800 miles of shoreline. Enjoy water sports, boating and other recreation or surround yourself with natural beauty while exploring quiet

QUICK REFERENCE CHART FOR WOODALL'S FEATURED PARKS

	Green Friendly	RV Lots for Sale	Park Models-Onsite Ownership	Park Membership for Sale	Big Rigs Welcome	Internet Friendly	Pets Welcome
URBANNA							
Bethpage Camp-Resort			*		▲	●	■
VIRGINIA BEACH							
Holiday Trav-L-Park of Virginia Beach					▲	●	■
WILLIAMSBURG							
American Heritage RV Park					▲	●	■
Anvil Campground					▲	●	■
KOA-Colonial Central	🍃				▲	●	■
KOA-Williamsburg	🍃				▲	●	■
WINCHESTER							
Candy Hill Campground					▲	●	■
WYTHEVILLE							
Fort Chiswell RV Park					▲	●	■
KOA-Wytheville Kampground	🍃				▲	●	■

Green Friendly 🍃; RV Lots for Sale ✖; Park Models/Onsite Onwership ✱; Park Memberships for Sale ✔; Big Rigs Welcome ▲; Internet Friendly ●; Internet Friendly-WiFi ●; Pets Welcome ■

coves and wooded shorelines. Camping at the site is available in the bordering **Occoneechee State Park**, which also extends 39 miles up the **Roanoke River**.

Danville Museum of Fine Arts and History, Danville. William T. Sutherlin home where Jefferson Davis stayed in April 1865 when Confederate government fled Richmond.

The Staunton River Battlefield State Park, Randolph, features a 3,800 square foot visitor center, battlefield exhibits, earthworks, nature trails, wildlife observation towers and prehistoric Native American artifacts.

TIDEWATER AND HAMPTON ROADS REGION

Colonial brick paths, the victory at Yorktown, and the birth of the space age come together in this area. Hampton Roads is known as "America's first region", with a hand in nearly every era of the nation's history.

Hampton. See an exceptional collection of African, African-American and American Indian art at the **Hampton University Museum**. The **Hampton History Museum** chronicles Hampton's history from first settlers through the 20th century.

Air Power Park & Museum, Hampton. This major cultural and educational facility houses an IMAX® theater, full-sized air and spacecraft, an observation deck and interactive exhibits.

Jamestown Settlement. First permanent settlement in North America. Seventeenth-century tower and reconstructed church. Ranger and living history tours. Archaeological and environmental exhibits, costumed glassblowers, wildlife, film and museum store.

Newport News. Located on the James River, this maritime community offers unique museums and historic homes:

Lee Hall Mansion. Historic antebellum home used as Confederate headquarters during the 1862 Peninsula Campaign.

Endview Plantation. A historic plantation home and grounds restored to its 1862 appearance.

Mariner's Museum. One of the largest maritime collections in the world showcases an international collection of ship models—including the **Crabtree Collection of Miniature Ships**, small crafts, paintings and decorative arts, working steam engines, scrimshaw, vintage boats and figureheads. Also featured are the **Chesapeake Bay Gallery** and historical interpreters.

Virginia War Museum houses more than 18,000 items depicting military history from pre-Revolutionary times to the Vietnam War.

Norfolk. Botanical gardens, historic homes and year-round waterfront festivals await visitors.

Nauticus, The National Maritime Center. See a virtual reality attraction, Aegis naval battle simulation, giant-screen movie and experience interactive exhibits and tour ships.

Battleship Wisconsin. Located next to Nauticus, this Iowa-class warship earned five battle stars during World War II.

Norfolk Naval Base. Take a narrated tour of the world's largest naval base.

Portsmouth. Highlights of this town situated on the world's largest natural harbor include the **Lightship Museum**, **Portsmouth Naval Shipyard Museum**, **Virginia Sports Hall of Fame and Museum** and **The Hill House**, a four-story English basement dwelling containing original furnishings.

Virginia Beach. Containing 29 miles of bright, sandy beaches, Virginia Beach is said to be the world's largest shore resort. More than a beach, it has historical attractions, golf, tennis, fishing and great restaurants.

Ocean Breeze Fun Park. Wild Water Rapids, Motorworld, Strike Zone and Shipwreck Golf are featured at this fun-filled park.

Virginia Aquarium & Marine Science Center, located in Virginia Beach, houses aquariums totaling 800,000 gallons in 2 exhibit areas depicting Virginia marineland habitats. The museum also provides hands-on activities, an IMAX® theatre and season boat trips.

Williamsburg. The restored Colonial capital of Virginia encompasses more than 80 original structures including the **Governor's Palace**, **Capital Building**, **Public Hospital of 1773**, an old jail, restaurants and pubs, plus shops in which costumed interpreters demonstrate colonial crafts.

Busch Gardens Williamsburg is a beautifully landscaped, 360-acre entertainment park with an Old Country theme. The park contains European-style hamlets including the new Ireland village.

Yorktown was the site of British General Cornwallis' surrender to General George Washington. **Yorktown Victory Center**, designed to let you see and feel the atmosphere of Revolutionary America, offers exhibits, a museum and films.

EASTERN SHORE REGION

Accessible via the 17.5 mile Chesapeake Bay Bridge, this area is filled with old railroad towns, and quaint fishing villages, and a unique old world accent can still be found here, especially by the Tangier Island residents.

Assateague Island National Seashore. Home to unique wild ponies, this area also features bicycle and hiking trails, seasonal programs, self-guided trails, swimming and a seasonal visitor center.

The Chesapeake Bay Bridge-Tunnel connects the Virginia mainland near Norfolk with Virginia's Eastern Shore. This 17.6-mile facility is an engineering marvel and is considered one of the seven man-made wonders of the world.

Chincoteague National Wildlife Refuge, Chincoteague. Known for its great abundance of migratory birds and wild horses, it is the perfect place to get away from it all. During the summer you can find crowded beaches or go for a little walk up the beach and find solitude. From Bird watching, surfing, swimming, fishing, crabbing or boating, the Chincoteague, Assateague area offers it all. Also known for the wild Chincoteague Ponies, you can see them and learn about their history. You can even go for a pony ride on a real Chincoteague Pony! If pony riding isn't for you, there are plenty of bike rental shops.

Kiptopeke State Park, Cape Charles, offers recreational access to the Chesapeake Bay as well as an opportunity to explore

CAMPCLUB USA

Where to Find CCUSA Parks

List City	Park Name	Map Coordinates
FRONT ROYAL		
	North Fork Resort	B-4
	Skyline Ranch Resort	B-4
GLOUCESTER POINT		
	Gloucester Point Family Campground	D-5
KING & QUEEN COURTHOUSE		
	Rainbow Acres Campground	D-5
LOUISA		
	Small Country Campground	C-4
MILFORD		
	R & D Family Campground	C-4
NATURAL BRIDGE		
	Yogi Bear's Jellystone Camp Resort At Natural Bridge	D-2

unique migratory bird habitat along the Atlantic flyway. The park offers camping, hiking, biking and a swimming beach.

NASA Visitor Center, Wallops Island, features model rocket launches, exhibits, films and other activities. The visitor center also provides information about current activities at Wallops Flight Facility, such as the sounding rockets, balloons and aircraft program. The outside grounds have rockets and aircraft used for space and aeronautical research including a full-scale four-stage reentry vehicle used to study the earth's atmosphere.

CENTRAL VIRGINIA REGION

This very large region of the state is rich in outdoor recreation opportunities, and home to some of the state's largest lakes and rivers. Civil War battlefields are found at nearly every turn in the road, as well as Colonial historic sites, including the home of Thomas Jefferson and Patrick Henry.

Appomattox Courthouse National Historic Park, Appomattox. The village with many original buildings where Lee surrendered to Grant in 1865, virtually ending the Civil War. The visitor center has fascinating exhibits, illustrated talks and audio-visual programs.

National D-Day Memorial, Bedford. A monument honoring all who fought in the D-Day invasion in World War II. Located in the village that lost more American soldiers per capita than any other U.S. locale.

Monticello. Located high on a hill overlooking the town of Charlottesville, Thomas Jefferson's magnificent estate is considered one of the most revered homes in America.

Pamplin Historical Park and National Museum of the Civil War Soldier, Petersburg. Visitors follow their chosen soldier guide, using a personal audio device, from training camp to the battlefield and beyond.

Richmond. This hub of central Virginia features many fine attractions, including:

Edgar Allan Poe Museum. View mementos, exhibit rooms and the enchanted garden of the imaginative author.

SHENANDOAH VALLEY REGION

Nicknamed "The Big Valley", this region stretches 200 miles across the Blue Ridge and Allegheny mountains. This area includes many sites devoted to the pioneers who traveled westward, settled and farmed the fertile valley. Several special sites are devoted to Civil War history of the region.

Dixie Caverns, Salem. Travel up into a mountain to see the magnificent cathedral room and many other formations. There is also an antique mall on-site.

George Washington's Office Museum, Winchester. View the office used by Washington while working as a surveyor and then a colonel in command of Virginia's troops.

Grand Caverns Regional Park, Grottoes. Fun for the family includes caverns, America's oldest show cave, swimming pool, mini-golf, tennis and picnicking.

Historic **Lexington** was home to Robert E. Lee and Stonewall Jackson. This restored 19th-century college town is home to **Washington & Lee University, Virginia Military Institute, Lee Chapel, Stonewall Jackson House, George C. Marshall Museum, VMI Museum, Virginia Horse Center**, country inns, carriage rides, specialty shops, a summer outdoor professional theatre and a summer-stock theatre.

Luray Caverns, Luray. Located just west of Skyline Drive, Luray Caverns has been fascinating visitors since its discovery in 1878. A one-hour guided tour leads spectators through a profusion of underground color. Hear the world's only Stalacpipe Organ. Also on the grounds is the **Garden Maze,** an ornamental garden featuring a half-mile pathway of puzzlement.

Natural Bridge. Located between the Appalachian and Blue Ridge Mountains, the town of Natural Bridge is home to 2 of nature's greatest creations.

Natural Bridge of Virginia. This serene bridge is one of the 7 natural wonders of the world. It was carved by nature from 36,000 tons of limestone and spans 90 feet.

Natural Bridge Wax Museum. More than 125 life-size replicas depict Native American legends and folklore.

Natural Chimneys Regional Park, Mt. Solon. Seven towering limestone columns are described as one of the great curiosities of nature in the eastern U.S.

New Market Battlefield Historical Park, New Market. Murals, life size models, rare artifacts and 3-dimensional dioramas help Civil War history unfold.

Roanoke. A variety of cultural establishments call Roanoke their home. The **O. Winston Link Museum** is located in the Norfolk and Western Passenger Station built in 1905. Link was an acclaimed 20th century photographer who portrayed trains and railroad towns in dramatic black and white photographs. Other Roanoke highlights include the **Harrison Museum of African-American Culture, Mill Mountain Zoo** and **Virginia's Explore Park.**

Shenandoah Caverns. Take the mile-long tour through numerous chambers as well as great rooms and halls. View the world famous Bacon Formations as well as the Grotto of the Gods and Rainbow Lake. The Caverns remain a cool 56° all year long.

Skyline Drive. Starting north at Front Royal, this meandering 105-mile long highway follows the crest of the Blue Ridge Mountains through Shenandoah National Park to Waynesboro at I-64, where it continues south at the Blue Ridge Parkway.

BLUE RIDGE HIGHLANDS REGION

The beautiful Blue Ridge Parkway runs through this region, and has been called "America's Most Scenic Drive". This region also has an abundance of outdoor recreational opportunities, and plenty of places to see wildlife.

Abingdon, Barter Theatre. The state theater of Virginia is nestled in the glorious mountains of Southwest Virginia. Enjoy comedies, musicals and drama on our two stages.

Booker T. Washington National Monument, Hardy (30 miles southeast of Roanoke). Birthplace of the noted educator, author and presidential adviser, the monument includes a replica of the slave cabin where he spent his early days and an audio-visual program illustrating his achievements.

Morgan McClure Motorsports Museum. Home of three-time Daytona 500 Champions. View actual racecars and exhibits. Authentic NASCAR apparel and collectibles for several drivers available.

Bastian. The Wolf Creek Indian Village & Museum is a recreated village with hands-on demonstrations and store. Experience a recreated village based on an actual archeological site. The village carbon dated almost 800 years ago, around the year 1215 A.D. The site was carefully excavated, mapped, and documented. It has been recreated so you may experience the actual layout of the wigwams and palisade. Interpretive guides lead you in a hands-on exploration of the early living skills, and skills that are still used today. Museum displays include artifacts from the site and other artifacts and replicas from not only Southwest Virginia, but also all of North America. Museum Store, picnic areas, picnic shelter, and nature trails are available.

Blue Ridge Parkway. Camping, fishing, hiking trails, picnicking, programs, restaurants and visitor centers.

Bristol. Birthplace of **Country Music Alliance Museum**. This town pays tribute to Bristol as the recognized "Birthplace of Country Music." **Bristol Motor Speedway**. World's fastest half-mile NASCAR track.

Virginia Creeper Trail. Scenic recreational trails for mountain biking, hiking, horseback riding and nature walks are available.

Wytheville. Come and be treated to blooming meadows and rich autumn colors. The **Homestead Museum** takes you on a journey through the 18th century. It features an authentic farm homestead, log buildings, a blacksmith shop, barn, weaving cabin and sorghum molasses mill.

CHESAPEAKE BAY REGION

This region is the birthplace of the nation's first president, George Washington, and is home to the estate of Confederate General Robert E. Lee, as well as the Pamunkey and Mattaponi native peoples. One of Virginia's most prestigious vineyards, Ingleside, can be found here, as well as Westmoreland Berry Farm and Orchard with its climbing goats.

Gloucester. Gloucester Historic District features an 18th-century courthouse, a debtor's prison, a tavern, a museum, shops and restaurants.

King George County. Caledon Natural Area is a bald eagle summer foraging area and forest designated national natural landmark.

West Point. Mattaponi Indian Museum and Minnie Ha Ha Educational Trading Post. An artifact that can be found here includes Pocahontas' necklace. A nature trail, participatory programs and a historical presentation are also available.

Lancaster County. Mary Ball Washington Museum and 1850s courthouse village offer exhibits, tours, a museum shop and a genealogy/research library.

Tangier and Chesapeake Cruises. Cruise from Reedville to quaint Tangier Island. May – October.

Westmoreland County, Stratford Hall Plantation is Robert E. Lee's birthplace, built in the late 1730s. Great house tours, a visitor center, a video, a museum, a dining room and a gift shop are offered.

ANNUAL EVENTS

JANUARY

Dino Day Festival at the Virginia Museum, Martinsville; Lexington Lee Jackson Day, Lexington.

FEBRUARY

Virginia Wine Showcase, Chantilly; African American Film Festival, Newport News; George Washington's Birthday Celebration, Alexandria/Mount Vernon; Mid-Atlantic Quilt Festival, Hampton; Virginia Wine Expo, Richmond.

MARCH

Highland Maple Festival, Monterey; Civil War Reenactment, Newport News; Daffodil Festival, Gloucester.

APRIL

Blue Ridge Bike Fest, Roanoke; Arts & Crafts Faire, Fredericksburg; Skirmish at Jeffersonville Civil War Reenactment, Tazewell; Revolutionary War Reenactment, Petersburg; Shakespeare's Birthday Festival, Staunton; Highlands Jazz Festival, Abingdon; Civil War History Weekend, Buchanan; Culpeper Remembrance Days, Culpeper; Virginia Arts Festival, Norfolk; Apple Blossom Festival, Winchester.

MAY

Antique Rose Festival, Lynchburg; Monacan Indian Pow Wow, Elon; American Indian Pow Wow, Virginia Beach; Faith Festival, Buchanan; Chesapeake Jubilee, Chesapeake; Tour de Chesapeake Bicycling Festival, Mathews; Spring Wine Festival, Mount Vernon; Strasburg Mayfest, Strasburg; Drummer's Call, Williamsburg; Magic in the Mountains, Clifton Forge; Monacan Indian Pow Wow, Elon; Loudoun County Spring Farm Tour, Leesburg; Battle of New Market Reenactment, New Market; Ralph Stanley Festival, Coeburn; Newtown Heritage Festival, Stephens City; Delaplane Strawberry Festival, Delaplane; Upper Mattaponi Spring Festival & Pow Wow, King William; Yorktown Civil War Weekend, Yorktown; Blessing of the Fleet, Chincoteague Island; Herndon Festival, Herndon; Virginia Regional Festival of Flight, Suffolk.

JUNE

Bluegrass Festival, Lanexa; Blackbeard Pirate Festival, Hampton; Celebrate Fairfax, Fairfax; Coalfields Folk Life Festival, Grundy; Clinch River Days, St. Paul; American Indian Festival, Chesapeake; Clinch Mountain Music Festival, Gate City; Hampton Jazz Festival, Hampton; Under the Redcoat, Williamsburg.

JULY

Blackbeard Pirate Festival & Ball, Hampton; Pony Swim & Auction, Assateague Island; Hot Air Balloon Rally, Lexington; Civil War Day Camps, New Market; Virginia Southern Gospel Jubilee, Buena Vista; Old time & Bluegrass Fiddlers' Convention, Tazewell; Daylily & Wine Festival, Fisherville; Renaissance Festival, Gloucester; Virginia Highlands Festival, Abingdon; Carter Family Traditional Music Festival, Hiltons.

AUGUST

Virginia's Peach Festival, Stuart; Fries Fiddlers' Convention, Fries; Staunton Music Festival, Staunton; Lucketts Fair, Lucketts; East Coast Surfing Championships, Virginia Beach.

SEPTEMBER

Mathews Market Days Festival, Mathews; Alexandria Festival of the Arts, Alexandria; Eastern Shore Birding & Wildlife Festival, Cape Charles; Bristol Rhythm & Roots Reunion, Bristol; Horray for Hopewell Festival, Hopewell; Umoja Festival, Portsmouth; Civil War Weekend, Winchester; Bluemont Fair, Bluemont; African American Heritage Festival, Staunton; Virginia Peanut Festival, Emporia; Chickahominy Fall Festival and Pow Wow, Charles City; Siege of Yorktown, Newport News.

OCTOBER

Chincoteague Oyster Festival, Chincoteague Island; Fall Festival, Vinton; Waterford Homes Tour, Waterford; Clarksville Hydroplane Challenge, Clarksville; Fall Festival of Folk Life, Newport News; Fredericksburg Area Wine Festival, Fredericksburg; Black Powder & Paint Living History Weekend, Gloucester; Mountain Foliage Festival, Independence; Rappahannock Tribal Pow Wow, Indian Neck; Virginia Wine & Garlic Festival, Amherst; Fall Farm Festival, Delaplane; Battle of Cedar Creek Reenactment, Middletown; Hot Air Balloon & Wine Festival, Millwood; Yorktown Victory Celebration, Yorktown.

NOVEMBER

Oyster Festival, Urbanna; Virginia Gourd Festival, Middletown; Assateague Island Waterfowl Week, Chincoteague Island; Foods & Feasts of Colonial Virginia, Williamsburg; 100 Miles of Lights, Newport News.

DECEMBER

Sugarloaf Crafts Festival, Chantilly; A Colonial Christmas, Williamsburg; Scottish Christmas Walk Parade, Alexandria; Christmas Tours at Belle Grove Plantation, Middletown; Centuries of Christmas at Berkeley Plantation, Charles City; Onancock Christmas Homes Tour, Onancock; Berkeley's Colonial Christmas, Charles City.

AMELIA—D-4

(E) Amelia Family Campground—(Amelia) *From jct US-360 & Hwy-153: Go 1/2 mi S on Hwy-153. Enter on R.* ◇◇◇FACILITIES: 88 sites, typical site width 20 ft, 50 full hkups, 20 W&E, (20/30/50 amps), 18 no hkups, 70 pull-thrus, family camping, tenting, dump, laundry, ltd groc. ◇◇◇RECREATION: swim pool, pond fishing, play equipment. Pets welcome. Open all yr. Rate in 2010 $21-24 for 2 persons. Member ARVC, VCA.

Phone: (804)561-3011
Address: 9720 Military Rd, Amelia, VA 23002
Lat/Lon: 37.35068/-77.88347
Email: ameliacampground@tds.net
Web: www.ameliafamilycampgrounds.com

APPOMATTOX—D-3

HOLLIDAY LAKE STATE PARK—(Appomattox) *From town: Go 9 mi E on Hwy-24, then 6 mi SE on Hwy-626 & 692.* FACILITIES: 30 sites, 25 ft max RV length, 30 W&E, (30 amps), tenting, dump. RECREATION: lake swim, boating, electric motors only, ramp, lake fishing, playground. Phone: (434)248-6308.

(N) Parkview MH & RV Park (RV SPACES) —(Appomattox) *From jct US 460 & Hwy 24 (2nd Appomatox exit on US 460 from either direction): Go 1 block N on Hwy 24, then 1 block E on Clover Lane. Enter on R.* FACILITIES: 33 sites, typical site width 25 ft, accepts self-contained units only, 33 full hkups, (20/30/50 amps), 30 pull-thrus. Pets welcome, breed restrict. No tents. Open all yr. Big rigs welcome. Rate in 2010 $32 for 2 persons. Phone: (434)352-2366.

ASHLAND—C-4

AMERICAMPS KOA RICHMOND-NORTH —(Hanover) *From jct I-95 (exit 89) & Hwy 802: Go 500 ft E on Hwy 802, then 1 mi S on Air Park Rd. Enter on L.*

WELCOME

◇◇◇◇FACILITIES: 200 sites, typical site width 30 ft, 200 full hkups, (20/30/50 amps), 50 amps ($), many extd stay sites, cable TV, WiFi Instant Internet at site, family camping, tenting, RV storage, dump, non-guest dump $, laundry, groceries, RV supplies, LP gas by weight/by meter, ice, picnic tables, patios, fire rings, grills, wood, controlled access.

◇◇RECREATION: rec room/area, coin games, swim pool, golf nearby, playground, sports field.

Pets welcome. Partial handicap access. Open all yr. Big rigs welcome. Escort to site. Clubs wel-

ASHLAND—Continued
AMERICAMPS KOA RICHMOND-NORTH—Continued

come. Rate in 2010 $30-57 for 2 persons. MC/VISA/DISC/AMEX/Debit. Member ARVC, VCA. FMCA discount.

Phone: (804)798-5298
Address: 11322 Air Park Rd, Ashland, VA 23005
Lat/Lon: 37.70992/-77.44733
Email: info@americampskoa.com
Web: www.americampskoa.com

SEE AD THIS PAGE AND AD TRAVEL SECTION PAGE 762

BASSETT—E-2

(W) GOOSE POINT (COE - Philpott Lake)—(Patrick) *From town: Go 8 mi N on Hwy-57, then 3-1/2 mi N on Hwy-822.* FACILITIES: 63 sites, 53 W&E, (20 amps), 10 no hkups, tenting, dump. RECREATION: lake swim, boating, ramp, dock, lake fishing, playground. Partial handicap access. Open all yr. Facilities fully operational Mar 25 - Oct 30. Phone: (276)629-2703.

BEDFORD—D-2

(N) BLUE RIDGE NAT'L PARKWAY (Peaks of Otter Campground)—(Bedford) *From town: Go 10 mi NW on Hwy 43. Blue Ridge Pkwy milepost 86.0.* FACILITIES: 141 sites, 35 ft max RV length, 141 no hkups, tenting, dump, ltd groc. RECREATION: lake fishing. Open May - Oct. Phone: (828)298-0398.

BIG ISLAND—D-3

(W) BLUE RIDGE NAT'L PARKWAY (Otter Creek)—(Carroll) *From town: Go 1 mi W, then 3 mi N on Blue Ridge Pkwy to milepost 60.9.* FACILITIES: 69 sites, 30 ft max RV length, 69 no hkups, tenting, dump. RECREATION: stream fishing. Open May - Oct. Phone: (540)377-2377.

BOWLING GREEN—C-5

MILITARY PARK (Fort A.P. Hill Campground)—(Caroline) *From town: Go 2 mi N on US 301, then W to Ft A.P. Hill. Report to Bldg. TT0106 or TT0101 before going to campground. On base.* FACILITIES: 48 sites, 48 full hkups, 10 pull-thrus, tenting, laundry. RECREATION: swim pool, boating, pond fishing. Open all yr. Phone: (804)633-8219.

BOYDTON—E-4

(S) NORTH BEND PARK (COE-John H Kerr Reservoir) —(Mecklenburg) *From town: Go 14 mi SE on US-58, then on Hwys-4 & 678.* FACILITIES: 249 sites, 88 E, 161 no hkups, tenting, dump, groceries. RECREATION: lake swim, boating, ramp, lake fishing, playground. Partial handicap access. Open all yr. Phone: (434)738-0059.

BOYDTON—Continued

(W) RUDDS CREEK CG (COE-John H Kerr Reservoir) —(Mecklenburg) *From town: Go 3 mi W on US-58.* FACILITIES: 99 sites, 75 W&E, (20/30 amps), 24 no hkups, tenting, dump. RECREATION: lake swim, boating, ramp, lake fishing, playground. Partial handicap access. Open all yr. Phone: (434)738-6143.

BRACEY—E-4

(SE) Americamps Lake Gaston—(Mecklenburg) *From jct I-85 (exit 4) & Hwy 903: Go 5 mi E on Hwy 903. Enter on R.* ◇◇◇FACILITIES: 112 sites, typical site width 25 ft, 15 full hkups, 97 W&E, (20/30/50 amps), 10 pull-thrus, family camping, tenting, dump, laundry, groceries. ◇◇◇◇RECREATION: swim pool, boating, canoeing, ramp, dock, lake fishing, playground. Pets welcome. Open all yr. Rate in 2010 $33-45 for 2 persons. Member ARVC, VCA. Phone: (434)636-2668.

BRISTOL—B-2

SUGAR HOLLOW RECREATION AREA (City Park)—(Washington) *From I-81 (exit 7): Go 1 mi N on US 11 (Robert E. Lee Hwy).* FACILITIES: 75 sites, 1 full hkups, 24 E, 50 no hkups, tenting, dump. RECREATION: swim pool, play equipment. Open Apr 15 - Nov 1. Phone: (276)645-7376.

BROADWAY—B-3

(SE) HARRISONBURG / SHENANDOAH VALLEY KOA—(Rockingham) *From jct I-81 (exit 257) & US 11; Go 100 yards N on US 11, then 3 mi E on Hwy 608. (Mauzy Athlone Rd) Entrance at end of Hwy 608. Use GPS coordinates, not physical address.*

WELCOME

AWARD WINNING KOA-OPEN ALL YEAR
I-81, Exit 257. In the Heart of the Shenandoah Valley near Skyline Drive. Heated Pool - Large, Wooded Pull-Thrus, Free Mini-Golf, Climate controlled Restrooms & kabins. Call 1-800-562-5406 or visit www.KOA.com/where/VA/46140

◇◇◇◇FACILITIES: 97 sites, typical site width 30 ft, 41 full hkups, 22 W&E, (20/30/50 amps), 34 no hkups, 23 pull-thrus, WiFi Internet central location, family camping, tenting, cabins, dump, non-guest dump $, laundry, groceries, RV supplies, LP gas by meter, ice, picnic tables, fire rings, wood.

HARRISONBURG / SHENANDOAH VALLEY KOA—Continued on next page

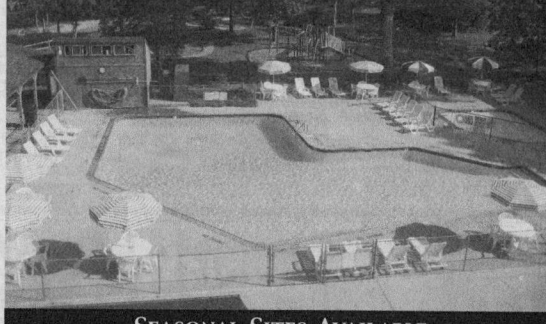

BROADWAY—Continued
HARRISONBURG / SHENANDOAH VALLEY KOA—Continued

◊◊◊◊RECREATION: rec room/area, pavilion, coin games, swim pool, pond fishing, fishing supplies, mini-golf, bsktball, playground, horseshoes, sports field, hiking trails, v-ball.

Pets welcome, breed restrict. Open all yr. Big rigs welcome. Escort to site. Clubs welcome. Rate in 2010 $35-45.50 for 2 persons. MC/VISA. Member ARVC, VCA. KOA discount.

Phone: (540)896-8929
Address: 12480 Mountain Valley Rd, Broadway, VA 22815
Lat/Lon: 38.53584/-78.70610
Email: shenandoahvalleykoa@yahoo.com
Web: www.koa.com/where/va/46140

SEE AD NEW MARKET PAGE 777 AND AD TRAVEL SECTION PAGE 762

BUCHANAN—D-2

(E) Middle Creek Campground—(Botetourt) *From jct I-81 (exit 168) & Hwy 614: Go 5 mi E on Hwy 614 (Arcadia Rd), then 1 mi SE on Middle Creek Rd. Enter on R.* ◊◊◊FACILITIES: 100 sites, 25 full hkups, 59 W&E, (30/50 amps), 50 amps ($), 16 no hkups, 15 pull-thrus, family camping, tenting, dump, laundry, ltd groc. ◊◊◊RECREATION: swim pool, saltwater swim, pond/stream fishing, playground. Pets welcome, breed restrict. Partial handicap access. Open all yr. Big rigs welcome. Rate in 2010 $32-36 for 4 persons. Phone: (540)254-2550.

BUENA VISTA—D-3

(S) GLEN MAURY PARK (Municipal)—(Rockbridge) *From jct I-81 (exit 188E) & US 60E: Go E on US 60, then S on US 501, then 1/4 mi W on 10th St.* FACILITIES: 52 sites, 22 full hkups, 27 W&E, (20/30 amps), 3 no hkups, 7 pull-thrus, tenting, dump. RECREATION: swim pool, river swim, canoeing, river fishing, playground. Pets welcome. Open Mar 15 - Nov 15. Phone: (540)261-7321.

CAPE CHARLES—D-6

KIPTOPEKE STATE PARK—(Northampton) *On Hwy 13, 3 mi N of Chesapeake Bay Bridge Tunnel.* FACILITIES: 141 sites, 40 full hkups, 54 W&E, (20/30 amps), 47 no hkups, tenting, dump, laundry, groceries. RECREATION: saltwater swim, boating, ramp, dock, saltwater fishing. Partial handicap access. Open all yr. Phone: (757)331-1040.

CENTREVILLE—B-4

(S) BULL RUN REGIONAL PARK—(Fairfax) *From jct I-66 (Exit 52) & US 29: Go 2 mi S on US 29, then 2 mi SW on Bull Run Post Office Rd. (Becomes Bull Run Dr). Enter on L.* FACILITIES: 150 sites, 45 full hkups, 56 W&E, (20/30/50 amps), 49 no hkups, 75 pull-thrus, family camping, tenting, dump, laundry, ltd groc. RECREATION: swim pool, stream fishing, playground. Pets welcome. Partial handicap access. Open all yr. Big rigs welcome. Phone: (703)631-0550.

CHARLOTTESVILLE—C-3

(NE) KOA-CHARLOTTESVILLE—(Albemarle) *From jct I-64 (exit 121): Go 8-1/2 mi S on Hwy 20, then 1-1/2 mi W on Hwy 708. Enter on R.*

WELCOME

◊◊◊◊FACILITIES: 64 sites, typical site width 25 ft, 32 full hkups, 20 W&E, (20/30/50 amps), 50 amps ($), 12 no hkups, 15 pull-thrus, WiFi Instant Internet at site, WiFi Internet central location, family camping, tenting, cabins, dump, laundry, groceries, RV supplies, LP gas by meter, ice, picnic tables, fire rings, wood.

◊◊◊◊RECREATION: rec room/area, pavilion, coin games, swim pool, pond fishing, fishing supplies, golf nearby, bsktball, playground, activities, horseshoes, sports field, hiking trails, v-ball.

Pets welcome, quantity restrict. Open Mid Mar - Mid Nov. Big rigs welcome. Clubs welcome. Rate in 2010 $30-41 for 2 persons. MC/VISA/DISC/ Debit. Member ARVC, VCA. KOA discount.

Roy Clark, entertainer, is from Virginia.

CHARLOTTESVILLE—Continued
KOA-CHARLOTTESVILLE—Continued

Phone: (434)296-9881
Address: 3825 Red Hill Rd, Charlottesville, VA 22903
Lat/Lon: 37.93180/-78.56601
Email: charlottesvillekoa@yahoo.com
Web: www.charlottesvillekoa.com

SEE AD THIS PAGE

CHERITON—D-6

(W) CHERRYSTONE FAMILY CAMPING RESORT—(Northampton) *From jct US 13 & Hwy 680 (Townfields Dr): Go 1-1/2 mi W on Hwy 680 (Townfields Dr). Enter at end.*

CHERRYSTONE FAMILY CAMPING RESORT
300 acres nestled along the beautiful lower Chesapeake Bay. Most of our sites are shaded by our tall growth pines and can accommodate almost any guest's rig or tent. Scenic water views with the best sunsets in Virginia.

◊◊◊◊◊FACILITIES: 725 sites, typical site width 28 ft, 403 full hkups, 303 W&E, (20/30/50 amps), 50 amps ($), 19 no hkups, 110 pull-thrus, WiFi Instant Internet at site, WiFi Internet central location, family camping, tenting, RV's/park model rentals, cabins, RV storage, dump, portable dump, laundry, full svc store, RV supplies, LP gas by weight/by meter, ice, picnic tables, wood, controlled access.

◊◊◊◊◊RECREATION: rec hall, equipped pavilion, coin games, 4 swim pools, spray ground, saltwater swim, boating, canoeing, kayaking, ramp, dock, 9 kayak/15 pedal boat/40 motorboat rentals, saltwater fishing, fishing supplies, fishing guides, mini-golf ($), golf nearby, bsktball, 60 bike rentals, playground, shuffleboard court 2 shuffleboard courts, activities, tennis, horseshoes, sports field, v-ball.

Pets welcome, breed restrict, quantity restrict. Partial handicap access. Open all yr. Big rigs welcome. Clubs welcome. Rate in 2010 $17-68 for 2 persons. MC/VISA/AMEX/Debit. ATM. Member ARVC, VCA.

Text 89808 to (440)725-8687 to see our Visual Tour.

Phone: (757)331-3063
Address: 1511 Townfield Dr, Cheriton, VA 23316
Lat/Lon: 37.28590/-76.01084
Email: info@cherrystoneva.com
Web: www.cherrystoneva.com

SEE AD NEXT PAGE AND AD TRAVEL SECTION PAGE 761 AND AD MD TRAVEL SECTION PAGE 327 AND AD DISCOVER SECTION PAGE 28

(W) MISS JENNIFER CHARTER FISHING—*From jct US 13 & Hwy 680 (Townfields Dr): Go 1-1/2 mi W on Hwy 680 (Townfields Dr).* Fifty foot Miss Jennifer is a charter boat specializing in family fishing with all equipment furnished. Also Sunset Cruises and Dolphin Searches. Open all yr.

WELCOME

Phone: (757)331-3740
Address: 1511 Townfields Dr, Cheriton, VA 23316
Web: www.missjennifercharterfishing.com

SEE AD NEXT PAGE AND AD TRAVEL SECTION PAGE 761 AND AD MD TRAVEL SECTION PAGE 327 AND AD DISCOVER SECTION PAGE 28

Virginia State Nicknames: Old Dominion; Mother of Presidents

CHESAPEAKE—E-6

(S) CHESAPEAKE CAMPGROUND—(City of Chesapeake) *From jct I-64 (exit 296) & Business US 17: Go 3-1/2 mi S on US 17. Enter on L.*

WELCOME

◊◊◊◊FACILITIES: 141 sites, typical site width 30 ft, 42 full hkups, 70 W&E, (20/30/50 amps), 50 amps ($), 29 no hkups, some extd stay sites, 66 pull-thrus, phone Internet central location, family camping, tenting, cabins, RV storage, dump, portable dump, laundry, ltd groc, RV supplies, LP gas by meter, ice, picnic tables, fire rings, wood, controlled access.

◊◊◊◊RECREATION: rec room/area, pavilion, equipped pavilion, coin games, 2 swim pools, boating, canoeing, kayaking, ramp, dock, 4 rowboat/12 canoe rentals, pond fishing, mini-golf, ($), golf nearby, bsktball, 20 bike rentals, playground, tennis, horseshoes, sports field, hiking trails, v-ball. Rec open to public.

Pets welcome, quantity restrict. Partial handicap access. Open all yr. Rate in 2010 $27.22-30.85 for 2 persons. MC/VISA/DISC. Member ARVC, VCA.

Phone: (757)485-0149
Address: 693 S. George Washington Hwy, Chesapeake, VA 23323
Lat/Lon: 36.71321/-76.35162

SEE AD PAGE 772

CHESAPEAKE BAY—D-6

See Listings at Gwynn & New Point

CHESTERFIELD—D-4

(W) POCAHONTAS STATE PARK—(Chesterfield) *From town: Go 4 mi SW on Hwy-655.* FACILITIES: 114 sites, 114 W&E, (20/30 amps), tenting, dump. RECREATION: swim pool, boating, electric motors only, canoeing, ramp, lake fishing, playground. Partial handicap access. Open all yr. Facilities fully operational May - Sep. Phone: (540)745-9662.

CHINCOTEAGUE—C-6

(E) Maddox Family Campground—(Accomack) *From jct US 13 & Hwy 175: Go 11 mi E on Hwy 175, then 1 mi SE on Maddox Blvd. Enter on R.* ◊◊◊FACILITIES: 340 sites, typical site width 25 ft, 180 full hkups, 160 W&E, (20/30/50 amps), 91 pull-thrus, family camping, tenting, dump, laundry, ltd groc. ◊◊◊RECREATION: swim pool, playground. Pets welcome, quantity restrict. Partial handicap access. Open Mar 1 - Nov 30. Big rigs welcome. Rate in 2010 $40.70-49.50 for 4 persons. Phone: (757)336-3111.

(N) Pine Grove Camground & Waterfowl Park—(Accomack) *From jct US 13 & Hwy 175: Go 11 mi E on Hwy 175, then 1/2 mi E on Maddox Blvd, then 3/4 mi N on Deep Hole Rd. Enter on L.* ◊◊FACILITIES: 150 sites, typical site width 25 ft, 72 full hkups, 45 W&E, (15/20/30 amps), 33 no hkups, 15 pull-thrus, tenting, dump, laundry, ltd groc. ◊◊RECREATION: swim pool, play equipment. Pets welcome, breed restrict, size restrict, quantity restrict. Open Apr - Dec. Rate in 2010 $36-40 per vehicle.

Phone: (757)336-5200
Address: 5283 Deep Hole Rd, Chincoteague, VA 23336
Lat/Lon: 37.93772/-75.35206
Email: WJT_shore@verizon.net
Web: www.pinegrovecampground.com

(S) Tom's Cove Park—(Accomack) *From jct US 13 & Hwy 175: Go 11 mi E on Hwy 175, then 2 mi S on Main St, then 1/2 mi E on Beebe Rd. Enter at end.* ◊◊◊◊FACILITIES: 888 sites, typical site width 35 ft, 633 full hkups, 200 W&E, (20/30/50 amps), 50 amps ($), 55 no hkups, 60 pull-thrus, family camping, tenting, dump, laundry, full svc store. ◊◊◊◊RECREATION: swim pool, boating, canoeing, ramp, dock, saltwater fishing, playground. Pets welcome. Open Mar 1 - Nov 30. Rate in 2010 $39.25-49 for 4 persons. Member ARVC, VCA. Phone: (757)336-6498.

CHRISTIANSBURG—D-2

BLUE RIDGE NAT'L PARKWAY (Rocky Knob Campground)—(Floyd) *From town: Go 17 mi SE on Hwy 8 (Floyd), then 6 mi S on Hwy 8, then 2 mi SW on Blue Ridge Pkwy to milepost 167.1.* FACILITIES: 109 sites, 35 ft max RV length, 109 no hkups, tenting, dump. RECREATION: Open May - Oct. Phone: (540)745-9662.

(E) Interstate Overnight Park (RV SPACES)—(Montgomery) *From jct I-81 (exit 118) & US 11/460: Go 1/2 mi E on US 11/460. Enter on R.* FACILITIES: 32 sites, 25 full hkups, 7 W&E, (30/50 amps), 50 amps ($), tenting, dump, laundry. Pets welcome, size restrict, quantity restrict. Open all yr. Rate in 2010 $24-27. Phone: (540)382-1554.

CLARKSVILLE—E-3

(SE) IVY HILL CAMPGROUND (COE-John H Kerr Reservoir)—(Macklenburg) *From town: Go 16 mi SE on US-15 & Hwy-825.* FACILITIES: 25 sites, 25 no hkups, tenting, dump. RECREATION: boating, ramp, lake fishing. Open Apr 1 - Oct 30. Phone: (434)738-6143.

CLARKSVILLE—Continued on next page

At Cherrystone, the fun never ends.

(except maybe when you have to go home.)

WHEN YOUR TALKING VACATIONS, Cherrystone Family Camping Resort just might have it all. Fishing, swimming, mini golf, you name it, all situated on 300 acres on **the Chesapeake Bay on Virginia's Eastern Shore**. So pitch a tent, pull up the RV or rent a cottage, but be ready to have a blast.

Fun on the water

(some activities are seasonal)

- Fishing
- Crabbing
- Clamming
- 4 piers
- Boat Ramp
- Boat Rentals
- Party Fishing Boat with Sunset Bay Cruises

Fun on land

(some activities are seasonal)

- NEW - Cherrystone Wet Zone
- 4 Pools
- Mini Golf
- Water Wars
- Pedal Boats
- Bike Rentals
- Game Room
- Playgrounds
- Horseshoe Courts
- Golf Course Nearby
- Shuffleboard, Tennis, Volleyball, Basketball
- Planned Activities
- Live Entertainment
- Church Services
- Pavilion
- Golf Cart Rentals

Camping Fun

- 725 Sites (open or shaded)
- Waterview Sites available
- Pull Thrus
- Full Hookups
- Wireless Hot Spots Available
- Free Smiles

Other Essentials

Bait & Tackle Shop

- Fishing Equipment
- Rental Equipment

General Store & Gift Shop

- RV supplies & accessories
- Clothing
- Groceries
- ATM

Cafe & Arcade

Laundry

50-amp Big Rig Sites
Deluxe Cottages
On-site Trailer Rentals
Camping Cabins
Wooded Tent Sites

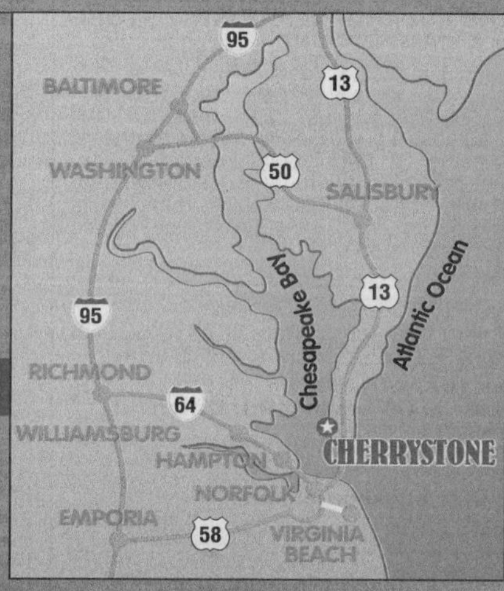

Cherrystone is located 11 miles North of the Chesapeake Bay Bridge Tunnel. Turn West at Cheriton at the traffic light off U.S. 13 onto VA 680. Follow the signs to the campground.

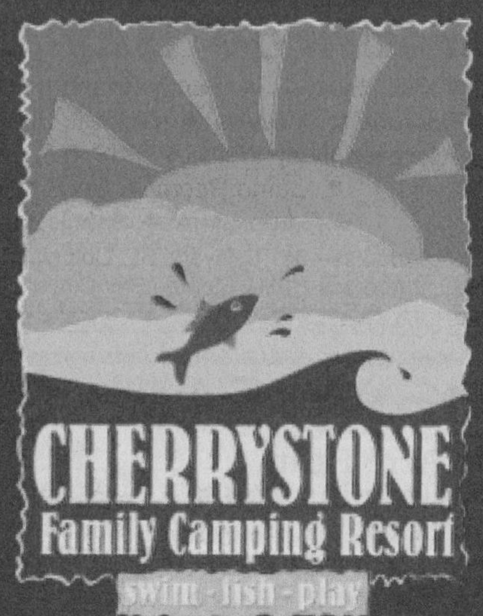

Call (757) 331-3063 for a Free Vacation Planner or visit our website at www.cherrystoneva.com

WOODALL RATED
Recreation: WWWWW
Facility: WWWWW

WHEELERS RATED
★★★★★

P.O. Box 545, Cheriton, Virginia 23316

See listing at Cheriton, VA

CLARKSVILLE—Continued

(S) LONGWOOD RECREATION AREA (COE-John H Kerr Reservoir)—(Mecklenburg) *From town: Go 4 mi S on US-15.* FACILITIES: 66 sites, 34 W&E, (15 amps), 32 no hkups, tenting, dump. RECREATION: lake swim, boating, ramp, lake fishing, playground. Open all yr. Phone: (434)738-6143.

OCCONEECHEE STATE PARK—(Mecklenburg) *From town: Go 1 mi E on US-58.* FACILITIES: 88 sites, 37 W&E, 51 no hkups, tenting, dump. RECREATION: boating, canoeing, ramp, lake fishing, playground. Partial handicap access. Open all yr. Phone: (804)374-2210.

CLIFTON FORGE—C-2

(N) DOUTHAT STATE PARK—(Bath) *From jct US-60 & Hwy-629: Go 2-1/2 mi N on Hwy-629.* FACILITIES: 74 sites, 55 W&E, (30 amps), 19 no hkups, tenting, dump, ltd groc. RECREATION: lake swim, boating, electric motors only, canoeing, ramp, lake fishing, playground. Partial handicap access. Facilities fully operational May - Sep. Phone: (540)862-8100.

(E) **THE BUCKHORNE COUNTRY STORE** —*From jct I-64 (exit 27) & Rte 629: Go 2 mi N on Rte 629. Enter on L.* Antiques, Country Kitchen, Ice Cream Parlor, fishing & camping supplies, video sales & rentals, handicap accessible kitchen & fenced-in playhouse for children while parents shop. Trout Stream. Amber Suzanne Beauty Salon. Open all yr. MC/VISA.

Phone: (540)862-4502
Address: 3508 Douthat Rd, Clifton Forge, VA 24422
Lat/Lon: 37.84873/-79.80427
Email: mrayallen@yahoo.com
Web: www.buckhorne.com

SEE AD THIS PAGE

(N) **THE BUCKHORNE COUNTRY STORE & CAMPGROUND**—(Alleghany) *From jct I-64 (exit 27) & Rte 629: Go 2 mi N on Rte 629. Enter on L.*

◆◆◆FACILITIES: 25 sites, 5 full hkups, 11 W&E, (20/30/50 amps), 9 no hkups, cable TV, WiFi Instant Internet at site, WiFi Internet central location, family camping, tenting, RV's/park model rentals, cabins, dump, non-guest dump $, ltd groc, RV supplies, ice, picnic tables, fire rings, wood.

◆RECREATION: horseshoes, sports field, hiking trails.

Pets welcome. Open all yr. Rate in 2010 $21-26 for 8 persons. MC/VISA. Member ARVC, VCA.

Phone: (877)301-3817
Address: 3508 Douthat Rd, Clifton Forge, VA 24422
Lat/Lon: 37.84912/-79.80406
Email: mrayallen@yahoo.com
Web: www.buckhorne.com

SEE AD THIS PAGE

Ella Fitzgerald, singer, was from Virginia.

CLINCHPORT—B-1

NATURAL TUNNEL STATE PARK—(Scott) *From jct US-23 & Hwy-871: Go 1/2 mi E on Hwy-871.* FACILITIES: 22 sites, 18 W&E, (20/30 amps), 4 no hkups, 18 pull-thrus, tenting, dump. RECREATION: swim pool, stream fishing, playground. Partial handicap access. Open all yr. Phone: (276)940-2674.

CLINTWOOD—A-2

CRANE NEST CAMPSITE (COE-John W Flannagan Reservoir)—(Dickenson) *From town: Go 2 mi E on Hwy 83, then 3 mi W on FR. Enter on L.* FACILITIES: 93 sites, 53 W&E, 40 no hkups, tenting, dump. RECREATION: river swim, boating, canoeing, ramp, dock, lake fishing, playground. Partial handicap access. Open mid May - early Sep. Phone: (276)835-9544.

COLLIERSTOWN—C-2

LAKE A. WILLIS ROBERTSON (Rockbridge County Park)—(Rockbridge) *From jct Hwy-251 & CR-770: Go 2 mi W on CR-770.* FACILITIES: 53 sites, 53 W&E, (30 amps), 7 pull-thrus, tenting, dump, laundry. RECREATION: swim pool, boating, electric motors only, canoeing, ramp, dock, lake fishing, playground. Open Apr 1 - Oct 30. Phone: (540)463-4164.

COLONIAL BEACH—C-5

(SE) **MONROE BAY CAMPGROUND**—(Westmoreland) *From jct Hwy 3 & Hwy 205: Go 4 mi N on Hwy 205, then 2 mi E on Hwy 628 (Monroe Bay Circle). Enter at end.*

◆◆◆FACILITIES: 310 sites, typical site width 25 ft, 140 full hkups, 170 W&E, (30 amps), mostly extd stay sites, 100 pull-thrus, family camping, tenting, dump, ltd groc, RV supplies, LP gas by weight/by meter, ice, picnic tables, wood.

◆◆◆◆RECREATION: rec room/area, coin games, saltwater swim, boating, canoeing, kayaking, ramp, dock, saltwater/pond fishing, fishing supplies, bsktball, playground.

Pets welcome. Open Apr 1 - Nov 1. Rate in 2010 $35 for 2 persons. MC/VISA. Member ARVC, VCA.

Phone: (804)224-7418
Address: 1412 Monroe Bay Cir, Colonial Beach, VA 22443
Lat/Lon: 38.23932/-76.96856

SEE AD THIS PAGE

OUTDOOR WORLD-HARBOR VIEW CAMPGROUND (CAMP RESORT)—(Westmoreland) *From jct Hwy 205 & Hwy 3: Go 2 mi SE on Hwy 3, then 3 mi N on Hwy 664. Enter on L.*

FACILITIES: 145 sites, 145 full hkups, (30/50 amps), 7 pull-thrus, family camping, tenting, RV's/park model rentals, dump, picnic tables, patios, fire rings, grills.

RECREATION: rec hall, rec room/area, pavilion, swim pool, wading pool, pond fishing, mini-golf, bsktball, playground, shuffleboard court shuffleboard court, horseshoes, sports field, v-ball.

Pets welcome. Partial handicap access. Open Mid-June - Mid-Sept. Clubs welcome. Member ARVC.

COLONIAL BEACH—Continued
OUTDOOR WORLD-HARBOR VIEW CAMPGROUND—Continued

Phone: (804)224-8164
Address: 15 Harbor View Circle, Colonial Beach, VA 22443
Lat/Lon: 38.20618/-76.97909
Web: www.1000trails.com

SEE AD ABINGDON PAGE 769

COVINGTON—C-2

(N) GEORGE WASHINGTON NATIONAL FOREST (Morris Hill Campground)—(Alleghany) *From jct US 220 & Hwy 687: Go 6 mi NW on Hwy 687, then 3 mi W on Hwy 641, then 5 mi N on Hwy 666.* FACILITIES: 55 sites, 55 no hkups, 1 pull-thrus, tenting, dump. RECREATION: lake swim, boating, canoeing, ramp, dock, lake fishing, playground. Partial handicap access. Open May 1 - Oct 31. Phone: (540)962-2214.

CUMBERLAND—D-4

BEAR CREEK LAKE STATE PARK—(Cumberland) *From town: Go 1/2 mi E on US-60, then 4-1/2 mi W on Hwy-622 & 629.* FACILITIES: 53 sites, 35 ft max RV length, 29 W&E, (20/30 amps), 24 no hkups, tenting, dump. RECREATION: lake swim, boating, electric motors only, canoeing, lake fishing. Pets welcome ($). Partial handicap access. Facilities fully operational May - Sep. Phone: (804)492-4410.

DAMASCUS—B-2

(E) JEFFERSON NATIONAL FOREST (Beartree Campground)—(Washington) *From town: Go 7 mi E on US-58.* FACILITIES: 84 sites, 25 ft max RV length, 84 no hkups, tenting, dump. RECREATION: lake swim, boating, no motors, lake/stream fishing, playground. Open all yr. Facilities fully operational Mar 15 - Dec 3. Phone: (276)388-3642.

DOSWELL—C-4

Kings Dominion Camp Wilderness—(Hanover) *From jct I-95 (exit 98) & Hwy 30: Go 1/2 mi E on Hwy 30. Enter on R.* ◆◆◆◆FACILITIES: 279 sites, 93 full hkups, 146 W&E, (20/30/50 amps), 40 no hkups, 37 pull-thrus, family camping, tenting, dump, laundry, groceries. ◆◆◆◆RECREATION: swim pool, playground. Pets welcome. Partial handicap access. Open all yr. Big rigs welcome. Rate in 2010 $36.83-42.25 for 4 persons. Member ARVC, VCA. Phone: (800)922-6710.

DRYDEN—B-1

(N) JEFFERSON NATIONAL FOREST (Cave Springs Campground)—(Lee) *From jct US-58A & Hwy-767: Go 3/4 mi N on Hwy-767, then 3-3/4 mi NE on Hwy-621, then 1/2 mi N on FR-1072.* FACILITIES: 40 sites, 40 no hkups, tenting, dump. RECREATION: Pets welcome. Open May 15 - Oct 15. Phone: (276) 328-2931.

DUBLIN—D-1

(E) CLAYTOR LAKE STATE PARK—(Pulaski) *From jct I-81 (exit 101) & Hwy 660: Go 2 mi E on Hwy 660.* FACILITIES: 110 sites, 35 ft max RV length, 40 W&E, (30 amps), 70 no hkups, tenting, dump. RECREATION: lake swim, boating, ramp, dock, lake fishing, playground. Partial handicap access. Facilities fully operational Mar - Dec. Phone: (540)643-2500.

DUMFRIES—B-5

TRAVEL TRAILER VILLAGE AT PRINCE WILLIAM FOREST PARK—(Prince William) *From jct I-95 (exit 152 B Manassas) & Hwy 234: Go 2-1/2 mi NW on Hwy 234. Enter on L.*

◆◆◆◆FACILITIES: 75 sites, typical site width 20 ft, 29 full hkups, 43 W&E, 3 E, (20/30 amps), 54 pull-thrus, WiFi Instant Internet at site, family camping, tenting, dump, laundry, LP gas by weight/by meter, picnic tables.

◆◆RECREATION: swim pool, golf nearby, playground, activities, (wkends), hiking trails.

Pets welcome, breed restrict. Partial handicap access. Open all yr. 14 day max stay. Green Friendly. Rate in 2010 $29-32 for 2 persons. MC/VISA/Debit. Member ARVC, VCA.

TRAVEL TRAILER VILLAGE AT PRINCE WILLIAM FOREST PARK—Continued on next page

Virginia was the 10th state admitted to the Union.

DUMFRIES—Continued
TRAVEL TRAILER VILLAGE AT PRINCE WILLIAM FOREST PARK—Continued

Phone: (703)221-2474
Address: 16058 Dumfries Rd, Dumfries, VA 22025
Lat/Lon: 38.60416/-77.35085
Email: traveltrailervillage@verizon.net
Web: www.traveltrailervillage.com

SEE AD TRAVEL SECTION PAGE 762 AND AD DC TRAVEL SECTION PAGE 61

EASTERN SHORE

See listings at Cheriton, Chincoteague & Temperanceville

ELKTON—C-3

SHENANDOAH NATIONAL PARK (Big Meadows Campground)—(Page) *From jct US 33 & Skyline Dr: Go 16 mi N on Skyline Dr to milepost 51.* FACILITIES: 217 sites, 217 no hkups, 32 pull-thrus, tenting, dump, laundry, groceries. RECREATION: stream fishing. Partial handicap access. Open all yr. Facilities fully operational May 24 - Dec 31. Phone: (800)365-CAMP.

(E) SHENANDOAH NATIONAL PARK (Lewis Mountain Campground)—(Madison) *From jct US 33 & Skyline Dr: Go 8 mi NE on Skyline Dr to milepost 57.5.* FACILITIES: 31 sites, 30 ft max RV length, 31 no hkups, tenting, laundry, ltd groc. RECREATION: stream fishing. Open May15 - Oct 31. Phone: (540)999-3273.

SHENANDOAH NATIONAL PARK (Loft Mountain Camp)—(Green) *From jct US 33 & Skyline Dr: Go 10 mi SW on Skyline Dr to milepost 79.5, then 1-1/2 mi E on park road.* FACILITIES: 219 sites, 30 ft max RV length, 219 no hkups, tenting, dump, laundry, ltd groc. RECREATION: stream fishing. Partial handicap access. Open May 25 - Oct 31. Phone: (703)823-4675.

EMPORIA—E-4

(N) YOGI BEAR'S JELLYSTONE PARK CAMP RESORT EMPORIA—(Greensville) *From I-95 (exit 17), then 1 mi S on US 301. Or from jct US 58 & I-95: Go 6 mi N on I-95 (exit 17), then 1 mi S on US 301. Enter on R.*

◇◇◇◇FACILITIES: 110 sites, typical site width 30 ft, 74 full hkups, 28 W&E, (20/30/50 amps), 8 no hkups, some extd stay sites, 54 pull-thrus, cable TV, WiFi Instant Internet at site, family camping, tenting, RV's/park model rentals, cabins, RV storage, dump, laundry, ltd groc, RV supplies, LP gas by weight/by meter, ice, picnic tables, fire rings, grills, wood.

◇◇◇◇RECREATION: rec room/area, pavilion, coin games, swim pool, golf nearby, bsktball, playground, activities, horseshoes, sports field, v-ball. Rec open to public.

Pets welcome. Open all yr. Big rigs welcome. Escort to site. Clubs welcome. Rate in 2010 $35-39 for 2 persons. MC/VISA/DISC/Debit. Member ARVC, VCA. FCRV discount. FMCA discount.

Phone: (434)634-3115
Address: 2940 Sussex Dr, Emporia, VA 23847
Lat/Lon: 36.74913/-77.48878
Email: info@campingbear.com
Web: www.campingbear.com

SEE AD THIS PAGE

Birthplace of eight presidents (more than any other state)—George Washington, Thomas Jefferson, James Madison, James Monroe, William Henry Harrison, John Tyler, Zachary Taylor, Woodrow Wilson

---

FAIRFAX—B-5

(S) BURKE LAKE PARK (Fairfax County Park Authority)—(Fairfax) *From jct I-95 (Exit 160) & Hwy 123: Go 7-1/2 mi N on Hwy-123 (Ox Rd). Enter on R.*

FACILITIES: 100 sites, 25 ft max RV length, 100 no hkups, family camping, tenting, dump, non-guest dump $, ltd groc, ice, picnic tables, fire rings, grills, wood.

RECREATION: boating, ramp, dock, 100 rowboat rentals, lake fishing, fishing supplies, mini-golf, ($), golf nearby, playground, hiking trails, v-ball. Rec open to public.

Pets welcome. Open Mid Apr - Last Weekend of Oct. Maximum 14 day consecutive stay Memorial Day to Labor Day. MC/VISA.

Phone: (703)323-6600
Address: 7315 Ox Rd, Fairfax Station, VA 22035-1118
Lat/Lon: 38.75932/-77.30750
Web: www.fairfaxcounty.gov/parks/burkelake

SEE AD THIS PAGE

LAKE FAIRFAX PARK (Fairfax County Park)—(Fairfax) *From jct I-495 (Exit 47A) & Hwy 7: Go 6-1/2 mi W on Hwy 7, then 1/2 mi SW on Hwy 606. Enter on L.*

FACILITIES: 136 sites, 35 ft max RV length, 54 E, (20/30/50 amps), 82 no hkups, tenting, dump, ltd groc, picnic tables, fire rings, grills.

RECREATION: swim pool, boating, canoeing, 15 pedal boat rentals, lake fishing, playground, sports field, hiking trails. Rec open to public.

Pets welcome. Open all yr. Maximum 14 day consecutive stay Memorial Day to Labor Day. MC/VISA.

Phone: (703)471-5415
Address: 1400 Lake Fairfax Drive, Reston, VA 20190
Lat/Lon: 38.96998/-77.31664
Web: www.fairfaxcounty.gov/parks/lakefairfax

SEE AD THIS PAGE

FANCY GAP—E-1

(S) Fancy Gap/Blueridge Parkway KOA—(Carroll) *From I-77 (Exit 8 Fancy Gap) & Hwy 148: Go 100 yrds W on Hwy 148, then 1/4 mi S on Pottery Rd, then 3/4 mi E on Frog Spur Rd (Follow Signs). Enter on L.* ◇◇◇◇FACILITIES: 76 sites, typical site width 25 ft, 76 full hkups, (20/30/50 amps), 50 amps ($), 20 pull-thrus, family camping, tenting, dump, laundry, groceries. ◇◇◇◇RECREATION: swim pool, boating, dock, pond fishing, playground. Pets welcome. Partial handicap access. Open Mar 1 - Nov 15. Big rigs welcome. Rate in 2010 $35-39 for 2 persons. Phone: (276)728-7776. KOA discount.

(N) Utt's Campground—(Carroll) *From jct Blueridge Pkwy & US 52: Go 1/2 mi N on US 52. Enter on R.* ◇◇◇FACILITIES: 104 sites, typical site width 22 ft, 72 full hkups, 6 W&E, (20/30/50 amps), 26 no hkups, 40 pull-thrus, tenting, dump, laundry. ◇◇RECREATION: play equipment. Pets welcome, breed restrict, size restrict. Open May 1 - Nov 1. Big rigs welcome. Rate in 2010 $23 for 2 persons. Phone: (276)728-7203.

FERRUM—E-2

(SW) HORSESHOE POINT (COE - Philpott Lake)—(Franklin) *From town: Go 7 mi SE on Hwy-767, then 3 mi W on Hwy-605, then 4 mi W on Hwy-903.* FACILITIES: 49 sites, 15 W&E, 34 no hkups, tenting, dump. RECREATION: lake swim, boating, ramp, lake fishing, playground. Open May 1 - Sep 29. Phone: (276)629-2703.

FERRUM—Continued

SALTHOUSE BRANCH (COE - Philpott Lake)—(Henry) *From town: Go 7 mi SE on Hwy-767, then 2-1/2 mi W on Hwy-605, then 2 mi SW on Hwy-798 and 773.* FACILITIES: 93 sites, 26 W&E, (30 amps), 67 no hkups, 45 pull-thrus, tenting, dump. RECREATION: lake swim, boating, ramp, lake fishing, playground. Partial handicap access. Open all yr. Phone: (540)365-7005.

FREDERICKSBURG—C-4

(S) KOA-FREDERICKSBURG/ WASHINGTON DC—(Spotsylvania) *Southbound: From jct I-95 (Spotsylvania exit 126) & US 1: Go 4 mi S on US 1, then 2-1/2 mi E on Hwy 607. Northbound: From jct I-95 (Thornburg exit 118) & US 1: Go 4 mi N on US 1, then 2-1/2 mi E on Hwy 607. Enter on R.*

◇◇◇◇FACILITIES: 117 sites, typical site width 30 ft, 52 full hkups, 34 W&E, (20/30/50 amps), 31 no hkups, 49 pull-thrus, cable TV, WiFi Instant Internet at site, family camping, tenting, cabins, RV storage, dump, non-guest dump $, laundry, groceries, RV supplies, LP gas by weight/by meter, ice, picnic tables, wood.

◇◇◇◇RECREATION: rec hall, rec room/area, pavilion, coin games, swim pool, boating, 6 pedal boat rentals, pond fishing, fishing supplies, golf nearby, bike rental 8 bike rentals, playground, activities, (wkends), horseshoes, sports field, hiking trails, v-ball.

Pets welcome, breed restrict. Partial handicap access. Open all yr. Big rigs welcome. Escort to site. Clubs welcome. Rate in 2010 $36-51 for 2 persons. MC/VISA/DISC/Debit. Member ARVC, VCA. KOA discount.

Phone: (800)562-1889
Address: 7400 Brookside Lane, Fredericksburg, VA 22408
Lat/Lon: 38.16882/-77.47495
Email: koainfo@fredericksburgkoa.com
Web: www.fredericksburgkoa.com

SEE AD NEXT PAGE AND AD DC TRAVEL SECTION PAGE 61

Jamestown was the first English settlement in the U.S. It was also the first capital of Virginia.

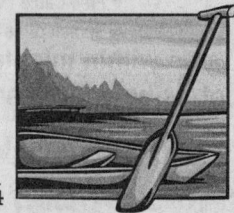

FRONT ROYAL—B-4

(S) FRONT ROYAL RV CAMPGROUND—(Warren) *From jct I-66 (exit 6) & US 340/522: Go 6 mi S on US 340, then 1 mi SE on KOA Dr. Enter on L.*

◆◆FACILITIES: 146 sites, typical site width 30 ft, 42 full hkups, 64 W&E, (20/30 amps), 40 no hkups, 28 pull-thrus, WiFi Instant Internet at site, WiFi Internet central location, family camping, tenting, cabins, dump, non-guest dump $, laundry, groceries, RV supplies, LP gas by weight/by meter, ice, picnic tables, patios, fire rings, wood.

◆◆◆RECREATION: rec hall, swim pool, hot tub, pond fishing, mini-golf, ($), bsktball, playground, horseshoes.

Pets welcome, quantity restrict. Open Apr 1 - Nov 1. Clubs welcome. Rate in 2010 $32-68 for 2 persons. MC/VISA. Member ARVC, VCA.

Phone: (540)635-2741
Address: 585 KOA Drive, Front Royal, VA 22630
Lat/Lon: 38.89751/-78.23119
Email: frrvcampground@aol.com
Web: www.frontroyalrvcampground.com

SEE AD THIS PAGE

(W) North Fork Resort—(Warren) *From jct I-66 & Hwy 340/522: Go 1 mi S on Hwy 55 W, then 2 mi W on Home Stead Rd. Enter at end.* ◆◆◆FACILITIES: 450 sites, typical site width 30 ft, 415 full hkups, 35 W&E, (20/30/50 amps), 59 pull-thrus, WiFi Instant Internet at site ($), WiFi Internet central location, family camping, tenting, dump, laundry, groceries, RV supplies, ice, picnic tables, patios, fire rings, wood. ◆◆◆◆RECREATION: rec hall, pavilion, 2 swim pools, wading pool, river fishing, mini-golf, bsktball, playground, shuffleboard court 4 shuffleboard courts, tennis, horseshoes, hiking trails, v-ball. Pets welcome, breed restrict. Partial handicap access. Open all yr. Big rigs welcome. CCUSA 50% Discount. CCUSA reservations Recommended, CCUSA max stay 14 days, CCUSA disc. not avail F,Sa, CCUSA disc. not avail holidays. 2 weeks between stays. No commercial trucks or converted school buses. WiFi surcharge. Limited facilities during winter.

Phone: (540)636-2295
Address: 301 North Fork Rd, Front Royal, VA 22630
Lat/Lon: 38.95658/-78.23181
Web: www.nfra.com

(W) Skyline Ranch Resort—(Warren) *From jct I-66 & Hwy 340: Go 5 mi S on Hwy 340, then 4-1/2 mi W on Rivermont Dr (Hwy 619), then 3/4 mi NW on Mountain Rd. Enter on R.* ◆◆◆FACILITIES: 92 sites, typical site width 35 ft, 78 full hkups, (20/30/50 amps), 14 no hkups, 2 pull-thrus, WiFi Internet central location ($), family camping, tenting, RV storage, dump, laundry, ltd groc, RV supplies, LP gas by meter, ice, picnic ta-

Shop with Dealers in Woodall's

FRONT ROYAL—Continued
Skyline Ranch Resort—Continued

bles, fire rings, wood. ◆◆◆◆RECREATION: rec hall, pavilion, swim pool, wading pool, hot tub, pond fishing, fishing supplies, mini-golf, ($), bsktball, playground, shuffleboard court 2 shuffleboard courts, activities horseshoes, v-ball. Pets welcome. Open all yr. Big rigs welcome. CCUSA 50% Discount. CCUSA reservations Accepted, CCUSA max stay 21 days, CCUSA disc. not avail F,Sa. Holiday weekends. July 4th (4 days around the 4th depending on when the 4th falls). Max 2 pets. $5 addl surcharge for more than 1 A/C. $2 charge for mini-golf. Wi-Fi surcharge $3. Catch & release fishing.

Phone: (540)635-4169
Address: 751 Mountain Rd, Front Royal, VA 22630
Email: rez@skylineranchresort.com
Web: www.skylineranchresort.com

GLOUCESTER—D-5

THOUSAND TRAILS-CHESAPEAKE BAY (CAMP RESORT)—(Gloucester) *From jct US 17 & Hwy 198: Go 5-1/2 mi E on Hwy 198, then 1/2 mi N on Dutton Rd. Enter on L.*

FACILITIES: 373 sites, typical site width 20 ft, 355 full hkups, 18 W&E, (30/50 amps), some extd stay sites, WiFi Internet central location, family camping, tenting, cabins, RV storage, dump, non-guest dump $, laundry, groceries, RV supplies, LP gas by weight/by meter, ice, picnic tables, fire rings, grills, wood, controlled access.

RECREATION: rec hall, rec room/area, pavilion, coin games, 2 swim pools, hot tub, boating, canoeing, kayaking, ramp, dock, 2 canoe/3 pedal boat rentals, saltwater/river/pond fishing, fishing supplies, mini-golf, golf nearby, bsktball, playground, shuffleboard court 2 shuffleboard courts, activities (wkends), tennis, horseshoes, sports field, hiking trails, v-ball.

Pets welcome, quantity restrict. Partial handicap access. Open all yr. Weekends only Dec - late Mar. Big rigs welcome. Clubs welcome. Rate in 2010 $32 for 2 persons. MC/VISA/DISC/AMEX.

Phone: (804)693-6924
Address: 12014 Trails Lane, Gloucester, VA 23061
Email: tripexpert@1000trails.com
Web: www.1000trails.com

SEE AD ABINGDON PAGE 769

Famous Virginians: Willa Cather, author (Back Creek Valley); Ella Fitzgerald, jazz singer (Newport News); Nat Turner, leader of slave uprising (Southhampton County)

GLOUCESTER POINT—D-5

(NE) GLOUCESTER POINT FAMILY CAMPGROUND—(Gloucester) *From jct Coleman Bridge & US 17: Go 2 mi N on US 17, then 1 mi E on Guinea Rd (Rt 216), then 1-1/2 mi N on Rt 641, then 1/4 mi E on Zack Rd, then 1/4 mi N on Campground Rd. Enter on R.*

◆◆◆◆FACILITIES: 230 sites, typical site width 30 ft, 165 full hkups, 65 W&E, (20/30/50 amps), some extd stay sites, 14 pull-thrus, WiFi Instant Internet at site, WiFi Internet central location, family camping, tenting, RV's/park model rentals, cabins, dump, laundry, groceries, RV supplies, LP gas by weight/by meter, marine gas, ice, picnic tables, fire rings, wood, controlled access.

◆◆◆◆RECREATION: rec room/area, pavilion, coin games, 2 swim pools, wading pool, boating, canoeing, kayaking, ramp, dock, 4 kayak rentals, saltwater fishing, fishing supplies, fishing guides, golf nearby, bsktball, 5 bike rentals, playground, activities, (wkends), horseshoes, v-ball.

Pets welcome. Partial handicap access. Open all yr. Facilities fully operational Apr 1 - Oct 30. Clubs welcome. Rate in 2010 $35-48 for 2 persons. MC/VISA/DISC. Member ARVC, VCA. CCUSA 50% Discount. CCUSA reservations Recommended, CCUSA max stay 3 days. Discount not offered on Fri & Sat Apr thru Oct or any day Memorial Day thru Labor Day & on premium dates. Call for details. Electric heater prohibited.

Phone: (800)332-4316
Address: 3149 Campground Rd, Hayes, VA 23072
Lat/Lon: 37.29804/-76.47373
Email: camping@gpfcampground.com
Web: www.gpfcampground.com

SEE AD THIS PAGE

GREEN BAY—D-4

TWIN LAKES STATE PARK—(Prime Edward) *W'bnd: From jct US 360 & Rte 621: Go N on Rte 621. E'bnd: Go from Hwy 360 to 613.* FACILITIES: 34 sites, 30 ft max RV length, 30 W&E, (20/30 amps), 4 no hkups, tenting, dump. RECREATION: lake swim, boating, electric motors only, canoeing, ramp, lake fishing, playground. Partial handicap access. Open all yr. Phone: (434) 392-3435.

GREENVILLE—C-3

(SE) Stoney Creek Resort Campground—(Augusta) *From I-81 (exit 217) & Rte 654 (White Hill Rd): Go 4 mi S on White Hill Rd, then 1/4 mi S on US 340, then 1-1/4 mi S on Indian Ridge Rd, then 4 mi SW on Cold Springs Rd. Enter on L.* ◆◆◆FACILITIES: 179 sites, 69 full hkups, 110 W&E, (30/50 amps), 40 pull-thrus, family camping, tenting, dump, laundry, ltd groc.

Stoney Creek Resort Campground—Continued on next page

GREENVILLE—Continued
Stoney Creek Resort Campground—Continued

◇◇◇◇RECREATION: swim pool, lake swim, boating, canoeing, dock, lake fishing, play equipment. Pets welcome. Partial handicap access. Open Apr 1 - Oct 31. Big rigs welcome. Green Friendly. Rate in 2010 $30-36 for 2 persons. Phone: (540)337-1510.

GREENWOOD—C-3

(SW) Misty Mountain Camp Resort—(Albermarle) *From jct I-64 (exit 107) & US 250: Go 1 mi W on US 250. Enter on L.* ◇◇◇◇FACILITIES: 105 sites, typical site width 20 ft, 51 full hkups, 49 W&E, (30/50 amps), 5 no hkups, 30 pull-thrus, family camping, tenting, dump, laundry, ltd groc. ◇◇◇◇RECREATION: swim pool, pond/stream fishing, playground. Pets welcome, breed restrict. Open all yr. Big rigs welcome. Rate in 2010 $30-40 for 2 persons. Member ARVC, VCA. Phone: (888)647-8900.

GREY'S POINT—D-5

(W) GREY'S POINT CAMP—(Middlesex) *From jct Hwy 33 & Hwy 3: Go 3 1/4 mi NE on Hwy 3. Enter on L.*

CHESAPEAKE BAY IN VIRGINIA!
Breathtaking views of the Rappahannock River and Chesapeake Bay from this waterfront RV resort. Complete recreational facility featuring New water park, pools, sandy beaches, marina & boat ramp. Pets welcome. Call (804)758-2485

◇◇◇◇◇FACILITIES: 700 sites, typical site width 50 ft, 700 full hkups, (30/50 amps), many extd stay sites, 36 pull-thrus, cable TV, WiFi Instant Internet at site, phone/cable on-site Internet (needs activ), WiFi Internet central location, family camping, RV storage, dump, non-guest dump $, laundry, full svc store, RV supplies, LP gas by weight/by meter, marine gas, ice, picnic tables, patios, fire rings, grills, wood, controlled access.

◇◇◇◇◇RECREATION: rec room/area, equipped pavilion, coin games, 2 swim pools, wading pool, spray ground, saltwater/river swim, boating, canoeing, kayaking, ramp, dock, 3 canoe/6 kayak/3 pedal boat rentals, saltwater/pond fishing, fishing supplies, golf nearby, bsktball, 8 bike rentals, playground, activities, tennis, horseshoes, sports field, hiking trails, v-ball.

Pets welcome. No tents. Open Apr 1 - Nov. 15. Big rigs welcome. Escort to site. Clubs welcome. Rate in 2010 $39.95-62.95 for 4 persons. MC/VISA. Member ARVC, VCA.

Phone: (804)758-2485
Address: 3601 Greys Point Rd, Topping, VA 23169
Lat/Lon: 37.61005/-76.43710
Email: greyspointcamp@oasisonline.com
Web: www.greyspointcamp.com

SEE AD URBANNA PAGES 782-783 AND AD TRAVEL SECTION PAGE 763 AND AD DC TRAVEL SECTION PAGE 62

RV ADVENTURES—*From jct Hwy 33 & Hwy 3: Go 3-3/4 mi NE on Hwy 3. Enter on L.* SALES: park models, pre-owned unit sales. SERVICES: Open Apr 1 - Nov 15.

Address: 3601 Grey's Point Rd, Topping, VA 23169
Lat/Lon: 37.61005/-76.43710
Web: www.greyspointcamp.com/rvadventures.html

SEE AD TRAVEL SECTION PAGE 763 AND AD DC TRAVEL SECTION PAGE 62

GWYNN—D-6

(E) Gwynn's Island RV Resort (Morgan RV Resorts)—(Mathews) *From jct Hwy 198 & Hwy 223: Go 1-1/2 mi NE on Hwy 223, then 2 mi NE on Hwy 633, then 1 mi SE on Old Ferry Rd, then 1/2 mi S on Buckschase Rd. Enter on L.* ◇◇FACILITIES: 120 sites, 120

GWYNN—Continued
Gwynn's Island RV Resort (Morgan RV Resorts)—Continued

W&E, (30/50 amps), 25 pull-thrus, family camping, tenting, dump, ltd groc. ◇◇◇RECREATION: saltwater swim, boating, canoeing, saltwater fishing, playground. Pets welcome, breed restrict, size restrict, quantity restrict. Partial handicap access. Open Apr 1 - Oct 31. Rate in 2010 $28-52 for 2 persons. Member ARVC, VCA. Phone: (804)725-5700.

HAMPTON—D-5

MILITARY PARK (The Colonies Travel Park)—(Independent City) *From I-64 (exit 268) south of town: Go E on Mallory St, then S on Mercury Blvd to Fort Monroe. On base.* FACILITIES: 13 sites, typical site width 12 ft, 35 ft max RV length, 13 full hkups, dump, laundry, ltd groc. RECREATION: 2 swim pools, saltwater swim, boating, canoeing, ramp, dock, saltwater fishing, play equipment. No tents. Open all yr. Phone: (757)788-2384.

HARRISONBURG—C-3

HARRISONBURG / SHENANDOAH VALLEY KOA—*From jct I-81 (exit 247) & US 33: Go 10 mi N on I-81 (Exit 257), then 100 yds N on US 11, then 3 mi E on SR 608 (Mauzy Athlone Rd). Enter at end of SR 608.*

SEE PRIMARY LISTING AT NEW MARKET AND AD NEW MARKET PAGE 777

HAYMARKET—B-4

(W) GREENVILLE FARM FAMILY CAMPGROUND—(Prince William) *From jct I-66 (exit 40) & US 15: Go 4 mi N on US 15, then 200 yards E on Hwy 234S, then 1 mi E on Hwy 601. Enter on L.*

◇◇◇FACILITIES: 150 sites, typical site width 30 ft, 38 ft max RV length, 30 full hkups, 95 W&E, (20/30/50 amps), 50 amps ($), 25 no hkups, 60 pull-thrus, family camping, tenting, dump, laundry, ltd groc, RV supplies, LP gas by weight/by meter, ice, picnic tables, wood.

◇◇◇RECREATION: rec room/area, pavilion, swim pool, wading pool, pond fishing, bsktball, playground. Rec open to public.

Pets welcome. Open all yr. Facilities fully operational Apr - Oct. No restrooms in the winter. Clubs welcome. Rate in 2010 $31-38 for 2 persons. MC/VISA/Debit. Member ARVC, VCA.

Phone: (703)754-7944
Address: 14004 Shelter Lane, Haymarket, VA 20169
Lat/Lon: 38.87600/-77.61085

SEE AD THIS PAGE AND AD DC TRAVEL SECTION PAGE 58

HAYSI—A-2

BREAKS INTERSTATE PARK—(Dickenson) *From town: Go 8 mi N on Hwy-80, then 2 mi NW on park road.* FACILITIES: 122 sites, 35 ft max RV length, 122 full hkups, (50 amps), 20 pull-thrus, tenting, dump. RECREATION: swim pool, boating, electric motors only, canoeing, dock, lake fishing, playground. Open Apr 1 - Oct 31. Phone: (276)865-4413.

LOWER TWIN CAMPGROUND (COE-John W Flannagan Reservoir)—(Dickenson) *From town: Go 3 mi SW on Hwy-63, then 1/2 mi S on Hwy-614, then 2 mi NW on Hwy-739, then W on Hwy-611. Enter on L.* FACILITIES: 32 sites, 15 E, (20/30 amps), 17 no hkups, tenting, dump. RECREATION: lake swim, boating, canoeing, ramp, dock, lake fishing, playground. Partial handicap access. Open May 11 - Early Sep. Phone: (270)835-9544.

HILLSVILLE—E-1

(N) Lake Ridge RV Resort—(Carroll) *From jct I-77 (exit 14) & US 221: Go 4-1/4 mi E on US 221, then 4-3/4 mi N on Hwy 100, then 3/4 mi NE on Deer Ridge Rd, then 1/4 mi E on Double Cabin Rd. Enter on L.* ◇◇◇◇FACILITIES: 134 sites, typical site width 30 ft, 85 full hkups, 49 W&E, (20/30/50 amps), 27 pull-thrus, family camping, tenting, dump, laundry, ltd groc. ◇◇◇◇◇RECREATION: 2 swim pools, boating, canoeing, lake fishing, playground. Pets welcome. Partial handicap access. Open Mar 15 - Nov 1. Big rigs welcome. Rate in 2010 $29-34 for 4 persons. Member ARVC, VCA. Phone: (276)766-3703.

HUDDLESTON—D-3

SMITH MOUNTAIN LAKE STATE PARK—(Bedford) *From jct Hwy 43 & Hwy 626: Go 14 mi SW on Hwy 626.* FACILITIES: 50 sites, 24 W&E, (20/30 amps), 26 no hkups, 5 pull-thrus, tenting, dump. RECREATION: lake/saltwater swim, boating, canoeing, ramp, saltwater/lake fishing. Open all yr. Phone: (540) 297-6066.

JAMESTOWN—D-5

(N) AMERICAN HERITAGE RV PARK—(James City) *From I-64 (exit 231 A -Norge): Go 1/4 mi S on Hwy 607, then 1/4 mi E on Maxton Lane. Enter on L.*

◇◇◇◇◇FACILITIES: 95 sites, typical site width 28 ft, 95 full hkups, (20/30/50 amps), 50 amps ($), 75 pull-thrus, cable TV, WiFi Instant Internet at site ($), WiFi Internet central location, family camping, tenting, RV's/park model rentals, RV storage, laundry, groceries, RV supplies, ice, picnic tables, patios, fire rings, wood.

◇◇◇◇RECREATION: rec hall, rec room/area, coin games, swim pool, wading pool, mini-golf, golf nearby, bsktball, playground, horseshoes, sports field, hiking trails, v-ball, local tours.

Partial handicap access. Age restrict may apply. Open all yr. Big rigs welcome. Escort to site. Clubs welcome. Rate in 2010 $44.95 for 4 persons. MC/VISA/DISC/AMEX/Debit. ATM. Member ARVC, VCA. FCRV discount.

Phone: (888)530-CAMP
Address: 146 Maxton Lane, Williamsburg, VA 23188
Lat/Lon: 37.37721/-76.76867
Email: americanheritagerv@verizon.net
Web: www.americanheritagervpark.com

SEE PRIMARY LISTING AT WILLIAMSBURG AND AD WILLIAMSBURG PAGE 785

KEELING—E-3

(NE) Paradise Hollow Lake & Campground—(Pittsylvania) *From jct US 29 & Hwy 726: Go 2-1/2 mi E on Hwy 726, then 1/2 mi N on Hwy 716. Enter on L.* ◇◇◇FACILITIES: 85 sites, typical site width 25 ft, 50 full hkups, 15 W&E, (20/30/50 amps), 20 no hkups, 10 pull-thrus, family camping, tenting, laundry, groceries. ◇◇◇◇RECREATION: swim pool, boating, canoeing, ramp, dock, lake fishing, playground. Pets welcome. Partial handicap access. Open all yr. Big rigs welcome. Rate in 2010 $23.50-30.50 Member ARVC, VCA. Phone: (434)836-2620.

KING & QUEEN COURTHOUSE—D-5

(N) RAINBOW ACRES CAMPGROUND—(King and Queen) *From jct Hwy 33 & Hwy 14: Go 13-3/4 mi NW on Hwy 14, then 1 mi SW on Fraizer Ferry Rd. (631). Enter on L.*

◇◇◇FACILITIES: 150 sites, typical site width 40 ft, 150 full hkups, (20/30/50 amps), many extd stay sites, 16 pull-thrus, WiFi Internet central location, family camping, tenting, cabins, RV storage, dump, non-guest dump $, laundry, groceries, RV supplies, LP gas by weight/by meter, marine gas, ice, picnic tables, fire rings, wood.

◇◇◇◇RECREATION: rec hall, pavilion, coin games, river swim, boating, canoeing, kayaking, ramp, dock, river fishing, fishing supplies, bsktball, play equipment, 2 shuffleboard courts, activities (wkends), horseshoes, v-ball.

Pets welcome, breed restrict, quantity restrict. Open all yr. Big rigs welcome. Escort to site. Clubs welcome. Rate in 2010 $30-35 for 2 persons. MC/VISA/DISC. Member ARVC, VCA. CCUSA 50% Discount. CCUSA reservations Recommended, CCUSA max stay 3 days, CCUSA disc. not avail

RAINBOW ACRES CAMPGROUND—Continued on next page

KING & QUEEN COURTHOUSE—Continued
RAINBOW ACRES CAMPGROUND—Continued

holidays. Discount not available Fri, Sat nights Apr thru Oct. Available anytime Nov thru Mar. Non-guest dump surcharge $6.

Text 107897 to (440)725-8687 to see our Visual Tour.

Phone: (804)785-9441
Address: 514 James Rd, King & Queen Courthouse, VA 23085
Lat/Lon: 37.66241/-76.88860
Email: rose@rainbowacrescampground.com
Web: www.rainbowacrescampground.com

SEE AD PAGE 775

LEXINGTON—C-3

(NE) Lee Hi Campground—(Rockbridge) *From Jct I-81 (exit 195) & US 11: Go 3/4 mi S on US 11. (Register at fuel desk). Enter on L.* ◊◊◊FACILITIES: 58 sites, 27 full hkups, 19 W&E, (20/30/50 amps), 12 no hkups, 12 pull-thrus, tenting, dump, laundry, groceries. ◊RECREATION: play equipment. Pets welcome. Partial handicap access. Open all yr. Big rigs welcome. Rate in 2010 $35 for 2 persons. Phone: (540)463-3478.

LORTON—B-4

(S) POHICK BAY REGIONAL PARK—(Fairfax) *From jct I-95 & Rt 1N (Lorton Rd): Go 1-1/2 mi E on Lorton Rd, then 1 mi S on Lorton Market Street, cross Rt 1, road changes to Gunston Rd. Go 3 mi S on Gunston Rd, then left on Pohick Bay Dr. Enter on L.* FACILITIES: 150 sites, 10 full hkups, 90 E, (30/50 amps), 50 no hkups, family camping, tenting, dump, laundry, ltd groc. RECREATION: swim pool, boating, canoeing, ramp. Pets welcome. Partial handicap access. Open all yr. Phone: (703)339-6104.

LOUISA—C-4

(W) Small Country Campground—(Louisa) *From jct I-64 (exit 143) & Hwy 208: Go 2 mi NE on Hwy 208, then 1/4 mi W on Hwy 640, then 4-1/2 mi N on Hwy 649 (Byrd Mill Rd). Enter on R.* ◊◊◊FACILITIES: 215 sites, typical site width 25 ft, 94 full hkups, 46 W&E, (30/50 amps), 75 no hkups, 25 pull-thrus, phone Internet central location, family camping, tenting, dump, laundry, ltd groc, RV supplies, picnic tables, fire rings, grills, wood. ◊◊◊◊RECREATION: rec hall, swim pool, lake swim, boating, canoeing, kayaking, ramp, dock, lake fishing, fishing supplies, bsktball, playground, activities, horseshoes. Pets welcome. Partial handicap access. Open all yr. Big rigs welcome. Rate in 2010 $30-50 for 2 persons. MC/VISA/DISC. CCUSA 50% Discount. CCUSA reservations Recommended, CCUSA max stay Unlimited, CCUSA disc. not avail holidays. Non guest dump surcharge $10.

Phone: (540)967-2431
Address: 4400 Byrd Mill Rd, Louisa, VA 23093
Lat/Lon: 38.02031/-78.09385
Email: camp@smallcountry.com
Web: smallcountry.com

Reserve Online at Woodalls.com

Stay with a Campground in Woodall's

LURAY—B-3

(N) LURAY RV RESORT -THE COUNTRY WAYE—(Page) *From jct US 211 & US 340: Go 2 mi N on US 340, then 1/4 mi E on Hwy 658 (Kimball Rd). Enter on L.*

WELCOME

◊◊◊◊FACILITIES: 82 sites, typical site width 40 ft, 82 full hkups, (30/50 amps), 34 pull-thrus, WiFi Instant Internet at site, family camping, tenting, laundry, ice, picnic tables, patios, fire rings, wood.

◊◊◊RECREATION: rec room/area, equipped pavilion, swim pool, playground, sports field, v-ball.

Pets welcome. Open Mar 15 - Nov 15. Big rigs welcome. Escort to site. Clubs welcome. Rate in 2010 $46 for 2 persons. MC/VISA/DISC/Debit. Member ARVC, VCA.

Phone: (540)743-7222
Address: 3402 Kimball Rd, Luray, VA 22835
Lat/Lon: 38.70069/-78.43811
Email: campers2@countrywaye.com
Web: www.lurayresort.com

SEE AD THIS PAGE

(E) Yogi Bear's Jellystone Park Camp-Resort—(Page) *From jct US 340 & US 211: Go 4 mi E on US 211. Enter on R.* ◊◊◊◊FACILITIES: 186 sites, typical site width 50 ft, 116 full hkups, 59 W&E, (20/30/50 amps), 11 no hkups, 92 pull-thrus, family camping, tenting, dump, laundry, full svc store. ◊◊◊◊◊RECREATION: 2 swim pools, boating, pond fishing, playground. Pets welcome. Partial handicap access. Open Apr 1 - Nov 15. Big rigs welcome. Rate in 2010 $37-64 for 4 persons. Member ARVC, VCA. Phone: (800)420-6679.

MADISON—C-4

(S) MADISON/SHENANDOAH HILLS KOA—(Madison) *From jct US 29 & Hwy 231: Go 1-1/2 mi S on US 29. Enter on R.*

WELCOME

◊◊◊◊FACILITIES: 64 sites, typical site width 30 ft, 56 full hkups, 8 W&E, (20/30/50 amps), 50 amps ($), some extd stay sites, 16 pull-thrus, cable TV, ($), WiFi Instant Internet at site, family camping, tenting, cabins, RV storage, shower$, dump, non-guest dump $, laundry, groceries, RV supplies, LP gas by weight/by meter, ice, picnic tables, fire rings, grills, wood, controlled access.

◊◊◊◊RECREATION: rec hall, rec room/area, pavilion, coin games, swim pool, pond fishing, golf nearby, bsktball, playground, activities, (wkends), tennis, horseshoes, sports field, v-ball.

Pets welcome, breed restrict. Partial handicap access. Open March - Dec. Big rigs welcome. Clubs welcome. Green Friendly. Rate in 2010 $34-48 for 2 persons. MC/VISA. Member ARVC, VCA. KOA discount. FMCA discount.

Phone: (540)948-4186
Address: 110 Campground Ln, Madison, VA 22727
Lat/Lon: 38.35258/-78.28036
Email: ateam143@msn.com
Web: www.shenandoahhills.com

SEE AD THIS PAGE

MARION—B-3

(N) HUNGRY MOTHER STATE PARK—(Smyth) *From town: Go 3 mi N on Hwy-16.* FACILITIES: 94 sites, 30 ft max RV length, 83 W&E, (20/30 amps), 11 no hkups, tenting, dump, ltd groc. RECREATION: lake swim, boating, no motors, lake fishing, playground. Partial handicap access. Open Mar 1 - Dec 1. Phone: (276)781-7400.

The College of William and Mary in Williamsburg is the second oldest in the United States, it was founded in 1693.

MEADOWS OF DAN—E-2

(S) MEADOWS OF DAN CAMPGROUND—(Patrick) *From jct Blue Ridge Pkwy (mp 177) & US 58 Bus: Go 1/4 mi W on US 58 Bus. Enter on L.*

WELCOME

◊◊◊◊FACILITIES: 38 sites, typical site width 30 ft, 26 full hkups, 11 E, (30/50 amps), 1 no hkups, 8 pull-thrus, WiFi Internet central location, family camping, tenting, cabins, dump, laundry, picnic tables, fire rings, grills, wood.

◊◊RECREATION: pond fishing, golf nearby, bsktball, play equipment, horseshoes, sports field, v-ball.

Pets welcome. Open all yr. Big rigs welcome. Clubs welcome. Rate in 2010 $28-30 for 2 persons. MC/VISA/DISC/AMEX/Debit. Member ARVC, VCA.

Phone: (276)952-2292
Address: 2182 JEB Stuart Highway, Meadows of Dan, VA 24120
Lat/Lon: 36.73449/-80.41609
Web: www.meadowsofdancampground.com

SEE AD THIS PAGE

MILFORD—C-4

(E) R & D FAMILY CAMPGROUND—(Caroline) *From jct I-95 (exit 98) & Rte 30 E (Kings Dominion): Go 6 mi E on Rte 30, then 13 mi N on US 301, then 4 mi E on Sparta Rd. Enter on L.*

WELCOME

◊◊◊◊FACILITIES: 35 sites, 35 full hkups, (20/30/50 amps), 50 amps ($), 20 pull-thrus, WiFi Internet central location, family camping, tenting, RV's/park model rentals, cabins, dump, non-guest dump $, laundry, ltd groc, RV supplies, LP gas by meter, ice, picnic tables, fire rings, wood.

CAMPCLUB USA

◊◊◊◊RECREATION: rec room/area, equipped pavilion, swim pool, golf nearby, bsktball, playground, horseshoes, sports field, hiking trails, v-ball.

Pets welcome, breed restrict, quantity restrict. Open all yr. Big rigs welcome. Clubs welcome. Rate in 2010 $33 for 2 persons. FCRV discount. FMCA discount. CCUSA 50% Discount. CCUSA reservations Not Accepted, CCUSA max stay 5 days, CCUSA disc. not avail F,Sa, CCUSA disc. not avail holidays. Discount not available special events. Call for availability. WiFi hotspot.

Phone: (804)633-9515
Address: 22085 Sparta Rd, Milford, VA 22514
Lat/Lon: 37.98732/-77.26550
Email: rdcampground@aol.com
Web: www.rdfamilycampground.homestead.com

SEE AD RICHMOND PAGE 779 AND AD TRAVEL SECTION PAGE 762

MINERAL—C-4

(N) Christopher Run Campground—(Jackson) *From jct Hwy-208 & US-522: Go 5 mi N on Hwy-208 & US-522, then 1-1/2 mi N on US-522. Enter on R.* ◊◊◊FACILITIES: 200 sites, typical site width 30 ft, 109 full hkups, 89 W&E, (20/30/50 amps), 2 no hkups, 4 pull-thrus, family camping, tenting, dump, laundry, full

Christopher Run Campground—Continued on next page

Virginia: Named in honor of Queen Elizabeth I, The Virgin Queen

MINERAL—Continued
Christopher Run Campground—Continued

svc store. ◆◆◆◆RECREATION: lake swim, boating, canoeing, ramp, dock, lake fishing, playground. Pets welcome, breed restrict. Open Apr 1 - Oct 31. Rate in 2010 $30-35 for 4 persons. Member ARVC, VCA. Phone: (540)894-4744.

MONROE—D-3

(NE) Wildwood Campground—(Amherst) *From jct Blue Ridge Parkway (MP 61-1/2) & Hwy 130: Go 1 mi E on Hwy 130. Enter on L.* ◆◆◆FACILITIES: 80 sites, typical site width 30 ft, 36 full hkups, 36 W&E, (20/30/50 amps), 8 no hkups, 45 pull-thrus, family camping, tenting, dump, laundry, ltd groc. ◆◆◆◆RECREATION: swim pool, pond fishing, playground. Pets welcome. Open all yr. Big rigs welcome. Rate in 2010 $32-34 for 2 persons. Member ARVC, VCA. Phone: (434)299-5228.

MONTEBELLO—C-3

(N) Montebello Camping & Fishing Resort—(Nelson) *From jct Blue Ridge Pky (milepost 27) & Hwy-56: Go 3-1/2 mi E on Hwy-56. Enter on R.* ◆◆◆FACILITIES: 74 sites, typical site width 35 ft, 40 full hkups, 17 W&E, (30/50 amps), 17 no hkups, 26 pull-thrus, family camping, tenting, dump, laundry, groceries. ◆◆◆RECREATION: lake swim, boating, canoeing, dock, lake/pond fishing, play equipment. Pets welcome. Open Apr 1 - Dec 1. Rate in 2010 $30-39 for 2 persons. Member ARVC, VCA. Phone: (540)377-2650.

MONTROSS—C-5

(N) WESTMORELAND STATE PARK—(Westmoreland) *N of town at jct Hwy 3 & Hwy 204.* FACILITIES: 116 sites, 42 W&E, (20/30 amps), 74 no hkups, tenting, laundry. RECREATION: swim pool, boating, ramp, saltwater/river/pond fishing, playground. Partial handicap access. Open all yr. Facilities fully operational May - Sep. Phone: (804)493-8821.

NATURAL BRIDGE—D-2

JEFFERSON NATIONAL FOREST (Cave Mountain Lake Rec. Area)—(Rockbride) *From jct Hwy-130 & Hwy-759: Go 3 mi SW on Hwy-759, then 1-1/2 mi W on Hwy-781, then 1 mi SW on FR-780.* FACILITIES: 42 sites, 42 no hkups, tenting, dump. RECREATION: lake swim. Partial handicap access. Open May 1 - Early Nov. Phone: (540)291-2189.

(W) KOA-Natural Bridge—(Rockbridge) *From jct I-81 (S'bound exit 180 B). Entrance to KOA at exit 180 B. (N' bound exit 180), then 1/4 mi NW on US 11. Enter on L.* ◆◆◆◆FACILITIES: 85 sites, typical site width 30 ft, 31 full hkups, 49 W&E, (20/30/50 amps), 50 amps ($), 5 no hkups, 63 pull-thrus, family camping, tenting, dump, laundry, groceries. ◆◆◆◆RECREATION: swim pool, playground. Pets welcome. Open Mar 1 - Nov 30. Big rigs welcome. Rate in 2010 $32.18-46.91 for 2 persons. Member ARVC, VCA. Phone: (540)291-2770. KOA discount.

(SE) YOGI BEAR'S JELLYSTONE CAMP RESORT AT NATURAL BRIDGE—(Rockbridge) *(Rockbridge) N'bnd from I-81 (Exit 175) & US 11 N: Go 1.25 mi N on US 11 or S'bnd I-81 (Exit 180A) Go 4 mi S on US 11, then 3 mi E on Hwy 130, R on Hwy 759 3/4 mi, then L on James River Rd. enter on L. Enter on L.*

◆◆◆◆FACILITIES: 215 sites, typical site width 30 ft, 155 full hkups, 57 W&E, (20/30/50 amps), 3 no hkups, 42 pull-thrus, cable TV, ($), WiFi Instant Internet at site, WiFi Internet central location, family camping, tenting, cabins, RV storage, dump, laundry, groceries, RV supplies, LP gas by weight/by meter, ice, picnic tables, fire rings, wood.

Check out our web site www.woodalls.com

NATURAL BRIDGE—Continued
YOGI BEAR'S JELLYSTONE CAMP RESORT AT NATURAL BRIDGE—Continued

◆◆◆◆◆RECREATION: rec hall, rec room/area, equipped pavilion, coin games, swim pool, spray ground, lake swim, boating, canoeing, kayaking, 6 canoe rentals, float trips, river/pond fishing, fishing supplies, mini-golf, ($), golf nearby, bsktball, playground, activities, horseshoes, sports field, hiking trails, v-ball.

Pets welcome, quantity restrict. Partial handicap access. Open mid Mar - Nov 30. Big rigs welcome. Escort to site. Clubs welcome. Rate in 2010 $50 for 2 persons. MC/VISA/DISC/Debit. Member ARVC, VCA. FCRV discount. FMCA discount. CCUSA 50% Discount. CCUSA reservations Recommended, CCUSA max stay 3 days, Cash only for CCUSA disc., CCUSA disc. not avail F,Sa, CCUSA disc. not avail holidays. Discount not available May 20 thru Labor Day.

Phone: (540)291-2727
Address: 16 Recreation Ln, Natural Bridge Station, VA 24579
Lat/Lon: 37.61247/-79.48699
Email: yogibearnb@comcast.net
Web: www.campnbr.com

SEE AD THIS PAGE

NEW MARKET—B-3

(SE) NASCAR RV Resorts at Endless Caverns (Morgan RV Resorts)—(Shenandoah) *From jct I-81 (exit 257) & US-11: Go 4 mi N on US 11, then 1-1/4 mi SE on Endless Caverns Rd. Enter at end.* ◆◆◆◆FACILITIES: 148 sites, typical site width 40 ft, 148 full hkups, (20/30/50 amps), 72 pull-thrus, family camping, tenting, laundry, ltd groc. ◆◆◆◆RECREATION: swim pool, pond fishing, play equipment. Pets welcome. Partial handicap access. Open all yr. Big rigs welcome. Rate in 2010 $36.99-59.99 for 2 persons. Member ARVC, VCA. Phone: (540)896-2283.

NEW POINT—D-6

(E) New Point RV Resort (Morgan RV Resorts)—(Matthews) *From jct Hwy 198 & Hwy 14E (at Matthews): Go 7 mi SE on Hwy 14 E, then 3/4 mi E on Hwy 602. Enter on R.* ◆◆◆FACILITIES: 330 sites, typical site width 30 ft, 300 full hkups, 30 W&E, (30/50 amps), 10 pull-thrus, family camping, tenting, laundry, ltd groc. ◆◆◆◆RECREATION: swim pool, saltwater swim,

NEW POINT—Continued
New Point RV Resort (Morgan RV Resorts)—Continued

boating, canoeing, ramp, dock, saltwater fishing, playground. Pets welcome, breed restrict, size restrict, quantity restrict. Open Apr 1 - Oct 31. Big rigs welcome. Rate in 2010 $28-47 for 2 persons. Member ARVC, VCA. Phone: (804)725-5120.

NEWPORT NEWS—E-5

(W) NEWPORT NEWS GOLF CLUB AT DEER RUN—*From jct I-64 (exit 250B) & Hwy 143 (Jefferson Ave): Go 1-1/4 mi E on Hwy 105 (Ft Eustis Blvd). Enter on L.* 36-holes of championship golf. Pro-shop, driving range, chipping & putting greens. Golf lessons with PGA Professionals. Deer Run Grille with full catering. Junior golf program. Tournaments. Open all yr. MC/VISA/DISC/AMEX.

Phone: (757)886-7925
Address: 901 Clubhouse Way, Newport News, VA 23608
Lat/Lon: 37.17738/-76.52757
Email: info@nngolfclub.com
Web: www.nngolfclub.com

SEE AD NEXT PAGE

(W) NEWPORT NEWS PARK CAMPGROUND (City Park)—(City of Newport News) *From jct I-64 (exit 250B) & Hwy 143 (Jefferson Ave): Go 1 mi NW on Hwy 143. Enter on R.*

FACILITIES: 188 sites, typical site width 15 ft, 121 W&E, 43 E, (20/30/50 amps), 24 no hkups, family camping, tenting, RV storage, dump, non-guest dump $, laundry, ltd groc, RV supplies, ice, picnic tables, grills.

RECREATION: pavilion, boating, canoeing, ramp, 22 rowboat/22 canoe/30 pedal boat rentals, lake fishing, fishing supplies, golf nearby, bike rental 20 bike rentals, playground, activities, sports field, hiking trails, v-ball. Rec open to public.

Pets welcome. Partial handicap access. Open all yr. Clubs welcome. MC/VISA. Member VCA.

NEWPORT NEWS PARK CAMPGROUND (City Park)—Continued on next page

NEWPORT NEWS—Continued
NEWPORT NEWS PARK CAMPGROUND (City Park)—Continued

Phone: (757)888-3333
Address: 13564 Jefferson Ave, Newport News, VA 23603
Lat/Lon: 37.18858/-76.55854
Email: kbarber@nngov.com
Web: www.nnparks.com/parks_nn.php

SEE AD THIS PAGE

(W) NEWPORT NEWS VISITORS CENTER —*From jct I-64 (exit 250B) & Hwy 143 (Jefferson Ave): Go 1/4 mi NW on Hwy 143. Enter on R.* Travel & Tourism information about the local and state areas. Brochures on places to stay, things to do, restaurants, visitors guides & more. Open all yr. MC/VISA/DISC/AMEX.

WELCOME

Phone: (888)493-7386
Address: 13560 Jefferson Ave, Newport News, VA 23603
Lat/Lon: 37.17988/-76.55135
Email: tourism-mailing@nngov.com
Web: www.newport-news.org

SEE AD THIS PAGE

15 minutes south of Williamsburg, VA
I-64 Exit 250B

Newport News Park
Campground

188 wooded sites with modern conveniences

- Picnic tables & grills
- Jon boat, canoe & paddleboat rentals
- Playground
- Geocaching
- Freshwater fishing
- Golf course
- 30 miles of hiking trails in an 8,000 acre park
- 24 hr. Security

13564 Jefferson Avenue
Newport News, VA 23603
(800) 203-8322
VISA/Mastercard
www.nngov.com
/parks-and-recreation

PETERSBURG—D-4

(S) BEAR'S DEN RESTAURANT—*From jct I-95 (exit 41) & Hwy 35: Go 1/2 mi E on Hwy 35 S. Enter on R.* Open daily at 5 pm. Closed Sun. From pizza & burgers to gourmet dinners. Open all yr. MC/VISA/DISC/AMEX/Debit.

WELCOME

Phone: (804)733-2066
Address: 2809 Courtland Rd, Petersburg, VA 23805
Lat/Lon: 37.07718/-77.35201
Web: www.southfortycampresort.com

SEE AD THIS PAGE

(SW) PICTURE LAKE CAMPGROUND—(Dinwiddie) *From jct I-95 & I-85: Go 4-1/2 mi SW on I-85 to exit 63A, then 3 mi S on US 1. Enter on R.*

WELCOME

◇◇◇FACILITIES: 237 sites, typical site width 30 ft, 105 full hkups, 102 W&E, (20/30/50 amps), 30 no hkups, some extd stay sites, 180 pull-thrus, WiFi Instant Internet at site, family camping, tenting, cabins, RV storage, dump, laundry, groceries, RV supplies, LP gas by meter, ice, picnic tables, fire rings, wood.

◇◇◇RECREATION: pavilion, swim pool, boating, canoeing, kayaking, ramp, dock, 2 rowboat/6 canoe/2 pedal boat rentals, lake fishing, golf nearby, bsktball, horseshoes, hiking trails, v-ball. Rec open to public.

EZ ON/OFF I-95, Exit 41
Good Sam Park
South Forty
Camp Resort
Bear's Den
Restaurant
Clubs Welcome
(877) 732-8345
2809 Courtland Rd.
See listing at Petersburg, VA

PETERSBURG—Continued
PICTURE LAKE CAMPGROUND—Continued

Pets welcome. Open all yr. Clubs welcome. Rate in 2010 $25-32 for 2 persons. MC/VISA/DISC/AMEX. Member ARVC, VCA. FMCA discount.

Phone: (804)861-0174
Address: 7818 Boydton Plank Rd, Petersburg, VA 23803
Lat/Lon: 37.16417/-77.51299
Email: contactus@picturelakecampgrounds.com
Web: www.picturelakecampgrounds.com

SEE AD THIS PAGE

(S) SOUTH FORTY CAMP RESORT—(Prince George) *From jct I-95 (exit 41) & Hwy 35: Go 1/2 mi E on Hwy 35S. Enter on R.*

WELCOME

◇◇◇FACILITIES: 114 sites, typical site width 20 ft, 46 full hkups, 61 W&E, (20/30/50 amps), 50 amps ($), 7 no hkups, some extd stay sites, 70 pull-thrus, cable TV, WiFi Instant Internet at site, WiFi Internet central location, family camping, tenting, cabins, RV storage, dump, laundry, ltd groc, RV supplies, LP gas by weight/by meter, ice, picnic tables, fire rings, grills, wood.

◇◇◇◇RECREATION: rec hall, rec room/area, coin games, swim pool, boating, dock, 2 rowboat/3 pedal boat rentals, lake fishing, fishing supplies, golf nearby, bsktball, playground, horseshoes, sports field, hiking trails, v-ball.

Pets welcome. Partial handicap access. Open all yr. Big rigs welcome. Escort to site. Clubs welcome. Rate in 2010 $32-35 for 2 persons. MC/VISA/DISC/AMEX/Debit. Member ARVC, VCA.

Phone: (877)732-8345
Address: 2809 Courtland Rd, Petersburg, VA 23805
Lat/Lon: 37.07718/-77.35101
Email: southfortycampresort@comcast.net
Web: www.southfortycampresort.com

SEE AD THIS PAGE AND AD TRAVEL SECTION PAGE 762

PETERSBURG—Continued on next page

Woodall's Tip... If you're ever lost in the forest, you can tell your direction from the trees. The bark will be thicker on the north side of trees.

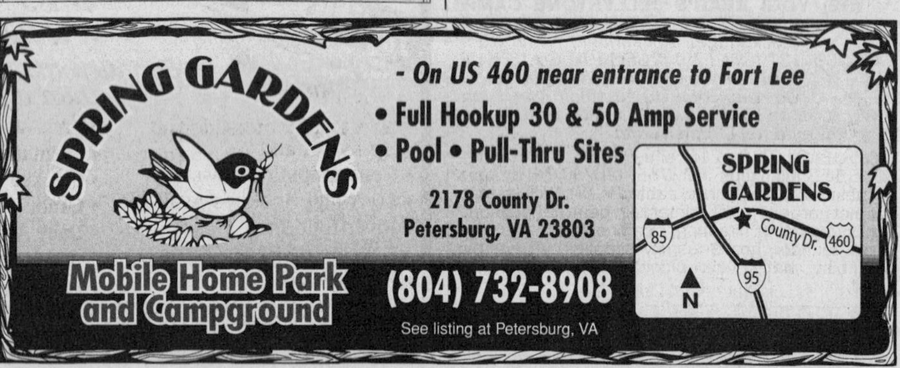

SPRING GARDENS
Mobile Home Park and Campground
- On US 460 near entrance to Fort Lee
• Full Hookup 30 & 50 Amp Service
• Pool • Pull-Thru Sites
2178 County Dr.
Petersburg, VA 23803
(804) 732-8908
SPRING GARDENS
County Dr.
85
95
460
N
See listing at Petersburg, VA

Picture Lake Campground
UNDER NEW MANAGEMENT
◆ Adjacent to VA Motorsports Park
◆ 15 Miles to Richmond International Raceway
◆ Waterfront tent sites ◆ Laundry ◆ Camp store
◆ 200 + sites ◆ Fishing & Boating
◆ Large 50A Pull-Thrus Avail. ◆ Cabins
◆ New Saltwater Pool ◆ New Concert Stage
www.picturelakecampgrounds.com
7818 Boydton Plank Rd., Petersburg, VA 23803
(804) 861-0174
◆ Open All Year ◆
From I-85 exit 63A take US Rte.1 South 4.5 Miles
To Richmond & Washington, DC
Petersburg National Battlefield Park
Exit 51
Petersburg
Lee Memorial Park
Exit 63A
Exit 61A
PICTURE LAKE
To North Carolina
To Emporia North Carolina
See listing at Petersburg, VA

(SE) SPRING GARDENS MOBILE HOME PARK (RV SPACES)—(City of Petersburg) *From jct I-95 (Fort Lee exit 50A) & US 460: Go 1 mi SE on US 460 E. Enter on R.*

FACILITIES: 44 sites, typical site width 25 ft, 44 full hkups, (20/30/50 amps), 50 amps ($), some extd stay sites, 5 pull-thrus, phone/cable on-site Internet (needs activ), cable Internet central location, laundry, picnic tables.

RECREATION: swim pool, horseshoes, v-ball.

Pets welcome, breed restrict, size restrict, quantity restrict. No tents. Open all yr. Rate in 2010 $30 for 2 persons.

Phone: (804)732-8908
Address: 2178 County Drive, Petersburg, VA 23803
Lat/Lon: 37.21552/-77.36505

SEE AD PAGE 778

POUND—A-2

(SW) JEFFERSON NATIONAL FOREST (Cane Patch Campground)—(Wise) *From jct US-23 & Hwy-671: Go 6 mi W on Hwy-671.* FACILITIES: 34 sites, 8 E, 26 no hkups, tenting, dump. RECREATION: playground. Open May 15 - Sept 15. Phone: (540) 328-2931.

POWHATAN—D-4

(W) Cozy Acres Campground/RV Resort—(Powhatan) *From jct US 522 & US-60: Go 4 mi W on US 60, then 2 mi S on Hwy 627 (Ridge Rd). Use printed directions - not GPS. Enter on R.* ◇◇◇◇FACILITIES: 99 sites, typical site width 25 ft, 90 full hkups, 9 W&E, (20/30/50 amps), 83 pull-thrus, family camping, tenting, dump, laundry, ltd groc. ◇◇◇◇RECREATION: swim pool, pond fishing, playground. Pets welcome. Open Apr 1 - Nov 15. Big rigs welcome. Rate in 2010 $37-41 for 2 persons. Member ARVC, VCA. Phone: (804)598-2470. FMCA discount.

QUANTICO—B-5

MILITARY PARK (Lunga Park Quantico-Marine Base) —(Prince William) *N'bound: From jct I-95 (exit 143B) & Hwy 610: Go 1 mi W on Hwy 610, then 2 mi N on Hwy 641, then 1 mi E on MCB 4. S'bound: From I-95 (exit 148) & Russell Rd: Go 7 mi W on MCB 1 & MCB 4. On base.* FACILITIES: 31 sites, 13 full hkups, 6 W&E, 12 no hkups, 4 pull-thrus, tenting. RECREATION: boating, canoeing, ramp, dock, lake fishing, playground. Open all yr. Facilities fully operational Apr 15 - Oct 15. Phone: (703)784-5270.

QUINBY—D-6

THOUSAND TRAILS-VIRGINIA LANDING (CAMP RESORT)—(Accomack) *From jct Hwy 182 & US 13: Go 3-1/2 mi E on Hwy 182 (Quinby Bridge Rd), then, 6-3/4 mi S on Hwy 605 (Upshur Neck Rd). Enter at end.*

FACILITIES: 200 sites, typical site width 30 ft, 200 W&E, (20/30/50 amps), some extd stay sites, heater not allowed, WiFi Internet central location, tenting, cabins, RV storage, dump, laundry, ltd groc, RV supplies, LP gas by weight/by meter, ice, picnic tables, patios, grills, controlled access.

RECREATION: rec hall, rec room/area, coin games, swim pool, river swim, boating, canoeing, kayaking, ramp, dock, saltwater/pond fishing, fishing supplies, mini-golf, playground, shuffleboard court 4 shuffleboard courts, horseshoes, sports field, hiking trails, v-ball.

Partial handicap access. Open Apr 1 - Oct 31. Clubs welcome. MC/VISA/DISC/AMEX.

Phone: (757)442-5489
Address: 40226 Upshur Neck Rd, Quinby, VA 23423
Lat/Lon: 37.47940/-75.79620
Email: vlmgr@1000trails.com
Web: www.1000trails.com

SEE AD ABINGDON PAGE 769

Visit a Dealer/Service Location in Woodall's.

REEDVILLE—C-6

(E) Chesapeake Bay Camp - Resort—(Northumberland) *From Jct Hwy & 200 US 360: Go 3-3/4 mi SE on US 360, then 2-1/2 mi E on SR 652 and SR 650,then 1/2 mi NE on Campground Rd. Enter on R.* ◇◇◇FACILITIES: 55 sites, typical site width 35 ft, 40 full hkups, 15 W&E, (30/50 amps), 55 pull-thrus, tenting, dump, laundry, ltd groc. ◇◇◇RECREATION: swim pool, boating, canoeing, ramp, dock, river fishing, playground. Pets welcome. Partial handicap access. Open 1st wknd of Apr - Nov 1. Big rigs welcome. Rate in 2010 $40-50 for 2 persons. Phone: (804)453-3430.

RICHMOND—D-4

AMERICAMPS KOA RICHMOND-NORTH —*From jct I-95 (exit 89) & Hwy 802: Go 200 yds E on Hwy 802, then 1 mi S on Air Park Rd. Enter on L.*

SEE PRIMARY LISTING AT ASHLAND AND AD ASHLAND PAGE 769 AND AD TRAVEL SECTION PAGE 762

ROANOKE—D-2

BLUE RIDGE NAT'L PARKWAY (Roanoke Mountain Campground)—(Roanoke) *From town: Go 5 mi S on US 220, then 1 mi N on Blue Ridge Pkwy to milepost 120.5, then 1 mi W on Mill Mt Spur.* FACILITIES: 105 sites, 30 ft max RV length, 105 no hkups, tenting, dump. RECREATION: river fishing. Open May - Oct. Phone: (540)745-9681.

DIXIE CAVERNS CAMPGROUND—*From jct I-81 (exit 143) & I-581: Go 11 mi S on I-81 (exit 132), then 1/4 mi S on US 460/US 11. Enter on R.*

SEE PRIMARY LISTING AT SALEM AND AD SALEM THIS PAGE

RURAL RETREAT—E-1

(S) RURAL RETREAT CAMPGROUND (Wythe County Park)—(Wythe) *From jct I-81 & Hwy 90: Go 4 mi S on Hwy 90 (becomes SR 749), then 1/2 mi W & S on SR 677, then 1/2 mi S on SR 678.* FACILITIES: 72 sites, 72 W&E, (20/30 amps), 5 pull-thrus, dump, ltd groc. RECREATION: swim pool, lake swim, boating, electric motors only, ramp, dock, lake fishing, playground. Open Apr - Oct. Phone: (276)686-4331.

RUSTBURG—D-3

(S) THOUSAND TRAILS-LYNCHBURG (CAMP RESORT)—(Campbell) *From jct US 501 & Hwy 24: Go 1 mi E on Hwy 24, then 6 mi S on Hwy 615, then 1/2 mi SW on Hwy 650. Enter on R.*

FACILITIES: 223 sites, typical site width 20 ft, 191 full hkups, 32 W&E, (30 amps), WiFi Internet central location, tenting, RV's/park model rentals, RV storage, dump, laundry, RV supplies, LP gas by weight/by meter, ice, picnic tables, grills, controlled access.

RECREATION: rec hall, rec room/area, pavilion, swim pool, wading pool, lake swim, hot tub, boating, electric motors only, canoeing, kayaking, dock, 3 rowboat/3 canoe/2 kayak rentals, lake fishing, mini-golf, ($), bsktball, playground, shuffleboard court 2 shuffleboard courts, activities (wkends), tennis, sports field, hiking trails, v-ball.

Pets welcome. Partial handicap access. Open May - Oct. MC/VISA/DISC/AMEX.

Phone: (434)332-6660
Address: 405 Mollies Creek Rd, Gladys, VA 24554
Lat/Lon: 37.21049/-79.04383
Email: jrttnlynch@aol.com
Web: 1000trails.com

SEE AD ABINGDON PAGE 769

Virginia's Bill of Rights was the model for the U.S. Bill of Rights.

SALEM—D-2

(SW) DIXIE CAVERNS—*From jct I-81 (exit 132) & Hwy 647: Go 1/4 mi S on Hwy 647, then 1/8 mi W on Hwy 11/460 (Main St). Enter on R.* The only underground caverns in SW Virginia, with rock shop, pottery, RV campground & antique mall. Open all yr. 9:30am-5pm. MC/VISA/DISC/AMEX.

Phone: (540)380-2085
Address: 5753 W Main St, Salem, VA 24153
Lat/Lon: 37.25437/-80.17395

SEE AD THIS PAGE

(SW) DIXIE CAVERNS CAMPGROUND—(Roanoke) *From jct I-81 (exit 132) & Hwy 647: Go 1/4 mi S on Hwy 647, then 1/4 mi W on Hwy 11/460 (Main St). Enter on R.*

◇◇◇FACILITIES: 92 sites, typical site width 25 ft, 62 full hkups, (20/30/50 amps), 30 no hkups, 32 pull-thrus, cable TV, WiFi Instant Internet at site, family camping, tenting, dump, ltd groc, LP gas by meter, picnic tables, fire rings.

◇RECREATION: golf nearby, horseshoes.

Pets welcome. Open all yr. Big rigs welcome. Clubs welcome. Rate in 2010 $26-28 for 2 persons. MC/VISA/DISC/AMEX/Debit.

Phone: (540)380-2085
Address: 5753 W Main St, Salem, VA 24153
Lat/Lon: 37.25437/-80.17395
Web: www.dixiecaverns.com

SEE AD THIS PAGE

SCOTTSBURG—E-3

STAUNTON RIVER STATE PARK—(Halifax) *From town: Go 9 mi SE on Hwy-344.* FACILITIES: 48 sites, 30 ft max RV length, 34 W&E, (20/30 amps), 14 no hkups, tenting, dump. RECREATION: swim pool, boating, canoeing, ramp, lake fishing, playground. Partial handicap access. Open all yr. Facilities fully operational May - Sep. Phone: (434)572-4623.

SPOUT SPRING—D-3

(W) Paradise Lake Family Campground—(Appomattox) *From jct Hwy 24 & US 460 (in Appomattox): Go 6 mi W on US 460, then 1 mi S West Lake (Private) Rd. Enter at end.* ◇◇◇FACILITIES: 133 sites, typical site width 35 ft, 43 full hkups, 63 W&E, (20/30/50 amps), 50 amps ($), 27 no hkups, 37 pull-thrus, tenting, dump, laundry, ltd groc. ◇◇◇◇RECREATION: lake swim, lake fishing, playground. Pets welcome. Open all yr. Rate in 2010 $29-34 for 2 persons. Member ARVC, VCA. Phone: (434)993-3332.

STAFFORD—C-4

AQUIA PINES CAMP RESORT—(Stafford) *From jct I-95 (Aquia-Garrisonville exit 143A) & Hwy 610: Go N (left) at light onto US 1, then 1/2 mi N on US 1. Enter on L.*

◇◇◇◇FACILITIES: 120 sites, typical site width 30 ft, 84 full hkups, 15 W&E, (20/30/50 amps), 21 no hkups, 93 pull-thrus, cable TV, phone/WiFi Instant Internet at site, WiFi Internet central location, family camping, tenting, cabins, RV storage, dump, non-guest dump $, laundry, groceries, RV supplies, LP gas by weight/by meter, ice, picnic tables, wood.

◇◇◇RECREATION: rec room/area, pavilion, swim pool, mini-golf, ($), golf nearby, bsktball, playground.

Pets welcome, quantity restrict. Open all yr. Big rigs welcome. Escort to site. Clubs welcome. Rate in 2010 $42-54.50 for 2 persons. MC/VISA/DISC/Debit. Member ARVC. FMCA discount.

AQUIA PINES CAMP RESORT—Continued on next page

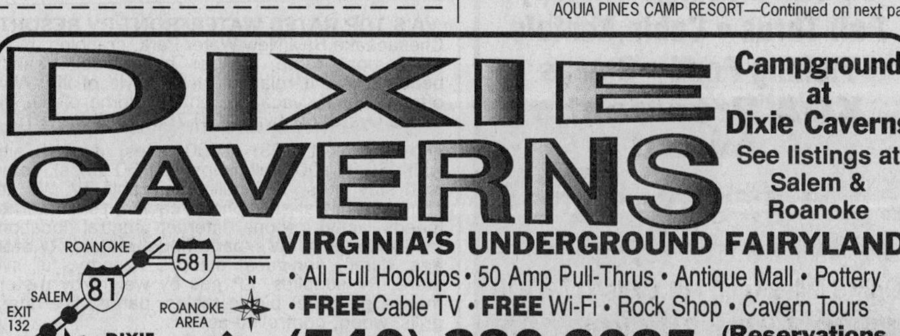

Phone: (540)659-3447
Address: 3071 Jefferson Davis Hwy, Stafford, VA 22554
Lat/Lon: 38.47051/-77.39976
Email: aquiapines@aol.com
Web: www.aquiapines.com

SEE AD DC TRAVEL SECTION PAGE 60

STANARDSVILLE—C-3

(NE) Heavenly Acres Campground—(Greene) *From jct US 33 & Hwy 230: Go 2 mi E on Hwy 230. Enter on R.* ◆◆FACILITIES: 54 sites, typical site width 25 ft, 23 full hkups, 8 W&E, (20/30/50 amps), 23 no hkups, 3 pull-thrus, family camping, tenting, dump. ◆◆◆RECREATION: swim pool, pond fishing, playground. Pets welcome. Open all yr. Facilities fully operational Mar - Nov. Rate in 2010 $28-38 for 2 persons. Member ARVC, VCA. Phone: (434)985-6601.

STAUNTON—C-3

(S) STAUNTON / WALNUT HILLS KOA—(Augusta) *S'bnd jct I-81 (exit 217) & Hwy 654: Go 1/2 mi N on Hwy 654, then 1-1/2 mi S on US 11, then 1 mi E on Hwy 655 (Walnut Hills Rd). Ent on L. N'bnd jct I-81 (exit 213) & US 11: Go 500 yds S on US 11, then 2-1/2 mi N on US 340, then 1/4 mi N on Hwy 655. Enter on R.*

SPEND A DAY / A WEEK / A VACATION
Easy On/Off I-81 & I-64. New Pool, Cabin & Cottage Rentals, Fishing, Lakeside Camping, On-Site Massage Therapy. Close to historical attractions. We cordially invite you and your family to share the beauty of this area with us.

◆◆◆◆FACILITIES: 149 sites, typical site width 25 ft, 63 full hkups, 64 W&E, (20/30/50 amps), 22 no hkups, 34 pull-thrus, cable TV, phone/WiFi Instant Internet at site, family camping, tenting, cabins, RV storage, dump, non-guest dump $, laundry, groceries, RV supplies, LP gas by weight/by meter, ice, picnic tables, fire rings, wood.

◆◆◆◆RECREATION: rec room/area, equipped pavilion, coin games, swim pool, wading pool, pond fishing, golf nearby, playground, activities, (wkends), horseshoes, v-ball. Rec open to public.

Pets welcome, quantity restrict. Partial handicap access. Open all yr. Big rigs welcome. Clubs welcome. Rate in 2010 $32-55 for 2 persons. MC/VISA/DISC/Debit. Member ARVC, VCA. KOA discount.

Text 82236 to (440)725-8687 to see our Visual Tour.

The first peanuts grown in the United States were grown in Virginia.

Phone: (540)337-3920
Address: 484 Walnut Hills Rd., Staunton, VA 24401
Lat/Lon: 38.04799/-79.10153
Email: stauntonkoa@yahoo.com
Web: www.walnuthillskoa.com

SEE AD THIS PAGE AND AD TRAVEL SECTION PAGE 762

STRASBURG—B-4

(N) GEORGE WASHINGTON NATIONAL FOREST (Elizabeth Furnace Campground)—(Shenandoah) *From jct Hwy-55 & Hwy-678: Go 4-1/2 mi S on Hwy-678.* FACILITIES: 32 sites, 32 no hkups, tenting, dump. RECREATION: stream fishing, playground. Open all yr. Phone: (540)984-4101.

STUART—E-2

FAIRY STONE STATE PARK—(Patrick) *From N jct US 58 & Hwy 8: go 4 mi N on Hwy 8, then 8 mi E on Hwy 57 (Fairystone Park Hwy), then 3/4 mi N on Hwy 346. Enter at end.* FACILITIES: 56 sites, 30 ft max RV length, 50 full hkups, (30 amps), 6 no hkups, family camping, tenting, dump. RECREATION: lake swim, boating, no motors, canoeing, ramp, lake fishing, playground. Partial handicap access. Open Mar 1 - Dec 1. Phone: (276)930-2424.

SUGAR GROVE—B-3

JEFFERSON NATIONAL FOREST (Hurricane Campground)—(Smyth) *From town: Go 5 mi S on Hwy-16, then 1-1/2 mi NW on Hwy-650, then 1/2 mi N on FR-84.* FACILITIES: 27 sites, 22 ft max RV length, 27 no hkups, 2 pull-thrus, tenting. RECREATION: Partial handicap access. Open Mid Mar - Oct 1. Phone: (276)783-5196.

TEMPERANCEVILLE—C-6

Tall Pines Harbor Waterfront Campground—(Accomack) *From jct US 13 & Hwy 695 (Saxis Rd): Go 6-3/4 mi W on Hwy 695 (Saxis Rd). Enter on R.* ◆◆◆◆FACILITIES: 177 sites, typical site width 25 ft, 98 full hkups, 69 W&E, (20/30/50 amps), 10 no hkups, 65 pull-thrus, family camping, tenting, dump, laundry, ltd groc. ◆◆◆◆RECREATION: swim pool, saltwater swim, boating, canoeing, dock, saltwater fishing, playground. Pets welcome. Open Mar 1 - Nov 1. Big rigs welcome. Rate in 2010 $28-65 for 2 persons. Member ARVC, VCA. Phone: (757)824-0777.

TOANO—D-5

(N) Williamsburg Christian Retreat Center—(James City) *From jct I-64 (exit 227) & Hwy 30: Go 1 mi NW on Hwy 30, then 1-1/4 mi SW on Barnes Rd. Enter on R.* ◆◆◆◆FACILITIES: 22 sites, typical site width 25 ft, 22 full hkups, (20/30/50 amps), family camping, tenting, dump, laundry. ◆◆◆RECREATION: swim pool, playground. Pets welcome. Partial handicap access. Open all yr. Rate in 2010 $30-35 for 2 persons. Phone: (757)566-2256.

TRIANGLE—B-5

(W) PRINCE WILLIAM FOREST PARK-NPS (Oak Ridge)—(PrinceWilliam) *From jct I-95 & Hwy-619: Go 1/4 mi W on Hwy-619 to park entrance, then follow signs 7 mi.* FACILITIES: 100 sites, 32 ft max RV length, 100 no hkups, tenting, dump. RECREATION: lake/stream fishing. Partial handicap access. Open all yr. Facilities fully operational Mar - Nov. Phone: (703)221-7181.

TROUTDALE—B-3

JEFFERSON NATIONAL FOREST (Grindstone Campground)—(Grayson) *From jct US-58 & Hwy-16: Go 7 mi N on Hwy-16, then 6-1/2 mi W on Hwy-603.* FACILITIES: 92 sites, 55 W&E, (30 amps), 37 no hkups, tenting, dump. RECREATION: playground. Partial handicap access. Open May 1 - Nov 30. Big rigs welcome. Phone: (276)388-3983.

URBANNA—D-5

(NW) BETHPAGE CAMP-RESORT—(Middlesex) *From jct US 17 & Hwy 602: Go 4 mi SE on Hwy 602, then 1/2 mi E on Browns Ln. Enter on L.*

VA'S TOP RATED WATERFRONT RV RESORT
Chesapeake Bay! New Water Park, crabbing, marina & boat ramp, charter boat, pools, sandy beaches and a relaxed "rivah" style of life. Also offering family vacation rentals. Home of the Urbanna Oyster Festival (804) 758-4349

◆◆◆◆◆FACILITIES: 1000 sites, typical site width 50 ft, 1000 full hkups, (30/50 amps), some extd stay sites, 100 pull-thrus, cable TV, WiFi Instant Internet at site, phone/cable on-site Internet (needs activ), phone Internet central location, family camping, RV's/park model rentals, RV storage, dump, non-guest dump $, laundry, full svc store, RV supplies, LP gas by weight/by meter, marine gas, ice, picnic tables, patios, fire rings, grills, wood, controlled access.

◆◆◆◆◆RECREATION: rec hall, rec room/area, equipped pavilion, coin games, 5 swim pools, wading pool, spray ground, lake swim, boating, canoeing, kayaking, ramp, dock, 3 canoe/6 kayak/6 pedal boat rentals, saltwater/lake fishing, fishing supplies, fishing guides, mini-golf ($), putting green, golf nearby, bsktball, 8 bike rentals, playground, activities, tennis, horseshoes, sports field, v-ball, local tours.

Pets welcome. Partial handicap access. No tents. Open Apr 1 - Nov 15. Big rigs welcome. Escort to site. Clubs welcome. Rate in 2010 $39.95-62.95 for 4 persons. MC/VISA. Member ARVC, VCA.

Text 81694 to (440)725-8687 to see our Visual Tour.

Phone: (804)758-4349
Address: 679 Browns Lane, Urbanna, VA 23175
Lat/Lon: 37.64891/-76.58525
Email: bethpage@oasisonline.com
Web: www.bethpagecamp.com

SEE AD PAGES 782-783 AND AD TRAVEL SECTION PAGE 763 AND AD DC TRAVEL SECTION PAGE 62 AND AD MAP PAGE 760 AND AD DISCOVER SECTION PAGE 27

(NW) BETHPAGE MINI-GOLF & ICE CREAMERY—*From jct US 17 & Hwy 602: Go 4-1/2 mi SE on Hwy 602. Enter on R.* 18-hole miniature golf course. Hershey's Old Fashioned Hand Dipped Ice Cream. Open to the public. Available for groups & Private parties. Open Apr 1 - Nov 15. MC/VISA.

Phone: (804)758-GOLF
Address: 679 Browns Ln, Urbanna, VA 23175
Lat/Lon: 37.64151/-76.59357
Email: bethpage@oasisonline.com
Web: www.bethpagecamp.com

SEE AD TRAVEL SECTION PAGE 763 AND AD DC TRAVEL SECTION PAGE 62

URBANNA—Continued on next page

Virginia State Nicknames: Old Dominion; Mother of Presidents

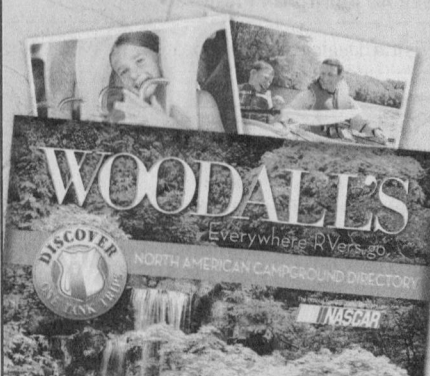

Both Resorts WWWWW

Woodall's Rated:
Fac: WWWWW
Rec: WWWWW

- Award Winning, Outstanding Facilities
- Marina and Boat Launch
- Crabbing, Biking, Swimming
- Unique Setting
- Quiet Evenings
- Superior Food
- Professional Staff
- Breathtaking Sunsets
- Perfect for Groups & Rallies
- Historical Attractions Nearby
- Cruises aboard the Bethpager, our authentic restored 48' Chesapeake Bay Deadrise

There is Always Plenty to do!

(804) 758-4349
P.O. Box 178, Urbanna, VA 23175
www.bethpagecamp.com

Woodall's Rated:
Fac: 
Rec: WWWWW

On the Rappahannock River in Virginia's River Country

- Minutes from Chesapeake Bay
- Acres of Woods with Walking Trails on a Meandering River
- Great Fishing, Crabbing and Boating
- Fun Events for Families and Groups
- Great Home Base for Virginia's Popular Attractions
- Enjoy Tennis, Basketball, Horseshoes and many other Recreational Activities

Enjoy our new Splash Point Water Complex!

Offering everything you need to unwind, relax and kick back "rivah style"

(804) 758-2485
P.O. Box 8, Topping, VA 23169
www.greyspointcamp.com

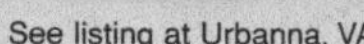
See listing at Urbanna, VA

URBANNA—Continued

✽ **(NW) RV ADVENTURES**—*From jct US 17 & Hwy 602: Go 4 mi SE on Hwy 602, then 1/2 mi E on Browns Ln. Enter on L.* SALES: park models, pre-owned unit sales. SERVICES: Open Apr 1 - Nov 15.

WELCOME

Phone: (804)758-0600
Address: 679 Browns Ln, PO Box 178, VA 23175
Lat/Lon: 37.64891/-76.58525
Web: www.bethpagecamp.com/RVAdventures.html

SEE AD TRAVEL SECTION PAGE 763 AND AD DC TRAVEL SECTION PAGE 62

VERONA—C-3

(N) Shenandoah Valley Campground—(Augusta) *From jct I-81 (exit 227) & Hwy 612: Go 1 mi W on Hwy 612, then 1/2 mi N on US 11, then 1 mi W on Hwy 781. Enter on L.* ◊◊◊◊FACILITIES: 150 sites, typical site width 25 ft, 25 full hkups, 105 W&E, (20/30/50 amps), 50 amps ($), 20 no hkups, 104 pull-thrus, family camping, tenting, dump, laundry, groceries. ◊◊◊◊RECREATION: swim pool, boating, canoeing, lake/river fishing, playground. Pets welcome. Partial handicap access. Open Apr 1 - Early 15. Big rigs welcome. Rate in 2010 $37-46 for 2 persons. Member ARVC, VCA. Phone: (800)310-2580.

VIRGINIA BEACH—E-6

AMERICAN HERITAGE RV PARK—*From jct I-264 & I-64: Go 53 mi NW on I-64, then 1/4 mi S on Hwy 607 (exit 231A), then 1/4 mi E on Maxto Ln. Enter on L.*

WELCOME

SEE PRIMARY LISTING AT WILLIAMSBURG AND AD WILLIAMSBURG NEXT PAGE

(N) FIRST LANDING-SEASHORE STATE PARK—(Virgina Beach) *From jct I-64 (exit 282) & Northampton Blvd/US 13: Go NE on US 13, then 5 mi E on Shore Dr/US 60.* FACILITIES: 218 sites, 103 W&E, 115 no hkups, tenting, dump, laundry. RECREATION: boating, ramp, saltwater fishing. Partial handicap access. Open Memorial Day - Labor day. Facilities fully operational Memorial Day - Labor Day. Phone: (757)412-2300.

The Blue Ridge Mountains are located in Virginia.

VIRGINIA BEACH—Continued

(S) HOLIDAY TRAV-L-PARK OF VIRGINIA BEACH—(City of Virginia Beach) *From Jct I-264 (exit 22) & Birdneck Rd: Go 3 mi SE on Birdneck Rd, then 1/4 mi S on General Booth Blvd. Enter on R.*

WELCOME

THERE'S SOMETHING FOR EVERYONE!
Bike path to the beach or use our free parking lot. Super sites-4 pools, new dog park, great seasonal entertainment & activities. We offer wooded, open & Big Rig sites. We're close to dozens of attractions-most just minutes away.

◊◊◊◊◊FACILITIES: 824 sites, typical site width 30 ft, 329 full hkups, 375 W&E, (20/30/50 amps), 120 no hkups, 625 pull-thrus, cable TV, WiFi Instant Internet at site ($), phone Internet central location, family camping, tenting, cabins, RV storage, dump, non-guest dump $, portable dump, laundry, full svc store, RV supplies, LP gas by meter, ice, picnic tables, patios, wood.

◊◊◊◊◊RECREATION: rec hall, pavilion, equipped pavilion, coin games, 4 swim pools, wading pool, mini-golf, ($), golf nearby, bsktball, 15 bike rentals, playground, activities, horseshoes, sports field, v-ball.

Pets welcome, breed restrict, quantity restrict. Partial handicap access. Open all yr. Big rigs welcome. Clubs welcome. Rate in 2010 $27-77 for 2 persons. MC/VISA/DISC. ATM. Member ARVC, VCA. FCRV discount. FMCA discount.

Phone: (866)850-9629
Address: 1075 General Booth Blvd, Virginia Beach, VA 23451-4828
Lat/Lon: 36.80285/-75.99699
Email: info@campingvb.com
Web: www.campingvb.com

SEE AD THIS PAGE

MILITARY PARK (Cape Henry Travel Camp-Ft. Story)—(Currituck) *From jct I-64 & US 13: Go 4-1/2 mi NE on US 13, then 4-1/2 mi E on US 60 to Ft. Story. On base.* FACILITIES: 24 sites, 24 W&E, tenting, dump, laundry, groceries. RECREATION: saltwater swim, saltwater/pond fishing, playground. Open all yr. Phone: (757)422-7601.

North Bay Shore Campground—(City of Virginia Beach) *From jct I-64 & I-264 (exit 22) Birdneck Rd: Go 3-1/2 mi SE on Birdneck Rd, then 7 mi S on General Booth Blvd, then 1 mi E on Princess Anne Rd, then*

VIRGINIA BEACH—Continued
North Bay Shore Campground—Continued

3-1/2 mi E on Sandbridge Rd, then 1-1/2 mi S on Colechester Rd. Enter on R. ◊◊◊FACILITIES: 87 sites, typical site width 35 ft, 5 full hkups, 71 W&E, (20/30/50 amps), 50 amps ($), 11 no hkups, 20 pull-thrus, family camping, tenting, dump, laundry. ◊◊◊◊RECREATION: swim pool, boating, canoeing, ramp, dock, stream fishing, play equipment. Pets welcome. Open May 1 - Oct 1. Rate in 2010 $35-45 for 2 persons. Member ARVC, VCA. Phone: (757)426-7911.

(S) North Landing Beach Riverfront Campground and Resort—(Virginia Beach City) *From jct I-64 (exit 286) & Indian River Rd: Go 12 mi SE on Indian River Rd, then 10 mi S on Princess Anne Rd. Enter on R.* ◊◊◊◊FACILITIES: 174 sites, typical site width 35 ft, 77 full hkups, 24 W&E, (20/30/50 amps), 73 no hkups, 66 pull-thrus, family camping, tenting, dump, laundry, ltd groc. ◊◊◊RECREATION: swim pool, river swim, boating, canoeing, ramp, dock, river fishing, playground. Pets welcome, breed restrict, quantity restrict. Open all yr. Big rigs welcome. Rate in 2010 $38-45 per family. Member ARVC, VCA. Phone: (757)426-6241.

(S) Virginia Beach KOA—(Princess Anne) *From jct I-264 (exit 22) & Birdneck Rd: Go 3 mi S on Birdneck Rd,, then 1 mi S on General Booth Blvd. Enter on L.* ◊◊◊◊FACILITIES: 376 sites, typical site width 30 ft, 130 full hkups, 150 W&E, (20/30/50 amps), 50 amps ($), 96 no hkups, 110 pull-thrus, family camping, tenting, dump, laundry, full svc store. ◊◊◊◊RECREATION: 2 swim pools, playground. Pets welcome, breed restrict. Partial handicap access. Open all yr. Rate in 2010 $45-71 for 2 persons. Phone: (800)KOA-4150. KOA discount.

VOLNEY—E-1

GRAYSON HIGHLANDS STATE PARK—(Grayson) *From jct Hwy-16 & US-58: Go 5 mi W on US-58.* FACILITIES: 96 sites, 60 W&E, (20/30 amps), 36 no hkups, tenting, dump, ltd groc. RECREATION: stream fishing. Partial handicap access. Open all yr. Phone: (276)579-7092.

WARM SPRINGS—C-2

GEORGE WASHINGTON NATIONAL FOREST (Bolar Mountain Campground)—(Bath) *From town: Go 13 mi W on Hwy-39, then 7 mi S on Hwy-600.* FACILITIES: 91 sites, 22 ft max RV length, 20 E, 71 no hkups, tenting, dump. RECREATION: lake swim, boating, canoeing, ramp, dock, lake fishing. Open Mar 29 - Dec 4. Phone: (540)839-2521.

WARM SPRINGS—Continued on next page

WARM SPRINGS—Continued

(N) GEORGE WASHINGTON NATIONAL FOREST (Hidden Valley Campground)—(Bath) *From jct Hwy-39 & Hwy-621: Go 1 mi N on Hwy-621, then 1-3/4 mi N on FR-24110.* FACILITIES: 30 sites, 30 no hkups, tenting, dump. RECREATION: river fishing. Open Mar 28 - Dec 1. Phone: (540)839-2521.

WAYNESBORO—C-3

GEORGE WASHINGTON NATIONAL FOREST (Sherando Lake Campground)—(Lynderst) *From town: Go 4 mi S on Hwy-624, then 10 mi SW on Hwy-664, then 2 mi W on FR-91.* FACILITIES: 63 sites, 35 ft max RV length, 30 E, 33 no hkups, tenting, dump. RECREATION: lake swim, boating, no motors, canoeing, ramp, playground. Partial handicap access. Open Apr 1 - Oct 31. Phone: (540)261-6105.

(N) Waynesboro North 340 Campground—(Augusta) *From Jct I-64 (exit 96) & US 340: Go 7 mi N on US 340. Enter on R.* ◇◇◇FACILITIES: 300 sites, typical site width 30 ft, 200 full hkups, 100 W&E, (20/30/50 amps), 30 pull-thrus, family camping, tenting, dump, laundry, ltd groc. ◇◇◇RECREATION: swim pool, playground. Pets welcome, breed restrict, quantity restrict. Open all yr. Big rigs welcome. Rate in 2010 $33.60 for 2 persons. Phone: (540)943-9573.

WILLIAMSBURG—D-5

(N) AMERICAN HERITAGE RV PARK—(James City) *From I-64 (exit 231A-Norge): Go 1/4 mi S on Hwy 607, then 1/4 mi E on Maxton Lane. Enter on L.*

GREAT CAMPING WITH LOTS TO SEE AND DO

Come celebrate the 400th anniversary of the first English settlement in America in nearby Jamestown. American Heritage RV Resort offers a great location for exploring your American heritage at all historic area attractions.

◇◇◇◇◇FACILITIES: 95 sites, typical site width 28 ft, 95 full hkups, (20/30/50 amps), 50 amps ($), 75 pull-thrus, cable TV, WiFi Instant Internet at site, WiFi Internet central location, family camping, tenting, RV's/park model rentals, RV storage, laundry, ltd groc, RV supplies, LP gas by weight/by meter, ice, picnic tables, patios, fire rings, wood.

◇◇◇◇RECREATION: rec hall, rec room/area, coin games, swim pool, wading pool, mini-golf, golf nearby, bsktball, playground, horseshoes, sports field, hiking trails, v-ball, local tours.

WILLIAMSBURG—Continued
AMERICAN HERITAGE RV PARK—Continued

Pets welcome. Partial handicap access. Open all yr. Big rigs welcome. Escort to site. Clubs welcome. Rate in 2010 $44.95 for 4 persons. MC/VISA/DISC/AMEX/Debit. Member ARVC, VCA.

Phone: (888)530-CAMP
Address: 146 Maxton Lane, Williamsburg, VA 23188
Lat/Lon: 37.37697/-76.76846
Email: americanheritagerv@verizon.net
Web: www.americanheritagervpark.com

SEE AD THIS PAGE

(N) ANVIL CAMPGROUND—(James City) *From I-64 (Colonial Williamsburg Camp Peary exit 238) & Hwy 143: Go 1 block S on Hwy 143, then 1-1/4 mi NW on Rochambeau Dr, Follow Blue Camping signs, then 2 mi SW on Hwy 645 (Airport Rd), then 1/2 mi S on Hwy 603, Mooretown Rd. Enter on R.*

◇◇◇◇FACILITIES: 62 sites, typical site width 20 ft, 50 full hkups, 12 W&E, (20/30/50 amps), 8 pull-thrus, cable TV, WiFi Instant Internet at site, phone Internet central location, family camping, tenting, cabins, dump, non-guest dump $, laundry, ltd groc, RV supplies, ice, picnic tables, fire rings, wood.

◇◇◇◇RECREATION: rec room/area, equipped pavilion, coin games, swim pool, golf nearby, bsktball, playground, activities, (wkends), horseshoes, local tours.

Pets welcome. Open all yr. Big rigs welcome. Clubs welcome. Rate in 2010 $29.99-49.99 for 2 persons. MC/VISA/AMEX. Member ARVC, VCA.

Phone: (800)633-4442
Address: 5243 Mooretown Rd, Williamsburg, VA 23188
Lat/Lon: 37.30788/-76.72888
Email: info@anvilcampground.com
Web: www.anvilcampground.com

SEE AD THIS PAGE

The American Revolution ended with the surrender of Lord Cornwallis in Yorktown.

WILLIAMSBURG—Continued

(NW) BETHPAGE CAMP-RESORT—(James City) *From I-64 (exit 220) & Hwy 33: Go 18-1/2 mi N on Hwy 33, then 2 mi N on US 17, then 2 1/2 mi NE on Hwy 33E, then 3 1/2 mi N on Hwy 227, then 1/2 mi E on Browns Ln. Enter on L.*

◇◇◇◇◇FACILITIES: 1000 sites, typical site width 50 ft, 1000 full hkups, (30/50 amps), some extd stay sites, 100 pull-thrus, cable TV, WiFi Instant Internet at site, phone/cable on-site Internet (needs activ), phone Internet central location, family camping, RV's/park model rentals, RV storage, dump, non-guest dump $, laundry, full svc store, RV supplies, LP gas by weight/by meter, marine gas, ice, picnic tables, patios, fire rings, grills, wood, controlled access.

◇◇◇◇◇RECREATION: rec hall, rec room/area, equipped pavilion, coin games, 5 swim pools, wading pool, spray ground, lake swim, boating, canoeing, kayaking, ramp, dock, 3 canoe/6 kayak/6 pedal boat rentals, saltwater/lake fishing, fishing supplies, fishing guides, mini-golf ($), putting green, golf nearby, bsktball, 8 bike rentals, playground, activities, tennis, horseshoes, sports field, v-ball, local tours.

Pets welcome. Partial handicap access. No tents. Open Apr 1 - Nov 15. Big rigs welcome. Escort to site. Clubs welcome. Rate in 2010 $39.95-62.95 for 4 persons. MC/VISA. Member ARVC, VCA.

Phone: (804)758-4349
Address: 679 Browns Lane, Urbanna, VA 23175
Lat/Lon: 37.64891/-76.58834
Email: bethpage@oasisonline.com
Web: www.bethpagecamp.com

SEE PRIMARY LISTING AT URBANNA AND AD URBANNA PAGES 782-783

WILLIAMSBURG—Continued on next page

Over 2,200 of the 4,000 battles fought in the civil war were fought in Virginia.

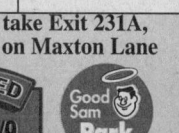

WILLIAMSBURG—Continued

GLOUCESTER POINT FAMILY CAMPGROUND—*From jct Hwy 199 & I-64 (exit 242): Go 8 mi SE on I-64 (exit 250B), then 4 mi N on US 17, then 1 mi E on Hwy 105, then N on Us 17, then 1 mi E on Guinea Rd (Hwy 216), then 1-1/2 mi N on Hwy 641, then 1/4 mi E on Zack Rd, then 1/4 mi N on Campground Rd. Enter on R.*

SEE PRIMARY LISTING AT GLOUCESTER POINT AND AD GLOUCESTER POINT PAGE 774

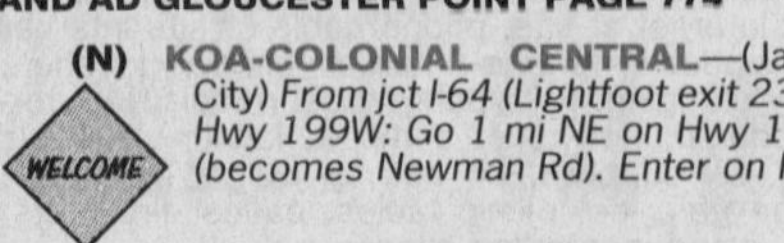

(N) KOA-COLONIAL CENTRAL—(James City) *From jct I-64 (Lightfoot exit 234) & Hwy 199W: Go 1 mi NE on Hwy 199W (becomes Newman Rd). Enter on R.*

COLONIAL WILLIAMSBURG KOA

Camp with us on our 180 acre, 370 site campground. We are close to Williamsburg, Busch Gardens, Water Country, Jamestown, Yorktown. For an easy get away try a kabin. Want all the comforts of home you will love our new lodges.

◊◊◊◊◊FACILITIES: 170 sites, typical site width 25 ft, 101 full hkups, 69 W&E, (20/30/50 amps), 180 pull-thrus, cable TV, WiFi Instant Internet at site, WiFi Internet central location, family camping, tenting, cabins, dump, laundry, groceries, RV supplies, LP gas by weight/by meter, ice, picnic tables, fire rings, grills, wood.

◊◊◊◊◊RECREATION: rec hall, pavilion, coin games, swim pool, wading pool, golf nearby, bsktball, 20 bike rentals, playground, activities, horseshoes, sports field, hiking trails, v-ball, local tours.

Pets welcome, breed restrict. Open Mar 1 - Dec. Big rigs welcome. Clubs welcome. Green Friendly. Rate in 2010 $34.95-61.95 for 2 persons. MC/VISA/DISC/Debit. Member ARVC, VCA. KOA discount.

Phone: (800)562-7609
Address: 4000 Newman Rd, Williamsburg, VA 23188
Lat/Lon: 37.36058/-76.71426
Email: camp@williamsburgkoa.com
Web: www.williamsburgkoa.com

SEE AD TRAVEL SECTION PAGE 762

(N) KOA-WILLIAMSBURG—(James City) *From jct I-64 (Lightfoot exit 234) & Hwy 199W: Go 1 mi NE on 199W (becomes Newman Rd). Enter on R.*

COLONIAL WILLIAMSBURG KOA

Camp with us on our 180 acre, 370 site campground. We are close to Williamsburg, Busch Gardens, Water Country, Jamestown, Yorktown. For an easy get away try a kabin. Want all the comforts of home you will love our new lodges.

◊◊◊◊◊FACILITIES: 150 sites, typical site width 30 ft, 71 full hkups, 74 W&E, (20/30/50 amps), 5 no hkups, 22 pull-thrus, cable TV, WiFi Instant Internet at site, WiFi Internet central location, family camping, tenting, cabins, dump, laundry, full svc store, RV supplies, ice, picnic tables, fire rings, wood.

◊◊◊◊◊RECREATION: rec hall, equipped pavilion, coin games, swim pool, golf nearby, bsktball, 12 bike rentals, playground, activities, horseshoes, sports field, hiking trails, v-ball, local tours.

WILLIAMSBURG—Continued
KOA-WILLIAMSBURG—Continued

Pets welcome, breed restrict. Open Mar 1 - Dec. Big rigs welcome. Clubs welcome. Green Friendly. Rate in 2010 $34.95-61.95 for 2 persons. MC/VISA/DISC/Debit. Member ARVC, VCA. KOA discount.

Text 107953 to (440)725-8687 to see our Visual Tour.

Phone: (800)562-1733
Address: 5210 Newman Rd, Williamsburg, VA 23188
Lat/Lon: 37.36511/-76.71519
Email: camp@williamsburgkoa.com
Web: www.williamsburgkoa.com

SEE AD TRAVEL SECTION PAGE 762

MILITARY PARK (Family Campground-Cheatham Annex)—(James City) *From jct I-64 (exit 242B) & Hwy 199: Go 2 mi E on Hwy 199 to FISC Cheatham Annex. On base.* FACILITIES: 19 sites, 19 full hkups, 1 pull-thrus, dump, laundry, ltd groc. RECREATION: 2 swim pools, boating, electric motors only, dock, lake/pond fishing, playground. No tents. Open all yr. Phone: (757) 887-7224.

(N) OUTDOOR WORLD-WILLIAMSBURG CAMPGROUND (CAMP RESORT) —(James City) *From jct I-64 (exit 231A) & Hwy 607: Go 1/4 mi S on Hwy 607, then 1/4 mi N on Rochambeau Rd (Hwy 30). Enter on L.*

FACILITIES: 155 sites, 132 full hkups, 17 W&E, (20/30/50 amps), 6 no hkups, 30 pull-thrus, WiFi Instant Internet at site, family camping, tenting, RV's/park model rentals, RV storage, dump, laundry, full svc store, RV supplies, ice, picnic tables, patios, fire rings, grills, wood.

RECREATION: rec hall, rec room/area, pavilion, coin games, 2 swim pools, wading pool, hot tub, mini-golf, bsktball, playground, shuffleboard court shuffleboard court, activities, horseshoes, sports field, v-ball.

Pets welcome. Partial handicap access. Open all yr. Facilities fully operational Mid Mar - Mid Dec. Big rigs welcome. Rate in 2010 $45 per family. MC/VISA/DISC/AMEX. Member ARVC, VCA.

Phone: (757)566-3021
Address: 4301 Rochambeau Dr, Williamsburg, VA 23188
Lat/Lon: 37.38827/-76.76772
Web: 1000trails.com

SEE AD ABINGDON PAGE 769

WINCHESTER—B-4

(SW) CANDY HILL CAMPGROUND—(Frederick) *N'bound from jct I-81 (exit 310) & Hwy 37: Go 5-1/2 mi N on Hwy 37, then 1 blk W on US 50, then 1/4 mi S on Ward Ave. S'bound from jct I-81 (exit 317) & Hwy 37: Go 4 mi S on Hwy 37, then 1 blk W on US 50. Enter on L.*

◊◊◊◊FACILITIES: 103 sites, typical site width 30 ft, 70 full hkups, 33 W&E, (30/50 amps), 50 amps ($), 25 pull-thrus, cable TV, WiFi Instant Internet at site ($), family camping, tenting, cabins, RV storage, dump, laundry, groceries, RV supplies, LP gas by weight/by meter, ice, picnic tables, fire rings, wood.

◊◊◊◊RECREATION: rec hall, rec room/area, coin games, swim pool, golf nearby, bsktball, 8 bike rentals, playground, shuffleboard court shuffleboard court, horseshoes, sports field, v-ball, local tours.

WINCHESTER—Continued
CANDY HILL CAMPGROUND—Continued

Pets welcome. Partial handicap access. Open all yr. Big rigs welcome. Escort to site. Clubs welcome. Rate in 2010 $35-50 for 4 persons. MC/VISA. Member ARVC, VCA.

Phone: (800)462-0545
Address: 165 Ward Ave, Winchester, VA 22602
Lat/Lon: 39.18746/-78.20373
Email: reservations@candyhill.com
Web: www.candyhill.com

SEE AD THIS PAGE

WOOLWINE—E-2

(E) Deer Run Campground—(Patrick) *From jct Hwy-8 & Hwy-40: Go 6 mi NE on Hwy-40, then 1-1/4 mi E on Hwy-622. Enter on R.* ◊◊◊FACILITIES: 121 sites, typical site width 35 ft, 28 ft max RV length, 52 full hkups, 69 W&E, (20/30/50 amps), 5 pull-thrus, family camping, tenting, dump, laundry, ltd groc. ◊◊◊RECREATION: swim pool, pond fishing, play equipment. Pets welcome, quantity restrict. Open all yr. Facilities fully operational May 1 - Oct 31. Rate in 2010 $24-27 for 2 persons. Member ARVC, VCA. Phone: (276)930-1235.

WYTHEVILLE—E-1

(E) FORT CHISWELL RV PARK—(Wythe) *From jct I-81 (exit 80) & US 52: Go 1/4 mi S on US 52. Enter on L.*

◊◊◊◊FACILITIES: 92 sites, typical site width 35 ft, 92 full hkups, (20/30/50 amps), 81 pull-thrus, cable TV, WiFi Instant Internet at site, WiFi Internet central location, family camping, cabins, RV storage, dump, non-guest dump $, laundry, ltd groc, RV supplies, LP gas by meter, ice, picnic tables, grills.

◊◊◊◊RECREATION: rec hall, rec room/area, pavilion, coin games, swim pool, pond fishing, fishing supplies, golf nearby, bsktball, playground, sports field, v-ball.

Pets welcome. No tents. Open all yr. Big rigs welcome. Clubs welcome. Rate in 2010 $29.50 for 2 persons. MC/VISA.

Phone: (276)637-6868
Address: 312 Ft Chiswell Rd., Max Meadows, VA 24360
Lat/Lon: 36.94012/-80.94348
Email: fcrv@psknet.com
Web: www.fcrvpark.com

SEE AD NEXT PAGE

(N) JEFFERSON NATIONAL FOREST (Stony Fork Campground)—(Wythe) *From jct I-77 & Hwy-717: Go 4 mi W on Hwy-717.* FACILITIES: 49 sites, 35 ft max RV length, 12 W&E, 21 E, (30/50 amps), 16 no hkups, tenting, dump. RECREATION: river fishing. Partial handicap access. Open Apr 1 - Oct 31. Phone: (540)228-5551.

(NE) KOA-WYTHEVILLE KAMPGROUND—(Wythe) *From jct I-77/I-81 (exit 77): Go 1 block S on exit road, then 1/4 mi W on Chapman Rd, then 1/4 mi S on Blue Sky Dr, then 1/4 mi W on KOA Rd. Enter at end.*

◊◊◊◊FACILITIES: 111 sites, typical site width 25 ft, 33 full hkups, 58 W&E, (20/30/50 amps), 20 no hkups, 50 pull-thrus, cable TV, WiFi Instant Internet at site, WiFi Internet central location, family camping, tenting, cabins, RV storage, dump, laundry, groceries, RV supplies, LP gas by weight/by meter, ice, picnic tables, fire rings, wood.

◊◊◊◊◊RECREATION: rec hall, rec room/area, equipped pavilion, coin games, swim pool, pond fishing, mini-golf, ($), golf nearby, bsktball, playground, shuffleboard court 2 shuffleboard courts, activities, horseshoes, sports field, hiking trails, v-ball. Rec open to public.

Pets welcome. Open all yr. Big rigs welcome. Clubs welcome. Green Friendly. Rate in 2010 $27.77-51.70 for 2 persons. MC/VISA/DISC/AMEX/Debit. Member ARVC, VCA. KOA discount.

Phone: (276)228-2601
Address: 231 KOA Rd, Wytheville, VA 24382
Lat/Lon: 36.93279/-81.00477
Email: wythevillekoa@embarqmail.com
Web: www.wythevillekoa.com

SEE AD NEXT PAGE

Woodall's Directory is split, East/West. You can buy a Directory with all of North America, or you can buy only the Eastern or Western editions. Browse our bookstore at www.woodalls.com/shop for more details.

We all know that one of the best parts about camping is the food! Woodall's Campsite Cookbook is a classic cookbook containing such fun campsite and RV recipes as Roadside Spuds, The Fastest Sauce in the West, and Hairy Squares (which taste a lot better than they sound!) To order your copy go to www.woodalls.com/shop.

• 30/50 Amp Service • Laundry • Pavilion • Free Cable TV • Large Bathhouse • RV Supplies • LP Gas • Wi-Fi • Enjoy Fishing, Walking Trails, Game Room

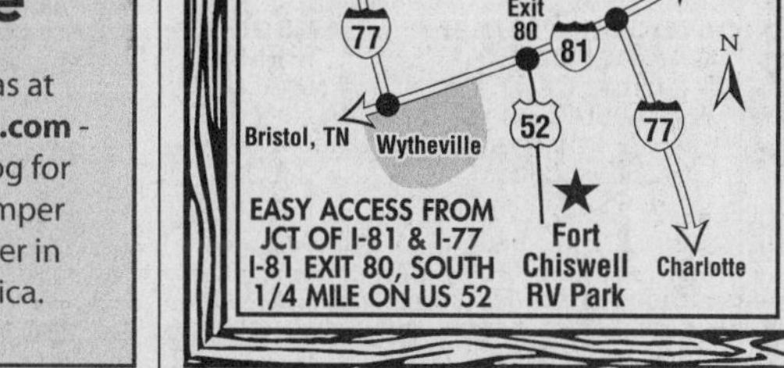

Please Call Cabins

(276) 637-6868

312 Ft. Chiswell Rd.

Max Meadows, VA 24360

www.fcrvpark.com

e-mail: fcrv@psknet.com

Specializing In All Your Outdoor & Camping Needs!

FANTASTIC RECREATION!

- Family Fun Center
- 50' Water Slide
- Heated Pool
- Gift Shop
- Kafe
- Mini-Golf
- LP-Gas
- Batting Cage
- Fishing Pond
- Music & More!

Woodall's Rated
FAC: ◇◇◇◇
REC: ◇◇◇◇◇

See listing at Wytheville, VA

Wytheville KOA

"Only One Minute off I-81/I-77 Exit #77"

FREE WI-FI • FREE CABLE • 30/50 Amp Pull-Thrus

...Near Canoe & Kayak, Rafting, Tubing, Boating, Go Carts, Gem Mining, Golf, Birding, Horseback Riding, Hiking & Bike Trails

Reservations: 1-800-562-3380

Information: 276-228-2601

231 KOA Road • WYTHEVILLE, VA 24382

Pet Playground

Large/Small Pet Areas

Deluxe Cottages & Kabins

Great people. Great camping.™
koa.com

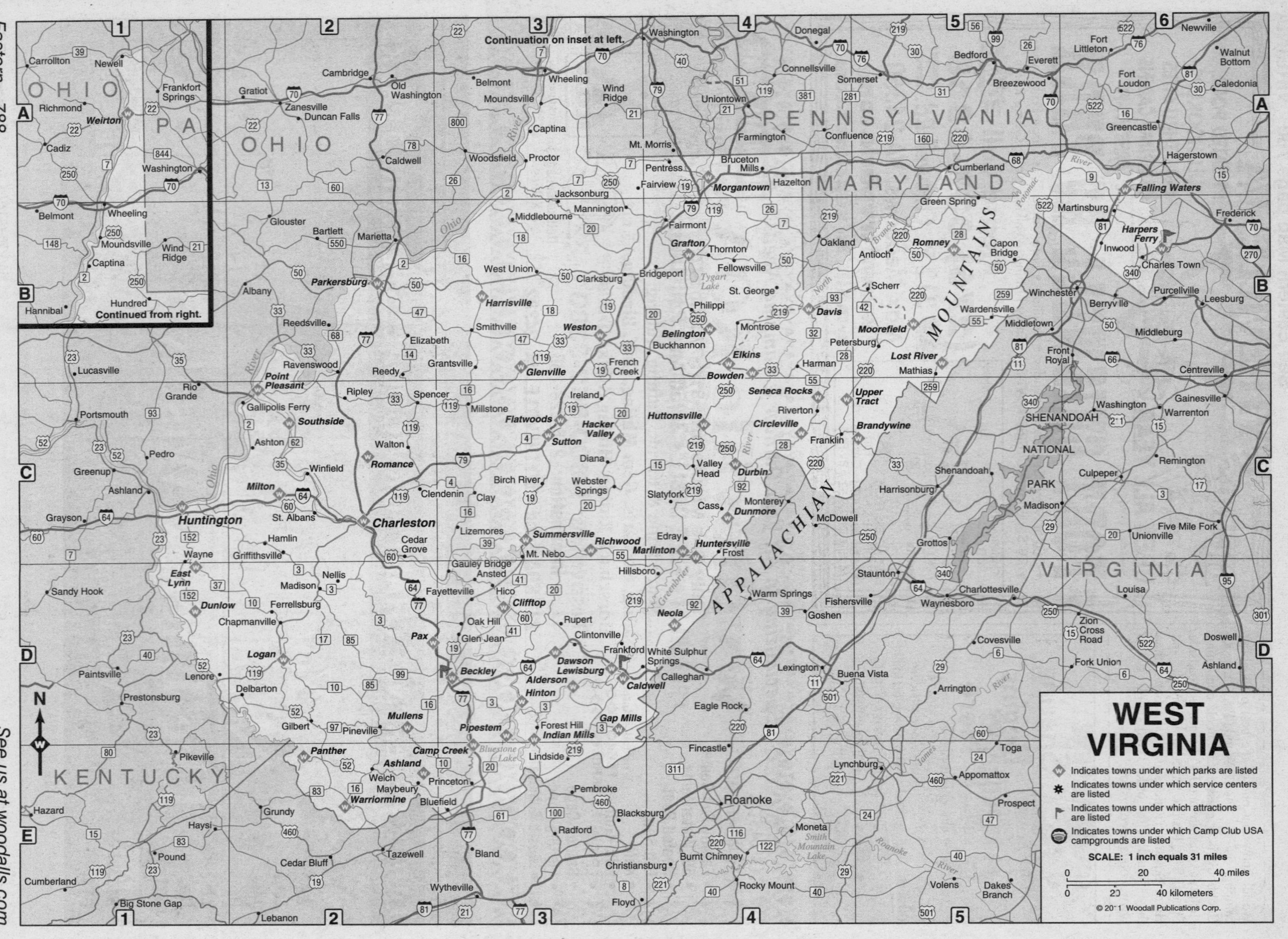

WEST VIRGINIA
Indicates towns under which parks are listed
Indicates towns under which service centers are listed
Indicates towns under which attractions are listed
Indicates towns under which Camp Club USA campgrounds are listed
SCALE: 1 inch equals 31 miles
0 20 40 miles
0 20 40 kilometers
© 20'1 Woodall Publications Corp.
PENNSYLVANIA
MARYLAND
OHIO
PA
VIRGINIA
KENTUCKY
APPALACHIAN
MOUNTAINS
SHENANDOAH NATIONAL PARK
Continuation on inset at left.
Continued from right.
Weirton
Falling Waters
Harpers Ferry
Morgantown
Grafton
Romney
Davis
Moorefield
Lost River
Belington
Elkins
Bowden
Seneca Rocks
Upper Tract
Brandywine
Huttonsville
Circleville
Durbin
Dunmore
Huntersville
Marlinton
Neola
Parkersburg
Harrisville
Weston
Glenville
Point Pleasant
Southside
Flatwoods
Sutton
Hacker Valley
Romance
Milton
Huntington
Charleston
Summersville
Richwood
East Lynn
Dunlow
Clifftop
Logan
Pax
Beckley
Dawson
Lewisburg
Alderson
Hinton
Caldwell
Mullens
Pipestem
Indian Mills
Gap Mills
Panther
Camp Creek
Ashland
Warriormine

TRAVEL SECTION West Virginia

TIME ZONE

West Virginia is in the Eastern Time Zone.

TOPOGRAPHY

West Virginia encompasses an area of 24,070 sq. miles; 75% of the area is forested. The terrain of the state is rugged, ranging from hilly to mountainous. The highest peaks (some over 4,000 feet) are located in the Allegheny Plateau in the east and cover about two-thirds of the state.

TEMPERATURE

West Virginia experiences four distinct seasons. January temperatures range from 24° to 41° and July temperatures range from 65° to 86°. Annual precipitation averages 40 to 60 inches per year.

TRAVEL & TOURISM INFO

State Agency:
West Virginia Division of Tourism
90 MacCorkle Ave. SW
South Charleston, WV 25303
(800/CALL-WVA)
www.wvtourism.com

Regional Agencies:
Cabell-Huntington CVB
210 11th St
Huntington, WV 25701
(800/635-6329 or 304/525-7333)
www.wvvisit.org

Jefferson Co. CVB
37 Washington Court
Harpers Ferry, WV 25425
(866/HELLO-WV or 304/535-2627)
www.hello-wv.com

Marion Co. CVB
110 Adams St.
P.O. Box 58
Fairmont, WV 26554
(304/368-1123)
www.marioncvb.com

Martinsburg/Berkeley Co. CVB
115 N. Queen St.
Martinsburg, WV 25401
(800/498-2386)
www.travelwv.com

Morgantown CVB
68 Donley St.
Morgantown, WV 26501
(800/458-7373)
www.tourmorgantown.com

Randolph Co. CVB
1035 N. Randolph Ave.
Elkins, WV 26241
(304/636-2780)
www.randolphcountywv.com

Southern West Virginia CVB
1406 Harper Rd.
Beckley, WV 25801
(800/847-4898)
www.visitwv.com

Tucker County CVB
P.O. Box 565
William Ave. & 4th St.

BUSINESSES OFFERING

	Things to See & Do	RV Sales	RV Service
BECKLEY			
Beckley Exhibition Coal Mine	⚑		
HARPERS FERRY			
River Riders	⚑		
LEWISBURG			
State Fair of West Virginia	⚑		

QUICK REFERENCE CHART FOR WOODALL'S FEATURED PARKS

	Green Friendly	RV Lots for Sale	Park Models-Onsite Ownership	Park Membership for Sale	Big Rigs Welcome	Internet Friendly	Pets Welcome
BECKLEY							
Lake Stephens Campground & Marina (Raleigh County Park)					▲		■
HARPERS FERRY							
Harpers Ferry/Civil War Battlefields KOA	🍃				▲	●	■
LEWISBURG							
State Fair of West Virginia Campground					▲	●	■
MILTON							
Huntington Fox Fire KOA					▲	●	■
ROMANCE							
Rippling Waters Church of God Campground					▲		■

Green Friendly 🍃; RV Lots for Sale ✖; Park Models/Onsite Onwership ✱; Park Memberships for Sale ✔; Big Rigs Welcome ▲; Internet Friendly ●; Internet Friendly-WiFi ●; Pets Welcome ■

Davis, WV 26260
(800/782-2775)
www.canaanvalley.org

West Virginia Mountain Highlands
P.O. Box 1456
Elkins, WV 26241
(877/WVA-MTNS)
www.mountainhighlands.com

Local Agencies:

Berkeley Springs CVB
127 Fairfax St.
Berkeley Springs, WV 25411
(800/447-8797)
www.berkeleysprings.com

Greater Bridgeport CVB
164 W. Main St.
Bridgeport, WV 26330
(800/368-4324)
www.greater-bridgeport.com

Greater Clarksburg CVB
P.O. Box 1226
Clarksburg, WV 26302
(304/622-2157)
www.cityofclarksburgwv.com

Charleston CVB
200 Civic Center Dr.
Charleston, WV 25301
(304/344-5075)
www.charlestonwv.com
(800/238-9488)
www.southcharlestonwv.org

Summersville CVB
1 Old Wilderness Rd, P.O. Box 231
Summersville, WV 26651
(304/872-3722)
www.summersvillecvb.com

Wheeling CVB
1401 Main St.
Wheeling, WV 26003
(304/233-7709)
www.wheelingcvb.com

RECREATIONAL INFO

Fishing & Hunting: For hunting and fishing licenses, call the West Virginia Div. of Natural Resources at (304/558-2758). For an online hunting or fishing license, contact: www.wvhunt.com/wizard/hflw000.asp

Hiking: West Virginia Scenic Trails Assn., (800/CALL WVA). www.wvscenictrails.org

Skiing: www.westvirginiaski.com

Whitewater Rafting: One of West Virginia's most popular pastimes provides a wonderful ride for experienced rafters as well as family and friends eager to relax and enjoy a gentle float trip. For more information, **West Virginia Professional River Outfitters Association**, P.O. Box 32, Fayetteville, West Virginia 25840 (877/4-A-WVPRO) www.americasbestwhitewater.com/

SHOPPING

Appalachian Gallery, 44 High St., Morgantown, WV. (304/296-0163) Finely handcrafted pottery, glass, basketry, jewelry and art by West Virginia artists.

Berdines 5 & Dime, Harrisville. You'll find almost anything at "America's Oldest 5 & Dime Store." 106 N. Court St., Harrisville, WV (304/643-2217).

Berkeley Springs is a treasure seeker's delight. Boutiques and specialty shops such as The **Bath House Day Spa and Bath Shop**, **Mountain Laurel Gallery** and **Jules** are packed with gifts, crafts and collectibles.

Black Gold Coal Crafts, Beaver. Specializing in crafts, collectibles and gifts made out of West Virginia coal. 257 Wayne St. (304/255-3110).

Centre Market Historic District, 2200 Market St., Wheeling, WV (304/234-3878). Unique shopping experience in a restored 1850s historic district. Antiques, art, handcrafts and restaurants.

The Fenton Glass Company in Williamson ranks among the world's foremost producers of handmade art glass. It is renowned for innovative glass colors as well as hand-painted decorations on pressed and blown glassware. In Milton you can find another West Virginia glass company, Blenko Glass, creating hand-blown glassware as well.

MountainMade Artisan Gallery & Country Store, 100 Front St., Circle Douglas Rd., Thomas, WV (877/686-6233). Shop for fine arts and crafts by 400 West Virginia artisans at retail galleries.

Poplar Forest, 82 Skidmore Lane, Sutton, WV. (304/765-3995) Craft cooperative gallery representing over 170 juried artists and craftsmen.

DESTINATIONS

Although small, this state has quite a bit to offer the outdoor enthusiast with 2,000 miles of mountain streams, perfect for fishing, kayaking, rafting and canoeing. From Civil War reenactments to Appalachian music and festivals, West Virginia offers some wonderful adventures to a variety of visitors.

NORTHERN PANHANDLE REGION

The Northern Panhandle region is an area steeped in history - from the ancient Adena people who once roamed this land, and the pioneers who traveled west along the National Road, to the debates during the Civil War that gave birth to this state. This vibrant history is still visible in many corners of this region today.

Benwood. The **Castle Halloween** is a totally unique museum with over 15,000 Halloween related artifacts from 1860 to the present.

Moundsville. The **Fostoria Glass Museum** celebrates the history and importance of quality glass making. Also in Moundsville is one of the largest and most famous Adena burial mounds at **Grave Creek Mound Archeology Complex.**

Wheeling. Once a pre-Revolutionary outpost, this river front town welcomes visitors with major recreational opportunities, historic areas and several days' worth of antiquing. Check out **Oglebay Park Resort's** 3 golf courses, nature center, boating, hiking, swimming, garden center, skiing and science theater. **Oglebay Good Zoo & Benedum Planetarium** offers 80 species of animals nestled in 30 acres of flowers, trees, hills and valleys. Learn about some of the most exciting wonders of nature and the universe at the on-site planetarium.

The Point Overlook Museum offers a full view of downtown Wheeling and the **Wheeling Suspension Bridge**, overlooking 12 miles of the Ohio River, 2 states and 3 counties. **Independence Hall** was built in 1859 as a customhouse, post office and federal court. Today, it houses a museum and is part of the Civil War Discovery Trail. The renovated **Wheeling Artisan Center** in the heart of downtown features arts and crafts, interactive exhibits, shows and festivals.

MOUNTAINEER COUNTRY REGION

This area is a wealth of woods, lakes, streams and trails, making it the perfect destination for outdoor enthusiasts. An intriguing mix of pioneer forts, covered bridges, ethnic foods, university sports, and antiques, this region would satisfy even the most fickle visitor.

Allegheny Trail, Morgantown. Pick up a guide for this 270-mile trail through state parks, forests and wilderness areas.

Coopers Rock State Forest, Morgantown. The magnificent West Virginia mountains and the beautiful Cheat River Gorge can be seen from the unusual lookout site atop a huge rock formation 1,200 feet above the river. Mountain biking, hiking, picnicking and camping are favorite activities in the rugged, boulder-strewn hardwood forest—a spectacular site in the fall.

Tygart Lake State Park, Grafton, is home to an 11-mile lake. Choose from scuba diving, fishing, boating, or swimming. Nearby there are hiking trails, a playground, a golf course, game courts and a seasonal recreation program.

Whitewater Trips. Whether you're an experienced rafter ready to take on the Class IV and V spring rapids of the Cheat and Tygart rivers, or just looking for a relaxing float down a scenic river, outfitters based in Rowlesburg and Albright can guide you.

EASTERN PANHANDLE REGION

This region is home to the restored 18th century town of Harpers Ferry, a once thriving town that was ravaged by the Civil War. This is also the region known as the starting point of Lewis & Clark. Being only an hour from the nation's capital, this area has become a favorite of those looking to get out of the city, and into the laid back pace of the Panhandle.

C&O Canal National Historical Park, located along the Potomac River. This former towpath canal was used to transport cargo from Cumberland, Md., to Georgetown in the District of Columbia, during the latter half of the 19th century. The canal runs 184.5 miles from DC to Cumberland.

Washington Heritage Trail. This designated Scenic Byway is a 112-mile loop driving tour throughout the Eastern Handle. Much of this area was surveyed by young Washington and he and his family owned thousands of acres in the region.

Harpers Ferry National Historic Park, Harpers Ferry. The town of Harpers Ferry was a lookout point for Colonial soldiers during the Revolutionary War. This was also the site where abolitionist John Brown staged his notorious raid on the federal arsenal and was later hanged for treason in nearby Charles Town.

POTOMAC HIGHLANDS REGION

Thanks to the natural snow belt created by the Allegheny Front, and plenty of snowmaking technology, this area is open for business for those looking for some great skiing, and other winter sports. A veritable skier's paradise, this area boasts 56 slopes and trails, and caters to those off all levels of experience.

Blackwater Falls State Park. Plunging from a height of five stories, the Blackwater River cuts a deep canyon that dominates this beautiful, densely wooded park.

Dolly Sods Wilderness Area. 10,200 acres of the Monongahela National Forest lies on a high plateau on Allegheny Mountain. Bogs, beaver ponds, streams and 25 miles of hiking trails are waiting to be explored.

Harper's Old Country Store, Seneca Rocks. In operation since 1902, this general store's appearance hasn't changed much over the years. Enjoy the majestic view of Seneca Rocks, against which the building is set.

Helvetia Historic District retains much of the character of the 19th century settlement of Swiss immigrants. Includes the Helvetia Museum, Hutte Restaurant, Beekeeper Inn, Cheese Haus and Woodshop.

Monongahela National Forest contains nearly 900,000 acres of outdoor fun. Travelers enjoy hunting, fishing and 850 miles of hiking trails. Special areas within the forest include Cranberry Area, Spruce Knob-Seneca Rocks National Recreation Area and Dolly Sods.

National Radio Astronomy Observatory at the Green Bank Science Center offers guided tours year-round and hands-on exhibits. Home of the world's largest fully steerable dish.

Potomac Eagle, Romney. Ride the rails along the south branch of the Potomac River to view bald eagles as well as mountain scenery and wilderness forests.

Seneca Caverns, Riverton. These caves are located in the beautiful German Valley and enclose the "Grand Ballroom."

Spruce Knob-Seneca Rocks National Recreation Area. Two prime recreation areas offer beautiful scenery surrounding fantastic rock formations. Stop by the visitor center for terrific views, exhibits and an excellent audio-visual presentation on rock climbing.

Smoke Hole Caverns, Seneca Rocks. See the world's largest ribbon stalactite.

MOUNTAIN LAKES REGION

This is a peaceful region of forested lakes, rivers, streams, and forested mountains. This area, much like the rest of the state, is rich in Civil War history, and is home to Stonewall Jackson's boyhood home, and Bulltown and Carnifex Ferry Battlefield State Park.

Cranberry Glades Botanical Area in Richwood is a unique open bog ecosystem within a forest including small Arctic tundra remnants, rare plants, wildlife and scenic views.

Stonewall's Home, Jackson's Mill. Part of the Civil War Discovery Trail, Confederate General Thomas "Stonewall" Jackson's boyhood home is now a year-round conference center and historical district.

Summersville Lake & Wildlife Management Area, Summersville. West Virginia's largest lake offers boating, swimming, fishing, scuba diving and waterskiing.

West Virginia State Wildlife Center, French Creek. Formerly French Creek Game Farm, this renovated center is home to a variety of wildlife native to West Virginia, including deer, elk, bald eagle, wild boar, river otter, mountain lion, bobcat, fox and bear.

NEW RIVER/ GREENBRIER VALLEY REGION

Each year, thousands come to whitewater raft, scale the walls of the ancient New River Gorge, or hike, bike, or ride the miles and miles of trail throughout the New River/Greenbrier Valley. This area is also rich in coal mining history, and visitors are sure to see a few abandoned mining towns as they explore the region.

Appalachian Trail. The famous Maine to Georgia footpath follows the crest of Peters Mountain for roughly 12 miles. Monroe and Jefferson counties are the only two West Virginia counties that contain a portion of the trail. This is America's first National Scenic Trail, stretches from Katahdin in Maine to Springer Mountain in Georgia. It was originally conceived as a greenway between these states in the 1920s and has become the most popular trail for day-hikers and thruhikers alike that want to see the scenic wonders of the Appalachian Mountains. This 2,160-mile well maintained, hiking-only trail has shelters conveniently spaced for overnight stays.

Beckley. After a recent expansion, the largest and most popular coal heritage destination in the region now offers a replica company store that houses a museum, visitor center and gift shop. Visit the **Exhibition Coal Mine**, where real miners take visitors for a 45-minute journey to the days of long ago. The **Coal Museum** is next door, portraying the history of this local industry. Filled with artifacts and photographs, this 3-room, furnished coal company house from the turn of the century is on the property.

ANNUAL EVENTS

JANUARY

Festival of Food and Wines, Morgantown.

APRIL

Glass Fest, Weston; Adventure Film & Photo Festival, Morgantown; Spring Mountain Festival, Petersburg; West Virginia Dance Festival, Charleston; Dogwood Arts & Crafts Festival, Huntington; Stonewall Resort Ramp Festival, Roanoke.

MAY

Strawberry Festival, Buckhannon; Scottish Festival & Celtic Gathering, Bridgeport; Spring Fest, Franklin; Battle of Rowlesburg Reenactment, Rowlesburg; Mullens Dogwood Festival, Mullens; Annual Bluegrass Festival, Cairo; Strawberry Festival, Buckhannon; Buffalo Heritage Days, Buffalo; Battle of Lewisburg Reenactment, Lewisburg; Elizabethtown Festival, Elizabethtown; Dandelion Festival, White Sulphur Springs; Three Rivers Festival, Fairmont; Wood Chopping Festival, Webster Springs; Snowshoe Mountain Memorial Day Celebration, Snowshoe; Wine & Arts Festival, Martinsburg; Matewan Massacre Reenactment, Matewan; Blue & Gray Reunion, Philippi; Cole Chevy Mountain Festival, Bluefield.

JUNE

Calhoun County Wood Festival, Grantsville; Gospel Jubilee, Ripley; Rail Trail Festival, Cairo; Ronceverte River Festival, Ronceverte; Woodland Indian Gathering, Fort Randolph; Heritage Arts & Crafts Festival, Charles Town; Lower West Fork River Fest, Worthington; Coal Festival, Madison; State Folk Festival, Glenville; FestivALL, Charleston; Hometown Mountain Heritage Festival, Amsted; Old Central City Days Festival, Huntington.

All privately owned campgrounds personally inspected by WOODALL'S Representatives

Dave and Femke Durham

ALDERSON—D-3

(E) Greenbrier River Campground—(Greenbrier) *From jct I-64 (exit 161) & Hwy 12: Go 10 mi S on Hwy 12, then 4 mi E on Hwy 63. Enter on R.* ◆◆◆◆FACILITIES: 50 sites, typical site width 37 ft, 37 full hkups, (20/30/50 amps), 13 no hkups, tenting, dump, laundry. ◆◆◆RECREATION: river swim, boating, canoeing, ramp, river fishing. Pets welcome. Partial handicap access. Open Apr 15 - Oct 15. Rate in 2010 $27.45-30.50 for 2 persons. Phone: (800)775-2203.

ASHLAND—E-2

(NW) Ashland West Virginia ATV Resort—(McDowell) *From jct I-77 (exit 1) & US 52 (Truck): Go 26 mi N on US 52, then (very sharp turn), 7 mi N on County Rd 17. Enter on L.* ◆◆◆◆FACILITIES: 54 sites, 23 full hkups, 24 W&E, (30/50 amps), 7 no hkups, 26 pull-thrus, tenting, dump, laundry, groceries. ◆◆◆RECREATION: playground. Pets welcome, breed restrict. Partial handicap access. Open all yr. Big rigs welcome. Rate in 2010 $23-49 for 4 persons. Phone: (304)862-3795.

BECKLEY—D-3

(W) BECKLEY EXHIBITION COAL MINE—*From jct I-77/64 (exit 44) & Hwy 3: Go 1-1/2 mi E on Hwy 3, then 1 mi N on Ewart Ave. Enter on R.* Tours through a real coal mine & mining museum guided by veteran certified miners. View coal mining from earliest manual stages to modern mechanized operation. Youth Museum. Restrooms available. City campground adjacent. Open Apr - Nov. Tours available 10 a.m.-6:00 p.m. MC/VISA/Debit.

WELCOME

Phone: (304)256-1747
Address: 513 Ewart AVe, Beckley, WV 25802
Lat/Lon: 37.78476/-81.19705
Email: info@beckleymine.com
Web: www.beckleymine.com

SEE AD THIS PAGE

(E) BECKLEY EXHIBITION COAL MINE CAMPGROUND—(Raleigh) *From jct I-77/I-64 (exit 44): Go 1-1/2 mi E on Hwy 3, then 6 blocks N on Ewart Ave. Entrance to campground on Willis St. (Caution - Narrow entry road, Steep hill with sharp turn at top). Enter on R.*

WELCOME

FACILITIES: 17 sites, 17 full hkups, (30 amps), tenting, picnic tables, fire rings, grills.

RECREATION: swim pool, bsktball, playground, tennis, horseshoes, sports field, hiking trails, v-ball.

Open Apr 1 - Nov 1.

BECKLEY—Continued
BECKLEY EXHIBITION COAL MINE CAMPGROUND—Continued

Phone: (304)256-1747
Address: 513 Ewart Ave, Beckley, WV 25802
Lat/Lon: 37.784889/-81.195417
Email: info@beckleymine.com
Web: www.beckleymine.com

SEE AD THIS PAGE

(W) LAKE STEPHENS CAMPGROUND & MARINA (Raleigh County Park)—(Raleigh) *From jct I-77/64 (exit 44) & Hwy 3: Go 9 mi W on Hwy 3. Enter on R.*

WELCOME

FACILITIES: 128 sites, typical site width 20 ft, 100 full hkups, (30/50 amps), 28 no hkups, some extd stay sites (summer), 100 pull-thrus, family camping, tenting, cabins, laundry, ltd groc, RV supplies, LP gas by weight/by meter, marine gas, ice, picnic tables, patios, fire rings, wood.

RECREATION: rec hall, rec room/area, pavilion, coin games, lake swim, boating, canoeing, kayaking, ramp, dock, lake fishing, fishing supplies, golf nearby, bsktball, playground, tennis, horseshoes, sports field, hiking trails, v-ball. Rec open to public.

Pets welcome. Partial handicap access. Open Apr 15 - Oct 15. Big rigs welcome. Clubs welcome. MC/VISA/DISC/AMEX/Debit.

Phone: (304)934-5323
Address: 1400 Lake Stephens Rd, Surveyon, WV 25932
Lat/Lon: 37.77076/-81.30683
Email: reservations@lakestephenswv.com
Web: www.lakestephenswv.com

SEE AD THIS PAGE

BELINGTON—B-4

AUDRA SP—(Barbour) *From jct US 250 & CR 11: Go 9 mi W on CR 11.* FACILITIES: 67 sites, 67 no hkups, 50 pull-thrus, family camping, tenting, dump, laundry. RECREATION: river swim, playground. Open mid Apr - Oct. Phone: (304)457-1162.

BOWDEN—B-4

(C) Revelle's River Resort—(Randolph) *From jct US 219 & US 33E: Go 10 mi E on US 33, then 200 yards N (left) to Faulkner Rd, then 1-1/4 mi E on Faulkner Rd. Enter on L.* ◆◆◆FACILITIES: 121 sites, typical site width 38 ft, 107 full hkups, 10 W&E, (20/30/50 amps), 4 no hkups, family camping, tenting, dump, laundry, ltd groc. ◆◆◆RECREATION: river swim, river fishing, play equipment. Pets welcome. Open all yr. Facilities fully operational Apr 1 - Nov 1. Big rigs welcome. Rate in 2010 $26-32 for 4 persons. Phone: (304)636-0023.

BRANDYWINE—C-5

(E) GEORGE WASHINGTON NF (Brandywine Lake Campground)—(Pendleton) *From town: Go 2 mi E on US 33. Enter on R.* FACILITIES: 34 sites, 22 ft max RV length, 34 no hkups, tenting, dump, ltd groc. RECREATION: lake swim, boating, electric motors only, canoeing, lake fishing. Partial handicap access. Open May 15 - Dec 10. Facilities fully operational May 15 - Sep 30. Phone: (703)828-2591.

CALDWELL—D-3

(S) GREENBRIER SF—(Greenbrier) *From jct I-64 (exit 175) & Harts Run Rd: Go 2 mi S on Harts Run Rd. Enter on R.* FACILITIES: 16 sites, 16 E, (30 amps), family camping, tenting. RECREATION: swim pool, play equipment. Partial handicap access. Open Mid Apr - Nov 30. Facilities fully operational Memorial Day - Labor Day. Phone: (304)536-1944.

CAMP CREEK—E-3

CAMP CREEK SP—(Mercer) *From I-77 (exit 20): Follow brown signs 2 mi into State Park, then continue 2 mi until Camp Creek State Park & Forest sign. Enter at end.* FACILITIES: 40 sites, 26 E, (30 amps), 14 no hkups, family camping, tenting, dump, laundry. RECREATION: stream fishing, play equipment. Partial handicap access. Open Mid Apr - Oct. Phone: (304)425-9481.

CHARLESTON—C-2

KANAWHA SF CAMPGROUND—(Kanawha) *From jct I-64 (exit 58A) & US 119: Go S on US 119, then E on Oakwood Rd, then follow signs for 6 mi.* FACILITIES: 46 sites, 26 ft max RV length, 25 W&E, (20 amps), 21 no hkups, family camping, tenting, dump, laundry. RECREATION: swim pool, pond fishing, playground. Open Mid Apr - Nov. Phone: (304)558-3500.

CIRCLEVILLE—C-4

MONONGAHELA NF (Spruce Knob Lake Campground) —(Randolph) *From town: Go 5 mi N on Hwy 28, then 4 mi W on CR 33/4, then 14 mi W on FR 112, then 1 mi NE on FR 1.* FACILITIES: 42 sites, 30 ft max RV length, 42 no hkups, 1 pull-thrus, tenting. RECREATION: boating, no motors, canoeing, ramp, lake/stream fishing. Partial handicap access. Open Apr 17 - Oct 12. Phone: (304)257-4488.

CLIFFTOP—D-3

(N) BABCOCK SP—(Fayette) *From jct US-60 & Hwy-41: Go 4 mi SW on Hwy-41.* FACILITIES: 52 sites, 26 E, (20/30 amps), 26 no hkups, family camping, tenting, dump, laundry. RECREATION: swim pool, boating, no motors, dock, lake/stream fishing, playground. Partial handicap access. Open mid Apr - Oct 15. Phone: (304)438-3004.

DAVIS—B-4

(SW) BLACKWATER FALLS SP—(Tucker) *From jct Hwy 32 & CR 29: Go 2 mi SW on CR 29. Enter on R.* FACILITIES: 65 sites, 25 ft max RV length, 30 E, (30 amps), 35 no hkups, 39 pull-thrus, family camping, tenting, dump, laundry. RECREATION: lake swim, boating, no motors, dock, river fishing, play equipment. Open Last Weekend of Apr - Oct 31. Phone: (304)259-5216.

(S) CANAAN VALLEY RESORT PARK (SP)—(Tucker) *From town: Go 9 mi S on Hwy 32.* FACILITIES: 34 sites, 34 full hkups, (30 amps), 19 pull-thrus, family camping, tenting, dump, laundry, ltd groc. RECREATION: 2 swim pools, stream fishing, playground. Open all yr. Phone: (304)866-4121.

DAWSON—D-3

Summer Wind RV Overnight Park—(Greenbriar) *From jct I-64 (exit 150) & SR 29: Go 200 yds E on SR 29 (Morris Branch Rd), then 200 yds S on sr 27 (Lawn Rd). Enter on L.* ◆◆FACILITIES: 21 sites, typical site width 25 ft, 11 full hkups, 10 W&E, (30/50 amps), 21 pull-thrus, tenting, dump, laundry. Pets welcome. Partial handicap access. Open May 1 - Oct 15. Rate in 2010 $22-24 per vehicle. Phone: (540)520-9935.

DUNLOW—D-1

CABWAYLINGO SF—(Wayne) *From town: Go S on Hwy 152, then 4 mi SE at Missouri Branch on local hwy.* FACILITIES: 31 sites, 6 W&E, 5 E, 20 no hkups, family camping, tenting, dump, laundry. RECREATION: swim pool, playground. Open Apr 1 - Oct 31. Phone: (304)385-4255.

DUNMORE—C-4

(S) SENECA SF—(Pocahontas) *From town: Go 4 mi S on Hwy 28.* FACILITIES: 10 sites, 10 no hkups, family camping, tenting. RECREATION: lake/stream fishing, playground. Open Apr 1 - early Dec. Phone: (304)799-6213.

DURBIN—C-4

(C) East Fork Campground & Horse Stables—(Pocahontas) *From center of town (Main St & US 250): Go 150 yards E on US 250, then 100' S on River Rd. Enter on R.* ◆◆FACILITIES: 30 sites, typical site width 30 ft, 24 full hkups, 6 W&E, (20/30/50 amps), 10 pull-thrus, tenting, dump. ◆◆◆RECREATION: river/canoeing, river fishing, play equipment. Pets welcome. Open all yr. Facilities fully operational Apr - Oct. Rate in 2010 $20-25 for 2 persons.

Phone: (304)456-3101
Address: 123 Main St., Durbin, WV 26264
Lat/Lon: 38.54428/-79.82408
Email: eastfork_campground@yahoo.com
Web: eastforkcampgrounddurbin.com

EAST LYNN—D-1

(E) EAST FORK CAMPGROUND (COE-East Lynn Lake) —*From town: Go 11 mi E on Hwy 37 to East Fork.* FACILITIES: 170 sites, 170 E, tenting, dump. RECREATION: boating, canoeing, ramp, dock, lake/stream fishing, playground. Partial handicap access. Open May 13 - Oct 9. Phone: (304)849-2355.

ELKINS—B-4

(E) MONONGAHELA NF (Stuart Campground)—(Randolph) *From jct US 219 & US 33: Go 4 mi E on US 33, then 2 mi NE on Old US 33, then 1/2 mi NW on Hwy 6, then 1/4 mi NW on FR 391.* FACILITIES: 26 sites, 30 ft max RV length, 26 E, 2 pull-thrus, tenting. RECREATION: river swim. Partial handicap access. Open Apr 17 - Oct 12. Phone: (304)478-3251.

(S) Pegasus Farm Campground—(Randolph) *From jct US 33/US 55 & US 219/US 250: Go 2 mi S on US 219/US 250, then 3/4 mi E on Country Club Rd, then 1/2 mi right on Arnold Hill Rd. Enter on R (narrow entry road). Enter on R.* ◆◆◆FACILITIES: 24 sites, typical site width 60 ft, 12 full hkups, 5 W&E, 3 E, 4 no hkups, 1 pull-thrus, family camping, tenting. Pets welcome, breed restrict, size restrict, quantity restrict. Rate in 2010 $25-35 for 2 persons. Phone: (800)768-2087.

FALLING WATERS—A-6

(N) Falling Waters Campsite—(Berkeley) *From jct I-81 (exit 23) & US 11: Go 1 mi S on US 11. Enter on R.* ◆◆◆FACILITIES: 50 sites, typical site width 37 ft, 20 full hkups, 30 W&E, (20/30/50 amps), 25 pull-thrus, tenting, laundry. Pets welcome. Open all yr. Big rigs welcome. Rate in 2010 $35-37 for 2 persons. Phone: (304)274-2791. FMCA discount.

FLATWOODS—C-3

(S) Flatwoods KOA—(Braxton) *From jct I-79 (exit 67) & US 19: Go 100 yards E on US 19, then 1 block S on Hwy 4, then 1 block NE on Days Dr, then 1 block E on Sutton Ln (behind Day's Inn Hotel). Enter on R.* ◆◆◆◆FACILITIES: 50 sites, 50 full hkups, (30/50 amps), 39 pull-thrus, laundry. ◆◆◆RECREATION: 2 swim pools, playground. Pets welcome. Partial handicap access. No tents. Open all yr. Big rigs welcome. Rate in 2010 $38-42 per family. Phone: (866)700-7284. KOA discount.

GAP MILLS—D-3

(N) MONCOVE LAKE SP—(Monroe) *From town: Go 6 mi N on Hwy 8.* FACILITIES: 48 sites, 25 E, (30 amps), 23 no hkups, family camping, tenting, dump, ltd groc. RECREATION: lake swim, boating, 5 hp limit, dock, lake fishing, playground. Open Apr 15 - Dec 31. Facilities fully operational Memorial Day - Labor Day. Phone: (304)772-3450.

GLENVILLE—B-3

(SW) CEDAR CREEK SP—(Gilmer) *From town: Go 3 mi SW on US-33, then 6 mi S on secondary road.* FACILITIES: 63 sites, 48 W&E, 9 E, (30 amps), 6 no hkups, family camping, tenting, dump, laundry, ltd groc. RECREATION: swim pool, boating, no motors, pond/stream fishing, playground. Open mid Apr - Oct 15. Facilities fully operational Memorial Day - Labor Day. Phone: (304) 462-7158.

GRAFTON—B-4

(S) TYGART LAKE SP—(Taylor) *From town: Go 3 mi SE on CR-9, then follow signs 1 mi SW. Enter at end.* FACILITIES: 40 sites, 30 ft max RV length, 14 E, (30 amps), 26 no hkups, family camping, tenting, dump. RECREATION: lake swim, boating, ramp, lake fishing, playground. Open mid Apr - mid Nov. Phone: (304) 265-6144.

HACKER VALLEY—C-3

(N) HOLLY RIVER SP—(Webster) *From town: Go 1 mi N on Hwy 20.* FACILITIES: 88 sites, 88 E, (30 amps), 24 pull-thrus, family camping, tenting, dump, laundry. RECREATION: swim pool, river/stream fishing, playground. Partial handicap access. Open Mid Apr - Oct. Facilities fully operational May 28 - Sep 16. Phone: (304)493-6353.

HARPERS FERRY—B-6

(W) HARPERS FERRY CAMPGROUND (NOT VISITED)—(Jefferson) *From jct Hwy 230 & US 340: Go 3/4 mi N on US 340, then 500 yds S on Millvile Rd, then 400 yds NE on Allstadts Hill Rd. Enter on R.*

FACILITIES: 21 sites, 21 no hkups, tenting, non-flush toilets only.

RECREATION: canoeing, kayaking, float trips, river fishing.

Open all yr. Rate in 2010 $25-35 for 4 persons.

Phone: (800)326-7238
Address: 1816 Potomac st, Harpers Ferry, WV 25425
Lat/Lon: 39.31356/-77.67942
Email: trips@riverriders.com
Web: www.campingharpersferry.com

SEE AD THIS PAGE

(W) HARPERS FERRY/CIVIL WAR BATTLEFIELDS KOA—(Jefferson) *From jct Hwy 230 & US 340: Go 2 mi N on US 340, then 25 feet S on Harpers Ferry entrance road, then 1/4 mi W on Campground Rd. Enter at end.*

◆◆◆◆◆FACILITIES: 311 sites, typical site width 35 ft, 142 full hkups, 67 W&E, (20/30/50 amps), 50 amps ($), 102 no hkups, some extd stay sites (summer), 104 pull-thrus, cable TV, WiFi Instant Internet at site, phone Internet central location, family camping, tenting, cabins, RV storage, dump, non-guest dump $, laundry, groceries, RV supplies, LP gas by meter, ice, picnic tables, fire rings, grills, wood, controlled access.

◆◆◆◆◆RECREATION: rec hall, rec room/area, pavilion, coin games, swim pool, wading pool, float trips, fishing supplies, mini-golf, golf nearby, bsktball, 35 bike rentals, playground, activities, (wkends), horseshoes, sports field, hiking trails, v-ball, local tours. Rec open to public.

Pets welcome ($), breed restrict. Partial handicap access. Open all yr. off season rates. Big rigs welcome. Escort to site. Clubs welcome. Green Friendly. Rate in 2010 $25-55 for 2 persons. MC/VISA/DISC/Debit. ATM. Member ARVC. KOA discount.

Phone: (800)KOA-9497
Address: 343 Campground Rd, Harpers Ferry, WV 25425
Lat/Lon: 39.31606/-77.76258
Email: hfkoa@aol.com
Web: www.harpersferrykoa.com

SEE AD THIS PAGE

(W) RIVER RIDERS—*From jct Hwy 230 & US 340: Go 3/4 mi N on US 340, then 500 yds S on Millville Rd, then 400 yds NE on Allstadts Hill Rd. Enter on R.* Guided kayaking and whitewater rafting trips down the Shenandoah & Potomapo Rivers. Also tubing, canoe & biking trips. Front porch cafe & gift store. Primitive camping available ((800)326-RAFT. Open Mar 1 - Oct 31. MC/VISA/DISC/AMEX/Debit. ATM.

Phone: (304)535-2663
Address: 408 Allstadts Hill Rd, Harpers Ferry, WV 25425
Lat/Lon: 39.31638/-77.76930
Email: trips@riverriders.com
Web: www.riverriders.com

SEE AD THIS PAGE

HARRISVILLE—B-3

NORTH BEND SP—(Ritchie) *From town: Go 3 mi W on paved narrow park road.* FACILITIES: 49 sites, 25 ft max RV length, 26 E, (30 amps), 23 no hkups, family camping, tenting, dump. RECREATION: swim pool, river/pond fishing, playground. Partial handicap access. Open mid Apr - Oct 31. Phone: (304) 643-2391.

HINTON—D-3

(S) BLUESTONE SP—(Summers) *From town: Go 4 mi S on Hwy 20.* FACILITIES: 87 sites, 18 ft max RV length, 22 E, (30 amps), 65 no hkups, family camping, tenting, dump. RECREATION: swim pool, boating, canoeing, ramp, dock, lake/stream fishing, playground. Open mid Apr - Oct. Phone: (304)466-2805.

HUNTERSVILLE—C-4

(S) WATOGA SP—(Pocahontas) *From town: Go 10 mi S on Beaver Creek Rd.* FACILITIES: 100 sites, 31 E, (30 amps), 69 no hkups, family camping, tenting, dump, laundry, ltd groc. RECREATION: swim pool, boating, electric motors only, dock, lake/river/stream fishing, playground. Open Apr 1 - End of deer season in Dec. Phone: (304)799-4087.

HUNTINGTON—C-1

BEECH FORK SP—(Wayne) *From jct I-64 (exit 11) & Hwy 10: Go S on Hwy 10, then W on Hughes Branch Rd.* FACILITIES: 275 sites, 49 full hkups, 189 E, (20/30/50 amps), 37 no hkups, 49 pull-thrus, tenting, dump, laundry, ltd groc. RECREATION: boating, 10 hp limit, canoeing, ramp, lake fishing, playground. Open Apr 15 - Oct 15. Phone: (304)528-5794.

HUNTINGTON—Continued on next page

We all know that one of the best parts about camping is the food! Woodall's Campsite Cookbook is a classic cookbook containing such fun campsite and RV recipes as Roadside Spuds, The Fastest Sauce in the West, and Hairy Squares (which taste a lot better than they sound!) To order your copy go to www.woodalls.com/shop.

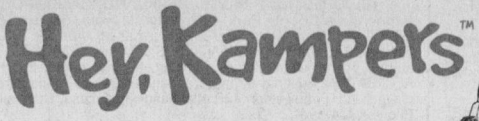

HUNTINGTON—Continued

HUNTINGTON FOX FIRE KOA—*From Huntington: Go 12 mi E on I-64 (exit 20B), then 1/4 mi S, then 5 mi E on Hwy 60, Enter on L on Fox Fire Rd. Enter on L.*

WELCOME

SEE PRIMARY LISTING AT MILTON AND AD THIS PAGE

HUTTONSVILLE—C-4

KUMBRABOW SF—(Randolph) *From town: Go 7 mi S on US 219, then 4 mi W on rock base access road.* FACILITIES: 13 sites, 13 no hkups, family camping, tenting, laundry. RECREATION: river fishing, playground. Open Mid Mar - Mid Dec. Phone: (304)335-2219.

INDIAN MILLS—D-3

BLUESTONE STATE WILDLIFE MGMT. AREA—(Summers) *From town: Go 2 mi S on Hwy 12, then 3 mi SW on Indian Mills Rd. Enter on R.* FACILITIES: 330 sites, 330 no hkups, family camping, tenting. RECREATION: lake/river swim, boating, canoeing, ramp, lake/river/stream fishing, playground. Partial handicap access. Open Mid Apr - Oct. Phone: (304)466-3398.

LEWISBURG—D-3

(S) STATE FAIR OF WEST VIRGINIA—*From jct I-64 (exit 169) & US 219: Go 3 mi S on US 219. Enter on L.* Annual State Fair held in Mid August. Carnival Exhibitions, Horse Track, Grandstands & Exhibition Bldgs. Free Parking. Special events year round. Open all yr. MC/VISA/DISC/Debit.

WELCOME

Phone: (304)645-1090
Address: 891 Maplewood Ave, Fairlea, WV 24902
Lat/Lon: 37.77903/-80.45703
Email: statefairofwv@statefairofwv.com
Web: www.statefairofwv.com

SEE AD THIS PAGE

(S) STATE FAIR OF WEST VIRGINIA CAMPGROUND—(Greenbriar) *From jct I-64 (exit 169) & US 219: Go 3 mi S on US 219.*

WELCOME

◆◆◆FACILITIES: 200 sites, typical site width 25 ft, 200 full hkups, (30/50 amps), 20 pull-thrus, WiFi Internet central location, family camping, tenting, dump, laundry, picnic tables.

◆RECREATION: pavilion, golf nearby, playground, sports field.

Pets welcome. Partial handicap access. Open all yr. Facilities fully operational Apr - Oct. Limited services in Winter. Big rigs welcome. Clubs welcome. Rate in 2010 $25 for 2 persons. MC/VISA/DISC/Debit.

Phone: (304)645-1090
Address: 891 Maplewood Ave, Fairlea, WV 24902
Lat/Lon: 37.77903/-80.45703
Email: statefairofwv@statefairofwv.com
Web: www.statefairofwv.com

SEE AD THIS PAGE

LOGAN—D-2

(N) CHIEF LOGAN SP—(Logan) *From town: Go 3 mi N on Hwy 10. Enter on L.* FACILITIES: 25 sites, 28 ft max RV length, 14 full hkups, 11 W&E, (30 amps), 7 pull-thrus, family camping, tenting, dump. RECREATION: swim pool, playground. Open Mid Apr - Oct. Phone: (304)792-7125.

West Virginia State Motto: "Montani semper liberi" (Mountaineers are always free)

LOST RIVER—B-5

(N) GEORGE WASHINGTON NF (Trout Pond Campground)—(Hardy) *From town: Go 6 mi E on Hwy 259-5, then 1 mi S on FR 500.* FACILITIES: 46 sites, 21 ft max RV length, 13 E, 33 no hkups, 2 pull-thrus, tenting, dump. RECREATION: lake swim, boating, no motors, canoeing, ramp, lake fishing, playground. Partial handicap access. Open late Apr - mid Dec. Phone: (877)444-6777.

MARLINTON—C-4

MONONGAHELA NF (Tea Creek Campground)—(Pocahontas) *From jct US 219 & Hwy 150: Go 7 mi W on Hwy 150, then 2 mi W on FR 86.* FACILITIES: 29 sites, 22 ft max RV length, 29 no hkups, tenting. RECREATION: stream fishing. Partial handicap access. Open Apr 1 - Nov 30. Phone: (304)799-4334.

MILTON—C-2

(W) HUNTINGTON FOX FIRE KOA—(Cabell) *From jct of I-64 (exit 28) & US 60: Go 3 mi W on US 60 (enter on right) Allow for sharp turn. From jct I-64 (exit 20B) & US 60: Go 5 mi E on US 60 (enter on left). Enter at end.*

WELCOME

◆◆◆◆FACILITIES: 110 sites, typical site width 35 ft, 110 full hkups, (30/50 amps), 50 amps ($), some extd stay sites, 70 pull-thrus, WiFi Instant Internet at site, family camping, tenting, cabins, RV storage, dump, non-guest dump $, laundry, ltd groc, RV supplies, LP gas by weight/by meter, ice, picnic tables, patios, wood, controlled access.

◆◆◆RECREATION: lake swim, lake fishing, fishing supplies, golf nearby, bsktball, 10 bike rentals, playground, activities, horseshoes, sports field.

Pets welcome. Partial handicap access. Open all yr. Big rigs welcome. Escort to site. Clubs welcome. Rate in 2010 $34-48 for 4 persons. MC/VISA/DISC/AMEX/Debit. KOA discount.

Phone: (304)743-5622
Address: 290 Fox Fire Rd, Milton, WV 25541
Lat/Lon: 38.43255/-82.16933
Email: information@foxfirekoa.com
Web: www.koa.com/where/wv/48118

SEE AD HUNTINGTON THIS PAGE

(W) Jim's Camping—(Cabell) *From jct I-64 (exit 28) & US 60: Go 1-1/2 mi W on US 60. Enter on L.* ◆◆FACILITIES: 81 sites, 41 full hkups, 40 W&E, (20/30/50 amps), tenting, dump. ◆RECREATION: river fishing. Pets welcome. Open all yr. Facilities fully operational Apr 1 - Oct 31. Rate in 2010 $20-25 per vehicle. Phone: (304)743-4560.

MOOREFIELD—B-5

(W) Riverside Cabins & RV Park—(Hardy) *From jct US 220 & SR 55: Go 3 mi W on SR 55, then 1-1/2 mi N on CR 13 (Fisher Rd), then 4 mi W on CR 10 (River Rd). Enter at end.* ◆◆◆FACILITIES: 80 sites, typical site width 30 ft, 70 full hkups, (30/50 amps), 10 no hkups, 14 pull-thrus, family camping, tenting. ◆◆◆RECREATION: swim pool, river fishing, playground. No pets. Open all yr. Big rigs welcome. Rate in 2010 $35 for 6 persons. Phone: (304)538-6467.

Reserve Online at Woodalls.com

MORGANTOWN—A-4

(E) CHESTNUT RIDGE PARK AND CAMPGROUND (Monongalia County Park)—(Monongalia) *From I-68 (exit 15) & CR 73: Go 1/4 mi E on CR 73, then 1-1/2 mi N on CR 1 (Sand Springs Rd). Enter on L.* FACILITIES: 70 sites, 20 W&E, (30 amps), 50 no hkups, family camping, tenting, dump, ltd groc. RECREATION: boating, no motors, canoeing, dock, pond fishing, playground. Pets welcome. Partial handicap access. Open all yr. Phone: (304)594-1773.

West Virginia State Bird: Cardinal

MORGANTOWN—Continued

COOPERS ROCK SF (McCollum Camping Area)—(Monongalia) *From town: Go 10 mi E on I-68 to exit 15, then 1-1/2 mi S on access road. Enter on L.* FACILITIES: 25 sites, 25 E, (30 amps), 7 pull-thrus, family camping, tenting, laundry. RECREATION: boating, electric motors only, pond fishing, playground. Partial handicap access. Open Apr 1 - Nov 30. Phone: (304)594-1561.

(E) Sand Springs Camping Area—(Monongalia) *From I-68 (exit 15) & CR 73: Go 1/4 mi E on CR 73, then 2 mi N on Chestnut Ridge Rd/Sand Springs Rd. Enter on L.* ◆◆FACILITIES: 77 sites, typical site width 30 ft, 40 ft max RV length, 30 full hkups, 5 W&E, (20/30/50 amps), 42 no hkups, 10 pull-thrus, tenting, dump, laundry, ltd groc. ◆◆RECREATION: swim pool. Pets welcome. Open May 1 - Oct 31. Rate in 2010 $29-37.10 for 4 persons. Phone: (304)594-2415.

MULLENS—D-2

(NW) TWIN FALLS RESORT SP—(Wyoming) *From jct Hwy 54 & Hwy 97: Go 5-1/2 mi W on Hwy 97.* FACILITIES: 50 sites, 30 ft max RV length, 25 E, (30 amps), 25 no hkups, 3 pull-thrus, family camping, tenting, dump, laundry, ltd groc. RECREATION: swim pool, playground. Partial handicap access. Open Mid Apr - Oct. Phone: (304)294-4000.

NEOLA—D-4

(N) MONONGAHELA NF (Lake Sherwood Recreation Area)—(Greenbrier) *From town: Go 11 mi NE on Hwy-14.* FACILITIES: 95 sites, 22 ft max RV length, 95 no hkups, tenting, dump. RECREATION: lake swim, boating, electric motors only, canoeing, ramp, lake fishing. Partial handicap access. Open all yr. Facilities fully operational mid May - early Sep. Phone: (304)536-2144.

PANTHER—E-2

PANTHER SF—(McDowell) *From US 52: Go 8 mi SW on CR 3 to Panther, then 3 mi S on CR 3/2.* FACILITIES: 6 sites, 6 E, (30 amps), family camping, tenting. RECREATION: swim pool, stream fishing. Partial handicap access. Open Mid Apr - Oct. Phone: (304)938-2252.

PARKERSBURG—B-2

MOUNTWOOD PARK CAMPGROUND (Wood County Park)—(Wood) *From jct I-77 & US 50: Go 14 mi E on US 50, then N on Borland Springs Rd. Follow signs.* FACILITIES: 124 sites, 88 W&E, 36 no hkups, tenting, dump. RECREATION: canoeing, lake fishing, play equipment. Open May - Nov. Phone: (304)679-3694.

PAX—D-2

PLUM ORCHARD LAKE STATE WILDLIFE MGMT. AREA—(Fayette) *From I-77 (Pax exit): Follow signs 4-1/2 mi NE on CR 23 & 23/1.* FACILITIES: 38 sites, 38 no hkups, family camping, tenting, dump. RECREATION: boating, ramp, dock, lake fishing. Open all yr. Phone: (304)469-9905.

PIPESTEM—D-3

PIPESTEM RESORT SP—(Summers) *From Hwy 20 & county road: Go 3 mi W on county road.* FACILITIES: 82 sites, 31 full hkups, 19 E, (30 amps), 32 no hkups, 23 pull-thrus, family camping, tenting, dump, laundry. RECREATION: 2 swim pools, canoeing, dock, lake/river fishing, playground. Open all yr. Phone: (304)466-1800.

POINT PLEASANT—C-2

KRODEL PARK (City Park)—(Mason) *From jct US 35 & Hwy 2: Cross the Shadle Bridge on Hwy 2, then 1/2 mi N on Hwy 2 to second park entrance for campground.* FACILITIES: 64 sites, typical site width 20 ft, 64 full hkups, (30 amps), 4 pull-thrus, tenting, dump, laundry. RECREATION: boating, electric motors only, ramp, dock, lake fishing, playground. Partial handicap access. Open Apr 1 - Oct 31. Phone: (304)675-1068.

RICHWOOD—C-3

MONONGAHELA NF (Bishop Knob Campground)—(Webster) *From town: Go 2 mi E on Hwy 39, then 3-1/2 mi E on Hwy 46, then 3 mi S on FR 101.* FACILITIES: 61 sites, 22 ft max RV length, 61 no hkups, tenting. RECREATION: Partial handicap access. Open Apr 1 - Dec 8. Phone: (304)846-2695.

(NE) MONONGAHELA NF (Cranberry Campground)—(Webster) *From town: Go 13 mi NE on FR-76.* FACILITIES: 30 sites, 22 ft max RV length, 30 no hkups, 1 pull-thrus, tenting. RECREATION: river fishing. Partial handicap access. Open all yr. Facilities fully operational Mar 15 - Dec 8. Phone: (304)846-2695.

(E) MONONGAHELA NF (Summit Lake Campground)—(Greenbrier) *From jct Hwy 39 & Hwy 77: Go 2 mi N on Hwy 77.* FACILITIES: 33 sites, 22 ft max RV length, 33 no hkups, 2 pull-thrus, tenting. RECREATION: lake swim, boating, electric motors only, ramp, lake fishing. Open Apr 10 - Nov 30. Phone: (304)846-2695.

ROMANCE—C-2

(S) RIPPLING WATERS CHURCH OF GOD CAMPGROUND—(Jackson) *From jct I-77 (exit 116) & Hwy 21: Go 100 ft E on Haines Branch Rd, then 1 mi N on CR 21, then 3 mi E on CR 42 (Rippling Waters/Middlefork Rd). For GPS use Lat/Lon only. Enter on L.*

◆◆◆◆FACILITIES: 29 sites, typical site width 28 ft, 20 full hkups, 9 W&E, (30/50 amps), 11 pull-thrus, phone Internet central location, tenting, cabins, dump, non-guest dump $, laundry, ltd groc, RV supplies, LP gas by weight, ice, picnic tables, patios, fire rings, wood.

◆◆◆RECREATION: pavilion, swim pool, 2 pedal boat rentals, lake/pond fishing, bsktball, playground, sports field, v-ball.

Pets welcome. Partial handicap access. Open all yr. Facilities fully operational Apr 15 - Nov 30. Big rigs welcome. Clubs welcome. Rate in 2010 $20-25 for 2 persons. MC/VISA.

Phone: (304)988-2607
Address: HC 62 (Middle Fork Rd), Romance, WV 25248
Lat/Lon: 38.57520/-81.60622
Email: rwcogcamp@hotmail.com

SEE AD THIS PAGE

ROMNEY—B-5

(W) Wapocoma Campground—(Hampshire) *From jct US 220 & US 50: Go 6 mi E on US 50, then 4 mi S on South Branch River Rd (HC 66). Enter on R.* ◆◆◆FACILITIES: 186 sites, typical site width 36 ft, 44 full hkups, 51 W&E, (20/30/50 amps), 91 no hkups, 50 pull-thrus, family camping, tenting, dump, ltd groc. ◆◆◆RECREATION: river swim, boating, canoeing, ramp, river fishing, playground. Pets welcome, quantity restrict. Partial handicap access. Facilities fully operational Apr 15 - Oct 31. Big rigs welcome. Rate in 2010 $23-25 per family. Phone: (304)822-5528.

SENECA ROCKS—C-4

MONONGAHELA NF (Seneca Shadows Campground)—(Pendleton) *From jct Hwy 28 & US 33: Go 1 mi S on US 33.* FACILITIES: 45 sites, 30 ft max RV length, 45 no hkups, 1 pull-thrus, tenting. RECREATION: stream fishing. Partial handicap access. Open Mar 13 - Oct 25. Phone: (304)257-4488.

(C) Yokum's Vacationland & Princess Snowbird's Indian Village—(Pendleton) *From jct US 33 & Hwy 28: Go 1/2 mi N on SR 28. Enter on R.* ◆◆FACILITIES: 200 sites, typical site width 37 ft, 28 ft max RV length, 18 full hkups, 32 W&E, (15/20/30 amps), 150

SENECA ROCKS—Continued
Yokum's Vacationland & Princess Snowbird's Indian Village—Continued

no hkups, tenting, laundry, groceries. ◆◆◆RECREATION: swim pool, river swim, river fishing. Pets welcome. Open all yr. Facilities fully operational Apr 1 - Oct 31. Rate in 2010 $16-20 for 2 persons. Phone: (800) 772-8342.

SOUTHSIDE—C-2

CHIEF CORNSTALK STATE PUBLIC HUNTING & FISHING AREA—*From town: Go 6 mi W on CR 29.* FACILITIES: 25 sites, 25 no hkups, tenting. RECREATION: boating, electric motors only, canoeing, lake/pond fishing. Open all yr. Phone: (304) 675-0871.

SUMMERSVILLE—C-3

(S) BATTLE RUN CAMPGROUND (COE-Summersville Lake)—(Nicholas) *From town: Go 7 mi S on US 19, then 4 mi W on Hwy 129.* FACILITIES: 117 sites, 110 E, 7 no hkups, tenting, dump, laundry. RECREATION: lake swim, boating, ramp, dock, lake fishing, playground. No pets. Partial handicap access. Open mid May - mid Oct. Phone: (304)872-3459.

(S) Mountain Lake Campground & Cabins—(Nicholas) *From jct US 19 & Hwy 39: Go 1-3/4 mi S on US 19, then 2 mi W on Airport Rd. Enter on R.* ◆◆◆FACILITIES: 251 sites, typical site width 50 ft, 197 W&E, (20/30/50 amps), 54 no hkups, 15 pull-thrus, tenting, dump, laundry, groceries. ◆◆◆RECREATION: swim pool, lake swim, boating, canoeing, lake fishing, playground. Pets welcome, breed restrict. Partial handicap access. Open Mar 1 - Nov 31. Green Friendly. Rate in 2010 $20-43 for 2 persons. Member ARVC. Phone: (877)686-6222.

(S) Summersville Lake Retreat—(Nicholas) *From jct US 19 & SR 129: Go 1/4 mi W on SR 129. Enter on R.* ◆◆◆FACILITIES: 65 sites, typical site width 30 ft, 12 full hkups, 20 W&E, (30/50 amps), 33 no hkups, 10 pull-thrus, tenting. ◆◆RECREATION: playground. Pets welcome. Partial handicap access. Open all yr. Big rigs welcome. Rate in 2010 $32-44 for 2 persons. Phone: (888)872-5580.

SUTTON—C-3

(S) BAKERS RUN CAMPGROUND (COE-Sutton Lake)—(Braxton) *In town from jct Main St & 2nd Ave: Go 4 mi S on Old US-19, then 10 mi E on CR-17. Enter on L.* FACILITIES: 130 sites, 28 E, 102 no hkups, tenting, dump, ltd groc. RECREATION: lake swim, boating, canoeing, ramp, lake fishing, playground. Partial handicap access. Open Apr 23 - Nov 31. Phone: (304)765-2816.

(E) GERALD R. FREEMAN CAMPGROUND (COE-Sutton Lake)—(Braxton) *From jct I-79 (exit 62) & Hwy 4: Go 5 mi NE on Hwy 4, then 11-1/2 mi E on CR 15.* FACILITIES: 158 sites, 77 E, (20/30 amps), 81 no hkups, tenting, dump, laundry, ltd groc. RECREATION: lake/river swim, boating, canoeing, ramp, lake/river fishing, playground. Partial handicap access. Open Apr 23 - Dec 5. Facilities fully operational May 15 - Sep 11. Phone: (304)765-2816.

UPPER TRACT—C-4

MONONGAHELA NF (Big Bend Campground)—(Grant) *From jct US 220 & CR 2: Go 9 mi N on CR 2.* FACILITIES: 45 sites, 16 ft max RV length, 45 no hkups, 1 pull-thrus, tenting, dump. RECREATION: boating, canoeing, river fishing. Open Apr 15 - Dec. Phone: (304)257-4488.

WARRIORMINE—E-2

BERWIND LAKE WMA—(McDowell) *From jct I-77 & Hwy 460W (exit 9): Stay on Hwy 460W to Tazwell, to Rte 16 N (exit 2) continue to end of city limits, left across the bridge, then 2 mi to park entrance. Enter on R.* FACILITIES: 8 sites, 2 W&E, 6 no hkups, family camping, tenting. RECREATION: swim pool, boating, electric motors only, ramp, dock, lake fishing. Pets welcome. Open all yr. Phone: (304)875-2577.

WEIRTON—A-1

TOMLINSON RUN SP—(Hancock) *From town: Go 6 mi N on Hwy-2, then 3 mi NE on Hwy-8.* FACILITIES: 54 sites, 39 E, (30 amps), 15 no hkups, 11 pull-thrus, family camping, tenting, dump, laundry. RECREATION: swim pool, lake swim, boating, no motors, dock, pond/stream fishing, playground. Partial handicap access. Open Apr - Oct 31. Facilities fully operational Memorial Day - Labor Day. Phone: (304)564-3651.

WESTON—B-3

(S) Broken Wheel Campground & Country Store—(Lewis) *From jct I-79 (SW on exit 96) & CR 30: Go 1-1/2 mi E on CR 30. Enter on R.* ◆◆◆FACILITIES: 53 sites, typical site width 40 ft, 36 W&E, 2 E, (30 amps), 15 no hkups, tenting, dump, groceries. ◆◆◆RECREATION: pond fishing, playground. Pets welcome. Open all yr. Rate in 2010 $27 for 4 persons. Phone: (304)269-6097.

STONEWALL JACKSON LAKE SP (Briar Point Campground)—(Lewis) *From town: Go 13 mi S on US 19. From I-79 (exit 91-Roanoke): Go 2-1/2 mi S on US 19.* FACILITIES: 46 sites, 40 full hkups, (20/30 amps), 6 no hkups, family camping, tenting, dump, ltd groc. RECREATION: boating, canoeing, ramp, dock, lake fishing, playground. Open Apr 1 - Dec 15. Facilities fully operational Apr 1 - Oct 31. Phone: (888)278-8150.

(SW) Whisper Mountain Campground & RV Park—(Lewis) *From jct I-79 (exit 91) & US 19: Go 200 yds N on US 19, then 5 mi W on Goosepen Rd (CR 21), then 100 ft S on Three Lick Rd. Enter on R.* ◆◆◆FACILITIES: 69 sites, typical site width 35 ft, 5 full hkups, 44 W&E, (20/30/50 amps), 50 amps ($), 20 no hkups, family camping, tenting, dump, laundry, ltd groc. ◆◆RECREATION: swim pool, pond fishing, playground. Pets welcome. Open all yr. Facilities fully operational Apr 1 - Nov 30. Rate in 2010 $25-28 for 4 persons. Phone: (304)452-9723.

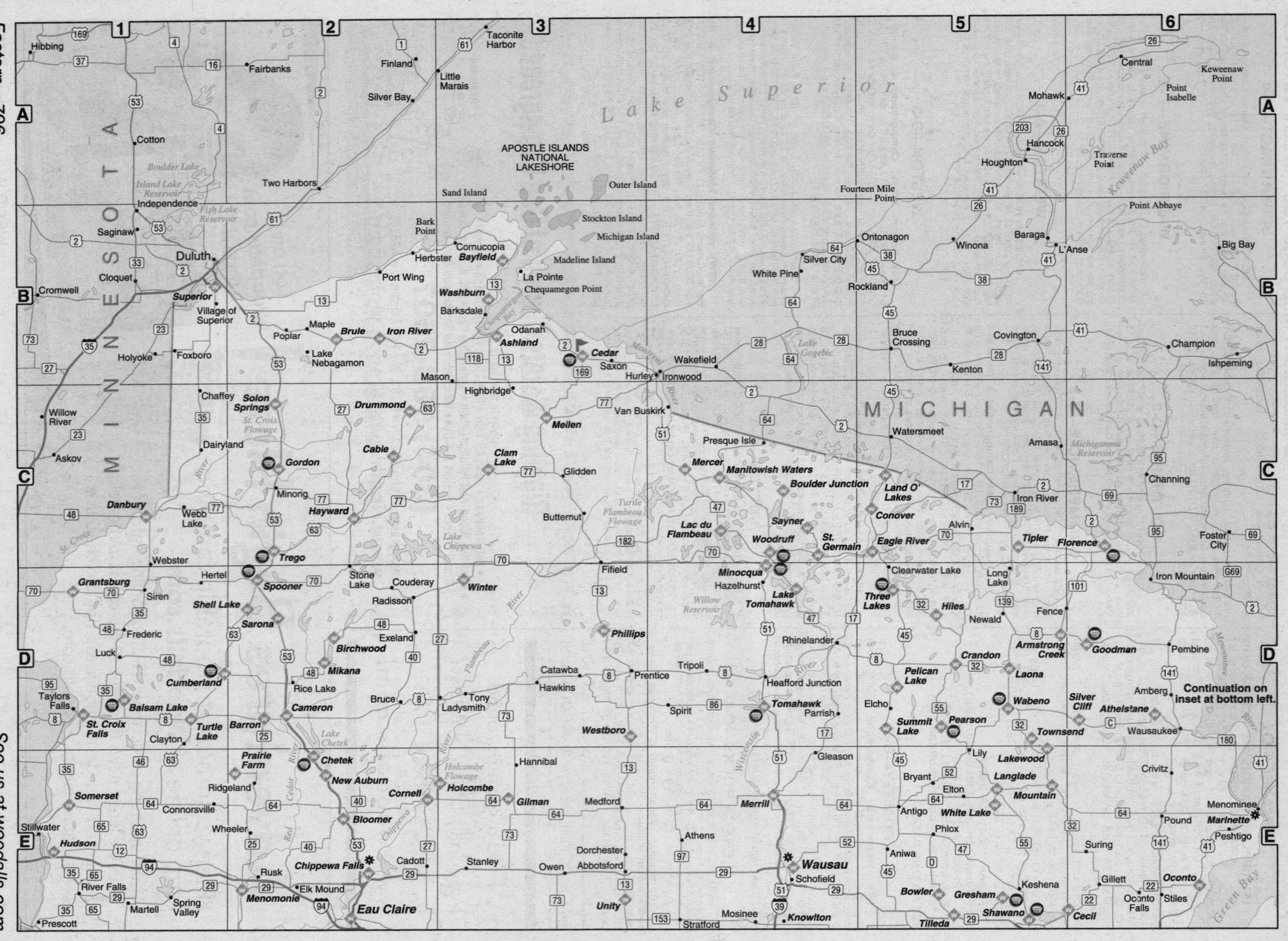
Lake Superior
MINNESOTA
MICHIGAN
APOSTLE ISLANDS NATIONAL LAKESHORE
Continuation on inset at bottom left.
Duluth
Superior
Ashland
Hayward
Rhinelander
Wausau
Eau Claire
Marinette
Green Bay

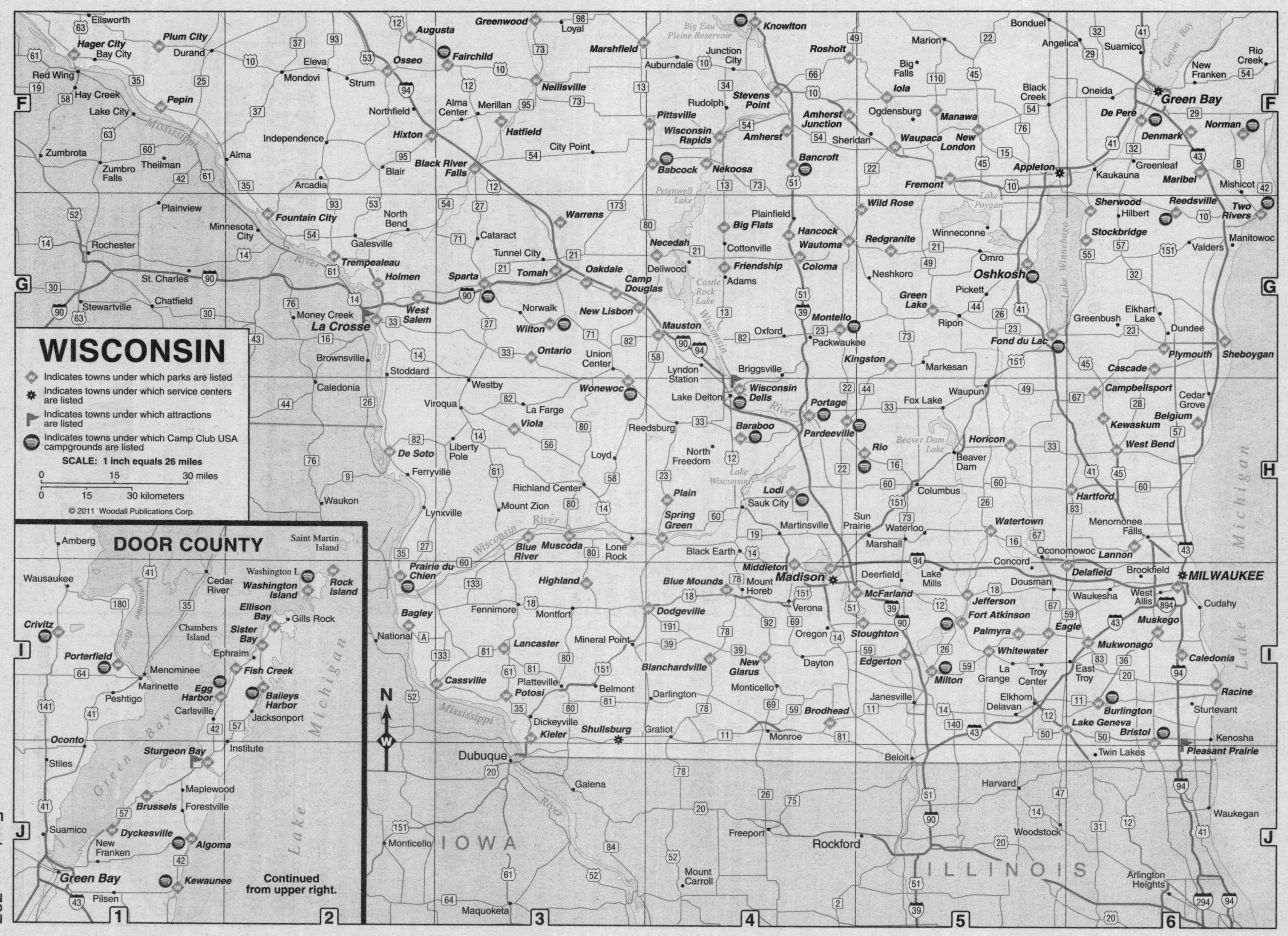
WISCONSIN
Indicates towns under which parks are listed
Indicates towns under which service centers are listed
Indicates towns under which attractions are listed
Indicates towns under which Camp Club USA campgrounds are listed
SCALE: 1 inch equals 26 miles
0 15 30 miles
0 15 30 kilometers
© 2011 Woodall Publications Corp.
DOOR COUNTY
Continued from upper right.
IOWA
ILLINOIS
Lake Michigan
MILWAUKEE
Madison
Green Bay
La Crosse
Oshkosh
Dubuque
Rockford

READER SERVICE INFO

The following businesses have placed an ad in the Wisconsin Travel Section. To receive free information, enter their Reader Service number on the Reader Service Card opposite page 48/Discover Section in the front of this directory:

Advertiser	RS#
Jelly Belly Candy Co.	4291
Truck Country	3456
Wisconsin Association of Campgrounds	3256

TIME ZONE

Wisconsin is in the Central Time Zone.

TOPOGRAPHY

The state's 56,154 square miles include 1,439 square miles of inland waters and 820 miles of Great Lakes shoreline, as well as two million acres of state and national forests. The northern half of the state contains over 14,000 lakes formed by the retreating glaciers of the Ice Age. Set among rolling hills heavily forested with hardwood and pine, these lakes are a source of abundant fishing and boating activity.

TEMPERATURE

January temperatures average around 19.5° and the average precipitation this month is 1.22 inches. July temperatures average around 73.6° and the average precipitation during this month is 3.74 inches.

TRAVEL & TOURISM INFO

State Agency:
Wisconsin Dept. of Tourism
201 W. Washington Ave.
Madison, WI 53708
(800/432-8747 or 608/266-2161)
www.travelwisconsin.com

Regional Agencies:
Door County Visitor Bureau
1015 Green Bay Rd.
Sturgeon Bay, WI 54235-0406
(800/52-RELAX or 920/743-4456)
www.doorcounty.com

Greater Green Bay CVB
1901 South Oneida St.
Green Bay, WI 54304
(888/867-3342 or 920/494-9507)
www.greenbay.com

Eagle River Chamber of Commerce
P.O Box 1917
Eagle River, WI 54521
(800/359-6315)
www.eagleriver.org

Green County Tourism
N3150 B Hwy. 81
Monroe, WI 53566
(888/222-9111)
www.greencounty.org

Chippewa Valley Convention & Visitors Bureau
3625 Gateway Drive
Eau Claire, WI 54701
(888/523-3866 or 715/831-2345)
www.chippewavalley.net/

Sheboygan County Chamber of Commerce
712 Riverfront Dr., Ste 101
Sheboygan, WI 53081
(920/457-9491)
www.sheboygan.org

Bayfield Chamber of Commerce
PO Box 138
42 S Broad Street
Bayfield, WI 54814
(715/779-3335 or 800/447-4094)
www.bayfield.org

Hayward Lakes Visitors & Convention Bureau
1585 US Hwy 63
P.O. Box 1055
Hayward, WI 54843
(800/724-2992)
www.haywardlakes.com

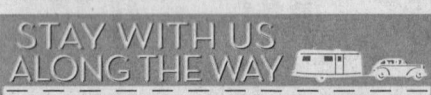

Lake Geneva
Convention and Visitors Bureau
201 Wrigley Drive
Lake Geneva, WI 53147
(262/248-4416)
www.lakegenevawi.com

Greater Tomah Area
Convention & Visitors Bureau
901 Kilbourn Avenue
P.O Box 625
Tomah, WI 54660
(608/372-2166 or 800/94-TOMAH)
www.tomahwisconsin.com

Local Agencies:
For information on areas not listed here, contact the Chamber of Commerce or Tourism Bureau for the locality you are interested in.

Visit Madison CVB
615 E. Washington Ave.
Madison, WI 53703
(800/373-6376 or 608/255-2537)
www.visitmadison.com

Visit Milwaukee CVB
648 N Plankinton Ave., Ste. 425
Milwaukee, WI 53203
(800/231-0903 or 414/273-3950)
www.milwaukee.org

Minocqua-Arbor Vitae-Woodruff Area Chamber of Commerce
8216 Hwy 51 S
Minocqua, WI 54548
(800/446-6784 or 715/356-5266)
www.minocqua.org

Stevens Point Area CVB
340 Division St. N.
Stevens Point, WI 54481
(800/236-4636 or 715/344-2556)
www.spacvb.com

Vilas County Tourism & Publicity
330 Court St.
Eagle River, WI 54521
(800/236-3649 or 715/479-3649)
www.vilas.org

Wisconsin Dells CVB
701 Superior St.
Wisconsin Dells, WI 53965
(800/223-3557 or 608/254-4636)
www.wisdells.com

RECREATIONAL INFO

All Terrain Vehicles: For a free Wisconsin ATV Guide, www.travelwisconsin.com or (800/432-8747). **The Wisconsin ATV Association.** (920/565-7531) www.watva.org

Bicycling: For a free Wisconsin Biking Guide, www.travelwisconsin.com or (800/432-8747). For a free TREK of the Northwoods Trails biking guide for the trails in Lincoln, Price and Vilas Counties, visit www.northwoodsbiking.com or call (800/236-3649).

Fishing & Hunting: Wisconsin Dept. of Natural Resources, P.O. Box 7921, Madison, WI 53707 (608/266-2621). For licenses: www.dnr.state.wi.us (877/945-4236)

Golf: For a free directory of Wisconsin Golf Courses, www.travelwisconsin.com. (800/432-8747). Golf Course Owners of Wisconsin, (800/348-2721) www.wisconsin4golf.com

Hiking: For a free Hiking/Biking/Birding/Cross-Country Ski/Snowshoe Trail Directory, visit www.vilas.org or call (800/236-3649).

Horseback Riding: For a guide of terrain maps, fees, stables, camps & riding trails, contact Wisconsin State Horse Council, 132 S. Ludington St., Columbus, WI 53925 (920/623-0393). www.wisconsinstatehorsecouncil.org

Snowmobiling: Association of Wisconsin Snowmobile Clubs, (920/734-5530) www.awsc.org

SHOPPING

Burnstad's European Village, Tomah. European-style shopping with 16 specialty stores. 701 E Clifton St. (608/372-4040) www.burnstads.com

Cedar Creek Settlement, Cedarburg. Village of shops in 1864 stone mill buildings on Cedar Creek. Winery Tours. (262/377-8020 or 866/626-7005).

Columbus Antiques Mall & Museum, Columbus. Antiques displayed and sold by 180 dealers at 400 booths. Known for having one of the largest collections of glassware in the USA. 239 Whitney St. (920/623-1992). www.columbusantiquemall.com

Dane Co. Farmers' Market on the Square, Madison. Every Saturday morning from early spring to late fall, Capitol Square is transformed into the largest open-air farmers' market in the country. Capitol Square, Madison, WI. www.dcfm.org

Fox River Mall, Appleton. Wisconsin's largest mall with 180 stores. 4301 W. Wisconsin Ave. (920/739-4100) ww.foxrivermall.com

Tanger Outlets 210 Gasser Road, Ste 105 Baraboo, WI 53913 (608/253-5380) www.tangeroutlet.com

Wisconsin Dairy State Cheese Company, Rudolph. Factory and retail outlet. 6860 State Rd. 34. (715/435-3144)

UNIQUE FEATURES

Apostle Islands National Lakeshore: National Geographic rated this lakeshore cluster of 21 islands as "the top park in the United States" because of its natural, breathtaking sites and close proximity to the town of Bayfield, which compliments the remote ambiance. The area, located along Lake Superior's shoreline, was designated as a National Lakeshore in 1970. The islands features six historic light stations, sea caves for exploring by kayak and many secluded beaches. The islands are also a center for deepwater fishing and sailing. Those who prefer to see the islands on foot can traverse more than 50 miles of hiking trails, which used to house abandoned quarries, historic logging sites and old farmsteads.

Great River Road. Named after history's great river, the mighty Mississippi, this scenic riverway traces a 200-mile path along Wisconsin's western boundary from Prescott in the north to the southwestern corner of the state near Dubuque, Iowa. The Great River Road is a gateway to adventure through picturesque towns, across breathtaking bluffs and panoramic overlooks. For a map of the entire Great River Road, write to: Great River Road Commission, Wisconsin Dept. of Transportation, P.O. Box 7910, 4802 Sheboygan Ave. Rm. 103, Madison, WI 53707 (715/836-4628).

DESTINATIONS

This great state is recognized as America's Dairyland, and a state that exudes natural beauty. Wisconsin attracts millions of vacationers every year to its lush green countryside, sparkling lakes and quiet valleys. Wisconsin boasts over 430 lakes, and 44,000 acres of wilderness areas, as well as 50 award winning state parks. The perfect place for endless outdoor recreation.

NORTHERN REGION

The early French explorers that first came to this region would be happily surprised that not much has changed since they first paddled their canoes through this region. This area is filled with picturesque roads, rolling hills and endless lakes. If ever there was an ideal place for fishing, canoeing, swimming and boating, this is it!

Bayfield and Madeline Island: Picturesque and charming, this small harbor town sits on the vast waters of Lake Superior surrounded by stunning rock formations and six historic lighthouses considered the finest collection in the country. Bayfield is also the gateway to the stunning Apostle Islands National Lakeshore – 22 gem-like coastal islands that are home to lighthouses, sea caves, hiking trails and terrific blue water sailing and kayaking. Visitors will find numerous types of lodging, cabins and restored Victorian mansions, bed and breakfasts and attractions such as Big Top Chautauqua, art galleries, museum and historic walking tours, charming shops and fine dining. And only a mile out of town, Bayfield's 15 orchards offer all types of berries, apples and flowers. The Madeline Island Ferry crosses the bay on a three-mile trip to Madeline Island, the home to Big Bay State Park, a historical museum and Robert Trent Jones Golf Course.

Brule River, Douglas County. This 30-mile river stretches from its source at Lake St. Croix to the mouth where it empties into Lake Superior, the largest freshwater lake in the world. The Brule River offers the best in trout fishing (rainbows, steelheads and brooks) and is a fine waterway for canoeing and boating, with scenic views along the banks.

Door County. Explore the outdoor activities and scenery where you can walk along sandy beaches and explore the wind-ravaged shoreline. Tour 10 towering lighthouses during the Festival of Blossoms in May. Charter a deepwater fishing boat, take a cruise on Sturgeon Bay, or explore scenic sea caves. As this county is known for its galleries, museums and performing arts troupes, painters, potters and performers abound. Among the many museums are **Door County Historical Museum, Door County Maritime Museum, Sturgeon Bay and Miller Art Museum**. Take a tour of the **Door Peninsula Winery**, where you can savor the flavor of wines made from local cherries, apples, cranberries and plums. Catch the ferry from Gillis Rock to Washington Island for a trolley or bicycle tour. Spend an evening enjoying an outdoor play at Peninsula State Park.

Eagle River. Take a tour of magnificent turn-of-the-century boathouses brimming with history and unique architecture. The Eagle River chain of 28 lakes offers guided and self-guided tours along its miles of waterways.

Lac du Flambeau. Visit Wa-Swa-Goning, a re-created Ojibwe village with birchbark lodges and canoes.

Rhinelander. With more than 230 lakes in a 12-mile radius, this area became a logging center. That heritage is preserved in the Logging Museum Complex located in Pioneer Park, including a full-scale reproduction of a 19th century logging camp with narrow-gauge railroad.

Vilas County. With more than 1,300 lakes and 73 rivers and streams, Vilas County offers one of the largest concentrations of freshwater lakes around for boating, fishing and paddling. Access to the Chequamegon-Nicolet-National Forest, the Northern Highland American Legion State Forest, and County Forest acres, as well as 48 designated trails, provide outstanding hiking, birdwatching and bicycling opportunities. Local museums present displays of the area's history. For outdoor adventure or peace and relaxation, the communities of Vilas County provide a sense of getting away from it all.

BUSINESSES OFFERING

	Things to See & Do	RV Sales	RV Service
APPLETON			
Truck Country			✱
CEDAR			
Frontier Bar	⚑		
CHIPPEWA FALLS			
North Point RV		🚌	✱
DOOR COUNTY			
Door County Visitor Bureau	⚑		
GREEN BAY			
Truck Country			✱
LA CROSSE			
La Crosse County Facilities Dept.	⚑		
MADISON			
Truck Country			✱
MARINETTE			
Truck Country			✱
MILWAUKEE			
Truck Country			✱
PLEASANT PRAIRIE			
Jelly Belly Center	⚑		
SHULLSBURG			
Truck Country			✱
WAUSAU			
Truck Country			✱
WISCONSIN DELLS			
Wisconsin Dells Visitor & Convention Bureau	⚑		

Waterfalls. Find dozens of waterfalls in Wisconsin, including the tallest waterfall east of the Rockies. Many more scattered throughout the Northwoods near Hurley and Superior and in northeast Wisconsin. Billed as the "Waterfall Capital of Wisconsin, Marinette is home to 14 waterfalls located in the county park system. View and download a waterfall tour map at http://therealnorth.com or call the Marinette County Tourism Office at 715/ 735-6681.

CENTRAL REGION

In the Central Region of the state, there are numerous cities and small towns to explore, with all of their historical and contemporary richness. Here, theme parks, museums and attractions of all kinds await.

Eau Claire. **The Chippewa Valley Museum** is an award-winning regional museum, which includes **Anderson Log House** and the one-room **Sunnyview School**. Other area attractions include **Paul Bunyan Logging Camp**, an authentic reproduction of an 1890s logging camp and **Dells Mills Museum**, a five-story, water-powered historic grist mill.

Ice Age Trail. A continuous 1000-mile footpath through diverse landscapes that provides outdoor recreation experiences, preserves geological features, serves as an educational resource and provides habitat for the movement of wildlife. Portions of this trail travel through Portage County.

International Crane Foundation. The International Crane Foundation is the only place in the world where visitors can view the 15 crane species. Over three miles of nature trails winding through a restored Wisconsin landscape of tall grass prairie and oak savanna. Guided and self-guided tours, gift shop, family education center and art gallery. www.savingcranes.org

National Railroad Museum. One of America's largest rail museums houses nearly 80 railroad cars and locomotives, including the world's largest steam locomotive.

Onalaska. River history, lumbering and Native American artifacts are featured at the **Onalaska Historical Museum**.

Sparta. See the progression of travel from the bicycle to air & space travel at the **Deke Slayton Memorial Space & Bike Museum**.

Sheboygan & Elkhart Lake. Located on the shores of Lake Michigan along Wisconsin's eastern border, Sheboygan is a city with small town charm. Its many restored buildings add to its quaint atmosphere. Visitors can meander along the picturesque riverfront boardwalk to explore fish shanties that have been turned into shops, galleries and restaurants or charter a boat for an afternoon of guided Great Lakes sport fishing. The new **Harbor Centre Marina and Lakeview Trail** offer spectacular waterfront views and **Kohler**

QUICK REFERENCE CHART FOR WOODALL'S FEATURED PARKS

	Green Friendly	RV Lots for Sale	Park Models-Onsite Ownership	Park Membership for Sale	Big Rigs Welcome	Internet Friendly	Pets Welcome
BAILEYS HARBOR							
Baileys Grove Campground					▲	●	■
BANCROFT							
Vista Royalle Campground					▲	●	■
BARABOO							
Fox Hill RV Park					▲	●	■
BAYFIELD							
Isle Vista Casino's Buffalo Bay Campground					▲	●	■
BRISTOL							
Happy Acres Kampground						●	■
CASCADE							
Hoeft's Resort & Campground							■
CEDAR							
Frontier RV Park & Campground						●	■
CHETEK							
Six Lakes Resort & RV Park					▲	●	■
CHIPPEWA FALLS							
O'Neil Creek Campground & RV Park					▲	●	■
DODGEVILLE							
Tom's Campground							■
EAGLE RIVER							
Hi-Pines Campground & Resort					▲	●	■
EDGERTON							
Hickory Hills Campground					▲		■
EGG HARBOR							
Door County Camping Retreat					▲	●	■
Egg Harbor Campground & RV Resort					▲	●	■
Frontier Wilderness Campground						●	■
ELLISON BAY							
Wagon Trail Campground Ltd.					▲	●	■
HIXTON							
KOA Hixton Alma Center					▲	●	■
KEWAUNEE							
Kewaunee Village RV Park & Campground					▲	●	■
KNOWLTON							
Lake DuBay Shores Campground & RV Park						●	■
LA CROSSE							
Goose Island Park (La Crosse County)					▲	●	■
Pettibone Resort						●	■
MADISON							
KOA Madison					▲	●	■
MAUSTON							
Castle Rock County Park (Juneau County)							■
MILTON							
Hidden Valley RV Resort & Campground					▲	●	■
MINOCQUA							
Patricia Lake RV Resort					▲	●	■
MUKWONAGO							
Country View Campground							■
NECEDAH							
Wilderness County Park (Juneau County)							■
NORMAN							
Maple View Campground					▲		■
OSSEO							
Stoney Creek RV Resort					▲	●	■

Green Friendly 🍃; RV Lots for Sale ✖; Park Models/Onsite Onwership ✱; Park Memberships for Sale ✔; Big Rigs Welcome ▲; Internet Friendly ●; Internet Friendly-WiFi ●; Pets Welcome ■

QUICK REFERENCE CHART FOR WOODALL'S FEATURED PARKS

	Green Friendly	RV Lots for Sale	Park Models-Onsite Ownership	Park Membership for Sale	Big Rigs Welcome	Internet Friendly	Pets Welcome
PORTAGE							
Pride of America Camping Resort					▲	●	■
REEDSVILLE							
Rainbows End Campground					▲	●	■
RIO							
Silver Springs Campsites, Inc.						●	■
Willow Mill Campsite LLC						●	■
SPARTA							
Leon Valley Campground					▲		■
SPRING GREEN							
Wisconsin Riverside Resort					▲	●	■
STURGEON BAY							
Harbour Village Resort						●	■
Yogi Bear Jellystone Park							■
SUPERIOR							
Northland Camping & RV Park					▲	●	■
TURTLE LAKE							
Turtle Lake RV Park					▲	●	■
TWO RIVERS							
Badger RV Park @ Village Inn on the Lake					▲	●	■
WATERTOWN							
River Bend Resort						●	■
WEST SALEM							
Veteran's Memorial Park (La Crosse County)					▲		■
WILD ROSE							
Evergreen Campsites & Resort	🍃				▲	●	■
WISCONSIN DELLS							
American World - Mt. Olympus Hotel & RV Resort					▲	●	■
Arrowhead Resort Campground					▲	●	■
Baraboo Hills Campground					▲	●	■
Bass Lake Campground							■
Bonanza Campground & RV Park					▲	●	■
Country Roads Motorhome & RV Park					▲	●	■
Dell Boo Campground					▲	●	■
Dells Timberland Camping Resort						●	■
Eagle Flats Campground & RV Park							■
Holiday Shores Campground & Resort					▲	●	■
KOA-Wisconsin Dells					▲	●	■
River Bay Resort Campground, Marina & RV Park					▲	●	■
Sherwood Forest Camping & RV Park					▲	●	■
Stand Rock Campground						●	■
Yogi Bear's Jellystone Park Camp-Resort					▲	●	■
Yukon Trails Camping						●	■
WOODRUFF							
Hiawatha Trailer Resort					▲	●	■
Indian Shores Camping, Cottages & RV Condominium Resort					▲	●	■

Green Friendly 🍃; RV Lots for Sale ✖; Park Models/Onsite Onwership ✱; Park Memberships for Sale ✔; Big Rigs Welcome ▲;
Internet Friendly ●; Internet Friendly-WiFi ●; Pets Welcome ■

Andrae State Park is a draw for outdoor enthusiasts. Nationally renowned for its innovative exhibitions, the **John Michael Kohler Arts Center** offers insightful displays. Nearby the village of Elkhart Lake is home to **Road America**, a premier motor sports racetrack, gives fans racing excitement from April to October.

Stevens Point. Interact with the natural world at the **Museum of Natural History**. Explore the origins of Earth, discover dinosaurs and witness natural habitats and rare collections of species. At the **Riverfront Arts Center** view ever-changing exhibits by area and regional artists.

Trempealeau. Located north of La Crosse on the shores of the Mississippi, historic Trempealeau features prime opportunities for viewing wildlife and simply enjoying some beautiful land. **Perrot State Park** is located at the confluence of the Trempealeau and Mississippi Rivers. Because the area was once considered sacred ground by Native Americans, visitors will find burial and ceremonial mounds as well as petroglyphs within the park. **Trempealeau National Wildlife Refuge** is home to a wide variety of flora and fauna. View the refuge along the 5-mile, self-guided auto trail, from a half-mile nature trail, or from the observation deck that overlooks river bluffs and marshes.

Wisconsin Rapids. At **Glacial Lake Cranberries** you can tour one of the oldest cranberry marshes in central Wisconsin with an actual grower.

SOUTHERN REGION

Much like the rest of the state, this area holds the same Midwestern charm and beauty. Travelers will find Devil's Lake State Park, a true geological gem created by glaciers, the park's spring fed lake is surrounded on three sides by 500-foot cliffs.

Aztalan State Park. This park contains one of Wisconsin's most important archaeological sites. It showcases an ancient Middle-Mississippian village and ceremonial complex that thrived between A.D. 1000 and 1300.

Baraboo. View scenic wooded trails and beautiful canyons. Guided trail rides are available from Dell View Riding Stables and from Hilltop Stable. Or visit the **Circus World Museum** and view memorabilia, miniature circus layouts and the world's largest collection of circus wagons.

Blue Mounds. Discovered in 1939 by quarry workers blasting limestone, **Cave of the Mounds** is a limestone cavern 20 feet high opening into other rooms and galleries containing numerous mineral formations.

Eagle. Explore Old World Wisconsin, the Midwest's largest outdoor museum of living history, located in Southern Kettle Moraine State Forest. Visit one of our diverse ethnic

Where to Find CCUSA Parks

List City	Park Name	Map Coordinates
ALGOMA		
	Ahnapee River Trails Campground	J-1
	Big Lake Campground	J-1
BABCOCK		
	Country Aire Camping Resort	F-4
BAILEYS HARBOR		
	Baileys Grove Campground	I-2
	Beantown Campground	I-2
BALSAM LAKE		
	D.N. (Do Nothing) Campground	D-1
BANCROFT		
	Vista Royalle Campground	F-4
BARABOO		
	Fox Hill RV Park	H-4
BRISTOL		
	Happy Acres Kampground	I-6
BURLINGTON		
	Meadowlark Acres Family Campground and Christian Fellowship Center	I-6
CEDAR		
	Frontier RV Park & Campground	B-3
CHETEK		
	Chetek River Campground	E-2
	Northern Exposure Resort & Campground	E-2
	Six Lakes Resort & RV Park	E-2
CRIVITZ		
	Crossroads Campground	I-1
CUMBERLAND		
	Country Quiet RV Park & Campground	D-1
DE PERE		
	Apple Creek Family Campground & Lodge	F-6
EGG HARBOR		
	Egg Harbor Campground & RV Resort	I-1
	Frontier Wilderness Campground	I-1
FAIRCHILD		
	Briarwood RV Park & Campground	F-3
FLORENCE		
	Keyes Lake Campground	C-6
FOND DU LAC		
	Westward Ho Camp Resort (Morgan Rv Resort)	G-5
FORT ATKINSON		
	Yogi Bear Jellystone Park/Fort Atkinson	I-5
GOODMAN		
	Lake Hilbert Campground	D-6
GORDON		
	Happy Ours RV Park	C-2
GRESHAM		
	Captain's Cove Resort and Country Club, LLC	E-5
KEWAUNEE		
	Kewaunee Village RV Park & Campground	J-1
KNOWLTON		
	Lake DuBay Shores Campground & RV Park	F-4
LODI		
	Smokey Hollow Campground	H-4
MILTON		
	Hidden Valley RV Resort & Campground	I-5
MINOCQUA		
	Patricia Lake RV Resort	D-4
MONTELLO		
	Buffalo Lake Camping Resort	G-4

Where to Find CCUSA Parks

List City	Park Name	Map Coordinates
	Ox Creek RV Park	G-4
NORMAN		
	Maple View Campground	F-6
OSHKOSH		
	Kalbus Country Harbor, Inc	G-5
PARDEEVILLE		
	Duck Creek Campground	H-4
PEARSON		
	Northern Hideaway RV Park & Campground	D-5
PORTAGE		
	Pride of America Camping Resort	H-4
	Sky High Camping Resort	H-4
PORTERFIELD		
	Diamond Lake Family Campground & Trout Farm	I-1
PRAIRIE DU CHIEN		
	Frenchman's Landing Campground	I-2
REEDSVILLE		
	Rainbows End Campground	G-6
RIO		
	Silver Springs Campsites, Inc.	H-5
	Willow Mill Campsite LLC	H-5
SHAWANO		
	Pine Grove Campground	E-5
SPARTA		
	Leon Valley Campground	G-3
SPOONER		
	Scenic View Campground	D-2
THREE LAKES		
	The Harbor Campground	D-5
TOMAHAWK		
	Terrace View Campsites	D-4
TREGO		
	Log Cabin Resort & Campground	C-2
TWO RIVERS		
	Badger RV Park @ Village Inn on the Lake	G-6
WABENO		
	S-J & W Ham Lake Campground LLC	D-5
WASHINGTON ISLAND		
	Washington Island Camping Retreat	I-2
WILTON		
	Tunnel Trail Campground	G-3
WISCONSIN DELLS		
	American World - Mt. Olympus Hotel & RV Resort	H-4
	Arrowhead Resort Campground	H-4
	Bonanza Campground & RV Park	H-4
	Yogi Bear's Jellystone Park Camp-Resort	H-4
WONEWOC		
	Chapparal Campground & Restaurant	H-3
WOODRUFF		
	Hiawatha Trailer Resort	C-4
	Indian Shores Camping, Cottages & RV Condominium Resort	C-4

farmsteads or stroll through an actual 1870s Crossroads Village where you can chat with merchants and townsfolk in authentic turn of the century homes and shops. You can experience interactive, hands-on activities and historic crafts such as quilting, wool rug braiding and blacksmithing.

Great Wisconsin Birding & Nature Trail. Dividing Wisconsin into five wildlife-viewing regions, the Great Wisconsin Birding and Nature Trail links important wildlife sites within each area. The entire driving trail encompasses five regional trails. A cooperative effort between more than 100 organizations and the Endangered Resource Program, these trails blend existing roads with customized maps to guide nature travelers to Wisconsin's best wildlife watching areas, as well as historic sites and bike trails. The five trails are: Lake Superior/Northwoods trail, Mississippi/Chippewa Rivers Birding and Nature Trail, Lake Michigan's Birding and Nature Trail, Central Sands Birding and Nature Trail and the Southern Savanna Birding and Nature Trail.

Lake Geneva is nicknamed the "Newport of the Midwest" for its many lovely homes, estates and cottages. The lake itself offers boating, sailing, swimming and water skiing. Visitors can take narrated boat tours of Geneva Lake to view the many mansions lining its shores and learn of the town's rich history. One of the most notable, **Black Point Estate**, is now open to the public for tours. Visitors arrive at the estate via boat, the same way the residents arrived at their summer home each year. The stately home includes 13 bedrooms and a four-story tower that can be seen from many points on the lake.

Madison. This capital city is home to the University of Wisconsin–Madison. On campus is the **Chazen Museum of Art**, with paintings, sculptures and decorative arts dating back to 2300 B.C. The campus is also home to the **University of Wisconsin Arboretum**, a 1,260-acre outdoor ecology laboratory in the heart of the city and the **Geology Museum** featuring minerals, fossils and dinosaur bones.

Milwaukee. The "City of Festivals" features concert performances, professional sports events, historical tours, charter boat fishing on Lake Michigan, brewery tours, ethnic restaurants and beautiful architectural structures. Also within Milwaukee:

Discovery World at Pier Wisconsin. Located on Milwaukee's waterfront this aquatic museum offers immersive and interactive experiences highlighting Wisconsin's freshwater marine life and nautical science. Several large aquariums, both fresh and salt water, provide close contact with many water creatures unique to our area. It is also home to the S/V Denis Sullivan, Wisconsin's flagship schooner.

Harley-Davidson. New Harley Davidson Museum just opened in Milwaukee, showcases exhibits from Harley Davidson's collection of more than 400 vehicles. The 130,000 square foot museum features a restaurant and café, a retail shop, meeting space and special event facilities.

Milwaukee Public Museum, IMAX Theatre and Planetarium includes "you are there" exhibits such as a tropical rain forest and the streets of old Milwaukee, as well as life-size dinosaur exhibits. The new expansion at the **Milwaukee Art Museum** has turned it into a world-class landmark. Highlights include a 250-foot suspended pedestrian bridge linking downtown Milwaukee to the Museum and lakefront. The permanent collection includes nearly 20,000 works, covering a wide spectrum of art dating from antiquity to the present. Adjacent to the Museum is the six-story Humphrey IMAX Dome Theatre and Daniel M. Soref Planetarium, which seat approximately 275 viewers.

Potosi Brewery Company Complex. For beer enthusiasts interested in breweriana and brewery history, the Potosi Brewery Complex is now open. The museum offers changing exhibits of breweriana: collections of beer labels, bottles, coasters and other memorabilia. In addition to the exhibits, the Potosi Brewery, which operated for 120 years (1852-1972), will again re open as a microbrewery and restaurant. Located right on the Great River Road.

Mineral Point. Charming old world town with art studios, galleries, antique and specialty shops. Local artists host Gallery Nights and workshops are offered year-round. **Pendarvis State Historic Site** provides a fascinating glimpse to early Wisconsin.

Spring Green. This sparkling town along the Wisconsin River has a reputation that far outranks its size, thanks to its most famous native son, architect Frank Lloyd Wright. **Taliesin,** Wright's 600-acre estate, is built into the hills of the Wisconsin River and Valley. The **American Players Theatre** presents classics in an open-air setting near the Wisconsin River. The **House on the Rock** is a world-famous museum with out-of-the-ordinary collections.

Wisconsin Dells is a popular tourist attraction area with such features as boat and amphibious vehicle trips to view unique rock formations. In and around the Wisconsin Dells and Lake Delton area, there are many family attractions. The extensive list includes **Dells Motor Speedway, Noah's Ark Waterpark, Family Land Waterpark, Original Wisconsin Ducks, Ripley's Believe It or Not! Museum, Riverside & Great Northern Railway, Riverview Park, Robot World, Tommy Bartlett's Legendary Thrill Show, Storybook Gardens** and a variety of tours of the Upper and Lower Dells. Another highlight of the Dells is **H.H. Bennett Studio and History Center,** opened as a studio in 1875 and now a state historic site.

ANNUAL EVENTS

JANUARY

Boat Show, Milwaukee; Waukesha JanBoree, Waukesha; Annual Kites on the River, Two Rivers; Winter Fest, Phillips; Polar Bear Swim, Jacksonport, Sheboygan & Nekoosa; Polar Bear Dip, Port Washington; Flake Out Festival, Wisconsin Dells; Annual World Championship Snowmobile Derby, Eagle River; Eagle Watching Days, Sauk City and Prairie du Sac.

FEBRUARY

Iola Winter Carnival, Iola; RV & Camping Show, Madison; Hot Air Affair, Hudson; Arti Gras, Green Bay; Ice Fisheree, Prairie du Chien; Orchid Quest, Madison; Winter Festival, Cedarburg; Snowflake International Ski Jump Tournament, Westby; Klondike Days Family Celebration, Eagle River; American Birkebeiner, Hayward to Cable.

MARCH

Maple Fest, Amery; Maypenny Madness Winter Carnival, Bayfield; Overture's International Festival, Madison; Model Train Show, LaCrosse; Winter Wine Fest & Craft Show, Jefferson; Custom Auto Show, LaCrosse.

APRIL

Yo-Yo Convention & Toy Celebration, Burlington; WPS Farm Show, Oshkosh; Wisconsin Film Festival, Madison; Wisconsin Deer & Turkey Expo, Madison; Latin American Film Series, Milwaukee; Springtime Polka Fest, Osseo.

MAY

Bloody Lake Rendezvous, Woodford; Going Green Expo, Madison; Apple Holler Festival, Sturtevant; Morel Mushroom Festival, Muscoda; Spring Expo, Park Falls; Annual Syttende Mai Festival, Westby; Janesville Renaissance, Janesville; Wisconsin State Polka Festival, Sullivan; Onalaska Sunfish Days, Onalaska; Ringelspiel Days, Boyd; Arcadia Broiler Days, Arcadia; Yesteryear Days, Albany; World's Largest Brat Fest, Madison; Asparagus Festival, Sturtevant; Chocolate Festival, Burlington; Ho-Chunk Nation Pow Wow, Black River Falls; Celebrate De Pere, De Pere; Ojibwe Pow Wow, Hayward.

JUNE

Cranberry Blossom Festival, Wisconsin Rapids; Cedarburg Strawberry Festival, Cedarburg; Big Gust Days, Grantsburg; Wisconsin Cheese Festival, Little Chute; Dairyfest, Marshfield; Annual Port Pirate Festival, Port Washington; Sawdust City Days, Eau Claire; Monroe Balloon Festival, Monroe; Prairie Villa Rendezvous, Prairie Du Chien; Czech-Slovak Festival, Phillips; Strawberry Fest, Waupaca.

JULY

Central Burnett County Fair, Webster; Riverfest, La Crosse; Sawdust Days, Oshkosh; Booster Days, Hudson; Wausau Area 4th of July Celebration, Wausau; Altrusa Polkafest, Black Creek; Mid-Western Rodeo, Manawa; Strawberries & Cream Festival, Medford; Oneida Pow Wow, Oneida; Northern Wisconsin State Fair, Chippewa Falls; Jefferson County Fair, Jefferson; Bastille Days, Milwaukee; Hodag Country Music Festival, Rhinelander; Colby Cheese Days, Colby; St. Albert's Fest, Sun Prairie; Mill Street Festival, Plymouth; Rock Fest, Cadott; Festa Italiana, Milwaukee; Outagamie County Fair, Seymour; Head of the Lakes Fair, Superior; Green County Fair, Monroe; Columbia County Fair, Portage.

AUGUST

Peninsula Music Festival, Fish Creek; Winnebago County Fair, Oshkosh; Wisconsin Valley Fair, Wausau; Fuddfest Country Festival, Deerbrook; Riverfest, Watertown; Utica Festival, Cambridge; Vilas County Fair, Eagle River; Adams County Fair, Friendship; Irish Fest, Milwaukee; Waushara County Fair, Wautoma; Dodge County Fair, Beaver Dam; Brown County Fair, De Pere; Rutabaga Festival, Cumberland; Sweet Corn Festival, Sun Prairie; Beef & Dairy Days, Whitehall; Blues Festival, Grafton.

SEPTEMBER

Wine & Harvest Festival, Cedarburg; The Warrens Cranberry Festival, Warrens; Central Wisconsin State Fair, Marshfield; Shawano County Fair, Shawano; Iowa County Fair, Mineral Point; Wisconsin State Cow Chip Throw, Prairie Du Sac; South Pier Festival, Sheboygan; Baraboo River Rendezvous, Baraboo; Calumet County Fair, Chilton; Rock River Thresheree, Edgerton.

OCTOBER

Audubon Days, Mayville; Mosquito Hill Nature Center Harvest Moon Festival, New London; Apple Affair, Galesville; Apple Festival, Bayfield; Fall Festival, Albany; Pumpkin Fest, Three Lakes; UFO Day, Belleville; Cranberry Festival, Stone Lake & Eagle River.

NOVEMBER

Swissfest, Monroe; Wisconsin Original Cheese Festival, Madison; Gem & Mineral Show, Madison; The Polar Express, Green Bay; Winter Magic, St. Germain.

DECEMBER

Holiday Parades, (throughout the state); Candlelight Stroll, Hudson; Bluegill Christmas Festival, Birchwood; Festival of the Trees, Whitehall; Holiday Ice Show, Pleasant Prairie.

ALGOMA—J-1

(NW) Ahnapee River Trails Campground—(Kewaunee) *From jct Hwy 54 & Hwy 42: Go 2 mi N on Hwy 42, then 1 mi W on Washington Rd, then 1 mi S on CR M to Wilson Rd, then 1 mi E (follow signs). Enter at end.* ◆◆◆FACILITIES: 65 sites, typical site width 40 ft, 45 W&E, (30 amps), 20 no hkups, 4 pull-thrus, WiFi Internet central location, family camping, tenting, dump, non-guest dump $, portable dump, laundry, ltd groc, RV supplies, ice, picnic tables, fire rings, wood. ◆◆◆RECREATION: swim pool, boating, canoeing, kayaking, river fishing, playground, horseshoes, hiking trails, v-ball. Pets welcome. Partial handicap access. Open May 1 - Mid Oct. Rate in 2010 $29-30 per family. MC/VISA/Debit. Member ARVC, WACO. CCUSA 50% Discount. CCUSA reservations Recommended, CCUSA max stay 4 days, CCUSA disc. not avail F,Sa, CCUSA disc. not avail holidays. Not available Memorial Day weekend thru Labor Day.

Phone: (920)487-5777
Address: E 6053 W. Wilson Rd., Algoma, WI 54201
Lat/Lon: 44.63179/-87.46941
Email: ahnapee@itol.com
Web: www.ahnapee.com

(C) Big Lake Campground—(Kewaunee) *From jct Hwy 54 & Hwy 42: Go 1 mi S on Hwy 42. Enter on R.* ◆◆FACILITIES: 86 sites, typical site width 30 ft, 42 full hkups, 30 W&E, (20/30/50 amps), 14 no hkups, 1 pull-thrus, WiFi Instant Internet at site, WiFi Internet central location, family camping, tenting, RV storage, dump, non-guest dump $, laundry, ice, picnic tables, fire rings, wood. ◆◆RECREATION: fishing supplies, fishing guides, play equipment, horseshoes. Pets welcome. Open May 1 - mid Oct. Rate in 2010 $33 for 4 persons. CCUSA 50% Discount. CCUSA reservations Recommended, CCUSA max stay 2 days, Cash only for CCUSA disc., CCUSA disc. not avail F,Sa. Not available Memorial Day weekend thru Labor Day.

Phone: (920)487-2726
Address: 2427 Lake St., Algoma, WI 54201
Lat/Lon: 44.59040/-87.44666
Email: mlthomas@itol.com
Web: www.biglakecampground.com

(NW) Timber Trail Campground—(Kewaunee) *From jct Hwy 54 & Hwy 42: Go 1/2 mi N on Hwy 42, then 1 mi W on CR-S, then 3/4 mi N on CR-M. Enter on R.* ◆◆◆◆FACILITIES: 100 sites, typical site width 40 ft, 95 W&E, (20/30/50 amps), 5 no hkups, 13 pull-thrus, family camping, tenting, dump, laundry, ltd groc. ◆◆◆◆RECREATION: swim pool, boating, canoeing, river fishing, playground. Pets welcome, breed restrict. Open Mid Apr - Mid Oct. Rate in 2010 $26-34 per family. Member ARVC, WACO. Phone: (920)487-3707.

AMHERST—F-4

(E) Wild West Campground & Corral—(Portage) *From jct Hwy 39/Hwy 51/Hwy 54: Go 12 mi E on Hwy 54. Enter on R.* FACILITIES: 54 sites, typical site width 30 ft, 54 W&E, (30 amps), family camping, tenting, dump, ltd groc. Pets welcome. Open all yr. Facilities fully operational Apr 15 - Oct 15. Rate in 2010 $30 per family. Member ARVC, WACO. Phone: (715)824-5112.

AMHERST JUNCTION—F-4

(W) LAKE EMILY PARK (Portage County Park)—(Portage) *From town: Go 1 mi W on Old US-18.* FACILITIES: 66 sites, 65 E, (20 amps), 1 no hkups, tenting, dump. RECREATION: lake swim, boating, ramp, dock, lake fishing, playground. Partial handicap access. Open May 1 - Oct 31. Phone: (715)346-1433.

APPLETON—F-5

See listings at DePere, Fremont, New London, Stockbridge & Waupaca

APPLETON—Continued

TRUCK COUNTRY—*From jct US 41 & CR J (exit 150): Go 300 yds N on CR J, then 1/2 mi W on Progress Way. Enter on L.* SERVICES: full-time mech, engine/chassis repair, body work/collision repair, 24-hr emerg rd svc, RV towing. Front end alignment. Open all yr. MC/VISA/DISC/AMEX/Debit.

Wisconsin State Motto: "Forward"

APPLETON—Continued
TRUCK COUNTRY—Continued

Phone: (800)236-5271
Address: 2401 Progress Way, Kaukauna, WI 54913
Lat/Lon: 44.30418/-88.25791
Web: www.truckcountry.com

SEE AD TRAVEL SECTION PAGE 798 AND AD IA TRAVEL SECTION PAGE 247

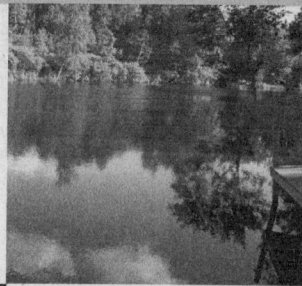

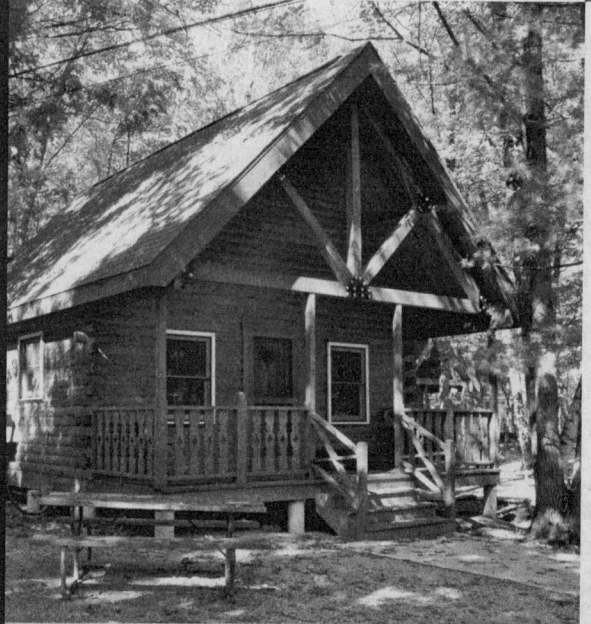

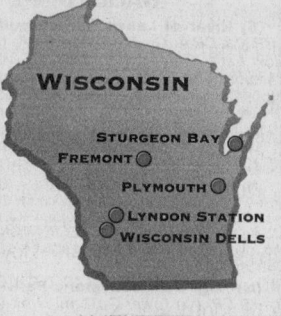

ARMSTRONG CREEK—D-5

(W) NICOLET NATIONAL FOREST (Laura Lake Campground)—(Forest) *From town: Go 2 mi W on US 8, then 5 mi N on FR 2163.* FACILITIES: 41 sites, 41 no hkups, tenting. RECREATION: lake swim, boating, electric motors only, ramp, lake fishing. Partial handicap access. Open May 2 - Oct 17. Phone: (715)674-4481.

ASHLAND—B-3

(NE) KREHER RV PARK (Municipal Park)—(Ashland) *In town on US 2.* FACILITIES: 28 sites, 28 no hkups, 2 pull-thrus, dump. RECREATION: lake swim, boating, ramp, dock, lake fishing, playground. Partial handicap access. No tents. Open May 15 - Oct 15. Phone: (715)682-7061.

PRENTICE PARK (Municipal Park)—(Ashland) *At West city limits on US-2.* FACILITIES: 19 sites, 9 E, 10 no hkups, tenting. RECREATION: lake swim, lake/pond fishing, playground. Open May 1 - Oct 30. Phone: (715)682-7061.

ATHELSTANE—D-6

(W) McCaslin Mountain Campground LLC—(Marinette) *From jct Hwy 32 & CR F (in Lakewood): Go 10 mi E on CR F. Enter on L.* ◆◆FACILITIES: 100 sites, typical site width 50 ft, 48 W&E, (20/30/50 amps), 52 no hkups, tenting, dump, ltd groc. ◆◆◆RECREATION: playground. Pets welcome, breed restrict. Open all yr. Facilities fully operational May 15 - Dec 1. Rate in 2010 $20-32 per family. Member ARVC, WACO. Phone: (715) 757-3734.

AUGUSTA—F-2

COON FORK LAKE PARK (Eau Claire County Park)—(Eau Claire) *From town: Go 1 mi E on US 12, then 4 mi N on CR CF.* FACILITIES: 88 sites, 37 E, 51 no hkups, tenting, dump. RECREATION: lake swim, boating, electric motors only, canoeing, ramp, dock, lake fishing, playground. Partial handicap access. Open May 1 - Sep 15. Phone: (715)839-4738.

BABCOCK—F-4

(S) Country Aire Camping Resort—(Wood) *From south jct Hwy 80 & Hwy 173: Go 1/8 mi S on Hwy 173. Enter on R.* ◆◆◆FACILITIES: 39 sites, 39 W&E, (20/30 amps), 7 pull-thrus, WiFi Internet central location, family camping, tenting, RV storage, dump, portable dump, ltd groc, RV supplies, ice, picnic tables, fire rings, wood. ◆◆◆RECREATION: swim pool, pond fishing, bsktball, playground, activities, horseshoes, hiking trails, v-ball. Pets welcome. Open Apr 1 - Dec 1. Rate in 2010 $30 per vehicle. Member ARVC, WACO. CCUSA 50% Discount. CCUSA reservations Recommended, CCUSA max stay 5 days, Cash only for CCUSA disc., CCUSA disc. not avail F,Sa, CCUSA disc. not avail holidays. Not available during deer season.

Phone: (715)884-2300
Address: 1221 Hwy 173, Babcock, WI 54413
Lat/Lon: 44.29324/-90.12978
Email: countryaire@tds.net
Web: www.countryairecampingresort.com

BAGLEY—I-2

(S) River of Lakes Campground—(Grant) *From jct CR-X & CR-A: Go 1 mi S on CR-A, then 3/4 mi W on Willow Lane. Enter on R.* ◆◆FACILITIES: 192 sites, 8 full hkups, 164 W&E, (20/30/50 amps), 20 no hkups, 30 pull-thrus, tenting, dump, ltd groc. ◆◆◆RECREATION: river swim, boating, canoeing, ramp, dock, river fishing, play equipment. Pets welcome. Open Mid Apr - Oct 31. Rate in 2010 $23-25 per family. Phone: (608) 996-2275.

(N) WYALUSING STATE PARK—(Grant) *From jct US 18/Hwy 12 & CR C: Go 3-1/4 mi W on CR C, then 1 mi W on CR CX, then 200 yds N on State Park Ln.* FACILITIES: 109 sites, 34 E, 75 no hkups, tenting, dump. RECREATION: boating, canoeing, ramp, playground. Partial handicap access. Open all yr. Phone: (608)996-2261.

(N) Yogi Bear Jellystone Park—(Grant) *From jct CR A & CR X in town: Go 1 mi N on CR X. Enter on R.* ◆◆◆◆FACILITIES: 204 sites, typical site width 40 ft, 103 full hkups, 86 W&E, (20/30/50 amps), 15 no hkups, 7 pull-thrus, family camping, tenting, dump, laundry, groceries. ◆◆◆◆◆RECREATION: swim pool, playground. Pets welcome. Open Apr 30 - Oct 10. Big rigs welcome. Rate in 2010 $23-50 per family. Member ARVC, WACO. Phone: (608)996-2201.

BAILEYS HARBOR—I-2

(W) BAILEYS GROVE CAMPGROUND—(Door) *From jct Hwy-57 & CR-EE/F: Go 1/2 mi W on CR-EE/F. Enter on R.*

◆◆◆◆FACILITIES: 95 sites, typical site width 40 ft, 55 full hkups, 40 W&E, (30/50 amps), some extd stay sites, 57 pull-thrus, WiFi Instant Internet at site, family camping, tenting, dump, non-guest dump $, portable dump, laundry, RV supplies, ice, picnic tables, fire rings, wood.

Wisconsin's Door County has five state parks and 250 miles of shoreline along Lake Michigan. This is more than any other county in the country.

BAILEYS HARBOR—Continued
BAILEYS GROVE CAMPGROUND—Continued

◆◆RECREATION: rec room/area, coin games, swim pool, golf nearby, bsktball, playground, horseshoes, sports field.

Pets welcome, breed restrict. Partial handicap access. Open May 1 - Mid Oct. Big rigs welcome. Escort to site. Clubs welcome. Rate in 2010 $30-36 per family. MC/VISA/DISC/Debit. CCUSA 50% Discount. CCUSA reservations Recommended, CCUSA max stay 1 day, Cash only for CCUSA disc., CCUSA disc. not avail Sa, CCUSA disc. not avail holidays. Discount available May 1-Jun 10 & Sep 1-Oct 1.

Phone: (866)839-2559
Address: 2552 CR F, Baileys Harbor, WI 54202
Lat/Lon: 45.07141/-87.13624
Email: campnowwi@yahoo.com
Web: www.baileysgrovecampground.com

SEE AD DOOR COUNTY PAGE 813

(W) Baileys Woods Campground—(Door County) *From jct Hwy 57 & CR EE/F: Go 3/4 mi W on CR EE/F, then 1/4 mi W on CR EE. Enter on L.* ◆◆◆FACILITIES: 79 sites, typical site width 20 ft, 30 ft max RV length, 25 W&E, 18 E, (30 amps), 36 no hkups, 2 pull-thrus, family camping, tenting, dump. ◆RECREATION: play equipment. Pets welcome. Partial handicap access. Open Mid May - Mid Oct. Rate in 2010 $25-30 per family. Member ARVC, WACO. Phone: (262)470-7091.

(NW) Beantown Campground—(Door) *From jct Hwy 57 & CR EE/F: Go 3/4 mi W on CR EE/F, then 1/2 mi N on CR F. Enter on R.* ◆◆◆FACILITIES: 85 sites, typical site width 30 ft, 62 full hkups, 7 W&E, (20/30/50 amps), 16 no hkups, 44 pull-thrus, cable TV, WiFi Instant Internet at site, family camping, tenting, RV storage, laundry, ltd groc, RV supplies, ice, picnic tables, fire rings, grills, wood. ◆◆◆RECREATION: rec hall, swim pool, playground, v-ball. Pets welcome. Partial handicap access. Open May 1 - Oct 31. Big rigs welcome. Rate in 2010 $30-35 per family. MC/VISA/AMEX/Debit. Member ARVC, WACO. CCUSA 50% Discount. CCUSA reservations Required, CCUSA max stay 1 day, CCUSA disc. not avail F,Sa, CCUSA disc. not avail holidays. Not available Jul & Aug.

Phone: (920)839-1439
Address: 8400 County Rd F, Baileys Harbor, WI 54202
Lat/Lon: 45.07583/-87.14061
Email: info@beantowncg@itol.com
Web: www.beantowncampground.com

BALSAM LAKE—D-1

(E) D.N. (Do Nothing) Campground—(Polk) *From jct of US/Hwy 46 & CR-H: Go 3-1/2 mi N on CR-H, then 1/2 mi E on 165th Ave. Enter on R.* ◆◆◆FACILITIES: 86 sites, typical site width 30 ft, 70 full hkups, 6 W&E, 10 E, (20/30 amps), 5 pull-thrus, family camping, tenting, dump, portable dump, ltd groc, ice, picnic tables, fire rings, wood. ◆◆◆RECREATION: pavilion, river swim, river fishing, bsktball, playground, horseshoes, v-ball. Pets welcome. Open all yr. Facilities fully operational Apr 1 - Oct 15. Rate in 2010 $25 for 4 persons. CCUSA 50% Discount.

Phone: (715)268-8980
Address: 956 165th Ave, Balsam Lake, WI 54810
Lat/Lon: 45.44621/-92.35725

BANCROFT—F-4

(N) VISTA ROYALLE CAMPGROUND—(Portage) *From jct I-39/US 51 (exit 143) & CR W: Go 3/4 mi E on CR W, then 1 mi N on Isherwood Rd. Enter on R.*

◆◆◆◆◆FACILITIES: 275 sites, typical site width 36 ft, 166 full hkups, 109 W&E, (30/50 amps), some extd stay sites, 20 pull-thrus, WiFi Internet central location, family camping, tenting, RV's/park model rentals, cabins, RV storage, dump, non-guest dump $, portable dump, laundry, ltd groc, RV supplies, LP gas by weight/by meter, ice, picnic tables, fire rings, wood.

◆◆◆◆◆RECREATION: rec room/area, equipped pavilion, coin games, pond fishing, fishing supplies, mini-golf, ($), golf nearby, bsktball, playground, shuffleboard court 2 shuffleboard courts, activities (wkends), horseshoes, sports field, hiking trails, v-ball.

Pets welcome. Partial handicap access. Open Mid Apr - Mid Oct. Big rigs welcome. Clubs welcome. Rate in 2010 $37-40 per family. MC/VISA/Debit. Member ARVC, WACO. CCUSA 50% Discount.

Visit Woodall's blog at blog.woodalls.com

BANCROFT—Continued
VISTA ROYALLE CAMPGROUND—Continued

Phone: (715)335-6860
Address: 8025 Isherwood Rd, Bancroft, WI 54921
Lat/Lon: 44.32615/-89.50795
Web: www.vistaroyalle.com

SEE AD STEVENS POINT PAGE 824 AND AD TRAVEL SECTION PAGE 798

(N) VISTA ROYALLE RV SALES—*From jct I-39/US 51 (exit 143) & CR W: Go 3/4 mi E on CR W, then 1 mi N on Sherwood Rd. Enter on R.* SALES: park models, pre-owned unit sales. SERVICES: LP gas by weight/by meter, dump station, RV storage, sells parts/accessories. Sales, Service, Parts and Accessories. Open all yr. MC/VISA/Debit.

Phone: (715)335-6860
Address: 8025 Isherwood Rd, Bancroft, WI 54921
Lat/Lon: 44.32615/-89.50795
Web: www.vistaroyalle.com

SEE AD STEVENS POINT PAGE 824

BARABOO—H-4

(S) DEVIL'S LAKE STATE PARK—(Sauk) *From jct I-90/94 (exit 92) & US 12: Go 10 mi S on US 12, then 2 mi E on Hwy 159.* FACILITIES: 407 sites, 121 E, (20/30 amps), 286 no hkups, tenting, dump, ltd groc. RECREATION: lake swim, boating, electric motors only, canoeing, ramp, lake fishing, playground. Pets welcome. Partial handicap access. Open all yr. Phone: (608)356-8301.

(SW) FOX HILL RV PARK—(Sauk) *From jct I-90/94 (exit 92) & US 12: Go 2-1/2 mi S on Hwy 12, then 1 mi E on Reedsburg Rd. Enter on R.*

◆◆◆◆FACILITIES: 125 sites, typical site width 30 ft, 45 full hkups, 44 W&E, (20/30/50 amps), 36 no hkups, some extd stay sites, 30 pull-thrus, WiFi Instant Internet at site, family camping, tenting, cabins, dump, non-guest dump $, portable dump, laundry, ltd groc, RV supplies, ice, picnic tables, fire rings, wood.

◆◆◆◆RECREATION: rec room/area, pavilion, swim pool, golf nearby, bsktball, playground, activities, (wkends), horseshoes, sports field, hiking trails, v-ball.

Pets welcome. Partial handicap access. Open May 1 - Mid Oct. Big rigs welcome. Clubs welcome. Rate in 2010 $36-45 for 4 persons. MC/VISA/DISC/Debit. Member ARVC, WACO. CCUSA 50% Discount. CCUSA reservations Recommended, CCUSA max stay 4 days, CCUSA disc. not avail F,Sa, CCUSA disc. not avail holidays. Max 6 persons/site. Not available with other coupons or discounts.

Phone: (888)236-9445
Address: E11371 N Reedsburg Rd, Baraboo, WI 53913
Lat/Lon: 43.52833/-89.75516
Email: foxhill@foxhillrvpark.com
Web: www.foxhillrvpark.com

Reserve Online at Woodalls.com

SEE AD WISCONSIN DELLS PAGE 829

(S) Merry Mac's Campground—(Sauk) *From jct I-90 & Hwy 78 (exit 108 A): Go 7 mi W on 78 to DL, then 8 mi SW on DL, then 1/2 mi S on Hwy 113, then EWR. Enter on R.* ◆◆◆◆FACILITIES: 250 sites, typical site width 40 ft, 106 full hkups, 144 W&E, (30/50 amps), 8 pull-thrus, family camping, tenting, dump, laundry, ltd groc. ◆◆◆◆RECREATION: swim pool, pond fishing, playground. Pets welcome, breed restrict. Partial handicap access. Open Mid Apr - Mid Oct. Big rigs welcome. Rate in 2010 $30-45 Member ARVC, WACO. Phone: (608)493-2367.

(SW) RED OAK CAMPGROUND—(Sauk) *From jct I-90/94 (exit 92) & US 12: Go 3/4 mi S on US 12. Enter on L.*

◆◆FACILITIES: 81 sites, typical site width 20 ft, 15 full hkups, 14 W&E, (20/30/50 amps), 52 no hkups, 24 pull-thrus, tenting, dump, laundry, ltd groc, ice, picnic tables, fire rings, wood.

◆◆RECREATION: pavilion, swim pool, golf nearby, bsktball, v-ball.

Pets welcome. Open May 1 - Nov 1. Open/close dates depend on weather. Clubs welcome. Rate in 2010 $30 for 2 persons.

RED OAK CAMPGROUND—Continued on next page

Famous Wisconsinites: Don Ameche, Harry Houdini, Douglas MacArthur, Frank Lloyd Wright

BARABOO—Continued
RED OAK CAMPGROUND—Continued

Phone: (608)356-7304
Address: S2350 Timothy Lane, Baraboo, WI 53913
Lat/Lon: 43.56125/-89.77760
Email: redoakcamp@centurytel.net
Web: www.redoakcampground.weebly.com

SEE AD WISCONSIN DELLS PAGE 829

(S) Wheeler's Campground—(Sauk) *From jct Hwy 33/136 & US-12: Go 2-1/2 mi S on E US 12, then 1/2 mi E on Hwy 159. Enter on R.* ◇◇◇FACILITIES: 139 sites, typical site width 30 ft, 29 full hkups, 34 W&E, (20/30/50 amps), 76 no hkups, 5 pull-thrus, family camping, tenting, dump, laundry, ltd groc. ◇◇◇RECREATION: pond fishing, playground. Pets welcome, quantity restrict. Partial handicap access. Open May 1 - Mid Oct. Rate in 2010 $35-41 per family. Phone: (608)356-4877.

BARRON—D-2

(C) Barron Motel & RV Campground—(Barron) *From jct US 53 (exit 135) & US 8: Go 4 mi W on US 8, then 100 ft N on 15th St. Check in at motel office. Enter on R.* ◇◇◇◇FACILITIES: 17 sites, typical site width 35 ft, 8 full hkups, 9 E, (20/30 amps), 8 pull-thrus, family camping, tenting, dump. Pets welcome. Open May 1 - Oct 1. Rate in 2010 $26.50 for 2 persons. Phone: (888)464-8819.

BAYFIELD—B-3

(S) Apostle Islands Area Campground—(Bayfield) *From jct Hwy 13 & CR-J: Go 1/4 mi W on CR-J, then 1/4 mi N on Trailer Court Rd. Enter on R.* ◇◇◇FACILITIES: 56 sites, typical site width 30 ft, 17 full hkups, 24 W&E, (30/50 amps), 50 amps ($), 15 no hkups, 3 pull-thrus, family camping, tenting, dump, ltd groc. ◇RECREATION: play equipment. Pets welcome, quantity restrict. Open early May - Early Oct. Rate in 2010 $26-38 per family. Member ARVC, WACO. Phone: (715)779-5524.

APOSTLE ISLANDS NATIONAL LAKESHORE (Presque Isle-Stockton)—(Bayfield) *Access by excursion boat (Jul & Aug) or private boat. 16 mi NE of Bayfield on Stockton Island.* FACILITIES: 21 sites, 21 no hkups, tenting. RECREATION: lake swim, boating, canoeing, dock, lake fishing. Open all yr. Phone: (715) 779-3397.

BIG BAY STATE PARK—(Ashland) *Ferry to Madeline Island, then go 5 mi E on CR-"H".* FACILITIES: 60 sites, 60 no hkups, tenting, dump. RECREATION: lake swim, boating, canoeing, lake fishing. Partial handicap access. Open all yr. Facilities fully operational Apr 15 - Oct 31. Phone: (715)747-6425.

(N) ISLE VISTA CASINO'S BUFFALO BAY CAMPGROUND—(Bayfield) *From jct CR J & Hwy 13: Go 3 mi N on Hwy 13. Enter on R.*

WELCOME

◇◇FACILITIES: 69 sites, typical site width 20 ft, 12 full hkups, 9 W&E, 18 E, (20/30/50 amps), 30 no hkups, WiFi Instant Internet at site, WiFi Internet central location, family camping, tenting, dump, non-guest dump $, laundry, ice, picnic tables, fire rings, wood.

◇◇RECREATION: lake swim, boating, canoeing, kayaking, ramp, dock, lake fishing, golf nearby, play equipment, activities (wkends). Rec open to public.

Pets welcome. Partial handicap access. Open May 1 - Mid Oct. Big rigs welcome. Escort to site. Rate in 2010 $30-35 per vehicle. MC/VISA/Debit.

Phone: (715)779-3743
Address: 37620 Red Cliff Campground Rd, Bayfield, WI 54814
Lat/Lon: 46.85526/-90.78675
Email: buffalobay@centurytel.net
Web: www.redcliffcasino.com

SEE AD THIS PAGE

BELGIUM—H-6

(E) HARRINGTON BEACH STATE PARK—(Ozaukee) *From jct I-43 (exit 107) & CR D: Go 2-1/4 mi E on CR D, then 3/4 mi S on Sauk Trail Rd. Enter on R.* FACILITIES: 75 sites, 29 E, (20/30 amps), 46 no hkups, family camping, tenting, dump. RECREATION: lake swim, lake fishing. Pets welcome. Open all yr. Facilities fully operational Memorial Day - Mid Oct. Phone: (262) 285-3015.

BIG FLATS—G-4

(NW) Pineland Camping Park—(Adams) *From jct US 51 & CR V: Go 2 mi S on CR V, then 10 mi W on CR C, then 1 mi N on Hwy 13. From jct Hwy 13 & CR C: Go 1 mi N on Hwy 13. Enter on R.* ◇◇◇FACILITIES: 190 sites, typical site width 40 ft, 54 full hkups, 136 W&E, (20/30/50 amps), 5 pull-thrus, family camping, tenting, dump, laundry, ltd groc. ◇◇◇RECREATION: swim pool, playground. Pets welcome, breed restrict. Partial handicap access. Open Apr 1 - Dec 1. Rate in 2010 $23-35 per family. Member ARVC, WACO. Phone: (608) 564-7818.

Woodall's — Trusted for Over 75 Years.

BIRCHWOOD—D-2

(N) DOOLITTLE CITY PARK—(Washburn) *From town: Go 2 mi N on CR-"D" & Main St, then E on Hinman Dr.* FACILITIES: 40 sites, 40 E, (15 amps), tenting, dump. RECREATION: lake swim, boating, ramp, lake fishing, playground. Partial handicap access. Open May 15 - Oct 15. Phone: (715)354-3300.

BLACK RIVER FALLS—F-3

(SE) BLACK RIVER STATE FOREST (Castle Mound Recreation Area)—(Jackson) *From town: Go 1-1/2 mi SE on US 12.* FACILITIES: 35 sites, 5 E, (30 amps), 30 no hkups, 12 pull-thrus, tenting, dump. RECREATION: playground. Partial handicap access. Open all yr. Phone: (715)284-4103.

BLACK RIVER STATE FOREST (Pigeon Creek Recreation Area)—(Jackson) *12 mi SE on US 12, then 3 mi NE on N Settlement Rd.* FACILITIES: 38 sites, 38 no hkups, tenting. RECREATION: lake swim, boating, canoeing, lake fishing, playground. Partial handicap access. Open all yr. Phone: (715)284-4103.

(SW) Lost Falls Campground—(Jackson) *From jct I-94 (exit 116) & Hwy 54: Go 10-1/2 mi W & S on Hwy 54, then 1/4 mi S on Sunnyvale Rd. Enter on L.* ◇◇◇FACILITIES: 40 sites, 12 full hkups, 7 W&E, 3 E, (20/30/50 amps), 18 no hkups, 2 pull-thrus, family camping, tenting, ltd groc. ◇◇◇RECREATION: river swim, canoeing, river fishing, play equipment. Pets welcome ($). Partial handicap access. Open Mid May - Oct 1. Rate in 2010 $30-37 per family. Member ARVC, WACO. Phone: (800)329-3911.

BLANCHARDVILLE—I-4

(SW) YELLOWSTONE LAKE STATE PARK—(Lafayette) *From jct Hwy 78 & CR F: Go 8 mi SW on CR F, then 1-1/2 mi S on Lake Rd.* FACILITIES: 128 sites, 38 E, (30 amps), 90 no hkups, tenting, dump, groceries. RECREATION: lake swim, boating, canoeing, ramp, lake fishing, playground. Partial handicap access. Open all yr. Facilities fully operational May 1 - Oct 31. Phone: (608)523-4427.

BLOOMER—E-2

(N) Willie's RV Center & Campground (RV SPACES)—(Chippewa) *From jct US 53 (exit 112) & Hwy 64: Go 500 feet E on Hwy 64. Enter on L.* FACILITIES: 11 sites, 5 full hkups, 6 W&E, (20/30 amps), tenting, laundry. Pets welcome. Open all yr. Facilities fully operational Apr 15 - Oct 15. Rate in 2010 $15 per family. Phone: (715)568-4947.

BLUE MOUNDS—I-4

(N) BLUE MOUND STATE PARK—(Iowa) *From jct US 18/151 & CR F: Go 1 mi N on CR F, then 3/4 mi W on CR ID, then 1 mi N on Mounds Rd. Enter at end.* FACILITIES: 78 sites, 17 E, (30/50 amps), 61 no hkups, 2 pull-thrus, tenting, dump. RECREATION: swim pool, playground. Partial handicap access. Open all yr. Phone: (608)437-5711.

(NE) BRIGHAM PARK (Dane County Park)—(Dane) *From jct US 18/151 & Cave of the Mounds Rd: Go N on Cave of the Mounds Rd, then 1 mi N on CR F.* FACILITIES: 25 sites, 25 no hkups, tenting. RECREATION: play equipment. Open May 15 - Oct 1. Phone: (608)246-3896.

BLUE RIVER—H-3

(N) Eagle Cave Resort LLC—(Richland) *From jct Hwy 193 & Hwy 60: Go 3 mi W on Hwy 60, then 2-1/2 mi N on Eagle Cave Rd. Follow signs. Enter on L.* ◇◇◇FACILITIES: 78 sites, typical site width 18 ft, 35 ft max RV length, 56 W&E, (30 amps), 22 no hkups, family camping, tenting, dump, ltd groc. ◇◇◇RECREATION: lake/river swim, canoeing, pond fishing, playground. Pets welcome. Open all yr. Facilities fully operational Memorial Day wknd - Labor Day wknd. Rate in 2010 $20 per family. Phone: (608)537-2988.

BOULDER JUNCTION—C-4

(W) Camp Holiday—(Vilas) *From jct US 51 & CR H: Go 3 mi NE on CR H, then 500 feet E on Rudolph Lake Lane. Enter on R.* ◇◇◇◇FACILITIES: 230 sites, typical site width 40 ft, 179 full hkups, 50 W&E, (20/30/50 amps), 50 amps ($), 1 no hkups, 28 pull-thrus, family camping, tenting, dump, laundry, ltd groc. ◇◇◇◇RECREATION: lake swim, boating, electric motors only, canoeing, ramp, dock, lake fishing, playground. Pets welcome, quantity restrict. Partial handicap access. Open May 1 - Nov 1. Big rigs welcome. Rate in 2010 $28-38 for 2 persons. Member ARVC, WACO. Phone: (715)385-2264.

NORTHERN HIGHLAND/AMERICAN LEGION SF (Big Lake)—(Vilas) *From town: Go 8 mi W on CR K, then 1 mi N on CR P.* FACILITIES: 72 sites, 72 no hkups, tenting. RECREATION: lake swim, boating, ramp, dock, lake fishing. Open all yr. Phone: (715) 385-2727.

(N) NORTHERN HIGHLAND/AMERICAN LEGION SF (South Trout Lake)—(Vilas) *From town: Go 6 mi S on CR M. Enter on R.* FACILITIES: 23 sites, 23 no hkups, tenting. RECREATION: lake swim, boating, canoeing, ramp, lake/river fishing. Open Memorial Day - Labor Day. Phone: (715)385-2727.

(SW) NORTHERN HIGHLAND/AMERICAN LEGION SF (Upper Gresham Lake)—(Vilas) *From jct US 51 & CR H: Go 1-1/2 mi NE on CR H.* FACILITIES: 27 sites, 27 no hkups, tenting. RECREATION: lake swim, boating, ramp, dock. Partial handicap access. Open all yr. Phone: (715)385-2727.

Gaylord Nelson, the founder of Earth Day, was born in Clear Lake, Wisconsin, on June 4, 1916.

BOWLER—E-5

(E) MOHICAN RV PARK—(Shawano) *From jct CR G & CR A in Gresham: Go 3 mi W on CR A: Check in at "Bus Stop" in casino. Enter on R.*

WELCOME

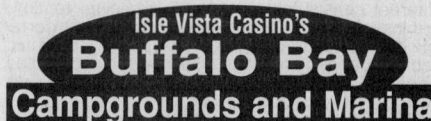

◇◇◇◇◇FACILITIES: 57 sites, typical site width 40 ft, accepts full hkup units only, 57 full hkups, (20/30/50 amps), 29 pull-thrus, phone Instant Internet at site, full svc store, RV supplies, LP bottle exch, ice, picnic tables, fire rings, wood.

RECREATION: golf nearby.

Pets welcome. Partial handicap access. No tents. Open all yr. Facilities fully operational Mid Apr - Mid Nov. Weather permitting. Big rigs welcome. Clubs welcome. Rate in 2010 $25-35 per vehicle. MC/VISA/DISC/Debit. ATM.

Phone: (715)787-2751
Address: W12180 CR A, Bowler, WI 54416-9401
Lat/Lon: 44.87324/-88.86159
Web: www.northstarcasinoresort.com

SEE AD NEXT PAGE

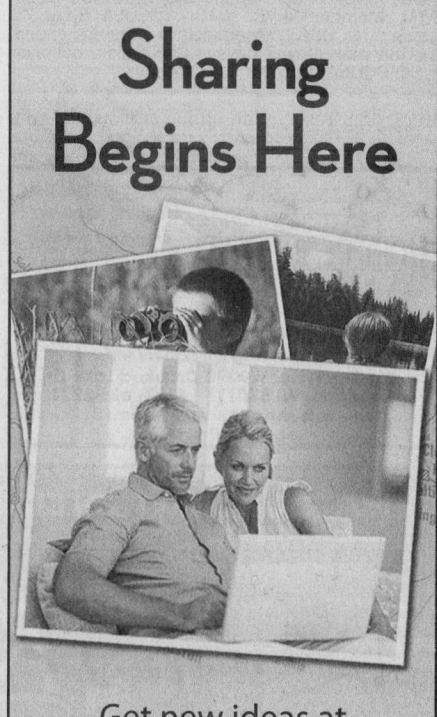

BOWLER—Continued on next page

Visit Woodall's Family Camping, RV destination and campground blog at blog.woodalls.com today!

BOWLER—Continued

(E) **NORTH STAR MOHICAN CASINO RESORT**—*From jct of CR G & CR A in Gresham: Go 3 mi W on CR A. Enter on R.*

YOUR VACATION DESTINATION

Mohican North Star is everyone's choice for year-round fun & RVing. Midwest Gaming & Travel Reader's Choice Awards recently recognized Mohican North Star as having the "Best Tribal Owned Golf Course" and "Best RV Park."

Full casino featuring blackjack, craps, roulette, bingo, slots & video poker. Also delicious food and free entertainment every weekend. Open all yr. MC/VISA/DISC/AMEX/Debit. ATM.

Phone: (800)775-CASH
Address: W12180 CR A, Bowler, WI 54416-9401
Lat/Lon: 44.87219/-88.86224
Web: www.northstarcasinoresort.com

SEE AD THIS PAGE

BRISTOL—I-6

(N) **HAPPY ACRES KAMPGROUND**—(Kenosha) *From jct Hwy 50 & US 45: Go 2 mi N on US 45, then 1-1/2 mi W on CR-"NN". Enter on R.*

◇◇◇FACILITIES: 224 sites, 191 W&E, (15/20/30/50 amps), 33 no hkups, some extd stay sites, 19 pull-thrus, WiFi Internet central location, family camping, tenting, cabins, shower$, dump, non-guest dump $, portable dump, laundry, ltd groc, RV supplies, ice, picnic tables, patios, fire rings, grills, wood, controlled access.

◇◇◇◇RECREATION: rec room/area, pavilion, equipped pavilion, coin games, swim pool, 3 kayak/9 pedal boat rentals, pond fishing, fishing supplies, mini-golf, ($), golf nearby, bsktball, 10 bike rentals, playground, activities, (wkends), horseshoes, sports field, hiking trails, v-ball. Rec open to public.

Pets welcome, breed restrict, size restrict. Partial handicap access. Open May 1 - Sep 30. Big rigs welcome. Escort to site. Clubs welcome. Rate in 2010 $36-47 per family. MC/VISA/DISC/Debit. ATM. Member ARVC, WACO. CCUSA 50% Discount. CCUSA reservations Recommended, CCUSA max stay 3 days, CCUSA disc. not avail F,Sa, CCUSA disc. not avail holidays.

Book your reservation online at woodalls.com

In Northern Kettle Moraine Area on Crooked Lake.

May 1 - Oct 1

• Sandy Beach • Tavern & Concession
• Canoe & Boat Rentals • Weekly Cottage Rentals
• Swimming • Good Fishing

For Brochure: W9070 Crooked Lake Dr. Cascade, WI 53011 (262) 626-2221
www.hoeftsresort.com
See listing at Cascade, WI

BRISTOL—Continued
HAPPY ACRES KAMPGROUND—Continued

Phone: (262)857-7373
Address: 22230 45th St., Bristol, WI 53104
Lat/Lon: 42.59755/-88.07795
Email: info@happyacres.com
Web: www.happyacres.com

SEE AD TRAVEL SECTION PAGE 799

BRODHEAD—I-4

(NW) **Crazy Horse Campground**—(Green) *From jct Hwy 11 and CR F: Go 1 mi W on CR F, then 1/2 mi S on Crazy Horse Lane. Enter on L.* ◇◇◇FACILITIES: 197 sites, typical site width 40 ft, 10 full hkups, 187 W&E, (20/30/50 amps), 12 pull-thrus, tenting, dump, laundry, ltd groc. ◇◇◇RECREATION: swim pool, river swim, boating, canoeing, river fishing, playground. Pets welcome. Open May 1 - Oct 31. Rate in 2010 $37-45 per family. Member ARVC, WACO. Phone: (608)897-2207.

BRULE—B-2

BRULE RIVER STATE FOREST (Bois Brule)—(Douglas) *From jct Hwy 27 & US 2: Go 1 mi W on US 2, then 1/2 mi W & 1 mi S on Ranger Rd.* FACILITIES: 20 sites, 20 no hkups, tenting. RECREATION: canoeing, river fishing. Pets welcome. Partial handicap access. Open all yr. Phone: (715)372-5678.

BRUSSELS—J-1

(NE) **Quietwoods South Camping Resort**—(Door) *From jct Hwy-57 & CR-C: Go 2-1/2 mi N on CR-C, then 1-1/2 mi E on CR-K, then 1/2 mi N on Lovers Lane. Enter on L.* ◇◇◇◇FACILITIES: 200 sites, typical site width 36 ft, 190 W&E, (30/50 amps), 10 no hkups, 8 pull-thrus, family camping, tenting, dump, laundry, ltd groc. ◇◇◇◇RECREATION: swim pool, pond fishing, playground. Pets welcome, breed restrict. Partial handicap access. Open last weekend April - End Oct. Big rigs welcome. Rate in 2010 $38-46 per family. Member ARVC, WACO. Phone: (920)825-7065.

BURLINGTON—I-6

BONG STATE RECREATION AREA—(Kenosha) *From jct Hwy 75 & Hwy 142: Go 1 mi W on Hwy 142.* FACILITIES: 217 sites, 54 E, (30 amps), 163 no hkups, tenting, dump. RECREATION: lake swim, boating, electric motors only, canoeing, ramp, lake fishing, play equipment. Partial handicap access. Open all yr. Phone: (262)878-5600.

(W) **Meadowlark Acres Family Campground and Christian Fellowship Center**—(Walworth) *From jct Hwys-36,83 & 11: Go 4 mi W on Hwy-11, then 1/2 mi S on North Rd. Enter on L.* ◇◇◇FACILITIES: 80 sites, 52 W&E, (20/30 amps), 28 no hkups, 24 pull-thrus, family camping, tenting, RV storage, dump, laundry, ltd groc, ice, picnic tables, fire rings, wood. ◇◇◇RECREATION: pavilion, swim pool, pond fishing, bsktball, 6 bike rentals, play equipment, activities horseshoes, hiking trails, v-ball. Pets welcome. Open May 1 - Oct 1. Rate in 2010 $25-45 per family. MC/VISA/DISC/Debit. Member ARVC, WACO. CCUSA 50% Discount. CCUSA max stay 2 days, CCUSA disc. not avail S,Th, CCUSA disc. not avail F,Sa, CCUSA disc. not avail holidays. Minimum stay 2 days.

Phone: (262)763-7200
Address: N 5146 North Road, Burlington, WI 53105
Lat/Lon: 42.67805/-88.35500
Email: info@meadowlarkacres.org
Web: www.meadowlarkacres.org

CABLE—C-2

CHEQUAMEGON NATIONAL FOREST (Namekagon Lake Campground)—(Bayfield) *From jct US-63 & CR-M: Go 12 mi E on CR-M, then 5-1/2 mi N on CR-D, then 1/3 mi SW on FR-209.* FACILITIES: 33 sites, 33 no hkups, tenting, ltd groc. RECREATION: lake swim, boating, ramp, lake fishing. Partial handicap access. Open May 1 - Oct 31. Phone: (715)634-4821.

CALEDONIA—I-6

(N) **Yogi Bear Jellystone Camp-Resort**—(Racine) *From I-94 (exit 326): Go 2 mi E on Seven Mile Rd, then 1/4 mi N on Hwy 38. Enter on R.* ◇◇◇◇◇FACILITIES: 244 sites, typical site width 40 ft, 116 full hkups, 97 W&E, (20/30/50 amps), 31 no hkups, 27 pull-thrus, family camping, tenting, dump, laundry, ltd groc. ◇◇◇◇◇RECREATION: swim pool, pond fishing, playground. Pets welcome. Partial handicap access. Open 1st Fri in May - Mid Oct. Big rigs welcome. Rate in 2010 $20-49 per family. Member ARVC, WACO. Phone: (262) 835-2565.

CAMERON—D-2

VETERANS MEMORIAL PARK (Barron County)—(Barron) *Go 1-1/2 mi S on CR-"SS", then 1 mi E on 12-1/2 Ave.* FACILITIES: 29 sites, 24 E, (20/30/50 amps), 5 no hkups, tenting, dump. RECREATION: lake swim, boating, ramp, dock, lake fishing, playground. Open May 1 - Oct 15. Phone: (715)458-4125.

CAMP DOUGLAS—G-3

(NE) MILL BLUFF STATE PARK—(Monroe) *From jct I-90 (exit 55) & US 12/16: Go 3 mi E on US 12/16.* FACILITIES: 21 sites, 6 E, 15 no hkups, tenting. RECREATION: playground. Partial handicap access. Open Memorial Day - Labor Day. Phone: (608)337-4775.

CAMPBELLSPORT—H-6

(E) **Benson's Century Camping Resort**—(Fond du Lac) *From jct US 45 & Hwy 67: Go 6 mi NE on Hwy 67. Enter on L.* ◇◇◇FACILITIES: 250 sites, typical site width 30 ft, 150 W&E, (20/30/50 amps), 100 no hkups, 1 pull-thrus, family camping, tenting, dump, ltd groc. ◇◇◇RECREATION: lake swim, boating, canoeing, ramp, dock, lake fishing, play equipment. Pets welcome. Open Mid May - Oct 15. Rate in 2010 $25 for 2 persons. Member ARVC, WACO. Phone: (920)533-8597.

(NE) KETTLE MORAINE SF-NORTHERN UNIT (Long Lake)—(Fond du Lac) *8 mi N via Hwy 67 & Kettle Moraine Dr. Entrance fee required.* FACILITIES: 200 sites, 200 no hkups, tenting, dump. RECREATION: lake swim, boating, canoeing, ramp, lake fishing. Partial handicap access. Open May 1 - Oct 15. Phone: (920)533-8612.

CASCADE—G-6

(W) **Hilly Haven Campground**—(Sheboygan) *From jct Hwy 57 & Hwy 28: Go 5 mi W on Hwy 28. Call ahead for reservation. Enter on L.* ◇◇◇FACILITIES: 100 sites, typical site width 35 ft, 75 full hkups, 25 W&E, (20/30/50 amps), 3 pull-thrus, family camping, tenting, dump, laundry, ltd groc. ◇◇◇RECREATION: swim pool, lake swim, boating, canoeing, ramp, dock, lake/river fishing, play equipment. Pets welcome. Open May 1 - 2nd Sun in Oct. Rate in 2010 $25 per family. Phone: (920)528-8966.

(SW) **HOEFT'S RESORT & CAMPGROUND**—(Sheboygan) *From jct Hwy 28 & CR-F: Go 6-1/4 mi W on CR-F, then 1-1/4 mi S on CR-W, then 1/2 mi S on Maple Tree Rd, then 3/4 mi W on Crooked Lake Dr. Enter on R.*

◇◇◇FACILITIES: 210 sites, 185 W&E, (20/30/50 amps), 25 no hkups, many extd stay sites, 0 pull-thrus, family camping, tenting, cabins, shower$, dump, portable dump, laundry, ltd groc, RV supplies, ice, picnic tables, fire rings, wood.

◇◇◇RECREATION: rec hall, coin games, lake swim, boating, 7.5 hp limit, canoeing, 13 rowboat/7 canoe/pedal boat rentals, lake fishing, golf nearby, bsktball, playground, horseshoes, hiking trails. Rec open to public.

HOEFT'S RESORT & CAMPGROUND—Continued on next page

PARK IT AT NORTH STAR MOHICAN CASINO RESORT

See listing at Bowler, WI

MOHICAN RV Park

1-800-775-CASH
or 1-715-RV-PARK-1

• North Star Mohican Casino Resort Next Door
• Open Year Round
• Full-Hookup Sites (50/30/20 amp services)
• Pull-Thru's Available
• Big Rig Friendly
• 24-Hour Security
• Pets Welcome
• Pine Hills Golf & Supper Club Nearby
• Satellite & Digital TV Friendly
• Woodall's ◇◇◇◇◇ Facilities
• GPS Coordinates: lat/long is 44"52'15.09 N\88"51'51.59 W

W12180 County Road A • Bowler, WI 54416
www.northstarcasinoresort.com

Pets welcome, quantity restrict. Open May 1 - Oct 1. Clubs welcome. Rate in 2010 $24-28 per family. MC/VISA/DISC/Debit. Member ARVC, WACO.

Phone: (262)626-2221
Address: W 9070 Crooked Lake Dr, Cascade, WI 53011
Lat/Lon: 43.62476/-88.15404
Email: hoeftsresort@aol.com
Web: www.hoeftsresort.com

SEE AD PAGE 810

CASSVILLE—I-3

(S) Big "H" Campground—(Clayton) *From jct Hwy 81 & Hwy 133: Go 9-1/2 mi S on Hwy 133, then 2 mi W on CR N. Enter on R.* ◇◇◇FACILITIES: 50 sites, typical site width 30 ft, 38 W&E, (20/30 amps), 12 no hkups, 8 pull-thrus, tenting, dump. ◇◇RECREATION: boating, canoeing, ramp, stream fishing, play equipment. Pets welcome. Open May 1 - Nov 1. Rate in 2010 $20-21 per vehicle. Phone: (608)725-5921.

(NW) NELSON DEWEY STATE PARK—(Grant) *From jct Hwy-133 & CR-VV: Go 1 mi NW on CR-VV. Enter on R.* FACILITIES: 45 sites, 16 E, (20/30 amps), 29 no hkups, tenting, dump. RECREATION: Partial handicap access. Open all yr. Facilities fully operational May 1 - Oct 31. Phone: (608)725-5374.

(S) Whitetail Bluff Camp & Resort, LLC—(Grant) *From jct Hwy 81 & Hwy 133: Go 9-1/2 mi S on Hwy 133, then 1-1/2 mi W on CR N, then 1-1/4 mi N on Irish Ridge Rd. Enter on R.* ◇◇◇FACILITIES: 108 sites, typical site width 30 ft, 92 full hkups, 16 E, (20/30/50 amps), 10 pull-thrus, tenting, dump, laundry, ltd groc. ◇◇◇◇RECREATION: swim pool, playground. Pets welcome. Partial handicap access. Open all yr. Facilities fully operational Apr 1 - Oct 1. Big rigs welcome. Rate in 2010 $28 per family. Member ARVC, WACO. Phone: (608)725-5577.

CECIL—E-6

CECIL LAKEVIEW PARK (Municipal Park)—(Shawano) *In town on Hwy 22.* FACILITIES: 40 sites, 40 W&E, tenting, dump. RECREATION: lake swim, boating, ramp, dock, lake fishing. Open May 1 - Sep 30. Phone: (715)745-4428.

CEDAR—B-3

(C) FRONTIER BAR—*At jct US 2 & Hwy 169.* Closed only on Christmas Day. We serve limited meals; burgers, chicken wings, nachos. Limited grocery with snacks in conjunction with a bar & gas station. Open all yr. Closed Christmas Day. MC/VISA.

Phone: (715)893-2461
Address: 11296 W US Hwy 2, Cedar, WI 54559
Lat/Lon: 46.51115/-90.50785

SEE AD THIS PAGE

(C) FRONTIER RV PARK & CAMPGROUND—(Iron) *At jct US-2 & Hwy-169.* ◇◇◇FACILITIES: 40 sites, typical site width 36 ft, 26 full hkups, 7 W&E, 2 E, (20/30/50 amps), 5 no hkups, some extd stay sites, 40 pull-thrus, WiFi Internet central location, family camping, tenting, shower$, laundry, ltd groc, LP bottle exch, ice, picnic tables, fire rings, grills, wood.

◇◇◇◇RECREATION: rec room/area, coin games, golf nearby, bsktball, playground, horseshoes, sports field, hiking trails.

Pets welcome. Open all yr. Facilities fully operational May 1 - Oct 15. Big rigs welcome. Rate in 2010 $26-31 for 2 persons. MC/VISA/DISC/AMEX/Debit. ATM. Member ARVC, WACO. CCUSA 50% Discount.

Phone: (715)893-2461
Address: 11296 W US Hwy 2, Cedar, WI 54559
Lat/Lon: 46.51115/-90.50785

SEE AD THIS PAGE

CHETEK—E-2

(SW) Chetek River Campground—(Barron) *From jct US 53 (exit 126) & CR I: Go 1/4 mi W on CR I, then 3/4 mi SW on River Rd. Enter on R.* ◇◇◇FACILITIES: 100 sites, typical site width 36 ft, 19 full hkups, 81 W&E, (20/30 amps), 4 pull-thrus, WiFi Instant Internet at site, family camping, tenting, shower$, dump, portable dump, ice, picnic tables, fire rings, wood. ◇◇◇◇RECREATION: swim pool, boating, no motors, canoeing, kayaking, dock, float trips, river fishing, mini-golf, ($), bsktball, 6 bike rentals, playground, shuffleboard court shuffleboard court, activities horseshoes, v-ball. Pets welcome. Open May 1 - Sept 30. Rate in 2010 $29-31 for 4 persons. MC/VISA/Debit. Member ARVC, WACO. CCUSA 50% Discount. CCUSA reservations

Recommended, CCUSA max stay Unlimited, CCUSA disc. not avail F,Sa, CCUSA disc. not avail holidays. Surcharges for A/C and electric heat.

Phone: (715)924-2440
Address: 590 24th St (River Road), Chetek, WI 54728
Lat/Lon: 45.29139/-91.66488
Email: camp@chetekriver.com
Web: www.chetekriver.com

(N) Northern Exposure Resort & Campground—(Barron) *From jct US 53 (exit 126) & CR I: Go 1/2 mi E on CR I, then 3/4 mi N on CR SS (Second St), then 2 mi N on CR M, then 1-1/2 mi NW on 10th Ave, then 1/2 mi E on 11th Ave, then 1/4 mi on 24-1/4 Ave. Enter at end.* ◇◇◇FACILITIES: 60 sites, 55 W&E, (20/30 amps), 5 no hkups, WiFi Instant Internet at site ($), tenting, shower$, dump, portable dump, ltd groc, ice, picnic tables, fire rings, wood. ◇◇◇RECREATION: lake swim, boating, canoeing, kayaking, ramp, dock, lake fishing, bsktball, playground. Pets welcome. Open Mid Apr - Oct 31. Rate in 2010 $25 per family. Member ARVC, WACO. CCUSA 50% Discount. CCUSA reservations Required, CCUSA max stay 3 days, Cash only for CCUSA disc., CCUSA disc. not avail F,Sa, CCUSA disc. not avail holidays. Maximum of 3 day advance reservation accepted prior to stays in Jun & Jul. Electric heater surcharge $3.

Phone: (800)731-2887
Address: 1075 24-1/4 Street, Cameron, WI 54728
Lat/Lon: 45.36075/-91.65923
Email: info@northernexposurevacation.com
Web: www.northernexposurevacation.com

(NE) SIX LAKES RESORT & RV PARK—(Barron) *From jct US 53 (exit 126) & CR I: Go 1/2 mi E on CR I, then 3/4 mi N on CR SS (Second St), then 1/2 mi E on CR D, then 1/2 mi N on 25th St. Enter at end.*

◇◇◇FACILITIES: 170 sites, typical site width 30 ft, 142 full hkups, 28 W&E, (30/50 amps), mostly extd stay sites, WiFi Internet central location, family camping, cabins, shower$, dump, non-guest dump $, portable dump, LP gas by weight, marine gas, ice, picnic tables, fire rings, wood.

◇◇◇◇RECREATION: rec room/area, coin games, lake swim, boating, canoeing, kayaking, dock, 3 pontoon/7 rowboat/pedal boat/4 motorboat rentals, lake fishing, golf nearby, bsktball, play equipment, sports field, v-ball. Rec open to public.

Pets welcome. No tents. Open May 1 - 1st wknd Oct. Big rigs welcome. Clubs welcome. Rate in 2010 $30-32 for 4 persons. MC/VISA/DISC/AMEX/Debit. CCUSA 50% Discount. CCUSA reservations Recommended, CCUSA max stay 5 days, CCUSA disc. not avail F,Sa, CCUSA disc. not avail holidays. Discount available before Memorial Day & after Labor Day weekends only.

Phone: (715)924-3680
Address: 2535 8 7/8th Ave, Chetek, WI 54728
Lat/Lon: 45.33460/-91.63873
Web: www.sixlakesresort.com

SEE AD TRAVEL SECTION PAGE 799

SOUTHWORTH MEMORIAL PARK (Barron County Park)—(Barron) *From town: Go 1-1/2 mi S on CR SS, then 1 mi E on 6th Ave, then 3/4 mi N on 26-1/2 St.* FACILITIES: 25 sites, 18 E, (20 amps), 7 no hkups, tenting. RECREATION: lake swim, boating, ramp, dock, lake/pond fishing, playground. Open May 1 - Oct 1. Phone: (715)537-6295.

CHIPPEWA FALLS—E-2

(NE) LAKE WISSOTA STATE PARK—(Chippewa) *From jct US 53 (exit 99) & CR S: Go 5-1/2 mi E on CR S, then 2 mi E on CR O. Enter on R.* FACILITIES: 81 sites, 17 E, (30/50 amps), 64 no hkups, 5 pull-thrus, tenting, dump. RECREATION: lake swim, boating, canoeing, ramp, dock, lake fishing, playground. Partial handicap access. Open Apr 1 - Nov. Phone: (715)382-4574.

(S) North Point RV—*From jct US 53 (exit 94) & CR 00: Go 1/4 mi W on CR 00, then 3/4 mi S on Bus 53. Enter on L.* SALES: travel trailers, park models, 5th wheels, toy hauler, Class A motorhomes, Class C motorhomes, pre-owned unit sales. SERVICES: full-time mech, RV appliance repair, LP gas by weight/by meter, dump station, RV rentals, sells parts/accessories, installs hitches. Open all yr. MC/VISA.

Phone: (800)962-4495
Lat/Lon: 44.88314/-91.42517
Email: pauld@northpointrv.com
Web: www.northpointrv.com

There are many ginseng growers in Marathon County, making it the Ginseng Capital of the world.

(N) O'NEIL CREEK CAMPGROUND & RV PARK—(Chippewa) *From jct US 53 (exit 99) & CR S: Go 2 mi E on CR S, then 2 mi N on Hwy 124, then 3/4 mi E on 105th Ave. Enter on L.*

◇◇◇◇FACILITIES: 391 sites, typical site width 28 ft, 101 full hkups, 288 W&E, (20/30/50 amps), 2 no hkups, many extd stay sites, 10 pull-thrus, WiFi Internet central location, family camping, tenting, cabins, dump, portable dump, laundry, ltd groc, RV supplies, LP gas by weight/by meter, ice, picnic tables, patios, fire rings, wood.

◇◇◇◇◇RECREATION: rec hall, rec room/area, coin games, river swim, boating, canoeing, kayaking, ramp, dock, 3 rowboat/3 canoe/3 pedal boat rentals, river fishing, fishing supplies, mini-golf, ($), golf nearby, bsktball, playground, activities, (wkends), horseshoes, hiking trails, v-ball.

Pets welcome. Partial handicap access. Open Apr 15 - Oct 15. Big rigs welcome. Clubs welcome. Rate in 2010 $29-35 per family. MC/VISA/DISC/AMEX/Debit. ATM.

Phone: (715)723-6581
Address: 14912 105th Ave, Chippewa Falls, WI 54729
Lat/Lon: 44.99531/-91.37009
Email: office@oneilcreek.com
Web: www.oneilcreek.com

SEE AD TRAVEL SECTION PAGE 799

(E) Pine Harbor Campground—(Chippewa) *From jct US 53 (exit 92) & Hwy 124: Go 3 mi N on Hwy 124, then 2 mi E on Hwy 29, then 2-3/4 mi E on CR X, then 1 mi N on 190th St, then 1/2 mi W on 70th Ave, then 1/4 mi N on 185th St. Enter on R.* ◇◇◇FACILITIES: 45 sites, typical site width 36 ft, 20 full hkups, 16 W&E, (20/30/50 amps), 9 no hkups, 6 pull-thrus, family camping, tenting, dump, laundry. ◇◇RECREATION: play equipment. Pets welcome. Open May 1 - Oct 15. Big rigs welcome. Rate in 2010 $25 per family. Member ARVC, WACO. Phone: (715)723-9865.

CLAM LAKE—C-3

(N) CHEQUAMEGON NATIONAL FOREST (Day Lake Campground)—(Ashland) *From town: Go 1 mi N on CR-GG, then 3/4 mi W on FR-1298.* FACILITIES: 52 sites, 52 no hkups, tenting, ltd groc. RECREATION: lake swim, boating, ramp, lake fishing, playground. Partial handicap access. Open May 1 - Oct 31. Phone: (715)264-2511.

COLOMA—G-4

(S) Coloma Camperland—(Waushara) *From jct US 51/I-39 & Hwy 21 (exit 124): Go 1/4 mi N on Hwy 21, then 1-1/2 mi S on CR CH. Enter on L.* ◇◇◇FACILITIES: 82 sites, typical site width 35 ft, 65 full hkups, 17 W&E, (30/50 amps), 3 pull-thrus, family camping, tenting, dump, laundry. ◇◇◇RECREATION: swim pool, playground. Pets welcome, breed restrict. Partial handicap access. Open all yr. Facilities fully operational mid Apr - Oct 15. Rate in 2010 $27-29 per family. Member ARVC, WACO. Phone: (715)228-3600.

CONOVER—C-5

NORTHERN HIGHLAND/AMERICAN LEGION SF (East Star Lake)—(Vilas) *From town: Go 9 mi W on CR N.* FACILITIES: 48 sites, 48 no hkups, tenting. RECREATION: lake swim, boating, ramp, lake fishing. Pets welcome. Open Memorial Day - Labor Day. Phone: (715)385-2727.

CORNELL—E-2

BRUNET ISLAND STATE PARK—(Chippewa) *From jct Hwy 27 & Hwy 64: Go 1/2 mi W on Hwy 64, then 3/4 mi N on Park Rd.* FACILITIES: 69 sites, 24 E, (30 amps), 45 no hkups, 5 pull-thrus, tenting, dump. RECREATION: river swim, boating, canoeing, ramp, dock, river fishing, playground. Partial handicap access. Open all yr. Facilities fully operational Mid Apr - Sep 1. Phone: (715)239-6888.

Wisconsin is known as "The Badger State" because many early settlers dug their homes into hills like badgers.

CRANDON—D-5

FOREST COUNTY VETERANS MEMORIAL PARK—(Forest) *From town: Go 4 mi S on East Shore Rd. Enter on R.* FACILITIES: 66 sites, 56 E, 10 no hkups, tenting, dump. RECREATION: lake swim, boating, canoeing, ramp, dock, lake/river/stream fishing, playground. Partial handicap access. Open May 1 - Oct 1. Phone: (715)478-2040.

CRIVITZ—I-1

(W) Crossroads Campground—(Marinette) *From jct US 141 & CR W: Go 12 mi W on CR W. Enter on R.* ◊◊◊FACILITIES: 21 sites, typical site width 40 ft, 7 full hkups, 14 W&E, (20/30/50 amps), 1 pull-thrus, family camping, tenting, shower$, dump, non-guest dump $, ice, picnic tables, fire rings, wood. RECREATION: Pets welcome. Open Mid May - Mid Nov. Rate in 2010 $20-25 per family. MC/VISA/DISC/Debit. CCUSA 50% Discount. CCUSA reservations Required, CCUSA max stay 5 days, CCUSA disc. not avail F,Sa, CCUSA disc. not avail holidays. Must call for availability.

Phone: (715)757-3877
Address: W11704 County Hwy W, Crivitz, WI 54114
Lat/Lon: 45.24191/-88.18674
Web: www.crossroadsbarandcampground.com

(S) Peshtigo River Campground, LLC—(Marinette) *From jct of CR A & Hwy 141: Go 2 mi S on Hwy 141, then 1/8 mi W on Airport Rd. Enter on R.* ◊◊◊FACILITIES: 112 sites, typical site width 40 ft, 103 W&E, (20/30/50 amps), 9 no hkups, 7 pull-thrus, family camping, tenting, dump, laundry, ltd groc. ◊◊◊◊RECREATION: river swim, canoeing, river fishing, playground. Pets welcome. Open May 1 - Oct 15. Rate in 2010 $29-31 per family. Member ARVC, WACO. Phone: (715)854-2986.

CUMBERLAND—D-1

(NE) Country Quiet RV Park & Campground—(Barron) *From jct of Hwy 48 & US 63: Go 2 mi N on US 63, then 4-1/4 mi E on CR-B, then 500 ft N on 11th St. Enter on R.* ◊◊◊FACILITIES: 102 sites, typical site width 50 ft, 98 W&E, 4 E, (30/50 amps), 85 pull-thrus, family camping, tenting, dump, non-guest dump $, portable dump, ltd groc, RV supplies, ice, picnic tables, fire rings, wood. ◊◊◊RECREATION: equipped pavilion, fishing supplies, bsktball, playground, activities, horseshoes, v-ball. Pets welcome. Partial handicap access. Open May 1 - Oct 1. Big rigs welcome. Rate in 2010 $30 per family. MC/VISA/Debit. CCUSA 50% Discount. CCUSA reservations Recommended, CCUSA max stay 1 day, Cash only for CCUSA disc., CCUSA disc. not avail F,Sa, CCUSA disc. not avail holidays. Not available Memorial Day thru Labor Day.

Phone: (715)822-2800
Address: 2535 11th St, Cumberland, WI 54829
Lat/Lon: 45.57290/-91.92952
Email: waltorgan@centurytel.net
Web: www.countryquiet.com

DANBURY—C-1

(C) Eagles Landing Campground—(Burnett) *From jct Hwy 77 & Hwy 35: Go 1/4 mi S on Hwy 35. Enter on L.* ◊◊◊FACILITIES: 46 sites, typical site width 15 ft, 35 ft max RV length, 36 full hkups, 10 E, (20/30 amps), family camping, tenting, dump, laundry. ◊◊RECREATION: river fishing, play equipment. Pets welcome. Open May 1 - Oct 15. Rate in 2010 $20 for 2 persons. Phone: (715)656-4402.

Voyager Village RV Park—(Burnett) *From jct of Hwy 77 & Hwy 35: Go 6 mi S on Hwy 35, then 9 mi E on CR-A, then 1-1/4 mi N on CR-C. Enter on L.* ◊◊FACILITIES: 45 sites, typical site width 25 ft, 32 ft max RV length, 40 W&E, (20/30 amps), 5 no hkups, tenting, dump. ◊◊◊RECREATION: play equipment. Pets welcome. Partial handicap access. Open mid May - Oct 1. Phone: (715)259-4161.

DE PERE—F-6

(S) Apple Creek Family Campground & Lodge—(Brown) *From jct US 41 & CR U: Go 1/4 mi W on CR U. Enter on R.* ◊◊◊◊FACILITIES: 138 sites, typical site width 30 ft, 133 W&E, (30/50 amps), 5 no hkups, 2 pull-thrus, WiFi Instant Internet at site, WiFi Internet central location, family camping, tenting, shower$, dump, non-guest dump $, portable dump, laundry, ltd groc, RV supplies, LP gas by weight/by meter, ice, picnic tables, fire rings, wood. ◊◊◊◊RECREATION: equipped pavilion, swim pool, pond/stream fishing, bsktball, playground, activities, v-ball. Pets welcome. Partial handicap access. Open Apr15 - Nov 1. Big rigs welcome. Rate in 2010 $32-34 per family. MC/VISA/DISC/Debit. Member ARVC, WACO. CCUSA 50% Discount. CCUSA reservations Accepted, CCUSA max stay 3 days. 4/15-10/15 CCUSA discount available Sun thru Thu, no weekends, no holidays, 3 day length of stay. 10/15-4/15 flat rate of $25, limited amenities.

Phone: (920)532-4386
Address: 3831 County Rd U, De Pere, WI 54115
Lat/Lon: 44.37582/-88.19168
Email: mail@applecreekcamping.com
Web: www.applecreekcamping.com

DE SOTO—H-2

BLACKHAWK PARK (COE-Mississippi River Pool #9)—(Vernon) *From jct Hwy 82 & Hwy 35: Go 3 mi N on Hwy 35.* FACILITIES: 165 sites, 65 E, 100 no hkups, tenting, dump. RECREATION: river swim, boating, canoeing, ramp, dock, river fishing, playground. Pets welcome. Partial handicap access. Open Apr 1 - Oct 31. Phone: (608)648-3314.

DELAFIELD—I-6

NAGA-WAUKEE PARK (Waukesha County Park)—(Waukesha) *From jct I-94 & Hwy-83: Go 1/2 mi N on Hwy-83, then 1/2 mi W on Mariner Dr.* FACILITIES: 33 sites, 33 no hkups, tenting. RECREATION: lake swim, boating, canoeing, ramp, dock, lake fishing. Open all yr. Facilities fully operational Apr - Nov 1. Phone: (262)548-7801.

DENMARK—F-6

(N) Shady Acres Campsites—(Brown) *From S I-43 (exit 171): Go 1 blk E on Hwy 96, 4 mi N on CR R, 300 yards W on Langes Corner Rd, then 1/4 mi S on Shady Acres Ln. From N I-43 & Hwy 172 (exit 178): Go 1-1/2 mi E on MM, 5 mi S on R, 1 blk E on Langes Corner Rd, then 1/4 mi S on Shady Acres Ln. Enter on L.* ◊◊FACILITIES: 26 sites, typical site width 28 ft, 22 W&E, (15/20/30/50 amps), 4 no hkups, 5 pull-thrus, family camping, tenting, dump. ◊◊RECREATION: play equipment. Pets welcome. Open Apr 15 - Oct 1. Rate in 2010 $25 per family. Phone: (920)863-8143.

DODGEVILLE—I-4

(N) GOVERNOR DODGE STATE PARK—(Iowa) *From jct US 18 & Hwy 23: Go 3 mi N on Hwy 23. Enter on R.* FACILITIES: 269 sites, 80 E, (30 amps), 189 no hkups, tenting, dump, ltd groc. RECREATION: lake swim, boating, electric motors only, canoeing, ramp, dock, playground. Partial handicap access. Open all yr. Phone: (608)935-2315.

(E) TOM'S CAMPGROUND—(Iowa) *From jct US 18 & US 151: Go 4 mi E on US 18/151, then 2-1/2 mi S on CR BB, then 1/4 mi E on Hwy 191. Enter on R.*

◊◊◊FACILITIES: 96 sites, typical site width 45 ft, 60 W&E, (30/50 amps), 36 no hkups, 25 pull-thrus, family camping, tenting, cabins, shower$, dump, non-guest dump $, ltd groc, ice, picnic tables, fire rings, wood.

◊◊RECREATION: equipped pavilion, bsktball, horseshoes, sports field, v-ball.

Pets welcome, breed restrict. Open Apr 1 - Oct 31. Facilities fully operational Apr 15 - Oct 31. Big rigs welcome. Clubs welcome. Rate in 2010 $20-22 per vehicle. Member ARVC, WACO.

Phone: (608)935-5446
Address: 2626 Spring Rd, Dodgeville, WI 53533
Lat/Lon: 42.94136/-90.02655
Web: www.tomscampground.com

SEE AD TRAVEL SECTION PAGE 799

DOOR COUNTY—I-2

See listings at Baileys Harbor, Brussels, Egg Harbor, Ellison Bay, Fish Creek, Kewaunee, Sister Bay, Sturgeon Bay, Washington Island.

(S) DOOR COUNTY VISITOR BUREAU—*From jct CR-C & Hwy-42/57: Go 1/2 mi SW on Hwy-42/57. Enter on L.* Agency for promotion of tourism in Door County. Brochures, maps & area information. RV parking. Lobby and restrooms open 24 hours a day 7 days a week. Open all yr.

Phone: (920)743-4456
Address: 1015 Green Bay Rd, Sturgeon Bay, WI 54235
Lat/Lon: 44.82054/-87.40062
Email: mary@doorcounty.com
Web: www.doorcounty.com

SEE AD NEXT PAGE

DRUMMOND—C-2

(SE) CHEQUAMEGON NATIONAL FOREST (Two Lakes Campground)—(Bayfield) *From town: Go 5 mi SE on FR 213, then 1/2 mi S on FR 214.* FACILITIES: 93 sites, 93 no hkups, 6 pull-thrus, tenting, dump. RECREATION: lake swim, boating, ramp, lake fishing. Partial handicap access. Open May 1 - Oct 10. Phone: (715)373-2667.

DYCKESVILLE—J-1

BAYSHORE CAMPGROUND (Brown County Park)—(Brown) *From town: Go 3-1/2 mi S on Hwy 57.* FACILITIES: 115 sites, 85 W&E, (20/30 amps), 30 no hkups, tenting, dump, laundry. RECREATION: boating, ramp, dock, lake fishing, playground. Pets welcome. Partial handicap access. Open May 1 - Oct 15. Phone: (920)448-4466.

EAGLE—I-5

(W) KETTLE MORAINE SF-SOUTHERN UNIT (Ottawa Lake)—(Waukesha) *From jct Hwy 99 & Hwy 67: Go 5 mi N on Hwy 67 to CR "ZZ".* FACILITIES: 100 sites, 49 E, (30/50 amps), 51 no hkups, tenting, dump. RECREATION: lake swim, canoeing, ramp, dock, lake fishing, playground. Partial handicap access. Open all yr. Phone: (262)594-6200.

KETTLE MORAINE SF-SOUTHERN UNIT (Pine Woods)—(Waukesha) *From town: Go 5 mi N on Hwy 67 to CR ZZ, then 3 mi N on CR G.* FACILITIES: 101 sites, 101 no hkups, tenting, dump. RECREATION: No pets. Partial handicap access. Open mid May - mid Nov. Phone: (262)594-6200.

EAGLE RIVER—C-5

(E) Chain O' Lakes KOA Resort—(Vilas) *From jct Hwy 45S & Hwy 70: Go 4 mi E on Hwy 70, then 1-3/4 mi S on Cranberry Lake Rd, then 1/2 mi E on East Bass Lake Rd, then 20 ft S on Nine Mile Rd, then 1/4 mi W on Campground Rd. Enter at end.* ◊◊◊FACILITIES: 180 sites, 180 W&E, (20/30 amps), 60 pull-thrus, family camping, tenting, dump, laundry, ltd groc. ◊◊◊RECREATION: swim pool, lake swim, boating, canoeing, ramp, dock, lake fishing, playground. Pets welcome. Partial handicap access. Open May 1 - Oct 1. Rate in 2010 $32 per vehicle. Phone: (715)479-6708.

(N) HI-PINES CAMPGROUND & RESORT—(Vilas) *From jct Hwy 70 & Hwy 45: Go 2 mi N on Hwy 45. Enter on L.*

◊◊◊◊FACILITIES: 183 sites, typical site width 38 ft, 40 full hkups, 85 W&E, (20/30/50 amps), 58 no hkups, some extd stay sites, 40 pull-thrus, WiFi Instant Internet at site, family camping, tenting, RV storage, dump, non-guest dump $, portable dump, laundry, ltd groc, LP bottle exch, ice, picnic tables, fire rings, wood.

◊◊◊◊RECREATION: rec room/area, pavilion, coin games, swim pool, pond fishing, golf nearby, bsktball, 2 bike rentals, playground, activities, horseshoes, hiking trails, v-ball.

Pets welcome, quantity restrict. Partial handicap access. Open May 1 - Oct 31. Big rigs welcome. Clubs welcome. Rate in 2010 $25-35 for 4 persons. MC/VISA/DISC/AMEX/Debit. Member ARVC, WACO.

Phone: (715)479-9124
Address: 1919 Hwy 45N, Eagle River, WI 54521
Lat/Lon: 45.94533/-89.24910
Email: contact@hipines.net
Web: www.hipines.net

SEE AD THIS PAGE

NICOLET NATIONAL FOREST (Franklin Lake Campground)—(Forest) *From town: Go 9 mi E on Hwy-70, then 2 mi S on FR-2178, then 6 mi E on FR-2181.* FACILITIES: 75 sites, typical site width 15 ft, 75 no hkups, tenting. RECREATION: lake swim, boating, ramp, lake fishing. Partial handicap access. Open May 2 - Oct 20. Phone: (715)479-2827.

NICOLET NATIONAL FOREST (Luna-White Deer Campground)—(Forest) *From town: Go 14-1/2 mi E on Hwy-70, then 4-1/2 mi S on FR-2176, then 1 mi NW on FR-2188.* FACILITIES: 35 sites, 35 no hkups, tenting. RECREATION: lake swim, boating, no motors, canoeing, ramp, lake fishing. Open May 2 - Oct 20. Phone: (715)479-2827.

NICOLET NATIONAL FOREST (Spectacle Lake Campground)—(Vilas) *From town: Go 8 mi E on Hwy 70, then 3 mi N on FR 2178, then 2 mi N on FR 2465, then 2 mi N on FR 2196, then 1 mi E on FR 2572.* FACILITIES: 33 sites, 33 no hkups, tenting. RECREATION: lake swim, boating, ramp, lake fishing. Open May 26 - Sep 8. Phone: (715)479-2827.

EAU CLAIRE—E-2

See listings at Bloomer, Chippewa Falls, Menomonie & Osseo

(SE) Elmer's Camping & Overnite Trailer Park—(Eau Claire) *From jct US 53 (exit 87) & US 12: Go 4-1/2 mi E on US 12. Enter on R.* ◊◊FACILITIES: 35 sites, typical site width 20 ft, 12 full hkups, 10 W&E, 8 E, (20/30 amps), 5 no hkups, 20 pull-thrus, family camping, tenting, dump, laundry. RECREATION: play equipment. Pets welcome. Open Apr 15 - Oct 30. Rate in 2010 $19-21 per family. Phone: (715)832-6277.

Can you trust the Woodall's ratings? 25 evaluation teams have scoured North American campgrounds to provide you with accurate, up to date information & ratings. Find a rating you don't agree with? Send a letter or email our way, and we'll give it extra attention for 2012.

EDGERTON—I-5

(NE) HICKORY HILLS CAMPGROUND—(Dane) *From jct I-90 (exit 160) & Hwy-73: Go 1/2 mi N on Hwy-73, then 3/4 mi E on Hwy-106, then 3/4 mi N on Hillside Rd. Enter on R.*

◊◊◊FACILITIES: 277 sites, 10 full hkups, 267 W&E, (20/30/50 amps), 50 amps ($), many extd stay sites, 11 pull-thrus, family camping, tenting, cabins, shower$, dump, non-guest dump $, ltd groc, RV supplies, LP bottle exch, ice, picnic tables, wood.

◊◊◊◊RECREATION: rec room/area, coin games, swim pool, lake swim, boating, no motors, canoeing, kayaking, dock, 3 rowboat/3 canoe rentals, lake fishing, fishing supplies, mini-golf, ($), golf nearby, bsktball, playground, shuffleboard court 2 shuffleboard courts, activities (wkends), horseshoes, sports field, v-ball.

Pets welcome. Partial handicap access. Open May 1 - Oct 15. Big rigs welcome. Clubs welcome. Rate in 2010 $39-52 per family. MC/VISA/DISC/Debit. Member ARVC, WACO.

Phone: (608)884-6327
Address: 856 Hillside Rd, Edgerton, WI 53534
Lat/Lon: 42.89508/-89.03944
Email: contactus@camphickoryhills.com
Web: www.CampHickoryHills.com

SEE AD THIS PAGE

EGG HARBOR—I-1

(S) DOOR COUNTY CAMPING RETREAT—(Door) *From jct Hwy 57 & Hwy 42: Go 10 mi N on Hwy 42, then 1/4 mi SE on Sunny Point Rd, then 1/2 mi E on Court Rd. Enter on L.*

◊◊◊◊FACILITIES: 270 sites, 29 full hkups, 201 W&E, (30/50 amps), 40 no hkups, some extd stay sites, 18 pull-thrus, WiFi Internet central location, family camping, tenting, cabins, RV storage, dump, portable dump, laundry, ltd groc, RV supplies, LP gas by weight/by meter, ice, picnic tables, fire rings, wood, controlled access.

◊◊◊◊RECREATION: rec room/area, equipped pavilion, coin games, swim pool, golf nearby, bsktball, 11 bike rentals, playground, horseshoes, sports field, hiking trails, v-ball.

Pets welcome, quantity restrict. Partial handicap access. Open May 1 - Mid Oct. Big rigs welcome. Clubs welcome. Rate in 2010 $28-39 for 3 persons. MC/VISA. Member ARVC, WACO.

Phone: (920)868-3151
Address: 4906 Court Rd, Egg Harbor, WI 54209
Lat/Lon: 45.00235/-87.29602
Email: office@doorcountycamp.com
Web: www.doorcountycamp.com

SEE AD DOOR COUNTY PAGE 813

(N) EGG HARBOR CAMPGROUND & RV RESORT—(Door) *From jct CR-E & Hwy-42: Go 1-1/2 mi N on Hwy-42. Enter on R.*

◊◊◊◊FACILITIES: 162 sites, typical site width 30 ft, 39 full hkups, 106 W&E, (20/30/50 amps), 17 no hkups, some extd stay sites, 22 pull-thrus, WiFi Internet central location, family camping, tenting, cabins, dump, portable dump, laundry, ltd groc, RV supplies, LP bottle exch, ice, picnic tables, fire rings, wood.

◊◊◊RECREATION: rec room/area, equipped pavilion, coin games, swim pool, golf nearby, playground, activities, (wkends), sports field, hiking trails, v-ball.

Pets welcome, breed restrict. Partial handicap access. Open Mid May - Mid Oct. Big rigs welcome. Escort to site. Clubs welcome. Rate in 2010 $37-46 per family. MC/VISA/DISC/Debit. Member ARVC, WACO. CCUSA 50% Discount. CCUSA reservations Required, CCUSA max stay 4 days,

EGG HARBOR—Continued
EGG HARBOR CAMPGROUND & RV RESORT—Continued

CCUSA disc. not avail F,Sa, CCUSA disc. not avail holidays. Not available months of Jul & Aug or Columbus Day weekend.

Phone: (920)868-3278
Address: 8164 Hwy 42, Egg Harbor, WI 54209
Lat/Lon: 45.06681/-87.26387
Email: eggharborcg@aol.com
Web: www.eggharborcampground.com

SEE AD DOOR COUNTY PAGE 813

(S) FRONTIER WILDERNESS CAMPGROUND—(Door) *From jct CR-E & Hwy 42: Go 2-1/2 mi S on Hwy 42, then 1-1/2 mi E on Hillside Rd. Enter on R.*

◊◊◊◊FACILITIES: 240 sites, typical site width 36 ft, 240 W&E, (20/30/50 amps), many extd stay sites, 4 pull-thrus, WiFi Instant Internet at site, cable Internet central location, family camping, tenting, cabins, shower$, dump, portable dump, laundry, ltd groc, RV supplies, LP bottle exch, ice, picnic tables, fire rings, wood.

◊◊◊◊RECREATION: rec hall, rec room/area, pavilion, equipped pavilion, coin games, swim pool, mini-golf, ($), golf nearby, bsktball, 14 bike rentals, playground, activities, (wkends), horseshoes, sports field, v-ball.

Pets welcome. Open May 1 - Oct 31. Big rigs welcome. Clubs welcome. Rate in 2010 $31-36 per family. MC/VISA/DISC/AMEX/Debit. Member ARVC, WACO. CCUSA 50% Discount. CCUSA reservations Recommended, CCUSA max stay 2 days. Not available Memorial Day weekend thru Labor Day.

Phone: (920)868-3349
Address: 4375 Hillside Rd, Egg Harbor, WI 54209
Lat/Lon: 45.02380/-87.25938
Email: traz_rasmunssen@yahoo.com
Web: www. frontierwildernesscampground.com

SEE AD DOOR COUNTY PAGE 813

(S) Monument Point Camping—(Door) *From north jct Hwy 42 & 57 near Sturgeon Bay: Go 8 mi N on Hwy 42, then 1-1/4 mi NW on Monument Point Rd. Enter on R.* ◊◊◊FACILITIES: 84 sites, typical site width 50 ft, 84 E, (30 amps), 5 pull-thrus, family camping, tenting, dump, ltd groc. ◊◊RECREATION: play equipment. Pets welcome. Partial handicap access. Open May 1 - Mid-Oct. Rate in 2010 $28 per family. Phone: (920)743-9411.

ELLISON BAY—I-2

(SW) Hy-Land Court RV Park—(Door) *From jct Hwy 57 & Hwy 42 (Sister Bay): Go 3-1/2 mi N on Hwy 42. Enter on L.* ◊◊◊◊FACILITIES: 30 sites, typical site width 35 ft, 19 full hkups, 11 W&E, (20/30/50 amps), 5 pull-thrus, family camping, tenting, dump. Pets welcome. Open May 1 - Nov 1. Big rigs welcome. Rate in 2010 $29-34 for 2 persons. Phone: (920)854-4850.

(SE) WAGON TRAIL CAMPGROUND LTD.—(Door) *From jct Hwy 42 & CR ZZ (in Sister Bay): Go 6 mi NE on CR ZZ. Enter on L.*

◊◊◊◊FACILITIES: 140 sites, typical site width 25 ft, 12 full hkups, 110 W&E, (20/30/50 amps), 50 amps ($), 18 no hkups, some extd stay sites, 9 pull-thrus, WiFi Internet central location, family camping, tenting, cabins, dump, non-guest dump $, portable dump, laundry, ltd groc, RV supplies, LP gas by weight/by meter, ice, picnic tables, fire rings, grills, wood.

◊◊◊◊RECREATION: rec hall, rec room/area, coin games, lake swim, lake fishing, fishing guides, golf nearby, playground, horseshoes, sports field, hiking trails, v-ball.

Say you saw it in Woodall's!

ELLISON BAY—Continued
WAGON TRAIL CAMPGROUND LTD.—Continued

Pets welcome. Partial handicap access. Open Mid May - Mid Oct. Big rigs welcome. Clubs welcome. Rate in 2010 $36-49 for 2 persons. MC/VISA/DISC/Debit. Member ARVC, WACO.

Phone: (920)854-4818
Address: 1190 County Road 22, Ellison Bay, WI 54210
Lat/Lon: 45.22015/-87.04228
Email: wtc@dcwis.com
Web: www.wagontrailcampground.com

SEE AD DOOR COUNTY PAGE 813

FAIRCHILD—F-3

(N) Briarwood RV Park & Campground—(Eau Claire) *From jct I-94 (exit 88) & US 10: Go 10 mi E on US 10, then 1/4 mi N on CR-YY, then 3/4 mi E on E Main, then 3/4 mi N on Camp Rd, then E on Tioga Rd. Enter on L.* ◊◊◊FACILITIES: 45 sites, typical site width 40 ft, 30 full hkups, (30/50 amps), 15 no hkups, WiFi Instant Internet at site, family camping, tenting, dump, non-guest dump, RV supplies, picnic tables, fire rings, wood. ◊◊RECREATION: pavilion, playground, v-ball. Pets welcome. Open May 1 - Oct 1. Big rigs welcome. Rate in 2010 $30-33 per vehicle. MC/VISA/Debit. CCUSA 50% Discount. CCUSA reservations Recommended, CCUSA max stay 1 day, CCUSA disc. not avail F,Sa, CCUSA disc. not avail holidays.

Phone: (715)206-0361
Address: 627 Tioga Rd, Fairchild, WI 54741
Lat/Lon: 44.60717/-90.94602
Email: slbuchholz@clearwire.net
Web: www.briarwoodgocamping.com

FISH CREEK—I-2

FISH CREEK CAMPGROUND (NOT VISITED)—(Door County) *Jct Hwy 42 & CR F: Go 3/4 mi E on CR F. Enter on R.*

FACILITIES: 80 sites, typical site width 40 ft, 80 W&E, (30 amps), some extd stay sites, 30 pull-thrus, cable TV, WiFi Instant Internet at site, family camping, tenting, dump, non-guest dump $, portable dump, laundry, RV supplies, ice, picnic tables, fire rings, wood.

RECREATION: rec room/area, pavilion, coin games, golf nearby, bsktball, playground, shuffleboard court shuffleboard courts, sports field.

Pets welcome, breed restrict. Partial handicap access. Open May 1st - Mid Oct. Big rigs welcome. Escort to site. Clubs welcome. Rate in 2010 $28-33 per family. MC/VISA/DISC.

Phone: (920)495-CAMP
Address: 3709 County Road F, Fish Creek, WI 54212
Email: info@fishcreekcampground.com
Web: www.fishcreekcampground.com

SEE AD DOOR COUNTY PAGE 813

(N) PENINSULA STATE PARK—(Door) *From jct CR A & Hwy 42: Go 1/2 mi N on Hwy 42. Enter on L.* FACILITIES: 468 sites, 103 E, (20/30 amps), 365 no hkups, tenting, dump, ltd groc. RECREATION: lake swim, boating, canoeing, ramp, lake fishing, playground. Partial handicap access. Open all yr. Facilities fully operational May 1 - Mid Oct. Phone: (920)868-3258.

FLORENCE—C-6

(S) Keyes Lake Campground—(Florence) *From jct of Hwy 70 & Hwy 101: Go 1 mi S on Hwy 101. Enter on L.* ◊◊FACILITIES: 33 sites, 31 W&E, (20/30 amps), 2 no hkups, 3 pull-thrus, WiFi Internet central location, family camping, tenting, dump, non-guest dump $, portable dump, laundry, ltd groc, RV supplies, LP gas by weight, ice, picnic tables, fire rings, wood. ◊◊RECREATION: fishing supplies, mini-golf, ($), bsktball, play equipment, horseshoes, v-ball. Pets welcome. Open all yr. Facilities fully operational May 1 - Oct 31. Rate in 2010 $21 per family. MC/VISA/Debit. Member ARVC, WACO. CCUSA 50% Discount.

Phone: (800)264-8071
Address: N4918 Hwy 101, Florence, WI 54121
Lat/Lon: 45.89336/-88.29961
Email: klcamp@borderlandnet.net
Web: www.keyeslakecampground.com

FOND DU LAC—G-5

(S) KOA-Fond du Lac Kampground—(Fond du Lac) *From jct US 41 (exit 92) & CR B: Go 1-1/2 mi E on CR B, then 200 yds N on Cearns Ln. Enter on L.* ◊◊◊◊FACILITIES: 94 sites, typical site width 40 ft, 15 full hkups, 70 W&E, (20/30/50 amps), 9 no hkups, 37 pull-thrus, family camping, tenting, dump, laundry, ltd groc. ◊◊◊◊RECREATION: swim pool, pond fishing, playground. Pets welcome, breed restrict. Partial handicap access. Open Mid Apr - Mid Oct. Big rigs welcome. Green Friendly. Rate in 2010 $30-45 per family. Member ARVC, WACO. Phone: (920)477-2300. KOA discount.

FOND DU LAC—Continued on next page

FOND DU LAC—Continued

(E) Westward Ho Camp Resort (Morgan Rv Resort)—(Fond du Lac) *From jct US 41 & Hwy 23: Go 16 mi E on Hwy 23, then 3 mi S on CR G, then 1/2 mi E on CR T and follow signs. Enter on R.* ◆◆◆◆FACILITIES: 338 sites, typical site width 40 ft, 218 full hkups, 110 W&E, (20/30/50 amps), 10 no hkups, 4 pull-thrus, WiFi Instant Internet at site ($), WiFi Internet central location, family camping, tenting, dump, non-guest dump $, portable dump, laundry, ltd groc, RV supplies, LP gas by weight/by meter, ice, picnic tables, patios, fire rings, wood. ◆◆◆◆◆RECREATION: rec hall, equipped pavilion, 3 swim pools, wading pool, pond fishing, mini-golf, ($), bsktball, playground, shuffleboard court 2 shuffleboard courts, activities, horseshoes, hiking trails, v-ball. Pets welcome. Partial handicap access. Open Mid Apr - Mid Oct. Big rigs welcome. Rate in 2010 $28-45 per family. MC/VISA/DISC/Debit. ATM. Member ARVC, WACO. CCUSA 50% Discount. CCUSA reservations Required, CCUSA max stay 4 days, CCUSA disc. not avail F,Sa, CCUSA disc. not avail holidays. Not available Jul, Aug.

Phone: (920)526-3407
Address: N5456 Division Rd, Glenbeulah, WI 53023
Lat/Lon: 43.73766/-88.16071
Email: info@westwardhocampresort.com
Web: www.westwardhocampresort.com

FORT ATKINSON—I-5

(W) Pilgrim's Campground—(Jefferson) *From jct Hwy 26 & US 12: Go 1 mi NW on US 12, then 1 mi W on CR C, then 1/4 mi S on Kunz Rd. Enter on L.* ◆◆FACILITIES: 89 sites, typical site width 35 ft, 59 full hkups, 18 W&E, (30/50 amps), 12 no hkups, 9 pull-thrus, family camping, tenting, dump. ◆◆RECREATION: swim pool, playground. Pets welcome. Open May 1 - Mid Oct. Rate in 2010 $28-32 per family. Member ARVC, WACO. Phone: (920)563-8122.

(S) Yogi Bear Jellystone Park/Fort Atkinson—(Jefferson) *From jct US 12 & Hwy 26: Go 5-1/4 mi SW on Hwy 26, then 3/4 mi W on Koshkonong Lake Rd, then 1/4 mi S on Wishing Well Dr. Enter on L.* ◆◆◆◆FACILITIES: 569 sites, 568 W&E, (20/30/50 amps), 1 no hkups, WiFi Internet central location, family camping, tenting, dump, portable dump, laundry, ltd groc, RV supplies, LP gas by weight/by meter, ice, picnic tables, patios, fire rings, wood. ◆◆◆◆◆RECREATION: rec hall, pavilion, equipped pavilion, 2 swim pools, wading pool, pond fishing, mini-golf, ($), bsktball, playground, shuffleboard court 4 shuffleboard courts, activities tennis, horseshoes, hiking trails, v-ball. Pets welcome. Partial handicap access. Open Mid May - Oct 1. Rate in 2010 $41 per family. MC/VISA/DISC/Debit. Member ARVC, WACO. FCRV discount. FMCA discount. CCUSA 50% Discount. CCUSA reservations Required, CCUSA max stay 5 days, CCUSA disc. not avail holidays. Discounts not available weekends between Memorial Day and Oct 1 with the exception of the weekend after Labor Day, also not available week of 4th of July. Add'l vehicle surcharge $9.

Phone: (920)568-4100
Lat/Lon: 42.86258/-88.91204
Email: info@jellystonefort.com
Web: www.jellystonefort.com

FOUNTAIN CITY—G-2

(N) MERRICK STATE PARK—(Buffalo) *3 mi N on Hwy-35.* FACILITIES: 67 sites, 22 E, (30 amps), 45 no hkups, tenting, dump. RECREATION: boating, canoeing, ramp, dock. Partial handicap access. Open all yr. Phone: (608)687-4936.

FREMONT—F-5

(W) Blue Top Resort & Campground—(Waupaca) *From jct Hwy 10 & Hwy 110 (Fremont exit): Go 1/2 mi E on Hwy 110, then 500 feet N on Wolf River Dr. Enter on L.* ◆◆◆FACILITIES: 65 sites, typical site width 30 ft, 30 ft max RV length, 20 full hkups, 27 W&E, 18 E, (20/30 amps), 9 pull-thrus, tenting, dump, laundry. ◆◆◆RECREATION: boating, canoeing, ramp, dock, lake/river fishing, playground. Pets welcome. Partial handicap access. Open Mid Apr - Mid Oct. Rate in 2010 $22-28.50 for 2 persons. Member ARVC, WACO. Phone: (920)446-3343.

(W) YOGI BEAR JELLYSTONE PARK CAMP-RESORT—(Waupaca) *From jct Hwy 10 & Hwy 110 (Freemont exit): Go 1/4 mi E on Hwy 110. Enter on L.*

◆◆◆◆FACILITIES: 286 sites, typical site width 50 ft, 73 full hkups, 167 W&E, 11 E, (30/50 amps), 35 no hkups, some extd stay sites, 28 pull-thrus, WiFi Internet central location ($), family camping, tenting, cabins, dump, non-guest dump $, portable dump, laundry, ltd groc, RV supplies, LP gas by weight, ice, picnic tables, fire rings, wood.

◆◆◆◆RECREATION: rec room/area, pavilion, equipped pavilion, coin games, swim pool, wading pool, boating, canoeing, ramp, dock, 4 pontoon/3 rowboat/2 canoe/10 pedal boat/19 motorboat rentals, lake/river/pond fishing, fishing supplies,

FREMONT—Continued
YOGI BEAR JELLYSTONE PARK CAMP-RESORT—Continued

mini-golf, ($), golf nearby, bsktball, 15 bike rentals, playground, shuffleboard court 4 shuffleboard courts, activities, horseshoes, sports field, hiking trails, v-ball.

Pets welcome. Open Mid Apr - Mid Oct. Clubs welcome. Rate in 2010 $32-68 per family. MC/VISA/DISC/AMEX/Debit. ATM. Member ARVC, WACO.

Phone: (800)258-3315
Address: E6506 State Road 110, Fremont, CA 54940
Lat/Lon: 44.26554/-88.90166
Email: info@fremontjellystone.com
Web: www.fremontjellystone.com

Reserve Online at Woodalls.com

SEE AD THIS PAGE AND AD ALGOMA PAGE 807

FRIENDSHIP—G-4

CASTLE ROCK PARK (Adams County)—(Adams) *From jct CR J & Hwy 13 (in town): Go 3-1/2 mi S on Hwy 13, then 6 mi W on CR F, then 1/2 mi S on CR Z.* FACILITIES: 200 sites, 150 E, 50 no hkups, tenting, dump. RECREATION: lake swim, boating, canoeing, ramp, dock, lake fishing, playground. Pets welcome. Open all yr. Phone: (608)339-7713.

(NW) PETENWELL PARK (Adams County)—(Adams) *From jct Hwy 13 & Hwy 21: Go 6 mi W on Hwy 21, then 5 mi N on CR Z, then 1 mi W on Bighorn Dr.* FACILITIES: 500 sites, 350 E, (20/30 amps), 150 no hkups, tenting, dump. RECREATION: lake swim, boating, canoeing, ramp, dock, lake fishing, playground. Partial handicap access. Open all yr. Phone: (608)564-7513.

(N) ROCHE-A-CRI SP—(Adams) *From town: Go 2 mi N on Hwy 13.* FACILITIES: 41 sites, 41 no hkups, tenting, dump. RECREATION: stream fishing, playground. Partial handicap access. Open May 1 - Oct 1. Phone: (608)339-6881.

GILMAN—E-3

CHEQUAMEGON NATIONAL FOREST (Chippewa Campground)—(Taylor) *From jct Hwy-73 & CR-M: Go 5 mi E on CR-M, then 1 mi S on FR-1417, then 1/2 mi W on FR-1455.* FACILITIES: 78 sites, typical site width 12 ft, 35 ft max RV length, 78 no hkups, 4 pull-thrus, tenting, dump. RECREATION: lake swim, boating, ramp, lake fishing, playground. Partial handicap access. Open May 14 - Sep 6. Phone: (715)748-4875.

GOODMAN—D-6

(N) Lake Hilbert Campground—(Marinette) *From jct of Hwy 8 & CR-H: Go 3 mi N on CR-H. Enter on L.* ◆◆◆FACILITIES: 105 sites, 105 W&E, (20/30/50 amps), 8 pull-thrus, family camping, tenting, dump, non-guest dump $, portable dump, laundry, ltd groc, RV supplies, ice, picnic tables, fire rings, wood. ◆◆RECREATION: fishing supplies, play equipment, horseshoes. Pets welcome. Open all yr. Facilities fully operational May 1 - Dec 1. Rate in 2010 $28 per family. MC/VISA/DISC/Debit. Member ARVC, WACO. CCUSA 50% Discount. CCUSA reservations Required, CCUSA max stay 2 days, CCUSA disc. not avail F,Sa, CCUSA disc. not avail holidays. Fully operational May 1-Dec 1.

GOODMAN—Continued
Lake Hilbert Campground—Continued

Phone: (715)336-3013
Address: N20470 Town Park Rd., Fence, WI 54120
Lat/Lon: 45.70729/-88.39964
Email: campgroundlady@centurytel.net
Web: www.lakehilbertcampground.com

GORDON—C-2

(W) Adventureland—(Douglas) *From jct of Hwy 53 & CR-Y: Go 5-1/4 mi W on CR-Y. Enter on L.* ◆◆FACILITIES: 50 sites, typical site width 36 ft, 50 W&E, (20/30 amps), 9 pull-thrus, family camping, tenting. ◆◆RECREATION: river fishing, play equipment. Pets welcome. Open May 1 - Oct 1. Rate in 2010 $24-26 per family. Phone: (715)376-4528.

(W) GORDON DAM COUNTY PARK (Douglas County Park)—(Douglas) *From town: Go 7 mi W on CR-Y to St. Croix Dam.* FACILITIES: 33 sites, 12 E, 21 no hkups, tenting. RECREATION: boating, canoeing, ramp, river fishing, playground. Partial handicap access. Open May 20 - Sep 30. Phone: (715)378-2219.

(E) Happy Ours RV Park—(Douglas) *From Jct of Hwy 53 & CR-Y: Go 7 mi E on CR-Y, then 2-1/2 mi S on McCumber Rd. Enter on R.* ◆◆◆FACILITIES: 70 sites, typical site width 30 ft, accepts self-contained units only, 70 full hkups, (20/30/50 amps), family camping, RV storage, picnic tables, fire rings. ◆RECREATION: hiking trails. Pets welcome, breed restrict. No tents. Open May 1 - Sept 30. Big rigs welcome. Rate in 2010 $25 for 2 persons. Member ARVC, WACO. CCUSA 50% Discount. CCUSA reservations Accepted, CCUSA max stay 2 days. Call for availability. No restrooms.

Phone: (715)376-2302
Address: 12601 E Mail Rd, Gordon, WI 54838
Lat/Lon: 46.23582/-91.65636

GRANTSBURG—D-1

(W) JAMES N MCNALLY CAMPGROUND (City Park)—(Burnett) *From Hwy 70/48/87: Go 7 blocks N, then 1 block W on Main St.* FACILITIES: 38 sites, 38 full hkups, (50 amps), tenting, dump. RECREATION: playground. Open May - Oct. Phone: (715)463-2405.

GREEN BAY—F-6

See listings at Algoma, Brussels, DePere, Kewaunee & Maribel.

(S) TRUCK COUNTRY—*From jct US 41 & Hwy 29: Go 4-1/2 mi S on US 41, then 1/2 mi SW on Oneida St (exit 164), then 1/8 mi S on Allied St, then 1/8 mi W on Parkview Rd. Enter on L.* SERVICES: full-time mech, engine/chassis repair, body work/collision repair, 24-hr emerg rd svc, mobile RV svc, RV towing. 5 Service Bays. Open all yr. MC/VISA/DISC/AMEX/Debit.

TRUCK COUNTRY—Continued on next page

The Republican Party was founded in Ripon in 1854.

GREEN BAY—Continued
TRUCK COUNTRY—Continued

Phone: (800)622-6962
Address: 1101 Parkview Ry, Green Bay, WI 54304
Lat/Lon: 44.47237/-88.10209
Web: www.truckcountry.com

SEE AD TRAVEL SECTION PAGE 798 AND AD IA TRAVEL SECTION PAGE 247

GREEN LAKE—G-5

(W) Green Lake Campground—(Green Lake) *From west jct Hwy 23 & Hwy 49: Go 3-1/2 mi W on Hwy 23. Enter on R.* ◇◇◇FACILITIES: 360 sites, typical site width 36 ft, 200 full hkups, 150 W&E, (20/30/50 amps), 10 no hkups, 15 pull-thrus, family camping, tenting, dump, laundry, ltd groc. ◇◇◇◇◇RECREATION: 3 swim pools, lake swim, lake/pond fishing, playground. Pets welcome. Partial handicap access. Open Apr 15 - Oct 15. Rate in 2010 $36-52 per family. Member ARVC, WACO. Phone: (920)294-3543.

(SW) HATTIE SHERWOOD CAMPGROUND—(Green Lake) *In town on S Lawson Dr.* FACILITIES: 37 sites, 24 ft max RV length, 37 E, (20/50 amps), tenting, dump. RECREATION: lake swim, boating, ramp, lake/pond fishing, playground. Pets welcome. Partial handicap access. Open May 1 - Oct 15. Phone: (920)294-6380.

GREENWOOD—F-3

NORTH MEAD PARK (Clark County)—(Clark) *From jct Hwy-73 & CR-G: Go 3 mi N on CR-G, then 2 mi N on CR-O, then 5 mi W on CR-MM.* FACILITIES: 71 sites, 71 E, tenting, dump. RECREATION: lake swim, boating, lake fishing, play equipment. Open May 1 - Nov 30. Phone: (715)743-5140.

ROCK DAM PARK CAMPGROUND (Clark County Park)—(Clark) *From town: Go 16 mi W on CR G & CR GG, then 2-1/2 mi W on Willard Rd.* FACILITIES: 150 sites, 8 full hkups, 17 W&E, 111 E, (20/30 amps), 14 no hkups, tenting, dump, laundry, groceries. RECREATION: lake swim, boating, ramp, lake fishing. Pets welcome. Partial handicap access. Open May 1 - Dec 1. Phone: (715)743-5140.

GRESHAM—E-5

(N) Captain's Cove Resort and Country Club, LLC—(Shawano) *From Shawano & Hwy 47/55: Go 7-1/2 mi N to CR-G, then 1/2 mi W to Spur Rd, then 3/4 mi to office. Enter on R.* ◇◇FACILITIES: 208 sites, typical site width 40 ft, 105 full hkups, 103 W&E, (30/50 amps), 3 pull-thrus, WiFi Instant Internet at site, WiFi Internet central location, family camping, tenting, dump, laundry, ice, picnic tables, fire rings, wood. ◇◇◇RECREATION: pavilion, swim pool, lake swim, hot tub, boating, electric motors only, canoeing, dock, lake fishing, mini-golf, bsktball, play equipment, shuffleboard court, activities horseshoes, hiking trails, v-ball. Pets welcome. Open all yr. Facilities fully operational May 1 - Nov 1. Big rigs welcome. MC/VISA/DISC/Debit. CCUSA 50% Discount. CCUSA reservations Required, CCUSA max stay Unlimited, CCUSA disc. not avail holidays. 2 night minimum stay, unlimited max stay based on availability. Rate does not include tax.

Phone: (715)787-3535
Address: N 9099 Big Lake Rd, Gresham, WI 54128
Lat/Lon: 44.92151/-88.76647
Web: www.captaincove.com

HAGER CITY

(S) Island Campground & Marina—(Pierce) *Enter on L.* ◇◇◇FACILITIES: 108 sites, typical site width 25 ft, 108 W&E, (20/30/50 amps), 11 pull-thrus, family camping, tenting, dump, laundry. ◇◇RECREATION: boating, canoeing, ramp, dock, river fishing, play equipment. Pets welcome. Open May 1 - Oct 31. Big rigs welcome. Rate in 2010 $32 for 4 persons. Phone: (715)222-1808.

HANCOCK—G-4

(S) Tomorrow Wood Campground—(Waushara) *From jct of I-39/Hwy 51 (exit 131) & CR-V: Go 1-1/4 mi E on CR-V, then 2 mi SE on CR-GG, then 1/2 mi S on 7th Dr. Enter on R.* ◇◇FACILITIES: 170 sites, typical site width 40 ft, 28 ft max RV length, 100 full hkups, 50 W&E, (20/30/50 amps), 20 no hkups, family camping,

HANCOCK—Continued
Tomorrow Wood Campground—Continued

tenting, dump, laundry, ltd groc. ◇◇RECREATION: lake swim, canoeing, dock, lake fishing, play equipment. Pets welcome. Partial handicap access. Open May 1 - Oct 15. Rate in 2010 $29 per family. Member ARVC, WACO. Phone: (800)457-3418.

VILLAGE OF HANCOCK CAMPGROUND—(Warshara) *From jct US 51 & CR V: Go 1-1/4 mi E on CR V, then 1/2 mi E on CR GG.* FACILITIES: 30 sites, 30 E, tenting, dump. RECREATION: lake swim, boating, canoeing, ramp, lake fishing, playground. Open Apr 15 - Dec 1. Phone: (715)249-5521.

HARTFORD—H-6

(E) KETTLE MORAINE SF-PIKE LAKE UNIT—(Washington) *From town: Go 2 mi E on Hwy 60.* FACILITIES: 32 sites, 11 E, 20 no hkups, tenting, dump. RECREATION: lake swim, lake fishing, playground. Pets welcome. Partial handicap access. Open 1st Wkend May - 3rd Wkend Oct. Phone: (262)670-3400.

HATFIELD—F-3

BLACK RIVER SF (East Fork Rec Area)—(Jackson) *From town: Go 1 mi SE on CR-K, then 2 mi E on West Clay Rd, then 1 mi N.* FACILITIES: 24 sites, 24 no hkups, 3 pull-thrus. RECREATION: canoeing, ramp, river fishing. Partial handicap access. No tents. Open May 1 - Oct 1. Phone: (715)284-4103.

RUSSELL MEMORIAL PARK (Clark County Park)—(Clark) *From jct Hwy 95 & CR J: Go 3 mi S on CR J.* FACILITIES: 230 sites, 8 full hkups, 13 W&E, 169 E, (20/30 amps), 37 no hkups, tenting, dump, laundry, ltd groc. RECREATION: lake swim, boating, ramp, lake fishing, playground. Partial handicap access. Open May 1 - Dec 1. Phone: (715)743-5140.

HAYWARD—C-2

(S) Camp Namekagon—(Washburn) *From jct of Hwy 27 & US 63: Go 5 mi SW on US 63, then 1 mi S on CR-E, then 1-3/4 mi W on Larson Rd. Enter on R.* ◇◇FACILITIES: 44 sites, typical site width 40 ft, 34 full hkups, (30/50 amps), 10 no hkups, 1 pull-thrus, family camping, tenting, ltd groc. ◇◇◇RECREATION: canoeing. Pets welcome, breed restrict. Partial handicap access. Open Mid Apr - Mid Oct. Big rigs welcome. Rate in 2010 $30 per family. Member ARVC, WACO. Phone: (715)766-2277.

(N) Hayward-KOA—(Sawyer) *From jct Hwy 27 & US 63: Go 3 mi NE on US 63. Enter on R.* ◇◇◇◇FACILITIES: 195 sites, typical site width 20 ft, 45 full hkups, 116 W&E, 8 E, (20/30/50 amps), 26 no hkups, 100 pull-thrus, family camping, tenting, dump, laundry, ltd groc. ◇◇◇◇◇RECREATION: 2 swim pools, canoeing, river fishing, playground. Pets welcome, breed restrict. Partial handicap access. Open May 1 - Mid Oct. Big rigs welcome. Rate in 2010 $37.40-57.60 for 2 persons. Member ARVC, WACO. Phone: (715)634-2331. KOA discount.

(E) Lake Chippewa Campground—(Sawyer) *From jct US-63 & Hwy-27: Go 1/2 mi S on Hwy-27, then 13 mi E on CR-B, then 5 mi S on CR-CC. Enter on L.* ◇◇◇FACILITIES: 200 sites, typical site width 30 ft, 105 full hkups, 91 W&E, 4 E, (20/30/50 amps), 10 pull-thrus, family camping, tenting, dump, laundry, ltd groc. ◇◇◇RECREATION: lake swim, boating, canoeing, ramp, dock, lake fishing, playground. Pets welcome. Partial handicap access. Open May 1 - Nov 1. Big rigs welcome. Rate in 2010 $25-42 per family. Member ARVC, WACO. Phone: (715)462-3672.

(SW) River Road RV Campground—(Washburn) *From jct Hwy 63 & Hwy 27: Go 4 mi S on Hwy 63. Enter on L.* ◇◇◇FACILITIES: 24 sites, typical site width 45 ft, 24 full hkups, (20/30/50 amps), 24 pull-thrus, family camping, tenting, dump. Pets welcome. Partial handicap access. Open Apr 1 - Mid Oct. Big rigs welcome. Rate in 2010 $30 per family. Phone: (715)634-2054.

(E) Sisko's Pine Point Resort—(Sawyer) *From jct US-63 & Hwy-27: Go 1/2 mi S on Hwy-27, then 13-1/4 mi E on CR-B, then 3-1/2 mi S on CR-CC. Enter on R.* ◇◇FACILITIES: 33 sites, typical site width 20 ft, 32 ft max RV length, 15 full hkups, 18 W&E, (20/30 amps), tenting, dump, laundry, ltd groc. ◇◇◇RECREATION: lake swim, boating, canoeing, ramp, dock, lake fishing, play equipment. Pets welcome. Open 1st Sat in May - Oct 15. Rate in 2010 $23-28.25 per family. Phone: (715)462-3700.

(NW) Sunrise Bay Campgrounds & RV Park—(Sawyer) *From jct US 63 & Hwy 77/27: Go 3-1/2 mi N on Hwy 27, then 1 block E on Jolly Fisherman Rd. Enter on R.* ◇◇FACILITIES: 50 sites, typical site width 26 ft, 25 full hkups, 12 W&E, 13 E, (20/30 amps), 2 pull-thrus, family camping, tenting, dump, ltd groc. ◇◇◇RECREATION: lake swim, boating, canoeing, ramp, dock, lake fishing, play equipment. Pets welcome. Partial handicap access. Open May 1 - Oct 1. Rate in 2010 $25 for 2 persons. Phone: (715)634-2213.

HIGHLAND—I-3

(S) BLACKHAWK LAKE RECREATION AREA (Iowa County Park)—(Iowa) *From jct Hwy-80 & CR-BH: Go 2-1/2 mi E on CR-BH.* FACILITIES: 150 sites, 78 E, 72 no hkups, 2 pull-thrus, tenting, dump, ltd groc, groceries. RECREATION: lake swim, boating, canoeing, ramp, dock, lake fishing, playground. Partial handicap access. Open all yr. Facilities fully operational Apr - Nov. Phone: (608)623-2707.

HILES—D-5

(E) Hiles Pine Lake Campground—(Forest) *From jct US 8 & Hwy 32: Go 14 mi N on Hwy 32, then 1/2 mi S on West Pine Lake Rd. Enter on L.* ◇◇◇FACILITIES: 80 sites, typical site width 35 ft, 7 full hkups, 60 W&E, (20/30/50 amps), 13 no hkups, 1 pull-thrus, tenting, dump, ltd groc. ◇◇◇RECREATION: lake swim, boating, canoeing, ramp, dock, lake fishing, play equipment. Pets welcome. Partial handicap access. Open all yr. Facilities fully operational May 1 - Oct 1. Rate in 2010 $23-26 per family. Member ARVC, WACO. Phone: (715)649-3319.

HIXTON—F-2

(E) KOA HIXTON ALMA CENTER—(Jackson) *From jct I-94 (exit 105) & Hwy 95: Go 3-1/2 mi E on Hwy 95. Enter on L.* ◇◇◇◇FACILITIES: 101 sites, typical site width 36 ft, 56 full hkups, 32 W&E, (30/50 amps), 50 amps ($), 13 no hkups, 45 pull-thrus, cable TV, WiFi Instant Internet at site, WiFi Internet central location, family camping, tenting, cabins, dump, non-guest dump $, laundry, groceries, RV supplies, ice, picnic tables, fire rings, wood.

◇◇◇◇RECREATION: rec room/area, equipped pavilion, coin games, swim pool, pond fishing, fishing supplies, golf nearby, bsktball, 8 bike rentals, playground, activities, (wkends), horseshoes, sports field, hiking trails, v-ball. Rec open to public.

Pets welcome. Open May 1 - Nov 1. Big rigs welcome. Escort to site. Clubs welcome. Rate in 2010 $25-50 for 2 persons. MC/VISA/DISC/Debit. Member ARVC, WACO. KOA discount.

Phone: (800)562-2680
Address: N 9657 St Hwy 95, Alma Center, WI 54611
Lat/Lon: 44.42113/-90.94999
Email: hixtonkoa@triwest.net
Web: hixtonkoa.com

SEE AD THIS PAGE

HOLCOMBE—E-3

(W) PINE POINT COUNTY PARK (Chippewa County)—(Chippewa) *From town: Go 2-1/2 mi NW on CR M. Enter on R.* FACILITIES: 48 sites, 48 E, (20 amps), 4 pull-thrus, tenting, dump. RECREATION: lake swim, boating, ramp, dock, lake fishing, playground. Pets welcome. Open 1st May weekend - Nov 1. Phone: (715)726-7880.

HOLMEN—G-2

(N) Whispering Pines Campground—(La Crosse) *From South jct Hwy 35 & US 53: Go 7-1/2 mi N on US 53. Enter on L.* ◇◇◇◇FACILITIES: 189 sites, typical site width 50 ft, 31 full hkups, 156 W&E, (30/50 amps), 2 no hkups, 13 pull-thrus, family camping, tenting, dump, laundry, ltd groc. ◇◇◇◇RECREATION: pond fishing, play equipment. Pets welcome, breed restrict. Open Mid Apr - Mid Oct. Big rigs welcome. Rate in 2010 $28-39 per family. Phone: (608)526-4956.

HORICON—H-5

(W) The Playful Goose—(Dodge) *From jct Hwy 26 & Hwy 33: Go 3 mi E on Hwy 33, then 1/2 mi S on Main St. Enter on L.* ◇◇FACILITIES: 199 sites, typical site width 40 ft, 90 full hkups, 83 W&E, (20/30/50 amps), 26 no hkups, 36 pull-thrus, tenting, dump, laundry. ◇◇◇RECREATION: swim pool, boating, no motors, canoeing, river/pond fishing, playground. Pets welcome. Partial handicap access. Open May 1 - Columbus Day (obs). Rate in 2010 $29-38 for 2 persons. Member ARVC, WACO. Phone: (920)485-4744.

HUDSON—E-1

(NE) WILLOW RIVER SP—(St. Croix) *From jct Hwy 35 & CR A: Go 5-1/2 mi E on CR A. Enter on L.* FACILITIES: 120 sites, 56 E, (20/30 amps), 64 no hkups, tenting, dump. RECREATION: lake swim, boating, canoeing, ramp, river fishing, playground. Partial handicap access. Open all yr. Phone: (715)386-5931.

IOLA—F-5

(NE) Iola Pines Campground—(Waupaca) *From jct Hwy 161/49 & CR-G/J: Go 1 mi NE on CR-G/J, then 1 block E on Fairway Dr. Enter on L.* ◇◇FACILITIES: 65 sites, 30 ft max RV length, 10 full hkups, 55 W&E, (20/30 amps), family camping, tenting, dump, ltd groc. ◇◇RECREATION: swim pool, playground. Pets welcome, breed restrict. Open May 1 - Late Nov. Facilities fully operational May 1 - Mid Oct. Member ARVC, WACO. Phone: (715)445-3489.

IRON RIVER—B-2

DELTA LAKE PARK (Bayfield County Park)—(Bayfield) *From jct US 2 & CR H: Go 5 mi S on CR H, then 5 mi S on Scenic Drive Rd.* FACILITIES: 31 sites, 31 no hkups, tenting, dump. RECREATION: lake swim, boating, canoeing, ramp, dock, lake fishing, playground. Pets welcome. Partial handicap access. Open May 1 - Oct 31. Phone: (715)372-8767.

IRON RIVER—Continued on next page

IRON RIVER—Continued

(SW) Top O The Morn Resort & Campground—(Bayfield) *From W jct CR "A" & US 2: Go 2 mi W on US 2, then 2 mi S on E Deep Lake Rd. From East: From jct CR "A" & US 2: Go 1 mi S on CR "A", then 1-1/4 mi W on Iron Lake road. Enter on R.* ◆◆FACILITIES: 61 sites, typical site width 30 ft, 15 full hkups, 46 W&E, (20/30/50 amps), 50 amps ($), 8 pull-thrus, tenting, dump, laundry. ◆◆◆RECREATION: lake swim, boating, canoeing, ramp, dock, lake fishing, playground. Pets welcome. Open May 1 - Oct 15. Rate in 2010 $29-30 for 2 persons. Phone: (715)372-4546.

TWIN BEAR PARK (Bayfield County Park)—(Bayfield) *From jct US 2 & CR H: Go 7 mi S on CR H.* FACILITIES: 48 sites, 40 E, 8 no hkups, tenting, dump, ltd groc. RECREATION: lake swim, boating, canoeing, ramp, dock, lake fishing, playground. Open May 1 - Oct 31. Phone: (715)372-8610.

JEFFERSON—I-5

(SE) Bark River Campground & Resort—(Jefferson) *From jct Hwy 106 & CR F: Go 3/4 mi N on CR F, then 1-1/2 mi W on Hanson Rd. Enter on R.* ◆◆FACILITIES: 317 sites, typical site width 30 ft, 30 full hkups, 212 W&E, (20/30/50 amps), 75 no hkups, 17 pull-thrus, family camping, tenting, dump, laundry, ltd groc. ◆◆◆RECREATION: swim pool, canoeing, river/pond fishing, playground. Pets welcome. Open Apr 2 - Oct 23. Rate in 2010 $30 per family. Phone: (262) 593-2421.

KEWASKUM—H-6

(NE) KETTLE MORAINE SF-NORTHERN UNIT (Mauthe Lake)—(Fond du Lac) *From jct Hwy 28 & Hwy 5: Go N 6 ;mi on Hwy 5 to 666, N 1 mi to Mauthe Lake Entrance. Entrance fee required.* FACILITIES: 137 sites, 51 E, (20 amps), 86 no hkups, tenting, dump. RECREATION: lake swim, boating, no motors, canoeing, ramp, lake fishing, playground. Partial handicap access. Open all yr. Phone: (262)626-2116.

KEWAUNEE—J-1

(N) Cedar Valley Campground—(Kewaunee) *From jct Hwy 42 & Hwy 29: Go 3/4 mi W on Hwy 29, then 5 mi NW on CR C, then 3/4 mi N on Cedar Valley Rd. Enter on R.* ◆◆◆◆FACILITIES: 240 sites, typical site width 30 ft, 240 W&E, (20/30 amps), 6 pull-thrus, family camping, tenting, dump, laundry, ltd groc. ◆◆◆RECREATION: swim pool, river fishing, playground. Pets welcome. Open Apr 25 - Mid-Oct. Rate in 2010 $30-40 per family. Phone: (920)388-4983.

KEWAUNEE MARINA CAMPGROUNDS (City Park)—(Kewaunee) *From jct Hwy 29 & Hwy 42: Go 1/4 mi N on Hwy 42. Enter on L.* FACILITIES: 36 sites, typical site width 30 ft, 24 W&E, 12 no hkups, tenting, dump. RECREATION: lake swim, boating, ramp, dock, lake fishing. Open May 1 - Oct 1. Phone: (920)388-3300.

(N) KEWAUNEE VILLAGE RV PARK & CAMPGROUND—(Kewaunee) *From jct Hwy 29 & Hwy 42: Go 1-1/4 mi N on Hwy 42, then 1/8 mi W on Terraqua Dr. Enter on R.*

WELCOME

◆◆◆FACILITIES: 85 sites, typical site width 40 ft, 50 full hkups, 24 W&E, (20/30/50 amps), 11 no hkups, some extd stay sites, 64 pull-thrus, WiFi Internet central location, family camping, tenting, cabins, RV storage, dump, non-guest dump $, laundry, ltd groc, RV supplies, LP gas by weight/by meter, ice, picnic tables, fire rings, wood.

CAMPCLUB USA

◆◆◆◆RECREATION: rec room/area, equipped pavilion, coin games, swim pool, mini-golf, golf nearby, bsktball, playground, shuffleboard court shuffleboard court, horseshoes, sports field, v-ball. Rec open to public.

Pets welcome, breed restrict, quantity restrict. Partial handicap access. Open May 1 - Early Oct. Big rigs welcome. Escort to site. Clubs welcome. Rate in 2010 $28-35 per family. MC/VISA/Debit. Member ARVC, WACO. CCUSA 50% Discount.

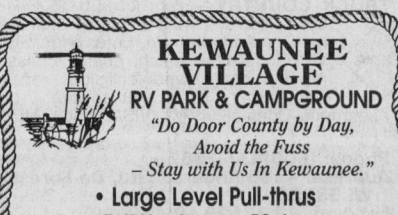

KEWAUNEE—Continued
KEWAUNEE VILLAGE RV PARK & CAMPGROUND—Continued

CCUSA reservations Required, CCUSA max stay 2 days, Cash only for CCUSA disc., Check only for CCUSA disc., CCUSA disc. not avail F,Sa, CCUSA disc. not avail holidays. Water and electric sites (30 amp) only discounted.

Phone: (920)388-4851
Address: 333 Terraqua Drive, Kewaunee, WI 54216
Lat/Lon: 44.47577/-87.50401
Email: camp@kewauneevillage.com
Web: www.kewauneevillage.com

SEE AD THIS PAGE

KIELER—I-3

(N) Rustic Barn Campground—(Grant) *From jct US 61/US 151/Hwy 35 & CR H: Go 1/2 mi S on CR H, then 2 blocks W on Dry Hollow Rd. Enter on R.* ◆◆◆◆FACILITIES: 68 sites, typical site width 35 ft, 2 full hkups, 56 W&E, (20/30/50 amps), 50 amps ($), 10 no hkups, 20 pull-thrus, tenting, dump, laundry. ◆◆◆RECREATION: play equipment. Pets welcome. Partial handicap access. Open Mid Apr - Oct 31. Big rigs welcome. Rate in 2010 $27-30 per family. Member ARVC, WACO. Phone: (608)568-7797.

KINGSTON—G-5

(S) Grand Valley Campground—(Green Lake) *From jct Hwy 44 & Westbound CR-B: Go 2-1/2 mi W on CR-B. Enter on L.* ◆◆◆◆FACILITIES: 200 sites, typical site width 30 ft, 200 W&E, (30/50 amps), 8 pull-thrus, family camping, tenting, dump, laundry, ltd groc. ◆◆◆◆RECREATION: swim pool, river swim, pond/stream fishing, playground. Pets welcome, breed restrict. Partial handicap access. Open Apr 1 - Dec 1. Big rigs welcome. Rate in 2010 $32 per family. Member ARVC, WACO. Phone: (920)394-3643.

KNOWLTON—F-4

(SW) LAKE DUBAY SHORES CAMPGROUND & RV PARK—(Marathon) *From jct I-39 & Hwy 51(exit 175): Go 2 mi S on Hwy 34, then 500 feet E on DuBay Dr. Enter on R.*

RELAX, HAVE FUN AT LK DUBAY SHORES
Bring your family to play in the water or kick back on the shores of beautiful Lake DuBay. The kids can keep busy in the game room, playground, or on our 32-ft wooden train. Adults can play on a CRAIGCAT as seen on RV Today.

◆◆◆FACILITIES: 219 sites, typical site width 45 ft, 20 full hkups, 183 W&E, (20/30/50 amps), 50 amps ($), 16 no hkups, some extd stay sites, 10 pull-thrus, WiFi Instant Internet at site, family camping, tenting, dump, portable dump, laundry, ltd groc, RV supplies, LP gas by weight/by meter, ice, picnic tables, fire rings, wood.

The town of Two Rivers is the home of the ice cream sundae.

KNOWLTON—Continued
LAKE DUBAY SHORES CAMPGROUND & RV PARK—Continued

◆◆◆◆RECREATION: rec room/area, pavilion, coin games, lake swim, boating, canoeing, kayaking, ramp, dock, 2 pontoon/5 canoe/5 pedal boat/6 motorboat rentals, float trips, lake/river fishing, fishing supplies, golf nearby, bsktball, playground, activities, (wkends), horseshoes, hiking trails, v-ball. Rec open to public.

Pets welcome. Open all yr. Facilities fully operational Apr 1 - Nov 30. Weather permitting. Big rigs welcome. Clubs welcome. Rate in 2010 $23-32 per family. MC/VISA/Debit. Member ARVC, WACO. CCUSA 50% Discount. CCUSA reservations Recommended, CCUSA max stay 2 days, CCUSA disc. not avail F,Sa, CCUSA disc. not avail holidays. Discount not available Memorial Day weekend thru Labor Day. Fully operational Apr 1 thru Nov 30.

Phone: (715)457-2484
Address: 1713 DuBay Drive, Mosinee, WI 54455
Lat/Lon: 44.71020/-89.69595
Email: camp@dubayshores.com
Web: www.dubayshores.com

SEE AD THIS PAGE

LA CROSSE—G-2

(S) Bluebird Springs Recreation Area—(La Crosse) *From jct I-90 (exit 4) & Hwy 57: Go 1/2 mi SE on Hwy 157, then 3/4 mi SW on US 16, then 1-1/4 mi E on CR-B, then 2-3/4 mi S on Smith Valley Rd (To the end). Enter on R.* ◆◆FACILITIES: 148 sites, typical site width 20 ft, 32 ft max RV length, 37 full hkups, 62 W&E, (20/30/50 amps), 49 no hkups, 6 pull-thrus, family camping, tenting, dump, ltd groc. ◆◆RECREATION: pond fishing, play equipment. Pets welcome. Open Mid Apr - Mid Oct. Rate in 2010 $15-27 for 2 persons. Phone: (608)781-2267.

(S) GOOSE ISLAND PARK (La Crosse County)—(La Crosse) *From south jct US 14/16 & Hwy 35: Go 1-1/2 mi S on Hwy 35, then 1 mi W on CR GI. Enter on R.*

WELCOME

FACILITIES: 400 sites, 130 W&E, 101 E, (30/50 amps), 169 no hkups, 10 pull-thrus, WiFi Internet central location, family camping, tenting, shower$, dump, non-guest dump $, portable dump, laundry, ltd groc, RV supplies, LP gas by weight/by meter, ice, picnic tables, fire rings, wood.

RECREATION: rec room/area, pavilion, coin games, river swim, boating, canoeing, kayaking, ramp, dock, 6 canoe/kayak rentals, river fishing,

GOOSE ISLAND PARK (La Crosse County)—Continued on next page

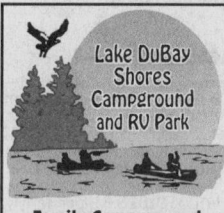

LA CROSSE—Continued
GOOSE ISLAND PARK (La Crosse County)—Continued

fishing supplies, mini-golf, ($), golf nearby, bsktball, playground, activities, (wkends), horseshoes, sports field, hiking trails, v-ball. Rec open to public.

Pets welcome. Partial handicap access. Open Mid Apr - end of Oct. 5 sites open - no bathrooms. Big rigs welcome. MC/VISA/Debit.

Phone: (608)788-7018
Address: W6488 County Rd GI, Stoddard, WI 54658
Lat/Lon: 43.72900/-91.20138
Web: www.co.la-crosse.wi.us

SEE AD PAGE 817

(C) LA CROSSE COUNTY FACILITIES DEPT.—*From jct I-90 & Hwy 53: Go 2 mi S on Hwy 53. Enter on L.* Two County parks: Goose Island Park located at Stoddard, WI & Veterans Memorial Park located at West Salem, WI Open all yr.

WELCOME

Phone: (608)785-9770
Address: 400 N 4th St Rm 1370, La Crosse, WI 54601
Lat/Lon: 43.81506/-91.24903
Email: facilities@lacrossecounty.org
Web: www.co.la-crosse.wi.us

SEE AD PAGE 817

(W) PETTIBONE RESORT—(La Crosse) *From jct I-90 (exit 275-Minn. side of river) & US 14/61: Go 5 mi S on US 14/61. Enter on R.*

WELCOME

◆◆◆◆FACILITIES: 160 sites, typical site width 40 ft, 130 W&E, (30/50 amps), 30 no hkups, many extd stay sites, 14 pull-thrus, cable TV, WiFi Instant Internet at site ($), family camping, tenting, RV storage, dump, non-guest dump $, portable dump, laundry, ltd groc, RV supplies, LP bottle exch, ice, picnic tables, patios, fire rings, wood, controlled access.

◆◆◆◆RECREATION: rec hall, pavilion, coin games, river swim, boating, canoeing, 3 canoe rentals, river fishing, fishing supplies, golf nearby, bsktball, playground, horseshoes, sports field.

Pets welcome. Partial handicap access. Open Mid Apr - Nov 1. Weather permitting. Big rigs welcome. Clubs welcome. Rate in 2010 $33 per vehicle. MC/VISA/DISC/Debit. ATM. Member ARVC, WACO.

Phone: (800)738-8426
Address: 333 Park Plaza Dr., La Crosse, WI 54601
Lat/Lon: 43.81299/-91.26648
Email: pettibone_resort@yahoo.com
Web: www.pettiboneresort.com

SEE AD THIS PAGE

LAC DU FLAMBEAU—C-4

(W) Lac Du Flambeau Tribal Campground—(Vilas) *From west jct CR D & Hwy 47 (in town): Go 1 mi NW on Hwy 47. Enter on L.* ◆◆FACILITIES: 70 sites, typical site width 40 ft, 17 full hkups, 53 W&E, (20/30 amps), 3 pull-thrus, family camping, tenting, dump, laundry, ltd groc. ◆◆RECREATION: lake swim, boating, canoeing, ramp, dock, lake fishing. Pets welcome. Open May1 - Oct 1. Rate in 2010 $28-31 per family. Phone: (715)588-9611.

LAKE GENEVA—I-6

(S) BIG FOOT BEACH SP—(Walworth) *From town: Go 1-1/2 mi S on Hwy 120.* FACILITIES: 100 sites, 14 E, (50 amps), 86 no hkups, tenting, dump. RECREATION: lake swim, boating, canoeing, lake fishing, playground. Partial handicap access. Open mid May - Oct. Phone: (262)248-2528.

LAKE TOMAHAWK—D-4

(NE) NORTHERN HIGHLAND/AMERICAN LEGION SF (Cunard Lake)—(Oneida) *From jct CR-D & CR-E: Go 2 mi N and 2 mi W on CR-E.* FACILITIES: 32 sites, 32 no hkups, tenting. RECREATION: lake swim, boating, canoeing, ramp, dock, lake fishing. Open Memorial Day - Labor Day. Phone: (715)356-5211.

LAKEWOOD—E-5

(E) Heaven's Up North Family Campground—(Oconto) *From jct Hwy 32 & CR F in Lakewood: Go 2 mi NE on CR F, then 3 mi N on Lake John Rd. (Stay right at "Y" in road). Enter on R.* ◆◆◆FACILITIES: 116 sites, typical site width 20 ft, 40 ft max RV length, 96 W&E, 19 E, (20/30/50 amps), 1 no hkups, 8 pull-thrus, family camping, tenting, dump, laundry, ltd groc. ◆◆◆RECREATION: swim pool, playground. Pets welcome. Partial handicap access. Open all yr. Facilities fully operational Mid May - Mid Oct. Rate in 2010 $20-28 per family. Member ARVC, WACO. Phone: (715)276-6556.

(N) Maple Heights Campground—(Oconto) *From jct of CR F & Hwy 32: Go 2 mi N on Hwy 32, then 500 feet NW on Chain Lake Rd. Enter on L.* ◆◆◆FACILITIES: 100 sites, typical site width 30 ft, 73 W&E, 25 E, (30/50 amps), 50 amps ($), 2 no hkups, 76 pull-thrus, family camping, tenting, dump, laundry, ltd groc. ◆◆◆◆RECREATION: swim pool, stream fishing, playground. Pets welcome. Partial handicap access. Open May 1 - Oct 31. Rate in 2010 $21-31 per family. Member ARVC, WACO. Phone: (715)276-6441.

LANCASTER—I-3

(NW) Klondyke Secluded Acres—(Grant) *From jct Hwy 61 & CR K: Go 1/2 mi N on CR K, then 2-1/2 mi W on Pine Knob Rd. Enter on R.* ◆◆FACILITIES: 87 sites, 50 W&E, (20/30/50 amps), 37 no hkups, 15 pull-thrus, family camping, tenting, dump. ◆◆RECREATION: canoeing, pond fishing, playground. Pets welcome. Open mid Apr - mid Oct. Facilities fully operational Memorial Day - Labor Day. Rate in 2010 $18 per vehicle. Phone: (608)723-2844.

LAND O'LAKES—C-5

NICOLET NATIONAL FOREST (Lac Vieux Desert Campground)—(Vilas) *From jct US-45 & CR-E: Go 3 mi E on CR-E, then 1-3/4 mi N on FR-2205.* FACILITIES: 31 sites, 31 no hkups, tenting. RECREATION: lake swim, boating, ramp, dock, lake fishing. Open May 2 - Oct 20. Phone: (715)479-2827.

LANGLADE—E-5

NICOLET NATIONAL FOREST (Boulder Lake Campground)—(Langlade) *From town: Go 5 mi SE on Hwy 55, then E on CR WW to FR 2116.* FACILITIES: 88 sites, 88 no hkups, tenting. RECREATION: lake swim, boating, ramp, dock, lake fishing. Open Apr 29 - Nov 1. Phone: (715)276-6333.

LANNON—H-6

MENOMONEE PARK (Waukesha County Park)—(Waukesha) *From jct Hwy 74 & CR V: Go 1-1/2 mi N on CR V.* FACILITIES: 33 sites, 33 no hkups, tenting. RECREATION: lake swim, lake fishing. Partial handicap access. Facilities fully operational Apr - Nov 1. Phone: (262)548-7801.

LAONA—D-5

(E) NICOLET NATIONAL FOREST (Bear Lake Campground)—(Forest) *From jct US-8 & CR-T: Go 3 mi E on CR-T, then 1/2 mi N on CR-H, then 4 mi E on FR-2136.* FACILITIES: 27 sites, 27 no hkups, tenting. RECREATION: lake swim, boating, ramp, lake fishing. Open Apr 29 - Nov 30. Phone: (715)674-4481.

LODI—H-4

(E) Crystal Lake RV Resort (Morgan RV Resort)—(Columbia) *From jct I-90/94 (exit 119) & Hwy 60: Go 11-1/2 mi W on Hwy 60, then 1 mi S on Gannon Rd. Enter at end.* ◆◆◆FACILITIES: 430 sites, typical site width 30 ft, 368 full hkups, 62 W&E, (30/50 amps), 9 pull-thrus, family camping, tenting, dump, laundry, ltd groc. ◆◆◆RECREATION: swim pool, lake swim, boating, canoeing, ramp, dock, lake fishing, playground. Pets welcome, quantity restrict. Partial handicap access. Open Apr 15 - Oct 15. Rate in 2010 $30-80 per family. Member ARVC, WACO. Phone: (608)592-5607.

LODI—Continued

(N) Smokey Hollow Campground—(Columbia) *From jct Hwy-60 & I-90/94: Go 4 mi N on I-90/94 (exit 115), then 3/4 mi W on County CS, then 1-1/2 mi S on County J, then 200 yards E on McGowan Rd. Enter on R.* ◆◆◆◆◆FACILITIES: 250 sites, typical site width 36 ft, 250 W&E, (20/30/50 amps), 12 pull-thrus, WiFi Internet central location, family camping, tenting, RV storage, shower$, dump, non-guest dump $, portable dump, laundry, ltd groc, RV supplies, LP gas by weight, ice, picnic tables, patios, fire rings, wood.

CAMPCLUB USA

◆◆◆◆◆RECREATION: equipped pavilion, swim pool, mini-golf, ($), bsktball, 56 bike rentals, playground, shuffleboard court shuffleboard court, activities, horseshoes, hiking trails, v-ball. Pets welcome, breed restrict, quantity restrict. Partial handicap access. Open all yr. Facilities fully operational Apr 15 - Oct 15. Big rigs welcome. Rate in 2010 $42-52 per family. MC/VISA/Debit. ATM. Member ARVC, WACO. CCUSA 50% Discount. CCUSA reservations Accepted, CCUSA max stay 4 days, CCUSA disc. not avail F,Sa, CCUSA disc. not avail holidays. Limited wireless.

Phone: (608)635-4806
Address: W9935 McGowan Rd, Lodi, WI 53555
Lat/Lon: 43.37017/-89.49354
Email: camp@smokeyhollowcampground.com
Web: www.smokeyhollowcampground.com

MADISON—I-4

See listings at Middleton, Stoughton, Milton & Edgerton.

(N) KOA MADISON—(Dane) *From jct I-39/90/94 (exit 126) & CR-V: Go 1/4 mi E on CR-V. Enter on R.*

WELCOME

CLOSE TO IT ALL!

Centrally located to Univ of WI & Wis Dells. Free Wi-Fi, satellite friendly, 81 Full-Hookup pull-through sites, big rigs welcome. Tent sites with W/E. Make this your hdqtrs for all So WI attractions. Enjoy "Outdoor Heated Pool"!

◆◆◆◆FACILITIES: 99 sites, typical site width 35 ft, 81 full hkups, 18 W&E, (20/30/50 amps), 81 pull-thrus, WiFi Instant Internet at site, phone Internet central location, family camping, tenting, RV's/park model rentals, RV storage, dump, non-guest dump $, laundry, groceries, RV supplies, LP gas by weight/by meter, ice, picnic tables, fire rings, wood.

◆◆◆RECREATION: rec room/area, coin games, swim pool, golf nearby, bike rental 7 bike rentals, playground, horseshoes, sports field, v-ball.

Pets welcome. Partial handicap access. Open Apr 1 - Oct 31. For reservations - (800)562-5784. Big rigs welcome. Clubs welcome. Rate in 2010 $30-45 for 2 persons. MC/VISA/DISC/AMEX/Debit. Member ARVC, WACO. KOA discount. FMCA discount.

Phone: (608)846-4528
Address: 4859 County Road V, De Forest, WI 53532
Lat/Lon: 43.24986/-89.37015
Email: madisonwikoa@centurytel.net
Web: www.madisonwikoa.com

SEE AD THIS PAGE AND AD TRAVEL SECTION PAGE 798

(NE) TOKEN CREEK PARK (Dane Couty Park)—(Dane) *From jct I-90/94 (exit 132) & US 51: Go 1/2 mi N on US 51, then 500 feet E on paved road.* FACILITIES: 38 sites, 25 E, (30 amps), 13 no hkups, tenting, dump. RECREATION: pond fishing, playground. Partial handicap access. Open May 1 - Sep 1. Phone: (608)246-3896.

TRUCK COUNTRY—*From jct I-90/39/94 & US 51: Go 1/2 mi S on US 51 then 1/4 mi E on Anderson Rd. Enter on R.* SERVICES: full-time mech, engine/chassis repair, body work/collision repair, 24-hr emerg rd svc, RV towing. Front end alignment. Open all yr. MC/VISA/DISC/AMEX/Debit.

WELCOME

Phone: (800)837-7367
Address: 4195 Anderson Rd, De Forest, WI 53532
Lat/Lon: 43.17129/-89.32082
Web: www.truckcountry.com

SEE AD TRAVEL SECTION PAGE 798 AND AD IA TRAVEL SECTION PAGE 247

MANAWA—F-5

(S) Bear Lake Campground—(Waupaca) *From jct CR-N & Hwy 22/110: Go 4 mi S on Hwy 22/110. Enter on R.* ◆◆◆FACILITIES: 200 sites, 30 ft max RV length, 188 W&E, (20/30 amps), 12 no hkups, 25 pull-thrus,

Bear Lake Campground—Continued on next page

MANAWA—Continued
Bear Lake Campground—Continued

family camping, tenting, dump, laundry, ltd groc. ◆◆◆RECREATION: lake swim, boating, canoeing, dock, lake fishing, playground. Pets welcome. Open May 1 - Oct 15. Rate in 2010 $24-31.50 per family. Member ARVC, WACO. Phone: (920)596-3308.

MANITOWISH WATERS—C-4

NORTHERN HIGHLAND/AMERICAN LEGION SF (Sandy Beach Lake)—(Iron) *From jct US-51 & Hwy-47: Go 8 mi SE on Hwy-47.* FACILITIES: 33 sites, 33 no hkups, tenting, dump. RECREATION: lake swim, boating, ramp, lake fishing. Open Memorial Day - Labor Day. Phone: (715)356-5211.

MARIBEL—F-6

(NE) Devils River Campground—(Manitowoc) *From jct I-43 (exit 164) & Hwy 147: Go 1/4 mi E on Hwy 147, then 1-1/4 mi N on CR-R. Enter on L.* ◆◆◆FACILITIES: 125 sites, 125 W&E, (30 amps), 11 pull-thrus, family camping, tenting, dump, laundry, ltd groc. ◆◆◆RECREATION: swim pool, river fishing, play equipment. Pets welcome. Open May 1 - Sept 30. Rate in 2010 $30 for 4 persons. Phone: (920)863-2812.

MARINETTE—E-6

✱ **(C) TRUCK COUNTRY**—*From jct US 41 & Cleveland Ave: Go 200 ft E on Cleveland Ave. Enter on R.* SERVICES: full-time mech, engine/chassis repair, body work/collision repair, 24-hr emerg rd svc, mobile RV svc, RV towing. 8 Service Bays. Open all yr. MC/VISA/DISC/AMEX/Debit.

Phone: (888)315-5995
Address: 2830 Cleveland Ave, Marinette, WI 54143
Lat/Lon: 45.08592/-87.64670
Web: www.truckcountry.com

SEE AD TRAVEL SECTION PAGE 798 AND AD IA TRAVEL SECTION PAGE 247

MARSHFIELD—F-3

NORTH WOOD COUNTY PARK (Wood County)—(Wood) *From jct US-10 & Hwy-13S: Go 10 mi SE on Hwy-13, then 2 mi E on CountyTrunk N, then 1 mi S on CR-A.* FACILITIES: 99 sites, 78 E, (20/30/50 amps), 21 no hkups, 30 pull-thrus, tenting, dump. RECREATION: lake swim, canoeing, playground. Partial handicap access. Open May 1 - Oct 31. Phone: (715)421-8422.

MAUSTON—G-4

(N) CASTLE ROCK COUNTY PARK (Juneau County)—(Juneau) *From jct I-90/94 (exit 69) & Hwy 82: Go 1/2 mi W on Hwy 82, then 6 mi N on CR 58, then E 5 mi on CR G. Enter on L.*

FACILITIES: 300 sites, typical site width 60 ft, 200 E, (20/30/50 amps), 100 no hkups, tenting, shower$, dump, non-guest dump $, ice, picnic tables, fire rings, grills, wood.

RECREATION: pavilion, lake swim, boating, canoeing, kayaking, ramp, dock, lake fishing, playground, horseshoes, sports field, hiking trails, v-ball. Rec open to public.

Pets welcome. Partial handicap access. Open May 1 - Oct 31. Clubs welcome. MC/VISA/DISC/Debit.

MAUSTON—Continued
CASTLE ROCK COUNTY PARK (Juneau County)—Continued

Phone: (608)847-7089
Address: 650 Prairie, Mauston, WI 53948
Lat/Lon: 43.88490/-89.97570

SEE AD THIS PAGE

MCFARLAND—I-5

BABCOCK CAMPGROUND (Dane County Park)—(Dane) *In town, S on Hwy-51.* FACILITIES: 25 sites, 25 E, (30 amps), tenting, dump. RECREATION: boating, canoeing, ramp, dock, lake fishing, playground. Partial handicap access. Open May 1 - Oct. Phone: (608)242-4576.

MELLEN—C-3

(NE) COPPER FALLS SP—(Ashland) *From jct Hwy 13 & Hwy 169: Go 2 mi NE on Hwy 169.* FACILITIES: 54 sites, 23 E, (30/50 amps), 31 no hkups, tenting, dump, ltd groc. RECREATION: lake swim, canoeing, lake/river fishing, playground. Partial handicap access. Open all yr. Facilities fully operational Mid Apr - Mid Oct. Phone: (715)274-5123.

MENOMONIE—E-2

(N) Twin Springs Camping Resort—(Dunn) *From jct I-94 (exit 41) & Hwy 25: Go 1 block N on Hwy 25, then 2 mi E on Cedar Falls Rd. Enter on R.* ◆◆FACILITIES: 75 sites, typical site width 30 ft, 30 full hkups, 45 W&E, (20/30/50 amps), 44 pull-thrus, family camping, tenting, dump. ◆◆◆RECREATION: swim pool, boating, canoeing, ramp, dock, lake fishing, playground. Pets welcome, breed restrict. Partial handicap access. Open Apr 1 - Oct 31. Facilities fully operational May 1 - Oct 1. Big rigs welcome. Rate in 2010 $36-42 for 2 persons. Member ARVC, WACO. Phone: (715)235-9321.

MERCER—C-4

(W) Loon Lagoon RV Resort & Campground—(Iron) *From jct Hwy-51 & Clinic St (S end of town): Go 1 block NE on Clinic St, then 1 block W on Margaret Rd. Enter on R.* ◆◆FACILITIES: 40 sites, typical site width 36 ft, 26 full hkups, 14 W&E, (20/30 amps), 9 pull-thrus, tenting, dump, laundry. ◆◆◆RECREATION: boating, canoeing, dock, lake fishing, play equipment. Pets welcome. Open May 1 - Oct 1. Rate in 2010 $20-22 for 2 persons. Phone: (715)476-2466.

MERRILL—E-4

(W) COUNCIL GROUNDS SP—(Lincoln) *From jct Hwy 64 & Hwy 107: Go 2 mi W on Hwy 107, then 1 mi S on Council Grounds Rd.* FACILITIES: 55 sites, 19 E, (30 amps), 36 no hkups, tenting, dump. RECREATION: river swim, boating, canoeing, ramp, dock, late/river fishing, playground. Partial handicap access. Open late/Apr - Oct 31. Phone: (715)536-8773.

MIDDLETON—I-4

MENDOTA PARK (Dane County Park)—(Dane) *From north jct US 142 & US 12: Go 1 mi N on US 12, then 2-1/4 mi E on CR M (Century Ave).* FACILITIES: 30 sites, 30 E, tenting. RECREATION: lake swim, boating, canoeing, ramp, dock, lake fishing, playground. Pets welcome. Partial handicap access. Open May 1 - Nov 1. Phone: (608)246-3896.

MIKANA—D-2

WALDO CARLSON PARK (Barron County Park)—(Barron) *From jct Hwy 48 & 29th Ave: Go 1/4 mi E on 29th Ave.* FACILITIES: 35 sites, 33 E, (20/30/50 amps), 2 no hkups, tenting. RECREATION: lake swim, boating, ramp, dock, lake fishing, playground. Open May 1 - Oct 15. Phone: (715)354-3353.

MILTON—I-5

(NW) Blackhawk Camping Resort—(Rock) *From jct Hwy 26 & Hwy 59 Westbound: Go 2-1/2 mi NW on Hwy 59, then 1/2 mi W on Clear Lake Rd & Blackhawk Rd. Enter at end.* ◆◆FACILITIES: 515 sites, typical site width 50 ft, 480 full hkups, 27 W&E, (20/30/50 amps), 8 no hkups, 2 pull-thrus, family camping, tenting, dump, laundry, ltd groc. ◆◆◆◆RECREATION: swim pool, lake swim, boating, canoeing, lake fishing, playground. Pets welcome. Partial handicap access. Open Mid Apr - Mid Oct. Rate in 2010 $35-54 for 2 persons. Member ARVC, WACO. Phone: (608)868-2586.

(W) HIDDEN VALLEY RV RESORT & CAMPGROUND—(Rock) *From jct I-90 (exit 163) & Hwy 59: Go 3/4 mi E on Hwy 59. Enter on R.*

◆◆◆◆◆FACILITIES: 232 sites, typical site width 40 ft, 180 full hkups, 52 W&E, (20/30/50 amps), some extd stay sites, 32 pull-thrus, WiFi Instant Internet at site ($), family camping, tenting, cabins, dump, non-guest dump $, laundry, ltd groc, RV supplies, LP gas by weight/by meter, ice, picnic tables, patios, fire rings, wood.

◆◆◆◆◆RECREATION: rec hall, rec room/area, coin games, swim pool, hot tub, golf nearby, bsktball, 13 bike rentals, playground, activities, horseshoes, sports field, hiking trails, v-ball.

Pets welcome. Partial handicap access. Open 4th wk in Apr - 3rd wk in Oct. Big rigs welcome. Escort to site. Clubs welcome. Rate in 2010 $34-64 per family. MC/VISA/Debit. Member ARVC, WACO. CCUSA 50% Discount. CCUSA reservations Recommended, CCUSA max stay 1 day, Cash only for CCUSA disc., CCUSA disc. not avail F,Sa, CCUSA disc. not avail holidays. Not available Memorial Day weekend thru Labor Day.

Phone: (800)469-5515
Address: 872 E Hwy 59, Milton, WI 53563
Lat/Lon: 42.82670/-89.01642
Web: www.hiddenvalleyrvresort.com

SEE AD THIS PAGE AND AD TRAVEL SECTION PAGE 798

MILTON—Continued on next page

MILTON—Continued

(W) Lakeland Camping Resort—(Rock) *From jct I-90 (exit 163) & Hwy 59: Go 2-1/4 mi E on Hwy 59. Enter on L.* ◇◇◇FACILITIES: 752 sites, typical site width 30 ft, 550 full hkups, 202 W&E, (30/50 amps), 8 pull-thrus, tenting, dump, laundry, ltd groc. ◇◇◇RECREATION: swim pool, lake swim, boating, canoeing, ramp, dock, lake/pond fishing, playground. Pets welcome. Partial handicap access. Open Apr 15 - Oct 15. Big rigs welcome. Rate in 2010 $44-50 per family. Member ARVC, WACO. Phone: (608)868-4700.

MILWAUKEE—I-6

See listings at Caledonia, Delafield, Hartford, Lannon, Mukwonago, Racine & West Bend.

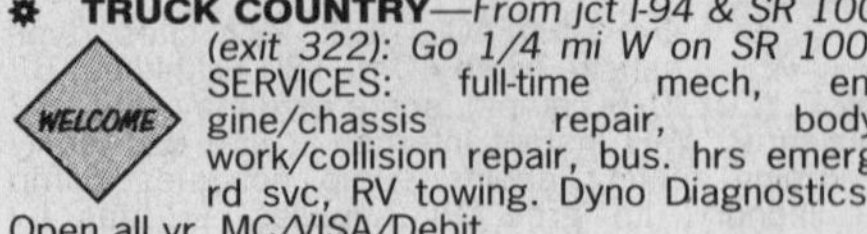

TRUCK COUNTRY—*From jct I-94 & SR 100 (exit 322): Go 1/4 mi W on SR 100.* SERVICES: full-time mech, engine/chassis repair, body work/collision repair, bus. hrs emerg rd svc, RV towing. Dyno Diagnostics. Open all yr. MC/VISA/Debit.

Phone: (800)236-6061
Address: 2222 W. Ryan Rd, Oak Creek, WI 53154
Lat/Lon: 42.87354/-87.94454
Web: www.truckcountry.com

SEE AD TRAVEL SECTION PAGE 798 AND AD IA TRAVEL SECTION PAGE 247

(W) WISCONSIN STATE FAIR RV PARK—(Milwaukee) *At I-94 (exit 306-84th St): Go 50 yards S on 84th St. Enter at gate 6. From 76th St, enter at gate 8. Enter on L.* FACILITIES: 241 sites, typical site width 40 ft, 70 full hkups, 50 W&E, 121 E, (20/30/50 amps), 41 pull-thrus, dump, laundry. RECREATION: Pets welcome. Partial handicap access. No tents. Open all yr. Big rigs welcome. Phone: (414)266-7035.

MINOCQUA—D-4

See listings at Boulder Junction, Eagle River, Lac du Flambeau, Tomahawk, St. Germain & Woodruff

(W) PATRICIA LAKE RV RESORT—(Oneida) *From south jct US 51 & Hwy 70: Go 2-1/2 mi W on Hwy 70, then 1/2 mi S on Camp Pinemere Rd. Enter on L.*

◇◇◇◇FACILITIES: 100 sites, typical site width 50 ft, 87 full hkups, 9 W&E, (15/20/30/50 amps), 4 no hkups, many extd stay sites, 3 pull-thrus, cable TV, WiFi Internet central location, family camping, tenting, shower$, dump, portable dump, laundry, ltd groc, RV supplies, ice, picnic tables, fire rings, wood.

◇◇◇◇RECREATION: rec room/area, equipped pavilion, coin games, lake swim, boating, electric motors only, canoeing, kayaking, ramp, dock, 3 rowboat/3 pedal boat rentals, lake fishing, fishing supplies, golf nearby, bsktball, playground, shuffleboard court shuffleboard court, horseshoes, sports field, hiking trails, v-ball.

Pets welcome, quantity restrict. Open May 1 - Oct 15. Big rigs welcome. Clubs welcome. Rate in 2010 $32-35 per family. MC/VISA/DISC/Debit. Member ARVC, WACO. CCUSA 50% Discount. CCUSA reservations Recommended, CCUSA max stay 2 days, Cash only for CCUSA disc., Check only for CCUSA disc., CCUSA disc. not avail F,Sa. Not available Memorial Day weekend thru Labor Day.

Phone: (715)356-3198
Address: 8508 Camp Pinemere Rd, Minocqua, WI 54548
Lat/Lon: 45.87687/-89.75646
Email: patlake@charter.net
Web: www.patricialakecampground.com

SEE AD TRAVEL SECTION PAGE 799

Visit Woodall's Attractions

MONTELLO—G-4

(W) Buffalo Lake Camping Resort—(Marquette) *From jct Hwy 22 & Hwy 23: Go W on Hwy 23, then 1 mi W on CR C. Enter on R.* ◇◇◇FACILITIES: 110 sites, typical site width 40 ft, 28 full hkups, 82 W&E, (20/30/50 amps), 8 pull-thrus, cable TV, WiFi Instant Internet at site, WiFi Internet central location, family camping, tenting, shower$, dump, portable dump, laundry, ltd groc, RV supplies, LP gas by weight/by meter, ice, picnic tables, fire rings, grills, wood. ◇◇◇RECREATION: rec hall, equipped pavilion, swim pool, lake swim, boating, canoeing, kayaking, ramp, dock, lake fishing, fishing supplies, bsktball, 13 bike rentals, playground, activities, horseshoes, v-ball. Pets welcome. Partial handicap access. Open Apr 15 - Oct 15. Big rigs welcome. Green Friendly. Rate in 2010 $32-43 per family. MC/VISA/DISC/Debit. Member ARVC, WACO. CCUSA 50% Discount. CCUSA reservations Recommended, CCUSA max stay 4 days, CCUSA disc. not avail F,Sa, CCUSA disc. not avail holidays.

Phone: (608)297-2915
Address: 555 Lake Ave, Montello, WI 53949
Lat/Lon: 43.79128/-89.34514
Email: info@buffalolakecamping.com
Web: www.buffalolakecamping.com

(NW) Kilby Lake Campground—(Marquette) *From jct Hwy 22 & Hwy 23: Go 2 mi W on Hwy 23, then 1/2 mi N on Fern Ave. Enter on R.* ◇◇◇FACILITIES: 123 sites, typical site width 40 ft, 64 full hkups, 59 W&E, (20/30/50 amps), 2 pull-thrus, family camping, tenting, dump, laundry, ltd groc. ◇◇◇RECREATION: swim pool, lake swim, boating, canoeing, dock, lake fishing, playground. Pets welcome, breed restrict, quantity restrict. Partial handicap access. Open Apr 15 - Oct 15. Rate in 2010 $32-40 per family. Member ARVC, WACO. Phone: (877)497-2344.

Lake Arrowhead Campground—(Marquette) *From jct Northbound Hwy 22 & Hwy 23: Go 1/8 mi E on Hwy 23, then 6 mi E on CR-C, then 1000 feet E on Fox Ct. Enter on R.* ◇◇◇◇FACILITIES: 237 sites, typical site width 50 ft, 40 ft max RV length, 159 full hkups, 78 W&E, (20/30/50 amps), 18 pull-thrus, family camping, tenting, dump, laundry, groceries. ◇◇◇◇RECREATION: swim pool, lake swim, boating, canoeing, ramp, dock, lake/river/pond fishing, playground. Pets welcome, breed restrict, quantity restrict. Open Apr 15 - Oct 15. Rate in 2010 $36-53 per family. Member ARVC, WACO. Phone: (920)295-3000.

(W) Ox Creek RV Park—(Marquette) *From the jct of Hwy 22 & Hwy 23: Go 1 mi W on Hwy 23, then 5 mi W on CR-C. Enter on L.* ◇◇◇FACILITIES: 30 sites, 10 full hkups, 8 W&E, (30/50 amps), 12 no hkups, 4 pull-thrus, WiFi Internet central location, family camping, tenting, dump, non-guest dump $, picnic tables, fire rings, wood. ◇◇RECREATION: boating, canoeing, kayaking, dock, lake fishing, bsktball, play equipment, horseshoes. Pets welcome. Open Apr 15 - Oct 15. Rate in 2010 $20-24 per family. Member ARVC, WACO. CCUSA 50% Discount. CCUSA reservations Recommended, CCUSA max stay 2 days, Cash only for CCUSA disc., CCUSA disc. not avail F,Sa, CCUSA disc. not avail holidays.

Phone: (608)589-5390
Address: W5303 CR-C, Montello, WI 53949
Lat/Lon: 43.77419/-89.42590
Email: dcfritz@yahoo.com
Web: www.oxcreekcampground.com

(S) Wilderness Campground—(Marquette) *From jct Hwy 23 & Hwy 22 Southbound: Go 7 mi S on Hwy 22, then 1/4 mi W on Wilderness Rd. Enter on R.* ◇◇◇FACILITIES: 338 sites, typical site width 45 ft, 167 full hkups, 171 W&E, (20/30/50 amps), 75 pull-thrus, family camping, tenting, dump, laundry, groceries. ◇◇◇RECREATION: swim pool, lake swim, boating, no motors, canoeing, ramp, lake fishing, playground. Pets welcome. Partial handicap access. Open Mid Apr - Mid Oct. Big rigs welcome. Rate in 2010 $36-46 per family. Member ARVC, WACO. Phone: (608) 297-2002.

Visit our website www.woodalls.com

MOUNTAIN—E-5

CHUTE PARK (Fischer Memorial Park)—(Oconto) *From town: Go 5 mi S on Hwy-32/64.* FACILITIES: 115 sites, 60 E, 55 no hkups, tenting, dump, groceries. RECREATION: lake swim, boating, ramp, dock, playground. Open all yr. Phone: (715)276-6261.

NICOLET NATIONAL FOREST (Bagley Rapids Campground)—(Oconto) *From town: Go 2 mi S on Hwy 32, then 1/2 mi W on FR 2111.* FACILITIES: 30 sites, 22 ft max RV length, 30 no hkups, tenting. RECREATION: river swim, canoeing, river fishing. Open Apr 29 - Nov 1. Phone: (715)276-6333.

MUKWONAGO—I-6

(W) COUNTRY VIEW CAMPGROUND—(Waukesha) *From jct I-43 (exit 43) & Hwy 83: Go 1/4 mi SE on Hwy 83, then 1/4 mi E on Wolf Run, then 1 mi SE on Maple, then 1-1/2 mi S on Craig Dr. Enter on L.*

◇◇◇◇FACILITIES: 159 sites, typical site width 40 ft, 37 full hkups, 104 W&E, (20/30 amps), 18 no hkups, 60 pull-thrus, family camping, tenting, dump, non-guest dump $, portable dump, laundry, ltd groc, RV supplies, LP gas by weight/by meter, ice, picnic tables, fire rings, wood.

◇◇◇◇RECREATION: rec room/area, equipped pavilion, coin games, swim pool, golf nearby, playground, activities, (wkends), sports field, v-ball. Rec open to public.

Pets welcome. Partial handicap access. Open mid Apr - mid Oct. Clubs welcome. Rate in 2010 $27-30 for 2 persons. MC/VISA/Debit.

Phone: (262)662-3654
Address: S110 W26400 Craig Ave., Mukwonago, WI 53149
Lat/Lon: 42.84218/-88.27528
Web: www.countryviewcamp.com

SEE AD MILWAUKEE THIS PAGE

MUKWONAGO PARK (Waukesha County Park)—(Waukesha) *From jct US-83 & US-99: Go 3 mi W on US-99.* FACILITIES: 33 sites, 33 no hkups, tenting. RECREATION: lake fishing. Open all yr. Facilities fully operational Apr - Nov 1. Phone: (262) 548-7801.

MUSCODA—H-3

RIVERSIDE CAMPGROUND (City Park)—(Grant) *From Hwy-80 north of town, follow signs.* FACILITIES: 36 sites, 31 E, 5 no hkups, tenting. RECREATION: boating, canoeing, ramp, river fishing, playground. Open May 1 - Oct 30. Phone: (608)739-3786.

MUSKEGO—I-6

MUSKEGO PARK (Waukesha County Park)—(Waukesha) *From jct I-43 & CR Y(Racine Ave): Go 2-1/2 mi S on CR Y, then 3/4 mi W on CR L (Janesville Rd).* FACILITIES: 24 sites, 24 no hkups, tenting. RECREATION: pond fishing. Open all yr. Phone: (262)548-7801.

NECEDAH—G-4

(S) Buckhorn Campground Resort—(Juneau) *From jct Hwy 21 & CR G: Go 7 mi S on CR G. Enter on L.* ◇◇◇FACILITIES: 147 sites, typical site width 45 ft, 27 full hkups, 120 W&E, (20/30/50 amps), 3 pull-thrus, family camping, tenting, dump. ◇◇RECREATION: swim pool, playground. Pets welcome. Partial handicap access. Open all yr. Facilities fully operational Mid Apr - Mid Oct. Rate in 2010 $30 for 4 persons. Phone: (608) 565-2090.

(SE) BUCKHORN SP—(Juneau) *From jct Hwy 21 & Hwy 80/CR Q: Go 3-1/4 mi S on Hwy 80/CR Q, then 4-1/2 mi E on CR G. Enter on L.* FACILITIES: 54 sites, 1 E, (50 amps), 53 no hkups, tenting. RECREATION: lake swim, boating, canoeing, ramp, dock, lake fishing, play equipment. Partial handicap access. Open all yr. Phone: (608)565-2789.

(N) Moonlite Trails Campground LLC—(Juneau) *From jct Hwy 21 & CR-G: Go 8 mi N on CR-G, then 2 mi E on 9th St. Enter on R.* ◇◇◇FACILITIES: 34 sites, typical site width 40 ft, 31 W&E, (30/50 amps), 3 no hkups, family camping, tenting, dump, ltd groc. ◇◇RECREATION: playground. Pets welcome. Partial handicap access. Open Mid Apr - Nov 30. Rate in 2010 $22 per family. Member ARVC, WACO. Phone: (608) 565-6936.

(C) St. Joseph Motel & Resort—(Juneau) *From jct Hwy 80 & Hwy 21: Go 1 mi E on Hwy 21. Enter on L.* ◇◇◇FACILITIES: 40 sites, typical site width 60 ft, 40 W&E, (20/30/50 amps), 20 pull-thrus, tenting, dump, laundry. ◇◇RECREATION: playground. Pets welcome. Open Apr 15 - Nov 30. Rate in 2010 $19 per family. Member ARVC, WACO. Phone: (608)565-7258.

NECEDAH—Continued on next page

Can you trust the Woodall's ratings? 25 evaluation teams have scoured North American campgrounds to provide you with accurate, up to date information & ratings. Find a rating you don't agree with? Send a letter or email our way, and we'll give it extra attention for 2012.

NECEDAH—Continued

(N) WILDERNESS COUNTY PARK (Juneau County)—(Juneau) *From jct CR 58 & Hwy 21: Go 1 mi E on Hwy 21, then 9 mi N on CR G, then 4 mi E on 8th St. Enter on R.*

WELCOME

FACILITIES: 128 sites, typical site width 60 ft, 110 E, (20/30 amps), 18 no hkups, tenting, shower$, dump, non-guest dump $, ice, picnic tables, fire rings, grills, wood.

RECREATION: pavilion, lake swim, boating, canoeing, kayaking, ramp, lake fishing, playground, horseshoes, hiking trails, v-ball. Rec open to public.

Pets welcome. Partial handicap access. Open all yr. Facilities fully operational May 1 - Nov 30. Clubs welcome. MC/VISA/DISC/Debit.

Phone: (608)565-7285
Address: 14054 21st Ave, Necedah, WI 54646
Lat/Lon: 44.15426/-89.98511

SEE AD MAUSTON PAGE 819

NEILLSVILLE—F-3

(SE) SHERWOOD COUNTY PARK (Clark County)—(Clark) *17 mi SE via Hwy-73 and CR-"Z".* FACILITIES: 36 sites, 20 E, (20/30 amps), 16 no hkups, 4 pull-thrus, tenting, dump. RECREATION: lake swim, boating, ramp, lake fishing, playground. Pets welcome. Open May 1 - Dec. Phone: (715)743-5140.

(W) SNYDER PARK (Clark County)—(Clark) *From jct Hwy 73 & US 10: Go 6 mi W on US 10.* FACILITIES: 32 sites, 20 E, (20/30 amps), 12 no hkups, 15 pull-thrus, tenting, dump. RECREATION: lake/river swim, boating, ramp, lake/river fishing, playground. Partial handicap access. Open May 1 - Dec. Phone: (715) 743-5140.

NEKOOSA—F-4

(S) Deer Trail Park Campground—(Wood) *From Hwy 173 & Hwy 73: Go 1/2 mi S on Hwy 73, then 3 mi S on CR-Z. Enter on R.* ◆◆FACILITIES: 170 sites, typical site width 45 ft, 167 W&E, (20/30/50 amps), 3 no hkups, 24 pull-thrus, family camping, tenting, dump, laundry, ltd groc. ◆◆◆RECREATION: swim pool, boating, canoeing, lake fishing, playground. Pets welcome. Open Apr 25 - Nov 30. Rate in 2010 $25-35 per family. Member ARVC, WACO. Phone: (715)886-3871.

NEW AUBURN—E-2

MORRIS-ERICKSON COUNTY PARK—(Chippewa) *From town: Go 8 mi NE on CR M & Hwy 40.* FACILITIES: 28 sites, 28 E, tenting, dump. RECREATION: lake swim, boating, ramp, dock, lake fishing, playground. Open 1st May weekend - Oct 15. Phone: (715)726-7880.

NEW GLARUS—I-4

NEW GLARUS WOODS SP—(Green) *From jct Hwy 69 & CR NN: Go 1/8 mi W on CR NN.* FACILITIES: 32 sites, 32 no hkups, tenting. RECREATION: Partial handicap access. Open all yr. Facilities fully operational Apr 1 - Oct 31. Phone: (608)527-2335.

NEW LISBON—G-3

(N) Lil' Yellow River RV Park & Campground—(Juneau) *From I-90/94 (exit 61) & Hwy-80: Go 4-1/3 mi N on Hwy-80. Enter on L.* ◆◆◆FACILITIES: 155 sites, typical site width 30 ft, 125 W&E, (20/30/50 amps), 30 no hkups, 20 pull-thrus, family camping, tenting, dump, ltd groc. ◆◆◆RECREATION: playground. Pets welcome. Open Apr 1 - End of Nov. Rate in 2010 $15-20 for 2 persons. Phone: (608)562-5355.

NEW LONDON—F-5

(S) Hucklberry Acres Campground—(Waupaca) *From jct US 45 & Hwy 54: Go 1/2 mi W on Hwy 54, then 4-1/2 mi S on CR D, then 2 mi W on Manske Rd, then 1/2 mi S on CR-W, then 1/2 mi E on Hucklberry Rd. Enter at end.* ◆◆◆FACILITIES: 184 sites, typical site width 40 ft, 170 W&E, (20/30/50 amps), 14 no hkups, family camping, tenting, dump, ltd groc. ◆◆◆RECREATION: lake swim, boating, no motors, canoeing, lake fishing. Pets welcome, breed restrict. Open all yr. Facilities fully operational May 1 - Oct 15. Rate in 2010 $31-32 per vehicle. Member ARVC, WACO. Phone: (920)982-4628.

(W) Wolf River Campgrounds—(Waupaca) *From jct US 45 & Hwy 54: Go 4 mi W on Hwy 54, then 1 mi S on Larry Rd, then 2 blocks W on CR X. Enter on L.* ◆◆◆FACILITIES: 198 sites, typical site width 24 ft, 48 full hkups, 106 W&E, (20/30/50 amps), 44 no hkups, 50 pull-thrus, tenting, dump, laundry, ltd groc. ◆◆◆◆RECREATION: river swim, boating, canoeing, ramp, dock, river fishing, playground. Pets welcome. Partial handicap access. Open May 1 - Oct 1. Rate in 2010 $29-32 per family. Member ARVC, WACO. Phone: (920)982-2458.

Wisconsin is the dairy capital of the United States and produces more milk than any other state.

NORMAN—F-6

(S) MAPLE VIEW CAMPGROUND—(Kewaunee) *From jct Hwy-42 & CR-G: Go 3 mi W on CR-G, then 500 feet S on Norman Rd. Enter on R.*

WELCOME

◆◆◆FACILITIES: 100 sites, typical site width 36 ft, 25 full hkups, 65 W&E, (20/30/50 amps), 10 no hkups, some extd stay sites, 5 pull-thrus, family camping, tenting, cabins, dump, non-guest dump $, portable dump, laundry, ltd groc, RV supplies, ice, picnic tables, fire rings, wood.

CAMPCLUB USA

◆◆◆RECREATION: equipped pavilion, coin games, lake swim, boating, no motors, canoeing, kayaking, 6 pedal boat rentals, lake fishing, golf nearby, bsktball, 5 bike rentals, playground, activities, (wkends), horseshoes, sports field, hiking trails, v-ball. Rec open to public.

Pets welcome, breed restrict. Partial handicap access. Open May 1 - Oct 15. Big rigs welcome. Clubs welcome. Rate in 2010 $28-35 per family. Member ARVC, WACO. CCUSA 50% Discount. CCUSA reservations Recommended, CCUSA max stay 4 days, Cash only for CCUSA disc., CCUSA disc. not avail F,Sa, CCUSA disc. not avail holidays.

Phone: (920)776-1588
Address: N 1267 Norman Rd, Kewaunee, WI 54216
Lat/Lon: 44.36909/-87.60399

SEE AD KEWAUNEE PAGE 817

OAKDALE—G-3

(E) KOA Oakdale—(Monroe) *From jct I-90/94 (exit 48) & CR PP: Go 1 block N on CR PP, then 2 blocks E on Woody Dr, then 1 block S on Jay St. Enter at end.* ◆◆◆◆FACILITIES: 74 sites, typical site width 40 ft, 48 full hkups, 12 W&E, 8 E, (20/30/50 amps), 6 no hkups, 38 pull-thrus, family camping, tenting, dump, laundry, ltd groc. ◆◆◆◆RECREATION: swim pool, playground. Pets welcome, breed restrict. Open Late Apr - Mid Oct. Big rigs welcome. Green Friendly. Rate in 2010 $29-45 for 2 persons. Member ARVC, WACO. Phone: (800)562-1737. KOA discount.

OCONTO—E-6

(S) HOLTWOOD CAMPSITE (Municipal Park)—(Oconto) *From jct Hwy 41 & McDonald St in town: Go 4 blocks W on McDonald St, then 1/2 mi N on Holtwood Way. Enter at end.* FACILITIES: 130 sites, 95 full hkups, 15 E, (30/50 amps), 20 no hkups, tenting, dump, laundry. RECREATION: swim pool, river swim, boating, electric motors only, canoeing, ramp, dock, lake/river fishing, playground. Pets welcome. Partial handicap access. Open May 1 - Oct 31. Phone: (920)834-7732.

NORTH BAY SHORE (Oconto County Park)—(Oconto) *From town: Go 9 mi NE on CR-Y.* FACILITIES: 33 sites, 33 E, tenting, dump. RECREATION: lake swim, boating, ramp, dock, lake fishing, playground. Partial handicap access. Open May 15 - Sep 15. Phone: (920)834-6825.

ONEIDA COUNTY—

See listings at Minocqua, Three Lakes, Tomahawk & Woodruff

ONTARIO—G-3

(SE) WILDCAT MOUNTAIN SP—(Vernon) *From town: Go 3 mi E on Hwy 33.* FACILITIES: 30 sites, 30 no hkups, tenting, dump. RECREATION: canoeing, river/stream fishing, playground. Partial handicap access. Open May 1 - Oct 14. Phone: (608)337-4775.

OSHKOSH—G-5

Circle R Campground—(Winnebago) *From jct Hwy 41 & Hwy 26 (exit 113): Go 1 mi E on CR N, then 1-1/4 mi S on Old Knapp Rd. Enter on R.* ◆◆FACILITIES: 132 sites, typical site width 33 ft, 42 full hkups, 37 W&E, 24 E, (20/30 amps), 29 no hkups, 22 pull-thrus, family camping, tenting, dump, laundry, ltd groc. ◆◆RECREATION: playground. Pets welcome. Open May 1 - Oct 15. Rate in 2010 $22-28 for 2 persons. Phone: (920)235-8909.

(N) Hickory Oaks Campground—(Winnebago) *From jct US 41 (exit 120) & Hwy 45: Go 1/8 mi S on Hwy 45 to Snell Rd: Go approx 2 mi E on Snell Rd, then 1/2 mi S on Vinland Rd. Enter on R.* ◆◆◆FACILITIES: 77 sites, typical site width 30 ft, 28 W&E, 11 E, (20/30/50 amps), 38 no hkups, 3 pull-thrus, family camping, tenting, dump, laundry. ◆◆RECREATION: boating, no motors, canoeing, dock, pond fishing. Pets welcome, breed restrict, quantity restrict. Partial handicap access. Open May 1 - Nov 1. Rate in 2010 $23-27 per family. Member ARVC, WACO. Phone: (920)235-8076.

(E) Kalbus Country Harbor, Inc—(Winnebago) *From jct US 41 (exit 113) & Hwy 26/CR N: Go 3 mi E on CR N (becomes Fisk Rd), then 1-1/2 mi S on US 45, then 1/2 mi E on Nekimi Ave, then 1/4 mi N on Lake Rd. Enter on R.* ◆◆◆◆FACILITIES: 78 sites, typical site width 35 ft, 8 full hkups, 45 W&E, 10 E, (20/30/50 amps), 15 no hkups, 7 pull-thrus, WiFi Instant Internet at site, family camping, tenting, RV storage, shower$, dump, non-guest dump $, portable dump, laundry, RV

OSHKOSH—Continued
Kalbus Country Harbor, Inc—Continued

supplies, marine gas, ice, picnic tables, fire rings, wood. ◆◆◆RECREATION: lake swim, boating, ramp, dock, lake fishing, bsktball, horseshoes. Pets welcome. Open May 1 - Oct 31. Big rigs welcome. Rate in 2010 $30-43 per vehicle. MC/VISA/Debit. Member ARVC, WACO. CCUSA 50% Discount. CCUSA reservations Required, CCUSA max stay 3 days, CCUSA disc. not avail Th, CCUSA disc. not avail F,Sa, CCUSA disc. not avail holidays.

CAMPCLUB USA

Phone: (920)426-0062
Address: 5309 Lake Rd, Oshkosh, WI 54902
Lat/Lon: 43.94087/-88.47924
Web: www.kalbuscountryharbor.com

OSSEO—F-2

(E) STONEY CREEK RV RESORT—(Trempealeau) *From jct I-94 (exit 88) & US 10: Go 100 yds E on US 10, then 1/4 mi S on Oak Grove Rd. Enter on R.*

WELCOME

◆◆◆◆◆FACILITIES: 122 sites, typical site width 50 ft, 83 full hkups, 39 W&E, (20/30/50 amps), 22 pull-thrus, cable TV, WiFi Instant Internet at site, phone on-site Internet (needs activ), phone Internet central location, family camping, tenting, cabins, dump, non-guest dump $, laundry, ltd groc, RV supplies, ice, picnic tables, patios, fire rings, wood.

◆◆◆◆◆RECREATION: rec hall, rec room/area, coin games, 2 swim pools, wading pool, spray ground, mini-golf, ($), golf nearby, bsktball, playground, activities, (wkends), horseshoes, sports field, hiking trails, v-ball.

Pets welcome, breed restrict. Partial handicap access. Open Apr 1 - Nov 1. Big rigs welcome. Escort to site. Clubs welcome. Rate in 2010 $23-45 per family. MC/VISA/DISC/Debit. Member ARVC, WACO.

Phone: (715)597-2102
Address: 50483 Oak Grove Rd, Osseo, WI 54758
Lat/Lon: 44.57536/-91.19619
Email: stoneycreek@triwest.net
Web: www.stoneycreekrvresort.com

SEE AD TRAVEL SECTION PAGE 799

PALMYRA—I-5

KETTLE MORAINE SF-SOUTHERN UNIT (Horserider's Campground)—(Jefferson) *From jct US 12 & Hwy 67: Go 5 mi NE on US 67, then 4 mi W on CR NN/EW. Camping for horse campers only.* FACILITIES: 55 sites, 55 no hkups, tenting. RECREATION: Open Apr 1 - Dec 1. Phone: (262)594-6200.

PARDEEVILLE—H-4

(W) Deer Creek Campground—(Columbia) *From jct Hwy 22 & Hwy 44: Go 3 mi N on Hwy 44, then 3 mi E on Hwy 33, then 1/8 mi N on Larson Rd. Enter on L.* ◆◆◆FACILITIES: 60 sites, typical site width 45 ft, 50 W&E, (30 amps), 10 no hkups, tenting, dump, ltd groc. ◆◆RECREATION: playground. Pets welcome, breed restrict. Open Last wknd Apr - Nov 2. Rate in 2010 $29 per family. Member ARVC, WACO. Phone: (920)348-6413.

(W) Duck Creek Campground—(Columbia) *From jct Hwy 16 & Hwy 22: Go 1/2 mi N on Hwy 22, then 1 mi W on CR-G. Enter on R.* ◆◆◆FACILITIES: 130 sites, typical site width 30 ft, 130 W&E, (20/30 amps), 3 pull-thrus, family camping, tenting, shower$, dump, portable dump, laundry, ltd groc, RV supplies, ice, picnic tables, fire rings, wood. ◆◆◆◆RECREATION: rec hall, equipped pavilion, pond/stream fishing, fishing supplies, bsktball, playground, activities, horseshoes, hiking trails, v-ball. Pets welcome, quantity restrict. Partial handicap access. Open Apr - Oct. Rate in 2010 $25-35 for 2 persons. MC/VISA/Debit. ATM. Member ARVC, WACO. CCUSA 50% Discount. CCUSA reservations Recommended, CCUSA max stay 5 days, CCUSA disc. not avail F,Sa, CCUSA disc. not avail holidays. $2.50 surcharge for electric heaters.

CAMPCLUB USA

Phone: (608)429-2425
Address: W6560 Co Hwy G, Pardeeville, WI 53954
Lat/Lon: 43.49934/-89.32890
Email: duckcrcg@palacenet.net
Web: www.duckcreekcampground.com

(N) Indian Trails Campground—(Columbia) *From jct Hwy 44 & Hwy 22 in Pardeeville: Go 1-1/4 mi N on Hwy 22, then 1 mi W on Haynes Rd. Enter on L.* ◆◆◆◆FACILITIES: 327 sites, typical site width 40 ft, 151 full hkups, 171 W&E, (30/50 amps), 19 pull-thrus, family camping, tenting, dump, laundry, ltd groc. ◆◆◆◆RECREATION: swim pool, lake/river swim, boating, electric motors only, canoeing, lake/river fishing, playground. Pets welcome ($). Partial handicap access. Open Mid Apr - Mid Oct. Rate in 2010 $25.50-49.50 per family. Member ARVC, WACO. Phone: (608)429-3244.

PEARSON—D-5

(NE) Northern Hideaway RV Park & Campground—(Langlade) *From jct of CR DD & Hwy 55: Go 5 mi N on Hwy 55, then 1 mi E on Pickeral Lake Rd, then 1/4 mi E on E Shore Rd.* ◆◆◆FACILITIES: 31 sites, 3 full hkups, 28 W&E, (20/30/50 amps), 50 amps ($), 29 pull-thrus, tenting, RV storage, dump, non-guest dump $, portable dump, laundry, picnic tables, fire rings, wood. ◆RECREATION: pavilion, bsktball, horseshoes, v-ball. Pets welcome. Open May 1 - Oct 31. Rate in 2010 $20 per family. CCUSA 50% Discount. CCUSA reservations Accepted, CCUSA max stay 4 days, Cash only for CCUSA disc., CCUSA disc. not avail F,Sa, CCUSA disc. not avail holidays.

Phone: (715)484-3373
Address: N10692 E Shore Rd, Pearson, WI 54462
Lat/Lon: 45.41366/-88.94272

PELICAN LAKE—D-5

(N) Pelican Lake Campground—(Oneida) *From jct US 45 & CR B: Go 2 mi N on US 45, then 1-1/2 mi W on CR Q. Enter on R.* ◆◆◆FACILITIES: 100 sites, typical site width 40 ft, 70 full hkups, 30 W&E, (20/30/50 amps), family camping, tenting, dump, laundry, ltd groc. ◆◆◆RECREATION: lake swim, boating, canoeing, ramp, dock, lake fishing, playground. Pets welcome. Open May 1 - Mid Oct. Rate in 2010 $28 per vehicle. Member ARVC, WACO. Phone: (715)487-4600.

PEPIN—F-1

(W) Lake Pepin Campground—(Pepin) *From Hwy 35 & Locust: Go 1 block N on Locust. Enter on L.* ◆◆◆FACILITIES: 130 sites, 130 full hkups, (20/30/50 amps), 25 pull-thrus, family camping, tenting, dump, laundry. Pets welcome. Open Apr 15 - Oct 15. Big rigs welcome. Rate in 2010 $24 per vehicle. Member ARVC, WACO. Phone: (715)442-2110.

PHILLIPS—D-3

(N) SOLBERG LAKE CAMPGROUND (Price County Park)—(Price) *From town: Go 1/4 mi N on Hwy 13, then 2-1/2 mi NE on Old Hwy 13, then 2-1/2 mi E on W Solberg Lake Rd.* FACILITIES: 60 sites, 54 E, (50 amps), 6 no hkups, tenting, dump. RECREATION: lake swim, boating, canoeing, ramp, dock, lake fishing, playground. Pets welcome. Partial handicap access. Open all yr. Phone: (715)339-6371.

PITTSVILLE—F-4

DEXTER PARK (Wood County Park)—(Wood) *From jct Hwy 80 & Hwy 54: Go 1/2 mi W on Hwy 54.* FACILITIES: 96 sites, 86 E, 10 no hkups, tenting, dump. RECREATION: lake swim, boating, canoeing, ramp, lake/river fishing, playground. Partial handicap access. Open May 1 - Nov 30. Phone: (715)421-8422.

PLAIN—H-4

WHITE MOUND CAMPGROUND (Sauk County Park)—(Sauk) *From jct Hwy 23 & CR GG: Go 2 mi W on CR GG, then 1/2 mi N on Lake Rd.* FACILITIES: 59 sites, 38 E, 21 no hkups, tenting. RECREATION: lake swim, boating, electric motors only, canoeing, ramp, dock, lake fishing. Partial handicap access. Open Apr - Nov. Phone: (608)546-5011.

PLEASANT PRAIRIE—J-6

JELLY BELLY CENTER—*From jct I-94 (exit 34) & Hwy 165: Go 3 mi E on Hwy 165, then 1/8 mi N on Jelly Belly Lane. Enter on L.* Free guided tour via rides on Jelly Belly Express indoor-train to learn the secret of making Jelly Belly jelly beans in Video presentations. Store 9am-5pm Daily. Tours 9 am-4 pm Daily. Candy store & Snack bar. Open all yr.

In 1882, the first hydroelectric plant in the United States was built at Fox River.

PLEASANT PRAIRIE—Continued
JELLY BELLY CENTER—Continued

Phone: (866)868-7522
Address: 10100 Jelly Belly Lane, Pleasant Prairie, WI 53158
Lat/Lon: 42.52727/-87.89260
Web: www.jellybelly.com

SEE AD TRAVEL SECTION PAGE 800 AND AD CA TRAVEL SECTION PAGE 87

PLUM CITY—F-1

NUGGET LAKE COUNTY PARK (Pierce County Park)—(Pierce) *From center of town: Go 3-1/2 mi W on US 10, then 3 mi N on CR CC, then 2 mi E on CR HH.* FACILITIES: 55 sites, 42 E, 13 no hkups, tenting, dump. RECREATION: lake swim, boating, electric motors only, canoeing, ramp, dock, lake fishing, playground. Pets welcome. Open all yr. Phone: (715)639-5611.

PLYMOUTH—G-6

(N) PLYMOUTH ROCK CAMPING RESORT—(Sheboygan) *From jct Hwy 23 & Hwy 67: Go 3 mi N on Hwy 67, then 1 block E on Lando St. Enter on R.*

◆◆◆◆FACILITIES: 667 sites, typical site width 30 ft, 450 full hkups, 167 W&E, (20/30/50 amps), 50 no hkups, many extd stay sites, 44 pull-thrus, cable TV, WiFi Internet central location, family camping, tenting, cabins, RV storage, dump, non-guest dump $, portable dump, laundry, ltd groc, RV supplies, LP bottle exch, ice, picnic tables, wood, controlled access.

◆◆◆◆RECREATION: rec hall, rec room/area, coin games, 2 swim pools, lake swim, hot tub, boating, no motors, canoeing, kayaking, dock, 2 rowboat/4 canoe/16 pedal boat rentals, lake fishing, fishing supplies, mini-golf, ($), golf nearby, bsktball, 20 bike rentals, playground, shuffleboard court 2 shuffleboard courts, activities (wkends), horseshoes, sports field, v-ball.

Pets welcome, breed restrict. Partial handicap access. Open Mid Apr - Mid Oct. Big rigs welcome. Clubs welcome. Rate in 2010 $37-58 per family. MC/VISA/Debit. Member ARVC, WACO.

Phone: (920)892-4252
Address: N7271 Lando St, Plymouth, WI 53073
Lat/Lon: 43.80344/-87.98161
Email: plymouthrock@equitylifestyle.com
Web: www.plymouthrock-resort.com

SEE AD ALGOMA PAGE 807

PORTAGE—H-4

(E) PRIDE OF AMERICA CAMPING RESORT—(Columbia) *From jct I-90/94 (exit 106) & Hwy 33: Go 4 mi E on Hwy 33, then 2-3/4 mi SE on CR P, then 1/2 mi S on CR G, then 1/8 mi E on W Bush Rd. Enter on L.*

THE ONE FOR FUN
On beautiful Lake George, Sandy Beach, Water Trampoline, Sprayground, Skate Park & Pool. Themed weekends and weekly activities. Bar & Grill. Karaoke Friday nights. Golf cart rental. Seasonable sites available.

◆◆◆◆◆FACILITIES: 365 sites, typical site width 40 ft, 293 full hkups, 72 W&E, (20/30/50 amps), many extd stay sites, 16 pull-thrus, WiFi Instant Internet at site ($), family camping, tenting, cabins, shower$, dump, non-guest dump $, portable dump, laundry, ltd groc, RV supplies, LP gas by weight/by meter, ice, picnic tables, patios, fire rings, grills, wood.

◆◆◆◆◆RECREATION: rec hall, rec room/area, equipped pavilion, coin games, 2 swim pools, wading pool, spray ground, lake swim, boating, electric motors only, canoeing, kayaking, ramp, dock, 5 rowboat/canoe/5 kayak/9 pedal boat rentals, lake/pond fishing, fishing supplies, golf nearby, bsktball, 40 bike rentals, playground, activities, horseshoes, sports field, v-ball. Rec open to public.

Pets welcome. Partial handicap access. Open Apr - Oct. Big rigs welcome. Escort to site. Clubs welcome. Rate in 2010 $35-57.50 for 4 persons. MC/VISA/DISC/Debit. ATM. Member ARVC, WACO. CCUSA 50% Discount. CCUSA reservations Recommended, CCUSA max stay 5 days, CCUSA disc. not avail F,Sa, CCUSA disc. not avail holidays. Boats with electric motors only.

Phone: (800)236-6395
Address: W 7520 W Bush Rd, Pardeeville, WI 53954
Lat/Lon: 43.52180/-89.37538
Email: info@camppoa.com
Web: www.camppoa.com

SEE AD THIS PAGE

PORTAGE—Continued

(W) Sky High Camping Resort—(Columbia) *From jct I-90/94 (exit 106) & Hwy 33: Go 1/2 mi W on Hwy 33, then 1/4 mi S on CR W, then 1-3/4 mi E on Rowley Rd. Enter on R.* ◆◆◆◆FACILITIES: 224 sites, typical site width 45 ft, 103 full hkups, 121 W&E, (20/30/50 amps), 20 pull-thrus, WiFi Internet central location, family camping, tenting, RV storage, dump, non-guest dump $, portable dump, laundry, ltd groc, RV supplies, LP gas by weight, ice, picnic tables, fire rings, wood. ◆◆◆◆RECREATION: rec hall, equipped pavilion, swim pool, wading pool, mini-golf, ($), bsktball, 8 bike rentals, playground, shuffleboard court 2 shuffleboard courts, activities horseshoes, hiking trails, v-ball. Pets welcome. Partial handicap access. Open all yr. Rate in 2010 $28-47 for 2 persons. MC/VISA/Debit. Member ARVC, WACO. CCUSA 50% Discount. CCUSA reservations Accepted, CCUSA max stay 7 days, CCUSA disc. not avail holidays. Not available Fri & Sat in Jul & Aug.

Phone: (608)742-2572
Address: N5740 Sky High Dr., Portage, WI 53901
Lat/Lon: 43.48449/-89.51271
Web: www.skyhighcampingresort.com

PORTERFIELD—I-1

(W) Diamond Lake Family Campground & Trout Farm—(Marinette) *From jct of Hwy 141 & CR W: Go 4-1/2 mi E on CR W, then 3-1/2 mi E on Loomis Rd. Enter on R.* ◆◆◆FACILITIES: 52 sites, typical site width 40 ft, 3 full hkups, 47 W&E, (30/50 amps), 2 no hkups, 3 pull-thrus, heater not allowed, family camping, tenting, shower$, dump, non-guest dump $, portable dump, ltd groc, RV supplies, ice, picnic tables, fire rings, wood. ◆◆◆RECREATION: lake swim, lake fishing, fishing supplies, playground, activities, horseshoes. Pets welcome. Open May 1 - Oct 31. Big rigs welcome. Rate in 2010 $26-30 per family. MC/VISA/Debit. Member ARVC, WACO. CCUSA 50% Discount. CCUSA reservations Accepted, CCUSA max stay 4 days, CCUSA disc. not avail S, CCUSA disc. not avail F,Sa, CCUSA disc. not avail holidays.

Phone: (715)789-2113
Address: 5449 Loomis Rd, Porterfield, WI 54159
Lat/Lon: 45.17219/-87.87052
Email: diamondlakewi@gmail.com
Web: www.campdiamondlakewi.com

POTOSI—I-3

(S) GRANT RIVER (COE - Lock & Dam 11)—(Grant) *From Hwy 133 S of town: Go 2 mi E on local road.* FACILITIES: 73 sites, 63 E, (20/30 amps), 10 no hkups, tenting, dump. RECREATION: boating, canoeing, ramp, dock, river fishing, playground. Partial handicap access. Open Apr 9 - Oct 24. Phone: (563)582-0881.

PRAIRIE DU CHIEN—I-2

(N) Frenchman's Landing Campground—(Crawford) *From jct US 18 & Hwy 35/60/27: Go 7 mi N on Hwy 35 (Sharp right turn southbound). Enter on L.* ◆◆◆FACILITIES: 52 sites, 1 full hkups, 51 W&E, (20/30/50 amps), 5 pull-thrus, WiFi Instant Internet at site, tenting, dump, portable dump, ice, picnic tables, fire rings, wood. ◆◆◆RECREATION: pavilion, river swim, boating, canoeing, kayaking, ramp, dock, river fishing, play equipment. Pets welcome. Partial handicap access. Open May 1 - Oct 1. Big rigs welcome. Rate in 2010 $26 per family. CCUSA 50% Discount. CCUSA reservations Recommended, CCUSA max stay 5 days, Cash only for CCUSA disc., CCUSA disc. not avail F,Sa, CCUSA disc. not avail holidays.

Phone: (608)874-4563
Address: 28741 Frenchman's Landing Dr., Eastman, WI 54626
Lat/Lon: 43.15175/-91.14046
Web: www.frenchmanslanding.tripod.com

(N) Sports Unlimited Campground & Hunters Slough—(Crawford) *From jct US 18 & Hwys 35/60/27: Go 1 3/4 mi N on Hwy 35, then 1/2 mi W on Cliffwood Dr, then 1 mi N on County Rd K. Enter on R.* ◆◆◆FACILITIES: 462 sites, typical site width 30 ft, 462 full hkups, (20/30/50 amps), family camping, tenting, laundry, ltd groc. ◆◆◆◆RECREATION: swim pool, boating, canoeing, ramp, dock, river fishing, playground. Pets welcome. Partial handicap access. Open Apr 15 - Oct 15. Big rigs welcome. Rate in 2010 $28-38 per family. Member ARVC, WACO. Phone: (608)326-2141.

PRAIRIE FARM—E-2

PIONEER PARK (Village Park)—(Barron) *From town: Go 1/4 mi W on CR A to 8-1/2 St. Enter on L.* FACILITIES: 32 sites, 24 E, 8 no hkups, tenting. RECREATION: boating, canoeing, ramp, river/pond fishing, play equipment. Open May 1 - Oct 1. Phone: (715)369-5121.

Wisconsin snowmobile trails total 15,210 miles of signed and groomed snow highways.

RACINE—I-6

CLIFFSIDE PARK (Racine County Park)—(Racine) *From jct I-94 (exit 326) & 7 Mile Rd: Go 6-1/2 mi E on 7 Mile Rd, then 1/2 mi S on Michna Rd. Enter on L.* FACILITIES: 92 sites, 53 W&E, 39 E, (30/50 amps), tenting, dump. RECREATION: playground. Open Apr 15 - Oct 15. Phone: (262)886-8440.

(SW) SANDERS PARK (Racine County Park)—(Racine) *From jct I-94 (exit 337) & CR KR: Go 5-1/2 mi E on CR KR, then 1/2 mi N on Wood Rd. Enter on R.* FACILITIES: 27 sites, 35 E, 27 no hkups, tenting, dump. RECREATION: playground. Open Apr 15 - Oct 15. Phone: (262)886-8440.

REDGRANITE—G-5

(N) Flanagan's Pearl Lake Campsites—(Waushara) *From jct Hwy 21 & CR EE/E: Go 3 mi N on CR EE, then 500 feet W on S. Pearl Lake Rd. Enter on L.* ◆◆FACILITIES: 250 sites, typical site width 36 ft, 245 W&E, (20/30/50 amps), 5 no hkups, family camping, tenting, dump, laundry, ltd groc. ◆◆◆RECREATION: swim pool, playground. Pets welcome, breed restrict. Partial handicap access. Open Apr 15 - Oct 15. Rate in 2010 $29-32 per family. Member ARVC, WACO. Phone: (920)566-2758.

REEDSVILLE—G-6

(E) RAINBOWS END CAMPGROUND—(Manitowoc) *From jct I-43 (exit 154) & US 10: Go 10 mi W on US 10. Enter on L.*

◆◆◆FACILITIES: 89 sites, typical site width 35 ft, 89 W&E, (20/30/50 amps), many extd stay sites, 17 pull-thrus, WiFi Instant Internet at site, WiFi Internet central location, family camping, tenting, RV's/park model rentals, shower$, dump, non-guest dump $, portable dump, laundry, LP gas by meter, ice, picnic tables, fire rings, wood.

◆◆◆RECREATION: rec hall, rec room/area, coin games, pond fishing, mini-golf, ($), golf nearby, bsktball, playground, horseshoes, sports field, v-ball.

Pets welcome, breed restrict. Partial handicap access. Open May 1 - Mid Oct. Big rigs welcome. Escort to site. Clubs welcome. Rate in 2010 $25 per family. Member ARVC, WACO. CCUSA 50% Discount. CCUSA reservations Recommended, CCUSA max stay 2 days, Cash only for CCUSA disc., CCUSA disc. not avail F,Sa, CCUSA disc. not avail holidays.

Phone: (920)754-4142
Address: 18227 US Highway 10, Reedsville, WI 54230
Lat/Lon: 44.15315/-87.93748
Email: rainbowscamp@tm.net
Web: www.wisconsincampgrounds.com

SEE AD TRAVEL SECTION PAGE 799

RIO—H-5

(S) Little Bluff Campground—(Columbia) *From jct Hwy 16 & CR B (west edge of town): Go 4-3/4 mi W on CR B, then 1-1/4 mi S on Traut Rd. Enter on R.* ◆◆FACILITIES: 135 sites, typical site width 35 ft, 80 full hkups, 55 W&E, (20/30 amps), 6 pull-thrus, tenting, dump, ltd groc. ◆◆RECREATION: swim pool, play equipment. Pets welcome. Open Mid Apr - Mid Oct. Rate in 2010 $32 per family. Member ARVC, WACO. Phone: (920)992-5157.

(N) SILVER SPRINGS CAMPSITES, INC.—(Columbia) *From jct Hwy 16 & CR B: Go 4-1/4 mi N & E on CRB, then 1 mi N on Ludwig Rd. Enter on R.*

◆◆◆◆◆FACILITIES: 300 sites, typical site width 40 ft, 116 full hkups, 184 W&E, (20/30/50 amps), many extd stay sites, 50 pull-thrus, WiFi Instant Internet at site, family camping, tenting, cabins, shower$, dump, non-guest dump $, portable dump, laundry, ltd groc, RV supplies, LP gas by weight, ice, picnic tables, fire rings, wood.

◆◆◆◆RECREATION: rec hall, rec room/area, coin games, swim pool, lake swim, boating, no motors, canoeing, kayaking, dock, canoe/4 pedal boat rentals, lake fishing, fishing supplies, golf nearby, bsktball, playground, activities, (wkends), horseshoes, sports field, hiking trails, v-ball.

Pets welcome ($). Partial handicap access. Open Apr 15 - Sep 30. Big rigs welcome. Clubs welcome. Rate in 2010 $36-46 per family. MC/VISA/DISC/Debit. Member ARVC, WACO. CCUSA 50% Discount. CCUSA reservations Recommended, CCUSA max stay 1 day, CCUSA disc. not avail S, CCUSA disc. not avail F,Sa, CCUSA disc. not avail holidays.

RIO—Continued
SILVER SPRINGS CAMPSITES, INC.—Continued

Phone: (920)992-3537
Address: N 5048 Ludwig Rd., Rio, WI 53960
Lat/Lon: 43.47017/-89.17590
Email: sscamp@centurytel.net
Web: www.silverspringscamp.com

SEE AD THIS PAGE

(N) WILLOW MILL CAMPSITE LLC—(Columbia) *From jct of Hwy 16 & CR B: Go 1-1/2 mi N & E on CR B, then 3 mi N on CR SS. Enter on R.*

◆◆◆FACILITIES: 220 sites, typical site width 38 ft, 38 ft max RV length, 12 full hkups, 208 W&E, (20/30 amps), mostly extd stay sites, WiFi Internet central location, family camping, tenting, cabins, shower$, dump, portable dump, laundry, ltd groc, RV supplies, LP bottle exch, ice, picnic tables, fire rings, wood.

◆◆◆RECREATION: rec hall, rec room/area, coin games, swim pool, boating, no motors, canoeing, 2 canoe/2 kayak/2 pedal boat rentals, lake fishing, fishing supplies, mini-golf, ($), golf nearby, bsktball, playground, activities, (wkends), horseshoes, sports field, hiking trails, v-ball.

Pets welcome. Partial handicap access. Open May 1 - Oct 1. Clubs welcome. Rate in 2010 $32-34 for 2 persons. MC/VISA/DISC/Debit. ATM. Member ARVC, WACO. CCUSA 50% Discount. CCUSA reservations Required, CCUSA max stay 2 days, CCUSA disc. not avail Th, CCUSA disc. not avail F,Sa, CCUSA disc. not avail holidays.

Phone: (920)992-5355
Address: N 5830 CH Hwy SS, Rio, WI 53960
Lat/Lon: 43.49038/-89.22675
Web: www.willowmillcampsite.com

SEE AD TRAVEL SECTION PAGE 799

ROCK ISLAND—I-2

(C) ROCK ISLAND SP—(Door) *Take passenger ferry from Washington Island. Accessible by boat only.* FACILITIES: 40 sites, 40 no hkups, tenting. RECREATION: lake swim, boating, canoeing, dock, lake fishing. Open Memorial Day - Mid Oct. Phone: (920)847-2235.

ROSHOLT—F-4

COLLINS PARK (Portage County Park)—(Portage) *From jct Hwy 66 & CR I: Go 1-1/2 mi S on CR I.* FACILITIES: 27 sites, 35 ft max RV length, 27 E, (20 amps), tenting, dump. RECREATION: lake swim, boating, canoeing, ramp, dock, lake fishing, play equipment. Partial handicap access. Open May 15 - Sep 30. Phone: (715)346-1433.

ST. CROIX FALLS—D-1

INTERSTATE SP—(Polk) *From jct US 8 & MN Hwy 95: Go 1/2 mi S on MN Hwy 95. Enter on L.* FACILITIES: 85 sites, 5 E, (50 amps), 80 no hkups, tenting, dump. RECREATION: lake swim, boating, canoeing, ramp, lake/river fishing. Partial handicap access. Open Apr 1 - Nov 15. Facilities fully operational May 15 - Oct 15. Phone: (715)483-3747.

ST. GERMAIN—C-4

(W) Lynn Ann's Campground—(Vilas) *From jct Hwy 70 & Hwy 155: Go 2 mi W on Hwy 70, then 1/2 mi N on Normandy Ct, then 1/4 mi E on South Shore Dr. Note: If you have over 34, please call ahead to ensure adequate space. Enter on L.* ◆◆FACILITIES: 93 sites, typical site width 36 ft, 34 ft max RV length, 45 full hkups, 43 W&E, 5 E, (20/30 amps), family camping, tenting, dump, laundry, ltd groc. ◆◆◆RECREATION: lake swim, boating, canoeing, ramp, dock, lake fishing, playground. Pets welcome. Open May 7 - Oct 10. Rate in 2010 $29-35 for 5 persons. Member ARVC, WACO. Phone: (715)542-3456.

SARONA—D-2

(SW) Whitetail Ridge Campground/RV Park—(Washburn) *From jct of US Hwy 53 & CR-D: Go 3-1/2 mi W on CR-D, then 2-1/2 mi S on Shallow Lake Rd.* ◆◆◆FACILITIES: 110 sites, typical site width 50 ft, 106 W&E, (20/30/50 amps), 4 no hkups, 3 pull-thrus, family camping, tenting, dump. ◆◆◆RECREATION: playground. Pets welcome. Open all yr. Facilities fully operational May 1 - Mid Oct. Big rigs welcome. Rate in 2010 $30 per vehicle. Member ARVC, WACO. Phone: (715)469-3309.

SAYNER—C-4

NORTHERN HIGHLAND/AMERICAN LEGION SF (Firefly Lake)—(Vilas) *From town: Go 3 mi W on CR N.* FACILITIES: 70 sites, 70 no hkups, tenting, dump. RECREATION: lake swim, boating, lake fishing. Open May - Oct. Phone: (715)356-5211.

(NW) NORTHERN HIGHLAND/AMERICAN LEGION SF (Razorback Lake)—(Vilas) *2 mi W on CR-N, then 5 mi N on Razorback Road.* FACILITIES: 55 sites, 55 no hkups, tenting, dump. RECREATION: lake swim, boating, ramp, dock, lake fishing. Open all yr. Phone: (715)356-5211.

(SE) NORTHERN HIGHLAND/AMERICAN LEGION SF (Starrett Lake)—(Vilas) *2 mi W on CR-"N," then 3 mi NW on Razorback and Musky Road.* FACILITIES: 46 sites, 46 no hkups, tenting, dump. RECREATION: lake swim, boating, ramp, dock, lake fishing. Open Memorial Day - Labor Day. Phone: (715)356-5211.

SHAWANO—E-5

(W) Pine Grove Campground—(Shawano) *From jct Hwy 22S & Hwy 29: Go 13-1/2 mi W on Hwy 29, then 1 mi N on Campground Rd. Enter on L.* ◆◆◆◆FACILITIES: 246 sites, typical site width 50 ft, 25 full hkups, 220 W&E, (20/30/50 amps), 50 amps ($), 1 no hkups, 18 pull-thrus, WiFi Internet central location, family camping, tenting, shower$, dump, non-guest dump $, portable dump, laundry, ltd groc, RV supplies, LP gas by weight/by meter, ice, picnic tables, fire rings, wood. ◆◆◆◆RECREATION: equipped pavilion, lake swim, boating, no motors, canoeing, kayaking, dock, lake fishing, fishing supplies, mini-golf, ($), bsktball, 2 bike rentals, playground, shuffleboard court 2 shuffleboard courts, activities horseshoes, v-ball. Pets welcome. Partial handicap access. Open Apr 15 - Nov 1. Facilities fully operational Mid May - Mid Oct. Big rigs welcome. Rate in 2010 $29-36.50 per family. MC/VISA/Debit. Member ARVC, WACO. CCUSA 50% Discount. CCUSA reservations Accepted, CCUSA max stay 3 days, CCUSA disc. not avail F,Sa, CCUSA disc. not avail holidays. Space limited in Jul & Aug.

Phone: (715)787-4555
Address: N5999 Campground Rd, Shawano, WI 54166
Lat/Lon: 44.80763/-88.86874
Email: pinegrovewis@frontiernet.net
Web: www.pinegrovecampgroundwis.com

SHEBOYGAN—G-6

(S) KOHLER-ANDRAE SP—(Sheboygan) *From jct I-43 (exit 120) & CR V/OK: Go 2 mi E on CR V, then E on Beach Park Lane.* FACILITIES: 105 sites, 49 E, (30 amps), 56 no hkups, 10 pull-thrus, tenting, dump, laundry. RECREATION: lake swim, boating, lake fishing, playground. Partial handicap access. Open all yr. Phone: (920)451-4080.

SHELL LAKE—D-2

(NE) Red Barn Campground—(Washburn) *From center of town: Go 1/2 mi N on US 63, then 2 mi E on CR B. Enter on L.* ◆◆◆FACILITIES: 65 sites, typical site width 30 ft, 33 full hkups, 27 W&E, (20/30/50 amps), 5 no hkups, 6 pull-thrus, family camping, tenting, dump. ◆◆◆RECREATION: playground. Pets welcome, breed restrict. Open May 1 - Oct 1. Big rigs welcome. Rate in 2010 $32-35 per family. Member ARVC, WACO. Phone: (877)468-2575.

(W) SHELL LAKE MEMORIAL PARK (Municipal Park)—(Washburn) *In town off US-63 at foot of Main Street.* FACILITIES: 41 sites, 41 W&E, (30 amps), 11 pull-thrus, tenting, dump. RECREATION: lake swim, boating, ramp, dock, lake fishing, playground. Pets welcome. Partial handicap access. Open May 1 - Oct 15. Phone: (715)468-7846.

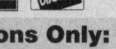

SHERWOOD—G-6

(SW) HIGH CLIFF SP—(Calumet) *From jct Hwy 114/55 & Clifton Rd: Go 3/4 mi S on Hwy 114/55, then 1-1/2 mi W on High Cliff Rd, then 3/4 mi W on State Park Rd.* FACILITIES: 112 sites, 32 E, (20/30 amps), 80 no hkups, tenting, dump, ltd groc. RECREATION: lake swim, boating, canoeing, ramp, dock, lake fishing, playground. Partial handicap access. Open all yr. Facilities fully operational May 1 - Mid Oct. Phone: (920)989-1106.

SHULLSBURG—I-3

✱ **(W) TRUCK COUNTRY**—*From jct of CR O & Hwy 11: Go 1/2 mi W on Hwy 11.* SERVICES: full-time mech, engine/chassis repair, body work/collision repair, 24-hr emerg rd svc, mobile RV svc, RV towing. 8 body shop bays. Open all yr. MC/VISA/DISC/AMEX/Debit.

Phone: (608)965-4462
Address: 119 Hwy 11, Shullsburg, WI 53586
Lat/Lon: 42.57708/-90.23489
Web: www.truckcountry.com

SEE AD TRAVEL SECTION PAGE 798 AND AD IA TRAVEL SECTION PAGE 247

SILVER CLIFF—D-6

(S) Kosir's Rapid Rafts & Campground—(Marinette) *From jct Hwy 141 & CR A: Go 15 mi W & N on CR A, then 10 mi W on CR C. Enter on L.* ◇◇◇FACILITIES: 38 sites, typical site width 36 ft, 32 ft max RV length, 11 W&E, (20/30 amps), 27 no hkups, family camping, tenting, dump. ◇◇◇RECREATION: river swim, boating, canoeing, ramp, river fishing. Pets welcome. Open Apr 1 - Sep 30. Rate in 2010 $16-21 for 2 persons. Phone: (715)757-3431.

SISTER BAY—I-2

(SW) Aqualand Camp Resort—(Door) *From jct Hwy 42 & Hwy 57: Go 2-1/4 mi S on Hwy 57, then 1/4 mi E on CR-Q. Enter on R.* ◇◇◇FACILITIES: 150 sites, typical site width 40 ft, 150 W&E, (20/30 amps), 3 pull-thrus, family camping, tenting, dump. ◇◇◇RECREATION: swim pool, pond fishing, play equipment. Pets welcome. Partial handicap access. Open May 15 - Oct 20. Rate in 2010 $29.95 per family. Member ARVC, WACO. Phone: (920)854-4573.

SOLON SPRINGS—C-2

LUCIUS WOODS (Douglas County Park)—(Douglas) *From jct CR A & US 53: Go 1/4 mi S, then 1/10 mi E on Marion Ave.* FACILITIES: 24 sites, 13 E, 11 no hkups, tenting, dump. RECREATION: lake swim, boating, canoeing, lake fishing, playground. Open May 20 - Sep 30. Phone: (715)378-4528.

SOMERSET—E-1

(N) Apple River Family Campground—(St Croix) *From jct US 64 & US 35: Go 3/4 mi NW on US 64, then 1/2 mi N on Church Hill Rd.* ◇◇◇FACILITIES: 105 sites, typical site width 35 ft, 105 W&E, (20/30 amps), 20 pull-thrus, family camping, tenting, dump, ltd groc. ◇◇◇RECREATION: 2 swim pools, river swim, river fishing. Pets welcome. Open all yr. Facilities fully operational May 15 - Oct 1. Rate in 2010 $25-50 per vehicle. Phone: (715)247-3600.

SOMERSET—Continued

(E) River's Edge Campground—(St. Croix) *From jct Hwy 35 & Hwy 64: Go 2 mi E on Hwy 64. Enter on L.* ◇◇◇FACILITIES: 422 sites, typical site width 30 ft, 75 W&E, (30 amps), 347 no hkups, 20 pull-thrus, family camping, tenting, dump, laundry, ltd groc. ◇◇◇◇RECREATION: swim pool, river fishing, playground. Pets welcome, breed restrict, size restrict. Partial handicap access. Open Memorial Day - Labor Day. Rate in 2010 $30-35 for 4 persons. Phone: (715)247-3305.

SPARTA—G-3

(S) LEON VALLEY CAMPGROUND—(Monroe) *From jct I-90 (exit 25) & Hwy 27: Go 3 mi S on Hwy 27, then 1-1/4 mi E on Jancing Ave. Enter on L.*

◇◇◇FACILITIES: 125 sites, typical site width 40 ft, 125 W&E, (20/30/50 amps), some extd stay sites, 10 pull-thrus, phone Internet central location, family camping, tenting, cabins, RV storage, dump, non-guest dump $, portable dump, ltd groc, RV supplies, ice, picnic tables, fire rings, wood.

◇◇◇RECREATION: rec room/area, equipped pavilion, coin games, swim pool, golf nearby, bsktball, playground, activities, (wkends), horseshoes, sports field, hiking trails, v-ball. Rec open to public.

Pets welcome. Partial handicap access. Open Apr 1 - Oct 31. Big rigs welcome. Clubs welcome. Rate in 2010 $25-35 per family. MC/VISA/DISC/Debit. Member ARVC, WACO. CCUSA 50% Discount. CCUSA reservations Recommended, CCUSA max stay 3 days, CCUSA disc. not avail F,Sa, CCUSA disc. not avail holidays.

Phone: (608)269-6400
Address: 9050 Jancing Ave, Sparta, WI 54656
Lat/Lon: 43.88178/-90.80951
Email: leonvalley@centurytel.net
Web: www.campleonvalley.net

SEE AD TRAVEL SECTION PAGE 799

MILITARY PARK (Pine View Recreation Area-Fort McCoy)—(Monroe) *From jct I-90W (exit 25) & Hwy 27: Go 1-1/2 mi N on Hwy 27, then 10 mi E on Hwy 21. On base.* FACILITIES: 132 sites, typical site width 10 ft, 35 full hkups, 5 W&E, 71 E, 21 no hkups, 4 pull-thrus, tenting, dump, laundry, ltd groc. RECREATION: lake swim, boating, electric motors only, canoeing, ramp, dock, lake/river/stream fishing, playground. Open all yr. Phone: (608)388-3517.

SPOONER—D-2

(S) Country House Motel & RV Park—(Washburn) *From jct US 53 & Hwy 70: Go 1 mi W on Hwy 70, then 1/2 mi S on US 63. Enter on R.* ◇◇◇◇FACILITIES: 21 sites, typical site width 35 ft, accepts self-contained units only, 21 W&E, (20/30/50 amps), 7 pull-thrus, family camping, dump. ◇◇RECREATION: swim pool. Pets welcome. No tents. Facilities fully operational Mid Apr - Mid Oct. Big rigs welcome. Rate in 2010 $30 for 2 persons. Member ARVC, WACO. Phone: (715)635-8721.

SPOONER—Continued
Country House Motel & RV Park—Continued

(W) Scenic View Campground—(Burnett) *From jct US 63 & Hwy 70: Go 9-1/4 mi W on Hwy 70, then 1/2 mi S on Scenic View Ln. Enter at end.* ◇◇FACILITIES: 45 sites, 34 ft max RV length, 40 W&E, (30 amps), 5 no hkups, WiFi Internet central location, family camping, tenting, dump, ice, picnic tables, fire rings, wood. ◇◇◇RECREATION: lake swim, boating, canoeing, ramp, dock, lake fishing, bsktball, play equipment, horseshoes, hiking trails, v-ball. Pets welcome. Partial handicap access. Open May 1 - Sep 30. Member ARVC, WACO. CCUSA 50% Discount.

Phone: (715)468-2510
Address: 24560 Scenic View Ln, Spooner, WI 54801
Lat/Lon: 45.80844/-92.07517
Email: scenicview@centurytel.net
Web: www.scenicview.com

SPRING GREEN—H-4

(N) River Valley RV Park—(Sauk) *From west jct Hwy 23 & Hwy 14: Go 3 blocks E on Hwy 14. Entrance on left. From east jct Hwy 23 & Hwy 14: Go 1 block W on Hwy 14. Enter on R.* ◇◇◇FACILITIES: 23 sites, typical site width 18 ft, 15 full hkups, 8 W&E, (20/30 amps), family camping, tenting, laundry. Pets welcome. Open all yr. Facilities fully operational May 1 - Nov 1. Rate in 2010 $20-25 for 2 persons. Phone: (608)588-4797.

TOWER HILL SP—(Iowa) *3 mi SE via US-14 and Hwy-23.* FACILITIES: 15 sites, 15 no hkups, tenting. RECREATION: boating, canoeing, river fishing. Partial handicap access. Open May - Oct 31. Phone: (608)588-2116.

(W) WISCONSIN RIVERSIDE RESORT—(Sauk) *From jct US 14/Hwy 23 & CR G: Go 1 mi S on CR G, then 1/4 mi W on Madison St, then 3/4 mi S on Shifflet Rd. Enter at end.*

◇◇◇◇FACILITIES: 174 sites, typical site width 30 ft, 137 full hkups, (20/30/50 amps), 37 no hkups, some extd stay sites, 9 pull-thrus, WiFi Instant Internet at site, family camping, tenting, cabins, shower$, dump, non-guest dump $, laundry, ltd groc, LP bottle exch, ice, picnic tables, patios, fire rings, wood.

◇◇◇◇◇RECREATION: rec hall, rec room/area, pavilion, coin games, swim pool, wading pool, river swim, boating, canoeing, kayaking, 120 canoe/10 kayak rentals, float trips, river fishing, fishing supplies, bsktball, playground, shuffleboard court shuffleboard court, activities, sports field, hiking trails, v-ball. Rec open to public.

Pets welcome. Partial handicap access. Open Apr 1 - Oct 31. Facilities fully operational Apr 15 - Oct 31. Big rigs welcome. Clubs welcome. Rate in 2010 $32-36 per vehicle. MC/VISA/Debit. Member ARVC, WACO.

Phone: (608)588-2826
Address: S13220 Shifflet Rd, Spring Green, WI 53588
Lat/Lon: 43.16384/-90.07905
Email: info@wiriverside.com
Web: www.wiriverside.com

SEE AD THIS PAGE

STEVENS POINT—F-4

See listings at Amherst Junction, Bancroft, Knowlton, Wausau, & Wisconsin Rapids

(NW) DUBAY PARK (Portage County)—(Portage) *From jct US 10 & Hwy 34: Go N on Hwy 34.* FACILITIES: 31 sites, 31 E, (20 amps), dump. RECREATION: lake swim, boating, canoeing, ramp, dock, lake fishing, playground. Partial handicap access. Open May 1 - Oct 31. Phone: (715)346-1433.

(NE) JORDAN PARK (Portage County)—(Portage) *From town: Go 4 mi NE on Hwy-66, then 1/4 mi N on CR-Y.* FACILITIES: 22 sites, 22 E, (20 amps), tenting, dump. RECREATION: lake/river swim, boating, canoeing, ramp, lake/river/pond fishing, playground. Partial handicap access. Open May 1 - Oct 31. Phone: (715)346-1433.

(N) Rivers Edge Campground & Marina (Not Visited)—(Portage) *From jct Hwy 51/I-39 & Casimir (Exit 163): Go E 1/2 mi, then 2.2 mi N on H 2nd St, then 2.4 mi N on Sunset Dr, then 1/4 mi W on Maple Dr (across Hwy 51/I-39), then 1/2 mi N on Campsite Dr. Enter on Left. Enter at end.* ◇◇◇◇FACILITIES: 190 sites, typical site width 36 ft, 184 W&E, (20/30/50 amps), 6 no hkups, 33 pull-thrus, family camping, tenting, dump, laundry, ltd groc. ◇◇◇◇RECREATION: swim pool, boating, canoeing, ramp, dock, river fishing, playground. Pets welcome. Open May 1 - Oct 15. Big rigs welcome. Rate in 2010 $35-42 per family. Member ARVC, WACO. Phone: (715)344-8058.

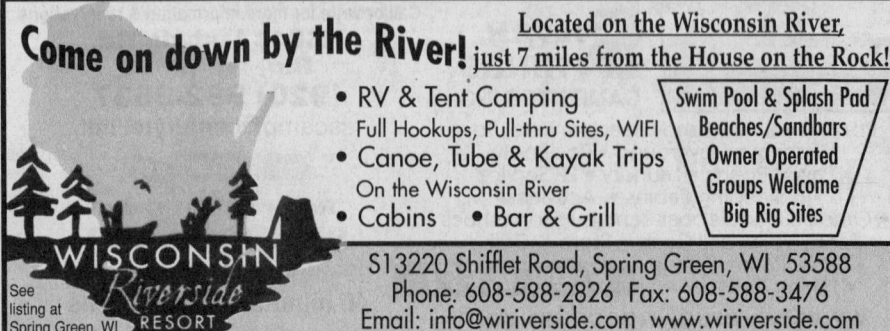

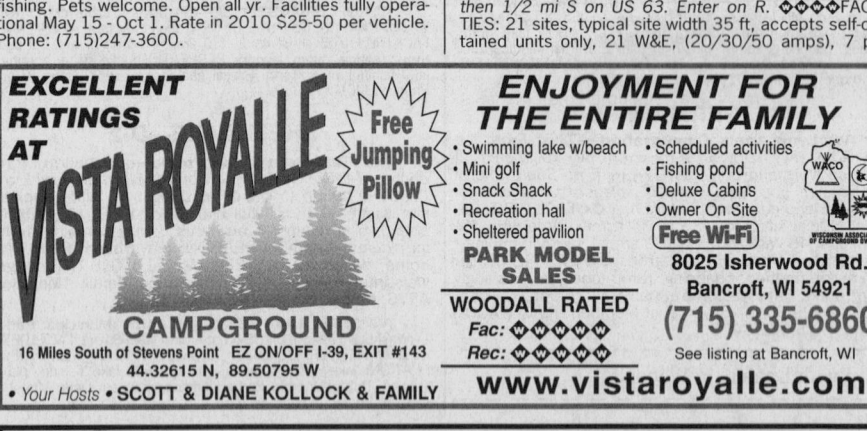

STOCKBRIDGE—G-6

(NW) CALUMET COUNTY PARK—(Calumet) *From town: Go 2 mi N on Hwy 55, then 2 mi W on CR EE.* FACILITIES: 71 sites, typical site width 40 ft, 59 E, (20/30 amps), 12 no hkups, tenting, dump, laundry, ltd groc. RECREATION: boating, ramp, dock, lake fishing, playground. Pets welcome. Partial handicap access. Open Apr 1 - Nov 1. Phone: (920)439-1008.

(S) Lakeview Campground—(Calumet) *From jct Hwy 55 & CR-F: Go 1-1/2 mi E on CR-F, then 3/4 mi N on Ledge Rd. Enter on L.* ◊◊◊FACILITIES: 110 sites, typical site width 40 ft, 96 W&E, 14 E, (20/30/50 amps), 0 pull-thrus, family camping, tenting, dump, laundry, ltd groc. ◊◊◊◊RECREATION: swim pool, play equipment. Pets welcome. Partial handicap access. Open Apr 1 - Nov 1. Big rigs welcome. Rate in 2010 $35 per family. Member ARVC, WACO. Phone: (920)439-1495.

STOUGHTON—I-5

(NW) LAKE KEGONSA SP—(Dane) *From jct US 51 & CR N: Go 4 mi N on CR N, then 1-1/2 mi W on Circle Dr, then 1 blk on Door Creek Rd.* FACILITIES: 80 sites, 25 E, (50 amps), 55 no hkups, tenting, dump. RECREATION: lake swim, boating, canoeing, ramp, dock, lake fishing, playground. Partial handicap access. Open May 1 - Oct 31. Phone: (608)873-9695.

(NE) Viking Village Campground & Resort—(Dane) *From jct I-90 (exit 147) & CR-N: Go 4-1/2 mi S on CR-N. Enter on L.* ◊◊◊◊FACILITIES: 71 sites, typical site width 40 ft, 71 full hkups, (20/30/50 amps), dump, laundry. ◊◊◊RECREATION: swim pool, playground. Pets welcome. Partial handicap access. No tents. Age restrict may apply. Open May 1 - Oct 1. Big rigs welcome. Rate in 2010 $41-45 for 5 persons. Member ARVC, WACO. Phone: (608)873-6601.

STURGEON BAY—J-1

(N) HARBOUR VILLAGE RESORT—(Door) *From jct Hwy 57 & 42: Go 5-3/4 mi N on Hwy 42. Enter on R.*

WELCOME

◊◊◊FACILITIES: 439 sites, 439 W&E, (30/50 amps), many extd stay sites, 10 pull-thrus, WiFi Internet central location, family camping, tenting, RV's/park model rentals, dump, portable dump, laundry, ltd groc, RV supplies, LP gas by weight/by meter, ice, picnic tables, fire rings, wood, controlled access.

◊◊◊◊RECREATION: rec room/area, equipped pavilion, coin games, 2 swim pools, wading pool, spray ground, hot tub, pond fishing, mini-golf, ($), golf nearby, bsktball, bike rental, playground, shuffleboard court 3 shuffleboard courts, activities (wkends), tennis, horseshoes, sports field, hiking trails, v-ball.

Pets welcome. Open Mid May - Mid Oct. Big rigs welcome. Rate in 2010 $35-47 per family. MC/VISA/Debit. ATM. Member ARVC, WACO.

Phone: (920)743-0274
Address: 5840 Hwy 42 N, Sturgeon Bay, WI 54235
Lat/Lon: 44.95383/-87.33681
Email: info@harbourvillageresort.net
Web: www.harbourvillageresort.net

SEE AD DOOR COUNTY PAGE 813

(NW) POTAWATOMI SP—(Door) *From jct Hwy 57 & CR PD: Go N 2-1/2 mi on CR PD.* FACILITIES: 123 sites, 40 E, (20 amps), 73 no hkups, tenting, dump, ltd groc. RECREATION: boating, canoeing, ramp, dock, lake fishing. Partial handicap access. Open all yr. Phone: (920)746-2890.

(NW) TRANQUIL TIMBERS CAMPING RETREAT—(Door) *From jct Hwy 42/57 & CR PD: Go 1-1/4 mi N on CR PD, then 1 mi E on CR C, then 3/4 mi N on Grondin Rd. Enter on R.*

WELCOME

◊◊◊FACILITIES: 270 sites, typical site width 32 ft, 40 full hkups, 208 W&E, (20/30/50 amps), 22 no hkups, many extd stay sites, 5 pull-thrus, WiFi Instant Internet at site, WiFi Internet central location, family camping, tenting, cabins, dump, portable dump, laundry, ltd groc, RV supplies, ice, picnic tables, fire rings, wood, controlled access.

◊◊◊◊RECREATION: rec room/area, pavilion, equipped pavilion, swim pool, wading pool, mini-golf, ($), golf nearby, bsktball, 6 bike rentals, playground, activities, horseshoes, sports field, hiking trails, v-ball.

Pets welcome, quantity restrict. Partial handicap access. Open Apr 15 - Oct 31. Big rigs welcome. Clubs welcome. Rate in 2010 $34-52 per family. MC/VISA/DISC/Debit. Member ARVC, WACO.

Phone: (800)986-2267
Address: 3668 Grondin Rd, Sturgeon Bay, WI 54235
Lat/Lon: 44.84895/-87.40780
Email: tranquil-timbers@equitylifestyle.com
Web: www.tranquiltimbers.com

Reserve Online at Woodalls.com

SEE AD ALGOMA PAGE 807

STURGEON BAY—Continued

(SW) YOGI BEAR JELLYSTONE PARK—(Door) *From jct Hwy 57/42 & County Rd MM: Go 3-1/4 mi N on MM, then 1-1/2 mi W on County Rd C, then 1-3/4 mi N on May Rd. Enter on L.*

WELCOME

◊◊◊FACILITIES: 274 sites, typical site width 40 ft, 20 full hkups, 254 W&E, (20/30/50 amps), some extd stay sites, 5 pull-thrus, family camping, tenting, cabins, dump, portable dump, laundry, ltd groc, RV supplies, LP bottle exch, ice, picnic tables, fire rings, wood.

◊◊◊RECREATION: rec room/area, pavilion, coin games, 3 swim pools, wading pool, mini-golf, ($), golf nearby, bsktball, 3 bike rentals, playground, shuffleboard court 4 shuffleboard courts, activities (wkends), horseshoes, sports field, hiking trails, v-ball. Rec open to public.

Pets welcome. Open Mid May - Mid Sep. Seasonal campers extended stay. Clubs welcome. Rate in 2010 $31.50-49.50 for 2 persons. MC/VISA/DISC/Debit. Member ARVC, WACO.

Phone: (920)743-9001
Address: 3677 May Rd, Sturgeon Bay, WI 54235
Lat/Lon: 44.84804/-87.50019
Email: camp@doorcountyjellystone.com
Web: www.doorcountyjellystone.com

SEE AD DOOR COUNTY PAGE 813

SUMMIT LAKE—D-5

VETERANS MEMORIAL PARK (Langlade County Park) —(Langlade) *4-1/2 mi SE via US-45 and 47, then 2 mi E on CR-"J".* FACILITIES: 41 sites, 26 ft max RV length, 31 E, 10 no hkups, tenting, dump. RECREATION: lake swim, boating, ramp, dock, lake fishing, playground. Open May 1 - Dec 1. Phone: (715)623-6214.

SUPERIOR—B-1

(E) AMNICON FALLS SP—(Douglas) *From town: Go 10 mi E on US 2, then 1/2 mi N on CR U.* FACILITIES: 36 sites, 36 no hkups, tenting. RECREATION: river fishing, playground. Partial handicap access. Open May 1 - Oct 1. Phone: (715)398-3000.

(C) Nemadji Mobile Home & RV Park—(Douglas) *From jct Hwy-13 & US-2/53: Go 4 mi NW on US-2/53, then 1/4 mi SW on 31st Ave E. Enter on L.* ◊◊◊FACILITIES: 47 sites, typical site width 26 ft, 11 full hkups, 13 W&E, 3 E, (20/30/50 amps), 20 no hkups, 3 pull-thrus, family camping, tenting, dump, laundry. RECREATION: river fishing, play equipment. Pets welcome. Open May 15 - Oct 15. Big rigs welcome. Rate in 2010 $20-24 for 2 persons. Phone: (715)398-6366.

(E) NORTHLAND CAMPING & RV PARK—(Douglas) *From jct US 2/53 & Hwy 13: Go 1000 feet E on South 13. Enter on L.*

WELCOME

◊◊◊FACILITIES: 85 sites, typical site width 36 ft, 65 full hkups, (20/30/50 amps), 20 no hkups, 40 pull-thrus, WiFi Instant Internet at site, WiFi Internet central location, family camping, tenting, laundry, ice, picnic tables, fire rings, wood.

◊◊◊RECREATION: rec room/area, swim pool, hot tub, golf nearby, play equipment, sports field, hiking trails, v-ball.

Pets welcome. Partial handicap access. Open May 15 - Oct 15. Big rigs welcome. Clubs welcome. Rate in 2010 $30 for 4 persons.

Phone: (715)398-3327
Address: 6377 E State Rd 13, South Range, WI 54874
Lat/Lon: 46.64783/-91.97479
Web: www.northlandcamprv.com

SEE AD DULUTH, MN PAGE 419

(S) PATTISON SP—(Douglas) *From jct US 2/53 & Hwy 35: Go 13 mi S on Hwy 35. Enter on L.* FACILITIES: 62 sites, 18 E, (30 amps), 44 no hkups, tenting, dump. RECREATION: lake swim, canoeing, river fishing, playground. Partial handicap access. Open all yr. Facilities fully operational Mid May - Mid Oct. Phone: (715)399-3111.

THREE LAKES—D-5

NICOLET NATIONAL FOREST (Sevenmile Lake Campground)—(Forest) *From town: Go 5-1/2 mi E on Hwy 32, then 4 mi N on FR 2178, then 2 mi E on FR 2179, then 1 mi S on FR 2435.* FACILITIES: 27 sites, 27 no hkups, tenting. RECREATION: lake swim, boating, ramp, dock, lake fishing. Partial handicap access. Open May 26 - Sep 8. Phone: (715)479-2827.

(E) The Harbor Campground—(Oneida) *From jct US 45 & Hwy 32: Go 2-3/4 mi S on Hwy 32. Enter on R.* ◊◊FACILITIES: 150 sites, typical site width 30 ft, 5 full hkups, 140 W&E, (20/30/50 amps), 5 no hkups, 10 pull-thrus, cable TV, ($), WiFi Internet central location, tenting, dump, portable dump, ice, picnic tables, fire rings, grills, wood. ◊◊RECREATION: lake swim, boating, canoeing, kayaking, ramp, dock, lake fishing, fishing guides, playground. Pets welcome. Partial handicap access. Open all yr. Facilities fully operational May 1 - Oct 1. Big rigs welcome. Rate in 2010

CAMPCLUB USA

THREE LAKES—Continued
The Harbor Campground—Continued

$30-50 for 4 persons. MC/VISA/Debit. Member ARVC, WACO. CCUSA 50% Discount. CCUSA reservations Accepted, CCUSA disc. not avail S, CCUSA disc. not avail F,Sa, CCUSA disc. not avail holidays.

Phone: (715)546-3520
Address: 1021 State Hwy 32E, Three Lakes, WI 54562
Lat/Lon: 45.79524/-89.11615
Email: theharborcampground@yahoo.com
Web: www.theharborcampground.com

TILLEDA—E-5

(W) Tilleda Falls Campground—(Shawano) *From jct Hwy 29 & CR D: Go 1 mi N on CR D. Enter on L.* ◊◊◊FACILITIES: 43 sites, typical site width 30 ft, 37 W&E, (20/30 amps), 6 no hkups, family camping, tenting, dump, ltd groc. ◊◊◊◊RECREATION: river swim, boating, electric motors only, canoeing, dock, river/pond fishing, playground. Pets welcome, breed restrict, quantity restrict. Open May 1 - Oct 15. Rate in 2010 $27-31 per family. Member ARVC, WACO. Phone: (715)787-4143.

TIPLER—C-5

NICOLET NATIONAL FOREST (Lost Lake Campground) —(Florence) *From town: Go 3-1/2 mi SE on FR 2156.* FACILITIES: 27 sites, 22 ft max RV length, 27 no hkups, tenting. RECREATION: lake swim, boating, no motors, canoeing, ramp, lake fishing. Partial handicap access. Open May 2 - Dec 1. Phone: (715) 528-4464.

TOMAH—G-3

(E) Holiday Lodge Golf Resort & RV Park—(Monroe) *From jct I-94 & Hwy 21: Go 6 mi E on Hwy 21, then 3/4 mi S on Excelsior Ave. Enter on L.* ◊◊FACILITIES: 27 sites, typical site width 36 ft, 23 full hkups, 4 W&E, (20/30 amps), 11 pull-thrus, family camping, tenting, dump, laundry. Pets welcome, breed restrict. Open May 1 - Mid Oct. Rate in 2010 $27 for 2 persons. Phone: (608)372-9314.

TOMAHAWK—D-4

(S) Birkensee Camping—(Lincoln) *From jct US 8 & US 51: Go 5 mi S on US 51 (exit 229), then 4 mi E on CR D, then 1-1/2 mi S on CR H. Enter on L.* ◊◊FACILITIES: 62 sites, typical site width 30 ft, 30 ft max RV length, 14 full hkups, 44 W&E, (20/30 amps), 4 no hkups, 2 pull-thrus, family camping, tenting, dump, laundry, ltd groc. ◊◊◊RECREATION: swim pool, pond fishing, playground. Pets welcome, breed restrict. Open all yr. Facilities fully operational May 1 - Oct 1. Rate in 2010 $30-35 per family. Phone: (715)453-5103.

(E) Northforest Campgrounds—(Lincoln) *From jct US 8 & US 51: Go 2 mi S on US 51, then 7-1/2 mi E on CR A, then 3/4 mi S on Pickerel Creek Rd, then continue 1/2 mi on Northforest Rd. Enter on L.* ◊◊FACILITIES: 152 sites, typical site width 30 ft, 124 full hkups, 28 W&E, (20/30/50 amps), family camping, tenting, dump, laundry, ltd groc. ◊◊◊RECREATION: lake swim, boating, canoeing, ramp, dock, lake fishing, playground. Pets welcome. Partial handicap access. Open May 1 - Oct 15. Rate in 2010 $22-32 per family. Member WACO. Phone: (715)453-2522.

OTTER LAKE RECREATION AREA (Lincoln County Park)—(Lincoln) *From town: Go 3 mi S on US-51, then 7 mi E on CR-S, Stevenson Rd, Grundy Rd, Bear Trail Rd & Otter Lake Rd.* FACILITIES: 25 sites, 30 ft max RV length, 25 no hkups, tenting. RECREATION: lake swim, boating, ramp. Open all yr. Phone: (715)536-0327.

(N) Terrace View Campsites—(Lincoln) *From jct US 51 & US 8: Go 1 mi W on US 8, then 2/10 mi S on Wolff Rd, then 2/10 mi E on Terrace View Rd. Enter at end.* ◊◊◊FACILITIES: 45 sites, typical site width 25 ft, 32 ft max RV length, 3 full hkups, 38 W&E, 4 E, (20/30 amps), WiFi Internet central location, tenting, shower$, dump, portable dump, ltd groc, ice, picnic tables, fire rings, wood. ◊◊◊◊◊RECREATION: lake swim, boating, canoeing, kayaking, ramp, dock, lake fishing, fishing supplies, bsktball, playground, horseshoes, v-ball. Pets welcome. Open Apr 1 - Dec 1. Rate in 2010 $26-28 for 4 persons. Member ARVC, WACO. CCUSA 50% Discount. CCUSA reservations Accepted, CCUSA max stay 1 day, Cash only for CCUSA disc., CCUSA disc. not avail F,Sa, CCUSA disc. not avail holidays. Not available Harley Colorama weekend (approx 3rd weekend of Sep-call for details).

CAMPCLUB USA

Phone: (715)453-8352
Lat/Lon: 45.53652/-89.68857
Email: tvcken@charter.net
Web: www.terraceviewcampsite.com

(N) Tomahawk Campground & RV Park—(Lincoln) *From jct US 8 & US 51: Go 2 mi S on US 51, then 3 mi W on CR A. Enter on L.* ◊◊FACILITIES: 80 sites, 19 full hkups, 20 W&E, (20/30/50 amps), 41 no hkups, 6 pull-thrus, family camping, tenting, dump. Pets welcome ($). Open Mid Apr - Mid Oct. Rate in 2010 $20-25 per family. Phone: (715)525-9600.

Green Bay is Wisconsin's oldest city and the second oldest city is Prairie du Chien.

TOWNSEND—D-5

NICOLET NATIONAL FOREST (Boot Lake Campground)—(Ocanto) *From town: Go 5-1/2 mi SW on CR-T.* FACILITIES: 32 sites, 22 ft max RV length, 32 no hkups, tenting. RECREATION: lake swim, boating, ramp, lake fishing. Open Apr 29 - Nov 30. Phone: (715)276-6333.

TREGO—C-2

(C) Log Cabin Resort & Campground—(Washburn) *From jct US 53 & US 63: Go 150 yards N on US 63. Enter on L.* ◇◇◇FACILITIES: 25 sites, typical site width 30 ft, 26 ft max RV length, 3 full hkups, 22 W&E, (30 amps), 1 pull-thrus, WiFi Internet central location, family camping, tenting, shower$, dump, ltd groc, ice, picnic tables, fire rings, wood. ◇◇◇RECREATION: river swim, boating, canoeing, kayaking, float trips, river/pond fishing, fishing supplies, bike rental 8 bike rentals, playground, horseshoes, v-ball. Pets welcome. Open May 1 - Oct 1. Rate in 2010 $30-35 for 4 persons. MC/VISA. Member ARVC, WACO. CCUSA 50% Discount. CCUSA reservations Required, CCUSA max stay 1 day, CCUSA disc. not avail F,Sa. Not available Memorial Day weekend thru Labor Day.

Phone: (715)635-2959
Address: N7470 Log Cabin Dr, Trego, WI 54888
Lat/Lon: 45.90654/-91.82568
Web: www.logcabin-resort.com

TREMPEALEAU—G-2

(W) PERROT SP—(Trempealeau) *From jct Hwy 35 & First St: Go W on First St and follow signs.* FACILITIES: 98 sites, 36 E, (20 amps), 62 no hkups, tenting, dump. RECREATION: boating, canoeing, ramp, dock, river fishing, playground. Partial handicap access. Open all yr. Facilities fully operational Memorial Day Wknd - Labor Day Wknd. Phone: (608)534-6409.

TURTLE LAKE—D-1

(C) St. Croix Casino & Hotel RV Park (RV SPACES)—(Barron) *From jct of US 63N & US 8: Go 500 yards W on US 8. Facing the Casino, the RV Park is behind and to the right. Enter on R.* FACILITIES: 28 sites, typical site width 20 ft, 18 W&E, (20/30/50 amps), 10 no hkups, family camping, tenting, dump, laundry. RECREATION: swim pool. Pets welcome. Open May 1 - Oct 31. Big rigs welcome. Rate in 2010 $15-25 per vehicle. Phone: (800)846-8946.

(W) TURTLE LAKE RV PARK—(Polk) *At the jct of US 63S & US 8 (southeast corner). Enter on L.*

◇◇◇FACILITIES: 70 sites, typical site width 30 ft, 70 full hkups, (20/30/50 amps), some extd stay sites, 29 pull-thrus, WiFi Instant Internet at site, family camping, tenting, RV supplies, ice, picnic tables, fire rings, grills, wood.

◇RECREATION: swim pool, golf nearby, sports field.

Pets welcome. Partial handicap access. Open mid April - mid Oct. Big rigs welcome. Clubs welcome. Rate in 2010 $24 per family. MC/VISA/DISC/Debit.

Phone: (715)986-4140
Address: 750 US Hwy 8, Turtle Lake, WI 54889
Lat/Lon: 45.39490/-92.16191
Email: tlrvpark@gmail.com
Web: www.turtlelakervpark.com

SEE AD TRAVEL SECTION PAGE 799

Can you trust the Woodall's ratings? 25 evaluation teams have scoured North American campgrounds to provide you with accurate, up to date information & ratings. Find a rating you don't agree with? Send a letter or email our way, and we'll give it extra attention for 2012.

TWO RIVERS—G-6

(C) BADGER RV PARK @ VILLAGE INN ON THE LAKE—(Manitowoc) *From jct Hwy 147 & Hwy 42: Go 1-1/2 mi S. Enter on R.*

◇◇◇◇◇FACILITIES: 24 sites, typical site width 35 ft, accepts self-contained units only, 24 full hkups, (20/30/50 amps), 12 pull-thrus, WiFi Instant Internet at site, family camping, laundry, ice, picnic tables, fire rings, grills, wood.

◇◇◇◇RECREATION: rec room/area, coin games, swim pool, lake swim, hot tub, fishing guides, mini-golf ($), golf nearby, bike rental 16 bike rentals, play equipment.

Pets welcome. Partial handicap access. No tents. Open all yr. Facilities fully operational Apr 1 - Mid Nov. Winter-electric only. Big rigs welcome. Clubs welcome. Rate in 2010 $35-45 per vehicle. MC/VISA/DISC/Debit. ATM. Member WACO. CCUSA 50% Discount. CCUSA reservations Required, CCUSA max stay 4 days, CCUSA disc. not avail holidays. Self-contained units only.

Phone: (920)794-8818
Address: 3310 Memorial Dr, Two Rivers, WI 54241
Lat/Lon: 44.13242/-87.60148
Email: info@villageinnwi.com
Web: www.villageinnwi.com

SEE AD THIS PAGE

(N) POINT BEACH SF—(Manitowoc) *From jct Hwy 42 & CTH O: Go 4 mi NE on CTH O.* FACILITIES: 127 sites, 23 W&E, 70 E, (20 amps), 34 no hkups, tenting, dump, ltd groc. RECREATION: lake swim, playground. Pets welcome. Partial handicap access. Open all yr. Facilities fully operational Apr 15 - Oct 15. Phone: (920)794-7480.

(C) Seagull Marina & Campground—(Manitowoc) *From jct Hwy 147 & Hwy 42: Go 2/3 mi S on Hwy 42. Enter on L.* ◇◇◇FACILITIES: 100 sites, typical site width 40 ft, 82 full hkups, 18 E, (20/30/50 amps), family camping, tenting, ltd groc. ◇◇RECREATION: lake swim, boating, canoeing, ramp, dock, lake fishing. Pets welcome. Open May 1 - Oct 1. Rate in 2010 $19-27 for 4 persons. Phone: (920)794-7533.

UNITY—E-3

(E) Monster Hall Campground—(Marathon) *From jct Hwy 13 & CR P: Go 4-3/4 mi E on CR P, then 1/4 mi N on CR F. Enter on R.* ◇◇FACILITIES: 193 sites, typical site width 48 ft, 193 W&E, (15/20/30/50 amps), 50 amps ($), 30 pull-thrus, tenting, dump, laundry, ltd groc. ◇◇RECREATION: swim pool, lake swim, boating, no motors, canoeing, lake fishing, play equipment. Pets welcome. Partial handicap access. Open Mid Apr - Mid Nov. Big rigs welcome. Rate in 2010 $28-31 for 2 persons. Phone: (715)223-4336. FMCA discount.

VIOLA—H-3

BANKER PARK (Municipal Park)—(Vernon) *At jct Hwy-131 & Hwy-56.* FACILITIES: 12 sites, 12 no hkups, tenting. RECREATION: canoeing, playground. Open May 1 - Oct 1. Phone: (608) 627-1831.

WABENO—D-5

(W) NICOLET NATIONAL FOREST (Richardson Lake)—(Forest) *From jct Hwy-32 & Hwy-52: Go 2 mi SW on Hwy-52, then 1/3 mi N on FR-2880.* FACILITIES: 26 sites, 22 ft max RV length, 26 no hkups, tenting. RECREATION: lake swim, boating, ramp, lake fishing. Open May 2 - Nov 30. Phone: (715)674-4481.

(N) S-J & W Ham Lake Campground LLC—(Forest) *From jct US 8 & Hwy 32: Go 4 mi S on Hwy 32. Enter on L.* ◇◇FACILITIES: 44 sites, 28 full hkups, 16 W&E, (30/50 amps), 11 pull-thrus, family camping, tenting, dump, non-guest dump $, laundry, ltd groc, RV supplies, ice, picnic tables, fire rings, wood. ◇◇RECREATION: lake swim, boating, electric motors only, canoeing, kayaking, dock, lake fishing, fishing supplies, mini-golf, ($), bsktball, play equipment, horseshoes, v-ball. Pets welcome. Open May 1 - Oct 15. Rate in 2010 $28-31 per family. CCUSA 50% Discount.

WABENO—Continued
S-J & W Ham Lake Campground LLC—Continued

CCUSA reservations Recommended, CCUSA max stay 2 days, Cash only for CCUSA disc., CCUSA disc. not avail F,Sa, CCUSA disc. not avail holidays. Not available Memorial Day weekend thru Labor Day.

Phone: (715)674-2201
Address: 3490 State Hwy 32, Wabeno, WI 54566
Lat/Lon: 45.49968/-88.67516
Web: www.hamlakecampgroundwi.com

WARRENS—G-3

(N) Jellystone Park Camp Resort—(Monroe) *From jct I-94 (exit 135) & CR EW: Go 1/2 mi E on CR EW. Enter on L.* ◇◇◇◇FACILITIES: 458 sites, typical site width 40 ft, 458 full hkups, (20/30/50 amps), 150 pull-thrus, family camping, tenting, dump, laundry, ltd groc. ◇◇◇◇◇RECREATION: 3 swim pools, pond fishing, playground. Pets welcome, breed restrict, quantity restrict. Partial handicap access. Open Apr - Oct. Big rigs welcome. Rate in 2010 $51-75 for 2 persons. Member ARVC, WACO. Phone: (608)378-2010.

WASHBURN—B-3

MEMORIAL PARK (Municipal Park)—(Bayfield) *From town: Go N on Memorial Park Lane.* FACILITIES: 51 sites, 51 E, tenting, dump. RECREATION: lake swim, boating, canoeing, lake fishing, playground. Open May 15 - Oct 15. Phone: (715)373-6160.

(W) WEST END THOMPSON PARK (Municipal Park)—(Bayfield) *From jct Hwy-13 & 8th Ave: Go 4 blocks S on 8th Ave.* FACILITIES: 51 sites, 51 E, (20/50 amps), tenting, dump. RECREATION: lake swim, boating, canoeing, ramp, dock, lake fishing, playground. Partial handicap access. Open Apr 15 - Oct 15. Phone: (715)373-6160.

WASHINGTON ISLAND—I-2

(SE) Washington Island Camping Retreat—(Door) *From Ferry Landing: Go 1-3/4 mi NE on Lobdells Point Rd, then 1/3 mi N on Main Rd, then 2 mi E on Lake View Rd, then 1/2 mi S on East Side Rd. Enter on R.* ◇◇◇FACILITIES: 101 sites, typical site width 25 ft, 47 W&E, (20/30/50 amps), 54 no hkups, 3 pull-thrus, family camping, tenting, dump, non-guest dump $, portable dump, laundry, ltd groc, ice, picnic tables, fire rings, grills, wood. ◇◇◇RECREATION: rec hall, mini-golf, bsktball, playground, tennis, horseshoes, hiking trails, v-ball. Pets welcome. Partial handicap access. Open May 1 - Nov 1. Big rigs welcome. Rate in 2010 $33 per family. MC/VISA/DISC/Debit. Member ARVC, WACO. CCUSA 50% Discount. CCUSA reservations Required, CCUSA max stay Unlimited. Discount not available Jun 18-Sep 4. Not valid on camping cabins or pop-up campers.

Phone: (920)847-2622
Address: 745 East Side Rd, Washington Island, WI 54246
Lat/Lon: 45.35667/-86.88895
Email: campingretreat@yahoo.com
Web: www.washingtonislandcamping.com

WATERTOWN—H-5

(W) RIVER BEND RESORT—(Jefferson) *From jct Hwy 26 & Hwy 19: Go 5-1/2 mi W on Hwy 19, then 1 mi S on CR Q, then 1 mi W on Hubbleton, then 1 mi S on River Bend Rd, then Rubidell Rd. Enter at end.*

◇◇◇◇FACILITIES: 602 sites, typical site width 45 ft, 432 full hkups, 170 W&E, (20/30/50 amps), many extd stay sites, 6 pull-thrus, WiFi Internet central location, family camping, tenting, RV's/park model rentals, RV storage, shower$, dump, portable dump, laundry, ltd groc, RV supplies, LP gas by weight/by meter, ice, picnic tables, patios, fire rings, wood, controlled access.

RIVER BEND RESORT—Continued on next page

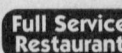

WATERTOWN—Continued
RIVER BEND RESORT—Continued

◊◊◊◊◊RECREATION: rec hall, rec room/area, equipped pavilion, coin games, swim pool, wading pool, spray ground, river swim, hot tub, boating, canoeing, kayaking, ramp, dock, 6 canoe rentals, river/pond fishing, fishing supplies, mini-golf, ($), golf nearby, bsktball, 40 bike rentals, playground, shuffleboard court 4 shuffleboard courts, activities (wkends), tennis, horseshoes, sports field, v-ball. Rec open to public.

Pets welcome. Partial handicap access. Open all yr. Facilities fully operational Mid Apr - Mid Oct. Big rigs welcome. Clubs welcome. Rate in 2010 $30-75 for 6 persons. MC/VISA/DISC/AMEX/Debit. ATM. Member ARVC, WACO.

Phone: (920)261-7505
Address: W 6940 Rubidell Rd, Watertown, WI 53094
Lat/Lon: 43.16369/-88.87304
Email: info@rbresort.com
Web: www.rbresort.com

SEE AD PAGE 826

WAUPACA—F-5

(W) HARTMAN CREEK SP—(Waupaca) *From jct Hwy 49 & Hwy 54: Go 4-1/2 mi W on Hwy 54, then 2-1/4 mi S on Hartman Creek Rd.* FACILITIES: 103 sites, 24 E, (15 amps), 79 no hkups, tenting, dump. RECREATION: lake swim, canoeing, ramp, lake fishing, playground. Partial handicap access. Open Apr 2 - Nov 30. Phone: (715)258-2372.

(S) Rustic Woods Campground—(Waupaca) *From jct US 10 & Hwy 49 & CR-A: Go 3 mi S on CR-A, then 1/4 mi W on CR-EE, then 2-1/4 mi W on Lake Spencer Rd, then 1/2 mi S on CR-E, then 500 feet E on Southwood Dr. Enter on R.* ◊◊FACILITIES: 180 sites, typical site width 40 ft, 87 full hkups, 93 W&E, (20/30 amps), tenting, dump, laundry. ◊◊◊RECREATION: swim pool, boating, no motors, canoeing, dock, lake fishing, playground. Pets welcome. Partial handicap access. Open all yr. Facilities fully operational Apr 15 - Oct 15. Phone: (715)258-2442.

(W) Waupaca Camping Park, LLC—(Waupaca) *From jct Hwy 10/22S & CR K: Go 1/3 mi S on Hwy 22S, then 1/3 mi W on S Western Ave, then 1/2 mi W on Holmes. Enter on R.* ◊◊◊FACILITIES: 114 sites, typical site width 36 ft, 38 full hkups, 76 W&E, (20/30/50 amps), 3 pull-thrus, family camping, tenting, dump, laundry, ltd groc. ◊◊◊RECREATION: swim pool, lake fishing, playground. Pets welcome. Partial handicap access. Open mid Apr - mid Oct. Big rigs welcome. Rate in 2010 $28-35 for 2 persons. Member ARVC, WACO. Phone: (715)258-8010.

WAUSAU—E-4

See listings at Amherst Junction, Bancroft, Knowlton, Stevens Point & Wisconsin Rapids

(SW) RIB MOUNTAIN SP—(Marathon) *5 mi SW on US-51.* FACILITIES: 30 sites, 30 no hkups, tenting, ltd groc. RECREATION: playground. Pets welcome. Partial handicap access. Open Apr 15 - Oct 31. Phone: (715)842-2522.

✽ **TRUCK COUNTRY**—*From jct I-39 (exit 185) & US 51 Bus: Go 100 yds N on US 51 Bus, then 1/2 mi S on CR XX, then 100 yds S on Trailwood Ln. Enter on R.* SERVICES: full-time mech, engine/chassis repair, body work/collision repair. Computerized alignment, quick lube pit. Open all yr. MC/VISA/DISC/AMEX/Debit.

Phone: (715)359-9989
Address: 2435 Trailwood Ln, Mosinee, WI 54474
Lat/Lon: 44.85542/-89.63512
Web: www.truckcountry.com

SEE AD TRAVEL SECTION PAGE 798 AND AD IA TRAVEL SECTION PAGE 247

WAUTOMA—G-4

(S) Lake of the Woods Campground—(Marquette) *From jct Hwys-73,21 & 22: Go 8 mi S on Hwy-22, then 1 mi W on CR JJ, then 1-1/4 mi S on 14th Ave. Enter on L.* ◊◊◊FACILITIES: 300 sites, typical site width 35 ft, 6 full hkups, 294 W&E, (20/30/50 amps), 12 pull-thrus, family camping, tenting, dump, laundry, ltd groc. ◊◊◊◊◊RECREATION: 2 swim pools, river swim, boating, no motors, canoeing, river/pond/stream fishing, playground. Pets welcome. Partial handicap access. Open all yr. Facilities fully operational Mid Apr - Oct 15. Rate in 2010 $26-38 for 4 persons. Member ARVC, WACO. Phone: (920)787-3601.

WEST BEND—H-6

(NE) Lake Lenwood Beach & Campground—(Washington) *From jct US 45 & Hwy D: Go 1 mi E on Hwy D, then 1 mi N on Hwy 144, then 200 feet E on Wallace Lake Rd. Enter on R.* ◊◊◊FACILITIES: 133 sites, typical site width 45 ft, 91 full hkups, 42 W&E, (20/30/50 amps), 8 pull-thrus, family camping, tenting, dump. ◊◊◊RECREATION: lake swim, boating, electric

WEST BEND—Continued
Lake Lenwood Beach & Campground—Continued

motors only, canoeing, lake fishing, playground. Pets welcome, breed restrict, quantity restrict. Open Apr 15 - Oct 9. Big rigs welcome. Rate in 2010 $34.50-38.50 per family. Member ARVC, WACO. Phone: (262)334-1335.

(NE) Lazy Days Campground—(Washington) *From jct US 45 & Eastbound Hwy 144: Go 2-3/4 mi NE on Hwy 144, then 2 mi E on CR-A, then 1/2 mi S on Lakeview Rd. Enter at end.* ◊◊FACILITIES: 355 sites, typical site width 50 ft, 26 full hkups, 295 W&E, (20/30 amps), 34 no hkups, 13 pull-thrus, family camping, tenting, dump, laundry, groceries. ◊◊RECREATION: lake swim, boating, 10 hp limit, dock, lake fishing, playground. Pets welcome. Partial handicap access. Open Apr 1 - Oct 31. Rate in 2010 $32-35 per family. Phone: (262)675-6511.

(N) Timber Trail Campground—(Washington) *From jct US 45 (exit 73) & CR-D: Go 1-1/2 mi W on CR-D, then 3/4 mi N on Good Luck Ln. Enter on R.* ◊◊FACILITIES: 122 sites, typical site width 45 ft, 35 ft max RV length, 40 full hkups, 80 W&E, (30 amps), 2 no hkups, family camping, tenting, dump, laundry, ltd groc. ◊◊◊RECREATION: swim pool, pond fishing, playground. Pets welcome. Open May 15 - Oct 15. Rate in 2010 $25-35 per family. Member ARVC, WACO. Phone: (262)338-8561.

WEST SALEM—G-2

(NE) Neshonoc Lakeside Camp Resort—(La Crosse) *From jct I-90 (exit 12) & CR-C: Go 1 mi N on CR-C, then 1-1/4 mi E on Hwy 16. Enter on R.* ◊◊◊◊FACILITIES: 285 sites, typical site width 50 ft, 264 full hkups, 21 W&E, (20/30/50 amps), 43 pull-thrus, family camping, tenting, dump, laundry, ltd groc. ◊◊◊◊◊RECREATION: 2 swim pools, lake swim, boating, canoeing, ramp, dock, lake fishing, playground. Pets welcome. Partial handicap access. Open Mid Apr - Mid Oct. Big rigs welcome. Rate in 2010 $45-59 per family. Member ARVC, WACO. Phone: (608) 786-1792.

(E) VETERAN'S MEMORIAL PARK (La Crosse County)—(La Crosse) *From jct I-90 (exit 12) & CR C: Go 1-1/2 mi N & W on CR C, then 2 mi W on Hwy 16. Enter on L.*

FACILITIES: 120 sites, typical site width 40 ft, 56 W&E, 55 E, (20/30/50 amps), 9 no hkups, 9 pull-thrus, family camping, tenting, showerS, dump, non-guest dump $, laundry, ltd groc, ice, picnic tables, fire rings, wood.

RECREATION: pavilion, boating, canoeing, river/pond fishing, fishing supplies, golf nearby, bsktball, playground, shuffleboard court 2 shuffleboard courts, activities (wkends), horseshoes, sports field, hiking trails, v-ball. Rec open to public.

Pets welcome. Partial handicap access. Open Mid Apr - mid Oct. Big rigs welcome.

Phone: (608)786-4011
Address: N4668 County Rd VP, West Salem, WI 54669
Lat/Lon: 43.89853/-91.11464
Email: facilities@lacrossecounty.org
Web: www.co.la-crosse.wi.us

SEE AD LA CROSSE PAGE 817

WESTBORO—D-3

CHEQUAMEGON NATIONAL FOREST (Spearhead Point Campground)—(Taylor) *From jct Hwy-13 & CR-D: Go 6-3/4 mi W on CR-D, then 1 mi S on FR-104, then 2 mi W on FR-106.* FACILITIES: 26 sites, 32 ft max RV length, 26 no hkups, tenting, dump, ltd groc. RECREATION: lake swim, boating, ramp, dock, lake fishing, playground. Partial handicap access. Open May 1 - Oct 31. Phone: (715)748-4875.

WHITE LAKE—E-5

(N) 9 Mile All Sport Resort—(Langlade) *From jct Hwy 64 & Hwy 55: Go 4 mi N on Hwy 55. Enter on R.* ◊◊◊FACILITIES: 100 sites, typical site width 35 ft, 50 full hkups, 35 W&E, (30/50 amps), 15 no hkups, 10 pull-thrus, tenting, laundry, ltd groc. ◊◊RECREATION: play equipment. Pets welcome. Open all yr. Big rigs welcome. Rate in 2010 $19-22 per family. Member ARVC, WACO. Phone: (715)484-8908.

(S) Raft N' Rest Campground—(Langlade) *From jct Hwy 64 & Hwy 55: Go 1/3 mi S on Hwy 55. Enter on L.* ◊◊FACILITIES: 46 sites, typical site width 30 ft, 30 ft max RV length, 15 W&E, (20/30 amps), 31 no hkups, 5 pull-thrus, tenting, dump. ◊◊RECREATION: play equipment. Pets welcome. Open Memorial Day - Labor Day. Rate in 2010 $12 for 1 persons. Member ARVC, WACO. Phone: (715)882-5613.

(S) River Forest Rafting Campground—(Langlade) *From jct Hwy 64 & Hwy 55: Go 6 mi S on Hwy 55. Enter on L.* ◊◊FACILITIES: 52 sites, 24 ft max RV length, 12 E, (20/30 amps), 40 no hkups, 2 pull-thrus, tenting, dump, ltd groc. Pets welcome. Open all yr. Facilities fully operational May 1 - Oct 1. Rate in 2010 $8 for 1 persons. Member ARVC, WACO. Phone: (715) 882-3351.

WHITEWATER—I-5

KETTLE MORAINE SF-SOUTHERN UNIT (Whitewater Lake)—(Walworth) *From jct US-12 & CR-P: Go SE on CR-P, then 1 mi W on Kettle Moraine Dr.* FACILITIES: 63 sites, 63 no hkups, tenting, dump. RECREATION: lake swim, boating, lake fishing. Open mid May - mid Oct. Phone: (262)594-6200.

WILD ROSE—G-5

(E) EVERGREEN CAMPSITES & RESORT—(Waushara) *From jct Hwy 22 & CR H: Go 3 mi E on Hwy H, then 1-1/2 mi E on Archer Ln. Enter on R.*

◊◊◊◊◊FACILITIES: 482 sites, typical site width 45 ft, 313 full hkups, 169 W&E, (20/30/50 amps), many extd stay sites, 33 pull-thrus, WiFi Instant Internet at site, tenting, RV's/park model rentals, cabins, RV storage, showerS, dump, non-guest dump $, laundry, groceries, RV supplies, LP gas by weight, ice, picnic tables, fire rings, wood.

◊◊◊◊◊RECREATION: rec room/area, equipped pavilion, coin games, 2 swim pools, wading pool, spray ground, lake swim, boating, canoeing, kayaking, ramp, dock, 2 pontoon/6 rowboat/4 canoe/6 pedal boat rentals, lake fishing, fishing supplies, mini-golf, ($), golf nearby, bsktball, 10 bike rentals, playground, activities (wkends), horseshoes, sports field, hiking trails, v-ball. Rec open to public.

Pets welcome. Partial handicap access. Open all yr. Facilities fully operational Apr 15 - Oct 15. Big rigs welcome. Clubs welcome. Green Friendly. Rate in 2010 $46 per family. MC/VISA/Debit. ATM. Member ARVC, WACO.

Phone: (866)450-2267
Address: W5449 Archer Lane, Wild Rose, WI 54984
Lat/Lon: 44.17368/-89.15616
Email: evergreencampsites@gmail.com
Web: www.evergreencampsites.com

SEE AD TRAVEL SECTION PAGE 799

WILTON—G-3

(S) Tunnel Trail Campground—(Monroe) *From east jct Hwy 131 & Hwy 71: Go 1 mi E on Hwy 71. Enter on R.* ◊◊◊◊FACILITIES: 80 sites, typical site width 30 ft, 75 W&E, (20/30/50 amps), 5 no hkups, 12 pull-thrus, WiFi Internet central location, family camping, tenting, dump, laundry, ltd groc, RV supplies, ice, picnic tables, fire rings, wood. ◊◊◊◊RECREATION: pavilion, 1 swim pools, wading pool, mini-golf, ($), bsktball, 75 bike rentals, playground, horseshoes, hiking trails, v-ball. Pets welcome, quantity restrict. Partial handicap access. Open May 1 - Oct 15. Rate in 2010 $35-40 for 2 persons. MC/VISA/Debit. Member ARVC, WACO. CCUSA 50% Discount. CCUSA reservations Recommended, CCUSA max stay 2 days, Cash only for CCUSA disc., CCUSA disc. not avail F,Sa. Not available Memorial Day weekend thru Labor Day.

Phone: (608)435-6829
Address: 26983 St. Highway 71, Wilton, WI 54670
Lat/Lon: 43.82530/-90.45268
Email: reservations@tunneltrail.com
Web: www.tunneltrail.com

WINTER—D-3

CHEQUAMEGON NATIONAL FOREST (Black Lake Campground)—(Sawyer) *From town: Go 11 mi NE on Hwy 70, then 8-1/2 mi N on FR 32, then 4 mi W on FR 172, then 1/2 mi N on FR 173, then 1/2 mi NE on FR 1666.* FACILITIES: 29 sites, 29 no hkups, tenting. RECREATION: lake swim, boating, ramp, lake fishing. Partial handicap access. Open May 1 - Oct 31. Phone: (715)634-4821.

(SE) FLAMBEAU RIVER SF (Connor's Lake)—(Sawyer) *From town: Go 15 mi SE on CR W.* FACILITIES: 35 sites, 35 no hkups, tenting, dump. RECREATION: lake swim, boating, canoeing, ramp, lake fishing. Partial handicap access. Open May - Sep. Phone: (715)332-5271.

(SE) FLAMBEAU RIVER SF (Lake of the Pines)—(Sawyer) *From town: Go 15 mi SE on CR W.* FACILITIES: 30 sites, 30 no hkups, tenting. RECREATION: lake swim, boating, canoeing, ramp, dock, lake fishing. Partial handicap access. Open Apr 15 - Dec 15. Phone: (715)332-5271.

WISCONSIN DELLS—H-4

See listings at Baraboo, Lake Delton, Portage & Wonowoc.

WISCONSIN DELLS—Continued on next page

Can you trust the Woodall's ratings? 25 evaluation teams have scoured North American campgrounds to provide you with accurate, up to date information & ratings. Find a rating you don't agree with? Send a letter or email our way, and we'll give it extra attention for 2012.

WISCONSIN DELLS AREA MAP

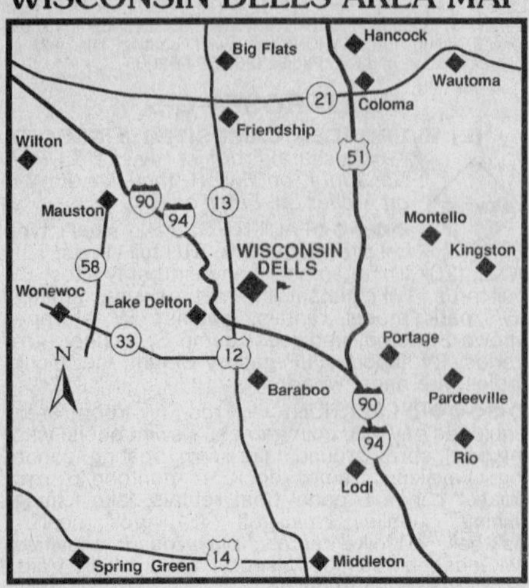

Symbols on map indicate towns within a 50 mi radius of Wisconsin Dells where campgrounds (diamonds), attractions (flags), & RV service centers & camping supply outlets (gears) are listed. Check listings for more information.

(C) AMERICAN WORLD - MT. OLYMPUS HOTEL & RV RESORT—(Sauk) *From jct I-90/94 (exit 87) & Hwy 13: Go 1/2 mi E on Hwy 13, then 1/2 mi S on Hwy 12, then 500 ft on CR A. Enter on L.*

WELCOME

◊◊◊FACILITIES: 60 sites, typical site width 20 ft, accepts full hkup units only, 60 full hkups, (30/50 amps), 12 pull-thrus, cable TV, WiFi Instant Internet at site, WiFi Internet central location, laundry, ltd groc, RV supplies, LP bottle exch, ice, picnic tables, fire rings, grills, wood.

CAMPCLUB USA

◊◊◊◊RECREATION: rec room/area, equipped pavilion, coin games, 3 swim pools, hot tub, golf nearby, bsktball, play equipment, tennis, v-ball.

Pets welcome. No tents. Open all yr. Big rigs welcome. Clubs welcome. Rate in 2010 $29-79 for 2 persons. MC/VISA/DISC/AMEX/Debit. ATM. Member ARVC, WACO. CCUSA 50% Discount. CCUSA reservations Recommended, CCUSA max stay 21 days, CCUSA disc. not avail holidays. Not available Polish fest weekend or when 80% full.

Phone: (608)253-4451
Address: 400 CRA & Hwy 12, Wisconsin Dells, WI 53965
Lat/Lon: 43.61818/-89.78282
Email: info@americanworld.com
Web: www.americanworld.com

SEE AD NEXT PAGE

(W) ARROWHEAD RESORT CAMPGROUND—(Juneau) *From jct I-90/94 (exit 85) & Hwy 12/16: Go 1 mi W on Hwy 12/16, then 1-1/4 mi S on Arrowhead Rd. Enter on R.*

WELCOME

◊◊FACILITIES: 333 sites, typical site width 30 ft, 180 full hkups, 86 W&E, (20/30/50 amps), 67 no hkups, some extd stay sites, 12 pull-thrus, WiFi Instant Internet at site, WiFi Internet central location, family camping, tenting, RV's/park model rentals, shower$, dump, non-guest dump $, laundry, ltd groc, RV supplies, LP gas by weight/by meter, ice, picnic tables, fire rings, wood.

CAMPCLUB USA

◊◊◊◊RECREATION: rec room/area, equipped pavilion, coin games, 2 swim pools, mini-golf, ($), golf nearby, bsktball, playground, shuffleboard court 2 shuffleboard courts, activities, tennis, horseshoes, sports field, hiking trails, v-ball.

Pets welcome, quantity restrict. Partial handicap access. Open Mid Apr - Mid Oct. Big rigs welcome. Escort to site. Clubs welcome. Rate in 2010 $41-52 per family. MC/VISA/DISC/AMEX/Debit. Member ARVC, WACO. CCUSA 50% Discount. CCUSA reservations Recommended, CCUSA max stay 4 days, CCUSA disc. not avail F,Sa, CCUSA disc. not avail holidays.

Phone: (608)254-7344
Address: W1530 Arrowhead Rd, Wisconsin Dells, WI 53965
Lat/Lon: 43.66310/-89.85014
Email: arrowheadrv@equitylifestyle.com
Web: www.ARROWHEADCAMPRESORT.com

Reserve Online at Woodalls.com

SEE AD NEXT PAGE AND AD ALGOMA PAGE 807

(SW) BARABOO HILLS CAMPGROUND—(Sauk) *From jct I-90/I-94 (exit 92) & US 12: Go 5-1/4 mi E on US 12, then 1-1/4 mi W on Terrytown Rd. Enter on L.*

WELCOME

◊◊◊◊FACILITIES: 133 sites, typical site width 50 ft, 36 full hkups, 97 W&E, (20/30/50 amps), some extd stay sites, 6 pull-thrus, WiFi Instant Internet at site, WiFi Internet central location, family camping, tenting, RV's/park model rentals, cabins, dump, portable dump, laundry, ltd groc, RV supplies, LP bottle exch, ice, picnic tables, fire rings, wood.

◊◊◊◊RECREATION: rec room/area, equipped pavilion, coin games, swim pool, pond fishing, fishing supplies, mini-golf, ($), golf nearby, bsktball, 40 bike rentals, playground, activities, (wkends), horseshoes, sports field, v-ball.

Pets welcome. Partial handicap access. Open Apr 15 - Oct 15. Big rigs welcome. Clubs welcome. Rate in 2010 $44-54 for 2 persons. MC/VISA/DISC/Debit. ATM. Member ARVC, WACO.

Phone: (800)226-7242
Address: E 10545 Terrytown Rd, Baraboo, WI 53913
Lat/Lon: 43.49477/-89.79591
Email: camp@baraboohillscampground.com
Web: www.baraboohillscampground.com

SEE AD NEXT PAGE AND AD TRAVEL SECTION PAGE 799

(N) BASS LAKE CAMPGROUND—(Juneau) *From jct I-90/94 (exit 79) & CR-HH: Go 1/2 mi S on CR-HH, then 2 mi SE on US 12/16, then 500 feet S on Southern Rd. Enter on R.*

WELCOME

◊◊◊◊FACILITIES: 68 sites, typical site width 25 ft, 36 full hkups, 21 W&E, 4 E, (20/30 amps), 7 no hkups, some extd stay sites, 21 pull-thrus, tenting, RV's/park model rentals, cabins, dump, portable dump, laundry, ltd groc, RV supplies, LP bottle exch, ice, picnic tables, fire rings, wood.

◊◊◊◊RECREATION: rec room/area, pavilion, coin games, swim pool, lake swim, boating, no motors, canoeing, kayaking, dock, rowboat/canoe/4 kayak/2 pedal boat rentals, lake/pond fishing, fishing supplies, golf nearby, bsktball, 12 bike rentals, playground, activities, (wkends), horseshoes, sports field, hiking trails, v-ball. Rec open to public.

Pets welcome. Open May 1 or last weekend in Apr. - end of Sep. Clubs welcome. Rate in 2010 $38-42 per family. MC/VISA/Debit. Member ARVC, WACO.

Phone: (608)666-2311
Address: N 1497 Southern Rd, Lyndon Station, WI 53944
Lat/Lon: 43.69120/-89.86857
Email: info@basslakecampground.com
Web: www.basslakecampground.com

SEE AD NEXT PAGE

(C) BONANZA CAMPGROUND & RV PARK—(Sauk) *From jct I-90/94 (exit 87) & Hwy-13: Go 1 mi E on Hwy-13, then 1 mi S on US-12. Enter on L.*

WELCOME

◊◊◊◊FACILITIES: 157 sites, typical site width 35 ft, 67 full hkups, 65 W&E, (20/30/50 amps), 25 no hkups, 77 pull-thrus, WiFi Internet central location, family camping, tenting, cabins, shower$, dump, laundry, ltd groc, RV supplies, LP bottle exch, ice, picnic tables, fire rings, wood.

CAMPCLUB USA

◊◊◊RECREATION: rec room/area, equipped pavilion, coin games, 2 swim pools, wading pool, mini-golf, ($), golf nearby, bsktball, playground, activities, (wkends), v-ball.

Pets welcome, quantity restrict. Open all yr. Facilities fully operational Apr 15 - Oct 1. Big rigs welcome. Escort to site. Clubs welcome. Rate in 2010 $25-44 for 4 persons. MC/VISA/DISC/Debit. Member ARVC, WACO. CCUSA 50% Discount. CCUSA reservations Recommended,

CCUSA max stay Unlimited, CCUSA disc. not avail F,Sa. Not available Memorial Day weekend thru Labor Day. Fully operational Apr 15-Oct 1.

Phone: (800)438-8139
Address: 1770 Wisconsin Dells Pkwy, Wisconsin Dells, WI 53965
Lat/Lon: 43.61168/-89.78723
Email: info@bonanzacamping.com
Web: www.bonanzacamping.com

SEE AD NEXT PAGE

(SW) COUNTRY ROADS MOTORHOME & RV PARK—(Sauk) *From jct I-90/94 & Hwy 23 (exit 89): Go 1/2 mi W on Hwy 23. Enter on R.*

WELCOME

◊◊◊◊FACILITIES: 100 sites, typical site width 35 ft, 38 full hkups, 62 W&E, (20/30/50 amps), 65 pull-thrus, WiFi Instant Internet at site, RV storage, dump, portable dump, laundry, ltd groc, RV supplies, LP gas by weight/by meter, ice, picnic tables, fire rings, wood.

◊◊RECREATION: rec room/area, equipped pavilion, golf nearby, play equipment, horseshoes, sports field, hiking trails.

Pets welcome. Partial handicap access. No tents. Open May 1 - Oct 1. Big rigs welcome. Escort to site. Clubs welcome. Rate in 2010 $30-35 for 2 persons. MC/VISA/Debit.

Phone: (608)253-2132
Address: S 1633 Hwy 23, Lake Delton, WI 53940
Lat/Lon: 43.58589/-89.82167
Email: cntryrdsrv@aol.com
Web: www.4countryroads.com

SEE AD TRAVEL SECTION PAGE 799

(N) Crockett's Resort Camping and RV Park—(Juneau) *From jct I-90 (exit 79) & Hwy HH: Go 3 mi N on Hwy HH, then 1 mi E on 58th St. Enter at end.* ◊◊◊FACILITIES: 226 sites, typical site width 50 ft, 146 full hkups, 44 W&E, (20/30/50 amps), 36 no hkups, 10 pull-thrus, family camping, tenting, dump, laundry, ltd groc. ◊◊◊RECREATION: swim pool, river swim, boating, no motors, canoeing, ramp, river/pond fishing, playground. Pets welcome, breed restrict. Partial handicap access. Open all yr. Facilities fully operational Mid Apr - Mid Oct. Big rigs welcome. Rate in 2010 $32-39 per family. Phone: (888)621-4711.

(S) DELL BOO CAMPGROUND—(Sauk) *From jct I-90/94 & US 12 (exit 92): Go 1-1/4 mi SE on US 12, then 3/4 mi W on Shady Lane Rd. Enter on R.*

WELCOME

◊◊◊◊FACILITIES: 151 sites, typical site width 35 ft, 54 full hkups, 97 W&E, (20/30/50 amps), some extd stay sites, 8 pull-thrus, WiFi Instant Internet at site, WiFi Internet central location, family camping, tenting, RV's/park model rentals, cabins, RV storage, dump, portable dump, laundry, ltd groc, RV supplies, LP bottle exch, ice, picnic tables, fire rings, wood, controlled access.

◊◊◊◊RECREATION: rec hall, equipped pavilion, coin games, swim pool, golf nearby, bsktball, 12 bike rentals, playground, shuffleboard court 2 shuffleboard courts, activities (wkends), tennis, horseshoes, sports field, hiking trails, v-ball.

Pets welcome, quantity restrict. Partial handicap access. Open May 1 - Sep 30. Big rigs welcome. Clubs welcome. Rate in 2010 $39-47 for 4 persons. MC/VISA/Debit. Member ARVC, WACO.

Phone: (608)356-5898
Address: E 10562 Shady Lane Rd, Baraboo, WI 53913
Lat/Lon: 43.54715/-89.79489
Email: dairystate@centurytel.net
Web: www.Dellboo.com

SEE AD NEXT PAGE

(NW) DELLS TIMBERLAND CAMPING RESORT—(Juneau) *From I-90/94 (exit 85): Go 2 mi NW on Hwy 12. Enter on L.*

WELCOME

FACILITIES: 145 sites, typical site width 30 ft, 103 full hkups, 31 W&E, (30/50 amps), 11 no hkups, many extd stay sites, 8 pull-thrus, WiFi Instant Internet at site, WiFi Internet central location, family camping, tenting, RV storage, dump, laundry, ltd groc, RV supplies, LP gas by weight, ice, picnic tables, fire rings, wood, controlled access.

RECREATION: rec hall, rec room/area, equipped pavilion, coin games, swim pool, mini-golf, golf nearby, bsktball, playground, shuffleboard court shuffleboard court, activities, horseshoes, v-ball.

DELLS TIMBERLAND CAMPING RESORT—Continued on page 830

See listing at Wisconsin Dells, WI

WISCONSIN DELLS—Continued
DELLS TIMBERLAND CAMPING RESORT—Continued

Pets welcome. Open Apr 15 - Oct 15. Escort to site. Clubs welcome. Rate in 2010 $30-52 per family. MC/VISA/DISC/Debit. Member ARVC, WACO.

Phone: (800)774-0535
Address: N 1005 US 12, Wisconsin Dells, WI 53965
Lat/Lon: 43.67451/-89.84117
Email: info@dellstimberland.com
Web: www.dellstimberland.com

SEE AD PAGE 829

(W) EAGLE FLATS CAMPGROUND & RV PARK—(Juneau) *From jct I-90/94 (exit 85) & US 12/16: Go 1/4 mi NW on US 12/16, then 300 feet S on CR-J. Enter on R.*

◇◇◇FACILITIES: 129 sites, typical site width 55 ft, 112 W&E, 7 E, (15/20/30 amps), 10 no hkups, many extd stay sites, 4 pull-thrus, family camping, tenting, RV's/park model rentals, dump, portable dump, laundry, ltd groc, RV supplies, ice, picnic tables, fire rings, wood.

◇◇RECREATION: equipped pavilion, swim pool, golf nearby, bsktball, play equipment, sports field, v-ball.

Pets welcome. Partial handicap access. Open May 1 - Oct 15. Clubs welcome. Rate in 2010 $26 per family.

Phone: (608)254-2764
Address: W 864 Hwy J, Wisconsin Dells, WI 53965
Lat/Lon: 43.65045/-89.81884
Web: www.dells.com/eagleflt

SEE AD PAGE 829

(NW) HOLIDAY SHORES CAMPGROUND & RESORT—(Adams) *From jct I-90/94 (exit 87) & Hwy 13: Go 7 mi E & N on Hwy 13, then 100 ft NW (left) on CR-Q, then 500 feet N on River Rd. Enter on L.*

◇◇◇◇FACILITIES: 500 sites, 186 full hkups, 303 W&E, (30/50 amps), 11 no hkups, many extd stay sites, 14 pull-thrus, WiFi Internet central location, family camping, tenting, RV's/park model rentals, cabins, RV storage, dump, portable dump, laundry, ltd groc, RV supplies, LP bottle exch, marine gas, ice, picnic tables, fire rings, wood, controlled access.

◇◇◇◇◇RECREATION: rec hall, rec room/area, equipped pavilion, coin games, swim pool, wading pool, river swim, boating, canoeing, ramp, dock, 20 pontoon/7 rowboat/6 canoe/4 pedal boat/30 motorboat rentals, river/pond fishing, fishing supplies, golf nearby, bsktball, playground, shuffleboard court 2 shuffleboard courts, activities, horseshoes, sports field, hiking trails, v-ball.

Pets welcome, quantity restrict. Partial handicap access. Open May 1 - Mid Oct. Big rigs welcome. Clubs welcome. Rate in 2010 $36-45 per family. MC/VISA/DISC/AMEX/Debit. ATM. Member ARVC, WACO.

Phone: (608)254-2717
Address: 3901 River Rd, Wisconsin Dells, WI 53965
Lat/Lon: 43.68332/-89.80612
Email: hsboat@earthlink.net
Web: www.holiday-shores.com

SEE AD PAGE 829

(NE) K & L Campground—(Adams) *From jct Hwy 13/16 & Hwy 23: Go 5 mi E on Hwy 23, then 7 mi N on CR G. Enter on L.* ◇◇◇FACILITIES: 100 sites, typical site width 40 ft, 73 full hkups, 23 W&E, (20/30 amps), 4 no hkups, family camping, tenting, dump, ltd groc. ◇◇◇RECREATION: swim pool, lake swim, boating, no motors, canoeing, dock, lake fishing, playground. Pets welcome, breed restrict, quantity restrict. Open May 1 - Sept 15. Rate in 2010 $25 per family. Member ARVC, WACO. Phone: (608)586-4720.

(W) KOA-WISCONSIN DELLS—(Sauk) *From jct I90/I94 (exit 87) & Hwy 13: Go 1-1/4 mi E on Hwy 13, then 1/4 mi N on Stand Rock Rd. Enter on L.*

◇◇◇◇FACILITIES: 123 sites, typical site width 25 ft, 48 full hkups, 60 W&E, (20/30/50 amps), 15 no hkups, 20 pull-thrus, cable TV, WiFi Instant Internet at site, family camping, tenting, RV's/park model rentals, cabins, dump, laundry, ltd groc, RV supplies, LP gas by weight/by meter, ice, picnic tables, patios, fire rings, grills, wood.

◇◇◇◇RECREATION: rec room/area, pavilion, equipped pavilion, coin games, swim pool, spray ground, golf nearby, bsktball, 6 bike rentals, playground, activities, (wkends), horseshoes, sports field, v-ball.

WISCONSIN DELLS—Continued
KOA-WISCONSIN DELLS—Continued

Pets welcome, breed restrict. Partial handicap access. Open Mid Apr - Mid Oct. Big rigs welcome. Escort to site. Clubs welcome. Rate in 2010 $31-59 for 2 persons. MC/VISA/DISC/Debit. Member ARVC, WACO. KOA discount.

Phone: (800)254-4177
Address: S235A Stand Rock Rd, Wisconsin Dells, WI 53965
Lat/Lon: 43.63677/-89.78710
Email: wd.koa@verizon.net
Web: www.WISDELLSKOA.com

SEE AD PAGE 829

(S) MIRROR LAKE SP—(Sauk) *From jct I-90/94 (exit 92) & US 12: Go 1/2 mi S on US 12, then 1-1/2 mi W on Fern Dell Rd. Enter on R.* FACILITIES: 166 sites, 47 E, (20/30 amps), 119 no hkups, tenting, dump. RECREATION: lake swim, boating, canoeing, ramp, lake fishing, playground. Partial handicap access. Open all yr. Phone: (608)254-2333.

(W) RIVER BAY RESORT CAMPGROUND, MARINA & RV PARK—(Juneau) *From jct I-90/94 (exit 85) & US 12/16: Go 2-1/2 mi NW on US 12/16, then 3/4 mi NE on 63rd St, then 1/4 mi NE on CR N. Enter on R.*

◇◇◇◇FACILITIES: 325 sites, typical site width 40 ft, 200 full hkups, 73 W&E, (20/30/50 amps), 52 no hkups, some extd stay sites, 32 pull-thrus, WiFi Instant Internet at site, family camping, tenting, RV's/park model rentals, cabins, RV storage, shower$, dump, portable dump, laundry, ltd groc, RV supplies, LP gas by weight/by meter, LP bottle exch, ice, picnic tables, fire rings, wood.

◇◇◇◇RECREATION: rec hall, rec room/area, pavilion, coin games, swim pool, river swim, boating, canoeing, kayaking, ramp, dock, 3 pontoon/6 rowboat rentals, river fishing, fishing supplies, golf nearby, bsktball, 8 bike rentals, playground, activities, (wkends), horseshoes, sports field, hiking trails, v-ball, local tours.

Pets welcome. Partial handicap access. Open Mid Apr - Mid Oct. Big rigs welcome. Clubs welcome. Rate in 2010 $41-44 per family. MC/VISA/DISC/Debit. ATM. Member ARVC, WACO.

Phone: (800)443-1112
Address: W1147 River Bay Rd, Lyndon Station, WI 53944
Lat/Lon: 43.68554/-89.83025
Email: riverbay@dells-camping.com
Web: www.dells-camping.com

SEE AD PAGE 829

ROCKY ARBOR SP—(Sauk) *From jct I-90/94 (exit 92) & US 12: Go 200 yds W on US 12, then 2 mi W on Fern Dell Rd. Enter on R.* FACILITIES: 90 sites, 19 E, 71 no hkups, tenting, dump. RECREATION: Partial handicap access. Open Memorial Wkend - Labor Day Wkend. Phone: (608)254-8001.

(W) SHERWOOD FOREST CAMPING & RV PARK—(Sauk) *From jct I-90/94 (exit 87) & Hwy 13: Go 1 mi E on Hwy 13, then 1/2 mi NW on Hwy 12/16. Enter on R.*

◇◇◇◇FACILITIES: 203 sites, typical site width 40 ft, 32 full hkups, 122 W&E, (20/30/50 amps), 49 no hkups, 23 pull-thrus, WiFi Instant Internet at site, family camping, tenting, cabins, dump, laundry, ltd groc, RV supplies, LP bottle exch, ice, picnic tables, fire rings, wood.

◇◇◇◇RECREATION: rec hall, coin games, 2 swim pools, wading pool, golf nearby, bsktball, playground, activities, (wkends), horseshoes, sports field, v-ball.

Pets welcome. Partial handicap access. Open May 1 - Oct 1. Big rigs welcome. Clubs welcome. Rate in 2010 $35-50 per family. MC/VISA/DISC/Debit. ATM. Member ARVC, WACO.

Phone: (608)254-7080
Address: S 352 Hwy 12/16, Wisconsin Dells, WI 53965
Lat/Lon: 43.63155/-89.78873
Email: info@sherwoodforestcamping.com
Web: www.sherwoodforestcamping.com

SEE AD PAGE 829

(NW) STAND ROCK CAMPGROUND—(Juneau) *From jct I-90/94 (exit 85) & US-12/16: Go 600 feet E on US-12/16, then 1mi NE on 60th St, then 600 feet N on Standrock Rd. Enter on R.*

◇◇◇◇FACILITIES: 251 sites, typical site width 40 ft, 144 full hkups, 97 W&E, (20/30/50 amps), 10 no hkups, some extd stay sites, 20 pull-thrus, WiFi Internet central location, family camping, tenting, RV storage, dump, laundry, ltd groc, RV supplies, LP gas by weight/by meter, ice, picnic tables, fire rings, wood, controlled access.

WISCONSIN DELLS—Continued
STAND ROCK CAMPGROUND—Continued

◇◇◇◇◇RECREATION: rec hall, coin games, 1 swim pools, lake/pond fishing, fishing supplies, mini-golf, ($), putting green, golf nearby, bsktball, playground, activities, (wkends), horseshoes, sports field, hiking trails, v-ball.

Pets welcome. Open Apr 15 - Oct 15. Clubs welcome. Rate in 2010 $40-43 per family. MC/VISA/DISC/Debit. Member ARVC, WACO.

Phone: (608)253-2169
Address: N570 Hwy N, Wisconsin Dells, WI 53965
Lat/Lon: 43.65812/-89.80318
Web: www.standrock.com

SEE AD PAGE 829

(NW) SUMMER BREEZE RESORT—(Juneau) *From jct I-90/94 (exit 85) & Hwy 12/16: Go 1/2 mi NW on US 12/16. Enter on R.*

◇◇◇FACILITIES: 25 sites, typical site width 30 ft, 5 full hkups, 5 W&E, (20/30/50 amps), 15 no hkups, some extd stay sites, WiFi Internet central location, family camping, tenting, dump, ice, picnic tables, fire rings, wood.

◇◇◇RECREATION: rec room/area, coin games, swim pool, golf nearby, bsktball, playground, horseshoes, hiking trails, v-ball.

Pets welcome. Open May 1 - Oct 1. Rate in 2010 $35-48 for 2 persons. MC/VISA/DISC/Debit.

Phone: (608)254-6220
Address: N530 Hwy 12 & 16, Wisconsin Dells, WI 53965
Lat/Lon: 43.65644/-89.82265
Email: summerbreezeresort@comcast.net
Web: www.summerbreezedells.com

SEE AD PAGE 829

(W) Wanna Bee Campground & RV Resort—(Columbia) *From jct I-90/94 (exit 87) & Hwy 13: Go 1/4 mi E on Hwy 13, then 2 mi SW on Trout Rd. Enter on R.* ◇◇◇FACILITIES: 109 sites, typical site width 30 ft, 37 full hkups, 28 W&E, (20/30/50 amps), 44 no hkups, 3 pull-thrus, family camping, tenting, dump, laundry, ltd groc. ◇◇◇RECREATION: swim pool, pond fishing, playground. Pets welcome. Partial handicap access. Open Mid Apr - Mid Oct. Rate in 2010 $34-43 per family. Member ARVC, WACO. Phone: (608)253-3122.

(W) WISCONSIN DELLS VISITOR & CONVENTION BUREAU—*From jct I-90/94 (exit 87) & Hwy 13: Go 1-3/4 mi E on Hwy 13, then 3 blocks S on Superior St. Enter on R.* Visitor center for the Wisconsin Dells region. Brochures, maps, schedules of events & other information available on this major tourist attraction area. Open all yr.

Phone: (608)254-8088
Address: 701 Superior St, Wisconsin Dells, WI 53965
Lat/Lon: 43.62649/-89.77541
Email: info@wisdells.com
Web: www.wisdells.com

SEE AD PAGE 829

(SW) YOGI BEAR'S JELLYSTONE PARK CAMP-RESORT—(Sauk) *From jct I-90/94 (exit 92) & US 12: Go 1/2 mi NW on US 12, then 1 mi W on Gasser Rd. Enter on R.*

◇◇◇◇◇FACILITIES: 263 sites, typical site width 50 ft, 49 full hkups, 155 W&E, (20/30/50 amps), 59 no hkups, 8 pull-thrus, WiFi Instant Internet at site, WiFi Internet central location, family camping, tenting, RV's/park model rentals, cabins, RV storage, dump, portable dump, laundry, full svc store, RV supplies, LP gas by weight/by meter, ice, picnic tables, patios, fire rings, grills, wood, controlled access.

◇◇◇◇◇RECREATION: rec hall, rec room/area, pavilion, equipped pavilion, coin games, 2 swim pools, wading pool, spray ground, lake swim, hot tub, boating, 5 hp limit, electric motors only, canoeing, dock, 8 canoe/6 pedal boat/2 motorboat rentals, lake fishing, mini-golf, ($), golf nearby, bsktball, playground, shuffleboard court 2 shuffleboard courts, activities, horseshoes, sports field, hiking trails, v-ball. Rec open to public.

Pets welcome. Partial handicap access. Open May 6 - Oct 31. Big rigs welcome. Clubs welcome. Rate in 2010 $35-109 for 4 persons. MC/VISA/DISC/Debit. ATM. Member ARVC, WACO. CCUSA 50%

YOGI BEAR'S JELLYSTONE PARK CAMP-RESORT—Continued on next page

Discount. CCUSA reservations Required, CCUSA max stay Unlimited, CCUSA disc. not avail F,Sa, CCUSA disc. not avail holidays.

Phone: (800)462-9644
Address: S 1915 Ishnala Rd., Baraboo, WI 53913
Lat/Lon: 43.7660/-89.80135
Email: reservations@dellsjellystone.com
Web: www.dellsjellystone.com

Reserve Online at Woodalls.com

SEE AD PAGE 829

(N) YUKON TRAILS CAMPING—(Juneau) *From jct I-90/94 (exit 79) & CR-HH: Go 1/2 mi N on CR-HH. Enter on R.*

◇◇◇FACILITIES: 204 sites, typical site width 50 ft, 40 ft max RV length, 134 full hkups, 61 W&E, (20/30/50 amps), 9 no hkups, many extd stay sites, 10 pull-thrus, WiFi Internet central location, family camping, tenting, cabins, RV storage, shower$, dump, portable dump, ltd groc, RV supplies, LP gas by weight, ice, picnic tables, fire rings, wood.

◇◇◇◇RECREATION: rec hall, rec room/area, equipped pavilion, coin games, swim pool, wading pool, pond fishing, mini-golf, ($), golf nearby, bsktball, playground, activities, (wkends), horseshoes, sports field, hiking trails, v-ball. Rec open to public.

Pets welcome. Open mid Apr - mid Oct. Clubs welcome. Rate in 2010 $38 per family. MC/VISA/Debit. Member ARVC, WACO.

Phone: (608)666-3261
Address: N2330 Co Rd HH, Lyndon Station, WI 53944
Lat/Lon: 43.72443/-89.88520
Email: yukon_trails@equitylifestyle.com
Web: www.yukontrailscamping.com

Reserve Online at Woodalls.com

SEE AD PAGE 829 AND AD ALGOMA PAGE 807

WISCONSIN RAPIDS—F-4

(E) SOUTH WOOD COUNTY PARK (Wood County)—(Wood) *From town: Go 5 mi SE on Hwy 13 & CR W.* FACILITIES: 73 sites, 54 E, (20/30/50 amps), 19 no hkups, 20 pull-thrus, tenting, dump. RECREATION: lake swim, boating, canoeing, ramp, lake fishing, playground. Partial handicap access. Open May 1 - Oct 31. Phone: (715)421-8422.

WONEWOC—H-3

(SE) Chapparal Campground & Restaurant—(Sauk) *From jct Hwy 58 & Hwy 33: Go 3-1/2 mi W on Hwy 33. Enter on R.* ◇◇◇◇FACILITIES: 101 sites, typical site width 40 ft, 45 full hkups, 56 W&E, (30/50 amps), 30 pull-thrus, WiFi Instant Internet at site, WiFi Internet central location, family camping, tenting, dump, laundry, ltd groc, RV supplies, ice, picnic tables, fire rings, wood. ◇◇◇◇RECREATION: rec hall, pavilion, equipped pavilion, swim pool, canoeing, float trips, river/pond fishing, bsktball, 8 bike rentals, playground, shuffleboard court shuffleboard court, activities horseshoes, hiking trails, v-ball. Pets welcome. Partial handicap access. Open Apr - Oct 31. Big rigs welcome. Rate in 2010 $29-39 for 2 persons. MC/VISA/Debit. Member ARVC, WACO. CCUSA 50% Discount. CCUSA max stay 2 days, CCUSA disc. not avail F,Sa, CCUSA disc. not avail holidays.

Phone: (888)283-0755
Address: S320 State Highway 33, Wonewoc, WI 53968
Lat/Lon: 43.63394/-90.17490
Email: chapparal@centurytel.net
Web: www.chapparal.com

WOODRUFF—C-4

(NE) Arbor Vitae Campground—(Vilas) *From jct US Hwy 51 & Hwy 70: Go 1-1/2 mi E on Hwy 70, then 1/2 mi N on Big Arbor Vitae Dr. Enter on R.* ◇◇FACILITIES: 102 sites, typical site width 20 ft, 77 full hkups, 6 W&E, 12 E, (20/30/50 amps), 7 no hkups, 14 pull-thrus, family camping, tenting, ltd groc. ◇◇◇RECREATION: lake swim, boating, dock, lake fishing, playground. Pets welcome. Open May 1 - Oct 15. Big rigs welcome. Rate in 2010 $24-28 per vehicle. Member ARVC, WACO. Phone: (715)356-5146.

(E) HIAWATHA TRAILER RESORT—(Vilas) *From jct US 51 & Hwy 47: Go 1/4 mi E on Hwy 47, then 1/2 mi N on Old Hwy 51. Enter on L.*

◇◇◇◇FACILITIES: 170 sites, typical site width 30 ft, 170 full hkups, (30/50 amps), mostly extd stay sites, 10 pull-thrus, cable TV, WiFi Internet central location, family camping, laundry, ltd groc, RV supplies, LP bottle exch, ice, picnic tables, patios, fire rings, grills, wood.

◇◇◇◇RECREATION: rec hall, rec room/area, coin games, lake swim, boating, canoeing, kayaking, ramp, dock, 2 rowboat/canoe/2 motorboat rentals, lake fishing, golf nearby, bsktball, playground, activities, horseshoes, sports field, hiking trails.

Pets welcome. Partial handicap access. No tents. Open May 1 - Oct 15. Big rigs welcome. Escort to site. Clubs welcome. Rate in 2010 $34-39 per family. MC/VISA/DISC/Debit. Member ARVC, WACO. CCUSA 50% Discount. CCUSA reservations Recommended, CCUSA max stay 2 days, CCUSA disc. not avail F,Sa. Not available Memorial Day weekend thru Labor Day or with other discounts..

Phone: (715)356-6111
Address: 1077 Old Hwy 51S, Woodruff, WI 54568
Lat/Lon: 45.90240/-89.68631
Email: info@hiawathatrailerresort@verizon.net
Web: www.hiawathatrailerresort.com

SEE AD THIS PAGE

(SE) INDIAN SHORES CAMPING, COTTAGES & RV CONDOMINIUM RESORT—(Oneida) *From jct US-51 & Hwy-47: Go 4-3/4 mi SE on Hwy-47. Enter on R.*

◇◇◇◇FACILITIES: 263 sites, typical site width 36 ft, 233 full hkups, 30 W&E, (20/30/50 amps), some extd stay sites, 11 pull-thrus, cable TV, WiFi Instant Internet at site ($), WiFi Internet central location, family camping, tenting, RV's/park model rentals, cabins, RV storage, dump, non-guest dump $, laundry, ltd groc, RV supplies, LP gas by weight/by meter, marine gas, ice, picnic tables, patios, fire rings, wood, controlled access.

◇◇◇◇◇RECREATION: rec hall, rec room/area, coin games, swim pool, lake swim, boating, canoeing, kayaking, ramp, dock, 2 pontoon/3 rowboat/6 canoe/2 pedal boat/6 motorboat rentals, lake fishing, fishing supplies, mini-golf, ($), golf nearby, bsktball, play equipment, 4 shuffleboard courts, activities, tennis, horseshoes, sports field, hiking trails, v-ball.

Pets welcome. Partial handicap access. Open May 1 - Nov 1. Big rigs welcome. Escort to site. Clubs welcome. Rate in 2010 $32-77 for 2 persons. MC/VISA/DISC/Debit. Member ARVC, WACO. CCUSA 50% Discount. CCUSA reservations Recommended, CCUSA max stay 2 days, CCUSA disc. not avail F,Sa. Not available Memorial Day weekend thru Labor Day or with other discounts..

Phone: (715)356-5552
Address: 7880 Indian Shores, Woodruff, WI 54568
Lat/Lon: 45.83908/-89.64547
Email: info@indian-shores.com
Web: www.indian-shores.com

SEE AD THIS PAGE

(SE) NORTHERN HIGHLAND/AMERICAN LEGION SF (Buffalo Lake)—(Oneida) *From town: Go 6 mi E on CR J.* FACILITIES: 52 sites, 20 ft max RV length, 52 no hkups, tenting. RECREATION: lake swim, boating, ramp, dock, lake fishing. Open all yr. Phone: (715)385-3352.

(SE) NORTHERN HIGHLAND/AMERICAN LEGION SF (Clear Lake)—(Oneida) *4 mi SE on Hwy-47.* FACILITIES: 98 sites, 98 no hkups, tenting, dump. RECREATION: lake swim, boating, ramp, dock, lake fishing. Partial handicap access. Open all yr. Phone: (715)385-3352.

Wisconsin State Flower: Wood Violet

NORTHERN HIGHLAND/AMERICAN LEGION SF (Crystal-Muskie)—(Vilas) *6 mi NE via US-51, then 3 mi NE on CR-"M", then 2 mi E on CR-"N".* FACILITIES: 181 sites, 181 no hkups, tenting. RECREATION: lake swim, boating, ramp, dock, lake fishing. Partial handicap access. Open all yr. Facilities fully operational Apr - Dec. Phone: (715)385-3352.

(SE) NORTHERN HIGHLAND/AMERICAN LEGION SF (Indian Mounds)—(Oneida) *5 mi SE on Hwy-47.* FACILITIES: 39 sites, 39 no hkups, tenting. RECREATION: lake swim, boating, ramp, dock, lake fishing. Open Apr - Dec. Phone: (715)385-3352.

NORTHERN HIGHLAND/AMERICAN LEGION SF (North Trout Lake)—(Vilas) *From town: Go 6 mi N on US 51, then 6 mi N on CR M.* FACILITIES: 48 sites, 48 no hkups, tenting, dump. RECREATION: lake swim, boating, lake fishing. Open all yr. Phone: (715)385-2727.

Visit Cave of the Mounds, near Blue Mounds, to see beautiful underground rock formations.

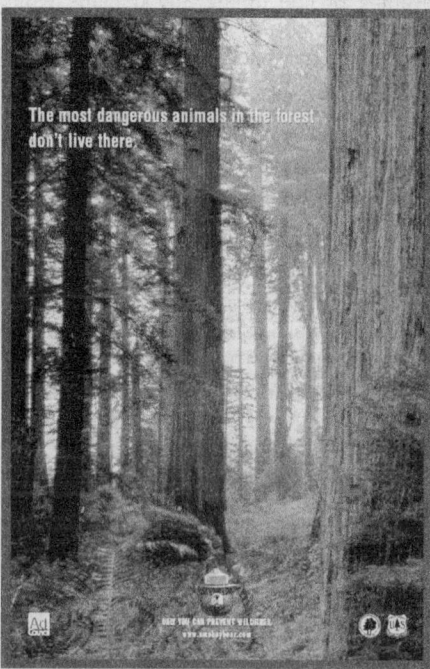

CROSSING INTO Canada

So... you're planning a visit to our neighbors up north. From the rugged sea-swept coastlines to the beautiful Canadian Rockies, you'll find unlimited avenues of adventure. Cosmopolitan cities greet visitors with an evening of fine dining and dancing while charming homespun villages sell intricate arts and crafts particular to their cultural heritage.

It is indeed a different country. One certainly worth exploration. But before you and your rig hit the road, we'd like to clarify a few of the requirements associated with traveling to another country.

Is identification required?

Visitors from all countries including the U.S. need a valid passport to enter Canada by air or sea travel. The Western Hemisphere Travel Initiative will require all Western Hemisphere travelers including land border travelers to have a passport or other accepted form of documentation to enter or re-enter the United States by June 1, 2009. Start your application early as there is a long wait. Other documentation may be required, such as a visa or alien card. Check with a Canadian embassy for more information. Currently, U.S. land border travelers are required to provide proof of citizenship upon entry into Canada. Please ensure you have either a valid passport or picture ID along with either a birth certificate or a voter registration card. Photocopies are not accepted. If under 18 you must be with a legal adult who has a signed letter of consent from your parents or legal guardian stating who you are traveling with, how long you will be there, where you are going, etc. Customs on both sides of the border will ask for this letter. Customs may want to contact the parent back home as well. Both the U.S. and Canadian governments urge frequent travelers to join the NEXUS trusted traveler program. NEXUS members receive a special travel card that allows expedited border crossings for both private and commercial travelers through both U.S. and Canadian border controls very quickly.

For more information contact: **Canada Immigration Division, Canada Employment and Immigration Centre**, Ottawa, ON, K1A 0J9 or the U.S. National Passport Information Center: (877) 4USA-PPT.

Is auto insurance required? Will I need a vehicle permit?

A valid driver's license from any country is good in Canada for three months. Car insurance is mandatory. Many visitors choose to carry a Canadian Non-Resident Insurance Card. Valid anywhere in Canada, the card is proof of financial responsibility and is available only in the U.S. through insurance companies.

Motor vehicle and RV registration cards should be carried with you. If the vehicle is registered to someone else, you should have a letter from that person stating authorization of use.

If you plan to leave your vacation trailer in Canada when returning home, ask Canada Customs for an E99 permit. Make a note of the expiration date and post the permit in the window of the trailer so it can be easily seen. Keep in mind, you cannot store a vacation trailer in Canada during the off-season.

If you need to leave your boat or boat trailer during the off-season, be prepared to prove that maintenance work is being undertaken by a bona fide marina or service depot. Customs will require a copy of a work order from the establishment handling the repairs. This work order must contain a description of the article, owner's name and address, type of work to be done and the time and location at which the work will be effected.

Will my health insurance be honored at Canadian hospitals?

You will not be refused treatment at Canadian hospitals; however, you may be liable for the cost. Most health coverage does not extend outside the country of residence. Visitors to Canada should obtain insurance before leaving home.

Are there any restrictions as to what I can bring across the border?

Personal baggage (in reasonable quantities) is duty-free, provided all items are declared upon entry and are for your own personal use (not intended for resale). Personal items include camping, fishing and other recreational equipment, boats & motors, cameras, typewriters, musical instruments and consumable goods. Any gasoline or oil imported, beyond the normal capacity of your vehicle, is subject to duty. Americans may bring up to $60 in gifts per recipient (excluding alcohol and tobacco.) All drugs and medicinals must be declared when crossing the border. A good rule of thumb is to only take with you what you will need while you are on your trip. These items must be carried in their original containers, and carrying a prescription or written statement from your physician that the substances are being used under a doctor's supervision, and are necessary for your physical well being is strongly recommended. Travelers must take note, in virtually all instances; individual citizens are prohibited from importing prescription drugs into the U.S. For further information regarding this, travelers are urged to call 202-307-2414 prior to crossing the border.

Alcohol and tobacco products

Visitors may import with a minimum of 48 hrs. length of absence, duty free, the following: a maximum of 1.5 liters (40 ounces) of liquor, 1.5 liters of wine, or 8.5 liters of beer or ale. If you're 18 or over, you can transport duty-free 100 cigars (not of Cuban origin), 200 cigarettes, 200 grams of tobacco and 200 tobacco sticks. Federal taxes and duties will apply on additional goods brought into Canada. Visitors who include tobacco products in personal exemptions will still have to pay a minimum duty on these products unless they are marked "Canada Duty Paid – Droit Acquitte." All provincial taxes and duties will also be levied on all foreign tobacco products.

Fireworks

All fireworks need authorization to be imported into Canada. An Explosives Importation Permit can be acquired by contacting: Chief Inspector of Explosives, Explosives Branch, Energy, Mines & Resources Canada, 580 Booth St., Ottawa, ON, Canada K1A 0E4.

Is money the same in Canada as in the U.S.?

The unit of currency is the Canadian dollar, which amounts to 100 cents. Monetary units are 1 and 2 dollar coins, 5, 10, 20, 50 and 100 dollar bill denominations. Banking hours vary, but are generally Monday-Friday, 9 a.m. to 5 p.m.; however, some banks are open on Saturday. Banks are not open on official Canadian holidays. At any bank or ATM machine, you can withdraw Canadian funds from a foreign currency account.

To get the best rate of exchange, change your traveler's checks into Canadian currency at a Canadian bank just after you cross the border. For the latest exact exchange rates, go to http://www.gocanada.com.

Credit Card & Debit Cards

Many stores, restaurants and accommodations in Canada accept major credit cards (e.g. Visa, MasterCard, American Express) as well as debit cards.

Credit and debit card charges will appear on your statement converted to your home currency. Be prepared for a pleasant surprise—the currency exchange rate is usually one of the best.

What is "duty" and "GST"?

"Duty" is the same as tax. Duty-free means you won't be taxed on the items.

The Goods and Services Tax (GST) is a Canada-wide 7% tax charged on non-essential items. Visitors to Canada can apply for a GST rebate if they are not residents of Canada and they made the eligible purchases while in Canada. Goods qualify for a rebate if: 1) You have original receipts with proof of export 2) Your purchase amounts (before taxes) total at least $200 Canadian. 3) Each individual receipt shows a minimum purchase amount (before taxes) on which you paid GST of $50. There is no rebate on items such as meals, entertainment, liquor, tobacco and gasoline. There are time limits for applying and as the visitor rebate program is being revised, check for further information before applying for a refund at 800/668-4748 (in Canada) or 902/432-5608 (outside Canada) or www.rc.gc.ca.

Are there limitations as to what I can bring home?

When re-entering the U.S., be sure to list your purchases, have your sales receipts handy and pack your purchases separately for convenience of inspection.

If you've been in Canada more than 48 hours, you may bring back, duty-free, $800 (based on fair retail value in Canada) worth of articles for personal or household use. If less than 48 hours, the maximum is $200. If purchases exceed the $200 exemption, you lose the exemption and all purchases become subject to duty. Also considered duty-free are 100 non-Cuban cigars, one liter of alcohol and one carton of cigarettes.

Any purchases in excess of the allowances may be subject to duties and taxes.

There are restrictions on exporting objects over 50 years old that are of historical, cultural or scientific significance. Items subject to export permit requirements include fossils, archaeological artifacts, fine and decorative art, technological objects, books and archival material.

If you plan to bring fresh fruits, vegetables or meat into the United States, contact APHIS (Animal and Plant Inspection Service) and get a copy of Traveler's Tips, which lists what you can and can't bring and also items for which you'll need a permit. The plants, cuttings, seeds, unprocessed plant products and certain endangered species that are allowed into the United States require import permits; some are prohibited entirely. Every single plant or plant product must be declared to the Customs officer and must be presented for USDA inspection.

For more information contact:

USDA-APHIS Veterinary Services, National Center for Import/Export (NCIE), 4700 River Road, Unit 40, Riverdale, MD 20737-1231; 301/734-7830/8295.

We live in Canada and are returning home from the States. What are we allowed to bring back?

That depends on how long you've been gone. If you've been out of Canada for 24 hours you may bring back goods worth up to CAN$50, duty-free. If you've been away for 48 hours or more you can bring back up to CAN$400 and after 7 days away you can bring in duty-free goods worth up to CAN$750. A minimum duty will apply to cigarettes, tobacco sticks and loose tobacco.

What about sending gifts to our friends in the States?

Mark the package "Unsolicited Gift" and list the contents and fair retail value. If the retail value isn't over CAN$60, you can send it tax-free. If it's over CAN $60, you will have to pay duties and taxes on the excess amount. You cannot claim alcoholic beverages, tobacco products, or advertising matter as gifts.

Do the RV parks in Canada differ from those in the U.S.?

Not really. Canada has an extensive system of RV parks and campgrounds ranging from rustic fishing and hunting camps to fully-equipped luxury resorts.

Where available, electrical hookups are usually of the 15-amp, two-wire type, furnishing 115 volt, 60 cycle AC. Many parks offer full 30-amp electrical service and some offer 50-amp. Water taps are standard thread and sewer drops and will usually accept the standard 3-inch hose, although a cushion seal or a threaded adapter may be required in some instances.

Parks Canada allows campers to make reservations in multiple national park campgrounds through one toll-free phone call or Web site visit. To find out about participating national parks and make reservations, visit their website at: www.pccamping.ca or call 877/737-3783 (877/RESERVE), a toll-free number to a call-centre (in operation 12 hours a day).

Are traffic rules the same?

Yes and no. In some provinces, the use of radar warning devices is illegal. In some provinces, even the possession of radar warning devices is illegal. Police officers can confiscate such devices and fine violators.

Seat belt use is mandatory for all drivers and passengers in Canada. Don't forget car seats for youngsters. In Yukon, children under 48 lbs. or 6 years of age must use an approved child restraint device. While traveling on Yukon highways, the law requires the use of headlights at all times.

Could you explain the Metric System?

Distance & Speed Limits (Kilometers):

Kilometers refer to both distance and speed. A kilometer is approximately 5/8 mile. To convert miles to kilometers: number of miles x 1.6 = kilometers; and number of kilometers x 0.62 = miles.

Temperature (Celsius):

9/5 x 0C + 32 = Fahrenheit

F - 32 x 5/9 = Celsius

Gasoline: Gas and oil are sold in Canada by the liter. One U.S. gallon is approximately 3.8 liters. (One Imperial gallon is approximately 4.5 liters.)

What about firearms?

All firearms and weapons must be declared to Customs at the first point of entry. A non-restricted firearm is a regular sporting rifle or a shotgun with a barrel over 470 mm (18.5 in.) and an overall of 660 mm (26 in.) which does not fall into the category of a prohibited or restricted firearm. It is illegal to import any revolvers, pistols, replica firearms or fully automatic firearms into Canada. A non-restricted firearm may only be imported for sporting or hunting use while in Canada, for use in competitions, or for an in-transit move through Canada. Any restricted firearms may be shipped in bond via a commercial carrier to the person's destination. Visitors bringing non-restricted firearms into Canada must complete a Firearms Declaration Form. For more information regarding restricted and unrestricted firearms, please contact: Canadian Firearms Centre, 239 Wellington, Ottawa, ON K1A 0H8, 800/731-4000 or www.cfc.gc.ca.

Am I allowed to bring my pet?

All pets must be accompanied by their owners and must have a certificate issued by a licensed veterinarian clearly identifying the pet and certifying that it has been vaccinated against rabies within the preceding 36 months. Collar tags alone don't count. Exceptions are made for Seeing-eye dogs and puppies or kittens younger than 3 months old. If your family pet is somewhat unusual (a ferret, for example), check if a permit is required.

Provincial Veterinary Service, Government of Newfoundland, PO Box 7400, St. John's West, NL AIE 3Y5.

Where can I write for more information?

For information on joining a Canadian auto club (or whether or not your current club is an affiliate member–qualifying you for membership services):

Canadian Automobile Assn., 1775 Courtwood Crescent, Ottawa, ON K2C 3J2.

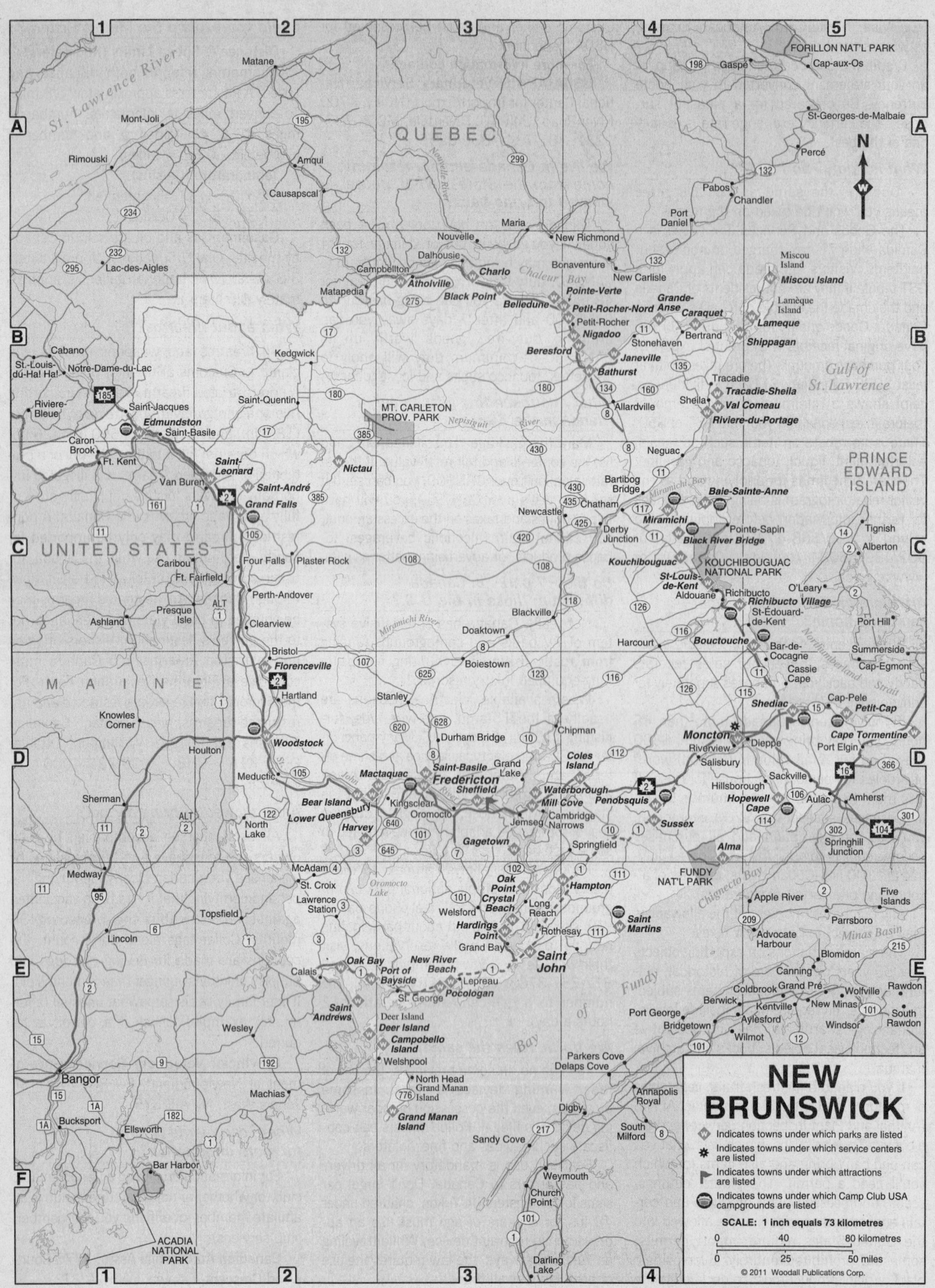
NEW BRUNSWICK
Indicates towns under which parks are listed
Indicates towns under which service centers are listed
Indicates towns under which attractions are listed
Indicates towns under which Camp Club USA campgrounds are listed
SCALE: 1 inch equals 73 kilometres
0 40 80 kilometres
0 25 50 miles
© 2011 Woodall Publications Corp.
QUEBEC
UNITED STATES
MAINE
PRINCE EDWARD ISLAND
St. Lawrence River
Gulf of St. Lawrence
Chaleur Bay
Miramichi Bay
Northumberland Strait
Chignecto Bay
Minas Basin
Bay of Fundy
Nouvelle River
Nepisiguit River
Miramichi River
St. John River
Oromocto Lake
FORILLON NAT'L PARK
Cap-aux-Os
Gaspé
St-Georges-de-Malbaie
Percé
Chandler
Pabos
Port Daniel
Matane
Mont-Joli
Rimouski
Amqui
Causapscal
Lac-des-Aigles
Maria
New Richmond
Nouvelle
Bonaventure
New Carlisle
Campbellton
Dalhousie
Matapedia
Atholville
Charlo
Black Point
Belledune
Pointe-Verte
Petit-Rocher-Nord
Petit-Rocher
Nigadoo
Beresford
Janeville
Bathurst
Allardville
Grande-Anse
Caraquet
Bertrand
Stonehaven
Miscou Island
Lamèque Island
Lameque
Shippagan
Tracadie
Tracadie-Sheila
Sheila
Val Comeau
Riviere-du-Portage
Neguac
Cabano
St.-Louis-du-Ha! Ha!
Notre-Dame-du-Lac
Riviere-Bleue
Saint-Jacques
Edmundston
Saint-Basile
Caron Brook
Ft. Kent
Van Buren
Saint-Leonard
Saint-André
Grand Falls
Kedgwick
Saint-Quentin
MT. CARLETON PROV. PARK
Nictau
Bartibog Bridge
Chatham
Newcastle
Baie-Sainte-Anne
Miramichi
Derby Junction
Pointe-Sapin
Black River Bridge
KOUCHIBOUGUAC NATIONAL PARK
Kouchibouguac
St-Louis-de-Kent
Aldouane
Richibucto
Richibucto Village
St-Édouard-de-Kent
Bouctouche
Bar-de-Cocagne
Cassie Cape
Tignish
Alberton
O'Leary
Port Hill
Summerside
Cap-Egmont
Caribou
Ft. Fairfield
Four Falls
Plaster Rock
Perth-Andover
Presque Isle
Ashland
Clearview
Blackville
Doaktown
Harcourt
Bristol
Florenceville
Boiestown
Hartland
Stanley
Knowles Corner
Woodstock
Houlton
Durham Bridge
Chipman
Shediac
Petit-Cap
Cape Tormentine
Port Elgin
Moncton
Dieppe
Riverview
Salisbury
Meductic
Saint-Basile
Fredericton
Mactaquac
Sheffield
Grand Lake
Coles Island
Waterborough
Mill Cove
Penobsquis
Sussex
Hillsborough
Hopewell Cape
Sackville
Aulac
Amherst
Springhill Junction
Sherman
Bear Island
Lower Queensbury
Harvey
Kingsclear
Oromocto
North Lake
Jemseg
Cambridge Narrows
Gagetown
Springfield
Alma
FUNDY NAT'L PARK
Medway
McAdam
St. Croix
Lawrence Station
Oak Point
Crystal Beach
Hampton
Long Reach
Welsford
Hardings Point
Rothesay
Grand Bay
Saint John
Saint Martins
Apple River
Five Islands
Parrsboro
Advocate Harbour
Topsfield
Lincoln
Calais
Oak Bay
Port of Bayside
New River Beach
Lepreau
St. George
Pocologan
Saint Andrews
Blomidon
Canning
Grand Pré
Coldbrook
Wolfville
Rawdon
Berwick
Kentville
New Minas
South Rawdon
Port George
Aylesford
Windsor
Bridgetown
Wilmot
Deer Island
Campobello Island
Welshpool
Wesley
Parkers Cove
Delaps Cove
Bangor
North Head
Grand Manan Island
Machias
Annapolis Royal
Digby
Bucksport
Ellsworth
South Milford
Sandy Cove
Bar Harbor
Weymouth
Church Point
ACADIA NATIONAL PARK
Darling Lake

CAMPING FEES

Camping fees in New Brunswick listings are stated in Canadian dollars. Fees are quoted before taxes. Call each location for details as they vary from province to province.

TIME ZONE

New Brunswick is in the Atlantic Time Zone.

TOPOGRAPHY

The largest of the three Maritime provinces, New Brunswick has a land area of 28,354 square miles. In the northern part of the province, the terrain is largely mountainous. The interior portion of the province is mostly rolling plateau, the north and east are fairly flat and the south is rugged. The highest point in New Brunswick is 2,690-foot Mount Carleton in Mount Carleton Provincial Park.

TEMPERATURE

New Brunswick has a blend of climates typical of a coastal area and an island province. Summers are typically warm and comfortable—but not too hot. Many pleasant but cooler days are experienced in spring and autumn.

TRAVEL & TOURISM INFO

Provincial Agency:

New Brunswick Dept. of Tourism and Parks
PO Box 12345
Campbellton, NB E3N 3T6
(800/561-0123)
www.TourismNewBrunswick.ca

Regional Agencies:

Albert County Tourism Assn.
5526 Route 114
Hopewell Hill, NB E4H 3N5
(506/882-2349)
www.albertcountytourism.com

Association Touristique de la Péninsule Acadienne
35 Avenue du Carrefour
Caraquet, NB E1W 1B6
(506/726-2676)
www.peninsuleacadienne.ca

Association Touristique de la Région de Kent
59 Irving Boulevard, Suite 201
Bouctouche, NB E4S 3J6
(506/743-7337)
www.kent.nb.ca

Association Touristique du Restigouche
P.O. Box / C.P. 114
Campbellton, NB E3N 3G1
www.destinationrestigouche.ca

Office Du Tourisme Edmundston Madawaska
121 Victoria Street
Edmundston, NB E3V 2H5
(506/737-1850)
www.republiquemadawaska.com

Grand Manan Tourism Association
1141 Route 776
Grand Manan, NB E5G 4E9
(506/662-3442)
www.grandmanannb.com

Greater Woodstock T ourism Partnership
Woodstock, NB E7M 1A1
(506/325-4600)
www.town.woodstock.nb.ca

Deer Island Tourism Association
C/o Brenda M Cline
21 Cedar Grove Road
Fairhaven, Deer Island, NB E5V 1N3
www.deerisland.nb.ca

Local Agencies:

City of Dieppe
333 Avenue Acadie
Dieppe, NB E1A 1G9
(506/877-7900)
www.dieppe.ca

QUICK REFERENCE CHART FOR WOODALL'S FEATURED PARKS

	Green Friendly	RV Lots for Sale	Park Models-Onsite Ownership	Park Membership for Sale	Big Rigs Welcome	Internet Friendly	Pets Welcome
EDMUNDSTON							
Camping Panoramic 86					▲	●	■
HARDINGS POINT							
Hardings Point Campground					▲	●	■
HOPEWELL CAPE							
Ponderosa Pines Campground					▲	●	■
SAINT-JOHN							
Rockwood Park Campground						●	■
SHEDIAC							
South Cove Rive - Sud Camping & Golf					▲	●	■
SHEFFIELD							
Casey's Campground							■

Green Friendly ; RV Lots for Sale ✖; Park Models/Onsite Onwership ✱; Park Memberships for Sale ✔; Big Rigs Welcome ▲; Internet Friendly ●; Internet Friendly-WiFi ●; Pets Welcome ■

City of Fredericton
PO Box 130, 11 Carleton St.
Fredericton, NB E3B 4Y7
(506/460-2041 or 888/888-4768)
www.tourismfredericton.ca

City of Miramichi/Community Dev. Tourism
141 Henry Street
Miramichi, NB E1V 2N5
(506/623-2200)
www.miramichi.org

City of Moncton
655 Main St.
Moncton, NB E1C 1E8
(800/363-4558)
www.gomoncton.com

City of Saint John
PO Box 1971
Saint John, NB E2L 4L1
(866/463-8639)
www.tourismsaintjohn.com

Where to Find CCUSA Parks

List City	Park Name	Map Coordinates
BAIE SAINTE-ANNE		
	Escuminac Beach & Family Park	C-4
	Sandy Point Park	C-4
BLACK RIVER BRIDGE		
	Camping Near Miramichi	C-4
BOUCTOUCHE		
	Bouctouche Bay Campground & Chalets	C-5
EDMUNDSTON		
	Riverside (Iroquois) RV Park	B-1
FREDERICTON		
	Woolastook Park	D-3
GRAND FALLS		
	Mulherin's Campground	C-2
HOPEWELL CAPE		
	Ponderosa Pines Campground	D-5
MIRAMICHI		
	Enclosure Campground	C-4
PENOBSQUIS		
	Lone Pine Park Campground & Cabins	D-4
PETIT CAP		
	Silver Sands Family Camping	D-5
RICHIBOUCTOU-VILLAGE		
	Camping Cap Lumiere Beach (Not Visited)	C-4
SHEDIAC		
	Etoile Filante Camping Wishing Star	D-5
	Ocean View Park	D-5
	South Cove Rive - Sud Camping & Golf	D-5
ST. MARTINS		
	Sea Side Tent & Trailer Park	E-4
WOODSTOCK		
	Cosy Cabins Campground	D-2

BUSINESSES OFFERING

	Things to See & Do	RV Sales	RV Service
MONCTON			
Ed's Travel Trailer Parts & Service		🚌	✻
SHEDIAC			
South Cove Rive-Sud Golf	⚑		
SHEFFIELD			
Casey's Artisans	⚑		
Casey's Museum	⚑		
Casey's Restaurant	⚑		

RECREATIONAL INFO

Bicycling: For information on competitive cycling, contact Velo NB Inc., 536 McAllister Road, Riverview, NB E1B 4G1. www.velo.nb.ca

Canoeing: Canoe New Brunswick, www.canoekayaknb.org

Fishing & Hunting: Dept. of Natural Resources, Box 6000, Fredericton, NB E3B 5H1 (506/453-2207). www.gnb.ca/0078/index-e.asp

Golf New Brunswick: (877/TEE-IN-NB) www.golfnb.com

DESTINATIONS

ACADIAN COASTAL DRIVE

From the southern town of Aulac all the way up the coast to Campbellton, travelers will not only enjoy fantastic seascapes, tempting seafood and sandy beaches, but will also be treated to a rich and unique culture.

Aquarium & Marine Centre, Shippagan. Learn about the marine animals that inhabit the Gulf of St. Lawrence through aquarium displays and a "Please Touch Me Tank."

Cape Jourimain Nature Centre is an environmental education facility with an interpretation centre, observation tower, lighthouse and exhibits. Walk out on an ice flow with an iceboat crew or take part in an interactive exhibit at the bird theatre.

Caraquet. This lovely coastal town is home to many artists and artisans. Caraquet also has one of the largest commercial fishing fleets in New Brunswick.

Village Historique Acadien near Caraquet. Costumed "residents" carry on the daily tasks of yesteryear within this working village. Watch the blacksmith, cobbler, weaver, wheelwright, broom maker and printer demonstrate their skills.

Irving Eco-Centre, La Dune de Bouctouche is located north of Bouctouche. Part of New Brunswick's Great Outdoors, this eco-tourism site is one of the few remaining great sand dunes on the northeastern coast of North America. A boardwalk allows you to observe a variety of plants, animals and birds, while protecting its fragile ecology.

Kingsbrae Garden, St. Andrews. This enchanting horticulture masterpiece on Passamaquoddy Bay was named one of Canada's top 10 public gardens.

Kouchibouguac National Park. The largest park in the province, encompassing 92-square miles of forests, salt marshes, beaches and miles of shoreline dunes. Open year-round, this park entices hikers, birdwatchers, cyclists, campers, canoeists and swimmers. Wide boardwalks allow visitors to get close to nature without disturbing habitats.

Le Pays de la Sagouine, Bouctouche. Discover the unique Acadian culture in this natural village setting alive with theatre, music, comedy and dance.

Plage de L'Aboiteau is located at the western end of Cap-Pelé. You'll have an unforgettable adventure at this entertainment and eco-tourism center. Observe waterfowl as you stroll along the marshes on the boardwalk. Enjoy the beach complex, live entertainment and Acadian hospitality.

Parlee Beach Provincial Park, Shediac area. Swim in the warmest salt water north of Virginia. Volleyball, touch football tournaments, golf and the annual sand-sculpture contest and triathlon are all here for your enjoyment.

RIVER VALLEY SCENIC DRIVE

One of the great wonders of the region, the St. John River encompasses 250 miles of rolling water that nourishes some of the most fertile farm land in Canada. Following the American Revolution, thousands of Loyalist refugees arrived from the colonies in the U.S. in order to remain loyal to the British establishment, and settled in this region.

Edmundston, capital of the mythical "Republic of Madawaska," is located among the hills where the Madawaska River flows into the St. John. The Madawaska Museum presents local history, traveling displays and the **Galerie Colline**.

Fredericton. Walking tours of New Brunswick's capital feature costumed tour guides. Noteworthy attractions include: **Christ Church Cathedral**, the **Legislative Assembly of New Brunswick**, the **University of New Brunswick** and the historic **Garrison District** and officers' barracks.

Grand Falls Gorge, Grand Falls/Grand Sault. The largest waterfalls in New Brunswick have carved out a most unique natural feature known simply as the "gorge," encircling half the town. Take time to explore the walking trails around the gorge.

Kings Landing Historical Settlement is located west of Fredericton. This living museum re-creates the sights, sounds and society of rural New Brunswick in the 1800s. See furnishings, tools and fashions of the period and try your hand at churning butter or pitching hay.

Saint-Jacques, just 7 km north of Edmundston, is home to the **New Brunswick Botanical Garden**. Spread over 7 hectares, over 80,000 plants are represented.

St. Stephen is the home of **Ganong's Chocolate Factory**, originators of the first 5¢ wrapped milk chocolate bar back in 1910. A chocolate festival is held every August.

MIRAMICHI RIVER ROUTE

Atlantic Salmon Museum, Doaktown. Extensive collection of artifacts connected with the salmon including artificial flies, fishing rods, accessories and clothing. Children can learn casting, fly tying and fishing.

Central New Brunswick Woodmen's Museum, Boiestown. Explores the woodman's way of life by visiting16 buildings including a 100-year-old trapper's cabin and a cookhouse-bunkhouse-dingle. Stories of the Miramichi Fire, Peter Emberley, the Dungarvon Whooper and the TBM Avenger 14.

City of Miramichi. Home to the Atlantic salmon, the mighty Miramichi River has attracted anglers from all over the world. Outfitters are plentiful along the river system.

Historic Garrison District, Fredericton. Set back behind a wrought iron and stone fence, this National Historic Site includes museums, galleries, shops, daily changing of the guards and more.

Sackville Waterfowl Park, Sackville. Boardwalks and walkways provide a means of viewing the marsh environment.

FUNDY COASTAL DRIVE

Twice daily, 100 billion tons of tidal water flow in and out of the Bay's funnel-like opening – an amount of water equal to all the rivers on the planet!

Cape Enrage. Enjoy one of the best views in Canada from atop 150-foot cliffs. There is a panoramic view of the entire bay from Apple River to Dorchester to Quaco. Outdoor adventures include cliff climbing, kayaking and cave exploration.

Fundy Isles. Composed of Grand Manan, Deer and Campobello Islands, the Fundy Isles offer unlimited recreation. "Must do" attractions include bird and whale-watching expeditions. Thousands of aquatic and bird species and over 15 types of whales are in this area. Other scenic options include pleasure cruises and bicycle or kayak rentals.

Fundy National Park. Discover the beaches, forest and the history of the Fundy Coast; or for the more active, experience camping, golf, swimming, tennis and lawn bowling.

Hartland Covered Bridge "National Historic Site," over 100-years old, is the longest covered bridge in the world (1282 feet), crossing the St. John River.

Moncton is the home of incredible natural attractions. The Tidal Bore occurs twice daily and is best seen from **Tidal Bore Park** on Main Street (at the corner of King). Watch as the waters in the bay cause the water in the placid Petitcodiac River to roll back upstream. For family fun, visit **Magic Mountain Water Theme Park** and tube the lazy river, ride a kamikaze waterslide or bob in the wave pool.

The Hopewell Rocks is located near Hopewell Cape, just south of Moncton. It offers a fantastic view of giant rock formations shaped by years of Fundy Tides. When the tide is out, you can actually walk along the floor of the bay and explore caves and tunnels at the base of the "flowerpot" rocks.

Magnetic Hill escapes the law of gravity. Put your vehicle in neutral, release the brake and watch in amazement as you coast uphill! Visit **Magnetic Hill Zoo** – 400+ animals from over 90 different species in a 40-acre facility.

Saint John. Canada's oldest incorporated city provides a good vantage point for watching the Bay of Fundy tides meet the waters of the St. John River. When the Fundy tides peak, the St. John retreats, creating one of the few places in the world where you can see a river actually reverse its flow at **Reversing Falls**. Walking tours of the city produce such sights as **Barbour's General Store Museum**, an authentic 19th-century general store, the **Saint John City Market** (built in 1875-76); the **Loyalist House & Burial Ground**; the **New Brunswick Museum**; **Cherry Brook Zoo**; and **Market Square**, a shopping and convention center. **Irving Nature Park** is a year-round naturalists' paradise with 600 acres of winding roads, nature trails and rugged coastline.

APPALACHIAN RANGE ROUTE

This region of Canada is maple syrup country, and travelers will find themselves amidst a breathtaking landscape older than the Himalayas.

Sugarloaf Provincial Park. The recreational opportunities of Sugarloaf Park include a chairlift, which travels 155 meters up the ski-hill for a breathtaking view. The lift also enhances the park's many bird watching opportunities.

Mount Carleton. Part of the famed Appalachian Range and the highest peak in the Maritimes, Mt. Carleton features extraordinary fishing, boating and bird watching opportunities. An extensive network of hiking trails challenges both novices and experts.

ANNUAL EVENTS

FEBRUARY

Hubcap Comedy Festival, Moncton; Regional Sno-Fest, Campbellton.

MARCH

Dalhousie's Winterfest, Dalhousie.

APRIL

Maple Sugar Festival, Riverview; Greater Moncton Music Festival, Moncton; Wine and Food Fest, Fredericton; Frye Festival, Moncton; New Brunswick Competitive Festival of Music, Various locations.

New Brunswick

ALMA—D-4

(W) FUNDY NATIONAL PARK (Chignecto North)—(Albert) *From town: Go 4 km/2-1/2 mi W on Hwy 114.* FACILITIES: 264 sites, 10 full hkups, 127 W&E, 127 no hkups, tenting, dump, laundry. RECREATION: canoeing, playground. Pets welcome. Partial handicap access. Open May 15 - Oct 12. Phone: (506)887-6000.

(W) FUNDY NATIONAL PARK (Headquarters Campground)—(Albert) *From town: Go 3/4 km/1/2 mi E on Hwy 114.* FACILITIES: 124 sites, 29 full hkups, 95 no hkups, 29 pull-thrus, tenting, dump, laundry. RECREATION: swim pool, canoeing, playground. Partial handicap access. Open Jun 25 - Sep 7. Phone: (506)887-6000.

(W) FUNDY NATIONAL PARK (Point Wolfe Campground)—*From jct Hwy 114 & Point Wolfe Rd: Go 8-3/4 km/5-1/2 mi S on Point Wolfe Rd.* FACILITIES: 178 sites, 24 ft max RV length, 178 no hkups, tenting. RECREATION: saltwater swim, canoeing, playground. Partial handicap access. Open Jun 25 - Sep 7. Phone: (506)887-6000.

(NW) FUNDY NATIONAL PARK (Wolfe Lake Campground)—*From town: Go 19-1/4 km/12 mi W on Hwy 114 to west entrance to park.* FACILITIES: 20 sites, 20 no hkups, tenting. RECREATION: lake swim. Open May 1 - Oct 31. Phone: (506) 887-6000.

ATHOLVILLE—B-3

SUGARLOAF PROVINCIAL PARK—(Restigouche) *From town: Go 3/4 km/1/2 mi S on Rte 270. Enter on L.* FACILITIES: 76 sites, typical site width 10 ft, 21 ft max RV length, 8 full hkups, 57 W&E, (15/30 amps), 11 no hkups, 5 pull-thrus, tenting, dump, laundry, ltd groc. RECREATION: play equipment. Pets welcome. Partial handicap access. Open all yr. Member COA of NB. Phone: (506)789-2366.

BAIE SAINTE-ANNE—C-4

(E) Escuminac Beach & Family Park—(Northumberland) *On Hwy 117 & jct Escuminac Point: Go 3 km/2 mi E on Escuminac Point. Enter on L.* ◆◆FACILITIES: 45 sites, 25 W&E, (15 amps), 20 no hkups, tenting, dump, non-guest dump $, portable dump, laundry, ice, picnic tables, fire rings, wood. ◆◆RECREATION: saltwater swim, saltwater fishing, play equipment, horseshoes, v-ball. Pets welcome. Open May 17 - Oct 10. Rate in 2010 $24 for 4 persons. VISA. Member COA of NB. CCUSA 50% Discount. CCUSA reservations Recommended, CCUSA max stay 2 days, Cash only for CCUSA disc. Discount not available Jul & Aug.

CAMPCLUB USA

Phone: (506)228-4532
Address: 301 Escuminac Point Rd, Baie Sainte-Anne, NB E9A 1V6
Lat/Lon: 47.07299/-64.80221
Email: famipark@nbnet.nb.ca
Web: www.escuminacbeach.com

(NE) Sandy Point Park—(Northumberland) *From Hwy 117 N at city limit: Go 1.5 km/1 mi S on Hwy 117, then 1.6 km/1 mi E on Chemin Pointe au Sable. Enter at end.* ◆◆FACILITIES: 68 sites, 8 full hkups, 40 W&E, (15 amps), 20 no hkups, tenting, dump, non-guest dump $, portable dump, laundry, ice, picnic tables, fire rings, wood. ◆◆RECREATION: rec hall, equipped pavilion, swim pool, saltwater/river swim, boating, canoeing, kayaking, saltwater fishing, play equipment, horseshoes. Pets welcome. Open May 19 - Sep 15. Rate in 2010 $23-25 for 4 persons. VISA. CCUSA 50% Discount.

CAMPCLUB USA

Phone: (506)228-1122
Address: 160 Chemin Pointe au Sable Rd, Baie Sainte - Anne, NB E9A 1J7
Lat/Lon: 47.05469/-64.99661
Web: www.sandypointpark.com

BATHURST—B-4

(SE) Berry Patch Campground & RV Park—*From Hwy 11 (exit 311): Go 1.4 km/1 mi W on Sunset Dr. Enter on R.* ◆◆◆FACILITIES: 40 sites, 38 full hkups, (15/30/50 amps), 50 amps ($), 2 no hkups, 15 pull-thrus, tenting, laundry, ltd groc. ◆RECREATION: play equipment. Pets welcome. Open May 15 - Oct 15. Facilities fully operational Jun 1 - Sep 15. Rate in 2010 $26 for 4 persons. Phone: (506)546-8987.

BEAR ISLAND—D-2

(N) Great Bear Camping—(York) *From Hwy 2 (exit 231), then Rte 105, South go 20 km. Enter on R.* ◆◆FACILITIES: 90 sites, typical site width 25 ft, 80 W&E, (15/30 amps), 10 no hkups, 15 pull-thrus, tenting, dump, laundry. ◆◆RECREATION: swim pool, boating, canoeing, ramp, lake fishing, play equipment. Pets welcome. Open May 19 - Oct 3. Rate in 2010 $25-31 for 4 persons. Phone: (506)575-8151.

BELLEDUNE—B-3

JACQUET RIVER PARK (Village Park)—*From Hwy 11 (exit 351): Go 2.6 km/1-1/2 mi E on Jacquet River Rd, then 90 meters/100 yards S on Hwy 134. Enter on L.* FACILITIES: 31 sites, 31 W&E, (50 amps), tenting, dump, laundry. RECREATION: saltwater swim, playground. Pets welcome. Open Jun 15 - Sep 2. Phone: (506)237-3239.

BERESFORD—B-4

(SE) Malybel Park Camping (Not Visited)—(Gloucester) *From Hwy 11 (exit 318): Go 1.2 km/3/4 mi E on the Beresford Rd, then 4.3 km/2-3/4 mi S on Hwy 134, then 1.7 km/1 mi E on Kent Lodge Rd, then 1 km/1/2 mi N on Bryar Rd. Enter on R.* ◆◆◆◆FACILITIES: 240 sites, typical site width 35 ft, 149 full hkups, 63 W&E, (15/30/50 amps), 50 amps ($), 28 no hkups, 12 pull-thrus, tenting, dump, laundry, ltd groc. ◆◆◆◆RECREATION: swim pool, playground. Pets welcome, quantity restrict. Partial handicap access. Open May 1 - Sep 30. Facilities fully operational May 15 - Sep 30. Big rigs welcome. Rate in 2010 $29-34 for 4 persons. Member COA of NB. Phone: (506)545-6888.

BLACK POINT—B-3

(S) Camping by the Bay—(Gloucester) *From city limits on Hwy 134 N: Go 1.5 km/1 mi S on Hwy 134, then 1.4 km/3/4 mi on Ch. Blackpoint Rd. Enter on R.* ◆◆FACILITIES: 40 sites, 32 full hkups, 8 W&E, (15/30 amps), tenting, dump, laundry. ◆RECREATION: saltwater swim, boating, canoeing, saltwater fishing. Pets welcome. Open Jun 1 - Sep 15. Rate in 2010 $20-22 for 4 persons. Member COA of NB. Phone: (506)237-5291.

BLACK RIVER BRIDGE—C-4

(SE) Camping Near Miramichi—(Northumberland) *At S Miramichi City Limit: Go S on Hwy 11, then 1.2 km/3/4 mi E on Ch. N Black River Rd. Enter on L.* ◆◆◆FACILITIES: 50 sites, 7 full hkups, 15 W&E, 7 E, (15/30 amps), 21 no hkups, WiFi Instant Internet at site, tenting, dump, non-guest dump $, laundry, ice, picnic tables, fire rings, wood. ◆◆RECREATION: swim pool, canoeing, play equipment, horseshoes. Pets welcome. Open May 15 - Oct 15. Rate in 2010 $25-27 for 4 persons. MC/VISA/Debit. CCUSA 50% Discount.

CAMPCLUB USA

Phone: (506)773-6252
Address: 116 North Black River Rd, Black River Bridge, NB E1N 5S4
Lat/Lon: 46.97729/-65.32077
Web: www.campingnearmiramichi.com

BOUCTOUCHE—C-5

(N) Bouctouche Bay Campground & Chalets—(Kent) *From jct Hwy 134 & Hwy 475: Go 8 km/5 mi N on Hwy 475. Enter on L.* ◆◆◆◆FACILITIES: 182 sites, typical site width 30 ft, 80 full hkups, 60 W&E, (15/30 amps), 42 no hkups, 40 pull-thrus, WiFi Internet central location, tenting, RV storage, dump, non-guest dump $, laundry, ice, picnic tables, fire rings, wood. ◆◆◆◆RECREATION: rec hall, equipped pavilion, swim pool, saltwater swim, playground, activities, horseshoes. Pets welcome. Open May 15 - Sep 15. Facilities fully operational Jun 15 - Sep 1. Rate in 2010 $27-35 per family. MC/VISA. CCUSA 50% Discount. CCUSA reservations Recommended, CCUSA max stay 5 days, CCUSA disc. not avail F,Sa, CCUSA disc. not avail holidays. Not available Jul & Aug. Fully operational Jun 15-Sept 1.

CAMPCLUB USA

Phone: (506)743-8883
Address: 2239 Route 475, Saint-Edouard-de-Kent, NB E4S-2J2
Lat/Lon: 46.47851/-64.70969
Email: reservation@bouctouchecamping.com
Web: www.bouctouchecamping.com

Canada's national animal is the beaver.

CAMPOBELLO ISLAND—E-3

(N) HERRING COVE PROVINCIAL PARK—(Charlotte) *US Rte 1 via 189 or by ferry from Deer Island. Follow signs. Enter on R.* FACILITIES: 88 sites, typical site width 30 ft, 40 E, (15/30 amps), 48 no hkups, 21 pull-thrus, tenting, dump, laundry, groceries. RECREATION: saltwater swim, saltwater/pond fishing, playground. Pets welcome. Partial handicap access. Open May 21 - Sep 25. Member COA of NB. Phone: (506)752-7010.

CAPE TORMENTINE—D-5

MURRAY BEACH PROVINCIAL PARK—(Westmorland) *From town: Go 13.4 km/8-1/3 mi W on Rte 955 (Murray Corner).* FACILITIES: 111 sites, 57 E, (15/30 amps), 54 no hkups, 51 pull-thrus, tenting, dump, laundry. RECREATION: saltwater swim, saltwater fishing, play equipment. Pets welcome. Partial handicap access. Open May 21 - Sep 19. COA of NB. Phone: (506)538-2628.

CARAQUET—B-4

Camping Caraquet—(Gloucester) *From town: Go 4-3/4 km/3 mi W on Hwy 11. Enter on L.* ◆◆◆FACILITIES: 120 sites, 22 full hkups, 40 W&E, (15 amps), 58 no hkups, tenting, dump, laundry, ltd groc. ◆RECREATION: saltwater swim, playground. Pets welcome. Partial handicap access. Open Jun 1 - Oct 15. Rate in 2010 $30. Phone: (506)726-2696.

(SW) Camping & Motel Colibri (Not Visited)—(Gloucester) *From jct Hwy 325 & Hwy 11: Go 1.5 km/1 mi S on Hwy 11. Enter on R.* ◆◆◆FACILITIES: 300 sites, typical site width 30 ft, 230 full hkups, 60 W&E, (15/30/50 amps), 50 amps ($), 10 no hkups, 24 pull-thrus, tenting, dump, laundry, ltd groc. ◆◆◆RECREATION: swim pool, playground. Pets welcome. Open May 15 - Sep 30. Facilities fully operational Jun 15 - Aug 25. Big rigs welcome. Rate in 2010 $25-40 per family. Member COA of NB. Phone: (506)727-2222.

CHARLO—B-3

(NW) BLUE HERON CAMPING (Town Park)—(Restigouche) *At jct Hwy 280 & Hwy 134.* FACILITIES: 172 sites, typical site width 50 ft, 135 full hkups, 10 W&E, (15/30 amps), 27 no hkups, tenting, dump, laundry, ltd groc. RECREATION: swim pool, playground. Pets welcome. Open Jun 1 - Sep 30. Phone: (506)684-7850.

COLES ISLAND—D-4

(NE) T.N.T. Campground (Not Visited)—(Queens) *From jct Hwy 10 & Route 112: Go 2.6 km/1-3/4 mi E on Hwy 112, then 1.3 km/3/4 mi S on Boyd Loop Rd. Enter on L.* ◆◆◆FACILITIES: 261 sites, 200 full hkups, 30 W&E, (15/30 amps), 31 no hkups, 10 pull-thrus, tenting, dump, laundry, ltd groc. ◆◆◆RECREATION: river swim, boating, canoeing, ramp, dock, river fishing, playground. Pets welcome. Open May 20 - Sept 30. Rate in 2010 $35 for 2 persons. Member COA of NB. Phone: (506)362-5372.

CRYSTAL BEACH—E-3

(NE) Crystal Beach Campground (Not Visited)—(Kings) *From east landing of Westfield Ferry & Hwy 845: Go 1.6 km/1 mi N on Hwy 845, then 0.8 km/1/2 mi W on Crystal Beach Road. Enter at end.* ◆◆FACILITIES: 40 sites, typical site width 21 ft, 30 ft max RV length, 30 full hkups, (15/30 amps), 10 no hkups, 10 pull-thrus, tenting, dump, ltd groc. ◆◆RECREATION: river swim, boating, canoeing, river fishing, play equipment. Pets welcome. Open Jun 1 - Sep 4. Rate in 2010 $29-35 per family. Phone: (506)763-2379.

DEER ISLAND—E-2

DEER ISLAND POINT CAMPGROUND—(Charlotte) *Located at Campobello-Eastport ferry dock. Enter on R.* FACILITIES: 79 sites, typical site width 30 ft, 39 E, 40 no hkups, tenting, dump, laundry, ltd groc. RECREATION: saltwater swim, playground. Open Jun 1 - Sep 20. Member COA of NB. Phone: (506) 747-2423.

New Brunswick was named for the German duchy of Brunswick-Luneburg (the electorate of Hanover when New Brunswick became a colony in 1784).

EDMUNDSTON—B-1

(NE) CAMPING PANORAMIC 86—(Madawaska) *From Trans Canada Hwy 2 (exit 8) & rue Principale: Go .08 km/1/2 mi E on Hwy 144 (rue Principale), then .04 km/1/3 mi NE on Ch. St. Joseph, then follow signs S for 1.8 km/1 mi, then .05 km/1/3 mi W on Chemin Albert. (also exit 16 then follow the sign). Enter on R.*

◇◇◇◇FACILITIES: 177 sites, typical site width 40 ft, 150 full hkups, 25 W&E, (15/30 amps), 2 no hkups, mostly extd stay sites, 15 pull-thrus, WiFi Instant Internet at site, phone Internet central location, tenting, dump, non-guest dump $, laundry, ltd groc, ice, picnic tables, fire rings, wood, controlled access.

◇◇◇◇RECREATION: rec hall, equipped pavilion, swim pool, wading pool, boating, canoeing, kayaking, ramp, golf nearby, bsktball, playground, activities, (wkends), horseshoes, sports field, hiking trails.

Pets welcome. Open May 1 - Oct 30. Facilities fully operational May 15 - Sep 15. Escort to site. Clubs welcome. Rate in 2010 $30 for 6 persons. MC/VISA/AMEX/Debit. Member COA of NB.

Phone: (506)739-6544
Address: 86 Chemin Albert, Edmundston (Saint-Jacques), NB E7B 1Z5
Lat/Lon: 47.41941/-68.37503
Email: campingpanoramic@NB.AIBN.com
Web: www.SN2000.Nb.ca/comp/camping-panoramic

SEE AD THIS PAGE

DE LA REPUBLIQUE PROVINCIAL PARK—(Madawaska) *From Edmundston: Go 9.8 km/6 mi W on Hwy 2 (exit 8). Enter on R.* FACILITIES: 150 sites, typical site width 24 ft, 100 E, (30 amps), 50 no hkups, 16 pull-thrus, tenting, dump. RECREATION: swim pool, boating, canoeing, ramp, dock, river fishing, playground. Pets welcome. Partial handicap access. Open May 20 - Sep 15. Member COA of NB. Phone: (506)735-2525.

Riverside (Iroquois) RV Park—*From Trans Canada Hwy 2 (exit 21): Go .06 km/1/4 mi S on Boul. Centre Madawaska, then .08 km/1/2 mi W on Hwy 144. Enter on L.* ◇◇◇FACILITIES: 61 sites, 22 full hkups, 21 W&E, (15/20/30/50 amps), 50 amps ($), 18 no hkups, 6 pull-thrus, WiFi Instant Internet at site, tenting, dump, non-guest dump, ice, picnic tables, fire rings, wood. ◇RECREATION: river swim, river fishing, bike rental 3 bike rentals, play equipment, horseshoes. Pets welcome, breed restrict. Open May 15 - Oct 12. Big rigs welcome. Rate in 2010 $28-39 per family. CCUSA 50% Discount. CCUSA reservations Accepted, CCUSA max stay 2 days, Cash only for CCUSA disc., Check only for CCUSA disc. Minimum stay 2 days.

Phone: (506)739-9060
Address: 1318 Principale, Saint-Basile, Edmundston, NB E7C 1L9
Lat/Lon: 47.36679/-68.27734
Email: owners@riversidervpark.ca
Web: www.riversidervpark.ca

FLORENCEVILLE—D-2

(W) River Country Campground—(Carleton) *From E'bnd on Hwy 2 (exit 115) & Hwy 130: Go .8 km on Rte 109, then go .5 km. Enter on L.* ◇◇◇FACILITIES: 89 sites, typical site width 30 ft, 25 full hkups, 49 W&E, (30 amps), 15 no hkups, 15 pull-thrus, tenting, dump, laundry. ◇◇◇RECREATION: river swim, boating, canoeing, ramp, dock, river fishing, playground. Pets welcome. Open May 1 - Oct 15. Rate in 2010 $24-30 for 4 persons. Member COA of NB. Phone: (506)278-3700.

FOUR FALLS—C-2

(N) Spring Water Campground—(Victoria) *From jct Hwy 2 & Route 130 (Exit 99): Go 1 km/3/4 mi N on Route 130. Enter on R.* ◇◇◇FACILITIES: 90 sites, typical site width 22 ft, 67 full hkups, 23 W&E, (15/30 amps), 25 pull-thrus, tenting, dump, laundry, ltd groc. ◇◇◇RECREATION: swim pool, playground. Pets welcome. Open May 1 - Oct 15. Facilities fully operational Jun 23 - Sep 7. Rate in 2010 $31 for 6 persons. Member COA of NB. Phone: (506)273-3682.

FREDERICTON—D-3

(W) Hartt Island RV Resort—(York) *From Hwy 8 (exit 3) & Hwy 102/Hwy 640: Go 5 km/3 mi NW on Hwy 102. Enter on R.* ◇◇◇FACILITIES: 118 sites, typical site width 28 ft, 69 full hkups, 45 W&E, (15/30/50 amps), 50 amps ($), 4 no hkups, tenting, dump, laundry, ltd groc. ◇◇◇◇RECREATION: swim pool, boating, canoeing, ramp, dock, river fishing, playground. Pets welcome. Partial handicap access. Open May 1 - Oct 30. Big rigs welcome. Rate in 2010 $25-45 for 4 persons. Member COA of NB. Phone: (866)462-9400.

Woolastook Park—(York) *From Hwy 2 (exit 258) & Rte 102: Go 3 km/2 mi E on Rte 102. Enter on R.* ◇◇◇FACILITIES: 284 sites, typical site width 30 ft, 156 full hkups, 15 W&E, 101 E, (15/30 amps), 6 no hkups, 60 pull-thrus, tenting, dump, non-guest dump $, portable dump, laundry, ice, picnic tables, fire rings, wood. ◇◇◇RECREATION: rec hall, equipped pavilion, lake swim, boating, canoeing, kayaking, ramp, lake fishing, mini-golf, putting green, bike rental 10 bike rentals, playground, activities, horseshoes, hiking trails, v-ball. Pets welcome. Partial handicap access. Open May 15 - Mid Oct. Rate in 2010 $25-29 for 4 persons. MC/VISA/Debit. Member COA of NB. CCUSA 50% Discount. CCUSA reservations Recommended, CCUSA max stay Unlimited, CCUSA disc. not avail F,Sa, CCUSA disc. not avail holidays. Not available Jul & Aug.

Phone: (506)472-5584
Address: 5171 Rte 102, Kingsclear, NB E3E 1P9
Lat/Lon: 45.87300/-66.91366
Email: info@woolastookpark.com
Web: www.woolastookpark.com

GAGETOWN—D-3

(NE) Coy Lake Camping—(Queens) *From jct Hwy 2 (exit 330) & Rte 102: Go 1.8 km/1 mi S on Rte 102. Enter on L.* ◇◇◇FACILITIES: 49 sites, typical site width 25 ft, 41 full hkups, (15/30/50 amps), 50 amps ($), 8 no hkups, 20 pull-thrus, tenting, dump, laundry, ltd groc. ◇◇RECREATION: swim pool, play equipment. Pets welcome. Partial handicap access. Open May 21 - Oct 15. Rate in 2010 $22-31 for 4 persons. Phone: (506)488-2567.

GALLAGHER RIDGE—D-4

(N) Pine Ridge Campground (Not Visited)—*From Hwy 2 (exit 450) & Hwy 126: Go 13 km/8 mi N on Hwy 126 N. Enter on R.* ◇◇FACILITIES: 52 sites, 8 full hkups, 14 W&E, (15 amps), 30 no hkups, tenting, dump, laundry. ◇RECREATION: swim pool, play equipment. Pets welcome. Open May 30 - Sep 3. Rate in 2010 $22-25 for 4 persons. Phone: (506)855-6938.

GRAND FALLS—C-2

(S) Mulherin's Campground—(Victoria) *From Hwy 2 (Exit 88) & Route 130: Go 1.8 km/1 mi N on Route 130, then 1.6 km/1 mi NW on McCluskey Rd. Enter on L.* ◇◇◇FACILITIES: 130 sites, typical site width 25 ft, 90 full hkups, 30 W&E, (30 amps), 10 no hkups, 12 pull-thrus, tenting, shower$, dump, non-guest dump $, laundry, ice, picnic tables, fire rings, wood. ◇◇◇RECREATION: rec hall, swim pool, no motors, canoeing, kayaking, bsktball, playground, activities, horseshoes, hiking trails, v-ball. Pets welcome. Open May 16 - Sep 14. Facilities fully operational Jun 5 - Sep 10. Rate in 2010 $29 for 4 persons. MC/VISA/Debit. Member COA of NB. CCUSA 50% Discount. CCUSA reservations Required, CCUSA max stay 14 days, CCUSA disc. not avail F,Sa, CCUSA disc. not avail holidays. Not available Jul & Aug.

Phone: (506)473-3050
Address: 170 McCluskey Rd, Grand Falls, NB E3Z 1L3
Lat/Lon: 46.98584/-67.76183
Email: mulherinscampground@hotmail.com
Web: www.mulherincampground.com

(S) Rapid Brook Camping (Not Visited)—(Victoria) *From jct Hwy 2 & Route 130 (Exit 83) Go 1 km/3/4 mi W on Route 130, then .02 km/1/8 mi S on Michaud Rd. Enter on L.* ◇◇◇FACILITIES: 47 sites, typical site width 20 ft, 20 full hkups, 8 W&E, (15/30 amps), 19 no hkups, 6 pull-thrus, tenting, dump, laundry. ◇◇RECREATION: swim pool, river fishing, play equipment. Pets welcome. Open May 15 - Oct 15. Rate in 2010 $19-27 for 2 persons. Phone: (506)473-1036.

GRAND MANAN ISLAND—F-3

THE ANCHORAGE PROVINCIAL PARK—(Charlotte) *From Rte 776 in town: Go SE on access road. On Grand Manan Island.* FACILITIES: 97 sites, typical site width 15 ft, 25 E, (15/30 amps), 72 no hkups, 6 pull-thrus, tenting, dump, laundry. RECREATION: saltwater swim, canoeing, pond fishing, play equipment. Pets welcome. Partial handicap access. Open mid May - mid Sep. Member COA of NB. Phone: (506)662-7022.

GRANDE-ANSE—B-4

(NE) Motel & Camping Baie des Chaleurs (Not Visited)—(Gloucester) *From jct Hwy 330 & Hwy 11: Go 2 km/1-1/4 mi S on Hwy 11. Enter on L.* ◇◇FACILITIES: 50 sites, typical site width 24 ft, 30 full hkups, 20 W&E, (15/30 amps), tenting, laundry. ◇RECREATION: swim pool. Pets welcome. Open May 1 - Sep 30. Facilities fully operational Jun 1 - Sep 1. Rate in 2010 $23-26 for 4 persons. Phone: (506)732-2948.

HAMPTON—E-4

(W) Hidden Valley Campground (Not Visited)—(Kings) *From Hwy 1 & Road 121 (exit 158): Go 4.3 km/2-3/4 mi E on Road 121, then 9.8 km/6 mi W on road 845, then 400 m/1/8 mi SE on Woodhaven, then 1 km/3/4 mi N on gravel road. Enter on L.* ◇◇FACILITIES: 45 sites, typical site width 25 ft, 33 full hkups, 5 W&E, (15 amps), 7 no hkups, 5 pull-thrus, tenting, laundry, ltd groc. ◇◇RECREATION: lake swim, boating, no motors, canoeing, lake fishing, play equipment. Pets welcome. Open May 1 - Oct 15. Rate in 2010 $20-28 for 5 persons. Phone: (506)832-4994.

HARDINGS POINT—E-3

(W) Hardings Point Campground—(Kings) *Located at east landing of Westfield Ferry & Hwy 845.* ◇◇◇FACILITIES: 150 sites, typical site width 30 ft, 118 full hkups, 13 W&E, (15/30/50 amps), 19 no hkups, 14 pull-thrus, tenting, dump, laundry, ltd groc. ◇◇◇RECREATION: swim pool, boating, ramp, dock, river fishing, playground. Pets welcome ($). Partial handicap access. Open May 15 - Sep 30. Big rigs welcome. Rate in 2010 $38 per family. Phone: (506)763-2517.

(W) HARDINGS POINT CAMPGROUND—*Located at east landing of Westfield Ferry & Hwy 845. Enter at end.*

◇◇◇FACILITIES: 150 sites, typical site width 30 ft, 118 full hkups, 13 W&E, (15/30/50 amps), 50 amps ($), 19 no hkups, many extd stay sites, 14 pull-thrus, WiFi Instant Internet at site, tenting, shower$, dump, non-guest dump, laundry, ltd groc, RV supplies, ice, picnic tables, fire rings, wood, controlled access.

◇◇◇RECREATION: rec room/area, pavilion, coin games, swim pool, boating, kayaking, ramp, dock, river fishing, fishing supplies, fishing guides, golf nearby, bsktball, playground, activities, (wkends), horseshoes, hiking trails, v-ball.

Pets welcome. Partial handicap access. Open May 15 - Sep 30. Big rigs welcome. Escort to site. Clubs welcome. Rate in 2010 $38-40 for 4 persons. MC/VISA/Debit. Member COA of NB.

Phone: (506)763-2517
Address: 71 Hardin's Point Landing Rd, Harding Point, NB E5S 1N8
Lat/Lon: 45.35200/-66.21767
Web: www.hardingspointcampground.com

SEE AD SAINT-JOHN PAGE 842

HARVEY—D-2

(NW) LAKE GEORGE FAMILY CAMPGROUND (City Park)—(York) *From jct Hwy 3 & Hwy 636: Go 12.8 km/8 mi N on Hwy 636. Enter on R.* FACILITIES: 62 sites, typical site width 20 ft, 16 full hkups, 30 W&E, 16 no hkups, tenting, dump, laundry, ltd groc. RECREATION: lake swim, boating, canoeing, ramp, lake fishing, play equipment. Pets welcome. Partial handicap access. Open May 30 - Sep 30. Phone: (506)366-2933.

HAWKSHAW—D-2

(E) Sunset View Campground & Cottages (Not Visited)—(York) *From jct Hwy 2 & Rte. 105 (exit 232): Go 0.5 km/1/3 mi E on Hwy 2, then 0.5 km/1/3 mi SE on Hawkshaw Rd. Enter on R.* ◇◇◇FACILITIES: 65 sites, typical site width 40 ft, 27 full hkups, 23 W&E, (15/30 amps), 15 no hkups, 12 pull-thrus, tenting, dump, laundry. ◇◇RECREATION: swim pool, play equipment. Pets welcome. Open Jun 1 - Sep 25. Rate in 2010 $28 for 4 persons. Phone: (506)575-2592.

New Brunswick became a Canadian province July 1, 1867.

HOPEWELL CAPE—D-5

(N) PONDEROSA PINES CAMPGROUND —(Albert) *From E at jct Hwy 114 & Hopewell Rocks ent: Go 1.7 km/1 mi W on Hwy 114. Enter on L.*

◇◇◇◇FACILITIES: 127 sites, typical site width 27 ft, 59 full hkups, 30 W&E, 5 E, (15/30/50 amps), 50 amps ($), 33 no hkups, 10 pull-thrus, WiFi Instant Internet at site, WiFi Internet central location, tenting, tent rentals, cabins, dump, non-guest dump $, laundry, ltd groc, RV supplies, ice, picnic tables, fire rings, wood, controlled access.

◇◇◇◇RECREATION: rec room/area, coin games, swim pool, lake swim, boating, canoeing, kayaking, ramp, 3 canoe/2 kayak/3 pedal boat rentals, lake fishing, golf nearby, playground, activities, horseshoes, sports field, hiking trails, v-ball. Rec open to public.

Pets welcome. Partial handicap access. Open Apr 15 - Oct 31. Facilities fully operational May 1 - Oct 31. Big rigs welcome. Escort to site. Clubs welcome. Rate in 2010 $32-43 per family. MC/VISA/AMEX/Debit. Member COA of NB. FMCA discount. CCUSA 50% Discount. CCUSA reservations Recommended, CCUSA max stay Unlimited, Cash only for CCUSA disc., CCUSA disc. not avail F,Sa, CCUSA disc. not avail holidays. Not available Jul & Aug. Rate applies to 20 amp only.

Phone: (800)822-8800
Address: 4325 Rte 114, Hopewell Cape, NB E4H 4W7
Lat/Lon: 45.81909/-64.59626
Email: ponderosa@nb.aibn.com
Web: www.ponderosapines.ca

SEE AD THIS PAGE

JANEVILLE—B-4

(N) Chapman's Tent & Trailer Park—(Gloucester) *From north city limit on Hwy 11: Go 1 km/3/4 mi S on Hwy 11. Enter on L.* ◇◇FACILITIES: 65 sites, 35 full hkups, 16 W&E, (15 amps), 14 no hkups, tenting, dump. RECREATION: saltwater swim, play equipment. Pets welcome. Open Jun 1 - Sep 30. Rate in 2010 $20-23 for 4 persons. Member COA of NB. Phone: (506)543-2710.

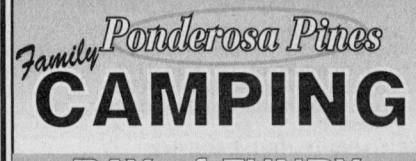

KOUCHIBOUGUAC—C-4

KOUCHIBOUGUAC NATIONAL PARK (Cote A Fabian) *—From Hwy 11 in town: Go 6-1/2 km/4 mi N, then 6-1/2 km/4 mi NE on gravel road.* FACILITIES: 32 sites, 32 no hkups, tenting. RECREATION: saltwater swim, boating, no motors, canoeing, dock, saltwater/river fishing, playground. Pets welcome. Open Jun 13 - Sep 1. Phone: (506)876-2443.

LAMEQUE—B-5

(NW) CAMPING ILE LAMEQUE (Municipal Park)—(Gloucester) *From town: Go 4-3/4 km/3 mi NW on Hwy 113, then 1-1/2 km/1 mi W on campground road. Enter at end.* FACILITIES: 52 sites, 18 full hkups, 14 W&E, (15/30 amps), 20 no hkups, tenting, dump, laundry, ltd groc. RECREATION: saltwater swim, boating, ramp, playground. Pets welcome. Partial handicap access. Open Jun 15 - Sep 15. Phone: (506)344-3292.

LOWER QUEENSBURY—D-2

Heritage Country Camping (Not Visited)—(York) *From N town city limit: Go 3.6 km/2-1/3 mi S on Hwy 105. Enter on L.* ◇◇FACILITIES: 109 sites, typical site width 30 ft, 49 full hkups, 59 W&E, (15/30 amps), 1 no hkups, tenting, dump, laundry. ◇◇RECREATION: swim pool, playground. Pets welcome. Open Mid May - Oct 5. Rate in 2010 $25-33 for 5 persons. Member COA of NB. Phone: (506)363-3338.

MACTAQUAC—D-3

Everett's Campground—(York) *From jct Rte 105 & Rte 102 at the Dam: Cross the dam, then 14.5 km/9 mi N on Rte 105. Enter on L.* ◇◇◇FACILITIES: 56 sites, typical site width 26 ft, 43 full hkups, 13 W&E, (15/30 amps), tenting, dump, laundry. ◇◇RECREATION: lake/boating, canoeing, lake fishing. Pets welcome. Open May 19 - Sept 30. Rate in 2010 $23-30 for 4 persons. Member COA of NB.

Phone: (506)363-3248
Address: 2137 Rt 105, Lower Queensbury, NB E6L 1E6
Lat/Lon: 45.89454/-66.93203
Email: pann@nb.sympatico.ca

(N) MACTAQUAC PROVINCIAL PARK—(York) *Route 105: Go 24 km / 15 mi W from Fredericton.* FACILITIES: 303 sites, 235 E, (30 amps), 68 no hkups, 97 pull-thrus, tenting, dump, laundry, ltd groc. RECREATION: river swim, boating, canoeing, ramp, dock, river fishing, play equipment. Pets welcome. Partial handicap access. Open May 21 - Oct 31. Member COA of NB. Phone: (506)363-4747.

MILL COVE—D-3

(N) Lakeside Campground and Recreation Park—(Queens) *From jct Hwy 2 & Rte 105 (exit 347): Go 3.8 km/2-1/3 mi E on Rte 105. Enter on L.* ◇◇◇FACILITIES: 150 sites, 19 full hkups, 44 W&E, (15/30 amps), 87 no hkups, 54 pull-thrus, tenting, dump, laundry, ltd groc. ◇◇◇RECREATION: lake swim, boating, canoeing, ramp, lake fishing, playground. Pets welcome. Open May 15 - Oct 10. Rate in 2010 $28-38 for 4 persons. Member COA of NB. Phone: (506)488-2321.

MIRAMICHI—C-4

(SW) Enclosure Campground—(Northumberland) *From Hwy 8 (exit 163): Go .04 km/1/4 mi E on 108, then follow signs. Enter at end.* ◇◇◇FACILITIES: 99 sites, typical site width 30 ft, 34 full hkups, 57 W&E, (15/30 amps), 8 no hkups, tenting, dump, non-guest dump $, laundry, ice, picnic tables, fire rings, wood.

◇◇◇RECREATION: equipped pavilion, swim pool, playground, activities, horseshoes, hiking trails, v-ball. Pets welcome, breed restrict. Partial handicap access. Open Jun 1 - Sep 30. Facilities fully operational Jun 20 - Sep 3. Rate in 2010 $28-30 for 2 persons. MC/VISA/AMEX/Debit. Member COA of NB. CCUSA 50% Discount. CCUSA reservations Recommended, CCUSA max stay 4 days, Cash only for CCUSA disc., CCUSA disc. not avail F,Sa, CCUSA disc. not avail holidays. Not available Jul & Aug.

MIRAMICHI—Continued
Enclosure Campground—Continued

Phone: (800)363-1733
Address: 8 Enclosure Rd, Miramichi, NB E1V 5B2
Lat/Lon: 46.57692/-65.35614
Email: enclosur@nbnet.nb.ca

(NE) Family Land Campground (Not Visited) —(Northumberland) *From jct Hwy 11 & Hwy 117: Go 11.2 km/7 mi S on Hwy 117, then 1.6 km/1 mi E on East Point Rd. Enter on L.* ◇◇◇FACILITIES: 140 sites, typical site width 40 ft, 66 full hkups, 74 W&E, (15/30 amps), tenting, dump, laundry, ltd groc. ◇◇◇RECREATION: swim pool, saltwater swim, play equipment. Pets welcome. Open May 24 - Sep 30. Facilities fully operational Jun 20 - Aug 30. Rate in 2010 $26 for 4 persons. Phone: (506)773-6666.

(NE) Oak Point Family Campground (Not Visited)—*From jct Hwy 8 & Hwy 11 (at Centennial Bridge): Go 18-3/4 km/11-1/2 mi N on Hwy 11, then 2 km/1-1/4 mi E on Ch.Oak Point Rd. Enter on L.* ◇◇◇FACILITIES: 50 sites, 31 full hkups, 8 W&E, (15/30 amps), 11 no hkups, tenting, dump, laundry. ◇◇RECREATION: swim pool, canoeing, play equipment. Pets welcome. Open May 15 - Oct 15. Rate in 2010 $20 for 4 persons. Member COA of NB. Phone: (506)778-9400.

(NE) Sunrise Campground—(Northumberland) *From jct Hwy 8 & Hwy 11 (at the Centennial Bridge): Go 11-1/4 km/7 mi N on Hwy 11. Enter on R.* ◇◇◇FACILITIES: 94 sites, typical site width 30 ft, 86 full hkups, 8 W&E, (15/30 amps), 30 pull-thrus, tenting, dump, laundry, ltd groc. ◇◇◇RECREATION: swim pool, canoeing, river fishing, playground. Pets welcome. Open May 15 - Oct 9. Rate in 2010 $28-29 for 4 persons. Member COA of NB.

Phone: (506)778-2282
Address: 504 Route 11, Lower Newcastle, NB E1V-7G1
Lat/Lon: 47.08918/-65.37025
Web: www.mightymiramichi.com

MISCOU ISLAND—B-5

Miscou Island Camping Cabins—(Gloucester) *From the Miscou Island bridge: Go 5 km/3 mi N on Hwy 113. Enter on R.* ◇◇FACILITIES: 39 sites, typical site width 20 ft, 25 ft max RV length, 9 full hkups, 18 W&E, (15 amps), 12 no hkups, tenting. ◇RECREATION: lake swim, play equipment. Open Jun 15 - Sep 15. Rate in 2010 $24-26 per family. Phone: (506)344-1881.

(N) Plage Miscou Camping (Not Visited)—(Gloucester) *From the Miscou Island Bridge: Go 14 km/8-3/4 mi N on Hwy 113, then follow signs. Enter on L.* ◇◇FACILITIES: 47 sites, typical site width 25 ft, 47 full hkups, (15 amps), tenting, laundry. ◇◇RECREATION: saltwater swim, play equipment. Pets welcome. Open Jun 15 - Sep 15. Rate in 2010 $28 per family. Member COA of NB. Phone: (506)344-1015.

MONCTON—D-4

(NW) CAMPER'S CITY RV/RESORT—(Westmorland) *From Hwy 2 & Mapleton Rd (exit 454): Go 100 meters/300 ft N on Mapleton Rd, then .04 km/1/4 mi E on Queens Way Dr. Enter at end.*

◇◇◇◇◇FACILITIES: 221 sites, 180 full hkups, 22 E, (15/20/30/50 amps), 50 amps ($), 20 no hkups, some extd stay sites, 73 pull-thrus, WiFi Instant Internet at site, phone Internet central location, tenting, cabins, shower$, dump, non-guest dump $, laundry, ltd groc, RV supplies, LP gas by weight/by meter, ice, picnic tables, controlled access.

CAMPER'S CITY RV/RESORT—Continued on next page

MONCTON—Continued
CAMPER'S CITY RV/RESORT—Continued

◆◆◆◆RECREATION: rec hall, pavilion, equipped pavilion, coin games, swim pool, golf nearby, bsktball, playground, activities, horseshoes, sports field, hiking trails, v-ball. Rec open to public.

Pets welcome ($). Partial handicap access. Open May 1 - Oct 15. Big rigs welcome. Clubs welcome. Rate in 2010 $25-44 for 2 persons. MC/VISA/Debit. Member COA of NB. FMCA discount.

Phone: (877)512-7868
Address: 138 Queensway Dr, Moncton, NB E1G 2L2
Lat/Lon: 46.13152/-64.82757
Email: camperscity@killamproperties.com
Web: www.killamleisureliving.com

SEE AD PAGE 840

(E) ED'S TRAVEL TRAILER PARTS & SERVICE—*From jct Hwy 2 & Hwy 134 (exit 465): Go .04 km/1/4 mi S on Hwy 134. Enter on L.* SALES: pre-owned unit sales. SERVICES: full-time mech, RV appliance repair, bus. hrs emerg rd svc, mobile RV svc, RV storage, sells parts/accessories, installs hitches. Open all yr. MC/VISA/AMEX/Debit.

WELCOME

Phone: (506)856-5001
Address: 1500 Shediac Rd, Moncton, NB E1A 7A7
Lat/Lon: 46.07490/-64.42193
Email: edd@rogers.com
Web: www.edstraveltrailer.com

SEE AD THIS PAGE

(NW) Stonehurst Trailer Park—(Westmorland) *From Hwy 2 (exit 450): Go one block on Mountain Road, then 2 mi E on Rte 128 E (Ensley Dr). Enter on R.* ◆◆◆FACILITIES: 151 sites, typical site width 30 ft, 72 full hkups, 58 W&E, (15/20/30/50 amps), 50 amps ($), 21 no hkups, tenting, dump, laundry, ltd groc. ◆◆RECREATION: swim pool, playground. Pets welcome. Partial handicap access. Open May 20 - Oct 15. Rate in 2010 $28-34 per family. Member COA of NB. Phone: (506)852-4162.

NEW RIVER BEACH—E-3

NEW RIVER BEACH PROVINCIAL PARK—(Charlotte) *From Saint-John: Go 38 1/2 km/24 mi W on Rte 1 (Follow signs).* FACILITIES: 99 sites, typical site width 12 ft, 60 E, (15/30 amps), 39 no hkups, 1 pull-thrus, tenting, dump, laundry. RECREATION: saltwater swim, play equipment. Pets welcome. Partial handicap access. Open May 21 - Oct 12. Member COA of NB. Phone: (506)755-4079.

NICTAU—C-2

(E) MOUNT CARLETON PROVINCIAL PARK—(Restigouche) *From Hwy 385 in town: Go 32 km/20 mi N.* FACILITIES: 88 sites, typical site width 12 ft, 88 no hkups, 10 pull-thrus, tenting, dump. RECREATION: lake/river swim, boating, 10 hp limit, canoeing, ramp, dock, lake/river fishing, playground. Pets welcome. Partial handicap access. Open May 14 - Oct 12. Member COA of NB. Phone: (506)235-0793.

NIGADOO—B-4

(C) Motel & Camping Hache (Not Visited)—(Gloucester) *From Hwy 11 (exit 321): Go 2.4 km/1-1/2 mi E to Hwy 134, then .08 km/1/2 mi N on Hwy 134. Enter on L.* ◆◆◆FACILITIES: 167 sites, typical site width 30 ft, 137 full hkups, 1 W&E, (15/30 amps), 29 no hkups, 4 pull-thrus, tenting, dump, laundry, groceries. ◆◆◆RECREATION: swim pool, playground. Pets welcome. Open May 15 - Sep 27. Facilities fully operational Jun 15 - Sep 5. Rate in 2010 $27-29 per family. Member COA of NB. Phone: (506)783-3739.

OAK BAY—E-2

(E) OAK BAY PROVINCIAL PARK—(Charlotte) *From E town city limit on Hwy 1: Go 8 km/5 mi E on Hwy 1. Enter on R.* FACILITIES: 115 sites, typical site width 20 ft, 31 full hkups, 50 W&E, (15/30 amps), 34 no hkups, 11 pull-thrus, tenting, dump, laundry, ltd groc. RECREATION: saltwater swim, playground. Pets welcome. Partial handicap access. Open May 15 - Oct 31. Member COA of NB. Phone: (506)466-4999.

OAK POINT—E-3

(S) OAK POINT KIWANIS PARK—(Kings) *From S city town limit on Hwy 102: Go .08 km/3/4 mi N on Hwy 102, then .06 km/1/2 mi SE on Oak Point Beach Rd. Enter on L.* FACILITIES: 77 sites, typical site width 30 ft, 35 full hkups, 31 W&E, 11 E, (15/30 amps), tenting, dump, laundry. RECREATION: swim pool, river swim, boating, canoeing, river fishing, playground. Pets welcome. Partial handicap access. Open May 16 - Sep 21. Phone: (506)468-2266.

PENOBSQUIS—D-4

(W) Lone Pine Park Campground & Cabins (Not Visited)—(Kings) *From jct Hwy 1 (exit 211) & Hwy 114: Go 1.4 km/3/4 mi W on Hwy 114, then 4 km/2-1/2 mi NE on ch. Portage Vale Rd, then .08 km/1/2 mi N on Gray Cross Rd. Enter at end.* ◆◆◆◆FACILITIES: 59 sites, typical site width 26 ft, 41 full hkups, (15/30 amps), 18 no hkups, 7 pull-thrus, phone Internet central location, tenting, dump, non-guest dump $, laundry, ltd

PENOBSQUIS—Continued
Lone Pine Park Campground & Cabins (Not Visited)—Continued

CAMPCLUB USA

groc, ice, picnic tables, fire rings, wood. ◆◆◆RECREATION: pavilion, swim pool, canoeing, kayaking, river fishing, mini-golf, bsktball, playground, activities, hiking trails, v-ball. Pets welcome. Partial handicap access. Open May 19 - Sep 25. Rate in 2010 $34 for 5 persons. MC/VISA/Debit. CCUSA 50% Discount. CCUSA reservations Accepted, CCUSA max stay 4 days, CCUSA disc. not avail S, CCUSA disc. not avail F,Sa.

Phone: (506)432-4007
Address: 45 Lone Pine Rd, Penobsquis, NB E4E 5T3
Lat/Lon: 45.80665/-65.30035
Email: cindy886@nb.sympatico.ca
Web: www.sn2000.nb.ca/comp/lone_pine

(W) Pine Cone Camping (Not Visited)—(Kings) *From jct Hwy 1 (exit 211) & Hwy 114: Go 9.6 km/6 mi W on Hwy 114. Enter on R.* ◆◆◆◆FACILITIES: 292 sites, typical site width 35 ft, 258 full hkups, 34 W&E, (15/30 amps), 10 pull-thrus, tenting, dump, laundry, ltd groc. ◆◆◆◆RECREATION: 2 swim pools, playground. Pets welcome. No tents. Open May 1 - Oct 10. Rate in 2010 $35 for 4 persons. Member COA of NB. Phone: (506) 433-4389.

(w) Three Bears Family Camping & RV Park—(Kings) *From Hwy 1 (exit 211) & Hwy 114: Go 2 km/1-1/4 mi W on Hwy 114. Enter on L.* ◆◆◆◆FACILITIES: 217 sites, 130 full hkups, 56 W&E, (15/30 amps), 31 no hkups, 15 pull-thrus, tenting, dump, laundry, ltd groc. ◆◆◆◆RECREATION: swim pool, river fishing, playground. Pets welcome. Partial handicap access. Open May 1 - Oct 1. Rate in 2010 $30-32 per family.

Phone: (506)433-2870
Address: 12049 Rte 114, Penobsquis, NB E4G 2Y2
Lat/Lon: 45.78552/-65.34943
Web: www.threebearscamping.com

PETIT CAP—D-5

(NE) Silver Sands Family Camping—(Westmorland) *From jct Route 133 & Route 950: Go 9.6 km/6 mi E on Route 950, then .06 km/1/2 mi NE on Ch Du Camp Rd. Enter at end.* ◆◆◆FACILITIES: 102 sites, typical site width 36 ft, 52 full hkups, (15/30 amps), 50 no hkups, 43 pull-thrus, tenting, dump, non-guest dump $, laundry, ice, picnic tables, wood. ◆◆RECREATION: equipped pavilion, saltwater swim, saltwater fishing, bsktball, play equipment, horseshoes, v-ball. Pets welcome. Open May 22 - Sep 30. Facilities fully operational Jun 15 - Sep 15. Rate in 2010 $20-30 per family. Member COA of NB. CCUSA 50% Discount. CCUSA max stay 4 days. Discount not available Fri, Sat & Sun during Jul & Aug.

CAMPCLUB USA

Phone: (506)577-6771
Address: 64 Ch.Du Camp Rd, Petit Cap, NB E4N-2W2
Lat/Lon: 46.20104/-64.19013

PETIT ROCHER NORD—B-4

(N) Camping Murraywood (Not Visited)—(Gloucester) *From S town limits: Go 2.4 km/1-1/2 mi N on Hwy 134. Enter on R.* ◆◆◆◆FACILITIES: 140 sites, typical site width 40 ft, 107 full hkups, 9 W&E, (15/30/50 amps), 50 amps ($), 24 no hkups, 12 pull-thrus, tenting, dump, laundry, ltd groc. ◆◆◆RECREATION: swim pool, saltwater swim, playground. Pets welcome, breed restrict, size restrict, quantity restrict. Open May 15 - Sep 23. Facilities fully operational Jun 15 - Aug 20. Big rigs welcome. Rate in 2010 $29-34 for 4 persons. Member COA of NB. Phone: (506)783-2137.

POCOLOGAN—E-3

(W) Ocean View Camping—(Charlotte) *From E on Hwy 1 at the City limits: Go 2.9 km/1-3/4 mi W on Hwy 1. Enter on R.* ◆◆FACILITIES: 50 sites, typical site width 20 ft, 18 full hkups, 23 W&E, (15/30 amps), 9 no hkups, 14 pull-thrus, tenting, dump, laundry. RECREATION: play equipment. Pets welcome. Open May 15 - Oct 15. Rate in 2010 $22-24 per family. Member COA of NB. Phone: (506)755-1818.

POINTE-VERTE—B-4

(S) Cedar Cove Camping (Not Visited)—(Gloucester) *From N city limit on Hwy 134: Go 1 km/3/4 mi S on Hwy 134. Enter on L.* ◆◆◆FACILITIES: 127 sites, 91 full hkups, 36 W&E, (30 amps), tenting, dump, laundry, ltd groc. ◆◆RECREATION: saltwater swim, canoeing, play equipment. Pets welcome. Partial handicap access. Open May 15 - Sep 15. Rate in 2010 $22-23 for 4 persons. Phone: (506)783-2648.

PORT OF BAYSIDE—E-2

(E) Island View Camping (Not Visited)—(Charlotte) *From Hwy 1 (exit 39) & Hwy 127 loop: Go 8 km/5mi W on Hwy 127 Loop. Enter on R.* ◆◆◆FACILITIES: 177 sites, typical site width 20 ft, 144 full hkups,

PORT OF BAYSIDE—Continued
Island View Camping (Not Visited)—Continued

19 W&E, (30 amps), 14 no hkups, 20 pull-thrus, tenting, dump, laundry, ltd groc. ◆◆RECREATION: swim pool, playground. Pets welcome. Partial handicap access. Open May 15 - Sep 30. Rate in 2010 $23-27 for 5 persons. Phone: (506)529-3167.

RICHIBOUCTOU-VILLAGE—C-4

(4) Camping Cap Lumiere Beach (Not Visited)—*On New Brunswick Hwy 11, (exit 42 or 53), follow Rte 505 to Chemin Cap Lumiere Rd, then Cap Lumiere Rd to the lighthouse, campground is at the lighthouse. Enter on L.* FACILITIES: 18 sites, 7 full hkups, 11 W&E, (20/30/50 amps), 6 pull-thrus, tenting, dump, laundry, ice, picnic tables, fire rings, grills, wood. RECREATION: boating, canoeing, kayaking, saltwater fishing, horseshoes, hiking trails, v-ball. Pets welcome. Open May 25 - Oct 16. Rate in 2010 $25-32 per vehicle. CCUSA 50% Discount.

CAMPCLUB USA

Phone: (506)523-0994
Address: 239 Ch Cap Lumiere, Richibouctou-Village, NB E4W 1C9
Lat/Lon: 46.6693/-64.7117
Email: acadian22@rogers.com
Web: http://caplumiere.info.ca

RIVIERE DU PORTAGE—B-4

(N) Tracadie Beach Campground—(Northumberland) *From north city limit on Hwy 11: Go 0.5 km/1/4 mi S on Hwy 11, then 0.8 km/1/2 mi W on gravel road. Enter at end.* ◆◆FACILITIES: 115 sites, 77 full hkups, 38 W&E, (15/30 amps), 30 pull-thrus, tenting, dump, laundry, ltd groc. ◆◆RECREATION: river swim, boating, canoeing, ramp, dock, river/pond fishing, playground. Pets welcome. Open May 15 - Sep 15. Facilities fully operational Jun 20 - Sep 3. Rate in 2010 $28-35 per family. Phone: (506)395-4010.

SACKVILLE—D-5

(E) Marshview Trailer Park & Tenting (Not Visited)—(Westmorland) *From Hwy 2 (exit 506) & Hwy 106: Go 30 meters/100 ft NW on the ramp. Enter on R.* ◆◆FACILITIES: 74 sites, typical site width 30 ft, 9 full hkups, 65 W&E, (15/30 amps), tenting, dump, laundry. RECREATION: play equipment. Pets welcome. Partial handicap access. Open May 1 - Oct 15. Rate in 2010 $20 for 6 persons. Member COA of NB. Phone: (506) 536-2880.

ST. ANDREWS—E-2

KIWANIS OCEAN FRONT CAMPING—(Charlotte) *From east jct Hwy 1 & Hwy 127: Go 17.6 km/11 mi S on Hwy 127, then 2 blocks SW on Harriet St, then 2.4 km/1-1/2 mi E on Water St. Enter on L.* FACILITIES: 82 sites, typical site width 28 ft, 31 full hkups, 24 W&E, (30 amps), 27 no hkups, 10 pull-thrus, tenting, dump, laundry, ltd groc. RECREATION: canoeing, saltwater fishing, playground. Pets welcome. Partial handicap access. Open May 1 - Mid Oct. Phone: (506)529-3439.

ST. MARTINS—E-4

(C) Century Farm Family Campground—(St. John) *From jct Hwy 111 & Main St: Go 1 km/1/2 mi E on Main St. Enter on R.* ◆◆◆◆FACILITIES: 190 sites, typical site width 30 ft, 160 full hkups, 15 W&E, (15/30 amps), 15 no hkups, 50 pull-thrus, tenting, dump, laundry. ◆◆◆RECREATION: saltwater/saltwater fishing, playground. Pets welcome, breed restrict. Partial handicap access. Open May 1 - Sep 30. Rate in 2010 $28 for 2 persons. Member COA of NB.

Phone: (866)394-4400
Address: 67 Ocean Wave Dr, St Martins, NB E5R 2E8
Lat/Lon: 45.35271/-65.54356
Email: cenfarcg@nbnet.nb.ca
Web: www.centuryfarmcampground.com

ST. MARTINS—Continued on next page

ST. MARTINS—Continued

(C) Sea Side Tent & Trailer Park—(St. John) *From jct Hwy 111 & Main St: Go 1.3 km/1-1/4 mi E on Main St. Enter on R.* ◇◇◇FACILITIES: 88 sites, typical site width 22 ft, 53 full hkups, 25 W&E, (15/30 amps), 10 no hkups, 12 pull-thrus, cable TV, ($), WiFi Instant Internet at site, tenting, RV storage, dump, non-guest dump $, laundry, RV supplies, ice, picnic tables, fire rings, wood. ◇◇◇RECREATION: rec hall, swim pool, saltwater swim, kayaking, mini-golf, ($), playground, activities, horseshoes. Pets welcome. Open May 15 - Oct 15. Rate in 2010 $30 per family. MC/VISA/AMEX/Debit. Member COA of NB. FMCA discount. CCUSA 50% Discount. CCUSA reservations Recommended, CCUSA max stay 2 days, Cash only for CCUSA disc. Discount not available Jun 15-Sep 15.

Phone: (877)833-4413
Address: 234 Main St, St Martins, NB E5R-1B8
Lat/Lon: 45.35283/-65.54061
Email: mikegill@nbnet.nb.ca
Web: www.sn2000.nb.ca/comp/seaside-trailer-park

SAINT-ANDRE—C-2

(N) Paradis de la P'tite Montagne (Not Visited)—(Victoria) *From Hwy 2 (Exit 69): Go 3.5 km/2 mi N on Ch. Bourgoin, then 1/2 km/1/4 mi E on Ch. P'tite Montagne. Enter on R.* ◇◇◇FACILITIES: 221 sites, typical site width 30 ft, 153 full hkups, 43 W&E, (15/30 amps), 25 no hkups, 6 pull-thrus, tenting, dump, laundry, ltd groc. ◇◇◇RECREATION: lake swim, playground. Pets welcome. Open all yr. Facilities fully operational May 15 - Nov 30. Rate in 2010 $26-28 for 4 persons. Member COA of NB. Phone: (506)473-6683.

SAINT-BASILE—D-3

(SE) Camping St Basile—(Madawaska) *From E Town City Limit: Go 4 km/2-1/4 mi W on Rte 144. Enter on L.* ◇◇FACILITIES: 76 sites, typical site width 40 ft, 31 full hkups, 13 W&E, 2 E, (15/30 amps), 30 no hkups, tenting, dump, ltd groc. ◇RECREATION: swim pool, play equipment. Pets welcome. Open May 15 - Sep 15. Facilities fully operational Jun 20 - Sep 6. Rate in 2010 $22 for 4 persons. Phone: (506)263-1183.

SAINT-JOHN—E-3

(C) ROCKWOOD PARK CAMPGROUND—(St. John) *From E on Hwy 1 (exit 125): At the light go 300 meters/1000 ft NW on Mt. Pleasant Rd, then .4 km/1/8 mi NE on Lake Drive S. From W on Hwy 1 (Exit 122) follow the sign. Enter at end.*

WELCOME

◇◇◇◇FACILITIES: 213 sites, typical site width 20 ft, 56 full hkups, 107 W&E, 8 E, (15/30 amps), 42 no hkups, 48 pull-thrus, WiFi Instant Internet at site, phone Internet central location, tenting, dump, non-guest dump $, laundry, ice, picnic tables, fire rings, wood, controlled access.

◇◇◇◇RECREATION: pavilion, equipped pavilion, lake swim, canoeing, kayaking, lake fishing, golf nearby, playground, activities, (wkends), hiking trails, local tours. Rec open to public.

SAINT-JOHN—Continued
ROCKWOOD PARK CAMPGROUND—Continued

Pets welcome. Partial handicap access. Open May 15 - Oct 15. Clubs welcome. Rate in 2010 $32 for 4 persons. MC/VISA/Debit. Member COA of NB.

Phone: (506)652-4050
Address: 142 Lake Drive South, Saint John, NB E2K 5S2
Lat/Lon: 45.29101/-66.05302
Email: SJhort@nb.aibn.com
Web: www.sn2000.nb.ca/comp/rockwood-park-campground

SEE AD THIS PAGE

SAINT-LEONARD—C-2

(NE) Camping St-Leonard—(Madawaska) *From jct Hwy 2 & Route 17: Go 3.8 km/2 mi N on Rte 17. Enter on L.* ◇◇◇FACILITIES: 100 sites, 63 full hkups, 12 W&E, 5 E, (15/30/50 amps), 20 no hkups, 39 pull-thrus, tenting, dump, laundry. ◇◇◇RECREATION: swim pool, canoeing, lake fishing, playground. Pets welcome. Partial handicap access. Open May 15 - Sep 15. Big rigs welcome. Rate in 2010 $20-30 for 4 persons. Phone: (506)423-6536.

(NW) Grande Riviere Camping—(Madawaska) *From Hwy 2 (exit 56) & Rte 144: Go 1 km/3/4 mi W on Rte 144 W. Enter on L.* ◇◇FACILITIES: 97 sites, typical site width 40 ft, 45 full hkups, 25 W&E, (15/30 amps), 27 no hkups, 68 pull-thrus, tenting, dump, laundry. ◇◇◇RECREATION: swim pool, canoeing, river fishing, playground. Pets welcome. Open May 15 - Oct 15. Rate in 2010 $27-29 for 4 persons. Phone: (506) 423-6292.

SAINT-LOUIS-DE-KENT—C-4

KOUCHIBOUGUAC NATIONAL PARK (South Kouchibouguac)—*From Hwy 11 in town: Go 9-1/2 km/6 mi NE on access road.* FACILITIES: 311 sites, 46 E, 265 no hkups, tenting, dump, ltd groc. RECREATION: saltwater/river swim, boating, no motors, canoeing, ramp, saltwater/river fishing, playground. Pets welcome. Open May 15 - Oct 19. Phone: (506)876-2443.

(N) PARC DAIGLE PARK—(Kent) *From jct Hwy 117 & Hwy 134: Go 2.4 km/1-1/2 mi S on Hwy 134. Enter on L.* FACILITIES: 214 sites, typical site width 28 ft, 71 full hkups, 64 W&E, (15/20/30 amps), 79 no hkups, 93 pull-thrus, family camping, tenting, dump, laundry, ltd groc. RECREATION: swim pool, playground. Pets welcome, breed restrict, quantity restrict. Open May 15 - Sep 13. Member COA of NB. Phone: (506)876-4540.

SHEDIAC—D-5

(S) Beausejour Camping—(Westmorland) *At jct Hwy 140 (exit 37) & Hwy 15 (follow signs). Enter on L.* ◇◇◇FACILITIES: 255 sites, typical site width 30 ft, 86 full hkups, 123 W&E, (15/30 amps), 46 no hkups, 11 pull-thrus, tenting, dump, laundry, ltd groc. ◇◇◇RECREATION: swim pool, playground. Pets welcome. Open May 1 - Oct 30. Facilities fully operational Jun 1 - Sep 15. Rate in 2010 $30-35 for 4 persons. Member COA of NB. Phone: (506)532-5885.

(NW) Camping Oceanic—*From Hwy 15 (Exit 37) & Hwy 140: Go .08 km/3/4 mi N on Hwy 140. Enter on L.* ◇◇◇FACILITIES: 240 sites, 220 full hkups, 20 W&E, (30 amps). ◇RECREATION: swim pool, play equipment. Pets welcome, breed restrict. Partial handicap access. No tents. Open May 15 - Oct 15. Rate in 2010 $27-35 per family. Phone: (506)533-7006.

(NE) Etoile Filante Camping Wishing Star—(Westmorland) *From west town limits: Go 0.4 km/1/4 mi W on Hwy 133. Enter on R.* ◇◇◇FACILITIES: 130 sites, typical site width 30 ft, 130 full hkups, (15/30 amps), cable TV, WiFi Instant Internet at site, WiFi Internet central location, dump, non-guest dump, laundry, ice, picnic tables, fire rings, wood. ◇RECREATION: rec hall, play equipment. Pets welcome. Open May 1 - Oct 20. Rate in 2010 $35 for 4 persons. Debit. Member COA of NB. CCUSA 50% Discount.

Phone: (506)532-6786
Lat/Lon: 46.21886/-64.55841
Email: info@etoilefilante.ca
Web: www.etoilefilante.ca

(E) Ocean Surf Trailer Park—(Westmorland) *From east town limits: Go .08 km/1/2 mi E on Hwy 133. Enter on L.* ◇◇◇FACILITIES: 350 sites, typical

SHEDIAC—Continued
Ocean Surf Trailer Park—Continued

site width 20 ft, 350 full hkups, (15/30 amps), dump, laundry, ltd groc. ◇◇RECREATION: saltwater swim, playground. Pets welcome. No tents. Open May 1 - Oct 1. Facilities fully operational Jun 15 - Sep 5. Rate in 2010 $34-36 per family. Member COA of NB. Phone: (506)532-5480.

(E) Ocean View Park—(Westmorland) *From east city limits: Go 8 km/5 mi E on Hwy 133. Enter on L.* ◇◇◇FACILITIES: 128 sites, typical site width 20 ft, 69 full hkups, 53 W&E, (15/30 amps), 6 no hkups, WiFi Instant Internet at site, tenting, shower$, dump, non-guest dump, laundry, ltd groc, ice, picnic tables, fire rings, wood. ◇◇◇RECREATION: pavilion, saltwater swim, mini-golf, ($), bsktball, playground, activities, horseshoes. Pets welcome. Open May 20 - Oct 1. Rate in 2010 $26-37 per family. Debit. Member COA of NB. CCUSA 50% Discount. CCUSA reservations Accepted, CCUSA max stay Unlimited, Cash only for CCUSA disc., CCUSA disc. not avail F,Sa, CCUSA disc. not avail holidays. Not available Jul & Aug.

Phone: (506)532-3520
Address: 1586 Route 133, Grand-Barachois, NB E4P 8H2
Lat/Lon: 46.21981/-64.39371
Web: www.oceanviewcamping.ca

(NE) Parasol Camping—(Westmorland) *From west town limits: Go 180 m/200 yards W on Hwy 133. Enter on L.* ◇◇◇FACILITIES: 120 sites, 95 full hkups, 15 W&E, (15/30 amps), 10 no hkups, 20 pull-thrus, tenting, dump, laundry. ◇RECREATION: swim pool, canoeing, play equipment. Pets welcome. Open May 15 - Oct 15. Rate in 2010 $29-36 per family. Member COA of NB. Phone: (506)532-8229.

(NE) PARLEE BEACH PROVINCIAL PARK—(Westmorland) *From east town limits: Go .8 km/1/2 mi E on Hwy 133. Enter on L.* FACILITIES: 170 sites, 53 full hkups, 34 E, (15/30/50 amps), 83 no hkups, tenting, dump, laundry, ltd groc. RECREATION: saltwater swim, canoeing, playground. Pets welcome. Partial handicap access. Open May 29 - Sep 4. Big rigs welcome. Member COA of NB. Phone: (506)533-3363.

(C) SOUTH COVE RIVE-SUD CAMPING & GOLF—(Westmorland) *From town center: Go .08 km/1/2 mi E on Hwy 133, then 304 meters/1000 feet N on South Cove Rd. Enter on L.*

WELCOME

◇◇◇◇FACILITIES: 138 sites, typical site width 33 ft, 130 full hkups, (30/50 amps), 50 amps ($), 8 no hkups, some extd stay sites, 14 pull-thrus, cable TV, WiFi Instant Internet at site, phone/cable on-site Internet (needs activ), WiFi Internet central location, family camping, tenting, dump, non-guest dump $, laundry, ltd groc, RV supplies, ice, picnic tables, fire rings, wood, controlled access.

SOUTH COVE RIVE-SUD CAMPING & GOLF—Continued on next page

New Brunswick is known as the "Picture Province".

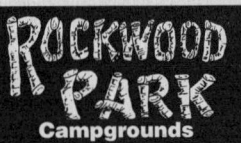

SHEDIAC—Continued
SOUTH COVE RIVE-SUD CAMPING & GOLF—Continued

◇◇◇RECREATION: rec hall, rec room/area, pavilion, putting green, golf nearby, playground, activities, (wkends), horseshoes, sports field, hiking trails. Rec open to public.

Pets welcome, quantity restrict. Partial handicap access. Open May 15 - Oct 18. Big rigs welcome. Escort to site. Clubs welcome. Rate in 2010 $30-40 per family. MC/VISA/Debit. Member COA of NB. CCUSA 50% Discount. CCUSA reservations Recommended, CCUSA max stay 5 days, CCUSA disc. not avail F,Sa, CCUSA disc. not avail holidays. Not available Jul & Aug.

Phone: (506)532-6713
Address: 55 South Cove Rd, Shediac, NB E4P 2T4
Lat/Lon: 46.22442/-64.52139
Email: reservations@shediacsouthcove.com
Web: www.shediacsouthcove.com

SEE AD PAGE 842

(C) SOUTH COVE RIVE-SUD GOLF—*From town center: Go .08 km/1/2 mi E on Hwy 133, then 300 m/1000 ft N on South Cove Rd. Enter on L.* 9 hole Par 3 Golf Course. Perfect for a quick round. Discounts every Tuesday and 20% campers discount. Open May15 - Oct 15. MC/VISA/Debit.

Phone: (506)532-6713
Address: 55 South Cove Rd, Shediac, NB E4P 2T4
Lat/Lon: 46.22442/-64.52139
Web: www.shediacsouthcove.com

SEE AD PAGE 842

SHEFFIELD—D-3

(E) CASEY'S ARTISANS—*From Fredericton on Hwy 105: Go 28 km. Enter on R.* Over 300 local New Brunswick artisans; Christmas & Halloween specialties, quilts, wooden items, hand made clothing, knitting & nostalgia. Summer hours: 8:30 am - 8 pm 7 days a week. Winter hours: 8:30 am - 7 pm Thur - Sun. Open all yr. MC/VISA/AMEX/Debit.

Phone: (506)357-8592
Address: 2511 Rte 105, Sheffield, NB E3A 9K3
Lat/Lon: 45.89141/-66.30782

SEE AD FREDERICTON PAGE 839

(E) CASEY'S CAMPGROUND—(York) *From Moncton on Hwy 2 (exit 333) & Rte 105: Go 13.2 km/8 mi N on Rte 105. Enter on R.*

◇◇◇FACILITIES: 34 sites, 18 full hkups, 16 W&E, (15/30 amps), some extd stay sites, tenting, dump, non-guest dump $, ltd groc, ice, picnic tables, fire rings, wood.

◇◇RECREATION: river swim, boating, canoeing, kayaking, ramp, dock, river fishing, golf nearby, sports field.

Pets welcome. Open May 20 - Oct 28. Clubs welcome. Rate in 2010 $22-30 for 4 persons. MC/VISA/AMEX/Debit.

Canada's national colors are red and white.

SHEFFIELD—Continued
CASEY'S CAMPGROUND—Continued

Phone: (506)357-8592
Address: 2511 Rte 105, Sheffield, NB E3A 9K3
Lat/Lon: 45.89141/-66.30782
Email: jsowers1@hotmail.com

SEE AD FREDERICTON PAGE 839

(E) CASEY'S MUSEUM—*From Moncton on Hwy 2 (exit 333) & Rte 105: Go 13.2 km/8 mi N on Rte 105. Enter on R.* Nostalgic museum (cars, tractors, toys, trains & service station memorabilia). Antiques for sale. Tourism info. Summer hours: 8:30 am - 8 pm 7 days a week. Winter hours: 8:30 am - 7 pm. Open all yr. MC/VISA/AMEX/Debit.

Phone: (506)357-8792
Address: 2511 Rte 105, Sheffield, NB E3A 9K3
Lat/Lon: 45.89141/-66.30782

SEE AD FREDERICTON PAGE 839

(E) CASEY'S RESTAURANT—*From Fredericton on Hwy 105: Go 28 km. Enter on R.* Breakfast, dinner, supper, home cooking. Home baking, home made desserts. Tourism information. Summer hours: 8:30 am - 8 pm 7 days a week. Winter hours: 8:30 am - 7 pm. Open all yr. MC/VISA/AMEX/Debit.

Phone: (506)357-8592
Address: 2511 Rte 105, Sheffield, NB E3A 9K3
Lat/Lon: 45.89141/-66.30782

SEE AD FREDERICTON PAGE 839

SHIPPAGAN—B-4

(NE) Camping Gite Janine & Auberge du Havre (Not Visited)—(Gloucester) *From N end town limit on Hwy 113 at bridge: Go 1.3 km/3/4 mi NE on Hwy 113, then 1000 ft/304 m S on Ch. Chiasson Rd. Enter on R.* ◇◇◇FACILITIES: 42 sites, 14 full hkups, 28 W&E, (15/30 amps), tenting, dump, laundry. ◇◇RECREATION: swim pool, boating, canoeing, ramp, play equipment. Pets welcome. Open May 15 - Oct 15. Facilities fully operational Jun 15 - Sep 15. Rate in 2010 $25-28 for 5 persons. Phone: (506)336-8884.

(W) CAMPING SHIPPAGAN (Town Park)—(Gloucester) *From jct Hwy 11 & Hwy 113: Go 17.5 km/11 mi N on Hwy 113, then 2.5 km/1-1/2 mi W on Upper Shippagan Rd. Enter on R.* FACILITIES: 153 sites, typical site width 25 ft, 38 full hkups, 73 W&E, (15/30 amps), 42 no hkups, 2 pull-thrus, tenting, dump, laundry, ltd groc. RECREATION: saltwater swim, boating, canoeing, ramp, saltwater fishing, playground. No pets. Partial handicap access. Open Jun - End of Sep. Phone: (506)336-3960.

SUSSEX—D-4

(NE) Town & Country Campark—(Kings) *From Hwy 1 (exit 195): Go 100 meters/300 ft N on Hwy 890, then 1 km/3/4 mi E on Wheeler Rd. Enter on L.* ◇◇◇◇FACILITIES: 350 sites, typical site width 25 ft, 250 full hkups, 40 W&E, (15/30 amps), 60 no hkups, 64 pull-thrus, family camping, tenting, dump, laundry. ◇◇◇RECREATION: swim pool, playground. Pets welcome. Open May 15 - Sep 26. Member COA of NB.

Phone: (506)432-9114
Address: 133 Alton Rd, Sussex, NB E4E 5L5
Lat/Lon: 45.73412/-65.48551
Email: sussexrivein@nb.aibn.com
Web: sussexdrivein.com

Canada's national animal is the beaver.

TRACADIE-SHEILA—B-4

(SW) Chalets et Camping de la Pointe (Not Visited)—(Gloucester) *From Hwy 11 & Hwy 370 (exit 192): Go 3.7km/2-1/4 mi W on Hwy 370, then 1/2 km/1/3 mi SE on Chemin A Comeau, then 1/3 km/1/4 mi E on Chemin Agnee Rd. Enter on R.* ◇◇◇FACILITIES: 107 sites, typical site width 35 ft, 80 full hkups, 7 W&E, (15/30 amps), 20 no hkups, 2 pull-thrus, tenting, dump, laundry, ltd groc. ◇◇◇RECREATION: 2 swim pools, river swim, boating, canoeing, dock, river fishing, playground. Pets welcome. Partial handicap access. Open May 15 - Sep 15. Facilities fully operational Jun 15 - Sep 5. Rate in 2010 $25-30 for 5 persons. Member COA of NB. Phone: (506)393-0987.

VAL COMEAU—B-4

(NE) VAL COMEAU PROVINCIAL PARK—*From jct Hwy 11 & 320: Go 2.7 km/1-3/4 mi S on Hwy 11, then 1.4 km/3/4 mi SE on Ch Val Comeau Rd, then 2.5 km/1-3/4 mi N on Val Ch Parc Val Comeau. Enter at end.* FACILITIES: 138 sites, 80 full hkups, 12 W&E, (15/30 amps), 46 no hkups, 50 pull-thrus, tenting, dump, laundry, ltd groc. RECREATION: saltwater/river swim, boating, canoeing, ramp, play equipment. Pets welcome. Partial handicap access. Open Jun 1 - Oct 1. Member COA of NB. Phone: (506)393-7150.

WATERBOROUGH—D-3

(NE) Mohawk Camping—(Queens) *From jct Hwy 2 (exit 347) & Hwy 105: Go 6.6 km/4 mi NE on Hwy 105. Enter on L.* ◇◇◇FACILITIES: 85 sites, typical site width 20 ft, 75 full hkups, (20/30 amps), 10 no hkups, 4 pull-thrus, tenting, dump, laundry, ltd groc. ◇◇◇RECREATION: lake swim, boating, canoeing, ramp, dock, lake fishing, playground. Pets welcome. Open May 15 - Oct 15. Rate in 2010 $32 per family. Phone: (506)362-5250.

WOODSTOCK—D-2

(S) Cosy Cabins Campground—*From Hwy 2 (exit 191) & Beardsley Rd: Go 1.5 km/1 mi E on Beardsley, then 30 m/100 ft N on Road 165. Enter on R.* ◇◇◇FACILITIES: 25 sites, 21 full hkups, 4 W&E, (15/30/50 amps), 12 pull-thrus, WiFi Internet central location, tenting, ice, picnic tables. RECREATION: canoeing, kayaking, river fishing. Pets welcome. Open May 1 - Nov 30. Big rigs welcome. Rate in 2010 $30 per family. MC/VISA/AMEX/Debit. CCUSA 50% Discount. CCUSA reservations Recommended, CCUSA max stay Unlimited. Discount not available holiday week-ends & special events unless approved by management. Pets must be on a leash.

Phone: (506)328-3344
Address: 2335 Rte 165, Woodstock, NB E7M 4A4
Lat/Lon: 46.13003/-67.57920
Email: cosycab@nbnet.nb.ca
Web: www.cosycabins.ca

(S) Yogi Bear's Jellystone Park at Kozy Acres—(Carleton) *From jct Hwy 2 (exit 191) & Beardsley Rd: Go .02 km/1/4 mi E on Beardsley Rd, then .04 km/1/4 mi W on Hemlock St. Enter on R.* ◇◇◇◇FACILITIES: 160 sites, typical site width 25 ft, 140 W&E, (15/30/50 amps), 50 amps ($), 20 no hkups, 92 pull-thrus, tenting, dump, laundry, ltd groc. ◇◇◇◇◇RECREATION: 2 swim pools, playground. Pets welcome. Partial handicap access. Open Jun 1 - Labor Day. Big rigs welcome. Rate in 2010 $38 per family. Member COA of NB. Phone: (888)222-9644.

Book your reservation online at woodalls.com

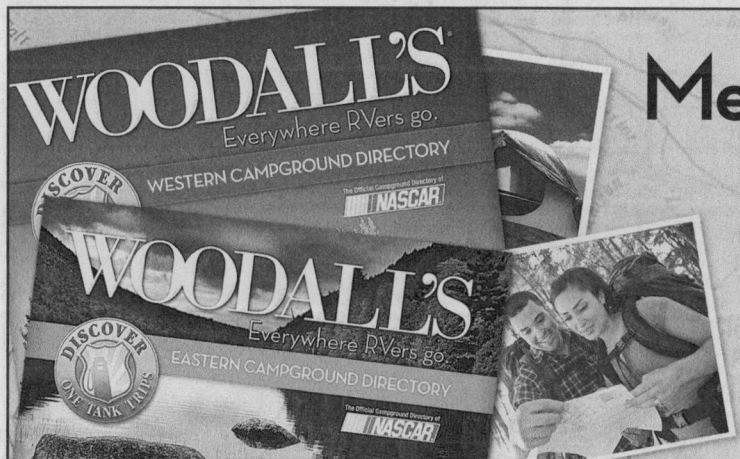

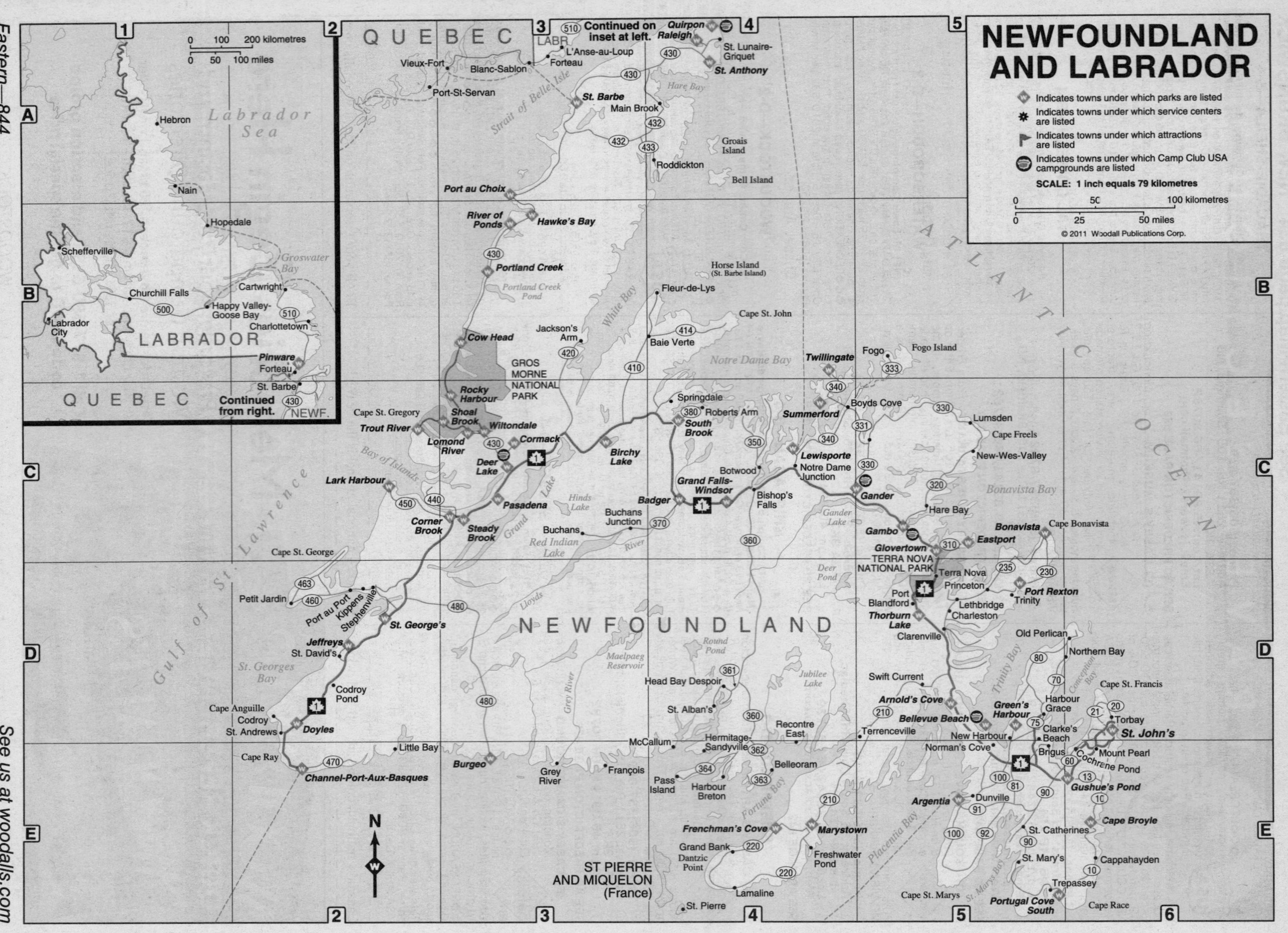

NEWFOUNDLAND AND LABRADOR
Indicates towns under which parks are listed
Indicates towns under which service centers are listed
Indicates towns under which attractions are listed
Indicates towns under which Camp Club USA campgrounds are listed
SCALE: 1 inch equals 79 kilometres
0 50 100 kilometres
0 25 50 miles
© 2011 Woodall Publications Corp.
Continued on inset at left.
Continued from right.
QUEBEC
LABRADOR
Labrador Sea
ATLANTIC OCEAN
Gulf of St. Lawrence
NEWFOUNDLAND
ST PIERRE AND MIQUELON (France)
GROS MORNE NATIONAL PARK
TERRA NOVA NATIONAL PARK
Hebron
Nain
Hopedale
Schefferville
Churchill Falls
Happy Valley-Goose Bay
Cartwright
Charlottetown
Labrador City
Pinware
Forteau
St. Barbe
Vieux-Fort
Blanc-Sablon
L'Anse-au-Loup
Port-St-Servan
Quirpon
Raleigh
St. Lunaire-Griquet
St. Anthony
Main Brook
Roddickton
Port au Choix
River of Ponds
Hawke's Bay
Portland Creek
Cow Head
Rocky Harbour
Shoal Brook
Wiltondale
Trout River
Lomond River
Cormack
Deer Lake
Lark Harbour
Corner Brook
Steady Brook
Pasadena
Birchy Lake
Springdale
Roberts Arm
South Brook
Baie Verte
Fleur-de-Lys
Twillingate
Fogo
Summerford
Boyds Cove
Lewisporte
Notre Dame Junction
Botwood
Grand Falls-Windsor
Badger
Bishop's Falls
Buchans
Buchans Junction
Gander
Gambo
Glovertown
Terra Nova
Bonavista
Eastport
Port Rexton
Trinity
Port Blandford
Thorburn Lake
Clarenville
Arnold's Cove
Bellevue Beach
Green's Harbour
Harbour Grace
Clarke's Beach
Brigus
Torbay
St. John's
Mount Pearl
Gushue's Pond
Cape Broyle
Argentia
Dunville
St. Catherines
St. Mary's
Trepassey
Portugal Cove South
Cape Race
Marystown
Frenchman's Cove
Grand Bank
Lamaline
St. Pierre
Burgeo
Grey River
François
Head Bay Despoir
St. Alban's
Hermitage-Sandyville
Harbour Breton
St. George's
Stephenville
Jeffreys
St. David's
Codroy Pond
Doyles
Cape Anguille
Codroy
St. Andrews
Cape Ray
Channel-Port-Aux-Basques
Little Bay

TRAVEL SECTION

Newfoundland and Labrador

CAMPING FEES

Camping fees in Newfoundland & Labrador listings are stated in Canadian dollars. Fees are quoted before taxes. Call each location for more details, as they vary from province to province.

TIME ZONE

Newfoundland and Labrador south of Black Tickle is in the Newfoundland Time Zone, which is one half hour later than Atlantic Time and 90 minutes later than Eastern Time.

TOPOGRAPHY

The island portion of the province has a rugged coastline and the interior is very scenic, consisting of heavily forested areas with rolling barren areas and innumerable lakes and ponds, rivers and fjords.

TEMPERATURE

Average summer temperatures range from about 69° F (20° C) during the day to around 54° F (12° C) at night. Winter temperatures are not extreme, as compared to inland continental areas. The coldest spells in St. John's range from 29° F to 32° F during the day and 18° F to 20° F at night. Temperature ranges are more pronounced in the inland and northern areas of the province.

TRAVEL & TOURISM INFO

Provincial Agency:
Newfoundland and Labrador Tourism
P.O. Box 8700
St. John's, NL A1B 4J6 Canada
(800/563-6353)
www.newfoundlandlabrador.com

Regional Agencies:

Coast of Bays Tourism Association
P.O. Box 310
St. Alban's, NL Canada A0H 2E0
(709/538-3552)
www.coastofbays.nl.ca

Destination St. John's
P.O. Box 205, Suite 201
Murray Premises
5 Beck's Cove
St. John's, NL Canada A1C 6H1
(709/739-8899 or 877/739-8899)
www.destinationstjohns.com

Dorset Trail Tourism Association
P.O. Box 419
Baie Verte, NL Canada A0K 1B0
(709/532-4242)

Western Newfoundland DMO
P.O. Box 130
Rocky Harbour, NL A0K 4N0
(709/458-3604)
www.westernnl.com

Combined Councils of Labrador
P.O. Box 479
North West River, NL Canada A0P 1M0
(709/497-3512)
www.combinedcouncils.ca/home/ or
www.ourlabrador.ca/

RECREATIONAL INFO

Fishing & Hunting: Dept. of Tourism, Culture and Recreation (709/729-3723). To order a copy of the **Guide to Hunting and Fishing Outfitters**, call 800/563-6353.

Icebergs: For those interested in finding where the icebergs are, there's a new website- icebergfinder.com.

SHOPPING

Chapel Arm Woodcrafts, Chapel Arm. You'll find handcrafted wood items including candleholders, bowls, vases and collapsible baskets. Rte 201, Chapel Arm, NF A0B 1L0 (709/592-2240).

King's Point Pottery, King's Point. Browse through pottery that highlights Newfoundland's environment and traditions, specializing in whale motifs on stoneware clay. Rte 391 Dr., P.O. Box 36, King's Point, NF A0J 1H0. (709/268-2216)

Where to Find CCUSA Parks

List City	Park Name	Map Coordinates
BELLEVUE BEACH		
	Bellevue Beach Campground (Not visited)	D-5
DEER LAKE		
	Gateway to the North RV Park	C-3
GAMBO		
	Square Pond Friends and Family RV Park	C-5
GANDER		
	Country Inn RV Park	C-5
QUIRPON		
	Viking RV Park	A-4

QUICK REFERENCE CHART FOR WOODALL'S FEATURED PARKS

	Green Friendly	RV Lots for Sale	Park Models-Onsite Ownership	Park Membership for Sale	Big Rigs Welcome	Internet Friendly	Pets Welcome
DOYLES							
Grand Codroy R.V. Camping Park Craft Shop						●	■

Green Friendly ; RV Lots for Sale ✖; Park Models/Onsite Onwership ✱; Park Memberships for Sale ✔; Big Rigs Welcome ▲; Internet Friendly ●; Internet Friendly-WiFi ●; Pets Welcome ■

Newfoundland Emporium, St. George's. Shop for unique Newfoundland crafts, folk art, antiques, rare books and more. Rte 1, P.O. Box 472, Corner Brook, NL A2H 4C2. (709/634-9376)

UNIQUE FEATURES

ICEBERGS

From the northern tip of Labrador down to the eastern coasts of Newfoundland the sea is nicknamed Iceberg Alley. Bergs born 10,000 years ago on the Greenland icecap are propelled by wind and tide into fantastic shapes before melting in the warm waters of the Gulf Stream. In the past, during certain times of the year, the alley has been thick with the largest and most beautiful icebergs found anywhere in the world. It is possible to wake up and see pure white and blue towers of ice rising out of the ocean. If you'd like a closer view, get as safely possible on a kayak or boating expedition to icebergs, whales and other marine life.

WHALES

The waters around Newfoundland and Labrador are home to whales of all kinds - humpback, minke, sperm, pothead, fin, blue and many more. Between May and September, these whales can be seen breaching the surface of the water and playing along our shores. Catching a single glimpse of these huge and majestic mammals is an exciting and awesome experience whether it is from the rail of a boat, the side of your sea kayak, or the seaside trail on land.

DESTINATIONS

Sprawling with natural beauty, and rich with history and culture, visitors will find the area rife with icebergs, whales, birds and wildlife. Hiking trails, parks and historic sites abound in this region. Around every bend, travelers will find a piece of heaven.

Access to the Island of Newfoundland is via plane or passenger/vehicle ferry. Motorists can cross Newfoundland on the fully paved Trans-Canada Highway, a distance of 565 miles (905 kilometers) from Port aux Basques to St. John's.

WESTERN REGION

This little corner of the island, which stretches from Channel-Port aux Basques to the Viking site of the Great Northern Peninsula, is anything but tiny. Ancient mountains, fjords, and thousands of miles of coastline create a unique geological history going back 1.25 billion years, little of which has been uncovered. Here, travelers will discover the first European settlement of the new world at L'Anse aux Meadows. A Viking village, and a World Heritage Site, featuring reconstructed sod huts that give visitors a glimpse into a day in the life of Nordic visitors who came to the area a thousand years ago - half a millennium before Columbus.

Corner Brook. One of the province's most scenic areas, Corner Brook is a bustling industrial center located at the mouth of the Humber River. The summit of the **Captain James Cook Memorial** provides an excellent view of Corner Brook and of the Bay of Islands. A large and growing colony of Arctic Terns can be viewed just a hundred meters from shore. The birds nest on a two-acre island rock and can be seen from several shoreline vantage points.

Gros Morne National Park. Located on the west coast of Newfoundland's Great Northern Peninsula, on the Gulf of St. Lawrence, Gros Morne is a scenic mixture of mountains, fjords, lakes, bays and abundant wildlife. The park offers a developed trail system and interpreter-guided nature hikes.

Labrador Lookout. This is a wonderful panoramic lookout over the Strait of Belle Isle to Labrador. The site has an interpretation panel detailing the area's natural and human history.

CENTRAL REGION

Literally the heart of Newfoundland, visitors will fall in love with the natural beauty and aboriginal history that goes back 5,000 years, including the Dorset people who carved soapstone pots at Newfoundland's first quarry. Notre Dame Bay is teeming with humpback whales and icebergs, and travelers can see these amazing creatures from the coast, or from a tour boat. For the more adventurous, explore the coastline from the seat of a kayak.

Dorset Trail, Baie Verte Peninsula. Visit the **Soapstone Quarry** at Fleur-de-Lys and learn first-hand how the Dorset Eskimos used soapstone for cooking pots and lamps. At the **Baie Verte Miners Museum** located at the site of the old Terra Nova copper mine you can learn about the mining history and geological formations of the region. Boat tours are available from Baie Verte, Nipper's Harbour and La Scie and Fleur-de-Lys. On the water you can see gigantic icebergs as they make their way south, whales, seabirds and seals. Tours from Nipper's Harbour also allow you to visit the now abandoned **Betts Cove Mine Site**.

EASTERN REGION

The Eastern Region stretches from John Cabot's historical landing place on the Bonavista Peninsula to the gateway of France on the Burin Peninsula. Here, visitors can explore villages established in the 16th century during the expansion of the British migratory fishery.

Cape Bonavista Lighthouse. First lit in 1842, the lighthouse is now restored to the 1870 period when the lightkeeper, his assistant and the assistant's family were all living there. Guides in period dress will help you explore this unique shaped house built around a central circular tower. The revolving light is the only known remaining one of its type in North America.

Also, on-site is a more recent lightkeeper's residence which houses an interpretation centre. This centre deals with the history and technology of lighthouses, along with an emphasis on the history behind the families that worked at the Cape Bonavista Lighthouse.

Bonavista is the landfall of John Cabot, the famous explorer who discovered Newfoundland.

AVALON

It was in this region that Alcock and Brown took off on the very first non-stop air crossing of the Atlantic in 1919, and it was here that Marconi ushered in the modern era of long distance wireless communications in 1901. History runs deep in the capital city of St. John's, inhabited since the 1620's. Today, the lively city that grew up around the harbor continues to thrive. Some of the best whale watching territory in the province can be found along the Irish Loop.

Cape Spear National Historic Site, located on Rt. 11, south of St. John's. Perched on North America's most easterly point, Cape Spear is the oldest lighthouse in Newfoundland. It has been restored to the 1839-1840 period.

Castle Hill National Historic Site, southwest of St. John's. See the remains of barracks, a powder magazine, guard rooms and a blockhouse.

St. John's. The capital of Newfoundland is a colorful town with both modern and Victorian architecture, museums, churches and historic sites and many shops selling Newfoundland handicrafts. Popular attractions include: **Memorial University Botanical Garden** at Oxen Pond, home to 90 acres of flowers, plants and rock gardens and **Commissariat House**, located near the downtown area. **Signal Hill National Historic Site** is the site of the last battle of the Seven Years' War in North America. A visitor's interpretation center offers displays and audio-visual presentations.

Witless Bay Ecological Reserve. This seabird sanctuary located off the east coast of the Avalon Peninsula, south of St. John's, is home to millions of puffins, gannets and kittiwakes, as well as playful whales and icebergs in the distance. There are several whalewatching tour companies in the Bay Bulls area to transport you to the bird islands as well as the summer home of the humpback whale.

All privately owned campgrounds personally inspected by
WOODALL'S
Representatives
John and Michele Pynenburg

ARGENTIA—E-5

(NW) Fitzgerald's Pond Park (Not visited)—*From Argentia Ferry Dock: Go 25 km/15-1/2 mi N on Hwy 100. Enter on R.* ◇◇FACILITIES: 47 sites, typical site width 18 ft, 47 no hkups, tenting, dump. ◇◇RECREATION: lake swim, canoeing, ramp, lake fishing. Pets welcome. Open all yr. Rate in 2010 $15 for 6 persons. Phone: (709)227-4488.

ARNOLD'S COVE—D-5

(SE) Putt 'N' Paddle Campground—*From W jct Arnold's Cove & Hwy 1: Go 5 km/3 mi E on Hwy 1. Enter on R.* ◇◇◇FACILITIES: 200 sites, typical site width 18 ft, 100 W&E, (20 amps), 100 no hkups, tenting, dump, laundry, ltd groc. ◇◇RECREATION: lake swim, boating, canoeing, ramp, lake fishing, playground. Pets welcome. Open Mid May - Sep 30. Rate in 2010 $24 for 4 persons. Phone: (709)685-6767.

BADGER—C-4

(NW) Catamaran Park—*From west town limits on Hwy 1: Go 8.4 km/5-1/4 mi W on Hwy 1. Enter on R.* ◇◇FACILITIES: 102 sites, typical site width 20 ft, 96 W&E, (15 amps), 6 no hkups, tenting, dump, laundry, ltd groc. ◇◇RECREATION: swim pool, lake swim, canoeing, ramp, lake fishing, play equipment. Pets welcome. Open May 19 - Sep 4. Rate in 2010 $18 for 4 persons. Phone: (709)539-5115.

BELLEVUE BEACH—D-5

(W) Bellevue Beach Campground (Not visited)—*From W on Hwy 1 & jct 201: Go 7.3 km/4-1/2 mi NE on Hwy 201. Enter on L.* ◇◇◇FACILITIES: 111 sites, typical site width 16 ft, 47 W&E, (15/30 amps), 64 no hkups, 6 pull-thrus, tenting, dump, non-guest dump $, ice, picnic tables, fire rings, wood. ◇◇RECREATION: lake swim, boating, canoeing, kayaking, ramp, lake fishing, play equipment, hiking trails. Pets welcome. Open May 15 - Labor Day. Rate in 2010 $23-31 for 2 persons. MC/VISA. CCUSA 50% Discount. CCUSA reservations Recommended, CCUSA max stay 2 days, Cash only for CCUSA disc. Discount not available Jul & Aug.

Phone: (709)442-4536
Address: 239 Main Road, Bellevue Beach, NL A0B 1B0
Lat/Lon: 47.63584/-53.78178
Email: maxineanderson@bellevuebeach.com
Web: www.bellevuebeach.com

BIRCHY LAKE—C-3

(SW) Fort Birchy Park & Campground—*Eastbound from jct Hwy 420 & Hwy 1: Go 32 km/20 mi E on Hwy 1. Or if westbound go 17 km/12 mi W on Hwy 1.* ◇◇FACILITIES: 100 sites, typical site width 28 ft, 34 full hkups, 14 W&E, 13 E, (15 amps), 39 no hkups, 4 pull-thrus, tenting, dump, laundry, ltd groc. ◇◇RECREATION: lake swim, boating, canoeing, ramp, dock, lake fishing, playground. Pets welcome. Partial handicap access. Open Jun 15 - Sep 15. Rate in 2010 $17-18-20 for 4 persons. Phone: (709)636-3678.

BONAVISTA—C-5

(S) Paradise Farm Trailer Park—*From jct Hwy 238 & Hwy 230: Go 2.5 km/1-1/2 mi S on Hwy 230. Enter on R.* ◇◇FACILITIES: 30 sites, typical site width 20 ft, 22 W&E, (15/30 amps), 8 no hkups, tenting, dump. ◇◇RECREATION: canoeing, lake fishing. Pets welcome. Open Mid May - Mid Sep. Rate in 2010 $15-18 for 4 persons. Phone: (709)468-8811.

Check out our web site www.woodalls.com

BURGEO—E-3

SANDBANKS (Provincial Park)—*In town on Hwy 480.* FACILITIES: 30 sites, 30 no hkups, tenting, dump, laundry. RECREATION: saltwater swim, saltwater fishing, playground. Pets welcome. Partial handicap access. Open Mid May - Mid Sep. Phone: (709)635-4520.

CAPE BROYLE—E-6

LA MANCHE (Provincial Park)—*From town: Go 11.5 km/7 mi N on Hwy 10.* FACILITIES: 69 sites, 69 no hkups, tenting, dump, laundry. RECREATION: river swim, canoeing, river fishing, playground. Pets welcome. Partial handicap access. Open Mid May - Mid Sep. Phone: (709)635-4520.

CHANNEL-PORT-AUX-BASQUES—E-2

JT CHEESEMAN (Provincial Park)—*From town: Go 8 km/5 mi W on Hwy 1.* FACILITIES: 101 sites, 21 E, 80 no hkups, tenting, dump. RECREATION: saltwater swim, saltwater fishing, playground. Pets welcome. Partial handicap access. Open Mid May - Mid Sep. Phone: (709)635-4520.

(NW) Little Paradise Park—*From jct Hwy 1 & Hwy 408: Go 11.5 km/7 mi E on Hwy 1. Enter on L.* ◇◇FACILITIES: 78 sites, typical site width 20 ft, 15 W&E, (15/30 amps), 63 no hkups, tenting, dump, laundry. RECREATION: canoeing. Pets welcome. Open Jun 1 - Sep 15. Rate in 2010 $18 for 4 persons. Phone: (709)955-2682.

CORMACK—C-3

(SW) Funland Resort—*From jct TCH 1 & Hwy 430: Go 7km/4-1/4 mi NW on Hwy 430, then at jct Hwy 430 & Hwy 422 go .08 km/1/4 mi NE on Hwy 422. Enter on R.* ◇◇◇FACILITIES: 96 sites, typical site width 30 ft, 84 full hkups, (30 amps), 12 no hkups, 17 pull-thrus, tenting, dump, laundry, ltd groc. ◇◇◇◇RECREATION: swim pool, playground. Pets welcome. Partial handicap access. Open all yr. Facilities fully operational May 15 - Oct 15. Rate in 2010 $22-28 for 6 persons. Phone: (709)635-7227.

CORNER BROOK—C-3

(SE) Family Adventure Park CG—*From TCH 1 (exit 4) & Hwy 450: Go 7.3 km/4-1/2 mi W on Hwy 450. Enter on L.* ◇◇◇FACILITIES: 37 sites, 29 full hkups, (30/50 amps), 8 no hkups, 4 pull-thrus, laundry, ltd groc. ◇◇◇RECREATION: swim pool, playground. Pets welcome, breed restrict, quantity restrict. Partial handicap access. No tents. Open May 15 - Sep 15. Big rigs welcome. Rate in 2010 $28 for 4 persons. Phone: (709)634-4719.

(W) Kinsman Prince Edward Park (Not visited)—*From jct Hwy TCH #1 & Hwy 440 (exit 7): Go 2.7 km/1-3/4 mi NW on Hwy 440. Enter on L.* ◇◇◇FACILITIES: 86 sites, 28 full hkups, 18 W&E, (30/50 amps), 40 no hkups, 9 pull-thrus, tenting, dump, laundry, ltd groc. ◇◇RECREATION: playground. Pets welcome. Open June 15 - Sep 5. Rate in 2010 $18-23 for 4 persons. Phone: (709)637-1580.

COW HEAD—B-3

GROS MORNE NATIONAL PARK (Shallow Bay)—*From Hwy-430: Go W on access road through town.* FACILITIES: 62 sites, 62 no hkups, tenting, dump. RECREATION: saltwater swim, saltwater/river fishing, playground. Partial handicap access. Open Jun 11 - Sep 20. Phone: (709)458-2417.

DEER LAKE—C-3

DEER LAKE MUNICIPAL PARK—*From Hwy 1 (exit 16): Go 2 km/1.3 mi N on Hwy 430, then left on Nicolson Rd 2.4 km/1.5 mi. Enter on R.* FACILITIES: 33 sites, typical site width 24 ft, 33 no hkups, tenting, dump. RECREATION: river swim, river fishing. Open Jul 1 - Sep 15. Phone: (709)635-5885.

(SE) Gateway to the North RV Park—*From jct TCH 1 (exit 16) & Hwy 430: Go .08 km/1/2 mi NW on Hwy 430. Enter on L.* ◇◇◇◇FACILITIES: 59 sites, typical site width 35 ft, 59 full hkups, (15/30/50 amps), 50 amps ($), 29 pull-thrus, WiFi Instant Internet at site,

DEER LAKE—Continued
Gateway to the North RV Park—Continued

tenting, laundry, ice, picnic tables, fire rings, wood. ◇◇RECREATION: pavilion, river swim, boating, canoeing, river fishing, hiking trails. Pets welcome. Partial handicap access. Open Mid May - Oct 1. Big rigs welcome. Rate in 2010 $29-35 for 4 persons. MC/VISA/AMEX/Debit. CCUSA 50% Discount. CCUSA reservations Required, CCUSA max stay 2 days. Discount available Jun 1-30 & Sep1-30.

Phone: (888)818-8898
Address: 1 Bonne Bay Hwy 430, Deer Lake, NL A8A 2Z4
Lat/Lon: 49.19436/-57.43459
Email: geribeaulieu@hotmail.com
Web: www.gatewaytothenorthrvpark.com

Reserve Online at Woodalls.com

SIR RICHARD SQUIRES MEMORIAL (Provincial Park)—*From town: Go 12.7 km/8 mi NW on Hwy 430, then 27.3 km/17 mi NE on Hwy 422.* FACILITIES: 159 sites, 159 no hkups, tenting, dump, laundry. RECREATION: canoeing, river fishing, playground. Pets welcome. Partial handicap access. Open Jun 1 - Mid Sep. Phone: (709)635-4520.

DOYLES—D-2

(NW) GRAND CODROY R.V. CAMPING PARK CRAFT SHOP—*From the ferry dock at Port aux Basques: Go 38 km/23-1/2 mi E on Trans Canada Hwy (Hwy 1), then 1.4 km/3/4 mi NW on Hwy 406 (Doyles Station Rd), then 1 km/3/4 mi E. Enter on L.*

◇◇◇◇FACILITIES: 85 sites, typical site width 25 ft, 38 full hkups, 32 W&E, (15/30 amps), 15 no hkups, 3 pull-thrus, WiFi Internet central location, tenting, dump, non-guest dump $, laundry, picnic tables, grills, wood, controlled access.

◇◇◇RECREATION: rec hall, river swim, canoeing, kayaking, river fishing, fishing guides, playground, hiking trails.

Pets welcome. Open Mid May - Sep 30. Escort to site. Clubs welcome. Rate in 2010 $20-28 per family.

Phone: (877)955-2520
Address: 5 Doyles Station Rd, Doyles, NL AON 1JO
Lat/Lon: 47.83346/-59.20500
Email: grandcodroyrvcamping@nf.sympatico.ca
Web: www3.nf.sympatico.ca/dennis.keeping

SEE AD THIS PAGE

EASTPORT—C-5

(W) HAROLD W DUFFSETT SHRINERS RV PARK—*From jct Hwy 1 & Hwy 310 (Eastport Peninsula Rd) at the west entrance to Terra Nova National Park: Go 13.6 km/8-1/2 mi E on Eastport Peninsula Rd. Enter on L.*

◇◇◇FACILITIES: 111 sites, typical site width 30 ft, 71 full hkups, 30 W&E, (20/30/50 amps), 50 amps ($), 10 no hkups, some extd stay sites, 6 pull-thrus, WiFi Instant Internet at site, phone Internet central location, family camping, tenting, cabins, dump, non-guest dump $, laundry, RV supplies, ice, picnic tables, controlled access.

HAROLD W DUFFSETT SHRINERS RV PARK—Continued on next page

EASTPORT—Continued
HAROLD W DUFFSETT SHRINERS RV PARK—Continued

◇◇◇RECREATION: rec hall, rec room/area, pavilion, coin games, mini-golf, ($), golf nearby, bsktball, playground, shuffleboard court shuffleboard court, horseshoes, hiking trails.

Pets welcome. Open May 15 - Oct 16. Big rigs welcome. Escort to site. Clubs welcome. MC/VISA/Debit.

Phone: (709)677-2438
Address: Route #310, Eastport, NL A0G 1Z0
Lat/Lon: 48.65224/-53.76079
Email: eastportrvpark@nf.aibn.com
Web: www.shrinesparkeastport.com

SEE AD PAGE 847

FRENCHMAN'S COVE—E-4

FRENCHMAN'S COVE (Provincial Park)—*From town: Go 1 km/1/2 mi S on Hwy 210.* FACILITIES: 75 sites, 75 no hkups, tenting, dump. RECREATION: saltwater swim, canoeing, saltwater fishing, playground. Pets welcome. Partial handicap access. Open Mid May - Mid Sep. Phone: (709)635-4520.

GAMBO—C-5

DAVID SMALLWOOD PARK (Town Park)—*From jct Hwy 1 & Hwy 320: Go 7.1 km/4.3 mi N on Hwy 320. Enter on L.* FACILITIES: 42 sites, 15 W&E, (20/30 amps), 27 no hkups, tenting. RECREATION: river fishing. Open Jun - Sep. Phone: (709)674-0122.

(NW) Square Pond Friends and Family RV Park —*From jct Hwy 320 & Hwy 1: Go 12 km/7-1/2 mi W on Hwy 1. Enter on L.* ◇◇◇◇FACILITIES: 110 sites, typical site width 50 ft, 1 full hkups, 60 W&E, (30 amps), 49 no hkups, cable TV, ($), WiFi Instant Internet at site, WiFi Internet central location, tenting, RV storage, dump, non-guest dump $, laundry, ltd groc, ice, picnic tables, fire rings, wood. ◇◇◇◇RECREATION: equipped pavilion, boating, canoeing, kayaking, ramp, dock, river/pond fishing, fishing supplies, bsktball, playground, activities, horseshoes, hiking trails, v-ball. Pets welcome. Partial handicap access. Open May 21 - Oct 11. Rate in 2010 $20-25 per vehicle. MC/VISA/Debit. CCUSA 50% Discount. CCUSA reservations Recommended, CCUSA max stay 2 days, Cash only for CCUSA disc., CCUSA disc. not avail F,Sa, CCUSA disc. not avail holidays. Not available Jun 26-Sep 2.

CAMPCLUB USA

Phone: (709)674-7566
Address: Glovertown, NL A0G 2L0
Lat/Lon: 48.80433/-54.29460
Email: info@squarepondpark.ca
Web: www.squarepondpark.ca

GANDER—C-5

(C) Country Inn RV Park—*From Hwy 1 & Hwy 330: Go 4.8 km/3 mi N on Hwy 330. Enter on L.* ◇◇◇FACILITIES: 64 sites, typical site width 22 ft, 30 full hkups, 34 W&E, (15/30 amps), 10 pull-thrus, WiFi Instant Internet at site, phone Internet central location, tenting, RV storage, dump, non-guest dump $, ice, picnic tables. ◇◇RECREATION: pavilion, equipped pavilion, fishing guides, playground, horseshoes, hiking trails. Pets welcome. Partial handicap access. Open May 15 - Oct 15. Rate in 2010 $23-26 per family. MC/VISA/Debit. CCUSA 50% Discount. CCUSA reservations Recommended, CCUSA max stay 2 days, Cash only for CCUSA disc., CCUSA disc. not avail F,Sa, CCUSA disc. not avail holidays. Not available Jul or Aug.

CAMPCLUB USA

Phone: (709)256-4005
Address: 315 Magee Rd, Gander, NL A1V 1W6
Lat/Lon: 48.98482/-54.60620
Email: fredguzz@hotmail.com

(N) Jonathan's Pond Campground (Not visited) —*From jct Hwy 1 & Hwy 330: Go 16.1 km/10 mi N on Hwy 330. Enter on R.* ◇◇FACILITIES: 155 sites, 100 W&E, 55 E, (30 amps), 20 pull-thrus, tenting, dump, laundry, ltd groc. ◇◇RECREATION: lake swim, boating, canoeing, ramp, dock, lake fishing, playground. Pets welcome. Open May 24 - Sep 30. Rate in 2010 $21-25 per family. Phone: (709)651-2492.

GLOVERTOWN—C-5

(SE) TERRA NOVA NATIONAL PARK (Madalay Head) —*Down Hwy 130.4 Kilometers from TransCanada Hwy 1, Ent. on Right.* FACILITIES: 99 sites, 99 no hkups, dump. RECREATION: canoeing, ramp, saltwater fishing, playground. Open Jun - Sep. Phone: (800)414-6765.

TERRA NOVA NP (Newman Sound Campground)—*From jct Trans Canada Hwy 1 & Hwy 310: Go 22.5 km/14 mi E on Hwy 1. Enter on L.* FACILITIES: 356 sites, typical site width 20 ft, 107 E, (20 amps), 249 no hkups, tenting, dump, laundry, ltd groc. RECREATION: lake swim, boating, canoeing, ramp, saltwater/lake/stream fishing, playground. Partial handicap access. Open all yr. Facilities fully operational May 15 - Oct 10. Phone: (709)533-3186.

GRAND FALLS-WINDSOR—C-4

(W) Beothuck Park (Not visited)—*On Hwy 1 (exit 17): Go 30m/100 ft N, then 2 Km/1-1/4 mi W on Main St. Enter on R.* ◇◇FACILITIES: 75 sites, typical site width 30 ft, 30 ft max RV length, 70 W&E, (15/30 amps), 5 no hkups, 8 pull-thrus, tenting. ◇◇RECREATION: lake swim, boating, canoeing, ramp, lake fishing, play equipment. Pets welcome. Partial handicap access. Open Jun 1 - Sep 20. Rate in 2010 $25 for 4 persons. Phone: (709)489-9832.

Sanger Memorial RV Park—*From Hwy 1 (exit 20): Go 2.5 km/1-1/2 mi SW on Industrial Access Rd/Scott Ave. Enter on L.* ◇◇◇◇FACILITIES: 47 sites, typical site width 30 ft, 43 full hkups, 4 W&E, (15/30/50 amps), 50 amps ($), 6 pull-thrus. ◇◇RECREATION: river swim, canoeing. Pets welcome. Partial handicap access. No tents. Open Jun 14 - Labour Day. Big rigs welcome. Rate in 2010 $26 for 6 persons. Phone: (709)489-8780.

GREEN'S HARBOUR—D-5

(C) Golden Arm Trailer Park—*From jct Hwy 1 & Hwy 80 (exit 28): Go 24 km/15 mi N on Hwy 80. Enter on R.* ◇◇◇FACILITIES: 140 sites, typical site width 30 ft, 90 full hkups, 50 W&E, (15/30 amps), 15 pull-thrus, tenting, dump, laundry, ltd groc. ◇◇◇RECREATION: swim pool, canoeing, pond fishing, playground. Pets welcome. Partial handicap access. Open May 1 - Oct 20. Rate in 2010 $20 per family. Phone: (709)582-3600.

GUSHUE'S POND—E-6

Gushue's Pond Park (Not visited)—*From jct Hwy 70 & Hwy 1 (exit 32): Go 1.6 km/1 mi SE on Service road to Gushue's Pond signs. Enter at end.* ◇◇◇FACILITIES: 137 sites, typical site width 20 ft, 74 W&E, (15/30 amps), 63 no hkups, 10 pull-thrus, tenting, dump, laundry, ltd groc. ◇◇RECREATION: no motors, canoeing, pond fishing, playground. Pets welcome. Open May 16 - Sep 5. Rate in 2010 $17-25 per family. Phone: (709)229-4003.

HAWKE'S BAY—B-3

(N) Torrent River Nature Park—*From E Town City Limit on Hwy 430: Go 1 km/3/4 mi W on Hwy 430. Enter on R.* ◇◇◇FACILITIES: 26 sites, typical site width 18 ft, 22 ft max RV length, 19 W&E, (15 amps), 7 no hkups, tenting, dump. ◇RECREATION: river swim, river fishing. Pets welcome. Partial handicap access. Open Jun 18 - Sep 7. Rate in 2010 $25 per family. Phone: (709)248-5344.

JEFFREYS—D-2

(SE) Wishingwell Campground (Not visited)—*From Codroy Pond overpass: Go 6.5 km/4 mi E on Hwy 1. Enter on R.* ◇◇FACILITIES: 67 sites, typical site width 20 ft, 27 full hkups, (15 amps), 40 no hkups, 11 pull-thrus, tenting, dump. RECREATION: play equipment. Pets welcome. Open Mid May - Mid Oct. Rate in 2010 $15 for 6 persons. Phone: (709)645-2501.

LARK HARBOUR—C-2

BLOW ME DOWN (Provincial Park)—*Southeast of town on Hwy 450.* FACILITIES: 28 sites, 28 no hkups, tenting, dump, laundry. RECREATION: saltwater swim, canoeing, saltwater fishing, playground. Pets welcome. Partial handicap access. Open May - Mid Sep. Phone: (709)635-4520.

LEWISPORTE—C-4

(NE) NOTRE DAME (Provincial Park)—*From town: Go 11.4 km/7 mi S on Hwy 340, then 3.4 km/2 mi W on Hwy 1.* FACILITIES: 100 sites, 100 no hkups, tenting, dump, laundry, ltd groc. RECREATION: canoeing, pond fishing, playground. Pets welcome. Partial handicap access. Open Mid May - Mid Sep. Phone: (709)635-4520.

LOMOND RIVER—C-3

(SE) Lomond River Lodge and RV Park—*From Hwys 430 & Hwy 431: Go 10 km/ 6-1/4 mi NW on Hwy 431. Enter on R.* ◇◇◇FACILITIES: 40 sites, typical site width 20 ft, 28 full hkups, (15/30 amps), 12 no hkups, tenting, dump, laundry, ltd groc. ◇◇RECREATION: boating, canoeing, river fishing, play equipment. Pets welcome. Partial handicap access. Open May 15 - Oct 15. Rate in 2010 $23 for 2 persons.

Phone: (877)456-6663
Address: Route 431, Lomond River, NL A0K 3V0
Lat/Lon: 49.40623/-57.72879
Email: info@lomond-river-lodge.com
Web: www.lomond-river-lodge.com

MARYSTOWN—E-4

(SW) Golden Sands Trailer Park (Not Visited) —*From jct Hwy 210 & Hwy 222: Go 3.2 km/2 mi SE on Hwy 222, then 1.6 km/1 mi on gravel road. Enter on R.* ◇◇FACILITIES: 110 sites, typical site width 20 ft, 41 W&E, 14 E, (15 amps), 55 no hkups, 21 pull-thrus, tenting, dump, laundry. ◇◇◇RECREATION: boating, canoeing, pond fishing, playground. Pets welcome. Partial handicap access. Open all yr. Phone: (709)891-2400.

Newfoundland produces half of Canada's iron ore.

PASADENA—C-3

(N) Pineridge Cabins & Campground (Not visited)—*From Hwy 1 (exit 13): Go .08 km/1/2 mi SE on service road. Enter on R.* ◇◇FACILITIES: 140 sites, typical site width 25 ft, 140 full hkups, (30 amps), tenting, dump, ltd groc. ◇◇◇RECREATION: swim pool, playground. Pets welcome. Open May 24 - Sep 30. Rate in 2010 $20-30 per family. Phone: (709)686-2541.

PINWARE—B-2

PINWARE RIVER (Provincial Park)—(Labrador) *Located in Labrador.* FACILITIES: 22 sites, 22 no hkups, tenting, dump, laundry. RECREATION: saltwater swim, canoeing, saltwater fishing. Pets welcome. Partial handicap access. Open Jun 1 - Mid Sep. Phone: (709)635-4520.

PORT REXTON—D-5

LOCKSTON PATH (Provincial Park)—*From town: Go 6.8 km/4 mi N on Hwy 236.* FACILITIES: 56 sites, 20 W&E, (15/30 amps), 36 no hkups, tenting, dump, laundry. RECREATION: boating, no motors, canoeing, ramp, river/pond fishing, playground. Pets welcome. Partial handicap access. Open Mid May - Mid Sep. Phone: (709)635-4520.

PORT-AU-CHOIX—A-3

(SW) Oceanside RV Park—*From jct Hwy 430 & Hwy 430-28: Go 13 km/8 mi NW on Hwy 430-28. Enter on L.* ◇◇◇FACILITIES: 46 sites, 26 W&E, (15/30 amps), 20 no hkups, tenting, dump. Pets welcome. Open May 20 - Sep 30. Rate in 2010 $25 per family. Phone: (709)861-2133.

(SW) Sea Echo Motel (Not visited) (RV SPACES)—*From jct Hwy 430 & jct 430-28: Go 14 km/8-3/4 mi W on 430-28. Enter on L.* FACILITIES: 20 sites, typical site width 20 ft, accepts self-contained units only, 10 W&E, (15 amps), 10 no hkups. Pets welcome. No tents. Open May 1 - Oct 1. Rate in 2010 $17 per vehicle. Phone: (709)861-3777.

PORTLAND CREEK—B-3

(NE) Mountain Waters Resort (Not visited)—*From W Town City Limit on Hwy 430: Go 4.8 km/3 mi E on Hwy 430, then 1.6 km/1 mi SE on dirt road. Enter at end.* ◇◇◇FACILITIES: 53 sites, typical site width 22 ft, 30 full hkups, (30 amps), 23 no hkups, 15 pull-thrus, tenting, dump, laundry, ltd groc. ◇◇◇RECREATION: lake swim, boating, canoeing, dock, lake fishing, play equipment. Pets welcome. Partial handicap access. Open June 1 - Sept 30. Rate in 2010 $25 per family. Phone: (709)898-2490.

PORTUGAL COVE SOUTH—E-5

CHANCE COVE (Provincial Park)—*From town: Go 10 km/6-1/4 mi S on Hwy 10.* FACILITIES: 25 sites, 25 no hkups, tenting. RECREATION: saltwater swim, canoeing, saltwater fishing. Pets welcome. Open Apr 15 - Oct 1. Phone: (709)635-4520.

QUIRPON—A-4

(W) Viking RV Park—*From jct Hwy 430 & 436:Go 24 km/15 mi E on Hwy 436, then 100 m/300 ft NE on Quirpon Intersection. Enter on L.* ◇◇◇FACILITIES: 35 sites, 26 ft max RV length, 17 W&E, (15/30 amps), 18 no hkups, 2 pull-thrus, WiFi Internet central location ($), tenting, dump, non-guest dump $, laundry, ice, picnic tables, fire rings, wood. RECREATION: play equipment. Pets welcome. Open May 24 - Sept 30. Rate in 2010 $22-25 per family. VISA/Debit. CCUSA 50% Discount. CCUSA reservations Recommended, CCUSA max stay 2 days, Cash only for CCUSA disc. Discount not available Jul & Aug. No credit cards. Not valid with any other discounts. Discount not available on tent sites.

CAMPCLUB USA

Phone: (709)623-2425
Address: Route 436, Quirpon, NL A0K 2X0
Lat/Lon: 51.56780/-55.48019
Email: vikingrvpark@hotmail.com

RALEIGH—A-4

PISTOLET BAY (Provincial Park)—*From town: Go 4.8 km/3 mi S on Hwy 437.* FACILITIES: 30 sites, 30 no hkups, tenting, dump, laundry. RECREATION: lake swim, river fishing. Pets welcome. Partial handicap access. Open Jun 1 - Mid Sep. Phone: (709)635-4520.

RIVER OF PONDS—B-3

(SW) River of Ponds Park (Not visited)—*From E Town City Limit on Hwy 430: Go .06 km/1/4 mi W on Hwy 430. Enter on L.* ◇◇FACILITIES: 54 sites, typical site width 15 ft, 15 W&E, (30 amps), 39 no hkups, tenting, dump, laundry, ltd groc. RECREATION: canoeing, ramp, pond fishing. Pets welcome. Open May 24 - Sep 16. Rate in 2010 $12.50-21 for 4 persons. Phone: (709)225-3130.

ROCKY HARBOUR—C-3

GROS MORNE NATIONAL PARK (Berry Hill)—*From town: Go 4 km/2-1/2 mi N on Hwy 430.* FACILITIES: 152 sites, 152 no hkups, tenting, dump. RECREATION: saltwater fishing, playground. Partial handicap access. Open Jun 19 - Sep 13. Phone: (709)458-2417.

(C) Gros Morne RV Campground & Motel—*From jct Hwy 430 and West Link Road: Go .08 km/1/2 mi west on West Link Road. Enter on L.* ◇◇◇◇FACILI-

Gros Morne RV Campground & Motel—Continued on next page

ROCKY HARBOUR—Continued
Gros Morne RV Campground & Motel—Continued

TIES: 74 sites, typical site width 30 ft, 53 full hkups, 18 W&E, (15/30/50 amps), 50 amps ($), 3 no hkups, 8 pull-thrus, tenting, dump, laundry, ltd groc. ◇◇RECREATION: playground. Pets welcome. Partial handicap access. Open mid May - mid Oct. Big rigs welcome. Rate in 2010 $22-28 for 4 persons. Phone: (877)488-3133. FMCA discount.

(S) Gros Morne/Norris Point KOA—*From jct Hwy 430 & Norris Point access road (National Park Visitor Center): Go 2.4 km/1-1/2 mi W on Norris Point access road. Enter on L.* ◇◇◇◇FACILITIES: 91 sites, typical site width 21 ft, 32 full hkups, 34 W&E, (15/30/50 amps), 50 amps ($), 25 no hkups, 11 pull-thrus, tenting, dump, laundry, ltd groc. ◇◇◇RECREATION: no motors, canoeing, pond fishing, playground. Pets welcome. Partial handicap access. Open May 15 - Oct 15. Big rigs welcome. Rate in 2010 $28-36 for 4 persons. Phone: (800)562-3441. KOA discount.

ST. ANTHONY—A-4

(NE) Triple Falls RV Park (Not visited)—*From jct Hwy 430 & Hwy 436: Go 1.6 km/1 mi E on Hwy 430. Enter on L.* ◇◇◇FACILITIES: 104 sites, typical site width 30 ft, 102 W&E, (15/30 amps), 2 no hkups, tenting, dump, laundry, ltd groc. ◇RECREATION: canoeing, play equipment. Pets welcome. Partial handicap access. Open May 28 - Sep 10. Rate in 2010 $25 per family. Phone: (709)454-2599.

ST. BARBE—A-3

(C) St. Barbe RV Park (Not visited)—*From Hwy 430 & St Barbe: Go 2 km/1-1/4 mi NW to St. Barbe. Enter on L.* ◇◇FACILITIES: 44 sites, 6 E, (15/30 amps), 38 no hkups, tenting, dump, laundry. RECREATION: canoeing. Pets welcome. Partial handicap access. Open mid June - mid Sep. Rate in 2010 $15-20 for 2 persons. Phone: (709)877-2515.

ST. GEORGE'S—D-2

BARACHOIS POND (Provincial Park)—*From town: Go 4.8 km/3 mi SE on paved road, then 14.8 km/9 mi N on Hwy 1.* FACILITIES: 150 sites, 150 no hkups, tenting, dump, laundry, full svc store. RECREATION: lake swim, canoeing, ramp, lake fishing, playground. Pets welcome. Partial handicap access. Open Mid May - Mid Sep. Phone: (709)635-4520.

ST. JOHN'S—D-6

(NW) Blue Fin RV Trailer Park—*From jct Hwy 1 & Hwy 62 (exit 36 on Hwy 1), then 1 block S. Enter on R.* ◇◇◇◇FACILITIES: 98 sites, typical site width 30 ft, 80 full hkups, 18 W&E, (30/50 amps), 50 amps ($), 6 pull-thrus, dump, laundry. ◇◇◇RECREATION: lake swim, boating, canoeing, lake fishing, playground. Pets welcome. Partial handicap access. No tents. Open May 7 - Sept 25. Big rigs welcome. Rate in 2010 $50 for 2 persons. Phone: (709)229-5500.

BUTTER POT (Provincial Park)—*From town: Go 32 km/20 mi SW on Hwy 1.* FACILITIES: 175 sites, 175 no hkups, tenting, dump, laundry. RECREATION: boating, canoeing, ramp, pond fishing, playground. Pets welcome. Partial handicap access. Open all yr. Facilities fully operational Mid May - Mid Sep. Phone: (709)635-4520.

(C) PIPPY PARK CAMPGROUND—*From jct TCH Hwy 1 (exit 46) & Allandale Rd: Go 1-1/2 km/1 mi S on Allandale Rd. Enter on R.* FACILITIES: 216 sites, typical site width 22 ft, 134 full hkups, 30 W&E, (15/30/50 amps), 50 amps ($), 26 no hkups, tenting, dump, laundry, ltd groc. RECREATION: pond fishing, playground. Pets welcome. Partial handicap access. Open May - Sep. Big rigs welcome. Phone: (709)737-3669.

SHOAL BROOK—C-3

THE WATERS EDGE CAMPGROUND—*From Hwy 430 & 431: Go 33.4 km/20 3/4 mi W on 431. Enter on L.* FACILITIES: 15 sites, typical site width 22 ft, 10 W&E, (15/30 amps), 5 no hkups, tenting, ltd groc. RECREATION: saltwater swim, boating, canoeing, dock, saltwater fishing, play equipment. Open Jun 1 - Oct 15. Phone: (709)453-2020.

SOUTH BROOK—C-4

(S) Kona Beach Trailer Park—*From jct Hwy 380 & Hwy 1: Go 1.6 km/1 mi E on Hwy 1. Enter on R.* ◇◇◇FACILITIES: 97 sites, typical site width 25 ft, 75 W&E, 9 E, (15/20/30 amps), 13 no hkups, 24 pull-thrus, tenting, dump, laundry. ◇◇◇RECREATION: lake swim, boating, canoeing, ramp, lake/river fishing, play equipment. Pets welcome. Open May 24 - Sep 23. Rate in 2010 $17-19 for 4 persons. Phone: (709)657-2400.

STEADY BROOK—C-3

(SE) Georges Mountain Village Trailer (Not visited)—*From Trans Canada Hwy 1 (exit 8): Go 30 M/100 ft NE on Service Rd. Enter on R.* ◇◇FACILITIES: 12 sites, typical site width 18 ft, 28 ft max RV length, 12 full hkups, (15 amps), tenting, laundry, ltd groc. Pets welcome. Open May 01 - Oct 31. Rate in 2010 $20 per family. Phone: (709)639-8168.

SUMMERFORD—C-4

DILDO RUN (Provincial Park)—*From town: Go 15.4 km/9-1/2 mi NW on Hwy 340 (on New World Island).* FACILITIES: 55 sites, 55 no hkups, tenting, dump, laundry. RECREATION: saltwater swim, canoeing, ramp, saltwater fishing. Pets welcome. Partial handicap access. Open May - Sep. Phone: (709)635-4520.

THORBURN LAKE—D-5

(NW) Tucker's Trailer Park (Not Visited)—*From jct Hwy 233 & Hwy 1: Go 11.4 km/2-1/4 mi E on Hwy 1. Enter on R.* ◇◇◇FACILITIES: 42 sites, typical site width 25 ft, 25 W&E, (15/30 amps), 17 no hkups, tenting, dump, laundry, ltd groc. ◇◇RECREATION: swim pool, lake swim, canoeing, lake fishing, playground. Pets welcome. Partial handicap access. Open Jun 30 - Labor Day. Rate in 2010 $30 for 4 persons. Phone: (709)427-7668.

TROUT RIVER—C-2

GROS MORNE NATIONAL PARK (Trout River Campground)—*From town: Go 2.75 km/1-3/4 mi on S Road 431.* FACILITIES: 44 sites, 44 no hkups, tenting. RECREATION: lake swim, boating, canoeing, dock, saltwater/river fishing, playground. Partial handicap access. Open Jun 11 - Sep 20. Phone: (709)458-2417.

TWILLINGATE—B-4

(C) Peyton's Woods RV Park and Campground—*From E Town City Limit on Hwy 340: Go 4 km/2-1/2 mi W on Hwy 340. Enter on R.* ◇◇◇FACILITIES: 60 sites, typical site width 30 ft, 22 full hkups, 27 W&E, (30/50 amps), 50 amps ($), 35 no hkups, tenting, dump, laundry. Pets welcome. Partial handicap access. Open May 1 - Oct 30. Rate in 2010 $25 per family. Phone: (709)884-2000.

WILTONDALE—C-3

GROS MORNE NATIONAL PARK (Lomond Campground)—*From jct Hwy 430 & Hwy 431: Go 17-1/2 km/11 mi W on Hwy 431.* FACILITIES: 29 sites, 23 W&E, 6 E, tenting, dump, laundry. RECREATION: saltwater swim, boating, ramp, dock, saltwater fishing, playground. Open May 21 - Oct 12. Phone: (709) 458-2417.

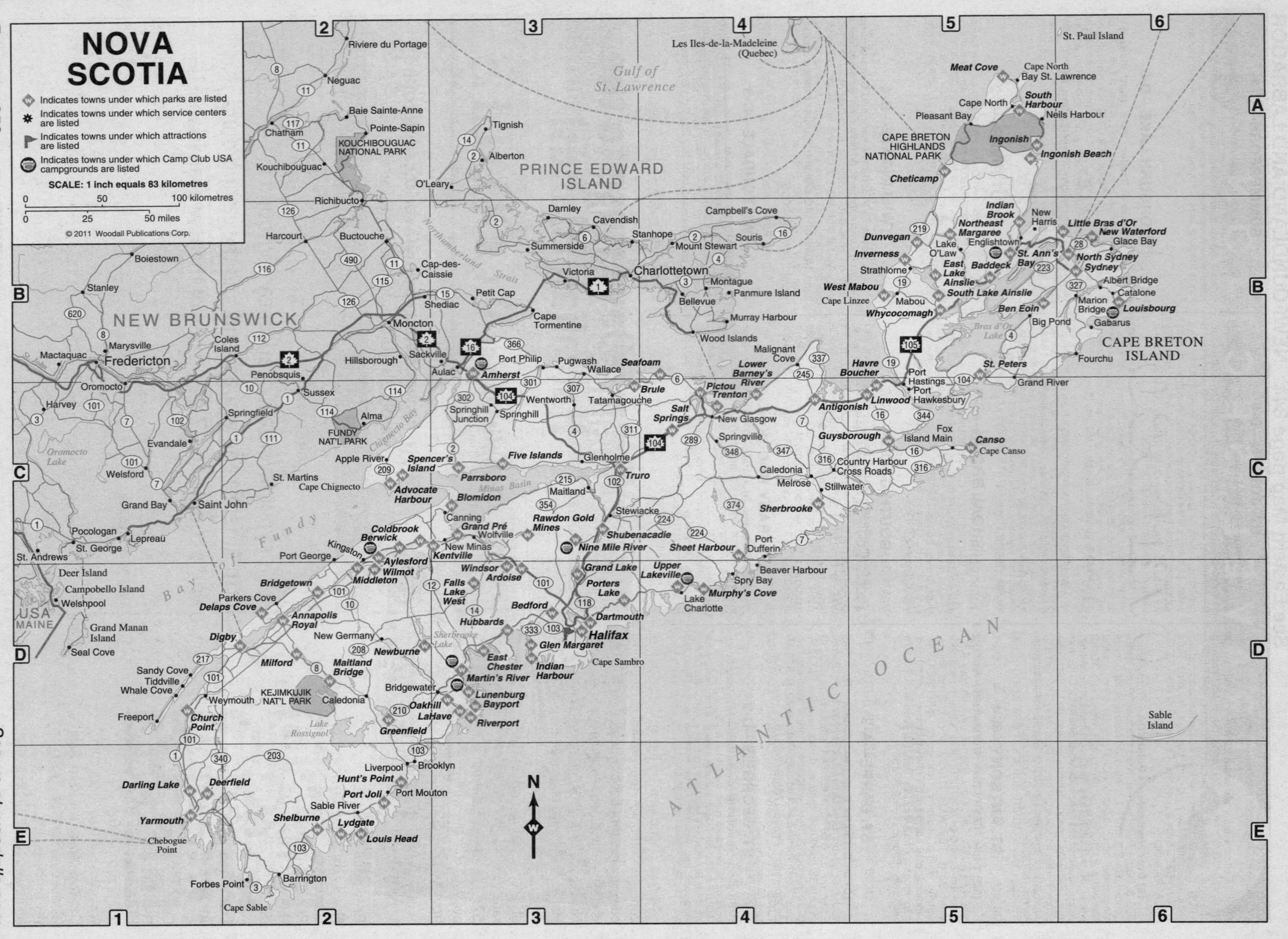
NOVA SCOTIA
Indicates towns under which parks are listed
Indicates towns under which service centers are listed
Indicates towns under which attractions are listed
Indicates towns under which Camp Club USA campgrounds are listed
SCALE: 1 inch equals 83 kilometres
0 50 100 kilometres
0 25 50 miles
© 2011 Woodall Publications Corp.
NEW BRUNSWICK
PRINCE EDWARD ISLAND
CAPE BRETON ISLAND
CAPE BRETON HIGHLANDS NATIONAL PARK
KOUCHIBOUGUAC NATIONAL PARK
FUNDY NAT'L PARK
KEJIMKUJIK NAT'L PARK
Gulf of St. Lawrence
Northumberland Strait
Bay of Fundy
Minas Basin
Chignecto Bay
ATLANTIC OCEAN
Les Iles-de-la-Madeleine (Quebec)
St. Paul Island
Sable Island
USA MAINE
Fredericton
Saint John
Moncton
Charlottetown
Halifax
Dartmouth
Truro
Amherst
Antigonish
Sydney
North Sydney
Louisbourg
Yarmouth
Digby
Lunenburg
Cheticamp
Ingonish
Baddeck
Inverness
Pictou
New Glasgow
Kentville
Wolfville
Windsor
Bridgewater
Liverpool
Shelburne
Annapolis Royal
Port Hastings
Canso
Guysborough
Sherbrooke
A B C D E
1 2 3 4 5 6

CAMPING FEES

Camping fees in Nova Scotia listings are stated in Canadian dollars. Fees are quoted before taxes. Call each location for more details, as they vary from province to province.

TIME ZONE

Nova Scotia is in the Atlantic Time Zone.

TOPOGRAPHY

Nova Scotia's 4,625-mile coastline features rugged granite cliffs, colonial towns and large bays. Canso Causeway connects the mainland to Cape Breton Island.

CLIMATE

Nova Scotia lies in the mid-temperate zone, and though the province is almost completely surrounded by water, the climate is closer to continental rather than maritime. Nova Scotia is very foggy in places, with Halifax averaging approximately 196 foggy days a year, and Yarmouth a close second at 191. Spring temperatures on average range from 36° F to 61° F. Summer from 57° F to 79° F. Fall from 43° F to 68° F on average, and the winter temperatures range from 10° F to 39° F.

TRAVEL & TOURISM INFO

Provincial Agency:

Nova Scotia Department of Tourism, Culture & Heritage
P.O. Box 456
Halifax, NS B3J 2R5
(902/425-5781)
www.novascotia.com

Local Agencies:

Antigonish Eastern Shore Tourist Assn.
9042 #7 Highway
General Delivery
Head Jeddore
HRM, NS B0J 2L0
(800/565-0000)
www.rewardyoursenses.com

Central Nova Tourism Assn., (Glooscap/Sunrise Trail)
65 Treaty Trail
Millbrook, NS B6L 1W3
(902/893-8782)
www.cnta.ns.ca

Destinations Southwest Nova Scotia
(877/552-4040)
www.destinationssouthwestnova.com

Evangeline Trail Tourism Assn.
244 Main St.
Kentville, NS B4N 1L7
(800/565-0000)
www.destination-ns.com

Pictou County Tourist Association
980 East River Road
New Glasgow, NS B2H 3S8
(902/752-6383 or 877/81-OCEAN)
www.tourismpictoucounty.com

Seaside Tourism Association
P.O. Box 52
Musquodoboit Harbour, NS B0J 2L0
(866/736-8217)
www.seacoasttrail.com

St. Margaret's Bay Regional Tourism Development Association
103 Highway 3, P.O. Box 398
Hubbards, NS B0J 1T0
(902/857-3249)
www.peggyscovearea.com

SHOPPING

Amos Pewter, 589 Main St., Mahone Bay. Handcrafted pewter gifts and keepsakes in an open studio.

Crafts of the Country, 726 Hwy 2, Elmsdale. Selection of Atlantic Canada crafts including local woodworking, quilts, jewelry, pottery and iron works.

Flora's Gift Shop, Point Cross. Features Cheticamp Hooked Rugs and huge selection of Maritime, Acadian and Cape Breton souvenirs. Open May-Oct.

BUSINESSES OFFERING

	Things to See & Do	RV Sales	RV Service
HALIFAX			
Nova Scotia Dept of Tourism and Culture	⚑		

Where to Find CCUSA Parks

List City	Park Name	Map Coordinates
AMHERST		
	Gateway Parklands	B-3
AYLESFORD		
	Klahanie Kamping	C-2
LOUISBOURG		
	Lake View Treasures (Not Visited)	B-6
LUNENBURG		
	Little Lake Family Campground	D-3
MARTIN'S RIVER		
	Rayport Campground	D-3
NINE MILE RIVER		
	Riverland Campground	C-3
ST. ANN'S BAY		
	St. Anns Bay Campark	B-5
UPPER LAKEVILLE		
	E & F Webber Lakeside Park	D-4

Gifts and Good Taste, 184 Silverbirch Drive, Hubley. Unique gift and craft shop specializes in tole painting.

Jennifer's of Nova Scotia, 5635 Spring Garden Rd., Halifax. Features ironwork, sailor's ropecraft, rug hooking, steam-bent woodwork, quilts, jewelry and more from native Nova Scotia craftspeople.

Train Station Gift Shop, 5401 St. Margaret's Bay Rd., St. Margaret's Bay. Housed in a unique 99-year-old train station and caboose, the shop has everything from kitchenware to art, train memorabilia and books on area history.

Wood N Wool Gift Shop, Hwy 333, Indian Harbour. Pure 100% wool in a full range of colors, hand-knit items, quilts and wooden Adirondack chairs.

DESTINATIONS

EVANGELINE TRAIL

The Evangeline Trail, paralleling the Fundy coast, is a combination of French Acadian fishing villages, the Bay of Fundy's world's highest tides, whale watching, Digby's world's largest inshore scallop fleet and the beautiful Annapolis Valley with its red African soil, lush vineyards, thoroughbred horse farms and North America's oldest apple orchards. A naturalist's paradise, the trail traverses salt marshes, rocky shores and fertile farmlands. Once home to the Cajuns, Grand Pré National Historic Park and Gardens honor their great Expulsion of 1755. This was the birthplace of New France in 1605 at Port Royal and the birthplace of Hockey at Windsor in 1800.

Annapolis Royal. Attractions within Annapolis Royal include:

Annapolis Royal Historic Gardens. In a beautiful setting overlooking a tidal river valley, the Historic Gardens is a premiere Nova Scotia attraction showcasing gardening methods, designs and materials representing more than four hundred years of local history. Enjoy 10 acres of themed gardens that include the Victorian Garden, Rose and Acadian Collection, Acadian Cottage and Garden and Governor's Garden.

Digby. Homeport to a large scallop fleet. View the colourful scallop-draggers on Digby's floating marina, which rises and falls almost 3 stories every few hours. The historic waterfront is lined with shops, cafes and restaurants and features live entertainment in the summer.

Fundy Geological Museum, Parrsboro. Discover an ancient world and see some of the oldest dinosaur bones in Canada with fossils dating back millions of years. See the mineral treasures exposed when the great Fundy Tides washed away the sea cliffs and a collection of beautiful amethyst and agate gemstones.

Grand Pré National Historic Site, Grand Pré. This memorial site marks the location of Acadian Village (1680-1755), which served as the setting for Longfellow's poem Evangeline.

Kejimkujik National Park, Maitland Bridge. Located between Annapolis Royal and Liverpool, this lovely wilderness country features island-studded lakes, an extensive network of waterways, varied wildlife, swimming, canoe rentals, fishing, cross-country skiing, camping, cycling and lecture tours.

Whale Watching Expeditions, Tiverton. Set sail in search of humpback, minke, fin and right whales, dolphins, porpoises and puffins. Charter boat companies are located around the Tiverton Ferry.

Fort Anne National Historic Site of Canada features well-preserved earthwork fortifications, an early 18th-century gunpowder magazine and 1797 British field officers' quarters, displays relating site significance and area history. The first fort was erected on this site about 1629. The French erected four forts subsequently, beginning in 1643. Impressive Heritage Tapestry depicts 400 years of area's history.

The **Charles MacDonald Concrete House** in **Centreville** is known as "the cement house with the deer statues." This artful property is surrounded by a garden full of original concrete sculptures of deer, mushrooms and other garden figures. Inside, the house is as it was built: every surface lovingly decorated in painted relief sculptures, paintings and exhibits.

GLOOSCAP TRAIL

Next along the Bay of Fundy is the Glooscap Trail, which is a coastal mosaic of soaring red cliffs, Fundy "flower pots," and a treasure of Jurassic and Triassic dinosaur fossils ending at the spectacular Cape Chignecto Provincial Park (Nova Scotia's largest), with its old growth forest hiking trails. Cliffs tower 600 feet in the air while below the world's highest tides flow from the Bay of Fundy. The Fundy Shore along the Glooscap Trail has the world's highest and most dramatic tides, along with a phenomenon called a Tidal Bore. Twice a day the tides send a wall of water into all the bays and rivers.

Amherst, located on the Trans Canada Highway near the New Brunswick border, is the gateway to Nova Scotia. Rich in history, Amherst is home to 4 Fathers of Confederation.

Cobequid Mountains Waterfalls. The Mountains stretch from Truro to Cape Chignecto. Headwaters originating in the mountain lakes and springs flow towards the Minas Basin, spilling over escarpments created by major fault lines in the rock. The abundant rivers found along this coastline can be traced inland to one or more spectacular waterfalls.

Parrsboro. This is one of eastern North America's most unique geological sites, where tides in the Bay of Fundy have eroded the cliff face to expose dinosaur footprints. Rockhounds and dinosaur buffs won't want to miss the Fundy Geological Museum.

Springhill Miners' Museum, Springhill. Experienced miners guide explorers through a real coalmine. The museum includes exhibits that depict the tragic history of coal mining in Springhill.

QUICK REFERENCE CHART FOR WOODALL'S FEATURED PARKS

	Green Friendly	RV Lots for Sale	Park Models-Onsite Ownership	Park Membership for Sale	Big Rigs Welcome	Internet Friendly	Pets Welcome
HAVRE BOUCHER							
Hyclass Campground						●	■
TRURO							
Scotia Pine Campground						●	■
UPPER LAKEVILLE							
E & F Webber Lakeside Park					▲	●	■

Green Friendly ; RV Lots for Sale ✖; Park Models/Onsite Onwership ✱; Park Memberships for Sale ✔; Big Rigs Welcome ▲; Internet Friendly ●; Internet Friendly-WiFi ●; Pets Welcome ■

Victoria Park, Truro. This 1,000-acre park features hiking trails, an outdoor pool, a playground, tennis courts, picnic grounds, waterfalls and Jacobs Ladder—200 steps leading to the top of a rocky gorge.

SUNRISE TRAIL

The **Northumberland Strait's Sunrise Trail** leads visitors past vineyards and superior beaches that are legendary—boasting the warmest fog free summer ocean north of Virginia. Celebrations and festivals are everywhere from Canada's Birthplace of Scottish Culture in Pictou to North America's oldest Highland Games at Antigonish. Have a Scottish fling!

Cape George Lighthouse. Located at **Cape George Point** and overlooking **St. George's Bay**, the present lighthouse was built in 1968 and it is the third lighthouse built on this site. It stands approximately 360 feet above the bay and both Cape Breton and Prince Edward Island are visible with a clear horizon. The original lighthouse was built in 1861 and set on top of a wooden house; the first lighthouse was destroyed by a fire in 1907. A second lighthouse and keeper's homestead complete with some farm and a vegetable garden was constructed in 1908. The 1908 lighthouse was rebuilt in 1968 and it is a white, concrete octagonal structure and red octagonal lantern, which stands on the site today. This lighthouse is one of the structural features on the Cape George route, also known locally as the "mini Cabot trail".

Pictou. In the comfort of your vehicle, knowledgeable guides lead you through museums, historic sites and picturesque scenery. Hector Heritage Quay, located on the Pictou waterfront, is a replica of the immigrant ship Hector and reminds tourists and residents of that date in 1773 when the original vessel brought the first of the Scottish Highlanders.

River John. Lismore Sheep Farm is a working farm that is open for visitors to see the sheep and lambs up close. Approximately 300 sheep roam the beautiful fields overlooking the Northumberland Strait. Interpretive displays and locally- made wool products.

Tatamagouche. The **Intercolonial Railway Station**, erected in 1887, is one of Canada's oldest standing railway stations. The station houses railway artifacts, china, photographs and stationmaster residence. Rolling stock includes a dining car, cabooses, & 2 boxcars. Guided and self-guided tours.

CAPE BRETON ISLAND

Alexander Graham Bell National Historic Site, Baddeck. View the world's largest collection of artifacts, photographs and personal mementos of the inventor of the telephone. Hands-on experiments and kite making programs.

Cabot Trail. Named for famous explorer John Cabot, today vacationers can enjoy the trail's magnificent scenery along Cape Breton's northern shore, which leads them to Cape Breton Highlands National Park. The scenic overlook provides views of the rugged coastline where you may spot a pod of whales or bald eagles soaring overhead. At Cheticamp, stop at the Acadian Museum, featuring a small display of relics of the Acadian people of this area. See demonstrations of wool carding, spinning, weaving and rug hooking. Craft shop features locally made hooked rugs. Acadian-style food served; French spoken.

Cape Breton Highlands National Park, located along the Cabot Trail. Experience magnificent highland plateaus, wind-swept lands, deep-walled canyons, beaches, cliffs and waterfalls.

Fortress of **Louisbourg National Historic Site**. Relive the glory days of New France in 1744 at the largest historical reconstruction in North America. Visit townsfolk in their homes and converse with soldiers at local pubs as they discuss their war with the British.

LIGHTHOUSE ROUTE

The **Lighthouse Trail** along Nova Scotia's South Shore is considered by many to be the most scenic of all the coastal trails and the only rival to America's Cape Cod for its historic ship building towns, pretty fishing villages, beaches and seaside church spires. In addition to over 20 lighthouses, you'll find quiet country roads where ox teams still haul lumber, and coastal villages where fishermen still row wooden dories out to sea. Lunenburg's unique colonial architecture has earned it UNESCO designation, while Shelburne's wonderful Loyalist attractions fascinate everyone. Peggy's Cove fishing village and lighthouse are the world's most photographed. Lobsters and beautiful scenery are plentiful.

ANNUAL EVENTS

JANUARY

Eagle Watch, Sheffield Mills; Seaside Folk Concerts, Broad Cove.

FEBRUARY

International Boat Show, Halifax; Winter Carnival, Pictou; Winter Sports Carnival, Springhill; Flight of the Silver Dart, Cape Breton Island.

MARCH

Jam Sessions, Cape Breton; Antique & Craft Show, Halifax.

APRIL

Modelmakers Showcase, Halifax; Maple Syrup Festival, Maplewood/Dean.

MAY

Edwardian Fair and Dinner, Amherst; First Nations Pow Wow, Yarmouth; Lobster Festival, Hubbards; Lighthouse Festival, West Pubnico/Lunenburg; Scotia Festival of Music, Halifax; Scottish Concert, Mabou; Cape Breton International Drum Festival, Cape Breton Island; Lobsterpalooza, Cape Breton Island (thru July).

JUNE

Lobsterpalooza, Cape Breton Island (thru July); Annapolis Valley Apple Blossom Festival, Kentville; Admiral Digby Regatta, Digby; Blossom Craft Show, Kentville; Cabot Day Celebrations, Dingwall; Ceilidh on the Cove, Hubbards; Fox Mountain Bluegrass Festival; Multicultural Festival, Dartmouth.

JULY

Digby Scallop Days, Digby; Privateer Days, Liverpool; Royal Nova Scotia International Tattoo, Halifax; Stan Rogers Folk Festival, Canso; Pictou Lobster Carnival, Pictou; Canada Trust Atlantic Jazz Festival, Halifax; Tall Ships Nova Scotia, Halifax; Antigonish Highland Games, Antigonish; Halifax Pride Week Festival, Halifax; Festival Acadien de Clare, Church Point; Halifax Highland Games and Scottish Festival, Halifax; Rose Show, Halifax; Age of Sail Festival, Parrsboro; Dominion Seaside Daze, Dominion; Dragon Boat Festival, Dartmouth; Minudie Day, Minudie; Maritime Fiddle Festival, Halifax; Muddy Bottom Blues Festival, Windsor; Park's Day, Maitland Bridge; SAILabration, Digby; Yarmouth Seafest, Yarmouth; Mahone Bay Classic Boat Festival, Mahone Bay; riverfront Music Jubilee, New Glasgow.

AUGUST

Aviation Day, Baddeck; Blessing of the Crops Festival, Minudie; Boardwalk Busker Festival, Sydney; Clark's Harbour Island Days, Cape Sable Island; Crab Festival, Louisbourg; Gem & Fossil Days, Parrsboro; Halifax Antique Car Show, Halifax; Hector Festival, Pictou; Highland Village Day, Iona; Mackerel Tournament, LeHave; Mahone Bay Classic Boat Festival, Mahone Bay; Nova Scotia Fold Art Festival, Lunenburg; Shark Scramble, Yarmouth; Alexander Keith's Natal Day Festival, Halifax; Digby Scallop Days, Digby; Lunenburg Folk Festival, Lunenburg; International Busker Festival, Halifax; Blueberry Harvest Festival, Province wide.

SEPTEMBER

Acadian Festival, Halifax; Atlantic Fringe Festival, Halifax; Ciderfest, Bridgetown; Dockside Ceilidh, North Sydney; Fall Fair, Louisdale; Great Canadian Lumberjack Challenge, Liverpool; Halifax Harbour Festival, Halifax; Kirk Logan Fiddling Contest, Musquodoboit.

ADVOCATE HARBOUR—C-2

CAPE CHIGNECTO PP—(Cumberland) *From town: Go 2.5 km/1-1/2 mi W on Hwy 209, then 1 km/1/2 mi S on West Advocate Rd.* FACILITIES: 59 sites, 59 no hkups, tenting. RECREATION: saltwater swim, canoeing. Pets welcome. Open May - Oct. Phone: (902)392-2085.

(C) Fundy Tides Campground—*From Town Centre & Mills Rd: Go .5 km/1/4 mi N on Mills Rd. Enter on L.* ◆◆FACILITIES: 32 sites, typical site width 30 ft, 20 full hkups, (15/30 amps), 12 no hkups, tenting, dump, laundry, ltd groc. ◆◆RECREATION: play equipment. Pets welcome. Partial handicap access. Open May 10 - Sep 30. Rate in 2010 $28 per family. Phone: (902)392-2606.

AMHERST—B-3

AMHERST SHORE PROVINCIAL PARK—(Cumberland) *From jct Hwy 6 & Hwy 366: Go 24 km/15 mi NE on Hwy 366.* FACILITIES: 42 sites, 42 no hkups, tenting, dump. RECREATION: saltwater swim, ramp, playground. Pets welcome. Partial handicap access. Open Jun 18 - Oct 11. Phone: (902)661-6002.

(NE) Gateway Parklands—(Cumberland) *From Hwy 104 (exit 1) & Fort Lawrence Rd: Go 100 meters/400 ft E on Fort Lawrence Rd. Enter on R.* ◆◆◆FACILITIES: 123 sites, typical site width 30 ft, 98 full hkups, (15/30 amps), 25 no hkups, 80 pull-thrus, tenting, RV storage, dump, non-guest dump $, laundry, ice, picnic tables, fire rings, wood. ◆RECREATION: rec hall, bsktball, play equipment, horseshoes, v-ball. Pets welcome, breed restrict. Open May 15 - Oct 15. Rate in 2010 $23 for 2 persons. MC/VISA/Debit. Member COA of NS. CCUSA 50% Discount. CCUSA max stay 2 days. Must stay 2 days to receive 50% discount. Any stay longer than 2 days will be at 20% discount.

Phone: (902)667-1106
Address: 1434 Fort Lawrence Rd, Amherst, NS B4H 3Z5
Lat/Lon: 45.85530/-64.25316
Email: mmms1963@hotmail.com
Web: www.gatewayparklandcampground.ca

(S) Loch Lomond Campground—(Cumberland) *From Hwy 104 (exit 4) & Hwy 2: Go 0.4 km/1/8 mi S on Hwy 2. Enter on R.* ◆◆FACILITIES: 150 sites, typical site width 30 ft, 108 full hkups, 29 W&E, (15/30/50 amps), 50 amps ($), 13 no hkups, 18 pull-thrus, tenting, dump, laundry. ◆◆◆RECREATION: swim pool, boating, canoeing, lake fishing, playground. Pets welcome. Open May 11 - Oct 15. Big rigs welcome. Rate in 2010 $22-29 for 4 persons. Member COA of NS. Phone: (902)667-3890.

Nova Scotia Provincial Tree: Red Spruce

ANNAPOLIS ROYAL—D-2

(NE) Dunromin Campsites—(Annapolis) *From east town limits: Go 2.4 km/1-1/2 mi E on Hwy 1. Enter on R.* ◆◆◆◆FACILITIES: 210 sites, 82 full hkups, 83 W&E, (15/30/50 amps), 50 amps ($), 45 no hkups, 30 pull-thrus, tenting, dump, laundry, ltd groc. ◆◆◆◆RECREATION: swim pool, saltwater swim, boating, canoeing, ramp, dock, saltwater fishing, playground. Pets welcome. Open May 1 - Oct 15. Big rigs welcome. Rate in 2010 $28-40.50 for 4 persons. Member COA of NS. Phone: (902)532-2808.

ANTIGONISH—C-4

(C) Oasis Motel & Campground (Not visited)—(Antigonish) *From E town limits on Hwy 104: Go 4 km/2-1/2 mi E on Hwy 104. Enter on L.* ◆◆◆FACILITIES: 41 sites, typical site width 25 ft, 33 full hkups, (30 amps), 8 no hkups, tenting, dump, laundry. ◆RECREATION: swim pool. Pets welcome. Open May 15 - Oct 15. Rate in 2010 $25 for 4 persons. Member COA of NS. Phone: (902)863-3557.

SALSMAN PROVINCIAL PARK—(Guysborough) *From jct Hwy 104 (exit 35) & Hwy 316: Go 56 km/35 mi S on Hwy 316.* FACILITIES: 40 sites, 40 no hkups, tenting, dump. RECREATION: saltwater/river swim, boating, ramp, dock, saltwater fishing. Pets welcome. Open Jun 18 - Sep 13. Phone: (902)328-2999.

(C) Whidden's Campground—(Antigonish) *On Hwy 245 at center Town: Go 30 m/100 ft S on Hawthorne St. Enter on L.* ◆◆◆FACILITIES: 174 sites, typical site width 20 ft, 128 full hkups, 24 W&E, (30 amps), 22 no hkups, 30 pull-thrus, tenting, dump, laundry. ◆◆◆RECREATION: 2 swim pools, playground. Pets welcome. Partial handicap access. Open May 15 - Oct 15. Rate in 2010 $34 for 4 persons. Member COA of NS. Phone: (902)863-3736.

ARDOISE—D-3

(W) Beechbrook Campground—*From jct Hwy 215 & Hwy 11: Go 2 km/1-1/3 mi S on Hwy 1, then .03 km/1/3 mi E on Rockwell Rd, then 1.1 km/3/4 mi N on Beechbrook Rd. Enter at end.* ◆◆FACILITIES: 157 sites, typical site width 35 ft, 135 full hkups, 15 W&E, (15 amps), 7 no hkups, tenting, dump, laundry. ◆RECREATION: swim pool, play equipment. Pets welcome. Open May 1 - Oct 10. Rate in 2010 $25 for 5 persons. Phone: (902)757-2211.

AYLESFORD—C-2

(E) Klahanie Kamping—(Kings) *From Hwy 101 (Exit 16): Go 1.6 km/1 mi S. Enter on L.* ◆◆◆FACILITIES: 150 sites, typical site width 40 ft, 85 full hkups, 23 W&E, (15/30 amps), 42 no hkups, cable TV, ($), WiFi Instant Internet at site, phone Internet central location, tenting, RV storage, dump, non-guest dump $, laundry, ltd groc, LP gas by weight, ice, picnic tables, fire rings, wood. ◆◆◆◆RECREATION: 2 swim pools, canoeing, pond fishing, mini-golf, bsktball, playground, shuffleboard court 2 shuffleboard courts, activities horseshoes, hiking trails, v-ball. Pets welcome. Partial handicap access. Open Apr 15 - Oct 30. Facilities fully operational May 15 - Oct 15. Rate in 2010 $26-31 for 4 persons. MC/VISA/AMEX/Debit. Member COA of NS. CCUSA 50% Discount. CCUSA reservations Accepted, CCUSA max stay 3 days, CCUSA disc. not avail S, CCUSA disc. not avail F,Sa, CCUSA disc. not avail holidays. Not available Labour Day, National Day. Cable available @ $2/night surcharge.

Visit a Dealer/Service Location in Woodall's.

AYLESFORD—Continued
Klahanie Kamping—Continued

Phone: (902)847-9316
Address: 1144 Victoria Rd, Aylesford, NS B0P 1C0
Lat/Lon: 45.02419/-64.83424
Email: klahaniekamping@av.eastlink.ca
Web: www.klahaniekamping.com

Reserve Online at Woodalls.com

BADDECK—B-5

(W) Adventures East Campground & Cottages—(Victoria) *From Baddeck: Go 8 km/5 mi W on Hwy 105. Enter on L.* ◆◆FACILITIES: 82 sites, typical site width 24 ft, 26 full hkups, 47 W&E, (30/50 amps), 9 no hkups, tenting, dump, laundry. ◆◆RECREATION: swim pool, playground. Pets welcome. Open Jun 4 - Oct 17. Rate in 2010 $28-30 per family. Member COA of NS. Phone: (902)295-2417.

(W) BADDECK CABOT TRAIL CAMPGROUND—(Victoria) *From W Town City Limit at Baddeck on Hwy 105: Go 8 km/5 mi W on Hwy 105 (between exit 7 & 8).*

WELCOME

◆◆◆◆◆FACILITIES: 174 sites, typical site width 24 ft, 98 full hkups, 28 W&E, 6 E, (15/30/50 amps), 50 amps ($), 42 no hkups, some extd stay sites, 53 pull-thrus, WiFi Instant Internet at site, phone Internet central location, tenting, cabins, RV storage, dump, non-guest dump, laundry, groceries, RV supplies, ice, picnic tables, fire rings, grills, wood.

◆◆◆◆RECREATION: rec room/area, coin games, swim pool, boating, canoeing, kayaking, dock, rowboat/2 canoe rentals, saltwater/river fishing, golf nearby, bsktball, playground, activities, (wkends), horseshoes, sports field, hiking trails, v-ball, local tours. Rec open to public.

Pets welcome. Open May 15 - Oct 15. Clubs welcome. Rate in 2010 $24-39 for 4 persons. MC/VISA/Debit. Member COA of NS.

Phone: (902)295-2288
Address: 9584 Hwy 105, Baddeck, NS B0E 1B0
Lat/Lon: 46.10046/-60.75214
Email: camp@baddeckcabottrailcampground.com
Web: www.baddeckcabottrailcampground.com

SEE AD THIS PAGE

(W) Bras D'or Lakes Campground—(Victoria) *From west town limits: Go 5 km/3 mi W on Hwy 105. (Between exit 7 and 8 on TCH105). Enter on L.* ◆◆FACILITIES: 95 sites, typical site width 30 ft, 75 full hkups, (30/50 amps), 20 no hkups, 8 pull-thrus, tenting, dump, laundry, ltd groc. ◆◆◆RECREATION: swim pool, lake swim, boating, canoeing, ramp, lake fishing, playground. Pets welcome. Partial handicap access. Open Jun 15 - Sep 30. Big rigs welcome. Rate in 2010 $32-38 for 2 persons. Member ARVC, COA of NS. Phone: (902)295-2329.

BAYPORT—D-3

(S) Shore Boat View Campground (Not visited)—(Lunenburg) *From NE Town City Limit: Go 2.6 km/1-3/4 mi SW on Hwy 332, (Lighthouse Route). Enter on R.* ◆◆FACILITIES: 55 sites, typical site width 25 ft, 25 ft max RV length, 17 full hkups, 38 W&E, (15 amps), tenting, dump, laundry, ltd groc. ◆RECREATION: play equipment. Pets welcome. Open May 15 - Oct 15. Rate in 2010 $27 per family. Phone: (902)766-4873.

BEDFORD—D-3

DOLLAR LAKE PROVINCIAL PARK—(Halifax) *From Hwy 102 (exit 5A) N of town: Go 22-1/2 km/14 mi NE on Old Guysborough Rd to Wyse Corner.* FACILITIES: 119 sites, 119 no hkups, tenting, dump. RECREATION: lake swim, boating, canoeing, ramp, lake fishing, playground. Pets welcome. Open Jun 18 - Oct 11. Phone: (902)384-2770.

BEN EOIN—B-5

(SW) Ben Eoin Beach RV Resort & Campground.—(Cape Breton) *From East City Town limit on Hwy 4: Go 8.3 km/5 mi W on Hwy 4. Enter on R.* ◆◆◆FACILITIES: 210 sites, typical site width 28 ft, 204 full hkups, (30/50 amps), 50 amps ($), 6 no hkups,

Ben Eoin Beach RV Resort & Campground.—Continued on next page

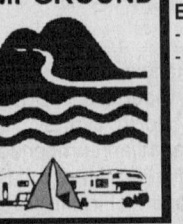

12 pull-thrus, tenting, dump, laundry, ltd groc. ◆◆◆◆RECREATION: lake swim, boating, canoeing, ramp, dock, lake fishing, playground. Pets welcome. Partial handicap access. Open May 15 - Sep 30. Facilities fully operational Jun 15 - Sep 15. Rate in 2010 $38-43.70 for 5 persons. Member COA of NS. Phone: (902)828-3100.

BERWICK—C-2

(SW) Fox Mountain Camping Park—(Kings) *From Hwy 101, (Exit 15) & Hwy 360: Go 2.7 km/1-3/4 mi S on Hwy 360, then 7.6 km/4-3/4 mi S to Windermere Town Sign, then to Lake George Sign 1.8km/1 mi SE. Enter on L.* ◆◆FACILITIES: 347 sites, typical site width 25 ft, 62 full hkups, (15 amps), 285 no hkups, 216 pull-thrus, tenting, dump, ltd groc. ◆RECREATION: playground. Pets welcome. Partial handicap access. Open May 1 - Oct 30. Rate in 2010 $22-30 per family. Phone: (902)847-3747.

(NE) Plantation Campground—(Kings) *From Hwy 101 (exit 15) & Hwy 360: Go .04 km/1/4 mi N on Hwy 360, then .04 km/1/4 mi E, then 2.2 km/1-1/4 mi N on Pleasant Valley, then 1 km/3/4 mi SE on Shaw Rd, 1 km/3/4 mi E on West Steadman Rd. Enter on R.* ◆◆◆◆FACILITIES: 250 sites, typical site width 32 ft, 215 full hkups, 23 W&E, (15/30/50 amps), 50 amps ($), 12 no hkups, 14 pull-thrus, tenting, laundry, ltd groc. ◆◆◆◆RECREATION: swim pool, playground. Pets welcome. Partial handicap access. Open May 15 - Oct 15. Big rigs welcome. Rate in 2010 $34-40 per family. Member COA of NS. Phone: (888)363-8882.

BLOMIDON—C-3

BLOMIDON PROVINCIAL PARK—(Kings) *From town: Go 4-3/4 km/3 mi N Hwy 358.* FACILITIES: 70 sites, 70 no hkups, tenting, dump. RECREATION: saltwater swim, playground. Pets welcome. Partial handicap access. Open May 21 - Sep 6. Phone: (902)582-7319.

BRIDGETOWN—D-2

(C) Annapolis River Campground (Not visited)—(Annapolis) *From W on Hwy 1 City Town Limit: Go 1 km/3/4 mi E on Hwy 1, then .08 km/1/4 mi S on Hwy 201. Enter on L.* ◆◆FACILITIES: 71 sites, typical site width 28 ft, 48 full hkups, (15/30/50 amps), 23 no hkups, 4 pull-thrus, tenting, dump, laundry. ◆◆RECREATION: boating, canoeing, play equipment. Pets welcome. Open Apr 15 - Oct 15. Rate in 2010 $30 per family. Member COA of NS. Phone: (902)665-2801.

(N) VALLEYVIEW PROVINCIAL PARK—(Annapolis) *From town: Go 4-3/4 km/3 mi N off Hwy 1.* FACILITIES: 30 sites, 30 no hkups, tenting, dump. RECREATION: Pets welcome. Partial handicap access. Open Jun 18 - Sep 6. Phone: (902)665-2559.

BRULE—C-3

(W) Sunset Watch Family Campground (Not Visited)—(Colchester) *From jct Hwy 6 & Brule Point Rd: Go 4.6 km/3 mi N on Brule Point Rd, then 1.2 km/3/4 mi W on Peninsula Point (gravel road). Enter at end.* FACILITIES: 84 sites, 41 full hkups, 31 W&E, (15/30 amps), 12 no hkups, tenting, dump, ltd groc. RECREATION: saltwater swim, play equipment. Pets welcome. Partial handicap access. Open May 18 - Oct 8. Rate in 2010 $28 for 4 persons. Member COA of NS. Phone: (902)657-0009.

CANSO—C-5

(E) Cape Canso RV Park & Marina (Not visited)—(Guysborough) *From jct Hwy 316 & Hwy 16: Go 6.4 km/4 mi SE to Fox Island, then 1.6 km/1 mi E on gravel road. Enter at end.* ◆◆FACILITIES: 33 sites, typical site width 20 ft, 33 full hkups, (15/30 amps), 6 pull-thrus, tenting, dump, laundry, ltd groc. ◆◆RECREATION: saltwater swim, boating, canoeing, saltwater fishing, playground. Pets welcome. Open Jun 1 - Oct 30. Rate in 2010 $22 per family. Member COA of NS. Phone: (902) 366-2937.

CHETICAMP—A-5

(N) CAPE BRETON HIGHLANDS NATIONAL PARK (Cheticamp Campground)—(Inverness) *From town: Go 4-3/4 km/3 mi N on the Cabot Trail.* FACILITIES: 162 sites, 24 full hkups, 13 E, (15/30 amps), 125 no hkups, tenting, dump. RECREATION: playground. Partial handicap access. Open May - Oct. Phone: (902)224-2306.

CAPE BRETON HIGHLANDS NATIONAL PARK (Corney Brook Campground)—(Inverness) *From town: Go 8-3/4 km/5-1/2 mi N on the Cabot Trail.* FACILITIES: 20 sites, 20 no hkups, tenting. RECREATION: saltwater swim, saltwater fishing, playground. Open May - Oct. Phone: (902)224-2306.

(SW) Plage St.-Pierre Beach & Campground (Not Visited)—(Inverness) *From S town limits on Cabot Trail: Go 3.2 Km/ 2 mi NW on Cheticamp Island Rd. Enter on L.* ◆◆◆FACILITIES: 147 sites, 86 full hkups, 26 W&E, (15/30 amps), 35 no hkups, 22 pull-thrus, tenting, dump, laundry, ltd groc. ◆◆◆RECREATION: saltwater swim, playground. Pets welcome. Open May 15 - Oct 15. Rate in 2010 $30-33 for 4 persons. Member COA of NS. Phone: (902)224-2112.

CHURCH POINT—D-1

(NE) Belle Baie Park (Not Visited)—(Digby) *From Hwy 101 (exit 28): Go 11 km/6 mi W on Hwy 1. Enter on R.* ◆◆◆FACILITIES: 156 sites, typical site width 28

ft, 143 full hkups, 13 W&E, (30 amps), 7 pull-thrus, tenting, dump, laundry. ◆◆◆RECREATION: swim pool, boating, play equipment. Pets welcome. Partial handicap access. Open May 10 - Sep 30. Rate in 2010 $25-45 per family. Member COA of NS. Phone: (902) 769-3160.

COLDBROOK—C-2

(C) Sherwood Forest Camping Park (Not visited)—(Kings) *From Hwy 101 (exit 14): Go 1.5 km/1 mi W on Hwy 1. Enter on L.* ◆◆◆FACILITIES: 223 sites, typical site width 25 ft, 151 full hkups, 69 W&E, 1 E, (15/30 amps), 2 no hkups, 15 pull-thrus, tenting, dump, laundry, ltd groc. ◆◆◆RECREATION: 2 swim pools, pond fishing, playground. Pets welcome. Open May 15 - Sep 30. Rate in 2010 $30-36 for 4 persons. Member COA of NS. Phone: (902)679-6632.

DARLING LAKE—E-1

(N) Lake Breeze Campground & Cottages (Not visited)—(Yarmouth) *From W Town City Limit on Hwy 1: Go .06 km/1/4 mi W on Hwy 1. Enter on L.* ◆◆FACILITIES: 50 sites, typical site width 18 ft, 4 full hkups, 46 W&E, (15/30 amps), 22 pull-thrus, tenting, dump, laundry. ◆RECREATION: lake swim, boating, canoeing, lake fishing, play equipment. Pets welcome. Open May 15 - Oct 15. Rate in 2010 $19.25-31.54 per family. Member COA of NS. Phone: (902)649-2332.

DARTMOUTH—D-3

(NE) Shubie Park Campground—*From Hwy 111 (exit 6A) & Hwy 318: Go 2.8 km/1-3/4 mi N on Hwy 318, then 0.3 km/1/3 mi W on Jaybee St. Enter at end.* ◆◆◆FACILITIES: 101 sites, 6 full hkups, 70 W&E, (15/30/50 amps), 50 amps ($), 25 no hkups, 16 pull-thrus, tenting, dump, laundry, ltd groc. ◆◆◆RECREATION: lake swim, canoeing, lake fishing, playground. Pets welcome. Partial handicap access. Open Mid May - Mid Oct. Big rigs welcome. Rate in 2010 $32-50 for 6 persons. Member COA of NS. Phone: (902)435-8328. FMCA discount.

DEERFIELD—E-1

ELLENWOOD LAKE PROVINCIAL PARK—(Yarmouth) *From town: Go 1-1/2 km/1 mi S off Hwy 340.* FACILITIES: 87 sites, 87 no hkups, tenting, dump. RECREATION: lake swim, boating, canoeing, ramp, lake fishing, playground. Pets welcome. Partial handicap access. Open May 21 - Sep 6. Phone: (902)761-2400.

DELAPS COVE—D-2

(W) Fundy Trail Campground & Cottages—(Annapolis) *From E Delaps Cove City Limit: Go 2.1 km/1-1/3 mi W on Delaps Cove Rd. Enter at end.* ◆◆◆FACILITIES: 73 sites, typical site width 35 ft, 30 full hkups, 20 W&E, (15/20/30 amps), 23 no hkups, tenting, dump, laundry, ltd groc. ◆◆◆RECREATION: swim pool, canoeing, ramp, saltwater fishing, playground. Pets welcome. Open May 15 - Sep 30. Rate in 2010 $26-30 per family. Member COA of NS. Phone: (902)532-7711.

DIGBY—D-2

(C) Digby Campground (Not visited)—(Digby) *From jct Hwy 101 & Hwy 303 (exit 26): Go 3 km/2 mi on Hwy 303 N, then 1 km/.6 mi W on Saint John Ferry Rd & follow St. John Ferry Signs. Enter on R.* ◆◆◆FACILITIES: 48 sites, typical site width 28 ft, 12 full hkups, 21 W&E, (15/30 amps), 15 no hkups, tenting, dump, laundry. ◆RECREATION: swim pool. Pets welcome. Open May 15 - Oct 15. Rate in 2010 $25-30 per family. Phone: (902)245-1985.

(E) Jaggar's Point Oceanside Camping (Not Visited)—(Digby) *From jct Hwy 101 (exit 24) & Hwy 1: Go 2.4 km/1-1/2 mi W on Hwy 1. Enter on R.* ◆◆◆FACILITIES: 141 sites, typical site width 25 ft, 41 full hkups, 70 W&E, (15/30 amps), 30 no hkups, 15 pull-thrus, tenting, dump, laundry, ltd groc. ◆◆RECREATION: swim pool, saltwater swim, saltwater fishing, playground. Pets welcome. Open May 15 - Sep 30. Rate in 2010 $25-28 per family. Member COA of NS. Phone: (902)245-4814.

DUNVEGAN—B-5

(W) MacLeod's Campsite (Not visited)—(Inverness) *From S Town City Limit on Hwy 19: Go 1.1 km/3/4 mi N on Hwy 19, then 1.2 km/3/4 mi W on Broad Cove Marsh Rd (gravel road). Enter on R.* ◆◆◆FACILITIES: 172 sites, typical site width 25 ft, 60 full hkups, 12 W&E, (15/30 amps), 100 no hkups, 12 pull-thrus, tenting, dump, laundry, ltd groc. ◆◆RECREATION: saltwater swim, canoeing, saltwater fishing, play equipment. Pets welcome, quantity restrict. Open Jun 15 - Oct 20. Rate in 2010 $27.50-30.50 for 4 persons. Member COA of NS. Phone: (902)258-2433.

EAST CHESTER—D-3

GRAVES ISLAND PROVINCIAL PARK—(Lunenburg) *From town: Go 3-1/4 km/2 mi E on Hwy 3.* FACILITIES: 84 sites, 84 no hkups, tenting, dump. RECREATION: saltwater swim, boating, ramp, dock, playground. Pets welcome. Partial handicap access. Open May 21 - Oct 11. Phone: (902)275-4425.

EAST LAKE AINSLIE—B-5

(W) MacKinnon's Campground (Not visited)—(Inverness) *From jct Hwy 105 (exit 5) & Hwy 252: Go 3 km/2 mi N on Hwy 252, then 12.6 km/8 mi NE on Route 395. Enter on L.* ◆◆FACILITIES: 75 sites, 55 full hkups, 20 W&E, (15/30 amps), 10 pull-thrus, tenting, dump, laundry, ltd groc. ◆◆RECREATION: swim pool, lake swim, boating, canoeing, lake fishing, play equipment. Pets welcome. Partial handicap access. Open May 1 - Oct 15. Rate in 2010 $24-26 per vehicle. Phone: (902)756-2790.

ENGLISHTOWN—B-5

(S) Englishtown Ridge Campground (Not Visited)—(Victoria) *From jct Hwy 105 (exit 12) & Hwy 312: Go 7.2 km/4-1/2 mi N on Hwy 312. Enter on R.* ◆◆◆FACILITIES: 73 sites, typical site width 24 ft, 62 full hkups, (15/30 amps), 11 no hkups, 6 pull-thrus, tenting, laundry, ltd groc. ◆◆◆RECREATION: swim pool, playground. Pets welcome. Partial handicap access. Open May 19 - Oct 15. Rate in 2010 $21-24 for 4 persons. Phone: (902)929-2598.

FALLS LAKE WEST—D-3

FALLS LAKE RECREATIONAL FACILITY—(Hants) *From Hwy 101 (exit 5): Go 24.1 km/15 mi on Hwy 14 W, then R on New Ross Rd, 3.2 km/2 mi (watch for signs), then R 3.2 km/2 mi on Pioneer (dirt) Rd. From Hwy 103 (exit 8): Go N 30 km/17 mi on Hwy 14, then L on New Ross Rd 3.2 km, then R on Pioneer Rd. Enter at end.* FACILITIES: 30 sites, typical site width 28 ft, 15 full hkups, (30 amps), 15 no hkups, tenting, dump, laundry, groceries. RECREATION: lake swim, boating, canoeing, ramp, dock, lake fishing, playground. Pets welcome. Partial handicap access. Open May 1 - Oct 16. Phone: (877)325-5253.

FIVE ISLANDS—C-3

(W) FIVE ISLANDS PROVINCIAL PARK—(Colchester) *From town: Go 3-1/4 km/2 mi E off Hwy 2.* FACILITIES: 90 sites, 90 no hkups, tenting, dump. RECREATION: saltwater swim, saltwater fishing, playground. Pets welcome. Open May 21 - Sep 6. Phone: (902)254-2980.

GLEN MARGARET—D-3

(S) Wayside Park (Not visited)—(Halifax) *From N Town City Limit on Hwy 333: Go 1.7 km/1 mi S on Hwy 333. Enter on L.* ◆◆◆FACILITIES: 150 sites, typical site width 30 ft, 50 full hkups, 75 W&E, (15/30/50 amps), 50 amps ($), 25 no hkups, 8 pull-thrus, tenting, dump, laundry. RECREATION: play equipment. Pets welcome. Partial handicap access. Open May 1 - Oct 31. Rate in 2010 $32 per vehicle. Member COA of NS. Phone: (902)823-2547.

GRAND LAKE—D-3

LAURIE PROVINCIAL PARK—(Halifax) *In town on Hwy-2.* FACILITIES: 71 sites, 71 no hkups, tenting, dump. RECREATION: lake swim, boating, ramp, lake fishing. Pets welcome. Partial handicap access. Open Jun 19 - Sep 14. Phone: (902)861-1623.

GRAND PRE'—C-3

(NW) Land of Evangeline-Family Camping Resort—(Kings) *From Hwy 101 (exit 10): Go 1.2 km/3/4 mi W on Hwy 1, then 3.6 km/2 1/3 mi N on Grand Pre Rd, then .07 km/1/2 mi W on Evangeline Beach Rd. Enter on R.* ◆◆◆◆FACILITIES: 230 sites, typical site width 30 ft, 182 full hkups, 21 W&E, (15/30/50 amps), 50 amps ($), 15 no hkups, 50 pull-thrus, tenting, dump, laundry, ltd groc. ◆◆◆◆RECREATION: swim pool, saltwater fishing, playground. Pets welcome, breed restrict. Partial handicap access. Open May 1 - Oct 1. Big rigs welcome. Rate in 2010 $27-38 per family. Member COA of NS. Phone: (902)542-5309.

GREENFIELD—D-2

Ponhook Lodge Campground (Not Visited)—(Queens) *From E city town limit on Hwy 210: Go 1.8 km/1 mi W on 210, then 1.8 km/1 mi N on Ponhook Lodge Rd (gravel road). Enter at end.* ◆◆◆FACILITIES: 150 sites, typical site width 25 ft, 135 full hkups, (30 amps), 15 no hkups, 3 pull-thrus, tenting, dump, laundry, ltd groc. ◆◆◆RECREATION: lake swim, boating, canoeing, ramp, dock, lake fishing, playground. Pets welcome. Open Jun 15 - Sep 15. Rate in 2010 $28 per family. Member COA of NS. Phone: (902)685-2346.

GUYSBOROUGH—C-5

(E) BOYLSTON PROVINCIAL PARK—(Guysborough) *From town: Go 6-1/2 km/4 mi N on Hwy 16.* FACILITIES: 35 sites, 35 no hkups, tenting, dump. RECREATION: saltwater swim, saltwater fishing. Pets welcome. Partial handicap access. Open Jun 18 - Sep 13. Phone: (902)533-3326.

HALIFAX—D-3

(NW) Halifax West KOA—(Halifax) *From jct Hwy 102 & Hwy 101 (exit 4B): Go 15.2 km/9-1/2 mi W on Hwy 101 (exit 3), then 2 km/1-1/4 mi E on Hwy 1. Enter on R.* ◆◆◆◆FACILITIES: 97 sites, typical site width 30 ft, 29 full hkups, 60 W&E, (30/50 amps), 50 amps ($), 8 no hkups, 15 pull-thrus, tenting, dump, laundry, ltd groc. ◆◆◆◆RECREATION: swim pool, canoeing, dock, river fishing, playground. Pets welcome. Partial handicap access. Open May 14 - Oct 15. Big rigs welcome. Rate in 2010 $31-51 per family. Member COA of NS. Phone: (888)562-4705. KOA discount.

HALIFAX—Continued on next page

HALIFAX—Continued

NOVA SCOTIA DEPT OF TOURISM AND CULTURE—*In city on Argyle St (World Trade Centre-6th Floor).* With such diverse landscapes & amazing scenery, the journey will quickly become your destination when you visit Nova Scotia. Go online or call to order your free 400 page Doers' and Dreamers' Guide. (800)565-0000. Open all yr.

Phone: (902)424-4581
Address: Halifax, NS B3J 2R7
Web: www.novascotia.com/road

SEE AD DISCOVER SECTION PAGE 109

(NW) Woodhaven RV Park of Halifax—(Halifax) *From jct Hwy 102 (exit 3) & Hwy 213: Go 6.5 km/4 mi W on Hwy 213. Enter on R.* ◇◇◇◇FACILITIES: 200 sites, typical site width 30 ft, 156 full hkups, 34 W&E, (15/30/50 amps), 50 amps ($), 73 pull-thrus, tenting, dump, laundry, ltd groc. ◇◇◇◇RECREATION: swim pool, playground. Pets welcome. Partial handicap access. Open May 1 - Oct 15. Big rigs welcome. Rate in 2010 $32-34 per family. Member COA of NS. Phone: (902)835-2271.

HAVRE BOUCHER—C-5

(SW) HYCLASS CAMPGROUND—(Antigonish) *From jct Hwy 104 (exit 37) & Frankville Rd: Go 7 km/4-1/4 mi E on Hwy 4. Enter on L.*

◇◇◇FACILITIES: 75 sites, typical site width 25 ft, 18 full hkups, 30 W&E, (15/30 amps), 27 no hkups, some extd stay sites, 11 pull-thrus, WiFi Instant Internet at site, WiFi Internet central location, family camping, tenting, cabins, shower$, dump, non-guest dump, laundry, ltd groc, ice, picnic tables, fire rings, wood, controlled access.

◇◇◇RECREATION: saltwater swim, boating, canoeing, kayaking, dock, 2 canoe/4 kayak/3 pedal boat rentals, saltwater fishing, fishing supplies, golf nearby, playground, horseshoes, hiking trails, v-ball.

Pets welcome. Open May 15 - Sep 15. Clubs welcome. Rate in 2010 $22-35 for 4 persons. MC/VISA/AMEX/Debit. Member COA of NS.

Phone: (902)232-3117
Address: 11370 Highway 4, Havre Boucher, NS B0H 1P0
Lat/Lon: 45.64645/-61.57707
Email: info@hyclass-campground.com
Web: www.hyclass-campground.com

SEE AD THIS PAGE

HUBBARDS—D-3

(E) Hubbards Beach Campground—(Halifax) *From jct Hwy 103 (exit 6) & Hwy 3: Go 3.2 km/2 mi E on Hwy 3, then .08 km/1/2 mi S on Shore Club Rd. Enter on L.* ◇◇◇◇FACILITIES: 129 sites, typical site width 25 ft, 127 full hkups, (15/30 amps), 2 no hkups, 2 pull-thrus, tenting, dump, laundry, ltd groc.

HUBBARDS—Continued
Hubbards Beach Campground—Continued

◇◇◇◇RECREATION: saltwater swim, canoeing, saltwater fishing, playground. Pets welcome. Partial handicap access. Open May 15 - Oct 1. Rate in 2010 $32-38.95 for 4 persons. Member COA of NS. Phone: (902)857-9460.

HUNT'S POINT—E-2

(W) Fisherman's Cove RV & Campground (Not visited)—(Queens) *From E City Town City limit on Hwy 3: Go 1 km/3/4 mi W on Hwy 3. Enter on R.* ◇◇FACILITIES: 20 sites, 10 W&E, (15/30 amps), 10 no hkups, 4 pull-thrus, tenting, dump, laundry, ltd groc. RECREATION: play equipment. Pets welcome. Partial handicap access. Open May 1 - Oct 31. Rate in 2010 $27-32 for 4 persons. Member COA of NS. Phone: (902)683-2772. FMCA discount.

INDIAN BROOK—B-5

(N) Pipers Campground & Trailer Park—(Victoria) *From S Town City Limit on Cabot Trail: Go 4 km/2-1/2 mi N on Cabot Trail. Enter on R.* ◇◇◇FACILITIES: 67 sites, typical site width 20 ft, 30 full hkups, 24 W&E, (15 amps), 13 no hkups, 10 pull-thrus, tenting, dump, laundry, groceries. ◇◇RECREATION: saltwater swim, play equipment. Pets welcome. Open May 15 - Oct 15. Rate in 2010 $25-28 for 2 persons. Member COA of NS. Phone: (902)929-2233.

INDIAN HARBOUR—D-3

(S) King Neptune Campground (Not Visited)—(Halifax) *From N Town City Limit on Hwy 333: Go 2.8 km/1-3/4 mi S on Hwy 333. Enter on R.* ◇◇FACILITIES: 65 sites, 11 full hkups, 34 W&E, (15/30 amps), 20 no hkups, tenting, dump. RECREATION: boating, ramp, dock, saltwater fishing, play equipment. Pets welcome. Open Jun 1 - Oct 15. Rate in 2010 $23 per vehicle. Phone: (902)823-2582.

INGONISH—A-5

(N) Dino's One Stop (Not visited)—(Victoria) *From S Town City Limit: Go 2 km/1-1/4 mi N on Cabot Trail. Enter on L.* ◇◇FACILITIES: 23 sites, 15 full hkups, 5 W&E, (15 amps), 3 no hkups, tenting, dump, laundry, groceries. RECREATION: play equipment. Pets welcome. Open Jun 1 - Oct 1. Rate in 2010 $20 per family. Member COA of NS. Phone: (902)285-2614.

INGONISH BEACH—A-5

(N) CAPE BRETON HIGHLANDS NATIONAL PARK (Broad Cove Campground)—(Victoria) *From town: Go 9-1/2 km/6 mi N on Cabot Trail.* FACILITIES: 256 sites, 83 full hkups, (30 amps), 173 no hkups, tenting, dump. RECREATION: saltwater swim, saltwater fishing, playground. Partial handicap access. Open May - Oct. Phone: (902)224-2306.

(N) CAPE BRETON HIGHLANDS NATIONAL PARK (Ingonish Beach)—(Victoria) *From town: Go 1-1/2 km/1 mi N on Cabot Trail.* FACILITIES: 90 sites, 90 no hkups, tenting. RECREATION: lake/saltwater swim, saltwater/lake fishing, playground. Partial handicap access. Open Jun - Sep. Phone: (902)224-2306.

INVERNESS—B-5

(N) Inverness Beach Village & Campground (Not visited)—(Inverness) *From N town limits on Hwy 19: Go .08 km/1/2 mi N on Hwy 19. Enter on R.* ◇◇◇FACILITIES: 40 sites, typical site width 20 ft, 25 W&E, (15 amps), 15 no hkups, tenting, dump, laundry. ◇◇RECREATION: saltwater swim, play equipment. Pets welcome, breed restrict, quantity restrict. Open Jun 15 - Oct 20. Rate in 2010 $26.50-29.50 for 4 persons. Member COA of NS. Phone: (902)258-2653.

KENTVILLE—C-3

(SE) Highbury Gardens Tent & Trailer Park—(Kings) *From Hwy 101 (exit 12): Go 1 km/3/4 mi S on New Canaan Rd (after stop). Enter on R.* ◇◇◇◇FACILITIES: 100 sites, typical site width 35 ft, 28 full hkups, 53 W&E, (20/30/50 amps), 19 no hkups, 35 pull-thrus, tenting, dump, laundry, ltd groc. ◇◇◇RECREATION: swim pool, playground. Pets welcome. Open May 15 - Oct 15. Rate in 2010 $34-38 for 4 persons. Member COA of NS.

Tides can reach up to 50 feet along the Fundy coast.

KENTVILLE—Continued
Highbury Gardens Tent & Trailer Park—Continued

Phone: (877)678-8011
Address: 121 New Canaan Rd, Kentville, NS B4N 4K1
Lat/Lon: 45.04950/-64.47757
Email: highburygardens@ns.sympatico.ca
Web: www.annapolisvalleycamping.com

(SW) South Mountain Park Family Camping & RV Resort Inc (Not Visited)—(Kings) *From jct Hwy 101 (exit 13) & Hwy 12: Go 9.6 km/6 mi S on Hwy 12. Enter on L.* ◇◇◇◇FACILITIES: 210 sites, typical site width 30 ft, 175 full hkups, (30 amps), 35 no hkups, 133 pull-thrus, tenting, dump, laundry, ltd groc. ◇◇◇◇RECREATION: swim pool, playground. Pets welcome. Partial handicap access. Open May 15 - Oct 15. Rate in 2010 $30 per family. Member COA of NS. Phone: (902)678-0152.

KINGSTON—C-2

(NW) Yogi Bear's Jellystone Park (Not Visited)—(Kings) *E'bound from Hwy 101 (exit 17W): Go .07 km/1/2 mi N on Marshall Rd, then .02 km/1/3 mi W on Brooklyn Rd. W'bound from Hwy 101 (exit 17E): Go 1 km/3/4 mi N Bishop Mtn Rd, then 2 km/1-1/3 mi W on Brooklyn Rd. Enter on R.* ◇◇◇◇FACILITIES: 229 sites, typical site width 30 ft, 120 full hkups, 90 W&E, (15/30/50 amps), 50 amps ($), 19 no hkups, 12 pull-thrus, tenting, dump, laundry, ltd groc. ◇◇◇◇◇RECREATION: swim pool, playground. Pets welcome. Partial handicap access. Open May 11 - Sep 16. Rate in 2010 $39-51 for 5 persons. Member ARVC, COA of NS. Phone: (888)225-7773.

LAHAVE—D-3

RISSER'S BEACH PROVINCIAL PARK—(Lunenburg) *In town on Hwy-331.* FACILITIES: 90 sites, 90 no hkups, tenting, dump. RECREATION: saltwater swim, boating, ramp, saltwater fishing, playground. Pets welcome. Partial handicap access. Open May 21 - Oct 11. Phone: (902)688-2034.

LINWOOD—C-5

(NW) Linwood Harbour Campground—*From Hwy 104 (exit 37): Follow Linwood Town sign 5.2 Km/3-1/4 mi (Hwy 4). Enter on L.* ◇◇◇FACILITIES: 40 sites, 30 full hkups, (30/50 amps), 50 amps ($), 10 no hkups, 10 pull-thrus, tenting, dump, laundry. Pets welcome. Partial handicap access. Open May 15 - Oct 15. Rate in 2010 $20-32 per family. Member COA of NS. Phone: (866)820-9550.

LITTLE BRAS D'OR—B-6

(S) Driftwood Tent & Trailer Park (Not visited)—(Cape Breton) *Hwy 105 (exit 18) & Georges River Rd: Go 2.5 km/1.5 mi S on Georges River Rd. Enter on R.* ◇◇FACILITIES: 75 sites, 30 full hkups, 32 W&E, (15 amps), 13 no hkups, tenting, dump, laundry. RECREATION: lake swim. Pets welcome. Open Jun 1 - Sep 30. Rate in 2010 $25 for 6 persons. Phone: (902)794-4519.

LOUIS HEAD—E-2

(C) Louis Head Beach Campground (Not Visited)—(Shelburne) *From Hwy 103 (exit 23): Go 4 km/2-1/2 mi W on Hwy 3, then 8.8 km/5-1/2 mi E on Louis Head Rd. Enter on R.* ◇◇FACILITIES: 35 sites, typical site width 20 ft, 15 full hkups, 17 W&E, (15/30 amps), 3 no hkups, tenting, dump, laundry, ltd groc. RECREATION: play equipment. Pets welcome. Open May 30 - Sep 30. Rate in 2010 $21-25 per family. Phone: (902)656-3129.

LOUISBOURG—B-6

(N) Lake View Treasures (Not Visited)—(Cape Breton) *From jct Hwy 125 (exit 8) & Hwy 22: Go 22.4 km/14 mi S on Hwy 22. Enter on L.* ◇◇◇FACILITIES: 150 sites, typical site width 30 ft, 35 full hkups, 40 W&E, (15/30 amps), 75 no hkups, tenting, shower$, dump, non-guest dump $, laundry, ice, picnic tables, fire rings, wood. ◇◇◇RECREATION: pavilion, swim pool, lake swim, boating, canoeing, kayaking, ramp, lake/river fishing, fishing guides, mini-golf, play equipment, horseshoes. Pets welcome. Open May 1 - Oct 5. Rate in 2010 $25-40 for 4 persons. MC/VISA/Debit. CCUSA 50% Discount. CCUSA reservations Recommended, CCUSA max stay 2 days, Cash only for CCUSA disc., CCUSA disc. not avail holidays. Not available month of Jul.

Phone: (902)733-2058
Address: 5785 Louisbourg Highway, Catalone, NS B1C 2G4
Lat/Lon: 45.98633/-59.99306
Web: www.lakeviewtreasures.com

(C) Louisbourg Motorhome RV Park & Campground (Not visited)—(Cape Breton) *From N Town City Limits on Hwy 22: Go 1.3 km/3/4 mi S on Hwy 22, then 30 meters/1000 ft E on Mitchell Crescent. Enter on L.* ◇◇◇FACILITIES: 57 sites, typical site width 16 ft, 39 full hkups, (30 amps), 18 no hkups, tenting. RECREATION: canoeing, saltwater fishing. Pets welcome. Partial handicap access. Open Jun 15 - Oct 15. Rate in 2010 $22-26 for 2 persons. Phone: (866)733-3631.

LOUISBOURG—Continued on next page

LOUISBOURG—Continued

(C) Point of View RV Park & Suites (Not visited) —(CapeBreton) *From N City Limit on Hwy 22: Go 2.4 km/1-1/2 mi S on Hwy 22. Enter on L.* ◇◇◇FACILITIES: 24 sites, typical site width 30 ft, 24 full hkups, (15/30 amps), 3 pull-thrus, laundry. Pets welcome. No tents. Open May 15 - Oct 15. Rate in 2010 $26 for 2 persons. Member COA of NS. Phone: (902)733-2080.

(C) Riverdale RV Park (Not visited)—*From N Town City Limit on Hwy 22: Go 2.2 km/1-1/4 mi S on Hwy 22, then 30 m/100 ft N on Riverdale St. Enter on L.* ◇◇◇FACILITIES: 30 sites, 30 full hkups, (30 amps), tenting, groceries. RECREATION: play equipment. Pets welcome. Partial handicap access. Open May 15 - Oct 31. Rate in 2010 $28 per family. Member COA of NS. Phone: (902)733-2531.

LOWER BARNEY'S RIVER—C-4

(W) Cranberry Campground (Not visited)—(Pictou) *From jct Barney's River & Hwy 245: Go 1 km/3/4 mi W on Hwy 245. Enter on R.* ◇◇◇FACILITIES: 46 sites, typical site width 30 ft, 29 full hkups, (15/30 amps), 17 no hkups, 4 pull-thrus, tenting, dump, laundry. ◇◇RECREATION: swim pool, saltwater swim, canoeing, saltwater fishing, play equipment. Pets welcome. Open May 14 - Oct 9. Rate in 2010 $20-32 for 4 persons. Phone: (902)926-2571.

LUNENBURG—D-3

(W) Little Lake Family Campground—(Lunenburg) *From jct Hwy 3 & Hwy 332 in Lunenberg: Go 1.6 km/1 mi W on Hwy 3. Enter on L.* ◇◇◇FACILITIES: 100 sites, typical site width 25 ft, 70 full hkups, 30 W&E, (30 amps), 2 pull-thrus, WiFi Instant Internet at site ($), WiFi Internet central location, tenting, dump, non-guest dump, laundry, ltd groc, ice, picnic tables, fire rings, wood. ◇◇◇RECREATION: swim pool, bsktball, playground, activities, v-ball. Pets welcome. Open Apr 15 - Oct 15. Rate in 2010 $32-35 per family. MC/VISA/Debit. Member COA of NS. CCUSA 50% Discount. CCUSA reservations Recommended, CCUSA max stay 2 days, CCUSA disc. not avail F,Sa, CCUSA disc. not avail holidays. Not available Jul thru Aug.

CAMPCLUB USA

Phone: (902)634-4308
Address: 11677 Hwy 3, Lunenburg, NS B0J 2C0
Lat/Lon: 44.37856/-64.36315
Email: murdot@ns.aliantzinc.ca
Web: www.littlelake-campground.piczo.com

LYDGATE—E-2

(W) Lockeport Cottages & Campgrounds ((Not visited)—*From E Town City Limit on Hwy 3: Go 1 km/3/4 mi W on Hwy 3. Enter on R.* ◇◇◇FACILITIES: 46 sites, 16 full hkups, (30 amps), 30 no hkups, tenting, dump, laundry. ◇◇RECREATION: swim pool, play equipment. Pets welcome. Open May 1 - Oct 15. Rate in 2010 $20-25 for 4 persons. Member COA of NS. Phone: (902)656-2876.

MAITLAND BRIDGE—D-2

(N) KEJIMKUJIK NATIONAL PARK (Jeremys Bay Campground)—(Annapolis) *From Hwy 8 in town: Go 8 km/5 mi S at National Park Entrance.* FACILITIES: 360 sites, 360 no hkups, tenting, dump, ltd groc. RECREATION: lake swim, boating, canoeing, lake/river fishing, playground. Partial handicap access. Open all yr. Phone: (902)682-2772.

MARTIN'S RIVER—D-3

(N) Rayport Campground—(Lunenburg) *From jct Hwy 103 (exit 10) & Hwy 3: Go 3.5 km/2 mi E on Hwy 3, then .08 km/1/2 mi N on Shingle Rd. Enter at end.* ◇◇◇◇FACILITIES: 70 sites, 60 W&E, (15/30/50 amps), 50 amps ($), 10 no hkups, 6 pull-thrus, cable TV, WiFi Instant Internet at site ($), tenting, dump, non-guest dump $, portable dump, laundry, ltd groc, ice, picnic tables, fire rings, wood. ◇◇◇RECREATION: swim pool, river fishing, playground, activities, hiking trails. Pets welcome. Partial handicap access. Open May 15 - Oct 15. Big rigs welcome. Rate in 2010 $29-33 for 4 persons. MC/VISA/AMEX/Debit. Member COA of NS. CCUSA 50% Discount. CCUSA reservations Accepted, CCUSA max stay Unlimited, Cash only for CCUSA disc., CCUSA disc. not avail F,Sa. Not available Thu thru Sun during peak season, Canadian holidays.

CAMPCLUB USA

Phone: (902)627-2678
Address: 165 Shingle Mill Rd, Martin's River, NS B0J 2E0
Lat/Lon: 44.48873/-64.34222
Email: rayport@hotmail.com
Web: www.rayport.ca

MEAT COVE—A-5

(C) Meat Cove Camping (Not Visited)—(Inverness) *From jct Cabot Trail & the Meat Cove Rd (Cape North Village): Go 16.5 km/10 mi to St Margaret's Village, then take the L fork (paved road) for 5.9 km/3-1/2 mi, then 7.5 km/5 mi on a winding, narrow, gravel road.*

MEAT COVE—Continued
Meat Cove Camping (Not Visited)—Continued

Enter at end. FACILITIES: 25 sites, 25 no hkups, tenting. RECREATION: saltwater swim, ramp, saltwater/river fishing. Pets welcome. Open Jun 1 - Oct 31. Rate in 2010 $20-23 per vehicle. Phone: (902)383-2379.

MIDDLETON—D-2

(E) Orchard Queen Motel & Campground—(Annapolis) *From jct Hwy 1 & Hwy 10: Go .08 km/3/4 mi E on Hwy 1. Enter on L.* ◇◇◇FACILITIES: 66 sites, typical site width 30 ft, 61 full hkups, (30/50 amps), 50 amps ($), 5 no hkups, tenting, dump, laundry. ◇RECREATION: swim pool, play equipment. Pets welcome. Open May 1 - Oct 9. Rate in 2010 $30 for 4 persons. Phone: (902)825-4801.

MILFORD—D-2

(SW) RAVEN HAVEN BEACHSIDE FAMILY PARK (City Town)—*From jct Hwy 101 (exit 22) & Rt 8: Go 20 km/12 mi S on Rt 8, then 5 km/3 mi W on Virginia St. Enter on R.* FACILITIES: 15 sites, 4 W&E, (20 amps), 11 no hkups, tenting, ltd groc. RECREATION: lake swim, canoeing, ramp, play equipment. Pets welcome. Open Jun 13 - Sep 3. Phone: (902)532-7320.

MURPHY'S COVE—D-4

(SW) Murphy's Camping on the Ocean (Not visited)—(Halifax) *From E Town City Limit on Hwy 7: Go 2.1 Km/1-1/3 mi W on Hwy 7, then 1.3 Km/3/4 mi S on Murphy Road. Enter at end.* ◇◇◇FACILITIES: 40 sites, typical site width 30 ft, 23 W&E, (15/30 amps), 17 no hkups, 6 pull-thrus, tenting, dump, laundry. ◇◇RECREATION: saltwater swim, canoeing, saltwater fishing, play equipment. Pets welcome. Open May 15 - Oct 15. Rate in 2010 $30 for 4 persons. Member COA of NS. Phone: (902)772-2700.

N.E. MARGAREE—B-5

(SE) The Lakes Campground (Not visited)—(Inverness) *From jct Hwy 19 & Cabot Trail: Go 16 km/10 mi S on Cabot Trail. Enter on R.* ◇◇FACILITIES: 42 sites, typical site width 32 ft, 30 ft max RV length, 10 full hkups, 24 W&E, (15/30 amps), 8 no hkups, tenting, dump, laundry, ltd groc. ◇◇RECREATION: lake swim, boating, canoeing, dock, lake fishing, play equipment. Pets welcome. Open May 15 - Oct 21. Rate in 2010 $23-25 per family. Phone: (902)248-2360.

NEW WATERFORD—B-6

(S) River Ryan Campground (Not visited)—(Cape Breton) *From jct Hwy 125 (exit 9) & Hwy 4: Go 5-3/4 km/3-1/2 mi E on Hwy 4, then 4 km/2-1/2 mi N on Gardiner Mines Rd, then 2 km/1-1/4 mi W on Hwy 28. Enter on R.* ◇◇FACILITIES: 42 sites, typical site width 25 ft, 35 full hkups, 5 W&E, (15 amps), 2 no hkups, tenting, laundry. ◇RECREATION: saltwater swim, saltwater fishing, play equipment. Pets welcome. Open May 1 - Oct 31. Rate in 2010 $25 for 4 persons. Phone: (902)862-8367.

NEWBURNE—D-2

(C) LaHave River Campground (Not Visited)—(Lunenburg) *From jct Hwy 103 (exit 11) & Hwy 324: Go 25.5 km/15-1/2 mi N on Hwy 324. Enter on L.* ◇◇FACILITIES: 58 sites, typical site width 30 ft, 58 W&E, (15 amps), tenting, dump, laundry. ◇◇RECREATION: river swim, river fishing, play equipment. Pets welcome. Open May 15 - Oct 1. Rate in 2010 $23 per family. Member COA of NS. Phone: (902)644-2654.

NINE MILE RIVER—C-3

(SW) Renfrew Campground (Not visited)—(Hants) *From jct Hwy 214 & Hwy 14: Go 3.5 km/2-1/3 mi W on Hwy 14, then 2 km/1-1/3 mi SW on Renfrew Road. Enter on L.* ◇◇◇FACILITIES: 185 sites, typical site width 44 ft, 60 full hkups, 87 W&E, (15/30 amps), 38 no hkups, 9 pull-thrus, tenting, dump, laundry, ltd groc. ◇◇◇RECREATION: swim pool, river swim, river fishing, playground. Pets welcome. Partial handicap access. Open May 18 - Oct 8. Rate in 2010 $33 per family. Member COA of NS. Phone: (902)883-1681.

(W) Riverland Campground—(Hants) *From jct Hwy 14 & 214 : Go 5.3 km/3-1/3 mi W on Hwy 14, then 2.1 km/1-1/3 mi SW on Thompson Road (gravel road). Enter at end.* ◇◇◇FACILITIES: 272 sites, typical site width 25 ft, 263 full hkups, 9 W&E, (15/30/50 amps), 50 amps ($), 24 pull-thrus, phone Internet central location, tenting, RV storage, shower$, dump, non-guest dump $, laundry, ltd groc, ice, picnic tables, fire rings, wood. ◇◇◇RECREATION: swim pool, river swim, boating, canoeing, river fishing, bsktball, playground, activities, horseshoes, hiking trails, v-ball. Pets welcome, breed restrict, size restrict. Open May 15 - Oct 15. Rate in 2010 $40 for 2 persons. MC/VISA/Debit. Member COA of NS. CCUSA 50% Discount. CCUSA reservations Required, CCUSA max stay 4 days, Cash only for CCUSA disc., CCUSA disc. not avail S, CCUSA disc. not avail F,Sa. Discount not available Labor Day or weekends unless authorized by personnel.

CAMPCLUB USA

NINE MILE RIVER—Continued
Riverland Campground—Continued

Phone: (902)883-7115
Address: 419 CP Thompson Rd, Nine Mile River, NS B2S 2X8
Lat/Lon: 45.04739/-63.61314
Email: riverlandcamp@aol.com
Web: www.riverlandcamping.com

NORTH SYDNEY—B-6

(N) Arm of Gold Campground (Not Visited)—(Cape Breton) *From jct Hwy 105 (exit 18) & Georges River Rd: Go .02 km/1/8 mi S on Georges River Rd. Enter on R.* ◇◇◇◇FACILITIES: 136 sites, typical site width 28 ft, 116 full hkups, (30/50 amps), 50 amps ($), 20 no hkups, 48 pull-thrus, tenting, dump, laundry. ◇◇◇RECREATION: river swim, canoeing, river fishing, playground. Pets welcome. Partial handicap access. Open Jun 1 - Oct 15. Big rigs welcome. Rate in 2010 $33.95 for 4 persons. Member COA of NS. Phone: (866)736-6516.

(NE) North Sydney/Cabot Trail KOA—(Victoria) *From Baddeck: Go 35.2 km/22 mi E on Hwy 105 to the western approach to Seal Island Bridge. Enter on R.* ◇◇◇◇FACILITIES: 152 sites, typical site width 25 ft, 103 full hkups, 24 W&E, (15/30/50 amps), 50 amps ($), 25 no hkups, 38 pull-thrus, tenting, dump, laundry, ltd groc. ◇◇◇◇RECREATION: lake/saltwater swim, boating, canoeing, ramp, saltwater/lake fishing, playground. Pets welcome. Open May 15 - Oct 15. Big rigs welcome. Rate in 2010 $27-38 for 2 persons. Phone: (800)562-7452. KOA discount.

OAKHILL—D-3

Oakhill Pines Camp & Trailer Park (Not visited) —(Lunenburg) *From S on Hwy 325 Town City limit: Go .08 km/ 1/4 mi N on Hwy 325, then 1.2 km/ 3/4 mi E on Oakhill Rd. Enter on L.* ◇◇FACILITIES: 143 sites, 100 full hkups, 32 W&E, (15/30 amps), 11 no hkups, 30 pull-thrus, tenting, dump, laundry, ltd groc. ◇◇◇RECREATION: swim pool, playground. Pets welcome. Open May 15 - Oct 1. Facilities fully operational Jul 1 - Sept 5. Rate in 2010 $23-33 for 4 persons. Member COA of NS. Phone: (902)543-2885.

PARRSBORO—C-3

(S) GLOOSCAP CAMPGROUND & RV—(Cumberland) *From the Parrsboro Town Centre Drive: Go 3.5 mi South on the "Two Islands" Road. Enter on R.* FACILITIES: 73 sites, typical site width 25 ft, 6 full hkups, 67 W&E, 6 pull-thrus, tenting, dump, ltd groc. RECREATION: saltwater swim, saltwater fishing, play equipment. Pets welcome. Open May 10 - Sept 30. Member COA of NS. Phone: (902)254-2529.

PICTOU—C-4

(SW) Birchwood Campground (Not visited)—(Pictou) *From Hwy 104 (exit 22) & Hwy 106: Go 12.2 km/7-1/2 mi N on Hwy 106 to Pictou Rotary, then take Lyon's Brook exit off Rotary, then 3.2 km/2 mi W on Hwy 376. Enter on R.* ◇◇◇FACILITIES: 70 sites, typical site width 28 ft, 40 full hkups, 15 W&E, (15/30 amps), 15 no hkups, 1 pull-thrus, tenting, dump, ltd groc. ◇◇◇RECREATION: swim pool, playground. Pets welcome. Open May 15 - Sep 30. Rate in 2010 $28-32 for 5 persons. Member COA of NS. Phone: (902)485-8565.

CARIBOU/MUNROES ISLAND PP—(Pictou) *From town: Go 8 km/5 mi N on Hwy 106, then 4.6 km/3 mi E on paved road.* FACILITIES: 95 sites, 95 no hkups, tenting, dump. RECREATION: saltwater swim, saltwater fishing. Pets welcome. Open Jun 18 - Oct 11. Phone: (902)485-6134.

(NE) Harbour Light Trailer Court & Campground—(Pictou) *From Pictou Rotary (Pictou exit): Go 1.5 km/1 mi E through town, then E fork at Y in center of Pictou, then follow signs 4.5 km/2-3/4 mi beyond Golf Course. Enter on R.* ◇◇◇FACILITIES: 180 sites, typical site width 30 ft, 85 full hkups, 65 W&E, (15/30/50 amps), 50 amps ($), 30 no hkups, 60 pull-thrus, tenting, dump, laundry, ltd groc. ◇◇◇RECREATION: swim pool, saltwater swim, canoeing, saltwater fishing, playground. Pets welcome. Partial handicap access. Open May 10 - Oct 15. Rate in 2010 $29-32 for 4 persons. Phone: (902)485-5733. FMCA discount.

PORT JOLI—E-2

(S) THOMAS RADDALL PP—(Queens) *From Hwy 103, west of Port Joli: Go 4 km/2-1/2 mi S on East Port l'Hebert Rd.* FACILITIES: 82 sites, 82 no hkups, tenting, dump. RECREATION: saltwater swim, boating, ramp, saltwater fishing, playground. Pets welcome. Partial handicap access. Open May 21 - Oct 11. Phone: (902)683-2664.

PORTERS LAKE—D-3

PORTERS LAKE PROVINCIAL PARK—(Halifax) *From Hwy 7 in town: Go 5-1/2 km/3-1/2 mi S on West Porter's Lake Rd.* FACILITIES: 80 sites, 80 full hkups, (15 amps), tenting, dump. RECREATION: lake/saltwater swim, boating, ramp, lake fishing, playground. Pets welcome. Partial handicap access. Open May 21 - Oct 11. Phone: (902)827-2250.

RAWDON GOLD MINES—C-3

(E) Rawdon Gold Mines Campground (Not visited)—(Hants) *From jct Hwy 101 (exit 5) & Hwy 14: Go 30 km/19 mi E on Hwy 14. Enter on R.* ◇◇◇FACILI-

Rawdon Gold Mines Campground (Not visited)—Continued on next page

RAWDON GOLD MINES—Continued
Rawdon Gold Mines Campground (Not visited)—Continued

TIES: 96 sites, typical site width 20 ft, 43 full hkups, 28 W&E, (15/30 amps), 25 no hkups, 10 pull-thrus, tenting, laundry, groceries. ◆◆◆RECREATION: swim pool, lake swim, boating, canoeing, ramp, dock, lake fishing, playground. Pets welcome. Open May 15 - Oct 15. Rate in 2010 $25-30 for 6 persons. Member COA of NS. Phone: (902)632-2050.

RIVERPORT—D-3

(NE) Ovens Natural Park (Not visited)—(Lunenburg) *From jct 332 NF & Hwy 3: Go 16 km/10 mi SW on Hwy 332, then 2.4 Km/1-1/5 mi S on Feltzen South Rd, then 1.5 Km/1 mi S on Ovens Rd (gravel road). Enter at end.* ◆◆FACILITIES: 158 sites, typical site width 25 ft, 30 full hkups, 45 W&E, (15/30 amps), 83 no hkups, tenting, dump, ltd groc. ◆◆RECREATION: swim pool, saltwater swim, playground. Pets welcome. Open May 18 - Oct 1. Rate in 2010 $33-45 for 4 persons. Phone: (902)766-4621.

ST. ANN'S BAY—B-5

(E) St. Anns Bay Campark—(Victoria) *Cross Englishtown Ferry: Go 3 km/1 3/4 mi N on Route 312 Or: From jct Hwy 105 & Cabot Trail (eixt 11): Go 30 km N on Cabot Trail, then 36 km S on Hwy 312. Enter on R.* ◆◆◆FACILITIES: 120 sites, 77 full hkups, 20 W&E, (30/50 amps), 23 no hkups, WiFi Instant Internet at site, tenting, shower$, dump, non-guest dump $, laundry, ltd groc, ice, picnic tables, fire rings, wood. ◆◆RECREATION: rec hall, pavilion, saltwater swim, play equipment, activities. Pets welcome. Partial handicap access. Open May 15 - Oct 19. Rate in 2010 $28-40 for 4 persons. Member COA of NS. CCUSA 50% Discount. CCUSA reservations Recommended, CCUSA max stay Unlimited. Call for availability weekends & holidays. 25% discount available Jul & Aug.

Phone: (866)791-9960
Address: 1762 Route 312, Englishtown, NS B0C 1H0
Email: katannya@ns.sympatico.ca
Web: www.stannsbaycampark.com

ST. PETERS—B-5

BATTERY PROVINCIAL PARK—(Richmond) *From town: Go 3/4 km/1/2 mi E on Hwy 4.* FACILITIES: 56 sites, 56 no hkups, tenting, dump. RECREATION: saltwater swim, boating, ramp, saltwater fishing, playground. Pets welcome. Partial handicap access. Open Jun 18 - Sep 13. Phone: (902)535-3094.

SALT SPRINGS—C-4

(W) Brookside Park and U-Fish (Not visited)—(Pictou) *From Hwy 104 (exit 19): Go .05 km/1/4 mi N, then 5.5 km/3-1/4 mi W on Six Mile Brook Road. Enter on L.* ◆◆FACILITIES: 29 sites, 16 W&E, (15 amps), 13 no hkups, tenting, ltd groc. RECREATION: pond fishing, playground. Pets welcome. Partial handicap access. Open May 1 - Oct 15. Rate in 2010 $18-20 per family. Phone: (902)485-1872.

SEAFOAM—B-4

(W) Seafoam Campground (Not Visited)—(Pictou) *From jct Hwy 106 & Hwy 6 (Rotary of Pictou): Go 24 km/15 mi W on Hwy 6. Enter on R.* ◆◆◆◆FACILITIES: 130 sites, typical site width 28 ft, 86 full hkups, 21 W&E, (30 amps), 23 no hkups, 35 pull-thrus, tenting, dump, laundry, ltd groc. ◆◆◆◆RECREATION: saltwater swim, canoeing, saltwater fishing, playground. Pets welcome. Partial handicap access. Open mid May - Oct 1. Rate in 2010 $26-33 per family. Member COA of NS. Phone: (902)351-3122.

SHEET HARBOUR—C-4

(NE) East River Lodge Campground & Trailer Park (Not visited)—(Halifax) *From W Town City Limit on Hwy 7: Go 5.5 km/3-1/2 mi E on Hwy 7, then .08 km/1/2 mi NE on West-East River Rd. Enter on R.* ◆◆◆FACILITIES: 40 sites, typical site width 25 ft, 28 full hkups, 11 W&E, (15/30 amps), 1 no hkups, tenting, dump, laundry. ◆◆RECREATION: river swim, canoeing, ramp, dock, river fishing, play equipment. Pets welcome. Open May 1 - Oct 31. Rate in 2010 $25 for 4 persons. Member COA of NS. Phone: (902)885-2057.

SHELBURNE—E-2

(SW) THE ISLANDS PROVINCIAL PARK—(Shelburne) *From town: Go 4-3/4 km/3 mi W off Hwy 3.* FACILITIES: 70 sites, 70 no hkups, tenting, dump. RECREATION: saltwater swim, boating, ramp, dock, saltwater fishing. Pets welcome. Partial handicap access. Open May 21 - Sep 6. Phone: (902)875-4304.

SHERBROOKE—C-4

(NE) Nimrods Campground (Not visited)—(Guysborough) *From jct Hwy 7 & Hwy 211: Go .08 km/1/2 mi SE on Hwy 211. Enter on L.* ◆◆FACILITIES: 60 sites, typical site width 25 ft, 45 W&E, (15/30/50 amps), 15 no hkups, tenting, dump, laundry. ◆◆RECREATION: lake swim, boating, canoeing, dock, lake/stream fishing, playground. Pets welcome. Open May 15 - Oct 15. Rate in 2010 $21-27 for 6 persons. Phone: (902)522-2441.

(NE) St. Mary's Riverside Campground (Not visited)—(Guysborough) *From W Town City Limit on Hwy 7: Go 2.6 km/1-3/4 mi E on Hwy 7, then 1.8 km/1 mi S on Sonora Rd. Enter on R.* ◆◆FACILITIES: 24 sites, typical site width 30 ft, 12 W&E, (30 amps), 12 no hkups, 2 pull-thrus, tenting, dump, laundry, ltd groc. ◆RECREATION: swim pool, playground. Pets welcome. Open May 15 - Oct 31. Rate in 2010 $25-30 for 4 persons. Phone: (902)522-2913.

SHUBENACADIE—C-3

(W) Whispering Winds (Not Visited)—(Hants) *From jct Hwy 102 & Hwy 215 (exit 10): Go 1 km/1/2 mi N on Hwy 215. Enter on R.* ◆◆FACILITIES: 256 sites, typical site width 30 ft, 15 full hkups, 201 W&E, (15/30/50 amps), 40 no hkups, 14 pull-thrus, tenting, dump, laundry, ltd groc. ◆◆◆RECREATION: swim pool, boating, canoeing, ramp, dock, river fishing, play equipment. Pets welcome. Open May 5 - Oct 15. Rate in 2010 $30 for 5 persons. Member COA of NS. Phone: (902)483-0995.

(S) Wild Nature Campground (Not Visited)—(Colchester) *From jct Hwy 224 & Hwy 2: Go 5.3 km/3-1/3 mi S on Hwy 2. Enter on L.* ◆◆FACILITIES: 45 sites, typical site width 30 ft, 15 full hkups, (30 amps), 30 no hkups, 5 pull-thrus, tenting, dump. ◆RECREATION: play equipment. Pets welcome. Open May 19 - Sept 30. Rate in 2010 $20 per family. Phone: (902) 758-1631.

SOUTH HARBOUR—A-5

(NW) Hideaway Campground & Oyster Market (Not visited)—(Victoria) *From Cabot Trail at South Harbour: Go 2km/1 1/2 mi N on Shore Roads. Enter on L.* ◆◆FACILITIES: 37 sites, 6 E, (15 amps), 31 no hkups, tenting, dump, laundry. RECREATION: saltwater/river swim, ramp, river fishing, play equipment. Pets welcome. Open May 20 - Oct 15. Rate in 2010 $20-25 per family. Member COA of NS. Phone: (902)383-2116.

SOUTH LAKE AINSLIE—B-5

(NE) Ainslie Village Camping—(Inverness) *From jct Hwy 105 (exit 5) & Hwy 252: Go 3 km/2 mi N on Hwy 252, then 6 km/3 3/4 mi NE on Rte 395. Enter on L.* ◆◆FACILITIES: 90 sites, typical site width 22 ft, 80 full hkups, (15/30 amps), 10 no hkups, tenting, dump, laundry, ltd groc. ◆◆RECREATION: swim pool, lake swim, boating, canoeing, ramp, lake fishing, play equipment. Pets welcome. Open May 15 - Oct 15. Rate in 2010 $16-23 for 5 persons. Phone: (902)756-2255.

SOUTH RAWDON—C-3

(E) Boutiliers Glen—(Hants) *From jct Hwy 215 & Hwy 14: Go 4 km/2-1/2 mi E on Hwy 14, then 6.4 km/4 mi S on South Rawdon Rd (either Ashdale Rd). Enter on L.* ◆◆◆FACILITIES: 80 sites, typical site width 35 ft, 61 full hkups, 11 W&E, (15/30/50 amps), 8 no hkups, 10 pull-thrus, tenting, dump, laundry, ltd groc. ◆◆◆RECREATION: river swim, river fishing, playground. Pets welcome. Partial handicap access. Open May 18 - Oct 9. Rate in 2010 $20-23 per family. Phone: (902)757-2401.

SPENCER'S ISLAND—C-2

(C) The Old Shipyard Beach Campground (Not visited)—(Cumberland) *From E City Town limit on Hwy 209: Go .05km/1/3 mi W on Hwy 209, then 1.2 km/3/4 mi SW on Spencer Beach Road, then 60 meters/200 ft SE on Beach Road. Enter at end.* ◆◆FACILITIES: 28 sites, 9 full hkups, 14 W&E, (30 amps), 5 no hkups, tenting, laundry. ◆◆RECREATION: saltwater swim, boating, canoeing, ramp, saltwater fishing. Pets welcome. Open Jun 1 - Sep 30. Rate in 2010 $23-30 for 5 persons. Phone: (902)392-2487.

SPRY BAY—D-4

(W) SpryBay Campground & Cabins (Not Visited)—(Halifax) *From E town city limit on Hwy 7: Go 13 km/8 mi W on Hwy 7. Enter on R.* ◆◆◆FACILITIES: 41 sites, typical site width 30 ft, 18 W&E, (15/30/50 amps), 50 amps ($), 23 no hkups, 8 pull-thrus, tenting, dump, laundry, groceries. ◆◆RECREATION: swim pool, play equipment. Pets welcome. Partial handicap access. Open May 15 - Oct 30. Big rigs welcome. Rate in 2010 $20-23 per family. Member COA of NS. Phone: (902)772-2554.

SYDNEY—B-6

MIRA RIVER PROVINCIAL PARK—(Cape Breton) *From town: Go 22-1/2 km/14 mi S on Hwy 22.* FACILITIES: 148 sites, 148 no hkups, tenting, dump. RECREATION: saltwater swim, boating, canoeing, ramp, saltwater fishing, playground. Pets welcome. Partial handicap access. Open Jun 11 - Sep 13. Phone: (902)563-3373.

TRENTON—C-4

(SW) TRENTON PARK CAMPGROUND (City Park)—*From Hwy 106 (exit 1A): Go E. In town. Enter on L.* FACILITIES: 43 sites, 43 full hkups, (30 amps), tenting, dump, laundry. RECREATION: swim pool, lake fishing, playground. Pets welcome. Open May 20 - Sep 12. Phone: (902)752-1019.

TRURO—C-3

Elm River Park—(Colchester) *From jct Hwy 104 & Hwys 2 & 4 (exit 12-Glenholme Loop): Go 1 km/1/2 mi W on Hwy 4 & Hwy 2 N. Enter on R.* ◆◆◆◆FACILITIES: 118 sites, typical site width 30 ft, 80 full hkups, 26 W&E, (15/30/50 amps), 50 amps ($), 12 no hkups, 70 pull-thrus, tenting, dump, laundry, ltd groc. ◆◆◆RECREATION: swim pool, river swim, river fishing, play equipment. Pets welcome. Partial handicap access. Open Apr 1 - Nov 30. Facilities fully operational Jun 1 - Oct 1. Big rigs welcome. Rate in 2010 $35.65 per family. Phone: (888)356-4356.

(NW) Hidden Hilltop Campground—(Colchester) *From Hwy 104 (exit 11) & Hwy 4: Go 3 km/2 mi W on Hwy 4. Enter on L.* ◆◆◆FACILITIES: 180 sites, typical site width 30 ft, 119 full hkups, 43 W&E, (20/30 amps), 18 no hkups, 6 pull-thrus, tenting, dump, laundry, ltd groc. ◆◆◆◆RECREATION: swim pool, play equipment. Pets welcome. Open May 15 - Oct 15. Rate in 2010 $27-32 for 6 persons. Member COA of NS. Phone: (902)662-3391.

(S) SCOTIA PINE CAMPGROUND—(Colchester) *From jct Hwy 102 (exit 13) & Hwy 2: Go 9.6 km/6 mi S on Hwy 2. Enter on L.*

◆◆◆◆FACILITIES: 160 sites, typical site width 25 ft, 80 full hkups, 15 W&E, (15/30/50 amps), 50 amps ($), 65 no hkups, some extd stay sites, 40 pull-thrus, cable TV, ($), WiFi Instant Internet at site, WiFi Internet central location, family camping, tenting, cabins, shower$, dump, non-guest dump $, laundry, ltd groc, RV supplies, LP gas by weight, ice, picnic tables, wood, controlled access.

◆◆◆RECREATION: pavilion, swim pool, golf nearby, bsktball, playground, shuffleboard court 2 shuffleboard courts, horseshoes, sports field, hiking trails.

Pets welcome, breed restrict. Partial handicap access. Open Jun 1 - Oct 15. Big rigs welcome. Clubs welcome. Rate in 2010 $32-36 for 2 persons. MC/VISA. Member COA of NS.

Phone: (877)893-3666
Address: 1911 Hwy 2, RR 1, Brookfield, NS B0N 1C0
Lat/Lon: 45.28645/-63.28925
Email: info@scotiapine.ca
Web: www.scotiapine.ca

SEE AD HALIFAX PAGE 856

UPPER LAKEVILLE—D-4

(NW) E & F WEBBER LAKESIDE PARK—(Halifax) *From Metro Halifax E on Hwy 107 to Musquodoboit HbR (38 km/23 mi), then 20 km/12 mi E on Hwy 7 to Upper Lakeville Rd, then 3.7 km/2-1/4 mi N on Upper Lakeville Rd. Enter at end.*

◆◆◆◆FACILITIES: 66 sites, typical site width 35 ft, 47 full hkups, 4 W&E, (15/30/50 amps), 15 no hkups, many extd stay sites, 7 pull-thrus, WiFi Instant Internet at site, tenting, cabins, laundry, ltd groc, LP bottle exch, marine gas, ice, picnic tables, fire rings, wood, controlled access.

◆◆◆RECREATION: rec hall, lake swim, boating, canoeing, kayaking, ramp, dock, 4 canoe/3 kayak/6 pedal boat rentals, lake fishing, golf nearby, play equipment, activities (wkends), horseshoes, hiking trails, v-ball. Rec open to public.

Pets welcome. Partial handicap access. Open May 15 - Oct 15. Big rigs welcome. Clubs welcome. Rate in 2010 $27-37 per family. MC/VISA/AMEX/Debit. Member COA of NS. CCUSA 50% Discount. CCUSA reservations Recommended, CCUSA max stay 4 days, CCUSA disc. not avail F,Sa, CCUSA disc. not avail holidays.

E & F WEBBER LAKESIDE PARK—Continued on next page

Nova Scotia is located on the eastern seaboard of Canada.

UPPER LAKEVILLE—Continued
E & F WEBBER LAKESIDE PARK—Continued

Phone: (902)845-2340
Address: 738 Upper Lakeville Rd, Upper Lakeville, NS B0J 1W0
Lat/Lon: 44.79903/-62.96394
Email: info@webberslakesideresort.com
Web: www.webberslakesideresort.com

SEE AD PAGE 858

WEST MABOU—B-5

(NW) Ceilidh Cottages, RV Sites & Campground—(Inverness) *From S Mabou Sign City limit on Hwy 19: Go .04 km/1/3 mi N o Hwy 19, then 5 km/2-1/2 mi W on West Mabour Road. Enter on L.* ◇◇◇FACILITIES: 17 sites, typical site width 35 ft, 35 ft max RV length, 10 full hkups, (15/30 amps), 7 no hkups, tenting, dump, laundry, ltd groc. ◇◇RECREATION: swim pool, play equipment. Pets welcome. Partial handicap access. Open May 1 - Oct 31. Rate in 2010 $25-35 per vehicle. Member COA of NS. Phone: (902)945-2992.

Nova Scotia Provincial Tree: Red Spruce

WHYCOCOMAGH—B-5

(C) Glenview Campground—(Inverness) *From jct Hwy 105 & Hwy 252 (exit 5): Go 500 feet N on Hwy 252. Enter on L.* ◇◇◇FACILITIES: 100 sites, typical site width 30 ft, 79 full hkups, 6 W&E, (15/30/50 amps), 50 amps ($), 15 no hkups, 17 pull-thrus, tenting, dump, laundry, ltd groc. ◇◇◇RECREATION: swim pool, canoeing, river fishing, playground. Pets welcome. Open May 15 - Oct 15. Rate in 2010 $25-30 per family. Member COA of NS. Phone: (888)691-8053.

(N) WHYCOCOMAGH PROVINCIAL PARK—(Inverness) *From town: Go 1/2 km/1/4 mi E on Hwy 105.* FACILITIES: 62 sites, 62 no hkups, tenting, dump. RECREATION: lake swim, boating, ramp, lake fishing. Pets welcome. Partial handicap access. Open Jun 18 - Oct 18. Phone: (902)756-2448.

WILMOT—D-2

(NE) Vidito Family Campground & Cottages LTD (TOO NEW TO RATE)—(Annapolis) *From W Town (city limit) on Hwy #1: Go .08 km/1/2 mi E on Hwy #1. Enter on R.* FACILITIES: 50 sites, 30 full hkups, 20 no hkups, family camping, tenting, dump, laundry. RECREATION: swim pool, river swim, playground. Pets welcome. Partial handicap access. Rate in 2010 $20 per family. Phone: (902)825-4380.

WINDSOR—D-3

(E) SMILEY'S PROVINCIAL PARK—(Hants) *From town: Go 12-3/4 km/8 mi E on Hwy 14.* FACILITIES: 86 sites, 86 no hkups, tenting, dump. RECREATION: river swim, river fishing, playground. Pets welcome. Partial handicap access. Open Jun 18 - Sep 27. Phone: (902)757-3131.

YARMOUTH—E-1

(SE) Camper's Haven—(Yarmouth) *From jct Hwy 1 & Hwy 3: Go 7.3 km/4-1/2 mi SE on Hwy 3. Enter on L.* ◇◇◇FACILITIES: 215 sites, typical site width 30 ft, 101 full hkups, 45 W&E, (15/30/50 amps), 50 amps ($), 69 no hkups, 37 pull-thrus, tenting, dump, laundry, ltd groc. ◇◇◇RECREATION: swim pool, lake/lake fishing, playground. Pets welcome. Partial handicap access. Open Jun 1 - Oct 1. Big rigs welcome. Rate in 2010 $31-37-43 for 4 persons. Member COA of NS. FCRV discount. FMCA discount.

Phone: (902)742-4848
Address: 9700 Hwy 3 East, arcadia, NS B5A 4A8
Lat/Lon: 43.82911/-66.03857
Email: campers@ns.sympatico.ca
Web: www.campershavencampground.com

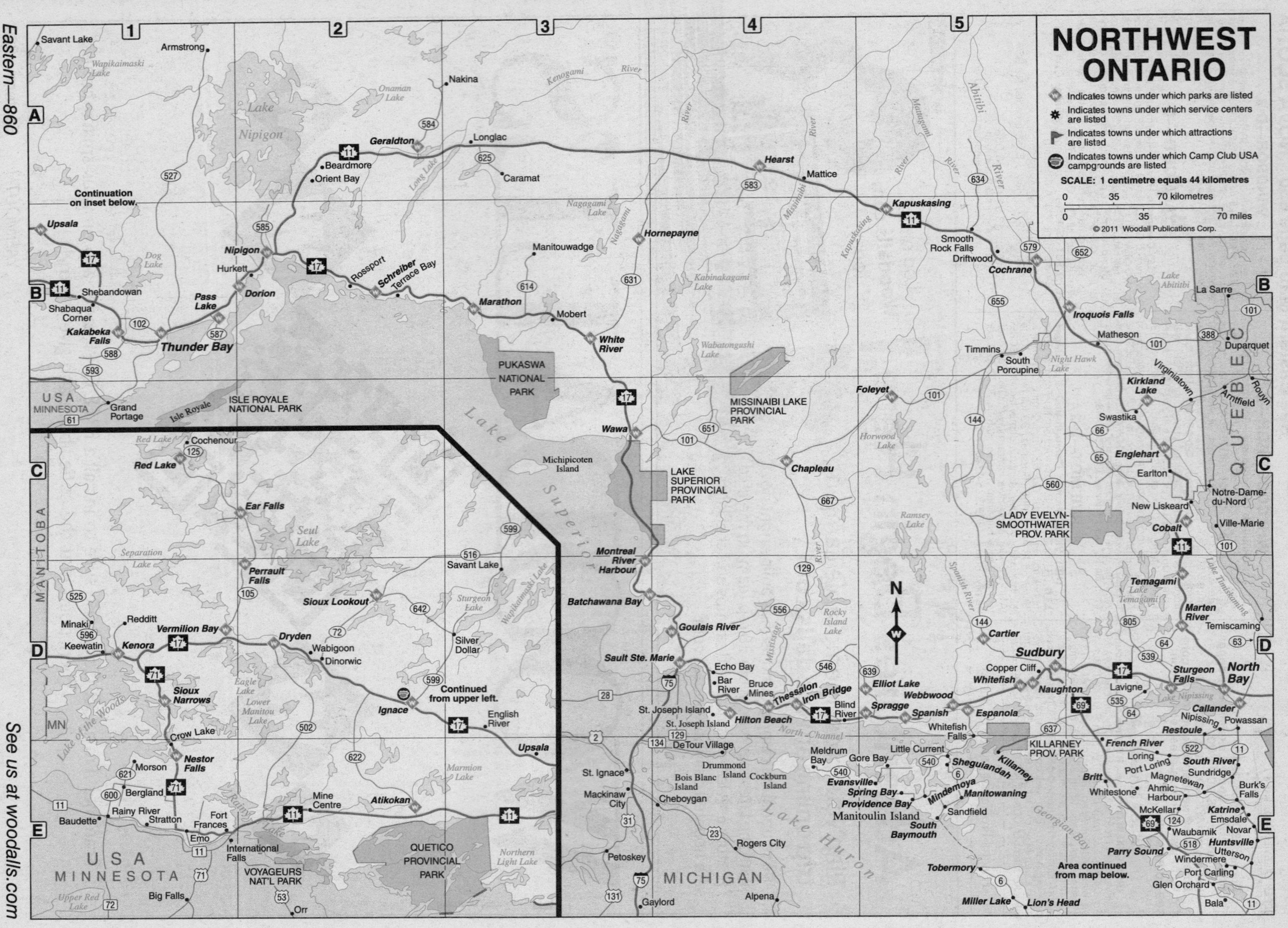
NORTHWEST ONTARIO
Indicates towns under which parks are listed
Indicates towns under which service centers are listed
Indicates towns under which attractions are listed
Indicates towns under which Camp Club USA campgrounds are listed
SCALE: 1 centimetre equals 44 kilometres
70 kilometres
70 miles
© 2011 Woodall Publications Corp.
Continuation on inset below.
Continued from upper left.
Area continued from map below.
PUKASWA NATIONAL PARK
ISLE ROYALE NATIONAL PARK
MISSINAIBI LAKE PROVINCIAL PARK
LAKE SUPERIOR PROVINCIAL PARK
LADY EVELYN-SMOOTHWATER PROV. PARK
KILLARNEY PROV. PARK
QUETICO PROVINCIAL PARK
VOYAGEURS NAT'L PARK
Thunder Bay
Sault Ste. Marie
Sudbury
North Bay
Kenora
Dryden
Wawa
Kapuskasing
Cochrane
Timmins
Lake Superior
Lake Huron
MICHIGAN
USA MINNESOTA
MANITOBA
QUEBEC

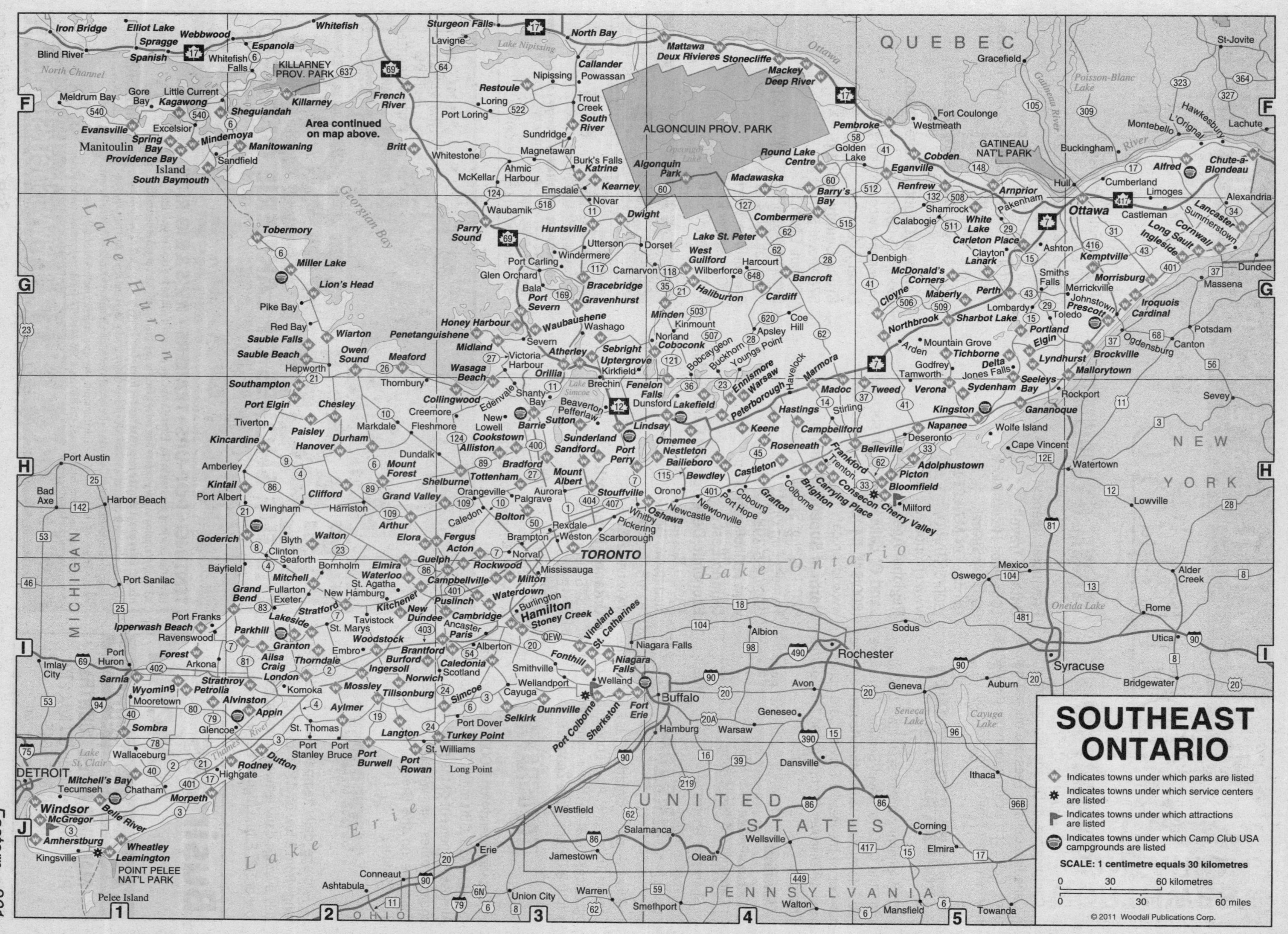
SOUTHEAST ONTARIO
Indicates towns under which parks are listed
Indicates towns under which service centers are listed
Indicates towns under which attractions are listed
Indicates towns under which Camp Club USA campgrounds are listed
SCALE: 1 centimetre equals 30 kilometres
0 30 60 kilometres
0 30 60 miles
© 2011 Woodall Publications Corp.
QUEBEC
NEW YORK
MICHIGAN
OHIO
PENNSYLVANIA
UNITED STATES
ALGONQUIN PROV. PARK
GATINEAU NAT'L PARK
KILLARNEY PROV. PARK
POINT PELEE NAT'L PARK
Lake Ontario
Lake Huron
Lake Erie
Georgian Bay
Area continued on map above.

TRAVEL SECTION

Ontario

CAMPING FEES

Camping fees in Ontario listings are stated in Canadian dollars. Fees are quoted before taxes. Call each location for more details, as they vary from province to province.

READER SERVICE INFO

The following businesses have placed an ad in the Ontario Travel Section. To receive free information, enter the Reader Service number on the Reader Service Card opposite page 48/Discover Section in the front of this directory:

Advertiser	RS#
Ontario Private Campground Association	466
Sherkston Shores	4325

TIME ZONE

Most of Ontario is in the Eastern Time Zone. About one quarter of the province, at the western end, is in the Central Time Zone.

TOPOGRAPHY

Ontario extends for 1,000 miles from east to west and 1,050 miles from north to south. Almost 20 percent of the province—68,490 square miles—is water. The freshwater shoreline on the Great Lakes extends for 2,362 miles.

TEMPERATURE

Average daily temperatures in January range from a low of -18° F to a high of 31° F. July average daily temperatures range from a low of 52° F to a high of 81° F.

TRAVEL & TOURISM INFO

Provincial Agency:

Ontario Travel
10th Floor, Hearst Block
900 Bay Street
Toronto, ON M7A 2E1
(800/ONTARIO)
www.ontariotravel.net

Regional Agencies:

Land O' Lakes Tourist Association
(800/840-4445 or 613/336-8818)
www.lol.on.ca/

North of Superior Tourism
920 Tungsten St., Suite 206A
Thunder Bay, ON P7B526
(800/265-3951)
www.northofsuperior.org

Ontario East
Economic Development Commission
18980 Beaverbrook Rd.
Marintown, ON K0C 1S0
(613/528-1472)
www.onteast.com

Ontario's Near North
1375 Seymour St.
P.O. Box 351
North Bay, ON P1B 8H5
(800/387-0516 or 705/474-6634)
www.ontariosnearnorth.on.ca

Niagara Falls Tourism
5400 Robinson St.
Niagara Falls, ON L2G 2A6
(905/356-6061)
www.niagarafallstourism.com

Norfolk County – South Coast Tourism
30 Peel St. South
Simcoe, ON N3Y 1R9
(519/426-9497 or 800/699-9038)
www.norfolktourism.ca

Rainbow Country Travel Assn.
(800/465-6655)
www.rainbowcountry.com

Local Agencies:

Bruce County Tourism
578 Brown St.
Wiarton, ON N0H 2T0
(800/268-3838 or 519/534-5344)
www.naturalretreat.com

Cambridge Tourism
750 Hespeler Road
Cambridge, ON N3H 5L8

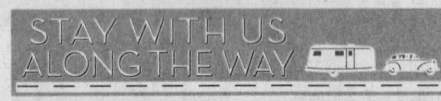

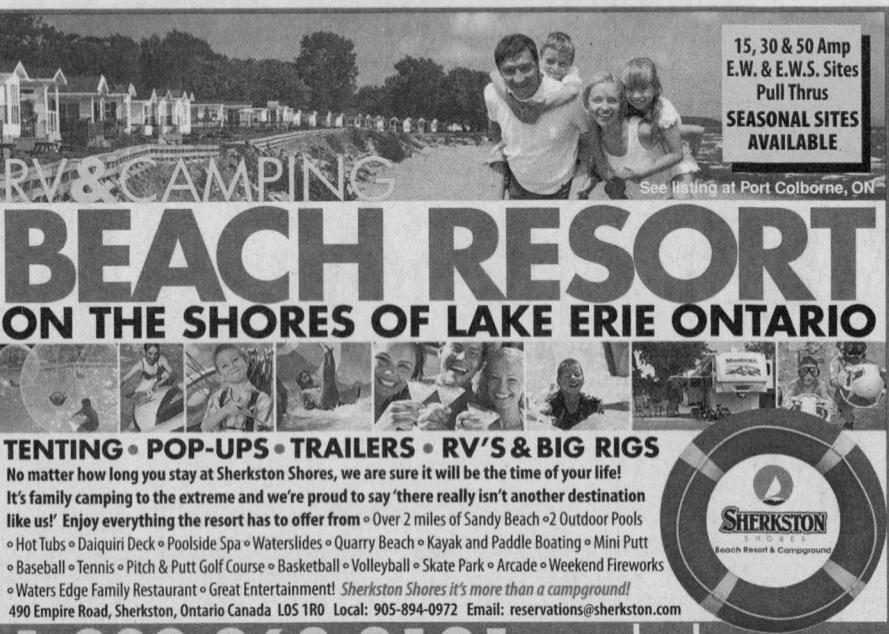

(519/622-2336 or 800/749-7560)
www.cambridgetourism.com

County of Lennox and Addington Economic Development
97 Thomas Street East
P.O. Box 1000
Napanee, ON K7R 3S9
(613/354-4883)
www.lennox-addington.on.ca

Tourism London
696 Wellington Road South
London, ON N6C 4R2
(519/661-5000 or 800/265-2602)
www.londontourism.ca

Town of Milton
Visitor & Community Information Service
43 Brown St.
Milton, ON L9T 5H2
(905/878-7252 or 800/418-5494)
www.town.milton.on.ca

Northumberland Tourism
555 Courthouse Rd
Cobourg, ON K9A 5J6
(866/401-3278 or 905/372-3329)
www.northumberlandtourism.com

Rainbow Country Travel Association
2726 Whippoorwill Ave.
Sudbury, ON P3G 1E9
(800/465-6655 or 705/522-0104)
www.rainbowcountry.com

Sioux Narrows/Nestor Falls Tourism Association
P.O. Box 236
Sioux Narrows, ON P0X 1N0
(807/226-5293 or 800/501-4430)
www.lakeofthewoodsvacations.com

Owen Sound Tourism
808-2nd Avenue East
Owen Sound, On N4K 2H4
(519/371-9833 or 888/675-5555)
www.owensound.ca

BUSINESSES OFFERING

	Things to See & Do	RV Sales	RV Service
CHERRY VALLEY			
Quinte's Isle Campark & Trailer Sale		🚌	✹
Quinte's Isle Diamond "J" Ranch	⚑		
LEAMINGTON			
Sturgeon Woods RV Sales & Services		🚌	✹
MCGREGOR			
Wildwood Golf & RV Resort	⚑		
PORT COLBORNE			
Sherkston Shores Park Model Sales		🚌	
Sherkston Shores Water Park	⚑		

The easy way to reserve a little piece of paradise...

Call 866 211 6841 or
go to www.campinginontario.ca

Create memories ... go camping ... reserve online!

FREE INFO! Enter #466 on Reader Service Card

The Bay of Quinte Tourist Council
(613/962-4597)
www.bayofquintecountry.com/

Temagami and District Chamber of Commerce
P.O. Box 57, Dept. T
Temagami, ON P0H 2H0
(800/661-7609)
www.temagamiinformation.com

Toronto Convention & Visitors Association
207 Queen's Quay W.
P.O. Box 126
Toronto, ON M5J 1A7
(800/499-2514 or 416/203-2600)
www.torontotourism.com

RECREATIONAL INFO

Bicycling: Ontario Cycling Assn., 1185 Eglinton Ave., E., Ste. 408, North York, ON M3C 3C6 (416/426-7416). www.ontariocycling.org

Canoeing & Kayaking: Paddling Ontario, 214 Munroe Ave., Peterborough, ON K9H 1H8 (705/745-9343) www.paddlingontario.com

Fishing & Hunting: Ministry of Natural Resources Information Centre, 300 Water St., Peterborough, ON K9J 8M5 (800/667-1940) www.fishontario.com or www.huntontario.com or www.mnr.gov.on.ca

Golf: Oakville, Ontario, Canada www.ontgolf.ca

Hiking: Hike Ontario, (postal mail only, no walk-ins please) 165 Dundas St. West, Suite 400, Mississauga, ON L5B 2N6 (800/894-7249 or 905/277-4453). www.hikeontario.com

SHOPPING

Toronto Eaton Centre, 220 Yonge St. A three-block-long shopping center with over 250 shops and services.

Vaughan Mills, Vaughan. Over 200 specialty shops and 15 anchor stores including Tommy Hilfiger, Hudson Bay and Bass Pro Shops. Over a mile long.

Locke Street, Hamilton. Known as "Antique Alley," this picturesque street is lined with unique antique and specialty stores. Located in southwest Hamilton below the Niagara Escarpment.

Village of St. Jacobs, St. Jacobs. Over 100 unique shops and restaurants, antiques, furniture and the Mennonite Story, Maple Syrup and Quilt museums.

Motorists crossing the U.S./Ontario border at 11 major points are able to enjoy duty-free shopping on the Ontario side for goods that are to be taken with them directly into the United States. Following is a list of Ontario's Duty-Free Shops open year-round; centres that are open 24 hours a day are indicated.

QUICK REFERENCE CHART FOR WOODALL'S FEATURED PARKS

	Green Friendly	RV Lots for Sale	Park Models-Onsite Ownership	Park Membership for Sale	Big Rigs Welcome	Internet Friendly	Pets Welcome
AMHERSTBURG							
Jellystone Park & Camp Resort							■
CHERRY VALLEY							
Martin's River Country						◍	■
Quinte's Isle Campark					▲	◍	■
KINCARDINE							
Fisherman's Cove Tent & Trailer Park	🍃					◍	■
KINGSTON							
Rideau Acres Campground						◍	■
LEAMINGTON							
Sturgeon Woods Campground & Marina						◍	■
MILTON							
Milton Heights Campground	🍃					◍	■
NIAGARA FALLS							
Knight's Hide-Away Park	🍃				▲	◍	■
Shalamar Lake Niagara						◍	■
Yogi Bear's Jellystone Park Camp-Resort	🍃				▲	◍	■
NORTH BAY							
Dreany Haven Campground (Not Visited)							■
OTTAWA							
Camp Hither Hills					▲	◍	■
Poplar Grove Tourist Camp					▲	◍	■
PEMBROKE							
Pine Ridge Park & Resort							■
PORT COLBORNE							
Sherkston Shores					▲	◍	■
PRESCOTT							
Grenville Park						◍	■
PUSLINCH							
Emerald Lake Trailer Resort & Water Park					▲	◍	■
RED LAKE							
South Bay on Gull Rock (Not Visited)					▲	◍	■
SAUBLE BEACH							
Woodland Park	🍃					●	■
SUDBURY							
Carol Campsite (Not Visited)						◍	■
THUNDER BAY							
Happy Land Campground & Cabins (Not Visited)						◍	■
TOBERMORY							
Tobermory Village Campground						●	■
WHEATLEY							
Lakeside Village Motel and Campground	🍃					◍	■

Green Friendly 🍃; RV Lots for Sale ✖; Park Models/Onsite Onwership ✱; Park Memberships for Sale ✔; Big Rigs Welcome ▲; Internet Friendly ●; Internet Friendly-WiFi ◍; Pets Welcome ■

Fort Erie (24 hours): Peace Bridge Plaza, at the Peace Bridge (905/871-5400)

Rainy River: 402 Atwood Ave. (807/852-3886)

Fort Frances: At the International Bridge, 401 Mowat Ave. (807/274-7151)

Point Edward (24 hours): At the Bluewater Bridge, 1 Bridge St. (519/332-4680)

Lansdowne (24 hours): Hill Island, at the Thousand Islands Bridge (613/659-2133)

Sault Ste. Marie: At the International Bridge Plaza, 127 Huron St. (705/759-6333)

Niagara Falls: 5726 Falls Avenue, at the Rainbow Bridge (905/374-3700)

Windsor: Location: 707 Patricia Street, Windsor (519/977-9100)

Queenston (24 hours): At the Lewiston-Queenston Bridge (905/262-5363)

Windsor-Ambassador Bridge (24 hours): 707 Patricia St. at the Ambassador Bridge (519/977-9100)

DESTINATIONS

SOUTHWESTERN ONTARIO

This region is home to a large part of Ontario's population. Here, travelers will find fertile farmlands, bustling cities and some of Canada's mildest climates.

Amherstburg is one of the oldest settlements in this region with numerous historic sites. Among these places is the **North American Black Historical Museum**, tracing the history of African Americans from slavery to emancipation. The **Fort Malden National Historic Site** contains several stone buildings displaying artifacts of Indians, French, British and Americans who all controlled the area at various times.

Brantford was the hometown of Alexander Graham Bell. Visit his home, the **Bell Homestead**, furnished just as it was when he lived there—complete with inventions. Also in Brantford is the **Kanata Village**, a 26 acre Iroquoian village and Interpretive Centre. Representing a 17th century village, it provides interactive learning experiences.

Hamilton. Popular attractions include **Hamilton Place**, a multi-million-dollar cultural center; Dundurn Castle, a 19th-century, 35-room mansion restored to its former splendor; the **Royal Botanical Gardens**; and 2,500 acres of colorful flower displays, a wildlife sanctuary and winding nature trails. For thrills and chills visit the **Canadian Warplane Heritage Museum** and slip inside a fighter jet or take flight in a simulator.

London. This growing town on the River Thames has 1,500 acres of parks and has been called the "Forest City." The **Springbank Park** alone contains 350 acres of lawns and flowers. A charming mix of old and new, London's quaint Victorian neighborhoods are complimented by modern shopping facilities, cultural activities and a major university. Dig back into local history at the **London Museum of Archeology** and explore a re-creation of a 500-year old Aboriginal hamlet at the Iroquoian Village.

Fanshawe Pioneer Village. This complex of 22 restored buildings brings to life Ontario's rural origins. Costumed interpreters show visitors what it was like to live in the pioneer era.

Niagara Falls is a bustling tourist town featuring one of the natural wonders of the world. The roar of the awe-inspiring majestic falls can be heard for dozens of miles. They are illuminated nightly year round and free fireworks shows run every Friday and Sunday throughout the summer season. Plenty of man made attractions abound here also. Highlights include:

Maid of the Mist. These world-famous boats have provided a close-up look (and feel) of the American and Horseshoe Falls since 1846. The boats pass directly in front of the American Falls, Rock of the Ages and Cave of Winds and enter Horseshoe Falls for a spectacular view.

IMAX® Theatre Niagara Falls. Experience Niagara's fascinating history on a giant six-story screen.

Marineland. Experience non-stop activities at Canada's largest theme park. Attractions include the Aqua Theatre Show, amusement rides, indoor aquarium and game farm.

Niagara Helicopters Limited. This is an exciting way to see Niagara Falls as well as other attractions.

Niagara-on-the-Lake, situated on Lake Ontario at the mouth of the Niagara River. Highlights include **Fort George National Historic Park** (restored in 1939), including officer's quarters, barracks, guard room, kitchen and huge ramparts; and **McFarland House**, an early 1800's Georgian brick house decorated with period furnishings.

Niagara Parks Botanical Garden. This beautiful 80-acre garden features a giant floral clock, made entirely of plants. The park is also home to 2,000 butterflies at the **Niagara Parks Butterfly Conservatory**.

Niagara Spanish Aero Car takes wide-eyed visitors across the whirlpool in a cable car suspended above the falls.

CENTRAL ONTARIO

Travelers to the Central Region of Ontario will find an endless number of outdoor activities, no matter the season. Glorious lakes, sandy beaches, rocky islands and stunning scenery tucked around every inlet and cove

CAMP CLUB USA — Where to Find CCUSA Parks

List City	Park Name	Map Coordinates
ALFRED		
	Evergreen Campground	F-6
APPIN		
	Jefferson Junction	I-2
BARRIE		
	Heidis' Campground	H-3
BELLE RIVER		
	Rochester Place RV, Golf & Marine Resort	J-1
FORT ERIE		
	Windmill Point Park	I-3
GODERICH		
	Auburn Riverside Retreat (Not visited)	H-2
GRANTON		
	Prospect Hill Camping Grounds	I-2
IGNACE		
	Davy Lake Campground & Resort	D-2
KINGSTON		
	Rideau Acres Campground	H-5
LINDSAY		
	Riverwood Park (Not visited)	H-4
MILLER LAKE		
	Summer House Park	G-2
PRESCOTT		
	Grenville Park	G-6
SUNDERLAND		
	Trout Water Family Camping	H-3

make for an incredible backdrop, no matter what the activity.

Chi-Cheemaun Ferry Service, Tobermory-Manitoulin. This ferry service between Manitoulin Island and Tobermory transports passenger vehicles of all kinds. Open seasonally.

Collingwood Air & Sightseeing Tours. View the beautiful area of Bruce Peninsula and Georgian Bay from the air. Half-hour to 2-hour tours available.

Collingwood Scenic Caves Nature Preserve. Located on the top of Blue Mountain, these caves plunge hundreds of feet into the depths. Above ground, nature trails feature rare and exotic plants.

TORONTO AND AREA

One of Canada's most cosmopolitan cities is a joy to explore. From the parks, gardens and lakefront boardwalks to the soaring glass towers of the commercial area, Toronto features fun around every corner. Cultural enthusiasts browse through galleries such as the **Art Gallery of Ontario & the Grange** and the **McMichael Canadian Art Collection**. Canada's largest public museum is the **Royal Ontario Museum**, with a vast collection of objects and specimens—everything from dinosaurs to totem poles, insects and Egyptian mummies to one of the greatest Chinese collections in the western world. Rich in ethnic diversity, the neighborhoods of Toronto portray authentic old world charm.

Art Gallery of Ontario. View a collection of 15,000 works including Oldenburg's "Hamburger," over 600 works of Henry Moore's sculptures and over 40 special exhibitions throughout the year.

Black Creek Pioneer Village. Journey back in time to discover life in early Ontario of the 1800s. 40 restored heritage homes, shops & gardens bring history alive as interpreters and artisans in period dress help you discover how settlers lived, worked and played.

EASTERN ONTARIO

Visitors to this region will immediately feel the rich sense of history faithfully preserved in the towns and villages that dot the region. Rolling hills, rocky highlands and soaring sand dunes make up the landscape here, and make for a spectacular show in the fall, when the trees change colors. Travelers will fall in love with the many charming, rural French communities throughout this region.

Cullen Gardens & Miniature Village, Whitby. View miniature reproductions in over 100 historic buildings, all from southern Ontario, in a garden setting. Entertainment and dining facilities available.

Kingston is a lovely city at the confluence of the St. Lawrence and Lake Ontario. It is architecturally unique due to the concentration of 19th-century limestone buildings. Known to be the birthplace of organized hockey, the first league game was played in 1885. The **International Hockey Hall of Fame and Museum** follows the game's development. Other attractions in Kingston include the **Marine Museum of the Great Lakes**, **Miller Museum of Geology and Mineralogy** and the **Pump House Steam Museum**.

Ottawa. The capital of Canada features acres of greenery that create a park-like setting anytime of year. Don't miss the changing of the guard on **Parliament Hill** (10 a.m. daily). Here on **Parliament Hill** stand the **Royal Canadian Mint** and the **Supreme Court of Canada**. Museums in Ottawa include the **National Museum of Science & Technology** (with hands-on exhibits and an observatory), the **National Aviation Museum** (housing over 100 aircraft), the **Canadian Museum of Nature** (featuring hands-on exhibits, live animals and mini-theater presentations); and the **Canadian Museum of Civilization** (with an IMAX®/ OMNIMAX® theater and children's museum). **Aboriginal Experiences** is a new cultural attraction in Ottawa that affords visitors a rare opportunity to experience the rich culture, teachings and history of Canada's First People from their own perspective.

NORTHEASTERN ONTARIO

Algonquin Provincial Park. One through-road (Hwy. 60) cuts across the southwest corner of this 3,000 square-mile park. Leaving your vehicle behind allows you to experience excellent fishing and unpopulated canoeing areas. Explore 2 overnight hiking trails or stroll along 1 of 2 short nature trails.

Aubrey Falls is the mid-point between Chapleau and Thessalon. The Falls are a spectacular attraction on the Mississagi River, just one mile off Hwy 129.

French River. This 70-mile (112-kilometer) shallow, swift-moving, freshwater river connects Lake Nipissing with Georgian Bay. The shores of the French River are the source for numerous water sports.

Rainbow Country. Rainbow Country, nestled against northern Georgian Bay, is the place where great vacation traditions happen. Its natural splendor and variety of lodging options offer tranquility, comfort and value for those who want to connect with others. Whether you're planning a family vacation, a romantic retreat, a getaway with friends or a simple camping trip, Rainbow Country has all of the ingredients to ensure that your adventure is a memorable one. Breathtaking scenery, adventurous recreation opportunities and the chance to enjoy one another's company in a fun and relaxed setting is what keeps our visitors coming back year after year.

NORTHWESTERN ONTARIO

Aviation & Fire Management Centre, Dryden. Tour the command center for fire suppression strategy and see the fleet of fire detection aircraft, including the CL-215, the only aircraft in the world designed specifically for firefighting.

Fort Vermilion, Vermilion Bay. This replica of an early log fort has an information center.

Kenora. Tour Boise Cascade's pulp and paper mill (June-August), or charter a boat to take you through the islands of Lake of the Woods.

Lake of the Woods. Explore nearly 15,000 islands and 65,000 miles of jagged shoreline at Ontario's second largest inland lake.

Nipigon. A popular tourist center on Lake Superior at the mouth of the Nipigon River, it is an excellent area for trout fishing. Once the home of the ancient Ojibwa Native Americans, Nipigon was also the site of the first white settlement on the North Shore.

Thunder Bay is Canada's third largest port. Highlights of the city include amethyst mines where visitors can mine for the gems in open pits; **Old Fort William**, the reconstructed 19th-century fort that looks just as it did 170 years ago and **Thunder Bay Historical Museum**.

Eagle Canyon Adventures is located on the sheer cliffs of Eagle Canyon. This outdoor paradise is surrounded with spectacular scenery, beautiful landscapes and serene surroundings. They are open year-round.

ANNUAL EVENTS

JANUARY

Boat Show, Toronto; Snowball Winter Carnival, Dorset; Festival of Northern Lights, Owen Sound; Niagara Icewine Festival, Niagara Region; Green Reel Environmental Film Festival, Vaughn.

FEBRUARY

Barrie Winterfest & Festival of Ice, Barrie; ByWard Markey Mardi Gras, Ottawa; Barry's Bay Timberfest, Barry's Bay; Gravenhurst Winter Carnival, Gravenhurst; WinterCity, Toronto; Wiarton Willie Festival, Wiarton; Welland Winter Carniaval, Welland; Pembroke Snospree Winter Carnival, Pembroke; PolarFest, Lakefield; Bon Soo Winter Carnival, Sault Ste. Marie; Winterlude, Ottawa; Temiskaming Shores Snowfest, Haileybury; Winterama, Penetanguishene; Porquis Winter Carnival, Porquis Junction.

MARCH

Home & Garden Show, Toronto; Winterfest, Elliot Lake; Maple in the County, Prince Edward County; Wildlife Festival & Adventure Show, Simcoe; Warkworth Maple Syrup Festival, Warkworth.

All privately owned campgrounds personally inspected by WOODALL'S Representatives **John and Michele Pynenburg**

ACTON—H-3

Nor-Halton Park—(Halton) *From south jct Hwy 7 & Hwy 25: Go 1.6 km/1 mi S on Hwy 25, then 2 km/1-1/4 mi W on Regional Rd 12. Enter on L.* ◇◇◇FACILITIES: 153 sites, typical site width 40 ft, 125 full hkups, 3 W&E, (30 amps), 25 no hkups, 17 pull-thrus, tenting, dump, laundry, ltd groc. ◇◇◇◇RECREATION: swim pool, playground. Pets welcome. Open Mar 1 - Nov 30. Facilities fully operational May 15 - Mid Oct. Rate in 2010 $35-40 per family. Member OPCA. Phone: (519)853-2959.

ADOLPHUSTOWN—H-5

Uel Heritage Centre & Park—*In town on Hwy-33. Enter on R.* ◇◇FACILITIES: 161 sites, typical site width 50 ft, 50 W&E, 51 E, (15/30 amps), 60 no hkups, 54 pull-thrus, tenting, dump. ◇◇◇RECREATION: lake swim, boating, canoeing, ramp, dock, lake fishing, playground. Pets welcome. Partial handicap access. Open May 1 - mid Oct. Rate in 2010 $31-39 per family. Member OPCA. Phone: (613)373-2196.

AILSA CRAIG—I-2

Shady Pines Campground (Not visited)—(Middlesex) *From jct Hwy 7 & CR 19 (business centre of town): Go 3.2 km/2 mi S on CR 19. Enter on R.* ◇◇◇FACILITIES: 247 sites, typical site width 39 ft, 220 full hkups, (15/30 amps), 27 no hkups, 12 pull-thrus, tenting, dump, laundry, groceries. ◇◇◇◇RECREATION: swim pool, boating, canoeing, river fishing, playground. Pets welcome. Partial handicap access. Open May 1 - mid Oct. Rate in 2010 $32-38 per vehicle. Member OPCA. Phone: (519)232-4210.

ALFRED—F-6

Evergreen Campground—*From west side of town: Go 3.2 km/2 mi W on Hwy 17. Enter on L.* ◇◇◇FACILITIES: 160 sites, typical site width 60 ft, 60 full hkups, 60 W&E, (15/30/50 amps), 40 no hkups, 12 pull-thrus, tenting, RV storage, shower$, dump, laundry, groceries, RV supplies, ice, picnic tables, fire rings, wood. ◇◇◇◇RECREATION: rec hall, swim pool, lake swim, hot tub, bsktball, playground, shuffleboard court 2 shuffleboard courts, activities horseshoes, hiking trails, v-ball. Pets welcome. Open May 1 - Oct 1. Rate in 2010 $30-37 per family. MC/VISA/AMEX/Debit. Member OPCA. CCUSA 50% Discount. CCUSA reservations Required, CCUSA max stay 4 days, CCUSA disc. not avail F,Sa, CCUSA disc. not avail holidays. Discount is valid May-Jun & Sep ONLY, Sun thru Thu nights only. Discount not valid on holiday Mondays.

Phone: (613)679-4059
Address: 5279 County Rd 17, Alfred, ON K0B 1A0
Lat/Lon: 45.54078/-74.55464

ALGONQUIN PARK—F-4

CANISBAY LAKE CAMPGROUND (Algonquin PP)—*From town: Go 24 km/15 mi E of west park gate on Hwy 60, then 1-1/2 km/1 mi N.* FACILITIES: 242 sites, 66 E, 176 no hkups, tenting, dump, laundry, ltd groc. RECREATION: lake swim, boating, canoeing, lake fishing. Partial handicap access. Open May - Nov. Phone: (705)633-5572.

(NW) KEARNEY LAKE CAMPGROUND (Algonquin PP)—*From town: Go 38-1/2 km/24-1/2 mi E of west park gate on Hwy 60.* FACILITIES: 103 sites, 103 no hkups, tenting, dump, laundry. RECREATION: lake swim, boating, canoeing, ramp, lake fishing. Open late Jun - early Sep. Phone: (705)633-5572.

(NW) LAKE OF TWO RIVERS CAMPGROUND (Algonquin PP)—*From town: Go 33-1/2 km/21 mi E of west park gate on Hwy 60.* FACILITIES: 241 sites, 160 E, 81 no hkups, tenting, dump, laundry, ltd groc. RECREATION: lake swim, boating, canoeing, lake fishing. Partial handicap access. Open mid May - mid Oct. Phone: (705)633-5572.

ALGONQUIN PARK—Continued

(NW) MEW LAKE CAMPGROUND (Algonquin PP)—*From town: Go 32 km/20 mi E of west park gate on Hwy 60.* FACILITIES: 131 sites, 66 E, 65 no hkups, tenting, dump, laundry. RECREATION: lake swim, boating, no motors, canoeing, lake fishing. Partial handicap access. Open Jun 14 - Oct 17. Phone: (705) 633-5572.

(NW) POG LAKE CAMPGROUND (Algonquin PP)—*From town: Go 36-3/4 km/23 mi E of west park gate on Hwy 60.* FACILITIES: 286 sites, 83 E, 203 no hkups, tenting, dump, laundry, ltd groc. RECREATION: lake swim, boating, no motors, canoeing, ramp, lake fishing. Open late Jun - early Sep. Phone: (705)633-5572.

(NW) ROCK LAKE CAMPGROUND (Algonquin PP)—*From town: Go 48 km/30 mi E of west park gate on Hwy 60.* FACILITIES: 121 sites, 72 E, 49 no hkups, tenting, dump, laundry. RECREATION: boating, canoeing, ramp, lake fishing. Open late Apr - mid Oct. Phone: (705)633-5572.

(W) TEA LAKE CAMPGROUND (Algonquin PP)—*From town: Go 12 km/7-1/2 mi E of west park gate on Hwy 60.* FACILITIES: 42 sites, 42 no hkups, tenting, dump, ltd groc. RECREATION: boating, canoeing, ramp, lake fishing. Open late Apr - Sep. Phone: (705)633-5572.

ALLISTON—H-3

(W) EARL ROWE PROVINCIAL PARK—*From town: Go 3-1/4 km/2 mi W on Hwy 89, then 3/4 km/1/2 mi N on Concession 1.* FACILITIES: 365 sites, 183 E, (15 amps), 182 no hkups, 10 pull-thrus, tenting, dump, laundry, ltd groc. RECREATION: no motors, canoeing, ramp, lake fishing, playground. Partial handicap access. Open May 2 - Oct 9. Phone: (705)435-2498.

Nicolston Dam Campground—(Simcoe) *From jct Hwy 400 & 89: Go 11 km/7 mi W on Hwy 89. Enter on R.* ◇◇◇FACILITIES: 109 sites, typical site width 50 ft, 99 W&E, (15/30 amps), 10 no hkups, 15 pull-thrus, tenting, dump, laundry. ◇◇◇◇RECREATION: swim pool, boating, no motors, canoeing, dock, river fishing, playground. Pets welcome. Open May 1 - Oct 31. Rate in 2010 $28.75-40.95 per family. Member OPCA. Phone: (705)435-7946.

ALVINSTON—I-1

(E) A.W. CAMPBELL (St. Clair Region Cons Auth.)—(Lambton) *From north city limits: Go 3/4 km/1/2 mi N on Hwy 79, then 3-1/4 km/2 mi E on Concession 1.* FACILITIES: 140 sites, 140 W&E, tenting, dump, laundry. RECREATION: swim pool, lake swim, no motors, canoeing, lake fishing, playground. Open Victoria Day - Thanksgiving. Phone: (519)847-5357.

AMHERSTBURG—J-1

JELLYSTONE PARK & CAMP RESORT—(Essex) *From east city limits: Go 3.2 km/2 mi E on Pike Rd (CR 18, Simcoe St). Enter on L.*

WELCOME

◇◇◇◇FACILITIES: 312 sites, typical site width 50 ft, 35 full hkups, 259 W&E, (30/50 amps), 18 no hkups, some extd stay sites, 5 pull-thrus, tenting, RV's/park model rentals, cabins, RV storage, dump, portable dump, laundry, full svc store, RV supplies, LP bottle exch, ice, picnic tables, fire rings, wood.

◇◇◇◇◇RECREATION: rec room/area, pavilion, equipped pavilion, coin games, swim pool, wading pool, spray ground, mini-golf, ($), golf nearby, bsktball, 20 bike rentals, playground, shuffleboard court 2 shuffleboard courts, activities, horseshoes, sports field, hiking trails, v-ball.

Pets welcome. Partial handicap access. Open Apr 15 - Oct 15. Clubs welcome. Rate in 2010 $31-49 per family. MC/VISA/AMEX/Debit. ATM. Member OPCA.

Phone: (519)736-3201
Address: RR 1 4610 Essex Ct Rd 18, Amherstburg, ON N9V 2Y7
Lat/Lon: 42.05917/-83.03308
Email: fun@campybear.com
Web: www.campybear.com

SEE AD WINDSOR PAGE 890

APPIN—I-2

Jefferson Junction—(Middlesex) *From jct Hwy 401 (exit 149) & CR 8: Go 12.6 km/8 mi N on CR 8, then 1.6 km/1 mi W on Switzer Rd. Enter on R.* ◇◇◇FACILITIES: 130 sites, typical site width 45 ft, 105 full hkups, 14 W&E, (15/30 amps), 11 no hkups, phone Internet central location, tenting, shower$, dump, portable dump, ltd groc, RV supplies, LP gas by weight, ice, picnic tables, fire rings, wood. ◇◇◇RECREATION: rec hall, swim pool, pond fishing, mini-golf, ($), bsktball, playground, shuffleboard court shuffleboard court, activities tennis, horseshoes, hiking trails, v-ball. Pets welcome. Open May 1 - mid Oct. Rate in 2010 $29-31 per family. MC/VISA/Debit. Member OPCA. FMCA discount. CCUSA 50% Discount. CCUSA reservations Recommended, CCUSA max stay 7 days, CCUSA disc. not avail holidays.

APPIN—Continued
Jefferson Junction—Continued

Phone: (519)289-2100
Address: 4838 Switzer Dr RR 4, Appin, ON N0L 1A0
Email: ronter8797@execulinr.com
Web: www.jeffersonjunction.ca

ARNPRIOR—F-5

FITZROY PROVINCIAL PARK—*From Hwy 17 in town: Go 11.2 km/7 mi NE on paved, local roads to Fitzroy Harbour.* FACILITIES: 235 sites, 107 E, (15/30 amps), 128 no hkups, 20 pull-thrus, tenting, laundry, ltd groc. RECREATION: river swim, boating, canoeing, ramp, lake fishing, playground. Partial handicap access. Open mid May - end Oct. Phone: (613)623-5159.

ARTHUR—H-2

Conestoga Family Campgrounds (Not visited)—(Wellington) *From jct Hwy 6 & CR 109 (formerly Hwy 9): Go 11.2 km/7 mi W on CR 109, then 2.4 km/1-1/2 mi N on Con 9. Enter on L.* ◇◇◇FACILITIES: 250 sites, typical site width 30 ft, 210 full hkups, 30 W&E, (30 amps), 10 no hkups, 10 pull-thrus, tenting, dump, laundry, groceries. ◇◇◇◇RECREATION: swim pool, lake swim, boating, electric motors only, canoeing, dock, pond fishing, playground. Pets welcome. Partial handicap access. Open May 15 - Oct 15. Rate in 2010 $35-40 per family. Member OPCA. Phone: (519)829-8115.

ATHERLEY—G-3

(S) MARA PROVINCIAL PARK—*From town: Go 4-3/4 km/3 mi E on Hwy 12, then 1-1/2 km/1 mi S on Courtland St.* FACILITIES: 105 sites, 36 E, (15/30 amps), 69 no hkups, tenting, dump. RECREATION: boating, canoeing, ramp, playground. Partial handicap access. Open mid Jun - Sep. Phone: (705)326-4451.

ATIKOKAN—E-2

(E) QUETICO PROVINCIAL PARK—*From town: Go 40 km/25 mi E on Hwy 17.* FACILITIES: 107 sites, 49 E, 58 no hkups, 28 pull-thrus, tenting, dump, laundry, ltd groc. RECREATION: lake swim, boating, no motors, canoeing, ramp, lake fishing, playground. Partial handicap access. Open all yr. Facilities fully operational May - Oct. Phone: (807)597-2735.

AYLMER—I-2

SPRINGWATER CONSERVATION AREA (Catfish Creek Cons Auth.)—(Elgin) *From town: Go 5 km/3 mi W on Hwy 3, then 3 km/1-3/4 mi S on Springwater Rd at Orwell. Enter on R.* FACILITIES: 264 sites, typical site width 45 ft, 182 W&E, 82 no hkups, tenting, dump, laundry, groceries. RECREATION: boating, no motors, canoeing, dock, pond/stream fishing, playground. Partial handicap access. Open May - Nov. Phone: (519)773-9037.

BAILIEBORO—H-4

Bensfort Bridge Resort—*From jct Hwy 28 & CR 2: Go 6.4 km/4 mi E on CR 2, then 6.4 km/4 mi N to park.* ◇◇◇FACILITIES: 50 sites, typical site width 40 ft, 48 full hkups, 2 W&E, (30 amps), tenting, dump, laundry, ltd groc. ◇◇◇◇RECREATION: river swim, boating, canoeing, ramp, dock, river fishing, playground. Pets welcome. Open May 5 - Oct 15. Rate in 2010 $29-32 per family. Member OPCA. Phone: (705) 939-6515.

BANCROFT—G-4

Bancroft Campground—*From jct Hwy 28 & Hwy 62: Go 6.4 km/4 mi N on Hwy 62, then .4 km/1/4 mi W on S Baptiste Lake Rd, then .4 km/1/4 mi N on Bird Lake Rd. Enter on R.* ◇◇◇FACILITIES: 85 sites, typical site width 50 ft, 32 full hkups, 18 W&E, (15/30 amps), 35 no hkups, 28 pull-thrus, tenting, dump, laundry. ◇◇◇RECREATION: swim pool, lake swim, boating, electric motors only, canoeing, dock, lake fishing, playground. Pets welcome. Open all yr. Facilities fully operational Apr 1 - Oct 15. Rate in 2010 $23-30 per family. Member OPCA. Phone: (877)404-4160.

Bancroft Tent & Trailer Camp (Not Visited)—*From jct Hwy 28 & Hwy 62: Go 3.2 km/2 mi S on Hwy 62. Enter on L.* FACILITIES: 100 sites, typical site width 30 ft, 75 full hkups, 15 W&E, (15/30 amps), 10 no

Bancroft Tent & Trailer Camp (Not Visited)—Continued on next page

BANCROFT—Continued
Bancroft Tent & Trailer Camp (Not Visited)—Continued

hkups, tenting, dump, laundry, ltd groc. RECREATION: lake swim, boating, no motors, canoeing, dock, lake fishing, playground. Pets welcome. Open May 1 - Oct 15. Rate in 2010 $26-37 for 2 persons. Member OPCA. Phone: (613)332-2183.

SILENT LAKE PROVINCIAL PARK—*From town: Go 22-1/2 km/14 mi S on Hwy 28.* FACILITIES: 167 sites, typical site width 20 ft, 10 E, (15/30 amps), 157 no hkups, tenting, dump, laundry. RECREATION: lake swim, no motors, canoeing, lake fishing. Partial handicap access. Open May - Sep. Phone: (613)339-2807.

BARRIE—H-3

HEIDIS' CAMPGROUND—(Simcoe) *From jct Hwy 400 & Hwy 11: Go 14.4 km/9 mi N on Hwy 11 (exit Oro-Medonte CR 11-Hawkestone). Enter on L.*

WELCOME

◆◆◆◆FACILITIES: 180 sites, typical site width 40 ft, 160 full hkups, 20 W&E, (15/30 amps), many extd stay sites, 10 pull-thrus, WiFi Instant Internet at site ($), WiFi Internet central location ($), tenting, RV's/park model rentals, RV storage, laundry, groceries, RV supplies, ice, picnic tables, fire rings, wood, controlled access.

◆◆◆◆◆RECREATION: rec hall, rec room/area, coin games, swim pool, hot tub, lake/stream fishing, golf nearby, bsktball, playground, activities, horseshoes, sports field, hiking trails, v-ball. Rec open to public.

Pets welcome. Partial handicap access. Open all yr. Facilities fully operational May 1 - Oct 15. Clubs welcome. Rate in 2010 $29.50-36.95 per family. MC/VISA/Debit. ATM. Member ARVC, OPCA. FCRV discount. FMCA discount. CCUSA 50% Discount. CCUSA reservations Recommended, CCUSA max stay 4 days, CCUSA disc. not avail F,Sa, CCUSA disc. not avail holidays. Not available Jul & Aug. WiFi surcharge $6/hr.

Phone: (705)487-3311
Address: 3982 Hwy 11 South RR2, Hawkestone, ON L0L 1T0
Lat/Lon: 44.30376/-79.28860
Email: heidis@heidisrv.com
Web: www.heidisrv.com

SEE AD THIS PAGE

KOA-Barrie—(Simcoe) *From jct Hwy 11 & Hwy 93: Go 11.2 km/7 mi N on Hwy 93. Enter on L.* ◆◆◆◆FACILITIES: 146 sites, typical site width 32 ft, 116 full hkups, 29 W&E, (15/30/50 amps), 1 no hkups, 29 pull-thrus, tenting, dump, laundry, groceries. ◆◆◆◆◆RECREATION: 2 swim pools, pond fishing, play equipment. Pets welcome. Partial handicap access. Open May 1 - Oct 15. Big rigs welcome. Rate in 2010 $48-80 for 2 persons. Member OPCA. Phone: (705)726-6128. KOA discount.

Oro Family Campground (Not visited)—(Simcoe) *From jct Hwy 400 & Hwy 11 Go: 15 km/9 mi N on Hwy 11, then exit on Oro Township Line 9, then go 2.5 km/1-1/2 mi S on Hwy 11.* ◆◆◆FACILITIES: 76 sites, typical site width 32 ft, 36 ft max RV length, 50 W&E, (15/30 amps), 26 no hkups, 3 pull-thrus, tenting, dump, laundry, ltd groc. ◆◆◆◆RECREATION: swim pool, playground. Pets welcome. Open May 15 - October 15. Rate in 2010 $24-30 per family. Member OPCA. Phone: (705)487-2267.

The Canadian Shield has many metamorphic rocks.

BARRY'S BAY—F-4

(S) EASY LIVING CAMPING & RV PARK & CHIPPAWA RESORT (Not Visited)—(Renfrew) *From jct Hwy 60 & CR 62: Go 11 km/7 mi S on CR 62, then 3km/2 mi W on Chippawa Rd. Follow signs. Enter on L.*

WELCOME

◆◆◆FACILITIES: 40 sites, typical site width 40 ft, 25 full hkups, (30 amps), 15 no hkups, some extd stay sites, 4 pull-thrus, family camping, tenting, cabins, RV storage, dump, laundry, marine gas, ice, picnic tables, fire rings, wood.

◆◆◆◆RECREATION: rec room/area, lake swim, boating, canoeing, kayaking, ramp, dock, 6 rowboat/6 canoe/2 kayak/3 motorboat rentals, lake fishing, golf nearby, bsktball, 8 bike rentals, playground, activities, (wkends), tennis, horseshoes, sports field, hiking trails, v-ball.

Pets welcome. Partial handicap access. Open May 1 - Oct 18. Clubs welcome. Rate in 2010 $35-50 per family. MC/VISA/AMEX/Debit. Member OPCA.

Phone: (800)267-8507
Address: RR 1 835 Chippawa Rd, Barry's Bay, ON K0J 1B0
Lat/Lon: 45.50513/-77.99094
Email: chippawa@igs.net
Web: www.chippawaresort.com

SEE AD THIS PAGE

BATCHAWANA BAY—D-3

(N) PANCAKE BAY PROVINCIAL PARK—*From town: Go 6-1/2 km/4 mi W on Hwy 60.* FACILITIES: 325 sites, 160 E, 165 no hkups, tenting, dump, laundry, ltd groc. RECREATION: canoeing, lake fishing, playground. Open early May - early Oct. Phone: (705)882-2209.

The Sunset Shores Resort (Not Visited)—(Algoma) *From jct of Hwy 17 & CR 563: Go S on Hwy 17 5.1 KM/3mi. Enter on R.* ◆◆◆FACILITIES: 104 sites, 58 full hkups, 45 W&E, (15/30 amps), 1 no hkups, 9 pull-thrus, family camping, tenting, dump, laundry, ltd groc. ◆◆◆◆RECREATION: lake swim, boating, canoeing, ramp, dock, lake fishing, playground. Pets welcome. Partial handicap access. Open Mid May - Mid Oct. Rate in 2010 $30-34 per family. Member OPCA. Phone: (705)882-2231.

BELLE RIVER—J-1

Rochester Place RV, Golf & Marine Resort—(Essex) *From jct Hwy 401 (exit 40) & CR 31: Go 4.3km/2-3/4 mi N on CR 31, then 0.1km/100 yds mi E on CR 42, then 2.7km/1-3/4 mi N on CR 31, then 0.3km/1/4 mi W on CR 2. Enter on R.* ◆◆◆◆FACILITIES: 274 sites, typical site width 30 ft, 274 full hkups, (20/30 amps), 2 pull-thrus, WiFi Instant Internet at site, WiFi Internet central location, tenting, RV storage, dump, non-guest dump $, RV supplies, ice, picnic tables, fire rings, wood. ◆◆◆◆◆RECREATION: rec hall, swim pool, boating, canoeing, kayaking, ramp, dock, lake/river/pond fishing, putting green, bsktball, playground, activities, horseshoes, hiking trails, v-ball. Pets welcome. Partial handicap access. Open May 1 - Oct 31. Rate in 2010 $30-40 per family. MC/VISA/Debit. Member OPCA. CCUSA 50% Discount. CCUSA reservations Required, CCUSA max stay 30 days, CCUSA disc. not avail F,Sa, CCUSA disc. not avail holidays. Discount available May 1 to Jun 15 & Labor Day to Oct 31. 10% surcharge for addl. persons & for 30 amp.

CAMPCLUB USA

Phone: (800)563-5940
Address: 981-991 CCR2, Belle River, ON N0R 1A0
Lat/Lon: 42.17711/-82.37746
Email: info@rochesterplace.com
Web: www.rochesterplace.com

BELLEVILLE—H-5

Carleton Cove Tourist Trailer Park and Camping (Not Visited)—*From jct Hwy 401 (exit 543B) & Hwy 62: Go 4 km/2-1/2 mi N on Hwy 62, then .4 km/1/4 mi E on Carleton's Cove Rd. Enter on L.* ◆◆◆FACILITIES: 69 sites, typical site width 40 ft, 69 W&E, (15/30/50 amps), 8 pull-thrus, tenting, dump. ◆◆◆RECREATION: river swim, boating, canoeing, river fishing, playground. Pets welcome. Open May 26 - Mid Oct. Rate in 2010 $20-26 for 2 persons. Member OPCA. Phone: (800)574-9597.

BEWDLEY—H-4

Sunrise Tourist Trailer Park—*From jct Hwy 401 (exit 464) & Hwy 28: Go 11 km/8 mi N on Hwy 28, pass Northumberland Rd #9 to Concession Rd 9, then 90 meters/100 yards E on Concession Rd 9.* ◆◆◆FACILITIES: 58 sites, typical site width 30 ft, 35 ft max RV length, 53 full hkups, 5 W&E, (15 amps), tenting, dump, groceries. ◆◆◆RECREATION: swim pool, boating, ramp, dock, lake fishing, playground. Pets welcome. Open May 3 - Oct 14. Rate in 2010 $25-30 for 2 persons. Member OPCA. Phone: (905)797-2456.

Tower Manor Lodge—*From jct Hwy 28 & Northumberland CR 9: Go 6.5 km/4 mi E on Northumberland CR 9, then follow signs 1.6 km/1 mi N, then left down lane to park. Enter on L.* ◆◆◆FACILITIES: 50 sites, typical site width 40 ft, 50 full hkups, (30/50 amps), 3 pull-thrus, tenting, ltd groc. ◆◆◆RECREATION: swim pool, lake swim, boating, ramp, dock, lake fishing, play equipment. Pets welcome. Open mid May - mid Oct. Rate in 2010 $28 for 2 persons. Member OPCA. Phone: (905)342-2078.

BLOOMFIELD—H-5

Hideaway Trailer Park—*From jct Hwy 33 & CR 12: Go 6.4 km/4 mi S on CR 12. Enter on R.* ◆◆◆FACILITIES: 233 sites, typical site width 50 ft, 143 full hkups, 40 W&E, (15/30 amps), 50 no hkups, tenting, dump, ltd groc. ◆◆◆RECREATION: lake swim, boating, canoeing, ramp, lake fishing, playground. Pets welcome. Open mid May - mid Oct. Rate in 2010 $33-39 per family. Phone: (613)393-2267.

SANDBANKS PROVINCIAL PARK—*From town: Go 12-3/4 km/8 mi S on West Lake Rd (CR 12), follow signs.* FACILITIES: 549 sites, typical site width 21 ft, 140 E, (15 amps), 409 no hkups, 26 pull-thrus, tenting, laundry, ltd groc. RECREATION: lake swim, boating, canoeing, ramp, lake fishing, playground. Partial handicap access. Open mid May - mid Oct. Phone: (613) 393-3319.

BOLTON—H-3

ALBION HILLS CONSERVATION AREA (Toronto & Region Cons. Auth.)—(Peel) *From jct King Rd & Hwy 50: Go 8 km/5 mi NW on Hwy 50. Enter on L.* FACILITIES: 234 sites, typical site width 35 ft, 234 W&E, (15/30 amps), tenting, dump, laundry, ltd groc. RECREATION: lake/river swim, boating, no motors, lake/river fishing, playground. Pets welcome. Open Apr 28 - Oct 8. Phone: (800)838-9921.

Leisure Time Park (Not visited)—(Peel) *From north end of town: Go 17 km/10-1/2 mi N on Hwy 50, then 1.6 km/1 mi W on Hwy 9, entrance on Duffy's Lane. Enter on L.* ◆◆◆FACILITIES: 227 sites, typical site width 50 ft, 10 full hkups, 208 W&E, (15/30 amps), 9 no hkups, 12 pull-thrus, tenting, dump, laundry, ltd groc. ◆◆◆◆RECREATION: swim pool, no motors, pond fishing, playground. Pets welcome. Partial handicap access. Open May 1 - End Oct. Rate in 2010 $20.80-44 per family. Member OPCA. Phone: (888) 280-0018. FCRV discount. FMCA discount.

BRACEBRIDGE—G-3

Bonnie Lake Camping—(Muskoka) *From jct Hwy 11 and Muskoka CR 117 (exit 193): Go 2.5 km/2 mi E on Muskoka CR 117, then 4.5 km/2 3/4 mi N on Bonnie Lake Rd., then 1.6 km/1 mi E on Bonnie Lake Camp Rd. Enter at end.* ◆◆◆FACILITIES: 400 sites, typical site width 35 ft, 300 W&E, (15/30 amps), 100 no hkups, 50

Bonnie Lake Camping—Continued on next page

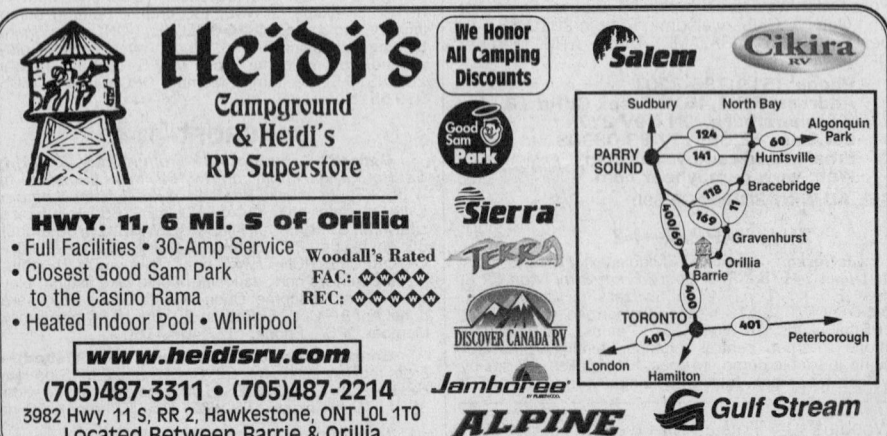

BRACEBRIDGE—Continued
Bonnie Lake Camping—Continued

pull-thrus, family camping, tenting, dump, laundry, ltd groc. ◆◆◆◆RECREATION: lake swim, boating, 10 hp limit, canoeing, ramp, dock, lake/pond fishing, play equipment. Pets welcome. Open Mid May - Mid Oct. Rate in 2010 $24-41 per family. Member OPCA. Phone: (705)645-4511.

(SW) Muskoka Ridge Trailer Park (Not Visited) *—From jct Hwy 11 & Hwy 118 (exit 182): Go 4.5 km/2-3/4 mi N on Hwy 118, then 3.8 km/2.4 mi W on Beaumont Dr: Go left on Stephens Bay Rd. Enter on L.* FACILITIES: 102 sites, typical site width 35 ft, 80 full hkups, 10 W&E, (15/30 amps), 12 no hkups, 26 pull-thrus, tenting, dump, laundry, groceries. RECREATION: swim pool, river swim, boating, canoeing, dock, river fishing, playground. Pets welcome. Open May 15 - Oct 15. Rate in 2010 $40-50 per family. Phone: (705)646-1259.

BRADFORD—H-3

Yogi Bear's Jellystone Park Camp-Resort—*From jct Hwy 400 (exit 64 B) & Simcoe Rd. 88: Go .4 km/1/4 mi W on 88. Enter on R.* ◆◆◆◆FACILITIES: 130 sites, typical site width 35 ft, 24 full hkups, 50 W&E, (20/30/50 amps), 56 no hkups, 54 pull-thrus, tenting, dump, laundry, ltd groc. ◆◆◆◆RECREATION: swim pool, playground. Pets welcome. Partial handicap access. Open May 1 - Sep 15. Rate in 2010 $49.95-76.95 for 2 persons. Member OPCA. Phone: (905)775-1377.

BRANTFORD—I-3

(W) BRANT CONSERVATION AREA (Grand River Cons Auth)—(Brant) *From town: Go 1-1/2 km/1 mi W on Hwy 53, follow signs. Enter on R.* FACILITIES: 387 sites, 31 full hkups, 126 E, (15/30 amps), 230 no hkups, tenting, dump, ltd groc. RECREATION: swim pool, no motors, canoeing, river fishing, playground. Open May 1 - Oct 15. Phone: (519)752-2040.

BRIGHTON—H-4

KOA-Brighton/401—*From jct Hwy 401 (exit 509) & Hwy 30: Go 152 m/500 feet N of Hwy 401 on Hwy 30, then 1.6 km/1 mi W on Telephone Rd. Enter on L.* ◆◆◆FACILITIES: 103 sites, typical site width 40 ft, 35 full hkups, 57 W&E, (30/50 amps), 11 no hkups, 57 pull-thrus, tenting, dump, laundry, groceries. ◆◆RECREATION: swim pool, playground. Pets welcome. Open Apr 20 - Oct 19. Rate in 2010 $38-50 per family. Member OPCA. Phone: (800)562-0906. KOA discount.

BRIGHTON—Continued

(S) PRESQU'ILE PROVINCIAL PARK—*From town: Go 3/4 km/1/2 mi W on Hwy 2, then 3-1/4 km/2 mi S on Ontario St.* FACILITIES: 394 sites, typical site width 20 ft, 118 E, 276 no hkups, tenting, dump, laundry, ltd groc. RECREATION: lake swim, boating, canoeing, ramp, lake fishing. Partial handicap access. Open May - mid Oct. Phone: (613)475-4324.

BRITT—F-2

(N) GRUNDY LAKE PROVINCIAL PARK—*From town: Go 14-1/2 km/9 mi N on Hwy 69.* FACILITIES: 475 sites, 138 E, (15/30 amps), 337 no hkups, 37 pull-thrus, tenting, dump, laundry, ltd groc. RECREATION: boating, no motors, canoeing, ramp, lake fishing. Partial handicap access. Open mid May - mid Oct. Phone: (705)383-2286.

KILLBEAR PROVINCIAL PARK—*From town: Go 12-3/4 km/8 mi N on Hwy 69, then 19-1/4 km/12 mi W on Hwy 559, then 9-1/2 km/6 mi W on Dillon Rd.* FACILITIES: 881 sites, 186 E, (15/30 amps), 695 no hkups, tenting, dump, laundry. RECREATION: lake swim, boating, canoeing, ramp, lake fishing. Partial handicap access. Open mid May - mid Oct. Phone: (705)342-5492.

STURGEON BAY PROVINCIAL PARK—*From town: Go 27-1/4 km/17 mi S on Hwy 69, then 1-1/2 km/1 mi on Hwy 644 (Pointe au Baril).* FACILITIES: 81 sites, 31 E, (15/30 amps), 50 no hkups, tenting, dump, ltd groc. RECREATION: boating, canoeing, ramp, dock, lake fishing. Open early May - mid Oct. Phone: (705)366-2521.

BROCKVILLE—G-6

Happy Green Acres Tent & Trailer Park—*From jct Hwy 401 (exit 687) & Hwy 2: Go 1.6 km/1 mi W on Hwy 2. Enter on L.* ◆◆◆FACILITIES: 150 sites, typical

BROCKVILLE—Continued
Happy Green Acres Tent & Trailer Park—Continued

site width 25 ft, 100 full hkups, 50 W&E, (15/30 amps), 40 pull-thrus, tenting, dump, laundry, ltd groc. ◆◆RECREATION: swim pool, playground. Pets welcome. Open all yr. Facilities fully operational Apr 15 - Oct 15. Rate in 2010 $30-40 per family. Phone: (613)342-9646.

Pleasure Park Campground and RV Resort (Not visited)—*From jct Hwy 401 & Hwy 29: Go 10.4 km/6-1/2 mi N on Hwy 29, then 1.2 km/3/4 mi W on CR 46, then 4 km/2-1/2 mi N on Graham Lake Rd. Enter on R.* ◆◆◆FACILITIES: 300 sites, typical site width 35 ft, 270 W&E, (15/30/50 amps), 30 no hkups, 40 pull-thrus, tenting, dump, laundry, groceries. ◆◆◆◆RECREATION: lake swim, boating, canoeing, ramp, dock, lake fishing, playground. Pets welcome. Partial handicap access. Open May 15 - Sep 15. Rate in 2010 $30-40 for 2 persons. Member OPCA. Phone: (613)923-5490.

(SW) ST. LAWRENCE PARK (City Park)—*From town: Go 3.2 km/2 mi W on Hwy 2.* FACILITIES: 30 sites, 10 W&E, (15 amps), 20 no hkups, tenting, laundry. RECREATION: river swim, boating, ramp, river fishing, playground. Partial handicap access. Open mid May - mid Sep. Phone: (613)345-1341.

BURFORD—I-2

Lyons Little Austria Family Campground (Not Visited)—(Brant) *From jct Hwy 403 & Brant Rd 25: Go 3.5 km/2 mi S on Brant Rd 25, then 3.3 km/2 mi E on*

Lyons Little Austria Family Campground (Not Visited)—Continued on next page

6th Conc. Rd. Enter on R. ◆◆◆FACILITIES: 220 sites, typical site width 35 ft, 180 full hkups, 10 W&E, (30 amps), 30 no hkups, 2 pull-thrus, tenting, dump, ltd groc. ◆◆◆RECREATION: swim pool, stream fishing, playground. Pets welcome. Open May 1 - Mid Oct. Rate in 2010 $25 per family. Member OPCA. Phone: (905) 536-3876. FCRV discount.

CALEDONIA—I-3

(N) LA FORTUNE (Haldimand County)—(Haldimand) *From West town limits: Go 3 km/2 mi W on Hwy 54, then 609 meters/2000 feet N on Onondaga Town line. Enter on R.* FACILITIES: 190 sites, 80 W&E, (15/30 amps), 110 no hkups, 5 pull-thrus, tenting, dump. RECREATION: swim pool, boating, canoeing, ramp, dock, river fishing, playground. Partial handicap access. Open May 1 - Oct 15. Phone: (905)765-4993.

CALLANDER—D-6

(SW) Bayview Camp & Cottages (Not Visited) —(Parry Sound) *From jct Hwy 11 (exit 329) & Hwy 654: Go 4.4 km/2-3/4 mi W on Hwy 654, then .8 km/1/2 mi N on Lighthouse Rd: E on Bayview Camp Rd go 1.9 km/1 mi NE on Bayview Camp Rd. Enter on R.* ◆◆◆FACILITIES: 54 sites, typical site width 30 ft, 46 full hkups, (30 amps), 8 no hkups, tenting, laundry. ◆◆◆◆RECREATION: lake swim, boating, canoeing, ramp, dock, lake fishing, playground. Pets welcome. Open mid May - Oct 15. Rate in 2010 $30-40 per family. Phone: (877)752-2095.

CAMBRIDGE—I-3

Pine Valley Park—(Hamilton-Wentworth) *From jct Hwy 5 & Hwy 8: Go 4.8 km/3 mi NW on Hwy 8, then 3.2 km/2 mi N on Valens Rd. Enter on L.* ◆◆◆FACILITIES: 270 sites, typical site width 45 ft, 260 W&E, (30 amps), 10 no hkups, tenting, dump, laundry, ltd groc. ◆◆◆RECREATION: swim pool, pond fishing, playground. Pets welcome. Open mid May - mid Oct. Rate in 2010 $27-40 per family. Member OPCA. Phone: (866)926-7787.

VALENS CONSERVATION AREA—(Hamilton Wentworth) *From jct Hwy 6 S & Regional Rd 97: Go 8 kms/5 mi W on RR 97. Enter on R.* FACILITIES: 200 sites, 61 W&E, (15/30 amps), 139 no hkups, tenting, dump, laundry, ltd groc. RECREATION: lake swim, boating, electric motors only, canoeing, ramp, dock, lake fishing, playground. Pets welcome. Partial handicap access. Open all yr. Phone: (519)621-6029.

(E) VALENS (Hamilton Reg. Cons Auth)—(Hamilton-Wentworth) *From town: Go 14-1/2 km/9 mi E on Regional Rd 97. Enter on L.* FACILITIES: 220 sites, 83 W&E, (15/30 amps), 137 no hkups, tenting, dump, laundry. RECREATION: lake swim, boating, electric motors only, canoeing, ramp, lake fishing, playground. Open all yr. Phone: (905)525-2183.

CAMPBELLFORD—H-4

(S) FERRIS PROVINCIAL PARK—*From town: Go 6-1/2 km/4 mi S on CR.* FACILITIES: 163 sites, 163 no hkups, tenting, laundry, ltd groc. RECREATION: boating, canoeing, ramp, playground. Partial handicap access. Open Apr - early Sep. Phone: (705)653-3575.

Woodland Estate (Not Visited)—*In town, from jct Hwy 30 & Queen St (CR 50): Go 9.6 km/6 mi N on CR 50, then .8 km/1/2 mi on a gravel road. Enter at end.* FACILITIES: 53 sites, typical site width 38 ft, 53 full hkups, (15/30 amps), tenting, dump, ltd groc. RECREATION: swim pool, lake swim, boating, canoeing, ramp, dock, lake fishing, playground. Pets welcome. Open mid May - mid Oct. Member OPCA. Phone: (705)653-1317.

CAMPBELLVILLE—I-3

Milton RV Park (KOA) (Not Visited)—(Halton) *From jct Hwy 401 (exit 312) & Guelph Line: Go 1.6 km/1 mi N on Guelph Line, then 1.6 km/1 mi W on 10th Side Rd, then 1.6 km/1 mi S on Second Line Nassagaweya. Enter on L.* FACILITIES: 152 sites, typical site width 30 ft, 64 full hkups, 40 W&E, (30/50 amps), 50 amps ($), 48 no hkups, 54 pull-thrus, family camping, tenting, dump, laundry, groceries. RECREATION: swim pool, playground. Pets welcome. Partial handicap access. Open Apr 10 - Oct 30. Rate in 2010 $44 per family. Member OPCA. Phone: (800)562-1523. KOA discount.

CARDIFF—G-4

Parkwood Beach—*From jct Hwy 121 & Inlet Bay Rd (at Cardiff): Go 1.6 km/1 mi S on Inlet Bay Rd. Enter on L.* ◆◆◆FACILITIES: 98 sites, typical site width 30 ft, 30 full hkups, 68 W&E, (15/20/30 amps), tenting, dump, laundry. ◆◆◆RECREATION: lake swim, boating, ramp, dock, lake fishing, playground. Pets welcome. Open mid May - mid Oct. Rate in 2010 $25-30 per vehicle. Phone: (613)339-2718.

CARDINAL—G-6

KOA-Cardinal Kampground—*From jct Hwy 401 (exit 730) & Shanly Rd (CR 22): Go 6.4 km/4 mi N on CR 22, then .4 km/1/4 mi E on Pitston Rd. Enter on R.* ◆◆◆FACILITIES: 90 sites, typical site width 40 ft, 79 W&E, (30/50 amps), 50 amps ($), 11 no hkups, 47

pull-thrus, tenting, dump, laundry, full svc store. ◆◆◆◆RECREATION: swim pool, playground. Pets welcome. Partial handicap access. Open May 1 - Oct 15. Big rigs welcome. Rate in 2010 $33-55 per family. Member OPCA. Phone: (800)562-3643. KOA discount.

CARLETON PLACE—G-5

Tranquil Acres Camping (Not visited)—*From jct Hwy 15 & Hwy 7: Go 3 mi E on Hwy 7, then 1 mi N on Appleton Side Road (17). Enter on L.* ◆◆◆FACILITIES: 55 sites, typical site width 50 ft, 53 full hkups, (15/30 amps), 2 no hkups, 2 pull-thrus, tenting, dump, ltd groc. ◆◆◆RECREATION: river swim, boating, canoeing, ramp, dock, river fishing, playground. Pets welcome. Open May 15 - Oct 15. Rate in 2010 $26-36 per family. Member OPCA. Phone: (613)257-4757.

CARRYING PLACE—H-4

Camp Barcovan Tent & RV Park—*From Hwy 401 (exit 522): Go 6.4 km/4 mi S on CR 40 (Wooler Rd), then 3.2 km/2 mi S on Hwy 33, then 5.6 km/3-1/2 mi W on CR 64 to Carter Rd, then follow signs. Enter on L.* ◆◆◆◆FACILITIES: 150 sites, typical site width 40 ft, 114 full hkups, 26 W&E, (30 amps), 10 no hkups, 20 pull-thrus, tenting, laundry, groceries. ◆◆◆◆RECREATION: swim pool, boating, canoeing, ramp, dock, lake fishing, playground. Pets welcome. Open May 1 - Oct 31. Rate in 2010 $30-37 per vehicle. Member OPCA. Phone: (888)859-2369.

(S) CEDARDALE FAMILY CAMPGORUND & COTTAGE RESORT (TOO NEW TO RATE)—*From jct Hwy's 401 & 30 (exit 509): Go 2 mi S on Hwy 30, then 4.8 mi on CR 64, then .3 mi S on Barcovan Beach Rd, then .6 mi SW on Stoney Pt. Rd, then .2 mi S on Cedardale Rd.*

FACILITIES: 218 sites, 188 full hkups, 16 W&E, 14 no hkups, many extd stay sites, family camping, tenting, cabins, laundry, ltd groc, RV supplies, ice, picnic tables, fire rings, wood, controlled access.

RECREATION: rec hall, swim pool, lake swim, lake fishing, golf nearby, bsktball, playground, activities, (wkends), horseshoes, hiking trails, v-ball, local tours.

Pets welcome, quantity restrict. Partial handicap access. Open May 9 - Oct 24. Clubs welcome. Rate in 2010 $26-40 per family. MC/DISC/Debit.

Phone: (613)475-1105
Address: 107 Cedardale Rd RR #2, Carying Place, ON K0K 1L0
Email: cedardale@killamproperties.com
Web: www.killamleisureliving.com/cedardale

SEE AD BRIGHTON PAGE 869

Wellers Bay Campground—*From jct Hwy 33 & CR 64: Go 5.6 km/3-1/2 mi W on CR 64, then 1.2 km/3/4 mi S on Carter Rd. Enter on L.* ◆◆◆FACILITIES: 50 sites, typical site width 35 ft, 47 full hkups, (15/30/50 amps), 3 no hkups, tenting, laundry, groceries. ◆◆◆RECREATION: lake swim, boating, canoeing, ramp, dock, lake fishing, playground. Pets welcome. Open May 1 - Oct 15. Rate in 2010 $32.50-35.50 per family. Member OPCA. Phone: (613)475-3113.

CARTIER—D-5

HALFWAY LAKE PROVINCIAL PARK—*From town: Go 25-1/2 km/16 mi N on Hwy 144.* FACILITIES: 215 sites, 120 E, (15 amps), 95 no hkups, tenting, laundry, ltd groc. RECREATION: lake swim, boating, canoeing, ramp, lake fishing, playground. Partial handicap access. Open mid May - late Sep. Phone: (705) 965-2702.

CASTLETON—H-4

Castleton Hills Trailer Park—*From jct Hwy 401 & Interchange 497: Go 9.6 km/6 mi N, then follow signs. Enter on R.* ◆◆◆FACILITIES: 90 sites, typical site width 40 ft, 70 full hkups, (30 amps), 20 no hkups, tenting, dump, laundry, ltd groc. ◆◆◆RECREATION: lake swim, no motors, canoeing, lake fishing, playground. Pets welcome. Open mid May - mid Oct. Rate in 2010 $28-30 per family. Member OPCA. Phone: (905)344-7838. FMCA discount.

CHAPLEAU—C-4

(SE) WAKAMI LAKE PROVINCIAL PARK—*From jct Hwy 129 & FR 667 (Forest Access Rd): Go 32 km/20 mi E on FR 667.* FACILITIES: 65 sites, 65 no hkups, tenting, dump, ltd groc. RECREATION: lake swim, boating, canoeing, ramp, dock, lake fishing. Open mid May - late Sep. Phone: (705)233-2853.

CHERRY VALLEY—H-5

Fairfield's Resort & Family Camping—*From town at jct CR 10 & CR 18: Go 2.4 km/1-1/2 mi S on CR 18.* ◆◆◆FACILITIES: 249 sites, typical site width 40 ft, 220 full hkups, 60 W&E, (20/30 amps), 10 pull-thrus, family camping, tenting, dump, laundry, ltd groc. ◆◆◆◆RECREATION: swim pool, lake swim, boating, canoeing, ramp, dock, lake fishing, playground. Pets welcome. Open May 30 - Sep 12. Facilities fully operational Jun 15 - Sep 5. Rate in 2010 $36-40 per family. Member OPCA. Phone: (613)476-2810.

Lake Avenue Park—*In town from jct CR 10 & CR 18: Go 4.8 km/3 mi W on CR 18. Enter on L.* ◆◆◆FACILITIES: 116 sites, typical site width 35 ft, 92 full hkups, 24 W&E, (15/30 amps), 15 pull-thrus, tenting, laundry, groceries. ◆◆◆◆RECREATION: swim pool, lake swim, boating, ramp, dock, lake fishing, playground. Pets welcome. Open May 1 - Oct 15. Rate in 2010 $35-45 per family. Member OPCA. Phone: (800) 371-5885.

MARTIN'S RIVER COUNTRY—*From town at jct CR 10 & CR 18: Go 9.6 km/6 mi S on CR 18. Enter on R.*

WELCOME

◆◆◆FACILITIES: 151 sites, typical site width 40 ft, 85 full hkups, 60 W&E, (15/30/50 amps), 6 no hkups, many extd stay sites, WiFi Instant Internet at site ($), WiFi Internet central location, family camping, tenting, shower$, dump, non-guest dump $, ltd groc, LP gas by weight, ice, picnic tables, fire rings, wood.

◆◆◆◆RECREATION: rec hall, rec room/area, coin games, lake/river swim, boating, canoeing, kayaking, ramp, dock, 3 canoe/kayak/3 motorboat rentals, lake/river fishing, golf nearby, bsktball, playground, activities, horseshoes, hiking trails, v-ball.

Pets welcome. Open May 1 - Oct 16. Clubs welcome. Rate in 2010 $28.99-35.99 per family. MC/VISA/Debit. Member OPCA.

Phone: (613)393-5645
Address: #1854 RR #1, Picton, ON K0K 2T0
Lat/Lon: 43.90125/-77.22162
Email: mrc@on.aibn.com
Web: www.martinsrivercountry.ca

SEE AD TRAVEL SECTION PAGE 862

QUINTE'S ISLE CAMPARK—*From town at jct CR 10 (Lake St) & CR 18: Go 9.6 km/6 mi S on CR 18, then .4 km/1/4 mi E on Salmon Point Rd (follow signs). Enter on L.*

WELCOME

◆◆◆◆◆FACILITIES: 245 sites, typical site width 50 ft, 210 full hkups, (30/50 amps), 50 amps ($), 35 no hkups, mostly extd stay sites, 36 pull-thrus, WiFi Instant Internet at site ($), WiFi Internet central location, family camping, tenting, RV's/park model rentals, RV storage, shower$, dump, laundry, groceries, RV supplies, LP gas by weight, ice, picnic tables, fire rings, wood, controlled access.

◆◆◆◆◆RECREATION: rec hall, rec room/area, pavilion, coin games, swim pool, wading pool, spray ground, lake swim, boating, canoeing, kayaking, ramp, dock, lake fishing, mini-golf, ($), golf nearby, bsktball, playground, shuffleboard court 2 shuffleboard courts, activities, tennis, horseshoes, sports field, hiking trails, v-ball. Rec open to public.

Pets welcome. Partial handicap access. Open Apr 15 - Nov 1. Big rigs welcome. Clubs welcome. Rate in 2010 $45-55 per family. MC/VISA/AMEX/Debit. ATM. Member ARVC, OPCA. FCRV discount. FMCA discount.

Text 107954 to (440)725-8687 to see our Visual Tour.

Phone: (613)476-6310
Address: RR 1 237 Salmon Pt Rd, Cherry Valley, ON K0K 1P0
Lat/Lon: 43.87248/-77.20690
Email: info@qicampark.com
Web: www.qicampark.com

SEE AD KINGSTON PAGE 875

✱ QUINTE'S ISLE CAMPARK & TRAILER SALE—*From town at jct CR 10 (Lake St) & CR 18: Go 9.6 km/6 mi S on CR 18, then 4 km/1/4 mi E on Salmon Point Rd. (Follow Signs).* SALES: travel trailers, park models, fold-down camping trailers, pre-owned unit sales. SERVICES: full-time mech, RV appliance repair, mobile RV svc, LP gas by weight, dump station, RV storage, sells parts/accessories. Open all yr. MC/VISA/AMEX/Debit. ATM.

Phone: (613)476-6310
Address: RR 1 237 Salmon Pt Rd, Cherry Valley, ON K0K 1P0
Lat/Lon: 43.87248/-77.20690
Email: info@qicampark.com
Web: www.qicampark.com

SEE AD KINGSTON PAGE 875

CHERRY VALLEY—Continued on next page

Rivers of southern Ontario drain into the Great Lakes.

QUINTE'S ISLE DIAMOND "J" RANCH—*From town at jct CR 10 (Lake St) & CR 18: Go 9.6 km/6 mi S on CR 18, then 4 km/1/4 mi E on Salmon Point Rd (Follow Signs).* Western style guided horse back riding trips thru hardwood bush along scenic shore of Lake Ontario. Open May 15 - Oct 15. MC/VISA/AMEX/Debit. ATM.

Phone: (613)476-6310
Address: RR 1 237 Salmon Pt. Rd, Cherry Valley, ON K0K 1P0
Lat/Lon: 43.87248/-77.20690
Email: info@qicampark.com

SEE AD KINGSTON PAGE 875

CHESLEY—H-2

Cedar Rail Camp (Not Visited)—(Grey) *From jct CR 10 & CR 25 (Scone Rd.): Go .7 km/1/4 mi N on Grey Bruce Line. Enter on R.* ◇◇◇FACILITIES: 196 sites, typical site width 40 ft, 160 full hkups, 36 W&E, (30 amps), 9 pull-thrus, tenting, dump, laundry, ltd groc. ◇◇◇◇RECREATION: swim pool, river swim, boating, 5 hp limit, canoeing, ramp, dock, river fishing, playground. Pets welcome. Partial handicap access. Open May 1 - Oct 15. Rate in 2010 $31 per family. Member OPCA. Phone: (519)363-3387.

CHUTE-A-BLONDEAU—F-6

VOYAGEUR PROVINCIAL PARK—*From town: Go 8 km/5 mi E on Hwy 17.* FACILITIES: 416 sites, typical site width 30 ft, 110 E, (15/30 amps), 306 no hkups, 45 pull-thrus, tenting, dump, laundry, ltd groc. RECREATION: river swim, boating, canoeing, ramp, dock, river fishing, playground. Partial handicap access. Open May - Oct. Phone: (613)674-2825.

CLIFFORD—H-2

Driftwood Beach Park (Not Visited)—(Huron) *From jct Hwy 9 & Allan St (in town): Go 3 blocks W on Allan St, then 6 km/4 mi N on CR 30 (Minto). Enter on R.* ◇◇◇◇FACILITIES: 407 sites, typical site width 45 ft, 307 full hkups, 20 W&E, (30/50 amps), 80 no hkups, tenting, dump, laundry, ltd groc. ◇◇◇◇RECREATION: lake swim, boating, canoeing, ramp, lake fishing, playground. Pets welcome. Partial handicap access. Age restrict may apply. Open all yr. Facilities fully operational Apr 15 - Oct 15. Rate in 2010 $37 per family. Phone: (519)327-8536.

CLOYNE—G-5

Bishop Lake Trailer Park (Not Visited)—*From south town limits: Go 1.6 km/1 mi S on Hwy 41. Enter on L.* FACILITIES: 95 sites, typical site width 50 ft, 65 full hkups, (15/30 amps), 30 no hkups, 6 pull-thrus, tenting, dump, laundry, ltd groc. RECREATION: lake swim, boating, electric motors only, canoeing, dock, lake fishing, playground. Pets welcome. Open all yr. Facilities fully operational mid May - mid Oct. Rate in 2010 $24-28 per family. Member OPCA. Phone: (613) 336-2311.

(N) BON ECHO PROVINCIAL PARK—*From town: Go 9-1/2 km/6 mi N on Hwy 41.* FACILITIES: 528 sites, 132 E, (15/30 amps), 396 no hkups, 33 pull-thrus, tenting, dump, laundry, ltd groc. RECREATION: boating, canoeing, ramp, playground. Partial handicap access. Open Apr - mid Oct. Phone: (613)336-2228.

Sherwood Park Campground—*From jct Hwy 41 & Hwy 506: Go .4 km/1/4 mi E on Hwy 506. Enter on L.* ◇◇◇FACILITIES: 100 sites, typical site width 40 ft, 80 W&E, (15/30 amps), 20 no hkups, tenting, dump, laundry, ltd groc. ◇◇◇RECREATION: lake swim, boating, canoeing, ramp, dock, lake fishing, playground. Pets welcome. Open May 1 - mid Oct. Rate in 2010 $28.25-41.24 per family. Member OPCA. Phone: (613) 336-8844.

COBALT—C-6

Marsh Bay Resort Tent & Trailer Park (Not Visited)—(Timiskaming) *From jct Hwy 11B & Hwy 11: Go 90 m/100 yards S on Hwy 11, then 2.4 km/1-1/2 mi E on Marsh Bay Rd. Enter at end.* FACILITIES: 24 sites, typical site width 30 ft, 25 full hkups, (15/20 amps), 5 no hkups, 5 pull-thrus, tenting, ltd groc. RECREATION: river swim, boating, canoeing, ramp, dock, river fishing, play equipment. Pets welcome. Open May 1 - Oct 31. Facilities fully operational mid May - mid Oct. Rate in 2010 $25-32 per family. Phone: (705)679-8810.

COBDEN—F-5

Cedar Haven Tent & Trailer Park (Not Visited)—(Renfrew) *From town: Go 1 km/3/4 mi E on Hwy 17, then 2 km/ 1.2 mi N on Forester Falls, then 2 km/1.2 mi N on Cedar Haven Park Rd. Enter on L.* FACILITIES: 130 sites, typical site width 40 ft, 80 full hkups, 20 W&E, (15/30 amps), 30 no hkups, 1 pull-thrus, tenting, dump, laundry, ltd groc. RECREATION: lake swim, boating, canoeing, ramp, dock, lake fishing, play equipment. Pets welcome. Open mid May - early Oct. Rate in 2010 $26-40 per family. Member OPCA. Phone: (613) 646-7989.

(W) COBDEN MUNICIPAL PARK—*In town on Hwy 417.* FACILITIES: 34 sites, 4 W&E, 8 E, (15 amps), 22 no hkups, tenting. RECREATION: lake swim, boating, canoeing, ramp, dock, lake fishing. Pets welcome. Partial handicap access. Open May 24 - Oct. Phone: (613)646-7188.

Logos Land Resort (Not Visited)—(Renfrew) *From jct Main St & Hwy 17: Go 3 km/1-3/4 mi SE on Hwy 17. Enter on L.* FACILITIES: 110 sites, 60 full hkups, (15/30 amps), 50 no hkups, 5 pull-thrus, tenting, laundry, ltd groc. RECREATION: swim pool, lake swim, boating, no motors, canoeing, lake fishing, playground. Pets welcome. Partial handicap access. Age restrict may apply. Open May long wkend - mid Oct. Rate in 2010 $32-39 for 6 persons. Phone: (613)646-9765.

COBOCONK—G-4

BALSAM LAKE PROVINCIAL PARK—*From town: Go 9-1/2 km/6 mi W on Hwy 46.* FACILITIES: 505 sites, 213 E, (15/30 amps), 292 no hkups, 64 pull-thrus, tenting, dump, laundry, ltd groc. RECREATION: boating, canoeing, ramp, dock, playground. Partial handicap access. Open May 12 - Oct 9. Phone: (705)454-3324.

COBOURG—H-4

See listing at Grafton

COCHRANE—B-5

(NE) GREENWATER PROVINCIAL PARK—*From town: Go 36-3/4 km/23 mi W on Hwy 11, then 12-3/4 km/8 mi N on Old Hwy 11.* FACILITIES: 66 sites, 32 E, (15/30 amps), 34 no hkups, 15 pull-thrus, tenting, dump, laundry. RECREATION: lake swim, boating, canoeing, ramp, lake fishing, playground. Partial handicap access. Open mid May - mid Sep. Phone: (705)272-6335.

COLLINGWOOD—H-3

(W) CRAIGLEITH PROVINCIAL PARK—*From town: Go 12-3/4 km/8 mi W on Hwy 26.* FACILITIES: 172 sites, 66 E, (15/30 amps), 106 no hkups, 12 pull-thrus, tenting, dump, ltd groc. RECREATION: playground. Partial handicap access. Open mid Apr - late Oct. Phone: (705)445-4467.

COMBERMERE—G-4

Sand Bay Camp—*From Combermere: Go 3.5 km/2 mi S on Hwy 62, then 1.8 km/1-1/4 mi W on Kamaniskeg Rd, then .4 km/1/4 mi on Sand Bay Rd. Enter on R.* ◇◇FACILITIES: 50 sites, typical site width 30 ft, 30 full hkups, 15 W&E, (15/30/50 amps), 5 no hkups, 5 pull-thrus, tenting, groceries. ◇◇◇RECREATION: lake swim, boating, canoeing, ramp, dock, lake fishing. Pets welcome. Open May 1 - Oct 15. Rate in 2010 $31.50-36.75 per family. Member OPCA. Phone: (613)756-5060.

CONSECON—H-4

Lake Consecon Resort—*From jct Hwy 33 & CR 1: Go 3.2 km/2 mi E on CR 1.* ◇◇◇FACILITIES: 70 sites, typical site width 40 ft, 70 W&E, (15/30 amps), tenting, dump, laundry, ltd groc. ◇◇◇RECREATION: swim pool, lake swim, boating, canoeing, ramp, dock, lake fishing. Pets welcome. Open May 1 - mid Oct. Rate in 2010 $26-40 per family. Member OPCA. Phone: (613)399-5518.

COOKSTOWN—H-3

KOA-Toronto North Cookstown—(Simcoe) *From jct Hwy 400 (exit 75) & Hwy 89: Go .4 km/1/4 mi N on Reive Blvd (NE corner). Enter on R.* ◇◇◇◇◇FACILITIES: 112 sites, typical site width 35 ft, 53 full hkups, 54 W&E, (15/30/50 amps), 5 no hkups, 65 pull-thrus, tenting, dump, laundry, groceries. ◇◇◇◇◇RECREATION: swim pool, playground. Pets welcome. Partial handicap access. Open May 1 - mid-Oct. Big rigs welcome. Rate in 2010 $28-51.55 for 2 persons. Phone: (705)458-2267. KOA discount.

CORNWALL—G-6

Maples RV Park—*From jct Hwy 401 (exit 789) & Brookdale: Go 1.8 km S on Brookdale, then 1.4 km W on Tollgate, then .3 km/ SW on Vincent Massey Dr (Hwy 2). Enter on L.* ◇◇◇FACILITIES: 26 sites, typical site width 40 ft, 20 full hkups, (30 amps), 6 no hkups, 2 pull-thrus, tenting, dump, laundry. Pets welcome. Open all yr. Rate in 2010 $32 per family. Member OPCA. Phone: (877)870-4160.

DEEP RIVER—F-4

DRIFTWOOD PROVINCIAL PARK—*From town: Go 27-1/4 km/17 mi W on Hwy 17 (Stonecliffe).* FACILITIES: 80 sites, 20 E, (15/30 amps), 60 no hkups, tenting, dump, laundry. RECREATION: boating, canoeing, ramp, dock, playground. Partial handicap access. Open mid May - early Sep. Phone: (613)586-2553.

Ryan's Campsite (Not visited)—(Renfrew) *From west city limits: Go 4.8 km/3 mi W on Hwy 17. Enter on R.* ◇◇FACILITIES: 100 sites, typical site width 50 ft, 2 full hkups, 98 W&E, (15/30 amps), 6 pull-thrus, family camping, tenting, dump, laundry, ltd groc. ◇◇◇RECREATION: river swim, boating, canoeing, ramp, dock, river/pond fishing, playground. Pets welcome. Open all yr. Facilities fully operational May 15 - Oct 15. Rate in 2010 $35-40 for 4 persons. Phone: (613)584-3453.

DELTA—G-5

(N) LOWER BEVERLEY LAKE TOWNSHIP PARK—*In town on Lower Beverley Lake Rd.* FACILITIES: 215 sites, 187 W&E, (15/30 amps), 28 no hkups, tenting, dump, laundry, ltd groc. RECREATION: lake swim, boating, canoeing, ramp, dock, playground. Open May 15 - Oct 15. Phone: (613)928-2881.

DEUX RIVIERES—F-4

Antler's Kingfisher Lodge (Not Visited) (RV SPACES)—(Renfrow) *East of Town on Hwy 17. Enter on L.* FACILITIES: 43 sites, typical site width 20 ft, 19 full hkups, 24 W&E, (15/30 amps), 18 pull-thrus, tenting, groceries. RECREATION: river swim, boating, canoeing, ramp, dock, river fishing, play equipment. Pets welcome. Open May 1 - Oct 15. Rate in 2010 $36-32 per vehicle. Member OPCA. Phone: (705)747-0851.

DORION—B-2

(NE) Eagle Canyon Adventures (Not Visited)—*From Hwy 11/17: Go 4 km/2.5 mi N on Ouimet Canyon Rd, then 2km/11.5 mi E on Valley Rd. Enter on L.* FACILITIES: 30 sites, typical site width 45 ft, 30 W&E, (30 amps), dump. Pets welcome. Partial handicap access. No tents. Open all yr. Facilities fully operational May - Oct. Rate in 2010 $25 per family. Phone: (807) 857-1475.

DRYDEN—D-2

Birchland Trailer Park (Not Visited)—(Kenora) *From jct Hwy 665 & Hwy 17: Go 1.2 km/3/4 mi W on Hwy 17. Enter on L.* FACILITIES: 60 sites, typical site width 35 ft, 33 full hkups, 9 W&E, 5 E, (30 amps), 13 no hkups, 4 pull-thrus, tenting, dump, laundry. RECREATION: playground. Pets welcome. Open all yr. Facilities fully operational May 1 - Oct 30. Rate in 2010 $24-28 per family. Phone: (807)937-4938.

Twin Towers Restaurant, Gas Bar & Camping (Not visited) (RV SPACES)—(Kenora) *10 Kms/6 mi E of Dryden on Hwy 17. Enter on R.* FACILITIES: 10 sites, 5 full hkups, (15 amps), 5 no hkups, tenting, ltd groc. RECREATION: lake swim, boating, lake fishing, playground. Pets welcome. Open all yr. Facilities fully operational May - Oct. Rate in 2010 $20 per family. Phone: (807)938-6569.

DUNNVILLE—I-3

(S) BYNG ISLAND (Grand River Cons Auth)—*From town: Go 1/2 km/1/4 mi W across bridge. Enter on R.* FACILITIES: 380 sites, 145 W&E, 235 no hkups, tenting, dump, ltd groc. RECREATION: swim pool, boating, canoeing, ramp, river fishing, playground. Open May 1 - Oct 15. Phone: (905)774-5755.

CHIPPAWA CREEK (Niagara Peninsula Cons Auth.)—*From east city limits: Go 9-1/2 km/6 mi E on Hwy 3, then 4-3/4 km/3 mi N on Wellandport Rd.* FACILITIES: 156 sites, 106 W&E, (15/30 amps), 50 no hkups, 110 pull-thrus, tenting, dump. RECREATION: lake/river swim, boating, canoeing, ramp, lake/river fishing, playground. Partial handicap access. Open May 16 - Sep 7. Phone: (905)386-6387.

Highland Trailer Park & RV Resort—*From jct Main St & CR 3: Go 11 km/7 mi E on CR 3 (Lakeshore Rd). Enter on R.* ◇◇◇◇FACILITIES: 181 sites, typical site width 35 ft, 171 full hkups, 10 W&E, (30 amps), 8 pull-thrus, tenting, dump, laundry, ltd groc. ◇◇◇◇RECREATION: swim pool, lake swim, lake fishing, playground. Pets welcome. Open May 1 - mid Oct. Rate in 2010 $40 for 4 persons. Member OPCA. Phone: (905)774-8082.

Knight's Beach (Not visited)—*From bridge in business center: Go 14.5 km/9 mi W on Regional Rd 3, then 1.6 km/1 mi S on Regional Rd 50, then 1.2 km/3/4 mi W on Lakeshore Rd. Enter on L.* ◇◇◇FACILITIES: 380 sites, typical site width 36 ft, 200 full hkups, 30 W&E, (15/30 amps), 150 no hkups, 12 pull-thrus, tenting, dump, laundry, ltd groc. ◇◇◇◇RECREATION: lake swim, boating, ramp, dock, lake fishing, playground. Pets welcome. Open May 1 - mid Oct. Rate in 2010 $42-45 per family. Member OPCA. Phone: (905)774-4566. FCRV discount.

(W) ROCK POINT PROVINCIAL PARK—*From town: Go 3/4 km/1/2 mi E on Hwy 3, then 12-3/4 km/8 mi S on Haldimand Rd 20.* FACILITIES: 178 sites, typical site width 40 ft, 81 E, (15/30 amps), 97 no hkups, tenting, dump, laundry, ltd groc. RECREATION: lake swim, canoeing, lake fishing, playground. Partial handicap access. Open mid May - early Sep. Phone: (905)774-6642.

DURHAM—H-2

(N) DURHAM CONSERVATION AREA (Saugeen Valley Cons Auth.)—*From jct Hwy 4 & Hwy 6: Go .8 km/1/2 mi N on Hwy 6, then 1.6 km/1 mi E on Old Durham Rd.* FACILITIES: 205 sites, 94 W&E, (15/30 amps), 111 no hkups, tenting, dump. RECREATION: river swim, boating, canoeing, ramp, river fishing, playground. Open late Apr - Nov 30. Phone: (519)364-1255.

DUTTON—J-2

Duttona Trailer Park—(Elgin) *From Hwy 401 (exit 149): Go 4.8 km/3 mi S at exit 149, then 3.2 km/2 mi W on Hwy 3, then S on Coyne Rd. Enter on L.* ◇◇◇FACILITIES: 150 sites, typical site width 35 ft, 150 full hkups, (15/30 amps), 4 pull-thrus, tenting, laundry, groceries. ◇◇◇◇RECREATION: swim pool, lake swim, canoeing, lake fishing, playground. Pets welcome. Open May 13 - Oct 20. Rate in 2010 $30 per family. Phone: (519)762-3643.

DWIGHT—G-3

(E) Algonquin Trails Camping Resort (Not Visited)—(Muskoka) *From the jct Hwy 60 & Hwy 35: Go E on Hwy 60 .8 km/1/2 mi. Enter on L.* FACILITIES: 143 sites, typical site width 40 ft, 15 full hkups, 98 W&E, (15/30 amps), 30 no hkups, 43 pull-thrus, tenting, dump, laundry, ltd groc. RECREATION: swim pool, playground. Pets welcome. Open May 1 - Oct 15. Rate in 2010 $28-39 per family. Member OPCA. Phone: (705) 638-1262.

EAR FALLS—C-2

(SE) Goose Bay Camp (Not Visited) (RV SPACES)—(Kenora) *From town: Go 5 km/3 mi S on Hwy 105, then 1 km/.6 mi E on Goose Bay Rd. Enter at end.* FACILITIES: 12 sites, typical site width 50 ft, 6 full hkups, (15/30 amps), 6 no hkups, tenting, laundry, ltd groc. RECREATION: lake swim, boating, canoeing, ramp, dock, lake fishing, playground. Pets welcome. Open mid May - end of Oct. Rate in 2010 $32 for 2 persons. Member OPCA. Phone: (800)667-5208.

Whitewing Resort and Floating Lodges (Not visited) (RV SPACES)—*From town: Go 8 km/5 mi S on Hwy 105, then .8 km/1/2 mi E on Whitewing Rd. Enter on L.* FACILITIES: 27 sites, 7 full hkups, (15 amps), 20 no hkups, tenting. RECREATION: lake swim, boating, canoeing, ramp, dock, lake fishing. Pets welcome. Open mid May - mid Oct. Rate in 2010 $20 for 1 persons. Member OPCA. Phone: (800)265-1764.

EGANVILLE—F-5

Lake Dore Tent & Trailer Park (Not Visited)—(Renfrew) *From jct Hwy 60 & Hwy 41 (4.8 km/3 mi W of town): Go 100 ft N on 41N then 3 km/1-1/2 mi W on Germanicus Rd. Enter on R.* FACILITIES: 144 sites, typical site width 35 ft, 107 full hkups, 21 W&E, (15/30 amps), 16 no hkups, 3 pull-thrus, tenting, dump, ltd groc. RECREATION: lake swim, boating, canoeing, ramp, dock, lake fishing, playground. Pets welcome. Open 1st week of May - Sep 30. Rate in 2010 $27-36 per family. Member OPCA. Phone: (613)628-2615.

ELGIN—G-5

Skycroft Campground and Cottages—*From jct Hwy 15 & CR 9: Go 14.4 km/9 mi W on CR 9. Enter on L.* ◇◇◇FACILITIES: 65 sites, typical site width 25 ft, 30 ft max RV length, 22 full hkups, 42 W&E, (15/30 amps), 1 no hkups, tenting, laundry, ltd groc. ◇◇◇RECREATION: lake swim, boating, canoeing, ramp, dock, lake fishing, playground. Pets welcome. Open May 15 - Oct 15. Rate in 2010 $38-49 for 2 persons. Member OPCA. Phone: (877)359-5491.

ELLIOT LAKE—D-5

(N) MISSISSAGI PROVINCIAL PARK—*From town: Go 17-1/2 km/11 mi N on Hwy 639.* FACILITIES: 90 sites, 21 ft max RV length, 90 no hkups, 62 pull-thrus, tenting, dump, ltd groc. RECREATION: boating, canoeing, ramp. Open mid May - early Sep. Phone: (705)848-2806.

ELMIRA—I-2

(NW) CONESTOGO LAKE (Grand River Cons Auth)—*From town: Go 16 km/10 mi W on Hwy 86, follow signs. Enter on R.* FACILITIES: 181 sites, 95 W&E, 86 no hkups, tenting, dump, ltd groc. RECREATION: lake swim, boating, canoeing, ramp, lake/river fishing, playground. Pets welcome. Open all yr. Facilities fully operational May 1 - Thanksgiving. Phone: (519)638-2873.

ELORA—H-2

(W) ELORA GORGE (Grand River Cons Auth)—*From west town limits: Go 1/2 km/1/4 mi W. Enter on R.* FACILITIES: 546 sites, 69 full hkups, 165 W&E, (15/30 amps), 312 no hkups, tenting, dump, laundry, ltd groc. RECREATION: lake swim, boating, no motors, canoeing, lake fishing, playground. Open all yr. Facilities fully operational May 1 - Thanksgiving. Phone: (519)846-9742.

ENGLEHART—C-6

KAP-KIG-IWAN PROVINCIAL PARK—*From town: Go 3/4 km/1/2 mi W on Hwy 11, then 2-1/2 km/1-1/2 mi S on 5th St.* FACILITIES: 62 sites, 32 E, (15 amps), 30 no hkups, 32 pull-thrus, tenting, dump, laundry, ltd groc. RECREATION: playground. Open May - Sep. Phone: (705)544-2050.

ENNISMORE—H-4

Anchor Bay Camp—*From business centre: Go 11.2 km/7 mi N on CR 16. Enter on R.* ◇◇FACILITIES: 196 sites, typical site width 50 ft, 161 full hkups, 17 W&E, (30 amps), 18 no hkups, 10 pull-thrus, tenting, dump, laundry, ltd groc. ◇◇◇RECREATION: swim pool, lake swim, boating, canoeing, ramp, dock, lake fishing, playground. Pets welcome. Open May 1 - Oct 8. Rate in 2010 $14-36 for 2 persons. Member OPCA. Phone: (705)657-8439.

Woodland Camp Site—*From jct CR 14 & CR 16: Go 16 km/10 mi N on CR 16, then follow signs for .4 km/1/4 mi E. Enter on L.* ◇◇◇FACILITIES: 175 sites, typical site width 40 ft, 150 W&E, (15/30 amps), 25 no hkups, tenting, dump. ◇◇◇RECREATION: lake swim, boating, canoeing, ramp, dock, lake fishing, playground. No pets. Open May 1 - Oct 31. Rate in 2010 $28-37 per family. Member OPCA. Phone: (705)657-8946.

ESPANOLA—D-5

Lake Apsey Resort & Trailer Park (Not Visited)—(Sudbury) *From jct Hwy 17 & Hwy 6: Go 9.6 km/6 mi S on Hwy 6, then 1 km/1/2 mi W on Lake Apsey Rd. Enter on R.* FACILITIES: 30 sites, typical site width 30 ft, 20 W&E, (15 amps), 10 no hkups, tenting, dump, ltd groc. RECREATION: lake swim, boating, canoeing, ramp, dock, lake fishing, playground. Pets welcome. Open mid May - mid Oct. Rate in 2010 $25-33 per family. Phone: (800)559-6583.

EVANSVILLE—F-1

Lake Wolsey Obejewung Park (Not Visited)—(Manitoulin) *From jct Hwy 540 & Indian Point Rd: Go 3.7 km/2-1/4 mi S on Indian Point Rd, then 1 km/2/3 mi on Lake Wolsey Rd. Enter at end.* ◇◇FACILITIES: 120 sites, typical site width 35 ft, 85 W&E, (15 amps), 35 no hkups, tenting, dump, laundry. ◇◇◇RECREATION: lake swim, boating, canoeing, ramp, dock, lake fishing, play equipment. Pets welcome. Open Mid May - Mid Oct. Rate in 2010 $24-26.50 per family. Phone: (705)282-2174.

FENELON FALLS—H-4

Fenelon Valley Trailer Park & Trailer Sales (Not visited)—*From jct Hwy 35A (center of town) & Hwy 121: Go 11.2 km/7 mi N on Hwy 121. Enter on R.* ◇◇◇FACILITIES: 111 sites, typical site width 50 ft, 66 full hkups, 25 W&E, (15/20/30 amps), 20 no hkups, tenting, dump, laundry, ltd groc. ◇◇◇RECREATION: 3 swim pools, playground. Pets welcome. Open May 1 - end Oct. Rate in 2010 $25-30 per vehicle. Member OPCA. Phone: (705)887-3251.

Log Chateau Park (Not visited)—*From jct Hwy 35A (center of town) & Hwy 121: Go 10.4 km/6-1/2 mi N on Hwy 121, then 1/2 km/1/3 mi W on Log Chateau Park Rd. Enter on L.* ◇◇◇FACILITIES: 288 sites, typical site width 40 ft, 240 full hkups, 32 W&E, 5 E, (15/30 amps), 47 no hkups, 5 pull-thrus, tenting, dump, laundry, ltd groc. ◇◇◇◇RECREATION: swim pool, river swim, boating, ramp, dock, lake/river fishing, playground. Pets welcome. Partial handicap access. Open May 1 - Oct 15. Rate in 2010 $34 for 2 persons. Member OPCA. Phone: (705)887-3960.

Sandy Beach Resort & Trailer Court (Not Visited)—*From jct Hwy 35A & Hwy 35: Go 4.8 km/3 mi N, follow signs.* ◇◇◇FACILITIES: 171 sites, typical site width 50 ft, 171 full hkups, (30 amps), 2 pull-thrus. ◇◇◇RECREATION: lake swim, boating, canoeing, ramp, dock, lake fishing, playground. Pets welcome. No tents. Open mid May - mid Oct. Rate in 2010 $30 per family. Member OPCA. Phone: (705)887-2550.

Sunny Acres (Not visited)—*From jct Hwy 35A & Hwy 35: Go 1.2 km/3/4 mi N on Hwy 35.* ◇◇◇FACILITIES: 100 sites, typical site width 40 ft, 52 full hkups, 42 W&E, (15/30 amps), 6 no hkups, tenting, dump, ltd groc. ◇◇◇RECREATION: lake swim, boating, canoeing, ramp, dock, lake fishing, playground. Pets welcome. Open May 10 - Oct 15. Rate in 2010 $30.25-32.50 per family. Member OPCA. Phone: (705)887-3416.

FERGUS—H-3

HIGHLAND PINES CAMPGROUND—(Wellington) *From jct Hwy 6 & CR 19: Go 9 km/5-1/2 mi E on CR 19. Enter on R.*

WELCOME

◇◇◇◇FACILITIES: 559 sites, typical site width 35 ft, 484 full hkups, 75 W&E, (30 amps), mostly extd stay sites, WiFi Internet central location, tenting, cabins, RV storage, dump, non-guest dump $, ltd groc, RV supplies, ice, picnic tables, patios, fire rings, wood, controlled access.

◇◇◇◇◇RECREATION: rec hall, equipped pavilion, swim pool, wading pool, spray ground, lake swim, boating, canoeing, kayaking, ramp, dock, lake fishing, golf nearby, bsktball, 4 bike rentals, playground, shuffleboard court 2 shuffleboard courts, activities (wkends), horseshoes, sports field, hiking trails, v-ball.

Pets welcome. Partial handicap access. Open First wk of May - Mid Oct. Rate in 2010 $42 per family. MC/VISA/Debit. Member ARVC, OPCA.

Phone: (519)843-2537
Address: RR 1 8523 Wellington Rd 19, Belwood, ON N0B 1J0
Lat/Lon: 43.46609/-80.20522
Email: camping@highlandpines.com
Web: www.highlandpines.com

SEE AD THIS PAGE

FOLEYET—C-5

(W) IVANHOE LAKE PROVINCIAL PARK—*From town: Go 12-3/4 km/8 mi NW on Hwy 101, then 4-3/4 km/3 mi S on Park Rd.* FACILITIES: 120 sites, 64 E, (15/30 amps), 56 no hkups, 75 pull-thrus, tenting, dump, laundry, ltd groc. RECREATION: lake swim, boating, canoeing, ramp, lake fishing, playground. Partial handicap access. Open mid May - early Sep. Phone: (705)899-2644.

FONTHILL—I-3

BISSELL'S HIDEAWAY RESORT—*From west city limits: Go .4 km/1/4 mi W on Hwy 20, then 2.4 km/1-1/2 mi N on Effingham Rd, then .8 km/1/2 mi E on Metler Rd. Enter on L.*

WELCOME

◇◇◇◇FACILITIES: 360 sites, typical site width 45 ft, 290 full hkups, (20/30/50 amps), 70 no hkups, many extd stay sites, 14 pull-thrus, WiFi Instant Internet at site, family camping, tenting, cabins, RV storage, shower$, dump, portable dump, laundry, ltd groc, RV supplies, LP gas by weight, ice, picnic tables, fire rings, wood, controlled access.

◇◇◇◇◇RECREATION: rec hall, rec room/area, equipped pavilion, coin games, swim pool, wading pool, spray ground, boating, 10 pedal boat rentals, pond fishing, fishing supplies, mini-golf, ($), golf nearby, bsktball, playground, shuffleboard court 2 shuffleboard courts, activities, tennis, horseshoes, sports field, hiking trails, v-ball. Rec open to public.

Pets welcome. Open Apr 30 - Oct 11. Waterpark open from Mid Jun - Sep 6. Big rigs welcome. Clubs welcome. Rate in 2010 $45-75 per family. MC/VISA/AMEX/Debit. ATM. Member ARVC, OPCA.

Phone: (888)236-0619
Address: RR 1 205 Metler Rd, Ridgeville, ON L0S 1M0
Lat/Lon: 43.03730/-79.18201
Email: izanded@aol.com
Web: www.bissellshideaway.com

SEE AD NIAGARA FALLS PAGE 881

FOREST—I-1

Carolinian Forest Campground (Not Visited)—(Lambton) *From jct Hwy 21 & Ipperwash Rd: Go 1.6 km/1 mi W on Ipperwash Rd. Enter on L.* FACILITIES: 143 sites, typical site width 40 ft, 127 full hkups, 8 W&E, (30 amps), 8 no hkups, 6 pull-thrus, tenting, dump, laundry. RECREATION: swim pool, lake swim, lake fishing, playground. Pets welcome, breed restrict, quantity restrict. Open May 1 - mid Oct. Rate in 2010 $32-45 per family. Member OPCA. Phone: (519)243-2258.

Lakewood Christian Campground (Not Visited)—(Lambton) *From jct Hwy 21 & CR 11: Go 12.8 km/8 mi W on CR 11, then .8 km/1/2 mi N on CR 7. Enter on R.* ◇◇◇◇FACILITIES: 350 sites, typical site width 35 ft, 35 ft max RV length, 334 full hkups, 16 W&E, (15/30 amps), tenting, dump, laundry, ltd groc. ◇◇◇◇◇RECREATION: swim pool, lake swim, boating, no motors, canoeing, dock, lake/pond fishing, playground. Pets welcome. Partial handicap access. Open May 1 - mid Oct. Rate in 2010 $27-41 per family. Member ARVC, OPCA. Phone: (519)899-4415.

Lambton Centre Family Campground—(Lambton) *From jct County Rd 21 & County Rd 7: Go 3.8km/2-1/2 mi SW on County Rd 7. Enter on R.* ◇◇FACILITIES: 103 sites, typical site width 50 ft, 12 full hkups, 87 W&E, (20/30 amps), 4 no hkups, tenting, dump, laundry, ltd groc. ◇◇◇◇RECREATION: swim pool, canoeing, lake fishing, playground. Pets welcome. Partial handicap access. Age restrict may apply. Open May 1 - Oct 15. Rate in 2010 $30-34 per family. Member OPCA. Phone: (519)786-5663.

Our Ponderosa Family Campground & Golf Resort (Not Visited)—(Lambton) *From town: Go 9.6 km/6 mi N on Hwy 21, then 90 m/100 yards W on Lambton CR 7, then 1.6 km/1 mi N on West Ipperwash Rd. Enter on R.* FACILITIES: 395 sites, typical site width 40 ft, 360 full hkups, 35 W&E, (30/50 amps), 9 pull-thrus, tenting, dump, laundry, groceries. RECREATION: 2 swim pools, pond fishing, playground. Pets welcome. Partial handicap access. Open all yr. Facilities fully operational May 1 - Oct 15. Rate in 2010 $48 per family. Member ARVC, OPCA. Phone: (888)786-CAMP.

FOREST—Continued on next page

FOREST—Continued

PARADISE VALLEY CAMPGROUND (Not visited)—*Directions: From jct Hwy 402 & Oil Heritage Rd. (exit 25): Go 13 km/8mi N on Oil Heritage Rd. (Con Rd 30), then 1 km/1/2 mi SW on Lakeshore Rd. (CR 7). Enter on L.*

◇◇◇FACILITIES: 350 sites, typical site width 40 ft, 290 full hkups, (30 amps), 60 no hkups, many extd stay sites, 14 pull-thrus, phone Internet central location, tenting, cabins, RV storage, dump, laundry, groceries, LP gas by weight, ice, picnic tables, fire rings, wood, controlled access.

◇◇◇◇◇RECREATION: rec hall, equipped pavilion, 2 swim pools, wading pool, hot tub, boating, no motors, 4 pedal boat rentals, pond fishing, mini-golf, ($), golf nearby, bsktball, playground, activities, horseshoes, sports field, hiking trails, v-ball. Rec open to public.

Pets welcome. Partial handicap access. Open all yr. Facilities fully operational May 1 - Oct 15. Pool opens Mid May. Clubs welcome. Rate in 2010 $36-46 per family. MC/VISA/Debit. Member ARVC, OPCA.

Phone: (519)899-4080
Address: RR5, 4895 Lakeshore Rd, Forest, ON N0N 1J0
Lat/Lon: 43.05645/-82.07668
Email: paradisevalley@killamproperties.com
Web: www.killamleisureliving.com/paradisevalley

SEE AD BRIGHTON PAGE 869

(S) WOOD HAVEN (EXTENDED STAY ONLY)—*From jct Hwy 21 (Rawlings Rd) & Hwy 7 (Lakeshore Rd): Go 1.2 mi NE on Hwy 21, then .7 mi N on Ipperwash Rd. Enter on L.*

FACILITIES: 100 sites, 100 full hkups, (30 amps), mostly extd stay sites, laundry, fire rings, wood.

RECREATION: rec hall, pavilion, swim pool, mini-golf, golf nearby, playground, activities, (wkends), horseshoes, sports field, hiking trails, v-ball.

Pets welcome. Partial handicap access. No tents. Open May 1 - Oct 30. Member OPCA.

Phone: (519)243-2405
Address: 9385 Ipperwash Road RR #2, Forest, ON N0N 1J0
Email: woodhaven@killamproperties.com
Web: www.killamleisureliving.com/woodhaven

SEE AD BRIGHTON PAGE 869

FORT ERIE—I-3

Windmill Point Park—*From jct QEW & Thompson Rd (1 mi north of Peace Bridge): Go 1/2 mi S on Thompson Rd, then 4 km/2-1/2 mi W on Hwy 3, then 2 km/1-1/4 mi S on Stonemill Rd (Reg Rd 120), then .4 km/1/4 mi W on Dominion Rd, then .4 km/1/4 mi S on paved road. Enter at end.* ◇◇FACILITIES: 205 sites, typical site width 50 ft, 95 W&E, 10 E, (30 amps), 100 no hkups, WiFi Internet central location, tenting, RV storage, dump, laundry, ice, picnic tables, fire rings, wood. ◇◇◇◇RECREATION: pavilion, equipped pavilion, lake swim, boating, no motors, canoeing, kayaking, ramp, dock, lake fishing, fishing supplies, bsktball, playground, activities, horseshoes, hiking trails, v-ball. Pets welcome. Partial handicap access. Age restrict may apply. Open May 1 - Oct 15. Rate in 2010 $39-45 per family. MC/VISA/AMEX/Debit. Member OPCA. CCUSA 50% Discount. CCUSA reservations Required, CCUSA max stay 5 days, CCUSA disc. not avail holidays. No discount on holiday weekends, weekly rate or site extras. Repeat guests may revisit w/discount after 3 days. May not be combined w/other offers. Glass alcohol containers & fireworks NOT permitted. Pet rules apply. Aggressive dog breeds not accepted.

Phone: (888)977-8888
Address: 2409 Dominion Rd, Ridgeway, ON L0S 1N0
Lat/Lon: 42.88463/-79.00300
Email: wpp@vaxxine.com
Web: www.windmillpointpark.com

FRANKFORD—H-4

Iroquois Trail Campsite—*From jct Hwy 401 (exit 526) & Glen Miller Rd: Go 8 km/4-3/4 mi N on Glen Miller Rd, then 3 km/1-3/4 mi N on CR 33 (Frankford Stirling Rd). Enter on R.* ◇◇◇◇FACILITIES: 81 sites, typical site width 40 ft, 69 full hkups, 10 W&E, (15/30 amps), 2 no hkups, 22 pull-thrus, family camping, tenting, dump, laundry, ltd groc. ◇◇◇RECREATION: river swim, boating, canoeing, ramp, dock, river fishing. Pets welcome. Open May 1 - Oct 15. Rate in 2010 $33 for 4 persons. Member OPCA. Phone: (877)246-4200. FMCA discount.

FRENCH RIVER—F-2

Loon's Landing (Not Visited)—(Sudbury) *From jct Hwy 69 & Hwy 607: Go .4 Km/1/4 mi on Hwy 607 to 607 A, then S on 607 A .8 kms/1/2 mi to Hass Rd ,then E on Hass Rd. Enter at end.* FACILITIES: 50 sites, typical site width 35 ft, 22 full hkups, 8 W&E, (15/30 amps), 20 no hkups, tenting, laundry, ltd groc. RECREATION: river swim, boating, canoeing, ramp, dock, river fishing, play equipment. Pets welcome. Open May 15 - Oct 15. Rate in 2010 $25-30 per family. Phone: (705) 857-2175.

GANANOQUE—H-5

1000 Island-Ivy Lea-KOA—*From jct Hwy 401 (exit 659) & Reynolds Rd: Go 2.4 km/1-1/2 mi S on Reynolds Rd, then 3.2 km/2 mi W on Thousand Island Pkwy. Enter on R.* ◇◇◇◇FACILITIES: 154 sites, typical site width 40 ft, 52 full hkups, 74 W&E, (15/30/50 amps), 50 amps ($), 28 no hkups, 36 pull-thrus, family camping, tenting, dump, laundry, groceries. ◇◇◇◇◇RECREATION: swim pool, pond fishing, playground. Pets welcome. Open May 9 - Oct 13. Big rigs welcome. Rate in 2010 $52-90 for 4 persons. Member OPCA. Phone: (800)562-2471. KOA discount.

1000 Islands Camping Resort—*From jct Hwy 401 (exit 647/648): Go 5 mi E on the 1000 Island Pkwy. Enter on L.* ◇◇◇FACILITIES: 173 sites, typical site width 40 ft, 25 full hkups, 100 W&E, (15/30/50 amps), 48 no hkups, 3 pull-thrus, family camping, tenting, dump, laundry, groceries. ◇◇◇◇RECREATION: swim pool, playground. Pets welcome. Open May 15 - Oct 15. Big rigs welcome. Rate in 2010 $30-48 per family. Member OPCA. Phone: (613)659-3058. FCRV discount. FMCA discount.

IVY LEA CAMPSITE (Parks of the St. Lawrence)—*From east city limits: Go 12-3/4 km/8 mi E on Thousand Islands Pkwy. Just west of the Ivy Lea Bridge.* FACILITIES: 163 sites, 14 W&E, 33 E, (15/30 amps), 116 no hkups, tenting, dump, laundry, ltd groc. RECREATION: river swim, boating, canoeing, ramp, dock, river fishing, playground. Open May 15 - Oct 12. Phone: (800)437-2233.

The Landon Bay Centre (Not visited)—*From Hwy 401 (exit 659): Go 2.4 km/1-1/2 mi S, then 8 km/5 mi W on the 1000 Islands Pkwy. Enter on R.* ◇◇◇FACILITIES: 125 sites, typical site width 35 ft, 75 W&E, (15/30 amps), 50 no hkups, tenting, dump, ltd groc. ◇◇RECREATION: swim pool, lake swim, lake fishing, playground. Pets welcome. Open mid May - Mid Oct. Rate in 2010 $24-32 per family. Member OPCA. Phone: (613)382-2719.

GERALDTON—A-2

(SE) MACLEOD PROVINCIAL PARK—*From jct Hwy 584 & Hwy 11: Go 2-3/4 km/1-3/4 mi E on Hwy 11.* FACILITIES: 85 sites, 28 E, (15/30 amps), 57 no hkups, 28 pull-thrus, tenting, dump, laundry. RECREATION: lake swim, boating, canoeing, ramp, lake fishing, playground. Partial handicap access. Open May - early Sep. Phone: (807)854-0370.

Wild Goose Lake Campground (Not Visited)—(Thunder Bay) *From jct of CR 584 & Hwy 11: Go 19.3 km/12 mi W on Hwy 11, then 1.2 km/3/4 mi N on Kueng's Rd. Enter on L.* FACILITIES: 61 sites, typical site width 30 ft, 52 full hkups, (15/30 amps), 9 no hkups, 7 pull-thrus, tenting, dump, laundry, ltd groc. RECREATION: lake swim, boating, canoeing, ramp, dock, lake fishing, play equipment. Pets welcome. Open May 15 - Sep 30. Rate in 2010 $18-33 per family. Member OPCA. Phone: (866)465-4404.

GODERICH—H-2

Auburn Riverside Retreat (Not visited)—(Huron) *From jct of Hwy 21 & CR 25: Go 12.8 km/8 mi E on CR 25. Enter on L.* ◇◇◇FACILITIES: 89 sites, typical site width 40 ft, 47 full hkups, 14 W&E, 12 E, (15/30 amps), 16 no hkups, 4 pull-thrus, tenting, RV storage, dump, laundry, ltd groc, ice, picnic tables, fire rings, wood. ◇◇◇◇RECREATION: rec hall, swim pool, river swim, canoeing, kayaking, river fishing, fishing supplies, bsktball, playground, activities, horseshoes, hiking trails, v-ball. Pets welcome. Open May 1 - Thanksgiving Monday. Rate in 2010 $26-32 per family. Debit. Member OPCA. CCUSA 50% Discount. CCUSA reservations Recommended, CCUSA max stay Unlimited, Cash only for CCUSA disc. Discount available 5/1-6/15 and 9/15-Thanksgiving Mon. Discount not available 6/15-9/15, Victoria Day.

Phone: (519)526-7238
Address: 38382 Blyth Rd, Auburn, ON N0M 1E0
Lat/Lon: 43.46517/-81.32267
Email: auburnriverside@hurontel.on.ca
Web: www.campground.org/auburnriverside

Lake Huron Resort—*From jct Hwy 8 and Hwy 21: Go 5 mi N on Hwy 21. Enter on L.* ◇◇◇◇FACILITIES: 210 sites, typical site width 50 ft, 60 full hkups, 140 W&E, (15/30 amps), 10 no hkups, tenting, dump, laundry, ltd groc. ◇◇◇RECREATION: swim pool, lake swim, lake fishing, playground. Pets welcome. Partial handicap access. Facilities fully operational May 10 - Oct 15. Rate in 2010 $28-37 Member OPCA. Phone: (519)524-5343.

(N) POINT FARMS PROVINCIAL PARK—*From town: Go 4-3/4 km/3 mi N on Hwy 21.* FACILITIES: 200 sites, 131 E, (15/30 amps), 69 no hkups, tenting, dump, laundry. RECREATION: lake swim, river fishing, playground. Partial handicap access. Open May - Oct. Phone: (519)524-7124.

GODERICH—Continued

Shelter Valley Tent & Trailer Park (Not visited)—(Huron) *From center of town at jct Hwy 21 & Hwy 8: Go 8 km/5 mi SE on Hwy 8. Enter on L.* ◇◇◇◇FACILITIES: 173 sites, typical site width 40 ft, 104 full hkups, 68 W&E, (15/30/50 amps), 1 no hkups, 7 pull-thrus, tenting, dump, laundry, ltd groc. ◇◇◇◇RECREATION: swim pool, river swim, canoeing, river/pond fishing, play equipment. Pets welcome. Partial handicap access. Open mid May - mid Oct. Rate in 2010 $32 per family. Member OPCA. Phone: (519)524-4141.

GOULAIS RIVER—D-4

(N) Blueberry Hill Motel & Campground (Not Visited)—(Algoma) *From jct Hwy 552 & Hwy 17: Go 3.6 km/2-1/4 mi S on Hwy 17. Enter on L.* ◇◇◇FACILITIES: 100 sites, typical site width 25 ft, 12 full hkups, 42 W&E, 6 E, (15/30 amps), 40 no hkups, 28 pull-thrus, family camping, tenting, dump, laundry, ltd groc. ◇◇◇◇RECREATION: swim pool, river swim, canoeing, river fishing, playground. Pets welcome. Open all yr. Rate in 2010 $22-35 for 2 persons. Member OPCA. Phone: (800)811-4411.

GRAFTON—H-4

Cobourg East Campground—*From jct Hwy 401 (exit 487) & Aird St: Go S on Aird St, then 1.6 km/1 mi E on Hwy 2, then .8 km/1/2 mi S on Benlock Rd.* ◇◇◇FACILITIES: 146 sites, typical site width 40 ft, 17 full hkups, 108 W&E, (30 amps), 21 no hkups, 26 pull-thrus, tenting, dump, laundry, ltd groc. ◇◇◇◇RECREATION: swim pool, river fishing, playground. Pets welcome. Open May 1 - mid Oct. Rate in 2010 $25-32 for 2 persons. Member OPCA. Phone: (905)349-2594. FCRV discount. FMCA discount.

GRAND BEND—I-2

Birch Bark Tent & Trailer Park—(Huron) *From jct Hwy 21 & Thames Rd (CR 83): Go 3.2 km/2 mi E on Thames Rd (Hwy 83). Enter on R.* ◇◇◇FACILITIES: 118 sites, typical site width 35 ft, 35 ft max RV length, 118 full hkups, (30 amps), 3 pull-thrus, tenting, laundry, ltd groc. ◇◇◇RECREATION: swim pool, playground. Pets welcome. Open May 1 - mid Oct. Rate in 2010 $42 per family. Member OPCA. Phone: (519)238-8256.

Oak Ridge Resort (Not Visited)—(Lambton) *From jct Hwy 81 & Hwy 21: Go 11 km/7 mi S on Hwy 21, then .4 km/1/4 mi W on Northville Crescent. Enter on L.* FACILITIES: 250 sites, typical site width 45 ft, 150 full hkups, 26 W&E, (15/30 amps), 74 no hkups, 6 pull-thrus, tenting, dump, laundry, ltd groc. RECREATION: 3 swim pools, river fishing, playground. Pets welcome. Open May 1 - Mid Oct. Rate in 2010 $31-36 per family. Member OPCA. Phone: (519)243-2500.

(S) PINERY PROVINCIAL PARK—*From town: Go 8 km/5 mi S on Hwy 21.* FACILITIES: 1000 sites, 404 E, (15/30 amps), 596 no hkups, tenting, dump, laundry, ltd groc. RECREATION: boating, no motors, canoeing. Partial handicap access. Open early Apr - late Oct. Phone: (519)243-2220.

Rus-Ton Family Campground & RV Resort (Not Visited)—*From jct Hwy 81 & Hwy 21: Go 6.4 km/4 mi S on Hwy 21. Enter on L.* ◇◇◇◇FACILITIES: 240 sites, typical site width 40 ft, 235 full hkups, 5 W&E, (30 amps), tenting, dump, laundry, groceries. ◇◇◇◇RECREATION: 2 swim pools, play equipment. Pets welcome. Open May 1 - Mid Oct. Rate in 2010 $45 per family. Member OPCA. Phone: (519)243-2424.

GRAND VALLEY—H-3

Summer Place (Not Visited)—(Dufferin) *From jct Hwy 109 & CR 25: Go 9.2 km/5-3/4 mi N on CR 25. Enter on L.* FACILITIES: 332 sites, typical site width 40 ft, 25 ft max RV length, 295 full hkups, 25 W&E, (15/30 amps), 12 no hkups, tenting, dump, laundry, ltd groc. RECREATION: swim pool, river swim, boating, no motors, canoeing, river fishing, playground. Pets welcome. Partial handicap access. Open mid May - mid Oct. Rate in 2010 $30-34 per family. Member OPCA. Phone: (519)928-5408.

GRANTON—I-2

Prospect Hill Camping Grounds—(Perth) *From jct Hwy 4 & Hwy 7: Go 10 km/6-1/4 mi E on Hwy 7, then 2.8 km/1-3/4 mi N on Prospect Rd (Middlesex CR 50). Enter on L.* ◇◇◇FACILITIES: 168 sites, typical site width 40 ft, 140 W&E, (30 amps), 28 no hkups, tenting, RV storage, dump, portable dump, laundry, ltd groc, RV supplies, LP gas by weight, ice, picnic tables, patios, fire rings, wood. ◇◇◇◇RECREATION: rec hall, swim pool, canoeing, stream fishing, bsktball, playground, activities, horseshoes, v-ball. Pets welcome. Open mid May - mid Oct. Rate in 2010 $27-36 per family. MC/VISA. Member OPCA. CCUSA 50% Discount.

Phone: (519)225-2405
Lat/Lon: 43.13218/-81.14194
Email: prospecthill@quadro.net
Web: www.prospecthillcamping.com

Ontario shares four out of the five Great Lakes with the United States.

GRAVENHURST—G-3

(S) Camp Hillbilly Estates (Not Visited)—(Muskoka) *From jct Hwy 11 & Kilworthy Rd: Go S on Hwy 11 .7 km/4/10 mi. Enter on R.* FACILITIES: 242 sites, typical site width 40 ft, 190 full hkups, 30 W&E, 2 E, (15/30 amps), 20 no hkups, 2 pull-thrus, tenting, ltd groc. RECREATION: swim pool, river swim, river fishing, playground. Pets welcome. Rate in 2010 $28-42 per family. Member OPCA.

(NE) KOA-Gravenhurst Muskoka (Not Visited)—(Muskoka) *From N jct Hwy 169 & Hwy 11: Go 4km/2.5 mi N on Hwy 11, then 30m/100 yds. E on Doelake Rd. (exit 175), then 4km/2,5 mi N on Graven hurst Parkway (Muskoka Rd.1), then .4km/ 1/4 mi E on Reay Rd. Enter on L.* ◊◊◊FACILITIES: 160 sites, typical site width 35 ft, 40 full hkups, 118 W&E, 6 E, (15/30 amps), 13 no hkups, 38 pull-thrus, family camping, tenting, dump, laundry, groceries. ◊◊◊◊RECREATION: swim pool, boating, no motors, canoeing, lake/pond fishing, playground. Pets welcome. Open all yr. Facilities fully operational May 1 - Oct 31. Rate in 2010 $34-66 for 2 persons. Member OPCA. Phone: (705)687-2333. KOA discount.

GUELPH—I-3

See listings at Acton, Cambridge, Campbellville, Milton, Waterloo, Kitchener & Fergus

(N) GUELPH LAKE (Grand River Cons Auth)—*From north town limits: Go 1-1/2 km/1 mi N on Hwy 6, then 1-1/2 km/1 mi E on CR 6. Enter on L.* FACILITIES: 294 sites, 104 W&E, 190 no hkups, tenting, dump, ltd groc. RECREATION: lake swim, boating, no motors, canoeing, ramp, lake fishing, playground. Open May 1 - Thanksgiving. Phone: (519)824-5061.

HALIBURTON—G-4

Sleepy Hollow Resort (Not visited)—*From jct Hwy 121 & Hwy 118: Go 11 km/7 mi W on Hwy 118, then .8 km/1/2 mi N on Kennisis Lake Rd. (Follow signs). Enter on L.* ◊◊◊FACILITIES: 100 sites, typical site width 40 ft, 20 full hkups, 50 W&E, (15/30 amps), 30 no hkups, tenting, dump, ltd groc. ◊◊◊RECREATION: lake swim, boating, canoeing, ramp, dock, lake fishing, playground. Pets welcome. Open May 15 - mid Oct. Rate in 2010 $24.38-34.98 per family. Member OPCA. Phone: (705)754-2057.

HAMILTON—I-3

CONFEDERATION PARK—(Hamilton-Wentworth) *From jct Queen Elizabeth Way (Q.E.W.), Hwy 20: Go 1/2 km/3/10mi N on Hwy 20 then 1/2 km 3/10 mi W on Van Wagners Beach Rd. Enter on R.* FACILITIES: 100 sites, 51 W&E, (30 amps), 49 no hkups, 55 pull-thrus, tenting, dump, laundry. RECREATION: lake swim, boating, ramp, lake/pond fishing, playground. Pets welcome. Partial handicap access. Open May 1 - Oct 9. Phone: (905)578-1641.

(E) CONFEDERATION PARK (Hamilton Reg. Cons Auth.)—*From jct Queen Elizabeth Way & Hwy 20: Go 1/2 km/1/4 mi N on Hwy 20, then 1/2 km/1/4 mi W on Van Wagners Beach Rd. Enter on R.* FACILITIES: 100 sites, 50 W&E, (15/30 amps), 50 no hkups, 55 pull-thrus, tenting, dump, laundry. RECREATION: lake swim, boating, ramp, lake/pond fishing, playground. Open May 1 - Oct 9. Phone: (905)578-1644.

Flamboro Valley Camping Resort—(Flamborough) *From jct Hwy 401 & Hwy 6: Go 6 mi SE on Hwy 6, then 3-1/2 km/ 2.3 mi W on Hwy 97. Enter on L.* ◊◊◊◊FACILITIES: 206 sites, typical site width 40 ft, 136 full hkups, 40 W&E, (30/50 amps), 50 amps ($), 30 no hkups, 9 pull-thrus, family camping, tenting, dump, laundry, ltd groc. ◊◊◊◊RECREATION: swim pool, pond fishing, play equipment. Pets welcome. Partial handicap access. Age restrict may apply. Open May 1 - Oct 15. Big rigs welcome. Rate in 2010 $31-34 per family. Member OPCA. Phone: (905)659-5053. FCRV discount.

HANOVER—H-2

Saugeen Cedars Campground (Not visited)—(Grey) *From jct Hwy 6 & Hwy 4: Go 14.5 km/9 mi W on Hwy 4 to campground on N. Enter on R.* ◊◊◊FACILITIES: 105 sites, typical site width 40 ft, 90 W&E, (15 amps), 15 no hkups, 4 pull-thrus, tenting, dump, laundry. ◊◊◊RECREATION: river swim, canoeing, river fishing, playground. Pets welcome. Partial handicap access. Open Apr 25 - Oct 15. Rate in 2010 $27-32 per family. Member OPCA. Phone: (519)364-2069.

Saugeen Springs RV Park—(Grey) *From east city limits: Go 10.8 km/6-3/4 mi E on Hwy 4, then 4.8 km/3 mi N on Mulock Rd. Enter on L.* ◊◊◊FACILITIES: 171 sites, typical site width 50 ft, 52 full hkups, 104 W&E, (30/50 amps), 15 no hkups, tenting, dump, laundry, ltd groc. ◊◊◊◊RECREATION: river swim, boating, canoeing, river/pond fishing, playground. Pets welcome. Partial handicap access. Open Apr 1 - Dec 30. Facilities fully operational May 1 - Oct 15. Rate in 2010 $26-43 per family. Member OPCA. Phone: (519)369-5136.

HASTINGS—H-4

Birdsall Beach Park—*From jct Hwy 45 & Albert St (CR 2) (at west city limits): Go 9.6 km/6 mi W on CR 2, then 2.4 km/1-1/2 mi S & follow signs. Enter on R.* ◊◊FACILITIES: 214 sites, typical site width 50 ft, 210 full hkups, (15/30 amps), 4 no hkups, 2 pull-thrus, tenting, laundry, ltd groc. ◊◊◊RECREATION: swim pool, lake swim, boating, canoeing, ramp, dock, lake fishing, playground. Pets welcome. Open May 1 - Oct 15. Rate in 2010 $36-42 for 4 persons. Member OPCA. Phone: (866)350-9395.

HEARST—A-4

Cecile's Campsite (Not Visited) (RV SPACES)—(Thunder Bay) *From east jct Hwy 583 & Hwy 11: Go 2.4 km/1-1/2 mi E on Hwy 11. Enter on L.* FACILITIES: 55 sites, typical site width 30 ft, 30 full hkups, (30 amps), 25 no hkups, 18 pull-thrus, tenting, laundry. RECREATION: play equipment. Pets welcome. Open May 1 - Oct 30. Rate in 2010 $22-38 for 3 persons. Phone: (705)362-8118.

(NW) FUSHIMI LAKE PROVINCIAL PARK—*From town: Go 24 km/15 mi W on Hwy 11, then 12-3/4 km/8 mi N on Fushimi Forest access road.* FACILITIES: 46 sites, 39 E, (30 amps), 7 no hkups, 10 pull-thrus, tenting, laundry. RECREATION: lake swim, boating, canoeing, ramp, dock, lake fishing. Open mid May - late Sep. Phone: (705)362-4164.

HILTON BEACH—D-4

Busy Beaver Campground (Not Visited)—(Algoma) *From jct Hwy 17 & Hwy 548: Go 4.8 km/3 mi S on Hwy 548, then 9.6 km/6 mi E on Hwy 548 E, then 4.8 km/3 mi W on Hilton Rd. Enter on L.* FACILITIES: 62 sites, typical site width 30 ft, 24 full hkups, 38 W&E, (15 amps), 1 pull-thrus, tenting, dump, laundry. RECREATION: lake swim, boating, canoeing, ramp, dock, lake fishing, play equipment. Pets welcome. Open mid May - end of Sep. Rate in 2010 $35 per vehicle. Phone: (705)246-2636.

Hilton Beach Tourist Park (Not Visited)—(Algoma) *From jct Hwy 17 & Hwy 548: Go 4.8 km/3 mi S on Hwy 548, then go 9.6 km/6 mi E on Hwy 548E, then go 1 km/.6 mi E on Hilton Rd, then go .3 km/.2 mi N on Marks St, then go .2 km/.1 mi W on Bowker St. Enter at end.* FACILITIES: 100 sites, typical site width 35 ft, 100 full hkups, (15/30 amps), tenting, dump, laundry. RECREATION: lake swim, boating, canoeing, play equipment. Pets welcome. Open May 1 - mid Oct. Rate in 2010 $39 per family. Phone: (705)246-2586.

HONEY HARBOUR—G-3

GEORGIAN BAY ISLANDS NATIONAL PARK (Cedar Spring)—*Take water taxi or private boat to Beausoleil Island. Info available at mainland park office on Muskoka Rd #5 off Hwy 69.* FACILITIES: 87 sites, 87 no hkups, tenting. RECREATION: lake swim, boating, dock, lake fishing. Partial handicap access. Open all yr. Phone: (705)756-2415.

HORNEPAYNE—B-3

(S) NAGAGAMISIS PROVINCIAL PARK—*From town: Go 25-1/2 km/16 mi N on Hwy 631.* FACILITIES: 107 sites, 107 no hkups, 25 pull-thrus, tenting, dump, laundry. RECREATION: lake swim, boating, canoeing, ramp, dock, lake fishing. Partial handicap access. Open mid May - mid Oct. Phone: (807)868-2254.

HUNTSVILLE—G-3

(N) ARROWHEAD PROVINCIAL PARK—*From town: Go 4-3/4 km/3 mi N on Hwy 11.* FACILITIES: 378 sites, 115 E, (15/30 amps), 263 no hkups, tenting, dump, ltd groc. RECREATION: lake swim, no motors, canoeing, lake fishing. Partial handicap access. Open all yr. Phone: (705)789-5105.

(NW) Deerlake Park & Muskoka RV Centre (Not Visited)—(Muskoka) *From jct Hwy 60 & Hwy 11: Go 1.6 km/1 mi S on Hwy 11 (exit 221), then 1.6 km/1 mi N on Muskoka Rd 2, then .8 km/1/2 mi S on Hutchinson Beach Rd. Enter on L.* FACILITIES: 251 sites, typical site width 35 ft, 240 W&E, (15/30 amps), 11 no hkups, 2 pull-thrus, tenting, dump, laundry, ltd groc. RECREATION: swim pool, lake swim, boating, canoeing, ramp, dock, lake fishing, playground. Pets welcome. Open all yr. Facilities fully operational mid May - mid Oct. Rate in 2010 $40-45 per family. Member OPCA. Phone: (705) 789-3326.

Lagoon Tent & Trailer Park (Not visited)—(Muskoka) *From jct Hwy 60 & Hwy 11 (exit 226): Go 4 km/2-12/ mi N on Hwy 11 to exit 226, then follow signs. Enter on L.* ◊◊◊FACILITIES: 87 sites, typical site width 35 ft, 27 full hkups, 24 W&E, (20/30 amps), 36 no hkups, 29 pull-thrus, tenting, dump, laundry, ltd groc. ◊◊◊RECREATION: river swim, boating, no motors, canoeing, river fishing, play equipment. Pets welcome. Open May 15 - Oct 15. Rate in 2010 $28.50-46.50 per family. Member OPCA. Phone: (705)789-5011.

IGNACE—D-2

Davy Lake Campground & Resort—*From Hwy 17, turn S onto Davy Lake Rd. Follow road into campground.* FACILITIES: 62 sites, 30 full hkups, 15 W&E, (20/30 amps), 17 no hkups, 20 pull-thrus, cable TV, WiFi Internet central location, tenting, dump, groceries, ice, picnic tables, fire rings, grills, wood. RECREATION: rec hall, pavilion, boating, lake fishing, playground, horseshoes, hiking trails. Pets welcome. Partial handicap access. Open May 15 - Oct 15. Rate in 2010 $24-32 per vehicle. CCUSA 50% Discount. CCUSA reservations Recommended, CCUSA max stay 1 day, CCUSA disc. not avail M,T,W,Th, CCUSA disc. not avail F.

CAMP CLUB USA

Address: Ignace, ON P0T 1T0
Lat/Lon: 49.4100/-91.6500
Email: reservations@davylakecampground.com
Web: www.davylakecampground.com

(N) SANDBAR LAKE PROVINCIAL PARK—*From town: Go 1-1/2 km/1 mi E on Hwy 17, then 11-1/4 km/7 mi N on Hwy 599.* FACILITIES: 74 sites, 28 E, 46 no hkups, tenting, laundry, ltd groc. RECREATION: lake swim, boating, canoeing, ramp, dock, lake fishing, playground. Partial handicap access. Open May - Sep. Phone: (807)934-2233.

INGERSOLL—I-2

Casey's Park—(Oxford) *From jct Hwy 401 (exit 218) & Hwy 19: Go 5 km/3 mi S on Hwy 19. Enter on R.* ◊◊◊FACILITIES: 70 sites, typical site width 35 ft, 30 ft max RV length, 5 full hkups, 30 W&E, 12 E, (15 amps), 23 no hkups, tenting, dump, laundry, ltd groc. ◊◊◊RECREATION: pond fishing, playground. Pets welcome. Open May 1 - Oct 31. Rate in 2010 $22-33 per family. Phone: (519)485-3992.

Spring Lake R.V. Resort—(Oxford) *From jct Hwy 401 (exit 216) & Culloden Rd: Go 10.4 km/6-1/2 mi S on Culloden Rd, then .4 km/1/4 mi W on CR 27 (Prouse Rd). Enter on R.* ◊◊◊◊◊FACILITIES: 298 sites, typical site width 35 ft, accepts full hkup units only, 298 full hkups, (30/50 amps), 4 pull-thrus, laundry, groceries. ◊◊◊◊◊RECREATION: lake swim, boating, electric motors only, canoeing, lake fishing, playground. Pets welcome. No tents. Open May 1 - Oct 31. Rate in 2010 $38-44 per family. Member ARVC, OPCA. Phone: (877) 877-9265.

INGLESIDE—G-6

FARRAN PARK (Township Park)—*From west town limits: Go 4-1/4 km/2-3/4 mi W on Hwy 2. Enter on L.* FACILITIES: 169 sites, 50 E, (30/50 amps), 119 no hkups, tenting, dump. RECREATION: boating, canoeing, ramp, lake fishing, playground. Partial handicap access. Open May 15 - Labor Day. Phone: (613)537-8600.

UPPER CANADA MIGRATORY BIRD SANCTUARY (Parks of the St. Lawrence)—*From west town limits: Go 3-1/4 km/2 mi W on Hwy 2. Enter on L.* FACILITIES: 69 sites, 32 E, (15/30 amps), 37 no hkups, tenting, dump. RECREATION: river swim, boating, canoeing, ramp, river fishing. Pets welcome. Open May 15 - Oct 25. Phone: (613)537-2024.

IPPERWASH BEACH—I-1

Birch Pine Park (Not visited)—(Lambton) *From jct County Rd 21 & County Rd 7: Go 90m/100yds W on County Rd 7, then go 2.9/km/1-3/4 mi N on West Ipperwash Beach Rd. Enter on L.* ◊◊◊FACILITIES: 244 sites, typical site width 40 ft, 35 ft max RV length, 200 full hkups, 4 W&E, (15/30 amps), 40 no hkups, 3 pull-thrus, tenting, dump. ◊◊◊RECREATION: lake swim, lake/pond fishing, playground. Pets welcome. Age restrict may apply. Open May 1 - Mid Oct. Rate in 2010 $30-40 for 2 persons. Member OPCA. Phone: (519)786-4289.

Silver Birches Campground (Not Visited)—(Lambton) *From jct Hwy 81 & Hwy 21: Go 16.7 km/10-1/2 mi S on Hwy 21, then 1.6 km/1 mi W on Army Camp Rd. Enter on L.* FACILITIES: 175 sites, typical site width 40 ft, 35 ft max RV length, 143 full hkups, 13 W&E, (15/30 amps), 19 no hkups, tenting, dump, laundry. RECREATION: swim pool, playground. Pets welcome. Partial handicap access. Open all yr. Facilities fully operational May 1 - Oct 31. Rate in 2010 $25-28 per family. Member OPCA.

IRON BRIDGE—D-4

Delmar Campground (Not visited)—(Algoma) *From east city limits: Go 6.4 km/4 mi W on Hwy 17. Enter on L.* FACILITIES: 35 sites, typical site width 45 ft, 4 full hkups, 17 W&E, (15 amps), 14 no hkups, 6 pull-thrus, tenting, dump, laundry, ltd groc. RECREATION: swim pool, play equipment. Pets welcome. Open mid Apr - mid Sep. Rate in 2010 $15-25 for 2 persons. Phone: (705)843-2098.

Viking Tent & Trailer Park (Not Visited)—*From west city limits: Go 2.4 km/1-1/2 mi W on Hwy 17. Enter on L.* ◊◊◊FACILITIES: 50 sites, typical site width 40 ft, 13 full hkups, 10 W&E, 8 E, (15/30 amps), 19 no hkups, 5 pull-thrus, tenting, dump, laundry, ltd groc. ◊RECREATION: swim pool. Pets welcome. Open May 1 - Oct 15. Rate in 2010 $25-27 per vehicle. Phone: (705)843-2834.

IROQUOIS—G-6

IROQUOIS MUNICIPAL PARK—*From jct Hwy 401 & Hwy 2 (Carman Rd): Go 3/4 km/1/2 mi S on Hwy 2.* FACILITIES: 122 sites, 2 W&E, 60 E, 60 no hkups, tenting, dump. RECREATION: river swim, boating, canoeing, ramp, dock, river fishing, playground. Open May 24 - Oct. Phone: (613)652-2506.

IROQUOIS FALLS—B-6

Cameron's Beach Trailer Park (Not Visited)—(Cochrane) *From jct Hwy 11 & Jacobs Hill Rd (formerly Hwy 578): Go 61 meters/200 feet E on Jacobs Hill Rd, then 1.6 km/1 mi N on Big Nellie Lake Rd. Enter on R.* FACILITIES: 120 sites, typical site width 40 ft, 60 full

Cameron's Beach Trailer Park (Not Visited)—Continued on next page

IROQUOIS FALLS—Continued
Cameron's Beach Trailer Park (Not Visited)—Continued

hkups, 60 W&E, (20/30 amps), 10 pull-thrus, tenting, dump, laundry, ltd groc. RECREATION: lake swim, boating, canoeing, dock, lake fishing, playground. Pets welcome. Open mid May - mid Sep. Rate in 2010 $30 per family. Member OPCA. Phone: (705)232-4905.

KETTLE LAKES PROVINCIAL PARK—*From town: Go 19-1/4 km/12 mi W on Hwy 67.* FACILITIES: 137 sites, 93 E, (15/30 amps), 44 no hkups, 41 pull-thrus, tenting, dump, laundry. RECREATION: lake swim, boating, no motors, canoeing, lake fishing, playground. Partial handicap access. Open mid May - early Oct. Phone: (705)363-3511.

KAGAWONG—F-1

Norm's Tent & Trailer Park (Not visited)—(Manitoulin) *From jct Hwy 540 & Lakeshore Rd: Go 1.6 km/1 mi S on Lakeshore Rd. Enter on R.* ◇◇◇FACILITIES: 60 sites, typical site width 30 ft, 40 W&E, (15/30 amps), 20 no hkups, 10 pull-thrus, tenting, dump, laundry, ltd groc. ◇◇◇RECREATION: lake swim, boating, canoeing, lake fishing, play equipment. Pets welcome. Partial handicap access. Open May 10 - Oct 10. Rate in 2010 $26-32 per family. Phone: (705)282-2827.

KAKABEKA FALLS—B-1

(W) KAKABEKA FALLS PROVINCIAL PARK—*In town on Hwy-17.* FACILITIES: 169 sites, 90 E, 79 no hkups, tenting, dump, laundry, ltd groc. RECREATION: canoeing, playground. Open mid May - early Oct. Phone: (807)473-9231.

KAPUSKASING—B-5

RENE BRUNELLE PROVINCIAL PARK—*From town: Go 20-3/4 km/13 mi E on Hwy 11, then 9-1/2 km/6 mi N on Hwy 581.* FACILITIES: 88 sites, 60 E, (15/30 amps), 28 no hkups, 20 pull-thrus, tenting, dump, laundry. RECREATION: boating, canoeing, ramp, dock, playground. Partial handicap access. Open mid May - late Sep. Phone: (705)367-2692.

KATRINE—F-3

Almaguin Parklands Campground (Not visited)—(ParrySound) *From jct Hwy 11 & 3 Mile Lake Rd: Go .4 km/1/4 mi E on 3 Mile Lake Rd, then 2 km/1-1/4 mi S on Owl Lake Rd. Enter on L.* ◇◇FACILITIES: 170 sites, typical site width 35 ft, 75 full hkups, 35 W&E, (15/30 amps), 60 no hkups, 20 pull-thrus, family camping, tenting, dump, laundry, ltd groc. ◇◇◇RECREATION: swim pool, lake swim, boating, no motors, canoeing, dock, lake fishing, playground. Pets welcome. Open Mid May - Mid Oct. Rate in 2010 $30-40 per family. Phone: (705)382-3802.

KEARNEY—F-3

Granite Ridge Campground (Not Visited)—(Parry Sound) *From jct Hwy 11 & Hwy 518 E: Go 14 km/8.6 mi E on Hwy 518. Enter on L.* FACILITIES: 141 sites, typical site width 40 ft, 16 full hkups, 45 W&E, (15/30 amps), 80 no hkups, 60 pull-thrus, tenting, dump. RECREATION: lake swim, boating, canoeing, ramp, dock, lake/river fishing, playground. Pets welcome. Open all yr. Facilities fully operational May 15 - Oct 15. Rate in 2010 $20-40 per family. Member OPCA. Phone: (705)636-1474.

KEENE—H-4

HOPE MILL (Otonabee Region Cons Auth)—*From town: Go 3-1/4 km/2 mi N on CR 34.* FACILITIES: 65 sites, 20 E, (15/30 amps), 45 no hkups, tenting. RECREATION: river swim, canoeing, river/pond fishing. Open Jun 27 - Sep 4. Phone: (705) 750-0545.

KEMPTVILLE—G-6

(N) RIDEAU RIVER PROVINCIAL PARK—*From town: Go 6-1/2 km/4 mi N on Hwy 16.* FACILITIES: 184 sites, typical site width 35 ft, 46 E, (15 amps), 138 no hkups, 14 pull-thrus, tenting, dump, ltd groc. RECREATION: boating, canoeing, ramp, dock, river fishing, playground. Partial handicap access. Open May - Sept. Phone: (613)258-2740.

Wildwood Campground—*From jct Hwy 416 & CR 20 (exit 24): Go 1 km/1/2 mi E on CR 20, then 4.4 km/2-1/4 mi S on CR 44. Enter on L.* ◇◇◇FACILITIES: 83 sites, typical site width 51 ft, 24 full hkups, 59 W&E, (15/20/30/50 amps), 50 amps ($), 10 pull-thrus, family camping, tenting, dump, laundry. ◇◇◇RECREATION: swim pool, playground. Pets welcome. Partial handicap access. Open May 15 - Oct 15. Big rigs welcome. Rate in 2010 $30-35 per family. Member OPCA.

Phone: (800)391-9616
Address: 9197 County Rd 44, Oxford Station, ON K0G 1T0
Lat/Lon: 44.91738/-75.55442
Email: info@wildwoodontario.com
Web: www.wildwoodontario.com

KENORA—D-1

See listings at Ear Falls, Nestor Falls, Perrault Falls, Red Lake, Sioux Narrows & Vermilion Bay

Anicinabe RV Park & Campground (Not Visited)—(Kenora) *From jct Hwy 17 E or W & Miikana Way: Go 1 km/6/10 mi S on Miikana Way. Enter at end.* FACILITIES: 77 sites, 26 full hkups, 30 W&E, (15/30 amps), 21 no hkups, tenting, dump, laundry, ltd groc. RECREATION: lake swim, boating, canoeing, ramp, dock, lake fishing, playground. Pets welcome. Open May 1 - mid Oct. Rate in 2010 $22.50-34 per vehicle. Member OPCA. Phone: (877)318-2267.

Longbow Lake Camp & Trailer Park (Not Visited)—(Kenora) *From jct Hwy 17A & Hwy 17: Go 1 km/1/2 mi W on Hwy 17. Enter on L.* FACILITIES: 99 sites, typical site width 30 ft, 83 full hkups, 16 W&E, (30 amps), 5 pull-thrus, tenting, dump, laundry. RECREATION: lake swim, boating, canoeing, ramp, dock, lake fishing, playground. Pets welcome. Open May 15 - Oct 1. Rate in 2010 $34 for 2 persons. Phone: (807)548-5444.

(E) RUSHING RIVER PROVINCIAL PARK—*From town: Go 25-1/2 km/16 mi E on Hwy 17, then 6-1/2 km/4 mi S on Hwy 71.* FACILITIES: 217 sites, 75 E, (15/30 amps), 142 no hkups, tenting, dump, laundry, ltd groc. RECREATION: lake swim, boating, canoeing, ramp, dock, lake fishing, playground. Partial handicap access. Open mid May - mid Sep. Phone: (807)548-4351.

KILLARNEY—F-2

(NE) KILLARNEY PROVINCIAL PARK—*From jct Hwy 69 & Hwy 637: Go 61-1/2 km/38-1/2 mi W on Hwy 637.* FACILITIES: 126 sites, 126 no hkups, 11 pull-thrus, tenting, laundry. RECREATION: lake swim, boating, canoeing, ramp, lake fishing. Open May - Sep. Phone: (705)287-2900.

KINCARDINE—H-2

Aintree Trailer Park—(Bruce) *From jct Hwy 9 & Hwy 21: Go 4.6 km/2 mi S on Hwy 21, then 2.0 km/1-1/2 mi W on Huron Con 12. Enter on L.* ◇◇◇FACILITIES: 171 sites, typical site width 30 ft, 35 ft max RV length, 159 full hkups, 12 W&E, (30 amps), 6 pull-thrus, tenting, dump, laundry. ◇◇◇◇RECREATION: lake swim, playground. Pets welcome. Open mid Apr - mid Oct. Rate in 2010 $30.50-35 per family. Member OPCA. Phone: (519)396-8533.

KINCARDINE—Continued

BLUEWATER TRAILER PARK (City Park)—(Bruce) *From jct Hwy 9 & Hwy 21: Go 1/2 km/1/4 mi S on Hwy 21, then 1/2 km/1/4 mi W on Durham St.* FACILITIES: 44 sites, 32 ft max RV length, 44 full hkups, (30 amps), tenting, dump, laundry. RECREATION: lake swim, boating, canoeing, ramp, dock, lake fishing, playground. Open May 11 - Oct 14. Phone: (519)396-8698.

FISHERMAN'S COVE TENT & TRAILER PARK—(Bruce) *From jct Hwy 21 & Hwy 9: Go 18 km/11-1/4 mi E on Hwy 9,then 1.6 km/1 mi S on Bruce Rd 1, then 1.6 km/1 mi E on Southline Ave. Enter at end.*

WELCOME

◇◇◇◇◇FACILITIES: 570 sites, typical site width 40 ft, 570 full hkups, (15/30/50 amps), many extd stay sites, 10 pull-thrus, WiFi Instant Internet at site ($), WiFi Internet central location, family camping, tenting, RV's/park model rentals, cabins, RV storage, shower$, dump, non-guest dump $, laundry, RV supplies, LP gas by weight, ice, picnic tables, fire rings, wood, controlled access.

◇◇◇◇◇RECREATION: rec hall, rec room/area, coin games, 2 swim pools, lake swim, hot tub, boating, 10 hp limit, canoeing, kayaking, ramp, dock, rowboat/3 canoe/kayak/4 pedal boat/6 motorboat rentals, lake fishing, fishing supplies, golf nearby, bsktball, 3 bike rentals, playground, shuffleboard court shuffleboard court, activities, horseshoes, hiking trails, v-ball. Rec open to public.

Pets welcome. Partial handicap access. Open May 15 - Oct 1. Clubs welcome. Green Friendly. Rate in 2010 $46-56 for 2 persons. MC/VISA/Debit. Member OPCA.

Text 108022 to (440)725-8687 to see our Visual Tour.

Phone: (519)395-2757
Address: 13 Southline Ave RR 4, Kincardine, ON N2Z 2X5
Lat/Lon: 44.04457/-81.24874
Email: info@fishermanscove.com
Web: www.fishermanscove.com

SEE AD THIS PAGE

Green Acres Campground & RV Park—(Bruce) *From jct Hwy 9 & Hwy 21: Go 4.6 km/2 mi S on Hwy 21,then .4 km/1/4 mi W on Huron Conc. 12 Rd. Enter on R.* ◇◇◇FACILITIES: 192 sites, typical site width 40 ft, 179 full hkups, 13 W&E, (15/30 amps), 16 pull-thrus, tenting, dump, laundry. ◇◇◇◇RECREATION: swim pool, playground. Pets welcome. Open May 1 - mid Oct. Rate in 2010 $30-37 per family. Member OPCA. Phone: (519)395-2808.

KINGSTON—H-5

See listings at Sydenham

KOA-Kingston—*From jct Hwy 401 (exit 611) & Hwy 38: Go .8 km/1/2 mi N on Hwy 38, then .8 km/1/2 mi E on Cordukes Rd. Enter on L.* ◇◇◇◇FACILITIES: 112 sites, typical site width 40 ft, 112 W&E, (30/50

KOA-Kingston—Continued on next page

KINGSTON—Continued
KOA-Kingston—Continued

amps), 44 pull-thrus, tenting, dump, laundry, groceries. ◊◊◊◊RECREATION: swim pool, playground. Pets welcome. Partial handicap access. Open May 1 - Oct 15. Big rigs welcome. Rate in 2010 $47-78 for 2 persons. Member OPCA. Phone: (800)562-9178. KOA discount.

RIDEAU ACRES CAMPGROUND—*From jct Hwy 401 (exit 623) & Hwy 15: Go 1.6 km/1 mi N on Hwy 15, then .4 km/1/4 mi W on Cunningham Rd. Enter at end.*

WELCOME

◊◊◊FACILITIES: 365 sites, typical site width 50 ft, 173 full hkups, 142 W&E, (15/30/50 amps), 50 amps ($), 50 no hkups, some extd stay sites, 71 pull-thrus, WiFi Instant Internet at site ($), WiFi Internet central location, family camping, tenting, RV's/park model rentals, RV storage, dump, portable dump, laundry, groceries, RV supplies, LP gas by weight/by meter, ice, picnic tables, fire rings, wood, controlled access.

CAMPCLUB USA

◊◊◊◊◊RECREATION: rec hall, rec room/area, coin games, swim pool, lake swim, boating, canoeing, kayaking, ramp, dock, pontoon/9 rowboat/8 canoe/4 kayak/3 pedal boat rentals, lake fishing, fishing supplies, mini-golf, ($), golf nearby, bsktball, 14 bike rentals, playground, activities, horseshoes, sports field, hiking trails, v-ball. Rec open to public.

Pets welcome. Partial handicap access. Open all yr. Facilities fully operational Apr 15 - Nov 15. Big rigs welcome. Clubs welcome. Rate in 2010 $29-43 per family. MC/VISA/Debit. Member ARVC, OPCA. FCRV discount. CCUSA 50% Discount. CCUSA reservations Accepted, CCUSA max stay 5 days. Discount not available holiday weekends or in months of Jul & Aug.

Phone: (800)958-5830
Address: 1014 Cunningham Rd, Kingston, ON K7L 4V3
Lat/Lon: 44.21889/-76.01423
Email: info@rideauacres.com
Web: www.rideauacres.com

SEE AD THIS PAGE

KINTAIL—H-2

MacKenzie's Trailer Park (Not Visited)—(Bruce) *From N town limits (Hwy 20) and MacKenzie Park Rd: Go 2 km/1-1/4 mi W on MacKenzie Park Rd. Enter at end.* FACILITIES: 125 sites, typical site width 35 ft, 35 ft max RV length, 91 full hkups, 11 W&E, (15/30 amps), 23 no hkups, tenting, dump. RECREATION: lake swim, canoeing, playground. Pets welcome. Open May 9 - Oct 13. Rate in 2010 $22-30 per family. Member OPCA. Phone: (519)529-7536.

KIRKLAND LAKE—C-6

(E) ESKER LAKES PROVINCIAL PARK—*From town: Go 20-3/4 km/13 mi NE on Provincial Rd.* FACILITIES: 103 sites, 64 E, (15 amps), 39 no hkups, tenting, dump, laundry, ltd groc. RECREATION: lake swim, boating, no motors, canoeing, ramp, dock, lake fishing, playground. Partial handicap access. Open mid May - mid Sep. Phone: (705)568-7677.

KITCHENER—I-2

See listings at Cambridge & Waterloo.

Bingemans Camping Resort—(Waterloo) *From Exit 278B, Hwy 401: Go 2.5 km/1-1/2 mi N on King St, then 5.9 km/3-3/4 mi W on Hwy 8, then 2.9 km/1-3/4 mi N on Hwy 85, then 0.6 km/1/2 mi E on Wellington St, then 1.6 km/1 mi on Shirley Ave. Enter on L.* ◊◊◊FACILITIES: 450 sites, typical site width 35 ft, 163 full hkups, 214 W&E, (30/50 amps), 73 no hkups, 14 pull-thrus, family camping, tenting, dump, laundry, ltd groc. ◊◊◊◊◊RECREATION: 2 swim pools, boating, no motors, canoeing, ramp, river fishing, playground. Pets welcome. Open all yr. Facilities fully operational Mid May - Oct 31. Big rigs welcome. Rate in 2010 $40-55 per family. Member ARVC, OPCA.

KITCHENER—Continued
Bingemans Camping Resort—Continued

Phone: 1(800)565-4631
Address: 425 Bingemans Centre Dr, Kitchener, ON N2B 3X7
Lat/Lon: 43.28424/-80.26665
Email: camping@bingemans.com
Web: www.bingemans.com/camping

LAKE ST. PETER—G-4

LAKE SAINT PETER PROVINCIAL PARK—*From town: Go 1-1/2 km/1 mi N on Hwy 127, then 1-1/2 km/1 mi E on North Rd.* FACILITIES: 65 sites, 65 no hkups, tenting, dump, laundry, ltd groc. RECREATION: boating, canoeing, ramp, dock, lake fishing. Open mid May - Oct. Phone: (613)338-5312.

LAKEFIELD—H-4

Lakefield Campground—*From jct CR 33 & CR 20 (Bridge St): Go 1/2 km W on CR 29, then 1/4 km N on Clement St, then follow signs on Hague St. Enter at end.* ◊◊FACILITIES: 117 sites, 53 full hkups, 42 W&E, 12 E, (30 amps), 10 no hkups, tenting, dump. ◊◊◊RECREATION: river swim, boating, ramp, dock, river fishing, playground. Pets welcome. Open all yr. Facilities fully operational May 1 - Oct 1. Rate in 2010 $33-38 Member OPCA. Phone: (705)652-8610.

(N) LAKEFIELD PARK & CAMPGROUND (City Park)—*From jct Hwy 7 & Hwy 28: Go 12-3/4 km/8 mi N on Hwy 28. Enter at end.* FACILITIES: 117 sites, typical site width 40 ft, 53 full hkups, 42 W&E, 12 E, (15/30 amps), 10 no hkups, 40 pull-thrus, tenting, dump, ltd groc. RECREATION: lake/river swim, boating, canoeing, ramp, lake/river fishing, playground. Pets welcome. Partial handicap access. Open May 2 - Oct 1. Phone: (705)652-8610.

LAKESIDE—I-2

Happy Hills Family Campground—(Oxford) *From jct CR 119 & CR 92: Go 6.1 km/3-3/4 mi E on CR 92. Enter on R.* ◊◊◊FACILITIES: 450 sites, 435 full hkups, (30 amps), 15 no hkups, tenting, dump, laundry, ltd groc. ◊◊◊◊◊RECREATION: swim pool, playground. Pets welcome. Open May 1 - Oct 1. Rate in 2010 $42-44 per vehicle. Member OPCA. Phone: (519) 475-4471.

Lakeside Resort—(Oxford) *From jct CR 119 & CR 92: Go 2.7 km/1-3/4 mi E to Brock St (Sunova Cres), then 1.2 km/3/4 mi S on Brock St. Enter on L.* ◊◊◊FACILITIES: 130 sites, typical site width 35 ft, 67 full hkups, 63 W&E, (15/30/50 amps), 4 pull-thrus, tenting, dump, laundry. ◊◊◊◊RECREATION: swim pool, lake swim, boating, canoeing, lake fishing, playground. Pets welcome. Partial handicap access. Open May 1 - Mid Oct. Rate in 2010 $35-39 per family. Member OPCA. Phone: (519)349-2820.

LANARK—G-5

Mal's Camping (Not visited)—*At south edge of town on Hwy 511: Go 2.4 km/1-1/2 mi E on CR 15. Enter on R.* ◊◊◊FACILITIES: 155 sites, typical site width 35 ft, 145 W&E, (15/30/50 amps), 10 no hkups, 20 pull-thrus, tenting, dump, laundry, full svc store. ◊◊◊◊RECREATION: river swim, boating, canoeing, ramp, dock, river fishing, playground. Open Mid May - Sep 30. Rate in 2010 $27-30 per family. Member OPCA. Phone: (613)259-5636.

LANCASTER—G-6

(E) GLENGARRY PARK (Parks of the St. Lawrence)—*From jct Hwy 401 (exit 814) & Hwy 2: Go 3-1/4 km/2 mi E on S service road. Enter on R.* FACILITIES: 169 sites, 17 W&E, 50 E, (15/30 amps), 102 no hkups, tenting, dump. RECREATION: lake swim, boating, canoeing, ramp, lake fishing, playground. Open May 15 - Sep 7. Phone: (613)347-2595.

Lancaster Park Outdoor Resort—*From jct Hwy 401 (exit 814) & Hwy 2: Go 3.2 km/2 mi E on S Service Rd. Enter on R.* ◊◊◊FACILITIES: 423 sites, typical site width 40 ft, 96 full hkups, 280 W&E, (15 amps), 47 no hkups, 15 pull-thrus, tenting, dump, laundry, ltd groc. ◊◊◊◊RECREATION: lake swim, boating, canoeing, ramp, dock, lake fishing, playground. Pets welcome, breed restrict. Open May 15 - Sep 15. Rate in 2010 $24-35 per family. Member OPCA. Phone: (613)347-3452.

LANGTON—I-2

(SW) DEER CREEK AREA (Long Point Region Cons Auth.)—*From town: Go 4-3/4 km/3 mi S on Hwy 59, then 1/2 km/1/4 mi W on Regional Rd 45.* FACILITIES: 40 sites, 7 W&E, (15/30 amps), 33 no hkups, tenting, dump. RECREATION: lake swim, boating, no motors, canoeing, ramp, dock, lake fishing, playground. Partial handicap access. Open May 1 - Oct 31. Phone: (519)875-2874.

LEAMINGTON—J-1

Leisure Lake Campground (Essex) *From Hwy 401 (exit 40): Go 16 km/9-1/2 mi S on CR 31 (Albuna Townline Rd). Enter on L.* ◊◊◊FACILITIES: 400 sites, typical site width 35 ft, 329 full hkups, 50 W&E, (20/30/50 amps), 21 no hkups, 5 pull-thrus, tenting, dump, laundry, groceries. ◊◊◊◊◊RECREATION: lake swim, boating, no motors, lake fishing, playground. Pets welcome. Open mid Apr - Oct 9. Facilities fully operational May 1 - mid Oct. Rate in 2010 $32-57 per family. Member ARVC, OPCA. Phone: (519)326-1255.

STURGEON WOODS CAMPGROUND & MARINA—(Essex) *From jct Hwy 3 & Hwy 77: Go 1.6 km/1 mi S on CR 20, then 3.2 km/2 mi SE on Essex CR 33 to Point Pelee, look for signs. Enter on L.*

WELCOME

◊◊◊◊◊FACILITIES: 318 sites, typical site width 35 ft, 280 full hkups, 38 W&E, (30/50 amps), many extd stay sites, 20 pull-thrus, heater not allowed, WiFi Instant Internet at site ($), WiFi Internet central location, tenting, cabins, RV storage, dump, laundry, ltd groc, LP gas by weight, ice, picnic tables, fire rings, wood, controlled access.

◊◊◊◊◊RECREATION: rec hall, rec room/area, pavilion, coin games, 2 swim pools, wading pool, lake swim, boating, canoeing, kayaking, ramp, dock, lake fishing, fishing supplies, golf nearby, bsktball, playground, shuffleboard court 3 shuffleboard courts, activities, horseshoes, sports field, hiking trails, v-ball. Rec open to public.

Pets welcome. Partial handicap access. Open Apr 15 - Oct 15. Clubs welcome. Rate in 2010 $36-41 per family. MC/VISA/Debit. Member OPCA.

Phone: (877)521-4990
Address: 1129 Concession C, Leamington, ON N8H 3V4
Lat/Lon: 42.00436/-82.34007
Web: www.sturgeonwoods.com

SEE AD THIS PAGE

✲ **STURGEON WOODS RV SALES & SERVICES**—*From jct Hwy 3 & Hwy 77: Go 1.6 km/1 mi S on CR 20, then 3.2 km/2 mi SE on Essex CR 33 to Point Pelee, look for signs. Enter on L.*

WELCOME

SALES: travel trailers, park models, 5th wheels, toy hauler, pre-owned unit sales. SERVICES: full-time mech, RV appliance repair, mobile RV svc. Open all yr.

Phone: (877)521-4990
Address: 1129 Concession C, Leamington, ON N8H 3V4
Lat/Lon: 42.00436/-82.34007
Web: www.sturgeonwoodsrv.com

SEE AD THIS PAGE

LINDSAY—H-4

Double "M" RV Resort & Campground—*From south jct Hwy 35 & Hwy 7: Go 1.2 km/3/4 mi W on Hwy 7, then .4 km/1/4 mi S on Little Britain Rd (4). Enter at end.* ◊◊◊FACILITIES: 199 sites, typical site width 40 ft, 169 full hkups, 20 W&E, (30/50 amps), 10 no hkups, tenting, dump, laundry, ltd groc. ◊◊◊◊RECREATION: river swim, boating, ramp, dock, river fishing, playground. Pets welcome. Open Apr 1 - Nov 30. Facilities fully operational May 15 - Oct 15. Rate in 2010 $33-40 per family. Member OPCA. Phone: (705)324-9317.

Riverwood Park (Not visited)—*From jct Hwy 7 & Hwy 35: Go .4 km/1/4 mi S on Hwy 35, then .8 km/1/2 mi W on Riverwood Rd. Enter on R.* ◊◊◊FACILITIES: 296 sites, typical site width 40 ft, 286 full hkups, 10 W&E, (15/30 amps), 7 pull-thrus, tenting, RV storage,

Riverwood Park (Not visited)—Continued on next page

LINDSAY—Continued
Riverwood Park (Not visited)—Continued

dump, laundry, ltd groc, RV supplies, ice, picnic tables, fire rings, wood. ◆◆◆RECREATION: rec hall, pavilion, swim pool, wading pool, river swim, boating, ramp, dock, river/stream fishing, fishing supplies, bsktball, playground, activities, horseshoes, hiking trails, v-ball. Pets welcome. Open May 20 - Oct 15. Rate in 2010 $32.39 per family. MC/VISA/Debit. Member OPCA. CCUSA 50% Discount. CCUSA reservations Recommended, CCUSA max stay Unlimited, CCUSA disc. not avail S, CCUSA disc. not avail F,Sa, CCUSA disc. not avail holidays.

Phone: (705)324-1655
Lat/Lon: 44.31938/-78.72337
Email: camping@riverwoodpark.net
Web: www.riverwoodpark.ca

LION'S HEAD—G-2

LION'S HEAD BEACH PARK—(Bruce) *From jct Hwy 6 & CR 9 at Ferndale: Go 4km/2 1/2 mi E on CR9A, then .4 km/ 1/4 mi N on Main St. Then 1 block E on Webster St. Enter on R.* FACILITIES: 34 sites, 34 W&E, (15 amps), tenting, dump. RECREATION: lake swim, boating, canoeing, ramp, dock, lake fishing, playground. Open May 15 - Thanksgiving. Phone: (519)793-3522.

LONDON—I-2

See listings at Dutton, Glencoe, Ingersoll, Lakeside, St. Thomas, Strathroy & Thorndale

(N) FANSHAWE CONSERVATION AREA (Upper Thames River Cons Auth)—*From jct Hwy 401 & Hwy 100: Go N on Hwy 100, then W on Oxford St, then 2 km/1-1/4 mi N on Clarke Sideroad.* FACILITIES: 650 sites, typical site width 30 ft, 420 W&E, (15/30 amps), 230 no hkups, 36 pull-thrus, tenting, dump, laundry, ltd groc. RECREATION: swim pool, lake swim, boating, 10 hp limit, canoeing, ramp, dock, lake fishing, playground. Pets welcome. Open all yr. Phone: (519)451-2800.

London KOA Campground—(Middlesex) *From jct Hwy 401 (exit 195) & Hwy 74: Go .4 km/1/4 mi E on Cromarty Dr. Enter on L.* ◆◆◆FACILITIES: 120 sites, typical site width 35 ft, 24 full hkups, 78 W&E, (15/30 amps), 18 no hkups, 55 pull-thrus, family camping, tenting, dump, laundry, groceries. ◆◆◆◆RECREATION: swim pool, playground. Pets welcome. Open May 1 - Oct 19. Rate in 2010 $30-54 for 2 persons. Member OPCA. Phone: (800)KOA-7398. KOA discount.

LONG SAULT—G-6

MCLAREN CAMPSITE (Parks of the St. Lawrence)—*From east town limits: Go 3/4 km/1/2 mi E on Hwy 2, then 3/4 km/1/2 mi E on Long Sault Pkwy. Enter at end.* FACILITIES: 141 sites, 15 W&E, 50 E, 76 no hkups, tenting, dump. RECREATION: lake swim, boating, canoeing, ramp, lake fishing, playground. Open May 16 - Oct 13. Phone: (800)437-2233.

(S) MILLE ROCHES CAMPSITE (Parks of the St. Lawrence)—*From east town limits: Go 3/4 km/1/2 mi E on Hwy 2, then 8 km/5 mi E on Long Sault Pkwy. Enter at end.* FACILITIES: 215 sites, 61 full hkups, 45 E, (15/30 amps), 109 no hkups, tenting, dump. RECREATION: lake swim, boating, canoeing, ramp, lake fishing, playground. Open Jun 11 - Sep 9. Phone: (800)437-2233.

(SW) WOODLANDS CAMPSITE (Parks of the St. Lawrence)—*From east town limits: Go 3/4 km/1/2 mi E on Hwy 2, then 1-1/2 km/1 mi E on Long Sault Pkwy. Enter at end.* FACILITIES: 172 sites, 17 W&E, 45 E, 110 no hkups, tenting, dump. RECREATION: lake swim, boating, canoeing, ramp, lake fishing, playground. Open Jun 18 - Sep 4. Phone: (800)437-2233.

LYNDHURST—G-5

CHARLESTON LAKE PROVINCIAL PARK—*From town: Go 11-1/4 km/7 mi S on CR 3 (outlet).* FACILITIES: 238 sites, 86 E, (15/30 amps), 152 no hkups, tenting, dump, laundry. RECREATION: lake swim, boating, canoeing, ramp, dock, lake fishing, playground. Partial handicap access. Open May 12 - Oct 29. Phone: (613)659-2065.

Singleton Lake Family Campground—*From west city limits at jct CR 33 & CR 3: Go 3.2 km/2 mi S on CR 3. Enter on L.* ◆◆◆FACILITIES: 106 sites, typical site width 40 ft, 100 W&E, (15/30 amps), 6 no hkups, 5 pull-thrus, tenting, dump, laundry, groceries. ◆◆◆RECREATION: lake swim, boating, canoeing, ramp, dock, lake fishing, playground. Pets welcome. Open May 7 - Oct 1. Rate in 2010 $27-32 per family. Member OPCA. Phone: (613)387-3230.

Wilson's Tent & Trailer Park—*From jct Hwy 15 & CR 33 (Lyndhurst Rd): Go 5-1/2 mi N on CR-33. Enter on R.* ◆◆◆FACILITIES: 128 sites, 110 W&E, (15/20 amps), 18 no hkups, tenting, dump, laundry, ltd groc. ◆◆◆RECREATION: lake swim, ramp, dock, lake/pond fishing, playground. Pets welcome. Open May 1 - Sep 30. Rate in 2010 $18-23 per family. Phone: (613)928-2557.

MABERLY—G-5

McGowan Lake Campground—*From jct RR 36 & Hwy 7: Go 1-3/4 mi E on Hwy 7. Enter on R.* ◆◆◆FACILITIES: 226 sites, 201 full hkups, (15/30 amps), 25 no hkups, tenting, dump, laundry, groceries. ◆◆◆◆RECREATION: lake swim, boating, canoeing, ramp, dock, lake fishing, playground. Pets welcome. Open May 1 - Oct 1. Rate in 2010 $25-34 per family. Member OPCA. Phone: (613)268-2234.

MABERLY—Continued

(W) SILVER LAKE PROVINCIAL PARK—*In town on Hwy-7.* FACILITIES: 148 sites, typical site width 20 ft, 26 E, (20 amps), 122 no hkups, 18 pull-thrus, tenting, dump, ltd groc. RECREATION: lake swim, boating, canoeing, ramp, dock, lake fishing, playground. Partial handicap access. Open mid May - early Sep. Phone: (613)268-2000.

MACKEY—F-4

Lakeview Trailer Park (Not Visited)—*From west city limits: Go 1.6 km/1 mi W on Hwy 17. Enter on R.* ◆◆◆FACILITIES: 54 sites, typical site width 40 ft, 30 full hkups, 24 W&E, (15/30 amps), 8 pull-thrus, tenting, dump. ◆◆◆RECREATION: lake swim, boating, canoeing, ramp, dock, river fishing. Pets welcome. Open Mid May - Mid Oct. Rate in 2010 $28-32 per family. Member OPCA. Phone: (613)586-2380.

MADAWASKA—F-4

(N) All Star Resort Tent & Trailer Park (Not visited)—(Nipissing) *From jct Hwy 523 & Hwy 60: Go .4 km/1/4 mi N on Major Lake Rd. Enter on R.* ◆◆◆FACILITIES: 72 sites, typical site width 60 ft, 35 ft max RV length, 57 W&E, (15/30 amps), 15 no hkups, 10 pull-thrus, tenting, dump. ◆◆◆RECREATION: lake swim, boating, canoeing, ramp, dock, lake fishing, play equipment. Open all yr. Facilities fully operational mid May - mid Oct. Rate in 2010 $31-38 per family. Phone: (613)637-5592.

(S) Red Deer Lodge & Campground (Not Visited)—*From jct Hwy 60 & Hwy 523: Go 2 km/1.2 mi S on Hwy 523. Enter on R.* FACILITIES: 40 sites, 12 W&E, (15 amps), 28 no hkups, 4 pull-thrus, tenting, dump. RECREATION: river swim, boating, canoeing, river fishing. Pets welcome. Open May 1 - Nov 1. Rate in 2010 $35-45 per family. Member OPCA. Phone: (613)637-5215.

Riverland Lodge and Camp (Not Visited)—(Nipissing) *At jct Hwy-60 & Hwy-523. Enter on R.* FACILITIES: 155 sites, typical site width 40 ft, 120 W&E, (15/30 amps), 35 no hkups, 15 pull-thrus, tenting, dump, laundry, ltd groc. RECREATION: river swim, boating, canoeing, ramp, dock, river fishing, play equipment. Pets welcome. Open May 1 - Mid Oct. Rate in 2010 $30 per family. Member OPCA. Phone: (613)637-5338.

MADOC—H-4

Loon Lake—*From jct Hwy 7 & Hwy 62: Go 6 km/3-3/4 mi S on Hwy 62, then 1.6 km/1 mi E on Quin-Mo-Lac Rd. Enter on R.* ◆◆◆FACILITIES: 135 sites, typical site width 35 ft, 110 full hkups, 25 W&E, (30 amps), 2 pull-thrus, tenting, dump, laundry. ◆◆◆RECREATION: swim pool, lake swim, boating, no motors, dock, lake fishing, playground. Pets welcome. Open May 1 - Mid Oct. Rate in 2010 $25-35 per family. Member OPCA. Phone: (613)473-0766.

MALLORYTOWN—G-6

KOA-Thousand Islands—*From jct Hwy 401 (exit 675) & Mallorytown Rd: Go .8 km/1/2 mi N on Mallorytown Rd, then .8 km/1/2 mi W on Hwy 2. Enter on L.* ◆◆◆◆FACILITIES: 120 sites, typical site width 35 ft, 24 full hkups, 78 W&E, (15/30/50 amps), 18 no hkups, 58 pull-thrus, tenting, dump, laundry, groceries. ◆◆◆◆RECREATION: swim pool, playground. Pets welcome. Partial handicap access. Open Apr 16 - Oct 31. Rate in 2010 $30-57.75 per family. Member OPCA. Phone: (800)562-9725. KOA discount.

MANITOULIN ISLAND—F-1

See listings at Espanola, Evansville, Manitowaning, Meldrum Bay, Mindemoya, Providence Bay, Sheguiandah, South Bayouth & Spring Bay.

MANITOWANING—F-2

Black Rock Resort (Not Visited) (RV SPACES)—(Manitoulin) *9.6 km/6 mi S on Hwy 6, then 1.6 km/1 mi E on Cowans Side Rd (formerly Black Rock Rd). Enter at end.* FACILITIES: 20 sites, typical site width 20 ft, 32 ft max RV length, 12 W&E, (15 amps), 8 no hkups, tenting, dump, laundry, ltd groc. RECREATION: lake swim, boating, canoeing, ramp, dock, lake fishing, play equipment. No pets. Open all yr. Facilities fully operational mid May - mid Oct. Rate in 2010 $22-29 per family. Phone: (705)859-3262.

Manitoulin Resort—(Manitoulin) *From jct Hwy 6 & Bidwell Rd (north of town): Go .8 km/1/2 mi W on Bidwell Rd, then .8 km/1/2 mi W on Holiday Haven Rd. Enter on L.* ◆◆◆FACILITIES: 125 sites, typical site width 40 ft, 105 W&E, (20/30 amps), 20 no hkups, 4 pull-thrus, family camping, tenting, dump, laundry, ltd groc. ◆◆◆◆RECREATION: lake/boating, canoeing, ramp, dock, lake fishing, playground. Pets welcome. Open May 1 - Sep 26. Rate in 2010 $28-36 for 4 persons. Member ARVC, OPCA.

Phone: (888)790-9165
Address: RR 1 152 Holiday Haven Rd, Manitowaning, ON P0P 1N0
Lat/Lon: 45.75869/-81.84738
Email: info@manitoulinresort.com
Web: www.manitoulinresort.com

MANITOWANING—Continued

Uncle Steve's Park & Cabins (Not visited) (REBUILDING)—(Manitoulin) *From jct Hwy 6 & Bidwell Rd (north of town): Go 8 km/5 mi W on Bidwell Rd. Enter on L.* FACILITIES: 46 sites, typical site width 30 ft, 26 ft max RV length, 26 W&E, 20 no hkups, 3 pull-thrus, tenting, laundry, ltd groc. RECREATION: lake swim, boating, canoeing, ramp, dock, lake fishing. Pets welcome. Open May 1 - Oct 1. Rate in 2010 $18-26.50 for 4 persons. Phone: (705)859-3488.

MARATHON—B-3

NEYs Lunch & Campground (Not Visited) (RV SPACES)—(Thunder Bay) *From west city limits: Go 20 km/12 mi W on Hwy 17. Enter on R.* FACILITIES: 14 sites, 9 full hkups, 5 W&E, (15 amps), tenting, groceries. RECREATION: play equipment. Pets welcome. Open all yr. Facilities fully operational Apr 30 - Oct 28. Rate in 2010 $20-30 per family. Member OPCA. Phone: (807)229-1869.

(W) NEYS PROVINCIAL PARK—*From town: Go 30-1/2 km/19 mi W on Hwy 17.* FACILITIES: 144 sites, 61 E, (15/30 amps), 83 no hkups, 27 pull-thrus, tenting, dump, laundry. RECREATION: boating, canoeing, ramp, lake fishing, playground. Partial handicap access. Open mid May - mid Sep. Phone: (807)229-1624.

MARMORA—H-4

BOOSTER PARK (City Park)—*From town: Go 2-1/2 km/1-1/2 mi W on Hwy 7, then 1-1/2 km/1 mi N on Crowe Lake Rd.* FACILITIES: 60 sites, 30 full hkups, 10 W&E, 20 no hkups, 6 pull-thrus, tenting, dump, ltd groc. RECREATION: lake swim, boating, canoeing, ramp, dock, lake fishing, playground. Open Victoria Day - Thanksgiving. Phone: (613)472-3127.

Glen Allan Park—*From jct Hwy 7 & Hwy 14: Go 1 block N on McGill St, then 4.8 km/3 mi W & N on CR 3, then 2 km/1-1/4 mi W on Glen Allan Rd. Enter on L.* ◆◆◆FACILITIES: 235 sites, typical site width 30 ft, 175 full hkups, 50 W&E, (15/20/30 amps), 10 no hkups, 6 pull-thrus, tenting, dump, laundry, ltd groc. ◆◆◆◆RECREATION: lake swim, boating, canoeing, ramp, dock, lake fishing, playground. Pets welcome. Open May 15 - Oct 15. Rate in 2010 $25-40 per family. Member OPCA. Phone: (613)472-2415.

KOA-Marmora—*From business center: Go 3.2 km/2 mi E on Hwy 7, then .8 km/1/2 mi S on KOA Campground Rd. Enter on R.* ◆◆◆FACILITIES: 180 sites, typical site width 40 ft, 3 full hkups, 167 W&E, (15/30 amps), 10 no hkups, 22 pull-thrus, tenting, dump, laundry, full svc store. ◆◆◆RECREATION: 2 swim pools, canoeing, pond fishing, playground. Pets welcome. Open May 1 - Oct 15. Rate in 2010 $25-45 per family. Member OPCA. Phone: (800)562-9156. KOA discount.

MARTEN RIVER—D-6

(W) MARTEN RIVER PROVINCIAL PARK—*From town: Go on Hwy-11.* FACILITIES: 190 sites, 62 E, (15/30 amps), 128 no hkups, tenting, dump, ltd groc. RECREATION: lake swim, boating, canoeing, ramp, dock, lake fishing, playground. Partial handicap access. Open mid May - late Sep. Phone: (705)892-2200.

MATTAWA—F-4

(W) SAMUEL DE CHAMPLAIN PROVINCIAL PARK—*From town: Go 14-1/2 km/9 mi W on Hwy 17.* FACILITIES: 215 sites, 106 E, (15/30 amps), 109 no hkups, 30 pull-thrus, tenting, dump, laundry, ltd groc. RECREATION: lake swim, boating, canoeing, ramp, dock, lake fishing, playground. Partial handicap access. Open mid May - late Sep. Phone: (705)744-2276.

(W) Sid Turcotte Park (Not Visited)—(Nipissing) *From business center: Go 1.6 km/1 mi W on Hwy 17, then .4 km/1/4 mi N on Turcotte Pk Rd. Enter on L.* ◆◆◆FACILITIES: 139 sites, typical site width 40 ft, 66 full hkups, 54 W&E, (15/30 amps), 19 no hkups, 30 pull-thrus, family camping, tenting, dump, laundry, ltd groc. ◆◆◆RECREATION: river swim, boating, canoeing, ramp, dock, river fishing, playground. Pets welcome. Open all yr. Facilities fully operational May 15 - Mid Oct. Rate in 2010 $25-33 per family. Member OPCA. Phone: (705)744-5375.

MCDONALD'S CORNERS—G-5

Paul's Creek Campsite (Not visited)—*From town: Go 5.6 km/3-1/2 mi W on CR 12. Enter on R.* ◆◆◆FACILITIES: 80 sites, typical site width 35 ft, 62 W&E, (15/30 amps), 18 no hkups, 4 pull-thrus, tenting, dump, laundry, ltd groc. ◆◆◆RECREATION: swim pool, stream fishing, playground. Pets welcome. Open May 1 - Oct 15. Rate in 2010 $10-12 for 2 persons. Member OPCA. Phone: (613)278-2770.

MCGREGOR—J-1

WILDWOOD GOLF & RV RESORT—(Essex) *From the Jct of Hwy 401 (exit 21) & Cty Rd 19 (Manning Rd) Go S on Cty Rd 19 4.6 km/3 mi to the Jct of Cty Rd 3, then Go SE on Cty Rd 3 4.8 km/3 mi to N Malden Rd, then Go SW on N Malden Rd 9.1 km/5-3/4 mi to Conc 11, then Go W on Conc 11 0.6 km/1/2 mi. Enter on R.*

◆◆◆◆◆FACILITIES: 385 sites, typical site width 35 ft, accepts full hkup units only, 385 full hkups,

WILDWOOD GOLF & RV RESORT—Continued on next page

MCGREGOR—Continued
WILDWOOD GOLF & RV RESORT—Continued

(30/50 amps), 50 amps ($), many extd stay sites, 83 pull-thrus, cable TV, ($), WiFi Internet central location, laundry, ice, picnic tables, patios, fire rings, wood, controlled access.

◇◇◇◇◇RECREATION: rec hall, 2 swim pools, putting green, golf nearby, bsktball, playground, shuffleboard court 2 shuffleboard courts, activities, horseshoes, sports field, hiking trails. Rec open to public.

Pets welcome. Partial handicap access. No tents. Open May 1 - Oct 31. Big rigs welcome. Clubs welcome. Rate in 2010 $40 for 2 persons. MC/VISA/Debit. Member OPCA. FMCA discount.

Phone: (866)994-9699
Address: 11112 Concession Rd 11, McGregor, ON N0R 1J0
Lat/Lon: 42.08395/-82.56986
Email: joelucier@aol.com
Web: www.wildwoodgolfandrvresort.com

SEE AD WINDSOR PAGE 889

WILDWOOD GOLF & RV RESORT—*From jct Hwy 401 (exit Manning Rd) CR 19: Go S on CR 19 to Kings Hwy 3 to N Malden Rd. Turn right, then go 10 km/6 mi. Follow tourist signs. Enter on R.* An 18-hole executive par four golf course, practice chipping green & sand trap, located in beautiful Essex County. Fully licensed clubhouse and restaurant with a full menu. Well-equipped pro shop with rental carts & clubs. Open May 1 - Oct 31. MC/VISA/Debit.

Phone: (519)726-6176
Address: 11112 Concession Rd 11, McGregor, ON N0R 1J0
Email: joelucier@aol.com
Web: www.wildwoodgolfandrvresort.com

SEE AD WINDSOR PAGE 889

MEAFORD—G-2

(E) MEAFORD MEMORIAL PARK (City Park)—*From jct Hwy 26 (Sykes) & Edwin St: Go 2 km/1-1/4 mi E on Edwin, continuing on Aiken & Grant. Enter at end.* FACILITIES: 140 sites, 30 full hkups, 110 W&E, (15/30 amps), 24 pull-thrus, tenting, dump, ltd groc. RECREATION: lake swim, boating, canoeing, lake/river fishing, play equipment. Open May 1 - Oct. Phone: (519)538-2530.

MIDLAND—G-3

Smith's Camp (Not visited)—(Simcoe) *From jct Hwy 93 & Hwy 12: Go 3.2 km/2 mi E on Hwy 12, then .8 km/1/2 mi N on King St. Enter on L.* ◇◇◇FACILITIES: 150 sites, typical site width 40 ft, 120 full hkups, 30 W&E, (15/30 amps), tenting, dump, groceries. ◇◇◇RECREATION: swim pool, lake swim, boating, 10 hp limit, canoeing, ramp, dock, lake fishing, playground. Pets welcome. Open mid May - mid Oct. Rate in 2010 $29-33.50 per family. Member OPCA. Phone: (705)526-4339.

MILLER LAKE—G-2

SUMMER HOUSE PARK—(Bruce) *From jct Hwy 6 & Miller Lake Rd: Go 3.2 km/2 mi E on Miller Lake Rd. Enter at end.* ◇◇◇◇FACILITIES: 248 sites, typical site width 30 ft, 169 full hkups, 62 W&E, (15/30/50 amps), 50 amps ($), 17 no hkups, many extd stay sites, 13 pull-thrus, WiFi Instant Internet at site ($), WiFi Internet central location, tenting, RV's/park model rentals, cabins, RV storage, dump, non-guest dump $, portable dump, laundry, full svc store, RV supplies, LP gas by weight, ice, picnic tables, fire rings, grills, wood, controlled access.

◇◇◇◇RECREATION: rec hall, equipped pavilion, coin games, lake swim, boating, canoeing, kayaking, ramp, dock, rowboat/6 canoe/4 kayak/4 pedal boat/7 motorboat rentals, lake fishing, fishing supplies, golf nearby, bsktball, 5 bike rentals, playground, shuffleboard

MILLER LAKE—Continued
SUMMER HOUSE PARK—Continued

court 2 shuffleboard courts, activities, tennis, horseshoes, sports field, hiking trails, v-ball, local tours.

Pets welcome. Partial handicap access. Open May 1 - Mid Oct. Escort to site. Clubs welcome. Green Friendly. Rate in 2010 $39-46 for 2 persons. MC/VISA/AMEX/Debit. Member ARVC, OPCA. CCUSA 50% Discount. CCUSA reservations Recommended, CCUSA max stay 7 days. Discount not available Jun 19-Sep 7.

Phone: (800)265-5557
Address: 197 Miller Lake Shore Rd, Miller Lake, ON N0H 1Z0
Lat/Lon: 45.09889/-81.40213
Email: darci@summerhousepark.ca
Web: www.summerhousepark.ca

SEE AD THIS PAGE

MILTON—I-3

MILTON HEIGHTS CAMPGROUND—*From jct Hwy 401 (exit 320) & Hwy 25: Go 1.6 km/1 mi N on Hwy 25, then 2.4 km/1-1/2 mi W on S Side Rd, then 90 meters/100 yards S on Tremaine. Enter on R.*

◇◇◇◇FACILITIES: 206 sites, typical site width 40 ft, 118 full hkups, 48 W&E, (30/50 amps), 40 no hkups, some extd stay sites, 30 pull-thrus, WiFi Instant Internet at site ($), phone Internet central location, tenting, RV's/park model rentals, RV storage, dump, non-guest dump $, laundry, groceries, RV supplies, ice, picnic tables, fire rings, wood, controlled access.

◇◇◇◇RECREATION: rec room/area, equipped pavilion, coin games, swim pool, golf nearby, bsktball, playground, activities, (wkends), horseshoes, sports field, v-ball.

Pets welcome. Partial handicap access. Open all yr. Clubs welcome. Green Friendly. Rate in 2010 $28-34 for 2 persons. MC/VISA/AMEX/Debit. Member OPCA. FMCA discount.

Phone: (800)308-9120
Address: RR 3 8690 Tremaine Rd, Milton, ON L9T 2X7
Lat/Lon: 43.31371/-79.56197
Email: miltonheightscampground@on.aibn.com
Web: www.miltonhgtscampgrd.com

SEE AD TORONTO PAGE 888

MINDEMOYA—F-1

Mindemoya Court Cottages & Campground (Not Visited)—*From town at jct CR 542 & CR 551: Go 1.2 km/3/4 mi N, then 400 meters/1600 feet W on Old 551, then 1.6 km/1 mi W on Ketchankookem Trail. Enter on R.* ◇◇◇FACILITIES: 16 sites, typical site width 25 ft, 16 full hkups, (20/30 amps), tenting, ltd groc. ◇◇◇◇RECREATION: lake swim, boating, canoeing, dock, lake fishing, play equipment. Pets welcome. Open mid May - Sept 15. Rate in 2010 $28-31 for 4 persons. Phone: (705)377-5778.

MINDEN—G-4

Buckslide Tent and Trailer Park (Not Visited)—*From jct Hwy 35 & Hwy 118: Go 3.2 km/2 mi W on Hwy 118, then .8 km/1/2 mi W on Kushog Lake Rd, then 1.6 km/1 mi N on Buckslide Rd. Enter on L.* ◇◇FACILITIES: 85 sites, typical site width 35 ft, 28 ft max RV length, 81 W&E, (15/20/30 amps), 4 no hkups, tenting, laundry, groceries. ◇◇RECREATION: lake swim, boating, canoeing, ramp, dock, lake fishing, play equipment. Pets welcome. Open May 15 - Oct 15. Rate in 2010 $20-30 per family. Phone: (705)489-2808.

Jay Lake Campground & RV Park—*From jct Hwy 35 & Hwy 121 (Haliburton): Go 4 km/2-1/2 mi E on Hwy 121. Enter on L.* ◇◇◇FACILITIES: 100 sites, 42 full hkups, 49 W&E, (30/50 amps), 9 no hkups, tenting, dump, laundry, ltd groc. ◇◇◇◇RECREATION: swim pool, lake swim, boating, no motors, canoeing, dock, lake fishing, playground. Pets welcome. Partial handicap access. Open May 11 - Oct 19. Rate in 2010 $30-35 per family. Member OPCA. Phone: (866)637-6607.

South Lake Tent and Trailer Park (Not visited)—*From jct Hwy 121 (Kinmount) & CR 16 at south city limits: Go 3.6 km/2-1/4 mi E on CR 16, then 2.4 km/1-1/2 mi S on Hospitality Rd, then .4 km/1/4 mi E on gravel road. Enter on L.* ◇◇FACILITIES: 153 sites, typical site width 35 ft, 70 full hkups, 25 W&E, (15 amps), 58 no hkups, tenting, dump, laundry, groceries. ◇◇◇RECREATION: lake swim, boating, canoeing, ramp, dock, lake fishing, playground. Pets welcome. Open May 14 - Oct 14. Rate in 2010 $30 per family. Member OPCA. Phone: (705)286-2555.

Visit our website www.woodalls.com

MITCHELL—I-2

Windmill Family Campground (Not Visited)—(Perth) *From jct Hwy 23 & County Rd 163: Go S 9.2 km/5-3/4 mi. Enter on R.* FACILITIES: 220 sites, typical site width 40 ft, 208 full hkups, (15/30 amps), 12 no hkups, tenting, dump, laundry, ltd groc. RECREATION: swim pool, playground. Pets welcome. Partial handicap access. Open May 1 - Oct 1. Rate in 2010 $30-32 for 2 persons. Member OPCA. Phone: (519)229-8982.

Woodland Lake RV Resort(Not Visited)—(Perth) *From jct Hwy 8 & Hwy 23: Go 10 km/6-1/4 mi N on Hwy 23 (Rd 164), then 5.1 km/3 mi W on Logan Line 46 to park. Enter on R.* FACILITIES: 196 sites, typical site width 40 ft, 161 full hkups, 19 W&E, (15/30 amps), 16 no hkups, 22 pull-thrus, tenting, laundry, ltd groc. RECREATION: swim pool, lake swim, boating, no motors, canoeing, dock, lake fishing, playground. Pets welcome. Partial handicap access. Open May 1 - mid Oct. Rate in 2010 $25-40 per family. Member OPCA. Phone: (877)952-7275. FMCA discount.

MITCHELL'S BAY—J-1

(N) MARINE PARK (St. Clair Parkway Commission)—(Chatham/Kent) *From jct Hwy 40 & Mitchell Bay Rd: Go 8 km/5 mi W on Mitchell Bay Rd. Enter on R.* FACILITIES: 108 sites, 100 W&E, (15/30 amps), 8 no hkups, tenting, dump, laundry. RECREATION: lake swim, boating, ramp, dock, lake/river fishing, play equipment. Open mid May - mid Oct. Phone: (519)354-8423.

MONTREAL RIVER HARBOUR—D-3

Twilight Resort (Not Visited)—(Algoma) *In town on Hwy 17 & Twilight Rd. Enter on L.* ◇◇FACILITIES: 42 sites, typical site width 25 ft, 4 full hkups, 17 W&E, (15 amps), 21 no hkups, 4 pull-thrus, family camping, tenting, dump, laundry, ltd groc. ◇◇RECREATION: lake swim, boating, canoeing, lake fishing, play equipment. Pets welcome. Open Apr 15 - Oct 31. Rate in 2010 $25-29 per family. Phone: (705)882-2183.

MORPETH—J-1

(S) RONDEAU PROVINCIAL PARK—(Kempt) *From town: Go 7-1/4 km/4-1/2 mi S on CR 17.* FACILITIES: 262 sites, typical site width 40 ft, 152 E, (15/30 amps), 110 no hkups, 60 pull-thrus, tenting, dump, laundry, ltd groc. RECREATION: lake swim, boating, canoeing, ramp, lake fishing, playground. Partial handicap access. Open Apr 1 - late Oct. Phone: (519)674-1750.

Rondeau Shores Trailer Park—(Kent) *From jct Hwy 3, Hwy 21 & CR 17 (Kent/Hill Rd): Go 2 km/1-1/4 mi S on CR 17, then .8 km/1/2 mi E on Scotland Ln. Enter on R.* ◇◇◇FACILITIES: 123 sites, typical site width 30 ft, 35 ft max RV length, 109 full hkups, 14 W&E, (15/20/30 amps), tenting, dump, laundry, groceries. ◇◇◇RECREATION: swim pool, lake swim, lake fishing, playground. Pets welcome. Open May 15 - Oct 15. Rate in 2010 $36 per vehicle. Member OPCA. Phone: (519)674-3330.

MORRISBURG—G-6

(NE) RIVERSIDE/CEDAR CAMPSITE (Parks of the St. Lawrence)—*From jct Hwy 401 (exit 750) & Hwy 31: Go 1-1/2 km/1 mi S on Hwy 31, then 6-1/2 km/4 mi E on Hwy 2.* FACILITIES: 322 sites, typical site width 20 ft, 50 W&E, 113 E, (15/30 amps), 159 no hkups, tenting, dump. RECREATION: lake swim, boating, canoeing, ramp, dock, lake fishing, playground. Open May 15 - Oct 12. Phone: (613)543-3287.

Upper Canada Campground—*From jct Hwy-401 (exit 758) & Upper Canada Rd: Go 100 yards N on Upper Canada Rd. Enter on R.* ◇◇◇FACILITIES: 150 sites, typical site width 40 ft, 140 W&E, (15/30 amps), 10 no hkups, 5 pull-thrus, family camping, tenting, dump, laundry, ltd groc. ◇◇◇◇RECREATION: swim pool, pond fishing, playground. Pets welcome. Open May 1 - Oct 1. Rate in 2010 $27-32 for 2 persons. Member OPCA. Phone: (613)543-2201.

MOSSLEY—I-2

Golden Pond RV Resort (Not Visited)—*From jct Hwy 401 (exit 208) & Putnam Rd: Go S 0.8km/1/2 mi on Putnam Rd, then E 400 meters on Cromarty Rd. Enter on L.* ◇◇◇◇FACILITIES: 298 sites, typical site width 35 ft, 240 full hkups, 8 W&E, (30/50 amps), 50 amps ($), 50 no hkups, 16 pull-thrus, tenting, laundry, ltd groc. ◇◇◇◇RECREATION: swim pool, canoeing, pond fishing, playground. Pets welcome. Partial handicap access. Open all yr. Facilities fully operational Apr 1 - Oct 30. Big rigs welcome. Rate in 2010 $34-40 per family. Member OPCA. Phone: (519)485-0679.

MOUNT ALBERT—H-3

Ponderosa Campground (Not Visited)—*From jct CR 13 & Hwy 48: Go .8 km/1/2 mi N on Hwy 48. From Hwy 404 & Green Ln (Hwy 19): Go .6 mi E, then 1-1/4 mi N on Hwy 8 (Woodbine Ave), then 5 mi E on York Rd 13, then .6 mi N on Hwy 48. Enter on L.* ◇◇◇◇FACILITIES: 261 sites, typical site width 30 ft, 181 full hkups, 35 W&E, (15/30 amps), 45 no hkups, 6 pull-thrus, tenting, dump, laundry, ltd groc. ◇◇◇◇RECREATION: 2 swim pools, stream fishing, playground. Pets welcome. Open Apr 1 - Nov 1. Rate in 2010 $31-40 per family. Member OPCA. Phone: (905)473-2607.

MOUNT ELGIN—I-6

See listing Ingersoll

MOUNT FOREST—H-2

River Place Park (Not Visited)—(Gray) *From jct Hwy 89 & Hwy 6: Go 13.6 km/8-1/2 mi N on Hwy 6, then 2.5 km/1-1/2 mi W on Normandy Concession Rd 12. Enter on L.* FACILITIES: 267 sites, typical site width 35 ft, 152 full hkups, 50 W&E, (30 amps), 65 no hkups, tenting, dump, laundry, ltd groc. RECREATION: swim pool, river fishing, playground. Pets welcome. Open May 15 - Oct 15. Rate in 2010 $35 per family. Member OPCA. Phone: (519)665-2228.

Silent Valley Park (Not Visited)—(Grey) *From jct 6 & 89: Go 9 km/5-1/2 mi N on Hwy 6, then go 2.3 km/1-1/2 mi W on County Road 9, then go 2.1 km/1-1/4 mi N on Township Rd 35. Enter on R.* FACILITIES: 307 sites, typical site width 40 ft, 284 full hkups, 12 W&E, (30 amps), 11 no hkups, 6 pull-thrus, tenting, dump, laundry, ltd groc. RECREATION: swim pool, lake swim, boating, no motors, canoeing, ramp, dock, lake fishing, playground. Pets welcome. Open May 1 - Oct 15. Rate in 2010 $32-42 for 2 persons. Member OPCA. Phone: (519)665-7787.

Spring Valley Resort (Not Visited)—(Wellington) *From jct Hwy 89 & Hwy 6: Go 8 km/5 mi S on Hwy 6, then 3-1/4 km/2 mi E on Sideroad 5. Enter on R.* FACILITIES: 225 sites, typical site width 35 ft, 220 full hkups, (30 amps), 5 no hkups, tenting, laundry, ltd groc. RECREATION: swim pool, lake swim, boating, no motors, canoeing, dock, lake fishing, playground. Pets welcome. Open Mid May - Mid Oct. Rate in 2010 $29-50 per family. Member OPCA. Phone: (519)323-2581.

NAPANEE—H-5

Pickerel Park (Not visited)—*From jct Hwy 401 (exit 579) & Hwy 41: Go 10 mi S on Hwy 41, then follow signs. Enter on L.* ◆◆◆FACILITIES: 240 sites, typical site width 40 ft, 35 ft max RV length, 176 W&E, (15/30 amps), 64 no hkups, tenting, dump, laundry, groceries. ◆◆◆RECREATION: swim pool, lake swim, boating, canoeing, ramp, dock, lake fishing, playground. Pets welcome. Open May 1 - Oct 15. Rate in 2010 $28-37 per family. Member OPCA. Phone: (613)373-2812.

NAUGHTON—D-5

Holiday Beach Campground (Not Visited) (REBUILDING)—(Sadbury) *From West jct Hwy 17 & Regional Rd 55 (Old Hwy 17): Go 4.8 km/3 mi E on Regional Rd 55. Enter on R.* FACILITIES: 130 sites, 90 W&E, (15/20 amps), 40 no hkups, 40 pull-thrus, tenting, dump, laundry, ltd groc. RECREATION: lake swim, boating, canoeing, ramp, dock, lake fishing, play equipment. Pets welcome. Open mid May - mid Oct. Rate in 2010 $21 per family. Phone: (705)866-0303.

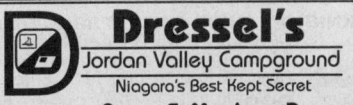

NESTLETON—H-4

Springwater RV Resort (Not visited)—*From town: Go 1.6 km/1 mi E on Hwy 7A. Enter on L.* ◆◆◆FACILITIES: 98 sites, typical site width 30 ft, 40 full hkups, 46 W&E, (20/30 amps), 12 no hkups, tenting, dump, laundry, ltd groc. ◆◆◆RECREATION: playground. Pets welcome. Open mid May - mid Oct. Rate in 2010 $27-32 per family. Member OPCA. Phone: (905)986-0274.

NESTOR FALLS—E-1

(S) CALIPER LAKE PROVINCIAL PARK—*From town: Go 6-1/2 km/4 mi S on Hwy 71, then 1-1/2 km/1 mi W on Park Rd.* FACILITIES: 83 sites, 26 E, (15/30 amps), 57 no hkups, tenting, dump. RECREATION: lake swim, boating, canoeing, ramp, dock, lake fishing, playground. Partial handicap access. Open mid May - mid Sep. Phone: (807)484-2181.

Clarke & Crombie Camps and C & C Motel (Not Visited)—(Kenora) *At south edge of town on Hwy 71. Enter on R.* FACILITIES: 45 sites, typical site width 20 ft, 30 full hkups, (15 amps), 15 no hkups, 8 pull-thrus, tenting, dump, groceries. RECREATION: lake swim, boating, canoeing, ramp, dock, lake fishing. Pets welcome. Open all yr. Facilities fully operational May 1 - Nov 1. Rate in 2010 $28 for 2 persons. Phone: (807) 484-2114.

Lecuyer's Tru-Tail Lodge (Not Visited)—*From jct Hwy 71 & Airport Rd at north edge of town: Go 1 km/3/4 mi W on Sabaskong Rd. Enter on R.* FACILITIES: 60 sites, typical site width 16 ft, 29 full hkups, 20 W&E, (15/30 amps), 11 no hkups, 18 pull-thrus, tenting, dump. RECREATION: lake swim, boating, canoeing, ramp, dock, lake fishing, play equipment. Pets welcome. Open May 1 - Oct 1. Rate in 2010 $30 for 4 persons. Phone: (807)484-2448.

NEW DUNDEE—I-2

Country Gardens RV Park—(Waterloo) *From jct Hwy 401 & Homer Watson Blvd (exit 275): Go 15 meters/50 feet N on Homer Watson Blvd, then 12 km/12 mi on CR 12, then 4.5 km N on Queen, then E 1km on Witmer Rd. Enter on R.* ◆◆◆◆FACILITIES: 254 sites, 250 full hkups, 4 W&E, (30 amps), tenting, dump, ltd groc. ◆◆◆◆RECREATION: swim pool, canoeing, pond fishing, playground. Pets welcome. Partial handicap access. Open May 1st - Mid Oct. Rate in 2010 $39 per family. Member OPCA. Phone: (519)696-3230.

Animals of Ontario include: moose, otter, mink & caribou.

NIAGARA FALLS—I-3

NIAGARA FALLS AREA MAP

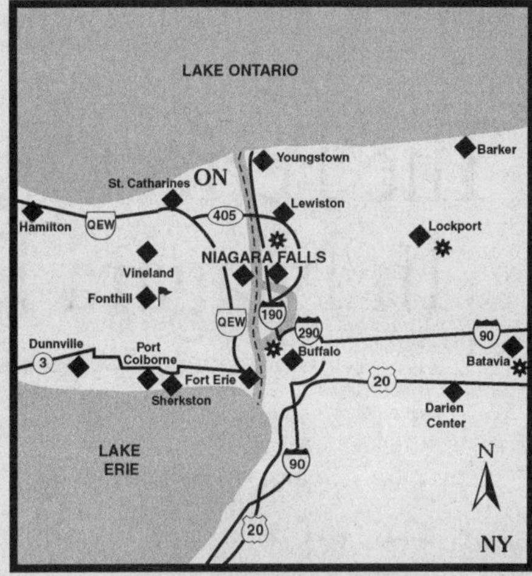

Symbols on map indicate towns within a 64 km/40 mi radius of Niagara Falls where campgrounds (diamonds), attractions (flags), & RV service centers & camping supply outlets (gears) are listed. Check listings for more information.

Tell Them Woodall's Sent You!

NIAGARA FALLS—Continued on next page

The world's largest deposits of nickel & copper were discovered in Sudbury in 1883.

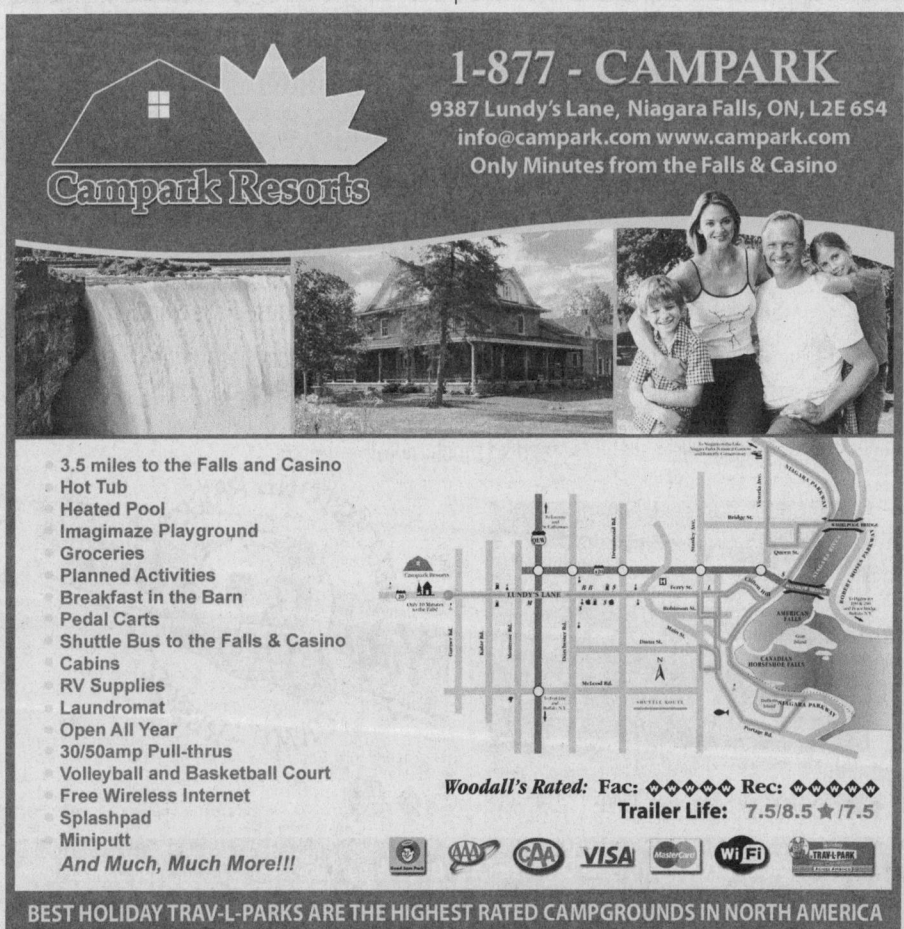

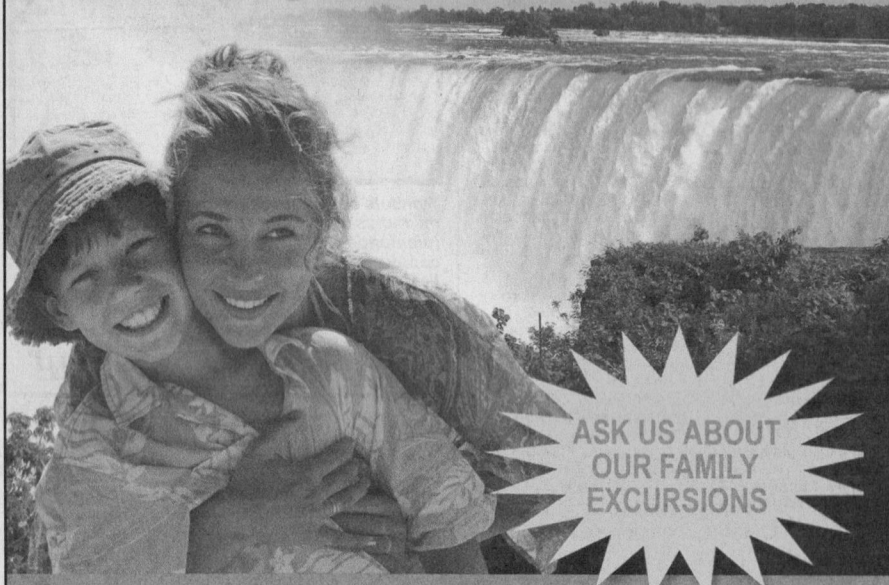

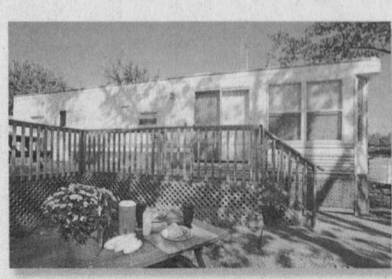

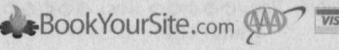

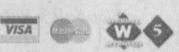

NIAGARA FALLS—Continued

CAMPARK RESORTS—*From jct Queen Elizabeth Way & Hwy 420 (exit Lundy's Lane, Hwy 20): Go 100 yards W, then .8 km/1/2 mi S on Montrose, then 2.4 km/1-1/2 mi W on Lundy's Lane. Enter on R.*

ACTIVITIES & FACILITIES SECOND TO NONE
A warmer welcome would be hard to find. Many campers are return visitors from around the world, brought back by the value and friendliness and fun we provide. Daily planned activities. Shuttle to falls, casinos. Open all year.

◊◊◊◊◊FACILITIES: 345 sites, typical site width 36 ft, 255 full hkups, 26 W&E, (15/20/50 amps), 50 amps ($), 64 no hkups, some extd stay sites, 43 pull-thrus, cable TV, WiFi Instant Internet at site, family camping, tenting, cabins, dump, laundry, groceries, RV supplies, ice, picnic tables, fire rings, wood, controlled access.

◊◊◊◊◊RECREATION: rec hall, rec room/area, pavilion, coin games, swim pool, spray ground, hot tub, mini-golf, ($), golf nearby, bsktball, 12 bike rentals, playground, activities, horseshoes, sports field, hiking trails, v-ball, local tours. Rec open to public.

Pets welcome. Partial handicap access. Open all yr. Facilities fully operational May 1 - Oct 31. Pool open end of May. Big rigs welcome. Clubs welcome. Rate in 2010 $41-56 per family. MC/VISA/Debit. ATM. Member ARVC, OPCA.

Phone: (877)226-7275
Address: 9387 Lundys Ln, Niagara Falls, ON L2E 6S4
Lat/Lon: 43.08532/-79.15313
Email: info@campark.com
Web: www.campark.com

SEE AD PAGE 879 AND AD NIAGARA FALLS, NY PAGE 557 AND AD DISCOVER SECTION PAGE 112

King Waldorf's Tent & Trailer Park—*From jct Hwy 420 & Queen Elizabeth Way: Go 7.2 km/4-1/2 mi S on QEW (exit 21), then 2.4 km/1-1/2 mi E on Lyons Creek Rd, then .8 km/1/2 mi N on Stanley Ave. Enter on R.* ◊◊◊◊FACILITIES: 210 sites, typical site width 35 ft, 28 full hkups, 182 W&E, (20/30/50 amps), 83 pull-thrus, family camping, tenting, dump, laundry, ltd groc. ◊◊◊◊RECREATION: swim pool, boating, canoeing, ramp, dock, river fishing, playground. Pets welcome. Open mid May - Oct 8. Big rigs welcome. Rate in 2010 $45-60 for 4 persons. Member OPCA. Phone: (905) 295-8191.

KNIGHT'S HIDE-AWAY PARK—*From jct QEW (at Peace Bridge) & Hwy 3: Go 11.9 km/7-1/2 mi W on Hwy 3. (At jct Hwy 3 & Regional Rd 116). Enter on R.*

◊◊◊FACILITIES: 171 sites, typical site width 35 ft, 19 full hkups, 132 W&E, (15/30/50 amps), 50 amps ($), 20 no hkups, some extd stay sites, 69 pull-thrus, WiFi Internet central location, family camping, tenting, RV's/park model rentals, RV storage, dump, non-guest dump $, portable dump, laundry, ltd groc, RV supplies, ice, picnic tables, fire rings, wood, controlled access.

◊◊◊◊RECREATION: rec room/area, pavilion, coin games, swim pool, golf nearby, bsktball, 10 bike rentals, playground, activities, (wkends), horseshoes, sports field, v-ball, local tours.

Pets welcome. Open May 1 - Oct 30. Pool opens 6-1. Big rigs welcome. Green Friendly. Rate in 2010 $22.50-39 per family. MC/VISA/Debit. Member OPCA.

Phone: (905)894-1911
Address: 1154 Gorham Rd, Ridgeway, ON L0S 1N0
Lat/Lon: 42.54349/-79.03430
Email: camping@lastmilenet.ca
Web: www.knightsfamilycamping.com

SEE AD PAGE 879

KOA-Niagara Falls—*From jct Queen Elizabeth Way & Hwy 20 (Lundys Lane): Go 100 yards W, then .8 km/1/2 mi S on Montrose, then 2 km/1-1/4 mi W on Hwy 20. Enter on R.* ◊◊◊◊FACILITIES: 357 sites, typical site width 35 ft, 104 full hkups, 161 W&E, 22 E, (15/30/50 amps), 70 no hkups, 46 pull-thrus, tenting, dump, laundry, groceries. ◊◊◊◊◊RECREATION: 2 swim pools, playground. Pets welcome. Open Apr 1 - Oct 31. Big rigs welcome. Rate in 2010 $50-90 for 2 persons. Member ARVC, OPCA. Phone: (800)562-6478. KOA discount.

Riverside Park Motel & Campground—*From jct Queen Elizabeth Way (exit 12) & Netherby Rd: Go 1.2 km/3/4 mi E on Netherby Rd, then 500 feet N on Niagara River Pkwy. Enter on L.* ◊◊◊◊FACILITIES: 102 sites, typical site width 30 ft, 38 ft max RV length,

Riverside Park Motel & Campground—Continued on next page

55 full hkups, 29 W&E, (15/20/30 amps), 18 no hkups, 10 pull-thrus, tenting, dump, laundry, ltd groc. ◇◇◇◇RECREATION: swim pool, boating, dock, river fishing, playground. Pets welcome. Open May 1 - Oct 15. Rate in 2010 $33-44 per family. Member OPCA. Phone: (905)382-2204.

Scott's Tent & Trailer Park—*From jct Queen Elizabeth Way & Hwy 420: Go 100 yards W, then .8 km/1/2 mi S on Montrose, then 2 km/1-1/4 mi W on Hwy 20. Enter on R.* ◇◇◇◇FACILITIES: 270 sites, typical site width 35 ft, 168 full hkups, 50 W&E, (30/50 amps), 50 amps ($), 52 no hkups, 20 pull-thrus, family camping, tenting, dump, laundry, groceries. ◇◇◇RECREATION: swim pool, playground. Pets welcome. Open all yr. Facilities fully operational mid Apr - Nov 1. Big rigs welcome. Rate in 2010 $36-42 for 2 persons. Member OPCA. Phone: (800)649-9497.

WELCOME

SHALAMAR LAKE NIAGARA—*From jct Rainbow & Niagara River Pkwy (River Rd): Go 12.4 km/7-3/4 mi N on Niagara River Pkwy, then .4 km/1/4 mi W on Line 8 Rd. Enter on R.*

◇◇◇◇FACILITIES: 354 sites, typical site width 35 ft, 214 full hkups, 20 W&E, (15/30 amps), 120 no hkups, some extd stay sites, 6 pull-thrus, WiFi Instant Internet at site, tenting, RV's/park model rentals, RV storage, dump, portable dump, laundry, ltd groc, RV supplies, LP gas by weight, ice, picnic tables, fire rings, grills, wood, controlled access.

◇◇◇◇RECREATION: rec hall, rec room/area, pavilion, coin games, swim pool, golf nearby, bsktball, playground, activities, horseshoes, sports field, hiking trails, v-ball, local tours. Rec open to public.

Pets welcome. Open May 1 - Oct 15. Clubs welcome. Rate in 2010 $32-51 per family. MC/VISA/AMEX/Debit. ATM. Member OPCA.

Phone: (888)968-6067
Address: 1501 Line 8, Niagara Falls, ON 55723
Lat/Lon: 43.10396/-79.03762
Email: shalamar@allstream.net
Web: www.shalamarlake.com

SEE AD PAGE 879

WELCOME

YOGI BEAR'S JELLYSTONE PARK CAMPRESORT—*From jct Hwy 420 & QEW: Go 3.2 km/2 mi S on QEW, then 183 meters/200 yards E on McLeod Rd, then 2.4 km/1-1/2 mi S on Oakwood Dr. Enter on L.*

THE CLOSEST CAMPGROUND TO NIAGARA FALLS

Yogi Bears Jellystone Park in Niagara Falls, Ontario Canada offers fun & affordable camping for the whole family. Large wooded sites, big rig pull-thru sites, furnished cabins & rental trailers, just minutes from the falls!

◇◇◇◇◇FACILITIES: 230 sites, typical site width 35 ft, 149 full hkups, 22 W&E, (15/30/50 amps), 50 amps ($), 59 no hkups, 37 pull-thrus, WiFi Instant Internet at site, family camping, tenting, RV's/park model rentals, cabins, RV storage, dump, laundry, full svc store, RV supplies, LP gas by weight, ice, picnic tables, fire rings, grills, wood, controlled access.

◇◇◇◇◇RECREATION: rec hall, rec room/area, equipped pavilion, coin games, swim pool, wading pool, mini-golf, ($), golf nearby, bsktball, 15 bike rentals, playground, shuffleboard court shuffleboard court, activities, horseshoes, sports field, hiking trails, v-ball, local tours. Rec open to public.

Pets welcome. Open Apr 25 - Oct 15. Big rigs welcome. Clubs welcome. Green Friendly. Rate in 2010 $36-67 for 2 persons. MC/VISA/AMEX/Debit. Member ARVC, OPCA.

Text 82060 to (440)725-8687 to see our Visual Tour.

Dreany Haven
Campground
Pull-Thru 30 Amp Sites
Pool • Boating • Canoeing
(866) 808-3488
RR 2 1859 2 Hwy 17E, Corbell, ON P0H 1K0
See listing at North Bay, ON

Phone: (905)354-1432
Address: 8676 Oakwood Dr, Niagara Falls, ON L2E 6S5
Lat/Lon: 43.03058/-79.07289
Email: yogibear@jellystoneniagara.ca
Web: www.jellystoneniagara.com

SEE AD PAGE 880 AND AD DISCOVER SECTION PAGE 114

NIPIGON—B-2

(N) Stillwater Tent & Trailer Park (Not Visited)—(Thunder Bay) *From jct Hwy 11 & Hwy 17: Go 4.8 km/3 mi W on Hwy 11/17. Enter on R.* ◇◇◇FACILITIES: 77 sites, typical site width 20 ft, 17 full hkups, 54 W&E, (30/50 amps), 50 amps ($), 6 no hkups, 43 pull-thrus, family camping, tenting, dump, laundry, ltd groc. ◇◇RECREATION: river swim, stream fishing, playground. Pets welcome. Open May 15 - Oct 15. Big rigs welcome. Rate in 2010 $22-29 for 2 persons. Member OPCA. Phone: (877)887-3701.

NORTH BAY—D-6

See listings at Callander, Mattawa, Sturgeon Falls

(S) Champlain Tent & Trailer Park (Not Visited)—(Nipissing) *From jct Hwys 11, 17 & Lakeshore Dr (exit 338): Go 8.8 km/5-1/2 mi W on Lakeshore Dr, then 1.6 km/1 mi S on Premier Rd. Enter on L.* FACILITIES: 55 sites, typical site width 20 ft, 30 full hkups, 12 W&E, (15 amps), 13 no hkups, 12 pull-thrus, tenting, dump, laundry, ltd groc. RECREATION: lake swim, canoeing, river fishing. Pets welcome. Open May 1 - Oct 31. Rate in 2010 $20-30 per family. Phone: (705)474-4669.

WELCOME

(NE) DREANY HAVEN CAMPGROUND (Not Visited)—(Nipissing) *From south jct Hwy 11 & Hwy 17: Go 6.4 km/4 mi E on Hwy 17. Enter on R.*

◇◇◇FACILITIES: 70 sites, typical site width 40 ft, 28 full hkups, 35 W&E, (15/20/30 amps), 7 no hkups, many extd stay sites, 6 pull-thrus, tenting, RV storage, dump, ltd groc, ice, picnic tables, fire rings, wood.

◇◇◇RECREATION: swim pool, boating, canoeing, ramp, dock, lake fishing, golf nearby, bsktball, playground, activities, (wkends), horseshoes, sports field, hiking trails, v-ball.

Pets welcome. Open Mid May - Sep 30. Pool opens mid June. Rate in 2010 $30 per family. MC/VISA.

Phone: (705)752-2800
Address: RR 2 Hwy 17E 1859, Corbeil, ON P0H 1K0
Email: dreanyhaven@bellnet.ca
Web: dreanyhaven.ca

SEE AD THIS PAGE

Fairview Park Camping & Marina—(Nipissing) *From jct Hwy 11 & 11B (South) Lakeshore Dr (exit 338): Go 4 Km/1/4 mi S on Pinewood Pk to Decaire, W on Decaire 1.2 Km/3/4 mi to Riverbend, then S on Riverbend 1 Km/6/10 mi. Enter on R.* ◇◇◇FACILITIES: 48 sites, typical site width 35 ft, 21 full hkups, 19 W&E, (15/30 amps), 8 no hkups, 8 pull-thrus, tenting, laundry, ltd groc. ◇◇◇RECREATION: swim pool, boating, canoeing, ramp, dock, river fishing. Pets welcome. Open May 15 - Oct 15. Rate in 2010 $26-30 for 4 persons. Member OPCA. Phone: (705)474-0903.

Franklin Motel Tent & Trailer Park (Not Visited)—(Nipissing) *From jct Hwy 11 & 17 (south side of Northbay) Go: 5.3 km/3.3 mi S on Hwy 11, then 6.4 km/4 mi W on Lakeshore Dr. Enter on R.* FACILITIES: 55 sites, typical site width 35 ft, 30 full hkups, 25 W&E, (15/30 amps), 5 pull-thrus, tenting, dump, laundry. RECREATION: swim pool, boating, canoeing, play equipment. Pets welcome. Open mid May - mid Oct. Rate in 2010 $32-37 for 2 persons. Phone: (705)472-1360.

NORTHBROOK—G-5

Woodcrest Resort Park—*From jct Hwy 7 & Hwy 41: Go 16 km/10 mi N on Hwy 41, then 6.4 km/4 mi E on Harlowe Rd and follow signs. Enter on R.* ◇◇◇FACILITIES: 131 sites, typical site width 35 ft, 100 W&E, (20/30/50 amps), 31 no hkups, 12 pull-thrus, tenting, dump, laundry, ltd groc. ◇◇◇◇RECREATION: lake swim, boating, canoeing, ramp, dock, lake fishing, playground. Pets welcome. Open all yr. Facilities fully operational May 1 - Oct 31. Rate in 2010 $29-42 per family. Member OPCA. Phone: (613)336-2966.

NORWICH—I-2

(SE) LITTLE LAKE AREA (Long Point Cons Auth.)—*From town: Go 4-3/4 km/3 mi S on Hwy 59, then 9-1/2 km/6 mi E on CR 19.* FACILITIES: 55 sites, 29 W&E, (15/30 amps), 26 no hkups, tenting, dump. RECREATION: lake swim, boating, 10 hp limit, ramp, dock, playground. Partial handicap access. Open May 1 - Oct 31. Phone: (877)990-9935.

OMEMEE—H-4

(NE) EMILY PROVINCIAL PARK—*From town; Go 4 km/2-1/2 mi E on Hwy 7, then 3-1/4 km/2 mi N on Emily Park Rd. Enter on L.* FACILITIES: 299 sites, 170 E, (15/30/50 amps), 129 no hkups, 50 pull-thrus, tenting, dump, laundry, ltd groc. RECREATION: river swim, boating, canoeing, ramp, dock, river fishing, playground. Partial handicap access. Open May 10 - Oct 14. Phone: (705)799-5170.

ORILLIA—G-3

(W) BASS LAKE PROVINCIAL PARK—*From jct Hwy 12 & Concession 2: Go 6-1/2 km/4 mi W on Concession 2.* FACILITIES: 182 sites, 92 E, (15/30 amps), 90 no hkups, tenting, dump. RECREATION: lake swim, boating, canoeing, ramp, dock, lake fishing, playground. Open mid May - early Sep. Phone: (705)326-7054.

Hammock Harbour Resort (Not Visited)—(Simcoe) *From jct Hwy 11 & Hwy 12: Go 7.2 km/4-1/2 mi S on Hwy 12, crossing bridge, then .8 km/1/2 mi N on CR 44. (Rama Rd). Enter on L.* FACILITIES: 208 sites, typical site width 30 ft, 208 W&E, (30 amps), 6 pull-thrus, tenting, dump, laundry. RECREATION: swim pool, boating, canoeing, ramp, dock, lake fishing, play equipment. Pets welcome. Open May 1 - Oct 15. Member OPCA. Phone: (705)326-7885.

OSHAWA—H-4

DARLINGTON PROVINCIAL PARK—*From Hwy 401 (exit 425): Go 3/4 km/1/2 mi S on Courtice Rd.* FACILITIES: 315 sites, 135 E, (15/30 amps), 180 no hkups, 102 pull-thrus, tenting, dump, laundry, ltd groc. RECREATION: lake swim, boating, canoeing, ramp, dock, lake fishing, playground. Partial handicap access. Open May 4 - Oct 28. Phone: (905)436-2036.

HEBER DOWN CONSERVATION AREA (Central Lake Cons. Auth.)—*From jct Hwy 401 & Hwy 12 (Interchange 410): Go 11-1/4 km/7 mi N on Hwy 12, then 3-1/4 km/2 mi W on Hwy 7, then follow signs.* FACILITIES: 48 sites, 48 W&E, 3 pull-thrus, tenting, dump, laundry. RECREATION: stream fishing, playground. Open May 1 - Nov. Phone: (905)579-0411.

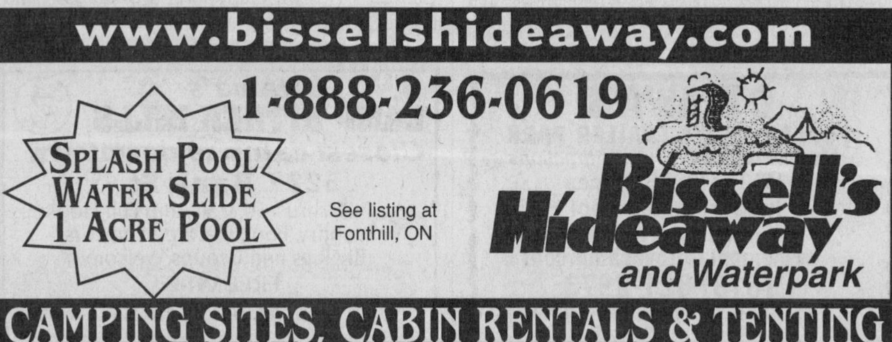

OTTAWA—G-6

OTTAWA AREA MAP

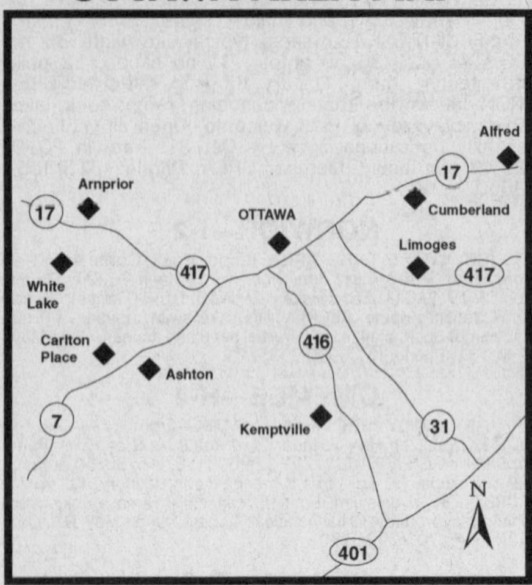

Symbols on map indicate towns within a 50 mi radius of Ottawa where campgrounds (diamonds), attractions (flags), & RV service centers & camping supply outlets (gears) are listed. Check listings for more information.

Tell Them Woodall's Sent You!

CAMP HITHER HILLS—*From jct Hwy 416 & Hwy 8 (exit 57): Go 2-3/4 mi E on Hwy 8, then 1/4 mi S on Manotick Main St (Hwy 13), then 8 mi E on Hwy 8, then 3/4 mi on Bank St. Enter on R.*

WELCOME

◇◇◇◇FACILITIES: 125 sites, typical site width 32 ft, 70 full hkups, 28 W&E, (30/50 amps), 27 no hkups, 17 pull-thrus, WiFi Instant Internet at site, phone Internet central location, family camping, tenting, RV storage, dump, non-guest dump, laundry, ltd groc, ice, picnic tables, fire rings, wood.

◇◇◇RECREATION: rec hall, swim pool, golf nearby, bsktball, 4 bike rentals, playground, horseshoes, sports field, hiking trails, v-ball.

Pets welcome. Open May 1 - Oct 15. Big rigs welcome. Clubs welcome. Rate in 2010 $24-35 per family. Member OPCA.

Phone: (613)822-0509
Address: 5227 Bank St, Ottawa, ON K1X 1H2
Lat/Lon: 45.28777/-75.57183
Email: terry@camphitherhills.com
Web: www.camphitherhills.com

SEE AD THIS PAGE

Grainger's Tent & Trailer Park (Not Visited)—*From jct Hwy 417 (exit 163) & Panmure Rd: Go 1 km S on Panmure Rd, then 3 km W on Breezy Heights Rd, then 1 km/1/2 mi on Grainger Park Rd. Enter on R.* ◇◇◇FACILITIES: 100 sites, typical site width 40 ft, 100 W&E, (15/30 amps), 30 pull-thrus, tenting, dump. ◇◇RECREATION: swim pool, pond fishing, playground. Pets welcome. Open May 1 - Oct 30. Rate in 2010 $27.50-32.50 for 4 persons. Phone: (613)839-5202.

OTTAWA MUNICIPAL CAMPGROUND—*From jct Hwy 417 (Queensway-exit 138) & March Rd: Go 1/2 km/1/3 mi N on March Rd, then 1 km/.8 mi E on CR 18 (Corkstown Rd). Enter on L.* FACILITIES: 176 sites, typical site width 60 ft, 1 full hkups, 105 W&E, 45 E, (15/30 amps), 25 no hkups, 1 pull-thrus, tenting, dump, laundry, ltd groc. RECREATION: playground. Pets welcome. Open May 1 - Oct 15. Phone: (613)828-6632.

OTTAWA—Continued

POPLAR GROVE TOURIST CAMP—*From East city limit jct Hwy 417 (exit 96) & Boundary Rd: Go .5 km/1/4 mi S on Boundary Rd, then 14.6 km/8-3/4 mi W on Mitch Owens Rd, then 3 km/1-3/4 mi S on Bank St. Enter on R.*

WELCOME

◇◇◇◇FACILITIES: 125 sites, typical site width 50 ft, 110 full hkups, 15 W&E, (20/30/50 amps), 30 no hkups, 70 pull-thrus, WiFi Instant Internet at site ($), phone Internet central location, family camping, tenting, RV storage, dump, laundry, ltd groc, ice, picnic tables, fire rings, grills, wood, controlled access.

◇◇◇◇◇RECREATION: rec hall, equipped pavilion, coin games, swim pool, mini-golf, ($), golf nearby, bsktball, playground, activities, tennis, horseshoes, sports field, hiking trails, v-ball. Rec open to public.

Pets welcome. Partial handicap access. Open May 1 - Oct 31. Big rigs welcome. Clubs welcome. Rate in 2010 $26-40 for 2 persons. MC/VISA/Debit. Member OPCA.

Phone: (613)821-2973
Address: 6154 Bank St, Greely, ON K4P 1B4
Lat/Lon: 45.15557/-75.33057
Email: info@poplargrovecamp.com
Web: www.poplargrovecamp.com

SEE AD THIS PAGE

Recreationland Tent & Trailer Park—*From jct Hwy 417 & Hwy 17: Go 26.5 km/16-1/2 mi E on Hwy 17, then .4 km/1/4 mi S on Canaan Rd. Enter on R.* ◇◇◇FACILITIES: 100 sites, typical site width 35 ft, 50 full hkups, 26 W&E, (15/30/50 amps), 50 amps ($), 24 no hkups, 30 pull-thrus, tenting, dump, laundry, ltd groc. ◇◇RECREATION: swim pool, playground. Pets welcome. Open May 1 - Oct 15. Big rigs welcome. Rate in 2010 $25-33 for 2 persons. Phone: (613)833-2974.

OWEN SOUND—G-2

(SE) HARRISON PARK (City Park)—*From jct Hwy 6 & 2nd Ave E: Go 3/4 km/1/2 mi S on 2nd Ave E.* FACILITIES: 108 sites, 108 W&E, (15/30 amps), 20 pull-thrus, tenting, dump, ltd groc. RECREATION: swim pool, river swim, boating, no motors, river fishing, playground. Open May 1 - Sep 30. Phone: (519)371-9734.

KELSO BEACH (City Park)—*From town: Go 3/4 km/1/2 mi W on Hwy 21, then 2-1/2 km/1-1/2 mi N on 4th Ave West.* FACILITIES: 40 sites, 40 W&E, tenting. RECREATION: lake swim, boating, lake fishing, playground. Open Jun - Sep. Phone: (519) 371-9734.

Kilsyth Country Campground (Not visited)—(Grey) *From jct Hwy 21 & CR 18: Go 4.8 km/3 mi S on CR 18, then go 3.8 km/2-1/2 mi W on Grey Rd 5. Enter on R.* ◇◇◇FACILITIES: 50 sites, typical site width 35 ft, 45 W&E, (15/30 amps), 5 no hkups, 3 pull-thrus, tenting, dump, laundry, ltd groc. ◇◇◇RECREATION: swim pool, playground. Pets welcome. Open mid May - mid Oct. Rate in 2010 $28-34 for 2 persons. Member OPCA. Phone: (519)371-3856.

KOA-Owen Sound (Not Visited)—(Grey) *From jct Hwy 26 & Hwy 6 & 10: Go .4 km/1/4 mi S on Hwy 6 & 10, then 3.2 km/2 mi E on 8th St., then .4 km/1/4 mi S on 28th Ave E (CR 5) then follow signs. Enter on L.* FACILITIES: 150 sites, typical site width 35 ft, 70 full hkups, 70 W&E, (15/30 amps), 10 no hkups, 8 pull-thrus, tenting, dump, laundry, ltd groc. RECREATION: swim pool, pond fishing, playground. Pets welcome. Open May 1 - mid Oct. Rate in 2010 $34-36 for 2 persons. Member ARVC, OPCA. Phone: (519)371-1331. KOA discount.

Sunny Valley Park (Not visited)—(Grey) *From jct Hwy 10 & Hwy 6: Go 10 km/6 mi S on Hwy 6, then .7 km/1/2 mi W on Sunny Valley Rd. Enter on R.* ◇◇◇FACILITIES: 75 sites, typical site width 40 ft, 35 ft max RV length, 75 W&E, (15/30 amps), 2 pull-thrus, tenting, dump, laundry, ltd groc. ◇◇◇◇RECREATION: swim pool, pond fishing, playground. Pets welcome. Open May 1 - End of Oct. Rate in 2010 $29 per family. Member OPCA. Phone: (519)794-3297.

Canada's two official sports are lacrosse and hockey.

PAISLEY—H-2

(NW) SAUGEEN BLUFFS (Saugeen Valley Cons Auth.)—*From town: Go 4 km/2-1/2 mi N on CR 3, follow signs.* FACILITIES: 212 sites, 68 W&E, 30 E, (30 amps), 114 no hkups, tenting, dump, laundry, ltd groc. RECREATION: river swim, boating, canoeing, dock, river fishing, playground. Pets welcome. Open May 15 - Oct 15. Phone: (519)353-7206.

PARIS—I-3

(N) PINEHURST LAKE (Grand River Cons Auth)—(Brant) *From north town limits: Go 9-1/2 km/6 mi N on Brant Hwy 24A. Enter on R.* FACILITIES: 273 sites, 179 W&E, 94 no hkups, tenting, dump, ltd groc. RECREATION: lake swim, boating, no motors, canoeing, lake fishing, playground. Open all yr. Facilities fully operational May 1 - Oct 15. Phone: (519)243-8563.

PARKHILL—I-2

Great Canadian Hideaway—(Middlesex) *From jct 7 & 81: Go 1.3km/3/4 mi N on Centre Rd & follow signs. Enter at end.* ◇◇◇FACILITIES: 162 sites, typical site width 35 ft, 2 full hkups, 120 W&E, 10 E, (15/30 amps), 30 no hkups, tenting, dump, laundry, ltd groc. ◇◇◇◇◇RECREATION: swim pool, lake swim, boating, electric motors only, canoeing, dock, lake fishing, playground. Pets welcome. Open May 1 - Mid Oct. Rate in 2010 $30-39 per family. Member OPCA. Phone: (519)294-6333.

PARRY SOUND—G-3

Horseshoe Lake Camp & Cottages (Not Visited)—(ParrySound) *From jct Hwy 400 (exit 207) & Hwy 141: Go 1.6 km/1 mi E on Hwy 141, then 4.3 km/2.7 mi N on North Sandy Plains Rd. Enter on L.* FACILITIES: 190 sites, typical site width 60 ft, 135 full hkups, 50 W&E, (30 amps), 5 no hkups, 8 pull-thrus, tenting, dump, laundry, ltd groc. RECREATION: lake swim, boating, canoeing, ramp, dock, lake fishing, playground. Pets welcome. Open all yr. Facilities fully operational May 1 - mid Oct. Rate in 2010 $25-45 per family. Member OPCA. Phone: (705)732-4928.

(S) OASTLER LAKE PROVINCIAL PARK—*From town: Go 8 km/5 mi S on Hwy 69.* FACILITIES: 148 sites, 24 E, (15 amps), 124 no hkups, 21 pull-thrus, tenting, dump, ltd groc. RECREATION: boating, canoeing, ramp, lake fishing. Partial handicap access. Open mid May - mid Oct. Phone: (705)378-2401.

Parry Sound-KOA Kampground (Not Visited)—(Parry Sound) *From jct Hwy 69 & Seguin Trail Rd/Horseshoe Lake Rd (exit 214): Go 1 mi S on Horseshoe Lake Rd to Black Rd, then 1/2 mi W to Rankin Lake Rd, then 1/2 mi N to the KOA. Enter on R.* FACILITIES: 111 sites, typical site width 35 ft, 67 W&E, (15/30/50 amps), 44 no hkups, 12 pull-thrus, tenting, dump, laundry, ltd groc. RECREATION: swim pool, playground. Pets welcome. Open May 1 - Oct 15. Rate in 2010 $32-50 for 2 persons. Member OPCA. Phone: (800) 562-2681. KOA discount.

PASS LAKE—B-1

(S) SLEEPING GIANT PROVINCIAL PARK—*From town: Go 19-1/4 km/12 mi S on Hwy 587.* FACILITIES: 200 sites, 85 E, (15 amps), 115 no hkups, 20 pull-thrus, tenting, dump, laundry, ltd groc. RECREATION: lake swim, boating, canoeing, ramp, dock, lake fishing, playground. Partial handicap access. Open May - Oct. Phone: (807)977-2526.

PEMBROKE—F-5

See listings at Cobden, Eganville & Round Lake Centre

(SE) PINE RIDGE PARK & RESORT—(Renfrew) *From jct Hwy 17 & CR 26 (Doran Rd): Go 1 km/1/2 mi N to Airport Rd, then 2.4 km/1-1/2 mi E on Airport Rd to Petawawa Blvd, then 2.4 km/1-1/2 mi E on Radtke Rd to River Rd, then 500 ft S on River Rd. Enter on R.*

WELCOME

◇◇◇FACILITIES: 38 sites, typical site width 40 ft, 26 full hkups, 1 W&E, (30 amps), 11 no hkups, mostly extd stay sites, 2 pull-thrus, family camping, tenting, cabins, dump, non-guest dump $, laundry, groceries, ice, picnic tables, fire rings, wood.

◇◇◇RECREATION: river swim, boating, canoeing, kayaking, ramp, dock, 4 canoe/2 kayak rentals, river fishing, golf nearby, bsktball, play equip-

PINE RIDGE PARK & RESORT—Continued on next page

PEMBROKE—Continued
PINE RIDGE PARK & RESORT—Continued

ment, shuffleboard court, activities (wkends), horseshoes, hiking trails, v-ball. Rec open to public.

Pets welcome. Open all yr. Facilities fully operational May 1 - Sep 30. Call ahead May,Jun, & Sep for reservations. Rate in 2010 $30 per family. MC/VISA/Debit. Member OPCA.

Phone: (888)746-3743
Address: RR 6 419 River Dr, Pembroke, ON K8A 6W7
Lat/Lon: 45.52883/-76.68583
Email: joshlin@sympatico.ca
Web: www.pineridgepark.com

SEE AD PAGE 882

(N) RIVERSIDE PARK (City Park)—*From jct Hwy 417 & Hwy 62: Go 8 km/5 mi N on Hwy 62, then 3/4 km/1/2 mi W on Pembroke St.* FACILITIES: 75 sites, 50 W&E, (30 amps), 25 no hkups, 28 pull-thrus, tenting, dump, laundry. RECREATION: river swim, river fishing, playground. Pets welcome. Open May 8 - Thanksgiving. Facilities fully operational Victoria Day - Labour Day. Phone: (613)735-6821.

PENETANGUISHENE—G-3

(W) AWENDA PROVINCIAL PARK—*From town: Go N on Hwy-35, then W.* FACILITIES: 233 sites, 102 E, (15/30 amps), 131 no hkups, tenting, dump, laundry. RECREATION: lake swim, canoeing, lake fishing, playground. Partial handicap access. Open mid May - Oct. Phone: (705)549-2231.

LaFontaine Resort Park (Not Visited)—(Simcoe) *From jct Hwy 93 & CR 25: Go 6.4 km/4 mi W on CR 25, then 8.5 km/5 mi N on CR 6, then 1.6 km/1 mi E on CR 26 (LaFontaine Rd). Enter on L.* FACILITIES: 300 sites, typical site width 45 ft, 152 full hkups, 44 W&E, (15/30 amps), 104 no hkups, 1 pull-thrus, tenting, dump, laundry, ltd groc. RECREATION: swim pool, saltwater swim, playground. Pets welcome. Open May 1 - Oct 15. Rate in 2010 $29-40 per family. Member OPCA. Phone: (705)533-2961.

PERRAULT FALLS—D-2

Gawley's Parkview Camp (Not Visited)—(Kenora) *From Hwy 105: Go .4 km/1/4 mi W on Camp Rd. S. of Bridge. Enter on L.* FACILITIES: 36 sites, 36 full hkups, (30 amps), tenting, laundry. RECREATION: lake swim, boating, canoeing, ramp, dock, lake fishing. Pets welcome. Open mid May - mid Sep. Rate in 2010 $24 for 2 persons. Phone: (807)529-3147.

PERTH—G-5

McCreary's Beach Vacation Resort—*From jct Hwy 43 & Hwy 7: Go 12 km/7-1/2 mi E on Hwy 7, then 1.6 km/1 mi S on Mississippi Lake W Shore Dr. Enter on L.* ◇◇◇FACILITIES: 150 sites, typical site width 35 ft, 130 full hkups, 20 W&E, (20/30 amps), 5 pull-thrus, tenting, dump, laundry, ltd groc. ◇◇◇◇RECREATION: swim pool, lake swim, boating, canoeing, ramp, dock, lake fishing, playground. Pets welcome. Open all yr. Facilities fully operational May 1 - Oct 15. Rate in 2010 $38-42 for 4 persons. Member OPCA. Phone: (613) 267-4450.

McCullough's Landing—*From jct Hwy 43 & Hwy 7: Go 12 km/7-1/2 mi N on Hwy 7 (east), then 1.6 km/1 mi E on Mississippi Lake W Shore Dr. Enter on R.* ◇◇◇FACILITIES: 200 sites, typical site width 30 ft, 35 ft max RV length, 180 W&E, (20 amps), 20 no hkups, 6 pull-thrus, tenting, dump, ltd groc. ◇◇◇◇RECREATION: lake swim, boating, canoeing, ramp, dock, lake fishing, playground. Pets welcome. Open May 1 - Sep 30. Rate in 2010 $28-35 per family. Member OPCA. Phone: (613)267-4310.

(S) MURPHY'S POINT PROVINCIAL PARK—*From town: Go 16 km/10 mi S on Hwy 10, then 4-3/4 km/3 mi SE on Hwy 14.* FACILITIES: 160 sites, 27 E, (15/30 amps), 133 no hkups, tenting, dump, laundry, ltd groc. RECREATION: lake swim, boating, canoeing, ramp, lake fishing, playground. Partial handicap access. Open mid May - mid Oct. Phone: (613)267-5060.

Tay River Tent & Trailer Camp—*From jct Hwy 43 & Christie Lake Rd (CR 6) in town: Go 14.4 km/9 mi W on Christie Lake Rd (CR 6). Enter on L.* ◇◇◇FACILITIES: 100 sites, typical site width 50 ft, 100 W&E, (30 amps), tenting, dump, laundry, ltd groc. ◇◇◇RECREATION: swim pool, river swim, boating, ramp, dock, lake/river fishing, playground. Pets welcome. Open mid May - mid Oct. Rate in 2010 $20-28 per family. Member OPCA. Phone: (613)267-3955.

PETERBOROUGH—H-4

See listings at Bailieboro, Bewdley & Ennismore

Bailey's Bay Resort (Not Visted)—*From jct Hwy 7 & Hwy 7B: Go 305 m/1000 feet E on Hwy 7B. Enter on L.* FACILITIES: 364 sites, typical site width 50 ft, 364 full hkups, (20/30 amps), dump, laundry, ltd groc. RECREATION: swim pool, lake swim, boating, ramp, dock, lake fishing, playground. Pets welcome. No tents. Open May 2 - Oct 19. Rate in 2010 $37.80 per family. Phone: (705)748-9656.

PETROLIA—I-1

LORNE C. HENDERSON AREA (St. Clair Region Cons Auth.)—(Lambton) *From town: Go 2 km/1-1/4 mi W on CR 4.* FACILITIES: 126 sites, 126 W&E, (15/30 amps), tenting, dump. RECREATION: swim pool, boating, no motors, canoeing, stream fishing, playground. Open late May - mid Oct. Phone: (519)882-2280.

PICTON—H-5

See listings at Adolphustown, Bloomfield, Cherry Valley & Milford

Smugglers Cove Campground (Not visited)—*From jct Hwy 49 & CR 8: Go 1-3/4 mi E on CR 8, then 4 mi SE on CR 17, then 3/4 mi E on CR 16, then 7-1/4 mi S on CR 13. Enter on L.* ◇◇◇FACILITIES: 128 sites, typical site width 45 ft, 12 full hkups, 92 W&E, (15/30 amps), 24 no hkups, tenting, dump, laundry, ltd groc. ◇◇◇RECREATION: lake swim, boating, canoeing, ramp, dock, lake fishing, playground. Pets welcome. Open May 1 - End of Sep. Rate in 2010 $31-40 per family. Member OPCA. Phone: (613)476-4125.

PORT BURWELL—J-2

Big Otter Marina & Campground (Not visited)—(Elgin) *From north end of town & Bridge St (CR 42): Go 500 feet N on CR 42. Enter on R.* ◇◇◇FACILITIES: 62 sites, typical site width 35 ft, 35 ft max RV length, 43 full hkups, 5 W&E, (15 amps), 14 no hkups, tenting, dump. ◇◇◇RECREATION: lake swim, boating, canoeing, ramp, dock, lake/river fishing, play equipment. Pets welcome. Open mid May - mid Oct. Member OPCA. Phone: (519)874-4034.

(W) PORT BURWELL PROVINCIAL PARK—*From town: Go 4-3/4 km/3 mi W on Lakeshore Rd.* FACILITIES: 232 sites, 123 E, (15/30 amps), 109 no hkups, tenting, dump, laundry, ltd groc. RECREATION: boating, canoeing, ramp, lake fishing, playground. Partial handicap access. Open mid May - early Sep. Phone: (519)874-4691.

Sand Hill Park (Not visited)—(Elgin) *From east town limits: Go 14.4 km/9 mi E on Lakeshore Rd (CR 42). Enter on R.* ◇◇◇FACILITIES: 290 sites, typical site width 40 ft, 50 full hkups, 100 W&E, (15/30 amps), 140 no hkups, tenting, dump, ltd groc. ◇◇◇RECREATION: lake swim, boating, canoeing, lake/pond/stream fishing, playground. Pets welcome. Partial handicap access. Open May 1 - mid Oct. Rate in 2010 $17 per vehicle. Phone: (519)586-3891.

PORT COLBORNE—I-3

LONG BEACH (Niagara Peninsula Cons Auth.) (Not Visited)—*From town: Go 16 km/10 mi W on Hwy 3 to Lake Shore Rd.* FACILITIES: 275 sites, 200 W&E, (15/30 amps), 75 no hkups, 275 pull-thrus, tenting, dump, ltd groc. RECREATION: lake swim, boating, canoeing, ramp, lake fishing, playground. Open May 15 - Sep 20. Phone: (905)899-3462.

WELCOME **SHERKSTON SHORES**—*From jct Hwy 140 & Hwy 3: Go 8 km/5 mi E on Hwy 3, then 2.4 km/1-1/2 mi S on Empire Rd (Regional Rd 98). Enter at end.*

FAMILY CAMPING ON LAKE ERIE SHORES

A 560 acre lakeside location full of amenities from outdoor pools, splash pool, hot tubs, sandy beach, waterslides, mini putt, tennis & more. Camping sites, EW & EWS RV Sites, Vacation Home Rentals.

◇◇◇◇◇FACILITIES: 246 sites, typical site width 40 ft, 156 full hkups, 70 W&E, (15/30/50 amps), 20 no hkups, some extd stay sites, 41 pull-thrus, cable TV, WiFi Instant Internet at site, WiFi Internet central location, tenting, dump, laundry, full svc store, RV supplies, LP gas by weight, LP bottle exch, ice, picnic tables, patios, fire rings, wood, controlled access.

◇◇◇◇◇RECREATION: rec hall, rec room/area, equipped pavilion, coin games, 2 swim pools, wading pool, spray ground, lake swim, hot tub, boating, canoeing, kayaking, 6 canoe/6 kayak/6 pedal boat rentals, lake/pond fishing, fishing supplies, mini-golf, putting green, golf nearby, bsktball, playground, activities, tennis, horseshoes, sports field, hiking trails, v-ball, local tours. Rec open to public.

Pets welcome. Partial handicap access. Open May 1 - Oct 31. Big rigs welcome. Clubs welcome. Rate in 2010 $19-91 per family. MC/VISA/Debit. ATM. Member ARVC, OPCA.

Phone: (877)482-3224
Address: 490 Empire Rd, Sherkston, ON LOS 1R0
Lat/Lon: 42.87012/-79.13407
Email: reservations@sherkston.com
Web: www.sherkston.com

SEE AD TRAVEL SECTION PAGE 862

WELCOME **SHERKSTON SHORES PARK MODEL SALES**—*From jct Hwy 140 & Hwy 3: Go 8 km/5 mi E on Hwy 3, then 2.4 km/1-1/2 mi S on Empire Rd (Regional Rd 98). Enter at end.* SALES: park models, pre-owned unit sales. SERVICES:

PORT COLBORNE—Continued
SHERKSTON SHORES PARK MODEL SALES—Continued

Phone: (877)482-3224
Lat/Lon: 42.87012/-79.13407
Email: reservation@sherkston.com
Web: www.sherkston.com

SEE AD TRAVEL SECTION PAGE 862

WELCOME **SHERKSTON SHORES WATER PARK**—*From jct Hwy 140 & Hwy 3: Go 8 km/5 mi E on Hwy 3, then 2.4 km/1-1/2 mi S on Empire Rd (Regional Rd 98). Enter at end.* Waterpark part of camping resort.

Address: Sherkston, ON LOS 1RO
Lat/Lon: 42.87012/-79.13407
Email: reservation@sherkston.com
Web: www.sherkston.com

SEE AD TRAVEL SECTION PAGE 862

PORT DOVER—I-3

See listings at: Port Burwell, Port Rowan, St. Williams, Turkey Point

PORT ELGIN—H-2

BRUCEDALE CONSERVATION AREA (Saugeen Valley Cons Area)—*From town: Go 13 km/8 mi S on Hwy 21, then 8 km/5 mi W on Concession Rd 10. Enter on L.* FACILITIES: 54 sites, 25 E, 29 no hkups, tenting, dump. RECREATION: lake swim, boating, canoeing, dock, lake fishing, playground. Partial handicap access. Open mid May - Sep 1. Phone: (519)364-1255.

(S) MACGREGOR POINT PROVINCIAL PARK—*From town: Go 4-3/4 km/3 mi S on Hwy 21.* FACILITIES: 360 sites, 140 E, (15/30 amps), 220 no hkups, 45 pull-thrus, tenting, dump, laundry, ltd groc. RECREATION: lake swim, canoeing, playground. Partial handicap access. Open mid May - mid Oct. Phone: (519) 389-9056.

(E) PORT ELGIN MUNICIPAL TOURIST CAMP—*In town at corner of Bruce St & Johnson Ave.* FACILITIES: 344 sites, 35 full hkups, 309 W&E, (30 amps), 3 pull-thrus, tenting, dump. RECREATION: lake swim, boating, ramp, dock, lake/river fishing, playground. Partial handicap access. Open May 1 - Oct 31. Phone: (519)832-2512.

PORT PERRY—H-3

Goreski's Landing (Not visited)—*From jct Hwy 12 & Hwy 7A: Go 6.4 km/4 mi E on Hwy 7A, then 6.4 km/4 mi N on Island (7), then follow signs. Enter on R.* ◇◇◇FACILITIES: 460 sites, typical site width 40 ft, 440 full hkups, 20 W&E, (15/30 amps), tenting, dump, ltd groc. ◇◇◇◇RECREATION: swim pool, lake swim, boating, ramp, dock, lake fishing, playground. Pets welcome. Open May 15 - Oct 12. Rate in 2010 $43-53 for 4 persons. Member OPCA. Phone: (905)985-9763.

PORT ROWAN—J-2

(N) BACKUS HERITAGE CONSERVATION AREA (Long Point Region Cons Auth.)—*From town: Go 2-1/2 km/1-1/2 mi N on Regional Rd 42.* FACILITIES: 150 sites, 50 W&E, (15 amps), 100 no hkups, tenting, dump, laundry. RECREATION: swim pool, boating, no motors, dock, pond fishing, playground. Open May 1 - Oct 15. Phone: (519)586-2201.

(S) LONG POINT PROVINCIAL PARK—*From town: Go 4-3/4 km/3 mi S on Hwy 59.* FACILITIES: 256 sites, 78 E, (15/30 amps), 178 no hkups, 52 pull-thrus, tenting, dump, laundry, ltd groc. RECREATION: boating, canoeing, ramp, playground. Partial handicap access. Open May 12 - Oct 9. Phone: (519)586-2133.

PORT SEVERN—G-3

(N) SIX MILE LAKE PROVINCIAL PARK—*From town: Go 9-1/2 km/6 mi N on Hwy 103.* FACILITIES: 217 sites, 53 E, (15/30 amps), 164 no hkups, tenting, dump, laundry, ltd groc. RECREATION: lake swim, boating, canoeing, ramp, dock, playground. Partial handicap access. Open May - Oct. Phone: (705) 756-2746.

PORTLAND—G-5

Moonlight Bay Campground (Not Visited)—*From jct Hwy 42 & Hwy 15: Go 15.2 km/9-1/2 mi N on Hwy 15, then 153 m/500 feet W on Briton-Houghton Bay Rd (CR 38).* ◇◇◇FACILITIES: 125 sites, typical site width 30 ft, 105 full hkups, 20 W&E, (30 amps), 10 pull-thrus, tenting, dump, laundry, ltd groc. ◇◇◇RECREATION: swim pool, lake swim, boating, canoeing, ramp, dock, lake fishing, playground. Pets welcome. Open May 15 - Oct 1. Rate in 2010 $36-38 per family. Member OPCA. Phone: (613)283-8659. FMCA discount.

PRESCOTT—G-6

WELCOME **GRENVILLE PARK**—*From jct Hwy 16 (Johnstown-Ogdensburg Bridge) S'bnd (Exit 1) & Hwy 401. E'bnd (Exit 721B) Or Hwy 401. W'bnd (Exit 721): Go 1 km/1/2 mi S on Hwy 16, then .4 km/1/4 mi E on Hwy 2. Enter on R.*

◇◇◇◇FACILITIES: 175 sites, typical site width 40 ft, 160 W&E, (15/30 amps), 15 no hkups, many extd stay sites, 8 pull-thrus, WiFi Instant Internet at site ($), family camping, tenting, RV's/park model rentals, cabins, RV storage, dump, non-

GRENVILLE PARK—Continued on next page

PRESCOTT—Continued
GRENVILLE PARK—Continued

guest dump $, portable dump, laundry, full svc store, RV supplies, ice, picnic tables, fire rings, grills, wood, controlled access.

◆◆◆◆◆RECREATION: rec hall, rec room/area, equipped pavilion, coin games, river swim, boating, canoeing, kayaking, ramp, 3 canoe/3 kayak/2 pedal boat rentals, river fishing, fishing supplies, golf nearby, bsktball, 15 bike rentals, playground, activities, horseshoes, sports field, hiking trails, v-ball. Rec open to public.

Pets welcome. Partial handicap access. Open Apr 1 - Oct 31. Clubs welcome. Rate in 2010 $31-36 per family. MC/VISA/Debit. ATM. Member OPCA. CCUSA 50% Discount. CCUSA reservations Accepted, CCUSA max stay 3 days, CCUSA disc. not avail F,Sa, CCUSA disc. not avail holidays. All stays based on availability. Cancellation policy: 1 night cancellation fee at regular price will apply.

Phone: (613)925-2000
Address: 2323 Hwy 2 RR #3, Prescott, ON K0E 1T0
Lat/Lon: 44.45057/-75.27162
Email: Grenvillepark@xplornet.com
Web: www.grenvillepark.com

SEE AD BROCKVILLE PAGE 869

PROVIDENCE BAY—F-1

Providence Bay Tent & Trailer Park (Not visited)—(Manitoulin) *From town: Go .8 km/1/2 mi E on Hwy 551. Enter on L.* ◆◆◆FACILITIES: 250 sites, typical site width 40 ft, 210 W&E, (15/20/30 amps), 40 no hkups, 2 pull-thrus, tenting, dump, ltd groc. ◆◆RECREATION: lake swim, boating, canoeing, lake/river fishing. Pets welcome. Open May 1 - Oct 1. Rate in 2010 $27-31 per family. Phone: (877)269-2018.

PUSLINCH—I-3

EMERALD LAKE TRAILER RESORT & WATER PARK—(Wellington) *From jct Hwy 401 and Hwy 6: Go 5 km/3 mi S on Hwy 6, then go 5 km/3 mi W on Con Rd 11. (Gore Rd). Enter on R.*

◆◆◆◆◆FACILITIES: 270 sites, typical site width 46 ft, 210 full hkups, 30 W&E, (30/50 amps), 30 no hkups, many extd stay sites, 10 pull-thrus, heater not allowed, WiFi Internet central location, family camping, tenting, cabins, RV storage, dump, non-guest dump $, laundry, ltd groc, ice, picnic tables, fire rings, wood, controlled access.

◆◆◆◆◆RECREATION: rec hall, pavilion, equipped pavilion, swim pool, wading pool, spray ground, lake swim, hot tub, boating, kayaking, 4 kayak/9 pedal boat rentals, golf nearby, bsktball, playground, activities, (wkends), horseshoes, sports field, hiking trails, v-ball. Rec open to public.

Pets welcome. Partial handicap access. Open May 1 - Oct 15. Big rigs welcome. Clubs welcome. Rate in 2010 $50-65 per family. MC/VISA/Debit. Member OPCA.

Phone: (800)679-1853
Address: 7248 Gore Rd RR 2, Puslinch, ON N0B 2J0
Lat/Lon: 43.41137/-80.12915
Email: emeraldlake@bellnet.ca
Web: www.emeraldlake.ca

SEE AD TORONTO PAGE 888

EMERALD LAKE WATER PARK—*From jct Hwy 401 and Hwy 6: Go 5 km/3 mi S on Hwy 6, then 5 km/3 mi W on Con Rd 11. (Gore Rd). Enter on R.* 4 acre spring fed lake with slides, splash park, whirlpool, wading pool. Open May 24 - Sep 5. MC/VISA/Debit.

Save Money—Plan Ahead with WOODALL'S!

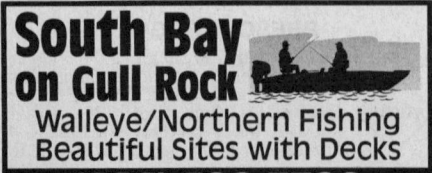

PUSLINCH—Continued
EMERALD LAKE WATER PARK—Continued

Phone: (800)679-1853
Address: 7248 Gore Rd RR 2, Puslinch, ON N0B 2J0
Email: emeraldlake@bellnet.ca
Web: www.emeraldlake.ca

SEE AD TORONTO PAGE 888

RED LAKE—C-1

(SE) SOUTH BAY ON GULL ROCK (Not Visited)—(Kenora) *From south city limits: Go 13 km/8 mi S on Hwy 105, then .8 km/1/2 mi E on Hopperstad Rd. Enter on R.*

FACILITIES: 16 sites, typical site width 50 ft, 12 full hkups, 4 W&E, (15/30/50 amps), 8 pull-thrus, WiFi Instant Internet at site, tenting, cabins, dump, laundry, ltd groc, marine gas, ice, picnic tables, fire rings, wood.

RECREATION: rec room/area, lake swim, boating, canoeing, ramp, dock, 2 pedal boat/5 motorboat rentals, lake fishing, fishing supplies, activities, horseshoes.

Pets welcome. Open May 15 - Oct 1. Big rigs welcome. Rate in 2010 $35 for 2 persons.

Phone: (866)300-5330
Address: #1 Hopperstad Rd, Red Lake, ON P0V 2M0
Lat/Lon: 50.55593/-93.44782
Email: spenceley@xplornet.com
Web: www.southbaygullrock.com

SEE AD THIS PAGE

RENFREW—F-5

(NW) Canadian Timberland Campground—(Renfrew) *From Hwy 17 & Castleford Rd: Go 5km/3mi E on Castleford Rd. Enter on R.* ◆◆◆FACILITIES: 74 sites, typical site width 40 ft, 62 full hkups, 12 W&E, (15/30/50 amps), 9 pull-thrus, family camping, tenting, dump, laundry, ltd groc. ◆◆◆RECREATION: swim pool, river fishing, playground. Pets welcome. Partial handicap access. Open May 1 - Mid Oct. Big rigs welcome. Rate in 2010 $29-45 per family. Member OPCA. Phone: (613)432-5767.

(NW) KOA-Renfrew—*From jct Hwy 17 & Hwy 60: Go 9.6 km/6mi W on Hwy 17, then .4 km/1/4 mi N on Storyland Rd (CR 4), then .4 km/1/4 mi S on Johnston Rd. Enter on L.* ◆◆◆◆FACILITIES: 100 sites, typical site width 35 ft, 67 full hkups, 11 W&E, (30 amps), 22 no hkups, 10 pull-thrus, tenting, dump, laundry, groceries. ◆◆◆◆RECREATION: lake swim, boating, no motors, canoeing, dock, lake fishing, playground. Pets welcome. Open May 1 - Oct 15. Rate in 2010 $30-45 for 2 persons. Phone: (800)562-3980. KOA discount.

RESTOULE—F-3

(W) RESTOULE PROVINCIAL PARK—*From town: Go 4-3/4 km/3 mi W on Hwy 534.* FACILITIES: 278 sites, 99 E, (15/30 amps), 179 no hkups, tenting, dump, laundry. RECREATION: boating, canoeing, ramp, dock, playground. Partial handicap access. Open Apr - Nov. Phone: (705)729-2010.

RICE LAKE—H-4

See listings at Bailieboro, Bewdley & Roseneath

ROCKWOOD—I-3

(W) ROCKWOOD (Grand River Cons Auth)—*From town: Go 11-1/4 km/7 mi E on Hwy 7. Enter on L.* FACILITIES: 100 sites, 50 W&E, (15/30 amps), 50 no hkups, tenting, dump. RECREATION: lake swim, boating, no motors, canoeing, lake fishing, playground. Open May 1 - Oct 15. Phone: (519)856-9543.

RODNEY—J-2

Lakewood Trailer Estates—(Aldborough) *From jct Hwy 401 & Furnival Rd (exit 129): Go 10.4 km/6-1/2 mi S on Furnival Rd. Enter on L.* ◆◆◆◆FACILITIES: 250 sites, 250 full hkups, (30 amps), laundry, ltd groc. ◆◆◆◆RECREATION: swim pool, lake swim, boating, lake fishing, playground. Pets welcome. Partial handicap access. No tents. Open May 1 - Oct 31. Rate in 2010 $28 per family. Member OPCA. Phone: (519)785-2020.

(SE) PORT GLASGOW TENT & TRAILER PARK (Township Park)—*From jct Hwy 3 & Elgin CR 3: Go 2 km/1-1/4 mi S on CR 3.* FACILITIES: 200 sites, 4 full hkups, 50 W&E, (30/50 amps), 146 no hkups, tenting, dump, ltd groc. RECREATION: lake swim, boating, lake fishing, playground. Partial handicap access. Open May - Oct. Phone: (519)785-0069.

ROSENEATH—H-4

Golden Beach Resort and Trailer Park (Not Visited)—*From jct Hwy 401 (exit 464) & Hwy 28: Go 12 km/7-1/2 mi N on Hwy 28, then 15.2 km/9-1/2 mi E on CR 9, then 1.6 km/1 mi N on Lilac Valley Rd (gravel road). Enter on L.* ◆◆◆FACILITIES: 329 sites, typical site width 40 ft, 289 full hkups, (30/50 amps), 40 no

Shop with Dealers in Woodall's

ROSENEATH—Continued
Golden Beach Resort and Trailer Park (Not Visited)—Continued

hkups, 40 pull-thrus, tenting, laundry, groceries. ◆◆◆◆RECREATION: swim pool, lake swim, boating, canoeing, ramp, dock, lake fishing, playground. Pets welcome. Open May 1 - Oct 15. Rate in 2010 $28-30 for 2 persons. Member OPCA. Phone: (905)342-5366.

ROUND LAKE CENTRE—F-4

BONNECHERE PROVINCIAL PARK—*From town: Go 6-1/2 km/4 mi N on Hwy 62.* FACILITIES: 128 sites, 24 E, (15/30 amps), 104 no hkups, tenting, dump, laundry. RECREATION: boating, canoeing, ramp, playground. Partial handicap access. Open mid May - mid Nov. Phone: (613)757-2103.

Covered Bridge Park (Not visited)—(Renfrew) *From jct CR 67 & CR 58: Go 5 km/3 mi S on CR 58 (Round Lake Rd). Enter on L.* FACILITIES: 57 sites, typical site width 30 ft, 47 full hkups, (15/30 amps), 10 no hkups, 6 pull-thrus, family camping, tenting, dump, laundry. RECREATION: lake/river swim, boating, canoeing, ramp, dock, lake/river fishing. Pets welcome. Open Mid May - Last week of Oct. Rate in 2010 $25-30 per family. Phone: (613)757-3368.

ST. CATHARINES—I-3

JORDAN VALLEY CAMPGROUND—*From jct QEW (exit 57) & Regional Rd 24: Go 2.4 km/1-1/2 mi E on South Service Rd, then 3 km/1-3/4 mi S on 21st St. Enter on R.*

◆◆◆FACILITIES: 116 sites, typical site width 40 ft, 50 full hkups, 9 W&E, (15/30 amps), 57 no hkups, some extd stay sites, 16 pull-thrus, cable TV, WiFi Internet central location, family camping, tenting, RV storage, dump, laundry, ice, picnic tables, fire rings, wood.

◆◆◆◆RECREATION: rec hall, coin games, swim pool, canoeing, 4 canoe/pedal boat rentals, river fishing, fishing supplies, golf nearby, bsktball, bike rental, playground, activities, (wkends), horseshoes, sports field, hiking trails, v-ball, local tours.

Pets welcome. Open May 1 - Oct 15. Green Friendly. Rate in 2010 $30.70-38.81 for 2 persons. MC/VISA/AMEX/Debit. Member OPCA.

Phone: (866)526-2267
Address: 3902 21st St RR 1, Jordan, ON L0R 1S0
Lat/Lon: 43.15122/-79.37183
Email: jvc@campingniagara.com
Web: www.campingniagara.com

SEE AD NIAGARA FALLS PAGE 879

Shangri-La Park Campground—*From jct QEW (exit 55) & Jordan Rd: Go 4.8 km/3 mi S on Jordan Rd, then 500 feet E on Regional Rd 81, then 1.6 km/1 mi S on 17th St. Enter on L.* ◆◆◆FACILITIES: 300 sites, typical site width 40 ft, 200 W&E, 50 E, (15/30/50 amps), 50 no hkups, 12 pull-thrus, tenting, dump, laundry, ltd groc. ◆◆◆RECREATION: swim pool, playground. Pets welcome. Open May 15 - Oct 15. Rate in 2010 $28-36 for 2 persons. Member OPCA. Phone: (905)562-5851.

ST. JOSEPH'S ISLAND—D-4

See listings at Hilton Beach

SANDFORD—H-3

Grangeways Trailer Park (Not visited)—*From jct Hwy 48 & Herald Rd.: Go 4 mi E on Herald Rd., then N on Rd. 30, then 1/2 mi N on 3rd Conc. Enter on L.* ◆◆◆◆FACILITIES: 300 sites, typical site width 30 ft, 300 full hkups, (30 amps), tenting, dump, laundry, ltd groc. ◆◆◆◆RECREATION: swim pool, river swim, river/pond fishing, playground. Pets welcome. Open May 1 - Mid Oct. Rate in 2010 $43.05 per family. Member OPCA. Phone: (905)852-3260.

SARNIA—I-1

See listings at Forest, Grand Bend, Strathroy & Wyoming.

WARWICK AREA (St. Clair Region Cons Auth.)—(Lambton) *From east city limits: Go 28-3/4 km/18 mi E on Hwy 7.* FACILITIES: 181 sites, 181 W&E, tenting, dump, laundry. RECREATION: swim pool, boating, no motors, canoeing, lake fishing, playground. Open mid May - mid Oct. Phone: (519)849-6770.

SAUBLE BEACH—G-2

Carson's Camp—(Bruce) *From south city limits: Go 1 km/1/2 mi S on CR 13 (Southhampton Pkwy). Enter on R.* ◆◆◆◆◆FACILITIES: 700 sites, typical site width 38 ft, 700 full hkups, (30/50 amps), 34 pull-thrus, family camping, tenting, laundry, groceries. ◆◆◆◆◆RECREATION: swim pool, lake swim, boating, no motors, canoeing, dock, lake/pond fishing, playground. Pets welcome. Partial handicap access. Open May 1 - mid Oct. Big rigs welcome. Rate in 2010 $38-44 for 2 persons. Member ARVC, OPCA. Phone: (519) 422-1143.

SAUBLE BEACH—Continued on next page

SAUBLE BEACH—Continued

Fiddlehead Resort Camp (Not visited)—(Bruce) *From jct Hwy 8 & CR 13: Go 11.3 km/6-1/2 mi N on (Bruce Rd 13) Sauble Falls Pkwy, then go 1.1 km W on Oliphant Way. Enter on L.* ◆◆◆FACILITIES: 37 sites, typical site width 50 ft, 22 full hkups, 2 W&E, (15/30 amps), 13 no hkups, tenting, dump. ◆◆◆RECREATION: lake swim, canoeing, lake fishing, playground. Pets welcome. Open May 1 - Mid Sep. Rate in 2010 $32-40 per family. Member OPCA. Phone: (519) 534-0405.

Sauble Beach Resort Camp—(Bruce) *From east city limits: Go 1.6 km/1 mi E on CR 8. Enter on L.* ◆◆FACILITIES: 295 sites, typical site width 35 ft, 200 full hkups, 89 W&E, (15/30 amps), 6 no hkups, 12 pull-thrus, family camping, tenting, laundry, ltd groc. ◆◆RECREATION: 2 swim pools, playground. Pets welcome. Open May 15 - Oct 15. Rate in 2010 $42 for 2 persons. Member ARVC, OPCA. Phone: (519)422-1101.

(N) SAUBLE FALLS PROVINCIAL PARK—*From town: Go 4 km/2-1/2 mi N on CR 21.* FACILITIES: 152 sites, typical site width 15 ft, 36 ft max RV length, 49 E, (15/30 amps), 103 no hkups, 22 pull-thrus, tenting, dump, laundry. RECREATION: river swim, boating, canoeing, ramp, river fishing, playground. Partial handicap access. Open late Apr - late Oct. Phone: (519)422-1952.

WOODLAND PARK—(Bruce) *From jct CR-8 & CR-13 (traffic light): Go .4 km/-1/4 mi N on CR 13 (Sauble Falls Rd). Enter on R.*

WELCOME

◆◆◆◆◆FACILITIES: 730 sites, typical site width 40 ft, 700 full hkups, 23 W&E, (30/50 amps), 7 no hkups, mostly extd stay sites, 13 pull-thrus, cable TV, cable Instant Internet at site ($), phone Internet central location ($), family camping, tenting, RV's/park model rentals, shower$, laundry, groceries, RV supplies, LP gas by weight, ice, picnic tables, patios, fire rings, wood, controlled access.

◆◆◆◆◆RECREATION: rec hall, rec room/area, coin games, swim pool, hot tub, golf nearby, bsktball, playground, activities, horseshoes, sports field, hiking trails, v-ball.

Pets welcome. Partial handicap access. Open May 1 - Mid Oct. Clubs welcome. Green Friendly. Rate in 2010 $32-51 for 2 persons. MC/VISA/Debit. Member OPCA.

Text 108023 to (440)725-8687 to see our Visual Tour.

Phone: (519)422-1161
Address: RR 1, 47 Sauble Falls Parkway, Sauble Beach, ON N0H 2G0
Lat/Lon: 44.63442/-81.26408
Email: info@woodlandpark.on.ca
Web: www.woodlandpark.on.ca

SEE AD THIS PAGE

SAUBLE FALLS—G-2

Sauble Falls Tent & Trailer Park (Not visited)—(Bruce) *From jct Hwy 8 & CR 13: Go 4 mi N on Sauble Falls Parkwy (Bruce Rd 13). Enter on R.* ◆◆◆◆FACILITIES: 350 sites, typical site width 40 ft, 230 full hkups, 60 W&E, (15/30 amps), 60 no hkups, 3 pull-thrus, tenting, laundry, ltd groc. ◆◆◆RECREATION: playground. Pets welcome. Open May 1 - Oct 15. Rate in 2010 $28-40 per family. Member ARVC, OPCA. Phone: (519) 422-1322.

SAULT STE. MARIE—D-4

See listings at Goulais River, Hilton Beach, Iron Bridge & Thessalon

(N) Glenview Cottages & Campground (Not Visited)—(Algoma) *Located on Hwy 17N 15.4 km/9.6 mi N of International Bridge and city center. Enter on L.* ◆◆◆FACILITIES: 60 sites, typical site width 35 ft, 19 full hkups, 26 W&E, (30 amps), 15 no hkups, 23 pull-thrus, family camping, tenting, dump, laundry, ltd groc. ◆◆◆RECREATION: swim pool, pond fishing, playground. Pets welcome. Open May 15 - Oct 15. Rate in 2010 $27-40 for 2 persons. Member OPCA. Phone: (705)759-3436. FMCA discount.

KOA-Sault Ste. Marie (Not Visited)—(Algoma) *From jct Hwy 550, Hwy 17-B & Hwy 17: Go 4.8 km/3 mi N on Hwy 17, then .8 km/1/2 mi W on 5th Line Rd. Enter on L.* ◆◆◆FACILITIES: 155 sites, typical site width 35 ft, 29 full hkups, 74 W&E, (30/50 amps), 52 no hkups, 86 pull-thrus, family camping, tenting, dump, laundry, ltd groc. ◆◆◆◆RECREATION: swim pool, playground. Pets welcome. Open May 1 - Oct 15. Big rigs welcome. Rate in 2010 $34-58 for 2 persons. Phone: (705)759-2344. KOA discount.

SCHREIBER—B-2

RAINBOW FALLS PROVINCIAL PARK—*From town: Go 12-3/4 km/8 mi W on Hwy 17.* FACILITIES: 36 sites, 23 E, 13 no hkups, 6 pull-thrus, tenting, dump, laundry, ltd groc. RECREATION: boating, canoeing, ramp, playground. Partial handicap access. Open May - Sep. Phone: (807)824-2298.

Travel Rest Tent & Trailer Park (Not Visited) (RV SPACES)—(Algoma) *At west end of town on Hwy-17. Enter on R.* FACILITIES: 40 sites, typical site width 40 ft, 18 full hkups, 14 W&E, (15/30 amps), 8 no hkups, 20 pull-thrus, tenting, dump. RECREATION: swim pool, play equipment. Pets welcome. Open mid May - mid Oct. Rate in 2010 $18-22 for 2 persons.

SEELEYS BAY—G-5

Cranberry Park—*From jct Hwy 32 & Hwy 15: Go 6.8 km/4-1/4 mi S on Hwy 15, then .8 km/1/2 mi W on Leo Lake Rd. Caution: Low overhead wire at entrance road. Enter on R.* ◆◆◆FACILITIES: 85 sites, typical site width 50 ft, 30 full hkups, 50 W&E, (20 amps), 5 no hkups, tenting, dump, laundry, ltd groc. ◆◆◆RECREATION: lake swim, boating, canoeing, ramp, dock, lake fishing, playground. Pets welcome. Open mid May - mid Oct. Rate in 2010 $30-35 per family. Member OPCA. Phone: (613)387-2004.

SELKIRK—I-3

(SW) HALDIMAND AREA (Long Point Region Cons Auth.)—*From town: Go 4-3/4 km/3 mi W on Regional Rd 3, then 4-3/4 km/3 mi S on Regional Rd 62, then W on Lakeshore Rd.* FACILITIES: 235 sites, 178 full hkups, (15/30 amps), 57 no hkups, tenting, dump, laundry. RECREATION: lake swim, boating, lake fishing, playground. Partial handicap access. Open May 1 - Oct 15. Phone: (905)776-2700.

(N) SELKIRK PROVINCIAL PARK—*From town: Go 3-1/4 km/2 mi W off Rainham Rd.* FACILITIES: 142 sites, typical site width 20 ft, 62 E, (15 amps), 80 no hkups, 40 pull-thrus, tenting, dump, laundry, ltd groc. RECREATION: boating, canoeing, ramp, playground. Partial handicap access. Open May 1 - mid Oct. Phone: (905)776-2600.

SHARBOT LAKE—G-5

(W) SHARBOT LAKE PROVINCIAL PARK—*From jct Hwy 7 & Hwy 38: Go 4-3/4 km/3 mi W on Hwy 7.* FACILITIES: 185 sites, typical site width 15 ft, 29 E, (15 amps), 156 no hkups, tenting, dump, laundry, ltd groc. RECREATION: lake swim, boating, canoeing, ramp, dock, lake fishing, playground. Partial handicap access. Open mid May - early Sep. Phone: (613)335-2814.

SHEGUIANDAH—F-1

BATMAN'S COTTAGES, CAMPGROUND—(Manitoulin) *From Sheguiandah: Go 3.2 km/2 mi S on Hwy 6. Enter on L.*

WELCOME

◆◆◆◆FACILITIES: 142 sites, typical site width 40 ft, 35 full hkups, 85 W&E, (15/30 amps), 22 no hkups, some extd stay sites, WiFi Internet central location, family camping, tenting, cabins, RV storage, dump, non-guest dump $, portable dump, laundry, full svc store, RV supplies, marine gas, ice, picnic tables, fire rings, grills, wood.

◆◆◆◆RECREATION: rec hall, coin games, lake swim, boating, canoeing, ramp, dock, 3 canoe/3 kayak/pedal boat/5 motorboat rentals, lake fishing, fishing supplies, fishing guides, golf nearby, bsktball, playground, shuffleboard court shuffleboard court, activities, horseshoes, sports field, hiking trails, v-ball. Rec open to public.

Pets welcome. Open May 1 - Mid Oct. Cottages open May 1. Clubs welcome. Rate in 2010 $26-39 per family. MC/VISA/Debit. Member ARVC, OPCA.

Phone: (877)368-2180
Address: 11408 Hwy 6, Sheguiandah, Manitoulin Island, ON P0P 1W0
Lat/Lon: 45.88415/-81.89930
Email: info@batmanscamping.com
Web: www.batmanscamping.com

SEE AD THIS PAGE

Green Acres Tent & Trailer Park (Not visited)—(Manitoulin) *On Hwy 6 & Limit St at S End of Sheguiandah.* ◆◆FACILITIES: 95 sites, typical site width 40 ft, 70 W&E, (15 amps), 25 no hkups, 3 pull-thrus, tenting, dump, laundry, ltd groc. ◆◆RECREATION: lake swim, boating, canoeing, lake fishing, playground. Pets welcome. Partial handicap access. Open May 17 - Oct 10. Rate in 2010 $29-30 per family. Member OPCA. Phone: (705)368-2428.

SHELBURNE—H-3

Primrose Park (Not Visited)—(Dufferin) *From east jct Hwy 89 & Hwy 10: Go .4 km/1/4 mi S on Hwy 10. Enter on L.* FACILITIES: 137 sites, typical site width 35 ft, 72 full hkups, 35 W&E, (15 amps), 30 no hkups, 8 pull-thrus, tenting, dump, laundry, groceries. RECREATION: swim pool, playground. Pets welcome. Open May 15 - Oct 15. Rate in 2010 $25-29 per family. Member OPCA. Phone: (519)925-2848.

SHERKSTON—I-3

Pleasant Beach Campground (Not visited)—*From Peace Bridge: Go 19 km/12 mi W on Hwy 3, then 4.8 km/3 mi S on Pleasant Beach Rd to park. Enter on R.* ◆◆◆FACILITIES: 73 sites, 50 W&E, 3 E, (15/30 amps), 20 no hkups, 5 pull-thrus, tenting, dump. ◆◆RECREATION: playground. Pets welcome. Open May 1 - Oct 15. Rate in 2010 $20-25 per family. Phone: (905)894-4249.

SIMCOE—I-3

NORFOLK AREA CONSERVATION AREA (Long Point Region Cons Auth)—*From town: Go 8 km/5 mi S on Hwy 24, follow signs to Lakeshore Rd.* FACILITIES: 164 sites, 51 full hkups, 113 W&E, (15 amps), tenting, dump, laundry. RECREATION: lake swim, boating, play equipment. Partial handicap access. Open May 1 - Oct 31. Phone: (519)428-1460.

TURKEY POINT PROVINCIAL PARK—*From town: Go 8 km/5 mi S on Hwy 24, then 6-1/2 km/4 mi SW on Hwy 24, then 3-1/4 km/2 mi SE on CR 10 (Turkey Point).* FACILITIES: 235 sites, typical site width 18 ft, 35 ft max RV length, 104 E, (15/30 amps), 131 no hkups, tenting, dump, laundry, ltd groc. RECREATION: lake swim, lake fishing, playground. Partial handicap access. Open early May - Oct. Phone: (519)426-3239.

SIOUX LOOKOUT—D-2

Abram Lake Tent and Trailer Park (Not Visited)—(Kenora) *From jct Hwy 664 & Hwy 72: Go 1.2 km/3/4 mi N on Hwy 72,(look for Abram Trails sign). Enter on R.* FACILITIES: 90 sites, typical site width 40 ft, 16 full hkups, 46 W&E, (15/30 amps), 28 no hkups, 37 pull-thrus, tenting, laundry, ltd groc. RECREATION: lake swim, boating, canoeing, ramp, dock, lake fishing, play equipment. Pets welcome. Open all yr. Facilities fully operational May 15 - mid Oct. Rate in 2010 $30-36 for 2 persons. Phone: (807)737-1247.

SIOUX LOOKOUT—Continued on next page

SIOUX LOOKOUT—Continued

(S) OJIBWAY PROVINCIAL PARK—*From town: Go 20-3/4 km/13 mi S on Hwy 72.* FACILITIES: 45 sites, 22 E, (15/30 amps), 23 no hkups, tenting, dump. RECREATION: boating, canoeing, ramp, dock, lake fishing. Partial handicap access. Open May - Sep. Phone: (807)737-2033.

SIOUX NARROWS—D-1

Paradise Point RV Park & Marina (Not Visited) —(Kenora) *From south city limits: Go 1.6 km/1 mi S on Hwy 71, then 1.6 km/1 mi W on Fickas Rd. Enter on L.* FACILITIES: 32 sites, typical site width 35 ft, 30 full hkups, (15/30 amps), 2 no hkups, tenting, ltd groc. RECREATION: lake swim, boating, canoeing, ramp, dock, lake fishing, play equipment. Pets welcome. Open May 1 - Sep 30. Rate in 2010 $23-25 for 2 persons. Phone: (807)226-5269.

Tomahawk Trailer Park Resort (Not Visited)—(Kenora) *From south city limits: Go 1.6 km/1 mi S on Hwy 71, then .8 km/1/2 mi E on Tomahawk Rd. Enter on R.* FACILITIES: 60 sites, typical site width 35 ft, 45 full hkups, 10 W&E, (30 amps), 5 no hkups, 20 pull-thrus, tenting, laundry. RECREATION: lake swim, boating, canoeing, ramp, dock, lake fishing, play equipment. Pets welcome. Open May 1 - Oct 1. Rate in 2010 $38-50 for 4 persons. Phone: (807)226-5622.

SOMBRA—I-1

(N) BRANTON-CUNDICK (St. Clair Parkway Commission)—(Lambton) *From town: Go 2 km/1-1/4 mi N on St. Clair Pkwy. Enter on R.* FACILITIES: 55 sites, 55 full hkups, (15/30 amps), tenting, dump. RECREATION: boating, ramp, river fishing. Open May - Oct. Phone: (519)892-3968.

(N) CATHCART PARK (St. Clair Parkway Commission) —(Lambton) *From town: Go 3-1/4 km/2 mi N on St. Clair Pkwy. Enter on L.* FACILITIES: 73 sites, 7 full hkups, 66 W&E, (15/30 amps), 1 pull-thrus, tenting, dump. RECREATION: boating, ramp, dock, river fishing, playground. Open May 24 - Oct 15. Phone: (519)892-3342.

SOUTH BAYMOUTH—F-1

South Bay Resort (Not visited)—(Manitoulin) *From ferry dock at South Baymouth & Hwy 6: Go .8 km/1/2 mi N on Hwy 6. Enter on R.* ◊◊◊FACILITIES: 77 sites, typical site width 35 ft, 60 W&E, (15/30 amps), 17 no hkups, 5 pull-thrus, tenting, dump, laundry. ◊◊◊RECREATION: lake swim, boating, canoeing, ramp, dock, lake fishing, playground. Pets welcome. Open mid May - Oct 31. Rate in 2010 $27-39 for 2 persons. Member OPCA. Phone: (705)859-3106.

SOUTH RIVER—F-3

(W) MIKISEW PROVINCIAL PARK—*From Hwy 11 in town: Go 16 km/10 mi W on Township Rd.* FACILITIES: 265 sites, 62 E, 203 no hkups, 11 pull-thrus, tenting, laundry. RECREATION: lake swim, boating, canoeing, ramp, lake fishing, playground. Open mid Jun - late Sep. Phone: (705)386-7762.

SOUTHAMPTON—H-2

Dreamaker Family Campground (Not Visited) —(Bruce) *From jct CR 13 & Hwy 21: Go 6.7 km/4-1/2 mi N on Hwy 21. Enter on R.* FACILITIES: 118 sites, typical site width 50 ft, 84 full hkups, 34 W&E, (15/30 amps), 19 pull-thrus, tenting, ltd groc. RECREATION: swim pool, lake swim, boating, no motors, canoeing, lake fishing, playground. Pets welcome. Partial handicap access. Open May 15 - Oct 15. Rate in 2010 $28-38 per family. Member OPCA. Phone: (519)797-9956.

(S) HOLIDAY PARK (TOO NEW TO RATE)—*Intown from jct Hwy 21 & High St: Go 100 Meters E on High St. Enter on R.*

WELCOME

FACILITIES: 286 sites, typical site width 25 ft, 35 ft max RV length, 282 full hkups, 2 W&E, 2 E, mostly extd stay sites, cable TV, WiFi Internet central location, family camping, RV's/park model rentals, shower$, laundry, ltd groc, RV supplies, ice, picnic tables, fire rings, wood, controlled access.

RECREATION: rec hall, rec room/area, coin games, swim pool, wading pool, saltwater swim, golf nearby, bsktball, 4 bike rentals, playground, shuffleboard court 8 shuffleboard courts, activities (wkends), horseshoes, sports field.

Partial handicap access. No tents. Open May 6 - Oct 24. Rate in 2010 $24-40 per family.

SOUTHAMPTON—Continued
HOLIDAY PARK—Continued

Phone: (519)797-2328
Address: 552 High Street, Southampton, On N0H 2L0
Email: holidaypark@killamproperties.com
Web: www.killamleisureliving.com/holidaypark

SEE AD BRIGHTON PAGE 869

SPANISH—D-5

Mitchells' Camp (Not Visited) (RV SPACES) —(Algoma) *From town: Go .8 km/1/2 mi S to Spanish River & follow signs. Enter at end.* FACILITIES: 20 sites, typical site width 35 ft, 15 W&E, (30 amps), 5 no hkups, 2 pull-thrus, tenting, dump. RECREATION: lake swim, boating, canoeing, ramp, dock, lake fishing. Pets welcome. Open mid May - Sep 30. Rate in 2010 $22-27 per family. Phone: (705)844-2202.

SPRAGGE—D-5

Spragge-KOA (Not Visited)—(Algoma) *From jct Hwy 108 & Hwy 17: Go 1.6 km/1 mi W on Hwy 17. Enter on L.* ◊◊◊◊FACILITIES: 114 sites, 10 full hkups, 89 W&E, (15/30 amps), 15 no hkups, 55 pull-thrus, family camping, tenting, dump, laundry, groceries. ◊◊◊◊RECREATION: swim pool, boating, canoeing, ramp, dock, river fishing, playground. Pets welcome. Open May 1 - Mid Oct. Rate in 2010 $28-39 for 2 persons. Member OPCA. Phone: (705)849-2210. KOA discount.

SPRING BAY—F-1

Santa Maria Trailer Resort (Not visited)—(Manitoulin) *From jct Hwy 551, Hwy 542 & Beaver Rd: Go 8 km/5 mi W on Beaver Rd, then 1 km/1/2 mi S on Square Bay Rd (gravel road). Enter on L.* ◊◊◊◊FACILITIES: 102 sites, typical site width 50 ft, 102 full hkups, (30 amps), 6 pull-thrus, laundry, ltd groc. ◊◊◊◊◊RECREATION: swim pool, lake swim, boating, canoeing, ramp, dock, lake/pond fishing, playground. Pets welcome. Partial handicap access. No tents. Open all yr. Facilities fully operational Mid Apr - End of Sep. Rate in 2010 $40 per family. Member OPCA. Phone: (705)377-5870.

STONECLIFFE—F-4

Morning Mist Resort (Not Visited)—(Renfrew) *From east village limits: Go .8 km/1/2 mi E on Hwy 17, then .3 km/.1 mi S on Pine Valley Rd. Enter on R.* ◊◊◊◊FACILITIES: 54 sites, typical site width 40 ft, 40 full hkups, 11 W&E, (30/50 amps), 3 no hkups, 3 pull-thrus, tenting, dump, laundry. ◊◊◊◊RECREATION: river swim, boating, canoeing, ramp, dock, river fishing, playground. Pets welcome. Open May 1 - End Oct. Big rigs welcome. Rate in 2010 $30-37 for 2 persons. Member OPCA. Phone: (613)586-1900.

Pine Valley Resort & Campground (Not Visited) —*From east village limits: Go .8 km/1/2 mi E on Hwy 17, then follow signs. Enter on L.* ◊◊◊FACILITIES: 25 sites, typical site width 35 ft, 25 full hkups, (20/30 amps), 12 pull-thrus, family camping, tenting, dump, laundry. ◊◊◊RECREATION: river swim, boating, canoeing, ramp, dock, river fishing, play equipment. Pets welcome. Open May 5 - mid Oct. Rate in 2010 $29-33 per family. Member OPCA. Phone: (613)586-2621.

STONEY CREEK—I-3

FIFTY POINT CONSERVATION AREA & MARINA—(Hamilton-Wentworth) *From QEW & Fifty Rd: Go 270 m/300 yds N on Fifty then 270 m/300 yds E on N Service Rd then 1/2 km/1/4 mi N on Baseline Rd.* FACILITIES: 47 sites, 47 full hkups, (30 amps), 30 pull-thrus, tenting, dump, laundry. RECREATION: lake swim, boating, canoeing, ramp, dock, lake/pond fishing, playground. Pets welcome. Partial handicap access. Open Spring - Oct 31. Phone: (905)525-2187.

FIFTY POINT (Hamilton Reg. Cons Auth.)—*From jct QEW & Fifty Rd: Go 270 meters/300 yards N on Fifty Rd, then 270 meters/300 yards E on N Service Rd, then 1/2 km/1/4 mi E on Baseline Rd. Enter on L.* FACILITIES: 47 sites, 47 full hkups, (30 amps), 30 pull-thrus, tenting, dump, laundry. RECREATION: lake swim, boating, canoeing, ramp, dock, lake/pond fishing, playground. Partial handicap access. Open Spring - Oct 31. Phone: (905)643-2103.

STOUFFVILLE—H-3

Cedar Beach Park (Not visited)—*Fron jct Hwy 48 & Aurora Rd. 15: Go 2 km/1-1/4 mi E on Aurora Rd. 15 then go 1/4 mile. Enter on R.* ◊◊◊FACILITIES: 570 sites, typical site width 40 ft, 519 full hkups, 41 W&E, (15/30/50 amps), 50 amps ($), 10 no hkups, 16 pull-thrus, tenting, dump, groceries. ◊◊◊◊RECREATION: 2 swim pools, lake swim, boating, no motors, canoeing, dock, lake fishing, playground. Pets welcome. Open Apr 1 - Oct 31. Rate in 2010 $35-45 per family. Member OPCA. Phone: (877)588-8828.

STRATFORD—I-2

WILDWOOD CONSERVATION AREA (Upper Thames River Cons Auth)—*From west city limits: Go 11-1/4 km/7 mi W on Hwy 7.* FACILITIES: 470 sites, 110 W&E, 360 E, tenting, dump, laundry, ltd groc. RECREATION: swim pool, lake swim, boating, canoeing, ramp, dock, lake fishing, playground. Pets welcome. Open May 1 - Oct 12. Phone: (519)284-2931.

STRATHROY—I-2

Trout Haven Park (Not visited)—(Middlesex) *From jct Hwy 402 (exit 65) & Hwy 81: Go 5.6 km/3-1/2 mi S on Hwy 81, then 1.2 km/3/4 mi W on Carroll St, then .4 km/1/4 mi N on Park St. Enter on L.* ◊◊◊FACILITIES: 70 sites, typical site width 35 ft, 60 full hkups, 10 W&E, (15/30 amps), 2 pull-thrus, tenting, dump, laundry. ◊◊◊RECREATION: swim pool, pond fishing, playground. Pets welcome. Partial handicap access. Open May 1 - Mid Oct. Rate in 2010 $25-30 per family. Member OPCA. Phone: (519)245-4070.

STURGEON FALLS—D-6

Big Oak Tent & Trailer Park (Not Visited)—(Nipissing) *From jct Hwy 17 & Nipissing St: Go 3.2 km/2 mi S on Nipissing St, then 2.4 km/1-1/4 mi W on Marleau, then .8 km/1/4 mi S on Malette Rd. Enter on L.* FACILITIES: 75 sites, typical site width 40 ft, 55 full hkups, 10 W&E, (15/30 amps), 10 no hkups, 5 pull-thrus, tenting, dump, laundry, ltd groc. RECREATION: lake swim, boating, canoeing, ramp, dock, lake fishing. Pets welcome. Open May 15 - Oct 15. Rate in 2010 $21.75-26.25 for 5 persons. Member OPCA. Phone: (705)753-0679.

Cache Bay Tent & Trailer Park (Not Visited)—(Nipissing) *From west city limits: GO 3.2 km/2 mi W on Hwy 17, then .4 km/1/4 mi S on Levac Rd., then 1.2 km/3/4 mi S on Cache St., then 100 yds. W on Old Mill Rd., then follow signs. Enter on L.* FACILITIES: 67 sites, typical site width 30 ft, 40 full hkups, 12 W&E, (15/30 amps), 15 no hkups, 12 pull-thrus, tenting, dump, laundry. RECREATION: swim pool, boating, canoeing, ramp, dock, lake fishing, playground. Pets welcome. Open mid May - mid Oct. Rate in 2010 $20-25 per family. Phone: (705)753-2592.

Glenrock Cottages & Trailer Park (Not Visited) —(Nipissing) *From jct Hwy 17 & Nipissing St: Go 3.2 km/2 mi S on Nipissing, then 1.6 km/1 mi W on Marleau Rd, then .4 km/1/4 mi S on Glenrock Rd. Enter on L.* FACILITIES: 86 sites, 67 full hkups, 11 W&E, (15/30 amps), 8 no hkups, 6 pull-thrus, tenting, dump, laundry, groceries. RECREATION: lake swim, boating, ramp, dock, lake fishing, playground. Pets welcome. Open May 15 - Oct 15. Rate in 2010 $26-36 per family. Member OPCA.

Sunshine Motel & RV (Not Visited) (RV SPACES) —(Nipissing) *From west city limits: Go 1.6 km/1 mi W on Hwy 17. Enter on R.* FACILITIES: 40 sites, typical site width 25 ft, 14 full hkups, (15 amps), 26 no hkups, 18 pull-thrus, tenting, laundry. Pets welcome. Open all yr. Facilities fully operational mid May - mid Oct. Rate in 2010 $15-25 per family. Phone: (705)753-0560.

SUDBURY—D-5

(S) CAROL CAMPSITE (Not Visited)—(Sudbury) *From jct Hwy 17 & Hwy 69: Go 4 km/2-1/2 mi S on Hwy 69. Enter on L.*

WELCOME

FACILITIES: 155 sites, typical site width 25 ft, 110 full hkups, 35 W&E, (15/30 amps), 10 no hkups, some extd stay sites, 40 pull-thrus, WiFi Instant Internet at site ($), tenting, RV storage, dump, non-guest dump $, portable dump, ltd groc, RV supplies, ice, picnic tables, fire rings, wood.

RECREATION: equipped pavilion, lake swim, boating, canoeing, ramp, dock, 2 canoe/2 pedal boat rentals, lake fishing, bsktball, play equipment, horseshoes, sports field.

Pets welcome. Open May 15 - Oct 15. Escort to site. Clubs welcome. Rate in 2010 $35 for 4 persons. MC/VISA/Debit. Member OPCA.

Phone: (705)522-5570
Address: 2388 Richard Lake Dr, Sudbury, ON P3E 4N1
Lat/Lon: 46.43225/-80.91664
Email: charb0@hotmail.com
Web: www.carolscampsite.com

SEE AD THIS PAGE

(N) WINDY LAKE PROVINCIAL PARK—*From town: Go 43-1/4 km/27 mi N on Hwy 144, then 1-1/2 km/1 mi E on Hwy 544 (Levack).* FACILITIES: 93 sites, 56 E, (15/30 amps), 37 no hkups, tenting, dump, laundry. RECREATION: boating, canoeing, ramp, lake fishing, playground. Partial handicap access. Open mid May - early Sep. Phone: (705)966-2315.

SUNDERLAND—H-3

Trout Water Family Camping—*From jct Hwy 12 & Hwy 7: Go 2 km/1-1/2 mi E on Hwy 7. Enter on R.* ◊◊FACILITIES: 150 sites, typical site width 40 ft, 75 full hkups, 35 W&E, (15/30 amps), 40 no hkups, 10 pull-thrus, WiFi Instant Internet at site ($), phone Internet

Trout Water Family Camping—Continued on next page

SUNDERLAND—Continued
Trout Water Family Camping—Continued

central location, family camping, tenting, RV storage, dump, non-guest dump $, laundry, ltd groc, ice, picnic tables, patios, fire rings, wood. ◊◊◊◊RECREATION: rec hall, 2 swim pools, boating, no motors, canoeing, kayaking, dock, river fishing, fishing supplies, putting green, bsktball, playground, activities, horseshoes, hiking trails, v-ball. Pets welcome. Open Apr 18 - mid Oct. Rate in 2010 $25-29 per family. MC/VISA/Debit. Member OPCA. CCUSA 50% Discount. CCUSA reservations Accepted, CCUSA max stay 7 days, CCUSA disc. not avail holidays. Best available sites Jun 15-Aug 15.

Phone: (866)454-8889
Address: Sunderland, ON L0C 1H0
Lat/Lon: 44.17650/-79.02552
Email: camping@troutwatercamping.com
Web: www.troutwatercamping.com

SUTTON—H-3

SIBBALD POINT PROVINCIAL PARK—*From town: Go 8 km/5 mi E on Hwy 48, then 3-1/4 km/2 mi N on CR 18.* FACILITIES: 604 sites, typical site width 50 ft, 284 E, (15/30 amps), 320 no hkups, 10 pull-thrus, tenting, dump, ltd groc. RECREATION: lake swim, boating, canoeing, ramp, dock, lake fishing, playground. Partial handicap access. Open May - Oct. Phone: (905)722-8061.

SYDENHAM—H-5

Glen-Lor Lodge (Not Visited)—*From Hwy 401 (exit 613) & CR 9: Go 16 km/10 mi N on CR 9 to end, then 3.2 km/2 mi E on CR 5. Follow signs. Enter on R.* FACILITIES: 45 sites, typical site width 30 ft, 36 ft max RV length, 25 full hkups, 10 W&E, (15/30 amps), 10 no hkups, tenting, dump, laundry, groceries. RECREATION: lake swim, boating, canoeing, ramp, dock, lake fishing, playground. Open Early May - Oct 1. Rate in 2010 $35-45 per family. Phone: (613)376-3020.

TEMAGAMI—D-6

(S) FINLAYSON POINT PROVINCIAL PARK—*From town: Go 1-1/2 km/1 mi S on Hwy 11, then 3/4 km/1/2 mi W on Finlayson.* FACILITIES: 117 sites, 33 E, (15/30 amps), 84 no hkups, 14 pull-thrus, tenting, dump, laundry. RECREATION: lake swim, boating, canoeing, ramp, dock, lake fishing, playground. Partial handicap access. Open mid May - early Sep. Phone: (705) 569-3205.

THESSALON—D-4

Brownlee Lake Park Resort & Campground (Not Visited)—(Algoma) *From jct Hwy 129 & Hwy 17: Go 9.6 km/6 mi E on Hwy 17, then 2.5 km/1-1/2 mi N on Brownlee Rd. Enter at end.* FACILITIES: 40 sites, typical site width 30 ft, 40 full hkups, (15/30 amps), 8 pull-thrus, tenting, laundry. RECREATION: lake swim, boating, canoeing, ramp, dock, lake fishing. Pets welcome. Partial handicap access. Open June 1 - Oct 15. Rate in 2010 $24-36 per family. Phone: (705)842-2118.

Pine Crest Campground (Not Visited)—(Algoma) *From jct Hwy 129 & Hwy 17: Go 3.2 km/2 mi W on Hwy 17. Enter on L.* ◊◊◊FACILITIES: 52 sites, typical site width 35 ft, 1 full hkups, 46 W&E, (15/30 amps), 5 no hkups, 10 pull-thrus, family camping, tenting, dump, laundry, ltd groc. ◊◊◊RECREATION: lake swim, boating, canoeing, lake fishing, playground. Pets welcome. Open mid May - mid Oct. Rate in 2010 $25-28 per family. Phone: (705)842-2635.

THORNDALE—I-2

River View Campground (Not Visited)—(Middlesex) *From jct of CR 28 & 27: Go 1.4 km/1 mi W on CR 28, then 2 km/1-1/4 mi N on Valley View Rd. Enter on R.* ◊◊◊FACILITIES: 106 sites, typical site width 40 ft, 95 W&E, (30 amps), 11 no hkups, 7 pull-thrus, family camping, tenting, dump, laundry, ltd groc. ◊◊◊RECREATION: swim pool, river swim, boating, canoeing, river fishing, playground. Pets welcome. Partial handicap access. Open May 1 - mid Oct. Rate in 2010 $33-35 per family. Member OPCA. Phone: (866)447-7197.

Woodall's RV Owner's Handbook—essential information you need to "get to know" your RV.

THUNDER BAY—B-1

(S) CHIPPEWA PARK (City Park)—(Thunder Bay) *From jct Hwy 61 & Chippewa Rd: Go 3.2 km/2 mi SE on Chippewa Rd to City Rd, E on City Rd 6.5 km/4 mi. Enter on L.* FACILITIES: 30 sites, 16 E, (15 amps), 14 no hkups, 16 pull-thrus, tenting, laundry, ltd groc. RECREATION: lake swim, canoeing, lake fishing, playground. Pets welcome. Partial handicap access. Open Mid May - Mid Sep. Phone: (807)623-3912.

HAPPY LAND CAMPGROUND & CABINS (Not Visited)—(Thunder Bay) *From west city limits: Go 25.6 km/16 mi W on Hwy 11-17. Enter on R.*

◊◊◊◊FACILITIES: 100 sites, typical site width 35 ft, 37 full hkups, 23 E, (15/30/50 amps), 50 amps ($), 40 no hkups, 85 pull-thrus, WiFi Instant Internet at site, WiFi Internet central location, family camping, tenting, cabins, RV storage, laundry, ltd groc, RV supplies, ice, picnic tables, grills, wood.

◊◊◊◊RECREATION: rec room/area, swim pool, hot tub, golf nearby, bsktball, playground, horseshoes, sports field, hiking trails, v-ball.

Pets welcome. Partial handicap access. Open May 1 - Oct 1. Phone for Availability. Clubs welcome. Rate in 2010 $28-38 for 2 persons. MC/VISA/Debit. Member OPCA.

Phone: (866)473-9003
Address: 4650 Hwy 11-17, Thunder Bay, ON P7C 5M9
Lat/Lon: 48.39294/-89.59896
Email: taltmann@tbaytel.net
Web: www.happylandpark.com

SEE AD THIS PAGE

(E) KOA-Thunder Bay—(Thunder Bay) *From jct Hwy 11-17 & Hwy 527: Go .4 km/1/4 mi S on Spruce River Rd. Enter on L.* ◊◊◊◊◊FACILITIES: 179 sites, typical site width 35 ft, 100 full hkups, 55 W&E, (30/50 amps), 50 amps ($), 24 no hkups, 133 pull-thrus, tenting, dump, laundry, ltd groc. ◊◊◊◊◊RECREATION: swim pool, pond fishing, playground. Pets welcome. Open Apr 15 - Oct 15. Rate in 2010 $33-39 for 2 persons. Phone: (807)683-6221. KOA discount.

(E) TROWBRIDGE FALLS (City Park)—(Thunder Bay) *From jct Hwys 11 & 17 & Hodder Ave (Hwy 11B & 17B): Go 4 km/1/4 mi N on Copenhagen Rd. Enter on L.* FACILITIES: 150 sites, 16 W&E, 58 E, (15 amps), 76 no hkups, 20 pull-thrus, tenting, dump, laundry, ltd groc. RECREATION: river swim, river fishing, playground. Pets welcome. Open May 16 - Labour Day. Phone: (807)683-6661.

TICHBORNE—G-5

Sunset Country Campgrounds (Not Visited)—*From south town limits: Go 6.4 km/4 mi E on Fish Creek Rd, then follow signs. Enter on L.* FACILITIES: 114 sites, typical site width 40 ft, 85 full hkups, 23 W&E, (20/30 amps), 6 no hkups, tenting, dump, laundry, groceries. RECREATION: lake swim, boating, canoeing, ramp, dock, lake fishing, playground. Pets welcome. Open May 15 - Oct 15. Rate in 2010 $40-55 for 2 persons. Member OPCA. Phone: (613)375-6649.

TILLSONBURG—I-2

Red Oak Travel Park—(Elgin) *From jct Hwy 19 & Hwy 3: Go 13 km/8 mi W on Hwy 3. Enter on R.* ◊◊◊◊FACILITIES: 100 sites, typical site width 30 ft, 60 full hkups, 30 W&E, (15/30/50 amps), 10 no hkups, 8 pull-thrus, tenting, dump, laundry, ltd groc. ◊◊◊◊RECREATION: swim pool, playground. Pets welcome. Open May 1 - Oct 15. Rate in 2010 $20-33 per family. Member OPCA. Phone: (519)866-3504.

TOBERMORY—G-2

Happy Hearts Tent & Trailer Park (Not visited)—(Bruce) *From south city limits: Go 90 m/100 yards N on Hwy 6, then 1.2 km/3/4 mi W on Cape Hurd Rd. Enter on L.* ◊◊◊FACILITIES: 133 sites, typical site width 25 ft, 24 full hkups, 9 W&E, (15/30 amps), 100 no hkups, tenting, dump, laundry, ltd groc. ◊◊◊RECREATION: swim pool, playground. Pets welcome. Open mid May - mid Oct. Rate in 2010 $32-39 per family. Member OPCA. Phone: (519)596-2455.

Lands End Park (Not Visited)—(Bruce) *From south city limits: Go 1.6 km/1 mi N on Hwy 6, then 2.4 km/1-1/2 mi W on Hay Bay Rd. Enter on L.* ◊◊◊FACILITIES: 108 sites, typical site width 40 ft, 86 W&E, (30 amps), 23 no hkups, 19 pull-thrus, tenting,

TOBERMORY—Continued
Lands End Park (Not Visited)—Continued

dump, ltd groc. ◊◊◊RECREATION: lake swim, boating, canoeing, ramp, dock, lake fishing, playground. Pets welcome. Open May 1 - Oct 15. Rate in 2010 $29-50 per family. Member OPCA. Phone: (519)596-2523.

TOBERMORY VILLAGE CAMPGROUND—(Bruce) *On Hwy 6 (3.2 km/2 mi S of Ferry). Enter on R.*

◊◊◊◊FACILITIES: 200 sites, typical site width 40 ft, 100 full hkups, 30 W&E, (15/30/50 amps), 70 no hkups, 12 pull-thrus, phone Internet central location, tenting, cabins, RV storage, dump, non-guest dump $, portable dump, laundry, ltd groc, RV supplies, ice, picnic tables, fire rings, wood, controlled access.

◊◊◊◊RECREATION: rec hall, swim pool, boating, no motors, canoeing, dock, 2 canoe/pedal boat rentals, pond fishing, golf nearby, bsktball, 15 bike rentals, playground, activities, sports field, hiking trails, v-ball, local tours. Rec open to public.

Pets welcome. Open May 1 - mid Oct. Escort to site. Clubs welcome. Rate in 2010 $27-48 per family. MC/VISA/Debit. Member ARVC, OPCA.

Phone: (519)596-2689
Address: RR 1, 7159 Hwy 6, Tobermory, ON N0H 2R0
Lat/Lon: 45.14183/-81.38445
Email: contact@tobermoryvillagecamp.com
Web: www.tobermoryvillagecamp.com

SEE AD THIS PAGE

TORONTO—H-3

TORONTO AREA MAP

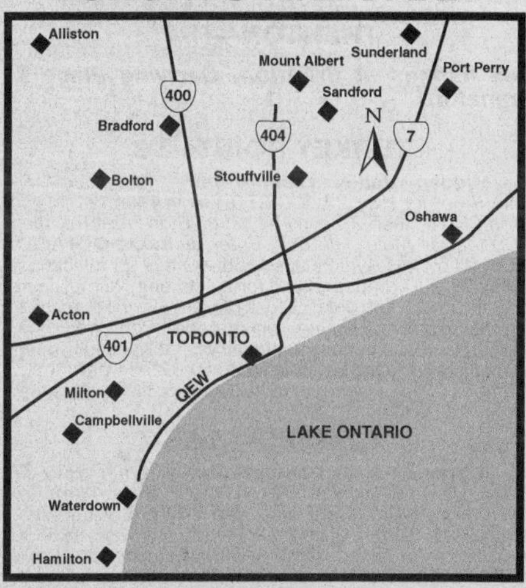

Symbols on map indicate towns within a 64km/40 mi radius of Toronto where campgrounds (diamonds), attractions (flags), & RV service centers & camping supply outlets (gears) are listed. Check listings for more information.

Tell Them Woodall's Sent You!

TORONTO—Continued on next page

Find a park or campground Woodall's does not list? Tell us about it! Use Reader Comment Forms located after the Alphabetical Quick Reference pages.

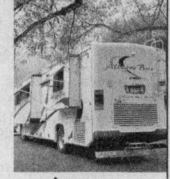

TORONTO—Continued

(NE) GLEN ROUGE CAMPGROUND (City of Toronto Park)—*From Hwy 401 (E'bound exit 390-Port Union Rd. W'bound exit 394-Whites Rd): Go 2 km/1 mi E on Kingston Rd.*

WELCOME

FACILITIES: 125 sites, 103 W&E, (20/30/50 amps), 22 no hkups, tenting, dump, ice, picnic tables, fire rings, grills, wood.

RECREATION: wading pool, spray ground, river swim, boating, canoeing, kayaking, lake/river fishing, playground, activities, horseshoes, sports field, hiking trails.

Pets welcome. Open May 7 - Oct 13. Clubs welcome. MC/VISA/Debit.

Phone: (416)338-2267
Address: ON L2E 6V5
Lat/Lon: 43.80554/-79.13675
Email: camping@toronto.ca
Web: www.toronto.ca/parks

SEE AD PAGE 887

INDIAN LINE CAMPGROUND (Toronto & Region Cons. Auth.)—*From jct Hwy 401 (exit 348) & Hwy 427: Go 5 km/3 mi N on Hwy 427, then 1/2 km/3/10 mi W on Finch. Enter on R.* FACILITIES: 246 sites, typical site width 35 ft, 41 full hkups, 162 W&E, (15/30/50 amps), 43 no hkups, 90 pull-thrus, tenting, dump, laundry, ltd groc. RECREATION: swim pool, boating, no motors, pond fishing, playground. Pets welcome. Open Apr. 29 - Oct 31. Phone: (800)304-9728.

TOTTENHAM—H-3

TOTTENHAM CONSERVATION AREA (Town of New Tecumseth)—*From jct Hwy 9 & CR 10: Go 6.4 km/4 mi N on CR 10, then 1/2 km/1/4 mi W on Mill St. Enter on L.* FACILITIES: 76 sites, 76 W&E, (15/30 amps), tenting, dump. RECREATION: boating, no motors, canoeing, pond fishing. Open mid May - mid Oct. Phone: (905)729-1260.

TRENTON—H-4

See listings at Brighton, Carrying Place & Frankford

TURKEY POINT—I-3

Hidden Valley Campground—(Haldimand-Norfolk) *From jct Hwy 24 & CR 10: Go 4.4 km (2-3/4 mi) S on CR 10, then 2.2 km (1-1/2 mi) E on Front Rd, then 500 feet on Mole Sideroad. Enter on R.* ◊◊◊◊FACILITIES: 215 sites, typical site width 40 ft, 195 full hkups, 20 W&E, (30 amps), 3 pull-thrus, tenting, dump, laundry, ltd groc. ◊◊◊◊RECREATION: swim pool, canoeing, lake/stream fishing, playground. Pets welcome. Partial handicap access. Open all yr. Facilities fully operational May 1 - Oct 15. Rate in 2010 $25-34 per family. Member OPCA. Phone: (519)426-5666. FCRV discount.

TWEED—H-5

Tipper's Family Campground—*From jct Hwy 37 & Hwy 7: Go 6.4 km/4 mi E on Hwy 7, then .4 km/1/4 mi N on Varty Rd. Enter on L.* ◊◊FACILITIES: 54 sites, typical site width 50 ft, 2 full hkups, 38 W&E, (15/30 amps), 14 no hkups, tenting, dump, laundry, ltd groc. ◊◊◊RECREATION: river swim, boating, no motors, canoeing, river fishing, playground. Pets welcome. Open mid May - mid Oct. Rate in 2010 $26-36 per family. Member OPCA. Phone: (613)478-6844.

UPSALA—B-1

Camp Sawmill Bay (Not Visited)—(Thunder Bay) *From town: Go 17 km/10.5 mi E on Hwy 17, then .4 km/1/4 mi S on Sawmill Bay Rd. Enter on R.* FACILITIES: 57 sites, typical site width 30 ft, 35 full hkups, 12 W&E, (15/30 amps), 10 no hkups, 4 pull-thrus, tenting, dump. RECREATION: lake swim, boating, ramp, dock, lake fishing. Pets welcome. Open all yr. Facilities fully operational May 15 - Oct 1. Rate in 2010 $30 per family. Phone: (807)986-2427.

G & G Service Upsala Campground (Not Visited)—(Thunder Bay) *Hwy 17 City Limits Upsala. Enter on R.* FACILITIES: 40 sites, 18 full hkups, 10 W&E, (15/30 amps), 12 no hkups, 10 pull-thrus, tenting, dump, ltd groc. RECREATION: lake swim, boating, lake fishing, playground. Pets welcome. Open all yr. Rate in 2010 $22 per vehicle. Phone: (807)986-2201.

UPSALA—Continued

Open Bay Cottages & Campground (Not Visited)—(Thunder Bay) *From east town limits on Hwy 17: Go 6.4 km/4 mi E on Hwy 17, then 16.8 km/10-1/2 mi S on Lac Des Mille Lac Rd. Enter on R.* FACILITIES: 32 sites, 32 W&E, (15/30 amps), tenting, dump, laundry, groceries. RECREATION: lake swim, boating, canoeing, ramp, dock, lake fishing, play equipment. Pets welcome. Open mid May - Mid Oct. Rate in 2010 $27 per vehicle. Phone: (807)986-2356.

Pine Point Resort (Not Visited)—(Thunder Bay) *From east town limits: Go 6.4 km/4 mi E on Hwy 17, then 27.2 km/17 mi S on Lac Des Mille Lac Rd. Enter at end.* FACILITIES: 82 sites, typical site width 35 ft, 23 full hkups, 55 W&E, (20/30 amps), 4 no hkups, 26 pull-thrus, tenting, dump, laundry, ltd groc. RECREATION: lake swim, boating, canoeing, ramp, dock, lake fishing. Pets welcome. Open all yr. Facilities fully operational May 1 - Sep 30. Rate in 2010 $30-33 for 2 persons. Phone: (807)986-1300.

Savanne River Resort (Not Visited)—(Thunder Bay) *From town: Go 19.3 km/12 mi E on Hwy 17. Enter on R.* FACILITIES: 85 sites, typical site width 40 ft, 85 W&E, (15/30 amps), 10 pull-thrus, tenting, laundry, groceries. RECREATION: river swim, boating, canoeing, ramp, dock, lake/river fishing. Pets welcome. Open all yr. Facilities fully operational May 1 - Oct 31. Rate in 2010 $23.50-31 per family. Phone: (800)663-5852.

Thousand Lakes Resort (Not Visited)—(Thunder Bay) *From east town limits on Hwy 17: Go 6.4 km/4 mi E on Hwy 17, then 9 km/7 mi S on Lac Des Mille Lac Rd. Enter on L.* FACILITIES: 64 sites, typical site width 20 ft, 53 W&E, (15/30 amps), 11 no hkups, 6 pull-thrus, tenting, dump, laundry, ltd groc. RECREATION: lake swim, boating, canoeing, dock, lake fishing, playground. Pets welcome. Open all yr. Facilities fully operational Mid May - Mid Oct. Rate in 2010 $15-35 for 2 persons. Phone: (877)986-1633.

UPTERGROVE—G-3

MCRAE POINT PROVINCIAL PARK—*From jct Hwy 12 & Muley Point Rd: Go 16 km/10 mi SE on Muley Point Rd.* FACILITIES: 203 sites, 166 E, (15/30 amps), 37 no hkups, 125 pull-thrus, tenting, dump, ltd groc. RECREATION: lake swim, boating, canoeing, ramp, dock, lake fishing, playground. Pets welcome. Partial handicap access. Open May - Oct. Phone: (705)325-7290.

VERMILION BAY—D-1

(N) BLUE LAKE PROVINCIAL PARK—*From jct Hwy 17 & Hwy 647: Go 8 km/5 mi NW on Hwy 647.* FACILITIES: 198 sites, 104 E, (15/30 amps), 94 no hkups, 60 pull-thrus, tenting, dump, laundry. RECREATION: lake swim, boating, canoeing, ramp, lake fishing, playground. Partial handicap access. Open mid May - mid Sep. Phone: (807)227-2601.

VERONA—H-5

Desert Lake Family Resort—*From jct Hwy 401 (exit 611) & Hwy 38: Go 27.2 km/17 mi N on Hwy 38, then 9.6 km/6 mi E on Desert Lake Rd. Enter on L.* ◊◊◊FACILITIES: 145 sites, typical site width 35 ft, 120 W&E, (20 amps), 25 no hkups, 30 pull-thrus, tenting, dump, laundry, full svc store. ◊◊◊◊RECREATION: lake swim, boating, canoeing, ramp, dock, lake fishing, playground. Pets welcome. Open all yr. Facilities fully operational Apr 15 - Oct 15. Rate in 2010 $29-34.50 for 2 persons. Member OPCA. Phone: (613) 374-2196.

VINELAND—I-3

N.E.T. Camping Resort—*From jct QEW (exit 57) & Regional Rd 24: Go 17.7 km/11 mi S on Regional Rd 24. Enter on L.* ◊◊◊◊FACILITIES: 407 sites, typical site width 30 ft, 307 full hkups, (15/30/50 amps), 100 no hkups, 12 pull-thrus, tenting, dump, laundry, ltd groc. ◊◊◊◊◊RECREATION: swim pool, boating, no motors, canoeing, dock, lake/pond fishing, playground. Pets welcome. Open May 1 - Mid Oct. Big rigs welcome. Rate in 2010 $36-55 per family. Member OPCA. Phone: (866)490-4745.

Woodall's Tip... If you think Woodall's Ratings mean Good, Better, Best...think again. See the "How to Use" section in the front of this Directory for an explanation of our Rating System.

WALTON—H-2

(S) FAMILY PARADISE CAMPGROUND (TOO NEW TO RATE)—*From jct Hwy 8 & CR 12: Go 7 mi NE on CR 12, then 3.2 mi SE on Hullett-McKillop Line Rd.*

WELCOME

FACILITIES: 217 sites, typical site width 30 ft, 189 full hkups, 28 W&E, (30 amps), mostly extd stay sites, 2 pull-thrus, WiFi Internet central location, family camping, tenting, RV's/park model rentals, dump, non-guest dump $, laundry, groceries, RV supplies, LP gas by weight, ice, picnic tables, fire rings, wood, controlled access.

RECREATION: rec hall, pavilion, swim pool, lake swim, no motors, dock, pond fishing, fishing supplies, golf nearby, bsktball, playground, shuffleboard court 2 shuffleboard courts, activities, horseshoes, sports field, hiking trails, v-ball.

Pets welcome, breed restrict, quantity restrict. Partial handicap access. Open May 1 - Oct 31. Clubs welcome. Rate in 2010 $22-41 per family. MC/VISA/Debit. Member OPCA.

Phone: (877)-591-1961
Address: 43835 Hullet McKillop Line RR #4, Walton, ON NOK 1ZO
Email: familyparadise@killamproperties.com
Web: www.killamleisureliving.com/familyparadise

SEE AD BRIGHTON PAGE 869

Family Paradise Campground (Not Visited)—(Huron) *From jct Hwy 8 & County Rd 12: Go N 11.2km/7mi on County Rd 12, then go E 5.11km/3-1/4 mi on Hullett-McKillop Rd. Enter on R.* FACILITIES: 190 sites, typical site width 40 ft, 158 full hkups, 32 W&E, (15/30 amps), 2 pull-thrus, tenting, dump, laundry, ltd groc. RECREATION: swim pool, lake swim, canoeing, lake fishing, playground. Partial handicap access. Open May 1 - Oct 15. Rate in 2010 $30-35 for 2 persons. Member OPCA. Phone: (877)591-1961.

WARSAW—H-4

WARSAW CAVES (Otonabee Region Cons Auth)—*From town: Go 4 km/2-1/2 mi N on CR 4.* FACILITIES: 50 sites, 50 no hkups, tenting. RECREATION: lake/river swim, canoeing, river fishing. Open May 1 - Oct 31. Phone: (705)652-3161.

WASAGA BEACH—H-3

Cedar Grove Park (Not visited)—(Simcoe) *Located on Hwy 26 at the W city limits. Enter on R.* ◊◊◊FACILITIES: 160 sites, 145 full hkups, 15 W&E, tenting, laundry, ltd groc. ◊◊◊RECREATION: lake swim, playground. Pets welcome. Open May 1 - Oct 1. Rate in 2010 $40-80 per family. Phone: (705)429-2134.

Jell-E-Bean Campground (Not visited)—(Simcoe) *Located on Hwy 26 at the W city limits. Enter on L.* ◊◊◊FACILITIES: 150 sites, typical site width 35 ft, 120 full hkups, 30 W&E, (15/30 amps), 3 pull-thrus, tenting, laundry, ltd groc. ◊◊◊RECREATION: swim pool, playground. Pets welcome. Open May 1 - Oct 1. Rate in 2010 $40-60 per family. Member OPCA. Phone: (705)429-5418.

Klondike Park (Not Visited)—(Simcoe) *From jct Hwy 92 & Zoo Park Rd: Go 0.8 km/1/2 mi S on Zoo Park Rd, then 2.3 km/1-1/2 mi W on Golf Course Rd, then 3.4 km/2 mi NW on Klondike Rd. Enter on L.* FACILITIES: 190 sites, typical site width 35 ft, 35 ft max RV length, 170 full hkups, 20 W&E, (15/30 amps), 2 pull-thrus, tenting, laundry. RECREATION: swim pool, playground. Pets welcome. Open May 15 - Oct 15. Rate in 2010 $37-43 per family. Member OPCA. Phone: (866)875-2537.

Wasaga Dunes Family Campground (Not Visited)—(Simcoe) *From jct Hwy 92 & CR 29: Go 7.1 km/4-1/4 mi N on CR 29. Enter on L.* FACILITIES: 202 sites, typical site width 35 ft, 160 full hkups, 5 W&E, (30 amps), 37 no hkups, tenting. RECREATION: swim pool, playground. Pets welcome. Open Mid May - Mid Oct. Rate in 2010 $31-41 per family. Member OPCA. Phone: (888)357-8755.

Wasaga Pines Family Campground (Not Visited)—(Simcoe) *From jct Hwy 92 & CR 29: Go 1-1/2 mi E on Hwy 92. Enter on L.* FACILITIES: 247 sites, typical site width 45 ft, 218 full hkups, 29 W&E, (15/30/50 amps), 35 pull-thrus, tenting, dump, laundry, groceries. RECREATION: swim pool, playground. Pets welcome. Open mid May - mid Oct. Rate in 2010 $45-48 per family. Member OPCA. Phone: (888)274-8817.

WATERDOWN—I-3

Olympia Village Trailer Park—*From jct Hwy 403 & Hwy 6: Go 3.2 km/2 mi N on Hwy 6, then 9.6 km/6 mi W on 4th Concession Rd. Enter on R.* ◊◊◊FACILITIES: 171 sites, typical site width 40 ft, 161 full hkups, 5 W&E, (30/50 amps), 5 no hkups, 14 pull-thrus, tenting, dump, laundry, ltd groc. ◊◊◊RECREATION: swim pool, pond fishing, playground. Pets welcome. Open Apr 15 - Oct 31. Rate in 2010 $28-35 per family. Member OPCA. Phone: (905)627-1923.

WATERLOO—I-2

Green Acre Park—(Waterloo) *From jct Hwy 401 & Hwy 8: Go 8 km/5 mi W on Hwy 8, then 10.4 km/6-1/2 mi N on Hwy 85, (frmly Hwy 86) then 3.2 km/2 mi W on Northfield Dr, then .8 km/1/2 mi N on Westmount Rd, then 1.6 km/1 mi W on Conservation Dr, then 90m/100 yards S on Beaver Creek Rd. Enter on L.* ◊◊◊◊FACILITIES: 357 sites, typical site width 30 ft, 320 full hkups, 37 W&E, (30/50 amps), 47 pull-thrus, family camping, dump, laundry, ltd groc. ◊◊◊◊RECREATION: swim pool, pond fishing, playground. Pets welcome. Partial handicap access. No tents. Open all yr. Facilities fully operational Apr 1 - Nov 30. Rate in 2010 $30-48 per family. Member ARVC, OPCA. Phone: (877)885-7275. FMCA discount.

(NW) LAUREL CREEK (Grand River Cons Auth)—*From town: Go 8 km/5 mi N on Conestogo Pkwy, then 3-1/4 km/2 mi W on Northfield Dr. Enter on L.* FACILITIES: 130 sites, 76 W&E, (15/30 amps), 54 no hkups, tenting, dump. RECREATION: lake swim, boating, no motors, canoeing, ramp, lake fishing, playground. Open May 1 - Oct 15. Phone: (519)884-6620.

WAUBAUSHENE—G-3

Mariner's Paradise (Not Visited)—(Simcoe) *From jct Hwy 12 & Hwy 400: Go 2.0 km/1-1/4 mi N on Hwy 400 (exit 149 Quarry Rd), then .4 km/1/4 mi S on Mayhew Rd. Enter on L.* FACILITIES: 89 sites, typical site width 40 ft, 74 full hkups, (15 amps), 15 no hkups, 1 pull-thrus, tenting, dump, laundry, ltd groc. RECREATION: lake swim, boating, canoeing, ramp, dock, lake fishing, play equipment. Pets welcome. Open mid May - mid Oct. Rate in 2010 $29-37 per family. Member OPCA. Phone: (705)538-2590.

WAWA—C-3

(S) AGAWA BAY CAMPGROUND (Lake Superior PP) —*From town: Go 88 km/55 mi S on Hwy 17.* FACILITIES: 164 sites, 38 E, (15/30 amps), 126 no hkups, 21 pull-thrus, tenting, dump, laundry. RECREATION: canoeing, lake fishing. Partial handicap access. Open mid May - late Sep. Phone: (705)856-2284.

CRESCENT LAKE CAMPGROUND (Lake Superior PP) —*From town: Go 96 km/60 mi S on Hwy 17.* FACILITIES: 36 sites, 36 no hkups, 15 pull-thrus, tenting, dump, laundry. RECREATION: boating, no motors, canoeing, ramp, lake fishing. Open late Jun - early Sep. Phone: (705)856-2284.

RABBIT BLANKET LAKE CAMPGROUND (Lake Superior PP)—*From town: Go 30-1/2 km/19 mi S on Hwy 17.* FACILITIES: 20 sites, 20 E, (15/30 amps), 6 pull-thrus, tenting, dump, laundry. RECREATION: boating, canoeing, lake fishing. Partial handicap access. Open early May - late Oct. Phone: (705)856-2284.

Wawa RV Resort & Campground (Not Visited) —(Algoma) *From jct Hwy 101 & Hwy 17: Go 1.6 km/1 mi W on Hwy 17. Enter on L.* ◊◊◊FACILITIES: 100 sites, typical site width 35 ft, 17 full hkups, 59 W&E, (15/30 amps), 24 no hkups, 24 pull-thrus, family camping, tenting, dump, laundry, groceries. ◊◊◊RECREATION: swim pool, boating, canoeing, dock, river fishing, playground. Pets welcome. Open Mid May - mid Oct. Rate in 2010 $25-35 for 2 persons. Phone: (705)856-4368.

WEBBWOOD—D-5

CHUTES PROVINCIAL PARK—*From town: Go 16 km/10 mi W on Hwy 17, then 3-1/4 km/2 mi N on Hwy 553 (Massey).* FACILITIES: 130 sites, 56 E, (15/30 amps), 74 no hkups, tenting, dump, laundry, ltd groc. RECREATION: lake swim, boating, canoeing, playground. Partial handicap access. Open mid May - late Sep. Phone: (705)865-2021.

WEST GUILFORD—G-4

Haliburton Forest & Wild Life Reserve—*From jct Hwy 118 & CR 7 (Kennisis Lake Rd): Go 19.2 km/12 mi N. Enter at end.* ◊◊FACILITIES: 340 sites, 340 no hkups, tenting, ltd groc. ◊◊◊RECREATION: lake swim, boating, 15 hp limit, canoeing, lake fishing. Pets welcome. Open all yr. Facilities fully operational May - mid Oct. Phone: (705)754-2198.

WHEATLEY—J-1

Campers Cove—(Essex) *From center of town (jct Erie S. & Hwy 3): Go 3.6 km/2-1/4 mi E on Hwy 3, then .8 km/1/2 mi S on Campers Cove Rd. Enter on L.* ◊◊◊◊FACILITIES: 324 sites, typical site width 50 ft, 311 full hkups, 13 W&E, (20/30/50 amps), 8 pull-thrus, family camping, tenting, dump, laundry, groceries.

Stay with a Campground in Woodall's

WHEATLEY—Continued
Campers Cove—Continued

◊◊◊◊RECREATION: lake swim, boating, canoeing, lake fishing, playground. Pets welcome. Partial handicap access. Open May 1 - Sep 30. Rate in 2010 $37-46 per family. Member ARVC, OPCA. Phone: (519)825-4732.

HOLIDAY HARBOUR RESORT—(Kent) *From jct Hwy 3 & Erie St: Go 5 blocks S on Erie St, then E on Middleton Line, then S on Pier Rd. Enter on L.*

WELCOME

◊◊◊◊FACILITIES: 188 sites, 185 W&E, (30 amps), 3 no hkups, some extd stay sites, 10 pull-thrus, tenting, RV's/park model rentals, RV storage, dump, non-guest dump $, portable dump, laundry, groceries, RV supplies, ice, picnic tables, fire rings, wood.

◊◊◊◊RECREATION: rec hall, lake swim, canoeing, kayaking, lake/river fishing, fishing supplies, golf nearby, playground, activities, (wkends), horseshoes, sports field, hiking trails, v-ball. Rec open to public.

Pets welcome. Open 1st week of May - Oct 28. Rate in 2010 $22-48 per family. MC/VISA/Debit. Member OPCA.

Phone: (800)997-7809
Address: 20951 Pier Rd, Wheatley, ON N0P 2P0
Email: holidayharbour@killamproperties.com
Web: www.holidayharbour.com

SEE AD BRIGHTON PAGE 869

LAKESIDE VILLAGE MOTEL AND CAMPGROUND—(Kent) *From Wheatley: Go 9 km/5-1/2 mi E on Talbot Trail (Hwy 3). Enter on R.*

WELCOME

◊◊◊FACILITIES: 71 sites, typical site width 30 ft, 61 full hkups, (20/30 amps), 10 no hkups, some extd stay sites, 2 pull-thrus, WiFi Instant Internet at site ($), family camping, tenting, RV storage, laundry, ice, picnic tables, fire rings, wood, controlled access.

◊◊◊RECREATION: rec room/area, coin games, lake swim, boating, canoeing, kayaking, lake fishing, golf nearby, horseshoes, v-ball.

Pets welcome. Open May 1 - Oct 10. Clubs welcome. Green Friendly. Rate in 2010 $30.75-34.75 per family. MC/VISA/Debit. Member ARVC, OPCA.

Phone: (888)505-4550
Address: 2416 Talbot Trail RR #1, Wheatley, ON N0P 2P0
Lat/Lon: 42.08288/-82.21644
Email: info@lakesidevillage.on.ca
Web: www.lakesidevillage.on.ca

SEE AD THIS PAGE

(E) WHEATLEY PROVINCIAL PARK—*From town: Go 1-1/2 km/1 mi E on Hwy 3, then 3/4 km/1/2 mi S on Lake St.* FACILITIES: 220 sites, 96 E, (15/30 amps), 124 no hkups, tenting, dump. RECREATION: lake swim, canoeing, playground. Partial handicap access. Open Apr - early Oct. Phone: (519)825-4659.

WHITE LAKE—G-5

Cedar Cove Resort (Not visited)—*From jct Hwy 17 & White Lake Rd: Go 12.4 km/7-1/2 mi W on White Lake Rd, then 8.8 km/5-1/2 mi E on Bellamy Rd, then 4.8 km/3 mi S, then follow signs. Enter on L.* ◊◊◊FACILITIES: 300 sites, typical site width 45 ft, 293 full hkups, (20/30/50 amps), 7 no hkups, 8 pull-thrus, family camping, tenting, dump, laundry, ltd groc.

Check out our web site www.woodalls.com

WHITE LAKE—Continued
Cedar Cove Resort (Not visited)—Continued

◊◊◊◊RECREATION: swim pool, lake swim, boating, canoeing, ramp, dock, lake fishing, playground. Pets welcome. Open all yr. Facilities fully operational May 1 - Oct 15. Big rigs welcome. Rate in 2010 $44-49 per family. Member OPCA. Phone: (888)650-8572.

WHITE RIVER—B-3

(SE) OBATANGA PROVINCIAL PARK—*From town: Go 35-1/4 km/22 mi S on Hwy 17.* FACILITIES: 130 sites, 20 E, (15/30 amps), 110 no hkups, tenting, dump, laundry, ltd groc. RECREATION: boating, canoeing, ramp, playground. Partial handicap access. Open early Jun - early Sep. Phone: (807)822-2592.

(NW) WHITE LAKE PROVINCIAL PARK—*From town: Go 36-3/4 km/23 mi N on Hwy 17.* FACILITIES: 187 sites, typical site width 30 ft, 60 E, (15/30 amps), 127 no hkups, tenting, dump, laundry, ltd groc. RECREATION: lake swim, boating, canoeing, ramp, lake fishing, playground. Partial handicap access. Open May - Sep. Phone: (807)822-2447.

WHITEFISH—D-5

FAIRBANK PROVINCIAL PARK—*From town: Go 4-3/4 km/3 mi W on Hwy 17, then 20-3/4 km/13 mi N on Hwy 658 (Worthington).* FACILITIES: 160 sites, 40 E, (30 amps), 120 no hkups, 30 pull-thrus, tenting, dump, laundry. RECREATION: boating, canoeing, ramp, playground. Partial handicap access. Open May 19 - Sep 4. Phone: (705)866-0530.

WIARTON—G-2

(N) BLUEWATER PARK (City Park)—(Bruce) *From jct Hwy 6 & William St: Go 1/2 km/1/4 mi E on William St. Enter on L.* FACILITIES: 117 sites, typical site width 16 ft, 33 ft max RV length, 63 full hkups, 34 W&E, (15 amps), 20 no hkups, 37 pull-thrus, tenting, dump, laundry, ltd groc. RECREATION: swim pool, lake swim, boating, canoeing, ramp, dock, lake fishing, playground. Partial handicap access. Open May 15 - Oct 15. Phone: (519)534-2592.

Hope Bay Campground (Not visited)—(Bruce) *From north city limits: Go 1.6 km/1 mi N on Hwy 6, then 17.6 km/11 mi N on Bruce Rd 9, to Beech St, then .8 km/1/2 mi E on Hope Bay Rd. Enter at end.* ◊◊◊FACILITIES: 92 sites, typical site width 50 ft, 50 full hkups, 4 W&E, 3 E, (15/20/30 amps), 35 no hkups, 2 pull-thrus, tenting, dump, laundry, groceries. ◊◊◊RECREATION: lake swim, boating, canoeing, dock, lake fishing, play equipment. Pets welcome. Open May 1 - Mid Oct. Rate in 2010 $35-40 per family. Member OPCA. Phone: (519)534-1208.

Roth Park (Not Visited)—(Bruce) *From north city limits: Go 1.6 km/1 mi N on Hwy 6, then .4 km/1/4 mi E on Bruce Rd 9, then 5 mi N on Berford Lake Rd. Enter on R.* ◊◊FACILITIES: 126 sites, typical site width 50 ft, 34 ft max RV length, 115 W&E, (15 amps), 11 no hkups, 1 pull-thrus, tenting, dump, laundry, ltd groc. ◊◊RECREATION: lake swim, boating, canoeing, ramp, dock, lake fishing, play equipment. Pets welcome. Open May 1 - mid Oct. Rate in 2010 $23-33 per family. Phone: (519)534-0145.

WINDSOR—J-1

See listings at Amherstburg, Leamington, McGregor & Wheatley

WINDSOR—Continued on next page

Woodall's Camping Life magazine is the perfect family camping companion to any of Woodall's Directories and Guides. With 7 monthly issues per year, containing camping stories, destination articles, buyer's guides and more, Camping Life is a valuable resource for any family camper. Visit www.campinglife.com for more info.

Discover our Modern R.V. Facility and Challenging Golf Course
Phone: 519-726-6176 • Toll-Free 1-866-994-9699 • Fax: 519-726-5833
www.wildwoodgolfandrvresort.com
11112, 11th Concession Rd., McGregor, Ontario N0R 1J0
See listing at McGregor, ON

WINDSOR—Continued

Windsor Campground (Not visited)—(Essex) *From jct Hwy 401 & Essex Rd 46 (exit 14): Go 1-3/4 mi E on Essex Rd 46, then 3/4 mi N on Ninth Conc. Rd. Enter on L.* ◇◇◇◇FACILITIES: 239 sites, typical site width 30 ft, 175 full hkups, 10 W&E, (15/30/50 amps), 50 amps ($), 54 no hkups, 67 pull-thrus, tenting, dump, laundry, ltd groc. ◇◇◇◇RECREATION: swim pool, pond fishing, playground. Pets welcome, breed restrict. Partial handicap access. Open Apr 15 - Oct 15. Rate in 2010 $31-37 per family. Phone: (866)258-5554.

WOODSTOCK—I-2

(NE) PITTOCK CONSERVATION AREA (Upper Thames River Cons Auth)—*From jct Hwy 401 (exit 28) & Hwy 59: Go 4-3/4 km/3 mi N on Hwy 59.* FACILITIES: 250 sites, 230 E, (15/30 amps), 20 no hkups, tenting, dump, ltd groc. RECREATION: swim pool, lake swim, boating, canoeing, ramp, dock, lake fishing, playground. Pets welcome. Open Apr 20 - Oct 12. Phone: (519)539-5088.

WOODSTOCK—Continued

Willow Lake Park—(Oxford) *From jct Hwy 401 (exit 230) & Sweaburg Rd: Go 3.2 km/2 mi N on Mill St, then 30 meters/100 feet E on Hwy 2, then 5.1 km/3 mi N on Hwy 59. Enter on L.* ◇◇◇FACILITIES: 97 sites, typical site width 40 ft, 70 full hkups, 20 W&E, (30/50 amps), 50 amps ($), 7 no hkups, 17 pull-thrus, family camping, tenting, dump, laundry, ltd groc. ◇◇◇◇RECREATION: swim pool, playground. Pets welcome. Partial handicap access. Open May 1 - Oct 15. Big rigs welcome. Rate in 2010 $30-37 per family.

Phone: (519)537-7301
Address: RR6, 595487 Hwy 59 N, Woodstock, ON N4S 7W1
Email: willowlake@xplornet.com
Web: www.willowlakepark.on.ca

Visit a Dealer/Service Location in Woodall's.

WYOMING—I-1

Country View Motel & RV Camping Resort (Not visited)—(Lambton) *From jct Hwy 402 (exit 25) & CR 21: Go 1 km/1/2 mi S on CR 21, then 305 meters/1000 feet E on CR 22 (Hwy 7). Enter on R.* ◇◇◇◇FACILITIES: 136 sites, typical site width 30 ft, 72 full hkups, 32 W&E, (15/30/50 amps), 50 amps ($), 32 no hkups, 23 pull-thrus, family camping, tenting, dump, laundry. ◇◇◇◇RECREATION: swim pool, dock, pond fishing, playground. Pets welcome. Open mid Apr - end Oct. Big rigs welcome. Rate in 2010 $30-35 per family. Member OPCA. Phone: (888)610-0874. FCRV discount. FMCA discount.

Woodall's listings for public campgrounds are based upon information supplied by the appropriate government agency.

Unless otherwise noted all listed campgrounds have hot showers & flush toilets.

TRAVEL SECTION

Prince Edward Island

CAMPING FEES

Camping fees in Prince Edward Island listings are stated in Canadian dollars. Fees are quoted before taxes. Call each location for more details, as they vary from province to province.

READER SERVICE INFO

The following business has placed an ad in the Ontario Travel Section. To receive free information, enter the Reader Service number on the Reader Service Card opposite page 48/Discover Section in the front of this directory:

Advertiser	RS#
PEI Provincial Parks	4294

TIME ZONE

Prince Edward Island is on Atlantic Time.

TOPOGRAPHY

Cradled in the Gulf of St. Lawrence between New Brunswick and Nova Scotia, Prince Edward Island is a relaxing maritime province with a total population of only 140,000 residents. Its 2,000 square miles are filled with rural beauty, unbounded seascapes and miles of sandy beaches.

TEMPERATURE

Cool evenings, light breezes and low humidity are characteristic of the island. Summer temperatures have been known to be as high as 86° F, but generally are closer to 73° F. Winter temperatures are fairly cold, with an average temperature of 19° F.

TRAVEL & TOURISM INFO

Provincial: Tourism PEI, Box 2000, Charlottetown, PEI C1A 7N8 (800/463-4734). www.gov.pe.ca/

Visitor Information Centres:

Borden-Carleton Visitor Information Centre
100 Abegweit Dr.,Borden-Carleton
(902/437-8570)

Cavendish Visitor Information Centre
7591 Cawnpore Lane, Cavendish
(902/963-7830)

Charlottetown Visitor Information Centre
6 Prince St., Charlottetown
(902/368-4444)

St. Peters Visitor Information Centre
1915 Greenwich Rd., St. Peters
(902/961-3540)

Souris Visitor Information Centre
95 Main St, Souris
(902/687-7030)

Summerside Visitor Information Centre
(800/463-4734)

West Prince Visitor Information Centre
Rte 2 West, Mount Pleasant
(902/831-7930)

Wood Islands Visitor Information Centre
(902/962-7411)

RECREATIONAL INFO

Bicycling: The Confederation Trail is a 350-kilometre-long recreation path created along an abandoned railway. Information regarding the trail, bike rentals, repair shops, etc. can be found at www.peiplay.com/trail.

Where to Find CCUSA Parks

List City	Park Name	Map Coordinates
DARNLEY		
	Twin Shores Camping Area	C-3
MILL COVE		
	Winterbay Tent & Trailer Park (Not Visited)	C-4
MURRAY HARBOUR NORTH		
	Seal Cove Campground	D-5
NORTH RUSTICO		
	White Sands Cottages and Campground Resort	C-3

BUSINESSES OFFERING

	Things to See & Do	RV Sales	RV Service
CHARLOTTETOWN			
PEI Provincial Parks	▶		

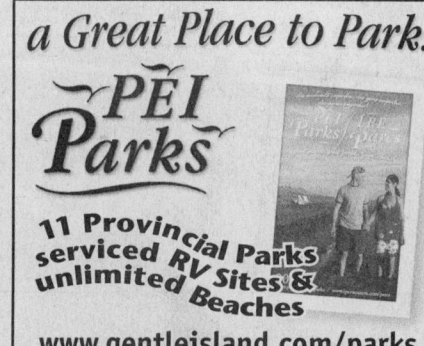

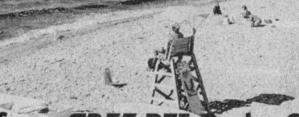

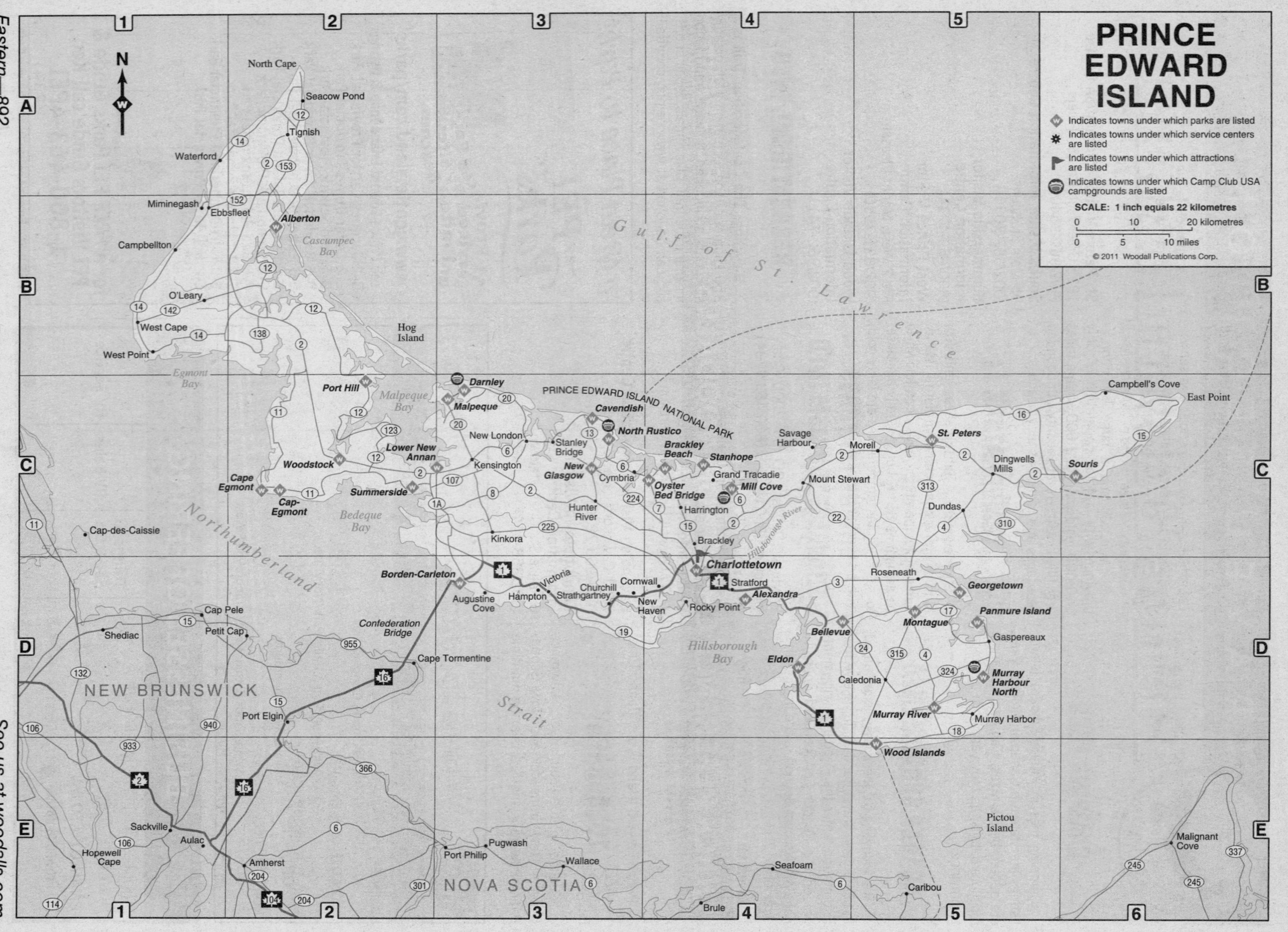
PRINCE EDWARD ISLAND
Indicates towns under which parks are listed
Indicates towns under which service centers are listed
Indicates towns under which attractions are listed
Indicates towns under which Camp Club USA campgrounds are listed
SCALE: 1 inch equals 22 kilometres
0 10 20 kilometres
0 5 10 miles
© 2011 Woodall Publications Corp.
Gulf of St. Lawrence
Northumberland Strait
PRINCE EDWARD ISLAND NATIONAL PARK
NEW BRUNSWICK
NOVA SCOTIA
North Cape
Seacow Pond
Tignish
Waterford
Miminegash
Ebbsfleet
Alberton
Cascumpec Bay
Campbellton
O'Leary
West Cape
West Point
Egmont Bay
Hog Island
Port Hill
Malpeque Bay
Darnley
Malpeque
Lower New Annan
Woodstock
Cape Egmont
Cap-Egmont
Summerside
Bedeque Bay
New London
Kensington
Stanley Bridge
Cavendish
North Rustico
Brackley Beach
Stanhope
New Glasgow
Cymbria
Oyster Bed Bridge
Grand Tracadie
Mill Cove
Harrington
Hunter River
Kinkora
Brackley
Hillsborough River
Charlottetown
Stratford
Alexandra
Borden-Carleton
Augustine Cove
Hampton
Victoria
Churchill
Strathgartney
Cornwall
New Haven
Rocky Point
Hillsborough Bay
Savage Harbour
Morell
St. Peters
Mount Stewart
Dingwells Mills
Souris
Campbell's Cove
East Point
Dundas
Roseneath
Georgetown
Panmure Island
Montague
Gaspereaux
Bellevue
Eldon
Caledonia
Murray Harbour North
Murray River
Murray Harbor
Wood Islands
Pictou Island
Malignant Cove
Cap-des-Caissie
Cap Pele
Shediac
Petit Cap
Confederation Bridge
Cape Tormentine
Port Elgin
Sackville
Aulac
Hopewell Cape
Amherst
Port Philip
Pugwash
Wallace
Seafoam
Caribou
Brule

Birding: For information on the over 300 species of birds, www.peiplay.com/birds or ask for the field checklist at one of the Visitor Information Centres.

Geocaching: To find out about the almost 200 Geocache sites in PEI visit: www.geocachingpei.com/geocaching

Golf: Golf season usually runs from May through October. (866/465-3734) www.golfpei.com

SHOPPING

The PEI Crafts council publishes a Craft and Gift Shop Guide, available at all Visitor Information centres. Among the traditional, quilts, pottery and knitted goods, you will find handmade shoes, soaps, furniture and more.

Anne of Green Gables Store, 110 Queen St., Charlottetown. www.annestore.ca. Dolls, clothing, books, posters, plates and more in a restored General Mercantile.

Charlottetown Mall, 670 University Ave. Charlottetown. More than 60 of Prince Edward Island's most-wanted stores and services under one roof.

The Shops of Confederation Court Mall, 134 Kent St. Charlottetown. www.confedcourtmall.com. Over 90 shops and services featuring independently owned and operated specialty stores in Atlantic Canada.

Gateway Village, Borden-Carleton. Many visitor services and a large collection of unique Island craft products.

Prince Edward Island Preserve Co., New Glasgow. This 1913 butter factory is one of PEI's special places. Includes an array of handcrafted items, preserves, specialty foods and homemade ice cream. Live entertainment.

Spinnakers' Landing, Summerside. www.summersidewaterfront.com. Waterfront shops for gifts, antiques, crafts, music and Island wear.

UNIQUE FEATURES

TRANSPORTATION

Northumberland Ferries: Car ferries depart from Caribou, Nova Scotia and Wood Islands, Prince Edward Island every hour and a half. The 75-minute trip is often considered a vacation highlight. www.nfl-bay.com (888/249-7245)

Les Îles-de-la-madeleine: C.T.M.A. offers regular ferry service from Cap-aux-Meules, Îles-de-la-madeleine, Québec to Souris, Prince Edward Island. (888/986-3278) The ferry does not operate from February to the end of March.

Confederation Bridge: A 13-kilometre engineering marvel, this bridge connects New Brunswick to the town of Borden-Carleton. It is a tourist attraction in itself. www.confederationbridge.com

Air: Air Canada Jazz, the regional affiliate of Air Canada, offers daily flights from Halifax, Montréal and Toronto. Air Canada has daily non-stop service from Toronto. www.aircanada.ca or www.flyjazz.ca

Daily flights from Toronto with WestJet and from Detroit with Northwest Airlines.

Train: Take the train as far as Moncton and continue on to PEI by bus or rental car. www.viarail.ca

QUICK REFERENCE CHART FOR WOODALL'S FEATURED PARKS

	Green Friendly	RV Lots for Sale	Park Models-Onsite Ownership	Park Membership for Sale	Big Rigs Welcome	Internet Friendly	Pets Welcome
ALBERTON							
Jacques Cartier Provincial Park							■
CAPE EGMONT							
Cedar Dunes Provincial Park							■
DARNLEY							
Twin Shores Camping Area	🍃				▲	●	■
ELDON							
Lord Selkirk Provincial Park							■
GEORGETOWN							
Brudenell River Provincial Park							■
MALPEQUE							
Cabot Beach Provincial Park							■
PANMURE ISLAND							
Panmure Island Provincial Park							■
PORT HILL							
Green Park Provincial Park							■
SOURIS							
Red Point Provincial Park							■
SUMMERSIDE							
Linkletter Provincial Park							■
WOOD ISLANDS							
Northumberland Provincial Park							■
WOODSTOCK							
Mill River Provincial Park							■

Green Friendly 🍃; RV Lots for Sale ✖; Park Models/Onsite Onwership ✱; Park Memberships for Sale ✔; Big Rigs Welcome ▲; Internet Friendly ●; Internet Friendly-WiFi ●; Pets Welcome ■

DESTINATIONS

NORTH CAPE COASTAL DRIVE

The name says it all for this region dominated by red sandstone cliffs, dunes and white lighthouses against a backdrop of breathtaking sunsets. A shallow strip of water along the region's north shore surrounded by sand dunes is called the "inland waterway" and offers spectacular views and birdwatching. An area of antiques, history and stately heritage homes, this region is perfect for walking tours and days spent browsing in museums.

Acadian Museum of P.E.I., Miscouche. This modern facility for the preservation of Acadian heritage features a historical museum, a documentation center and an audio-visual presentation in the museum theater.

Lennox Island Aboriginal Ecotourism. Surrounded by the rich and tranquil waters of Malpeque Bay, activities include a 10-km walking trail, sea kayaking, deep-sea fishing, authentic native craft shops, a nature store, as well .as PEI's only Aboriginal History Museum. Eat traditional Mi'kmaq food at the Minegoo Café. An excellent bird watching destination.

North Cape. Watch for seals when you visit the **Reef at North Cape**, the longest natural rock reef in North America. **North Cape Lighthouse,** built in 1866, warns ships of the 2-mile long rock reef. Also the home of **Wind Energy Interpretive Centre, North Cape Wind Farm** and **Black Marsh Nature Trail.**

West Point Lighthouse, West Point. Visit Canada's only inn located within a functioning Coast Guard lighthouse. In operation since 1875, West Point Lighthouse is one of the Island's tallest lighthouses. There is also a museum and craft shop.

RED SANDS SHORE

Visitors crossing the Confederation Bridge are first greeted by the rolling hills and red cliffs of Red Sands Shore, the economic and political centre of the province. It also has a thriving cultural community with theatres, nightclubs and musical entertainment from Celtic to jazz.

Gateway Village. Borden-Carleton. **Gateway Village**, located at the foot of the Confederation Bridge, gives a perfect introduction to PEI, by offering visitor services and information to help plan an itinerary.

Charlottetown. Attractions within the capital city include: **Founders' Hall, Province HousSt. Dunstan's Basilica, Peakes Wharf, Victoria Park, Confederation Centre of the Arts** and **Mackenzie Theatre**.

POINTS EAST COASTAL DRIVE

This area is largely rural, consisting of farmsteads, fishing ports and lighthouses. Many of the residents can trace their roots back to Scotland, which is evident in the festivals and music of the area. This is also an excellent area if you are looking for outdoor recreation such as hiking and cycling or golfing. The best of Prince Edward Island's natural features are here— landscape, fishing ports, beaches and trails.

Cape Bear Lighthouse & Marconi Museum, Cape Bear. Built in 1881, this is the site of the first Canadian Marconi station to hear the S.O.S. distress call from the Titanic. Magnificent view of Northumberland Strait.

Greenwich Interpretation Centre. Prince Edward Island National Park. Parks Canada protects a rare system of parabolic sand dunes and sites of Aboriginal, French and Acadian occupation. Learn about this unique ecosystem through multi-media program, exhibits and 3D floor model. It also includes three interpretive trails and a beach facility.

Montague. Newly developed, scenic waterfront offers shopping, dining and seal-watching tours. Visit **Garden of the Gulf Museum**, PEI's oldest museum, depicting pioneer and early 20th century life.

Northumberland Ferries. Taking the ferry from Pictou, NS to Wood Islands, PEI, is the shortest way to PEI from Nova Scotia and adds a delightful 1 hour and 15 minute sea voyage to your trip.

Wood Islands Lighthouse & Interpretive Museum. Stand in the 54-ft. tower and experience a breathtaking 360-degree view of coastal shores. Guided tour lets you experience life as it was in 1876.

ANNE'S LAND

This area has great family appeal as it has something for everyone, from amusement parks to quiet beaches and delicate dunes. Visit man-made tourist attractions or explore the history of the area.

Green Gables was the setting for L.M. Montgomery's beloved novel *Anne of Green Gables*. The house is furnished in period setting.

Lucy Maud Montgomery Birthplace, New London. The birthplace of this famous author of Anne of Green Gables is decorated with authentic Victorian period pieces. View the writer's wedding dress and her personal scrapbooks containing copies of her many stories and poems.

ANNUAL EVENTS

FEBRUARY

Charlottetown Winter Carnival, Charlottetown.

MAY

Scottish Ceilidh Concerts (thru Oct), Ceili at the Irish Hall (thru Oct), Charlottetown; Charlottetown Festival (thru Oct), Charlottetown.

JUNE

Come Fly a Kite Event, Port-la-Joye; Summerside Highland Gathering; Evening Frolic concerts (thru Aug), Cavendish; Victoria Playhouse Festival (thru Sept), Victoria; Natal Day Weekend, Charlottetown; Atlantic Superstore Festival of Lights, Charlottetown; Tour de PEI, Prince Edward Island.

JULY

Summerside Lobster Carnival, Summerside; British Car Days Across the Bridge, Rustico; Charlottetown Yacht Club Race Week, Charlottetown; Georgetown Summer Days, Georgetown; Celtic Festival (thru Aug), Summerside; Cardigan Canada Day, Cardigan; PEI Bluegrass & Oldtime Music Festival, Rollo Bay; Annual PEI Street Rod Association Show 'N Shine, Montague; Kinkora Somerset Festival, Kinkora; Evangeline Bluegrass & Traditional Music Festival, Abram-Village; Souris Regatta; Take a Hike Event, Cavendish; Emerald Junction Irish Festival, Kensington; Festival Rendez-vous Rustico Festival, Rustic; Anne of Green Gables Country Fair, Cavendish.

AUGUST

Annual Highland Games, Eldon; Old Home Week/PEI Provincial Exhibition, Charlottetown; L.M. Montgomery Festival, Cavendish; Gold Cup Parade, Charlottetown; PEI Tractor Pull Championships, Crapaud; Atlantic Fiddlers Jamboree, Abram-Village; Fiddlers & Followers Weekend, Cavendish; Tyne Valley Oyster Festival, Tyne Valley; PEI Lighthouse Festival, Island-wide; Tyne Valley Oyster Festival, Tyne Valley; West Prince Red Clay Bluegrass Festival, Tignish.

SEPTEMBER

Annual Cymbria Music Fest, Rustico; Cornwall Cornfest Festival, Cornwall; Mt. Stewart Heritage River Festival, Mount Stewart; PEI International Shellfish Festival, Charlottetown; Come to the Ceilidh, Charlottetown; Annual 70 Mile Coastal Yard Sale, Southeastern PEI; Prince Edward Island Studio Tour, Island-wide; Fall Flavours, Island wide.

OCTOBER

Prince Edward Island Marathon, Charlottetown to North Shore.

NOVEMBER

Charlottetown Christmas Parade.

DECEMBER

Christmas Lights Across Canada, Charlottetown; Capital New Year in the Park, Charlottetown; Consolidated Credit Union New Year's Eve Outdoor Community Celebration, Summerside.

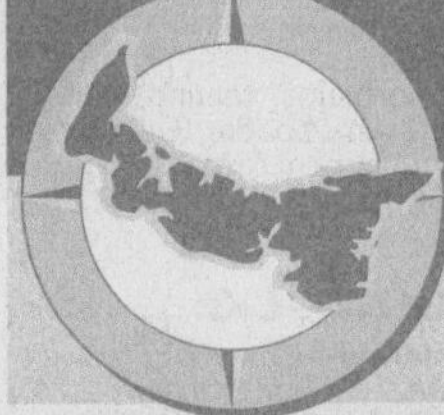

Prince Edward Island

All privately owned campgrounds personally inspected by
WOODALL'S
Representatives
John and Michele Pynenburg

ALBERTON—B-2

(NE) JACQUES CARTIER PROVINCIAL PARK—(Prince) *From town: Go 4.75 km/3 mi N on Hwy 12 and follow signs. Enter on R.*

FACILITIES: 74 sites, 34 W&E, (15 amps), 40 no hkups, tenting, dump, non-guest dump $, laundry, ltd groc, ice, picnic tables, fire rings, wood, controlled access.

RECREATION: rec hall, equipped pavilion, saltwater swim, canoeing, kayaking, golf nearby, activities, v-ball. Rec open to public.

Pets welcome. Partial handicap access. Open Mid Jun - End Sep. Clubs welcome. MC/VISA.

Phone: (902)853-8632
Address: 16448 Rt 12 Kildare, Aberton, PE C0B 1V0
Web: www.peiplay.com/parks

SEE AD TRAVEL SECTION PAGE 891

ALEXANDRA—D-4

(E) Vistabay Chalets RV Park & Golf Course—(Queens) *From West jct of Hwy 1 & 1A at Alexandra: Go 4-3/4 km/3 mi SE on Hwy 1A (Either Rte 26). Enter on L.* ◇◇◇FACILITIES: 15 sites, 15 full hkups, (15/30/50 amps), tenting, laundry. Pets welcome. Partial handicap access. Open May 1 - Oct 31. Big rigs welcome. Rate in 2010 $25-30 for 5 persons. Phone: (902)569-2252.

AUGUSTINE COVE—D-3

Cumberland Cove Campground (Not Visited)—(Prince) *From W town city limit on Hwy 10: Go 4.5 km/2-3/4 mi E on Hwy 10, then 1 km/1/2 mi S on Cumberland Cove Rd (dirt road). Enter at end.* ◇◇FACILITIES: 24 sites, typical site width 30 ft, 9 W&E, (15/20 amps), 15 no hkups, tenting, dump, ltd groc. ◇RECREATION: saltwater swim, canoeing, play equipment. Pets welcome. Open End Jun - Labor Day. Rate in 2010 $13-16 for 4 persons. Phone: (902)855-2961.

BELLEVUE—D-4

(SE) Ben's Lake Campground & Trout Fishing—(Queens) *From jct Hwy 3 and Hwy 24: Go 15.7 km/9-1/2 mi S on Hwy 24; or from Wood Island Ferry: Go 12 km/7-1/2 mi N on Hwy 315, then 3 km/2 mi NW on Hwy 24. Enter on R.* ◇◇◇FACILITIES: 30 sites, typical site width 24 ft, 35 ft max RV length, 14 full hkups, 6 W&E, (15 amps), 10 no hkups, tenting, dump, laundry. ◇◇RECREATION: electric motors only, canoeing, ramp, dock, lake fishing. Pets welcome. Open May 5 - Sep 30. Rate in 2010 $20-27 for 5 persons. Phone: (902)838-2706.

BORDEN-CARLETON—D-3

(NE) Sun-N-Shade Campground—(Prince) *From PEI end of the Confederation Bridge: Go 2.4 km/1-1/2 mi E on Hwy 1. Enter on L.* ◇◇◇FACILITIES: 99 sites, typical site width 24 ft, 71 full hkups, 19 W&E, (15/30 amps), 9 no hkups, 33 pull-thrus, family camping, tenting, dump, laundry. Pets welcome. Partial handicap access. Open May 13 - Oct 4. Rate in 2010 $28 for 2 persons.

Phone: (902)855-3492
Address: 23714 Hwy 1, Borden-Carleton, PE C0B 1X0
Lat/Lon: 46.25500/-63.67330
Email: info@sun-n-shade.com
Web: www.sun-n-shade.com

The Island's first residents were the Mi'kmaq.

BRACKLEY BEACH—C-4

PRINCE EDWARD ISLAND NATIONAL PARK (Robinsons Island)—(Queens) *From National Park entrance on Hwy 15: Go 4 km/2-1/2 mi W on Gulf Shore Pkwy.* FACILITIES: 148 sites, 148 no hkups, tenting. RECREATION: saltwater swim, canoeing, playground. Open late Jun - Labour day. Phone: (902)672-6350.

(NE) Vacationland RV Park—(Queens) *From jct Hwy 6 & Hwy 15: Go N 2 km/1-1/4 mi on Hwy 15, then 1.6 km/1 mi E on Britain Shore Rd. Enter at end.* ◇◇◇◇FACILITIES: 345 sites, 245 full hkups, 100 W&E, (15/30/50 amps), 50 amps ($), 73 pull-thrus, tenting, dump, laundry, ltd groc. ◇◇◇◇RECREATION: swim pool, canoeing, river fishing, playground. Pets welcome. Partial handicap access. Open May 15 - Sep 15. Big rigs welcome. Rate in 2010 $36-44 per family. Member PEI Assn. Phone: (800)529-0066.

CAP-EGMONT—C-2

(W) Moonlight Camping (Not Visited)—(Prince) *From jct Hwy 124 & Hwy 11: Go 11.2 km/7 mi E on Hwy 11. Enter on L.* ◇◇FACILITIES: 100 sites, typical site width 30 ft, 50 full hkups, (15 amps), 50 no hkups, 10 pull-thrus, tenting, laundry, ltd groc. ◇◇RECREATION: saltwater swim, play equipment. Pets welcome. Open May 15 - Sep 30. Rate in 2010 $23 for 4 persons. Phone: (902)854-2746.

CAPE EGMONT—C-2

CEDAR DUNES PROVINCIAL PARK—(Prince) *From jct Hwys 11 and 124: Go 15 km/8 mi W on Hwy 11. Enter on L.*

FACILITIES: 59 sites, 39 W&E, (15 amps), 20 no hkups, tenting, dump, non-guest dump $, laundry, ice, picnic tables, fire rings, wood, controlled access.

RECREATION: equipped pavilion, saltwater swim, saltwater fishing, golf nearby, playground, activities, hiking trails. Rec open to public.

Pets welcome. Partial handicap access. Open June 23 - Sep 30. Clubs welcome. MC/VISA.

Phone: (902)859-8785
Address: 265 Cedar Dunes Park Rd, Cape Egmont, PE C0B 1V0
Web: www.peiplay.com/parks

SEE AD TRAVEL SECTION PAGE 891

CAVENDISH—C-3

(C) Cavendish KOA—(Queens) *From jct Hwy 13 & Hwy 6: Go 1.2 km/3/4 mi W on Hwy 6. Enter on L.* ◇◇◇◇FACILITIES: 225 sites, typical site width 28 ft, 146 full hkups, 67 W&E, (15/30/50 amps), 50 amps ($), 12 no hkups, 31 pull-thrus, family camping, tenting, dump, laundry, groceries. ◇◇◇◇RECREATION: swim pool, playground. Pets welcome. Partial handicap access. Open Jun 1 - Oct 15. Big rigs welcome. Green Friendly. Rate in 2010 $27-42 per family. Phone: (902) 963-2079. KOA discount.

(C) Cavendish Sunset Campground—(Queens) *From jct Hwy 13 & Hwy 6: Go 2.4 km/1-1/2 mi W on Hwy 6. Enter on L.* ◇◇◇◇FACILITIES: 460 sites, typical site width 40 ft, 140 full hkups, 100 W&E, (15/30/50 amps), 50 amps ($), 220 no hkups, 75 pull-thrus, family camping, tenting, dump, laundry, groceries. ◇◇◇◇RECREATION: swim pool, playground. Pets welcome. Partial handicap access. Open mid Jun - Labor Day. Rate in 2010 $36-41 for 4 persons. Phone: (902)963-2440.

(C) Marco Polo Land—(Queens) *From jct Hwy 6 & Hwy 13: Go 1.6 km/1 mi S on Hwy 13. Enter on L.* ◇◇◇◇FACILITIES: 524 sites, typical site width 40 ft, 301 full hkups, 200 W&E, (15/30/50 amps), 50 amps ($), 23 no hkups, 25 pull-thrus, tenting, dump, laundry, full svc store. ◇◇◇◇RECREATION: 2 swim pools, pond fishing, playground. Pets welcome. Partial handicap access. Open May 31 - Sept 20. Big rigs welcome. Rate in 2010 $30-40 for 4 persons. Phone: (800)665-2352.

(NW) PRINCE EDWARD ISLAND NATIONAL PARK (Cavendish Campground)—(Queens) *From jct Hwy 13 & Hwy 6: Go 3-1/4 km/2 mi W on Hwy 6, then 2 km/1-1/4 mi N on Grahams Lane.* FACILITIES: 302 sites, 83 full hkups, 78 E, (15/20/50 amps), 78 no hkups, tenting, laundry. RECREATION: swim pool, saltwater swim, canoeing, playground. Open all yr. Facilities fully operational Late Jun - Late Aug. Phone: (902)672-6350.

CHARLOTTETOWN—D-4

(SW) Holiday Cornwall KOA—(Queens) *From jct Hwy 1 & Hwy 248 (at Cornwall): Go S 3.7km/2 mi to Ferry Rd, then 2 km/1/4 mi on Ferry Rd. Enter on L.* ◇◇◇◇FACILITIES: 271 sites, typical site width 27 ft, 185 full hkups, 76 W&E, (20/30/50 amps), 50 amps

CHARLOTTETOWN—Continued
Holiday Cornwall KOA—Continued

($), 10 no hkups, 78 pull-thrus, tenting, dump, laundry, ltd groc. ◇◇◇RECREATION: swim pool, river swim, playground. Pets welcome. Open Jun 1 - Sep 24. Facilities fully operational Jul 1 - Labour Day. Rate in 2010 $31-53 per family. Phone: (902)566-2421. KOA discount.

PEI PROVINCIAL PARKS—11 province parks, Heritage sites, day parks & golf courses. (800)463-4PEI (734). Open all yr.

Phone: (902)368-6556
Address: 105 Rochford St, 3rd floor, Charlottetown, PE C1A 7N8
Lat/Lon: 46.234117/-63.133258
Email: klmaclaren@gov.pe.ca
Web: www.peiplay.com/parks

SEE AD TRAVEL SECTION PAGE 891

(NW) Pine Hills RV Park—(Queens) *From jct Hwy 1 and Arterial Hwy (Charlottetown bypass): Go 3 km/1-3/4 mi on Arterial Hwy to Route 15, then 9 km /6 mi N. Enter on L.* ◇◇◇◇FACILITIES: 200 sites, 134 full hkups, 66 W&E, (15/30/50 amps), 28 pull-thrus, dump, laundry, ltd groc. ◇◇◇RECREATION: swim pool, playground. Pets welcome. No tents. Open mid May - mid Sep. Rate in 2010 $33-40 for 2 persons. Phone: (877)226-2267.

(E) Southport RV Park Motel—(Queens) *From jct Hwy 1 & Stratford Rd (Hwy 1A): Go 90 meters/100 yards S on Stratford Rd. Enter on R.* ◇◇◇FACILITIES: 45 sites, typical site width 30 ft, accepts full hkup units only, 45 full hkups, (15/30/50 amps), 50 amps ($), 28 pull-thrus, laundry. Pets welcome. No tents. Open Apr 1 - Oct 31. Big rigs welcome. Rate in 2010 $34-52 per family. Phone: (902)569-2287.

DARNLEY—C-3

(NW) TWIN SHORES CAMPING AREA—(Prince) *From jct Hwy 20 & Hwy 6: Go 17.3 km/10-3/4 mi W on Hwy 20, thend 3.2 km/2 mi N on Darnley Point Rd. Enter at end.*

◇◇◇◇◇FACILITIES: 600 sites, typical site width 30 ft, 370 full hkups, 113 W&E, (15/20/30/50 amps), 127 no hkups, some extd stay sites, 127 pull-thrus, WiFi Instant Internet at site, WiFi Internet central location, family camping, tenting, shower$, dump, non-guest dump, laundry, groceries, RV supplies, LP bottle exch, ice, picnic tables, fire rings, wood, controlled access.

◇◇◇◇◇RECREATION: rec hall, rec room/area, pavilion, equipped pavilion, coin games, saltwater swim, boating, canoeing, kayaking, saltwater fishing, fishing supplies, golf nearby, bsktball, playground, shuffleboard court 3 shuffleboard courts, activities, tennis, horseshoes, sports field, hiking trails, v-ball, local tours.

Pets welcome. Partial handicap access. Open Jun 1 - Oct 2. Big rigs welcome. Escort to site. Clubs welcome. Green Friendly. Rate in 2010 $29-36 per family. MC/VISA/Debit. ATM. CCUSA 50% Discount. CCUSA reservations Recommended, CCUSA max stay 21 days. Discount not available Jul or Aug.

Phone: (877)PEI-CAMP
Address: 702 Lower Darnley Rd, Kensington, PE C0B 1M0
Lat/Lon: 46.5615/-63.6623
Email: info@twinshores.com
Web: www.twinshores.com

SEE AD NEXT PAGE

Can you trust the Woodall's ratings? 25 evaluation teams have scoured North American campgrounds to provide you with accurate, up to date information & ratings. Find a rating you don't agree with? Send a letter or email our way, and we'll give it extra attention for 2012.

ELDON—D-4

LORD SELKIRK PROVINCIAL PARK—(Queens) *From the village: Go 2 km/1-1/4 mi E on Hwy 1. Enter on R.*

FACILITIES: 77 sites, 56 W&E, (15/30 amps), 21 no hkups, tenting, dump, non-guest dump $, laundry, ice, picnic tables, fire rings, wood, controlled access.

RECREATION: equipped pavilion, swim pool, river swim, golf nearby, playground, sports field, v-ball. Rec open to public.

Pets welcome. Partial handicap access. Open Jun 7 - Sep 27. Clubs welcome. MC/VISA.

Phone: (902)659-7221
Address: Parks Division East Box 370, Montague, PE C0A 1R0
Web: www.peiplay.com/parks

SEE AD TRAVEL SECTION PAGE 891

GEORGETOWN—D-5

BRUDENELL RIVER PROVINCIAL PARK—(Kings) *From jct of Hwy 4 and Hwy 3: Go 1.5 km/1 mi E and follow signs. Enter at end.*

FACILITIES: 95 sites, typical site width 28 ft, 25 full hkups, 18 W&E, (15/30 amps), 52 no hkups, tenting, dump, non-guest dump $, laundry, ice, picnic tables, fire rings, wood, controlled access.

RECREATION: rec hall, equipped pavilion, river swim, boating, canoeing, kayaking, dock, 20 canoe/15 kayak rentals, golf nearby, bsktball, playground, activities, tennis, sports field, v-ball, local tours. Rec open to public.

Pets welcome. Partial handicap access. Open End May - Oct 15. Clubs welcome. MC/VISA.

Phone: (902)652-8966
Address: 283 Brudenedl River Blvd, Georgetown, PE C0A 1R0
Web: www.peiplay.com/parks

SEE AD TRAVEL SECTION PAGE 891

LOWER NEW ANNAN—C-2

(NE) Crystal Beach Campground—(Prince) *From jct Hwy 2 & Waterview Rd (Rt 120N): Go .08 km/1/2 mi N on 120 N Lower New Annan Rd, then .04 km/1/4 mi E on Barbara Weit Rd, then .08 km/ 1/2 mi N on Chrystal Drive. Enter at end.* ◆◆◆FACILITIES: 250 sites, typical site width 28 ft, 130 full hkups, 60 W&E, (15/30/50 amps), 50 amps ($), 60 no hkups, 65 pull-thrus, family camping, tenting, dump, laundry, ltd groc. ◆◆◆RECREATION: swim pool, saltwater/playground. Pets welcome. Partial handicap access. Open May 20 - Sep 27. Rate in 2010 $26-29 per family.

Phone: (877)433-2267
Address: 178 Crystal Dr, New Annan, PE C1N 4J8
Lat/Lon: 46.43294/-63.71063
Email: stay@crystalbeachcampground.net
Web: www.crystalbeachcampground.net

MALPEQUE—C-3

CABOT BEACH PROVINCIAL PARK—(Prince) *From town: Go 16 km/10 mi N on Hwy 20. Enter on L.*

FACILITIES: 163 sites, 28 full hkups, 30 W&E, (15/30 amps), 105 no hkups, tenting, dump, non-guest dump $, laundry, ice, picnic tables, fire rings, wood, controlled access.

RECREATION: rec hall, equipped pavilion, saltwater swim, canoeing, kayaking, golf nearby, playground, activities, sports field. Rec open to public.

Pets welcome. Partial handicap access. Open June 9 - Sept 6. Clubs welcome. MC/VISA.

MALPEQUE—Continued
CABOT BEACH PROVINCIAL PARK—Continued

Phone: (902)836-8945
Address: 449 Malpeque Rt 20, Malpeque, PE C1E 1V4
Web: www.peiplay.com/parks

SEE AD TRAVEL SECTION PAGE 891

MILL COVE—C-4

(C) Wintorbay Tent & Trailer Park (Not Visited)—(Queens) *From jct Hwy 219 & Hwy 6: Go 0.5 klm/1/4 mi SE on Hwy 219. Enter on L.* ◆◆◆FACILITIES: 68 sites, typical site width 22 ft, 39 full hkups, 18 W&E, (15/30 amps), 11 no hkups, cable Internet central location ($), tenting, dump, non-guest dump, laundry, ltd groc, ice, picnic tables, fire rings, wood. ◆◆RECREATION: swim pool, saltwater swim, canoeing, kayaking, play equipment, horseshoes. Pets welcome, breed restrict, quantity restrict. Open May 15 - Sep 15. Rate in 2010 $28-32 per family. VISA. CCUSA 50% Discount. CCUSA reservations Recommended, CCUSA max stay 2 days, Cash only for CCUSA disc., CCUSA disc. not avail F,Sa, CCUSA disc. not avail holidays. Not available Jul & Aug.

Phone: (902)672-2834
Address: 95 Donaldston Rd Hwy 219, Mill Cove, PE C0A 1T0
Lat/Lon: 46.37178/-63.03005

MONTAGUE—D-5

Lane's Cottages & Suites—(Kings) *From jct Hwy 1 & Hwy 210: Go 9.7 km W on Hwy 210, then 90.3 km N on Hwy 4. Enter on R.* ◆◆◆◆FACILITIES: 15 sites, 5 full hkups, (30 amps), 10 no hkups, tenting, laundry. ◆◆RECREATION: playground. Rate in 2010 $31 per family.

Phone: (800)268-7532
Address: 33 Brook St, Montague, PE C0A 1R0
Lat/Lon: 46.16719/-62.64418
Email: info@lanescottages.com
Web: www.lanescottages.com

(C) Montague Recreation Park (Not Visited)—(Kings) *From jct Hwy 326 & Hwy 17: Go 30 meters/100 ft N on Hwy 17. Enter on L.* ◆◆FACILITIES: 33 sites, typical site width 50 ft, 19 full hkups, (15/30 amps), 14 no hkups, tenting, dump. ◆RECREATION: saltwater swim, canoeing, dock. Pets welcome. Partial handicap access. Open May 1 - Oct 15. Rate in 2010 $22 per family. Phone: (902)838-2074.

MURRAY HARBOUR NORTH—D-5

(E) Seal Cove Campground (Not Visited)—(Kings) *From jct 17 & 17A: Go .08 km/1/2 mi S on Hwy 17, then 100 meter/400 feet W on Mink River Rd. Enter on L.* ◆◆◆FACILITIES: 124 sites, typical site width 25 ft, 87 full hkups, 20 W&E, (15/30 amps), 17 no hkups, 25 pull-thrus, tenting, dump, non-guest dump, laundry, ltd groc, LP gas by weight, ice, picnic tables, fire rings, wood. ◆◆◆RECREATION: equipped pavilion, swim pool, saltwater swim, boating, canoeing, kayaking, ramp, saltwater fishing, mini-golf, ($), play equipment, shuffleboard court, horseshoes, v-ball. Pets welcome. Open Jun 3 - Sep 19. Rate in 2010 $31-37 for 4 persons. MC/VISA/AMEX/Debit. CCUSA 50% Discount. CCUSA reservations Accepted, CCUSA max stay 3 days, CCUSA disc. not avail F,Sa, CCUSA disc. not avail holidays. Not available Jul & Aug.

Phone: (902)962-2745
Address: 87 Mink River Road, Murray Harbour North, PE C0A 1R0
Lat/Lon: 46.04955/-62.52412
Email: mcnairn@pei.sympatico.ca
Web: www.sealcovecampground.ca

MURRAY RIVER—D-5

(N) River RV Campground (Not Visited)—(Kings) *From jct Hwy 24 & Hwy 4: Go .08 km/1/4 mi N on Hwy 4. Enter on R.* ◆◆FACILITIES: 23 sites, 20

MURRAY RIVER—Continued
River RV Campground (Not Visited)—Continued

full hkups, (15/30 amps), 3 no hkups, tenting, dump, laundry. ◆RECREATION: river swim, boating, canoeing, dock, saltwater fishing, play equipment. Pets welcome. Open May 1 - Oct 15. Rate in 2010 $23-25 for 2 persons. Phone: (902)962-3738.

NEW GLASGOW—C-3

(E) New Glasgow Highlands—(Queens) *From jct Hwy 13 & Hwy 224: Go 1.9 km/1-1/4 mi E on Hwy 224. Enter on R.* ◆◆◆◆FACILITIES: 18 sites, 12 full hkups, (30/50 amps), 50 amps ($), 6 no hkups, 3 pull-thrus, tenting, dump, laundry, ltd groc. ◆◆◆RECREATION: swim pool, playground. Pets welcome. Open May 1 - Oct 31. Rate in 2010 $35 for 4 persons. Phone: (902) 964-3232.

NORTH RUSTICO—C-3

(W) White Sands Cottages and Campground Resort—(Queens) *From jct Hwy 6 & Hwy 269: Go 4.5 Km/2-3/4 mi W on Hwy 6, then 1.2 Km/3/4 mi E on Cape Rd (dirt road). Enter on R.* ◆◆◆FACILITIES: 55 sites, typical site width 30 ft, 2 full hkups, 24 W&E, (15/30 amps), 29 no hkups, cable Internet central location, family camping, tenting, dump, non-guest dump $, laundry, ltd groc, ice, picnic tables, fire rings, wood. ◆◆RECREATION: swim pool, play equipment, horseshoes, v-ball. Pets welcome ($), breed restrict, size restrict, quantity restrict. Open Jun 1 - Sep 15. Rate in 2010 $34-39 per family. MC/VISA/Debit. CCUSA 50% Discount. CCUSA reservations Recommended, CCUSA max stay 3 days, Cash only for CCUSA disc., CCUSA disc. not avail F,Sa, CCUSA disc. not avail holidays.

Phone: (902)963-2532
Address: 226 Cape Rd, North Rustico/Cavendish, PE C0B 1M0
Lat/Lon: 46.48679/-63.32401
Email: whitesands@pei.albn.com
Web: www.whitesandspei.com

OYSTER BED BRIDGE—C-4

(N) Bayside RV Campground—(Queens) *From jct Hwy 7 & Hwy 6: Go 1.3 km/3/4 mi W on Hwy 6, then 0.8 km/1/2 mi N on Camp Rd. Enter on R.* ◆◆◆FACILITIES: 110 sites, typical site width 30 ft, 81 full hkups, 19 W&E, (15/30 amps), 10 no hkups, 22 pull-thrus, family camping, tenting, dump, laundry, ltd groc. ◆◆◆RECREATION: swim pool, canoeing, playground. Pets welcome, breed restrict, quantity restrict. Open May 28 - Sep 26. Rate in 2010 $29-23 for 2 persons.

Phone: (877)445-2489
Address: 112 Camp Road, Charlottetown, PE C1E 1Z4
Lat/Lon: 46.40298/-63.23940
Email: baysiderv@pei.sympatico.ca
Web: www.baysidervcampground.com

PANMURE ISLAND—D-5

PANMURE ISLAND PROVINCIAL PARK—(Kings) *From jct Hwy 17 and Hwy 347: Go 3 km/2 mi N on Hwy 347. Enter on R.*

FACILITIES: 44 sites, 22 W&E, (15 amps), 22 no hkups, tenting, dump, non-guest dump $, laundry, ice, picnic tables, fire rings, wood, controlled access.

RECREATION: equipped pavilion, saltwater swim, boating, canoeing, kayaking, ramp, saltwater fishing, golf nearby, bike rental 8 bike rentals, activities. Rec open to public.

Pets welcome. Partial handicap access. Open late Jun - Mid Sep. Clubs welcome. MC/VISA.

Phone: (902)838-0668
Address: Parks Div East, Montague, PE C0A IR0
Web: www.peiplay.com/parks

SEE AD TRAVEL SECTION PAGE 891

PORT HILL—C-2

GREEN PARK PROVINCIAL PARK—(Prince) *From the Village: Go 2.5 km/1-1/2 mi N on Hwy 12.*

FACILITIES: 58 sites, 18 W&E, (15 amps), 40 no hkups, tenting, cabins, dump, non-guest dump $, laundry, ice, picnic tables, fire rings, wood, controlled access.

RECREATION: equipped pavilion, river swim, golf nearby, bsktball, playground, activities.

Pets welcome. Open Mid Jun - Sep 6. Clubs welcome. MC/VISA.

GREEN PARK PROVINCIAL PARK—Continued on next page

PORT HILL—Continued
GREEN PARK PROVINCIAL PARK—Continued

Phone: (902)831-7912
Address: 364 Greenpark Rd, Port Hill, PE C0B 1V0
Web: www.peiplay.com/parks

SEE AD TRAVEL SECTION PAGE 891

ST. PETERS—C-5

ST. PETERS PARK (Community of St. Peters)—*From Int Hwy 2 Go 1 km/.06 mi E on Hwy 2. Enter on R.* FACILITIES: 68 sites, 44 full hkups, (20 amps), 24 no hkups, dump, laundry. RECREATION: swim pool, playground. Open June 15 - Sept 19. Phone: (902)961-2786.

SOURIS—C-6

RED POINT PROVINCIAL PARK—(Kings) *From town: Go 12.75 km/8 mi NE on Hwy 16. Enter on R.*

WELCOME

FACILITIES: 97 sites, 43 full hkups, 22 W&E, (15/30 amps), 32 no hkups, tenting, dump, non-guest dump $, laundry, picnic tables, fire rings, wood, controlled access.

RECREATION: rec hall, equipped pavilion, saltwater swim, canoeing, kayaking, golf nearby, bsktball, playground, activities, sports field. Rec open to public.

Pets welcome. Partial handicap access. Open end of May - Sept 30. Clubs welcome. MC/VISA.

Phone: (902)357-3075
Address: Parks Division East, Montague, PE C0A 1R0
Web: www.peiplay.com/parks

SEE AD TRAVEL SECTION PAGE 891

STANHOPE—C-4

(N) PRINCE EDWARD ISLAND NATIONAL PARK (Stanhope Campground)—(Queens) *From jct Hwy 6 & Hwy 25: Go 3-1/4 km/2 mi NW on Hwy 25, then 1-1/2 km/1 mi E on Gulf Shore Pkwy.* FACILITIES: 125 sites, 30 ft max RV length, 14 full hkups, (15/20 amps), 111 no hkups, tenting, laundry. RECREATION: saltwater swim, canoeing, playground. Partial handicap access. Open Jun 15 - Oct 8. Phone: (902)672-6350.

Woodall's Tip... Get FREE Information—Use the Reader Service card.

SUMMERSIDE—C-2

LINKLETTER PROVINCIAL PARK—(Prince) *From town: Go 8 km/5 mi W on Hwy 11. Enter on L.*

WELCOME

FACILITIES: 93 sites, typical site width 26 ft, 25 full hkups, 17 W&E, (15/30/50 amps), 51 no hkups, tenting, dump, non-guest dump $, laundry, ice, picnic tables, fire rings, wood, controlled access.

RECREATION: equipped pavilion, saltwater swim, canoeing, kayaking, golf nearby, playground. Rec open to public.

Pets welcome. Partial handicap access. Open May 30 - Sept 30. Clubs welcome. MC/VISA.

Phone: (902)888-8366
Address: 437 Linkletter Rd, Summerside, PE C0B 1V0
Web: www.peiplay.com/parks

SEE AD TRAVEL SECTION PAGE 891

TRACADIE CROSS—C-4

(SW) Confederation Trailside Tourist Grounds (Not Visited)—(Queens) *From jct Hwy 218 & Hwy 2: Go 2 km/1-1/4 mi W on Hwy 2. Enter on R.* ◇FACILITIES: 45 sites, 10 full hkups, 10 W&E, (15/30 amps), 25 no hkups, tenting. Pets welcome. Open Jun 1 - Sep 15. Rate in 2010 $25 for 2 persons. Phone: (902)940-3630.

WATERFORD—A-1

(S) Waterford Campground (Not Visited)—(Prince) *From Tignish: Go 21 klms. 13 mi on Hwy 14 S. Enter on R.* ◇◇FACILITIES: 58 sites, 30 full hkups, 12 W&E, (15/30 amps), 16 no hkups, tenting, dump, laundry, ltd groc. ◇◇RECREATION: swim pool, saltwater swim, play equipment. Pets welcome. Partial handicap access. Open Jun 15 - Sep 15. Rate in 2010 $23-25 per vehicle. Phone: (902)882-2644.

Canada's two official sports are lacrosse and hockey.

WOOD ISLANDS—E-5

(E) NORTHUMBERLAND PROVINCIAL PARK—(Queens) *From Wood Islands Ferry: Go 3 km/2 mi E on Hwy 4. Enter on L.*

WELCOME

FACILITIES: 60 sites, 10 full hkups, 28 W&E, (15/30 amps), 22 no hkups, tenting, cabins, dump, non-guest dump $, laundry, ice, picnic tables, fire rings, wood, controlled access.

RECREATION: equipped pavilion, saltwater swim, canoeing, kayaking, golf nearby, bsktball, playground, activities, (wkends), hiking trails. Rec open to public.

Pets welcome. Partial handicap access. Open May 30 - Sep 30. Clubs welcome. MC/VISA.

Phone: (902)962-7418
Address: Park Division East, Montague, PE C0A 1R0
Web: www.peiplay.com/parks

SEE AD TRAVEL SECTION PAGE 891

WOODSTOCK—C-2

(NE) MILL RIVER PROVINCIAL PARK—(Prince) *From Hwy 2 North of town: Go 1/2 mi E and follow signs on RT 136. Enter on L.*

WELCOME

FACILITIES: 72 sites, typical site width 28 ft, 36 full hkups, 18 W&E, (15/30 amps), 18 no hkups, tenting, dump, non-guest dump $, laundry, picnic tables, fire rings, grills, wood, controlled access.

RECREATION: rec hall, rec room/area, equipped pavilion, river swim, canoeing, kayaking, dock, 12 canoe/4 kayak rentals, golf nearby, playground, activities, sports field.

Pets welcome. Partial handicap access. Open Mid May - Mid Oct. Clubs welcome. MC/VISA.

Phone: (902)859-8786
Address: 3 Mill River Resort Rd, Woodstock, PE C0B 1V0
Web: www.peilplay.com/parks

SEE AD TRAVEL SECTION PAGE 891

Prince Edward Island joined Confederation in 1873 and is the smallest province in Canada.

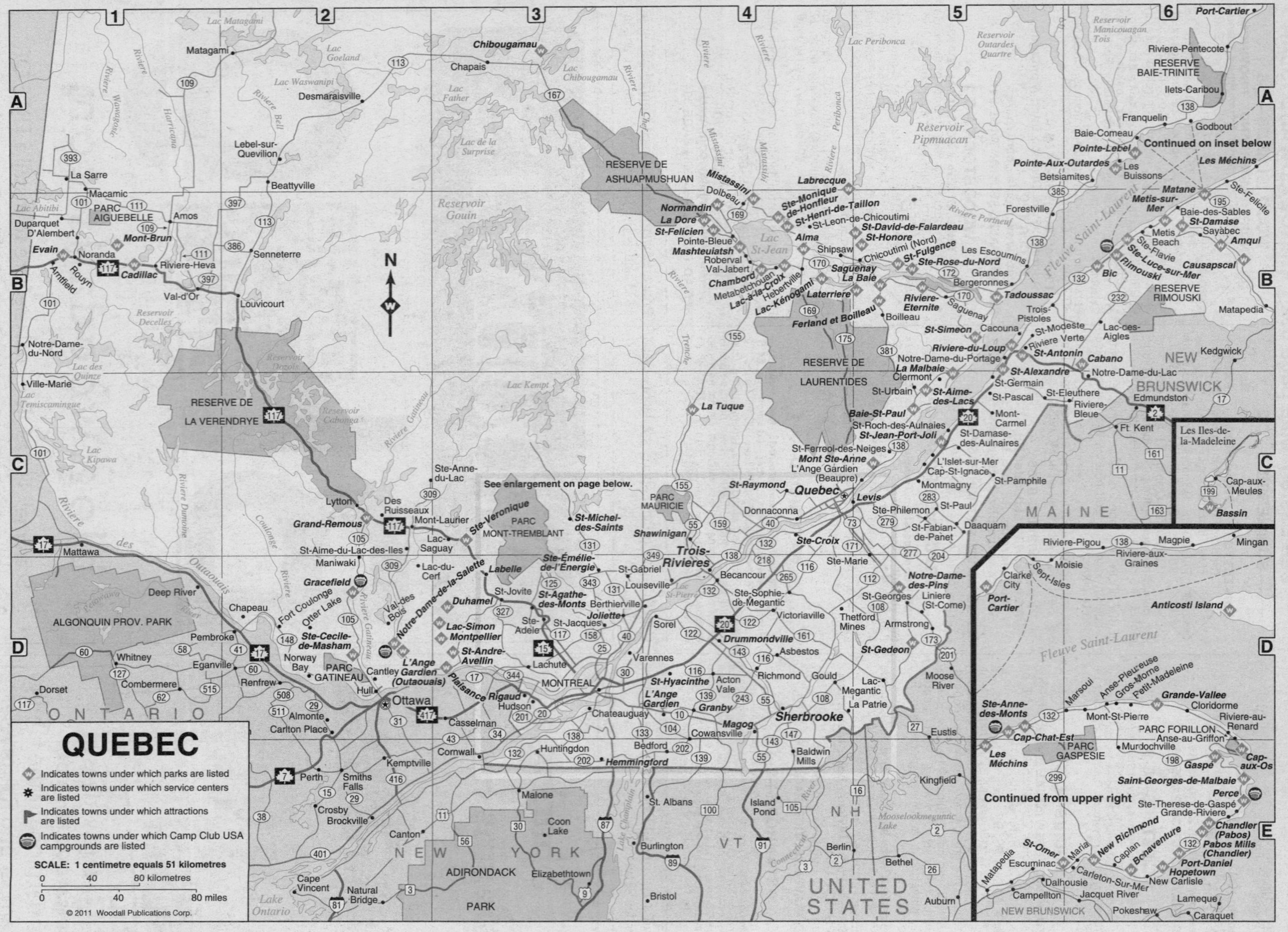
QUEBEC
Indicates towns under which parks are listed
Indicates towns under which service centers are listed
Indicates towns under which attractions are listed
Indicates towns under which Camp Club USA campgrounds are listed
SCALE: 1 centimetre equals 51 kilometres
0 40 80 kilometres
0 40 80 miles
© 2011 Woodall Publications Corp.
See enlargement on page below.
Continued on inset below
Continued from upper right
Les Iles-de-la-Madeleine
UNITED STATES
ONTARIO
NEW BRUNSWICK
MAINE
NEW YORK
RESERVE DE LA VERENDRYE
RESERVE DE ASHUAPMUSHUAN
RESERVE DE LAURENTIDES
ALGONQUIN PROV. PARK
ADIRONDACK PARK
Quebec
Montreal
Ottawa
Sherbrooke
Trois-Rivieres

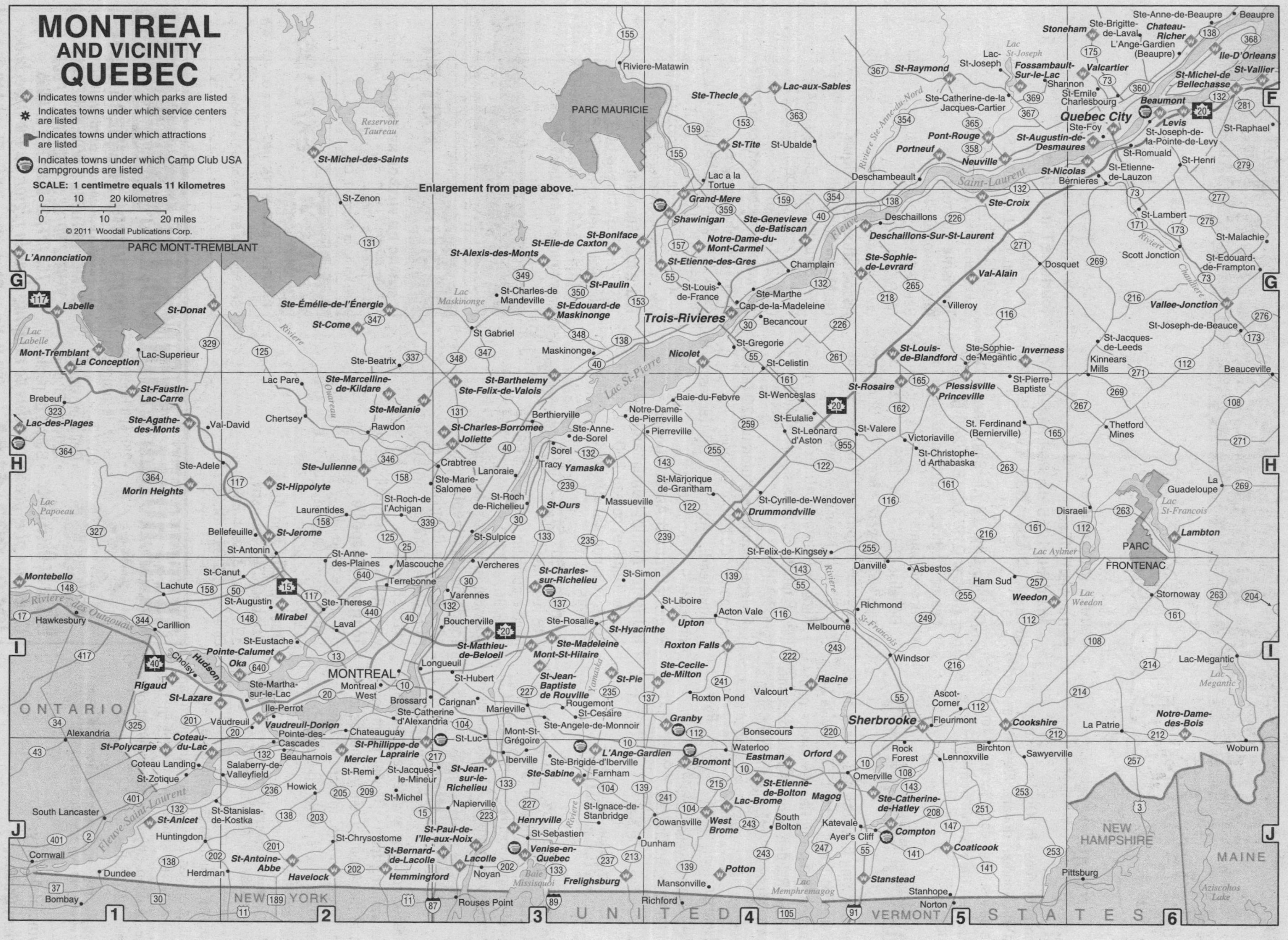
MONTREAL AND VICINITY QUEBEC
Indicates towns under which parks are listed
Indicates towns under which service centers are listed
Indicates towns under which attractions are listed
Indicates towns under which Camp Club USA campgrounds are listed
SCALE: 1 centimetre equals 11 kilometres
0 10 20 kilometres
0 10 20 miles
© 2011 Woodall Publications Corp.
Enlargement from page above.
PARC MONT-TREMBLANT
PARC MAURICIE
PARC FRONTENAC
MONTREAL
Quebec City
Trois-Rivieres
Sherbrooke
ONTARIO
NEW YORK
VERMONT
NEW HAMPSHIRE
MAINE
UNITED STATES

CAMPING FEES

Camping fees in Québec listings are stated in Canadian dollars. Fees are quoted before taxes. Call each location for more details, as they vary from province to province.

READER SERVICE INFO

The following business has placed an ad in the Québec Travel Section. To receive free information, enter the Reader Service number on the Reader Service Card opposite page 48/Discover Section in the front of this directory:

Advertiser	RS#
Conseil De Development du Camping au Quebec	627
Okeechobee Landings	4231

TIME ZONE

Québec is in the Eastern Time Zone, with the exception of Iles-de-la-Madeleine (a series of islands located in the Gulf of St. Lawrence), which are on Atlantic Time.

TOPOGRAPHY

Québec contains a wide variety of landscapes ranging from a fluvial plain in the north to the Appalachian Mountains in the south. Forest, tundra, millions of lakes and thousands of rivers make up Québec's geographic features.

TEMPERATURE

Québec's climate is temperate. Annual rainfall averages 15 inches in the north and 40 inches in the south. In the high plateau above Québec City, annual snowfall often exceeds 120 inches.

TRAVEL & TOURISM INFO

Provincial Agency:
Tourism Québec
PO Box 979, Montréal, Québec H3C 2W3
(514/873-2015 or 877/266-5687)
www.bonjourquebec.com

Centres Infotouriste
Permanent offices:

Montréal: 1255 rue Peel, bureau 100, Montreal, Quebec H3B 4V4 (877/266-5687)

Québec City: 12 rue Sainte-Anne, Quebec, Quebec G1R 3X2 (877/266-5687)

Seasonal offices, located near major highway access points:

Dégelis: 1373 rte 185 S., C.P. 398 (access via Highway 2 from New Brunswick)

Lacolle: Autoroute 15 (access via Interstate 87 from New York State)

Rigaud: Autoroute 40, exit 9, 100 rue St-Jean-Baptiste E., (access via Highway 417 from Ontario)

Riviére-Beaudette: Autoroute 20 (access via Highway 401 from Ontario)

Stanstead: Autoroute 55 (access via Interstate 91 from Vermont)

Regional Tourist Associations:

Tourisme, Abitibi-Témiscamingue
155 av. Dallaire, bureau 100
Rouyn Noranda, QC J9X 4T3
(819/762-8181)

Tourisme Bas-St. Laurent
148 rue Fraser,
Rivière-du-Loup, QC G5R 1C8
(418/867-1272)
www.tourismebas-st-laurent.com

Tourisme Charlevoix
495, Boul. de Comporté
La Malbaie, Québec G5A 3G3
(418/665-4454)
www.tourisme-charlevoix.com/

Tourisme Gaspésie
357 route de la Mer
Sainte-Flavie Québec, GOJ 2L0
(418/775-2223)

Québec City and Area:
Québec City Tourism
399, Saint-Joseph Est
Québec, QC G1K 8E2
(418/641-6654)
www.regiondequebec.com

Tourisme Lanaudière
3568 rue Church
Rawdon, Québec, J0K 1S0
(450/834-2535)
www.lanaudiere.ca

Tourisme Laurentides
Aut. 15 sortie 51
Saint-Jérôme, Québec, J5L 2S4
(450/224-7007)
www.laurentides.com

Association touristique de Manicouagan
337, boul. La Salle Bureau 304
Baie-Comeau, Québec, G4Z 2Z1
(418/294-2876)
www.tourismecote-nord.com

Tourisme Montérégie
2001 boul de rome, 3e etage
Brossard, QC J4W 3K5
(450/466-4666 or 866/469-0069)
www.tourisme-monteregie.qc.ca

Tourisme Montréal
1555 rue Peel, bureau 600
Montréal, Québec, H3A 3L8
(514/844-5400 or 877/266-5687)
www.tourisme-montreal.org

Tourisme Saguenay - Lac-Saint-Jean
412 boul. du Saguenay E., bureau 100,
Chicoutimi, Québec, G7H 7Y8
(418/543-9778)
www.promotionsaguenay.qc.ca

RECREATIONAL INFO

Golf: Golf Quebec, 415 av. Bourke, bureau 110, Dorval, Québec, H9S 3W9 (514/633-1088)

Hunting/Fishing: Ressources naturelles et Faune Québec, 880, chemin Sainte-Foy, RC 120-C, Québec, Québec G1S 4X4 (418/627-8600)

Hiking/Canoeing/Kayaking/Dogsledding: Aventure Écotourisme Québec, 4981 boul. Lévesque E., Laval, Québec, H7C 1N3 (450/661-2225 or 866/278-5923)

Skiing: Québec Ski Areas Association, 7665 rue Larrey, bureau 100, Anjou, Québec, H1J 2T7 (514/493-1810)

Snowmobiling: Fédération des clubs de motoneigistes du Québec, 4545 av. Pierre-De-Coubertin, C.P. 1000 succ. M, Montréal, Québec, H1V 3R2 (514/252-3076)

SHOPPING

Antiques and Memorabilia: Amherst Street and Notre-Dame West in Montreal both contain a wealth of fascinating shops. Quebec City's Saint-Paul Street in the lower part of town is home to several shops offering traditional furnishings. Hwy 20, running between both these cities, contains many artisan shops.

Centre Eaton, Montreal. Over 175 retailers are located in this underground pedestrian mall network at McGill metro station.

Les Galeries de la Capitale, Quebec City. Mall with over 280 stores including Simons. Also includes an indoor amusement park and movie theaters. 5401 boul. des Galeries.

Place Fleur-de-Lys, Quebec City. Shopping center containing over 250 shops. On 550 boul Wilfrid-Hamel.

DESTINATIONS

ABITIBI-TÉMISCAMINGUE

Centrale Robert-Bourassa, Radisson. This is the largest underground power station in the world. Guided tours are by reservation only. You'll be treated to an introduction of the production and transportation of electricity.

Malartic. "Boom Town" boasted seven gold mining operations during the Rush of the 1940s. **Musé régional des mines** is a museum that gives its visitors a better understanding of the mining process.

Refuge Pageau, Amos. The Pageau family provides care for injured wildlife. Hundreds of animals have found shelter at the center—moose, deer, bears, foxes, raccoons and wolves, to name a few. Make tour reservations one week prior to your arrival.

BAS-SAINT-LAURENT

There's no shortage of good reasons to make a stop in this region! Charming villages rich in architectural heritage, museums, lighthouses, sampling local specialties, like smoked fish, or just the incredibly fresh air. The serenity of this area is just what the doctor ordered to blow off the every day stress, and get to some good relaxation.

Institut maritime du Québec. Rimouski. Canada's foremost marine training institution includes an exhibition on marine shipping, electronic navigation simulators, commercial diving training centre, hyperbaric chambers and the only submarine emergency evacuation simulator of its kind.

Kamouraska. This town, rich in architecture, contains narrow winding streets, a shoreline promenade, a wharf and a boat launch. Take time to read the plaques along Rue LeBlanc. You'll learn about the islands, plant and animal life and the unusual tide which retreats twice daily, revealing huge saltwater flats. **Musé de Kamouraska** teaches ethnology, history and folklore through permanent and temporary exhibitions. At **Berceau de Kamouraska** you'll find a commemorative chapel and the graves of 1,300 settlers.

Lighthouses. Ile Verte, Ile du Pot a l'Eau-de-Vie and **Pointe-au-Pere** are three of the lighthouses on the local section of the Route des Phares. Across from Pointe-au-Pere is the **Empress of Ireland** museum, which takes a look at life aboard the ship, salvaged objects and underwater photos.

Saguenay-St. Lawrence Marine Park. Covering part of the St. Lawrence estuary and most of the Saguenay fjord, the park offers excursions to the islands, marine life observation, hiking, diving and sea kayaking. View fin whale, minke and beluga whales and grey, harbour and harp seals.

CENTRE-DU-QUÉBEC

This region, balanced between Montreal and Québec City, is the economic hub of the province. Four scenic routes help you discover the beauty and diversity of this area: **Drummond to the Bois-Francs, The Maple Route, Shores of the St. Lawrence** and **Snow Goose Country.**

Drummondville. Born out of the War of 1812 and named for the governor of 1815, this thriving community has a great deal to offer visitors as well as residents.

Le Village québecois d'antan. Over 70 buildings will transport you through a century of history (1810-1910).

Pavillon thématique et multifonctionnel. This 10,000-sq. ft. museum houses magnificent models of old cars. Also on display are a dentist's office, a photographer's studio, a barbershop and some 1,500 various items from the 1900s to the 1950s.

Le Musée du Bronze d'Inverness. This economuseum displays and sells works of bronze in addition to educating people about bronze and the process of making bronze art.

Nicolet. A wonderful testament to human spirituality is the **Musée des Religions,** or **Museum of Religions.** Here, faith and cultures meet to develop themed presentations dealing with the world's religions.

QUÉBEC CITY AND AREA

Thousands of visitors fall under Quebec's spell every year. The only fortified city in North America, its winding streets, and old neighborhoods will enrapture travelers, and keep them coming back again and again.

Québec. A walking tour of Old Québec unveils a marvelous historic richness. Copper rooftops overhang cobblestone streets. 17th- and 18th-century buildings have been restored and converted for residential and commercial use. Historical treasures of art and architecture can be found at **Domaine Maizerets**, **Maison des Jesuites**, the **Trail-Carré** and the **Maison Hamel-Bruneau**. The **Musée national des beaux-arts du Québec** contains Québec art from the 17th century to the present. For themed exhibits head to the Musée de la Civilisation near the Old Port.

Get a bird's eye view of Québec and the St. Lawrence from the **Château Frontenac**, a fairy tail structure with towers, turrets, copper roof and dormers.

Villa Bagatelle, an interpretation centre, is an exceptional example of 19th century neo-gothic country architecture. More than 300 varieties of indigenous and exotic plant species are grown in its English garden.

Québec Expérience. This multimedia 3-D sound and light show takes you into the heart of Québec's history.

Sainte-Anne-de-Beaupré. The **Sanctuary,** a superb medieval-style monument to St. Anne, shelters a multitude of art treasures, including the polychrome mosaics of its central nave.

CHARLEVOIX

Mountains and sea combine in this region to form a setting that can only be described as spellbinding. Capes and outcroppings flank the coast, villages nestle at the foot of the mountains, and fertile fields offer a stunning glimpse of the backcountry peaks. This region combines top resort destinations with an unusual range of outdoor activities. Artists have flocked to this region for generations to try and capture the unique mixture of serenity and grandeur of the area.

Baie-Saint-Paul. Take a walking tour of one of the oldest towns in Québec. Features 200-year-old houses, quaint boutiques and sidewalk cafés. Art galleries are plentiful. You'll see works by the masters, as well as by local artists. Rent a bicycle and explore picturesque country roads throughout the valley.

Centre d'histoire naturelle de Charlevoix. The center presents an excellent overview of the entire Charlevoix region—in all its uniqueness. Original displays and a colorful slide show unveil the region's exceptional diversity.

CHAUDIÈRE-APPALACHES

The string of riverside villages in this region are some of the loveliest in Quebec. Bordered by the Appalachians and Maine to the south, this region is a natural habitat of craftspeople and sculptors. The fall brings dazzling color to the backcountry maple trees, and the banks of the St. Lawrence area, a refuge for snow geese.

Massif du Sud Park, surrounded by Buckland, Saint-Philémon, Saint-Luc and Saint-Magloire. This regional park encompasses the most elevated sector of the Appalachian mountains. Re-live the gold rush era at Ranch du Massif du Sud. Activities include snowmobiling, skiing, biking and hiking.

Vin artisanal Le Ricaneux, Saint-Charles-de-Bellechasse. Vineyards process fresh fruit into wine and other tasteful products.

EASTERN TOWNSHIPS

"Picturesque" is the only word to describe this region. This area rubs elbows with the U.S. border, and is brimming with holiday resorts. Its Wine Route, agrotourism, fine dining and many cozy B&Bs make for an irresistible invitation for those seeking a gourmet getaway.

Bromont. Shoppers will enjoy a large flea market located on auto route 10. Exciting water slides and over 15 activities keep the

QUICK REFERENCE CHART FOR WOODALL'S FEATURED PARKS

	Green Friendly	RV Lots for Sale	Park Models-Onsite Ownership	Park Membership for Sale	Big Rigs Welcome	Internet Friendly	Pets Welcome
BROMONT							
Camping du Village Bromont RV Resort					▲	●	■
SAINT-ANTONIN							
Camping Lido						●	■
SAINT-BARTHELEMY							
Camping Du Vieux Moulin							■
SAINT-ETIENNE-DE-BOLTON							
Domaine du Lac Libby							■
SAINT-MATHIEU-DE-BELOEIL							
Camping Alouette Inc	🍃				▲	●	■
VALCARTIER							
Camping Valcartier							■

Green Friendly 🍃; RV Lots for Sale ✖; Park Models/Onsite Onwership ✱; Park Memberships for Sale ✔; Big Rigs Welcome ▲; Internet Friendly ●; Internet Friendly-WiFi ●; Pets Welcome ■

whole family busy at Bromont Aquatic Park. Explore nine acres of forests, trails, flowerbeds, stone walls, a small lake and a waterfall at Jardin Marisol.

Domaine Bleu Lavande. Discover the peaceful haven of the Domaine Bleu Lavande lavender farm. Close to the village of Fitch Bay on a hill more than 300 metres high. View a short film on the history and culture of lavender, enjoy a picnic and stroll through the fields filled with more than 200,000 lavender plants!

Granby. Interesting period houses and Lac Boivin fountain grace the city.

Magog-Orford. The Magog-Orford Tourist Station incorporates three municipalities and offers lots of recreational opportunities.

GASPÉSIE

This maritime peninsula boasts activities as varied as any can imagine. From whale watching, to fishing in lakes and rivers, taking time at a spa, or sampling the delectable maritime cuisine.

Bonaventure. Stroll along the clearest river in Quebec along more than 50 km of waymarked trails that take you by cascades, waterfalls, lookouts and salmon pools.

Cap Chat. Moose watching with a guide-interpreter. Also kayaking, hiking and a lighthouse.

Vallie la Matapédia. The western section of the Gaspésie region will take you inward, where forestry and farming are the major occupations. The valley was named "Capitale forestière canadienne" (Canadian forestry capital) for 1993. From Lac Matapédia runs the Rivière Matapédia, known for its excellent salmon fishing. The covered bridges, which span the river and the brilliant fall foliage, create a postcard-worthy picture.

LANAUDIÈRE

Right on the doorstep of Montreal, lies this gem of a region. To the south lies fertile lands that line the St. Lawrence, and to the north, vast open spaces and forest cloaked hills that make this a snowmobiler's dream - not to mention hikers, cyclists, ATVers and skiers.

Rawdon, Arbraska tree top adventure trekking for the whole family. Move from one tree to another, doing over 100 different activities in complete safety: rope bridges, Tyroleans, nets, Tarzan-style vines and much more. An adventure you're family will be talking about for years.

Terrebonne, l'île des Moulins. Become acquainted with the life and times of a 19th-century pre-industrial complex.

LAURENTIDES

This region of mountains, lakes and resorts draws travelers, winter and summer, who are searching for a little elbow room, and a lot of fresh air. Just north of Montreal, this region is renowned for its ski hills, vast network of cross country ski trails, and first class golf facilities.

Mirabel. One of Québec's largest municipalities has two beautiful regional parks, several golf courses, campgrounds, cycling and cross-country trails, equestrian centers and traditional sugar shacks. Mirabel is home to two very unique attractions: **Intermiel and Miramiel** – both involved in the process of bee-keeping and honey-making.

Saint-Eustache. Visit this agricultural area known for its historical heritage, dating back to 1739. Globensky Manor houses the Patriotes de Saint-Eustache—a museum that presents themed exhibitions.

MAURICIE

The highlight of this region is the immense Lac-Saint-Jean, with Saguenay-lac-St. Jean and of course, all the recreation that comes with such huge bodies of water. Take a starlight cruise on either the Lac-Saint-Jean or Saguenay River, or explore the incredibly beautiful Saguenay fjord via a sea-kayak. Fish sparkling rivers for salmon, walleye and pike. The rivière Saguenay flows from Lac-Saint-Jean to the Saint Lawrence river. Scenic boat cruises are plentiful along the breathtaking fjord.

Notre-Dame-du-Cap Shrine, Cap-de-la-Madeleine. Modern-style basilica is renowned for its stained-glass windows and its organ, one of the most impressive in the country.

Sanctuaire Notre-Dame-du-Cap, Cap-de-la-Madeleine. This sanctuary is the third most frequented pilgrimage site in Québec.

Trois-Rivières. Named for the three channels at the mouth of the Saint-Maurice river, Trois-Rivières was founded in 1634. The ambience of the region's capital is exemplified with walking tours such as the Heritage Tour and the Promenade de la poésie. Also see the **Cathédrale de l'Assomption.** Beautiful Westminster style cathedral with 125 stained glass windows created by Guido Nencheri between 1925 and 1954. The **Maison Hertel-d-la-Fresnière**, built in the 1820s, offers a historical exhibit during the peak season.

Where to Find CCUSA Parks

List City	Park Name	Map Coordinates
BROMONT		
	Camping du Village Bromont RV Resort	J-4
CAP CHAT-EST		
	Camping Au Bord de la Mer (Not Visited)	D-5
COMPTON		
	Camping de Compton	J-5
GRACEFIELD		
	Camping Pionnier (Not visited)	D-2
GRANBY		
	Camping Tropicana	I-4
L'ANGE-GARDIEN		
	Camping Plage Fortier (K.F.A.)	J-3
LAC-DES-PLAGES		
	Camping Lac des Plages (Not Visited)	H-1
LEVIS		
	Camping La Jolie Rochelle	F-6
	Camping Transit	F-6
NOTRE-DAME-DE-LA-SALETTE		
	Camping Royal Papineau du Lac de l'Argile	D-2
PERCE		
	Camping Tete d'Indien	E-6
RIMOUSKI		
	Camping Motel de l'Anse (Not Visited)	B-6
SAINT-CHARLES-SUR-RICHELIEU		
	Camping Domaine Madalie (Not Visited)	I-3
SAINT-PHILIPPE-DE-LAPRAIRIE		
	Camping Amerique Montreal	J-2
SHAWINIGAN		
	Camping KEA Otamac	G-4
VENISE-EN-QUEBEC		
	Camping Champlain 2003	J-3

ALMA—B-4

(NW) Camping Colonie Notre Dame (Not visited)—*From S city town limit: Go 5 km/3 mi N on Hwy 169, then 11 km/7 mi W on Rue Melancon. Enter on L.* ◊◊◊FACILITIES: 200 sites, 148 full hkups, 13 W&E, (15/30/50 amps), 39 no hkups, tenting, dump, laundry, ltd groc. ◊◊◊RECREATION: lake swim, boating, canoeing, ramp, dock, lake fishing, playground. Pets welcome, breed restrict, size restrict, quantity restrict. Open May 26 - Sep 3. Facilities fully operational Jun 20 - Aug 23. Rate in 2010 $20-28 for 6 persons. Member CQ. Phone: (418)662-9113.

RESERVE FAUNIQUE DES LAURENTIDES, CAMPING BELLE-RIVIERE—(Saguenay Lac St-Jean) *From jct Hwy 175 & Hwy 169: Go NW on Hwy 169 N to Laurentides Wildlife Reserve.* FACILITIES: 30 sites, 30 no hkups, tenting, dump, laundry, ltd groc. RECREATION: lake swim, canoeing, lake fishing, playground. Pets welcome. Open May - Sep. Phone: (418)864-2161.

AMQUI—B-6

(W) CAMPING AMQUI (Municipal Park)—(Gaspesie) *From jct Hwy 195 & Hwy 132: Go 4.5 km/2-3/4 mi W on Hwy 132.* FACILITIES: 146 sites, 30 full hkups, 66 W&E, (15/30 amps), 50 no hkups, tenting, dump, laundry. RECREATION: swim pool, boating, 200 hp limit, canoeing, ramp, dock, lake/river fishing, playground. Pets welcome. Open Jun 17 - Sep 5. Member ARVC, CQ. Phone: (418)629-3433.

ANTICOSTI ISLAND—D-6

PARC NATIONAL D'ANTICOSTI/BAIE-DE-LA-TOUR—*Take ferry from Rimouski or Sept-Iles, also by plane from Montreal, Quebec, Mont-Joli or Sept-Iles.* FACILITIES: 12 sites, 12 no hkups, tenting. RECREATION: saltwater/river swim. No pets. Open June - Sept. Phone: (418)535-0231.

SEPAQ ANTICOSTI/CAMPING WILCOX & CHICOTTE—(Duplessis) *Take the ferry boat from Rimouski or Sept-Iles, also by plane from Montreal, Quebec, Mont-Joli or Sept-Iles.* FACILITIES: 27 sites, 27 no hkups, tenting, dump, laundry, ltd groc. RECREATION: saltwater swim, canoeing, lake fishing. No pets. Open Jun - Aug 25. Phone: (418)535-0231.

BAIE-SAINT-PAUL—C-5

(E) Camping du Gouffre—(Charlevoix) *From jct Hwy 138 & Hwy 362: Go 2.8 km/1-3/4 mi E on Hwy 362, then 4.8 km/3 mi N on Rang St-Laurent. Enter on L.* ◊◊◊FACILITIES: 128 sites, 46 full hkups, 25 W&E, (15/30 amps), 57 no hkups, 11 pull-thrus, family camping, tenting, dump, laundry, ltd groc. ◊◊◊◊RECREATION: swim pool, river fishing, play equipment. Pets welcome. Open May 18 - Oct 7. Facilities fully operational Jun 20 - Sep 1. Rate in 2010 $32 per family. Member CQ.

Phone: (866)435-2143
Address: 439 St-Laurent CP 3164, Baie St-Paul, QC G3Z 3B6
Lat/Lon: 47.48990/-70.50778
Email: info@campingdugouffre.com
Web: www.campingdugouffre.com

BAIE-SAINT-PAUL—Continued

(E) le Genevrier—(Charlevoix) *From jct Hwy 362 & Hwy 138: Go 4-3/4 km/3 mi E on Hwy 138. Enter on L.* ◊◊◊◊FACILITIES: 430 sites, 261 full hkups, 169 W&E, (15/30/50 amps), 50 amps ($), 14 pull-thrus, tenting, dump, laundry, ltd groc. ◊◊◊RECREATION: lake swim, river fishing, playground. Pets welcome. Partial handicap access. Open all yr. Facilities fully operational May 1 - Oct 30. Big rigs welcome. Rate in 2010 $30-45 for 6 persons. Member CQ. Phone: (877)435-6520.

PARC NATIONAL DES GRANDS-JARDINS—(Charlevoix) *From Hwy 138 & 381 N.* FACILITIES: 107 sites, 107 no hkups, tenting, dump. RECREATION: canoeing, lake fishing. No pets. Open May - Sept. Phone: (418)439-1227.

BASSIN—C-6

Camping Plage du Golfe (Not Visited)—*On Hwy 199W. On Madeleine Islands.* FACILITIES: 72 sites, 30 ft max RV length, 50 full hkups, 10 W&E, 12 no hkups, tenting, dump, laundry, groceries. RECREATION: saltwater swim, boating, ramp, playground. Pets welcome. Open Jun 1 - Labor Day. Rate in 2010 $25 for 4 persons. Phone: (418)937-5224.

BEAUMONT—F-6

(NE) Camping Carol—(Chaudiere-Appalaches) *From I-20 (exit 341) & Rte Beaumont: Go 1.6 km/1 mi N on Beaumont, then .04 km/1/4 mi W on Hwy 132. Enter on R.* ◊◊◊FACILITIES: 138 sites, 119 full hkups, 18 W&E, (15/30 amps), 1 no hkups, 19 pull-thrus, tenting, dump, laundry, ltd groc. ◊◊◊RECREATION: swim pool, playground. Pets welcome. Open May 17 - Sep 24. Facilities fully operational Jun 15 - Sep 1. Rate in 2010 $40 for 5 persons. Member CQ. Phone: (888) 557-2942.

(SW) Camping Parc Beaumont (Not Visited)—(Chaudiere-Appalaches) *From I-20 (exit 337) & Hwy 279: Go 1.2 km/3/4 mi N on Hwy 279, then 0.8 km/1/2 mi W on Hwy 132. Enter on R.* ◊◊◊◊FACILITIES: 163 sites, 159 full hkups, (15/30 amps), 4 no hkups, tenting, dump, laundry, ltd groc. ◊◊◊◊RECREATION: swim pool, playground. Pets welcome, breed restrict. Partial handicap access. Open May 1 - Aug 10. Rate in 2010 $37 for 4 persons. Member CQ. Phone: (418) 837-3787.

BIC—B-6

PARC NATIONAL DU BIC/CAMPING RIOUX—(Bas St-Laurent) *On Hwy 132 E.* FACILITIES: 196 sites, 41 W&E, 12 E, (30/50 amps), 143 no hkups, tenting, laundry, ltd groc. RECREATION: dock, play equipment. No pets. Open May - Oct. Phone: (800)665-6527.

PARC NATIONAL DU BIC/CAMPING RIVIERE-DU-SUD-OUEST—(Basse-Laurentide) *On Hwy 132 E.* FACILITIES: 138 sites, 41 W&E, 12 E, (15/30/50 amps), 85 no hkups, tenting, dump, laundry, ltd groc. RECREATION: ramp. No pets. Open May - Oct. Phone: (418)736-5035.

BONAVENTURE—E-6

(W) CAMPING PLAGE BEAUBASSIN (Municipal Park)—(Gaspesie) *From jct Grand Pre Ave & Hwy 132: Go 1/2 km/1/4 mi E on Hwy 132.* FACILITIES: 252 sites, 150 full hkups, 58 W&E, 44 E, (15/30 amps), 22 pull-thrus, tenting, dump, laundry, ltd groc. RECREATION: saltwater swim, boating, canoeing, dock, saltwater fishing, playground. Pets welcome. Partial handicap access. Open June 1 - Sep 30. Member ARVC, CQ. Phone: (418) 534-3246.

Quebec Provincial Motto: "Je me souviens" (I remember)

BROMONT—J-4

(SW) CAMPING DU VILLAGE BROMONT RV RESORT—(Canton-de-l'est) *From I-10 (exit 74): Go 5.6 km/3-1/2 mi S on Boul Pierre Laporte, then 152 m/500 ft E on Shefford. Enter on R.*

◊◊◊◊◊FACILITIES: 275 sites, 245 full hkups, (15/30/50 amps), 30 no hkups, some extd stay sites, 40 pull-thrus, WiFi Instant Internet at site, phone on-site Internet (needs activ), family camping, tenting, dump, non-guest dump $, laundry, LP gas by weight, ice, picnic tables, fire rings, wood, controlled access.

◊◊◊◊◊RECREATION: rec hall, pavilion, coin games, swim pool, lake swim, mini-golf, ($), golf nearby, bsktball, 10 bike rentals, playground, activities, (wkends), tennis, horseshoes, sports field, hiking trails, v-ball. Rec open to public.

Pets welcome. Partial handicap access. Open Apr 15 - Oct 25. Big rigs welcome. Escort to site. Clubs welcome. Rate in 2010 $40-47 per family. MC/VISA/AMEX/Debit. Member CQ. CCUSA 50% Discount. CCUSA reservations Recommended, CCUSA max stay Unlimited, CCUSA disc. not avail holidays. Discount available Apr 15 thru Jun 15 & Aug 15 thru Oct 15.

Text 107944 to (440)725-8687 to see our Visual Tour.

Phone: (450)534-2404
Address: 1699 Shefford, Bromont, QC J2L 3N8
Lat/Lon: 45.29302/-72.70235
Email: m.f.poulin@hotmail.com
Web: www.campingbromont.ca

SEE AD THIS PAGE AND AD TRAVEL SECTION PAGE 900

(N) Camping Parc Bromont—*From Hwy 10 (exit 78) & Boul Bromont: Go .04 km/1/4 mi S on Boul Bromont, then 100 meters/ 325 ft E on Rue St-Denis, then 100 meters/325 ft S on Rue Lafontaine. Enter at end.* ◊◊◊FACILITIES: 195 sites, 131 full hkups, 36 W&E, (15/30 amps), 28 no hkups, 35 pull-thrus, tenting, dump, laundry, groceries. ◊◊◊RECREATION: swim pool, playground. Pets welcome, quantity restrict. Open Apr 27 - Oct 14. Rate in 2010 $36-40 per family. Member CQ. Phone: (450)534-2712.

(N) Camping Vacances Bromont (Not Visited)—*From Hwy 10 (exit 78) & boul Bromont: Go .05 km/1/4 mi S on Boul. Bromont, then 130 meters/425 feet E on Rue Bleury. Enter on R.* ◊◊◊FACILITIES: 305 sites, 243 full hkups, 56 W&E, (15/30 amps), 6 no hkups, 29 pull-thrus, tenting, dump, laundry. ◊◊◊RECREATION: swim pool, playground. Pets welcome. Partial handicap access. Open May 1 - Oct 31. Facilities fully operational Jun 15 - Sep 5. Rate in 2010 $32-45 per family. Member CQ. Phone: (450)534-4434.

CABANO—B-6

(N) Camping Temilac—*From jct Hwy 185 & Hwy 232: Go 2 km/1-1/4 mi N on Commerciale, then .2 km/1/4 mi E on du Quai, then 0.4 km/1/4 mi N on de La Plage. Enter on L.* ◊◊◊◊FACILITIES: 131 sites, 32 ft max RV length, 91 full hkups, 20 W&E, (15/30 amps), 20 no hkups, tenting, laundry. ◊◊◊◊RECREATION: lake swim, boating, canoeing, ramp, dock, playground. Pets welcome, breed restrict. Open May 15 - Sep 30. Facilities fully operational Jun 20 - Aug 20. Rate in 2010 $25-28 for 6 persons. Member CQ. Phone: (418)854-7660.

CADILLAC—B-1

Camping Lac Normand (Not Visited)—*From jct Hwy 117 N & Born 580: Go .8 km/1/2 mi NW on gravel road. Enter on R.* FACILITIES: 143 sites, 32 ft max RV length, 83 full hkups, 40 W&E, (15/30 amps), 20 no hkups, tenting, dump. RECREATION: lake swim, no motors, canoeing, play equipment. Pets welcome. Open May 19 - Sep 4. Rate in 2010 $22 for 4 persons. Member CQ. Phone: (819)759-8444.

CANTLEY—D-2

(SE) Camping Cantley (Not Visited)—(Outaouais) *From jct Hwy 50 (exit 138) & Hwy 307: Go 14 km/8-3/4 mi N on Hwy 307, then 1.6 km/1 mi E on*

Camping Cantley (Not Visited)—Continued on next page

CANTLEY—Continued
Camping Cantley (Not Visited)—Continued

Chemin Ste-Elizabeth. Enter on R. ◊◊◊FACILITIES: 305 sites, 206 full hkups, 40 W&E, (15/30/50 amps), 50 amps ($), 59 no hkups, tenting, dump, laundry, ltd groc. ◊◊◊◊RECREATION: 2 swim pools, pond fishing, playground. Pets welcome. Partial handicap access. Open May 15 - Sep 15. Big rigs welcome. Rate in 2010 $33-35 for 5 persons. Member CQ. Phone: (819)827-1056.

CAP CHAT-EST—D-5

(E) Camping Au Bord de la Mer (Not Visited) *—From west town limits on Hwy 132: Go 5 km/3 mi E on Hwy 132. Enter on L.* ◊◊◊FACILITIES: 82 sites, 15 full hkups, 36 W&E, (15/30 amps), 31 no hkups, 2 pull-thrus, tenting, dump, non-guest dump $, laundry, ice, picnic tables, fire rings, grills, wood. RECREATION: play equipment. Pets welcome. Partial handicap access. Open June 15 - Sep 15. Rate in 2010 $25 for 4 persons. Member CQ. CCUSA 50% Discount. CCUSA reservations Recommended, CCUSA max stay 2 days, Cash only for CCUSA disc. Discount not available Jul & Aug. Minimum stay 2 days. 15 amp standard rate.

Phone: (418)786-2251
Address: 173 Notre-Dame Est, Cap Chat-est, QC G0J 1G0
Lat/Lon: 49.01143/-66.64854
Email: info@campinguaborddelamer.com
Web: www.campinguaborddelamer.com

(E) Camping Fleur de Lys (Motel) (Not Visited) *—From west town limits on Hwy 132: Go 5.2 km/3-1/4 mi E on Hwy 132. Enter on R.* ◊FACILITIES: 25 sites, 8 full hkups, 6 W&E, (15 amps), 11 no hkups, tenting, dump. Pets welcome. Open May 15 - Sept 30. Rate in 2010 $18 per family. Phone: (418)786-5518.

CAP-AUX-OS—E-6

Camping 4 Vents (Not visited)*—From church: Go 1.6 km/1 mi E on Hwy 132. Enter on R.* ◊◊FACILITIES: 30 sites, 36 ft max RV length, 15 full hkups, 15 no hkups, tenting, dump, laundry, ltd groc. ◊◊RECREATION: playground. Pets welcome. Open May 1 - Oct 31. Phone: (418)892-5256.

CAPLAN—E-6

(E) Camping Ruisselet (Not Visited)*—From east town limits: Go 1.6 km/1 mi W on Hwy 132. Enter on L.* ◊◊◊FACILITIES: 150 sites, 150 full hkups, (15/30 amps), 4 pull-thrus, tenting, laundry, ltd groc. ◊◊◊RECREATION: 2 swim pools, playground. Pets welcome. Open Jun 1 - Labor Day. Rate in 2010 $24 for 4 persons. Phone: (418)388-2138.

CAUSAPSCAL—B-6

(N) CAMPING DE CAUSAPSCAL (Municipal Park)—(Gaspesie) *From west town limits on Hwy-132: Go 1/4 mi E on Hwy-132.* FACILITIES: 65 sites, 30 full hkups, 18 W&E, (15/30 amps), 17 no hkups, 2 pull-thrus, tenting, dump, laundry. RECREATION: swim pool. Pets welcome. Open Jun 9 - Sep 4. Member ARVC, CQ. Phone: (418)756-5621.

CHAMBORD—B-4

VILLAGE HISTORIQUE DE VAL-JALBERT—(Saguenay Lac St-Jean) *Halfway between Chambord & Roberval on Hwy 169 N.* FACILITIES: 190 sites, 60 full hkups, 30 W&E, (15/30 amps), 100 no hkups, tenting, dump, laundry, ltd groc. RECREATION: swim pool, playground. Pets welcome. Open May - Oct. Phone: (418)275-3132.

CHANDLER (PABOS)—E-6

(NE) Centre de Plain air La Seig Neurie*—From east of town: Go 5 km E on Hwy 132, then 1 k N on Rue de L'Eglise. Enter on L.* ◊◊◊FACILITIES: 60 sites, typical site width 30 ft, 40 full hkups, 3 W&E, (15/30 amps), 17 no hkups, 4 pull-thrus, family camping, tenting, dump, laundry. ◊◊◊◊RECREATION: playground. Pets welcome. Partial handicap access. Open May 15 - Sep 15. Rate in 2010 $26 for 4 persons. Phone: (418)689-4000.

CHATEAU-RICHER—F-6

(E) Camping Lac Aux Flambeaux (Not visited) *—On Hwy 138 E at St-Anne de Beaupre. Enter on L.* ◊◊◊FACILITIES: 200 sites, 30 ft max RV length, 175 full hkups, 15 W&E, (15/30 amps), 10 no hkups, tenting, dump, laundry. ◊◊◊RECREATION: swim pool, canoeing, playground. Pets welcome. Open Apr 25 - Oct 15. Facilities fully operational Jun 20 - Sep 3. Rate in 2010 $30-35 for 4 persons. Member CQ. Phone: (418)827-3977.

CHIBOUGAMAU—A-3

RESERVE FAUNIQUE ASSINICA ET DES LACS-ALBANEL-MISTASSINI-ET WACONICHI/CAMPING BAIE PENICOU—(Saguenay Lac St-Jean) *Road 167 N.* FACILITIES: 27 sites, 12 W&E, (15 amps), 15 no hkups, tenting, dump. RECREATION: boating, 25 hp limit, canoeing, ramp, lake/river fishing. No pets. Open Jun - Sep. Phone: (418)748-7748.

COATICOOK—J-5

(S) Camping du Lac Lyster (Piskiart-la Sequiniere)*—From town: Go 1.6 km/1 mi S on paved road around Lake Lyster on Chemin Des Chalets to Chemin*

COATICOOK—Continued
Camping du Lac Lyster (Piskiart-la Sequiniere)—Continued

Seguin. Enter on R. ◊◊◊FACILITIES: 100 sites, 52 full hkups, 18 W&E, 8 E, (15/30 amps), 22 no hkups, 7 pull-thrus, tenting, dump. ◊RECREATION: playground. Pets welcome. Open Jun 1 - Sep 1. Member CQ. Phone: (819)849-3929.

COMPTON—J-5

(C) Camping de Compton*—From jct Hwy 208 W & Hwy 147: Go 65 meters/215 ft N on Hwy 147, then 0.3 km/1/4 mi W on Rue de la Station. Enter on L.* ◊◊◊◊FACILITIES: 300 sites, 254 full hkups, 46 W&E, (15/30/50 amps), 50 amps ($), 38 pull-thrus, WiFi Instant Internet at site, phone on-site Internet (needs activ), tenting, dump, non-guest dump $, portable dump, laundry, ltd groc, ice, picnic tables, fire rings, wood. ◊◊◊◊RECREATION: rec hall, equipped pavilion, swim pool, hot tub, bsktball, playground, shuffleboard court 2 shuffleboard courts, activities horseshoes, hiking trails, v-ball. Pets welcome, breed restrict, size restrict. Partial handicap access. Open April 15 - Nov 1. Facilities fully operational May 15 - Oct 1. Big rigs welcome. Rate in 2010 $37-42 per family. MC/VISA/Debit. Member CQ. CCUSA 50% Discount. CCUSA reservations Recommended, CCUSA max stay Unlimited, CCUSA disc. not avail F,Sa, CCUSA disc. not avail holidays. Not available Jul 19-Aug 3. $5 WiFi surcharge.

Phone: (800)563-5277
Address: 24 Chemin de la Station, Compton, QC J0B 1L0
Lat/Lon: 45.24297/-71.83199
Email: info@campingcompton.com
Web: www.campingcompton.com

COOKSHIRE—I-5

(SE) Camping Coop Familiale du Prevert de Birchton*—From jct Hwy 108 & Hwy 210: Go .04 km/1/4 mi SE on Hwy 210, then .04 km/1/4 mi E on Chemin Chute. Enter at end.* ◊◊◊FACILITIES: 317 sites, 250 full hkups, 67 W&E, (15/30 amps), tenting, dump, laundry, ltd groc. ◊◊◊RECREATION: swim pool, lake swim, lake fishing, playground. Pets welcome. Partial handicap access. Open May 1 - Sep 30. Facilities fully operational Jun 15 - Sep 5. Rate in 2010 $25 for 5 persons. Member CQ. Phone: (819)875-3186.

COTEAU DU LAC—J-1

(NE) KOA Montreal West*—From jct I-20 (exit 14) & Hwy 201: Go 1.6 km/1 mi S on Hwy 201, then 1.2 km/3/4 mi E on Hwy 338. Enter on L.* ◊◊◊FACILITIES: 102 sites, 72 full hkups, 15 W&E, (15/30/50 amps), 50 amps ($), 15 no hkups, 44 pull-thrus, tenting, dump, laundry, ltd groc. ◊◊◊RECREATION: swim pool, play equipment. Pets welcome. Open Apr 20 - Oct 20. Big rigs welcome. Rate in 2010 $35-45 for 4 persons. Member CQ. Phone: (450)763-5625. KOA discount.

DESCHAILLONS-SUR-SAINT-LAURENT—G-5

(W) Camping Cap a la Roche*—From jct Hwy 20 (exit 253) & Hwy 265: Go 29 km/18 mi N on Hwy 265, then 1.5 km/1 mi W on Hwy 132. Enter on R.* ◊◊FACILITIES: 195 sites, 181 full hkups, 5 W&E, (15/30 amps), 9 no hkups, 20 pull-thrus, tenting, dump, laundry, ltd groc. ◊RECREATION: ramp, lake fishing, play equipment. Pets welcome. Partial handicap access. Open May 11 - Oct 15. Rate in 2010 $24-44 for 4 persons. Member CQ. Phone: (819)292-1212.

DRUMMONDVILLE—H-4

CAMPING DES VOLTIGEURS—(Centre-du-Quebec) *From Hwy 20 (exit 181): Go W on boul Montplaisir. Enter on R.* FACILITIES: 290 sites, 118 full hkups, 58 W&E, 94 E, (15/30 amps), 20 no hkups, tenting, dump, laundry, ltd groc. RECREATION: swim pool, lake swim, lake fishing, playground. Pets welcome. Open May - Sep. Phone: (819)477-1360.

(NE) Camping "Domaine Du Repos"—(Centre-du-Quebec) *From Hwy 20 (exit 181): Go 1.2 km/3/4 mi SE on Boul Foucault, then 1.6 km/1 mi NE on Hwy 122, then 7.2 km/4-1/2 mi S on 3 Rg. Simpson, then 1.6 km/1 mi W on Du Repos. Enter at end.* ◊◊◊FACILITIES: 83 sites, 80 full hkups, 3 W&E, (15/30 amps), tenting, dump, laundry. ◊◊◊RECREATION: swim pool, boating, canoeing, river fishing, play equipment. Pets welcome. Partial handicap access. Open May 1 - Oct. 15. Rate in 2010 $25 for 4 persons. Member CQ. Phone: (819)478-1758.

(E) Camping La Detente*—From Hwy 20 (exit 181-Boul Foucault): Go 1.2 km/3/4 mi SE on Boul Foucault, then 1.6 km/1 mi N on Hwy 122, then 8.8 km/5-1/2 mi S on 3e Rang Simson, then 0.4 km/1/4 mi E on Chemin Hemming.* ◊◊◊FACILITIES: 376 sites, 352 full hkups, 24 W&E, (15 amps), tenting, dump, laundry. ◊◊◊RECREATION: swim pool, playground. Pets welcome. Open May 1 - Sep 30. Rate in 2010 $28.50 for 4 persons. Member CQ. Phone: (819)478-0651.

Quebec Provincial Bird: The Snowy Owl

DUHAMEL—D-3

CENTRE TOURISTIQUE DU LAC-SIMON—(Outaouais) *2 km/1-1/4 mi from Duhamel on Hwy 321 N.* FACILITIES: 400 sites, 162 full hkups, 141 W&E, (15 amps), 97 no hkups, tenting, dump, laundry, ltd groc. RECREATION: lake swim, boating, canoeing, ramp, lake fishing, playground. No pets. Open Jun - Sep. Phone: (819)428-7931.

EASTMAN—J-4

(C) Camping Do Re Mi*—From jct Hwy 10 (exit 106) & Hwy 245: Go 200 meters/700 feet N on Hwy 245, then 0.4 km/1/4 mi W on Hwy 112 (either rue Principale). Enter on R.* ◊◊◊FACILITIES: 45 sites, 19 full hkups, 26 W&E, (15/30 amps), tenting, dump, laundry, ltd groc. ◊◊◊RECREATION: swim pool, lake swim, boating, no motors, canoeing, ramp, lake fishing, play equipment. Pets welcome. Partial handicap access. Open May 12 - Oct 15. Facilities fully operational May 15 - Oct 15. Rate in 2010 $32-40 for 4 persons. Member CQ. Phone: (450)297-2983.

(S) Camping La Mine de Cuivre (Not Visited) *—From I-10 (exit 106): Go 354 meters/1100 feet S on Hwy 245. Enter on L.* ◊◊◊FACILITIES: 146 sites, 113 full hkups, 12 W&E, (15/30 amps), 21 no hkups, tenting, dump, laundry, ltd groc. ◊◊◊RECREATION: swim pool, playground. Pets welcome ($). Open May 12 - Sep 17. Facilities fully operational Jun 15 - Sep 10. Rate in 2010 $35 for 4 persons. Member CQ. Phone: (450) 297-3226.

EVAIN—B-1

Camping aux Petits Trembles (Lac Flavrian) (Not Visited)*—From jct Hwy 101 & Hwy 117: Go 5.5 km/3-1/2 mi N on Hwy 117, then 152 meters/500 feet NW on Beauchastel, then 305 meters/1000 feet W on Principale, then 3.4 km/2 mi N on Ave Eglise, then 9.8 km/6 mi W on Rang 10 W (gravel road). Enter on L.* FACILITIES: 70 sites, 30 ft max RV length, 26 full hkups, 40 W&E, (15/30 amps), 4 no hkups, tenting, dump, laundry, ltd groc. RECREATION: lake swim, boating, 6 hp limit, canoeing, dock, lake fishing, play equipment. Pets welcome. Open Jun 1 - Sep 15. Facilities fully operational Jun 20 - Aug 15. Rate in 2010 $20-22 for 5 persons. Phone: (819)768-3759.

FERLAND ET BOILLEAU—B-5

DOMAINE DU LAC HA! HA! (Municipal Park)—(Saguenay Lac St-Jean) *From church at Boilleau: Go 12 km/7-1/2 mi S on Hwy 381. Enter on L.* FACILITIES: 71 sites, 65 full hkups, 6 W&E, (30 amps), tenting, dump, laundry, ltd groc. RECREATION: lake swim, boating, 6 hp limit, canoeing, ramp, dock, lake fishing, play equipment. Pets welcome. Open May 19 - Sep 7. Phone: (418)676-2373.

FOSSAMBAULT-SUR-LE-LAC—F-5

(N) Plage Lac Saint-Joseph—(Quebec) *From jct Hwy 369 S & Hwy 367: Go 3.5 km/2 mi N on Hwy 367N, then 8 km/5 mi NE on Rte de Fossam bault. Enter on L.* ◊◊◊FACILITIES: 245 sites, 75 full hkups, 128 W&E, (15/30/50 amps), 50 amps ($), 42 no hkups, 5 pull-thrus, tenting, dump, laundry, groceries. ◊◊◊◊RECREATION: lake swim, boating, canoeing, ramp, dock, lake fishing, playground. Pets welcome ($). Open Jun 15 - Sep 3. Big rigs welcome. Rate in 2010 $50-53 per family. Member CQ. Phone: (877)522-3224.

FRELIGHSBURG—J-3

(SE) Camping Ecologique de Frelighsburg*—From jct Hwy 213 & Hwy 237: Go 4.4 km/2-3/4 mi S on Hwy 237. Enter on R.* ◊◊FACILITIES: 100 sites, 30 ft max RV length, 44 full hkups, 36 W&E, (15/30 amps), 20 no hkups, tenting, dump, laundry. ◊◊RECREATION: swim pool, play equipment. No pets. Open May 15 - Sep 15. Facilities fully operational Jun 1 - Sep 1. Rate in 2010 $27 for 5 persons. Member CQ. Phone: (450) 298-5259.

GASPE—E-6

CAMPING AUBERGE FORT PREVEL—(Gaspesie) *Road 132 E.* FACILITIES: 28 sites, 28 W&E, (30 amps), tenting, dump, laundry, ltd groc. RECREATION: swim pool, playground. Pets welcome. Open May 23 - Oct 13. Phone: (418)368-2281.

(NE) Camping Baie de Gaspe (Not visited)—(Gaspesie) *From church on Hwy 132 in town: Go 3.2 km/2 mi W on Hwy 132. Enter on L.* ◊◊◊FACILITIES: 100 sites, 80 full hkups, 5 W&E, (15/30 amps), 15 no hkups, 20 pull-thrus, tenting, dump, laundry. ◊RECREATION: play equipment. Pets welcome. Open Jun 1 - Sep 30. Facilities fully operational Jun 20 - Aug 20. Rate in 2010 $28-32 for 4 persons. Member CQ. Phone: (418) 892-5503.

(SE) Camping Gaspe (Not visited)—(Gaspesie) *From east town limits: Go 9.6 km/6 mi E on Hwy 132. Enter on L.* 1 E, ◊◊◊FACILITIES: 48 sites, 23 full hkups, 10 W&E, 1 E, (15/30 amps), 14 no hkups, tenting, dump, laundry. ◊◊RECREATION: canoeing, river fishing, play equipment. Pets welcome, quantity restrict. Open Jun 1 - Sep 30. Rate in 2010 $20.04-25.71 for 4 persons. Member CQ. Phone: (418)368-4800.

(NE) Camping Griffon (Not Visited)*—From jct Hwy 197 & Hwy 132: Go 8 km/5 mi W on Hwy 132. Enter on L.* ◊◊FACILITIES: 75 sites, 30 ft max RV

Camping Griffon (Not Visited)—Continued on next page

GASPE—Continued
Camping Griffon (Not Visited)—Continued

length, 30 full hkups, 27 W&E, (15/30 amps), 18 no hkups, tenting, dump, laundry, ltd groc. ◇RECREATION: play equipment. Pets welcome, breed restrict. Open Jun 1 - Sep 30. Facilities fully operational Jun 20 - Aug 20. Rate in 2010 $23 for 4 persons. Member CQ. Phone: (418)892-5938.

(NW) Camping Motel Fort Ramsay—(Gaspesie) *From west town limits at the bridge: Go 3.6 km/2-1/4 mi W on Hwy 132. Enter on R.* ◇◇◇◇FACILITIES: 42 sites, 21 full hkups, (15/30 amps), 21 no hkups, tenting, laundry. ◇◇RECREATION: boating, canoeing, river fishing, playground. Pets welcome. Open May 22 - Sep 30. Facilities fully operational Jun 1 - Sep 30. Rate in 2010 $30-32 per family. Member CQ. Phone: (418) 368-5094.

FORILLON NP (Cap-Bon-Ami)—(Gaspesie) *From jct Hwy 197 & Hwy 132: Go 24 km/15 mi E on Hwy 132.* FACILITIES: 41 sites, 41 no hkups, tenting. RECREATION: Open Jun 6 - Sep 1. Phone: (418)368-5505.

FORILLON NP (Des-Rosiers)—(Gaspesie) *From jct Hwy 197 & Hwy 132: Go 20-3/4 km/13 mi E on Hwy 132.* FACILITIES: 155 sites, 42 E, (30 amps), 113 no hkups, tenting, dump. RECREATION: playground. No pets. Partial handicap access. Open May 18 - Oct 13. Phone: (418)368-5505.

FORILLON NP (Petit Gaspe)—(Gaspesie) *From town: Go 29 km/18 mi NE on Hwy 132.* FACILITIES: 171 sites, 35 E, 136 no hkups, tenting, dump, laundry, ltd groc. RECREATION: playground. No pets. Partial handicap access. Open May 16 - Oct 15. Phone: (418)368-5505.

GRACEFIELD—D-2

(S) Camping Pionnier (Not visited)—(Outaouais) *From S city limit on Hwy 105: Go 3.7 km/2-1/4 mi S on Hwy 105. Enter on L.* ◇◇◇FACILITIES: 125 sites, 125 full hkups, (15/30 amps), tenting, RV storage, shower$, dump, non-guest dump $, laundry, ltd groc, ice, picnic tables, fire rings, wood. ◇◇◇RECREATION: equipped pavilion, swim pool, boating, canoeing, kayaking, ramp, dock, river fishing, bsktball, playground, shuffleboard court 2 shuffleboard courts, activities horseshoes, v-ball. No pets. Open May 15 - Oct 15. Facilities fully operational Jun 15 - Sep 15. Rate in 2010 $28 for 4 persons. Member CQ. CCUSA 50% Discount. CCUSA reservations Recommended, CCUSA max stay 4 days, CCUSA disc. not avail S, CCUSA disc. not avail F,Sa, CCUSA disc. not avail holidays. Not available Jun 15 thru Sep 10.

Phone: (819)463-4163
Lat/Lon: 46.05590/-76.05434

GRANBY—I-4

(C) Camping Bon-Jour—(Canton-de-l'est) *From Hwy 10 (exit 68) & Hwy 139: Go 8 km/5 mi N on Hwy 139, then 4 km/2-1/2 mi W on Hwy 112 (Principale St). Enter on R.* ◇◇◇◇FACILITIES: 220 sites, 198 full hkups, 12 W&E, 10 E, (15/30 amps), tenting, dump, laundry, ltd groc. ◇◇◇◇RECREATION: swim pool, playground. Pets welcome ($). Partial handicap access. Open May 9 - Oct 15. Rate in 2010 $35-42 for 2 persons. Member CQ. Phone: (450)378-0213.

(C) Camping Tropicana—*From Hwy 10 (exit 68) & Hwy 139: Go 8 km/5 mi N on Hwy 139, then 4.4 km/2-3/4 mi W on Hwy 112 (Principale St). Enter on L.* ◇◇◇◇FACILITIES: 1000 sites, 925 full hkups, 75 W&E, (15/30/50 amps), 50 amps ($), 25 pull-thrus, WiFi Instant Internet at site ($), phone Internet central location, tenting, shower$, dump, non-guest dump $, laundry, full svc store, LP gas by weight, ice, picnic tables, fire rings, wood. ◇◇◇◇RECREATION: rec hall, swim pool, lake swim, no motors, mini-golf, ($), bsktball, playground, shuffleboard court 2 shuffleboard courts, activities horseshoes, v-ball. Pets welcome. Partial handicap access. Open Apr 25 - Oct 13. Facilities fully operational Jun 20 - Sep 6. Big rigs welcome. Rate in 2010 $35-38 for 4 persons. MC/VISA/Debit. Member CQ. CCUSA 50% Discount. CCUSA reservations Accepted, CCUSA max stay 4 days, Cash only for CCUSA disc., CCUSA disc. not avail S, CCUSA disc. not avail F,Sa. Not valid Jul 10-Aug 10.

Phone: (450)378-9410
Address: 1680 Principale St, Granby, QC J2G 8C8
Lat/Lon: 45.25600/-72.49189
Email: info@campingtropicana.com
Web: www.campingtropicana.com

GRAND-MERE—G-4

LA MAURICIE NATIONAL PARK (Riviere-a-la-Peche)—(Mauricie Bois-Francs) *From Hwy 55 (exit 226): Go 16 km/10 mi N. 4-8/10 km/3 mi NW of St-Jean des Piles entrance.* FACILITIES: 254 sites, 62 E, 192 no hkups, tenting, dump. RECREATION: lake swim, canoeing, lake fishing, playground. No pets. Open May 11 - Oct 14. Phone: (819)533-7272.

GRAND-REMOUS—C-2

RESERVE FAUNIQUE LA VERENDRYE OUTAOUAIS-CAMPING LAC RAPIDE—(Outaouais) *Hwy 15/Hwy 117N.* FACILITIES: 50 sites, 50 no hkups, tenting, dump, ltd groc. RECREATION: lake swim, canoeing, ramp, lake fishing. Pets welcome. Open May - Sep. Phone: (819)435-2246.

GRAND-REMOUS—Continued

RESERVE FAUNIQUE LA VERENDRYE-OUTAOUAIS-CAMPING DE LA VIEILLE—(Outaouais) *Hwy 15N/117N.* FACILITIES: 187 sites, 43 full hkups, (15/30 amps), 144 no hkups, tenting, dump. RECREATION: lake swim, boating, canoeing, ramp, lake fishing, playground. No pets. Open May - Sep. Phone: (819)438-2017.

RESERVE FAUNIQUE LA VERENDRYE-OUTAOUAIS-CAMPING LAC SAVARY—(Outaouais) *Hwy 15 N, then at Sainte-Agathe-des-Monts follow 117 N.* FACILITIES: 59 sites, 10 W&E, 49 no hkups, tenting, dump. RECREATION: lake swim, canoeing, ramp, lake fishing. No pets. Open May - Sep. Phone: (819)438-2017.

GRANDE-VALLEE—D-6

(E) Camping Au Soleil Couchant (Not Visited)—(Gaspesie) *From west town limits on Hwy 132: Go 2.8 km/1-3/4 mi E on Hwy 132. Enter on L.* ◇◇◇FACILITIES: 93 sites, 36 full hkups, 21 W&E, (15/30 amps), 36 no hkups, tenting, dump, laundry, ltd groc. ◇◇RECREATION: playground. Pets welcome. Partial handicap access. Open June 1 - Sep 30. Rate in 2010 $20-23 for 4 persons. Member CQ. Phone: (418) 393-2489.

HAVELOCK—J-2

(SW) Camping Domaine de la Frontiere Enchantee—(Monteregie) *From jct Hwy 202 & Hwy 203: Go 2.8 km/1-3/4 mi S on Hwy 203, then .04 km/1/4 mi W on Covey Hill Rd. Enter on L.* ◇◇◇FACILITIES: 330 sites, 320 full hkups, 10 W&E, (15/30 amps), tenting, dump, laundry, groceries. ◇◇◇◇RECREATION: swim pool, no motors, canoeing, playground. Pets welcome, breed restrict. Open May 1 - Sep 30. Rate in 2010 $40 for 4 persons. Member CQ. Phone: (450)826-4490.

HEMMINGFORD—J-2

(C) Camping Canne De Bois—(Monteregie) *From jct Hwy 202 & Hwy 219: Go 1.6 km/1 mi S on Hwy 219. Enter on L.* ◇◇◇FACILITIES: 420 sites, 36 ft max RV length, 359 full hkups, (15/30 amps), 61 no hkups, family camping, tenting, dump, laundry, ltd groc. ◇◇◇RECREATION: swim pool, lake swim, no motors, canoeing, playground. Pets welcome. Open May 7 - Sep 19. Rate in 2010 $31-40 per family. Member CQ. Phone: (800)770-7977.

HENRYVILLE—J-3

(W) Oasis du Richelieu—*From jct Hwy 202 & Hwy 225: Go 5.2 km/3-1/4 mi N on Hwy 225, then .08 km/1/2 mi NE on Rang Goyette. Enter on L.* ◇◇FACILITIES: 78 sites, 38 ft max RV length, 68 full hkups, 10 W&E, (15/30 amps), tenting, laundry. ◇◇RECREATION: swim pool, river swim, boating, canoeing, ramp, dock, river fishing, play equipment. Pets welcome. Open May 15 - Sep 30. Rate in 2010 $31 for 4 persons. Member CQ. Phone: (450)294-2332.

HOPETOWN—E-6

(W) Camping des Etoiles (Not visited)—*From E. City limit: Go 4.2 km/2-3/4 mi W on Hwy 132. Enter on L.* ◇◇◇FACILITIES: 76 sites, 76 full hkups, (15/30/50 amps), 50 amps ($), 5 pull-thrus, tenting, laundry, ltd groc. RECREATION: play equipment. Pets welcome, breed restrict, quantity restrict. Partial handicap access. Open May 1 - Oct 15. Rate in 2010 $27 for 4 persons. Member CQ. Phone: (418)752-6553.

HUDSON—I-1

(SW) Camping Choisy—(Monteregie) *From Hwy 40 (exit 17) & Hwy 201: Go 3 km/2 mi S on Hwy 201. Enter on L.* ◇◇◇FACILITIES: 399 sites, 360 full hkups, 35 W&E, (15/30 amps), 4 no hkups, 13 pull-thrus, tenting, dump, laundry, groceries. ◇◇◇◇RECREATION: 2 swim pools, playground. Pets welcome. Partial handicap access. Open all yr. Facilities fully operational May 1 - Oct 10. Rate in 2010 $37 for 4 persons. Member CQ. Phone: (450)458-4900.

ILE D'ORLEANS—F-6

(W) Camping Ile Orleans (Not Visited)—*From Hwy 138 (Ile d'Orlean Bridge) & Hwy 368: Go 33.2 km/20-3/4 mi E on Hwy 368 E. Enter on L.* ◇◇◇FACILITIES: 154 sites, typical site width 25 ft, 19 full hkups, 84 W&E, (15/30 amps), 51 no hkups, 10 pull-thrus, tenting, dump, laundry, ltd groc. ◇◇◇RECREATION: swim pool, canoeing, playground. Pets welcome. Partial handicap access. Open May 18 - Oct 8. Facilities fully operational Jun 20 - Sep 15. Rate in 2010 $42 per family. Member CQ. Phone: (418)829-2953.

INVERNESS—G-5

(NE) Camping Inverness (Not Visited)—*From jct Hwy 267 & Gosford St (in town): Go 8.3 km/5 mi N on Gosford St. Enter on R.* ◇◇FACILITIES: 76 sites, 32 full hkups, 40 W&E, (15/30 amps), 4 no hkups, tenting, dump, laundry. ◇◇RECREATION: swim pool, river fishing, play equipment. Pets welcome. Partial handicap access. Open May 26 - Sep 5. Facilities fully operational Jun 15 - Sep 1. Rate in 2010 $25-28 for 4 persons. Member CQ. Phone: (418)453-2400.

JOLIETTE—H-3

(NE) Camping Belle-Maree—*From jct Hwy 158 & Hwy 131: Go 3.6 km/2 1/4 mi N on Hwy 131, then .04 km/ 1/4 mi W on Boul Ant. Barette, then 1 km/1/2 mi N on Rang Ste Julie, then .07 km/1/2 mi W on Chemin 4 (Notre Dame des Prairies). Enter on L.* ◇◇FACILITIES: 99 sites, 89 full hkups, 10 W&E, (15/30 amps), tenting, dump, laundry. ◇◇RECREATION: lake swim, canoeing. Pets welcome. Partial handicap access. Open May 15 - Sep 15. Rate in 2010 $30 for 4 persons. Member CQ. Phone: (450)756-2542.

LA CONCEPTION—G-1

(N) Camping Parc La Conception (Not Visited)—*From jct Hwy 117 & Rue Principale: Go 0.8 km/1/2 mi SW on Rue Principale, then 0.8 km/1/2 mi W on des Erables, then 2.4 km/1-1/2 mi S on des Ormes. Enter on L.* ◇◇◇FACILITIES: 225 sites, 86 full hkups, 119 W&E, (15 amps), 20 no hkups, tenting, dump, laundry, ltd groc. ◇◇◇RECREATION: swim pool, lake swim, electric motors only, canoeing, river fishing, playground. Pets welcome ($), breed restrict. Open May 11 - Oct 8. Facilities fully operational Jun 15 - Sep 5. Rate in 2010 $31-42 for 5 persons. Member CQ. Phone: (819)686-5596.

LA DORE—B-4

RESERVE FAUNIQUE ASHUAPMUSHUAN CAMPING LAC CHIBOUBICHE—(Saguenay Lac St-Jean) *From Road 175 N & Hwy 169: Go 33 km on Hwy 167.* FACILITIES: 33 sites, 33 no hkups, tenting, dump. RECREATION: lake swim, lake/river fishing. No pets. Open May - Sep. Phone: (418)256-3806.

LA MALBAIE—C-5

(NW) Camping Chutes Fraser—(Charlevoix) *From jct Hwy 362 & Hwy 138: Go 153 m/500 feet E on Hwy 138, then 3.2 km/2 mi N on Chemin de la Vallee. Enter on R.* ◇◇◇FACILITIES: 325 sites, 112 full hkups, 100 W&E, (15/30 amps), 163 no hkups, 10 pull-thrus, tenting, dump, laundry, full svc store. ◇◇◇◇RECREATION: swim pool, river fishing, playground. Pets welcome. Open May 15 - Oct 30. Rate in 2010 $28-38 for 4 persons. Member CQ. Phone: (418) 665-2151.

(NW) Domaine Riviera Au Bord De a Riviere—*From jct Hwy 362 & Hwy 138 (bridge): Go 1.2 km/3/4 mi W on Hwy 138. Enter on R.* ◇◇FACILITIES: 140 sites, 89 full hkups, 26 W&E, (15/30 amps), 25 no hkups, tenting, dump, laundry. ◇◇RECREATION: swim pool, river swim, boating, 9 hp limit, canoeing, river fishing, playground. Pets welcome, breed restrict. Open May 15 - Oct 10. Facilities fully operational Jun 15 - Sep 15. Rate in 2010 $30 for 4 persons. Member CQ. Phone: (418)665-4991.

LA TUQUE—C-4

LA TUQUE MUNICIPAL CAMPGROUND—(Mauricie Bois-Francs) *In town at Hwy 155 N.* FACILITIES: 424 sites, 228 full hkups, 196 W&E, (30 amps), tenting, dump, laundry, ltd groc. RECREATION: swim pool, river swim, boating, canoeing, ramp, dock, river fishing, playground. Pets welcome. Partial handicap access. Open May 27 - Sep 11. Member CQ. Phone: (819)523-4561.

LABELLE—G-1

(C) Camping Chutes Aux Iroquois—(Laurentides) *From jct Hwy 117 & Rue DuPont: Go E over bridge on DuPont, then 0.2 km/1/10 mi E on Du Moulin, then 0.2 km/1/10 mi SE on Rue Du Camping. Enter at end.* ◇◇◇◇FACILITIES: 159 sites, 35 ft max RV length, 100 full hkups, 15 W&E, 27 E, (15/30 amps), 17 no hkups, 8 pull-thrus, tenting, dump, laundry, ltd groc. ◇◇◇RECREATION: swim pool, river swim, canoeing, river fishing, playground. Pets welcome ($). Open May 4 - Sep 26. Rate in 2010 $35.90 per family. Member CQ. Phone: (819)686-2337.

LABRECQUE—A-4

(NE) Camping Domaine Lemieux (Not Visited)—*From chruch in town: Go 2 km/1-1/4 mi N on Rue Principale. Enter on R.* FACILITIES: 85 sites, 44 full hkups, 41 W&E, (15 amps), tenting, dump, laundry. RECREATION: lake swim, boating, canoeing, lake fishing, play equipment. Pets welcome, breed restrict. Open Jun 9 - Aug 20. Rate in 2010 $25 for 4 persons. Phone: (418)481-2442.

LAC SIMON—D-3

(NE) Camping Haut-des-Cotes (Not Visited)—*From jct Hwy 315 & Hwy 321: Go 1.8 km/1 mi N on Hwy 321, then 2.8 km/1-3/4 mi NE on Chemin Haut-des-Cotes. Enter on R.* ◇◇FACILITIES: 127 sites, 80 full hkups, 21 W&E, (15/30 amps), 26 no hkups, tenting, dump, laundry, ltd groc. ◇◇RECREATION: lake swim, electric motors only, canoeing, lake fishing, play equipment. Pets welcome. Open May 18 - Oct 8. Facilities fully operational Jun 15 - Sep 2. Rate in 2010 $35-38 for 4 persons. Member CQ. Phone: (819)428-3712.

Woodall's Tip... Understand our ratings—Turn to the "How to Use" pages in the front of this Directory.

LAC-A-LA-CROIX—B-4

(NE) Camping Villa des Sables—*From jct Hwy 169 & Hwy 170: Go 1.6 km/1 mi E on Hwy 170. Enter on L.* ◆◆FACILITIES: 175 sites, 24 ft max RV length, 110 full hkups, 35 W&E, (15/30 amps), 30 no hkups, tenting, dump, laundry, ltd groc. ◆◆RECREATION: lake swim, boating, canoeing, lake fishing, play equipment. Pets welcome, breed restrict. Open May 20 - Sep 20. Rate in 2010 $35 for 4 persons. Member CQ. Phone: (418)345-2655.

LAC-AUX-SABLES—F-4

(NE) Camping Lac-aux-Sables (Not Visited)—*From jct Hwy 153 & Hwy 363: Go 1.2 km/3/4 mi N on Hwy 153, then 153 m/500 feet W on rue Cloutier. Enter on R.* ◆◆FACILITIES: 292 sites, 208 full hkups, 79 W&E, (15/30 amps), 5 no hkups, tenting, dump, laundry, ltd groc. ◆◆◆RECREATION: lake swim, boating, canoeing, lake fishing, play equipment. Pets welcome, breed restrict. Open May 18 - Sep 16. Facilities fully operational Jun 24 - Sep 3. Rate in 2010 $40 for 5 persons. Member CQ. Phone: (418)336-2488.

LAC-BROME—J-4

(NW) Camping Fairmount (Not Visited)—*From Hwy 10 (exit 78) & boul.de Bromont: Go 7 Km/4-1/3 mi SE on boul de Bromont, then 7 km/4-1/3 mi S on rue Brome, then 2 Km/1-1/4 mi W on Ch Fairmont. Enter on L.* ◆◆FACILITIES: 112 sites, 24 ft max RV length, 75 full hkups, 15 W&E, (15/30 amps), 22 no hkups, tenting, dump, laundry, ltd groc. ◆◆◆RECREATION: playground. Pets welcome, breed restrict, quantity restrict. Open May 1 - Sep 23. Rate in 2010 $26-31.95 for 4 persons. Member CQ. Phone: (450)266-0928.

(NE) Domaine des Erables (Lac Brome)—(Canton-de-l'est) *From Hwy 10 (exit 90) & Hwy 243: Go 3.2 km/2 mi S on Hwy 243, then 0.4 km/1/4 mi S on Hwy 215 (Bondville St). Enter on L.* ◆◆◆FACILITIES: 185 sites, 125 full hkups, 50 W&E, (15/30/50 amps), 50 amps ($), 10 no hkups, 3 pull-thrus, tenting, dump, laundry, groceries. ◆◆◆RECREATION: swim pool, boating, canoeing, ramp, dock, lake fishing, play equipment. Pets welcome, breed restrict. Open all yr. Facilities fully operational May 1 - Oct 31. Rate in 2010 $32.75-38.75 for 6 persons. Member CQ.

Phone: (450)242-8888
Address: 688 Bondville (Foster), Lac Brome, QC J0E 1R0
Lat/Lon: 45.27799/-72.50921

LAC-DES-PLAGES—H-1

(N) Camping Lac des Plages (Not Visited)—*From south town limits on Hwy 323: Go 2.1 km/1-1/4 mi N on Hwy 323, then 2.2 km/1-1/4 mi W on chemin Tour du Lac, then 152 meters/500 feet N on Chenail du Moine (gravel road). Enter on L.* ◆◆◆FACILITIES: 100 sites, 51 full hkups, 23 W&E, (15/30 amps), 26 no hkups, heater not allowed, tenting, dump, non-guest dump $, portable dump, laundry, ltd groc, LP gas by weight, ice, picnic tables, fire rings, wood. ◆◆◆RECREATION: rec hall, swim pool, lake swim, boating, canoeing, kayaking, ramp, dock, lake fishing, bsktball, playground, activities, horseshoes, hiking trails, v-ball. Pets welcome. Open May 16 - Sep 28. Facilities fully operational Jun 15 - Sep 1. Rate in 2010 $35-44 for 4 persons. MC/VISA/Debit. Member CQ. CCUSA 50% Discount. CCUSA reservations Required, CCUSA max stay 4 days, Cash only for CCUSA disc., CCUSA disc. not avail S, CCUSA disc. not avail F,Sa. No dogs. Heater not allowed.

Phone: (819)426-2576
Address: 10 Chenail du Moine, Lac des Plages, QC J0T 1K0
Lat/Lon: 46.00882/-74.89996
Web: www.lacdesplages.com

LAC-KENOGAMI—B-4

CENTRE TOURISTIQUE DU LAC KENOGAMI—(Saguenay Lac St-Jean) *From jct Hwy 175 & Hwy 169: Go N on Hwy 169.* FACILITIES: 149 sites, 60 full hkups, 48 E, (15/30/50 amps), 41 no hkups, tenting, dump, laundry, ltd groc. RECREATION: lake swim, canoeing, lake fishing, playground. Pets welcome. Open Jun - Sep. Phone: (418)344-1142.

LACOLLE—J-3

(NE) Camping Gregoire (Not Visited)—*From jct Hwy 202 & Hwy 221: Go 6 km/3-3/4 mi N on Hwy 221. Enter on R.* ◆◆◆FACILITIES: 380 sites, 300 full hkups, 40 W&E, (15/30/50 amps), 40 no hkups, 8 pull-thrus, tenting, dump, laundry, ltd groc. ◆◆◆RECREATION: swim pool, lake swim, canoeing, playground. Pets welcome. Open May 15 - Sep 15. Facilities fully operational Jun 15 - Sep 5. Big rigs welcome. Rate in 2010 $38 for 6 persons. Member CQ. Phone: (450)246-3385.

LAMBTON—H-6

PARC NATIONAL DE FRONTENAC, BAIE SAUVAGE—(Canton-de-l'est) *From Hwy 112 or 108.* FACILITIES: 205 sites, 44 W&E, 45 E, (15/30 amps), 116 no hkups, tenting, dump, laundry, ltd groc. RECREATION: lake swim, boating, canoeing, ramp, dock, lake fishing. No pets. Open May - Oct. Phone: (418) 486-2300.

L'ANGE GARDIEN (OUTAOUAIS)—D-2

(C) Camping Ange Gardien—(Outaouais) *From jct Hwy 50 (exit 159) & Blvd Laurentides: Go 1 km/3/4 mi N on Blvd Laurentides, then 0.4 km/1/4 mi W on Chemin Fillion, then 1.2 km/3/4 mi N on Lamarche. Enter on L.* ◆◆◆FACILITIES: 79 sites, 68 full hkups, 6 W&E, (15/30 amps), 5 no hkups, tenting, dump, laundry, ltd groc. ◆◆◆RECREATION: swim pool, play equipment. Pets welcome. Partial handicap access. Facilities fully operational May 1 - Oct 31. Rate in 2010 $26-37 for 4 persons. Member CQ. Phone: (819)281-5055.

(N) Domaine de l'Ange Gardien (Not Visited)—*From I-50 (exit 159): Go 2.4 km/1-1/2 mi N on Blvd des Laurentides, then .04 km/1/4 mi W on Chemin Fillion, then 2.4 km/1-1/2 mi N on Lamarche, then .06 km/1/2 mi W on ch. Pierre Laporte. Enter on R.* ◆◆◆FACILITIES: 83 sites, 35 ft max RV length, 54 full hkups, 11 W&E, (15/30 amps), 18 no hkups, tenting, dump, laundry, ltd groc. ◆◆RECREATION: play equipment. Pets welcome. Open Apr 15 - Oct 15. Rate in 2010 $26-30 for 4 persons. Member CQ. Phone: (819) 281-0299.

L'ANGE-GARDIEN—J-3

(N) Camping Plage Fortier (K.F.A.)—(Quebec) *From Hwy 138 (at L'Ange-Gardien) & Hwy 360: Go 1.3 km/3/4 mi NW on Hwy 360, then 6.8 km/4-1/4 mi N on Chemin Lefrancois. Enter on L.* ◆◆◆FACILITIES: 286 sites, 156 full hkups, 88 W&E, (15/30/50 amps), 42 no hkups, 10 pull-thrus, phone on-site Internet (needs activ), phone Internet central location, tenting, RV storage, dump, non-guest dump $, laundry, ltd groc, LP gas by weight, ice, picnic tables, fire rings, wood. ◆◆◆◆RECREATION: pavilion, lake swim, bsktball, playground, activities, tennis, horseshoes, v-ball. Pets welcome. Partial handicap access. Open May 1 - Oct 14. Facilities fully operational Jun 25 - Aug 30. Big rigs welcome. Rate in 2010 $37-41 for 2 persons. MC/VISA/Debit. Member CQ. CCUSA 50% Discount. CCUSA reservations Required, CCUSA max stay 3 days. Minimum stay 2 days. Discount not available weekends only Jul 1-Aug 15/available Sun-Thu. Fully operational Jun 25-Aug 30.

Phone: (888)226-7387
Lat/Lon: 46.96341/-71.12765
Email: info@campingplagefortier.ca
Web: www.campingplagefortier.ca

L'ANNONCIATION—G-1

RESERVE FAUNIQUE/ROUGE MATAWIN-CAMPING LAC DES SUCRERIES—(Laurentides) *North on Hwy 117.* FACILITIES: 160 sites, 35 E, 125 no hkups, tenting, dump, laundry, ltd groc. RECREATION: lake swim, canoeing, lake fishing. No pets. Open May - Sep. Phone: (819)275-1811.

LATERRIERE—B-5

(W) Domaine de Vacances la Rocaille—*From jct Hwy 175 & Rue du Boulevard: Go .04 km/1/4 mi N on Rue du Boulevard, then 5.6 km/3-1/2 mi W on St-Pierre. Enter on R.* ◆◆FACILITIES: 140 sites, 30 ft max RV length, 115 full hkups, 5 W&E, (15/30 amps), 20 no hkups, tenting, dump, laundry. ◆RECREATION: lake swim, river fishing, play equipment. Pets welcome, breed restrict. Open Jun 1 - Sep 15. Rate in 2010 $17-27 for 8 persons. Member CQ. Phone: (418)678-2657.

LES MECHINS—E-5

Camping aux Pignons Verts (Not Visited)—*From W city limit: Go 2.8 km/1-1/2 mi E on Hwy 132. Enter on R.* ◆◆◆FACILITIES: 42 sites, typical site width 20 ft, 42 full hkups, (30 amps), tenting, laundry. Pets welcome, breed restrict. Partial handicap access. Open Jun 1 - Sep 15. Rate in 2010 $30 for 2 persons. Member CQ. Phone: (418)729-3423.

LEVIS—F-6

(E) Camping du Fort de la Martiniere (Not Visited)—*From jct Hwy 20 (exit 330)& Lallemand Rd: Go 1.6 km/1 mi N on rue Lallemand, then 1.2 km/3/4 mi E on Hwy 132. Enter on L.* ◆◆◆FACILITIES: 28 sites, 21 full hkups, 2 W&E, (15/30 amps), 5 no hkups, tenting, dump, laundry. ◆◆RECREATION: swim pool, play equipment. Pets welcome ($). Open May 1 - Oct 15. Rate in 2010 $36 for 2 persons. Phone: (418)835-9060.

(SE) Camping La Jolie Rochelle—(Bellechase) *From jct Hwy 20 & 281: Go 19 km S on 281, then .5 km W on Rang, then 90 2.4 km S on God Bout. Enter at end.* ◆◆◆◆FACILITIES: 120 sites, typical site width 35 ft, 92 full hkups, 18 W&E, (15/30 amps), 10 no hkups, tenting, shower$, dump, laundry, ice, picnic tables, fire rings, wood. ◆◆RECREATION: swim pool, river swim, river fishing, playground, horseshoes, hiking trails, v-ball. Pets welcome ($), breed restrict, size restrict, quantity restrict. Open May 15 - Oct 15. Rate in 2010 $34 per family. MC/VISA/Debit. CCUSA 50% Discount. CCUSA reservations Recommended, CCUSA max stay 2 days, Cash only for CCUSA disc., CCUSA disc. not avail F,Sa, CCUSA disc. not avail holidays. Not available Jul & Aug.

Phone: (418)243-1320
Address: 135 Petite Troisieme, Saint Raphael de Bellechase, QC G0R 4C0
Lat/Lon: 46.76432/-70.69817
Email: lajolierochelle@videotron.ca
Web: www.lajolierochelle.com

(SE) Camping Transit—*From Hwy 20 (exit 330) & Chemin St-Roch: Go 3.6 km/2-1/4 mi E on Chemin St-Roch. Enter on L.* ◆◆◆◆FACILITIES: 184 sites, 134 full hkups, 30 W&E, (15/30/50 amps), 50 amps ($), 20 no hkups, 100 pull-thrus, WiFi Instant Internet at site ($), phone Internet central location, tenting, RV storage, shower$, dump, non-guest dump $, laundry, ltd groc, RV supplies, LP gas by weight, ice, picnic tables, fire rings, wood. ◆◆◆◆RECREATION: rec hall, equipped pavilion, swim pool, hot tub, playground, shuffleboard court 2 shuffleboard courts, horseshoes, hiking trails, v-ball. Pets welcome ($). Partial handicap access. Open Apr 15 - Oct 25. Facilities fully operational Jun 15 - Sep 15. Big rigs welcome. Rate in 2010 $40-50 for 4 persons. MC/VISA/Debit. Member CQ. FMCA discount. CCUSA 50% Discount. CCUSA reservations Recommended, CCUSA max stay Unlimited, Cash only for CCUSA disc., CCUSA disc. not avail holidays. Fully operational Jun 15-Sep 15. Not available Jun 20-Sep 8.

Phone: (888)882-0948
Address: 600 Chemin St-Roch, Levis, QC G6V 6N4
Lat/Lon: 46.81190/-71.05125
Email: info@campingtransit.com
Web: www.campingtransit.com

MADELEINE ISLANDS—D-6

See Maritime Provinces map (F-5), Also see listing at Bassin

MAGOG—J-4

See listings at Bromont, Granby, Lac Brome, & Magog-Orford.

(E) Camping Domaine Parc Estrie—(Canton-de-l'est) *From Hwy 10-55 (exit 123): Go 0.8 km/1/2 mi W on Boul Bourque (Hwy 112), then 0.8 km/1/2 mi S on rue du Domaine. Enter on L.* ◆◆◆◆FACILITIES: 446 sites, 316 full hkups, 88 W&E, (15/30 amps), 42 no hkups, 11 pull-thrus, tenting, dump, laundry, ltd groc. ◆◆◆◆RECREATION: swim pool, pond fishing, playground. Pets welcome. Partial handicap access. Open Apr 29 - Oct 29. Rate in 2010 $30.79-36.32 per family. Member CQ.

Phone: (819)868-6944
Address: 19 rue du Domaine, Magog, QC J1X 5Z3
Lat/Lon: 45.29408/-72.10445
Email: camping@domaineparc-estrie.qc.ca
Web: www.domaineparc-estrie.qc.ca

(NW) Camping Magog - Orford—(Canton-de-l'est) *From Hwy 10 (exit 118) & Hwy 141: Go 2.3 km/1-1/2 mi N on Hwy 141, then 5.5 km/3-1/2 mi E on Ch. Alfred Desrochers. Enter on R.* ◆◆◆◆FACILITIES: 300 sites, 161 full hkups, 74 W&E, (15/30 amps), 65 no hkups, 24 pull-thrus, tenting, dump, laundry. ◆◆◆◆RECREATION: swim pool, pond fishing, playground. Pets welcome. Partial handicap access. Open May 12 - Oct 9. Rate in 2010 $27-31 for 6 persons. Member CQ. Phone: (819)843-2500.

MASHTEUIATSH—B-4

(SE) Camping Plage Robertson—*From south town limits: Go 5.2 km/3.2 mi N on a paved road. Enter on R.* ◆◆FACILITIES: 150 sites, 30 ft max RV length, 120 full hkups, 15 W&E, (15/30 amps), 15 no hkups, 2 pull-thrus, tenting, dump, laundry, ltd groc. ◆RECREATION: lake swim, boating, canoeing, lake fishing, play equipment. Pets welcome ($), breed restrict. Open May 25 - Oct 8. Facilities fully operational Jun 20 - Aug 20. Rate in 2010 $35 for 4 persons. Member CQ. Phone: (418)275-1375.

MATANE—B-6

(W) Camping Parc Sirois La Baleine—(Gaspesie) *From jct Hwy 195 & Hwy 132: Go 4 km/2-1/2 mi W on Hwy 132. Enter on L.* ◆◆◆FACILITIES: 100 sites, 60 full hkups, 10 W&E, (15/30 amps), 30 no hkups, tenting, dump, laundry, ltd groc. ◆◆RECREATION: playground. Pets welcome. Open May 15 - Oct 15. Facilities fully operational Jun 1 - Sep 30. Rate in 2010 $28 for 4 persons. Member CQ. Phone: (418) 562-2242.

RESERVE FAUNIQUE DE MATANE ET DE DUNIERE/CAMPING ETANG A LA TRUITE—(Gaspesie) *Hwy I-20 E & 195 S.* FACILITIES: 20 sites, 4 W&E, (15 amps), 16 no hkups, tenting, dump. RECREATION: lake swim, canoeing, lake fishing. No pets. Open Jun - Sep. Phone: (418)562-3700.

RESERVE FAUNIQUE DE MATANE/CAMPING JOHN—(Gaspesie) *From jct Hwy 132 & Hwy 195: Go S on Hwy 195.* FACILITIES: 16 sites, 8 full hkups, (15 amps), 8 no hkups, tenting, dump. RECREATION: lake swim, boating, canoeing, ramp, lake/river fishing. No pets. Open Jun - Sep. Phone: (418)224-3345.

MERCIER—J-2

(C) Domaine du Bel Age (Not Visited)—*From jct Hwy 132 & Hwy 138: Go 2 km/1-1/4 mi SW on Hwy 138. Enter on R.* ◇◇◇FACILITIES: 42 sites, 33 full hkups, (15/20/30/50 amps), 9 no hkups, tenting, dump, laundry. ◇◇RECREATION: swim pool, play equipment. Pets welcome. Open Apr 15 - Oct 31. Rate in 2010 $23-35 for 4 persons. Member CQ. Phone: (450)691-0306.

METIS-SUR-MER—B-6

(W) Camping Annie—*From jct Hwy 234 & Hwy 132: Go 8.8 km/5-1/2 mi E on Hwy 132. Enter on R.* ◇◇◇◇FACILITIES: 195 sites, 86 full hkups, 53 W&E, (15/30 amps), 56 no hkups, 6 pull-thrus, tenting, dump, laundry. ◇◇◇RECREATION: swim pool, playground. Pets welcome ($). Partial handicap access. Open May 4 - Oct 1. Facilities fully operational Jun 20 - Sep 3. Rate in 2010 $30-33 per family. Member CQ. Phone: (418) 936-3825.

MIRABEL—I-2

(SE) Camping Mirabel (Not Visited)—(Laurentides) *From Hwy 15 (exit 23) & Chemin de la Cote Nord: Go 6.4 km/4 mi W on Chemin de la Cote-Nord. Enter on L.* ◇◇◇FACILITIES: 387 sites, 345 full hkups, 42 W&E, (15/30/50 amps), 50 amps ($), tenting, dump,

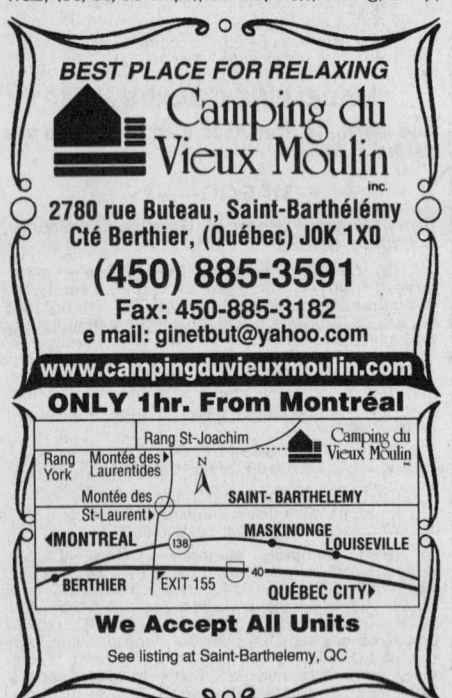

MIRABEL—Continued
Camping Mirabel (Not Visited)—Continued

laundry, ltd groc. ◇◇◇◇RECREATION: 2 swim pools, playground. No pets. Open May 1 - Oct 31. Facilities fully operational Jun 15 - Sep 5. Big rigs welcome. Rate in 2010 $33-45 for 2 persons. Member CQ. Phone: (450)475-7725.

MISTASSINI—B-4

(NE) Camping St Louis—*From north town limits: Go .08 km/1/2 mi N on Rang St-Louis. Enter on L.* ◇◇◇FACILITIES: 165 sites, 135 full hkups, (15/30 amps), 30 no hkups, tenting, dump, laundry, ltd groc. ◇◇RECREATION: swim pool, play equipment. Pets welcome, breed restrict. Open Jun 1 - Sep 10. Facilities fully operational Jun 20 - Aug. Rate in 2010 $24 for 5 persons. Phone: (418)276-4670.

MONT SAINTE-ANNE—C-5

(NE) Camping Mont Sainte Anne—*At Beaupre jct Hwy 138 & Hwy 360: Go 9-1/3 km/5-3/4 mi E on Hwy 360, then 1 km/3/4 mi N on Rang Saint-Julien.* ◇◇◇◇FACILITIES: 166 sites, typical site width 25 ft, 48 full hkups, 47 W&E, 31 E, (15/30/50 amps), 40 no hkups, family camping, tenting, dump, laundry, ltd groc. ◇◇◇◇RECREATION: lake/river swim, river fishing, playground. Pets welcome. Open May 11 - Oct 8. Rate in 2010 $41-44 for 5 persons. Member CQ. Phone: (800)463-1568.

MONT ST HILAIRE—I-3

(E) Camping Laurier—*From jct Hwy 229 & Hwy 116: Go .06km/1/4 mi W on Hwy 116. Enter on R.* ◇◇FACILITIES: 330 sites, 330 full hkups, (15/30 amps), tenting, dump, laundry. ◇◇◇RECREATION: swim pool, playground. Pets welcome ($). Open May 15 - Sept 15. Rate in 2010 $28-31 for 4 persons. Member CQ. Phone: (450)467-2518.

MONT-BRUN—B-1

PARC NATIONAL AIGUEBELLE/CAMPING ABIJEVIS—(Abitibi) *From Hwy 117-111 or 101 Follow signs.* FACILITIES: 47 sites, 26 W&E, (30 amps), 21 no hkups, tenting, dump, laundry, ltd groc. RECREATION: lake/river swim, canoeing, lake fishing, play equipment. No pets. Partial handicap access. Open June - Sep. Phone: (819)637-2480.

MONT-TREMBLANT—G-1

PARC NATIONAL DU MONT-TREMBLANT/CAMPING SECTEUR DE LA DIABLE—(Laurentides) *From Hwy 117-125-329- or 343.* FACILITIES: 577 sites, 39 full hkups, (15/30 amps), 538 no hkups, tenting, dump, laundry, ltd groc. RECREATION: lake swim, canoeing, ramp, lake fishing, play equipment. No pets. Partial handicap access. Open May - Oct. Phone: (877)688-2281.

PARC NATIONAL DU MONT-TREMBLANT/LAC CACHE—(Laurentides) *From Hwy 117-125-329 or 343.* FACILITIES: 29 sites, 29 no hkups, tenting, dump. RECREATION: canoeing, lake fishing. No pets. Open May - Oct. Phone: (877)688-2289.

MONTEBELLO—I-1

(C) MARINA CAMPING MONTABELLO (City Park)—(Outaouais) *From jct Hwy 148 & rue Laurier in town: Go 152 m/500 feet S on rue Laurier. Enter at end.* FACILITIES: 41 sites, 18 full hkups, 2 W&E, (30 amps), 21 no hkups, tenting, dump, laundry. RECREATION: boating, canoeing, ramp, dock, river fishing. Pets welcome. Open May 15 - Oct 15. Phone: (819)423-5070.

Woodall's — Trusted for Over 75 Years.

MONTPELLIER—D-3

RESERVE FAUNIQUE DE PAPINEAU-LABELLE/LAC ECHO—(Outaouais) *From jct Hwy 148 & Hwy 315: Go N on Hwy 315 to Montpellier (Accueil Mulet).* FACILITIES: 56 sites, 56 no hkups, tenting, dump, laundry. RECREATION: lake swim, canoeing, ramp, lake fishing, playground. No pets. Partial handicap access. Open May - Sep. Phone: (819)454-2011.

MONTREAL—I-2

See listings at Bernard-de-Lacolle, Bromont, Granby, LacBrome, Montreal, Mont St-Hilaire, Mont-Tremblant, Sainte-Agathe-des-Monts, Saint-Antoine-Abbe, Saint-Bathelemy, Saint-Bernard-de-Lacolle, Saint-Jerome, Saint-Mathieu-de-Beloeil, Sainte-Madeleine, & Sainte-Sabine.

MONTREAL AREA MAP

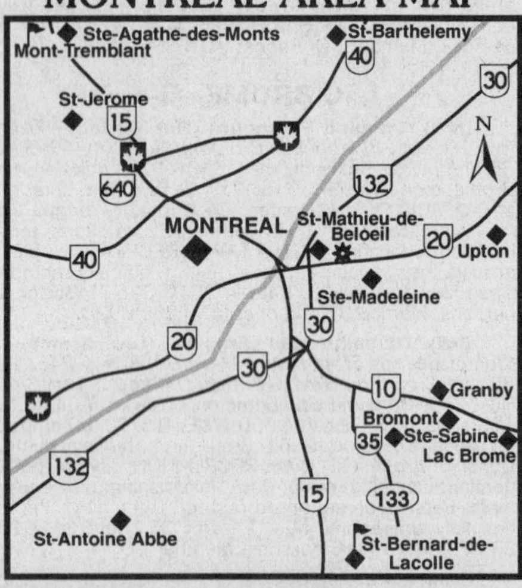

Symbols on map indicate towns within an 80km/50 mi radius of Montreal where campgrounds (diamonds), attractions (flags), & RV service centers & camping supply outlets (gears) are listed. Check listings for more information.

Tell Them Woodall's Sent You!

MORIN HEIGHTS—H-1

(SW) Camping & Cabines Nature Morin Heights (Not visited)—*From jct Hwy 15 (exit 60) & Hwy 364: Go 9.5 km/6 mi W on Hwy 364, then 1 km/3/4 mi S on rue Bennett. Enter on R.* ◇◇◇FACILITIES: 104 sites, 27 ft max RV length, 51 W&E, (15/30 amps), 53

Camping & Cabines Nature Morin Heights (Not visited)—Continued on next page

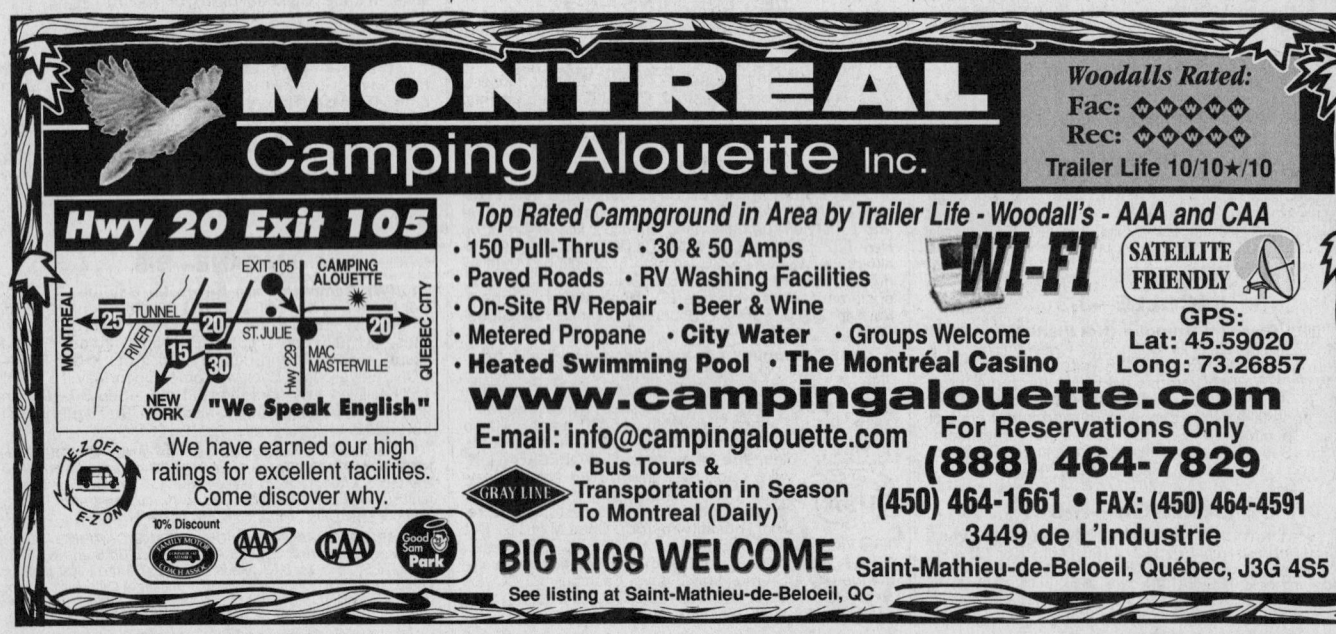

MORIN HEIGHTS—Continued
Camping & Cabines Nature Morin Heights (Not visited)—Continued

no hkups, tenting, dump, laundry, ltd groc. ◆◆◆RECREATION: swim pool, playground. Pets welcome. Partial handicap access. Open all yr. Facilities fully operational May 20 - Oct 15. Rate in 2010 $25-35 for 4 persons. Member CQ. Phone: (450)227-2020.

NEUVILLE—F-5

(NW) Riv-O-Pom (Not Visited)—*From jct Hwy 40 (exit 281) & Hwy 365: Go 1 km/3/4 mi N on Hwy 365. Enter on L.* ◆◆◆FACILITIES: 150 sites, 98 full hkups, 27 W&E, (15/30/50 amps), 50 amps ($), 25 no hkups, 30 pull-thrus, tenting, dump, laundry, ltd groc. ◆◆◆RECREATION: swim pool, river fishing, play equipment. Pets welcome. Open May 15 - Sep 15. Facilities fully operational Jun 20 - Sep 3. Rate in 2010 $27 for 4 persons. Member CQ. Phone: (418)561-5061.

NEW RICHMOND—E-6

(W) Camping New Richmond (Not Visited)—*At jct Hwy 132 & Hwy 299: Go 3/4 Km/1/2 mi SW on Hwy 132. Enter on R.* ◆◆◆FACILITIES: 100 sites, 100 full hkups, (15/30 amps), tenting, laundry. ◆RECREATION: boating, canoeing, dock, saltwater/river fishing. Pets welcome. Open Jun 1 - Sep 15. Rate in 2010 $22-27 for 5 persons. Member CQ. Phone: (418)392-6060.

NICOLET—G-4

(NE) Camping Port St-Francois—*From jct I-55 & Hwy 132 (Sainte-Angele): Go 13.2 km/8 mi W on Hwy 132, then 3.7 km/2-1/4 mi N on Rte du Port. Enter on L.* ◆◆◆FACILITIES: 217 sites, 166 full hkups, 21 W&E, (15/30 amps), 30 no hkups, tenting, dump, laundry, ltd groc. ◆◆◆RECREATION: swim pool, lake fishing, playground. Pets welcome, breed restrict. Partial handicap access. Open Apr 15 - Oct 15. Facilities fully operational Jun 15 - Sep 7. Rate in 2010 $34 for 4 persons. Member CQ. Phone: (819)293-5091.

NORMANDIN—B-4

SITE TOURISTIQUE CHUTE A L'OURS (Municipal Park) —(SaguenayLac St-Jean) *From St-Felicien at jct Hwy 167N & 169N: Go 1 km/3/4 mi NE on Hwy 169, then 15 km/9-1/4 mi N on Rang St-Eusebe, then 2.7 km/1-3/4 mi W on CR LS Ovide Bouchard. Enter at end.* FACILITIES: 184 sites, 101 full hkups, 48 W&E, (15 amps), 35 no hkups, tenting, dump, laundry, ltd groc. RECREATION: swim pool, playground. Pets welcome ($). Partial handicap access. Open May 19 - Sep 24. Member ARVC, CQ. Phone: (418)274-3411.

NOTRE-DAME-DE-LA-SALETTE—D-2

(NE) Camping Royal Papineau du Lac de l'Argile (Not Visited)—*From S Town City Limit: Go 1 km/3/4 mi N on Hwy 309, then 12 km/7-1/2 mi E on Chemin Thomas. Enter at end.* ◆◆◆FACILITIES: 366 sites, 266 full hkups, (15/30/50 amps), 50 amps ($), 100 no hkups, heater not allowed, tenting, dump, non-guest dump $, laundry, ltd groc, ice, picnic tables, patios, fire rings, wood. ◆◆◆◆◆RECREATION: swim pool, lake swim, boating, canoeing, kayaking, ramp, dock, lake fishing, bsktball, playground, activities, tennis, horseshoes, hiking trails, v-ball. Pets welcome. Partial handicap access. Open May 2 - Sep 28. Facilities fully operational Jun 15 - Sep 5. Big rigs welcome. Rate in 2010 $36-40 for 4 persons. MC/VISA/AMEX/Debit. CCUSA 50% Discount. Cash only for CCUSA disc., CCUSA disc. not avail F,Sa, CCUSA disc. not avail holidays. Not available Jun 15-Aug 15. Heater not allowed.

CAMPCLUB USA

Phone: (819)766-2626
Lat/Lon: 45.83179/-75.53169
Email: info@lacargile.com
Web: www.lacargile.com

NOTRE-DAME-DES-BOIS—I-6

PARC NATIONAL DU MONT-MEGANTIC—(Canton-de-l'est) *On Hwy 212.* FACILITIES: 13 sites, 13 no hkups, tenting, ltd groc. RECREATION: No pets. Open Jun - Sept. Phone: (819) 888-2941.

NOTRE-DAME-DES-PINS—D-5

(N) Camping La Roche D'Or (Not Visited)—*From jct Hwy 204 & Hwy 173: Go 7.2 km/4-1/2 mi N on Hwy 173. Enter on R.* FACILITIES: 300 sites, 225 full hkups, 55 W&E, (15/30 amps), 20 no hkups, tenting, dump, laundry, ltd groc. RECREATION: swim pool, playground. Pets welcome. Open May 12 - Sep 10. Facilities fully operational Jun 20 - Aug 20. Rate in 2010 $27-38 for 5 persons. Member CQ. Phone: (418)774-9191.

NOTRE-DAME-DU-MONT-CARMEL—G-4

(NE) Camping Lac Morin (Not Visited)—(Mauricie Bois-Francs) *From jct I-40 & Hwy 157N: Go 15 km/9-1/4 mi N on Hwy 157 to Notre-Dame-du-Mont-Carmel, then 1-1/3 km/3/4 mi E on Rang Saint-Flavien. Enter on R.* ◆◆◆FACILITIES: 182 sites, 166 full hkups, 6 W&E, (15/30/50 amps), 50 amps ($), 10 no hkups, 1 pull-thrus, tenting, dump, laundry, ltd groc.

NOTRE-DAME-DU-MONT-CARMEL—Continued
Camping Lac Morin (Not Visited)—Continued

◆◆◆RECREATION: lake swim, no motors, canoeing, ramp, playground. Pets welcome, breed restrict. Open all yr. Facilities fully operational May 15 - Oct 31. Rate in 2010 $31 for 5 persons. Member CQ. Phone: (819) 376-1479.

(NE) Camping Paradiso (Not Visited)—*From jct Hwy 40 & Hwy 157: Go 15 km/9-1/4 mi N on Hwy 157 to Notre-Dame-du-Mont-Carmel, then 1 km/1/2 mi E on Rang Saint-Flavien. Enter on L.* ◆◆◆FACILITIES: 185 sites, 185 full hkups, (15/30 amps), tenting, dump, laundry, ltd groc. ◆◆◆RECREATION: swim pool, lake swim, play equipment. Pets welcome, breed restrict. Open May 11 - Oct 9. Facilities fully operational Jun 24 - Sep 5. Rate in 2010 $31 for 6 persons. Member CQ. Phone: (819)375-1569.

OKA—I-2

(SW) PARC NATIONAL D'OKA—(Laurentides) *From Hwy 640 or 344.* FACILITIES: 891 sites, 301 full hkups, (15/30 amps), 590 no hkups, tenting, dump, laundry, ltd groc. RECREATION: lake swim, canoeing, ramp, lake fishing. No pets. Partial handicap access. Open May - Oct. Phone: (450)479-8365.

ORFORD—J-4

PARC NATIONAL DU MONT-ORFORD/CAMPING LAC FRASER—(Canton-de-l'est) *From Hwy 220 & I-10 follow signs.* FACILITIES: 149 sites, 50 E, (15/50 amps), 99 no hkups, tenting, dump, laundry, ltd groc. RECREATION: lake swim, boating, 9.9 hp limit, canoeing, ramp, lake fishing, play equipment. No pets. Partial handicap access. Open May - Sep. Phone: (819)843-9855.

PARC NATIONAL DU MONT-ORFORD/CAMPING LAC STUKELY—(Canton-de-l'est) *From I-10 or Hwy 220, follow signs.* FACILITIES: 321 sites, 54 full hkups, 9 W&E, 64 E, (15/30/50 amps), 194 no hkups, tenting, dump, laundry, ltd groc. RECREATION: lake swim, boating, 9.9 hp limit, canoeing, ramp, lake fishing, playground. No pets. Partial handicap access. Open May - Oct. Phone: (819)843-9855.

PABOS MILLS (CHANDLER)—E-6

(NE) Camping le Bourg de Pabos—*From E town City limit on Hwy 132: Go 7 km/4-1/4 mi W on Hwy 132, then 300 meters/1000 feet S on Anse aux Canards, then 2 km/1-1/4 mi E on rue de la Plage. Enter on L.* ◆◆◆◆FACILITIES: 110 sites, typical site width 25 ft, 62 full hkups, 24 W&E, (15/30/50 amps), 24 no hkups, 5 pull-thrus, tenting, dump, laundry. ◆◆◆RECREATION: playground. Pets welcome. Open June 1 - Sep 30. Facilities fully operational Jun 15 - Sep 1. Rate in 2010 $28-34 for 4 persons. Member CQ. Phone: (418)689-6043.

PERCE—E-6

(W) Camping Cote Surprise—*From west city limits: Go .04 km/1/4 mi W on Hwy 132. Enter on L.* ◆◆◆FACILITIES: 100 sites, 50 full hkups, (15/30/50 amps), 50 amps ($), 50 no hkups, tenting, dump, laundry. RECREATION: play equipment. Pets welcome, breed restrict. Open May 15 - Oct 30. Big rigs welcome. Rate in 2010 $32 for 8 persons. Member CQ. Phone: (418)782-5443.

(N) CAMPING DE LA BAIE-DE-PERCE—(Gaspesie) *In town on Hwy 132.* FACILITIES: 166 sites, 33 W&E, 16 E, (15 amps), 117 no hkups, tenting, dump, laundry. RECREATION: swim pool, saltwater fishing, playground. No pets. Open Jun - Sep. Phone: (418)782-5102.

(E) Camping Havre de la Nuit (Not Visited)—(Gaspesie) *From jct Hwy 132 & Rue Biard (in town): Go 304 meters/1000 feet N on Rue Biard. Enter on L.* ◆◆◆FACILITIES: 25 sites, typical site width 30 ft, 20 full hkups, 5 W&E, (15/30 amps), tenting, dump, laundry. Pets welcome. Open May 1 - Oct 15. Rate in 2010 $25-35 for 4 persons. Phone: (418)782-2924.

(NE) Camping Tete d'Indien (Not Visited)—(Gaspesie) *In town of Perce: Go 28 Km/17 mi NE on Hwy 132. Enter on R.* ◆◆◆◆FACILITIES: 42 sites, 19 full hkups, 16 W&E, (15/30/50 amps), 50 amps ($), 7 no hkups, cable TV, ($), WiFi Instant Internet at site ($), tenting, dump, non-guest dump $, laundry, ice, picnic tables, fire rings, wood. ◆◆RECREATION: equipped pavilion, boating, canoeing, kayaking, saltwater fishing, fishing guides, play equipment, horseshoes, v-ball. Pets welcome. Partial handicap access. Open Jun 1 - Oct 15. Facilities fully operational Jun 1 - Oct 1. Big rigs welcome. Rate in 2010 $24-35 for 4 persons. MC/VISA. Member ARVC, CQ. FCRV discount. FMCA discount. CCUSA 50% Discount. CCUSA reservations Required, CCUSA max stay 7 days, Cash only for CCUSA disc. Discount not available Jul 1-Aug 15. Reservations absolutely required. $14 discounted rate applies only to standard sites. Premium sites /w private decks overlooking ocean are $8 surcharge. Wifi surcharge $3/day. Kennel surcharge $7/day.

CAMPCLUB USA

Phone: (877)530-8383
Address: 1669 Rte 132 Est, Perce, QC G0C 2X0
Lat/Lon: 48.63435/-64.17994
Email: info@gaspecamping.com
Web: www.gaspecamping.com

PERCE—Continued

(W) Du Village—*From west town limits on Hwy 132: Go 1.2 km/3/4 mi E on Hwy 132. Enter on L.* ◆◆FACILITIES: 100 sites, 68 full hkups, (15/30 amps), 32 no hkups, tenting. Pets welcome, breed restrict. Open May 1 - Oct 1. Facilities fully operational Jun 20 - Sep 1. Rate in 2010 $30 for 6 persons. Member CQ. Phone: (418)782-2020.

PLAISANCE—D-3

PARC NATIONAL DE PLAISANCE—*On Hwy 148, follow signs 8 km/5mi.* FACILITIES: 152 sites, 63 W&E, (15/30 amps), 89 no hkups, tenting, dump, laundry, ltd groc. RECREATION: swim pool, lake swim, boating, canoeing, ramp, river fishing, playground. No pets. Open May - midOct. Phone: (819)427-5334.

PLESSISVILLE—H-5

(S) Camping Mon Plaisir (Not Visited)—*From south city limits: Go 2.3 km/1-1/2 mi S on Hwy 165, then 0.8 km/1/2 mi W on Rd. Ste-Sophie. Enter on R.* ◆◆◆FACILITIES: 200 sites, typical site width 39 ft, 138 full hkups, 40 W&E, (15/30 amps), 22 no hkups, tenting, dump, laundry, ltd groc. ◆◆◆RECREATION: swim pool, lake fishing, play equipment. Pets welcome. Open May 11 - Sep 10. Facilities fully operational Jun 20 - Sep 1. Rate in 2010 $34 for 4 persons. Member CQ. Phone: (819)362-7591.

POINTE-AUX-OUTARDES—A-6

Camping Parc de la Rive (Not Visited)—*From jct Hwy 138 & Les Buissons: Go 6.8 km/4-1/4 mi SW on Les Buissons (Rue Principale), then 3.8 km/2-1/4 mi S on de la Baie. Enter at end.* FACILITIES: 195 sites, 174 full hkups, 15 W&E, (15/30 amps), 6 no hkups, tenting, dump, laundry, ltd groc. RECREATION: swim pool, lake swim, play equipment. Pets welcome. Open Jun 1 - Sep 16. Facilities fully operational Jun 20 - Aug 20. Rate in 2010 $24 for 6 persons. Member CQ. Phone: (418) 567-4021.

POINTE-CALUMET—I-2

(W) Camping L'Escale (Not Visited)—*From jct Hwy 640 & Hwy 334: Go 1.2 km/3/4 mi SE on Hwy 344, then 1.2 km/3/4 mi S on Montee De La Baie, then .04 km/1/4 mi W on Andre-Soucy. Enter on R.* ◆◆◆◆FACILITIES: 230 sites, 188 full hkups, 42 W&E, (15/30 amps), 11 pull-thrus, tenting, dump, laundry. ◆◆◆RECREATION: lake swim, lake fishing, playground. Pets welcome. Open Apr 15 - Oct 15. Facilities fully operational Jun 5 - Sep 5. Rate in 2010 $34-40 for 6 persons. Member CQ. Phone: (450)472-6789.

POINTE-LEBEL—A-6

Camping de la Mer (Not Visited)—*From jct Hwy 138 & Pointe Lebel: Go 11.4 km/7 mi NE on Rue Granier, then .8 km/1/2 mi E on Rue Chouinard. Enter on R.* FACILITIES: 174 sites, 124 full hkups, 28 W&E, (15/30 amps), 22 no hkups, tenting, dump, laundry, ltd groc. RECREATION: swim pool, play equipment. Pets welcome. Open May 18 - Oct 8. Facilities fully operational Jun 24 - Aug 20. Rate in 2010 $30 for 6 persons. Member CQ. Phone: (418)589-6576.

PONT-ROUGE—F-5

(E) Un Air d'ete 2005—*From jct Hwy 40 (exit 281) & Hwy 365: Go 4.8 km/3 mi N on Hwy 365, then 6 km/3-3/4 mi E on Hwy 358. Enter on R.* ◆◆◆FACILITIES: 231 sites, 196 full hkups, 25 W&E, (15/30 amps), 10 no hkups, 16 pull-thrus, tenting, dump, laundry, ltd groc. ◆◆◆RECREATION: swim pool, playground. Pets welcome. Open May 1 - Oct 1. Rate in 2010 $28 for 4 persons. Member CQ. Phone: (877) 873-4791.

PORT-CARTIER—D-5

RESERVE FAUNIQUE DE PORT-CARTIER-SEPT-ILES/CAMPING LAC WALKER—(Duplessis) *From Hwy 138 E follow sign for Reserve.* FACILITIES: 50 sites, 9 W&E, 8 E, (15/30 amps), 33 no hkups, tenting, dump. RECREATION: lake swim, boating, canoeing, ramp, lake/river fishing, play equipment. Pets welcome. Open Jun - Sep. Phone: (418)766-4743.

PORT-DANIEL—E-6

RESERVE FAUNIQUE DE/CAMPING PORT-DANIEL—(Gaspesie) *In town, at church: Go 1 km/3/4 mi E on Hwy 132.* FACILITIES: 38 sites, 13 full hkups, 12 E, (15/30 amps), 13 no hkups, tenting, dump, laundry. RECREATION: lake swim, canoeing, ramp, lake fishing, playground. Pets welcome. Partial handicap access. Open Jun - Sep. Phone: (418)396-2789.

PORTNEUF—F-5

(W) Camping Panoramique (Not Visited)—*From Hwy 40 (exit 261): Go 1.6 km/1 mi S on Rue Provencher, then 1 km/3/4 mi W on Hwy 138, then .04 km/1/4 mi N on Francois Gignac. Enter on L.* ◆◆◆FACILITIES: 425 sites, 380 full hkups, 16 W&E, (15/30 amps), 29 no hkups, 46 pull-thrus, tenting, dump, laundry, ltd groc. ◆◆◆RECREATION: swim pool, play equipment. Pets welcome ($). Open May 1 - Oct 1. Facilities fully operational Jun 20 - Sep 1. Rate in 2010 $35 per family. Member CQ. Phone: (418)286-3655.

PORTNEUF—Continued on next page

PORTNEUF—Continued

RIVIERE FAUNIQUE DE PORTNEUF/CAMPING LAC BELLEVUE—(Quebec) *From Hwy 40 (exit 281): Go N on Hwy 365 to Saint-Raymond, then NW on Hwy 367 to Wildlife Reserve.* FACILITIES: 55 sites, 55 no hkups, tenting, dump. RECREATION: lake swim, canoeing, ramp, lake fishing, playground. No pets. Open May - Sep. Phone: (418)323-2021.

POTTON—J-4

(W) Camping Carrefour des Campeurs (Not Visited)—*From N town city limit on Hwy 243: Go 5 km/3 mi S on Hwy 243, then 1.2 km/ 3/4 mi W on Chemin Vallee Missisquoi. Enter on L.* ◆FACILITIES: 125 sites, 70 full hkups, 26 W&E, (15/30 amps), 29 no hkups, tenting, dump, laundry, ltd groc. ◆RECREATION: canoeing, play equipment. Pets welcome ($). Open May 4 - Sep 16. Rate in 2010 $33 for 4 persons. Member CQ. Phone: (450)292-3737.

PRINCEVILLE—H-5

(W) Camping Plage des Sables—*From jct Hwy 263 & Hwy 116: Go 7.2 km/4-1/2 mi W on Hwy 116. Enter on L.* ◆◆FACILITIES: 224 sites, 160 full hkups, 34 W&E, (15/30 amps), 30 no hkups, tenting, dump, laundry, ltd groc. ◆◆◆RECREATION: lake swim, playground. Pets welcome. Partial handicap access. Open May 11 - Sep 9. Rate in 2010 $33 for 4 persons. Member CQ. Phone: (819)364-5769.

QUEBEC CITY—F-6

See listings at L'Ange-Gardien (Beaupre), Levis, Neuville, Quebec City, Saint-Apollinaire, Saint-Nicholas & Valcartier.

QUEBEC CITY AREA MAP

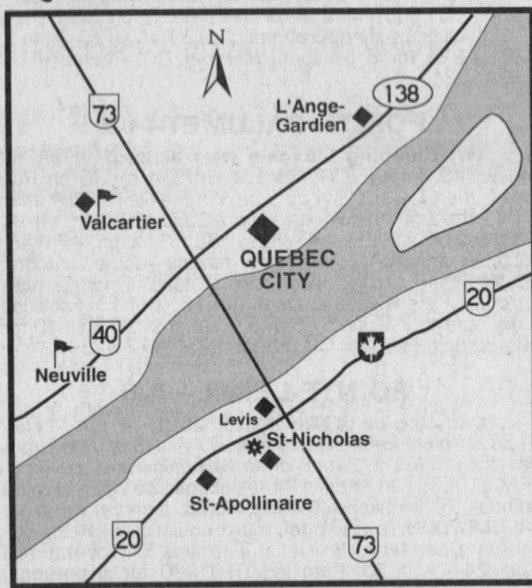

Symbols on map indicate towns within an 80 km/ 50 mi radius of Quebec City where campgrounds (diamonds), attractions (flags), & RV service centers & camping supply outlets (gears) are listed. Check listings for more information.

(N) Camping Aeroport—(Quebec) *From jct Hwy 138 & Route de l'Aeroport (either Hwy Duplessis): Go 4.8 km/3 mi N on Route de l'Aeroport. Enter on L.* ◆◆◆◆FACILITIES: 200 sites, 120 full hkups, 49 W&E, (15/30/50 amps), 50 amps ($), 31 no hkups, 24 pull-thrus, tenting, dump, laundry, ltd groc. ◆◆◆◆RECREATION: swim pool, playground. Pets welcome. Partial handicap access. Open Apr 15 - Oct 31. Facilities fully operational May 1 - Sep 30. Big rigs welcome. Rate in 2010 $36-45 Member CQ. Phone: (800)294-1574.

QUEBEC CITY—Continued

PARC NATIONAL RUSTIQUE DE LA JACQUES-CARTIER SECTEUR DE LA PALLIC—(Quebec) *On Hwy 175 N.* FACILITIES: 158 sites, 82 E, (15/30 amps), 76 no hkups, tenting, dump, ltd groc. RECREATION: river swim, canoeing, ramp, lake/river fishing, playground. No pets. Open May - Sep. Phone: (418)848-3169.

RESERVE FAUNIQUE DES LAURENTIDES-CAMPING LA LOUTRE—(Quebec) *On 175 N.* FACILITIES: 126 sites, 36 full hkups, 11 W&E, (15/30 amps), 79 no hkups, tenting, dump, laundry, ltd groc. RECREATION: lake swim, canoeing, ramp, lake fishing. Pets welcome ($). Open May - Sep. Phone: (418)846-2201.

RACINE—I-4

(E) Camping Plage McKenzie—(Canton-de-l'est) *From jct Hwy 249 & Hwy 222: Go 1.6 km/1 mi W on Hwy 222. Enter on L.* ◆◆◆FACILITIES: 255 sites, 230 full hkups, 25 W&E, (15/30 amps), tenting, dump, laundry, ltd groc. ◆◆◆RECREATION: lake swim, boating, canoeing, ramp, dock, lake fishing, playground. Pets welcome ($). Open May 12 - Sep 19. Rate in 2010 $32-44 per family. Member CQ. Phone: (819)846-2011.

RIGAUD—I-1

(W) Camping Trans-Canadien (Not Visited)—(Monteregie) *From Hwy 40 (exit 9) & Hwy 342: Go 4 km/2-1/2 mi W on Hwy 342. Enter on R.* ◆◆◆FACILITIES: 300 sites, 300 full hkups, (15/30 amps), 6 pull-thrus, tenting, dump, laundry, ltd groc. ◆◆◆RECREATION: swim pool, boating, canoeing, dock, river fishing, playground. Pets welcome. Open all yr. Facilities fully operational May 1 - Nov 1. Rate in 2010 $35 for 6 persons. Member CQ. Phone: (514)867-4515.

RIMOUSKI—B-6

(W) Camping Motel de l'Anse (Not Visited)—*From jct Hwy 20 & Hwy 132 after Bic: Go 8 km E on Hwy 132 E. Enter on R.* ◆◆◆FACILITIES: 114 sites, 72 full hkups, 4 E, (15/30 amps), 50 amps ($), 45 no hkups, WiFi Instant Internet at site, tenting, dump, non-guest dump $, laundry, ice, picnic tables. ◆RECREATION: bsktball, play equipment, horseshoes. Pets welcome, breed restrict, quantity restrict. Open April 15 - Nov 15. Facilities fully operational May 1 - Oct 31. Big rigs welcome. Rate in 2010 $28.95-37.95 for 3 persons. MC/VISA/Debit. Member CQ. CCUSA 50% Discount. CCUSA reservations Recommended, CCUSA max stay 2 days, CCUSA disc. not avail F,Sa, CCUSA disc. not avail holidays. Fully operational May 1-Oct 31. Discount not available Jun 24 thru Labor Day.

CAMPCLUB USA

Phone: (418)721-0322
Address: 1105 Boul St-Germain Ouest (Rte 132), Rimouski, QC G5L 8Y9
Lat/Lon: 48.41736/-68.61277
Email: campingmoteldelanse@hotmail.com
Web: www.guidecamping.ca/anse

RESERVE FAUNIQUE DE RIMOUSKI/CAMPING LAC RIMOUSKI—(Bas St-Laurent) *From jct Hwy 20 & Hwy 232: Go E on Hwy 232.* FACILITIES: 26 sites, 10 full hkups, 4 W&E, (15/30/50 amps), 12 no hkups, tenting, dump, ltd groc. RECREATION: lake swim, canoeing, ramp, lake fishing. No pets. Open May - Sep. Phone: (418)735-5672.

RIVIERE-DU-LOUP—B-5

(C) Camping du Quai—(Bas St-Laurent) *From I-20 (exit 507): Go .05km/1/4 mi N on Boul Cartier, then .07 km/1/2 mi W on Rue de l'Ancrage. Enter on R.* ◆◆◆◆FACILITIES: 150 sites, typical site width 25 ft, 80 full hkups, 46 W&E, 10 E, (15/30/50 amps), 50 amps ($), 14 no hkups, 44 pull-thrus, tenting, dump, laundry, ltd groc. ◆◆◆◆RECREATION: playground. Pets welcome. Partial handicap access. Open May 15 - Oct 15. Big rigs welcome. Rate in 2010 $24-29 for 4 persons. Member CQ. Phone: (418)860-3111.

(N) CAMPING MUNICIPAL DE LA POINTE—(Bas St-Laurent) *At Hwy 20 (exit 507) or Road 185, exit at Fraserville Rd. (Hwy 132).* FACILITIES: 113 sites, 98 full hkups, 15 W&E, (15/30 amps), tenting, dump, laundry, ltd groc. RECREATION: river swim, canoeing, playground. Pets welcome. Open May 21 - Oct 4. Phone: (418)862-4281.

Woodall's Tip... Turn to the Travel Section for "at-a-glance" RV Sales & Service Locations.

RIVIERE-ETERNITE—B-5

PARC NATIONAL DU SAGUENAY, BAIE-ETERNITE—(Saguenay Lac St-Jean) *From Hwy 138 & Hwy 170: Go NE on Hwy 170 to Riviere Eternite.* FACILITIES: 106 sites, 19 W&E, (15 amps), 87 no hkups, tenting, dump, laundry, ltd groc. RECREATION: canoeing, ramp, river fishing, playground. No pets. Open Jun - Sept. Phone: (877)272-1556.

ROXTON FALLS—I-4

(C) Camping De L'Ile—*From jct Hwy 139 & Hwy 241: Go .03 km/1/8 mi N on Hwy 139, then 1 km/3/4 mi E o de la Riviera, then 0.4 km/1/4 mi SE on Chemin Pepin. Enter at end.* ◆◆◆FACILITIES: 156 sites, 91 full hkups, 59 W&E, (15/30/50 amps), 50 amps ($), 6 no hkups, 3 pull-thrus, tenting, dump, laundry, ltd groc. ◆◆◆RECREATION: swim pool, playground. Pets welcome, breed restrict, quantity restrict. Partial handicap access. Open May 2 - Oct 11. Facilities fully operational Jun 15 - Sep 3. Rate in 2010 $29-34 for 6 persons. Member CQ. Phone: (450)548-2495.

SAGUENAY-LA BAIE—B-5

(SW) Camping Au Jardin De Mon Pere—(Saguenay Lac St-Jean) *From jct Hwy 381 & Hwy 170: Go 2.5 km/1-1/2 mi W on Hwy 170, then 1.5 km/1 mi S on Ave du Port, then 150 meters/500 feet SE on Joseph-Gagne, then 1.3 km/1 mi S on St-Louis. Enter on R.* ◆◆◆◆◆FACILITIES: 169 sites, 142 full hkups, 19 W&E, (15/30/50 amps), 50 amps ($), 8 no hkups, 9 pull-thrus, tenting, dump, laundry, ltd groc. ◆◆◆◆◆RECREATION: swim pool, river/pond fishing, playground. Pets welcome, quantity restrict. Partial handicap access. Open May 18 - Sep 16. Facilities fully operational Jun 10 - Sep 5. Rate in 2010 $22-34 for 4 persons. Member CQ. Phone: (877)544-6486.

SAINT BONIFACE—G-3

Camping Saint Boniface (Not Visited)—*From jct Hwy 153 & Hwy 55 (exit 211): Go W 1 km on Hwy 153. Enter on R.* ◆◆FACILITIES: 30 sites, 40 ft max RV length, 28 full hkups, 2 W&E, (30 amps), family camping, tenting, dump, laundry. ◆◆◆RECREATION: swim pool. Pets welcome. Partial handicap access. Open May 1 - Oct 12. Rate in 2010 $26-31 for 4 persons. Phone: (877)535-7047.

SAINT-AIME-DES-LACS—C-5

PARC NATIONAL HAUTES-GORGES-DE-LA-RIVIERE-MALBAIE—(Charlevoix) *Hwy 138 & 172.* FACILITIES: 103 sites, 103 no hkups, tenting, dump, ltd groc. RECREATION: river swim, canoeing, ramp, river fishing. No pets. Partial handicap access. Open May - Sep. Phone: (418)439-1227.

SAINT-ALEXANDRE—B-5

(NE) Camping le Rayon de Soleil—*From Hwy 20 (exit 488): Go 230 meters/760 feet S, then 1.6 km/1 mi W on Rang St-Edouard Quest. Enter on L.* ◆◆◆FACILITIES: 120 sites, 46 full hkups, 27 W&E, 4 E, (15/30/50 amps), 50 amps ($), 43 no hkups, 84 pull-thrus, family camping, tenting, dump, laundry, ltd groc. ◆◆◆RECREATION: swim pool, playground. Pets welcome. Open May 14 - Oct 7. Rate in 2010 $25-29 per family. Member CQ.

Phone: (418)495-2677
Address: 571 Rang St-Edouard Ouest, Saint-Alexandre de Kamouraska, QC G0L 2G0
Lat/Lon: 47.69849/-69.66077
Email: campinglerayondesoleil@bellnet.ca
Web: www.campinglerayondesoleil.com

SAINT-ALEXIS-DES-MONTS—G-3

RESERVE FAUNIQUE MASTIGOUCHE/LAC SAINT-BERNARD—(Mauricie Bois-Francs) *From jct Hwy 40 & Hwy 348: Go N on Hwy 348 to Saint-Alexis-des-Monts.* FACILITIES: 95 sites, 95 no hkups, tenting, dump, laundry, ltd groc. RECREATION: lake swim, boating, canoeing, ramp, lake fishing, play equipment. No pets. Open Jun - Sep. Phone: (819)265-6055.

SAINT-ANDRE-AVELLIN—D-3

(NW) Camping au Petit Lac Simon (Not Visited)—*From north city limits: Go 8.8 km/5-1/2 mi N on Hwy 321. Enter on L.* ◆◆FACILITIES: 266 sites, 190 full hkups, 58 W&E, (15/30 amps), 18 no hkups, tenting, dump, laundry. ◆◆RECREATION: 2 swim pools, canoeing, lake fishing, play equipment. Pets welcome. Open May 1 - Oct 15. Facilities fully operational Jun 15 - Sep 3. Rate in 2010 $35 for 4 persons. Member CQ. Phone: (819)983-6584.

(C) Camping Saint-Andre-Avellin (Not Visited)—*From jct Hwy 148 & Hwy 321: Go 13.2 km/8-1/4 mi N on Hwy 321, then .04 km/1/4 mi E on Du Moulin (Duquette). Enter on L.* ◆◆◆FACILITIES: 169 sites, 148 full hkups, (15/30 amps), 21 no hkups, 1 pull-thrus, tenting, dump, laundry, ltd groc. ◆◆◆◆RECREATION: swim pool, boating, 9 hp limit, canoeing, dock, river fishing, playground. Pets welcome. Open May 9 - Oct 7. Facilities fully operational Jun 23 - Sep 1. Rate in 2010 $34.16 for 4 persons. Member CQ. Phone: (819) 983-3777.

Woodall's Tip... For details on how to read the listings, turn to the "How to Use" pages in the front of the Directory.

SAINT-ANICET—J-1

(W) Camping Le Dauphin (Not Visited)—*From west town limits: Go 3.2 km/2 mi W on Hwy 132. Enter on R.* ◇◇◇FACILITIES: 116 sites, 67 full hkups, 10 W&E, (15/30 amps), 39 no hkups, tenting, dump, laundry, ltd groc. ◇◇◇RECREATION: swim pool, playground. Pets welcome. Open May 1 - Oct 31. Facilities fully operational Jun 15 - Sep 5. Rate in 2010 $25-30 for 2 persons. Member CQ. Phone: (450)264-4310.

SAINT-ANTOINE-ABBE—J-2

(NW) Camping Lac Des Pins—(Monteregie) *From jct Hwy 202 & Hwy 201: Go 4.8 km/3 mi NW on Hwy 201. Enter on R.* ◇◇◇◇FACILITIES: 1116 sites, 1076 full hkups, 40 W&E, (15/30 amps), tenting, dump, laundry, full svc store. ◇◇◇◇◇RECREATION: 2 swim pools, lake swim, play equipment. Pets welcome. Open May 15 - Oct 1. Rate in 2010 $33 per family. Member CQ. Phone: (450)827-2353.

SAINT-ANTONIN—B-5

(C) Camping Chez Jean (Not Visited)—*From West on I-20 (exit 499) & Hwy 85: Go 12 km/9 mi S on Hwy 85, then at Hwy 185 (exit 89), then 4 km/2-1/2 mi W on rue Principale. Enter on R.* ◇◇◇FACILITIES: 185 sites, 158 full hkups, 27 W&E, (15/30 amps), 66 pull-thrus, tenting, dump, laundry. ◇◇◇RECREATION: swim pool, playground. Pets welcome. Partial handicap access. Open May 1 - Oct 1. Facilities fully operational Jun 15 - Sep 5. Rate in 2010 $28 for 4 persons. Member CQ. Phone: (418)862-3081.

(NW) CAMPING LIDO—*From W on I-20 & Hwy 185 (exit 499): Go 17 km/10-1/2 mi S on Hwy 185, then 1 km/3/4 mi N on Chemin Riviere-Verte. Enter on L.*

WELCOME

◇◇◇◇FACILITIES: 156 sites, 152 full hkups, 4 W&E, (15/30/50 amps), 50 amps ($), many extd stay sites, 10 pull-thrus, WiFi Instant Internet at site, phone on-site Internet (needs activ), tenting, shower$, dump, non-guest dump $, laundry, ltd groc, LP gas by weight, ice, picnic tables, fire rings, wood.

◇◇◇◇RECREATION: rec hall, pavilion, coin games, swim pool, spray ground, mini-golf, ($), golf nearby, bsktball, playground, shuffleboard court shuffleboard court, activities (wkends), horseshoes, v-ball. Rec open to public.

Pets welcome. Open May 1 - Oct 15. Facilities fully operational May 15 - Sep 15. Escort to site. Clubs welcome. Rate in 2010 $29.68 per family. MC/VISA/Debit. Member CQ.

Phone: (866)493-6933
Address: 928 Chemin Riviere-Verte,
Saint Antonin, QC G0L 2J0
Lat/Lon: 47.76827/-69.43830
Email: info@camping-lido.net
Web: www.camping-lido.net

SEE AD RIVIERE-DU-LOUP PAGE 910

SAINT-APOLLINAIRE—G-5

(E) Camping Domaine de la Chute (Not Visited)—(Chaudiere-Appalaches) *From I-20 (exit 296) & Rte du Cap: Go 1 km/1/2 mi S on Rt du Cap, then 2.2 km/1-1/2 mi E on Chemin de la Chute. Enter at end.* ◇◇◇◇FACILITIES: 600 sites, typical site width 40 ft, 550 full hkups, 50 W&E, (15/30/50 amps), 50 amps ($), 16 pull-thrus, dump, laundry, groceries. ◇◇◇◇◇RECREATION: swim pool, lake swim, no motors, canoeing, pond fishing, playground. Pets welcome. Partial handicap access. No tents. Open May 1 - Oct 30. Facilities fully operational May 15 - Sep 30. Big rigs welcome. Rate in 2010 $35 for 4 persons. Member CQ. Phone: (418)831-1311.

SAINT-AUGUSTIN-DE-DESMAURES—F-6

(E) Camping Canadien & Americain (Not Visited)—*From Hwy 40 (exit 298W) & Hwy 138: Go 1.2 km/3/4 mi W on Hwy 138. Enter on L.* ◇FACILITIES: 50 sites, 50 full hkups, (15/30 amps), tenting, dump, laundry. ◇RECREATION: play equipment. Pets welcome, breed restrict. Open May 1 - Oct 2. Facilities fully operational Jun 1 - Oct 10. Rate in 2010 $26 for 4 persons. Member CQ. Phone: (418)878-4254.

(E) Camping Juneau—*From jct Hwy 40 (exit 300) & Chemin du Lac: Go 1 km/3/4 mi W on Chemin du Lac. Enter on L.* ◇◇◇◇FACILITIES: 125 sites, 71 full hkups, 14 W&E, 36 E, (15/30/50 amps), 50 amps ($), 4 no hkups, 4 pull-thrus, tenting, dump, laundry, ltd groc. ◇◇◇◇RECREATION: boating, canoeing, ramp, dock, lake fishing, play equipment. Pets welcome. Partial handicap access. Open Apr 25 - Oct 31. Facilities fully operational Jun 1 - Sep 30. Big rigs welcome. Rate in 2010 $31.01 for 2 persons. Member CQ. Phone: (418)871-9090.

Quebec Provincial Flower: The Blue Flag is an indigenous spring flower that grows on over half of Quebec's territory, from St. Lawrence Valley to the shores of James Bay.

SAINT-BARTHELEMY—H-3

(NE) CAMPING DU VIEUX MOULIN—(Lanaudiere) *From Hwy 40 & Saint-Barthelemy (exit 155): Go 4.4 km/2-3/4 mi N on Mte. St-Laurent, then 30 meters/50 ft E on York, then 3.4 km/2-1/4 mi N on Montee des Laurentides, then 2 km/1-1/4 mi E on Rang St-Joachim. Enter at end.*

WELCOME

◇◇◇◇FACILITIES: 400 sites, 363 full hkups, 37 W&E, (15/30 amps), mostly extd stay sites, tenting, RV storage, shower$, dump, non-guest dump $, laundry, ltd groc, ice, picnic tables, fire rings, wood, controlled access.

◇◇◇◇RECREATION: rec hall, equipped pavilion, swim pool, boating, no motors, canoeing, kayaking, 3 kayak rentals, lake fishing, golf nearby, bsktball, playground, activities, (wkends), tennis, horseshoes, sports field, v-ball. Rec open to public.

Pets welcome ($). Partial handicap access. Open May 15 - Sep 30. Facilities fully operational Jun 15 - Labor Day. Clubs welcome. Rate in 2010 $31.01 for 4 persons. MC/VISA/AMEX/Debit. Member CQ.

Phone: (450)885-3591
Address: 2780 Rue Buteau,
Saint-Barthelemy, QC J0K 1X0
Lat/Lon: 46.22400/-73.13788
Email: ginetbut@yahoo.com
Web: www.campingduvieuxmoulin.com

SEE AD MONTREAL PAGE 908

SAINT-BERNARD-DE-LACOLLE—J-3

(C) Camping Premier RV Park—(Monteregie) *Just at NY State (US I-87) & Canadian (I-15) border: Go to exit 1 on I-15. Enter on L.* ◇◇◇FACILITIES: 90 sites, 50 full hkups, 40 W&E, (15/30/50 amps), 10 pull-thrus, tenting, laundry. ◇RECREATION: swim pool. Pets welcome. Open May 30 - Sep 30. Big rigs welcome. Rate in 2010 $30-35 for 4 persons. Phone: (450)246-4000.

(SW) Cool Breeze Camping (Not Visited)—(Monteregie) *From jct Hwy 15 (exit 1) & Montee Glass: Go 1.2 km/ 3/4 mi on Montee Glass. Enter on R.* ◇◇◇FACILITIES: 110 sites, 70 full hkups, 40 W&E, (15/30 amps), tenting, dump, laundry, ltd groc. ◇◇◇RECREATION: playground. Pets welcome. Open Mar 1 - Sep 30. Rate in 2010 $28-35 for 2 persons. Phone: (450)246-3785.

SAINT-CHARLES-BORROMEE—H-3

(NW) Camping de la Rive (Not Visited)—*From jct Hwy 158 & end Hwy 31: Go 2 km/1-1/4 mi N on Boul Dollard, then 1.7 km/1 mi N on rue St-Charles-Borromee, then 2.5 km/1-1/2 mi NW on rue de la Visitation, then 152 meters/500 feet E on Sansregret. Enter on R.* ◇◇◇FACILITIES: 91 sites, 81 full hkups, 10 W&E, (15/30/50 amps), 50 amps ($), tenting, dump, laundry. ◇◇RECREATION: swim pool, river swim, river fishing, play equipment. Pets welcome, breed restrict. Partial handicap access. Open Apr 15 - Oct 30. Rate in 2010 $33-36 for 4 persons. Member CQ. Phone: (450) 755-6555.

SAINT-CHARLES-SUR-RICHELIEU—I-3

(NE) Camping Domaine Madalie (Not Visited)—*From I-20 (exit 115): Go 10 km/6-1/4 mi N on Rang 3. Enter on R.* ◇◇◇FACILITIES: 150 sites, 130 full hkups, 10 W&E, (15/30/50 amps), 10 no hkups, phone Internet central location, tenting, shower$, dump, non-guest dump $, laundry, ltd groc, ice, picnic tables, fire rings, wood. ◇◇◇RECREATION: lake swim, boating, electric motors only, canoeing, kayaking, lake fishing, bsktball, 3 bike rentals, play equipment, activities horseshoes, v-ball. Pets welcome ($), breed restrict, quantity restrict. Open May 1 - Oct 15. Rate in 2010 $36 for 4 persons. VISA/Debit. Member CQ. CCUSA 50% Discount. CCUSA reservations Recommended, CCUSA max stay 4 days, Cash only for CCUSA disc., CCUSA disc. not avail S, CCUSA disc. not avail F,Sa. Not available Jun 15-Aug 15.

CAMPCLUB USA

Phone: (450)584-2444
Address: 512 3 Rang N.,
Saint-Charles-Sur-Richelieu, QC J0H 2G0
Lat/Lon: 45.67881/-73.14571
Email: info@domaine-madalie.com
Web: www.domaine-madalie.com

SAINT-COME—G-2

(N) Camping Fort Apache—*From jct Hwy 343 & Hwy 347: Go 5.5 km/3-1/2 mi N on Hwy 347. Enter on R.* ◇◇FACILITIES: 128 sites, 42 full hkups, 48 W&E, (15/30 amps), 38 no hkups, 12 pull-thrus, tenting, dump, laundry, ltd groc. ◇◇◇RECREATION: swim pool, river fishing, playground. Pets welcome ($). Partial handicap access. Open all yr. Facilities fully operational May 15 - Sep 30. Rate in 2010 $28 for 4 persons. Member CQ. Phone: (450)883-1968.

Say you saw it in Woodall's!

SAINT-COME—Continued

PARC NATIONAL DU MONT-TREMBLANT/CAMPING SECTEUR DE L'ASSOMPTION—(Laurentides) *From Hwy 117-125-329 or 343.* FACILITIES: 88 sites, 88 no hkups, tenting, dump, ltd groc. RECREATION: lake swim, canoeing, lake fishing. No pets. Partial handicap access. Open May - Oct. Phone: (877) 688-2281.

SAINT-DAMASE—B-6

(N) Base Plein Air Saint-Damase—*From jct Hwy 132 & Hwy 297: Go 10.3 km/6-1/4 mi S on Hwy 297. Enter on L.* ◇◇◇FACILITIES: 159 sites, 80 full hkups, 30 W&E, (15/30 amps), 49 no hkups, tenting, dump, laundry. ◇◇◇RECREATION: lake swim, boating, no motors, canoeing, lake fishing, play equipment. Pets welcome, breed restrict. Partial handicap access. Open all yr. Facilities fully operational May 15 - Sep 15. Rate in 2010 $28 for 4 persons. Member CQ. Phone: (418) 776-2828.

SAINT-DAVID-DE-FALARDEAU—B-5

Municipal L'Oasis (Not Visited)—*From jct Blvd St-David & Blvd Desgagme: Go 1.4 km/1 mi N on Blvd Desgagme, then 152 meters/500 feet SE on Lac Clair. Enter on L.* ◇FACILITIES: 60 sites, 20 full hkups, 34 W&E, (15/30 amps), 6 no hkups, tenting, laundry. ◇RECREATION: lake swim, boating, 50 hp limit, canoeing, lake fishing, play equipment. Pets welcome, breed restrict. Open Jun 1 - Sep 3. Rate in 2010 $26 for 6 persons. Phone: (418)673-3066.

SAINT-DONAT—G-1

PARC NATIONAL DU MONT-TREMBLANT/CAMPING SECTEUR DE LA PIMBINA—(Laurentides) *From Hwy 117-125-329 or 343.* FACILITIES: 284 sites, 284 no hkups, tenting, dump, laundry, ltd groc. RECREATION: lake swim, canoeing, ramp, lake fishing, playground. No pets. Open May - Oct. Phone: (877)688-2281.

SAINT-EDOUARD-DE-MASKINONGE—G-3

(NW) Camping du Zoo de Saint-Edouard—(Mauricie Bois-Francs) *From jct I-40 (exit 166-Louiseville) & Hwy 348: Go 19km/12 mi W on Hwy 348. Enter on L.* ◇◇◇FACILITIES: 315 sites, 265 full hkups, 25 W&E, (15/30/50 amps), 25 no hkups, 25 pull-thrus, tenting, dump, laundry. ◇◇◇RECREATION: swim pool, lake swim, lake/pond fishing, playground. Pets welcome, breed restrict. Partial handicap access. Open May 11 - Sep 16. Facilities fully operational Jun 24 - Sep 5. Rate in 2010 $35 for 4 persons. Member CQ. Phone: (819)268-2422.

SAINT-ELIE-DE-CAXTON—G-3

(NW) Floribell (Not Visited)—*From church in town: Go 1.6 km/1 mi NE on Hwy 351, then 1.6 km/1 mi S on St Boniface Rd, then 1.2 km/3/4 mi E on Rang 7 (Lac Bell). Enter at end.* ◇◇◇FACILITIES: 136 sites, 120 full hkups, 12 W&E, (15/30 amps), 4 no hkups, tenting, dump, laundry, ltd groc. ◇◇◇RECREATION: lake swim, boating, no motors, canoeing, playground. Pets welcome, breed restrict. Partial handicap access. Open May 5 - Sep 23. Facilities fully operational Jun 20 - Aug 20. Rate in 2010 $37 for 4 persons. Member CQ. Phone: (819)221-5731.

SAINT-ETIENNE DES GRES—G-4

(S) Camping du Lac Blais (Not Visited)—*From Hwy I-55 (exit 202) & Rue Principale: Go 3.2 km/2 mi NW on Rue Principale. Enter on L.* ◇FACILITIES: 200 sites, 29 ft max RV length, 100 full hkups, 67 W&E, (15/30 amps), 33 no hkups, tenting, dump, laundry. ◇RECREATION: swim pool, playground. Pets welcome, breed restrict. Open May 15 - Sep 15. Facilities fully operational Jun 24 - Sep 5. Rate in 2010 $30 for 4 persons. Member CQ. Phone: (819)535-2783.

SAINT-ETIENNE-DE-BOLTON—J-4

(NW) Domaine des Cantons—*From Hwy I-10 (exit 100): Go 30 meters/100 ft N on Ch. du Grand Bois, then .05 km/1/4 mi E on Hwy 112. Enter on L.* ◇◇◇◇FACILITIES: 137 sites, 137 full hkups, (15/30 amps), dump, laundry. ◇◇◇RECREATION: swim pool. Pets welcome. Partial handicap access. No tents. Age restrict may apply. Open May 1 - Oct 31. Rate in 2010 $36 for 2 persons. Member CQ. Phone: (450)297-2444.

(NW) Domaine du Lac Libby—*From Hwy 10 & exit 100: Go S .5 km on Grand Boies, then E 4.0 km on Rang #1. Enter on R.* ◇◇◇FACILITIES: 300 sites, 196 full hkups, 92 W&E, (15/30 amps), 12 no hkups, tenting, dump, laundry, ltd groc. ◇◇◇◇RECREATION: lake/boating, electric motors only, canoeing, lake fishing, playground. Pets welcome, quantity restrict. Open May 12 - Sep 10. Facilities fully operational Jun 24 - Aug 24. Rate in 2010 $35.50-38.50 for 4 persons. Member CQ.

Phone: (450)297-2221
Address: 426 Rang 1, Saint-Etienne-de-Bolton, QC J0E 2E0
Lat/Lon: 45.28113/-72.36406
Email: libby@campinglaclibby.com
Web: www.campinglaclibby.com

SAINT-FAUSTIN-LAC-CARRE—H-1

(W) Domaine Desjardins—*From jct Hwy 117 & Boul St Faustin (Parc Mt Tremblant exit): Go 0.8 km/1/2 mi NE on Boul St Faustin, then 152 m/300 feet N on Chemin De La Pisciculture, then 152 m/300 feet E on Chemin Desjardins. Enter on R.* ◆◆◆FACILITIES: 100 sites, 30 ft max RV length, 65 full hkups, 20 W&E, (15/30 amps), 15 no hkups, tenting, dump, laundry. ◆◆RECREATION: lake swim, lake fishing, play equipment. Pets welcome ($). Open May 15 - Sep 3. Facilities fully operational Jun 20 - Sep 5. Rate in 2010 $31 for 4 persons. Member CQ. Phone: (819)688-2179.

SAINT-FELICIEN—B-4

CAMPING MUNICIPAL ST-FELICIEN—*From jct Hwy 169 & Hwy 167: Go .5 km/1/4 mi N on Hwy 167 (Boul St-Felicien), then 5.5 km/3-1/2 mi NW on du Jardin. Enter on R.* FACILITIES: 283 sites, 156 full hkups, 94 W&E, (30 amps), 33 no hkups, tenting, dump, laundry, ltd groc. RECREATION: swim pool, playground. No pets. Partial handicap access. Open Jun 4 - Sep 6. Member ARVC, CQ. Phone: (418)679-1719.

SAINT-FELIX-DE-KINGSEY—H-4

(SW) Camping Parc Central (Not Visited)—*From jct Hwy 243 & Hwy 255: Go 2 km/1-1/4 mi N on Hwy 255, then 1.6 km/1 mi NW on Chemin de la Chapelle, then 30 meters/100 feet S on Chemin des Domaines. Enter on L.* ◆◆◆FACILITIES: 140 sites, 123 full hkups, 17 W&E, (15/30 amps), tenting, dump, laundry. ◆◆◆RECREATION: swim pool, play equipment. Pets welcome. Open May 14 - Sep 18. Facilities fully operational Jun 24 - Labor Day. Rate in 2010 $34-36 for 4 persons. Member CQ. Phone: (819)848-2564.

SAINT-FELIX-DE-VALOIS—H-3

(NE) Camping Aux Bouleaux Argentes—*From jct Hwy 348 & Hwy 131: Go 3.6 km/2-1/4 mi N on Hwy 131, then 3.2 km/2 mi E on Rang St Leon Est. Enter on R.* ◆◆◆FACILITIES: 214 sites, 149 full hkups, 45 W&E, (15/30 amps), 20 no hkups, 10 pull-thrus, tenting, dump, laundry, ltd groc. ◆◆◆RECREATION: swim pool, play equipment. Pets welcome ($), breed restrict. Open May 11 - Sep 16. Facilities fully operational Jun 24 - Aug 15. Rate in 2010 $34 for 6 persons. Member CQ. Phone: (450)889-5809.

(NW) Camping Globe Trotter—*From jct Hwy 348 & Hwy 131: Go 2.4 km/1 1/2 mi N on Hwy 131, then 3.5 km/2 1/4 mi E on Rang Des Forges, then .04 km/1/4 mi N on Chewin Brandon. Enter on L.* ◆◆◆FACILITIES: 200 sites, 84 full hkups, 116 W&E, (15/30/50 amps), 8 pull-thrus, tenting, dump, laundry, ltd groc. ◆◆◆RECREATION: lake swim, boating, ramp, lake fishing, playground. Pets welcome ($). Partial handicap access. Open May 15 - Sep 16. Facilities fully operational Jun 1 - Sep 1. Rate in 2010 $29 for 4 persons. Member CQ. Phone: (450)889-5832.

SAINT-FULGENCE—B-5

PARC NATIONAL DES MONTS-VALIN—(Saguenay Lac St-Jean) *On Hwy 172 follow Parc des Monts-Valin.* FACILITIES: 10 sites, 10 no hkups, tenting. RECREATION: river swim, canoeing, lake/river fishing. No pets. Open Jun - Sep. Phone: (418)674-1200.

SAINT-GEDEON—D-5

Camping 2 Rivieres (Not Visited)—*From jct Hwy-269 & 204: Go 15 mi W on Hwy-204.* FACILITIES: 96 sites, 48 full hkups, 36 W&E, 12 no hkups, 6 pull-thrus, tenting, dump, laundry, ltd groc. RECREATION: swim pool, river fishing, playground. Open May 15 - Sep 15. Facilities fully operational Jun 14 - Sep 1. Rate in 2010 $20-26 for 4 persons. Phone: (418)582-3278.

SAINT-GEORGES-DE-MALBAIE—E-6

AUBERGE FORT - PREVEL—(Gaspesie) *Hwy 132 E.* FACILITIES: 28 sites, 28 W&E, (15/30 amps), tenting, dump, laundry. RECREATION: swim pool. No pets. Open Jun - Sep. Phone: (418)368-2281.

(E) Camping Cap Rouge (Not Visited)—*From west town limits on Hwy 132: Go 2 km/1-1/4 mi E on Hwy 132. Enter on L.* ◆◆FACILITIES: 85 sites, 28 ft max RV length, 60 full hkups, 20 W&E, (15 amps), 5 no hkups, tenting, dump, laundry. ◆RECREATION: play equipment. Pets welcome, breed restrict. Open May 30 - Sep 30. Facilities fully operational Jun 20 - Sep 20. Rate in 2010 $27 for 4 persons. Phone: (418)645-3804.

SAINT-HENRI-DE-TAILLON—B-4

(SE) Camping Belley (Not visited)—*From north town limits: Go 3.2 km/2 mi S on Hwy 169, then 2.2 km/1-1/4 mi W on Chemin Wilson, then 1 km/3/4 mi NW on Chemin Belley. Enter at end.* ◆◆◆FACILITIES: 285 sites, 165 full hkups, 69 W&E, (15/30/50 amps), 51 no hkups, 23 pull-thrus, tenting, dump, laundry. ◆◆RECREATION: lake swim, boating, canoeing, lake fishing, playground. Pets welcome, breed restrict. Partial handicap access. Open May 25 - Oct 14. Rate in 2010 $43 for 6 persons. Member CQ. Phone: (418) 347-3612.

PARC NATIONAL DE LA POINTE-TAILLON—(Saguenay Lac St-Jean) *From Hwy 169.* FACILITIES: 75 sites, 75 no hkups, tenting, ltd groc. RECREATION: lake swim, canoeing, lake/river fishing, playground. No pets. Open June - Sept. Phone: (418)347-5371.

SAINT-HIPPOLYTE—H-2

(NW) Camping L'Iris (Not Visited)—*From jct church in town & Chemin Lac Pin Rouge: Go 4.4 km/2-3/4 mi NW on Chemin Lac Pin Rouge. Enter on R.* ◆◆FACILITIES: 96 sites, 28 ft max RV length, 55 full hkups, 23 W&E, (15/30/50 amps), 18 no hkups, tenting, dump, laundry, ltd groc. ◆◆RECREATION: swim pool, lake swim, no motors, canoeing, lake fishing, play equipment. Pets welcome ($). Open May 15 - Sep 15. Rate in 2010 $26-36 for 5 persons. Member CQ. Phone: (450)563-4000.

SAINT-HONORE—B-5

(E) Camping Lac Joly (Not Visited)—*From church in town: Go 1 km/3/4 mi NE on Boul. Martel, then 5 km/3 mi E on Chemin du Cap, then .04 km/1/4 mi S on gravel road. Enter at end.* FACILITIES: 230 sites, 215 full hkups, (15 amps), 15 no hkups, tenting, dump, laundry, ltd groc. RECREATION: swim pool, no motors, canoeing, playground. Pets welcome, breed restrict. Open May 20 - Sep 5. Facilities fully operational Jun 20 - Aug 20. Rate in 2010 $23 per family. Phone: (418)673-4777.

SAINT-HYACINTHE—I-3

(E) Camping Belle Rose—*From jct Hwy I-20 (exit 141) & Hwy 116: Go 3.6 km/2-1/4 mi W on Hwy 116, then 1.6 km/1 mi N on 4e Rang. Enter on L.* ◆◆◆FACILITIES: 138 sites, 119 full hkups, 19 W&E, (15/30 amps), tenting, dump, laundry, ltd groc. ◆◆◆RECREATION: swim pool, playground. Pets welcome. Partial handicap access. Open Apr 20 - Oct 30. Rate in 2010 $22-32 per family. Member CQ. Phone: (450)799-5169.

SAINT-JEAN-BAPTISTE-DE-ROUVILLE—I-3

(SW) Camping Auclair—(Monteregie) *From jct Hwy 229 & rue Rouville: Go 1.2 km/3/4 mi N on rue Rouville, then 1.2 km/3/4 mi W on Rang Des Etangs. Enter on R.* ◆◆FACILITIES: 172 sites, 172 full hkups, (15/30 amps), tenting, dump, laundry, ltd groc. ◆◆RECREATION: swim pool, play equipment. Pets welcome. Open May 1 - Sep 30. Facilities fully operational Jun 20 - Sep 1. Rate in 2010 $28-35 for 2 persons. Member CQ. Phone: (450)467-1898.

(NW) Domaine de Rouville (Not Visited)—*From jct Hwy 229 & rue Rouville: Go .08 km/1/2 mi N on rue Rouville. Enter on L.* ◆◆◆FACILITIES: 1869 sites, 1756 full hkups, 50 W&E, 63 E, (15/30 amps), tenting, dump, laundry, full svc store. ◆◆◆◆RECREATION: swim pool, lake swim, playground. Pets welcome. Partial handicap access. Open May 18 - Oct 1. Facilities fully operational Jun 10 - Sep 5. Rate in 2010 $49 for 6 persons. Member CQ. Phone: (450)467-6867.

SAINT-JEAN-PORT-JOLI—C-5

(C) Camping Au Bonnet Rouge—*From jct Hwy 20 (exit 414) & Hwy 204: Go 3.6 km/2-1/4 mi N on Hwy 204, then 0.4 km/1/4 mi E on Hwy 132. Enter on R.* ◆◆FACILITIES: 47 sites, 16 full hkups, 31 W&E, (15/30 amps), 2 pull-thrus, tenting, dump, laundry. ◆RECREATION: swim pool. Pets welcome, breed restrict. Open May 1 - Oct 31. Facilities fully operational Jun 20 - Sep 5. Rate in 2010 $27 for 4 persons. Member CQ. Phone: (418)598-3088.

(E) Camping de La Demi-Lieue—(Chaudiere-Appalaches) *From jct Hwy 20 (exit 414) & Hwy 204: Go 3.6 km/2-1/4 mi NE on Hwy 204, then 4 km/2-1/2 mi E on Hwy 132. Enter on L.* ◆◆◆◆FACILITIES: 359 sites, 247 full hkups, 92 W&E, (15/30 amps), 20 no hkups, 39 pull-thrus, tenting, dump, laundry, groceries. ◆◆◆◆◆RECREATION: swim pool, play equipment. Pets welcome. Partial handicap access. Open May 8 - Sep 26. Rate in 2010 $23-40 for 4 persons. Member CQ. Phone: (418)598-6108.

SAINT-JEAN-SUR-LE-RICHELIEU—J-3

(SW) Camping Les Cedres—*From jct Hwy 223 & Hwy 219: Go 5.6 km/3-1/2 mi SW on Hwy 219. Enter on R.* ◆◆◆◆FACILITIES: 600 sites, 542 full hkups, 8 W&E, (15/30/50 amps), 50 amps ($), 50 no hkups, tenting, dump, laundry, groceries. ◆◆◆◆RECREATION: 2 swim pools, lake/playground. No pets. Partial handicap access. Open May 1 - Sep 30. Rate in 2010 $36-40 per family. Member CQ.

Phone: (450)346-9276
Address: 658 Route 219,
Saint-Jean-Sur-le-Richelieu, QC J2Y 1C4
Lat/Lon: 45.29411/-73.33057
Email: info@campinglescedres.com
Web: www.campinglescedres.com

SAINT-JEROME—H-2

(W) Camping Lac Lafontaine—(Laurentides) *N'bnd from I-15 (exit 41): Go .03 km/1/4 mi SW on John F. Kennedy, then .03 km/1/4 mi S on Daniel Johnson, then .02 km/200 yds W on boul. du Grand Heron. Enter on R.* ◆◆◆◆FACILITIES: 360 sites, 252 full hkups, 69 W&E, (15/30/50 amps), 50 amps ($), 39 no hkups, 29 pull-thrus, tenting, dump, laundry, groceries.

SAINT-JEROME—Continued
Camping Lac Lafontaine—Continued

◆◆◆◆◆RECREATION: lake swim, playground. Pets welcome ($), breed restrict, quantity restrict. Partial handicap access. Open all yr. Facilities fully operational Apr 15 - Nov 15. Rate in 2010 $28-32 for 4 persons. Member CQ. Phone: (450)431-7373.

SAINT-LAZARE—I-1

(C) Camping Lac des Cedres (Not Visited)—(Monteregie) *From Hwy 20 (exit 26) & Hwy 338: Go 5 km/3 mi N on Hwy 338, then 3.2 km/2 mi W on chemin Ste-Angelique, then 0.4 km/1/4 mi N on Denis. Enter at end.* ◆◆◆FACILITIES: 405 sites, 380 full hkups, (15/30/50 amps), 50 amps ($), 25 no hkups, 8 pull-thrus, tenting, dump, laundry, ltd groc. ◆◆◆RECREATION: swim pool, lake swim, playground. Pets welcome ($), quantity restrict. Partial handicap access. Open Apr 15 - Oct 30. Facilities fully operational Jun 20 - Oct 15. Big rigs welcome. Rate in 2010 $40 for 4 persons. Member CQ. Phone: (450)455-2131.

SAINT-LOUIS-DE-BLANDFORD—G-5

(N) Domain du Lac Louise (Not visited)—(Centre-du-Quebec) *From Hwy I-20 (exit 235) & Hwy 263: Go 1.6 km/1 mi N on Hwy 263, then 1.2 km/3/4 mi E on dirt road. Enter on R.* ◆◆◆FACILITIES: 285 sites, 273 full hkups, 12 W&E, (15/30 amps), 30 pull-thrus, tenting, dump, laundry, ltd groc. ◆◆◆RECREATION: swim pool, lake swim, playground. Pets welcome. Open May 5 - Oct 15. Facilities fully operational Jun 20 - Sep 3. Rate in 2010 $33 for 4 persons. Member CQ. Phone: (819)364-7002.

SAINT-MATHIEU-DE-BELOEIL—I-3

(N) CAMPING ALOUETTE INC—(Monteregie) *From Hwy I-20 (exit 105): Go 1.6 km/1 mi NE on service road (ch.de l'Industrie). Enter on L.*

WELCOME

◆◆◆◆◆FACILITIES: 400 sites, 344 full hkups, 33 W&E, (15/30/50 amps), 50 amps ($), 23 no hkups, some extd stay sites, 150 pull-thrus, WiFi Instant Internet at site ($), phone Internet central location, tenting, RV storage, shower$, dump, non-guest dump $, laundry, groceries, RV supplies, LP gas by weight/by meter, ice, picnic tables, fire rings, wood, controlled access.

◆◆◆◆◆RECREATION: rec hall, rec room/area, swim pool, golf nearby, bsktball, playground, shuffleboard court shuffleboard court, activities, horseshoes, sports field, hiking trails, v-ball, local tours. Rec open to public.

Pets welcome ($). Partial handicap access. Open all yr. Facilities fully operational Apr 15 - Oct 15. Big rigs welcome. Escort to site. Clubs welcome. Green Friendly. Rate in 2010 $39.50 for 2 persons. MC/VISA/Debit. Member CQ. KOA discount. FMCA discount.

Phone: (450)464-1661
Address: 3449 De L'Industrie,
Saint-Mathieu-de-Beloeil, QC J3G 4S5
Lat/Lon: 45.59020/-73.26857
Email: info@campingalouette.com
Web: www.campingalouette.com

SEE AD MONTREAL PAGE 908 AND AD TRAVEL SECTION PAGE 900

SAINT-MICHEL-DE-BELLECHASSE—F-6

(E) Camping Parc St-Michel—(Chaudiere-Appalaches) *From jct I 20 (exit 348) & Hwy 281: Go 1.6 km/1 mi N on Hwy 281, then 2.5 km/1-1/2 mi E on Hwy 132. Enter on L.* ◆◆◆FACILITIES: 85 sites, 75 full hkups, 10 W&E, (15/30/50 amps), 50 amps ($), 7 pull-thrus, tenting, dump, laundry, ltd groc. ◆◆◆RECREATION: swim pool, playground. Pets welcome. Open May 15 - Oct 15. Rate in 2010 $32 for 4 persons.

Phone: (418)884-2621
Address: Road 132, 7 route des Camping,
Saint-Michel-de-Bellechasse, QC G0R 3S0
Lat/Lon: 46.88681/-70.88557

SAINT-MICHEL-DES-SAINTS—F-2

Domaine Lac des Pins (Not Visited)—*From church in town: Go 4 mi NE on Hwy-131, then 1-1/2 mi N on Chemin St. Benoit.* FACILITIES: 20 sites, 18 ft max RV length, 8 full hkups, 12 no hkups, tenting, ltd groc. RECREATION: lake swim, boating, ramp, dock, lake/river fishing. No pets. Open all yr. Facilities fully operational Jun 24 - Labor Day. Phone: (514)833-6675.

SAINT-NICOLAS—F-6

(SW) Camping Au Sous Bois Du Campeur (Not Visited)—*From Hwy 20 (exit 305): Go 4 km/2-1/2 mi W on Chemin Filteau. Enter on R.* ◆◆◆FACILITIES: 140 sites, 90 full hkups, 40 W&E, (15/30 amps), 10 no

Camping Au Sous Bois Du Campeur (Not Visited)—Continued on next page

SAINT-NICOLAS—Continued
Camping Au Sous Bois Du Campeur (Not Visited)—Continued

hkups, 8 pull-thrus, tenting, dump, laundry, ltd groc. ◇◇◇RECREATION: swim pool, playground. Pets welcome. Open May 1 - Oct 1. Facilities fully operational May 15 - Sep 15. Rate in 2010 $22-38 for 4 persons. Member CQ. Phone: (418)831-1788.

(sw) KOA-Quebec City—(Chaudiere-Appalaches) *1 mi W of I-73: Go W on I-20 (exit 311), then left at traffic light going E on I-20, (exit 311). Cross over I-20. Turn left at Oliver Rd (service road). Enter on R.* ◇◇◇◇FACILITIES: 220 sites, 96 full hkups, 56 W&E, 12 E, (15/30/50 amps), 50 amps ($), 56 no hkups, 134 pull-thrus, tenting, dump, laundry, groceries. ◇◇◇◇RECREATION: swim pool, playground. Pets welcome ($), quantity restrict. Open May 1 - Oct 12. Big rigs welcome. Rate in 2010 $40-60 for 2 persons. Member CQ. KOA discount.

Phone: (418)831-1813
Address: 684 Chemin Olivier, Saint-Nicolas, QC G7A 2N6
Lat/Lon: 46.69880/-71.30122
Email: koaquebec@gmail.com
Web: www.koaquebec.com

SAINT-OMER—E-5

(W) Camping Aux Flots Bleus (Not Visited)—*From west town limits: Go 153 meters/500 feet E on Hwy 132. Enter on R.* ◇◇◇FACILITIES: 96 sites, 54 full hkups, 22 W&E, (15/30 amps), 20 no hkups, tenting, dump, laundry. ◇RECREATION: play equipment. Pets welcome. Open May 1 - Oct 30. Facilities fully operational May 20 - Oct 30. Rate in 2010 $20-30 for 4 persons. Member CQ. Phone: (418)364-3659.

SAINT-OURS—H-3

(N) Camping & Marina Parc Bellerive—*From jct Hwy 239 & Hwy 133: Go 5.2 km/3-1/4 mi S on Hwy 133. Enter on R.* ◇◇◇◇FACILITIES: 309 sites, 306 full hkups, 3 W&E, (15/30/50 amps), 2 pull-thrus, tenting, dump, laundry, ltd groc. ◇◇◇◇RECREATION: 2 swim pools, boating, canoeing, ramp, dock, river fishing, playground. Pets welcome ($). Open Apr 25 - Oct 12. Facilities fully operational Jun 10 - Sep 4. Rate in 2010 $38-49 for 4 persons. Member CQ. Phone: (450) 785-2272.

SAINT-PAUL-DE-l'ILE-AUX-NOIX—J-3

(N) Domaine Riviera—*From jct Hwy 133 & 67th Ave: Go 0.4 km/1/4 mi E on 67 Ave, then 0.8 km/1/2 mi N on 1 Rue. Enter on R.* ◇◇FACILITIES: 160 sites, 24 ft max RV length, 160 full hkups, (15 amps), tenting, dump, laundry. ◇RECREATION: swim pool, boating, ramp, dock, river fishing, play equipment. Pets welcome. Open May 15 - Sep 15. Rate in 2010 $25 for 4 persons. Member CQ. Phone: (450)291-5444.

SAINT-PAULIN—G-3

(N) Camping Belle Montagne (Not Visited)—*From jct Hwy 350 & Hwy 349: Go 4 km/2-1/2 mi N on Hwy 349, then .04 km/1/4 mi E on Belle Montagne. Enter on L.* ◇◇◇FACILITIES: 119 sites, 76 full hkups, 36 W&E, (15/30 amps), 7 no hkups, tenting, dump, laundry, ltd groc. ◇◇RECREATION: swim pool, canoeing, river fishing, playground. Pets welcome, breed restrict. Partial handicap access. Open May 18 - Oct 14. Facilities fully operational Jun 24 - Sep 7. Rate in 2010 $34-55 for 6 persons. Member CQ. Phone: (819)268-2881.

SAINT-PHILIPPE-DE-LAPRAIRIE—J-2

(W) Camping Amerique Montreal—(Monteregie) *From Hwy 15 (exit 38): Go 1.6 km/1 mi E on Boul Monette, then 0.4 km/1/4 mi S on Rang St-Andre. Enter on R.* ◇◇FACILITIES: 112 sites, 92 full hkups, 12 W&E, (15/30 amps), 8 no hkups, 2 pull-thrus, WiFi Instant Internet at site, WiFi Internet central location, tenting, dump, non-guest dump $, laundry, ltd groc, ice, picnic tables, fire rings, wood. ◇◇◇RECREATION: rec hall, swim pool, play equipment, shuffleboard court, activities horseshoes. Pets welcome ($), breed restrict, size restrict, quantity restrict. Open Apr 1 - Oct 31. Facilities fully operational Apr 20 - Oct 31. Rate in 2010 $23-29 per family. Member CQ. CCUSA 50% Discount. CCUSA reservations Recommended, CCUSA max stay 7 days, Cash only for CCUSA disc., CCUSA disc. not avail F,Sa, CCUSA disc. not avail holidays. Heater not allowed. WIFI charge-call for details.

CAMPCLUB USA

Phone: (450)659-8282
Address: 40 Rang St. Andre, Saint-Philippe-de-Laprairie, QC J0L 2K0
Lat/Lon: 45.34006/-73.49138
Email: campingameriquemontreal@videotron.ca
Web: www.campingameriquemontreal.ca

(W) Camping Bon Air Inc—(Monteregie) *From I-15 (exit 38): Go 1.6 km/1 mi E on Boul Monette, then 2.4 km/1-1/2 mi S on St-Andre. Enter on R.* ◇◇◇FACILITIES: 400 sites, 265 full hkups, 22 W&E, (15/30 amps), 113 no hkups, 5 pull-thrus, tenting, dump, laundry, ltd groc. ◇◇RECREATION: swim pool. Pets welcome. Partial handicap access. Open Apr 25 - Oct 25. Rate in 2010 $27-34 per family. Member CQ. Phone: (450)659-8868.

SAINT-PHILIPPE-DE-LAPRAIRIE—Continued

(E) Camping la Cle des Champs (Not Visited)—(Monteregie) *From Hwy 30 (exit 104): Go 2.5 km/1-1/2 mi E on Hwy 104, then 3.5 km/2 mi S on Rang St-Raphael, then 1 km/3/4 mi W on Montee St-Claude. Enter on R.* ◇◇◇FACILITIES: 170 sites, 142 full hkups, 28 W&E, (15/30 amps), laundry, ltd groc. ◇◇◇RECREATION: swim pool, play equipment. Pets welcome. No tents. Open Apr 22 - Oct 22. Rate in 2010 $30-35 for 6 persons. Member CQ. Phone: (450) 659-3389.

(W) KOA Montreal South—(Monteregie) *From Hwy 15 (exit 38): Go 1.6 km/1 mi E on Boul Monette. Enter on L.* ◇◇◇◇FACILITIES: 190 sites, 105 full hkups, 50 W&E, (20/30/50 amps), 50 amps ($), 35 no hkups, 160 pull-thrus, tenting, dump, laundry, groceries. ◇◇◇RECREATION: swim pool, playground. Pets welcome. Partial handicap access. Open May 14 - Oct 4. Big rigs welcome. Rate in 2010 $32-75 for 2 persons. Phone: (450)659-8626. KOA discount.

SAINT-PIE—I-3

(NE) Camping Au Vieux Foyer—*From jct Hwy 235 & Chemin St-Dominique: Go 2.4 km/1-1/2 mi E on Chemin St-Dominique. Enter on R.* ◇◇◇FACILITIES: 160 sites, 160 full hkups, (15/30 amps), tenting, dump, laundry. ◇◇◇RECREATION: swim pool, playground. Pets welcome. Open May 15 - Sep 15. Facilities fully operational Jun 5 - Sep 5. Rate in 2010 $29-32 for 5 persons. Member CQ. Phone: (450)772-5177.

SAINT-POLYCARPE—J-1

(SW) Camping Saint-Polycarpe (Not Visited)—*From Hwy 20 (exit 6) & Chemin St-Thomas: Go 4.5 km/2-3/4 mi N on Chemin St-Thomas. Enter on R.* ◇◇◇FACILITIES: 225 sites, 179 full hkups, 16 W&E, (15/30 amps), 30 no hkups, tenting, dump, laundry, ltd groc. ◇◇◇RECREATION: 2 swim pools, lake swim, playground. Pets welcome. Partial handicap access. Open May 2 - Sep 15. Facilities fully operational Jun 1 - Sep 15. Rate in 2010 $25-35 for 2 persons. Member CQ. Phone: (450)265-3815.

SAINT-RAYMOND—F-5

(S) Camping Claire Fontaine—(Quebec) *From jct Hwy 354 & Hwy 365: Go 2.5 km/1-1/2 mi S on Hwy 365. Enter on R.* ◇◇◇FACILITIES: 200 sites, 185 full hkups, (15 amps), 15 no hkups, tenting, dump, laundry, ltd groc. ◇◇◇◇RECREATION: swim pool, playground. Pets welcome. Partial handicap access. Open May 15 - Sep 15. Rate in 2010 $24-29 for 4 persons. Member CQ. Phone: (418)337-2744.

SAINT-ROCH-DE-L'ACHIGAN—H-2

(SW) Camping Horizon (Not Visited)—*From jct Hwy 25 & Ruisseau des Anges (St-Roch-de-l'Achigan): Go 1.6 km/1 mi W on Ruisseau des Anges, then 1.2 km/3/4 mi S on Hwy 125. Enter on R.* ◇◇◇FACILITIES: 170 sites, 145 full hkups, 20 W&E, (15/30/50 amps), 50 amps ($), 5 no hkups, tenting, dump, laundry, ltd groc. ◇◇◇RECREATION: 2 swim pools, playground. Pets welcome, breed restrict. Open May 7 - Sep 15. Facilities fully operational Jun 20 - Sep 1. Rate in 2010 $29 for 4 persons. Member CQ. Phone: (450) 588-5607.

SAINT-ROSAIRE—H-5

(NE) Camping Domaine du Lac Cristal (Not visited)—*From jct Hwy 20 (exit 228) & Hwy 165: Go 5.6 km/3-1/2 mi S on Hwy 165, then 6.4 km/4 mi W on Hwy 162. Enter on R.* ◇◇◇FACILITIES: 543 sites, 543 full hkups, (15/30 amps), 100 pull-thrus, tenting, dump, laundry, ltd groc. ◇◇◇RECREATION: swim pool, lake swim, playground. Pets welcome. Open May 1 - Nov 1. Rate in 2010 $31-39 for 4 persons. Member CQ. Phone: (819)752-4275.

SAINT-SIMEON—B-5

(E) Camping Levesque—*From jct Hwy 170 & Hwy 138: Go 1.6 km/1 mi E on Hwy 138. Enter on R.* ◇◇◇FACILITIES: 36 sites, 7 full hkups, 18 W&E, (15/30 amps), 11 no hkups, tenting, dump, laundry, ltd groc. ◇◇RECREATION: play equipment. Pets welcome. Open May 18 - Oct 15. Rate in 2010 $24-28 per family.

Phone: (418)638-5220
Address: Rte 138 (40 Port aux Quilles), Saint-Simeon, QC G0T 1X0
Lat/Lon: 47.86274/-69.86740
Email: campinglevesque@hotmail.com
Web: www.quebecweb.com/campinglevesque

(W) Camping Maurice—*From jct Hwy 170 & Hwy 138: Go 5.6 km/3-1/2 mi W on Hwy 138. Enter on R.* ◇◇FACILITIES: 33 sites, 19 full hkups, 1 W&E, (15 amps), 13 no hkups, tenting, dump, laundry. ◇◇RECREATION: swim pool, play equipment. Pets welcome. Open Jun 1 - Sep 30. Facilities fully operational Jun 20 - Sep 3. Rate in 2010 $22 for 8 persons. Member CQ. Phone: (418)638-2716.

SAINT-TITE—F-4

(N) Camping La Gervaisie (Not Visited)—*From jct Hwy 159 & Hwy 153: Go 2.4 km/1-1/2 mi N on Hwy 153, then 2.8 km/1-3/4 mi W on Route des Pointes.*

SAINT-TITE—Continued
Camping La Gervaisie (Not Visited)—Continued

Enter on R. ◇◇◇FACILITIES: 118 sites, 118 full hkups, (15/30 amps), tenting, dump, laundry, ltd groc. ◇◇◇RECREATION: swim pool, lake swim, no motors, canoeing, playground. Pets welcome. Partial handicap access. Open May 15 - Sep 15. Facilities fully operational Jun 24 - Sep 1. Rate in 2010 $35 for 2 persons. Member CQ. Phone: (418)365-7171.

SAINT-VALLIER—F-6

(S) Camping Le Domaine Champetre (Not Visited)—*From Hwy 20E (exit 356): Go .04 km/1/4 mi E, then 2.8 km/1-3/4 mi S on Montee de la Station. Enter on L.* ◇◇FACILITIES: 150 sites, 84 full hkups, 36 W&E, (15/30 amps), 30 no hkups, tenting, dump, laundry, ltd groc. ◇◇RECREATION: swim pool, play equipment. Pets welcome. Open May 12 - Sep 15. Facilities fully operational Jun 21 - Sep 4. Rate in 2010 $23-35 for 5 persons. Member CQ. Phone: (418)884-2270.

SAINTE-AGATHE-DES-MONTS—H-1

(N) Camping Domaine Lausanne—(Laurentides) *From jct Hwy 329 & Hwy 117: Go 9.6 km/6 mi N on Hwy 117. Enter on R.* ◇◇◇◇FACILITIES: 316 sites, 90 full hkups, 149 W&E, (15/30 amps), 77 no hkups, 10 pull-thrus, tenting, dump, laundry, ltd groc. ◇◇◇◇RECREATION: lake swim, boating, electric motors only, canoeing, ramp, dock, lake/river fishing, playground. Pets welcome ($), breed restrict, quantity restrict. Partial handicap access. Open May 12 - Sep 17. Rate in 2010 $38 for 5 persons. Member CQ. Phone: (819)326-3550.

SAINTE-ANNE-DES-MONTS—D-5

(W) Camping du Rivage (Not visited)—(Gaspesie) *From west on Hwy 132: Go 5.7 km/3-1/2 mi E on Hwy 132E, then 30 meters/100 feet NW on 29c Avenue Quest, then 10 meters/30 feet on 1c Avenue Quest. Enter on R.* ◇◇◇FACILITIES: 29 sites, 24 W&E, (15/30 amps), 5 no hkups, dump, laundry. RECREATION: saltwater swim. Pets welcome. Partial handicap access. No tents. Open May 15 - Oct 30. Rate in 2010 $17-25 for 4 persons. Member CQ. Phone: (418)763-3529.

Centre Recreo-Touristique Camping des Monts—(Gaspesie) *From west town limits: Go 3.2 km/2 mi E on Hwy 132. Enter on R.* ◇◇FACILITIES: 150 sites, 98 full hkups, 12 W&E, (15 amps), 40 no hkups, tenting, laundry, ltd groc. ◇◇RECREATION: river fishing, playground. Open May 31 - Sep 22. Rate in 2010 $18-19 for 4 persons. Member CQ. Phone: (418) 763-3240.

PARC NATIONAL DE LA GASPESIE—(Gaspesie) *From Hwy 132 & Hwy 299: Go S on Hwy 299 to Gite Mont-Albert.* FACILITIES: 209 sites, 13 W&E, (15/50 amps), 196 no hkups, tenting, dump. RECREATION: canoeing, lake fishing. No pets. Open Jun - Sep. Phone: (418)763-7494.

PARC NATIONAL DE LA GASPESIE, LAC CASCAPEDIA—(Gaspesie) *From Hwy 132 in Sainte-Anne-des-Monts: Go S on Hwy 299 to Gite Mont-Albert.* FACILITIES: 50 sites, 50 no hkups, tenting. RECREATION: lake swim, boating, canoeing, lake/river fishing. No pets. Open Jun 4 - Oct 3. Phone: (866)727-2427.

PARC NATIONAL DE LA GASPESIE, MONT-ALBERT—(Gaspesie) *From Hwy 132 E in Sainte-Anne-des-Monts: Go S on Hwy 299 to Gite du Mont-Albert.* FACILITIES: 122 sites, 122 no hkups, tenting, dump, laundry, ltd groc. RECREATION: lake swim, canoeing, lake/river fishing. No pets. Open May 28 - Sep 19. Phone: (866)727-2427.

SAINTE-CATHERINE-DE-HATLEY—J-5

(SW) Camping Chez Ben 2000—*From jct Hwy 55 (exit 29) & Hwy 108: Go 1.6 km/1 mi E on Hwy 108. Enter on L.* ◇◇FACILITIES: 218 sites, 91 full hkups, 51 W&E, (15/30 amps), 76 no hkups, 8 pull-thrus, tenting, dump, laundry, ltd groc. ◇◇◇RECREATION: lake swim, boating, canoeing, ramp, dock, lake fishing, playground. Pets welcome. Partial handicap access. Open May 11 - Sep 16. Rate in 2010 $30 for 4 persons. Member CQ. Phone: (819)843-5337.

SAINTE-CECILE-DE-MASHAM—D-2

GATINEAU PARK (La Peche Lake)—*From jct Hwy 105 & Hwy 366: Go 12-3/4 km/8 mi W on Hwy 366, then S on Eardley Rd. Sites accessible by boat or canoe only.* FACILITIES: 299 sites, 299 no hkups, tenting, dump, laundry, ltd groc. RECREATION: lake swim, boating, 10 hp limit, canoeing, ramp, lake fishing. No pets. Partial handicap access. Open May 21 - Oct 11. Phone: (819)456-3016.

GATINEAU PARK (Philippe Lake)—*From jct Hwy 105 & Hwy 366: Go 8 km/5 mi W on Hwy 366.* FACILITIES: 250 sites, 250 no hkups, tenting, dump, ltd groc. RECREATION: lake swim, boating, no motors, canoeing, lake fishing. No pets. Partial handicap access. Open mid May - Oct. Phone: (819)456-3016.

SAINTE-CECILE-DE-MILTON—I-4

(W) Camping Oasis (Not Visited)—*From jct Hwy 112 & Hwy 137: Go 6 km/3-3/4 mi N on Hwy 137, then 3.6 km/2-1/4 mi W on Rang 1 Ouest. Enter on R.* ◇◇◇◇FACILITIES: 441 sites, 409 full hkups, 7 W&E, (15/30 amps), 25 no hkups, tenting, dump, laundry,

Camping Oasis (Not Visited)—Continued on next page

SAINTE-CECILE-DE-MILTON—Continued
Camping Oasis (Not Visited)—Continued

groceries. ◆◆◆RECREATION: lake swim, playground. Pets welcome. Partial handicap access. Open May 1 - Oct 15. Facilities fully operational Jun 20 - Sep 1. Rate in 2010 $26-36 for 4 persons. Member CQ. Phone: (450)378-2181.

SAINTE-CROIX—G-5

(NW) Camping Belle-Vue—*From jct Hwy 271 & Hwy 132: Go 8 km/5 mi W on Hwy 132, then .04 km/1/4 mi NW on Route Pointe au Platon. Enter on R.* ◆◆◆FACILITIES: 302 sites, 271 full hkups, 12 W&E, (15/30 amps), 19 no hkups, 14 pull-thrus, tenting, dump, laundry, ltd groc. ◆◆◆◆◆RECREATION: swim pool, boating, canoeing, ramp, river fishing, playground. Pets welcome. Partial handicap access. Open May 1 - Oct 15. Facilities fully operational May 15 - Sep 15. Rate in 2010 $45 for 7 persons. Member CQ. Phone: (418)926-3482.

SAINTE-EMILIE-DE-L'ENERGIE—G-2

(SE) Camping Sainte-Emilie (Not Visited)—*From jct Hwy 347 N & Hwy 131: Go 6 km/3-3/4 mi S on Hwy 131. Enter on L.* ◆◆◆FACILITIES: 175 sites, 91 full hkups, 37 W&E, (15/30 amps), 47 no hkups, tenting, dump, laundry, ltd groc. ◆◆◆RECREATION: swim pool, lake swim, boating, no motors, canoeing, river fishing, playground. Pets welcome. Open May 11 - Sep 30. Facilities fully operational Jun 24 - Sep 1. Rate in 2010 $27-43 for 4 persons. Member CQ. Phone: (450)886-5879.

SAINTE-FLAVIE—B-6

(W) Camping Capitaine Homard (Not Visited)—*From west city limits: Go 1.6 km/1 mi E on Hwy 132. Enter on L.* ◆◆FACILITIES: 50 sites, 50 full hkups, (15/30 amps), tenting, dump. Pets welcome, breed restrict. Open May 30 - Sep 15. Facilities fully operational Jun 20 - Aug 20. Rate in 2010 $25 for 2 persons. Phone: (418)775-8046.

SAINTE-GENEVIEVE-DE-BATISCAN—G-4

(W) Parc de la Peninsule—*From Bridge & Church: Go 1.6 km/1 mi N on rue de L'Eglise, then .08 km/1/2 mi NW on Rang des Forges, then .08 km/1/2 mi NW on des Pointes. Enter on L.* ◆◆FACILITIES: 578 sites, 405 full hkups, 139 W&E, (15/30 amps), 34 no hkups, tenting, dump, laundry, ltd groc. ◆◆◆RECREATION: swim pool, river swim, ramp, playground. Pets welcome, breed restrict. Partial handicap access. Open May 4 - Sep 16. Facilities fully operational Jun 20 - Sep 5. Rate in 2010 $34 for 6 persons. Member CQ. Phone: (418) 362-2043.

SAINTE-JULIENNE—H-2

(N) Camping Kelly (Not Visited)—*From jct Hwy 346 & Hwy 125: Go 2 km/1-1/4 mi N on Hwy 125. Enter on L.* ◆◆◆FACILITIES: 320 sites, 320 full hkups, (15/30 amps), 25 pull-thrus, laundry. ◆◆◆RECREATION: 2 swim pools, playground. Pets welcome, breed restrict, quantity restrict. Partial handicap access. No tents. Open May 15 - Sep 15. Facilities fully operational Jun 20 - Sep 2. Rate in 2010 $29-30 for 4 persons. Member CQ. Phone: (450)831-2422.

SAINTE-LUCE-SUR-MER—B-6

(E) Camping la Luciole—*From jct Hwy 298 & Hwy 132: Go 1/2 Km/1/3 mi W on Hwy 132. Enter on R.* ◆◆FACILITIES: 57 sites, 22 full hkups, 15 W&E, (15/30 amps), 20 no hkups, 5 pull-thrus, tenting, dump, laundry. ◆RECREATION: play equipment. Pets welcome ($). Open May 15 - Oct 15. Rate in 2010 $31-33 for 2 persons. Member CQ. Phone: (418)739-3258.

SAINTE-MADELEINE—I-3

(NW) Camping Ste-Madeleine—(Monteregie) *From Hwy 20 (exit 120) & Hwy 227: Go .04 km/1/4 mi S on Hwy 227. Enter on R.* ◆◆◆◆FACILITIES: 210 sites, 200 full hkups, (15/30 amps), 10 no hkups, tenting, dump, laundry, groceries. ◆◆◆RECREATION: swim pool, playground. Pets welcome. Partial handicap access. Open May 1 - Oct 1. Rate in 2010 $34 for 4 persons. Member CQ. Phone: (450)795-3888.

SAINTE-MARCELLINE-DE-KILDARE—H-2

(SW) Camping Sol Air (Not Visited)—*From church in town: Go 1 km/3/4 mi S on Hwy 343, then 1.6 km/1mi W on Rang 9, then .04 km/1/4 mi NW on Chemin Lac Andy. Enter on L.* ◆◆◆FACILITIES: 198 sites, 35 ft max RV length, 179 full hkups, 19 W&E, (15/30 amps), tenting, laundry, ltd groc. ◆◆RECREATION: swim pool, lake swim, playground. Pets welcome, breed restrict. Open May 1 - Sep 30. Facilities fully operational Jun 24 - Sep 1. Rate in 2010 $32-38 for 4 persons. Member CQ. Phone: (450)883-3400.

SAINTE-MELANIE—H-2

(SE) Camping Bernard—*From Hwy 131 at Notre Dame de Lourdes: Go 6 km/3-3/4 mi NW on Principale St (Rg 2), then 1 km/1/2 mi W on Rang 1, then 1 km/1/2 mi S on Boul Bernard. Enter at end.* ◆◆◆FACILITIES: 318 sites, 304 full hkups, 4 W&E, (15/30 amps), 10 no hkups, 10 pull-thrus, tenting,

SAINTE-MELANIE—Continued
Camping Bernard—Continued

dump, laundry, ltd groc. ◆◆◆RECREATION: 2 swim pools, boating, 50 hp limit, canoeing, ramp, river fishing, playground. Pets welcome, breed restrict, quantity restrict. Open May 1 - Sep 15. Facilities fully operational Jun 8 - Sep 5. Rate in 2010 $32 for 4 persons. Member CQ. Phone: (450)756-2560.

(N) Camping Campus (Not Visited)—*From church in town: Go 3.6 km/2-1/4 mi W on Hwy 348, then 4.3 km/2-3/4 mi N on Rte Ste Beatrix. Enter on L.* ◆◆◆FACILITIES: 240 sites, 240 full hkups, (15/30 amps), 5 pull-thrus, tenting, laundry, ltd groc. ◆◆◆RECREATION: swim pool, lake swim, lake fishing, playground. No pets. Open May 10 - Sep 9. Facilities fully operational Jun 20 - Sep 1. Rate in 2010 $32 for 6 persons. Member CQ. Phone: (450)883-2337.

SAINTE-MONIQUE-DE-HONFLEUR—B-4

(SW) CENTRE TOURISTIQUE SAINTE-MONIQUE—*From S City Limit on Hwy 169: Go .05 km/1/4 mi S on Hwy 169, then 1 km/3/4 mi W on Rang 6 Ouest. Enter on L.* FACILITIES: 80 sites, 34 full hkups, 12 W&E, (15/30 amps), 34 no hkups, tenting, dump, laundry. RECREATION: swim pool, pond fishing, play equipment. Pets welcome. Open May 23 - Sep 1. Member CQ. Phone: (418)347-3124.

SAINTE-ROSE-DU-NORD—B-5

(S) Camping la Descente des Femmes (Not Visited)—*From jct Hwy 172 & Rue du Quai: Go 2.7 km/1-1/2 mi S on Rue du Quai, then 172 meters/568 feet W on Rue de la Montagne. Enter on R.* ◆FACILITIES: 46 sites, 26 full hkups, (15 amps), 20 no hkups, tenting, dump, laundry. Pets welcome, breed restrict. Open Jun 1 - Oct 12. Facilities fully operational Jun 20 - Sep 1. Rate in 2010 $23 for 4 persons. Member CQ. Phone: (418)675-2581.

SAINTE-SABINE—J-3

(E) Camping Caravelle—(Canton-de-l'est) *From jct Hwy 104 & Hwy 235: Go 4.8 km/3 mi S on Hwy 235, then .08 km/1/2 mi W on Rang de la Gare. Enter on L.* ◆◆◆◆FACILITIES: 412 sites, 412 full hkups, (15/30/50 amps), 50 amps ($), 35 pull-thrus, tenting, dump, laundry, groceries. ◆◆◆◆◆RECREATION: 2 swim pools, playground. Pets welcome ($), breed restrict. Partial handicap access. Open Apr 20 - Oct 20. Facilities fully operational May 15 - Sep 15. Big rigs welcome. Rate in 2010 $32 for 4 persons. Member CQ. Phone: (450)293-7637.

SAINTE-SOPHIE-DE-LEVRARD—G-5

(W) Camping Plage Paris—*From south jct Hwy 218 & Hwy 226: Go 6.4 km/4 mi W on Hwy 226. Enter on R.* ◆◆FACILITIES: 178 sites, 90 full hkups, 88 W&E, (15/30 amps), dump, laundry, ltd groc. ◆◆RECREATION: swim pool, play equipment. Pets welcome. No tents. Open May 15 - Sep 17. Facilities fully operational Jun 15 - Sep 1. Rate in 2010 $27-32 for 4 persons. Member CQ. Phone: (819)288-5948.

SAINTE-THECLE—F-4

(NW) Domaine Lac et Foret (Not Visited)—*From S City town limit on Hwy 153: Go 2.4 km/1-1/2 mi N on Hwy 153, then .03 km/1/4 mi W on 12 Avenue. Enter on L.* FACILITIES: 179 sites, 77 full hkups, 96 W&E, (15/30 amps), 6 no hkups, tenting, dump, laundry, ltd groc. RECREATION: swim pool, lake swim, boating, canoeing, ramp, dock, lake fishing, playground. Pets welcome ($). Open May 18 - Sept 19. Facilities fully operational Jun 15 - Sep 1. Rate in 2010 $19-32 for 5 persons. Member CQ. Phone: (418)289-3871.

SAINTE-VERONIQUE—C-3

CAMPING MUNICIPAL SAINTE-VERONIQUE—(Laurentides) *From jct Hwy 117 & Blvd Lafontaine: Go 2 km/1-1/4 mi E on Blvd. Lafontaine. Enter at end.* FACILITIES: 185 sites, 169 full hkups, (30/50 amps), 50 amps ($), 16 no hkups, 50 pull-thrus, tenting, dump, laundry, ltd groc. RECREATION: lake/river swim, boating, canoeing, ramp, dock, lake/river fishing, playground. Pets welcome. Open May 5 - Oct 10. Phone: (819)275-2155.

SHAWINIGAN—G-4

(E) Camping KEA Otamac—(Mauricie Bois-Francs) *From jct Hwy 153 & Hwy 359: Go 2.4 km/1-1/2 mi S on Hwy 359, then 1.2 km/3/4 mi E on 49 Avenue. Enter on R.* ◆◆◆◆FACILITIES: 400 sites, 249 full hkups, 46 W&E, (15/30/50 amps), 105 no hkups, WiFi Instant Internet at site, WiFi Internet central location ($), tenting, RV storage, dump, non-guest dump $, laundry, ltd groc, RV supplies, LP gas by weight, ice, picnic tables, patios, fire rings, wood. ◆◆◆◆◆RECREATION: rec hall, pavilion, equipped pavilion, swim pool, wading pool, hot tub, boating, canoeing, kayaking, lake fishing, mini-golf, ($), bsktball, playground, shuffleboard court 2 shuffleboard courts, activities tennis, horseshoes, v-ball. Pets welcome. Partial handicap access. Open May 15 - Sep 15. VISA/Debit. Member CQ. CCUSA 50% Discount. CCUSA reservations Recommended, CCUSA max stay 4 days, Cash only for CCUSA disc., CCUSA disc. not avail S, CCUSA disc. not avail F,Sa. Not allowed Jun 22-Aug 12.

CAMPCLUB USA

SHAWINIGAN—Continued
Camping KEA Otamac—Continued

Phone: (819)538-9697
Address: 5431 Ave Tour du Lac, Shawinigan, QC G0X 1L0
Lat/Lon: 46.61201/-72.61774
Web: www.campingotamac.com

(E) Camping Rouillard 2000—*From jct Hwy 153 & Hwy 359 (Lac a la Tortue): Go 2.4 km/1-1/2 mi S on Hwy 359, then 2km/1/4 mi E on 49th Ave. Enter on R.* ◆◆◆FACILITIES: 250 sites, typical site width 35 ft, 170 full hkups, 40 W&E, (15/30 amps), 40 no hkups, tenting, dump, laundry. ◆◆◆◆RECREATION: swim pool, boating, canoeing, dock, lake fishing, playground. Pets welcome. Open May 4 - Oct 1. Facilities fully operational Jun 10 - Sep 6. Rate in 2010 $33 for 2 persons. Member CQ. Phone: (819)538-2159.

LA MAURICIE NATIONAL PARK (Mistagance)—*From jct Hwy 55 (exit 217) & Hwy 351 S: Go 24 km/15 mi N on Hwy 351.* FACILITIES: 90 sites, 90 no hkups, tenting, dump. RECREATION: lake swim, canoeing, ramp, lake fishing, playground. No pets. Open May 11 - Oct 8. Phone: (819)538-3232.

LA MAURICIE NATIONAL PARK (Wapizagonke)—*From jct Hwy 55 (exit 217) & Hwy 351: Go 48 km/30 mi N on Hwy 351. North of Lake Wapizagonka.* FACILITIES: 219 sites, 219 no hkups, tenting, dump, ltd groc. RECREATION: lake swim, canoeing, lake fishing. No pets. Open Jun 21 - Sep 3. Phone: (819)538-3232.

RESERVE FAUNIQUE DU SAINT-MAURICE/LAC NORMAND—(Mauricie Bois-Francs) *From jct I-40 & Hwy 55: Go N on Hwy 55, then N on Hwy 155.* FACILITIES: 68 sites, 8 E, (15 amps), 60 no hkups, tenting, dump, ltd groc. RECREATION: lake swim, canoeing, ramp, lake/river fishing. No pets. Open May - Sep. Phone: (819)646-5687.

SHERBROOKE—I-5

(E) Camping Beau-Lieu—*From jct Hwy 216 & Chemin St-rock: Go 1.2km / 3/4mi W on Hwy 216. Enter on R.* ◆◆◆FACILITIES: 475 sites, 435 full hkups, 40 W&E, (15/30 amps), 5 pull-thrus, tenting, dump, laundry, ltd groc. ◆◆◆RECREATION: 2 swim pools, playground. Pets welcome, breed restrict. Open May 1 - Sep 28. Facilities fully operational Jun 1 - Sep 1. Rate in 2010 $26-32 per family. Member CQ. Phone: (819) 864-4531.

(N) Camping de l'Ile Marie (Not Visited)—*From jct Hwy 143 & Hwy 108: Go 0.8 km/1/2 mi E on Hwy 108 (past bridge), then 2 km/1-1/4 mi on St-Francis. (Bridge entrance to campground max 10 tons.). Enter on L.* ◆◆◆FACILITIES: 225 sites, 32 ft max RV length, 158 full hkups, 57 W&E, (15/30 amps), 10 no hkups, tenting, dump, laundry, ltd groc. ◆◆◆RECREATION: swim pool, playground. Pets welcome. Open May 15 - Sep 15. Rate in 2010 $27 for 4 persons. Member CQ. Phone: (819)820-0330.

(E) Camping Lac Magog—*From jct Hwy 216 & Chemin St-rock: Go 1 km / 3/4 mi N on Chemin St-Rock, then 4 km / 2-1/2 mi W on Chemin Blanchette. Enter on L.* ◆◆◆FACILITIES: 162 sites, 107 full hkups, 30 W&E, (15/30 amps), 25 no hkups, tenting, dump, laundry, ltd groc. ◆◆◆RECREATION: swim pool, lake swim, boating, canoeing, ramp, dock, lake fishing, playground. Pets welcome, quantity restrict. Open May 4 - Sep 30. Facilities fully operational Jun 15 - Aug 20. Rate in 2010 $27-35 per family. Member CQ. Phone: (819) 864-4401.

STANSTEAD—J-5

(SE) Camping Lac Frontiere (Border Lake)—(Canton-de-l'est) *From Hwy 55 (exit 2) & Hwy 143: Go 1.2 km/3/4 mi NE on Hwy 143. Enter on R.* ◆◆FACILITIES: 127 sites, 85 full hkups, 26 W&E, (15/30 amps), 16 no hkups, 61 pull-thrus, tenting, dump, laundry, ltd groc. ◆◆◆RECREATION: swim pool, boating, electric motors only, canoeing, lake fishing, playground. Pets welcome. Open May 15 - Oct 15. Facilities fully operational Jun 1 - Sep 5. Rate in 2010 $28-32 for 6 persons. Member CQ. Phone: (819)876-5505.

STONEHAM—F-6

(N) Camping Stoneham—*From Hwy 175 N (exit Saint-Adolphe at Stoneham): Go 300 meters/990 feet. Enter on R.* ◆◆◆FACILITIES: 259 sites, 98 full hkups, 56 W&E, 27 E, (15/30 amps), 78 no hkups, 10 pull-thrus, tenting, dump, laundry, ltd groc. ◆◆◆◆RECREATION: swim pool, lake fishing, playground. Pets welcome ($), breed restrict. Open May 11 - Sep 9. Facilities fully operational Jun 20 - Aug 20. Rate in 2010 $35 per family. Member CQ. Phone: (418)848-2233.

TADOUSSAC—B-5

Camping Tadoussac (Not Visited)—(Manicouagan) *From Saquenay ferry boat landing: Go .8 km/1/2 mi E on Hwy 138 (Bateau Passeur St). Enter on R.* FACILITIES: 198 sites, 53 full hkups, 123 W&E, (15/30/50 amps), 50 amps ($), 22 no hkups, tenting, dump, laundry. RECREATION: play equipment. Pets welcome. Partial handicap access. Open Jun 1 - Sep 16. Rate in 2010 $29 for 4 persons. Member CQ. Phone: (418)235-4501.

Woodall's Tip... Find free Tourism Information in the Travel Section

TERREBONNE—I-2

(W') Camping au Plateau 5 Etoiles (Not Visited) —*From south jct Hwy 25 (exit 22W) & Hwy 344: Go 6 km/3-3/4 mi W on Hwy 344 (Cote Terrebonne). Enter on L.* ◆◆◆◆FACILITIES: 222 sites, 216 full hkups, 6 W&E, (15/30 amps), 8 pull-thrus, dump, laundry, ltd groc. ◆◆◆◆RECREATION: 3 swim pools, playground. Pets welcome ($), breed restrict. Partial handicap access. No tents. Open Apr 15 - Oct 15. Rate in 2010 $45 for 2 persons. Member CQ. Phone: (450)471-6266.

TROIS-RIVIERES—G-4

See listings at Saint-Barthelemy & Shaivinigan.

(NE) Camping Domaine au Grand "R" (Not Visited)—*From jct I-40 (exit 203) & Hwy 157: Go 1.2 km/3/4 mi N on Hwy 157, then 2.4 km/1-1/2 mi W on boul des Prairies. Enter on R.* ◆◆FACILITIES: 399 sites, 352 full hkups, 7 W&E, (15/30 amps), 40 no hkups, 13 pull-thrus, tenting, laundry, ltd groc. ◆◆◆RECREATION: swim pool, lake swim, playground. No pets. Open May 19 - Sep 25. Facilities fully operational Jun 20 - Aug 20. Rate in 2010 $35 for 4 persons. Member CQ. Phone: (819)378-3723.

(NE) Camping La Rochelle—*From jct Hwy I-40 (exit 203) & Hwy 157: Go 8.8 km/5-1/2 mi N on Hwy 157, then 1.2 km/3/4 mi W on Blvd Ste-Marguerite. Enter on R.* ◆◆◆FACILITIES: 228 sites, 190 full hkups, 4 W&E, (15/30 amps), 34 no hkups, tenting, dump, laundry, ltd groc. ◆◆◆◆RECREATION: swim pool, playground. Pets welcome ($), breed restrict. Partial handicap access. Open May 5 - Sept 23. Facilities fully operational Jun 18 - Sep 1. Rate in 2010 $28-35 for 4 persons. Member CQ. Phone: (819)372-9636.

(N) Camping Lac St-Michel des Forges—(Mauricie Bois-Francs) *From Hwy I 55 (exit 191): Go 2.4 km/1 1/2 mi E on Boul St. Michel, then 3.6 km/2 1/4 mi N on Boul des Forges, then .04 km/1/4 mi E on rue des Pignons. Enter at end.* ◆◆◆FACILITIES: 150 sites, 95 full hkups, 39 W&E, (15/30 amps), 16 no hkups, 12 pull-thrus, tenting, dump, laundry, ltd groc. ◆◆◆RECREATION: 2 swim pools, playground. Pets welcome. Open May 11 - Sep 15. Facilities fully operational Jun 15 - Sep 5. Rate in 2010 $30-34 for 4 persons. Member CQ. Phone: (877)374-8474.

UPTON—I-4

(C) Camping Wigwam—(Monteregie) *From Hwy 20 (exit 147) & Hwy 116: Go 10.4 km/6-1/2 mi SE on Hwy 116. Enter on L.* ◆◆◆◆FACILITIES: 270 sites, typical site width 40 ft, 260 full hkups, 10 W&E, (15/30 amps), tenting, dump, laundry, groceries. ◆◆◆◆◆RECREATION: swim pool, electric motors only, canoeing, dock, river fishing, playground. Pets welcome. Partial handicap access. Open May 1 - Oct 20. Rate in 2010 $31-34 for 5 persons. Member CQ. Phone: (450)549-4513.

VAL-ALAIN—G-5

(W) Camping Lac Georges (Not Visited)—*From Hwy 20 (exit 256): Go .08 km/1/2 mi E on 5e Rang, then 1.2 km/3/4 mi N on Rte Seigneuriale. Enter on R.* ◆◆◆FACILITIES: 340 sites, 270 full hkups, 70 W&E, (15/30 amps), 48 pull-thrus, tenting, dump, laundry, ltd groc. ◆◆◆RECREATION: lake swim, no motors, canoeing, play equipment. Pets welcome. Partial handicap access. Open May 10 - Oct 8. Rate in 2010 $38-44 for 5 persons. Member CQ. Phone: (418)744-3510.

VAL-DES-BOIS—D-2

(C) Camping Lac Vert (Not Visited)—(Outaouais) *From jct Hwy 307 & Hwy 309: Go 2.2 km/1-1/4 mi S on Hwy 309, then .05 km/1/4 mi NW on Chemin du Pont de Bois. Enter on R.* ◆◆◆FACILITIES: 196 sites, 196 full hkups, (15/30 amps), tenting, dump, laundry, ltd groc. ◆◆◆RECREATION: lake swim, electric motors only, canoeing, dock, lake fishing, playground. No pets. Open May 4 - Sep 3. Rate in 2010 $32 for 4 persons. Member CQ. Phone: (819) 454-2210.

VALCARTIER—F-6

(NE) CAMPING VALCARTIER—(Quebec) *From jct Hwy 40 E (Henri IV) & Hwy 573: Go 11 Km/7 mi NE on Hwy 573, then 10 Km/6-1/4 mi NE on Hwy 371 (Boul. Valcartier). Enter on R.*

◆◆◆◆◆FACILITIES: 705 sites, typical site width 30 ft, 124 full hkups, 301 W&E, 280 E, (15/30/50 amps), 50 amps ($), 80 pull-thrus, RV's/park model rentals, dump, non-guest dump, laundry, ltd groc, ice, picnic tables, fire rings, wood, controlled access.

◆◆◆◆◆RECREATION: rec room/area, equipped pavilion, coin games, swim pool, spray ground, canoeing, kayaking, river fishing, mini-golf, ($), golf nearby, playground, activities, horseshoes, v-ball.

Pets welcome. Partial handicap access. No tents. Open Jun 16 - Aug 27. Clubs welcome. Rate in 2010 $30.95-48.95 for 4 persons. MC/VISA/Debit. ATM. Member CQ.

Phone: (888)384-5524
Address: 1860 boulevard Valcartier, Valcartier, QC G0A 4S0
Lat/Lon: 46.94000/-71.47353
Email: informations@valcartier.com
Web: www.valcartier.com

SEE AD QUEBEC CITY PAGE 910

VALLEE-JONCTION—G-6

(NW) Camping A La Belle Etoile—(Beauce) *From jct Hwy 173 & Hwy 112 W: Go 0.4 km/1/4 mi W on Hwy 112, then 1.6 km/1 mi N on de L'Ecore. Enter on L.* ◆◆◆FACILITIES: 103 sites, 55 full hkups, 15 W&E, (15/30 amps), 33 no hkups, tenting, dump. ◆◆◆RECREATION: swim pool, boating, canoeing, dock, river fishing, play equipment. Pets welcome. Open May 15 - Sep 15. Facilities fully operational Jun 20 - Sep 1. Rate in 2010 $28 for 4 persons. Phone: (418)253-5630.

VAUDREUIL-DORION—I-2

(E) Camping D'Aoust—(Monteregie) *From Montreal: Take Hwy 40 (exit 26) & Hwy 342: Go 2.8 km/1-3/4 mi W on Hwy 342. Entrance on left. From Ottawa: Take Hwy 40 E (exit 22) & Hwy 342: Go 1.3 km/3/4 mi N on St Charles, then 2.6 km/1-1/2 mi E on Hwy 342. Entrance on right.* ◆◆◆FACILITIES: 211 sites, 131 full hkups, 50 W&E, (15/30 amps), 30 no hkups, 5 pull-thrus, family camping, tenting, dump, laundry, ltd groc. ◆◆◆RECREATION: 2 swim pools, playground. Pets welcome ($). Open May 1 - Oct 30. Facilities fully operational Jun 20 - Sep 10. Rate in 2010 $29-35 for 4 persons. Member CQ. Phone: (450)458-7301.

VENISE-EN-QUEBEC—J-3

(C) Camping Champlain 2003—*From jct Hwy 202 & Hwy 227: Go 0.8 km/1/2 mi E on Hwy 202. Enter on L.* ◆◆◆FACILITIES: 192 sites, 125 full hkups, 20 W&E, 6 E, (15/30 amps), 41 no hkups, tenting, shower$, dump, non-guest dump $, laundry, groceries, LP gas by weight/by meter, ice, picnic tables, fire rings, wood. ◆◆◆◆RECREATION: swim pool, lake swim, boating, canoeing, kayaking, lake fishing, bsktball, play equipment, 2 shuffleboard courts, activities horseshoes, v-ball. Pets welcome. Open May 15 - Sep 15. Rate in 2010 $34 for 5 persons. MC/VISA/Debit. Member CQ. CCUSA 50% Discount. CCUSA reservations Recommended, CCUSA max stay Unlimited, Cash only for CCUSA disc., CCUSA disc. not avail S, CCUSA disc. not avail F,Sa, CCUSA disc. not avail holidays. Not valid Ste John Baptiste.

Phone: (450)244-5317
Address: 29 Venise Ave E, Venise-En-Quebec, QC J0J 2K0
Lat/Lon: 45.08580/-73.14206
Email: nanroc@videotron.ca
Web: www.campingquebec.com/plagechamplain

(C) Camping Plage Kirkland (Not Visited)—*From jct Hwy 227 & Hwy 202: Go .08 km/1/2 mi E on Hwy 202. Enter on L.* ◆◆FACILITIES: 182 sites, 131 full hkups, 39 W&E, (15/30 amps), 12 no hkups, tenting, dump, laundry. ◆◆◆RECREATION: lake swim, boating, canoeing, lake fishing, playground. Pets welcome. Open May 1 - Sep 30. Rate in 2010 $26 for 4 persons. Member CQ. Phone: (450)244-5337.

(C) Camping Plage Venise (Not Visited)—*From jct Hwy 227 & Hwy 202: Go 1.2 km/3/4 mi E on Hwy 202. Enter on L.* ◆◆◆FACILITIES: 114 sites, 74 full hkups, 40 W&E, (15/30 amps), tenting, dump, laundry. ◆◆◆RECREATION: swim pool, lake swim, boating, canoeing, ramp, lake fishing, playground. Pets welcome, breed restrict, quantity restrict. Open May 15 - Sep 30. Rate in 2010 $22-30 for 4 persons. Member CQ. Phone: (450)244-5325.

WEEDON—I-5

(NW) Camping Beau-Soleil (Not Visited)—*From jct Hwy 257 & Hwy 112: Go 6.8 km/4-1/4 mi W on Hwy 112. Enter on R.* ◆◆◆FACILITIES: 157 sites, 116 full hkups, 7 W&E, (15/30 amps), 34 no hkups, tenting, dump, laundry, ltd groc. ◆◆◆RECREATION: swim pool, no motors, canoeing, play equipment. Pets welcome. Open May 11 - Sep 16. Rate in 2010 $27-30 for 6 persons. Member CQ. Phone: (819)877-5000.

WEST BROME—J-4

(NW) Camping Vallee Bleue—*From jct Hwy 139 & Hwy 104: Go 5 km/3-1/4 mi E on Hwy 104, then .05 km/1/4 mi S on Haman. Enter at end.* ◆◆◆◆FACILITIES: 215 sites, 193 full hkups, 12 W&E, (15/30 amps), 10 no hkups, 5 pull-thrus, tenting, dump, laundry. ◆◆◆◆RECREATION: lake swim, playground. Pets welcome, breed restrict. Partial handicap access. Open May 15 - Sep 15. Facilities fully operational Jun 15 - Sep 15. Rate in 2010 $30-36 for 5 persons. Member CQ. Phone: (450)263-4804.

YAMASKA—H-3

PARC NATIONAL DE LA YAMASKA—(Canton-de-l'est) *From I-10 (exit 68) & Hwy 139: Go on Hwy 139.* FACILITIES: 120 sites, 34 W&E, (15/30 amps), 86 no hkups, tenting, dump, laundry, ltd groc. RECREATION: lake swim, canoeing, ramp, lake fishing, playground. No pets. Partial handicap access. Open Jun - Sep. Phone: (450)776-7182.

WOODALL'S ALPHABETICAL QUICK REFERENCE

For Your Convenience Facilities are Listed Alphabetically by Name within each State/Province.

Types of Facilities Listed:

Campground/RV Parks ★ RV Sales/Service Centers ● Attractions & Tourism Locations

A Name in Bold Type indicates Advertisers who want your business

Campground/RV Parks Special Services Indicated:

□ Cabin Rentals, ® RV/Park Trailer Rentals, △ Tent Rentals

ALABAMA

AAA RV Park — FOLEY F-2
Anchors Aweigh RV Resort — FOLEY F-2
● **Auburn University** — AUBURN D-4
● **Auburn-Opelika Convention & Visitors Bureau** — AUBURN D-4
Autauga Creek Landing RV Campground — PRATTVILLE D-3
Azalea Acres RV Park — ROBERTSDALE F-2
B & B RV Park — VALLEY C-5
Bankhead NF (Clear Creek Rec Area) — JASPER B-2
Bankhead NF (Corinth Rec Area) — DOUBLE SPRINGS B-2
Bankhead NF (Houston Rec Area) — DOUBLE SPRINGS B-2
Barclay RV Parking — BOAZ B-4
®□ Bay Breeze RV On the Bay — GULF SHORES F-2
□ Bear Creek Dev Auth (Elliott Branch) — RUSSELLVILLE A-2
Bear Creek Dev Auth (Horseshoe Bend) — HODGES A-2
Bear Creek Dev Auth (Slickrock) — RUSSELLVILLE A-2
Beech's Camping MHP — ORANGE BEACH F-2
Bella Terra of Gulf Shores — GULF SHORES F-2
□ Birmingham South Campground — PELHAM C-3
Bladon Springs State Park — BLADON SPRINGS E-1
□ Blakeley State Park — SPANISH FORT F-2
Blue Heron Paradise — GUNTERSVILLE A-4
Blue Springs SP — CLIO E-4
Bluff Creek Park (COE-Walter F. George Lake) — COTTONTON D-5
Buck's Pocket SP — GROVE OAK A-4
Cane 9 Creek RV Park & Campground — HEFLIN B-4
Capital City RV Park — MONTGOMERY D-4
Carson Village Mobile Home Community — BIRMINGHAM B-3
Cathedral Caverns SP — WOODVILLE A-4
□ Cheaha SP and Cheaha Lodge — DELTA C-4
Cherokee Campground — HELENA C-3
□ Chesnut Bay Campground — LEESBURG B-4
□ **Chewacla SP** — AUBURN D-4
Chickasabogue Park & CG (Mobile County Pk) — MOBILE F-1
Chickasaw SP — GALLION D-2
Chilatchee Creek Park (COE-Alabama River Lakes) — ALBERTA D-2
Citronelle Lakeview RV Park (City Park) — CITRONELLE E-1
□ Claude D. Kelley SP — ATMORE E-2
Coastal Haven RV Park — FAIRHOPE F-2
Cochrane Campground (COE-Tennessee/Tombigbee Waterway) — COCHRANE C-1
Conecuh NF (Open Pond Campground) — ANDALUSIA E-3
Corinth Recreation Area — DOUBLE SPRINGS B-2
Country Court RV Park — ANNISTON B-4
Country Sunshine RV Park — CASTLEBERRY E-3
Country View RV Park — HANCEVILLE B-3
Crawford RV Park — SCOTTSBORO A-4
Cullman Campground — CULLMAN B-3
® Dandy RV Park — CLANTON C-3
Dauphin Island Campground (City Park) — DAUPHIN ISLAND F-1
□ De Soto SP — FORT PAYNE A-4
□ Dead Lake Marina & CG — CREOLA F-2
Deer Run RV Park — TROY E-4
Deerlick Creek (COE-Holt Lake) — TUSCALOOSA C-2
DeSoto Caverns Park Campground — CHILDERSBURG C-3
□ DeSoto State Park Lodge — FORT PAYNE A-4
Ditto Landing Marina Campground (City/County Park) — HUNTSVILLE A-3
Doc's RV Park — GULF SHORES F-2
Driftwood RV Park — FAIRHOPE F-2
® **Eagles Landing RV Park** — AUBURN D-4
East Bank Access Area (COE-Alabama River Lakes)/Millers Ferry Campground — CAMDEN D-2
Escapees Rainbow Plantation — SUMMERDALE F-2
□ Escatawpa Hollow Campground — WILMER F-1
Florala SP — FLORALA E-4
Forkland Park (COE-Demopolis Lake) — DEMOPOLIS D-2
Fort Morgan RV Park — GULF SHORES F-2
Fort Toulouse/Jackson Park (Ala. State Historical Commission) — WETUMPKA D-4
Foscue Park (COE-Demopolis Lake) — DEMOPOLIS D-2
Frank Jackson SP — OPP E-4
□ Goose Pond Colony (City Park) — SCOTTSBORO A-4
®□ **Gulf Breeze Resort** — GULF SHORES F-2
□ Gulf Shores/Pensacola West KOA — LILLIAN F-2
□ Gulf SP — GULF SHORES F-2
Gunter Hill Park (COE-Alabama River Lakes) — MONTGOMERY D-4
Hardridge Creek Park (COE-Walter F. George Lake) — SHORTERVILLE E-5
Heritage Acres RV Park — TUSCUMBIA A-2
Heritage Motorcoach & Marina — ORANGE BEACH F-2
® Hidden Cove Outdoor Resort — ARLEY B-2
Hilltop RV Park — ROBERTSDALE F-2
● **Hodge's Vineyard** — AUBURN D-4
Hoover RV Park — HOOVER C-3
I-10 Kampground — MOBILE F-1
I-65 RV Campground — MOBILE F-1
Isaac Creek Park (COE - Alabama River Lakes) — MONROEVILLE E-2
Island Retreat RV Park — GULF SHORES F-2
□ Joe Wheeler SP — ROGERSVILLE A-2
□ Joe Wheeler State Park Lodge — ROGERSVILLE A-2
Johnny's Lakeside RV Resort — FOLEY F-2
□ **Johnny's RV Resort** — MOBILE F-1
John's Campground & Grocery — CENTRE B-4
● **Jule Collins Smith Museum of Fine Art** — AUBURN D-4
Koestler Parks — BAY MINETTE F-2
□ Lake Guntersville State Lodge and State Park — GUNTERSVILLE A-4
Lake Lurleen SP — TUSCALOOSA C-2
Lake Osprey RV Country Club — ELBERTA F-2
□ Lakepoint Resort Lodge — EUFAULA D-5
□ Lakepoint SP — EUFAULA D-5
Lakeside Landing RV Park & Marina — PELL CITY B-4
Lakeside Retreat RV Resort — LANGSTON A-4
Lakeside RV Park — OPELIKA C-5
Lazy Acres — ELBERTA F-2
Lazy Lake RV Park — GULF SHORES F-2
Leisure Time Campgrounds — AUBURN D-4
□ **Little Mountain Marina Camping Resort** — LANGSTON A-4
Luxury RV Resort — GULF SHORES F-2
M & J RV Park — BIRMINGHAM B-3
Magnolia Springs RV Hideaway — FOLEY F-2
Mallard Creek (TVA-Wheeler Lake) — DECATUR A-3

ALABAMA — Continued

Mc Farland Park (City Park) — FLORENCE A-2
□ **McCalla Campground** — MCCALLA C-3
Meaher SP — SPANISH FORT F-2
MILITARY PARK (Fort Rucker Campground) — OZARK E-4
MILITARY PARK (Redstone Arsenal Travel Camp) — HUNTSVILLE A-3
□ Monte Sano SP — HUNTSVILLE A-3
□ **Montgomery Campground** — MONTGOMERY D-4
® **Montgomery South RV Park** — MONTGOMERY D-4
Moundville Archaeological Park (Univ of Alabama) — MOUNDVILLE C-2
Mountain Breeze RV Park — HUNTSVILLE A-3
® Mr. D's — OZARK E-4
● **Noccalula Falls** — GADSDEN B-4
□ **Noccalula Falls Park & Campground (City Park)** — GADSDEN B-4
Northgate RV Travel Park — ATHENS A-3
Northshore Campground at the Big Rock — LANGSTON A-4
□ Oak Mountain SP — PELHAM C-3
Ozark Travel Park — OZARK E-4
Pala Verde RV Park — MOBILE F-1
□ **Parnell Creek RV Park** — WOODVILLE A-4
Paul M. Grist SP — SELMA D-3
Payne's RV Park — MOBILE F-1
Peach Park RV Park — CLANTON C-3
Peach Queen Campground — JEMISON C-3
Pecan Point RV Park — DOTHAN E-5
Pickensville Campground (COE-Tennessee/Tombigbee Waterway) — PICKENSVILLE C-1
Plantation Harbor RV Resort (Wolf Bay Plantations) — ELBERTA F-2
Point Mallard Campground (City Park) — DECATUR A-3
Ponderosa RV Park — URIAH E-2
Prairie Creek Park (COE-Alabama River Lakes) — LOWNDESBORO D-3
★ **Prattville Auto & RV Repair Center** — MONTGOMERY D-4
Rickwood Caverns SP — WARRIOR B-3
River Country Campground — GADSDEN B-4
● **Robert Trent Jones Grand Nat'l Golf Course** — OPELIKA C-5
□ Roland Cooper SP — CAMDEN D-2
Rolling Hills RV Park — CALERA C-3
Seibold Campground — GUNTERSVILLE A-4
Service Park (COE-Coffeeville Lake) — COFFEEVILLE E-1
Shady Acres Campground — MOBILE F-1
□ **Shallow Creek RV Park** — ASHFORD E-5
Sharon Johnston Park — NEW MARKET A-3
Sherling Lake Park & Campground (City Park) — GREENVILLE D-3
Six Mile Creek (COE-Alabama River Lakes) — SELMA D-3
®□ **Sleepy Holler Campground** — JASPER B-2
● **Soldiers Creek Golf Course** — ELBERTA F-2
South Sauty Creek Resort — LANGSTON A-4
Southport Campgrounds — GULF SHORES F-2
□ Southwind RV Park — MAGNOLIA SPRINGS F-2
® Styx River Resort — ROBERTSDALE F-2
Sun-Runners RV Park — GULF SHORES F-2
Sunset Travel Park — TUSCALOOSA C-2
Swan Creek Community — TANNER A-3
□ **Talladega Creekside Resort** — TALLADEGA C-4
Talladega NF (Coleman Lake) — HEFLIN B-4
Talladega NF (Payne Lake West Side) — CENTREVILLE C-3
Talladega NF (Pine Glen) — HEFLIN B-4
□ Tannehill Ironworks Historical State Park — MCCALLA C-3
● **The Quick Exxon** — AUBURN D-4
The Woods RV Park and Campground — MONTGOMERY D-4
® **University Station Motorcoach & RV Resort** — AUBURN D-4
● **U.S. Army Aviation Museum** — FORT RUCKER E-4
US Space & Rocket Center RV Campground — HUNTSVILLE A-3
Veterans Memorial Park (City Park) — FLORENCE A-2
Wales West RV Resort & Light Railway — FAIRHOPE F-2
Wheeler Reservation Campground — ROGERSVILLE A-2
White Oak Creek Park (COE-Walter F. George Lake) — EUFAULA D-5
Wilderness RV Park — ROBERTSDALE F-2
Wills Creek RV Park — FORT PAYNE A-4
Wilson Dam/Rockpile (TVA-Wilson Lake) — MUSCLE SHOALS A-2
□ Wind Creek SP — ALEXANDER CITY C-4
Wind Drift Campground — SHORTER D-4

ARKANSAS

®□ **Arkadelphia Campground & RV Park** — ARKADELPHIA D-3
□ **Arkansas Fiddlers Valley RV Resort** — MOUNTAIN VIEW B-4
Aux Arc Park (COE - Ozark Lake) — OZARK B-2
□ Beaver Lake Hide A Way Campground & RV Park — ROGERS A-2
Bidwell Point Rec. Area (COE-Norfork Lake) — MOUNTAIN HOME A-3
® Blue Clouds RV and Cabin Resort — EDGEMONT B-3
△□ **Blue Heron Campground and Resort** — FLIPPIN A-3
Blue Sky RV Park — MOUNTAIN VIEW B-4
Buck Creek Rec. Area (COE-Bull Shoals Lake) — PEEL A-3
Buffalo National River (Buffalo Point Campground) — YELLVILLE A-3
Buffalo National River (Tyler Bend Campground) — ST. JOE A-3
□ Bull Shoals SP — BULL SHOALS A-3
Bullfrog Marina & RV Park — ASHDOWN D-2
Burns Park (City Park) — NORTH LITTLE ROCK C-3
Cane Creek SP — STAR CITY D-4
Catherine's Landing at Hot Springs — HOT SPRINGS C-3
Chateau Aux Arc RV Park — ALTUS B-2
Cherokee Park (COE-Toad Suck Ferry) — MORRILTON B-3
Cherokee Recreation Area (COE-Greers Ferry Lake) — DRASCO B-4
Choctaw Recreation Area (COE-Greers Ferry Lake) — CHOCTAW B-3
Citadel Bluff (COE-Ozark Lake) — CECIL B-2
Clear Creek (COE-Ozark Lake) — ALMA B-2
Cloud Nine RV Park — HOT SPRINGS C-3
□ **Coffee Creek Motel and RV Park** — PERRYVILLE C-3
Cove Creek (COE-Greers Ferry Lake) — QUITMAN B-3
Crabtree RV Park — ALMA B-2
Craighead Forest Park (City Park) — JONESBORO B-5
Cranfield Campground (COE-Norfork Lake) — MOUNTAIN HOME A-3
Crater of Diamonds SP — MURFREESBORO D-2
Cricket Creek Rec. Area (COE-Table Rock Lake) — OMAHA A-3

ARKANSAS — Continued

Crossett RV Park & Campground (Crossett Port Auth) — CROSSETT E-4
□ Crowley's Ridge SP — PARAGOULD A-5
Crystal Hill RV Park — NORTH LITTLE ROCK C-3
Daisy SP — DAISY D-2
Dam Site Rec Area (COE-Beaver Lake) — EUREKA SPRINGS A-2
Dam Site Recreation Area (COE-Bull Shoals Lake) — BULL SHOALS A-3
Dam Site Recreation Area (COE-Greers Ferry Lake) — HEBER SPRINGS B-4
DeGray Lake Resort SP — ARKADELPHIA D-3
Denton Ferry RV Park Resort — COTTER A-3
△□ Devil's Den SP — WEST FORK A-2
Devil's Fork Rec. Area (COE-Greers Ferry Lake) — GREERS FERRY B-3
Downtown Riverside RV Park — NORTH LITTLE ROCK C-3
Fair Park RV Park (City Park) — HOPE D-2
Fairfield Bay Campground — FAIRFIELD BAY B-3
● **Fort Smith Visitors Center** — FORT SMITH B-1
Four States Fairgrounds RV Park — TEXARKANA E-2
★ **Fred & Jack Trailer Sales** — LITTLE ROCK C-3
Gamaliel Recreation Area (COE-Norfork Lake) — MOUNTAIN HOME A-3
Golden Pond RV Park — SHIRLEY B-3
Grand Marais (Union County Park) — FELSENTHAL E-3
Green Acres RV Park — MOUNTAIN VIEW B-4
□ Green Tree Lodge & RV Park — EUREKA SPRINGS A-2
Greentree RV Park — SILOAM SPRINGS A-1
Hardy Camper Park (City Park) — HARDY A-4
Harrison Village Campground & RV Park — HARRISON A-3
Heber Springs Recreation Area (COE-Greers Ferry Lake) — HEBER SPRINGS B-4
Henderson Rec. Area (COE-Norfork Lake) — HENDERSON A-3
Heritage Inn and RV Park — BRINKLEY C-4
Hickory Creek Recreation Area (COE-Beaver Lake) — SPRINGDALE A-2
Highway 125 Recreation Area (COE - Bull Shoals Lake) — PEEL A-3
Hill Creek Public Use Area (COE-Greers Ferry Lake) — DRASCO B-4
®□ **Holiday Mountain Resort** — MOUNTAIN VIEW B-4
Horseshoe Bend Recreation Area (COE-Beaver Lake) — ROGERS A-2
®□ **Hot Springs National Park - KOA** — HOT SPRINGS C-3
Hot Springs NP (Gulpha Gorge Campground) — HOT SPRINGS C-3
I-30 Travel Park — BENTON C-3
Indian Creek Recreation Area (COE-Beaver Lake) — GATEWAY A-2
Ivy's Cove RV Retreat — RUSSELLVILLE B-3
J & J RV Park — HOT SPRINGS C-3
Jacksonport SP — JACKSONPORT B-4
JB's RV Park & Campground — BENTON C-3
John F. Kennedy (COE-Greers Ferry Lake) — HEBER SPRINGS B-4
Jordan Recreation Area (COE-Norfork Lake) — JORDAN A-3
★ **Jordan's RV Service** — HARRISON A-3
®□ Kettle Campground, Cabins & RV Park — EUREKA SPRINGS A-2
□ KOA-Eureka Springs — EUREKA SPRINGS A-2
□ **KOA-Fort Smith/Alma** — ALMA B-2
□ KOA-Little Rock North — NORTH LITTLE ROCK C-3
□ KOA-Morrilton/Conway — MORRILTON B-3
△□ Lake Catherine SP — MALVERN D-3
Lake Charles SP — BLACK ROCK A-4
Lake Chicot County Park — LAKE VILLAGE E-4
□ Lake Chicot SP — LAKE VILLAGE E-4
Lake Dardanelle SP — RUSSELLVILLE B-3
Lake Hamilton RV Resort — HOT SPRINGS C-3
□ Lake Leatherwood City Park — EUREKA SPRINGS A-2
□ Lake Ouachita SP — HOT SPRINGS C-3
Lake Poinsett SP — HARRISBURG B-5
Lakeside RV Park — TUMBLING SHOALS B-4
Lakeview Public Use Area (COE-Bull Shoals Lake) — LAKEVIEW A-3
Lead Hill Public Use Area (COE-Bull Shoals Lake) — LEAD HILL A-3
Leisure Landing RV Park — HOT SPRINGS C-3
□ Lindsey's Resort on the Little Red River — HEBER SPRINGS B-4
Lost Bridge Park (COE-Beaver Lake) — GARFIELD A-2
Maumelle (COE-Toad Suck Ferry) — LITTLE ROCK C-3
□ **Memphis KOA** — MARION B-5
Merrisach Lake (COE-Pine Bluff River Area) — TICHNOR D-4
MILITARY PARK (Little Rock AFB FAMCAMP) — JACKSONVILLE C-4
Mill Creek Rec. Area (COE-Greers Ferry Lake) — GREERS FERRY B-3
Millwood SP — ASHDOWN D-2
□ **Miner's Camping & Rock Shop** — MURFREESBORO D-2
Mission RV Park — RUSSELLVILLE B-3
Moro Bay SP — EL DORADO E-3
□ Mt. Nebo SP — DARDANELLE B-3
□ Mt. View RV Park/Guest House Motel — MOUNTAIN VIEW B-4
Narrows Recreation Area (COE-Greers Ferry Lake) — GREERS FERRY B-3
● **North Little Rock Visitors Bureau** — NORTH LITTLE ROCK C-3
Notrebes Bend (COE-Arkansas Post River Area) — TICHNOR D-4
Oakland Public Use Area (COE-Bull Shoals Lake) — OAKLAND A-3
Old Davidsonville SP — POCAHONTAS A-5
Old Hwy-25 Campground (COE-Greers Ferry Lake) — HEBER SPRINGS B-4
Old Post Road Park (COE-Lake Dardanelle) — RUSSELLVILLE B-3
Ouachita National Forest (Albert Pike Campground) — LANGLEY D-2
Ouachita National Forest (Charlton Rec. Area) — HOT SPRINGS C-3
Ouachita National Forest (Mill Creek Rec. Area) — Y CITY C-2
Ouachita National Forest (Shady Lake Rec. Area) — ATHENS D-2
★ **Outdoor Living Center** — RUSSELLVILLE B-3
★ **Outdoor Living Center** — VAN BUREN B-1
Outdoor Living Center RV Park — RUSSELLVILLE B-3
Outdoor Resorts of the Ozarks — BLUE EYE A-2
Outlet Area (COE-Blue Mountain Lake) — WAVELAND B-2
Overland RV Park — VAN BUREN B-1
Ozark Isle Park (COE-Bull Shoals Lake) — OAKLAND A-3
Ozark National Forest (Blanchard Springs Rec. Area) — FIFTY-SIX A-3
Ozark National Forest (Cove Lake Campground) — PARIS B-2
Ozark National Forest (Gunner Pool Rec. Area) — FIFTY-SIX A-3
Ozark National Forest (Redding Campground) — OZARK B-2
□ **Ozark RV Park** — MOUNTAIN VIEW B-4
® **Ozark View RV Park & Campground** — BURLINGTON A-2

Panther Bay (COE-Norfork Lake) — MOUNTAIN HOME A-3
Park Ridge RV Campground — VAN BUREN B-1
Parkers RV Park — HARRISON A-3
Parkway Travel Park — HARRISON A-3
□ Pecan Grove RV Park — LAKE VILLAGE E-4
Perkins RV Park — JONESBORO B-5
△□ Petit Jean SP — MORRILTON B-3
Pilgrims's Rest RV Park — SPRINGDALE A-2
● Pine Bluff Parks & Recreation — PINE BLUFF D-4
Piney Bay (COE - Dardanelle Lake) — PINEY B-2
Prairie Creek Recreation Area (COE-Beaver Lake) — ROGERS A-2
Quarry Cove (COE-Nimrod Lake) — OLA C-2
Quarry Cove/Dam Park (COE - Norfork Lake) — MOUNTAIN HOME A-3
Queen Wilhelmina SP — MENA C-2
★ Razorback Camper Sales — HOT SPRINGS C-3
Rising Star (COE-Pine Bluff River Area) — LINWOOD D-4
Robinson Point (COE-Norfork Lake) — MOUNTAIN HOME A-3
Rocky Branch Park (COE-Beaver Lake) — ROGERS A-2
□ Rogers/Pea Ridge Garden RV and Campground — GARFIELD A-2
St. Francis National Forest (Boundary Campground) — MARIANNA C-5
Saracen Trace RV Park (City Park) — PINE BLUFF D-4
□ Shadow Mountain RV Park — MENA C-2
®□ Shady Oaks Campground & RV Park — HARRISON A-3
®□ Sherwood Forest RV Park & Campground — YELLVILLE A-3
Shiloh Recreation Area (COE-Greers Ferry Lake) — GREERS FERRY B-3
Shoal Bay (COE-Lake Dardanelle) — NEW BLAINE B-2
Silver Eagle RV Campground — HAMPTON E-3
Southgate RV Park of Fayetteville — FAYETTEVILLE A-2
Spadra (COE-Lake Dardanelle) — CLARKSVILLE B-2
Speedway RV Park — BATESVILLE B-4
Springhill (COE - Ozark Lake) — BARLING B-1
Starkey Recreation Area (COE - Beaver Lake) — EUREKA SPRINGS A-2
Sugar Loaf Rec. Area (COE-Greers Ferry Lake) — GREERS FERRY B-3
Sunlight Bay (COE-Nimrod Lake) — PLAINVIEW C-2
Sunrise RV Park — TEXARKANA E-2
Sweeden Island (COE-Lake Dardanelle) — ATKINS B-3
□ Sylamore Creek Camp — MOUNTAIN VIEW B-4
T Ricks RV Park — HAZEN C-4
Tar Camp (COE-Pine Bluff River Area) — REDFIELD C-3
● The Creeks Golf Resort — CAVE SPRINGS A-2
The Creeks RV Resort — CAVE SPRINGS A-2
Timbercrest RV & Mobile Home Park — HOT SPRINGS C-3
Toad Suck Ferry Park (COE-Toad Suck Ferry) — CONWAY C-3
Tom Sawyer's Mississippi River RV Park — WEST MEMPHIS B-5
□ Trails End RV Park — NORTH LITTLE ROCK C-3
□ Treasure Isle RV Park — HOT SPRINGS C-3
Tucker Hollow (COE-Bull Shoals Lake) — LEAD HILL A-3
□ Village Creek SP — FORREST CITY C-5
□ Wanderlust RV Park — EUREKA SPRINGS A-2
War Eagle Public Use Area (COE-Beaver Lake) — SPRINGDALE A-2
Waveland Park (COE-Blue Mountain Lake) — WAVELAND B-2
★ Wheels RV — SPRINGDALE A-2
® Whispering Pines RV Park — CLINTON B-3
White Oak SP — BLUFF CITY D-3
Whitewater Bluegrass RV Park — MOUNTAIN VIEW B-4
Wiederkehr Wine Cellars RV — ALTUS B-2
● Wild Horse Theatre — MOUNTAIN VIEW B-4
□ Wilderness Hills Park & Campground — SILOAM SPRINGS A-1
Willow Beach (Corp of Engineers - Pine Bluff River Area) — NORTH LITTLE ROCK C-3
Withrow Springs SP — HUNTSVILLE A-2
Woolly Hollow SP — CONWAY C-3
Young's Lakeshore RV Resort — HOT SPRINGS C-3

CONNECTICUT

□ Aces High RV Park — EAST LYME D-5
®□ Acorn Acres Campsites — NORWICH C-5
American Legion State Forest (Austin F. Hawes Memorial Campground) — PLEASANT VALLEY A-3
Black Rock State Park — THOMASTON B-2
Branch Brook Campground — THOMASTON B-2
® Brialee RV & Tent Park — ASHFORD A-5
Camp Niantic Family Campground — NIANTIC D-5
® Chamberlain Lake Campground — WOODSTOCK A-6
Charlie Brown Campground — EASTFORD A-5
□ Circle C Campground — VOLUNTOWN C-6
Countryside RV Park — GRISWOLD C-6
□ Cozy Hills Campground — BANTAM B-2
★ Cusson Automotive, Inc — SOUTH WINDSOR B-4
Deer Haven Campground — LISBON B-6
Devil's Hopyard State Park — EAST HADDAM C-4
Hammonasset Beach State Park — MADISON D-4
Hemlock Hill Camp Resort — LITCHFIELD B-2
®□ Hidden Acres Family Campground — PRESTON C-6
Highland Campground — SCOTLAND B-5
★ Highland Orchards RV — NORTH STONINGTON C-6
Hopeville Pond State Park — JEWETT CITY B-6
Housatonic Meadows State Park — CORNWALL BRIDGE B-2
Kettletown State Park — SOUTHBURY C-2
®□ KOA - Sterling — STERLING B-6
● Lake Compounce Family Theme Park — BRISTOL B-3
Lake Waramaug State Park — NEW PRESTON B-2
Little City Campground — HIGGANUM C-4
®□ Lone Oak Campsites — CANAAN A-2
Macedonia Brook State Park — KENT B-1
Mashamoquet Brook State Park — ABINGTON A-6
● Mashantucket Pequot Museum — MASHANTUCKET C-6
□ Mineral Springs Family Campground — STAFFORD SPRINGS A-5
Moosemeadow Camping Resort — WILLINGTON A-5
®□ Mystic KOA Campground — NORTH STONINGTON C-6
□ Nature's Campsites — VOLUNTOWN C-6
® Nelson's Family Campground — EAST HAMPTON C-4
Nickerson Park Family Campground — CHAPLIN B-5
□ Odetah Camping Resort — BOZRAH C-5
Pachaug State Forest (Green Falls Campground) — VOLUNTOWN C-6
Pachaug State Forest (Mount Misery Campground) — VOLUNTOWN C-6
Peppertree Camping — EASTFORD A-5
®□ River Bend Campground — ONECO B-6
®□ Riverdale Farm Campsite — CLINTON D-4
Rocky Neck State Park — NIANTIC D-5
□ Ross Hill Park — LISBON B-6
Salem Farms Campground — SALEM C-5
★ Scranton Motors, Inc — VERNON B-4
®△ Seaport Campground (Morgan RV Resorts) — MYSTIC D-6
®□ Stateline Campresort & Cabins — EAST KILLINGLY A-6
® Strawberry Park Resort Campground — PRESTON C-6
®□ Water's Edge Campground — LEBANON B-5
West Thompson Lake (COE-West Thompson Lake) — THOMPSON A-6
White Memorial Family Campground (Point Folly) — LITCHFIELD B-2
□ White Pines Campsites — BARKHAMSTED A-3
Wilderness Lake Park — WILLINGTON A-5
Witch Meadow Lake Campground — SALEM C-5
®□ Wolf's Den Family Campground — EAST HADDAM C-4

DELAWARE

®□ Big Oaks Family Campground — REHOBOTH BEACH E-4
Cape Henlopen SP — LEWES E-4
Cedar Creek Landing Campground — LINCOLN E-3
Delaware Seashore SP — REHOBOTH BEACH E-4

DELAWARE — Continued

□ G & R Campground — HARRINGTON D-2
□ Killens Pond SP — FELTON D-2
Lums Pond SP — GLASGOW B-2
□ Tall Pines Campground Resort — LEWES E-4
□ Trap Pond SP — LAUREL F-2
Treasure Beach RV Park — FENWICK ISLAND F-4

DISTRICT OF COLUMBIA

FLORIDA

7 Oaks RV Park & Sales — HUDSON C-3
® Adelaide Shores RV Resort — AVON PARK D-4
● Ah-Tah-Thi-Ki Museum — CLEWISTON D-4
Alligator Park — PUNTA GORDA D-3
Anastasia State Park — ST. AUGUSTINE B-4
Apalachicola National Forest (Wright Lake Campground) — SUMATRA F-3
® Aqua Isles Mobile Home & RV Resort (Morgan RV Resorts) — LA BELLE D-4
Arbor Terrace RV Resort — BRADENTON D-3
Arcadia Peace River Campground — ARCADIA D-3
□ Arrowhead Campsites — MARIANNA E-3
★ Arrowhead RV Sales — MARIANNA E-3
Aruba RV Park — MOORE HAVEN D-4
Avalon Landing RV Park — MILTON F-1
Aztec RV Resort — MARGATE E-5
□ Bahia Honda State Park — BAHIA HONDA KEY F-4
Baker Acres RV Resort — ZEPHYRHILLS C-3
® Barrington Hills RV Resort — HUDSON C-3
Bay Aire Travel Trailer Park — PALM HARBOR C-3
Bay Bayou RV Resort — TAMPA C-3
Beaver Lake Campground — QUINCY A-1
®□ Bee's RV Resort — CLERMONT C-3
Belle Glade Campground (City Park) — BELLE GLADE D-5
®□ belle parc RV Resort — BROOKSVILLE C-3
□ Beverly Beach Camptown RV Resort — FLAGLER BEACH B-4
□ Big Cypress RV Resort — CLEWISTON D-4
Big Lagoon State Park — PENSACOLA F-1
Big Oak RV Park — TALLAHASSEE A-1
● Big Pine Key & Florida's Lower Keys — KEY WEST F-4
Big Tree RV Resort — ARCADIA D-3
□ Bill Frederick Park at Turkey Lake (City Park) — ORLANDO C-4
Blackwater River State Park — HOLT E-1
Blair's Jungle Den — ASTOR B-4
Blue Jay RV Park — DADE CITY C-3
□ Blue Spring State Park — ORANGE CITY B-4
Bluewater Key RV Resort — KEY WEST F-4
Bonita Lake RV Resort — BONITA SPRINGS E-4
Bonnet Lake RV Resort — AVON PARK D-4
Boyd's Key West Campground — KEY WEST F-4
Breezy Hill RV Resort — POMPANO BEACH E-5
Breezy Oaks RV Park — BUSHNELL C-3
Breezy Palms RV Park — MELBOURNE C-5
® Breezy Pines RV Estates — BIG PINE KEY F-4
● Broward County Parks & Recreation Division — FORT LAUDERDALE E-5
Buckhead Ridge Marina Resort — OKEECHOBEE D-4
Bull Creek Campground & Marina — BUNNELL B-4
Bullock's Landing RV Park & Storage Facility — LAKE WALES C-4
®□ Bulow Plantation RV Resort — FLAGLER BEACH B-4
Buttonwood Bay — SEBRING D-4
Buttonwood Inlet RV Resort (Formerly Key Way) — CORTEZ D-3
Caladesi RV Park — PALM HARBOR C-3
® Calusa Campground Condominium Association — KEY LARGO F-3
Camelot RV Park — MALABAR C-5
® Camp Florida Resort — LAKE PLACID D-4
Camp Lemora RV Park — THONOTOSASSA C-3
□ Camp Macks River Resort — LAKE WALES C-4
Camp Nebraska — TAMPA C-3
Camper Village — OCALA B-3
Campers Holiday — BROOKSVILLE C-3
□ Campers Inn — PANAMA CITY BEACH F-2
□ Camping on the Gulf — DESTIN F-2
Camp'n Aire RV Resort — LAKE WALES C-4
□ Carrabelle Beach Outdoor Destinations — CARRABELLE BEACH B-1
Casey Jones' RV Park — LAKE CITY A-3
Cattail Creek RV Park — YANKEETOWN B-3
C.B. Smith Park (Broward County Park) — PEMBROKE PINES E-5
Cedar Key RV Resort — CEDAR KEY B-2
Cedar Key Sunset Isle RV Park — CEDAR KEY B-2
Cedar Pines Campground — MILTON F-1
® Central Park of Haines City — HAINES CITY C-4
★ Charlotte RV Center — PORT CHARLOTTE D-3
Chassahowitzka River Campground (City Park) — CHASSAHOWITZKA C-3
Chokoloskee Island Park & Campground — CHOKOLOSKEE E-4
® Christmas RV Park — TITUSVILLE C-4
Citrus Hill Park & Sales — DADE CITY C-3
Citrus Hills RV Park — DOVER C-3
□ Clark Family Campground — ORANGE CITY B-4
Clearwater Travel Resort — CLEARWATER C-3
Clearwater-Tarpon Springs RV Campground — PALM HARBOR C-3
®□ Clerbrook Golf & RV Resort Encore — CLERMONT C-3
®□ Clewiston/Lake Okeechobee KOA Kampground — CLEWISTON D-4
Cloverleaf Forest RV Resort — BROOKSVILLE C-3
Club Naples RV Resort (Morgan RV Resorts) — NAPLES E-4
Collier-Seminole State Park — NAPLES E-4
★ Como RV & Truck Sales — HOMOSASSA C-3
★ Como RV & Truck Sales, Service & RV Collision Center — INVERNESS C-3
Countryside RV Park — LAKE PANASOFFKEE C-3
Covered Wagon Campground — HOMOSASSA C-3
Craig's RV Park — ARCADIA D-3
® Crooked Hook RV Resort — CLEWISTON D-4
Cross Creek Country Club & RV Resort — ARCADIA D-3
□ Crystal Isles — CRYSTAL RIVER B-3
Crystal Lake RV Park — MIMS C-4
® Crystal Lake RV Resort — NAPLES E-4
® Crystal Lake Village — WAUCHULA D-3
Cypress Campground & RV Park — WINTER HAVEN C-4
□ Cypress Isle RV Park & Marina — LAKE PLACID D-4
★ Cypress RV Sales — WINTER HAVEN C-4
Cypress Woods RV Resort — FORT MYERS D-3
Daytona Beach KOA — PORT ORANGE B-4
® Daytona Beach RV Resort — PORT ORANGE B-4
Daytona Speedway KOA — DAYTONA BEACH B-4
Dead Lakes State Recreation Area — WEWAHITCHKA F-3
® Deer Creek Golf & RV Resort — DAVENPORT C-4
Deerwood Madison Campground & Motel — MADISON A-2
Del Raton RV Park — DELRAY BEACH E-5
□ Destin Recreation Area — DESTIN F-2
Destin Village RV Resort — DESTIN F-2
®□ Devil's Den Springs Resort — WILLISTON B-3
□ Disney's Fort Wilderness Resort & Campground — LAKE BUENA VISTA C-4
★ Dixie Trailer Supply — FORT LAUDERDALE E-5
® Dove Rest RV Park & Campground — MARIANNA E-3
Dunedin RV Resort — DUNEDIN C-3
★ Eagle's Pride at the Great Outdoors — TITUSVILLE C-4
East Haven RV Park — WINTER HAVEN C-4
□ East Lake RV Resort Restaurant & Marina — KISSIMMEE C-4
Easterlin Park (Broward County Park) — OAKLAND PARK E-5

FLORIDA — Continued

® Elite Resorts at Citrus Valley — CLERMONT C-3
□ Elite Resorts At Salt Springs — SALT SPRINGS B-3
Ellenton Gardens Travel Resort — ELLENTON D-3
□ Emerald Beach RV Park — NAVARRE F-1
Emerald Coast RV Beach Resort — PANAMA CITY BEACH F-2
Encore Lake Magic RV Resort — CLERMONT C-3
® Encore Manatee RV Resort — BRADENTON D-3
® Encore Royal Coachman — NOKOMIS D-3
Encore Winter Quarters-Pasco RV Park — LUTZ C-3
Endless Summer RV Park — NAPLES E-4
Everglades Isle Motorcoach Retreat — EVERGLADES CITY E-4
Everglades National Park (Long Pine Key) — HOMESTEAD E-5
Falling Waters State Park — CHIPLEY E-2
Faver-Dykes State Park — ST. AUGUSTINE B-4
Fiesta Grove RV Resort — PALMETTO D-3
® Fiesta Key RV Resort — FIESTA KEY F-5
®□ Fisheating Creek Campground — PALMDALE D-4
® Fisherman's Cove Golf Marina & RV Resort — TAVARES C-3
Fishermans Cove RV Resort — PALMETTO D-3
Flagler by the Sea Campground — FLAGLER BEACH B-4
● Flagler County Chamber of Commerce — PALM COAST B-4
□ Flamingo Lake RV Resort — JACKSONVILLE A-3
● Florida Association of RV Parks and Campgrounds — TALLAHASSEE A-1
□ Florida Camp Inn — DAVENPORT C-4
Florida Caverns State Park — MARIANNA E-3
Florida City Campsite (City Park) — FLORIDA CITY E-5
® Florida Gateway Resort — JASPER A-2
Florida Grande Motor Coach Resort — WEBSTER C-3
Florida Pines Mobile Home Court & RV — VENICE D-3
® Florida Springs RV Resort & Campgrounds — BONIFAY E-2
Forest Lake Estates RV Resort — ZEPHYRHILLS C-3
Fort Clinch State Park — FERNANDINA BEACH A-4
® Fort Myers Beach RV Resort — FORT MYERS BEACH E-3
Fred Gannon Rocky Bayou State Recreation Area — NICEVILLE F-2
® Frog Creek Campground — PALMETTO D-3
Gamble Rogers Memorial State Park at Flagler Beach — FLAGLER BEACH B-4
Gator Park — MIAMI E-5
Geronimo RV Resort — DESTIN F-2
□ Ginnie Springs Outdoors LLC — HIGH SPRINGS B-3
Glen Haven RV Resort — ZEPHYRHILLS C-3
® Goethe Trailhead Ranch & RV Park — DUNNELLON B-3
Goldcoaster Mobile Home & RV Resort — HOMESTEAD E-5
® Good Life RV Resort — BARTOW C-3
Gracious RV Park — OKEECHOBEE D-4
□ Grand Lake RV & Golf Resort (Morgan RV Resorts) — ORANGE LAKE B-3
Grassy Key RV Park & Resort — MARATHON F-4
□ Grayton Beach State Park — GRAYTON BEACH F-2
® Great Oak Campgrounds — KISSIMMEE C-4
® Grove Ridge RV Resort — DADE CITY C-3
Groves RV Resort — FORT MYERS D-3
® Gulf Air RV Resort — FORT MYERS BEACH E-3
Gulf Islands National Seashore (Fort Pickens) — PENSACOLA F-1
□ Gulf Pines KOA — MILTON F-1
® Gulf View RV Resort — PUNTA GORDA D-3
Gulf Waters RV Resort — FORT MYERS BEACH E-3
Haines Creek RV Village — LEESBURG C-3
□ Hammondell Campsites & RV Sales — WINTER HAVEN C-4
□ Hanna Park (City Park) — JACKSONVILLE A-3
® Happy Days RV Park — ZEPHYRHILLS C-3
®□ Happy Traveler RV Park — THONOTOSASSA C-3
Harbor Lakes — PORT CHARLOTTE D-3
®□ Harris Village RV Park — ORMOND BEACH B-4
Hickory Point Mobile Home & RV Park — TARPON SPRINGS C-3
Hidden River Travel Resort — RIVERVIEW C-3
Hidden Valley Campground — BROOKSVILLE C-3
Hide-A-Way RV Resort — RUSKIN D-3
High Springs Campground — HIGH SPRINGS B-3
® Highbanks Marina & Campresort — DEBARY B-4
Highland Oaks RV Resort — SEBRING D-4
Highland Pines RV Resort — POMPANO BEACH E-5
® Highland Wheel Estates — SEBRING D-4
Highland Woods — POMPANO BEACH E-5
Highlands Hammock State Park — SEBRING D-4
Hillcrest RV Resort — ZEPHYRHILLS C-3
Hillsborough River State Park — THONOTOSASSA C-3
Ho-Hum RV Park — CARRABELLE B-1
Holiday Campground — PANACEA A-1
Holiday Cove RV Resort — BRADENTON D-3
Holiday Park — HALLANDALE E-5
Holiday Trav-L-Park RV Resort — OCALA B-3
Holiday Travel Resort — LEESBURG C-3
□ Homosassa Carefree RV Resort(formerly Turtle Creek) — HOMOSASSA SPRINGS C-3
® Horseshoe Cove RV Resort — BRADENTON D-3
Hunter's Run RV Resort — ZEPHYRHILLS C-3
Imperial Bonita Estates RV Resort — BONITA SPRINGS E-4
Indian Creek Resort — FORT MYERS BEACH E-3
Indian Forest Campground — ST. AUGUSTINE B-4
□ Indian River Shores Mobile Home Park — MICCO C-5
□ Inn & Out RV Park — LAKE CITY A-3
International RV Park & Campground — DAYTONA BEACH B-4
★ J. D. Sanders RV Center — GAINESVILLE B-3
Ja-Mar North Travel Park — PORT RICHEY C-3
Ja-Mar Travel Park — PORT RICHEY C-3
Jennings Outdoor Resort Campground — JENNINGS A-2
Jetty Park (Canaveral Port Auth) — CAPE CANAVERAL C-5
Jim's RV Park — ZEPHYRHILLS C-3
John Pennekamp Coral Reef State Park — KEY LARGO F-5
John Prince Memorial Park (Palm Beach County Park) — LAKE WORTH D-5
Jolly Roger Travel Park — MARATHON F-4
□ Jonathan Dickinson State Park — HOBE SOUND D-5
® Juno Ocean Walk RV Resort — JUNO BEACH D-5
Kelly's Countryside RV Park — CALLAHAN A-3
Key RV Park — MARATHON F-4
□ Kings Kamp, RV, Tent & Marina — KEY LARGO F-5
Kissimmee South (formerly Three Worlds Resort) — DAVENPORT C-4
®□ KOA Naples — NAPLES E-4
□ KOA Orlando/Kissimmee — KISSIMMEE C-4
□ KOA-Cape Kennedy — TITUSVILLE C-4
□ KOA-Chattahoochee/Tallahassee West — CHATTAHOOCHEE A-1
□ KOA-St. Petersburg — ST. PETERSBURG C-3
® KOA-Sugarloaf Key West — SUGARLOAF KEY F-4
□ KOA-Tallahassee East/Monticello — MONTICELLO A-2
®□ KOA-Wildwood — WILDWOOD B-3
Koreshan State Park — ESTERO E-3
Kozy Kampers RV Park — FORT LAUDERDALE E-5
® Labonte's Garden RV Park — FORT MYERS D-3
® Lake Bryant MH & RV Park — OCKLAWAHA B-3
®□ Lake City Campground — LAKE CITY A-3
® Lake Glenada RV Park — AVON PARK D-4
Lake Griffin State Park — FRUITLAND PARK B-3
Lake Josephine RV Resort — SEBRING D-4
Lake Kissimmee State Park — LAKE WALES C-4
Lake Letta RV Park — AVON PARK D-4
Lake Manatee State Recreation Area — BRADENTON D-3
□ Lake Marian Paradise Marina & RV Resort — KENANSVILLE C-4
Lake Monroe Park (Volusia County Park) — DEBARY B-4
□ Lake Okeechobee Outpost KOA — PAHOKEE D-5
Lake San Marino RV Resort — NAPLES E-4
Lake Toho RV Resort — ST. CLOUD C-4
Lake Trinity Estates — HOLLYWOOD E-5
Lake Waldena Resort — SILVER SPRINGS B-3
Lake Wales RV & Campsites — LAKE WALES C-4

ALPHABETICAL LISTINGS CONTINUED

FLORIDA — Continued

□ Lakeland RV Resort — LAKELAND C-3
® Lakemont Ridge Home & RV Park — FROSTPROOF C-4
★ Land Yachts — JUPITER D-5
Larry & Penny Thompson Park & Campground — MIAMI E-5
Lazy Dazy Retreat — LAKELAND C-3
® Lazy Lakes RV Resort — SUGARLOAF KEY F-4
Lazydays RV Campground — TAMPA C-3
★ Lazydays Sales & Service — TAMPA C-3
• Lee County Visitor & Convention — FORT MYERS D-3
Lee's Country Campground — WHITE SPRINGS A-3
Lee's Travel Park — LARGO C-3
® Leisure Days RV Resort — ZEPHYRHILLS C-3
LeLynn RV Resort — POLK CITY C-3
Lettuce Lake Travel Resort — PORT CHARLOTTE D-3
□ Lion Country Safari KOA — WEST PALM BEACH D-5
® Little Charlie Creek RV Park — WAUCHULA D-3
Little Manatee River State Recreation Area — WIMAUMA D-3
Little Talbot Island State Park — JACKSONVILLE A-3
Little Willies RV Resort — ARCADIA D-3
Live Oak Landing — FREEPORT F-2
Long Key State Park — LONG KEY F-4
Long Point Park (Brevard County Park) — SEBASTIAN C-5
® M RV Resort — MOORE HAVEN D-4
Majestic Oaks RV Resort — ZEPHYRHILLS C-3
Manatee Hammock Park (Brevard County Park) — TITUSVILLE C-4
Manatee Springs State Park — CHIEFLAND B-2
® Many Mansions RV Park — DADE CITY C-3
Marco Naples Hitching Post Travel Resort — NAPLES E-4
® Marina RV Resort — MOORE HAVEN D-4
Markham Park (Broward County Park) — SUNRISE E-5
Melbourne Beach Mobile Park — MELBOURNE BEACH C-5
Merry "D" RV Sanctuary — KISSIMMEE C-4
□ Miami Everglades Campground — MIAMI E-5
□ Mike Roess Gold Head Branch State Park — KEYSTONE HEIGHTS B-3
□ MILITARY PARK (Destin Recreation Area-Fort Benning GA) — DESTIN F-2
MILITARY PARK (FAMCAMP-Eglin AFB) — VALPARAISO F-2
MILITARY PARK (Jacksonville NAS) — JACKSONVILLE A-3
MILITARY PARK (Key West NAS-Sigsbee Park) — KEY WEST F-4
MILITARY PARK (Lake Pippin Rec Area-Maxwell/Gunter AFB AL) — NICEVILLE F-2
MILITARY PARK (Manatee Cove Campground-Patrick AFB) — COCOA BEACH C-5
®△□ MILITARY PARK (Oak Grove Fam-Camp-Pensacola NAS) — PENSACOLA F-1
MILITARY PARK (Tyndall AFB FAMCAMP) — PANAMA CITY F-2
Mill Creek RV Resort — KISSIMMEE C-4
Mouse Mountain RV Camping Resort — DAVENPORT C-4
□ Myakka River State Park — SARASOTA D-3
Myakka RV Resort - KOA — VENICE D-3
Naples Gardens - Morgan RV Resorts (formerly Kountree Kampinn) — NAPLES E-4
Nascar RV Resorts at Blueberry Hill — BUSHNELL C-3
Nature Coast Landings Resort — CRYSTAL RIVER B-3
□ Nature's Resort & Marina — HOMOSASSA C-3
□ Navarre Beach Campground — NAVARRE F-1
Neapolitan Cove RV Resort — NAPLES E-4
® Nettles Island Resort & RV Park — JENSEN BEACH D-5
□ New Smyrna Beach RV Park — NEW SMYRNA BEACH B-4
□ North Beach Camp Resort — ST. AUGUSTINE B-4
North Coast RV Park & Marina — FORT LAUDERDALE E-5
North Lake Estates RV Resort (Morgan RV Resorts) — MOORE HAVEN D-4
★ North Trail RV — FORT MYERS D-3
★ North Trail RV Center — FORT LAUDERDALE E-5
®□ Nova Family Campground — DAYTONA BEACH B-4
Oak Haven MH & RV Park — PORT CHARLOTTE D-3
Oak Tree Village Campground — OCALA B-3
®□ Oaks 'N Pines RV Campground — LAKE CITY A-3
Ocala National Forest (Alexander Springs Rec. Area) — ALTOONA B-4
Ocala National Forest (Big Bass Campground) — ALTOONA B-4
Ocala National Forest (Big Scrub Campground) — ALTOONA B-4
Ocala National Forest (Clearwater Lake Campground) — UMATILLA B-4
Ocala National Forest (Fore Lake Campground) — SILVER SPRINGS B-3
Ocala National Forest (Juniper Springs Rec. Area) — ASTOR B-4
Ocala National Forest (Lake Dorr Campground) — UMATILLA B-4
Ocala National Forest (Salt Springs Rec. Area) — SALT SPRINGS B-3
Ocala North RV Park — REDDICK B-3
□ Ocala RV Camp Resort — OCALA B-3
Ocala Sun RV Resort — OCALA B-3
Ocean Grove RV Resort — ST. AUGUSTINE B-4
Ochlockonee River State Park — SOPCHOPPY A-1
• Okeechobee County Tourism Development Council — OKEECHOBEE D-4
Okeechobee Landings — CLEWISTON D-4
®□ Okeechobee Resort KOA — OKEECHOBEE D-4
® Old Town Campground N' Retreat — OLD TOWN B-2
□ O'Leno State Park/River Rise — HIGH SPRINGS B-3
★ Open Road RV Center — FORT WALTON BEACH F-2
Orange Blossom Adult RV Park — BOWLING GREEN D-3
Orange City RV Resort — ORANGE CITY B-4
Orange Grove Campground — KISSIMMEE C-4
® Orange Grove Mobile Home & RV Park — FORT MYERS D-3
Orbit RV Park — GRANT C-5
Orchid Lake RV Resort — NEW PORT RICHEY C-3
□ Orlando SW - Fort Summit-KOA — DAVENPORT C-4
□ Orlando/Lake Whippoorwill KOA Campground — ORLANDO C-4
Oscar Scherer State Park — OSPREY D-3
Osceola National Forest (Ocean Pond Campground) — OLUSTEE A-3
Osprey First In Florida RV Park — YULEE A-3
Otter Springs Park & Campground — TRENTON B-2
® Outdoor Resorts At Orlando — CLERMONT C-3
Outdoor Resorts St. Lucie West Motorcoach Resort — PORT ST. LUCIE D-5
□ Outdoor Resorts/Chokoloskee Island — CHOKOLOSKEE E-4
Outdoor Resorts/Melbourne Beach — MELBOURNE BEACH C-5
□ Pacetti's Marina RV Park & Fishing Resort — ST. AUGUSTINE B-4
★ Palm Beach RV — WEST PALM BEACH D-5
Palm Beach Traveler Park — LANTANA D-5
Panama City Beach RV Resort — PANAMA CITY BEACH F-2
Paradise Island — FORT LAUDERDALE E-5
Paradise Oaks Golf & RV Resort — BUSHNELL C-3
Paradise Pointe Luxury RV Resort — NAPLES E-4
□ Parramore's Campground — ASTOR B-4
Paynes Prairie Preserve State Park — GAINESVILLE B-3
□ Peace River - Thousand Trails — WAUCHULA D-3
Pecan Park RV Resort — JACKSONVILLE A-3
Pelican Lake Motorcoach Resort — NAPLES E-4
Pelican Palms RV Park — MILTON F-1
□ Pelican's Landing Resort — SEBASTIAN C-5
Pensacola RV Park — PENSACOLA F-1
Perdido Cove RV Resort & Marina — PERDIDO KEY F-1
®□ Perry KOA — PERRY A-2
®□ Pine Island Resort — ST. JAMES CITY E-3
Pine Isle Mobile Home Park — HOMESTEAD E-5
®□ Pine Lake RV Park — FOUNTAIN F-3
Pineglen RV Park — PANAMA CITY BEACH F-2
® Pioneer Village RV Resort (Encore) — FORT MYERS D-3
Playa del Rio RV Resort — PERDIDO KEY F-1
Playground RV Park — FORT WALTON BEACH F-2
Pleasant Lake RV Resort — BRADENTON D-3
® Ponderosa RV Park — KISSIMMEE C-4
Port St. Lucie RV Resort — PORT ST. LUCIE D-5
• Princess Place Preserve — PALM COAST B-4
Punta Gorda RV Resort — PUNTA GORDA D-3
Quail Run RV Resort — WESLEY CHAPEL C-3

FLORIDA — Continued

△ Quiet Waters Park (Broward County Park) — DEERFIELD BEACH E-5
Raccoon River Campground — PANAMA CITY BEACH F-2
Rainbow Country RV Campground — CEDAR KEY B-2
Rainbow Resort — FROSTPROOF C-4
Rainbow Springs State Park — DUNNELLON B-3
Rainbow Village RV Resort — LARGO C-3
® Rainbow Village RV Resort — ZEPHYRHILLS C-3
Raintree RV Resort — FORT MYERS D-3
Ralph's Travel Park — ZEPHYRHILLS C-3
Ramblers Rest Resort Campground — VENICE D-3
□ Red Coconut RV Resort on the Beach — FORT MYERS BEACH E-3
Red Oaks RV Resort — BUSHNELL C-3
Redfish RV Park — STEINHATCHEE B-2
★ Revels Nationwide RV Sales — STARKE B-3
Ridgecrest RV & Mobile Home Resort — LEESBURG C-3
River Lodge RV Resort — INGLIS B-3
Riverbend Motorcoach Resort — FORT MYERS D-3
River's Edge RV Campground — HOLT E-1
□ Riverside Lodge — INVERNESS C-3
® Riverside RV Resort & Campground — PORT CHARLOTTE D-3
□ Road Runner Travel Resort — FORT PIERCE D-5
Robert's Mobile Home & RV Resort — ST. PETERSBURG C-3
Rock Creek RV Resort — NAPLES E-4
Rock Crusher Canyon RV Park — CRYSTAL RIVER B-3
Rodman (COE - Lake Ocklawaha) — PALATKA B-4
Rolling Ridge RV Resort — CLERMONT C-3
® Rose Bay Travel Park — PORT ORANGE B-4
® Sabal Palm RV Resort & Campground — PALMDALE D-4
St. Andrews State Recreation Area — PANAMA CITY BEACH F-2
□ St. Augustine Beach KOA Kampground Resort — ST. AUGUSTINE B-4
St. George Island State Park — ST. GEORGE ISLAND B-1
St. John's RV Park — ST. AUGUSTINE B-4
□ St. Joseph Peninsula State Park — PORT ST. JOE F-3
® St. Mary's River Fish Camp & Campground — HILLIARD A-3
Salt Springs Resort — SALT SPRINGS B-3
® San Carlos Island Resort — FORT MYERS BEACH E-3
® Sandy Oaks RV Resort — BEVERLY HILLS B-3
Sanlan RV Park — LAKELAND C-3
Sarasota Bay RV Park — BRADENTON D-3
Sarasota Lakes Camping Resort — SARASOTA D-3
® Sarasota Sunny South RV Park — SARASOTA D-3
Scruftys Riverwood RV Park — GEORGETOWN B-4
Seasons in the Sun — TITUSVILLE C-4
Sebastian Inlet State Park — SEBASTIAN C-5
Sebring Grove RV Resort — SEBRING D-4
® Seminole Campground — FORT MYERS D-3
Settlers Rest RV Park — ZEPHYRHILLS C-3
Seven Springs Travel Park — NEW PORT RICHEY C-3
® Shady Acres RV Park — FORT MYERS D-3
Shady Brook Golf & RV Resort — SUMTERVILLE C-3
Shady Oaks RV & Mobile Home Park, Inc — CROSS CITY B-2
Shell Creek RV Resort — PUNTA GORDA D-3
Sherwood Forest RV Resort — KISSIMMEE C-4
Sherwood Forest Travel RV Park — PALM HARBOR C-3
Siesta Bay RV Resort — FORT MYERS BEACH E-3
Signature Motorcoach Resort at Naples — NAPLES E-4
Silver Dollar RV and Golf Resort — ODESSA C-3
Silver Lakes RV Resort and Golf Club — NAPLES E-4
Silver Palms RV Village — OKEECHOBEE D-4
® Sonrise Palms Christian RV Park — COCOA C-4
® Sonrise Village RV Resort — COCOA C-4
South Bay RV Campground (Palm Beach County Park) — SOUTH BAY D-4
Southern Charm RV Resort — ZEPHYRHILLS C-3
® Southern Oaks RV Resort — SUMMERFIELD B-3
® Southern Palms RV Resort — EUSTIS B-4
Space Coast RV Resort — ROCKLEDGE C-4
Spanish Main RV Resort — THONOTOSASSA C-3
® Sportsman's Cove Resort — MCINTOSH B-3
Stage Stop Campground — WINTER GARDEN C-4
Stagecoach RV Park — ST. AUGUSTINE B-4
□ Starke/Gainesville NE KOA — STARKE B-3
□ Stephen Foster Folk Culture Center State Park — WHITE SPRINGS A-3
□ Sugar Mill Ruins Travel Park — NEW SMYRNA BEACH B-4
Sumter Oaks RV Park — BUSHNELL C-3
Sun Lake RV Resort — RUSKIN D-3
Sun 'N' Shade Campground — PUNTA GORDA D-3
Sun Resort — APOPKA C-4
® Sun-N-Fun RV Resort — SARASOTA D-3
Suncoast RV Resort — PORT RICHEY C-3
Sundance Lakes RV Resort — PORT RICHEY C-3
Sunnier Palms (Nudist) — FORT PIERCE D-5
Sunny Pines — SEBRING D-4
® Sunseeker's RV Park — FORT MYERS D-3
Sunset Isle RV & Yacht Club Resort — CARRABELLE B-1
®□ Sunset King Lake RV Resort — DEFUNIAK SPRINGS E-2
®□ Sunshine Coast Resorts & Retreats — INGLIS B-3
Sunshine Holiday RV Park — FORT LAUDERDALE E-5
□ Sunshine Holiday RV Park — ORMOND BEACH B-4
® Sunshine Key Resort — BIG PINE KEY F-4
® Sunshine RV Resort — LAKE PLACID D-4
Sunshine Travel-Encore — VERO BEACH D-5
Sunshine Village RV Resort — WEBSTER C-3
Suwannee River Hideaway Campground, Inc. — OLD TOWN B-2
□ Suwannee River State Park — LIVE OAK A-2
®□ Suwannee Valley Campground — WHITE SPRINGS A-3
• Swamp House Grill — DEBARY B-4
Swan Lake Village Manufactured Homes & RV Resort — FORT MYERS D-3
Sweetwater RV Park — ZEPHYRHILLS C-3
Tallahassee RV Park — TALLAHASSEE A-1
Tamiami RV Park — FORT MYERS D-3
Tampa East RV Resort — DOVER C-3
® Tampa South RV Resort — RUSKIN D-3
Terra Ceia Village — PALMETTO D-3
The Boardwalk — HOMESTEAD E-5
The Floridian RV Resort — ST. CLOUD C-4
®□ The Glades RV, Golf & Marina Resort — LA BELLE D-4
The Great Outdoors RV-Nature & Golf Resort — TITUSVILLE C-4
® The Harbor RV Resort & Marina — LAKE WALES C-4
The Outback RV Resort at Tanglewood — SEBRING D-4
The Recreation Plantation RV Resort — LADY LAKE B-3
Themeworld RV Resort — DAVENPORT C-4
® Thousand Palms RV Resort — WILDWOOD B-3
® Thousand Trails-Orlando — CLERMONT C-3
® Three Flags RV Resort — WILDWOOD B-3
Three Lakes RV Resort (Morgan RV Resorts) — HUDSON C-3
□ Three Rivers State Park — SNEADS E-3
® Thunder Gulch Campground — BUNNELL B-4
Tiki House RV Park on Pensacola Beach — PENSACOLA F-1
Toby's RV Resort — ARCADIA D-3
Tomoka State Park — ORMOND BEACH B-4
Topeekeegee Yugnee (T.Y.) Park (Broward County Park) — HOLLYWOOD E-5
Topics RV Community — SPRING HILL C-3
□ Topsail Hill Preserve State Park — SANTA ROSA BEACH F-2
Torrey Oaks RV & Golf Resort — BOWLING GREEN D-3
Torreya State Park — BRISTOL F-3
Town and Country RV Resort — DADE CITY C-3
Travel World — CLEARWATER C-3
Travelers Campground — ALACHUA B-3
Travelers Rest Resort — DADE CITY C-3
Treasure Coast RV Park — FORT PIERCE D-5
Treasure Village MH/RV Park — ST. PETERSBURG C-3
Tropic Breeze — PORT RICHEY C-3
® Tropical Gardens RV Park — BRADENTON D-3
□ Tropical Palms Resort — KISSIMMEE C-4
Turtle Beach Campground at Turtle Beach Park — SARASOTA D-3

FLORIDA — Continued

®□ Turtleback RV Resort — LAKE PANASOFFKEE C-3
Twelve Oaks RV Resort — SANFORD C-4
Twin Lakes Travel Park — FORT LAUDERDALE E-5
Upriver RV Resort — FORT MYERS D-3
Vacation Inn Resort — WEST PALM BEACH D-5
Vacation Village (Formerly Sunburst RV Park) — LARGO C-3
□ Vero Beach Kamp Inc — SEBASTIAN C-5
□ Vortex Spring Camping and Diving Resort — PONCE DE LEON E-2
• Walt Disney World Resort — LAKE BUENA VISTA C-4
Water's Edge RV Resort — ZEPHYRHILLS C-3
Water's Edge RV Resort of Punta Gorda — PUNTA GORDA D-3
® Webster Travel Park — WEBSTER C-3
Wekiva Falls Resort — SANFORD C-4
Wekiwa Springs State Park — APOPKA C-4
® West Jupiter Camping Resort — JUPITER D-5
Whisper Creek RV Resort — LA BELLE D-4
Whispering Palms RV Resort — SEBASTIAN C-5
Whispering Pines RV Park — SILVER SPRINGS B-3
Whispering Pines Village — SEBRING D-4
Wickham Park (Brevard County Park) — MELBOURNE C-5
® Wild Frontier Rally Park & Campground — OCALA B-3
® Wilderness RV Park Estates — SILVER SPRINGS B-3
Williston Crossings RV Resort — WILLISTON B-3
Winter Garden RV Resort - Encore — WINTER GARDEN C-4
Winterset RV Resort — PALMETTO D-3
□ Withlacoochee Backwaters RV Park — DUNNELLON B-3
® Woodall's Mobile Home Village & RV Park — LAKELAND C-3
® Woodsmoke Camping Resort — FORT MYERS D-3
Woody's RV Resort — SEBRING D-4
Yacht Haven Park & Marina — FORT LAUDERDALE E-5
Yankee Traveler RV Park — LARGO C-3
□ Yellow Jacket Campground Resort — OLD TOWN B-2
□ Yogi Bear's Jellystone Park Camp Resort — MADISON A-2
□ Zachary Taylor RV Resort — OKEECHOBEE D-4

GEORGIA

Agrirama RV Park — TIFTON E-3
Albany RV Resort — ALBANY E-2
□ Alexander H. Stephens State Historic Park — CRAWFORDVILLE C-3
® Allatoona Landing Marine Resort & Campground — CARTERSVILLE B-1
□ Amicalola Falls State Park & Lodge — DAWSONVILLE B-2
Amity Park (West Point Lake COE) — WEST POINT C-1
□ Amy's South Georgia RV Park — TIFTON E-3
Atlanta - Marietta RV Resort — ATLANTA B-2
□ Atlanta South RV Resort — MCDONOUGH C-2
Atlanta-Marietta RV Resort — MARIETTA B-2
Back to Nature Campground — DANVILLE D-3
□ Bald Mountain Camping Resort — HIAWASSEE A-2
Bald Ridge Creek Campground (COE-Lake Sidney Lanier) — CUMMING B-2
• Bargainville Flea Market — LAKE PARK F-3
□ Best Holiday Trav-L-Park — ROSSVILLE A-1
Big Hart Camp Area (COE - J. Strom Thurmond Lake) — THOMSON C-4
Big Oak RV Park — TALLAPOOSA B-1
Biltmore Gardens RV Park — SAVANNAH D-5
□ Black Rock Mountain State Park — MOUNTAIN CITY A-3
Blanton Creek Park (Georgia Power) — COLUMBUS D-1
Blythe Island Regional Park Campground — BRUNSWICK E-5
Bobby Brown State Park — ELBERTON B-3
Boland's RV Park — PERRY D-2
Bolding Mill (COE-Lake Sidney Lanier) — CUMMING B-2
Boss's RV Park — WRENS C-4
• Brickyard Plantation Golf Club — AMERICUS D-2
Brickyard Plantation RV Park — AMERICUS D-2
□ Cartersville KOA — CARTERSVILLE B-1
Cat Head Creek RV Park — DARIEN E-5
Cecil Bay RV Park — CECIL E-3
® Cedar Creek RV Park & Outdoor Center — CAVE SPRING B-1
Chattahooche National Forest (Mulky) — BLUE RIDGE A-2
Chattahoochee-Oconee National Forest-Tallulah River — CLAYTON A-3
△ Chattahoochee National Forest (Lake Conasauga Campground) — CHATSWORTH A-1
Chattahoochee National Forest (Lake Russell Campground) — CORNELIA B-3
Chattahoochee National Forest (Lake Winfield Scott Campground) — BLAIRSVILLE A-2
Chattahoochee National Forest (Morganton Point Campground) — MORGANTON A-2
Chattahoochee National Forest (Rabun Beach Campground) — CLAYTON A-3
Chattahoochee National Forest (The Pocket Campground) — LA FAYETTE A-1
Chattahoochee-Oconee National Forest-Sandy Bottom — CLAYTON A-3
Chattahoochee-Oconee National Forest-Tate Branch — CLAYTON A-3
Cherokee Campground — HELEN A-2
Chestnut Ridge Park (COE-Lake Sidney Lanier) — BUFORD B-2
City Campground — ANDERSONVILLE D-2
Clark Creek North (Allatoona Lake COE) — ACWORTH B-1
□ Cloudland Canyon State Park — RISING FAWN A-1
Coastal Georgia RV Resort — BRUNSWICK E-5
Coosa River Campground (Rome-Floyd County Park) & Nature Center — ROME B-1
□ Cordele KOA — CORDELE D-2
Cotton Hill Park (COE-Walter F George Lake) — FORT GAINES E-1
□ Country Boy's RV Park — COMMERCE B-3
Country Boy's RV Park — MADISON C-3
Country Oaks Campground & RV Park — KINGSLAND F-5
® Creekside Plantation RV Campground — ALBANY E-2
□ Creekwood Resort Campground & Cabins — HELEN A-2
□ Crooked River State Park — ST. MARYS F-5
Cross Creek Campground — MOUNTAIN CITY A-3
Crossroads Holiday Trav-L-Park — PERRY D-2
Dames Ferry Park (Georgia Power) — JULLIETTE C-2
Doll Mountain Campground (COE-Carters Lake) — ELLIJAY A-2
Duckett Mill (COE - Lake Sidney Lanier) — GAINESVILLE B-2
Eagles Roost RV Resort — LAKE PARK F-3
□ Elijah Clark State Park — LINCOLNTON B-4
□ Emerald Lake RV Park — COLQUITT E-1
□ Enota Mountain Retreat — HELEN A-2
□ F. D. Roosevelt State Park — PINE MOUNTAIN C-1
Fair Harbor RV Park & Campground — PERRY D-2
Flint River KOA — BAINBRIDGE F-1
□ Florence Marina State Park — OMAHA D-1
Flynn's Inn Camping Village — AUGUSTA C-4
Forest Glen Mobile Home & RV Park — JACKSON C-2
□ Forsyth KOA — FORSYTH C-2
□ Fort McAllister State Historic Park — RICHMOND HILL D-5
□ Fort Mountain State Park — CHATSWORTH A-1
□ Fort Yargo State Park — WINDER B-2
• Fran's Place Restaurant — BRUNSWICK E-5
□ General Coffee State Park — DOUGLAS E-3
□ George L. Smith State Park — TWIN CITY D-4
Georgia Mountain Fairgrounds Campground (County Park) — HIAWASSEE A-2
• Georgia Mountain Fairgrounds & Music Hall — HIAWASSEE A-2
□ Georgia Veterans Memorial State Park — CORDELE D-2
□ Golden Isles RV Park — BRUNSWICK E-5
Gordonia-Alatamaha State Park — REIDSVILLE D-4
Hamburg State Park — WARTHEN C-3
□ Hard Labor Creek State Park — RUTLEDGE C-3
□ Hart State Park — HARTWELL B-3

GEORGIA — Continued

Hesters Ferry Camp Area (COE - J. Strom Thurmond Lake) — ***LINCOLNTON B-4***
High Falls State Park — ***HIGH FALLS C-2***
□ **Hillside Bluegrass RV Park — *COCHRAN D-3***
□ Holiday Harbor Marina & Resort — ***ACWORTH B-1***
Holiday Park (West Point Lake COE) — ***LA GRANGE C-1***
□ Indian Springs State Park — ***FLOVILLA C-2***
Inland Harbor RV Park — ***DARIEN E-5***
Interstate RV Campground — ***BYRON D-2***
□ Jacksonville North/Kingsland KOA — ***KINGSLAND F-5***
□ James H. Floyd State Park — ***SUMMERVILLE B-1***
Jekyll Island Campground — ***JEKYLL ISLAND E-5***
John Tanner State Park — ***CARROLLTON C-1***
Jones RV Park — *NORCROSS B-2*
King George RV Resort — *WOODBINE E-4*
□ KOA-Calhoun — ***CALHOUN B-1***
□ KOA-Savannah South — ***RICHMOND HILL D-5***
Kolomoki Mounds State Park — ***BLAKELY E-1***
Lake Harmony RV Park & Campground — *TOWNSEND E-5*
Lake Lanier Islands Campground — *BUFORD B-2*
• **Lake Pines Event Center — *COLUMBUS D-1***
®□ **Lake Pines RV Park & Campground — *COLUMBUS D-1***
Lake Tobesofkee Recreation Area (Bibb Co.) — *MACON C-2*
□ Laura S. Walker State Park — ***WAYCROSS E-4***
Lawrence Shoals Park (Georgia Power) — *EATONTON C-3*
Leisure Acres Campground — ***CLEVELAND A-2***
□ Little Ocmulgee State Park — ***MCRAE D-3***
Little River Park Campground & Marina — *MILLEDGEVILLE C-3*
□ Lookout Mountain KOA-Chattanooga West — ***TRENTON A-1***
□ Magnolia Springs State Park — ***MILLEN C-4***
McIntosh Lake RV Park — ***TOWNSEND E-5***
McKaskey Campground (COE-Allatoona Lake) — ***CARTERSVILLE B-1***
McKinney Campground (Allatoona Lake COE) — ***ACWORTH B-1***
△ MILITARY PARK (Dobbins ARB Family Campground) — ***MARIETTA B-2***
®□ MILITARY PARK (Fort Gordon Rec. Area) — ***LEAH B-4***
□ MILITARY PARK (Ft. McPherson-Lk Allatoona Army Rec Area) — ***CARTERSVILLE B-1***
□ MILITARY PARK (Grassy Pond Rec. Area) — ***LAKE PARK F-3***
MILITARY PARK (Hunter Army Airfield Trailer Camp) — ***SAVANNAH D-5***
MILITARY PARK (Robins AFB FAMCAMP) — ***WARNER ROBINS D-3***
®□ MILITARY PARK (Uchee Creek Army Campground/Marina) — ***FORT BENNING D-1***
□ MILITARY PARK (World Famous Navy Lake Site-Atlanta NAS) — ***ACWORTH B-1***
Milltown Campground (COE - Hartwell Lake) — ***HARTWELL B-3***
□ Mistletoe State Park — ***APPLING C-4***
Moccasin Creek State Park — ***CLARKESVILLE A-3***
Mossy Oaks RV Park & Campground (Not visited) — *JESUP E-4*
Oconee National Forest (Lake Sinclair Campground) — ***EATONTON C-3***
□ Oconee Springs Park (Putnam County Park) — ***EATONTON C-3***
Old 41 No. 3 Campground (COE Allatoona Lake) — ***ACWORTH B-1***
Old Federal Road Park (COE-Lake Sidney Lanier) — ***GAINESVILLE B-2***
Old Salem Park (Georgia Power) — *GREENSBORO C-3*
Parks Ferry Park (Georgia Power) — *GREENSBORO C-3*
□ **Parkwood RV Park & Cottages — *STATESBORO D-4***
Paulk Park RV Park & Campground — ***FITZGERALD E-3***
Payne Campground (COE-Allatoona Lake) — ***ACWORTH B-1***
Paynes Creek Campground (COE - Hartwell Lake) — ***HARTWELL B-3***
Petersburg Camp Area (COE - J. Strom Thurmond Lake) — ***LEAH B-4***
Pine Lake RV Campground — ***BISHOP B-3***
□ **Pine Mountain RV Resort — *PINE MOUNTAIN C-1***
□ **Plum Nelly Campground — *ELLIJAY A-2***
Ponderosa Park Campground — ***FORT VALLEY D-2***
Poteete Creek (Union County Park) — ***BLAIRSVILLE A-2***
R. Shaefer Heard (COE - West Point Lake) — ***WEST POINT C-1***
Ramsey RV Park — *WARM SPRINGS C-1*
Raysville Bridge Camp Area (COE - J. Strom Thurmond Lake) — ***THOMSON C-4***
Red Gate CG & RV Resort — *SAVANNAH D-5*
□ Red Top Mountain State Park — ***CARTERSVILLE B-1***
Reed Bingham State Park — ***ADEL E-3***
□ Richard B Russell State Park — ***ELBERTON B-3***
Ridge Road Camp Area (COE-J. Strom Thurmond Lake) — ***LEAH B-4***
Ringer Park (COE - West Point Lake) — ***LA GRANGE C-1***
River Bend Campground — ***HIAWASSEE A-2***
River Forks Park and Campground — ***GAINESVILLE B-2***
River Park RV Park — *VALDOSTA F-3*
□ **River Vista Mountain Village — *DILLARD A-3***
□ **River's End Campground & RV Park — *SAVANNAH D-5***
□ **River's End Campground & RV Park — *TYBEE ISLAND D-5***
□ **Savannah Oaks RV Resort — *SAVANNAH D-5***
Sawnee Campground (COE-Lake Sidney Lanier) — ***CUMMING B-2***
®□ **Scenic Mountain RV Park — *MILLEDGEVILLE C-3***
□ Seminole State Park — ***DONALSONVILLE E-1***
Shady Grove Park (COE-Lake Sidney Lanier) — ***CUMMING B-2***
Skidaway Island State Park — ***SAVANNAH D-5***
South Oaks Mobile Home & RV Community — ***PALMETTO C-1***
®□ Southern Gates RV Park & Campground — ***ARABI E-2***
□ **Southern Trails RV Resort — *UNADILLA D-2***
State Line Park (COE - West Point Lake) — ***LA GRANGE C-1***
□ Stephen C. Foster State Park — ***FARGO F-4***
Stone Mountain Family Campground — *STONE MOUNTAIN B-2*
Sugar Mill Plantation RV Park — ***OCHLOCKNEE E-2***
Sweetwater Campground (Allatoona Lake COE) — ***CANTON B-2***
Tallulah Gorge State Park — ***TALLULAH FALLS A-3***
® Talona Creek Campground — ***TALKING ROCK B-2***
★ **Team RV Inc — *ALBANY E-2***
The Parks at Chehaw Campground (City Park) — ***ALBANY E-2***
The Pines Campground — ***TIFTON E-3***
• **Three Oaks Farm — *BRUNSWICK E-5***
Toccoa RV Park — *TOCCOA B-3*
□ **Trackrock Campground & Cabins — *BLAIRSVILLE A-2***
Traders Hill Recreation Area & Campground (Charlton County) — ***FOLKSTON F-4***
□ Tugaloo State Park — ***LAVONIA B-3***
Twin Lakes RV Park — *CUMMING B-2*
□ **Twin Oaks RV Park — *ELKO D-2***
□ Unicoi State Park — ***HELEN A-2***
□ Valdosta/Lake Park KOA — ***LAKE PARK F-3***
Victoria Bryant State Park — ***ROYSTON B-3***
Victoria Campground (Allatoona Lake COE) — ***WOODSTOCK B-2***
□ Vogel State Park — ***BLAIRSVILLE A-2***
Watsadler Campground (COE - Hartwell Lake) — ***HARTWELL B-3***
Watson Mill Bridge State Park — ***COMER B-3***
Whitetail Ridge (COE - West Point Lake) — ***LA GRANGE C-1***
Whitewater Creek Park (Macon County Park) — ***OGLETHORPE D-2***
Wildwood Park (Columbia County Park) — ***APPLING C-4***
Winfield Camp Area (COE - J. Strom Thurmond Lake) — ***WINFIELD C-4***
Woodring Branch Public Use Area (COE-Carters Lake) — ***CHATSWORTH A-1***
□ **Yogi Bear's Jellystone Park of Georgia — *BREMEN B-1***

ILLINOIS

Andalusia Slough (COE-Mississippi River Rec Areas-Muscatine Area) — ***ANDALUSIA B-2***
Anderson Lake State Conservation Area — ***HAVANA C-2***
Apple River Canyon State Park — ***STOCKTON A-3***
Arcola Camper Stop — ***ARCOLA D-4***
Argyle Lake State Park — ***COLCHESTER C-2***
Arrowhead Lake Campground (City Park) — ***JOHNSTON CITY F-4***
Bear Creek (COE - Lock & Dam 21) — ***URSA C-1***
□ Beaver Dam State Park — ***CARLINVILLE D-3***
□ Benton KOA — ***BENTON E-4***
Best Holiday Lehman's Lakeside RV Resort — *MARENGO A-4*
Big River State Forest — ***OQUAWKA B-2***
★ **Bigfoot Construction Equipment — *WOODSTOCK A-4***

ILLINOIS — Continued

Black Hawk Valley Campground — ***ROCKFORD A-3***
Blanchard Island (COE-Mississippi River Rec Areas-Muscatine Area) — ***ILLINOIS CITY B-2***
Blanding Landing (COE - Lock & Dam 11) — ***HANOVER A-2***
Boulder Access Area (Lake Carlyle-Corp of Engineers) — ***BOULDER E-3***
Burrell Park Campground (City Park) — ***CARMI E-4***
®□ **Cahokia RV Parque — *CAHOKIA E-2***
□ **Camp Lakewood — *EFFINGHAM D-4***
□ Casey KOA Kampground & RV Service — ***CASEY D-4***
Casino Queen RV Park — ***EAST ST. LOUIS E-2***
□ Cave-In-Rock State Park — ***CAVE IN ROCK F-4***
□ Cedarbrook RV Park and Campground — ***MULBERRY GROVE D-3***
□ Chain O' Lakes State Park — ***FOX LAKE A-4***
Champaign Sportsmen's Club — ***MAHOMET C-4***
Channahon State Park — ***CHANNAHON B-4***
®□ Circle G Campground — ***CARTHAGE C-1***
Clinton Lake-Mascoutin State Recreation Complex — ***DE WITT C-4***
Coles Creek Recreation Area (Lake Carlyle - COE) — ***BOULDER E-3***
Condit's Ranch — ***PUTNAM B-3***
Coon Creek (COE-Shelbyville Lake) — ***SHELBYVILLE D-4***
Crab Orchard Campground — ***CARBONDALE F-3***
Crazy Horse Campground — ***JACKSONVILLE D-2***
• **Crossties Christian Ministries — *ANNAPOLIS D-5***
Crow Valley Campground — ***STERLING A-3***
D & W Lake Camping and RV Park — ***CHAMPAIGN C-4***
Dam West Recreation Area (Lake Carlyle-COE) — ***CARLYLE E-3***
Delabar State Park — ***OQUAWKA B-2***
Des Plaines State Fish & Wildlife Area — ***WILMINGTON B-4***
Dixon Springs State Park — ***GOLCONDA F-4***
★ **Double J RV Sales & Service — *SPRINGFIELD C-3***
Driftwood Campground — ***QUINCY C-1***
Du Quoin State Fair Campground — ***DU QUOIN E-3***
Eagle Creek State Park — ***FINDLAY D-4***
□ Eldon Hazlet State Park — ***CARLYLE E-3***
Emerald Acres Campground — ***PEARL CITY A-3***
Emerald Trails Campground — ***CRETE B-5***
□ Evening Star Camping Resort — ***TOPEKA C-3***
Ferne Clyffe State Park — ***GOREVILLE F-3***
Fish Lake Beach Camping Resort — ***VOLO A-4***
Fishermens Corner Rec. Area (COE-Thomson Park) — ***HAMPTON B-2***
Forest Glen Preserve (Vermilion County Park) — ***WESTVILLE C-5***
Forrest W. BO Woods Recreation Area (COE-Lake Shelbyville) — ***SULLIVAN D-4***
Fort Massac State Park — ***METROPOLIS F-4***
®□ **Fossil Rock Recreation Area — *WILMINGTON B-4***
□ **Four Seasons Campground — *HERRIN F-3***
Four Star Campground — ***MARSEILLES B-4***
□ Fox Ridge State Park — ***CHARLESTON D-4***
Francis Park (City Park) — ***KEWANEE B-3***
Friends Creek Regional Park (Macon County Park) — ***ARGENTA C-4***
□ **Galesburg East Best Holiday Trav-L-Park — *GALESBURG B-2***
Gebhard Woods State Trail Access — ***MORRIS B-4***
□ **Geneseo Campground — *GENESEO B-2***
□ Giant City State Park — ***CARBONDALE F-3***
Great River Road Campground (City Park) — ***PLEASANT HILL D-2***
® Green River Oaks Camping Resort — ***AMBOY A-3***
Green River State Wildlife Area — ***OHIO B-3***
Gun Creek Recreation Area (COE - Rend Lake) — ***BENTON E-4***
□ Hamilton County State Conservation Area — ***MCLEANSBORO E-4***
Hansen's Hide Away Ranch & Family Campground — ***OREGON A-3***
□ Hebron Hills Camping — ***OAKLAND D-4***
Henderson County State Conservation Area. — ***OQUAWKA B-2***
□ Hi-Tide Recreation — ***SOMONAUK B-4***
Hickory Grove Campground — ***SHEFFIELD B-3***
Hickory Hill Campground — *EL PASO B-3*
Hickory Holler Campground — *ANNAPOLIS D-5*
□ Hickory Hollow Campground — ***UTICA B-3***
□ **Hickory Shores Resort — *CARLYLE E-3***
® **Hide-A-Way Lakes — *YORKVILLE B-4***
Hilltop Campgrounds — ***GOREVILLE F-3***
□ Holiday Acres Camping Resort — ***GARDEN PRAIRIE A-4***
Hononegah Forest Preserve (Winnebago County) — ***ROCKTON A-3***
Horseshoe Lake State Conservation Area — ***OLIVE BRANCH F-3***
Horseshoe Lake State Park — ***GRANITE CITY E-2***
Illinois Beach State Park — ***ZION A-4***
Illinois State Fair Grounds — ***SPRINGFIELD C-3***
Johnson Sauk Trail State Park — ***KEWANEE B-3***
△ Jubilee College State Park — ***BRIMFIELD B-3***
Kamp Komfort — *CARLOCK C-3*
Kamper Kompanion Campground — ***LITCHFIELD D-3***
★ **Kamper's Supply — *MARION F-4***
□ Kankakee River State Park — ***BOURBONNAIS B-4***
Katchewan Lakes RV Resort — ***STREATOR B-4***
Kickapoo State Park — ***DANVILLE C-5***
□ KOA-Chicago Northwest — ***MARENGO A-4***
□ KOA-Kankakee South — ***KANKAKEE B-4***
□ **KOA-LaSalle/Peru — *UTICA B-3***
®□ KOA-Lena — ***LENA A-3***
□ KOA-St. Louis Area — ***GRANITE CITY E-2***
□ KOA-Springfield — ***SPRINGFIELD C-3***
Lake De Pue City Park — ***DE PUE B-3***
□ Lake LaDonna Family Campground — ***OREGON A-3***
□ Lake Le-Aqua-Na State Park — ***LENA A-3***
□ **Lake Louise Campground — *BYRON A-3***
Lake Murphysboro State Park — ***MURPHYSBORO F-3***
® Lankels Lazy Days Campground — ***LITCHFIELD D-3***
Leisure Lake Campground — ***ROCK FALLS A-3***
® **Leisure Lake Membership Resort — *JOLIET B-4***
Leisure Oaks Park — *BARTONVILLE C-3*
Lincoln Trail State Park — ***MARSHALL D-5***
Lincoln's New Salem Park (IL Historic Preservation Agency) — ***PETERSBURG C-3***
Lithia Springs Access Area (COE-Shelbyville Lake) — ***SHELBYVILLE D-4***
Little Grassy Lake Campground & Marina — ***CARBONDALE F-3***
Lone Point Access Area (Corp of Engineers - Lake Shelbyville) — ***FINDLAY D-4***
□ Lowden Memorial State Park — ***OREGON A-3***
Lundeen's Landing — ***EAST MOLINE B-2***
□ Mallard Bend Campground & RV Park — ***SHERIDAN B-4***
Marion Campground & RV Park — ***MARION F-4***
Marshall State Fish & Wildlife Area — ***LACON B-3***
Martin Campground — ***JOLIET B-4***
McMillen's Camp-A-While — ***LINCOLN C-3***
McNair Campground (Lake Carlyle-Corp of Engineers) — ***CARLYLE E-3***
® Mendota Hills Campground — ***AMBOY A-3***
□ MGM Campground — ***GRANITE CITY E-2***
Middle Fork State Fish & Wildlife Area — ***OAKWOOD C-4***
MILITARY PARK (Scott AFB FAMCAMP) — ***BELLEVILLE E-3***
□ Mill Creek Park Campground (Clark County Park) — ***MARSHALL D-5***
Millpoint Park — *EAST PEORIA C-3*
△ Mississippi Palisades State Park — ***SAVANNA A-2***
Moraine View State Park — ***LE ROY C-4***
Morrison-Rockwood State Park — ***MORRISON A-3***
Nauvoo State Park — ***NAUVOO C-1***
North Sandusky Creek Rec. Area (COE - Rend Lake) — ***BENTON E-4***
Oasis RV Park — ***JOLIET B-4***
®□ **O'Connell's Yogi Bear's Jellystone Park Camp-Resort — *AMBOY A-3***
□ **Okaw Valley Kampground — *VANDALIA D-3***
Opossum Creek Rec. Area (COE - Lake Shelbyville) — ***SHELBYVILLE D-4***
□ **Palace Campground — *GALENA A-2***
Pearl Lake Campground — ***SOUTH BELOIT A-3***
Pecatonica River Forest Preserve (Winnebago County) — ***PECATONICA A-3***
Percival Springs Airport Campground — ***WATSON D-4***
□ Pere Marquette State Park — ***GRAFTON D-2***
□ Pine Lakes Resort — ***PITTSFIELD D-2***

ILLINOIS — Continued

® **Pine View Campground — *AMBOY A-3***
△ Prairie Pines Campground (City Park) — ***RANTOUL C-4***
Prophetstown State Park — ***PROPHETSTOWN B-3***
Pyramid State Park — ***PINCKNEYVILLE E-3***
Quality Times — *MT VERNON E-4*
Ramsey Lake State Park — ***RAMSEY D-3***
Randolph County State Fish & Wildlife Area — ***CHESTER E-3***
Red Barn Rendezvous RV Park — ***EDWARDSVILLE E-3***
Red Hills Lake State Park — ***LAWRENCEVILLE E-5***
Rice Lake (State Cons Area) — ***CANTON C-2***
Riversedge Campground and Restaurant — ***ROCKTON A-3***
□ Robin Hood Woods Campground & Resort — ***SHELBYVILLE D-4***
□ **Rock Island/Quad Cities-KOA — *ROCK ISLAND B-2***
□ Rock-Cut State Park — ***ROCKFORD A-3***
Rolling Oaks Campground — *SHERIDAN B-4*
Ruffit Park — ***STERLING A-3***
Saline County State Conservation Area — ***EQUALITY F-4***
Sam Dale Lake (State Cons Area) — ***CISNE E-4***
Sam Parr State Park — ***NEWTON D-4***
□ Sangchris Lake State Park — ***ROCHESTER D-3***
• **Sawmill BBQ — *CAHOKIA E-2***
Schuy-Rush Park — ***RUSHVILLE C-2***
Seward Bluffs Forest Preserve (Winnebago County) — ***SEWARD A-3***
□ Shabbona Lake State Park — ***SHABBONA A-4***
®□ Shady Lakes Camping & Recreation — ***ALPHA B-2***
Shawnee National Forest (Buck Ridge Campground) — ***VIENNA F-4***
Shawnee National Forest (Johnson Creek Campground) — ***AVA F-3***
Shawnee National Forest (Lake Glendale-Oak Point Campground) — ***VIENNA F-4***
Shawnee National Forest (Pine Ridge-Pounds Hollow Recreation Area) — ***KARBERS RIDGE F-4***
Shawnee National Forest (Tower Rock Campground) — ***CAVE IN ROCK F-4***
□ Siloam Springs State Park — ***QUINCY C-1***
South Marcum Recreation Area (COE - Rend Lake) — ***BENTON E-4***
South Park Municipal Campground — *GIBSON CITY C-4*
South Sandusky Creek Rec. Area (COE - Rend Lake) — ***BENTON E-4***
South Shore State Park — ***CARLYLE E-3***
Spring Lake Park Campground (City Park) — ***MACOMB C-2***
Spring Lake (State Cons Area) — ***PEKIN C-3***
□ Starved Rock State Park — ***UTICA B-3***
□ Stephen A. Forbes State Park — ***SALEM E-3***
Sugar River Forest Preserve (Winnebago County) — ***SHIRLAND A-3***
Sugar Shores RV Resort — ***DURAND A-3***
Sullivan Marina & Campgrounds Resort — ***SULLIVAN D-4***
□ **Sunset Lakes Resort — *JOSLIN B-2***
Sycamore RV Resort — ***SYCAMORE A-4***
The Double J Campground & RV Park — *SPRINGFIELD C-3*
The Old Timber RV Park — *CAMBRIDGE B-2*
Thomson Causeway (COE-Thomson Park) — ***THOMSON A-2***
□ Timber Lake Resort & Campground — ***MT. CARROLL A-3***
Timber Trails Campground — *MULBERRY GROVE D-3*
Timberview Lakes Campground — *BUSHNELL C-2*
Tincup RV Park — ***MAHOMET C-4***
Twin River Campground & Retreat Center — *AROMA PARK B-5*
Walnut Point State Park — ***OAKLAND D-4***
Washington County Lake (State Cons Area) — ***NASHVILLE E-3***
□ Wayne Fitzgerrell State Park — ***SESSER E-3***
Weldon Springs State Park — ***CLINTON C-3***
□ White Pines Forest State Park — ***OREGON A-3***
Whitley Creek Recreation Area (COE - Lake Shelbyville) — ***SULLIVAN D-4***
□ **Whittington Woods Campground — *WHITTINGTON E-4***
Willow Creek Resort (Not Visited) — ***ROCKFORD A-3***
□ Wolf Creek State Park — ***WINDSOR D-4***
World Shooting & Recreational Complex — ***SPARTA E-3***
®□ Yogi Bear Jellystone Camp-Resort Chicago-Millbrook — ***MILLBROOK B-4***
®□ Yogi Bear Jellystone/Goodfield — ***GOODFIELD C-3***

INDIANA

Acorn Oaks Campground — ***FRANCESVILLE B-2***
Add-More RV Park — ***CLARKSVILLE F-4***
□ Atwood Lake Campground — ***WOLCOTTVILLE A-4***
Bass Lake State Beach — ***KNOX A-3***
Beaver Ridge Family Camping Inc. — *LAKEVILLE A-3*
Big Oak Park — ***MUNCIE C-4***
□ Bill Monroe Memorial Music Park & Campground — ***NASHVILLE D-3***
Bixler Lake Campground (City Park) — ***KENDALLVILLE A-4***
□ Blackhawk Campground — ***CLOVERDALE D-2***
®□ Blue Lake Resort Campground — ***CHURUBUSCO A-4***
Broadview Lake and Campground — ***COLFAX C-3***
®□ Broken Arrow Campground — ***WINAMAC B-3***
Brookville Lake (State Lake) — ***BROOKVILLE D-5***
Brown County SP — ***NASHVILLE D-3***
®□ **Caboose Lake Campground — *REMINGTON B-2***
Camp Sack-In — *ANGOLA A-5*
Camp Shore Campground — ***AURORA D-5***
□ Captain Carl's Famous Buck Lake Ranch — ***ANGOLA A-5***
□ Chain O'Lakes SP — ***ALBION A-4***
Charlestown State Park — ***CHARLESTOWN E-4***
®□ Circle B Park — ***ANGOLA A-5***
Clark SF — ***HENRYVILLE E-4***
Clifty Falls SP — ***MADISON E-4***
Cloverdale RV Park — *CLOVERDALE D-2*
Columbus Woods-N-Waters — *COLUMBUS D-3*
Deam Lake SF Rec Area — ***HAMBURG E-4***
Deer Ridge Camping Resort — *RICHMOND C-5*
Donna Jo Camping & Recreation Area — ***KOUTS A-2***
Earl Park Rest Area (City Park) — ***EARL PARK B-2***
□ Eby's Pines RV Park & Campground — ***BRISTOL A-4***
□ **Elkhart Campground — *ELKHART A-3***
Elkhart Co. 4-H & Agriculture Exposition, Inc. — ***GOSHEN A-3***
®□ **Elkhart County, Middlebury Exit KOA — *MIDDLEBURY A-4***
EZ Kamp — *GROVERTOWN A-3*
®□ Fallen Rock Park Campground — ***BRAZIL D-2***
Ferdinand SF — ***FERDINAND F-2***
□ Fireside Resort at Kruse Park — ***AUBURN A-4***
Follow the River RV Resort — *FLORENCE E-5*
Fowler Park (Vigo County) — ***TERRE HAUTE D-2***
△ France Park (Cass County Park) — ***LOGANSPORT B-3***
□ Free Spirit RV Resort — ***BEDFORD E-3***
Glendale State Fish & Wildlife Area Camp Ground — ***WASHINGTON E-2***
Glo Wood Campground — *PENDLETON C-4*
®□ Gordon's Camping — ***WOLCOTTVILLE A-4***
□ Grand Trails RV Park (Not Visited) — ***CORYDON F-3***
Grand View Bend — *HOWE A-4*
Grandpa's Farm — ***RICHMOND C-5***
Greene-Sullivan SF — ***DUGGER D-2***
Hardy Lake (State Lake) — ***SCOTTSBURG E-4***
□ Harmonie SP — ***NEW HARMONY F-1***
Harrison-Crawford SF — ***CORYDON F-3***
Hawthorn Park — ***TERRE HAUTE D-2***
Heartland Resort — *GREENFIELD C-4*
Hickory Grove Lakes Campground — *PORTLAND C-5*
® Hickory Hills Campground at Bass Lake — ***BASS LAKE B-3***
□ **Hidden Paradise Campground — *ST. PAUL D-4***
Hillside Camp Grounds — ***JAMESTOWN C-3***
□ **Hoffman Lake Camp — *WARSAW A-3***
• **Holiday World & Splashin' Safari — *SANTA CLAUS F-2***
□ **Honey Bear Hollow Family Campground — *PERU B-3***
Hoosier NF (Celina Campground) — ***ST. CROIX F-3***
Hoosier NF (Hardin Ridge Rec. Area) — ***BLOOMINGTON D-3***

INDIANA — Continued

Hoosier NF (Tipsaw Lake Campground) — ST. CROIX F-3
Horseshoe Lakes — CLINTON D-2
Huntington State Lake — HUNTINGTON B-4
Indian Lakes Campground — WOLCOTTVILLE A-4
Indian Lakes-NACO — BATESVILLE D-4
®□ Indian Springs Campground — GARRETT A-4
□ Indiana Beach Camp Resort (Morgan RV Resorts) — MONTICELLO B-2
Indiana Dunes SP — CHESTERTON A-2
Indiana State Fairgrounds Campground — INDIANAPOLIS D-3
Jackson-Washington SF — BROWNSTOWN E-3
®□ Jellystone Park Camp Resort (Morgan RV Resorts) — MONTICELLO B-2
Johnny Appleseed Park (Municipal Park) — FORT WAYNE B-4
Johnson County Park & Recreation Area — FRANKLIN D-3
□ KOA-Crawfordsville — CRAWFORDSVILLE C-2
□ **KOA-Indiana Ohio Kampground — RICHMOND C-5**
□ KOA-Indianapolis — GREENFIELD C-4
□ **KOA-Louisville Metro Campground — CLARKSVILLE F-4**
□ KOA-South Bend East — SOUTH BEND A-3
Lake Haven Retreat — INDIANAPOLIS D-3
®□ Lake Monroe Village — BLOOMINGTON D-3
®□ **Lake Rudolph Campground & RV Resort — SANTA CLAUS F-2**
® **Lakeside RV Resort — NEW CARLISLE A-3**
Lakeview Campground — ROCHESTER B-3
Lane Motel — FRENCH LICK E-3
Last Resort Campground — HANNA A-2
Lieber SRA (Cagles Mill Lake) — CLOVERDALE D-2
□ Lincoln SP — DALE F-2
®□ **Little Farm on the River Camping Resort — RISING SUN E-5**
Lost Acres RV Park — MONTICELLO B-2
Lynnville Park (City Park) — LYNNVILLE F-2
□ **Manapogo Park — ORLAND A-4**
Mar-Brook Campground — GAS CITY B-4
Martin SF — SHOALS E-2
□ McCormick's Creek SP — SPENCER D-2
Mendenhall's RV/Mobile Park — BLUFFTON B-4
Miami Camp — FRANKTON C-4
□ **Michigan City Campground — MICHIGAN CITY A-2**
® Mini Mountain Campground — NEW CARLISLE A-3
Mississinewa Lake (State Lake) — PERU B-3
□ Misty Morning Campground — CLOVERDALE D-2
Monroe Lake SRA — BLOOMINGTON D-3
□ Morgan-Monroe SF — MARTINSVILLE D-3
Mounds SP — ANDERSON C-4
Muscatatuck (Jennings County Park) — NORTH VERNON E-4
□ New Lisbon Family Campground LLC — NEW CASTLE C-4
New Vision RV Park, LLC — OAKTOWN E-2
Norway Campground — MONTICELLO B-2
□ **Oak Lake Family Campground — FAIR OAKS B-2**
Ouabache SP — BLUFFTON B-4
□ Ouabache (Wabash) Trails Park (Knox County Park) — VINCENNES E-1
Owen-Putnam SF — SPENCER D-2
Patoka Lake SRA — WICKLIFFE E-2
®□ Pic-A-Spot Campground — WARSAW A-3
Pigeon River State Fish & Wildlife Area — LAGRANGE A-4
Pike Lake Campground (City Park) — WARSAW A-3
Pike SF — WINSLOW E-2
□ Pine Lakes Camping and Fishing — PENDLETON C-4
Pla-Mor Campground — BREMEN A-3
Pokagon SP — ANGOLA A-5
□ Potato Creek SP — LAKEVILLE A-3
Prairie Creek Park (Vigo County) — TERRE HAUTE D-2
Prophetstown State Park — WEST LAFAYETTE C-2
Raccoon SRA (Cecil M Hardin Lake) — ROCKVILLE D-2
Rising Sun Campground — BASS LAKE B-3
Riverside Campground — SHIPSHEWANA A-4
Rupert's Resort Campground — BREMEN A-3
®□ **S & H Campground — GREENFIELD C-4**
Salamonie Lake (State Lake) — HUNTINGTON B-4
Salamonie River SF — LAGRO B-4
□ **Sand Creek Campground — CHESTERTON A-2**
□ Scales Lake Park (Warrick County Park) — BOONVILLE F-2
Shades State Park — WAVELAND C-2
□ Shakamak SP — JASONVILLE D-2
□ Shipshewana Campground-North — SHIPSHEWANA A-4
Shipshewana Campground-South — SHIPSHEWANA A-4
Shipshewana Trading Place RV Park — SHIPSHEWANA A-4
Ski World — NASHVILLE D-3
Sports Lake Campground — GAS CITY B-4
Spring Mill SP — MITCHELL E-3
Starve Hollow Lake SF — VALLONIA E-3
Sugar Creek Campground of Crawfordsville — CRAWFORDSVILLE C-2
Summers-Carroll Campground — ATTICA C-2
Summit Lake SP — NEW CASTLE C-4
□ Terre Haute KOA — TERRE HAUTE D-2
□ **The Last Resort RV Park & Campground — NASHVILLE D-3**
Thrasher's Woods — MONON B-2
△ Tippecanoe River SP — WINAMAC B-3
Turkey Run State Park — MARSHALL C-2
®□ **Twin Mills Camping Resort — HOWE A-4**
Vanderburgh 4H Center Campground (Vanderburgh County Park) — EVANSVILLE F-1
Versailles SP — VERSAILLES D-4
Walnut Ridge Campground — NEW CASTLE C-4
□ West Boggs Park (Daviess-Martin County) — LOOGOOTEE E-2
□ **Westward Ho Campground — NASHVILLE D-3**
Westwood Park (Big Blue River Conservancy Dist.) — NEW CASTLE C-4
□ White Oaks On the Lake A Western Horizon Property — MONTICELLO B-2
White River Campground — CICERO C-3
Whitewater Memorial SP — LIBERTY D-5
Wildwood Acres Campground — HARTFORD CITY C-4
Willow Slough State Fish & Wildlife Area — MOROCCO B-2
Wolfe's Leisure Time Campground — LAFAYETTE C-2
Wyandotte Woods SF Rec Area — CORYDON F-3
Yellowwood SF — NASHVILLE D-3
□ **Yogi Bear Jellystone at Raintree Lake — SCOTTSBURG E-4**
□ Yogi Bear's Jellystone Park — PIERCETON A-4
□ Yogi Bear's Jellystone Park at Barton Lake — FREMONT A-5
®□ Yogi Bear's Jellystone Park Camp Resort — PLYMOUTH A-3
□ **Yogi Bear's Jellystone Park Camp-Resort — PORTAGE A-2**
□ **Yogi Bear's Jellystone Park-Knightstown — KNIGHTSTOWN C-4**

IOWA

4th Pumping Plant Recreation Park (Des Moines County Park) — KINGSTON D-5
Acorn Valley (COE - Saylorville Lake) — DES MOINES D-3
Adventureland Campground — ALTOONA D-3
Alcock Park (Bremer County Park) — FREDERIKA B-4
Amana Colonies RV Park — AMANA C-5
• **Amana Colonies Visitors Center — AMANA C-5**
Ambrose A. Call SP — ALGONA B-3
Arnolds Park (City Park) — ARNOLDS PARK A-2
□ Arrowhead Park (Pottawattamie County Park) — NEOLA D-1
□ Backbone SP — STRAWBERRY POINT B-5
Bailey Ford (Delaware County Park) — MANCHESTER B-5
Bankston Park (Dubuque County Park) — HOLY CROSS B-5
Beeds Lake SP — HAMPTON B-3
Bellevue SP — BELLEVUE C-6
Bells Mill Park (Hamilton County Park) — STRATFORD C-3
Benton City-Fry Campground (Benton County Park) — VINTON C-4
Black Hawk SP — LAKE VIEW C-2
Bluffs Run RV Park — COUNCIL BLUFFS D-1
Bob Shetler Campground (COE - Saylorville Lake) — DES MOINES D-3

IOWA — Continued

Bobwhite SP — ALLERTON E-3
Botna Bend Park (Pottawattamie County Park) — HANCOCK D-2
Boy Scout Campground — GUTTENBERG B-5
Bridge View (COE - Rathbun Lake) — MORAVIA E-4
Bridgeport Campground — SIGOURNEY D-4
□ Briggs Woods Park (Hamilton County Park) — WEBSTER CITY C-3
□ Brown's Lake Bigelow Park (Woodbury County Park) — SALIX C-1
Brushy Creek SRA — LEHIGH C-3
Buck Creek (COE - Rathbun Lake) — MORAVIA E-4
Buffalo Creek Park-Walnut Grove Campground (Linn County Park) — COGGON C-5
Buffalo Shores (Scott County Park) — BUFFALO D-6
Bulgers Hollow Rec Area (COE-Thomson Park) — CLINTON C-6
Camp Crescent (Municipal Park) — LAKE VIEW C-2
Casey City Park — CASEY D-2
Cass County Fairgrounds Campground — ATLANTIC D-2
Cedar Bend Park (Bremer County Park) — WAVERLY B-4
Cedar View Park (Municipal Park) — NASHUA B-4
Cen La RV Park — SPIRIT LAKE A-2
Cherokee City Park — CHEROKEE B-1
Cherry Glen Campground (COE - Saylorville Lake) — DES MOINES D-3
Clark's Ferry (COE-Mississippi River Rec Areas-Muscatine) — DAVENPORT D-6
Clayton Hills Campground — GARNAVILLO B-5
Clear Lake SP — CLEAR LAKE B-3
Cobb Park & Campground — IDA GROVE C-2
Coffins Grove (Delaware County Park) — MANCHESTER B-5
Colony Country Campground — NORTH LIBERTY C-5
Country Court RV Park — CRESTON D-2
□ **Country Home Campground & Motel — SIOUX CENTER B-1**
□ Crawford Creek Recreation Area (Ida County Park) — BATTLE CREEK C-1
Crossroads RV Campground — MOUNT PLEASANT E-5
®□ **Cutty's Des Moines Camping Club — GRIMES D-3**
Dallas County Fair Campgrounds — ADEL D-3
Deer Valley Lodge CG — CLEAR LAKE B-3
Deerwood Park (City Park) — EVANSDALE B-4
□ **Des Moines West KOA — ADEL D-3**
Diamond Lake Park (Poweshiek County Park) — MONTEZUMA D-4
Dickson Timber — GLIDDEN
□ Doggs RV Park — MORAVIA E-4
□ Dolliver Memorial SP — LEHIGH C-3
E. Pott Co. Fairgrounds Campground — AVOCA D-2
Elinor Bedell SP — LAKE OKOBOJI A-2
Elk Rock SP — KNOXVILLE D-4
Emerson Bay SRA — MILFORD A-2
Fairport SRA/Wildcat Den State Park — MUSCATINE D-5
Ferry Landing (COE-Mississippi River Rec Areas-Muscatine) — OAKVILLE D-5
Fieldstone RV Park — ARNOLDS PARK A-2
Fillmore Recreation Area (Dubuque County Park) — CASCADE C-5
Finley's Landing (Dubuque County Park) — DUBUQUE B-6
Fontana Park (Buchanan County Park) — HAZLETON B-5
Fort Defiance SP — ESTHERVILLE A-2
Fountain Springs (Delaware County Park) — GREELEY B-5
F.W. Kent Park (Johnson County Park) — TIFFIN C-5
Geode SP — DANVILLE E-5
George Wyth Memorial SP — CEDAR FALLS B-4
Grant Park (Sac County Park) — AUBURN C-2
Great Western Park — MANNING C-2
□ Green Valley SP — CRESTON D-2
Griffs Valley View RV — ALTOONA D-3
Gull Point SP — MILFORD A-2
□ Hagge Park (Sac County Park) — SAC CITY C-2
Hannen Park (Benton County Park) — BLAIRSTOWN C-4
□ Harvest Farm Campground — KENDALLVILLE A-4
Hickory Grove Breezy Bay (Story County Park) — COLO C-3
Hickory Haven Campground — KEOKUK E-5
Hildreth Lighthouse Campground — WHITING C-1
Honey Creek SP — MORAVIA E-4
Howell Station (COE - Red Rock Lake) — PELLA D-4
Hunts Cedar River Campground — TIPTON C-5
• **Indian Hills Inn — ALBIA D-4**
Indian Hills RV Park — ALBIA D-4
Interstate RV Park — DAVENPORT D-6
Iowa State Fair Campgrounds — DES MOINES D-3
• **Iowa's Best Burger Cafe — KELLOGG D-4**
Island View (COE - Rathbun Lake) — CENTERVILLE E-4
Jakway Area (Buchanan County Park) — AURORA B-5
Jester Park (Polk County Park) — GRANGER C-3
John F. Kennedy Memorial Park (Webster County Park) — FORT DODGE B-3
Kellogg RV Park & Campground-Interstate 80 — KELLOGG D-4
□ KOA-Onawa/Blue Lake — ONAWA C-1
□ Lacey-Keosauqua SP — KEOSAUQUA E-5
□ Lake Ahquabi SP — INDIANOLA D-3
Lake Anita SP — ANITA D-2
□ Lake Cornelia Park (Wright County Park) — CLARION B-3
□ Lake Darling SP — BRIGHTON D-5
Lake Keomah SP — OSKALOOSA D-4
Lake Macbride SP — SOLON C-5
Lake Manawa SP — COUNCIL BLUFFS D-1
□ Lake of Three Fires SP — BEDFORD E-2
□ Lake Wapello SP — DRAKESVILLE E-4
Lakeside Marina and Campground — LAKESIDE B-2
Lakeside RV Park & Campground — DAVENPORT D-6
★ **Lasso E RV — ANAMOSA C-5**
★ **Lasso E RV — ANAMOSA C-5**
®□ **Lazy Acres RV Park — URBANA C-5**
Leach Park Campground — SPENCER B-2
Ledges SP — BOONE C-3
Lewis & Clark SP — ONAWA C-1
Lime Creek Area (Buchanan County Park) — BRANDON C-5
Linder Point (COE - Coralville Lake) — IOWA CITY D-5
□ Little Sioux Park (Woodbury County Park) — CORRECTIONVILLE B-1
Little Wall Lake Campground (Hamilton County Park) — JEWELL C-3
Lost Island-Huston Park (Palo Alto County Park) — RUTHVEN B-2
Lower Skunk River Access (Des Moines County Park) — AUGUSTA E-5
M. MacNider Park (Municipal Park) — MASON CITY B-3
Marble Beach SRA — ORLEANS A-2
Massey Marina (Dubuque County Park) — DUBUQUE B-6
McIntosh Woods SP — VENTURA B-3
Meskwaki Casino RV Park — TAMA C-4
□ Miami Park — ALBIA D-4
Minne Estema Campground (Benton County Park) — VINTON C-4
Morgan Creek Campground (Linn County Park) — CEDAR RAPIDS C-5
Morman Trail Park (Adair County Park) — BRIDGEWATER D-2
□ Morwood Campground & Resort — HAZLETON B-5
Mud Lake Campground (Dubuque County Park) — DUBUQUE B-6
Nelson Park (Crawford County Park) — DOW CITY C-2
New Wine Park (Dubuque County Park) — DYERSVILLE B-5
Newton KOA — NEWTON D-4
Nielsen RV Park — HARLAN D-2
Nine Eagles SP — DAVIS CITY E-3
North Cedar Park (Bremer County Park) — PLAINFIELD B-4
North Overlook (COE - Red Rock Lake) — PELLA D-4
North Woods Park (Bremer County Park) — SUMNER B-4
□ Oak Grove County Park (Sioux County Park) — HAWARDEN B-1
Oakwood RV Park — CLEAR LAKE B-3
Oelwein City Park Campground — OELWEIN B-5
On-Ur-Wa RV Park — ONAWA C-1
□ Palisades-Kepler SP — MOUNT VERNON C-5
Pikes Peak SP — MCGREGOR B-5
Pilot Knob SP — FOREST CITY A-3
□ Pine Lake SP — ELDORA C-4
Pinicon Ridge Flying Squirrel Campground (Linn county Park) — CENTRAL CITY C-5
Pleasant Creek (COE - Lock & Dam 11) — BELLEVUE C-6
□ Pleasant Creek SRA — PALO C-5
Prairie Flower (COE - Saylorville Lake) — DES MOINES D-3

IOWA — Continued

Prairie Ridge (COE - Rathbun Lake) — MORAVIA E-4
Prairie Rose SP — HARLAN D-2
Pulpit Rock Campground (City Park) — DECORAH A-5
R Campground — CHARLES CITY B-4
® Red Barn Resort — LANSING A-5
Red Haw SP — CHARITON D-3
Richey Park — GLIDDEN
□ River Ranch Camping — NASHUA B-4
Riverside Park — COON RAPIDS
□ Rock Creek Marina & Campground (Clinton County Park) — CAMANCHE C-6
Rock Creek SP — KELLOGG D-4
Rodgers Park (Benton County Park) — VINTON C-4
Rolling Cove (COE - Rathbun Lake) — CENTERVILLE E-4
Sac City Park — SAC CITY C-2
Sandy Beach (COE - Coralville Lake) — SHUEYVILLE C-5
Scales Pointe Camping and Boating — NORTH LIBERTY C-5
Scott County Park — DAVENPORT D-6
Shady Creek (COE-Mississippi River Rec Areas-Muscatine) — MUSCATINE D-5
□ Shady Oaks Camping — MARSHALLTOWN C-4
Shelby Country Inn and RV Park — SHELBY D-2
®□ **Skip-A-Way RV Park & Campground — CLERMONT B-5**
• **Sleepy Hollow Pizza and Ice Cream — OXFORD C-5**
Sleepy Hollow RV Park & Campground — OXFORD C-5
Smith Lake Park (Kossuth County Park) — ALGONA B-3
Snyder Bend Park (Woodbury County Park) — SALIX C-1
South Sabula Lakes Park (Jackson County Park) — SABULA C-6
Southwood Conservation Area (Woodbury County Park) — SMITHLAND C-1
□ Spook Cave and Campground — MCGREGOR B-5
Spring Lake (Greene County Park) — JEFFERSON C-2
□ Springbrook SP — GUTHRIE CENTER D-2
Spruce Creek (Jackson County Park) — BELLEVUE C-6
Squaw Creek Park (Linn County Park) — MARION C-5
Stone SP — SIOUX CITY B-1
Sudbury Court Motel & RV Park — MARENGO C-4
Sugar Bottom (COE - Coralville Lake) — NORTH LIBERTY C-5
Sunrise Campground — STORM LAKE B-2
Swan Lake State Park — CARROLL
Swiss Valley Campground (Dubuque County Park) — DUBUQUE B-6
Tailwater West (COE - Coralville Lake) — IOWA CITY D-5
Terrible's Lakeside Casino RV Park Osceola, IA — OSCEOLA D-3
The Grotto of the Redemption RV Park — WEST BEND B-2
• **The White Buffalo Restaurant & Lounge — ALBIA D-4**
□ **Timberline Campground — WAUKEE D-3**
Tomes RV Park — COUNCIL BLUFFS D-1
★ **Truck Country — CEDAR RAPIDS C-5**
★ **Truck Country — DAVENPORT D-6**
★ **Truck Country — DECORAH A-5**
★ **Truck Country — DUBUQUE B-6**
Turtle Creek River Access (Delaware County Park) — DELHI C-5
® Twin Anchors Campground — COLO C-3
Twin Bridges (Delaware County Park) — COLESBURG B-5
Union Grove SP — GLADBROOK C-4
□ Upper Iowa Resort & Rental — DORCHESTER A-5
Vick's Corner — SPIRIT LAKE A-2
Victory Park & Hubinger Landing Camping (City Parks) — KEOKUK E-5
Viking Lake SP — STANTON D-2
Volga River SRA — FAYETTE B-5
Wallashuck (COE - Red Rock Lake) — PELLA D-4
□ Walnut Acres Campground — MONTICELLO C-5
Walnut Woods SP — DES MOINES D-3
Wapsipinicon SP — ANAMOSA C-5
Waubonsie SP — SIDNEY E-1
West Lake Park (Scott County Park) — DAVENPORT D-6
□ **West Liberty RV Park — WEST LIBERTY D-5**
West Overlook (COE - Coralville Lake) — IOWA CITY D-5
Whispering Oaks RV Park & Campground — STORY CITY C-3
Whitebreast (COE-Red Rock Lake) — KNOXVILLE D-4
Wildcat Bluff (Benton County Park) — URBANA C-5
Wildcat Den SP — MUSCATINE D-5
□ Willow Lake (Harrison County Park) — WOODBINE C-1
□ Wilson Island SRA — MISSOURI VALLEY D-1
Winterset City Park Campground — WINTERSET D-3
Woodland Campground — LITTLE SIOUX C-1
Yellow Banks Park (Polk County Park) — PLEASANT HILL D-3
Yellow Smoke Park (Crawford County Park) — DENISON C-2

KENTUCKY

□ Aurora Oaks Campground — AURORA B-2
Axtel Campground (COE - Rough River Lake) — MCDANIELS D-2
Bailey's Point Campground (COE-Barren River Lake) — SCOTTSVILLE E-2
□ Barren River Lake State Resort Park — GLASGOW E-3
□ Big Bear Resort — BENTON B-2
Big Bone Lick State Park — WALTON B-4
Big South Fork Nat'l River & Rec. Area (Blue Heron Campground) — STEARNS E-4
Birmingham Ferry (LBL) National Recreation Area — GRAND RIVERS B-2
Blue Licks Battlefield State Park — MOUNT OLIVET C-4
®□ **Bluegrass Music RV Park — FRANKLIN E-2**
□ Breaks Interstate Park — ELKHORN CITY D-6
Buckhorn Dam Recreation Area (COE-Buckhorn Lake) — BUCKHORN D-5
Canal Recreation Area (COE-Lake Barkley) — GRAND RIVERS B-2
Carr Creek State Park — SASSAFRAS D-5
□ Carter Caves State Resort Park — OLIVE HILL C-5
Cave Country RV Campground — CAVE CITY D-3
Cave Creek (COE-Rough River Lake) — FALLS OF ROUGH D-2
□ Cincinnati South Rose Garden Resort — CRITTENDEN B-4
(COE-Fishtrap Lake) Fish Trap Lake Shelters — PIKEVILLE D-6
Columbus - Belmont State Park — COLUMBUS B-1
®□ Corbin-KOA — CORBIN E-4
Cravens Bay (LBL) National Recreation Area — GRAND RIVERS B-2
Crockett Frontier Campground — GRAND RIVERS B-2
□ Cumberland Falls State Resort Park — CORBIN E-4
Cumberland Gap National Historical Park (Wilderness Road Campground) — MIDDLESBORO E-5
Cumberland Point Public Use Area (COE-Lake Cumberland) — SOMERSET E-4
Cypress Lakes RV Park — CALVERT CITY B-2
Dale Hollow Lake State Park — BURKESVILLE E-3
Daniel Boone National Forest (Grove Boat-In Campground) — CORBIN E-4
Daniel Boone National Forest (Grove Campground) — CORBIN E-4
Daniel Boone National Forest (Holly Bay Rec. Area) — LONDON D-4
Daniel Boone National Forest (Koomer Ridge Campground) — SLADE D-5
Daniel Boone National Forest (Twin Knobs Rec. Area) — MOREHEAD C-5
Daniel Boone National Forest (White Oak Boat-In Campground) — LONDON D-4
Daniel Boone National Forest (Zilpo Recreation Area) — SALT LICK C-5
□ **Diamond Caverns Resort & Golf Club — PARK CITY E-3**
® Diamond Lake Resort Campground (Not Visited) — OWENSBORO D-2
Dog Creek (COE - Nolin River Lake) — LEITCHFIELD D-2
□ Dogwood Lakes Camping & Resort (Not Visited) — DUNMOR E-2
® **Duck Creek RV Park — PADUCAH B-1**
Eagle Falls Lodge — PARKERS LAKE E-4
□ Eagle Valley Camping Resort — SANDERS B-4

KENTUCKY — Continued

□ Elizabethtown Crossroads Campground — ***ELIZABETHTOWN D-3***
Elkhorn Campground — *FRANKFORT C-4*
Energy Lake (LBL) National Recreation Area — ***GOLDEN POND E-1***
Exit 31 RV Park — *GRAND RIVERS B-2*
Fall Creek Campground (Corps of Engineers) — ***MONTICELLO E-4***
Fenton (LBL) National Recreation Area — ***GOLDEN POND E-1***
Fern Lake Campground — *PADUCAH B-1*
Fishing Creek Public Use Area (COE-Lake Cumberland) — ***SOMERSET E-4***
Fort Boonesborough State Park — ***RICHMOND D-4***
General Burnside State Park — ***BURNSIDE E-4***
□ General Butler State Resort Park — ***CARROLLTON B-3***
German Bridge Camping Area — ***PRESTONSBURG D-6***
Glendale Campground — *ELIZABETHTOWN D-3*
□ **Grandma's RV Park — *SHEPHERDSVILLE C-3***
Grayson Lake State Park — ***GRAYSON C-5***
Green River Lake State Park — ***CAMPBELLSVILLE D-3***
Greenbo Lake State Resort Park — ***GREENUP B-6***
Gregory Lake RV Park — ***DRAKESBORO D-2***
Hillman Ferry Campground (LBL) — ***GOLDEN POND E-1***
Hillman Ferry (LBL) National Recreation Area — ***GRAND RIVERS B-2***
□ Holiday Hills Resort — ***EDDYVILLE D-1***
Holmes Bend Recreation Area (COE-Green River Lake) — ***CAMPBELLSVILLE D-3***
Holt's Campground (Not Visited) — ***BARDSTOWN D-3***
Hurricane Creek Recreational Area (COE-Lake Barkley) — ***CADIZ E-1***
□ I-75 Camper Village — ***DRY RIDGE B-4***
□ Indian Ridge Campground — ***CAMPBELLSVILLE D-3***
□ Jenny Wiley State Resort Park — ***PRESTONSBURG D-6***
□ John James Audubon State Park — ***HENDERSON C-1***
Kendall Recreation Area (COE-Lake Cumberland) — ***JAMESTOWN E-3***
□ Kenlake State Resort Park — ***AURORA B-2***
□ Kentucky Dam Village State Resort Park — ***GILBERTSVILLE B-2***
Kentucky Horse Park (SP) — ***LEXINGTON C-4***
□ Kentucky Lakes KOA at Prizer Point — ***CADIZ E-1***
Kincaid Lake State Park — ***FALMOUTH B-4***
□ KOA Ashland/West Huntington — ***ASHLAND C-6***
□ KOA-Bowling Green (Not Visited) — ***BOWLING GREEN E-2***
□ KOA-Horse Cave (Not Visited) — ***HORSE CAVE D-3***
□ KOA-Indian Hills — ***RUSSELL SPRINGS E-3***
□ KOA-KY Lake Dam/Paducah — ***CALVERT CITY B-2***
®□ KOA-Renfro Valley — ***RENFRO VALLEY D-4***
□ Lake Barkley State Resort Park — ***CADIZ E-1***
Lake Cumberland RV Park — ***BURNSIDE E-4***
□ Lake Cumberland State Resort Park — ***JAMESTOWN E-3***
Lake Malone State Park — ***DUNMOR E-2***
Lakeside Campground & Marina — ***AURORA B-2***
Laurel Branch Campground (COE- Rough River Lake) — ***MCDANIELS D-2***
Levi Jackson Wilderness Road State Park — ***LONDON D-4***
★ **Louisville RV Center — *LOUISVILLE C-3***
®□ Louisville South KOA (Not Visited) — ***SHEPHERDSVILLE C-3***
□ Mammoth Cave Jellystone Park Camp Resort — ***CAVE CITY D-3***
Mammoth Cave NP (Headquarters Campground) — ***PARK CITY E-3***
□ MILITARY PARK (Camp Carlson Army Travel Camp) — ***MULDRAUGH C-3***
□ MILITARY PARK (Eagle's Rest Army Travel Camp-Fort Campbell) — ***HOPKINSVILLE E-1***
● **Miss Scarlett's Restaurant — *GRAND RIVERS B-2***
Moutardier (COE-Nolin River Lake) — ***LEITCHFIELD D-2***
● **Mt. Vernon-Rock Castle County Tourist Commission — *RENFRO VALLEY D-4***
★ **Murphy's RV's — *EDDYVILLE D-1***
My Old Kentucky Home SP — ***BARDSTOWN D-3***
□ Natural Bridge State Resort Park — ***SLADE D-5***
Nolin Lake State Park — ***LEITCHFIELD D-2***
North Fork (Corps of Engineers-Rough River Lake) — ***MCDANIELS D-2***
Oak Creek Campground — *WALTON B-4*
Oh Kentucky Campground — *BEREA D-4*
Ohio County Park — ***HARTFORD D-2***
Outback RV Resort — *EDDYVILLE D-1*
Paintsville Lake State Park — ***STAFFORDSVILLE C-6***
□ Pennyrile Forest State Resort Park — ***DAWSON SPRINGS D-1***
Pike Ridge (COE-Green River Lake) — ***CAMPBELLSVILLE D-3***
□ Renfro Valley RV Park — ***RENFRO VALLEY D-4***
□ Rough River Dam State Resort Park — ***FALLS OF ROUGH D-2***
Rushing Creek (LBL) National Recreation Area — ***GOLDEN POND E-1***
Singing Hills Campground and RV Park — *CAVE CITY D-3*
□ Smith Ridge (COE - Green River Lake) — ***CAMPBELLSVILLE D-3***
Still Waters Campground — ***FRANKFORT C-4***
®□ Sulphur Creek Resort (Not Visited) — ***BURKESVILLE E-3***
Tailwater Campground (COE-Buckhorn Lake) — ***BUCKHORN D-5***
Taylorsville Lake State Park — ***TAYLORSVILLE C-3***
□ The Falls Campground — ***LOUISA C-6***
The Narrows (COE-Barren River Lake) — ***GLASGOW E-3***
The Tailwater Below Dam (COE-Barren River Lake) — ***SCOTTSVILLE E-2***
Trace Branch (COE-Buckhorn Lake) — ***HYDEN D-5***
Union County Fair & Expo Center — ***STURGIS A-2***
Valley Breeze RV Campground — ***GRAYSON C-5***
Victory RV Park & Campground, Inc — *PADUCAH B-1*
Waitsboro Rec Area (COE-Lake Cumberland) — ***SOMERSET E-4***
Walnut Meadow RV Park — *BEREA D-4*
Wax Site (COE-Nolin River Lake) — ***LEITCHFIELD D-2***
Western Kentucky RV Park (Not Visited) — ***CENTRAL CITY D-2***
Westgate RV Camping — *LONDON D-4*
White Acres Campground (Not Visited) — ***BARDSTOWN D-3***
Wildcat Creek Rec Area — ***MURRAY C-2***
®□ **Windy Hollow Campground & Recreation Area (Not Visited) — *OWENSBORO D-2***
Wrangler (LBL) National Recreation Area — ***GOLDEN POND E-1***
Wranglers Campground (LBL) — ***GOLDEN POND E-1***
Yatesville Lake SP — ***LOUISA C-6***

LOUISIANA

A +Motel & RV Park — ***LAKE CHARLES D-2***
Abbeville RV Park — ***ABBEVILLE D-3***
Ajax Country Livin' at I-49 Rv Park, LLC — *AJAX B-2*
● **Avoyelles Parish Tourism Commission — *MARKSVILLE C-3***
B & B RV Park — *DONALDSONVILLE D-4*
□ **Baton Rouge KOA — *BATON ROUGE D-4***
● **Bayou LaFourche Area CVB — *THIBODAUX D-4***
□ Bayou Segnette State Park — ***WESTWEGO D-5***
Bayou Wilderness RV Resort — *CARENCRO D-3*
Betty's RV Park — *ABBEVILLE D-3*
□ Bonnie & Clyde Trade Days & Campground — ***ARCADIA A-2***
● **Cajun Coast Visitors & Convention Bureau — *MORGAN CITY E-4***
Cajun Country Campground — ***PORT ALLEN D-4***
® Cajun Haven RV Park — ***EGAN D-3***
□ Calloway RV & Campground — ***HAMMOND D-5***
Capri Court MHP — *HOUMA E-4*
□ Cash Point Landing — ***BOSSIER CITY A-2***
□ **Catfish Heaven Aqua Farm & Campground — *ST. MARTINVILLE D-3***
Chase's RV Park — ***NEW IBERIA D-3***
□ Chemin-A-Haut State Park — ***BASTROP A-3***
□ Chicot State Park — ***VILLE PLATTE C-3***
Cinnamon Creek RV Park — *MINDEN A-2*
City of Rayne RV Park — ***RAYNE D-3***
Colfax Recreation Area RV Park & Campground — ***COLFAX B-3***
● **Coushatta Casino Resort — *KINDER D-3***
Coushatta Luxury RV Resort At Red Shoes Park — *KINDER D-3*
□ Crooked Creek Rec. Area — ***PINE PRAIRIE C-3***
□ Cypress Bend Park/Toledo Bend Lake (Sabine River Auth. Site 11) — ***MANY B-2***
® **Cypress Bend RV Park — *IOWA D-2***
□ Cypress Black Bayou Recreation Area — ***BENTON A-2***
Diamond Jacks RV Park — ***BOSSIER CITY A-2***

LOUISIANA — Continued

Earl Williamson Park/Caddo Lake Park (Caddo Parish) — ***OIL CITY A-2***
Fairview-Riverside State Park — ***MADISONVILLE D-5***
® **Fanz RV Park — *ST. BERNARD D-5***
Farr Park Campground & Horse Activity Center — ***BATON ROUGE D-4***
Fountainebleau State Park — ***MANDEVILLE D-5***
French Quarter RV Resort — *NEW ORLEANS D-5*
□ Frenchman's Wilderness — ***HENDERSON D-3***
★ **G & J Mobile Home & RV Supplies — *LAFAYETTE D-3***
★ **Gauthier's RV Service Center — *LAFAYETTE D-3***
□ Grand Bayou Resort — ***COUSHATTA B-2***
Grand Isle State Park — ***GRAND ISLE E-5***
□ Hidden Oaks Family Campground — ***HAMMOND D-5***
□ **Hidden Ponds RV Park — *LAKE CHARLES D-2***
Hodges Gardens — ***FLORIEN C-2***
□ Hodges Wilderness Camp Ground — ***MANY B-2***
★ **Hope's Camper Corner RV Center — *MONROE A-3***
● **Houma Area Convention & Visitors Bureau — *HOUMA E-4***
I-10 Mobile Village & RV Campground — ***LAKE CHARLES D-2***
● **Iberia Parish Convention & Visitors Bureau — *NEW IBERIA D-3***
□ Indian Creek Campground & RV Park — ***INDEPENDENCE C-5***
Indian Creek Recreation Area (Alexander SF) — ***WOODWORTH C-3***
□ Jimmy Davis State Park — ***CHATHAM A-3***
Jude Travel Park of New Orleans — ***NEW ORLEANS D-5***
Kemper Williams Park (St. Mary Parish Park) — ***MORGAN CITY E-4***
Kisatchie National Forest (Kincaid Rec. Site) — ***GARDNER C-3***
□ **KOA-Lafayette — *LAFAYETTE D-3***
KOA-New Orleans West — ***NEW ORLEANS D-5***
● **Koasati Pines At Coushatta — *KINDER D-3***
KOC Kampground — *NEW IBERIA D-3*
LaBoulaie RV Park & Campground — ***BROUSSARD D-3***
● **Lafayette Convention & Visitors Commission — *LAFAYETTE D-3***
□ Lake Bistineau State Park — ***DOYLINE A-2***
Lake Bruin State Park — ***ST. JOSEPH B-4***
● **Lake Charles/Southwest Louisiana Convention & Visitors Bureau — *LAKE CHARLES D-2***
□ Lake Claiborne State Park — ***HOMER A-2***
□ Lake D'Arbonne State Park — ***FARMERVILLE A-3***
Lake End RV Campground (Municipal Park) — ***MORGAN CITY E-4***
□ Lake Fausse Pointe State Park — ***ST. MARTINVILLE D-3***
□ **Lakeside RV Park — *LIVINGSTON D-4***
□ **Lakeview RV Park — *EUNICE D-3***
Lamar Dixon Expo Center RV Park — ***GONZALES D-4***
®□ Land-O-Pines Family Campground — ***COVINGTON D-5***
Lincoln Parish Park — ***RUSTON A-3***
● **Louisiana Culinary Trails — *BATON ROUGE D-4***
● **Louisiana Travel Promotion Association — *BATON ROUGE D-4***
Maxie's Campground — *BROUSSARD D-3*
MILITARY PARK (Barksdale AFB FAMCAMP) — ***BOSSIER CITY A-2***
® MILITARY PARK (New Orleans NAS Travel Camp) — ***BELLE CHASSE D-5***
□ MILITARY PARK (Toledo Bend Rec Site-Fort Polk) — ***LEESVILLE C-2***
Nakatosh Campground — *NATCHITOCHES B-2*
● **Natchitoches Parish Tourist Commission — *NATCHITOCHES B-2***
□ **New Orleans East Kampground — *SLIDELL D-5***
● **New Orleans Plantation Country — *NEW ORLEANS D-5***
● **New Rockdale Radio Shop LLC — *MANSFIELD B-2***
New Rockdale RV Park/Radioshop LLC — *MANSFIELD B-2*
□ North Toledo Bend State Park — ***ZWOLLE B-2***
Opelousas City Park — ***OPELOUSAS D-3***
● **Paragon Casino — *MARKSVILLE C-3***
□ **Paragon Casino RV Resort — *MARKSVILLE C-3***
□ Pavilion RV Park — ***WEST MONROE A-3***
Peaceful Pines RV Park — *ST. FRANCISVILLE C-4*
Pine Crest RV Park — *SLIDELL D-5*
□ Pleasure Point/Toledo Bend Lake (Sabine River Auth. Site 15) — ***HORNBECK C-2***
● **Poche Plantation — *GONZALES D-4***
□ **Poche Plantation RV Resort — *GONZALES D-4***
□ **Poche's Fish-N-Camp — *BREAUX BRIDGE D-3***
● **Poche's Market, Restaurant & Smokehouse — *BREAUX BRIDGE D-3***
®□ **Pontchartrain Landing — *NEW ORLEANS D-5***
Punkin Park Campground — ***HAMMOND D-5***
Quiet Oaks RV Park — *FENTON D-2*
Rapides Coliseum (Parish Park) — ***ALEXANDRIA C-3***
River View RV Park — *VIDALIA B-4*
Riverboat RV Park — *NEW ORLEANS D-5*
● **Ruston/Lincoln Convention & Visitors Bureau — *RUSTON A-3***
● **Sabine Parish — *MANY B-2***
Saint Bernard State Park — ***VIOLET D-5***
● **St. Landry Parish Tourist Commission — *OPELOUSAS D-3***
● **St. Tammany Parish Tourist & Convention Commission — *MANDEVILLE D-5***
□ Sam Houston Jones State Park — ***LAKE CHARLES D-2***
□ San Miguel Park/Toledo Bend Lake (Sabine River Auth. Site 7-A) — ***ZWOLLE B-2***
□ **Shiloh Campground & RV Resort — *MONROE A-3***
● **Shreveport/Bossier Convention & Tourist Bureau — *SHREVEPORT A-2***
□ **Silver Creek Campground — *MT. HERMON C-5***
□ South Toledo Bend State Park — ***ANACOCO C-2***
Springhill RV Park (City Park) — ***SPRINGHILL A-2***
Sugar Hill RV Park — ***GONZALES D-4***
□ Sweetwater Campground & RV Park — ***LORANGER C-5***
□ **Tall Pines RV Park — *SHREVEPORT A-2***
□ **Tchefuncte Campground — *FOLSOM C-5***
□ Tickfaw State Park — ***SPRINGFIELD D-5***
Travel America's RV Park — ***GREENWOOD A-1***
Twelve Oaks RV Park — *LAKE CHARLES D-2*
□ V RV Park-Lake Charles/Vinton — ***VINTON D-2***
● **Vernon Parish Tourist Information Center — *LEESVILLE C-2***
® **Whispering Meadow RV Park — *LAKE CHARLES D-2***
□ Yogi Bear's Jellystone Park Camp Resort — ***HAMMOND D-5***
□ Yogi Bear's Jellystone Park Camp-Resort — ***LAKE CHARLES D-2***

MAINE

Acadia National Park (Blackwoods Campground) — ***BAR HARBOR E-4***
Acadia National Park (Seawall Campground) — ***SOUTHWEST HARBOR E-4***
®□ **Acres of Wildlife — *STEEP FALLS E-1***
□ **Arndt's Aroostook River Lodge & Campground — *PRESQUE ISLE B-4***
Aroostook State Park — ***PRESQUE ISLE B-4***
® **Augusta-West Lakeside Resort Kampground — *WINTHROP E-2***
★ **Augusta-West Lakeside RV Sales & Service — *WINTHROP E-2***
®□ Balsam Cove Campground — ***ORLAND D-3***
®□ **Balsam Woods Campground — *ABBOT D-3***
Bar Harbor Campground — ***BAR HARBOR E-4***
® Bar Harbor KOA — ***BAR HARBOR E-4***
□ Bar Harbor Woodlands KOA — ***BAR HARBOR E-4***
□ Bass Harbor Campground — ***BASS HARBOR E-4***
® **Bayley's Camping Resort — *OLD ORCHARD BEACH F-2***
®□ **Bayley's Camping Resort — *SCARBOROUGH F-2***
Beach Acres Campground — *WELLS F-1*
®□ Beaver Brook Campground — ***NORTH MONMOUTH E-2***
□ **Beaver Dam Campground — *BERWICK F-1***
Bethel Outdoor Adventure and Campground — ***BETHEL E-1***
□ Birch Point Lodge Campground & Cottage Resort — ***ISLAND FALLS B-4***
□ **Blueberry Pond Campground — *FREEPORT E-2***
Bradbury Mountain State Park — ***POWNAL E-2***
□ Camden Hills RV Resort (Morgan RV Resorts) — ***ROCKPORT E-3***
Camden Hills State Park — ***CAMDEN E-3***
Camp Eaton — ***YORK HARBOR F-1***
Cascadia Park — ***SACO F-2***
Cathedral Pines (Stratton-Eustis Dev. Corp.) — ***STRATTON D-2***
Chewonki Campgrounds — ***WISCASSET E-2***

MAINE — Continued

□ Christie's Campground & Cottages — ***NEWPORT D-3***
Cobscook Bay State Park — ***DENNYSVILLE D-5***
®□ Colonial Mast Campground — ***NAPLES E-1***
□ Deer Farm Camps & Campground — ***KINGFIELD D-2***
Desert Dunes of Maine Campground — *FREEPORT E-2*
● **Desert of Maine — *FREEPORT E-2***
Dixon's Coastal Maine Campground — ***CAPE NEDDICK F-1***
□ Duck Puddle Family Campground — ***NOBLEBORO E-3***
® **Family and Friends Campground — *STANDISH E-1***
®□ Flat Rock Bridge Family Resort — ***LEBANON F-1***
® Four Seasons Camping Area — ***NAPLES E-1***
Freeport Village Campground — *FREEPORT E-2*
®□ Freeport/Durham KOA — ***FREEPORT E-2***
□ Gray Homestead Oceanfront Camping — ***BOOTHBAY HARBOR E-2***
Greenland Cove Campground — ***DANFORTH C-4***
Hadley's Point Campground — *BAR HARBOR E-4*
□ Happy Horseshoe Campground — ***NORTH NEW PORTLAND D-2***
® Hemlock Grove Campground — ***ARUNDEL F-1***
● **Hermon Family Resaurant — *BANGOR D-3***
Hid'n Pines Family Campground — ***OLD ORCHARD BEACH F-2***
Hilltop Campground — *ROBBINSTON D-5*
Holden Family Campground — *HOLDEN D-3*
□ Katahdin Shadows Campground & Cabins — ***MEDWAY C-4***
®□ KOA-Augusta/Gardiner — ***RICHMOND E-2***
□ KOA-Skowhegan-Canaan — ***SKOWHEGAN D-2***
® **Kokatosi Campground — *RAYMOND E-2***
□ **Lake Pemaquid Camping — *DAMARISCOTTA E-3***
Lake St. George State Park — ***LIBERTY E-3***
®□ Lakeside Pines Campground — ***BRIDGTON E-1***
Lakeview Camping Resort — ***ST. AGATHA A-4***
Lamoine State Park — ***ELLSWORTH D-4***
Libby's Oceanside Camp — *YORK HARBOR F-1*
Lily Bay State Park (Moosehead Lake) — ***GREENVILLE C-3***
□ Littlefield Beaches Lakeside Campground — ***GREENWOOD E-1***
® Loon's Haven Family Campground — ***NAPLES E-1***
□ **Meadowbrook Camping — *BATH E-2***
□ Mic Mac Cove — ***UNION E-3***
△ MILITARY PARK (Sprague Neck Campsites) — ***EAST MACHIAS D-5***
□ MILITARY PARK (Winter Harbor Rec Area) — ***WINTER HARBOR E-4***
□ **Moose River Campground & Cabins — *JACKMAN C-2***
Moosehead Family Campground — ***GREENVILLE C-3***
®□ More to Life Family Campground — ***WINTHROP E-2***
Mount Blue State Park — ***WELD D-2***
®□ Mountain View Campground — ***DIXFIELD D-2***
□ **Mountainview Campground — *SULLIVAN D-4***
® **Mt. Desert Narrows Camping Resort — *BAR HARBOR E-4***
®□ **My Brothers Place Campground — *HOULTON B-4***
® Naples Campground — ***NAPLES E-1***
®□ **Narrows Too Camping Resort — *BAR HARBOR E-4***
□ Nascar RV Resort at Meguntlcook (Morgan RV Resorts) — ***ROCKPORT E-3***
NASCAR RV Resort at Virginia Park (Morgan RV Resorts) — ***OLD ORCHARD BEACH F-2***
Nascar RV Resort at Wagon Wheel (Morgan RV Resorts) — ***OLD ORCHARD BEACH F-2***
® Nascar RV Resort at Wild Acres (Morgan RV Resorts) — ***OLD ORCHARD BEACH F-2***
Neil E Michaud Campground — ***PRESQUE ISLE B-4***
NE'RE Beach Family Campground — ***OLD ORCHARD BEACH F-2***
□ Ocean View Cottages & Camping — ***WELLS F-1***
Palmyra Golf Course & Campground — ***PALMYRA D-3***
®□ Papoose Pond Resort & Campground — ***WATERFORD E-1***
® Paradise Park Resort Campground — ***OLD ORCHARD BEACH F-2***
®□ **Patten Pond Camping Resort — *ELLSWORTH D-4***
Paul Bunyan Campground — *BANGOR D-3*
Peaks-Kenny State Park — ***DOVER-FOXCROFT D-3***
□ **Pine Grove Campground & Cottages — *MEDWAY C-4***
Pinederosa Camping Area — ***OGUNQUIT F-1***
Pinehirst RV Resort — ***OLD ORCHARD BEACH F-2***
® **Pleasant Hill RV Park & Campground — *BANGOR D-3***
® Pleasant River Campground — ***BETHEL E-1***
★ **Point Sebago — *CASCO E-1***
□ **Point Sebago Golf and Beach RV Resort — *CASCO E-1***
® **Poland Spring Campground — *POLAND SPRING E-2***
Powder Horn Family Camping Resort — ***OLD ORCHARD BEACH F-2***
Pumpkin Patch RV Resort — *BANGOR D-3*
® **Range Pond Campground — *POLAND E-2***
Rangeley (Lake) State Park — ***RANGELEY D-1***
®□ **Red Apple Campground — *KENNEBUNKPORT F-2***
Red Barn Campground — *HOLDEN D-3*
● **Red Barn Diner — *HOLDEN D-3***
Riverbend Campground — *LEEDS E-2*
Riverside Park Campground — ***WELLS F-1***
®□ **Saco/Old Orchard Beach KOA — *SACO F-2***
® Sagadahoc Bay Campground — ***GEORGETOWN E-2***
® Salmon Falls River Camping Resort — ***LEBANON F-1***
□ **Saltwater Farm Campground — *THOMASTON E-3***
Salty Acres Campground — ***KENNEBUNKPORT F-2***
Scott's Cove Camping Area — *ALFRED F-1*
Sea Vu Campground — *WELLS F-1*
★ **Seacoast RV's — *SACO F-2***
□ Seaview Campground — ***EASTPORT D-5***
Sebago Lake State Park — ***NAPLES E-1***
□ **Sebasticook Lake Campground — *NEWPORT D-3***
®□ Sennebec Lake Campground — ***APPLETON E-3***
□ **Shady Oaks Campground and Cabins — *ORLAND D-3***
Shannons Sanctuary — ***BROWNFIELD E-1***
□ Sherwood Forest Campsite & Cabins — ***NEW HARBOR E-3***
□ **Shore Hills Campground & RV Park — *BOOTHBAY E-2***
□ **Silver Springs Campground — *SACO F-2***
□ Smuggler's Den Campground — ***SOUTHWEST HARBOR E-4***
□ **South Arm Campground — *ANDOVER D-1***
®□ **Stony Brook Recreation — *HANOVER D-1***
□ **Sunset Point Campground — *HARRINGTON D-4***
Sunset Point RV Trailer Park — ***LUBEC D-5***
The Casey's Stadig Campground — ***WELLS F-1***
The Moorings — ***BELFAST E-3***
□ **The Waltons Campground — *EDDINGTON D-3***
Timberland Acres RV Park — *TRENTON E-4*
®□ Two Lakes Camping Area — ***OXFORD E-1***
Two Rivers Campground — *SKOWHEGAN D-2*
□ **Walnut Grove Campground — *ALFRED F-1***
Wassamki Springs Campground — *SCARBOROUGH F-2*
® **Wells Beach Resort — *WELLS F-1***
® Wheeler Stream Campground — ***BANGOR D-3***
® **Wild Duck Adult Campground — *SCARBOROUGH F-2***
Woodland Acres Campground & Canoe — ***BROWNFIELD E-1***
Yellowstone Park — ***SANFORD F-1***
□ Yogi Bear's Jellystone Park — ***SKOWHEGAN D-2***
York Beach Camper Park — *YORK BEACH F-1*

MARYLAND

Assateague Island National Seashore (Bayside Campground) — ***BERLIN D-6***
Assateague SP — ***OCEAN CITY D-6***
Assateague Island National Seashore (Oceanside Campground) — ***BERLIN D-6***
® **Bar Harbor RV Park & Marina — *ABINGDON A-4***
● **Bay Breeze Cafe at Castaways — *OCEAN CITY D-6***
Big Run SP — ***GRANTSVILLE D-1***
□ **Capitol KOA/Washington D.C. Northeast — *MILLERSVILLE B-4***
®□ **Castaways RV Resort & Campground — *OCEAN CITY D-6***
Catoctin Mountain NP (Owens Creek) — ***THURMONT A-2***
®□ **Cherry Hill Park — *COLLEGE PARK B-3***

ALPHABETICAL LISTINGS CONTINUED

MARYLAND — Continued

☐ Cunningham Falls SP (Houck Area) — ***THURMONT A-2***
Cunningham Falls SP (Manor Area) — ***THURMONT A-2***
Deep Creek Lake SP — ***OAKLAND E-1***
®☐ **Duncan's Family Campground — *LOTHIAN C-4***
☐ Elk Neck SP — ***NORTH EAST A-5***
Fort Frederick SP — ***HAGERSTOWN A-2***
Fort Whaley Campground — *WHALEYVILLE D-6*
®☐ **Frontier Town Campground — *OCEAN CITY D-6***
• **Frontier Town Water Park — *OCEAN CITY D-6***
• **Frontier Town Western Theme Park — *OCEAN CITY D-6***
☐ Gambrill SP — ***FREDERICK A-2***
Greenbelt NP (Greenbelt Campground) — ***GREENBELT B-3***
Greenbrier SP — ***HAGERSTOWN A-2***
☐ Hagerstown/Antietam Battlefield-KOA — ***WILLIAMSPORT A-2***
☐ Happy Hills Campground — ***HANCOCK A-1***
☐ **Hidden Springs Campground — *FLINTSTONE D-2***
® **Holiday Park Campground — *GREENSBORO B-5***
☐ Island Resort Campground — ***NEWARK D-6***
☐ Janes Island SP — ***CRISFIELD E-5***
△ Little Bennett Regional Park (Montgomery County Park) — ***CLARKSBURG B-3***
☐ Martinak SP — ***DENTON C-5***
®△☐ MILITARY CAMPGROUND (Solomons Navy Rec Center) — ***SOLOMONS D-4***
MILITARY PARK (FAMCAMP-Andrews AFB) — ***MORNINGSIDE C-3***
• **Miss Alice's Ice Cream Parlor — *OCEAN CITY D-6***
• **Morris Meadows Historic Preservation Museum — *FREELAND A-4***
☐ **Morris Meadows Recreation Farm — *FREELAND A-4***
☐ New Germany SP — ***GRANTSVILLE D-1***
• **Painted Pony Saloon — *OCEAN CITY D-6***
☐ Patapsco Valley SP (Hilton Area) — ***CATONSVILLE B-3***
Patapsco Valley SP (Hollofield Area) — ***ELLICOTT CITY B-3***
Pocomoke River SP (Milburn Landing Area) — ***POCOMOKE CITY E-5***
☐ Pocomoke River SP (Shad Landing Area) — ***SNOW HILL D-6***
☐ Point Lookout SP — ***SCOTLAND E-4***
• **Pony Island Arcade & Gifts — *OCEAN CITY D-6***
☐ **Ramblin' Pines Family Campground & RV Park — *WOODBINE B-3***
Rocky Gap SP — ***FLINTSTONE D-2***
Sandy Hill Family Camp — *QUANTICO D-5*
☐ Susquehanna SP — ***HAVRE DE GRACE A-4***
△ Swallow Falls SP — ***OAKLAND E-1***
Take-It-Easy Campground — ***CALLAWAY D-4***
☐ Tuckahoe SP — ***QUEEN ANNE C-5***
☐ **Yogi Bear's Jellystone Park Camp-Resort-Williamsport-Hagerstown — *WILLIAMSPORT A-2***

MASSACHUSETTS

® Adventure Bound Camping Resorts - Cape Cod (Formerly North Truro Camping Area) — ***NORTH TRURO C-6***
® **Atlantic Oaks — *EASTHAM C-6***
Bay View Campgrounds — *BOURNE D-5*
Beach Rose RV Park — *SALISBURY BEACH A-5*
Beartown SF — ***MONTEREY C-1***
Black Bear Campground — *SALISBURY A-5*
Bonny Rigg Camping Club — *BECKET B-1*
Boston Harbor Islands State Park — ***HINGHAM B-5***
☐ **Boston Minuteman Campground — *LITTLETON B-4***
☐ Boston/Cape Cod KOA — ***MIDDLEBORO C-5***
☐ **Bourne Scenic Park (Municipal Park) — *BOURNE D-5***
☐ Camp Coldbrook RV Resort (Morgan RV Resort) — ***BARRE B-3***
Camp Overflow Campground & Marina — ***OTIS C-1***
Camper's Haven RV Resort — *DENNISPORT D-6*
Canoe River Campground — *MANSFIELD C-4*
Cape Ann Camp Site — *GLOUCESTER B-5*
☐ **Cape Cod Campresort & Cabins — *EAST FALMOUTH D-5***
Circle CG Farm Family Camping & RV Park — *BELLINGHAM C-4*
Clarksburg State Park — ***CLARKSBURG A-1***
Coastal Acres Camping Court — ***PROVINCETOWN C-6***
Country Aire Campground — *CHARLEMONT A-2*
D.A.R. State Forest — ***GOSHEN B-2***
Dunes' Edge Campground — ***PROVINCETOWN C-6***
☐ **Dunroamin' Cottages & Trailer Park — *SANDWICH D-5***
☐ Ellis Haven Campground — ***PLYMOUTH C-5***
Erving State Forest — ***ERVING B-2***
Granville State Forest — ***GRANVILLE C-2***
Harold Parker State Forest — ***NORTH ANDOVER A-4***
® **Hidden Valley Campground — *LANESBOROUGH B-1***
Historic Valley Campground (Municipal Park) — ***NORTH ADAMS A-1***
Horseneck Beach State Reservation — ***WESTPORT D-5***
® **Indian Ranch Campground — *WEBSTER C-3***
® Indianhead Resort — ***PLYMOUTH C-5***
John's Pond Campground/Otis Trailer Village — ***MASHPEE D-5***
® King's Family Campground — ***SUTTON C-3***
Lake Dennison State Recreation Area — ***WINCHENDON A-3***
®☐ Lamb City Campground — ***PHILLIPSTON B-3***
☐ **Martha's Vineyard Family Campground — *MARTHA'S VINEYARD D-5***
Massasoit State Park — ***TAUNTON C-4***
☐ Maurice's Campground — ***WELLFLEET C-6***
☐ MILITARY PARK (Fourth Cliff Rec. Area-Hanscom AFB) — ***HUMAROCK C-5***
MILITARY PARK (Hanscom AFB FAMCAMP) — ***BEDFORD B-4***
☐ Mohawk Trail State Forest — ***CHARLEMONT A-2***
Myles Standish State Forest — ***SOUTH CARVER C-5***
Nickerson SP — ***BREWSTER D-6***
☐ **Normandy Farms Family Camping Resort — *FOXBORO C-4***
Oak Haven Family Campground — ***WALES C-3***
★ **Oakham Trailer Sales & Service — *OAKHAM B-3***
October Mountain State Forest — ***LEE B-1***
Old Chatham Road RV Resort — ***SOUTH DENNIS D-6***
Otter River State Forest — ***WINCHENDON A-3***
Partridge Hollow Camping Area — ***MONSON C-2***
Pearl Hill State Park — ***WEST TOWNSEND A-3***
Peppermint Park Camping Resort — ***PLAINFIELD B-1***
®☐ Peters Pond RV Resort (Morgan RV Resorts) — ***SANDWICH D-5***
®☐ **Pine Acres Family Camping Resort — *OAKHAM B-3***
Pines Camping Area — ***SALISBURY A-5***
®☐ **Pinewood Lodge Campground — *PLYMOUTH C-5***
★ **Pinewood Lodge RV Service — *PLYMOUTH C-5***
Pittsfield State Forest — ***PITTSFIELD B-1***
☐ Prospect Lake Park — ***NORTH EGREMONT C-1***
☐ Prospect Mountain Campground & RV Park — ***GRANVILLE C-2***
®☐ Quinebaug Cove Campground — ***BRIMFIELD C-3***
® **Rusnik Family Campground — *SALISBURY A-5***
Salisbury Beach State Reservation — ***SALISBURY A-5***
®☐ Sandy Pond Campground — ***PLYMOUTH C-5***
☐ Savoy Mountain SF — ***FLORIDA A-1***
Scusset Beach State Park — ***SANDWICH D-5***
Shady Knoll Campground — *BREWSTER D-6*
®☐ Shady Pines Campground — ***SAVOY B-1***
Shawme Crowell State Forest — ***SANDWICH D-5***
☐ Sippewissett Cabins & Campground — ***FALMOUTH D-5***
® Summit Hill Campground — ***WASHINGTON B-1***
Sunsetview Farm Camping Area — *MONSON C-2*
Sweetwater Forest Family Camping Resort — ***BREWSTER D-6***
The Old Holbrook Place — ***WEST SUTTON C-3***
The Old Sawmill Campground — *WEST BROOKFIELD C-3*
The Pines Campground — *ASHBY A-3*
Tolland State Forest — ***OTIS C-1***
Travelers Woods of New England — ***BERNARDSTON A-2***
Village Green Family Campground — ***BRIMFIELD C-3***
® Walker Island Family Camping — ***CHESTER B-1***
Waquoit Bay Nat'l. Estuarine Reserve (SP) — ***FALMOUTH D-5***
Webster/Sturbridge Family Camp — *WEBSTER C-3*
Wells State Park — ***STURBRIDGE C-3***

MASSACHUSETTS — Continued

® White Birch Campground — ***WHATELY B-2***
Willard Brook State Forest — ***ASHBY A-3***
Windsor State Forest — ***WINDSOR B-1***
Winter Island Park (City Park) — ***SALEM B-5***
Wompatuck State Park — ***HINGHAM B-5***
® Yogi Bear's Jellystone Park Cape Cod at Maple Park — ***EAST WAREHAM D-5***
®☐ **Yogi Bear's Jellystone Park-Sturbridge — *STURBRIDGE C-3***

MICHIGAN

6 Lakes Campground — ***HILLSDALE J-4***
☐ Albert E. Sleeper State Park — ***CASEVILLE G-5***
☐ Alcona County Park — ***GLENNIE F-5***
Algonac State Park — ***ALGONAC I-6***
® Alice Springs RV Park & Resort — ***IONIA H-3***
★ **All Seasons RV Supercenter — *MUSKEGON H-2***
Allegan State Game Area — ***ALLEGAN I-3***
®☐ **Allendale/Grand Rapids West KOA — *ALLENDALE H-2***
Aloha State Park — ***CHEBOYGAN D-5***
Alpine Campground — *BESSEMER A-5*
Angel Cove (Branch County) — ***COLDWATER J-3***
★ **Annie Rae RV — *DEWITT H-4***
Antrim 131 RV Campground — ***MANCELONA E-4***
®☐ **Apple Creek Campground & RV Park — *GRASS LAKE I-4***
Au Gres City Riverfront Park & Campground — *AU GRES F-5*
Au Sable SF (Ambrose Lake) — ***WEST BRANCH F-4***
Au Sable SF (Black Creek) — ***SANFORD G-4***
Au Sable SF (Canoe Harbor) — ***GRAYLING E-5***
Au Sable SF (Houghton Lake) — ***HOUGHTON LAKE F-4***
Au Sable SF (House Lake) — ***MEREDITH F-4***
Au Sable SF (Jones Lake) — ***FREDERIC E-5***
Au Sable SF (Lake Margrethe) — ***GRAYLING E-5***
Au Sable SF (Manistee River Bridge) — ***GRAYLING E-5***
Au Sable SF (McCollum Lake) — ***CURRAN E-6***
Au Sable SF (Mio Pond) — ***MIO E-5***
Au Sable SF (Reedsburg Dam) — ***HOUGHTON LAKE F-4***
Au Sable SF (Shupac Lake) — ***LOVELLS E-5***
Au Sable SF (Trout Lake) — ***MEREDITH F-4***
Au Sable SF (Upper Manistee River) — ***FREDERIC E-5***
Au Sable SF (Van Etten Lake) — ***OSCODA F-5***
Aune-Osborn RV Park — *SAULT STE. MARIE C-5*
☐ Back Forty RV Park — ***ROTHBURY G-2***
Baldwin Oaks Campground — ***HUDSONVILLE H-3***
☐ Baraga State Park — ***BARAGA B-1***
☐ Battle Creek Michigan Campground — ***BATTLE CREEK I-3***
☐ Bay City State Recreation Area — ***BAY CITY G-5***
• **Bay Mills Resort & Casinos — *BRIMLEY C-5***
Bay Mills RV Campground — *BRIMLEY C-5*
• **Beachside Bike Rentals — *HOLLAND I-2***
☐ **Bear Cave Resort — *BUCHANAN J-2***
Beaver Trail Campground — *WEST BRANCH F-4*
®☐ **Ber-Wa-Ga-Na Campground — *VASSAR H-5***
☐ Betsie River Campsite — ***FRANKFORT E-3***
Bewabic State Park — ***CRYSTAL FALLS C-1***
• **Big Bend Canoe Livery — *OMER F-5***
® **Big Bend Family Campground — *OMER F-5***
Big Bend Park (Big Prairie Township) — ***WHITE CLOUD G-3***
Big Cedar Campground & Canoe Livery — *GERMFASK C-4*
Blue Lake County Park (Muskegon County Park) — ***HOLTON H-2***
Branch County Memorial Park — ***COLDWATER J-3***
☐ Brighton Recreation Area (SP) — ***BRIGHTON I-5***
Brimley State Park — ***BRIMLEY C-5***
• **Bronner's Christmas Wonderland — *FRANKENMUTH H-5***
☐ Brower Park (Mecosta County) — ***STANWOOD G-3***
☐ Burt Lake State Park — ***INDIAN RIVER D-5***
☐ **Cadillac Woods Campground — *CADILLAC F-3***
Calhoun Campground (City Park) — ***BEAVERTON G-4***
® Camelot Campground — ***JONES J-3***
☐ **Camp Cadillac — *CADILLAC F-3***
® Camp Lord Willing Management RV Park & Campground — ***MONROE J-5***
Camp Withii — ***HARRISON F-4***
®☐ **Campers Cove RV Park & Canoe Livery — *ALPENA E-6***
® Camper's Haven Family Campground — ***BAD AXE G-6***
Campers Paradise, Inc. — *GRAND HAVEN H-2*
Caseville County Park — *CASEVILLE G-5*
Castle Rock Lakefront Campark — *ST. IGNACE C-5*
Cedarville RV Park — *CEDARVILLE C-5*
®☐ **Chain O'Lakes Campground — *BELLAIRE E-4***
Chandler Hill Campground — *BOYNE FALLS E-5*
Chapel in the Pines Campground — *HUDSONVILLE H-3*
Charles Mears State Park — ***PENTWATER G-2***
☐ Cheboygan State Park — ***CHEBOYGAN D-5***
Chinook Camping — ***GRANT H-3***
Chippewa Landing Campground — ***MANTON F-3***
☐ Chippewa Landing of Bay Mills — ***BRIMLEY C-5***
Clear Lake Campground — ***DAFTER C-5***
☐ Clear Lake State Park — ***ATLANTA E-5***
®☐ **Clearwater Campground — *ORTONVILLE H-5***
☐ **Clementz's Northcountry Campground and Cabins — *NEWBERRY C-4***
Cold Brook County Park — ***CLIMAX I-3***
☐ Coldwater Lake Family Park (Isabella County) — ***WEIDMAN G-4***
® **Conestoga Grand River Campground — *COOPERSVILLE H-2***
Copper Country SF (Big Eric's Bridge) — ***SKANEE B-1***
Copper Country SF (Glidden Lake) — ***CRYSTAL FALLS C-1***
☐ Country Village RV Park — ***ISHPEMING C-2***
☐ **Countryside Campground — *HARRISON F-4***
☐ **Covenant Hills Camp — *OTISVILLE H-5***
®☐ **Covered Wagon Camp Resort — *OTTAWA LAKE J-5***
☐ Covert Park Beach & Campground — ***COVERT I-2***
☐ **Cran-Hill Ranch Family Campground — *BIG RAPIDS G-3***
Creek Valley — ***BATTLE CREEK I-3***
Crittenden Park (Osceola County Park) — ***SEARS G-3***
Crooked Lake Park (Missaukee County Park) — ***LAKE CITY F-3***
Croton Township Park — ***NEWAYGO H-3***
Crystal Lake Campground — ***SCOTTVILLE G-2***
Deerfield Nature Park — ***MOUNT PLEASANT G-4***
®☐ **Detroit/Greenfield RV Park — *YPSILANTI I-5***
®☐ **Double R Ranch Resort — *BELDING H-3***
Downhour's Shady Acres Campground — *HARRISON F-4*
Drews Country Camping — ***HOLLAND I-2***
Duck Creek RV Resort — ***MUSKEGON H-2***
Duggan's Campground — ***PORT AUSTIN F-6***
®☐ **Duke Creek Campground — *CEDAR SPRINGS H-3***
® Dumont Lake Campground — ***ALLEGAN I-3***
☐ **Dune Lake Campground — *COLOMA J-2***
Dutch Treat Camping & Recreation — *ZEELAND H-2*
East Branch River RV Park — *TAWAS CITY F-5*
East Jordan Tourist Park (City of East Jordan) — ***EAST JORDAN E-4***
®☐ East Lake Camping — ***HOPKINS I-3***
East Tawas City Park — ***EAST TAWAS F-5***
Ed Henning Park (Newaygo County Park) — ***NEWAYGO H-3***
Eden Springs Park & Campground (formerly House of Davids) — ***BENTON HARBOR J-2***
®☐ **Elkwood Campground — *WOLVERINE D-5***
Emerick Park — *HILLMAN E-6*
®☐ **Emmett KOA — *EMMETT H-6***
Escanaba River SF (Forest Lake) — ***FOREST LAKE C-3***
Escanaba SF (Little Lake) — ***LITTLE LAKE C-2***
® Everflowing Waters Campground — ***WILLIAMSBURG E-4***
Evergreen Park — ***CASS CITY G-5***
Fayette Historic State Park — ***GARDEN D-3***
Finn Road Campground & Boat Launch (Hampton Township) — ***ESSEXVILLE G-5***
Fisherman's Island State Park — ***CHARLEVOIX D-4***
☐ F.J. McLain State Park — ***HANCOCK A-1***
☐ Forester Park — ***PORT SANILAC G-6***

MICHIGAN — Continued

☐ Fort Custer State Recreation Area — ***BATTLE CREEK I-3***
☐ Fort Wilkins State Park — ***COPPER HARBOR A-2***
• **Frankenmuth Bavarian Inn Restaurant — *FRANKENMUTH H-5***
®☐ **Frankenmuth Jellystone Park Camp-Resort — *FRANKENMUTH H-5***
®☐ **Fuller's Resort & Campground on Clear Lake — *BUCHANAN J-2***
☐ Gammy Woods Campground — ***WEIDMAN G-4***
®☐ **Gateway Park Campground — *HILLSDALE J-4***
☐ **Gaylord KOA — *GAYLORD E-5***
★ **Gillette's Interstate RV — *EAST LANSING I-4***
☐ Gitche Gumee RV Park & Campground — ***MARQUETTE B-2***
Gladstone Bay Campground (City Park) — ***GLADSTONE D-2***
Gladwin City Park & Campground — ***GLADWIN G-4***
• **Go Karts Plus — *MONROE J-5***
Grand Haven State Park — ***GRAND HAVEN H-2***
Grand Rogue Campgrounds and Paddlesports — ***GRAND RAPIDS H-3***
☐ **Great Circle Campground — *HIGGINS LAKE F-4***
☐ Green Valley Campground — ***STURGIS J-3***
Greenwood Acres Family Campground — *JACKSON I-4*
• **Greenwood Acres Golf — *JACKSON I-4***
Haas Lake Park — *NEW HUDSON I-5*
Hancock Recreation Area (City Park) — ***HANCOCK A-1***
☐ Happi Days Campground & Diner — ***FREDERIC E-5***
☐ **Harbortown RV Resort — *MONROE J-5***
☐ Harrisville State Park — ***HARRISVILLE E-6***
☐ Hartwick Pines State Park — ***GRAYLING E-5***
☐ **Heart of the Forest RV Park — *WELLSTON F-2***
Hearthside Grove Luxury Motorcoach Resort — ***PETOSKEY D-5***
® **Heartland Woods Family RV — *STOCKBRIDGE I-4***
☐ Herrick Recreation Area (Isabella County) — ***CLARE G-4***
Hiawatha National Forest (Au Train Lake Campground) — ***AU TRAIN C-3***
Hiawatha National Forest (Bay Furnace Campground) — ***MUNISING C-3***
Hiawatha National Forest (Brevoort Lake Campground) — ***ST. IGNACE C-5***
Hiawatha National Forest (Camp Seven Lake) — ***MANISTIQUE C-3***
Hiawatha National Forest (Carp River Campground) — ***ST. IGNACE C-5***
Hiawatha National Forest (Colwell Lake Campground) — ***SHINGLETON C-3***
Hiawatha National Forest (Foley Creek Campground) — ***ST. IGNACE C-5***
Hiawatha National Forest (Island Lake Campground) — ***WETMORE C-3***
Hiawatha National Forest (Lake Michigan Campground) — ***ST. IGNACE C-5***
Hiawatha National Forest (Little Bay de Noc Rec. Area) — ***RAPID RIVER C-2***
Hiawatha National Forest (Monocle Lake Campground) — ***BRIMLEY C-5***
Hiawatha National Forest (Petes Lake Campground) — ***WETMORE C-3***
Hiawatha National Forest (Soldier Lake Campground) — ***STRONGS C-4***
Hiawatha National Forest (Three Lakes Campground) — ***STRONGS C-4***
Hiawatha National Forest (Widewaters Campground) — ***WETMORE C-3***
Hidden Hill Family Campground — ***HARRISON F-4***
Hidden Ridge RV Resort — *HOPKINS I-3*
Hide Away Park — ***LINDEN H-5***
☐ Hideaway Campground & Resort — ***MEARS G-2***
Hideaway RV Park — ***JACKSON I-4***
® Higgins Lake Family Campground — ***ROSCOMMON F-4***
☐ Higgins Lake KOA — ***HIGGINS LAKE F-4***
Hill and Hollow Campground — ***PENTWATER G-2***
Hilltop Campground — ***LAPEER H-5***
☐ **Holiday Camping Resort — *NEW ERA G-2***
Holiday Park Campground — *TRAVERSE CITY E-4*
Holiday Shores — ***DURAND H-5***
Holland State Park — ***HOLLAND I-2***
☐ Holly KOA Fun Park — ***HOLLY I-5***
☐ Holly State Recreation Area — ***HOLLY I-5***
Holt's RV Sites & Mobile Home Court — ***FLINT H-5***
®☐ **Honcho Rest Campground — *ELK RAPIDS E-4***
Hopkins Park Campground (City Park) — ***BEAR LAKE F-2***
☐ **Horseshoe Lake Campground & RV Park — *GWINN C-2***
☐ **Houghton Lake Travel Park — *HOUGHTON LAKE F-4***
Houghton RV Park (City Park) — ***HOUGHTON A-1***
☐ **Hungry Horse Campground — *DORR I-3***
Huron National Forest (Jewell Lake Campground) — ***BARTON CITY E-6***
Huron National Forest (Kneff Lake Campground) — ***GRAYLING E-5***
Huron National Forest (Mack Lake Campground) — ***MIO E-5***
Huron National Forest (Round Lake Campground) — ***TAWAS CITY F-5***
☐ **Indian Creek Camp & Conference Center — *TECUMSEH J-5***
☐ Indian Lake State Park (South Shore) — ***MANISTIQUE C-3***
Indian Lake State Park (West Shore) — ***MANISTIQUE C-3***
Indian Lake Travel Resort — *MANISTIQUE C-3*
☐ Indian River RV Resort & Campground — ***INDIAN RIVER D-5***
®☐ **Indian Valley Campground Canoe Livery — *CALEDONIA I-3***
• **Indian Valley Canoe Livery & Campground — *CALEDONIA I-3***
☐ Indigo Bluffs Rally Park (Formerly Sleepy Bear Campground) — ***EMPIRE E-3***
Indigo Bluffs Resort — ***EMPIRE E-3***
®☐ **Insta-Launch Campground & Marina — *MANISTEE F-2***
• **Insta-Launch Marina & Campground — *MANISTEE F-2***
△☐ Interlochen State Park — ***INTERLOCHEN E-4***
☐ Ionia State Recreation Area — ***IONIA H-3***
☐ Irish Hills Kampground — ***CEMENT CITY J-4***
Iron River RV Park (City Park) — ***IRON RIVER C-1***
☐ J. W. Wells State Park — ***CEDAR RIVER D-2***
Ja Do Park Campground — *TIPTON J-4*
☐ Jack's Landing Resort — ***HILLMAN E-6***
John Gurney Park (Municipal) — ***HART G-2***
★ **Just Trucks — *TRAVERSE CITY E-4***
☐ Just-In-Time Campground — ***ITHACA H-4***
K C Campground — *MILAN J-5*
☐ **Kalkaska RV Park & Campground — *KALKASKA E-4***
Kampvilla RV Park & Family Campground — ***BEAR LAKE F-2***
Kestelwoods Campground — *WELLSTON F-2*
Kewadin Casino Park — ***SAULT STE. MARIE C-5***
® **Kibby Creek Campground — *LUDINGTON G-2***
Kinross RV Park East — *KINROSS C-5*
Kinross RV Park East (Township Park) — ***KINROSS C-5***
Kinross RV Park West (Township Park) — ***KINROSS C-5***
Kleinke Park (Menominee County Park) — ***CEDAR RIVER D-2***
☐ KOA Newberry/Tahquamenon — ***NEWBERRY C-4***
®☐ KOA-Coloma/St. Joseph — ***COLOMA J-2***
☐ **KOA-Mackinaw City/Mackinac Island — *MACKINAW CITY D-5***
☐ **KOA-Port Huron — *PORT HURON H-6***
®☐ Krystal Lake Campground — ***VASSAR H-5***
Lake Billings Campground (Municipal Park) — ***MANTON F-3***
Lake Chemung Outdoor Resort — *HOWELL I-5*
☐ Lake Fanny Hooe Resort & Campground — ***COPPER HARBOR A-2***
®☐ **Lake George Campground — *HARRISON F-4***
Lake Gogebic State Park — ***BERGLAND A-6***
Lake Hudson State Recreation Area — ***CLAYTON J-4***
☐ Lake Huron Campground — ***PORT SANILAC G-6***
☐ Lake Leelanau RV Park — ***LAKE LEELANAU E-4***
☐ Lake of Dreams Campground — ***MERRILL G-4***
☐ **Lake Sch-Nepp-A-Ho Campground — *MUSKEGON H-2***
Lake Shore Park Campground — *ST. IGNACE C-5*
Lake Superior SF (Andrus Lake) — ***PARADISE B-4***
Lake Superior SF (Big Knob) — ***NAUBINWAY C-4***
Lake Superior SF (Blind Sucker No. 2) — ***GRAND MARAIS B-3***
Lake Superior SF (Bodi Lake) — ***PARADISE B-4***
Lake Superior SF (Culhane Lake) — ***PARADISE B-4***
Lake Superior SF (Hog Island Point) — ***NAUBINWAY C-4***
Lake Superior SF (Little Brevort Lk-North Unit) — ***BREVORT C-4***

MICHIGAN — Continued

Lake Superior SF (Milakokia Lake) — NAUBINWAY C-4
Lake Superior SF (Mouth of Two Hearted River) — NEWBERRY C-4
Lake Superior SF (Munuscong River) — PICKFORD C-5
Lake Superior SF (Perch Lake) — NEWBERRY C-4
Lake Superior SF (Pike Lake) — PARADISE B-4
Lake Superior SF (South Manistique Lake) — CURTIS C-4
□ Lakeport State Park — PORT HURON H-6
★ Lakeshore RV Center — MUSKEGON H-2
Lakeside Camp Park — CEDAR SPRINGS H-3
Lansing Cottonwood Campground — LANSING I-4
Leelanau Pines Campground — CEDAR E-4
□ Leelanau State Park — NORTHPORT E-4
★ Leisure Days Travel Trailer Sales — CLIO H-5
□ Leisure Lake Family Campground — SUMNER H-4
®□ Leisure Time Campground — IRONS F-3
Leisure Valley RV Resort & Campground — DECATUR J-2
Lexington Park — LEXINGTON H-6
□ Lighthouse County Parks — PORT HOPE G-6
Lighthouse Family Camping Resort — MECOSTA G-3
□ Lincoln Pines Resort — GOWEN H-3
Linwood Beach Marina & Campground — LINWOOD G-4
● Little River Casino — MANISTEE F-2
Little River Resort — MANISTEE F-2
★ Lloyd Bridges Traveland — CHELSEA I-5
□ Log Cabin Resort & Campground — CURTIS C-4
□ Loons Point RV Park & Campground — CEDARVILLE C-5
® Loranger Pines RV Park — WEST BRANCH F-4
Lost Haven Campground — BEAVERTON G-4
□ Ludington State Park — LUDINGTON G-2
®□ Lyons' Landing & Travel Trailer Park — HILLMAN E-6
● Mackinaw Club Golf Course — MACKINAW CITY D-5
□ Mackinaw Mill Creek Camping — MACKINAW CITY D-5
Mackinaw SF (Beaver Island) — ST. JAMES D-4
Mackinaw SF (Big Bear Lake) — VIENNA E-5
Mackinaw SF (Big Oaks) — ATLANTA E-5
Mackinaw SF (Black Lake) — ONAWAY D-5
Mackinaw SF (Jackson Lake) — ATLANTA E-5
Mackinaw SF (Little Wolf Lake) — LEWISTON E-5
Mackinaw SF (Maple Bay) — ALANSON D-5
Mackinaw SF (Ossineke) — OSSINEKE E-6
Mackinaw SF (Pickerel Lake) — VANDERBILT E-5
Mackinaw SF (Shoepac Lake) — ONAWAY D-5
Mackinaw SF (Tomahawk Creek Flooding) — ATLANTA E-5
Magnus Municipal Park — PETOSKEY D-5
Manistee National Forest (Lake Michigan Rec. Area) — MANISTEE F-2
Manistee National Forest (Nichols Lake Campground) — BROHMAN G-3
Manistee National Forest (Pines Point Campground) — HESPERIA G-2
Manistee National Forest (Sand Lake Campground) — WELLSTON F-2
● Manistee Paddlesport Adventures — MANISTEE F-2
Manistique KOA — MANISTIQUE C-3
®□ Maple River Campground — PEWAMO H-4
Marble Springs Campground — ALLEN J-4
Markin Glen County Park — KALAMAZOO I-3
Marquette Tourist Park (City Park) — MARQUETTE B-2
Mason County Campground & Picnic Area — LUDINGTON G-2
®□ Matson's Big Manistee River Campground — MANISTEE F-2
□ Mecosta Pines Campground — MORLEY G-3
□ Merrill Lake Park (Mecosta County) — BARRYTON G-3
□ Metamora-Hadley State Recreation Area — LAPEER H-5
□ Michawana Campground — HASTINGS I-3
□ Michigamme Shores Campground Resort — CHAMPION B-1
★ Midland RV Sales — MIDLAND G-4
Miller Lake Campground — HOPKINS I-3
Minnow Lake Campground — BRIMLEY C-5
□ Mio Pine Acres Campground — MIO E-5
Missaukee Lake Park (Missaukee County Park) — LAKE CITY F-3
®□ Monroe County KOA — PETERSBURG J-5
Moscow Maples RV Park — MOSCOW J-4
Munising Tourist Park Campground — MUNISING C-3
Muskallonge Lake State Park — NEWBERRY C-4
□ Muskegon State Park — NORTH MUSKEGON H-2
□ Muskegon-KOA — MUSKEGON H-2
□ Myers Lake Campground — BYRON H-5
Newaygo State Park — NEWAYGO H-3
□ North Higgins Lake State Park — ROSCOMMON F-4
North Park Campground (City Park) — HARBOR BEACH G-6
□ Northern Exposure Campground — MESICK F-3
Oak Beach County Park — PORT AUSTIN F-6
®□ Oak Grove Campground Resort — HOLLAND I-2
®□ Oak Knoll Family Campground — HOLTON H-2
®□ Oak Shores Campground — DECATUR J-2
O.B. Fuller Park (Delta County Park) — ESCANABA D-2
Ojibwa Casino RV Park — MARQUETTE B-2
Ojibwa RV Park — BARAGA B-1
□ Old Orchard Park (Iosco County Park) — OSCODA F-5
Onaway State Park — ONAWAY D-5
□ Orchard Beach State Park — MANISTEE F-2
Oscoda County Park — MIO E-5
®□ Oscoda KOA — OSCODA F-5
□ Otsego Lake State Park — GAYLORD E-5
Ottawa National Forest (Black River Harbor Campground) — BESSEMER A-5
Ottawa National Forest (Clark Lake Campground) — WATERSMEET B-6
Ottawa National Forest (Lake Ottawa Campground) — IRON RIVER C-1
Ottawa National Forest (Lake Ste. Kathryn Campground) — SIDNAW B-1
Ottawa National Forest (Marion Lake Campground) — WATERSMEET B-6
Ottawa National Forest (Norway Lake Campground) — SIDNAW B-1
□ Otter Lake Campground — MUNISING C-3
Otter Lake Campground (Village Park) — OTTER LAKE H-5
Oxbow Park (Big Prairie Township) — WHITE CLOUD G-3
®□ Paddle Brave Canoe & Campground Resort — ROSCOMMON F-4
□ Paris Park (Mecosta County) — PARIS G-3
Park Place of the North — ESCANABA D-2
★ Parshallburg Campers — CHESANING H-4
□ Paul Bunyan Family Kamp — OSSINEKE E-6
Pere Marquette SF (Arbutus No. 4) — TRAVERSE CITY E-4
Pere Marquette SF (Baxter Bridge) — MANTON F-3
Pere Marquette SF (CCC Bridge) — KALKASKA E-4
Pere Marquette SF (Goose Lake) — LAKE CITY F-3
Pere Marquette SF (Guernsey Lake) — KALKASKA E-4
Pere Marquette SF (Lake Ann) — LAKE ANN E-4
Pere Marquette SF (Long Lake) — LAKE CITY F-3
Pere Marquette SF (Old US 131) — MANTON F-3
Pere Marquette SF (Platte River) — HONOR E-3
Pere Marquette SF (Scheck's Place) — WILLIAMSBURG E-4
Pere Marquette SF (Silver Creek) — LUTHER F-3
Pere Marquette SF (Spring Lake) — FIFE LAKE F-3
Pere Marquette SF (Veteran's Memorial) — HONOR E-3
△ Perkins Park (Marquette County Park) — BIG BAY B-2
□ Petoskey KOA — PETOSKEY D-5
□ Petoskey State Park — PETOSKEY D-5
□ P.H. Hoeft State Park — ROGERS CITY D-6
● Pictured Rocks Cruises — MUNISING C-3
Pinckney State Rec. Area (Bruin Lake Campground) — PINCKNEY I-5
® Pine Haven Campground — WALKERVILLE G-2
Pine Ridge RV Campground — BIRCH RUN H-5
□ Pine River Paddlesport Center and Campground — WELLSTON F-2
Pioneer Park (Muskegon County) — NORTH MUSKEGON H-2
Pioneer Trail Park (Delta County) — ESCANABA D-2
Pirolli Park RV Resort — PETERSBURG J-5
P.J. Hoffmaster State Park — MUSKEGON H-2
PJ's Family Campground — STOCKBRIDGE I-4
Poncho's Pond — LUDINGTON G-2
Pontiac Lake State Recreation Area — WATERFORD I-5
Porcupine Mtns. State Park (Presque Isle Unit) — WAKEFIELD A-5

MICHIGAN — Continued

□ Porcupine Mtns. State Park (Union Bay Campground) — SILVER CITY A-6
□ Port Crescent State Park — PORT AUSTIN F-6
Potawatomie Recreation Area — UNION CITY J-3
□ Proud Lake State Recreation Area — WIXOM I-5
□ Pt Au Gres Marina & Campground — AU GRES F-5
Quincy Marble Lake (Branch County Park) — QUINCY J-4
□ Rifle River State Recreation Area — LUPTON F-5
Rippling Waters Campground — OMER F-5
River Park Campground — GRAYLING E-5
River Park Campground (City Park) — MENOMINEE E-2
□ River Ridge Campground — MIDLAND G-4
® River Ridge RV Resort — STANWOOD G-3
River Road RV Park & Campground — ONTONAGON A-6
□ River Valley RV Park — GLADWIN G-4
□ River View Campground & Canoe Livery — STERLING F-5
● River View Canoe Livery — STERLING F-5
Rivers Bend Campground — IRON MOUNTAIN D-1
®□ Rockeys Campground — ALBION I-4
Rose Lake Park (Osceola County Park) — LE ROY F-3
□ Ruby Campground — PORT HURON H-6
□ St. Ignace/Mackinac Island KOA — ST. IGNACE C-5
□ Salmon Run Campground and Vic's Canoes — GRANT H-3
Sandy Beach (Newaygo County Park) — WHITE CLOUD G-3
®□ Sandy Pines RV Resort & Campground — HOPKINS I-3
Sandy Shores Campground — MEARS G-2
● Sawmill City — PORT HURON H-6
□ Scalley Lake Park — GRATTAN H-3
□ School Section Lake (Mecosta County) — MECOSTA G-3
Scottville Riverside Park (City Park) — SCOTTVILLE G-2
□ Sebewaing County Park — SEBEWAING G-5
Seven Lakes State Park — HOLLY I-5
Shady Bend Campground and Canoe Livery — AUGUSTA I-3
Shakey Lakes Park (Menominee County Park) — STEPHENSON D-2
★ Signature Ford of Perry — PERRY H-4
Signature Motorcoach Resort at Bay Harbor — BAY HARBOR D-4
Silver Creek RV Resort — MEARS G-2
®□ Silver Hills Camp Resort — MEARS G-2
□ Silver Lake Resort & Campground — MEARS G-2
Silver Lake State Park — SHELBY G-2
Sleeping Bear Dunes National Lakeshore (D.H. Day Campground) — GLEN ARBOR E-3
Sleeping Bear Dunes National Lakeshore (Platte River Campground) — HONOR E-3
Sleepy Hollow State Park — LAINGSBURG H-4
□ Sno-Trac Camper Village — GRAYLING E-5
□ Snow Lake Kampground — FENWICK H-3
● Snow Lake Kampground & Restaurant — FENWICK H-3
□ Somerset Beach Campground — SOMERSET CENTER J-4
Soo Locks Campground & RV Park — SAULT STE. MARIE C-5
□ South Haven Family Campground — SOUTH HAVEN I-2
□ South Haven KOA RV Resort — COVERT I-2
□ South Higgins Lake State Park — ROSCOMMON F-4
Spaulding Lake Campground — NILES J-2
Spring Lake Tourist Park (Municipal Park) — SPRING LAKE H-2
□ Stafford County Park — PORT HOPE G-6
Sterling State Park — MONROE J-5
□ Stony Haven Campground & Cabins — NEW ERA G-2
□ Straits State Park — ST. IGNACE C-5
□ Sturgeon River Campground & Resort — WOLVERINE D-5
□ Sugar Bush Campground — HILLSDALE J-4
Summer Breeze Campground & RV Park — IRON MOUNTAIN D-1
Sunday Lake Campground — WAKEFIELD A-5
Sunny Brook RV Resort — SOUTH HAVEN I-2
□ Sunset Bay Campground & RV Resort — AHMEEK A-1
Sutter's Recreation Area — NORTH BRANCH H-5
Sweet Lake Resort Community — STURGIS J-3
Tahquamenon Falls State Park — PARADISE B-4
□ Tawas Point State Park — EAST TAWAS F-5
® Taylor's Beach Campground — HOWELL I-5
Tee Pee Campground — MACKINAW CITY D-5
★ Terry Town Travel Center — GRAND RAPIDS H-3
The Campground — MANTON F-3
The Oaks Resort — MUNITH I-4
Thousand Trails Saint Clair Campground — SAINT CLAIR H-6
Thunder Bay Campground — ALPENA E-6
□ Thunder Bay RV & Golf Resort — HILLMAN E-6
Tiki RV Park & Campground — ST. IGNACE C-5
®□ Timber Ridge RV & Recreation Resort — TRAVERSE CITY E-4
Timber Surf Camping Resort — WALHALLA G-2
® Timber Trails RV Park — DECATUR J-2
Timberline Campground — BENZONIA F-2
□ Totem Pole Park — PETERSBURG J-5
Trailway Campground — MONTAGUE G-2
Traverse Bay RV Resort — TRAVERSE CITY E-4
□ Traverse City KOA — BUCKLEY F-3
□ Traverse City State Park — TRAVERSE CITY E-4
Tri Lake Trails Campground — MARSHALL I-4
□ Tri Ponds Family Camp Resort — ALLEGAN I-3
□ Troll Landing Canoe Livery & Campground — WEST BRANCH F-4
□ Twin Lakes State Park — MASS CITY A-6
Twin Pines Campground & Canoe Livery — CONCORD J-4
□ Tyler Creek Campground & Golf — ALTO H-3
□ Uhricks Motel & RV Park — CHARLEVOIX D-4
®□ Vacation Station RV Resort — LUDINGTON G-2
®□ Vacation Trailer Park — BENZONIA F-2
□ Vagabond Resort — RAPID RIVER C-2
Valley Plaza Resort RV Park — MIDLAND G-4
Van Buren State Park — SOUTH HAVEN I-2
□ Van Riper State Park — CHAMPION B-1
Veterans Memorial Park (Village Park) — MARION F-3
□ W. J. Hayes State Park — ONSTED J-4
Waffle Farm Camp — COLDWATER J-3
□ Wagener County Park — HARBOR BEACH G-6
□ Wandering Wheels Campground — MUNISING C-3
□ Warner Camp RV Park — GRAND JUNCTION I-2
Washakie Campground & Golf — NORTH BRANCH H-5
Water Tower Travel Trailer Park (City Park) — LAPEER H-5
Waterloo State Rec. Area (Green Lake Unit) — CHELSEA I-5
Waterloo State Rec. Area (Portage Unit) — CHELSEA I-5
Waterloo State Rec. Area (Sugarloaf Lake Unit) — CHELSEA I-5
△ Waterways Campground — CHEBOYGAN D-5
Wayne County Fairgrounds & RV Park — BELLEVILLE I-5
□ Welcome Woods Campground — HASTINGS I-3
□ Wesleyan Woods Campground — VASSAR H-5
West Branch RV Park (Ogemaw County Pk) — WEST BRANCH F-4
®□ West Houghton Lake Campground — HOUGHTON LAKE F-4
Wheel Inn Campground and White Tail Acres Archery — LESLIE I-4
□ Whispering Oaks Campground & Cabins — BALDWIN G-3
®□ Whispering Pines Family Campground — MANCELONA E-4
Whispering Surf Camping Resort — PENTWATER G-2
□ Whispering Valley Campground & RV Park — RAPID RIVER C-2
Whispering Waters Campground and Kayak Rental — HASTINGS I-3
● Whispering Waters Kayak Rental — HASTINGS I-3
® White River RV Park & Campground — MONTAGUE G-2
® Whitefish Hill RV Park — RAPID RIVER C-2
● Whitetail Acres Archery — LESLIE I-4
● Wild Bluff Golf Course — BRIMLEY C-5
Wild Cherry RV Resort — SUTTONS BAY E-4
□ Wilderness Campground — DUNDEE J-5
□ Wilderness State Park — MACKINAW CITY D-5
Wildwood Acres — JONESVILLE J-4
□ William Mitchell State Park — CADILLAC F-3
△□ Wilson State Park — HARRISON F-4
□ Witz's Marina & Campground — SKANEE B-1
Wolverine Campground (Genesee County Park) — DAVISON H-5
® Woodchip Campground — GRAND RAPIDS H-3
□ Wooded Acres Campground — HOUGHTON LAKE F-4

MICHIGAN — Continued

Wooden Shoe Park (Village Park) — EAST JORDAN E-4
Woodland Park (Burt Twp Park) — GRAND MARAIS B-3
® Woodlands on the Lake — WHITE CLOUD G-3
Woodstar Beach Campground — MANISTIQUE C-3
□ Yankee Springs State Rec. Area (Deep Lake Campground) — MIDDLEVILLE I-3
Yankee Springs State Rec Area (Gun Lake Campground) — MIDDLEVILLE I-3
®□ Yogi Bear's Jellystone Camp Resort — GRAYLING E-5
Yogi Bear's Jellystone Park Grand Haven (Morgan RV Resorts) — GRAND HAVEN H-2
□ Yogi Bear's Jellystone Park Indian River — INDIAN RIVER D-5
□ Yogi Bear's Jellystone Park Silver Lake — MEARS G-2
®□ Yoreplace RV Resort — LAWRENCE I-2
□ Young State Park — BOYNE CITY E-4

MINNESOTA

A-J Acres Campground — CLEARWATER D-3
Adrian Campground (Municipal Park) — ADRIAN F-1
Afton State Park — HASTINGS E-4
Akeley City Campground — AKELEY C-2
□ Albert Lea/Austin KOA Kampground — ALBERT LEA F-3
Alexandria Shooting Park & RV Campground — ALEXANDRIA D-2
Arnold's Campground & RV Park — INTERNATIONAL FALLS A-3
Autumn Woods RV Park — ROCHESTER F-4
□ Banning State Park — SANDSTONE D-4
Barsness Park-Chalet Campground (Municipal Park) — GLENWOOD D-2
□ Bear Head Lake State Park — TOWER B-4
Beaver Creek Valley State Park — CALEDONIA F-5
®□ Beaver Trails Jellystone Park Camp-Resort — AUSTIN F-4
Bent Trout Lake Campground — BARNUM C-4
Big Stone Lake State Park — ORTONVILLE E-1
Birch Lake State Forest (Birch Lake Campground) — MELROSE D-2
Blue Mounds State Park — LUVERNE F-1
Bluff Valley Campground — ZUMBRO FALLS F-4
Bray Park (Blue Earth County Park) — MADISON LAKE F-3
□ Breeze Camping & RV Resort — PARK RAPIDS C-2
Brookside Campground — BLOOMING PRAIRIE F-4
Buffalo River State Park — GLYNDON C-1
Buffalo Valley Camping — DULUTH C-4
Burlington Bay Campground (City Park) — TWO HARBORS C-5
Camden State Park — LYND E-1
Camp Faribo — FARIBAULT F-4
□ Camp Holiday Resort & Campground — GARRISON D-3
Camp Maiden Rock West — MORRISTOWN F-3
Camp RnL RV Park/Campground — LONG PRAIRIE D-2
Camp Waub-O-Jeeg — TAYLORS FALLS D-4
● Canal House Restaurant & Bar — CASS LAKE B-2
Cannon Falls Campground — CANNON FALLS E-4
□ Canoe Country Campground & Cabins — ELY B-5
□ Captain Dan's Crow's Nest Resort — MORA D-4
Carley State Park — PLAINVIEW F-4
Cascade River State Park — GRAND MARAIS A-5
Charles A Lindbergh State Park — LITTLE FALLS D-3
□ Checkers Welcome Campground — WELCOME F-2
Chengwatana State Forest (Snake River Campground) — PINE CITY D-4
Chippewa National Forest (Chippewa Campground) — CASS LAKE B-2
Chippewa National Forest (Clubhouse Lake Campground) — MARCELL B-3
Chippewa National Forest (Deer Lake Campground) — SQUAW LAKE B-3
Chippewa National Forest (North Star Campground) — MARCELL B-3
Chippewa National Forest (Norway Beach Campground) — CASS LAKE B-2
Chippewa National Forest (O-ne-gum-e Campground) — SQUAW LAKE B-3
Chippewa National Forest (Stony Point Campground) — WALKER C-3
Chippewa National Forest (Tamarack Point Campground) — BENA C-3
Chippewa National Forest (Wanaki Campground) — CASS LAKE B-2
Chippewa National Forest (Winnie Dam Campground) — CASS LAKE B-2
Cloquet Valley State Forest (Indian Lake Campground) — TWO HARBORS C-5
□ Cloquet/Duluth KOA — CLOQUET C-4
Cokato Lake RV Resort — COKATO E-3
Country Campground — DETROIT LAKES C-2
Country Camping RV Park — ISANTI D-4
Crow Wing State Forest (Greer Lake Campground) — CROSBY C-3
□ Crow Wing State Park — BRAINERD D-3
Crystal Springs RV Resort — ALBERT LEA F-3
Dakotah Meadows RV Park & Campground — PRIOR LAKE E-3
Daly Park (Blue Earth County Park) — MAPLETON F-3
Don & Mayva's Crow Wing Lake Campground — BRAINERD D-3
Eagle Cliff Campground & Lodging — LANESBORO F-5
El Rancho Manana — AVON D-3
Fairgrounds Campground (Isanti Co. Agricultural Society) — CAMBRIDGE D-4
Father Hennepin State Park — ISLE D-3
Finland State Forest (Eckbeck Campground) — FINLAND B-5
Finland State Forest (Finland Campground) — FINLAND B-5
Fisherman's Point Campground (City Park) — HOYT LAKES B-4
Flandrau State Park — NEW ULM F-3
Flying Goose Campground — FAIRMONT F-3
Fond du Lac Campground & Boat Landing — DULUTH C-4
Forest Hills Golf & RV Resort — DETROIT LAKES C-2
Forestville-Mystery Cave State Park — WYKOFF F-4
Fort Ridgely State Park — FAIRFAX E-2
● Fortune Bay Resort Casino — TOWER B-4
Fortune Bay Resort, Casino & RV Park — TOWER B-4
□ Fritz's Resort, Campground & Golf Course — NISSWA C-3
Frontenac State Park — LAKE CITY E-4
General C.C. Andrews State Forest (Willow River Campground) — WILLOW RIVER D-4
George Crosby Manitou State Park — FINLAND B-5
George Washington State Forest (Bear Lake Campground) — TOGO B-4
George Washington State Forest (Owen Lake Campground) — BIGFORK B-3
George Washington State Forest (Thistledew Lake Campground) — TOGO B-4
Glacial Lakes State Park — STARBUCK D-2
Gooseberry Falls State Park — TWO HARBORS C-5
□ Grand Casino Hinckley RV Resort — HINCKLEY D-4
Grand Marais Recreation Area (Municipal Park) — GRAND MARAIS A-5
Great River Bluffs State Park — NODINE F-5
Gull Lake Recreation Area (COE) — BRAINERD D-3
□ Gunflint Pines Resort & Campground — GRAND MARAIS A-5
□ Ham Lake Campground — HAM LAKE E-4
Hamilton's Fox Lake Campground — BEMIDJI B-2
Haycreek Valley Campground — RED WING E-4
□ Hayes Lake State Park — WANNASKA A-2
Hickory Lake Campground — AITKIN C-3
Hidden Meadows RV Park — PINE ISLAND F-4
Highview Campground & RV Park — BREEZY POINT C-3
Highway 250 Campground — LANESBORO F-5
Hoodoo Point Campground (City Park) — TOWER B-4
Huntersville State Forest (Huntersville Landing) — MENAHGA C-2
Indian Point Campground — DULUTH C-4
Interstate State Park — TAYLORS FALLS D-4
Iron Trail RV Park & Campground — CHISHOLM B-4
□ Itasca State Park — PARK RAPIDS C-2

MINNESOTA — Continued

Jackpot Junction RV Park — **MORTON E-2**
□ Jackson-KOA — **JACKSON F-2**
□ Jay Cooke State Park — **CARLTON C-4**
Judge C R Magney State Park — **GRAND MARAIS A-5**
Kabetogama State Forest (Wakemup Bay Campground) — **COOK B-4**
Kabetogama State Forest (Woodenfrog Campground — **KABETOGAMA LAKE A-4**
□ Kamp Dels — **WATERVILLE F-3**
Kandiyohi County Park Number 1 — **LAKE LILLIAN E-2**
Kandiyohi County Park Number 2 — **LAKE LILLIAN E-2**
Kandiyohi County Park Number 3 — **ATWATER E-2**
Kandiyohi County Park Number 5 — **SPICER E-2**
Kandiyohi County Park Number 7 — **NEW LONDON E-2**
Kiesler's Campground & R.V. Resort — WASECA F-3
Kilen Woods State Park — **LAKEFIELD F-2**
Knife Island Campground — **SCANLON C-4**
Knife River Campground — **TWO HARBORS C-5**
□ KOA-Bemidji Kampground — **BEMIDJI B-2**
□ KOA-Fargo-Moorhead — **MOORHEAD C-1**
□ **KOA-Minneapolis Southwest — MINNEAPOLIS E-4**
□ **KOA-Rochester/Marion — ROCHESTER F-4**
Kozy Oaks Kamp — **NORTH BRANCH D-4**
Lac Qui Parle State Park — **MONTEVIDEO E-2**
Lake Bemidji State Park — **BEMIDJI B-2**
Lake Bronson State Park — **LAKE BRONSON A-1**
Lake Byllesby Campground (Dakota County Park) — CANNON FALLS E-4
Lake Carlos State Park — **CARLOS D-2**
Lake Elmo Park Reserve (Washington County Park) — **LAKE ELMO E-4**
Lake Louise State Park — **LE ROY F-4**
Lake Pepin Campgrounds & Trailer Court — LAKE CITY E-4
□ Lake Shetek State Park — **CURRIE F-2**
Lake-of-the-Woods Campground — **BAUDETTE A-3**
Lakehead Boat Basin, Inc — DULUTH C-4
Lakes Area Motel & RV Park — **ALEXANDRIA D-2**
® Lakeshore RV Park, Inc — **ORTONVILLE E-1**
®□ Lamb's Campground — **SCHROEDER B-5**
Land O'Lakes State Forest (Clint Converse Memorial Campground) — **OUTING C-3**
□ **Lazy D Campground & Trail Rides — ST. CHARLES F-5**
● **Lazy D Trail Rides — ST. CHARLES F-5**
Lazy Days Campground — MILTONA D-2
Lebanon Hills Campground (Dakota County Park) — APPLE VALLEY E-4
Leech Lake Recreation Area (COE Leech Lake Reservoir) — **FEDERAL DAM C-3**
Long Lake Campsite & RV Resort — **DETROIT LAKES C-2**
Lowry Grove — MINNEAPOLIS E-4
Maple Springs Campground — **PRESTON F-5**
□ Maplewood State Park — **PELICAN RAPIDS C-1**
□ Marclay Point Resort Campground/RV Park — **CASS LAKE B-2**
McCarthy Beach State Park — **SIDE LAKE B-4**
McKinley Park Campground (Breitung Twp Park) — **SOUDAN B-4**
□ Mille Lacs Kathio State Park — **ONAMIA D-3**
□ **Minneapolis NW KOA Campground — MINNEAPOLIS E-4**
□ Minneopa State Park — **MANKATO F-3**
Minnesota Valley State Park — **JORDAN E-3**
Money Creek Haven, Inc. — **HOUSTON F-5**
Monson Lake State Park — **SUNBURG E-2**
Moose Lake City Park — **MOOSE LAKE C-4**
Moose Lake State Park — **MOOSE LAKE C-4**
□ Myre-Big Island State Park — **ALBERT LEA F-3**
Nerstrand Big Woods State Park — **NERSTRAND E-4**
Oak Park Kampground — **GARFIELD D-2**
Ogston's RV Park — **DULUTH C-4**
Old Barn Resort — **PRESTON F-5**
Old Mill State Park — **ARGYLE A-1**
Olson Park Campground (Municipal Park) — **WORTHINGTON F-2**
Paul Bunyan State Forest (Mantrap Lake Campground) — **PARK RAPIDS C-2**
Penmarallter Campsite — **TWO HARBORS C-5**
Pete's Retreat Family Campground & RV Park — MALMO C-3
Pillsbury State Forest (Rock Lake Campground) — **PILLAGER D-3**
□ Pine Acres Resort & Campground — **ORR B-4**
Pine Creek RV Park — **WALKER C-3**
Pioneer Campsite Resort — WABASHA E-5
Pipestone RV Campground — PIPESTONE F-1
®□ PLA-Mor Campground — **WINONA F-5**
Pokegama Lake RV Park & Golf Course — PINE CITY D-4
Prairie Cove Campground & RV Park — **ASHBY D-2**
Prairie Island Campground (City Park) — **WINONA F-5**
Prairie Lake Campground — **GRAND RAPIDS C-3**
Prairie View RV Park & Campground — GRANITE FALLS E-2
● **Prairie's Edge Casino Resort — GRANITE FALLS E-2**
Quadna Mountain Campground & RV Park — **HILL CITY C-3**
Red Lake State Forest (Waskish Campground) — **WASKISH B-3**
Rice Lake State Park — **OWATONNA F-4**
River Terrace Park — MONTICELLO E-3
□ Riverview Campground — **OWATONNA F-4**
Ronald Louis Cloutier Rec Area (COE-Crosslake) — **CROSS LAKE C-3**
Rothenburg Campground — **SPRINGFIELD F-2**
Royal Oaks RV Park — **BEMIDJI B-2**
Saginaw Campground — **SAGINAW C-4**
St. Cloud Campground & RV Park — **ST. CLOUD D-3**
□ St. Cloud/Clearwater RV Park — **CLEARWATER D-3**
St. Croix Bluffs Regional Park (Washington County Park) — **HASTINGS E-4**
St. Croix Haven Campground — **HINCKLEY D-4**
□ St. Croix State Park — **HINCKLEY D-4**
□ **St. Paul East RV Park — ST. PAUL E-4**
□ Sakatah Lake State Park — **WATERVILLE F-3**
Sand Dunes State Forest (Ann Lake Campground) — **ZIMMERMAN D-3**
Sandy Lake Recreation Area (COE Sandy Lake Reservoir) — **MCGREGOR C-4**
□ Savanna Portage State Park — **MCGREGOR C-4**
Savanna State Forest (Hay Lake Campground) — **JACOBSON C-4**
□ Scenic State Park — **BIGFORK B-3**
Schoolcraft State Park — **DEER RIVER C-3**
Schreier's on Shetek — **CURRIE F-2**
Shades of Sherwood Campground — **ZUMBROTA F-4**
Shady Oaks Campground — **GARDEN CITY F-3**
Shakopee Valley RV Park — **SHAKOPEE E-3**
Sherin Memorial Campground (City Park) — **PELICAN RAPIDS C-1**
Sherwood Forest Campground (City Park) — **GILBERT B-4**
Shooting Star RV Park and Casino — **MAHNOMEN C-1**
Sibley State Park — **WILLMAR E-2**
Silver Lake Motorcoach Resort — **ROCHESTER F-4**
Sinclair Lewis Campground (City Park) — **SAUK CENTRE D-2**
South Isle Family Campground — **ISLE D-3**
Spirit Mountain Campground (City Park) — **DULUTH C-4**
Split Rock Creek State Park — **IHLEN F-1**
Split Rock Lighthouse State Park — **BEAVER BAY C-5**
Stonehill Regional Park (Lac Qui Parle Yellow Bank Watershed) — **CANBY E-1**
□ **Stony Point Resort Trailer Park & Campground — CASS LAKE B-2**
Sugar Bay Campground/Resort — **GRAND RAPIDS C-3**
□ Summer Haven RV Resort — **BEMIDJI B-2**
Superior National Forest (Birch Lake Campground) — **ELY B-5**
Superior National Forest (Crescent Lake Campground) — **TOFTE B-5**
Superior National Forest (East Bearskin Lake Campground) — **GRAND MARAIS A-5**
Superior National Forest (Echo Lake Campground) — **ORR B-4**
Superior National Forest (Fenske Lake Campground) — **ELY B-5**
Superior National Forest (Sawbill Lake Campground) — **TOFTE B-5**
Superior National Forest (South Kawishiwi River Campground) — **ELY B-5**
Superior National Forest (Trails End Campground) — **GRAND MARAIS A-5**

MINNESOTA — Continued

Superior National Forest (Two Island Lake Campground) — **GRAND MARAIS A-5**
Superior NF (Fall Lake Campground) — **ELY B-5**
Temperance River State Park — **SCHROEDER B-5**
□ Tettegouche State Park — **SILVER BAY C-5**
Tilly's American Traveler's RV Resort — ROCHESTER F-4
Town & Country Campground & RV Park — **MINNEAPOLIS E-4**
Trails RV Park — WALKER C-3
● **Treasure Island Resort & Casino — RED WING E-4**
Treasure Island RV Park — RED WING E-4
Two Rivers Campground & Tubing — **ROYALTON D-3**
Upper Sioux Agency State Park — **GRANITE FALLS E-2**
Vagabond Village Campground — **PARK RAPIDS C-2**
Valley View Campground, Inc — **PRESTON F-5**
□ Wabasha Motel & RV — **WABASHA E-5**
Warroad Municipal Park — **WARROAD A-2**
Watona Park (City Park) — **MADELIA F-3**
□ Whitewater State Park — **ELBA F-5**
□ Wild River State Park — **NORTH BRANCH D-4**
Wildwood Campground — **TAYLORS FALLS D-4**
● **Willard Munger Inn — DULUTH C-4**
□ William O'Brien State Park — **STILLWATER E-4**
Zippel Bay State Park — **BAUDETTE A-3**

MISSISSIPPI

Ameristar RV Park — **VICKSBURG D-2**
□ Archusa Creek Water Park (Pat Harrison Waterway District) — **QUITMAN D-4**
Atwood Water Park (Pearl River Basin Dev. Dist.) — **MONTICELLO E-3**
Bay Hide Away RV & Camping Resort — BAY ST. LOUIS F-4
® **Baywood RV Park and Campground, Inc. — GULFPORT F-4**
Benchmark Coach and RV Park — MERIDIAN D-4
Bienville National Forest (Marathon Campground) — **FOREST D-3**
□ Big Creek Water Park (Pat Harrison Waterway District) — **SOSO E-4**
Blue Bluff Campground (COE-Tennessee/Tombigbee Waterway) — **ABERDEEN B-4**
□ Bogue Chitto Water Park Campground (Pearl River Basin Dev. Dist.) — **MCCOMB E-2**
Buccaneer SP — WAVELAND F-3
Buck Island MHC — ROBINSONVILLE A-3
Cajun RV Park — BILOXI F-4
★ **Camper City — TUPELO B-4**
Campgrounds at Barnes Crossing — TUPELO B-4
Chickasaw Hill Campground (COE-Enid Lake) — **ENID B-3**
● **Clark Creek Nature Park — WOODVILLE E-1**
□ **Clarkco SP — QUITMAN D-4**
□ Clearwater RV Park — **PICAYUNE F-3**
Coal Bluff Park (Pearl River Valley Water Supply District) — **LUDLOW D-3**
Country Side RV Park — GULFPORT F-4
□ Cypress Hill RV Park — **HATTIESBURG E-4**
Dewayne Hayes Campground (COE-Tennessee/Tombigbee Waterway) — **COLUMBUS B-5**
□ D'Lo Water Park (Pearl River Basin Dev. Dist.) — **MENDENHALL D-3**
Dry Creek Water Park (Pat Harrison Waterway District) — **MOUNT OLIVE E-3**
Dub Patton Campground (COE-Arkabutla Lake) — **COLDWATER A-3**
□ Dunn's Falls Water Park (Pat Harrison Waterway District) — **ENTERPRISE D-4**
Elvis Presley Lake & Campground (County Park) — **TUPELO B-4**
EZ Daze RV Park — SOUTHAVEN A-3
□ Flint Creek Water Park (Pat Harrison Waterway District) — **WIGGINS F-4**
● **Florewood State Park — GREENWOOD B-3**
Frog Hollow Campground/RV Park — **GRENADA B-3**
Frog Level RV Park — **PHILADELPHIA C-4**
□ **George Payne Cossar SP — OAKLAND B-3**
Golden Memorial State Park — WALNUT GROVE D-3
Goshen Springs Campground (Pearl River Valley Water Supply District) — **JACKSON D-3**
Grand Gulf Military Park Campground (State) — **PORT GIBSON D-2**
Great River Road SP — ROSEDALE B-2
Gulf Islands National Seashore (Davis Bayou Area) — **OCEAN SPRINGS F-4**
Harrah's Casino RV Resort — TUNICA A-2
● **Harrah's Casino Tunica — TUNICA A-2**
Harrison County Fairgrounds — **GULFPORT F-4**
Hernando Point (COE - Arkabutla Lake) — **COLDWATER A-3**
□ **Hidden Springs Resort — TYLERTOWN E-3**
Holly Springs National Forest (Chewalla Lake Campground) — **HOLLY SPRINGS A-3**
Hollywood Casino RV Park — **BAY ST. LOUIS F-4**
Hollywood Casino RV Resort — **TUNICA A-2**
□ **Holmes County SP — DURANT C-3**
□ **Hugh White SP — GRENADA B-3**
®□ **Indian Point RV Resort — GAUTIER F-4**
Isle of Capri RV Park — **LULA A-2**
□ **John Kyle SP & Mallard Point Golf Course — SARDIS A-3**
□ **JP Coleman SP — IUKA A-5**
Lake Lincoln SP — WESSON E-2
□ **Lake Lowndes SP — COLUMBUS B-5**
Leake County Water Park (Pearl River Valley Water Supply District) — **LENA D-3**
LeFleur's Bluff SP & Golf Course — JACKSON D-3
□ **Legion SP — LOUISVILLE C-4**
□ **Leroy Percy SP — HOLLANDALE C-2**
□ Little Black Creek Water Park (Pat Harrison Waterway District) — **LUMBERTON E-3**
Low Head Dam (Pearl River Valley Water Supply District) — **LENA D-3**
Magnolia RV Park Resort — VICKSBURG D-2
Majestic Oaks RV Resort — **BILOXI F-4**
□ Maynor Creek Water Park (Pat Harrison Waterway District) — **WAYNESBORO E-4**
®□ **Mazalea Travel Park — BILOXI F-4**
McLeod Water Park — **BAY ST. LOUIS F-4**
□ Memphis Jellystone Camp Resort — **HORN LAKE A-3**
Memphis South campground & RV Park — COLDWATER A-3
MILITARY PARK (Lake Walker Family Campground-Camp Shelby) — **HATTIESBURG E-4**
Mississippi State Parks — JACKSON D-3
Morgan's Landing Park — ABERDEEN B-4
®□ Movietown RV Resort — **CANTON D-3**
Nanabe Creek Campground — MERIDIAN D-4
□ **Natchez SP — NATCHEZ E-1**
Natchez Trace Parkway (Rocky Springs Campground) — **PORT GIBSON D-2**
Natchez Trace RV Park — TUPELO B-4
Oaklawn RV Park — BILOXI F-4
□ Okatibbee Water Park (Pat Harrison Waterway District) — **MERIDIAN D-4**
Okatoma Resort & RV Park — HATTIESBURG E-4
□ **Parker's Landing RV Park — BILOXI F-4**
□ **Paul B Johnson SP — HATTIESBURG E-4**
□ **Percy Quin SP & Quail Hollow Golf Course — MCCOMB E-2**
Persimmon Hill-South Abutment (COE-Enid Lake) — **ENID B-3**
Piney Grove Campground (COE-Tennessee/Tombigbee Waterway) — **BURTON A-5**
River Town Campground — **VICKSBURG D-2**
□ **Roosevelt SP — MORTON D-3**
Sam's Town RV Park — **TUNICA A-2**
® **Santa Maria RV Park — GAUTIER F-4**
□ **Shepard SP — GAUTIER F-4**
South Abutment Campground (COE-Arkabutla Lake) — **COLDWATER A-3**
Southaven RV Park — **SOUTHAVEN A-3**
★ **Southaven RV Supercenter — SOUTHAVEN A-3**
Southern Comfort Camping Resort — BILOXI F-4
Springridge RV Park — **CLINTON D-2**

MISSISSIPPI — Continued

□ **Sun Roamers RV Resort — PICAYUNE F-3**
Swinging Bridge RV Park — BYRAM D-3
Timberlake Campground (Pearl River Valley Water Supply District) — **JACKSON D-3**
□ **Tishomingo SP — TISHOMINGO A-5**
Tombigbee National Forest (Davis Lake Campground) — **HOUSTON B-4**
□ **Tombigbee SP — TUPELO B-4**
Town Creek Campground (COE-Tennessee/Tombigbee Waterway) — **COLUMBUS B-5**
□ **Trace SP — TUPELO B-4**
□ Turkey Creek Water Park (Pat Harrison Waterway District) — **DECATUR D-4**
Twiltley Branch Camping Area (COE-Okatibbee Lake) — **MERIDIAN D-4**
□ **Wall Doxey SP — HOLLY SPRINGS A-3**
Wallace Creek (COE-Enid Lake) — **ENID B-3**
Warfield Point Park (Washington County Park) — **GREENVILLE C-2**
Water Valley Landing Campground (COE-Enid Lake) — **ENID B-3**
Wendy Oaks RV Resort — FLORENCE D-3
Whitten Park — **FULTON A-5**
®□ Yogi On The Lake — **PELAHATCHIE D-3**

MISSOURI

370 Lakeside Park RV & Campground — ST. PETERS C-5
□ **Acorn Acres RV Park & Campground — BRANSON E-3**
□ **America's Best Campground — BRANSON E-3**
Arrow Rock State Historic Site — ARROW ROCK B-3
□ Arrowhead Point RV Park & Campground — **COLLINS D-2**
Aunts Creek Park (COE Table Rock Lake) — **KIMBERLING CITY E-2**
Babler State Park — CHESTERFIELD C-5
® Ballards Campground — **CARTHAGE E-2**
□ **Bass' River Resort — STEELVILLE D-4**
● **Bass' River Resort Canoe Rental — STEELVILLE D-4**
□ Basswood Country Resort — **PLATTE CITY B-2**
Battle of Athens State Historic Site — **REVERE A-4**
Baxter Park (COE Table Rock Lake) — **BLUE EYE E-3**
Beacon RV Park — ST. JOSEPH B-1
Beaver Creek Campground (COE Bull Shoals Lake) — **FORSYTH E-3**
Belleville Mobile Home and RV Estates — **FENTON C-5**
□ **Bennett Spring State Park — BENNETT SPRINGS D-3**
Berry Bend (COE - Harry S. Truman Reservoir) — **WARSAW C-3**
® **Big Creek RV Park — ANNAPOLIS D-5**
Big Elk Camp & Canoe Rental — PINEVILLE E-2
□ **Big Lake State Park — BIGELOW A-1**
Big M Boat Dock & Park (COE - Table Rock Lake) — **CASSVILLE E-2**
® **Big Red Barn RV Park — CARTHAGE E-2**
□ Big Spring RV Camp — **VAN BUREN E-4**
Blue Springs Lake Campground (Jackson County Park) — **BLUE SPRINGS C-2**
Bluff View Park (COE Clearwater Lake) — **PIEDMONT E-5**
® **Boiling Spring Campground — DIXON D-4**
● **Boomland — CHARLESTON E-6**
Boomland RV Park & Campground — CHARLESTON E-6
®□ Branson KOA — **BRANSON E-3**
● **Branson Lakes Area Chamber of Commerce & Convention & Visitors Bureau — BRANSON E-3**
Branson Lakeside RV Park (City Park) — **BRANSON E-3**
Branson Shenanigans RV Park — BRANSON E-3
Branson Stagecoach RV Park — BRANSON E-3
Branson View Campground (Not visited) — BRANSON E-3
Branson View Estates — BRANSON E-3
Branson's Ozark Country Campground — BRANSON E-3
Buck Creek Park (COE - Bull Shoals Lake) — **THEODOSIA E-3**
Bucksaw Point (COE - Harry S. Truman Reservoir) — **TIGHTWAD C-2**
★ **Byerly RV Center — EUREKA C-5**
Camelot RV Campground — **POPLAR BLUFF E-5**
Camp Branch Campground & Marina (Clay County Park) — **SMITHVILLE B-2**
Campbell Point Boat Dock & Park (COE Table Rock Lake) — **SHELL KNOB E-2**
Campus RV Park — **INDEPENDENCE B-2**
Cape Camping & RV Park — **CAPE GIRARDEAU D-6**
Cape Fair Dock & Park (COE Table Rock Lake) — **CAPE FAIR E-2**
Cedar Ridge Area (COE Stockton Lake) — **BONA D-2**
City of Canton Mississippi River Park — CANTON A-4
Coachlight Campground — CARTHAGE E-2
★ **Coachlight RV Sales — CARTHAGE E-2**
□ **Compton Ridge Campground — BRANSON E-3**
□ **Cooper Creek Campground — BRANSON E-3**
Cottonwoods RV Park — COLUMBIA C-3
Country Gardens RV Park — ODESSA C-2
Countryside Adult & Senior RV Park — **SEDALIA C-3**
Cow Creek Park (COE Table Rock Lake) — **BLUE EYE E-3**
Cozy C RV Campground — BOWLING GREEN B-4
□ Cozy Corner RV Park — **CLINTON C-2**
Crabtree Cove (COE Stockton Lake) — **STOCKTON D-2**
□ **Cross Creek RV Park — LAKE OZARK C-3**
Crowder State Park — TRENTON A-2
Crows Creek (Clay County Park) — **SMITHVILLE B-2**
Cuivre River State Park — TROY C-4
Damsite Camp Area (COE Pomme de Terre Lake) — **HERMITAGE D-3**
DeerRest CampPark — WARSAW C-3
● **Division of State Parks Missouri — JEFFERSON CITY C-3**
Eagle Ridge RV Park — EAGLEVILLE A-2
Eagle Rock Boat Dock & Park (COE Table Rock Lake) — **EAGLE ROCK E-2**
Finger Lakes State Park — COLUMBIA C-3
Frank Russell Rec. Area (COE - Mark Twain Lake) — **PERRY B-4**
□ Gasconade Hills Resort — **HAZELGREEN D-3**
● **Glore Psychiatric Museum — ST. JOSEPH B-1**
Graham Cave State Park — DANVILLE C-4
Greenville (COE - Wappapello Lake) — **GREENVILLE E-5**
®△ **Hanson Hills Campground — KINGDOM CITY C-4**
● **Hanson Hills Campground Kitchen — KINGDOM CITY C-4**
★ **Happy Trails RV Center — LEBANON D-3**
□ **Happy Trails RV Park — LEBANON D-3**
Harry S. Truman State Park — WARSAW C-3
□ **Hava Space RV Park — GRAVOIS MILLS C-3**
Hawker Point (COE - Stockton Lake) — **STOCKTON D-2**
Hawn State Park — WEINGARTEN D-5
□ **Hayti-Portageville KOA — HAYTI A-6**
Hermann RV & Trailer Park (City Park) — **HERMANN C-4**
Highway K Park (COE Clearwater Lake) — **ANNAPOLIS D-5**
Hinton Park — SIKESTON E-6
□ **Huzzah Valley Resort — STEELVILLE D-4**
● **Huzzah Valley Resort Canoe Rental — STEELVILLE D-4**
Hwy 160 RV Park — HIGHLANDVILLE E-3
Hwy 60 RV Park — GRANBY E-2
Indian Creek (COE - Mark Twain Lake) — **MONROE CITY B-4**
Indian Point Boat Dock & Park (COE Table Rock Lake) — **BRANSON E-3**
Injun Joe Campground — HANNIBAL B-4
Jacks Fork Canoe Rental & Campground — **EMINENCE E-4**
Jacomo Campground at Fleming Park (Jackson County Park) — **LEE'S SUMMIT C-2**
□ Jason Place Campground — **AKERS FERRY D-4**
Johnson's Shut-ins State Park — LESTERVILLE D-5
Kan-Do Kampground & RV Park — DANVILLE C-4
□ **Kansas City East KOA — OAK GROVE C-2**
Knob Noster State Park — KNOB NOSTER C-2
□ **KOA St. Louis West/Historic Rt 66 — EUREKA C-5**
□ KOA-Joplin — **JOPLIN E-2**
● **Lady Luck Casino Caruthersville — CARUTHERSVILLE A-6**
Lady Luck RV Park and Nature Trail — CARUTHERSVILLE A-6

MISSOURI — Continued

Ladybug RV Park & Campground — CUBA D-4
□ Lake of the Ozarks State Park — OSAGE BEACH D-3
□ Lake Paradise Resort — OAK GROVE C-2
□ Lake Wappapello State Park — WILLIAMSVILLE E-5
Laurie RV Park — LAURIE C-3
Lazy Day Campground — DANVILLE C-4
Lazy Day Camping — MARSHALL B-3
Lewis & Clark State Park — RUSHVILLE B-1
Lightfoot Public Use Area (COE Pomme de Terre Lake) — ELKTON D-3
Long Branch State Park — MACON B-3
Long Creek Boat Dock & Park (COE Table Rock Lake) — BRANSON E-3
Longshoal (COE - Harry S Truman Reservoir) — WARSAW C-3
Longview Lake Campground (Jackson County Park) — KANSAS CITY B-2
®□ Majestic Oaks Park — LAKE OZARK C-3
• Mark Twain Cave — HANNIBAL B-4
Mark Twain Cave and Campground — HANNIBAL B-4
□ Mark Twain Landing Resort — MONROE CITY B-4
Mark Twain National Forest (Big Bay Campground) — SHELL KNOB E-2
Mark Twain National Forest (Council Bluff Lake Campground) — BELGRADE D-5
Mark Twain National Forest (Lane Spring Campground) — ROLLA D-4
Mark Twain National Forest (Marble Creek Campground) — IRONTON D-5
Mark Twain National Forest (Markham Springs Campground) — WILLIAMSVILLE E-5
Mark Twain National Forest (Red Bluff Campground) — DAVISVILLE D-4
Mark Twain National Forest (Silver Mines Campground) — FREDERICKTOWN D-5
Mark Twain National Forest (Sutton Bluff Campground) — CENTERVILLE D-4
Mark Twain State Park — STOUTSVILLE B-4
Masters Area (COE Stockton Lake) — STOCKTON D-2
□ Meramec State Park — SULLIVAN C-4
® Meramec Valley RV Camp Resort — CUBA D-4
®□ MILITARY PARK (Lake of the Ozarks Rec Area-Fort Leonard Wood) — LINN CREEK D-3
Mill Creek Park (COE Table Rock Lake) — BLUE EYE E-3
Miller's Kampark — LIBERTY B-2
• Missouri Division of Tourism — JEFFERSON CITY C-3
Missouri Park & Campground — MOUNTAIN GROVE E-3
Missouri State Fair RV Park — SEDALIA C-3
Montauk State Park — SALEM D-4
Mutton Creek (COE Stockton Lake) — STOCKTON D-2
• National Military Heritage Museum — ST. JOSEPH B-1
Nemo Park (COE Pomme de Terre Lake) — HERMITAGE D-3
Oak Grove RV Resort — BRANSON E-3
□ Oak Hill Court & RV Park — CASSVILLE E-2
• Oceans of Fun — KANSAS CITY B-2
Old Highway 86 Park (COE Table Rock Lake) — BLUE EYE E-3
• One Good Taste Country Store — ODESSA C-2
Onondaga Cave State Park — LEASBURG D-4
Orleans Trail Marina & Public Use Area (COE Stockton Lk) — STOCKTON D-2
□ Osage Beach RV Park — OSAGE BEACH D-3
Osage Bluff (COE - Harry S Truman Reservoir) — WARSAW C-3
Osage Campground & More — JEFFERSON CITY C-3
□ Osage Prairie RV Park — NEVADA D-2
Osceola RV Park — OSCEOLA D-2
Outlet Area (COE Pomme de Terre Lake) — HERMITAGE D-3
Ozark National Scenic Riverways (Akers) — SALEM D-4
Ozark National Scenic Riverways (Alley Spring) — EMINENCE E-4
Ozark National Scenic Riverways (Big Spring) — VAN BUREN E-4
Ozark National Scenic Riverways (Pulltite) — ROUND SPRING D-4
Ozark National Scenic Riverways (Round Spring Campground) — ROUND SPRING D-4
®□ Ozark Outdoors/Riverfront Resort — LEASBURG D-4
Ozark RV Park — OZARK E-3
□ Ozark Trails RV Park — LINN CREEK D-3
□ Ozarks Mountain Springs RV Park — MOUNTAIN VIEW E-4
□ Paradise Cove Camping Resort — EAGLE ROCK E-2
Paradise In The Woods RV Park & Campground — STRAFFORD E-3
• Patee House Museum & Jesse James Home — ST. JOSEPH B-1
Pea Patch RV Park — BRANSON E-3
Peculiar Park Place RV Park — PECULIAR C-2
Peoples Creek Campground (COE Wappapello Lake) — WAPPAPELLO E-5
®□ Perryville Campground — PERRYVILLE D-5
Pershing State Park — LACLEDE B-3
Piedmont Park (COE Clearwater Lake) — PIEDMONT E-5
□ Pin Oak Creek RV Park — VILLA RIDGE C-5
Pittsburg Park (COE Pomme de Terre Lake) — PITTSBURG D-3
Pomme de Terre State Park — PITTSBURG D-3
Pontiac Park (COE Bull Shoals Lake) — GAINESVILLE E-3
• Pony Express National Museum — ST. JOSEPH B-1
Pony Express RV Park & Campground — MAYSVILLE A-2
Ray Behrens Recreation Area (COE - Mark Twain Lake) — PERRY B-4
Red Maples Community — FULTON C-4
Redman Creek Campgrounds (COE Wappapello Lake) — WAPPAPELLO E-5
★ Reliable RV Center — SPRINGFIELD E-3
□ River Ranch RV Park & Campground — NOEL E-2
River Road Park (COE Clearwater Lake) — PIEDMONT E-5
River Run Park (COE Bull Shoals Lake) — FORSYTH E-3
Riverview RV Park — LAKE OZARK C-3
Road Runner RV Park — WEST PLAINS E-4
Roaring River State Park — CASSVILLE E-2
Robertsville State Park — ROBERTSVILLE C-5
• Robidoux Row Museum — ST. JOSEPH B-1
Rothwell Park Campground (City Park) — MOBERLY B-3
Roubidoux Springs Campground (City Park) — WAYNESVILLE D-3
Ruark Bluff (COE Stockton Lake) — STOCKTON D-2
RV Park Strafford — STRAFFORD E-3
Saint Francois State Park — BONNE TERRE D-5
Saint Joe State Park — BISMARCK D-5
• St. Joseph Visitors Bureau — ST. JOSEPH B-1
• St. Peters Rec-Plex — ST. PETERS C-5
□ Sam A Baker State Park — PATTERSON E-5
★ Sam's Trailer Service — BRANSON E-3
Shadow Rock Park & Campground (City Park) — FORSYTH E-3
Shoemaker RV Park — BEVIER B-3
Smith's Fork Campground — SMITHVILLE B-2
Sparrowfoot (COE - Harry S. Truman Reservoir) — CLINTON C-2
Speedway RV Park — BOLIVAR D-3
®□ Springfield/Route 66 KOA — SPRINGFIELD E-3
Stadium RV Park — INDEPENDENCE B-2
Stage Stop Campground — NEOSHO E-2
Stage Stop RV Park — OZARK E-3
□ Stanton/Meramec KOA — STANTON C-4
Stockton State Park — STOCKTON D-2
• Sundermeier Banquet & Conference Center — ST. CHARLES C-5
• Sundermeier Beef Eaters Restaurant — ST. CHARLES C-5
□ Sundermeier RV Park & Conference Center — ST. CHARLES C-5
Table Rock State Park — BRANSON E-3
□ Tall Pines Campground — BRANSON E-3
Talley Bend (COE - Harry S. Truman Reservoir) — LOWRY CITY D-2
Taneycomo Lakefront Resort/RV Park — BRANSON E-3
Taum Sauk State Park — IRONTON D-5
• Terrible's St. Jo Frontier Casino — ST. JOSEPH B-1
• The Black Archives of St. Joseph — ST. JOSEPH B-1
® The Great Escape RV & Camp Resort — HIGGINSVILLE B-2
• The Lone Wolf — CARUTHERSVILLE A-6
• The St. Joseph Museum — ST. JOSEPH B-1
®□ The Wilderness at Silver Dollar City — BRANSON E-3
Theodosia Park (COE Bull Shoals Lake) — THEODOSIA E-3
Thibaut Point (COE - Harry S. Truman Reservoir) — WARSAW C-3

MISSOURI — Continued

★ Thomas & Sons RV Supply — SPRINGFIELD E-3
□ Thousand Hills State Park — KIRKSVILLE A-3
Three Springs RV Park & Campground — ROLLA D-4
Town & Country RV Resort — SIKESTON E-6
Trail of Tears State Park — CAPE GIRARDEAU D-6
Trailside RV Park — GRAIN VALLEY C-2
® Treasure Lake RV Resort — BRANSON E-3
Turkey Creek RV Village — BRANSON E-3
Van Meter State Park — MARSHALL B-3
Viney Creek Park (COE Table Rock Lake) — GOLDEN E-2
Viola Boat Dock & Park (COE Table Rock Lake) — SHELL KNOB E-2
□ Wakonda State Park — LA GRANGE A-4
Wallace State Park — CAMERON B-2
□ Washington State Park — DE SOTO D-5
□ Water's Edge on Table Rock Lake — KIMBERLING CITY E-2
Watkins Woolen Mill State Park — LAWSON B-2
Webb Creek Park (COE - Clearwater Lake) — ELLINGTON E-4
Weston Bend State Park — WESTON B-1
Wheatland Park (COE Pomme de Terre Lake) — HERMITAGE D-3
• Whistle Stop Cafe — BRANSON E-3
Wildwood — STEEDMAN C-4
Wildwood RV Park — DEXTER E-5
Windsor Crossing (COE - Harry S Truman Reservoir) — TIGHTWAD C-2
• Worlds of Fun — KANSAS CITY B-2
□ Worlds of Fun Village — KANSAS CITY B-2
• Wyeth-Tootle Museum — ST. JOSEPH B-1
® Yogi Bear's Jellystone Park At Van Buren — VAN BUREN E-4
△□ Yogi Bear's Jellystone Park Resort at Six Flags — EUREKA C-5

NEW HAMPSHIRE

Ames Brook Campground — ASHLAND D-3
Ammonoosuc Campground — TWIN MOUNTAIN C-3
Autumn Hills Campground — WEARE E-3
□ Ayers Lake Farm Campground — BARRINGTON E-4
□ Barrington Shores Campground — BARRINGTON E-4
Beach Camping Area — NORTH CONWAY C-4
Bear Brook SP — ALLENSTOWN E-4
® Beaver Hollow Campground — OSSIPEE D-4
®□ Beech Hill Campground — TWIN MOUNTAIN C-3
® Bethel Woods Campground — HOLDERNESS D-3
□ Blake's Brook Family Campground — EPSOM E-4
® Branch Brook Campground — CAMPTON D-3
®□ Chocorua Camping Village KOA — CHOCORUA D-4
Circle 9 Ranch — EPSOM E-4
• Clark's Trading Post — NORTH WOODSTOCK C-3
□ Clearwater Campground — MEREDITH D-3
□ Cold Springs Camp Resort — WEARE E-3
Coleman SP — COLEBROOK B-3
Connecticut Lakes SF (Deer Mountain Campground) — PITTSBURG A-3
• Conway Scenic Railroad — NORTH CONWAY C-4
□ Country Bumpkins Campground & Cabins — LINCOLN C-3
Cove Camping Area on Conway Lake — CONWAY C-4
Cozy Pond Camping Resort — WEBSTER E-3
Crawford Notch SP (Dry River Campground) — BARTLETT C-4
® Crazy Horse Campground & RV Park — LITTLETON C-3
Crown Point Campground — STRAFFORD E-4
®△□ Crow's Nest Campground — NEWPORT E-2
®□ Danforth Bay Camping & RV Resort — FREEDOM D-4
□ Davidson's Countryside Campground — BRISTOL D-3
Ellacoya SP — GILFORD D-4
Epsom Valley Campground — EPSOM E-4
®□ Exeter Elms Family Campground — EXETER F-4
Ferndale Acres Campground — LEE E-4
Field and Stream RV Park — BROOKLINE F-3
Forest Lake Campground, Inc — WINCHESTER F-2
• Forest Lake Pitch and Putt — WINCHESTER F-2
Fort Jefferson Campground at Six Gun City — JEFFERSON C-3
Franconia Notch SP (Echo Lake RV Park) — FRANCONIA C-3
Franconia Notch SP (Lafayette Place Campground) — FRANCONIA C-3
® Fransted Family Campground — FRANCONIA C-3
Friendly Beaver Campground — NEW BOSTON F-3
® Glen Ellis Family Campground — GLEN C-4
Goose Hollow Camp & RV Park — THORNTON D-3
Great Bay Camping/Shell — NEWFIELDS F-4
Green Meadow Camping Area — GLEN C-4
Greenfield SP — GREENFIELD F-3
□ Gunstock Mountain Resort — GILFORD D-4
Hack-Ma-Tack Family Campground — LACONIA E-3
Hampton Beach SP — HAMPTON BEACH F-5
®□ Harbor Hill Camping Area — MEREDITH D-3
□ Hillcrest Campground — CHICHESTER E-3
Hinsdale Campground — HINSDALE F-2
® Keyser Pond Campground — HENNIKER E-3
Lake Francis SP — PITTSBURG A-3
® Lake Ivanhoe Campground — EAST WAKEFIELD D-4
® Lantern Resort Motel & Campground — JEFFERSON C-3
Laurel Lake Campground — FITZWILLIAM F-2
Lazy River Family Campground — EPSOM E-4
□ Littleton/Lisbon KOA — LISBON C-3
□ Living Water Campground — TWIN MOUNTAIN C-3
®□ Long Island Bridge Campground — MOULTONBOROUGH D-4
• Loon Mountain — LINCOLN C-3
• Lost River Gorge & Boulder Caves — NORTH WOODSTOCK C-3
□ Lost River Valley Campground — NORTH WOODSTOCK C-3
□ Maple Haven Camping, Cottages, & Lodge — NORTH WOODSTOCK C-3
□ Meredith Woods 4 Season Camping Area — MEREDITH D-3
□ Mi-Te-Jo Campground — MILTON E-4
Mile Away Campground — HENNIKER E-3
Mohawk Valley Camping Area — COLEBROOK B-3
Mollidgewock SP — ERROL B-4
Monadnock SP — JAFFREY F-2
Moose Brook SP — GORHAM C-4
□ Moose Hillock Campground — WARREN D-3
□ Mountain Lake Campground & RV Park — LANCASTER B-3
• Mt. Washington Auto Road — GORHAM C-4
• Museum of Family Camping — RICHMOND F-2
Newfound RV Park — BRIDGEWATER D-3
Northstar Campground — NEWPORT E-2
□ Notch View Country Inn & RV Resort — COLEBROOK B-3
Old Stage Campground — MADBURY E-4
□ Oxbow Campground — HILLSBORO E-3
Paugus Bay Campground — WEIRS BEACH D-3
Pawtuckaway SP — RAYMOND F-4
Pillsbury SP — WASHINGTON E-2
□ Pine Acres RV Resort, LLC (Morgan RV Resorts) — RAYMOND F-4
Pine Haven Campground — WENTWORTH D-3
Pine Hollow Park — WEIRS BEACH D-3
Riverbend RV Resort — TAMWORTH D-4
®□ Roger's Campground — LANCASTER B-3
® Saco River Camping Area — NORTH CONWAY C-4
□ Sandy Beach RV Resort — CONTOOCOOK E-3
• Santa's Village — JEFFERSON C-3
□ Scenic View Campground — WARREN D-3
Seven Maples Campground — HANCOCK F-2
® Shel-Al Campground — NORTH HAMPTON F-5
□ Shir-Roy Camping Area — RICHMOND F-2
□ Silver Lake Park Campground — LACONIA E-3
Storrs Pond Recreation Area — HANOVER D-2
• Story Land — GLEN C-4
Sun River Campground — BARNSTEAD E-4
□ Swanzey Lake Camping Area — SWANZEY F-2
® Tamworth Camping Area — TAMWORTH D-4
□ Tarry-Ho Campground & Cottages — TWIN MOUNTAIN C-3
□ Terrace Pines — CENTER OSSIPEE D-4

NEW HAMPSHIRE — Continued

The Bluffs Adult RV Resort — FREEDOM D-4
• The Flume/Franconia Notch State Park — FRANCONIA NOTCH C-3
The Green Gate Camping Area — EXETER F-4
The Pastures — ORFORD D-2
• The Whale's Tale Water Park — LINCOLN C-3
Thousand Acres Family Campground — FRANKLIN E-3
Tidewater Campground — HAMPTON F-5
Timberland Campground — GORHAM C-4
□ Tuxbury Pond Resort — SOUTH HAMPTON F-4
□ Twin Mountain KOA — TWIN MOUNTAIN C-3
®□ Twin River RV Park & Cottages — BATH C-2
®□ Twin Tamarack Family Camping and RV Resort — MEREDITH D-3
□ Umbagog Lake Campground SP — ERROL B-4
Wadleigh Falls Campground — LEE E-4
® Wakeda Campground — HAMPTON FALLS F-5
□ White Birches Camping Park — GORHAM C-4
White Lake SP — WEST OSSIPEE D-4
• White Mountain Attractions Visitors Center — NORTH WOODSTOCK C-3
White Mountain National Forest (Big Rock Campground) — LINCOLN C-3
White Mountain National Forest (Blackberry Crossing Campground) — CONWAY C-4
White Mountain National Forest (Campton Campground) — CAMPTON D-3
White Mountain National Forest (Covered Bridge Campground) — CONWAY C-4
White Mountain National Forest (Dolly Copp Campground) — GORHAM C-4
White Mountain National Forest (Hancock Campground) — LINCOLN C-3
White Mountain National Forest (Jigger Johnson Campground) — BARTLETT C-4
White Mountain National Forest (Passaconaway Campground) — CONWAY C-4
White Mountain National Forest (Russell Pond Campground) — NORTH WOODSTOCK C-3
White Mountain National Forest (Sugarloaf I Campground) — TWIN MOUNTAIN C-3
White Mountain National Forest (Sugarloaf II Campground) — TWIN MOUNTAIN C-3
White Mountain National Forest (Waterville Campground) — CAMPTON D-3
White Mountain National Forest (White Ledge Campground) — CONWAY C-4
White Mountain National Forest (Wildwood Campground) — NORTH WOODSTOCK C-3
Wolfeboro Campground — WOLFEBORO D-4
□ Woodmore Family Campground & RV Park — RINDGE F-2
®□ Woodstock KOA — WOODSTOCK D-3
□ Yogi Bear's Jellystone Park Camp Resort — ASHLAND D-3

NEW JERSEY

Acorn Campground — GREEN CREEK F-3
□ Adventure Bound Camping Resorts - Cape May — CAPE MAY COURT HOUSE F-3
□ Allaire State Park — FARMINGDALE C-4
® Atlantic City Blueberry Hill RV Park (Morgan RV Resorts) — PORT REPUBLIC E-4
®□ Avalon Campground — CLERMONT F-3
□ Baker's Acres Campground — LITTLE EGG HARBOR E-4
□ Bass River State Forest — NEW GRETNA E-4
®□ Beachcomber Camping Resort — CAPE MAY F-3
Belleplain State Forest — WOODBINE F-3
□ Best Holiday Trav-L-Park/Holly Acres — EGG HARBOR CITY E-3
®□ Big Timber Lake Camping Resort — CAPE MAY COURT HOUSE F-3
Birch Grove Park (City Park) — NORTHFIELD E-3
® Brookville Campground — BARNEGAT D-4
• Buck Stop Gift Shop — COLUMBIA B-2
□ Buena Vista Camping Resort (Morgan RV Resorts) — BUENA E-3
□ Butterfly Camping Resort — JACKSON D-4
□ Byrne State Forest — PEMBERTON D-3
®□ Camp Taylor Campground — COLUMBIA B-2
®□ Cedar Creek Campground — BAYVILLE D-4
Cheesequake State Park — MATAWAN C-4
Chestnut Lake Campground — PORT REPUBLIC E-4
□ Country Oaks Campground — DOROTHY E-3
Delaware and Raritan Canal State Park (Bull's Island Section) — STOCKTON C-3
®□ Delaware River Family Campground — DELAWARE B-2
Egg Harbor City Lake and Campground — EGG HARBOR CITY E-3
Evergreen Woods Lakefront Resort — POMONA E-3
□ Four Seasons Campground — WOODSTOWN E-2
□ Frontier Campground — OCEAN VIEW F-3
★ George's RV Repair — HOPE B-3
□ Goodland Country Club & Spa — HACKETTSTOWN B-3
□ Harmony Ridge Campground — BRANCHVILLE A-3
□ High Point State Park — COLESVILLE A-3
®□ Holly Shores Campground — CAPE MAY F-3
□ Indian Rock Resort — JACKSON D-4
□ Jenny Jump State Forest — GREAT MEADOWS B-3
® Jugtown Mountain Campsites — WEST PORTAL B-2
□ King Nummy Trail Campground — CAPE MAY COURT HOUSE F-3
®□ Kymer's Camping Resort — BRANCHVILLE A-3
® Lake and Shore — OCEAN VIEW F-3
Lake Laurie Campground (Morgan RV Resorts) — CAPE MAY F-3
• Lakota Wolf Preserve at Camp Taylor — COLUMBIA B-2
Liberty Harbor RV Park — JERSEY CITY B-4
□ Long Beach Carefree RV Resort — BARNEGAT D-4
Long Beach Island Trailer Park — BEACH HAVEN E-4
Mahlon Dickerson Reservation (Morris County Park) — WOODPORT A-3
®□ Nascar at May's Landing RV Resort (Morgan RV Resorts) — MAYS LANDING E-3
®□ Ocean View Resort Campground — OCEAN VIEW F-3
★ Ocean View Trailer Sales — OCEAN VIEW F-3
□ Old Cedar Campground — MONROEVILLE E-2
□ Oldman's Creek Campground — MONROEVILLE E-2
® Outdoor World-Sea Pines Campground — SWAINTON F-3
®□ Panther Lake Camping Resort — ANDOVER A-3
□ Parvin State Park — CENTERTON E-2
□ Pine Cone Resort — FREEHOLD C-4
®□ Pleasant Acres Farm Campground — SUSSEX A-3
□ Pleasant Valley Family Campground — ESTELL MANOR E-3
® Pomona RV Park — POMONA E-3
Round Valley State Recreation Area — CLINTON B-3
®□ Sea Grove Camping Resort — OCEAN VIEW F-3
□ Sea Pirate Campground — WEST CREEK E-4
Seashore Campsites — CAPE MAY F-3
® Shady Pines Carefree RV Resort — ABSECON E-4
□ Shellbay Campground — CAPE MAY COURT HOUSE F-3
• Shore Gate Golf Club — OCEAN VIEW F-3
Spruce Run State Recreation Area — CLINTON B-3
Stephens State Park — HACKETTSTOWN B-3
□ Stokes State Forest — BRANCHVILLE A-3
□ Swartswood State Park — NEWTON A-3
□ Tamerlane Campground — OCEAN VIEW F-3
® The Depot Travel Park — CAPE MAY F-3
□ Timberland Lake Campground — JACKSON D-4
□ Timberlane Campground — CLARKSBORO D-2
®□ Timberline Lake Camping Resort — NEW GRETNA E-4

NEW JERSEY — Continued

Tip Tam Camping Resort — *JACKSON D-4*
Triplebrook Camping Resort — *HOPE B-3*
Turkey Swamp (Monmouth County Park) — ***FREEHOLD C-4***
Turtle Run Campground — *EGG HARBOR CITY E-3*
Voorhees State Park — ***HIGH BRIDGE B-3***
Wading Pines Camping Resort — *CHATSWORTH D-3*
Wharton State Forest (Atsion Rec. Area) — ***HAMMONTON E-3***
Wharton State Forest (Godfrey Bridge Camp) — ***HAMMONTON E-3***
Whippoorwill Campground — ***MARMORA F-3***
Winding River Campground — *MAYS LANDING E-3*
• **Winding River Canoeing & Kayaking — *MAYS LANDING E-3***
Worthington State Forest — ***COLUMBIA B-2***
Yogi Bear Jellystone Park at Tall Pines Resort — ***ELMER E-2***

NEW YORK

1000 Islands Campground — *ALEXANDRIA BAY B-6*
AA Royal Campground & Motel — *NIAGARA FALLS D-2*
Adirondack 1000 Islands Campground — *NATURAL BRIDGE C-7*
Adirondack Adventure Resorts-Saratoga Springs — *SARATOGA SPRINGS D-9*
Adirondack Adventure Resorts-Schroon River — *LAKE GEORGE D-9*
Adirondack Camping Village — *LAKE GEORGE D-9*
Adirondack Gateway Campground & Lodge — *POLAND D-7*
Adirondack Gateway RV Resort (Morgan RV Resorts) — ***GANSEVOORT D-9***
Adventure Bound Camping Resort at Deer Run — ***MECHANICVILLE E-9***
Allegany State Park (Quaker Area) — ***SALAMANCA F-2***
Allegany State Park (Red House Area) — ***SALAMANCA F-2***
Alpine Lake RV Resort, LLC — *CORINTH D-9*
Alps Family Campground — *AVERILL PARK E-10*
American Family Campground, Inc — ***GODEFFROY B-1***
Arrowhead Camping Area — ***DELEVAN E-2***
Arrowhead Marina & RV Park — *SCHENECTADY E-9*
Association Island RV Resort & Marina — *HENDERSON HARBOR C-6*
• **Ausable Chasm — *AUSABLE CHASM B-10***
Ausable Chasm Campground — ***AUSABLE CHASM B-10***
Ausable Point Campground (Adirondack SF) — ***PERU B-9***
Ausable River Campsite — *AUSABLE CHASM B-10*
Babbling Brook RV Park — *WESTVILLE CENTER A-8*
Babcock Hollow Campground — ***BATH F-4***
Battle Row Campground (Nassau County Park) — ***OLD BETHPAGE C-3***
Bear Spring Mountain (Catskill SF) — ***WALTON F-7***
Beaver Meadow Family Campground — *JAVA CENTER E-3*
Beaver Spring Lake Campground — *DAVENPORT E-8*
Beaverkill Campground (Catskills SF) — ***LIVINGSTON MANOR F-8***
Bedford Creek Marina & Campground — ***SACKETS HARBOR C-6***
Belden Hill Campground — ***HARPURSVILLE F-7***
Belvedere Lake Campground — ***CHERRY VALLEY E-8***
Black Bear Campground — *FLORIDA B-2*
Black River Bay Campground — ***DEXTER C-6***
Blue Mountain Campground — *SAUGERTIES F-9*
Blydenburgh Park (Suffolk County Park) — ***SMITHTOWN B-4***
Bowman Lake State Park — ***OXFORD F-7***
Branches of Niagara Campground & Resort — *NIAGARA FALLS D-2*
Brennan Beach RV Resort — *PULASKI D-6*
Bristol Woodlands Campground — ***CANANDAIGUA E-4***
Brook N Wood Family Campground — *ELIZAVILLE F-9*
Brookside Beach Campground — *WESTFIELD F-1*
Brown Tract Pond Campground (Adirondack SF) — ***RAQUETTE LAKE C-8***
Buck Pond (Adirondack SF) — ***GABRIELS B-9***
★ **Bull's RV Center — *PLATTSBURGH B-10***
Bulwagga Bay Campground & RV Park — ***PORT HENRY C-10***
Burnham Point State Park — ***CAPE VINCENT C-6***
Buttermilk Falls State Park — ***ITHACA F-5***
Camp Bell Campground — *CAMPBELL F-4*
Camp Chautauqua Camping Resort — *CHAUTAUQUA F-1*
Camp Waubeeka Family Campground (Morgan RV Resorts) — ***COPAKE F-10***
Campers Haven — ***BATH F-4***
Camping at Mariposa Ponds — *HOUGHTON F-3*
Caroga Lake Campground (Adirondack SF) — ***CAROGA LAKE D-8***
Cayuga Lake State Park — ***SENECA FALLS E-5***
Cedar Point State Park — ***CLAYTON B-6***
Cedar Point (Suffolk County Park) — ***EAST HAMPTON B-5***
Cedar Valley Campsite — ***MORRISVILLE E-7***
Chautauqua Heights Camping Resort — *DEWITTVILLE F-1*
★ **Chautauqua Lake RV & Park Model Sales — *DEWITTVILLE F-1***
Cheerful Valley Campground — *PHELPS E-5*
Chenango Valley State Park — ***BINGHAMTON F-6***
Cherry Grove Campground — ***WOLCOTT D-5***
Cherrystone Family Camping Resort — *ALBANY E-9*
Chittenango Falls State Park — ***CAZENOVIA E-6***
Cinderella Campsite & Motel — ***NIAGARA FALLS D-2***
Clarence Fahnestock Memorial State Park — ***COLD SPRING B-2***
Cliff and Ed's Trailer Park — ***CUTCHOGUE B-5***
Clute Memorial Park & Campground — *WATKINS GLEN F-5*
Coldbrook RV Resort (Morgan RV Resorts) — ***GANSEVOORT D-9***
Coles Creek State Park — ***WADDINGTON A-7***
Conesus Lake Campground — ***LAKEVILLE E-4***
Cool-Lea Camp — *ODESSA F-5*
Cooperstown Beaver Valley Cabins & Campsites — ***COOPERSTOWN E-8***
Cooperstown Famous Family Tent & Trailer Campground — ***COOPERSTOWN E-8***
Cooperstown Ringwood Farms Campground — ***COOPERSTOWN E-8***
Cooperstown Shadow Brook Campground — *COOPERSTOWN E-8*
Cortland's Country Music Park & Campground — ***CORTLAND E-6***
Country Roads Campground — *GILBOA F-8*
Cranberry Lake Campground (Adirondack SF) — ***CRANBERRY LAKE B-8***
Crown Point Reservation Campground (Adirondack SF) — ***CROWN POINT C-10***
Crystal Grove Diamond Mine & Campground — ***ST. JOHNSVILLE E-8***
Cumberland Bay State Park — ***PLATTSBURGH B-10***
Darien Lakes State Park — ***DARIEN CENTER E-3***
Deer River Campsite — ***DUANE B-8***
Delta Lake State Park — ***ROME D-7***
★ **Doug's RV Repairs — *CAMBRIDGE D-10***
Eagle Point Campground (Adirondack SF) — ***POTTERSVILLE C-9***
Eastern Long Island Kampground — *GREENPORT B-5*
Eighth Lake (Adirondack SF) — ***RAQUETTE LAKE C-8***
Evangola State Park — ***ANGOLA E-2***
Evergreen Trails Campground — ***ANGELICA F-3***
Fair Haven Beach State Park — ***FAIR HAVEN D-5***
Ferenbaugh Campground — *CORNING F-4*
Fillmore Glen State Park — ***MORAVIA E-5***
• **Finger Lakes Wellness Center & Health Spa — *BATH F-4***
Fire Island Nat'l Seashore (Watch Hill Campground) — ***PATCHOGUE C-4***
Fish Creek Ponds Campground (Adirondack SF) — ***TUPPER LAKE B-8***
Flint Creek Campgrounds — ***MIDDLESEX E-4***
Forest Lake Campground — *WINDSOR F-7*
Forked Lake Campground (Adirondack SF) — ***DEERLAND C-8***
Fort Niagara SP (Four Mile Campsite) — ***YOUNGSTOWN D-2***
Four Winds Campground — *PORTAGEVILLE E-3*
Frost Ridge Campground — *LE ROY E-3*
• **Gems Along the Mohawk — *HERKIMER D-7***
Genesee Country Campground — ***CALEDONIA E-3***
Gilbert Lake State Park — ***ONEONTA E-7***
Glimmerglass State Park — ***EAST SPRINGFIELD E-8***
Golden Beach (Adirondack SF) — ***RAQUETTE LAKE C-8***

NEW YORK — Continued

Golden Hill State Park — ***BARKER D-2***
Grass Point State Park — ***ALEXANDRIA BAY B-6***
Green Lakes State Park — ***FAYETTEVILLE E-6***
Half Mile Ranch Camping Resort — ***LAKE LUZERNE D-9***
Hamlin Beach State Park — ***HAMLIN D-3***
Harriman SP (Beaver Pond Campground) — ***STONY POINT B-2***
Hartwick Highlands Campground — *COOPERSTOWN E-8*
Hearthstone Point Campground (Adirondack SF) — ***LAKE GEORGE D-9***
Heckscher State Park — ***EAST ISLIP C-4***
Hejamada Campground and RV Park — ***MONTEZUMA E-5***
• **Herkimer Crystal Chandelier Restaurant — *HERKIMER D-7***
• **Herkimer Diamond Mines — *HERKIMER D-7***
Hickory Hill Camping Resort — *BATH F-4*
Hickory Ridge Golf & RV Resort — ***ALBION D-3***
Hidden Valley Camping Area — ***JAMESTOWN F-1***
Hide-A-Way Campsites — *CENTRAL BRIDGE E-8*
Higley Flow State Park — ***SOUTH COLTON B-8***
Hither Hills State Park — ***MONTAUK B-5***
Holiday Hill Campground — *SPRINGWATER E-4*
Ideal Campground — ***POTTERSVILLE C-9***
Indian Island Park (Suffolk County Park) — ***RIVERHEAD B-4***
Indian Ridge Campground — ***CATSKILL F-9***
Interlake RV Park & Sales — *RHINEBECK F-9*
★ **Interlake Trailer Sales — *RHINEBECK F-9***
Iroquois RV Park & Campground — ***PERU B-9***
Jacques Cartier State Park — ***MORRISTOWN B-7***
Junius Ponds Cabins & Campgrounds — *PHELPS E-5*
Kayuta Lake Campground — ***FORESTPORT D-7***
Keewaydin State Park — ***ALEXANDRIA BAY B-6***
Kellystone Park Campsite — *AFTON F-7*
Kenneth L. Wilson Campground (Catskills SF) — ***PHOENICIA F-8***
Keuka Lake State Park — ***KEUKA PARK E-4***
King Phillip's Campground & Resort — *LAKE GEORGE D-9*
Kittatinny Campgrounds — ***BARRYVILLE A-1***
KOA Copake — *COPAKE F-10*
KOA-Warsaw/Dream Lake — ***WARSAW E-3***
KOA-Canandaigua/Rochester — ***FARMINGTON E-4***
KOA-Cooperstown — ***COOPERSTOWN E-8***
KOA-Herkimer Diamond Resort — *HERKIMER D-7*
KOA-Lake Placid Whiteface Mountain — ***WILMINGTON B-9***
KOA-Medina/Wildwook Lake — ***MEDINA D-3***
KOA-Newburgh/New York City North — *NEWBURGH A-2*
KOA-Niagara Falls — ***NIAGARA FALLS D-2***
KOA-Niagara Falls North — *NIAGARA FALLS D-2*
KOA-Saugerties/Woodstock — *SAUGERTIES F-9*
KOA-UNADILLA/Delaware Valley — ***UNADILLA F-7***
KOA-Watkins Glen/Corning Resort — ***WATKINS GLEN F-5***
KOA-Westfield-Lake Erie — ***WESTFIELD F-1***
Korn's Campgrounds — ***MIDDLETOWN B-2***
Kring Point State Park — ***ALEXANDRIA BAY B-6***
Lake Bluff Campground — ***WOLCOTT D-5***
Lake Chalet Campground & Motel — ***BRIDGEWATER E-7***
Lake Durant (Adirondack SF) — ***BLUE MOUNTAIN LAKE C-8***
Lake Eaton Campground (Adirondack SF) — ***LONG LAKE C-8***
Lake Erie State Park — ***BROCTON F-1***
Lake George Battleground Campground (Adirondack SF) — ***LAKE GEORGE D-9***
Lake George Campsites (Morgan RV Resorts) — ***LAKE GEORGE D-9***
Lake George Escape Resort — *LAKE GEORGE D-9*
Lake George RV Park — *LAKE GEORGE D-9*
Lake George/Schroon Valley Resort — *WARRENSBURG D-9*
Lake Harris Campground (Adirondack SF) — ***LONG LAKE C-8***
Lake Lauderdale Campground — *CAMBRIDGE D-10*
Lake Taghkanic State Park — ***HUDSON F-9***
Lakeside Beach State Park — ***ALBION D-3***
Lakeside Campground — *WINDSOR F-7*
Lazy K RV Ranch — ***CLEVELAND D-6***
Lebanon Reservoir Campground — ***HAMILTON E-7***
Ledgeview RV Park — *LAKE GEORGE D-9*
LEI-TI Campground — ***BATAVIA E-3***
Letchworth State Park — ***MT. MORRIS E-3***
Lewey Lake Public Campground (Adirondack SF) — ***INDIAN LAKE C-8***
Limekiln Lake (Adirondack SF) — ***INLET C-8***
Lisbon Beach and Campground — ***OGDENSBURG B-7***
Little Pond Campground (Catskill SF) — ***LIVINGSTON MANOR F-8***
Little Sand Point (Adirondack SF) — ***LAKE PLEASANT D-8***
Locust Park — ***CENTRAL BRIDGE E-8***
Long Point State Park (Thousand Islands Region) — ***THREE MILE BAY C-6***
Luzerne Public Campground (Adirondack SF) — ***LAKE LUZERNE D-9***
Macomb Reservation State Park — ***SCHUYLER FALLS B-9***
Magic Pines Family Campground — ***LEWIS B-9***
Maple Lane Campground & RV Park — ***CUBA F-3***
Massena International Kampground — *MASSENA A-8*
Max V. Shaul State Park — ***MIDDLEBURGH E-8***
Mayfair Campground — ***SYLVAN BEACH D-6***
McConchies Heritage Acres — ***GALWAY D-9***
McLear's Cottage Colony & Campground — ***HAMMOND B-6***
Meacham Lake Campground (Adirondack SF) — ***DUANE B-8***
Meadow-Vale Campsites — ***COOPERSTOWN E-8***
Meadowbrook Campground (Adirondack SF) — ***SARANAC LAKE B-9***
Merry Knoll 1000 Islands Campground — ***CLAYTON B-6***
△ MILITARY CAMPGROUND (Round Pond Recreation Area-West Point USMA) — ***NEWBURGH A-2***
Mills-Norrie State Park — ***POUGHKEEPSIE A-2***
Moffitt Beach Campground (Adirondack SF) — ***LAKE PLEASANT D-8***
Mongaup Pond (Catskills SF) — ***LIVINGSTON MANOR F-8***
Moreau Lake State Park — ***GLENS FALLS D-9***
Mt. Kenyon Family Campground — *LAKE LUZERNE D-9*
• **New York City Tours - KOA-Newburgh/New York City North — *NEWBURGH A-2***
• **New York City Tours-Black Bear Campground — *FLORIDA B-2***
Niagara County Camping Resort — *LOCKPORT D-2*
Niagara Falls Campground — ***NIAGARA FALLS D-2***
Niagara Hartland RV Resort — ***GASPORT D-2***
Niagara Woodland Campground & RV Service Center — *RANSOMVILLE D-2*
★ **Niagara Woodland Service Center — *RANSOMVILLE D-2***
Niagara's Lazy Lakes Camping Resort — *NIAGARA FALLS D-2*
Nickerson Park Campground — *GILBOA F-8*
Nick's Lake Campground (Adirondack SF) — ***OLD FORGE C-7***
North Pole Camping Resort — *WILMINGTON B-9*
North/South Lake Campground (Catskills SF) — ***HAINES FALLS F-9***
Northampton Beach Campground (Adirondack SF) — ***NORTHVILLE D-9***
Oak Orchard Marina & Campground — *SENECA FALLS E-5*
Oakland Valley Campground — ***CUDDEBACKVILLE B-1***
Onoville Marina and Campground — ***STEAMBURG F-2***
Oquaga Creek State Park — ***BAINBRIDGE F-7***
Paradise Bay Park — ***FINDLEY LAKE F-1***
Paradise Park Campground — ***WATKINS GLEN F-5***
Paradox Lake Campground (Adirondack SF) — ***TICONDEROGA C-10***
Pine Crest Campground — ***WINDSOR F-7***
Pine Valley RV Park and Campground — ***ENDICOTT F-6***
Pinecreek Campground — *ITHACA F-5*
Pixley Falls State Park — ***BOONVILLE D-7***
Plattsburgh RV Park — ***PLATTSBURGH B-10***
Point Comfort Campground (Adirondack SF) — ***LAKE PLEASANT D-8***
Poke-O-Moonshine Campground (Adirondack SF) — ***KEESEVILLE B-10***
Pope Haven Campground — *RANDOLPH F-2*
Pop's Lake Campground — ***GALWAY D-9***
Port Henry Champ Beach Campground & RV Park — ***PORT HENRY C-10***
Putnam Pond Campsite (Adirondack SF) — ***TICONDEROGA C-10***
Rancho Pines — ***CHESTERTOWN C-9***
Red Rock Ponds RV Resort — *HOLLEY D-3*
Rip Van Winkle Campgrounds — *SAUGERTIES F-9*
★ **Rip Van Winkle RV Sales — *SAUGERTIES F-9***
River Road Campground — ***CORINTH D-9***
River View Campground — ***LAKE GEORGE D-9***

NEW YORK — Continued

Riverforest Park — ***WEEDSPORT D-5***
Riverside RV Camping — ***BAINBRIDGE F-7***
Robert H Treman State Park — ***ITHACA F-5***
Robert Moses State Park — ***MASSENA A-8***
Rogers Rock Campground (Adirondack SF) — ***TICONDEROGA C-10***
Rolling Acres Golf Course & Campground — ***PIKE E-3***
Rollins Pond Campground (Adirondack SF) — ***TUPPER LAKE B-8***
Rondout Valley Resort — *ACCORD A-2*
Royal Mountain Campsite — ***JOHNSTOWN E-8***
Russell Brook Campsite — ***ROSCOE F-8***
Sacandaga Campground (Adirondack SF) — ***NORTHVILLE D-9***
St. Johnsville Campsite & Marina (City Park) — ***ST. JOHNSVILLE E-8***
Sampson State Park — ***KENDAIA E-5***
Saratoga RV Park — ***GANSEVOORT D-9***
Schroon River Campsites — *WARRENSBURG D-9*
Sears Bellows (Suffolk County Park) — ***HAMPTON BAYS B-5***
Selkirk Shores State Park — ***PULASKI D-6***
Shady Oaks RV Park — ***PLATTSBURGH B-10***
Sharp Bridge Campground (Adirondack SF) — ***SCHROON LAKE C-9***
Singing Waters Campground — ***OLD FORGE C-7***
Skybrook Campground — ***DANSVILLE E-4***
Skyline Resort Campground — *DARIEN CENTER E-3*
★ **Skyline RV Sales & Service — *DARIEN CENTER E-3***
Skyway Camping Resort — *ELLENVILLE A-2*
★ **Skyway RV Sales — *ELLENVILLE A-2***
Sleepy Hollow Lake Campground — *AKRON E-2*
Smith Point Park (Suffolk County Park) — ***SHIRLEY C-4***
Sned-Acres Family Campground — ***OVID E-5***
So-Hi Campground — ***STONE RIDGE A-2***
Southhaven County Park — ***BROOKHAVEN C-4***
Southwick Beach State Park — ***WOODVILLE C-6***
Southwoods RV Resort — ***BYRON D-3***
Spruce Row Campground — ***ITHACA F-5***
Stony Brook State Park — ***DANSVILLE E-4***
Streamside RV Park & Golf Course — ***PULASKI D-6***
Sugar Creek Glen Campground — ***DANSVILLE E-4***
• **Sullivan County Visitors Association — *FERNDALE A-1***
Sun Valley Campsites — ***ARKPORT F-4***
Sunset RV Park — ***OSWEGO D-5***
Susquehanna Trail Campground — *ONEONTA E-7*
Ta-Ga-Soke Campgrounds — ***SYLVAN BEACH D-6***
Taconic SP (Copake Falls Area) — ***MILLERTON F-10***
Taconic SP (Rudd Pond) — ***MILLERTON F-10***
Tall Pines Riverfront Campground, Canoeing & Country Store — ***BAINBRIDGE F-7***
Taughannock Falls State Park — ***ITHACA F-5***
The Landing Campground — *SYLVAN BEACH D-6*
The Villages at Turning Stone RV Park — *VERONA D-7*
The Willows on the Lake RV Park & Resort — ***HENDERSON HARBOR C-6***
Thompson's Lake State Park — ***ALTAMONT E-9***
Timberline Lake Park — ***LE ROY E-3***
Treasure Isle RV Park — *SYLVAN BEACH D-6*
Triple R Camping Resort & Trailer Sales — ***FRANKLINVILLE F-3***
Tumble Hill Campground — *COHOCTON E-4*
• **Turning Stone Resort & Casino — *VERONA D-7***
Twin Ells Campsites — ***WEST CHAZY A-9***
Verona Beach State Park — ***ONEIDA D-7***
Warrensburg Travel Park — ***WARRENSBURG D-9***
Watkins Glen State Park — ***WATKINS GLEN F-5***
Wellesley Island State Park — ***ALEXANDRIA BAY B-6***
★ **W.E.S. Trailer Sales Inc. — *WADING RIVER B-4***
Wescott Beach State Park — ***SACKETS HARBOR C-6***
West Canada Creek Campsites — ***POLAND D-7***
Whetstone Gulf State Park — ***LOWVILLE C-7***
Whip-O-Will Campsite — ***ACRA F-9***
Whippoorwill Campground — ***LAKE GEORGE D-9***
Whispering Pines Campground — ***LAKE PLACID B-9***
Whispering Pines Campsites — ***SARATOGA SPRINGS D-9***
Wildwood State Park — ***WADING RIVER B-4***
Wilmington Notch Campground (Adirondack SF) — ***WILMINGTON B-9***
Winding Hills Park (Orange County Park) — ***MONTGOMERY A-2***
Woodland Hills Campground — *AUSTERLITZ F-10*
Woodland Valley Campground (Catskill SF) — ***PHOENICIA F-8***
Woodstream Campsite — *GAINESVILLE E-3*
Yellow Lantern Kampground — ***CORTLAND E-6***
Yogi Bear's Jellystone Park at Birchwood Acres — *ELLENVILLE A-2*
Yogi Bear's Jellystone Park at Crystal Lake — ***COOPERSTOWN E-8***
Yogi Bear's Jellystone Park at Paradise Pines — *NORTH HUDSON C-9*
Yogi Bear's Jellystone Park Camp Resort at Mexico — *MEXICO D-6*
Yogi Bear's Jellystone Park Camp-Resort at Lazy River — *GARDINER A-2*
Yogi Bear's Jellystone Park of Western New York — ***NORTH JAVA E-3***

NORTH CAROLINA

70 East Mobile Acres & RV Park — ***GARNER B-4***
Adventure Village & Lodgings — *BREVARD E-2*
Asheville East-KOA — *SWANNANOA E-2*
Asheville West KOA — ***CANDLER E-2***
Asheville-Bear Creek RV Park — *ASHEVILLE E-2*
Bandit's Roost Park (COE-W. Kerr Scott Reservoir) — ***WILKESBORO A-1***
Bass Lake — *SALISBURY B-2*
• **Battleship North Carolina — *WILMINGTON D-4***
Beachcomber Campground — ***OCRACOKE C-6***
Bear Den Campground — ***SPRUCE PINE D-3***
Birchwood RV Park — *DURHAM A-3*
Black Forest Family Camping Resort — *CEDAR MOUNTAIN E-2*
Blue Ridge National Parkway (Crabtree Meadows Campground) — ***LITTLE SWITZERLAND D-3***
Blue Ridge National Parkway (Doughton Park Campground) — ***SPARTA A-1***
Blue Ridge National Parkway (Julian Price Memorial Campground) — ***BLOWING ROCK A-1***
Blue Ridge National Parkway (Linville Falls Campground) — ***LINVILLE FALLS D-3***
Blue Ridge National Parkway (Mt. Pisgah) — ***ASHEVILLE E-2***
• **Buck Creek Driving Range — *MARION E-3***
Buck Creek RV Park Campground — *MARION E-3*
Cabin Creek Campground — *JACKSONVILLE C-5*
Camp Adventure Family Campground — ***LAKE JUNALUSKA E-2***
Camp Hatteras — *RODANTHE B-6*
Campfire Lodgings — *ASHEVILLE E-2*
Cane Creek Park (Union County Park) — ***MONROE C-2***
Cape Hatteras KOA — ***RODANTHE B-6***
Cape Hatteras National Seashore (Cape Point Campground) — ***BUXTON B-6***
Cape Hatteras National Seashore (Frisco Campground) — ***FRISCO B-6***
Cape Hatteras National Seashore (Ocracoke Campground) — ***OCRACOKE C-6***
Cape Hatteras National Seashore (Oregon Inlet Campground) — ***NAGS HEAD A-6***
Cape Pointe RV Park — *HARKERS ISLAND C-5*
Cape Woods Campground — *BUXTON B-6*
Cardinal Ridge Farm RV & B — *FRANKLIN E-1*
Carolina Beach State Park — ***CAROLINA BEACH D-4***
• **Carowinds — *CHARLOTTE B-2***
Carowinds Camp Wilderness Resort — *CHARLOTTE B-2*
Carrollwoods RV Park at Grapefull Sisters Vineyard — *TABOR CITY D-3*
Cartoogechaye Creek Campground — *FRANKLIN E-1*

NORTH CAROLINA — Continued

Cascade Lake Recreation Area — **PISGAH FOREST E-2**
Charlotte Motor Speedway Camping — CHARLOTTE B-2
Charlotte Motor Speedway Camping — CONCORD B-2
Cliffs of the Neuse State Park — **GOLDSBORO B-4**
Cooper's Mobile Home Park & RV's — CLAYTON B-4
Country Girl's RV Park — BRYSON CITY E-1
Country Woods RV Park — FRANKLIN E-1
□ **Crawford's Campground & Cabin Rentals — MURPHY E-1**
□ Creekwood Farm RV Park — **WAYNESVILLE E-2**
★ **Crisp RV Center — WASHINGTON B-5**
Croatan National Forest (Cedar Point Campground) — **SWANSBORO C-5**
Cross Country Campground — **DENVER B-1**
Cross Winds Family Campground — LEXINGTON B-2
★ **Daly RV — GOLDSBORO B-4**
□ Dan Nicholas Park (Rowan County Park) — **SALISBURY B-2**
Dan River Campground — **STONEVILLE A-2**
□ Deep Creek Tube Center & Campground — **BRYSON CITY E-1**
□ **Deep River Campground & RV Park — ASHEBORO B-2**
Down By The River Campground — **PINEOLA D-3**
®□ **Ela Campground — BRYSON CITY E-1**
Elmore Mobile Home & RV Park — CHARLOTTE B-2
● **Emerald Isle Wine Market — EMERALD ISLE C-5**
Falls Lake State Rec. Area (Holly Point Campground) — **RALEIGH B-4**
Falls Lake State Rec. Area (Rollingview Campground) — **RALEIGH B-4**
□ **Fayetteville KOA — WADE C-3**
Fayetteville Spring Valley Park — **HOPE MILLS C-3**
□ **Flintlock Campground — BOONE A-1**
®□ **Fort Wilderness Campground and RV Resort — CHEROKEE E-1**
Four Oaks RV Resort — FOUR OAKS B-4
®□ **Four Paws Kingdom — RUTHERFORDTON E-3**
Franklin RV Park & Campground — FRANKLIN E-1
□ **Frisco Woods Campground — FRISCO B-6**
□ **Ft. Tatham RV Park (Carefree RV Resort) — SYLVA E-2**
Goose Creek Resort Family Campground — **CAPE CARTERET C-5**
□ **Grandfather Campground — BANNER ELK A-1**
Great Smokey Mountain RV Camping Resort — CHEROKEE E-1
Great Smoky Mountains National Park (Balsam Mountain Campground) — **CHEROKEE E-1**
Great Smoky Mountains National Park (Cataloochee Campground) — **COVE CREEK E-2**
Great Smoky Mountains National Park (Deep Creek Campground) — **BRYSON CITY E-1**
Great Smoky Mountains National Park (Smokemont Campground) — **CHEROKEE E-1**
□ **Green Acres Family Campground — WILLIAMSTON B-5**
□ **Greensboro Campground — GREENSBORO A-2**
□ Hanging Rock State Park — **WALNUT COVE A-2**
□ Happy Holiday RV Village — **CHEROKEE E-1**
Hawkins Creek Campground — HUBERT C-5
□ High Rock Lake Marina & Campground — **LEXINGTON B-2**
Holiday Trav-L-Park Resort For Campers — EMERALD ISLE C-5
Holly Bluff Family Campground — ASHEBORO B-2
□ **Holly Ridge Family Campground — BOONVILLE A-2**
□ **Honey Bear Campground — BOONE A-1**
□ Hot Springs Campground & Suites — **HOT SPRINGS D-2**
Jaymar Travel Park — HENDERSONVILLE E-2
Jones Lake State Park — **ELIZABETHTOWN C-4**
Jordan Lake State Rec. Area (Crosswinds Campground) — **APEX B-3**
Jordan Lake State Rec. Area (Parkers Creek) — **APEX B-3**
Jordan Lake State Rec. Area (Poplar Point) — **APEX B-3**
Jordan Lake State Rec. Area (Vista Point) — **APEX B-3**
Kerr State Rec. Area (Bullocksville) — **HENDERSON A-4**
Kerr State Rec. Area (County Line Park) — **NORLINA A-4**
Kerr State Rec. Area (Henderson Point) — **HENDERSON A-4**
Kerr State Rec. Area (Hibernia) — **HENDERSON A-4**
Kerr State Rec. Area (Kimball Point Park) — **NORLINA A-4**
Kerr State Rec. Area (Nutbush Bridge) — **HENDERSON A-4**
□ Kerr State Rec. Area (Satterwhite Points) — **HENDERSON A-4**
KOA Shallotte/Brunswick Beaches — **SUNSET BEACH D-4**
□ **KOA-Boone — BOONE A-1**
□ KOA-Cherokee Great Smokies — **CHEROKEE E-1**
□ KOA-Enfield-Rocky Mt. — **ENFIELD A-4**
Lake James State Park — **MARION E-3**
□ Lake Myers RV Resort — **MOCKSVILLE B-2**
Lake Norman State Park — **STATESVILLE B-2**
Lake Reidsville Recreation Park (City Park) — **REIDSVILLE A-3**
Lake Waldo's Beach Campground — HOPE MILLS C-3
Lakewood RV Resort — HENDERSONVILLE E-2
Lanier's Campground — SURF CITY D-5
Lazy Acres Campground — FAYETTEVILLE C-3
□ **Linville Falls Trailer Lodge & Campground — LINVILLE FALLS D-3**
® **Long Leaf Pine Oasis — ABERDEEN C-3**
□ **Mama Gertie's Hideaway Campground — SWANNANOA E-2**
△□ McDowell Nature Preserve Campground — **CHARLOTTE B-2**
Merchants Millpond State Park — **GATESVILLE A-5**
Miles Motors RV Campground — **SWANNANOA E-2**
MILITARY PARK (Cherry Point MCAS Travel Camp) — **HAVELOCK C-5**
□ MILITARY PARK (Fort Bragg Travel Camp) — **FAYETTEVILLE C-3**
□ MILITARY PARK (Fort Fisher Air Force Rec. Area) — **KURE BEACH D-4**
MILITARY PARK (New River Rec. Area) — **JACKSONVILLE C-5**
MILITARY PARK (Onslow Beach Recreation Area-Camp Lejeune MCB) — **JACKSONVILLE C-5**
□ **Moonshine Creek Campground — BALSAM E-2**
□ Morrow Mountain State Park — **ALBEMARLE B-2**
Mountain Stream RV Park — MARION E-3
Nantahala National Forest (Cable Cove Campground) — **FONTANA VILLAGE E-1**
Nantahala National Forest (Cheoah Point Rec. Area) — **ROBBINSVILLE E-1**
Nantahala National Forest (Hanging Dog Campground) — **MURPHY E-1**
Nantahala National Forest (Jackrabbit Mountain Campground) — **HAYESVILLE E-1**
Nantahala National Forest (Standing Indian Campground) — **FRANKLIN E-1**
Nantahala National Forest (Tsali Recreational Area) — **ALMOND E-1**
□ NASCAR RV Resorts at Stonebridge — **MAGGIE VALLEY E-2**
□ New Bern KOA — **NEW BERN C-5**
□ **North River Campground & RV Park — SHILOH A-6**
Oak Hollow Family Campground — HIGH POINT B-2
Ocean Waves Campground — RODANTHE B-6
□ **Orchard Lake Campground & RV Park — SALUDA E-2**
● **Outer Banks Visitors Bureau — MANTEO A-6**
□ Peace Valley KOA at Murphy — **MURPHY E-1**
Pilot Mountain State Park — **PINNACLE A-2**
®□ **Pine Lake RV Resort — ABERDEEN C-3**
□ **Pines RV Park — FRANKLIN E-1**
Pisgah Nantahala National Forest (Carolina Hemlock Park) — **MICAVILLE D-2**
Pisgah National Forest (Black Mountain Campground) — **MICAVILLE D-2**
Pisgah National Forest (Davidson River Campground) — **BREVARD E-2**
Pisgah National Forest (Lake Powhatan Rec. Area) — **ASHEVILLE E-2**
Pisgah National Forest (North Mills River Rec. Area) — **ASHEVILLE E-2**
Pisgah National Forest (Rocky Bluff Campground) — **HOT SPRINGS D-2**
□ **Pride RV Resort — WAYNESVILLE E-2**
® **Raccoon Holler Campground — GLENDALE SPRINGS A-1**
□ **River Vista Mountain Village — FRANKLIN E-1**
□ **RiverCamp USA RV Park & Campground — PINEY CREEK A-1**
Rivers Edge Mountain RV Resort — MURPHY E-1
Rocky Hock Campground — EDENTON A-5
®□ **Rutledge Lake RV Park — FLETCHER E-2**
RVacation Campground — SELMA B-4
□ **Sands of Time Campground — AVON B-6**
®□ **Sleepy Bear's RV Park — LUMBERTON C-3**
□ Smithfield KOA — **FOUR OAKS B-4**
Spring Hill Park — CHAPEL HILL B-3
□ Statesville East I-40/Winston Salem KOA — **STATESVILLE B-2**
□ Statesville/I-77 KOA — **STATESVILLE B-2**
□ **Steele Creek Park — MORGANTON B-1**
Stone Mountain State Park — **ROARING GAP A-1**
Taps RV Park — **ASHEVILLE E-2**
The Campground at Tom Johnson Camping Center — MARION E-3
The Great Outdoors RV Resort — **FRANKLIN E-1**
The Refuge — MANTEO A-6
The RV Resort at Carolina Crossroads — ROANOKE RAPIDS A-4
Timberlake Campground — CHEROKEE E-1
★ **Tom Johnson Camping Center — CONCORD B-2**
★ **Tom Johnson Camping Center — MARION E-3**
Trails End Family Camping — ASHEBORO B-2
Trails End RV Park — WAYNESVILLE E-2
△□ **Tranter's Creek Resort & Campground — WASHINGTON B-5**
Tuckaseegee R.V. Resort — WHITTIER E-1
®□ Tumbling Waters Campground — **ALMOND E-1**
□ Twin Lakes Camping Resort and Yacht Basin — **WASHINGTON B-5**
® Twin Ponds RV Park — **HENDERSONVILLE E-2**
Twin Rivers Family Campground — **CRUMPLER A-1**
□ Van Hoy Farms Family Campground — **UNION GROVE A-2**
Vanderpool Campground — VILAS A-1
Warrior Creek Park (COE-W. Kerr Scott Reservoir) — **WILKESBORO A-1**
Whispering Pines RV Park — MOREHEAD CITY C-5
White Oak Shores Camping & RV Resort — **STELLA C-5**
Wildlife Woods Campground — **TERRELL B-1**
William B Umstead State Park — **RALEIGH B-4**
□ Wilmington KOA — **WILMINGTON D-4**
□ Winngray Family Campground — **WAYNESVILLE E-2**
□ **Yogi Bear's Jellystone Park at Daddy Joe's — TABOR CITY D-3**
□ Yogi Bear's Jellystone Park Camp Resort — **MARION E-3**
□ Yogi in the Smokies — **CHEROKEE E-1**

OHIO

® A1 Twin Valley Campground — **CARROLLTON C-5**
□ **ABC Country Camping & Cabins — CARROLLTON C-5**
Alton RV Park — COLUMBUS D-3
□ Alum Creek State Park — **DELAWARE C-3**
□ **American Wilderness Campground — CLEVELAND B-4**
□ **American Wilderness Campground — GRAFTON B-4**
Amish Country Campsites — WINESBURG C-4
Archway Campground — **NEW PARIS D-1**
®□ **Arrowhead Campground — NEW PARIS D-1**
□ Atwood Lake Park (Muskingum Watershed Conservancy Dist) — **MINERAL CITY C-4**
Auburn Lake Park — **NEW WASHINGTON B-3**
Austin Lake Park and Campground — TORONTO C-5
□ Autumn Lakes Family Campground — **SUNBURY C-3**
A.W. Marion State Park — **CIRCLEVILLE D-3**
□ **Back Forty Ltd — BELLEFONTAINE C-2**
△□ Barkcamp State Park — **BELMONT D-5**
□ Bay Shore Resort — **ANDOVER B-5**
Baylor Beach Park — WILMOT C-4
● **Baylor Beach Water Park — WILMOT C-4**
Beaver Creek State Park — **EAST LIVERPOOL C-5**
□ **Beaver Valley Resort — SPRINGFIELD D-2**
□ **Beechwood Acres Camping Resort — WILMINGTON E-2**
Berkshire Lake Campgrounds — GALENA C-3
□ Big Sandy Toledo/Maumee Campground — **SWANTON B-2**
△□ Blue Rock State Park — **DUNCAN FALLS D-4**
Buccaneer Campsites — **ASHTABULA A-5**
□ Buck Creek State Park — **SPRINGFIELD D-2**
□ **Buckeye Lake/Columbus East KOA Kamping Resort — BUCKEYE LAKE D-3**
△□ Burr Oak State Park — **GLOUSTER D-4**
®□ Caesar Creek State Park — **WAYNESVILLE D-1**
□ **Camp Toodik Family Campground Cabins & Canoeing — LOUDONVILLE C-3**
□ **Cardinal Center Campground — MARENGO C-3**
Carthage Gap Campground — **COOLVILLE E-4**
□ **Cedar Point Camper Village/Lighthouse Point — SANDUSKY B-3**
□ Cedarbrook Campground — **LEBANON E-1**
®□ **Cedarlane RV Park — PORT CLINTON B-3**
Chaparral Family Campground — **SALEM C-5**
□ Charles Mill Lake Park (Muskingum Watershed Conservancy Dist) — **MANSFIELD C-3**
Cherokee Park Campground — AKRON B-4
Chestnut Ridge Park & Campground — **HUBBARD B-5**
□ Chet's Place — **PORT CLINTON B-3**
® Clare-Mar Lakes Campground — **WELLINGTON B-3**
□ **Clay's Park Resort — CANAL FULTON C-4**
● **Clearwater Park — UNIONTOWN B-4**
® **Clearwater Park Camping Resort — UNIONTOWN B-4**
□ Clendening Marina (Muskingum Watershed Conservancy Dist) — **FREEPORT C-5**
Clinton Lake Camping — REPUBLIC B-3
Cottonwood Lakes — **VERSAILLES C-1**
®□ **Country Acres Campground — RAVENNA B-5**
□ **Country Lakes Family Campground — MONTVILLE B-5**
Country Stage Campground — **NOVA B-3**
® **Countryside Campground — AKRON B-4**
□ Cowan Lake State Park — **WILMINGTON E-2**
Cozy Ridge Campground — CARROLLTON C-5
®□ **Cross Creek Camping Resort — COLUMBUS D-3**
□ Crystal Rock Campground — **SANDUSKY B-3**
Cutty's Sunset Camping Resort — LOUISVILLE C-5
★ **Cutty's Sunset RV Service — LOUISVILLE C-5**
△□ Deer Creek State Park — **MOUNT STERLING D-2**
Delaware State Park — **DELAWARE C-3**
□ Dillon State Park — **ZANESVILLE D-4**
® **Dogwood Valley Camping Resort — MOUNT GILEAD C-3**
Eagle Creek Marina (COE) — **RIPLEY E-2**
□ East Fork State Park — **BATAVIA E-1**
®□ East Harbor State Park — **PORT CLINTON B-3**
Easy Campground — **ST. MARYS C-1**
□ **Enon Beach Campground — ENON D-2**
□ **Evergreen Lake Park — CONNEAUT A-5**
★ **Evergreen Lake RV Sales — CONNEAUT A-5**
□ **Evergreen Park RV Resort — MT. EATON C-4**
□ **Findlay/Van Buren KOA — VAN BUREN B-2**
□ Findley State Park — **WELLINGTON B-3**
® Flying Finn Campground — **UNITY C-5**
△□ Forked Run State Park — **REEDSVILLE E-4**
Friendship Acres Park, Inc. — **RANDOLPH B-5**
□ Geneva State Park — **GENEVA A-5**
△□ Grand Lake St. Mary's State Park — **ST. MARYS C-1**
Great Seal State Park — **CHILLICOTHE E-3**
Green Acres Lake Park Resort — **LAKE MILTON B-5**
Guilford Lake State Park — **LISBON C-5**
● **Hamilton County Park District — CINCINNATI E-1**
□ Happy Hills Campground & Cabins — **NELSONVILLE D-4**
□ Harrison Lake State Park — **FAYETTE B-1**
Heritage Hills Family Campground — THOMPSON A-5
Heritage Springs Campground — VANLUE B-2
● **Hickey's Barber Shop — CINCINNATI E-1**
® **Hickory Grove Lake Campground — MARION C-2**
□ **Hickory Lakes Campground — ASHLAND C-3**
Hidden Hill Campground — **NEWARK D-3**
Hidden Lakes Community Assoc. — **MOUNT GILEAD C-3**
Hidden Valley Mobile Home Park — CINCINNATI E-1
Hide-A-Way Lakes Campground — **ASHTABULA A-5**
□ Hillview Acres Campground — **CAMBRIDGE D-4**
®□ **Hocking Hills KOA — LOGAN D-3**
□ Hocking Hills State Park (Old Man's Cave) — **LOGAN D-3**
Honey-Do Campground — **CHATHAM B-4**
® Hubbard's Haven Family Campground — **HUBBARD B-5**
□ Hueston Woods State Park — **OXFORD D-1**

OHIO — Continued

□ Huggy Bear Campground — **VAN WERT C-1**
Huron River Valley Campground & Marina — HURON B-3
★ Hy-Tek Truck & Auto Center, LTD — **NORWALK B-3**
Independence Dam State Park — **DEFIANCE B-1**
Indian Creek Camping Resort (Morgan RV Resorts) — **GENEVA-ON-THE-LAKE A-5**
□ Indian Lake State Park — **LAKEVIEW C-2**
Indian Springs Campground — CINCINNATI E-1
□ Indian Trail Campground — **FITCHVILLE B-3**
□ Jackson Lake Park — **CANAL WINCHESTER D-3**
Jackson Lake State Park — **OAK HILL E-3**
John Bryan State Park — **YELLOW SPRINGS D-2**
□ Kamp Kozy — **MARBLEHEAD B-3**
△ Kelleys Island State Park (Lake Erie Islands SP) — **PORT CLINTON B-3**
Kenisee's Grand River Camp & Canoe — **GENEVA A-5**
□ Kiser Lake State Park — **ROSEWOOD D-2**
□ **KOA-Bear Creek Resort Ranch — CANTON C-4**
□ KOA-Butler/Mohican — **BUTLER C-3**
□ **KOA-Dayton Tall Timbers Resort — BROOKVILLE D-1**
Kokosing Valley Camp & Canoe — **HOWARD C-3**
□ Kool Lakes Family Campground — **PARKMAN B-5**
®□ **Kountry Resort — RACINE E-4**
Kozy Kamp Ground — CELINA C-1
□ Lake Alma State Park — **WELLSTON E-3**
△□ Lake Hope State Park — **ZALESKI E-3**
△ Lake Loramie State Park — **FORT LORAMIE C-1**
Lake Park Recreation Area (County Park) — **COSHOCTON C-4**
Lake Snowden Educational and Recreation Park — **ALBANY E-4**
□ Lake Timberlin Camp Resort — **BELLVILLE C-3**
®□ Lake Wapusun Campground — **LOUDONVILLE C-3**
Lakeview RV Park — **LANCASTER D-3**
Lancaster RV Camp Ground — **LANCASTER D-3**
□ Lazy Dog Camp Resort — **JACKSON E-3**
□ **Lazy J RV Resort — BELLEVUE B-3**
□ **Lazy River at Granville — NEWARK D-3**
□ Lazy River Resort Campground — **PIONEER B-1**
□ Lazy Village Campground & RV Park — **PORTSMOUTH E-3**
□ **Leafy Oaks Campground — CLYDE B-3**
Lock 30 Woodlands RV Resort — **LISBON C-5**
□ Long's Retreat Family Resort — **SINKING SPRING E-2**
Loveberry's Funny Farm Campground — PIONEER B-1
Malabar Farm State Park — **MANSFIELD C-3**
® **Maple Lakes Recreational Park — SEVILLE B-4**
□ Mary Jane Thurston State Park — **GRAND RAPIDS B-2**
△□ Maumee Bay State Park — **OREGON B-2**
Meadow Lake Park — **WOOSTER C-4**
Miami Whitewater Forest Campground (Hamilton County Park) — CINCINNATI E-1
Middle Bass Island State Park — **PORT CLINTON B-3**
®□ Milan Travel Park — **MILAN B-3**
®△ MILITARY PARK (Wright-Patterson AFB FAMCAMP) — **DAYTON D-1**
Mill Creek Recreation Area (COE - Berlin Reservoir) — **DEERFIELD B-5**
□ **Millbrook Outdoor Resort (Formerly Wagon Trail Resort) — JEFFERSON A-5**
®□ **Mohican Adventures Camp and Cabins — LOUDONVILLE C-3**
● **Mohican Adventures Canoe & Fun Center — LOUDONVILLE C-3**
△□ **Mohican Reservation Campgrounds and Canoeing — LOUDONVILLE C-3**
★ Mohican RV Center — **LOUDONVILLE C-3**
□ Mohican State Park — **LOUDONVILLE C-3**
□ Mohican Wilderness — **LOUDONVILLE C-3**
Mosquito Lake State Park — **CORTLAND B-5**
△□ Mt. Gilead State Park — **MOUNT GILEAD C-3**
Muskingum River Parkway State Park — **ZANESVILLE D-4**
□ National Road Campground — **ZANESVILLE D-4**
®□ **Natural Springs Resort — NEW PARIS D-1**
New London Village Reservoir Park — **NEW LONDON B-3**
Oak Crest Campground — **WEST LIBERTY C-2**
● **Ohio Department of Natural Resources (Div. of Parks & Rec.) — COLUMBUS D-3**
□ **Ohio State Eagles Family Recreation Park — BELLEFONTAINE C-2**
● **Ole Farmstead Inn — MARENGO C-3**
△□ Paint Creek State Park — **BAINBRIDGE E-2**
Paradise Lake Park — **EAST ROCHESTER C-5**
Paradise Lakes Family Campground — **BRISTOLVILLE B-5**
□ Petersburg Marina (Muskingum Conservancy District) — **CARROLLTON C-5**
□ **Philabaun's Hidden Cove Resort — DEERFIELD B-5**
Piedmont Marina (Muskingum Watershed Conservancy Dist) — **SMYRNA D-5**
Pier-Lon Park — **MEDINA B-4**
□ Pike Lake State Park — **BAINBRIDGE E-2**
Pine Lakes Campground — **ORWELL B-5**
□ Pleasant Hill Lake Park (Muskingum Watershed Conservancy Dist) — **PERRYSVILLE C-3**
Portage Lakes State Park — **AKRON B-4**
★ **Post's Traveland — COLUMBUS D-3**
□ Punderson State Park — **NEWBURY B-5**
□ Pymatuning State Park — **ANDOVER B-5**
®□ **Ridge Ranch Campground — NEWTON FALLS B-5**
Rippling Stream Campground — **BALTIMORE D-3**
River Bend Family Campground — **MARION C-2**
River Run Family Campground & Canoe Livery — **LOUDONVILLE C-3**
River Trail Crossing RV Park — **BUTLER C-3**
Rocky Fork State Park — **HILLSBORO E-2**
□ **Rustic Knolls Campground — MOUNT VERNON C-3**
Rustic Lakes Campgrounds Inc. — **SULLIVAN B-4**
★ **RV Wholesalers — LAKEVIEW C-2**
□ St. Hazards Village (Not Visited) — **PORT CLINTON B-3**
△□ Salt Fork State Park — **CAMBRIDGE D-4**
® **Sandusky Bayshore KOA — SANDUSKY B-3**
● **Sauder Village — ARCHBOLD B-1**
Sauder Village Campground — ARCHBOLD B-1
Scenic Hills RV Park — BERLIN C-4
Schaun Acres Campground — **OBERLIN B-3**
□ Scioto Trail State Park — **CHILLICOTHE E-3**
□ Seneca Lake Park (Muskingum Watershed Conservancy Dist) — **SENECAVILLE D-4**
Seneca Marina Point (Muskingum Watershed Conservancy Dist) — **SENECAVILLE D-4**
®□ Shade Acres Campground & Cottages — **PORT CLINTON B-3**
△□ Shawnee State Park — **PORTSMOUTH E-3**
□ **Shelby/Mansfield KOA (Wagon Wheel Campground) — SHELBY C-3**
□ Smith's Pleasant Valley Campground & Cabins — **LOUDONVILLE C-3**
□ South Bass Island State Park (Lake Erie Islands SP) — **PORT CLINTON B-3**
□ **Spring Valley Campground — CAMBRIDGE D-4**
Steamboat Bend (Hamilton County Park) — CINCINNATI E-1
△□ Stonelick State Park — **BLANCHESTER E-2**
□ **Streetsboro/Cleveland SE KOA (Mar-Lynn lake Park) — STREETSBORO B-4**
△□ Strouds Run State Park — **ATHENS E-4**
Sun Valley Campground — CHILLICOTHE E-3
Sun Valley Family Campground — **LIMA C-1**
Sunny's Campground — WAUSEON B-1
Sunset Lake Campground — **SPENCER B-4**
Surf Motel & RV Campground — MARBLEHEAD B-3
® **Tall Timbers Campground — PORT CLINTON B-3**
□ Tappan Lake Park (Muskingum Watershed Conservancy Dist) — **CADIZ C-5**
Tar Hollow State Park — **LAURELVILLE D-3**
®□ Terrace Lakes — **ROGERS C-5**
Timashamie Family Campground — **SALEM C-5**
Timberwoods Camping Resort — VAN WERT C-1
□ Toledo East/Stony Ridge KOA — **STONY RIDGE B-2**

ALPHABETICAL LISTINGS CONTINUED

OHIO — Continued

Tomorrow's Stars RV Resort — *SPRINGFIELD D-2*
Town & Country Camp Resort — *WEST SALEM B-4*
Tree Haven Campground — ***WESTERVILLE D-3***
Twin Acres Campground — ***WHITEHOUSE B-2***
□ Twin Lakes Park — ***BLUFFTON C-2***
Valley Lake Park — ***WARREN B-5***
Van Buren State Park — ***VAN BUREN B-2***
Village Green Campground (City Park) — ***NORTH KINGSVILLE A-5***
Wally World Camping Resort — *LOUDONVILLE C-3*
□ **Walnut Grove Campground — *TIFFIN B-2***
□ **Wapakoneta/Lima South - KOA — *WAPAKONETA C-1***
Washington County Fair Park — ***MARIETTA D-4***
Wayne National Forest (Iron Ridge Campground) — ***PEDRO F-3***
Wayne National Forest (Lake Vesuvius Campground) — ***IRONTON F-3***
West Branch State Park — ***RAVENNA B-5***
□ Whispering Hills Family Campground — ***SHREVE C-4***
□ **Wild Wood Lakes Campground — *HOMERVILLE B-4***
Wildwood Acres Family Campground — ***ANDOVER B-5***
® Willow Lake Park — ***CHAMPION B-5***
Willow Lake Park Inc. — *BRUNSWICK B-4*
Windy Hill Golf Course & Campground — *CONNEAUT A-5*
Winona Lake Campground — ***LIMA C-1***
□ **Winton Woods Campground (Hamilton County Park) — *CINCINNATI E-1***
Wolf Run State Park — ***CALDWELL D-4***
®□ **Wolfies Campground — *ZANESVILLE D-4***
Wolford's Landing Campground — *PORTSMOUTH E-3*
Woodbridge Campground — ***PAULDING B-1***
□ **Wood's Tall Timber Lake Resort — *NEW PHILADELPHIA C-4***
□ **Woodside Lake Park — *STREETSBORO B-4***
®□ Yogi Bear's Jellystone Park (Morgan RV Resorts) — ***AURORA B-4***

PENNSYLVANIA

764 Campground — ***DUNCANSVILLE D-4***
□ Adventure Bound Camping Resort at Eagles Peak — ***ROBESONIA D-8***
● **Adventure Golf at Granite Hill — *GETTYSBURG F-6***
Allegheny National Forest (Beaver Meadows Campground) — ***MARIENVILLE B-3***
Allegheny National Forest (Buckaloons Campground) — ***WARREN B-3***
Allegheny National Forest (Dewdrop Campground) — ***WARREN B-3***
Allegheny National Forest (Hearts Content Campground) — ***WARREN B-3***
Allegheny National Forest (Kiasutha Campground) — ***KANE B-4***
Allegheny National Forest (Loleta Campground) — ***MARIENVILLE B-3***
Allegheny National Forest (Red Bridge Campground) — ***KANE B-4***
Allegheny National Forest (Tracy Ridge Campground) — ***BRADFORD A-4***
Allegheny National Forest (Twin Lakes Campground) — ***KANE B-4***
● **Allegheny National Forest Vacation Bureau — *KANE B-4***
Allegheny National Forest (Willow Bay Campground) — ***BRADFORD A-4***
□ Allegheny River Campground — ***COUDERSPORT B-5***
®□ **Appalachian Campsites — *SHARTLESVILLE D-8***
®□ **Artillery Ridge Camping Resort — *GETTYSBURG F-6***
®□ **Austin Campground — *AUSTIN B-5***
Bald Eagle State Park (Russel P. Letterman Campground) — ***HOWARD C-5***
● **Barnwell Cafe' — *KNOX C-2***
□ **Beacon Hill Camping — *INTERCOURSE E-8***
®□ **Bear Run Campground — *PORTERSVILLE C-1***
● **Bear Run Campground Canoe Rental — *PORTERSVILLE C-1***
□ Beaver Valley Family Campground — ***OTTSVILLE D-10***
● **Bedford County Conference & Visitors Bureau — *BEDFORD E-4***
Ben Franklin RV Park — *YORK E-7*
□ Benner's Meadow Run Camping & Cabins — ***FARMINGTON F-2***
□ Birchview Farm Campground — ***COATESVILLE E-8***
□ Black Moshannon State Park — ***PHILIPSBURG C-4***
Blue Knob State Park — ***PAVIA E-4***
□ Blue Ridge Campground — ***ASHFIELD D-9***
®□ **Blue Rocks Family Campground — *LENHARTSVILLE D-8***
Bluefalls Grove Waterpark & Campground — ***READING D-8***
® Boulder Woods Campground — ***GREEN LANE D-9***
★ **Boyer RV Center — *ERIE A-1***
□ **Brookdale Family Campground — *MEADVILLE C-2***
®□ Bucktail Camping Resort — ***MANSFIELD B-6***
□ Buttercup Woodlands Campground — ***BUTLER C-2***
®□ Buttonwood Campground — ***MEXICO D-6***
□ Caledonia State Park — ***CALEDONIA E-6***
Camp Eriez Campground — *LAKE CITY A-1*
Camp-A-While Inc — ***HEGINS D-7***
□ Campers Paradise Campground & Cabins — ***SIGEL C-3***
□ **Canyon Country Campground — *WELLSBORO B-6***
Cayman Landing at Treasure Lake — ***DU BOIS C-4***
® **Cedar Lake Campground — *DOVER E-7***
□ Chapman State Park — ***CLARENDON B-3***
□ Cherry Ridge Campsites & Lodging — ***HONESDALE B-9***
Cherry Springs State Park — ***COUDERSPORT B-5***
Chestnut Lake Campground — ***BRODHEADSVILLE C-9***
® **Choice Camping Court — *BEDFORD E-4***
□ Christmas Pines Campground — ***AUBURN D-8***
Circle M - Outdoor World — *LANCASTER E-8*
® **Clayton Park Recreation Area — *MT. COBB B-9***
□ Clear Creek State Park — ***SIGEL C-3***
® **Clearview Campground — *DU BOIS C-4***
Codorus State Park — ***HANOVER F-7***
Colonel Denning State Park — ***NEWVILLE E-6***
®□ **Colonial Woods Family Camping Resort — *REVERE D-10***
Colton Point State Park — ***WELLSBORO B-6***
® Conewago Isle Campground — ***EAST BERLIN E-7***
□ **Country Acres Campground — *LANCASTER E-8***
Country Haven Campground — *NEW HOLLAND E-8*
®□ **Countryside Family Campground — *HONESDALE B-9***
□ Cowans Gap State Park — ***FORT LOUDON E-5***
Crawford's Camping Park — ***DARLINGTON D-1***
Creekside Campground — ***NORTH EAST A-2***
★ **Dale Smith's Camper Sales — *BROOKVILLE C-3***
Day's End Campground — ***MESHOPPEN B-8***
Deer Meadow Campground — *COOK FOREST C-3*
□ Deer Run Campgrounds — ***CARLISLE E-6***
Deihl's Camping Resort, Inc — ***BLOOMSBURG C-7***
®□ **Delaware Water Gap/Pocono Mt. KOA — *STROUDSBURG C-9***
®□ **Dogwood Acres Campground — *CARLISLE E-6***
Don Laine Campground — *PALMERTON D-9*
Donegal Campground — ***DONEGAL E-3***
Driftstone on the Delaware — *MOUNT BETHEL C-10*
□ Drummer Boy Camping Resort — ***GETTYSBURG F-6***
Dusty Rhodes Mobile Home Village — *NORTH HUNTINGDON E-2*
□ **Dutch Cousin Campground — *ADAMSTOWN E-8***
®□ **Echo Valley Campground — *RAVINE D-7***
®□ Elizabethtown/Hershey KOA — ***ELIZABETHTOWN E-7***
Evergreen Lake Campground — *BATH D-9*
Family Affair Campground — ***NORTH EAST A-2***
□ **Fantasy Island Campground — *SUNBURY D-7***
□ Farma Family Campground — ***GREENVILLE B-1***
□ Ferryboat Campsites — ***LIVERPOOL D-6***
Firehouse RV Campground — ***JEFFERSON E-1***
®□ **Flory's Cottages & Camping — *LANCASTER E-8***
Folly's End Campground — ***GIRARD A-1***
®□ **Forest Ridge Campground (Not Visited) — *MARIENVILLE B-3***
Four Seasons Campgrounds — ***SCOTRUN C-9***
Fox Den Acres Campground — *NEW STANTON E-2*
®□ Foxwood Family Campground — ***STROUDSBURG C-9***
Frances Slocum State Park — ***WILKES-BARRE C-8***
□ French Creek State Park — ***ELVERSON E-9***
□ **Friendship Village Campground & RV Park — *BEDFORD E-4***
● **Gettysburg Bluegrass Festival — *GETTYSBURG F-6***
□ **Gettysburg Campground — *GETTYSBURG F-6***
Gettysburg Farm - Outdoor World — *DOVER E-7*

PENNSYLVANIA — Continued

□ Gifford Pinchot State Park — ***ROSSVILLE E-7***
®□ Goddard Park Vacationland Campground — ***SANDY LAKE C-1***
□ **Granite Hill Camping Resort — *GETTYSBURG F-6***
Greenwood Furnace State Park — ***BELLEVILLE D-5***
Gretna Oaks Camping — ***MANHEIM E-8***
□ Happy Acres Resort — ***WATERVILLE C-6***
®□ Harecreek Campground — ***CORRY A-2***
Harrisburg East Campground — ***HARRISBURG E-7***
Harts Content Campground — ***BEAVER FALLS D-1***
□ **Hemlock Campground & Cottages — *TOBYHANNA C-9***
®□ Hemlock Hideaway Campground — ***ENTRIKEN D-5***
□ **Heritage Cove Resort — *BEDFORD E-4***
□ **Hershey Conewago Campground — *ELIZABETHTOWN E-7***
®□ **Hershey Highmeadow Campground — *HERSHEY E-7***
Hershey-Thousand Trails — *LEBANON E-7*
Hershey's Fur Center Camping Area (Not Visited) — ***YORK SPRINGS E-6***
□ **Hickory Hollow Campground — *SOMERSET E-3***
□ Hickory Run Family Camping Resort — ***DENVER E-8***
Hickory Run State Park — ***WHITE HAVEN C-8***
Hidden Acres Camping Grounds — *COATESVILLE E-8*
□ Hidden Valley Camping Resort — ***LEWISBURG C-7***
□ Hills Creek State Park — ***WELLSBORO B-6***
®□ **Hill's Family Campground — *ERIE A-1***
®□ Holiday Pines Campground — ***LOGANTON C-6***
Homestead Campground — *QUAKERTOWN D-9*
Huntingdon Fairgrounds Campground — ***HUNTINGDON D-5***
□ Hyner Run State Park — ***RENOVO C-5***
□ Indian Brave Campground — ***HARMONY***
Indian Head Recreational Campgrounds — *BLOOMSBURG C-7*
Indian Rock Campground — ***YORK E-7***
Ironwood Point Recreation Area (PPL) — ***GREENTOWN C-9***
Ives Run Recreation Area (COE-Hammond Lake) — ***TIOGA A-6***
J and D Campground — ***CATAWISSA C-7***
□ **Jim Thorpe Camping Resort — *JIM THORPE C-9***
□ Kalyumet Camping & Cabins — ***COOK FOREST C-3***
®□ **Keen Lake Camping & Cottage Resort — *WAYMART B-9***
®□ **Kenshire Campground — *GAINES B-6***
Kettle Creek State Park — ***RENOVO C-5***
Keystone RV Campground — ***GREENCASTLE F-5***
□ Keystone State Park — ***NEW ALEXANDRIA D-2***
□ Knoebels Grove Campground — ***ELYSBURG D-7***
□ Knoebels Lake Glory Campground — ***CATAWISSA C-7***
□ **KOA-Allentown-Lehigh Valley Kampground — *ALLENTOWN D-9***
□ **KOA-Bellefonte/State College — *BELLEFONTE C-5***
®□ **KOA-Erie — *ERIE A-1***
□ KOA-Gettysburg — ***GETTYSBURG F-6***
□ **KOA-Jonestown — *JONESTOWN D-7***
®□ KOA-Madison/Pittsburgh — ***NEW STANTON E-2***
□ KOA-Mercer/Grove City — ***MERCER C-1***
□ KOA-Philadelphia/West Chester — ***WEST CHESTER E-9***
□ KOA-Washington — ***WASHINGTON E-1***
□ Kooser State Park — ***DONEGAL E-3***
□ **Kozy Rest Kampground — *GROVE CITY C-1***
Lackawanna State Park — ***EAST BENTON B-9***
®□ **Lake In Wood Resort — *BOWMANSVILLE E-8***
□ Lake Raystown Resort and Lodge — ***ENTRIKEN D-5***
Lampe Marina Campground — *ERIE A-1*
Laurel Highlands Campland — *DONEGAL E-3*
△□ Laurel Hill State Park — ***SOMERSET E-3***
Laurel Lake Campsites — ***NEW RINGGOLD D-8***
® **Lazy-K Campground — *BOYERTOWN E-9***
Ledgedale Recreation Area (PPL) — ***GREENTOWN C-9***
Lehigh Gorge Campground — *WHITE HAVEN C-8*
★ **Lehigh Gorge RV Center — *WHITE HAVEN C-8***
Leonard Harrison State Park — ***WELLSBORO B-6***
□ **Lickdale Campground — *LICKDALE D-7***
● **Lickdale Campground & Canoe Rentals — *LICKDALE D-7***
®□ Little Buffalo Family Camping — ***NEWPORT D-6***
®□ **Little Mexico Campground — *LEWISBURG C-7***
□ Little Pine State Park — ***WATERVILLE C-6***
Little Red Barn Campgrounds, LLC — ***QUAKERTOWN D-9***
Locust Lake State Park — ***MAHANOY CITY D-8***
Lyman Run State Park — ***GALETON B-5***
® Mallards Landing Family Campground — ***LINESVILLE B-1***
★ **Mellott Brothers Trailer Sales — *LANCASTER E-8***
Merritt Pond Campground — ***BEDFORD E-4***
● **Mill Bridge Village — *LANCASTER E-8***
□ **Mill Bridge Village & Campresort — *LANCASTER E-8***
®□ Milton Loop Campground — ***DAYTON C-3***
Montrose Campsites — ***NEW MILFORD B-9***
® Mount Pocono Campground — ***MOUNT POCONO C-9***
®□ **Mountain Creek Campground — *CARLISLE E-6***
□ Mountain Pines RV Resort (Morgan Rv Resorts) — ***CHAMPION E-3***
□ Mountain Springs Camping Resort — ***SHARTLESVILLE D-8***
Mountain Top Campground — *TARENTUM D-2*
□ **Mountain Vista Campground — *STROUDSBURG C-9***
®□ Moyer's Grove Campground — ***HOBBIE C-8***
Mt. Morris Travel Trailer Park — ***MOUNT MORRIS F-1***
Muddy Run Recreation Park (Exelon Energy) — ***HOLTWOOD F-8***
● **National Riding Stables — *GETTYSBURG F-6***
□ Oak Creek Campground — ***BOWMANSVILLE E-8***
Oak Grove Park & Sales — ***HATFIELD E-9***
△□ Ohiopyle State Park — ***OHIOPYLE E-2***
®□ **Oil Creek Family Campground — *TITUSVILLE B-2***
Old Mill Stream Campground — *LANCASTER E-8*
□ Ole Bull State Park — ***GALETON B-5***
Orchard Grove Campsites — ***BEAVER D-1***
®□ Otter Creek Campground (PPL) — ***AIRVILLE F-8***
Otter Lake Camp Resort — *STROUDSBURG C-9*
Outflow Camping Area (COE-Tionesta Lake) — ***TIONESTA B-3***
Outflow Recreation Area (COE-Youghioheny Lake) — ***CONFLUENCE F-3***
PA Dutch County - Outdoor World — *MANHEIM E-8*
□ **Paradise Stream Family Campground — *LOYSVILLE E-6***
□ Parker Dam State Park — ***PENFIELD C-4***
Penn Avon Campground — *SELINSGROVE D-7*
Pennsylvania Dutch Campsite — ***SHARTLESVILLE D-8***
● **Pennsylvania Dutch Convention & Visitors Bureau — *LANCASTER E-8***
Pequea Creek Campground (PPL) — *PEQUEA E-8*
□ Pettecote Junction Campground — ***CEDAR RUN B-6***
□ **Pinch Pond Family Campground & RV Park — *MANHEIM E-8***
Pine Cove Beach & RV Park — *WASHINGTON E-1*
□ Pine Cradle Lake Family Campground — ***ROME B-8***
Pine Grove Furnace State Park — ***CENTERVILLE E-6***
□ Pine Hill RV Park — ***KUTZTOWN D-9***
Pineview Camplands, LLC — ***LINESVILLE B-1***
□ **Pioneer Campground — *LAPORTE B-7***
□ Pioneer Park Campground — ***SOMERSET E-3***
□ **Pleasant Hills Resort — *HESSTON D-5***
Pocono Raceway Campground — ***BLAKESLEE C-9***
Pocono Vacation Park — *STROUDSBURG C-9*
Poe Paddy State Park — ***POTTERS MILLS D-5***
Poe Valley State Park — ***POTTERS MILLS D-5***
□ **Ponderosa Pines Campground — *HONESDALE B-9***
®□ Potter County Family Campground — ***COUDERSPORT B-5***
Primitive Campground at Bald Eagle State Park — ***HOWARD C-5***
□ Prince Gallitzin State Park — ***FRUGALITY D-4***
□ Promised Land State Park — ***GREENTOWN C-9***
□ Pymatuning State Park (Jamestown Camp) — ***JAMESTOWN B-1***
Pymatuning State Park (Linesville Camp) — ***LINESVILLE B-1***
□ Pymatuning State Park (Tuttle Camp) — ***ESPYVILLE B-1***
®□ **Quakerwoods Campground — *QUAKERTOWN D-9***
□ R. B. Winter State Park — ***LEWISBURG C-7***
□ Raccoon Creek State Park — ***FRANKFORT SPRINGS D-1***
Ravensburg State Park — ***JERSEY SHORE C-6***
★ Ray Wakley's RV Center — ***NORTH EAST A-2***
®□ Red Oak Campground — ***SCANDIA A-3***
□ **Red Run Campground — *NEW HOLLAND E-8***
□ Ricketts Glen State Park — ***BENTON C-7***

PENNSYLVANIA — Continued

□ Ride Campground-Cook State Forest — ***COOKSBURG C-3***
□ Ringing Rocks Family Campground — ***UPPER BLACK EDDY D-10***
River Beach Campsites on the Delaware-Kittatinny Canoes — ***MILFORD C-10***
®□ River Edge RV Camp & Marina — ***LEWISBURG C-7***
□ Rivers Edge Camping and Cabins — ***CONNELLSVILLE E-2***
□ Riverside Acres Campground — ***TOWANDA B-7***
®□ Riverside Campground — ***MONTGOMERY C-7***
□ Roamers' Retreat Campground — ***KINZERS E-8***
□ **Robin Hill Camping Resort — *LENHARTSVILLE D-8***
□ **Rose Point Cabins & Camping — *PORTERSVILLE C-1***
□ **Rosemount Camping Resort — *TAMAQUA D-8***
□ Round Top Campground — ***GETTYSBURG F-6***
® Rustic Acres Campgrounds — ***CLARION C-3***
RV Village Camping Resort — ***MERCER C-1***
□ Ryerson Station State Park (McNay Ridge Campground) — ***WIND RIDGE E-1***
□ S B Elliott State Park — ***CLEARFIELD C-4***
Sara's Campground — ***ERIE A-1***
Saunderosa Park Inc — ***MERCERSBURG F-5***
Scotrun - Outdoor World — *SCOTRUN C-9*
®□ Scottyland Camping Resort — ***SOMERSET E-3***
Secluded Acres Campground — ***LAKEVILLE B-9***
®□ Seven Mountains Campground — ***POTTERS MILLS D-5***
□ **Shady Grove Campground — *DENVER E-8***
□ **Shawnee Sleepy Hollow Campground — *BEDFORD E-4***
Shawnee State Park — ***SCHELLSBURG E-4***
△ Shenango Public Use Area (COE-Shenango Lake) — ***SHARON C-1***
Shenango Valley RV Park — *SHARON C-1*
Sheshequin Campground — *TROUT RUN B-6*
Shoops Country Campground — ***PORT ROYAL D-6***
□ **Shore Forest Campground — *HOP BOTTOM B-8***
□ Sill's Family Campground — ***ADAMSTOWN E-8***
□ Silver Canoe Campground — ***ELDERTON D-3***
®□ **Silver Valley Campsites — *BRODHEADSVILLE C-9***
□ Sinnemahoning State Park — ***SINNEMAHONING C-5***
Sizerville State Park — ***EMPORIUM B-4***
□ Slumber Valley Campground — ***MESHOPPEN B-8***
Snow Shoe Park (City Park) — ***SNOW SHOE C-5***
□ **Sparrow Pond Family Campground — *ERIE A-1***
®□ **Spring Gulch Resort Campground — *NEW HOLLAND E-8***
Starlite Camping Resort — ***EPHRATA E-8***
★ Starr's Trailer Sales — ***BROCKWAY C-4***
® Stoneybrook Estates — ***LEHIGHTON D-9***
®□ **Stony Fork Creek Campground — *WELLSBORO B-6***
□ **Sun Valley Campground — *BOWMANSVILLE E-8***
®□ Sunsational Family Campground — ***GLEN IRON C-6***
□ Susquehanna Campground — ***JERSEY SHORE C-6***
□ Tanglewood Camping — ***COVINGTON B-6***
□ The Camp at East Lake — ***NEW MILFORD B-9***
□ **The Foote Rest Campground — *KANE B-4***
The Loose Caboose Campground — ***KINZERS E-8***
● **The National Toy Train Museum — *STRASBURG E-8***
□ **Timberlane Campground — *PHILADELPHIA E-10***
Timothy Lake North - Outdoor World — *EAST STROUDSBURG C-9*
Timothy Lake South - Outdoor World — *EAST STROUDSBURG C-9*
□ Tioga Heritage Campground — ***TIOGA A-6***
△ Tionesta Recreation Area (COE - Tionesta Lake) — ***TIONESTA B-3***
Tobyhanna State Park — ***TOBYHANNA C-9***
Tohickon Family Campground — ***QUAKERTOWN D-9***
Tompkins Rec Area (COE - Cowanesque Lake) — ***LAWRENCEVILLE A-6***
Tri-State RV Park — ***MATAMORAS B-10***
□ Trough Creek State Park — ***ENTRIKEN D-5***
Tub Run Recreation Area (COE-Youghiogheny Lake) — ***CONFLUENCE F-3***
□ **Tucquan Park Family Campground — *HOLTWOOD F-8***
Twin Bridge Meadow Family Campground — ***CHAMBERSBURG E-5***
● **Twin Grove Amusement Park — *PINE GROVE D-8***
□ **Twin Grove Resort KOA at Pine Grove — *LICKDALE D-7***
● **Twin Grove Restaurant — *LICKDALE D-7***
□ Twin Streams Campground — ***WELLSBORO B-6***
Two Log Campground — ***HONEY BROOK E-8***
Two Mile Run County Park — ***FRANKLIN B-2***
®□ **Valleyview Farm & Campground — *WAYMART B-9***
Village Scene Park — *HATFIELD E-9*
□ Virginia's Beach Campground — ***NORTH SPRINGFIELD A-1***
® **W T Family Camping — *BLAKESLEE C-9***
★ **W T Family RV Sales & Service — *BLAKESLEE C-9***
Walmar Manor Campground — ***DILLSBURG E-6***
□ **WaterSide Campground & RV Park — *LEWISTOWN D-6***
West Haven at Lake Erie RV Park and Family Campground — *ERIE A-1*
□ **Western Village RV Park, Inc. — *CARLISLE E-6***
Wheel-In Campground — *INDIANA D-3*
®□ **Whispering Pines Camping Estates — *BENTON C-7***
Whispering Pines Family Campground — *WASHINGTON E-1*
Whispering Winds Campground — ***SHEFFIELD B-3***
White Oak Campground — *STRASBURG E-8*
□ White's Haven Campground & Cabins — ***CLARINGTON C-3***
□ Williamsport South/Nittany Mountain KOA — ***NEW COLUMBIA C-7***
Wilsonville Recreation Area (PPL) — ***HAWLEY B-9***
®□ **Wolfs Camping Resort — *KNOX C-2***
□ Woodhaven Acres — ***BRADFORD A-4***
®□ **Woodland Campground — *WOODLAND C-4***
Woodland Campsites — ***SOMERSET E-3***
Woodland Park Inc — ***EBENSBURG D-4***
□ Worlds End State Park — ***FORKSVILLE B-7***
Wright's Orchard Station Campground — ***ALTOONA D-4***
® **Ye Olde Mill Campground — *FORT LITTLETON E-5***
□ Yellow Creek Campground — ***INDIANA D-3***
□ Yogi At Shangri-La On the Creek — ***MILTON C-7***
□ **Yogi Bear's Jellystone Park Camp-Resort-Lancaster South/Quarryville — *QUARRYVILLE E-8***
®□ Yogi Bear's Jellystone Park Camp-Resort-Mill Run — ***MILL RUN E-2***

RHODE ISLAND

Bowdish Lake Camping Area — ***CHEPACHET A-2***
□ Burlingame State Park — ***CHARLESTOWN E-2***
Charlestown Breachway (State Camping Area) — ***CHARLESTOWN E-2***
Fishermen's Memorial State Park — ***NARRAGANSETT D-3***
George Washington Management Area (SP) — ***CHEPACHET A-2***
Ginny-B Family Campground — *FOSTER B-2*
Holiday Acres Camping Resort — *HARMONY A-3*
Meadowlark RV & Mobile Home Park — ***MIDDLETOWN D-4***
Melville Ponds Campground (City Park) — ***PORTSMOUTH C-4***
Oak Embers Campground — ***WEST GREENWICH C-2***
Wawaloam Campground — ***WEST KINGSTON D-3***
□ **Whispering Pines Campground — *HOPE VALLEY D-2***

SOUTH CAROLINA

Aiken RV Park — *AIKEN C-3*
Aiken State Natural Area — ***AIKEN C-3***
®□ Anderson/Lake Hartwell KOA — ***ANDERSON B-2***
Andrew Jackson State Park — ***LANCASTER A-4***
® **Apache Family Campground — *MYRTLE BEACH C-6***
April Valley RV Park — ***EASLEY A-2***
Baker Creek State Park — ***MCCORMICK C-2***
□ Barnwell State Park — ***BLACKVILLE C-3***

SOUTH CAROLINA — Continued

• Barnyard Flea Market — COLUMBIA B-3
Barnyard RV Park — COLUMBIA B-3
Bass Lake RV Campground — DILLON B-5
Big Cypress Lake RV Park & Fishing Retreat — CONWAY C-6
® Briarcliffe RV Resort, Inc — MYRTLE BEACH C-6
Calhoun Falls State Recreation Area — CALHOUN FALLS B-2
Camp Pedro — DILLON B-5
□ Campground at James Island County Park — CHARLESTON D-5
Cedar Pond Campground — LEESVILLE C-3
□ Charlotte/Fort Mill KOA — FORT MILL A-4
□ Cheraw State Recreation Area — CHERAW A-5
Chester State Park — CHESTER A-3
Colleton State Park — CANADYS D-4
Coneross Campground (COE-Hartwell Lake) — TOWNVILLE B-1
Croft State Natural Area — SPARTANBURG A-2
Crooked Creek RV Park — SENECA A-1
Cross/Santee Cooper Lakes KOA — CROSS C-4
Crown International Campground — FORT MILL A-4
Cunningham RV Park — SPARTANBURG A-2
□ Devils Fork State Park — WALHALLA A-1
□ Dreher Island State Recreation Area — CHAPIN B-3
Ebenezer Park — ROCK HILL A-3
□ Edisto Beach State Park — EDISTO ISLAND E-4
□ Givhans Ferry State Park — SUMMERVILLE D-4
Hamilton Branch State Recreation Area — MCCORMICK C-2
Hardeeville RV-Thomas' Parks and Sites — HARDEEVILLE E-3
Hawe Creek Campground (COE-J. Strom Thurmond Lake) — MCCORMICK C-2
□ Hickory Knob State Resort Park — MCCORMICK C-2
Hilton Head Harbor RV Resort & Marina — HILTON HEAD ISLAND E-4
Hilton Head Island Motorcoach Resort — HILTON HEAD ISLAND E-4
□ Hunting Island State Park — BEAUFORT E-4
Huntington Beach State Park — MURRELLS INLET C-6
Ivy Acres RV Park — PIEDMONT A-2
® Jolly Acres RV Park & Storage — ST. GEORGE D-4
Keowee Falls Rv Park (Not Visited) — WEST UNION A-1
□ Keowee-Toxaway State Natural Area — PICKENS A-2
Kings Mountain State Park — YORK A-3
□ KOA-Charleston — CHARLESTON D-5
®□ KOA-Myrtle Beach — MYRTLE BEACH C-6
□ KOA-Point South — POINT SOUTH D-4
Lake Aire RV Park and Campground — CHARLESTON D-5
Lake Greenwood State Recreation Area — GREENWOOD B-2
®□ Lake Hartwell Camping & Cabins — ANDERSON B-2
□ Lake Hartwell RV Park — FAIR PLAY B-1
Lake Hartwell State Recreation Area — FAIR PLAY B-1
Lake Wateree State Recreation Area — WINNSBORO B-3
®□ Lakewood Camping Resort — MYRTLE BEACH C-6
Lee State Natural Area — BISHOPVILLE B-4
Little Pee Dee State Park — DILLON B-5
□ Magnolia RV Park & Campground — JOANNA B-3
△ MILITARY PARK (Shady Oaks Family Campground-Charleston AFB) — CHARLESTON D-5
MILITARY PARK (Short Stay Rec Area-Charleston Naval Sta.) — BONNEAU C-5
®□ MILITARY PARK (Wateree Recreation Area and FAMCAMP-Shaw AFB) — SUMTER C-4
□ MILITARY PARK (Weston Lake Rec. Area-Ft. Jackson) — COLUMBIA B-3
Modoc Campground (COE-J. Strom Thurmond Lake) — CLARKS HILL C-2
Moon Landing RV Park & Marina — GREENWOOD B-2
Mt. Carmel Campground (COE-J. Strom Thurmond Lake) — MCCORMICK C-2
□ Mt. Pleasant/Charleston KOA — CHARLESTON D-5
• Myrtle Beach Campground Association — MYRTLE BEACH C-6
□ Myrtle Beach State Park — MYRTLE BEACH C-6
® Myrtle Beach Travel Park — MYRTLE BEACH C-6
New Green Acres R.V. Park — WALTERBORO D-4
Oak Plantation Campground — CHARLESTON D-5
□ Ocean Lakes Family Campground — MYRTLE BEACH C-6
Oconee Point Campground (COE - Hartwell Lake) — TOWNVILLE B-1
□ Oconee State Park — WALHALLA A-1
Paris Mountain State Park — GREENVILLE A-2
® Pine Acres Campground — AIKEN C-3
®□ Pine Ridge Campground — ROEBUCK A-2
® Pirateland Family Camping Resort — MYRTLE BEACH C-6
□ Poinsett State Park — WEDGEFIELD C-4
Rainbow RV Park — GREENVILLE A-2
® Rocks Pond Campground & Marina — EUTAWVILLE C-4
Sadlers Creek State Recreation Park — ANDERSON B-2
St. George RV Park — ST. GEORGE D-4
Santee Lakes Campground — SANTEE C-4
□ Santee State Park — SANTEE C-4
Scuffletown USA Campground — GREENVILLE A-2
Sesquicentennial State Park — COLUMBIA B-3
Shuman's RV Trailer Park — CANADYS D-4
□ Solitude Pointe — CLEVELAND A-2
• South of the Border — DILLON B-5
Spartanburg NE/Gaffney KOA — GAFFNEY A-3
• Splash Zone Waterpark — CHARLESTON D-5
Springfield Campground (COE-Hartwell Lake) — ANDERSON B-2
Springwood RV Park — GREENVILLE A-2
Sumter National Forest (Parson's Mountain Lake Campground) — ABBEVILLE B-2
Sumter NF (Cherry Hill Campground) — WALHALLA A-1
Sumter NF (Woods Ferry Campground) — CHESTER A-3
□ Table Rock State Park — PICKENS A-2
The Farm Campground — MCBEE B-4
® The Oaks at Point South RV Resort — POINT SOUTH D-4
• The Pink Pig — HARDEEVILLE E-3
□ Tiger Cove Campground — ANDERSON B-2
★ Tony's RV Parts & Service — COLUMBIA B-3
Tuck In The Wood Campground — BEAUFORT E-4
Twin Lakes Campground (COE-Hartwell Lake) — CLEMSON A-2
□ Valley Park Resort — TRAVELERS REST A-2
□ WillowTree Resort — LONGS B-6
□ WillowTree Resort — MYRTLE BEACH C-6
Woodsmoke Family Campground — IRMO B-3
□ Yogi Bear's Jellystone Park @ River Bottom Farms — SWANSEA C-3

TENNESSEE

AAA RV Park — UNION CITY A-2
□ Adventure Bound Camping Resort Gatlinburg (formerly Crazy Horse Camping & RV Resort) — GATLINBURG E-5
Agricenter RV Park — MEMPHIS C-1
Anderson Road Campground (Corps of Engineers) — ANTIOCH B-4
□ Arrow Creek Campground — GATLINBURG E-5
Athens I-75 Campground — ATHENS B-6
□ Baileyton RV Park — BAILEYTON D-5
□ Bean Pot Campground — CROSSVILLE B-5
Beech Bend (Decatur County Pk) — PERRYVILLE B-3
□ Beech Lake Family Camping Resort — LEXINGTON B-2
□ Best Holiday Trav-L-Park — CHATTANOOGA C-5
□ Big Buck Camping Resort — HORNSBY C-2
Big Hill Pond State Park — POCAHONTAS C-2
Big Meadow Family Campground — TOWNSEND E-5
□ Big Ridge State Park — NORRIS A-6
Big South Fork Nat'l. River & Rec. Area (Bandy Creek Campground) — ONEIDA A-6
□ Birdsong Resort, Marina & Lakeside Campground — CAMDEN B-3
Bledsoe Creek State Camping Park — GALLATIN A-4
Blue Water Marina/Campground — DAYTON B-5
□ Buchanan Resort — PARIS A-2
Bumpus Mills Recreational Area (COE-Lk Barkley) — DOVER A-3

TENNESSEE — Continued

Cages Bend Campground (COE-Old Hickory Lake) — GALLATIN A-4
□ Camp on the Lake Campground — GUILD C-5
□ Campers RV Park — COLUMBIA B-4
Camping in the Smokies — GATLINBURG E-5
Caney Creek RV Resort & Marina — HARRIMAN B-6
Cedar Creek Campground (COE-Old Hickory Lake) — MT. JULIET B-4
□ Cedars of Lebanon State Park — LEBANON B-4
□ Chattanooga's Raccoon Mtn. Caverns & Campground — CHATTANOOGA C-5
• Chattanooga's Raccoon Mtn. Crystal Caverns — CHATTANOOGA C-5
Cherokee National Forest (Cardens Bluff Campground) — HAMPTON D-6
Cherokee National Forest (Chilhowee Campgrounds) — CLEVELAND C-6
Cherokee National Forest (Indian Boundary A & Overflow Areas) — TELLICO PLAINS C-6
Cherokee National Forest (Jacobs Creek Campgrounds) — SHADY VALLEY D-6
Cherokee National Forest (Little Oak Campground) — BRISTOL D-6
Cherokee National Forest (Parksville Lake Campground) — PARKSVILLE C-6
Cherokee National Forest (Rock Creek Campgrounds) — ERWIN D-6
Chester Frost Park (Hamilton County Park) — CHATTANOOGA C-5
□ Chickasaw State Park — HENDERSON C-2
□ Clabough's Campground & RV Resort — PIGEON FORGE E-5
□ Clarksville RV Park & Campground — CLARKSVILLE A-3
Countryside RV Resort — LEBANON B-4
Cove Lake State Park — CARYVILLE A-6
Cove Mountain Resorts RV Park — PIGEON FORGE E-5
Creekside RV Park — PIGEON FORGE E-5
□ Crossville KOA Campground — CROSSVILLE B-5
★ Cullum & Maxey Camping Center — NASHVILLE B-4
□ Cumberland Mountain State Park — CROSSVILLE B-5
Dale Hollow Dam Campground (COE-Dale Hollow Lake) — CELINA A-5
David Crockett State Park — LAWRENCEBURG C-3
★ Davis Motorhome/D & N Camper Sales — MEMPHIS C-1
Davy Crockett Birthplace Historical SP — GREENEVILLE D-5
®□ Deer Run RV Resort — CROSSVILLE B-5
Defeated Creek Park (Corps of Engineers) — CARTHAGE A-5
□ Dickson RV Park — DICKSON B-3
Douglas Dam Tailwater (TVA - Douglas Reservoir) — SEVIERVILLE E-5
Douglas Headwater (TVA - Douglas Reservoir) — SEVIERVILLE E-5
Eagles Nest Campground — PARIS A-2
□ Eagle's Nest Campground — PIGEON FORGE E-5
□ Edgar Evins State Rustic Park — SMITHVILLE B-5
Elvis Presley Blvd RV Park — MEMPHIS C-1
Escapees Raccoon Valley RV Park — KNOXVILLE B-6
Express RV Park — LOUDON B-6
□ Fall Creek Falls State Park — PIKEVILLE B-5
Floating Mill (COE-Center Hill Reservoir) — SILVER POINT B-5
Fooshee Pass — TEN MILE B-6
□ Foothills RV Park & Cabins — PIGEON FORGE E-5
Fort Pillow State Historic Area — HENNING B-1
Foster Falls (TVA) — TRACY CITY C-5
□ Fox Inn Campground/Norris — CLINTON B-6
Frozen Head State Park — WARTBURG B-6
Gatlin Point (LBL) National Recreation Area (Lake Access Site Only) — DOVER A-3
• Graceland — MEMPHIS C-1
□ Great Smoky Jellystone Park Camp Resort — GATLINBURG E-5
Great Smoky Mountains National Park (Cades Cove Campground) — TOWNSEND E-5
Great Smoky Mountains National Park (Cosby Campground) — COSBY E-5
Great Smoky Mountains National Park (Elkmont Campground) — GATLINBURG E-5
Great Smoky Mountains National Park (Look Rock Campground) — WALLAND E-5
Greenbrier Island Campground — GATLINBURG E-5
□ Greenlee of May Springs — JEFFERSON CITY D-5
Harrison Bay State Park — CHATTANOOGA C-5
□ Henry Horton State Park — CHAPEL HILL B-4
Heron Point Marina & Campground — MORRISTOWN D-5
Hiawassee State Scenic River & Ocoee River (Gee Creek Campground) — DELANO C-6
Hornsby Hollow (Watts Bar Lake) — TEN MILE B-6
Indian Mountain State Park — JELLICO A-6
Jackson RV Park — JACKSON B-2
Joy-O RV Park — JACKSON B-2
King's Holly Haven RV Park — PIGEON FORGE E-5
Kinser Park (City Park) — GREENEVILLE D-5
□ KOA Tellico Plains — TELLICO PLAINS C-6
□ KOA-Bristol/Kingsport — KINGSPORT D-6
□ KOA-Buffalo — BUFFALO B-3
□ KOA-Chattanooga North/Cleveland — CLEVELAND C-6
□ KOA-Manchester — MANCHESTER B-4
®□ KOA-Newport I-40/Smoky Mtns — NEWPORT D-5
□ KOA-Paris Landing — PARIS A-2
□ KOA-Pigeon Forge/Gatlinburg — PIGEON FORGE E-5
□ KOA-Sweetwater Valley — SWEETWATER B-6
Lake Cove Resort — DANDRIDGE D-5
® Lakeview RV Park — BRISTOL D-6
□ Lazy Daze Campground — TOWNSEND E-5
Lillydale Campground (COE-Dale Hollow Lake) — LIVINGSTON A-5
□ Little Eagle RV Park — PARIS A-2
Lock A Campground (COE - Cheatham Lake) — ASHLAND CITY A-4
Long Branch (COE - Center Hill Reservoir) — SILVER POINT B-5
□ Loretta Lynn's Ranch — HURRICANE MILLS B-3
Lotterdale Cove — GREENBACK B-6
Loyston Point (TVA - Norris Reservoir) — NORRIS A-6
Lynchburg Wilderness RV Park — LYNCHBURG C-4
Maple Grove Campground — GRANVILLE A-5
Maple Hill RV Park — JAMESTOWN A-5
□ Meeman-Shelby Forest State Park — MILLINGTON C-1
Melton Hill Dam (TVA-Melton Hill Reservoir) — LENOIR CITY B-6
□ Memphis East Campground — MEMPHIS C-1
□ Memphis/Graceland RV Park & Campground — MEMPHIS C-1
®△ MILITARY PARK (FAMCAMP-Arnold AFB) — MANCHESTER B-4
□ Misty River Cabins & RV Resort, LLC — TOWNSEND E-5
□ Montgomery Bell State Park — WHITE BLUFF B-3
Mountain Glen RV Park — PIKEVILLE B-5
□ Mountain Lake Marina & Campground — LAKE CITY A-6
□ Mountaineer Campground — TOWNSEND E-5
Mousetail Landing State Park — PERRYVILLE B-3
®□ Nashville Country RV Park — NASHVILLE B-4
□ Nashville I-24 Campground — SMYRNA B-4
□ Nashville KOA — NASHVILLE B-4
□ Nashville Shores RV Campground — NASHVILLE B-4
• Nashville Shores Water Park — NASHVILLE B-4
□ Nashville's Jellystone Park — NASHVILLE B-4
Natchez Trace Campground — HOHENWALD B-3
Natchez Trace Parkway (Meriwether Lewis Campground) — HOHENWALD B-3
□ Natchez Trace State Park — CLARKSBURG B-2
□ Nathan Bedford Forrest State Park — CAMDEN B-3
□ Norris Dam State Park — NORRIS A-6
Notchy Creek — VONORE B-6
Obey River Campground (COE-Dale Hollow Lake) — LIVINGSTON A-5
Old Stone Fort State Archaeological Area — MANCHESTER B-4
Over-Niter RV Park — ATHENS B-6
Panther Creek State Park — MORRISTOWN D-5
□ Paris Landing State Park — PARIS A-2
□ Parker's Crossroads RV Park & Campground — PARKERS CROSSROADS B-2
Parkway Village — JACKSON B-2
□ Pickett State Park — JAMESTOWN A-5
Pickwick Dam (TVA-Pickwick Lake) — COUNCE C-2
□ Pickwick Landing State Resort Park — SAVANNAH C-2
• Pigeon Forge Department of Tourism — PIGEON FORGE E-5
® Pine Mountain RV Park — PIGEON FORGE E-5

TENNESSEE — Continued

□ Piney (LBL) National Recreation Area — DOVER A-3
Ragland Bottom (COE - Center Hill Reservoir) — SMITHVILLE B-5
Redwood Estates — MEMPHIS C-1
□ Reelfoot Lake State Park — TIPTONVILLE A-1
□ Ripplin' Waters Campground — SEVIERVILLE E-5
□ River Plantation RV Park — PIGEON FORGE E-5
Riverbend Campground — PIGEON FORGE E-5
□ Riveredge RV Park — PIGEON FORGE E-5
®□ Riverside RV Park & Resort — SEVIERVILLE E-5
□ Roan Mountain State Resort Park — ROAN MOUNTAIN D-6
□ Rock Island State Park — ROCK ISLAND B-5
□ Rocky Top Campground & RV Park — BLOUNTVILLE D-6
Salt Lick Creek Campground (Corps of Engineers) — GAINESBORO A-5
Seven Points Campground (Corps of Engineers) — HERMITAGE B-4
Shady Acres Campground — LEBANON B-4
□ Shady Oaks Campground Pigeon Forge/Gatlinburg — PIGEON FORGE E-5
Shady Oaks Community — MILLINGTON C-1
Shauan's RV Park — HARTFORD E-5
Shellmound-Nickajack Dam Reservation (TVA-Nickajack Lake) — JASPER C-5
Shipp's RV Campground — CHATTANOOGA C-5
Smoker Holler RV Resort — PIGEON FORGE E-5
□ Smoky Bear Campground — GATLINBURG E-5
Soaring Eagle Campground & RV Park — LENOIR CITY B-6
Southlake RV Park — KNOXVILLE B-6
Spring Lake RV Resort — CROSSVILLE B-5
□ Standing Stone State Park — LIVINGSTON A-5
Stonegate RV Park — NASHVILLE B-4
Stoney Creek RV Park — ELIZABETHTON D-6
★ Tennessee RV Camping World — KNOXVILLE B-6
• Tennessee State Parks Department of Environment and Conservation — NASHVILLE B-4
□ Texas "T" Campground — CORNERSVILLE C-4
□ Tims Ford State Rustic Park — WINCHESTER C-4
T.O. Fuller State Park — MEMPHIS C-1
Toqua Beach Campground — VONORE B-6
□ Townsend Great Smokies KOA — TOWNSEND E-5
□ Tremont Outdoor Resort — TOWNSEND E-5
TVA/Cherokee Dam - Cherokee Lake — JEFFERSON CITY D-5
□ Twin Creek RV Resort — GATLINBURG E-5
Twin Lakes Catfish Farm & Campground — BAXTER B-5
Twin Mountain RV Park and Campground — PIGEON FORGE E-5
Two Rivers Campground — NASHVILLE B-4
Two Rivers Landing Resort — SEVIERVILLE E-5
• US Army Corps of Engineers/Volunteer Clearing House — NASHVILLE B-4
® Volunteer Park — KNOXVILLE B-6
Waldens Creek Campground — PIGEON FORGE E-5
Warrior's Path State Park — KINGSPORT D-6
Whispering Pines RV Park — JACKSON B-2
Willow Grove (COE-Dale Hollow Lake) — LIVINGSTON A-5
Woodsmoke Campground — UNICOI D-6

VERMONT

Abel Mountain Campground — BRAINTREE C-2
®□ Apple Island Resort — SOUTH HERO B-1
Ascutney SP — ASCUTNEY E-3
Bald Mountain Campground — TOWNSHEND F-3
Barrewood Campground — WESTFIELD A-3
Bomoseen SP — BOMOSEEN D-2
Branbury SP — SALISBURY C-2
®□ Brattleboro North-KOA — DUMMERSTON F-3
□ Brighton SP — ISLAND POND A-4
Burton Island SP — ST. ALBANS BAY A-2
Button Bay SP — VERGENNES C-1
® Camping on The Battenkill — ARLINGTON E-2
® Caton Place Campground — CAVENDISH E-3
Coolidge SP — PLYMOUTH UNION D-2
Country Village Campground — BRANDON D-2
Crown Point Camping Area — PERKINSVILLE E-3
DAR SP — ADDISON C-1
Dorset RV Park — DORSET E-2
Elmore SP — ELMO B-3
Emerald Lake SP — NORTH DORSET E-2
Fort Dummer SP — BRATTLEBORO F-3
® Getaway Mountain Campground — ASCUTNEY E-3
□ Gifford Woods SP — KILLINGTON D-2
Gold Brook Campground (at Nichols Lodge). — STOWE B-3
□ Grand Isle SP — GRAND ISLE A-1
Green Mountain NF (Hapgood Pond Campground) — PERU E-2
Greenwood Lodge and Campsites — BENNINGTON F-1
® Groton Forest Road Campground — MARSHFIELD B-3
□ Half Moon Pond SP — HUBBARDTON D-2
Hidden Acres Campground — DUMMERSTON F-3
® Homestead Campground — GEORGIA A-2
Horseshoe Acres Campground — ANDOVER E-2
Jamaica SP — JAMAICA E-2
Kenolie Village Campground — NEWFANE F-3
®□ Lake Bomoseen Campground — BOMOSEEN D-2
□ Lake Carmi SP — ENOSBURG FALLS A-2
® Lake Champagne Campground — RANDOLPH CENTER C-3
®□ Lake Dunmore Kampersville — MIDDLEBURY C-2
Lake St. Catherine SP — POULTNEY D-1
Lakeside Campground — ISLAND POND A-4
® Lakeview Camping Area — EDEN MILLS A-3
®□ Lazy Lions Campground — BARRE C-3
®□ Limehurst Lake Campground — BARRE C-3
Little River SP — WATERBURY B-2
Lone Pine Campsites — COLCHESTER B-2
Maidstone SP — BLOOMFIELD A-5
Malletts Bay Campgrounds — COLCHESTER B-2
Molly Stark SP — WILMINGTON F-2
®□ Mountain View Campground — MORRISVILLE B-3
New Discovery Campground (Groton SF) — GROTON C-4
North Beach Campground — BURLINGTON B-2
North Hero SP — NORTH HERO A-1
Pine Hollow Campground — BENNINGTON F-1
Prouty Beach Campground (City Park) — NEWPORT A-4
Quechee Gorge SP — QUECHEE D-3
®□ Quechee Pine Valley KOA — QUECHEE D-3
Rest N' Nest Campground — EAST THETFORD D-3
□ Ricker Campground (Groton SF) — GROTON C-4
® Rivers Bend Campground — MIDDLEBURY C-2
® Running Bear Camping Area — ASCUTNEY E-3
® Shelburne Camping Area — SHELBURNE B-1
Silver Lake SP — BARNARD D-3
Smoke Rise Campground — BRANDON D-2
Smugglers Notch Campground (Mount Mansfield SF) — STOWE B-3
Stillwater Campground (Groton SF) — GROTON C-4
® Sugar Ridge RV Village & Campground — DANVILLE B-4
Thetford Hill SP — THETFORD HILL D-3
Townshend SF — TOWNSHEND F-3
□ Tree Corners Family Campground — IRASBURG A-3
Tree Farm Campground — SPRINGFIELD E-3
□ Wilgus SP — ASCUTNEY E-3
Will-O-Wood Campground — ORLEANS A-4
Winhall Brook Camping Area (COE-Ball Mountain Lake) — SOUTH LONDONDERRY E-2
Woodford SP — BENNINGTON F-1

VIRGINIA

Amelia Family Campground — *AMELIA D-4*
Americamps KOA Richmond-North — *ASHLAND C-4*
□ Americamps Lake Gaston — ***BRACEY E-4***
® **American Heritage RV Park — *JAMESTOWN D-5***
® **American Heritage RV Park — *WILLIAMSBURG D-5***
□ **Anvil Campground — *WILLIAMSBURG D-5***
□ **Aquia Pines Camp Resort — *STAFFORD C-4***
Bear Creek Lake State Park — ***CUMBERLAND D-4***
• **Bear's Den Restaurant — *PETERSBURG D-4***
® **Bethpage Camp-Resort — *URBANNA D-5***
® **Bethpage Camp-Resort — *WILLIAMSBURG D-5***
• **Bethpage Mini-Golf & Ice Creamery — *URBANNA D-5***
Blue Ridge Nat'l Parkway (Otter Creek) — ***BIG ISLAND D-3***
Blue Ridge Nat'l Parkway (Peaks of Otter Campground) — ***BEDFORD D-2***
Blue Ridge Nat'l Parkway (Roanoke Mountain Campground) — ***ROANOKE D-2***
Blue Ridge Nat'l Parkway (Rocky Knob Campground) — ***CHRISTIANSBURG D-2***
Breaks Interstate Park — ***HAYSI A-2***
□ Bull Run Regional Park — ***CENTREVILLE B-4***
Burke Lake Park (Fairfax County Park Authority) — *FAIRFAX B-5*
□ **Candy Hill Campground — *WINCHESTER B-4***
®□ **Cherrystone Family Camping Resort — *CHERITON D-6***
□ Chesapeake Bay Camp - Resort — ***REEDVILLE C-6***
□ **Chesapeake Campground — *CHESAPEAKE E-6***
®□ Christopher Run Campground — ***MINERAL C-4***
□ Claytor Lake State Park — ***DUBLIN D-1***
□ Cozy Acres Campground/RV Resort — ***POWHATAN D-4***
Crane Nest Campsite (COE-John W Flannagan Reservoir) — ***CLINTWOOD A-2***
□ Deer Run Campground — ***WOOLWINE E-2***
• **Dixie Caverns — *SALEM D-2***
Dixie Caverns Campground — *SALEM D-2*
□ Douthat State Park — ***CLIFTON FORGE C-2***
□ Fairy Stone State Park — ***STUART E-2***
®□ Fancy Gap/Blueridge Parkway KOA — ***FANCY GAP E-1***
□ First Landing-Seashore State Park — ***VIRGINIA BEACH E-6***
□ **Fort Chiswell RV Park — *WYTHEVILLE E-1***
□ **Front Royal RV Campground — *FRONT ROYAL B-4***
George Washington National Forest (Bolar Mountain Campground) — ***WARM SPRINGS C-2***
George Washington National Forest (Elizabeth Furnace Campground) — ***STRASBURG B-4***
George Washington National Forest (Hidden Valley Campground) — ***WARM SPRINGS C-2***
George Washington National Forest (Morris Hill Campground) — ***COVINGTON C-2***
George Washington National Forest (Sherando Lake Campground) — ***WAYNESBORO C-3***
Glen Maury Park (Municipal) — ***BUENA VISTA D-3***
®□ **Gloucester Point Family Campground — *GLOUCESTER POINT D-5***
Goose Point (COE - Philpott Lake) — ***BASSETT E-2***
Grayson Highlands State Park — ***VOLNEY E-1***
Greenville Farm Family Campground — *HAYMARKET B-4*
Grey's Point Camp — *GREY'S POINT D-5*
Gwynn's Island RV Resort (Morgan RV Resorts) — ***GWYNN D-6***
□ **Harrisonburg / Shenandoah Valley KOA — *BROADWAY B-3***
®□ Heavenly Acres Campground — ***STANARDSVILLE C-3***
□ **Holiday Trav-L-Park of Virginia Beach — *VIRGINIA BEACH E-6***
Holliday Lake State Park — ***APPOMATTOX D-3***
Horseshoe Point (COE - Philpott Lake) — ***FERRUM E-2***
□ Hungry Mother State Park — ***MARION B-3***
Interstate Overnight Park — ***CHRISTIANSBURG D-2***
Ivy Hill Campground (COE-John H Kerr Reservoir) — ***CLARKSVILLE E-3***
Jefferson National Forest (Beartree Campground) — ***DAMASCUS B-2***
Jefferson National Forest (Cane Patch Campground) — ***POUND A-2***
Jefferson National Forest (Cave Mountain Lake Rec. Area) — ***NATURAL BRIDGE D-2***
Jefferson National Forest (Cave Springs Campground) — ***DRYDEN B-1***
Jefferson National Forest (Grindstone Campground) — ***TROUTDALE B-3***
Jefferson National Forest (Hurricane Campground) — ***SUGAR GROVE B-3***
Jefferson National Forest (Stony Fork Campground) — ***WYTHEVILLE E-1***
□ Kings Dominion Camp Wilderness — ***DOSWELL C-4***
® Kiptopeke State Park — ***CAPE CHARLES D-6***
□ **KOA-Charlottesville — *CHARLOTTESVILLE C-3***
□ **KOA-Colonial Central — *WILLIAMSBURG D-5***
□ **KOA-Fredericksburg/Washington DC — *FREDERICKSBURG C-4***
®□ KOA-Natural Bridge — ***NATURAL BRIDGE D-2***
□ **KOA-Williamsburg — *WILLIAMSBURG D-5***
□ **KOA-Wytheville Kampground — *WYTHEVILLE E-1***
Lake A. Willis Robertson (Rockbridge County Park) — ***COLLIERSTOWN C-2***
Lake Fairfax Park (Fairfax County Park) — *FAIRFAX B-5*
□ Lake Ridge RV Resort — ***HILLSVILLE E-1***
Lee Hi Campground — ***LEXINGTON C-3***
Longwood Recreation Area (COE-John H Kerr Reservoir) — ***CLARKSVILLE E-3***
Lower Twin Campground (COE-John W Flannagan Reservoir) — ***HAYSI A-2***
Luray RV Resort -The Country Waye — *LURAY B-3*
Maddox Family Campground — ***CHINCOTEAGUE C-6***
□ **Madison/Shenandoah Hills KOA — *MADISON C-4***
□ **Meadows of Dan Campground — *MEADOWS OF DAN E-2***
□ Middle Creek Campground — ***BUCHANAN D-2***
□ MILITARY PARK (Cape Henry Travel Camp-Ft. Story) — ***VIRGINIA BEACH E-6***
MILITARY PARK (Family Campground-Cheatham Annex) — ***WILLIAMSBURG D-5***
□ MILITARY PARK (Fort A.P. Hill Campground) — ***BOWLING GREEN C-5***
MILITARY PARK (Lunga Park Quantico-Marine Base) — ***QUANTICO B-5***
MILITARY PARK (The Colonies Travel Park) — ***HAMPTON D-5***
• **Miss Jennifer Charter Fishing — *CHERITON D-6***
□ Misty Mountain Camp Resort — ***GREENWOOD C-3***
Monroe Bay Campground — *COLONIAL BEACH C-5*
□ Montebello Camping & Fishing Resort — ***MONTEBELLO C-3***
NASCAR RV Resorts at Endless Caverns (Morgan RV Resorts) — ***NEW MARKET B-3***
Natural Tunnel State Park — ***CLINCHPORT B-1***
New Point RV Resort (Morgan RV Resorts) — ***NEW POINT D-6***
• **Newport News Golf Club at Deer Run — *NEWPORT NEWS E-5***
Newport News Park Campground (City Park) — *NEWPORT NEWS E-5*
• **Newport News Visitors Center — *NEWPORT NEWS E-5***
□ North Bay Shore Campground — ***VIRGINIA BEACH E-6***
North Bend Park (COE-John H Kerr Reservoir) — ***BOYDTON E-4***
®□ **North Fork Resort — *FRONT ROYAL B-4***
□ North Landing Beach Riverfront Campground and Resort — ***VIRGINIA BEACH E-6***
Occoneechee State Park — ***CLARKSVILLE E-3***
® **Outdoor World-Harbor View Campground — *COLONIAL BEACH C-5***
® **Outdoor World-Williamsburg Campground — *WILLIAMSBURG D-5***
® Paradise Hollow Lake & Campground — ***KEELING E-3***
®□ Paradise Lake Family Campground — ***SPOUT SPRING D-3***
Parkview MH & RV Park — ***APPOMATTOX D-3***
□ **Picture Lake Campground — *PETERSBURG D-4***
Pine Grove Campground & Waterfowl Park — *CHINCOTEAGUE C-6*
Pocahontas State Park — ***CHESTERFIELD D-4***
□ Pohick Bay Regional Park — ***LORTON B-4***
Prince William Forest Park-NPS (Oak Ridge) — ***TRIANGLE B-5***
®□ **R & D Family Campground — *MILFORD C-4***
□ **Rainbow Acres Campground — *KING & QUEEN COURTHOUSE D-5***
Rudds Creek CG (COE-John H Kerr Reservoir) — ***BOYDTON E-4***

VIRGINIA — Continued

Rural Retreat Campground (Wythe County Park) — ***RURAL RETREAT E-1***
★ **RV Adventures — *GREY'S POINT D-5***
★ **RV Adventures — *URBANNA D-5***
Salthouse Branch (COE - Philpott Lake) — ***FERRUM E-2***
Shenandoah National Park (Big Meadows Campground) — ***ELKTON C-3***
Shenandoah National Park (Lewis Mountain Campground) — ***ELKTON C-3***
Shenandoah National Park (Loft Mountain Camp) — ***ELKTON C-3***
®□ Shenandoah Valley Campground — ***VERONA C-3***
®□ **Skyline Ranch Resort — *FRONT ROYAL B-4***
®□ **Small Country Campground — *LOUISA C-4***
□ Smith Mountain Lake State Park — ***HUDDLESTON D-3***
□ **South Forty Camp Resort — *PETERSBURG D-4***
Spring Gardens Mobile Home Park — *PETERSBURG D-4*
□ **Staunton / Walnut Hills KOA — *STAUNTON C-3***
□ Staunton River State Park — ***SCOTTSBURG E-3***
®□ Stoney Creek Resort Campground — ***GREENVILLE C-3***
Sugar Hollow Recreation Area (City Park) — ***BRISTOL B-2***
® Tall Pines Harbor Waterfront Campground — ***TEMPERANCEVILLE C-6***
• **The Buckhorne Country Store — *CLIFTON FORGE C-2***
®□ **The Buckhorne Country Store & Campground — *CLIFTON FORGE C-2***
□ **Thousand Trails-Chesapeake Bay — *GLOUCESTER D-5***
® **Thousand Trails-Lynchburg — *RUSTBURG D-3***
□ **Thousand Trails-Virginia Landing — *QUINBY D-6***
Tom's Cove Park — ***CHINCOTEAGUE C-6***
Travel Trailer Village at Prince William Forest Park — *DUMFRIES B-5*
□ Twin Lakes State Park — ***GREEN BAY D-4***
Utt's Campground — ***FANCY GAP E-1***
®□ Virginia Beach KOA — ***VIRGINIA BEACH E-6***
Waynesboro North 340 Campground — ***WAYNESBORO C-3***
□ Westmoreland State Park — ***MONTROSS C-5***
□ Wildwood Campground — ***MONROE D-3***
Williamsburg Christian Retreat Center — ***TOANO D-5***
□ **Yogi Bear's Jellystone Camp Resort At Natural Bridge — *NATURAL BRIDGE D-2***
®□ **Yogi Bear's Jellystone Park Camp Resort Emporia — *EMPORIA E-4***
□ Yogi Bear's Jellystone Park Camp-Resort — ***LURAY B-3***

WEST VIRGINIA

□ Ashland West Virginia ATV Resort — ***ASHLAND E-2***
Audra SP — ***BELINGTON B-4***
□ Babcock SP — ***CLIFFTOP D-3***
Bakers Run Campground (COE-Sutton Lake) — ***SUTTON C-3***
Battle Run Campground (COE-Summersville Lake) — ***SUMMERSVILLE C-3***
• **Beckley Exhibition Coal Mine — *BECKLEY D-3***
Beckley Exhibition Coal Mine Campground — *BECKLEY D-3*
□ Beech Fork SP — ***HUNTINGTON C-1***
Berwind Lake WMA — ***WARRIORMINE E-2***
□ Blackwater Falls SP — ***DAVIS B-4***
□ Bluestone SP — ***HINTON D-3***
Bluestone State Wildlife Mgmt. Area — ***INDIAN MILLS D-3***
Broken Wheel Campground & Country Store — ***WESTON B-3***
□ Cabwaylingo SF — ***DUNLOW D-1***
Camp Creek SP — ***CAMP CREEK E-3***
□ Canaan Valley Resort Park (SP) — ***DAVIS B-4***
Cedar Creek SP — ***GLENVILLE B-3***
□ Chestnut Ridge Park and Campground (Monongalia County Park) — ***MORGANTOWN A-4***
Chief Cornstalk State Public Hunting & Fishing Area — ***SOUTHSIDE C-2***
Chief Logan SP — ***LOGAN D-2***
Coopers Rock SF (McCollum Camping Area) — ***MORGANTOWN A-4***
East Fork Campground (COE-East Lynn Lake) — ***EAST LYNN D-1***
East Fork Campground & Horse Stables — *DURBIN C-4*
Falling Waters Campsite — ***FALLING WATERS A-6***
Flatwoods KOA — ***FLATWOODS C-3***
George Washington NF (Brandywine Lake Campground) — ***BRANDYWINE C-5***
George Washington NF (Trout Pond Campground) — ***LOST RIVER B-5***
Gerald R. Freeman Campground (COE-Sutton Lake) — ***SUTTON C-3***
® Greenbrier River Campground — ***ALDERSON D-3***
□ Greenbrier SF — ***CALDWELL D-3***
Harpers Ferry Campground — *HARPERS FERRY B-6*
□ **Harpers Ferry/Civil War Battlefields KOA — *HARPERS FERRY B-6***
□ Holly River SP — ***HACKER VALLEY C-3***
□ **Huntington Fox Fire KOA — *MILTON C-2***
Jim's Camping — ***MILTON C-2***
Kanawha SF Campground — ***CHARLESTON C-2***
Krodel Park (City Park) — ***POINT PLEASANT C-2***
□ Kumbrabow SF — ***HUTTONSVILLE C-4***
□ **Lake Stephens Campground & Marina (Raleigh County Park) — *BECKLEY D-3***
Moncove Lake SP — ***GAP MILLS D-3***
Monongahela NF (Big Bend Campground) — ***UPPER TRACT C-4***
Monongahela NF (Bishop Knob Campground) — ***RICHWOOD C-3***
Monongahela NF (Cranberry Campground) — ***RICHWOOD C-3***
Monongahela NF (Lake Sherwood Recreation Area) — ***NEOLA D-4***
Monongahela NF (Seneca Shadows Campground) — ***SENECA ROCKS C-4***
Monongahela NF (Spruce Knob Lake Campground) — ***CIRCLEVILLE C-4***
Monongahela NF (Stuart Campground) — ***ELKINS B-4***
Monongahela NF (Summit Lake Campground) — ***RICHWOOD C-3***
Monongahela NF (Tea Creek Campground) — ***MARLINTON C-4***
®□ Mountain Lake Campground & Cabins — ***SUMMERSVILLE C-3***
Mountwood Park Campground (Wood County Park) — ***PARKERSBURG B-2***
□ North Bend SP — ***HARRISVILLE B-3***
Panther SF — ***PANTHER E-2***
Pegasus Farm Campground — ***ELKINS B-4***
□ Pipestem Resort SP — ***PIPESTEM D-3***
Plum Orchard Lake State Wildlife Mgmt. Area — ***PAX D-2***
□ Revelle's River Resort — ***BOWDEN B-4***
□ **Rippling Waters Church of God Campground — *ROMANCE C-2***
• **River Riders — *HARPERS FERRY B-6***
□ Riverside Cabins & RV Park — ***MOOREFIELD B-5***
Sand Springs Camping Area — ***MORGANTOWN A-4***
□ Seneca SF — ***DUNMORE C-4***
• **State Fair of West Virginia — *LEWISBURG D-3***
State Fair of West Virginia Campground — *LEWISBURG D-3*
□ Stonewall Jackson Lake SP (Briar Point Campground) — ***WESTON B-3***
Summer Wind RV Overnight Park — ***DAWSON D-3***
□ Summersville Lake Retreat — ***SUMMERSVILLE C-3***
Tomlinson Run SP — ***WEIRTON A-1***
□ Twin Falls Resort SP — ***MULLENS D-2***
□ Tygart Lake SP — ***GRAFTON B-4***
Wapocoma Campground — ***ROMNEY B-5***
□ Watoga SP — ***HUNTERSVILLE C-4***
□ Whisper Mountain Campground & RV Park — ***WESTON B-3***
□ Yokum's Vacationland & Princess Snowbird's Indian Village — ***SENECA ROCKS C-4***

WISCONSIN

□ 9 Mile All Sport Resort — ***WHITE LAKE E-5***
□ Adventureland — ***GORDON C-2***
Ahnapee River Trails Campground — *ALGOMA J-1*

WISCONSIN — Continued

American World - Mt. Olympus Hotel & RV Resort — *WISCONSIN DELLS H-4*
Amnicon Falls SP — ***SUPERIOR B-1***
□ Apostle Islands Area Campground — ***BAYFIELD B-3***
Apostle Islands National Lakeshore (Presque Isle-Stockton) — ***BAYFIELD B-3***
□ **Apple Creek Family Campground & Lodge — *DE PERE F-6***
Apple River Family Campground — ***SOMERSET E-1***
Aqualand Camp Resort — ***SISTER BAY I-2***
□ Arbor Vitae Campground — ***WOODRUFF C-4***
® **Arrowhead Resort Campground — *WISCONSIN DELLS H-4***
Babcock Campground (Dane County Park) — ***MCFARLAND I-5***
Badger RV Park @ Village Inn on the Lake — *TWO RIVERS G-6*
Baileys Grove Campground — *BAILEYS HARBOR I-2*
Baileys Woods Campground — ***BAILEYS HARBOR I-2***
Banker Park (Municipal Park) — ***VIOLA H-3***
®□ **Baraboo Hills Campground — *WISCONSIN DELLS H-4***
Bark River Campground & Resort — ***JEFFERSON I-5***
Barron Motel & RV Campground — ***BARRON D-2***
®□ **Bass Lake Campground — *WISCONSIN DELLS H-4***
Bayshore Campground (Brown County Park) — ***DYCKESVILLE J-1***
®□ **Beantown Campground — *BAILEYS HARBOR I-2***
Bear Lake Campground — ***MANAWA F-5***
Benson's Century Camping Resort — ***CAMPBELLSPORT H-6***
Big Bay State Park — ***BAYFIELD B-3***
Big Foot Beach SP — ***LAKE GENEVA I-6***
Big "H" Campground — ***CASSVILLE I-3***
® **Big Lake Campground — *ALGOMA J-1***
Birkensee Camping — ***TOMAHAWK D-4***
Black River SF (East Fork Rec Area) — ***HATFIELD F-3***
Black River State Forest (Castle Mound Recreation Area) — ***BLACK RIVER FALLS F-3***
Black River State Forest (Pigeon Creek Recreation Area) — ***BLACK RIVER FALLS F-3***
®□ Blackhawk Camping Resort — ***MILTON I-5***
□ Blackhawk Lake Recreation Area (Iowa County Park) — ***HIGHLAND I-3***
Blackhawk Park (COE-Mississippi River Pool #9) — ***DE SOTO H-2***
□ Blue Mound State Park — ***BLUE MOUNDS I-4***
□ Blue Top Resort & Campground — ***FREMONT F-5***
Bluebird Springs Recreation Area — ***LA CROSSE G-2***
□ **Bonanza Campground & RV Park — *WISCONSIN DELLS H-4***
□ Bong State Recreation Area — ***BURLINGTON I-6***
□ **Briarwood RV Park & Campground — *FAIRCHILD F-3***
Brigham Park (Dane County Park) — ***BLUE MOUNDS I-4***
Brule River State Forest (Bois Brule) — ***BRULE B-2***
Brunet Island State Park — ***CORNELL E-2***
Buckhorn Campground Resort — ***NECEDAH G-4***
□ Buckhorn SP — ***NECEDAH G-4***
®□ **Buffalo Lake Camping Resort — *MONTELLO G-4***
Calumet County Park — ***STOCKBRIDGE G-6***
Camp Holiday — ***BOULDER JUNCTION C-4***
□ Camp Namekagon — ***HAYWARD C-2***
®□ **Captain's Cove Resort and Country Club, LLC — *GRESHAM E-5***
Castle Rock County Park (Juneau County) — *MAUSTON G-4*
Castle Rock Park (Adams County) — ***FRIENDSHIP G-4***
Cecil Lakeview Park (Municipal Park) — ***CECIL E-6***
Cedar Valley Campground — ***KEWAUNEE J-1***
® Chain O' Lakes KOA Resort — ***EAGLE RIVER C-5***
□ **Chapparal Campground & Restaurant — *WONEWOC H-3***
Chequamegon National Forest (Black Lake Campground) — ***WINTER D-3***
Chequamegon National Forest (Chippewa Campground) — ***GILMAN E-3***
Chequamegon National Forest (Day Lake Campground) — ***CLAM LAKE C-3***
Chequamegon National Forest (Namekagon Lake Campground) — ***CABLE C-2***
Chequamegon National Forest (Spearhead Point Campground) — ***WESTBORO D-3***
Chequamegon National Forest (Two Lakes Campground) — ***DRUMMOND C-2***
Chetek River Campground — *CHETEK E-2*
Chute Park (Fischer Memorial Park) — ***MOUNTAIN E-5***
Circle R Campground — ***OSHKOSH G-5***
Cliffside Park (Racine County Park) — ***RACINE I-6***
Collins Park (Portage County Park) — ***ROSHOLT F-4***
Coloma Camperland — ***COLOMA G-4***
Coon Fork Lake Park (Eau Claire County Park) — ***AUGUSTA F-2***
□ Copper Falls SP — ***MELLEN C-3***
Council Grounds SP — ***MERRILL E-4***
Country Aire Camping Resort — *BABCOCK F-4*
Country House Motel & RV Park — ***SPOONER D-2***
□ **Country Quiet RV Park & Campground — *CUMBERLAND D-1***
Country Roads Motorhome & RV Park — *WISCONSIN DELLS H-4*
Country View Campground — *MUKWONAGO I-6*
□ Crazy Horse Campground — ***BRODHEAD I-4***
□ Crockett's Resort Camping and RV Park — ***WISCONSIN DELLS H-4***
□ **Crossroads Campground — *CRIVITZ I-1***
®□ Crystal Lake RV Resort (Morgan RV Resort) — ***LODI H-4***
Deer Creek Campground — ***PARDEEVILLE H-4***
®□ Deer Trail Park Campground — ***NEKOOSA F-4***
®□ **Dell Boo Campground — *WISCONSIN DELLS H-4***
Dells Timberland Camping Resort — *WISCONSIN DELLS H-4*
Delta Lake Park (Bayfield County Park) — ***IRON RIVER B-2***
Devil's Lake State Park — ***BARABOO H-4***
Devils River Campground — ***MARIBEL F-6***
Dexter Park (Wood County Park) — ***PITTSVILLE F-4***
□ **Diamond Lake Family Campground & Trout Farm — *PORTERFIELD I-1***
D.N. (Do Nothing) Campground — *BALSAM LAKE D-1*
Doolittle City Park — ***BIRCHWOOD D-2***
□ **Door County Camping Retreat — *EGG HARBOR I-1***
• **Door County Visitor Bureau — *DOOR COUNTY I-2***
DuBay Park (Portage County) — ***STEVENS POINT F-4***
□ **Duck Creek Campground — *PARDEEVILLE H-4***
□ Eagle Cave Resort LLC — ***BLUE RIVER H-3***
® **Eagle Flats Campground & RV Park — *WISCONSIN DELLS H-4***
Eagles Landing Campground — ***DANBURY C-1***
□ **Egg Harbor Campground & RV Resort — *EGG HARBOR I-1***
Elmer's Camping & Overnite Trailer Park — ***EAU CLAIRE E-2***
®□ **Evergreen Campsites & Resort — *WILD ROSE G-5***
□ **Fish Creek Campground — *FISH CREEK I-2***
Flambeau River SF (Connor's Lake) — ***WINTER D-3***
Flambeau River SF (Lake of the Pines) — ***WINTER D-3***
Flanagan's Pearl Lake Campsites — ***REDGRANITE G-5***
Forest County Veterans Memorial Park — ***CRANDON D-5***
□ **Fox Hill RV Park — *BARABOO H-4***
Frenchman's Landing Campground — *PRAIRIE DU CHIEN I-2*
• **Frontier Bar — *CEDAR B-3***
Frontier RV Park & Campground — *CEDAR B-3*
□ **Frontier Wilderness Campground — *EGG HARBOR I-1***
Goose Island Park (La Crosse County) — *LA CROSSE G-2*
Gordon Dam County Park (Douglas County Park) — ***GORDON C-2***
Governor Dodge State Park — ***DODGEVILLE I-4***
®□ Grand Valley Campground — ***KINGSTON G-5***
Grant River (COE - Lock & Dam 11) — ***POTOSI I-3***
Green Lake Campground — ***GREEN LAKE G-5***
□ **Happy Acres Kampground — *BRISTOL I-6***
Happy Ours RV Park — *GORDON C-2*
® **Harbour Village Resort — *STURGEON BAY J-1***
Harrington Beach State Park — ***BELGIUM H-6***
Hartman Creek SP — ***WAUPACA F-5***
Hattie Sherwood Campground — ***GREEN LAKE G-5***
□ Hayward-KOA — ***HAYWARD C-2***
□ Heaven's Up North Family Campground — ***LAKEWOOD E-5***
Hi-Pines Campground & Resort — *EAGLE RIVER C-5*
Hiawatha Trailer Resort — *WOODRUFF C-4*
□ **Hickory Hills Campground — *EDGERTON I-5***

®□ Hickory Oaks Campground — OSHKOSH G-5
□ **Hidden Valley RV Resort & Campground — MILTON I-5**
□ High Cliff SP — SHERWOOD G-6
® Hiles Pine Lake Campground — HILES D-5
Hilly Haven Campground — CASCADE G-6
□ **Hoeft's Resort & Campground — CASCADE G-6**
□ Holiday Lodge Golf Resort & RV Park — TOMAH G-3
®□ **Holiday Shores Campground & Resort — WISCONSIN DELLS H-4**
Holtwood Campsite (Municipal Park) — OCONTO E-6
Huckleberry Acres Campground — NEW LONDON F-5
Hy-Land Court RV Park — ELLISON BAY I-2
®□ **Indian Shores Camping, Cottages & RV Condominium Resort — WOODRUFF C-4**
□ Indian Trails Campground — PARDEEVILLE H-4
Interstate SP — ST. CROIX FALLS D-1
Iola Pines Campground — IOLA F-5
Island Campground & Marina — HAGER CITY
Isle Vista Casino's Buffalo Bay Campground — BAYFIELD B-3
James N McNally Campground (City Park) — GRANTSBURG D-1
• **Jelly Belly Center — PLEASANT PRAIRIE J-6**
®□ Jellystone Park Camp Resort — WARRENS G-3
Jordan Park (Portage County) — STEVENS POINT F-4
□ K & L Campground — WISCONSIN DELLS H-4
Kalbus Country Harbor, Inc — OSHKOSH G-5
Kettle Moraine SF-Northern Unit (Long Lake) — CAMPBELLSPORT H-6
Kettle Moraine SF-Northern Unit (Mauthe Lake) — KEWASKUM H-6
Kettle Moraine SF-Pike Lake Unit — HARTFORD H-6
Kettle Moraine SF-Southern Unit (Horserider's Campground) — PALMYRA I-5
Kettle Moraine SF-Southern Unit (Ottawa Lake) — EAGLE I-5
Kettle Moraine SF-Southern Unit (Pine Woods) — EAGLE I-5
Kettle Moraine SF-Southern Unit (Whitewater Lake) — WHITEWATER I-5
Kewaunee Marina Campgrounds (City Park) — KEWAUNEE J-1
□ **Kewaunee Village RV Park & Campground — KEWAUNEE J-1**
□ **Keyes Lake Campground — FLORENCE C-6**
□ Kilby Lake Campground — MONTELLO G-4
□ Klondyke Secluded Acres — LANCASTER I-3
□ **KOA Hixton Alma Center — HIXTON F-2**
® **KOA Madison — MADISON I-4**
□ KOA Oakdale — OAKDALE G-3
□ KOA-Fond du Lac Kampground — FOND DU LAC G-5
®□ **KOA-Wisconsin Dells — WISCONSIN DELLS H-4**
△ Kohler-Andrae SP — SHEBOYGAN G-6
Kosir's Rapid Rafts & Campground — SILVER CLIFF D-6
Kreher RV Park (Municipal Park) — ASHLAND B-3
• **La Crosse County Facilities Dept. — LA CROSSE G-2**
Lac Du Flambeau Tribal Campground — LAC DU FLAMBEAU C-4
□ Lake Arrowhead Campground — MONTELLO G-4
®□ Lake Chippewa Campground — HAYWARD C-2
Lake DuBay Shores Campground & RV Park — KNOWLTON F-4
△ Lake Emily Park (Portage County Park) — AMHERST JUNCTION F-4
□ **Lake Hilbert Campground — GOODMAN D-6**
Lake Kegonsa SP — STOUGHTON I-5
Lake Lenwood Beach & Campground — WEST BEND H-6
®□ Lake of the Woods Campground — WAUTOMA G-4
Lake Pepin Campground — PEPIN F-1
Lake Wissota State Park — CHIPPEWA FALLS E-2
□ Lakeland Camping Resort — MILTON I-5
® Lakeview Campground — STOCKBRIDGE G-6
® Lazy Days Campground — WEST BEND H-6
□ **Leon Valley Campground — SPARTA G-3**
® Lil' Yellow River RV Park & Campground — NEW LISBON G-3
Little Bluff Campground — RIO H-5
□ **Log Cabin Resort & Campground — TREGO C-2**
Loon Lagoon RV Resort & Campground — MERCER C-4
□ Lost Falls Campground — BLACK RIVER FALLS F-3
Lucius Woods (Douglas County Park) — SOLON SPRINGS C-2
® Lynn Ann's Campground — ST. GERMAIN C-4
® Maple Heights Campground — LAKEWOOD E-5
□ **Maple View Campground — NORMAN F-6**
®□ McCaslin Mountain Campground LLC — ATHELSTANE D-6
Meadowlark Acres Family Campground and Christian Fellowship Center — BURLINGTON I-6
Memorial Park (Municipal Park) — WASHBURN B-3
Mendota Park (Dane County Park) — MIDDLETON I-4
Menomonee Park (Waukesha County Park) — LANNON H-6
Merrick State Park — FOUNTAIN CITY G-2
®□ Merry Mac's Campground — BARABOO H-4
®△□ MILITARY PARK (Pine View Recreation Area-Fort McCoy) — SPARTA G-3
Mill Bluff State Park — CAMP DOUGLAS G-3
□ Mirror Lake SP — WISCONSIN DELLS H-4
Mohican RV Park — BOWLER E-5
□ Monster Hall Campground — UNITY E-3
Monument Point Camping — EGG HARBOR I-1
Moonlite Trails Campground LLC — NECEDAH G-4
Morris-Erickson County Park — NEW AUBURN E-2
Mukwonago Park (Waukesha County Park) — MUKWONAGO I-6
Muskego Park (Waukesha County Park) — MUSKEGO I-6
Naga-Waukee Park (Waukesha County Park) — DELAFIELD I-6
Nelson Dewey State Park — CASSVILLE I-3
Nemadji Mobile Home & RV Park — SUPERIOR B-1
□ Neshonoc Lakeside Camp Resort — WEST SALEM G-2
New Glarus Woods SP — NEW GLARUS I-4
Nicolet National Forest (Bagley Rapids Campground) — MOUNTAIN E-5
Nicolet National Forest (Bear Lake Campground) — LAONA D-5
Nicolet National Forest (Boot Lake Campground) — TOWNSEND D-5
Nicolet National Forest (Boulder Lake Campground) — LANGLADE E-5
Nicolet National Forest (Franklin Lake Campground) — EAGLE RIVER C-5
Nicolet National Forest (Lac Vieux Desert Campground) — LAND O'LAKES C-5
Nicolet National Forest (Laura Lake Campground) — ARMSTRONG CREEK D-5
Nicolet National Forest (Lost Lake Campground) — TIPLER C-5
Nicolet National Forest (Luna-White Deer Campground) — EAGLE RIVER C-5
Nicolet National Forest (Richardson Lake) — WABENO D-5
Nicolet National Forest (Sevenmile Lake Campground) — THREE LAKES D-5
Nicolet National Forest (Spectacle Lake Campground) — EAGLE RIVER C-5
North Bay Shore (Oconto County Park) — OCONTO E-6
North Mead Park (Clark County) — GREENWOOD F-3
★ North Point RV — CHIPPEWA FALLS E-2
• **North Star Mohican Casino Resort — BOWLER E-5**
North Wood County Park (Wood County) — MARSHFIELD F-3
®□ **Northern Exposure Resort & Campground — CHETEK E-2**
Northern Hideaway RV Park & Campground — PEARSON D-5
Northern Highland/American Legion SF (Big Lake) — BOULDER JUNCTION C-4
Northern Highland/American Legion SF (Buffalo Lake) — WOODRUFF C-4
Northern Highland/American Legion SF (Clear Lake) — WOODRUFF C-4
Northern Highland/American Legion SF (Crystal-Muskie) — WOODRUFF C-4
Northern Highland/American Legion SF (Cunard Lake) — LAKE TOMAHAWK D-4
Northern Highland/American Legion SF (East Star Lake) — CONOVER C-5
Northern Highland/American Legion SF (Firefly Lake) — SAYNER C-4
Northern Highland/American Legion SF (Indian Mounds) — WOODRUFF C-4
Northern Highland/American Legion SF (North Trout Lake) — WOODRUFF C-4
Northern Highland/American Legion SF (Razorback Lake) — SAYNER C-4

WISCONSIN — Continued

Northern Highland/American Legion SF (Sandy Beach Lake) — MANITOWISH WATERS C-4
Northern Highland/American Legion SF (South Trout Lake) — BOULDER JUNCTION C-4
Northern Highland/American Legion SF (Starrett Lake) — SAYNER C-4
Northern Highland/American Legion SF (Upper Gresham Lake) — BOULDER JUNCTION C-4
Northforest Campgrounds — TOMAHAWK D-4
Northland Camping & RV Park — SUPERIOR B-1
Nugget Lake County Park (Pierce County Park) — PLUM CITY F-1
□ **O'Neil Creek Campground & RV Park — CHIPPEWA FALLS E-2**
Otter Lake Recreation Area (Lincoln County Park) — TOMAHAWK D-4
®□ **Ox Creek RV Park — MONTELLO G-4**
Patricia Lake RV Resort — MINOCQUA D-4
Pattison SP — SUPERIOR B-1
Pelican Lake Campground — PELICAN LAKE D-5
Peninsula State Park — FISH CREEK I-2
Perrot SP — TREMPEALEAU G-2
□ Peshtigo River Campground, LLC — CRIVITZ I-1
Petenwell Park (Adams County) — FRIENDSHIP G-4
Pettibone Resort — LA CROSSE G-2
Pilgrim's Campground — FORT ATKINSON I-5
□ **Pine Grove Campground — SHAWANO E-5**
Pine Harbor Campground — CHIPPEWA FALLS E-2
Pine Point County Park (Chippewa County) — HOLCOMBE E-3
®□ Pineland Camping Park — BIG FLATS G-4
Pioneer Park (Village Park) — PRAIRIE FARM E-2
□ **Plymouth Rock Camping Resort — PLYMOUTH G-6**
□ Point Beach SF — TWO RIVERS G-6
□ Potawatomi SP — STURGEON BAY J-1
Prentice Park (Municipal Park) — ASHLAND B-3
□ **Pride of America Camping Resort — PORTAGE H-4**
®□ Quietwoods South Camping Resort — BRUSSELS J-1
Raft N' Rest Campground — WHITE LAKE E-5
® **Rainbows End Campground — REEDSVILLE G-6**
Red Barn Campground — SHELL LAKE D-2
Red Oak Campground — BARABOO H-4
Rib Mountain SP — WAUSAU E-4
®□ **River Bay Resort Campground, Marina & RV Park — WISCONSIN DELLS H-4**
® **River Bend Resort — WATERTOWN H-5**
□ River Forest Rafting Campground — WHITE LAKE E-5
®□ River of Lakes Campground — BAGLEY I-2
River Road RV Campground — HAYWARD C-2
River Valley RV Park — SPRING GREEN H-4
□ River's Edge Campground — SOMERSET E-1
Rivers Edge Campground & Marina (Not Visited) — STEVENS POINT F-4
Riverside Campground (City Park) — MUSCODA H-3
Roche-A-Cri SP — FRIENDSHIP G-4
Rock Dam Park Campground (Clark County Park) — GREENWOOD F-3
Rock Island SP — ROCK ISLAND I-2
Rocky Arbor SP — WISCONSIN DELLS H-4
Russell Memorial Park (Clark County Park) — HATFIELD F-3
Rustic Barn Campground — KIELER I-3
□ Rustic Woods Campground — WAUPACA F-5
®□ **S-J & W Ham Lake Campground LLC — WABENO D-5**
St. Croix Casino & Hotel RV Park — TURTLE LAKE D-1
□ St. Joseph Motel & Resort — NECEDAH G-4
Sanders Park (Racine County Park) — RACINE I-6
® **Scenic View Campground — SPOONER D-2**
Seagull Marina & Campground — TWO RIVERS G-6
Shady Acres Campsites — DENMARK F-6
Shell Lake Memorial Park (Municipal Park) — SHELL LAKE D-2
Sherwood County Park (Clark County) — NEILLSVILLE F-3
□ **Sherwood Forest Camping & RV Park — WISCONSIN DELLS H-4**
□ **Silver Springs Campsites, Inc. — RIO H-5**
□ Sisko's Pine Point Resort — HAYWARD C-2
□ **Six Lakes Resort & RV Park — CHETEK E-2**
□ **Sky High Camping Resort — PORTAGE H-4**
®□ **Smokey Hollow Campground — LODI H-4**
Snyder Park (Clark County) — NEILLSVILLE F-3
Solberg Lake Campground (Price County Park) — PHILLIPS D-3
South Wood County Park (Wood County) — WISCONSIN RAPIDS F-4
Southworth Memorial Park (Barron County Park) — CHETEK E-2
□ Sports Unlimited Campground & Hunters Slough — PRAIRIE DU CHIEN I-2
Stand Rock Campground — WISCONSIN DELLS H-4
□ **Stoney Creek RV Resort — OSSEO F-2**
Summer Breeze Resort — WISCONSIN DELLS H-4
Sunrise Bay Campgrounds & RV Park — HAYWARD C-2
Terrace View Campsites — TOMAHAWK D-4
□ **The Harbor Campground — THREE LAKES D-5**
The Playful Goose — HORICON H-5
□ Tilleda Falls Campground — TILLEDA E-5
® Timber Trail Campground — ALGOMA J-1
Timber Trail Campground — WEST BEND H-6
Token Creek Park (Dane County Park) — MADISON I-4
Tomahawk Campground & RV Park — TOMAHAWK D-4
Tomorrow Wood Campground — HANCOCK G-4
□ **Tom's Campground — DODGEVILLE I-4**
®□ Top O The Morn Resort & Campground — IRON RIVER B-2
Tower Hill SP — SPRING GREEN H-4
□ **Tranquil Timbers Camping Retreat — STURGEON BAY J-1**
★ **Truck Country — APPLETON F-5**
★ **Truck Country — GREEN BAY F-6**
★ **Truck Country — MADISON I-4**
★ **Truck Country — MARINETTE E-6**
★ **Truck Country — MILWAUKEE I-6**
★ **Truck Country — SHULLSBURG I-3**
★ **Truck Country — WAUSAU E-4**
□ **Tunnel Trail Campground — WILTON G-3**
Turtle Lake RV Park — TURTLE LAKE D-1
Twin Bear Park (Bayfield County Park) — IRON RIVER B-2
□ Twin Springs Camping Resort — MENOMONIE E-2
Veterans Memorial Park (Barron County) — CAMERON D-2
Veteran's Memorial Park (La Crosse County) — WEST SALEM G-2
Veterans Memorial Park (Langlade County Park) — SUMMIT LAKE D-5
Viking Village Campground & Resort — STOUGHTON I-5
Village of Hancock Campground — HANCOCK G-4
®□ **Vista Royalle Campground — BANCROFT F-4**
★ **Vista Royalle RV Sales — BANCROFT F-4**
Voyager Village RV Park — DANBURY C-1
□ **Wagon Trail Campground Ltd. — ELLISON BAY I-2**
Waldo Carlson Park (Barron County Park) — MIKANA D-2
□ Wanna Bee Campground & RV Resort — WISCONSIN DELLS H-4
®□ **Washington Island Camping Retreat — WASHINGTON ISLAND I-2**
□ Waupaca Camping Park, LLC — WAUPACA F-5
West End Thompson Park (Municipal Park) — WASHBURN B-3
□ **Westward Ho Camp Resort (Morgan Rv Resort) — FOND DU LAC G-5**
Wheeler's Campground — BARABOO H-4
□ Whispering Pines Campground — HOLMEN G-2
White Mound Campground (Sauk County Park) — PLAIN H-4
□ Whitetail Bluff Camp & Resort, LLC — CASSVILLE I-3
Whitetail Ridge Campground/RV Park — SARONA D-2
Wild West Campground & Corral — AMHERST F-4
Wildcat Mountain SP — ONTARIO G-3
®□ Wilderness Campground — MONTELLO G-4
Wilderness County Park (Juneau County) — NECEDAH G-4
Willie's RV Center & Campground — BLOOMER E-2
□ **Willow Mill Campsite LLC — RIO H-5**
Willow River SP — HUDSON E-1
• **Wisconsin Dells Visitor & Convention Bureau — WISCONSIN DELLS H-4**
□ **Wisconsin Riverside Resort — SPRING GREEN H-4**
Wisconsin State Fair RV Park — MILWAUKEE I-6
Wolf River Campgrounds — NEW LONDON F-5
Wyalusing State Park — BAGLEY I-2

WISCONSIN — Continued

Yellowstone Lake State Park — BLANCHARDVILLE I-4
□ Yogi Bear Jellystone Camp-Resort — CALEDONIA I-6
□ Yogi Bear Jellystone Park — BAGLEY I-2
□ **Yogi Bear Jellystone Park — STURGEON BAY J-1**
□ **Yogi Bear Jellystone Park Camp-Resort — FREMONT F-5**
□ **Yogi Bear Jellystone Park/Fort Atkinson — FORT ATKINSON I-5**
®□ **Yogi Bear's Jellystone Park Camp-Resort — WISCONSIN DELLS H-4**
□ **Yukon Trails Camping — WISCONSIN DELLS H-4**

NEW BRUNSWICK

Beausejour Camping — SHEDIAC D-5
Berry Patch Campground & RV Park — BATHURST B-4
Blue Heron Camping (Town Park) — CHARLO B-3
Boutouche Bay Campground & Chalets — BOUCTOUCHE C-5
□ **Camper's City RV/Resort — MONCTON D-4**
Camping by the Bay — BLACK POINT B-3
Camping Cap Lumiere Beach (Not Visited) — RICHIBOUCTOU-VILLAGE C-4
Camping Caraquet — CARAQUET B-4
Camping Gite Janine & Auberge du Havre (Not Visited) — SHIPPAGAN B-4
Camping Ile Lameque (Municipal Park) — LAMEQUE B-5
Camping & Motel Colibri (Not Visited) — CARAQUET B-4
Camping Murraywood (Not Visited) — PETIT ROCHER NORD B-4
□ **Camping Near Miramichi — BLACK RIVER BRIDGE C-4**
Camping Oceanic — SHEDIAC D-5
Camping Panoramic 86 — EDMUNDSTON B-1
Camping Shippagan (Town Park) — SHIPPAGAN B-4
Camping St Basile — SAINT-BASILE D-3
Camping St-Leonard — SAINT-LEONARD C-2
• **Casey's Artisans — SHEFFIELD D-3**
Casey's Campground — SHEFFIELD D-3
• **Casey's Museum — SHEFFIELD D-3**
• **Casey's Restaurant — SHEFFIELD D-3**
Cedar Cove Camping (Not Visited) — POINTE-VERTE B-4
®□ **Century Farm Family Campground — ST. MARTINS E-4**
□ Chalets et Camping de la Pointe (Not Visited) — TRACADIE-SHEILA B-4
Chapman's Tent & Trailer Park — JANEVILLE B-4
□ **Cosy Cabins Campground — WOODSTOCK D-2**
□ Coy Lake Camping — GAGETOWN D-3
Crystal Beach Campground (Not Visited) — CRYSTAL BEACH E-3
De la Republique Provincial Park — EDMUNDSTON B-1
Deer Island Point Campground — DEER ISLAND E-2
★ **Ed's Travel Trailer Parts & Service — MONCTON D-4**
Enclosure Campground — MIRAMICHI C-4
Escuminac Beach & Family Park — BAIE SAINTE-ANNE C-4
Etoile Filante Camping Wishing Star — SHEDIAC D-5
Everett's Campground — MACTAQUAC D-3
Family Land Campground (Not Visited) — MIRAMICHI C-4
Fundy National Park (Chignecto North) — ALMA D-4
Fundy National Park (Headquarters Campground) — ALMA D-4
Fundy National Park (Point Wolfe Campground) — ALMA D-4
Fundy National Park (Wolfe Lake Campground) — ALMA D-4
□ Grande Riviere Camping — SAINT-LEONARD C-2
Great Bear Camping — BEAR ISLAND D-3
Hardings Point Campground — HARDINGS POINT E-3
Hardings Point Campground — HARDINGS POINT E-3
Hartt Island RV Resort — FREDERICTON D-3
Heritage Country Camping (Not Visited) — LOWER QUEENSBURY D-2
Herring Cove Provincial Park — CAMPOBELLO ISLAND E-3
Hidden Valley Campground (Not Visited) — HAMPTON E-4
Island View Camping (Not Visited) — PORT OF BAYSIDE E-2
Jacquet River Park (Village Park) — BELLEDUNE B-3
Kiwanis Ocean Front Camping — ST. ANDREWS
Kouchibouguac National Park (Cote A Fabian) — KOUCHIBOUGUAC C-4
Kouchibouguac National Park (South Kouchibouguac) — SAINT-LOUIS-DE-KENT C-4
Lake George Family Campground (City Park) — HARVEY D-2
Lakeside Campground and Recreation Park — MILL COVE D-3
®□ **Lone Pine Park Campground & Cabins (Not Visited) — PENOBSQUIS D-4**
Mactaquac Provincial Park — MACTAQUAC D-3
□ Malybel Park Camping (Not Visited) — BERESFORD B-4
Marshview Trailer Park & Tenting (Not Visited) — SACKVILLE D-5
□ Miscou Island Camping Cabins — MISCOU ISLAND B-5
® Mohawk Camping — WATERBOROUGH D-3
Motel & Camping Baie des Chaleurs (Not Visited) — GRANDE-ANSE B-4
□ Motel & Camping Hache (Not Visited) — NIGADOO B-4
Mount Carleton Provincial Park — NICTAU C-2
□ **Mulherin's Campground — GRAND FALLS C-2**
Murray Beach Provincial Park — CAPE TORMENTINE D-5
New River Beach Provincial Park — NEW RIVER BEACH E-3
Oak Bay Provincial Park — OAK BAY E-2
Oak Point Family Campground (Not Visited) — MIRAMICHI C-4
Oak Point Kiwanis Park — OAK POINT E-3
Ocean Surf Trailer Park — SHEDIAC D-5
Ocean View Camping — POCOLOGAN E-3
Ocean View Park — SHEDIAC D-5
□ Paradis de la P'tite Montagne (Not Visited) — SAINT-ANDRE C-2
Parasol Camping — SHEDIAC D-5
□ Parc Daigle Park — SAINT-LOUIS-DE-KENT C-4
Parlee Beach Provincial Park — SHEDIAC D-5
® Pine Cone Camping (Not Visited) — PENOBSQUIS D-4
Pine Ridge Campground (Not Visited) — GALLAGHER RIDGE D-4
Plage Miscou Camping (Not Visited) — MISCOU ISLAND B-5
△□ **Ponderosa Pines Campground — HOPEWELL CAPE D-5**
®□ Rapid Brook Camping (Not Visited) — GRAND FALLS C-2
River Country Campground — FLORENCEVILLE D-2
Riverside (Iroquois) RV Park — EDMUNDSTON B-1
Rockwood Park Campground — SAINT-JOHN E-3
Sandy Point Park — BAIE SAINTE-ANNE C-4
® **Sea Side Tent & Trailer Park — ST. MARTINS E-4**
Silver Sands Family Camping — PETIT CAP D-5
South Cove Rive-Sud Camping & Golf — SHEDIAC D-5
• **South Cove Rive-Sud Golf — SHEDIAC D-5**
Spring Water Campground — FOUR FALLS C-2
Stonehurst Trailer Park — MONCTON D-4
Sugarloaf Provincial Park — ATHOLVILLE B-3
Sunrise Campground — MIRAMICHI C-4
Sunset View Campground & Cottages (Not Visited) — HAWKSHAW D-2
The Anchorage Provincial Park — GRAND MANAN ISLAND F-3
□ **Three Bears Family Camping & RV Park — PENOBSQUIS D-4**
T.N.T. Campground (Not Visited) — COLES ISLAND D-4
Town & Country Campark — SUSSEX D-4
Tracadie Beach Campground — RIVIERE DU PORTAGE B-4
Val Comeau Provincial Park — VAL COMEAU B-4
□ **Woolastook Park — FREDERICTON D-3**
□ Yogi Bear's Jellystone Park at Kozy Acres — WOODSTOCK D-2

NEWFOUNDLAND AND LABRADOR

Barachois Pond (Provincial Park) — ST. GEORGE'S D-2
Bellevue Beach Campground (Not visited) — BELLEVUE BEACH D-5
Beothuck Park (Not visited) — GRAND FALLS-WINDSOR C-4
Blow Me Down (Provincial Park) — LARK HARBOUR C-2

NEWFOUNDLAND AND LABRADOR — Continued

Blue Fin RV Trailer Park — ST. JOHN'S D-6
Butter Pot (Provincial Park) — ST. JOHN'S D-6
Catamaran Park — BADGER C-4
Chance Cove (Provincial Park) — PORTUGAL COVE SOUTH E-5
Country Inn RV Park — GANDER C-5
David Smallwood Park (Town Park) — GAMBO C-5
Deer Lake Municipal Park — DEER LAKE C-3
Dildo Run (Provincial Park) — SUMMERFORD C-4
Family Adventure Park CG — CORNER BROOK C-3
Fitzgerald's Pond Park (Not visited) — ARGENTIA E-5
Fort Birchy Park & Campground — BIRCHY LAKE C-3
Frenchman's Cove (Provincial Park) — FRENCHMAN'S COVE E-4
□ Funland Resort — CORMACK C-3
□ **Gateway to the North RV Park — DEER LAKE C-3**
Georges Mountain Village Trailer (Not visited) — STEADY BROOK C-3
□ Golden Arm Trailer Park — GREEN'S HARBOUR D-5
Golden Sands Trailer Park (Not Visited) — MARYSTOWN E-4
Grand Codroy R.V. Camping Park Craft Shop — DOYLES D-2
Gros Morne National Park (Berry Hill) — ROCKY HARBOUR C-3
Gros Morne National Park (Lomond Campground) — WILTONDALE C-3
Gros Morne National Park (Shallow Bay) — COW HEAD B-3
Gros Morne National Park (Trout River Campground) — TROUT RIVER C-2
Gros Morne RV Campground & Motel — ROCKY HARBOUR C-3
®□ Gros Morne/Norris Point KOA — ROCKY HARBOUR C-3
Gushue's Pond Park (Not visited) — GUSHUE'S POND E-6
□ **Harold W Duffsett Shriners RV Park — EASTPORT C-5**
Jonathan's Pond Campground (Not visited) — GANDER C-5
JT Cheeseman (Provincial Park) — CHANNEL-PORT-AUX-BASQUES E-2
Kinsman Prince Edward Park (Not visited) — CORNER BROOK C-3
Kona Beach Trailer Park — SOUTH BROOK C-4
La Manche (Provincial Park) — CAPE BROYLE E-6
Little Paradise Park — CHANNEL-PORT-AUX-BASQUES E-2
Lockston Path (Provincial Park) — PORT REXTON D-5
□ **Lomond River Lodge and RV Park — LOMOND RIVER C-3**
□ Mountain Waters Resort (Not visited) — PORTLAND CREEK B-3
Notre Dame (Provincial Park) — LEWISPORTE C-4
Oceanside RV Park — PORT-AU-CHOIX A-3
Paradise Farm Trailer Park — BONAVISTA C-5
□ Peyton's Woods RV Park and Campground — TWILLINGATE B-4
□ Pineridge Cabins & Campground (Not visited) — PASADENA C-3
Pinware River (Provincial Park) — PINWARE B-2
Pippy Park Campground — ST. JOHN'S D-6
Pistolet Bay (Provincial Park) — RALEIGH A-4
Putt 'N' Paddle Campground — ARNOLD'S COVE D-5
River of Ponds Park (Not visited) — RIVER OF PONDS B-3
St. Barbe RV Park (Not visited) — ST. BARBE A-3
Sandbanks (Provincial Park) — BURGEO E-3
Sanger Memorial RV Park — GRAND FALLS-WINDSOR C-4
□ Sea Echo Motel (Not visited) — PORT-AU-CHOIX A-3
Sir Richard Squires Memorial (Provincial Park) — DEER LAKE C-3
Square Pond Friends and Family RV Park — GAMBO C-5
Terra Nova National Park (Madalay Head) — GLOVERTOWN C-5
Terra Nova NP (Newman Sound Campground) — GLOVERTOWN C-5
The Waters Edge Campground — SHOAL BROOK C-3
Torrent River Nature Park — HAWKE'S BAY B-3
Triple Falls RV Park (Not visited) — ST. ANTHONY A-4
Tucker's Trailer Park (Not Visited) — THORBURN LAKE D-5
Viking RV Park — QUIRPON A-4
Wishingwell Campground (Not visited) — JEFFREYS D-2

NOVA SCOTIA

□ Adventures East Campground & Cottages — BADDECK B-5
Ainslie Village Camping — SOUTH LAKE AINSLIE B-5
Amherst Shore Provincial Park — AMHERST B-3
Annapolis River Campground (Not visited) — BRIDGETOWN D-2
□ Arm of Gold Campground (Not Visited) — NORTH SYDNEY B-6
□ **Baddeck Cabot Trail Campground — BADDECK B-5**
Battery Provincial Park — ST. PETERS B-5
Beechbrook Campground — ARDOISE D-3
Belle Baie Park (Not Visited) — CHURCH POINT D-1
®□ Ben Eoin Beach RV Resort & Campground. — BEN EOIN B-5
□ Birchwood Campground (Not visited) — PICTOU C-4
Blomidon Provincial Park — BLOMIDON C-3
□ Boutiliers Glen — SOUTH RAWDON C-3
Boylston Provincial Park — GUYSBOROUGH C-5
□ Bras D'or Lakes Campground — BADDECK B-5
Brookside Park and U-Fish (Not visited) — SALT SPRINGS C-4
®△ **Camper's Haven — YARMOUTH E-1**
Cape Breton Highlands National Park (Broad Cove Campground) — INGONISH BEACH A-5
Cape Breton Highlands National Park (Cheticamp Campground) — CHETICAMP A-5
Cape Breton Highlands National Park (Corney Brook Campground) — CHETICAMP A-5
Cape Breton Highlands National Park (Ingonish Beach) — INGONISH BEACH A-5
Cape Canso RV Park & Marina (Not visited) — CANSO C-5
□ Cape Chignecto PP — ADVOCATE HARBOUR C-2
Caribou/Munroes Island PP — PICTOU C-4
□ Ceilidh Cottages, RV Sites & Campground — WEST MABOU B-5
Cranberry Campground (Not visited) — LOWER BARNEY'S RIVER C-4
Digby Campground (Not visited) — DIGBY D-2
Dino's One Stop (Not visited) — INGONISH A-5
Dollar Lake Provincial Park — BEDFORD D-3
Driftwood Tent & Trailer Park (Not visited) — LITTLE BRAS D'OR B-6
□ Dunromin Campsites — ANNAPOLIS ROYAL D-2
□ **E & F Webber Lakeside Park — UPPER LAKEVILLE D-4**
East River Lodge Campground & Trailer Park (Not visited) — SHEET HARBOUR C-4
Ellenwood Lake Provincial Park — DEERFIELD E-1
Elm River Park — TRURO C-3
Englishtown Ridge Campground (Not Visited) — ENGLISHTOWN B-5
□ Falls Lake Recreational Facility — FALLS LAKE WEST D-3
Fisherman's Cove RV & Campground (Not visited) — HUNT'S POINT E-2
Five Islands Provincial Park — FIVE ISLANDS C-3
®□ Fox Mountain Camping Park — BERWICK C-2
Fundy Tides Campground — ADVOCATE HARBOUR C-2
□ Fundy Trail Campground & Cottages — DELAPS COVE D-2
Gateway Parklands — AMHERST B-3
Glenview Campground — WHYCOCOMAGH B-5
Glooscap Campground & RV — PARRSBORO C-3
Graves Island Provincial Park — EAST CHESTER D-3
□ Halifax West KOA — HALIFAX D-3
Harbour Light Trailer Court & Campground — PICTOU C-4
® Hidden Hilltop Campground — TRURO C-3
□ Hideaway Campground & Oyster Market (Not visited) — SOUTH HARBOUR A-5
Highbury Gardens Tent & Trailer Park — KENTVILLE C-3
□ Hubbards Beach Campground — HUBBARDS D-3
□ **Hyclass Campground — HAVRE BOUCHER C-5**
□ Inverness Beach Village & Campground (Not visited) — INVERNESS B-5
® Jaggar's Point Oceanside Camping (Not Visited) — DIGBY D-2
Kejimkujik National Park (Jeremys Bay Campground) — MAITLAND BRIDGE D-2
King Neptune Campground (Not Visited) — INDIAN HARBOUR D-3
Klahanie Kamping — AYLESFORD C-2
LaHave River Campground (Not Visited) — NEWBURNE D-2
□ Lake Breeze Campground & Cottages (Not visited) — DARLING LAKE E-1
Lake View Treasures (Not Visited) — LOUISBOURG B-6
Land of Evangeline-Family Camping Resort — GRAND PRE' C-3
Laurie Provincial Park — GRAND LAKE D-3

NOVA SCOTIA — Continued

Linwood Harbour Campground — LINWOOD C-5
®□ **Little Lake Family Campground — LUNENBURG D-3**
Loch Lomond Campground — AMHERST B-3
□ Lockeport Cottages & Campgrounds ((Not visited) — LYDGATE E-2
Louis Head Beach Campground (Not Visited) — LOUIS HEAD E-2
Louisbourg Motorhome RV Park & Campground (Not visited) — LOUISBOURG B-6
MacKinnon's Campground (Not visited) — EAST LAKE AINSLIE B-5
MacLeod's Campsite (Not visited) — DUNVEGAN B-5
Meat Cove Camping (Not Visited) — MEAT COVE A-5
Mira River Provincial Park — SYDNEY B-6
® Murphy's Camping on the Ocean (Not visited) — MURPHY'S COVE D-4
Nimrods Campground (Not visited) — SHERBROOKE C-4
□ North Sydney/Cabot Trail KOA — NORTH SYDNEY B-6
● **Nova Scotia Dept of Tourism and Culture — HALIFAX D-3**
Oakhill Pines Camp & Trailer Park (Not visited) — OAKHILL D-3
Oasis Motel & Campground (Not visited) — ANTIGONISH C-4
® Orchard Queen Motel & Campground — MIDDLETON D-2
□ Ovens Natural Park (Not visited) — RIVERPORT D-3
Pipers Campground & Trailer Park — INDIAN BROOK B-5
® Plage St.-Pierre Beach & Campground (Not Visited) — CHETICAMP A-5
□ Plantation Campground — BERWICK C-2
Point of View RV Park & Suites (Not visited) — LOUISBOURG B-6
Ponhook Lodge Campground (Not Visited) — GREENFIELD D-2
Porters Lake Provincial Park — PORTERS LAKE D-3
Raven Haven Beachside Family Park (City Town) — MILFORD D-2
Rawdon Gold Mines Campground (Not visited) — RAWDON GOLD MINES C-3
Rayport Campground — MARTIN'S RIVER D-3
Renfrew Campground (Not visited) — NINE MILE RIVER C-3
Risser's Beach Provincial Park — LAHAVE D-3
River Ryan Campground (Not visited) — NEW WATERFORD B-6
□ Riverdale RV Park (Not visited) — LOUISBOURG B-6
Riverland Campground — NINE MILE RIVER C-3
® **St. Anns Bay Campark — ST. ANN'S BAY B-5**
St. Mary's Riverside Campground (Not visited) — SHERBROOKE C-4
Salsman Provincial Park — ANTIGONISH C-4
□ **Scotia Pine Campground — TRURO C-3**
Seafoam Campground (Not visited) — SEAFOAM B-4
Sherwood Forest Camping Park (Not visited) — COLDBROOK C-2
®□ Shore Boat View Campground (Not visited) — BAYPORT D-3
Shubie Park Campground — DARTMOUTH D-3
Smiley's Provincial Park — WINDSOR D-3
□ South Mountain Park Family Camping & RV Resort Inc (Not Visited) — KENTVILLE C-3
□ SpryBay Campground & Cabins (Not Visited) — SPRY BAY D-4
Sunset Watch Family Campground (Not Visited) — BRULE C-3
The Islands Provincial Park — SHELBURNE E-2
□ The Lakes Campground (Not visited) — N.E. MARGAREE B-5
The Old Shipyard Beach Campground (Not visited) — SPENCER'S ISLAND C-2
Thomas Raddall PP — PORT JOLI E-2
Trenton Park Campground (City Park) — TRENTON C-4
Valleyview Provincial Park — BRIDGETOWN D-2
□ Vidito Family Campground & Cottages LTD — WILMOT D-2
Wayside Park (Not visited) — GLEN MARGARET D-3
□ Whidden's Campground — ANTIGONISH C-4
Whispering Winds (Not Visited) — SHUBENACADIE C-3
Whycocomagh Provincial Park — WHYCOCOMAGH B-5
Wild Nature Campground (Not Visited) — SHUBENACADIE C-3
Woodhaven RV Park of Halifax — HALIFAX D-3
□ Yogi Bear's Jellystone Park (Not Visited) — KINGSTON C-2

ONTARIO

□ 1000 Island-Ivy Lea-KOA — GANANOQUE H-5
® 1000 Islands Camping Resort — GANANOQUE H-5
□ Abram Lake Tent and Trailer Park (Not Visited) — SIOUX LOOKOUT D-2
Agawa Bay Campground (Lake Superior PP) — WAWA C-3
Aintree Trailer Park — KINCARDINE H-2
Albion Hills Conservation Area (Toronto & Region Cons. Auth.) — BOLTON H-3
Algonquin Trails Camping Resort (Not Visited) — DWIGHT G-3
□ All Star Resort Tent & Trailer Park (Not visited) — MADAWASKA F-4
□ Almaguin Parklands Campground (Not visited) — KATRINE F-3
□ Anchor Bay Camp — ENNISMORE H-4
Anicinabe RV Park & Campground (Not Visited) — KENORA D-1
□ Antler's Kingfisher Lodge (Not Visited) — DEUX RIVIERES F-4
Arrowhead Provincial Park — HUNTSVILLE G-3
Auburn Riverside Retreat (Not visited) — GODERICH H-2
A.W. Campbell (St. Clair Region Cons Auth.) — ALVINSTON I-1
Awenda Provincial Park — PENETANGUISHENE G-3
Backus Heritage Conservation Area (Long Point Region Cons Auth.) — PORT ROWAN J-2
® Bailey's Bay Resort (Not Visted) — PETERBOROUGH H-4
□ Balsam Lake Provincial Park — COBOCONK G-4
Bancroft Campground — BANCROFT G-4
®□ Bancroft Tent & Trailer Camp (Not Visited) — BANCROFT G-4
Bass Lake Provincial Park — ORILLIA G-3
□ **Batman's Cottages, Campground — SHEGUIANDAH F-1**
Bayview Camp & Cottages (Not Visited) — CALLANDER D-6
□ Bensfort Bridge Resort — BAILIEBORO H-4
Big Oak Tent & Trailer Park (Not Visited) — STURGEON FALLS D-6
® Big Otter Marina & Campground (Not visited) — PORT BURWELL J-2
□ **Bingemans Camping Resort — KITCHENER I-2**
® Birch Bark Tent & Trailer Park — GRAND BEND I-2
® Birch Pine Park (Not visited) — IPPERWASH BEACH I-1
Birchland Trailer Park (Not Visited) — DRYDEN D-2
Birdsall Beach Park — HASTINGS H-4
Bishop Lake Trailer Park (Not Visited) — CLOYNE G-5
□ **Bissell's Hideaway Resort — FONTHILL I-3**
□ Black Rock Resort (Not Visited) — MANITOWANING F-2
Blue Lake Provincial Park — VERMILION BAY D-1
®□ Blueberry Hill Motel & Campground (Not Visited) — GOULAIS RIVER D-4
Bluewater Park (City Park) — WIARTON G-2
Bluewater Trailer Park (City Park) — KINCARDINE H-2
□ Bon Echo Provincial Park — CLOYNE G-5
□ Bonnechere Provincial Park — ROUND LAKE CENTRE F-4
Bonnie Lake Camping — BRACEBRIDGE G-3
Booster Park (City Park) — MARMORA H-4
Brant Conservation Area (Grand River Cons Auth) — BRANTFORD I-3
Branton-Cundick (St. Clair Parkway Commission) — SOMBRA I-1
□ Brownlee Lake Park Resort & Campground (Not Visited) — THESSALON D-4
Brucedale Conservation Area (Saugeen Valley Cons Area) — PORT ELGIN H-2
Buckslide Tent and Trailer Park (Not visited) — MINDEN G-4
Busy Beaver Campground (Not Visited) — HILTON BEACH D-4
Byng Island (Grand River Cons Auth) — DUNNVILLE I-3
Cache Bay Tent & Trailer Park (Not Visited) — STURGEON FALLS D-6
Caliper Lake Provincial Park — NESTOR FALLS E-1
Cameron's Beach Trailer Park (Not Visited) — IROQUOIS FALLS B-6
®□ Camp Barcovan Tent & RV Park — CARRYING PLACE H-4
□ Camp Hillbilly Estates (Not Visited) — GRAVENHURST G-3
Camp Hither Hills — OTTAWA G-6
□ Camp Sawmill Bay (Not Visited) — UPSALA B-1
□ **Campark Resorts — NIAGARA FALLS I-3**
□ Campers Cove — WHEATLEY J-1
® Canadian Timberland Campground — RENFREW F-5
Canisbay Lake Campground (Algonquin PP) — ALGONQUIN PARK F-4
Carleton Cove Tourist Trailer Park and Camping (Not Visited) — BELLEVILLE H-5
Carol Campsite (Not Visited) — SUDBURY D-5
Carolinian Forest Campground (Not Visited) — FOREST I-1

ONTARIO — Continued

®□ Carson's Camp — SAUBLE BEACH G-2
Casey's Park — INGERSOLL I-2
Castleton Hills Trailer Park — CASTLETON H-4
Cathcart Park (St. Clair Parkway Commission) — SOMBRA I-1
Cecile's Campsite (Not Visited) — HEARST A-4
Cedar Beach Park (Not visited) — STOUFFVILLE H-3
®□ Cedar Cove Resort (Not visited) — WHITE LAKE G-5
Cedar Grove Park (Not visited) — WASAGA BEACH H-3
® Cedar Haven Tent & Trailer Park (Not Visited) — COBDEN F-5
□ Cedar Rail Camp (Not Visited) — CHESLEY H-2
□ **Cedardale Family Campgorund & Cottage Resort — CARRYING PLACE H-4**
® Champlain Tent & Trailer Park (Not Visited) — NORTH BAY D-6
Charleston Lake Provincial Park — LYNDHURST G-5
Chippawa Creek (Niagara Peninsula Cons Auth.) — DUNNVILLE I-3
□ Chippewa Park (City Park) — THUNDER BAY B-1
Chutes Provincial Park — WEBBWOOD D-5
□ Clarke & Crombie Camps and C & C Motel (Not Visited) — NESTOR FALLS E-1
Cobden Municipal Park — COBDEN F-5
Cobourg East Campground — GRAFTON H-4
Conestoga Family Campgrounds (Not visited) — ARTHUR H-2
Conestogo Lake (Grand River Cons Auth) — ELMIRA I-2
Confederation Park — HAMILTON I-3
Confederation Park (Hamilton Reg. Cons Auth.) — HAMILTON I-3
Country Gardens RV Park — NEW DUNDEE I-2
®□ Country View Motel & RV Camping Resort (Not visited) — WYOMING I-1
□ Covered Bridge Park (Not visited) — ROUND LAKE CENTRE F-4
Craigleith Provincial Park — COLLINGWOOD H-3
□ Cranberry Park — SEELEYS BAY G-5
Crescent Lake Campground (Lake Superior PP) — WAWA C-3
Darlington Provincial Park — OSHAWA H-4
Davy Lake Campground & Resort — IGNACE D-2
Deer Creek Area (Long Point Region Cons Auth.) — LANGTON I-2
® Deerlake Park & Muskoka RV Centre (Not Visited) — HUNTSVILLE G-3
Delmar Campground (Not visited) — IRON BRIDGE D-4
□ Desert Lake Family Resort — VERONA H-5
Double "M" RV Resort & Campground — LINDSAY H-4
® Dreamaker Family Campground (Not visited) — SOUTHAMPTON H-2
Dreany Haven Campground (Not Visited) — NORTH BAY D-6
Driftwood Beach Park (Not Visited) — CLIFFORD H-2
Driftwood Provincial Park — DEEP RIVER F-4
Durham Conservation Area (Saugeen Valley Cons Auth.) — DURHAM H-2
Duttona Trailer Park — DUTTON J-2
Eagle Canyon Adventures (Not Visited) — DORION B-2
Earl Rowe Provincial Park — ALLISTON H-3
□ **Easy Living Camping & RV Park & Chippawa Resort (Not Visited) — BARRY'S BAY F-4**
Elora Gorge (Grand River Cons Auth) — ELORA H-2
□ **Emerald Lake Trailer Resort & Water Park — PUSLINCH I-3**
● **Emerald Lake Water Park — PUSLINCH I-3**
Emily Provincial Park — OMEMEE H-4
Esker Lakes Provincial Park — KIRKLAND LAKE C-6
□ **Evergreen Campground — ALFRED F-6**
Fairbank Provincial Park — WHITEFISH D-5
Fairfield's Resort & Family Camping — CHERRY VALLEY H-5
®□ Fairview Park Camping & Marina — NORTH BAY D-6
® **Family Paradise Campground — WALTON H-2**
Family Paradise Campground (Not Visited) — WALTON H-2
Fanshawe Conservation Area (Upper Thames River Cons Auth) — LONDON I-2
Farran Park (Township Park) — INGLESIDE G-6
Fenelon Valley Trailer Park & Trailer Sales (Not visited) — FENELON FALLS H-4
Ferris Provincial Park — CAMPBELLFORD H-4
□ Fiddlehead Resort Camp (Not visited) — SAUBLE BEACH G-2
Fifty Point Conservation Area & Marina — STONEY CREEK I-3
Fifty Point (Hamilton Reg. Cons. Auth.) — STONEY CREEK I-3
Finlayson Point Provincial Park — TEMAGAMI D-6
®□ **Fisherman's Cove Tent & Trailer Park — KINCARDINE H-2**
Fitzroy Provincial Park — ARNPRIOR F-5
□ Flamboro Valley Camping Resort — HAMILTON I-3
Franklin Motel Tent & Trailer Park (Not visited) — NORTH BAY D-6
Fushimi Lake Provincial Park — HEARST A-4
G & G Service Upsala Campground (Not Visited) — UPSALA B-1
□ Gawley's Parkview Camp (Not Visited) — PERRAULT FALLS D-2
Georgian Bay Islands National Park (Cedar Spring) — HONEY HARBOUR G-3
□ Glen Allan Park — MARMORA H-4
Glen Rouge Campground (City of Toronto Park) — TORONTO H-3
Glen-Lor Lodge (Not Visited) — SYDENHAM H-5
Glengarry Park (Parks of the St. Lawrence) — LANCASTER G-6
Glenrock Cottages & Trailer Park (Not Visited) — STURGEON FALLS D-6
□ Glenview Cottages & Campground (Not Visited) — SAULT STE. MARIE D-4
□ Golden Beach Resort and Trailer Park (Not Visited) — ROSENEATH H-4
®□ Golden Pond RV Resort (Not Visited) — MOSSLEY I-2
□ Goose Bay Camp (Not Visited) — EAR FALLS C-2
Goreski's Landing (Not visited) — PORT PERRY H-3
Grainger's Tent & Trailer Park (Not Visited) — OTTAWA G-6
Grangeways Trailer Park (Not visited) — SANDFORD H-3
Granite Ridge Campground (Not Visited) — KEARNEY F-3
® Great Canadian Hideaway — PARKHILL I-2
® Green Acre Park — WATERLOO I-2
® Green Acres Campground & RV Park — KINCARDINE H-2
Green Acres Tent & Trailer Park (Not visited) — SHEGUIANDAH F-1
Greenwater Provincial Park — COCHRANE B-5
®□ **Grenville Park — PRESCOTT G-6**
Grundy Lake Provincial Park — BRITT F-2
Guelph Lake (Grand River Cons Auth) — GUELPH I-3
Haldimand Area (Long Point Region Cons Auth.) — SELKIRK I-3
Halfway Lake Provincial Park — CARTIER D-5
□ Haliburton Forest & Wild Life Reserve — WEST GUILFORD G-4
Hammock Harbour Resort (Not Visited) — ORILLIA G-3
Happy Green Acres Tent & Trailer Park — BROCKVILLE G-6
®□ Happy Hearts Tent & Trailer Park (Not visited) — TOBERMORY G-2
Happy Hills Family Campground — LAKESIDE I-2
□ **Happy Land Campground & Cabins (Not Visited) — THUNDER BAY B-1**
Harrison Park (City Park) — OWEN SOUND G-2
Heber Down Conservation Area (Central Lake Cons. Auth.) — OSHAWA H-4
® **Heidis' Campground — BARRIE H-3**
Hidden Valley Campground — TURKEY POINT I-3
Hideaway Trailer Park — BLOOMFIELD H-5
□ **Highland Pines Campground — FERGUS H-3**
Highland Trailer Park & RV Resort — DUNNVILLE I-3
□ Hilton Beach Tourist Park (Not Visited) — HILTON BEACH D-4
Holiday Beach Campground (Not Visited) — NAUGHTON D-5
® **Holiday Harbour Resort — WHEATLEY J-1**
® **Holiday Park — SOUTHAMPTON H-2**
Hope Bay Campground (Not visited) — WIARTON G-2
Hope Mill (Otonabee Region Cons Auth) — KEENE H-4
□ Horseshoe Lake Camp & Cottages (Not Visited) — PARRY SOUND G-3
Indian Line Campground (Toronto & Region Cons. Auth.) — TORONTO H-3
Iroquois Municipal Park — IROQUOIS G-6
Iroquois Trail Campsite — FRANKFORD H-4
Ivanhoe Lake Provincial Park — FOLEYET C-5
Ivy Lea Campsite (Parks of the St. Lawrence) — GANANOQUE H-5
Jay Lake Campground & RV Park — MINDEN G-4
® **Jefferson Junction — APPIN I-2**

ONTARIO — Continued

Jell-E-Bean Campground (Not visited) — WASAGA BEACH H-3
®□ Jellystone Park & Camp Resort — AMHERSTBURG J-1
Jordan Valley Campground — ST. CATHARINES I-3
Kakabeka Falls Provincial Park — KAKABEKA FALLS B-1
Kap-Kig-Iwan Provincial Park — ENGLEHART C-6
Kearney Lake Campground (Algonquin PP) — ALGONQUIN PARK F-4
Kelso Beach (City Park) — OWEN SOUND G-2
Kettle Lakes Provincial Park — IROQUOIS FALLS B-6
Killarney Provincial Park — KILLARNEY F-2
Killbear Provincial Park — BRITT F-2
Kilsyth Country Campground (Not visited) — OWEN SOUND G-2
King Waldorf's Tent & Trailer Park — NIAGARA FALLS I-3
Klondike Park (Not Visited) — WASAGA BEACH H-3
Knight's Beach (Not visited) — DUNNVILLE I-3
® Knight's Hide-Away Park — NIAGARA FALLS I-3
□ KOA-Barrie — BARRIE H-3
□ KOA-Brighton/401 — BRIGHTON H-4
□ KOA-Cardinal Kampground — CARDINAL G-6
□ KOA-Gravenhurst Muskoka (Not Visited) — GRAVENHURST G-3
□ KOA-Kingston — KINGSTON H-5
®□ KOA-Marmora — MARMORA H-4
®□ KOA-Niagara Falls — NIAGARA FALLS I-3
□ KOA-Owen Sound (Not Visited) — OWEN SOUND G-2
®□ KOA-Renfrew — RENFREW F-5
□ KOA-Sault Ste. Marie (Not Visited) — SAULT STE. MARIE D-4
□ KOA-Thousand Islands — MALLORYTOWN G-6
□ KOA-Thunder Bay — THUNDER BAY B-1
□ KOA-Toronto North Cookstown — COOKSTOWN H-3
La Fortune (Haldimand County) — CALEDONIA I-3
®□ LaFontaine Resort Park (Not Visited) — PENETANGUISHENE G-3
Lagoon Tent & Trailer Park (Not visited) — HUNTSVILLE G-3
□ Lake Apsey Resort & Trailer Park (Not Visited) — ESPANOLA D-5
®□ Lake Avenue Park — CHERRY VALLEY H-5
□ Lake Consecon Resort — CONSECON H-4
Lake Dore Tent & Trailer Park (Not Visited) — EGANVILLE F-5
® Lake Huron Resort — GODERICH H-2
Lake of Two Rivers Campground (Algonquin PP) — ALGONQUIN PARK F-4
Lake Saint Peter Provincial Park — LAKE ST. PETER G-4
® Lake Wolsey Obejewung Park (Not Visited) — EVANSVILLE F-1
Lakefield Campground — LAKEFIELD H-4
Lakefield Park & Campground (City Park) — LAKEFIELD H-4
Lakeside Resort — LAKESIDE I-2
Lakeside Village Motel and Campground — WHEATLEY J-1
Lakeview Trailer Park (Not Visited) — MACKEY F-4
□ Lakewood Christian Campground (Not Visited) — FOREST I-1
Lakewood Trailer Estates — RODNEY J-2
Lambton Centre Family Campground — FOREST I-1
Lancaster Park Outdoor Resort — LANCASTER G-6
□ Lands End Park (Not Visited) — TOBERMORY G-2
Laurel Creek (Grand River Cons Auth) — WATERLOO I-2
□ Lecuyer's Tru-Tail Lodge (Not Visited) — NESTOR FALLS E-1
® Leisure Lake Campground — LEAMINGTON J-1
Leisure Time Park (Not visited) — BOLTON H-3
Lion's Head Beach Park — LION'S HEAD G-2
Little Lake Area (Long Point Cons Auth.) — NORWICH I-2
□ Log Chateau Park (Not visited) — FENELON FALLS H-4
® Logos Land Resort (Not Visited) — COBDEN F-5
□ London KOA Campground — LONDON I-2
Long Beach (Niagara Peninsula Cons Auth.) (Not Visited) — PORT COLBORNE I-3
Long Point Provincial Park — PORT ROWAN J-2
□ Longbow Lake Camp & Trailer Park (Not Visited) — KENORA D-1
Loon Lake — MADOC H-4
Loon's Landing (Not Visited) — FRENCH RIVER F-2
Lorne C. Henderson Area (St. Clair Region Cons Auth.) — PETROLIA I-1
□ Lower Beverley Lake Township Park — DELTA G-5
Lyons Little Austria Family Campground (Not Visited) — BURFORD I-2
MacGregor Point Provincial Park — PORT ELGIN H-2
MacKenzie's Trailer Park (Not Visited) — KINTAIL H-2
MacLeod Provincial Park — GERALDTON A-2
Mal's Camping (Not visited) — LANARK G-5
□ Manitoulin Resort — MANITOWANING F-2
Maples RV Park — CORNWALL G-6
Mara Provincial Park — ATHERLEY G-3
Marine Park (St. Clair Parkway Commission) — MITCHELL'S BAY J-1
Mariner's Paradise (Not Visited) — WAUBAUSHENE G-3
□ Marsh Bay Resort Tent & Trailer Park (Not Visited) — COBALT C-6
Marten River Provincial Park — MARTEN RIVER D-6
Martin's River Country — CHERRY VALLEY H-5
□ McCreary's Beach Vacation Resort — PERTH G-5
□ McCullough's Landing — PERTH G-5
McGowan Lake Campground — MABERLY G-5
McLaren Campsite (Parks of the St. Lawrence) — LONG SAULT G-6
McRae Point Provincial Park — UPTERGROVE G-3
Meaford Memorial Park (City Park) — MEAFORD G-2
Mew Lake Campground (Algonquin PP) — ALGONQUIN PARK F-4
Mikisew Provincial Park — SOUTH RIVER F-3
Mille Roches Campsite (Parks of the St. Lawrence) — LONG SAULT G-6
® Milton Heights Campground — MILTON I-3
□ Milton RV Park (KOA) (Not Visited) — CAMPBELLVILLE I-3
□ Mindemoya Court Cottages & Campground (Not Visited) — MINDEMOYA F-1
Mississagi Provincial Park — ELLIOT LAKE D-5
□ Mitchells' Camp (Not Visited) — SPANISH D-5
Moonlight Bay Campground (Not Visited) — PORTLAND G-5
®□ Morning Mist Resort (Not Visited) — STONECLIFFE F-4
Murphy's Point Provincial Park — PERTH G-5
Muskoka Ridge Trailer Park (Not Visited) — BRACEBRIDGE G-3
Nagagamisis Provincial Park — HORNEPAYNE B-3
□ N.E.T. Camping Resort — VINELAND I-3
□ NEYs Lunch & Campground (Not Visited) — MARATHON B-3
Neys Provincial Park — MARATHON B-3
®□ Nicolston Dam Campground — ALLISTON H-3
Nor-Halton Park — ACTON H-3
Norfolk Area Conservation Area (Long Point Region Cons Auth) — SIMCOE I-3
□ Norm's Tent & Trailer Park (Not visited) — KAGAWONG F-1
®□ Oak Ridge Resort (Not Visited) — GRAND BEND I-2
Oastler Lake Provincial Park — PARRY SOUND G-3
Obatanga Provincial Park — WHITE RIVER B-3
Ojibway Provincial Park — SIOUX LOOKOUT D-2
Olympia Village Trailer Park — WATERDOWN I-3
□ Open Bay Cottages & Campground (Not Visited) — UPSALA B-1
□ Oro Family Campground (Not visited) — BARRIE H-3
Ottawa Municipal Campground — OTTAWA G-6
®□ Our Ponderosa Family Campground & Golf Resort (Not Visited) — FOREST I-1
Pancake Bay Provincial Park — BATCHAWANA BAY D-3
Paradise Point RV Park & Marina (Not Visited) — SIOUX NARROWS D-1
□ Paradise Valley Campground (Not visited) — FOREST I-1
□ Parkwood Beach — CARDIFF G-4
®□ Parry Sound-KOA Kampground (Not Visited) — PARRY SOUND G-3
®□ Paul's Creek Campsite (Not visited) — MCDONALD'S CORNERS G-5
®□ Pickerel Park (Not visited) — NAPANEE H-5
□ Pine Crest Campground (Not Visited) — THESSALON D-4
□ Pine Point Resort (Not Visited) — UPSALA B-1
□ Pine Ridge Park & Resort — PEMBROKE F-5
® Pine Valley Park — CAMBRIDGE I-3
Pine Valley Resort & Campground (Not Visited) — STONECLIFFE F-4
Pinehurst Lake (Grand River Cons Auth) — PARIS I-3
Pinery Provincial Park — GRAND BEND I-2
Pittock Conservation Area (Upper Thames River Cons Auth) — WOODSTOCK I-2
□ Pleasant Beach Campground (Not visited) — SHERKSTON I-3
Pleasure Park Campground and RV Resort (Not visited) — BROCKVILLE G-6
Pog Lake Campground (Algonquin PP) — ALGONQUIN PARK F-4

ONTARIO — Continued

Point Farms Provincial Park — GODERICH H-2
□ Ponderosa Campground (Not Visited) — MOUNT ALBERT H-3
Poplar Grove Tourist Camp — OTTAWA G-6
Port Burwell Provincial Park — PORT BURWELL J-2
Port Elgin Municipal Tourist Camp — PORT ELGIN H-2
Port Glasgow Tent & Trailer Park (Township Park) — RODNEY J-2
Presqu'ile Provincial Park — BRIGHTON H-4
Primrose Park (Not Visited) — SHELBURNE H-3
Prospect Hill Camping Grounds — GRANTON I-2
®□ Providence Bay Tent & Trailer Park (Not visited) — PROVIDENCE BAY F-1
Quetico Provincial Park — ATIKOKAN E-2
® Quinte's Isle Campark — CHERRY VALLEY H-5
★ Quinte's Isle Campark & Trailer Sale — CHERRY VALLEY H-5
● Quinte's Isle Diamond "J" Ranch — CHERRY VALLEY H-5
Rabbit Blanket Lake Campground (Lake Superior PP) — WAWA C-3
Rainbow Falls Provincial Park — SCHREIBER B-2
Recreationland Tent & Trailer Park — OTTAWA G-6
□ Red Deer Lodge & Campground (Not Visited) — MADAWASKA F-4
® Red Oak Travel Park — TILLSONBURG I-2
Rene Brunelle Provincial Park — KAPUSKASING B-5
Restoule Provincial Park — RESTOULE F-3
® Rideau Acres Campground — KINGSTON H-5
Rideau River Provincial Park — KEMPTVILLE G-6
River Place Park (Not Visited) — MOUNT FOREST H-2
□ River View Campground (Not Visited) — THORNDALE I-2
® Riverland Lodge and Camp (Not Visited) — MADAWASKA F-4
Riverside Park (City Park) — PEMBROKE F-5
Riverside Park Motel & Campground — NIAGARA FALLS I-3
□ Riverside/Cedar Campsite (Parks of the St. Lawrence) — MORRISBURG G-6
Riverwood Park (Not visited) — LINDSAY H-4
Rochester Place RV, Golf & Marine Resort — BELLE RIVER J-1
Rock Lake Campground (Algonquin PP) — ALGONQUIN PARK F-4
Rock Point Provincial Park — DUNNVILLE I-3
Rockwood (Grand River Cons Auth) — ROCKWOOD I-3
Rondeau Provincial Park — MORPETH J-1
□ Rondeau Shores Trailer Park — MORPETH J-1
®□ Roth Park (Not Visited) — WIARTON G-2
□ Rus-Ton Family Campground & RV Resort (Not Visited) — GRAND BEND I-2
Rushing River Provincial Park — KENORA D-1
Ryan's Campsite (Not visited) — DEEP RIVER F-4
St. Lawrence Park (City Park) — BROCKVILLE G-6
Samuel De Champlain Provincial Park — MATTAWA F-4
®□ Sand Bay Camp — COMBERMERE G-4
Sand Hill Park (Not visited) — PORT BURWELL J-2
Sandbanks Provincial Park — BLOOMFIELD H-5
Sandbar Lake Provincial Park — IGNACE D-2
□ Sandy Beach Resort & Trailer Court (Not Visited) — FENELON FALLS H-4
□ Santa Maria Trailer Resort (Not visited) — SPRING BAY F-1
® Sauble Beach Resort Camp — SAUBLE BEACH G-2
Sauble Falls Provincial Park — SAUBLE BEACH G-2
□ Sauble Falls Tent & Trailer Park (Not visited) — SAUBLE FALLS G-2
Saugeen Bluffs (Saugeen Valley Cons Auth.) — PAISLEY H-2
® Saugeen Cedars Campground (Not visited) — HANOVER H-2
®□ Saugeen Springs RV Park — HANOVER H-2
□ Savanne River Resort (Not visited) — UPSALA B-1
Scott's Tent & Trailer Park — NIAGARA FALLS I-3
Selkirk Provincial Park — SELKIRK I-3
Shady Pines Campground (Not visited) — AILSA CRAIG I-2
® Shalamar Lake Niagara — NIAGARA FALLS I-3
Shangri-La Park Campground — ST. CATHARINES I-3
Sharbot Lake Provincial Park — SHARBOT LAKE G-5
□ Shelter Valley Tent & Trailer Park (Not visited) — GODERICH H-2
Sherkston Shores — PORT COLBORNE I-3
★ Sherkston Shores Park Model Sales — PORT COLBORNE I-3
● Sherkston Shores Water Park — PORT COLBORNE I-3
Sherwood Park Campground — CLOYNE G-5
Sibbald Point Provincial Park — SUTTON H-3
□ Sid Turcotte Park (Not Visited) — MATTAWA F-4
Silent Lake Provincial Park — BANCROFT G-4
Silent Valley Park (Not Visited) — MOUNT FOREST H-2
□ Silver Birches Campground (Not Visited) — IPPERWASH BEACH I-1
Silver Lake Provincial Park — MABERLY G-5
□ Singleton Lake Family Campground — LYNDHURST G-5
Six Mile Lake Provincial Park — PORT SEVERN G-3
□ Skycroft Campground and Cottages — ELGIN G-5
Sleeping Giant Provincial Park — PASS LAKE B-1
®□ Sleepy Hollow Resort (Not visited) — HALIBURTON G-4
Smith's Camp (Not visited) — MIDLAND G-3
□ Smugglers Cove Campground (Not visited) — PICTON H-5
□ South Bay on Gull Rock (Not Visited) — RED LAKE C-1
□ South Bay Resort (Not visited) — SOUTH BAYMOUTH F-1
South Lake Tent and Trailer Park (Not visited) — MINDEN G-4
□ Spragge-KOA (Not Visited) — SPRAGGE D-5
® Spring Lake R.V. Resort — INGERSOLL I-2
Spring Valley Resort (Not Visited) — MOUNT FOREST H-2
Springwater Conservation Area (Catfish Creek Cons Auth.) — AYLMER I-2
Springwater RV Resort (Not Visited) — NESTLETON H-4
Stillwater Tent & Trailer Park (Not Visited) — NIPIGON B-2
Sturgeon Bay Provincial Park — BRITT F-2
□ Sturgeon Woods Campground & Marina — LEAMINGTON J-1
★ Sturgeon Woods RV Sales & Services — LEAMINGTON J-1
®□ Summer House Park — MILLER LAKE G-2
® Summer Place (Not Visited) — GRAND VALLEY H-3
□ Sunny Acres (Not visited) — FENELON FALLS H-4
Sunny Valley Park (Not visited) — OWEN SOUND G-2
®□ Sunrise Tourist Trailer Park — BEWDLEY H-4
®□ Sunset Country Campgrounds (Not Visited) — TICHBORNE G-5
Sunshine Motel & RV (Not Visited) — STURGEON FALLS D-6
®□ Tay River Tent & Trailer Camp — PERTH G-5
Tea Lake Campground (Algonquin PP) — ALGONQUIN PARK F-4
The Landon Bay Centre (Not visited) — GANANOQUE H-5
□ The Sunset Shores Resort (Not Visited) — BATCHAWANA BAY D-3
□ Thousand Lakes Resort (Not Visited) — UPSALA B-1
® Tipper's Family Campground — TWEED H-5
□ Tobermory Village Campground — TOBERMORY G-2
□ Tomahawk Trailer Park Resort (Not Visited) — SIOUX NARROWS D-1
Tottenham Conservation Area (Town of New Tecumseth) — TOTTENHAM H-3
®□ Tower Manor Lodge — BEWDLEY H-4
Tranquil Acres Camping (Not visited) — CARLETON PLACE G-5
Travel Rest Tent & Trailer Park (Not Visited) — SCHREIBER B-2
®□ Trout Haven Park (Not visited) — STRATHROY I-2
Trout Water Family Camping — SUNDERLAND H-3
Trowbridge Falls (City Park) — THUNDER BAY B-1
Turkey Point Provincial Park — SIMCOE I-3
□ Twilight Resort (Not Visited) — MONTREAL RIVER HARBOUR D-3
Twin Towers Restaurant, Gas Bar & Camping (Not visited) — DRYDEN D-2
Uel Heritage Centre & Park — ADOLPHUSTOWN H-5
□ Uncle Steve's Park & Cabins (Not visited) — MANITOWANING F-2
Upper Canada Campground — MORRISBURG G-6
Upper Canada Migratory Bird Sanctuary (Parks of the St. Lawrence) — INGLESIDE G-6
Valens Conservation Area — CAMBRIDGE I-3
Valens (Hamilton Reg. Cons Auth) — CAMBRIDGE I-3
Viking Tent & Trailer Park (Not Visited) — IRON BRIDGE D-4
Voyageur Provincial Park — CHUTE-A-BLONDEAU F-6
Wakami Lake Provincial Park — CHAPLEAU C-4
Warsaw Caves (Otonabee Region Cons Auth) — WARSAW H-4
Warwick Area (St. Clair Region Cons Auth.) — SARNIA I-1
® Wasaga Dunes Family Campground (Not Visited) — WASAGA BEACH H-3
Wasaga Pines Family Campground (Not Visited) — WASAGA BEACH H-3
®□ Wawa RV Resort & Campground (Not Visited) — WAWA C-3
®□ Wellers Bay Campground — CARRYING PLACE H-4

ONTARIO — Continued

Wheatley Provincial Park — WHEATLEY J-1
White Lake Provincial Park — WHITE RIVER B-3
□ Whitewing Resort and Floating Lodges (Not visited) — EAR FALLS C-2
® Wild Goose Lake Campground (Not Visited) — GERALDTON A-2
Wildwood Campground — KEMPTVILLE G-6
Wildwood Conservation Area (Upper Thames River Cons Auth) — STRATFORD I-2
Wildwood Golf & RV Resort — MCGREGOR J-1
● Wildwood Golf & RV Resort — MCGREGOR J-1
□ Willow Lake Park — WOODSTOCK I-2
□ Wilson's Tent & Trailer Park — LYNDHURST G-5
® Windmill Family Campground (Not Visited) — MITCHELL I-2
Windmill Point Park — FORT ERIE I-3
□ Windsor Campground (Not visited) — WINDSOR J-1
Windy Lake Provincial Park — SUDBURY D-5
Wood Haven — FOREST I-1
® Woodcrest Resort Park — NORTHBROOK G-5
Woodland Camp Site — ENNISMORE H-4
□ Woodland Estate (Not Visited) — CAMPBELLFORD H-4
Woodland Lake RV Resort(Not Visited) — MITCHELL I-2
® Woodland Park — SAUBLE BEACH G-2
Woodlands Campsite (Parks of the St. Lawrence) — LONG SAULT G-6
Yogi Bear's Jellystone Park Camp-Resort — BRADFORD H-3
®□ Yogi Bear's Jellystone Park Camp-Resort — NIAGARA FALLS I-3

PRINCE EDWARD ISLAND

Bayside RV Campground — OYSTER BED BRIDGE C-4
®□ Ben's Lake Campground & Trout Fishing — BELLEVUE D-4
Brudenell River Provincial Park — GEORGETOWN D-5
Cabot Beach Provincial Park — MALPEQUE C-3
®□ Cavendish KOA — CAVENDISH C-3
Cavendish Sunset Campground — CAVENDISH C-3
Cedar Dunes Provincial Park — CAPE EGMONT C-2
Confederation Trailside Tourist Grounds (Not Visited) — TRACADIE CROSS C-4
□ Crystal Beach Campground — LOWER NEW ANNAN C-2
Cumberland Cove Campground (Not Visited) — AUGUSTINE COVE D-3
□ Green Park Provincial Park — PORT HILL C-2
Holiday Cornwall KOA — CHARLOTTETOWN D-4
Jacques Cartier Provincial Park — ALBERTON B-2
□ Lane's Cottages & Suites — MONTAGUE D-5
Linkletter Provincial Park — SUMMERSIDE C-2
Lord Selkirk Provincial Park — ELDON D-4
Marco Polo Land — CAVENDISH C-3
Mill River Provincial Park — WOODSTOCK C-2
Montague Recreation Park (Not Visited) — MONTAGUE D-5
□ Moonlight Camping (Not Visited) — CAP-EGMONT C-2
□ New Glasgow Highlands — NEW GLASGOW C-3
□ Northumberland Provincial Park — WOOD ISLANDS E-5
Panmure Island Provincial Park — PANMURE ISLAND D-5
● PEI Provincial Parks — CHARLOTTETOWN D-4
®□ Pine Hills RV Park — CHARLOTTETOWN D-4
Prince Edward Island National Park (Cavendish Campground) — CAVENDISH C-3
Prince Edward Island National Park (Robinsons Island) — BRACKLEY BEACH C-4
Prince Edward Island National Park (Stanhope Campground) — STANHOPE C-4
Red Point Provincial Park — SOURIS C-6
River RV Campground (Not Visited) — MURRAY RIVER D-5
St. Peters Park (Community of St. Peters) — ST. PETERS C-5
Seal Cove Campground (Not Visited) — MURRAY HARBOUR NORTH D-5
Southport RV Park Motel — CHARLOTTETOWN D-4
□ Sun-N-Shade Campground — BORDEN-CARLETON D-3
Twin Shores Camping Area — DARNLEY C-3
® Vacationland RV Park — BRACKLEY BEACH C-4
□ Vistabay Chalets RV Park & Golf Course — ALEXANDRA D-4
□ Waterford Campground (Not Visited) — WATERFORD A-1
□ White Sands Cottages and Campground Resort — NORTH RUSTICO C-3
Winterbay Tent & Trailer Park (Not Visited) — MILL COVE C-4

QUEBEC

□ Auberge Fort - Prevel — SAINT-GEORGES-DE-MALBAIE E-6
Base Plein Air Saint-Damase — SAINT-DAMASE B-6
Camping 2 Rivieres (Not Visited) — SAINT-GEDEON D-5
Camping 4 Vents (Not visited) — CAP-AUX-OS E-6
Camping A La Belle Etoile — VALLEE-JONCTION G-6
Camping Aeroport — QUEBEC CITY F-6
Camping Alouette Inc — SAINT-MATHIEU-DE-BELOEIL I-3
Camping Amerique Montreal — SAINT-PHILIPPE-DE-LAPRAIRIE J-2
Camping Amqui (Municipal Park) — AMQUI B-6
® Camping Ange Gardien — L'ANGE GARDIEN (OUTAOUAIS) D-2
Camping Annie — METIS-SUR-MER B-6
Camping Au Bonnet Rouge — SAINT-JEAN-PORT-JOLI C-5
Camping Au Bord de la Mer (Not Visited) — CAP CHAT-EST D-5
Camping Au Jardin De Mon Pere — SAGUENAY-LA BAIE B-5
Camping au Petit Lac Simon (Not Visited) — SAINT-ANDRE-AVELLIN D-3
Camping au Plateau 5 Etoiles (Not Visited) — TERREBONNE I-2
Camping Au Soleil Couchant (Not Visited) — GRANDE-VALLEE D-6
Camping Au Sous Bois Du Campeur (Not Visited) — SAINT-NICOLAS F-6
Camping Au Vieux Foyer — SAINT-PIE I-3
□ Camping Auberge Fort Prevel — GASPE E-6
Camping Auclair — SAINT-JEAN-BAPTISTE-DE-ROUVILLE I-3
Camping Aux Bouleaux Argentes — SAINT-FELIX-DE-VALOIS H-3
®□ Camping Aux Flots Bleus (Not Visited) — SAINT-OMER E-5
Camping aux Petits Trembles (Lac Flavrian) (Not Visited) — EVAIN B-1
® Camping aux Pignons Verts (Not Visited) — LES MECHINS E-5
Camping Baie de Gaspe (Not visited) — GASPE E-6
Camping Beau-Lieu — SHERBROOKE I-5
Camping Beau-Soleil (Not Visited) — WEEDON I-5
Camping Belle Montagne (Not Visited) — SAINT-PAULIN G-3
Camping Belle Rose — SAINT-HYACINTHE I-3
Camping Belle-Maree — JOLIETTE H-3
Camping Belle-Vue — SAINTE-CROIX G-5
Camping Belley (Not visited) — SAINT-HENRI-DE-TAILLON B-4
Camping Bernard — SAINTE-MELANIE H-2
Camping Bon Air Inc — SAINT-PHILIPPE-DE-LAPRAIRIE J-2
Camping Bon-Jour — GRANBY I-4
□ Camping & Cabines Nature Morin Heights (Not visited) — MORIN HEIGHTS H-1
Camping Campus (Not Visited) — SAINTE-MELANIE H-2
Camping Canadien & Americain (Not Visited) — SAINT-AUGUSTIN-DE-DESMAURES F-6
®□ Camping Canne De Bois — HEMMINGFORD J-2
® Camping Cantley (Not Visited) — CANTLEY D-2
Camping Cap a la Roche — DESCHAILLONS-SUR-SAINT-LAURENT G-5
Camping Cap Rouge (Not Visited) — SAINT-GEORGES-DE-MALBAIE E-6
Camping Capitaine Homard (Not Visited) — SAINTE-FLAVIE B-6
Camping Caravelle — SAINTE-SABINE J-3
Camping Carol — BEAUMONT F-6
Camping Carrefour des Campeurs (Not Visited) — POTTON J-4
Camping Champlain 2003 — VENISE-EN-QUEBEC J-3

ALPHABETICAL LISTINGS CONTINUED

QUEBEC — Continued

Camping Chez Ben 2000 — ***SAINTE-CATHERINE-DE-HATLEY J-5***
Camping Chez Jean (Not Visited) — ***SAINT-ANTONIN B-5***
Camping Choisy — ***HUDSON I-1***
△□ Camping Chutes Aux Iroquois — ***LABELLE G-1***
□ Camping Chutes Fraser — ***LA MALBAIE C-5***
® Camping Claire Fontaine — ***SAINT-RAYMOND F-5***
Camping Colonie Notre Dame (Not visited) — ***ALMA B-4***
Camping Coop Familiale du Prevert de Birchton — ***COOKSHIRE I-5***
Camping Cote Surprise — ***PERCE E-6***
® Camping D'Aoust — ***VAUDREUIL-DORION I-2***
Camping de Causapscal (Municipal Park) — ***CAUSAPSCAL B-6***
□ **Camping de Compton** — ***COMPTON J-5***
Camping de la Baie-de-Perce — ***PERCE E-6***
Camping de La Demi-Lieue — ***SAINT-JEAN-PORT-JOLI C-5***
Camping de la Mer (Not Visited) — ***POINTE-LEBEL A-6***
Camping de la Rive (Not Visited) — ***SAINT-CHARLES-BORROMEE H-3***
△ Camping De L'Ile — ***ROXTON FALLS I-4***
Camping de l'Ile Marie (Not Visited) — ***SHERBROOKE I-5***
Camping des Etoiles (Not visited) — ***HOPETOWN E-6***
Camping des Voltigeurs — ***DRUMMONDVILLE H-4***
Camping Do Re Mi — ***EASTMAN J-4***
Camping Domaine au Grand "R" (Not Visited) — ***TROIS-RIVIERES G-4***
® Camping Domaine de la Chute (Not Visited) — ***SAINT-APOLLINAIRE G-5***
Camping Domaine de la Frontiere Enchantee — ***HAVELOCK J-2***
Camping Domaine du Lac Cristal (Not visited) — ***SAINT-ROSAIRE H-5***
Camping "Domaine Du Repos" — ***DRUMMONDVILLE H-4***
Camping Domaine Lausanne — ***SAINTE-AGATHE-DES-MONTS H-1***
Camping Domaine Lemieux (Not Visited) — ***LABRECQUE A-4***
Camping Domaine Madalie (Not Visited) — ***SAINT-CHARLES-SUR-RICHELIEU I-3***
Camping Domaine Parc Estrie — ***MAGOG J-4***
Camping du Fort de la Martiniere (Not Visited) — ***LEVIS F-6***
®□ **Camping du Gouffre** — ***BAIE-SAINT-PAUL C-5***
Camping du Lac Blais (Not Visited) — ***SAINT-ETIENNE DES GRES G-4***
Camping du Lac Lyster (Piskiart-la Sequiniere) — ***COATICOOK***
® Camping du Quai — ***RIVIERE-DU-LOUP B-5***
Camping du Rivage (Not visited) — ***SAINTE-ANNE-DES-MONTS D-5***
Camping Du Vieux Moulin — ***SAINT-BARTHELEMY H-3***
Camping du Village Bromont RV Resort — ***BROMONT J-4***
Camping du Zoo de Saint-Edouard — ***SAINT-EDOUARD-DE-MASKINONGE G-3***
Camping Ecologique de Frelighsburg — ***FRELIGHSBURG J-3***
Camping Fairmount (Not Visited) — ***LAC-BROME J-4***
□ Camping Fleur de Lys (Motel) (Not Visited) — ***CAP CHAT-EST D-5***
® Camping Fort Apache — ***SAINT-COME G-2***
Camping Gaspe (Not visited) — ***GASPE E-6***
Camping Globe Trotter — ***SAINT-FELIX-DE-VALOIS H-3***
Camping Gregoire (Not Visited) — ***LACOLLE J-3***
Camping Griffon (Not Visited) — ***GASPE E-6***
Camping Haut-des-Cotes (Not Visited) — ***LAC SIMON D-3***
Camping Havre de la Nuit (Not Visited) — ***PERCE E-6***
Camping Horizon (Not Visited) — ***SAINT-ROCH-DE-L'ACHIGAN H-2***
Camping Ile Orleans (Not Visited) — ***ILE D'ORLEANS F-6***
Camping Inverness (Not Visited) — ***INVERNESS G-5***
□ Camping Juneau — ***SAINT-AUGUSTIN-DE-DESMAURES F-6***
Camping KEA Otamac — ***SHAWINIGAN G-4***
Camping Kelly (Not Visited) — ***SAINTE-JULIENNE H-2***
Camping la Cle des Champs (Not Visited) — ***SAINT-PHILIPPE-DE-LAPRAIRIE J-2***
Camping la Descente des Femmes (Not Visited) — ***SAINTE-ROSE-DU-NORD B-5***
Camping La Detente — ***DRUMMONDVILLE H-4***
Camping La Gervaisie (Not Visited) — ***SAINT-TITE F-4***
Camping La Jolie Rochelle — ***LEVIS F-6***
Camping la Luciole — ***SAINTE-LUCE-SUR-MER B-6***
Camping La Mine de Cuivre (Not Visited) — ***EASTMAN J-4***
Camping La Roche D'Or (Not Visited) — ***NOTRE-DAME-DES-PINS D-5***
Camping La Rochelle — ***TROIS-RIVIERES G-4***
Camping Lac Aux Flambeaux (Not visited) — ***CHATEAU-RICHER F-6***
□ Camping Lac des Cedres (Not Visited) — ***SAINT-LAZARE I-1***
Camping Lac Des Pins — ***SAINT-ANTOINE-ABBE J-2***
Camping Lac des Plages (Not Visited) — ***LAC-DES-PLAGES H-1***
Camping Lac Frontiere (Border Lake) — ***STANSTEAD J-5***
Camping Lac Georges (Not Visited) — ***VAL-ALAIN G-5***
Camping Lac Joly (Not Visited) — ***SAINT-HONORE B-5***
Camping Lac Lafontaine — ***SAINT-JEROME H-2***
Camping Lac Magog — ***SHERBROOKE I-5***
Camping Lac Morin (Not Visited) — ***NOTRE-DAME-DU-MONT-CARMEL G-4***
Camping Lac Normand (Not Visited) — ***CADILLAC B-1***
□ Camping Lac St-Michel des Forges — ***TROIS-RIVIERES G-4***
Camping Lac Vert (Not Visited) — ***VAL-DES-BOIS D-2***
Camping Lac-aux-Sables (Not Visited) — ***LAC-AUX-SABLES F-4***
Camping Laurier — ***MONT ST HILAIRE I-3***
® Camping le Bourg de Pabos — ***PABOS MILLS (CHANDLER) E-6***
Camping Le Dauphin (Not Visited) — ***SAINT-ANICET J-1***
Camping Le Domaine Champetre (Not Visited) — ***SAINT-VALLIER F-6***
□ **Camping le Rayon de Soleil** — ***SAINT-ALEXANDRE B-5***
Camping Les Cedres — ***SAINT-JEAN-SUR-LE-RICHELIEU J-3***

QUEBEC — Continued

Camping L'Escale (Not Visited) — ***POINTE-CALUMET I-2***
Camping Levesque — ***SAINT-SIMEON B-5***
Camping Lido — ***SAINT-ANTONIN B-5***
Camping L'Iris (Not Visited) — ***SAINT-HIPPOLYTE H-2***
□ Camping Magog - Orford — ***MAGOG J-4***
® Camping & Marina Parc Bellerive — ***SAINT-OURS H-3***
Camping Maurice — ***SAINT-SIMEON B-5***
Camping Mirabel (Not Visited) — ***MIRABEL I-2***
Camping Mon Plaisir (Not Visited) — ***PLESSISVILLE H-5***
Camping Mont Sainte Anne — ***MONT SAINTE ANNE C-5***
Camping Motel de l'Anse (Not Visited) — ***RIMOUSKI B-6***
□ Camping Motel Fort Ramsay — ***GASPE E-6***
Camping Municipal de la Pointe — ***RIVIERE-DU-LOUP B-5***
Camping Municipal Sainte-Veronique — ***SAINTE-VERONIQUE C-3***
Camping Municipal St-Felicien — ***SAINT-FELICIEN B-4***
Camping New Richmond (Not Visited) — ***NEW RICHMOND E-6***
Camping Oasis (Not Visited) — ***SAINTE-CECILE-DE-MILTON I-4***
Camping Panoramique (Not Visited) — ***PORTNEUF F-5***
Camping Paradiso (Not Visited) — ***NOTRE-DAME-DU-MONT-CARMEL G-4***
□ Camping Parc Beaumont (Not Visited) — ***BEAUMONT F-6***
Camping Parc Bromont — ***BROMONT J-4***
® Camping Parc Central (Not Visited) — ***SAINT-FELIX-DE-KINGSEY H-4***
Camping Parc de la Rive (Not Visited) — ***POINTE-AUX-OUTARDES A-6***
Camping Parc La Conception (Not Visited) — ***LA CONCEPTION G-1***
Camping Parc Sirois La Baleine — ***MATANE B-6***
Camping Parc St-Michel — ***SAINT-MICHEL-DE-BELLECHASSE F-6***
® **Camping Pionnier (Not visited)** — ***GRACEFIELD D-2***
Camping Plage Beaubassin (Municipal Park) — ***BONAVENTURE E-6***
Camping Plage des Sables — ***PRINCEVILLE H-5***
Camping Plage du Golfe (Not Visited) — ***BASSIN C-6***
® **Camping Plage Fortier (K.F.A.)** — ***L'ANGE-GARDIEN J-3***
Camping Plage Kirkland (Not Visited) — ***VENISE-EN-QUEBEC J-3***
Camping Plage McKenzie — ***RACINE I-4***
Camping Plage Paris — ***SAINTE-SOPHIE-DE-LEVRARD G-5***
Camping Plage Robertson — ***MASHTEUIATSH B-4***
Camping Plage Venise (Not Visited) — ***VENISE-EN-QUEBEC J-3***
Camping Port St-Francois — ***NICOLET G-4***
□ Camping Premier RV Park — ***SAINT-BERNARD-DE-LACOLLE J-3***
Camping Rouillard 2000 — ***SHAWINIGAN G-4***
® **Camping Royal Papineau du Lac de l'Argile (Not Visited)** — ***NOTRE-DAME-DE-LA-SALETTE D-2***
Camping Ruisselet (Not Visited) — ***CAPLAN E-6***
△ Camping Saint Boniface (Not Visited) — ***SAINT BONIFACE G-3***
Camping Saint-Andre-Avellin (Not Visited) — ***SAINT-ANDRE-AVELLIN D-3***
Camping Saint-Polycarpe (Not Visited) — ***SAINT-POLYCARPE J-1***
Camping Sainte-Emilie (Not Visited) — ***SAINTE-EMILIE-DE-L'ENERGIE G-2***
Camping Sol Air (Not Visited) — ***SAINTE-MARCELLINE-DE-KILDARE H-2***
Camping St-Louis — ***MISTASSINI B-4***
Camping Ste-Madeleine — ***SAINTE-MADELEINE I-3***
Camping Stoneham — ***STONEHAM F-6***
Camping Tadoussac (Not Visited) — ***TADOUSSAC B-5***
□ Camping Temilac — ***CABANO B-6***
Camping Tete d'Indien (Not Visited) — ***PERCE E-6***
®□ Camping Trans-Canadien (Not Visited) — ***RIGAUD I-1***
Camping Transit — ***LEVIS F-6***
® **Camping Tropicana** — ***GRANBY I-4***
Camping Vacances Bromont (Not Visited) — ***BROMONT J-4***
® **Camping Valcartier** — ***VALCARTIER F-6***
Camping Vallee Bleue — ***WEST BROME J-4***
Camping Villa des Sables — ***LAC-A-LA-CROIX B-4***
□ Camping Wigwam — ***UPTON I-4***
Centre de Plain air La Seig Neurie — ***CHANDLER (PABOS) E-6***
Centre Recreo-Touristique Camping des Monts — ***SAINTE-ANNE-DES-MONTS D-5***
□ Centre Touristique du Lac Kenogami — ***LAC-KENOGAMI B-4***
□ Centre Touristique du Lac-Simon — ***DUHAMEL D-3***
□ Centre Touristique Sainte-Monique — ***SAINTE-MONIQUE-DE-HONFLEUR B-4***
Cool Breeze Camping (Not Visited) — ***SAINT-BERNARD-DE-LACOLLE J-3***
Domain du Lac Louise (Not visited) — ***SAINT-LOUIS-DE-BLANDFORD G-5***
Domaine de l'Ange Gardien (Not Visited) — ***L'ANGE GARDIEN (OUTAOUAIS) D-2***
Domaine de Rouville (Not Visited) — ***SAINT-JEAN-BAPTISTE-DE-ROUVILLE I-3***
Domaine de Vacances la Rocaille — ***LATERRIERE B-5***
Domaine des Cantons — ***SAINT-ETIENNE-DE-BOLTON J-4***
Domaine des Erables (Lac Brome) — ***LAC-BROME J-4***
Domaine Desjardins — ***SAINT-FAUSTIN-LAC-CARRE H-1***
® Domaine du Bel Age (Not Visited) — ***MERCIER J-2***
Domaine du Lac Ha! Ha! (Municipal Park) — ***FERLAND ET BOILLEAU B-5***
Domaine du Lac Libby — ***SAINT-ETIENNE-DE-BOLTON J-4***
Domaine Lac des Pins (Not Visited) — ***SAINT-MICHEL-DES-SAINTS F-2***
Domaine Lac et Foret (Not Visited) — ***SAINTE-THECLE F-4***

QUEBEC — Continued

Domaine Riviera — ***SAINT-PAUL-DE-l'ILE-AUX-NOIX J-3***
Domaine Riviera Au Bord De a Riviere — ***LA MALBAIE C-5***
Du Village — ***PERCE E-6***
Floribell (Not Visited) — ***SAINT-ELIE-DE-CAXTON G-3***
Forillon NP (Cap-Bon-Ami) — ***GASPE E-6***
Forillon NP (Des-Rosiers) — ***GASPE E-6***
Forillon NP (Petit Gaspe) — ***GASPE E-6***
Gatineau Park (La Peche Lake) — ***SAINTE-CECILE-DE-MASHAM D-2***
Gatineau Park (Philippe Lake) — ***SAINTE-CECILE-DE-MASHAM D-2***
□ KOA Montreal South — ***SAINT-PHILIPPE-DE-LAPRAIRIE J-2***
KOA Montreal West — ***COTEAU DU LAC J-1***
□ **KOA-Quebec City** — ***SAINT-NICOLAS F-6***
La Mauricie National Park (Mistagance) — ***SHAWINIGAN G-4***
La Mauricie National Park (Riviere-a-la-Peche) — ***GRAND-MERE G-4***
La Mauricie National Park (Wapizagonke) — ***SHAWINIGAN G-4***
La Tuque Municipal Campground — ***LA TUQUE C-4***
□ le Genevrier — ***BAIE-SAINT-PAUL C-5***
Marina Camping Montebello (City Park) — ***MONTEBELLO I-1***
Municipal L'Oasis (Not Visited) — ***SAINT-DAVID-DE-FALARDEAU B-5***
Oasis du Richelieu — ***HENRYVILLE J-3***
Parc de la Peninsule — ***SAINTE-GENEVIEVE-DE-BATISCAN G-4***
□ Parc National Aiguebelle/Camping Abijevis — ***MONT-BRUN B-1***
□ Parc National d'Anticosti/Baie-de-la-Tour — ***ANTICOSTI ISLAND D-6***
□ Parc National de Frontenac, Baie Sauvage — ***LAMBTON H-6***
□ Parc National de la Gaspesie — ***SAINTE-ANNE-DES-MONTS D-5***
Parc National de la Gaspesie, Lac Cascapedia — ***SAINTE-ANNE-DES-MONTS D-5***
Parc National de la Gaspesie, Mont-Albert — ***SAINTE-ANNE-DES-MONTS D-5***
Parc National de la Pointe-Taillon — ***SAINT-HENRI-DE-TAILLON B-4***
Parc National de la Yamaska — ***YAMASKA H-3***
□ Parc National de Plaisance — ***PLAISANCE D-3***
□ Parc National des Grands-Jardins — ***BAIE-SAINT-PAUL C-5***
□ Parc National des Monts-Valin — ***SAINT-FULGENCE B-5***
Parc National d'Oka — ***OKA I-2***
Parc National du Bic/Camping Rioux — ***BIC B-6***
Parc National du Bic/Camping Riviere-du-Sud-Ouest — ***BIC B-6***
Parc National du Mont-Megantic — ***NOTRE-DAME-DES-BOIS I-6***
Parc National du Mont-Orford/Camping Lac Fraser — ***ORFORD J-4***
Parc National du Mont-Orford/Camping Lac Stukely — ***ORFORD J-4***
□ Parc National du Mont-Tremblant/Camping Secteur de la Diable — ***MONT-TREMBLANT G-1***
Parc National du Mont-Tremblant/Camping Secteur de la Pimbina — ***SAINT-DONAT G-1***
□ Parc National du Mont-Tremblant/Camping Secteur de l'Assomption — ***SAINT-COME G-2***
Parc National du Mont-Tremblant/Lac Cache — ***MONT-TREMBLANT G-1***
□ Parc National du Saguenay, Baie-Eternite — ***RIVIERE-ETERNITE B-5***
Parc National Hautes-Gorges-de-la-Riviere-Malbaie — ***SAINT-AIME-DES-LACS C-5***
□ Parc National Rustique de la Jacques-Cartier Secteur de la pallic — ***QUEBEC CITY F-6***
□ Plage Lac Saint-Joseph — ***FOSSAMBAULT-SUR-LE-LAC F-5***
□ Reserve Faunique Ashuapmushuan Camping Lac Chiboubiche — ***LA DORE B-4***
□ Reserve Faunique Assinica et des Lacs-Albanel-Mistassini-et Waconichi/Camping Baie Penicou — ***CHIBOUGAMAU A-3***
□ Reserve Faunique de Matane et de Duniere/Camping Etang a la Truite — ***MATANE B-6***
□ Reserve Faunique de Matane/Camping John — ***MATANE B-6***
□ Reserve Faunique de Papineau-Labelle/Lac Echo — ***MONTPELLIER D-3***
□ Reserve Faunique de Port-Cartier-Sept-Iles/Camping Lac Walker — ***PORT-CARTIER D-5***
□ Reserve Faunique de Rimouski/Camping Lac Rimouski — ***RIMOUSKI B-6***
□ Reserve Faunique de/Camping Port-Daniel — ***PORT-DANIEL E-6***
□ Reserve Faunique des Laurentides, Camping Belle-Riviere — ***ALMA B-4***
□ Reserve Faunique des Laurentides-Camping La Loutre — ***QUEBEC CITY F-6***
□ Reserve Faunique du Saint-Maurice/Lac Normand — ***SHAWINIGAN G-4***
□ Reserve Faunique La Verendrye Outaouais-Camping Lac Rapide — ***GRAND-REMOUS C-2***
□ Reserve Faunique La Verendrye-Outaouais-Camping de la Vieille — ***GRAND-REMOUS C-2***
Reserve Faunique La Verendrye-Outaouais-Camping Lac Savary — ***GRAND-REMOUS C-2***
□ Reserve Faunique Mastigouche/Lac Saint-Bernard — ***SAINT-ALEXIS-DES-MONTS G-3***
□ Reserve Faunique/Rouge Matawin-Camping Lac des Sucreries — ***L'ANNONCIATION G-1***
Riv-O-Pom (Not Visited) — ***NEUVILLE F-5***
□ Riviere Faunique de Portneuf/Camping Lac Bellevue — ***PORTNEUF F-5***
□ Sepaq Anticosti/Camping Wilcox & Chicotte — ***ANTICOSTI ISLAND D-6***
Site Touristique Chute a l'Ours (Municipal Park) — ***NORMANDIN B-4***
Un Air d'ete 2005 — ***PONT-ROUGE F-5***
□ Village Historique de Val-Jalbert — ***CHAMBORD B-4***

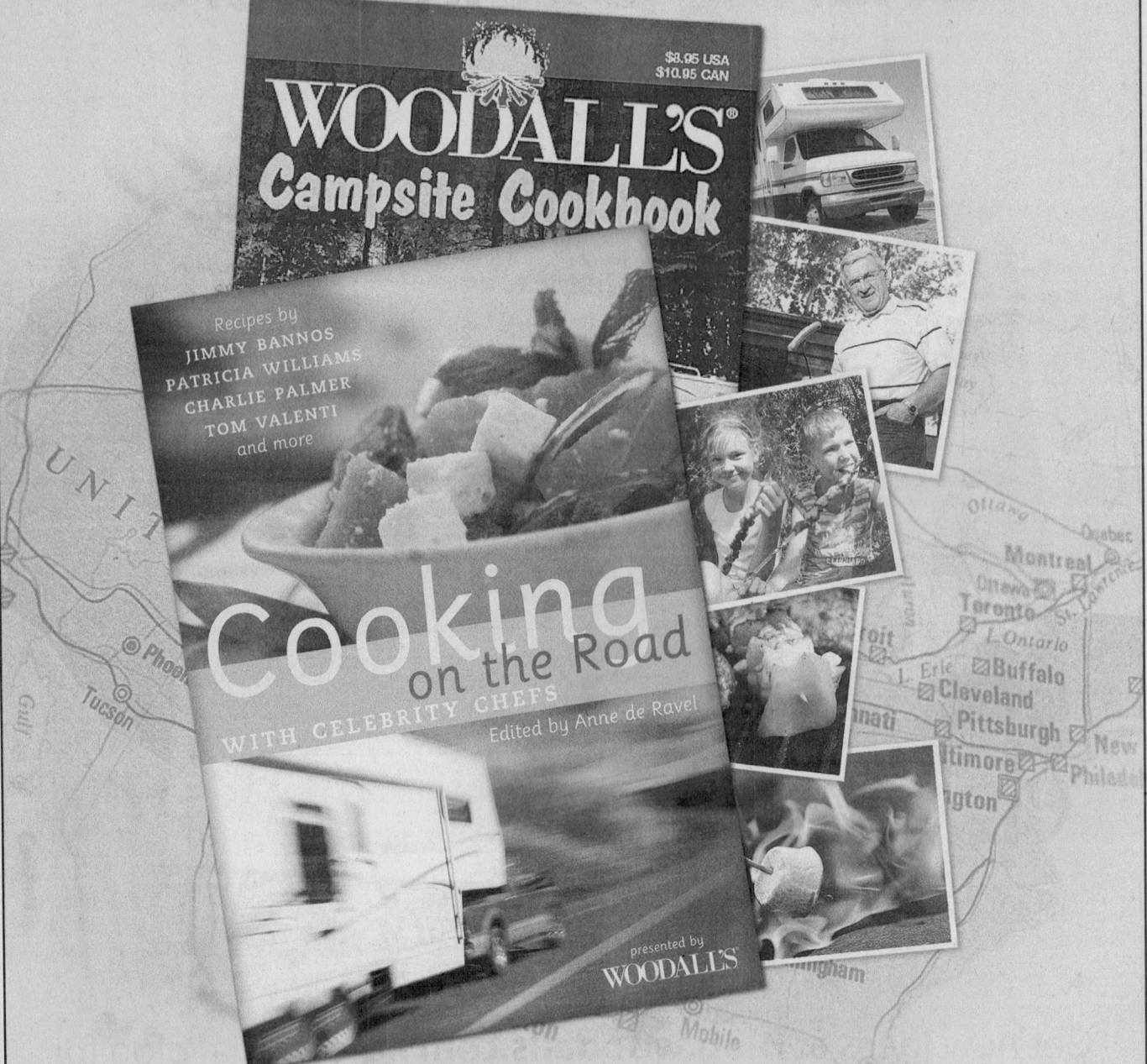

WOODALL'S® EXTENDED STAY

WEEKLY MONTHLY SEASONAL WEEKLY MONTHLY SEASONAL WEEKLY MONTHLY SEASONAL

SPRING SUMMER AUTUMN WINTER SPRING SUMMER AUTUMN WINTER SPRING

GUIDE TO RV PARKS/CAMPGROUNDS 2011

WOODALL'S 2011 EXTENDED STAY GUIDE TO RV PARKS/CAMPGROUNDS HELPS YOU MAKE YOUR PLANS!

If you'd like some great recommendations on where you can camp for a week, a month or an entire season, and which parks, RV dealerships and attractions cater to seasonal campers, then WOODALL'S 2011 EXTENDED STAY GUIDE TO RV PARKS/CAMPGROUNDS is for you! It has been specially designed for snowbirds, sunbirds and full-timers.

Throughout these pages, we have provided detailed listings and display advertising from RV parks and campgrounds that invite you to come stay with them.

The ADVERTISEMENTS show you what is unique about each listed facility. They may provide special seasonal rates, and tell you what attractions are nearby. They expand on the information in the listings. For example, the listing will tell you how many sites there are at an RV park. Their ad might say: Waterfront sites, or extra-wide pull-thrus. Additional information about hospital services, special entertainment programs, park trailer sales, distances to lakes and beaches is often provided, too. The LISTINGS tell you the "nuts and bolts" about the RV parks and campgrounds. They provide detailed driving directions, on-site facilities, and more. The reference line at the bottom of each advertiser listing tells you exactly where to find their ad.

The LISTINGS and ADVERTISEMENTS in this Guide are organized alphabetically, first by state in the United States, then by Canadian province. Within each state and province, the towns are listed in alphabetical order, and within each town, the facilities are also organized alphabetically.

WHAT DO THE NUMBERS MEAN AT THE BOTTOM OF EACH AD?

Reader Service Numbers are assigned to each advertiser in the EXTENDED STAY GUIDE. Look at the bottom of each ad for these numbers. Then, turn to the Reader Service Card following page 48 in the front of the book. In the spaces provided on the card, write the numbers of the facilities you are interested in. Drop the postage-paid card in the mail. It's that easy! You'll receive brochures and other information... sent directly to your home.

If you choose to inquire by phone, e-mail or web site, please let the RV Park/Campground know you found out about them by using WOODALL'S.

WHAT THE LISTINGS TELL YOU

PEACEFUL VALLEY – A-2

(NW) CAREFREE CAMPING RV PARK—(DuPage)

WELCOME

From jct I-94 (exit 24) & Hwy 120: Go 1/2 mi N on Hwy 120 (Golden Eagle Road), then 4 mi W on Hwy 80, then 1 mi N on Carefree Rd. Enter on R.

JUST LIKE NEW!

We've completely renovated our park for this season! Come relax in our new swimming pool or take advantage of our deluxe new bathhouses. Don't miss our annual festivities such as Christmas in July & end-of-season pig roast.

◊◊◊◊◊ FACILITIES: 320 sites, typical site width 40 ft, 175 full hkups, 100 W & E, 25 E, (20/30/50 amp), 50 amps ($), 20 no hkups, some extd stay sites, 50 pull-thrus, heater not allowed, cable TV, Wi-Fi Instant Internet at site ($), phone/cable on-site Internet (needs activ), cable Internet access central location, family camping, tenting, RV/park model rentals, cabins, dump, non-guest dump ($), laundry, groceries, LP gas by weight/meter, LP bottle exch, ice, picnic tables, wood.

◊◊◊◊◊ RECREATION: rec hall, equipped pavilion, coin games, 2 swim pools, wading pool, lake swim, hot tub, boating, 10 motorboat rentals, lake fish ing, fishing supplies, mini-golf ($), 25 bike rentals, playground, activities, tennis, hiking trails, local tours.

Pets welcome, breed restrict, size restrict, quantity restrict ($). Partial handicap access. Escort to site. Open all year. Big rigs welcome. Clubs welcome. Green friendly. Rate in 2010 $18.50-23.50 per family. MC/VISA/DISC/AMEX. ATM. Member of ARVC. FCRV discount. FMCA discount.

Phone: (999)555-6200.
Address: 27 Carefree Rd., Zephyr Hills, FL 34875
LAT/LON: 28.27213/-82.17965
Email: cmpn@carefree.com
Website: www.carefreecamping.com

SEE AD THIS PAGE

FACILITIES: All of the facilities listed are available on site.

INTERNET ACCESS: Phone and/or cable available upon activation by local phone company.

RECREATION: All of the recreation listed is available right at the campground.

SPECIAL INFORMATION: This area includes such information as no pets, age restrictions, and operating season. If the listing does not state "No Pets", pets are allowed. If you see "pet restrictions" in the listing, pets are allowed, but be sure to check with park management regarding stipulations they may have on pets.

E-MAIL ADDRESS: When available, advertiser listings contain e-mail addresses.

COUNTY: Appears in parentheses after park name. May be useful in the event of severe weather, since most broadcast weather warnings are given by county.

DRIVING DIRECTIONS: Detailed, easy-to-read driving information, including where the entrance to the campground is located.

PARTIAL HANDICAP ACCESS: Indicates the park has been adapted in one or more ways to accommodate RVers/campers with disabilities. If you or a family member has special needs, please call ahead to determine the type of services/facilities available.

ADVERTISER REFERENCE: This line will refer you to the specific page for this listing's advertisement.

Free Camping Information
Extended Stay Guide

SAVE HOURS OF RESEARCH!

The campgrounds/RV parks, RV service centers and attractions listed below want your business! Here is a quick and easy way to receive free information about seasonal camping, fun things to do, and where to service your RV or buy a new one. Simply enter their **Reader Service Number** (listed below) on the **Reader Service Card**, which is located opposite page 48 in the front of the **Discover Section**. Your request will be forwarded to the names you've indicated. Then, you'll receive brochures and/or pricing information, sent directly to your home. It's the no-hassle way to shop for the campground, attraction or RV dealership you are interested in!

Enter Number	
ARIZONA	
4207	Butterfield RV Resort
3835	Desert Gold RV Resort
3834	Holiday Palms RV Park
CALIFORNIA	
2677	La Pacifica RV Resort
3532	Morena Mobile Village
3590	Sunland RV Resorts (Formerly Golden Village Palms)
FLORIDA	
4033	Lakeland RV Resort
3554	Mill Creek RV Resort
3884	Paradise Island
4092	Riverbend Motorcoach Resort
906	Road Runner Travel Resort
3889	Sun 'N' Shade Campground
3656	The Glades
3885	Woodall's Mobile Home Village
439	Zachary Taylor Resort
GEORGIA	
3058	River's End Campground & RV Park
INDIANA	
4110	Indian Lakes Campground
MAINE	
1050	Beach Acres Campground
MICHIGAN	
2124	Clearwater Campground
1076	Greenwood Acres Family Campground
3441	Lake Chemung Outdoor Resort
4212	Shady Shores Resort
MISSISSIPPI	
3792	Indian Point RV Resort
CANADA	
ONTARIO	
3173	Rochester Place Resort Inc

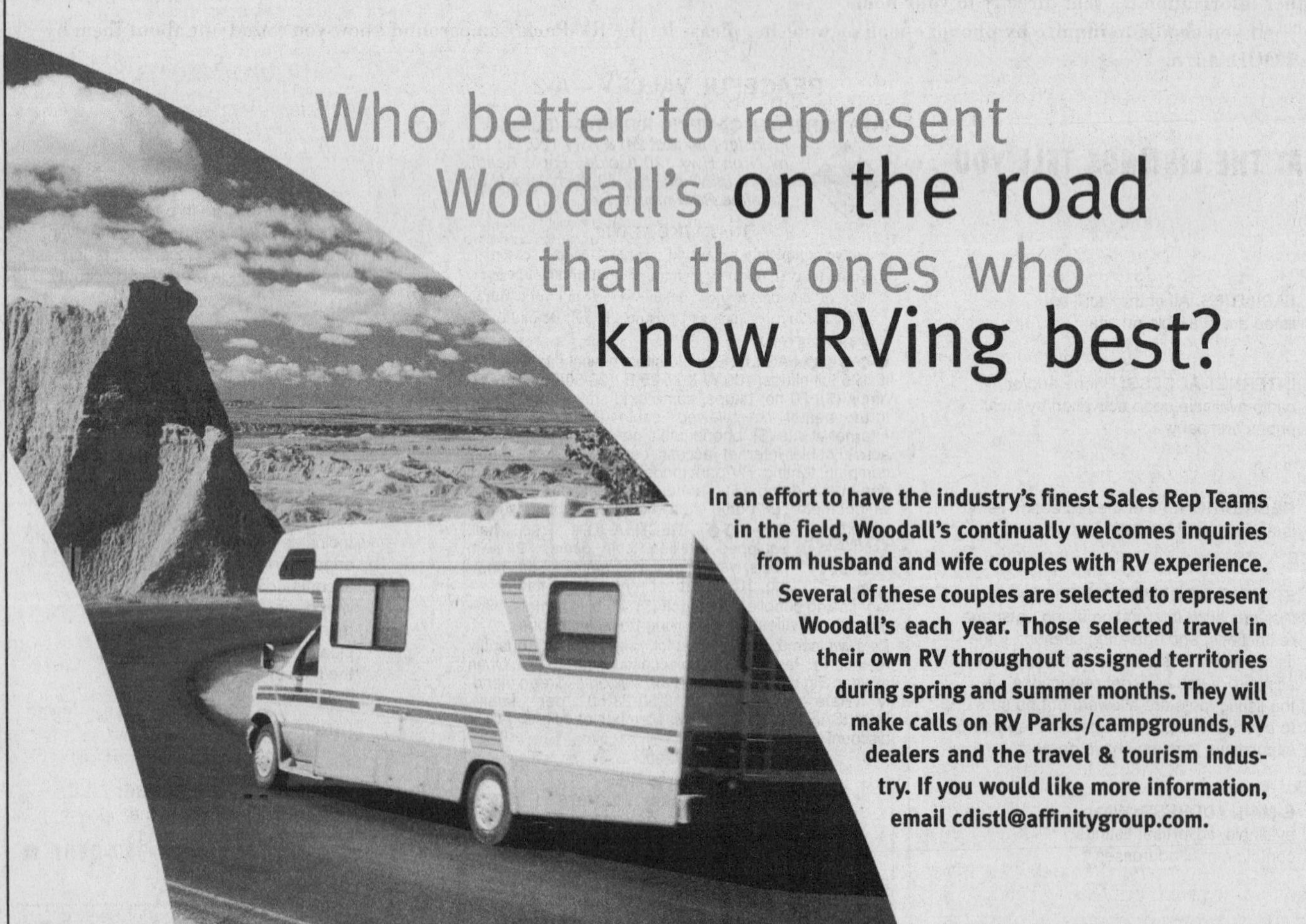

Who better to represent
Woodall's on the road
than the ones who
know RVing best?
In an effort to have the industry's finest Sales Rep Teams in the field, Woodall's continually welcomes inquiries from husband and wife couples with RV experience. Several of these couples are selected to represent Woodall's each year. Those selected travel in their own RV throughout assigned territories during spring and summer months. They will make calls on RV Parks/campgrounds, RV dealers and the travel & tourism industry. If you would like more information, email cdistl@affinitygroup.com.

EXTENDED STAY GUIDE TO RV PARKS/CAMPGROUNDS

ALASKA

VALDEZ

(E) Eagle's Rest RV Park & Cabins—(Valdez-Cordova) *From Hwy 4 (Richardson Hwy) Mile Post 0: Go 3-1/2 mi S on Hwy 4, then 200 feet W on E Pioneer Dr. Enter on R.* FACILITIES: 237 sites, typical site width 20 ft, 187 full hkups, (20/30/50 amps), 50 no hkups, 83 pull-thrus, family camping, cable TV, WiFi Instant Internet at site, phone Internet central location, cabins, RV storage, dump, non-guest dump, laundry, ltd groc, RV supplies, LP gas by meter, ice, picnic tables, fire rings, wood. RECREATION: float trips, fishing supplies, fishing guides, bike rental, horseshoes, local tours. Rec open to public. Pets welcome. Partial handicap access. Open all yr. Facilities fully operational May - Oct. Big rigs welcome. Member ARVC, ACOA. ATM.

Phone: (800)553-7275
Address: 139 East Pioneer Dr, Valdez, AK 99686
Lat/Lon: 61.13092/-146.34593
Email: rvpark@alaska.net
Web: www.eaglesrestrv.com

Reserve Online at Woodalls.com

ARIZONA

APACHE JUNCTION

(S) Superstition Sunrise RV Resort—(Pinal) *From jct Fwy 202 Loop & US 60 (Superstition Fwy): Go 3 mi E on US 60 (exit 193/Signal Butte Rd), then 1/2 mi N on Signal Butte Rd, then 1 mi E on Southern, then 1 mi N on Meridian. Enter on L.* FACILITIES: 1119 sites, typical site width 34 ft, accepts full hkup units only, 1119 full hkups, (30/50 amps), cable TV, WiFi Instant Internet at site ($), phone Internet central location ($), laundry, ice, patios, controlled access. RECREATION: rec hall, rec room/area, equipped pavilion, 2 swim pools, hot tub, putting green, golf nearby, 16 shuffleboard courts, activities, tennis, horseshoes, sports field, local tours. Pets welcome, quantity restrict. Partial handicap access. No tents. Age restrict may apply. Open all yr. Big rigs welcome. Member ARVC, AZ ARVC.

Phone: (800)624-7027
Address: 702 So Meridian, Apache Junction, AZ 85120
Lat/Lon: 33.40203/-111.58135
Email: info@superstitionsunrise.com
Web: superstitionsunrise.com

(E) VIP RV Resort—(Pinal) *From jct Fwy 202 Loop & US 60 (Superstition Fwy): Go 5 mi E on US 60 (exit 195/Ironwood Dr), then 1-3/4 mi N on Ironwood Dr. Enter on R.* FACILITIES: 128 sites, typical site width 30 ft, 40 ft max RV length, accepts full hkup units only, 128 full hkups, (30/50 amps), WiFi Instant Internet at site, WiFi Internet central location, RV storage, laundry, patios. RECREATION: rec hall, rec room/area, golf nearby, 2 shuffleboard courts, activities, horseshoes. Pets welcome, size restrict, quantity restrict. Partial handicap access. No tents. Age restrict may apply. Open all yr. Big rigs welcome. Member ARVC, AZ ARVC.

Phone: (480)983-0847
Address: 401 S Ironwood Dr, Apache Junction, AZ 85120
Lat/Lon: 33.41187/-111.56250
Web: www.viprvresort.com

BRENDA

(SE) DESERT GOLD RV RESORT—(La Paz) *From jct I-10 (exit 31) & US 60: Go 4 mi NE on US 60 (MP 35). Enter on R.*

WELCOME

FACILITIES: 550 sites, typical site width 35 ft, 550 full hkups, (20/30/50 amps), 42 pull-thrus, cable TV, WiFi Instant Internet at site, WiFi Internet central location, family camping, RV's/park model rentals, RV storage, laundry, LP gas by meter, picnic tables, patios.

RECREATION: rec hall, rec room/area, swim pool, hot tub, mini-golf, activities, horseshoes, hiking trails, local tours.

Pets welcome, breed restrict, quantity restrict. Partial handicap access. No tents. Open all yr. Big rigs welcome.

Woodall's — Trusted for Over 75 Years.

BRENDA—Continued
DESERT GOLD RV RESORT—Continued

Phone: (800)927-2101
Address: 46628 E US Highway 60, Salome, AZ 85348
Lat/Lon: 33.67887/-113.94718
Email: desertgoldrvresort@gmail.com
Web: grapevine7.com

SEE AD THIS PAGE

(E) Wagon West RV Park—(La Paz) *From jct I-10 (exit 31) & US 60: Go 7 mi E on US 60 (MP 39). Enter on R.* FACILITIES: 215 sites, typical site width 30 ft, 215 full hkups, (30/50 amps), 11 pull-thrus, WiFi Instant Internet at site ($), phone Internet central location, shower$, laundry, LP gas by meter, ice. RECREATION: rec hall, rec room/area, golf nearby, 3 shuffleboard courts, activities, horseshoes, hiking trails. Pets welcome, breed restrict, quantity restrict. No tents. Age restrict may apply. Open Oct - Apr. Big rigs welcome.

Phone: (928)927-7077
Address: 50126 E Hwy 60, Salome, AZ 85348
Lat/Lon: 33.69383/-113.88512
Email: wagonwest@tds.net
Web: www.wagonwestrvpark.com

MARANA

(SW) Valley of The Sun RV Resort—(Pima) *From jct I-10 (exit 236 Marana) & Sandario Rd: Go 1/2 mi S on Sandario Rd. Enter on R.* FACILITIES: 121 sites, typical site width 30 ft, 121 full hkups, (30/50 amps), 20 pull-thrus, family camping, cable TV ($), WiFi Instant Internet at site ($), WiFi Internet central location, laundry, LP gas by meter, patios. RECREATION: rec hall, rec room/area, equipped pavilion, swim pool, hot tub, golf nearby, shuffleboard court, activities, horseshoes. Pets welcome. Partial handicap access. No tents. Open all yr. Big rigs welcome.

Phone: (520)682-3434
Address: 13377 North Sandario Rd, Marana, AZ 85653
Lat/Lon: 32.45132/-111.21713
Email: smhrv@qwestoffice.net
Web: www.valleyofthesunrv.com

Reserve Online at Woodalls.com

MESA

(E) Venture Out at Mesa—(Maricopa) *From jct Loop 101 & US 60 (Superstition Fwy): Go 9 mi E on US 60 (exit 185) Greenfield Rd, then 2 mi N on Greenfield, then 3/4 mi E on E Main St. Enter on R.* FACILITIES: 1769 sites, typical site width 25 ft, accepts full hkup units only, 1769 full hkups, (30/50 amps), 12 pull-thrus, cable TV, WiFi Internet central location, RV's/park model rentals, dump, laundry, ice, patios, controlled access. RECREATION: rec hall, rec room/area, 2 swim pools, hot tub, putting green, golf nearby, bsktball, 20 shuffleboard courts, activities, tennis, horseshoes, sports field, local tours. No pets. Partial handicap access. No tents. Age restrict may apply. Open all yr. Big rigs welcome.

Phone: (480)832-0200
Address: 5001 E Main St, Mesa, AZ 85205
Lat/Lon: 33.41520/-111.72359
Email: ventureoutgm@qwestoffice.net
Web: www.ventureoutrvresort.com

PHOENIX

(N) Desert's Edge RV Village—(Maricopa) *From jct I-10 & I-17: Go 15 mi N on I-17 (exit 215 Deer Valley Rd), then 1/2 mi N on East Frontage Road, then 500 ft E on Williams Dr. Enter on L.* FACILITIES: 205 sites, typical site width 28 ft, 205 full hkups, (20/30/50 amps), 15 pull-thrus, family camping, WiFi Instant Internet at site, phone on-site Internet (needs activ), WiFi Internet central location, RV storage, laundry, RV supplies, LP gas by meter, picnic tables, patios. RECREATION: rec hall, rec room/area, pavilion, coin games, swim pool, hot tub, golf nearby, bsktball, playground, activities, horseshoes. Pets welcome, breed restrict, quantity restrict. Partial handicap access. No tents. Open all yr. Big rigs welcome. Green Friendly. Member ARVC, AZ ARVC.

Phone: (623)587-0940
Address: 22623 N. Black Canyon Hwy., Phoenix, AZ 85027
Lat/Lon: 33.69129/-112.11067
Email: info@desertsedgerv.com
Web: www.desertsedgerv.com

(N) Phoenix Metro RV Park—(Maricopa) *From jct Loop 101 & I-17: Go 1 mi N on I-17 (Deer Valley exit 215), then 3/4 mi N on east frontage road. Enter on R.* FACILITIES: 310 sites, typical site width 27 ft, accepts full hkup units only, 310 full hkups, (30/50 amps), WiFi Instant Internet at site, phone on-site Internet (needs activ), WiFi Internet central location, RV storage, laundry, ice, grills. RECREATION: rec hall, rec room/area, equipped pavilion, swim pool, hot tub, golf nearby, 2 shuffleboard courts, activities, horseshoes, local tours. Pets welcome, breed restrict, size restrict, quantity restrict. Partial handicap access. No tents. Age restrict may apply. Open all yr. Big rigs welcome. Member ARVC, AZ ARVC.

Phone: (877)582-0390
Address: 22701 N Black Canyon Hwy, Phoenix, AZ 85027
Lat/Lon: 33.69355/-112.11267
Email: info@phoenixmetrorvpark.com
Web: phoenixmetrorvpark.com

QUARTZSITE

(W) HOLIDAY PALMS—(La Paz) *From jct I-10 & Bus Loop 10 (exit 17): Go 1-1/4 mi E on Bus Loop 10 (Main St). Enter on L.*

WELCOME

FACILITIES: 243 sites, typical site width 25 ft, accepts full hkup units only, 243 full hkups, (20/30/50 amps), 14 pull-thrus, cable TV, WiFi Instant Internet at site, WiFi Internet central location, family camping, RV storage, laundry, LP gas by meter, patios.

RECREATION: rec hall, rec room/area, pavilion, hot tub, shuffleboard court, activities, horseshoes, local tours.

Pets welcome, breed restrict, size restrict, quantity restrict. No tents. Open all yr. Planned group activities Oct 1 - Apr 30. Big rigs welcome.

HOLIDAY PALMS—Continued on next page

QUARTZSITE—Continued
HOLIDAY PALMS—Continued

Phone: (800)635-5372
Address: 355 W Main, Quartzsite, AZ 85359
Lat/Lon: 33.66589/-114.22262
Email: holidaypalmsrvpark@gmail.com
Web: grapevine7.com

SEE AD PAGE 3

CALIFORNIA

BAKERSFIELD

(E) Bakersfield River Run RV Park—(Kern) *From jct Hwy 99 & Hwy 58 (Rosedale Hwy): Go 1/2 mi W on Hwy 58 (Rosedale Hwy), then 1/2 mi S on Gibson Street, then 1/2 mi E on Burr St. Enter at end.* FACILITIES: 123 sites, typical site width 29 ft, 123 full hkups, (20/30/50 amps), 31 pull-thrus, family camping, cable TV, WiFi Instant Internet at site, WiFi Internet central location, dump, non-guest dump $, laundry, groceries, RV supplies, LP gas by meter, ice, patios. RECREATION: rec hall, rec room/area, equipped pavilion, swim pool, hot tub, golf nearby, hiking trails. Pets welcome ($), breed restrict, size restrict, quantity restrict. Partial handicap access. No tents. Open all yr. Pool open during summer months. Spa open year round. Big rigs welcome. Green Friendly. Member ARVC, CALARVC.

Phone: (888)748-7786
Address: 3715 Burr St, Bakersfield, CA 93308
Lat/Lon: 35.37919/-119.04764
Email: reservations@riverrunrvpark.com
Web: www.riverrunrvpark.com

Reserve Online at Woodalls.com

DESERT HOT SPRINGS

(SE) Sam's Family Spa Resort—(Riverside) *From jct Hwy 62 & I-10: Go 6 mi E on I-10, then 3 mi N on Palm Dr, then 4.8 mi E on Dillon Rd. Enter on R.* FACILITIES: 170 sites, typical site width 25 ft, 170 full hkups, (20/30/50 amps), family camping, WiFi Instant Internet at site ($), laundry, ltd groc, ice, patios. RECREATION: rec hall, pavilion, equipped pavilion, swim pool, hot tub, golf nearby, bsktball, play equipment, activities, horseshoes, v-ball. Pets welcome. Open all yr. Planned group activities winter only. Big rigs welcome. Member ARVC, CALARVC.

Phone: (760)329-6457
Address: 70-875 Dillon Rd, Desert Hot Springs, CA 92241
Lat/Lon: 33.92325/-116.42552
Email: samsfamilyspa@aol.com
Web: www.samsfamilyspa.com

EL CAJON

(NE) CIRCLE RV RESORT-SUNLAND—(San Diego) *From jct I-15 & I-8: Go 12-3/4 mi E on I-8, then 1 block N on Greenfield Dr, then 1/4 mi E on E Main St. Enter on R.*

FACILITIES: 170 sites, typical site width 20 ft, 170 full hkups, (30/50 amps), 8 pull-thrus, cable TV, WiFi Instant Internet at site ($), family camping, laundry, LP gas by meter, ice, picnic tables, patios.

RECREATION: rec hall, rec room/area, equipped pavilion, swim pool, hot tub, golf nearby, activities (wkends), local tours.

Pets welcome ($), breed restrict, quantity restrict. Partial handicap access. No tents. Open all yr. Advanced Reservations Suggested. Big rigs welcome. Member ARVC, CALARVC.

Phone: (866)225-3650
Address: 1835 E. Main St, El Cajon, CA 92021
Lat/Lon: 32.81545/-116.91581
Email: circlerv@sunlandrvresorts.com
Web: www.circlerv.com

SEE AD PALM SPRINGS PAGE 6

(NE) OAK CREEK RV RESORT-SUNLAND—(SanDiego) *From jct I-15 & I-8: Go 16 mi E on I-8, then take Lake Jennings Park Rd exit, then 2-1/2 mi E (straight ahead) on Olde Hwy 80. Enter on L.*

FACILITIES: 121 sites, typical site width 20 ft, 121 full hkups, (30/50 amps), cable TV, WiFi Instant Internet at site ($), family camping, laundry, ice, picnic tables, patios.

RECREATION: rec hall, equipped pavilion, swim pool, hot tub, golf nearby, activities, horseshoes.

Pets welcome ($), breed restrict, quantity restrict. Partial handicap access. No tents. Open all yr. Advanced Reservations Suggested. Big rigs welcome. Member ARVC, CALARVC.

EL CAJON—Continued
OAK CREEK RV RESORT-SUNLAND—Continued

Phone: (866)225-1697
Address: 15379 Oak Creek Rd, El Cajon, CA 92021
Lat/Lon: 32.85659/-116.84375
Email: oakcreekrv@sunlandrvresorts.com
Web: www.oakcreekrv.com

SEE AD PALM SPRINGS PAGE 6

(E) THE VACATIONER RV RESORT-SUNLAND—(San Diego) *From jct Hwy I-15 & I-8: Go 12-3/4 mi E on I-8 (Greenfield Dr exit), then 1 block N on Greenfield Dr, then 1/2 mi SW on E Main St. Enter on L.*

FACILITIES: 147 sites, typical site width 20 ft, 38 ft max RV length, 147 full hkups, (20/30/50 amps), 13 pull-thrus, cable TV, WiFi Instant Internet at site ($), family camping, RV storage, laundry, LP gas by meter, ice, picnic tables, patios.

RECREATION: rec room/area, swim pool, hot tub, golf nearby, activities, horseshoes, local tours.

Pets welcome ($), breed restrict, quantity restrict. Partial handicap access. No tents. Open all yr. Advanced reservations suggested. Member ARVC, CALARVC.

Phone: (866)225-4831
Address: 1581 E Main, El Cajon, CA 92021
Lat/Lon: 32.80659/-116.92285
Email: vacationerrv@sunlandrvresorts.com
Web: www.vacationerrv.com

SEE AD PALM SPRINGS PAGE 6

ENCINITAS

(N) Trailer Rancho—(San Diego) *From jct Hwy 78 & I-5: Go 7-1/4 mi S on I-5, then 1/2 mi W on La Costa Ave, then 1/2 mi S on Vulcan Ave. Enter on L.* FACILITIES: 61 sites, typical site width 28 ft, 36 ft max RV length, accepts full hkup units only, 61 full hkups, (30/50 amps), WiFi Instant Internet at site, laundry, patios. RECREATION: rec room/area, golf nearby. Pets welcome, breed restrict, size restrict, quantity restrict. Partial handicap access. No tents. Open all yr. Member ARVC, CALARVC.

Phone: (760)753-2741
Address: 1549 Vulcan Ave, Encinitas, CA 92024
Lat/Lon: 33.07476/-117.30512
Email: trailerrancho@prodigy.net
Web: www.woodalls.com/a/CAW44241900.html

ESCONDIDO

(N) ESCONDIDO RV RESORT-SUNLAND—(San Diego) *From jct Hwy 78 & I-15: Go 1 mi N on I-15 (El Norte Pkwy exit), then 200 yds E on El Norte Pkwy, then 1 block N on Seven Oaks Rd. Enter on R.*

FACILITIES: 125 sites, typical site width 24 ft, 125 full hkups, (20/30/50 amps), cable TV, WiFi Instant Internet at site ($), family camping, laundry, LP gas by meter, patios.

RECREATION: rec room/area, swim pool, hot tub, golf nearby, playground, sports field, hiking trails, local tours.

Pets welcome ($), breed restrict, quantity restrict. Partial handicap access. No tents. Open all yr. Advanced Reservations Suggested. Big rigs welcome. Member ARVC, CALARVC.

Phone: (866)225-3620
Address: 1740 Seven Oaks Rd., Escondido, CA 92026
Lat/Lon: 33.14744/-117.10282
Email: escondidorv@sunlandrvresorts.com
Web: www.escondidorv.com

SEE AD PALM SPRINGS PAGE 6

HEMET

(W) GOLDEN VILLAGE PALMS RV RESORT - SUNLAND—(Riverside) *From jct Hwy 79/Sanderson & Hwy 74/Florida Ave: Go 1/4 mi W on Hwy 74/Florida Ave. Enter on R.*

FACILITIES: 1041 sites, typical site width 35 ft, 1041 full hkups, (20/30/50 amps), 103 pull-thrus, cable TV, WiFi Instant Internet at site ($), phone on-site Internet (needs activ), phone Internet central location, laundry, ice, patios, controlled access.

HEMET—Continued
GOLDEN VILLAGE PALSM RV RESORT - SUNLAND—Continued

RECREATION: rec hall, rec room/area, equipped pavilion, 3 swim pools, hot tub, putting green, golf nearby, 8 shuffleboard courts, activities, horseshoes, v-ball, local tours.

Pets welcome, breed restrict, quantity restrict. Partial handicap access. No tents. Age restrict may apply. Open all yr. Advanced Reservation Suggested. Big rigs welcome. Member ARVC, CALARVC.

Phone: (866)225-2239
Address: 3600 W Florida Ave, Hemet, CA 92545
Lat/Lon: 33.74745/-117.01124
Email: goldenrv@sunlandrvresorts.com
Web: www.goldenvillagepalms.com

SEE AD PALM SPRINGS PAGE 6

INDIO

(SE) Indian Wells RV Resort—(Riverside) *From jct Hwy 74 & I-10: Go 7-1/2 mi E on I-10, then 3 mi S on Jefferson St. Enter on L.* FACILITIES: 306 sites, typical site width 25 ft, 306 full hkups, (20/30/50 amps), 168 pull-thrus, family camping, cable TV, WiFi Instant Internet at site ($), RV storage, dump, laundry, ice, patios. RECREATION: rec hall, rec room/area, equipped pavilion, 3 swim pools, hot tub, putting green, golf nearby, 4 shuffleboard courts, activities, horseshoes, v-ball. Pets welcome, breed restrict, quantity restrict. Partial handicap access. No tents. Open all yr. Big rigs welcome.

Phone: (800)789-0895
Address: 47-340 Jefferson St, Indio, CA 92201
Lat/Lon: 33.70414/-116.26807
Email: indianwellsrv@dc.rr.com
Web: www.carefreervresorts.com

(N) Shadow Hills RV Resort—(Riverside) *From jct I-10 & Jefferson St (exit 139): Go 200 yds N on Jefferson, then 200 yds E on Varner, then 1/4 mi N on Jefferson. Enter on L.* FACILITIES: 120 sites, typical site width 32 ft, 116 full hkups, 4 W&E, (30/50 amps), 2 pull-thrus, family camping, cable TV, WiFi Instant Internet at site, RV's/park model rentals, RV storage, laundry, LP gas by meter, ice, picnic tables, patios. RECREATION: rec hall, rec room/area, pavilion, equipped pavilion, swim pool, hot tub, golf nearby, 4 shuffleboard courts, activities, horseshoes, local tours. Pets welcome ($), breed restrict, quantity restrict. Partial handicap access. Open all yr. Dog park open all year. Big rigs welcome. Member ARVC, CALARVC.

Phone: (760)360-4040
Address: 40-655 Jefferson, Indio, CA 92203
Lat/Lon: 33.75465/-116.26913
Email: info@shadowhillsrvresort.com
Web: www.shadowhillsrvresort.com

Woodall's Tip... Turn to the Travel Section for "at-a-glance" RV Sales & Service Locations.

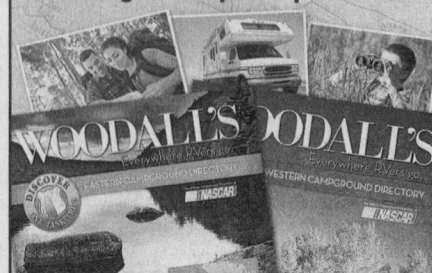

LA JOLLA

SUNLAND RV RESORTS—Experience the finest in Southern California! Emerald Desert in Palm Desert; Golden Village Palms in Hemet; San Diego in La Mesa; Escondido in Escondido; Oak Creek in El Cajon; Circle in El Cajon; Vacationer in El Cajon. Join us soon! Open all yr.

EXPERIENCE THE FINEST HOSPITALITY
Each of Sunland's 7 resorts offers the best on-site amenities in Southern California! Our friendly staff is ready to introduce you to mountains, desert, inland valleys, beaches, shopping, golf, casinos & restaurants. Join us!

Email: goldenrv@sunlandrvresorts.com
Web: www.sunlandrvresorts.com

SEE AD PALM SPRINGS NEXT PAGE

LA MESA

(W) SAN DIEGO RV RESORT - SUNLAND—(San Diego) *From jct I-15 & I-8: Go 3 mi on I-8 to 70th St/Lake Murrray Blvd exit, then stay in the Lake Murray Blvd/Alvarado Rd left lane to south side of I-8, then 1/2 mi E on Alvarado Rd. Enter on R.*

FACILITIES: 174 sites, typical site width 25 ft, 174 full hkups, (15/20/30/50 amps), 2 pull-thrus, cable TV, WiFi Instant Internet at site ($), family camping, laundry, LP gas by meter, patios.

RECREATION: rec hall, rec room/area, equipped pavilion, swim pool, hot tub, golf nearby, activities (wkends), local tours.

Pets welcome ($), breed restrict, quantity restrict. Partial handicap access. No tents. Open all yr. Advanced Reservations Suggested. Big rigs welcome. Member ARVC, CALARVC.

Phone: (866)225-3556
Address: 7407 Alvarado Rd, La Mesa, CA 91941
Lat/Lon: 32.77288/-117.03725
Email: Sandiegorv@sunlandrvresorts.com
Web: www.sdrvresort.com

SEE AD PALM SPRINGS NEXT PAGE

LAKE ELSINORE

(SW) LAKE ELSINORE WEST MARINA & RV RESORT—(Riverside) *From jct I-15 & Hwy 74: Go 1 blck SW on Central Ave (Hwy 74), then 1/4 mi NW on Collier (Hwy 74), then 4 mi SW on Riverside Dr (Hwy 74). Enter on L.*

FACILITIES: 181 sites, typical site width 30 ft, 181 full hkups, (30/50 amps), cable TV, phone Internet central location, family camping, RV storage, dump, non-guest dump $, laundry, ltd groc, RV supplies, LP gas by meter, ice, picnic tables, controlled access.

RECREATION: rec hall, pavilion, lake swim, boating, ramp, dock, lake fishing, fishing supplies, golf nearby, horseshoes. Rec open to public.

Pets welcome ($), breed restrict, size restrict. Partial handicap access. No tents. Open all yr. No pets allowed on beach area. Big rigs welcome. Member ARVC, CALARVC.

Phone: (800)328-6844
Address: 32700 Riverside Dr, Lake Elsinore, CA 92530
Lat/Lon: 33.66812/-117.37994
Email: info@lakeelsinoremarina.com
Web: www.lakeelsinoremarina.com

SEE AD THIS PAGE

NEWPORT BEACH

(S) Newport Dunes Waterfront Resort—(Orange) *From jct I-5 & Hwy 55: Go 5 mi S on Hwy 55, then 1-3/4 mi SE on I-405, then 5 mi SW on Jamboree Rd, then 1 block NW on Back Bay Rd. Enter on L.* FACILITIES: 378 sites, typical site width 20 ft, 378 full hkups, (20/30/50 amps), 12 pull-thrus, family camping, cable TV, WiFi Instant Internet at site, cabins, RV storage, laundry, full svc store, RV supplies, LP gas by meter, ice, picnic tables, patios, fire rings, grills, wood, controlled access. RECREATION: rec hall, rec room/area, pavilion, equipped pavilion, coin games, swim pool, saltwater swim, hot tub, boating, canoeing, kayaking, ramp, dock, 28 canoe/10 kayak/10 pedal boat rentals, saltwater fishing, fishing guides, golf nearby, bsktball, 15 bike rentals, playground, activities, horseshoes, hiking trails, v-ball, local tours. Rec open to public. Pets welcome ($), breed restrict, quantity restrict. Partial handicap access. Open all yr. Suri Tours, cottages & 2 electric boats to rent. Big rigs welcome. Member ARVC, CALARVC. ATM.

Phone: (800)765-7661
Address: 1131 Back Bay Dr, Newport Beach, CA 92660
Lat/Lon: 33.61486/-117.89222
Email: info@newportdunes.com
Web: www.newportdunes.com

PALM DESERT

(N) EMERALD DESERT GOLF & RV RESORT - SUNLAND—(Riverside) *From jct I-10 & Cook St: Go 3/4 mi S on Cook St, then 1 mi E on Frank Sinatra Dr. Enter on L.*

FACILITIES: 251 sites, typical site width 31 ft, 251 full hkups, (20/30/50 amps), 6 pull-thrus, cable TV, WiFi Instant Internet at site, RV storage, laundry, patios, controlled access.

RECREATION: rec hall, rec room/area, equipped pavilion, 2 swim pools, hot tub, putting green, golf nearby, activities, tennis, horseshoes, local tours.

Pets welcome ($), breed restrict, quantity restrict. Partial handicap access. No tents. Age restrict may apply. Open all yr. Advanced reservations suggested. Big rigs welcome. Member CALARVC.

Phone: (866)225-4982
Address: 76-000 Frank Sinatra Dr, Palm Desert, CA 92211
Lat/Lon: 33.77278/-116.33849
Email: info@emeralddesert.com
Web: www.emeralddesert.com

SEE AD PALM SPRINGS NEXT PAGE

PALM SPRINGS

See listings at Cathedral City, Desert Hot Springs, Indio, Palm Desert & Twentynine Palms

PARKER DAM

(W) Black Meadow Landing—(San Bernardino) *From jct Hwy 95 & Hwy 62: Go 16 mi E on Hwy 62, then 17 mi N on Parker Dam Rd, then 10 mi W on Black Meadow Rd (M.W.D. Rd). Enter at end.* FACILITIES: 398 sites, typical site width 25 ft, 350 full hkups, (30/50 amps), 50 amps ($), 48 no hkups, family camping, WiFi Instant Internet at site ($), cabins, RV storage, dump, laundry, full svc store, RV supplies, LP gas by meter, marine gas, ice, picnic tables, fire rings, controlled access. RECREATION: rec hall, lake/river swim, boating, canoeing, ramp, dock, river fishing, fishing supplies, golf nearby, playground, activities, horseshoes, hiking trails. Pets welcome, breed restrict, quantity restrict. Open all yr. Green Friendly. Member ARVC, CALARVC.

Phone: 800-742-8278
Address: 156100 Black Meadow Rd, Parker Dam, CA 92267
Lat/Lon: 34.34797/-114.20018
Email: info@blackmeadowlanding.com
Web: www.blackmeadowlanding.com

PETALUMA

(N) KOA-SAN FRANCISCO NORTH/PETALUMA—(Sonoma) *S'bnd: From Jct Hwy 101 & Petaluma Blvd N'bnd: Jct Hwy 101 & Old Redwood Hwy/Penngrove exit: Go 1/4 mi W on Petaluma Blvd, then 1/4 mi N on Stony Point Rd, then 200 yds W on Rainsville Rd. Enter on R.*

FACILITIES: 302 sites, typical site width 25 ft, 140 full hkups, 25 W&E, (20/30/50 amps), 137 no hkups, 161 pull-thrus, cable TV, WiFi Instant Internet at site, phone Internet central location, family camping, cabins, RV storage, dump, non-guest dump $, laundry, groceries, RV supplies, LP gas by meter, ice, picnic tables, fire rings, grills, wood, controlled access.

RECREATION: rec hall, pavilion, equipped pavilion, coin games, swim pool, hot tub, golf nearby, bsktball, 20 bike rentals, playground, activities, sports field, v-ball, local tours. Rec open to public.

Pets welcome, breed restrict. Partial handicap access. Open all yr. Big rigs welcome. Member ARVC, CALARVC.

Phone: (800)992-CAMP
Address: 20 Rainsville Rd, Petaluma, CA 94952
Lat/Lon: 38.27383/-122.67924
Email: sfkoa@aol.com
Web: www.sanfranciscokoa.com

SEE AD SAN FRANCISCO PAGE 7

SACRAMENTO

(E) Sacramento Shade RV Park—(Sacramento) *From jct I-80 & Bus I-80: Go 2 mi SW on Bus I-80, then 200 yds S on Fulton Ave, then 1 mi SW on Auburn Blvd. Enter on L.* FACILITIES: 90 sites, typical site width 35 ft, 90 full hkups, (30/50 amps), family camping, cable TV, WiFi Instant Internet at site, RV storage, laundry. RECREATION: rec room/area, swim pool, golf nearby. Pets welcome, breed restrict, quantity restrict. No tents. Open all yr.

Phone: (916)922-0814
Address: 2150 Auburn Blvd, Sacramento, CA 95821
Lat/Lon: 38.62382/-121.41634
Email: sacrv@comcast.net
Web: www.sacramentoshadervpark.com

SAN JOSE

(N) Coyote Valley RV & Golf Resort—(Santa Clara) *From jct of Hwy 101 & exit 367/Cochrane Rd: Go 1 mi W on Cochrane Rd, then 4 mi N on Monterey Rd. Enter on R.* FACILITIES: 126 sites, 126 full hkups, (30/50 amps), family camping, cable TV, WiFi Instant Internet at site, dump, laundry, groceries, RV supplies, LP gas by meter, ice, patios. RECREATION: rec hall, rec room/area, swim pool, hot tub, stream fishing, putting green, golf nearby, horseshoes, hiking trails, v-ball. Pets welcome, breed restrict, quantity restrict. Partial handicap access. No tents. Open all yr. Big rigs welcome. Green Friendly. Member ARVC, CALARVC.

Phone: (866)376-5500
Address: 9750 Monterey Rd, Morgan Hill, CA 95037
Lat/Lon: 37.19141/-121.71315
Email: info@coyotevalleyresort.com
Web: www.coyotevalleyresort.com

TWENTYNINE PALMS

(NE) TwentyNine Palms Resort: RV Park.Cottages.Golf—(San Bernardino) *From jct I-10 & Hwy 62: Go 44 mi E on Hwy 62, then 2 mi N on Adobe Rd, then 1/2 mi E on Amboy Rd, then 100 yds N on Desert Knoll Ave. Enter on L.* FACILITIES: 197 sites, typical site width 25 ft, 157 full hkups, 40 W&E, (30/50 amps), 31 pull-thrus, family camping, WiFi Instant Internet at site, phone on-site Internet (needs activ), cabins, RV storage, laundry, ltd groc, RV supplies, LP gas by meter, ice. RECREATION: rec hall, rec room/area, equipped pavilion, swim pool, hot tub, putting green, golf nearby, bsktball, 2 shuffleboard courts, activities, tennis, horseshoes. Pets welcome, breed restrict, size restrict. Partial handicap access. Open all yr. Big rigs welcome. Member ARVC, CALARVC.

Phone: (800)874-4548
Address: 4949 Desert Knoll Ave, Twentynine Palms, CA 92277
Lat/Lon: 34.16573/-116.04469
Email: info@29palmsresort.com
Web: www.29palmsresort.com

VAN NUYS

(W) Birmingham RV Park—(Los Angeles) *From jct I-405 & US 101 (Ventura Fwy): Go 2 mi W on US 101, then 2-3/4 mi N on Balboa Ave. Enter on R.* FACILITIES: 186 sites, 186 full hkups, (30/50 amps), family camping, cable TV, WiFi Internet central location, laundry, picnic tables, patios, controlled access. RECREATION: rec hall, golf nearby. Pets welcome, breed restrict. Partial handicap access. No tents. Open all yr.

Phone: (818)785-0949
Address: 7740 Balboa Blvd, Van Nuys, CA 91406
Lat/Lon: 34.21146/-118.50093
Email: birminghamrv7@yahoo.com
Web: www.birminghamrv.com

CONNECTICUT

GRISWOLD

(E) Countryside RV Park—(New London) *From jct Hwy-138 & Hwy-201: Go 1 mi S on Hwy-201, then 1/3 mi E on Cook Hill Rd. Enter on R.* FACILITIES: 118 sites, typical site width 50 ft, 118 full hkups, (30/50 amps), 7 pull-thrus, heater not allowed, family camping, WiFi Internet central location, RV storage, dump, non-guest dump $, portable dump, laundry, LP gas by meter, ice, picnic tables, fire rings, wood, controlled access. RECREATION: rec room/area, pavilion, lake swim, pond fishing, golf nearby, bsktball, playground, shuffleboard court, activities (wkends), horseshoes, sports field, hiking trails, v-ball. Pets welcome. Partial handicap access. No tents. Open May 1 - Oct 9. Big rigs welcome. Member ARVC, CCOA.

Phone: (860)376-0029
Address: 75 Cook Hill Rd., Griswold, CT 06351
Lat/Lon: 41.56715/-71.88523
Web: www.countrysidecampground.com

VOLUNTOWN

(NE) Nature's Campsites—(New London) *From jct Hwy-165 & Hwy-49: Go 1/2 mi N on Hwy-49. Enter on R.* FACILITIES: 150 sites, typical site width 35 ft, 20 full hkups, 75 W&E, (20/30/50 amps), 55 no hkups, 6 pull-thrus, heater not allowed, family camping, cabins, RV storage, dump, laundry, ltd groc, LP gas by weight/by meter, ice, picnic tables, fire rings, grills, wood, controlled access. RECREATION: rec room/area, pavilion, coin games, 2 swim pools, boating, canoeing, kayaking, 8 canoe/2 kayak rentals, river/pond fishing, fishing supplies, golf nearby, bsktball, playground, activities (wkends), sports field, hiking trails. Pets welcome. Open May 1 - Oct 15. Member ARVC, CCOA.

Phone: (860)376-4203
Address: 96 EKonk Hill Rd, Voluntown, CT 06384
Lat/Lon: 41.58202/-71.85339
Email: naturescampsites@hotmail.com
Web: www.naturescampsites.com

DELAWARE

LEWES

(W) Tall Pines Campground Resort—(Sussex) *From jct Hwy 1 & US 9: Go 2-3/4 mi SW on US 9, then 50 feet NW on Sweetbriar Rd, then 3/4 mi SW on Log Cabin Hill Rd. Enter on R.* FACILITIES: 524 sites, typical site width 50 ft, 484 full hkups, 24 W&E, (20/30/50 amps), 16 no hkups, 5 pull-thrus, family camping, WiFi Internet central location, cabins, dump, laundry, groceries, LP gas by weight/by meter, ice, picnic tables, fire rings, wood, controlled access. RECREATION: rec room/area, pavilion, coin games, swim pool, golf nearby, bsktball, playground, 2 shuffleboard courts, activities (wkends), horseshoes, sports field, v-ball. Pets welcome, breed restrict. Open all yr. Facilities fully operational Memorial Day - Labor Day. Big rigs welcome. Green Friendly. Member DCA.

Phone: (302)684-0300
Address: 29551 Persimmon Rd, Lewes, DE 19958
Lat/Lon: 38.73743/-75.23792
Email: tpinfo@tallpines-del.com
Web: www.tallpines-del.com

FLORIDA

ARCADIA

(E) Big Tree RV Resort—(DeSoto) *From jct US-17 & Hwy-70: Go 2-1/2 mi E on Hwy-70. Enter on L.* FACILITIES: 392 sites, typical site width 40 ft, 392 full hkups, (20/30/50 amps), WiFi Instant Internet at site ($), dump, laundry, LP gas by weight, picnic tables, patios. RECREATION: rec hall, rec room/area, swim pool, hot tub, golf nearby, 6 shuffleboard courts, activities, horseshoes, local tours. Pets welcome, breed restrict. Partial handicap access. No tents. Age restrict may apply. Open all yr. Big rigs welcome. Member ARVC, FLARVC.

Phone: (863)494-7247
Address: 2626 NE Hwy 70, Arcadia, FL 34266
Lat/Lon: 27.20900/-81.83057
Email: bigtreerv@embarqmail.com
Web: www.carefreervresorts.com

(N) Craig's RV Park—(DeSoto) *From jct Hwy 70 & US 17 N: Go 7 mi N on US 17 N, then 200 feet SW on Cubitis Ave. Enter on L.* FACILITIES: 349 sites, typical site width 35 ft, 40 ft max RV length, 349 full hkups, (20/30/50 amps), 64 pull-thrus, WiFi Instant Internet at site ($), RV storage, dump, non-guest dump $, laundry, RV supplies, LP gas by weight/by meter, patios. RECREATION: rec hall, rec room/area, pavilion, swim pool, putting green, golf nearby, bsktball, 8 shuffleboard courts, activities, horseshoes, hiking trails, local tours.

ARCADIA—Continued
Craig's RV Park—Continued

Pets welcome, quantity restrict. Partial handicap access. No tents. Open all yr. Church services & planned activities during Nov-Apr. Member ARVC, FLARVC.

Phone: (863)494-1820
Address: 7895 NE Cubitis Ave., Arcadia, FL 34266
Lat/Lon: 27.30908/-81.81987
Email: craigsrv@desoto.net
Web: www.craigsrv.com

BONITA SPRINGS

(E) IMPERIAL BONITA ESTATES RV RESORT—(Lee) *From jct I-75 (exit 116) & CR 865 (Bonita Beach Rd): Go 1/2 mi W on Bonita Beach Rd, then 1/4 mi N on Imperial St, then 2 blocks E on Dean St. Enter on L.*

WELCOME

FACILITIES: 312 sites, typical site width 30 ft, 312 full hkups, (20/30/50 amps), 30 pull-thrus, WiFi Instant Internet at site, RV storage, dump, non-guest dump $, laundry, LP gas by weight, ice, picnic tables, patios.

RECREATION: rec hall, rec room/area, pavilion, swim pool, boating, canoeing, kayaking, river fishing, putting green, golf nearby, bsktball, 8 shuffleboard courts, activities, tennis, horseshoes.

Pets welcome. Partial handicap access. No tents. Age restrict may apply. Open all yr. Big rigs welcome. Member ARVC, FLARVC.

Phone: (239)992-0511
Address: 27700 Bourbonniere Dr, Bonita Springs, FL 34135
Lat/Lon: 26.33512/-81.76079
Email: ibecoop@comcast.net
Web: www.imperialbonitaestates.com

SEE AD THIS PAGE

CLEWISTON

(SE) OKEECHOBEE LANDINGS—(Hendry) *From west jct Hwy 80 & US 27: Go 10 mi S on US 27, then 500 feet S on Holiday Isles Blvd. Enter on L.*

WELCOME

FACILITIES: 270 sites, 270 full hkups, (30/50 amps), heater not allowed, WiFi Instant Internet at site ($), RV storage, laundry, picnic tables, patios.

RECREATION: rec hall, swim pool, hot tub, lake fishing, golf nearby, bsktball, playground, 4 shuffleboard courts, activities, tennis, horseshoes, local tours.

Pets welcome, breed restrict, size restrict, quantity restrict. Partial handicap access. Open all yr. Activities in winter season only. Big rigs welcome. Member ARVC, FLARVC.

Phone: (863)983-4144
Address: 420 Holiday Blvd, Clewiston, FL 33440
Lat/Lon: 26.75193/-80.91358
Email: okeechobeelandings@embarqmail.com
Web: www.okeechobeelandingsrv.com

SEE AD THIS PAGE

Woodall's Tip... If you're ever lost in the forest, you can tell your direction from the trees. The bark will be thicker on the north side of trees.

DADE CITY

(SE) Blue Jay RV Park—(Pasco) *From jct Hwy 301 & US 98: Go 3/4 mi S on US 98. Enter on L.* FACILITIES: 56 sites, typical site width 20 ft, 38 ft max RV length, 56 full hkups, (20/30/50 amps), phone/cable on-site Internet (needs activ), RV storage, laundry. RECREATION: rec hall, swim pool, golf nearby, 4 shuffleboard courts, activities, horseshoes. Pets welcome, breed restrict, size restrict, quantity restrict. Partial handicap access. No tents. Age restrict may apply. Open all yr.

Phone: (352)567-9678
Address: 38511 Wilds Rd, Dade City, FL 33525
Lat/Lon: 28.31769/-82.17914
Email: bluejayrv@tampabay.rr.com
Web: www.carefreervresorts.com

DESTIN

(E) Camping on the Gulf—(Walton) *From Destin Mid Bay Bridge (293) & US 98: Go 5 mi E on US 98. Enter on R.* FACILITIES: 201 sites, typical site width 30 ft, 185 full hkups, 16 W&E, (30/50 amps), 18 pull-thrus, family camping, cable TV, WiFi Instant Internet at site, phone on-site Internet (needs activ), cable Internet central location, cabins, RV storage, dump, laundry, ltd groc, RV supplies, LP gas by weight/by meter, ice, picnic tables, patios, controlled access. RECREATION: rec hall, rec room/area, equipped pavilion, 2 swim pools, saltwater swim, hot tub, saltwater/lake fishing, fishing supplies, golf nearby, bsktball, playground, shuffleboard court, activities, horseshoes, v-ball. Pets welcome. Partial handicap access. Open all yr. Big rigs welcome. Member ARVC, FLARVC.

Phone: (877)226-7485
Address: 10005 W Emerald Coast Pkwy (US 98), Miramar Beach, FL 32550
Lat/Lon: 30.37674/-86.34245
Email: camp@campgulf.com
Web: www.campgulf.com

(E) Geronimo RV Resort—(Walton) *From jct US 98 & Hwy 293 (Mid Bay Bridge): Go 4 mi E on US 98, then 1/2 mi S on South Geronimo St, then 500 ft W on Arnett Ln.* FACILITIES: 34 sites, 29 full hkups, 5 W&E, (30/50 amps), family camping, cable TV, WiFi Instant Internet at site, dump, non-guest dump $, laundry, patios. RECREATION: golf nearby, sports field. Pets welcome, breed restrict. Partial handicap access. No tents. Open all yr. Big rigs welcome. Member ARVC, FLARVC.

Phone: (850)424-6801
Address: 75 Arnett Ln, Destin, FL 32550
Lat/Lon: 30.37851/-86.36099
Email: info@geronimorvresort.com
Web: www.geronimorvresort.com

Woodall's RV Owner's Handbook—essential information you need to "get to know" your RV.

FORT LAUDERDALE

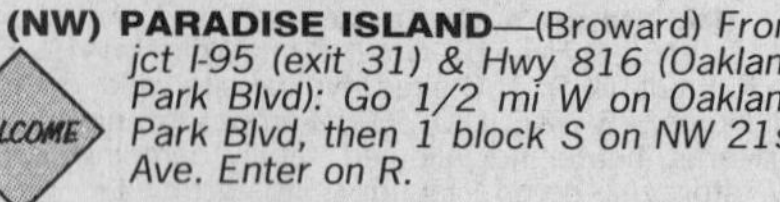

(NW) PARADISE ISLAND—(Broward) *From jct I-95 (exit 31) & Hwy 816 (Oakland Park Blvd): Go 1/2 mi W on Oakland Park Blvd, then 1 block S on NW 21st Ave. Enter on R.*

FACILITIES: 232 sites, typical site width 25 ft, 232 full hkups, (20/30/50 amps), 25 pull-thrus, WiFi Instant Internet at site ($), family camping, dump, non-guest dump $, laundry, RV supplies, ice, picnic tables, patios.

RECREATION: rec hall, rec room/area, equipped pavilion, swim pool, golf nearby, 2 shuffleboard courts, activities.

Pets welcome, breed restrict, size restrict. Partial handicap access. No tents. Open all yr. Group activities winter only. Big rigs welcome. Member ARVC, FLARVC.

Phone: (800)487-7395
Address: 2121 NW 29th Ct., Fort Lauderdale, FL 33311
Lat/Lon: 26.16344/-80.17124
Email: info@paradiserv.com
Web: www.paradiserv.com

SEE AD THIS PAGE

FORT MYERS

(NE) Seminole Campground—(Lee) *From jct Hwy 82 & I-75: Go 5-1/2 mi N on I-75 (exit 143), then 1/4 mi E on Hwy 78 (Bayshore Rd), then 1/4 mi N on Wells Rd, then 1/4 mi W on Triplett Rd. Enter on R.* FACILITIES: 129 sites, typical site width 25 ft, 129 full hkups, (30/50 amps), 5 pull-thrus, family camping, WiFi Instant Internet at site, RV's/park model rentals, RV storage, dump, non-guest dump $, laundry, ltd groc, RV supplies, LP bottle exch, ice, picnic tables, patios, fire rings, wood. RECREATION: rec hall, rec room/area, swim pool, stream fishing, golf nearby, 2 shuffleboard courts, activities, horseshoes, sports field, hiking trails, v-ball. Pets welcome. Partial handicap access. Open all yr. Big rigs welcome. Member ARVC, FLARVC.

Phone: (239)543-2919
Address: 8991 Triplett Rd, N Fort Myers, FL 33917
Lat/Lon: 26.71867/-81.80989
Email: info@seminolecampground.com
Web: www.seminolecampground.com

(NE) UPRIVER RV RESORT—(Lee) *From jct Hwy 82 & I-75: Go 5-1/2 mi N on I-75 (exit 143), then 1-3/4 mi E on Hwy 78 (Bayshore Rd). Enter on R.*

FACILITIES: 350 sites, typical site width 35 ft, 350 full hkups, (20/30/50 amps), 60 pull-thrus, heater not allowed, cable TV, WiFi Instant Internet at site ($), RV storage, laundry, RV supplies, LP gas by weight/by meter, ice, picnic tables, patios.

RECREATION: rec hall, rec room/area, pavilion, swim pool, hot tub, boating, canoeing, kayaking, ramp, dock, saltwater/river fishing, putting green, golf nearby, bsktball, 6 shuffleboard courts, activities, tennis, horseshoes, hiking trails, local tours.

Pets welcome ($), breed restrict, size restrict, quantity restrict. Partial handicap access. No tents. Age restrict may apply. Open all yr. Group activities during winter season only. Big rigs welcome. Member ARVC, FLARVC.

Phone: (800)848-1652
Address: 17021 Upriver Dr, North Fort Myers, FL 33917
Lat/Lon: 26.71480/-81.78496
Email: info@upriver.com
Web: www.upriver.com

SEE AD THIS PAGE

FORT MYERS—Continued

(S) WOODSMOKE CAMPING RESORT—(Lee) *From jct Hwy 82 & I-75: Go 14 mi S on I-75 (exit 123), then 2 mi W on Corkscrew Rd, then 2 mi N on US 41. Enter on R.*

FACILITIES: 300 sites, typical site width 35 ft, 300 full hkups, (20/30/50 amps), 16 pull-thrus, WiFi Instant Internet at site, WiFi Internet central location, family camping, RV's/park model rentals, RV storage, dump, non-guest dump $, laundry, RV supplies, picnic tables, patios.

RECREATION: rec hall, rec room/area, equipped pavilion, swim pool, hot tub, boating, no motors, canoeing, kayaking, lake fishing, golf nearby, bsktball, playground, 5 shuffleboard courts, activities, horseshoes, hiking trails.

Pets welcome, breed restrict, size restrict, quantity restrict. Partial handicap access. Open all yr. Planned group activities winter only. Big rigs welcome. Member ARVC, FLARVC.

Phone: (800)231-5053
Address: 19551 S. Tamiami Trail (US 41S), Ft Myers, FL 33908
Lat/Lon: 26.45625/-81.82414
Email: woodsmok@aol.com
Web: www.woodsmokecampingresort.com

SEE AD THIS PAGE

FORT PIERCE

(NW) ROAD RUNNER TRAVEL RESORT—(St. Lucie) *From jct Hwy 70 & I-95: Go 9 mi N on I-95 (exit 138), then 3 mi E on Hwy 614 (Indrio Rd), then 3 mi S on Hwy 713 (Kings Hwy), then 1-1/4 mi E on CR 608 (St. Lucie Blvd). Enter on L.*

FACILITIES: 452 sites, typical site width 30 ft, 452 full hkups, (20/30/50 amps), 10 pull-thrus, cable TV, WiFi Internet central location, family camping, cabins, RV storage, dump, non-guest dump $, laundry, full svc store, RV supplies, LP gas by weight/by meter, ice, picnic tables, patios, controlled access.

RECREATION: rec hall, rec room/area, pavilion, swim pool, pond fishing, fishing supplies, putting green, golf nearby, bsktball, 4 shuffleboard courts, activities, tennis, horseshoes, v-ball.

Pets welcome, breed restrict, quantity restrict. Partial handicap access. Open all yr. Big rigs welcome. Green Friendly. Member ARVC, FLARVC. ATM.

Phone: (800)833-7108
Address: 5500 Saint Lucie Blvd., Fort Pierce, FL 34946
Lat/Lon: 27.48413/-80.37983
Email: info@roadrunnerresort.com
Web: www.roadrunnertravelresort.com

SEE AD NEXT PAGE

Tell our advertisers you saw them in Woodall's!

HOMESTEAD

(NE) Pine Isle Mobile Home Park—(Dade) *From jct Hwy 9336 (Palm Dr) & US 1: Go 4 mi N on US 1, then 2 mi E on 288 St, then 500 ft N on 132 Ave. Enter on L.* FACILITIES: 257 sites, typical site width 50 ft, 257 full hkups, (30/50 amps), 20 pull-thrus, WiFi Internet central location, laundry, patios. RECREATION: rec hall, pavilion, swim pool, golf nearby, 3 shuffleboard courts, activities, horseshoes. Pets welcome, quantity restrict. No tents. Age restrict may apply. Open all yr. Planned activities in winter only. Big rigs welcome.

Phone: (305)248-0783
Address: 28600 SW 132 Ave, Homestead, FL 33033
Lat/Lon: 25.50157/-80.40436
Web: www.pineislepark.com

(E) THE BOARDWALK—(Dade) *From jct Hwy 9336 (Palm Dr) & US 1: Go 2 mi N on US 1, then 1 block E on 328th St, then 200 feet N on 6th Ave. Enter on R.*

WELCOME

FACILITIES: 130 sites, typical site width 40 ft, 130 full hkups, (30/50 amps), WiFi Internet central location, family camping, RV storage, laundry, picnic tables, patios, controlled access.

RECREATION: rec hall, rec room/area, swim pool, golf nearby, playground, 5 shuffleboard courts, activities, horseshoes, v-ball.

Pets welcome. Partial handicap access. No tents. Open all yr. Big rigs welcome. Member ARVC, FLARVC.

Phone: (305)248-2487
Address: 100 NE 6th Ave, Homestead, FL 33030
Lat/Lon: 25.47142/-80.46889
Email: boardwalkrv@gmail.com
Web: www.boardwalkrv.com

SEE AD THIS PAGE

JUNO BEACH

(N) Juno Ocean Walk RV Resort—(Palm Beach) *From jct Hwy 786 (PGA Blvd) & I-95: Go 3 mi N on I-95 (exit 83), then 4-1/2 mi E on Donald Ross Rd, then 3/4 mi N on US 1, then 1/4 mi W on Juno Ocean Walk. Enter at end.* FACILITIES: 246 sites, typical site width 30 ft, 246 full hkups, (30/50 amps), cable TV, WiFi Instant Internet at site, RV's/park model rentals, dump, non-guest dump $, laundry, picnic tables, patios. RECREATION: rec hall, rec room/area, swim pool, hot tub, golf nearby, playground, 2 shuffleboard courts, activities, v-ball. Pets welcome, quantity restrict. Partial handicap access. No tents. Open all yr. Big rigs welcome. Green Friendly. Member ARVC, FLARVC.

Phone: (561)622-7500
Address: 900 Juno Ocean Walk, Juno Beach, FL 33408
Lat/Lon: 26.89278/-80.06237
Email: Junorvresort@comcast.net
Web: www.junooceanwalkrvresort.com

FREE INFO! Enter #4365 on Reader Service Card

FREE INFO! Enter #906 on Reader Service Card

KISSIMMEE

(W) MILL CREEK RV RESORT—(Osceola) *From jct US 17/92 & US 192: Go 3/4 mi E on US 192, then 1-1/2 mi N on Hwy 531 (Michigan Ave). Enter on R.*

WELCOME

FACILITIES: 157 sites, typical site width 22 ft, 36 ft max RV length, 157 full hkups, (20/30/50 amps), phone/cable on-site Internet (needs activ), WiFi Internet central location, family camping, laundry, LP gas by weight/by meter, picnic tables, patios.

RECREATION: rec hall, swim pool, golf nearby, 4 shuffleboard courts, activities, horseshoes.

Pets welcome, breed restrict, quantity restrict. No tents. Open all yr. Planned group activities winter only. Office closed Sundays & holidays. Member ARVC, FLARVC.

Phone: (407)847-6288
Address: 2775 Michigan Ave, Kissimmee, FL 34744
Lat/Lon: 28.32881/-81.39083
Email: millcreekrv@cfl.com
Web: www.carefreervresorts.com

SEE AD ORLANDO NEXT PAGE

LAKELAND

(N) LAKELAND RV RESORT—(Polk) *From I-4 (exit 33 & Hwy 582): Go 1/4 mi NE on Hwy 582, then 1/4 mi E on Old Combee Rd. Enter on L.*

WELCOME

FACILITIES: 230 sites, typical site width 35 ft, 230 full hkups, (20/30/50 amps), 100 pull-thrus, WiFi Instant Internet at site ($), phone on-site Internet (needs activ), WiFi Internet central location ($), family camping, cabins, RV storage, dump, non-guest dump $, laundry, RV supplies, LP gas by weight/by meter, ice, picnic tables, patios, controlled access.

RECREATION: rec hall, rec room/area, swim pool, wading pool, hot tub, boating, 2 pedal boat rentals, pond fishing, mini-golf, golf nearby, bsktball, playground, 3 shuffleboard courts, activities, horseshoes, v-ball.

Pets welcome, breed restrict, quantity restrict. Open all yr. Church service & planned activities winter only. Discounts Apr - Dec. Big rigs welcome. Member ARVC, FLARVC.

Phone: (888)622-4115
Address: 900 Old Combee Rd, Lakeland, FL 33805
Lat/Lon: 28.10979/-81.93968
Email: lakelandrv@tampabay.rr.com
Web: www.carefreervresorts.com

SEE AD THIS PAGE

MARIANNA

(E) ARROWHEAD CAMPSITES—(Jackson) *From jct I-10 (exit 142) & Hwy 71: Go 2 mi N on Hwy 71, then 1/2 mi W on US 90. Enter on R.*

WELCOME

FACILITIES: 245 sites, typical site width 30 ft, 175 full hkups, 45 W&E, (20/30/50 amps), 175 pull-thrus, cable TV, WiFi Internet central location, family camping, cabins, dump, non-guest dump $, laundry, groceries, RV supplies, LP gas by weight/by meter, ice, picnic tables, controlled access.

RECREATION: pavilion, swim pool, boating, canoeing, kayaking, ramp, dock, lake fishing, fishing supplies, golf nearby, bsktball, playground.

Pets welcome. Partial handicap access. Open all yr. Member ARVC, FLARVC. ATM.

Phone: (800)643-9166
Address: 4820 Hwy 90 E, Marianna, FL 32446
Lat/Lon: 30.75512/-85.19437
Email: arrowhead@phonl.com
Web: www.arrowheadcamp.com

SEE AD THIS PAGE

MILTON

(S) Pelican Palms RV Park—(Santa Rosa) *From jct I-10 (exit 26) & Hwy 191: Go 200 yds S on Hwy 191. Enter on L.* FACILITIES: 51 sites, typical site width 30 ft, 49 full hkups, 2 E, (30/50 amps), 29 pull-thrus, family camping, WiFi Instant Internet at site, dump, non-guest dump $, laundry, RV supplies, LP gas by weight/by meter, ice. RECREATION: rec room/area, equipped pavilion, swim pool, horseshoes, hiking trails. Pets welcome. Open all yr. Big rigs welcome. Member ARVC, FLARVC.

Phone: (850)623-0576
Address: 3700 Garcon Point Rd, Milton, FL 32583
Lat/Lon: 30.56753/-87.03125
Email: pprvp@aol.com
Web: www.pelicanpalmsrvpark.com

FREE INFO! Enter #4033 on Reader Service Card

FREE INFO! Enter #3753 on Reader Service Card

OKEECHOBEE

(SE) ZACHARY TAYLOR RV RESORT—(Okeechobee) *From jct Hwy 78 & US 441/98: Go 2-1/4 mi SE on US 441/98, then 500 feet on 30th St. Enter on L.*

WELCOME

FACILITIES: 210 sites, typical site width 30 ft, 210 full hkups, (30/50 amps), 50 amps ($), 14 pull-thrus, WiFi Instant Internet at site, cabins, RV storage, laundry, RV supplies, ice, picnic tables, patios.

RECREATION: rec hall, swim pool, boating, canoeing, kayaking, ramp, dock, lake/river fishing, fishing supplies, fishing guides, golf nearby, 3 shuffleboard courts, activities, horseshoes, hiking trails.

Pets welcome ($), breed restrict, quantity restrict. Partial handicap access. No tents. Age restrict may apply. Open all yr. Big rigs welcome. Member ARVC, FLARVC.

Phone: (888)282-6523
Address: 2995 US Hwy 441 SE, Okeechobee, FL 34974
Lat/Lon: 27.21194/-80.79736
Email: info@flrvresort.com
Web: www.flrvresort.com

SEE AD THIS PAGE

PORT CHARLOTTE

(NE) Riverside RV Resort & Campground—(DeSoto) *From jct I-75 (exit 170) & Hwy 769 (Kings Hwy): Go 4-1/2 mi NE on Hwy 769. Enter on R.* FACILITIES: 350 sites, typical site width 35 ft, 350 full hkups, (30/50 amps), 50 amps ($), 4 pull-thrus, family camping, WiFi Instant Internet at site ($), RV's/park model rentals, RV storage, dump, non-guest dump $, laundry, groceries, RV supplies, LP gas by weight/by meter, ice, picnic tables, patios, fire rings, wood, controlled access. RECREATION: rec hall, rec room/area, equipped

PORT CHARLOTTE—Continued
Riverside RV Resort & Campground—Continued

pavilion, coin games, 2 swim pools, hot tub, boating, canoeing, kayaking, ramp, dock, 6 canoe rentals, river fishing, fishing supplies, golf nearby, bsktball, playground, 4 shuffleboard courts, activities, horseshoes, v-ball, local tours. Pets welcome. Partial handicap access. Open all yr. Big rigs welcome. Member ARVC, FLARVC.

Phone: (800)795-9733
Address: 9770 SW County Rd 769 Kings Hwy, Arcadia, FL 34269
Lat/Lon: 27.07961/-82.01331
Email: riverside@desoto.net
Web: www.riversidervresort.com

PUNTA GORDA

(SE) SUN 'N' SHADE CAMPGROUND—(Charlotte) *From jct US 17 & I-75: Go 6-1/2 mi S on I-75 (exit 158), then 1 mi W on Tucker Grade Rd, then 3-1/2 mi S on US 41. Enter on L.*

WELCOME

FACILITIES: 191 sites, typical site width 30 ft, 191 full hkups, (20/30/50 amps), heater not allowed, WiFi Instant Internet at site ($), family camping, RV storage, dump, non-guest dump $, laundry, RV supplies, ice, picnic tables, patios.

RECREATION: rec hall, swim pool, pond fishing, golf nearby, 2 shuffleboard courts, activities, horseshoes, hiking trails.

Pets welcome, breed restrict. Partial handicap access. No tents. Open all yr. Member ARVC, FLARVC.

Phone: (941)639-5388
Address: 14880 Tamiami Trail (Hwy 41), Punta Gorda, FL 33955
Lat/Lon: 26.81369/-81.95905
Email: parkinfo@sunnshade.com
Web: www.sunnshade.com

SEE AD THIS PAGE

TAMPA

(NW) Bay Bayou RV Resort—(Hillsborough) *N'bnd from jct I-275 (exit 47) & Hillsborough Ave (SR 580): Go 10-1/2 mi W on Hillsborough Ave (SR 580), then 1/2 mi N on Countryway Blvd, then 3/4 mi W on Memorial Hwy. Enter on L.* FACILITIES: 275 sites, typical site width 50 ft, 275 full hkups, (30/50 amps), family camping, cable TV, WiFi Instant Internet at site, phone/cable on-site Internet (needs activ), WiFi Internet central location, RV storage, dump, non-guest dump $, laundry, RV supplies, LP gas by weight/by meter, picnic tables, patios, controlled access. RECREATION: rec hall, rec room/area, equipped pavilion, swim pool, hot tub, boating, canoeing, kayaking, 2 kayak rentals, saltwater/pond fishing, golf nearby, 4 bike rentals, 2 shuffleboard courts, activities, horseshoes. Pets welcome, breed restrict, quantity restrict. Partial handicap access. No tents. Open all yr. Children accepted, 21 day limit. Big rigs welcome. Member ARVC, FLARVC.

Phone: (813)855-1000
Address: 12622 Memorial Hwy, Tampa, FL 33635
Lat/Lon: 28.02982/-82.63058
Email: info@baybayou.com
Web: www.baybayou.com

WESLEY CHAPEL

(W) QUAIL RUN RV RESORT—(Pasco) *From jct I-75 (Zepher Hills exit 279) & SR 54: Go 1/2 mi W on SR 54, then 2 mi N on Old Pasco Rd. Enter on R.*

WELCOME

FACILITIES: 291 sites, typical site width 35 ft, 291 full hkups, (20/30/50 amps), 53 pull-thrus, cable TV, WiFi Instant Internet at site, WiFi Internet central location, family camping, dump, non-guest dump $, laundry, full svc store, RV supplies, LP gas by weight/by meter, ice, picnic tables, patios, controlled access.

RECREATION: rec hall, rec room/area, equipped pavilion, swim pool, golf nearby, play equipment, 4 shuffleboard courts, activities, horseshoes.

Pets welcome, breed restrict. Partial handicap access. No tents. Open all yr. Planned activities winter only. Big rigs welcome. Member ARVC, FLARVC.

Phone: (800)582-7084
Address: 6946 Old Pasco Rd., Wesley Chapel, FL 33544
Lat/Lon: 28.25846/-82.34200
Email: qrrv@usa.net
Web: www.quailrunrv.com

SEE AD THIS PAGE

ZEPHYRHILLS

(NE) Baker Acres RV Resort—(Pasco) *From N jct US 301 & Hwy 54 West: Go 1/4 mi E on Hwy 54, then 1-1/2 mi N on Wire Rd. Enter on R.* FACILITIES: 353 sites, typical site width 30 ft, 40 ft max RV length, accepts full hkup units only, 353 full hkups, (20/30/50 amps), WiFi Instant Internet at site ($), phone/cable on-site Internet (needs activ), phone Internet central location, RV storage, dump, non-guest dump $, laundry, picnic tables, patios. RECREATION: rec hall, rec room/area, swim pool, golf nearby, 12 shuffleboard courts, activities, horseshoes. Pets welcome ($), breed restrict. No tents. Age restrict may apply. Open all yr. Church services winter only. No showers. Member ARVC, FLARVC.

Phone: (813)782-3950
Address: 7820 Wire Rd, Zephyrhills, FL 33540
Lat/Lon: 28.27113/-82.17962
Email: bakeracresrv@tampabay.rr.com
Web: www.carefreervresorts.com

ZEPHYRHILLS—Continued on next page

ZEPHYRHILLS—Continued

FOREST LAKE ESTATES RV RESORT—(Pasco) *From north jct US 301 & SR 54: Go 3 mi E on SR 54-East. Enter on R.*

WELCOME

FACILITIES: 268 sites, typical site width 35 ft, 40 ft max RV length, accepts full hkup units only, 268 full hkups, (30/50 amps), cable TV, WiFi Instant Internet at site, phone/cable on-site Internet (needs activ), WiFi Internet central location, laundry, LP gas by weight, patios.

RECREATION: rec hall, rec room/area, swim pool, hot tub, lake fishing, golf nearby, 6 shuffleboard courts, activities, horseshoes.

Pets welcome ($), size restrict. Partial handicap access. No tents. Age restrict may apply. Open all yr. Planned group activities winter season only. Restrooms limited hours.

Phone: (800)283-9715
Address: 41219 Hockey Dr, Zephyrhills, FL 33540
Lat/Lon: 28.25312/-82.13520
Email: forestlakerv@tampabay.rr.com
Web: www.forestlakes-estates.com/rv

SEE AD THIS PAGE

(SE) Majestic Oaks RV Resort—(Pasco) *From jct SR 54 West & US 301: Go 2 mi S on US 301, then 1-1/2 mi E on Chancey Rd. Enter on L.* FACILITIES: 252 sites, typical site width 40 ft, 252 full hkups, (30/50 amps), WiFi Instant Internet at site ($), phone/cable on-site Internet (needs activ), phone Internet central location, RV storage, laundry, patios. RECREATION: rec hall, pavilion, swim pool, golf nearby, 8 shuffleboard courts, activities, tennis, horseshoes. Pets welcome, breed restrict. Partial handicap access. No tents. Age restrict may apply. Open all yr. Planned activities in winter only. Big rigs welcome. Member ARVC, FLARVC.

Phone: (813)783-7518
Address: 3751 Laurel Valley Blvd, Zephyrhills, FL 33542
Lat/Lon: 28.21004/-82.16135
Email: majesticoaksrv@tampabay.rr.com
Web: www.carefreervresorts.com

(SW) Rainbow Village RV Resort—(Pasco) *From jct US 301 & Hwy 54 West: Go 1 mi W on Hwy 54 West, then 1 mi S on Lane Rd. Enter on L.* FACILITIES: 382 sites, typical site width 35 ft, accepts full hkup units only, 382 full hkups, (20/30/50 amps), WiFi Instant Internet at site ($), phone/cable on-site Internet (needs activ), WiFi Internet central location, RV's/park model rentals, laundry, picnic tables, patios. RECREATION: rec hall, rec room/area, swim pool, golf nearby, bsktball, 6 shuffleboard courts, activities, horseshoes, v-ball. Pets welcome, breed restrict. Partial handicap access. No tents. Age restrict may apply. Open all yr. Planned activities winter only. Free cable for summer only. Big rigs welcome.

Phone: (813)782-5075
Address: 4150 Lane Rd, Zephyrhills, FL 33541
Lat/Lon: 28.21822/-82.19641
Email: rainbowrv@tampabay.rr.com
Web: www.carefreervresorts.com

(SW) Southern Charm RV Resort—(Pasco) *From S jct Hwy 54 West & US 301: Go 2 mi S on US 301, then 1/4 mi W on Chancey Rd. Enter on R.* FACILITIES: 497 sites, typical site width 30 ft, 40 ft max RV length, accepts full hkup units only, 497 full hkups, (20/30/50 amps), WiFi Instant Internet at site ($), phone/cable on-site Internet (needs activ), phone Internet central location, RV storage, dump, laundry, picnic tables, patios. RECREATION: rec hall, swim pool, hot tub, golf nearby, 8 shuffleboard courts, activities, horseshoes, v-ball. Pets welcome, breed restrict, size restrict. Partial handicap access. No tents. Age restrict may apply. Open all yr. Planned activities winter only.

Phone: (813)783-3477
Address: 37811 Chancey Rd, Zephyrhills, FL 33541
Lat/Lon: 28.20848/-82.19115
Email: southerncharmrv@tampabay.rr.com
Web: www.carefreervresorts.com

GEORGIA

ALBANY

(S) Albany RV Resort—(Dougherty) *From jct US 82 & US 19/Hwy 300: Go 4-1/2 mi S on US 19/Hwy 300. Enter on L.* FACILITIES: 82 sites, typical site width 40 ft, 82 full hkups, (20/30/50 amps), 42 pull-thrus, family camping, cable TV, WiFi Instant Internet at site, phone on-site Internet (needs activ), WiFi Internet central location, RV storage, laundry, RV supplies, picnic tables, patios. RECREATION: rec hall, pavilion, pond fishing, horseshoes. Pets welcome. Partial handicap access. Open all yr. Big rigs welcome.

Phone: (866)792-1481
Address: 1202 Liberty Expwy SE, Albany, GA 31705
Lat/Lon: 31.52048/-84.11515
Email: info@albanyrvresort.com
Web: www.albanyrvresort.com

AMERICUS

(E) Brickyard Plantation RV Park—(Sumter) *From jct Hwy 27 & US 280: Go 7 mi E on US 280, then 1/2 mi S on Parkers Crossing. Enter on L.* FACILITIES: 48 sites, typical site width 30 ft, 48 full hkups, (30/50 amps), 32 pull-thrus, family camping, WiFi Instant Internet at site, WiFi Internet central location, laundry, picnic tables, patios. RECREATION: rec hall, pond fishing, golf nearby, activities. Pets welcome, breed restrict, quantity restrict. Partial handicap access. No tents. Open all yr. Big rigs welcome.

Phone: (229)874-1234
Address: 224 Parkers Crossing, Americus, GA 31709
Lat/Lon: 31.99779/-84.11437
Email: bpgcdeb@sowega.net
Web: www.brickyardgolfclub.com

AUGUSTA

(S) Flynn's Inn Camping Village—(Richmond) *From jct I-20 (exit 196 A) & I-520 (Bobby Jones Expressway): Go 7 mi S on I-520 (exit 7), then 3-1/2 mi S on US 25 (Peach Orchard Rd). Enter on L.* FACILITIES: 71 sites, typical site width 30 ft, 62 full hkups, (30/50 amps), 9 no hkups, 30 pull-thrus, family camping, laundry. RECREATION: golf nearby. Pets welcome. No tents. Open all yr. Big rigs welcome.

Phone: (706)798-6912
Address: 3746 Peach Orchard Rd, Augusta, GA 30906
Lat/Lon: 33.35861/-82.04316

BRUNSWICK

(W) Golden Isles RV Park—(Glynn) *From jct I-95 (exit 29) & US 17: Go 1/2 mi W on US 17, then 1/4 mi N on Hwy 303. Enter on L.* FACILITIES: 160 sites, typical site width 26 ft, 149 full hkups, 11 W&E, (20/30/50 amps), 102 pull-thrus, family camping, cable TV, WiFi Instant Internet at site, phone on-site Internet (needs activ), cable Internet central location, cabins, RV storage, dump, non-guest dump $, laundry, LP gas by weight/by meter, ice, picnic tables, wood. RECREATION: pavilion, swim pool, golf nearby, playground, horseshoes. Pets welcome. Partial handicap access. Open all yr. AAA & Passport Discounts. Big rigs welcome.

Phone: (912)261-1025
Address: 7445 Blythe Island Hwy, Brunswick, GA 31523
Lat/Lon: 31.14438/-81.57933
Email: goldenislesrv@bellsouth.net
Web: goldenislesrvpark.com

CAVE SPRING

(N) Cedar Creek RV Park & Outdoor Center—(Floyd) *From jct US 411 & US 27: Go 7 mi S on US 411. Enter on R.* FACILITIES: 62 sites, typical site width 30 ft, 62 full hkups, (20/30/50 amps), 10 pull-thrus, family camping, WiFi Instant Internet at site, WiFi Internet central location, RV's/park model rentals, RV storage, laundry, ltd groc, RV supplies, LP gas by weight/by meter, LP bottle exch, ice, picnic tables, fire rings, grills, wood. RECREATION: pavilion, river swim, boating, canoeing, kayaking, 5 canoe/5 kayak rentals, float trips, river fishing, fishing supplies, golf nearby, bsktball, activities (wkends), horseshoes, sports field, v-ball. Pets welcome. Partial handicap access. Open all yr. Big rigs welcome. Member ARVC.

Phone: (706)777-3030
Address: 6770 Cave Spring Rd SW, Cave Spring, GA 30124
Lat/Lon: 34.13332/-85.30839
Email: camp@bigcedarcreek.com
Web: bigcedarcreek.com

CECIL

(W) CECIL BAY RV PARK—(Cook) *From jct I-75 (exit 32) & Old Coffee Rd: Go 150 yds W on Old Coffee Rd. Enter on R.*

WELCOME

FACILITIES: 104 sites, typical site width 30 ft, 98 full hkups, 6 W&E, (30/50 amps), 104 pull-thrus, cable TV, WiFi Instant Internet at site, RV storage, dump, non-guest dump $, laundry.

RECREATION: rec hall, pond fishing.

Pets welcome. Open all yr. Big rigs welcome.

Phone: (229)794-1484
Address: 1787 Old Coffee Rd, Cecil, GA 31627
Lat/Lon: 31.04415/-83.39865
Web: www.cecilbayrv.com

SEE AD VALDOSTA NEXT PAGE

COLUMBUS

(E) Lake Pines RV Park & Campground—(Muscogee) *From jct I-185 & US 80: Go 9-1/2 mi E on US 80, between milepost 12 & 13, then 1/4 mi S on Garrett Rd. Enter on L.* FACILITIES: 85 sites, typical site width 25 ft, 76 full hkups, 9 W&E, (20/30/50 amps), 37 pull-thrus, family camping, WiFi Instant Internet at site, phone on-site Internet (needs activ), cable Internet central location, RV's/park model rentals, cabins, RV storage, dump, non-guest dump $, laundry, LP gas by weight/by meter, picnic tables, patios, wood. RECREATION: rec hall, swim pool, pond fishing, golf nearby, 8 bike rentals, playground, horseshoes, hiking trails. Pets welcome, breed restrict, quantity restrict. Open all yr. Big rigs welcome. Member ARVC.

Phone: (706)561-9675
Address: 6404 Garrett Rd, Midland, GA 31820
Lat/Lon: 32.53812/-84.82727
Email: info@lakepines.net
Web: www.lakepines.net

DILLARD

(N) River Vista Mountain Village—(Rabun) *From jct US 441/23 & Hwy 246: Go 1 mi E on Hwy 246. Enter on R.* FACILITIES: 144 sites, typical site width 35 ft, 144 full hkups, (20/30/50 amps), 27 pull-thrus, family camping, cable TV, WiFi Instant Internet at site, WiFi Internet central location, cabins, laundry, ltd groc, LP gas by weight/by meter, ice, picnic tables, grills. RECREATION: rec hall, pavilion, 2 swim pools, hot tub, pond fishing, golf nearby, bsktball, play equipment, activities, horseshoes. Pets welcome. Partial handicap access. No tents. Open all yr. Big rigs welcome. Member GARVC.

Phone: (888) 850-7275
Address: 20 River Vista Dr, Dillard, GA 30537
Lat/Lon: 34.98600/-83.36850
Email: relax@rvmountainvillage.com
Web: www.rvmountainvillage.com

MARIETTA

(S) Atlanta-Marietta RV Resort—(Cobb) *From N'bnd jct I-75 (exit 261) & Hwy 280: Go 3/4 mi W on Hwy 280, then 1/2 mi N on US 41, then 1 block E on Wylie Rd. Enter on right. From S'bnd jct I-75 (exit 263) & Hwy 120: Go 1-1/2 mi W on Hwy 120, then 1 mi S on Wylie Rd. Enter on L.* FACILITIES: 70 sites, typical site width 25 ft, 70 full hkups, (30/50 amps), cable TV, WiFi Instant Internet at site, cable Internet central location, laundry, LP gas by weight/by meter, ice, picnic tables, patios. RECREATION: swim pool, golf nearby. Pets welcome, breed restrict. Partial handicap access. No tents. Open all yr. Big rigs welcome. Member ARVC, GARVC.

Phone: (877)727-5787
Address: 1031 Wylie Rd SE, Marietta, GA 30067
Lat/Lon: 33.92826/-84.50668
Email: information@amrvresort.com
Web: www.amrvresort.com

MCDONOUGH

(N) Atlanta South RV Resort—(Henry) *From jct I-75 (exit 222) & Jodeco Rd: Go 1/2 block W on Jodeco Rd, then 1/4 mi S on Mt. Olive Rd. Enter at end.* FACILITIES: 170 sites, typical site width 25 ft, 170 full hkups, (30/50 amps), 80 pull-thrus, family camping, WiFi Instant Internet at site, phone Internet central location, cabins, RV storage, dump, laundry, RV supplies, LP gas by meter, ice, picnic tables, fire rings. RECREATION: rec hall, rec room/area, pavilion, swim pool, pond fishing, golf nearby, bsktball, playground. Pets welcome. Partial handicap access. Open all yr. Big rigs welcome. ATM.

Phone: (800)778-0668
Address: 281 Mt Olive Rd, McDonough, GA 30253
Lat/Lon: 33.47482/-84.21613
Email: atlrvresort@gmail.com
Web: atlantasouthrvresort.com

NORCROSS

(E) Jones RV Park—(Gwinnett) *From jct I-85 (exit 101) & Indian Trl/Lilburn Rd: Go 400 ft E on Indian Trl/Lilburn Rd, then 1 block S on Willowtrail Pkwy. Enter at end.* FACILITIES: 173 sites, typical site width 24 ft, 173 full hkups, (20/30/50 amps), 55 pull-thrus, WiFi Instant Internet at site ($), RV storage, dump, non-guest dump $, laundry, LP gas by weight/by meter. RECREATION: golf nearby. Pets welcome, breed restrict. Partial handicap access. No tents. Open all yr. Big rigs welcome.

NORCROSS—Continued
Jones RV Park—Continued

Phone: (770)923-0911
Address: 2200 Willowtrail Pkwy., Norcross, GA 30093
Lat/Lon: 33.92555/-84.17652
Email: info@jonesrvpark.com
Web: www.jonesrvpark.com

PERRY

(N) Crossroads Holiday Trav-L-Park—(Houston) *From I-75 (exit 136) & US 341: Go 500 ft W on US 341. Enter on L.* FACILITIES: 64 sites, typical site width 28 ft, 58 full hkups, 6 W&E, (20/30/50 amps), 34 pull-thrus, family camping, cable TV, phone on-site Internet (needs activ), phone Internet central location, RV storage, laundry, ltd groc, RV supplies, LP gas by weight/by meter, ice, picnic tables. RECREATION: pavilion, swim pool, golf nearby, bsktball, play equipment. Pets welcome. Open all yr. Big rigs welcome.

Phone: (478)987-3141
Address: 1513 Sam Nunn Blvd, Perry, GA 31069
Lat/Lon: 32.47374/-83.74644
Email: crossroadscampground@windstream.net

SAVANNAH

(W) Savannah Oaks RV Resort—(Chatham) *From jct I-95 (exit 94) & Hwy 204: Go 2 1/2 mi W on Hwy 204. (Fort Argyle Rd). Enter on L.* FACILITIES: 139 sites, typical site width 30 ft, 111 full hkups, 28 W&E, (30/50 amps), 76 pull-thrus, family camping, cable TV, WiFi Instant Internet at site, WiFi Internet central location, cabins, dump, non-guest dump $, laundry, groceries, RV supplies, LP gas by weight/by meter, marine gas, ice, picnic tables, grills, controlled access. RECREATION: rec room/area, pavilion, coin games, swim pool, boating, canoeing, kayaking, ramp, dock, 2 kayak rentals, lake fishing, golf nearby, playground, local tours. Pets welcome. Partial handicap access. No tents. Open all yr. Big rigs welcome. Member ARVC.

Phone: (800)851-0717
Address: 805 Fort Argyle Rd., Savannah, GA 31419
Lat/Lon: 32.02647/-81.31989
Email: campinginsavannah@yahoo.com
Web: www.savannahoaks.net

TYBEE ISLAND

(W) RIVER'S END CAMPGROUND & RV PARK—(Chatham) *From jct I-95 & I-16: Go 9 mi E on I-16 to(exit 167A), then 3/4 mi N on MLK Jr Blvd, then 1 mi E on Bay St (stay in left hand lane), then 15 mi E on President St (Becomes Island Expwy then into US 80 to Tybee Island), then 2 blks N on Polk St. Enter on L.*

WELCOME

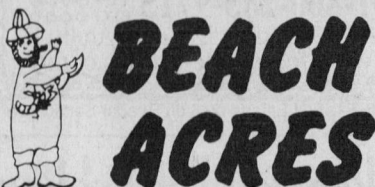

FACILITIES: 150 sites, typical site width 20 ft, 91 full hkups, 19 W&E, (30/50 amps), 40 no hkups, 44 pull-thrus, cable TV, cable Internet central location, family camping, cabins, dump, non-guest dump $, laundry, ltd groc, RV supplies, LP gas by weight/by meter, ice, picnic tables, wood.

RECREATION: rec hall, rec room/area, pavilion, swim pool, golf nearby, 7 bike rentals, activities, horseshoes, hiking trails.

Pets welcome, breed restrict, size restrict, quantity restrict. Partial handicap access. Open all yr. Big rigs welcome. Member ARVC.

Phone: (800)786-1016
Address: Five Fort Ave, Tybee Island, GA 31328
Lat/Lon: 32.02313/-80.85165
Email: riversend1@aol.com
Web: www.riversendcampground.com

SEE AD THIS PAGE

VALDOSTA

(W) River Park RV Park—(Lowndes) *From jct I-75 (exit 18) & Hwy 133: Go 300 yds W on Hwy 133. Enter on R.* FACILITIES: 118 sites, typical site width 25 ft, 118 full hkups, (30/50 amps), 57 pull-thrus, family camping, cable TV, WiFi Instant Internet at site, phone on-site Internet (needs activ), dump, non-guest dump $, laundry, picnic tables, patios. RECREATION: golf nearby. Pets welcome. No tents. Open all yr. Big rigs welcome.

Phone: (229)244-8397
Address: 1 Suwanee Dr., Valdosta, GA 31602
Lat/Lon: 30.84756/-83.33459
Email: info@riverparkvaldosta.com
Web: www.riverparkvaldosta.com

LOUISIANA

MT. HERMON

(E) Silver Creek Campground—(Washington) *From jct I-55 (exit 61) & Hwy 38: Go 15 mi E on Hwy 38, then 1-1/4 mi E on Hwy 1055. Enter on L.* FACILITIES: 297 sites, typical site width 35 ft, 111 full hkups, 186 W&E, (30/50 amps), 187 pull-thrus, family camping, phone Internet central location, cabins, RV storage, dump, non-guest dump $, laundry, ltd groc, RV supplies, ice, picnic tables, wood. RECREATION: rec room/area, pavilion, swim pool, pond/stream fishing, fishing supplies, golf nearby, bsktball, playground, activities, horseshoes, hiking trails, v-ball, local tours. Pets welcome. Partial handicap access. Open all yr. Big rigs welcome. Member ARVC, LCOA.

Phone: (985)877-4256
Address: 37567 Hwy 1055, Mt. Hermon, LA 70450
Lat/Lon: 30.957665/-90.270292
Email: silvercreekcamp@bellsouth.net
Web: www.silvercreekcamp.com

MAINE

WELLS

(S) BEACH ACRES CAMPGROUND—(York) *From jct I 95 (exit 19) & Hwy 109: Go 1-1/2 mi E on Hwy 109, then 2 mi S on US 1, then 1 block E on Eldridge Rd. Enter on L.*

WELCOME

FACILITIES: 400 sites, typical site width 40 ft, 320 full hkups, 20 W&E, 11 E, (20/30/50 amps), 49 no hkups, cable on-site Internet (needs activ), family camping, RV storage, shower$, dump, non-guest dump $, laundry, ice, picnic tables, fire rings, wood, controlled access.

RECREATION: swim pool, golf nearby, bsktball, playground, shuffleboard court, activities (wkends), horseshoes, sports field.

No pets. Open late May - mid Sep. Big rigs welcome. Member ARVC, MECOA.

Phone: (207)646-5612
Address: 76 Eldridge, Wells, ME 04090
Lat/Lon: 43.29105/-70.58719
Email: beachacres@beachacres.com
Web: www.beachacres.com

SEE AD THIS PAGE

MARYLAND

ABINGDON

(S) Bar Harbor RV Park & Marina—(Harford) *From jct I-95 (exit 80) & Hwy 543: Go 1-1/2 mi S on Hwy 543, then 1-1/2 mi W on US 40, then 3/4 mi S on*

Bar Harbor RV Park & Marina—Continued on next page

ABINGDON—Continued
Bar Harbor RV Park & Marina—Continued

Long Bar Harbor Rd, then 1/2 mi E on Baker Ave. Enter at end. FACILITIES: 93 sites, typical site width 30 ft, 93 full hkups, (30/50 amps), 7 pull-thrus, family camping, cable TV, WiFi Instant Internet at site, phone/cable on-site Internet (needs activ), WiFi Internet central location, RV's/park model rentals, dump, non-guest dump $, laundry, ltd groc, RV supplies, LP gas by weight/by meter, ice, picnic tables, patios, fire rings, grills, wood, controlled access. RECREATION: rec hall, rec room/area, coin games, swim pool, boating, canoeing, kayaking, ramp, dock, 2 kayak/pedal boat rentals, saltwater/river fishing, fishing supplies, golf nearby, playground. Pets welcome. No tents. Open all yr. Facilities fully operational Mar 1 - Dec 31. Dec 31 thru Mar 1, self-contained units only. Member ARVC, MAC. ATM.

Phone: (800)351-2267
Address: 4228 Birch Ave, Abingdon, MD 21009
Lat/Lon: 39.46075/-76.24387
Web: barharborrvpark.com

QUANTICO

(W) Sandy Hill Family Camp—(Wicomico) *From jct US 50 (Bus) & Hwy 349: Go 10 mi W on Hwy 349, then 3-1/2 mi N on Royal Oak Rd, then 3/4 mi E on Sandy Hill Rd. Enter at end.* FACILITIES: 99 sites, typical site width 25 ft, 99 W&E, (20/30 amps), 3 pull-thrus, family camping, dump, portable dump, laundry, ltd groc, RV supplies, LP gas by weight, ice, picnic tables, fire rings, wood. RECREATION: rec hall, river swim, boating, ramp, dock, river fishing, fishing supplies, golf nearby, playground, activities (wkends), hiking trails. Pets welcome. Partial handicap access. Open Mar 1 - Dec 15. Member ARVC, MAC.

Phone: (410)873-2471
Address: 5752 Sandy Hill Rd, Quantico, MD 21856
Lat/Lon: 38.35385/-75.85321
Email: sandyhill@sandyhillfamilycamp.com
Web: www.sandyhillfamilycamp.com

WOODBINE

(E) Ramblin' Pines Family Campground & RV Park—(Carroll) *From jct I-70 (exit 76) & Hwy-97: Go 2-1/2 mi N on Hwy-97, then 1/2 mi NW on Hoods Mill Rd. (Do not turn right on first Hoods Mill Rd; go across railroad tracks & up hill, then turn left on Hoods Mill Rd). Enter on L.* FACILITIES: 200 sites, typical site width 42 ft, 200 full hkups, (20/30/50 amps), 15 pull-thrus, family camping, WiFi Instant Internet at site, phone on-site Internet (needs activ), cabins, RV storage, dump, non-guest dump $, laundry, groceries, RV supplies, LP gas by weight/by meter, ice, picnic tables, patios, fire rings, grills, wood, controlled access. RECREATION: rec hall, rec room/area, equipped pavilion, coin games, swim pool, pond fishing, fishing supplies, mini-golf ($), golf nearby, bsktball, playground, 2 shuffleboard courts, activities (wkends), horseshoes, sports field, hiking trails, v-ball. Pets welcome, breed restrict. Partial handicap access. Open all yr. Discounts not available on Holiday weekends. Big rigs welcome. Member ARVC, MAC. ATM.

Phone: (800)550-8733
Address: 801 Hoods Mill Rd, Woodbine, MD 21797
Lat/Lon: 39.36704/-77.02533
Email: rpines@qis.net
Web: www.ramblinpines.com

Say you saw it in Woodall's!

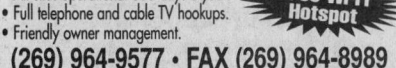

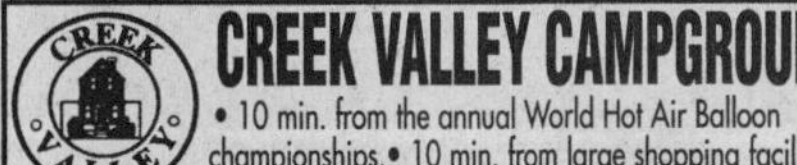

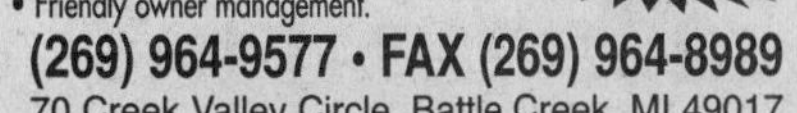

MICHIGAN

BATTLE CREEK

(N) CREEK VALLEY—(Calhoun) *From jct I-94 (exit 95) & Hwy 37: Go 8-1/2 mi N on Hwy 37. Enter on L.*

WELCOME

FACILITIES: 22 sites, typical site width 25 ft, accepts full hkup units only, 22 full hkups, (20/30 amps), 1 pull-thrus, WiFi Internet central location, family camping, RV storage, picnic tables.

Pets welcome, breed restrict. No tents. Open all yr. No restrooms.

Phone: (269)964-9577
Address: 70 Creek Valley Circle, Battle Creek, MI 49017
Lat/Lon: 42.36041/-85.23280

SEE AD THIS PAGE

DOWAGIAC

(NW) SHADY SHORES RESORT—(Cass) *From jct Hwy 51 & Hwy 152: Go 4 mi W on Hwy 152, then 1 mi S on Garret Rd. Enter on R.*

WELCOME

FACILITIES: 28 sites, typical site width 30 ft, 28 full hkups, (20/30 amps), heater not allowed, family camping, cabins, RV storage, picnic tables.

RECREATION: rec hall, lake swim, boating, canoeing, kayaking, 7 rowboat rentals, lake fishing, golf nearby, bsktball, 8 bike rentals, playground, 4 shuffleboard courts, tennis, horseshoes, sports field, v-ball.

No pets. No tents. Open May - Oct.

Phone: (269)424-5251
Address: 51256 Garrett Rd, Dowagiac, MI 49047
Lat/Lon: 42.05269/-86.19033

SEE AD THIS PAGE

HASTINGS

(NW) Whispering Waters Campground and Kayak Rental—(Barry) *From west jct Hwy 43 & Hwy 37: Go 3 mi N on Hwy 37, then 1/4 mi N on Irving Rd. Enter on L.* FACILITIES: 88 sites, typical site width 35 ft, 47 full hkups, 13 W&E, 15 E, (20/30/50 amps), 13 no hkups, 20 pull-thrus, family camping, RV storage, dump, portable dump, laundry, groceries, RV supplies, LP gas by weight/by meter, ice, picnic tables, fire rings, wood. RECREATION: rec room/area, equipped pavilion, swim pool, canoeing, kayaking, 28 canoe/70 kayak rentals, float trips, river fishing, fishing supplies, golf nearby, playground, activities (wkends), horseshoes, sports field, hiking trails, v-ball. Rec open to public. Pets welcome, breed restrict. Partial handicap access. Open Apr (last) - Sep (last). Member ARVC, ARVC MI.

Phone: (269)945-5166
Address: 1805 Irving Rd, Hastings, MI 49058
Lat/Lon: 42.67656/-85.38380
Email: whisper1805@gmail.com
Web: www.whisperingwatersonline.com

HOUGHTON LAKE

(NW) HOUGHTON LAKE TRAVEL PARK—(Roscommon) *From jct US 127 & Hwy 55: Go 200 yards E on Hwy 55, then 1/4 mi S on Cloverleaf Lane. Enter on R.*

WELCOME

FACILITIES: 85 sites, 27 full hkups, 45 W&E, (20/30/50 amps), 13 no hkups, 72 pull-thrus, cable TV, WiFi Instant Internet at site, family camping, cabins, RV storage, dump, non-guest dump $, portable dump, laundry, ltd groc, RV supplies, LP gas by weight/by meter, ice, picnic tables, fire rings, wood.

HOUGHTON LAKE—Continued
HOUGHTON LAKE TRAVEL PARK—Continued

RECREATION: rec room/area, coin games, swim pool, golf nearby, bsktball, playground, horseshoes, sports field, v-ball. Rec open to public.

Pets welcome. Open Apr 1 - Oct 1. Big rigs welcome. Member ARVC, ARVC MI.

Phone: (800)659-9379
Address: 370 Cloverleaf Lane, Houghton Lake, MI 48629
Lat/Lon: 44.32919/-84.80350
Email: hltp89@charter.net
Web: www.houghtonlaketravelpark.com

SEE AD THIS PAGE

HOWELL

(SE) LAKE CHEMUNG OUTDOOR RESORT—(Livingston) *From jct US 23 & I-96: Go 3 mi W on I-96 (exit 145), then 3 mi NW on Grand River Ave, then 2 mi N on Hughes Rd. Enter on L.*

WELCOME

FACILITIES: 340 sites, typical site width 30 ft, 340 full hkups, (30/50 amps), WiFi Internet central location, family camping, laundry, groceries, LP bottle exch, ice, picnic tables, patios, fire rings, wood, controlled access.

RECREATION: rec hall, rec room/area, pavilion, swim pool, lake swim, boating, canoeing, kayaking, lake/pond fishing, fishing supplies, mini-golf, golf nearby, bsktball, playground, 2 shuffleboard courts, activities, tennis, horseshoes, sports field, v-ball.

Pets welcome, quantity restrict. Partial handicap access. No tents. Open all yr. Facilities fully operational Memorial Day - Labor Day. Mid May thru mid Sep daily rates apply. Big rigs welcome. Member ARVC, ARVCMI.

Phone: (517)546-6361
Address: 320 S Hughes Rd, Howell, MI 48843
Lat/Lon: 42.59304/-83.85342
Email: lcori@comcast.net
Web: www.lcori.com

SEE AD THIS PAGE

JACKSON

(E) GREENWOOD ACRES FAMILY CAMPGROUND—(Jackson) *From jct US 127 S & I-94: Go 5 mi E on I-94 (exit 147), then 1 block S on Race Rd, then 3/4 mi W on Ann Arbor Rd, then 1-1/4 mi S on Portage Rd, then 1/2 mi E on Greenwood Rd, then N on Hilton. Enter on L.*

WELCOME

FACILITIES: 1080 sites, typical site width 40 ft, 500 full hkups, 580 W&E, (20/30/50 amps), 35 pull-thrus, heater not allowed, WiFi Instant Internet at site, WiFi Internet central location, family camping, dump, portable dump, laundry, ltd groc, RV supplies, LP gas by weight/by meter, ice, picnic tables, fire rings, wood, controlled access.

RECREATION: rec hall, rec room/area, pavilion, coin games, swim pool, lake swim, boating, 5 hp limit, canoeing, kayaking, ramp, dock, lake fishing, fishing supplies, mini-golf, golf nearby, bsktball, playground, activities (wkends), tennis, horseshoes, sports field, hiking trails, v-ball.

Pets welcome. Partial handicap access. Open April 1 - Oct 31. Facilities fully operational Memorial Day - Labor Day. Member ARVC, ARVC MI. ATM.

GREENWOOD ACRES FAMILY CAMPGROUND—Continued on next page

JACKSON—Continued
GREENWOOD ACRES FAMILY CAMPGROUND—Continued

Phone: (517)522-8600
Address: 2401 Hilton Rd, Jackson, MI 49201
Lat/Lon: 42.26571/-84.26070
Email: office@greenwoodacrescampground.com
Web: www.greenwoodacrescampground.com

SEE AD THIS PAGE

ORTONVILLE

(SW) Clearwater Campground—(Oakland) *From jct I-75 (exit 91) & Hwy 15: Go 6-1/4 mi N on Hwy 15. Enter on L.* FACILITIES: 114 sites, typical site width 25 ft, 114 full hkups, (20/30/50 amps), 12 pull-thrus, family camping, WiFi Internet central location, RV's/park model rentals, cabins, RV storage, dump, non-guest dump $, laundry, ltd groc, RV supplies, ice, picnic tables, patios, fire rings, wood, controlled access. RECREATION: rec hall, pavilion, lake swim, boating, electric motors only, canoeing, kayaking, 3 rowboat rentals, lake fishing, fishing supplies, golf nearby, bsktball, playground, activities (wkends), horseshoes, hiking trails, v-ball. Pets welcome, breed restrict. Partial handicap access. Open Apr 15 - Oct 15. No credit cards. Big rigs welcome.

ORTONVILLE—Continued
Clearwater Campground—Continued

Phone: (248)627-3820
Address: 1140 S Ortonville Rd (Hwy 15), Ortonville, MI 48462
Lat/Lon: 42.83638/-83.44762
Email: clearwatercampground1140@yahoo.com
Web: www.campsmore.com

MISSISSIPPI

BAY ST. LOUIS

(W) Bay Hide Away RV & Camping Resort—(Hancock) *From jct I-10 W (exit 13) & Hwy 43/603: Go 6 mi S on Hwy 43/603, then 4.8 mi W on US 90, then 1/2 mi S on Lakeshore Rd. Enter on L.* FACILITIES: 46 sites, typical site width 30 ft, 46 full hkups, (20/30/50 amps), 41 pull-thrus, WiFi Instant Internet at site, phone Internet central location, laundry, RV supplies, ice, picnic tables, patios, fire rings, wood. RECREATION: rec hall, equipped pavilion, swim pool, pond fishing, golf nearby, playground, activities (wkends), horseshoes, sports field, hiking trails, v-ball. Pets welcome. Partial handicap access. No tents. Open all yr. Big rigs welcome. Green Friendly. Member ARVC.

Phone: (228)466-0959
Address: 8374 Lakeshore Rd, Bay St Louis, MS 39520
Lat/Lon: 30.29193/-89.45654
Email: bhacamping@aol.com
Web: www.bayhideaway.com

BILOXI

(C) Southern Comfort Camping Resort—(Harrison) *From jct I-10 (exit 46A) & I-110: Go 2 mi S on I-110 (exit 1B), then 2-3/4 mi W on US 90. Enter on R.* FACILITIES: 129 sites, typical site width 30 ft, 86 full hkups, 43 W&E, (20/30/50 amps), 57 pull-thrus, cable TV, WiFi Instant Internet at site, phone Internet central location, RV storage, dump, laundry, RV supplies, LP gas by weight/by meter, ice, picnic tables, patios. RECREATION: rec hall, rec room/area, coin games, swim pool, wading pool, golf nearby, local tours. Pets welcome, breed restrict. Partial handicap access. Open all yr. Big rigs welcome.

Phone: (877)302-1700
Address: 1766 Beach Blvd, Biloxi, MS 39531
Lat/Lon: 30.39426/-88.94124

GAUTIER

(NW) INDIAN POINT RV RESORT—(Jackson) *From I-10 (exit 61) & Gautier/VanCleave Rd: Go 3/4 mi S on Gautier/VanCleave Rd, then E on Indian Point Rd to gate. Enter at end.*

WELCOME

FACILITIES: 200 sites, typical site width 40 ft, 200 full hkups, (20/30/50 amps), 13 pull-thrus, cable TV, WiFi Instant Internet at site, WiFi Internet central location, RV's/park model rentals, cabins, RV storage, dump, non-guest dump $, laundry, RV supplies, LP gas by weight/by meter, ice, picnic tables, patios, wood.

RECREATION: rec hall, rec room/area, equipped pavilion, 2 swim pools, boating, canoeing, ramp, dock, river fishing, fishing guides, mini-golf, golf nearby, bsktball, playground, 2 shuffleboard courts, activities (wkends), horseshoes, sports field, hiking trails.

Pets welcome, breed restrict. Partial handicap access. No tents. Open all yr. Big rigs welcome. Member ARVC.

GAUTIER—Continued
INDIAN POINT RV RESORT—Continued

Phone: (228)497-1011
Address: 1600 Indian Point Parkway, Gautier, MS 39553
Lat/Lon: 30.41235/-88.62956
Email: ip@indianpt.com
Web: www.indianpt.com

SEE AD THIS PAGE

(N) SANTA MARIA RV PARK—*From I-10 (exit 61) & Gautier/Van Cleave Rd: Go 1/2 mi S on Gautier/Van Cleave Rd, then 1-1/2 mi E on Martin Bluff Rd.*

WELCOME

FACILITIES: 142 sites, 142 full hkups, (30/50 amps), WiFi Instant Internet at site, family camping, RV's/park model rentals, laundry, LP gas by weight/by meter, ice.

RECREATION: swim pool, lake/river fishing, golf nearby, bsktball, playground, horseshoes, sports field, v-ball.

Pets welcome. Partial handicap access. No tents. Open all yr. Big rigs welcome.

Phone: (228)522-3009
Address: 5800 Martin Bluff Rd, Gautier, MS 39553
Lat/Lon: 30.42820/-88.63155
Web: santamariarvpark.com

SEE AD THIS PAGE

GULFPORT

(N) Country Side RV Park—(Harrison) *From jct I-10 (exit 34B) & US 49: Go 10 mi N on US 49. Enter on R.* FACILITIES: 32 sites, typical site width 29 ft, 32 full hkups, (20/30/50 amps), 2 pull-thrus, cable TV, laundry, RV supplies, LP gas by weight/by meter, ice, picnic tables. RECREATION: rec room/area, pavilion, swim pool, pond fishing, golf nearby, activities, local tours. Pets welcome. Partial handicap access. Open all yr. Big rigs welcome.

Phone: (228)539-0807
Address: 20278 US Highway 49, Saucier, MS 39574
Lat/Lon: 30.57507/-89.12514
Email: csrv@bellsouth.net
Web: www.countrysidervpark.com

MERIDIAN

(E) NANABE CREEK CAMPGROUND—(Lauderdale) *From jct US 45 & I-20/59 (exit 157): Go 3-1/2 mi E on I-20/59 (exit 160), then 1 mi N on Russell Rd. Enter on R.*

WELCOME

FACILITIES: 75 sites, typical site width 28 ft, 55 full hkups, 10 W&E, (20/30/50 amps), 50 amps ($), 10 no hkups, 30 pull-thrus, WiFi Instant Internet at site, phone Internet central location, RV storage, laundry, RV supplies, LP gas by weight/by meter, ice, picnic tables, fire rings, wood.

RECREATION: rec room/area, pavilion, swim pool, pond fishing, golf nearby, play equipment, sports field, v-ball. Rec open to public.

Pets welcome. Open all yr. Big rigs welcome.

Phone: (601)485-4711
Address: 1933 Russell-Mt. Gilead Rd., Meridian, MS 39301
Lat/Lon: 32.40286/-88.59116
Email: maryjo@nanabervpark.com
Web: nanabervpark.com

SEE AD NEXT PAGE

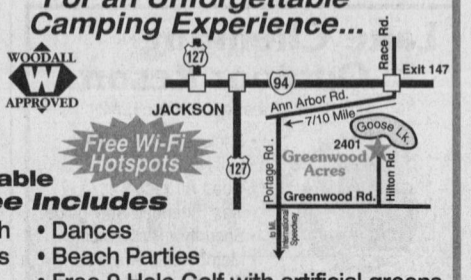

VICKSBURG

(S) RIVER TOWN CAMPGROUND—(Warren) *From I-20 (exit 1B) & US Hwy 61 S: Go 6 mi S on Hwy 61 S. Enter on L.* WELCOME FACILITIES: 148 sites, typical site width 45 ft, 148 full hkups, (20/30/50 amps), 60 pull-thrus, cable TV, WiFi Instant Internet at site, phone Internet central location, dump, laundry, RV supplies, LP gas by weight/by meter, ice, picnic tables.

RECREATION: rec hall, swim pool, playground, local tours.

Pets welcome. Partial handicap access. Open all yr. Big rigs welcome.

Phone: (866)442-2267
Address: 5900 Hwy 61 S, Vicksburg, MS 39180
Lat/Lon: 32.23791/-90.92373
Email: rt5900@bellsouth.net
Web: www.rivertown-campground.com

SEE AD THIS PAGE

MISSOURI

BRANSON

(N) America's Best Campground—(Taney) *From jct US 65 & Hwy 248 (Shepherd of the Hills Expwy): Go 1-3/4 mi W on Hwy 248 (Shepherd of the Hills Expwy), then keep right to Hwy 248 (1/2 mi N of Tri-Lake Center), then 1-1/4 mi N on Hwy 248, then 300 yards W on Buena Vista Rd. Enter on L.* FACILITIES: 161 sites, typical site width 30 ft, 159 full hkups, 2 W&E, (30/50 amps), 136 pull-thrus, family camping, cable TV, phone/WiFi Instant Internet at site, phone Internet central location, cabins, RV storage, dump, non-guest dump $, laundry, groceries, RV supplies, LP gas by meter, ice, picnic tables, patios, grills. RECREATION: rec hall, rec room/area, coin games, swim pool, hot tub, golf nearby, bsktball, playground, activities, horseshoes, v-ball, local tours. Pets welcome. Partial handicap access. Open all yr. Facilities fully operational Mid Mar - Mid Dec. Planned activities in season only. Rental units open Mid Mar - Mid Dec. Big rigs welcome. Member ARVC, MOARC.

Phone: (800)671-4399
Address: 499 Buena Vista Rd, Branson, MO 65616
Lat/Lon: 36.68326/-93.26055
Email: fun4uabc@aol.com
Web: www.abc-branson.com

MONTANA

ANACONDA

(E) Fairmont RV Park—(Silver Bow) Altitude 5286 ft. *From I-90 (exit 211) & Fairmont Rd/Hwy 441: Go 2-1/2 mi W on Fairmont Rd/Hwy 441. Enter on L.* FACILITIES: 140 sites, typical site width 30 ft, 100 full hkups, 40 W&E, (30/50 amps), 50 amps ($), 36 pull-thrus, family camping, WiFi Instant Internet at site, WiFi Internet central location, cabins, RV storage, dump, non-guest dump $, laundry, ltd groc, RV supplies, ice, picnic tables, grills. RECREATION: rec hall, pavilion, coin games, golf nearby, playground, horseshoes, sports field, v-ball. Pets welcome. Partial handicap access. Open Apr 15 - Oct 15. Big rigs welcome. Member COAM. ATM.

Phone: (406)797-3505
Address: 1700 Fairmont Rd, Anaconda, MT 59711
Lat/Lon: 46.04273/-112.80529
Email: fairmontrvpark@aol.com
Web: www.fairmontrvresort.com

BILLINGS

(S) Yellowstone River RV Park & Campground—(Yellowstone) *From jct I-90 (exit 450) & Hwy 3/27th St: Go 1 block S on 27th St, then 1/4 mi SW on Garden Ave. Enter on L.* FACILITIES: 136 sites, typical site width 20 ft, 76 full hkups, 30 W&E, (20/30/50 amps), 30 no hkups, 83 pull-thrus, family camping, cable TV, WiFi Instant Internet at site, WiFi Internet central location, cabins, RV storage, dump, laundry, ltd groc, RV supplies, ice, picnic tables. RECREATION: rec room/area, equipped pavilion, coin games, swim pool, hot tub, river fishing, golf nearby, bsktball, playground, horseshoes, sports field, hiking trails, local tours. Pets welcome. Partial handicap access. Open all yr. Facilities fully operational Apr 1 - Nov 1. Nov 2 - Mar 31 - Accepts Self-Contained Units only. Big rigs welcome. Member COAM.

Phone: (800)654-0878
Address: 309 Garden Ave, Billings, MT 59101
Lat/Lon: 45.76384/-108.48385
Web: www.yellowstonerivercampground.com

ENNIS

(N) Ennis RV Village—(Madison) Altitude 4995 ft. *From jct Hwy 287 & US 287: Go 3/4 mi N on US 287. Enter on R.* FACILITIES: 90 sites, typical site width 30 ft, 76 full hkups, 14 W&E, (20/30/50 amps), family camping, WiFi Instant Internet at site, phone on-site Internet (needs activ), phone Internet central location, dump, non-guest dump $, laundry, ltd groc, RV supplies, ice, picnic tables, patios, grills. RECREATION: rec hall, fishing supplies, fishing guides, golf nearby, horseshoes, hiking trails. Pets welcome. Partial handicap access. Open Apr 1 - Nov. 15. Big rigs welcome. Member COAM.

Phone: (866)682-5272
Address: 15 Geyser St, Ennis, MT 59729
Lat/Lon: 45.36749/-111.72896
Email: info@ennisrv.com
Web: www.ennisrv.com

NEVADA

CARSON CITY

(S) Camp-N-Town RV Park—(Carson) Altitude 4600 ft. *S'bound from jct of Hwy 395 & N Carson St exit: Go 1-3/4 mi S on N Carson St. Enter on R.* FACILITIES: 157 sites, typical site width 26 ft, 157 full hkups, (30/50 amps), 100 pull-thrus, family camping, cable TV ($), WiFi Instant Internet at site, dump, non-guest dump $, laundry, picnic tables. RECREATION: rec room/area, coin games, golf nearby, horseshoes. Pets welcome ($). Partial handicap access. Open all yr. Big rigs welcome.

Phone: (775)883-1123
Address: 2438 N Carson St, Carson City, NV 89706
Lat/Lon: 39.18180/-119.76836

(W) Silver City RV Resort—(Douglas) Altitude 4500 ft. *From south jct US 50 & US 395 (Carson St): Go 3-1/2 mi S on US 395 (Carson St) (8 mi N of Minden). Enter on L.* FACILITIES: 206 sites, typical site width 35 ft, 206 full hkups, (20/30/50 amps), 80 pull-thrus, family camping, cable TV ($), WiFi Instant Internet at site, WiFi Internet central location, RV storage, dump, non-guest dump $, laundry, full svc store, RV supplies, LP gas by meter, ice, picnic tables, fire rings, wood. RECREATION: rec hall, rec room/area, pavilion, coin games, swim pool, hot tub, pond fishing, fishing supplies, mini-golf, golf nearby, bsktball, playground, horseshoes. Pets welcome, breed restrict. Partial handicap access. Open all yr. Big rigs welcome. ATM.

Phone: (800)997-6393
Address: 3165 Highway 395, Minden, NV 89423
Lat/Lon: 39.06933/-119.77947
Email: manager@silvercityrvresort.com
Web: www.silvercityrvresort.com

ELY

(SE) KOA of Ely—(White Pine) Altitude 6607 ft. *From center of town at jct US-50/93 & US-6: Go 3 mi SE on Pioche Hwy (US-6-50 E & 93 S). Enter on R.* FACILITIES: 134 sites, typical site width 26 ft, 90 full hkups, 26 W&E, (20/30/50 amps), 50 amps ($), 18 no hkups, 54 pull-thrus, family camping, cable TV ($), WiFi Instant Internet at site ($), WiFi Internet central location, cabins, RV storage, dump, non-guest dump $, laundry, groceries, RV supplies, LP gas by meter, ice, picnic tables, grills, wood. RECREATION: rec hall, golf nearby, bsktball, playground, horseshoes, hiking trails, v-ball. Pets welcome. Partial handicap access. Open all yr. Big rigs welcome.

Phone: (800)562-3413
Address: 1593 S US 93, Ely, NV 89301
Lat/Lon: 39.21541/-114.85432
Email: elykoa@mwpower.net
Web: koa.com

FALLON

(W) Fallon RV Park & Country Store & Gift Shop—(Churchill) *From Westside of town: Go 6 mi W on Hwy 50 (Reno Hwy). Enter on L.* FACILITIES: 70 sites, typical site width 20 ft, 63 full hkups, 7 W&E, (30/50 amps), 30 pull-thrus, family camping, cable TV, WiFi Internet central location, RV storage, dump, non-guest dump $, laundry, full svc store, RV supplies, LP gas by meter, ice, picnic tables. RECREATION: golf nearby, playground, horseshoes. Pets welcome, breed restrict. Partial handicap access. Open all yr. Big rigs welcome. ATM.

Phone: (775)867-2332
Address: 5787 Reno Hwy, Fallon, NV 89406
Lat/Lon: 39.48642/-118.87309
Email: fallonrv@gmail.com
Web: www.fallonrv.com

LAS VEGAS

(E) Arizona Charlie's Boulder Hotel, Casino & RV Park—(Clark) *From jct I-515 (US 93/95 Expwy) & Boulder Hwy (exit 70): Go 1-1/4 mi S on Boulder Hwy. Enter on L.* FACILITIES: 221 sites, typical site width 18 ft, accepts full hkup units only, 221 full hkups, (30/50 amps), 100 pull-thrus, family camping, WiFi Instant Internet at site, laundry. RECREATION: rec room/area, swim pool, hot tub, golf nearby. Pets welcome, breed restrict, size restrict. Partial handicap access. No tents. Open all yr. No vans, station wagons, pick-up campers. Big rigs welcome. ATM.

Phone: (800)970-7280
Address: 4445 Boulder Highway, Las Vegas, NV 89121
Lat/Lon: 36.12465/-115.07732
Web: www.arizonacharlies.com

(N) Hitchin' Post RV Park—(Clark) *From jct I-15 (exit 50) & Lamb Blvd: Go 2 mi S on Lamb Blvd, then 300 yds SW on Las Vegas Blvd. N'bnd from I-15 & exit 48 (Craig Rd): Go 1 mi E on Craig Rd, then 1 mi S on Lamb Rd, then 300 yds SW on Las Vegas Blvd. Enter on L.* FACILITIES: 196 sites, typical site width 30 ft, accepts full hkup units only, 196 full hkups, (30/50 amps), 107 pull-thrus, cable TV, WiFi Instant Internet at site, phone Internet central location, laundry, RV supplies, LP gas by meter, ice, picnic tables, controlled access. RECREATION: rec room/area, coin games, swim pool, golf nearby, horseshoes. Pets welcome, breed restrict, quantity restrict. Partial handicap access. No tents. Open all yr. Big rigs welcome. ATM.

Phone: (888)433-8402
Address: 3640 Las Vegas Blvd N, Las Vegas, NV 89115
Lat/Lon: 36.22323/-115.08312
Web: www.hprvp.com

LAUGHLIN

(S) Laughlin/AVI Casino KOA—(Clark) *From jct Hwy 95 & Hwy 163: Go 2 mi W on Hwy 163 (Laughlin Bridge), then 9 mi S on Needles Hwy, then 4-1/2 mi SE on Aha Macav Pkwy. Enter on L.* FACILITIES: 260 sites, typical site width 18 ft, 260 full hkups, (30/50 amps), 191 pull-thrus, family camping, cable TV, WiFi Instant Internet at site, WiFi Internet central location, dump, non-guest dump $, laundry, RV supplies, marine gas, ice, picnic tables, grills. RECREATION: pavilion, coin games, swim pool, river swim, hot tub, boating, canoeing, kayaking, ramp, dock, 30 motorboat rentals, float trips, river fishing, golf nearby, playground, horseshoes, sports field, v-ball. Pets welcome, breed restrict. Partial handicap access. No tents. Open all yr. Big rigs welcome. ATM.

Phone: (800)562-4142
Address: 10000 Aha Macav Parkway, Laughlin, NV 89028
Lat/Lon: 35.16682/-114.57207
Email: westl@avicasino.com
Web: www.avicasino.com

PAHRUMP

(N) Nevada Treasure RV Resort & Spa—(Nye) *From jct SR 372 & SR 160: Go 7-1/2 mi NW on SR 160. Enter on L.* FACILITIES: 202 sites, typical site width 25 ft, 202 full hkups, (30/50 amps), phone/WiFi Instant Internet at site, WiFi Internet central location, RV storage, laundry, RV supplies, LP gas by meter, ice, picnic tables, patios, grills, controlled access. RECREATION: rec hall, rec room/area, coin games, 2 swim pools, hot tub, putting green, golf nearby, shuffleboard court, ac-

Nevada Treasure RV Resort & Spa—Continued on next page

PAHRUMP—Continued
Nevada Treasure RV Resort & Spa—Continued

tivities, horseshoes, hiking trails, local tours. Pets welcome, quantity restrict. Partial handicap access. No tents. Open all yr. Big rigs welcome. ATM.

Phone: (775)751-1174
Address: 301 W Leslie Rd, Pahrump, NV 89060
Lat/Lon: 36.31207/-116.01859
Email: frontdesk@nevadatreasurervresort.com
Web: www.nevadatreasurervresort.com

NEW HAMPSHIRE

FREEDOM

(NW) DANFORTH BAY CAMPING & RV RESORT—(Carroll) *From jct Hwy 16 & Hwy 41: Go 1/2 mi N on Hwy 41, then 4-3/4 mi E on Ossippee Lake Rd, then 1 mi NE on Shawtown Rd. Enter on R.*

FACILITIES: 300 sites, typical site width 30 ft, 254 full hkups, 46 W&E, (30/50 amps), 24 pull-thrus, cable TV, WiFi Instant Internet at site, WiFi Internet central location, family camping, RV's/park model rentals, cabins, RV storage, shower$, dump, non-guest dump $, laundry, groceries, RV supplies, LP gas by weight/by meter, LP bottle exch, ice, picnic tables, fire rings, grills, wood, controlled access.

RECREATION: rec hall, rec room/area, equipped pavilion, coin games, 2 swim pools, wading pool, lake swim, boating, canoeing, kayaking, ramp, dock, 2 rowboat/8 canoe/15 kayak/3 pedal boat/2 motorboat rentals, lake/river fishing, fishing supplies, golf nearby, bsktball, playground, activities, tennis, horseshoes, sports field, hiking trails, v-ball.

Pets welcome, quantity restrict. Partial handicap access. Open all yr. Facilities fully operational Memorial Day - Columbus Day. Big rigs welcome. Member NE-HA-CA. ATM.

Phone: (603)539-2069
Address: 196 Shawtown Rd, Freedom, NH 03836
Lat/Lon: 43.83204/-71.11036
Email: reservations@danforthbay.com
Web: www.danforthbay.com

SEE AD THIS PAGE

(NW) THE BLUFFS ADULT RV RESORT—(Carroll) *From jct Hwy 16 & Hwy 41: Go 1/2 mi N on Hwy 41, then 4-3/4 mi E on Ossipee Lake Rd, then 1-1/4 m NE on Shawtown Rd. Enter on R.*

FACILITIES: 240 sites, typical site width 50 ft, 240 full hkups, (20/30/50 amps), cable TV, WiFi Instant Internet at site, WiFi Internet central location, shower$, laundry, groceries, RV supplies, LP gas by weight/by meter, LP bottle exch, ice, picnic tables, fire rings, grills, wood, controlled access.

RECREATION: rec hall, rec room/area, coin games, 5 swim pools, lake swim, boating, canoeing, kayaking, ramp, dock, 2 rowboat/8 canoe/15 kayak/3 pedal boat/2 motorboat rentals, lake/river fishing, fishing supplies, golf nearby, bsktball, playground, activities, tennis, horseshoes, sports field, hiking trails, v-ball.

Pets welcome, quantity restrict. Partial handicap access. No tents. Age restrict may apply. Open Mid-April - Mid-November. Facilities fully operational May 1 - October 31. Min 1 week stay. Big rigs welcome. Member NE-HA-CA. ATM.

Phone: (603)539-2069
Address: 196 Shawtown Rd., Freedom, NH 03836
Lat/Lon: 43.83204/-71.11036
Email: seasonal@danforthbay.com
Web: www.nhrvresort.com

SEE AD THIS PAGE

HAMPTON

(S) Tidewater Campground—(Rockingham) *From jct Hwy 101 & US 1: Go 160 yards S on US 1. Enter on R.* FACILITIES: 225 sites, typical site width 30 ft, 185 full hkups, (20/30/50 amps), 50 amps ($), 40 no hkups, 4 pull-thrus, heater not allowed, family camping, WiFi Instant Internet at site, shower$, ltd groc, RV supplies, ice, picnic tables, fire rings, wood, controlled access. RECREATION: rec hall, coin games, swim pool, golf nearby, bsktball, playground, horseshoes, sports field. No pets. Partial handicap access. Open May 15 - Oct 15. Big rigs welcome. Member ARVC, NE-HA-CA.

Phone: (603)926-5474
Address: 160 Lafayette Rd, Hampton, NH 03842
Lat/Lon: 42.93074/-70.84512
Web: www.ucampnh.com/tidewater

NEW BOSTON

(W) Friendly Beaver Campground—(Hillsborough) *From jct Hwy 77 & Hwy 136 & Hwy 13: Go 100 feet S on Hwy 13, then 2 mi W on Old Coach Rd. Enter on R.* FACILITIES: 278 sites, typical site width 40 ft, 213 full hkups, 62 W&E, (20/30/50 amps), 3 no hkups, heater not allowed, family camping, WiFi Instant Internet at site ($), WiFi Internet central location ($), dump, portable dump, laundry, groceries, RV supplies, ice, picnic tables, fire rings, grills, wood. RECREATION: rec hall, rec room/area, pavilion, coin games, 4 swim pools, wading pool, golf nearby, bsktball, playground, activities, horseshoes, sports field, hiking trails, v-ball. Pets welcome. Partial handicap access. Open all yr. Entire facility fully operational during Winter months. Big rigs welcome. Member ARVC, NE-HA-CA. ATM.

Phone: (603)487-5570
Address: 88 Cochran Hill Rd, New Boston, NH 03070
Lat/Lon: 42.96871/-71.72274
Email: reservations@friendlybeaver.com
Web: www.friendlybeaver.com

NEW JERSEY

CAPE MAY

(N) The Depot Travel Park—(Cape May) *From jct Garden State Pkwy (exit 0) & Hwy 109: Go 1 mi W on Hwy 109/US 9, then 1 mi S on CR 626 (Seashore Rd). From jct Cape May - Lewes Ferry & US 9: Go 2 mi E on US 9, then 1-3/4 mi S on CR 626 (Seashore Rd). Enter on R.* FACILITIES: 135 sites, typical site width 40 ft, 100 full hkups, 35 W&E, (20/30/50 amps), heater not allowed, family camping, cable TV, WiFi Internet central location, RV's/park model rentals, dump, non-guest dump $, laundry, LP gas by weight/by meter, ice, picnic tables. RECREATION: pavilion, golf nearby, playground, horseshoes, sports field. Pets welcome. Partial handicap access. Open May 1 - Columbus Day. Big rigs welcome. Member ARVC, NJCOA.

Phone: (609)884-2533
Address: 800 Broadway, West Cape May, NJ 08204
Lat/Lon: 38.94386/-74.92944
Web: www.thedepottravelpark.com

CLARKSBORO

(S) Timberlane Campground—(Gloucester) *N'bnd from jct I-295 & Timberlane Rd (exit 18): Go 3/4 mi SE on Timberlane Rd. Ent on rt. S'bnd from I-295 (exit 18AB):Go 1 mi S on Hwy 667 (Cohawkin Rd), then 1/4 mi SW on Friendship Rd, then 1/4 mi NW on Timberlane Rd.* FACILITIES: 96 sites, typical site width 30 ft, 82 full hkups, (20/30/50 amps), 14 no hkups, 51 pull-thrus, family camping, cable TV, WiFi Internet central location, cabins, RV storage, dump, non-guest dump $, laundry, RV supplies, LP gas by weight/by meter, ice, picnic tables, fire rings, wood. RECREATION: rec room/area, pavilion, coin games, swim pool, wading pool, pond fishing, fishing supplies, golf nearby, bsktball, playground, shuffleboard court, horseshoes, sports field, v-ball. Pets welcome. Partial handicap access. Open all yr. Big rigs welcome. Member ARVC, NJCOA.

Phone: (856)423-6677
Address: 117 Timberlane Road, Clarksboro, NJ 08210
Lat/Lon: 39.80458/-75.23582
Email: info@timberlanecampground.com
Web: www.timberlanecampground.com

HOPE

(S) Triplebrook Camping Resort—(Warren) *From jct I-80 (exit 12) & CR 521: Go 1 mi S on CR 521, then 3 mi W on CR 609, then 1 mi N on Nightingale Rd, then 1/2 mi E on Honey Run Rd. Enter on L.* FACILITIES: 217 sites, typical site width 40 ft, 110 full hkups, 101 W&E, (20/30/50 amps), 6 no hkups, 6 pull-thrus, family camping, WiFi Instant Internet at site, WiFi Internet central location, cabins, RV storage, dump, non-guest dump $, portable dump, laundry, ltd groc, RV supplies, LP gas by weight/by meter, ice, picnic tables, wood.

HOPE—Continued
Triplebrook Camping Resort—Continued

RECREATION: rec room/area, equipped pavilion, coin games, 2 swim pools, hot tub, boating, canoeing, kayaking, 6 rowboat/4 pedal boat rentals, pond fishing, fishing supplies, mini-golf ($), golf nearby, bsktball, playground, shuffleboard court, activities, tennis, horseshoes, sports field, hiking trails, v-ball. Pets welcome. Open all yr. 3 day min. stay holiday wkends with reservations. Dec 1-Mar 31 by reservation only. Big rigs welcome. Green Friendly. Member ARVC, NJCOA.

Phone: (908)459-4079
Address: 58 Honey Run Rd, Blairstown, NJ 07825
Lat/Lon: 40.91177/-75.01913
Email: info@triplebrook.com
Web: www.triplebrook.com

MAYS LANDING

(N) Winding River Campground—(Atlantic) *From jct Hwy 50 & Hwy 40 & Hwy 616: Go 1/4 mi N on Hwy 616, then 4 mi NE on Hwy 559. Enter on R.* FACILITIES: 133 sites, 105 full hkups, 28 W&E, (20/30 amps), family camping, phone Internet central location, RV's/park model rentals, cabins, RV storage, shower$, dump, non-guest dump $, laundry, ltd groc, LP gas by weight, ice, picnic tables, fire rings, wood. RECREATION: rec room/area, pavilion, coin games, swim pool, boating, 20 hp limit, canoeing, kayaking, ramp, 34 canoe/40 kayak rentals, float trips, river/pond fishing, fishing supplies, golf nearby, bsktball, playground, activities (wkends), horseshoes, v-ball. Pets welcome. Open May 1 - Oct 15. 3 day min. stay Holiday Weekends with Reservations. Member ARVC, NJCOA. ATM.

Phone: (609)625-3191
Address: 6752 Weymouth Rd, Mays Landing, NJ 08330
Lat/Lon: 39.48858/-74.76993
Email: windingrivercampgroundnj@msn.com
Web: www.windingrivercamping.com

OCEAN VIEW

(S) Ocean View Resort Campground—(Cape May) *From jct Garden State Pkwy South (exit 17) & Hwy 625 (Sea Isle Blvd): Go 1/4 mi W on Hwy 625, then 1/4 mi N on US 9. Enter on L.* FACILITIES: 1175 sites, 1175 full hkups, (20/30/50 amps), 40 pull-thrus, heater not allowed, family camping, cable TV, WiFi Instant Internet at site, WiFi Internet central location, RV's/park model rentals, cabins, RV storage, shower$, laundry, full svc store, RV supplies, LP gas by weight/by meter, ice, picnic tables, fire rings, wood, controlled access. RECREATION: rec hall, rec room/area, equipped pavilion, coin games, swim pool, wading pool, lake swim, boating, 6 pedal boat rentals, pond fishing, fishing supplies, mini-golf ($), golf nearby, bsktball, playground, 2 shuffleboard courts, activities, tennis, sports field, v-ball, local tours. Pets welcome. Partial handicap access. Open Mid Apr - Sep 30. Weekends only early season. Big rigs welcome. Green Friendly. Member ARVC, NJCOA. ATM.

Phone: (609)624-1675
Address: 2555 Shore Rd (US9), Ocean View, NJ 08230
Lat/Lon: 39.17467/-74.72440
Email: camp@ovresort.com
Web: www.ovresort.com

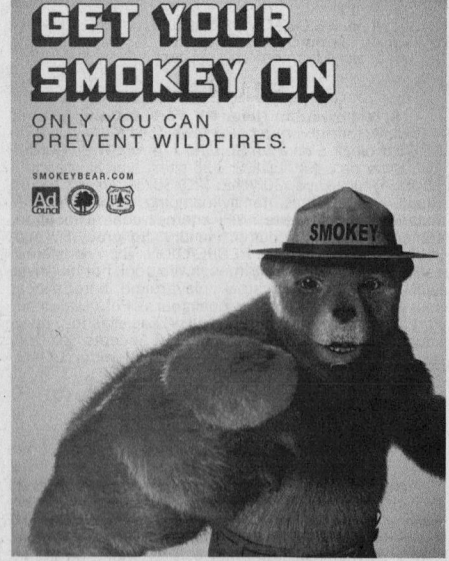

NEW MEXICO

BERNARDO

(S) KIVA RV PARK AND HORSE MOTEL —(Socorro) Altitude 5000 ft. *From jct I-25 (exit 175) & US 60: Go 1/10 mi W on US 60. Enter on L.*

WELCOME

FACILITIES: 36 sites, typical site width 30 ft, 36 full hkups, (30/50 amps), 50 amps ($), 36 pull-thrus, WiFi Instant Internet at site, WiFi Internet central location, family camping, RV storage, dump, non-guest dump $, laundry.

RECREATION: rec room/area, equipped pavilion.

Pets welcome. Partial handicap access. Open all yr. Big rigs welcome.

Phone: (505)861-0693
Address: 21 Old Highway 60W, Bernardo, NM 87006
Lat/Lon: 34.41621/-106.84305
Email: admin@kivarvparkandhorsemotel.com
Web: www.kivarvparkandhorsemotel.com

SEE AD THIS PAGE

NEW YORK

CUTCHOGUE

(C) Cliff and Ed's Trailer Park—(Suffolk) *From jct I-495 (exit 73) & Hwy 25: Go 15-1/4 mi E on Hwy 25, then 1 block N on Depot Lane, then 1 block W on Schoolhouse Rd. Enter on R.* FACILITIES: 24 sites, typical site width 36 ft, accepts full hkup units only, 24 full hkups, (20/30/50 amps), family camping, cable TV, phone/cable on-site Internet (needs activ), shower$, picnic tables, patios. RECREATION: golf nearby. Pets welcome, breed restrict. Partial handicap access. No tents. Open Apr 1 - Nov 1. Big rigs welcome. Member ARVC, CONY.

Phone: (631)298-4091
Address: 395 Schoolhouse Rd, Cutchogue, NY 11935
Lat/Lon: 41.01262/-72.48799
Email: cliffandeds@optonline.net

FLORIDA

(W) Black Bear Campground—(Orange) *From jct Hwy 17 (exit 124) & Hwy 17A: Go 5-1/2 mi SW on Hwy 17A, turn right at light (Bridge St), then 1-1/2 mi W on CR 41. Enter on L.* FACILITIES: 160 sites, typical site width 30 ft, 154 full hkups, 6 W&E, (20/30/50 amps), 10 pull-thrus, family camping, cable TV, WiFi Instant Internet at site, RV's/park model rentals, cabins, dump, portable dump, laundry, ltd groc, RV supplies, ice, picnic tables, fire rings, grills, wood. RECREATION: equipped pavilion, coin games, swim pool, mini-golf, golf nearby, bsktball, playground, activities (wkends), horseshoes, sports field, v-ball, local tours. Pets welcome, breed restrict. Partial handicap access. No tents. Open all yr. Big rigs welcome. Member ARVC, CONY.

Phone: (845)651-7717
Address: 197 Wheeler Rd, Florida, NY 10921
Lat/Lon: 41.32225/-74.37359
Email: topcamp@warwick.net
Web: www.blackbearcampground.com

HENDERSON HARBOR

(W) Association Island RV Resort & Marina—(Jefferson) *From I-81 (exit 41) & Hwy 178: Go 12 mi W on Hwy 178, then 2 mi N on Snowshoe Rd, cross bridge to 2nd Island. Enter at end.* FACILITIES: 305 sites, typical site width 40 ft, 305 full hkups, (20/30/50 amps), 29 pull-thrus, family camping, cable TV, WiFi Instant Internet at site ($), WiFi Internet central location ($), cabins, dump, laundry, ltd groc, RV supplies, ice, picnic tables, fire rings, wood, controlled access. RECREATION: rec hall, rec room/area, coin games, swim pool, lake swim, boating, canoeing, kayaking, ramp, dock, 4 kayak rentals, lake fishing, fishing supplies, fishing guides, golf nearby, bsktball, playground, shuffleboard court, activities (wkends), tennis, sports field, hiking trails. Pets welcome, breed restrict, quantity restrict. Partial handicap access. No tents. Open May 15 - Columbus Day. Big rigs welcome. Member ARVC, CONY. ATM.

Phone: (800)393-4189
Address: 15530 Snowshoe Rd, Henderson, NY 13650
Lat/Lon: 43.88696/-76.23008
Email: info@airesort.com
Web: www.associationislandresort.com

ITHACA

(W) Pinecreek Campground—(Tompkins) *From jct Hwy 13 & Hwy 79: Go 7 mi S on Hwy 79, then 3-1/2 mi S on CR 327 (Hulsey Valley), then 1/4 mi S on Hines Rd, then 500 ft W on Rockwell Rd. Enter on R.* FACILITIES: 162 sites, typical site width 40 ft, 57 full hkups, 56 W&E, (20/30/50 amps), 49 no hkups, 5 pull-thrus, family camping, RV's/park model rentals, cabins, RV storage, dump, non-guest dump $, ltd groc, ice, picnic tables, fire rings, wood. RECREATION: rec room/area, pavilion, coin games, swim pool, pond/stream fishing, golf nearby, bsktball, playground, horseshoes, sports field, v-ball. Pets welcome, breed restrict. Open May 1 - Oct 15. Big rigs welcome. Member ARVC, CONY.

Phone: (607)273-1974
Address: 28 Rockwell Rd, Newfield, NY 14867
Lat/Lon: 42.40734/-76.61138
Email: info@pinecreekcampground.com
Web: www.pinecreekcampground.com

WARRENSBURG

(NE) Schroon River Campsites—(Warren) *From jct I-87 (exit 23-Warrensburg) & Diamond Point Rd: Go 200 feet W on Diamond Point Rd, then 1/2 mi N on US 9, then 3 mi N on Horicon Ave/Schroon River Rd. Enter on R.* FACILITIES: 300 sites, typical site width 30 ft, 250 full hkups, 50 W&E, (15/20/30/50 amps), heater not allowed, family camping, cable TV, WiFi Internet central location, cabins, dump, non-guest dump $, laundry, groceries, RV supplies, LP gas by weight, ice, picnic tables, fire rings, wood. RECREATION: rec room/area, coin games, swim pool, river swim, boating, canoeing, kayaking, 2 rowboat/7 canoe/2 kayak rentals, float trips, river fishing, fishing supplies, golf nearby, bsktball, playground, activities (wkends), horseshoes, sports field, v-ball. Pets welcome. Open May 13 - Oct 2. Member ARVC, CONY.

Phone: (518)623-2171
Address: 686 Schroon River Rd, Warrensburg, NY 12885
Lat/Lon: 43.53123/-73.75544
Email: info@schroonrivercampsites.com
Web: www.schroonriver.com

NORTH CAROLINA

GREENSBORO

(E) Greensboro Campground—(Guilford) *From jct I-40 & Bus 85: Go 4-1/4 mi NE on Bus I-40/Bus 40 (exit 224), then 1/4 mi SE on E Lee St, then 1 mi W on Sharpe Rd, then 1/4 mi N on Trox St. Enter on L.* FACILITIES: 76 sites, accepts full hkup units only, 76 full hkups, (20/30/50 amps), 70 pull-thrus, family camping, WiFi Instant Internet at site, WiFi Internet central location, cabins, RV storage, dump, non-guest dump $, laundry, ltd groc, RV supplies, LP gas by weight/by meter, ice, picnic tables, fire rings, wood, controlled access. RECREATION: rec room/area, pavilion, swim pool, golf nearby, playground, horseshoes. Pets welcome, breed restrict. Partial handicap access. No tents. Open all yr. Big rigs welcome. Member ARVC, CARVC.

Phone: (336)274-4143
Address: 2300 Montreal Ave, Greensboro, NC 27406
Lat/Lon: 36.04701/-79.74672
Email: greensborocampgr@bellsouth.net
Web: www.GreensboroCampground.com

JACKSONVILLE

(SW) Cabin Creek Campground—(Onslow) *From west jct Hwy 24 & US 17: Go 4 3/4 mi S on US 17. Enter on R.* FACILITIES: 100 sites, typical site width 30 ft, 93 full hkups, (30/50 amps), 7 no hkups, 30 pull-thrus, family camping, cable TV, WiFi Instant Internet at site, WiFi Internet central location, RV's/park model rentals, cabins, RV storage, laundry, RV supplies, LP gas by weight/by meter, ice, picnic tables. RECREATION: rec hall, rec room/area, pavilion, mini-golf ($), golf nearby, play equipment, hiking trails. Pets welcome, quantity restrict. Open all yr. Big rigs welcome. Member ARVC, CARVC.

Phone: (910)346-4808
Address: 3200 Wilmington Hwy, Jacksonville, NC 28540
Lat/Lon: 34.69154/-77.47894
Email: cabincreekcampground@yahoo.com
Web: www.cabincreekcampground.com

OHIO

LIMA

(SE) Sun Valley Family Campground—(Allen) *From jct US 33 & Hwy 196: Go 8 mi N on Hwy 196, then 3 mi E on Amherst Rd, then 2 mi N on Hay Rd, then 1 blk W on Faulkner Rd. Enter on R.* FACILITIES: 242 sites, typical site width 30 ft, 242 full hkups, (20/30/50 amps), 5 pull-thrus, family camping, phone Internet central location, laundry, ltd groc, RV supplies, LP gas by weight/by meter, ice, picnic tables, fire rings, wood. RECREATION: rec room/area, pavilion, lake swim, boating, electric motors only, dock, lake/pond fishing, fishing supplies, golf nearby, bsktball, playground, shuffleboard court, activities (wkends), horseshoes, sports field, v-ball. Rec open to public. Pets welcome, breed restrict, size restrict. Partial handicap access. Open Apr 1 - Oct 31. Big rigs welcome. Member ARVC, OCOA.

Phone: (419)648-2235
Address: 9779 Faulkner Rd, Harrod, OH 45850
Lat/Lon: 40.68112/-83.92283
Email: info@sunvalley.com
Web: www.sunvalleycampground.com

OREGON

FAIRVIEW

(W) Rolling Hills RV Park—(Multnomah) *From I-84 (exit 13): Go 3 blocks N on 181st Ave, then 1 mi E on NE Sandy Blvd. Enter on L.* FACILITIES: 101 sites, typical site width 28 ft, 101 full hkups, (20/30/50 amps), 88 pull-thrus, family camping, cable TV, WiFi Instant Internet at site, phone on-site Internet (needs activ), RV's/park model rentals, laundry, picnic tables, patios. RECREATION: rec hall, swim pool, golf nearby. Pets welcome, breed restrict, size restrict. No tents. Open all yr. Pool open on a seasonal basis. Big rigs welcome. Member ORCA.

Phone: (503)666-7282
Address: 20145 NE Sandy #31, Fairview, OR 97024
Lat/Lon: 46.54476/-123.45480
Email: rollinghillsmobileterrace@yahoo.com
Web: www.rollinghillsmobileterrace.com

PENNSYLVANIA

BOYERTOWN

(N) Lazy-K Campground—(Berks) *From jct SR 73 & SR 100: Go 2-1/2 mi N on SR 100, then 200 yds E on Township Line Rd. Enter on R.* FACILITIES: 84 sites, typical site width 25 ft, 84 full hkups, (20/30/50 amps), 50 amps ($), family camping, cable TV, WiFi Instant Internet at site, WiFi Internet central location, RV's/park model rentals, RV storage, dump, laundry, RV supplies, ice, picnic tables, fire rings, wood. RECREATION: golf nearby, playground. Pets welcome. Open all yr. Call for water availability in Winter. Big rigs welcome. Member ARVC, PCOA.

Phone: (610)367-8576
Address: 61 Washington Rd, Bechtelsville, PA 19505
Lat/Lon: 40.35884/-75.62530
Email: camp@lazycamping.com
Web: www.lazykcamping.com

JEFFERSON

(NE) Firehouse RV Campground—(Greene) *From jct I-79 (exit 19) & SR-19: Go 300 yds S on SR-19, then 4 mi E on SR-221, then 4 mi E on SR-188. Enter on L.* FACILITIES: 48 sites, typical site width 30 ft, 48 full hkups, (30/50 amps), 20 pull-thrus, cable TV, WiFi Instant Internet at site, phone on-site Internet (needs activ), laundry, ice, picnic tables, patios. RECREATION: golf nearby, horseshoes. Pets welcome. Open all yr. Big rigs welcome. ATM.

Phone: (724)883-1955
Address: 1483 Jefferson Rd, Jefferson, PA 15344
Lat/Lon: 39.93335/-80.05511
Email: jvfc@atlanticbbn.net

SHARON

(NE) Shenango Valley RV Park—(Mercer) *From jct of I-80 & SR18 (exit 4B): Go 11 mi N on SR 18 then 1/2 mi E on Reynolds Industrial Park Rd, then 1 mi SE on Crestview Dr, then left at Y intersetion onto East Crestview Dr. Enter on L.* FACILITIES: 198 sites, typical site width 40 ft, 189 full hkups, 9 W&E, (20/30/50 amps), 5 pull-thrus, family camping, cable TV, WiFi Instant Internet at site, WiFi Internet central location, shower$, dump, laundry, ltd groc, RV supplies, LP gas by weight/by meter, LP bottle exch, ice, picnic tables, fire rings, wood, controlled access. RECREATION: rec hall, rec room/area, coin games, swim pool, river swim, canoeing, kayaking, 2 canoe/6 kayak rentals, river fishing, fishing supplies, putting green, golf nearby, bsktball, playground, shuffleboard court, activities (wkends), horseshoes, sports field, hiking trails, v-ball.

Shenango Valley RV Park—Continued on next page

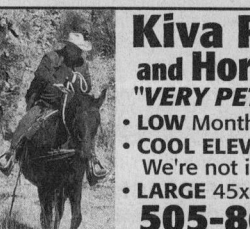

Pets welcome, breed restrict, quantity restrict. Partial handicap access. Open May 1 - Oct 15. Big rigs welcome. Member ARVC, PCOA.

Phone: (724)962-9800
Address: 559 E Crestview Dr, Transfer, PA 16154
Lat/Lon: 41.33323/-80.37746
Email: info@shenangovalleyrvpark.com
Web: www.shenangovalleyrvpark.com

SOUTH CAROLINA

ANDERSON

(NW) Lake Hartwell Camping & Cabins—(Anderson) *From jct I-85 (exit 11) & Hwy 24: Go 2-1/2 mi W on Hwy 24, then 1/2 mi N on O'Neal Ferry Rd, then 1/2 mi E on Ponderosa Rd. Enter at end.* FACILITIES: 120 sites, typical site width 35 ft, 80 full hkups, 40 W&E, (20/30/50 amps), 45 pull-thrus, family camping, WiFi Instant Internet at site, WiFi Internet central location, RV's/park model rentals, cabins, RV storage, dump, non-guest dump $, laundry, ltd groc, RV supplies, LP gas by weight/by meter, ice, picnic tables, fire rings, grills, wood. RECREATION: rec hall, pavilion, swim pool, wading pool, boating, canoeing, kayaking, ramp, dock, 2 pontoon/6 canoe/2 motorboat rentals, lake fishing, mini-golf, bsktball, playground, tennis, horseshoes, hiking trails, v-ball. Rec open to public. Pets welcome. Open all yr.

Phone: (888)427-8935
Address: 400 Ponderosa Pt Rd, Townville, SC 29689
Lat/Lon: 34.56366/-82.85731
Email: info@camplakehartwell.com
Web: camplakehartwell.com

COLUMBIA

(W) Barnyard RV Park—(Lexington) *From jct I-26 (exit 111A) & US 1: Go 3 mi SW on US 1. Enter on R. Or from jct I-20 (exit 58) & US 1: Go 2 mi NE on US 1. Enter on L.* FACILITIES: 129 sites, typical site width 40 ft, 129 full hkups, (30/50 amps), 82 pull-thrus, cable TV, WiFi Instant Internet at site ($), phone on-site Internet (needs activ), phone Internet central location, RV storage, dump, non-guest dump $, laundry, RV supplies, ice, picnic tables, patios. RECREATION: pavilion, horseshoes. Pets welcome. Partial handicap access. No tents. Open all yr. Big rigs welcome.

Phone: (803)957-1238
Address: 201 Oak Dr, Lexington, SC 29073
Lat/Lon: 33.97660/-81.15818
Email: barnyardrvpark@sc.rr.com
Web: www.barnyardrvpark.com

HARDEEVILLE

(SE) Hardeeville RV-Thomas' Parks and Sites—(Jasper) *From I-95 (exit 5) & jct US 17: Go N 1 mi on US 17, then E 5 mi on Hwy 46, then 1/4 mi W on Hwy 170 and continue straight on Hwy 170-A for 3 mi. Enter on L.* FACILITIES: 100 sites, typical site width 35 ft, accepts full hkup units only, 100 full hkups, (30/50 amps), 50 amps ($), 30 pull-thrus, cable TV, WiFi Instant Internet at site, laundry, ice, picnic tables, fire rings, wood. RECREATION: hiking trails. Pets welcome. No tents. Open all yr. No restrooms. Big rigs welcome. Member ARVC, CARVC.

Phone: (843)784-6210
Address: 2942 S Okatie Hwy, Hardeeville, SC 29927
Lat/Lon: 32.18878/-81.02996
Web: www.hardeevillerv.com

LONGS

(SE) WillowTree Resort—(Horry) *From jct SC-9 and SC 905: Go 1-3/4 mi NE on SC 905, then 1-1/2 mi N on Old Buck Creek Rd. Enter on R.* FACILITIES: 106 sites, typical site width 45 ft, 106 full hkups, (20/30/50 amps), 98 pull-thrus, family camping, WiFi Instant Internet at site, WiFi Internet central location, cabins, RV storage, dump, non-guest dump $, laundry, ltd groc, RV supplies, LP gas by meter, ice, picnic tables, patios, fire rings, grills, wood, controlled access. RECREATION: rec hall, rec room/area, coin games, swim pool, wading pool, lake swim, hot tub, boating, electric motors only, canoeing, canoe/6 pedal boat/5 motorboat rentals, lake fishing, fishing supplies, golf nearby, bsktball, 12 bike rentals, playground, activities, horseshoes, hiking trails, v-ball. Pets welcome. Partial handicap access. No tents. Open all yr. Big rigs welcome. Member ARVC, CARVC.

Phone: (866)207-2267
Address: 520 Southern Sights Drive, Longs, SC 29568
Lat/Lon: 33.97505/-78.71937
Email: reservations@willowtreervr.com
Web: www.willowtreervr.com

MYRTLE BEACH

(N) Apache Family Campground—(Horry) *From jct US 501 & US 17: Go 9-3/4 mi N on US 17, then 1/2 mi E on Chestnut Rd, then 1/4 mi S on Kings Rd. Enter on L.* FACILITIES: 937 sites, typical site width 32 ft, 931 full hkups, 6 W&E, (30/50 amps), 18 pull-thrus, family

camping, cable TV, WiFi Instant Internet at site ($), phone Internet central location, RV's/park model rentals, RV storage, dump, laundry, full svc store, RV supplies, LP gas by weight/by meter, ice, picnic tables, controlled access. RECREATION: rec room/area, equipped pavilion, coin games, swim pool, wading pool, saltwater swim, saltwater fishing, fishing supplies, golf nearby, bsktball, playground, activities, v-ball. Rec open to public. Pets welcome, breed restrict, quantity restrict. Partial handicap access. Open all yr. Big rigs welcome. Member ARVC, CARVC.

Phone: (800)553-1749
Address: 9700 Kings Rd, Myrtle Beach, SC 29572
Lat/Lon: 33.76909/-78.78801
Web: www.apachefamilycampground.com

(N) Briarcliffe RV Resort, Inc—(Horry) *From jct US 501 & US 17: Go 11 mi N on US 17. Enter on L.* FACILITIES: 174 sites, typical site width 35 ft, 174 full hkups, (30/50 amps), cable TV, WiFi Instant Internet at site, WiFi Internet central location, RV's/park model rentals, laundry, ice, picnic tables, patios, controlled access. RECREATION: rec hall, swim pool, mini-golf, golf nearby, bsktball, play equipment, 2 shuffleboard courts, activities, horseshoes. Pets welcome. Partial handicap access. No tents. Age restrict may apply. Open all yr. Big rigs welcome.

Phone: (843)272-2730
Address: 10495 N Kings Hwy, Myrtle Beach, SC 29572
Lat/Lon: 33.79548/-078.75097
Email: briarcliffervresort@sc.rr.com
Web: www.briarcliffervresort.com

(S) Lakewood Camping Resort—(Horry) *From jct US 501 & 544: Go E 14 mi on Hwy 544, then N 1/2 mi on US 17 Bus. Enter on R.* FACILITIES: 1900 sites, typical site width 34 ft, 1874 full hkups, 26 W&E, (20/30/50 amps), 45 pull-thrus, family camping, cable TV, WiFi Instant Internet at site, WiFi Internet central location, RV's/park model rentals, cabins, RV storage, dump, laundry, full svc store, RV supplies, LP gas by weight/by meter, ice, picnic tables, wood, controlled access. RECREATION: rec hall, rec room/area, equipped pavilion, coin games, 2 swim pools, wading pool, saltwater swim, hot tub, canoeing, kayaking, 9 canoe/10 kayak/20 pedal boat rentals, saltwater/lake/pond fishing, fishing supplies, mini-golf ($), golf nearby, bsktball, 40 bike rentals, playground, 3 shuffleboard courts, activities, horseshoes, v-ball, local tours. Pets welcome, breed restrict. Partial handicap access. Open all yr. Big rigs welcome. Green Friendly. Member ARVC, CARVC. ATM.

Phone: (843)238-5161
Address: 5901 S Kings Hwy, Myrtle Beach, SC 29575-4997
Lat/Lon: 33.63420/-78.95652
Email: info@lakewoodcampground.com
Web: www.lakewoodcampground.com

(NE) Myrtle Beach Travel Park—(Horry) *From jct US-501 & US-17: Go 9-3/4 mi on US-17, then 1/2 mi E on Chestnut Rd, then 1/4 mi N on Kings Rd. Enter on R.* FACILITIES: 1100 sites, typical site width 35 ft, 1080 full hkups, 20 W&E, (20/30/50 amps), 500 pull-thrus, family camping, cable TV, WiFi Instant Internet at site ($), phone Internet central location, RV's/park model rentals, RV storage, dump, non-guest dump, laundry, full svc store, RV supplies, LP gas by weight, ice, picnic tables, controlled access. RECREATION: rec room/area, pavilion, coin games, 3 swim pools, wading pool, saltwater swim, hot tub, dock, saltwater/pond fishing, golf nearby, bsktball, playground, activities, hiking trails, v-ball, local tours. Pets welcome. Partial handicap access. Open all yr. Big rigs welcome. Member ARVC, CARVC.

Phone: (800)255-3568
Address: 10108 Kings Rd, Myrtle Beach, SC 29572
Lat/Lon: 33.77757/-78.77362
Email: timbryant@scrr.com
Web: www.myrtlebeachtravelpark.com

(S) Ocean Lakes Family Campground—(Horry) *From jct US-501 & SC Hwy 544: Go 14 mi E on SC Hwy 544. Enter at end.* FACILITIES: 3447 sites, typical site width 40 ft, 3447 full hkups, (20/30/50 amps), 893 pull-thrus, family camping, cable TV, phone/WiFi Instant Internet at site ($), WiFi Internet central location, cabins, RV storage, laundry, full svc store, RV supplies, LP gas by weight/by meter, ice, picnic tables, controlled access. RECREATION: rec hall, rec room/area, equipped pavilion, coin games, 3 swim pools, wading pool, saltwater swim, saltwater/lake fishing, fishing supplies, mini-golf ($), golf nearby, bsktball, 15 bike rentals, playground, 3 shuffleboard courts, activities, horseshoes, v-ball, local tours. Pets welcome, breed restrict. Partial handicap access. Open all yr. Big rigs welcome. Green Friendly. Member ARVC, CARVC. ATM.

Phone: (800)876-4306
Address: 6001 S. Kings Highway, Myrtle Beach, SC 29575
Lat/Lon: 33.62897/-78.96236
Email: camping@oceanlakes.com
Web: www.oceanlakes.com

(S) Pirateland Family Camping Resort—(Horry) *From jct US 17 & US 544: Go 2 mi E on US 544, then 1 mi N on US 17 Bus. Enter on R.* FACILITIES:

1493 sites, typical site width 40 ft, 1493 full hkups, (30/50 amps), 39 pull-thrus, family camping, cable TV, WiFi Instant Internet at site ($), WiFi Internet central location, RV's/park model rentals, RV storage, laundry, full svc store, RV supplies, LP gas by weight/by meter, ice, picnic tables, controlled access. RECREATION: rec hall, rec room/area, equipped pavilion, coin games, 3 swim pools, wading pool, saltwater swim, 4 canoe/15 pedal boat rentals, saltwater/lake/pond fishing, fishing supplies, mini-golf ($), golf nearby, bsktball, playground, activities, local tours. Pets welcome, breed restrict. Partial handicap access. Open all yr. Facilities fully operational Easter Wknd, then memorial Day - Labor Day. Big rigs welcome. Green Friendly. Member ARVC, CARVC. ATM.

Phone: (800)443-2267
Address: 5401 S Kings Hwy, Myrtle Beach, SC 29575
Lat/Lon: 33.64191/-78.94713
Email: pirateland@pirateland.com
Web: www.pirateland.com

SENECA

(NW) Crooked Creek RV Park—(Oconee) *From jct I-85 & US 76 W/SC 28 (exit 19B): Go 11 mi W on US 76 W/SC 28, then 9 mi W on US 76/US 123/SC 28, then 1-1/4 mi NW on SC 28, then 3-1/4 mi NE on SC 188 (Keowee School Rd), then 1-3/4 mi N on Ebenezer Rd to Arvee Ln. Enter on R.* FACILITIES: 110 sites, typical site width 35 ft, 97 full hkups, 13 W&E, (20/30/50 amps), 97 pull-thrus, family camping, cable TV, phone/WiFi Instant Internet at site, WiFi Internet central location, RV storage, laundry, ltd groc, RV supplies, LP gas by weight/by meter, marine gas, ice, picnic tables, wood. RECREATION: rec room/area, pavilion, coin games, swim pool, wading pool, lake swim, boating, canoeing, kayaking, ramp, dock, pontoon/2 kayak/pedal boat rentals, lake fishing, fishing supplies, golf nearby, bsktball, playground, horseshoes, v-ball. Pets welcome, breed restrict. Partial handicap access. Open all yr. Big rigs welcome. ATM.

Phone: (864)882-5040
Address: 777 Arvee Lane, West Union, SC 29696
Lat/Lon: 34.76172/-82.97798
Email: ccrvp@trivergent.net
Web: www.crookedcreekrvpark.com

SWANSEA

(SW) Yogi Bear's Jellystone Park @ River Bottom Farms—(Lexington) *From jct US 321 & S.C. 3: Go W 6-1/2 mi on S.C. 3, then NW 1/2 mi on US 178, then W 1/2 mi on Cedar Creek Rd. Enter on L.* FACILITIES: 70 sites, typical site width 40 ft, 52 full hkups, 14 W&E, 4 E, (30/50 amps), 25 pull-thrus, family camping, WiFi Instant Internet at site, WiFi Internet central location, cabins, RV storage, laundry, RV supplies, LP gas by weight/by meter, ice, picnic tables, fire rings, grills, wood. RECREATION: rec hall, pavilion, coin games, swim pool, river/pond fishing, fishing supplies, play equipment, activities (wkends), horseshoes, sports field, hiking trails, v-ball. Pets welcome. Partial handicap access. Open all yr. Big rigs welcome. Member ARVC, CARVC.

Phone: (803)568-4182
Address: 357 Cedar Creek Rd, Swansea, SC 29160
Lat/Lon: 33.68947/-81.19251
Email: rbfrvresort@pbtcomm.net
Web: www.columbiajellystone.com

SOUTH DAKOTA

PIEDMONT

(E) Lazy JD RV Park—(Meade) *From jct US 16 Truck/Hwy 79 & I-90 (exit 61): Go 6 mi W on I-90 (exit 55), then 3 mi N on Deadwood Ave, then 3-1/4 mi E on Peaceful Pines. Enter on R.* FACILITIES: 42 sites, typical site width 20 ft, 22 full hkups, (50 amps), 20 no hkups, 22 pull-thrus, family camping, RV storage, dump, non-guest dump $, laundry, picnic tables. RECREATION: golf nearby, sports field. Pets welcome. Open May 1 - Oct 1. Water dependant on weather. Big rigs welcome. Member ARVC, SDCOA.

Phone: (605)787-7036
Address: 12336 Erickson Ranch Rd, Piedmont, SD 57769
Lat/Lon: 44.19930/-103.28713
Email: adbeckham@juno.com
Web: www.lazyjdgroup.com

TENNESSEE

LAKE CITY

(N) Mountain Lake Marina & Campground—(Anderson) *From jct I-75 (exit 128) & US 441: Go 1-1/4 mi SE on US 441, then 2 mi NE on Oak Grove Rd, then 3/4 mi E on Lindsey Mill Circle/Campground Rd. Follow signs. Enter at end.* FACILITIES: 196 sites, 180 full

Mountain Lake Marina & Campground—Continued on next page

hkups, 16 W&E, (20/30/50 amps), 50 amps ($), 24 pull-thrus, cable TV ($), WiFi Instant Internet at site, phone Internet central location, cabins, RV storage, dump, laundry, ltd groc, RV supplies, LP bottle exch, ice, picnic tables, patios, fire rings, wood. RECREATION: rec hall, rec room/area, coin games, swim pool, boating, canoeing, ramp, dock, 2 pontoon/motorboat rentals, lake fishing, fishing supplies, fishing guides, golf nearby, 2 shuffleboard courts, activities (wkends), horseshoes, v-ball. Pets welcome. Partial handicap access. Open all yr. Big rigs welcome. Member ARVC, TNARVC.

Phone: (877)686-2267
Address: 136 Campground Rd, Lake City, TN 37769
Lat/Lon: 36.25901/-84.15082
Email: mountainlakemarina@comcast.net
Web: www.mountainlakemarina.com

SEVIERVILLE

(N) Riverside RV Park & Resort—(Sevier) *From jct I-40 (exit 407) & Hwy 66: Go 4 mi S on Hwy 66, then 1/4 mi W on Boyds Creek Rd (turn right at Marathon). Enter on R.* FACILITIES: 316 sites, typical site width 30 ft, 296 full hkups, 20 W&E, (30/50 amps), 50 amps ($), 101 pull-thrus, family camping, cable TV, WiFi Instant Internet at site, RV's/park model rentals, cabins, RV storage, laundry, groceries, RV supplies, LP gas by weight/by meter, ice, picnic tables, patios, fire rings, grills, wood. RECREATION: rec room/area, equipped pavilion, coin games, swim pool, boating, ramp, river fishing, fishing supplies, golf nearby, bsktball, playground, activities. Pets welcome. No tents. Open all yr. Big rigs welcome.

Phone: (800)341-7534
Address: 4280 Boyds Creek Hwy, Sevierville, TN 37876
Lat/Lon: 35.92848/-83.58674
Email: KVOLUNTEER@aol.com
Web: www.riversidecamp.com

TEXAS

ALPINE

(N) Lost Alaskan RV Park—(Brewster) Altitude 4481 ft. *From jct US 90 & Hwy 118: Go 1-1/4 mi N on Hwy 118. Enter on L.* FACILITIES: 91 sites, typical site width 28 ft, 91 full hkups, (30/50 amps), 50 amps ($), 69 pull-thrus, family camping, cable TV, WiFi Instant Internet at site, dump, non-guest dump $, laundry, RV supplies, picnic tables, patios. RECREATION: rec hall, swim pool, spray ground, golf nearby, playground, horseshoes. Pets welcome. Partial handicap access. Open all yr. Big rigs welcome. Member ARVC, TACO.

Phone: (800)837-3604
Address: 2401 North Hwy 118, Alpine, TX 79830
Lat/Lon: 30.37995/-103.67018
Email: lostalaskanrv@gmail.com
Web: www.lostalaskan.com

ARLINGTON

(S) Treetops RV Village—(Tarrant) *From jct I-20 (exit 449) & Hwy 157: Go 1/2 mi N on Hwy 157, then 1/4 mi W on Arbrook. Enter on R.* FACILITIES: 165 sites, typical site width 40 ft, accepts self-contained units only, 165 full hkups, (30/50 amps), 50 amps ($), 63 pull-thrus, family camping, cable TV, phone/WiFi Instant Internet at site, phone on-site Internet (needs activ), phone Internet central location, dump, non-guest dump $, laundry, RV supplies, LP gas by weight/by meter, picnic tables, patios. RECREATION: swim pool, golf nearby, activities (wkends). Pets welcome, breed restrict. No tents. Open all yr. Big rigs welcome. Member ARVC, TACO.

Phone: (800)747-0787
Address: 1901 W Arbrook, Arlington, TX 76015
Lat/Lon: 32.68501/-97.13934
Email: treetopsrv@sbcglobal.net
Web: www.carefreervresorts.com

ATHENS

(W) Windsor Place RV Estates—(Henderson) *From jct Bus US 175, Hwy 19 & Bus Hwy 31: Go 3/4 mi W on Bus Hwy 31 (Corsicana St). Enter on R.* FACILITIES: 46 sites, typical site width 44 ft, accepts full hkup units only, 46 full hkups, (30/50 amps), family camping, cable TV, phone/cable on-site Internet (needs activ), WiFi Internet central location, RV storage, laundry, picnic tables, patios, controlled access. RECREATION: rec hall, pavilion, golf nearby, activities (wkends). Pets welcome, breed restrict, size restrict. Partial handicap access. No tents. Age restrict may apply. Open all yr. No restrooms. Big rigs welcome. Member ARVC, TACO.

Phone: (903)477-4001
Address: 1506 W Corsicana, Athens, TX 75751
Lat/Lon: 32.20124/-95.88137
Email: stay@windsorplacerv.com
Web: windsorplacerv.com

AUSTIN

(NE) La Hacienda RV Park—(Travis) *From jct Hwy 71 & RM 620: Go 7-1/2 mi NE on RM 620, then 1-1/2 mi N on Hudson Bend. Enter on L.* FACILITIES: 240 sites, typical site width 40 ft, accepts full hkup units only, 240 full hkups, (20/30/50 amps), 88 pull-thrus, family camping, cable TV, phone/WiFi Instant Internet at site, RV's/park model rentals, RV storage, dump, non-guest dump $, laundry, RV supplies, LP gas by meter, ice, picnic tables, patios. RECREATION: rec hall, rec room/area, equipped pavilion, 2 swim pools, spray ground, hot tub, golf nearby, bsktball, playground, activities (wkends), horseshoes, hiking trails, v-ball. Pets welcome. Partial handicap access. No tents. Open all yr. Big rigs welcome. Member ARVC, TACO.

Phone: (512)266-8001
Address: 5320 Hudson Bend Rd, Austin, TX 78734
Lat/Lon: 30.41556/-97.92966
Email: lahaciendarvpark@yahoo.com
Web: www.lahaciendarvpark.com

CONCAN

(N) PARKVIEW RIVERSIDE RV PARK—(Uvalde) *From jct Hwy 127 & US 83: Go 8 mi N on US 83, then 1 mi E on FM 1050, then 1 1/2 mi S on CR 350. Enter on R.*

WELCOME

FACILITIES: 94 sites, typical site width 30 ft, 94 full hkups, (20/30/50 amps), 17 pull-thrus, cable TV, WiFi Instant Internet at site ($), family camping, RV storage, dump, non-guest dump $, laundry, groceries, RV supplies, LP gas by weight/by meter, ice, picnic tables, fire rings, grills, wood.

RECREATION: rec hall, pavilion, river swim, canoeing, kayaking, float trips, river fishing, fishing supplies, golf nearby, shuffleboard court, activities, horseshoes, sports field, hiking trails, v-ball, local tours.

Pets welcome. Partial handicap access. No tents. Open all yr. Big rigs welcome. Member ARVC, TACO.

Phone: (877)374-6748
Address: 2651 CR 350, Concan, TX 78838
Lat/Lon: 29.58274/-99.72745
Email: parkviewrv@gmail.com
Web: www.parkviewriversiderv.com

Reserve Online at Woodalls.com

SEE AD THIS PAGE

CORPUS CHRISTI

(E) Laguna Shore Village—(Nueces) *From jct I-37 & Hwy 358 (S. Padre Island Dr): Go 15 mi SE on S. Padre Island Dr (Hwy 358), then 3-1/2 mi S on Flour Bluff Dr, then 1-1/2 mi E on Yorktown, then 200 ft N on Laguna Shores Dr. Enter on L.* FACILITIES: 45 sites, typical site width 15 ft, 45 full hkups, (30/50 amps), 20 pull-thrus, cable TV, WiFi Instant Internet at site, phone Internet central location, dump, non-guest dump $, laundry, picnic tables, patios. RECREATION: rec room/area, saltwater fishing, golf nearby, activities, local tours. Pets welcome. Partial handicap access. No tents. Open all yr. Big rigs welcome. Member ARVC, TACO.

Phone: (888)221-4009
Address: 3828 Laguna Shores Rd, Corpus Christi, TX 78418
Lat/Lon: 27.61864/-97.29745
Email: jennieashmore@hotmail.com
Web: www.lagunashorevillage.com

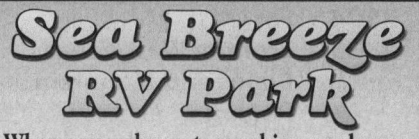

LUBBOCK

(W) Camelot Village RV & MHP—(Lubbock) *From jct US 84 W & Loop 289 W: Go 4-1/2 mi S on Loop 289 (34th St exit), then 500 feet W on 34th St.. Enter on L.* FACILITIES: 157 sites, typical site width 45 ft, 157 full hkups, (20/30/50 amps), 8 pull-thrus, family camping, phone Internet central location, RV storage, laundry, picnic tables, patios, grills. RECREATION: pavilion, swim pool, golf nearby, bsktball, v-ball. Pets welcome, breed restrict, size restrict. No tents. Open all yr. Big rigs welcome. Member ARVC, TACO.

Phone: (806)792-6477
Address: 6001 34th, Lubbock, TX 79407
Lat/Lon: 33.56300/-101.94682
Web: www.commanderspalacelubbock.com

MCALLEN

(E) McAllen Mobile Park—(Hidalgo) *From jct Hwy 336 & US 83: Go 1-3/4 mi E on US 83, then 3-1/2 mi N on McColl Rd (2061). Enter on R.* FACILITIES: 318 sites, typical site width 25 ft, 318 full hkups, (30/50 amps), 50 amps ($), 70 pull-thrus, heater not allowed, WiFi Instant Internet at site, RV storage, laundry, RV supplies, ice, patios. RECREATION: rec hall, rec room/area, swim pool, hot tub, golf nearby, 6 shuffleboard courts, activities, horseshoes, local tours. Pets welcome, size restrict, quantity restrict. Partial handicap access. No tents. Open all yr. Big rigs welcome.

Phone: (956)682-3304
Address: 4900 N. McColl Rd, McAllen, TX 78504
Lat/Lon: 26.24491/-98.20509
Email: mcallenmobile@aol.com
Web: www.mcallenmobilepark.com

PORTLAND

(SW) SEA BREEZE RV PARK—(San Patricio) *From jct Hwy 181 & Moore Ave (FM 893): Go 1 mi W on Moore Ave (FM 893), then 1/2 mi SW on Marriot, then 3 blocks S on CR 3669. Enter on R.*

FACILITIES: 142 sites, typical site width 24 ft, 140 full hkups, 2 W&E, (30/50 amps), 34 pull-thrus, WiFi Instant Internet at site, phone Internet central location, RV storage, laundry, RV supplies, ice, picnic tables.

RECREATION: rec hall, rec room/area, swim pool, wading pool, hot tub, boating, canoeing, kayaking, dock, saltwater fishing, fishing guides, golf nearby, activities, horseshoes, local tours.

Pets welcome, breed restrict, quantity restrict. Partial handicap access. No tents. Open all yr. Planned activities winter only. Big rigs welcome. Member ARVC, TACO.

Phone: (361)643-0744
Address: 1026 Seabreeze Lane, Portland, TX 78374
Lat/Lon: 27.88514/-97.34345
Email: seabreezerv@aol.com
Web: www.seabreezerv.com

SEE AD THIS PAGE

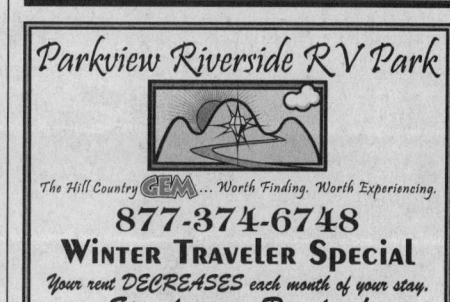

SCHULENBURG

(N) Schulenburg RV Park—(Fayette) *From jct I-10 (exit 674) & US 77: Go 1/4 mi S on US 77. Enter on R.* FACILITIES: 49 sites, typical site width 30 ft, 49 full hkups, (20/30/50 amps), 50 amps ($), 45 pull-thrus, family camping, cable TV, WiFi Instant Internet at site, dump, non-guest dump $, laundry, RV supplies, picnic tables, grills. RECREATION: rec hall, rec room/area, equipped pavilion, pond fishing, fishing supplies, golf nearby, bsktball, activities, local tours. Pets welcome, breed restrict. Partial handicap access. Open all yr. Big rigs welcome. Member ARVC, TACO.

Phone: (979)743-4388
Address: 65 N Kessler Ave, Schulenburg, TX 78956
Lat/Lon: 29.68962/-96.90108
Email: camp@schulenburgrvpark.com
Web: www.schulenburgrvpark.com

TOMBALL

(S) Corral RV Park of Tomball—(Harris) *From jct FM 2920 & Hwy 249: Go 1-1/2 mi S on Hwy 249, then 3/4 mi E on Holderreith St, then 1 mi N on South Cherry St. Enter on L.* FACILITIES: 160 sites, typical site width 35 ft, 160 full hkups, (20/30/50 amps), 38 pull-thrus, family camping, phone on-site Internet (needs activ), WiFi Internet central location, RV storage, shower$, laundry, ltd groc, RV supplies, LP gas by weight/by meter, LP bottle exch, ice, patios. RECREATION: rec hall, rec room/area, coin games, pond fishing, golf nearby, sports field, hiking trails. Pets welcome, breed restrict, size restrict, quantity restrict. Partial handicap access. No tents. Open all yr. Big rigs welcome. Member ARVC, TACO. ATM.

Phone: (281)351-2761
Address: 1402 S Cherry, Tomball, TX 77375
Lat/Lon: 30.08309/-95.61169
Email: corralrv@houstonrvpark.com
Web: www.corralrvpark.com

Woodall's Directory is split, East/West. You can buy a Directory with all of North America, or you can buy only the Eastern or Western editions. Browse our bookstore at www.woodalls.com/shop for more details.

UTAH

ST. GEORGE

(S) McArthur's Temple View RV Resort—(Washington) *From jct I-15 (exit 6) & Bluff St: Go 1/2 block N on Bluff St, then 1/4 mi N on Main St. Enter on R.* FACILITIES: 276 sites, typical site width 29 ft, 266 full hkups, 10 W&E, (20/30/50 amps), 40 pull-thrus, family camping, cable TV, WiFi Instant Internet at site, phone on-site Internet (needs activ), WiFi Internet central location, RV storage, dump, non-guest dump $, laundry, RV supplies, ice, picnic tables, patios. RECREATION: rec hall, rec room/area, swim pool, hot tub, putting green, golf nearby, 4 shuffleboard courts, activities, horseshoes, sports field, v-ball, local tours. Pets welcome, breed restrict. Partial handicap access. Open all yr. Big rigs welcome. Member ARVC.

Phone: (800)381-0321
Address: 975 S Main St, St. George, UT 84770
Lat/Lon: 37.09164/-113.58334
Email: mcarthur@templeviewrv.com
Web: www.templeviewrv.com

WASHINGTON

CASTLE ROCK

(N) Toutle River RV Resort—(Cowlitz) *From jct I-5 (exit 52) & Barnes Drive: Go 1 blk W on Barnes Drive, then 1/2 mi S on Happy Trails Rd. Enter at end.* FACILITIES: 306 sites, typical site width 40 ft, 300 full hkups, (20/30/50 amps), 6 no hkups, 270 pull-thrus, family camping, WiFi Instant Internet at site, phone Internet central location, dump, laundry, groceries, RV supplies, ice, picnic tables, patios, fire rings, grills, wood, controlled access. RECREATION: rec hall, rec room/area, pavilion, equipped pavilion, coin games, swim pool, river swim, hot tub, kayaking, river fishing, fishing supplies, golf nearby, bsktball, playground, activities, tennis, horseshoes, sports field, hiking trails, v-ball, local tours. Rec open to public. Pets welcome. Partial handicap access. Open all yr. Big rigs welcome.

Phone: (360)274-8373
Address: 150 Happy Trails Rd, Castle Rock, WA 98611
Lat/Lon: 46.31252/-122.76273
Email: greatrvresort@aol.com
Web: www.greatrvresort.com

BRITISH COLUMBIA

SURREY

(S) Hazelmere RV Park & Campground—*From jct Hwy 10 & Hwy 15/176 St (Cloverdale): Go 9.8 km /6mi S on Hwy 15, then 2.5 km/1-1/2 mi E on 8 Ave. Enter on L.* FACILITIES: 200 sites, typical site width 22 ft, 172 full hkups, 20 W&E, (15/30 amps), 8 no hkups, family camping, cable TV, WiFi Instant Internet at site, phone Internet central location ($), cabins, shower$, dump, non-guest dump $, laundry, groceries, RV supplies, LP gas by weight, ice, picnic tables, fire rings, grills, wood. RECREATION: rec room/area, swim pool, hot tub, mini-golf, golf nearby, bsktball, 8 bike rentals, playground, activities, horseshoes, sports field, hiking trails, v-ball. Pets welcome. Partial handicap access. Open all yr. Member BCLCA.

Phone: (877)501-5007
Address: 18843 8th Ave, Surrey, BC V3S9R9
Lat/Lon: 49.01670/-122.70070
Email: camping@hazelmere.ca
Web: www.hazelmere.ca

Woodall's Tip... To be considered a "Big Rig Friendly" park, the campground must meet the following requirements: minimum of 50 amps, adequate road width, overhead access clearance, site clearance to accommodate the tallest and widest rigs built. Often not every site can accommodate a big rig, so we recommend that you call ahead for availability.

Can you trust the Woodall's ratings? 25 evaluation teams have scoured North American campgrounds to provide you with accurate, up to date information & ratings. Find a rating you don't agree with? Send a letter or email our way, and we'll give it extra attention for 2012.

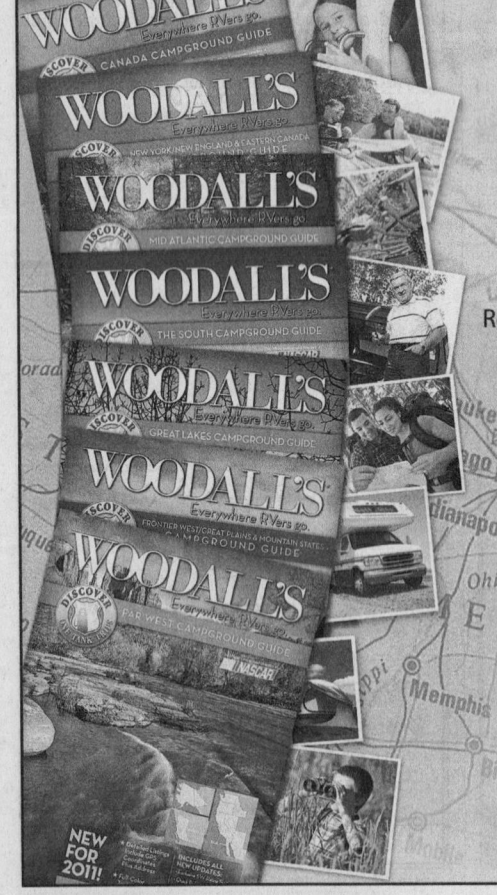

t's not 's fault

by TheShelterPetProject.org